THE WRITERS
DIRECTORY 1990-92

THE WRITERS
DIRECTORY 1990-92

NINTH EDITION

St J
St James Press

Chicago and London

For further information, write:
ST. JAMES PRESS
233 East Ontario Street
Chicago 60611, U.S.A.
        or
3 Percy Street
London W1P 9FA, England

British Cataloguing in Publication Data
The Writers Directory. — 1990-92
  1. Literature — Directories
  808'.02'05   PN12

  ISBN 1-55862-032-X

First published in the U.S.A. and U.K. 1990

Filmsetting by A.L. Publishing Services
London

CONTENTS

PREFACE

The Writers Directory 1990–92 is the completely revised and expanded ninth edition of this biennial reference work. It lists more than 17,000 living writers from Australia, Canada, Ireland, New Zealand, South Africa, the United Kingdom and the United States, as well as others who write in English.

The main section of the book lists fiction and nonfiction writers who have published at least one full-length book in English. To ensure accuracy, the editors use information provided by the writers themselves whenever possible. Each entry contains name (and pseudonyms); citizenship and year of birth; subject categories; current and past appointments; a complete bibliography; and address. The unique "yellow pages" section lists writers under their various writing categories. This section is especially useful to students, bibliographers and others who need a list of writers on a particular subject.

The 17,000 entrants include all of the writers featured in the special-subject books published by St. James Press—6,000 writers in all from *Contemporary Poets, Contemporary Novelists, Contemporary Dramatists, Contemporary Literary Critics, 20th Century Children's Writers, 20th Century Crime and Mystery Writers, 20th Century Science-Fiction Writers, 20th Century Romance and Historical Fiction Writers, and 20th Century-Western Writers.* The remaining 11,000 entrants include the best-known, best-selling authors of fiction as well as the most prominent non-fiction writers.

Although suggestions for inclusion from librarians, literary agents and publishers are welcome, entry in *The Writers Directory* is at the discretion of the editors.

ABBREVIATIONS USED IN THE WRITERS DIRECTORY

ABC	American Broadcasting Company	Glam.	Glamorgan
A.C.T.	Australian Capital Territory	G.L.C.	Greater London Council (U.K.)
A.D.C.	Aide de Camp	Glos.	Gloucestershire
Add.	Address	Gov.	Governor
Admin.	Administration	Govt.	Government
AFL-CIO	American Federation of Labor Congress of Industrial Organizations	G.P.O.	General Post Office (U.K.)
		Grad.	Graduate
Ala.	Alabama	Hants.	Hampshire
Alta.	Alberta	H.E.	His Eminence; His/Her Excellency
APO	Armed Forces Post Office (U.S.)	Herts.	Hertfordshire
Apt.	Apartment	H.M.	His/Her Majesty('s)
Ariz.	Arizona	H.M.S.	His/Her Majesty's Ship; His/Her Majesty's Service
Ark.	Arkansas		
Assn.	Association	Hon.	Honourable; Honorary
Assoc.	Associate	Hosp.	Hospital
Asst.	Assistant	I.B.M.	International Business Machines
Ave.	Avenue	Ill.	Illinois
b.	born	Inc.	Incorporated
BBC	British Broadcasting Corporation	Ind.	Indiana
B.C.	British Columbia	Inst.	Institute
Bd.	Board	Instn.	Institution
Beds.	Bedfordshire	Instr.	Instructor
Berks.	Berkshire	Intnl.	International
BFPO	British Forces Post Office	Ire.	Ireland
Bldg.	Building	Jr.	Junior
Blvd.	Boulevard	Kans.	Kansas
Brig.	Brigadier	Ky.	Kentucky
Bros.	Brothers	La.	Louisiana
Bucks.	Buckinghamshire	Lab.	Laboratory
Calif.	California	Lancs.	Lancashire
Cambs.	Cambridgeshire	Lectr.	Lecturer
Can.	Canada	Leics.	Leicestershire
Capt.	Captain	L.I.	Long Island
CBS	Columbia Broadcasting System (U.S.)	Lincs.	Lincolnshire
Chmn.	Chairman	Lt.	Lieutenant
Cia.	Company	Ltd.	Limited
C.I.A.	Central Intelligence Agency (U.S.)	Ltee.	Limited
Cie.	Company	Mag.	Magazine
Co.	Company; County	Maj.	Major
Co-ed.	Co-editor	Man.	Manitoba
Col.	Colonel	Mass.	Massachusetts
Coll.	College	Md.	Maryland
Colo.	Colorado	Me.	Maine
Comdg.	Commanding	Mgr.	Manager
Comdr.	Commander	Mich.	Michigan
Commn.	Commission	Middx.	Middlesex
Commnr.	Commissioner	Minn.	Minnesota
Conn.	Connecticut	Miss.	Mississippi
Contrib.	Contributor; contributing	Mo.	Missouri
Corp.	Corporation	Mont.	Montana
Corresp.	Correspondent	Mt.	Mount
Co-trans.	Co-translator	N.	North
Cres.	Crescent	NASA	National Aeronautics and Space Administration (U.S.)
Ct.	Court		
Cttee.	Committee	NATO	North Atlantic Treaty Organization
D.C.	District of Columbia	N.B.	New Brunswick
Del.	Delaware	NBC	National Broadcasting Company (U.S.)
Dept.	Department	N.C.	North Carolina
Dir.	Director	N.D.	North Dakota
Div.	Division	N.E.	North East
Dr.	Drive	Nebr.	Nebraska
E.	East	Nev.	Nevada
Ed.	Editor; Edition	cfld.	Newfoundland
E.E.C.	European Economic Community	N.H.	New Hampshire
Exec.	Executive	N. Ire.	Northern Ireland
F.B.I.	Federal Bureau of Investigation (U.S.)	N.J.	New Jersey
Fedn.	Federation	N.M.	New Mexico
Fla.	Florida	No.	Number
Foundn.	Foundation	Northants.	Northamptonshire
FPO	Fleet Post Office (U.S.)	Notts.	Nottinghamshire
Ft.	Fort	Nr.	Near
Ga.	Georgia	N.S.	Nova Scotia
Gen.	General	N.S.W.	New South Wales

N.T.	Northern Territory	Secty.	Secretary
N.W.	North West	SHAPE	Supreme Headquarters Allied Powers, Europe
N.W.T.	Northwest Territories	Soc.	Society
N.Y.	New York	Sq.	Square
NYC	New York City	Sr.	Senior
O.E.C.D.	Organization for Economic Cooperation and Development	St.	Saint; Street
		Staffs.	Staffordshire
Okla.	Oklahoma	Supt.	Superintendent
Ont.	Ontario	Supvr.	Supervisor
Orch.	Orchestra	S.W.	South West
Ore.	Oregon	Tas.	Tasmania
Org.	Organization	Tenn.	Tennessee
Oxon	Oxfordshire	Terr.	Terrace
Pa.	Pennsylvania	Tex.	Texas
P.E.I.	Prince Edward Island	Trans.	Translator
P.E.N.	Poets, Playwrights, Essayists, Editors, Novelists (organization)	Treas.	Treasurer
		T.U.C.	Trades Union Congress (U.K.)
Pl.	Place	U.K.	United Kingdom
P.O.	Post Office	U.N.	United Nations
Pres.	President	Unesco	United Nations Educational, Scientific and Cultural Organization
Prof.	Professor		
Prog.	Program	Unicef	United Nations Children's Emergency Fund
Pseud.	Pseudonym	Univ.	University
Pty.	Proprietary	U.S.	United States
Qld.	Queensland	U.S.A.	United States of America
Que.	Quebec	U.S.S.	United States Ship; United States Service
R.A.F.	Royal Air Force (U.K.)	U.S.S.R.	Union of Soviet Socialist Republics
R.C.A.	Radio Corporation of America	Va.	Virginia
Rd.	Road	Vic.	Victoria
R.D.	Rural Delivery	vol.	Volume
Rep.	Representative	Vt.	Vermont
Rev. ed.	Revised edition	W.	West
R.F.D	Rural Free Delivery	W.A.	Western Australia
R.I.	Rhode Island	Warwicks.	Warwickshire
R.R.	Rural Route	Wash.	Washington
Rt.	Route	tsWHO	World Health Organization
S.	South	Wilts.	Wiltshire
S.A.	Sociedad Anonima (Corp.)	tsWisc.	Wisconsin
S.A.	South Australia	Worcs.	Worcestershire
S. Africa	South Africa	W. Va.	West Virginia
Salop.	Shropshire	Wyo.	Wyoming
Sask.	Saskatchewan	YMCA	Young Men's Christian Association
S.C.	South Carolina	YM-YWHA	Young Men's—Young Women's Hebrew Association
Sch.	School		
S.D.	South Dakota	Yorks.	Yorkshire
S.E.	South East	YWCA	Young Women's Christian Association
SEATO	South East Asia Treaty Organization		

INDEX TO WRITING CATEGORIES

CONTENTS

CREATIVE WRITING

Novels/short stories

Abbas, Ahmad
Abbensetts, Michael
Abish, Walter
Ableman, Paul
Abrahams, Peter
Abrams, Linsey
Abse, Dannie
Achebe, Chinua
Ackroyd, Peter
Acland, Alice
Acton, (Sir) Harold
Adams, Alice
Adams, Douglas
Adams, Hazard
Adams, Richard •
Addison, Doris Maureen
Adlard, Mark
Adleman, Robert H.
Adler, Renata
Adler, Warren
Agnew, Spiro T.
Aidoo, Ama Ata
Albert, Marvin
Aldiss, Brian
Aldridge, James
Aldridge, John W.
Alexander, Joan
Alexander, Lloyd
Alexander, Patrick James
Ali, Ahmed
Allan, Mabel Esther
Allan, Ted
Allbeury, Ted
Allen, Steve
Allen, Walter
Allen, Woody
Allsop, Bruce
Alphonso-Karkala, John B.
Alter, Judith
Alther, Lisa
Aluko, T.M.
Alvarez, A.
Amadi, Elechi
Ambler, Eric
Ames, Delano L.
Amis, Kingsley
Amis, Martin
Anand, Mulk Raj
Anania, Michael
Anaya, Rudolfo A.
Andersen, Doris
Anderson, Chester
Anderson, Colin
Anderson, (Lady) Flavia
Anderson, Jessica
Anderson, John
Anderson, Rachel
Anderson, Robert
Anderson, Verily
Andrew, Prudence
Andrews, Allen
Angelou, Maya
Aniebo, I.N.C.
Anthony, Michael
Appiah, Peggy
Apple, May
Appleman, Philip
Archer, Jeffrey
Archibald, Douglas
Arden, John
Aresty, Esther Bradford
Armah, Ayi Kwei
Armstrong, William H.
Arrighi, Mel
Ash, William Franklin
Ashbery, John
Ashby, Cliff
Asinof, Eliot
Astley, Thea
Athas, Daphne

Atkins, John Alfred
Atkins, Meg Elizabeth
Atwood, Margaret
Auchincloss, Louis
Auel, Jean
Auster, Paul
Austin, Richard
Avallone, Michael
Awoonor, Kofi
Axelrod, George
Ayrton, Elisabeth
Babb, Sanora
Bach, Richard
Bache, Ellen
Bacon, Margaret
Bacon, R.L.
Badeni, June
Bahr, Jerome
Bail, Murray
Bailey, Anthony
Bailey, Charles Waldo
Bailey, F. Lee
Bailey, Paul
Bainbridge, Beryl
Baird, Thomas
Baker, Elliott
Baker, Howard
Baker, Lucinda
Baker, Peter
Ball, Brian N.
Banks, Russell
Banville, John
Barba, Harry
Barber, Benjamin
Bardis, Panos D.
Barich, Bill
Barker, A.L.
Barker, Dennis
Barker, Garry
Barker, George
Barker, Pat
Barkin, Carol
Barlay, Stephen
Barnes, Julian
Barnett, Correlli
Barr, Densil
Barr, Patricia
Barrio, Raymond
Barris, Chuck
Barry, Clive
Barry, Jane
Barstow, Stan
Bart, Peter
Barth, John
Barthelme, Donald
Barthelme, Frederick
Batchelor, David
Batchelor, John
Batchelor, John Calvin
Bates, (Sir) Darrell
Bates, Peter Watson
Baumbach, Jonathan
Bawden, Nina
Bax, Martin
Baxter, John
Baybars, Taner
Bayer, William
Bayley, John
Beach, Edward L.
Beagle, Peter S.
Beattie, Ann
Beatty, Patricia
Beaty, David
Beausay, Florence E.
Beaver, Bruce
Bechervaise, John Mayston
Becker, Jillian
Becker, Stephen
Beckett, Samuel
Beckham, Barry
Beckwith, Lillian
Beddington, Roy
Bedford, Sybille

Beekman, Allan
Beer, Patricia
Behr, Edward
Bell, Charles G.
Bell, Madison Smartt
Bell, Quentin
Bellow, Saul
Bemmy, Karen
Benasutti, Marion
Bence-Jones, Mark
Benchley, Peter
Benedict, Rex
Benedictus, David
Bennett, Hal
Benton, Patricia
Beresford-Howe, Constance
Berge Carol
Berger, John
Berger, Thomas
Bergonzi, Bernard
Berkoff, Steven
Bermant, Chaim
Bernard, Kenneth
Bernstein, Burton
Berry, Francis
Berry, James
Berry, Ron
Berry, Wendell
Bhatia, Jamunadevi
Bickham, Jack M.
Billing, Graham
Billington, Rachel
Bingham, Charlotte
Bingham, Sally
Bingley, David Ernest
Birmingham, Stephen
Birney, Earle
Birstein, Ann
Bishop, Claire Huchet
Blackwood, Caroline
Blaise, Clark
Blamires, Harry
Blatty, William
Blechman, Burt
Blishen, Edward
Block, Lawrence
Block, Thomas H.
Blond, Anthony
Blood, Marje
Bloomfield, Anthony John
    Westgate
Blume, Judy
Blythe, Ronald
Boardman, Arthur
Bodett, Thomas Edward
Bodsworth, Fred
Bogarde, Dirk
Bogner, Norman
Bogue, Lucile Maxfield
Bond, C.G.
Bond, Michael
Boore, Walter Hugh
Booth, Martin
Borland, Kathryn
Boston, L.M.
Bourjaily, Vance
Bowen, John
Bowen, Robert O.
Bowering, George
Bowering, Marilyn
Bowers, John
Bowles, Paul
Boyd, John
Boyd, William
Boylan, Clare
Boyle, Kay
Bradbury, Malcolm
Bradbury, Ray
Braddon, Russell
Bradley, David
Bradley, Marion Zimmer
Bragg, Melvyn
Braithwaite, E.R.

Bramble, Forbes
Brand, Mona
Brandi, John
Branfield, John
Brata, Sasthi
Bratby, John Randall
Braithwaite, Errol
Brashler, William
Brawley, Ernest
Braybrooke, Neville
Brennan, Joseph Payne
Brenneman, Helen Good
Breslin, Jimmy
Bretnor, Reginald
Brewster, Elizabeth
Bridgers, Sue Ellen
Briley, John
Brink, André
Briskin, Jacqueline
Bristow, Robert O'Neil
Brock, Edwin
Broderick, John
Brodeur, Paul
Brodkey, Harold
Bromell, Henry
Bromige, David
Broner, E.M.
Brooke, Dinah
Brooke-Rose, Christine
Brookner, Anita
Brooks, Gwendolyn
Brooks, Jeremy
Brooks, Richard
Brophy, Brigid
Brossard, Chandler
Broughton, T. Alan
Brown, George Mackay
Brown, Jamie
Brown, Kenneth H.
Brown, Michael Douglas
Brown, Rita Mae
Browne, Howard
Brownstein, Michael
Bruchac, Joseph
Bruff, Nancy
Brunner, John
Bryans, Robin
Bryant, Dorothy
Buchan, Tom
Buchanan, George
Buchanan, Marie
Buckman, Peter
Budbill, David
Budd, Lillian
Buechner, Frederick
Bukowski, Charles
Bulla, Clyde Robert
Buller, Herman
Bullins, Ed
Bullock, Michael
Bulmer, Henry Kenneth
Burgess, Anthony
Burke, John
Burke, Kenneth
Burland, Brian
Burley, W.J.
Burmeister, Jon
Burnett, Hallie
Burns, Alan
Burns, Carol
Burns, Joan Simpson
Burnshaw, Stanley
Burroughs, William S
Burroway, Janet Gay
Burt, Nathaniel
Burton, Elizabeth
Burton, Anthony
Busch, Frederick
Busch, Niven
Buscheister, Patt
Butler, Richard
Buzo, Alexander
Byatt, A.S.

Byrne, Robert
Cacciatore, Vera
Caidin, Martin
Caillou, Alan
Calder-Marshall, Arthur
Calisher, Hortense
Callaghan, Morley
Callard, Maurice
Callison, Brian
Callow, Philip
Cameron, Silver Donald
Campbell, Judith
Campbell, Ramsey
Candy, Edward
Caputi, Anthony
Card, Orson Scott
Carew, Jan Rynveld
Carey, Ernestine Gilbreth
Carey, Peter
Carkeet, David
Carlino, Lewis John
Carlson, Andrew R.
Carlson, Ron
Carr, Glynn
Carr, J.L.
Carr, Jess
Carr, Margaret
Carrier, Warren
Carroll, Gladys Hasty
Carroll, James
Carter, Angela
Carter, Felicity
Casey, Kevin
Casper, Leonard
Cassill, R.V.
Causley, Charles
Caute, David
Cavallo, Diana
Cave, Emma
Cavendish, Richard
Chaffin, Lillie D.
Chamberlin, Mary
Chantler, David T.
Chapman, Ronald
Chapman-Mortimer, William
   Charles
Charles, Gerda
Charlier, Roger Henri
Charlwood, D.E.
Charteris, Leslie
Charters, Samuel
Charyn, Jerome
Chastain, Thomas
Cheavens, Frank
Cheever, Susan
Cheng, James K.
Cherry, Kelly
Childress, Alice
Chisholm, Matt
Chitty, Susan
Christesen, C.B.
Christian, Carol Cathay
Christopher, John
Christopher, Matt
Cicellis, Kay
Clancy, Laurie
Clark, Ann Nolan
Clark Eleanor
Clark, Eric
Clark, Laurence
Clark, LaVerne Harrell
Clark, Margaret Goff
Clark, Tom
Clarke, Austin C.
Clarke, Hugh Vincent
Clavell, James
Cleary, Jon
Cleaver, Vera
Cleeve, Brian
Clemo, Jack
Clewes, Dorothy
Clifford, Derek
Clifton, Lucille

Clutterbuck, Richard
Coates, Austin
Codrescu, Andrei
Coetzee, J.M.
Coffin, Tristram
Cohen, Leonard
Cohen, Matt
Cohen, Stanley I.
Cole, Barry
Cole, John Alfred
Cole, Sheila R
Colegate, Isabel
Coleman, Terry
Collier, Peter
Collier, Richard
Collier, Zena
Collings, I.J.
Collins, Jackie
Collins, Larry
Collinson, Laurence
Collis, Louise
Colquhoun, Keith
Colter, Cyrus
Comfort, Alex
Comfort, Iris Tracy
Condon, Richard
Connell, Evan S., Jr.
Conner, Rearden
Connolly, Ray
Connors, Bruton
Conot, Robert E.
Conquest, Ned
Conran, Shirley
Cook, David
Cook, Glen
Cook, Lennox
Cook, Robin
Coomer, Joc
Cooper, Bryan
Cooper, Dominic
Cooper, Lettice
Cooper, Susan Mary
Cooper, William
Coover, Robert
Cope, Jack
Coppel, Alfred
Copper, Basil
Corbett, Scott
Cordell, Alexander
Coren, Alan
Corey, Paul
Cormier, Robert
Corrington, John William
Corso, Gregory
Cosh, Mary
Cotterell, Geoffrey
Coulter, Stephen
Couper, J.M.
Courter, Gay
Cowan, Peter
Cowasjee, Saros
Cowlin, Dorothy
Cox, Richard
Crane, Caroline
Crawford, Christian
Crawley, Aidan
Creeley, Robert
Cregan, David
Crews, Harry
Crichton, Michael
Crichton, Robert
Crick, Donald Herbert
Cronin, Anthony
Crosby, John
Cross, Ian
Crowther, Harold Francis
Crozier, Brian
Cruickshank, Charles Greig
Crump, Barry
Cuddon, J.A.
Cullingford, Guy
Curteis, Ian
Curtis, Tony

Cussler, Clive
Cutler, Ivor
Dabydeen, Cyril
Dahl, Roald
Daley, Robert
Daly, Leo
Daly, Maureen
Danby, Mary
Daniels, Norman A.
Das, Kamala
Dathorne, O.R.
Davenport, Guy
Davenport, Marcia
Davidson, Basil
Davidson, Lionel
Davidson, Sol M.
Davies, Hunter
Davies, L.P.
Davies, Margaret
Davies, Robertson
Davin, Dan
Davis, Burke
Davis, Christopher
Davis, Hope Hale
Davis, Julia
Davis, Margaret Thomson
Davis, Patti
Davis, Richard
Davis, Robert Prunier
Dawe, Bruce
Dawson, Jennifer
Day, Stacey B.
DeAndrea, William L.
DeBlasis, Celeste
de Boissière, Ralph
de Camp, L. Sprague
de Chair, Somerset
Deford, Frank
Deighton, Len
Deiss, Joseph Jay
Delano, Anthony
Delbanco, Nicholas F.
Delillo, Don
Delius, Anthony
Demetillo, Ricaredo
deMille, Richard
Demott, Benjamin
Dempsey, David
Denholm, David
Denker, Henry
Dennis, Nigel
Desai, Anita
de St. Jorre, John
Desani, G.V.
Dethier, Vincent G.
de Trevino, Elizabeth
Deveraux, Jude
Devlin, Anne
De Vries, Peter
de Vries, Rachel
DeWeese, Gene
Dewhurst, Keith
D'Hondt, John Patrick
Dibble, J. Birney
DiCerto, J.J.
Dick, Kay
Dickens, Monica
Dickey, James
Dickinson, Peter
Didion, Joan
Dilke, Caroline
Dillard, Annie
Dillard, R.H.W.
Dillon, Eilis
Dintenfass, Mark
di Prima, Diane
Disch, Thomas M.
Dixon, Roger
Dixon, Stephen
Dobyns, Stephen
Doctorow, E.L.
Dodd, Susan
Dodd, Wayne D.

Dodson, Daniel B.
Donleavy, J.P.
Donovan, John
Doubtfire, Dianne
Downs, Robert
Doyle, Richard
Drabble, Margaret
Drake, Albert Dee
Drake, David A.
Draper, Alfred Ernest
Drewe, Robert
Drexler, Rosalyn
Driver, Charles Jonathan
Drucker, Peter
Drury, Allen
Dubus, Andre
Duffy, Maureen
Duke, Madelaine
Duncan, David
Duncan, Lois
Dundy, Elaine
Dunmore, Spencer S.
Dunn, Nell
Dunne, John Gregory
Dunnett, Alastair MacTavish
Dupre, Catherine
Durham, Marilyn
Durrell, Gerald
Durrell, Lawrence
Dutton, Geoffrey
Dyer, Charles
Dyer, Wayne W.
Dykeman, Wilma
Earnshaw, Anthony
Easmon, R. Sarif
Eastlake, William
Easton, Robert
Eaton, Charles Edward
Ebbett, Eve
Ebersohn, Wessel
Ebert, Alan
Edmonds, Walter D.
Edwards, Anne
Edwards, Page, Jr.
Effinger, George Alec
Egan, Ferol
Egbuna, Obi
Ehle, John
Eigner, Larry
Eisenberg, Larry
Ekwensi, Cyprian
Elbert, Joyce
Elegant, Robert
Elkin, Stanley
Elliot, Brian Robinson
Elliott, Janice
Elliott, Sumner Locke
Ellis, Bret Easton
Ellis, Ella T.
Ellis, Mark
Ellis, Royston
Ellison, Harlan
Ellison, Ralph
Elmslie, Kenward
Elstob, Peter
Ely, David
Emecheta, Buchi
Emerson, David
Engel, Monroe
England, Barry
Engle, Eloise
Engle, Paul
English, Brenda H.
English, Isobel
Enright, D.J.
Epp, Margaret Agnes
Epstein, Seymour
Erdrich, Louise
Erhard, Tom
Eri, Vincent
Erickson, Steve
Erno, Richard B.
Esler, Anthony James

Lykiard, Alexis
Lynam, Shevawn
Lynds, Dennis
Lynn, Jonathan
Lynne, James Broom
Lytle, Andrew
Maas, Peter
Macauley, Robie
MacBeth, George
MacGibbon, Jean
Mackworth, Cecily
MacLennan, Hugh
Macleod, Alison
Macleod, Alistair
MacLeod, Sheila
MacMahon, Bryan Michael
Macvean, Jean
Macvicar, Angus
Madden, David
Maddocks, Margaret
Maddy, Y.A.
Maguire, Michael
Mailer, Norman
Mairowitz, David
Major, Clarence
Malgonkar, Manohar
Mallik, Umesh
Malone, Michael
Malouf, David
Malpass, Eric
Manchester, William
Mandel, Oscar
Manfred, Frederick Feikema
Mangione, Jerre
Mankowitz, Wolf
Mann, Anthony
Mann, Peggy
Manning, Rosemary
Markandaya, Kamala
Markfield, Wallace
Marks, Stan
Markson, David M.
Markus, Julia
Marlatt, Daphne
Marlow, Joyce
Marlowe, Derek
Maron, Margaret
Marr-Johnson, Diana
Marshall, Elizabeth Margaret
Marshall, Paule
Marshall, Tom
Martelli, George Ansley
Martin, David
Martin, Judith
Martin, Rhona
Martin, Robert Bernard
Martin, Valerie
Martin, Victoria Carolyn
Martini, Teri
Marx, Arthur
Marzani, Carl
Mason, Bobbie Ann
Mason, Philip
Mason, Ronald Charles
Massie, Allan
Masterton, Graham
Mathers, Peter
Mathew, Ray
Mathis, Roland
Mathis, Sharon Bell
Matthew, Christopher C.F.
Matthews, Jack
Matthews, Patricia
Matthews, Thomas Stanley
Matthiessen, Peter
Mavor, Elizabeth
Maxwell, William
May, Derwent
Maynard, Nan
McCabe, Eugene
McCarry, Charles
McCarthy, Mary
McCaughrean, Geraldine

McClure, James
McClure, Michael
McConkey, James Rodney
McConnell, J.D.R.
McCord, David
McCount, James
McCullough, Colleen
McCutchan, Philip
McCutcheon, Hugh Davie-Martin
McDonald, Gregory
McDowell, Edwin Stewart
McDowell, Michael
McElroy, Colleen J.
McElroy, Joseph
McEwan, Ian
McFadden, David
McGahern, John
McGarrity, Mark
McGill, Angus
McGrath, Thomas M.
McGraw, Eloise Jarvis
McGuane, Thomas
McIlvanney, Mark
McInerny, Jay
McInerny, Ralph Mathew
McKillip, Patricia
McLean, Allan Campbell
McManus, Kay
McMurtry, Larry
McNair, Kate
McNamara, Eugene Joseph
McNeill, Janet
McNeish, James
McPherson, James A.
McQuay, Mike
McWhirter, George
Meacham, Ellis K.
Mead, Shepherd
Megged, Aharon
Meggs, Brown
Mehta, Ved
Meinke, Peter
Melchior, Ib
Meltzer, David
Merrill, James
Metcalf, John
Mewshaw, Michael
Meyer, Michael
Meyerowitz, Patricia
Michaels, Fern
Michaels, Leonard
Michel, Milton Scott
Michener, James A.
Middleton, O.E.
Middleton, Stanley
Millar, George
Miller, Arthur
Miller, Christian
Miller, Hugh
Miller, Jim Wayne
Miller, Orlo
Mills, James
Mills, Mervyn
Millum, Trevor
Millward, Eric
Milne, John
Milton, John R.
Minghella, Anthony
Minot, Stephen
Minot, Susan
Minshall, Vera
Mirabelli, Eugene, Jr.
Mirsky, Mark
Mitchell, Adrian
Mitchell, Elyne
Mitchell, Joseph
Mitchell, Julian
Mitchell, W.O.
Mitchison, Naomi
Mitgang, Herbert
Mitson, Eileen N.
Mo, Timothy
Moat, John

Moggach, Deborah
Momaday, N. Scott
Montague, John
Montgomery, Marion
Moorcock, Michael
Moore, Barbara
Moore, Brian
Moore, Raylyn
Moreau, David Merlin
Morey, Walt
Morressy, John
Morris, Desmond
Morris, Jean
Morris, Katharine
Morris, Michael
Morris, Willie
Morris, Wright
Morrison, Theodore
Morrison, Toni
Morritt, Hope
Mortimer, John
Mortimer, Penelope
Mosley, Leonard
Mosley, Nicholas
Moss, Rose
Moynahan, Julian
Mphahlele, Ezekiel
Mucha, Jiri
Mueller, Robert Emmett
Muggeson, Margaret Elizabeth
Mukherjee, Bharati
Muller, Robert
Mullins, Edwin
Mullins, Helene
Mundis, Hester
Munonye, John
Munro, Alice
Murdoch, Iris
Murphy, Lawrence Agustus
Murphy, Sylvia
Murphy, Walter Francis
Murray, Albert
Murray, Linda
Murray, Rona
Murray, William Hutchinson
Murry, Colin Middleton
Musser, Joe
Musto, Barry
Myers, John Myers
Nahal, Chaman
Naipaul, Shiva
Naipaul, V.S.
Najarian, Peter
Narayan, R.K.
Nassauer, Rudolf
Nathan, David
Nathan, Norman
Nathan, Robert
Naughton, Bill
Naylor, Gloria
Naylor, Phyllis Reynolds
Neame, Alan John
Neely, William J.
Neighbour, Ralph W., Sr.
Nelson, Cordner
Nelson, Ray
Nemerov, Howard
Neugeboren, Jay
Newby, P.H.
Newman, Andrea
Newman, Charles
Newman, Coleman J.
Newman, Daisy
Newman, Edwin
Newman, Gordon F.
Newton, Norman Lewis
Ngugi, J.T.
Nichols, John
Nichols, Ruth
Nicholson, Hubert
Nicol, Abioseh
Nicolaysen, Bruce
Nicole, Christopher

Nissenson, Hugh
Nkosi, Lewis
Noakes, Vivien
Noel-Hume, Ivor
Nolan, Christopher
Norman, Marsha
Norris, Phyllis Irene
North, Elizabeth
Nott, Kathleen
Nourse, Alan E.
Novak, Michael
Nowra, Louis
Noyes, Stanley
Nuttall, Jeff
Nuwer, Hank
Nwapa, Flora
Nye, Robert
Oakes, Philip
Oates, Joyce Carol
O'Brien, Edna
O'Brien, Tim
Odaga, Asenath
O'Daniel, Janet
O'Dell, Scott
O'Donovan, Joan Mary
O'Faolain, Julia
O'Faolain, Sean
Okara, Gabriel
Oldsey, Bernard S.
Oleck, Howard L.
Olsen, Tillie
Olson, Toby
Ondaatje, Michael
Onyeama, Dillibe
Opie, June
Ordish, George
O'Rourke, Frank
O'Rourke, William
Osbourne, Ivor
Osofisan, Femi
Owen, Roderic
Oz, Amos
Ozick, Cynthia
Pace, Eric
Padfield, Peter
Padgett, Ron
Paetro, Maxine
Page, Geoff
Page, Kathy
Painter, Charlotte
Paley, Grace
Palmer, C. Everard
Palmer, Carey
Palmer, Diana
Park, Ruth
Parker, Gordon
Parker, Richard
Parker, Robert B.
Parkes, Roger Graham
Parkin, Molly
Parkinson, Cyril Northcote
Parks, Gordon
Parks, Tim
Parotti, Phillip
Parry, Hugh Jones
Pascal, Francine
Patchett, Mary Elwyn
Paterson, Neil
Patten, Brian
Patterson, Orlando
Paulsen, Gary
Pawel, Ernst
Payne, Donald Gordon
Pearce, Brian Lovis
Pearce, Mary E.
Pearson, Bill
Pearson, Diane
Pearson, John (1)
Pearson, John (2)
Peck, Robert Newton
Peden, William
Peel, H.M.
Peeples, Edwin A.

Pemberton, Margaret
Pendleton, Don
Percy, Douglas C.
Percy, Walker
Perkins, Michael
Perutz, Kathrin
Peterkiewicz, Jerzy
Peters, Lenrie
Petrakis, Harry Mark
Petry, Ann
Phelps, Gilbert
Phillips, Caryl
Phillips, James Atlee
Phillips, Jayne Anne
Phillips, Louis Cristopher
Phillips, Robert
Phillpotts, Adelaide
Phipson, Jean
Pickering, Robert Easton
Pierce, Joe E.
Piercy, Marge
Pincher, Chapman
Pinchot, Ann
Pinner, David
Pirie, David
Plagemann, Bentz
Plain, Belva
Plante, David
Plater, Alan
Plunkett, James
Podgórecki, Adam
Pohl, Frederik
Poland, Marguerite
Polland, Madeleine A.
Polley, Judith Anne
Pollock, Seton
Poole, Josephine
Popham, Hugh
Porteous, Leslie
Posner, Richard
Potok, Chaim
Potter, Dennis
Pournelle, Jerry
Powe, Bruce
Powell, Anthony
Powell, Padgett
Powell, Talmage
Powers, Anne
Powers, J.F.
Pownall, David
Poyer, Joe
Pratt, John Clark
Prebble, John
Price, Reynolds
Price, Stanley
Price, Victor
Priest, Christopher
Prince, Peter
Prior, Allan
Pritchett, (Sir) V.S.
Proctor, George W.
Prose, Francine
Prosser, Harold Lee
Pryce-Jones, David
Pryor, Adel
Puechner, Ray
Pullein-Thompson, Dian
Pulvertaft, Lalage
Purdy, James
Purser, Philip
Puzo, Mario
Pye, Michael
Pye, Virginia
Pynchon, Thomas
Quantrill, Malcom
Quinn, Derry
Radcliff-Umstead, Douglas
Raddall, Thomas Head
Rae, Doris
Rae, Hugh C.
Rae, John Malcolm
Ransley, Peter
Rao, Rajo

Raphael, Frederick
Rathbone, Julian
Rathmell, Neil
Ratner, Rochelle
Raucher, Herman
Raven, Simon
Raworth, Tom
Ray, David
Raymond, Diana Joan
Raymond, Patrick
Rayner, William
Read, Miss
Read, Piers Paul
Read, Sylvia Joan
Reaver, J. Russell
Rechy, John
Redgrove, Peter
Reed, Ishmael
Reed, Kit
Reed, Rex
Reeman, Douglas
Rees, Barbara
Rees, David Bartlett
Reeve, F.D.
Reid, Meta Mayne
Reid, Vic
Reile, Louis
Reilly, Robert Thomas
Reveley, Edith
Reyburn, Wallace
Reynolds, William J.
Rhodes, Anthony
Rice, Anne
Richard, Adrienne
Richardson, Henry V.M.
Richardson, Jack
Richie, Donald
Richler, Mordecai
Richmond, Roe
Richter, Harvena
Ricketts, Ralph Robert
Riding, Laura
Rigoni, Orlando
Riley, Dick
Riley, Madeleine
Robbards, Karen
Robbins, Harold
Robbins, Tom
Roberts, Denys
Roberts, Keith
Roberts, Kevin
Roberts, Nora
Robertson, Keith
Robinson, Derek
Robinson, Marilynne
Robinson, Philip
Robinson, Robert
Robison, Mary
Roche, Paul
Roddy, Lee
Rodgers, Mary
Rohrbach, Peter Thomas
Roiphe, Anne Richardson
Rooke, Daphne
Root, William Pitt
Rosen, Gerald
Ross, Sam
Ross, Sinclair
Ross-Macdonald, Malcolm
Rossner, Judith
Rosten, Leo
Roth, Henry
Roth, Philip
Rothenstein, (Sir) John
Rothweiler, Paul R.
Roueche, Berton
Rounds, Glen
Rovit, Earl
Rowbotham, David
Rowse, A.L.
Roy, Archie E.
Rubens, Bernice
Rubin, Larry

Ruhen, Olaf
Rule, Jane
Rumaker, Michael
Rumens, Carol
Rush, Christopher
Rushdie, Salman
Rushing, Jane Gilmore
Russell, Ray
Russell Taylor, Elizabeth
Ryan, William
Sachs, Judith
Saddler, K. Allen
Sahgal, Nayantara
St. John, Nicole
St. John, Robert
St. Omer, Garth
Sakol, Jeannie
Salazar, Rachel
Sale, Richard
Salinger, J.D.
Salinger, Pierre
Salkey, Andrew
Sambrot, William Anthony
Samelson, William
Sandburg, Helga
Sanders, Ed
Sanders, James Edward
Sanders, Lawrence
Sandford, Jeremy
Saroyan, Aram
Sarton, May
Sasser, Charles W.
Saunders, Jean
Sava, George
Savery, Constance Winifred
Sayles, John
Scannell, Vernon
Scarfe, Wendy Elizabeth
Schaeffer, Susan Fromberg
Schevill, James
Schlee, Ann
Schlossstein, Steven
Schoen, Barbara
Scholefield, Alan
Schott, Penelope
Schreiner, Samuel
Schroeder, Andreas
Schulberg, Budd
Schulze, Hertha
Schuyler, James
Schwamm, Ellen
Schwartz, Barry
Schwartz, Lynne Sharon
Scott, Bill
Scott, Gavin
Seaman, Sylvia Sybil
Searls, Hank
Sederberg, Arelo
See, Carolyn
Seelye, John
Sefton, Catherine
Segal, Erich
Segal, Harriet
Segal, Lore
Selby, Hubert, Jr.
Self, Margaret Cabell
Selvon, Samuel
Serling, Robert J.
Servadio, Gaia
Seth, Vikram
Sethna, M.J.
Seward, William W., Jr.
Seymour, Alan
Seymour, Miranda
Shadbolt, Maurice
Shaffer, Peter
Shagan, Steve
Shahane, Vasant
Shange, Ntozake
Shank, Margarethe Erdahl
Shannon, Doris
Shapiro, Karl
Shapiro, Stanley

Sharp, Margery
Sharpe, Tom
Shaw, Bob
Shaw, Bynum G.
Shaw, Felicity
Shecter, Ben
Sheed, Wilfrid
Sheffield, Charles
Sheldon, Sidney
Shepard, Sam
Sherman, Steve
Sherrin, Ned
Sherry, Sylvia
Sherwin, Judith Johnson
Shine, Francis L.
Shirley, John
Shirreffs, Gordon Donald
Shobin, David
Shockley, Ann Allen
Shreve, Susan R.
Shrimsley, Bernard
Shubin, Seymour
Shulman, Irving
Shulman, Milton
Shuttle, Penelope
Sidney, Neilma
Siegel, Benjamin
Sigal, Clancy
Silko, Leslie
Sillitoe, Alan
Silman, Roberta
Sim, Katharine Phyllis
Simon, Edith
Simon, Roger L.
Simpson, N.F.
Sinclair, Olga Ellen
Singer, Isaac Bashevis
Singh, Khushwant
Sisson, C.H.
Sisson, Rosemary Anne
Skelton, Peter
Skinner, B.F.
Skvorecky, Josef
Slaughter, Carolyn
Slavitt, David
Slesar, Henry
Slosberg, Mike
Slote, Alfred
Smith, Bert Kruger
Smith, Dodie
Smith, Ella
Smith, Emma
Smith, Frederick E.
Smith, Gregory
Smith, Iain Crichton
Smith, Kathleen J.
Smith, Mark
Smith, Martin Cruz
Smith, Peter Charles Horstead
Smith, Wilbur
Smither, Elizabeth
Smithson, Alison
Snow, Helen Foster
Snow, Richard F.
Snyder, Cecil
Snyder, Zilpha Keatley
Sontag, Susan
Sorensen, Virginia
Sorrentino, Gilbert
Souster, Raymond
Southern, Terry
Soyinka, Wole
Spacks, Barry
Spann, Weldon Oma
Spark, Muriel
Speicher, Helen Ross
Spence, William John Duncan
Spencer, Colin
Spencer, Elizabeth
Spencer, Scott
Spender, (Sir) Stephen
Spielberg, Peter
Spicer, Bart

Adams, Clifton
Aird, Catherine
Albert, Marvin H.
Allbeury, Ted
Allen, Henry Wilson
Allison, Eric W.
Ames, Delano L.
Amis, Kingsley
Anderson, James
Anderson, Poul
Anthony, Evelyn
Ardies, Tom
Asimov, Isaac
Audemars, Pierre
Avallone, Michael
Babson, Marian
Ball, Doris Bell
Barnard, Robert
Barnes, Julian
Bawden, Nina
Baxt, George
Bayer, William
Behn, Noel
Benton, Kenneth
Bergman, Andrew
Bickham, Jack M.
Biggle, Lloyd, Jr.
Birmingham, Maisie
Blackburn, John
Blackstock, Charity
Blair, Walter
Blanc, Suzanne
Block, Lawrence
Bonham, Barbara
Borgenicht, Miriam
Bourquin, Paul Henry James
Branson, H.C.
Bredsdorff, Elias Lunn
Breen, Jon L.
Brennan, Joseph Payne
Brett, Michael
Brett, Simon
Browne, Howard
Bruton, Eric
Buchanan, Marie
Buckley, William F.
Burke, John
Burley, W.J.
Burns, Rex
Busby, Roger
Butler, Gwendoline
Caillou, Alan
Caird, Janet
Cameron, Lou
Candy, Edward
Carr, Glyn
Carr, Margaret
Carter, Felicity
Caudwell, Sarah
Charbonneau, Louis
Charles, Theresa
Charteris, Leslie
Chastain, Thomas
Christian, Frederick H.
Clark, Douglas
Clark, Margaret Goff
Clarke, Anna
Cleary, Jon
Cleeve, Brian
Coburn, Andrew
Cohen, Susan
Collins, Max Allan
Compton, D.G.
Condon, Richard
Constantine, K.C.
Constiner, Merle
Cook, Robin
Cooper, Brian
Coppel, Alfred
Copper, Basil
Cosgrave, Patrick
Coulson, John H.A.
Coulson, Robert

Coulter, Stephen
Cowen, Frances
Cox, William R.
Craig, Mary
Cruickshank, Charles Greig
Crumley, James
Cullingford, Guy
Cunningham, Chet
Daniels, Dorothy
Daniels, Norman A.
Davidson, Lionel
Davies, L.P.
Davis, Dorothy Salisbury
Davis, Mildred
Davison, Geoffrey
De Andrea, William L.
Deighton, Len
Lelahaye, Michael
de la Torre, Lillian
Demaris, Ovid
Dewey, Thomas B.
Dexter, Colin
Dickinson, Peter
Diment, Adam
Disney, Dorothy Cameron
Dodge, David
Donaldson, Stephen R.
Driscoll, Peter
Drummond, June
Duke, Madelaine
Duncan, Lois
Duncan, Robert L.
Dunne, John Gregory
Dunnett, Dorothy
Durbridge, Francis
Durst, Paul
Eberhart, Mignon G.
Ebersohn, Wessel
Edmondson, G.C.
Egleton, Clive
Ehrlich, Jack
Emerson, Earl W.
Epstein, Charlotte
Erdman, Paul E.
Erskine, Margaret
Estleman, Loren D.
Estridge, Robin
Eustis, Helen
Evans, Julia
Fairburn, Eleanor
Fantoni, Barry
Fast, Howard
Fenwick, Elizabeth
Ferrars, Elizabeth
Finney, Jack
Fischer, Bruno
Fitzgerald, Nigel
Fletcher, Lucille
Floren, Lee
Follett, Ken
Forbes, Stanton
Forrest, Richard
Forsyth, Frederick
Francis, Dick
Francis, Dorothy Brenner
Fraser, (Lady) Antonia
Freedgood, Morton
Freeling, Nicolas
Freeman, Lucy
Freemantle, Brian
Fremlin, Celia
Frewer, Glyn
Fuller, Roy
Fuller, Samuel
Gadney, Reg
Gainham, Sarah
Gardner, John
Garfield, Brian
Garner, William
Garve, Andrew
Gash, Jonathan
Gaskin, Catherine
Gaston, William James

Gault, William Campbell
Gifford, Thomas
Gilbert, Michael
Gillespie, Robert B.
Gilman, Dorothy
Gilman, George G.
Goodman, Jonathan
Gordon, Gordon
Gores, Joe
Gosling, Paula
Goulart Ron
Graham, Winston
Granger, Bill
Gray, Dulcie
Grayland, Valerie
Greene, Graham
Greenleaf, Stephen
Gribble, Leonard
Haiblum, Isidore
Hall, Angus
Hallahan, William H.
Hansen, Joseph
Harcourt, Palma
Hardison, Osborne B.
Harris, Herbert
Harris, John
Harrison, Michael
Hartland, Michael
Harvey, John B.
Heald, Tim
Healey, Ben
Heilbrun, Carolyn G.
Hensley, Joe L.
Herron, Shaun
Higgins, George V.
Highsmith, Patricia
Hildick, E.W.
Hill, Reginald
Hillerman, Tony
Hilton, John Buxton
Hoch, Edward D.
Hodder-Williams, Christopher
Holt, Victoria
Hone, Joseph
Hough, S.B.
Howard, Clark
Hoyt, Richard
Hughes, Dorothy B.
Hunter, Alan
Hunter, Evan
Hunter, Jack D.
Huxley, Elspeth
Hyland, Stanley
Iams, Jack
Iannuzzi, John N.
Ingate, Mary
Isaacs, Susan
Jackman, Stuart
Jakes, John
James, P.D.
Janifer, Laurence M.
Jarvis, Frederick G.H.
Jay, Geraldine Mary
Jeffries, Roderic
Johns, Veronica Parker
Johnson, E. Richard
Johnston, Velda
Joscelyn, Archie
Kallen, Lucille
Kaminsky, Stuart
Kane, Henry
Kaye, M.M.
Keating, H.R.F.
Kelly, Mary
Kemelman, Harry
Kenrick, Tony
Kent, Arthur
Kenyon, Michael
Kienzle, William X.
Knight, Bernard
Knott, William C.
Knox, William
Kurland, Michael

Kyle, Duncan
Labern, Arthur
Lambert, Derek
Langton, Jane
Larson, Charles
Lathen, Emma
La Tourette, Jacqueline
Laumer, Keith
Leasor, James
Le Carré, John
Lejeune, Anthony
Lemarchand, Elizabeth
Leonard, Constance
Leonard, Elmore
Lescroart, John T.
Lewin, Michael Z.
Lewis, J.R.
Ley, Alice Chetwynd
Littell, Robert
Longmate, Norman Richard
Longrigg, Roger
Lovesey, Peter
Low, Dorothy Mackie
Luard, Nicholas
Ludlum, Robert
Lutz, John
Lyall, Gavin
Lynds, Dennis
Lyons, Arthur
MacKenzie, Donald
MacLeod, Charlotte
Mair, George Brown
Maling, Arthur
Malzberg, Barry Norman
Mann, Jessica
Markstein, George
Marlowe, Derek
Marlowe, Stephen
Maron, Margaret
Marsh, Jean
Marshall, William
Masur, Harold Q.
Mather, Berkely
Maxwell, Patricia Anne
McAuliffe, Frank
McCarthy, Shaun
McCloy, Helen
McClure, James
McConnell, J.D.R.
McCurtin, Peter
McCutcheon, Hugh
McDonald, Gregory
McDowell, Michael
McElfresh, Adeline
McGarrity, Mark
McIlvanney, William
McMullen, Mary
McShane, Mark
Meggs, Brown
Melville, James
Merwin, Sam, Jr.
Meyer, Lawrence
Meyer, Nicholas
Michael, I. D. L.
Michaels, Barbara
Michel, Milton Scott
Millar, Margaret
Millhiser, Marlys
Milne, John
Mitchell, James
Moffat, Gwen
Moore, C.L.
Moyes, Patricia
Muller, Marcia
Myers, Paul
Naha, Ed
Neely, Richard
Nevins, Francis M.
Nichols, Beverley
Nicole, Christopher
Nielsen, Helen
Nolan, William F.
Norway, Kate

Nuwer, Hank
O'Donnell, Lillian
O'Donnell, Peter
Ogilvie, Elisabeth
Ormerod, Roger
O'Rourke, Frank
Pace, Eric
Page, Emma
Palmer, Madelyn
Parker, Robert B.
Pargeter, Edith
Parry, Hugh Jones
Patterson, Henry
Payne, Laurence
Pendleton, Don
Perry, Thomas
Peters, Maureen
Phillips, James Atlee
Porter, Joyce
Posner, Richard
Potter, Jeremy
Potter, Margaret
Potts, Jean
Powell, Talmage
Powell-Smith, Vincent
Prather, Richard Scott
Price, Anthony
Prickett, Stephen
Prior, Alan
Pronzini, Bill
Pullein-Thompson, Josephine
Purtill, Richard L.
Pyle, A. M.
Rae, Hugh C.
Rafferty, S.S.
Randisi, Robert J.
Raphael, Chaim
Raphael, Rick
Rathbone, Julian
Rendell, Ruth
Riefe, Alan
Rifkin, Shepard
Roberts, Irene
Roberts, Willo Davis
Robinson, Sheila
Rook, Tony
Roos, William
Roosevelt, Elliott
Ross, Angus
Ross, Sam
Ross, Zola
Rossiter, John
Royce, Kenneth
Russell, Martin
Russell, Ray
St. John, Nicole
Sale, Richard
Sanders, Lawrence
Sasser, Charles W.
Savage, Ernest
Schofield, Sylvia Anne
Schorr, Mark
Scotti, R. A.
Selwyn, Francis
Seymour, Gerald
Seymour, Henry
Sharkey, Jack
Shaw, Felicity
Sheckley, Robert
Sherwood, John H.
Simon, Roger L.
Simpson, Dorothy
Sims, George
Siodmak, Curt
Sladek, John
Slesar, Henry
Smith, Kay Nolte
Smith, Martin Cruz
Smith, Norman Edward Mace
Smith, Shelley
Sohl, Jerry
Somerville-Large, Peter
Speed, F. Maurice

Spencer, Ross H.
Spicer, Bart
Spillane, Mickey
Stern, Richard Martin
Stewart, J.I.M.
Stewart, Mary
Storey, Margaret
Straker, J.F.
Stuart, Ian
Stubbs, Jean
Symons, Julian
Teller, Neville
Tennant, Emma
Thomas, Craig
Thomas, Ross
Thomey, Tedd
Thompson, Neil
Thomson, June
Timms, Kathleen
Treat, Lawrence
Trench, John
Trenhaile, John Stevens
Trevanian
Trevor, Elleston
Trimble, Barbara Margaret
Tripp, Miles
Trotman, Jack
Truman, Margaret
Tubb, E.C.
Tucker, Wilson
Tyre, Nedra
Uhnak, Dorothy
Underwood, Michael
Valin, Jonathan
Vance, Jack
Van De Wetering, Janwillem
van Vogt, A.E.
Wainwright, John
Wallace, F.L.
Waugh, Hillary
Webb, Jean Francis
Welcome, John
Westlake, Donald E.
Whalley, Peter
White, Lionel
Whitney, Phyllis A.
Whittington, Harry
Wiegand, William
Wilcox, Collin
Williams, David
Williams, Gordon
Willis, Ted
Willock, Colin
Wilson, Jacqueline
Winslow, Pauline Glen
Winston, Daoma
Woods, Frederick
Worboys, Anne
Wright, Stephen
Yaffe. James
Yarrow, Arnold
York, Helen
Yorke, Margaret

Historical/Romance

Acland, Alice
Aiken, Joan
Ainsworth, Patricia
Allan, Mabel Esther
Allen, Charlotte Vale
Andrews, Lucilla
Anthony, Evelyn
Arbor, Jane
Armstrong, William H.
Ashton, Elizabeth
Asquith, Nan
Avallone, Michael
Bancroft, Iris
Barr, Patricia
Barrie, Susan
Bassett, Ronald Leslie

Beardsworth, Millicent Monica
Beaty, Betty
Belfrage, Cedric
Belle, Pamela
Beresford, Elisabeth
Bevan, Gloria
Binchy, Maeve
Black, Laura
Blackmore, Jean
Blackstock, Charity
Blair, Kathryn
Blake, Stephanie
Bonham, Barbara
Borland, Kathryn
Bourquin, Paul Henry James
Bowden, Jean
Boyle, Ann
Bradford, Barbara Taylor
Bradley, Marion Zimmer
Bradshaw, Gillian
Brandewyne, Rebecca
Brent, Madeleine
Briggs, Jean
Britt, Katrina
Bromige, Iris
Brown, Sandra
Browning, Dixie Burns
Burford, Lolah
Burghley, Rose
Busbee, Shirlee
Buscheister, Patt
Butler, Gwendoline
Cadell, Elizabeth
Caird, Janet
Carr, Margaret
Carr, Robyn
Cartland, Barbara
Case, David
Chace, Isobel
Chappell, Mollie
Charles, Theresa
Clarke, Brenda
Cleeve, Brian
Cockrell, Marian
Coffman, Virginia
Cohen, Susan
Collin, Marion
Compton, D.G.
Cook, Dorothy Mary
Cookson, Catherine
Cooper, Jilly
Copper, Basil
Coulson, Juanita
Courtney, Caroline
Cowen, Frances
Craig, Mary
Crowe, Cecily
Cushman, Dan
Dailey, Janet
Danbury, Iris
Daniels, Dorothy
Darcy, Clare
Darrell, Elizabeth
Davis, Dorothy Salisbury
Debreczeny, Paul
de Camp, L. Sprague
Delinsky, Barbara
Delmar, Vin
DeWeese, Gene
Dingwell, Joyce
Dodson, Kenneth
Donnelly, Jane
Dunnett, Dorothy
Dwyer-Joyce, Alice
Dymoke, Juliet
Ebel, Suzanne
Eberhart, Mignon
Edmondson, G.C.
Edwards, Anne
Ellerbeck, Rosemary
Ellis, Julie
Elsna, Hebe
Fairburn, Eleanor

Farnes, Eleanor
Fellows, Catherine
Fink, Merton
Finley, Glenna
Fitzgerald, Valerie
Floren, Lee
Francis, Dorothy Brenner
Franken, Rose
Fuchs, Lucy
Gallagher, Patricia
Gann, Ernest K.
Garfield, Brian
Gaskin, Catherine
Gaston, William James
Gattey, Charles Neilson
Gavin, Catherine
Geach, Christine
Gellis, Roberta
Gilbert, Anna
Gladstone, Arthur M.
Glover, Judith
Gluyas, Constance
Gordon, Ethel E.
Gordon, Katherine
Gower, Iris
Graham, Winston
Grimstead, Hettie
Haines, Pamela
Hall, Marjory
Hampson, Anne
Hansen, Joseph
Hardwick, Mollie
Harris Marilyn
Harris, Rosemary
Harrison, Elizabeth
Harrod-Eagles, Cynthia
Harwood, Alice
Hastings, Brooke
Hastings, Phyllis
Heaven, Constance
Hill, Pamela
Hilton, Margery
Hintze, Naomi, A.
Hodge, Jane Aiken
Hodges, C. Walter
Hoffman, Lee
Holland, Isabelle
Holland, Sheila
Holt, Victoria
Hooper, Kay
Hoskins, Robert
Howard, Linda
Howard, Mary
Howatch, Susan
Howe, Doris
Howe, Muriel
Ibbotson, Eva
Irwin, Constance
Jakes, John
Janifer, Laurence M.
Jarman, Rosemary
Jennings, Gary
Joscelyn, Archie
Johnson, Barbara Ferry
Johnson, Susan
Kimbrough, Katheryn
Knight, Alanna
Krentz, Jayne Ann
Lafferty, R.A.
Laker, Rosalind
Larkin, Rochelle
Latham, Jean Lee
La Tourrette, Jacqueline
Lee, Elsie
Lewty, Marjorie
Ley, Alice Chetwynd
Lindsay, Rachel
Lindsey, Johanna
Llywelyn, Morgon
London, Laura
Long, Freda Margaret
Lorin, Amii
Lorrimer, Claire

Dunlop, Eileen
Dunn, Hugh Patrick
Dunn, Nell
Durack, (Dame) Mary
Durrell, Gerald
Dutton, Geoffrey
Dymoke, Juliet
Eckblad, Edith G.
Edmonds, Walter D.
Edwards, Harvey
Edwards, Monica
Ekwensi, Cyprian
Elder, Michael Aiken
Elkin, Benjamin
Elliott, Janice
Ellis, Ella T.
Ellison, Virginia Howell
Elwood, Ann
Engdahl, Sylvia L.
Ephron, Delia
Epp, Margaret Agnes
Erno, Richard B.
Espeland, Pamela
Estes, Eleanor
Ets, Marie Hall
Evans, Alan
Evans, Julia
Evans, Mari
Evansen, Virginia B.
Evarts, Hal
Evernden, Margery
Fairman, Joan Alexandra
Farley, Carol
Farley, Walter
Farmer, Penelope
Fatchen, Max
Fatio, Louise
Faulknor, Clifford Vernon
Fenner, Carol
Fenton, Edward
Figes, Eva
Fine, Anne
Fink, Augusta
Finlay, Winifred
Finnigan, Joan
Fisher, Aileen
Fisher, Leonard Everett
Fisk, Nicholas
Fitzgerald, John D.
Fleischman, Paul
Fleischman, Sid
Fleming, Alice
Flesch, Y.
Flora, James
Foley, Louise Munro
Folsom, Franklin Brewster
Fontenot, Mary Alice
Foon, Dennis
Forbes, Bryan
Forbus, Ina B.
Foreman, Michael
Forest, Antonia
Forman, Joan
Foster, Malcolm Burton
Foulds, Elfrida Vipont
Fox, M.W.
Fox, Paula
Frame, Janet
Francis, Dorothy Brenner
Fraser, (Lady) Antonia
Fraser, Conon
Frazee, Steve
Freeman, Barbara
Freeman, Bill
French, Fiona
French, Simon
Freud, Clement
Frewer, Glyn
Friermood, Elisabeth H.
Fritz, Jean
Fry, Rosalie K.
Fuchs, Lucy
Fuller, Roy

Fyson, J.G.
Galbraith, Jean
Gannett, Ruth Stiles
Gard, Joyce
Gardam, Jane
Garden, Nancy
Gardner, Richard A.
Garfield, Leon
Garner, Alan
Garnett, Eve C.R.
Garnett, Richard
Gasperini, Jim
Gathorne-Hardy, Jonathan
Gault, William Campbell
Gay, Kathlyn R.
Gee, Maurice
Geisart, Arthur
Gentle, Mary
Gentleman, David
George, Jean Craighead
Geras, Adele
Gessner, Lynne
Gibson, Charles E.
Gilman, Dorothy
Giovanni, Nikki
Gliewe, Unada G.
Glovach, Linda
Godden, Rumer
Goldman, William
Goodacre, Elizabeth Jane
Gordon, Ethel
Gordon, Giles
Gordon, John
Gould, Jean R.
Grace, Patricia
Graham, Bob
Graham, John
Graham, Lorenz
Grayland, Valerie
Greaves, Margaret
Green, Roger James
Greene, Bette
Greene, Constance C.
Greene, Graham
Greenfield, Eloise
Greenwood, Ted
Gregor, Arthur
Griffith, Helen V.
Griffiths, Helen
Grohskopf, Bernice
Guinness, Bryan
Guthrie, A.B.,Jr.
Guy, Rosa
Hahn, Mary Downing
Halam, Ann
Haley, Gail E.
Hall, Aylmer
Hall, Donald
Hall, Lynn
Hall, Marjory
Hall, Willis
Hallin, Emily Watson
Halvorson, Marilyn
Hamilton, Mary
Hamilton, Virginia
Hammond Innes, Ralph
Hampton, Christopher
Hamre, Leif
Hanley, Clifford
Hansen, Joyce
Hanson, Joan
Hardcastle, Michael
Harding, Lee
Harris, Christie
Harris, Geraldine
Harris, John
Harris, Marilyn
Harris, Rosemary
Harrison, Harry
Harrison, Sarah
Harvey, John B.
Harwood, David
Haugaard, Erik

Hautzig, Esther
Hawes, Judy
Hawthorne, Jennie
Hayden, Eric William
Hays, Wilma Pitchford
Haywood, Carolyn
Heath, Veronica
Heaven, Constance
Heckelmann, Charles N.
Hedderwick, Mairi
Heerwagen, Paul K.
Hegeler, Sten
Heide, Florence Parry
Hein, Lucille Eleanor
Henri, Adrian
Henry, Marguerite
Hentoff, Nat
Herrmanns, Ralph
Hewett, Anita
Higdon, Hal
Highwater, Jamake
Hildick, E.W.
Hill, Douglas
Hill, Elizabeth Starr
Hill, Lorna
Hill, Susan
Hillerman, Tony
Hinckley, Helen
Hinton, S.E.
Hintze, Naomi A.
Hoban, Russell
Hochman, Sandra
Hodges, C. Walter
Hodges, Margaret
Hoff, Syd
Hoffmann, Peggy
Hogarth, Grace
Hogner, Dorothy Childs
Holland, Cecelia
Holland, Isabelle
Hollander, John
Holman, Felice
Holt, Michael
Holyer, Ernie
Hope, Christopher
Hope-Simpson, Jacynth
Hopkins, Antony
Hopkins, Lee Bennett
Horgan, Paul
Horvath, Betty
Hough, Charlotte
Hough, Richard
Houghton, Eric
Houston, James A.
Howe, Fanny
Howe, James
Hoyle, Geoffrey
Hughes, Monica
Hughes, Shirley
Hughes, Ted
Hull, Eleanor
Hunkin, Tim Mark Trelawney
Hunt, Bernice Kohn
Hunt, Irene
Hunt, Patricia Joan
Hunt, Peter
Hunter, Evan
Hunter, Kristin
Hunter, Mollie
Hunter, Norman
Hurwitz, Johanna
Hutchins, Hazel J.
Hutchins, Pat
Hyde, Michael
Ibbotson, Eva
Ilsley, Velma E.
Irwin, Constance
Jackson, Rosemary Elizabeth
Jacobs, Helen Hull
Jaffe, Rona
Janes, J. Robert
Jauss, Anne Marie
Jeffries, Roderic

Jennings, Gary
Jennings, Paul
Jeppson, J.O.
Johnson, Annabell
Johnson, James Ralph
Jones, Adrienne
Jones, Diana Wynne
Jones, Mary Voell
Jones, Raymond F.
Joose, Barbara M.
Jordan, June
Joscelyn, Archie
Joslin, Sesyle
Judah, Aaron
Juster, Norton
Kamm, Josephine
Katz, Bobbi
Katz, Welwyn
Kay, Mara
Kaye, Geraldine
Keesing, Nancy
Keith, Harold
Kelleher, Victor
Kelley, Leo P.
Kellogg, Steven
Kemp, Gene
Kendall, Carol
Keneally, Thomas
Kennedy, Richard
Kennemore, Tim
Kenward, Jean
Kerr, Judith
Kerr, M.E.
Kesselman, Wendy
Kilworth, Garry
Kimenye, Barbara
Kimmel, Eric A.
Kindred, Wendy
King, Clive
Kingman, Lee
King-Smith, Dick
Klein, Robin
Knight, Frank
Knott, William C.
Knowles, Anne
Knudsen, Margrethe June
Knudson, R.R.
Konigsburg, E.L.
Konkle, Janet Everest
Korfker, Dena
Kotzwinkle, William
Krantz, Hazel
Krasilovsky, Phyllis
Kraus, Joanna Halpert
Kraus, Robert
Krauss, Ruth
Kudian, Mischa
Kumin, Maxine
Kushner, Donn
Kuskin, Karla
Lamplugh, Lois
Landis, J.D.
Landon, Lucinda
Lane, Carolyn
Langton, Jane
Lanier, Sterling E.
Latham, Jean Lee
Laughlin, Florence
Lavin, Mary
Lawrence, Louise
Lawrence, Steven C.
Lee, Benjamin
Lee, Mildred
Lee, Tanith
Leeson, Robert
Le Guin, Ursula
Leibold, Jay
Leitch, Adelaide
L'Engle, Madeleine
Lent, Blair
Leonard, Constance
Lester, Julius
Levin, Betty

Levitin, Sonia
Levoy, Myron
Lewis, Claudia Louise
Lewis, Janet
Lewis, Judith Mary
Lewis, Thomas P
Lexau, Joan M.
Lifton, Betty Jean
Liggett, Thomas
Lillington, Kenneth
Lingard, Joan
Lipsyte, Robert
Lionni, Leo
List, Ilka
Little, Jean
Littledale, Freya
Lively, Penelope
Livingston, Myra Cohn
Llewelyn Owens, Joan
Lloyd, Marjorie
Lobel, Arnold
Locke, Elsie
Loeper, John J.
Lord, Douglas
Lord, John Vernon
Lorrimer, Clair
Lowry, Lois
Lucas, Celia
Lunn, Janet
Lurie, Alison
Lynds, Dennis
Lyon, Elinor
Lyons, Dorothy Marawee
MacBeth, George
MacDonald, Caroline
MacGibbon, Jean
MacGuire, Gregory
MacIntyre, Elisabeth
Mackay, Claire
MacLachlan, Patricia
MacLeod, Ellen Jane
MacMahon, Bryan Michael
MacPherson, Margaret
Macvicar, Angus
Maddock, R.B.
Maestro, Giulio
Magee, Wes
Mahy, Margaret
Major, Kevin
Mamet, David
Mango, Karin N.
Mann, Peggy
Manning, Rosemary
Maples, Evelyn Palmer
Mark, Jan
Marko, Katherine D.
Markoosie
Marlow, Joyce
Marsh, Jean
Marshall, James
Martin, David
Martin, Marjorie
Martini, Teri
Marvin, Blanche
Mason, Philip
Matthews, Patrica
Mattingley, Cristobel
Mayhar, Ardath
Maynard, Christopher
Mayne, William
Mazer, Norma Fox
McCaba, Eugene
McCall, Edith
McCaughrean, Geraldine
McCaughren, Tom
McCloskey, Robert
McClung, Robert Marshall
McClure, Gillian Mary
McCord, David
McDonnell, Lois Eddy
McElfresh, Adeline
McGough, Roger
McGrath, Thomas M.

McGraw, Eloise Jarvis
McGregor, Iona
McKee, David
McKillip, Patricia
McKinley, Robin
McLeish, Kenneth
McManus, Kay
McNeil, Florence
McNeill, Janet
McNulty, Faith
McQuay, Mike
Meeks, Esther MacBain
Mellanby, Kenneth
Melton, David
Meltzer, David
Melwood, Mary
Melzack, Ronld
Merriam, Eve
Merrill, Jean
Meyers, Susan
Middleton, O.E.
Miklowitz, Gloria D.
Miles, Betty
Miller, Arthur
Miller, Frances A.
Milton, Joyce
Minarik, Else H.
Mitchell, Elyne
Mitchison, Naomi
Moore, Patrick
Moorhead, Diana
Moray Williams, Ursula
Morey, Walt
Morgan, Alison M.
Morgan, Helen
Morressy, John
Morris, Jean
Morriss, Frank
Moss, Peter
Moss, Robert
Mowat, Farley
Muehl, Lois Baker
Munsch, Robert
Murphy, Jill
Murphy, Shirley R.
Murray, Frances
Musgrave, Susan
Myers, Walter Dean
Naughton, Bill
Naylor, Phyllis Reynolds
Needle, Jan
Neumeyer, Peter
Neville, Emily Cheney
Nevin, Evelyn C.
Newby, P.H.
Newman, Daisy
Newman, Sharan
Newton, Suzanne
Nichols, Ruth
Nicoll, Helen
Nimmo, Jenny
Nixon, Joan Lowry
Norman, Lilith
Norris, Phyllis Irene
North, Joan Marian
Norton, Andre Alice
Norton, Mary
Norway, Kate
Nourse, Alan E.
Nwapa, Flora
Nye, Robert
Oakley, Graham
O'Brien, Anne Sibley
O'Brien, Edna
Odaga, Asenath
O'Daniel, Janet
O'Dell, Scott
Ogilvie, Elisabeth
O'Gorman, Ned
Okoro, Anezi
Oldfield, Jenny
Oldfield, Pamela
Olmsted, Robert W.

Oneal, Elizabeth
O'Neill, Judith
Opie, Iona
Orgel, Doris
Ormondroyd, Edward
O'Shea, Pat
Ovard, Glen F.
Overton, Jenny
Owen, Gareth
Pack, Robert
Palmer, C. Everard
Papas, William
Pardoe, M.
Park, Ruth
Parker, Nancy W.
Parker, Richard
Patridge, Jenny
Pascal, Francine
Patchett, Mary Elwyn
Paterson, Katherine
Paton Walsh, Jill
Patten, Brian
Paulsen, Gary
Pearce, A. Philippa
Pearson, Gayle
Peck, Richard
Peck, Robert Newton
Peel, H.M.
Peeples, Edwin A.
Peet, Bill
Pender, Lydia
Peppé, Rodney
Petrie, Catherine
Petry, Ann
Peyton, K.M.
Pfeffer, Susan Beth
Phipson, Joan
Picard, Barbara Leonie
Pierce, Meredith Ann
Pilkington, Frances Meredyth
Pilling, Ann
Pinkwater, Daniel Manus
Pinto, Jacqueline
Plowman, Stephanie
Poland, Marguerite
Politi, Leo
Pollack, Reginald
Polland, Madeleine A.
Poole, Josephine
Pope, Ray
Porter, Sheena
Posner, Richard
Potter, Margaret
Potts, Richard
Powers, Bill
Powling, Chris
Pownall, David
Prelutsky, Jack
Price, Susan
Prieto, Mariana Beeching
Prime, Derek James
Primmer, Phyllis
Prince, Alison
Pullein-Thompson, Christine
Pullein-Thompson, Diana
Pullein-Thompson, Josephine
Puzo, Mario
Pye, Virginia
Rabe, Berniece
Rabinowitz, Sandy
Radin, Ruth Yaffe
Rae, John Malcolm
Randall, Florence Engel
Randell, Beverley
Ransom, Candice F.
Ray, Mary
Rayner, Mary
Rayner, William
Read, Brian
Read, Elfreida
Read, Miss
Reaney, James
Reed, Kit

Rees, David Bartlett
Rees, Leslie
Reid, Alastair
Reid, Meta Mayne
Reid, Vic
Reilly, Robert Thomas
Renier, Elizabeth
Rey, Margret
Rhinehart, Susan Oneacre
Rich, Elaine Sommers
Richards, Christine-Louise
Richmond, Robert P.
Riordan, James
Roberts, Eric
Roberts, Irene
Roberts, Nancy Correll
Robertson, Keith
Rockwell, Anne
Rockwell, Thomas
Roddy, Lee
Rodgers, Mary
Rogers, Pamela
Rolfe, Sheila Constance
Romano, Louis
Rooke, Daphne
Roop, Connie
Roop, Peter
Roose-Evans, James
Root, Phyllis
Roseman, Kenneth David
Rosen, Michael
Rosen, Sidney
Ross, Diana
Ross, Tony
Ross, Zola
Rossel, Seymour
Rothman, Joel
Rounds, Glen
Rubinstein, Gillian
Rundle, Anne
Rush, Philip
Russell, Franklin
Russell Taylor, Elisabeth
Ryan, John
Rydberg, Ernie
Rylant, Cynthia
Sachs, Marilyn Stickle
St. George, Judith
St. John, Nicole
St. John, Patricia Mary
Salkey, Andrew
Sanchez, Sonia
Sandburg, Helga
Sanderlin, Owenita
Sanger, Marjory Bartlett
Saunders, Jean
Savery, Constance Winifred
Savitt, Sam
Scarry, Richard
Schlee, Ann
Schlein, Miriam
Scholey, Arthur
Scott, Bill
Sebestyen, Ouida
Seed, Jennie
Sefton, Catherine
Segun, Mabel D.
Seidler, Ann
Seidler, Tor
Selden, George
Self, Margaret Cabell
Sendak, Maurice
Serraillier, Ian
Serventy, Vincent Noel
Seton, Anya
Seuss, Dr.
Sharmat, Marjorie Weinman
Sharp, Margery
Sheppard-Jones, Elisabeth
Sherry, Sylvia
Shirreffs, Gordon Donald
Shotwell, Louisa R.
Shrand, David

Buckman, Peter
Budbill, David
Buller, Herman
Bullins, Ed
Bullock, Michael
Burns, Alan
Burnshaw, Stanley
Burroughs, William S
Burrows, John
Butler, Guy
Butler, Ivan
Butler, Richard
Buttitta, Tony
Buzo, Alexander
Byrne, John
Caillou, Alan
Caldwell, Erskine
Callaghan, Morley
Callard, Maurice
Callow, Philip
Campbell, Alistair
Campbell, Donald
Campton, David
Cannan, Denis
Card, Orson Scott
Carew, Jan Rynveld
Carlino, Lewis John
Carmichael, Fred Walker
Carter, Angela
Casey, Kevin
Castle, Charles
Causley, Charles
Caute, David
Chambers, Aidan
Chapman-Mortimer, William
  Charles
Charteris, Leslie
Charyn, Jerome
Childress, Alice
Chilton, Charles
Chodorov, Jerome
Churchill, Caryl
Cimino, Michael
Clapp, Patricia
Clark, Brian
Clark, John Pepper
Clark, Tom
Clarke, Joan L.
Clavell, James
Cleary, Jon
Cochrane, Peggy
Cohen, Leonard
Cohen, Peter Zachary
Cole, E.R.
Collins, Barry
Collinson, Laurence
Comfort, Alex
Condon, Richard
Conn, Stewart
Connolly, Ray
Connor, Tony
Conquest, Ned
Cook, Albert
Cook, Michael
Coolidge, Clark
Cooney, Ray
Cooper, Colin Symons
Cooper, Susan Mary
Cooper, William
Coover, Robert
Cope, Jack
Coren, Alan
Corlett, William
Corrington, John William
Corso, Gregory
Corwin, Norman
Costley, Bill
Cowasjee, Saros
Cowen, Ron
Cox, Constance
Coxe, Louis
Crane, Richard
Crawley, Aidan

Creeley, Robert
Cregan, David
Crichton, Michael
Crick, Donald Herbert
Cristofer, Michael
Cronin, Anthony
Cross, Beverley
Crouse, William H.
Crowley, Mart
Cuddon, J.A.
Curnow, Allen
Curteis, Ian
Curto, Josephine
Cutler, Ivor
Dahl, Roald
D'Amato, Anthony A.
Daniels, Sarah
Darke, Nick
Davies, Piers Anthony David
Davies, Robertson
Davis, Jack
Davis, Julia
Davis, Ossie
Davis, Robert Prunier
Davison, Dennis
Day, Stacey B.
Dean, Phillip Hayes
Delaney, Shelagh
de la Torre, Lillian
Delbanco, Nicholas F.
Delius, Anthony
Delmar, Vin
Demetillo, Ricaredo
Denker, Henry
Dennis, Nigel
Desani, G.V.
Devlin, Anne
De Vries, Peter
Dewhurst, Keith
Dickey, James
Dickinson, Patric
Dillard, R.H.W.
Dillon, Eilis
di Prima, Diane
Dixon, Roger
Dizenzo, Charles
Doctorow, E.L.
Dodd, Arthur Edward
Donald, William
Donleavy, J.P.
Drabble, Margaret
Drexler, Rosalyn
Duberman, Martin
Duberstein, Helen
Duffy, Maureen
Dunbar, Andrea
Duncan, David
Dundy, Elaine
Dunn, Nell
Dunnett, Alastair MacTavish
Durang, Christopher
Durbridge, Francis
Durrell, Lawrence
Dyer, Charles
Easmon, R. Sarif
Eastaugh, Kenneth
Eberhart, Richard
Ebert, Roger
Edgar, David
Edson, Russell
Egbuna, Obi
Elder, Lonne III
Elkin, Stanley
Elliott, Sumner Locke
Elsmlie, Kenward
Elsna, Hebe
Elsom, John
England, Barry
Engle, Paul
English, Isobel
Erhard, Tom
Essex, Harry J.
Evans, Marie

Eveling, Stanley
Everett, Peter
Exton, Clive
Eyen, Tom
Ezekiel, Nissim
Fainlight, Ruth
Fast, Howard
Fast, onathan
Fedder, Norman Joseph
Feiffer, Jules
Fellows, Malcolm Stuart
Fenn, Charles
Fennario, David
Ferlinghetti, Lawrence
Ferlita, Ernest
Ferris, Paul
Fielding, Raymond
Fierstein, Harvey
Filosa, Gary
Findley, Timothy
Finnigan, Joan
Fischer, Edward A.
Fisher, Aileen
Fisher, David E.
Fitzsimons, Raymond
Fjelde, Rolf
Fleischman, Sid
Fletcher, Lucille
Fletcher, Ronald
Foote, Horton
Foote, Shelby
Forbes, Bryan
Ford, Jesse Hill
Foreman, Richard
Foreman, Joan
Fornés, Maria Irene
Forsyth, James
Foster, Paul
Fox, Hugh
Franken, Rose
Franklin, Alexander John
Fraser, George MacDonald
Fratti, Mario
Frayn, Michael
Freeman, David
Freeman, Gillian
French, David
Freund, Philip
Frewer, Glyn
Friedberg, Gertrude
Friedman, Bruce Jay
Friel, Brian
Frisby, Terence
Fry, Christopher
Fuchs, Daniel
Fugard, Athol
Fuller, Charles
Fuller, John
Fuller, Samuel
Furth, George
Gagliano, Frank
Gallacher, Tom
Gallagher, Tess
Galwey, Geoffrey
Gann, Ernest K.
Gardner, Herb
Garfield, Brian
Garrett, George
Gartner, Chloe Maria
Gascoyne, David
Gattey, Charles Neilson
Gay, Kathlyn R.
Gébler, Ernest
Gee, Shirley
Gelbart, Larry
Gelber, Jack
Gems, Pam
Gibson, William
Gill, Peter
Gilliatt, Penelope
Gilroy, Frank D.
Gittings, Robert
Glaskin, G.M.

Glaze, Andrew Louis
Gliauda, Jurgis
Gloag, Julian
Glyn, (Sir) Anthony
Godber, John
Golding, William
Goldman, James
Goldman, William
Gooch, Steve
Goodman, Jonathan
Gordone, Charles
Gorman, Clem
Gourlay, David
Gow, Ronald
Gratus, Jack
Gray, Alasdair
Gray, Dulcie
Gray, Jack
Gray, John
Gray, Simon
Gray, Spalding
Greenberger, Howard
Greene, Graham
Greenwood, Duncan
Gregg, Hubert
Gregor, Arthur
Grenville, John A.S.
Griffiths, Trevor
Gross, Joel
Guare, John
Guest, Barbara
Guest, Harry
Guinness, Bryan
Gurney, A.R., Jr.
Guy, Rosa
Hailey, Arthur
Hailey, Oliver
Haire, Wilson John
Hale, Allean Lemmon
Hale, John
Hall, Oakley
Hall, Roger
Hall, Willis
Halliwell, David
Hampton, Christopher
Hanley, Clifford
Hanley, Gerald
Hanley, James
Hanley, William
Harding, John
Hardwick, Michael
Hardwick, Mollie
Hare, David
Harris, Leonard
Harris, Mark
Harrison, Tony
Harron, Don
Hartmann, Michael
Harwood, Ronald
Hastings, Michaelhp
Hauptmann, WilliamhX
Hawkes, John
Hayes, Joseph
Hearne, John
Hearne, Reginald
Heath-Stubbs, John
Heifetz, Harold
Heller, Joseph
Hendry, Thomas
Henley, Beth
Henschel, Elizabeth Georgie
Henshaw, James Ene
Herbert, Ivor
Herbert, John
Herlihy, James Leo
Hernton, Calvin C.
Herrmanns, Ralph
Hewett, Dorothy
Hibberd, Jack
Higgins, Dick
Hignett, Sean
Hill, Carol
Hill, Errol

Hill, Reginald
Hill, Susan
Hillman, Barry
Hine, Daryl
Hines, Barry
Hiro, Dilip
Hitchcock, George
Hitchcock, Raymond John
Hivnor, Robert
Hochman, Sanda
Hoff, Syd
Hoffman, William M.
Hogan, Robert
Hoggard, James
Holden, Joan
Holles, Robert
Hollingsworth, Margaret
Holmes, Martin
Home, William Douglas
Honeycombe, Gordon
Honig, Edwin
Hood, Christopher
Hopcraft, Arthur
Hopkins, John
Horgan, Paul
Horovitz, Israel
Hotchner, A.E.
Howard, Elizabeth
Howard, Roger
Howarth, Donald
Howe, Tina
Howlett, John
Hoyle, Trevor
Hubler, Richard G.
Hufana, Alejandrino G.
Huggett, Frank Edward
Huggett, Richard
Hughes, Dusty
Hughes, Ted
Humphreys, Emyr
Hunter, Evan
Hunter, Kristin
Hunter, Mollie
Hurley, John
Hutchinson, Ron
Hwang, David Henry
Hyams, Joe
Innaurato, Albert
Ireland, David
Isaacs, Susan
Israel, Charles
Jacker, Corinne
James, J. Robert
Jellicoe, Ann
Jenkin, Len
Jenkins, Alan
Jhabvala R. Prawer
Johns, Richard A.
Johnson, Terry
Johnston, Jennifer
Johnstone, Keith
Jonas, George
Jones, Bob, Jr.
Jones, Diana Wynne
Jones, Gayle
Jones, Julia
Jones, LeRoi
Jones-Evans, Eric
Jordan, Neil
Josipovici, Gabriel
Judson, John
Kalcheim, Lee
Kallen, Lucille
Kanin, Garson
Karp, David
Kauffmann, Stanley
Kavanagh, P.J.
Kaye, Marvin
Keane, John B.
Keeffe, Barrie
Kelly, Robert
Kelly, Tim
Kempenski, Tom

Kenna, Peter
Kennedy, Adrienne
Kerr, Jean
Kerr, Walter
Kershaw, H.V.
Kesselman, Wendy
Kessler, Jascha
Kiefer, Warren
Kilroy, Thomas
King, Larry L.
Kingsley, Sidney
Kirkup, James
Klein, Alexander
Kneale, Nigel
Knight, Bernard
Koch, Kenneth
Kondoleon, Harry
Konig, Hans
Konvitz, Jeffrey
Kopit, Arthur
Kops, Bernard
Krasner, William
Kraus, Joanna Halpert
Krauss, Ruth
Kreisel, Henry
Kresh, Paul
Kubly, Herbert
Kubrick, Stanley
Kureishi, Hanif
Laffan, Kevin
Lambert, Gavin
Lan, David
Lane, Carolyn
Langford, Gary R.
Lantz, J. Edward
Lapine, James
Lasky, Jesse Louis, Jr.
Latham, Jean Lee
Laurence, Dan H.
Laurents, Arthur
Lavery, Bryony
Lawler, Lucille
Lawler, Ray
Lawrence, Jerome
Lee, Laurie
Lee, Maryat
Lee, Robert E.
Lehmann, Rosamond
Leigh, Mike
Leisy, James Franklin
L'Engle, Madelaine
Lengyel, Cornel
Leonard, Hugh
Leslie, Aleen
Leslie, Desmond
Lessing, Doris
Levin, Ira
Levy, Alan
Lieberman, Herbert
Lifton, Betty Jean
Lillington, Kenneth
Lima, Robert F., Jr.
Lingard, Joan
Linney, Romulus
Litvinoff, Emanuel
Lively, Penelope
Livings, Henry
Livingstone, Douglas
Lochhead, Liz
Lockerbie, D. Bruce
Lodge, David
Logue, Christopher
Loney, Glenn Meredith
Longstreet, Stephen
Lord, Robert
Lowden, Desmond Scott
Lowe, Stephen
Lucas, Barbara
Lucie, Doug
Ludwig, Jack
Luke, Peter
Lurie, Morris
Lynn, Jonathan

Lynne, James Broom
MacBeth, George
MacLean, Katherine
Macleod, Alison
MacLeod, Ellen Jane
Mac Low, Jackson
MacMahon, Bryan Michael
Macvear, Jean
Macvicar, Angus
Madden, David
Maddy, Y.A.
Mailer, Norman
Mairowitz, David
Mallik, Provash
Mallik, Umesh
Mamet, David
Mandel, Oscar
Mankowitz, Wolf
Mann, Emily
Marchant, Tony
Marcus, Frank
Marks, Stan
Markson, David M.
Marlowe, Derek
Marshall, Henry
Marvin, Blanche
Marx, Arthur
Mastrosimone, William
Mather, Berkely
Mathew, Ray
Matura, Mustapha
May, Elaine
Mayhew, Christopher
McCabe, Eugene
McCallum, Phyllis
McCaslin, Nellie
McClure, Michael
McElroy, Colleen J.
McEwan, Ian
McGahern, John
McGee, Greg
McGough, Roger
McGrath, John
McGrath, Tom
McGraw, Eloise Jarvis
McKee, David
McLure, James
McManus, Kay
McNair, Kate
McNally, Terrence
McNeil, Florence
McNeish, James
Mednick, Murray
Medoff, Mark
Megged, Aharon
Melchior, Ib
Melfi, Leonard
Melwood, Mary
Merriam, Eve
Merrill, James
Merwin, W.S.
Meserve, Walter Joseph, Jr.
Meudt, Edna
Meyer, Michael Leverson
Meyer, Nicholas
Michel, Milton Scott
Milgate, Rodney Armour
Millar, (Sir) Ronald
Miller, Arthur
Miller, Jason
Miller, Lynn H.
Miller, Orlo
Miller, Susan
Milligan, Spike
Mills, Mervyn
Milner, Ron
Minghella, Anthony
Mitchell, Adrian
Mitchell, Julian
Mitchell, Loften
Mitchell, W.O.
Mitgang, Herbert
Moe, Christian H.

Moggach, Deborah
Molloy, Michael
Montague, John
Moore, Brian
Moore, Mavor
Morgan, Pete
Morgan, Robert
Morris, Jean
Morrison, Bill
Mortimer, John
Mosel, Tad
Mowat, David
Mucha, Jiri
Muller, Robert
Munro, Ian S.
Murdoch, Iris
Murphy, Arthur Lister
Murphy, Thomas
Murray, Rona
Murrell, John
Musaphia, Joseph
Musser, Joe
Naiden, James
Nathan, David
Naughton, Bill
Nelson, Richard
Newman, Coleman J.
Newman, Gordon F.
Newton, Norman Lewis
Ngugi, J.T.
Nicolaeff, Ariadne
Nicolaysen, Bruce
Nkosi, Lewis
Nolan, Paul T.
Noonan, John Ford
Norman, Bruce
Norman, Lilith
Norman, Marsha
North, Elizabeth
Nowra, Louis
Nuttall, Jeff
Nye, Robert
Oakes, Philip
Oates, Joyce Carol
O'Brien, Edna
Odaga, Asenath
O'Faolain, Sean
Okpaku, Joseph
Olson, Elder
O'Malley, Mary
Ondaatje, Michael
Ornstein, Robert
Osborne, John
Osofisan, Femi
Owen, Alun
Owen, Roderic
Owens, Rochelle
Padgett, Ron
Page, Louise
Park, Ruth
Parker, Gordon
Parkinson, Thomas
Pascal, Francine
Paterson, Neil
Patrick, John
Patrick, Robert
Patten, Brian
Paulin, Tom
Payne, J. Gregory
Pearce, Brian Louis
Peck, Robert Newton
Pertwee, Michael
Peterkiewicz, Jerzy
Peters, Robert
Petrakis, Harry Mark
Phelps, Gilbert
Phillips, Caryl
Phillpotts, Adelaide
Pielmeier, John
Piercy, Marge
Pilcher, Rosamunde
Pinner, David
Pinter, Harold

Barzelay, Walter Moshe
Baybars, Taner
Bayley, John
Beaver, Bruce
Bechervaise, John Mayston
Beckett, Samuel
Beer, Patricia
Beer, Stafford
Beissel, Henry
Belitt, Ben
Bell, Charles G.
Bell, Marvin
Bell, Robin
Beloof, Robert Lawrence
Benedict, Rex
Benedikt, Michael
Bennett, John
Bennett, John M.
Bennett, Louise
Bentley, Beth
Benton, Patricia
Benveniste, Asa
Beresford, Anne
Berg, Stephen
Bergé Carol
Bergonzi, Bernard
Berkson, Bill
Bernard, Oliver
Bernard, Sidney
Bernstein, Charles
Berrigan, Daniel J.
Berry, Francis
Berry, James
Berry, Wendell
Bertolino, James
Bertram, James
Bielski, Alison
Billing, Graham
Birney, Earle
Bishop, Michael
Bissett, Bill
Black, Charles Lund, Jr.
Black, David
Blamires, David
Blaser, Robin
Blight, John
Boalch, Donald Howard
Bode, Carl
Boer, Charles
Bogue, Lucile Maxfield
Bold, Alan
Bond, Harold
Boore, Walter Hugh
Booth, Martin
Booth, Philip
Borenstein, Emily
Bosley, Keith
Bottrall, Ronald
Bowden, Roland Heywood
Bowering, George
Bowering, Marilyn
Bowers, Edgar
Bowles, Paul
Boyle, Kay
Bradbury, Malcolm
Bradbury, Ray
Brandi, John
Brata, Sasthi
Braun, Richard Emil
Bray, John Jefferson
Braybrooke, Neville
Bremser, Ray
Brennan, Joseph Payne
Brenton, Howard
Brew, O.H. Kwesi
Brewer, Wilmon
Brewster, Elizabeth
Brilliant, Alan
Bringhurst, Robert
Brinnin, John Malcolm
Brock, Edwin
Brodine, Karen
Brodribb, Gerald

Brodsky, Joseph
Bromige, David
Bronk, William
Brooks, Gwendolyn
Broughton, James
Broughton, T. Alan
Broumas, Olga
Brown, George Mackay
Brown, Marel
Brown, Rita Mae
Brown, Wayne
Browne, Michael Dennis
Brownjohn, Alan
Brownlow, Timothy
Brownstein, Michael
Bruce, George
Bruce, Lennart
Bruchac, Joseph
Bruff, Nancy
Brunner, John
Brutus, Dennis
Bryans, Robin
Budbill, David
Buchan, Tom
Buchanan, George
Buckley, Vincent
Buddee, Paul Edgar
Buell, Frederick
Bukowski, Charles
Bullock, Michael
Burden, Jean
Burford, William
Burke, Kenneth
Burnett, Alfred David
Burns, Jim
Burns, Joan Simpson
Burnshaw, Stanley
Burroughs, William S.
Burroway, Janet Gay
Burt, Nathaniel
Butler, Guy
Buxbaum, Martin
Buxton, John
Cage, John
Caire, Janet
Callow, Philip
Campbell, Alistair
Campbell, Donald
Carew, Jan Rynveld
Carew, (Sir) Rivers
Carrier, Constance
Carrier, Warren
Carroll, Paul
Carruth, Hayden
Carson, Ciaran
Carter, Angela
Carter, Martin
Casey, Michael
Cassity, Turner
Causley, Charles
Chaffin, Lillie D.
Champkin, Peter
Chapman, Ronald George
Charlier, Roger Henri
Charters, Samuel
Cheavens, Frank
Cherry, Kelly
Chesham, Sallie
Cheyney-Coker, Syl
Christensen, J.A.
Christensen, Paul
Christesen, C.B.
Clampitt, Amy
Clare, William
Clark of Herriotshall,
    Arthur Melville
Clark, David Ridgley
Clark, John Pepper
Clark, Laurence
Clark, Robert
Clark, Tom
Clarke, Gillian
Clarkson, E. Margaret

Clemo, Jack
Cleveland, Leslie
Clifford, Derek Plint
Clifton, Lucille
Cluysenaar, Anne
Cobbing, Bob
Codrescu, Andrei
Cogswell, Fred
Cohen, Leonard
Cohen, Matt
Cole, Barry
Cole, E.R.
Coleman, Terry
Coles, Robert
Collinson, Laurence
Colombo, John Robert
Comfort, Alex
Conn, Stewart
Conners, Kenneth Wray
Connor, Tony
Connors, Bruton
Conquest, Robert
Conran, Anthony
Cook, Albert
Cook, Stanley
Cooke, William
Coolidge, Clark
Cooper, Jane
Cooperman, Hasye
Cope, Jack
Corman, Cid
Corn, Alfred
Cornish, Sam
Corrington, John William
Corso, Gregory
Corwin, Norman
Costley, Bill
Cotton, John
Couper, J.M.
Couzyn, Jeni
Cox, Charles Brian
Coxe, Louis
Creeley, Robert
Crew, Louie
Crews, Judson
Cronin, Anthony
Crossley-Holland, Kevin
Crozier, Andrew
Cruz, Victor Hernandez
Cumberlege, Marcus
Cunningham, J.V.
Curnow, Allen
Currey, R.N.
Curtis, Tony
Dabydeen, Cyril
Dacey, Philip
Dale, Peter
Dallas, Ruth
Dana, Robert
Dann, Jack
Das, D.K.
Das, Kamala
Dathorne, O.R.
Davenport, Guy
Davey, Frank
Davidson, Michael
Davie, Donald
Davie, Ian
Davies, Piers Anthony David
Davis, Dick
Davis, Jack
Davison, Peter
Dawe, Bruce
Day, Stacey B.
de Camp, L. Sprague
de Chair, Somerset
DeFrees, Madeline
Delius, Anthony
Demetillo, Ricardo
Den Boer, James D.
Dennis, Nigel
de Regniers, Beatrice Schenk
de Vinck, José M.G.A.

de Vries, Rachel
Dewhirst, Ian
Dickey, James
Dickey, William
Dickinson, Patric
Dickinson, Peter
Dillard, Annie
Dillard, R.H.W.
di Prima, Diane
Disch, Thomas M.
Dobson, Rosemary
Dobyns, Stephen
Dodd, Arthur Edward
Dodd, Wayne D.
Dorman, Sonya
Dorn, Ed
Dowling, Basil
Downie, Freda
Doyle, Charles
Drake, Albert Dee
Driver, Charles Jonathan
Duberstein, Helen
Dubie, Norman
Dudek, Louis
Dufault, Peter Kane
Duffy, Maureen
Dugan, Alan
Dugdale, Norman
Duncan, Anthony Douglas
Duncan, Robert
Dunn, Douglas
Dunn, Stephen
Durrell, Lawrence
Dutton, Geoffrey
Dylan, Bob
Earley, Tom
Eastlake, William
Eaton, Charles Edward
Eberhart, Richard
Echeruo, Michael
Eckels, Jon
Economou, George
Eddins, Dwight
Edmond, Lauris
Edson, Russell
Edwards, Michael
Eigner, Larry
Einbond, Bernard Lionel
Eisenberg, Larry
Elliot, Alistair
Ellis, Royston
Elmslie, Kenward
Emanuel, James A.
Engels, John
Engle, Paul
Enright, D.J.
Enslin, Theodore
Eshleman, Clayton
Espeland, Pamela
Espino, Federico
Essop, Ahmed
Etter, Dave
Evans, Hubert
Evans, Mari
Everson, Ronald
Everson, William
Everwine, Peter
Every, George
Ewart, Gavin
Ezekiel, Nissim
Fainlight, Ruth
Fairfax, John
Falck, Colin
Fanthorpe, U.A.
Farmiloe, Dorothy
Fatchen, Max
Fea, James Lyon
Federman, Raymond
Feinberg, Barry
Feinstein, Elaine
Feldman, Irving
Fenton, Edward
Fenton, James

Ferlinghetti, Lawrence
Fetherling, Doug
Fiacc, Padraic
Field, Edward
Fielder, Mildred
Figueroa, John
Finch, Peter
Finch, Robert
Finkel, Donald
Finlay, Ian Hamilton
Finnigan, Joan
Fisher, Allen
Fisher, A. Stanley T.
Fisher, Aileen
Fisher, Roy
FitzGerald, Robert D.
Fjelde, Rolfe
Fletcher, Ronald
Forbes, John
Forché Carolyn
Ford, Charles Henri
Ford, R.A.D.
Fossum, Robert H.
Foster, Don
Foster, M.A.
Fowler, Alastair
Fowler, Gene
Fowles, John
Fox, Hugh
Fox, Len
Frame, Janet
Francis, Marilyn
Frankhouser, Floyd Richard
Fraser, Douglas
Fraser, Kathleen
Fratti, Mario
Freund, Philip
Friedman, Jacob Horace
Friedman, Norman
Friedrich, Paul
Friend, Robert
Frumkin, Gene
Fry, Christopher
Fuller, Jean Overton
Fuller, John
Fuller, Roy
Fulton, Robin
Galbraith, Jean
Gallagher, Tess
Galvin, Brendan
Garfitt, Roger
Garlick, Raymond
Garrett, Florence Rome
Garrett, George
Gascoyne, David
Gatenby, Greg
Gavronsky, Serge
Geddes, Gary
Geiger, Don Jesse
Geras, Adele
Gershon, Karen
Gesner, Carol
Ghiselin, Brewster
Ghose, Zulfikar
Giannaris, George
Gibbons, Stella
Gibbs, Alonzo
Gibson, Miles
Gibson, William
Gilbert, Ruth
Gilchrist, Ellen
Gildner, Gary
Gill, Brendan
Gill, David
Gill, Myrna Lakshmi
Gillies, Valerie
Gillon, Adam
Ginsberg, Allen
Giovanni, Mikki
Gittings, Robert
Glaze, Andrew Louis
Glen, Duncan
Gliauda, Jurgis

Gluck, Louise
Gnarowski, Michael
Goacher, Denis
Godden, Rumer
Goedicke, Patricia
Gokak, Vinayak Krishna
Goldbarth, Albert
Golding, William
Goodman, Jonathan
Gordopn, Giles
Gotlieb, Phyllis
Graham, Henry
Graham, Jorie
Grant, James Russell
Gray, Robert
Green. Dorothy
Green, Frederick Pratt
Green, J.C.R.
Greenberg, Alvin
Greene, Graham
Greene, Jonathan
Gregor, Arthur
Gresser, Seymour
Grier, Eldon
Griffin, Jonathan
Griffiths, Bryn
Griffiths, John Gwyn
Guenther, Charles
Guest, Barbara
Guest, Harry
Guinness, Bryan
Gullans, Charles
Gunn, Thom
Gustafson, Ralph
Gutteridge, Don
Hacker, Marilyn
Haines, John
Haldeman, Jack C.
Hall, Donald
Hall, J.C.
Hall, James B.
Hall, Rodney
Hamburger, Michael
Halpern, Daniel
Hamilton, Franklin W.
Hamilton, Ian
Hamilton, Mary
Hamilton-Edwards, Gerald
Hammond, Mac
Hanson, Kenneth O.
Hanson, Pauline
Hardman, David Rennie
Harper, Michael S.
Harrell, Irene Burk
Harris, Jana
Harris, Wilson
Harrison, Jim
Harrison, Keith
Harrison, Tony
Harsent, David
Hart, Kevin
Hartman, Geoffrey H.
Hartnett, Michael
Hart-Smith, William
Harvey, John B.
Harwood, Gwen
Harwood, Lee
Hasluck, Nicholas
Hasluck, (Sir) Paul
Hass, Robert
Hassler, Donald M.
Hastings, Michael
Haviaras, Stratis
Hawley, Richard A.
Hayman, Carol Bessent
Hazo, Samuel
Heaney, Seamus
Heath-Stubbs, John
Hecht, Anthony
Hejinian, Lyn
Heller, Michael D.
Hellyer, Jill
Helwig, David

Henderson, Hamish
Henderson Smith, Stephen Lane
Hendriks, A.L.
Henri, Adrian
Hernton, Calvin C.
Hesketh, Phoebe
Hewett, Dorothy
Hewitt, Geof
Heyen, William
Heyer, Paul
Hibbs, John
Hidden, Norman
Higgins, Dick
Higham, Charles
Higson, Philip
Hilberry, Conrad Arthur
Hill, Geoffrey
Hillman, Barry
Hindus, Milton
Hine, Daryl
Hiro, Dilip
Hirschman, Jack
Hitchcock, George
Hoare, Merval Hannah
Hobsbaum, Philip
Hochman, Sandra
Hoffman, Daniel
Hofmann, Michael
Hoggard, James
Holbrook, David
Hollander, John
Hollo, Anselm
Holloway, Geoffrey
Holloway, John
Holloway, Mark
Holman, Felice
Home, William Douglas
Honig, Edwin
Hooker, Jeremy
Hooper, Peter
Hope, A.D.
Hope, Christopher
Hopkins, Lee Bennett
Horovitz, Israel
Horovitz, Michael
Houédard, dom Sylvester
Howard, Richard
Howard, Roger
Howe, Fanny
Howell, Anthony
Howes, Barbara
Hoyem, Andrew
Hoyland, Michael
Hubler, Richard G.
Hufana, Alejandrino G.
Huff, Robert
Hughes, Dorothy B.
Hughes, Glyn
Hughes, Ted
Hull, William D.
Hulme, Keri
Humphrey, James
Humphreys, Emyr
Hunt, Sam
Hurley, John
Hutchinson, Pearse
Ignatow, David
Igo, John
Inez, Colette
Ingalls, Jeremy
Ingham, R.A.
Irby, Kenneth
Ireland, Kevin
Irion, Mary Jean
Ivens, Michael William
Jacobsen, Josephine
Jacobus, Lee A.
Jaffin, David
James, Clive
Janowitz, Tama
Jay, Peter
Jennings, Elizabeth
Jerome, Judson

Johnson, Denis
Johnson, Josephine
Johnson, Ronald
Johnson, Stowers
Johnston, George
Jonas, George
Joners, Bob, Jr.
Jones, Brian
Jones, D.G.
Jones, Evan
Jones, Gayle
Jones, Glyn
Jones, LeRoi
Jones, Peter
Jones, Sally Roberts
Jong, Erica
Jordan, June
Joseph, Stephen M.
Joslin, Sesyle
Judson, John
Juergensen, Hans
Junkins, Donald
Justice, Donald
Kahn, Sy M.
Kandel, Lenore
Karanikas, Alexander
Katz, Bobbi
Katz, Menke
Katz, Steve
Kauffman, Janet
Kavanagh, P.J.
Kavanaugh, James
Kawin, Bruce F.
Kaye, Barrington
Kearns, Lionel
Keesing, Nancy
Kell, Richard
Kelly, Robert
Kennedy, X.J.
Kennelly, Brendan
Kenward, Jean
Kessler, Jascha
Kessler, Milton
Kgositsile, Keorapetse
Kherdian, David
Kiely, Jerome
Kilbracken, Baron: John
  Raymond Godley
Kilgore, James C.
King, Francis
King-Hele, Desmond
Kinnell, Galway
Kinsella, Thomas
Kirkup, James
Kirsten, Lincoln
Kizer, Carolyn
Klappert, Peter
Knight, Etheridge
Knoepfle, John
Knott, Bill
Knowles, Susanne
Koch, Kenneth
Koehler, G. Stanley
Kogawa, Joy Nozomi
Kolatkar, Arun
Koller, James
Kondoleon, Harry
Kops, Bernard
Kostelanetz, Richard
Kramer, Aaron
Kroetsch, Robert
Kudian, Mischa
Kumar, Shiv K.
Kumin, Maxine
Kunitz, Stanley
Kuskin, Karla
Kyger, Joanne
Lachs, John
Laffin, John
La Fortune, Knolly Stephen
Lake, David
Lal, P.
Lamantia, Philip

Lamb, Elizabeth Searle
Lamont, Corliss
Lamplugh, Lois
Lamppa, William R.
Lande, Lawrence
Lane, Patrick
Langford, Gary R
Langland, Joseph
Latham, Jean Lee
Laughlin, James
Layton, Irving
Lazarus, A.L.
Lee, Dennis
Lee, Don L.
Lee, Laurie
Leed, Jacob
Leeds, Morton Harold
Legler, Philip
Le Guin, Ursula K.
Lehmann, Geoffrey
Leiber, Fritz
LeMaster, J.R.
L'Engle, Madeleine
Lengyel, Cornel
Lennox-Short, Alan
Leonard, Tom
LePan, Douglas
Lepore, Dominick James
Lerner, Laurence
Lessing, Doris
Lester, Julius
Levenson, Christopher
Levertov, Denise
Levi, Peter
Levine, Norman
Levine, Philip
Levis, Larry
Lewis, Hywel David
Lewis, Janet
Lewis-Smith, Anne
L'Heureux, John
Liddy, James
Lieberman, Laurence
Lifshin, Lyn
Lima, Robert F., Jr.
Lindsay, Maurice
Lipsitz, Lou
Lister, R.P.
Little, Jean
Litvinoff, Emanuel
Livesay, Dorothy
Livingston, Myra Cohn
Livingstone, Douglas
Liyong, Taban lo
Lochhead, Douglas
Lochhead, Liz
Locklin, Gerald Ivan
Loewinsohn, Ron
Logue, Christopher
Long, Frank Belknap
Longley, Michael
Lorde, Audre
Lorrimer, Claire
Lowbury, Edward
Lucas, John
Lucie-Smith, Edward
Lykiard, Alexis
Lyons, W.T.
MacAdams, Lewis
Macainsh, Noel Leslie
MacBeth, George
MacCaig, Norman
Mackie, Alastair
Mackworth, Cecily
Maclean, Alasdair
MacLeod, Alistair
Mac Low, Jackson
Macnab, Roy
Macpherson, Jay
MacSweeney, Barry
Macvean, Jean
Madden, David
Madge, Charles

Madgett, Naomi Long
Magee, Wes
Mahon, Derek
Mahy, Margaret
Mainone, Robert Franklin
Major, Clarence
Malouf, David
Mandel, Eli
Mandel, Oscar
Manfred, Frederick Feikema
Manhire, Bill
Mankowitz, Wolf
Mann, Chris
Maples, Evelyn Palmer
Mariah, Paul
Marlatt, Daphne
Marshall, Jack
Marshall, Tom
Martin, David
Martin, Marjorie
Marty, Sid
Marvin, Blanche
Masefield, Geoffrey
Massingham, Harold
Matchett, William H.
Mathew, Ray
Mathias, Roland
Matthews, Jack
Matthews, Patricia
Matthews, Thomas Stanley
Matthews, William
Matthias, John
Mayer, Bernadette
Mayer, Gerda
Mayne, Seymour
Mazer, Norma Fox
Mazzaro, Jerome
McAuley, James J.
McCarthy, Eugene
McClatchy, J.D.
McCloskey, Mark
McClure, Michael
McCord, David
McDonald, Roger
McElroy, Colleen J.
McFadden, David
McFadden, Roy
McGaughey, Florence Helen
McGough, Roger
McGrath, Thomas M.
McGukian, Medbh
McHugh, Heather
McIllvanney, William
McKee, David
McKeown, Tom
McKuen, Rod
McNamara, Eugene Joseph
McNeil, Florence
McNeill, Anthony
McPherson, Sandra
McWhirter, George
Mead, Matthew
Measham, Donald Charles
Mednick, Murray
Mehrotra, Arvind
Meinke, Peter
Melton, David
Meltzer, David
Meredith, William
Merriam, Eve
Merrill, James
Merwin, W.S.
Meudt, Edna
Mezey, Robert
Michie, James
Middleton, Christopher
Middleton, O.E.
Minhinnick, Robert
Milgate, Rodney Armour
Miller, Jim Wayne
Miller, Vassar
Millett, John
Milligan, Spike

Mills, Paul
Mills, Ralph J., Jr.
Millward, Eric
Milton, John R.
Minarik, Else
Mintz, Ruth Finer
Mitchell, Adrian
Mitchell, David
Mitchell, Margaretta
Mitchell, Robby K.
Mitchell, Roger
Moat, John
Moffett, Judith
Mokashi-Punekar, Shankar
Mole, John
Momaday, N. Scott
Montag, Tom
Montague, John
Montgomery, Marion
Moore, Mavor
Moore, Nicholas
Moore, Richard
Moraes, Dom
Morgan, Edwin
Morgan, Frederick
Morgan, Helen
Morgan, Pete
Morgan, Robert
Morris, Harry
Morris, Michael
Morris, Stephen
Morrison, Blake
Morrison, Theodore
Moss, Stanley
Motion, Andrew
Mtshali, Oswald
Mucha, Jiri
Mueller, Lisel
Mueller, Robert Emmett
Muldoon, Paul
Mullins, Helene
Murdoch, Iris
Murphy, Richard
Murray, Les A.
Murray, Rona
Musgrave, Susan
Myers, Jack
Myers, John Myers
Naiden, James
Najarian, Peter
Nandy, Pritish
Nassauer, Rudolf
Nathan, Leonard
Nathan, Norman
Naudé Adèle
Nelson, Geoffrey Kenneth
Nelson, Harry William
Nemerov, Howard
Neumeyer, Peter
Newcomer, James W.
Newlin, Margaret Rudd
Newlove, John
Newton, Norman Lewis
Nichols, John Gordon
Nicholson, Hubert
Nims, John Frederick
Nissman, Albert
Nitchie, George Wilson
Nolan, Christopher
Nolan, William F.
Norris, Leslie
Norse, Harold
Notley, Alice
Nott, Kathleen
Noyes, Stanley
Nunn, William Curtis
Nuttall, Jeff
Nye, Robert
Oakes, Philip
Oates, Joyce Carol
O'Brien, Katharine E.
O'Connor, Francis V.
O'Farrell, Padraic

O'Gorman, Ned
O'Grady, Desmond
Okai, John
Okara, Gabriel
Oliver, Kenneth A.
Oliver, Mary
Olmsted, Robert W.
Olson, Elder
Olson, Toby
Ondaatje, Michael
Ormond, John
Ormsby, Frank
Orr, Gregory
Ortiz, Simon J.
Osborne, Charles
O'Sullivan, Vincent
Ovard, Glen F.
Owen, Gareth
Owens, Rochelle
Oxley, William
Pack, Robert
Padgett, Ron
Page, Geoff
Page, P.K.
Palmer, Michael
Parker, Barrett
Parker, Derek
Parkinson, Thomas
Parks, Gordon
Parthasarathy, R.
Parvin, Betty
Pastan, Linda
Paterson, Alistair
Patten, Brian
Patterson, Raymond R.
Paulin, Tom
Paust, Marian
Pearce, Brian Louis
Peck, John
Peck, Robert Newton
Pender, Lydia
Perkins, Michael
Peskett, William
Petaja, Emil
Peterkiewicz, Jerzy
Peters, Lenrie
Peters, Robert
Petersen, Donald
Petrie, Paul
Petty, W.H.
Phillips, Louis Christopher
Phillips, Michael Joseph
Phillips, Robert
Phillpotts, Adelaide
Phoenice, Jay
Pickard, Tom
Piercy, Marge
Pilling, Christopher
Pinsker, Sanford S.
Pinsky, Robert
Pinter, Harold
Pitchford, Kenneth S.
Pitter, Ruth
Plantz, Allen
Platt, Charles
Platt, Eugene
Pleasants, Ben
Plumly, Stanley
Pocock, Hugh
Pomeroy, Ralph
Popham, Hugh
Porter, Bern
Porter, Joshua Roy
Porter, Peter
Poulin, A., Jr.
Powell, Craig
Powell, Enoch
Powell, Neil
Pownall, David
Prelutsky, Jack
Press, John
Price, Reynolds
Price, Victor

Prince, F.T.
Prosser, Harold Lee
Prynne, J.H.
Prys-Jones, A.G.
Purcell, Sally
Purdy, A.W.
Purdy, James
Purser, John W.
Pybus, Rodney
Raine, Craig
Raine, Kathleen
Rajan, Tilottama
Rakosi, Carl
Ramanujan, A.K.
Ramsey, Jarold
Ramsey, Paul
Randall, Dudley
Randall, Julia
Randall, Margaret
Ratcliffe, Eric Hallam
Ratner, Rochelle
Raworth, Tom
Ray, David
Ray, Judy
Ray, Sib Narayan
Read, Sylvia Joan
Reade, Brian Edmund
Reading, Peter
Reaney, James
Rebert, M. Charles
Redgrove, Peter
Redmond, Eugene B.
Reed, Ishmael
Reed, Robert Rentoul, Jr.
Reed, Thomas Thornton
Reeve, F.D.
Reghaby, Heydar
Reid, Alastair
Reid, Christopher
Reid, Frances P.
Reid, Meta Mayne
Reynolds, Ernest Randolph
Rich, Adrienne
Richards, Mark
Riding, Laura
Ridler, Anne
Rivenburgh, Viola K.
Roberts, Kevin
Roberts, Philip Davies
Robins, Patricia
Robinson, Roland
Robson, Jeremy
Roche, Paul
Roddick, Alan
Rodefer, Stephen
Rodgers, Carolyn M.
Roditi, Edouard
Rodriguez, Judith
Rodway, Allan Edwin
Rolls, Eric Charles
Rook, Alan
Root, William Pitt
Rootham, Jasper St. John
Rosberg, Rose
Rose, Elinor K.
Rosen, Michael
Rosen, Stanley Howard
Rosenblatt, Joseph
Rosensaft, Menachem Z.
Rosenthal, M.L.
Ross, Alan
Rothenberg, Jerome
Rowbotham, David
Rowland, J.R.
Rowse, A.L.
Rubin, Larry
Rucker, Rudy
Rumens, Carol
Rush, Christopher
Russell, Norman H.
Russell, Peter
Russell, Ray
Rutsala, Vern A.

Ryan, William
Sabine, William Henry Waldo
Sail, Laurence
St. John, Bruce
Salinger, Herman
Salkey, Andrew
Sanchez, Sonia
Sandburg, Helga
Sanders, Ed
Sandy, Stephen
Saner, Reg
Saroyan, Aram
Sarton, May
Scannell, Vernon
Scarfe, Wendy Elizabeth
Schaeffer, Susan Fromberg
Schechter, Ruth Lisa
Scheele, Roy
Schevill, James
Schmidt, Michael
Schmitz, Dennis
Schroeder, Andreas
Schuyler, James
Schwartz, Barry
Schwerner, Armand
Scott, Alexander
Scott, Bill
Scott, Tom
Scovell, E.J.
Scully, James
Scupham, Peter
Seager, Ralph William
Segun, Mabel D.
Seidel, Frederick
Seidman, Hugh
Sellin, Eric
Serraillier, Ian
Seth, Vikram
Sethi, Narendra Kumar
Seymour, A.J.
Seymour-Smith, Martin
Shahane, Vasant
Shange, Ntozake
Shapcott, Thomas W.
Shapiro, David
Shapiro, Karl
Sharat Chandra, G.S.
Shelton, Richard
Sherman, Arnold
Sherman, Ingrid
Sherwin, Judith Johnson
Shuttle, Penelope
Siebrasse, Glen
Silk, Dennis
Silkin, Jon
Silko, Leslie
Sillitoe, Alan
Silverstein, Shel
Simic, Charles
Simmons, James
Simpson, Louis
Simpson, R.A.
Simpson, Ruth M.
Sinclair, Keith
Singer, Sarah Beth
Sisler, Harry Hall
Sisson, C.H.
Skelton, Robin
Skinner, Knute
Skinner, Martyn
Slavitt, David
Slavutych, Yar
Slesinger, Warren
Smith, Dave
Smith, Iain Crichton
Smith, John
Smith, Kathleen J.
Smith, Ken
Smith, Michael
Smith, Vivian
Smith, William Jay
Smither, Elizabeth
Smithyman, Kendrick

Snodgrass, W.D.
Snow, Helen Foster
Snow, Richard F.
Snyder, Gary
Sobin, Gustaf
Solt, Mary Ellen
Sorley Walker, Kathrine
Sorrentino, Gilbert
Soto, Gary
Souster, Raymond
Soyinka, Wole
Spacks, Barry
Spark, Muriel
Sparshott, Francis
Spears, Heather
Spender, Stephen
Spivack, Kathleen
Squires, Radcliffe
Stafford, William
Stanford, Derek
Stanford, Donald Elwin
Stanier, Maida
Stapleton, Laurence
Starbuck, George
Stead, C.K.
Stepanchev, Stephen
Stephens, Alan
Stephens, Meic
Stern, Gerald
Sternlicht, Sanford
Stevens, Peter
Stewart, Harold Frederick
Stiles, Lindley J.
Storey, Edward
Stow, Randolph
Strand, Mark
Stranger, Joyce
Straub, Peter
Street, Julia Montgomery
Strong, Eithne
Stryk, Lucien
Stuart, Dabney
Stuart, Francis
Suknaski, Andrew, Jr.
Summers, Hal
Summers, Hollis
Sutherland, James
Sutton, David John
Swaim, Alice Mackenzie
Sward, Robert S.
Sweetman, David
Swenson, May
Swetman, Glenn Robert
Szirtes, George
Tagliabue, John
Talbot, Norman Clare
Tarn, Nathaniel
Tate, James
Taylor, Andrew
Taylor, Henry
Thiele, Colin
Thomae, Betty Kennedy
Thomas, D.M.
Thomas, R.S.
Thompson, Robert Bruce
Thomson, Derick S.
Thwaite, Anthony
Tipton, David
Toczek, Nick
Toledano, Ralph de
Tomlinson, Charles
Tong, Raymond
Tonogbanua, Francisco G.
Toulson, Shirley
Towle, Tony
Tranter, John
Trewin, John Courtenay
Trickett, Joyce
Trivelpiece, Laurel
Trypanis, Constantine
Tschumi, Raymond
Tucker, Martin
Tudor, Tasha

Turco, Lewis
Turk, Frances
Turnbull, Gael
Turner, Darwin T.
Tuwhare, Hone
Updike, John
Urdang, Constance
Valentine, Jean
Vallis, Val
Van Duyn, Mona
Varma, Monika
Vas Dias, Robert
Vaughan Williams, Ursula
Vesey, Paul
Viereck, Peter
Villa, José Garcia
Viorst, Judith
Waddington, Miriam
Waddington-Feather, John Joseph
Wagner, Linda
Wagoner, David
Wahl, Jan
Wain, John
Wainwright, Jeffrey
Wakoski, Diane
Walcott, Derek
Waldman, Anne
Walker, Alice
Walker, Margaret
Walker, Ted
Wallace-Crabbe, Christopher
Walsh, Chad
Wandor, Michelene
Wang, Hui-Ming
Ward, Donald
Ward, John Powell
Ward, Philip
Warner, Francis
Warner, Val
Warren, James E., Jr.
Warren, Robert Penn
Warsh, Lewis
Waterman, Andrew
Watkins, William Jon
Watson, James Wreford
Watson, Robert
Watson, Roderick
Way, Peter
Wayman, Tom
Webb, Bernice
Webb, Harris
Webb, Phyllis
Weber, Richard
Wedde, Ian
Weinstein, Arnold
Weiss, Theodore
Weissbort, Daniel
Weisstub, David N.
Welch, James
Welcher, Rosalind
Wendt, Albert
Whalen, Philip
Wheatcroft, John Stewart
Whister, Laurence
White, E.B.
White, Ivan
White, Jon Manchip
White, Kenneth
White, Patrick
Whitehead, James
Whitman, Ruth
Whittemore, Reed
Whitten, Leslie Hunter, Jr.
Whone, Herbert
Wieners, John
Weinman, Irving
Wilbur, Richard
Wild, Peter
Willetts, Ronald Frederick
Williams, C.K.
Williams, Emmett
Williams, Gwyn
Williams, Herbert

Poetry—*cont.*

Williams, Heathcote
Williams, Hugo
Williams, John
Williams, John Stuart
Williams, Jonathan
Williams, Miller
Williams, Thomas
Williamson, Robin
Willy, Margaret
Wilmer, Clive
Wilson, Keith
Wilson, Pat
Wingfield, Sheila
Winston, Sarah
Wise, Charles Conrad, Jr.
Witheford, Hubert
Witt, Harold Vernon
Wittlin, Thaddeus
Woiwode, Larry
Wojciechowska, Maia
Wolfe, Michael
Wong, May
Wood, Marguerite N.
Woodcock, George
Woods, John
Worner, Philip
Wright, A.J.
Wright, Celeste Turner

Poetry—*cont.*

Wright, Charles
Wright, Charles (P., Jr.)
Wright, David
Wright, Judith Arundell
Wright, Kit
Yates, J. Michael
Yolen, Jane
Young, Al
Young, David
Young, Elizabeth
Young, Ian
Young, Marguerite
Zeldis, Chayym
Zimmer, Paul J.
Zinnes, Harriet
Zolotow, Charlotte

Songs/Lyrics/Libretti

Austin, James C.
Bart, Lionel
Bond, Edward
Brand, Oscar
Browne, Michael Dennis
Brunner, John
Causley, Charles
Chodorov, Jerome
Cohen, Leonard

Songs/Lyrics/Libretti—*cont.*

Corwin, Norman
Crane, Richard
Cross, Beverley
Cutler, Ivor
Dickinson, Patric
Disch, Thomas M.
Durack, (Dame) Mary
Dylan, Bob
Elmslie, Kenward
Ferlita, Ernest
Franklin, Alexander John
Friedlander, Albert H.
Fry, Christopher
Galwey, Geoffrey
Garner, Alan
Gibbs, Alonzo
Greenberg, Alvin
Gregg, Hubert
Harwood, Gwen
Holbrook, David
Hurd, Michael John
Kessler, Jascha
Lawrence, Jerome
Lapine, James
Levy, Alan
Lewis, Janet
Marshall, Henry
McGaughey, Florence Helen

Songs/Lyrics/Libretti—*cont.*

Meredith, William
Millar, Ronald
Miller, Jim Wayne
Moore, Richard
Nelson, Harry William
Ramsey, Jarold
Ray, Mary
Richards, Christine-Louise
Ridler, Anne
Rodgers, Mary
Rose, Al
Rowell, George
Sarno, Ronald Anthony
Scott, Bill
Shapcott, Thomas W.
Sherrin, Ned
Stavis, Barrie
Stow, Randolph
Swann, Donald
Thomae, Betty Kennedy
Valency, Maurice
Vaughan Williams, Ursula
Williamson, Robin
Wilson, Geoffrey
Wilson, Sandy
Wise, Charles Conrad, Jr.

NON-FICTION

Admin./Management

Allison, Eric W.
Anderson, Courtney
Antill, J.M.
Armstrong, John Alexander
Athos, Anthony G.
Bakewell, Kenneth
Barrington, Thomas Joseph
Bartels, Robert
Bass, Bernard M.
Bates, James
Baum, Bernard H.
Beer, Stafford
Bennis, Warren
Blum, Albert A.
Blum, Albert A.
Bosticco, Mary
Brown, Robert G.
Bruns, William John, Jr.
Buell, Victor P.
Burack, Elmer H.
Cairncross, (Sir) Alexander
Chambers, Raymond John
Chorafas, Dimitris N.
Cojeen, Robert Henry
Copeman, George Henry
Daughtrey, Anne Scott
Davis, Keith
Dawes, Edward Naasson
DeBoer, John C.
de Bono, Edward
Diebold, John
Drucker, Peter
Dyer, Frederick C.
Eilon, Samuel
Ewing, David Walkley
Exton, William, Jr.
Fiedler, Fred E.
Field, John
Ford, Robert N.
Fox, Alan
Fremgen, James Morgan
George, Claude S., Jr.
Goldschmidt, Yaaqov
Gole, Victor Leslie
Goode, Kenneth G.
Granick, David
Grundstein, Nathan
Hague, (Sir) Douglas
Haney, William Valentine Patrick
Harris, Philip Robert
Hedrick, Floyd
Hodgetts, Richard M.
Hollander, Stanley C.
Janger, Allen R.
Jay, Antony
Johnson, H. Webster
Karger, Delmar William
King, William Richard
Lazer, William
Levinson, Harry
Linowes, David Francis
Ludlow, Howard Thomas
Lyden, Fremont James
Macbeath, Innis
Mantel, Samuel J., Jr.
Margolis, Diane Rothbard
Martin, Roderick
Martyn, Howe
Marvin, Philip
Massie, Joseph Logan
Mayer, Raymond
McCraw, Thomas K.
McFarland, C.K.
McFarland, Dalton E.
McGuire, Joseph William
Meltzer, Morton Franklin
Moreau, David Merlin
Mundel, Marvin Everett
Musolf, Lloyd D.
Negandhi, Anant R.

Nelson, Daniel
Noltingk, Bernard Edward
O'Connell, Jeremiah J.
Ovard, Glen F.
Owen, Charles
Pacifico, Carl
Parkinson, Cyril Northcote
Pasewark, William Robert
Paul, Thomas Francis
Payne, Bruce
Polach, Jaroslav G.
Reeves, Elton T.
Roos, Noralou P.
Sarnat, Marshall
Scheer, Wilbert E.
Schroeter, Louis C.
Schuller, Robert H.
Sethi, Narendra Kumar
Sigband, Norman Bruce
Simon, Herbert A.
Sizer, John
Smith, Howard Ross
Snow, Philip
Solomons, David
Steel, D.R.
Steiner, George A.
Steinmetz, Lawrence Leo
Stewart, Rosemary
Stillman, Richard Joseph
Thierauf, Robert James
Thorelli, Hans B.
Votaw, Dow
Vroom, Victor H.
Wadia, Maneck S.
Walker, William George
Warmington, William Allan
Wasserman, Paul
Webber, Ross A.
Wettenhall, Roger
Wolfle, Dael
Woll, Peter
Wynn, Dale Richard
Zacher, Robert Vincent

Advertising/Public relations

Arnold, Edmond Clarence
Ayars, Albert Lee
Baker, Stephen
Baus, Herbert Michael
Bernays, Edward L.
Buell, Victor P.
Butterfield, William H.
Davis, Martyn P.
Denenberg, Herbert
Derriman, James Parkyns
Diamant, Lincoln
Dunn, S. Watson
Firestone, O.J.
Fox, Stephen R.
Jefkins, Frank William
Lesly, Philip
Pompian, Richard
Simon, Julian L.
Stewart, Daniel Kenneth
Zacher, Robert Vincent

Agriculture/Forestry

Allaby, Michael
Baseley, Godfrey
Berry, Wendell
Bonham-Carter, Victor
Breimyer, Harold F.
Britton, Denis
Cracknell, Basil Edward
Cumberland, Kenneth B.
Dalton, G.E.
Dethier, Vincent G.
Donaldson, Frances
Farrington, Ian S.

Fussell, George Edwin
Gates, Paul W.
Hallett, Graham
Hardin, Clifford M.
Harris, Helen
Harvey, Nigel
Haythorne, George Vickers
James, Noel David Glaves
Jones, Eric Lionel
Lamb, F. Bruce
MacEwan, J.W. Grant
Masefield, Geoffrey
Mellor, John W.
Millett, Mervyn
Ordish, George
Perry, Peter John
Roy, James
Ryder, M.L.
Schuh, G. Edward
Scott, Roy Vernon
Tarrant, John Rex
Teller, Walter Magnes
Tracy, Michael Alec
Upton, Martin
Usher, George
Wearin, Otha Donner
Whittingham, Charles Percival
Wills, Walter J.
Wright, Philip Arthur
Wrigley, Gordon

Air/Space topics

Abbott, John Patrick
Allward, Maurice
Argyris, John
Bach, Richard
Barlay, Stephen
Berman, Arthur I.
Brooks, Peter Wright
Bueschel, Richard
Caidin, Martin
Clarke, Arthur C.
Delear, Frank J.
Di Certo, J.J.
Fishlock, David J.
Gann, Ernest K.Q.
Gatland, Kenneth William
Godwin, John
Grey, Jerry
Gunston, Bill
Hadingham, Evan
Hooper, Meredith Jean
Hopkins, George Emil
King-Hele, Desmond
Lunan, Duncan
Macvey, John Wishart
Mason, Francis K.
Mason, Herbert
Miele, Angelo
O'Connor, William E.
Ordway, Frederick I., III
Powers, Robert M.
Rollo, Vern Foster
Serling, Robert J.
Sherman, Arnold
Stambler, Irwin
Stine, G. Harry
Storer, James Donald
Tanner, John
Taylor, John William Ransom
Turnill, Reginald
Wagner, Wenceslas J.
Wood, Derek Harold
Wragg, David W.

Animals/Pets

Abbott, May Laura
Adler, Helmut E.
Allen, Durward L.

Berry, Barbara
Bone, J.F.
Bridges, William
Burden, Jean
Burgess, Warren E.
Bush, Barry
Campbell, Judith
Clements, Ellen Catherine
Corcoran, Barbara
Daniels, Mary
Delderfield, Eric R.
Downey, Fairfax Davis
Durrell, Gerald
Durrell, Jacqueline
Fairbairn, Douglas
Fairley, James S.
Farley, Walter
Ford, Lee Ellen
Fox, M.W.
Gaddis, Vincent Hayes
Gordon, John Fraser
Halsall, Eric
Heath, Veronica
Heim, Alice W.
Henschel, Elizabeth Georgie
Herriot, James
Holmes, John
Kevles, Bettyann
Le Roi, David
Mallinson, Jeremy
McNulty, Faith
Money, Keith
Mundis, Hester
Necker, Claire
Neufeld, Peter Lorenz
Nye, Nelson
Pinkwater, Daniel Manus
Pond, Grace
Prince, Alison
Rabinowitz, Sandy
Ponsonby, D.A.
Savitt, Sam
Scheffer, Victor B.
Serventy, Vincent Noel
Singer, Peter
Stranger, Joyce
Taylor, David
Walker, Stella Archer
Watkins-Pitchford, D.J.
Willock, Colin
Wolters, Richard A.
Worrell, Eric

Anthropology/Ethnology

Abrahams, Roger D.
Adams, Robert McCormick, Jr.
Anati, Emmanuel
Bailey Frederick George
Baldwin, Gordon C.
Barnes, John Arundel
Barnett, S. Anthony
Bascom, William Russel
Basham, Richard
Beattie, John Hugh Marshall
Berger, Arthur A.
Berndt, Ronald Murray
Bharati, Agehananda
Biebuyck, Daniel P.
Bock, Philip Karl
Bohannan, Paul
Boissevain, Jeremy
Bruemmer, Fred
Castaneda, Carlos
Chafe, Wallace L.
Clark, J. Desmond
Clark, John Grahame Douglas
Coe, Michael
Cole, Edmund Keith
Colson, Elizabeth
Cook, Warren Lawrence
Count, Earl W.

Crocombe, Ronald Gordon
Dames, Michael
Danaher, Kevin
Davies, Nigel
Dillon, Wilton Sterling
Divale, William T.
Dobyns, Henry F.
Dorn, Ed
Edmonson, Munro S.
Emeneau, Murray Barnson
Evans, E. Estyn
Fagan, Brian Murray
Faulkner, Charles Herman
Fell, Barry
Firth, (Sir) Raymond
Fitzgerald, Charles Patrick
Flynn, Frank
Forde Johnston, James
Fowler, Don D.
Friedrich, Paul
Gallaher, Art, Jr.
Gamst, Frederick Charles
Gayre of Gayre and Nigg, Robert
Geertz, Clifford
Gmelch, George
Gmelch, Sharon
Goodenough, Ward Hunt
Goody, John R.
Greenberg, Joseph
Gwaltney, John Langston
Heath, Dwight B.
Hemming, John Henry
Heyerdahl, Thor
Himmelfarb, Milton
Hinds, Margery
Hockett, Charles F.
Hoffman, Michael A.
Hogbin, Herbert Ian
Holmes, Lowell D.
Houston, James A.
Howell, F. Clark
Howells, William White
Hudson, Charles
Ishwaran, K.
Jett, Stephen Clinton
Johanson, Donal C.
Johnson, Colin
Keesing, Roger M.
Kilson, Marion D. de B.
Kuper, Adam
La Barre, Weston
Landes, Ruth
Leakey, Richard
Lewis, Claudia Louise
Lewis, Herbert S.
Lloyd, Peter Cutt
Luzbetak, Louis J.
Manners, Robert Alan
Maranda, Pierre
Marwick, Max Gay
Matthiessen, Peter
Maude, H.E.
Mead, Sidney Moko
Meggars, Betty J.
Meggitt, Mervyn John
Metge, Alice Joan
Money, Keith
Montagu, Ashley
Morgan, Lael
Morris, Desmond
Mowat, Farley
Murray, Robert Allen
Newell, William H.
Norbeck, Edward
Oakley, Ann
Oliver, Chad
Ortiz, Alfonso A.
Ottenberg, Simon
Patai, Raphael
Phillipson, David W.
Pitt, David Charles
Pospisil, Leopold Jaroslav
Quimby, George

Ransom, Jay Ellis
Rapoport, Robert Norman
Rauch, Irmengard
Ray, Dorothy Jean
Redgrove, Peter
Reynolds, Barrie
Richardson, Miles
Richie, Donald
Riley, Carroll L.
Robinson, Marguerite S.
Robinson, Roland
Rogler, Lloyd Henry
Rohner, Ronald P.
Rosenthal, Bernard G.
Rouse, Irving
Sahlins, Marshall
Schusky, Ernest L.
Sebeok, Thomas A.
Shapiro, Harry L.
Shiloh, Ailon
Simmons, David Roy
Snow, Philip
Spencer, Paul
Spindler, George Dearborn
Stover, Leon
Sunderland, Eric
Symmons-Symonolewicz,
   Konstantin
Taylor, John Vernon
Thomas, David H.
Thompson, Laurence Graham
Tiger, Lionel
Trigger, Bruce Graham
Turnbull, Colin M.
Tyler, Stephen Albert
Vayda, Andrew P.
Warwick, Roger
Waters, Frank
Watson, Lyall
Wax, Murray L.
Weinrich, A.K.H.
Whitten, Norman E., Jr.
Willet, Frank
Willey, Peter Robert Everard
Zinkin, Taya

Antiques/Furnishings

Benedictus, David
Bennion, Elisabeth
Bishop, Robert
Brunner, Marguerite Ashworth
Bruton, Eric
Butler, Joseph T.
Charleston, Robert Jesse
Clutton, Cecil
Cooper, Jeremy
Cross, Wilbur L.
Franklin, Linda
Gabriel, Jü
Godden, Geoffrey Arthur
Grant, Neil
Hillier, Bevis
Ketchum, William C.
Klamkin, Marian
Kovel, Ralph Mallory
Kovel, Terry Horvitz
Mackay, James Alexander
Mankowitz, Wolf
Mebane, John Harrison
Mullenix, Dennis
Noel-Hume, Ivor
Pearsall, Ronald
Philip, Peter
Reilly, Robin
Reynolds, Ernest Randolph
Rodd, John
Sabine, Ellen S.
Scott, Amoret
Scott, Christopher
Symons, Scott
Woodforde, John Ffooks

Archaeology/Antiquities

Anati, Emmanuel
Anderson, Richard Lloyd
Ashmore, Owen
Atthill, Robin
Awdry, W.
Baughan, Peter Edward
Bell, Robert Eugene
Boardman, John
Bodey, Hugh
Borer, Mary Cathcart
Bracegirdle, Brian
Branigan, Keith
Brilliant, Richard
Brodribb, Gerald
Buchanan, Robert Angus
Burton, Anthony
Butzer, Karl W.
Capon, Edmund
Clark, John Grahame Douglas
Coleman, Shalom
Coles, John Morton
Cunliffe, Barry
Davies, Nigel
Day, Michael Herbert
Deiss, Joseph Jay
Drower, Margaret Stefana
Dyer, James
Edwards, Iorwerth
Evans, E. Estyn
Fagan, Brian Murray
Farrington, Ian S.
Faulkner, Charles Herman
Field, John
Finegan, Jack
Folsom, Franklin Brewster
Forde-Johnston, James
Fox, Aileen
Frere, S.S.
Frye, Richard Nelson
Guido, Cecily Margaret
Hadingham, Evan
Hallo, William W.
Hammond, Nicholas
Harden, Donald B.
Harris, Helen
Hawkes, Jacquetta
Hawkins, Gerald Stanley
Haynes, Sybille
Henshall, Audrey Shore
Heyerdahl, Thor
Higgins, Reynold Alleyne
Hoddinott, R.F.
Hoffman, Michael A.
Hood, Martin Sinclair Frankland
Horn, Siegfried H.
Hume, John Robert
Irwin, Constance
Johnson, Stephen
Johnston, Alan
Kapelrud, Arvid Schou
Kendall, Aubyn
Lancaster Brown, Peter
Larn, Richard James Vincent
Lavine, Sigmund Arnold
Leaky, Mary
Lester, G.A.
MacDonald, William L.
Maclagen, Michael
Magnusson, Magnus
Malet, Hugh
Marsden, Peter Richard Valentine
Marx, Robert
Mason, Edmund
McDonald, William Andrew
McKay, Alexander Gordon
McLeod, Wallace
Meggers, Betty J.
Michaels, Barbara
Millard, Alan Ralph
Moorey, Peter Roger Stuart
Mourant, A.E.
Murphy, Richard Thomas
Murray, Robert Allen

Noel-Hume, Ivor
Norman, Bruce
North, Robert
Pearlman, Mosche
Phillipson, David W.
Platt, Colin
Porten, Bezalel
Quimby, George
Renfrew, Colin
Riley, Carroll L.
Rivet, Albert Lionel Frederick
Roe, Derek Arthur
Rook, Tony
Romer, (Louis) John
Rouse, Irving
Russell, Ronald
Ryder, M.L.
Saggs, Henry
Saunders, Ann Loreille
Schofield, Sylvia Anne
Shaw, Thurstan
Snodgrass, Anthony McElrea
Snow, Philip
Stevenson, Dwight Eshelman
Thomas, Charles
Thomas, David H.
Tigerman, Stanley
Trench, John
Trendall, Arthur Dale
Trever, John Cecil
Trigger, Bruce Graham
Tushingham, A. Douglas
Vermeule, Emily Dickinson
   Townsend
Walton, James
Wilkinson, Donald
Willey, Peter Robert Everard
Wilson, David M.
Wiseman, Donald John

Architecture

Addison, (Sir) William
Alexander, Christopher
Allsopp, Bruce
Angus, Margaret
Aveling, J.C.H.
Ayrton, Elisabeth
Bacon, Edmund N.
Baxter, Brian
Bayley, Stephen
Beard, Geoffrey
Bence-Jones, Mark
Biermann, Barrie
Blake, Peter
Bonham-Carter, Victor
Braham, Allan
Brawne, Michael
Brooks, H. Allen
Brown, Theodore M.
Brunskill, Ronald William
Butler, Joseph T.
Buxton, David Roden
Carver, Norman Francis, Jr.
Casson, (Sir) Hugh
Colvin, H.M.
Condit, Carl
Cook, Jeffrey
Cormack, Patrick
Crawford, Alan
Crook, Joseph
Curl, James Stevens
Curtis, William J.R.
Dale, Antony
Damaz, Paul F.
Davis, Douglas
Downs, Kerry
Drew, Philip
Dunlop, Ian
Durrant, David
Eckbo, Garrett
Eisenman, Peter D.

Art—cont.

Ramsden, E.H.
Ratcliff, Carter
Reade, Brian Edmund
Reilly, Robin
Rewald, John
Reynolds, Graham
Rinhart, Floyd
Rinhart, Marion
Robinson, Basil William
Roditi, Edouard
Rosand, David
Rosenblum, Robert
Roskill, Mark Wentworth
Roston, Murray
Rothenstein, (Sir) John
Russell, John
Russell, Ronald
Rykwert, Joseph
Sabine, Ellen S.
Sandler, Irving
Saver, Gordon C.
Schapiro, Meyer
Scharf, Aaron
Schulze, Franz
Selz, Peter
Shapcott, Thomas W.
Shapiro, David
Shearman, John
Shikes, Ralph Edmund
Short, Robert Stuart
Slive, Seymour
Smart, Alastair
Smith, Bernard
Spector, Jack Jerome
Spencer, Charles
Statler, Oliver
Stearn, William Thomas
Steinberg, Leo
Stevens, Mark
Strand, Kenneth A.
Strauss, Walter L.
Strong, (Sir) Roy
Sullivan, Michael
Summerson, (Sir) John
Surtees, Virginia
Sutton, Denys
Tancock, John
Thomas, Denis
Thomas, Paul
Thomson, Francis Paul
Tomkins, Calvin
Truitt, Anne
Tushingham, A. Douglas
Walker, John
Waller, Irene Ellen
Wang, Hui-Ming
Wearin, Otha Donner
Wedgewood, (Dame) C.V.
Weintraub, Stanley
Weismann, Donald L.
Weiss, Paul
Wertenbaker, Lael Tucker
Whalley, Joyce Irene
White, Christopher
White, John Edward
Willett, Frank
Willett, John
Wilmerding, John
Wilson, David M.
Wilson, David S.
Wolterstorff, Nicholas
Young, Sheila

Astronomy

Aller, Lawrence Hugh
Ashe, Russell
Barrow, John David
Bash, Frank N.
Batten, James William
Berry, Adrian M.
Bonnor, William Bowen

Astronomy—cont.

Chapman, Robert
Clarke, Arthur C.
Clotfelter, Beryl E.
Davies, P.C.W.
Evans, David Stanley
Ferris, Timothy
Gallant, Roy Arthur
Hawkins, Gerald Stanley
Henbest, Nigel
Hodge, Paul William
Holdstock, Robert
Hoyle, (Sir) Fred
Jastrow, Robert
Kaufmann, William J.
Kopal, Zdenek
Lancaster Brown, Peter
Longair, Malcolm
Lovell, (Sir) Bernard
Lunan, Duncan
Macvey, John Wishart
McCrea, (Sir) William
Moore, Patrick
Nakayama, Shigeru
Newton, Robert R.
Osterbrock, Donald E.
Powers, Robert M.
Ronan, Colin Alistair
Roy, Archie E.
Shipman, Henry Longfellow
Silk, Joseph
Spitzer, Lyman
Swihart, Thomas L.
Taylor, John
Vaizey, Marina
van de Kamp, Peter
Vermeule, Emily Dickinson Townsend
Weinberg, Steven
Whitcomb, John C.
Wickramasinghe, Nalin Chandra
Wood, Fergus James
Zeilik, Michael

Biology

Anastasiou, Clifford
Ayala, Francisco Jose
Barnett, S. Anthony
Beadle, George W.
Berrill, Norman John
Bigelow, Robert Sydney
Blakemore, Colin Brian
Bodmer, Walter Fred
Bonner, James
Bonner, John Tyler
Bracegirdle, Brian
Burges, Norman Alan
Butler, Colin G.
Causey, Gilbert
Chinery, Michael
Clarke, (Sir) Cyril
Cloudsley-Thompson, John
Cox, Christopher Barry
Crick, F.H.C.
Dowdeswell, Wilfrid Hogarth
Edey, Maitland A.
Ehrlich, Paul
Farish, Donald J.
Fogg, Gordon Elliott
Ford, Brian John
Fruton, Joseph S.
Gallant, Roy Arthur
Gaze, R. Michael
Gibbs, R. Darnley
Gooch, Stanley
Goodwin, Trevor W.
Gould, Stephen Jay
Grant, Verne
Gregory, Richard Langton
Grey-Wilson, Christopher
Griffin, Donald R.
Hanson, Earl D.

Biology—cont.

Harrison, (Sir) Richard
Harrison, Roger
Harrison, Ronald George
Hickin, Norman
Hirons, Montague
Holdgate, Martin W.
Holmes, Robert Lewis
Howells, William White
Ingram, Vernon Martin
Jacker, Corinne
Johnsgard, Paul A.
Kabat, Elvin Abraham
Kendrew, (Sir) John
Kevles, Bettyann
Kimball, John
King, Robert C.
Kormondy, Edward J.
Kramer, Paul J.
Kushner, Donn
Lanfranco, Guido Gaetan
Lubar, Joel F.
Luria, Salvador
MacDonald, Simon Gavin George
Macfadyen, Amyan
McGuigan, F.J.
Medvedev, Zhores
Milne, Lorus J.
Milne, Margery
Mitchell, George Archibald Grant
Moore, John A.
Morgan, Elaine
Morowitz, Harold J.
Morris, Desmond
Moss, Cynthia J.
Nahas, Gabriel G.
Nelson, J. Bryan
Noble, William Charles
Parsons, Peter Angas
Perry, Gordon Arthur
Perutz, Max
Peterson, Randolph Lee
Pianka, Eric R.
Pincher, Chapman
Powell, Eric
Preston, Reginald Dawson
Quinn, Peter
Ransom, Jay Ellis
Rowett, Helen
Ryder, M.L.
Salisbury, Frank B.
Sanger, Marjory Bartlett
Shneour, Elie Alexis
Shock, Nathan W.
Smith, C.U.M.
Smith, Hobart Muir
Smyth, Harriet Rucker
Snow, Keith Ronald
Solbrig, Otto Thomas
Stent, Gunther S.
Sunderland, Eric
Thimann, Kenneth Vivian
Thomas, Lewis
Trainor, Francis
Usher, George
Velardo, Joseph Thomas
Wallace, Bruce
Warwick, Roger
Waters, John F.
Watson, James D.
Welles, Samuel P.
Wells, Martin John
Whittingham, Charles Percival
Willmer, Edward Nevill
Wilson, Edward O.
Wilson, (Sir) Graham
Wiseman, Alan
Worthington, Edgar Barton
Young, John Zachary
Yoxen, Edward

Botany

Alexopoulos, Constantine John
Allison, R. Bruce
Audus, Leslie John
Bellamy, David James
Benson, Lyman
Bowen, Humphrey J.M.
Burges, Norman Alan
Dowden, Anne Ophelia Todd
Fahn, Abraham
Fogg, Gordon Elliott
Galbraith, Jean
Gibbs, R. Darnley
Grant, Verne
Greulach, Victor A.
Grey-Wilson, Christopher
Headstrom, Richard
Heady, Harold
Heiser, Charles B., Jr.
Holttum, Richard Eric
Huxley, Anthony Julian
Jackson, William
James, Noel David Glaves
Kastner, Joseph
Kramer, Paul J.
Millett, Mervyn
Milne, Lorus J.
Milne, Margery
Polunin, Nicholas
Preston, Reginald Dawson
Richardson, David
Russell, Norman H.
Salisbury, Frank B.
Sharr, Francis, Aubie
Solbrig, Otto Thomas
Stearn, William Thomas
Usher, George
Whittingham, Charles Percival

Business/Trade/Industry

Adair, John
Allison, Eric W.
Ammer, Christine
Aurner, Robert Ray
Bailey, Nathan A.
Bannock, Graham
Bartels, Robert
Bates, James
Bauer, Peter Thomas
Baum, Bernard H.
Beaver, Patrick
Beckinsale, Robert Percy
Beer, Stafford
Behrens, John C.
Behrman, Jack Newton
Billmeyer, Fred W., Jr.
Blond, Anthony
Blotnick, Srully
Blumberg, Phillip Irvin
Bodey, Hugh
Bolles, Richard Nelson
Bosticco, Mary
Bowyer, Mathew Justice
Branch, Alan E.
Cashin, James A.
Chapman, Stanley David
Chazanof, William
Cochran, Thomas
Cohn, Jules
Cojeen, Robert Henry
Corley, Thomas Anthony Buchanan
Cox, Roger
Crispo, John
Daughtrey, Anne Scott
Davidson, Frank Geoffrey
Davidson, Jeffrey P.
Davis, Keith
Davis, William
De Leeuw, Adèle
Dell, Edmund
Dessauer, John Paul

Business/Trade/Industry—*cont.*

Dimock, Marshall Edward
Donnelly, Austin S.
Duncan, William
Dyer, John M.
Espey, John
Flower, John Matthew
Gowing, Margaret Mary
Grant, Julius
Gray, Harold James
Greener, Michael John
Harris, Marjorie
Harrison, Brian Fraser
Henkel, Stephen Charles
Higham, Robert R.A.
Hollander, Stanley C.
Hume, John Robert
Hunker, Henry L.
Ilersic, Aldred Roman
Ivens, Michael William
Jaeger, Harry Kenneth
Jay, Antony
Jenkins, Alan
Josephy, Alvin M., Jr.
Joy, Thomas Aldred
Jones, Billy Mac
Karger, Delmar William
King, William Richard
Klein, Lawrence R.
Koplin, H.T.
Lang, William Rawson
Lesly, Philip
Lewis, W. David
Lyons, Nick
Marsh, Robert Mortimer
Martyn, Howe
Marvin, Philip
Massie, Joseph Logan
McDonald, Forrest
McFadzean of Kelvinside, Baron
McQuown, Judith H.
Metzger, Stanley D.
Minsky, Betty Jane
Moore, Carl Leland
Moss, Rose
Mundel, Marvin Everett
Myers, Walter Dean
Naisbitt, John
Negandhi, Anant R.
Nehrt, Lee C.
Newell, William T.
Nierenberg, Gerald I.
Nixson, Frederick Ian
Oakley, Charles Allen
O'Connell, Jeremiah J.
Ordish, George
Paetro, Maxine
Pascarella, Perry
Pasewark, William Robert
Paul, Thomas Francis
Paxton, John
Pilarski, Laura P.
Prochnow, Herbert Victor
Proctor, William Gilbert, Jr.
Ringer, Robert J.
Robens, (Baron)
Robinson, G Mel
Rockley, L.E.
Rostow, Eugene V.
Sarnat, Marshall
Scharff, Edward E.
Schlossstein, Steven
Sharp, Doreen Maud
Shillinglaw, Gordon
Shone, Ronald
Shultz, George P.
Siegel, Irving H.
Silk, Leonard S.
Sims, Bernard John
Sizer, John
Skupsky, Donald S.
Smith, Howard Ross
Solomons, David
Stacey, Nicholas

Business/Trade/Industry—*cont.*

Steiner, George A.
Steinmetz, Lawrence Leo
Terpstra, Vern
Thierauf, Robert James
Tobias, Andrew P.
Tugendhat, Christopher
Turner, Louis Mark
Ullmann, John E.
Vesper, Karl H.
Vidger, Leonard Perry
Votaw, Dow
Webb, James
Weidenbaum, Murray
Wellington, Richard Anthony
Westcott Jones, Kenneth
White, Lawrence J.
Whitehead, Geoffrey Michael
Williams, C. Arthur, Jr.
Williams, Clifford Glyn
Wills, Walter J.
Wilson, George Wilton
Winter, Elmer L.
Zentner, Peter
Zimpel, Lloyd

Chemistry

Albert, Adrien
Allen, R.L.M.
Amend, John R.
Andrews, Edgar Harold
Bacon, George Edward
Beadle, George W.
Billmeyer, Fred W., Jr.
Bloom, Harry
Bowen, Humphrey J.M.
Boyland, Eric
Brown, Herbert C.
Buttrey, Douglas Norton
Calvin, Melvin
Dainton, (Sir) Frederick
Davies, Mansel Morris
Davis, John Gilbert
Dewar, Michael J.
Dodge, Bertha Sanford
Donaldson, Norman
Eaborn, Colin
Ebert, James D.
Ellis, Gwynn Pennant
Everdell, M.H.
Everett, Douglas Hugh
Ferry, John Douglass
Fruton, Joseph S.
Gallant, Roy Arthur
Gaydon, Aldred Gordon
Gibbs, R. Darnley
Giddings, John Calvin
Golding, Raymund Marshall
Goodwin, Trevor W.
Grant, Julius
Greenwood, Norman Neill
Gregg, Sidney John
Gunstone, Frank Denby
Harrison, Roger
Herzberg, Gerhard
Hiller, Lejaren
Horne, R.A.
Kendrew, (Sir) John
Laidler, Keith James
Leaney, Aldred Robert Clare
Lipscomb, William Nunn
Luckey, T.D.
Lunt, George
March, N.H.
McGlashan, M.L.
McIlwain, Henry
Mellon, Melvin Guy
Neville, Kris
Overend, William George
Pauling, Linus
Perutz, Max
Pimentel, George C.

Chemistry—*cont.*

Polya, John Béla
Porter, (Sir) George
Rees, Albert Lloyd George
Roberts, Iolo Francis
Robertson, John Monteath
Schroeter, Louis C.
Seaborg, Glenn
Sisler, Harry Hall
Streitwieser, Andrew, Jr.
Tarnoky, Andras Laszlo
Taylor, Edward C.
Tedder, John M.
Trotman-Dickenson, Aubrey
　Fiennes

Children's non-fiction

Aardema, Verna
Agle, Nan Hayden
Albert, Marvin H.
Allan, Robin
Altman, Frances
Anand, Mulk Raj
Ancona, George
Anderson, John
Anderson, Verily
Appiah, Peggy
Archer, John Hall
Arkley, Arthur James
Arnold, Arnold F.
Ashby, Gwynneth Margaret
Ashley, Bernard
Atwood, Ann
Averill, Esther
Baerg, Harry John
Baldwin, Gordon C.
Ballard, Martin
Barkin, Carol
Bauer, Caroline Feller
Beckles Willson, Robina Elizabeth
Beddington, Roy
Beebe, B.F.
Beery, Mary
Bere, Rennie Montague
Berg, Leila
Berger, Terry
Berry, Barbara
Bishop, Claire Huchet
Blair, Ruth Van Ness
Bloch, Marie Halun
Boardman, Fon W., Jr.
Bond, Ruskin
Bonham, Barbara
Borer, Mary Cathcart
Borland, Kathryn
Borten, Helen
Brand, Mona
Brandenberg, Aliki
Brandreth, Gyles
Breinburg, Petronella
Briggs, Jean
Brown, Marc
Brown, Marcia
Buck, Margaret Waring
Butcher, Thomas Kennedy
Butler, Dorothy
Bye, Beryl
Byers, Irene
Caidin, Martin
Campton, David
Carr, Glyn
Carlson, Bernice Wells
Carter, Frances Tunnell
Carter, John Thomas
Cebulash, Mel
Chambers, Aidan
Chang, Isabelle C.
Chilton, Charles
Christian, Frederick H.
Clark, Mavis Thorpe
Clarkson, Ewan
Clifford, Mary Louise

Children's non-fiction—*cont.*

Cloudsley, Thompson John
Clymer, Eleanor
Coakley, Mary Lewis
Coates, Doreen Frances
Cobb, Vicki
Cockett, Mary
Coen, Rena Neumann
Coerr, Eleanor Beatrice
Cohen, Daniel
Cohen, Susan
Colbeck, Maurice
Cole, William
Collier, Zena
Collins, David R.
Colloms, Brenda
Comfort, Iris Tracy
Cone, Molly
Cooper, Lettice
Copp, Jim
Corbett, Scott
Corlett, William
Cosby, Bill
Cousins, Margaret
Cowie, Evelyn Elizabeth
Cowlin, Dorothy
Crouch, Marcus S.
Crystal, David
Danby, Mary
Davenport, Marcia
Davies, Hunter
Davis, Burke
Davis, Julia
Dean, Anabel
de Camp, Catherine Crook
del Rey, Lester
dePaola, Tomie
de Regniers, Beatrice Schenk
de Trevino, Elizabeth
Dickey, James
Dickson, Naida
Dinhofer, Alfred D.
Doan, Eleanor Lloyd
Dodson, Kenneth
Dotts, Maryann J.
Downie, Mary Alice
Drackett, Phil
Draper, Cena C.
Drury, Maxine Cole
Dyer, James
Eckblad, Edith G.
Edwards, Anne
Elkin, Benjamin
Ellis, Harry Bearse
Ellison, Virginia Howell
Elwood, Ann
Englehardt, (Sister) M. Veronice
Ephron, Delia
Espekna, Pamela
Ets, Marie Hall
Farson, Daniel
Fenten, D.X.
Finnegan, Joan
Fisher, Leonard Everett
Fisk, Nicholas
Fleming, Alice
Flesch, Y.
Flowerdew, Phyllis
Folsom, Franklin Brewster
Foon, Dennis
Foulds, Elfrida Vipont
Fox, Aileen
Frazee, Steve
Freeman, Gillian
Fritz, Jean
Galbraith, Jean
Gallant, Roy Arthur
Garden, Nancy
Gardner, Richard A.
Garnett, Eve C.R.
George, Jean Craighead
Glovach, Linda
Goaman, Muriel
Goldin, Augusta

Goodacre, Elizabeth Jane
Gordon, Sydney
Gould, Jean R.
Graham, Ada
Graham, Bob
Graham, Frank, Jr.
Graham, Lorenz
Grant, Neil
Gray, Nicolete
Green, Peter
Gregory, James Stothert
Grohskopf, Bernice
Haines, Gail Kay
Hallin, Emily Watson
Hammontree, Marie
Hanson, Joan
Hardcastle, Michael
Harris, Aurand
Harris, Dudley Arthur
Harris, Geraldine
Harris, Jonathan
Harris, Marion
Harwood, David
Haskins, Jim
Haughton, Rosemary
Hautzig, Esther
Hawes, Judy
Hawkesworth, Eric
Hays, Wilma Pitchford
Heady, Harold
Heath, Veronica
Heaven, Constance
Heerwagen, Paul K.
Hein, Lucille Eleanor
Helfman, Elizabeth S.
Helfman, Harry Carmozin
Henbest, Nigel
Henkel, Steve
Herman, George Richard
Hewett, Anita
Hieatt, Constance B.
Higdon, Hal
Highwater, Jamake
Hilton, Suzanne
Hinckley, Helen
Hirsch, S. Carl
Hobley, Leonard Frank
Hodges, Margaret
Hoffmann, Peggy
Hogner, Dorothy Childs
Holt, Victoria
Holyer, Ernie
Hopkins, Lee Bennett
Hough, Charlotte
Howe, James
Hoyland, Michael
Hoyle, Geoffrey
Huffaker, Clair
Humphrys, Leslie George
Hunkin, Tim Mark Trelawney
Hunt, Bernice Kohn
Hunt, Patricia Joan
Hurd, Edith Thacher
Hurwitz, Johanna
Ingman, Nicholas
Ipsen, D.C.
Jacker, Corinne
James, Alan
James, Elizabeth
James, J. Robert
Jauss, Ann Marie
Jenkins, Ray
Jennings, Gary
Johnson, James Ralph
Johnson, Joan J.
Johnson, William Weber
Jones, Raymond F.
Kamm, Josephine
Kettelkamp, Larry Dale
Knudsen, Margrethe June
Korfker, Dena
Krantz, Hazel
Kraus, Robert

Kupferberg, Herbert
Lamb, Elizabeth Searle
Lamb, Geoffrey Frederick
Larrick, Nancy
Latta, Richard J.
Lavine, Sigmund Arnold
Leaney, Alfred Robert Clare
Leeson, Robert
Le Roi, David
Levine, Isreal E.
Lewis, Claudia Louise
List, Ilka
Liversidge, Henry Douglas
Llewelyn Owens, Joan
Locke, Elsie
Loeper, John J.
Macanlay, David
Mackay, Claire
Mail, Audrey Maureen
Mann, Peggy
Martin, Marjorie
Martini, Teri
Maughan, Joyce Bowen
Maynard, Christopher
McCall, Edith
McClung, Robert Marshall
McCord, Anne
McGregor, Iona
McLeish, Kenneth
McNulty, Faith
Meadow, Charles T.
Miklowitz, Gloria D.
Miles, Betty
Milne, Lorus J.
Milne, Margery
Milotte, Alfred George
Milton, Joyce
Mitchison, Naomi
Myers, Elisabeth P.
Nabokov, Peter
Naylor, Phyllis Reynolds
Neumeyer, Peter
Nissman, Blossom S.
Nixon, Joan Lowry
Nwapa, Flora
Olney, Ross R.
Orgel, Doris
Palmer, Juliette
Paradis, Adrian Alexis
Parker, Nancy W.
Paterson, Katherine
Paulsen, Gary
Peterson, Helen Stone
Petry, Ann
Phelan, Mary Kay
Picard, Barbara Leonie
Pilarski, Laura P.
Pilkington, Roger Windle
Pinto, Jacqueline
Plagemann, Bentz
Pluckrose, Henry
Polking, Kirk
Powers, Bill
Priest, Christopher
Prieto, Mariana Beeching
Prince, Alison
Ray, Mary
Read, Brian
Redman, Lister Appleton
Reed, Stanley
Reeves, Marjorie E.
Rey, Margaret
Richardson, Midge Turk
Ridgway, John
Ridout, Ronald
Robottom, John
Rockwell, Anne
Roddy, Lee
Rofes, Eric Edward
Roland Smith, Gordon
Rolls, Eric Charles
Romano, Louis
Ronan, Colin Alistair

Roop, Cannie
Roop, Peter
Roseman, Kenneth David
Rossel, Seymour
Rothman, Joel
Rush, Philip
Russell, Helen Ross
Rydell, Wendy
Saddler, Allen
St. George. Judith
St. John, Nicole
Sanderlin, Owenita
Sanger, Marjory Bartlett
Sauvain, Philip Arthur
Scarf, Maggi
Schlein, Miriam
Scott, Tom
Sealey, Leonard
Serraillier, Ian
Serventy, Vincent Noel
Shirreffs, Gordon Donald
Shoesmith, Kathleen A.
Shotwell, Louisa R.
Silverberg, Robert
Simon, Seymour
Sinclair, Olga Ellen
Smith, Evelyn E.
Smith, Howard E., Jr.
Smith, Howard K.
Smith, Vivian
Snow, Keith Ronald
Sobol, Donald J.
Sobol, Ken
Softly, Barbara
Somerset Fry, Plantagenet
Southall, Ivan
Speare, Elizabeth George
Speicher, Helen Ross
Steele, Harwood E.
Stern, Ellen Norman
Stirling, Nora B.
Stuart, Forbes
Sullivan, George Edward
Sumner, Aurea
Sutherland, Efua
Sweetman, David
Syme, Ronald
Tate, Joan
Taylor, Theodore
Temple, Nigel
Thompson, Brenda
Tyler-Whittle, Michael
Ushida, Yoshiko
Van Riper, Guernsey, Jr.
Vansittart, Peter
Verral, Charles Spain
Wachter, Oralee
Waller, Leslie
Wallower, Lucille
Walton, Richard J.
Ward, Elizabeth Honor
Waters, John F.
Weems, John Edward
Welles, Samuel P.
West, Wallace
Whitlock, Ralph
Williams, Guy R.
Wilson, Barbara Ker
Wiseman, Bernard
Worcester, Donald E.
Yashima, Taro
Young, Bernice Elizabeth
Zinkin, Taya

Cinema

Adler, Renata
Affron, Charles
Allan, Elkan
Alloway, Lawrence
Alpert, Hollis
Armes, Roy

Barnouw, Erik
Basinger, Jeanine
Baxter, John
Bayer, William
Beja, Morris
Berger, Arthur A.
Bergman, Andrew
Bogdanovich, Peter
Brakhage, Stan
Braudy, Leo
Brownlow, Kevin
Butler, Ivan
Callenbach, Ernest
Casty, Alan Howard
Chanan, Michael
Chantler, David T.
Chatman, Seymour
Chipman, Bruce Lewis
Colloms, Brenda
Cooke, Alistair
Craig, Edward Anthony
Crist, Judith
Dardis, Thomas
Dick, Bernard
Burgnat, Raymond Eric
Eastaugh, Kenneth
Ebert, Roger
Erens, Patricia
Fellows, Malcom Stuart
Ferlita, Ernest
Fielding, Raymond
Finch, Christopher
Fischer, Edward A.
Fordin, Hugh
French, Philip
French, Warren G.
Fumento, Rocco
Garfield, Brian
Gifford, Denis
Gilliatt, Penelope
Glut, Don F.
Greene, Graham
Guiles, Fred Lawrence
Hénault, Marie
Higham, Charles
Hillier, Jim
Hirschhorn, Clive
Hull, David Stewart
Hunnings, Neville March
Kael, Pauline
Kaminsky, Stuart
Kanin, Garson
Katz, Ephraim
Kauffmann, Stanley
Kawin, Bruce F.
Lambert, Gavin
Lax, Eric
Leab, Daniel Josef
Lee, M. Owen
Limbacher, James L.
Lipton, Lenny
Low, Rachael
Manchel, Frank
Mapp, Edward
McCabe, John C. III
McCarty, Clifford
Mellen, Joan
Monaco, James
Morley, Sheridan
Naha, Ed
O'Leary, Liam
Parish, James
Perry, George
Pirie, David
Poague, Leland
Prawer, S.S.
Pye, Michael
Reed, Joseph W., Jr.
Reed, Stanley
Reile, Louis
Renan, Sheldon
Richie, Donald
Robinson, W.R.

Cinema—*cont.*

Rotsler, William
Schickel, Richard
Seelye, John
Sheratsky, Rodney E.
Shipman, David
Sklar, Robert
Skvorecky, Josef
Slide, Anthony
Smith, Ella
Southern, Terry
Speed, F. Maurice
Taylor, John Russell
Temple, Philip
Tilley, Patrick
Trevanian
Tudor, Andrew Frank
Underwood, Peter
Walker, Alexander
Willis, John A.
Young, William

Civil liberties/Human rights

Abraham, Henry J.
Archer, Peter Kingsley
Bedau, Hugo Adam
Berger, Nan
Blaustein, Albert P.
Bosmajian, Haig
Bozeman, Adda
Breckenridge, Adam Carlyle
Cleaver, Eldridge
Conot, Robert E.
Cray, Edward
Dershowitz, Alan M.
Dorsen, Norman
Emerson, Thomas I.
Fleischman, Harry
Fliess, Peter Joachim
Friendly, Fred W.
Garrow, David
Gaylin, Willard
Gotlieb, Allan
Gregory, Dick
Hanbury-Tenison, Robin
Hentoff, Nat
Janowsky, Oscar I.
Konvitz, Milton R.
Lamont, Corliss
Luker, Kristin
Lyons, Thomas Tolman
MacEoin, Gary
McMullen, Jeremy
Nagel, Stuart
O'Higgins, Paul
O'Rourke, William
Powledge, Fred
Rendon, Armando B.
Rothman, David J.
Sandford, Jeremy
Sawyer, Roger
Schmeiser, Douglas A.
Schofield, Michael
Smith, Robert Ellis
Sperlich, Peter Werner
Teal, G. Donn
Ungar, Stanford J.
Wellman, Carl Pierce
Whitaker, Ben

Classics

Adkins, Arthur William Hope
Arrowsmith, William
Bailey, D. R. Shackleton
Baldry, Harold Caparne
Barrow, Robin
Boardman, John
Brumbaugh, Robert S.
Burn, Andrew Robert
Chadwick, John

Classics—*cont.*

Chase, Alston Hurd
Clarke, Martin Lowther
Colledge, Malcolm
Dilke, Oswald Ashton Wentworth
Dover, (Sir) K.J.
Evans, James Allan S.
Galinsky, G. Karl
Gerber, Douglas E.
Goheen, Robert
Grant, Michael
Green, Peter
Griffiths, John Gwyn
Hamilton, James Robertson
Hammond, Nicholas
Handley, Eric Walter
Harris, Bruce Fairgray
Kelly, Maurice
Kirk, Geoffrey Stephen
Laurence, Dan H.
Lee, (Sir) Desmond
Lee, M. Owen
Ling, Roger
Lloyd-Jones, Peter Hugh Jefferd
Long, A.A.
MacDowell, Douglas Maurice
McCall, Marsh Howard, Jr.
McDonald, William Andrew
McDowell, Douglas Maurice
McDowell, John
McGregor, Malcolm Francis
McKay, Alexander Gordon
McLeish, Kenneth
McLeod, Wallace
Moore, John Michael
Norman, Bruce
O'Meara, John Joseph
Osborn, Eric Francis
Pack, Roger A.
Pearson, Lionel
Powell, Enoch
Quinn, Kenneth
Rankin, Herbert David
Rivet, Albert Lionel Frederick
Segal, Erich
Simpson, David Penistan
Smart, Ninian
Smith, Morton
Sullivan, John Patrick
Syme, (Sir) Ronald
Thompson, William B.
Todd, James Maclean
Trypanis, Constantine
Vermeule, Emily Dickinson
  Townsend
Walbank, Frank William
Walsh, P.G.
Watson, Alan
Webb, Timothy
Wellesley, Kenneth
Whitefield, John Humphreys
Willetts, Ronald Frederick
Winterbottom, Michael

Communications media

Adams, William C.
Atkinson, Frank
Allan, Elkan
Alley, Robert S.
Ayerst, David
Bachman, John W.
Bagdikian, Ben Haig
Baker, Thomas Harrison
Baird, Russell
Barnouw, Erik
Beaver, Patrick
Bell, Raymond M.
Bergreen, Laurence
Califano, Joseph A. Jr.
Casty, Alan Howard
Codding, George A.
Cole, John Alfred

Communications Media—*cont.*

Coppa, Frank John
Cronkite, Walter
Davis, Martyn P.
Day, (Sir) Robin
Denisoff, R. Serge
Di Certo, J.J.
Dudek, Louis
Eisenson, Jon
Farrar, Ronald T.
Fielding, Raymond
Gabriel, Juri
Gifford, Dennis
Goldfarb, Ronald
Golding, Peter
Hoggart, Richard
Hotzenberg, John
Hubbell, Richard Whittaker
Hutteng, John L.
Jefkins, Frank William
Johnson, Nicholas
Lang, Gladys Engel
Lang, Kurt
Lang, William Rawson
Lee, Robert E.
Lent, John A.
Lewis, Peter
Lofton, John M.
Melly, George
Millum, Trevor
Minow, Newton N.
Monaco, James
Morgan, Janet
Parish, James
Pateman, Trevor John
Paulu, Burton
Post, Steve
Pye, Michael
Reston, James
Schrank, Jeffrey
Shulman, Milton
Singer, Benjamin D.
Skornia, Harry Jay
Slide, Anthony
Smith, Alfred G.
Smith, Ralph Lee
Stewart, Daniel Kenneth
Swallow, Norman
Taylor, John Russell
Temple, Philip
Thomas, Denis
Tilley, Patrick
Tunstall, C. Jeremy
Turner, David
Watson, James
Wedell, Eberhard George
Wickham, Glynne
Wilden, Anthony
Willis, Edgar E.
Willis, John A.
Young, Jack

Crafts

Adair, Ian
Alexander, Eugenie
Angus-Butterworth, Lionel
Armstrong, Nancy
Arnold, Arnold F.
Barker, Dennis
Barker, Theodore Cardwell
Beard, Geoffrey
Beckwith, John Gordon
Bell, Robert Charles
Betts, Victoria Bedford
Bishop, Robert
Blair, Claude
Blandford, Percy
Brears, Peter C.D.
Brunner, Marguerite Ashworth
Bullard, Helen
Charleston, Robert Jesse
Crawford, Alan

Crafts—*cont.*

Creager, Clara
Dean, Beryl
De Weese, Gene
Dickerson, John
Doan, Eleanor, Lloyd
Dodd, Arthur Edward
Entwisle, Eric Arthur
Epple, Anne Orth
Finlay, Ian
Fishburn, Angela Mary
Fraser, Harry
Gottshall, Franklin H.
Grimwade, Arthur Girling
Harris, John F.
Hatcher, John
Hirst-Smith, Ann
Hodin, Josef Paul
Howard, Constance
Hutton, Warwick
Irwin, John Conran
Isenberg, Seymour
Jenkins, John Geraint
Ketchum, William C. Jr.
Lewis, John N.C.
Lister, Raymond George
Loomes, Brian
Madden-Work, Betty
McLaughlin, Terence Patrick
Morton, Brenda
Muir, Richard
Peake, Pamela
Pugh, Patterson David Gordon
Rendell, Joan
Roland Smith, Gordon
Sparnon, Norman
Treves, Ralph
Turner, Ralph
Waller, Irene Ellen
Whalley, Joyce Irene
Whitlock, Ralph
Wilson, David M.
Wright, Dorothy

Criminology

Andrews, Allen
Arnold, Peter
Babington, Anthony Patrick
Bagdikian, Ben Haig
Brandreth, Gyles
Butler, Ivan
Carleton, Mark Thomas
Carlson, Ron
Chapman, Samuel Greeley
Cohen, Henry
Collier, Richard
Conklin, John E.
Cooper, William
Critchley, Thomas Alan
Crown, David Allan
Davies, Christie
Dershowitz, Alan M.
Fisher, David
Fox, Stephen R.
Fraenkel, Jack R.
Goodman, Jonathan
Gordon, Gordon
Hepworth, Mike
Howard, Clark
Hoyles, J. Arthur
Hyde, H. Montgomery
Johnson, Elmer Hubert
Jonas, George
Kelly, Nora Hickson
Kennedy, Ludovic
Keve, Paul W.
Kirkham, George L.
Klare, Hugh J.
Lefebure, Molly
Lipton, Dean
Macdonald, John M.
Macmillan, John Angus David

Criminology—*cont.*

Marx, Gary T.
Mayo, Patricia Elton
McDonald, Lynn
Moenssens, Andre A.
Moldea, Dan E.
Morgan, Patricia
Nettler, Gwynn
Odell, Robin Ian
Quinney, Richard
Radzinowicz, (Sir) Leon
Rolph, C.H.
Rothman, David J.
Ruchelman, Leonard I.
Russell, Kenneth Victor
Schmeiser, Douglas A.
Schwarz, Louis Brown
Servadio, Gaia
Slovenko, Ralph
Smith, Kathleen J.
Soothill, Keith
Stead, Philip John
Stebbins, Robert A.
Stotland, Ezra
Tobias, John Jacob
Turner, Merfyn
Turner, William Weyand
Wagner, Diane
Walker, Nigel
Walker, Samuel
Wambaugh, Joseph
West, Donald James
Whitaker, Ben
Williams, Guy R.
Wilson, Harriet C.
Wright, A. J.
Yee, Min S.
Young, Jock

Cultural/Ethnic topics

Abrahams, Roger D.
Ackley, Randall William
Anand, Mulk Raj
Anees, Munawar Ahmad
Asante, Molefi K.
Banks, James Albert
Basham, Richard
Beier, Ulli
Bermant, Chaim
Biebuyck, Daniel P.
Bierhorst, John
Brown, Dee
Brown, Mark H.
Buday, George
Clark, LaVerne Harrell
Dodge, Bertha Sanford
Edwards, Ronald George
Farren, Mick
Feuerstein, Georg.
Flier, Michael Stephen
Fontenot, Mary Alice
Goldman, Albert
Hamburger, Philip
Highwater, Jamake
Himmelfarb, Milton
Holli, Melvin George
Howard, Helen Addison
Jones, Jaqueline
Josephy, Alvin M. Jr.
Lang, David Marshall
Lemons, James Stanley
Liptzin, Sol
Liyong, Taban lo
Marks, Stan
McDarrah, Fred W.
Mellers, Wilfrid
Milton, J.R.
Monsarrat, Ann Whitelaw
Murie, Margaret E.
Ogawa, Dennis
Oliver, Paul
Ong, Walter J.

Cultural/Ethnic topics—*cont.*

Panichas, George A.
Peterson, Edwin Loose
Peterson, Richard Austin
Pilarski, Laura P.
Raju, Poolla Tirupati
Randall, Francis Ballard
Ray, Dorothy Jean
Reynolds, Barrie
Rosenthal, Bernard G.
Schermerhorn, Richard A.
Scott, Bill
Shah, Idries
Sklar, Robert
Sklare, Marshall
Smith, Alfred G.
Tennant, (Sir) Peter
Thomas, Denis
Thomas, Paul
Thomey, Tedd
Travis, Dempsey J.
van Peursen, Cornelis A.
Wallace, Irving
Watkins, Floyd C.
Wright, Helen L.
Wright, Robert Lee
Wytrwal, Joseph A.
Ziff, Larzer
Zimpel, Lloyd

Dance/Ballet

Austin, Richard
Barnes, Clive
Bowden, Jean
Buckle, Richard
Buday, George
Clarke, Mary
Cohen, Selma Jeanne
Cunningham, Merce
Grey, Beryl
Guest, Ivor
Kerensky, Oleg
Kirstein, Lincoln
Lawson, Joan
Money, Keith
Riordan, James
Russell, Joan Mercedes
Sorley Walker, Kathrine
Swift (Sister) Mary Grace

Demography

Appleman, Philip
Borrie, Wilfred
Cassedy, James H.
Chandler, Tertius
Cipolla, Carlo M.
Goldstein, Sidney
Heer, David MacAlpine
Jones, Landon Y.
Keyfitz, Nathan
Organski, A.F.K.
Parsons, Jack
Simon, Julian L.
Spencer, Paul
Sunderland, Eric
Udry, J. Richard
Westoff, Charles F.

Design

Bayley, Stephen
Benveniste, Asa
Buday, George
Conran, Shirley
Crawford, Alan
Ellinger, John Henry
Gourdie, Thomas
Gray, Nicolete
Gullans, Charles
Harling, Robert

Design—*cont.*

Kouwenhoven, John A.
Lewis, John N.C.
Lionni, Leo
Lynes, Russell
Margolin, Victor
McLean, Ruari
Nelson, Roy P.
Overy, Paul
Pavey, Don
Smith, C. Ray
Waller, Irene Ellen
Wilson, Trevor Frederick
Yates, Frank

Earth sciences

Ager, Derek Victor
Anderson, Alan, Jr.
Backus, George Edward
Baird, David McCurdy
Batten, James William
Bhatt, Jagdish J.
Bolt, Bruce
Butzer, Karl W.
Charlier, Roger Henri
Chesterman, Charles W.
Comfort, Iris Tracy
Cooper, Bryan
DeSeyn, Donna E.
Dixon, Dougal
Dunham, (Sir) Kingsley
Elder, John
Evans, Anthony Meredith
Fea, James Lyon
Fleming, (Sir) Charles
Gallant, Roy Arthur
Gass, Ian
Gould, Stephen Jay
Gregory, Cedric E.
Harness, Charles L.
Hurlbut, Cornelius Searle, Jr.
Jacobs, John
James, J. Robert
Kirkaldy, John Francis
Krauskopf, Konrad
Mourant, A.E.
Odell, Peter R.
Ollier, Cliff David
Orr, Clyde
Peters, William C.
Ransom, Jay Ellis
Sinkankas, John
Tufty, Barbara
Vita-Finzi, Claudio
Waltham, Tony
Weisberg, Joseph
Welles, Samuel P.
Whitcomb, John C.
Whitmore, Raymond Leslie
Wood, Fergus James
Wyllie, Peter J.

Economics

Aaronvitch, Sam
Adams, Walter
Adelman, Irma Glicman
Aitken, Hugh
Aldcroft, Derek Howard
Alexander, Robert J.
Alford, B.W.E.
Ambirajan, Srinivasa
Ammer, Christine
Arkin, Marcus
Arndt, Heinz Wolfgang
Arnold, H.J.P.
Arrow, Kenneth
Atkinson, Anthony Barnes
Avramovic, Dragoslav
Baker, Christopher John
Balassa, Bela

Economics—*cont.*

Bangs, Robert B.
Bannock, Graham
Barker, Theodore Cardwell
Barlowe, Raleigh
Barratt Brown, Michael
Barrett, Nancy Smith
Bartlett, Bruce R.
Bates, James
Batson, Edward
Bauer, Peter Thomas
Baumol, William J.
Becker, Gary S.
Beckerman, Wilfred
Beckwith, Burnham Putnam
Beer, Samuel
Bellan, Ruben Carl
Beresford, Maurice
Bergson, Abram
Bird, Richard
Birmingham, Walter
Black, Robert Perry
Blase, Melvin G.
Blatt, John Markus
Blau, Francine D.
Bleakley, David Wylie
Bolino, August C.
Boltho, Andrea
Boot, John C.G.
Bosland, Chelcie Clayton
Boulding, Kenneth Ewart
Bowen, Howard R.
Bowen, William
Bowley, Marian E.A.
Bracewell-Milnes, Barry
Brahmananda, Palahally Ramaiya
Brems, Hans J.
Brenner, Yehojachin Simon
Breton, Albert
Briggs, Asa
Brittan, Samuel
Brown, (Sir) Henry Phelps
Brown, Murray
Bruns, William John, Jr.
Buchanan, James M.
Burnett, John
Burtt, Everett J.
Button, Kenneth J.
Cagan, Phillip
Cairncross, (Sir) Alexander
Cameron, Rondo
Campbell, Robert
Candilis, Wray, O.
Carter, (Sir) Charles
Caves, Richard Earl
Chambers, Raymond John
Champernowne, David
Chapman, Stanley David
Chenery, Hollis
Chiplin, Brian
Chisholm, Michael
Cipolla, Carlo M.
Cleveland, Harlan
Cohen, Bernard Lande
Cochran, Thomas
Cooper, Bryan
Cooper, Richard Newell
Copeman, George Henry
Corden, Warner Max
Corley, Thomas Anthony
  Buchanan
Crispo, John
Culyer, A.J.
Dahl, Robert
Daugherty, Anne Scott
Davidson, Frank Geoffrey
Davies, Robert William
Davis, Horace Bancroft
Dawson, George Glenn
Debreu, Gerald
Dell, Sidney
Denison, Edward Fulton
Denman, Donald Robert
Domar, Evsey D.

A33

Anderson, Vernon E.
Aptheker, Bettina
Armstrong, William H.
Arnold, Arnold F.
Ashby, Eric
Atkinson, Frank
Aukerman, Robert C.
Austin, Cedric Ronald Jonah
Ayars, Albert Lee
Ayerst, David
Ballard, Martin
Banks, James Albert
Bantock, Geoffrey Herman
Barba, Harry
Barnes, Douglas
Barrow, Robin
Beck, Earl Ray
Beckham, Barry
Beeby, Clarence Edward
Belknap, Robert L.
Bellman, Samuel I.
Benne, Kenneth Dean
Bennett, Neville
Berg, Leila
Bestor, Arthur E.
Biddle, Bruce Jesse
Bigge, Morris L.
Biggs, John Burville
Blackstone, Tessa
Blair, Glenn Myers
Blake, Leslie James
Blishen, Edward
Boles, Harold Wilson
Bossone, Richard
Bowen, Howard R.
Bowley, Rex Lyon
Bradley, R.C.
Brandt, Richard M.
Briggs, Jean
Briggs, Kenneth
Brookover, Wilbur
Brown, Frederick G.
Brown, Marcia
Brubacher, John Seiler
Bruner, Jerome S.
Bull, Norman John
Burgess, Charles
Burke, Arvid James
Burrell, Thomas William
Butland, Gilbert J.
Butler, Dorothy
Cameron, James Munro
Carr, William George
Carter, (Sir) Charles
Cass, Joan Evelyn
Cassel, Russell N.
Caws, Peter
Chilver, Peter
Clarke, Martin Lowther
Clarkson, E. Margaret
Cleveland, Harlan
Coggin, Philip A.
Collier, Kenneth
Colman, John Edward
Connell, William
Coombs, Philip
Corcoran, Gertrude B.
Cornett, R. Orin
Cottle, Thomas J.
Cowan, Gordon
Cox, Charles Brian
Craig, Robert Charles
Cramer, Stanley H.
Cratty, Bryant J.
Cremin, Lawrence
Crighton, John Clark
Cross, K. Patricia
Cross, Wilbur L.
Dainton, (Sir) Frederick
Davies, Daniel R.
Davies, E.T.
DeCrow, Karen
Dent, Harold Collett

Dexter, Lewis Anthony
Dierenfield, Richard Bruce
Doll, Ronald C.
Doman, Glenn
Donoghue, Mildred R.
Dotts, Maryann J.
Downing, John Allen
Downs, Robert B.
Drucker, Daniel Charles
Dunleavy, Patrick
Dunmore, John
Dupuis, Adrian M.
Durr, William K.
Espeland, Pamela
Ehlers, Henry James
Epstein, Charlotte
Evans, Kathleen Marianne
Fenwick, Ian
Figueroa, John
Filosa, Gary
Fink, Merton
Flew, Antony
Flinders, Neil J.
Ford, Boris
Fraenkel, Jack R.
Freedman, Mervin Burton
Fry, Edward
Fuchs, Lucy
Garforth, Francis William
Gearheart, Bill R.
Gibberd, Kathleen
Gillett, Margaret
Glock, Marvin David
Godwin, John
Goheen, Robert
Goldin, Augusta
Goldstein, Harvey
Good, Carter V.
Goodacre, Elizabeth Jane
Goode, Kenneth Gregory
Goodlad, John I.
Gotz, Ignacie L.
Grant, Nigel
Green, Donald Ross
Gross, Richard
Halls, Wilfred Douglas
Hannam, Charles, Lewis
Harrington, Elbert W.
Harris, Philip Robert
Haslegrave, Herbert Leslie
Hawley, Richard A.
Heater, Derek Benjamin
Heath, G. Louis
Hechinger, Fred M.
Hegeman, (Sister) Mary Theodore
Hendershot, Carl H.
Herbst, Jurgen
Herron, Orley Rufus
Heslep, Robert Durham
Highet, John
Hildebrand, Verna
Hill, Barrington Julian Warren
Hills, Philip James
Hines, Paul D.
Hodgkin, Robin A.
Holbrook, David
Hollingsworth, Paul M.
Hollis, Lucile Ussery
Holtzman, Wayne Harold
Hoppock, Robert
Horowitz, Irving Louis
Hostrop, Richard W.
Houle, Cyril O.
Houston, W. Robert
Howat, Gerald Malcolm David
Hughes, Phillip William
Hunt, J. McVicker
Hutchison, Henry
Hyman, Ronald T.
Itzkoff, Seymour William
Jackson, Peter
Jacobus, Lee A.
James, David Edward

Jarman, Thomas Leckie
Jensen, Arthur Robert
Joseph, Stephen M.
Judge, Harry George
Karmel, Peter Henry
Kaye, Barrington
Keenleyside, Hugh Llewellyn
Keeton, Morris Teuton
Kellaway, George Percival
Kelly, Thomas
Kerr, Clark
King, Francis P.
Kirk, Russell
Kirkendall, Lester A.
Knox, Henry Macdonald
Knudson, Danny Alan
Knudson, R.R.
Koch, Kenneth
Koerner, James D.
Kozol, Jonathan
Kraushaar, Otto F.
Krieghbaum, Hillier
Kurzweil, Erich Zvi
LaGrand, Louis E.
Lamb, Geoffrey Frederick
Lawlor, John James
Lecht, Leonard A.
Lee, (Sir) Desmond
Lee, W. Storrs III
Lee, William Rowland
Leedy, Paul D.
LeGrand, Louis E.
Lehrer, Stanley
Lewis, William Russell
Lifton, Walter
Liggero, John
Llewelyn Owens, Joan
Lockerbie, Donald Bruce
Logan, Lillian
Logan, Virgil G.
London, Herbert I.
Longmate, Worman Richard
Lucas, Christopher John
Lysaught, Jerome P.
Mabey, Richard Thomas
Mackie, Margaret Davidson
Mallinson Vernon
Marland, Michael
Marshak, Robert Eugene
Massialas, Byron G.
McCaughrean, Geraldine
McCullagh, Sheila Kathleen
McCullough, Constance M.
McDonnell, Lois Eddy
McKeachie, Wilbert J.
McLaren, John
Mellanby, Kenneth
Mellander, Gustavo A.
Melton, David
Melvin, A. Gordon
Midwinter, Eric
Miel, Alice Marie
Miles, Margaret
Milgram, Gail Gleason
Millar, James
Miller, Randolph Crump
Miller, Wilma Hildruth
Millgram, Abraham E.
Millington, Alaric
Moffat, John Lawrence
Mollenkott, Virginia Ramey
Moore-Rinvolucri, Mina
Morris, Benjamin Stephen
Morrish, Ivor
Morrison, Arnold
Morse, J. Mitchell
Murphy, Sylvia
Musgrove, Frank
Muuss, Rolf Eduard
Nash, Paul
Neagley, Ross
Nelson, Jack Lee
Neumeyer, Peter

Newsome, George Lane
Newton, Kenneth
Niblett, William Roy
Nissman, Albert
Nissman, Blossom S.
Noah, Harold J.
Nursten, Jean Patricia
O'Connell, Brian
O'Doherty, Eamonn
O'Gorman, Ned
Oinas, Felix J.
Ollerenshaw, (Dame) Kathleen
Olson, David Richard
Orem, Reginald Calvert
Orlans, Harold
Ovard, Glen F.
Painter, Helen
Palmer, (John) Carey
Parker, Franklin
Parsons, C.J.
Pasewark, William Robert
Passow, A. Harry
Pateman, Trevor
Paterson, Ronald
Pauk, Walter
Paulston, Rolland G.
Peacock, Alan Turner
Pearce, Brian Louis
Perkins, James
Peter, Laurence
Peters, Richard Stanley
Phenix, Philip Henry
Phillips, Dewi Zephaniah
Phillips, Gerald M.
Phillips, John Lawrence, Jr.
Phythian, Brian A.
Pluckrose, Henry
Poster, Cyril Dennis
Price, Kingsley Blake
Price, Ronald Francis
Pulaski, Mary Ann
Rapoport, Roger Dale
Reeves, Marjorie E.
Renfield, Richard Lee
Roberts, Iolo Francis
Roberts, Joan Ila
Robson, Derek Ian
Roe, Ernest
Rogers, William
Romano, Louis
Rose, Peter Isaac
Ross, Murray George
Ross, Ralph Gilbert
Rowntree, Derek
Rupp, Richard H.
Russell, Helen Ross
Sahakian, William S.
Sanderlin, Owenita
Saylor, John Galen
Schilpp, Paul Arthur
Schrag, Peter
Schrank, Jeffrey
Schwartz, Sheila R.
Scott, John Anthony
Sealey, Leonard
Segal, S.S.
Seifman, Eli
Shafer, Robert
Shallcrass, John James
Silberman, Charles Eliot
Silver, Harold
Silvern, Leonard C.
Sizer, Theodore Ryland
Slade, Peter
Slaughter, Eugene Edward
Sloman, Albert Edward
Smart, Ninian
Smith, Bert Kruger
Smith, Edwin H.
Soltis, Jonas F.
Souper, Patrick C.
Southgate, Vera
Southworth, Warren H.

Food and Wine—*cont.*

McCullough, Colleen
McWilliams, Margaret
Melville, James
Morgan, Marabel
Neely, Martina
Neely, William J.
Nilson, Bee
Norman, Barbara
Ray, Cyril
Read, Jan
Rook, Alan
Rose, Evelyn Gita
Roth, June
Sanctuary, Brenda
Scott, Amoret
Shippen, Zoè
Slater, Mary
Smith, Delia
Spencer, Colin
Taylor, Fred James
Thompson, Neil
Ungerer, Miriam
Vondra, Josef Gert
Weir, Molly
Whitehorn, Katharine
Wilson, Trevor Frederick
Worth, Helen
Younie, William J.

Genealogy/Heraldry

Abbott, John Patrick
Addington, Arthur Charles
Andrews, Allen
Beausay, Florence E.
Bell, Raymond M.
Boles, Harold Wilson
Brooke-Little, John
Christie-Murray, David
Dunboyne, Lord
Eilers, Hazel Kraft
Filby, P. William
Gayre of Gayre and Nigg, Robert
Hamilton-Edwards, Gerald
Maclagan, Michael
Pama, Cornelis
Powell-Smith, Vincent
Snow, Helen Foster
Tanner, John
Wagner, (Sir) Anthony
Wise, Terence

Geography

Ackah, Christian Abraham
Adamec, Ludwig W.
Addison, (Sir) William
Backus, George Edward
Balchin, William George Victor
Barrett, John Henry
Berry, Brian J.L.
Bird, James Harold
Brooks, Edwin
Butland, Gilbert J.
Carpenter, Allan
Carter, Harold
Chisholm, Michael
Chorley, John J.
Cox, Kevin Robert
Cumberland, Kenneth B.
Cumming, William P.
Darby, Henry Clifford
de Blij, Harm J.
De Vorsey, Louis, Jr.
Dewdney, John Christopher
Dodgshon, Robert A.
Doughty, Robin W.
Douglas, John
Dukert, Joseph Michael
East, William Gordon
Evans, E. Estyn

Geography—*cont.*

Eyre, S. Robert
Farmer, Bertram Hughes
Franklin, Samuel Harvey
Gilbert, Alan
Gleave, John T.
Hall, Peter Geoffrey
Harris, Chauncy D.
Harris, Geraldine
Hart, John Fraser
Harvey, P.D.A.
Henderson, William Otto
Higbee, Edward
Hobley, Leonard Frank
Hodgkin, Robin A.
Hodgkiss, Alan Geoffrey
Hope, Ronald
Horton, Frank E.
Hunker, Henry L.
Huxley, Anthony Julian
Irwin, Peter George
Jackson, John N.
Jett, Stephen Clinton
Johnson, James Henry
Johnston, R.J.
Jones, Emrys
Kaiser, Ward L.
Kasperson, Roger E.
Kay, George
Kellaway, George Percival
Kimble, George
Laffin, John
Lamb, Hubert Horace
Lancaster Brown, Peter
Learmonth, Andrew
Lee, W. Storrs III
Lefebure, Molly
Lydolph, Paul Edward
Macaulay, John Ure
MacLennan, Hugh
Manners, Gerald
Martin, Geoffrey John
Maude, H.E.
McGee, Terence Gary
McKnight, Tom Lee
Michelson, William Michael
Minshull, Roger
Money, David Charles
Moore, W.G.
Morgan, Neil
Morris, John W.
Murphey, Rhoads
Nader, G.A.
O'Connor, Anthony Michael
Odell, Peter R.
Oliver, John Edward
Ollier, Cliff David
Palmer, Peter John
Parker, W.H.
Pask, Raymond Frank
Pedler, (Sir) Frederick
Perry, Peter John
Peterson, Edwin Loose
Phillips, Robert
Popple, James
Porteous, Leslie
Prescott, J.R.V.
Pugh, John Charles
Rees, Henry
Richardson, Geoffrey Alan
Robinson, J. Lewis
Robson, Brian Turnbull
Rodgers, (Sir) John
Rollo, Vera Foster
Ruhen, Olaf
Sauvain, Philip Arthur
Scargill, David Ian
Shackleton, (Baron)
Smith, Clifford Thorpe
Smith, David Marshall
Smith, Peter J.
Symons, Leslie John
Tarrant, John Rex
Thomas, David

Geography—*cont.*

Thompson, Francis George
Thompson, Ian Bentley
Toulson, Shirley
Tregear, Thomas R.
Turnock, David
Tushingham, A. Douglas
Ward, David
Ward, Ralph Gerard
Warren, Kenneth
Watson, James Wreford
Webb, Kempton Evans
Young, Eric William
Zelinsky, Wilbur
Zimmermann, Arnold Walter

History

Abrams, Alan
Abrams, Richard M.
Abzug, Robert Henry
Acton, (Sir) Harold
Adair, John
Adamec, Ludwig W.
Adams, Kenneth Menzies
Adams, Michael Evelyn
Adam-Smith, Patsy
Addington, Larry Holbrook
Addison, (Sir) William
Adler, Mortimer J.
Africa, Thomas W.
Aitken, Hugh
Akrigg, George Philip Vernon
Alberts, Robert Carman
Albertson, Dean
Alden, John Richard
Alexander, John Thorndike
Alexander, Robert J.
Alford, B.W.E.
Allen, Harry Cranbrook
Allen, Louis
Allen, William Sheridan
Alley, Robert S.
Altick, Richard Daniel
Ambrose, Stephen
Amery, Julian
Anders, Leslie
Anderson, (Lady) Flavia
Anderson, Malcolm
Anderson, Matthew Smith
Anderson, Olive Ruth
Anderson, Richard Lloyd
Andrews, Allen
Angus, J. Colin
Angus, Margaret
Angus-Butterworth, Lionel
Annan, Noel Gilroy
Anthony, Michael
Antill, J.M.
Archer, John Hall
Archer, Jules
Arkin, Marcus
Armstrong, John Alexander
Arnade, Charles W.
Arndt, Karl
Arnold, Guy
Arnold, Rollo Davis
Aronson, Theo
Ash, Russell
Ash, William Franklin
Ashe, Geoffrey Thomas
Ashley, Maurice
Ashmore, Owen
Ashton, Robert
Asimov, Isaac
Atthill, Robin
Austin, M.M.
Aveling, J.C.H.
Axelson, Eric
Ayerst, David
Aylmer, G.E.
Badeni, June
Badian, Ernst

History—*cont.*

Bagley, John Joseph
Bailey, Alfred Goldsworthy
Bailey, D.R. Shackleton
Bailey, Norman
Bailyn, Bernard
Baker, Christopher John
Baker, Paul R.
Baker, Thomas Francis Timothy
Balfour, Michael
Ballard, Martin
Barber, John
Barber, Richard
Bardis, Panos D.
Barfield, Owen
Barkow, Al
Barlow, Frank
Barmann, Lawrence
Barnes, James J.
Barnie, John
Barnouw, Erik
Barr, Alwyn
Barratt Brown, Michael
Barrett, John G.
Barrie, Alexander
Barrow, Robin
Barry, Hugh Collis
Barry, James P.
Bartholomew, Paul Charles
Bartlett, Christopher John
Barzun, Jacques
Bates, (Sir) Darrell
Bates, Peter Watson
Batten, T.R.
Battenhouse, Roy W.
Bauer, Yehuda
Baur, John Edward
Baxter, Craig
Baylen, Joseph O.
Bayley, Charles Calvert
Baynes, (Sir) John
Baynham, Henry Wellesley Forster
Beach, Edward L.
Beales, D.E.D.
Beasley, William Gerald
Beaver, Paul
Bechervaise, John Mayston
Beck, Earl Ray
Beck, Warren Albert
Beckingham, Charles Fraser
Bedford, Henry Frederick
Bedini, Silvio A.
Beebe, Ralph K.
Beekman, Allan
Beers, Burton Floyd
Beisner, Robert L.
Belfrage, Cedric
Bell, Raymond M.
Beloff, Lord
Bence-Jones, Mark
Bender, Thomas
Bennett, Edward M.
Beresford, Maurice
Berghahn, Volker R.
Berlin, (Sir) Isaiah
Berndt, Ronald Murray
Bernstein, Barton Jannen
Berry, Don
Berton, Pierre
Bestor, Arthur E.
Bethell, Nicholas
Betts, Raymond Frederick
Bhagat, Goberdhan
Biddiss, Michael Denis
Billias, George Athan
Bingham, Caroline
Binion, Rudolph
Bird, Vivian
Birn, Raymond Francis
Bishop, James Drew
Bissoondoyal, Basdeo
Black, Clinton Vane De Brosse
Blainey, Geoffrey Norman
Blair, Kay Kimery Reynolds

Blake, Brian
Blake, Leslie James
Blake, Robert
Bleakley, David Wylie
Bluhm, Heinz
Blum, Jerome
Blumberg, Arnold
Boalch, Donald Howard
Bode, Carl
Bodey, Hugh
Boller, Paul F., Jr.
Bonham-Carter, Victor
Bonner, Brian
Boorstin, Daniel J.
Borer, Mary Cathcart
Borrie, John
Boskin, Joseph
Boswell, John
Bosworth, Allan R.
Bosworth, R.J.B.
Bott, George
Botting, Douglas
Boulton, David
Bourdeaux, Michael Alan
Bourne, Kenneth
Bowd, Douglas Gordon
Bowker, Margaret
Bowley, Rex Lyon
Boyd, Elizabeth French
Boyd, W. Harland
Bradbrook, Muriel Clara
Braddon, Russell
Bradford, M.E.
Bradlow, Frank Rosslyn
Brandes, Joseph
Branigan, Keith
Brasher, Norman Henry
Brathwaite, Edward
Braithwaite, Errol
Brears, Peter C.D.
Briggs, Asa
Brinkley, Alan
Broadfield, Aubrey Alfred
Brock, Michael
Brock, Peter de Beauvoir
Brock, William Hodson
Brock, William Ranulf
Brome, Vincent
Bromhead, Peter Alexander
Bronner, Edwin Blaine
Brooke, Christopher N.L.
Brooke-Little, John
Brookes, Pamela
Brooks, George E., Jr.
Brooks, John
Brown, Dee
Brown, Mark H.
Brown, Peter Douglas
Brown, Ralph Adams
Brown, Robert L.
Brown, Terence
Browne, Henry
Browning, Robert
Bruce, Dickson Davies, Jr.
Brundage, James A.
Buchanan, Robert Angus
Buckley, Thomas
Buckman, Peter
Budd, Lillian
Bueler, William Merwin
Bullard, Helen
Bullock, (Baron)
Bullus, (Sir) Eric E.
Bulpin, Thomas Victor
Bumsted, J.M.
Buranelli, Vincent
Burchell, R.A.
Burgess, Robert Herrmann
Burke, James
Burke, Ulick Peter
Burman, Jose Lionel
Burn, Andrew Robert
Burnett, John

Burnette, O. Lawrence, Jr.
Burns, James MacGregor
Burton, Elizabeth
Burton, Hester
Burton, Ivor Flower
Burtschi, Mary Pauline
Busch, Briton Cooper
Bushman, Richard Lyman
Byrnes, Robert Francis
Cady, John Frank
Calder, Angus
Calhoun, Richard J.
Calvert, Peter
Calvocoressi, Peter
Cameron, Rondo
Cameron Watt, Donald
Capps, Benjamin
Carew, Jan
Carleton, Mark Thomas
Carlson, Andrew R.
Carmichael, Joel
Carpenter, Allan
Carr, Jess
Carr, Raymond
Carrington, Charles Edmund
Carsten, Francis Ludwig
Carswell, John Patrick
Carter, Gwendolen Margaret
Carter, Samuel, III
Caruso, John Anthony
Carver, (Lord)
Cash, Anthony
Cassels, Alan
Caute, David
Chadwick, Owen
Chalfont, (Lord)
Chandler, George
Chandler, Tertius
Channing, Steven A.
Chapple, John Alfred Victor
Charlwood, D.E.
Chatfield, E. Charles
Chazanof, William
Chen, Joseph T.
Cheng, J. Chester
Chesham, Sallie
Chew, Allen F.
Chibnall, Marjorie McCallum
Childs, David
Childs, Marquis
Chipman, Donald
Chitham, Edward
Chiu, Hungdah
Christian, Roy Cloberry
Christie, Ian
Churchill, E. Richard
Churchward, Lloyd Gordon
Chute, Marchette
Clabby, John
Clark, Charles E.
Clark, J.C.
Clarke, Mary Stetson
Clarke, Mary Whatley
Cleeve, Brian
Cleveland, Ray L.
Clough, Shepard
Clouse, Robert Gordon
Clubb, O. Edmund
Coates, Austin
Cobb, Richard
Cochran, Thomas
Coffin, Tristram
Coffman, Barbara Frances
Coffman, Edward M.
Cohen, Stephen F.
Cohen, William Benjamin
Cohn, Norman
Cole, Edmund Keith
Cole, Wayne S.
Coleman, Terry
Colish, Marcia Lillian
Colledge, Malcolm
Collier, Richard

Collins, Robert O.
Collis, Louise
Colton, Joel
Commager, Henry Steele
Compton, James Vincent
Cone, Carl B.
Connell, Brian Reginald
Connolly, Peter
Conot, Robert E.
Conquest, Robert
Conway, Alan
Cook, Chris
Cook, Warren Lawrence
Cooke, Jacob Ernest
Cooley, John Kent
Coolidge, Olivia
Cooper, Bryan
Coox, Alvin D.
Coppa, Frank John
Cosgrave, Patrick
Cosh, Mary
Coughlan, Robert
Costigan, Daniel M.
Covington, James W.
Cowan, Edward
Cowan, Ian
Cowie, Hamilton Russell
Cowie, Leonard Wallace
Cox, Alfred Bertram
Cox, (Sir) Geoffrey
Crawley, Aidan
Cremin, Lawrence
Crews, Harry
Crighton, John Clark
Cronen, William
Crosby, Alfred W., Jr.
Cross, Anthony Glenn
Cross, Claire
Cross, Wilbur L.
Crouch, Marcus S.
Crowson, P.S.
Cruickshank, John
Cumming, William P.
Cunliffe, Marcus
Curry, Richard O.
Cushman, Dan
Dabney, Joseph Earl
Dabney, Virginius
Daiches, David
Dale, Antony
Daly, Lowrie J.
Daniel, Pete
Daniels, Elizabeth Adams
Daniels, Robert
Darby, John
Darnton, Robert
Dary, David Archie
Davidson, Basil
Davidson, Eugene
Davies, E.T.
Davies, Nigel
Davies, Norman
Davin, Dan
Davis, Allen F.
Davis, Burke
Davis, David Brion
Davis, Ralph Henry Carless
Davis, Richard Whitlock
Dawidowicz, Lucy S.
Deak, Istvan
Deakin, (Sir) William
De Camp, L. Sprague
De Crespigny, Rafe
Deighton, Len
Delderfield, Eric R.
Delzell, Charles F.
Dempsey, David
Denholm, David
Dercfler, Leslie
Derry, John
Derry, Thomas Kingston
de St. Jorre, John
De Santis, Vincent P.

Devlin, (Lord)
Dewey, Donald O.
Dewhirst, Ian
Dickens, Arthur Geoffrey
Dickinson, Harry Thomas
Dinnerstein, Leonard
Divine, Robert A.
Dobbs, Betty Jo
Dobson, Richard
Dobyns, Henry F.
Dodge, Peter
Dodgshon, Robert A.
Dohan, Mary Helen
Donaldson, Frances
Donaldson, Gordon
Donnachie, Ian
Donnelly, James S.
Donnison, Frank Siegfried Vernon
Donovan, John
Dornberg, John
Dorset, Phyllis Flanders
Douglas-Hamilton, James
Alexander
Draper, Hal
Dresner, Samuel
Drower, Margaret Stefana
Druks, Herbert
Duberman, Martin
Ducjham, Baron Frederick
Duffield, Gervase E.
Dukes, Paul
Duncan, A.A.M.
Dunlop, Eileen
Dunmore, John
Dupuy, Trevor Nevitt
Durack, (Dame) Mary
Durden, Robert F.
Durst, Paul
Dyer, James
Dymoke, Juliet
East, William Gordon
Easton, Robert
Eaton, Richard Behrens
Ebbett, Eve
Ebert, Roger
Edmonds, Walter Dumaux
Edwards, Iorwerth
Egan, Ferol
Ehret, Christopher
Ehrman, John
Eisenhower, John S.D.
Ekirch, Arthur A., Jr.
Elath, Eliahu
Elcock, Howard
Eldridge, Colin Clifford
Elegant, Robert
Elliott, John Huxtable
Elliott, William Rowcliffe
Ellis, Edward Robb
Ellis, Harry Bearse
Ellis, Keith
Ellis, Richard N.
Elstob, Peter
Elton, Geoffrey Rudolph
English, Barbara
Epstein, Helen
Erickson, Charlotte J.
Ernst, Robert
Esler, Anthony James
Evans, E. Estyn
Evans, Eric J.
Evans, James Allan S.
Evans, William McKee
Evarts, Hal
Everest, Allan S.
Everitt, Alan Milner
Eyck, Frank
Fagan, Brian Murray
Fage, John Donnelly
Fancutt, Walter
Faridi, Shah Nasir
Fast, Howard
Faulk, Odie B.

Fehrenbach, T.R.
Fehrenbacher, Don Edward
Feldman, Gerald D.
Fennell, John Lister Illingworth
Fenton, James
Feuerwerker, Albert
Fielder, Mildred
Fieldhouse, David K.Filby, P. William
Fine, Sidney
Fink, Augusta
Finlay, Ian
Finlayson, Roderick
Firkins, Peter Charles
Fisher, A. Stanley T.
Fisher, Alan W.
Fisher, Marrin
Fisher, Ralph Talcott, Jr.
Fitzgerald, Charles Patrick
Fladeland, Betty
Fleming, Thomas
Flexner, James Thomas
Fliess, Peter Joachim
Flint, John Edgar
Flood, Charles Bracelen
Florence, Ronald
Folsom, Franklin Brewster
Foner, Eric
Foner, Philip S.
Fontenot, Mary Alice
Foot, Michael
Foot, Michael Richard Daniell
Foote, Shelby
Ford, Herbert
Forder, Charles Robert
Forrest, William George Grieve
Foster, Elizabeth Read
Fothergill, Brian
Fowler, Don D.
Fox, C. P.
Fox, Levi
Fox, Robert
Fox, Stephen R.
Fox-Genovese, Elizabeth
Frakes, George Edward
Franck, Frederick
Franey, Ros
Frank, André Gunder
Franklin, John Hope
Frantz, Joe B.
Fraser, (Lady) Antonia
Freeborn, Richard
Freeman-Grenville, Greville Stewart Parker
French, Alfred
Frere, S.S.
Friis, Erik Johan
Frost, Alan
Frost, Stanley Brice
Frye, Alton
Frye, Richard Nelson
Fryer, Jonathan
Fuller, Edmund
Fuller, Jean Overton
Fussell, George Edwin
Fussner, Frank Smith
Gadney, Reg
Gagliardo, John G.
Gamble, Andrew Michael
Gann, Lewis Henry
Gardner, Brian
Garfield, Brian F.W.
Garlinski, Jozef
Garrett, Richard
Gascoigne, Bamber
Gash, Norman
Gaskell, Philip
Gates, Paul W.
Gathorne-Hardy, Jonathan
Gavin, Catherine
Gavronsky, Serge
Gay, Peter
Gentry, Curt

Gerlach, Don R.
Gibson, Charles E.
Gifford, Edward Stewart, Jr.
Gilbert, Benjamin Franklin
Gilbert, Bentley Brinkerhoff
Gilbert, Martin
Giles, John
Gill, Joseph
Gill, Ronald Crispin
Gittings, Robert
Glover, Janet Reaveley
Glover, Judith
Glover, Michael
Goaman, Muriel
Godbold, E. Stanly, Jr.
Goen, Clarence C.
Goff, Martyn
Golant, William
Goldman, Eric Frederick
Goldsmith, Barbara
Goldstein, Jonathan Amos
Gooch, Brison D.
Goode, Kenneth Gregory
Gopal, Sarvepalli
Gordon, Cyrus Herzl
Gordon, Donald C.
Goulden, Joseph C.
Gracy, David Bergen II
Graff, Henry Franklin
Graham, Alexander John
Graham, Hugh
Grant, Michael
Grant, Neil
Gray, Alfredo O.
Gray, Clayton
Gray, Francine du Plessix
Gray, Tony
Grayland, Valerie Merle
Green, Vivian
Greene, A.C.
Greene, Nathanael
Greene, Victor
Greenfield, Jerome
Greenhill, Basil Jack
Gregg, Pauline
Grenville, John A.S.
Grey, Ian
Grieb, Kenneth J.
Grierson, Edward
Grierson, Philip
Grigg, John
Grimble, Ian
Grimes, Alan P.
Grindrod, Muriel
Grob, Gerald N.
Grose, Peter
Gross, Richard
Gutman, Judith Mara
Guttmann, Allen
Haac, Oscar A.
Hackett, John
Haley, Alex
Haley, Kenneth
Hall, Aylmer
Hall, Marie Boas
Hall, Trevor Henry
Hallam, Elizabeth M.
Hallett, Robin
Hallo, William W.
Halls, Wilfred Douglas
Hamby, Alonzo Lee
Hamilton, Bernard
Hamilton, Charles
Hamilton, James Robertson
Hamilton, Ronald
Hamilton-Edwards, Gerald
Hammond, Nicholas
Hammond Innes, Ralph
Hampson, Norman
Hand, Geoffrey Joseph Philip
Hansen, Ann Natalie
Hansen, Chadwick
Hardie, Frank

Hardman, David Rennie
Hareven, Tamara K.
Hargreaves, John D.
Harkness, David W.
Harnack, Curtis
Harrel, David Edwin, Jr.
Harris, Bruce Fairgray
Harris, John
Harris, Jonathan
Harris, Ronald Walter
Harris, Sheldon H.
Harrison, John F.C.
Harrison, Lowell H.
Harrison, Royden John
Hart-Davis, Duff
Hartley, Marie
Harvey, P.D.A.
Haskins, George Lee
Hasluck, (Sir) Paul
Hassall, William Owen
Hastings, Max M.
Hastings, Robert Paul
Haswell, Chetwynd John Drake
Hatch, John
Hatcher, John
Hatton, Ragnhild
Havighurst, Alfred
Havran, Martin Joseph
Hawkes, Jacquetta
Hay, Denys
Hayes, Paul Martin
Haynes, Renée Oriana
Haythornthwaite, Philip John
Haywood, Richard Mowbray
Hazlehurst, Cameron
Healy, David Frank
Heater, Derek Benjamin
Heath, Dwight B.
Hedley, Olwen
Hellie, Richard
Helmreich, Ernst Christian
Hemming, John Henry
Hendricks, George David, Sr.
Hendrickson, James E.
Hennessy, Peter
Herbst, Jurgen
Heren, Louis
Hersey, John
Hess, Robert L.
Hibbert, Christopher
Hicken, Victor
Higginbotham, Jay
Higham, Robin
Higham, Roger Stephen
Highwater, Jamake
Higson, Philip
Hilberg, Raul
Hill, Christopher
Hill, Douglas
Hill, Rosalind Mary Theodosia
Hillgarth, J.N.
Hills, George
Hilton, Ronald
Himmelfarb, Gertrude
Hine, Robert V.
Hines, Paul D.
Hinsley, Francis H.
Hintz, Orton Sutherland
Hirsch, Morris Isaac
Hoare, Merval Hannah
Hobbs, Cecil
Hobley, Leonard Frank
Hobsbawm, Eric
Hoddinott, R.F.
Hodges, Donald Clark
Hoffman, Robert Louis
Hoffmann, Ann Marie
Hoffmann, Peter
Hohenberg, John
Holbo, Paul Sothe
Holdgate, Martin W.
Holland, Francis, Jr.
Holley, Irving Brinton, Jr.

Holli, Melvin George
Holloway, David
Holloway, Mark
Holmes, Geoffrey Shorter
Holmes, Jay
Holmes, Martin
Holt, James Clarke
Holt, Victoria
Holtby, Robert Tinsley
Honoor, Hugh
Hooper, Meredith Jean
Hoover, Dwight Wesley
Hope, Ronald
Hopkinson, (Sir) Thomas
Horgan, Paul
Horne, Alistair,
Horne, Donald Richmond
Horsman, Reginald
Hough, Henry
Hough, Richard
Houn, Franklin W.
Hovannisian, Richard G.
Howard, A.E. Dick
Howard, Helen Addison
Howard, (Sir) Michael
Howarth, Patrick
Howat, Gerald Malcolm David
Howe, Irving
Howell, Roger, Jr.
Hubbard, Robert Hamilton
Huber, Richard Miller
Hudson, Charles
Hudson, Derek
Huggett, Frank Edward
Hughes, H. Stuart
Hughes, Judith M.
Hull, Eleanor
Hulse, James Warren
Hundley, Norris C., Jr.
Hunt, Edward H.
Hutchins, Francis Gilman
Huthmacher, J. Joseph
Huxley, George Leonard
Hyam, Ronald
Hyde, H. Montgomery
Hyland, Stanley
Hyman, Harold M.
Iggers, Georg G.
Ingham, Kenneth
Ingilby, Joan Alicia
Inglis, Brian
Iremonger, Lucille
Irvine, Keith
Irwin, Constance
Irwin, John Conran
Israel, John
Jackman, Sydney Wayne
Jackson, Kenneth T.
Jackson, (Sir) William
Jacobs, Wilbur Ripley
Jacobson, Jon
James, Louis
James, R.V.Rhodes
James, Sydney V.
Janowsky, Oscar I.
Jarman, Thomas Leckie
Jenkins, Alan
Jenkins, John Geraint
Jenkins, Roy
Jensen, De Lamar
Jessup, Frank W.
Jha, Akhileshwar
Johnson, Paul
Johnson, Robert Erwin
Johnson, Stephen
Johnson, William Weber
Johnston, William Murray
Joll, James
Jones, Billy Mac
Jones, Douglas C.
Jones, Gwyn
Jones, Jaqueline
Jones, Landon Y.

Jones, Richard Allan
Jones, Richard Benjamin
Jones, Sally Roberts
Jones, Trevor
Jones, Wilbur Devereux
Josephs, Ray
Josephy, Alvin M., Jr.
Judd, Denis
Judge, Harry George
Kamen, Henry
Kamm, Josephine
Kammen, Michael
Kapelrud, Arvid Schou
Karp, Abraham J.
Karpat, Kemal H.
Katz, William Loren
Kavenagh, W. Deith
Kay, Geoffrey
Kay, Robin Langford
Kaye, Barrington
Kealey, Edward J.
Keating, Bern
Kedourie, Elie
Kee, Robert
Keegan, John
Keenleyside, Hugh Llewellyn
Keeton, George Williams
Keith-Lucas, Bryan
Kellett, Arnold
Kelley, Robert
Kelly, Maurice
Kelton, Elmer
Kemp, Betty
Kennan, George
Kennedy, David Michael
Kennedy, Joseph
Kennedy, Ludovic
Kennedy, Paul Michael
Kent, Dale Vivienne
Kenyon, John
Kerr, K. Austin
Ketcham, Ralph Louis
Ketchum, Richard M.
Kevles, Daniel J.
Kiely, Benedict
Kilbourn, William
Kim, Young
King, Betty
Kingdon, Robert McCune
Kinnear, Michael Steward Read
Kirk, David Peter
Kirk, Russell
Kirk-Greene, Anthony Hamilton
 Millard
Kissinger, Henry
Kitchen, Martin
Klamkin, Marian
Klehr, Harvey
Klein, Frederic Shriver
Kleine-Ahlbrandt, William Laird
Klement, Frank L.
Knapton, Ernest John
Knecht, Robert Jean
Knight, Frank
Knight, Hardwicke
Knightley, Phillip
Knox, Robert Buick
Knudson, Danny Alan
Kochan, Miriam
Koenigsberger, Helmut Georg
Kogan, Norman
Kohler, (Sister) Mary Hortense
Koskoff, David E.
Kotker, Norman R.
Kouwenhoven, John A.
Kraehe, Enno Edward
Kranzberg, Melvin
Krieger, Leonard
Kuehl, Warren F.
Kurzman, Dan
Kusin, Vladimir V.
Lacey, Robert
LaFeber, Walter Frederick

Lam, Truong Buu
Lamar, Howard Roberts
Lamb, Geoffrey Frederick
Lamont-Brown, Raymond
Lande, Lawrence Montague
Lander, Ernest McPherson, Jr.
Lander, Jack Robert
Langdon, Robert A.
Langley, Lester D.
Lapping, Brian
Laqueur, Walter
Larkin, Maurice
Larn, Richard James Vincent
Larsen, Egon
Lawler, Lucille
Lawrence, Berta
Lea, Tom
Leach, Douglas Edward
Leary, Edward A.
Leasor, James
Leder, Lawrence H.
Lee, W. Storrs, III
Lee, Wayne C.
Leeds, Christopher
Legge, John David
Lehmberg, Stanford Eugene
Leighton, Albert C.
Leitch, Adelaide
Leitch, David Bruce
LeKai, Louis J.
LeMay, G.H.L.
Lemons, James Stanley
Lendvai, Paul
Lengyel, Cornel Adam
Lerner, Max
Lerner, Robert Earl
Lester, Julius
Levine, Mortimer
Levinson, Olga May
Lewin, Moshe
Lewis, Lesley
Lewis, Roy
Leyser, Karl
Li Tien-yi
Liddle, Peter
Lindsay, Jack
Lingenfelter, Richard Emery
Link, Arthur S.
Lipman, Vivian David
Lisk, Jill
Little, Bryan
Litwack, Leon
Liu Wu-chi
Liversidge, Henry Douglas
Livingood, James Weston
Livings, Henry
Lloyd, Howell Arnold
Lloyd, Peter Cutt
Lloyd, T.O.
Loades, David Michael
Locke, Elsie
Locke, Hubert G.
Lockyer, Roger Walter
Loeper, John Joseph
Lofton, John M.
Loh, Pichon P.Y.
Lollis, Lorraine
Longford, Elizabeth
Longford, Lord
Longmate, Norman Richard
Longstreet, Stephen
Longworth, Philip
Loomie, Albert Joseph
Lorant, Stefan
Lord, Walter
Lott, Arnold
Low, Alfred D.
Lucia, Ellis
Luebke, Frederick Carl
Lukas, Richard Conrad
Lunderberg, Philip
Lunn, Janet
Lunt, James Doiran

Luttwak, Edward
Lycan, Gilbert L.
Lynch, John
Lyons, Thomas Tolman
Mabbett, Ian William
Mabee, Carleton
MacEwan, J.W. Grant
MacGregor, James Grierson
Machin, George Ian Thom
Macintosh, Joan
Mackay, James Alexander
Mackenzie, Andrew Carr
MacKenzie, David
Mackerras, Colin Patrick
Mackesy, Piers Gerald
Macksey, K.J.
Mack Smith, Denis
Maclagan, Michael
Maclean, (Sir) Fitzroy
MacLennan, Hugh
MacMahon, Byron Michael
Macnab, P.A.
Macnab, Roy
Maddox, Robert James
Magnusson, Magnus
Mahon, John K.
Mahy, Margaret
Mair, Craig
Major, J. Russell
Maland, David
Malefakis, Edward
Malet, Hugh
Malgonkar, Manohar
Malkiel, Yakov
Manchester, William
Mangione, Jerre
Mango, C.A.
Mann, Anthony
Mansergh, Nicholas
Mansfield, Bruce Edgar
Mapp, Alf Johnson, Jr.
Marcus, Harold G.
Marlow, Joyce
Marr, David George
Marsh, Jean
Marsh, Peter T.
Marshall, Helen Edith
Marshall, Rosalind Kay
Marszalek, John F.
Martelli, George Ansley
Martin, Ernest Walter
Martin, F.X.
Martin, Geoffrey Haward
Martin, Ralph G.
Marty, Martin E.
Marty, Sid
Marwick, Arthur
Marx, Robert
Marzani, Carl
Masao, Maruyama
Masefield, Geoffrey
Mason, Francis Kenneth
Mason, Herbert
Mason, Nicholas
Mason, Philip
Massie, Joseph Logan
Mastny, Vojtech
Mathias, Peter
Mathias, Roland
Mattingley, Christobel
Maude, H.E.
Maxwell, Kenneth Robert
May, Henry F.
May, Robin
Mayne, Richard
McCall, Edith
McCauley, Martin
McClelland, Charles Edgar
McClelland, Vincent Alan
McConica, James Kelsey
Mc Cormack, Gavan
McCormick, Donald
McCormick, Eric Hall

McCraw, Thomas K.
McCrea, (Sir) William (Hunter)
McCurtin, Peter
McCutcheon, William Alan
McDonald, Forrest
McEvedy, Colin
McFarland, C.K.
McGregor, Malcolm Francis
McIntyre, W. David
McKenna, Marian Cecilia
McKinlay, Brian John
McLaren, Ian Francis
McLean, Ruari
McLeod, Wallace
McMillen, Neil Raymond
McNeill, William Hardy
McPherson, James Munro
McRae, Kenneth Douglas
Medvedev, Roy
Medvedev, Zhores
Mehrotra, Sriiram
Mellander, Gustavo
Mendenhall, George Emery
Meserve, Walter Joseph, Jr.
Meyendorff, John
Middlebrook, Martin
Miles, Michael Wade
Millar, George
Miller, Douglas T.
Miller, Frederick
Miller, Helen Hill
Miller, Orlo
Miller, Stuart Creighton
Mills, Mervyn
Milsom, Charles H.
Milsom, Strond
Milton, Joyce
Milward, Alan S.
Minear, Richard Hoffman
Mingay, G.E.
Mitchell, Broadus
Mitchell, David John
Mitchell, Memory F.
Mitchison, Naomi
Mitchison, Rosalind
Monet, Jacques
Moore, Rayburn Sabatzky
Moore, Wilbert E.
Moore-Rinvolucri, Mina
Moorhouse, Geoffrey
Moote, A. Lloyd
Morgan, Neil
Morgan-Witts, Max
Morpurgo, J.E.
Morris, Jan
Morris, Jean
Morrison, James Frederic
Morrison, Wilbur H.
Morse, Richard McGee
Mosley, Leonard
Mosley, Nicholas
Mosse, George L.
Mould, Daphne
Moulton, James Louis
Mowat, Farley
Moxon, Roland James
Mrazek, James Edward
Munford, William Arthur
Munro, John M.
Munz, Peter
Murdock, Eugene C.
Murphey, Rhoads
Murphy, Richard Thomas
Murray, John Joseph
Murray, Robert Allen
Murray-Smith, Stephen
Muse, Benjamin
Myers, John Myers
Myrick, David F.
Nabokov, Peter
Nagel, Paul C.
Naipaul, V.S.
Nanda, Bal Ram

Nasatir, Abraham Phineas
Nash, Gary B.
Nash, Gerald D.
Nash, Roderick
Natusch, Sheila
Neal, Fred Warner
Neal, Harry Edward
Neilson, James Warren
Nelson, Cordner
Nelson, Daniel
Neufeld, Peter Lorenz
Newby, P.H.
Newman, Daisy
Newsome, David Hay
Newton, Norman Lewis
Nicholas, Herbert George
Nicholson, Ranald
Nicol, Abioseh
Nicol, Donald MacGillivray
Nicole, Christopher
Nicholas, David M.
Nicholson, Nigel
Nish, Ian Hill
Nitske, W. Robert
Nock, O.S.
Nolen, Claude
Norling, Bernard
Norman, Barbara
Norman, Bruce
Norman, John
Norman, Lilith
Norton, Philip
Norwich, John Julius
Nuge t, Walter T.K.
Nunis, Doyce B., Jr.
Nunn, Frederick McKinley
Nunn, William Curtis
Nutting, (Sir) Anthony
Nye, Russel
Oakes, James
Oakley, Charles Allen
Oakley, Stewart Philip
Oates, Stephen B.
Oatts, Lewis Balfour
O'Ballance, Edgar
O'Briant, Walter H.
O'Brien, Conor Cruise
O'Brien, Patrick
OBroin, Leon
O'Connor, Francis V.
O'Connor, Raymond G.
O'Faolain, Sean
O'Farrell, Patrick
Ogburn, Charlton, Jr.
Okpaku, Joseph
Oleck, Howard L.
Oliva, L. Jay
Oliver, Egbert
Oliver, Robert Tarbell
Oliver, Roland Anthony
Ollard, Richard
Olsen, Otto H.
Olson, James Clifton
O'Neill, Robert John
O'Neill, William L.
Ordish, George
Osborne, Milton
Overholser, Wayne D.
Owen, Charles
Owen, Roderic
Packett, Charles Neville
Padfield, Peter
Paget, Julian
Painter, John
Pakenham, Thomas
Palmer, Alan Warwick
Palmer, Michael Denison
Palmer, Peter John
Pama, Cornelis
Pankhurst, Richard
Parfitt, Tudor
Parker, Barrett
Parkinson, Cyril Northcote

Parmet, Herbert S.
Parrish, William E.
Parry, Albert
Patterson, Alfred Temple
Pavlowitch, Stevan K.
Paxton, John
Payne, J. Gregory
Pearlman, Moshe
Pedler, (Sir) Frederick Johnson
Peel, Bruce Braden
Pelling, Henry Mathison
Penick, James Lal, Jr.
Pennington, Donald Henshaw
Percival, Alicia C.
Perkins, Dwight Heald
Perrett, Bryan
Perry, George
Persico, Joseph E.
Pessen, Edward
Peterson, John Eric
Peterson, Merrill D.
Pethybridge, Roger William
Philips, (Sir) Cyril Henry
Phillips, Robert
Philmus, Robert M.
Phythian, Brian A.
Picard, Barbara Leonie
Pierce, Richard Austin
Pierson, George Wilson
Pipes, Richard
Pitt, Barrie
Pittenger, Norman
Platt, Colin
Plaut, W. Gunther
Plimpton, George
Plowden, Alison
Plumb, John Harold
Pocock, Hugh
Pogue, Forrest Carlisle
Polakoff, Keith
Pole, Jack Richon
Polenberg, Richard
Pollard, John
Pollard, Sidney
Pollock, John Charles
Pollock, Seton
Polonsky, Antony
Pope, Dudley
Popham, Hugh
Poppino, Rollie E.
Porch, Douglas
Porter, Bernard
Porter, Brian
Potter, Jeremy
Powell, Enoch
Powell, Geoffrey
Powell, Gordon George
Powell, Sumner Chilton
Poynter, John Riddoch
Prall, Stuart E.
Prebble, Joh
Preston, Richard
Price, Roger
Pritchard, R. John
Pugh, Patterson David Gordon
Pulleybank, Edwin George
Pulman, Michael Barraclough
Pulzer, Peter George Julius
Pundeff, Marin V.
Pye, Michael
Quale, G. Robina
Quarrie, Bruce
Quinn, David
Rabb, Theodore K.
Rabinowicz, Mordka Harry
Raddall, Thomas Head
Radzinowicz, (Sir) Leon
Rae, John Bell
Raeburn, Antonia
Raeff, Marc
Ramsden, John Andrew
Ramsey, Gordon Clark
Randall, Francis Ballard

Ransford, Oliver
Raphael, Chaim
Rapson, Richard L.
Ratner, Lorman
Ravitch, Norman
Rawley, James A.
Ray, Cyril
Ray, Sib Narayan
Read, Anthony
Read, Donald
Read, Jan
Reader, William Joseph
Reed, Joseph W.
Reed, Thomas Thornton
Reeves, Marjorie E.
Reeves, Thomas C.
Reid, Helen Evans
Reid, John P.
Reid, Loren
Reid, Robert
Reilly, Robin
Reischauer, Edwin O.
Rembar, Charles
Rhodes, Anthony
Riasanovsky, Nicholas
Rice, C. Duncan
Rice, Otis Kermit
Richards, Denis George
Richmond, Robert P.
Ridgway, Matthew B.
Ridley, Anthony
Ridley, Jasper
Riley, Carroll L.
Rinhart, Floyd
Rinhart, Marion
Rippley, La Vern J.
Rischin, Moses
Riste, Olav
Rivenburgh, Viola K.
Rivkin, Ellis
Roberts, Brian
Roberts, John Morris
Roberts, Michael
Robertson, James I., Jr.
Robertson, Marian
Robinson, A.M. Lewin
Robottom, John
Robson, Derek Ian
Rockland, Michael Aaron
Roddy, Lee
Rodes, John Edward
Rodgers, (Sir) John
Rodney, William
Rohrbough, Malcolm Justin
Roll, Eric
Rolle, Andrew
Rollo, Vera Foster
Rolls, Eric Charles
Rolo, Paul Jacques Victor
Romer, (Louis) John
Ronan, Colin Alistair
Roosevelt, Elliott
Rose, Kenneth
Rose, Norman Anthony
Rose, Paul
Rosenberg, J. Mitchell
Rosenthal, Erwin
Ross, Angus
Rossabi, Morris
Rostow, Walt W.
Rothman, David J.
Rothschild, Joseph
Rothwell, Victor Howard
Rowe, D. Trevor
Rowell, Douglas Geoffrey
Rowen, Herbert H.
Rowland, Arthur Ray
Rowland, Peter Kenneth
Rowse, A.L.
Rubenstein, Richard Lowell
Rubin, Stanley
Ruby, Robert H.
Rudy, Willis

Ruhen, Olaf
Rulon, Philip Reed
Runciman, (Sir) Steven
Rushing, Jane Gilmore
Russell, Brian Fitzgerald
Russell, Conrad
Russell, Francis
Russell, Jeffrey Burton
Rutman, Darrett Bruce
Ryder, Arthur John
Ryder, M.L.
Sabine, William Henry Waldo
Saggs, Henry
Sahgal, Nayantara
Salaman, Raphael A.
Salmon, Edward Togo
Salmon, John
Salmond, John
Salsbury, Stephen
Salvadori, Max William
Sanborn, Margaret
Sanderlin, George
Sanders, James Edward
Sanders, Peter
Sanders, Ronald
Sanjian, Avedis K.
Saricks, Ambrose
Sarna, Jonathan D.
Sarno, Ronald Anthony
Saunders, Ann Loreille
Sauvain, Philip Arthur
Sava, George
Sawyen, Roger
Scanlan, Arthur Brian
Scarborough, William Kauffmann
Schama, Simon Michael
Schapsmeier, Edward Lewis
Scharff, Edward E.
Schedvin, Carl Boris
Scheiber, Harry N.
Schlesinger, Arthur, Jr.
Schmokel, Wolfe W.
Schoenfeld, Maxwell Philip
Scholefield, Alan
Schuettinger, Robert Lindsay
Schwarz, Henry G.
Scott, Arthur Finley
Scott, Franklin D.
Scott, John Anthony
Scott, Roy Vernon
Seale, William
Searle, Graham William
Seifman, Eli
Seldes, George
Sellman, Roger Raymond
Serle, Alan Geoffrey
Severin, Timothy
Shankland, Peter Macfarlane
Shaw, Henry I., Jr.
Shaw, Stanford Jay
Shennan, Joseph Hugh
Shenton, James
Shepperson, Wilbur
Sherlock, (Sir) Philip
Sherman, Richard B.
Sherwood, Morgan Bronson
Shirer, William L.
Shneidman, J. Lee
Shorter, Edward
Shukman, Harold
Shulman, Milton
Shumaker, Wayne
Silver, Harold
Silverberg, Robert
Simmonds, Jack
Simmons, Marc
Simon, Edith
Simpson, A.W. Brian
Simpson, Ervin
Simpson, Jacqueline
Sinclair, Andrew
Sinclair, Keith
Singh, Khushwant

Sinor, Denis
Skendi, Stavro
Skinner, Quentin
Skipp, Victor
Sklar, Kathryn Kish
Slonim, Reuben
Smith, Anna Hester
Smith, Duane Allan
Smith, Dwight L.
Smith, Lacey Baldwin
Smith, Morton
Smith, Page
Smith, Peter Charles Horstead
Smith, Ralph Bernard
Snellgrove, Laurence Ernest
Snow, Helen Foster
Snow, Philip
Snow, Richard F.
Snowman, Daniel
Snyder, Louis L.
Socolofsky, Homer Edward
Solberg, Richard William
Somerset Fry, Plantagenet
Somerville-Large, Peter
Sonnichsen, C.L.
Soper, Eileen Louise
Sorrenson, Maurice Peter Keith
Speaight, George
Spear, Allan Henry
Spector, Sherman David
Spence, William John Duncan
Spencer, William
Spitz, Lewis William
Staff, Frank William
Spink, Reginald
Stadtman, Verne August
Stampp, Kenneth M.
Standen, John Derek
Stansky, Peter David Lyman
Stark, (Dame) Freya
Stark, Werner
Starke, Joseph Gabriel
Starr, Chester G.
Statler, Oliver
Stavis, Barrie
Stavrianos, Leften
Steel, Ronald
Stegner, Wallace Earle
Stein, Peter Gonville
Steinberg, Jonathan
Stephens, William Peter
Stern, Clarence A.
Stern, Fritz
Stern, Madeleine B.
Sternlicht, Sanford
Stevens, James R.
Stevens, Richard P.
Stevenson, David
Stevenson, Dwight Eshelman
Stewart, Donald H.
Still, William N.
Stone, Gerald
Stone, Irving
Stone, Lawrence
Storey, Robin Lindsay
Stout, Joseph A., Jr.
Stover, John Ford
Stover, Leon
Straight, Michael
Strong, (Sir) Roy Colin
Stuart, Forbes
Stubbs, Peter Charles
Suda, Zdenek Ludvik
Sulzberger, C.L.
Summers, Anthony
Supple, Barry E.
Sutcliff, Rosemary
Swanberg, William Andrew
Swierenga, Robert P.
Sword, Wiley
Sydenham, Michael John
Syers, William
Syme, (Sir) Ronald

Symonds, Richard
Synan, Vinson
Syrop, Konrad
Szulc, Tad
Tait, George Edward
Talbot, Godfrey Walker
Tames, Richard Lawrence
Tanner, John
Tarling, Nicholas
Tarr, Joel Arthur
Taylor, A.J.P.
Taylor, John Stephen
Taylor, John William Ransom
Taylor, Telford
Taylor, Welford Dunaway
Temple, Robert
Temple, Wayne C.
Terraine, John Alfred
Thaden, Edward Carl
Thiele, Colin
Thirsk, Irene Joan
Thomas, Charles
Thomas, David Arthur
Thomas, Gordon
Thomas, Hugh
Thomas, Keith
Thompson, Laurence Graham
Thompson, Roger Francis
Thompson, William Irwin
Thomson, George Malcolm
Thorne, Christopher
Thubron, Colin Gerald Dryden
Till, Barry Dorn
Tinker, Hugh
Titley, David Paul
Tobias, John Jacob
Toland, John
Toliver, Raymond Frederick
Tompkins, Edwin
Torrance, Thomas Forsyth
Tours, Hugh Berthold
Townsend, Peter
Tragle, Henry Irving
Tranter, Nigel
Trattner, Walter I.
Treadgold, Donald Warren
Trease, Geoffrey
Trefousse, Hans Louis
Trench, John
Trengove, Alan Thomas
Trevor-Roper, Hugh
Trinkaus, Charles
Tulchin, Joseph S.
Tullett, James Stuart
Turnbull, Stephen
Turner, E.S.
Turner, John Frayn
Turner, Katharine Charlotte
Tushingham, A. Douglas
Tute, Warren
Tuttle, William McCullough, Jr.
Tyson, Joseph B.
Ulam, Adam Bruno
Ullendorff, Edward
Unterberger, Betty Miller
Usherwood, Stephen
Utley, Robert M.
Vale, Malcolm Graham Allan
Vandiver, Frank Everson
Vansittart, Peter
Vasil, Raj Kumar
Vatikiotis, P.J.
Vaughan, Alden T.
Vaughan-Thomas, Wynford
Vermes, Geza
Vermuele, Emily Dickinson
  Townsend
Verney, Peter
Vital, David
Von Laue, Theodore H.
Waagenaar, Sam
Waddington-Feather, John Joseph
Waddy, Charis

Waddy, Lawrence Heber
Wade, Mason
Wagenknecht, Edward
Waite, Peter
Wakeman, Frederic Evans, Jr.
Walker, Alan
Walker, Benjamin
Walker, Kenneth Roland
Walker, Samuel E.
Wall, Joseph Frazier
Waller, George Macgregor
Walshe, R.D.
Walters, John Beauchamp
Walton, Richard J.
Walvin, James
Walworth, Arthur
Ward, Alan J.
Ward, David
Ward, Harry Merrill
Ward, John Manning
Ward, Russel Braddock
Warmington, William Alan
Warner, Marina
Warner, Philip
Warren, Harris Gaylord
Warren, Robert Penn
Warren, Sidney
Warren, Wilfred Lewis
Waters, David Watkin
Waters, Frank
Watney, John Basil
Watson, David Robin
Watt, Ian
Watt, William Montgomery
Watts, Anthony John
Wearin, Otha Donner
Webb, Jean Francis
Weber, David Joseph
Weber, Eugen
Weber, Ralph E.
Webster, Norman William
Wedgwood, (Dame) C.V.
Weeks, Jeffrey
Weems, John Edward
Weinberg, Meyer
Weinstein, Allen
Weiss, John
Wellard, James Howard
Weller, George Anthony
Wellesley, Kenneth
West, Francis James
West, John Frederick
Westbrook, Perry D.
Westfall, Richard S.
Weston, Corinne Comstock
Westwood, John Norton
Whitcomb, John C.
White, Jon Manchip
White, Stanhope
White, Terence de Vere
Whitlock, Ralph
Whitmore, Raymond Leslie
Whitnah, Donald Robert
Whitworth, Rex
Wiener, Joel Howard
Wilkinson-Latham, Robert John
Willett, John
Willetts, Ronald Frederick
Williams, Barry
Williams, David Alden
Williams, Herbert
Williams, John A.
Williams, Trevor Illtyd
Williams, William A.
Wills, Alfred John
Wilson, Brian R.
Wilson, Geoffrey
Wilson, Richard
Wilson, Trevor Gordon
Wiltgen, Ralph
Wingate, John
Winkler, Henry Ralph
Winstone, Reece

Winterbotham, Frederick William
Wise, Terence
Wiseman, Donald John
Wittlin, Thaddeus
Wittner, Lawrence Stephen
Woloch, Isser
Wolpert, Stanley Albert
Wolters, Oliver William
Wolters, Raymond
Wood, Arthur Skevington
Wood, Charles Tuttle
Wood, Derek Harold
Wood, Kerry
Wood, Leonard C.
Wood, Neal
Woodberry, Joan Merle
Woodcock, George
Woodford, Peggy
Woodhouse, Montague
Woodman, Harold David
Woodward, C. Vann
Woodward, Ralph Lee, Jr.
Woolf, Harry
Woolf, Stuart Joseph
Woollcombe, Robert
Woolrych, Austin Herbert
Wootton, Graham
Worcester, Donald E.
Workman, William D., Jr.
Worrall, Ralph Lyndal
Wragg, David W.
Wright, Christopher
Wright, Esmond
Wright, Patricia
Wright, Philip Arthur
Wright, Robert Lee
Wright, William Edward
Wroughton, John Presbury
Wykeham, (Sir) Peter
Wykes, Alan
Wynes, Charles E.
Wytrwal, Joseph A.
Yost, Nellie Snyder
Young, Janet Randall
Young, Marguerite
Youngblood, Ronald Fred
Zacek, Joseph Frederick
Zahn, Gordon C.
Zeldin, Theodore
Ziegler, Philip
Ziemke, Earl F.
Ziff, Larzer
Zimmermann, Arnold Walter
Zinkin, Taya
Zinn, Howard
Zohn, Harry
Zornow, William Frank
Zucker, Norman Livingston
Zuckerman, Michael

Homes/Gardens

Clifford, Derek Plint
Corey, Paul
Courter, Gay
Downie, Mary Alice
Fenton, D.X.
Fishburn, Angela Mary
Flesch, Y.
Harris, John F.
Harris, Marion
Hellyer, Arthur George Lee
Herwig, Rob
Hogner, Dorothy Childs
Kidder, Tracey
Kilvert, B. Cory, Jr.
Lee, Elsie
Paulsen, Gary
Prockter, Noel James
Russell Taylor, Elizabeth
Sanecki, Kay Naylor
Temple, Nigel

Homes/Gardens—*cont.*

Treves, Ralph
Van Der Spuy, Una
Waugh, Dorothy
Yarwood, Doreen

Horticulture

Bailey, Lee
Boddy, Frederick Arthur
Clifford, Derek Plint
Cowles, Fleur
Fenten, D.X.
Grounds, Roger
Harvey, John
Hellyer, Arthur George Lee
Herwig, Rob
Holttum, Richard Eric
Huxley, Anthony Julian
Lothian, Thomas Robert Noel
Money, Keith
Sanecki, Kay Naylor
Stearn, William Thomas
Thomas, Alfred Strickland
Thomas, Graham Stuart
Walls, Ian G.
Webber, E. Ronald

Human relations

Albert, Marvin H.
Atkinson, Ronald Field
Bailey, Anthony
Bardis, Panos D.
Berman, Claire
Beyfus, Drusilla
Bohannan, Paul
Bottel, Helen
Bowlby, John
Brown, Helen Gurley
Brownmiller, Susan
Buscaglia, Leo F.
Callenbach, Ernest
Cappon, Daniel
Cartland, Barbara
Cassidy, Michael
Charny, Israel
Cheavens, Frank
Cook, Mark
Constantelos, Demetrios J.
Cooper, Jilly
Cosby, Bill
Davidson, Sol M.
Deats, Richard
de Vinck, Jose
Dominian, Jack
Duhl, Leonard J.
Duvall, Evelyn Millis
Ebert, Alan
Ellis, Albert
Epstein, Charlotte
Flescher, Irwin
Flinders, Neil J.
Francoeur, Robert Thomas
Friday, Nancy
Fullerton, Gail
Gittelsohn, Roland B.
Gordon, Thomas
Gorman, Clem
Hacker, Rose
Holmes, Marjorie
Howell, John Christian
Hunt, Gladys M.
Johnson, Eric W.
Kirkendall, Lester A.
LaGrand, Louis E.
Lasswell, Marcia
Leshan, Eda J.
Lichtenberg, Philip
Lifton, Walter
Linkletter, Art
Lomas, Peter Eric Samuel

Human relations—*cont.*

Lowen, Alexander
Mace, David
Martin, Judith
Miel, Alice Marie
Morgan, Marabel
Morris, William Otis
Mudd, Emily Hartshorne
Nash, Paul
Nichols, Jack
O'Kelly, Elizabeth
Perutz, Kathrin
Phillips, Gerald M.
Pinson, William M., Jr.
Powledge, Fred
Rendon, Armando B.
Sampson, Ronald Victor
Sarnoff, Dorothy
Schuller, Robert H.
Schutz, Will
Sperlich, Peter Werner
Spock, Benjamin
Stamm, Martin L.
Staples, Robert Eugene
Steinmetz, Lawrence Leo
Swift, W. Porter
Trimmer, Ellen
Ulam, Adam Bruno
Verney, Stephen Edmund
West, Francis James
Worrall, Ralph Lyndal
Wrightsman, Lawrence Samuel

Humanities

Caplan, Arthur L.
Caras, Roger
Coggin, Philip A.
Comfort, Alex
Constantelos, Demetrios J.
Crispo, John
Dunleavy, Patrick
Inge, M. Thomas
Kuehnelt-Leddihn, Erik
Levi, Anthony H.T.
Martin, F. David
Meyer, Leonard B.
Montgomery, Marion
Murray, John Joseph
Niblett, William Roy
Oinas, Felix J.
Olsen, Otto H.
O'Meara, John Joseph
Ong, Walter J.
Pierson, George Wilson
Plumb, John Harold
Pollard, John
Prosch, Harry
Rapson, Richard L.
Sauvain, Philip Arthur
Staples, Robert Eugene
Weismann, Donald L.
Weiss, Paul

Industrial relations

Allaun, Frank
Arnold, Guy
Bealey, Frank
Bedford, Henry Frederick
Beebe, Ralph K.
Beynon, Huw
Blum, Albert A.
Carrothers, Alfred
Crispo, John
Davis, Horace Bancroft
De Caux, Len
Dunlop, John T.
Fine, Sidney
Fogarty, Michael Patrick
Foner, Philip S.
Fox, Alan

Industrial relations—*cont.*

Fraser, W. Hamish
Friedland, William H.
Galenson, Walter
Harris, Marjorie
Hopkins, George Emil
Hunt, Edward H.
Kerr, Clark
Ludlow, Howard Thomas
Macbeath, Innis
Mahoney, Thomas Arthur
Martin, Roderick
McCarthy, William E.J.
McMullen, Jeremy
Mortimer, James Edward
Moskow, Michael H.
Rezler, Julius
Roberts, Benjamin Charles
Ruppenthal, Karl M.
Schneider, B.V.H.
Scoville, James Griffin
Sheridan, Thomas
Shipler, David K.
Shultz, George P.
Sloane, Peter J.
Stein, Bruno
Turner, Herbert Arthur
van de Vall, Mark
Warmington, William Allan
Wigham, Eric

Information science/Computers

Aguolu, Christian Chukwunedu
Apter, Michael John
Bakewell, Kenneth
Beer, Stafford
Blatt, John Markus
Blotnick, Srully
Boden, Margaret A.
Brown, Robert G.
Burgess, Norman
Burrell, Thomas William
Cabaceiras, James
Chandler, George
Chorafas, Dimitris N.
Clifton, Harold Dennis
Cooper, Christopher
Costigan, Daniel M.
Diebold, John
Elliott, C. Orville
Flores, Ivan
Foskett, Douglas John
Gildersleeve, Thomas
Godman, Arthur
Haga, Enoch John
Hendershot, Carl H.
Hofstadter, Douglas
Johnson, George
Karplus, Walter J.
Kidder, Tracey
King, William Richard
Lamberton, Donald McLean
Laurie, Edward James
Meadow, Charles T.
Meltzer, Morton Franklin
Moss, Barbara
Mundel, Marvin E.
Murphy, Gordon J.
Ractliffe, John Fuller
Robinson, Philip
Rowntree, Derek
Sampson, Geoffrey
Skupsky, Donald S.
Thierauf, Robert James
Tomeski, Edward
Van Tassell, Dennie L.
Wasserman, Paul
Watkins, Wiliam John

Institutions/Organizations

Anderson, Peggy
Blau, Peter M.
Bowd, Douglas Gordon
Chadwick, John
Chatfield, E. Charles
Codding, George A., Jr.
Dell, Edmund
Goulden, Joseph C.
Huntley, James Robert
Hutchison, Sidney Charles
Jordan, Robert Smith
Martin, George Whitney
Nisbet, Stanley Donald
Nye, Joseph S., Jr.
Pearson, Keith David
Plano, Jack Charles
Schoenherr, Richard Anthony
Symonds, Richard
van de Vall, Mark
Wettenhall, Roger
Wynn, Dale Richard
Zald, Mayer Nathan

Intellectual history

Adkins, Arthur William Hope
Aveling, J.C.H.
Barnard, Frederick Mechner
Birn, Raymond Francis
Boller, Paul F., Jr.
Bowen, Barbara C.
Burke, Ulick Peter
Bush, Douglas
Chadwick, Owen
Crosland, Maurice P.
Davis, David Brion
Debreczeny, Paul
Debus, Allen George
Ekirch, Arthur A., Jr.
Fadiman, Clifton
Gay, Peter
Harris, Ronald Walter
Hartshorne, Thomas L.
Himmelfarb, Gertrude
Hunter, Michael
Karl, Frederick
King, Bruce
Knight, D.M.
Lane, Harlan
Langford, James Jerome
Leff, Gordon
Lottman, Herbert
Marshall, Margaret Lenore
McClelland, Charles Edgar
McCoy, Ralph E.
McIntosh, Christopher
McKeon, Richard
McLellan, David
Meeks, Wayne A.
Morowitz, Harold J.
Novak, Maximillian Erwin
Nove, Alec
O'Brien, Elmer
Ong, Walter J.
Petuchowski, Jakob Josef
Pipes, Richard
Pole, Jack Richon
Poster, Mark
Prosch, Harry
Quinton, (Lord)
Rapson, Richard L.
Ravitz, Abe Carl
Rickman, Hans Peter
Rivkin, Ellis
Roark, Dallas M.
Rogow, Arnold A.
Roston, Murray
Rousseau, George S.
Sampson, Ronald Victor
Screech, M.A.
Shapiro, Herman
Sigworth, Oliver F.

Intellectual History—*cont.*

Simpson, Lewis P.
Skinner, Quentin
Smith, Grover Cleveland
Sprigge, Timothy
Stigler, George J.
Stoessinger, John G.
Sweeney, Leo
Synan, Edward A.
Thomson, Robert
Toulmin, Stephen E.
Webb, Timothy
Weintraub, Stanley
Wellek, René
Welter, Rush
Willett, John

International relations/ Current affairs

Abrams, Richard M.
Absalom, Roger Neil Lewis
Abshire, David Manker
Ackroyd, Joyce Irene
Adamec, Ludwig W.
Adams, Michael Evelyn
Al-Azm, Sadik
Albinski, Henry Stephen
Alexander, Robert J.
Allen, Harry Cranbrook
Al-Marayati, Abid A.
Almond, Gabriel A.
Alport, Baron
Anglin, Douglas G.
Appleton, Sheldon Lee
Archer, Jules
Armstrong, John Alexander
Arnold, Guy
Bailey, Norman
Balfour, Michael
Ball, George
Barghoorn, Frederick C.
Barnaby, Charles Frank
Barnett, Arthur Doak
Baumann, Carol Edler
Baylen, Joseph O.
Bayley, Charles Calvert
Baylis, John
Beasley, William Gerald
Becker, Jillian
Beers, Burton Floyd
Behr, Edward
Bell, Roger
Beloff, Lord
Bennett, Edward M.
Benton, Kenneth
Bethell, Nicholas
Betts, Raymond Frederick
Biddiss, Michael Denis
Bircham, Deric
Bishop, Donald G.
Blackmer, Donald
Bloomfield, Lincoln Palmer
Booth, Ken
Bosworth, R.J.B.
Boyle, Andrew
Bozeman, Adda
Bradlee, Ben
Braunthal, Gerard
Brecher, Michael
Bromke, Adam
Brook, David
Brzezinski, Zbigniew
Bueler, William Merwin
Burton, John
Busch, Briton Cooper
Butland, Gilbert J.
Butow, Robert J.C.
Byrnes, Robert Francis
Cady, John Frank
Calvert, Peter
Calvocoressi, Peter
Cameron Watt, Donald

International relations/ Currrent affairs—*cont.*

Capelle, Russell Beckett
Carlton, David
Carr, William George
Carter, Gwendolen Margaret
Cassels, Alan
Cattan, Henry
Catudal, Honoré, Jr.
Chadwick, John
Chatfield, E. Charles
Chiu, Hungdah
Chomsky, Walter C., Jr.
Clapham, Christopher
Clark, Eric
Clemens, Walter C., Jr.
Cleveland, Harlan
Clutterbuck, Richard
Cohen, Bernard
Cole, Wayne S.
Compton, James Vincent
Conquest, Robert
Cooke, Alistair
Cooley, John Kent
Cooper, Richard Newell
Coox, Alvin D.
Copeland, Miles
Cox, Richard
Crocker, (Sir) Walter
Cronkite, Walter
Crowson, P.S.
Crozier, Brian
Dallek, Robert
Davidson, Basil
Davies, Norman
Davis, Vincent
Dawidowicz, Lucy S.
Dawisha, Adhid
Deane-Drummond, Anthony
Deats, Richard
Derry, Thomas Kingston
Dimbleby, Jonathan
Dornberg, John
Dowty, Alan K.
Druks, Herbert
East, William Gordon
Falk, Stanley Lawrence
Fatouros, Arghyrios A.
Feld, Werner J.
Finger, Seymour
Fisher, Roger
Fitzgerald, Charles Patrick
Fitzgerald, Stephen
Fliess, Peter Joachim
Foot, Michael Richard Daniell
Franck, Thomas Martin
Frank, Charles Raphael, Jr.
Frankel, Joseph
Friedberg, Maurice
Frye, Alton
Galante, Pierre
Galbraith, J. Kenneth
Garthoff, Raymond Leonard
Garve, Andrew
Geyen, Georgie Anne
Gil, Federico Guillermo
Gimbel, John
Ginsburgs, George
Girling, John
Gladwyn, Herbert Miles
Glaser, Kurt
Glick, Edward Bernard
Goldberg, Arthur J.
Goldwin, Robert
Gooding, Judson
Goodwin, Geoffrey
Gott, Richard
Graebner, Norman Arthur
Grant, Bruce
Gray, Richard Butler
Green, David E.
Grenville, John A.S.
Grieb, Kenneth J.
Griffith, William
Gutteridge, William Frank

International relations/ Current afffairs—*cont.*

Halberstam, David
Han, Suyin
Hapgood, David
Harbottle, Michael
Harris, Peter Bernard
Hart, Judith
Hayes, Paul Martin
Hayter, (Sir) William
Hazzard, Shirley
Healey, Denis
Healy, David Frank
Heater, Derek Benjamin
Henderson, William Otto
Henkin, Louis
Heren, Louis
Herzog, Arthur
Hess, Gary R.
Hewlett, Sylvia Ann
Higgins, Rosalyn
Hilsman, Roger
Hilton, Ronald
Hinsley, Francis H.
Hiro, Dilip
Hodson, Henry Vincent
Hoffmann, Stanley
Holbo, Paul Sothe
Holsti, Kalevi J.
Holsti, Ole Rudolf
Hope, Marjorie
Hopkins, Harry
Huck, Arthur
Hughes, R. John
Hunt, (Sir) David
Huntley, James Robert
Ikle, Fred C.
Ionescu, Ghita
Jacobs, Walter Darnell
Jay, Peter
Jensen, De Lamaar
John, Robert
Jonas, Manfred
Jones, Wilbur Devereux
Jordan, Robert Smith
Judd, Denis
Jukes, Geoffrey
Kaplan, Morton A.
Karpat, Kemal H.
Kavic, Lorne John
Kazemzadeh, Firuz
Keeton, George Williams
Kelman, Herbert Chanoch
Kennan, George
Kennedy, Edward
Kennedy, Gavin
Kennedy, Ludovic
Kennedy, Moorhead
Khadduri, Majid
Khouri, Fred John
Kim, Young
King, Robert R.
Kirk, Donald
Kirkman, William Patrick
Kissinger, Henry
Kitzinger, Uwe
Knorr, Klaus
Kogan, Norman
Kohler, Foy David
Kolinsky, Martin
Krejci, Jaroslav
Kriesberg, Louis
Kristol, Irving
Kuehl, Warren F.
Kuehnett-Leddihn, Eric
Kulski, Wladyslaw Wszebor
LeFeber, Walter Frederick
Lamont, Corliss
Lappe, Francis Moore
Larson, Arthur
Legum, Colin
Lewis, William Russell
Licklider, Roy E.
Lieber, Robert J.
Liss, Sheldon B.

International relations/ Current affairs—*cont.*

Lottman, Herbert
Low, Alfred D.
Lust, Peter
Luttwak, Edward Nicolae
Lycan, Gilbert L.
MacEoin, Gary
Mackerras, Colin Patrick
Maddox, Robert James
Mallin, Jay
Marcus, Harold G.
Marr, David George
Martin, Laurence
Mastny, Vojtech
Maxwell, Kenneth Robert
McGurn, Barrett
McIntyre, W. David
McLellan, David S.
McNamara, Robert
Mellander, Gustavo A.
Metzger, Stanley D.
Meyer, Lawrence
Mickolus, Edward
Middleton, Drew
Miller, John Donald Bruce
Miller, Kenneth E.
Miller, Stuart Creighton
Moore, John Norton
Morgan-Witts, Max
Morris, Christopher Hugh
Morrison, James Frederic
Moss, Robert John
Mowrer, Lilian T.
Neal, Fred Warner
Nehrt, Lee Charles
Newman, Peter
Nieburg, H.L.
Nish, Ian Hill
Norton, Augustus Richard
Nutting, (Sir) Anthony
Nye, Joseph S., Jr.
O'Ballance, Edgar
O'Brien, Lawrence F.
Odell, Peter R.
O'Kelly, Elizabeth
Organski, A.F.K.
Palmer, Norman D.
Parker, W.H.
Parry, Albert
Paxton, John
Perkins, Dwight Heald
Pipes, Richard
Plischke, Elmer
Podhoretz, Norman
Porter, Brian
Pranger, Robert
Prochnow, Herbert Victor
Prybyla, Jan S.
Quester, George
Rainey, Gene Edward
Randall, Francis Ballard
Ransom, Harry Howe
Ratiu, Ion
Reddaway, Peter
Rendon, Armando B.
Reynolds, Philip Alan
Riggs, Robert Edwon
Riordan, James
Rivkin, Ellis
Roberts, Adam
Roberts, Chalmers
Rose, Norman Anthony
Rose, Richard
Rosenaft, Menachem Z.
Rossabi, Morris
Rostow, Walt W.
Rotblat, Joseph
Roth, Andrew
Royster, Vermont
Russell, Jeremy
Russett, Bruce Martin
Said, Edward W.
Salisbury, Harrison
Sampson, Anthony

International relations/ Current affairs—*cont.*

Schell, Orville Hickok
Schelling, Thomas C.
Schoenbrun, David
Scott, Franklin D.
Segal, Ronald Michael
Shawcross, William
Sheehan, Neil
Shulman, Marshall Darrow
Simpson, R. Smith
Singer, J. David
Skendi, Stavro
Smith, Arthur L., Jr.
Smith, Hedrick
Smith, Howard K.
Solomon, Richard H.
Sorensen, Thomas Chaikin
Starke, Joseph Gabriel
Stavrianos, Leften
Steele, Harwood E.
Stegenga, James A.
Sterling, Claire
Stevens, Richard P.
Stoessinger, John G.
Stupak, Ronald Joseph
Suleiman, Michael Wadie
Sulzberger, C.L.
Swift, Richard Newton
Symonds, Richard
Szulc, Tad
Taborsky, Edward J.
Thompson, Kenneth W.
Thorne, Christopher
Tinker, Hugh
Townley, Ralph
Tugwell, Maurice A.J.
Tulchin, Joseph S.
Turner, Frederick C.
Turner, Louis Mark
Van Dyke, Vernon B.
Vatikiotis, P.J.
Vincent, John James
Viorst, Milton
von Glahn, Gerhard Ernst
Wakeman, Frederic Evans, Jr.
Wall, Patrick
Walton, Richard J.
Waltz, Kenneth N.
Waugh, Auberon
Weber, Ralph E.
Weiss, John
Wesson, Robert G.
West, Wallace
Weston, Burns H.
Wicker, Brian
Wilkinson, Paul
Willrich, Mason
Wilson, Andrew
Wilson, Wesley M.
Winterbotham, Frederick William
Wittenbach, Henry August
Wolfbein, Seymour L.
Wright, Esmond
Wright, Theodore Paul, Jr.
Wyatt, Woodrow
Yarshater, Ehsan
York, Herbert
Young, Elizabeth
Young, Wayland
Zawodny, J.K.

Language/Linguistics

Abrahams, Roger D.
Absalom, Roger Neil Lewis
Addison, (Sir) William
Alexander, Louis George
Algeo, John
Allen, W. Stannard
Anand, Mulk Raj
Asher, John Alexander
Barber, Charles Laurence
Bardis, Panos D.

Language/Linguistics—*cont.*

Barfield, Owen
Barnes, Douglas
Barr, James
Baus, Herbert Michael
Bender, Coleman
Bierhorst, John
Binham, Philip Frank
Bissoondoyal, Basdeo
Blake, Norman Francis
Bolinger, Dwight Le Merton
Bosmajian, Haig
Bossone, Richard
Bowen, Robert O.
Bredsdorff, Elias Lunn
Bronstein, Arthur G.
Brosnahan, L.F.
Broughton, Geoffrey
Brown, James I.
Brown, Roger William
Browning, Robert
Burchfield, Robert William
Cachia, Pierre
Cannon, Garland
Carrillo, Lawrence W.
Cassidy, Frederic Gomes
Cevasco, G.A.
Chadwick, John
Chafe, Wallace L.
Chomsky, Noam
Christ, Henry I.
Christophersen, Paul
Clark of Herriotshall, Arthur
  Melville
Close, Reginald Arthur
Clyne, Douglas
Coltharp, Lurline H.
Cook, Lennox
Copperud, Roy H.
Crocker, Lester G.
Croxton, C.A.
Crystal, David
Curran, Peter Malcolm
Davie, Donald
Dennis-Jones, Harold
DeVito, Joseph
Di Lella, Alexander Anthony
Di Pietro, Robert Joseph
Dohan, Mary Helen
Donoghue, Mildred R.
Dudley, Geoffrey A.
Dunn, Charles W.
Dyen, Isidore
Eaton, Trevor
Ehret, Christopher
Ehrlich, Eugene
Elgin, Suzette Haden
Ellis, Mark
Emeneau, Murray Barnson
Evans, David Ellis
Faridi, Shah Nasir
Fenwell, John Lister Illingworth
Finch, Peter
Flexner, Stuart B.
Flier, Michael Stephen
Ford, Gordon Buell, Jr.
Friedrich, Paul
Gilbert, Glenn Gordon
Glover, Judith
Gokak, Vinayak Krishna
Gordon, Cyrus Herzl
Gordon, Ian Alistair
Gorrell, Robert
Gray, Douglas
Greenbeaum, Sidney
Greenberg, Joseph
Greene, Judith
Greenlee, J. Harold
Griffith, Thomas Gwynfor
Gutteridge, Don
Hacikyan, Agop Jack
Harris, Roy
Haugen, Einar
Hayden, Donald E.

Language/Linguistics—*cont.*

Henderson, James
Herman, George Richard
Hetzron, Robert
Hewson, John
Hockett, Charles F.
Hoenigswald, Henry M.
Howard, Philip
Huppé Bernard F.
Jennings, Gary
Johnson, Eric W.
Johnson, Falk S.
Jones, Alan Griffith
Kaplan, Robert B.
Keating, L. Clark
Kellett, Arnold
Kelly, Louis Gerard
Kirk-Greene, Christopher
  Walter Edward
Klare, George Roger
Lane, Harlan
Lane, Ronald
Langdon, Robert Adrian
Langendoen, D. Terence
Lee, William Rowland
Leech, Geoffrey Neil
Leedy, Paul D.
Lennox-Short, Alan
Lester, G.A.
Lewis, Norman
Lockwood, W.B.
Luzbetak, Louis Joseph
Madgett, Naomi Long
Major, Clarence
Malkiel, Yakov
Mallinson, Vernon
Mansoor, Manahem
Martinet, André
Masson, David I.
Matthews, Peter
McConnell, J.D.R.
McDo ald, William Andrew
Miles, Leland
Millard, Alan Ralph
Miller, James Edwin
Miller, Randolph Crump
Moffat, John Lawrence
Moore-Rinvolucri, Mina Josephine
Morle, Albert Henry George
Moses, Elbert Raymond, Jr.
Narang, Gopi Ghand
Nelson, Lowry, Jr.
Newman, Edwin
Newmark, Leonard
Nierenberg, Gerald I.
Nostrand, Howard Lee
O'Doherty, Eamonn Feichin
Oinas, Felix J.
Oliver, Kenneth A.
Olson, David Richard
O'Neill, Patrick Geoffrey
Ong, Walter J.
Opie, Iona
Osgood, Charles E.
Paffard, Michael Kenneth
Palmer, Frank Robert
Parsons, C.J.
Partridge, Astley Cooper
Pateman, Trevor
Phythian, Brian A.
Pierce, Joe E.
Posner, Rebecca
Prawer, S.S.
Pride, John Bernard
Pulleybank, Edwin George
Quirk, Randolph
Rabin, Chaim
Ramsden, Herbert
Rauch, Irmengard
Riding, Laura
Ridout, Ronald
Rippley, La Vern J.
Roberts, Philip Davies
Robins, Robert Henry

Language/Linguistics—*cont.*

Robinson, Philip
Rutherford, Phillip R.
Ryan, William M.
Safine, William
Samelson, William
Sampson, Geoffrey Richard
Scaglione, Aldo
Schwartz, Joseph
Sebeok, Thomas A.
Sedwick, Frank
Semaan, Khalil I.H.
Shenker, Israel
Shieh, Francis
Simpson, Jacqueline
Slavutych, Yar
Smith, Elsdon Coles
Snellgrove, Laurence Ernest
Spalding, Keith
Spencer, John
Stack, Edward MacGregor
Steinberg, Erwin R.
Stewart, Ann Harleman
Stone, Gerald
Svartvik, Jan
Symonds, Pamela
Tregidgo, Philip Sillince
Tresidder, Argus John
Tryon, Darrell Trevor
Tschumi, Raymond
Turner, George William
Tyler, Stephen Albert
Ullendorff, Edward
Van Dusen, C. Raymond
Walford, A.J.
Walshe, R.D.
Wardhaugh, Ronald
Watkins, Floyd C.
Wells, Peter Frederick
Wilgus, D.K.
Willetts, Ronald
Wolverton, Robert E.
Zohn, Harry

Law

Abel-Smith, Brian
Abraham, Henry J.
Adler, Mortimer J.
Afterman, Allen Buddy
Akehurst, Michael
Alford, Neill Herbert, Jr.
Allen, Francis A.
Anderson, (Sir) Norman
Archer, Peter Kingsley
Areeda, Phillip
Atiyah, P.S.
Babington, Anthony Patrick
Bailey, F. Lee
Bamford, Brian Reginald
Beckman, Gail M.
Bedau, Hugo Adam
Bedford, Sybille
Black, Charles Lund, Jr.
Blaustein, Albert P.
Bloom, Murray Teigh
Bok, Derek
Bowett, Derek W.
Breckenridge, Adam
Brownlie, Ian
Bozeman, Adda
Campbell, Ian Barclay
Carlson, Ron
Carrington, Paul Dewitt
Cattan, Henry
Cavenagh, Winifred
Chiu, Hungdah
Claude, Richard Pierre
Cohen, Bernard Lande
Cohen, Maxwell
Countryman, Vern
Cowen, Zelman
Cox, Archibald

A45

Crawford, William P.
Cray, Edward
D'Amato, Anthony A.
Daube, David
Dawes, Edward Naasson
Denning, (Lord)
Derrett, Duncan
Derriman, James Parkyns
Dershowitz, Alan M.
Devlin, (Lord)
Dorsen, Norman
Downie, Leonard, Jr.
Drake, Charles D.
Dunboyne, (Lord)
Dworkin, Ronald
Eaton, Richard Behrens
Falkl, Ze'ev W.
Farndale, W.A.J.
Fatouros, Arghyrios A.
Fazal, Muhammad Abul
Fiss, Owen M.
Fonseca, John dos Reis
Ford, Lee Ellen
Forrester, William Ray
Fox, Samuel
Franck, Thomas Martin
Frankel, Sandor
Fraser, Walter Ian Reid
Fratcher, William Franklin
Friedman, Lawrence M.
Gaylin, Willard
Ginger, Ann F.
Gledhill, Alan
Goldberg, Arthur J.
Goldfarb, Ronald Lawrence
Goldsmith, Immanuel
Goldstein, Abraham S.
Goldstein, Joseph
Greener, Michael John
Grundstein, Nathan
Guest, Anthony Gordon
Gunther, Gerald
Hall, Jerome
Hanbury, Harold Grenville
Hand, Geoffrey Joseph Philip
Harrison, Brian Fraser
Hart, H.L.A.
Haskins, George Lee
Hazard, John Newbold
Heap, (Sir) Desmond
Henderson, Dan Fenno
Hendrickson, Robert A.
Henkin, Louis
Higgins, Rosalyn
Hoffmann, Malcolm A.
Hogg, Quintin
Holden, J. Milnes
Honoré Tony
Howard, A.E. Dick
Hyde, H. Montgomery
Hunnings, Neville March
Ianuzzi, John Nicholas
Inbau, Fred E.
Ivamy, Edward
Jackson, David Coop r
Jacobs, Francis G.
Jaffa, George
Jager, Martin Otto
James, Philip Seaforth
Jeffs, Julian
Jolowicz, J.A.
Jones, Gareth
Katz, Sanford N.
Keeton, George Williams
Khadduri, Majid
Kilpatrick, James Jackson
Konvitz, Milton R.
Kuh, Richard H.
Kunstler, William M.
La Forest, Gerard V.
Langbein, John Harriss
Larson, Arthur
Lebowitz, Albert

Levi, Edward Hirsch
Lewis, J.R.
Lipstein, Kurt
Lloyd, Dennis
Lofton, John M.
Loss, Louis
MacCormick, Neil
MacGuigan, Mark R.
Macneil, Ian Roderick
Magnus, Samuel Woolf
Manne, Henry G.
Marsh, Norman Stayner
Marshall, (Sir) Roy
Mather, Leonard
Mathieson, Donald Lindsay
McMullen, Jeremy
Meinhardt, Peter
Mellows, Anthony
Mendelsohn, Martin
Metzger, Stanley D.
Miller, Abraham
Miller, Charles A.
Milsom, S.F.C.
Moenssens, Andre A.
Mooney, Christopher Francis
Moore, E. Garth
Moore, John Norton
Morris, William Otis
Murphy, Walter Francis
Nagel, Stuart
Nash, Patrick Gerard
Northey, John Frederick
Oaks, Dallin H.
O'Higgins, Paul
Oleck, Howard L.
Podgorecki, Adam
Pollock, Seton
Pospisil, Leopold Jaroslav
Powell-Smith, Vincent
Reid, John P.
Rembar, Charles
Rhyne, Charles S.
Riggs, Robert Edwon
Ringer, Barbara Alice
Roebuck, Derek
Rolph, C.H.
Rose, Paul
Rosenberg, J. Mitchell
Rostow, Eugene V.
St. John-Stevas, Norman
Samuels, Warren J.
Sax, Joseph L.
Schmeiser, Douglas A.
Schmitthoff, Clive Macmillan
Schwartz, Louis Brown
Schwarzenberger, Georg
Sethna, M.J.
Sheridan, Lionel Astor
Shrand, David
Shuman, Samuel I.
Simon, Rita J.
Simpson, A.W. Brian
Sims, Bernard John
Skupsky, Donald S.
Slovenko, Ralph
Smith, Robert Ellis
Snyder, Francis Gregory
Sohn, Louis Bruno
Stanley, Olivere
Starke, Joseph Gabriel
Stein, Peter Gonville
Steiner, Kurt
Stone, Alan A.
Stumpf, Samuel
Szasz, Thomas Stephen
Taylor, Telford
Thomae, Betty Kennedy
Tierney, Kevin
Treitel, G.H.
Turner, (Sir) Alexander
Turner, Amédée Edward
Turner, William Weyand
Turow, L. Scott

Ungar, Sanford J.
Vachss, Andrew H.
von Mehren, Arthur Taylor
Wade, William
Wagner, Wenceslas J.
Walker, David
Warden, Lewis Christopher
Watson, Alan
Weisstub, David N.
Weston, Burns H.
Weston, Corinne Comstock
White, Gillian Mary
Wickens, Peter Charles
Williams, Glanville
Wilson, Wesley M.
Woll, Peter
Wortley, Ben Atkinson
Wren, Christopher G.
Wren, Jill Robinson
Wrottesley, John Francis
Yiannopoulos, A.N.

Librarianship

Aguolo, Christian Chukwunedu
Atkinson, Frank
Bakewell, Kenneth
Berman, Sanford
Black, Clinton V.
Bloomfield, Barry
Bobinski, George S.
Borko, Harold
Broadfield, Aubrey Alfred
Bryan, Harrison
Burnett, Alfred David
Burrell, Thomas William
Cabeceiras, James
Carroll, C. Edward
Chandler, George
Conant, Ralph W.
Corbett, Edmund Victor
Dalglish, Edward Russell
Davinson, Donald
Downs, Robert B.
Dunlap, Leslie W.
Ellis, Alec
Ellsworth, Ralph E.
Foskett, Douglas John
Gaskell, Philip
Harrison, Kenneth
Harvey, John F.
Hobson, Anthony Robert Alwyn
Holley, Edward Gailon
Horecky, Paul L.
Hostrop, Richard W.
Houle, Cyril O.
Hunter, Eric J.
Isaac, Peter
Jordan, Alma Theodora
Joy, Thomas Alfred
Kelly, Thomas
Keys, Thomas Edward
Lakritz, Esther
Limbacher, James L.
Line, Maurice Bernard
Masson, David I.
McCoy, Ralph E.
Mumford, William Arthur
Musiker, Reuben
Nunn, G. Raymond
Pafford, John Henry Pyle
Perry, Charles Stuart
Pinkett, Harold Thomas
Ray, Shiela G.
Ristow, Walter W.
Roe, Ernest
Rothstein, Samuel
Rowland, Arthur Ray
Sable, Martin Howard
Shaffer, Dale Eugene
Sharr, Francis Aubi
Simsova, Sylva

Thompson, James
Thornton, John Leonard
Walford, A.J.
Ward, Philip
Wasserman, Paul
Werkley, Caroline E.
Wheeler, Helen Rippier
Wren, Christopher
Wren, Jill Robinson

Literary Criticism/History

Abraham, Claude Kurt
Abrams, M.H.
Ackroyd, Peter
Adams, Hazard
Adams, Robert Martin
Adamson, Donald
Adler, Jacob Henry
Adrian, Arthur Allenffron, Charles
Akrigg, George Philip Vernon
Alaya, Flavia
Alazraki, Jaime
Aldiss, Brian
Aldridge, A. Owen
Aldridge, John W.
Alexander, M.J.
Alfred, William
Ali, Ahmed
Allen, Dick
Allen, Gay Wilson
Allen, John Jay
Allen, Walter
Allison, A.F.
Almansi, Guido
Alphonso-Karkala, John B.
Alter, Robert B.
Altick, Richard Daniel
Alvarez, A.
Amis, Kingsley
Anand, Mulk Raj
Anderson, David Daniel
Anderson, Donald K., Jr.
Anderson, Quentin
Anderson, Rachel
Andrews, Clarence Adelbert
Anees, Munawar Ahmad
Angus-Butterworth, Lionel
Appel, Alfred, Jr.
Appleton, Sarah
Araki, James Tomomasa
Andrew, John
Armour, Richard
Armstrong, Judith
Arndt, Karl
Arnold, Guy
Arnott, Peter Douglas
Ash, Brian
Asher, John Alexander
Ashley, Leonard R.N.
Asimov, Isaac
Atkins, John Alfred
Atkins, Stuart
Atkinson, Frank
Atwood, Margaret
Auchincloss, Louis
Auster, Paul
Austin, James C.
Avery, Gillian
Avni, Abraham
Badawi Mohamed Mustafa
Bahr, Ehrhard
Bailey, Arthur Goldsworthy
Baker, Houston Alfred, Jr.
Baker, Howard
Baker, James Rupert
Baker, Sheridan
Bantock, Geoffrey
Barasch, Frances K.
Barber, Charles Laurence
Bareham, Terence
Barfield, Owen

Barish, Jonas A.
Barker, Arthur E.
Barltrop, Robert
Barnard, Robert
Barnett, George Leonard
Barranger, M.S.
Barth, J. Robert
Barzun, Jacques
Batchelor, John
Bate, Walter Jackson
Battestin, Martin Carey
Baumbach, Jonathan
Bauer, Caroline Feller
Bayley, John
Bayley, Peter
Beardsley, Theodore S., Jr.
Beck, Evelyn Torton
Becker, George Joseph
Becker, Lucille Frackman
Beer, Patricia
Beja, Morris
Bell, Marvin
Bellman, Samuel I.
Bellow, Saul
Beloof, Robert Lawrence
Bender, Todd K.
Benkovitz, Miriam J.
Bennett, James Richard
Bennett, John
Bensen, Alice R.
Benson, Jackson J.
Benstock, Bernard
Benstock, Shari
Bentley, Eric
Bentley, Gerald Eades
Benzie, William
Berbrich, Joan D.
Berger, Arthur A.
Berger, John
Bergonzi, Bernard
Berry, Francis
Bertram, James
Betts, William Wilson, Jr.
Beyer, Werner W.
Biasin, Gian-Paolo
Bien, Peter A.
Bigsby, C.W.E.
Birney, Alice Lotvin
Birney, Earle
Bishop, Ferman
Bishop, Ian Benjamin
Bissoondoyal, Basdeo
Blair, Dorothy S.
Blair, Kay Kimery Reynolds
Blake, Leslie James
Blake, Norman Francis
Blamires, David
Blamires, Harry
Bloom, Edward A.
Bloom, Harold
Bloom, Lynn
Bloomfield, Barry
Blotner, Joseph
Bluhm, Heinz
Blumenthal, Gerda René
Blythe, Ronald
Bode, Carl
Boer, Charles
Bogard, Travis
Bold, Alan
Boll, Theophilus E.M.
Booth, Martin
Booth, Wayne Clayson
Borchardt, Frank L.
Bott, George
Bottrall, Margaret
Boulton, James T.
Bowden, Mary W.
Bowen, Barbara C.
Bowen, Zack
Bowers, Fredson
Boyd, Elizabeth French
Boyers, Robert

Bradbrook, Muriel Clara
Bradbury, Malcolm
Bradford, M.E.
Bradley, John Lewis
Bradley, Marion Zimmer
Branch, Edgar Marquess
Branden, Nathaniel
Bratton, J.S.
Braudy, Leo
Braybrooke, Neville
Bredsdorff, Elias Lunn
Brée, Germaine
Breen, Jon L.
Brennan, Neil F.
Brett, Michael
Brett, Raymond Laurence
Brewer, Wilmon
Brinnin, John Malcolm
Brissenden, Alan
Brittin, Norman Aylsworth
Brodsky, Joseph
Broer, Lawrence R.
Brombert, Victor
Brome, Vincent
Broner, E.M.
Brooke-Rose, Christine
Brooks, A. Russell
Brooks, Cleanth
Brophy, Brigid
Brotherston, Gordon
Brown, John Russell
Brown, Terence
Brownjohn, Alan
Bruccoli, Matthew J.
Bruce, George
Bruchac, Joseph
Bryant, Joseph Allen, Jr.
Buckler, William Earl
Buckley, Vincent
Bucknall, Barbara Jane
Buell, Frederick
Buitenhuis, Peter M.
Bull, Angela
Buranelli, Vincent
Burgess, Anthony
Burgess, C.F.
Burnshaw, Stanley
Burrow, J.A.
Busch, Frederick
Butler, Dorothy
Butler, Guy
Butler, Marilyn
Butter, Peter Herbert
Buxton, John
Byatt, A.S.
Cacciatore, Vera
Cachia, Pierre
Cadogan, Mary
Cady, Edwin Harrison
Calder, Angus
Calder-Marshall, Arthur
Calderwood, James Lee
Calhoun, Richard James
Cameron, Donald Silver
Campbell, Ian
Campbell, Paul N.
Caputi, Anthony
Carey, John
Carlsen, G. Robert
Carnall, Geoffrey Douglas
Carnochan, W.B.
Carpenter, Frederic I.
Carpenter, Nan Cooke
Carroll, Paul
Carson, Herbert L.
Carter, Everett
Carter, Lin
Cary, Richard
Casper, Leonard
Cate, Curtis
Cauthen, Irby Bruce, Jr.
Caws, Mary Ann
Cevasco, G.A.

Chalker, Jack L.
Chambers, Aidan
Champion, Larry S.
Chandler, George
Chandler, S. Bernard
Chapple, John Alfred Victor
Charles, Gerda
Charters, Ann
Chatman, Seymour
Chesters, Graham
Chitham, Edward
Christ, Henry I
Christ, Ronald
Christensen, Paul
Christesen, C.B.
Christophersen, Paul
Clare, William
Clark of Herriotshall, Arthur
  Melville
Clark, Bruce
Clark, David Ridgley
Clark, John Pepper
Clark, John R.
Clarke, Dorothy Clotelle
Cleall, Charles
Clemen, Wolfgang H.
Clements, Arthur L.
Clements, Robert
Closs, August
Clubbe, John L.E.
Cluysenaar, Anne
Cockshut, A.O.J.
Coe, Richard Nelson Caslon
Cogswell, Fred
Cohen, Morton N.
Collin, Marion
Collins, Carvel
Collins, Harold Reeves
Collins, Philip Arthur William
Colman, E. Adrian M.
Colmer, John Anthony
Comfort, Alex
Conran, Anthony
Conquest, Robert
Cook, Albert
Cooke, William
Cooperman, Hasye
Cope, Jack
Cope, Jackson I.
Corngold, Stanley
Cosgrave, Patrick
Cotter, James Finn
Cotton, John
Coughlan, Robert
Cousins, Norman
Cowan, James C.
Cowasjee, Saros
Cox, Charles Brian
Coxe, Louis
Craig, Patricia
Craik, T.W.
Craik, Wendy Ann
Creeley, Robert
Crews, Frederick C.
Crocker, Lester G.
Crompton, Louis
Cronin, Anthony
Crosland, Margaret
Cross, Anthony Glenn
Cross, Richard K.
Crossan, G.D.
Crouch, Marcus S.
Crowder, Richard H.
Cruickshank, John
Cubeta, Paul
Cuddon, J.A.
Cunliffe, Marcus
Cunningham, J.V.
Currey, R.N.
Curtis, Anthony
Curtis, Tony
Cutt, Margaret Nancy
Dace, Tish

Dahl, Curtis
Dahlie, Hallvard
Daiches, David
Daleski, H.M.
Daly, Leo
Darnton, Robert
Dathorne, O.R.
Davenport, Guy
Davey, Frank
Davidson, Michael
Davidson, Mildred
Davie, Donald
Davies, Horton Marlais
Davies, Margaret
Davies, Robertson
Davin, Dan
Davis, David Brion
Davis, Michael
Davis, Richard
Davison, Dennis
Dearden, James Shackley
Debreczeny, Paul
de Jonge, Alex
Dekker, George
Demetillo, Ricaredo
Deming, Robert H.
De Mordaunt, Walter Julius
Demott, Benjamin
Dennis, Nigel
Detweiler, Robert
De Waal, Ronald Burt
Di Cesare, Mario A.
Dick, Bernard
Dick, Kay
Dickey, James
Dilke, Oswald Ashton Wentworth
Dillard, Annie
Dillingham, William B.
Disch, Thomas M.
Donahue, Francis James
Donaldson, Scott
Donoghue, Denis
Dorn, Ed
Dow, Marguerite
Downes, David Anthony
Doyle, Paul A.
Drabble, Margaret
Draper, R.P.
Drew, Fraser
Duberman, Martin
Duchene, Louis-François
Dudek, Louis
Dunn, Charles W.
Dunn, Peter Norman
Durband, Alan
Dutton, Geoffrey
Dyson, A.E.
Eagleton, Terence
Eaton, Trevor
Echeruo, Michael
Echeverria, Durand
Economou, George
Eddins, Dwight
Edel, Leon
Edwards, Michael
Edwards, Philip
Edwards, Thomas R.
Eichner, Hans
Einbond, Bernard Lionel
Elliott, Brian Robinson
Ellis, Alec
Elsom, John
Emanuel, James A.
Engel, Bernard F.
Engel, Monroe
Engle, Paul
Enright, D.J.
Erhard, Tom
Espey, John
Esslin, Martin
Evans, Robert Owen
Everson, William
Every, George

Ezekiel, Nissim
Fairfax, John
Falk, Signi Lenea
Fedder, Norman Joseph
Federman, Raymond
Fein, Richard J.
Feinberg, Leonard
Fellows, Malcolm Stuart
Felver, Charles Stanley
Fennell, John Lister Illingworth
Fenton, James
Ferrar, Harold
Fiacc, Padraic
Fickert, Kurt J.
Fiedler, Leslie A.
Figueroa, John
Finch, Peter
Finch, Robert
Fine, Sidney
Finlayson, Roderick
Finneran, Richard J.
Fiore, Peter Amadeus
Firchow, Peter
Fisch, Harold
Fish, Stanley E.
Fisher, Marvin
FitzGerald, Robert D.
Fixler, Michael
Fjelde, Rolf
Flanagan, Thomas
Fleishman, Avrom
Fletcher, John Walter James
Flora, Joseph M.
Ford, George H.
Fossum, Robert H.
Foster, David William
Foster, Edward Halsey
Foster, Malcolm Burton
Foster, Ruel E.
Foulkes, Peter
Fowler, Alastair
Fox, Hugh
Fox, Levi
Foxe, Arthur Norman
Foxell, Nigel
Frame, Donald Murdoch
Francis, H.E., Jr.
Frank, Joseph
Frantzen, Allen J.
Fraser, Russell A.
Freeborn, Richard
French, Alfred
French, Marilyn
French, Philip
French, Warren G.
Freund, Philip
Friedberg, Maurice
Freidman, Alan Warren
Friedman, Melvin J.
Friedman, Norman
Fry, William Finley, Jr.
Frye, Northrop
Frye, Roland
Fuegi, John
Fuller, Edmund
Fuller, John
Fuller, Roy
Fulton, Robin
Furst, Lilian R.
Fuson, Ben W.
Fussell, Paul
Gans, Eric L.
Gardner, Ralph D.
Garlick, Raymond
Garrett, George
Gascoigne, Bamber
Gascoyne, David
Gaskell, Philip
Gass, William
Gaston, Edwin Willmer, Jr.
Gatch, Milton McCormick, Jr.
Gates, Henry Louis
Gates, Norman T.

Geering, R.G.
Geiger, Don Jesse
Gelpi, Albert
Gerber, Douglas E.
Gerber, John C.
Gerrold, David
Gerstenberger, Donna
Gesner, Carol
Ghiselin, Brewster
Ghose, Zulfikar
Gianakaris, Constantine John
Giannaris, George
Gibbs, Anthony Matthews
Gibson, Robert
Gifford, Denis
Gillespie, Gerald
Gillie, Christopher
Gillon, Adam
Gilman, Richard
Gindin, James
Ginsberg, Allen
Gittings, Robert
Glasrud, Clarence
Gleckner, Robert F.
Glen, Duncan
Glicksberg, Charles Irving
Glut, Don F.
Gnarowski, Michael
Goldberg, Samuel Louis
Goldfarb, Russell M.
Goldman, Albert
Goldman, Arnold
Goodheart, Eugene
Gordon, Cyrus Herzl
Gordon, Giles
Gordon, Ian Alistair
Gordon, Lois G.
Gorrell, Robert
Goulart, Ron
Gould, Jean R.
Graham, Bob
Graham, Desmond
Graham, John
Graham, Victor Ernest
Granger, Bruce Ingham
Graver, Lawrence Stanley
Gray, Douglas
Greaves, Margaret
Gregstein, Sheldon Norman
Green, D.H.
Green, Dorothy
Green, Martin
Gregg, Richard
Grieb, Kenneth J.
Griffith, Thomas Gwynfor
Griffiths, Richard Mathias
Gross, John
Gross Kurth, Phyllis
Grover, Philip
Grumbach, Doris
Grundy, Joan
Guenther, Charles
Guerard, Albert Joseph
Gunn, James Edwin
Gunn, Thom
Gurr, A.J.
Guttmann, Allen
Haac, Oscar A.
Hackett, Cecil Arthur
Haeberle, Erwin J.
Haines, John
Hall, Donald
Hall, J.C.
Hall, Kathleen Mary
Hall, Trevor Henry
Halls, Wilfred Douglas
Hamburger, Michael
Hamilton, Ian
Hamilton, Kenneth
Handley, Graham Roderick
Hanley, James
Harden, O. Elizabeth
Harding, D.W.

Harding, James
Harding, Walter
Hardman, David Rennie
Hardwick, Elizabeth
Hardwick, Michael
Hardwick, Mollie
Hardy, Barbara
Hardy, John Philips
Harmon, Maurice
Harper, George Mills
Harris, Wilson
Harrison, Bernard
Hart, Kevin
Hart-Davis, (Sir) Rupert
Hartman, Geoffrey
Haslam, Gerald William
Hassan, Ihab
Hassler, Donald M.
Haugen, Einar
Hayashi, Tetsumaro
Hayden, Donald E.
Hayman, David
Hayman, Ronald
Haynes, Renée Oriana
Hays, Peter L.
Hayter, Alethea
Hazo, Samuel
Heaney, Seamus
Heath, William Webster
Heath-Stubbs, John
Heilbrun, Carolyn G.
Heilman, Robert B.
Heitner, Robert R.
Heller, Erich
Heller, Michael D.
Hellstrom, Ward
Helms, Randel
Henault, Marie
Hewitt, (Lady) Alison Hope
Hibbert, Howard
Hidden, Norman
Hieatt, Constance Bartlett
Higgins, Dick
Hildick, E.W.
Hill, Douglas
Himelstein, Morgan Y.
Hindus, Milton
Hirsch, E.D., Jr.
Hobsbaum, Philip
Hobson, Fred Colby
Hodgart, Matthew
Hoffman, Arthur W.
Hoffman, Daniel
Hoffman, Michael J.
Hogan, Robert
Hoggart, Richard
Hohnen, David
Holbrook, David
Holdheim, William
Holland, Elizabeth Anne
Holland, Norman N.
Hollander, John
Hollindale, Peter
Hollingdale, Reginald John
Holloway, John
Holmes, Edward M.
Holroyd, Michael
Homberger, Eric
Honan, Park
Honig, Edwin
Hooker, Jeremy
Hope, A.D.
Hopkinson, (Sir) Thomas
Horovitz, Michael
Hough, Graham
Howarth, William
Howe, Irving
Howse, Ernest Marshall
Hudson Derek
Hufana, Alejandrino G.
Hughes, Ted
Hull, William D.
Hume, Robert D.

Hunt, Peter
Hunter, J. Paul
Hunter, Jim
Huppé Bernard F.
Hurley, John
Huxley, George Leonard
Hynes, Samuel
Igo, John
Ilie, Paul
Ingalls, Jeremy
Inge, M. Thomas
Irwin, Constance
Jack, Ian
Jacobsen, Josephine
Jacobson, Dan
Jacobus, Lee A.
Jacobus, Mary
James, Louis
Jeffares, A. Norman
Jenkins, Harold
Jennings, Elizabeth
Jerome, Judson
Johnson, Robert Vincent
Johnson, Wendell Stacy
Jones, Charles W.
Jones, D.G.
Jones, Evan
Jones, Glyn
Jones, John
Jones, Malcolm V.
Jones, Margaret E.W.
Jones, Peter
Jordan, John E.
Josipovici, Gabriel David
Kahn, Sy M.
Kain, Richard Morgan
Kallich, Martin
Kaminsky, Alice R.
Kaplan, Justin
Karanikas, Alexander
Karl, Frederick
Kato, Shuici
Katz, Michael Ray
Kauffmann, Stanley
Kawin, Bruce F.
Kazin, Alfred
Keating, H.R.F.
Keating, L. Clark
Keeley, Edmund LeRoy
Keene, Donald
Keesing, Nancy
Kelling, Hans-Wilhelm
Kellner, Bruce
Kelly, Linda
Kelly, Louis Gerard
Kelly, Richard
Kemp, Peter
Kennedy, X.J.
Kenner, Hugh
Kenworthy, Brian J.
Kermode, Frank
Kerr, Elizabeth Margaret
Kherdian, David
Kiely, Benedict
Kiernan, Brian
Kimbrough, Robert Alexander III
King, Betty
King, Bruce
King-Hele, Desmond
Kingman, Lee
Kinkead-Weekes, Mark
Kinnamon, Keneth
Kinnell, Galway
Kinney, Arthur F.
Kinsella, Thomas
Kirkham, E. Bruce
Klein, Marcus
Knight, Karl Frederick
Knight, William Nicholas
Knights, L.C.
Koch, Kenneth
Kopp, Richard L.
Korg, Jacob

Kort, Wesley A.
Kosinski, Jerzy
Kostelanetz, Richard
Koster, Donald Nelson
Kramer, Aaron
Kramer, Dale
Kramer, Leonie
Krieger, Murray
Krog, Eustace Walter
Kronegger, Maria Elisabeth
Kudian, Mischa
Kumar, Shiv K.
Kumin, Maxine
Kunitz, Stanley
LaHood, Marvin J.
Lake, David
Lal, P.
Lamb, Elizabeth Searle
Lane, Gary Martin
Lane, Richard
Lang, David Marshall
Langbaum, Robert
Lange, Victor
Langford, Gerald
Lanham, Richard Alan
Larrick, Nancy
Laurence, Dan H.
Lawlor, John James
Lazarus, A.L.
Leary, Lewis
Lee, Don L.
Lee, Peter H.
Leeds, Barry H.
Leeds, Christopher
Legat, Michael
Leggatt, Alexander
LeGuin, Ursula
Lemon, Lee Thomas
Lennox-Short, Alan
Lerner, Laurence
Lester, G.A.
Lester, Julius
Levi, Anthony H.T.
Levin, Gerald
Levin, Harry
Levin, Richard Louis
Levine, Stuart George
Lewis, Claudia Louise
Lewis, Peter
Lichtblau, Myron I.
Lichtenstadter, Ilse
Liddell, Robert
Liddy, James
Lieberman, Laurence
Lillington, Kenneth
Lima, Robert F., Jr.
Lind, Levi Robert
Lingemann, Richard
Link, Frederick M.
Liptzin, Sol
Liu Wu-chi
Lochhead, Douglas Grant
Lockerbie, Donald Bruce
Lodge, David
Loney, Glenn Meredith
Low, Anthony
Lowenthal, Leo
Lowndes, Robert A.W.
Lowry, Lois
Lucas, John
Ludwig, Jack
Lundwall, Sam J.
Lupoff, Richard A.
Lyons, Nick
Lytle, Andrew
Macbuire, Gregory
Mack, Maynard
Mackenzie, Norman H.
Mackerras, Colin Patrick
Mackworth, Cecily
MacLaine, Allan H.
Macpherson, Jay
MacQueen, John

MacShane, Frank
Madden, David
Maddison, Carol
Madgett, Naomi Long
Maes-Jelinek, Hena
Major, Clarence
Major, Kevin
Malek, James S.
Malin, Irving
Malkiel, Yakov
Mandel, Eli
Mandel, Oscar
Mango, C.A.
Manlove, Colin
Mansell, Darrell
Mapp, Alf Johnson, Jr.
Marchand, Leslie A.
Markovic, Vida E.
Markson, David M.
Marlatt, Daphne
Marsh, Derick Rupert Clement
Marshall, Tom
Martin, Ernest Walter
Martin, Robert Bernard
Martz, Louis
Mason, Haydn Trevor
Mason, Ronald Charles
Mathew, Ray
Matthias, John
Maxwell, D.E.S.
May, Derwent
Mazzaro, Jerome
McAlindon, Thomas
McBride, Robert
McCarthy, Mary
McClelland, Ivy Lilian
McConkey, James Rodney
McCormick, Eric Hall
McCormick, John O.
McDowell, Frederick P.W.
McFarlane, James Walter
McKenzie, Barbara
McLaren, John
McLean, Sammy
McMaster, Juliet Sylvia
McNamara, Eugene Joseph
Measham, Donald Charles
Medvedev, Roy
Meinke, Peter
Mellown, Elgin W.
Meltzer, David
Merrill, Thomas F.
Meserve, Walter
Metzger, Michael M.
Mewshaw, Michael
Meyerowitz, Patricia
Meyers, Jeffrey
Michael, I.D.L.
Mickel, Emanuel J., Jr.
Mikhail, Edward H.
Miles, Elton
Miles, Leland
Miller, J. Hillis
Miller, James Edwin
Miller, Jordan Yale
Millgram, Abraham E.
Mills, Ralph J.
Milne, W. Gordon
Milner, Ian Frank George
Milton, John R.
Miner, Earl
Miner, Ward L.
Minot, Stephen
Minter, David Lee
Mintz, Samuel I.
Mitchell, Jerome
Mitgang, Herbert
Mohl, Ruth
Mokashi-Punekar, Shankar
Mole, John
Mollenkott, Virginia Ramey
Montgomery, Marion
Moore, Mavor

Moore, Nicholas
Moore, Rayburn Sabatzky
Moore-Rinvolucri, Mina
Morgan, Dewi
Morpurgo, J.E.
Morris, Harry
Morris, Helen
Morris, Robert K.
Morrison, Blake
Morrison, Kristin Diane
Morrison, Theodore
Morse, Donald E.
Morse, J. Mitchell
Morton, Richard Everett
Moss, Leonard
Motion, Andrew
Moynahan, Julian Lane
Mueller, William R.
Muir, Kenneth
Munro, John M.
Murdy, Louise Baughan
Murray-Smith, Stephen
Myers, Robert Manson
Nahal, Chaman
Naiden, James
Nassar, Eugene Paul
Natanson, Maurice
Nathan, Leonard
Nathan, Norman
Needle, Jan
Nelson, James Graham
Nelson, Lowry, Jr.
Nemerov, Howard
Neumeyer, Peter
Nevins, Francis M., Jr.
Newby, P.H.
Newcomer, James W.
Newlin, Margaret Rudd
Ngugi, J.T.
Nichols, John Gordon
Niklaus, Robert
Nims, John Frederick
Nitchie, George Wilson
Niven, Alastair
Nolan, Paul T.
Norris, Leslie
Norwich, John Julius
Nostrand, Howard Lee
Novak, Maximillian Erwin
Oates, Joyce Carol
O'Brien, Conor Cruise
O'Connor, Patricia W.
O'Flaherty, James Carneal
Oldfield, Jenny
Oldsey, Bernard S.
Oliver, Egbert S.
Oliver, Kenneth A.
Olson, Elder
Ondaatje, Michael
O'Neill, Judith
Opie, Iona
Orel, Harold
Ornstein, Robert
Orr, Gregory
Osborne, Charles
Osofisan, Femi
O'Sullivan, Vincent
Owen, Douglas David Roy
Owen, Warwick
Pack, Robert
Paffard, Michael Kenneth
Page, Norman
Painter, Helen
Palmer, John Alfred
Palsson, Hermann
Panichas, George A.
Panshin, Alexei
Paris, Bernard Jay
Parkinson, Thomas
Parsons, Coleman O.
Partridge, Astley Cooper
Paterson, Katherine
Patrides, C.A.

Paulin, Tom
Paulson, Ronald
Peacock, Ronald
Pearce, Roy Harvey
Pearsall, Derek
Peckham, Morse
Peden, William
Perkins, George
Perkins, Michael
Perloff, Marjorie
Perrine, Laurence
Perry, Margaret
Peterkiewicz, Jerzy
Peters, Margot
Peters, Robert
Peterson, Elmer
Phelps, Gilbert
Phillips, Michael Joseph
Phillips, Robert
Phillips, William
Philmus, Robert Michael
Philp, Peter
Phythian, Brian A.
Pinion, F.B.
Pinsker, Sanford S.
Pinsky, Robert
Pitcher, Harvey John
Pittock, Joan
Plimpton, George
Podhoretz, Norman
Poirier, Richard
Pollard, Arthur
Poster, Cyril Dennis
Potoker, Edward Martin
Powell, Anthony
Powell, Neil
Powell, Violet
Pratt, John Clark
Prawer, S.S.
Press, John
Price, Cecil
Prickett, Stephen
Prince, F.T.
Pritchard, William H.
Pritchett, V.S.
Proctor, Thelwall
Prosser, Harold
Pullein-Thompson, Diana
Quayle, Eric
Quennell, Peter
Raban, Jonathan
Rabinovitz, Rubin
Radcliff-Umstead, Douglas
Raine, Kathleen
Raitt, Alan William
Rajan, Tilottama
Ralphs, Sheila
Ramsden, Herbert
Ramsey, Paul
Randall, Dale B.J.
Randall, Dudley
Ravenscroft, Arthur
Ravitz, Abe Carl
Rawson, Claude Julien
Ray, Shiela G.
Ray, Sib Narayan
Rayfield, Donald
Reade, Brian Edmund
Reaver, J. Russell
Reed, James
Reed, Joseph W.
Reed, Robert Rentoul, Jr.
Reed, T.J.
Reed, Thomas Thornton
Reeve, F.D.
Reichart, Walter A.
Richardson, Joanna
Richetti, John J.
Richmond, Hugh Macrae
Richter, Harvena
Ricks, Christopher
Riddel, Joseph Neill
Riding, Laura

Riley, Edward Calverley
Rippley, La Vern J.
Robbins, John Albert
Robinson, Kim Stanley
Robinson, W.R.
Rodway, Allan Edwin
Rogers, Katharine M.
Rogers, Pat
Rollin, Roger B.
Romeril, John
Ronsley, Joseph
Rook, Alan
Rose, Ernst
Rosen, Gerald
Rosenberg, John D.
Rosenberg, Marvin
Rosensaft, Menachem Z.
Rosenthal, M.L.
Roston, Murray
Rothwell, Kenneth Sprague
Rountree, Thomas J.
Rousseau, George S.
Rovit, Earl
Rowse, A.L.
Rubin, Larry Jerome
Rudrum, Alan William
Rule, Jane
Rumens, Carol
Rupp, Richard H.
Russell, Francis
Ryan, John
Ryan, William M.
Ryken, Leland
Sachs, Murray
Saddlemyer, Ann
Sage, Lorna
Said, Edward W.
Salinger, Herman
Salvan, Jacques, Léon
Sambrook, A.J.
Samelson, William
Sams, Eric
Sanders, David
Sanderson, Stewart F.
Sanjian, Avedis K.
Scaglione, Aldo
Scannell, Vernon
Schmidt, Michael Norton
Schneider, Ben Ross, Jr.
Schulz, Max Frederick
Schwartz, Joseph
Schwartz, Kessel
Schwartz, Sheila R.
Scott, Alexander
Scott, Arthur Finley
Scott, Nathan A., Jr.
Scott, Tom
Scouten, Arthur H.
Screech, M.A.
Scully, James
Sealts, Merton M., Jr.
Searles, Baird
Sedwick, Frank
Seelye, John
Sellin, Eric
Seltzer, Leon F.
Sewell, Brocard
Seyersted, Per
Seymour, A.J.
Seymour-Smith, Martin
Shahane, Vasant A.
Shapcott, Thomas W.
Shapiro, Karl
Shattuck, Roger
Shawcross, John T.
Sheaffer, Louis
Sherry, Norman
Shinagel, Michael
Shippey, T.A.
Shirley, Frances Ann
Short, Robert Stuart
Shugrue, Michael Francis
Shumaker, Wayne

Siegel, Paul N.
Sigworth, Oliver F.
Silkin, Jon
Silverstein, Theodore
Simmonds, Jack
Simonson, Harold P.
Simpson, Lewis P.
Simpson, Louis
Sinclair, Keith Val
Singh, Amritjit
Sisson, C.H.
Skelton, Robin
Sklar, Robert
Slavutych, Yar
Slesinger, Warren
Sloman, Albert Edward
Smith, Barbara Herrnstein
Smith, Elton Edward
Smith, Grover Cleveland
Smith, James L.
Smith, John
Smith, Maxwell Austin
Smith, Rowland
Smith, Vivian
Smith, William Jay
Smither, Elizabeth
Smithyman, Kendrick
Snodgrass, W.D.
Sonnichsen, C.L.
Sorrentino, Gilbert
Southam, B.C
Spacks, Patricia Meyer
Spalding, Keith
Spark, Muriel
Spear, Hilda D.
Spears, Monroe K.
Spector, Robert D.
Spencer, Christopher
Spender, Stephen
Spielberg, Peter
Spivack, Charlotte
Spurling, Hilary
Spurling, John
Squires, Radcliffe
Stade, George
Stafford, William
Stallworthy, Jon
Stanford, Barbara
Stanford, Derek
Stanford, Donald Elwin
Stansky, Peter David Lyman
Stapleton, Laurence
Stead, C.K.
Steane, John Barry
Steegmuller, Francis
Steele, Max
Steinberg, Erwin R.
Steiner, George
Stepanchev, Stephen
Stephens, Meic
Stephens, Robert Oren
Sternlicht, Sanford
Stevens, Joan
Stevens, John
Stevenson, Anne
Stevenson, Elizabeth
Stewart, Ann Harleman
Stewart, J.I.M.
Stillinger, Jack
Stoltzfus, Ben Franklin
Storey, Graham
Stover, Leon
Straumann, Heinrich
Stuart, Dabney
Styan, John Louis
Sukenick, Ronald
Sullivan, Alvin D.
Sullivan, John Patrick
Sultan, Stanley
Sultana, Donald Edward
Summers, Joseph Holmes
Super, Robert Henry
Sweetser, Wesley

Swenson, May
Talbot, Norman Clare
Tanner, Stephen L.
Tanner, Tony
Tanselle, G. Thomas
Taylor, Welford Dunaway
Tennant, (Sir) Peter
Tennyson, G.B.
Theroux, Paul
Thody, Philip
Thomas, Alan Gradon
Thomas, Clara McCandless
Thomas, R.S.
Thomson, Derick Smith
Thomson, George Henry
Thomson, Peter
Thorpe, James
Thwaite, Anthony
Tindall, Gillian
Timms, David
Tobias, Richard C.
Tomalin, Claire
Tomlinson, Charles
Tonogbanua, Francisco G.
Townsend, John Rowe
Tracy, Clarence
Traversi, Derek A.
Trawick, Buckner Beasley
Trickett, Rachel
Trilling, Diana
Trueblood, Paul Graham
Tschumi, Raymond
Tucker, James
Tucker, Martin
Turco, Lewis
Turner, Darwin T.
Turner, Paul
Tydeman, William
Tysdahl, Björn Johan
Ueda, Makoto
Unwin, Rayner
Updike, John
Usborne, Richard A.
Usherwood, Stephen
Valdes, Mario J.
Valency, Maurice
Vasta, Edward
Vendler, Helen
Voigt, Milton
Voitle, Robert
Voorhees, Richard J.
Waddington, Miriam
Waddington, Raymond B.
Waddington-Feather, John Joseph
Wagenknecht, Edward
Wagner, Linda C.
Waidson, Herbert Morgan
Wain, John
Wakoski, Diane
Wallace, John Malcolm
Wallace-Crabbe, Christopher Keith
Walsh, Chad
Walsh, P.G.
Walsh, William
Ward, John Powell
Ward, Russel Braddock
Warner, Alan
Warner, Marina
Warren, Austin
Warren, Robert Penn
Wasiolek, Edward
Watkins, Floyd C.
Watson, George
Watson, J.R.
Watt, Ian
Watts, Harold H.
Weales, Gerald
Weatherhead, A. Kingsley
Webb, Timothy
Weber, Brom
Wedgwood, (Dame) C.V.
Wegelin, Christof
Weinberg, Florence M.

Weinberg, Kerry
Weinstein, Mark Allen
Weintraub, Stanley
Weiss, Theodore
Weisstein, Ulrich W.
Wellek, René
Wells, Stanley
Wells, Walter
Wellwarth, George E.
Welsh, Alexander
Welty, Eudora
West, Paul
Westbrook, Perry D.
Weston, Susan
White, Edward M.
White, Ray Lewis
White, Robert Lee
White, William
White, William Luther
Whitehead, Frank
Whitfield, George
Whitfield, John Humphreys
Whittemore, Reed
Wicker, Brian John
Wieners, John
Wiesenfarth, Joseph
Wilbur, Richard
Wilding, Michael
Wilgus, D.K.
Willey, Peter Robert Everard
Williams, Gwyn
Williams, Ioan Miles
Williams, John
Williams, Thomas
Williamson, Jack
Wills, Garry
Willy, Margaret
Wilson, A.N.
Wilson, (Sir) Angus
Wilson, Robert Neal
Winegarten, Renee
Winnifrith, T.J.
Wiseman, Donald John
Witemeyer, Hugh Hazen
Wohlgelernter, Maurice
Wolfe, Peter
Wolverton, Robert E.
Wood, Marguerite N.
Woodress, James
Woodring, Carl
Woodward, Robert H.
Wright, Austin M.
Wright, Celeste Turner
Wright, David
Wright, George Thaddeus
Wright, Walter Francis
Wykes, Alan
Yarrow, Philip John
Young, David
Young, Philip
Young, T.D.
Yudkin, Leon Israel
Zall, Paul M.
Zants, Emily
Zietlow, Edward Robert
Ziff, Larzer
Ziolkowski, Theodore
Zohn, Harry

Local history/Rural topics

Alter, Judith
Archer, Fred
Baseley, Godfrey
Beddington, Roy
Blythe, Ronald
Bourjaily, Vance
Camp, John
Cushman, Dan
Faulknor, Cliff
Fussell, George Edwin
Goulding, Peter G.

Local history/Rural topics—cont.

Halsall, Eric
Harris, Helen
Harrey, Nigel
Hartley, Marie
Hedderwick, Mairi
Herriot, James
Huggett, Frank Edward
Ingilby, Joan Alicia
Jenkins, John Geraint
Lamplugh, Louis
Lunn, Janet
Martin, Ernest Walter
Muir, Richard
Page, Robin
Roberts, Nancy Correll
Russell, Ronald
Simpson, Ruth M.
Tranter, Nigel
Vaughan-Thomas, Wynford
Woodforde, John Ffooks

Marine science/Oceanography

Abbot, R. Tucker
Anderson, Alan, Jr.
Bhatt, Jagdish, J.
Burgess, Warren E.
Clarke, Arthur C.
Crawford, William P.
Doak, Wade
Dunbar, Maxwell
Eltringham, S.K.
Emery, Kenneth
Fell, Barry
Fogg, Gordon Elliott
Goldman, Charles R.
Horne, R.A
Limburg, Peter R.
Rudloe, Jack
Thomson, James Miln
Waters, David Watkin
Weisberg, Joseph
Young, John Zachary

Marketing

Baily, Nathan A.
Bauer, Peter Thomas
Blankenship, A.B.
Branch, Alan
Buell, Victor P.
Daenzer, Bernard J.
Davidson, Jeffrey P.
Davis, Martyn P.
Denenberg, Herbert
Dommermuth, William P.
Duncan, William
Dyer, John M.
Harness, Charles L.
Hocking, Anthony
Jefkins, Frank William
Johnson, H. Webster
Kotler, Philip
Kraushar, Peter Maximilian
Lazer, William
Mendelsohn, Martin
Montgomery, David Bruce
Pacifico, Carl
Redman, Lister Appleton
Simon, Julian L.
Still, Richard
Stone, Merlin
Talarzyk, W. Wayne
Teller, Neville
Terpstra, Vern
Thompson, Donald Neil
Tobias, Andrew P.
Wills, Walter J.

Mathematics/Statistics

Adams, John Frank
Bailey, Norman Thomas John
Baker, Alan
Bartz, Albert
Biggs, John Burville
Birkhoff, Garrett
Bochner, Salomon
Bolt, Bruce
Bonnor, William Bowen
Boot, John C.G.
Bradley, James Vandiver
Bulmer-Thomas, Ivor
Byrt, Edwin Andrew
Coleman, James
Conway, Freda
Cooper, Christopher
Edgington, Eugene Sinclair
Fruchter, Benjamin
Godman, Arthur
Goldstein, Harvey
Good, Irving John
Haberman, Richard
Hannan, Edward James
Hatcher, William S.
Hayman, Walter Kurt
Hilton, Peter
Hirsch, Werner Z.
Hollands, Roy
Horadam, Alwyn Francis
Houston, W. Robert
Hughes, Philip William
Johnson, David Lawrence
Jones, Stanley Bruce
Kaplansky, Irving
Kennedy, Gavin
Kingman, J.F.C.
Kilmister, Clive William
Kish, Leslie
Klare, George Roger
Kline, Morris
Lawden, Derek Frank
Layton, W.I.
Letchford, Stanley
Luchins, Edith Hirsch
Macdonald, Ian David
McCrea, (Sir) William Hunter
McKinlay, Brian John
Miele, Angelo
Millington, Alaric
Minium, Edward W.
Moore, Hal G.
Morton, Bruce Rutherfurd
Moss, Barbara
Mostert, Paul Stallings
Neal, Frank
Northcott, Douglas
O'Brien, Katharine E.
Ogilvy, C. Stanley
Oliver, Francis Richard
Ollerenshaw, (Dame) Kathleen
Omari, T. Peter
Pedoe, Daniel
Quine, Willard V.
Rennie, Basil Cameron
Ringenberg, Lawrence Albert
Robinson, Gilbert de Beauregard
Rogerson, Alan Thomas
Rowntree, Derek
Sealey, Leonard
Shackle, George Lennox Sharman
Siegel, Irving H.
Skemp, Richard Rowland
Sneddon, Ian Naismith
Taylor, John
Tranter, Clement John
Turner, John Christopher
Whittle, Peter
Wickramasinghe, Nalin
Wike, Edward L.
Williams, Walter E.
Woods, L.C.
Wybourne, Brian Garner
Yates, Frank

Mathematics/Statistics—cont

Zelinger, Geza
Zellner, Arnold

Medicine/Health

Abel-Smith, Brian
Abraham, Edward Penley
Adey, William Ross
Aikawa, Jerry K.
Aiken, Linda H.
Albert, Adrien
Ammer, Christine
Anderson, Ferguson
Anderson, Kenneth Norman
Anderson, Odin Waldemar
Anderson, Peggy
Anees, Munawar Ahmad
Arnold, Peter
Atkinson, R.S.
Autton, Norman
Azneer, J. Leonard
Bahr, Robert
Balint, Enid
Ballantyne, John
Baly, Monica Eileen
Bannister, (Sir) Roger
Barker, David J.P.
Barlow, Wilfred
Barnard, Christiaan
Barnes, (Dame) Josephine
Baron, Denis Neville
Barr, Patricia
Barry, Hugh Collis
Bax, Martin
Beadle, George W.
Begg, Neil Colquhoun
Bell, Robert Charles
Bender, Arnold
Bennet, Glin
Bevan, James
Beveridge, William
Bickerstaff, Edwin Robert
Bingham, June Rossbach
Birdwood, George F.B.
Black, (Sir) Douglas
Blake, John Ballard
Blakemore, Colin Brian
Blank, Robert H.
Bloom, Samuel W.
Bodmer, Walter Fred
Bonica, John Joseph
Boone, Daniel R.
Borrie, John
Boyland, Eric
Breathach, Aodan S.
Bright, Pamela
Brody, Jane
Brooke, Bryan Nicholas
Brookes, Murray
Bross, Irwin D.J.
Brown, Raymond George
Bullough, Vern L.
Burger, Robert
Bush, Barry
Busvine, James Ronald
Butterfield, (Sir) John
Caplan, Arthur L.
Carney, Richard E.
Carruthers, Malcolm
Carter, Frances Monet
Cartland, Barbara
Cassedy, James H.
Causey, Gilbert
Cerney, James V.
Christie, A.B.
Cipolla, Carlo M.
Clabby, John
Clarke, (Sir) Cyril
Clyne, Douglas
Cochrane, Peggy
Comfort, Alex
Conrow, Robert W.

Medicine/Health—cont.

Cooper, Wendy
Crabb, Henry Stuart Malcolm
Crichton, Michael
Cross, Wilbur L.
Crystal, David
Culyer, A.J.
Dally, Ann
Dalrymple, Willard
Davenport, John
Davies, David Margerison
Davis, John Gilbert
Day, Stacey B.
DeBakey, Michael Ellis
Debus, Allen George
Deloughery, Grace L.
Di Cyan, Erwin
Dinerman, Beatrice
Dixon, Bernard
Dixon, Eustace A.
Dobson, James C., Jr.
Dodge, Bertha Sanford
Doll, (Sir) Richard
Duhl, Leonard J.
Ebert, James D.
Eccles, (Sir) John
Edwards, Joseph Castro
Ellis, Harold
Epstein, Charlotte
Eskin, Frada
Essex-Cater, Antony John
Espeland, Pamela
Farndale, W.A.J.
Farr, Alfred Derek
Feder, Bernard
Feingold, Eugene
Felstein, Ivor
Fenner, Frank John
Ferris, Paul
Field, Mark G.
Fiennes, Richard
Fishlock, David Jocelyn
Fison, David Charles
Fitzgerald, Julia
Flynn, Frank
Francoeur, Robert Thomas
Franken, Rose
Gajdusek, D. Carleton
Gallagher, James Roswell
Gandevia, Bryan Harle
Garb, Solomon
Gardner, Richard A.
Geist, Harold
Geyman, John P.
Godman, Arthur
Goodheart, Barbara
Gordon, Richard
Graubard, Mark
Greenwalt, Tibor J.
Gross, Ludwik
Guirdham, Arthur
Hacker, Rose
Hamby, Wallace Bernard
Harthoorn, Antonie Marinus
Hastings, Robert Paul
Havard, Cyril
Henley, Arthur
Herriot, James
Hofstetter, Henry W.
Holmstrom, Lynda Lytle
Hughes, Edward Stuart Reginald
Hunton, Richard Edwin
Hutchin, Kenneth Charles
Illingworth, Ronald Stanley
Inglis, Brian
Ingram, Vernon Martin
Isaacs, Bernard
Isenberg, Seymour
Jackson, William
Jaco, E. Gartly
James, David Geraint
James, John Ivor Pulsford
Jaques, Louis Barker
Jeffcoate, (Sir) Norman

Medicine/Health—cont.

Kabat, Elvin, Abraham
Kaim-Caudle, Peter Robert
Keen, Martin Leon
Kent, Allegra
Kerner, Fred
Keys, Thomas Edward
Kistner, Robert William
Kitzinger, Sheila
Knight, Bernard
Knight, James Allen
Krasner, William
Kubler-Ross, Elizabeth
Lance, James Waldo
Larkin, Rochelle
Lax, Eric
Ledermann, Erich
Leech, Kenneth
Le Riche, William Harding
Le Vay, David
Lewis, Thomas L.T.
Linde, Shirley Motter
Lingeman, Richard
Llewellyn-Jones, Derek
Lodge, Thomas
Ludbrook, John
Luria, Salvador
Lysaught, Jerome P.
Mair, George Brown
Mann, Peggy
McCaffery, Margo
McGovern, John Phillip
McIlwain, Henry
McWilliams, Margaret
Medvei, Victor Cornelius
Mellanby, Kenneth
Melton, David
Metcalf, Donald
Miller, Jonathan
Mines, Samuel
Mitchell, George Archibald Grant
Mitchell, John Phillimore
Moreau, David Merlin
Morley, David
Morton, Robert Steel
Nahas, Gabriel G.
Nathan, Peter
Newill, Robert
Nilson, Bee
Noble, William Charles
Nossal, (Sir) Gustav
Okaro, Anezi
Oliver, Leslie Claremont
Owen, David
Parry, Wilfrid Hocking
Partridge, James W.
Percival, Robert C.
Phillipp, Elliot Elias
Philps, Richard
Pinchot, Ann
Pines, Maya
Polya, John Béla
Powell, Eric
Proctor, William Gilbert, Jr.
Pugh, Patterson David Gordon
Pyke, Magnus
Rachman, Stanley Jack
Rapoport, Robert Norman
Rapoport, Roger Dale
Raven, Ronald William
Rayner, Clair
Rees, William Linford
Rendle-Short, John
Renfroe, Earl W.
Restak, Richard M.
Rhodes, Philip
Richardson, Baron
Richardson, Frank McLean
Richardson, Robert Galloway
Roberts, Derek Harry
Roberts, Nancy Correll
Rodahl, Kaare
Roos, Noralou P.
Rotblat, Joseph

Medicine/Health—cont.

Roth, June
Rothenberg, Robert Edward
Roueche, Berton
Roy, James
Rubin, Stanley
Russell, Brian Fitzgerald
Sacks, Oliver
Sandler, Merton
Sauer, Gordon C.
Saunders, (Dame) C.M.
Sava, George
Scott, David L.
Scott, Donald Fletcher
Seaman, Sylvia Sybil
Shephard, Roy Jesse
Sherman, Ingrid
Shiloh, Ailon
Shock, Nathan W.
Shorter, Edward
Shubin, Seymour
Siegal, Bernie
Silber, Sherman J.
Simpson, Michael Andrew
Slaughter, Frank G.
Smith, David E.
Smith, Ralph Lee
Smythies, John R.
Snow, Keith Ronald
Soulsby, E.J.L.
Southworth, Warren H.
Spencer, Paul
Spock, Benjamin
Stallworthy, (Sir) John
Steele, Peter
Stephens, F. Douglas
Stoddard, Alan
Stoppard, Miriam
Strachan, J. George
Sunderland, (Sir) Sydney
Temin, Peter
Thornton, John Leonard
Trengove, Alan Thomas
Trevor-Roper, Patrick Dacre
Trimmer, Eric J.
Tyrrell, David Arthur John
Van Essen, W.
van Vogt, A.E.
Velardo, Joseph Thomas
Wachter, Oralee
Walsh, (Sir) John Patrick
Walton, (Sir) John
Warwick, Roger
Watkins, John Goodrich
Wells, Charles
Wertenbaker, Lael Tucker
Wessel, Helen S.
Wheeler, Penny Estes
Whitmore, Raymond Leslie
Wilson, (Sir) John
Wilson, Robert Anton
Wilson, Robert Neal
Woodruff, (Sir) Michael
Wunderlich, Ray Charles, Jr.
Young, Morris N.
Yudkin, John

Meteorology/Atmospheric sciences

Anthes, Richard A.
Byers, Horace
Crawford, William P.
Holford, Ingrid
Lamb, Hubert Horace
Namias, Jerome
Riehl, Herbert
Spilhaus, Athelstan
Sutcliffe, Reginald Cockcroft
Tufty, Barbara
Watts, Alan
Weisberg, Joseph
Welch, Ann Courtenay

Meteorology/Atmospheric sciences—cont

Whitnah, Donald Robert

Military/Defence

Addington, Larry Holbrook
Allaun, Frank
Andreski, Stanislav Leonard
Anglesey, Marquess of
Ashley, Leonard R.N.
Asprey, Robert Brown
Barker, Dennis
Barnaby, Charles Frank
Barnett, Correlli
Bassett, Ronald Leslie
Baur, John Edward
Baylis, John
Barnes, (Sir) John
Beach, Edward L.
Beauman, Katherine Bentley
Beaver, Paul
Blair, Clay Drewry
Bloomfield, Lincoln P.
Blumenson, Martin
Booth, Ken
Bretnor, Reginald
Caidin, Martin
Callinan, Bernard J.
Carman, William Young
Chalfont, (Lord)
Chandler, David
Coggins, Jack B.
Combe, Gordon Desmond
Cooper, Bryan
Coox, Alvin D.
Cruickshank, Charles Greig
Cunliffe, Marcus
David, Heather M.
de Chair, Somerset
Downey, Fairfax Davis
Dupuy, Trevor Nevitt
Engle, Eloise
English, Barbara
Falk, Stanley Lawrence
Farran, Roy Alexander
Fehrenbach, Theodore Reed
Firkins, Peter Charles
Fitzgerald, Frances
Frankland, Noble
Gayre of Gayre and Nigg, Robert
Glick, Edward Bernard
Glover, Michael
Goulden, Joseph C.
Gunston, Bill
Hackett, John
Harbottle, Michael Neale
Hartcup, Guy
Hastings, Max M.
Haswell, Chetwynd John Drake
Haythornthwaite, Philip John
Hicken, Victor
Higham, Robin
Holley, Irving Brinton, Jr.
Howard, (Sir) Michael
Howard, Philip
Howarth, David
Huntington, Samuel Philips
Jackson, (Sir) William
Jefferson, Alan
Johnson, Jesse J.
Kahn, David
Keegan, John
Kuenne, Robert Eugene
Laffin, John
Macksey, K.J.
Martin, Laurence
Middleton, Drew
Morris, Eric
Morrison, Wilbur H.
Mrazek, James Edward
Nieburg, H.L.
O'Connor, Raymond G.
O'Neill, Robert John

Military/Defence—cont.

Organski, A.F.K.
Owen, Charles
Perrett, Bryan
Pincher, Chapman
Pocock, Tom
Powell, Geoffrey
Pranger, Robert
Ransom, Harry Howe
Read, Anthony
Reedy, George E.
Russett, Bruce Martin
Shaw, Henry I., Jr.
Sherman, Arnold
Singer, J. David
Spector, Leonard S.
Speed, Frank Warren
Stillman, Richard Joseph
Strutton, Bill
Tanham, George Kilpatrick
Thomas, Charles
Thompson, (Sir) Robert
Tugwell, Maurice A.J.
Waltz, Kenneth N.
Watts, Anthony John
Way, Peter
Williams, Alan Lee
Wilson, Andrew
Winterbotham, Frederick William
Wood, Derek Harold
Woollcombe, Robert
Yarmolinsky, Adam
York, Herbert
Ziemke, Earl F.

Money/Finance

Aliber, Robert Z.
Arndt, Heinz Wolfgang
Barash, Samuel T.
Barkin, Carol
Baxter, William T.
Bird, Richard
Black, Robert Perry
Bloom, Murray Teigh
Bosland, Chelcie Clayton
Brockington, Raymond Berard
Browne, Harry
Cashin, James A.
Chambers, Raymond John
Clarkson, G.P.
Cowan, Tom Keith
Crawford, John Richard
Daenzer, Bernard John
Davis, William
Dell, Sydney
Denenberg, Herbert
Donnelly, Austin S.
Ellis, Keith
Erdman, Paul E.
Fehrenbach, T.R.
Field, John
Fonseca, John des Reis
Fox, Samuel
Frankel, Sandor
Fremgen, James Morgan
Ghosh, Arun Kumar
Goldberg, Louis
Gole, Victor Leslie
Green, Timothy
Gregg, Davis Weinert
Grierson, Philip
Harriss, C. Lowell
Hawthorne, Jennie
Hazlitt, Henry
Heller, Walter W.
Hepworth, Noel P.
Holck, Manfred, Jr.
Holden, J. Milnes
Jackson, Peter
Jaeger, Harry Kenneth
Jager, Martin Otto
Janeway, Eliot

Money/Finance—cont.

Johnson, Robert
Kamm, Jacob Oswald
Kedzie, Daniel Peter
King, Francis P.
Krefetz, Gerald Saul
Lindholm, Richard W.
Mather, Leonard
Mayer, Raymond
Mendelson, Morris
Moynihan, Maurice
Pesek, Boris Peter
Popovic, Nenad D.
Porter, Sylvia
Prochnow, Herbert Victor
Pugh, John Wilbur
Redwood, John
Renwick, Fred Blackwell
Revell, John Robert Stephen Jack
Robinson, G. Melville
Rockley, L.E.
Roll, Eric
Rosenberg, Claude N., Jr.
Rosenberg, Wolfgang
Sarnat, Marshall
Shafer, Neil
Sherwood, Hugh C.
Shrand, David
Smith, Ralph Lee
Sorensen, Thomas Chaikin
Sprinkel, Beryl Wayne
Stafford, David
Stanley, Oliver
Stillman, Richard Joseph
Sullivan, Clara K.
Thomson, Francis Paul
Tobias, Andrew P.
Toch, Henry
Tuccille, Jerome
van Vogt, A.E.
Vidger, Leonard Perry
Waller, Leslie
Walters, Alan Arthur
Whittington, Geoffrey
Wilson, Thomas
Winnikoff, Albert

Music

Ammer, Christine
Anthony, James R.
Asman, James
Atkins, Russell
Austin, William W.
Balliett, Whitney
Barzun, Jacques
Bernstein, Leonard
Berry, Wallace Taft
Blades, James
Blyth, Alan Geoffrey
Boalch, Donald Howard
Bostock, Donald Ivan
Brindle, Reginald Smith
Brown, Howard Mayer
Cage, John
Carpenter, Nan Cooke
Carrell, Norman Gerald
Carson, Ciaran
Charters, Samuel
Chissell, Joan Olive
Clapham, John
Cleall, Charles
Clutton, Cecil
Collier, Graham
Craft, Robert
Dance, Stanley
Debus, Allen George
Del Mar, Norman
Edwards, Ronald George
Feather, Leonard
Fenby, Eric
Fesperman, John T.
Fields, Victor Alexander

Music—cont.

Fleming, William
Fordin, Hugh
Fox, Ted
Garden, Edward
George, Graham Elias
Giannaris, George
Gillett, Charlie
Goff, Martyn
Goldman, Albert
Gorman, Clem
Green, Benny
Green, Elizabeth A.H.
Grunfield, Frederic V.
Haar, James
Harding, James
Hardwick, Michael
Harris, Sheldon H.
Haywood, Charles
Headington, Christopher
Heath, Edward
Heaton, Charles H.
Hentoff, Na
Hiller, Lejaren
Hobsbawm, Eric
Hoffmann, Peggy
Holland, James R.
Hollis, Helen Rice
Holmes, Lowell
Hopkins, Antony
Horder, Mervyn
Howard, Patricia
Hugill, Stan
Hunt, Edgar Hubert
Hurd, Michael John
Hutchings, Arthur
Ingman, Nicholas
Jackson, Barbara Ann Garvey Seagrave
Jackson, Clyde O.
Jacobs, Arthur David
Jefferson, Alan
Kennan, Kent Wheeler
Kennedy, Michael
Kerman, Joseph
Kettelkamp, Larry Dale
Kline, Peter
Kostelanetz, Richard
Kresh, Paul
Kupferberg, Herbert
Lande, Laurence Montague
Landon, H.C.
Last, Joan
Laurence, Dan H.
Lee, M. Owen
Leisy, James Franklin
Lester, Julius
Levey, Michael
Limbacher, James L.
Longstreet, Stephen
Magee, Bryan
Mann, William
Martin, George Whitney
Matthews, Denis
May, Robin
McCarty, Clifford
Mellers, Wilfrid
Menuhin, Yehudi
Meyer, Leonard B.
Moore, Carman
Mullett, John St. Hilary
Myers, Robert Manson
Naha, Ed
Nathan, Hans
Newman, William S.
Nichols, Roger
Norris, Geoffrey
Oja, Carol J.
Oliver, Paul
Osborne, Charles
Palmer, Cedric King
Parks, Edna Dorintha
Parrott, Ian
Peacock, Alan urner

Music—cont.

Pearsall, Ronald
Picker, Martin
Pleasants, Henry
Porter, Andrew
Previn, André
Raynor, Henry
Read, Gardner
Reed, H. Owen
Reynolds, Ernest Randolph
Rezits, Joseph
Rhys, Francis Stephen
Rose, Al
Routh, Francis John
Sadie, Stanley John
Sallis, James
Salter, Lionel
Sams, Eric
Scaduto, Tony
Schonberg, Harold C.
Schuller, Gunther
Schwartz, Elliott S.
Scott, Bill
Seaman, Gerald Roberts
Silverman, Jerry
Simpson, Robert
Skelton, Geoffrey
Snowman, Daniel
Spink, Ian
Stambler, Irwin
Steane, John Barry
Stevens, John
Taylor, Dorothy A.
Temperley, Nicholas
Terkel, Studs
Tischler, Hans
Toledano, Ralph de
Trevor-Roper, Patrick
Tureck, Rosalyn
Walsh, Stephen
Warrack, John
Weisstein, Ulrich W.
Whone, Herbert
Wilgus, D.K.
Williams, Harold
Williamson, Robin
Wolff, Konrad
Woodford, Peggy
Woods, Frederick
Wright, Helen L.
Yorke, Ritchie Ian
Zimmerman, Franklin

Mythology/Folklore

Alpers, Antony
Andrews, Allen
Ashe, Geoffrey Thomas
Asprin, Robert
Barber, Richard
Bascom, William Russel
Bennett, Louise
Bielski, Alison
Bierhorst, John
Blair, Walter
Bradley, Ramona K.
Buday, George
Campbell, Alistair
Campbell, Joseph
Cavendish, Richard
Christian, Roy Cloberry
Clark, LaVerne Harrell
Coffin, Tristram Potter
Cray, Edward
Cutt, Margaret Nancy
Emeneau, Murray Barnson
Espeland, Pamela
Fowke, Edith Margaret
Garner, Alan
Gifford, Edward Stewart, Jr.
Grumley, Michael
Harris, Christie
Harris, Geraldine

Mythology/Folklore—cont.

Harris, Rosemary
Haughton, Rosemary
Haywood, Charles
Hendricks, George David, Sr.
Hodges, Margaret
Hoffman, Daniel
Hugill, Stan
Igo, John
Irwin, John Conran
Jones, Gwyn
La Barre, Weston
Lester, Julius
Lingenfelter, Richard Emery
Macpherson, Jay
Mango, Karin N.
Maple, Eric William
Maranda, Pierre
Miles, Elton
Newall, Venetia June
Odaga, Asenath
Oinas, Felix J.
Opie, Iona
Owen, Douglas David Roy
Peterson, Harold Bruce
Picard, Barbara Leonie
Pilkington, Francis Meredyth
Reed, James
Rivenburgh, Viola K.
Robinson, Roland
Rosenberg, Bruce Alan
Ryan, William M.
St. J hn, Nicole
Sanderson, Stewart F.
Scott, Bill
Sebeok, Thomas A.
Shepard, Leslie Alan
Silverman, Jerry
Simpson, Jacqueline
Skendi, Stavro
Sonnichsen, C.L.
Spink, Reginald
Stanford, Barbara
Stevens, James R.
Synge, Ursula
Toulson, Shirley
Tresidder, Argus John
Tresselt, Alvin
Uchida, Yoshiko
Wang, Hui-Ming
Whitlock, Ralph
Wilgus, D.K.
Wilson, Barbara Ker
Wilson, David S.
Wolverton, Robert E.
Wright, Robert Lee

Natural history

Anastasiou, Clifford
Anderson, Alan, Jr.
Angel, Heather
Attenborough, David
Baerg, Harry John
Baird, David McCurdy
Banfield, A.W. Frank
Barrett, John Henry
Beckinsale, Robert Percy
Beddington, Roy
Beebe, B.F.
Beggs, David
Bellairs, Angus D'Albini
Bellamy, David James
Bere, Rennie Montague
Bodsworth, Fred
Breeden, Stanley
Brown, Vinson
Bruemmer, Fred
Burton, John Andrew
Burton, Maurice
Butler, Colin G.
Caras, Roger
Chinery, Michael

Lloyd, Geoffrey Ernest Richard
Long, A.A.
Long, Eugene Thomas
Lucas, John Randolph
Lukes, Steven M.
Lyons, David
MacGregor, John Geddes
Macintyre, Alasdair
Magee, Bryan
Malcolm, Norman
Manning, David
Mansfield, Walter Kenneth
Margenau, Henry
Margolis, Joseph
Martland, Thomas R.
Mascall, Eric Lionel
Masters, Roger D.
Matilal, B.K.
Matson, Wallace I.
McCreery, Charles Anthony Selby
McDonald, Hugh Dermot
McDowell, John
McInerny, Ralph Matthew
Meyendorff, John
Miles, Leland
Milhaven, John Giles
Miller, K. Bruce
Minogue, Kenneth Robert
Mintz, Samuel I.
Mirenburg, Barry L.
Mollenkott, Virginia Ramsey
Morlan, George K.
Morowitz, Harold J.
Mullan, Bob
Munson, Thomas Nolan
Munz, Peter
Murchie, Guy
Murdoch, Iris
Nahal, Chaman
Nahm, Milton C.
Nakhnikian, George
Nasr, Seyyed Hossein
Natanson, Maurice
Nerlich, Graham C.
Nettler, Gwynn
Neville, Robert C.
Nott, Kathleen
Novack, George
Novak, Michael
Nyanaponika
O'Briant, Walter H.
O'Brien, Elmer
Odell, Robin Ian
O'Flaherty, James Carneal
Ogletree, Thomas Warren
O'Meara, John Joseph
Oppenheim, Felix E.
Organ, Troy Wilson
Orr, Robert Richmond
Osborn, Eric Francis
Owens, Joseph
Ozmon, Howard
Panichas, George A.
Parker, W. Dale
Paterson, Ronald
Peters, Richard Stanley
Phenix, Philip Henry
Phillips, Dewi Zephaniah
Pilkington, Roger Windle
Pitcher, George
Pittenger, Norman
Plantinga, Alvin
Popper, (Sir) Karl
Porn, Ingmar
Porter, Burton F.
Potter, Vincent G.
Price, Kingsley Blake
Prosch, Harry
Purtill, Richard L.
Putnam, Hilary
Quine, Willard V.
Quinton, (Lord)
Raju, Poolla Tirupati

Rankin, Herbert David
Raphael, David Daiches
Rawls, John
Reardon, Bernard M.G.
Reck, Andrew Joseph
Reghaby, Heydar
Reichenbach, Bruce
Reid, Charles L.
Rickman, Hans Peter
Roberts, James Deotis, Sr.
Rosen, Stanley Howard
Rosenbloom, Noah H.
Roshwald, Mordecai
Ross, Ralph Gilbert
Roth, Robert Joseph
Royce, James E.
Russell, John Leonard
Ryan, Alan
Rychlak, Joseph F.
Sahakian, William S.
St. Aubyn, Giles
Sallis, John C.
Salvan, Jacques Léon
Sampson, Geoffrey Richard
Sandoz, G. Ellis
Sarkar, Anil Kumar
Schacht, Richard
Schilpp, Paul Arthur
Schuettinger, Robert Lindsay
Scott, Nathan A., Jr.
Scruton, Roger
Searle, John R.
Seidel, George Joseph
Sethna, M.J.
Shaffer, Jerome Arthur
Shah, Idries
Shapiro, Herman
Shaw, Russell B.
Sherburne, Donald W.
Shibles, Warren
Silver, Daniel J.
Silverstein, Theodore
Simon, Michael A.
Singer, Marcus George
Singer, Peter
Skemp, Joseph Bright
Skipp, Victor Henry Thomas
Skutch, Alexander F.
Smart, John Jamieson Carswell
Smart, Ninian
Smythies, John R.
Snyder, Gary
Solomon, Robert C.
Soltis, Jonas F.
Sparshott, Francis
Sprigge, Timothy
Stack, George
Stankiewicz, Wladyslaw Jozef
Steinkraus, Warren Edward
Stent, Gunther S.
Stern, Axel
Strawson, Peter Frederick
Stroup, Herbert
Stumpf, Samuel
Sweeney, Leo
Swinburne, Richard
Szasz, Thomas Stephen
Thompson, Laurence Graham
Tipton, Ian Charles
Todd, John Murray
Torrance, Thomas Forsyth
Toulmin, Stephen E.
Trepp, Leo
Trethowan, William Kenneth Illtyd
Trinkaus, Charles
Tschumi, Raymond
Valdes, Mario J.
van Fraassen, Bas C.
van Peursen, Cornelis A.
Vesey, Godfrey
Viereck, Peter
Vivas, Eliseo
von Leyden, Wolfgang Marius

Walters, John Beauchamp
Walzer, Michael
Ward, John Stephen Keith
Warnock, G.J.
Warnock, Mary
Weiss, Paul
Wellek, René
Wellman, Carl Pierce
White, Alan Richard
White, Morton
Whiteman, Michael
Whitfield, George
Wicker, Brian John
Wiener, Philip Paul
Wiggins, David
Wilden, Anthony
Williams, Bernard
Williams, C.J.F.
Wilson, John
Winch, Peter
Winetrout, Kenneth
Wirth, Arthur
Wolff, Robert P.
Wolstein, Benjamin
Wolterstorff, Nicholas
Yandell, Keith Edward
Young-Bruehl, Elizabeth

Photography

Ades, Dawn
Allen, Mary
Allsopp, Bruce
Angel, Heather
Arnold, H.J.P.
Avedon, Richard
Bracegirdle, Brian
Brown, Theodore M.
Cleare, John S.
Coleman, A.D.
Douglas, John
Edey, Maitland A.
Edgerton, Harold E.
Enyeart, James L.
Erith, John
Faber, John
Fowler, Don D.
Gernsheim, Helmut
Goldsmith, Arthur
Gutman, Judith Mara
Homer, William Innes
Hopkinson, (Sir) Thomas
Hunt, Robert
Knight, Hardwicke
Lucie-Smith, Edward
Macgregor, James Murdoch
McDarrah, Fred W.
Mitchell, Margaretta
Newhall, Beaumont
Nurnberg, Walter
Plowden, David
Rinhart, Floyd
Rinhart, Marion
Scharf, Aaron
Sethna, M.J.
Tucker, Anne W.
Van Essen, W.
Warham, John
Whone, Herbert
Williams, Jonathan
Wilson, Trevor Frederick

Physics

Aitchison, Ian J.R.
Andrew, Edward Raymond
Andrews, Edgar Harold
Atkins, Kenneth R.
Backus, George Edward
Bacon, George Edward
Batchelor, George Keith

Bell, Raymond M.
Betts, John
Billmeyer, Fred W., Jr.
Blatt, John Markus
Bloembergen, Nicholaas
Bonnor, William Bowen
Bube, Richard H.
Bueche, Frederick J.
Burcham, William Ernest
Chandrasekhar, Subrahmanyan
Clotfelter, Beryl E.
Coleman, James A.
Cook, Alan Hugh
Cottrell, (Sir) Alan
Croxton, C.A.
Dalitz, Richard Henry
Davies, Mansel Morris
Davies, P.C.W.
Dicke, Robert H.
Feinberg, Gerald
Fermi, Laura
Ford, Brian John
Gaydon, Alfred Gordon
Gell-Mann, Murray
Golding, Raymund Marshall
Gray, Harold James
Gwynne, Peter
Hawking, Stephen William
Heppenheimer, Thomas A.
Hodge, Paul William
Hodgson, Peter Edward
Holland, Leslie Arthur
Hoyle, (Sir) Fred
Hughes, William
Kilmister, Clive William
Lawden, Derek Frank
Llewellyn-Jones, Frank
Macdonald, Simon Gavin George
Macfadyen, Kenneth Alexander
March, N.H.
Margenau, Henry
Marshak, Robert Eugene
McCrea, (Sir) William (Hunter)
Messel, Harry
Newton, Robert R.
Nurnberg, Walter
Oldham, Frank
Prokhovnik, Simon Jacques
Prutton, Martin
Ramsey, Norman F.
Redman, Lister Appleton
Reimann, Arnold Leuhrs
Sachs, Mendel
Schwinger, Julian
Sciama, Dennis
Segre, Emilio
Sneddon, Ian Naismith
Spitzer, Lyman
Sprackling, Michael Thomas
Swihart, Thomas L.
Taylor, Charles
Trefil, James
Titterton, (Sir) Ernest William
Townes, Charles H.
Ward, Elizabeth Honor
Weart, Spencer R.
Weinberg, Steven
Wheeler, John Archibald
Wickramasinghe, Nalin Chandra
Wilkinson, Denys
Wilson, Arthur James Cochran

Politics/Government

Abraham, Henry J.
Abrams, Mark
Abshire, David Manker
Adler, Mortimer J.
Alba, Victor
Albinski, Henry Stephen
Alexander, Robert J.
Alisky, Marvin

Allen, Francis A.
Allen, Harry Cranbrook
Allison, R. Bruce
Al-Marayati, Abid A.
Almond, Gabriel A.
Alsop, Joseph Wright
Anders, Leslie
Anderson, Jack
Anderson, John B.
Anderson, Malcolm
Anglin, Douglas G.
Appleton, Sheldon Lee
Apter, David Ernest
Archer, Peter Kingsley
Arnold, Guy
Asbell, Bernard
Bachrach, Peter
Badgley, John Herbert
Baerwald, Hans H.
Bailey, Frederick George
Bailey, Norman
Ball, George
Barber, Benjamin R.
Barber, James David
Barber, John
Barghoorn, Frederick C.
Barltrop, Robert
Barnard, Frederick Mechner
Barnes, Samuel Henry
Barnett, Arthur Doak
Bartlett, Bruce R.
Bass, Jack
Baus, Herbert Michael
Baxter, Craig
Bealey, Frank
Beamish, Tufton Victor Hamilton
Beckwith, Burnham Putnam
Bedau, Hugo Adam
Beer, Samuel
Bell, Roger
Beloff, Lord
Beloff, Nora
Bendiner, Robert
Benn, Tony
Berghahn, Volker R.
Berman, Arthur I.
Bernstein, Barton Jannen
Bernstein, Carl
Berrington, Hugh Bayard
Birch, Anthony Harold
Birnbach, Martin
Bishop, Donald G.
Blake, Robert
Blank, Robert H.
Blondel, Jean
Bogdanor, Vernon
Boissevain, Jeremy
Bolles, Blair
Bolling, Richard
Bone, Hugh A.
Boorstin, Daniel J.
Booth, Ken
Boskoff, Alvin
Bottomore, Thomas
Boulton, David
Bradford, Peter Amory
Brandon, Henry
Brasher, Norman Henry
Braunthal, Gerard
Bray, Jeremy
Brecher, Michael
Breckenridge, Adam
Brewer, Garry D.
Brittan, Samuel
Bromhead, Peter Alexander
Bromke, Adam
Brookes, Pamela
Brown, Archibald Haworth
Brown, Bernard E.
Brzezinski, Zbigniew
Buchanan, James M.
Buckley, William F., Jr.
Buckman, Peter

Budge, Ian
Bulmer-Thomas, Ivor
Burns, James MacGregor
Burton, Ivor Flower
Butler, David
Buttinger, Joseph
Califano, Joseph A., Jr.
Calvert, Peter
Campbell, Peter Walter
Canovan, Margaret Evelyn
Carter, Jimmy
Casstevens, Thomas William
Carter, Douglas
Catudal, Honoré, Jr.
Caute, David
Chelf, Carl P.
Cheng, J. Chester
Childs, David
Childs, Marquis
Chomsky, Noam
Christoph, James B.
Churchward, Lloyd Gordon
Clancy, Thomas H.
Clark, Laurence
Clarke, Peter Frederick
Clecak, Peter
Clem, Alan L.
Cleveland, Leslie
Clutterbuck, Richard
Codding, George A., Jr.
Cohen, Maxwell
Cohen, Stephen F.
Collins, Larry
Combe, Gordon Desmond
Cone, Carl
Converse, Philip E.
Cook, Chris
Cook, Don
Copeland, Miles
Cormack, Patrick
Cosgrave, Patrick
Countryman, Vern
Cox, Alfred Bertram
Cranston, Maurice
Crick, Bernard R.
Crighton, John Clark
Crocker, (Sir) Walter
Crocombe, Ronald Gordon
Cummings, Milton C., Jr.
Cuomo, Mario
Dahl, Robert
Dale, Richard
Daly, Lowrie J.
D'Amato, Anthony A.
Davidson, Roger H.
Davis, David
Davis, Vincent
Degenhardt, Henry W.
Dell, Edmund
Deutsch, Karl
Dexter, Lewis Anthony
Dimock, Marshall Edward
Dinerman, Beatrice
Donoughue, Bernard
Dorman, Michael L.
Dornberg, John
Dowse, Robert Edward
Dowty, Alan K.
Doyle, Charles
Drucker, H.M.
Drury, Allen
Duchene, Louis-François
Dunleavy, Patrick
Eagleton, Terence
Easton, David
Edelman, Murray J.
Ehrlichman, John
Ekirch, Arthur A., Jr.
Elcock, Howard
Elliot, Jeffrey M.
Emerson, Thomas I.
Evans, Rowland, Jr.
Fazal, Muhammad Abul

Feld, Werner J.
Finer, Samuel
Finger, Seymour
Fireside, Harvey F.
Fisher, David
Fisher, Louise
Fisher, (Sir) Nigel
Fisher, Ralph Talcott, Jr.
Fitzgerald, Frances
Fitzgerald, Garret
Fitzgerald, Stephen
Fletcher-Cooke, (Sir) John
Flynn, James Robert
Fonseca, Aloysius
Foot, Michael
Foote, Geoffrey
Fox, Len
Fox, Samuel
Franck, Thomas Martin
Frank, André Gunder
Freeman, Bill
Freeman, Jo
Friedman, Lawrence M.
Frye, Alton
Fulbright, J. William
Gamble, Andrew Michael
Gamson, William Anthony
Garrow, David
Garthoff, Raymond Leonard
Geras, Norman
Gerber, William
Geyer, Georgie Anne
Gil, Federico Guillermo
Glaser, Kurt
Glick, Edward Bernard
Goldfarb, Ronald Lawrence
Goldwater, Barry M.
Goldwin, Robert
Goodman, Elliot R.
Gould, James A.
Gowing, Margaret Mary
Graebner, Norman Arthur
Graham, Hugh Davis
Grant, Bruce
Gray, Richard Butler
Gregory, Roy
Grieb, Kenneth J.
Griffith, Ernest S.
Grimes, Alan P.
Grimond, Jo
Grose, Peter
Gruberg, Martin
Gwyn, William Brent
Hacker, Andrew
Halberstam, David
Hall, Richard
Hampsch, George
Hampton, William
Hardie, Frank
Hargrove, Erwin C.
Harrington, Michael
Harris, Fred R.
Harris, Jonathan
Harris, Peter Bernard
Harris, Ronald Walter
Harris, Walter A.
Harrison, Royden John
Haskins, George Lee
Hart, H.L.A.
Hayden, Tom
Hayek, Friedrich August von
Hazlehurst, Cameron
Healey, Denis
Heater, Derek Benjamin
Heath, Edward
Held, Virginia P.
Hellyer, Paul T.
Hennessy, Peter
Hepworth, Noel P.
Herzog, Arthur
Hills, Denis
Hilsman, Roger
Hiscocks, Richard

Hodges, Donald Clark
Hoffman, Robert Louis
Hoffmann, Stanley
Hogg, Quintin
Holden, Matthew, Jr.
Holloway, Harry
Holsti, Ole Rudolf
Holtzman, Abraham
Honderich, Ted
Hope, Marjorie
Horn, Stephen
Horne, Alistair
Horowitz, Irving Louis
Houn, Franklin W.
Howard, A.E. Dick
Howard, J. Woodford, Jr.
Howard, Roger
Howell, David
Huck, Arthur
Hughes, Colin Anfield
Hughes, Judith M.
Huntington, Samuel Phillips
Ikle, Fred C.
Ingram, Derek Thynne
Ionescu, Ghita
Jacker, Corinne
Jackman, Sydney Wayne
Jackson, Robert J.
Jackson, William Keith
Jacobs, Clyde
Jacobs, Dan N.
Jacobs, Walter Darnell
Jarman, Thomas Leckie
Jenkins, Roy
Jensen, Richard
Jessup, Frank W.
Johnson, A. Ross
Johnson, George
Johnson, Nicholas
Johnston, Russell
Jones, Aubrey
Jordan, Robert Smith
Judd, Frank
Kaplan, Morton A.
Kariel, Henry S.
Kaufman, Gerald Bernard
Kedourie, Elie
Keith-Lucas, Bryan
Kennedy, Edward
Kessel, John Howard
Keyserling, Leon H.
Khadduri, Majid
Kilpatrick, James Jackson
King, Anthony
King, Larry L.
King, Robert R.
Kingdon, John W.
Kinnear, Michael Stewart Read
Kirk, Russell Amos
Kirkpatrick, Jeane
Kissinger, Henry
Kitzinger, Uwe
Klehr, Harvey
Kohler, Foy David
Kolinsky, Martin
Koning, Hans
Kornhauser, William
Kovel, Joel
Kresh, Paul
Kristol, Irving
Kulski, Wladyslaw Wszebor
Kusin, Vladimir V.
Laffin, John
Lakeman, Enid
Lamb, Karl A.
Landecker, Manfred
Lane, David Stuart
Langley, Lester D.
Laponce, Jean Antoine
Lapping, Brian
Laqueur, Walter
Larson, Arthur
Lasch, Christopher

A56

Lasky, Victor
Leder, Lawrence H.
Leeds, Christopher
Legge, John David
Legum, Colin
LeMay, G.H.L.
Lendvai, Paul
Levin, Peter
Lewin, Moshe
Lewis, (Sir) Arthur
Lewis, William Russell
Liebhafsky, Herbert Hugo
Lifton, Robert J.
Linder, Robert D.
Lindsay, John
Lipset, Seymour Martin
Lipsitz, Lou
Liss, Sheldon B.
Liu, Leo
Loh, Pichon P.Y.
Low, Alfred D.
Lukes, Steven M.
Luttwak, Edward Nicolae
Lycan, Gilbert L.
MacCormick, Neil
Macfarlane, Leslie John
MacGuigan, Mark R.
Maddox, Robert James
Maddox, Russell Webber
Madge, Charles
Magee, Bryan
Maheshwari, Shriram
Mairowitz, David
Mandel, Ernest
Manheim, Jarol B.
Manning, David
Mansergh, Nicholas
Marr, David George
Marsh, Peter T.
Martin, Boyd A.
Martin, Ralph G.
Masao, Maruyama
Massialas, Byron G.
Masters, Roger D.
Mastny, Vojtech
Mayhew, Christopher
Mayhew, David Raymond
Mayne, Richard
Mayo, Patricia Elton
McCarthy, Eugene
McCauley, Martin
McConnell, Grant
McCraw, Thomas K.
McGinniss, Joe
McLaren, John
McMillan, James
McNelly, Theodore Hart
McRae, Kenneth Douglas
Means, Gordon Paul
Medvedev, Roy
Medvedev, Zhores
Mehrotra, Sriram
Meller, Norman
Menard, Orville D.
Menendez, Albert
Merton, Robert K.
Mickolus, Edward
Middleton, Drew
Miles, Michael Wade
Miller, Abraham
Miller, David
Miller, Helen Hill
Miller, John Donald Bruce
Miller, Kenneth E.
Miller, Lynn H.
Miller, Warren E.
Minogue, Kenneth Robert
Minow, Newton N.
Mitchell, Joan E.
Mitchell, Memory F.
Moldea, Dan E.
Mollenhoff, Clark
Montgomery, John D.

Moodie, Graeme Cochrane
Moonman, Eric
Morgan, Donald Grant
Morgan, Janet
Morris-Jones, Wyndraeth Humphreys
Morrison, James Frederic
Morton, Henry W.
Moskow, Michael H.
Moss, Robert John
Muirden, Bruce Wallace
Mullard, Christopher Paul
Mundel, Marvin Everett
Murphy, Dervla Mary
Murphy, Walter Francis
Musolf, Lloyd Daryl
Nagel, Stuart
Navasky, Victor
Neal, Fred Warner
Neal, Harry Edward
Neustadt, Richard E.
Newman, Peter
Nicholas, Herbert George
Nieburg, H.L.
Nixon, Richard
Nogee, Joseph L.
Noonan, Lowell G.
Norman, John
Norton, Philip
Novack, George
Nunn, Frederick McKinley
Nye, Joseph S., Jr.
O'Brien, Conor Cruise
O'Brien, Lawrence F.
O'Connor, William E.
Oppenheim, Felix E.
Osborne, Milton
Owen, David
Page, Robin
Palumbo, Dennis
Panitch, Leo
Parker, Robert Stewart
Parker, Stanley R.
Parker, W. Dale
Parkinson, Cyril Northcote
Parry, Albert
Paxton, John
Peabody, Robert Lee
Pierce, Neal R.
Pelling, Henry Mathison
Pen, Jan
Pethybridge, Roger William
Phillips, William
Pierard, Richard V.
Pierce, Roy
Plischke, Elmer
Pogrebin, Letty C.
Pole, Jack Richon
Polonsky, Antony
Popovic, Nenad D.
Powell, Enoch
Pranger, Robert
Prescott, J.R.V.
Press, O. Charles
Prewitt, Kenneth
Pringle, John Martin Douglas
Pritchard, R. John
Pulzer, Peter George Julius
Pundeff, Marin V.
Punnett, Robert Malcolm
Qualter, Terence H.
Quandt, William Bauer
Rae, John Malcolm
Rainey, Gene Edward
Ramsden, John Andrew
Randall, Margaret
Ransom, Harry Howe
Ray, Sib Narayan
Raymond Ellsworth
Reddaway, Peter
Reedy, George E.
Rees, Ioan Bowen
Regenstreif, S. Peter

Reghaby, Heydar
Rejai, Mostafa
Rembar, Charles
Reynolds, Philip Alan
Richardson, Richard Judson
Riggs, Robert Edwon
Ripley, Randall Butler
Roazen, Paul
Robinson, Marguerite S.
Roche, John P.
Rodgers, (Sir) John
Rodney, William
Rogers, George William
Rogers, William
Rogow, Arnold A.
Roos, Noralou P.
Rose, Paul
Rose, Richard
Rosenberg, Wolfgang
Rosenthal, Donald B.
Rossabi, Morris
Rosten, Leo
Rostow, Eugene V.
Rostow, Walt W.
Roth, Andrew
Rothschild, Joseph
Rowat, Donald C.
Royster, Vermont
Rubenstein, Richard E.
Rubenstein, Richard Lowell
Ruchelman, Leonard I.
Ruppenthal, Karl M.
Rusher, William Allen
Russett, Bruce Martin
Ryder, Arthur John
Safire, William
Salisbury, Robert H.
Salvadori, Max William
Sampson, Anthony
Sampson, Geoffrey Richard
Sampson, Ronald Victor
Samuels, Warren J.
Sandoz, G. Ellis
Sargent, Lyman T.
Scalapino, Robert Anthony
Scammon, Richard M.
Scheiber, Harry N.
Schlesinger, Arthur, Jr.
Schmandt, Henry J.
Schrag, Peter
Schuettinger, Robert Lindsay
Schwartz, Mildred Anne
Schwarz, Henry G.
Schwarzenberger, Georg
Scott, John Anthony
Scruton, Roger
Seabury, Paul
Sears, David O.
Segal, Ronald Michael
Selbourne, David
Sharkansky, Ira
Shepherd, George W.
Short, Philip
Shrapnel, Norman
Shulman, Marshall Darrow
Shuman, Samuel I.
Silk, Leonard S.
Simon, Sheldon Weiss
Simpson, Dick
Singer, J. David
Skidmore, Max J.
Skolnikoff, Eugene B.
Smith, Brian
Smith, (Sir) Dudley
Smith, Howard E., Jr.
Smith, Howard K.
Smith, Ralph Lee
Snowman, Daniel
Snyder, Francis Gregory
Solomon, Richard H.
Sorensen, Theodore
Sorensen, Thomas Chaikin
Spear, T.G. Percival

Spector, Sherman David
Speed, Frank Warren
Spiro, Herbert
Staar, Richard F.
Stacey, Tom
Stankiewicz, Wladyslaw Jozef
Stapleton, Laurence
Stave, Bruce M.
Steel, D.R.
Steel, David
Steel, Ronald
Stein, Michael B.
Steiner, Kurt
Stern, Clarence A.
Stevens, Christopher
Stevens, Richard P.
Stevenson, William
Stewart of Fulham (Baron)
Stockman, David
Stockwin, Arthur
Stretton, Hugh
Stupak, Ronald Joseph
Suda, Zdenek Ludvik
Suleiman, Michael Wadie
Sulzberger, C.L.
Sundquist, James
Sussman, Barry
Symmons-Symonolewicz, Konstantin
Szulc, Tad
Taborsky, Edward J.
Target, George William
Taverne, Dick
Taylor, John Vernon
Teller, Neville
Theobald, Robert
Thompson, (Sir) Robert
Thompson, Robert Norman
Tinker, Hugh
Toland, John
Toledano, Ralph de
Tuccille, Jerome
Tucker, Robert C.
Tugendhat, Christopher
Tulchin, Joseph S.
Turner, Frederick C.
Turner, Henry A.
Ulam, Adam Bruno
Ungar, Sanford J.
Van Dyke, Vernon B.
Vasil, Raj Kumar
Vatikiotis, P.J.
Verney, Douglas
Viereck, Peter
Viorst, Milton
Vital, David
von Leyden, Wolfgang
Wagner, Wenceslas J.
Wakeman, Frederic Evans, Jr.
Wall, Patrick
Walton, Richard J.
Waltz, Kenneth N.
Walzer, Michael
Ward, Alan J.
Ward, Harry Merrill
Ward, Norman
Ward, Russel Braddock
Warren, Harris Gaylord
Warren, Sidney
Watkins, Alan
Waugh, Auberon
Wearin, Otha Donner
Weeks, Jeffrey
Weidenbaum, Murray
Weiss, Paul
Wesson, Robert G.
West, Francis James
Weston, Corinne Comstock
Wettenhall, Roger
Whale, John
Wheelwright, Edward Lawrence
Whitlam, Gough
Wicker, Tom

Politics/Government—cont.

Wilkinson, Paul
Williams, Alan Lee
Williams, Walter E.
Willrich, Mason
Wilson, Lord
Wilson, A. Jeyaratnam
Wilson, Des
Wilson, James Quinn
Wise, David
Wittner, Lawrence Stephen
Wolff, Robert P.
Woll, Peter
Wood, Neal
Wood, Robert
Woodward, Bob
Woolf, Stuart Joseph
Wootton, Graham
Workman, William D., Jr.
Wright, Theodore Paul, Jr.
Yglesias, Jose
Young, Donald
Young, James
Young, Wayland
Zacek, Joseph Frederick
Zentner, Peter
Zimmerman, Joseph Francis
Zinn, Howard
Zucker, Norman Livingston
Zuckerman, Michael

Psychiatry

Abse, David Wilfred
Apter, Michael John
Ban, Thomas Arthur
Barker, Philip
Browning, Don
Cappon, Daniel
Chesen, Eli S.
Coles, Robert
Comfort, Alex
Dally, Ann
Dershowitz, Alan M.
Dewald, Paul A.
Erikson, Erik H.
Eysenck, Hans
Fay, Allen
Fraser, Morris
Freeman, Lucy
Gardner, Richard A.
Geist, Harold
Goldenson, Robert M.
Green, Richard
Hartmann, Ernest L.
Heaton-Ward, William Alan
Hoenig, J.
Howells, John Gwilym
Kiev, Ari
Knight, James Allen
Kubler-Ross, Elizabeth
La Barre, Weston
Ledermann, Erich
Leighton, Alexander
Lester, David
Lichtenberg, Philip
Lidz, Theodore
Lifton, Robert Jay
Lowen, Alexander
Macdonald, John M.
May, Rollo
McGuigan, F. Joseph
Morgan, H.G.
Murphy, William Francis
Peterson, Bruce Henry
Pribram, Karl H.
Rees, William Linford
Reid, Andrew H.
Robertiello, Richard C.
Rogler, Lloyd Henry
Rogow, Arnold A.
Rubin, Theodore I.
Rutter, Michael

Psychiatry—cont.

Rycroft, Charles
Ryle, Anthony
Sahakian, William S.
Sainsbury, Maurice Joseph
Saul, Leon Joseph
Scarf, Maggie
Shepard, Martin
Shubin, Seymour
Siirala, Aarne Johannes
Slovenko, Ralph
Smythies, John R.
Starke, Joseph Gabriel
Stevenson, Ian
Stierlin, Helm
Stoller, Alan
Stone, Alan A.
Storr, Anthony
Szasz, Thomas Stephen
Viscott, David S.
Walsh, (Sir) John
Walton, Henry John
Willis, James
Wing, John K.
Wolman, Benjamin B.
Wolpe, Joseph
Yates, Aubrey James
Zubin, Joseph

Psychology

Abse, David Wilfred
Adams, James F.
Adler, Helmut E.
Ahsen, Akhter
Aiken, Lewis R., Jr.
Ainsworth, Mary D. Salter
Anstey, Edgar
Apter, Michael John
Ard, Ben Neal, Jr.
Argyle, Michael
Arnold, M.B.
Badcock, Christopher Robert
Bandura, Albert
Bardwick, Judith M.
Barlow, John
Barnett, S. Anthony
Barral, Mary-Rose
Bartek, Edward J.
Bass, Bernard M.
Beauchamp, Kenneth
Beech, H. Reginald
Bell, James Edward
Berger, Evelyn Miller
Berger, Terry
Berman, Claire
Bettelheim, Bruno
Biddle, Bruce Jesse
Biggs, John Burville
Birnbach, Martin
Black, Percy
Blackham, Garth
Blair, Glenn Myers
Boden, Margaret A.
Bowlby, John
Bradford, Leland Powers
Branden, Nathaniel
Brandt, Richard M.
Breakwell, Glynis M.
Breen, Dana
Broadbent, Donald
Brothers, Joyce
Brown, Frederick G.
Brown, Roger William
Browning, Don
Bruner, Jerome S.
Buck, Margaret Waring
Bugental, James F.T.
Byrne, Donn E.
Calder, Matthew Lewis
Candland, Douglas Keith
Cappon, Daniel
Cassel, Russell N.

Psychology—cont.

Cattell, Raymond Bernard
Chaplin, James Patrick
Chapman, J. Dudley
Clark, Kenneth Bancroft
Clinebell, Howard J., Jr.
Coan, Richard W.
Coe, William C.
Cole, Shiela R.
Coles, Robert
Conger, John
Cook, Mark
Cottle, Thomas J.
Craig, Robert Charles
Cratty, Bryant J.
Criscuolo, Anthony Thomas
Dally, Ann
Davis, John David
Day, James F.
Dempsey, David
Dichter, Ernest
Di Cyan, Erwin
Di Leo, Joseph
Dixon, Norman
Dobson, James C., Jr.
Doman, Glen
Dominian, Jack
Doob, Leonard W.
Downing, John Allen
Dreyfus, Edward A.
Dudley, Geoffrey A.
Duhl, Leonard J.
Dyer, Wayne W.
Edgington, Eugene-Sinclair
Edwards, Allen Jack
Eisenson, Jon
Elkins, Dov Peretz
Ellis, Albert
Ellis, Keith
Engle, Thelburn L.
Erikson, Erik H.
Estes, William
Eysenck, Hans
Fay, Allan
Feingold, S. Norman
Felstein, Ivor
Fiedler, Fred E.
Flescher, Irwin
Flint, Betty Margaret
Flynn, James Robert
Freedman, Mervin Burton
Friedman, Norman
Fruchter, Benjamin
Fullerton, Gail
Gallagher, James Roswell
Garner, Wendell
Gaylin, Willard
Geist, Harold
Goldenson, Robert M.
Gooch, Stanley
Green, Celia
Green, Donald Ross
Greenberg, Ira
Greene, Judith
Gregory, Richard Langton
Grossinger, Tania
Grossman, Sebastian P.
Hammer, Emanuel F.
Hammes, John A.
Handy, Rollo
Hannam, Charles Lewis
Harding, D.W.
Hardy, Richard Earl
Hare Duke, Michael
Harré Rom
Harris, Albert J.
Heim, Alice W.
Henley, Arthur
Herron, William
Hilgard, Ernest
Holland, Norman N.
Holtzman, Wayne Harold
Homans, Peter
Howells, John Gwilym

Psychology—cont.

Huber, Jack
Hudson, Liam
Hunt, J. McVicker
Hyde, Janet S.
James, David Edward
Jeeves, Malcolm A.
Jensen, Arthur Robert
Josephs, Ray
Kagan, Jerome
Keen, Ernest
Kelman, Herbert Chanoch
Kerner, Fred
Kessen, William
Kettelkamp, Larry Dale
Klare, George Roger
Klinger, Eric
Kovel, Joel
Kraft, William F.
Laing, R.D.
Lane, Harlan
Lasswell, Marcia
Lazarus, Richard S.
Leach, Penelope
LeBoeuf, Michael
Leeds, Morton Harold
Leshan, Eda J.
Lester, David
Levinson, Harry
Lichtenberg, Philip
Lidz, Theodore
Lifton, Robert J.
Lindgren, Henry Clay
Lomas, Peter Eric Samuel
Lowen, Alexander
Lubar, Joel F.
Lubin, Bernard
Luce, Gay
Lynn, Richard
Marcuse, Frederick Lawrence
Masterton, Graham
May, Rollo
McCall, Robert B.
McConnell, James Vernon
McCreery, Charles Anthony Selby
McGuigan, F. Joseph
McKeachie, Wilburt J.
McKinney, Fred
Mehrabian, Albert
Melzack, Ronald
Milgram, Stanley
Miller, John Gordon
Milner, Esther
Milner, Marion
Moore, Raymond S.
Moreno, Antonio
Morgan, Patricia
Morlan, George K.
Mouly, George Joseph
Moyer, K.E.
Mudd, Emily H.
Muuss, Rolf Eduard
Natchez, Gladys
Nathan, Peter
Nettler, Gwynn
Newman, Oscar
Nichols, R. Eugene
Nouwen, Henri J.
Odlum, Doris Maude
O'Doherty, Eamonn
Olson, David Richard
Osgood, Charles E.
Pacifico, Carl
Peck, M. Scott
Peel, Edwin
Peters, Richard Stanley
Peterson, Bruce Henry
Phillips, John Lawrence, Jr.
Pikunas, Justin
Pines, Maya
Powers, William
Pribram, Karl H.
Pulaski, Mary Ann
Randall, John L.

A58

Psychology—*cont.*

Rapoport, Robert Norman
Rees, William Linford
Reeves, Elton T.
Reger, Roger
Reid, Clyde Henderson, Jr.
Reuben, David
Roazen, Paul
Robertiello, Richard C.
Rogo, D. Scott
Rohner, Ronald P.
Roiphe, Anne Richardson
Rosenthal, Bernard G.
Royce, James E.
Royce, Joseph Russell
Rutter, Michael
Rychlak, Joseph F.
Ryle, Anthony
Sabine, William Henry Waldo
Sahakian, William S.
Sampson, Edward E.
Sarkar, Anil Kumar
Sarnoff, Irving
Scarf, Maggie
Schellenberg, James A.
Schrank, Jeffrey
Schuller, Robert H.
Schultz, Will
Scott, Donald Fletcher
Sears, David O.
Sexton, Linda Gray
Sexton, Virginia Staudt
Shah, Idries
Shepard, Martin
Sherman, Ingrid
Shibutani, Tamotsu
Shideler, Mary M.
Shock, Nathan W.
Shone, Ronald
Shontz, Franklin C.
Siirala, Aarne Johannes
Sime, Mary
Simon, Herbert A.
Skemp, Richard Rowland
Skinner, B.F.
Slade, Peter
Slovenko, Ralph
Smith, Bert Kruger
Smythies, John R.
Spatz, Kenneth Christopher, Jr.
Spector, Jack Jerome
Sperlich, Peter Werner
Stanley, Julian C., Jr.
Stenhouse, David
Sternberg, Robert J.
Stotland, Ezra
Straus, Murray A.
Strom, Robert
Suinn, Richard M.
Summers, Gene F.
Sutherland, Norman Stuart
Swartz, Jon David
Swift, W. Porter
Szasz, Thomas Stephen
Székely, Endre
Tallent, Norman
Tart, Charles T.
Terrace, Herbert S.
Thomson, Robert
Trasler, Gordon Blair
Tripodi, Tony
Vaughan, Richard Patrick
Vernon, Magdalen Dorothea
Vroom, Victor H.
Wagner, Rudolph Fred
Walker, Nigel
Walton, Henry John
Watkins, John Goodrich
Weaver, Carl Harold
Weinrich, A.K.H.
Westheimer, Ruth
Wike, Edward L.
Wilden, Anthony
Wilson, Colin

Psychology—*cont.*

Wilson, John
Winston, Sarah
Wolman, Benjamin B.
Wolstein, Benjamin
Wrightsman, Lawrence Samuel
Wunderlich, Ray Charles, Jr.
Yates, Aubrey James
Young, Chesley Virginia
Young, John Zachary
Zimbardo, Philip
Zubin, Joseph

Public/Social administration

Abel-Smith, Brian
Brown, Muriel
Critchley, Thomas Alan
Davidson, Roger H.
Dimock, Marshall Edward
Downes, Bryan
Fazal, Muhammad Abul
Forder, Anthony
Freeman, Roger A.
Glaser, Kurt
Hodgson, John Syner
Holden, Matthew, Jr.
Kash, Don C.
Lapping, Brian
Loney, Martin
Lyden, Fremont James
Maddox, Russell Webber
Maheshwari, Shriram
Mesa-Lago, Carmelo
Millar, James
Moskow, Michael H.
Mulligan, Raymond A.
Musolf, Lloyd Daryl
Nagel, Stuart
Nigro, Felix Anthony
Oram, Clifton
Parker, Robert Stewart
Phillips, Robert Arthur John
Popper, Frank James
Press, Otto Charles
Punnett, Robert Malcolm
Rees, Ioan Bowen
Ripley, Randall Butler
Roos, Noralou P.
Ross, Murray George
Rowat, Donald C.
Shivers, Jay Sanford
Simmie, James
Smith, Brian
Stein, Bruno
Steiner, George A.
Streeten, Paul Patrick
Toch, Henry
Wettenhall, Roger
Williams, Walter E.
Zimmerman, Joseph Francis

Race relations

Aptheker, Bettina
Banks, James Albert
Barr, Alwyn
Boskin, Joseph
Clark, Kenneth Bancroft
Clark, Mary T.
Egbuna, Obi
Foner, Eric
Foner, Philip S.
Frakes, George Edward
Franklin, John H.
Garrow, David
Giovanni, Nikki
Glazer, Nathan
Gray, Richard
Gwaltney, John Langston
Hall, Rodney
Heath, G. Louis

Race relations—*cont.*

Hellmann, Ellen
Hernton, Calvin C.
Hiro, Dilip
Holden, Matthew, Jr.
Hornsby, Alton, Jr.
Jackson, Clyde O.
Jones, Frank Lancaster
Jones, Jaqueline
Jones, LeRoi
Kilpatrick, James Jackson
Knopf, Terry Ann
Kovel, Joel
Krausz, Ernest
Kuper, Leo
Lee, Don L.
Loney, Martin
Lyons, Thomas Tolman
Marszalek, John F., Jr.
Marx, Gary T.
Mason, Philip
McPherson, James Munro
Melady, Thomas
Miller, Stuart Creighton
Mitchell, Loften
Morrish, Ivor
Mullard, Christopher Paul
Muse, Benjamin
Nabokov, Peter
Olsen, Otto H.
Onyeama, Dillibe
Pettigrew, Thomas Fraser
Pole, Jack Richon
Powledge, Fred
Rex, John Arderne
Rischin, Moses
Roberts, James Deotis, Sr.
Rose, Eliot Joseph Benn
St. John, Robert
Sanders, Ronald
Sawyer, Roger
Scarfe, Wendy Elizabeth
Schermerhorn, Richard A.
Schusky, Ernest L.
Schwartz, Mildred Anne
Segal, Ronald Michael
Shepherd, George W.
Sherman, Richard B.
Sorrenson, Maurice Peter Keith
Spear, Allan Henry
Staples, Robert Eugene
Tinker, Hugh
Vasil, Raj Kumar
Vincent, John James
Walker, Alan
Walvin, James
Weinrich, Anna Katharina
  Hildegard
Williams, Walter E.
Williamson, Joey
Workman, William D., Jr.
Wynes, Charles E.

Recreation

Abbot, May Laura
Adair, Ian
Allen, Edith Beavers
Bale, Don
Bechervaise, John Mayston
Bell, Robert Charles
Bennett, Hal
Blair, Claire Drewry
Blandford, Percy William
Bond, Nelson S.
Bowker, Robin Marsland
Bowyer, Mathew Justice
Brandreth, Gyles
Bueschel, Richard
Byrne, Robert
Churchill, E. Richard
Coffin, George Sturgis
Corbett, Scott

Recreation—*cont.*

Crawford, William P.
Cunningham, Chet
Davies, Hunter
Dick, Robert C.
Dickson, Paul
Dingle, Graeme
Dominy, Eric Norman
Dummett, M.A.E.
Forsberg, Gerald
Gardner, Paul
Goaman, Muriel
Goldstein-Jackson, Kevin
Goren, Charles H.
Greenhill, Basil Jack
Halliday, William R.
Hamilton, Charles
Hampton, Jack Fitz-Gerald
Hartson, William Roland
Hastings, Phyllis
Hawkesworth, Eric
Hegeler, Sten
Helmker, Judith A.
Henderson, Richard
Henkel, Steve
Hirst-Smith, Ann
Holt, Michael
Hunter, Norman
Hyams, Joe
James, Theodore, Jr.
Jensen, Clayne
Johnson, James Ralph
Kaye, Marvin
King, Teri
Lamb, Geoffrey Frederick
Latta, Richard J.
Laumer, Keith
Lewis, John N.C.
Mackay, James Alexander
Mason, Edmund
Mason, Francis K.
Matthews, Robert C.O.
Montagu of Beaulieu, Lord
Morgan-Grenville, Gerard
  Wyndham
Morton, Brenda
Moss, Stirling
Murray, William Hutchinson
New, Anthony
Nunn, John
Olney, Ross R.
Ord-Hume, Arthur W.J.G.
Pavey, Don
Pick, John Barclay
Quarrie, Bruce
Rees, Ioan Bowen
Rendell, Joan
Resnick, Mike
Ridgway, John
Ridout, Ronald
Riefe, Alan
Ryalls, Alan
Scott, Amorett
Scott, Christopher
Self, Margaret Cabell
Slater, Mary
Somerville, James Hugh Miller
Staff, Frank William
Stebbins, Robert A.
Stone, William S.
Taylor, Fred James
Tippette, Giles
Traver, Robert
Van Essen, W.
Verney, Michael Palmer
Waltham, Tony
Wang, Hui-Ming
Watts, Allan
Welch, Ann Courtenay
Wilkinson, Tim
Williams, Guy R.
Wise, Terence
Wykes, Alan
Yoder, Glee

Regional/Urban planning

Berry, Brian J.L.
Blair, Thomas
Blumenfeld, Hans
Bourne, Larry Stuart
Breese, Gerald
Chaplin, F. Stuart, Jr.
Frieden, Bernard J.
Gilbert, Alan
Gould, Peter
Haar, Charles Monroe
Hall, Peter Geoffrey
Heap, (Sir) Desmond
Hill, Michael J.
Hirsch, Werner Z.
Jackson, John N.
Jackson, Kenneth Terry
Jones, Emrys
Lewis, J. Parry
Mumford, Lewis
Munzer, Martha E.
Pawley, Martin
Plummer, (Sir) Desmond
Popper, Frank James
Pushkarev, Boris S.
Ravetz, Alison
Rees, Henry
Reps, John W.
Taylor, John
Warren, Kenneth
Weintraub, Dov

Sciences

Africa, Thomas W.
Anastasiou, Clifford
Andrews, Edgar Harold
Anees, Munawar Ahmad
Asimov, Isaac
Bedini, Silvio A.
Berry, Adrian M.
Bickel, Lennard
Blackwell, Richard J.
Bova, Ben
Boyd, Waldo T.
Brock, William Hodson
Buchdahl, Gerd
Burke, James
Bylinsky, Gene
Calder, Nigel
Caws, Peter
Chrstian, John Wyrill
Cole, Jonathan
Commoner, Barry
Cook, Melvin A.
Cottrell, (Sir) Alan
Crombie, Alistair Cameron
Crosland, Maurice P.
Cunningham, Chet
Davis, John Tasman
Davies, Mansel Morris
de Camp, L. Sprague
del Rey, Lester
de Mille, Richard
Denbigh, George Kenneth
Dixon, Bernard
Dukert, Joseph Michael
Engdahl, Silvia L.
Feder, Bernard
Ferris, Timothy.
Fisher, David E.
Fishlock, David Jocelyn
Ford, Brian John
Fox, Robert
George, Wilma
Godman, Arthur
Goodfield, June
Goran, Morris
Gowing, Margaret Mary
Graubard, Mark
Green, Celia
Gregory, Richard Langton
Grey, Jerry

Sciences—cont.

Gunther, A.E.
Habgood, John Stapylton
Harré, Rom
Hartcup, Guy
Hatcher, William S.
Hellman, Hal
Heminway, John Hylan, Jr.
Hesse, Mary Brenda
Hills, Philip James
Holmes, Jay
Holmes, Joseph Everett
Huston, Mervyn J.
Ipsen, D.C.
Isaacs, Alan
Jones, Raymond F.
Kettelkamp, Larry Dale
King-Hele, Desmond
Knight, Morris
Knight, D.M.
Koff, Richard M.
Kuhn, Thomas S.
Kushner, Donn
Larsen, Egon
Lear, John
Le Roi, David
McCreery, Charles Anthony
McDonnell, Kevin Lee
Milton, Joyce
Morgan-Grenville, Gerard
Morowitz, Harold J.
Nakayama, Shigeru
Nasr, Seyyed Hossein
Nourse, Alan E.
Parry, Albert
Patterson, Elizabeth Chambers
Pierce, John R.
Pizer, Vernon
Pyke, Magnus
Ramo, Simon
Rapoport, Roger Dale
Reid, Robert
Ridley, Anthony
Ronan, Colin Alistair
Rosen, Sydney
Ross-Macdonald, Malcolm
Rotblat, Joseph A.
Rucker, Rudy
Sachs, Mendel
Sagan, Carl
St. John, John
Saunders, (Sir) Owen
Sheffield, Charles
Silverberg, Robert
Simon, Michael A.
Skolnikoff, Eugene B.
Smith, Anthony
Spilhaus, Athelstan
Stearn, William Thomas
Sullivan, George Edward
Sullivan, Walter
Temple, Robert
Torrance, Thomas Forsythe
Tottle, Charles Ronald
van Fraassen, Bas C.
Victor, Edward
Viorst, Judith
Watts, Alan James
Wheeler, John Archibald
Whiteman, Michael
Williams, Alan
Williams, Trevor Illtyd
Wilson, Edward O.
Wolcfle, Dael
Woodruff, (Sir) Michael
Worrall, Ralph Lyndal
Wright, William David
Young, Louise B.
Young, Morris N.
Zuckerman, Edward
Zuckerman, Solly

Sex

Ableman, Paul
Altman, Dennis
Ard, Ben Neal, Jr.
Babbage, Stuart Barton
Bancroft, Iris
Barnett, Leonard
Blamires, David
Boyd, Malcolm
Brown, Helen Gurley
Bullough, Vern L.
Chapman, J. Dudley
Comfort, Alex
Cook, Mark
Dunn, Hugh Patrick
Durall, Evelyn Millis
Ellis, Albert
Felstein, Ivor
Francoeur, Robert Thomas
Friday, Nancy
Green, Richard
Haeberle, Erwin J.
Hegeler, Sten
Howell, John Christian
Humphreys, Laud
Hyde, Janet S.
Johnson, Eric W.
Johnson, Virginia
Kitzinger, Sheila
Lowen, Alexander
Masters, William H.
Masterton, Graham
Nelson, Jack Lee
Nichols, Jack
Pendleton, Don
Peterson, Bruce Henry
Philipp, Elliot Elias
Pilkington, Roger Windle
Pincher, Chapman
Reiss, Ira Leonard
Richardson, Frank McLean
Richie, Donald
Robertiello, Richard C.
Rofes, Eric Edward
Sarno, Ronald Anthony
Sarnoff, Irving
Schofield, Michael
Seymour-Smith, Martin
Wachter, Oralee
Wandor, Michelene
Weeks, Jeffrey
West, Donald James
Westheimer, Ruth
Wilson, Robert Anton
Woods, Richard
Wynn, J.C.

Social commentary

Abraham, Willie E.
Ackroyd, Peter
Adelman, Clifford
Alexander, Shana
Allaun, Frank
Altman, Dennis
Amory, Cleveland
Angell, Roger
Ashbolt, Allan Campbell
Asinof, Eliot
Astor, Gerald
Atkinson, Anthony
Austin, Henry Wilfred
Bache, Ellen
Bainbridge, John
Bass, Jack
Bayer, Cary Stuart
Beaver, Patrick
Beloff, Nora
Benniss, Warren
Bernard, Sidney
Berrigan, Daniel J.
Berton, Pierre
Beyfus, Drusilla

Social commentary—cont.

Bird, Caroline
Birenbaum, William M.
Birmingham, Stephen
Blair, Clay Drewry
Blake, Brian
Blanchard, William
Bok, Sissela
Boone, Pat
Boorstin, Daniel J.
Boswell, John
Brandon, Henry
Brooks, John
Brossand, Chandler
Bryant, Gay
Buchanan, George
Burger, Robert
Burns, Rex
Burt, Nathaniel
Buscaglia, Leo G.
Bush, Martin H.
Bylinsky, Gene
Callenbach, Ernest
Callwood, June
Carr, Jess
Cater, Douglass
Catherwood, (Sir) Frederick
Childs, Marquis
Chipman, Bruce Lewis
Clecak, Peter
Coles, Robert
Collier, Peter
Collins, Larry
Colombo, John Robert
Commoner, Barry
Cooke, Alistair
Cooper, Wendy
Cormack, Patrick
Cousins, Norman
Cray, Edward
Crick, Bernard R.
Critchfield, Richard
Dary, David Archie
Davenport, William H.
Davidson, Sol M.
Deford, Frank
Delaney, Mary Murray
Demaris, Ovid
Demott, Benjamin
Di Certo, J.J.
Dickson, Paul
Didion, Joan
Donaldson, Scott
Donleavy, J.P.
Dow, Marguerite
Draper, Hal
Driver, Christopher
Epstein, Joseph
Fairbairns, ZÖe
Feuerstein, Georg
Fiedler, Leslie A.
Fitzgerald, Fiances
Fleming, Alice
Franey, Ros
Frost, David
Fussell, Paul
Gardner, Paul
Gathorne-Hardy, Jonathan
Gattey, Charles William
Gay, Kathlyn R.
Gibberd, Kathleen
Gil, David George
Gittler, Joseph B.
Gliauda, Jurgis
Goldman, Albert
Goldman, Eric Frederick
Gordon, George N.
Gornick, Vivian
Gould, Lois
Grumley, Michael
Hanff, Helene
Harris, Jonathan
Haskins, Jim
Hawley, Richard A.

Krausz, Ernest
Kriesberg, Louis
Kubler-Ross, Elizabeth
Kuper, Leo
Lane, David Stuart
Lang, Gladys Engel
Lang, Kurt
Lee, Alfred McClung
Leech, Kenneth
Leeds, Moreton Harold
Lees, Ray
Lehrer, Stanley
Lichtenstadter, Ilse
Lincoln, C. Eric
Lipset, Seymour Martin
Lloyd, Peter Cutt
Lockwood, David
Loether, Herman John
London, Herbert I.
Loney, Martin
Lopez-Rey, Manuel
Lopreato, Joseph
Lowenthal, Leo
Lowry, Ritchie Peter
Luker, Kristin
Lukes, Steven M.
Maccoby, Michael
MacLaren, A. Allan
Macmillan, John Angus David
Macneil, Ian Roderick
Mace, David
Madge, Charles
Mandel, Ernest
Mangione, Jerre
Mann, Peter H.
Marden, Charles Frederick
Marsh, Robert Mortimer
Martin, David Alfred
Martin, Ernest Walter
Martin, Roderick
Marwick, Max Gay
Marx, Gary T.
Masters, Roger O.
Matsuba, Moshe
Mayo, Patricia Elton
McDonald, Lynn
McGuire, Joseph William
Menendez, Albert J.
Merton, Robert K.
Michelson, William Michael
Mihanovich, Clement Simon
Miller, Abraham
Milner, Esther
Mitchell, Geoffrey Duncan
Moberg, David O.
Mol, Johannis J.
Moore, Wilbert E.
Moorhouse, Geoffrey
Morrish, Ivor
Moreton, Henry W.
Mullan, Bob
Mullard, Christopher Paul
Mulligan, Raymond A.
Musgrove, Frank
Nahas, Gabriel G.
Neal, (Sister) Marie Augusta
Nelson, Geoffrey Kenneth
Nelson, Jack Lee
Nettler, Gwynn
Newell, William H.
Newton, Kenneth
Nicolas, David M.
Nursten, Jean Patricia
Oakley, Ann
Omari, T. Peter
Page, Charles H.
Parker, Stanley R.
Parry, Hugh Jones
Patterson, Orlando
Pessen, Edward
Peterson, Richard Austin
Petras, John W.
Phillips, Derek L.

Phillips, Gerald M.
Pitt, David Charles
Podgorecki, Adam
Pogrebin, Letty C.
Rapoport, Robert Norman
Reiss, Ira Leonard
Rex, John Arderne
Rice, Brian Keith
Richmond, Anthony Henry
Rieff, Philip
Riesman, David
Roazen, Paul
Robb, James Harding
Roby, Pamela Ann
Rogler, Lloyd Henry
Rose, Peter Isaac
Rosenberg, Morris
Russell, Kenneth Victor
Sampson, Edward E.
Sampson, Ronald Victor
Sandford, Jeremy
Schellenberg, James A.
Schlesinger, Benjamin
Schoenherr, Richard Anthony
Schrag, Peter
Schwartz, Mildred Anne
Seabrook, Jeremy
Sennett, Richard
Sewell, William
Sharot, Stephen
Shibutani, Tamotsu
Shotwell, Louisa R.
Silver, Harold
Simmie, James
Simon, Rita James
Singer, Benjamin D.
Sklare, Marshall
Skornia, Harry Jay
Smelser, Neil Joseph
Smith, David E.
Soothill, Keith
Spencer, Paul
Spindler, George Deaborn
Stacey, Margaret
Staples, Robert Eugene
Stark, Werner
Stebbins, Robert A.
Sterne, Richard Stephen
Straus, Murray A.
Stroup, Herbert
Suda, Zdenek Ludvik
Summers, Gene F.
Symmons-Symonolewicz, Konstantin
Thomas, Paul
Thorp, Roderick
Tripodi, Tony
Tudor, Andrew Frank
Tumin, Melvin M.
Tunstall, C. Jeremy
Turnbull, Colin M.
Turner, Bryan S.
Turner, Ralph
Udry, J. Richard
van de Vall, Mark
Walker, Alan
Walton, Ortiz
Ward, John Powell
Watt, William Montgomery
Wax, Murray L.
Weeks, Jeffrey
Weintraub, Dov
Whitaker, Ben
Whitworth, John McKelvie
Wilkinson, Paul
Willhelm, Sidney McLarty
Williamson, Robert C.
Willmott, Peter
Wilson, Bryan R.
Wilson, George Wilton
Wilson, Harriett C.
Wilson, (Sir) John
Wilson, Robert Neal

Wogaman, J. Philip
Wolff, Kurt H.
Woods, (Sister) Frances Jerome
Wootton, Graham
Wright, R. Selby
Wrightsman, Lawrence Samuel
Wykes, Alan
Yorburg, Betty
Young, Michael
Zahn, Gordon C.
Zald, Mayer Nathan

Speech/Rhetoric

Asante, Molefi K.
Azarowicz, Marjory
Bell, James Kenton
Bender, Coleman
Berry, Cicely
Bolding, Amy
Boone, Daniel R.
Booth, Wayne Clayson
Bosmajian, Haig
Braden, Waldo W.
Bronstein, Arthur J.
Brown, James I.
Bryant, Dorothy
Byars Brown, Betty
Corbett, Edward P.J.
Crystal, David
Detz, Joan
Dickson, Paul
Flinders, Neil J.
Hull, Raymond
Hurley, John
Ingham, R.A.
Kaplan, Robert B.
Laurie, Rona
Lewis, Norman
Marlow, Clark Strang
Moses, Elbert Raymond, Jr.
Oliver, Robert Tarbell
Phillips, Gerald M.
Prochnow, Herbert Victor
Reid, Loren
Sarnoff, Dorothy
Seidler, Ann
Van Dusen, C. Raymond
Weaver, Carl Harold

Sports/Fitness

Allen, (Sir) Peter Christopher
Alston, Rex
Alter, Judith
Anderson, Kenneth Norman
Ansell, (Sir) Michael
Arlott, John
Ashe, Arthur
Asinof, Eliot
Austin, Henry Wilfred
Balaskas, Arthur
Bannister, (Sir) Roger
Barkow, Al
Bartlett, Eric George
Bass, Howard
Beddington, Roy
Benaud, Richie
Bethel, Dell
Betts, Charles L.
Bircham, Deric
Bird, Dennis Leslie
Boycott, Geoffrey
Bradman, (Sir) Donald
Brasch, Rudolph
Brasher, Christopher
Brearley, Mike
Brodribb, Gerald
Bullus, (Sir) Eric E.
Carr, Raymond
Cerney, James V.

Charlton, Bobby
Christ, Henry I.
Clarke, H. Harrison
Colby, Jean Poindexter
Compton, Denis
Cowdrey, Colin
Cratty, Bryant J.
Creamer, Robert W.
Cruickshank, Charles Greig
Cuddon, J.A.
Curling, Bill
Daley, Robert
Deford, Frank
Dingle, Graeme
Dominy, Eric Norman
Drackett, Phil
Dudley, Geoffrey A.
Edwards, Harvey
Evanott, Vlad
Fichter, George S.
Filosa, Gary
Finn, R.L.
Fisher, David
Fitzgeorge-Parker, Tim
Fletcher, Colin
Fonda, Jane
Forrester, Rex
Gallwey, W. Timothy
Gardner, Paul
Glanville, Brian
Griffin, Henry
Guffmann, Allen
Hall, Willis
Harris, Jonathan
Heath, Edward
Heinz, W.C.
Heller, Mark
Helmker, Judith A.
Henschel, Elizabeth Georgie
Herbert, Ivor
Higdon, Hal
Hintz, Orton Sutherland
Hopcraft, Arthur
Howard-Williams, Jeremy
Huston, Mervyn J.
Hyams, Joe
Hyland, Ann
Jackson, Gordon Noel
Jacobs, Helen Hull
Jares, Joe
Jarvis, Frederick G.H.
Jensen, Clayne
Katchmer, George Andrew
Keith, Harold
King, Billie Jean
Krog, Eustace Walter
Langford, James R.
LeGrand, Louis E.
Levin, Gerald
Lipman, David
Lipsyte, Robert
Lovesey, Peter
Mason, Nicholas
Mason, Ronald Charles
McCormick, John O.
McIntosh, Peter C.
Mills, A.R.
Milsom, Charles Henry
Mitchell, Elyne
Moss, Stirling
Moynihan, John Dominic
Mrazek, James Edward
Nelson, Cordner
Nicholson, Geoffrey
Nicole, Christopher
Nolan, William F.
Nuwer, Hank
Oaksey, (Lord) John
Odd, Gilbert
Ogilvy, C. Stanley
Olney, Ross R.
Page, Charles H.
Parkinson, Michael

Sports/Fitness—cont.

Ramo, Siman
Redmond, Gerald
Resnick, Mike
Reyburn, Wallace
Riordan, James
Ross, Alan
Rydell, Wendy
Savitt, Sam
Schenck, Hilbert
Shepard, Richmond
Shephard, Roy Jesse
Sobol, Ken
Suinn, Richard M.
Sullivan, George Edward
Thomas, Vaughan
Tippette, Giles
Travers, Basil Holmes
Trengove, Alan Thomas
Verral, Charles Spain
Walker, Stella Archer
Walvin, James
Watkins-Pitchford, D.J.
Weiss, Paul
Welcome, John
Whittington, Richard Smallpiece
Wilkinson, Sylvia
Willock, Colin
Wolters, Richard A.
Yee, Min S.

Technology

Adams, Ernest Charles
Allen, John E.
Andrews, Allen
Antill, J.M.
Baker, C.
Ballard, Martin
Batchelor, George Keith
Baxter, Brian
Bennett, Ernest Walter
Benson, Frank Atkinson
Betts, John
Boorstin, Daniel J.
Bowley, Marian E.A.
Bradley, Ian
Bueschel, Richard
Buttrey, Douglas Norton
Coggin, Philip A.
Costigan, Daniel M.
Cowan, Henry
Crouse, William H.
de Bono, Edward
Diamant, R.M.E.
Diebold, John
Drucker, Daniel Charles
Dukert, Joseph Michael
Fenner, Roger T.
Fishlock, David Jocelyn
Gilpin, Alan
Gousing, Mary
Gregory, Cedric E.
Grey, Jerry
Gunston, Bill
Habakkuk, John Hrothgar
Hellman, Hal
Heppenheimer, Thomas A.
Hooper, Meredith Jean
Illich, Ivan
Kash, Don E.
Kouwenhoven, John A.
Kranzberg, Melvin
Laithwaite, Eric Roberts
Lang, William Rawson
Larsen, Egon
Leerburger, Benedict A.
Lewis, W. David
Macfadyen, Kenneth Alexander
Merdinger, Charles
Morris, George E.
Nash, William George
Nock, O.S.

Technology—cont.

Noltingk, Bernard Edward
Orchard, Dennis Frank
Overman, Michael
Perri, Joseph G.
Pournelle, Jerry
Pumphrey, William Idwal
Raudkivi, A.J.
Rybczynski, Witold
Scroggie, Marcus Graham
Seeley, Ivor Hugh
Shaw, David T.
Silvern, Leonard C.
Spector, Leonard S.
Stephen, David Douglas
Storer, James Donald
Taylor, Eric Openshaw
Thompson, Francis George
Tottle, Charles Ronald
Tribus, Myron
Vesper, Karl H.
Williams, Trevor Illtyd
Willrich, Mason
Wright, Philip Arthur
Zade, Hans Peter
Zelinger, Geza
Zuckerman, Edward

Theatre

Arnott, Peter Douglas
Ashley, Leonard R.N.
Aylen, Leo
Barranger, M.S.
Bentley, Eric
Bentley, Gerald Eades
Bigsby, C.W.E.
Billington, Michael
Bratton, J.S.
Brissenden, Alan
Brockett, Oscar Gross
Brown, John Russell
Brustein, Robert
Burian, Jarka M.
Butler, Ivan
Buttita, Tony
Campbell, Paul N.
Caputi, Anthony
Chilver, Peter
Clark, Brian
Clarke, Mary
Cohn, Ruby
Collier, Richard
Corrigan, Robert W.
Corson, Richard
Cotes, Peter
Craig, Edward Anthony
Dace, Tish
Dalrymple, Jean
Davies, Robertson
Denison, Michael
Donaldson, Frances
Dow, Marguerite
Dukore, Bernard F.
Durband, Alan
East, John
Elsom, John Edward
Esslin, Martin
Eveling, Stanley
Falk, Signi Lenea
Fedder, Norman Joseph
Fenton, James
Franklin, Alexander John
Gascoigne, Bamber
Gielgud, (Sir) John
Gilman, Richard
Goldman, William
Hagen, Uta
Hayman, Ronald
Hendry, Thomas
Hill, Errol
Hobson, Harold
Hodge, Francis

Theatre—cont.

Hodges, C. Walter
Holmes, Martin
Honri, Peter
Huggett, Richard
Kelly, Linda
Kerr, Walter
King, Larry L.
Kline, Peter
Kustow, Michael
Lahr, John
Laurie, Rona
Lawson, Joan
Lee, Maryat
Loney, Glenn Meredith
Mackinlay, Lelia
Macleod, Joseph
Marowitz, Charles
Marshall, Norman
May, Robin
May, Robert Stephen
McCabe, John C., III
McCaslin, Nellie
McGrath, John
McNaughton, H.D.
Meserve, Walter Joseph, Jr.
Miller, Jordan Yale
Mitchell, Loften
Moe, Christian H.
Morley, Sheridan Robert
Morrison, Kristin Diane
Morton, Richard Everett
Nathan, David
O'Connor, Patricia W.
O'Neill, Patrick Geoffrey
Patterson, Michael
Peters, Margot
Price, Cecil
Read, Anthony
Rees, Leslie
Reynolds, Ernest Randolph
Roose-Evans, James
Roston, Murray
Rowell, George
Sainer, Arthur
Schevill, James
Shank, Theodore
Shepard, Richmond
Skelton, Geoffrey
Slade, Peter
Slide, Anthony
Smith, C. Ray
Smith, Michael
Speaight, George
Styan, John Louis
Sykes, Alrene
Taylor, John Russell
Thomson, Peter
Toll, Robert Charles
Trussler, Simon
Turner, Darwin T.
Tydeman, William
Valdez, Luis
Wandor, Michelene
Wardle, Irving
Watkins, Ronald
Weales, Gerald
Webb, Jean Francis
Wells, Stanley
Wickham, Glynne
Willis, John A.
Young, William

Theology/Religion

Abbey, Merrill R.
Ackroyd, Peter
Adair, James R.
Adler, Mortimer J.
Allan, John David
Allen, Diogenes
Allen, Edith Beavers
Alley, Robert S.

Theology/Religion—cont.

Allison, A.F.
Ammerman, Leila T.
Anderson, (Sir) Norman
Anderson, Richard Lloyd
Anders-Richards, Donald
Andrews, Clarence Adelbert
Andrews, Edgar Harold
Andrus, Hyrum Leslie
Archer, Gleason Leonard
Ashbrook, James Barbour
Ashby, Philip H.
Atkinson, James
Austgen, Robert Joseph
Autton, Norman
Aveling, J.C.H.
Azneer, J. Leonard
Babbage, Stuart Barton
Bachman, John W.
Bahm, Archie J.
Baker, Frank
Bancroft, Anne
Barack, Nathan A.
Barbour, Hugh
Barmann, Lawrence
Barnett, Leonard Palin
Barr, James
Barrett, Charles Kingsley
Barth, Markus
Battenhouse, Roy W.
Beasley-Murray, George Raymond
Beck, Hubert Frederick
Beckelhymer, Hunter
Beebe, Ralph K.
Beeson, Trevor Randall
Berrigan, Daniel J.
Berry, Thomas
Bethmann, Erich
Bewes, Richard
Bharati, Agehananda
Bianchi, Eugene Carl
Billington, Ray
Binkley, Luther John
Bissondoyal, Basdeo
Blackwood, Andrew W.
Blamires, Harry
Blanch, Stuart Yarworth
Blenkinsopp, Joseph
Bloesch, Donald George
Boice, James Montgomery
Boone, Pat
Boswell, John
Bourdeaux, Michael Alan
Bourke, Vernon J.
Bowker, John Westerdale
Bowker, Margaret
Bowley, Rex Lyon
Bowyer, Mathew
Boyd, Malcolm
Brandt, Leslie F.
Brasch, Rudolph
Brauer, Jerald C.
Brenneman, Helen Good
Breward, Ian
Bromiley, Geoffrey William
Brown, Dale W.
Brown, Robert McAfee
Browning, Don
Browning, Wilfrid
Bruce, Frederick
Bruteau, Beatrice
Bryant, Robert Harry
Bube, Richard H.
Buchanan, Colin
Buck, Harry M.
Buckley, Francis Joseph
Buechner, Frederick
Bull, Norman John
Bulmer-Thomas, Ivor
Burtchaell, James Tunstead
Burtt, Edwin Arthur
Bye, Beryl
Cairns, David
Cairns, Earle E.

Calian, Carnegie Samuel
Callahan, Nelson J.
Campling, Christopher Russell
Capitan, William H.
Carnley, Peter Frederick
Carr, Jo Crisler
Carstenson, Roger
Cassidy, Michael
Catherwood, (Sir) Frederick
Cauthen, Kenneth
Cegielka, Francis
Cell, Edward Charles
Chadwick, Henry
Chadwick, Owen
Chambers, Jim Bernard
Champlin, Joseph M.
Cherry, Charles Conrad
Chibnall, Marjorie McCallum
Christie-Murray, David
Clarkson, E. Margaret
Cleall, Charles
Cleeve, Brian
Clemo, Jack
Clinebell, Howard J., Jr.
Clouse, Robert Gordon
Coad, Frederick Roy
Coats, George Wesley
Cockshut, A.O.J.
Coder, S. Maxwell
Coggan, (Lord)
Coggin, Philip A.
Cole, E.R.
Coleburt, James Russell
Coleman, Shalom
Colquhoun, Frank
Comay, Joan
Conners, Kenneth Wray
Connick, C. Milo
Constantelos, Demetrios J.
Cooke, Bernard
Coombs, Joyce
Copeland, Edwin
Coppa, Frank John
Cousins, Peter Edward
Cowie, Leonard Wallace
Cox, Harvey
Crabb, Edmund William
Cragg, Kenneth
Crago, Thomas Howard
Cranfield, Charles E.B.
Crawford, John Richard
Crenshaw, James L.
Crichton, James
Curran, Charles E.
Curran, Francis X.
Curry, Lerond
Dalglish, Edward Russell
Daly, Cahal Brendan
Daly, Lowrie J.
Daly, Mary
Danker, William J.
Daube, Davide
Davies, E.T.
Davies, Horton
Davies, John Gordon
Davies, Rupert E.
Davies, Walter Merlin
Dean, William Denard
Deats, Richard
DeBoer, John C.
Demaray, Donald E.
Derham, Arthur Morgan
Derrett, Duncan
de Vinck, Jose M.G.A.
Dewart, Leslie
Dhavamony, Mariasusai
Dierenfield, Richard Bruce
Di Lella, Alexander Anthony
Dillenberger, John
Ditterich, Keith
Doan, Eleanor Lloyd
Dotts, Maryann J.
Douglas, James Dixon

Dresner, Samuel
Droppers, Carl H.
Dudley-Smith, Timothy
Duffield, Gervase E.
Dulles, Avery E.
Duncan, Anthony Douglas
Dunne, John S.
Dupre, Louis
Durnbaugh, Donald F.
Dyrness, William A.
Earhart, H. Byron
Eaton, John Herbert
Eckardt, A. Roy
Elkins, Dov Peretz
Eller, Vernard
Elliott-Binns, Michael Ferres
Elson, Edward L.R.
Epp, Eldon Jay,
Every, George
Fackenheim, Emil L.
Fancutt, Walter
Fairey, Robert L.
Farmer William R.
Farr, Alfred Derek
Fenton, John Charles
Ferguson, Everett
Feuerstein Georg
Finegan, Jack
Fischer, Robert H.
Fisher, A. Stanley T.
Fitzgerald, Ernest Abner
Flinders, Neil J.
Flynn, Leslie Bruce
Ford, Douglas
Forder, Charles Robert
Forman, Charles William
Foulds, Elfrida Vipont
Franck, Frederick
Franke, Carl Wilfred
Fraser. Iam Watson
Fremantle, Anne
Frend, William
Friedlander, Albert H.
Friedman, Jacob Horace
Frost, Stanley Brice
Fuller, Reginald Horace
Furnish, Victor Paul
Galloway, Allan Douglas
Gardner, Edward Clinton
Garrard, Lancelot Austin
Gatch, Milton McCormick, Jr.
Geisler, Norman
Gerrish, Brian Albert
Gesch, Roy
Gill, Jerry H.
Gill, Joseph
Gittelsohn, Roland B.
Glasson, T. Francis
Glen, Frank Grenfell
Godsey, John Drew
Goen, Clarence C.
Gonzalez, Justo L.
Gordis, Robert
Gordon, Ernest
Goyder, George Armin
Graham, Billy
Graham, W. Fred
Grant, John Webster
Gratus, Jack
Green, Vivian
Greenlee, J. Harold
Greet, Kenneth Gerald
Grigg, John
Gritsch, Eric W.
Grubb, Norman Percy
Guffin, Gilbert Lee
Gundry, Dudley William
Gutteridge, Richard
Gyldenvand, Lily M.
Habgood, John Stapylton
Hall, Thor
Ham, Wayne Albert
Hamell, Patrick Joseph

Hamilton, Kenneth
Hammes, John A.
Hardon, John Anthony
Hare Duke, Michael
Häring, Bernard
Harrell, David Edwin, Jr.
Harrell, Irene Burk
Harrelson, Walter Joseph
Harrison, Everett F.
Hartshorne, Charles
Hatcher, William S.
Haughton, Rosemary
Hausmann, Winifred Wilkinson
Hayden, Eric William
Hayman, Carol Bessent
Haymes, Renee Oriana
Hays, Brooks
Heaton, Eric William
Hebblethwaite, Peter
Hein, Lucille Eleanor
Helmreich, Ernst Cristian
Herron, Orley Rufus
Herzog, Arthur
Hessert, Paul
Heywood, Thomas John
Hick, John
Hickinbotham, James
Hiebert, D. Edmond
Highet, John
Hill, Michael
Hill, William Joseph
Hillis, Dick
HimmelFarb, Milton
Hinchliff, Peter Bingham
Hinson, E. Glenn
Hobbs, Herschel H.
Hodgson, Peter C.
Hoehner, Harold W.
Holck, Manfred, Jr.
Holmer, Paul L.
Holmes, Arthur Frank
Holmes, Marjorie
Holtby, Robert Tinsley
Homans, Peter
Hong, Howard V.
Hooker, Morna Dorothy
Hopkins, Jasper
Horgan, Paul
Hovey, E. Paul
Howard, David M.
Howlett, Duncan
Howse, Ernest Marshall
Hoyles, J. Arthur
Huber, Jack
Huddleston, Trevor
Hudnut, Robert K.
Hudson, Winthrop S.
Hughes, Phillip E.
Hull, William E.
Hunt, Gladys M.
Hunt, Patricia Joan
Hunter, Archibald MacBride
Hutchison, Henery
Huxtable, John
Ice, Jackson Lee
Ikerman, Ruth C.
Inch, Morris Alton
Ingalls, Jeremy
Irion, Mary Jean
Jackman, Stuart
Jacobs, Louis
Jaffin, David
Jagger, Peter
Jaques, Louis Barker
Jay, Eric George
Jeeves, Malcolm A.
Johns, Richard A.
Johnson, Robert Clyde
Johnston, William
Jones, Bob, Jr.
Jones, (Abbot) Christopher
Jones, Clifford M.
Jones, Richard Granville

Joy, Donald Marvin
Kaiser, Ward L.
Kantonen, Taito Almar
Kapelrud, Arvid Schou
Karp, Abtraham J.
Kavanaugh, James
Kellett, Arnold
Kelsey, Morton T.
Kent, Homer Austin, Jr.
Kenton, Warren
Kereszty, Roch A.
Kingston, Frederick Temple
Kirby, Gilbert Walter
Knapp-Fisher, Edward George
Knight, George A.F.
Knight, James Allen
Knox, David Broughton
Knox, John
Koren, Henry Joseph
Kort, Wesley A.
Kossoff, David
Kraft, Robert A.
Krentz, Edgar Martin
Kuntz, John Kenneth
Kushner, Harold S.
Lacy, Creighton Boutelle
Lamirande, Emilien
Lane, William Lister
Lantz, J. Edward
Larson, Muriel Koller
Lash, N.L.A.
Leaney, Alfred Robert Clare
Lechner, Robert
Leech, Kenneth
Lehrer, Stanley
Lewis, Jack Pearl
Lichtenstadter, Ilse
Lindars, Frederick C.
Linder, Robert D.
Lindsey, Hal
Lochman, Jan Milic
Locke, Hubert G.
Lockerbie, Donald Bruce
Lofton, John M.
Long, Edward Leroy, Jr.
Long, Eugene Thomas
Lowry, Charles W.
Lucas, Barbara
Lund, Gerald N.
Luzbetak, Louis Joseph
Lynch, William E.
McEoin, Gary
MacGregory, Geddes
Macintyre, Alasdair
MacLaren, A. Allan
Macquarrie, John
Maggal, Moshe Morris
Maier, Paul Luther
Marsh, John
Marsh, Peter T.
Marshall, Elizabeth Margaret
Martin, David Alfred
Martland, Thomas R.
Marty, Martin E.
Mascall, Eric Lionel
Massey, James Earl
Matilal, B.K.
May, Rollo
Mayer, Herbert T.
McArthur, Harvey King
McBrien, Richard P.
McClelland, Vincent Alan
McDonald, Hugh Dermot
McDormand, Thomas Bruce
McGurn, Barrett
McHugh, J.F.
McKeating, Henry
Meeks, Wayne A.
Mendenhall, George Emery
Menendez, Albert J.
Metzger, Bruce Manning
Meyendorff, John
Meyer, Ben Franklin

Meyer, Charles Robert
Miles, Leland
Milhaven, John Giles
Milhouse, Paul William
Miller, Alan W.
Miller, Donald George
Miller, Randolph Crump
Millgram, Abraham E.
Minear, Paul Sevier
Moberg, David O.
Moffett, Samuel Hugh
Mohler, James Aylward
Mol, Johannis J.
Mollenkott, Virginia Ramey
Monk, Robert C.
Mooney, Christopher Francis
Moore, Carey Armstrong
Moore, E. Garth
Moore, Trevor Wyatt
Moorhouse, Geoffrey
Moreno, Antonio
Morgan, Dewi
Moriarty, Frederick L.
Morris, Leon Lamb
Morrish, Ivor
Morriss, Frank
Mosley, Nicholas
Mould, Daphne
Moule, Charles Francis Digby
Mueller, David L.
Mueller, William R.
Muggeridge, Malcolm
Mullett, John St. Hilary
Munson, Thomas Nolan
Munz, Peter
Murphy, Richard Thomas
Murphy, Roland Edmund
Myers, Jacob M.
Nasr, Seyyed Hossein
Neal, (Sister) Marie Augusta
Neame, Alan John
Neighbour, Ralph Webster, Sr.
Nelson, Geoffrey Kenneth
Nelson, J. Robert
Nelson, Martha
Neuhaus, Richard John
Neusner, Jacob
Neville, Robert C.
Newsome, David Hay
Nicholson, E.W.
Nielsen, Niels Christian, Jr.
Nineham, Dennis Eric
North, Robert
Nouwen, Henri J.
Novak, Michael
Nyanaponika
O'Brien, Elmer
O'Collins, Gerald Glynn
O'Doherty, Eammon
Oesterreicher, John M.
O'Flaherty, James Carneal
Ogletree, Thomas Warren
Osborn, Eric Francis
Osborn, Ronald Edwin
Owen, Derwyn
Packer, James Innell
Padovano, Anthony T.
Pagels, Elaine
Painter, John
Parfitt, Tudor
Parker, Thomas
Paton, David Macdonald
Pawlikowski, John Thaddeus
Peale, Norman Vincent
Pearson, Keith David
Pearson, Roy
Peck, M. Scott
Peel, Malcolm L.
Pelikan, Jaroslav
Percy, Douglas C.
Perry, Michael Charles
Peterson, Bruce Henry
Petuchowski, Jakob Josef

Phenix, Philip Henry
Phillips, Dewi Zephaniah
Phipps, William Eugene
Pierard, Richard V.
Pierson, Robert
Piet, John H.
Pike, Diane Kennedy
Pinson, William M., Jr.
Pittenger, Norman
Plantinga, Alvin
Plaut, W. Gunther
Plowman, Edward E.
Poganski, Donald John
Pollard, Thomas Evan
Pollock, John Charles
Poovey, William Arthur
Porten, Bezalel
Porter, Joshua Roy
Potter, Vincent G.
Powell, Gordon George
Price, Reynolds
Prime, Derek James
Prior, Kenneth
Proctor, William Gilbert, Jr.
Prosch, Harry
Purcell, William
Rabinowicz, Mordka Harry
Raju, Poolla Tirupati
Raphael, Chaim
Rayner, John Desmond
Read, David
Read, William M.
Reardon, Bernard M.G.
Redding, David A.
Rees, Paul Stromberg
Reid, Clyde Henderson, Jr.
Reid, John
Reindorp, George Edmund
Rhymes, Douglas Alfred
Rice, Brian Keith
Richard, Cliff
Rivkin, Ellis
Roark, Dallas M.
Roberts, James Deotis, Sr.
Robin, Arthur de Quetteville
Roddy, Lee
Rogerson, Alan Thomas
Roland Smith, Gordon
Rollins, Wayne Gilbert
Roseman, Kenneth David
Rosenbloom, Joseph R.
Rosenbloom, Noah H.
Rosenthal, Erwin
Roth, Robert Joseph
Rubinoff, Lionel
Ruef, John Samuel
Ruether, Rosemary Radford
Russell, David Syme
Russell, Jeffrey Burton
Russell, John Leonard
Russell, Kenneth Victor
St. John, John
St. John, Patricia Mary
Salisbury, Frank B.
Sarkar, Anil Kumar
Sarna, Jonathan D.
Sarna, Nahum, M.
Sarno, Ronald Anthony
Schilpp, Paul Arthur
Schuller, Robert H.
Schultz, Samuel J.
Scott, Nathan A., Jr.
Searle, Graham William
Shaw, Russell B.
Shideler, Mary M.
Siirala, Aarne Johannes
Silver, Daniel J.
Silverman, Hillel E.
Silverstein, Theodore
Simonson, Harold P.
Simpson, Ervin
Sklare, Marshall
Skoglund, John E.

Slonim, Reuben
Smalley, Stephen S.
Smith, Morton
Smith, Wilfred Cantwell
Snyder, Graydon
Solberg, Richard William
Soper, (Baron) Donald Oliver
Stagg, Frank
Stark, Werner
Stephens, William Peters
Stern, Jay B.
Stevenson, Dwight Eshelman
Stewart, Harold Frederick
Stewart, James Stuart
Stockwood, Arthur Merwyn
Stott, John Robert Walmsley
Stowe, David Metz
Stradling, Leslie Edward
Strand, Kenneth A.
Streng, Frederick John
Stroup, Herbert
Stuhlmueller, Carroll
Suelcflow, August Robert
Suggs, M. Jack
Swearer, Donald K.
Sweeney, Leo
Swinburne, Richard
Synan, Vinson
Taylor, John Vernon
Taylor, Michael J.
Temperley, Neville
Teselle, Eugene
Thomas, Keith
Thomas, Paul
Thompson, Laurence Graham
Thompson, William David
Tibbetts, Orlando L.
Till, Barry Dorn
Tinsley, Ernest John
Todd, John M.
Tomkins, Oliver Stratford
Torrance, Thomas Forsyth
Trepp, Leo
Trethowan, William
Trever, John Cecil
Trinkaus, Charles
Truman, Ruth
Tucker, William Edward
Turner, Bryan S.
Turner, Harold Walter
Tyson, Joseph B.
Ullendorff, Edward
Vahanian, Gabriel
Van De Wetering, Janwillem
Vaughan, Richard Patrick
Vermes, Geza
Verney, Stephen Edmund
Vidler, Alexander Roper
Vincent, John James
Vockler, John Charles
Wainwright, Geoffrey
Walker, Alan
Walker, Benjamin
Walsh, Chad
Walsh, (Sir) John Patrick
Walsh, P.G.
Ward, Elizabeth Honor
Ward, John Stephen Keith
Ware, Kallistos
Washington, Joseph R., Jr.
Watt, William Montgomery
Watts, Harold H.
Webster, Alan Brunskill
Wenger, J.C.
Wessel, Helen S.
Whale, John
Wheeler, Penny Estes
Whitcomb, John C.
White, James Floyd
White, Reginald
White, William Luther
Whitehouse, Walter Alexander
Whitfield, George

Whitworth, John McKelvie
Wicker, Brian John
Wickham, Edward Ralph
Wiesel, Elie
Wiles, Maurice Frank
Wilkinson, John
Williams, Harold
Wills, Garry
Wilson, A.N.
Wilson, Bryan R.
Wilson, John
Wilson, Robert McLachlan
Wiltgen, Ralph
Wingren, Gustaf Fredrik
Winter, David Brian
Winter, Michael Morgan
Wise, Charles Conrad, Jr.
Wiseman, Donald John
Wittenbach, Henry August
Witton-Davies, Carlyle
Wogaman, J. Philip
Wolcott, Leonard Thompson
Wood, Arthur Skevington
Wood, Maurice Arthur Posonby
Woods, Richard
Worlock, Derek
Wright, Christopher
Wright, Conrad
Wright, Philip Arthur
Wright, R. Selby
Wynn, Daniel Webster
Wynn, J.C.
Yandell, Keith Edward
Yoder, Glee
Young, Matt Norvel, Jr.
Youngblood, Ronald Fred
Zahn, Gordon C.
Zimmermann, Arnold Walter

Third World

Anees, Munawar Ahmad
Arnold, Guy
Birmingham, Walter
Cracknell, Basil Edward
Crozier, Brian
Deats, Richard
Douglas, John
Fieldhouse, David K.
Flint, John Edgard
Frank, André Gunder
Fryer, Jonathan
Fukuda, Haruko
Girling, John
Gott, Richard
Griffin, Keith B.
Hopcraft, Arthur
Karasz, Arthur
Klayman, Maxwell Irving
Lloyd, Peter Cutt
Madge, Charles
Melady, Thomas
Nixson, Frederick Ian
Norton, Augustas Richard
O'Kelly, Elizabeth
Palmer, Norman D.
Scarfe, Wendy Elizabeth
Simon, Sheldon Weiss
Stavrianos, Leften
Stevens, Christopher
Turner, Bryan S.
Turner, Louis Mark

Transportation

Allen, (Sir) Peter Christopher
Aldcroft, Derek Howard
Atthill, Robin
Awdry, W.
Barker, Theodore Cardwell
Baughan, Peter Edward

Travel/Exploration—cont.

Shackleton, (Baron)
Shadbolt, Maurice
Sherman, Steve
Sim, Katharine Phyllis
Simpson, Colin
Simpson, Myrtle Lillias
Skelton, Peter
Slater, Mary
Slonim, Reuben
Smith, Anthony
Smith, Dwight L.
Snow, Philip
Somerville-Large, Peter
Speaight, George
Speed, Frank Warren
Spencer, William
Spender, Stephen
Stacey, Tom
Stark, (Dame) Freya
Statler, Oliver
Steele, Peter
Stevenson, William
Stockwood, Arthur Mervyn
Stonehouse, Bernard
Storey, Edward
Straker, J.F.
Sullivan, Walter
Templeton, Edith
Theroux, Paul
Thesiger, Wilfred Patrick
Thomas, Leslie John
Thampson, E.V.
Thompson, Neil
Thubron, Colin Gerald Dryden
Thum, Marcella
Thwaite, Anthony
Tong, Raymond
Tonogbanua, Francisco G.
Tranter, Nigel
Tullett, James Stuart
Usherwood, Stephen
van der Post, Laurens
Van Til, William
Vaughan-Thomas, Wynford
Vondra, Josef Gert
Waagenaar, Sam
Walworth, Arthur
Ward, Philip
Waters, David Watkin
Weems, John Edward
Weidman, Jerome
Wellington, Richard Anthony
Westcott Jones, Kenneth
White, Terence de Vere
Willey, Peter Robert Everard
Williams, Guy R.
Williams, Gwyn
Williams, Hugo
Williams, Joy
Willock, Colin
Wilson, Trevor Frederick
Winch, Michael Bluett
Wollaston, Nicolas
Wolseley, Roland E.
Wolfe, Michael
Woodcock, George
Worthington, Edgar Barton
Wright, David
Yee, Min S.
Young, Wayland

Urban topics

Beckinsale, Robert Percy
Bellan, Ruben Carl
Bender, Thomas
Boskoff, Alvin
Bourne, Larry Stuart
Breese, Gerald
Carter, Harold
Catanese, Anthony James
Conant, Ralph W.

Urban Topics—cont.

Coppa, Frank John
Cullingworth, J. Barry
Cuomo, Mario
Curl, James Stevens
Dinerman, Beatrice
Downes, Bryan
Downie, Leonard, Jr.
Duhl, Leonard J.
Dunleay, Patrick
Finnegan, Frances
Glazer, Nathan
Glazer, Sidney
Horton, Frank E.
Hunker, Henry L.
Jackson, Kenneth T.
Jacobs, Jane
Jenkins, Simon
Johnson, James Henry
Kasperson, Roger E.
Lewis, J. Parry
Loewenstein, Louis Klee
Lynch, Kevin
Michelson, William Michael
Muth, Richard Ferris
Nader, G.A.
Powledge, Fred
Press, O. Charles
Ravetz, Alison
Robson, Brian Turnbull
Rodwin, Lloyd
Schmandt, Henry J.
Sekler, Eduard F.
Smerk, George M.
Smith, David Marshall
Smithson, Alison
Smithson, Peter
Spreiregen, Paul
Stave, Bruce M.
Stretton, Hugh
Sutton, S.B.
Tarr, Joel Arthur
Thrasher, Peter Adam
Tindall, Gillian
Watkins, William Jon
Willensky, Elliot
Wilson, James Quinn
Winestone, Reece
Wolman, Abel

Women's Studies

Agonito, Rosemary
Aptheker, Bettina
Arms, Suzanne
Bardwick, Judith
Barkin, Carol
Barr, Patricia
Beauman, Katharine Bentley
Berbrich, Joan D.
Berger, Nan
Bird, Caroline
Blau, Francine D.
Brown, Helen Gurley
Brownmiller, Susan
Bullough, Vern L.
Callwood, June
Chamberlain, Mary
Coakley, Mary Lewis
Conran, Shirley
Dally, Ann
Daly, Mary
DeCrow, Karen
Decter, Midge
Dunn, Nell
Epstein, Cynthia Fuchs
Erens, Patricia
Falk, Candace
Feingold, S. Norman
Fox-Genorese, Elizabeth
Freeman, Jo
Friday, Nancy
Friedan, Betty

Women's Studies—cont.

Gornick, Vivian
Greer, Germaine
Hale, Allean Lemmon
Heyman, Abigail
Johnston, Jill
Luker, Kristin
Lutzker, Edythe
Margolis, Diane Rothbard
Maughan, Joyce Bowen
Millett, Kate
Mitchell, Juliet
Morgan, Marabel
Nelson, Martha
Oakley, Ann
O'Faolain, Julia
Peters, Margot
Pogrebin, Letty Cottin
Raeburn, Antonia
Randall, Margaret
Rich, Elaine Sommers
Rover, Constance Mary
Rowbotham, Sheila
Ruether, Rosemary Radford
Sexton, Linda Gray
Sklar, Kathryn Kish
Stanford, Barbara
Stassinopoulos, Arianna
Tremain, Rose
Trilling, Diana
Truman, Ruth
Tuttle, Lisa
Waddy, Charis
Wandor, Michelene
Welburn, Vivienne C.
Wheeler, Helen Rippier
Wilson, Elizabeth
Winter, Elmer L.
Zapoleon, Marguerite Wykoff

Writing/Journalism

Adams, Julian
Adleman, Robert H.
Aiken, Joan
Alisky, Marvin
Alsop, Joseph Wright
Andrews, Clarence Adelbert
Arnold, Edmund Clarence
Ashe, Geoffrey Thomas
Austin, Cedric Ronald Jonah
Aurner, Robert Ray
Baird, Russell N.
Barba, Harry
Behrens, John C.
Bell, James Kenton
Bennett-England, Rodney
Berbrich, Joan D.
Bingley, Clive
Blackman, Victor
Bowen, Robert O.
Brittin, Norman Aylsworth
Brown, Leland
Burnett, Hallie Southgate
Bruchac, Joseph
Butterfield, William H.
Byrne, Robert
Cassill, R.V.
Christensen, J.A.
Copperud, Roy H.
Curto, Josephine
Damerst, William A.
De Mordaunt Walter Julius
Downie, Leonard, Jr.
Detz, Joan
Dyer, Frederick C.
Ehrlich, Eugene
Evans, Harold Matthew
Ferris, Timothy.
Friendly, Fred W.
Gerber, John C.
Geyer, Georgie Anne
Glicksberg, Charles Irving

Writing/Journalism—cont.

Goodheart, Barbara
Heckelmann, Charles N.
Hinkley, Helen
Hoffmann, Ann Marie
Holmes, Marjorie
Hulteng, John L.
Jeppson, J.O.
Johnson, Falk S.
Keating, H.R.F.
Kilpatrick, James Jackson
Knight, Karl Frederick
Knott, William C.
Koerner, James D.
Koontz, Dean R.
Krieghbaum, Hillier
Lanham, Richard Alan
Leab, Daniel Josef
Legat, Michael
Lesikar, Raymond Vincent
Loomis, Edward
Macauley, Robie
Madgett, Naomi Long
Meredith, Scott
Mirsky, Mark
Mitchell, John Howard
Moldea Dan E.
Morrison, Robert Haywood
Morse, J. Mitchell
Nathan, Norman
Neal, Harry Edward
Nelson, Roy P.
Oldsey, Bernard S.
Peeples, Edwin A.
Politella, Dario
Polking, Kirk
Pompian, Richard
Ransom, Jay Ellis
Rivenburgh, Viola K.
Ryan, Peter Allen
Sanders, Jean
Sandman, Peter Mark
Schwartz, Joseph
Seldes, George
Shenker, Israel
Sherwood, Hugh C.
Sigband, Norman Bruce
Spinrad, Norman
Stewart, Daniel Kenneth
Stewart, Donald Charles
Thomas, David St. John
Turner, Katharine Charlotte
Walshe, R.D.
Wells, Walter
Whale, John
White, Edward M.
Whitney, Phyllis A
Winkler, Anthony C.
Wolseley, Roland E.
Wright, Helen L.
Youngs, Betty F.
Zall, Paul M.

Zoology

Alexander, Robert McN.
Andrewartha, Herbert George
Andrews, John Henry
Banfield, A.W. Frank
Barnett, S. Anthony
Behle, William Harroun
Bellairs, Angus D'Albini
Berrill, Norman John
Bigelow, Robert Sydney
Binford, Laurence C.
Burgess, Warren E.
Burton, John Andrew
Burton, Maurice
Butler, Colin G.
Chinery, Michael
Cloudsley-Thompson, John
Colbert, Edwin Harris
Cox, Christopher Barry

Davis, Wayne Harry
DeSanto, Robert S.
Dethier, Vincent G.
Doughty, Robin W.
Edey, Maitland A.
Eltringham, S.K.
Fairley, James S.
Fiennes, Richard
Fossey, Dian
Gallant, Roy Arthur
Garnham, Percy Cyril Claude
George, Wilma
Gilbert, Douglas L.
Gould, Stephen Jay
Grant, Verne
Griffin, Donald R.
Headstrom, Richard
Hirons, Montague
Hoffmeister, Donald Frederick
Johnsgard, Paul A.
Lee, Donald
Lust, Peter
Main, Barbara York
Mech, L. David
Merne, Oscar James
Milne, Lorus J.
Milne, Margery
Moore, John A.
Morris, Desmond
Moss, Cynthia J.
Peterson, Randolph Lee
Pruitt, William O.
Ride, W.D.L.
Rowett, Helen
Smith, Hobart Muir
Smyth, James Desmond
Snow, Keith Ronald
Southwood, Richard Edmund
Stenhouse, David
Stonehouse, Bernard
Taylor, David
Thomson, James Miln
Turbott, Evan Graham
Van Lawick, Hugo
Warham, John
Watson, Lyall
Wells, Martin John
Williams, Roland
Willmer, Edward Nevill
Wilson, Edward O.
Young, John Zachary

OTHER

Autobiography/Memoirs

Abbas, Ahmad
Abbey, Edward
Abbott, George
Abse, Dannie
Ackland, Rodney
Adair, James R.
Adam-Smith, Patsy
Allen, Steve
Allen, Walter
Ambler, Eric
Amery, Julian
Andrews, Lucilla
Ansell, (Sir) Michael
Arlen, Michael J.
Ash, William Franklin
Ashley, Jack
Auchinloss, Louis
Austin, Henry Wilfred
Ayer, A.J.
Babington, Anthony Patrick
Bacall, Lauren
Bailey, Anthony
Bailey, Pearl
Baker, Russell

Ball, George
Bamford, Brian Reginald
Barich, Bill
Barnard, Christian
Bates, (Sir) Darrell
Baybars, Taner
Beckwith, Lillian
Beer, Patricia
Behr, Edward
Beier, Ulli
Bergen, Candice
Bernays, Edward L.
Berrigan, Daniel J.
Bingham, Charlotte
Bingham, Sally
Birney, Earle
Blades, James
Blanch, Lesley
Blashford-Snell, John Nicholas
Blishen, Edward
Blyth, Chay
Bogarde, Dirk
Bonington, Chris
Boone, Pat
Borland, Hal
Bosworth, Allan R.
Bowers, John
Bowles, Paul
Box, Muriel
Boyd, Malcolm
Brackhage, Stan
Braithwaite, E.R.
Brata, Sasthi
Brock, Edwin
Brooks, Gwendolyn
Brown, Michael Douglas
Brown, Robert McAfee
Bryans, Robin
Buchanan, George
Buckle, Richard
Budd, Mavis
Buechner, Frederick
Bukowski, Charles
Burchett, Wilfred G.
Burgess, Anthony
Burtschi, Mary Pauline
Butland, Gilbert J.
Butler, Guy
Buttitta, Tony
Buxbaum, Martin
Caillou, Alan
Calder-Marshall, Arthur
Calisher, Hortense
Callaghan, Morley
Capelle, Russell Beckett
Carey, Ernestine Gilbreth
Carrington, Charles Edmund
Carroll, Gladys Hasty
Carter, Jimmy
Cartland, Barbara
Caspary, Verna
Castle, Charles
Clare, George
Clarke, Austin C.
Clarke, Derrick Harry
Cleaver, Eldridge
Clemo, Jack
Clough, Shepard
Clyne, Douglas
Coates, Austin
Codrescu, Andrei
Collier, Richard
Cooke, Alistair
Cookson, Catherine
Cotes, Peter
Cowie, Mervyn
Cowles, Fleur
Cox, Alfred Bertram
Crawford, Christina
Crawford, John Richard
Crichton, Robert
Crocker, (Sir) Walter
Cronkite, Walter

Curry, Leonard
Dabney, Virginius
Dalrymple, Jean
D'Arcy, Margaretta
Davenport, Marcia
Davis, Patrick
Davison, Peter
Day, (Sir) Robin
Deane-Drummond, Anthony
DeFrees, Madeline
Delmar, Vin
Denison, Michael
Denson-Gerber, Judianne
deTrevino, Elizabeth
Dickens, Monica
Dickinson, Patric
Dillard, Annie
Dimock, Marhshall Edward
Divale, William
Donald, William
Donaldson, Frances
Drury, Allen
Dunnett, Alastair MacTavish
Durrell, Gerald
Durst, Paul
Dyson, Freeman
Earnshaw, Anthony
Edwards, Anne
Edwards, Donald
Ehrlichman, John
Eisenhower, John S. D.
Elath, Eliahu
Ellis, Ella Thorp
Emecheta, Buchi
Enright, D.J.
Epp, Margaret Agnes
Farmer, Philip Josë
Farson, Daniel
Fenby, Eric
Fennario, David
Fiennes, Ranulph
Finn, R.L.
FitzGibbon, Theodora
Fletcher-Cooke, (Sir) John
Flynn, Frank
Forbes, Bryan
Forrester, Rex
Fox, Hugh Bernard
Francis, Clare
Francis, Dick
Franken, Rose
Freedgood, Morton
Freeman, Lucy
Friedan, Betty
Friermood, Elisabeth H.
Fry, Christopher
Fuller, Roy
Gaan, Margaret
Gajdusek, D. Carleton
Gann, Ernest K.
Gardner, John
Garnett, Eve C.R.
Gascoyne, David
Gayre of Gayre and Nigg, Robert
Gellhorn, Martha
Geger, Georgie Anne
Ghose, Zulfikar
Gielaud, (Sir) John
Gifford, Edward Stewart, Jr.
Gilman, Richard
Ginsberg, Allen
Gish, Lillian
Glen, Frank Grenfell
Godden, Rumer
Gold, Herbert
Gordon, Ernest
Greene, A.C.
Greene, Graham
Grey, Anthony
Grossinger, Tania
Hahn, Emily
Haley, Alex
Hamburger, Michael

Hamilton, Elizabeth
Hanley, Clifford
Han Suyin
Harbottle, Michael Neal
Harkey, Ira Brown, Jr.
Harnack, Curtis
Harris, Mark
Harrison, Rex
Harrison, Rosina
Hart-Davis, (Sir) Rupert
Hasluck, (Sir) Paul
Hassan, Ihab
Hattersley, Roy
Hautzig, Esther
Hawley, Richard A.
Hayden, Tom
Hazo, Samuel
Hemphill, Paul
Heren, Louis
Herriot, James
Hesketh, Phoebe
Heyman, Abigail
Hickin, Norman
Hidden, Norman
Higginbotham, Jay
Higgins, Aidan
Hillary, (Sir) Edmund
Hillis, Dick
Hinde, Thomas
Hoffman, Malcolm A.
Holloway, John
Holmes, Edward M.
Home, Alec Douglas
Home, William Douglas
Hook, Sidney
Hopcraft, Arthur
Hope, Bob
Hopkins, Antony
Hopkinson, (Sir) Thomas
Horne, Donald Richard
Howard, Maureen
Hoyle, (Sir) Fred
Hudson, Liam
Huffaker, Clair
Humphrey, William
Hunt, (Sir) David
Hutchins, Francis Gilman
Huxley, Elspeth
Iacocca, Lee
Ignatow, David
Jacobs, Helen Hull
Jacobs, Lewis
James, Clive
Jeffery, Graham
Johnston, Jill
Jones, (Abbot) Christopher
Jones, Tristan
Jones-Evans, Eric
Joy, Thomas Alfred
Judson, John
Kanin, Garson
Kauffmann, Stanley
Kavanagh, P.J.
Kee, Robert
Kelly, (Lady) Marie-Noële
Kennedy, Moorhead
Kerr, Jean
Kilbracken, Baron
Kimbrough, Emily
King, Larry L.
Kingston, Maxine Hong
Kissinger, Henry
Klass, Sheila Solomon
Knox, John
Knox-Johnston, Robin
Koerner, James D.
Kopal, Zdene
Kops, Bernard
Kriegel, Leonard
Krim, Seymour
Kunstler, William M.
Lamplugh, Lois
Leakey, Mary

Lear, Martha Weinman
Ledwith, Frank
Lees-Milne, James
L'Engle, Madeleine
Leonard, Hugh
Le Pan, Douglas
Leslie, Robert Franklin
Lester, Julius
Levine, Norman
Levy, Alan
Lifton, Betty Jean
Lindbergh, Anne Morrow
Linkletter, Art
Longford, Lord
Longford, Elizabeth
Lorant, Stefan
Lowenthal, Leo
Luke, Peter
MacCracken, Mary
MacEoin, Gary
MacGregor, James Grierson
Macintosh, Joan
MacKenzie, Donald
MacLaine, Shirley
Maclean, (Sir) Fitzroy
Maddocks, Margaret
Mair, George Brown
Manfred, Frederick Feikema
Mangione, Jerre
Mann, Anthony
Marcus, Stanley
Marshak, Robert Eugene
Mason, Malcolm John
Mason, Philip
Matthews, Denis
Matthews, Thomas Stanley
Maxwell, William
Mayhew, Christopher
McCarthy, Mary
McConkey, James Rodney
McDormand, Thomas Bruce
McEldowney, Richard Dennis
McGurn, Barrett
Mehta, Ved Parkash
Melly, George
Meltzer, David
Meyer, Michael
Millar, George
Millar, Margaret
Miller, Arthur
Miller, Frances A.
Miller, Frederick Walter Gascoyne
Milne, Christopher Robin
Milner, Marion
Mitchell, Elyne
Mitford, Jessica
Mitson, Eileen N.
Morgan-Grenville, Gerard
Morris, Jan
Morris, Wright
Morritt, Hope
Mortimer, Penelope
Mould, Daphne
Mowat, Farley McGill
Mowrer, Lilian T
Moynihan, John Dominic
Mphahlele, Ezekiel
Mucha, Jiri
Muggeridge, Malcolm
Murie, Margaret E.
Naipaul, V.S.
Na ayan, R.K.
Natwar-Singh, K.
Naughton, Bill
Neugeboren, Jay
Newby, Eric
Nichols, John
Nichols, Peter
Nicholson, Hubert
Nolan, Christopher
Notley, Alice
Oatts, Lewis Balfour
O'Brien, Lawrence F.

Ogilvie, Elisabeth
Oliver, Egbert
Onyeama, Dillibe
Padfield, Peter
Parks, Gordon
Perl, Ruth June
Pertwee, Michael
Petrakis, Harry Mark
Piggott, Alan
Pike, Diane Kennedy
Plagemann, Bentz
Plaut, W. Gunther
Plimpton, George
Popper, (Sir) Karl
Powell, Anthony
Powell, Geoffrey
Powell, Violet
Preston, Ivy
Pringle, John
Pritchett, (Sir) V.S.
Purser, Philip
Raddall, Thomas Head
Raine, Kathleen
Ratcliffe, E. Jane
Raven, Simon
Rayburn, Robert G.
Read, Eifreida
Reile, Louis
Richardson, Jack
Richardson, Midge Turk
Ridgway, John
Ridgway, Matthew Bunker
Rivers, Joan
Robens, (Lord) Alfred
Robinson, Roland
Rolph, C.H.
Ross, Alan
Rothenstein, (Sir) John
Rubenstein, Richard Lowell
Ruhen, Olaf
St. John, John
Sanderlin, Owenita
Sanders, James Edward
Sanders, Ronald
Sarton, May
Sava, George
Scannell, Vernon
Schneebaum, Tobias
Schneider, Ben Ross, Jr.
Scott, Bill
Seabrook, Jeremy
Segal, Ronald Michael
Segun, Mabel D.
Sewell, Brocard
Shank, Margarethe Erdahl
Shapiro, Karl
Shattock, Ernest
Sheppard, Martin
Sheppard, David Stuart
Sheppard-Jones, Elisabeth
Sherrin, Ned
Simpson, Myrtle Lillias
Singer, Isaac Bashevis
Skarsten, Malvin Ola
Skinner, B.F.
Snow, Helen Foster
Soper, Eileen Louise
Spence, Eleanor
Spencer, Dora
Spender, Stephen
Stafford, William
Stark, (Dame) Freya
Stern, James
Stewart of Fulham (Baron)
Stone, Brian Ernest
Storey, Edward
Stott, Mary
Straight, Michael
Sulzberger, C.L.
Summers, Essie
Sutcliffe, Rosemary
Swann, Donald
Sypher, Lucy Johnston

Talbot, Godfrey Walker
Talese, Gay
Taylor, Fred James
Teller, Walter Magnes
Thomas, Leslie John
Thompson, Mervyn
Travell, Janet
Traver, Robert
Travis, Dempsey J.
Trawick, Buckner Beasley
Trease, Geoffrey
Trevelyan, (Lord) Humphrey
Trevelyan, Raleigh
Tripp, Miles
Truitt, Anne
Truman, Margaret
Truman, Ruth
Urch, Elizabeth
Ustinov, Peter
van Vogt, A.E.
Vaughan-Thomas, Wynford
Viscott, David S.
Ward, Russel
Watney, John Basil
Waugh, Auberon
Weidman, Jerome
Weir, Molly
Welch, Ann Courtney
Welk, Lawrence
Weller, George Anthony
Westheimer, Ruth
Whistler, Laurence
White, Kenneth
White, Patrick
White, Stanhope
Whitlock, Ralph
Wideman, John Edgar
Wilkinson, Tim
Williams, John A.
Williamson, Richard
Willis, Ted
Willock, Colin
Wilson, Dorothy Clarke
Wilson, Elizabeth
Wilson, (Sir) John
Wilson, Robert Anton
Wilson, Sandy
Windham, Donald
Wingfield, Sheila
Wood, Kerry
Wright, Celeste Turner
Wright, David
Wyatt, Lord
Yates, Elizabeth
Young, T.D.
Zetterling, Mai
Zinkin, Taya

Biography

Abbas, Ahmad
Abrams, Alan
Acland, Alice
Acton, (Sir) Harold
Adair, James R.
Adair, John
Adam-Smith, Patsy
Adamson, Donald
Adler, Renata
Adrian, Arthur Allen
Alaya, Flavia
Alberts, Robert Carman
Albertson, Dean
Alden, John Richard
Aldridge, A. Owen
Alexander, Robert J.
Allan, Ted
Allen, Gay Wilson
Allen, Walter
Alpers, Antony
Alphonso-Karkala, John B.
Alter, Judith

Alter, Robert B.
Amery, Julian
Amis, Kingsley
Anderson, Courtney
Anderson, David Daniel
Andrews, Allen
Anglesey, Marquess of
Angus-Butterworth, Lionel
Annan, Noel Gilroy
Archer, Jules
Armstrong, William H.
Arnold, H.J.P.
Arnott, Anne
Aronson, Theo
Ash, Russell
Ashley, Maurice
Ashton, Dore
Asprey, Robert Brown
Atkins, John Alfred
Atkinson, R.S.
Ayling, Stanley
Badeni, June
Bagley, John Joseph
Bahr, Ehrhard
Bahr, Robert
Bailey, Paul
Bainbridge, John
Baker, Margaret J.
Barlow, Frank
Barnett, Correlli
Barr, Patricia
Bartlett, Christopher John
Bartley, William Warren III
Batchelor, John
Bates, (Sir) Darrell
Battiscombe, Georgina
Baxter, John
Baylen, Joseph O.
Beck, Earl Ray
Beckelhymer, Hunter
Becker, Lucille Frackman
Becker, Stephen
Bedford, Sybille
Bedini, Silvio A.
Behle, William Harroun
Bell, Quentin
Benedictus, David
Benkovitz, Miriam J.
Bentley, Gerald Eades
Bergreen, Laurence
Berlin, (Sir) Isaish
Bernstein, Burton
Berry, Paul
Berton, Pierre
Bickel, Lennard
Bingham, Caroline
Bingham, Charlotte
Bingham, June Rossbach
Binion, Rudolph
Birmingham, Stephen
Birrell, James Peter
Bissoondoyal, Basdeo
Blackbourne, Neville
Blainey, Geoffrey Norman
Blair, Walter
Blake, Leslie James
Blake, Norman Francis
Blake, Robert
Blanch, Lesley
Blanchard, William
Bleakley, David Wylie
Bloom, Lynn
Blotner, Joseph
Blumenson, Martin
Blyth, Alan Geoffrey
Bode, Carl
Bogue, Lucile
Boll, Theophilus E.M.
Bonham-Carter, Victor
Booth, Edwin
Booth, Martin
Botting, Douglas
Bottrall, Margaret

Bourke, Vernon J.
Bowen, Zack
Boyd, Elizabeth French
Boyes, Megan
Boyle, Andrew
Brabazon, James
Braddon, Russell
Bradford, M.E.
Bradlow, Frank Rosslyn
Branch, Edgar Marquess
Bredsdorff, Elias Lunn
Brée, Germaine
Brendon, Piers
Brome, Vincent
Bronner, Edwin Blaine
Brooks, Paul
Brophy, Brigid
Bruce Lockhart, Robind
Buckle, Richard
Buckley, Thomas
Bulpin, Thomas Victor
Buranelli, Vincent
Burgesss, Charles
Burnett, Alistair
Burns, Joan Simpson
Burtschi, Mary Pauline
Busch, Niven
Butler, Iris Mary
Butter, Peter Herbert
Buston, John
Calder-Marshall, Arthur
Callahan, North
Callow, Philip
Cameron, James Munro
Campbell, Ian
Campbell, Judith
Cannon, Garland
Canovan, Margaret Evelyn
Carmichael, Joel
Carnall, Geoffrey Douglas
Caro, Robert A.
Carpenter, Humphrey
Carrington, Charles Edmund
Carswell, John Patrick
Cartland, Barbara
Cary, Richard
Castle, Charles
Cate, Curtis
Cathcart, Helen
Cegielka, Francis
Chalfton, (Lord)
Chandler, David
Chapman, Ronald
Charters, Ann
Chatfield, E. Charles
Cheever, Susan
Christ, Henry I.
Christenson, Cornelia V.
Christian, Carol Cathay
Chute, Marchette
Clark of Herriotshall, Arthur
  Melville
Clark, Mavis Thorpe
Clarke, Martin Lowther
Clarke, Mary Stetson
Clubbe, John L.E.
Coakley, Mary Lewis
Coates, Austin
Coder, S. Maxwell
Coffman, Barbara Francis
Cohen, Morton N.
Colbeck, Maurice
Cole, Edmund Keith
Cole, John Alfred
Coles, Robert
Collier, Peter
Collier, Richard
Collis, Louise
Colloms, Brenda
Comini, Alessandra
Condry, William
Connell, Brian Reginald
Conot, Robert E.

Conrow, Robert W.
Constant, Stephen
Cooke, Alistair
Cooke, Jacob Ernest
Cooke, William
Coolidge, Olivia
Coombs, Joyce
Cooper, Lettice
Cooper, William
Coox, Alvin D.
Cope, Jack
Coppa, Frank John
Corley, Thomas Anthony
  Buchanan
Cosgrave, Patrick
Cotes, Peter
Cousins, Margaret
Cousins, Norman
Cowan, Edward
Cowan, Peter
Cowie, Leonard Wallace
Cowles, Fleur
Cox, William R.
Coxe, Louis
Crago, Thomas Howard
Craig, Edward Anthony
Crandall, Norma
Crawley, Aidan
Creamer, Robert W.
Crick, Bernard R.
Crinkley, Richmond Dillard
Crocker, Lester G.
Crocker, (Sir) Walter
Crosland, Margaret
Crowder, Richard H.
Crozier, Brian
Curling, Bill
Dabney, Virginius
Dallek, Robert
Dally, Ann
Daniels, Elizabeth Adams
Danker, William J.
Davenport, Marcia
David, Heather M.
Davies, Hunter
Davis, Allen F.
Davis, Burke
de Camp, L. Sprague
Deiss, Joseph Jay
de Jonge, Alex
Delaney, Norman Conrad
de la Torre, Lillian
Demaray, Donald E.
Demaris, Ovid
de Mille, Richard
Dempsey, David
Derry, John
Dick, Kay
Dickinson, Harry Thomas
Dickson, Mora Agnes
Dimbleby, Jonathan
Dodson, Kenneth
Donaldson, Frances
Donaldson, Gordon
Donaldson, Norman
Donaldson, Scott
Donoughue, Bernard
Donovan, John
Dornberg, John
Downey, Fairfax Davis
Downs, Robert B.
Doyle, Charles
Drabble, Margaret
Drackett, Phil
Draper, Alfred Ernest
Drower, Margaret Stefana
Dundy, Elaine
Dunmore, John
Dupre, Catherine
Durant, David
Durden, Robert F.
Dutton, Geoffrey
Dykeman, Wilma

Eastaugh, Kenneth
Easton, Robert
Eaton, Charles Edward
Eaton, Richard Behrens
Ebon, Martin
Edel, Leon
Edwards, Anne
Egan, Ferol
Ehle, John
Ehrman, John
Elder, Michael Aiken
Elegant, Robert
Elliott, Brian Robinson
Elsmere, Jane Shaffer
Elsna, Hebe
Epp, Margaret Agnes
Ernst, Robert
Evans, Max
Evans, Rowland, Jr.
Everest, Allan S.
Falk, Candace
Falk, Signi Lenea
Farrar, Ronald T.
Fehrenbacher, Don Edward
Feinberg, Barry
Feinstein, Elaine
Felver, Charles Stanley
Fenn, Charles
Ferris, Paul
Fielder, Mildred
Finch, Christopher
Fink, Augusta
Fisher, (Sir) Nigel
Fitter, Richard
Fitzgeorge-Parker, Tim
Fitzgerald, Penelope
FitzSimons, Raymund
Fladeland, Betty
Fleming, Thomas
Flesch, Y.
Fletcher, Colin
Flexner, James Thomas
Flint, John Edgar
Flood, Charles
Floren, Lee
Fontenay, Charles Louis
Fontenot, Mary Alice
Foot, Michael
Forbes, Bryan
Ford, Herbert
Forster, Margaret
Forsyth, James
Foskett, Daphne
Foster, Malcolm Burton
Fothergill, Brian
Foxall, Raymond
Franck, Frederick
Franklin, Noble
Frantz, Joe B.
Fraser, (Lady) Antonia
Freedland, Michael
Freeman, Lucy
Fremantle, Anne
Friedlander, Albert
Friedman, B.H.
Fryer, Jonathan
Fuller, Edmund
Fuller, Jean Overton
Galante, Pierre P.
Gallant, Roy Arthur
Gardner, Brian
Gardner, Ralph D.
Garrett, Richard
Garrison, Omar V.
Gash, Norman
Gaston, Edwin Willmer, Jr.
Gattey, Charles Neilson
Gavin, Catherine
Gentry, Curt
George, Wilma
Gernsheim, Helmut
Gibson, Robert
Gilbert, Martin

Gill, Brendan
Ginger, Ann F.
Giovanni, Nikki
Gittings, Robert
Glasson, T. Francis
Glen, Frank Grenfell
Glover, Michael
Glyn, (Sir) Anthony
Godbold, E. Stanly, Jr.
Godwin, John
Goldman, Albert
Goldman, Eric Frederick
Gopal, Sarvepalli
Goran, Morris
Gordan, Ian Alistair
Gould, Jean R.
Graham, Desmond
Grant, R derick
Graver, Lawrence Stanley
Gray, Tony
Green, Benny
Green, J.C.R.
Green, Martin
Green, Peter
Greenberger, Howard
Greene, Graham
Gregg, Pauline
Grey, Ian
Grimble, Ian
Gross, John
Grosskurth, Phyllis
Grubb, Norman Percy
Grumbach, Doris
Guest, Barbara
Guiles, Fred Lawrence
Gunston, Bill
Gunther, A.E.
Gutman, Robert W.
Haac, Oscar A.
Hahn, Emily
Haight, Gordon
Halberstam, David
Haley, Kenneth
Hall, J.C.
Hall, Richard
Hall, Rodney
Haltrecht, Montague
Hamburger, Philip
Hamby, Alonzo
Hamilton, Elizabeth
Hamilton, Ian
Hamilton, Ronald
Hamilton, Virginia
Hamilton, William B.
Hamilton-Edwards, Gerald
Hampson, Norman
Harding, James
Hardwick, Michael
Hardwick, Mollie
Hareven, Tamara K.
Harkey, Ira Brown, Jr.
Harrison, Lowell H.
Harrison, Michael
Hartcup, Adeline
Hartcup, John
Hart-Davis, Duff
Hart-Davis, (Sir) Rupert
Harvey, John
Harwood, Ronald
Haskins, George Lee
Haskins, Jim
Hastings, Max M.
Hattersley, Roy
Havighurst, Alfred
Havran, Martin Joseph
Hayes, Paul Martin
Hayman, Ronald
Haynes, Renée Oriana
Hayter, Alethea
Hayter, (Sir) William
Haywood, Charles
Hazlehurst, Cameron
Heald, Tim

Heaven, Constance
Hedley, Olwen
Hemingway, John Hylan, Jr.
Hemlow, Joyce
Hendrickson, Robert A.
Herrmanns, Ralph
Hesketh, Phoebe
Hess, Gary R.
Hibbert, Christopher
Higham, Charles
Hill, Christopher
Hill, Lorna
Hills, George
Hinckley, Helen
Hinde, Wendy
Hirschhorn, Clive
Hodgart, Matthew
Hodge, Jane Aiken
Holden, Anthony
Holland, James R.
Holley, Edward Gailon
Holli, Melvin George
Holloway, David
Holloway, Mark
Holroyd, Michael
Holt, Victoria
Holtby, Robert Tinsley
Holyer, Ernie
Honan, Park
Honeycombe, Gordon
Horgan, Paul
Horner, John Curwen
Hotchner, A.E.
Hough, Richard
Houston, James D.
Howard, J. Woodford, Jr.
Howarth, David
Howarth, Patrick
Howat, Gerald
Howe, James
Howell, Roger, Jr.
Howlett, John
Huber, Richard Miller
Hubler, Richard G.
Hudson, Derek
Hudson, Wilma Jones
Hudson, Winthrop S.
Huggett, Richard
Hughes, Dorothy B.
Hull, Eleanor
Hunter, Michael
Hurd, Michael John
Hutchings, Arthur
Hyams, Joe
Hyde, H. Montgomery
Iremonger, Lucille
Itzhoff, Seymour William
Iwata, Masakazu
Jackman, Sydney Wayne
Jagger, Peter
James, Alan
James, R.V. Rhodes
Jarrett, Derek
Jarvis, Frederick G.H.
Jeal, Tim
Jeffares, A. Norman
Jeffs, Rae
Jenkins, Elizabeth
Jenkins, Michael
Jenkins, Roy
Johnson, Diane
Johnson, Robert Erwin
Johnson, William Weber
Jolly, W.P.
Jones, Billy Mac
Jones, Evan
Jordan, June
Jordan, Ruth
Judd, Denis
Kaminsky, Stuart
Kamm, Josephine
Kaplan, Justin
Karl, Frederick

Karp, David
Kastner, Joseph
Katz, Martin
Kealey, Edward J.
Kelen, Stephen
Kellner, Bruce
Kelly, Linda
Kennedy, Michael
Kerensky, Oleg
Ketcham, Ralph Louis
Ketchum, Richard M.
Kherdian, David
Khosla, Gopal Das
Kilbracken, Lord
King-Hele, Desmond
Kirby, Gilbert Walter
Kirk, Russell Amos
Kitchen, Paddy
Klement, Frank L.
Knapton, Ernest John
Knight, Hardwicke
Knightley, Phillip
Knowlton, Derrick
Knox, Robert Buick
Korda, Michael
Korfker, Dena
Korg, Jacob
Koskoff, David E.
Kresh, Paul
Kupferbrg, Herbert
Kurzman, Dan
Lacey, Robert
Lacy, Creighton Boutelle
Laffin, John
Lahr, John
Lamb, Geoffry
Langford, Gerald
Larsen, Egon
Lasky, Victor
Lasson, Kenneth
Laurence, Dan H.
Lavine, Sigmund Arnold
Lawrence, Berta
Lawrence, Jerome
Lax, Eric
Lea, Tom
Leasor, James
Leder, Lawrence H.
Lee, W. Storrs III
Leerburger, Benedict A.
Lees-Milne, James
Lefebure, Molly
Legge, John David
Lehrer, Stanley
Lendvai, Paul
Lengyel, Cornel Adam
Leonard, Maurice
Le Vay, David
Leverence, John
Levy, Alan
Lewis, William Russell
Li Tien-yi
Lindsay, Jack
Lindsay, Maurice
Link, Arthur S.
Little, Bryan
Liu, Wu-chi
Liversidge, Henry Douglas
Locke, Elsie
Lockyer, Roger Walter
Loh, Pichon, P.Y.
Long, Frank Belknap
Longford (Lord)
Longford, Elizabeth
Longstreet, Stephen
Loomes, Brian
Lorant, Stefan
Lorrimer, Claire
Lottman, Herbert
Lucas, Celia
Lucia, Ellis
Lunt, James Doiran
Lutyens, Mary

Lutzker, Edythe
Lynam, Shevawn
Lytle, Andrew
Maas, Peter
Mabee, Carleton
MacGregor, John Geddes
MacGregor, James Grierson
Mackay, James Alexander
MacKenzie, David
Macksey, K.J.
Mack Smith, Denis
Maclagan, Michael
MacLaine, Shirley
Maclean, (Sir) Fitzroy
Macnab, Roy
MacShane, Frank
Maier, Paul Luther
Mair, Craig
Malet, Hugh
Mallin, Jay
Manchester, William
Mann, Anthony
Mansfield, Bruce Edgar
Mapp, Alf Johnson, Jr.
Marshall, Helen Edith
Marshall, Rosalind Kay
Martelli, George Ansley
Martin, F.X.
Martin, Geoffrey John
Martin, George Whitney
Martin, Ralph G.
Marx, Arthur
Massey, James Earl
Mathis, Sharon Bell
Mavor, Elizabeth
Maxwell, D.E.S.
May, Gita
McCabe, John C., III
McCarry, Charles
McCormick, Donald
McCormick, Eric Hall
McDonald, Forrest
McDowell, Edwin Stewart
McEldowney, Richard Dennis
McKenna, Marian Cecilia
McLaren, Ian Francis
McLean, Ruari
McMillen, Neil Raymond
McNeish, James
Mehta, Ved Parkash
Menendez, Albert J.
Meredith, Scott
Merriam, Eve
Meserve, Walter Joseph, Jr.
Messer, Thomas M.
Meyer, Michael
Midwinter, Eric
Milford, Nancy
Milhouse, Paul William
Millar, George
Miller, Frances A.
Miller, Helen Hill
Miller, Jonathan
Miller, Karl
Mills, A.R.
Milton, John R.
Milton, Joyce
Miner, Ward L.
Mitchell, Broadus
Mitchell, David John
Mitchell, Julian
Mitchison, Rosalind
Mitgang, Herbert
Mohl, Ruth
Mollenhoff, Clark
Money, Keith
Monsarrat, Ann Whitelaw
Moore, Carman
Moore, Rayburn Sabatzky
Moore, Raylyn
Moore, Raymond S.
Moorehead, Caroline
Morgan, Donald Grant

Morgan, Janet
Morgan, Ted
Morley, Sheridan
Morris, Edmund
Morritt, Hope
Mosel, Tad
Mosley, Leonard
Mowrer, Lilian T.
Mucha, Jiri
Muggeridge, Malcolm
Muir, Kenneth
Mullan, Bob
Munford, William Arthur
Munz, Peter
Murray-Smith, Stephen
Myers, Elisabeth P.
Nabokov, Peter
Nanda, Bal Ram
Nash, Roderick
Nathan, David
Natusch, Sheila
Neely, William J.
Neilson, James Warren
Nelson, Cordner
Nelson, James Graham
Nelson-Humphries, Tessa
Neville, Pauline
Newman, Aubrey N.
Newsome, David Hay
Nicolson, Nigel
Nitske, W. Robert
Noakes, Vivien
Noble, William Charles
Nolan, William F.
Norman, John
Nunn, William Curtis
Nutting, (Sir) Anthony
Oakes, Philip
Oates, Stephen B.
O'Broin, Leon
O'Collins, Gerald Glyn
O'Faolain, Sean
O'Farrell, Patrick
Ogburn, Charlton, Jr.
Oldham, Frank
Ollard, Richard
Olney, Ross R.
Olsen, Tillie
Olson, James Clifton
Omari, T. Peter
O'Meara, John Joseph
O'Neill, Robert John
Osborn, Ronald Edwin
O'Sullivan, Timothy
Owen, Roderic
Padfield, Peter
Page, Norman
Palmer, Alan Warwick
Parham, William Thomas
Parker, Barrett
Parker, Derek
Parker, Franklin
Parkinson, Cyril Northcote
Parkinson, Michael
Parmet, Herbert S.
Parrish, William E.
Parry, Albert
Pascal, Francine
Partridge, Astley Cooper
Paterson, Ronald
Patterson, Elizabeth Chambers
Pawel, Ernst
Payne, Donald Gordon
Payne, J. Gregory
Pearson, John
Pelling, Henry Mathison
Percival, Alicia C.
Percy, Douglas C.
Peters, Maureen
Peters, Margot
Peterson, Merrill D.
Petrakis, Harry Mark
Philip, Eliot Elias

Pick, John Barclay
Pilapil, Vincente R.
Pinchot, Ann
Pinkett, Harold Thomas
Pipes, Richard
Pitrone, Jean Maddern
Pittenger, Norman
Plimpton, George
Plumb, John Harold
Pocock, Hugh
Pocock, Thomas Allcot Guy
Pogue, Forrest Carlistle
Pollard, John
Pollock, John Charles
Ponsonby, D.A.
Pope, Dudley
Porteous, Leslie Crichton
Potoker, Edward Martin
Powell, Violet
Powling, Chris
Poynter, John Riddoch
Prebble, John
Price, Cecil
Pritchard, William H.
Pundeff, Martin V.
Purcell, William
Quennell, Peter
Rabinowicz, Mordka Harry
Ramsey, Gordon Clark
Ratcliff, Carter
Ravitz, Abe Carl
Rawley, James A.
Rayfield, Donald
Raynor, Henry
Read, Anthony
Read, Donald
Reader, William Joseph
Reddaway, Peter
Reed, Joseph W.
Reed, Thomas Thornton
Reedy, George E.
Rees, Joan
Reeves, Thomas
Reid, Helen Evans
Reid, John
Reid, Loren
Reid, Robert
Reilly, Robert Thomas
Reilly, Robin
Rendle-Short, John
Richardson, Joanna
Richmond, Roe
Ridley, Jasper
Rischin, Moses
Rivenburgh, Viola K.
Roberts, Brian
Robertson, Barbara Anne
Robin, Arthur de Quetteville
Robinson, Gilbert de Beauregard
Roddy, Lee
Roditi, Edòuard
Rodney, William
Rogers, Pat
Rogow, Arnold A.
Rohmer, Richard
Rolle, Andrew
Rolo, Paul Jacques Victor
Ronan, Colin Alistair
Roosevelt, Elliott
Roper, Laura Wood
Rose, Kenneth
Rose, Marilyn Gaddis
Rose, Norman Anthony
Rosen, Sidney
Rose, Alan
Ross, Angus
Roth, Andrew
Rouse, Parke Shepherd, Jr.
Rowland, Peter Kenneth
Ruby, Robert H.
Ruether, Rosemary Radford
Rush, Philip
Russell, Francis

Ryan, Peter Allen
Saint, Andrew
St. Aubyn, Giles Rowan
St. John, John
St. John, Patricia Mary
St. John, Robert
St. John-Stevas, Norman
Salinger, Pierre
Salmon, John
Sambrook, A.J.
Sanborn, Margaret
Sanderlin, George
Sanders, Ronald
Sanecki, Kay Naylor
Sanger, Marjory Bartlett
Saricks, Ambrose
Sarna, Jonathan D.
Saroyan, Aram
Savery, Constance Winifred
Scarfe, Wendy Elizabeth
Schapsmeier, Edward Lewis
Schapsmeier, Frederick H.
Schneider, Robert W.
Schonberg, Harold C.
Schulberg, Budd
Scott, Alexander
Scott, Amoret
Scott, Christopher
Scott, Franklin D.
Scott, John Anthony
Seale, William
Sealts, Merton M., Jr.
Searls, Hank
Segre, Emilio
Selden, George
Seldes, George
Semmler, Clement William
Sewell, Brocard
Seymour-Smith, Martin
Shackleton (Baron)
Shankland, Peter Macfarlane
Sheaffer, Louis
Sheed, Wilfred
Shepperson, Wilbur
Sherrin, Ned
Shikes, Ralph Edmund
Short, Philip
Shulman, Irving
Sigworth, Oliver F.
Silver, Eric
Silverberg, Robert
Sim, Katharine Phyllis
Simonson, Harold P.
Simpson, Myrtle Lillias
Sinclair, Keith
Singh, Amritjit
Singh, Khushwant
Skarsten, Malvin Olai
Skelton, Geoffrey
Slatzer, Robert
Smart, Alastair
Smith, Bradley F.
Smith, Dodie
Smith, (Sir) Dudley
Smith, Ella
Smith, George H.
Smith, Hobart Muir
Smith, Lacey Baldwin
Smith, Page
Smith, Vivian
Smithers, (Sir) Peter
Snow, Philip
Sobol, Ken
Socolofsky, Homer Edward
Somerset Fry, Plantagenet
Sonnichsen, C.L.
Sorel, Nancy Caldwell
Sorley, Walker Katherine
Spalding, Ruth
Spencer, Christopher
Spitz, Lewis William
Spivack, Charlotte
Spurling, Hilary

Squires, Radcliffe
Stansky, Peter
Stead, Philip John
Stearn, Jess
Stearn, William Thomas
Steegmuller, Francis
Steel, Ronald
Stegner, Wallace Earle
Stern, Ellen Norman
Stern, Madeleine B.
Sternlicht, Sanford
Stevenson, Anne
Stevenson, Elizabeth
Stewart, Donald H.
Stirling, Nora B.
Stone, Irving
Storey, Anthony
Straight, Michael
Strickland, Margot
Sullivan, Marion F.
Sultana, Donald Edward
Super, Robert Henry
Surtees, Virginia
Sutton, Denys
Sutton, S.B.
Swallow, Norman
Swanberg, William Andrew
Sweetser, Wesley
Swift, (Sister) Mary Grace
Symonds, John
Symons, Geraldine
Symons, Julian Gustave
Talbot, Godfrey Walker
Tanner, Stephen L.
Target, George William
Taylor, Robert Lewis
Taylor Wedford, Dunaway
Teller, Walter Magnes
Thackray, Derek Vincent
Thiele, Colin
Thody, Philip
Thomas, Alan Gradon
Thomas, Clara McCandless
Thomas, Hugh
Thomey, Tedd
Thornton, John Leonard
Thornton, Michael
Thrasher, Peter Adam
Thwaite, Ann Barbara
Tindall, Gillian
Tipton, David
Todd, John M.
Tomalin, Ruth
Tomkins, Calvin
Tomkins, Oliver Stratford
Tours, Hugh Berthold
Tracy, Clarence
Travers, Basil Holmes
Travis, Dempsey J.
Trefousse, Hans Louis
Tremain, Rose
Trengove, Alan Thomas
Trevelyan, Raleigh
Trevor, Meriol
Trueblood, Paul Graham
Truman, Margaret
Trypanis, Constantine
Tucker, William Edward
Tullett, James Stuart
Tuohy, Frank
Turner, John Frayn
Turner, Paul
Tuttle, William McCullough, Jr.
Tyler-Whittle, Michael
Ueda, Makota
Underwood, Peter
Urquhart, Brian Edward
Vale, Malcolm Graham Allan
Vandiver, Frank Everson
Van Dusen, C. Raymond
Vaughan Williams, Ursula
Verney, Peter
Verral, Charles Spain

Vining, Elizabeth Gray
Voitle, Robert
von Hoffman, Nicholas
Waagenaar, Sam
Waddington, Miriam
Wade, Mason
Wagenknecht, Edward
Walbank, Frank William
Walker, Peter Benson
Wall, Joseph Frazier
Wallace, Ian
Waller, George Macgregor
Walters, John Beauchamp
Walworth, Arthur
Warden, Lewis Christopher
Wardle, Irving
Ware, Jean
Warner, Marina
Warren, Wilfred Lewis
Waters, Frank
Watney, John Basil
Waugh, Dorothy
Wearin, Otha Donner
Weatherhead, A. Kingsley
Webb, Bernice
Webb, Jean Francis
Webber, E. Ronald
Weber, Ralph E.
Webster, Norman William
Wedgwood, (Dame) C.V.
Weems, John Edward
Weinstein, Mark Allen
Weintraub, Stanley
Wertenbaker, Lael Tucker
West, Francis James
West, Gertrude
Westbrook, Perry D.
Westfall, Richard S.
White, Jon Manchip
White, Ray Lewis
White, Stanhope
White, Terence de Vere
Whitington, Richard
Whitlock, Ralph
Whitten, Leslie Hunter, Jr.
Whitworth, Rex
Wicker, Rom
Wilkinson, Burke
Willett, John
Williams, David Alden
Williams, John A.
Wilson, A.N.
Wilson, Dorothy Clarke
Wilson, Phillip
Winetrout, Kenneth
Winter, David Brian
Wittlin, Thaddeus
Wolfe, Burton H.
Wolff, Geoffrey
Wolrige Gordon, Anne
Wolseley, Roland E.
Wood, Arthur Skevington
Wood, Kerry
Woodcock, George
Woodford, Peggy
Woodhouse, Montague
Woods, Frederick
Wright, Esmond
Wright, Judith Arundell
Wykeham, (Sir) Peter
Wykes, Alan
Yarwood, Doreen
Yates, Elizabeth
Yost, Nellie Snyder
Young, Bernice Elizabeth
Young, Janet Randall
Young, Philip
Young, Scott
Young-Bruehl, Elisabeth
Zacek, Joseph Frederick
Zahn, Gordon C.
Zall, Paul M.
Zapoleon, Marguerite Wykoff

Biography—cont.

Zeldin, Theodore
Ziegler, Philip
Zochert, Donald
Zohn, Harry
Zolotow, Maurice
Zornow, William Frank

Documentation/Reportage

Abrahams, Peter
Abrams, Alan
Anderson, Jack
Bailey, Anthony
Borland, Hal
Brata, Sasthi
Breslin, Jimmy
Clare, George
Delano, Anthony
Finnegan, Joan
Friendly, Fred W.
Geyer, Georgie Anne
Godden, Rumer
Gratus, Jack
Hastings, Max M.
Honeycombe, Gordon
Jordan, Ruth
Katz, Ephraim
Krim, Seymour
Kurzman, Dan
Lax, Eric
MacAdams, Lewis
Mailer, Norman
Mallin, Jay
Martin, Ralph G.
Marzani, Carl
Menendez, Albert J.
Moorehead, Caroline
Mowrer, Lilian T.
Opie, June
Payne, Donald Gordon
Pearlman, Moshe
Pearson, John
Plowden, Alison
Popham, Hugh
Pryce-Jones, David
Read, Piers Paul
Reilly, Robert Thomas
Reston, James
Rusher, William Allen
Russell, Roy
Savitt, Sam
Schalk, Adolph F.
Schell, Jonathan
Short, Philip
Shubin, Seymour
Snyder, Louis L.
Sobol, Ken
Spalding, Ruth
Summers, Anthony
Syrop, Konrad
Toynbee, Polly
Walker, Joseph E.
Waugh, Auberon
Westlake, Donald E.
Wiessel, Elie
Winchester, Simon
Wood, Fergus James

Essays

Achebe, Chinua
Barich, Bill
Bernstein, Charles
Bodett, Thomas Edward
Brodsky, Joseph
Buckley, William F., Jr.
Comfort, Alex
Cooke, Alistair
Crew, Louie
de Vries, Rachel
Dunne, John Gregory

Essays—cont.

Eastlake, William
Ellison, Ralph
Epstein, Joseph
Fadiman, Clifton
Finger, Seymour
Gallagher, Tess
Gold, Herbert
Gould, Lois
Guest, Judith
Hamburger, Philip
Hawley, Richard A.
Hayden, Tom
Huie, William Bradford
Kunitz, Stanley
Lifton, Robert J.
Lurie, Morris
Mandel, Oscar
May, Gita
McCarthy, Mary
McCaslin, Nellie
McCord, David
McMurtry, Larry
McPhee, John
Middleton, Christopher
Mitchell, Joseph
Mohl, Ruth
Mokashi-Punekar, Shankar
Morgan, Edwin
Morris, Wright
Mphahlele, Ezekiel
Mueller, Robert Emmett
Mueller, William R.
Natwar-Singh, K.
Nkosi, Lewis
Nochlin, Linda Weinberg
Oldsey, Bernard S.
Ozick, Cynthia
Peeples, Edwin
Piercy, Marge
Poovey, William Arthur
Porter, Bern
Porter, Joshua Roy
Price, Reynolds
Pringle, John
Pritchard, William H.
Pryce-Jones, David
Quennell, Peter
Ratcliffe, Eric Hallam
Ratner, Rochelle
Raven, Simon
Rees, David Bartlett
Reile, Louis
Rooney, Andrew A.
Rosensaft, Menachem Z.
Rosten, Leo
Roth, Philip
Royster, Vermont
Rubenstein, Richard Lowell
Segun, Mabel D.
Shapiro, Karl
Sheed, Wilfrid
Sigworth, Oliver F.
Sisson, C.H.
Sontag, Susan
Stanford, Donald Elwin
Stark, (Dame) Freya
Stern, Richard G.
Stewart, Harold Frederick
Straumann, Heinrich
Thomas, Lewis
Thompson, William Irwin
Tonogbanua, Francisco G.
Travers, P.L.
Trilling, Diana
Tschumi, Raymond
Tucci, Niccolo
Tucker, Martin
Turco, Lewis
Vonnegut, Kurt, Jr.
Voorhees, Richard J.
Waddington, Miriam
Wallace-Crabbe, Christopher
Waugh, Auberon

Essays—cont.

Weidman, Jerome
Weinberg, Kerry
Wells, John
Wesker, Arnold
West, Paul
White, Edmund
White, Kenneth
White, Ray Lewis
Whitehorn, Katharine
Whittemore, Reed
Wiesel, Elie
Williams, Emmett
Williams, Jonathan
Williams, Thomas
Wright, Stephen
Wynes, Charles E.
Young-Bruehl, Elisabeth

Humor/Satire

Allen, Steve
Armour, Richard
Baker, Russell
Baker, Stephen
Bellairs, John
Bendiner, Robert
Bentine, Michael
Berg, Dave
Berton, Pierre
Betts, William Wilson, Jr.
Blair, Walter
Bombeck, Erma
Buchwald, Art
Burns, George
Buxbaum, Martin
Cleese, John
Cole, William
Colombo, John Robert
Cooper, Jilly
Coren, Alan
Cutler, Ivor
Davidson, Sol M.
Davies, Christie
Dinhofer, Alfred D
Dodge, David
Downey, Fairfax Davis
Eisenberg, Larry
Ellis, Alice T.
Ellis, Humphrey Francis
Fantoni, Barry
Feiffer, Jules
Fink, Merton
Ford, Brian J.
Frost, David
Freud, Clement
Goldstein-Jackson, Kevin
Gould, Lois
Green, Michael
Hamburger, Philip
Harron, Don
Hatch, Denison
Holles, Robert
Hoppe, Arthur Watterson
Huggett, Richard
Huston, Mervyn J.
Ingrams, Richard
James, Clive
Jennings, Paul
Kaufman, Gerald
Keane, John B.
Keillor, Garrison
Kimbrough, Emily
Lewis, William Russell
Linkletter, Art
Martin, Judith
Marx, Arthur
Matthew, Christopher C.F.
McConnell, James Vernon
Mead, Shepherd
Melly, George
Milligan, Spike
Mowat, Farley

Humor/Satire—cont.

Muir, Frank
Newman, Charles
Nunn, William Curtis
Papas, William
Pick, John Barclay
Pile, Stephen
Plimpton, George
Politella, Dario
Powe, Bruce
Rice, Donald L.
Rivers, Joan
Roberts, Denys
Robinson, Derek
Robinson, Robert
Rooney, Andrew A.
Rosten, Leo
Ryan, John
Saddler, Allen
Schulz, Charles Monroe
Seaman, Sylvia Sybil
Searle, Ronald
Shank, Margarethe Erdahl
Shenker, Israel
Sherman, Arnold
Silverstein, Shel
Slosberg, Mike
Taylor, Welford Dunaway
Trudeau, Garry
Truman, Ruth
Turner, E.S.
Ward, Norman
Wardroper, John Edmund
Waterhouse, Keith
Welcher, Rosalind
Westlake, Donald E.
Wilson, Sandy
Wiseman, Bernard
Wolfe, Burton H.

Translations

Abraham, Claude Kurt
Abraham, Willie E.
Adams, Robert Martin
Adamson, Donald
Adler, Helmut E.
Aiken, Joan
Alexander, M.J.
Alfred, William
Ali, Ahmed
Anderson, Malcolm
Antin, David
Araki, James Tomomasa
Archer, Gleason Leonard
Arnott, Peter Douglas
Ashbery, John
Asher, Harry
Atkins, Stuart
Auster, Paul
Austin, William W.
Bahr, Ehrhard
Bailey, D.R. Shackleton
Barzelay, Walter Moshe
Baybars, Taner
Becker, Stephen
Beckett, Samuel
Beckingham, Charles Fraser
Beissel, Henry
Belfrage, Cedric
Belitt, Ben
Benedict, Rex
Bentley, Eric
Benton, Peggie
Berg, Stephen
Bernard, Oliver
Bethell, Nicholas
Bien, Peter A.
Binham, Philip Frank
Blackwell, Richard J.
Blair, Dorothy S.
Blake, Norman Francis
Blaser, Robin

Bloch, Marie Halun
Bly, Robert
Boer, Charles
Bosley, Keith
Bourke, Vernon J.
Bowles, Paul
Bowlt, John Ellis
Bradley, Marion Zimmer
Braun, Richard Emil
Bretnor, Reginald
Brilliant, Alan
Bromiley, Geoffrey William
Brooke, Dinah
Brotherston, Gordon
Broumas, Olga
Brown, Rita Mae
Bruce, Lennart
Bulla, Clyde Robert
Bullock, Michael
Burford, William
Burgess, Anthony
Carmichael, Joel
Carrier, Constance
Carrier, Warren
Carter, Angela
Causley, Charles
Caws, Mary Ann
Caws, Peter
Chanan, Michael
Chase, Alston Hurd
Cheng, James K.
Christ, Ronald
Christian, Frederick H.
Christophersen, Paul
Cicellis, Kay
Clark, Eleanor
Coe, Richard N.
Coetzee, J.M.
Cogswell, Fred
Cohn, Norman
Cole, John Alfred
Comfort, Alex
Connell, Brian Reginald
Connor, Tony
Conran, Anthony
Cope, Jack
Corman, Cid
Corrigan, Robert W.
Cragg, Kenneth
Crosland, Margaret
Crossley-Holland, Kevin
Dale, Peter
Davenport, Guy
Davis, Dick
Davis, John David
Davison, Dennis
Dennis-Jones, Harold
de Vinck, José M.G.A.
Di Cesare, Mario A.
Dickinson, Patric
di Prima, Diane
Dobson, Rosemary
Dorn, Ed
Duffy, Maureen
Duncan, A.R.C.
Durrell, Lawrence
Edwards, Harvey
Enright, D.J.
Eshleman, Clayton
Ettinger, Elzbieta
Evans, Robert Owen
Fabry, Joseph B.
Fainlight, Ruth
Faulk, Odie B.
Federman, Raymond
Fenton, Edward
Fenton, James
Ferlita, Ernest
Feuerstein, Georg
Fielding, A.W.
Firchow, Peter
Fischer, Robert H.
Fjelde, Rolf

Fletcher, John Walter James
Ford, Gordon Buell, Jr.
Ford, R.A.D.
Fowles, John
Fox-Genovese, Elizabeth
Frame, Donald Murdoch
Francis, H.E., Jr.
Frayn, Michael
Fremantle, Anne
Friedberg, Maurice
Friedman, Jacob Horace
Friend, Robert
Friis, Erik Johan
Fry, Christopher
Fulton, Robin
Gard, Joyce
Garnett, Richard
Garrard, Lancelot Austin
Gascoyne, David
Gavronsky, Serge
Giannaris, George
Gilbert, Creighton Eddy
Gilbert, John Raphael
Gillespie, Gerald
Gillon, Adam
Goacher, Denis
Godden, Rumer
Goldstein, Jonathan Amos
Gonzàlez, Justo Luis
Grant, James Russell
Green, J.C.R.
Green, Peter
Gregory, James Stothert
Griffin, Jonathan
Griffith, Thomas Gwynford
Grigson, Jane
Grindrod, Muriel
Guenther, Charles
Gullans, Charles
Hacikyan, Agop Jack
Haines, John
Hamburger, Michael
Hamby, Wallace B.
Hamilton, Elizabeth
Hanson, Kenneth O.
Hapgood, David
Harrison, Tony
Hartcup, Adeline
Harwood, Lee
Haugen, Einar
Haviaras, Stratis
Haywood, Charles
Heath-Stubbs, John
Henderson, Hamish
Hibbett, Howard
Hieatt, Constance Bartlett
Higson, Philip
Hillier, Caroline
Himelstein, Morgan Y.
Hine, Daryl
Hirschman, Jack
Hohnen, David
Holden, Anthony
Holdheim, William
Hollingdale, Reginald John
Hollo, Anselm
Hong, Howard V.
Honig, Edwin
Hopkins, Jasper
Horovitz, Michael
Howard, Richard
Hoyem, Andrew
Hull, William D.
Hutchinson, Pearse
Ingalls, Jeremy
Jacobs, Arthur
Jay, Peter
Johnson, Ronald
Johnston, George
Jones, Charles W.
Jones, D.G.
Jones, Glyn
Jordan, Ruth

Kamen, Henry
Katz, Michael Ray
Keating, L. Clark
Keeley, Edmund LeRoy
Keene, Donald
Kellett, Arnold
Kelly, Louis Gerard
Kenworthy, Brian J.
Kessler, Jascha Frederick
Kinnell, Galway
Kinsella, Thomas
Kirkup, James
Knoepcfle, John
Kochan, Miriam
Kramer, Aaron
Kudian, Mischa
Kusin, Vladimir V.
Kustow, Michael
Lal, P.
Lane, Richard
Leaney, Alfred Robert Clare
Lee, Peter H.
Legat, Michael
Leigh Fermor, Patrick Michael
Le Vay, David
Levenson, Christopher
Levertov, Denise
Levi, Peter
Liddell, Robert
Lima, Robert F., Jr.
Lind, Levi Robert
Lindsay, Jack
Logue, Christopher
Lucie-Smith, Edward
MacKay, James Alexander
MacMahon, Bryan Michael
Magnusson, Magnus
Mandel, Oscar
Mansfield, Walter Kenneth
Mason, Edmund
Mayne, Seymour
Mazzaro, Jerome
McCaughrean, Geraldine
McFarlane, James Walter
McGrath, John
McHugh, J.F.
McLean, Ruari
McLeish, Kenneth
McWhirter, George
Mead, Matthew
Melchoir, Ib
Meredith, William
Merwin, W.,S.
Meyer, Michael
Mezey, Robert
Michie, James
Middleton, Christopher
Miller, Donald George
Miller, Jim Wayne
Milner, Ian Frank George
Minear, Richard Hoffman
Miner, Earl
Mintz, Ruth Finer
Moffett, Judith
Mokashi-Punekar, Shankar
Moore, Carey Armstrong
Moorehead, Caroline
Morgan, Edwin
Morris, Jean
Moyes, Patricia
Mucha, Jiri
Muir, Kenneth
Murphy, Richard Thomas
Nakayama, Shigeru
Nandy, Pritish
Nelson, Lowry, Jr.
Neusner, Jacob
Nicolaeff, Ariadne
Nims, John Frederick
Norman, Barbara
Nyanaponika
O'Faolain, Julia
O'Flaherty, James Carneal

O'Grady, Desmond
Oliva, L. Jay
Oliver, Kenneth A.
O'Neill, Patrick Geoffrey
Owen, Douglas David Roy
Padgett, Ron
Palsson, Hermann
Pargeter, Edith Mary
Parker, W.H.
Parks, Tim
Parry, Albert
Pawel, Ernst
Plante, David Robert
Potter, Vincent G.
Poulin, A., Jr.
Prelusky, Jack
Price, Victor
Prince, F.T.
Purcell, Sally
Raine, Kathleen
Ramanujan, A.K.
Randall, Margaret
Ratner, Rochelle
Rayfield, Donald
Reed, T.J.
Reeve, F.D.
Reid, Alastair
Reid, John
Renfield, Richard Lee
Roche, Paul
Rodefer, Stephen
Root, William Pitt
Rose, Ernst
Rose, Marilyn Gaddis
Rothenberg, Jerome
Rowen, Herbert H.
Rudkin, David
Russell, Peter
Salinger, Herman
Salter, Lionel
Sanders, Peter
Savory, Teo
Schroeder, Andreas
Scully, James
Sharat Chandra, G.S.
Shukman, Harold
Simic, Charles
Simon, Edith
Simpson, Jacqueline
Sinclair, Andrew
Singer, Isaac Bashevis
Singh, Khushwant
Sisson, C.H.
Skelton, Geoffrey
Slavitt, David
Slavutych, Yar
Smith, Kay Nolte
Smith, William Jay
Snodgrass, W.D.
Sobin, Gustaf
Soyinka, Wole
Sparnon, Norman
Spink, Reginald
Steinberg, Jonathan
Stephens, William Peters
Stern, James
Stewart, Harold Frederick
Stone, Brian Ernest
Strand, Mark
Stryk, Lucien
Stuart, Francis
Sullivan, John Patrick
Swenson, May
Syrop, Konrad
Tarn, Nathaniel
Taylor, Andrew
Taylor, Henry
Templeton, Edith
Todd, James Maclean
Trevelyan, Raleigh
Truitt, Anne
Turnell, Martin
Turner, Paul

Ueda, Makoto
Ure, Jean
Vahanian, Gabriel
van Itallie, Jean-Claude
Van Stockum, Hilda
Varma, Monika
Waidson, Herbert Morgan
Wainwright, Jeffrey
Walsh, P.G.
Walter, Elizabeth
Ward, Philip
Warner, Val

Warsh, Lewis
Wedde, Ian
Wedgewood, (Dame) C.V.
Weissbort, Daniel
Weisstein, Ulrich, W.
Wellwarth, George E.
West, John Frederick
White, Kenneth
Whitfield, John Humphreys
Whitman, Ruth
Whitten, Leslie Hunter, Jr.
Wilbur, Richard

Willett, John
Williams, C.K.
Williams, Emmett
Williams, Gwyn
Williams, Miller
Wilson, David Henry
Witton-Davies, Carlyle
Wojciechowska, Maia
Wolff Kurt H.
Wong, May
Wright, David
Wright, George Thaddeus

Yarrow, Philip John
Yashima, Taro
Yglesias, Jose
Young, Ian
Yudkin, Leon Israel
Zacek, Joseph Frederick
Zeldis, Chayym
Ziolkowski, Theodore
Zohn, Harry

A

AARDEMA, Verna. American, b.1911. Children's non-fiction. Elementary school teacher, Mona Shores Schs., and Corresp., The Muskegon Chronicle, both Michigan., 1951–73. *Publs:*Tales From the Story Hat, 1960; Otwe, 1960; The Na of Wa, 1960; The Sky-God Stories, 1960; More Tales from the Story Hat, 1966; Tales for the Third Ear: From Equatorial Africa, 1969; Behind the Back of the Mountain: Black Folktales from Southern Africa, 1973; Why Mosquitoes Buzz in People's Ears, 1975; Who's in Rabbit's House, 1977; Ji-Nango-Nango Means Riddles, 1978; The Riddle of the Drum: A Tale from Tizapan, Mexico, 1979; Half-a-Ball-of Kenki, 1979; Bringing the Rain to Kapiti Plain, 1981; What's So Funny, Ketu?, 1982; The Vinganane and the Tree Toad, 1983; Oh, Kojo! How Could You!, 1984; Bimwili and the Zimwi, 1985; Princess Gorilla and a New Kind of Water, 1988; Rabbit Makes a Monkey of Lion, 1989. Add: 784 Via Del Sol, N., Ft. Myers, Fla. 33903, U.S.A.

AARON, Chester. American, b. 1923. Novels/Short stories, Children's Fiction. Chief X-Ray Technician, Alta Bates Hosp., Berkeley, Calif., 1958–71; Technical Writer, MKI Engineering, San Francisco, 1971–72; Prof. of English, St. Mary's Coll., Moraga, Calif., 1972. *Publs:* About Us (novel), 1967; children's fiction – Better Than Laughter, 1972; An American Ghost, 1973; Hello to Bodega, 1975; Spill, 1977; Catch Calico!, 1979; Gideon, 1982; Duchess, 1982; Out of Sight, Out of Mind, 1984; Lackawanna, 1986. Add: P.O. Box 388, Occidental, Calif. 95465, U.S.A.

AARON, James E. American, b. 1927. Education. Admin. and Teacher, Southern Illinois Univ., Carbondale, since 1957. Consultant, Office of Supt. of Public Instruction, since 1960; Consultant, Office of the Illinois Secty. of State; Member, Traffic Education and Training Cttee., National Safety Council, since 1972. Teacher of Driver Education, New York Univ., NYC, 1956–57; Member, National Highway Safety Advisory Cttee., 1970–73. *Publs:* The Police Officer and Alcoholism, 1963; Driver and Traffic Safety Education: Content, Method, Organization, 1966, 1977; Driver Education: Learning to Drive Defensively, 1973; Driving Task Instruction: Dual Control, 1974; First Aid and Emergency Care, 1979; Fundamentals of Safety Education, 1981. Add: P.O. Box 3284, Carbondale, Ill. 62902, U.S.A.

AARONOVITCH, Sam. British, b. 1919. Economics, Sociology. Sr. Lectr. in Economics, Polytechnic of the South Bank, London, since 1972. Former Economic Researcher, Balliol Coll., Oxford, and Researcher, Dept. of Political Economy, Univ. Coll., London. *Publs:* (co-author) Crisis in Kenya, 1947; Monopoly, 1955; The Ruling Class: A Study of British Finance Capital, 1961, 1979; Economics for Trade Unionists, 1964; (with Malcolm C. Sawyer) Big Business, 1975; (with R. Smith) The Political Economy of British Capitalism: A Marxist Analysis, 1981; The Road from Thatcherism, 1981. Add: 19 Bromwich Ave., London N6 6QH, England.

ABBAS, (Khwaja) Ahmad. Indian, b. 1914. Novels/Short stories, Plays/Screenplays, Autobiography/Memoirs/Personal, Biography. Journalist; film dir. and producer; Contributing Columnist, Blitz Mag., Bombay, since 1947. Reporter and Sub-Ed., 1936–39, Ed. of Sunday Ed., and Columnist, 1939–47, The Bombay Chronicle. *Publs:* Outside India: The Adventures of a Roving Reporter, 1940; An Indian Looks at America, 1943; Tomorrow Is Ours!, 1943; Defeat for Death: A Story Without Names, 1944; (with N.G. Yog) Report to Gandhiji, 1944; Invitation to Immortality (play), 1946; Blood and Stones, 1947; Rice and Other Stories, 1947; I Write As I Feel, 1948; Kashmir Fights for Freedom, 1948; Cages of Freedom and Other Stories, 1952; In the Image of Mao Tse-Tung, 1953; Inqilab, 1955; One Thousand Nights on a Bed of Stones and Other Stories, 1957; Face to Face with Krushchev, 1960; Till We Reach the Stars: The Story of Yuri Gagarin, 1961; Black Sun and Other Stories, 1963; Indira Gandhi: Return of the Red Rose, 1966; The Most Beautiful Woman in the World, 1968; When Night Falls, 1968; Mera Naam Joker, 1970; Maria, 1971; That Woman: Her Seven Years in Power, 1973; I Am Not an Island, 1977; Indira Gandhi: The Last Post, 1985. Add: Philomena Lodge, Church Rd., Juhu, Bombay 54, India.

ABBENSETTS, Michael. British, b. 1938. Novels/Short stories, Plays/Screenplays. Dramatist-in-Residence, Royal Court Theatre, London, 1974; Visiting Prof. of Drama, Carnegie Mellon Univ., Pittsburgh, Pa., 1981. *Publs:* Sweet Talk, 1976; Empire Road (novelization of TV series), 1979; Samba, 1980; In the Mood, 1981; Outlaw, 1983; El Dorado, 1984. Add: c/o Anthony Sheil Assocs., 43 Doughty St., London WC1N 2LF, England.

ABBEY, Merrill R. American, b. 1905. Theology/Religion. Prof. Emeritus, Garrett-Evangelical Theological Seminary, Evanston, Ill., since 1973 (James E. MacMurray Prof. of Preaching, 1959–73). Pastor, Methodist churches in Minn. and Wisc., 1931–46, First-Univ. Methodist Church, Madison, Wisc., 1946–53, and First Methodist Church, Ann Arbor, Mich., 1953–59. *Publs:* Creed of Our Hope, 1954; Encounter with Christ, 1961; Preaching to the Contemporary Mind, 1963; Living Doctrine in a Vital Pulpit, 1964; The Word Interprets Us, 1967; The Shape of the Gospel, 1970; Man, Media and the Message, 1970; Communication in Pulpit and Parish, 1973; (with O.C. Edwards) Proclamation: Epiphany, 1974; Day Dawns in Fire: America's Quest for Meaning, 1976; The Epic of United Methodist Preaching: A Profile in American Social History, 1984. Add: 1113 Elm Cove, Luverne, Minn. 56156, U.S.A.

ABBOTT, Alice. *See* **BORLAND,** Kathryn.

ABBOTT, George (Francis). American, b. 1887. Plays/Screenplays, Autobiography/Memoirs/Personal. Stage, film and television dir. Co-Founder, Abbott-Dunning Inc., 1931–34. *Publs:* (with W. Smith) A Holy Terror: A None-Too-Serious Drama, 1926; (with J.V.A. Weaver) Love 'em and Leave 'em, 1926; (with P. Dunning) Broadway, 1927; (with D. Burnett) Four Walls, 1928; (with J. Gleason) The Fall Guy, 1928; (with A.P. Bridgers) Coquette, 1928; (with J.C. Holm) Three Men on a Horse, 1935; (with Richard Bissell) The Pajama Game, 1954; (with D. Wallop) Damn Yankees, 1958; (adaptor) New Girl in Town, 1958; (with Jerome Weidman) Fiorello!, 1950; (with J. Weidman) Tenderloin, 1961; Mister Abbott (autobiography), 1963; (adaptor) Where's Charley?, 1965; Tryout (novel), 1979. Add: 1270 Ave. of the Americas, New York, N.Y. 10020, U.S.A.

ABBOTT, John Patrick. British, b. 1930. Air/Space topics, Genealogy/Heraldry. Headmaster, St. Paul's V.C.J.M. Sch., Shepton Mallet, since 1970. Formerly teaching in Birmingham, Wiltshire and Nottinghamshire. *Publs:* Family Patterns, 1971; Airship, 1973. Add: Linden Alhampton, nr. Shepton Mallet, Somerset, England.

ABBOTT, May Laura (née Cox). British, b. 1916. Animals/Pets, Environment, Recreation/Leisure/Hobbies. Freelance journalist and writer since 1961. Founder-Dir., M. Cox Literary Competition Agency, 1937–40; Reporter and Chief Reporter, Westminster Press, Bedford, 1942–46; with News Staff, Daily Telegraph, London, 1946–55; News and Features Ed., Woman's Sunday Mirror, London, 1956–61. *Publs:* Working with

Animals, 1962, 3rd ed. 1967; Me and the Bee: The Battles of a Bumbling Beekeeper, 1965; Careers in Art and Design, 1969; The Daily Telegraph 50th Anniversary Crossword Book, 1975; How to Do Crosswords Better, 1975, as How to Do Crosswords Faster, 1984. Add: 26 York Court, Albany Park Rd, Kingston-upon-Thames, Surrey KT2 5ST, England.

ABBOTT, R(obert) Tucker. American, b. 1919. Marine Science/Oceanography, Natural History. Pres., American Malacologists Inc., Melbourne, Fla. Ed., The Nautilus, since 1959, and Monographs of Marine Mollusca since 1978. *Publs:* American Seashells, 1954, 1974; Introducing Seashells, 1955; How to Know the American Seashells, 1961; (with G.L. Warmke) Caribbean Seashells, 1961; Seashells of the World, 1962; Seashells of North America, 1968; (with H. & M. Stix) The Shell, 1968; Kingdom of the Seashell, 1972; (with S. Sandved) Shells in Color, 1973; (with R.J.L. Wagner) Standard Catalog of Shells, 1978; (with S. Peter Dance) Compendium of Seashells, 1982; Collectible Florida Shells, 1984; Collectible Shells of the South east United States, Bahamas and Caribbean, 1984. Add: Box 2255, Melbourne, Fla. 32902, U.S.A.

a'BEAR, Howard. *See* **BOALCH,** Donald Howard.

ABEL, Reuben. American, b. 1911. Philosophy. Faculty member, New Sch. for Social Research, NYC, since 1950 (Chmn. of Humanities, 1965–84; Adjunct Prof., 1967–84; Assoc. Dean, 1972–74). *Publs:* The Pragmatic Humanism of F.C.S. Schiller, 1955; (ed.) Humanistic Pragmatism, 1966; Man is the Measure, 1976. Add: 17 Monroe Ave., Larchmont, N.Y. 10538, U.S.A.

ABEL-SMITH, Brian. British, b. 1926. Law, Medicine/Health, Public/Social administration. Prof. of Social Admin., London Sch. of Economics, since 1967. Adviser to Secty. of State for Social Services, 1968–70, 1974–79. *Publs:* (with R.M. Titmuss) The Cost of the National Health Service in England and Wales, 1956; A History of the Nursing Profession, 1960; (with R.M. Titmuss) Social Policy and Population Growth in Mauritius, 1961; The Hospitals 1800-1948, 1964; (with R.B. Stevens) In Search of Justice, 1968; (with H. Rose) Doctors, Patients and Pathology, 1972; (with M. Zander & R. Brooke) Legal Problems and the Citizen, 1973; People Without Choice, 1974; Value for Money in Health Services, 1976; Poverty Development and Health Policy, 1978; National Health Service: The First Thirty Years, 1978; (with P. Grandjeat) Pharmaceutical Consumption, 1978; (with A. Maynard) The Organization, Financing and Cost of Health Care in the European Community, 1979; Sharing Health Care Costs, 1979; Cost Containment in Health Care, 1984. Add: London Sch. of Economics, Houghton St., London WC2, England.

ABELSON, Raziel (Alter). American, b. 1921. Philosophy. Prof. of Philosophy, New York Univ., NYC, since 1955; Visiting Prof., Columbia Univ., 1962, Univ. of Hawaii, 1965, State Univ. of New York, Buffalo, 1967, and Univ. of California at San Diego, 1970; Visiting Scholar, Inst. of Advanced Studies in Behavioral Sciences, Stanford Univ., 1965. *Publs:* Ethics and Metaethics, 1963; (with Marie-Louise Friquegnon) Ethics for Modern Life, 1975, 3rd ed., 1986; Persons: A Study in Philosophical Psychology, 1977; (with Friquegnon) The Philosophical Imagination: An Introduction to Philosophy, 1977; Lawless Mind, 1988. Add: 110 Bleecker St., New York, N.Y. 10012, U.S.A.

ABISH, Walter. American, b. 1931. Novels/Short stories, Poetry. Lectr. in English and Comparative Literature, Columbia Univ., NYC, since 1979. Writer-in-Residence, Wheaton Coll., Norton, Mass., 1976; Visiting Butler Prof. of English, State Univ. of New York at Buffalo, 1977; Visiting Prof., Yale Univ., New Haven, CT, 1986. *Publs:* Duel Site (verse), 1970; Alphabetical Africa (novel), 1974; Minds Meet (short fictions), 1975; In the Future Perfect (short fictions), 1977; How German Is It (novel), 1980. Add: P.O. Box 485, Cooper Station, New York, N.Y. 10003, U.S.A.

ABLEMAN, Paul. British, b. 1927. Novels/Short stories, Plays/Screenplays, Poetry, Sex. *Publs:* (with Gertrude Macauley) Even His Enemy, 1948; I Hear Voices, 1958; As Near As I Can Get, 1962; Green Julia (play), 1966; Tests (playlets), 1966; Vac, 1968; Blue Comedy: Madly in Love, Hawk's Night, 1968; The Twilight of the Vilp, 1969; Bits: Some Prose Poems, 1969; The Mouth and Oral Sex, 1969, reissued in U.K. as The Mouth, and in U.S. as The Sensuous Mouth, 1972; Tornado Pratt, 1977; Shoestring (novelization of TV play), 1979; Porridge (novelization of screenplay), 1979; Shoestring's Finest Hour, 1980; County Hall (novelization of TV series), 1981; The Anatomy of Nakedness, 1982; The Doomed Rebellion, 1983. Add: Flat 36, Duncan House, Fellows Rd., London NW3, England.

ABRAHAM, Claude Kurt. American, b. 1931. Literature. Prof. of French, Univ. of California at Davis, since 1975. Faculty member, Univ. of Illinois, 1959–64; Prof. of French, Univ. of Florida, Gainesville, 1964–75. *Publs:* Gaston d'Orléans et sa Cour, 1963, 1964; (ed.) Bourgeois Gentilhomme, 1966; Strangers: The Tragic World of Tristan L'Hermite, 1966; (trans. with M. Abraham) J. Mesnard: Pascal, 1969; Enfin Malherbe, 1971 (SAMLA Studies Award); Corneille, 1972; (ed. with J. Schweitzer & J. van Baelen) Tristan L'Hermite: Théâtre Complet, 1974; J. Racine, 1977; Tristan L'Hermite, 1980; Norman Satirists of the Age of Louis XIII, 1983; Molière's Comédies—Ballets, 1984, 1985. Add: 1604 Westshore St., Davis, Calif. 95616, U.S.A.

ABRAHAM, (Sir) Edward (Penley). British, b. 1913. Medicine/Health. Emeritus Prof. of Chemical Pathology, Oxford Univ. Fellow of Lincoln Coll., Oxford, 1948–60, Hon. Fellow, 1961. *Publs:* (with others) Antibiotics, 1949; (co-author) General Pathology, 1957, 4th ed. 1970; Biochemistry of some Peptide and Steroid Antibiotics, 1957; Howard Walter Florey, 1971; (co-author) Cephalosporins and Penicillins, 1972; Biosynthesis and Enzymic Hydrolysis of Penicillins and Cephalosporins, 1974; Hamno Umezawa, 1979; Leonard Colebrook, 1981; Ernst Boris Chain, 1983. Add: Sir William Dunn Sch. of Pathology, Oxford, England.

ABRAHAM, Henry J. American, b. 1921. Civil liberties/Human rights, Law, Politics/Government. James Hart Prof. of Govt. and Foreign Affairs, Univ. of Virginia, Charlottesville, since 1971. Asst. Prof., 1953–57, Assoc. Prof., 1957–62, and Prof. of Political Science, 1962–72, Univ. of Pennsylvania, Philadelphia. *Publs:* Compulsory Voting, 1955; Government as Entrepreneur and Social Servant, 1956; Courts and Judges: An Introduction to the Judicial Process, 1959; (with J.A. Corry) Elements of Democratic Government, 4th ed. 1964; (with J.C. Phillips) Essentials of American National Government, 1971; Freedom and the Court: Civil Rights and Liberties in the United States, 4th ed., 1982, 5th ed., 1988; The Judiciary: The Supreme Court in the Governmental Process, 6th ed., 1983, 7th ed., 1987; Justices and Presidents: A Political History of Appointments to the Supreme Court, 1975, 1985; (with W.E. Keefe) American Democracy, 9th ed., 1989; The Judicial Process: An Introductory Analysis of the Courts of the United States, England, and France, 5th ed. 1986. Add: 906 Fendall Terr., Charlottesville, Va. 22903, U.S.A.

ABRAHAM, Willard. American, b. 1916. Education. Prof., Dept. of Special Education, Arizona State Univ., Tempe, since 1953. Consultant, Grolier Educational Services. Writer and Editor, Parent Talk, since 1973. Syndicated column, Our Children, since 1972. Newspaper column, Your Special Child, Arizona Republic, and Job Hunter, Chicago Times. Assoc. Prof. of Education, Roosevelt Univ., Chicago, 1946–53. *Publs:* Your Post-War Career, 1945; Get the Job!, 1946; A Guide for the Study of Exceptional Children, 1956; A New Look at Reading, 1957; Barbara: A Prologue, 1958; Common Sense About Gifted Children, 1958; The Slow Learner, 1964; A Time for Teaching, 1964; (ed.) The Preparation of BIA Teacher and Dormitory Aides, 1968; A Study of the Devereux Foundation, 1970; Living with Pre-Schoolers, 1976; (co-author) A Dictionary of Special Education Terms, 1980; You Always Lag One Child Behind, 1980. Add: Coll. of Education, Arizona State Univ., Tempe, Ariz. 85287, U.S.A.

ABRAHAM, Willie E. (William Emmanuel Abraham). Ghanaian, b. 1934. Philosophy, Social commentary/phenomena, Translations. Prof. of Philosophy, Univ. of California, Berkeley, since 1973. Sr. Research Fellow, Stanford Univ., Calif., since 1974. Member of faculty, Univ. of Liverpool, 1959–60; Fellow, All Souls Coll., Oxford, 1959–62; member of faculty, 1962–70, and former acting Vice-Chancellor, Univ. of Ghana, Legon; member, Presidential Commn. with powers of Pres. of the Republic, Ghana, 1965–66. *Publs:* The Mind of Africa, 1962; (co-author) Encounter, 1963; (trans.) A.W. Amo: Apatheia humanae mentis. Add: Dept. of Philosophy, Univ. of California, Berkeley, Calif. 94720, U.S.A.

ABRAHAMS, Peter. South African, b. 1919. Novels/Short stories, Documentaries/Reportage. Regular Contrib., The Observer, London, and The Herald Tribune, NYC and Paris, 1952–64; Ed., West Indian Economist, and Controller, West Indian News, Jamaica, 1955–64; Chmn., Radio Jamaica, 1977–80. *Publs:* Dark Testament (short stories), 1942; Song of the City, 1945; Mine Boy, 1946; The Path of Thunder, 1948; Wild Conquest, 1950; Return to Goli (reportage), 1953; Tell Freedom: Memories of Africa, 1954: A Wreath for Udomo, 1956; A Night of Their Own, 1965; This Island Now, 1966; The View from Coyaba, 1985; Hard Rain, 1988. Add: Red Hills, St. Andrew, Jamaica.

ABRAHAMS, Roger D(avid). American, b. 1933. Anthropology/Ethnology, Cultural/Ethnic topics, Language/Linguistics. Rosen Chair of Folklore and Humanities, Univ. of Pennsylvania, Philadelphia, since 1989 (Prof. of Folklore and Folklife, 1985–89). Prof. of English and Anthropology, 1969–79, and Chmn., Dept. of English, 1974–79, Univ. of Texas, Austin. Kenan Prof. of Humanities and Anthropology, Scripps and Pitzer Colleges, Claremont, 1979–85. *Publs:* Deep Down in the Jungle, 1964, rev. ed. 1970; (with G.W. Foss, Jr.) Anglo-American Folksong Style, 1968; (ed.) Jump Rope Rhymes: A Dictionary, 1968; Positively Black, 1970; (ed.) A Singer and Her Songs, 1970; (ed. with R.C. Troike) Language and Cultural Diversity in American Education, 1972; Deep the Water, Shallow the Shore, 1974; Talking Black, 1975; (ed. with J. Szwed) Afro-American Folk Culture: An Annotated Bibliography, 1977; Between the Living and the Dead: Riddles Which Tell Stories, 1980; (ed. with Lois Rankin) Counting Out Rhymes: A Dictionary, 1980; (ed. with Richard Bauman) And Other Neighborly Names, 1981; Performers, Performances and Enactments, 1983; (ed. with John Szwed) After Africa, 1983; (ed.) African Folktales, 1983; The Man-of-Words in the West Indies, 1983; (ed.) Afro-American Folktales, 1985. Add: Dept. of Folklore and Folklife, 415 Logan Hall, Univ. of Pennsylvania, Philadelphia, Pa. 19104, U.S.A.

ABRAMS, Alan. American, b. 1941; Canadian Landed Immigrant, since 1981. History, Biography, Documentation/Reportage. Special Writer, Detroit Jewish News, since 1983; Special Writer, 1980–85, and General Assignment Reporter, since 1985, The Windsor Star. Public Relations Dir., Motown Record Corp., Detroit, 1959–66; Owner, Al Abrams Assocs., Detroit, 1966–74; Public Relations Dir., 1974–76, Head of Journalism Dept. and Ed. of Contemporary Journalists, 1976–81, Gale Research Co., Detroit; Special Writer, Detroit Free Press, 1983–85, and the Toronto Globe and Mail, 1984–85. *Publs:* Media Personnel Guide, 1979; Journalist Biographies Master Index, 1979; The Fourth Estate, 1980; Why Windsor? An Anecdotal History of the Jews of Windsor and Essex County, 1981; Special Treatment: The Untold Story of the Survival of Jews in Hitler's Third Reich, 1985. Add: 3154 Longfellow Ave., Windsor, Ont. N9E 2L5, Canada.

ABRAMS, Linsey. American, b. 1951. Novels. Professor of fiction writing, Sarah Lawrence Coll., Bronxville, N.Y. (Member of faculty since 1980). *Publs:* Charting by the Stars, 1979; Double Vision, 1984. Add: Writing Dept., Sarah Lawrence Coll., Bronxville, N.Y. 10708, U.S.A.

ABRAMS, Mark. British, b. 1906. Politics/Government, Social sciences (general). Research Dir., Age Concern, since 1976. Managing Dir., then Chmn., Research Services Ltd., 1946–70; Dir. of Survey Unit, Social Science Research Council, London, 1970–76. *Publs:* The Home Market, 1936, 3rd ed. 1950; (co-author) When We Build Again: Survey of Housing Conditions in Birmingham, 1941: The Population of Great Britain, 1945; The Condition of the British People 1911–1945, 1946; (ed.) Britain and Her Export Trade, 1947; Social Surveys and Social Action, 1951; (with R. Rose) Must Labour Lose?, 1960; Beyond Three Score and Ten, 1978; (with D. Gerard and N. Timms) Values and Social Change, 1985; The Elderly Shopper, 1986. Add: 12 Pelham Sq., Brighton, Sussex BN1 4ET, England.

ABRAMS, M(eyer) H(oward). American, b. 1912. Literature. Class of 1916 Prof. Emeritus, Cornell Univ., Ithaca, N.Y. (Asst. Prof., 1945–47, Assoc. Prof., 1947–53, Prof., 1953–60, and Frederic J. Whiton Prof., 1960–63). Advisory Ed., W.W. Norton and Co. Inc. (publishers), NYC, since 1961; Member, Council of Scholars, Library of Congress, since 1980. Instr., 1938–42, and Research Assoc., Psycho-Acoustic Lab., 1942–45, Harvard Univ., Cambridge, Mass.; Fulbright Lectr., Royal Univ. of Malta and Cambridge Univ., 1953; Roache Lectr., Univ. Of Indiana, Bloomington, 1963; Alexander Lectr., Univ. of Toronto, 1964; Ewing Lectr., Univ. of California at Los Angeles, 1974. *Publs:* The Milk of Paradise: The Effect of Opium Visions on the Works of DeQuincey, Crabbe, Francis Thompson and Coleridge, 1934, 1970; The Mirror and the Lamp: Romantic Theory and the Critical Tradition, 1953; A Glossary of Literary Terms, 1957, 1987; (ed.) Literature and belief, 1958; (ed.) The Poetry of Pope, 1958; (ed.) English Romantic Poets: Modern Essays in Criticism, 1960, 1975; (ed.) The Norton Anthology of English Literature, 1962, 1986; Natural Supernaturalism: Tradition and Revolution in Romantic Literature, 1971; (ed.) Wordsworth: A Collection of Critical Essays, 1972; (ed. with others) Wordsworth's Prelude 1799–1850, 1979; The Correspondent Breeze: Essays in English Romanticism, 1984, 1986. Add: 512 Highland Rd., Ithaca, N.Y. 14850, U.S.A.

ABRAMS, Richard M. American, b. 1932. History, International relations/Current affairs. Prof. of History, Univ. of California, Berkeley, since 1970 (Instr., 1961–62; Asst. Prof., 1962–66; Assoc. Prof., 1966–70).

Instr. in History, Columbia Univ., NYC, 1957–60. *Publs:* The Issue of Federal Regulation in the Progressive Era, 1963; Conservatism in a Progressive Era, 1964; (with L.W. Levine) The Shaping of 20th Century America, 1967, 1972; (co-author) The Unfinished Century, 1973; The Burdens of Progress, 1978. Add: Dept. of History, Univ. of California, Berkeley, Calif. 94720, U.S.A.

ABSALOM, Roger Neil Lewis. British, b. 1929. International relations/Current affairs, Language/Linguistics. Reader in Modern Languages, Sheffield City Polytechnic. Teacher of English, English Inst. of Naples, and British Council Sch., Milan, 1956–60; Sr. Lectr., 1966–70, and Principal Lectr. in Italian, 1970–73, Cambridgeshire Coll. of Arts and Technology. *Publs:* Modern English, 1958; Italian Phrase Book, 1960; 'A' Level French, 1965; (ed.) Passages for Translation from Italian, 1967; 'A' Level Italian, 1968; Mussolini and the Rise of Italian Fascism, 1969; (ed.) France, 1968; The May Events, 1970; (ed. with S. Potesta) Advanced Italian, 1970; Comprehension of Spoken Italian, 1978; Gli alleati e la ricostruzione in Toscana, 1988. Add: 5 The Mill, Edale, nr. Sheffield S30 2ZE, England.

ABSE, Dannie. British, b. 1923. Novels/Short stories, Plays/Screenplays, Poetry, Autobiography/Memoirs/Personal. Specialist in charge of Chest Clinic, Central London Medical Establishment, since 1954. Pres., Poetry Soc., London, since 1978. Visiting Writer-in-Residence, Princeton Univ., N.J., 1973–74. *Publs:* After Every Green Thing, 1949; Walking Under Water, 1952; Ash on a Young Man's Sleeve (novel), 1954; Some Corner of an English Field (novel), 1956; Fire in Heaven, 1956; Tenants of the House, 1957; (ed. with H. Sergeant) Mavericks, 1957; The Eccentric, 1961; Poems, Golders Green, 1962; Dannie Abse: A Selection, 1963; Is the House Shut?, 1964; (ed.) European Verse, 1964; Medicine on Trial, 1967; Three Quester Plays, 1967; A Small Desperation, 1968; The Dogs of Pavlov, 1969; Demo, 1969; O. Jones, O. Jones (novel), 1970; Selected Poems, 1970; Funland, 1973; A Poet in the Family (autobiography), 1974; (with D.J. Enright & M. Langley) Penguin Modern Poets No. 2, 1974; (ed.) Poetry Dimension 2, 1974; (ed.) Poetry Dimension Annual 3, 1975; Poetry Dimension Annual 4, 1976; Pythagoras (play), 1976; Poetry Dimension Annual 5, 1977; Collected Poems 1948–1976, 1977; Gone in January, 1978; Way Out in the Centre, 1981; Miscellany One, 1981; A Strong Dose of Myself, 1983; Ask the Bloody Horse (poems), 1986; Journals from the Ant-Heap, 1986; (ed. with J. Abse) Voices in the Gallery, 1986; (ed. with J. Abse) The Music Lover's Literary Companion, 1988; White Coat, Purple Coat: Collected Poems 1948–88, 1989. Add: 85 Hodford Rd., London NW11, England.

ABSE, David Wilfred. American, b. 1915. Psychiatry, Psychology. Prof. Emeritus, Univ. of Virginia, Charlottesville, since 1987 (Prof. of Psychiatry, 1962–87). Faculty Member, Washington Psychoanalytic Inst., Washington, D.C. since 1962, and Washington Sch. of Psychiatry (Group Psychotherapy Prog.) since 1971. Pres., Virginia Psychoanalytic Soc., since 1978. Assoc. Prof. of Psychiatry, and Dir., In-Patient Service, 1957–59, and Prof. of Psychiatry, 1959–62, Univ. of North Carolina, Chapel Hill. *Publs:* The Diagnosis of Hysteria, 1950; (co-ed. with Nash & Jessner) Marriage Counseling in Medical Practice, 1964; Hysteria and Related Mental Disorders, 1966, 2nd ed., 1987; Speech and Reason: Language Disorder in Mental Disease, 1971; (co-ed. with Nash and Louden) Marital and Sexual Counseling in Medical Practice, 2nd ed. 1974; Clinical Notes on Group Analytic Psychotherapy, 1974. Add: 1852 Winston Rd., Charlottesville, Va. 22903, U.S.A.

ABSHIRE, David Manker. American, b. 1926. International Relations, Politics. Permanent U.S. Representative to NATO, since 1983. Pres. 1982–83 and since 1988, Exec. Dir., 1962–70, and Chmn., 1973–82, Center for Strategic and Intnl. Studies, Georgetown Univ., Washington, D.C.; Asst. Secty. of State for Congressional Relations, 1970–73. Member, Congressional Cttee. on the Organization of Government for the Conduct of Foreign Policy, 1973–75; Chmn., U.S. Bd. for Intnl. Broadcasting, 1974–77; Dir., National Security Group, Transition Office of Pres.-Elect Reagan, 1980–81. *Publs:* (ed.) National Security, 1963; (with others) Detente, 1965; The South Rejects a Prophet: The Life of Senator D.M. Key, 1967; (ed.) Portuguese Africa, 1969; Research Resources for the Seventies, 1971; International Broadcasting: A New Dimension of Western Diplomacy, 1976; Vietnam Legacy, 1976; (ed.) Egypt and Israel: Prospects for a New Era, 1979; Foreign Policy Makers: President vs. Congress, 1981; Preventing WWIII: A Realistic Grand Strategy, 1988. Add: Ctr. Strategic & Intl. Studies, Suit 1014, 1800 K St., NW Washington D.C.

ABZUG, Robert Henry. American, b. 1945. History. Assoc. Prof. of History, Univ. of Texas at Austin, since 1984 (Asst. Prof., 1978–84).

Instr. in History, Univ. of California, Berkeley, 1976–77; Lectr. in History, Univ. of California at Los Angeles, 1977–78. Trustee, Carver Museum of Black History, 1981–83. *Publs:* Passionate Liberator: Theodore Dwight Weld and the Dilemma of Reform, 1980; Inside the Vicious Heart: Americans and the Liberation of the Nazi Concentration Camps, 1985; (ed. with Stephen Maizlish) New Perspectives on Race and Slavery in America, 1986. Add: Dept. of History, Univ. of Texas, Austin, Tex. 78712, U.S.A.

ACHEBE, Chinua. Nigerian, b. 1930. Novels/Short stories, Children's fiction, Poetry, Essays. Emeritus Prof., Univ. of Nigeria, Nsukka, since 1985 (Prof. of English, 1976–81; Sr. Research Fellow, 1967–72). Dir., Heinemann Educational Books (Nigeria) Ltd., and Nwamife & Co. (Publrs.) Ltd., Enugu, since 1970; Ed., Okike, Nigerian Journal of New Writing, since 1971. Talks Producer, Lagos, 1954–57, Controller, Enugu, 1958–61, and Dir., Lagos, 1961–66, Nigerian Broadcasting Corp.; Prof. of English, Univ. of Massachusetts, Amherst, 1972–75; Prof. of African Studies, Univ. of Connecticut, Storrs, 1987–88. Pro-Chancellor and Chairman of Council, Anambra State Univ. of Technology, Enugu, 1986–88. *Publs:* Things Fall Apart, 1958; No Longer at Ease, 1960; The Sacrificial Egg and Other Stories, 1962; Arrow of God, 1964; A Man of the People, 1966; Chike and the River, 1966; Beware Soul-Brother and Other Poems, 1971; Girls at War, 1972; How the Leopard Got His Claws, 1972; Morning Yet on Creation Day, 1975; The Flute, 1977; The Drum, 1977; (co-ed.) Don't Let Him Die, 1978; The Trouble with Nigeria, 1983; Anthills of the Savannah, 1987; Hopes and Impediments (essays), 1987; Nigerian Topics, 1989. Add: Univ. of Nigeria, P.O. Box 53, Nsukka, Nigeria.

ACKAH, Christian Abraham. Ghanaian, b. 1908. Geography, Philosophy. Asst. Master, Adisadel Coll., Cape Coast, 1926–36; Accountant, Ghana Govt. Treasury, 1937–51; Headmaster, Ghana National Coll., 1953–56; Supvr., Ghana Students in U.K. and Ireland, 1956–59; Principal, University Coll., Cape Coast, 1962–64, 1966–68. *Publs:* West Africa: A General Certificate Geography, 1959, 3rd ed. 1973; Akan Ethics, 1988. Add: Baffoa Lodge, P.O. Box 264, Cape Coast, Ghana.

ACKERMAN, Diane. American, b. 1948. Poetry. Freelance writer and journalist. Staff writer, The New Yorker, since 1988. Dir., Writer's Prog., Washington Univ., St. Louis, 1984–86. Visiting writer, Columbia Univ., New York, and Cornell Univ., Ithaca, N.Y., 1987. *Publs:* verse—The Planets: A Cosmic Pastoral, 1976; Wife of Light, 1978; Lady Faustus, 1983; Reverse Thunder, 1988; other—Twilight of the Tenderfoot: A Western Memoir, 1980; On Extended Wings, 1985, 1987. Add: c/o Janklow and Nesbitt, 598 Madison Ave., New York, N.Y. 10022, U.S.A.

ACKLAND, Rodney. British, b. 1908. Plays/Screenplays, Autobiography/Memoirs/Personal. Writer, actor and director. *Publs:* Improper People, 1930; Strange Orchestra, 1932; Dance with No Music, 1933; Birthday, 1935; The Old Ladies (adaptation of novel by Hugh Walpole), 1935; After October, 1936; The Dark River, 1942; The Diary of a Scoundrel (adaptation of play by A.N. Ostrovsky), 1948; Crime and Punishment (adaptation of novel by Dostoevsky), 1948; Before the Party (adaptation of story by W. Somerset Maugham), 1950; (with Elspeth Grant) The Celluloid Mistress; or, The Custard Pie of Dr. Caligari (autobiography), 1954; A Dead Secret, 1958; Farewell, Farewell, Eugene (adaptation of work by John Vari), 1960. Add: c/o Eric Glass Ltd., 28 Berkeley Sq., London W1X 8HD, England.

ACKLEY, Randall William. American, b. 1931. Poetry. Cultural/Ethnic topics. Teacher, Univ. of Alaska, Juneau, since 1977. Member of faculty, Univ. of Minnesota, Minneapolis, 1961–62, Univ. of Texas, Austin, 1965–66, and Univ. of Utah, 1966–67; Ed., Quetzal, QV Press, 1970–72. Dir., Southwest Poets Conference, 1969–75; Chmn., Assn. for Studies in American Indian Literatures, 1973–77. *Publs:* Troll Songs, 1971; Lord of All Dreams, 1974; Troll Erotica, Etc., 1975. Add: Univ. of Alaska, 11120 Glacier Highway, Juneau, Alaska 99803, U.S.A.

ACKRILL, John L(loyd). British, b. 1921. Philosophy. Prof. of the History of Philosophy, Oxford Univ., since 1966 (Univ. Lectr., 1951–52; Fellow and Tutor, Brasenose Coll., 1953–66). Asst. Lectr., Glasgow Univ., 1948–49; Visiting Prof., Princeton Univ., 1955, 1974. *Publs:* (trans.) Categories and De Interpretatione by Aristotle, 1963; Aristotle's Ethics, 1973; Aristotle the Philosopher, 1981; New Aristotle Reader, 1987. Add: 22 Charlbury Rd., Oxford, England.

ACKROYD, Joyce Irene. Australian. International relations/Current Affairs, Travel/Exploration/Adventure. Prof. and Head, Dept. of Japanese Language and Literature, Univ. of Queensland, 1965–83, now

Emerita. *Publs:* The Unknown Japanese, 1967; Japan Today, 1970; Discovering Japan, 1972; Your Journey into Japan, 1973; Told Round a Brushwood Fire, 1979; Lessons from History, 1982. Add: Vanwall Rd., Moggill, Qld., 4070, Australia.

ACKROYD, Peter. British, b. 1949. Novels, Poetry, Literature, Social Commentary. Chief Book Reviewer, The Times, London, since 1986. Literary Ed., The Spectator, London, 1973–77; television critic, The Times, London, 1977–81. *Publs:* London Lickpenny (poetry), 1973; Notes for a New Culture: An Essay on Modernism, 1976; Country Life (poetry), 1978; Dressing up: Transvestism and Drag: The History of an Obsession, 1979; Ezra Pound and His World, 1981; The Great Fire of London (novel), 1982; The Last Testament of Oscar Wilde (novel), 1983; T.S. Eliot, 1984; Hawksmoor (novel), 1985; Chatterton (novel), 1987; The Diversions of Purley (poetry), 1987; First Light (novel), 1989. Add: c/o Anthony Sheil Assocs. Ltd., 43 Doughty St., London WC1N 2LF, England.

ACKROYD, Peter (Runham). British, b. 1917. Theology/Religion. Samuel Davidson Prof. of Old Testament Studies 1961–82, Prof. Emeritus, 1982, and Fellow of King's Coll. since 1969, Univ. of London (Dean, Faculty of Theology, King's Coll., 1968–69). Minister, Roydon Congregational Church, Essex, 1943–47, and Balham Congregational Church, London, 1947–48; Lectr. in Old Testament and Biblical Hebrew, Univ. of Leeds, Yorks., 1948–52; Lectr. in Divinity, Cambridge Univ., 1952–61. Ordained Anglican priest, 1958. Pres., Soc. for Old Testament Study, 1972. *Publs:* Freedom in Action, 1951; The People of the Old Testament, 1959; Continuity, 1962; The Old Testament Tradition, 1963; Exile and Restoration, 1968; (ed.) Words and Meanings, 1968; (ed.) The Cambridge History of the Bible, 1970; Israel Under Babylon and Persia, 1970 (New Clarendon Bible); The Age of the Chronicler, 1970; I Samuel (Cambridge Bible Commentary), 1971; I and II Chronicles, Ezra, Nehemiah (Torch Bible Commentaries), 1973; II Samuel (Cambridge Bible Commentary), 1977; Doors of Perception, 1978, 1983; Studies in the Religious Tradition of the Old Testament, 1987. Add: Lavender Cottage, Middleton, Suffolk IP17 3NQ, England.

ACLAND, Alice. Also writes as Anne Marreco. British, b. 1912. Novels/Short stories, Historical/Romance/Gothic, Biography. Freelance writer. *Publs:* Caroline Norton, 1948; Templeford Park, 1954; A Stormy Spring, 1955; A Second Choice, 1956; A Person of Discretion, 1958; (as Anne Marreco) The Charmer and the Charmed, 1963; (as Anne Marreco) The Boat Boy, 1964; (as Anne Marreco) The Rebel Countess, 1967; The Corsican Ladies, 1974; The Secret Wife, 1975; The Ruling Passion, 1976. Add: c/o Curtis Brown Ltd., 162-168 Regent St., London W1, England.

ACORN, Milton. Canadian, b. 1923. Poetry. Freelance writer. Co-Ed., Momemt mag., 1960–62. *Publs:* In Love and Anger, 1957; The Brain's the Target, 1960; Against a League of Liars, 1960; Jawbreakers, 1963; I've Tasted My Blood: Poems 1956 to 1968, 1969; I Shout Love and Shaving Off His Beard, 1971; More Poems for People, 1972; Jackpine Sonnets, 1977; Captain MacDougal and the Naked Goddess, 1982; Dig Up My Heart: Selected Poems 1952–1983, 1983. Add: c/o McClelland and Stewart Ltd., 25 Hollinger Rd., Toronto, Ont. M4B 3G2, Canada.

ACTON, (Sir) Harold (Mario). British, b. 1904. Novels/Short stories, History, Biography. Vice-Chmn., The British Inst. of Florence. *Publs:* Aquarium, 1923; An Indian Ass, 1925; Five Saints and an Appendix, 1927; Humdrum, 1928; Cornelian, 1928; This Chaos, 1930; The Last Medici, 1932, 1958; (ed.) Modern Chinese Poetry, 1936; (ed.) Famous Chinese Plays, 1937; Peonies and Ponies, 1941; Glue and Lacquer, 1941, as Four Cautionary Tales, 1947; Memoirs of an Aesthete, 1948; Prince Isidore, 1950; The Bourbons of Naples, 1956; The Last Bourbons of Naples, 1961; Florence, 1961; Old Lamps for New, 1965; More Memoirs of an Aesthete, 1970; Tit for Tat, 1972; Tuscan Villas, 1973; Nancy Mitford, 1975; The Pazzi Conspiracy, 1979; The Soul's Gymnasium, 1982; Three Extraordinary Ambassadors, 1983; Florence: A Traveller's Companion, 1986. Add: Villa la Pietra, Florence, Italy.

ADAIR, Ian (Hugh). British, b. 1942. Crafts, Recreation/Leisure/Hobbies. Writer and Partner, Supreme Magic Co., Devon; Pres., Ideas Associated. Former television announcer and presenter, STV, and Westward Television, both U.K. *Publs:* Adair's Ideas, 1958; Magic with Doves, 1958; Dove Magic, Parts 1 & 2, 1959; Dove Magic Finale, 1960; Ideen, 1960; Television Dove Magic, 1961; Television Card Manipulations, 1962; Television Puppet Magic, 1963; Doves in Magic, 1964; Doves from Silks, 1964; New Doves from Silks, 1964; Dove Classics, 1964; More Modern Dove Classics, 1964; Further Dove Classics, 1964; Classical Dove Secrets, 1964; Diary of a Dove Worker, 1964; Magic on the

Wing, 1965; Balloon-o-Dove, 1965; Spotlite on Doves, 1965; Watch the Birdie, 1965; Dove Dexterity, 1965; Rainbow Dove Routines, 1965; Heads Off!, 1965; Tricks and Stunts with a Rubber Dove, 1965; Television Dove Steals, 1965; La Zombie, 1966; Pot Pourri, 1966; Magical Menu (3 vols.), 1967; Encyclopedia of Dove Magic, vols. 1 & 2, 1968, vol. 3, 1973, vol. 4, 1977, vol. 5, 1980; Magic with Latex Budgies, 1969; Paddle Antics, 1969; Conjuring as a Craft, 1970; Magic Step by Step, 1970; Party Planning and Entertainment, 1972; Oceans of Notions, 1973; Papercraft Step by Step, 1975; Card Tricks, 1975; Glove Puppetry, 1975; The Know How Book of Jokes and Tricks, 1977; Complete Party Planner, 1978; Complete Guide to Conjuring, 1978; Magic, 1979; Complete Guide to Card Conjuring, 1980; Swindles: The Cheating Game, 1980. Add: 20 Ashley Terr., Bideford, Devon, England.

ADAIR, James R(adford). American, b. 1923. Theology/Religion, Autobiography/Memoirs/Personal, Biography. Ed., Pacific Garden Mission News, since 1949; Sr. Ed., Victor Books Div., Scripture Press Publications Inc., Wheaton, since 1970 (Ed., Power for Living, Free Way, Teen Power and Counselor weekly churchpapers, 1949–77). *Publs:* Saints Alive, 1951; (ed.) God's Power Within, 1961; (ed. with T. Miller) We Found Our Way, 1964; (ed.) Teen with a Future, 1965; (ed.) God's Power to Triumph, 1965; The Old Lighthouse, 1966; The Man from Steamtown, 1967, 1988; (ed.) Tom Skinner, Top Man of the Lords and Other Stories, 1967; M.R. DeHaan: The Man and His Ministry, 1969; (ed.) Hooked on Jesus, 1971; (ed.) Unhooked, 1971; (ed.) Brothers Black, 1973; Surgeon on Safari, 1976, 1985; (ed. with Ted Miller) Escape from Darkness, 1982. Add: 703 Webster Ave., Wheaton, Ill. 60187, U.S.A.

ADAIR, John (Eric). British, b. 1934. Business/Trade/Industry, History, Biography. Freelance writer, lectr. and organisational consultant. Dir. of Studies, St. George's House, Windsor Castle, since 1968. Former Sr. Lectr., Royal Military Academy Sandhurst; Assoc. Dir., The Industrial Soc., 1969–73. *Publs:* (with P. Young) Hastings to Culloden, 1964; Training for Leadership, 1968; Roundhead General: The Life of Sir William Walker, 1969; Training for Decisions, 1971, 1978; Training for Communication, 1973; Action-Centered Leadership, 1973; Cheriton, 1644: The Campaign and the Battle, 1973; Management and Morality: The Problems and Opportunities of Social Capitalism, 1974; John Hampden, 1976; The Pilgrim's Way: Shrines & Saints in Britain and Ireland, 1978; Founding Fathers: The Puritans in England and America, 1982; Effective Leadership, 1983; The Skills of Leadership, 1984; Management Decision Making, 1985; Effective Teambuilding, 1986. Add: 1 Crockford Park Rd., Addlestone, Surrey, England.

ADAM, Helen (Douglas). American (b. British), b. 1909. Plays/Screenplays, Poetry. *Publs:* The Elfin Pedlar and Tales Told by Pixy Pool, 1923; Charms and Dreams from the Elfin Pedlar's Pack, 1924; Shadow of the Moon, 1929; The Queen o' Crow Castle, 1958; (with Pat Adam) San Francisco's Burning (play), 1963; Ballads, 1964; Counting-Out Rhyme, 1972; Selected Poems and Ballads, 1974; Ghosts and Grinning Shadows (short stories), 1977; Turn Again to Me and Other Poems, 1977; Gone Sailing, 1980; Songs with Music, 1982; The Bells of Dis, 1984; (with Auste Adam) Stone Cold Gothic, 1984. Add: 223 E. 82nd St., New York, N.Y. 10028, U.S.A.

ADAMEC, Ludwig W. American, b. 1924. Geography, History, International relations/Current affairs. Dir., Near Eastern Center, Univ. of Arizona, Tucson (Prof. since 1967). U.S. Ed., Afghanistan Journal, since 1973. *Publs:* Afghanistan 1900–1923: A Diplomatic History, 1967; (ed.) Afghanistan: Some New Approaches, 1969; Tarikh-e Ravabet-e Siya-si-ye Afghanistan az Zaman-e Amir Abdur Rahman ta Isteqlal, 1970; (ed.) Political and Historical Gazetteer of Afghanistan (6 vols.), 1972–74; Who is Who of Afghanistan, 1974; Afghanistan's Foreign Affairs in the 20th Century: Relations with the U.S.S.R., Germany, and Britain, 1974; Historical Gazetteer of Iran (4 vols.), 1976–88; Biographical Dictionary of Contemporary Afghanistan, 1987. Add: 3931 E. Whittier, Tucson, Ariz. 85711, U.S.A.

ADAMS, Alice. American, b. 1926. Novels/Short stories. *Publs:* Careless Love (in U.K. as The Fall of Daisy Duke), 1966; Families and Survivors, 1975; Listening to Billie, 1978; Beautiful Girl (short stories), 1979; Rich Rewards, 1980; Superior Women, 1984; Second Chances, 1988. Add: 2661 Clay St., San Francisco, Calif. 94115, U.S.A.

ADAMS, Bart. *See* **BINGLEY,** David Ernest.

ADAMS, Chuck. *See* **TUBB,** E.C.

ADAMS, Clifton. Also writes as Jonathan Gant, Matt Kinkaid, and Clay Randall. American, b. 1919. Mystery/Crime/Suspense, Westerns/Adventure. Professional jazz drummer, then freelance writer. *Publs:* western novels—The Desperado, 1950; A Noose for the Desperado, 1951; (as Clay Randall) Six-Gun Boss, 1952; The Colonel's Lady, 1952; (as Clay Randall) When Oil Ran Red, 1953; Two-Gun Law, 1954; Gambling Man, 1955; Law of the Trigger, 1956; Outlaw's Son, 1957; (as Clay Randall) Boomer, 1957; Killer in Town, 1959; Stranger in Town, 1960; The Legend of Lonnie Hall, 1960; Day of the Gun, 1962; Reckless Men, 1962; The Moonlight War, 1963; Hogan's Way, 1963; The Dangerous Days of Kiowa Jones, 1963; (as Clay Randall) The Oceola Kid, 1963; (as Clay Randall) Hardcase for Hire, 1963; (as Clay Randall) Amos Flagg series, 6 vols., 1963–69; Doomsday Creek, 1964; The Hottest Fourth of July in the History of Hangtree County, 1964, in U.K. as The Hottest Fourth of July, 1965; The Grabhorn Bounty, 1965; Shorty, 1966; A Partnership with Death, 1967; The Most Dangerous Profession, 1967; Dude Sheriff, 1969; Tragg's Choice, 1969; The Last Days of Wolf Garnett, 1970, in U.K. as Outlaw Destiny, 1972; Biscuit-Shooter, 1971; Rogue Cowboy, 1971; The Badge and Harry Cole, 1972, in U.K. as Lawman's Badge, 1973; Concannon, 1972; Hard Times and Arnie Smith, 1972; Once an Outlaw, 1973; The Hard Time Bunch, 1973; Hassle and the Medicine Man, 1973; crime novels—Whom Gods Destroy, 1953; (as Matt Kinkaid) Hardcase, 1953; Death's Sweet Song, 1955; (as Matt Kinkaid) The Race of Giants, 1956; (as Jonathan Gant) Never Say No to a Killer, 1956; The Very Wicked, 1960; (as Jonathan Gant) The Long Vendetta, 1963. Add: c/o Ace Books, Berkeley Publishing Group, 200 Madison Ave., New York, N.Y. 10016, U.S.A.

ADAMS, Don. American, b. 1925, Education. Prof. of Economic and Social Development since 1969, and Prof. of Educational Planning, Univ. of Pittsburgh, Pa. Asst. Prof. of Education, George Peabody Coll., Nashville, Tenn., 1958–61; Prof. of Education, Dir. of Center for Development Education, and Chmn., Cultural Foundns. of Education, Syracuse Univ., N.Y., 1961–69; Pres., Comparative Education Soc., 1965–66. *Publs:* (with I.N. Thut) Patterns of Education in Contemporary Societies, 1964 (National Book Award); (ed.) Educational Planning, 1965; (ed.) Introduction to Education: A Comparative Analysis, 1966; (with Robert M. Bjork) Education in Developing Areas, 1969 (National Book Award); Education and Modernization in Asia: A Systems Analysis, 1970; (ed.). Education and National Development, 1971; Education and Social Change in Modern America, 1972. Add: Intnl. & Devel. Edn. Prog., Univ. of Pittsburgh, 5AOI Forbes Quadrangle, Pittsburgh, Pa. 15260, U.S.A.

ADAMS, Douglas (Noel). British b. 1952. Novels/Short stories, Science Fiction Plays/Screenplays. Radio Producer, BBC, London, 1978; Script Ed., Doctor Who, BBC-TV, London, 1978–80. *Publs:* The Hitch Hiker's Guide to the Galaxy (radio series), 1978, novel, 1979; The Restaurant at the End of the Universe, 1980; Life, The Universe and Everything, 1982; (with John Lloyd) The Meaning of Life, 1983; So Long, and Thanks for All the Fish, 1985; (ed.) The Utterly Utterly Merry, 1986; (co-author) Comic Relief Christmas Book, 1986; Dirk Gently's Holistic Detective Agency, 1987; The Long Dark Tea-Time of the Soul, 1988. Add: c/o Ed Victor Ltd., 162 Wardour St., London W1, England.

ADAMS, Ernest Charles. British, b. 1926. Technology. Materials Testing and Concrete Engineer, George Wimpey & Co. Ltd., London, 1953–59; Lectr., Crawley Coll. of Further Education, 1959–71; Lectr., then Sr. Lectr., Leeds Polytechnic, 1971–84. *Publs:* Science in Building (3 vols.), 1964; Fundamentals of Building Science, 1980. Add: 10 Kenworthy Vale, Holt Park, Adel, Leeds LS16 7QG, England.

ADAMS, Hazard. American, b. 1926. Novels, Literature. Lockwood Prof. of Humanities in English and Comparative Literature, Univ. of Washington, Seattle, (Prof. since 1977). Instr., Cornell Univ., Ithaca, N.Y., 1952–56; Asst. Prof., Univ. of Texas, 1956–59; Assoc. Prof., and Prof., Michigan State Univ., East Lansing, 1959–64; Prof. of English, 1964–74, Chmn. of the Dept. of English, 1964–69, Dean of the Sch. of Humanities, 1970–72, and Vice-Chancellor for Academic Affairs, 1972–74, Univ. of California at Irvine. *Publs:* (ed.) Poems by Robert Simeon Adams, 1952; Blake and Yeats, 1955; William Blake: A Reading, 1963; The Contexts of Poetry, 1963; (ed.) Poetry: An Introductory Anthology, 1968; (ed.) Fiction as Process, 1968; The Horses of Instruction (novel), 1968; The Interests of Criticism, 1969; (ed.) William Blake, 1970; The Truth About Dragons (novel), 1971; (ed.) Critical Theory since Plato, 1972; Lady Gregory, 1973; The Academic Tribes, 1976; Philosophy of the Literary Symbolic, 1983; Joyce Cary's Trilogies, 1983; (ed.) Critical Theory since 1965, 1986; The Book of Yeats's Poems, 1989; Antithetical Essays, 1989. Add: 3930 N.E. 157th Pl., Seattle, Wash. 98155, U.S.A.

ADAMS, James F(rederick). American, b. 1927. Psychology. Asst.

Prof. of Psychology, Whitworth Coll., Spokane, Wash., 1952–55; Research Assoc., Experimental Study in Instructional Procedures, Miami Univ., Oxford, Ohio, 1957–59; Prof. of Psychology, 1959–80, Chmn. of Counseling Psychology, 1973–80, and Coordinator, Div. of Educational Psychology, 1974–80, Temple Univ., Philadelphia; Prof. of Psychology, and Dean of Grad. Sch., Univ. of Nevada, Las Vegas, 1980–85; Sr. Vice Pres. (Academic), Longwood Coll., Farmville, Va., 1985–86. *Publs:* Problems in Counseling, 1962; (ed.) Counseling and Guidance: A Summary View, 1965; (ed.) Understanding Adolescence, 1968, 4th ed. 1980; (ed.) The Philosophy of Human Nature, by Joseph Buchanan, 1972; (ed.) Human Behavior in a Changing Society, 1973; (ed.) Songs That Had to Be Sung, by B.N. Adams, 1979. Add: Rt. 1, Box 143, Cumberland, Va. 23040, U.S.A.

ADAMS, John Frank. British, b. 1930. Mathematics. Fellow of Trinity Coll., and Lowndean Prof. of Astronomy and Geometry, Cambridge Univ., since 1970. Jr. Lectr., Oxford Univ., 1955–56; Research Fellow, Trinity Coll., 1955–58, Dir. of Studies in Mathematics, Trinity Hall, 1958–61, and Asst. Lecturer, 1958–61, Cambridge Univ.; Reader, 1962–64, and Fielden Prof. of Pure Mathematics, Manchester Univ., 1964–71. *Publs:* Stable Homotopy Theory, 1964; Lectures on Lie Groups, 1969; Algebraic Topology, 1972; Stable Homotopy and Generalised Homology, 1974; Infinite Loop Spaces, 1978. Add: 7 Westmeare, Hemingford Grey, Huntingdon PE18 9BZ, England.

ADAMS, Julian. American, b. 1919. Writing/Journalism. Freelance writer. Personnel and Admin., Mare Island Navy Yard, 1940–48; Teacher and Counselor, Richmond Schs., Calif., 1950–74. *Publs:* Press Time, 1963, 4th ed. 1985; Student Journalist and Mass Communication, 1980; Freedom and Ethics in the Press, 1982. Add: 52 El Camino Real, Berkeley, Calif. 94705, U.S.A.

ADAMS, Justin. *See* **CAMERON,** Lou.

ADAMS, Kenneth Menzies. Australian, b. 1922. History. Retired from the Victoria Education Dept., 1983 (with Box Hill High Sch., 1949–51, Wangaratta High Sch., 1952–61, Mitcham High Sch., 1962–67, Nunawading High Sch., 1968–73, and Hallam High Sch., 1974–77; Principal, Doveton High Sch., 1977–82). *Publs:* Seeing History: Book 1, The First Australians, 1968, Book 2, Gaol to Colony, 1968, Book 3, Colonies to Commonwealth, 1971, Book 4, Twentieth Century Australia, 1972. Add: 20 Leoni Ave., Heathmont, Vic. 3135, Australia.

ADAMS, Laurie. American, b. 1941. Art. Prof. of Art History, John Jay Coll., City Univ. of New York. Psychoanalyst in private practice. Ed., Source: Notes in the History of Art. *Publs:* Art Cop, 1974; (ed.) Giotto in Perspective, 1974; Art on Trial: From Whistler to Rothko, 1976; also children's books. Add: 63 East 93rd St., New York, N.Y. 10128, U.S.A.

ADAMS, Michael Evelyn. British, b. 1920. History, International relations/Current affairs. Research Fellow, Dept. of Politics, Univ. of Exeter. Middle East Corresp., 1956–62, and Rome Corresp., 1961–62, The Guardian; Asst. to Dir. of Voluntary Service Overseas, 1964–67; Dir. of Information, Council for Advancement of Arab–British Understanding, 1968–78; Ed., Middle East Intnl., 1972–80. *Publs:* Suez and After, 1958; Umbria, 1964; Voluntary Service Overseas, 1968; Chaos or Rebirth, 1968; (ed.) Handbook to the Middle East, 1971, 1987; (with Christopher Mayhew) Publish It Not . . ., 1975; The Untravelled World, 1984. Add: 7 Moorlands Rd., Budleigh Salterton, Devon, England.

ADAMS, Perseus. (Peter Robert Charles Adams). South African, b. 1933. Poetry. *Publs:* The Land at My Door, 1965; Grass for the Unicorn, 1975. Add: 7 New End, Hampstead, London N.W.3, England.

ADAMS, Richard (George). British, b. 1920. Novels/Short stories, Children's fiction, Poetry. Freelance writer. Formerly a Higher Civil Servant with Dept. of the Environment. *Publs:* Watership Down, 1972 (Carnegie Medal: Guardian Award for Children's Fiction); Shardik, 1974; (with Max Hooper) Nature Through the Seasons, 1975; The Tyger Voyage, 1976; The Ship's Cat, 1977; The Plague Dogs, 1977; (with Max Hooper) Nature Day and Night, 1978; The Watership Down Film Picture Book, 1978; The Girl in a Swing (novel), 1980; The Iron Wolf and Other Stories, 1980; (with Ronald Lockley) Voyage Through the Antarctic, 1982; Maia, 1984; The Bureaucrats, 1985; The Bureaucats, 1985; A Nature Diary, 1985; (ed. and contrib.) Occasional Poets, 1986; The Legend of Te Tuna (narrative poem), 1986; Traveller, 1988. Add: 26 Church St., Whitchurch, Hants., England.

ADAMS, Robert Martin. American, b. 1915. Literature, Translations. Instr. in English, Univ. of Wisconsin, Madison, 1942–43; Instr. and Asst. Prof., Rutgers Univ., New Brunswick, N.J., 1947–50; Asst. Prof. and Prof. of English, Cornell Univ., Ithaca, N.Y., 1950–68; Formerly, Prof. of English, Univ. of California at Los Angeles. *Publs:* (as Robert Martin Krapp) Liberal Anglicanism 1636-1647: An Historical Essay, 1944; Ikon: John Milton and the Modern Critics, 1955; Strains of Discord: Studies in Literary Openness, 1958; Stendhal: Notes on a Novelist, 1959; Surface and Symbol: The Consistency of James Joyce's Ulysses, 1962; James Joyce: Common Sense and Beyond, 1966; Nil: Episodes in the Literary Conquest of the Void During the Nineteenth Century, 1966; (ed. & trans.) Candide, by Voltaire, 1966; (ed. & trans.) Red and Black, by Stendhal, 1969; (trans.) Circe, by Giovanni Battista Gelli, 1963; Proteus, His Lies, His Truth: Discussions of Literary Translation, 1973; The Roman Stamp: Frame and Facade in Some Forms of Neo-Classicism, 1974; Bad Mouth, 1977; (trans.) The Prince, by Nicolo Machiavelli, 1977; Decadent Societies, 1983; The Land and Literature of England: A Historical Account, 1986; Shakespeare, The Four Romances, 1989. Add: 813 Waldo St., Santa Fe, N. Mex. 87501, U.S.A.

ADAMS, Robert McCormick, Jr. American, b. 1926. Anthropology. Adjunct Prof., Johns Hopkins Univ., since 1984. Secty., Smithsonian Instn., Washington, D.C., since 1984. Prof. of Anthropology, Univ. of Chicago, since 1963 (Instr., 1955–57; Asst. Prof., 1957–61; Assoc. Prof., 1961–62; Prof., 1962; Dir., Oriental Inst., 1962–68, 1981–83; Dean of Social Sciences, 1970–74, 1979–80; University Provost, 1982–84). *Publs:* (ed. with C.H. Kraeling) City Invincible: A Symposium on Urbanization and Cultural Development in the Ancient Near East, 1960; Land Behind Baghdad: A History of Settlement on the Diyala Plains, 1965; The Evolution of Urban Society: Early Mesopotamia and Prehispanic Mexico, 1966; (with H.J. Nissen) The Uruk Countryside, 1972; (ed. with C.S. Schelling) Corners of a Foreign Field, 1979; Heartland of Cities, 1981; (with N.J. Smelser and D.J. Treiman) Behavioral and Social Science Research: A National Resource, 2 vols., 1982. Add: Smithsonian Instn., Office of the Secty., 1000 Jefferson Dr. SW, Washington, D.C. 20560, U.S.A.

ADAMS, Walter. American, b. 1922. Economics. Distinguished Univ. Prof. of Economics, Michigan State Univ., East Lansing, since 1970 (faculty member since 1947; Pres., 1969–70). *Publs:* (co-ed.) Reading in Economics, 1948; (ed. & co-author) The Structure of American Industry, 1950, 7th ed., 1985; (co-author) Monopoly in America, 1955; (co-author) From Main Street to the Left Bank, 1959; (co-author) Is the World Our Campus?, 1960; (ed. & co-author) The Brain Drain, 1968; The Test, 1971; (with others) Tariffs, Quotas and Trade: The Politics of Protectionism, 1979; (with James Brock) The Bigness Complex: Industry, Labor and Government in the American Economy, 1986. Add: 928 Lantern Hill Dr., East Lansing, Mich. 48823, U.S.A.

ADAMS, William C. American, b. 1948. Communications Media. Prof. of Public Admin., George Washington Univ., Washington, D.C., (member of the faculty since 1978). Member, Editorial Advisory Bd., Journal of Communication, Philadelphia, since 1983. *Publs:* (ed. with Fay Schreibman) Television Network News: Issues in Content Research, 1978; (ed.) Television Coverage of the Middle East, 1981; (ed.) Television Coverage of International Affairs, 1982; (ed.) Television Coverage of the 1980 Presidential Campaign, 1983. Add: Public Admin. Dept., George Washington Univ., Washington, D.C. 20052, U.S.A.

ADAM-SMITH, Patsy. (Patricia Jean Adam-Smith). Australian, b. 1926. History, Autobiography/Memoirs/Personal, Biography. Manuscripts Field Officer, State Library of Victoria, 1970–82; Adult Education Officer, Hobart, Tas., 1960–66; Pres., Federal Fellowship of Australian Writers, 1973–75. *Publs:* Hear the Train Blow, 1963; Moon-Bird People, 1964; There was a Ship, 1965; Tiger Country, 1966; The Rails Go Westward, 1967; Folklore of Australia's Railmen, 1969; No Tribesmen, 1970; Tasmania Sketchbook, 1972; Launceston Sketchbook, 1972; Port Arthur Sketchbook, 1973; Barcoo Salute, 1973; The Desert Railway, 1974; Romance of Australian Railways, 1974; The Anzacs, 1978; Outback Hero, 1981; The Shearers, 1982; Australian Women at War, 1984; Heart of Exile, 1986. Add: 47 Hawksburn Rd., South Yarra, Vic. 3141, Australia.

ADAMSON, Donald. British, b. 1939. History, Literature, Biography, Translations. Asst. Master, Manchester Grammar Sch., 1962–64; member of staff, J. Walter Thompson Co., Ltd., London, 1965–67; Head of Modern Languages, St. George's Sch., Gravesend, 1968; Lectr., 1969–70, Sr. Lectr., 1970–77, and Principal Lectr. in French, 1977–89, Goldsmith's Coll., London; Visiting Fellow, Wolfson Coll., Cambridge, 1989–90.

Publs: The Genesis of 'Le Cousin Pons', 1966; (trans.) The Black Sheep, by Balzac, 1970; Dusty Heritage: A National Policy for Museums and Libraries, 1971; (ed.) T.S. Eliot: A Memoir, by R. Sencourt, 1971; (with P. Dewar) The House of Nell Gwyn: The Fortunes of the Beauclerk Family, 1670-1974, 1974; (trans.) Ursule Mirouët, by Balzac, 1976; A Rescue Policy for Museums, 1980; Balzac: "Illusions Perdues," 1981; Les Romantiques francais devant la peinture espagnole, 1989. Add: Dodmore House, The Street, Meopham, Kent, England.

ADAMSON, Robert. Australian, b. 1943. Poetry. Founding Ed. and Dir., with Dorothy Hewett, Big Smoke Books, Sydney. Assoc. Ed., 1968–70, Ed., 1970–75, and Asst. Ed., 1975–77, New Poetry mag., Sydney; Ed. and Dir., Prism Books, Sydney, 1970–77. *Publs:* Canticles on the Skin, 1970; The Rumour, 1972; Swamp Riddles, 1974; (with Bruce Hanford) Zimmer's Essay (novel), 1974; Theatre I-XIX, 1976; Cross the Border, 1977; Selected Poems, 1977; Where I Come From, 1979; The Law at Heart's Desire, 1982. Add: 1/2 Billyard Ave., Elizabeth Bay, N.S.W. 2011, Australia.

ADCOCK, Fleur. British (b. New Zealander), 1934. Poetry. *Publs:* The Eye of the Hurricane, 1964; Tigers, 1967; High Tide in the Garden, 1971; The Scenic Route, 1974; The Inner Harbour, 1979; Below Loughrigg, 1979; (ed.) The Oxford Book of Contemporary New Zealand Poetry, 1982; Selected Poems, 1983; The Virgin and the Nightingale: Medieval Latin Poems, 1983; The Incident Book, 1986; (ed.) The Faber Book of 20th Century Women's Poetry, 1987. Add: 14 Lincoln Rd., London N2 9DL, England.

ADDINGTON, Arthur Charles. British, b. 1939. Genealogy/Heraldry. *Publs:* Royal House of Stuart: The Descendants of King James VI of Scotland, James I of England, vol. I, 1969, vol. II, 1971, vol. III, 1975; (ed.) The Lineage and Ancestry of H.R.H. Prince Charles, Prince of Wales, by Gerald Paget, 2 vols., 1977. Add: 6 Fairfield Close, Harpenden, Herts, England.

ADDINGTON, Larry Holbrook. American, b. 1932. History, Military/Defence. Prof. of History, The Citadel, The Military Coll. of South Carolina, Charleston, since 1970 (Asst. Prof. of History, 1964–66; Assoc. Prof., 1966–70). Asst. Prof. of History, San Jose State Coll., Calif., 1962–64; Consultant to the Inst. of Advanced Studies, U.S. Army War Coll., Carlisle, Pa., 1968–69. *Publs:* From Moltke to Hitler: The Evolution of German Military Doctrine, 1865-1939, 1967; The Blitzkrieg Era and the German General Staff, 1865-1941, 1971; The Patterns of War since the 18th Century, 1984. Add: History Dept., The Citadel, Charleston, S.C. 29409, U.S.A.

ADDISON, Doris Maureen. New Zealander, b. 1926. Novels/Short stories, Plays/Screenplays. *Publs:* Valley in the Clouds, 1963; Mara, 1964; Bird of Time, 1965; A Greenstone of Two Colours, 1965; Morning Tide, 1967; Jane, 1967; A Collection of Plays, 1970. Add: 7 Caughey Pl., Auckland 3, New Zealand.

ADDISON, (Sir) William (Wilkinson). British, b. 1905. Architecture, Geography, History, Language/Linguistics. Justice of the Peace for Essex since 1949; Deputy Lt. of Essex since 1973. Member, Lord Chancellor's Advisory Council for the Training of Magistrates, 1964–73; Chmn., Magistrates Assn. of England and Wales, 1970–76; Assessor to the Erroll Cttee. on Licensing, 1971. *Publs:* Epping Forest, 1945; The English Country Parson, 1947; Essex Heyday, 1949; Suffolk, 1950; English Spas, 1951; Worthy Dr. Fuller, 1951; Audley End, 1953; English Fairs and Markets, 1953; Thames Estuary, 1954; In the Steps of Charles Dickens, 1955; Essex Worthies, 1973; Portrait of Epping Forest, 1977; Understanding English Place-Names, 1978; Understanding English Surnames, 1978; The Old Roads to England, 1980; Local Styles of the English Parish Church, 1982; Farmhouses in the English Landscape, 1986. Add: Ravensmere, Epping, Essex, England.

ADELBERG, Doris. *See* **ORGEL,** Doris.

ADELMAN, Clifford. American b. 1942. Politics/Government, Social commentary/phenomena. Sr. Assoc., Office of Research, U.S. Dept. of Education, since 1979. Instr. and Lectr., City Coll. of New York, 1968–71; Visiting Fellow, Yale Univ., New Haven, Conn., 1972, 1973; Assoc. Dean for Academic Development and Research, and Assoc. Prof. of Communications, William Paterson (State) Coll. of New Jersey, Wayne, 1974–79. *Publs:* Generations: A Collage on Youthcult, 1972; No Loaves, No Parables: American Politics and the English Language, 1974; The Standardized Test Scores of College Graduates, 1985; Starting with Students, 1985; (ed.) Assessment in American Higher Education, 1986. Add:

10204 Clearbrook Pl., Kensington, Md. 20895, U.S.A.

ADELMAN, Irma Glicman. American, b. 1930. Economics. Prof. of Economics and Agricultural and Resource Economics, Univ. of California, Berkeley, since 1979. Consultant, U.S. Dept. of State, since 1963, also Intnl. Bank for Reconstruction and Development (IBRD), since 1968, and Intnl. Labor Org., Geneva, since 1973. Vice Pres., American Economic Assn. Prof., Stanford Univ., Calif., 1960–62; Assoc. Prof., Johns Hopkins Univ., Baltimore, Md., 1962–66; Prof. of Economics, Northwestern Univ., Evanston, Ill., 1967–72; Sr. Economist, Development Research Center, IBRD, 1971–72; Prof. of Economics, Univ. of Maryland, College Park, 1972–79; Fellow, Netherlands Inst. of Advanced Study, and Cleveringa Chair, Leiden Univ., Netherlands, 1977–78. *Publs:* Theories of Economic Growth and Development, 1964; (with C.T. Morris) Society, Politics and Economic Development, 1967; (with C.T. Morris) Economic Growth and Social Equity in Developing Countries, 1973; (with Sherman Robinson) Income Distribution Planning, 1978; (with C.T. Morris) Comparative Patterns of Economic Development 1850-1914, 1987. Add: 207 Gianninni Hall, Univ. of California, Berkeley, Calif. 94720, U.S.A.

ADES, Dawn. British, b. 1943. Art, Photography. Member of the Dept. of Art, University of Essex, Colchester, since 1968. *Publs:* Dada and Surrealism, 1974; Photomontage, 1976; Dada and Surrealism Reviewed, 1978; Salvador Dali, 1982. Add: Department of Art, University of Essex, Wivenhoe Park, Colchester, Essex, England.

ADEY, William Ross. American, b. 1922. Medicine/Health. Dir., Research and Development, Loma Linda VA Medical Center, since 1977. Reader in Anatomy, Univ. of Adelaide, 1951–53; Sr. Lectr. in Anatomy, Univ. of Melbourne, 1955–56; Prof. of Anatomy and Physiology, Univ. of California, Los Angeles, 1957–77. *Publs:* Stereotaxic Atlas of the Brain of the Chimpanzee, 1966; Problems of Molecular Coding, 1968; A Stereotaxic Brain Atlas for Macaca Nemestrina, 1970; Nonlinear Electrodynamics in Biomolecular Systems, 1984; Magnetic Resonance-Imaging of The Brain, Head, and Neck, 1985. Add: Res. Sve. (151), VA Medical Center, Loma Linda, Calif. 92357, U.S.A.

ADKINS, Arthur William Hope. British, b. 1929. Classics, Intellectual history. Successively Edward Olson Prof. of Greek, Prof. of Philosophy and Early Christian Literature, Univ. of Chicago, since 1974. Asst. in the Humanity Dept., Univ. of Glasgow, 1954–56; Lectr. in Greek, Bedford Coll., Univ. of London, 1956–61; Fellow in Classical Languages and Literature, Exeter Coll., Oxford, 1961–65; Prof. of Classics, Univ. of Reading, 1966–74; Visiting Sr. Fellow, Soc. for the Humanities, Cornell Univ., Ithaca, N.Y., 1969–70. *Publs:* Merit and Responsibility: A Study in Greek Values, 1960; From the Many to the One: Study of Personality and Views of Human Nature in the Context of Ancient Greek Society, Values and Beliefs, 1970; Moral Values and Political Behaviour in Ancient Greece, 1972; Poetic Craft in the Early Greek Elegists, 1985. Add: Dept. of Classics, Univ. of Chicago, 1050 E. 59th St., Chicago, Ill. 60637, U.S.A.

ADLARD, Mark. British, b. 1932. Novels/Short stories, Science Fiction/Fantasy. Teacher of economics, since 1985. Exec. in the steel industry, 1956–76. *Publs:* Interface, 1971; Volteface, 1972; Multiface, 1975; The Greenlander (novel), 1978. Add: 12 The Green, Seaton Carew, Hartlepool TS25 1AS, England.

ADLEMAN, Robert H. American, b. 1919. Novels/Short stories. Supernatural/Occult topics, Writing/Journalism. Freelance writer. *Publs:* (with G. Walton) The Devil's Brigade, 1967; (with G. Walton) Rome Fell Today, 1968; (with G. Walton) Champagne Campaign, 1969; The Bloody Benders, 1970; Annie Deane, 1972; Baker, 1972; What's Really Involved in Writing and Selling Your Book, 1973; Explanation of Occult, 1973; Alias Big Cherry, 1973; How to Write Anything, 1979; Best Seats in the House, 1980; Sweetwater Fever, 1984. Add: Sweetwater Ranch, Box 600, Jacksonville, Ore, 97530, U.S.A.

ADLER, C(arole) S(chwerdtfeger). American, b. 1932. Children's fiction. Advertising Asst., Worthington Corp., Harrison, N.J., 1952–54; English teacher, Niskayuna Middle Schs., N.Y., 1967–77. *Publs:* Juvenile—The Magic of the Glits, 1979; The Silver Coach, 1979; In Our House, Scott is My Brother, 1980; Shelter on Blue Barns Road, 1981; The Cat Was Left Behind, 1981; Down By the River, 1981; Footsteps on the Stairs, 1982; The Evidence that Wasn't There, 1982; The Once in a While Hero, 1982; Some Other Summer, 1982; Get Lost Little Brother, 1983; Roadside Valentine, 1983; The Shell Lady's Daughter, 1983; Shadows on Little Reef Bay, 1984; Fly Tree, 1984; With Westie and the Tin Man, 1985; Binding Ties, 1985; Good-bye, Pink Pig, 1985;

Split Sisters, 1986; Kiss the Clown, 1986; Carly's Buck, 1987; Always and Forever Friends, 1988; If You Need Me, 1988; Eddie's Blue Winged Dragon, 1988; One Sister Too Many, 1989; The Lump in the Middle, 1989. Add: 1350 Ruffner Rd., Schenectady, N.Y. 12309, U.S.A.

ADLER, Helmut E. American, b. 1920. Animals/Pets, Psychology, Translations. Prof. of Psychology, Yeshiva Univ., NYC, since 1964 (Instr., 1950–53; Asst. Prof. 1953–57; Assoc. Prof., 1957–64). Research Assoc., The American Museum of Natural History, NYC, since 1969 (Research Fellow, 1955–69). Research Assoc., Mystic Marinelife Aquarium, Mystic, Conn., since 1979; Asst. Ed., International Journal for the Study of Group Tensions, since 1980. Lectr., Columbia Univ., NYC, 1955–60. *Publs:* (with J.D. Macdonald & D. Goodwin) Bird Behavior, 1962, rev. ed. as Bird Life, 1969; (trans.) Elements of Psychophysics, vol. I, by G.T. Fechner, 1966; Fish Behavior: Why Fishes Do What They Do, 1975; (ed. with Nicholas Pastore) Helmholtz's Popular Lectures on Vision, 1986. Add: 162-14 86th Ave., Jamaica, N.Y. 11432, U.S.A.

ADLER, Jacob Henry. American, b. 1919. Literature. Prof. of English, Purdue Univ., W. Lafayette, Ind., since 1969 (Head, Dept. of English, 1969–81). Instr., Asst. Prof., Assoc. Prof., and Prof., 1949–50 and 1951–69, and Chmn., Dept. of English, 1964–69, Univ. of Kentucky, Lexington. *Publs:* The Reach of Art: A Study in the Prosody of Pope, 1964; Lillian Hellman, 1969. Add: Dept. of English, Purdue Univ., West Lafayette, Ind. 47907, U.S.A.

ADLER, Mortimer J(erome). American, b. 1902. Education, History, Law, Philosophy, Politics/Government, Theology/Religion. Dir., Inst. for Philosophical Research, Chicago, since 1952. Ed., The Great Ideas Today series, since 1962, Gateway to the Great Books series, since 1963, and The Annals of America series, since 1968, also Dir. of Editorial Planning since 1966, and Chmn. of the Bd. of Editors, since 1974, Encyclopaedia Britannica, Chicago. Secty. to the Ed., New York Sun, 1915–17; Instr. in Psychology, Columbia Univ., NYC, 1923–30; Assoc. Prof., 1930–42, and Prof. of the Philosophy of Law, 1942–52, Univ. of Chicago. *Publs:* Dialectic, 1927; (with Jerome Michael) Crime, Law, and Social Science, 1933; (with Maude Phelps Hutchins) Diagrammatics, 1935; Art and Prudence: A Study in Practical Philosophy, 1937, rev. ed. as Poetry and Politics, 1965; What Man Has Made of Man: A Study of the Consequences of Platonism and Positivism in Psychology, 1937; St. Thomas and the Gentiles, 1938; Problems for Thomists: The Problem of Species, 1940; (ed.) The Philosophy and Science of Man: A Collection of Texts as a Foundation for Ethics and Politics, 1940; How to Read a Book: The Art of Getting a Liberal Education, 1940, rev. ed. (with Charles Van Doren) 1972; Hierarchy, 1940; A Dialectic of Morals: Toward the Foundations of Political Philosophy, 1941; How to Think about War and Peace, 1944; (ed.) The Great Ideas: A Syntopicon of Great Books of the Western World (Encyclopaedia Britannica), 2 vols., 1952; (assoc. ed.) Great Books of the Western World, 54 vols.; The Democratic Revolution, 1956; The Capitalistic Revolution, 1957; Liberal Education in an Industrial Democracy, 1957; (with Louis O. Kelso) The Capitalist Manifesto, 1958; (with Milton Mayer) The Revolution in Education, 1958; The Idea of Freedom, 2 vols., 1958, 1961; Family Participation Plan for Reading and Discussing the Great Books of the Western World (Encyclopaedia Britannica), 1959; The Great Ideas Program (Encylopaedia Britannica), 10 vols., 1959–63; (with Louis O. Kelso) The New Capitalists: A Proposal to Free Economic Growth from the Slavery of Savings, 1961; The Conditions of Philosophy: Its Checkered Past, Its Present Disorder, and Its Future Promise, 1965; The Greeks, The West, and World Culture, 1966; The Difference of Man and the Difference It Makes, 1967; Freedom: A Study of the Development of the Concept in the English and American Traditions of Philosophy, 1968; (ed.) The Negro in American History, 3 vols., 1969; The Time of Our Lives: The Ethics of Common Sense, 1970; The Common Sense of Politics, 1971; (with William Gorman) The American Testament, 1975; Some Questions about Language, 1976; Philosopher at Large: An Intellectual Autobiography, 1977; Reforming Education, 1977; (with Charles Van Doren) Great Treasury of Western Thought, 1977; Aristotle for Everybody, 1978; How to Think about God: A Guide for the 20th Century Pagan, 1980; Six Great Ideas, 1981; The Angels and Us, 1982; The Paideia Proposal, 1982; How to Speak and How to Listen, 1983; A Vision of the Future: Twelve Ideas for a Better Life and a Better Society, 1984; Ten Philosophical Mistakes, 1985; A Guidebook to Learning: For the Lifelong Pursuit of Wisdom, 1986; We Hold These Truths: Understanding the Ideas and Ideals of the Constitution, 1987; Reforming Education: The Opening of the American Mind, 1989; Intellect: Mind over Matter, 1990. Add: Inst. for Philosophical Research, 101 E. Ontario St., Chicago, Ill. 60611, U.S.A

ADLER, Renata. American, b. 1938. Novels/Short stories, Film, Biography. Writer-Reporter, The New Yorker, since 1963. Member, Editorial Bd., American Scholar, 1968–73. Film critic, New York Times, 1968–69. Member, P.E.N. Exec. Bd., 1964–70; Judge in arts and letters, National Book Awards, 1969; Fellow, Trumbull Coll., Yale Univ. 1969–72. *Publs:* Toward A Radical Middle: Fourteen Pieces of Reporting and Criticism, 1970; A Year in the Dark: Journal of a Film Critic 1968–69, 1970; Speedboat, 1976; Pitch Dark (novel), 1984; Reckless Disregard: Westmoreland v. CBS et al., Sharon v. Time, 1986. Add: c/o The New Yorker, 25 West 43rd St., New York, N.Y. 10036, U.S.A.

ADLER, Warren. American, b. 1927. Novels/Short stories. Chmn. of Bd., Washington Dossier mag. *Publs:* Options, 1974; Banquet Before Dawn, 1976; The Henderson Equation, 1976; Trans-Siberian Express, 1977; The Sunset Gang, 1977; The Casanova Embrace, 1978; Blood Ties, 1979; The War of the Roses, 1981; American Sextet, 1982; American Quartet, 1982; Random Hearts, 1984; Twilight Child, 1986; We Are Holding the President Hostage, 1986. Add: 3301 Woodbine St., Chevy Chase, Md., 20015, U.S.A.

ADOFF, Arnold. American, b. 1935. Children's Poetry. Literary Agent, Yellow Springs, Ohio, since 1977. Teacher in the New York public schools, 1957–69. *Publs:* verse for children—Manda 1A, 1971; Black Is Brown Is Tan, 1973; Make a Circle, Keep Us In: Poems for a Good Day, 1975; My Sister Tells Me That I'm Black, 1976; Tornado!, 1977; Under the Early Morning Trees, 1978; Where Wild Willy, 1978; Eats, 1979; I Am the Running Girl, 1979; Friend Dog, 1980; Today We Are Brother and Sister, 1981; OUTside INside Poems, 1981; Birds, 1982; All the Colors of the Race, 1982; The Cabbages Are Chasing the Rabbits, 1985; Sports Pages, 1986; Greens, 1988; other—Malcolm X, 1970; editor—I am the Darker Brother: An Anthology of Modern Poems by Negro Americans, 1968; Black on Black: Commentaries by Negro Americans, 1968; City in All Directions: An Anthology of Modern Poems, 1969; Black Out Loud: An Anthology of Modern Poems by Black Americans, 1970; Brothers and Sisters: Modern Stories by Black Americans, 1970; It Is the Poem Singing into Your Eyes: An Anthology of New Young Poets, 1971; The Poetry of Black America: An Anthology of the 20th Century, 1973; My Black Me: A Beginning Book of Black Poetry, 1974; Celebrations: A New Anthology of Black American Poetry, 1977. Add: Box 293, Yellow Springs, Ohio 45387, U.S.A.

ADRIAN, Arthur Allen. American, b. 1906. Literature, Biography. Prof. Emeritus, Case Western Reserve Univ., Cleveland, Ohio, since 1974 (Asst. Prof. of English, 1946–51; Assoc. Prof., 1951–61; Prof., 1962–74). English teacher, high schs. in Kansas, 1929–35; Instr. in English, Univ. of Kansas, Lawrence, 1935–39, and Oregon State Coll., 1940–44. *Publs:* Georgina Hogarth and the Dickens Circle, 1957; Mark Lemon: First Editor of Punch, 1965; Charles Dickens and the Parent–Child Relationship, 1984. Add: 1099 Mt. Vernon Blvd., Cleveland Heights, Ohio 44112, U.S.A.

ADRIAN, Frances. *See* **POLLAND**, Madeleine.

AFFRON, Charles. American, b. 1935. Film, Literature. Prof. of French and Italian, New York Univ., NYC, since 1968 (Asst. Prof., 1965–68). Former Instr. and Asst. Prof. of Romance Languages, Brandeis Univ., Waltham, Mass. *Publs:* Patterns of Failure in La Comedie Humaine, 1966; A Stage for Poets: Studies in the Theatre of Hugo and Musset, 1971; Star Acting: Gish, Garbo, Davis, 1977; Cinema and Sentiment, 1982;Divine Garbo, 1985; Fellini's 8, 1987. Add: 180 Park Row, New York, N.Y. 10038, U.S.A.

AFRICA, Thomas W. American, b. 1927. History, Sciences. Prof. of History, State Univ. of New York at Binghamton, since 1969. Staff member, Univ. of California, Santa Barbara, 1959–60, Louisiana State Univ., New Orleans, 1960–61, and Univ. of Southern California, Los Angeles, 1961–69. *Publs:* Phylarchus and Spartan Revolution, 1961; Rome of the Caesars, 1965; Science and the State in Greece and Rome, 1968; The Ancient World, 1969; The Immense Majesty, 1974. Add: 421 African Rd., Vestal, N.Y. 13850, U.S.A.

AFTERMAN, Allen Buddy. American, b. 1941. Poetry, Law. Sr. Lectr. in Law, Melbourne Univ., Vic., 1970–73. *Publs:* Company Directors and Controllers, 1972; (with R. Baxt) Cases and Materials on Corporations and Associations, 1972, 3rd ed. 1980; The Maze Rose (poetry), 1974; (with R. Baxt) Casebook On Companies and Securities, 1976; Purple Adam (poetry), 1980. Add: Kfar Clil, D.N. Oshrat, Israel.

AGARD, John. British (born in Guyana). Poetry, Children's Fiction. Has worked as an actor and jazz performer. *Publs:* verse for adults—

Shoot Me with Flowers, 1973; Man to Pan, 1982; Limbo Dancer in the Dark, 1983; Mangoes and Bullets: Selected and New Poems 1972–84, 1985; fiction for children—Letters for Lettie and Other Stories, 1979; Dig Away Two-Hole Tim, 1981; poetry for children—I Did Do Nuttin and Other Poems, 1983; Say It Again, Granny!: Twenty Poems from Caribbean Proverbs, 1986; Lend Me Your Wings, 1987. Add: c/o Hodder and Stoughton, 47 Bedford Sq., London WC1B 3DP, England.

AGER, Derek Victor. British, b. 1923. Earth sciences. Research Prof., Dept. of Geology, University Coll., Swansea, since 1969. Pres., Geologists Assn. Ed.-in-Chief, Palaeogeography, Palaeoclimatology, and Palaeoecology. Demonstrator, 1951–52, Asst. Lectr., 1952–54, Lectr., 1954–59, and Reader, 1959–69, Imperial Coll., London; Visiting Prof., Univ. of Illinois, Urbana, 1958–59. *Publs:* Introducing Geology, 2nd ed. 1961; Principles of Paleoecology, 1963; The Nature of the Stratigraphical Record, 1973, 1981; The Geology of Europe, 1980. Add: Dept. of Geology, University Coll., Swansea SA2 8PP, Wales.

AGLE, Nan Hayden. American, b. 1905. Children's fiction, Children's non-fiction. Former Art Teacher, Baltimore Friends Sch. *Publs:* (with E. Wilson) Three Boys series, 6 vols., 1951–68; Constance and the Honeybee, 1959; Princess Mary of Maryland, 1960; Makon and the Dauphin, 1961; (with F.A. Bacon) The Lords Baltimore, 1962; Kate and the Apple Tree, 1965; (with F.A. Bacon) The Ingenious John Banvard, 1966; Joe Bean, 1967; Kish's Colt, 1968; Tarr of Belway Smith, 1969; Maple Street, 1970; My Animals and Me, 1970; K Mouse and Bo Bixby, 1972; Baney's Lake, 1972, Susan's Magic, 1973; A Promise Is to Keep (adult), 1985. Add: 221 Stony Rune Lane, Baltimore, Md. 21210, U.S.A.

AGNEW, Spiro T(heodore). American, b. 1918. Novels/Short stories. Former Claims Adjuster, Lumbermens Mutual Casualty Co.; Personnel Dir., Schreiber Food Stores; admitted to Maryland Bar, in private law practice in Baltimore and Baltimore Co., and Chmn., Baltimore Co. Bd. of Appeals, 1958–61; Member of Exec., Baltimore Co., 1962–66; Chmn., Transport Cttee., National Assn. of Counties, 1963; Gov. of Maryland, 1967–69; Vice President of the U.S., 1969–73 (resigned). *Publs:* The Canfield Decision, 1976; Go Quietly—or Else, 1980. Add: Kenwood, Chevy Chase, Md. 20015, U.S.A.

AGONITO, Rosemary. American, b. 1937. Women. Gender Equity Consultant since 1983. Taught at Maria Regina Coll., Syracuse, N.Y., 1966–68, Syracuse Univ., 1968–73, Colgate Univ., Hamilton, N.Y., 1973–75, and Eisenhower Coll., 1976–83. *Publs:* History of Ideas on Woman: A Source Book, 1977; Promoting Self Esteem in Young Women: A Teacher's Manual, 1988. Add: 4502 Broad Rd., Syracuse, N.Y. 13215, U.S.A.

AGUOLU, Christian Chukwunedu. Nigerian, b. 1940. Information Science, Librarianship. Head of Dept. of Library Science, since 1978, Prof. of Library Science, since 1982, and Dean of Education, 1979–82 and since 1984, Univ. of Maiduguri, Nigeria (Sr. Lectr., 1977–79; Assoc. Prof./Reader, 1979–82). French and Latin teacher, high sch., Oraukwu, Nigeria, 1965–66; Reference Librarian and Bibliographer, Univ. of California, Santa Barbara, 1968–72. *Publs:* Ghana in the Humanities and Social Sciences, 1900–1971: A Bibliography, 1973; Nigerian Civil War, 1967–70: An Annotated Bibliography, 1973; Nigeria: A Comprehensive Bibliography in the Humanities and Social Sciences, 1900–1971, 1973; Library Development in Borno State, 1984. Add: Dept. of Library Science, Univ. of Maiduguri, Maiduguri, Nigeria.

AHLBERG, Allan. British, b. 1938. Children's Fiction/Plays/Poetry. Has held various jobs; currently full-time writer. *Publs:* children's fiction—Brick Street Boys, 5 vols., 1975–76; Burglar Bill, 1977; Jeremiah in the Dark Woods, 1977; The Vanishment of Thomas Tull, 1977; The One and Only Two Heads, 1979; Son of a Gun, 1979; The Little Worm Book, 1979; Two Wheels, Two Heads, 1979; Funnybones, 1980; A Pair of Sinners, 1980; The Baby's Catalogue, 1982; Ten in a Bed, 1983; Woof, 1986; The Jolly Postman, 1986; The Clothes Horse and Other Stories, 1987; children's verse—Cops and Robbers, 1978; Each Peach Pear Plum, 1978; Peepo! (in U.S. as Peek-a-Boo!), 1981; Please, Mrs. Butler, 1983; Daisychains, 4 vols., 1983; other—The Old Joke Book, 1976; Happy Families (readers), 12 vols., 1980–81; The Ha Ha Bonk Book, 1982; Help Your Child to Read, 6 vols., 1982. Add: 20 Nether Hall Lane, Birstall, Leicester LE4 4DT, England.

AHLSWEDE, Ann. American, b. 1928. Westerns/Adventure. Independent Artist. *Publs:* Day of the Hunter, 1960; Hunting Wolf, 1960; The Savage Land, 1962. Add: 4616 Rancho Reposo, Del Mar, Calif. 92014, U.S.A.

AHSEN, Akhter. Indian, b. 1931. Psychology. Clinical Dir., The Eidetic Analysis Inst., Yonkers, N.Y., since 1969. Ed., Journal of Mental Imagery, since 1981. Chief Psychologist, The Eidetic Psychotherapy Inst., Philadelphia, 1966–69. *Publs:* Eidetic Psychotherapy: A Short Introduction, 1965; Basic Concepts in Eidetic Psychotherapy, 1968; Eidetic Parents Test and Analysis, 1972; Psycheye, 1977; Manhunt in the Desert, 1979; Oedipus at Thebes, 1984; Trojan Horse, 1984; Rhea Complex, 1984; The New Structuralism, 1986; ABC of Imagery, 1987; Aphrodite: The Psychology of Consciousness, 1988; Age Projection Test, 1988. Add: c/o Brandon House Inc., P.O. Box 240, Bronx, N.Y. 10471, U.S.A.

AIDOO, (Christina) Ama Ata. Ghanaian, b. 1942. Novels/Short stories, Plays/Screenplays. *Publs:* The Dilemma of a Ghost (play), 1965; Anowa (play), 1970; No Sweetness Here (short stories), 1970; Our Sister Killjoy (novel), 1977. Add: c/o Longman, 5 Bentinck St., London W1M 5RN, England.

AIKAWA, Jerry K(azuo). American, b. 1921. Medicine/Health. Assoc. Dean for Allied Health Prog. since 1983, Prof. of Medicine and Biometrics since 1967, and Assoc. Dean, Clin. Affairs, since 1974, Univ. of Colorado Sch. of Medicine, Denver (joined faculty, 1953). *Publs:* Myxedema, 1961; The Role of Magnesium in Biologic Processes, 1963; Rocky Mountain Spotted Fever, 1966; The Relationship of Magnesium to Disease in Domestic Animals and in Humans, 1972; (with E.R. Pinfield) Computerizing a Clinical Laboratory, 1973; Magnesium: Its Biological Significance, 1981. Add: Univ. of Colorado School of Medicine, 4200 East Ninth Ave., Denver, Colo. 80262, U.S.A.

AIKEN, Joan (Delano). British, b. 1924. Historical/Romance/Gothic, Children's fiction, Plays/Screenplays, Poetry, Writing/Journalism, Translations. Worked for the BBC, 1942–43; Librarian, U.N. Information Centre, London, 1943–49; Sub-Ed. and Features Ed., Argosy mag., London, 1955–60; Copywriter, J. Walter Thompson, London, 1960–61. *Publs:* All You've Ever Wanted and Other Stories, 1953; More Than You Bargained For and Other Stories, 1955; The Kingdom and the Cave, 1960; The Wolves of Willoughby Chase, 1962; Black Hearts in Battersea, 1964; The Silence of Herondale (romance), 1964; The Fortune Hunters (romance), 1965; Nightbirds on Nantucket, 1966; Trouble with Product X (romance) (in U.S as Beware of the Banquet), 1966; Hate Begins at Home (romance) (in U.S. as Dark Interval), 1967; The Ribs of Death (romance), 1967, in U.S. as The Crystal Crow, 1968; The Whispering Mountain, 1968; Necklace of Raindrops and Other Stories, 1968; Armitage, Armitage, Fly Away Home, 1968; A Small Pinch of Weather and Other Stories, 1969; Night Fall, 1969; The Windscreen Weepers and Other Tales of Horror and Suspense (for adults), 1969; Smoke from Cromwell's Time and Other Stories, 1970; The Embroidered Sunset (romance), 1970; The Green Flash and Other Tales of Horror, Suspense, and Fantasy, 1971; All and More, 1971; The Cuckoo Tree, 1971; The Kingdom under the Sea and Other Stories, 1971; A Harp of Fishbones and Other Stories, 1972; Arabel's Raven, 1972; Died on a Rainy Sunday (romance), 1972; The Butterfly Picnic (romance) (in U.S. as A Cluster of Separate Sparks), 1972; The Escaped Black Mamba, 1973; Winterthing, and the Mooncusser's Daughter (plays), 1973 (in U.S. published separately as Winterthing, 1972; The Mooncusser's Daughter, 1974); All But a Few, 1974; The Bread Bin, 1974; Midnight Is a Place, 1974; Not What You Expected: A Collection of Short Stories, 1974; Voices in an Empty House (romance), 1975; Castle Barebane (romance), 1976; Mortimer's Tie, 1976; A Bundle of Nerves, 1976; The Skin Spinners (poetry), 1976; (trans.) The Angel Inn, by Contessa de Ségur, 1976; The Faithless Lollybird and Other Stories, 1977; The Far Forests: Tales of Romance, Fantasy, and Suspense, 1977; Go Saddle the Sea, 1977; Last Movement (romance), 1977; The Five-Minute Marriage, 1977; The Smile of the Stranger (romance), 1978; Tale of a One-Way Street and Other Stories, 1978; Mice and Mendelson, 1978; Street (play), 1978; Mortimer and the Sword Excalibur, 1979; The Spiral Stair, 1979; A Touch of Chill (stories), 1979; Arabel and Mortimer, 1980; The Shadow Guests, 1980; Mortimer's Portrait on Glass, 1980; Mr. Jones's Disappearing Taxi, 1980; The Stolen Lake, 1981; A Whisper in the Night, 1982; The Lightning Tree (romance) (in U.S. as The Weeping Ash), 1980; The Young Lady from Paris (romance) (in U.S. as The Girl from Paris), 1982; The Way to Write for Children (for adults), 1982; Foul Matter, 1983; Mortimer's Cross, 1983; The Kitchen Warriors, 1984; Up the Chimney Down, 1984; Fog Hounds, Wind Cat, Sea Mice, 1984; Mansfield Revisited, 1984; Dido and Pa, 1986; Past Eight O'Clock, 1986; Deception, 1987. Add: The Hermitage, East St., Petworth, W. Sussex GU28 0AB, England.

AIKEN, Lewis R., Jr. American, b. 1931. Education, Psychology. Prof. of Psychology, Pepperdine Univ., Malibu, Calif., since 1979. Sch. Psychologist, N.C. Dept. of Public Instruction; Psychodiagnostician, N.C.

Dept of Human Resources; Research Psychologist Consultant, Veterans Admin. Former Dana Prof., and Chmn., Psychology Dept., Guildford Coll., N.C., 1966–74, and Former Assoc. Prof. of Psychology, and Dir. of Testing, Univ. of North Carolina, Greensboro 1960–65. Prof., Sacred Heart Coll., Belmont, N.C., 1974–76, and Univ. Pacific, Stockton, Calif., 1977–79. *Publs:* General Psychology: A Survey, 1969; Psychological and Educational Testing, 1971; (ed.) Readings in Psychological and Educational Testing, 1973; Psychological Testing and Assessment, 1975, 7th ed. 1982; Later Life, 2nd ed. 1982; Dying, Death and Bereavement, 1985; Assessment of Intellectual Functioning, 1986. Add: 1308 Knightwood Dr., Greensboro, N.C. 27410, U.S.A.

AIKEN, Linda H. American, b. 1943. Medicine/Health. Trustee Professor of Nursing and Sociology and Associate Director of Leonard Davis Institute of Health Economics, Univ. of Pennsylvania, Philadelphia, since 1989. Nurse, Univ. of Florida Medical Center, 1964–65; Instr., Sch. of Nursing, 1969–70, and Clinical Nurse Specialist, 1967–70, Univ. of Missouri; Lectr., Sch. of Nursing, Univ. of Wisconsin, Madison, 1973–74. Vice Pres., Robert Wood Johnson Foundn., Princeton, N.J., since 1981 (Prog. Officer, 1974–76; Dir. of Research, 1976–79; Asst. Vice Pres., 1979–81). *Publs:* (ed.) Nursing in the 1980s: Crises, Challenges, Opportunities, 1982; (co-ed. with B. Kehrer) Evaluation Studies Review Annual, 1985; (co-ed. with D. Mechanic) Applications of Social Science to Clinical Medicine and Health Policy, 1986. Add: University of Pennsylvania, Philadelphia, Pa. 19104-6096, U.S.A.

AINSWORTH, Harriet. *See* **CADELL,** Elizabeth.

AINSWORTH, Mary D(insmore) Salter. Has also written as Mary D. Salter. Canadian, b. 1913. Psychology. Emeritus Prof. of Psychology, Univ. of Virginia, Charlottesville, since 1984 (Commonwealth Prof., 1975–84). Sr. Research Psychologist, Tavistock Clinic, London, 1950–54; Sr. Research Fellow, East African Inst. of Social Research, Kampala, Uganda, 1954–55; Lectr., 1956–58, Assoc. Prof., 1958–63, and Prof., 1964–75, Johns Hopkins Univ., Baltimore, Md. *Publs:* (as Mary D. Salter with A.W. Ham) Doctor in the Making, 1943; (with B. Klopfer, W.F. Klopfer and R.R. Holt) Developments in the Rorschach Technique, vol. I, 1954; (with L.H. Ainsworth) Measuring Security in Personal Adjustment, 1958; (with J. Bowlby) Child Care and the Growth of Love, 1965; Infancy in Uganda, 1967; (with M.C. Blehar, E. Waters, and S. Wall) Patterns of Attachment, 1978. Add: 920 Rosser Ln., Charlottesville, Va. 22903, U.S.A.

AINSWORTH, Patricia. Pseud. for Patricia Nina Bigg. Australian, b. 1932. Historical/Romance/Gothic. Secty., 1948–55; Full-time writer since 1967. *Publs:* The Flickering Candle, 1968; The Candle Rekindled, 1969; Steady Burns the Candle, 1970; The Devil's Hole, 1970; Portrait in Gold, 1971; A String of Silver Beads, 1972; The Bridal Lamp, 1975; The Enchanted Cup, 1980. Add: 3/2 Lorraine Ave., Mitcham, S.A. 5062, Australia.

AINSWORTH, Ruth (Gallard). British, b. 1908. Children's fiction, Poetry. *Publs:* Tales about Tony, 1936; Mr. Popcorn's Friends, 1938; The Gingerbread House, 1938; The Ragamuffins, 1939; Richard's First Term, 1940; All Different (verse), 1947; Five and a Dog, 1949; "Listen with Mother" Tales, 1951; Rufty Tufty the Golliwog, 1952; The Evening Listens (verse), 1953; The Ruth Ainsworth Readers, 12 vols., 1953–55; Charles Stories and Others, from "Listen with Mother", 1954; More about Charles and Other Stories, from "Listen with Mother", 1954; Rufty Tufty at the Seashore, 1954; Three Little Mushrooms: Four Puppet Plays, 1955; More Little Mushrooms: Four Puppet Plays, 1955; The Snow Bear, 1956; Rufty Tufty Goes Camping, 1956; (with Ronald Ridout) Look Ahead Readers, 8 vols, 1956–57; Five "Listen with Mother" Tales about Charles, 1957; Rufty Tufty Runs Away, 1957; Nine Drummers Drumming, 1958; Rufty Tufty Flies High, 1959; Cherry Stones: A Book of Fairy Stories, 1960; Rufty Tufty's Island, 1960; Lucky Dip: A Selection of Stories and Verses, 1961; Far-Away Children, 1963; The Ten Tales of Shellover, 1963; The Wolf Who Was Sorry, 1964; Rufty Tufty Makes a House, 1965; Rufty Tufty and Hattie, 1965; (with Ronald Ridout) Books for Me to Read: Red Books, 6 vols., 1964, Blue Books, 6 vols. 1965, and Green Books, 6 vols., 1968; Daisy the Cow, 1966; Horse on Wheels, 1966; Jack Frost, 1966; Roly the Railway Mouse, 1967, in U.S. as Roly The Railroad Mouse, 1969; The Look about You Books, 6 vols., 1967–69; (ed.) Book of Colours and Sounds, 1968; The Aeroplane Who Wanted to See the Sea, 1968; Boris the Teddy Bear, 1968; Dougal the Donkey, 1968; More Tales of Shellover, 1968; Mungo the Monkey, 1968; The Old Fashioned Car, 1968; The Rabbit and His Shadow, 1968; The Noah's Ark, 1969; The Bicycle Wheel, 1969; Look, Do and Listen, 1969; The Ruth Ainsworth Book, 1970; Dandy the Donkey (reader), 1971; The Wild Wood

(reader), 1971; The Phantom Cyclist and Other Stories, 1971; Fairy Gold: Favourite Fairy Tales Retold for the Very Young, 1972; Another Lucky Dip, 1973; The Phantom Fisherboy: Tales of Mystery and Magic, 1974; Bedtime Book, 1974; Three's Company, 1974; Three Bags Full (miscellany), 1975; The Bear Who Liked Hugging People and Other Stories, 1976; The Phantom Roundabout and Other Stories, 1977; Up the Airy Mountain, 1977; The Phantom Carousel, 1978; Mr. Jumble's Toyshop, 1978; The Talking Rock, 1979; The Mysterious Baba and Her Magic Caravan, 1980; Mermaids' Tales, 1980; The Pirate Ship and Other Stories, 1980; The Little Yellow Taxi and His Friends, 1982. Add: Field End, Corbridge, Northumberland, England.

AIRD, Catherine. Pseud. for Kinn Hamilton McIntosh. British, b. 1930. Mystery/Crime/Suspense. Chmn., Finance Cttee., Girl Guides Assn., London, 1975–80, 1983–87. *Publs:* The Religious Body, 1966; A Most Contagious Game, 1967; Henrietta Who?, 1968; The Complete Steel, 1969 (in U.S. as The Stately Home Murder, 1970); A Late Phoenix, 1971; His Burial Too, 1973; Slight Mourning, 1976; Parting Breath, 1978; Some Die Eloquent, 1979; Passing Strange, 1980; Last Respects, 1982; Harm's Way, 1984; A Dead Liberty, 1986. Add: Invergordon, Sturry Hill, Sturry, Canterbury, Kent CT2 0NG, England.

AIRLIE, Catherine. *See* **MacLEOD,** Jean S.

AITCHISON, Ian J(ohnston) R(hind). British, b. 1936. Physics. Fellow, Worcester College, and Lectr. in Theoretical Physics, Oxford Univ., since 1966. Research Assoc., Brookhaven Natl. Laboratory, NYC, 1961–63; Collaborateur Temporaire Etranger, CEN Saclay, France, 1963–64; Research Assoc., Cavendish Laboratory, Cambridge, 1964–66. *Publs:* Relativistic Quantum Mechanics, 1972; (co-ed.) Rudolf Peierls and Theoretical Physics, 1977; (with A.J.G. Hey) Gauge Theories in Particle Physics, 1982; An Informal Introduction to Gauge Field Theories, 1982. Add: Dept. of Theoretical Physics, 1 Keble Rd., Oxford OX1 3NP, England.

AITKEN, Hugh (George Jeffrey). American, b. 1922. Economics, History. George D. Olds Prof. of Economics and American Studies, Amherst Coll., Mass., since 1964. Prof. of Economics, Univ. of California, Riverside, 1954–64. Ed., Journal of Economic History, 1966–69. *Publs:* The Welland Canal Company: A Study in Canadian Enterprise, 1954; (ed. and co-author) The Social Sciences in Historical Study, 1954; (ed. and co-author) The State and Economic Growth, 1959; (with W.T. Easterbrook) Canadian Economic History, 1956; Taylorism at Watertown Arsenal, 1960; American Capital and Canadian Resources, 1961; (ed.) The Canadian Commercial Revolution, by Gilbert N. Tucker, 1964; Explorations in Enterprise, 1965; Did Slavery Pay?: Readings in the Economics of Black Slavery in the United States, 1971; Syntony and Spark: The Origins of Radio, 1976; The Continuous Wave: Technology and American Radio 1900–1932, 1985. Add: 155 Amity St., Amherst, Mass. 01002, U.S.A.

AKEHURST, Michael (Barton). British, b. 1940. Law. Reader in Law, Keele Univ., since 1974 (Lectr., 1970–71; Sr. Lectr., 1971–74). Asst. Lectr., 1963–66, and Lectr., 1966–69, Manchester Univ. *Publs:* The Law Governing Employment in International Organizations, 1967; A Modern Introduction to International Law, 1970, 6th ed., 1987. Add: Law Dept., Keele University, Keele, Staffs. ST5 5BG, England.

AKERS, Alan Burt. *See* **BULMER,** Kenneth.

AKRIGG, George Philip Vernon. Canadian. History, Literature. Prof. Emeritus of English, Univ. of British Columbia, Vancouver (Instr., 1941–45; Asst. Prof., 1945–47; Assoc. Prof., 1947–58; Prof. 1958–79). *Publs:* Jacobean Pageant, or The Court of King James I, 1962; Shakespeare and the Earl of Southampton, 1968; (with H.B. Akrigg) 1001 British Columbia Place Names, 1969, 3rd ed. 1973; (co-author) British Columbia Chronicle, 1778-1846: Adventures by Sea and Land, 1975; (co-author) British Columbia Chronicle, 1847-1871: Gold and Colonists, 1977; (ed.) Letters of King James VI & I, 1984. Add: 4633 W. 8th Ave., Vancouver, B.C. V6R 2A6, Canada.

ALAYA, Flavia. American, b. 1935. Literature, Biography. Prof. of English and Comparative Literature, Ramapo Coll. of New Jersey, Mahwah, since 1973 (Assoc. Prof., and Dir., Sch. of Intercultural Studies, 1971–73). Instr., Univ. of North Carolina at Greensboro, 1959–60; Lectr. and Asst. in English, Barnard Coll., NYC, 1960–62; Lectr., Hunter Coll. of the City Univ. of New York, 1962–66; Instr., 1966–67, and Asst. Prof. of English, 1967–71, New York Univ., Bronx. Pres., Northeast Victorian Studies Assn., 1977–81. *Publs:* William Sharp—Fiona Macleod 1855-

1905, 1970; The Imagination Is a Square Wheel, 1977; Gaetano Federici: The Artist As Historian, 1980; Silk and Sandstone, 1984. Add: 520 East 28th St., Paterson, N.J. 07514, U.S.A.

AL-AZM, Sadik J. Syrian. International relations/Current affairs, Philosophy. Prof. of Philosophy, Univ. of Damascus, since 1977. Asst. in Instruction, Dept. of Philosophy, Yale Univ., New Haven, Conn., 1960–61; Instr. in Philosophy, Hunter Coll., NYC, 1961–62; Lectr. in Philosophy, Univ. of Damascus, 1962–63; Asst. Prof. of Philosophy, 1963–67, and Asst. Prof., Cultural Studies Prog., 1967–68, American Univ. of Beirut; Lectr. in Philosophy, Beirut Univ. Coll., 1965–68; Asst. Prof. of Philosophy, Univ. of Jordan, 1968–69. Ed., Arab Studies Review, 1969–73. *Publs:* Studies in Modern Western Philosophy, 1966; Kant's Theory of Time, 1967; Of Love and Arabic Courtly Love, 1968; Self-Criticism after the Defeat, 1968; Critique of Religious Thought, 1970; The Origins of Kant's Arguments in the Antinomies, 1972; A Critical Study of the Palestinian Resistance Movement, 1973. Add: Dept. of Philosophy, Damascus Univ., Damscus, Syria.

ALAZRAKI, Jaime. American, b. 1934. Literature. Prof. of Latin American Literature, Columbia Univ., New York, since 1987. Member, Editorial Bd., Hispanic Review, Latin American Literary Review, PMLA, Hispania, Hispanic Journal, Revista Iberoamericana, and Discurso Literario-revista de temas hispanicos. Instr., Columbia Univ., NYC, 1964–67; Asst. Prof., 1967–68, Assoc. Prof., 1968–71, and Prof. of Spanish Literature, 1972–77, Univ. of California at San Diego. Member, Exec. Council, International Inst. of Ibero-American Literature, 1975–77. Prof. of Latin American Literature, Harvard Univ., Cambridge, 1977–87. Co-ed., Revista Hispanica Moderna, 1987. *Publs:* Poetica y poesia de Pablo Neruda, 1965; La Prosa Narrativa de Jorge Luis Borges, 1968, rev. ed. 1974; Jorge Luis Borges, 1971; (co-ed.) Homenaje a Andres Iduarte, 1976; (ed.) Jorge Luis Borges: el escritor y la critica, 1976; Versiones/inversiones/reversiones: el espejo como modelo estructural del relato en los cuentos de Borges, 1977; (co-ed.) The Final Island: The Fiction of Julio Cortazar, 1980; (ed.) Antolog de la novela hispanoamericana, 2 vols., 1982; En busca del unicornio: les cuentos de Julio Cortazar, 1983; Critical Essays on Jorge Luis Borges, 1987; Borges and the Kabbalah and Other Essays, 1988. Add: Dept. of Spanish and Portuguese, Columbia Univ., 612 W. 116th St., New York. N.Y. 10027, U.S.A.

ALBA, Victor. American, b. 1916. Politics/Government. Prof., Dept. of Political Science, Kent State Univ., Ohio, since 1967, now Emeritus Prof. Dir., Galerias Excelsior, Mexico, 1957–60; Ed., Pan American Union, Washington D.C., 1960–62; Dir., Center for Social Education and Documentation, Mexico City, 1962–65; Lectr., American Univ., Washington, D.C., 1966–68. *Publs:* Sleepless Spain, 1948; Las ideas sociales en Mexico, 1958; Alliance Without Allies, 1966; The Mexicans, 1967; Nationalists Without Nations, 1968; Politics and the Labor Movement in Latin America, 1969; The Latin Americans, 1970; A Concise History of Mexico, 1972; Historia general del campesinado, 1973; Catalonia, 1974; Historia social de la mujer, 1974; El Maxisme a Catalunya, 1974; Catalonia Profile, 1976; Transition in Spain, 1978; Historia de la Resistencia Anti-franquista, 1978; El Partido Communista en Espana, 1979; Los Conservadores en Espana, 1981; Donde esta la Izquierda, 1982; The Communist Party in Spain, 1984; Spanish Marxism Versus Soviet Communism, 1988. Add: Apartat 214, 08870 Sitges (Barcelona), Spain.

ALBEE, Edward (Franklin). American, b. 1928. Plays/Screenplays. Producer, New Playwrights Unit Workshop, later Albarwild Theatre Arts, and Albar Productions, NYC. Pres., Edward F. Albee Foundn. Inc. *Publs:* The Zoo Story, The Death of Bessie Smith, The Sandbox: Three Plays (in U.K. as The Zoo Story and Other Plays), 1960; Fam and Yam, 1961; The American Dream, 1961; Who's Afraid of Virginia Woolf?, 1962; (adaptor) The Ballad of the Sad Cafe, 1963; Tiny Alice, 1965; (adaptor) Malcolm, 1966; A Delicate Balance, 1966; (adaptor) Everything in the Garden, 1968; Box and Quotations from Chairman Mao Tse-Tung, 1969; All Over, 1971; Seascape, 1975; Two Plays: Counting the Ways and Listening, 1977; The Lady from Dubuque, 1980; The Man with Three Arms, 1982; Walking, 1984; Marriage Play, 1986; Conversations with Edward Albee, 1988. Add: 14 Harrison St., New York, N.Y. 10013, U.S.A.

ALBERT, Adrien. Australian, b. 1907. Chemistry, Medicine/Health. Prof. Emeritus since 1972, and Visiting Fellow, Sch. of Chemistry, Australian National Univ. (First Prof. of Medical Chemistry, John Curtin Sch. of Medical Research, 1949–72). Member of Staff, Sydney Univ., 1938–47; Adviser on Drugs, Medical Directorate of the Australian Army, 1941–46; Wellcome Research Fellow, 1947–48. *Publs:* Selective Toxicity, 1951, 7th ed. 1985; The Acridines, 1951, 1966; Heterocyclic Chemistry, 1959, 1966; Ionization Constants, 1962, 3rd ed. 1984; The Selectivity of Drugs, 1975; Xenobiosis, 1987. Add: 15/13 Northbourne Flats, Braddon, Canberra 2601, Australia.

ALBERT, Marvin H. Also writes mystery novels as Nick Quarry and Anthony Rome. American. Novels, Mystery/Crime/Suspense, Westerns/Adventure, Children's non-fiction, Screenplays. Journalist, then freelance writer. *Publs:* Lie Down with Lions, 1955; The Law and Jake Wade, 1956; (with Theodore R. Seidman) Becoming a Mother (non-fiction), 1956, 3rd ed. 1978; Apache Rising, 1957, in U.K. as Duel at Diablo, 1966; Broadsides and Boarders (non-fiction), 1957; The Long White Road: Ernest Shackleton's Antarctic Adventures (juvenile non-fiction), 1957; Party Girl (novelization of screenplay), 1958; The Bounty Killer, 1958; Renegade Posse, 1958; (as Nick Quarry) The Hoods Come Calling, 1958; (as Nick Quarry) Trail of a Tramp, 1958; (as Nick Quarry) The Girl with No Place to Hide, 1959; Rider from Wind River, 1959; The Reformed Gun, 1959; That Girl from Maine, 1959; Pillow Talk (novelization of screenplay), 1959; All the Young Men (novelization of screenplay), 1960; (as Nick Quarry) No Chance in Hell, 1960; (as Nick Quarry) Till It Hurts, 1960; (as Nick Quarry) Some Die Hard, 1961; (as Anthony Rome) Miami Mayhem, 1961, in U.S. as Tony Rome, 1967; (as Anthony Rome) The Lady in Cement, 1962; (as Anthony Rome) My Kind of Game, 1962; Lover Come Back (novelization of screenplay), 1962; The VIP's (novelization of screenplay), 1963; Move Over, Darling (novelization of screenplay), 1963; Palm Springs Week-end, 1963; Under the Yum Yum Tree, 1963; Posse at High Pass, 1964; The Outrage (novelization of screenplay), 1964; Goodbye Charlie, 1964; The Pink Panther (novelization of screenplay), 1964; Honeymoon Hotel, 1964; What's New, Pussycat? (novelization of screenplay), 1965; Strange Bedfellows (novelization of screenplay), 1965; Do Not Disturb, 1965; The Great Race, 1965; A Very Special Flavor (novelization of screenplay), 1965; The Divorce (non-fiction), 1965; Come September, 1971; (as Nick Quarry) The Don is Dead, 1972; (as Nick Quarry) The Vendetta, 1973; The Gargoyle Conspiracy, 1975; The Dark Goddess, 1978; Clayburn, 1979; The Medusa Complex, 1982; Hidden Lives, 1982; Operation Lila, 1983; The Corsican, 1984; Stone Angel, 1986; Back In the Real World, 1986; Get Off At Babylon, 1987; Long Teeth, 1987; The Last Smile, 1988; The Midnight Sister, 1989. Add:c/o Fawcett Books, 201 East 50th St., New York, N.Y. 10022, U.S.A.

ALBERTS, Robert Carman. American, b. 1907. History, Biography. Vice Pres., Ketchum MacLeod & Grove Inc., Pittsburgh, Pa., 1956–69 (joined staff, 1942); Contrib. Ed., American Heritage mag., NYC, 1970–77. *Publs:* The Most Extraordinary Adventures of Major Robert Stobo, 1965; The Golden Voyage: The Life and Times of William Bingham, 1752-1804, 1969; The Good Provider: H.J. Heinz and His 57 Varieties, 1973; A Charming Field for an Encounter: The Story of George Washington's Fort Necessity, 1975; George Rogers Clark and the Winning of the Old Northwest, 1975; Benjamin West: A Biography, 1978; The Shaping of the Point: Pittsburgh's Renaissance Park, 1980; Pitt: The Story of the University of Pittsburgh 1787-1987, 1986. Add: 307 S. Dithridge St., Pittsburgh, Pa. 15213, U.S.A.

ALBERTSON, Dean. American, b. 1920. History, Biography. Prof. of History, Univ. of Massachusetts, Amherst, since 1965. Asst. Dir., Oral History Project, Columbia Univ., NYC, 1948–55; Exec. Asst., Cttee on Intnl. Exchange of Persons, Washington, D.C., 1956–59; Instr. to Assoc. Prof., Brooklyn Coll., NYC, 1959–65. *Publs:* Roosevelt's Farmer: Claude R. Wickard and the New Deal, 1961; Eisenhower as President, 1963; (with H.H. Quint and M. Cantor) Main Problems in American History (2 vols.), 1964, 4th ed. 1978; American History Visually, 1969; (ed. and contrib.) The Study of American History, 1974; Rebels or Revolutionaries: Student Movements of the Sixties, 1974. Add: Dept. of History, Univ. of Massachusetts, Amherst, Mass. 01003, U.S.A.

ALBINSKI, Henry Stephen. American, b. 1931. International relations/Current affairs, Politics/Government. Prof. of Political Science, and Dir. of the Australian Studies Center, Pennsylvania State Univ. (joined faculty, 1959). Consultant, Strategic Studies Div., Research Analysis Corp., Center for Strategic and Intnl. Studies, Georgetown Univ., Washington, D.C., 1972–73, and U.S. Dept. of State, 1978. *Publs:* Australia and the China Problem During the Korean War Period, 1964; Australian Policies and Attitudes Toward China, 1965; The Australian Labor Party and the Aid to Parochial Schools Controversy, 1966; (with L.K. Pettit) European Political Processes, 1968, rev. ed. 1974; Australia in Southeast Asia, 1970; Politics and Foreign Policy in Australia, 1970; (ed. and contrib.) Asian Political Processes, 1971; Canadian and Australian Politics in Comparative Perspective, 1973; Australian External

Policy under Labor, 1977; The Australian-American Security Relationship, 1982; ANZUS: The United States and Pacific Security, 1987. Add: Dept. of Political Science, Pennsylvania State Univ., University Park, Pa. 16802, U.S.A.

ALCOCK, Vivien (Dolores). British, b. 1926. Children's Fiction. Formerly commercial artist. *Publs:* The Haunting of Cassie Palmer, 1980; The Stonewalkers, 1981; The Sylvia Game, 1982; Travellers by Night, 1983; Ghostly Companions, 1984; The Cuckoo Sister, 1985; The Mysterious Mr. Ross, 1987; The Monster Garden, 1988. Add: 59 Wood Lane, London N6, England.

ALDCROFT, Derek Howard. British and Australian, b. 1936. Economics, Transportation. Prof. of Economic History, since 1976, and Head of Dept., Univ. of Leicester (Asst. Lectr., 1962–63, Sr. Lectr., 1967–70, and Reader, 1970–73). Member, Advisory Panel, The Economic Review, since 1982; Member, Advisory Bd., Independent Research Services, Oxford, since 1986. Teaching Asst., 1960–62, Lectr., 1964–67, Univ. of Glasgow; Prof. and Head, Dept. of Economic History, Univ. of Sydney, 1973–76. Chmn., Editorial Cttee., Journal of Transport History, 1969–73; Editorial Adviser, Business History Review, 1971–73. *Publs:* British Railways in Transition: The Economic Problems of Britain's Railways since 1914, 1968; (ed.) The Development of British Industry and Foreign Competition 1875-1914, 1968; (with H.W. Richardson) Building in the British Economy Between the Wars, 1968; (with H.W. Richardson) The British Economy, 1969; (ed. with P. Fearon) Economic Growth in Twentieth Century Britain, 1969; (with H.J. Dyos) British Transport: An Economic Survey from the Seventeenth Century to the Twentieth, 1969; The Inter-War Economy, Britain 1919–1939, 1970; (ed. with P. Fearon) British Economic Fluctuations 1790-1939, 1972; Studies in British Transport History 1879-1970, 1974; British Transport since 1914, 1975; From Versailles to Wall Street: The International Economy 1919–1929, 1977; The East Midlands Economy, 1979; The European Economy, 1914–80, 1980; Full Employment: The Elusive Goal, 1984; The British Economy: Vol. I, Years of Turmoil, 1920–1951, 1986. Add: 10 Linden Dr., Evington, Leicester LE5 6AH, England.

ALDEN, John Richard. American, b. 1908. History, Biography. Emeritus Prof. of History, Duke Univ., Durham, N.C., since 1976 (James B. Duke Prof., 1955–76). Prof. of History, Univ. of Nebraska, Lincoln, 1950–55. *Publs:* John Stuart and the Southern Colonial Frontier, 1944 (Albert Beveridge Prize); General Gage in America, 1948; General Charles Lee, 1951; (ed.) The War of the Revolution, 1952; The American Revolution, 1954; The South in the Revolution, 1957; (co-author) A History of the United States, 1960; The First South, 1961; Rise of the American Republic, 1963; Pioneer America 1966; A History of the American Revolution, 1969; Governor Robert Dinwiddie, 1973; Stephen Sayre, 1983; George Washington, 1984. Add: 2417 Persian Dr., Clearwater, Fla. 34623, U.S.A.

ALDEN, Sue. *See* **FRANCIS,** Dorothy Brenner.

ALDERSON, Sue Ann. American (born Canadian), b. 1940. Children's fiction. Instr. in English, Simon Fraser Univ., Vancouver, 1967–71, and Capilano Coll., Vancouver, 1972–80. *Publs:* Bonnie McSmithers You're Driving Me Dithers, 1974; Hurry Up, Bonnie!, 1976; The Adventures of Prince Paul, 1977; The Finding Princess, 1977; Bonnie McSmithers Is at It Again!, 1979; Comet's Tale, 1983; The Not Impossible Summer, 1983; The Something in Thurlo Darby's House, 1984; Ida and the Wool Smugglers, 1987. Add: 4004 W. 32nd Ave., Vancouver, B.C. V6S 1Z6, Canada.

ALDING, Peter. *See* **JEFFRIES,** Roderic.

ALDISS, Brian (Wilson). British, b. 1925. Novels/Short stories, Science fiction/Fantasy, Plays/Screenplays, Poetry, Literature, Travel/Exploration/Adventure. Literary Ed., Oxford Mail, 1958–69; Ed., Penguin Science Fiction, 1961–64. Pres., World SF, 1982–84. *Publs:* The Brightfount Diaries, 1955; Space Time and Nathaniel, 1957; Non-Stop (in U.S. as Starship), 1958; No Time Like Tomorrow, 1959; Vanguard from Alpha, 1959; Canopy of Time, 1959; Male Response, 1959; Bow Down to Nul, 1960; Galaxies Like Grains of Sand, 1960; Equator, 1961; (ed.) Penguin Science Fiction, 1961; Primal Urge, 1961; The Interpreter, 1961; Hothouse (in U.S. as Long Afternoon of Earth), 1962; (ed.) More Penguin Science Fiction, 1962: (ed.) Best Fantasy Stories, 1962; Airs of Earth, 1963; The Dark Light Years, 1964; (ed.) Yet More Penguin Science Fiction, 1964; Introducing SF, 1964; Greybeard, 1964; Starswarm, 1964; Earthworks, 1965; Best SF Stories of Brian W. Aldiss (in U.S. as Who Can Replace a Man?), 1965; The Saliva Tree and Other Strange Growths,

1966; Cities and Stones: A Traveller's Jugoslavia, 1966; An Age (in U.S. as Cryptozoic!) 1967; (ed. with H. Harrison) Nebula Award Stories II, 1967; Farewell Fantastic Venus (in U.S. as All About Venus), 1968; (ed. with H. Harrison) Best SF 1967 to 1975, 1968–76; Report on Probability A, 1968; A Brian Aldiss Omnibus, 1969; Intangibles Inc. and Other Stories, 1969; Barefoot in the Head, 1969; Neanderthal Planet, 1970; The Shape of Further Things, 1970; The Hand-Reared Boy, 1970; A Soldier Erect: or, Further Adventures of the Hand-Reared Boy, 1971; Brian Aldiss Omnibus 2, 1971; The Moment of Eclipse, 1971; The Comic Inferno, 1972; (ed. with H. Harrison) The Astounding-Analog Reader, vol. I, 1972; Frankenstein Unbound, 1973; (ed. with H. Harrison) The Astounding-Analog Reader, vol. II, 1973; (ed.) Penguin Science Fiction Omnibus, 1973; Billion Year Spree: The History of Science Fiction, 1973; The Eighty-Minute Hour, 1974; Space Opera, 1974; (ed.) Space Odysseys, 1975; (ed. with H. Harrison) Hell's Cartographers, 1975; Science Fiction Art: The Fantasies of SF, 1975; (ed.) Space Odysseys, 1975; (ed.) Evil Earths: An Anthology of Way-Back-When Futures, 1975; (ed. with C. Foss) Science Fiction Art, 1975; (ed. with H. Harrison) Decade: The 1940's, 1950's, 1960's, 1975–77; The Malacia Tapestry, 1976; (ed.) Galactic Empires, 1976; Last Orders, 1977; Brothers of the Head, 1977; A Rude Awakening, 1978; (ed.) Enemies of the System, 1978; Distant Encounters (play), 1978; Perilous Planets, 1978; New Arrivals, Old Encounters, 1979; This World and Nearer Ones, 1979; Pile (verse), 1979; Life in the West, 1980; Moreau's Other Island, 1980; Helliconia Spring, 1982; Helliconia Summer, 1983; Science Fiction Quiz, 1983; Seasons in Flight, 1984; ... and the Lurid Glare of the Comet, 1985; Helliconia Winter, 1985; Pale Shadow of Science, 1986; Trillion Year Spree, 1986; Cracken at Critical, 1987; Ruins, 1987; Forgotten Life, 1988; Science Fiction Blues, 1989. Add: Woodlands, Foxcombe Rd., Boars Hill, Oxford OX1 5DL, England.

ALDRIDGE, A. Owen. American, b. 1915. Literature, Philosophy, Biography. Prof. Emeritus of Comparative Literature, Univ. of Illinois, Urbana, 1967–86; Will and Ariel Durant Chair, St. Peter's Coll., Jersey City, 1986–87; Fulbright Prof., Korea, 1988. Ed., Comparative Literature Studies journal, since 1963. *Publs:* Shaftesbury and the Deist Manifesto, 1951; Benjamin Franklin and His French Contemporaries, 1957; Man of Reason: The Life of Thomas Paine, 1959; Essai sur les personnages des Liaisons Dangereuses en tant que types litteraires, 1960; Jonathan Edwards, 1964; Benjamin Franklin: Philosopher and Man, 1965; Benjamin Franklin and Nature's God, 1967; (ed.) Comparative Literature: Matter and Method, 1969; (ed.) The Iberoamerican Enlightenment, 1970; Voltaire and the Century of Light, 1975; Comparative Literature East-West, 1979; Thomas Paine's American Ideology, 1984; Fiction in Japan and the West, 1985; The Reemergence of World Literature: A Study of Asia and the West, 1986. Add: 101 East Chalmers St., Champaign, Ill. 61820, U.S.A.

ALDRIDGE, Gordon James. American (born Canadian), b. 1916. Sociology. Prof. of Social Work, Arizona State Univ., Tempe, since 1978. Consultant on Social Work Education, Teachers Coll., Columbia Univ., NYC, since 1962. Social Worker, Toronto Family Agency, Can., 1939–41; Lectr. in Psychology, Univ. of Toronto, and Exec. Dir., Toronto Family Agency, 1946–50; Assoc. Prof. of Social Work, and Dir., Human Relations Institute, Florida State Univ., Tallahassee, 1950–52; Prof. of Social Work, Michigan State Univ., East Lansing, 1952–77 (Dean, 1959–66). *Publs:* (with F.F. Fauri) Social Welfare and the Aged, 1959; (ed.) Social Issues and Psychiatric Social Work Practice, 1959; (ed. with J. Kaplan) Social Welfare of the Aging, 1962; (with E.J. McGrath) Liberal Education and Social Work, 1965; Undergraduate Social Work Education, 1972. Add: 7709 E. Sheridan, Scottsdale, Ariz., U.S.A.

ALDRIDGE, (Harold Edward) James. Australian, b. 1918. Novels/Short stories, Children's fiction, Plays/Screenplays, Travel/Exploration/Adventure. Writer, Melbourne Herald and Sun, 1937–38, and London Daily Sketch and Sunday Dispatch, 1939; European and Middle East War Corresp., Australian Newspaper Service and North American Newspaper Alliance, 1939–44. *Publs:* Signed with Their Honour, 1942; The Sea Eagle, 1944; Of Many Men, 1946; The 49th State (play), 1946; The Diplomat, 1950; The Hunter, 1951; Heroes of the Empty View, 1954; Underwater Hunting for Inexperienced Englishmen, 1955; I Wish He Would Not Die, 1957; Gold and Sand, 1960; The Last Exile, 1961; A Captive in the Land, 1962; The Statesman's Game, 1966; My Brother Tom (in U.S. as My Brother Tom: A Love Story), 1966; The Flying 19, 1966; (with P. Stand) Living Egypt, 1969; Cairo: Biography of a City, 1969; A Sporting Proposition, 1973; The Marvelous Mongolian, 1974; Mockery in Arms, 1974; The Untouchable Juli, 1975; One Last Glimpse, 1977; Goodbye Un-America, 1979; The Broken Saddle, 1983; The True Story of Lilli Stubeck, 1984; The True Story of Spit MacPhee, 1986.

Add: c/o Curtis Brown, 162-168 Regent St., London W1R 5TA, England.

ALDRIDGE, John W(atson). American, b. 1922. Novels, Literature. Prof. of English, Univ. of Michigan, Ann Arbor, since 1964. Member, National Book Critics Circle. Lectr. in Criticism, 1948–50, and Asst. Prof. of English, 1950–55, Univ. of Vermont, Burlington; Christian Gauss Lectr. in Criticism, Princeton Univ., N.J., 1953–54; Member of the Literature Faculty, Sarah Lawrence Coll., Bronxville, N.Y., and The New Sch. for Social Research, NYC; Prof. of English, Queens Coll., NYC, 1956–57; Berg Prof. of English, New York Univ., 1957–58; Fulbright Lectr., Univ. of Munich, 1958–59, and the Univ. of Copenhagen, 1962–63; Writer-in-Residence, Hollins Coll., Va., 1960–62; Book Critic, New York Herald Tribune Book Week, 1965–66, and Saturday Review, NYC, 1969–79; Special Adviser for American Studies, U.S. Embassy, Bonn, 1972–73; Book Commentator, MacNeil/Lehrer News Hour, 1983–84. *Publs:* After the Lost Generation: A Critical Study of the Writers of Two Wars, 1951; (ed.) Critiques and Essays on Modern Fiction 1920–1951, 1952; (ed.) Discovery 1, 1952; In Search of Heresy: American Literature in the Age of Conformity, 1956; (ed.) Selected Stories, by P.G. Wodehouse, 1958; The Party at Cranton (novel), 1960; Time to Murder and Create: The Contemporary Novel in Crisis, 1966; In the Country of the Young, 1970; The Devil in the Fire: Retrospective Essays on American Literature and Culture 1951–1972, 1972; The American Novel and the Way We Live Now, 1983. Add: 1050 Wall St., Ann Arbor, Mich. 48105, U.S.A.

ALDYNE, Nathan. *See* **McDOWELL,** Michael.

ALEXANDER, Baron, of Potterhill; William Picken Alexander. British, b. 1905. Education. Dir. of Education, Margate, Kent, 1935–39, and Sheffield, Yorks., 1939–44; Secty., Assn. of Education Cttees., London, 1944–77. *Publs:* Intelligence, Concrete and Abstract, 1935; The Educational Need of Democracy, 1940; A Performance Scale for the Measurement of Technical Ability, 1947; A Parents' Guide to the Education Act 1944, 1947; Education in England, 1953; (co-author) County and Voluntary Schools, 4th ed. 1967; Towards a New Education Act, 1969; (co-author) Education Acts Amended, 1969. Add: 3 Moor Park Gardens, Pembroke Rd., Moor Park, Herts., England.

ALEXANDER, Christopher. British, b. 1936. Architecture. Dir., Center for Environmental Structure, Berkeley, since 1967; Prof. of Architecture, Univ. of California, Berkeley, since 1970 (Asst. Prof., 1963; Prof. in the Humanities, 1965–66; Assoc. Prof. of Architecture, 1966–70). Worked for the Village Development Planning Dept. of the Govt. of Gujarat, India, 1962; Consultant in Urban Housing, Arthur D. Little Co., San Francisco, 1963; Consultant Architect, Bay Area Rapid Transit System, San Francisco, 1963–64; Consultant on User Needs, Ministry of Public Buildings and Works, London, 1965–66. *Publs:* (with Serge Chermayeff) Community and Privacy; Towards a New Architecture of Humanism, 1963; Notes on the Synthesis of Form, 1964; Systems Generating Systems, 1967; (with Sara Ishikawa and Murray Silverstein) A Pattern Language Which Generates Multi-Service Centers, 1968; (with others) Houses Generated by Patterns, 1969; Tres Aspectos de Matematica Desegno, 1969; Mosaic of Subcultures, 1969; A Human City, 1970; La Estructrua del Medio Ambiente, 1971; (with Walter Wendler) The New Apartment Building, 1975; The Oregon Experiment, 1975; A Pattern Language, 1977; The Timeless Way of Building, 1979; The Linz Cafe, 1981; (with Howard Davis) The Production of Houses, 1985; (with Hajo Neis, Artemis Anninou and Ingrid King) A New Theory of Urban Design, 1987. Add: Center for Environmental Structure, 2701 Shasta Rd., Berkeley, Calif. 94708, U.S.A.

ALEXANDER, Eugenie. British, b. 1919. Art, Crafts. Freelance writer and designer. Lectr., Goldsmiths' Coll. of Art, London, 1955–58. *Publs:* Art for Young People, 1958; Fabric Pictures, 1959; Museums and How to Use Them, 1974. Add: 56 King George St., Greenwich, London SE10 8QD, England.

ALEXANDER, Floyce. American, b. 1938. Poetry. Freelance Ed., Univ. of New Mexico Press, Albuquerque, since 1983. Editorial Asst., Washington State Univ. Press, Pullman, 1963–70; Teaching Asst., Washington State Univ., Pullman, 1970–71, Univ. of Massachusetts, Amherst, 1972–74, and Univ. of New Mexico, Albuquerque, 1978–81. *Publs:* Ravines, 1971; Machete, 1972; Bottom Falling out of the Dream, 1976; Red Deer, 1982; (ed. with Margaret Randall) Risking a Somersault in the Air: Conversations with Nicaraguan Writers, 1984; Love's Alibi, 1988. Add: 1502 Silver Ave. S.E., Albuquerque, N.M. 87106, U.S.A.

ALEXANDER, Joan. Pseud. for Lady Carwath. British, b. 1920. Novels/Short stories. *Publs:* Fly Away Paul, 1954; The Choice and the

Circumstance, 1956; Carola, 1957; Lewis's Wife, 1959; Thy People, My People, 1967; Strange Loyalty, 1969; Where Have All the Flowers Gone?, 1969; Bitter Wind, 1970; Whom the Gods Love, 1977; One Sunny Day, 1978; Voices and Echoes: Tales of Colonial Women, 1983. Add: Coachman's Cottage, 33 Grove Rd., Barnes, London SW13, England.

ALEXANDER, John Thorndike. American, b. 1940. History. Prof. of History and Slavic and Soviet Area Studies, Univ. of Kansas, since 1974 (Asst. Prof., 1966–70; Assoc. Prof., 1970–74). *Publs:* Autocratic Politics in National Crisis: The Imperial Russian Government and Pugachev's Revolt 1773-1775, 1969; (trans. & ed.) S.F. Platonov, The Time of Troubles, 1970; Emperor of the Cossacks: Pugachev and the Frontier Jacquerie of 1773-1775, 1973; Bubonic Plague in Early Modern Russia: Public Health and Urban Disaster, 1980; Catherine the Great: Life and Legend, 1989. Add: Dept. of History, Univ. of Kansas, Lawrence, Kans. 66045, U.S.A.

ALEXANDER, Lloyd (Chudley). American, b. 1924. Novels/Short stories, Children's fiction. Dir., Carpenter Lane Chamber Music Soc., Philadelphia, since 1970; Member, Editorial Advisory Bd., Cricket mag., La Salle, Ill., since 1973. Author-in-Residence, Temple Univ., Philadelphia, 1970–74. Recipient, Newbery Medal, 1968; National Book Award, 1970; American Book Award, 1981. *Publs:* (trans.) The Wall and Other Stories, by Jean-Paul Sartre, 1948, as Intimacy and Other Stories, 1949; (trans.) Nausea, by Jean-Paul Sartre, 1949; (trans.) Selected Writings, by Paul Eluard, 1951; (trans.) The Sea Rose, by Paul Vialar, 1952; And Let the Credit Go, 1955; My Five Tigers, 1956; Border Hawk: August Bondi, 1958; The Flagship Hope: Aaron Lopez, 1960; Janine Is French, 1960; My Love Affair with Music, 1960; (with Louis J. Camuti) Park Avenue Vet, 1962; Time Cat: The Remarkable Journeys of Jason and Gareth, 1963; The Book of Three, 1964; Fifty Years in the Doghouse, 1964; The Black Cauldron, 1965; Coll and His White Pig, 1965; The Castle of Llyr, 1966; Taran Wanderer, 1967; The High King, 1968; The Marvelous Misadventures of Sebastian, 1970; The King's Fountain, 1971; The Four Donkeys, 1972; The Cat Who Wished to Be a Man, 1973; The Foundling and Other Tales of Prydain, 1973; The Wizard in the Tree, 1975; The Town Cats and Other Tales, 1977; The First Two Lives of Lukas-Kasha, 1978; Westmark, 1981; The Kestrel, 1982; The Beggar Queen, 1984; The Illyrian Adventure, 1986; The El Dorado Adventure, 1987. Add: 1005 Drexel Ave., Drexel Hill, Pa. 19026, U.S.A.

ALEXANDER, Louis George. British, b. 1932. Language/Linguistics. Adviser, Longman Group, since 1966, and Deutsch Volkshochschul-Verband, since 1967. Member, Threshold Level Cttee., Council of Europe, since 1973. Head, English Dept., Protypon Lykeion, Athens, 1957–65. Chmn., Educational Writers Group, Soc. of Authors, 1975–77. *Publs:* Sixty Steps, 1962; Poetry and Prose Appreciation, 1963; A First Book in Comprehension, 1965; Essays and Letter Writing, 1965; The Carters of Greenwood, 1966; Detectives from Scotland Yard, 1966; April Fools Day, 1966; New Concept English (4 vols.), 1967; Worth A Fortune, 1967; Question and Answer, 1967; For and Against, 1968; Look, Listen and Learn, Sets 1-4, 1968–71; Reading and Writing English, 1969; Car Thieves, 1969; (with A. Evangelisti) Language and Life, 1970; Operation Mastermind, 1971; Guided Composition in ELT, 1971; Tell Us a Story, 1973; (with J. Tadman and R. Kingsbury) Target, Sets 1-3, 1972–74; Mainline Progress and B, 1973; (with C. Wilson) In Other Words, 1974; (with M. Vincent) Make Your Point, 1975; K's First Case, 1975; Good Morning, Mexico!, 1975; (with M. Vincent and R. Kingsbury) Mainline Skills A, 1975; (with W.S. Allen, R. Close, and R. O'Neill) English Grammatical Structure, 1975; (with R. Kingsbury) I Think, You Think, 1976; Operation Janus, 1976; Clint Magee, 1976; Dangerous Game, 1977; (with R. Kingsbury) Mainline Skills B, 1977; (with J. van Ek and A. Fitzpatrick) Waystage, Council of Europe, 1977; Some Methodological Implications of Waystage and Threshold Level, Council of Europe, 1977; (with K. Preis, F. Schimek, and A. Prochazka) Look, Listen and Learn for Austria, Sets 1-4, 1974–78; (with A. Evangelisti, et al) Way In, 1978; Mainline Beginners, A, 1978; Mainline Beginners B, 1979; Follow Me, 1979; Survive in French/Spanish/German/Italian, 1980; Conversational French/Spanish/German/Italian, 1981; Excel, 1985–87; Plain English, 1987–88; Longman English Grammar, 1987–88. Add: Garden House, Weydown Rd., Haslemere, Surrey, England.

ALEXANDER, M(ichael) J(oseph). British, b. 1941. Poetry, Literature, Translations. Berry Prof. of English Literature, Univ. of St. Andrews, Scotland, since 1985. Employed by William Collins, publishers, London, 1963–65; Fellow, Princeton Univ. Grad. Sch., New Jersey, 1965–66; Lectr., Univ. of California at Santa Barbara, 1966–67; Ed., Andre Deutsch, publishers, London, 1967–68; Lectr. in English, Univ. of East Anglia, Norwich, 1968–69; Lectr., 1969–77, Sr. Lectr., 1977–85, and Reader in English Studies, 1985, Univ. of Stirling, Scotland. *Publs:* (trans.) The Earliest English Poems, 1966, 1978; (trans.) Beowulf, 1973; The Poetic Achievement of Ezra Pound, 1979; Twelve Poems, 1980; The Prologue to the Canterbury Tales, 1980; (trans.) Old English Riddles from the Exeter Book, 1980; The Knight's Tale, 1981; A History of Old English Literature, 1983. Add: Dept. of English, The University, St. Andrews, Scotland.

ALEXANDER, Patrick James. British, b. 1926. Novels/Short stories, Plays/Screenplays. Freelance TV writer since 1957. Sub-Ed., Yorkshire Post, 1945–49, Daily Sketch, 1949–51, and Daily Mirror, 1952–54; Feature Writer, Woman's Mirror, 1954–56; Script Ed., Rediffusion TV, 1961–65, and BBC, 1966–69. *Publs:* Death of A Thin-Skinned Animal, 1976; Soldier on the Other Side, 1984; Show Me a Hero, 1986. Add: 2 Worcester Gardens, Worcester Park, Surrey KT4 7HN, England.

ALEXANDER, Robert J. American, b. 1918. Economics, History, International Relations/Current Affairs, Politics/Government, Biography. Prof. of Economics and Political Science, Rutgers Univ., New Brunswick, N.J., since 1961 (Instr., 1947–50; Asst. Prof., 1950–56; Assoc. Prof., 1956–61). Asst. Economist, Office of Inter-American Affairs, Washington, D.C., 1945–46. *Publs:* The Peron Era, 1951; Communism in Latin America, 1957; The Bolivian National Revolution, 1958; (with C.O. Porter) The Struggle for Democracy in Latin America, 1961; A Primer of Economic Development, 1962; Prophets of the Revolution, 1962; Labor Relations in Argentina, Brazil and Chile, 1962; Today's Latin America, 1962; Latin America, 1964; The Venezuelan Democratic Revolution, 1964; Organized Labor in Latin America, 1965; Latin American Politics and Goverment, 1965; An Introduction to Argentina; The Communist Party of Venezuela; Trotskyism in Latin America; Latin American Political Parties; Aprismo: The Ideas and Doctrines of Victor Raul Haya de la Tore; Agrarian Reform in Latin America; A New Development Strategy; Arturo Alessandri: A Biography; The Tragedy of Chile; Juan Peron: A History; The Right Opposition: The Lovestoneites and the International Communist Opposition of the 1930s; Romulo Betancourt and the Transformation of Venezuela; Bolivia: Past, Present and Future of its Politics, 1982; (ed.) Political Parties of the Americas, 1982; (ed.) Biographical Dictionary of Latin American and Caribbean Political Leaders, 1988. Add: 944 River Rd., Piscataway, N.J. 08854, U.S.A.

ALEXANDER, Robert McN(eill). British, b. 1934. Zoology. Prof. of Zoology, Univ. of Leeds, since 1969. Asst. Lectr., 1958–61, Lectr., 1961–68, and Sr. Lectr., 1968–69, University Coll. of North Wales, Bangor. *Publs:* Functional Design in Fishes, 1967, 3rd ed., 1974; Animal Mechanics, 1968, 1983; Size and Shape, 1971; The Chordates, 1975, 1981; Biomechanics, 1975; (with G. Goldspink) Mechanics and Energetics of Animal Locomotion, 1977; The Invertebrates, 1979; Locomotion of Animals, 1981; Optima for Animals, 1982; Elastic Mechanisms in Animal Movement, 1988. Add: Dept. of Pure and Applied Biology, Univ. of Leeds, Leeds LS2 9JT, England.

ALEXANDER, Shana. American, b. 1925. Social commentary/phenomena, Women. Member, New York State Council on the Arts, since 1978; Dir., American Film Inst. With Harper's Bazaar, 1946–47, and Flair mag., 1950; reporter, 1951–54, member of West Coast staff, 1954–61, staff writer, 1961–64, and columnist, The Feminine Eye, 1964–69, Life mag.; Ed.-in-Chief, McCall's mag., NYC, 1969–71; Vice Pres., Norton Simon Inc, 1971–72; radio and TV commentator, Spectrum, CBS News, 1972; Columnist, Newsweek mag., 1972–74; Commentator, Sixty Minutes, CBS-TV, 1974–79. *Publs:* The Feminine Eye, 1970; Shana Alexander's State-by-State Guide to Women's Rights, 1975; Talking Woman, 1976; Anyone's Daughter, 1979; Very Much a Lady: The Untold Story of Jean Harris and Dr. Herman Tarnower, 1983; Nutcracker: Money, Madness, Murder: A Family Album, 1985; The Pizza Connection, 1988. Add: c/o Joy Harris, The Lantz Office, 888 Seventh Ave., New York, N.Y. 10106, U.S.A.

ALEXANDER, Sue. American, b. 1933. Children's fiction, Plays. *Publs:* Small Plays for You and a Friend, 1973; Nadir of the Streets, 1975; Peacocks Are Very Special, 1976; Witch, Goblin and Sometimes Ghost, 1976; Small Plays for Special Days, 1977; Marc the Magnificent, 1978; More Witch, Goblin and Ghost Stories, 1978; Seymour the Prince, 1979; Finding Your First Job, 1980; Whatever Happened to Uncle Albert? and Other Puzzling Plays, 1980; Witch, Goblin and Ghost in the Haunted Woods, 1981; Witch, Goblin and Ghost's Book of Things to Do, 1982; Nadia the Willful, 1983; Dear Phoebe, 1984; World Famous Muriel, 1984; Witch, Goblin and Ghost Are Back, 1985; World Famous Muriel and the Scary Dragon, 1985; Lila on the Landing, 1987; There's More—Much

More, Said Squirrel, 1987; America's Own Holidays, 1988. Add: 6846 McLaren, Canoga Park, Calif. 91307, U.S.A.

ALEXOPOULOS, Constantine John. American, b. 1907. Botany. Prof. Emeritus of Botany, Univ. of Texas at Austin, since 1977 (Prof., 1962–77). Head, Dept. of Botany, Univ. of Iowa, Iowa City, 1956–62. *Publs:* Introductory Mycology, 1952, 1962, (with C.W. Mims) 1979; (with H.C. Bold) Algae and Fungi, 1967; (with W.D. Gray) Biology of the Myxomycetes, 1968; (with G.W. Martin) The Myxomycetes, 1969; (with H.C. Bold and T. Delevoryas) Morphology of Plants and Fungi, 1980; (with G.W. Martin and M.L. Farr) The Genera of Myxomycetes, 1983. Add: 917 Calithea Rd., Austin, Tex. 78746, U.S.A.

ALFORD, B(ernard) W(illiam) E(rnest). British, b. 1937. Economics, History. Prof. of Economic and Social History, Univ. of Bristol, since 1982 (Asst. Lectr., 1962–64, Lectr., 1964–73, Sr. Lectr., 1973–76, and Reader, 1976–82). Asst. Lectr. in Economic History, London Sch. of Economics, 1961–62. *Publs:* (with T.C. Barker) A History of the Carpenters' Company, 1968; Depression and Recovery? British Economic Growth 1918–1939, 1972; W.D. & H.O. Wills and the Development of the U.K. Tobacco Industry 1786-1965, 1973; British Economic Performance, 1945–75, 1987. Add: Dept. of Economic and Social History, Univ. of Bristol, Bristol BS8 1TB, England.

ALFORD, Neill Herbert, Jr. American, b. 1919. Law. Percy Brown Jr. Prof. of Law, Univ. of Virginia, Charlottesville, since 1976. Reporter, Supreme Ct. of Virginia, since 1977. Stockton Chair of Intnl. Law, Naval War Coll., Newport, R.I., 1961–62; Doherty Prof. of Law, 1966–74, and Special Counsel to the Pres., 1972–74, Univ. of Virginia, Charlottesville; Dean of the Law Sch., and Joseph Henry Lumpkin Prof. of Law, Univ. of Georgia, Athens, 1974–76. *Publs:* Modern Economic Warfare: Law and the Naval Participant, 1967; Cases and Text on Decedents Estates and Trusts, 5th ed., 1977. Add: The Law Sch., Univ. of Virginia, Charlottes-ville, Va. 22901, U.S.A.

ALFRED, William. American, b. 1922. Plays/Screenplays, Literature, Translations. Abbott Lawrence Lowell Prof. of the Humanities, Harvard Univ., Cambridge, Mass., since 1963 (Inst., 1954–57; Asst. Prof., 1957–59; Assoc. Prof., 1959–63). Ed., American Poet mag., 1942–44. *Publs:* The Annunciation Rosary, 1948; Agamemnon, 1953; (co-ed) Complete Prose Works of John Milton, vol. I, 1953; (trans.) Beowulf, 1963; Hogan's Goat, 1966; The Curse of an Aching Heart, 1983. Add: 31 Athens St., Cambridge, Mass. 02138, U.S.A.

ALGEO, John. American, b. 1930. Language/Linguistics. Alumni Foundation Distinguished Prof. of English, Univ. of Georgia, Athens (member of faculty since 1971; Head of the Dept. 1975–79). Asst. Prof., Prof., and Asst. Dean of Grad. Sch., Univ. of Florida, 1961–71. Ed. American Speech mag., 1971–81. *Publs:* Problems in the Origins and Development of the English Language, 1966, 1972, 1982; (with T. Pyles) English: An Introduction to Language, 1970; On Defining the Proper Name, 1973; Exercises in Contemporary English, 1974; (ed.) T. Pyles: Selected Essays on English Usage, 1979; (with T. Pyles) Origins and Development of the English Language, 1982. Add: Park Hall, Univ. of Georgia, Athens, Ga. 30602, U.S.A.

ALI, Ahmed. Pakistani, b. 1910. Novels/Short stories, Poetry, Literature, Translations. Managing Dir., Lomen Fabrics Ltd., Karachi, since 1970; Adviser, Akrash Publr., Karachi. Lectr., University of Lucknow, Agra and Allahabad, 1933–42; Rep. and Dir., BBC, India, 1942–44; Prof., Presidency Coll., Calcutta, 1944–48; British Council Visiting Prof. in China, 1947–48; with Pakistan Foreign Service, 1950–60; Visiting Prof., Michigan State Univ., East Lansing, 1975, and Univ of Karachi, 1977–79; Fulbright Prof., Western Kentucky Univ., Bowling Green, and Southern Illinois Univ., Carbondale, 1978–79. *Publs:* Land of Twilight, 1931; Break the Chains, 1932; (co-author) Angaray, 1932; Sholay, 1934; Hamari Gali, 1940; Twilight in Delhi, 1940; Mr. Eliot's Penny-World of Dreams, 1942; Qaidkhana, 1942; (ed.) Tomorrow, 1944; Maut Se Pahlay, 1945; Muslim China, 1949; (ed.) Indian Writing, 1949; Flaming Earth: Selected Poems from Indonesia, 1949; Purple Gold Mountain, 1960; Bulbul and the Rose, 1962; Ocean of Night, 1964; Ghalib: Selected Poems, 1969; Problem of Style and Technique in Ghalib, 1969; (ed. & trans.) The Golden Tradition: An Anthology of Urdu Poetry, 1973; (trans.) Al-Qur'an, 1984; The Prison House: Selected Short Stories, 1985; Rats and Diplomats, 1985, 1986; (ed.) Selected Short Stories from Pakistan, 1986; Selected poems, 1988. Add: 21A Faran, Hyder Ali Rd., Karachi 5, Pakistan.

ALIBER, Robert Z. American, b. 1930. Money/Finance. Prof. of

Intnl. Economics and Finance, and Dir., Center for Studies in Intnl. Finance, Grad. Sch. of Business, Univ. of Chicago. Staff Economist, Commn. on Money and Credit, 1959–61, and Cttee. for Economic Development, 1961–64; Sr. Economic Advisor, Agency for Intl. Development, U.S. Dept. of State, 1964–65. *Publs:* (ed. and contrib.) National Monetary Policies and the International Financial System, 1974; International Money Game, 1979, 1985; Exchange Risk and Corporate International Finance, 1979; (co-author) Money, Banking and Economic Activity, 1981, 1987; Your Money and Your Life, 1982. Add: Univ. of Chicago, Grad. Sch. of Business, 1101 East 58th St., Chicago, Ill. 60637, U.S.A.

ALIKI, *See* **BRANDENBERG,** Aliki.

ALISKY, Marvin (Michael Howard). American, b. 1923. Communications Media, Politics/Government, Writing/Journalism. Prof. of Political Science, Arizona State Univ., Tempe, since 1960 (Chmn., Dept. of Mass Communications, 1957–65; Dir., Center for Latin American Studies, 1965–72; Ed. and Publr., Latin America Digest, 1966–72). Editorial Page Columnist, Arizona Republic, Phoenix; Columnist, Tempe Daily News, both since 1972. News Corresp., NBC, Latin America, 1947–49. *Publs:* Latin American Journalism Bibliography, 1958; (with B.G. Barnett and K.F. Johnson) Political Forces in Latin America, 1968, 1970; Who's Who in Mexican Government, 1969; Uruguay: A Contemporary Survey, 1969; (with M.C. Needler) Political Systems of Latin America, 1970; Government of Mexican State of Nuevo Leon, 1971; Government of Mexican State of Sonora, 1971; Peruvian Political Perspective, 1972; Historical Dictionary of Peru, 1979; Historical Dictionary of Mexico, 1980; Latin American Media: Guidance and Censorship, 1981; Arms Production in Developing Countries, 1984; Latin American Biography, 1987; Handbook of International Broadcasting Systems, 1987. Add: Dept. of Political Science, Arizona State Univ., Tempe, Ariz. 85281, U.S.A.

ALLABY, (John) Michael. British, b. 1933. Agriculture/Forestry, Environmental science/Ecology. Freelance writer since 1973. Drama Student, then Actor, 1954–64; with the Editorial Dept. of the Soil Assn., 1964–72; Assoc. Ed., 1970–72, and Managing Ed., 1972–73, The Ecologist mag. *Publs:* The Eco-Activists, 1971; Who Will Eat?, 1972; (with Floyd Allen) Robots Behind the Plow, 1974; Ecology, 1975; (with others) The Survival Handbook, 1975; Inventing Tomorrow, 1975; (with Colin Tudge) Home Farm, 1977; (ed.) A Dictionary of the Environment, 1977; World Food Resources, Actual and Potential, 1977; Wildlife of North America, 1979; Animals That Hunt, 1979; Making and Managing a Smallholding, 1979; (with David Baldock and Colin Blythe) Food Policy and Self Sufficiency, 1979; (with Peter Bunyard) The Politics of Self Sufficiency, 1980; A Year in the Life of a Field, 1980; (with Peter Crawford) The Curious Cat, 1982; Animal Artisans, 1982; (with James Lovelock) The Great Extinction, 1983; (with James Lovelock) The Greening of Mars, 1984; The Food Chain, 1984; 2040, 1985; (with Jane Burton) Nine Lives, 1985; (ed.) The Oxford Dictionary of Natural History, 1986; The Woodland Trust Book of British Woodlands, 1986; Ecology Facts, 1986; (with Jane Burton) Dog's Life, 1986; The Ordnance Survey Outdoor Handbook, 1987; (with Jane Burton) A Pony's Tale, 1987; Conversation at Home, 1988. Add: "Penquite", Fernleigh Rd., Wadebridge, Cornwall PL27 7BB, England.

ALLAN, Elkan. British, b. 1922. Film, Media. Listings Ed., 1986–88, and since 1988 Sr. Ed., The Independent, London, since 1986. Writer, Odhams Press, 1950–55; Writer, Producer, Exec. and Head of Entertainment, Rediffusion Television, 1955–66; television columnist, Sunday Times, 1966–82; Ed., Video Viewer, 1982–83. *Publs:* Quiz Team, 1945; (ed.) Living Opinion, 1946; (with D.M. Robinson) Good Listening: A Survey of Broadcasting, 1948; (with A. Allan) The Sunday Times Guide to Movies on Television, 1973, 1980; (ed.) Video Yearbook, 1984, 1985. Add: 3 Crescent Rd., Ipswich IP1 2EX, England.

ALLAN, John (David). British, b. 1950. Theology/Religion. Assoc. Evangelist, British Youth for Christ, since 1974. Literary Adviser, Educational Vacations Ltd., since 1973. Scholar, Hertford Coll., Oxford, 1971–74. *Publs:* I Know Where I'm Going, 1975; The Gospel According to Science Fiction, 1975; Transcendental Meditation: A Cosmic Confidence Trick, 1980; Sure Thing, 1981; (with others) Conversations in Spirit, 1981; Yoga, 1983; The Healing Energy of Love: A Personal Journal, 1986; The Kingdom of God, 1987; Shopping for a God, 1987; (with Gus Eyre) A Field Guide to Christianity, 1987. Add: c/o Inter-Varsity, 38 De Montfort St., Leicester LE1 7GP, England.

ALLAN, Mabel Esther. Also writes as Jean Estoril, Priscilla Hagon and Anne Pilgrim. British, b. 1915. Novels/Short stories, Histori-

cal/Romance/Gothic, Children's fiction. *Publs:* author of over 130 books, some being: Shadow Over the Alps, 1960; A Summer in Brittany (in U.S. as Hilary's Summer on Her Own), 1960; Tansy of Tring Street, 1960; Holiday of Endurance, 1961; Home to the Island, 1962; Pendron Under the Water, 1962; Schooldays in Skye, 1962; Signpost to Switzerland, 1962; The Ballet Family, 1963; Kate Comes to England, 1963; New York for Nicola, 1963; The Sign of the Unicorn, 1963; It Happened in Arles (in U.S. as Mystery in Arles), 1964; The Ballet Family Again, 1964; Fiona on the Fourteenth Floor (in U.S. as Mystery on the Fourteenth Floor), 1964; The Way Over Windle, 1966; Skiing to Danger, 1966; Mystery of the Ski Slopes, 1966; It Started in Madeira (in U.S. as The Mystery Started in Madeira), 1967; Missing in Manhattan, 1967; The Dancing Garlands, 1968; Wood Street Series, 6 vols., 1968–79; Climbing to Danger (in U.S. as Mystery in Wales), 1969; The Kraymer Mystery, 1969; Dangerous Inheritance, 1970; Christmas at Spindle Bottom, 1970; The Secret Dancer, 1971; The May Day Mystery, 1971; Behind the Blue Gates, 1972; Time to Go Back, 1972; An Island in a Green Sea, 1972; Mystery in Rome, 1973; A Formidable Enemy, 1973; Crow's Nest, 1974; A Chill in the Lane, 1974; The Night Wind, 1974; Ship of Danger, 1974; The Secret Players, 1974; Bridge of Friendship, 1975; Romansgrove, 1975; The Flash Children, 1975; Trouble in the Glen, 1976; The Rising Tide, 1976; The Sound of Cowbells, 1977; My Family's Not Forever, 1977; The View Beyond My Father, 1977; Pine Street Pageant, 1978; Tomorrow Is a Lovely Day, 1979; Pine Street Goes Camping, 1980; The Mills Down Below, 1980; A Lovely Tomorrow, 1980; The Pine Street Problem, 1981; A Strange Enchantment, 1981; The Horns of Danger, 1982, 1985; Growing Up in Wood Street, 1982; Goodbye to Pine Street, 1982; Alone at Pine Street, 1983; The Crumble Line Adventure, 1983; A Dream of Hunger Moss, 1983, 1985; A Secret in Spindle Bottom, 1984; Friends at Pine Street, 1984; Trouble in Crumble Lane, 1984; The Flash Children in Winter, 1985; The Pride of Pine Street, 1985; The Crumble Lane Captives, 1986; A Mystery in Spindle Bottom, 1986; The Road to Huntingland, 1986; The Crumble Lane Mystery, 1987; as Jean Estoril—Drina series, 10 vols., 1957–65; We Danced in Bloomsbury Square, 1967; as Priscilla Hagon—Cruising to Danger, 1966; Dancing to Danger, 1967; Mystery at Saint-Hilaire, 1968; Mystery at the Villa Bianca, 1969; Mystery of the Secret Square, 1970; as Anne Pilgrim—The First Time I Saw Paris, 1961; Clare Goes to Holland, 1962; A Summer in Provence, 1963; Strangers in New York, 1964; Selina's New Family, 1967. Add: 11 Oldfield Way, Heswall, Wirral, L60 6RQ, England.

ALLAN, Robin. British, b. 1934. Children's fiction. Artistic Dir., InterTheatre, since 1987. Typographical Designer, Eyre and Spottiswoode Ltd., London, 1957–60; Lectr. in English, Kuwait, 1961–65, Television Officer in Malta, 1965–67, and Iran, 1967–70, Asst. Dir., Educational Aids Dept., London, 1970–71, all for British Council; Lectr. in Drama, Basingstoke Technical Coll., 1972–73; Lectr. in Drama and Film, Coll. of Adult Education, Manchester, 1973–87. Pres., Intnl. Theatre of Teheran, Iran, 1969–70; Chmn., Green Room Theatre, Manchester, 1975–77. *Publs:* Come Into My Castle, 1964; Beyond the Blue Mountains, 1979. Add: 10 Dale Rd., New Mills, Stockport SK12 4NW, England.

ALLAN, Ted. Also writes as William Maxwell. Canadian, b. 1916. Novels/Short stories, Children's fiction, Plays/Screenplays, Biography. *Publs:* This Time a Better Earth (novel), 1939; The Scalpel, The Sword: The Story of Dr. Norman Bethune, 1952; (with Roger MacDougall) Double Image, 1957; (as William Maxwell) Quest for Pajaro (novel), 1961; Oh What Lovely War, 1964; Fuse (screenplay), 1970; Chu Chem: A Zen Buddhist-Hebrew Novel, 1973; Lies My Father Told Me (novel), 1975; My Sister's Keeper, 1976; Willie the Squowse, (juvenile), 1977; Love Is A Long Shot (novel), 1985; Don't You Know Anybody Else (short stories), 1986. Add: c/o Mike Zimring, William Morris Agency, 151 El Camino, Beverly Hills, CA 90212, U.S.A.

ALLARDYCE, Paula. *See* **BLACKSTOCK,** Charity.

ALLAUN, Frank (Julian). British, b. 1913. Military/Defence, Social commentary/phenomena. Labour Member of Parliament (U.K.) for East Salford, 1955–83. Formerly on editorial staff, Manchester Evening News, and Daily Herald, London. *Publs:* Your Trade Union and You, 1950; Stop the H Bomb Race, 1959; Heartbreak Housing, 1966; No Place Like Home: Britain's Housing Tragedy, 1972; The 30 Billion Pounds Wasted on False Security, 1975; Questions on Nuclear Weapons, 1981; Spreading the News, 1988. Add: 1 South Dr., Manchester M21 2DX, England.

ALLBEURY, Ted. Also writes as Richard Butler and Patrick Kelly. British, b. 1917. Novels/Short stories, Mystery/Crime/Suspense.

Publs: Choice of Enemies, 1973; Snowball, 1974; Palomino Blonde, 1975; The Special Collection, 1975; Moscow Quadrille, 1976; The Only Good German, 1976; The Man with the President's Mind, 1976; The Lantern Network, 1977; The Alpha List, 1978; Consequence of Fear, 1979; The Twentieth Day of January, 1980; The Reaper, 1980; The Other Side of Silence, 1981; The Secret Whispers, 1981; Shadow of Shadows, 1982; All Our Tomorrows, 1982; Pay Any Price, 1983; The Girl from Addis, 1984; No Place to Hide, 1984; The Judas Factor, 1984; Children of Tender Years, 1985; The Choice, 1986; The Seeds of Treason, 1986; The Crossing, 1987; A Wilderness of Mirrors, 1988; Deep Purple, 1989; as Richard Butler—Where All the Girls are Sweeter, 1975; Italian Assets, 1976; as Patrick Kelly—Codeword Cromwell, 1980; The Lonely Margins, 1981. Add: Cheriton House, Furnace Lane, Lamberhurst, Kent, England.

ALLEN, Alex B. *See* **HEIDE,** Florence Parry.

ALLEN, Charlotte Vale. Also writes as Claire Vincent. Canadian, b. 1941. Historical/Romance. Actress and singer, London, 1961–64, Toronto, 1964–66, and in the United States, 1966–70; insurance broker, 1971–74. *Publs:* Hidden Meanings, 1976; Love Life, 1976; Sweeter Music, 1976; Another Kind of Magic, 1977; Becoming, 1977; Gentle Stranger, 1977; Mixed Emotions, 1977; Running Away, 1977; Gifts of Love, 1978; Julia's Sister, 1978; Meet Me in Time, 1978; (as Claire Vincent) Believing in Giants (in U.K. as Charlotte Vale Allen), 1978; (as Claire Vincent) Acts of Kindness, 1979; (as Claire Vincent) Moments of Meaning, 1979; (as Claire Vincent) Times of Triumph, 1979; (as Claire Vincent) Promises, 1980; Daddy's Girl (autobiography), 1980 (as Claire Vincent) Promises, 1980; (as Claire Vincent) The Marmalade Man (in U.K. as Destinies), 1981; (as Claire Vincent) Perfect Fools, 1981; (as Claire Vincent) Intimate Friends, 1983; (as Claire Vincent) Pieces of Dreams, 1984; Matters of the Heart, 1985, Time/Steps, 1986; Illusions, 1987; Dream Train, 1988; Night Magic, 1989. Add: 144 Rowayton Woods Dr., Norwalk, CT 06854, U.S.A.

ALLEN, Dick. American, b. 1939. Poetry, Literature. Dir. of Creative Writing since 1972, Prof. since 1976, and Dana Prof. of English since 1979, Dept. of English, Univ. of Bridgeport (Asst. Prof. of Creative Writing and American Literature, 1968–72; Assoc. Prof., 1971–76). Contrib. Ed., The American Poetry Review, since 1972; Reviewer, American Book Review, since 1982. Reviewer, Hudson Review, since 1986. Teaching Assoc., Brown Univ., Providence, R.I., 1962–64; Instr. in English and Creative Writing, Wright State Univ., 1964–68; Ed.-in-Chief, The Mad River Review, 1966–68. *Publs:* Anon and Various Time Machine Poets, 1971; (ed.) Science Fiction: The Future, 1971, 1982; (co-ed.) Detective Fiction: Crime and Compromise, 1974; Regions With No Proper Names (poetry), 1975; (co-ed.) Looking Ahead: The Vision of Science Fiction, 1975; Overnight in the Guest House of the Mystic (poetry), 1984; Flight and Pursuit, 1987; (ed.) Expansive Poetry: The New Formalism and the New Narrative, 1989. Add: Dept. of English, Univ. of Bridgeport, Bridgeport, Conn. 06601, U.S.A.

ALLEN, Diogenes. American, b. 1932. Theology/Religion. Clergyman: Stuart Prof. of Philosophy, Princeton Theological Seminary, N.J., since 1981 (Assoc. Prof., 1967–74; Prof., since 1974). Minister, Windham Presbyterian Church, N.H., 1958–61; Asst. Prof., 1964–66, and Assoc. Prof., 1966–67, Dept. of Philosophy, York Univ., Toronto. *Publs:* (ed.) Leibniz' Theodicy, 1966; The Reasonableness of Faith, 1968; Finding Our Father, 1974; Between Two Worlds, 1977, new ed. as Temptation, 1986; Traces of God, 1981; Three Outsiders: Pascal, Kierkegaard, and Simone Weil, 1983; Mechanical Explanations and the Ultimate Origins of the Universe According to Leibniz, 1983; Philosophy for Understanding Theology, 1985; Love: Christian Romance, Marriage, Friendship, 1987. Add: 133 Cedar Lane, Princeton, N.J. 08540, U.S.A.

ALLEN, Durward L(eon). American, b. 1910. Mammals, Birds, Environmental science/Ecology. Emeritus Prof. of Wildlife Ecology, Dept. of Forestry and Natural Resources, Purdue Univ., West Lafayette, since 1976 (Prof., 1954–76). Member of the Council, National Park System Advisory Bd. to the Secty. of the Interior, Washington, D.C., since 1971 (appointed to the Bd., 1966; Chmn., 1970–71); Member, Bd. of Dirs., American Forestry Assn., since 1983; Research Biologist, Game Div., Michigan Dept. of Conservation, Lansing, 1937–46; Research biologist, U.S. Fish and Wildlife Service, Laurel, Md., 1946–49; Assistant Chief, Branch of Wildlife Research, U.S. Fish and Wildlife Service, Washington, D.C., 1950–54. Member, National Council, Boy Scouts of America, 1951–69; Pres., The Wildlife Soc., 1954–55; Chmn., Research Cttee., Intnl. Assn. of Fish, Game, and Conservation Commissioners, 1971–72; Chmn., Cttee. on North American Wildlife Policy, Wildlife Management Inst., 1972–73; Chmn., National Science Advisory Cttee. for Fish and Wildlife

and Parks, Dept. of the Interior, 1975–76. *Publs:* Michigan Fox Squirrel Management, 1943; Pheasants Afield, 1953; Our Wildlife Legacy, 1954, 1962; (ed.) Pheasants in North America, 1956; The Life of Prairies and Plains, 1967; Wolves of Minong, 1979. Add: Dept. of Forestry and Natural Resources, Purdue Univ., West Lafayette, Ind. 47907, U.S.A.

ALLEN, Edith Beavers. American, b. 1920. Recreation/Leisure/Hobbies, Theology/Religion. Real estate broker, retired. *Publs:* New Testament Bible Games, 1964; 100 Bible Games, 1966; Bridal Showers, 1969; Better Bible Games, 1969; Get in the Game, 1971; Let's Plan a Bridal Shower, 1974. Add: 904 Sevard Ave., Clearwater, Fla. 33518, U.S.A.

ALLEN, Francis A. American, b. 1919. Law, Politics/Government. Prof. of Law, Univ. of Florida, Gainesville, since 1986. Edson R. Sunderland Prof. of Law, Univ. of Michigan, Ann Arbor, 1972–86 (Dean of Law Sch., 1966–71). *Publs:* The Borderland of Criminal Justice, 1964; The Crimes of Politics, 1974; Law, Intellect and Education, 1979; The Decline of the Rehabilitative Ideal, 1981. Add: 4414 NW 8th Pl., Gainesville, Fla. 32605, U.S.A.

ALLEN, Gay Wilson. American, b. 1903. Literature, Biography. Prof. of English Emeritus, New York Univ., NYC, since 1969 (Prof. of English, 1946–69). Ed. with Sculley Bradley, Collected Writings of Walt Whitman, New York Univ. Press, since 1963. *Publs:* American Prosody, 1935, 1966; (ed. with H.H. Clark) Literary Criticism: Pope to Croce, 1941; Walt Whitman Handbook, 1946, 1975; (ed. with H.A. Pochmann) Masters of American Literature, 1949; Walt Whitman: Man, Poet, Philosopher, 1955, 1978; The Solitary Singer: A Critical Biography of Walt Whitman, 1955; (ed.) Walt Whitman Abroad, 1955; (with C.T. Davis) Walt Whitman's Poems, 1955; Walt Whitman as Man, Poet and Legend, 1961; (ed. with W.B. Rideout and J.K. Robinson) American Poetry, 1965; William James: A Biography, 1967; A Reader's Guide to Walt Whitman, 1970; The World of Herman Melville, 1971; Aspects of Walt Whitman, 1971; (ed.) A William James Reader, 1971; Carl Sandburg, 1972; Studies in Leaves of Grass, 1972; The New Walt Whitman Handbook, 1975; 25 Years of Walt Whitman Bibliography 1918–1942, 1978; Waldo Emerson, A Biography, 1981; (with Roger Asselineau) St. John de Crèvecoeur: The Life of an American Farmer, 1987. Add: 454 Grove St., Oradell, N.J. 07649, U.S.A.

ALLEN, Grace. *See* **HOGARTH,** Grace.

ALLEN, Harry Cranbrook. British, b. 1917. History, International relations/Current affairs, Politics/Government. Prof. of American Studies, Univ. of East Anglia, Norwich, 1972–80, now Emeritus. Fellow, Lincoln Coll., Oxford, 1946–55; Commonwealth Fund Prof. of American History, 1955–71, and Dir., Inst. of U.S. Studies, 1966–71, Univ. of London. *Publs:* Great Britain and the United States: A History of Anglo-American Relations 1783-1952, 1954; (ed. with C.P. Hill) British Essays in American History, 1957; Bush and Backwoods: A Comparison of the Frontier in Australia and the United States, 1959; The Anglo-American Predicament: The British Commonwealth, The United States, and European Unity, 1960; The Anglo-American Relationship since 1783, 1959; The United States of America, 1964, later published as A Concise History of the United States; (ed. with Roger Thompson) Contrast and Connection: Bicentennial Essays in Anglo-American History, 1976. Add: 1 Shepard Way, Chipping Norton, Oxon OX7 5BE, England.

ALLEN, Henry Wilson. Also writes as Clay Fisher and Will Henry. American, b. 1912. Mystery/Crime/Suspense, Westerns/Adventure, Children's fiction. Freelance writer. *Publs:* Genesis Five, 1968; Tayopa!, 1970; See How They Run, 1970; as Will Henry—No Survivors, 1950; Wolf-Eye, The Bad One (juvenile), 1951; To Follow a Flag, 1953; Death of a Legend, 1954, as The Raiders, 1956, in U.K. as Jesse James, 1957; The Fourth Horseman, 1954; Who Rides with Wyatt, 1955; The North Star, 1956; Pillars of the Sky, 1956; The Texas Rangers (juvenile), 1957; Orphan of the North (juvenile), 1958; Reckoning at Yankee Flat, 1958; The Seven Men at Membres Springs, 1958; Where the Sun Now Stands, 1960; Journey to Shiloh, 1960; The Feleen Brand, 1962; San Juan Hill, 1962; The Gates of the Mountains, 1963; Mackenna's Gold, 1963; In the Land of the Mandans (juvenile), 1965; The Last Warpath, 1966; Songs of the Western Frontier (short stories), 1966, as Red Brother and White, and Outlaws and Legends, vols., 1969; Custer's Last Stand, 1966; One More River to Cross, 1967; Alias Butch Cassidy, 1968; Maheo's Children, 1968, as The Squaw Killers, 1968; (ed.) 14 Spurs, 1968; The Day Fort Larking Fell, 1968; Chiricahua, 1972; The Bear Paw Horses, 1973; I, Tom Horn, 1975; Summer of the Gun, 1978; as Clay Fisher—Red Blizzard, 1951; Santa Fe Passage, 1952; War Bonnet, 1953; Yellow Hair,

1953; The Tall Men, 1954; The Brass Command, 1955, in U.K. as Dull Knife, 1958; The Big Pasture, 1955; The Blue Mustang, 1956, in U.K. (as Will Henry) as Starbuck, 1972; Yellowstone Kelly, 1957; The Crossing, 1958, in U.K. as River of Decision, 1960; Nino: The Legend of Apache Kid, 1961, in U.K. as The Legend of Apache Kid, 1964, in U.S. paperback as The Apache Kid, 1973; The Return of the Tall Man, 1961; The Pitchfork Patrol, 1962; The Oldest Maiden Lady in New Mexico and Other Stories, 1962; Valley of the Bear (juvenile), 1964; Outcasts of Canyon Creek, 1972; Apache Ransom, 1974; Black Apache, 1976; Nine Lives West (short stores), 1978; Seven Card Stud (short stories), 1981 Add: c/o John K. Payne, Lenniger Literary Agency, 101 E. 40th St., New York, N.Y. 10016, U.S.A.

ALLEN, John E(lliston). Also writes as Paul M. Danforth. British, b. 1921. Engineering, Technology. Consultant to Rolls-Royce, Raychem, Ove Arup, etc. Chmn., Working Party on Transport, Watt Cttee. on Energy Ltd. Principal Scientific Officer, Royal Aircraft Establishment, Farnborough, 1950–54; Head of Aerodynamics, Projects and Assessment Dept., A.V. Roe & Co., Ltd., Weapons Research Div., Manchester, 1954–63; Deputy Chief Engineer, Advanced Projects Group, 1963–69, and Chief Future Projects Engineer, 1969–83, British Aerospace, Kingston upon Thames. *Publs:* (as Paul M. Danforth) Transport Control, 1970; (co-ed.) The Future of Aeronautics, 1970; (co-author) Energy and Humanity; Aeronautics in a Finite World, 1974; (as Paul M. Danforth) The Channel Tunnel, 1974; Have Energy, Will Travel, 1977; Aerodynamics, 1982. Add: The Gabriels, Angel Lane, Blythburgh, Suffolk, England.

ALLEN, John Jay. American b. 1932. Literature. Prof. of Spanish, Univ. of Kentucky, Lexington, since 1983. Asst. Prof., 1960–66, Assoc. Prof., 1966–72, and Prof. of Spanish, 1972–83, Univ. of Florida, Gainesville. *Publs:* Don Quixote: Hero or Fool?, 1969, part II, 1979; (ed.) Don Quijote de La Mancha, 1977; The Reconstruction of a Spanish Golden Age Playhouse: El Corral del Principe 1583-1744, 1983. Add: 424 Queensway Dr., Lexington, Ky. 40502, U.S.A.

ALLEN, Louis. British, b. 1922. History. Reader in French, Univ. of Durham. Member of Council, British Assn. for Japanese Studies, since 1975. Chmn., BBC North-East Region Advisory Council, and Member, BBC Gen. Advisory Council, 1969–75. *Publs:* (ed.) Le Barbier de Seville, by Beaumarchais, 1951; (ed.) Le Mariage de Figaro, by Beaumarchais, 1952; (trans.) The Frontier, by Regis Debray; (trans. with Hide Ishiguro) Prisoner of the British, by Yuji Aida, 1966; Japan: The Years of Triumph, 1971; Sittang: The Last Battle, 1973; (contrib.) Resistance in Europe, 1939–45, 1975; The End of the War in Asia, 1976; John-Henry Newman and the Abbe Jager, 1976; (contrib.) Decisive Battles of the Twentieth Century, 1976; Singapore, 1941–42, 1977; (contrib.) If I Had Been ..., 1977; Burma: The Longest War: 1941–1945, 1985; (with Jean Wilson) The Great Interpreter: An Anthology of Lafcadio Hearn, 1988. Add: Dun Cow Cottage, Durham DH1 3ES, England.

ALLEN, Mary (Charlotte Chocqueel). British, b. 1909. Photography. Lectr. and instr. on photography and some aspects of psychology. *Publs:* Portrait Photography: How and Why, 1973; Portrait Photography in Practice, 1985. Add: Melita, West Leigh, Ship St., East Grinstead, Sussex RH19 4DU, England.

ALLEN, (Sir) Peter (Christopher). British, b. 1905. Sports, Transportation. Company director, now retired. Vice Pres., British Assn. for Commercial and Industrial Education, since 1969; Advisory Dir., New Perspective Fund, since 1973. Pres., Univ. of Manchester Inst. of Science and Technology, 1968–71. *Publs:* The Railways of the Isle of Wight, 1928; Locomotives of Many Lands, 1954; On the Old Lines, 1957; (with P.B. Whitehouse) Narrow Gauge Railways of Europe, 1959; (with R.A. Wheeler) Steam on the Sierra, 1960; (with P.B. Whitehouse) Round the World on the Narrow Gauge, 1966; (with Consuelo Allen) The Curve of Earth's Shoulder, 1966; (with A.B. MacLeod) Rails on the Isle of Wight, 1967; Famous Fairways, 1968; Play the Best Courses, 1973; (with P.B. Whitehouse) Narrow Gauge the World Over, 1976; The 91 Before Lindbergh, 1985. Add: Telham Hill House, Battle, Sussex, England.

ALLEN, R(eginald) L(ancelot) M(ountford). British, b. 1909. Chemistry. Member, Research Dept., I.C.I. Ltd., Dyestuffs Div., 1932–71. *Publs:* Colour Chemistry, 1971; (with K.H. Saunders) Aromatic Diazo Compounds, 1985. Add: 22 Guest Rd., Prestwich, Manchester M25 7DL, England.

ALLEN, Steve. Has also written as William Christopher Stevens. American, b. 1921. Novels/Short stories, Social commentary/phenomena, Autobiography/Memoirs/Personal, Humor/Satire.

Television comedian, motion picture actor, recording artist, lyricist, composer and author. *Publs:* Bop Fables, 1955; 14 for Tonight, 1955; The Funny Men, 1956; Wry on the Rocks, 1956; The Girls on the 10th Floor, 1958; The Question Man, 1959; Mark It and Strike It, 1960; Not All of Your Laughter, Not All of Your Tears, 1962; Letter to a Conservative, 1965; The Ground is Our Table, 1966; Bigger Than a Breadbox, 1967; (as William Christopher Stevens) A Flash of Swallows, 1969; The Wake, 1972; Curses! . . . Or . . . How Never to Be Foiled Again, 1973; Princess Snip Snip and the Puppy Kittens, 1973; Schmock-Schmock, 1975; Meeting of Minds, 1978; Chopped-Up Chinese, 1978; Ripoff, 1979; Meeting of Minds, Second Series, 1979; Explaining China, 1980; The Talk Show Murders, 1982; Funny People, 1982; More Funny People, 1982; How to Make a Speech, 1985; How To Be Funny, 1987. Add: 15201 Burbank Blvd., Van Nuys, Calif. 91411, U.S.A.

ALLEN, Steve. Has also written as William Christopher Stevens. American, b. 1921. Novels/Short stories, Social commentary/phenomena, Autobiography/Memoirs/Personal, Humor/Satire. Television comedian, motion picture actor, recording artist, lyricist, composer and author. *Publs:* Bop Fables, 1955; 14 for Tonight, 1955; The Funny Men, 1956; Wry on the Rocks, 1956; The Girls on the 10th Floor, 1958; The Question Man, 1959; Mark It and Strike It, 1960; Not All of Your Laughter, Not All of Your Tears, 1962; Letter to a Conservative, 1965; The Ground is Our Table, 1966; Bigger Than a Breadbox, 1967; (as William Christopher Stevens) A Flash of Swallows, 1969; The Wake, 1972; Curses! . . . Or . . . How Never to Be Foiled Again, 1973; Princess Snip Snip and the Puppy Kittens, 1973; Schmock-Schmock, 1975; Meeting of Minds, 1978; Chopped-Up Chinese, 1978; Ripoff, 1979; Meeting of Minds, Second Series, 1979; Explaining China, 1980; The Talk Show Murders, 1982; Funny People, 1982; More Funny People, 1982; How to Make a Speech, 1985; How To Be Funny, 1987. Add: 15201 Burbank Blvd., Van Nuys, Calif. 91411, U.S.A.ALLEN

ALLEN, Walter (Ernest). British, b. 1911. Novels/Short stories, Literature, Autobiography/Memoirs/Personal, Biography. Asst. Literary Ed., 1959–60 and Literary Ed., 1960–61, New Statesman, London; Prof. and Chmn., Dept of English Studies, New Univ. of Ulster, Coleraine, 1968–73; Visiting Prof. of English, Dalhousie Univ., Halifax, N.S., 1973–74. *Publs:* Innocence is Drowned, 1938; Blind Man's Ditch, 1939; Living Space, 1940; Rogue Elephant, 1946; The Black Country (topography), 1946; Arnold Bennett, 1948; Reading a Novel, 1948; 1956; (ed.) Writers on Writing, 1948; Dead Man Over All (in U.S. as Square Peg), 1950; Joyce Cary, 1953, 3rd ed. 1971; The English Novel: A Short Critical History, 1954; Six Great Novelists: Defoe, Fielding, Scott, Dickens, Stevenson, Conrad, 1955; The Novel Today, 1955, 1960; All in a Lifetime (in U.S. as Threescore and Ten), 1959; George Eliot, 1964; Tradition and Dream: The English and American Novel from the Twenties to Our Time (in U.S. as The Modern Novel in Britain and the United States), 1964; The British Isles in colour 1965; The Urgent West: An Introduction to the Idea of the United States (in U.S. as the Urgent West: The American Dream and Modern Man), 1969; Transatlantic Crossing: American Visitor to Britain and British Visitor to America in the Nineteenth Century, 1971; Some Aspects of the American Short Story, 1973; (ed.) The Roaring Queen, by Wyndham Lewis, 1973; The Short Story in English, 1981; As I Walked Down New Grub Street: Memories of a Writing Life, 1981; Get Out Early, 1986. Add: 4B Alwyne Rd., London N1, England.

ALLEN, William Sheridan. American, b. 1932. History. Prof. of History, State Univ. of New York, Buffalo, since 1970. Instr., Bay City Jr. Coll., Mich., 1957–58, and Massachusetts Inst. of Technology, Cambridge, 1960–61; Asst. Prof. Univ. of Missouri, Columbia, 1961–67; Assoc. Prof., Wayne State Univ., Detroit, 1967–70. Pres., New York State Assn. of European Historians, 1983–84. *Publs:* The Nazi Seizure of Power, 1965, 1984; (ed. and trans.) The Infancy of Nazism, 1975. Add: 164 Woodward Ave., Buffalo, N.Y. 14214, U.S.A.

ALLEN, W(illiam) Stannard. British, b. 1913. Language/Linguistics. British Council Overseas Officer, 1940–60; member, British Council English Language Advisory Cttee., 1967–72. *Publs:* Living English Structure, 1947, 3rd ed. 1974; Living English Speech, 1954, 1966; Yugoslav Dances, 1956; Living English Structure for Schools, 1958, 1970; (with R.B. Cooke) Living English for Jordan, 1960–62; Keep Up Your English (radio course), 1961; (with R.B. Cooke) Living English for the Arab World, 1964; (with R.B. Cooke) New Living English for the Arab World, 1966; (with El-Anani and Y. Salah) New Living English for Jordan, 1971; Living English Secondary Course for the Arab World, 1971; Living English Revision Book, 1972; (with others) English Grammatical Structure, 1975; Progressive Living English for the Arab World, 1975, (with Alan C. McLean) books and 4, 1977; (with Alan C. McLean) Progressive

Living English, 1977–78. Add: c/o Longman Group, Harlow, Essex CM20 2JE, England.

ALLEN, Woody. American, b. 1935. Novels/Short stories, Plays/Screenplays. Comedian, actor, and film dir. Former staff writer for NBC. *Publs:* What's New, Pussycat (screenplay), 1965; What's Up, Tigerlily (screenplay), 1967; Don't Drink the Water, 1967; Play It Again, Sam, 1969, screenplay, 1972; Take the Money and Run (screenplay), 1969; Bananas (screenplay), 1970; Getting Even, 1971; Everything You Always Wanted to Know about Sex but Were Afraid to Ask (screenplay), 1972; Sleeper (screenplay), 1974; Without Feathers (novel), 1975; Love and Death (screenplay), 1975; Annie Hall (screenplay), 1978; Interiors (screenplay), 1978; Manhattan (screenplay), 1979; Stardust Memories (screenplay), 1980; Side Effects, 1980; The Floating Light Bulb, 1982; A Midsummer Night's Sex Comedy (screenplay), 1982; Zelig (screenplay), 1983; Broadway Danny Rose (screenplay), 1984; The Purple Rose of Cairo (screenplay), 1985; Hannah and Her Sisters (screenplay), 1986; Radio Days (screenplay), 1987; September (screenplay), 1988. Add: c/o Random House, 201 East 50th St., New York, N.Y. 10022, U.S.A.

ALLER, Lawrence Hugh. American, b. 1913. Astronomy. Prof. Emeritus of Astronomy, Univ. of California, Los Angeles, since 1984 (member of faculty since 1962). Asst. Prof., Indiana Univ., Bloomington, 1945–48; Assoc. Prof., 1948–54, and Prof., 1954–62, Univ. of Michigan, Ann Arbor. *Publs:* (with Leo Goldberg) Atoms, Stars and Nebulae, 1942, 1971; Nuclear Transformations, Stellar Interiors and Nebulae, 1954; Gaseous Nebulae, 1956; Abundance of Elements, 1961; Atmospheres of the Stars and Suns, 1963; (ed. with Dean B. McLauglin) Stellar Structure and Evolution, 1965; (ed. with Barbara Middlehurst) Interstellar Medium, 1967; Physics of Thermal Gaseous Nebulae, 1984. Add: c/o Astronomy Dept., University of California, Los Angeles, Calif. 90024, U.S.A.

ALLEY, Robert S. American, b. 1932. Communications Media, History, Theology/Religion. Prof. of Humanities, Univ. of Richmond, since 1973 (Asst. Prof., 1963–66; Assoc. Prof., 1966–73). *Publs:* Revolt Against the Faithful: A Biblical Case for Inspiration as Encounter, 1970; So Help Me God: Religion and the Presidency, Wilson to Nixon, 1972; Television: Ethnics for Hire?, 1977; (ed.) James Madison on Religious Liberty, 1985; The Supreme Court on Church and State, 1988. Add: Humanities Dept., Univ. of Richmond, Richmond, Va. 23173, U.S.A.

ALLISON, A(ntony) F(rancis). British, b. 1916. Literature, Theology/Religion. Gen. Ed., 1963–84, and since 1984 Chmn., Catholic Record Soc., London. Asst. Keeper, Dept. of Printed Books, British Library, London, 1946–72. *Publs:* (with D.M. Rogers) A Catalogue of Catholic Books in English Printed Abroad or Secretly in England 1558-1640, 1956; Thomas Dekker: (Thomas Lodge, Four Metaphysical Poets, Robert Greene): A Bibliographical Catalogue of the Early Editions, 4 vols., 1972–75; English Translations from the Spanish and Portuguese to the Year 1970: An Annotated Catalogue of the Extant Printed Versions, 1974; (with V.F. Goldsmith) Titles of English Books: An Alphabetical Finding-List, 2 vols., 1976–77; (with D.M. Rogers) The Contemporary Printed Literature of the English Counter-Reformation Between 1558 and 1640: vol. 1, Works in Languages Other Than English, 1989. Add: Kinnordy, Welcomes Rd., Kenley, Surrey, England.

ALLISON, E.M.A. *See* ALLISON, Eric W(illiam).

ALLISON, Eric W(illiam). Also writes as E.M.A. Allison (joint pseudonym with Mary Ann Allison). American, b. 1947. Mystery/Crime/Suspense, Business/Trade/Industry, Administration/Management. Full-time writer, since 1983. Community History Ed. and Dir., The Hill (quarterly publication), Brooklyn, N.Y. Account Exec., Paine Webber Jackson and Curtis, Garden City, NY, 1973–81; Account Exec., Merrill Lynch, Jericho, NY, 1981–83. *Publs:* (as E.M.A. Allison) Through the Valley of Death, 1983; (with Mary Ann Allison) Managing Up, Managing Down, 1984, 1986; The Raiders of Wall Street, 1986. Add: 152 Lafayette Ave., Brooklyn, NY 11238, U.S.A.

ALLISON, R(ichard) Bruce. American, b. 1949. Botany, politics, Travel. *Publs:* Humanizing Our Future, 1972; (ed.) Toward a Human Future, 1972; Democrats in Exile 1968-1972, 1974; Travel Journal: Europe and North Africa, 1978; (ed.) Wisconsin's Champion Trees, 1980; Tree Walks of Dane County, 1982; Tree Walks of Milwaukee County, 1983; Famous and Historic Trees of Wisconsin, 1983.Add: 2769 Marshall Parkway, Madison, Wis. 53713, U.S.A.

ALLOWAY, Lawrence. British, b. 1926. Art, Cinema. Teacher, Ben-

nington Coll., Vermont, 1961–62; curator, Guggenheim Museum, NYC, 1962–66; teacher, State Univ. of N.Y. at Stony Brook, 1968–81. Art Ed., The Nation, 1968–80; Assoc. Ed., Artforum, 1971–76. *Publs:* The Venice Biennale 1895–1968, 1978; Violent America: The Movies 1946–1964, 1971; American Pop Art, 1974; Topics in American Art since 1945, 1975; Roy Lichtenstein, 1983; Network-Art in the Complex Present, 1985. Add: 330 W. 30th St., New York, N.Y. 10011, U.S.A.

ALLSOPP, (Harold) Bruce. British, b. 1912. Novels/Short stories, Architecture, Art, Environmental science/Ecology, Philosophy, Photography. Lectr. in Architecture, 1946–55, Sr. Lectr., 1955–73, and Reader in the History of Architecture, 1973–77, Univ. of Newcastle upon Tyne; Chmn., Oriel Press Ltd., 1962–87; Dir., Routledge & Kegan Paul Books Ltd., 1974–86. Chmn., Soc. of Architectural Historians of Great Britain, 1959–65; Master, Art-Workers' Guild, 1972. *Publs:* Art and the Nature of Architecture, 1952; Decoration and Furniture (2 vols.), 1952; A General History of Architecture, 1955; Style in the Visual Arts, 1955; A History of Renaissance Architecture, 1956; The Future of the Arts, 1959, Possessed, 1959; The Naked Flame, 1962; (with U. Clark) Architecture of France, 1963; Architecture, 1964; (with U. Clark) Architecture of Italy, 1964; (with U. Clark) Architecture of England, 1964; To Kill a King, 1965; a History of Classical Architecture, 1965; (with H. Booton and U. Clark) The Great Tradition of Western Architecture, 1966; (with U. Clark) Photography for Tourists, 1966; (ed.) Historic Architecture of Newcastle upon Tyne, 1968; Civilization: The Next Stage, 1969; (with U. Clark) Historic Architecture of Northumberland, 1969; The Study of Architectural History, 1970; The Professional Artist in a Changing Society, 1970; (ed.) Inigo Jones on Palladio, 1970; (ed.) Modern Architecture of Northern England, 1970; Romanesque Architecture, 1971; Ecological Morality, 1972; The Garden Earth, 1972; Towards a Humane Architecture, 1974; Return of the Pagan, 1974; A Modern Theory of Architecture, 1977; (with Ursula Clark) English Architecture, 1979; Appeal to the Gods, 1980; Should Man Survive? 1982; Social Responsibility and the Responsible Society, 1984; The Country Life Companion to British and European Architecture, 1985; Guide de l'Architecture, 1985. Add: Stocksfield Studio, Branch End, Stocksfield, Northumberland NE43 7NA, England.

ALLWARD, Maurice (Frank). British, b. 1923. Air/Space topics. Chief Draughtsman, Palmer Tyre Co., London, 1946–56; Deputy Mgr., Technical Publs., Civil Aircraft Div., British Aerospace, 1957–88. Regular contributor, Air Pictorial, and Jane's All the World Aircraft. *Publs:* (with John Taylor) Spitfire; (with John Taylor) Wings for Tomorrow; (ed.) Encyclopaedia of Space; Daily Mirror Book of Space; Triumphs of Flight; Aircraft; Safety in the Air; Source Book of Aircraft; Story of Flight; Milestones in Science; Objective—Outer Space; Look It Up Book of Transport; Look It Up Book of Space; Marvels of Jet Aircraft; The Earth in Space; Hurricane Special; The Sabre Story; The Buccaneer; Gloster Javelin. Add: 14 Chantry Lane, Hatfield, Herts. AL10 9HP, England.

ALMANSI, Guido. British, b. 1931. Literature. Prof. of English and Comparative Literature, Univ. of East Anglia, Norwich. Asst. Lectr., then Lectr., Univ. of Glasgow, 1962–66; Lectr., and Sr. Lectr., Univ. of Kent, 1966–71; Visiting Assoc. Prof., Univ. of British Columbia, 1969–70; Prof. of Italian, University Coll., Dublin, 1972–74; Visiting Prof., Carleton Univ., Ottawa. *Publs:* The Writer as Liar, 1975; (ed.) Letters and Photographs of Lewis Carroll, 1975, (with B. Merry) E. Montale: The Private Language of Poetry, 1978; (with Simon Henderson) Harold Pinter, 1983. Add: Sch. of English and American Studies, Univ. of East Anglia, Norwich NOR 88C, England.

AL-MARAYATI, Abid A(min). American, b. 1931. International relations/Current affairs, Politics/Government. Prof. Dept. of Political Science, and Dir., Center for Intnl. Studies, Univ. of Toledo, since 1968. United Nations Intern. 1954; Secty., Delegation of Iraq 1955, and Delegation of Yemen 1956–60, U.N. Gen. Assembly; Instr., Dept. of Government, Univ. of Massachusetts, Amherst, 1960; Technical Assistancefficer, Div. of Economic and Technical Assistance, Intnl. Atomic Energy Agency, Vienna, Austria, 1960–62; Assoc. Prof. of Political Science, State Univ. Coll. of New York, Plattsburg, 1962–64; Research Fellow, Harvard Univ., Cambridge, Mass., 1964–65; Assoc. Prof., Arizona State Univ., Tempe, 1965–68; Lectr. and Intnl. Education Consultant, The American Inst. for Foreign Trade, Glendale, Ariz., 1965–68. *Publs:* A Diplomatic History of Modern Iraq, 1961; Middle Eastern Constitutions and Electoral Laws, 1968; (with others) The Middle East: Its Governments and Politics, 1972; (ed.) International Relations of the Middle East and North Africa, 1984; Add: 2109 Terrace View West, Toledo, Ohio 43607, U.S.A.

ALMOND, Gabriel A(braham). American, b. 1911. International relations/Current affairs, Politics/Government. Prof. of Political Science, Stanford Univ., since 1963 (Exec. Head, Dept. of Political Science, 1964–69). Member, Social Science Research Council. Instr. in Political Science, Brooklyn Coll., N.Y., 1939–42; served in Office of War Information, 1942–45, and War Dept., European Theater of Operations, 1945; Assoc. Prof., 1949–51, and Prof. of Political Science, 1959–63, Yale Univ., New Haven, Conn.; Assoc. Prof. of Intnl. Affairs, 1951–54; Prof., 1954–57, and Prof. of Politics, 1957–59, Princeton Univ., N.J. Consultant, Air Univ., 1948, Dept. of State, 1950, Office of Naval Research, 1951, and Rand Corp., 1954–55; Pres., American Political Science Assn., 1965–66. *Publs:* The American People and Foreign Policy, 1950; The Appeals of Communism, 1954; (co-author) The Struggle for Democracy in Germany, 1949; The Politics of the Developing Areas, 1960; (co-author) The Civic Culture, 1963; Comparative Politics: A Developmental Approach, 1966, 1978; Political Development, 1970; (co-author) Crisis, Choice and Change, 1973; Civic Culture Revisited, 1980; Progress and Its Discontents, 1982; (with others) Comparative Politics Today: A World View, 4th ed., 1988. Add: 4135 Old Trace Rd., Palo Alto, Calif. 94306, U.S.A.

ALPERS, Antony. New Zealander, b. 1919. Mythology/Folklore, Biography. Journalist and ed. in New Zealand, 1936–66; Prof. of English Queen's Univ., Kingston, Ont., 1966–82, now Emeritus. *Publs:* Katherine Mansfield: A Biography, 1953; Dolphins, 1960; Maori Myths and Tribal Legends, 1964; Legends of the South Sea, 1970, as The World of the Polynesians, 1987; The Life of Katherine Mansfield, 1980; (ed.) The Stories of Katherine Mansfield, 1984. Add: 46 Memorial Ave., Christchurch 5, New Zealand.

ALPERT, Hollis. Also writes as Robert Carroll. American, b. 1916. Film. Ed., American Film, since 1975. Book reviewer, Saturday Review, New York Times, etc., 1947–59; Film Critic, Woman's Day, 1953–60; Visiting Prof., Southern Methodist Univ., 1982. Chmn., National Soc. of Film Critics, 1972–73. *Publs:* The Summer Lovers, 1958; Some Other Time, 1960; The Dreams and the Dreamers, 1962; For Immediate Release, 1963; The Barrymores, 1964; The Claimant, 1968; The People Eaters, 1971; Smash, 1973; (as Robert Carroll) A Disappearance, 1974; (with Lana Turner) Lana: The Lady, The Legend, The Truth, 1982; Burton, 1986; Fellini: A Life, 1986. Add: Box 142, Shelter Island, N.Y. 11964, U.S.A.

ALPHONSO-KARKALA, John B. Indian, b. 1923. Novels/Short stories, Poetry, Literature, Biography. Prof. of Literature, State Univ. of New York at New Paltz, since 1969 (Asst. Prof., 1964–65; Assoc. Prof., 1965–68). Teaching Fellow, Oriental Studies Prog., Columbia Univ., NYC, 1962–64. Member, Indian Foreign Missions, Geneva, London, and United Nations, NYC, 1953–60. *Publs:* Indo-English Literature in the Nineteenth Century, 1970; (ed.) An Anthology of Indian Literature: Selections from Vedas to Tagore, 1972, 1987; Passions of the Nightless Nights (novel), 1974; (with Leena Karkala) Bibliography of Indo-English Literature, 1800-1966, 1974; Studies in Comparative Literature: Essays, 1974; Jawaharial Nehru: A Literary Portrait, 1975; (ed.) Vedic Vision, 1980; (with Leena Karkala) When Night Falls (verse), 1980; Joys of Jayamagara (novel), 1981. Add: 20 Millrock Rd., New Paltz, N.Y. 12561, U.S.A

ALPORT, Baron, of Colchester; Cuthbert James McCall Alport. British, b. 1912. International relations/Current affairs. Deputy Speaker, House of Lords, since 1972. Conservative M.P. (U.K.), 1950–61; Minister of State, Commonwealth Relations Office, 1958–61; High Comnr. for Rhodesia and Nyasaland (Malawi), 1961–63. *Publs:* Kingdoms in Partnership, 1937; Hope in Africa, 1955; The Sudden Assignment, 1964. Add: The Cross House, Layer de la Haye, Colchester, Essex, England.

ALSOP, Joseph Wright. American, b. 1910. Politics, Journalism. With New York Herald Tribune, New York, 1932–35, and Washington, D.C. 1936–37; syndicated columnist, with Robert Kitner, The Capital Parade, 1937–40; served WWII; syndicated columnist with brother Stewart Alsop, Matter of Fact, 1946–58, and sole author 1958–74. *Publs:* (with Turner Catledge) The 168 Days, 1938, 1973; (with Robert Kitner) Men Around the President, 1938, and The American White Paper, 1940; (with Stewart Alsop) We Accuse, 1955, and The Reporter's Trade, 1958; From the Silent Earth, 1964; The Life and Times of Franklin D. Roosevelt: A Centenary Remembrance 1882–1945, 1982. Add: 2806 N St., N.W., Washington, D.C. 20007, U.S.A.

ALSTON, Rex. British, b. 1901. Sports/Physical education/Keeping fit. Member of staff, Bedford Sch., 1924–41; with BBC, specialising in sports commentary and reporting, 1943–61; cricket and rugby writer, Daily Telegraph, London, from 1961; now retired. *Publs:* Taking of the Air, 1950; Test Commentary, 1956; Over to Rex Alston, 1953; Watching Cricket, 1962. Add: Garlands, Ewhurst, Cranleigh, Surrey GU6 7QA, England.

ALTER, Judy. (Judith MacBain Alter). American, b. 1938. Novels/Short stories, Children's fiction, Biography, Local history/Rural topics, Sports/Fitness. Dir., Texas Christian Univ. Press, Ft. Worth, since 1987 (Ed., 1982–87). Freelance writer, 1973–75; Columnist, Roundup mag. and Ft. Worth Star Telegram, 1974–75; Instr. of English as a Second Language, 1975–76; Assoc. Dir. of News and Information, Texas Coll. of Osteopathic Medicine, Ft. Worth, 1978–80 (Dir. of Publs., 1972). *Publs:* (with Phil Russell) The Quack Doctor, 1974; After Pa was Shot, 1978; (with Susan Pearson) Single Again, 1978; The Texas ABC Book, 1981; Surviving Exercise: Judy Alter's Safe and Sane Exercise Program, 1983; (with Joyce Roach) Texas and Christmas, 1983; Luke and the Van Zandt County War, 1984; Stretch and Strengthen, 1986; Mattie, 1988; Elmer Kelton, 1988; Thistle Hill: The History and the House, 1988. Add: c/o Ray Peekner Literary Agency, 3210 S. Seventh St., Milwaukee, Wisc. 53215, U.S.A.

ALTER, Robert B. American, b. 1935. Literature, Biography. Prof. of Hebrew and Comparative Literature, Univ. of California, Berkeley, since 1967. Contrib. Ed., Tri-Quarterly, since 1973. Instr., then Asst. Prof. of English, Columbia Univ., NYC, 1962–66; Contrib. Ed., Commentary, 1971–1987. *Publs:* Rogue's Progress: Studies in the Picaresque Novel, 1965; Fielding and the Nature of the Novel, 1968; After the Tradition (critical essays), 1969; Partial Magic: The Novel as a Self-Conscious Genre, 1975; (ed.) Modern Hebrew Literature, 1975; Defenses of the Imagination (critical essays), 1978; A Lion for Love: A Critical Biography of Stendhal, 1979; The Art of Biblical Narrative, 1981; Motives for Fiction, 1984; The Art of Biblical Poetry, 1985; The Invention of Hebrew Prose, 1988. Add: Dept. of Comparative Literature, Univ. of California, Berkeley, Calif. 94720, U.S.A.

ALTHER, Lisa. American, b. 1944. Novels/Short stories. Staff member, Atheneum Publishers, NYC, 1967, and Garden Way Publishers, Vermont, 1969–72. *Publs:* Kinflicks, 1976; Original Sins, 1981; Other Women, 1984. Add: c/o Alfred A. Knopf, 201 East 50th St., New York, N.Y. 10022, U.S.A.

ALTICK, Richard Daniel. American, b. 1915. Cultural topics, Literature. Regents' Prof. Emeritus of English, Ohio State Univ. Columbus, since 1982 (joined faculty, 1945; Regents' Prof. of English, 1968–82). *Publs:* Preface to Critical Reading, 1946, 6th rev. ed. 1984; The Cowden Clarkes, 1948; The Scholar Adventurers, 1950; The English Common Reader: A Social History of the Mass Reading Public, 1800-1900, 1957; The Art of Literary Research, 1963, 3rd ed. 1981; Lives and Letters: A History of Literary Biography in England and America, 1965; (ed.) Carlyle: Past and Present, 1965; (with J.F. Loucks) Browning's Roman Murder Story, 1968; To Be in England, 1969; Victorian Studies in Scarlet, 1970; (ed.) Browning: The Ring and the Book, 1971; Victorian People and Ideas: Companion for the Modern Reader of Victorian Literature, 1973; The Shows of London, 1978; Paintings from Books: Art and Literature in Britain 1760-1900, 1985; Deadly Encounters: Two Victorian Sensations (as Evil Encounters in UK), 1986; Writers, Readers, and Occasions: Selected Essays on Victorian Literature and Life, 1988. Add: Dept. of English, Ohio State Univ., 164 West 17th Ave., Columbus, Ohio 43210, U.S.A.

ALTMAN, Dennis. Australia, b. 1943. Sex, Social commentary/phenomena. Sr. Lectr., Politics, La Trobe Univ., Victoria, since 1986. Lectr., 1969–75, and Sr. Lectr., 1975–80, Govt. Dept., Univ. of Sydney; Regents Lectr., Univ. of California, Santa Cruz, 1983; Policy Fellow, Univ. of California, San Francisco, 1984–85. *Publs:* Homosexual: Oppression and Liberation, 1972, rev. ed. 1974; Coming Out in the Seventies, 1979; Rehearsals for Change, 1980; The Homosexualization of America, 1982; AIDS and the New Puritanism, 1986; AIDS in the Mind of America, 1986. Add: 17 South Terrace, Clifton Hill, Vic. 3068, Australia.

ALTMAN, Frances (Evelyn). American, b. 1937. Children's fiction, Children's non-fiction. Freelance writer, ed. and lectr.; Communications Mgr., Teepak, Inc. Promotions Dir., Paddock Publrs., Arlington Heights, Ill., 1970–72; Mgr. Ed., Suburban Week supplement to Chicago Daily News, 1972–74; Ed., Countryside Living mag., 1974. *Publs:* Reggie, the Goat, 1967; George Gershwin, 1967; The Something Egg, 1969; Herbert V. Prochnow, 1969; Dwight D. Eisenhower, 1970; Douglas A. MacArthur, 1974; Mr. Stibbs (documentary film). 1974; Add: 7026 Seminole, Darien, Ill. 60559, U.S.A.

ALUKO, T(imothy) M(ofolorunso). Nigerian, b. 1918. Novels/Short stories. Partner, Scott Wilson Kirkpatrick, Lagos, since 1979. Town Engineer, Lagos Town Council, 1956–60; Dir. and Permanent Secty., Ministry of Works and Transport, Western Nigeria, 1960–66; Sr. Research Fellow in Municipal Engineering, Univ. of Lagos, 1966–78; Assoc. Prof. of Public Health Engineering, Univ. of Lagos, 1978. *Publs:* One Man, One Wife, 1959; One Man, One Matchet, 1964; Kinsman and Foreman, 1966; Chief the Honourable Minister, 1970; His Worshipful Majesty, 1973; Wrong Ones in the Dock, 1982; A State of Our Own, 1986. Add: 53 Ladipo Oluwole Rd., Apapa, Lagos, Nigeria.

ALVAREZ, A(lfred). British, b. 1929. Novels/Short stories, Poetry, Literature. Advisory Poetry Ed., The Observer, London, 1956–66; Gauss Lectr., Princeton Univ., NJ., 1957–58; Drama Critic, New Statesman, London, 1958–60; Advisory Ed., Penguin Modern European Poets in Translation, 1965–75. *Publs:* (Poems), 1952; The End of It (poetry), 1958; The Shaping Spirit: Studies in Modern English and American Poets (in U.S. as Stewards of Excellence: Studies in Modern English and American Poets), 1958; The School of Donne, 1961; (ed.) The New Poetry: An Anthology, 1962, 1966; Under Pressure: The Artist and Society: Eastern Europe and the U.S.A., 1965; Beyond All This Fiddle: Essays, 1955–67, 1968; Twelve Poems, 1968; Lost (poetry), 1968; (with Roy Fuller and Anthony Thwaite) Penguin Modern Poets 18, 1970; Apparition (poetry), 1971; The Savage God: A Study of Suicide, 1971; The Legacy (poetry), 1972; Beckett, 1973; Hers (novel), 1974; Hunt (novel), 1978; Autumn to Autumn and Selected Poems 1953–1976, 1978; Life after Marriage: Scenes from Divorce (in U.S.A. as Life After Marriage: Love in an Age of Divorce), 1982; The Biggest Game in Town, 1983; Offshore: A North Sea Journey, 1986; Feeding the Rat: Profile of a Climber, 1988; (with Charles Blackman) Rainforest, 1988. Add: c/o Aitken & Stowe, 29 Fernshaw Rd., London SW10 0TG, England.

AMABILE, George. Canadian, b. 1936. Poetry. Assoc. Prof. of English, Univ. of Manitoba, Winnipeg, since 1971. Ed., Northern Light mag. *Publs:* Blood Ties, 1972; Open Country, 1976; Flower and Song, 1978; Ideas of Shelter, 1981; The Presence of Fire, 1982; (ed. with Kim Dales) No Feather, No Ink, 1985. Add: Dept. of English, Univ. of Manitoba, Winnipeg R3T 2N2, Canada.

AMADI, Elechi. Nigerian, b. 1934. Novels/Short stories, Plays/Screenplays. Govt. divisional officer, and Sr. Asst. Secty., Ahoada and Port Harcourt, Nigeria, since 1968; Permanent Secty., 1973. Science teacher, 1960–63, and army officer, 1963–67. *Publs:* The Concubine, 1966; The Great Ponds, 1969; Isiburu (play), 1973; Sunset in Biafra, 1974; Peppersoup, and The Road to Ibadan (plays), 1977; The Slave, 1978; Dancer of Johannesburg (play), 1979; Ethics in Nigerian Culture, 1982; Estrangement (novel), 1986. Add: Box 331, Port Harcourt, Nigeria.

AMBERLEY, Richard. *See* **BOURQUIN**, Paul Henry James.

AMBIRAJAN, Srinivasa. Indian, b. 1936. Economics. Prof. of Economics, Indian Inst. of Technology, Madras, since 1981. Hallsworth Research Fellow, Univ. of Manchester, 1963–64; Lectr. in Economics, Univ. of Queensland, 1964–66 and Sr. Lectr. and Assoc. Prof., Univ. of New South Wales, Kensington, 1966–81. *Publs:* A Grammar of Indian Planning, 1959; Malthus and Classical Economics, 1959; The Taxation of Corporate Income in India, 1964; Classical Political Economy and British Policy in India, 1978; Political Economy and Monetary Management in India 1766-1914, 1984. Add: Dept. of Humanities and Social Sciences, Indian Inst. of Technology, Madras 600 036, India.

AMBLER, Eric. With Charles Rodda also writes as Eliot Reed. British, b. 1909. Novels/Short stories, Plays/Screenplays, Autobiography. Freelance writer. Advertising copywriter, 1928–37; Dir., advertising agency, 1937–38. *Publs:* The Dark Frontier, 1936; Uncommon Danger (in U.S. as Background to Danger), 1937; Epitaph for a Spy, 1938; Cause for Alarm, 1938; The Mask of Dimitrios (in U.S. as Coffin for Dimitrios), 1939; Journey into Fear, 1940; The Way Ahead, 1944; United States, 1945; The October Man, 1948; One Woman's Story (The Passionate Friends), 1948; (with Charles Rodda as Eliot Reed) Skytip, 1950; (with Charles Rodda as Eliot Reed) Tender to Danger, 1951; Judgement on Deltchev, 1951; Highly Dangerous, 1951; The Magic Box, 1952; Gigolo and Gigolette, 1952; The Card (The Promoter), 1952; Roughshoot, 1953; The Cruel Sea, 1953; The Schirmer Inheritance, 1953; (with Charles Rodda as Eliot Reed) The Marasffair, 1953; (with Charles Rodda as Eliot Reed) Charter to Danger, 1954; Lease of Life, 1955; The Purple Plain, 1955; The Night Comers (in U.S. as State of Siege), 1956; Yangtse Incident, 1957; A Night to Remember, 1959; Passage of Arms, 1959; The Wreck of the Mary Deare, 1960; The Light of Day, 1962 (Edgar Award);

The Ability to Kill and Other Pieces, 1963; (ed.) To Catch a Spy: An Anthology of Favourite Spy Stories, 1964; A Kind of Anger, 1964; Topkapi, 1964; Dirty Story, 1967; The Intercom Conspiracy, 1969; Love Hate Love, 1970; The Levanter, 1972; Dr. Frigo, 1974; Send No More Roses (in the U.S. The Siege of the Villa Lipp), 1977; The Care of Time, 1981; Here Lies: An Autobiography, 1985. Add: c/o Campbell, Thomson and McLaughlin Ltd., 31 Newington Green, London NI6 9PY, England.

AMBROSE, Alice (Mrs. Morris Lazerowitz). American, b. 1906. Philosophy. Emeritus Prof. of Philosophy, Smith Coll., Northampton, Mass., since 1972 (joined faculty, 1937). *Publs:* (with Morris Lazerowitz) Fundamentals of Symbolic Logic, 1948, 1962; (with M. Lazerowitz) Logic: The Theory of Formal Inference, 1961, 1972; Essays in Analysis, 1966; (ed. with M. Lazerowitz and contrib.) G.E. Moore, Essays in Retrospect, 1970; (ed. with M. Lazerowitz and contrib.) Ludwig Wittgenstein, Philosophy and Language, 1972; (with M. Lazerowitz) Philosophical Theories, 1976; (ed.) Wittgenstein's Lectures, Cambridge 1932–35, 1979; (with M. Lazerowitz) Essays in the Unknown Wittgenstein, 1984; (with M. Lazerowitz) Necessity and Language, 1985. Add: 126 Vernon St., Northampton, Mass. 01060, U.S.A.

AMBROSE, Stephen (Edward). American, b. 1936. History. Prof. of History, Univ. of New Orleans, since 1971. Asst. Prof. of History, Univ. of New Orleans, 1960–64; Assoc. Prof., 1964–66, and Prof. of History, 1966–69, Johns Hopkins Univ., Baltimore; Ernest J. King Prof. of Maritime History, U.S. Naval War College, Newport, RI, 1969–70; Dwight D. Eisenhower Prof. of War and Peace, Kansas State Univ., Manhattan, 1970–71. *Publs:* (ed.) A Wisconsin Boy in Dixie, 1961; Lincoln's Chief of Staff, 1962; Upton and the Army, 1964; Duty, Honor, and the Country: A History of West Point, 1966; Eisenhower and Berlin 1945, 1967; (ed.) Institutions in Modern America: Innovation in Structure and Process, 1967; (asst. ed.) The Papers of Dwight D. Eisenhower: The War Years, 5 vols., 1970; The Supreme Commander: Eisenhower, 1970; Rise to Globalism: American Foreign Policy 1938–70, 1970, 1976; (with James A. Barber, Jr.) The Military and American Society, 1972; Ike: Abilene to Berlin, 1973; Crazy Horse and Custer: The Parallel Lives of Two American Warriors, 1975; Ike's Spies: Eisenhower and the Espionage Establishment, 1981; (with Richard H. Immerman) Milton S. Eisenhower, 1983; Eisenhower, 2 vols., 1983–84; Pegasus Bridge, 1985; Nixon: The Education of a Politician, 1987. Add: Dept. of History, Univ. of New Orleans, LA 70211, U.S.A.

AMEND, John R(obert). American, b. 1938. Chemistry. Prof. of Chemistry, Montana State Univ., Bozeman, since 1967. Electrical Engineer, Alaska Communications System, 1957–60; Physics/Chemistry Teacher and Dept. Head, University Place Schools, Tacoma, Wash., 1960–65; Research Assoc., Univ. of Texas at Austin, 1965–67. *Publs:* Investigations in Atomic and Nuclear Science, 1964; (with Ralph Olsen) Experimental Chemistry, 1977; Introductory Chemistry: Models and Basic Concepts, 1977; Add: Dept. of Chemistry, Montana State Univ., Bozeman, Mont. 59717, U.S.A.

AMERY, (Harold) Julian. British, b. 1919. History, Autobiography/Memoirs/Personal, Biography. Conservative M.P. for the Pavilion div. of Brighton, Sussex, since 1969 (M.P. for Preston, Lancs., 1950–66; Delegate to Consultative Assembly, Council of Europe, 1950–53 and 1956; Member, Round Table Conference on Malta, 1955; Parliamentary Under Secty. of State and Financial Secty., War Office, London, 1957–58; Parliamentary Under Secty. of State, Colonial Office, 1958–60; Secty. of State for Air, 1960–62; Minister of Aviation, 1962–64; Minister for Housing and Construction, 1970–72; Minister for Foreign and Commonwealth Affairs, 1972–74). *Publs:* Sons of the Eagle, 1948; The Life of Joseph Chamberlain: At the Height of His Power 1901–1903, vol. IV, 1951, Joseph Chamberlain and the Tariff Reform Campaign 1901–1924, vols. V and VI, 1969; Approach March (autobiography), 1973. Add: 112 Eaton Sq., London SW1, England.

AMES, Delano L. American, b. 1906. Novels/Short stories, Mystery/Crime/Suspense. *Publs:* novels. Uneasily to Bed, 1934; A Double Bed on Olympus, 1936; mystery novels—They Journey by Night (in U.S. as Not in Utter Nakedness), 1932; No Traveller Returns, 1934; The Cornish Coast Conspiracy, 1942; He Found Himself Murdered, 1947; She Shall Have Murder, 1948; Murder Begins at Home, 1949; Corpse Diplomatique, 1950; Death of a Fellow Traveller, 1950, (in U.S. as Nobody Wore Black), 1951; The Body on Page One, 1951; Murder, Maestro, Please, 1952; No Mourning for the Matador, 1953; Crime, Gentlemen, Please (in U.S. as Coffin for Christopher), 1954; Landscape with Corpse, 1955; Crime Out of Mind, 1956; She Wouldn't Say Who, 1957; Lucky Jane (in U.S. as For Old Crime's Sake), 1959; The Man in the Tricorn Hat, 1960; The Man with Three Jaguars, 1961; The Man with Three Chins, 1965; The Man with Three Passports, 1967; other—Contract Bridge Rhymes, 1933. Add: c/o Harper and Row Paperbacks, 10 E. 53rd St., New York, N.Y. 10022, U.S.A.

AMES, Felicia. *See* **BURDEN**, Jean.

AMES, Leslie. *See* **RIGONI**, Orlando.

AMES, Rachel. *See* **GAINHAM**, Sarah.

AMIS, Kingsley (William). Has also written as Robert Markham. British, b. 1922. Novels/Short stories, Mystery/Crime/Suspense, Science fiction/Fantasy, Poetry, Literature, Biography. Lectr. in English, Univ. Coll., Swansea, 1949–61; Fellow in English, Peterhouse Coll., Cambridge, 1961–63. *Publs*: Bright November, 1947; (ed. with J. Michie) Oxford Poetry 1949, 1949; A Frame of Mind, 1953; Lucky Jim, 1954; That Uncertain Feeling, 1955; A Case of Samples: Poems 1946–1956, 1956; Socialism and the Intellectuals, 1957; I Like It Here, 1958; New Maps of Hell: A Survey of Science Fiction, 1960; Take a Girl Like You, 1960; (ed. with Robert Conquest) Spectrum: A Science Fiction Anthology, 1961; The Evans Country, 1962; (with D. Moraes and P. Porter) Penguin Modern Poets 2, 1962; One Fat Englishman, 1963; (with R. Conquest) The Egyptologist, 1965; The James Bond Dossier, 1965; The Anti-Death League, 1966; A Look Round the Estate: Poems 1957–1967, 1967; (as Robert Markham) Colonel Sun: A James Bond Adventure, 1968; Lucky Jim's Politics, 1968; I Want It Now, 1968; The Green Man, 1969; What Became of Jane Austin?, 1970; Girl, 20, 1971; (ed.) Selected Short Stories of G.K. Chesterton, 1972; The Riverside Villa Murder, 1973; Ending Up, 1974; Rudyard Kipling and His World, 1975; The Alteration, 1976; The New Oxford Book of Light Verse, 1978; Jake's Thing, 1978; Collected Poems 1944–1979; Russian Hide-and-Seek, 1980; Selected Short Stories, 1980; (ed.) The Golden Age of Science Fiction, 1981; Every Day Drinking, 1983; How's Your Glass?, 1984; Stanley and the Women (novel), 1984; The Old Devils, 1986 (Booker Prize); Crime of the Century, 1987; Difficulties with Girls (novel), 1988. Add: c/o Jonathan Clowes, 22 Prince Albert Rd., London NW1 7ST, England.

AMIS, Martin (Louis). British, b. 1949. Novels/Short stories. Editorial Asst., Times Literary Supplement, London, 1972–75; Asst. Literary Ed., 1975–77, and Literary Ed., 1977–79, New Statesman, London. Contrib., Times Literary Supplement, Observer newspaper, and the New Statesman mag., Sunday Times, N.Y. Times, and Sunday Telegraph. *Publs*: The Rachel Papers, 1973; Dead Babies, 1975, as Dark Secrets, 1977; Success, 1978; Einstein's Monsters (short stories), 1987; Invasion of the Space Invaders, 1982; Other People: A Mystery Story, 1981; Money, 1984; The Moronic Inferno and Other Visits to America, 1986; Einstein's Monsters (short stories), 1987. Add: c/o A.D. Peters, The Chambers, Chelsea Harbour, Lots Road, London SW10 0XF, England.

AMMER, Christine (Parker). American, b. 1931. Business/Trade/Industry, Economics, Medicine/Health, Music. *Publs*: Harvard Dictionary of Music, 2nd ed., 1969; Musician's Handbook of Foreign Terms, 1971; Harper's Dictionary of Music, 1972; (with Dean S. Ammer) Dictionary of Business and Economics, 1977, 1984; Unsung: A History of Women in American Music, 1980; The A to Z of Women's Health: A Concise Encyclopaedia, 1982; (with Nathan T. Sidley) The Common Sense Guide to Mental Health Care 1982; The Harper Dictionary of Music, 1986; The A to Z of Investing, 1986; It's Raining Cats and Dogs ... and Other Beastly Expressions, 1988. Add: c/o Greenwood Press, 51 Riverside Ave., Westport, Conn. 06880, U.S.A.

AMMERMAN, Leila T(remaine). American, b. 1912. Theology/Religion. Freelance writer. Office Asst., Webb's City Inc., since 1973 (Receiving and Transfer Clerk, 1973–74; Service Secty., 1974). Exec. Dir., Girl's Club, Portsmouth, Va. 1963–65, and The Little Library, a philosophical venture, St. Petersburg, Fla. 1965–73. *Publs*: Ghost on Crutches (radio play), 1952 (Prize Award in Dr. Christian play contest); (compiler and ed.) Of Such is the Kingdom (poetry) 1954; Abingdon Promotion Rally Day Book, 1955; Abingdon Easter Programs, 1960; Abingdon Mother's Day Book, 1960; Abingdon Christmas Programs No. 2, 1960; Inspiring Devotional Programs for Women's Groups, 1960, 1969; Programs for Special Days, 1961, 1970; Golden Ladder of Stewardship, 1962, 1971; Inspiring Devotional Programs for Women's Groups, 1971; Be Still, and Know (meditation); Installation Services That Inspire, 1982; Stewardship Talks and Resources, 1988. Add: 200 57th Ave. South, St. Petersburg, Fla. 33705, U.S.A.

AMMONS, A(rchie) R(andolph). American, b. 1926. Poetry. Prof. of English since 1971, and Goldwin Smith Prof. of English since 1973, Cornell aUniv., Ithaca. N.Y. (joined faculty, 1964; Assoc. Prof., 1969–71). Prinuscipal, Hatteras Elementary Sch., N.C., 1949–50; Exec. Vice-Pres., Friedrich Dimmock Inc., Mellville, N.J., 1952–62; Visiting Prof., Wake Forest Univ., Winston-Salem, N.C., 1974–75. Recipient, National Book Award, 1973; National Book Critics Circle Award, 1981. *Publs*: Ommateum with Doxology, 1955; Expressions of Sea Level, 1964; Corsons Inlet: A Book of Poems, 1965; Tape for the Turn of the Year, 1965; Northfield Poems, 1966; Selected Poems, 1968; Uplands, 1970; Briefings: Poems Small and Easy, 1971; Collected Poems, 1951–1971, 1972; Sphere: The Form of a Motion, 1974: Diversifications, 1975; The Snow Poems, 1977; Selected Poems, 1977; Highgate Road, 1978; Six-Piece Suite, 1979; A Coast of Trees, 1981; Worldly Hopes, 1982; Lake Effect Country, 1983; Selected Poems, 1987; Sumerian Vistas, 1987. Add: Dept. of English, Cornell Univ., Ithaca, N.Y. 14850, U.S.A.

AMORY, Cleveland. American, b. 1917. Environmental science/Ecology, Social commentary/phenomena. Freelance writer since 1943. Syndicated Columnist, Animail; Pres., The Fund for Animals. *Publs*: The Proper Bostonians, 1947; Home Town, 1950; The Last Resorts, 1952; Who Killed Society?, 1960; (ed.) Vanity Fair (anthology), 1960; Man Kind? Our Incredible War on Wildlife, 1974; Animail, 1976; The Trouble with Nowadays, 1979; The Cat Who Came for Christmas, 1987. Add: 200 W. 57th St., New York, N.Y. 10019, U.S.A.

ANAND, Mulk Raj. Indian, b. 1905. Novels/Short stories, Art, Children's non-fiction, Cultural/Ethnic topics, Language/Linguistics, Literature. Pres., Lokayata Trust, New Delhi, since 1970. Ed., Marg mag., Bombay, since 1946. Lectr. at various univs., 1948–65; Tagore Prof. of Literature and Fine Art, Univ. of Punjab, 1963–66; Fine Art Chmn., Lalit Kala Akademi (National Academy of Art), New Delhi, 1965–70 *Publs*: Persian Painting, 1930; The Golden Breath: Studies in Five Poets of New India, 1933; The Hindu View of Art, 1933, rev. ed. 1957, 1978; Apology for Heroism: An Essay in Search of a Faith, 1934; The Lost Child and Other Stories, 1934; Untouchable, 1935; Coolie, 1936: Two Leaves and a Bud, 1937; The Village, 1939; Lament on the Death of a Master of Arts, 1939; Across the Black Waters, 1940; The Sword and the Sickle, 1942; Letters on India, 1942; The Barber's Trade Union and Other Stories, 1944; The Big Heart, 1945; Indian Fairy Tales: Retold, 1946; The Tractor and the Corn Goddess and Other Stories, 1947; (ed. with I. Singh) Indian Short Stories, 1947; On Education, 1947; (with K.N. Hutheesing) The Bride's Book of Beauty, 1947, 1974; The Story of India, 1958; The King Emperor's English: or, The Role of the English Language in the Free India, 1948; Lines Written to an Indian Air: Essays, 1949: Indian Theatre, 1950; Seven Summers, 1951; Private Life of an Indian Prince, 1953, rev. ed. 1970; Reflections on the Golden Bed, 1954; The Story of Man, 1954; More Indian Fairy Tales, 1956; Kama Kala: Some Notes on the Philosophical Basis of Hindu Erotic Sculpture, 1958; India in Colour, 1959; (with S. Kramrisch) Homage to Khajuraho, 1960; The Road, 1962; The Old Woman and the Cow, 1963; Is There a Contemporary Indian Civilisation?, 1963; Death of a Hero, 1964; The Power of Darkness, 1966; The Third Eye: A Lecture on Art, 1966; Morning Face, 1968; The Volcano: Lectures on the Painting of Rabindranath Tagore, 1968; Ajanta, 1971; Confession of a Lover, 1976; The Bubble, 1984. Add: 25 Cuffe Parade, Bombay 5, India.

ANANIA, Michael (Angelo). American, b. 1938. Novels/short stories, Poetry. Asst. Prof. of English, Univ. of Illinois, Chicago, since 1970 (Instr., 1968–70). Literary Ed., Swallow Press, Chicago, since 1968; member, Bd. of Dirs., since 1971 (Chmn of the Board and President 1974–76), and Exec. Cttee., since 1972, Coordinating Council of Literary Mags. Bibliographer, Lockwood Library, State Univ. of New York, Buffalo, 1963–64; Ed., Audit, 1963–64; Co-Ed., Audit/Poetry, Buffalo, 1963–67; Instr. in English, State Univ. of New York, Fredonia, 1964–65, and Northwestern Univ., Evanston, Ill., 1965–68. *Publs*: (ed.) New Poetry Anthology I and II, 1969, 1972; The Colour of Dust, 1970; Set/Sorts, 1974; Riversongs, 1978; The Red Menace (novel), 1984; Constructions/Variations, 1985; The Sky at Ashland, 1986. Add: Dept. of English, Univ. of Illinois at Chicago, Chicago, Ill. 60680, U.S.A.

ANASTASIOU, Clifford (John). Canadian, b. 1929. Biology, Natural History, Sciences. Prof. of Education, Univ. of British Columbia, Vancouver, since 1971 (joined faculty, 1962). *Publs*: Ascomycetes & Fungi Imperfecti from the Salton Sea, 1963; Reading about Science, 1968; Teachers, Children, and Things, 1971; The Stump Book, 1975; The Creek Book, 1978; The Estuary Book, 1980; The Wild Cells, 1980; Managing the Forest, 1985; Hurray for Me, 1985; It's Your Body, 1985. Add: c/o Dept. of Education, Univ. of British Columbia, Vancouver, B.C., Canada.

ANATI, Emmanuel. Italian, b. 1930. Anthropology/Ethnology, Archaeology/Antiquities, Art. Prof. of Palaeo-ethnology, Univ. of Lecce. Dir. and Ed.-in-Chief, Centro Camuno Di Studi Prehistorici, Capo Di Ponte, since 1964. Gen. Secty., Intnl. Assn. for the Study of Prehistoric and Primitive Religions. *Publs:* Camonica Valley, 1961; La Grande Roche de Naquane, 1961; Palestine Before the Hebrews, 1963; (with F. Roiter and C. Roy) Naquane: Découverte d'un Pays et d'une Civilisation, 1966; Arte Prehistorica in Valtellina, 1967; Origini della Civilta Camuna, 1968; Arte Rupestre nelle regioni Occidentali della Penisola Iberica, 1968; Rock Art in Central Arabia, 4 vols., 1968–75; Le Statue stele dell'-Italia Settentrionale, 1972; (with M. Avnimelech, N. Haas and E. Meyerhof) Hazorea I, 1973; Evolution and Style in Camunian Rock Art, 1976; Methods of Recording and Analysing Rock Engravings, 1977; L'art rupestre: Negev et Sinai, 1979; Le Statue Stele delle Lunigiana, 1981; I Camuni alle Radici della Civilta Europea, 1982; Gli Elementi: Fondamentali della Cultura, 1983. Add: Centro Camuno Di Studi Prehistorici, 25044 Capo Di Ponte, Italy.

ANAYA, Rudolfo A(lfonso). American, b. 1937. Novels/Short stories, Poetry. Dir. of Counseling, 1972–74, and since 1987. Prof. of English, Univ. of New Mexico, Albuquerque. Teacher in the Albuquerque public schools, 1963–70; Assoc. Ed., American Book Review, NYC, 1980–85. Vice-Pres., Coordinating Council of Literary Magazines, 1974–80. *Publs:* Bless Me, Ultima (novel), 1972; Heart of Aztlan (novel), 1976; Tortuga (novel), 1979; (ed. with Antonio Marquez) Cuentos Chicanos, 1980; (ed. with Simon J. Ortiz) A Ceremony of Brotherhood 1680-1980, 1981; The Silence of Llano (short stories), 1982; The Legend of La Llorona (novel), 1984; The Adventures of Juan Chicaspatas (poetry), 1985; Lord of the Dawn (novel), 1987. Add: 5324 Canada Vista N.W., Albuquerque, N.M. 87120, U.S.A.

ANCONA, George. American, b. 1929. Children's fiction, Children's non-fiction. Photographer and filmmaker, George Ancona, Inc., New York, since 1961. Illustrator, numerous children's books. *Publs:* Monsters on Wheels, 1974; (with Remy Charlip and Mary Beth) Handtalk: An ABC of Finger Spelling and Sign Language, 1974; And What Do You Do?, 1975; Feel: A Picture Book on Emotions, 1977; Growing Older, 1977; It's a Baby!, 1979; Dancing Is . . . , 1981; Monster Movers, 1984; Bananas, 1984; Teamwork, 1984; Freighter, 1985; Sheepdog, 1985; Helping Out, 1985; Handtalk Birthday, 1987; Turtlewatch, 1987. Add: 75 Crickettown Rd., Stony Point, N.Y. 10980, U.S.A.

ANDELSON, Robert V. American, b. 1931. Philosophy, Social sciences (general). Prof. of Philosophy, Auburn Univ., Ala., since 1973 (Asst. Prof., 1965–69; Assoc. Prof., 1969–73). Member, Editorial Bd., American Journal of Economics and Sociology, since 1969; Member, Academic Staff, Ludwig von Mises Inst., since 1983. Ordained Minister of Congregationalist Church, 1959. Faculty member, Arlington Coll., Calif., 1955–58; Exec. Dir., San Diego Extension, Henry George Sch. of Social Science, Calif., 1959–62; Instr. in Philosophy and Religion, Northland Coll., Wisconsin, 1962–63; Asst. Prof. of Philosophy and Government, Northwestern State Univ., Natchitoches, La., 1963–65. Member, Editorial Bd., The Personalist, 1975–80. *Publs:* Imputed Rights: An Essay in Christian Social Theory, 1971; (ed.) Critics of Henry George, 1979; (with James M. Dawsey) Wasteland/Promised Land: An Alternative Approach for Liberation Theology, 1989. Add: 534 Cary Dr., Auburn, Ala. 36830, U.S.A.

ANDERS, Leslie. American, b. 1922. History, Politics/Government. Prof. of History, Central Missouri State Univ., Warrensburg, since 1963, retired 1987 (Asst. Prof., 1955–58; Assoc. Prof., 1958–63). Historian, Engineer Historical Div., Dept. of the Army, 1951–55. *Publs:* The Ledo Road: General Joseph W. Stilwell's Highway to China, 1965; The Eighteenth Missouri, 1968; Education for Service: Centennial History of Central Missouri State College, 1971; The Twenty-First Missouri: From Home Guard to Union Regiment, 1975; Gentle Night: The Life and Times of Major General Edwin F. Harding, 1985. Add: Dept. of History, Central Missouri State Univ., Warrensburg, Mo. 64093, U.S.A.

ANDERSEN, Doris (Isabel Crompton). Canadian, b. 1909. Novels/Short stories, Children's fiction. Library Asst., Seattle Public Library, 1929–30; Librarian, Ottawa Public Library, 1940–43, and Canadian Legion Library, Ottawa, 1943–45; Children's Librarian, 1956–65, and Branch Head Librarian, 1965–74, Vancouver Public Library; Lectr. in Children's Literature, Capilano Coll., North Vancouver, 1969. *Publs:* Blood Brothers, 1967; Ways Harsh and Wild, 1973; Slave of the Haida, 1974; The Evergreen Islands, 1980; The Columbia Is Coming!, 1982; To Change the World: A Biography of Pauline Jewett, 1987. Add:

1232 Esquimalt Ave., W. Vancouver, B.C. V7T 1K3, Canada.

ANDERSON, Alan, Jr. American, b. 1943. Earth sciences, Marine science/Oceanography, Natural history. With the National Academy of Sciences, Washington, D.C., 1965–66, and NASA, Beltsville, Md., 1966; Time mag., NYC, 1969–71, Rio de Janeiro, 1971–72, and NYC, 1973–74; Saturday Review, San Francisco, 1972–73; Co-Founder, Illinois Times, Springfield, 1975–77; with the News-Record, Marshall, N.C., 1979–80. *Publs:* The Drifting Continents, 1971; (with John Sanders and Robert Carola) Physical Geology, 1976; (co-author) The Blue Reef, 1979; (co-author) Above Timberline, 1981. Add: P.O. Box 747, Mars Hill, N.C., 28754, U.S.A.

ANDERSON, Chester. Also writes as John Valentine. American, b. 1932. Novels/Short stories, Science fiction/Fantasy, Poetry. Ed., The Communication Company, 1967, and Crawdaddy mag., 1968–69. *Publs:* Colloquy (poetry), 1960; A Liturgy for Dragons (poetry), 1961; The Pink Palace (novel), 1963; (with Michael Kurland) Ten Years to Doomsday (science fiction), 1964; The Butterfly Kid (science fiction), 1967; Puppies (memoirs), 1979; Fox and Hare (novel), 1980 Add: P.O. Box 80, Rio Nido, Calif. 95471, U.S.A.

ANDERSON, Colin. British. Novels/Short stories, Science fiction/Fantasy. *Publs:* Boon (novel), 1964; Magellan, 1970. Add: c/o Gollancz, 14 Henrietta St., London WC2E 8QJ, England.

ANDERSON, Courtney. American, b. 1906. Administration/Management, Biography. Vice Pres., Research and Development, Elba Systems Corp., Denver, Colo., 1965–76. *Publs:* To the Golden Shore: The Life of Adoniram Judson, 1956; (with R.T. Hitt, C.S. Kilby and H.V. Coray) Heroic Colonial Christians, 1966; Letters to our Friends: A Discussion of Audiovisual Sales Systems, 1973. Add: 12427 Rochedale Lane, Los Angeles, Calif. 90049, U.S.A.

ANDERSON, David Daniel. American, b. 1924. Literature, Biography. Prof., Dept. of American Thought and Language, Michigan State Univ., East Lansing, since 1957. Ed., Midwestern Miscellany Annual. Exec. Secty., Soc. for the Study of Midwestern Literature (Pres., 1971–73). *Publs:* Louis Bromfield, 1964; Critical Studies in American Literature, 1964; Sherwood Anderson, 1967; Sherwood Anderson's Winesburg, Ohio, 1967; Brand Whitlock, 1968; (ed.-in-chief) The Black Experience, 1969; Abraham Lincoln, 1970; (ed.) The Literary Works of Abraham Lincoln, 1970; (ed. with R. Wright) The Dark and Tangled Path, 1971; (ed.) Sunshine and Smoke, 1971; Robert Ingersoll, 1972; (ed.) Mid-America I-XVI, 1974–89; (ed.) Sherwood Anderson: Dimensions of His Literary Art (essays), 1976; Woodrow Wilson, 1978; (ed.) Sherwood Anderson: The Writer at his Craft, 1979; Ignatius Donnelly, 1980; William Jennings Bryan, 1981; Critical Essays on Sherwood Anderson, 1981; Michigan: A State Anthology, 1982. Add: Dept. of American Thought and Language, Michigan State Univ., East Lansing, Mich. 48824, U.S.A.

ANDERSON, Donald K., Jr. American, b. 1922. Literature. Prof. of English Literature, Univ. of Missouri-Columbia, since 1967 (Assoc. Prof., 1965–67). Asst. and Assoc. Prof. of English Literature, Butler Univ., Indianapolis, Ind., 1958–65. *Publs:* Perkin Warbeck by John Ford, 1965, 1968; (ed.) The Broken Heart by John Ford, 1968; (ed. with Charles R. Hoffer) Performing Music with Understanding, 1971; John Ford, 1972; Concord in Discord: The Plays of John Ford 1586–1986, 1987. Add: c/o Dept. of English, Univ. of Missouri, Columbia, Mo. 65211, U.S.A.

ANDERSON, Ella. *See* **MacLEOD,** Ellen Jane.

ANDERSON, (William) Ferguson. British, b. 1914. Medicine/Health. Chmn., Scottish Retirement Council, since 1963. Physician in Geriatric Medicine, Stobhill Gen. Hosp., Glasgow, 1952–79; David Cargill Prof. of Geriatric Medicine, Univ. of Glasgow, 1965–79. Pres., British Medical Assn., 1977–78. *Publs:* (with B. Isaacs) An Introduction to Geriatrics, 1965; Practical Management of the Elderly, 1971, 5th ed. (with B. Williams) 1989; (ed. with T.G. Judge) Geriatric Medicine, 1974; (with others) Gerontology and Geriatric Nursing, 1982. Add: Rodel, Moor Rd., Strathblane, G63 9EX, Scotland.

ANDERSON, (Lady) Flavia. Has also written as Petronella Portobello. British, b. 1910. Novels/Short stories, History. *Publs:* Keep Thy Wife, 1931; Jezebel and the Dayspring, 1959; The Ancient Secret: In Search of the Holy Grail (history), 1955; (as Petronella Portobello) How to Be a Deb's Mum, 1957; The Rebel Emperor (history), 1958; Fire from the Sun: Latest Research of the Ancient Secret (history of the Grail), 1988. Add: 13 Carlton Terr., Edinburgh 7, Scotland.

ANDERSON, Jack (Northman). American, b. 1922. Politics/Government, Documentaries/Reportage. Newspaper columnist: writer of syndicated column, Washington Merry-Go-Round, since 1969 (Reporter, 1947–65; Partner, 1965–69); Washington Bureau Chief, Parade mag., since 1968. Reporter, Salt Lake Tribune, Utah, 1939–41; Missionary, Southern States, Church of Jesus Christ of Latter Day Saints, 1941–44. *Publs:* (with R. May) McCarthy the Man, the Senator, the Ism, 1952; (with F. Blumenthal) The Kefauver Story, 1956; (with Drew Pearson) U.S.A.: Second Class Power?, 1958; Washington Exposé, 1966; (with Drew Pearson) The Case Against Congress, 1968; (with Carl Kalvelage) American Government —Like It Is, 1972; (with G. Clifford) the Anderson Papers, 1973; Confessions of a Muckraker, 1979; (with Bill Pronzini) The Cambodia File, 1981; (with John Kidner) Alice in Blunderland, 1983; (with James Boyd) Fiasco, 1983. Add: c/o United Feature Syndicate, 200 Park Ave., New York, N.Y. 10166, U.S.A.

ANDERSON, James. British. Mystery/Crime/Suspense. *Publs:* Assasin, 1969; The Alpha List, 1972; The Abolition of Death, 1974; The Affair of the Blood-Stained Egg Cosy, 1975; Appearance of Evil, 1977; Angel of Death, 1978; Assault and Matrimony, 1980; The Affair of the Mutilated Mink, 1982; Auriol, 1982; The Murder of Sherlock Holmes, 1985; Hooray for Homicide, 1985; Lovers and Other Killers, 1986; Additional Evidence, 1988. Add: 4 Church Rd., Penarth, Glamorgan, Wales.

ANDERSON, James G. American, b. 1936. Education, Sociology. Prof. of Sociology, Dept. of Sociology and Anthropology, Purdue Univ., West Lafayette, Ind., since 1970. Instr. in Mathematics, Mount St. Agnes Coll., 1962–64; Administrative Asst. to the Dean, 1964–65, and Dir., Div. of Engineering, 1965–66, Evening Coll., Johns Hopkins Univ., Baltimore, Md.; Research Prof. of Educational Admin., New Mexico State Univ., Las Cruces, 1966–70. *Publs:* Bureaucracy in Education, 1968; (with S.J. Jay) Use and Impact of Computers in Clinical Medicine, 1987. Add: 4141 Black Forest Lane, West Lafayette, Ind. 47906, U.S.A.

ANDERSON, Jessica (Margaret). Australian. Novels/Short stories. *Publs:* An Ordinary Lunacy, 1963; The Last Man's Head, 1970; The Commandant, 1976; Tirra Lirra by the River, 1978; The Impersonators (in U.S. and U.K. as The Only Daughter), 1980; Stories from the Warm Zone, 1987. Add: c/o Elaine Markson, Agent, 44 Greenwich Ave., New York, N.Y. 10011, U.S.A.

ANDERSON, John. British, b. 1909. Novels/Short stories, Children's non-fiction. Librarian and Asst. Ed. of Children's Books, Oxford Univ. Press, London, 1932–39; Officer, London Fire Service, 1939–45; Headmaster, Haysbrook Sch., 1956–68. *Publs:* Big Book of Trains, 1934; Mr. Pippleberry, 1936; Let's Go Flying, 1937; Little Book of London, 1939; rev. ed. 1951; By Wheels, Wings and Water, 1943; Our Firefighters, 1944; Discovery Readers (14 vols.), 1949–64; Pioneer Books (5 vols.), 1951; The Fireman, 1952; Eight Religious Plays, 1952; Adventures in Work (12 vols.). 1954–57; (with Jack Plant) Discovery Plays (3 vols.), 1961–63; Discovery Books of Aircraft, Ships, Trains, Motors, 1964; Discovery Bible Plays, 1965; Tale of the Torrey Canyon, 1976; Glimpses of Colthouse Meeting During Three Centuries, 1988. Add: Dubber Beck, Oxen Park, Ulverston, Cumbria, England.

ANDERSON, John B(ayard). American, b. 1922. Politics/Government. Chmn., National Unity Party, Washington. Lectr. in Political Science, Bryn Mawr Coll., since 1980, and Nova Univ. Center for Study of Law, since 1987. Formerly, Member for the 16th district of Illinois (Republican), U.S. House of Representatives; Chmn., House Republican Conference, and Member, House Rules Cttee., and Joint Cttee. on Atomic Energy. Foreign Service Officer on staff of the U.S. High Commissioner to Germany, 1952–55; practised law, Rockford, Ill., 1955–60; State's Attorney, Winnebago County, Ill., 1956–60; Independent Candidate for President of the U.S. 1980. *Publs:* Between Two Worlds: A Congressman's Choice, 1970; (ed.) Congress and Conscience, 1970; Vision and Betrayal in America, 1976; The American Economy We Need—And Won't Get from the Republicans or the Democrats, 1984. Add: 2720 35th Pl. N.W., Washington, D.C. 20007, U.S.A.

ANDERSON, Jon (Victor). American, b. 1940. Poetry. Assoc. Prof., Univ. of Arizona, Tuscon, since 1978. Instr., later Asst. Prof. of Creative Writing, Univ. of Portland, Ore., 1968–72; Asst. Prof. of Creative Writing, Ohio Univ., Athens, 1972–73, and the Univ. of Pittsburgh, 1973–76; Asst. Prof. of Creative Writing, Univ. of Iowa, Iowa City, 1976–77. *Publs:* Looking for Jonathan, 1968; Death and Friends, 1970; In Sepia, 1974; Counting the Days, 1974; Cypresses, 1981; The Milky Way, 1983. Add: Dept. of English, Univ. of Arizona, Tuscon, Ariz. 85716, U.S.A.

ANDERSON, Kenneth Norman. American, b. 1921. Health, Keeping fit. Pres., Pubs. Editorial Services, Inc., Katonah, NY, since 1981. Exec. Ed., Publishers Editorial Services; Pres., Editorial Guild. Ed., Holt, Rinehart & Winston, Inc., New York, 1965–70; Exec. Dir., Coffee Information Inst., NYC, 1970–81. *Publs:* (co-author) Lawyer's Medical Cyclopedia, 1962; (with Robert Addison) The Family Physician, 1963; (with William Baver) Today's Health Guide, 1965; (with Robert Addison) Pictorial Medical Guide, 1967; Field and Stream Guide to Physical Fitness, 1969; (with Paul Kuhn) Home Medical Encyclopedia, 1973; Sterno Guide to the Outdoors, 1977; Eagle Claw Fish Cookbook, 1977; The Newsweek Encyclopedia of Family Health and Fitness, 1980; (with Walter Glanze) Bantam Medical Dictionary, 1980, 1982; How Long Will You Live, 1981; (with David Tver) Dictionary of Dangerous Pollutants, Ecology, and Environment, 1981; The Pocket Guide to Coffees and Teas, 1982; Orphan Drugs, 1983, 1988; (with Walter Glanze and Robert Goldenson) Longman Dictionary of Psychology and Psychiatry, 1984; (with Jack Murphy) History of the U.S. Marines, 1984; (with Lois Harmon Anderson) Prentice-Hall Dictionary of Nutrition and Health, 1985; (with Lois Harmon Anderson and Walter Glanze) Mosby Medical Encyclopedia, 1985; Symptoms After Forty, 1987. Add: 23 McQueen St., Katonah, NY 10536, U.S.A.

ANDERSON, Malcolm. British, b. 1934. History, Politics/Government, Translations. Prof. of Politics, Univ. of Edinburgh, since 1979. Lectr. in Government, Univ. of Manchester, 1960–64; Sr. Lectr., 1965–73, and Prof. of Politics, 1973–79, Univ. of Warwick. *Publs:* (co-author) The Right in France, 1890-1919, 1962; (trans.) An Introduction to the Social Sciences: With Special Reference to Their Methods, by Maurice Duverger, 1964; Government in France, 1971; Conservative Politics in France, 1974; Frontier Regions in Western Europe, 1983; Women, Equality and Europe, 1988; Policing the World: Interpol and the Politics of International Police Co-operation, 1989. Add: Dept. of Politics, Univ. of Edinburgh, Edinburgh EH8 9JT, Scotland.

ANDERSON, Matthew Smith. British, b. 1922. History. Lectr. in Political History, 1953–61, Reader, 1961–72, and Prof. of Intnl. History, 1972–85, London Sch. of Economics. *Publs:* Britain's Discovery of Russia, 1553-1815, 1958; Europe in the Eighteenth Century, 1713-1783, 1961, 1987; The Eastern Question, 1774-1923, 1966; Eighteenth Century Europe, 1713-1789, 1966; (ed.) The Great Powers and the Near East, 1774-1923, 1970; (ed.) Studies in Diplomatic History: Essays in Memory of David Bayne Horn, 1970; The Ascendancy of Europe, 1815-1914, 1972, 1985; Peter the Great, 1978; Historians and Eighteenth Century Europe, 1979. Add: 45 Cholmeley Cres., London N6 5EX, England.

ANDERSON, (Sir) (James) Norman (Dalrymple). British, b. 1908. Law, Theology/Religion. Prof. of Oriental Laws, 1953–75, Head of the Dept. of Law, Sch. of Oriental and African Studies, 1953–71, and Dean of the Faculty of Laws, 1965–69, Univ. of London; Dir., Inst. of Advanced Legal Studies, 1959–76. *Publs:* Islamic Law in Africa, 1954, 1970; Islamic Law in the Modern World, 1959; (ed.) Changing Law in Developing Countries, 1963; (ed.) Family Law in Asia and Africa, 1968; Christianity: The Witness of History, 1969; Christianity and Comparative Religion, 1970; Morality, Law and Grace, 1972; A Lawyer Among the Theologians, 1973; Law Reform in the Muslim World, 1976; Issues of Life and Death, 1976; Liberty, Law and Justice, 1978; The Mystery of the Incarnation, 1978; God's Law and God's Love, 1980; God's Word for God's World, 1981; The Teaching of Jesus, 1983; Christianity and World Religions: The Challenge of Pluralism, 1984; Jesus Christ: The Witness of History, 1984; An Adopted Son: The Story of My Life, 1985; Freedom under Law, 1988. Add: 9 Larchfield, Gough Way, Cambridge, England.

ANDERSON, Odin Waldemar. American, b. 1914. Health. Emeritus Prof. and Prof., part-time, since 1980, Grad. Sch. of Business and Dept. of Sociology, Univ. of Chicago (Assoc. Prof., 1962–64; Prof., 1964–80; Dir., Center for Health Administration Studies, 1972–80); Prof. of Sociology, Univ. of Wisconsin, Madison, since 1980. Instr., Sch. of Public Health, Univ. of Michigan, Ann Arbor, 1945–49; Assoc. Prof., Faculty of Medicine, Univ. of Western Ontario, London, 1949–52; Research Dir., Health Information Foundn., New York, 1952–62; Adjunct Assoc. Prof., Graduate Sch., New York Univ., 1953–57, and at Sch. of Public Health, Columbia Univ., New York, 1957–62. *Publs:* Health Care: Can There be Equity: The U.S., Sweden and England, 1972; Health Services in the U.S.: A Growth Enterprise since 1875, 1985; HMO Development, Patterns and Prospects: A Comparative Analysis of HMOs, 1985; Cross-National Comparisons of Health Services Systems: Observations and Generalizations, 1989. Add: Dept. of Sociology, Univ. of Wisconsin–Madison, Social Science Bldg., Madison, Wis. 53705, U.S.A.

ANDERSON, Olive Ruth. British, b. 1926. History. Prof. of History, Westfield Coll., Univ. of London, since 1986 (Asst. Lectr., 1949–57; Lectr., 1958–69; Reader, 1969–86). *Publs:* A Liberal State at War: English Politics and Economics during the Crimean War, 1967; Suicide in Victorian and Edwardian England, 1987. Add: 45 Cholmeley Cres., Highgate, London N6 5EX, England.

ANDERSON, Peggy. American, b. 1938. Institutions/Organizations, Medicine/Health. *Publs:* The Daughters: An Unconventional Look at America's Fan Club—The DAR, 1974; Nurse, 1978; Children's Hospital, 1985. Add: 322 S. Camac, Philadelphia, Pa. 19107, U.S.A.

ANDERSON, Poul. American, b. 1926. Mystery/Crime/Suspense, Science fiction/Fantasy. Pres., Science Fiction Writers of America, 1972–73. *Publs:* Vault of the Ages, 1952; Brain Wave, 1954; The Broken Sword, 1954; The Star Ways, 1957; Earthman's Burden, 1957; Virgin Planet, 1959; Perish by the Sword, 1959; The Enemy Stars, 1959; Murder in Black Letter, 1960; The Golden Slave, 1960; The High Crusade, 1960; Rogue Sword, 1960; Guardians of Time, 1960; Twilight World, 1960; Three Hearts and Three Lions, 1961; Orbit Unlimited, 1961; After Doomsday, 1962; Trader to the Stars, 1964; Time and Stars, 1964; The Star Fox, 1965; The Corridors of Time, 1965; Agent of the Terran Empire, 1965; Flandry of Terra, 1965; The Fox, the Dog, and the Griffin, 1966; Infinite Voyage, 1969; Operation Chaos, 1971; Byworlder, 1971; The Horn of Time, 1973; Hrolf Kraki's Saga, 1973; Tau Zero, 1973; A Midsummer Tempest, 1974; Fire Time, 1974; Knight of Ghosts and Shadows, 1975; Mirkheim, 1977; The Avatar, 1978; The Earth Book of Stormgate, 1978; Orion Shall Rise, 1983; The Year of the Ransom, 1988. Add: c/o Doubleday & Co. Inc., 666 Fifth Ave., New York, N.Y. 10104, U.S.A.

ANDERSON, Quentin. American, b. 1912. Literature. Emeritus Julian Levi Prof. in the Humanities, Columbia Univ., NYC, since 1981 (Instr. and Asst. Prof. of English, 1939–55; Assoc. Prof., 1955–61; Prof., 1961–78; Julian Levi Prof., 1978–81). Fulbright Lectr. in France, 1962–63; Visiting Prof., Univ. of Sussex, 1966–67, and Univ. of Barcelona, spring 1985. Fellow, New York Inst. for the Humanities, 1981–89. *Publs:* (ed.) Selected Short Stories by Henry James, 1950; The American Henry James, 1957; (ed. with Joseph A. Mazzeo) The Proper Study: Essays on Western Classics, 1962; The Imperial Self: An Essay in American Literary and Cultural History, 1971; (ed. with others) Art, Politics and Will: Essays in Honor of Lionel Trilling, 1977. Add: 29 Claremont Ave., New York, N.Y. 10027, U.S.A.

ANDERSON, Rachel. Pseud. for Rachel Bradby. British, b. 1943. Novels/Short stories, Plays/Screenplays, Literature. *Publs:* Pineapple, 1965; Tomorrow's Tomorrow (radio play), 1972; The Purple Heart Throbs, 1974; Moffatt's Road, 1978; Dream Lovers, 1978; Fairy Snow and the Disability Box (play for children), 1981; The Poacher's Son, 1982; Little Angel Comes to Stay, 1984; The War Orphan, 1986; Renard the Fox, 1986; French Lessons, 1988; Little Angel, Bonjour, 1988; The Bus People, 1989; The Boy Who Laughed, 1989. Add: Lower Damsels, Northrepps, Norfolk, England.

ANDERSON, Richard Lloyd. American, b. 1926. History, Theology/Religion. Prof. of Ancient Scripture, Brigham Young Univ., Provo, Utah, since 1962 (faculty member from 1955). Lectr. in Classical and Medieval Rhetoric, Univ. of California, 1960–61. *Publs:* Joseph Smith's New England Heritage, 1971; Investigating the Book of Mormon Witnesses, 1981; Understanding Paul, 1983. Add: 165 Joseph Smith Bldg., Brigham Young Univ., Provo, Utah 84602, U.S.A.

ANDERSON, Robert (Woodruff). American, b. 1917. Novels/Short stories, Plays/Screenplays. Vice-Pres., The Authors League of America, since 1981. Teacher of Playwriting, American Theatre Wing, 1946–50, Actors' Studio, 1955–56, Salzburg Seminar in American Studies, 1968, and Iowa Writers Workshop, 1976. Pres., Dramatists Guild, 1971–73, and Theatre Hall of Fame, 1981. *Publs:* Tea and Sympathy (play), 1953; All Summer Long (play), 1954; Silent Night, Lonely Night (play), 1959; The Nun's Story (screenplay), 1959; The Days Between (play), 1965; The Sand Pebbles (screenplay), 1966; You Know I Can't Hear You When the Water's Running (play), 1967; I Never Sang for My Father (play), 1968; screenplay 1970; Solitaire/Double Solitaire (play), 1971; After (novel), 1973; Getting Up and Going Home (novel), 1978; Free and Clear (play), 1983. Add: Roxbury, Conn. 06783, U.S.A.

ANDERSON, Verily. British, b. 1915. Novels/Short stories, Children's fiction, Plays/Screenplays, Children's non-fiction. Freelance writer, journalist and broadcaster. Ed., The Townsend, 1950–54. *Publs:* Spam Tomorrow: Our Square; Beware of Children, No Kidding (Film Version);

Daughters of Divinity; The Flo Affair: The Northreeps Grandchildren; Scrambled Eggs for Christmas; The Last of the Eccentrics; Nine Times Never; Friends and Relations; Vanload to Venice; The Yorks in London; Clover Coverdale; Friends and Relatives; The Persian Kitten (television play); Brownies and Their Animal Friends, 1974; Brownie Cookbook, 1975; Brownies and the Christening, 1979; Brownies and the Wedding Day, 1980; Brownies on Wheels, 1981. Add: Templeword, Northrepps, Cromer, Norfolk, England.

ANDERSON, Vernon E(llsworth). American, b. 1908. Education. Prof. Emeritus, Univ. of Maryland, College Park, since 1973 (Dean, Coll. of Education, 1955–70; Prof. of Education, 1970–73). Dean, Worthington Jr. Coll., Minn., 1937–40; Administrative Asst. to the Dean, Univ. of Colorado, Boulder, 1940–42; Curriculum Dir., State of Washington Dept. of Public Instruction. 1942–44; Dir of Curriculum, Portland, Oregon Public Schools, 1944–46; Dir. of Curriculum Center and Assoc. Prof. of Education. 1946–53, and Prof. 1953–55, Univ of Connecticut, Storrs; Prof. of Educational Leadership, U.S. Intnl. Univ., San Diego, Calif., 1974–79. *Publs:* (with P.R. Grim and W.T. Gruhn) Principles and Practices of Secondary Education, 1951, 1962; Principles and Procedures of Curriculum Improvement. 1956. 1965; Before You Teach Children, 1962; Teacher's Guide: Before You Teach Children, 1962; Curriculum Guide Lines in an Era of Change, 1969. Add: 25369 Carmel Knolls Dr., Carmel, Calif. 93923, U.S.A.

ANDERS-RICHARDS, Donald. British, b. 1928. Theology/Religion. Primary and secondary sch. teacher. 1951–57; Sr. Curate, St. Francis, Bournemouth, 1962–64; Asst. Chaplain, Quainton Hall Sch., Harrow, Middx., 1964–68; Lectr., 1968–71, and Sr. Lectr., 1971–76, Totley-Thornbridge Coll. of Education, Sheffield; Sr. Lectr. in Education, Sheffield City Polytechnic, 1976–88. *Publs:* The Drama of the Psalms, 1968. Add: Laburnum Cottage, Gwenn-y-Brenin, near Oswestry, Salop SY10 8AS, England.

ANDRE, Michael. Canadian, b. 1946. Poetry. Ed., Unmuzzled Ox, NYC, since 1971. Editorial Assoc., Art News, NYC, 1972–76; Lectr. in English, City Coll. of New York, 1973. *Publs:* Studying the Ground for Holes, 1978; Letters Home, 1979; The Poets' Encyclopedia, 1979 (ed.) Writings. Add: Unmuzzled Ox, 105 Hudson St., New York, N.Y. 10013, U.S.A.

ANDRESKI, Stanislav Leonard. British (born Polish), b. 1919. Military/Defence, Sociology. Prof. and Head, Dept. of Sociology. Univ. of Reading, Berks, since 1964. Lectr. in Sociology, Rhodes Univ., Grahamstown, South Africa, 1947–53; Sr. Research Fellow in Anthropology, Manchester Univ., Lancs., 1954–56; Lectr. in Economics, Acton Technical Coll., London, 1956–57; Lectr. in Management Studies, Brunel Coll. of Technology, London, 1957–60; Prof. of Sociology, Sch. of Social Sciences, Santiago, Chile, 1960–61; Sr. Research Fellow, Nigerian Inst. of Social and Economic Research, Ibadan, Nigeria, 1962–64; Visiting Prof. of Sociology and Anthropology, City Coll., City Univ. of New York, 1968–69. *Publs:* Military Organization and Society, 1954, 1968; (with Jan Ostaszewski et al) Class Structure and Social Development, 1964; Elements of Comparative Sociology, (in U.S. as The Uses of Comparative Sociology) 1964; Parasitism and Subversion: The Case of Latin America, 1966, 1970; The African Predicament; A Study in Pathology of Modernisation, 1968, 1969; (ed.) Herbert Spencer: Structure, Function and Evolution, 1971; Social Sciences as Sorcery, 1972; The Prospects of a Revolution in the U.S.A., 1973; (ed.) The Essential Comte, 1974; (ed.) Reflections on Inequality, 1975; (ed.) Max Weber on Capitalism, Bureaucracy and Religion, 1983; Max Weber's Insights and Errors, 1984; Syphilis, Puritanism and Witch-hunts: Historical Explanations in the Light of Medicine and Psychoanalysis with a Forecast about AIDS, 1989. Add: Faculty of Letters, Univ. of Reading, Reading, Berks, England.

ANDREW, Edward Raymond. British, b. 1921. Physics. Research Prof., Univ. of Florida, Gainesville, since 1983. Ed.-in-Chief, Magnetic Resonance in Medicine; Member, Advisory Editorial Bd., Magnetic Resonance Reviews since 1971; Member, Editorial Bd., Journal of Magnetic Resonance, since 1973; Ed. Physics Reports, since 1974. Lectr. in Physics, Univ. of St. Andrews, 1949–54; Prof. of Physics, Univ. of Wales, Bangor, 1954–63; Lancashire-Spencer Prof. of Physics, Univ. of Nottingham, 1964–83. *Publs:* Nuclear Magnetic Resonance, 1955, 4th ed. 1969; (ed.) Magnetic Resonance and Related Phenomena, 1975. Add: Dept. of Physics, Univ of Florida, Gainesville, Fla. 32611, U.S.A.

ANDREW, Prudence. British, b. 1924. Novels/Short stories, Children's fiction. *Publs:* The Hooded Falcon, 1960; Ordeal by Silence, 1961; Ginger Over the Wall, 1962; A Question of Choice, 1963; Ginger and Batty Billy, 1963; The Earthworms, 1964; Ginger and No. 10, 1964; The Constant Star, 1964; A Sparkle from the Coal (Novel), 1964; Christmas Card, 1966; Mr. Morgan's Marrow, 1967; Mister O'Brien, 1972; Rodge, Sylvie and Munch, 1973; Una and Grubstreet, 1973; Goodbye to the Rat, 1974; The Heroic Deeds of Jason Jones, 1975; Where Are You Going To, My Pretty Maid?, 1977; Robinson Daniel Crusoe, 1978, in U.S. as Close Within My Own Circle, 1980; The Other Side of the Park, 1984. Add: c/o Heinemann Ltd., 81 Fulham Rd., London SW3 6RB, England.

ANDREWARTHA, Herbert George. Australian, b. 1907.Environmental science/Ecology, Zoology. Former Prof. of Zoology, Univ. of Adelaide (Entomologist, 1936–53; Reader in Animal Ecology, 1953–61). *Publs:* (with L.C. Birch) Distribution and Abundance of Animals, 1954; Introduction to Study of Animal Populations, 1961, 1971; Selections From the Distribution and Abundance of Animals, 1982; (with L.C. Birch) The Ecological Web: More about the Distribution and Abundance of Animals, 1984. Add: 37 Claremont Ave., Netherby, S.A. 5062, Australia.

ANDREWS, Allen. Also writes as Billy Cotton. British, b. 1913. Novels/Short stories, Criminology/Law enforcement/Prisons, Engineering/Technology, Genealogy/Heraldry, History, Mythology/Folklore, Travel/Exploration/Adventure, Biography, Humor/Satire. Fleet Street feature writer and features ed., London, 1946. *Publs:* Proud Fortress: Gibraltar, 1958; Earthquake (sociology), 1963; The Mad Motorists (exploration), 1964; Sex and Marriage (sociology), 1964; Slimming, 1964; Relax and Sleep Well, 1965; (with Bill Richardson) Those Magnificent Men in their Flying Machines (humour), 1965; She Doubles Her Money (sociology), 1966; The Splendid Pauper: Moreton Frewen, 1968; The Prosecutor: Mervyn Pugh, 1968; Monte Carlo or Bust (humour), 1969; (ed. and compiler) Quotations for Speakers and Writers, 1969; (as Billy Cotton) I Did It My Way (biography), 1970; The Air Marshals (history), 1970; The Royal Whore: Barbara Castlemaine, 1970; Intensive Inquiries (criminology), 1973; (as Albert Pierrepoint) Executioner: Pierrepoint (biography), 1974; Lafavette in London (history), 1974; And This Is Me (biography), 1974; The Follies of King Edward VII, 1975; Kings and Queens of England and Scotland, 1976; The King Who Lost America, 1976; Exemplary Justice, The Stalag Luft III Investigation, 1976; Back to the Drawing Board, 1977; The Flying Machine, 1977; The Whisky Barons (biography), 1977; The Life of L.S. Lowry, 1977; The Meaning of Flowers, 1977; Curious Myths of the Middle Ages, 1977; Victorian Grotesque, 1977; An Illustrated Dictionary of Classsical Mythology, 1978; The Cards Can't Lie, 1978; Victorian Engineering, 1978; The Technology of Man, 1979; The Pig Plantagenet (novel), 1980; American Express in Europe, 1981; The Royal Coats of Arms of England, 1982; Castle Crespia (novel), 1982, Castle Crespin (novel), 1982; The People of Rome (verse), 1984; Straight Up, 1984; Impossible Loyalties (novel), 1985. Add: 4 Hazelmere Rd., London NW6 6PY, England.

ANDREWS, Clarence Adelbert. American b. 1912. Literature, Writing/Journalism. Publisher, Midwest Heritage Publishing Co., since 1979. Instr., Continuing Education Div., Univ. of Iowa, Iowa City, since 1982 (Lectr. in Journalism, 1976–82). Asst. Prof. of Technical Journalism, Colorado State Univ., Fort Collins 1060-61; Asst. Prof., 1963–66 and Assoc. Prof., 1967–69, Univ. of Iowa, Iowa City; Dir of Technical Communications and Prof. of Language and Literature, Michigan Technical Univ., Houghton, 1971–75. *Publs:* Technical and Scientific Writing, 1963; Writing: Growth Through Structure, 1972; A Literary History of Iowa, 1972; Technical and Business Writing, 1974; History of the First Presbyterian Church of Iowa City, Iowa 1840-1865; Growing Up in Iowa, 1978; Christmas in Iowa, 1979; Growing Up in the Midwest, 1981; Chicago in Story: A Literary History, 1983; This Is Iowa: A Cavalcade of the Tall Corn State, 1983; Christmas in the Midwest, 1984. Add: 108 Pearl St., Iowa City, Iowa 62240, U.S.A.

ANDREWS, Edgar Harold. British, b. 1932. Chemistry, Physics, Sciences, Theology/Religion. Prof. of Materials, Queen Mary Coll., Univ. of London, London, since 1968 (Reader in Materials Science, 1963–68). Pres., Bible Creation Soc., since 1978. Technical Officer, ICI Ltd., Welwyn Garden City, 1953–55; Sr. Physicist, Rubber Producers' Research Assn., Welwyn Garden City, 1955–63. *Publs:* (co-author) Chemistry and Physics of Rubberlike Substances, 1963; Fracture in Polymers (monograph), 1968; Is Evolution Scientific?, 1977; From Nothing to Nature (A Young People's Guide to Evolution and Creation), 1978; (ed. and co-author) Developments in Polymer Fracture, 1979; The Promise of the Spirit, 1982; Christ and the Cosmos, 1986. Add: Redcroft, 87 Harmer Green Lane, Welwyn, Herts., England.

ANDREWS, J(ames) S(ydney). Also writes as Jim Andrews. Irish, b.

1934. Children's fiction. *Publs:* The Bell of Nendrum, 1969, in U.S. as The Green Hill of Nendrum, 1970; The Man from the Sea, 1970; Cargo for a King, 1972; Catamarans for Cruising, 1974; publications for adults (as Jim Andrews) — Simple Sailing, 1975; (with Judy Andrews) Food for Arthritics, Based on Dr. Dong's Diet, 1982; Twelve Ships A-Sailing: Thirty-Five Years of Home-Water Cruising, 1986. Add: c/o David and Charles, Brunel House, Newton Abbot, Devon TQ12 4PU, England.

ANDREWS, Jim. *See* **ANDREWS, J.S.**

ANDREWS, John Henry. British, b. 1939. Zoology. Head of Conservation Planning Dept., Royal Soc. for the Protection of Birds, Sandy, Beds., since 1973. *Publs:* Birds and Their World, 1976; Birds, 1978; Birds of Prey, 1979; Adaptable Birds, 1982. Add: 28 Drake Rd., Eaton Socon, St. Neots, Cambs., England.

ANDREWS, Julie (Elizabeth). British, b. 1935. Children's fiction. Singer and Actress: Broadway stage—The Boy Friend, 1954; My Fair Lady, 1956; Camelot, 1960; films—Mary Poppins, 1963 (Academy Award); The Americanization of Emily, 1964; The Sound of Music, 1964; Hawaii, 1965; Torn Curtain, 1966; Thoroughly Modern Millie, 1966; Star, 1967; Darling Lili, 1970; The Tamarind Seed, 1973; 10, 1980; Little Miss Marker, 1980; S.O.B., 1981; Victor/Victoria, 1982; The Man Who Loved Women, 1983; That's Life, 1986; Duet for One, 1987. *Publs:* Mandy, 1972; The Last of the Really Great Whangdoodles, 1973. Add: c/o Triad Artists, 10100 Santa Monica Blvd. 16th Floor, Los Angeles, Calif. 90067, U.S.A.

ANDREWS, Lucilla (Mathew). Also writes as Diana Gordon and Joanna Marcus. British. Historical/Romance/Gothic, Autobiography/Memoirs/Personal. *Publs:* The Print Petticoat, 1954; The Secret Armour, 1955; The Quiet Wards, 1956; The First Year, 1957; A Hospital Summer, 1958; My Friend the Professor, 1960; Nurse Errant, 1961; The Young Doctors Downstairs, 1963; Flowers for the Doctor, 1963; The New Sister Theatre, 1964; The Light in the Ward, 1965; A House for Sister Mary, 1966; Hospital Circles, 1967; (as Diana Gordon) A Few Days in Endel, 1968; Highland Interlude, 1968; The Healing Time, 1969; Edinburgh Excursion, 1970; Ring o' Roses, 1972; Silent Song, 1973; In Storm and in Calm, 1975; No Time for Romance: An Autobiographical Account of a Few Moments in British and Personal History (non-fiction), 1977; The Crystal Gull, 1978; One Night in London, 1979; (as Joanna Marcus) Marsh Blood, 1980; A Weekend in the Garden, 1981; In an Edinburgh Drawing Room, 1983; After a Famous Victory, 1984; The Lights of London, 1985; The Phoenix Syndrome, 1987. Add: c/o Heinemann, 81 Fulham Rd., London SW3 6RB, England.

ANDREWS, Lyman. American, b. 1938. Poetry. Lectr. in American Literature, Univ. of Leicester, since 1965. Visiting Prof. of English, Indiana Univ., Bloomington, 1978–79. Poetry Critic, The Sunday Times, London, 1968–79. *Publs:* Ash Flowers, 1958; Fugitive Visions, 1962; The Death of Mayakovsky and Other Poems, 1968; Kaleidoscope: New and Selected Poems, 1973. Add: Dept. of English, Univ. of Leicester, University Rd., Leicester LE1 7RH, England.

ANDRUS, Hyrum Leslie. American, b. 1924. Theology/Religion. Formerly, Prof. of Church History and Doctrine, Brigham Young Univ., Provo, Utah. *Publs:* Helps for Missionaries, 1949; Doctrinal Themes of the Doctrine and Covenants, 1957; Joseph Smith and World Government, 1958; Joseph Smith the Man and Seer, 1960; The Glory of God and Man's Relation to Deity, 1965; Liberalism, Conservatism and Mormonism, 1965; Mormonism and the Rise of Western Civilization, 1966; Anticipation of the Civil War in Mormon Thought, 1966; Doctrinal Commentary on the Pearl of Great Price, 1967; God, Man and the Universe, 1968; Principles of Perfection, 1970; Doctrines of the Kingdom, 1973; (with Helen Mae Andrus) They Knew the Prophet, 1974. Add: 630 N. Patterson Lane, Alpine, Utah 84004, U.S.A.

ANEES, Munawar Ahmad. Pakistani, b. 1948; American immigrant since 1983. Cultural/Ethnic topics, Literary criticism, Medicine/Health, Sciences, Third World. Dir. of Research and Development, East–West Univ., Chicago, since 1986. Pres., Zahra Publications, San Antonio, TX, 1984; Dir., Asas Inc., Houston, 1984–85. *Publs:* Health Sciences in Early Islam, 1984; Guide to Sira and Hadith Literature, 1986; Islam and Biological Futures, 1987; Issues in Islamic Science, 1988; (with Ziaudden Sardar) Key Books in Islamic Resurgence, 1988. Add: 5400 N. Sheridan Rd., Chicago, Il 60640, U.S.A.

ANGEL, Heather. British, b. 1941. Photography, Natural history. Biological photographer and lectr. Pres. Royal Photographic Soc., 1984–

86. *Publs:* Your Book of Fishes, 1972; Nature Photography: Its Art and Techniques, 1972; The World of an Estuary, 1975; (with Martin Angel) All Colour Book of Ocean Life, 1975; Photographing Nature: Trees, Seashore, Insects, Flowers, Fungi, 5 vols., 1975; Seashore Life on Rocky Shores, 1975; Seashore Life on Sandy Beaches, 1975; The World of a Stream, 1976; Sea Shells of the Seashore, 1976; Wild Animals in the Garden, 1976; Life on the Seashore, 1976; Life in the Oceans, 1976; Life in Our Rivers, 1977; Life in Our Estuaries, 1977; British Wild Orchids, 1977; The Countryside of the New Forest, 1977; Seaweeds of the Seashore, 1977; The Countryside of South Wales, 1977; Fungi, 1979; Lichens, 1980; Mosses and Ferns, 1980; The Country Side of Devon, 1980; The Guiness Book of Seashore Life, 1981; The Book of Nature Photography, 1982; The Book of Close-Up Photography, 1983; Heather Angel's Countryside, 1983; A Camera in the Garden, 1984; A View from the Window, 1988; Nature in Focus, 1988. Add: Highways, Vicarage Hill, Farnham, Surrey GU9 8HJ, England.

ANGELL, Roger. American, b. 1920. Social commentary. Fiction Ed., The New Yorker, since 1956. Ed., Mag. X, 1946–47; Sr. Ed., Holiday, 1947–56. *Publs:* The Stone Arbor, 1961; A Day in the Life of Roger Angell, 1971; The Summer Game, 1972; Five Seasons, 1977; Late Innings, 1982. Add: 1261 Madison Ave., New York, N.Y. 10028, U.S.A.

ANGELOU, Maya. American, b. 1928. Novels/Short stories. Plays/Screenplays, Poetry. Member, Bd. of Trustees, American Film Inst., since 1975. Former stage and screen actor and dancer; Assoc. Ed., Arab Observer, Cairo, Egypt, 1962–63; writer, Ghanaian Times, Accra, 1963–65, and Ghanaian broadcasting Corp., 1963–65; Asst. Admin., Inst. of African Studies, Sch. of Music and Drama, Univ. of Ghana, Accra, 1963–65; Feature Ed., African Review, Accra, 1965–66; Lectr., Univ. of California, 1966. *Publs:* The Best of These, 1966; The Clawing Within, 1966; Adjoa Amissah, 1967; I Know Why the Caged Bird Sings, 1970, teleplay 1977; Just Give Me a Cool Drink of Water 'Fore I Diiie (poetry), 1971; Georgia Georgia (screenplay), 1972; Gather Together in My Name, 1974; Oh Pray My Wings are Gonna Fit Me Well (poetry), 1975; Singin' and Swingin' and Gettin' Merry Like Christmas, 1976; And Still I Rise (poetry), 1978; Sisters (teleplay), 1978; The Heart of a Woman, 1981; Shaker, Why Don't You Sing? (poetry), 1983; All God's Children Need Traveling Shoes (autobiog.), 1986; The Heart of a Woman, 1986; Now Sheba Sings the Song (poetry), 1987; Conversations with Maya Angelou, 1988. Add: c/o Random House, 201 East 50th St., New York, N.Y. 10017, U.S.A.

ANGLESEY, Marquess of; George Charles Henry Victor Paget. British, b. 1922. Military/Defence, Biography. *Publs:* (ed.) The Capel Letters 1814-1817, 1955; One-Leg: The Life and Letters of Henry William Paget, First Marquess of Anglesey, K.G., 1768-1854, 1961; (ed.) Sergeant Pearman's Memoirs, 1968; (ed.) Little Hodge, 1971; A History of the British Cavalry 1816-1919, 4 vols., 1978–86. Add: Plas Newydd, Llanfairpwll, Anglesey, North Wales.

ANGLIN, Douglas G(eorge). Canadian, b. 1923. International relations/Current affairs, Politics/Government. Prof. of Political Science, Carleton Univ., Ottawa, since 1958. Vice-Chancellor, Univ. of Zambia, 1965–69. *Publs:* The Political Pattern, 1961; The St. Pierre and Miquelonffaire of 1941, 1966, 1970; Conflict and Change in Southern Africa, 1978; Canada, Scandinavia and Southern Africa, 1978; Zambia's Foreign Policy: Studies in Diplomacy and Dependence, 1979; Canada and South Africa: Challenge and Response, 1986. Add: Dept. of Political Science, Carleton Univ., Ottawa, Ont. K1S 5B6, Canada.

ANGLUND, Joan Walsh. American, b. 1926. Children's fiction, Children's non-fiction. *Publs:* A Friend Is Someone Who Likes You, 1958; Look Out the Window, 1959; The Brave Cowboy, 1959; Love Is a Special Way of Feeling, 1960; In a Pumpkin Shell: A Mother Goose ABC, 1960; Christmas Is a Time of Giving, 1961; Cowboy and His Friend, 1961; Nibble Nibble Mousekin: A Tale of Hansel and Gretel, 1962; Cowboy's Secret Life, 1963; Spring Is a New Beginning, 1963: Childhood Is a Time of Innocence, 1964; A Pocketful of Proverbs (verse), 1964; (ed.) A Book of Good Tidings from the Bible, 1965; What Color Is Love?, 1966; A Year Is Round, 1966; A Cup of Sun: A Book of Poems, 1967; A Is for Always: An ABC Book, 1968; Morning Is a Little Child (verse), 1969; A Slice of Snow: A Book of Poems, 1970; Do You Love Someone?, 1971; The Cowboy's Christmas, 1972; A Child's Book of Old Nursery Rhymes, 1973; Goodbye, Yesterday: A Book of Poems, 1974; Storybook, 1978; Emily and Adam, 1979; Almost a Rainbow, 1980; A Gift of Love, 5 vols., 1980; A Christmas Cookie Book, 1982; Rainbow Love, 1982; Christmas Candy Book, 1983; A Christmas Book, 1983; See the Year,

1984; Coloring Book, 1984; Memories of the Heart, 1984; Teddy Bear Tales, 1985; Baby Brother, 1985; All About Me! 1986; Christmas is Here!, 1986; Tubtime for Thaddeus, 1986; The Song of Love, 1987; The Joan Anglund Book of Poetry, 1987; All about My Family, 1987; Christmas Is Love, 1988; How Many Days Has Baby to Play?, 1988. Add: c/o Random House, 201 E. 50th St., New York, N.Y. 10022, U.S.A.

ANGUS, Ian. *See* **MACKAY,** James Alexander.

ANGUS, J(ohn) Colin. Australian, b. 1907. Art, History. Professional artist. Historian associated with North-Eastern Historical Soc., Vic., since 1961, and Royal Historical Soc. of Victoria, Melbourne. *Publs:* Wangaratta Shire Centenary, 1967; Mining at El Dorado; (with Harley W. Forester) The Ovens Valley; (with Hilde Knorr) J. Colin Angus: Landscapes, 1955–1978, 1978. Add: Wandana, El Dorado, Vic. 3746, Australia.

ANGUS, Margaret (Sharp). Canadian, b. 1908. Architecture. Freelance historical consultant since 1960. With Queen's Univ., Ont., until retirement in 1968; Archivist and Historian, Kingston Gen. Hosp., Ont., 1968–70. *Publs:* The Old Stones of Kingston, 1966, 5th ed. 1984; Kingston General Hospital, 1973; (ed.) Buildings of Architectural and Historic Significance in Kingston, vols. I-VI, 1973–85; John A. Lived Here, 1984. Add: 191 King St. East, Kingston, Ont., Canada.

ANGUS-BUTTERWORTH, Lionel (Milner). British, b. 1900. Poetry, Crafts, History, Literature, Biography. Pres., Lancashire Author's Assn., 1972–88, now Emeritus. Governing Dir., Abercorn Publishing Co. Ltd., 1960–67; Pres., Manchester Literary Club, 1961–62, and Manchester Poetical Soc., 1968–72. *Publs:* Old Cheshire Families and Their Seats, 1934; The Manufacture of Glass, 1948; British Table and Ornamental Glass, 1956; Ten Master Historians, 1961, 1962; Pottery and Porcelain, 1964; The Chinese Kitchen, 1967; The Angus Poetical Tradition, 1968; Robert Burns and the 18th Century Revival in Scotish Vernacular Poetry, 1969; Scotish Folk-Song, 1971; Selected Poems, 1973; Belfield Papers, 1975; Poems of Life and Death, 1977; General W.J. Butterworth, Governor of Singapore (biography), 1978; Sir Alex K. Butterworth (biography), 1979; Lancashire Literary Worthies, 1980; Old Lancashire Halls, 1982. Add: St. Ann's Hotel, The Crescent, Buxton, Derbyshire, England.

ANIEBO, I(feanyichukwu) N(dubuisi) C(hikezie). Nigerian, b. 1939. Novels/Short stories. Sr. Lectr. in English, Univ. of Port Harcourt. Officer in the Nigerian Army, 1959–71. *Publs:* The Anonymity of Sacrifice (novel), 1974; The Journey Within (novel), 1978; Of Wives, Talismans and the Dead (short stories), 1983; (with W.F. Fenser) Essays in Comparitive African Literature, 1988. Add: Dept. of English, Univ. of Port Harcourt, P.M.B. 5523, Port Harcourt, Rivers State, Nigeria.

ANNAN, Noel Gilroy. (Lord Annan). British, b. 1916. History, Biography. Provost, King's Coll., Cambridge, 1956–66; Trustee, British Museum, London, 1963–81; Dir., Royal Opera House, London, 1965–78; member, Public Schs. Commn., 1966; Provost, University Coll., London, 1966–78; Vice-Chancellor of the Univ. of London, 1978–81; Chmn, of Trustees, National Gallery, London, 1980–85. *Publs:* Leslie Stephen: His Thought and Character in Relation to His Time, 1951, 1984; The Curious Strength of Positivism in English Political Thought, 1959; Roxburgh of Stowe, 1965. Add: 16 St. John's Wood Rd., London NW8 8RE, England.

ANNAND, James King. British, b. 1908. Poetry. Principal Teacher of History, Firrhill Secondary Sch., Edinburgh, 1962–71; Ed., Lallans, Scots Language mag., 1973–83. *Publs:* Sing It Aince for Pleisure, 1965; Two Voices, 1968; (ed.) Early Lyrics, by Hugh MacDiarmid, 1968; Twice for Joy, 1973; Poems and Translations, 1975; Songs from Carmina Burana 1978; Thrice Thrice to Show Ye, 1979; (ed.) A Scots Handsel, 1980; Dod and Davie, 1986. Add: 173/314 Comely Bank Rd., Edinburgh EH4 1DJ, Scotland.

ANNANDALE, Barbara. *See* **BOWDEN,** Jean.

ANSCOMBE, Gertrude (Elizabeth Margaret). British, b. 1919. Philosophy. Research studentships, Oxford and Cambridge univs., 1941–44; research fellowships, 1946–64, and Fellow, 1964–70, Somerville Coll., Oxford Univ; Fellow, New Hall, and Prof. of Philosophy, Cambridge Univ., 1970–86. *Publs:* Intention, 1957; An Introduction to Wittgenstein's Tractatus, 1959; (with Peter Geach) Three Philosophers, 1961; Collected Papers: 1. Parmenides to Wittgenstein, 2. Metaphysics and the Philosophy of Mind, 3. Ethics, Religion, and Politics, 1981; also trans. and ed. of posthumous works of Wittgenstein. Add: 3 Richmond

Rd., Cambridge, England.

ANSELL, (Col. Sir) Michael. British, b. 1905. Sports/Physical education/Keeping Fit, Autobiography/Memoirs/Personal. Dir., Royal Intnl. Horse Show and Horse of the Year Show, 1947–75; Pres. and Chmn., British Equestrian Fedn., 1972–76. *Publs:* Soldier On, 1973; Riding High, 1974; Leopard: The Story of My Horse, 1979. Add: Pillhead House, Bideford, N. Devon EX39 4NF, England.

ANSTEY, Edgar. British, b. 1917. Personnel management, Psychology. Principal, Research Unit, Civil Service Commn., 1945–51; Principal, Home Office, 1951–58; Sr. Principal Psychologist, Ministry of Defence, 1958–64; Chief Psychologist, Civil Service Selection Bd., 1964–69; Chief Psychologist, and Dir., Behavioural Sciences Research Div., Civil Service Dept., London, 1969–77. Maj., British Army, 1940–45. *Publs:* (with E.O. Mercer) Interviewing for the Selection of Staff, 1956; Staff Reporting and Staff Development, 1961; Committees: How They Work and How to Work Them, 1962; Psychological Tests, 1966; Techniques of Interviewing, 1968; Staff Appraisal and Development, 1976; An Introduction to Selection Interviewing, 1978. Add: Sandrock Higher Tristram, Polzeath, Cornwall PL27 6TF, England.

ANTHES, Richard A. American, b. 1944. Meteorology/Atmospheric sciences. President, University Corp. for Atmospheric Research, Boulder, since 1988. Research Meteorologist, National Hurricane Research Lab., Miami, 1968–71; Prof. of Meteorology, Pennsylvania State Univ., 1971–81; Consultant to the U.S. National Weather Service, 1972–81; Dir. of the Atmospheric Analysis and Prediction Div. 1981–86, and Dir. of the Center, 1986–88, National Center for Atmospheric Research, Boulder. *Publs:* (with A. Miller) Meteorology, 1967, 5th ed. 1985; (with others) The Atmosphere, 1975, 3rd ed. 1981; Weather Around Us, 1976. Add: University Corporation for Atmospheric Research, P.O. Box 3000, Boulder, Colo. 80307, U.S.A.

ANTHONY, C.L. *See* **SMITH,** Dodie.

ANTHONY, Evelyn. Pseud. for Evelyn Bridget Patricia Ward-Thomas. British, b. 1928. Mystery/Crime/Suspense, Historical/Romance/Gothic. *Publs:* Imperial Highness (in U.S. as Rebel Princess), 1953; Curse Not the King (in U.S. as Royal Intrigue), 1954; Far Flies the Eagle, 1955; Anne Boleyn, 1957; Victoria and Albert, 1958, as Victoria, 1959; Elizabeth (in U.S. as All the Queen's Men), 1960; Charles the King, 1961; Clandara, 1963; The Heiress, 1964, in U.S. as The French Bride, 1964; Valentina, 1966; The Rendezvous, 1967; Anne of Austria (in U.S. as The Cardinal and the Queen), 1968; The Legend, 1969; The Assassin, 1970; The Tamarind Seed, 1971; The Poellenberg Inheritance, 1972; The Occupying Power (in U.S. as Stranger at the Gates) 1973; The Malaspiga Exit (in U.S. as Mission to Malaspiga), 1974; The Persian Ransom (in U.S. as The Persian Price), 1975; The Silver Falcon, 1977; The Return, 1978; The Grave of Truth, 1979, in U.S as The Janus Imperative, 1980; The Defector, 1980; The Avenue of the Dead, 1981; Albatross, 1982; The Company of Saints, 1983; Voices on the Wind, 1985; No Enemy But Time, 1987, in U.S. as A Place to Hide, 1987; The House of Vandekar, 1988. Add: Horham Hall, Thaxted, Essex, England.

ANTHONY, James R. American, b. 1922. Music. Prof. of Musicology Univ. of Arizona, Tucson, since 1952. Contrib., Grove's Dictionary of Music and Musicians, since 1972; Consultant, National Endowment for the Humanities, since 1974. Regional Assoc., American Council of Learned Socs., 1956–60. *Publs:* French Baroque Music from Beaujoyeulx to Rameau, 1973, 1978; Cantatas, Book III, by Monteclair, 1978; De profundis, by Delalande, 1980; La Musique en France a l'-Epoque Baroque, 1981; Michel-Richard Delalande's "De Profundis", 1981; (with others) The New Grove French Baroque Masters, 1986. Add: Dept. of Music, Univ. of Arizona, Tucson, Ariz. 85721, U.S.A.

ANTHONY, Michael. Trinidadian, b. 1930. Novels/Short stories, History, Travel/Exploration/Adventure. Researcher, Ministry of Culture, since 1972. Journalist, Reuters News Agency, London, 1964–68; Asst. Ed., Texaco Trinidad, 1970–72. *Publs:* The Games Were Coming (novel), 1963; The Year in San Fernando (novel), 1965; Green Days by the River (novel), 1967; Cricket in the Road (short stories), 1973; Sandra Street and Other Stories, 1973; Glimpses of Trinidad and Tobago, 1974; (ed. with A. Carr) David Frost Introduces Trinidad and Tobago, 1975; Profile Trinidad, 1975; Streets of Conflict (novel), 1976; Folk Tales and Fantasies (short stories), 1976; The Making of the Port of Spain 1757-1939, 1978; All That Glitters (novel), 1982; Bright Road to El Dorado (novel), 1982; Port of Spain in a World at War, 1984. Add: 99 Long Circular Rd., St. James, Port of Spain, Trinidad.

ANTHONY, Piers. Pseud. for Anthony Dillingham Jacob. American, (b. British), b. 1934. Westerns/Adventure, Science fiction/Fantasy. *Publs:* Chthon, 1967; Omnivore, 1968, Orn, 1971, Ox, 1976 (novel trilogy); (with Robert E. Margroff) The Ring, 1968; Macroscope, 1969; (with Robert E. Margroff) The E.S.P. Worm, 1970; Prostho Plus, 1973; Race Against Time (juvenile), 1973; Rings of Ice, 1974; Triple Detente, 1974; martial arts adventure series (with Roberto Fuentes)—Kiai!, 1974, Mistress of Death, 1974, Bamboo Bloodbath, 1974, Ninja's Revenge, 1975, Amazon Slaughter, 1976; Phthor, 1975; Steppe, 1976; (with Robert Coulson) But What of Earth?, 1976; Hasan, 1977; Cluster, 1977; Chaining the Lady, 1978, Kirlian Quest, 1978, Thousandstar, 1980, Viscous Circle, 1982 (novel quintology); Xanth series—A Spell for Chameleon, 1977, The Source of Magic, 1979; Castle Roogna, 1979 (1st 3 vols. published as The Magic of Xanth, 1981), Centaur Aisle, 1982, Ogre, Ogre, 1982, Night Mare, 1983, Dragon on a Pedestal, 1983; Crewel Lye, 1985; Battle Circle, 1978 (novel trilogy; published separately as Sos the Rope, 1968, Var the Stick, 1973, Neq the Sword, 1975; (with Frances Hall) The Pretender, 1979; God of Tarot, 1979, Vision of Tarot, 1980, Faith of Tarot, 1980 (novel in 3 vols.); Mute, 1981; The Apprentice Adept, 1982 (novel trilogy; published separately as Split Infinity, 1980, Blue Adept, 1981, Juxtaposition, 1982); Incarnations of Immortality series—On a Pale Horse, 1983, Bearing an Hourglass, 1984, With a Tangled Skein, 1985, Wielding a Red Sword, 1986, Bio of a Space Tyrant quintology—Refugee, 1983, Mercenary, 1984, Politician, 1985, Executive, 1985, Statesman, 1986; Anthonology, 1985; Ghost, 1986; Shade of the Tree, 1986; Golem in the Gears, 1986; Out of Phaze, 1987; Wielding a Red Sword, 1987; Being a Green Mother, 1987; Biography of an Ogre (autobiography), 1988. Add: 3185 E. Pineleaf Lane, Inverness, Fla. 32652, U.S.A.

ANTILL, J(ames) M(acquarie). Australian, b. 1912. Administration/Management, Technology, History. Consulting Construction Engineer, Sydney, since 1958. Examiner and Visiting Lectr. in Engineering Construction and Management Univ. of Sydney and Univ. of New South Wales, 1956–84, and New South Wales Inst. of Technology, 1970–81; Visiting Prof. of Civil Engineering, Univ. of New South Wales, 1973–84. Engaged in supervision of construction works in Australia and Great Britain, 1932–58. *Publs:* History of Antill Family, 1944; (with W.A. Steel) History of All Saints College, Bathhurst, N.S.W., 1952, 1964; (with P.W.S. Ryan) Civil Engineering Construction, 1957, 6th ed. 1987; (with R.W. Woodhead) Critical Path Methods in Construction Practice, 1964, 3rd ed. 1982; Civil Engineering Management, 1970, 1973; (with R. Nagarajan) Australian Concrete Inspection Manual, 1978. Add: P.O. Box 100, Cremorne Junction, N.S.W. 2090, Australia.

ANTIN, David. American, b. 1932. Poetry, Translations. Prof. of Visual Arts, Univ. of California at San Diego, since 1972 (Dir. of the Univ. Art Gallery and Asst. Prof. of Visual Arts, 1968–72). Member, Editorial Bd., New Wilderness, since 1979. Freelance ed. and translator, 1956–57, Chief Ed. and Scientific Dir., Research Information Service, NYC, 1958–60; freelance ed. and consultant, Dover Press, NYC, 1959–64; Curator, Inst. of Contemporary Art, Boston, 1967. *Publs:* (trans.) 100 Great Problems of Elementary Mathematics: Their History and Solution, by Heinrich Doerrie, 1965; (trans.) The Physics of Modern Electronics, by W.A. Guenther, 1967; Definitions, 1967; Autobiography, 1967; Code of Flag Behavior, 1968; Meditations, 1971; Talking, 1972; After the War, 1973; Talking at the Boundaries, 1976; Who's Listening Out There?, 1980; Tuning, 1984; Selected Poems 1963–1973, 1989. Add: P.O. Box 1147, Del Mar, Calif. 92014, U.S.A.

ANTONINUS, Brother. *See* **EVERSON,** William.

ANTROBUS, John. British, b. 1933. Children's fiction, Plays/Screenplays. *Publs:* (with Spike Milligan) The Bed-Sitting Room, 1963, screenplay 1970; Trixie and Baba, 1969; Why Bournemouth? and Other Plays, 1970; Captain Oates' Left Sock, 1974; The Boy With Illuminated Measles (children's book), 1978; Help! I Am a Prisoner in a Toothpaste Factory (children's book), 1978; Hitler in Liverpool and Other Plays 1981; Captain Buttondown (children's book) 1983; Ronnie and the Great Knitted Robbery (children's book), 1984; Ronnie and the Haunted Rolls Royce (children's book), 1985. Add: c/o Blanche Marvin, 21a St. Johns Wood High St., London NW8 7NG, England.

ANVIL, Christopher. Pseud. for Harry C. Crosby, Jr. American. Science fiction. *Publs:* The Day the Machines Stopped, 1964; Strangers in Paradise, 1969; Pandora's Planet, 1972; Warlord's World, 1975; The Steel, the Mist, and the Blazing Sun, 1983. Add: c/o Ace Books, 200 Madison Ave., New York, NY 10016, U.S.A.

APPEL, Alfred, Jr. American, b. 1934. Literary Criticism/History.

Prof. of English, Northwestern Univ., Evanston, since 1974 (Asst.Prof., 1968–69; Assoc. Prof., 1969–74). Asst. Prof., Stanford Univ., California, 1963–68. *Publs:* A Season of Dreams, 1965; Nabokov's Dark Cinema, 1974; (with Simon Kazlinsky) The Bitter Air of Exile, 1977; Nabokov's Fifth Arc, 1982; Signs of Life, 1983. Add: 717 Greenleaf Ave., Wilmette, Ill. 60091, U.S.A.

APPIAH, Peggy. British, b. 1921. Novels, Children's fiction. *Publs:* Ananse the Spider, 1966; Tales of an Ashanti Father, 1967; The Pineapple Child and Other Tales from Ashanti, 1969; Children of Ananse, 1969; A Smell of Onions, 1971; Why Are There So Many Roads?, 1972; Gift of the Mmoatia, 1973; Ring of Gold, 1976; A Dirge Too Soon, 1976; Why the Hyena Does Not Care for Fish and Other Tales, 1977; Poems of Three Generations, 1978. Add: c/o David Higham Assocs., 5-8 Lower John St., London W1R 4HA, England.

APPLE, Max (Isaac). American, b. 1941. Novels/short stories. Prof. of English, Rice Univ., Houston, since 1980 (Asst. Prof., 1972–76; Assoc. Prof., 1976–80). *Publs:* (with others) Studies in English, 1975; The Oranging of America and Other Stories, 1976; Zip: A Novel of the Left and athe Right, 1978; (ed.) Southwest Fiction, 1980; Free Agents, 1984; The Propheteers, 1987. Add: c/o Dept. of English, Rice Univ., Houston, Tex. 77001, U.S.A.

APPLEGATE, James. American, b. 1923. Literature. Prof. and Chmn. of English, Wilson Coll., since 1965. *Publs:* Adventures in World Literature, 1970. Add: Wilson Coll., Chambersburg, Pa. 17201, U.S.A.

APPLEMAN, Philip (Dean). American, b. 1926. Novels, Poetry, Darwin studies, Demography. Distinguished Prof. of English Emeritus Indiana Univ., Bloomington, since 1986 (Instr., 1955–58; Asst. Prof., 1958–63; Assoc. Prof., 1963–67; Prof., 1967–82; Distinguished Prof., 1982–86). *Publs:* (co-ed.) 1859: Entering an Age of Crisis, 1959; The Silent Explosion, 1965; Kites on a Windy Day (poetry), 1967; Summer Love and Surf (poetry), 1968; In the Twelfth Year of the War (novel), 1970; (ed.) Darwin, 1970, 1979; (ed.) The Origin of Species, 1975; (ed.) Malthus: An Essay on the Principle of Population, 1976; Open Doorways (poetry), 1976; Shame the Devil (novel), 1981; Darwin's Ark (poetry), 1984; Darwin's Bestiary (poetry), 1986; Apes and Angels (novel), 1989. Add: P.O. Box 39, Sagaponack, N.Y. 11962, U.S.A.

APPLETON, Sarah (Sherman). American, b. 1930. Poetry, Literature. Teaching Asst., Ohio State Univ., Columbus, 1955–61; Instr. in English, Smith Coll., Northampton, Mass., 1962–65; Poetry Ed., Literature East and West, College Park, Md., 1966–68; Fellow, Bunting Inst., Radcliffe Coll., Cambridge, Mass., 1970–72; Member of the Adjunct Faculty, Syracuse Univ., New York, 1977. *Publs:* (as Sarah Appleton Weber) Theology and Poetry in the Middle English Lyric, 1969; The Plenitude We Cry For, 1972; Ladder of the World's Joy, 1977. Add: 124 Dorset Rd., Syracuse, N.Y. 13210, U.S.A.

APPLETON, Sheldon Lee. American, b. 1933. International relations/Current affairs, Politics/Government. Prof. of Political Science, since 1969, and Assoc. Dean, since 1979, Oakland Univ., Rochester, Mich. (Asst. Prof., 1960–64; Assoc. Prof., 1964–69). With Public Reports Office, U.S. AID, 1955–56; U.S. Foreign Service Officer, 1956–57; Visiting Prof. of Political Science, Univ. of Hawaii, 1969–70. *Publs:* The Eternal Triangle?: Communist China, the United States, and the United Nations, 1961; United States Foreign Policy, 1968. Add: Office of the Provost, Oakland Univ., Rochester, Mich. 48063, U.S.A.

APTER, David Ernest. American, b. 1924. Politics/Government. Henry J. Heinz Prof. of Comparative Political and Social Development, Yale Univ., New Haven, Conn., since 1969. Asst. Prof., Northwestern Univ., Evanston, IL, 1954–57; Assoc. Prof., Univ. of Chicago, 1957–61; Prof., Univ. of California, Berkeley, 1961–69, and Dir., Inst. of Intnl. Studies, Univ. of California, Berkeley, 1963–69. *Publs:* Ghana in Transition, 1955, 1972; The Political Kingdom in Uganda, 1961; (author and ed.) Ideology and Discontent, 1963; (ed. with H. Eckstein) Comparative Politics, 1963; The Politics of Modernization, 1965; Some Conceptual Approaches in the Study of Modernization, 1968; Choice and Politics of Allocation, 1971 (Woodrow Wilson Award); (ed. with C. Andrain) Contemporary Analytical Theory, 1972; (author and ed. with J. Joll) Anarchism Today, 1972; Political Change, 1974, 1975; (author and ed. with L. Goodman) The Multinational Corporation and Development, 1976; An Introduction to Political Analysis, 1977; (with Nagayo Sawa) Against the State: Politics and Social Protest In Japan, 1984; Rethinking Development: Modernization, Dependency, and Post-Modern Politics, 1987. Add: Dept. of Political Science, Yale Univ., New Haven, Conn. 19520, U.S.A.

APTER, Michael John. British, b. 1939. Information science/Computers, Psychiatry, Psychology. Sr. Lectr. in Psychology, Univ. Coll., Cardiff, since 1973 (Lectr., 1967–73). Head of Research and Validation Dept., Education and Scientific Developments Ltd., Bristol, 1964–67. *Publs:* Cybernetics and Development, 1966; An Introduction to Psychology, 1967; The New Technology of Education, 1968; The Computer Simulation of Behaviour, 1970; (ed. with G. Westby) The Computer in Psychology, 1973; The Experience of Motivation: The Theory of Psychological Reversals, 1982; (ed. with others) Reversal Theory: Applications and Development, 1985. Add: Alexandra Park Hotel, 2 Beach Rd., Penarth, South Glamorgan CF6 2AQ, Wales.

APTHEKER, Bettina. American, b. 1944. Education, Race relations, Women. Teacher, Women's Studies Program, Univ. of California at Santa Cruz. *Publs:* (with Robert Kaufman and Michael B. Folsom) FSM (Free Speech Movement), 1965; Big Business and the American University, 1966; Higher Education and the Student Rebellion in the United States 1960–69 (bibliography), 1969, 1972; (with Herbert Aptheker) Racism and Reaction in the United States: Two Marxian Studies, 1971; (with Angela Y. Davis) If They Come In The Morning: Voices of Resistance, 1971; The Academic Rebellion in the United States: A Marxist Appraisal, 1972; The Morning Breaks: The Trial of Angela Y. Davis, 1975; Mary Church Terrell and Ida B. Wells: A Comparative Rhetoric/Historical Analysis, 1976; (ed.) The Unfolding Drama: Studies in U.S. History by Herbert Aptheker, 1978; Woman's Legacy: Essays on Race, Sex and Class in American History, 1982; Tapestries of Life: Women's Work, Women's Consciousness, and the Meaning of Daily Experience, 1989. Add: Kresge Coll., Univ. of California, Santa Cruz, Calif. 95064, U.S.A.

APTHOMAS, Ifan. British, b. 1917. Poetry. Retired radiologist. *Publs:* Journey to the Silverless Island, 1957; Oakwoods of Love, 1960. Add: 7 Bryn Estyn Rd., Wrexham, Clwyd LL13 9ND, Wales.

ARAKI, James Tomomasa. American, b. 1925.Literature, Translations.us Prof. of Japanese Literature, Univ. of Hawaii, since 1964. Asst. Prof. of Oriental Languages, Univ. of California, Los Angeles, 1961–64. *Publs:* The Ballad-Drama of Medieval Japan, 1964; (trans. with D.M. Brown) Studies in Shinto Thought, by T. Muraoka, 1964; (trans.) The Roof Tile of Tempyo, by Y. Inoue, 1975; (trans. with E.G. Seidensticker) Lou-Ian and Other Stories, by Y. Inoue, 1979; (trans.) The Barren Zone, by T. Yamasaki, 1984; (trans.) Winds and Waves, by Y. Inoue, 1989. Add: Dept. of East Asian Literature, Univ. of Hawaii, Honolulu, Hawaii 96822, U.S.A.

ARBOR, Jane. British. Historical/Romance/Gothic. Freelance writer. Formerly owner of a book shop and circulating library. *Publs:* This Second Spring, 1948; Each Song Twice Over, 1948; Ladder of Understanding, 1949; Strange Loyalties, 1949; By Yet Another Door, 1950; No Lease for Love, 1950; The Heart Expects Adventure, 1951; Eternal Circle, 1952; Memory Serves My Love, 1952; Flower of the Nettle, 1953; Such Frail Armour, 1953; Jess Mawney, Queen's Nurse, 1954; Dear Intruder, 1955; Folly of the Heart, 1955; Towards the Dawn, 1956; City Nurse, 1956; Yesterday's Magic, 1957; Far Sanctuary, 1958; Nurse Harlowe, 1959; Sandflower, 1959; Consulting Surgeon, 1959; No Silver Spoon, 1959; Queen's Nurse, 1960; A Girl Named Smith, 1960; Nurse of All Work, 1962; Nurse in Waiting, 1962; Desert Nurse, 1963; Jasmine Harvest, 1963; Lake of Shadows, 1964; Kingfisher Tide, 1965; High Master of Clere, 1966; Summer Every Day, 1966; Golden Apple Island, 1967; Stranger's Trespass, 1968; The Cypress Garden, 1969; The Feathered Shaft, 1970; Walk into the Wind, 1970; The Other Miss Donne, 1971; The Linden Leaf 1971; The Flower on the Rock, 1972; Wildfire Quest, 1972; Roman Summer, 1973; The Velvet Spur, 1974; Meet the Sun Halfway, 1974; The Wide Fields of Home, 1975; Tree of Paradise, 1976; Smoke into Flame, 1976; Flash of Emerald, 1977; Two Pins in a Fountain, 1977; A Growing Moon, 1977; Late Rapture, 1978; Return to Silbersee, 1978; Pact Without Desire, 1979; The Devil Drives, 1979; One Brief Sweet Hour, 1980; Where the Wolf Leads, 1980; Invisible Wife, 1981; Handmaid to Midas, 1982; House of Discord, 1983. Add: c/o Mills and Boon, Eton House, 18-24 Paradise Rd., Richmond, Surrey, TW9 1SR, England.

ARCHER, Fred. British, b. 1915. Country life/Rural societies. Farmer's Asst., Archer & Bailey, since 1931. Self-employed farmer, 1939–73. *Publs:* The Distant Scene, 1967; Under the Parish Lantern, 1969; Hawthorne Hedge Country, 1970; The Secrets of Bredon Hill, 1971; A Lad of Evesham Vale, 1972; Muddy Boots and Sunday Suits, 1973; Golden Sheaves, Black Horses, 1974; The Countryman Cottage Life Book, 1974; Sir Lionel, 1980; By Hook and by Crook, 1980; When Adam Was a Boy, 1981; Fred Archer, Farmer's Son, 1986; Village Doctor, 1986.

Add: Cloud Hill Cottage, Guiting Power, nr. Cheltersham, Glos., England.

ARCHER, Gleason Leonard (Jr.). American, b. 1916. Theology/Religion, Translations. Prof. of Old Testament, Trinity Evangelical Divinity Sch., Deerfield, Ill., since 1965 (Chmn., Dept. of Old Testament, 1965–75). Prof. of Biblical Languages, 1948–65, and Acting Dean of aFaculty, 1948–49 and 1960–62, Fuller Theological Seminary, Pasadena, Calif.us *Publs:* The Epistle to the Hebrews: Study Manual, 1957; (trans.) Jerome's Commentary on Daniel, 1958; Epistle to the Romans: A Study Manual, 1959; Survey of Old Testament Introduction, 1964, 1974; (assoc. ed.) The Zondervan Pictorial Encyclopedia of the Bible, 1975; (assoc. ed.) Theological Wordbook of the Old Testament; (assoc. ed.) Theological Wordbook of the Old Testament, 1980; Job: God's Answer to Undeserved Suffering, 1982; Encyclopedia of Bible Difficulties, 1982; (with G.C. Chirichigno) Old Testament Quotations in the New Testament: a Complete Survey, 1983; Secret History (trans. from Danish of J. Ahmanson), 1984; The Rapture: Pre-, Mid-, or Post-Tribulation?, 1984. Add: 812 Castlewood Lane, Deerfield, Ill. 60015, U.S.A.

ARCHER, Jeffrey (Howard). British, b. 1940. Novels/Short stories. Member of the Greater London Council for Havering, 1966–69; Conservative Member of Parliament for Louth, 1969–74; Deputy Chmn. of the Conservative Party, 1985–86. *Publs:* Not a Penny More, Not a Penny Less, 1976; Shall We Tell the President?, 1978; Kane and Abel, 1980; A Quiver Full of Arrows (stories), 1981; The Prodigal Daughter, 1982; First Among Equals, 1984; A Matter of Honour, 1986; A Twist in the Tale (short stories), 1989. Add: The Old Vicarage, Grantchester, nr. Cambridge, England.

ARCHER, John Hall. Canadian, b. 1914. Children's non-fiction, History. Principal, Univ. of Saskatchewan, since 1970; Pres. Emeritus, Univ. of Regina, since 1976 (Pres. and Prof. of History, 1974–76). Legislative Librarian, Saskatchewan, 1951–64; Asst. Clerk of Legislature, Saskatchewan, 1956–61; Provincial Archivist, 1957–62; Dir. of Libraries McGill Univ., Montreal, 1964–67; Univ. Archivist and Assoc. Prof. of History, Queen's Univ., Kingston. *Publs:* Historic Saskatoon, 1948; (co-author) The Story of a Province: A Junior History of Saskatchewan, 1955; (co-author) The Hudson's Bay Route, 1957; (ed.) Search for Stability, 1958; (ed.) West of Yesterday, 1967; (co-author) Footprints in Time: Saskatchewan, 1967; (ed.) Land of Promise, 1970; (contrib.) Canadian Business History, 1972; (ed.) Saskatchewan History; (ed.) Americana; A History of Saskatchewan, 1980; Honoured with the Burden: History of Regina Board of Education, 1987. Add: 1530 MacPherson Ave., Regina, Sask. S4S 4C9, Canada.

ARCHER, Jules. American, b. 1915. History, International relations/Current affairs, Law, Biography. *Publs:* (with Abel Green) Show Biz, 1959; Front-Line General: Douglas MacArthur, 1963; Twentieth-Century Caesar: Benito Mussolini, 1964; Man of Steel: Joseph Stalin, 1965; Fighting Journalist: Horace Greeley, 1966; Laws That Changed America, 1967; The Dictators, 1967; World Citizen: Woodrow Wilson, 1967; Battlefield President: Dwight D. Eisenhower, 1967; Red Rebel: Tito of Yugoslavia, 1968; The Unpopular Ones, 1968; From Whales to Dinosaurs, 1968; African Firebrand: Kenyatta of Kenya, 1969; The Extremists: Gadflies of American Society, 1969; Angry Abolitionist: William Lloyd Garrison, 1969; Philippines' Fight for Freedom, 1970; Indian Foe, Indian Friend, 1970; Colossus of Europe: Metternich, 1970; Hawks, Doves, and the Eagle, 1970; Who's Running Your Life, 1971; 1968: Year of Crisis, 1971; Revolution in Our Time, 1971; Treason in America: Disloyalty Versus Dissent, 1971; Ho Chi Minh: The Legend of Hanoi, 1971; Uneasy Friendship: France and the United States, 1972; Strikes, Bombs, and Bullets: Big Bill Haywood and the I.W.W., 1972; Cho En-lai, 1973; Mexico and the United States, 1973; The Plot to Seize the White House, 1973; Resistance, 1973; They Made a Revolution, 1776, 1973; Trotsky: World Revolutionary, 1973; Famous Young Rebels, 1973; Mao Tse-tung: A Biography, 1973; China in the Twentieth Century, 1974; Washington Versus Main Street, 1974; Riot: A History of Mob Action in the United States, 1974; The Russians and the Americans, 1975; Watergate: America in Crisis, 1975; Legacy of the Desert, 1976; The Chinese and the Americans, 1976; Police State, 1976; Epidemic!, 1977; Hunger on Planet Earth, 1977; Superspies, 1977; You and the Law, 1978; You Can't Do That to Me, 1980; Winners and Losers: How Elections Work In America, 1984; Jungle Fighters: A.G.I. War Correspondent's Experiences in the New Guinea Campaign, 1985; The Incredible Sixties: The Stormy Years That Changed America, 1986. Add: 404 High St., Santa Cruz, Calif. 95060, U.S.A.

ARCHER, Mildred (Agnes). British, b. 1911. Art. In charge of the Prints and Drawings Section, India Office Library and Records, London,

1954–80. *Publs:* Patna Painting, 1947; (with W.G. Archer) Indian Painting for the British 1770-1880, 1955; Tippoo's Tiger, 1959; Natural History Drawings (British Drawings, Company Drawings, Indian Popular Painting, Indian Miniatures) in the India Office Library, 5 vols., 1962–81; Indian Miniatures and Folk Paintings, 1967; Indian Architecture and the British, 1968; Indian Paintings from Court, Town, and Village, 1970; Artist Adventurers in 18th Century India, 1974; India and British Portraiture 1770-1825, 1979; Early Views of India, 1980; Visions of India, 1986. Add: 18a Provost Rd., London NW3, England.

ARCHER, Peter Kingsley. British, b. 1926. Civil liberties/Human rights, Law, Politics/Government. Labour M.P. (U.K.) for Warley West since 1974, and Member of Shadow Cabinet, 1981–87, (Member for Rowley Regis and Tipton, 1966–74; Parliamentary Private Secty. to the Attorney Gen., 1967–70; Solicitor Gen., 1974–79). Chmn., Soc. of Labour Lawyers, and British Section of Amnesty Intnl., 1971–74. *Publs:* The Queen's Courts, 1956; (ed.) Social Welfare and the Citizen, 1957; Communism and the Law, 1963; (co-author) Freedom at Stake, 1966; Human Rights, 1969; (co-author) Purpose in Socialism, 1973; The Role of the Law Officers, 1978; (co-ed.) More Law Reform Now, 1984. Add: House of Commons, London SW1, England.

ARCHER, Ron. *See* **WHITE,** Ted.

ARCHIBALD, (Rupert) Douglas. Trinidadian, b. 1919. Novels/Short stories, Plays/Screenplays. Ed., Progress Mag., 1952; Member Editorial Bd., Clarion newspaper, 1954–56; Gen. Mgr., Trinidad and Tobago Telephone Service, 1963–68; Chmn., Railway Bd., Trinidad, 1963–65; Chmn., Central Water Distribution Authority, Trinidad and Tobago, 1964; Vice-Chmn., Public Transport Service Corp., Trinidad and Tobago, 1965–67; Managing Dir., Trinidad and Tobago Telephone Co. Ltd., 1968–69; Dir., Trinidad Engineering and Research Ltd., 1970–83. *Publs:* Junction Village, 1954; Anne Marie, 1958; The Bamboo Clump, 1962; The Rose Slip, 1962; Old Maid's Tale, 1965; Island Tide, 1972; Defeat with Honour, 1973; Isidore and the Turtle (novel), 1973. Add: 3 St. Andrew's Ave., Freeways, Maravel, Trinidad and Tobago, West Indies.

ARD, Ben Neal, Jr. American, b. 1922. Psychology, Sex. Prof. of Counseling, San Francisco State Univ., since 1963. Psychologist, and marriage, family and child counselor in private practice, San Francisco, since 1964. Asst. Prof. of Psychology, Michigan State Univ., East Lansing, 1956–59; Prof., Central Michigan Univ., Mount Pleasant, 1960–63. *Publs:* (ed.) Counseling and Psychotherapy, 1966, 1975; (ed. with Constance Ard) Handbook of Marriage Counseling, 1969, 1976; Treating Psychosexual Dysfunction, 1974; Rational Sex Ethics, 1978, 1989; Living Without Guilt and/or Blame: Conscience, Superego and Psychotherapy, 1983; Solving Sex Problems in the 1990s, 1989. Add: 125 Cambon Dr., Apt. M-H, San Francisco, Calif. 94132, U.S.A.

ARDEN, John. British, b. 1930. Novels/Short stories, Plays/Screenplays, Literature. Freelance writer and director. Architectural Asst., London, 1955–57; Fellow in Playwriting, Univ. of Bristol, 1959–60. *Publs:* Serjeant Musgrave's Dance: An Unhistorical Parable, 1960; (with M. D'Arcy) The Business of Good Government: A Christmas Play, 1963; The Workhouse Donkey: A Vulgar Melodrama, 1964; Three Plays: The Waters of Babylon, Live Like Pigs, The Happy Haven, 1964; Ironhand (adaptation of play by Goethe), 1965; Armstrong's Last Goodnight: An Exercise in Diplomacy, 1965; Left-Handed Liberty: A Play about Magna Carta, 1965; (with M. D'Arcy) The Royal Pardon: or, The Soldier Who Became an Actor, 1967; Soldier, Soldier and Other Plays, 1967; (with M. D'Arcy) The Hero Rises Up: A Romantic Melodrama, 1969; Two Autobiographical Plays: The True History of Squire Jonathan and His Unfortunate Treasure, and the Bagmanjor, The Impromptu of Muswell Hill, 1971; (with M. D'Arcy) The Island of the Mighty, 1974; (with M. D'Arcy) The Non-Stop Connolly Show, 5 vols., 1977–78; To Present the Pretence (essays), 1978; Pearl, 1979; (with M. D'Arcy) Vandaleur's Folly, 1981; Silence Among the Weapons: Some Events at the Time of the Failure of a Republic (novel), 1982, in U.S. as Vox Pop: The Last Days of the Roman Republic, 1983; Whose Is the Kingdom, 1988; Books of Bale, 1988; (with M. D'Arcy) Awkward Corners, 1988. Add: c/o Margaret Ramsay Ltd., 14a Goodwin's Ct., London WC2, England.

ARDEN, William. *See* **LYNDS,** Dennis.

ARDIES, Tom. American, b. 1931. Mystery/Crime/Suspense. Reporter, Columnist, and Editorial Writer, Vancouver Sun, 1950–64; Telegraph Ed., Honolulu Star Bulletin, 1964–65; Special Asst. to Gov. of Guam, 1965–67. *Publs:* Their Man in the White House, 1971; This

Suitcase Is Going to Explode, 1972; Pandemic, 1973; Kosygin Is Coming, 1974, in U.K. paperback as Russian Roulette, 1975; In a Lady's Service, 1976; Palm Springs, 1978. Add: c/o Doubleday, 666 Fifth Ave., New York, NY 10103, U.S.A.

AREEDA, Phillip. American, b. 1930. Law. Prof. of Law, Harvard Law Sch., Cambridge, since 1961. Asst. Special Counsel to Pres. of U.S., 1956–61; Exec. Dir., U.S. Cabinet Task Force on Oil Import Control, 1969; Counsel to Pres. of U.S., 1974–75. *Publs:* Antitrust Analysis: Problems, Text, Cases, 1967, 4th ed., 1988; Antitrust Law, 8 vols., 1978–89. Add: Harvard Law Sch., Cambridge, Mass. 02138, U.S.A.

ARESTY, Esther Bradford. Has also written as Elaine Arthur. American. Cookery/Gastronomy/Wine. *Publs:* The Grand Venture, 1964; The Delectable Past, 1964; The Best Behavior, 1970; The Exquisite Table, 1980; (as Elaine Arthur) Romance in Store, 1983. Add: 41 Armour Rd., Princeton, N.J. 08540, U.S.A.

ARETA, Mavis. *See* **WINDER**, Mavis Areta.

ARGYLE, Michael. British, b. 1925. Psychology. Reader in Social Psychology since 1969, and Professorial Fellow of Wolfson Coll. since 1966, Oxford Univ. (Univ. Lectr. in Social Psychology, 1952–69, Acting Head, Dept. of Experimental Psychology, 1978–80). Social Psychology Ed., British Journal of Social and Clinical Psychology, 1961–67; Ed., Pergamon Intnl. Series in Experimental Social Psychology. *Publs:* The Scientific Study of Social Behavior, 1947; Religious Behaviour, 1959; (with M. Kirton and T. Smith) Training Managers, 1962; (ed. with A.T. Welford, D. Glass and J.N. Morris) Society, 1962; (ed. with G. Humphrey) Social Psychology Through Experiment, 1962; Psychology and Social Problems, 1964; The Psychology of Interpersonal Behavior, 1967, 4th ed. 1983; Social Interaction, 1969; The Social Psychology of Work, 1972, 1989; (with E. Sidney and M. Brown) Skills with People: A Guide for Managers, 1973; (ed.) Social Encounters, 1973; Bodily Communication, 1974, 1988; (with B. Beit-Hallhmi) The Social Psychology of Religion, 1975; (with M. Cook) Gaze and Mutual Gaze, 1975; (with P. Trower and B. Bryant) Social Skills and Mental Health, 1978; (with P. Trower) Person to Person, 1979; (with A. Furnham and J.A. Graham) Social Situations, 1981; (ed. with A. Furnham) The Psychology of Social Situations, 1981; (ed.) Social Skills and Work (Health), 2 vols., 1981; (with M. Henderson) The Anatomy of Relationships, 1985; The Psychology of Happiness, 1987. Add: Dept. of Experimental Psychology, South Parks Rd., Oxford, England.

ARGYRIS, John. British, b. 1913. Air/Space topics. Visiting Prof. of Aeronautical Structures, Imperial Coll., Univ. of London, 1955–80, now Emeritus (Reader, 1950–55); Prof. and Dir., Inst. fur Statik und Dynamik der Luft und Raumfahrtkonstruktionen, Univ. of Stuttgart, since 1959. Ed., Computer Methods in Applied Mechanics and Engineering. Research and Technical Officer, Royal Aeronautical Soc., London, 1943–49. *Publs:* Energy Theorems and Structural Analysis, 1960, 3rd ed. 1971; (co-author) Modern Fuselage Analysis and the Elastic Aircraft, 1963; Recent Advances in Matrix Methods of Structural Analysis, 1964; Introduction into the Finite Element Method, 3 vols., 1986–87. Add: Dept. of Aeronautics, Imperial Coll., South Kensington, London SW7 2AZ, England.

ARKHURST, Joyce Cooper. American, b. 1921. Children's non-fiction. Librarian, New York City Public Schools, since 1983. Librarian, Chicago Public Library, 1967–69; Librarian and teacher, Fieldston Sch., Riverdale, N.Y., 1971–74. *Publs:* The Adventures of Spider, 1964, 1987; More Adventures of Spider, 1971. Add: c/o Little Brown Inc., 34 Beacon St., Boston, Mass. 02104, U.S.A.

ARKIN, Marcus. South African, b. 1926. Economics, History. Attached Dept. of Economics, Univ. of Durban-Westville. Contrib. and Consultant Ed., Dictionary of South African Biography. Prof. of Economics and Head of Dept. of Economics and Economic History, Rhodes Univ., Grahamstown, 1967–73; former Dir.-Gen., South African Zionist Fedn. *Publs:* John Company at the Cape, 1962 (Founders' Medal and prize, Economic Soc. of South Africa); Supplies for Napoleon's Gaolers, 1964; Agency and Island, 1965; South African Economic Development: An Outline Survey, 1966; Economists and Economic Historians, 1968; Introducing Economics: The Science of Scarcity, 1971; The Economist at the Breakfast Table, 1971; Storm in a Teacup: The Cape Colonists and the English East India Company, 1973; Aspects of Jewish Economic History, 1975; The Zionist Idea: A History and Evaluation, 1977; (ed.) South African Jewry, 1984; One People, One Destiny: Some Explorations in Jewish Affairs, 1989. Add: 22179 Glenashley, Natal,

4022 South Africa.

ARKLEY, Arthur James. British, b. 1919. Children's fiction, Children's non-fiction. Headmaster, Rossmere Co. Primary Sch., Hartlepool, 1974–81, now retired. Headmaster, Elwick Rd. Jr. Sch., Hartlepool, 1970–73. Contrib. Ed., The Nelson Contemporary English Dictionary, 1977. *Publs:* (ed.) Ten Short Stories of Today, 1960; (ed.) Modern Tales of Action and Suspense, 1961; A Children's Working Dictionary, 1963; Man Under the Sea, 1964; (ed.) Mystery and Suspense, 1964; The Hamish Hamilton Children's Dictionary, 1964; Man in the Air, 1966; (ed.) Strange to Relate, 1966; Let's Work with the Dictionary, 1970; (ed.) In Fear and Dread, 1974; (ed.) Far Out, 1974. Add: 15 The Grove, Hartlepool, Cleveland TS26 9NB, England.

ARLEN, Michael J. American, b. 1930. Novels/Short stories, Social commentary, Autobiography. Staff Writer, The New Yorker mag., since 1956. Reporter, Life mag., NYC, 1952–56. *Publs:* Living-Room War, 1969; Exiles, 1970; An American Verdict, 1973; Passage to Ararat, 1975; The View from Highway 1: Essays on Television, 1976; Thirty Seconds, 1980; The Camera Age, 1981; Say Goodbye to Sam, 1984. Add: c/o The New Yorker, 25 W. 43rd Street, New York, N.Y. 10036, U.S.A.

ARLOTT, John. British, b. 1914. Cookery/Gastronomy/Wine, Sports/Physical education/Keeping fit. Sport and wine coresp. and gen. writer, Guardian newspaper, London; cricket and gen. broadcaster, BBC, London. Pres., Cricketers' Assn. *Publs:* (with G. Hamilton) Landmarks, 1943; Of Period and Place, 1944; Clausentum, 1945; First Time in America, 1949; Concerning Cricket, 1949; English Cheeses of the South and West, 1954; Vintage Summer, 1967; Fred, 1971; The Ashes, 1972; Island Camera, 1973; Snuff Shop, 1974; Krug: House of Champagne, 1976; (with Christopher Fielden) Burgundy Vines and Wines, 1976; Jack Hobbs: Profile of The Master, 1981; A Word From Arlott, 1983; (ed.) Wine, 1984; Arlott on Cricket, 1984. Add: c/o The Guardian, 119 Farringdon Rd., London EC1R 3ER, England.

ARMAH, Ayi Kwei. Ghanaian, b. 1939. Novels/Short stories. Former Trans., Revolution Africaine mag., Algiers. Scriptwriter for Ghana Television, and English Teacher, Navrongo Sch., Ghana, 1966; Ed., Jeune Afrique mag., Paris, 1967–68. *Publs:* The Beautiful Ones Are Not Yet Born, 1968; Fragments, 1970; Why Are We So Blest?, 1972; The Two Thousand Seasons, 1973; The Healers, 1978. Add: c/o Heinemann Ltd., 10 Upper Grosvenor St., London W1X 9PA, England.

ARMES, Roy. British, b. 1937. Film. Reader in Film, Middlesex Polytechnic. Film Critic of London Mag. *Publs:* French Cinema since 1946 (2 vols.), 1966, 1970; The Cinema of Alain Resnais, 1968; French Film, 1970; Patterns of Realism, 1972; Film and Reality, 1974; The Ambiguous Image, 1975; A Critical History of British Cinema, 1978; The Films of Alain Robbe-Grillet, 1981; French Cinema, 1985; Patterns of Realism, 1985; Third World Film Making & the West, 1987; On Video, 1988. Add: 19 New End, Hampstead, London NW3, England.

ARMITAGE, Ronda (Jacqueline). New Zealander, b. 1943. Children's Fiction. Infant Teacher, Duvauchelles, 1964–66, and Auckland, 1968–69; Supply Teacher, London, 1966; Adviser on Children's Books, Dorothy Butler Ltd., booksellers, Auckland, 1970–71; Asst. Librarian, Lewes Priory Comprehensive Sch., Sussex, 1976–77; Supply teacher, East Sussex County Council, from 1978. *Publs:* The Lighthouse Keeper's Lunch, 1977; The Trouble with Mr. Harris, 1978; Don't Forget Matilda, 1979; The Bossing of Josie, 1980, as The Birthday Spell, 1981; Ice Creams for Rosie, 1981; One Moonlight Night, 1983; Grandma Goes Shopping, 1985; The Lighthouse Keepers Catastrophe, 1986; The Lighthouse Keeper's Rescue, 1987. Add: Old Tiles Cottage, Church Lane, Hellingly, E. Sussex BN27 4HA, England.

ARMOUR, Richard. American, b. 1906. Literature, Humor/Satire. Emeritus Prof. of English, and Dean of Faculty, Scripps Coll. and Claremont Grad. Sch., California. Trustee, Claremont McKenna College, since 1968. *Publs:* Barry Cornwall, 1935; (with R.F. Howes) Coleridge the Talker, 1940; (ed.) Young Voices, 1941; Yours for the Asking, 1942; (with B. Adams) To These Dark Steps, 1943; Privates' Lives, 1944; Leading With My Left, 1946; Golf Bawls, 1946; Writing Light Verse, 1947; For Partly Proud Parents, 1950; It All Started with Columbus, 1953, rev. ed. 1961; Light Armour, 1954; It All Started with Europa, 1955; It All Started with Eve, 1956; Twisted Tales from Shakespeare, 1957; It All Started with Marx, 1958; Nights with Armour, 1958; Drug Store Days, 1959; The Classics Reclassified, 1960; Golf is a Four-Letter Word, 1962; Armour's Almanac, 1962; The Medical Muse, 1963; American Lit Relit, 1964; An Armoury of Light Verse, 1964; The Year Santa Went Modern,

1964; Our Presidents, 1964; Through Darkest Adolescence: With Tongue in Cheek and Pen in Checkbook, 1964; The Adventures of Egbert the Easter Egg, 1965; Going Around in Academic Circles, 1965; Animals on the Ceiling, 1966; Punctured Poems, 1966; It All Started with Hippocrates, 1966; It All Started with Stones and Clubs, 1967; A Dozen Dinosaurs, 1967; Odd Old Mammals, 1968; My Life with Women, 1968; English Lit Relit, 1969; On Your Marks: A Package of Punctuation, 1969; A Diabolical Dictionary of Education, 1969; All Sizes and Shapes of Monkeys and Apes, 1970; A Short History of Sex, 1970; Who's in Holes?, 1971; Writing Light Verse and Prose Humor, 1971; All in Sport, 1972; Out of My Mind, 1972; The Strange Dreams of Rover Jones, 1973; It All Started with Freshman English, 1973; Going Like Sixty: A Lighthearted Look at the Later Years, 1974; Sea Full of Whales, 1974; The Academic Bestiary, 1974; The Spouse in the House, 1975; The Happy Bookers: A History of Librarians and Their World, 1976; It All Would Have Startled Columbus, 1976; It All Started with Nudes: An Artful History of Art, 1977; Strange Monsters of the Sea, 1979; Insects All Around Us, 1981; Anyone for Insomnia?, 1982; Educated Guesses, 1983; Have You Ever Wished You Were Something Else?, 1983. Add: 894 W. Harrison Ave., Claremont, Calif. 91711, U.S.A.

ARMS, Suzanne. American, b. 1944. Women. Photographer. *Publs:* A Season to be Born, 1973; (author and photographer) Immaculate Deception: A New Look at Women and Childbirth, 1975; (photographer) Build Your Own Playground, by Jeremy Hewes, 1975; (photographer) Birth Diary, by Sheila Kitzinger, 1981; (author and photographer) To Love and Let Go, 1983; (author and photographer) A Handful of Hope: The New Open Adoption, 1989; (co-author and photographer) Feeding Your Baby: A Woman's Guide to Breastfeeding Made Simple, 1989. Add: 2298 Cornell St., Palo Alto, Calif. 94306, U.S.A.

ARMSTRONG, David Malet. Australian, b. 1926. Philosophy. Challis Prof. of Philosophy, Univ. of Sydney, since 1964. Asst. Lectr. in Philosophy, Birbeck Coll., Univ. of London, 1954–55; Lectr. and Sr. Lectr. in Philosophy, Melbourne Univ., 1956–63. *Publs:* Berkeley's Theory of Vision, 1960; Perception and the Physical World, 1961; Bodily Sensations, 1961; (ed.) Berkeley's Philosophical Writings, 1965; (co-ed.) Locke and Berkeley, 1968; A Materialist Theory of the Mind, 1968; Belief, Truth and Knowledge, 1973; Universals and Scientific Realism, 1978; The Nature of Mind and Other Essays, 1980; What Is a Law of Nature?, 1983; (with Norman Malcolm) Consciousness and Causality, 1984; A Combinatorial Theory of Possibility, 1989; Universals, 1989. Add: c/o Dept. of Traditional and Modern Philosophy, Sydney Univ., N.S.W. 2006, Australia.

ARMSTRONG, John Alexander. American, b. 1922. Administration/Management, History, International relations/Current affairs. Emeritus Prof. of Political Science, Univ. of Wisconsin, Madison, since 1986 (Asst. Prof., 1954–57; Assoc. Prof., 1958–60; Prof., 1960–78; Exec. Secty., Russian Area Studies Prog., 1959–63 and 1964–65; Acting Chmn., Western European Area Prog. 1967; Philippe de Commynes Prof., 1978–86). Pres., American Assn. for the Advancement of Slavic Studies, 1965–67; Consultant, Bureau of Intelligence and Research, U.S. Dept of State, Washington, D.C., 1972–81 (member, Advisory Panel, Bureau of European Affairs, 1966–69). *Publs:* Ukrainian Nationalism, 1955, 1963; The Soviet Bureaucratic Elite, 1959, 1966; The Politics of Totalitarianism, 1961; Ideology, Politics and Government in the Soviet Union, 1962, 4th ed. 1979; (co-author and ed.) Soviet Partisans in World War II, 1964; The European Administrative Elite, 1973; Nations Before Nationalism, 1982. Add: 40 Water St., Saint Augustine, Fla. 32084, U.S.A.

ARMSTRONG, Judith (Mary). Australian, b. 1935. Literature, Member, Russian Dept., Univ. of Melbourne, since 1974. *Publs:* The Novel of Adultery, 1976; (trans.) In the Land of Kangaroos and Goldmines, by Oscar Comettant, 1980; (ed. with Rae Slonek) Essays to Honour Nina Christesen, 1980; The Unsaid Anna Karenina, 1988. Add: Russian Dept., Univ. of Melbourne, Parkville, Melbourne, Australia 3052.

ARMSTRONG, Nancy. British, b. 1924. Art, Crafts. Lectr., Victoria and Albert Museum, Univ. of London, NAD-FAS, National Trust, etc., since 1963. *Publs:* Jewellery: An Historical Survey of British Styles and Jewels, 1973; The Collector's History of Fans, 1974; Victorian Jewellery, 1976; Fans from the East, 1978; The Book of Fans, 1979; Fans, 1985; Otros Abanicos, 1985; Fans from the Fitzwilliam, 1985. Add: Priory Cottage, Prospect Pl., Porthleven, Cornwall TR13 9DS, England.

ARMSTRONG, Robert Laurence. American, b. 1926. Philosophy. Prof. and Chmn., Dept. of Philosophy and Religious Studies, Univ. of West Florida, Pensacola, since 1969 (Assoc. Prof., and Chmn., 1967–69).

Asst. Prof. of Philosophy, Univ. of Nevada, Reno, 1962–67. *Publs:* Metaphysics and British Empiricism, 1970. Add: Dept. of Philosophy and Religious Studies, Univ. of West Florida, Pensacola, Fla. 32514, U.S.A.

ARMSTRONG, William H(oward). American, b. 1914. Novels/Short stories, Historical/Romance/Gothic, Children's fiction, Education, Autobiography, Biography. Teacher, Kent Sch., Conn., since 1945. Virginia Episcopal Sch., 1939–44. *Publs:* Study is Hard Work (textbook), 1956; Through Troubled Waters (personal experiences), 1957; (with Joseph W. Swain) Peoples of the Ancient World (textbook), 1959; 87 Ways to Help Your Child In School, 1961; Tools of Thinking, 1968; Sounder (fiction), 1969; Barefoot in the Grass: The Story of Grandma Moses, 1970; Sour Land (fiction), 1971; The MacLeod Place (fiction),, 1972; Hadassah: Esther the Orphan Queen (historical fiction), 1972; The Mills of God (fiction), 1974; The Education of Abraham Lincoln (biography), 1974; My Animals (children's fiction), 1974; Joanna's Miracle (fiction), 1978; Tawny and Dingo (fiction), 1980. Add: Kimadee Hill, Kent, Conn. 06757, U.S.A.

ARNADE, Charles W. American, b. 1927. History. Prof. of Intnl. Studies, Univ. of South Florida, Tampa, since 1972 (Assoc. Prof. of History and Social Studies, 1960–63; Prof. of History and Coordinator of Intnl. Studies, 1963–66; Prof. of Social Science and American Ideas, 1966–69; Chmn. and Prof., American Ideas Dept. (American Instns.), 1969–72). Instr. in History and American Instns. 1952–56, and Asst. Prof. of History 1958–60, Univ. of Florida, Gainesville; Asst. Prof. of History and Political Science, Florida State Univ., Tallahassee, 1956–58. *Publs:* The Creation of the Republic of Bolivia, 1952; The Emergence of the Republic of Bolivia, 1957; The Trial of Florida 1593-1602, 1959; The Siege of St. Augustine in 1702 , 1959; (with Josef Kuhnel) El problema del humanista Tadeo Haenke, 1960; La Historia del Bolivia y de los Estados Unidos, 1962; La dramatica insurgencia de Bolivia, 1963. Add: 219 North Main St., San Antonio, Fla. 33576, U.S.A.

ARNDT, Heinz Wolfgang. Australian, b. 1915. Economics, Money/Finance. Prof. of Economics, Research Sch. of Pacific Studies, Australian National Univ., Canberra, 1963–80 (Prof. of Economics, Sch. of Gen. Studies, 1951–63). Ed., Asian-Pacific Economic Literature, since 1986. Pres., Economic Soc. for Australia and New Zealand, 1957–59, and Australian Assn. for Cultural Freedom, 1977–86; Economic Consultant, UN Economic Commn. for Europe, Geneva, 1960; Deputy Dir., Country Studies Div., OECD, Paris, 1972; Member, Governing Council, UN Asian Inst., Bangkok, 1969–76. Ed., Bulletin of Indonesian Economic Studies, 1965–84. *Publs:* The Economic Lessons of the Nineteen-Thirties, 1944; Labour and Economic Policy, 1956; The Australian Trading Banks, 1957, 3rd ed. with C.P. Harris, 1965; 4th Ed. with D.W. Stammer, 1973; 5th ed. with W.J. Blackert; The Banks and the Capital Market, 1960; (ed. with W.M. Corden) The Australian Economy: A Volume of Readings, 1963, 1972; (co-author) Taxation in Australia: Agenda for Reform, 1964; (co-author) Some Factors in Economic Growth in Europe During the 1950s, 1964; (with J. Panglaykin) The Indonesian Economy: Facing a New Era?, 1966; A Small Rich Industrial Country: Studies in Australian Development, Aid and Trade, 1968; Australia and Asia: Economic Essays 1972; (ed. with A.H. Boxer) The Australian Economy: A Second Volume of Readings, 1972; (co-author) Australia: OECD Annual Survey, 1973; The Rise and Fall of Economic Growth, 1978, 1984; The Indonesian Economy: Collected Papers, 1984; A Course through Life: Memoirs of an Australian Economist, 1985; Economic Development: The History of an Idea, 1987; Asian Diaries, 1987. Add: Australian National Univ., Canberra, A.C.T. 2600, Australia.

ARNDT, Karl (John Richard). American, b. 1903. History, Literature, Media. Prof. of German Language and Literature Clark Univ., Worcester, Mass., since 1950. Consultant, Historic New Harmony Inc., Ind. Prof. of German and Greek, Hartwick Coll., Oneonta, N.Y., 1933–35; Asst. Prof., 1935–42, and Assoc. Prof. of Germanics, 1942–45, Louisiana State Univ., Baton Rouge; Chief of Religious Affairs Branch, U.S. Military Govt. for Germany, 1946–50. *Publs:* (ed.) Early German American Narratives, 1941; (with M. Olson) German-American Newspapers and Periodicals: 1732-1955, 1961, rev. ed. 1965; George Rapp's Successors and Material Heirs: 1847-1916, 1971; George Rapp's Harmony Society: 1785-1847, 1972; (ed.-in chief) Charles Sealsfield: Greatest American Writer of the 1830s and 1840s, 28 vols., 1972—; The German Language Press of the Americas, 3 vols., 1976–80; A Documentary History of the Indiana Decade of the Harmony Society, 2 vols., 1975, 1978; The Treaty of Amity and Commerce of 1785 Between His Majesty the King of Prussia and the United States, 1977; The Annotated and Enlarged Edition of Ernst Steiger's Precentennial Bibliography The Periodical Literature of the United States, 1979; George Rapp's Separatists: The German Prelude to Rapp's American Harmony Society 1700-1805, 1980; Harmony on the Connoquenessing, George Rapp's First American Harmony: A Documentary History of the First American Decade of the Harmony Society 1803-1814, 1980; Harmony on the Wabash in Transition to Rapp's Divine Economy on the Ohio, and to Owen's New Moral World at New Harmony on the Wabash, 1824-1826, 1981; Economy on the Ohio 1826-1834, George Rapp's Third Harmony: A Documentary History, 1984; George Rapp's Years of Glory: Economy on the Ohio 1834-1847, 1987. Add: Dept. of German, Clark Univ., Worcester, Mass. 01610, U.S.A.

ARNHEIM, Rudolf. American, b. 1904. Art, Communications Media, Film, Psychology. Emeritus Prof., Psychology of Art, Harvard Univ., Cambridge, Mass. (Prof., 1968–74). Visiting Prof., Univ of Michigan, Ann Arbor, 1974–84. Member of Psychology Faculty, Sarah Lawrence Coll., Bronxville, N.Y., 1943–68. *Publs:* Art and Visual Perception, 1954, rev. ed. 1974; Film as Art, 1957; Genesis of a Painting, 1962; Toward a Psychology of Art, 1966; Entropy and Art, 1971; Radio: An Art of Sound, 1971; The Dynamics of Architectural Form, 1977; The Power of the Center, 1982; New Essays on the Psychology of Art, 1986. Add: 1133 S. Seventh St., Ann Arbor, Mich. 48103, U.S.A.

ARNOLD, Arnold F. American, b. 1929. Children's non-fiction, Education, Crafts. Graphic and industrial designer, since 1946; cyberneticist, writer and consultant in systems analysis and operational research, London, since 1976. Pres., Arnold Arnold Design, Inc., New York, 1960–66; Pres., Manuscript Press, Inc., New York, 1963–66. Consultant Ed. for Rutledge Books, New York, 1962–65. *Publs:* Your Child's Play, 1955; The Arnold Arnold Book of Toy Soldiers, 1963; Tongue Twisters and Double Talk, 1964; Look and Do Books Series, 1964; Games, 4 vols., 1965; Violence and Your Child, 1969; Pictures and Stores from Forgotten Children's Books, 1969; Your Child and You, 1970; The Yes and No Book, 1970; Teaching Your Child to Learn from Birth to School Age, 1971; The World Book of Children's Games, 1972; (ed.) Antique Paper Dolls, 1915–1920, 1975; The World Book of Arts and Crafts for Children, 1977; Winners, 1989; Nothing But a Machine, 1990. Add: c/o Grafton Books, 8 Grafton St., London W1X 3LA, England.

ARNOLD, Edmund Clarence. American, b. 1913. Advertising/Public relations, Communications Media, Design, Writing/Journalism Distinguished Prof. Emeritus, Virginia Commonwealth Univ., Richmond, since 1975. Dir., National Newspaper Inst., since 1983. Night Ed., State Journal, Lansing, Mich., 1952–54; Ed., Linotype News, 1954–60; Chmn., Graphic Arts Dept., Sch. of Public Communications, Syracuse Univ., N.Y., 1960–75. *Publs:* Functional Newspaper Design, 1956 (George Polk Memorial Award); Profitable Newspaper Advertising, 1960; Feature Photos That Sell, 1960; Ink on Paper: A Handbook of the Graphic Arts, 1963; The Student Journalist, 1963; Tipografia y Diagramados, 1965; The Yearbook, 1966; Copy Preparation, 1966; Graphic Arts Procedures, 1966; Layout for Advertising, 1966; Advertising Design, 1966; Type Handbook, 1966; Modern Newspaper Design, 1969; Ink on Paper 2, 1972; Editing the Yearbook, 1973; (with Hillier Kreigbaum) Handbook of Student Journalism, 1976; Arnold's Ancient Axioms, 1978; Designing the Total Newspaper, 1980; Editing the Organizational Publication, 1981; Fliers, Folders and Brochures, 1984; 34 Outstanding Organizational Publications, 1986; The Trailblazers: The Story of the 70th Infantry Division. Add: 3208 Hawthorn Ave., Richmond, Va. 23222, U.S.A.

ARNOLD, Guy. British, b. 1932. History, Industrial relations, International relations/Current affairs, Literature, Politics/Government, Third World problems. Freelance writer. Adviser on youth problems, Govt. of Northern Rhodesia, 1963–64; Researcher, Overseas Development Inst., London, 1965–66; Dir., Africa Bureau, London, 1968–72. *Publs:* Longhouse and Jungle, 1959; Towards Peace and a Multiracial Commonwealth, 1964; Economic Co-operation in the Commonwealth, 1967; Kenyatta and the Politics of Kenya, 1974; The Last Bunker, 1976; Modern Nigeria, 1977; (with Ruth Weiss) Strategic Highways of Africa, 1977; Britain's Oil, 1978; Aid in Africa, 1979; Held Fast for England: G.A. Henty, Imperialist Boys' Writer, 1980; The Unions, 1981; Modern Kenya, 1981; Datelines of World History, 1983; Aid and the Third World, 1985; Third World Handbook, 1989; Down the Danube: The Black Forest to the Black Sea, 1989. Add: 163 Seymour Place, London W1, England.

ARNOLD, H(arry) J(ohn) P(hilip) (Douglas). British, b. 1932. Economics, Photography, Biography. Managing Dir., Space Frontiers Ltd., since 1974. Foreign News Ed., Financial Times newspaper, London, 1956–60; Asst. to Managing Dir. and Public Relations Adviser,

Kodak Ltd., London, 1966–74. *Publs:* Aid to Developing Countries, 1961; Aid for Development, 1966; Photographer of the World: Biography of H.G. Ponting, 1969; Another World, 1975; William Henry Fox Talbot: Photographic Pioneer and Man of Science, 1977; Images from Space, 1979; Night Sky Photography, 1988. Add: 30 Fifth Ave., Denvilles, Havant, Hants. PO9 2PL, England.

ARNOLD, Janet. British, b. 1932. Fashion/Costume. Freelance work, BBC, since 1973. Jubilee Research Fellow, 1978–81, and Leverhulme Fellow, since 1982, Dept. of Drama and Theatre Studies, Royal Holloway Coll., Univ. of London. Sr. Lectr., Avery Hill Coll. of Education, 1962–70; Research Lectr., West Surrey Coll. of Art and Design, 1971–75. *Publs:* Patterns of Fashion I: Englishwomen's Dresses and Their Construction, 1660-1860, 1972, II: Englishwomen's Dresses and Their Construction, 1860-1940, 1972; III: The Cut and Construction of Clothes for Men and Women c.1560-1620, 1985; A Handbook of Costume, 1973; Lost from Her Majesties Back, 1980; Queen Elizabeth's Wardrobe Unlock'd, 1988. Add: Brayfield Terr., Islington, London N1, England.

ARNOLD, Joseph H. *See* **HAYES,** Joseph.

ARNOLD, M(agda) B(londiau). American, b. 1903. Psychology. Faculty member, Univ. of Toronto, 1942–47; Wellesley Coll., Mass., 1947–48; Bryn Mawr Coll., Pa., 1948–50; Barat Coll., Lake Forest, Ill., 1950–52; and Loyola Univ., Chicago, 1950–72; Prof. of Psychology, and Chmn. of the Social Sciences Div., Spring Hill Coll., Mobile, Ala., 1972–75. *Publs:* (co-author and co-ed.) The Human Person, 1954; Emotion and Personality (2 vols.), 1960. Story Sequence Analysis, 1962; (ed.) The Nature of Emotion, 1968; (ed.) Feelings and Emotions: The Loyola Symposium, 1970; Memory and the Brain, 1984. Add: 5863 Montfort Rd., Mobile, Ala. 36608, U.S.A.

ARNOLD, Peter. American, b. 1943. Criminology/Law enforcement/Prisons, Medicine/Health, Travel/Exploration/Adventure. *Publs:* (ed. with Jerry Lewis) The Total Filmmaker, 1971; Burgler-Proof Your Home and Car, 1971; Off the Beaten Track in Copenhagen, 1972; Lady Beware (crime prevention), 1974; Check List for Emergencies (health), 1974; Crime and Youth, 1976; How to Protect Your Child Against Crime, 1977; Emergency Handbook, 1980; (with Richard Germann) Bernard Haldane Associates' Job and Career Building, 1980; (with Richard Germann and Diane Blumenson) Working and Liking It, 1983; (with Ellen J. Wallach) The Job Search Companion, 1984; (with Bruce A. Percelay) Packaging Your House for Profit, 1985. Add: Writers House, Literary Agency, 21 West 26th St., New York, N.Y. 10010, U.S.A.

ARNOLD, Rollo Davis. New Zealander, b. 1926. Children's fiction, History. Emeritus Professor, Victoria Univ., Wellington, since 1987 (Sr. Lectr., 1965–75; Reader, 1975–77; Prof., 1977–87). Head of English Dept., Palmerston North Teachers' Coll., 1961–65. *Publs:* Bracken Block, 1967; The Freedom of Ariki, 1967; The Farthest Promised Land, 1981. Add: 15 Hauraki St., Wellington 5, New Zealand.

ARNOTT, (Margaret) Anne. British, b. 1916. Autobiography, Biography. Justice of the Peace, Newcastle upon Tyne, and Weston-Super-Mare Bench, 1964–73. Former teacher in grammar and high schs. *Publs:* The Brethren (in U.S. as Turbulent Waters) 1969; Journey into Understanding: Portrait of a Family, 1971; The Secret Country of C.S. Lewis, 1974; Wife to the Archbishop, 1976; Fruits of the Earth, 1979; The Unexpected Call, 1981; Valiant for Truth: The Story of John Bunyan, 1986. Add: c/o Mowbray, St Thomas House, Becket St., Oxford, OX1 1SJ, England.

ARNOTT, Peter Douglas. British, b. 1931. Classics, Literature, Theatre, Translations. Prof. and Chmn., Dept. of Drama, Tufts Univ., Medford, Mass., since 1969. Prof. Univ. of Iowa, Iowa City, 1958–69. *Publs:* Introduction to the Greek Theater, 1959; (trans.) Two Classical Comedies, 1959; (trans.) Oedipus, and Antigone, 1960; (trans.) Three Greek Plays for the Theater, 1961; Greek Scenic Conventions in the Fifth Century B.C., 1962; (trans.) Libation Bearers, and Eumenides, 1964; (trans.) Agamemnon, 1964; Plays without People, 1964; (trans.) Prometheus Vinctus and Seven Against Thebes, 1968; (trans.) Hecuba, and Heracles, 1969; Introduction to Greek World, 1969; Theaters of Japan, 1969; Introduction to the Roman World, 1970; Ancient Greek and Roman Theater, 1971; Ballet of Comedians, 1971; The Byzantines and Their World, 1973; Introduction to the French Theatre, 1977; (ed.) Thirteen Plays; (ed.) Twenty-Three Plays; The Theatre in Its Time. Add: 6 Herrick St., Winchester, Mass. 01890, U.S.A.

ARONSON, Theo(dore Ian Wilson). British, b. 1930. History, Biography. Freelance writer since 1964. Advertising Designer, J. Walter Thompson Co., London and South Africa, 1953–64. *Publs:* The Golden Bees, 1964; Royal Vendetta, 1966; The Coburgs of Belgium (in U.S. as Defiant Dynasty), 1968; The Fall of the Third Napoleon, 1970; The Kaisers, 1971; Queen Victoria and the Bonapartes, 1972; Grandmama of Europe, 1973; A Family of Kings, 1976; Victoria and Disraeli, 1977; Kings over the Water, 1979; Princess Alice, Countess of Athlone, 1981; Royal Family: Years of Transition, 1983; Crowns in Conflict, 1986; The King in Love, 1988. Add: North Knoll Cottage, 15 Bridge St., Frome, England.

ARRE, Helen. *See* **ROSS**, Zola.

ARRIGHI, Mel. American, b. 1933. Novels, Plays. Actor, 1956–62. *Publs:* novels—Freak Out, 1968; An Ordinary Man, 1970; Daddy Pig, 1974; The Death Collection, 1975; The Hatchet Man, 1975; Navono 1000, 1976; Turkish White, 1977; Delphine, 1978; On Tour, 1979; Alter Ego, 1983; Manhattan Gothic, 1985; plays—An Ordinary Man, 1969; The Castro Complex, 1971. Add: 344 East 79th St., New York, N.Y. 10021, U.S.A.

ARROW, Kenneth (Joseph). American, b. 1921. Economics. Joan Kenney Prof. of Economics, Stanford Univ., California, since 1979. Asst. Prof., Univ. of Chicago, 1948; Asst. Prof., 1949–50, Assoc. Prof., 1950–53, and Prof. of Economics, 1953–68, Stanford Univ.; Prof., 1968–74 and James Bryant Conant Univ. Prof., 1974–79, Harvard Univ., Cambridge, Mass. Fellow, Center for Advanced Study in the Behavioral Sciences, Palo Alto, Calif., 1956–57; Economist, Council of Economic Advisors, U.S. Govt., 1962; Fellow, Churchill Coll., Cambridge, 1963–64. Recipient, Nobel Prize in Economics, 1972. *Publs:* (with Selma G. Arrow) Methodological Problems in Airframe Cost-Performance Studies, 1950; Cost Quality Relations in Bomber Airframes, 1951; (with Selma G. Arrow) On Mandelbaum's Study of the Industrialization of Backward Areas, 1951; Social Choice and Individual Values, 1951; The Combination of Time Series and Cross-Section Data in Interindustry Flow Analysis, 1956; (with others) Studies in the Linear and Non-Linear Programming, 1958; (with others) Studies in the Mathematical Theory of Inventory and Production, 1958; (with William M. Capron) Dynamic Shortages and Price Rises: The Engineer-Scientist Case, 1958; A Time Series Analysis of Interindustry Demands, 1959; (with Alain C. Enthoven) Quasi-Concave Programming, 1959; (with Hirofumi Uzawa) Constraint Qualifications in Maximization Problems, II, 1960; Economic Welfare and the Allocation of Resources for Invention, 1960; (ed.) Mathematical Methods in the Social Sciences: Proceedings of the Stanford Symposium on Mathematical Methods in the Social Sciences, 1960; The Economic Implications of Learning by Doing, 1961; (with Marc Nerlove) Optimal Advertising Policy under Dynamic Conditions, 1961; (ed., with others) Studies in Applied Probability and Management Science, 1962; Control in Large Organizations, 1963; Statistical Requirements for Greek Economic Planning, 1965; Optimal Capital Policy with Irreversible Investment, 1966; (with David Levhari) Uniqueness of the Internal Rate of Return with Variable Life of Investment, 1968; (ed.) Readings in Welfare Economics, 1969; Essays in the Theory of Risk-Bearing, 1970; (with F.H. Hahn) General Competitive Analysis, 1971; Some Models of Racial Discrimination in the Labor Market, 1971; (ed.) Selected Readings in Economic Theory from Econometrica, 1971; Gifts and Exchanges, 1972; Information and Economic Behavior, 1973; Optimal Insurance and Generalized Deductibles, 1973; Theoretical Issues in Health Insurance, 1973; Welfare Analysis of Changes in Health Coinsurance Rates, 1973; The Limits of Organization, 1974; Two Notes on Inferring Long Run Behavior from Social Experiments, 1975; (ed., with Leonard Hurwicz) Studies in Resource Allocation Processes, 1977; (with others) Energy, the Next Twenty Years: A Report, 1979; (with Joseph P. Kalt) Petroleum Price Regulation: Should We Decontrol?, 1979; (ed. with others) Applied Research for Social Policy: The United States and the Federal Republic of Germany, 1979; (ed. with Michael D. Intriligator) Handbook of Mathematical Economics, 1981; Collected Papers, 6 vols, 1983–85. Add: Dept. of Economics, Stanford Univ., Stanford, Calif. 94305, U.S.A.

ARROW, William. *See* **ROTSLER**, William.

ARROWSMITH, William. American, b. 1924. Classics, Translations. Univ. Prof., and Prof. of Classics, Boston Univ., 1972–76, and since 1986. Commissioner, National Study Commn. on Undergrad. Education; Ed., Arion: A Journal of Classics and Humanities since 1962; Advisory Ed., Mosaic, since 1967; Contrib. Ed., American Poetry Review, 1972. Instr. in Classics, Princeton Univ., N.J., 1951–53; Instr. in Classics and Humanities, Wesleyan Univ., Middletown, Conn., 1953–54; Asst. Prof. of Classics and Humanities, Univ. of California at Riverside, 1954–56;

Assoc. Prof. of Classics, 1958–59, Prof. of Classics, 1959–70, Chmn, of the Dept. of Classics, 1965–66, and University Prof., 1967–70, Univ. of Texas at Austin; Prof. of Classics, Johns Hopkins Univ., Baltimore, 1977–82; Woodruff Prof. of Classics and Comparative Literature, Emory Univ., Atlanta, 1982–86. Founding Ed., Chimera, NYC, 1942–45, and The Hudson Review, NYC, 1948–60; Advisory Ed., Tulane Drama Review, New Orleans, 1958–68; Member of Bd., National Translation Center, 1964–69; Consultant, U.S. Office of Education, 1969–74, Ford Foundn., 1970–71, and Mass. Inst. of Technology, Cambridge, 1971–72. *Publs:* (trans.) The Satyricon of Petronius, 1958, 1962; (trans.) Euripides' Bacchae, Cyclops, Hecuba, Heracles, and Orestes, in The Complete Greek Tragedies, ed. Lattimore, 1960, 1967; (trans.) The Birds, by Aristophanes, 1960, 1965; (with R. Shattuck) The Craft and Context of Translation, 1960, 3rd ed., 1969 (trans.) The Clouds, by Aristophanes, 1961, 1966; (ed.) Image of Italy, 1962; (gen. ed.) The Complete Greek Comedy, 1962—; (ed.) Great Italian Novellas, 1965; (gen. ed.) The Greek Tragedy in New Translation, 33 vols., 1973—; (trans.) Alcestis, by Euripides, 1975; (ed.) Hard Labor: Poems by Cesare Pavese, 1979; (trans.) The Storm and Other Poems, 1984; (trans. with others) Four Plays, by Aristophanes, 1984; (trans.) That Bowling Alley on the Tiber, by Michelangelo Antonioni, 1986; (trans.) The Storm and Other Things, by Eugenio Montale, 1986; (trans.) The Occasions, by Eugenio Montale, 1987. Add: 275 Goddard Ave., Brookline, Mass. 02146, U.S.A.

ARTHUR, Elaine. *See* **ARESTY**, Esther Bradford.

ASANTE, Molefi K. (Arthur L. Smith). American. Poetry, Cultural/Ethnic topics, Speech/Rhetoric. Prof. and Chmn., African-American Studies, Temple Univ., Philadelphia. Ed., Journal of Black Studies, since 1970; Assoc. Ed., The Speech Teacher, since 1972. Prof., Purdue Univ., Lafayette, Ind., 1968–69; Prof., 1969 and Dir., Center for Afro-American Studies, 1970–73, Univ. of California, Los Angeles. *Publs:* Break of Dawn (poetry), 1964; Rhetoric of Black Revolution, 1969; Toward Transracial Communication, 1970; (with Andrea Rich) Rhetoric of Revolution, 1970; (ed. with Stephen Robb) The Voice of Black Rhetoric, 1971; (with Anne Allen and Deluvina Hernandez) How to Talk with People of Other Races, 1971; (ed.) Language, Communication and Rhetoric in Black America, 1972; Transracial Communication, 1973; Epic in Search of African Kings, 1978; Contemporary Black Thought, 1979; Mass Communication, 1979; Handbook of Intercultural Communication, 1979; Afrocentricity, 1980; The Afrocentric Idea, 1987. Add: Dept. of African-American Studies, Temple Univ., Philadelphia, Pa. 19122, U.S.A.

ASARE, Meshack (Yaw). Ghanaian, b. 1945. Children's fiction. Art Director and Illustrator, Educational Press and Manufacturers, Accra, since 1979. Teacher, elementary sch., Tema, 1966–68, and Lincoln Community Sch., Accra, 1969–70. *Publs:* Tawia Goes to Sea, 1970; I Am Kofi, 1972; Mansa Helps at Home, 1972; The Brassman's Secret, 1981; The Canoe's Story, 1982; Chipo and the Bird on the Hill: A Tale of Ancient Zimbabwe, 1984; Cat in Search of a Friend, 1986. Add: c/o Educational Press and Manufacturers, P.O. Box 9184, Airport, Accra, Ghana.

ASBELL, Bernard. Has also written as Nicholas Max. American, b. 1923. Politics/Government. Dir., New England Writers Center, since 1979; Assoc. Fellow, Trumbull Coll., Yale Univ., New Haven, Conn., since 1981. Reporter, Richmond, Virginia Times-Dispatch, 1945–47; in public relations, Chicago, 1947–55; Managing Ed., Chicago mag., 1955–56; Teacher of writing, Univ. of Chicago, 1956–60, Bread Loaf Writers Conference, Vermont, 1960–61, and Univ. of Bridgeport, Connecticut, 1961–63; Visiting Lectr., Yale Univ., 1979–80, Pennsylvania State Univ., 1984–85. *Publs:* When FDR Died, 1961; The New Improved American, 1965; What Lawyers Really Do, 1970; Careers in Urban Affairs, 1970; The FDR Memoirs, 1973; (as Nicholas Max) President McGovern's First Term, 1973; (with Clair F. Vough) Productivity, 1975; The Senate Nobody Knows, 1978; (with David Hartman) White Coat, White Cane, 1978; (ed.) Mother and Daughter: The Letters of Eleanor and Anna Roosevelt, 1982; Transit Point Moscow, 1985. Add: Box 522, State College, Pa. 16804, U.S.A.

ASCH, Frank. American, b. 1946. Children's fiction. Has worked as a Montessori school teacher and in children's theatre. *Publs:* George's Store, 1969; Linda, 1969; Elvira Everything, 1970; The Blue Balloon, 1971; Yellow Yellow, 1971; Rebecka, 1971; I Met a Penguin, 1972; In the Eye of the Teddy, 1973; Gia and the $100 Worth of Bubblegum, 1974; Good Lemonade, 1975; The Inside Kid, 1977; Monkey Face, 1977; Macgoose's Grocery, 1978; Moon Bear, 1978; Turtle Tale, 1978; City Sandwich, 1978; Country Pie, 1979; Little Devil's ABC, 1979; Popcorn, 1979; Sand Cake, 1979; Little Devil's One Two Three, 1979; Running with Rachel, 1979; The Last Puppy, 1980; Starbaby, 1980; Just Like

Daddy, 1981; Good Night, Horsey, 1981; Happy Birthday, Moon, 1982; Milk and Cookies, 1982; Bread and Honey, 1982; Mooncake, 1983; Moongame, 1984; Pearl's Promise, 1984; Skyfire, 1984; Bear Shadow, 1985; Bear's Bargain, 1985; Goodbye House, 1986; I Can Blink, 1986; I Can Roar, 1986; Pearl's Pirates, 1987; Oats and Wild Animals, 1988; Journey to Terezor, 1989. Add: c/o Holiday House, 18 E. 53rd St., New York, N.Y. 10022, U.S.A.

ASH, Brian. Pseud: Henry Dorland. British, b. 1936. Literature. Asst., Bank of England, London, 1953–58; Admin. Officer, Royal National Lifeboat Instn., London, 1959–65; Advertising Exec., Kodak Ltd., London, 1965–66; Head of Editorial Services, Esso Petroleum Co., London, 1966–70; Public Relations Officer, London Borough of Camden, London, 1971–72. Publicity Officer, H.G. Wells Centenary, London, 1966; Gen. Secty., H.G. Wells Soc., London, 1967–70. *Publs:* (ed.) H.G. Wells: A Comprehensive Bibliography, 1966; (ed.) The Last Books of H.G. Wells, 1968; Tiger in Your Tank, 1969; Faces of the Future: The Lessons of Science Fiction, 1975; Who's Who in Science Fiction, 1976; (ed.) The Visual Encyclopaedia of Science Fiction, 1977; Who's Who in H.G. Wells, 1977. Add: c/o Elek, 88 Islington High St., London N1 8EN, England.

ASH, John. British, b. 1948. Poetry. Primary school teacher, 1970–71; research assistant, 1971–75. *Publs:* Casino, 1978; The Bed and Other Poems, 1981; The Goodbyes, 1982; The Branching Stair, 1984; Disbelief, 1987. Add: c/o Carcanet New Press Ltd., 208 Corn Exchange Bldgs., Manchester M4 3BQ, England.

ASH, Russell (John). British, b. 1946. Art, History, Biography, Humor. Editorial consultant, Pavilion Books Ltd., London, since 1983. Dir., Ash and Grant Ltd., London, 1973–78; Dir., Weidenfeld & Nicolson, London, 1980–83. *Publs:* Discovering Highwaymen, 1970; Britain's Buried Treasures, 1972; Shipwrecks and Sunken Treasure, 1972; Fact or Fiction?, 1973; (ed.) Talking about the Family, 1973; Alma-Tadema, 1973; (with I. Grant) Comets, 1973; (ed.) John William Polidori's The Vampyre, 1974; The Wright Brothers, 1974; (ed.) Talking about Race, 1974; (ed. with I. Grant) Dead Funny, 1974, as Last Laughs, 1984; Impressionists and Their Art, 1980; The Cynic's Dictionary, 1984; Thefficial British Yuppie Handbook, 1984; Selections from the Reader's Digest Collection (exhibition catalogue), 1985; Howlers, 1985; The Londoner's Almanac, 1985; (with Brian Lake) Bizarre Books, 1985; The Pig Book, 1985; The Frog Book, 1986; Dear Cats: The Post Office Letters, 1986; The Daily Trivia Diary, 1986. Add: 4 Crieff Rd., London SW18 2EA, England.

ASH, William Franklin. British, b. 1917. Novels, History, Autobiography. Sr. Script Ed., BBC Radio Drama Dept., until 1980 (joined BBC, 1948). Adapted numerous novels to radio drama, including The Spoils of Poynton, The Golden Bowl, Wuthering Heights, and The Idiot. *Publs:* The Lotus in the Sky, 1961; Choice of Arms, 1962; The Longest Way Round, 1963; Marxism and Moral Concepts, 1964; Ride a Paper Tiger, 1968; Take Off, 1969; Pickaxe and Rifle: The Story of the Albanian People, 1974; Morals and Politics: The Ethics of Revolution, 1977; A Red Square (autobiography), 1978; Incorporated, 1979; Right Side Up, 1984; The Way to Write Radio Drama, 1985. Add: Flat 9, Chenies House, 43 Moscow Rd., London W.2, England.

ASHBERY, John (Lawrence). American, b. 1927. Poetry; also, Novels/Short stories, Plays/Screenplays, Translations. Prof. of English, and Co-Dir. of the MFA Program in Creative Writing, Brooklyn College, New York, since 1974. Copywriter, Oxford Univ. Press, NYC, 1951–54, and McGraw-Hill Book Co., NYC, 1954–55; Art Critic, European Ed. of New York Herald Tribune, Paris, 1960–65, and Art Intnl., Lugano, Switzerland, 1961–64; Ed., Locus Solus mag., Lans-en-Vercors, France, 1960–62; Ed., Art and Literature, Paris, 1963–66; Paris Corresp., 1964–65, and Exec. Ed., 1966–72, Art News, NYC; Poetry Ed., Partisan Review, NYC, 1976–80; Art Critic, New York mag., 1978–80; Art Critic, Newsweek, New York, 1980–85. *Publs:* Turandot and Other Poems, 1953; Some Trees, 1956, 1970, 1978; The Poems, 1960; (trans.) Melville, by Jean-Jacques Mayoux, 1960; The Tennis Court Oath, 1962; (trans.) Alberto Giacometti, by Jacques Dupin, 1963; The Philosopher (play), 1964; Rivers and Mountains, 1966, 1977; Selected Poems, 1967; (co-ed.) American Literary Anthology 1, 1968; Sunrise in Suburbia, 1968; Three Madrigals, 1968; Fragment, 1969; (with James Schuyler) A Nest of Ninnies (novel), 1969, 1976; The Double Dream of Spring, 1970, 1976; The New Spirit, 1970; (with Lee Harwood & Tom Raworth) Penguin Modern Poets 19, 1971; Three Poems, 1972; (ed.) Penguin Modern Poets 24, 1973; (ed.) Muck Arbour, by Bruce Marcus, 1974; The Vermont Notebook, 1975; Self-Portrait in a Convex Mirror, 1975; Houseboat Days, 1977; Three Plays, 1978; As We Know, 1979; Shadow Train, 1981; Fairfield

Porter (non-fiction), 1983; (with others) R.B. Kitaj (non-fiction), 1983; A Wave, 1984; Selected Poems, 1985; April Galleons, 1987. Add: c/o Georges Borchardt Inc., 136 E. 57th St., New York, N.Y. 10022, U.S.A.

ASHBOLT, Allan (Campbell). Australian, b. 1921. Social commentary/phenomena. Dir., Left Book Club Cooperative, since 1989. Dir., Mercury Theatre, Sydney, 1946–49; Lectr. and Writer, Victorian Council of Adult Education, 1949–51; Drama Critic, Sydney Morning Herald, 1951–56; Lectr. and Writer, Adult Education Dept., Sydney Univ., 1951–56; Book Reviewer, Sydney Morning Herald, 1951–57, 1961–70, 1984–88; Documentary Talks Producer, 1954–58, North American Corresp., 1958–61, Federal Talks Supvr., 1961–67; Head of Special Projects TV, 1967–69, and Dir. of Radio Special Projects, 1969–78, ABC, Sydney; Australian Corresp., New Statesman, London, 1969–78. Deputy Chmn. Council, Mitchell Coll. of Advanced Education, 1980–83; Chmn., Australian Soc. of Authors, 1981–84; Chmn., New South Wales Worker Cooperative Program, 1986–88. *Publs:* An American Experience, 1966; An Australian Experience, 1974. Add: 8 Monteith St., Turramurra, N.S.W., Australia 2074.

ASHBROOK, James Barbour. American, b. 1925. Theology/Religion. Prof. of Personality and Religion, Garrett-Evangelical Theological Seminary, Evanston, Ill., since 1982. Minister, South Congregational Church, Rochester, 1950–54, and First Baptist Church, Granville, Ohio, 1955–60; Prof. of Psychology and Theology, Colgate Rochester/Bexley Hall/Croxer Theological Schs., Rochester, N.Y., 1969–81 (Assoc. Prof., 1960–65); Prof. of Pastoral Theology, 1965–69). *Publs:* be/come Community (theology), 1971; In Human Presence—Hope (human relations), 1971; Humanitas: Human Becoming and Being Human, 1973; The Old Me and A New i (theology), 1974; Responding to Human Pain, 1975; (co-author) Christianity for Pious Skeptics, 1977; The Human Mind and the Mind of God: Theological Promise in Brain Research, 1984; (co-ed.) At the Point of Need: Living Human Experience, 1988; (ed.) Paul Tillich in Conversation, 1988; The Brain and Belief: Faith in the Light of Brain Research, 1988. Add: 2121 Sheridan Rd., Evanston, Ill, 60201, U.S.A.

ASHBY, Baron (of Brandon, Suffolk). Writes as Eric Ashby. British, b. 1904. Education, Engineering/Technology, Environmental science/Ecology. Lectr., Imperial Coll., London, 1931–35; Reader in Botany, Bristol Univ., 1935–37; Prof. of Botany, Univ. of Sydney, 1938–46; Harrison Prof. of Botany, and Dir. of the Botanical Labs., Univ. of Manchester, 1946–50; Pres. and Vice-Chancellor, Queen's Univ. of Belfast, 1950–59; Master of Clare Coll., Cambridge, 1959–75, and Vice-Chancellor of Cambridge Univ., 1967–69. Chmn., Australian National Research Council, 1940–42; Chmn., Northern Ireland Advisory Council for Education, 1953–58; Chmn., Scientific Grants Cttee., 1955–56, and Postgrad. Grants Cttee., 1956–60, Dept. of Scientific and Industrial Research; Vice Chmn., Assn. of Universities of the British Commonwealth, 1959–61; Member, Univ. Grants Cttee., 1959–67; Pres., British Assn. for the Advancement of Science, 1963; Member, Council of the Royal Soc., 1964–65; Chmn., Royal Commn. on Environmental Pollution, 1970–73; Trustee, British Museum, 1970–78. *Publs:* Environment and Plant Development, 1931; (with H. Ashby) English-German Botanical Terminology, 1938; Challenge to Education, 1946; Scientist in Russia, 1947; Science and the People, 1953; Technology and the Academics, 1958; Community of Universities, 1963; African Universities and Western Tradition, 1964; (with M. Anderson) Universities: British, Indian, African, 1966; (with M. Anderson) The Rise of the Student Estate, 1970; Masters and Scholars, 1970; Any Person, Any Study, 1971; Portrait of Haldane, 1974; Reconciling Man with the Environment, 1978; The Search for an Environmental Ethic, 1980; (with M. Anderson) The Politics of Clean Air, 1981. Add: 22 Eltisley Ave., Cambridge, England.

ASHBY, Cliff. (John Clifford Ashby). British, b. 1919. Novels/Short stories, Poetry. *Publs:* In the Vulgar Tongue (verse), 1968; The Old Old Story (novel), 1969; Howe and Why (novel), 1969; The Dogs of Dewsbury (verse), 1976; Lies and Dreams (verse), 1980; Plain Song (collected verse), 1985. Add: 27 Brunswick St., Heckmondwyke, W. Yorks, WF16 0LW, England.

ASHBY, Eric. *See* **ASHBY,** Baron.

ASHBY, Gwynneth Margaret. British, b. 1922. Children's fiction, Children's non-fiction. Freelance writer since 1945. *Publs:* Mystery of Coveside House, 1946; The Secret Ring, 1948; The Cruise of the Silver Spray, 1951; The Land and People of Sweden 1951; The Land and People of Belgium, 1955; Let's Look at Austria, 1966; Looking at Norway, 1967; Looking at Japan, 1969; Let's Go to Japan, 1980; Korean Village, 1986; A Family in South Korea, 1987. Add: 12D Blenheim Drive, De Havilland Way, Christchurch, Dorset, England.

ASHBY, Philip H(arrison). American, b. 1916. Theology/Religion. Prof. Emeritus, Princeton Univ., N.J., since 1978 (joined faculty, 1950; Asst. Dean of Coll., 1959–62; Chmn., Dept. of Religion, 1968–73; William H. Danforth Prof. of Religion, 1972–78). *Publs:* The Conflict of Religions, 1955; History and the Future of Religious Thought, 1963; Modern Trends in Hinduism, 1974. Add: 5216 Rockaway Beach, Bainbridge Island, Wash. 98110, U.S.A.

ASHE, Arthur (R., Jr.). American, b. 1943. Sports/Fitness. Former tennis star; currently, Lectr. and writer; Correspondent, ABC Sports. Pres., Players Enterprises Inc., since 1969. Tennis championships: U.S. Open, 1968; Australian Open, 1970; Wimbledon Men's Singles Championship, 1975. *Publs:* (with Clifford G. Gewecke, Jr.) Advantage Ashe, 1967; (with Frank Deford) Arthur Ashe: Portrait in Motion, 1975; (with Louie Robinson, Jr.) Getting Started in Tennis, 1977; (with Neil Amdur) Off the Court, 1981; A Hard Road to Glory: The History of the African–American Athlete since 1946, 3 vols., 1988. Add: 888 17th St. N.W., Washington, D.C. 20006, U.S.A.

ASHE, Geoffrey Thomas. British, b. 1923. History, Mythology/Folklore, Supernatural/Occult topics, Writing/Journalism. Secty., Camelot Research Cttee., London, since 1965. Lectr. in Polish, Univ. Coll., London, 1948–50; Administrative Asst., Ford Motor Co. of Canada, 1952–54; Lectr. in Mgmt. Studies Polytechnic, London, 1956–68. *Publs:* The Tale of the Tub, 1950; King Arthur's Avalon, 1957; From Caesar to Arthur, 1960; Land to the West, 1962; The Land and the Book, 1965; Gandhi, 1968; (ed.) The Quest for Arthur's Britain, 1968; All About King Arthur (in U.S. as King Arthur in Fact and Legend), 1969; Camelot and the Vision of Albion, 1971; The Art of Writing Made Simple, 1972; The Finger and the Moon, 1973; Do What You Will, 1974; The Virgin, 1976; The Ancient Wisdom, 1977; Miracles, 1978; A Guidebook to Arthurian Britain, 1980; Kings and Queens of Early Britain, 1982; Avalonian Quest, 1982; The Discovery of King Arthur, 1985; (assoc. ed.) The Arthurian Encyclopaedia, 1986; The Landscape of King Arthur, 1987; (with others) The Arthurian Handbook, 1988. Add: Chalice Orchard, Well House Lane, Glastonbury, Somerset BA6 8BJ, England.

ASHER, John Alexander. New Zealander, b. 1921. Language/Linguistics, Literature. Prof. of German, and Head of Dept. of Germanic Languages and Literature, Univ. of Auckland, since 1962 (Lectr., Sr. Lectr., Assoc. Prof. of German, 1948–62). Co-Ed. of Australisch-Neuseelandische Studien zur deutschen Sprache und Literatur. *Publs:* The Framework of German, 1951, 12th ed. 1985; Der guote Gerhart von Rudolf von Ems, 1962, 3rd ed. 1989; A Short Descriptive Grammar of Middle High German, 1967; 3rd ed. 1981. Add: 27 New Windsor Rd., Avondale, Auckland, New Zealand.

ASHFORD, Jeffrey. *See* **JEFFRIES,** Roderic.

ASHLEY, Bernard. British, b. 1935. Children's fiction, Children's non-fiction. Head-teacher, Charlton Manor Jr. Sch., London, since 1977. Served in the R.A.F., 1953–55; Teacher, Kent Education Cttee, Gravesend, 1957–65, Hertfordshire Education Cttee., Hertford Heath, 1965–71, and Hartley Jr. Sch., Newham, London, 1971–76. *Publs:* Don't Run Away (reader), 1965; Wall of Death (reader), 1966; Space Shot (reader), 1967; The Big Escape (reader), 1967; The Men and the Boats: Britain's Life-Boat Service, 1968; Weather Men, 1970, 1974; The Trouble with Donovan Croft, 1974; Terry on the Fence, 1975; All My Men, 1977; A Kind of Wild Justice, 1978; Break in the Sun, 1980; I'm Trying to Tell You (short stories), 1981; Dinner Ladies Don't Count, 1981; Dodgem, 1981; Linda's Lie, 1982; High Pavements Blues, 1983; Your Guess Is as Good as Mine, 1983; A Bit of Give and Take, 1984; Janey, 1985; Running Scared, 1986; Bad Blood, 1988; The Clipper Street series, 1988–89; The Country Boy, 1989. Add: 128 Heathwood Gardens, London SE7 8ER, England.

ASHLEY, Jack. British, b. 1922. Autobiography/Memoirs/Personal. Labour M.P. (U.K.) for Stoke-on-Trent South since 1966. Founder and Pres., Hearing Research Trust, 1985. Labourer and crane driver, 1936–46; Shop Steward, Convenor and National Exec. Member, Chemical Worker's Union, 1946; BBC radio producer 1951–57, and television producer. *Publs:* Journey into Silence, 1973. Add: c/o House of Commons, London SW1A 0AA, England.

ASHLEY, Leonard R(aymond) N(elligan). American, b. 1928. Language and Linguistics, Literature, Military/Defence. Prof. of English, Brooklyn Coll., City Univ. of New York, since 1972 (Instr., 1961–65; Asst. Prof., 1965–68; Assoc. Prof., 1968–71). Member, The Place Name Commn. of the United States, since 1987. Part-time faculty member, New Sch. for Social Research, NYC, 1962–72. Pres., American Soc. for Geolinguistics, 1984–85, and American Name Soc., 1979 and 1987; Member, Exec. Cttee., Intnl. Linguistics Assn., 1982–87. *Publs:* (with F.F. Liu) A Military History of Modern China, 1956; Colley Cibber, 1965; Nineteeth-Century British Drama, 1968, 1988; Authorship and Evidence: A Study of Attribution and the Renaissance Drama, 1968; (ed. with S.L. Astor) British Short Stories: Classics and Criticism, 1968; History of the Short Story, 1968; (ed.) A Narrative of the Life of Mrs. Charlotte Clarke, 1969; George Peele, 1970; Other People's Lives: 34 Stories, 1970; (ed.) Phantasms of the Living (2 vols.), 1970; (ed.) Reliques of Irish Poetry: A Memoir of Miss Brooke, 1970; (ed.) Shakespeare's Jest Book, 1970; (ed.) Suhrab and Rustam, 1972; (ed.) The Picture of Dorian Grey, 1972; (ed.) Ballad Poetry of Ireland, 1973; (ed.) Enriched Classics (11 vols. to date); Ripley's "Believe It or Not" Book of the Military, 1977; (ed.) Tales of Mystery and Melodrama, 1978; The Wonderful World of Superstition, Prophecy and Luck, 1983; The Wonderful World of Magic and Witchcraft, 1986; The Amazing World of Superstition, Prophecy, Luck, Magic and Witchcraft, 1988; Elizabethan Popular Culture, 1988. Add: 1901 Ave. H, Brooklyn, N.Y. 11230, U.S.A.

ASHLEY, Maurice. British, b. 1907. History, Biography. Historical Research Asst. to Sir Winston Churchill, 1929–33; Staff member, Manchester Guardian, 1933–37; Staff member, Times newspaper, 1937–39; Ed., Britain Today, 1939–40; Deputy Ed., 1946–58, and Ed. 1958–67, The Listener mag.; Research Fellow, Loughborough Univ. of Technology, 1968–70. *Publs:* Financial and Commercial Policy Under the Cromwellian Protectorate, 1934, 1962; Oliver Cromwell, 1937; Marlborough, 1939; Louis XVI and the Greatness of France, 1946; John Wildman: Plotter and Postmaster, 1947; Mr. President, 1948; England in the Seventeenth Century, 1952, 1978; Cromwell's Generals, 1954; The Greatness of Oliver Cromwell, 1957, 1967; Oliver Cromwell and the Puritan Revolution, 1958; Great Britain to 1688, 1966, 1968; Churchill as Historian, 1968; A Golden Century 1598-1715, 1969; (ed.) Cromwell: Great Lives Observed, 1969; Charles II: The Man and the Statesman, 1971; Oliver Cromwell and His World, 1972; The Life and Times of King John, 1972; The Life and Times of King William I, 1973; A History of Europe 1648-1815, 1973; The Age of Absolutism, 1974; Rupert of the Rhine, 1976; General Monck, 1977; James II, 1978; The House of Stuart, 1980; The People of England, 1982; Charles I and Oliver Cromwell, 1987. Add: 2 Elm Court, Cholmeley Park, London N6 5EJ, England.

ASHMORE, Owen. British, b. 1920. Archaeology/Antiquities, History. Dir. of Extra-Mural Studies, Univ. of Manchester, 1976–83 (Resident Staff Tutor, 1950–62; Deputy Dir., 1962–69; Assoc. Dir., 1969–73; Acting Dir., 1973–76). *Publs:* The Development of Power in Britain, 1967; Industrial Archaeology of Lancashire, 1969; The Industrial Archaeology of Stockport, 1975; (ed.) Historic Industries of Marple and Mellor, 1977; The Industrial Archaeology of North West England, 1982. Add: 5 Flowery Field, Woodsmoor, Stockport, Cheshire SK2 7ED, England.

ASHTON, Dore. American. Art, Biography. Prof. of Art History, The Cooper Union, NYC. Assoc. Ed., 1951–54, and Contrib. Ed., since 1965, Arts mag. (formerly Art Digest). Art Critic, New York Times, NYC, 1955–60; Art History Instr., Pratt Inst., 1962–64. *Publs:* Abstract Art Before Columbus, 1957; Poets and the Past, 1959; Philip Guston, 1960; (co-author) Redon, Moreau, Bresdin, 1961; The Unknown Shore, 1962; Rauschenberg's Dante, 1964; Modern American Sculpture, 1968; A Reading of Modern Art, 1969; Richard Lindner, 1969; The Sculpture of Pol Bury, 1971; Picasso on Art, 1972; The New York School: A Cultural Reckoning, 1973; A Joseph Cornell Album, 1974; Yes, But . . . A Critical Biography of Philip Guston, 1976; A Fable of Modern Art, 1980; (with Denise Browne Hare) Rosa Bonheur: A Life and a Legend, 1981; American Art since 1945, 1982; About Rothko, 1983; Twentieth Century Artists on Art, 1985; Out of the Whirlwind, 1987; Fragonard in the Universe of Painting, 1988. Add: 217 East 11th St., New York, N.Y. 10003, U.S.A.

ASHTON, Elizabeth. Historical/Romance/Gothic. *Publs:* The Pied Tulip, 1969; The Benevolent Despot, 1970; Parisian Adventure, 1970; Cousin Mark, 1971; The Enchanted Wood, 1971; Sweet Simplicity, 1971; Flutter of White Wings, 1972; A Parade of Peacocks, 1972; Scorched Wings, 1972; The Rocks of Arachenza, 1973; Sigh No More, 1973; The Bells of Bruges, 1973; Alpine Rhapsody, 1973; Errant Bride, 1973; Moorland Magic, 1973; Dark Angel, 1974; The House of the Eagles, 1974; Dangerous to Know, 1974; The Road to the Border, 1974; The Scent of Sandalwood, 1974; Miss Nobody from Nowhere, 1975; The Willing Hostage, 1975; Crown of Willow, 1975; The Player King, 1975; Sanctuary in the Desert, 1976; My Lady Disdain, 1976; Mountain Heritage, 1976; Lady in the Limelight, 1976; Aegean Quest, 1977; Voyage of Enchantment, 1977; Green Harvest, 1977; Breeze from the Bosphorous, 1978; The Garden of the Gods, 1978; The Golden Girl, 1978; The Questing Heart, 1978; Rendezvous in Venice, 1978; The Joyous Adventure, 1979; Moonlight on the Nile, 1979; Reluctant Partnership, 1979; Borrowed Plumes, 1980; The Rekindled Flame, 1980; Sicilian Summer, 1980; Silver Arrow, 1980; Rebel Against Love, 1981; Egyptian Honeymoon, 1981; White Witch, 1982. Add: c/o Mills and Boon Ltd., Eton House, 18-24 Paradise Rd., Richmond, Surrey TW9 1SR, England.

ASHTON, Robert. British, b. 1924. History. Prof. of English History, Univ. of East Anglia, Norwich, 1963–89 (Dean, Sch. of English Studies, 1964–67). Asst. Lectr. in Economic History, 1952–54, Lectr., 1954–61, and Sr. lectr., 1961, Univ. of Nottingham; Visiting Fellow, All Souls Coll., Oxford, 1973 and 1987. *Publs:* The Crown and the Money Market 1603-1640, 1960; James I by His Contemporaries, 1969; The English Civil War, 1978; The City and the Court 1603-1643, 1979; Reformation and Revolution 1558-1660, 1984. Add: The Manor Hse., Brundall, Norwich, England.

ASIMOV, Isaac. American, b. 1920. Mystery/Crime/Suspense, Science fiction/Fantasy, History, Literature, Sciences, Biography, Humor/Satire. *Publs:* novels—Pebble in the Sky, 1950; I Robot, 1950; The Stars, Like Dust, 1951; Foundation, 1951; Foundation and Empire, 1952; The Currents of Space, 1952; David Starr, Space Ranger, 1952; Second Foundation, 1953; Lucky Starr and the Pirates of the Asteroids, 1953; The Caves of Steel, 1954; Lucky Starr and the Oceans of Venus, 1954; The End of Eternity, 1955; Lucky Starr and the Big Sun of Mercury, 1956; The Naked Sun, 1957; Lucky Starr and the Moons of Jupiter, 1957; Lucky Starr and the Rings of Saturn, 1958; The Rest of the Robots, 1964; Fantastic Voyage, 1966; A Whiff of Death, 1968; The Gods Themselves, 1972; Murder at the ABA, 1976; Foundation's Edge, 1982; The Robots of Dawn, 1983; (with Janet Asimov) Norby, the Mixed-Up Robot, 1983; (with Janet Asimov) Norby's Other Secret, 1984; (with Janet Asimov) Norby and the Lost Princess, 1985; Robots and Empire, 1985; (with Janet Asimov) Norby and the Invaders, 1985; Foundation and Earth, 1986; (with Janet Asimov) Norby and the Queen's Necklace, 1986; short stories—The Martian Way and Other Stories, 1955; Earth Is Room Enough, 1957; Nine Tomorrows: Tale of the Near Future, 1959; Through a Glass, Clearly, 1967; Asimov's Mysteries, 1968; Nightfall and Other Stories, 1969; The Early Asimov: or, Eleven Years of Trying, 1972; Tales of the Black Widowers, 1974; Buy Jupiter and Other Stories, 1975; The Bicentennial Man, and Other Stories, 1976; More Tales of the Black Widowers, 1976; Casebook of the Black Widowers, 1980; The Winds of Change and Other Stories, 1983; The Union Club Mysteries, 1983; Banquets of the Black Widowers, 1984; The Edge of Tomorrow, 1985; The Disappearing Man and Other Stories, 1985; The Alternate Asimovs, 1986; Best Science Fiction of Isaac Asimov, 1986; Best Mysteries of Isaac Asimov, 1986; Robot Dreams, 1986; other—(with B. Walker and W. Boyd) Biochemistry and Human Metabolism, 1952; Chemicals of Life: Enzymes, Vitamins, Hormones, 1954; (with W. Boyd) Races and People, 1955; (with B. Walker and M. Nicholas) Chemistry and Human Health, 1956; Inside the Atom, 1956; Building Blocks of the Universe, 1957; Only a Trillion, 1957; The World of Carbon, 1958; The World of Nitrogen, 1958; The Clock We Live On, 1959; The Living River, 1959, rev. ed. as The Bloodstream: River of Life, 1961; The Realm of Numbers, 1959; Worlds of Science, 1959; Break-throughs in Science, 1960; The Kingdom of the Sun, 1960; The Realm of Measure, 1960; Satellites in Outer Space, 1960; The Double Planet, 1960; The Wellsprings of Life, 1960; The Realm of Algebra, 1961; Words from the Myths, 1961; Fact and Fancy, 1962; Life and Energy, 1962; The Search for the Elements, 1962; Words in Genesis, 1962; Words on the Map, 1962; View from a Height, 1963; The Genetic Code, 1963; The Human Body: Its Structure and Operation, 1963; The Kite That Won the Revolution, 1963; Words from the Exodus, 1963; Adding a Dimension: 17 Essays on the History of Science, 1964; The Human Brain: Its Capabilities and Functions, 1964; Quick and Easy Math, 1964; A Short History of Biology, 1964; (with S. Dole) Planets for Man, 1964; Asimov's Biographical Encyclopedia of Science and Technology, 1964, rev. ed. 1974; An Easy Introduction to the Slide Rule, 1964; The Greeks: A Great Adventure, 1965; Of Time and Space and Other Things, 1965; A Short History of Chemistry, 1965; The Neutrino: Ghost Particle of the Atom, 1966; The Genetic Effects of Radiation, 1966; The Noble Gases, 1966; The Roman Republic, 1966; Understanding Physics, 1966; The Universe: From Flat Earth to Quasar, 1966; The Roman Empire, 1967; The Moon, 1967; Is Anyone There?, 1967; To the Ends of the Universe, 1967, rev. ed. 1975; The Egyptians, 1967; Mars, 1967; From Earth to

Heaven: 17 Essays on Science, 1967; Environments Out There, 1968; Science Numbers and I: Essays on Science, 1968; The Near East: 10,000 Years of History, 1968; Asimov's Guide to the Bible Vol. I, The Old Testament, 1968, Vol. II, The New Testament, 1969; The Dark Ages, 1968; Galaxies, 1968; Stars, 1968; Words from History, 1968; Photosynthesis, 1969; Twentieth Century Discovery, 1969; Opus 100, 1969; ABCs of Space, 1969; Great Ideas of Science, 1969; The Solar System and Back, 1970; Asimov's Guide to Shakespeare (2 vols.) 1970; Constantinople, 1970; ABCs of the Ocean, 1970; Light, 1970; Stars in Their Courses, 1971; What Makes the Sun Shine, 1971; Isaac Asimov Treasury of Humor, 1971; The Sensuous Dirty Old Man, 1971; Possible Tomorrows: Science Fiction, 1972; How Did We Find Out the Earth Was Round?, 1972; The Story of Ruth, 1972; Today, Tomorrow, and . . ., 1973; Please Explain, 1973; The Best of Isaac Asimov (1939–1972), 1973; The Tragedy of the Moon, 1973; The Shaping of North America; From the Earliest Times to 1763, 1973; Jupiter the Largest Planet, 1973; Comets and Meteors, 1973; The Sun, 1973; Asimov on Astronomy, 1974; Asimov on Chemistry, 1974; Earth: Our Crowded Spaceship, 1974; The Birth of the United States 1763-1816, 1974; Birth and Death of the Universe, 1975; World is Room Enough, 1975; Eyes on the Universe: A History of the Telescope, 1975; Lecherous Limericks, 1975; Science Past—Science Future, 1975; The Ends of the Earth: The Polar Regions of the World, 1975; Before the Golden Age, 1975; The Heavenly Host, 1975; How Did We Find Out About Energy?, 1975; Our Federal Union: The United States from 1816 to 1865, 1975; Asimov Guide to Science (2 vols.), 1975; Asimov on Physics, 1976; The Collapsing Universe: The Story of Black Holes, 1976; Lecherous Limericks, 1976; More Lecherous Limericks, 1976; Murder at the A.B.A. (in UK as Authorised Murder), 1976; I, Rabbit (juvenile novel), 1976; How Did We Find Out about Atoms, 1976; Asimov on Physics, 1976; The Planet That Wasn't, 1976; How Did We Find Out about Nuclear Power, 1976; The Key Word and Other Mysteries (juvenile fiction), 1977; Still More Lecherous Lyrics, 1977; Asimov on Numbers, 1977; How Did We Find Out about Outer Space, 1977; The Beginning of the End, 1977; The Golden Door, 1977; Asimov's Sherlockian Limericks, 1978; (with John Ciardi) Limericks: Too Gross, 1978; Quasar, Quasar Burning Bright, 1978; Animals of the Bible, 1978; Life and Time, 1978; Asimov's Fantastic Facts, 1978; Worlds Within Worlds, 1978; In Memory Yet Green (autobiography), 1979; Extraterrestrial Civilizations, 1979; Opus 200, 1979; The Road to Infinity, 1979; In Joy Still Felt (autobiography), 1980; The Annotated Gulliver's Travels, 1980; How Did We Find Out About Coal, 1980; In the Beginning, 1981; Asimov on Science Fiction, 1981; Venus: Near Neighbor of the Sun, 1981; How Did We Find Out About Solar Power, 1981; How Did We Find Out About Volcanoes, 1981; Visions of the Universe, 1981; The Sun Shines Bright, 1981; Change!, 1981; (with John Ciardi) A Glossary of Limericks, 1981; How Did We Find Out About Life in the Deep Sea?, 1982; Exploring the Earth and the Cosmos, 1982; How Did We Find Out About the Beginning of Life, 1982; How Did We Find Out About the Universe, 1982; Counting the Eons, 1983; The Roving Mind, 1983; The Measure of the Universe, 1983; How Did We Find Out About Genes, 1983; X Stands For Unknown, 1984; How Did We Find Out About Computers, 1984; Opus 300, 1984; Limericks For Children, 1984; Asimov's New Guide to Science, 1984; How Did We Find Out About Robots, 1984; Asimov's Guide to Halley's Comet, 1985; Exploding Suns, 1985; How Did We Find Out About the Atmosphere, 1985; The Subatomic Monster, 1985; How Did We Find Out About DNA, 1985; The Dangers of Intelligence, 1986; How Did We Find Out About the Speed of Light, 1986; Future Days, 1986; Far as Human Eye Could See, 1987; How Did We Find Out About Blood, 1987; Past, Present and Future, 1987; How Did We Find Out About Sunshine, 1987; How to Enjoy Writing, 1987; Norby Finds a Villain, 1987; Fantastic Voyage II: Destination Brain, 1987; How Did We Find Out About the Brain, 1987; Did Comets Kill the Dinosaurs?, 1987; Beginnings, 1987; Asimov's Annotated Gilbert and Sullivan, 1988; How Did We Find Out About Superconductivity, 1988; Other Worlds of Isaac Asimov: Relativity of Wrong, 1988; Prelude to Foundation, 1988; Asteroids, 1988; Earth's Moon, 1988; Mars: Our Mysterious Neighbor, 1988; Our Milky Way and Other Galaxies, 1988; Quasars, Pulsars and Black Holes, 1988; Rockets, Probes and Satellites, 1988; Our Solar System, 1988; Sun, 1988; Uranus: The Sideways Planet, 1988; Azazel, 1988; Saturn: The Ringed Beauty, 1988; How Was the Universe Born?, 1988; Earth: Our Home Base, 1988; Ancient Astronomy, 1988; Unidentified Flying Objects, 1988; The Space Spotters Guide, 1988; Norby Down to Earth, 1988. Add: 10 W. 66th St., New York, N.Y. 10023, U.S.A.

ASINOF, Eliot. American, b. 1919. Novels/Short stories, Social commentary/phenomena, Sports/Physical education/Keeping fit. *Publs:* Man on Spikes, 1955; Eight Men Out, 1963, 1981; The Bedfellow, 1967; Seven Days to Sunday, 1968; The Name of the Game is Murder, 1968; People vs Blutcher, 1968; Craig and Joan, 1971; (with W. Hinckle and W. Turner) The Ten Second Jailbreak, 1973; The Fox is Crazy Too, 1976; Say It Ain't So, Gordon Littlefield, 1977; Bleeding Between the Lines, 1979; Eight Men Out: The Black Sox and the 1919 World Series, 1987. Add: 255 West End Ave., New York, N.Y. 10023, U.S.A.

ASMAN, James. British, b. 1914. Music. Company Dir., James Asman Ltd. (Gramophone Record Retailers), London. Record Critic and Writer, Records & Recording, London; National Secty., National Fedn. of Jazz Orgs. (Great Britain). Ed., Jazz Record mag., Jazz Appreciation Soc., 1943–46; former jazz and folkmusic columnist, Daily Mirror, Musical Express, Record Mirror, London Review, Jazz Journal, etc. *Publs:* (co-ed.) Jazz on Record, 1944; (co-ed.) Jazz, 1944; (co-ed) Jazz Writings, 1945; (co-ed.) Jazz Today, 1945; (co-ed.) American Jazz, vols. 1 and 2, 1945; (ed. and compiler) N.F.J.O. Blue Book, 1953; (with others) The Decca Book of Jazz, 1958; (with Martin Lindsay) Teach Yourself Jazz, 1964. Add: Flat 27, Clare Court, Judd St., London WC1, England.

ASPREY, Robert Brown. American, b. 1923. Military/Defence, Biography. *Publs:* The Panther's Feast, 1959; The First Battle of the Marne, 1962; (with A.A. Vandegrift) Once a Marine, 1964; At Belleau Wood, 1965; Semper Fidelis, 1967; War in the Shadows: The Guerrilla in History, 2 vols., 1977; Operation Prophet, 1977; The Magnificent Enigma: Frederick the Great of Prussia, 1986. Add: Apartamentos Tenis, Bloque 24-A-8, Sotogrande (Cadiz), Spain.

ASPRIN, Robert (Lynn). American, b. 1946. Sciencefiction/Fantasy, Mythology/Folklore. Freelance writer since 1978. Accounts Clerk, 1966–70, Payroll Analyst, 1970–74, and Cost Accountant, 1974–78, University Microfilm, Ann Arbor. *Publs:* The Cold Cash War, 1977; Another Fine Myth, 1978; The Bug Wards, 1979; Tambu, 1979; (with George Takei) Mirror Friend, Mirror Foe, 1979; (ed.) Thieve's World, 1979; Myth Conceptions, 1979; (ed.) Storm Season, 1982; Hit or Myth, 1983; Myth-ing Persons, 1984; The Face of Chaos, 1984; Shadows of Sanctuary, 1984; Tales from the Vulgar Unicorn, 1984; (ed. with Lynn Abbey) Birds of Prey, 1984; (ed. with Lynn Abbey) Wings of Omen, 1984; Myth Directions, 1985; Myth Adventures Two, 1986; (with Kay Reynolds) Myth Inc. Link, 1986; Thieve's World, 1986; Myth-Nomers and Im-Pervections, 1987; Duncan and Mallory: The Raiders, 1988. Add: c/o Kirby McCauley Ltd., 432 Park Ave., S., Suite 1509, New York, NY 10016, U.S.A.

ASQUITH, Nan. Pseud. for Nancy Evelyn Pattinson. British. Historical/Romance/Gothic. Has worked as advertising copywriter. *Publs:* My Dream Is Yours, in Can. as Doctor Robert Comes Around, 1965; With All My Heart, 1954; Believe in To-morrow, 1955; Only My Heart to Give, 1955; The Certain Spring, 1956; Honey Island, 1957; The House on Brinden Water, 1958, in Can. as The Doctor is Engaged, 1962; The Time for Happiness, 1959; Time May Change, 1961; The Way the Wind Blows, 1963; The Quest, 1964; The Summer at San Milo, 1965; Dangerous Yesterday, 1967; The Garden of Persephone, 1967; The Admiral's House, 1969; Turn the Page, 1970; Beyond the Mountain, 1970; Carnival at San Cristobal, 1971; Out of the Dark, 1972; The Girl from Rome, 1973; The Sun in the Morning, 1974. Add: c/o Mills and Boon Ltd., Eton House, 18-24 Paradise Road, Richmond, Surrey TW9 1SR, England.

ASTLEY, Thea (Beatrice May). Australian, b. 1925. Novels/Short stories. Sr. Tutor, then Fellow, Sch. of English, Macquarie Univ., Sydney, since 1968. *Publs:* Girl with a Monkey, 1959; A Descant for Gossips, 1960; The Well-Dressed Explorer, 1962; The Slow Natives, 1965; A Boat Load of Home Folk, 1968; (ed.) Coast to Coast, 1969–70, 1971; The Acolyte, 1972; A Kindness Cup, 1974; Hunting the Wild Pineapple, 1979; An Item from the Late News, 1983; Beachmasters, 1985; It's Raining in Mango, 1987. Add: P.O. Box 213, Kuranda, Qld. 4872, Australia.

ASTOR, Gerald. American. Sex, Social commentary/phenomena. *Publs:* The Charge is Rape, 1974; Capitol Hell, 1974; A Question of Rape, 1974; (with A. Villano) Brick Agent, 1978; The Disease Detectives: Deadly Medical Mysteries and the People Who Solve Them, 1983; The "Last" Nazi: The Life and Times of Dr. Joseph Mengele, 1985. Add: c/o Pinnacle Books, 1 Century Plaza, 2029 Century Park East, Los Angeles, Calif. 90067, U.S.A.

ATHAS, Daphne. American, b. 1923. Novels/Short stories. Lectr. in Creative Writing, Univ. of North Carolina, Chapel Hill, since 1966. Fulbright Prof. of American Literature, Tehran Univ., Iran, 1973–74.

Publs: Weather of the Heart, 1947; The Fourth World, 1956; (with G. Campbell) Sit on the Earth (play), 1957; Greece by Prejudice, 1963; Entering Ephesus, 1971; Cora, 1978. Add: Box 224, Chapel Hill, N.C. 27514, U.S.A.

ATHOS, Anthony G(eorge). American, b. 1934. Business. Consultant. With Sch. of Business Admn., Harvard Univ., Boston, Mass., 1966–82 (Prof. of Organizational Behavior, 1970–82). *Publs:* (with Robert E. Coffey) Behavior in Organizations: A Multi-Dimensional View, 1968, 1975; (with Lewis B. Ward) Student Expectation of Corporate Life: Implications for Management Recruiting, 1972; (with John J. Gabarro) Interpersonal Behavior: Communication and Understanding in Relationships, 1978; (with Richard Tanner Pascale) The Art of Japanese Management: Applications for American Executives, 1981. Add: 9 Norwood Heights, Gloucester, Mass. 01930, U.S.A.

ATIYAH, P(atrick) S(elim). British, b. 1931. Law. Prof. of English Law, Oxford Univ., from 1977, retired 1988. Asst. Lectr., London School of Economics, 1954–55; Lectr., Univ. of Khartoum, 1955–59; Legal Asst., Bd. of Trade, 1961–64; Fellow, New Coll., Oxford, 1964–69; Prof. of Law, Australian Natl. Univ., Canberra, 1970–73, and Warwick Univ., Coventry, 1973–77. *Publs:* The Sale of Goods, 1957, 7th ed., 1985; Introduction to the Law of Contract, 1961, 3rd ed., 1981; Vicarious Liability, 1967; Accidents, Compensation, and the Law, 1970, 3rd ed., 1980; The Rise and Fall of Freedom of Contract, 1979; Promises, Morals, and Law, 1981. Add: 9 Sheepway Court, Iffley, Oxford, England.

ATKIN, Flora B. American, b. 1919. Plays. Lectr. and consultant on children's theatre at universities and conferences, since 1979. Dir., Recreational Arts Dept., 1940–44, and Founding Dir., Creative Arts Day Camp, 1941–44, Jewish Community Center, Washington, D.C.; Instr. in Dance Education, Howard Univ., Washington, D.C., 1942–43; free-lance creative arts educator and children's theatre dir., 1953–80; Founding Dir. and Playwright, In-School Players, Adventure Theatre, Montgomery County, Md., 1969–79. *Publs:* Tarradiddle Tales, 1969; Tarradiddle Travels, 1970; Golliwhoppers!, 1972; Skupper-Duppers, 1974; Dig 'n Tel, 1977; Grampo/Scampo, 1981; Shoorik and Puffik, 1983; Hold That Tiger, 1986. Add: 5507 Uppingham St., Chevy Chase, Md. 20815, U.S.A.

ATKINS, John Alfred. British, b. 1916. Novels/Short stories, Science fiction/Fantasy, Literature, Biography. Lectr. in English, Univ. of Libya, Benghazi, 1968–70; Docent, Univ. of Lodz, Poland, 1970–76. *Publs:* Cat on Hot Bricks (novel), 1950; The Art of Ernest Hemingway, 1952; George Orwell, 1953; Rain and the River (novel), 1954; Arthur Koestler, 1956; Aldous Huxley, 1956; Tomorrow Revealed, 1957; Graham Greene, 1957; (with J.B. Pick) Land Fit for Eros (novel), 1957; Sex in Literature (4 vols.), 1970–82; Six Novelists Look at Society, 1977; J.B. Priestley, The Last of the Sages, 1981; The British Spy Novel, 1984. Add: Braeside Cottage, Birch Green, Birch, Colchester, Essex CO2 0NH, England.

ATKINS, Kenneth R(obert). British, b. 1920. Physics. Prof. of Physics, Univ. of Pennsylvania, Philadelphia, since 1954. Fellow of Trinity Coll., Cambridge, 1948–52; Assoc. Prof. of Physics, Univ. of Toronto, 1951–54. *Publs:* Liquid Helium, 1959; Physics, 1965, 3rd ed. 1976; Physics Once Over Lightly, 1972; (with John R. Holum and Arthur N. Strahler) Essentials of Physical Science, 1978. Add: 555 Colonel Dewees Rd., Wayne, Pa. 19087, U.S.A.

ATKINS, Meg Elizabeth. Has also written as Elizabeth Moore. British. us-Novels/Short stories, Children's fiction. *Publs:* (as Elizabeth Moore) Something to Jump For (children's fiction), 1960; The Gemini, 1963; Shadows of the House, 1968; By the North Door, 1975; Samain, 1976; Kestrels in the Kitchen, 1979; Haunted Warwickshire, 1981; Palimpsest, 1982; The Folly, 1987; Tangle, 1988. Add: 16 Hambleton Ave., Northallerton, N. Yorks. DL7 8SW, England.

ATKINS, Russell. American, b. 1926. Plays/Screenplays, Poetry, Music. Creative Writing Instr., Karamu House and Theatre, since 1971. Ed., Free Lance Mag., since 1950. Member, Ohio Arts Council, 1974–75. *Publs:* Psychovisual Perspective for Musical Composition, 1956, 3rd ed. 1969; Phenomena (poetry and play), 1961; Objects (poetry), 1963; Heretofore (poetry and play), 1968; Here In The (poetry), 1976; Whichever, 1978. Add: 6005 Grand Ave., Cleveland, Ohio 44104, U.S.A.

ATKINS, Stuart. American, b. 1914. Literature, Translations. Emeritus Prof. of German, Univ. of California, Santa Barbara, since 1984 (Prof., 1965–84). Staff member, Dartmouth Coll, Hanover, N.H., 1938–

41; Asst. Prof., Assoc. Prof., and Prof., Harvard Univ., Cambridge, Mass., 1941–65. Pres., Modern Language Assn. of America, 1972. *Publs:* The Testament of Werther in Poetry and Drama, 1949; Goethe's Faust: A Literary Analysis, 1958, 3rd ed. 1969; (ed.) Goethe's Faust: Bayard Taylor Translation, revised, 2 vols., 1962; (ed.) The Age of Goethe: An Anthology of German Literature, 1969; (ed. with O. Schoenberg) Heinrich Heine: Werke Band I, 1973; (ed. with O. Boeck) Heinrich Heine: Werke Band II, 1978; (ed.) Goethe: Torquato Tasso, 1977; (ed. and trans.) Goethe: Faust I and II, 1984. Add: Univ. of Calfornia, Santa Barbara, Calif. 93106, U.S.A.

ATKINSON, Anthony Barnes. British, b. 1944. Economics, Social Commentary. Prof. of Economics, London Sch. of Economics, since 1980. Ed., Journal of Public Economics, since 1972. Prof. of Economics, Univ. of Essex, 1970–76; Prof. and Head of Dept. of Political Economy, University College, London, 1976–79. *Publs:* Poverty in Britain and the Reform of Social Security, 1969; Unequal Shares, 1972; The Economics of Inequality, 1975; (with A.J. Harrison) Distribution of Personal Wealth in Britain, 1978; (with J.E. Stiglitz) Lectures on Public Economics, 1980; Social Justice and Public Policy, 1983; (with A. Maynard and C. Trinder) Parents and Children, 1985; (with J. Micklewright) Unemployment Benefits and Unemployment Duration, 1988; Poverty and Social Security, 1989. Add: 33 Hurst Green, Brightlingsea, Colchester, Essex, England.

ATKINSON, Frank. Also writes as Robert Shallow and Frank Curnow. British, b. 1922. Education, Librarianship, Literature, Media. Librarian, St. Paul's Cathedral, London, since 1981. Lending Librarian, Hampstead Central Library, London, 1953–60; Lectr., Brighton Sch. of Librarianship, 1960–61; Teacher, Kingston upon Hull Schools, 1961–65; Tutor-Librarian, Berkshire Coll. of Education, 1965–67; Librarian, City of London, 1967–81. *Publs:* The English Newspaper since 1900: A Bibliography, 1960; (with Derick Unwin) The Computer in Education, 1968; The Public Library, 1970; (with J. Fines) Yesterday's Money, 1971; Librarianship: An Introduction to the Profession, 1974; (with J. Matthews) Illustrated Teach Yourself Coin Collecting, 1975; Dictionary of Pseudonyms and Pen-Names, 1975, as Dictionary of Literary Pseudonyms, 1977, 1981, 1987; The Best of Robert Shallow, 1976; Fiction Librarianship, 1980; St. Paul's and the City, 1985. Add: The Library, St. Paul's Cathedral, London EC4M 8AE, England.

ATKINSON, James. British, b. 1914. Theology/Religion. Dir., Centre for Reformation Studies, Univ. of Sheffield; Canon Theologian of Sheffield Cathedral, since 1970. Reader in Theology, Univ. of Hull, 1956–67; Prof. of Biblical Studies, Univ. of Sheffield, 1967–79; Theological Adviser to Archbishop of Canterbury, 1955–79. *Publs:* Luther's Early Theological Works, 1962; Rome and Reformation, 1965; Luther and the Birth of Protestantism, 1968, 1982; The Reformation, 1968; The Trial of Luther, 1971; Erasmus of Rotterdam (television script), 1974; Martin Luther, Prophet to the Church Catholic, 1984; The Darkness of Faith, 1987. Add: Leach House, Hathersage, Derbyshire, England.

ATKINSON, R(ichard) S(tuart). British, b. 1927. Medicine, Psychology, Biography. Consultant Anaesthetist, North-East Thames Regional Health Authority, since 1961. *Publs:* (with J.A. Lee) A Synopsis of Anaesthesia, 7th ed. 1973, 9th ed. 1982, 10th ed. 1987; James Simpson and Chloroform, 1973; (co-ed.) Recent Advances in Anaesthesia and Analgesia—15, 1985; (with J.A. Lee) Sir Robert Macintosh's Lumbar Puncture and Spinal Analgesia, 5th ed. 1985. Add: 75 High Cliff Dr., Leigh on Sea, Essex SS9 1DQ, England.

ATKINSON, Ronald Field. British, b. 1928. Human relations, Philosophy. Prof. of Philosophy, Univ. of Exeter, since 1979. Lectr. in Philosophy, Univ. of Keele, Staffs., 1954–67; Prof. of Philosophy, Univ. of York, 1967–79. *Publs:* Sexual Morality, 1965; Conduct: An Introduction to Moral Philosophy, 1969; Knowledge and Explanation in History, 1978. Add: Dept. of Philosophy, University of Exeter, Exeter EX4 4QH, England.

ATLEE, Philip. *See* **PHILIPS,** James Atlee.

ATTENBOROUGH, (Sir) David (Frederick). British, b. 1926. Natural history, Travel/Exploration/Adventure. Broadcaster. Joined BBC, 1952: Zoological and filming expeditions in Sierra Leone, 1954, Indonesia, 1956, South West Pacific, 1959, Madagascar, 1960, Northern Australia, 1962, Zambesi, 1964, Bali, 1969, New Guinea, 1971, and Borneo, 1973; Controller, BBC 2 TV, 1965–68; Dir. of Progs., BBC TV, 1969–72. *Publs:* Zoo Quest to Guiana, 1956; Zoo Quest for a Dragon, 1957; Zoo Quest in Paraguay, 1959; Quest in Paradise, 1960; Zoo Quest in Madagascar, 1961; Quest Under Capricorn, 1963; The Tribal Eye, 1977;

Life on Earth, 1979; The Living Planet, 1984, 1985; The First Eden, 1987. Add: BBC TV Centre, London W12, England.

ATTHILL, Robin. (Robert Anthony Atthill). British, b. 1912. Poetry. Archaeology/Antiquities, History, Transportation. English Teacher, Downside Sch., Somerset, 1948–82. *Publs:* If Pity Departs (poetry), 1947; The Curious Past, 1955; Old Mendip, 1964; (with O.S. Nock) The Somerset and Dorset Railway, 1967; (with Ivo Peters) The Picture History of the Somerset and Dorset, 1970; Mendip: A New Study, 1976. Add: Stoneleigh Cottage, Oakhill, Bath, Somerset, England.

ATWOOD, Ann. American, b. 1913. Children's fiction, Children's non-fiction. *Publs:* The Little Circle, 1967; New Moon Cove, 1969; (with Elizabeth Hazelton) Sammy, The Crow Who Remembered, 1969; The Wild Young Desert, 1970; Haiku: The Mood of Earth, 1971; The Kingdom of the Forest, 1972; My Own Rhythm, 1973; For All That Lives, 1975; Haiku: Vision, 1977; (with Gunther Klinge) Drifting with the Moon, 1978; Fly with the Wind, 1979; (trans.) Day into Night: A Haiku Journey, by Gunther Klinge, 1980. Has also produced numerous educational filmstrips on nature and haiku poetry. Add: c/o Charles Scribner's Sons, 597 Fifth Ave., New York, N.Y. 10017, U.S.A.

ATWOOD, Margaret (Eleanor). Canadian, b. 1939. Novels/Short stories, Poetry, Literature. Lectr. in English, Univ. of British Columbia, Vancouver, 1964–65; Instr. in English, Sir George Williams Univ., Montreal, 1967–68. *Publs:* Double Persephone, 1961; The Circle Game, 1964, rev. ed. 1966; Talismans for Children, 1965; Kaleidoscopes: Baroque, 1965; Speeches for Doctor Frankenstein, 1966; The Animals in that Country, 1968; The Edible Women (novel), 1969; (with others) Five Modern Canadian Poets, 1970; The Journals of Susanna Moodie: Poems, 1970; Procedures for Underground, 1970; Power Politics, 1971; Surfacing (novel), 1972; Survival: A Thematic Guide to Canadian Literature, 1972; You Are Happy, 1974; Lady Oracle (novel), 1976; Selected Poems, 1976; Dancing Girls (stories), 1978; Two-Headed Poems, 1978; Life Before Man (novel), 1979; Bodily Harm (novel), 1981; True Stories (verse), 1981; Second Words: Selected Critical Prose, 1982; Encounters with the Element Man, 1982; Murder in the Dark (novel), 1983; Bluebeard's Egg (short stories), 1983; Interlunar (verse), 1984; Unearthing Suite, 1984; The Handmaid's Tale, 1986; Selected Poems II, 1986; Cat's Eye, 1988. Add: c/o Oxford Univ. Press, 70 Wynford Dr., Don Mills, Ont., Canada.

AUBERT, Alvin. American, b. 1930. Poetry. Prof. of English, Wayne State Univ., Detroit, since 1979. Founding Ed., Obsidian mag., Fredonia, N.Y. Instr., 1960–62, Asst. Prof., 1962–65, and Assoc. Prof. of English, 1965–70, Southern Univ., Baton Rouge, La; Assoc. Prof. of English, State Univ. of New York, Fredonia, 1970–79. *Publs:* Against the Blues, 1972; Feeling Through, 1975; New and Selected Poems, 1985. Add: 18234 Parkside, Detroit, Mich. 48221, U.S.A.

AUCHINCLOSS, Louis (Stanton). American, b. 1917. Novels/Short stories, Plays, Literature, Autobiography/Memoirs/Personal. Pres., Museum of the City of New York, since 1966. Assoc. Lawyer, Sullivan & Cromwell, NYC, 1941–51. Assoc., 1954–58, and Partner, 1958–86, Hawkins, Delafield & Wood, attorneys-at-law, NYC. *Publs:* (as Andrew Lee, later reprinted as Auchincloss) The Indifferent Children, 1947; The Injustice Collectors, 1950; Sybil, 1952; A Law for the Lion, 1952; The Romantic Egoists: A Reflection in Eight Minutes, 1954; The Great World and Timothy Colt, 1956; Venus in Sparta, 1958; Pursuit of the Prodigal, 1959; The House of Five Talents, 1960; Edith Wharton, 1961; Reflections of a Jacobite, 1961; Portrait in Brownstone, 1962; Powers of Attorney, 1963; The Rector of Justin, 1964; Ellen Glasgow, 1964; Pioneers and Caretakers: A Study of Nine American Women Novelists, 1965; (ed.) An Edith Wharton Reader, 1965; The Embezzler, 1966; Tales of Manhattan, 1967; The Club Bedroom, (play), 1967; A World of Profit, 1968; Motiveless Malignity, 1969; Second Chance, 1970; Henry Adams, 1971; Edith Wharton: A Woman in Her Time, 1971; I Come as a Thief, 1972; Richelieu, 1972; (ed.) Fables of Wit and Elegance, 1972; The Partners, 1974; Writer's Capital (autobiography), 1974; Reading Henry James, 1975; The Winthrop Covenant, 1976; The Dark Lady, 1977; The Country Cousin, 1978; Persons of Consequence, 1979; The House of the Prophet, 1980; Life, Law, and Letters, 1980; The Cat and the King, 1981; The Unseen Versailles, 1981; Watchfires, 1982; Narcissa and Other Fables, 1983; Exit Lady Masham, 1983; The Book Class, 1984; Honorable Men, 1985; Diary of a Yuppie, 1986; Skinny Island, 1987; The Golden Calves, 1988; Fellow Passengers, 1989; The Vanderbilt Era (essays), 1989. Add: 1111 Park Ave., New York, N.Y. 10028, U.S.A.

AUCHTERLONIE, Dorothy. *See* **GREEN,** Dorothy.

AUDEMARS, Pierre. Also writes as Peter Hodemart. British, b. 1909. Mystery/Crime/Suspense. Salesman, Louis Audemars and Co., London, 1928–39; Mgr., Camerer Cuss and Co., jewellers, London, 1949–56; Sales Mgr., Zenith Watch Co. Ltd., London, 1960–76. *Publs:* mystery novels—Night Without Darkness, 1936; Hercule and the Gods, 1944; The Temptations of Hercule, 1945; When the Gods Laughed, 1946; The Obligations of Hercule, 1947; The Confessions of Hercule, 1947; (non-mystery novel, as Peter Hodemart) Wrath of the Valley, 1947; The Thieves of Enchantment, 1956; The Two Imposters, 1958; The Fire and the Clay, 1959; The Turns of Time, 1961; The Crown of Night, 1962; The Dream and the Dead, 1963; The Wings of Darkness (in U.S., as The Street of Grass), 1963; Fair Maids Missing, 1964; Dead with Sorrow, 1964 (in U.S. as A Woven Web, 1965); Time of Temptation, 1966; A Thorn in the Dust, 1967; The Veins of Compassion, 1967; The White Leaves of Death, 1968; The Flame in the Mist, 1969; A Host for Dying, 1970; Stolen Like Magic Away, 1971; The Delicate Dust of Death, 1973; No Tears for the Dead, 1974; Nightmare in Rust, 1975; And One for the Dead, 1975; The Healing Hands of Death, 1977; Now Dead Is Any Man, 1978; A Sad and Savage Dying, 1978; Slay Me a Sinner, 1979; Gone to Her Death, 1981; The Bitter Path of Death, 1982; The Red Rust of Death, 1983; A Small Body Slain, 1985. Add: c/o John Johnson (Authors Agent) Ltd., 45-47 Clerkenwell Green, London EC1R 0HT, England.

AUDUS, Leslie John. British, b. 1911. Botany. Hildred Carlile Prof. of Botany, Bedford Coll., Univ. of London, 1948–79. *Publs:* Plant Growth Substances, 1953, 3rd ed. 1972; (ed.) Physiology and Biochemistry of Herbicides, 1964; Herbicides: Physiology, Biochemistry, and Ecology, 1975. Add: 38 Belmont Lane, Stanmore, Middx., England.

AUEL, Jean M(arie). American, b. 1936. Novels/Short stories. *Publs:* The Clan of the Cave Bear, 1980; The Valley of Horses, 1982; The Mammoth Hunters, 1985. Add: c/o Crown Publishers Inc., One Park Ave., New York, N.Y. 10016, U.S.A.

AUKERMAN, Robert C. American, b. 1910. Education (not textbooks on other subjects). Emeritus Prof. of Education, Univ. of Rhode Island, Kingston (joined faculty, 1954). Teacher, Detroit Public Schs., 1935–48; Dean of Instruction, Missouri State Teachers Coll., Kirksville, 1948–54. Pres., College Reading Assn., 1964–65; Ed., Journal of New England Reading Assn., 1965–73. *Publs:* Approaches to Beginning Reading, 1971, 1984; (ed.) Some Persistent Problems in Beginning Reading, 1972; Reading in the Secondary School Classroom 1972; (with Louise R. Aukerman) How Do I Teach Reading?, 1981; The Basal Reader Approach to Reading, 1981; (with Louise R. Aukerman) How Do I Teach Reading: Professor's Resource Manual, 1981. Add: 75 Clarke Lane, Kingston, R.I. 02881, U.S.A.

AURNER, Robert Ray. American, b. 1898. Business/Trade/Industry, Writing/Journalism. Chmn., Pres. and Chief Exec. Officer, Aurner & Assocs., Corporate Counsel, Carmel, Calif., since 1938; Vice-Pres. and Dir., Scott Inc., Wisconsin and California, since 1949; Vice-Pres. and Dir., Pacific Futures Inc., since 1962. Faculty member, Univ. of Wisconsin, Madison, 1925–48 (Sr. Research Prof. of Business Admin., and Chmn. of Courses in Admin., 1930–48); Dir., SAE Corp., Evanston, Ill., 1943–53 (Pres., Chmn. and CEO, 1951–53); Pres., Chmn. and CEO, Levere Memorial Foundn., Evanston, 1951–53; Dir., Carmel Savings and Loan Assn., 1960–71. Consultant to numerous businesses, including Intnl. Cellucotton Products Co., Chicago, 1947–52, and Fox River Paper Corp., Communications Div., Appleton, Wisc., 1947–60. *Publs:* Henry Fielding, Lucianist, 1920; A History of the Structure of the English Sentence from Caxton to Macaulay, 1922; (contrib. ed.) American Business Practice (4 vols.); 1940; (contrib. ed.) American Encyclopedia of the Social Sciences, 1950; Effective English for Colleges, 8th ed. 1984; Effective English for Business Communication, 8th ed. 1985; Effective Communication in Business with Management Emphasis, 9th ed. 1988. Add: P.O. Box 3434, Carmel, Calif. 93921, U.S.A.

AUSTER, Paul. American, b. 1947. Novels/Short stories, Poetry, Literary criticism, History, Translations. Teacher of Creative Writing, Princeton Univ., New Jersey, since 1986. Formerly, variously employed as a merchant seaman, census taker, tutor, telephone operator, translator and writer. *Publs:* (trans.) A Little Anthology of Surrealist Poems, 1972; (trans.) Fits and Starts: Selected Poems of Jacques Dupin, 1974; Unearth: Poems 1970–72, 1974; (trans. with Lydia Davis) Arabs and Israelis: A Dialogue by Saul Friedlander and Mahmoud Hussein, 1975; (trans.) The Uninhabited: Selected Poems of André de Bouchet, 1976; Wall Writing: Poems 1971–75, 1976; (trans. with Lydia Davis) Life Situations, by Sartre, 1978; (trans. with Lydia Davis) China: The People's Republic,

by Jean Chesneaux, 1979; (trans. with Lydia Davis) China from the 1911 Revolution to Liberation, by Chesneaux and others, 1979; Facing the Music, 1980; White Spaces, 1980; (ed.) The Random House Book of Twentieth–Century French Poetry, 1982; The Invention of Solitude, 1982; (ed. and trans.) The Notebooks of Joseph Joubert: A Selection, 1983; (trans.) A Tomb for Anatole, by Mallarmé, 1983; (trans.) Vicious Circles, by Maurice Blanchot, 1985; (trans.) On the High Wire, by Philippe Petit, 1985; City of Glass, 1985; Ghosts, 1986; (trans. with Margit Rowell) Selected Writings, by Joan Miro, 1986; The Locked Room, 1987; Squeeze Play, 1987; In the Country of Last Things, 1987; Moon Palace, 1989. Add: 458 Third St., Brooklyn, NY 11215, U.S.A.

AUSTGEN, Robert Joseph. American, b. 1932. Theology/Religion. Asst. Dean of the Coll. of Arts and Letters, Univ. of Notre Dame, since 1982 (Asst. Prof., 1955, 1964–69; Asst. Dean of the Grad. Sch., 1970–81). Pres., North Central Conference on Summer Schools, 1978–79; Pres., Assoc. of Univ. Summer Sessions, 1980–81. *Publs:* Natural Motivation in the Pauline Epistles, 2nd ed. 1969. Add: Box 200, Univ. of Notre Dame, Notre Dame, Ind. 46556, U.S.A.

AUSTIN, Brett. *See* **FLOREN,** Lee.

AUSTIN, Cedric Ronald Jonah. British, b. 1912. Cookery/Gastronomy/Wine, Education (not textbooks on other subjects), Writing/Journalism. Chmn., Assn. of Informed Drinkers; Founder Member, Amateur Winemakers National Guild of Judges. *Publs:* Read to Write, 1954; Reading Today, 1956; Enjoy These Stories, 1962; Reason for Reading, 1964; The Science of Wine, 1968; Whys and Wherefores of Winemaking, 1970; The Good Wines of Europe, 1972; 100 Winemaking Problems Answered, 1974. Add: 38 Mandeville Rd., Hertford, Herts., England.

AUSTIN, Henry Wilfred. British, b. 1906. Social commentary/phenomena, Sports/Physical education/Keeping fit, Autobiography/Memoirs/Personal. Lawn Tennis Feature Writer, Evening News, 1929–39. *Publs:* Bits and Pieces, 1929; (with Caulfield) Lawn Tennis Made Easy, 1935; Under the Heavens, 1936; Moral Re-Armament: The Battle for Peace, 1938; (with P.K. Austin) A Mixed Double, 1969; Frank Buchman As I Knew Him, 1975; To Phyll with Love, 1979. Add: 12 Palace St., London SW1, England.

AUSTIN, James C. American, b. 1923. Songs, lyrics and libretti, Literature. Prof. Emeritus of English, Southern Illinois Univ., Edwardsville, since 1960 (Head, Humanities Div., 1963–64). Prof. and Chmn. of English, Yankton Coll., S.D., 1954–60. *Publs:* Fields of the Atlantic Monthly, 1953; (Librettist, with F.A. McClain) Snack Shop, 1957; (Librettist, with F.A. McClain) The Princess and the Frog, 1958; (Librettist, with F.A. McClain) Dakota Dakota Dakota, 1961; (Librettist, with F.A. McClain) Shangri-Lost, 1962; Artemus Ward, 1964; Petroleum V. Nasby, 1965; Bill Arp, 1970; (ed. with D.A. Koch) Popular Literature in America, 1972; American Humor in France, 1978. Add: Dept. of English, Southern Illinois Univ., Edwardsville, Ill. 62026, U.S.A.

AUSTIN, M(ichel) M(ervyn). British, b. 1943. History. Lectr., 1968–85, and Sr. Lectr. in Ancient History, since 1985, Univ. of St. Andrews, Fife, Scotland. *Publs:* Greece and Egypt in the Archaic Age, 1970; (with Pierre Vidal-Naquet) Economies et sociétés en Grèce ancienne, 1972, 1973, as Economic and Social History of Ancient Greece: An Introduction, 1977; The Hellenistic World from Alexander to the Roman Conquest, 1981; (contributor) The Greek World, ed. by R. Browning, 1985 ; (contributor) Civilizations of the Ancient Mediterranean, by M. Grant and R. Kitzinger, 1988. Add: Dept. of Ancient History, Univ. of St. Andrews, St. Andrews, Fife, Scotland.

AUSTIN, Richard. British, b. 1926. Novels/Short stories, Poetry, Dance/Ballet. *Publs:* Night Bird, 1970; Carnival, 1972; Watchman, What of the Night, 1973; Nocturnes, 1973; The Ballerina, 1974; The Hour Before Twilight, 1974; Images of the Dance, 1975; Birth of a Ballet, 1976; Natalia Makarova, 1978; Dance and Ballet, 1979; Lynn Seymour, 1980; Anna Pavlova, 1980; The Art of the Dancer, 1982; The Seasons of Love, 1986; Selected Poems, 1989. Add: 57 Cathcart Rd., London SW10, England.

AUSTIN, William W. American, b. 1920. Music, Translations. Given Foundn. Prof. of Musicology, Cornell Univ., since 1969 (Asst. Prof., 1947–50; Assoc. Prof., 1950–60 Prof., 1960–69). *Publs:* Music in the Twentieth Century, 1966; (ed.) New Looks at Italian Opera, 1968; (ed.) Debussy's Prelude to the Afternoon of a Faun, 1970; Susanna, Jeanie, and the Old Folks at Home: The Songs of Stephen C. Foster from His

Time to Ours, 1975, 1987; (trans.) Esthetics of Music by Carl Dahlhaus, 1982. Add: Dept. of Music, Cornell Univ., Ithaca, N.Y. 14853, U.S.A.

AUTTON, Norman (William James). British, b. 1920. Medicine/Health, Theology/Religion. Chaplain, Univ. Hosp. of Wales, Cardiff, since 1972. Chaplain, St. George's Hosp., London, 1961–67; Dir. of Training, Hosp. Chaplaincies Council of Gen. Synod, London, 1967–72. *Publs:* The Pastoral Care of the Mentally Ill, 1963; The Pastoral Care of the Dying, 1964; The Pastoral Care of the Bereaved, 1967; The Pastoral Care in Hospitals, 1968; (ed.) From Fear to Faith, 1970; (ed.) Christianity and Change, 1971; When Sickness Comes, 1973; (contrib.) A Guide to Oncological Nursing, 1974; (contrib.) The Dying Patient, 1975; Visiting Ours, 1975; (compiler) Readings in Sickness, 1976; (compiler) Watch with the Sick, 1976; Getting Married, 1976; (contrib.) Understanding Cancer, 1977; Peace at the Last, 1978; Visiting the Sick, 1980; A Handbook of Sick Visiting, 1981; Doctors Talking, 1984; Pain: An Exploration, 1986. Add: Univ. Hosp. of Wales, Heath Park, Cardiff CF4 4XW, Wales.

AVALLONE, Michael (Angelo, Jr.). Also writes as Nick Carter; Troy Conway; Priscilla Dalton; Mark Dane; Jean-Anne de Pre; Dora Highland; Stuart Jason; Steve Michaels; Dorothea Nile; Edwina Noone; Vance Stanton; Sidney Stuart; Max Walker, and Lee Davis Willoughby. American, b. 1924. Novels/Short stories, Mystery/Crime/Suspense, Historical/Romance/Gothic. Full-time writer since 1960. Stationery salesman, 1946–55; Ed. for Republic Features, NYC, 1956–58, and Cape Magazines, 1958–60. Chmn., Television Cttee., 1963–65, and Movie Cttee., 1965–70, Mystery Writers of America. *Publs:* novels—All the Way, 1960; The Little Black Book, 1961; Stag Stripper, 1961; Women in Prison, 1961; Flight Hostess Rogers, 1962; Never Love a Call Girl, 1962; The Platinum Trap, 1962; Sex Kitten, 1962; Sinners in White, 1962; Lust at Leisure, 1963; And Sex Walked In, 1963; Station Six—Sahara (novelization of screenplay), 1964; Krakatoa, East of Java (novelization of screenplay), 1969; Beneath the Planet of the Apes (novelization of screenplay), 1970; The Doctors, 1970; Hornets' Nest (novelization of screenplay), 1970; The Haunted Hall, 1970; Keith, The Hero, 1970; The Partridge Family, 1970; (as Max Walker) The Last Escape, 1970; Love Comes to Keith Partridge, 1973; The Girls in Television, 1974; CB Logbook of the White Knight, 1977; Carquake, 1977; Name That Movie, 1978; Son of Name That Movie, 1978; (as Lee Davis Willoughby) The Gunfighters, 1981; A Woman Called Golda (novelization of screenplay), 1982; (as Amanda Jean Jarrett) Red Roses Forever, 1983; novels, as Troy Conway—Come One, Come All, 1968; The Man-Eater, 1968; The Big Broad Jump, 1969; A Good Peace, 1969; Had Any Lately?, 1969; I'd Rather Fight Than Swish, 1969; The Blow-Your-Mind Job, 1970; The Cunning Linguist, 1970; All Screwed Up, 1971; The Penetrator, 1971; A Stiff Proposition, 1971; mystery novels—The Spitting Image, 1953; The Tall Dolores, 1953; Dead Game, 1954; Violence in Velvet, 1956; The Case of the Bouncing Betty, 1957; The Case of the Violent Virgin, 1957; The Crazy Mixed-Up Corpse, 1957; The Voodoo Murders, 1957; Meanwhile Back at the Morgue, 1960; The Alarming Clock, 1961; The Bedroom Bolero, 1963, in U.K. as The Bolero Murders, 1972; (as Steve Michaels) The Main Attraction (novelization of screenplay), 1963; The Living Bomb, 1963; There Is Something about a Dame, 1963; Shock Corridor, 1963; The Doctor's Wife, 1963; Lust Is No Lady, 1964, in U.K. as The Brutal Kook, 1965; (as Mark Dane) Felicia (novelization of screenplay), 1964; The Thousand Coffins Affair, 1965; The Birds of a Feather Affair, 1966; The Blazing Affair, 1966; The Fat Death, 1966; Kaleidoscope (novelization of screenplay), 1966; The February Doll Murders, 1966; Madame X (novelization of screenplay), 1966; The Felony Squad, 1967; The Man from AVON, 1967; Assassins Don't Die in Bed, 1968; The Coffin Things, 1968; Hawaii Five-O, 1968; The Incident (novelization of screenplay), 1968; The Horrible Man, 1968; Mannix, 1968; The Flower-Covered Corpse, 1969; The Doomsday Bag, 1969, in U.K. as Killer's Highway, 1970; Hawaii Five-O: Terror in the Sun, 1969; The Killing Star, 1969; Missing!, 1969; A Bullet for Pretty Boy (novelization of screenplay), 1970; One More Time (novelization of screenplay), 1970; Death Dives Deep, 1971; Little Miss Murder (in U.K. as The Ultimate Client), 1971; When Were You Born?, 1971; The Night Before Chaos, 1971; Shoot It Again, Sam, 1982, in U.K. as The Moving Graveyard, 1973; The Girl in the Cockpit, 1972; London, Bloody London, 1972, in U.K. as Ed Noon in London, 1974; Kill Her—You'll Like It!, 1973; The Hot Body, 1973; Killer on the Keys, 1973; The X-Rated Corpse, 1973; (as Dora Highland) 153 Oakland Street, 1973; (as Dora Highland) Death is a Dark Man, 1974; Fallen Angel, 1974; The Werewolf Walks Tonight, 1974; Devil, Devil, 1985; Only One More Miracle, 1975; The Big Stiffs, 1977; Dark on Monday, 1978; Charlie Chan and the Curse of the Dragon Queen (novelization of screenplay), 1981; The Cannonball Run (novelization of screenplay), 1981; Friday the Thirteenth, Part Three (novelization of screenplay),

1982; (as Lee Davis Willoughby) The Rough Riders, 1984; (as Lee Davis Willoughby) The Sixgun Apostles, 1985; (as Edwina Noone) Tender Loving Fear, 1985; mystery novels, as Nick Carter—The China Doll, 1964; Run Spy Run, 1964; Saigon, 1964; mystery novels as Sidney Stuart—The Night Walker (novelization of screenplay), 1964; Young Dillinger (novelization of screenplay), 1965; The Beast with Red Hands, 1973; High Noon At Midnight, 1988; gothics, as Priscilla Dalton—The Darkening Willows, 1965; 90 Gramercy Park, 1965; The Silent, Silken Shadows, 1965; gothics, as Edwina Noone—Corridor of Whispers, 1965; Dark Cypress, 1965; Heirloom of Tragedy, 1965; Daughter of Darkness, 1966; The Second Secret, 1966; The Victorian Crown, 1966; Seacliffe, 1968; The Cloisonné Vase, 1970; The Craghold Legacy, 1971; The Craghold Creatures, 1972; The Craghold Curse, 1972; The Craghold Crypt, 1973; High Noon at Midnight, 1988; gothics, as Dorothea Nile—The Evil Men Do, 1966; Mistress of Farrondale, 1966; Terror at Deepcliff, 1966; The Vampire Cameo, 1968; The Third Shadow, 1973; gothics, as Jean-Anne de Pre—A Sound of Dying Roses, 1971; The Third Woman, 1971; Aquarius, My Evil, 1972; Die, Jessica, Die, 1972; Warlock's Woman, 1973; mystery novels as Vance Stanton—Keith Partridge, Master Spy, 1971; The Fat and Skinny Murder Mystery, 1972; The Walking Fingers, 1972; Who's That Laughing in the Grave, 1972; mystery novels as Stuart Jason—The Judas Judge, 1979; Slaughter in September, 1979; Coffin Corner, U.S.A., 1980; Death in Yellow, 1980; Kill Them Silently, 1980; The Hoodoo Horror, 1981; Go Die in Afghanistan, 1981; The Man from White Hat, 1982; Gotham Gore, 1982; short stories—Tales of the Frightened, 1963; Where Monsters Walk, 1978; Five Minute Mysteries, 1978. Add: 80 Hilltop Blvd., East Brunswick, N.J. 08816, U.S.A.

AVEDON, Richard. American, b. 1923. Photography. Staff Photographer for Junior Bazaar, 1945–47, Harper's Bazaar, 1946–65, and Vogue mag., since 1966. Special Visual Consultant for Paramount film Funny Face, 1957; Television Consultant and Advertising Photographer. *Exhibitions:* Smithsonian Inst., Washington, 1962; Minneapolis Inst. of Arts, 1970; Museum of Modern Art, NYC, 1974; Marlborough Gallery, NYC, 1975; Metropolitan Museum of Art, NYC, 1978; Dallas Museum of Fine Art, 1979; Univ. Art Museum, Berkeley, Calif. 1980; Amon Carter Museum, Fort Worth, Texas, 1985; Cororan Gallery of Art, Washington, D.C., 1986; San Francisco Museum of Modern Art, 1986; Art Inst. of Chicago, 1986; Phoenix Art Museum, 1986; Inst. of Contemporary Art, Boston, 1987; High Museum of Art, Atlanta, Ga., 1987. *Publs:* (with T. Capote) Observations, 1959; (with J. Baldwin) Nothing Personal, 1964; (ed.) Diary of a Century: Photographs by Jacques-Henri Lartigue, 1970; (with D. Arbus) Alice in Wonderland, 1973; Portraits, 1976; Avedon: Photographs 1947–77, 1978; In the American West, 1985. Add: 407 E. 75th St., New York, N.Y. 10021, U.S.A.

AVELING, J(ohn) C(edric) H(ugh). British, b. 1917. History, Intellectual history, Theology/Religion. Asst. Curate, All Souls Church, Leeds, 1940–44; Head of History, Ampleforth Coll., York, 1952–67; Asst. Curate, St. Peter's Church, Yaxley, Hunts., 1969–71; Chmn. of the Faculty, Garth Hill Comprehensive Sch., Bracknell, Berks., 1971 until retirement, 1982. *Publs:* Post-Reformation Catholicism in East Yorkshire, 1960; Catholic Recusancy in the West Riding of Yorkshire, 1963; Northern Catholics: Recusancy in the North Riding of Yorkshire, 1966; (ed. with A. Pantin) The Letter—Book of Robert Joseph of Evesham, 1966; Catholic Recusancy in York City, 1970; A History of St. Peter's, Yaxley, 1973; The Handle and the Axe: The Catholic Recusants in England from Reformation to Emancipation, 1976; The Jesuits, 1981; (with J.M. Loades and J. McAdoo) Catholics and Anglicans, 1982. Add: 14 Weycrofts, Priestwood, Bracknell, Berks. RG12 1TD, England.

AVERILL, Esther (Holden). American, b. 1902. Children's fiction, Children's non-fiction. *Publs:* The Cat Club, 1944; Daniel Boone, 1946; The School for Cats, 1947; Jenny's First Party, 1948; Jenny's Moonlight Adventure, 1949; King Philip: The Indian Chief, 1951; When Jenny Lost Her Scarf, 1951; Jenny's Adopted Brothers, 1952; How the Brothers Joined the Cat Club, 1953; Jenny's Birthday Book, 1954; Cartier Sails the St. Lawrence, 1956; Jenny Goes to Sea, 1957; Jenny's Bedside Book, 1959; The Fire Cat, 1960; The Hotel Cat, 1969; Eyes on the World, 1969; Captains of the City Streets, 1972. Add:30 Joralemon St., Brooklyn, N.Y. 11201, U.S.A.

AVERY, Gillian (Elise). British, b. 1926. Children's fiction, Literature. Jr. Reporter, Surrey Mirror, Redhill, Surrey, 1944–47; Staff Member, Chambers Encyclopedia, London, 1947–50; Asst. Illustrations Ed., Clarendon Press, Oxford, 1950–54. *Publs:* The Warden's Niece, 1957; Trespassers at Charlcote, 1958; James Without Thomas, 1959; (ed.) A Flat Iron for Farthing, by Juliana Horatia Ewing, 1959; The Elephant War, 1960; (ed.) Jan of the Windmill, by Juliana Horatia Ewing, 1960;

(ed.) The Sapphire Treasury of Stories for Boys and Girls, 1960; (ed.) In the Window Seat: A Selection of Victorian Stories, 1960; To Tame a Sister, 1961; The Greatest Gresham, 1962; (ed.) Father Phim, by Annie Keary, 1962; The Peacock House, 1963; The Italian Spring, 1964; Mrs. Ewing, 1964; (ed.) Unforgettable Journeys, 1965; (with Angela Bull) Nineteenth Century Children: Heroes and Heroines in English Children's Stories 1780-1900, 1965; Call of the Valley, 1966; (ed.) School Remembered, 1967; (ed.) A Great Emergency, and a Very Ill-Tempered Family, by Juliana Horatia Ewing, 1967; (ed.) The Gold of Fairnilee and Other Stories, by Andrew Lang, 1967; (ed.) Village Children, by Charlotte Yonge, 1967; (ed.) Banning and Blessing, by Margaret Roberts, 1967; (ed.) The Hole in the Wall and Other Stories, 1968; (ed.) Victoria Bess and Others, by Brenda, Mrs. Gatty and Frances Hodgson Burnett, 1968; (ed.) The Wallypug of Why, by G.E. Farrow, 1968; (ed.) Froggy's Little Brother, by Brenda, 1968; (ed.) My New Home, by Mary Louisa Molesworth, 1968; (ed.) The Life and Adventures of Lady Anne (anonymous), 1969; (ed.) Stephanie's Children, by Margaret Roberts, 1969; (ed.) Anne's Terrible Good Nature and Other Stories for Children, by E.V. Lucas, 1970; (ed.) The Rival Kings, by Annie Keary, 1970; Victorian People in Life and Literature, 1970; A Likely Lad, 1971; Ellen's Birthday, 1971; (ed. with others) Authors' Choice 1, 1971; (ed.) Red Letter Days, 1971; Jemima and the Welsh Rabbit, 1972; The Echoing Green Memories of Victorian and Regency Youth, 1974; Ellen and the Queen, 1974; Book of Strange and Odd, 1975; Childhood's Pattern A Study of the Heroes and Heroines of Children's Fiction 1770-1950, 1975; Freddie's Feet, 1976; Huck and Her Time Machine, 1977; Mouldy's Orphan, 1978; Sixpence, 1979; The Lost Railway, 1980; Onlookers, 1983. Add: 32 Charlbury Rd., Oxford OX2 6UU, England.

AVI. (Avi Wortis). American, b. 1937. Children's fiction. Staff Member, Lincoln Center Library of the Performing Arts, NYC, 1962–70, and Lambeth Public Library, London, 1968; Asst. Prof. and Humanities Librarian, Trenton State Coll., New Jersey, 1970–86. *Publs:* Things That Sometimes Happen, 1970; Snail Tale, 1972; No More Magic, 1975; Captain Grey, 1977; Emily Upham's Revenge, 1978; Night Journeys, 1979; Encounter at Easton, 1980; The History of Helpless Harry, 1980; Man from the Sky, 1980; A Place Called Ugly, 1981; Who Stole the Wizard of Oz?, 1981; Sometimes I Think I Hear My Name, 1982; Shadrach's Crossing, 1983; Devil's Race, 1984; The Fighting Ground, 1984; S.O.R. Losers, 1984; Bright Shadow, 1985; Wolf Rider, 1986; Romeo and Juliet — Together (and Alive!) — at Last, 1987; Something Upstairs: A Tale of Ghosts, 1988. Add: 15 Sheldon St., Providence, RI 02906, U.S.A.

AVISON, Margaret (Kirkland). Canadian, b. 1918. Poetry. *Publs:* Winter Sun, 1960 (Gov.-Gen.'s Award); (with Albert Rose) The Research Compendium, 1964; The Dumbfounding, 1966; Sunblue, 1978. Add: 17 Lascelles Blvd., Apt. 108, Toronto, Ont., M4V 2B6, Canada.

AVNI, Abraham. American, b. 1921. Literature. Prof. of English, Calforna State Univ., Long Beach, since 1971 (Asst. Prof., 1964–67; Assoc. Prof., 1968–71). Instr. in Hebrew and the Bible, Univ. of Wisconsin, Madison, 1962–64. *Publs:* The Bible and Romanticism: The Old Testament in German and French Romantic Poetry, 1969. Add: Dept. of English, California State Univ., Long Beach, Calif. 90840, U.S.A.

AVRAMOVIC, Dragoslav. Yugoslavian, b. 1919. Economics. Sr. Staff Member, Intnl. Bank for Reconstruction and Development, Washington 1953–77; Sr. Adviser, Office of the Secty.-Gen., UNCTAD, Geneva, 1980–84; Economic Adviser, Bank of Credit and Commerce Intnl., Washington, 1984. Lectr. in Economics, Univ. of Belgrade, 1947–53. *Publs:* Debt Servicing Capacity and Postwar Growth in International Indebtedness, 1958; Debt Servicing Problems of Low Income Countries, 1960; Economic Growth and External Debt, 1965; (ed.) Economic Growth of Colombia, 1972; (ed.) South–South Financial Cooperation: Approaches to the Current Crisis, 1983. Add: 13200 Cleveland Dr., North Glen Hills, Rockville, Md. 10850, U.S.A.

AWDRY, W(ilbert) V(ere). British, b. 1911. Children's fiction, Archaeology/Antiquities, Transportation. Anglican clergyman: Rector, Elsworth and Knapwell, Cambridge, 1946–53; Vicar of Emneth, Wisbech, 1953–65. *Publs:* The Three Railway Engines, 1945; Thomas the Tank Engine, 1946; James the Red Engine, 1948; Tank Engine Thomas Again, 1949; Troublesome Engines, 1950; Henry the Green Engine, 1951; Toby the Tram Engine, 1952; Gordon the Big Engine, 1953; Edward the Blue Engine, 1954; Four Little Engines, 1955; Percy the Small Engine, 1956; The Eight Famous Engines, 1957; Duck and the Diesel Engine, 1958; Belinda the Beetle, 1958; The Little Old Engine, 1959; The Twin Engines, 1960; Branch Line Engines, 1961; Belinda Beats the Band, 1961; Gallant Old Engine, 1962; Stepney the Blue Bell Engine, 1963; Mountain En-

gines, 1964; Very Old Engines,1965; Main Line Engines, 1966; Small Railway Engines, 1967; Duke the Lost Engine, 1970; Map of the Island of Sodor, 1971; Tramway Engines, 1972; (ed.) Industrial Archaeology in Gloucestershire, 1974, 3rd ed. 1983; (co-ed.) A Guide to Steam Railways of Great Britain, 1979, 3rd ed. 1984; (co-author) The Birmingham and Gloucester Railway, 1987; (co-author) The Island of Sodor, Its People, History and Railways, 1987. Add: Sodor, 30 Rodborough Ave., Stroud, Glos. GL5 3RS, England.

AWOONOR, Kofi. Ghanaian, b. 1935. Novels/Short stories, Plays/Screenplays, Poetry. Research Fellow, Inst. of African Studies, Legon, 1960–64; Dir., Ghana Ministry of Information Film Corp., 1964–67; Research Fellow, University Coll., London, 1967–68; Asst. Prof., 1968–72, and Assoc. Prof., 1973–75, State Univ. of New York at Stony Brook; Visiting Prof., Univ. of Texas, Austin, 1972–73; Prof., Univ. of Cape Coast, Ghana, 1977–82; Ambasssador of Ghana to Brazil, from 1983. Former Ed., Okyeame, Accra, and Co-Ed., Black Orpheus, Ibadan. *Publs:* Rediscovery and Other Poems, 1964; This Earth, My Brother: An Allegorical Tale of Africa, 1970; (ed. with G. Adali-Martty) Messages: Poems from Ghana, 1970; Night of My Blood (poetry), 1971; Ancestral Power (play), 1972; Lament (play), 1972; Ride Me, Memory (poetry), 1973; Guardians of the Sacred Word (poetry), 1974; The Breast of the Earth (essays), 1975; The House by the Sea (poetry), 1978; The Ghana Revolution (personal perspective), 1984; Fire in the Valley (folk stories), 1984. Add: Embassy of Ghana, SHIS QL. 10, Conjunto 08, Casa 02, Brasilia DF, Brazil.

AXELROD, George. American, b. 1922. Novels/Short stories, Plays/Screenplays. Stage and film dir. *Publs:* Beggar's Choice (novel), 1947, in U.K. as Hobson's Choice, 1951; Blackmailer (novel), 1952; The Seven Year Itch: A Romantic Comedy, 1953; Will Success Spoil Rock Hunter?, 1956; Goodbye Charlie, 1959; Where Am I Now—When I Need Me? (novel), 1971; (with Peter Viertel) Souvenir, 1975. Add: c/o Irving Paul Lazar Agency, 211 S. Beverly Dr., Beverly Hills, Calif. 90212, U.S.A.

AXELSON, Eric (Victor). South African, b. 1913. History, Travel/Exploration/Adventure. Asst. Ed., Union War Histories, 1946–49; Ed., Central African Archives, 1949–50; Chief Narrator, Union War Histories, 1951–55; Research Officer, Ernest Oppenheimer Inst. of Portuguese Studies, Univ. of Witwatersrand, 1955–62; Head, Dept. of History, 1962–74, Dean, Faculty of Arts, 1967–69, and Asst. Principal, 1972–78, Univ. of Cape Town. Gen. Ed., Brenthurst Series, 1974–84. *Publs:* South East Africa 1488-1530, 1940; (ed.) South African Explorers, 1954; Portuguese in South East Africa 1600-1700, 1960; Portugal and the Scramble for Africa 1875-1891, 1967; Portuguese in South East Africa 1488-1600, 1973; Congo to Cape: Early Portuguese Explorers, 1973; (co-ed.) Baines on the Zambezi 1858 to 1859, 1982; (ed.) Dias and His Successors, 1987. Add: P.O. Box 15, Constantia, Cape, 7848, South Africa.

AXTON, David. *See* **KOONTZ,** Dean R.

AYALA, Francisco Jose. American, b. 1934. Biology. Prof. of Biology, Univ. of Calif., Irvine, since 1987. Research Assoc., 1964–65, and Asst. Prof., 1967–71, Rockefeller Univ., New York; Asst. Prof., Providence Coll., R.I., 1965–67. Prof. of Genetics, Univ. of California, Davis (joined faculty 1971; Dir., Inst. of Ecology, 1977–81; Assoc. Dean of Environmental Studies, 1977–81). *Publs:* Studies in the Philosophy of Biology, 1974; Molecular Evolution, 1976; Evolution, 1977; Evolving: The Theory and Processes of Organic Evolution, 1979; Evolutionary and Population Genetics, 1982; Genetic Variation and Evolution, 1983; Origin of Species, 1983; Modern Genetics, 1984. Add: Univ. of Calif., Dept. of Ecology and Evolutionary Biology, Irvine, CA 92717, U.S.A.

AYARS, Albert Lee. American, b. 1917. Advertising/Public relations, Education. Supt. Emeritus, Norfolk Public Schs., Virginia, since 1983 (Supt., 1972–83). Teacher, Davenport High Sch., 1940–42; Principal, Colville High Sch., 1942–45, Supt., Omak Public Schs., 1945–49, and Sunnyside Public Schs., 1949–52, all Wash.; Assoc. Dir., Joint Council on Economic Education, NYC, 1952–53; Dir., Education Dept., Hill & Knowlton Inc., NYC, 1953–65; Vice-Pres., John W. Hill Foundn., 1956–65; Supt., Spokane Public Schs., Wash., 1965–72; Consulting Ed., Journal of National Open Education, and Editorial Advisory Bd.; member, Issues in Education, and Public Relations News, all 1960–65. *Publs:* How to Plan Your Community Resources Workshop, 1954; Administering the People's Schools, 1957; (with Gail Milgram) The Teenager and Alcohol, 1970; How to Plan a Community Resources Workshop, 1974; (with John Ryan) The Teenager and the Law, 1978. Add: 4827 102nd Ln. NE, Kirkland, Wash. 98033, U.S.A.

AYCKBOURN, Alan. British, b. 1939. Plays/Screenplays. Artistic Dir., Stephen Joseph Theatre-in-the-Round, Scarborough, Yorks., since 1971. BBC Radio Drama Producer, 1964–70; National Theatre Company Dir., 1986–87. *Publs:* The Norman Conquests, A Trilogy, 1975; Three Plays (Absurd Person Singular, Absent Friends, Bedroom Farce), 1977; Joking Apart and Other Plays (Ten Times Table, Just Between Ourselves), 1979; Sisterly Feelings/Taking Steps, 1981; A Chorus of Disapproval, 1986; Woman in Mind, 1986; A Small Family Business, 1987; Henceforth ..., 1988. Non-fiction: (with Ian Watson) Conversations with Ayckbourn, 1981. Add: c/o Margaret Ramsay Ltd., 14a Goodwin's Ct., St. Martin's Lane, London WC2N 4LL, England.

AYDY, Catherine. *See* **TENNANT,** Emma.

AYER, A.J. (Sir Alfred Jules Ayer). British b. 1910. Philosophy, Autobiography/Memoirs/Personal. Hon. Fellow, New Coll. Oxford, since 1978 (Lectr. in Philosophy, Christ Church, 1932–35; Fellow, 1944–46, and Dean, 1945–46. Wadham Coll.; Wykeham Prof. of Philosophy Univ. of Oxford, 1959–78). Grote Prof. of the Philosophy of Mind and Logic, Univ. of London, 1946–59. Pres., Humanist Assn., 1965–70, and Modern Languages Assn., 1966–67. *Publs:* Language, Truth and Logic, 1936, 1946; The Foundations of Empirical Knowledge, 1940; (ed. with Raymond Winch) British Empirical Philosophers, 1952; Philosophical Essays, 1954; The Problem of Knowledge, 1956; (ed.) Logical Positivism, 1959; The Concept of a Person and Other Essays, 1963; The Origins of Pragmatism, 1968; (ed.) The Humanist Outlook, 1968; Metaphysics and Common Sense, 1969; Russell and Moore: The Analytical Heritage, 1971; Probability and Evidence, 1972; Russell, 1972; The Central Questions of Philosophy, 1974; Part of My Life, 1977; Perception and Identity, 1979; Hume, 1980; Philosophy in the Twentieth Century, 1982; More of My Life, 1984; Freedom and Morality, 1984; Wittgenstein, 1985; Voltaire, 1986; Thomas Paine, 1988. *Deceased, 1989.*

AYER, Jacqueline (Brandford). American, b. 1932. Children's fiction. Freelance fabric designer, since 1975. Fashion Illustrator, Vogue and Jardin des Modes, both Paris, 1952–53, and Bonwit Teller, NYC, 1954; Exec. Fabric and Fashion Designer, Intnl. Basic Economy Corp., Bangkok, 1960–70; Adviser to the Indian Govt. on fabric fashion export, Delhi and Bombay, 1971–74. *Publs:* Nu Dang and His Kite, 1959; A Wish for Little Sister, 1960; The Paper-Flower Tree, 1962; Little Silk, 1970; Oriental Costume, 1974. Add: 10 East End Ave., New York, N.Y. 10020, U.S.A.

AYERST, David (George Ogilvy). British, b. 1904. Education. History, Media. Editorial staff member, 1929–34, and Historian, 1964–73, The Guardian, Manchester and London; H.M. Inspector of Schs., 1947–64. *Publs:* Europe in the 19th Century, 1940; Understanding Schools, 1967; (ed. with A.S.T. Fisher) Records of Christianity, 1970, 1977; Guardian; Biography of a Newspaper (in U.S. as The Manchester Guardian), 1971; (ed.) The Guardian Omnibus, 1973; Garvin of the Observer, 1985. Add: Littlecote, Burford, Oxford OX8 4RY, England.

AYLEN, Leo. British. Poetry, Theatre. Freelance writer and film dir. Poet-in-Residence, Fairleigh Dickinson Univ., N.J., 1972–74; Hooker Distinguished Visiting Prof., McMaster Univ., Ontario, 1982; former Producer for BBC TV. *Publs:* Greek Tragedy and the Modern World, 1964; Discontinued Design, 1969; I Odysseus, 1971; Greece for Everyone, 1976; Sunflower, 1976; Return to Zululand, 1980; The Apples of Youth, 1980; Red Alert: This Is a God Warning, 1981; Jumping-Shoes, 1983; The Greek Theater, 1985; Rhymoceros, 1989. Add: 13 St.

Saviour's Rd., London SW2, England.

AYLING, Stanley (Edward). British, b. 1909. Biography. Asst. Master, Parmiter's Sch. London, 1933–45; Sr. History Master, Sandown Grammar Sch., England, 1945–69. *Publs:* Twelve Portraits of Power, 1961, 5th ed. as Portraits of Power, 1971; Nineteenth Century Gallery, 1970; George the Third, 1972; The Elder Pitt, 1976; John Wesley, 1979; A Portrait of Sheridan, 1985; Edmund Burke: His Life and Opinions, 1988. Add: The Beeches, Middle Winterslow, Salisbury, Wilts., England.

AYLMER, G(erald) E(dward). British, b. 1926. History. Master of St. Peter's Coll., Oxford, since 1978. On Editorial Bd., History of Parliament, since 1968; Member, Royal Commn. on Historical Manuscripts, since 1977. J.E. Proctor Visiting Fellow, Princeton Univ., N.J., 1950–51; Jr. Research Fellow, Balliol Coll., Oxford, 1951–54; Asst. Lectr. in Modern History, 1954–57; Lectr., Univ. of Manchester, 1957–62; Prof. of History and Head of Dept., Univ. of York, 1963–78. Vice-Pres., 1973–77, and Pres., 1984–88, Royal Historical Soc. *Publs:* The King's Servants: The Civil Service of Charles I, 1625-1642, 1961, rev. ed. 1974; (ed.) The Diary of William Lawrence, 1961; The Struggle for the Constitution 1603-1689 (in U.S. as A Short History of 17th-Century England), 1963; (ed.) The Interregnum: The Quest for Settlement, 1646-1660, 1972; The State's Servants: The Civil Service of the English Republic, 1649-1660, 1973; The Levellers in the English Revolution, 1975; (ed., with R. Cant) A History of York Minster, 1977; Rebellion or Revolution? England 1640-1660, 1986. Add: St Peter's Coll., Oxford OX1 2DL, England.

AYRTON, Elisabeth. British, b. 1910. Novels/Short stories. Architecture, Cookery/Gastronomy/Wine. Freelance writer. *Publs:* The Cook's Tale, 1957; Sauce and Sensuality, 1957; Doric Temples, 1961; The Cretan (in U.S. as Silence in Crete), 1963; Two Years in My Afternoon, 1972; Cookery of England, 1974; Day Eight, 1978; English Provincial Cookery, 1980; The Pleasures of Vegetables, 1983; Good Simple Cooking, 1984. Add: The Maze House, Rockhampton, Berkeley, Glos., England.

AZAROWICZ, Marjory (Frances Brown). American, b. 1922. Speech/Rhetoric. Prof. of Education, George Mason Univ., since 1968. Teacher, Alberta, Canada, 1942–56; Assoc. Prof., State Univ. of New York at Buffalo, 1960–66; Teacher, Fairfax County Schs., 1966–68. *Publs:* A Handbook of Creative Choral Speaking, 1970; Individual and Group Assessment Procedures in Reading, 1982; Communication Skills for Parents Through Children's Literature, 1982; Analyses of the Individual, 1985. Add: Dept. of Education, George Mason Univ., Fairfax, Va., U.S.A.

AZNEER, J. Leonard. American, b. 1921. Medicine/Health, Theology/Religion. Pres., Univ. of Osteopathic Medicine and Health Services since 1971. Rabbi, Allentown, Pa., 1944–45, Bay City Mich., 1945–47, Schenectady, N.Y., 1947–50, and Temple Anshe E'meth, Youngstown, 1950–67; faculty member, Youngstown State Univ., Ohio, 1951–71; Adjunct Prof. of Philosophy, and Head, Dept of Hebrew, 1956–62; Assoc. Prof. of Education, 1967–71; Sr. Member of Grad. Faculty, 1971. *Publs:* Passover: A Programmed Text, 1967; Sukkot: A Programmed Text, 1968; (with Caccamo and Kessler) Diabetic Acidosis: A Programmed Text, 1968; (with Caccamo and Kesseler) Resuscitation: A Programmed Text, 1969. Add: Coll. of Osteopathic Medicine and Surgery, 3200 Grant Ave., Des Moines, Iowa 50312, U.S.A.

B

BABB, Sanora. American, b. 1907. Novels/Short stories. Teacher of Short Story Writing, Univ. of California, Los Angeles, 1958. *Publs:* The Lost Traveler, 1958; An Owl on Every Post, 1970; The Dark Earth (stories), 1987. Add: 1562 Queens Rd., Hollywood, Calif. 90069, U.S.A.

BABBAGE, Stuart Barton. New Zealander, b. 1916. Sex, Theology/Religion. Registrar, Australian Coll. of Theology, since 1974. Dean, St. Andrew's Cathedral, Sydney, 1947–53, and St. Paul's Cathedral, Melbourne, 1953–62; Principal, Ridley Coll., Univ. of Melbourne, 1953–63; Pres., Melbourne Coll. of Divinity, 1960–63, and Conwell Sch. of Theology, Temple Univ., Philadelphia, Pa., 1967–69; Vice Pres. and Dean, Gordon-Conwell Theological Seminary, South Hamilton, Mass., 1970–73; Master, New Coll. of New South Wales, Kensington, 1973–82. *Publs:* Hauhauism, or the Religion of Pai Marire, 1937; Man in Nature and in Grace, 1957; (with I. Siggins) Light Beneath the Cross, 1960; Puritanism and Richard Bancroft, 1962; Christianity and Sex, 1963; Sex and Sanity, 1965; The Mark of Cain; Studies in Literature and Theology, 1966; The Light of the Cross, 1966; The Vacuum of Unbelief, 1969. Add: 46 St. Thomas St., Waverley, N.S.W. 2024, Australia.

BABBITT, Natalie. American. Children's fiction. *Publs:* Dick Foote and the Shark, 1967; Phoebe's Revolt, 1968; The Search for the Delicious, 1969; Kneeknock Rise, 1970; The Something, 1970; Goody Hall, 1971; The Devil's Storybook, 1974; Tuck Everlasting, 1975; The Eyes of the Amaryllis, 1977; Herbert Rowbarge, 1982; The Devil's Other Storybook, 1984. Add: 26 Benefit St., Providence, RI 02904, U.S.A.

BABBITT, Robert. *See* **BANGS,** Robert B.

BABE, Thomas. American, b. 1941. Plays/Screenplays. Operated the Summer Players, Agassiz Theatre, Cambridge, Mass., with Timothy S. Mayer, 1966–68; speechwriter for John Lindsay, Mayor of New York, 1968–69. *Publs:* Rebel Women, 1976; A Prayer for My Daughter, 1977; Taken in Marriage, 1979; Kid Champion, 1980; Fathers and Sons, 1980; Salt Lake City Skyline, 1980; Great Solo Town, 1981; Buried Inside Extra, 1983; Planet Fires, 1985. Add: 103 Hoyt St., Darien, CT 06820, U.S.A.

BABINGTON, Anthony Patrick. British, b. 1920. Criminology/Law enforcement/Prisons, Law, Autobiography/Memoirs/Personal. Circuit Judge since 1972. Metropolitan Stipendiary Magistrate, London, 1964–72. *Publs:* No Memorial, 1954; The Power to Silence, 1968; A House in Bow Street, 1969; The English Bastille, 1971; The Only Liberty, 1975; For the Sake of Example, 1983. Add: 3 Gledhow Gardens, Kensington, London SW5 0BL, England.

BABSON, Marian. American. Mystery/Crime/Suspense. Secty., Crime Writers Assn., London, 1976–86. *Publs:* Cover-Up Story, 1971; Murder on Show, 1972; Pretty Lady, 1973; The Stalking Lamb, 1974; Unfair Exchange, 1974; Murder Sails at Midnight, 1975; There Must Be Some Mistake, 1975; Untimely Guest, 1976; The Lord Mayor of Death, 1977; Murder, Murder, Little Star, 1977; Tightrope for Three, 1978; So Soon Done For, 1979; the Twelve Deaths of Christmas, 1979; Dangerous to Know, 1980; Queue Here for Murder, 1980; Bejewelled Death, 1981; Death Warmed Up, 1982; Death Beside the Seaside, 1982; A Fool for Murder, 1983; The Cruise of a Deathtime, 1983; A Trail of Ashes, 1984; Death Swap, 1984; Death in Fashion, 1985; Weekend for Murder, 1985; Reel Murder, 1986; Fatal Fortune, 1987; Guilty Party, 1988. Add: c/o William Collins Sons and Co. Ltd., 8 Grafton St., London W1X 3LA,

England.

BACALL, Lauren. American, b. 1924. Autobiography/Memoirs/Personal. Actress in films since 1944, and on the stage and on television since the 1950s. Films include: To Have and Have Not, 1945; The Big Sleep, 1946; Dark Parkage, 1947; Key Largo, 1948; Young Man with a Horn, 1950; How to Marry a Millionarie, 1953; The Cobweb, 1955; Blood Alley, 1955; Written on the Wind, 1956; Designing Woman, 1957; The Gift of Love, 1958; Flame over India, 1959; Shock Treatment, 1964; Sex and the Single Girl, 1964; Harper, 1966; Murder on the Orient Express, 1974; The Shootist, 1976; Health, 1980; The Fan, 1981. *Publs:* Lauren Bacall By Myself, 1979. Add: c/o Johnnie Planco, William Morris Agency, 1350 Ave. of the Americas, New York, N.Y. 10019, U.S.A.

BACH, Richard. American, b. 1936. Novels/Short stories, Air/Space topics. U.S. Air Force pilot, 1956–59, 1961–62; Assoc. Ed., Flying mag., Calif., 1961–64. *Publs:* Stranger to the Ground, 1963; Biplane, 1966; Nothing by Chance: A Gypsy Pilot's Adventures in Modern America, 1969; Jonathan Livingston Seagull, 1970; A Gift of Wings, 1975; Illusions: The Adventures of a Reluctant Messiah, 1977; There's No Such Place as Far Away, 1979; The Bridge Across Forever: A Lovestory, 1984; One, 1988. Add: c/o William Morrow & Co., 105 Madison Ave., New York, N.Y. 10016, U.S.A.

BACHE, Ellen. Also writes as Ellen Matthews. American, b. 1942. Novels, Social commentary. Instr., North Carolina Writers Network, since 1986. Freelance journalist, Washington Post, Baltimore Sun, etc., 1974–85; Ed., Antietam Review, 1982–85. *Publs:* (as Ellen Matthews) Culture Clash, 1982; Safe Passage (novel), 1988. Add: 2314 Waverly Dr., Wilmington, NC 28403, U.S.A.

BACHMAN, John W(alter). American, b. 1916. Communications Media, Theology/Religion. Chmn., Lutheran World Fedn. Commn. on Communication. Assoc. Prof., to Prof. of Practical Theology, and Dir., Center for Communication and the Arts, Union Theological Seminary, NYC, 1952–64; Pres., Wartburg Coll., Waverly, Iowa, 1964–74; Dir. of Communication and Mission Support, American Lutheran Church, 1974–81. *Publs:* How to Use Audio-Visual Materials, 1956; The Church in the World of Radio-Television, 1960; (ed. with E.M. Browne) Better Plays for Today's Churches, 1964; Faith That Makes a Difference, 1984; Media: Wasteland or Wonderland, 1985. Add: 8549 Irwin Rd., No. 334, Minneapolis, Minn. 55437, U.S.A.

BACHMAN, Richard. *See* **KING,** Stephen.

BACHRACH, Peter. American, b. 1918. Politics/Government. Prof. of Political Science, Temple Univ., Philadelphia. *Publs:* The Theory of Democratic Elitism, 1967; (with M. Baratz) Power and Poverty, 1970; (ed.) Political Elites in a Democracy, 1971; (with E. Bergman) Power and Choice, 1973. Add: Dept. of Political Science, Temple Univ., Philadelphia, Pa., U.S.A.

BACKUS, George Edward. American, b. 1930. Earth sciences, Physics. Prof. of Geophysics, Univ. of California San Diego, at La Jolla, since 1962 (Assoc. Prof., 1960–62). Royal Soc. Arts Fellow, London, since 1970; Co-Chmn., Intl. Working Group on Magnetic Field Satellites, since 1983; member, visiting cttee., Institut de Physique du Globe de Paris, since 1987. Asst. Examiner, Univ. of Chicago, 1949–50; Jr. Mathematician, Inst. for Air Weapons Research, Univ. of Chicago, 1950–54;

Physicist, Project Matterhorn, Princeton Univ., N.J., 1957–58; Asst. Prof. of Mathematics, Massachusetts Inst. of Technology, Boston, 1959–60. *Publs:* Self-Sustaining Dissipative Kinematic Fluid Dynamo, 1958; Rotational Splitting of the Free Oscillations of the Earth, 1961; Propagation of Short Waves on a Slowly Rotating Earth, 1962; Magnetic Anomalies over Oceanic Ridges, 1964; Possible Forms of Seismic Anistropy, 1962, 3rd ed., 1970; Potentials for Tangent Tensor Fields in Spheroids, 1966; (with F. Gilbert) Inversion of Seismic Normal Mode Data, 1966; Geomagnetic Data and Core Motions, 1967; (with F. Gilbert) Inversion of Earth Normal Mode Data, 1968, 3rd ed., 1970; Inference from Inaccurate and Inadequate Data, 1971, 1972; Mathematical Representation of Seismic Sources, 1976; Computing Extrema of Multidimensional Polynomials, 1980; Relative Importance of Tectonic Plate-Driving Forces, 1981; Construction of Geomagnetic Field Models, 1982. Add: Inst. of Geophysics and Planetary Physics, Univ. of California, San Diego, A-025, La Jolla, Calif. 92093, U.S.A.

BACON, Edmund N(orwood). American, b. 1910. Architecture, Regional/Urban planning. Vice-Pres. of Design and Development, Mondev International Ltd., Montreal, since 1972. Adjunct Prof., Univ. of Pennsylvania, Philadelphia, since 1950. Exec. Dir., Philadelphia City Planning Commn., 1949–70. *Publs:* Design of Cities, 1967, rev. ed. 1974. Add: 2117 Locust St., Philadelphia, Pa. 19103, U.S.A.

BACON, George Edward. British, b. 1917. Chemistry, Physics. Prof. of Physics, Univ. of Sheffield, since 1963–81, now Emeritus. Ed., Zietschrift fur Kristallographie, since 1963. Deputy Chief Scientist, Atomic Energy Research Establishment, Harwell, 1946–63. *Publs:* Neutron Diffraction 1955, 3rd ed. 1975; Applications of Neutron Diffraction in Chemistry, 1963; X-ray and Neutron Diffraction, 1966; Neutron Physics, 1969; Neutron Scattering in Chemistry, 1977; The Architecture of Solids, 1981; (ed.) 50 Years of Neutron Diffraction, 1987. Add: Windrush Way, Guiting Power, Cheltenham GL54 5US, England.

BACON, Margaret. British. Novels, Travel. *Publs:* Journey to Guyana, 1970; The Episode, 1971; Kitty, 1972; The Unentitled, 1974; A Packetful of Trouble, 1974; The Package, 1975; Snow in Winter, 1978; The Kingdom of the Rose, 1982; The Chain, 1984; The Serpent's Tooth, 1987. Add: Hill House, Highworth, Wilts., England.

BACON, R(onald) L(eonard). New Zealander, b. 1924. Novels/Short stories, Children's fiction. Principal, Favona Primary Sch., Auckland. *Publs:* In the Sticks, 1963; Along the Road, 1964; The Boy and the Taniwha, 1966; Rua and the Sea People, 1968; Auckland: Gateway to New Zealand, 1968; Again the Bugles Blow, 1973; Auckland: Town and Around, 1973; The House of the People, 1977; Hatupatu and the Bird Woman, 1979; Wind, 1984; The Bay, 1986. Add: Unit 3, 16 Turama Rd., Royal Oak, Auckland, New Zealand.

BADAWI, Mohamed Mustafa. British, b. 1925. Literature. Lectr., Oxford Univ. and Brasenose Coll., both since 1964; Fellow, St. Antony's Coll., Oxford, since 1967. Co-ed., Journal of Arabic Literature, Leiden, since 1970; Advisory Bd. Member, Cambridge History of Arabic Literature, since 1971. Research Fellow, 1947–54, Lectr., 1954–60, and Asst. Prof. of English, 1960–64, Alexandria Univ., Egypt. Member, Cttees. of Ministry of Culture, Egypt, 1961; Unesco Expert on Modern Arabic Culture, 1974. *Publs:* (ed.) An Anthology of Modern Arabic Verse, 1970; Coleridge, Critic of Shakespeare, 1973; (trans.) The Saint's Lamp and Other Stories, by Yahya Haqqi, 1973; A Critical Introduction to Modern Arabic Poetry, 1975; (trans.) Sara, by A.M. El Aqqad, 1978; Background to Shakespeare, 1981; (co-trans.) The Thief and the Dogs, by Naguib Mahfouz, 1984; Modern Arabic Literature and the West, 1985; Modern Arabic Drama in Egypt, 1987; Early Arabic Drama, 1988. Add: St. Antony's Coll., Oxford, England.

BADCOCK, Christopher Robert. British, b. 1946. Psychology, Sociology. Reader in Sociology, London Sch. of Economics. Lectr. in Sociology, Polytechnic of the South Bank, London, 1969–73. *Publs:* Levi-Strauss: Structuralism and Sociological Theory, 1975; The Psychoanalysis of Culture, 1980; Madness and Modernity, 1984; The Problem of Altruism: Freudian-Darwinian Solutions, 1986. Add: London Sch. of Economics, Houghton St., London WC2A 2AE, England.

BADENI, June. Has also written as June Wilson. British, b. 1925. Novels/Short stories, History, Biography. *Publs:* as June Wilson—The Bitter Journey, 1947; One Foolish Heart, 1948; Second Hearing, 1949; Green Shadows: A Life of John Clare, 1951; as June Badeni—Wiltshire Forefathers, 1960; The Slender Tree: A Life of Alice Meynell, 1981. Add: Norton Manor, Malmesbury, Wilts., England.

BADGLEY, John Herbert. American, b. 1930. Politics/Government. Pres., Inst. of the Rockies, Missoula, since 1973. Asst. Prof., Miami Univ., Ohio, 1962–66; Assoc. Prof., 1967–70, and Dir. of Asian Studies, 1970–73, Johns Hopkins Univ., Washington, D.C. *Publs:* (co-ed.) Japan's Future in Southeast Asia, 1965; (with Osgood and Packard) U.S. and Japan in Asia, 1969; Politics Among Burmans, 1970; Asian Development, 1971; Burmese Strategists, 1985. Add: Inst. of the Rockies, 10300 O'Brien Creek, Missoula, Mont. 59801, U.S.A.

BADIAN, Ernst. New Zealander, b. 1925. History. Prof. of History, since 1971, and John Moors Cabot Prof. of History, since 1982, Harvard Univ., Cambridge, Mass. Ed., American Journal of Ancient History, since 1976. Prof. of Ancient History, Univ. of Leeds, 1964–69; Prof. of Classics and History, State Univ. of New York, Buffalo, 1969–71. *Publs:* Foreign Clientelae 264-270 B.C., 1958 (Conington Prize, Oxford Univ.); Studies in Greek and Roman History, 1964; (ed.) Polybius, 1966; (ed. and contrib.) Ancient Society and Institutions, 1966; Roman Imperialism in the Late Republic, 1967, 1968; Publicans and Sinners, 1972; (ed.) The Roman Stonecutter, by G. Susini, 1973; (ed.) Roman Papers by Ronald Syme, (2 vols.), 1979. Add: Dept. of History, Harvard Univ., Cambridge, Mass. 02138, U.S.A.

BAERG, Harry John. American, b. 1909. Children's fiction, Children's non-fiction, Natural history. Illustrator and Designer, Review & Herald Publishing Assn., since 1954 (Art Dir., 1968–70). Textbook coordinator, 1970–74; former freelance artist, writer, and teacher. *Publs:* Bright Eyes, 1952; Gray Ghosts, 1952; Western Trees, 1955; Chipmunk Willie, 1958; Humpy the Moose, 1963; Benny the Beaver, 1964; Tico the Coyote, 1970; Kari the Elephant, 1970; Billy the Buck, 1970; Molly Cottontail, 1971; Bill the Whooping Crane, 1971; Winnie the White Heron, 1971; Creation and Catastrophe, 1972; Coco the Range Pony, 1973; Bucky the Jack Rabbit, 1976; Prairie Boy, 1980; Birds that Can't Fly, 1983. Add: 11009 Lombardy Rd., Silver Spring, Md. 20901, U.S.A.

BAERWALD, Hans H. American, b. 1927. Politics/Government. Prof. of Political Science, Univ. of California at Los Angeles, since 1969 (Lectr., 1962–65; Assoc. Prof., 1965–69). Asst. Prof., 1956–61, and Assoc. Prof. of Govt., 1961–62, Miami Univ., Oxford, Ohio. *Publs:* The Purge of Japanese Leaders Under the Occupation, 1959, 1977; (with Peter H. Odegard) American Government: Structure, Problems, Policies, 1962; (with Dan N. Jacobs) Chinese Communism: Selected Documents, 1963; (with Odegard) The American Republic, Its Government and Politics, 1964, rev. ed. with William Havard, 1969; Japan's Parliament: An Introduction, 1974; Party Politics in Japan, 1986. Add: 914 Bluegrass Lane, Los Angeles, Calif. 90049, U.S.A.

BAGDIKIAN, Ben Haig. American, b. 1920. Communications media, Criminology/Law enforcement/Prisons, Sociology. Prof., Grad. Sch. of Journalism, Univ. of California, Berkeley, since 1977 (Dean, 1985–88). Chief Washington Corresp., The Providence Journal, R.I., 1947–61; Contrib. Ed., Saturday Evening Post, 1963–67; Asst. Managing Ed., for National News, Washington Post, 1970–72. *Publs:* (ed.) Man's Contracting World in an Expanding Universe, 1960; In the Midst of Plenty: The Poor in America, 1964; The Information Machines, 1970; The Shame of the Prisons, 1972; The Effete Conspiracy and Other Crimes by the Press, 1972; Caged, 1976; Bagdikian on Political Reporting, Newspaper Economics, Law, and Ethics, 1977; The Media Monopoly, 1983, 1987. Add: 25 Stonewall Rd., Berkeley, Calif. 94705, U.S.A.

BAGLEY, John Joseph. British, b. 1908. History, Biography. Hon. Ed., A History of Cheshire, Publs. Trust, Cheshire Community Council. Schoolmaster, Rochdale Grammar Sch., 1931–38, and Up Holland Grammar Sch., 1938–51; Hon. Ed., Transactions of the Historic Soc. of Lancashire and Cheshire, 1950–69; Lectr., 1951–60, Sr. Lectr., 1960–67, and Reader in History, Inst. of Extension Studies, 1967–75, Univ. of Liverpool. *Publs:* Margaret of Anjou, Queen of England, 1948; History of Lancashire with Maps and Pictures, 1956; Life in Medieval England, 1960; Henry VIII and His Times, 1962; (with P.B. Rowley) Documentary History of England, 1066-1540, 1966; Historical Interpretation (2 vols.), 1965, 1971; (with A.J. Bagley) The English Poor Law, 1966; State and Education in England and Wales, 1833-1968, 1969; Lancashire, 1972; Lancashire Diarists, 1974; (with A.S. Lewis) Lancashire at War, 1977; Medieval People, 1978; (with A.G. Hodgkiss) Lancashire: A History of the County Palatine in Early Maps, 1985; The Earls of Derby, 1485-1985, 1985. Add: 10 Beach Priory Gardens, Southport, Merseyside, England.

BAHM, Archie J(ohn). American, b. 1907. Philosophy, Theology/Religion. Prof. of Philosophy Emeritus, Univ. of New Mexico, Albuquerque, since 1973 (Prof., 1948–73). Instr., to Assoc. Prof. of

Philosophy and Sociology, Texas Technological Coll., 1934–46; Assoc. Prof. of Philosophy, Univ. of Denver, Colo., 1946–48. *Publs:* Philosophy: An Introduction, 1953; Philosophy of the Buddha, 1958; What Makes Acts Right?, 1958; Tao Teh Ching, by Lao Tzu, 1958; Logic for Beginners, 1958; Yoga: Union with the Ultimate, 1961; Types of Intuition, 1961; Directory of American Philosophers, Vols. I-IX, 1962–78; The World's Living Religions, 1964; Yoga for Business Executives, 1965; The Heart of Confucius, 1969; Bhagavad Gita: The Wisdom of Krishna, 1970; Polarity, Dialectic, and Organicity, 1970; Metaphysics: An Introduction, 1974; Ethics as a Behavioral Science, 1974; Comparative Philosophy, 1977; Interdependence, 1977; The Specialist, 1977; The Philosopher's World Model 1979; Why Be Moral?, 1980; Axiology: The Science of Values, 1980; Ethics: The Science of Oughtness, 1980. Add: 1915 Las Lomas Rd. N.E., Albuquerque, N.M. 87106, U.S.A.

BAHR, Ehrhard. German, b. 1932. Literature, Biography, Translations. Prof. of German. Univ. of California, Los Angeles, since 1972 (Acting Asst. Prof., 1966–68; Asst. Prof., 1968–70; Assoc. Prof., 1970–72; Chmn., Dept. of Germanic Languages, 1981–84). Teaching Asst., Univ. of California, Berkeley, 1962–66. *Publs:* (co-trans.) Nelly Sachs: Beryll Sees in the Night (play), 1969; Die Ironie in Goethes Spatwerk (criticism), 1972; (with Ruth G. Kunzer) Georg Lukacs (biography), 1972; Ernst Bloch (biography), 1974; (ed.) Kant: What Is Enlightenment, 1974; Nelly Sachs (biography), 1980; (ed. with others) Lessing Yearbook Supplement: Humanitat und Dialog, 1982. Add: Dept. of Germanic Languages. Univ. of California, Los Angeles, Calif. 90024, U.S.A.

BAHR, Jerome. American, b. 1909. Novels/Short stories. Reporter, Louisville Courier-Journal, Ky., 1929–30, and Minneapolis Star, Minn., 1931–33; Writing and odd jobs, NYC, 1933–42; Officer, U.S. Army Air Force and U.S. Air Force, 1942 until leaving with rank of Maj., 1950; Civilian Writer, U.S. Dept. of Defense, Washington, D.C.; 1951–58; Civilian Information Officer, U.S. Army, Berlin, Germany, 1958–64; Speech writer, Defense Supply Agency, U.S.A. 1964–68, and U.S. Office of Education 1968 until retirement in 1971. *Publs:* All Good Americans (short stories), 1937; The Platinum Tower, 1939; The Linen Suit and Other Stories, 1957; Wisconsin Tales, 1964; Holes in the Wall, 1970; The Perishing Republic (short stories), 1971; The Lonely Scoundrel (novella supplement to The Perishing Republic), 1974; Five Novellas, 1977. Add: 800 Hillcrest Dr., Santa Fe., N.M. 87501, U.S.A.

BAHR, Robert. American, b. 1940. Medicine/Health, Biography. Managing Ed. of Health Bulletin, 1965–67, Sr. Ed. of Prevention mag., 1967–69, Managing Ed. of Fitness For Living, 1969–71, and Dir. of Educational Services Div., 1971–72, Rodale Press., Emmaus, Pa. *Publs:* Man With a Vision (biography), 1961; Natural Way to a Healthy Skin, 1972; Physical Fitness in Business and Industry, 1973; The Virility Factor, 1976; (contrib.) Reader's Digest Practical Medical Health Guide, 1976; Least of All Saints, 1979; The Blizzard, 1980; Blizzard at the Zoo, 1982; Kreskin's Fun Way to Mind Expansion, 1984; Good Hands, 1984; The Hibernation Response, 1988. Add: 1070 Zurich St., Mobile, Ala. 36608, U.S.A.

BAIGELL, Matthew. American, b. 1933. Art. Distinguished Prof. of Art History, Rutgers: The State Univ. of New Jersey, New Brunswick, since 1978 (joined faculty, 1968). Inst., Asst. Prof., and Assoc. Prof., Ohio State Univ., Columbus, 1961–68. *Publs:* (ed.) A Thomas Hart Benton Miscellany, 1971; A History of American Painting, 1971; Thomas Hart Benton, 1974; Charles Burchfield, 1976; The American Scene: American Painting in the 1930s, 1974; Frederic Remington, 1976; Dictionary of American Art, 1979; Thomas Cole, 1981; Albert Bierstadt, 1981; A Concise History of American Painting and Sculpture, 1984; (ed.) The Papers of the American Artists' Congress (1936), 1985; The Western Art of Frederic Remington, 1980; 19th Century Painters of the Delaware Valley, 1983. Add: Art History Dept., Rutgers Univ., New Brunswick, N.J. 08903, U.S.A.

BAIL, Murray. Australian, b. 1941. Novels/Short stories. Member of the Council, Australian National Gallery, Canberra, 1976–81. *Publs:* Contemporary Portraits and Other Stories, 1975, in U.K. as The Drover's Wife, 1986; Homesickness (novel), 1980; Ian Fairweather, 1981; Holden's Performance (novel), 1987; (ed.) The Faber Book of Contemporary Australian Short Stories, 1988; Longhand, 1989. Add: 39/75 Buckland St., Chippendale, N.S.W. 2008, Australia.

BAILEY, Alfred Goldsworthy. Canadian, b. 1905. Poetry, History, Literature. Prof. Emeritus of History, Univ. of New Brunswick, Fredericton (Head, Dept. of History, 1938–69; Dean of Arts, 1946–64; Vice-Pres., Academic, 1965–70). *Publs:* Songs of the Saguenay (verse), 1927; Tao

(verse), 1930; (ed.) The University of New Brunswick Memorial Volume, 1950; Border River (verse), 1952; (ed., with others) The Literary History of Canada, 1965; The Conflict of European and Eastern Algonkian Culture 1504–1700: A Study in Canadian Civilisation, 2nd ed., 1969; Culture and Nationality, 1972; Thanks for a Drowned Island (verse), 1973; Miramichi Lightning: Collected Poems, 1981. Add: 2 Acacia Grove, Fredericton, N.B. E3B 1Y7, Canada.

BAILEY, Anthony. British, b. 1933. Novels/Short Stories, Human Relations, Travel/Exploration/Adventure, Autobiography, Documentaries/Reportage. Staff Writer, The New Yorker, since 1956. Chmn., The Burney St. Garden Project, London, since 1981. Chmn., The Greenwich Soc., London, 1979–81. *Publs:* Making Progress (novel), 1959; The Mother Tongue (novel), 1961; The Inside Passage (travel), 1965; Through the Great City (reportage), 1967; The Thousand Dollar Yacht (autobiography: boating), 1968; The Light in Holland (reportage), 1970; In the Village (human relations), 1971; A Concise History of the Low Countries, 1972; Rembrandt's House (biography), 1978; Acts of Union: Reports on Ireland, 1980; America, Lost and Found (autobiography), 1981; Along the Edge of the Forest: An Iron Curtain Journey, 1983; England, First and Last (autobiography), 1985; Spring Jaunts: Some Walks, Excursions, and Personal Explorations of City, Country, and Seashore, 1986; Major André, 1987; The Other Banks (travel), 1989. Add: c/o Candida Donadio and Associates, 231 W. 22nd St., New York, N.Y. 10011, U.S.A.

BAILEY, Charles Waldo (II). American, b. 1929. Novels/Short stories. Washington Ed., National Public Radio, since 1984. Former Ed., Minneapolis Star & Tribune. *Publs:* (contrib.) Candidates 1960, 1959; (with Fletcher Knebel) No High Ground, 1960; Seven Days in May, 1962; Convention, 1964; (contrib.) Exeter Remembered, 1965; (contrib.) The President's Trip to China, 1972; Conflicts of Interest: A Matter of Journalistic Ethics, 1984. Add: 3001 Albemarle St. N.W., Washington, D.C. 20008, U.S.A.

BAILEY, D(avid) R. Shackleton. British, b. 1917. Classics, History, Translations. Pope Prof. of Latin Language and Literature, Harvard Univ., Cambridge, Mass., since 1982, now Emeritus (Visiting Lectr., 1963; Prof. of Greek and Latin, 1975–82). Fellow, Caius Coll., 1944–55; Lectr. in Tibetan, Cambridge Univ., 1948–68; Fellow, Jesus Coll., 1955–64; Fellow, Deputy Bursar, and Sr. Bursar, Caius Coll., 1964–68; Prof. of Latin, Univ. Of Michigan, Ann Arbor, 1968–74. Ed., Harvard Studies in Classical Philology, 1980–85. *Publs:* (ed. and trans.) The Satapancasatka of Matrceta, 1951; Propertiana, 1951; (ed.) Ciceronis Epistulae ad Atticum IX-XVI, 1961; (ed. and trans.) Cicero's Letters to Atticus (7 vols.) 1965–70; Cicero, 1971; Two Studies in Roman Nomenclature, 1976; (ed.) Cicero; Letters to His Friends, 1977; (trans.) Cicero's Letters to Atticus, 1978; (trans.) Cicero's Letters to His Friends, 2 vols., 1978; Towards a Text of "Anthologia Latina," 1979; Cicero: Epistulae ad Q. Fratrem et M. Brutum, 1981; Profile of Horace, 1982; (ed.) Anthologia Latina I, 1982; (ed.) Horatius, 1985; (ed.) Cicero, Philippics, 1985; Ciceronis Epistulae, 4 vols., 1987–88; Lucanus, 1988; Onomasticon to Cicero's Speeches, 1988. Add: 303 N. Division, Ann Arbor, Mich. 48104, U.S.A.

BAILEY, F(rancis) Lee. American, b. 1933. Law, Novels. Admitted to the Bar of Massachusetts, 1960; partner in the law firm of Bailey, Alch and Gillis, Boston, Mass.; founder of private detective agency; host of weekly prog., "Good Company", ABC-TV, 1967; publisher of Gallery mag., since 1972; Pres. of Enstrom Helicopter Corp., since 1972. *Publs:* (with Harvey Aronson) The Defense Never Rests: The Art of Cross–Examination, 1971; (with John Greenya) For the Defense, 1975; (with Greenya) Cleared for Approach: F. Lee Bailey in Defense of Flying, 1977; Secrets (novel), 1978; (with Henry P. Rothblatt) Complete Manual of Criminal Forms: Federal and State, 2 vols., 1968, 1974, suppl. 1987; (with Rothblatt) Defending Business and White Collar Crimes: Federal and State, 1969, 1984, suppl. 1987; (with Rothblatt) Investigation and Preparation of Criminal Cases: Federal and State, 1970, 1986; (with Rothblatt) Successful Techniques for Criminal Trials, 1971, 1985; (with Rothblatt) Handling Narcotic and Drug Cases, 1972, suppl. 1987; (with Rothblatt) Crimes of Violence: Rape and Other Sex Crimes, 1973, suppl. 1988; (with Rothblatt) Crimes of Violence: Homicide and Assault, 1973, suppl. 1988; (with Rothblatt) Fundamentals of Criminal Advocacy, 1974; (with Rothblatt) Handling Misdemeanor Cases, 1976, suppl. 1987; (with Rothblatt) Handling Juvenile Delinquency Cases, vol. I, 1978, suppl. 1985; To Be a Trial Lawyer, 1985. Add: 1 Center Plaza, Boston, MA 02108, U.S.A.

BAILEY, Frederick George. British, b. 1924. Anthropology/Ethnology, Politics. Prof. of Anthropology, Univ. of California at San Diego, since 1971. Prof., Univ. of Sussex, Brighton, 1964–71. *Publs:* Caste and the Economic Frontier, 1957; Tribe, Caste and Nation: A Study of Political Activity and Political Change in Highland Orissa, 1960; Politics and Social Change: Orissa in 1959, 1963; Stratagems and Spoils: A Social Anthropology of Politics, 1969; (ed.) Gifts and Poisons: The Politics of Reputation, 1971; (ed.) Debate and Compromise: The Politics of Innovation, 1973; Morality and Expediency: The Folklore of Academic Politics, 1977; The Tactical Uses of Passion, 1983. Add: Dept. of Anthropology, Univ. of California at San Diego, La Jolla, CA 92093, U.S.A.

BAILEY, Gordon (Keith). British, b. 1936. Poetry. Voluntary youth worker since 1962; freelance broadcaster since 1968. Film Ed., 1956–59; Sales Mgr., 1959–62; Gordon Bailey series, ATV Network Ltd., Birmingham, 1973–75. *Publs:* Plastic World, 1971; Moth-balled Religion, 1972; Patchwork Quill, 1975; Can a Man Change?, 1979; 100 Contemporary Christian Poets, 1983; I Want to Tell You How I Feel, God, 1983. Add: 9 Wentworth Dr., Blackwell, nr. Bromsgrove, Worcs., England.

BAILEY, Lee. American, b. 1926. Cookery/Gastronomy/Wine, Horticulture. *Publs:* Lee Bailey's Country Weekends, 1983; City Food, 1984; Lee Bailey's Country Flowers, 1985; Good Parties, 1986; Country Desserts, 1988. Add: 10 W. 57th St., New York, N.Y. 10019, U.S.A.

BAILEY, Norman (Alishan). American, b. 1931. Plays/Screenplays, History, International relations/Current affairs, Politics/Government. Prof., Queen's Coll., NYC, since 1968 (Asst. Prof., 1962–64; Assoc. Prof., 1964–68). Dir., Cttee. for Monetary Research and Education, since 1971. Intnl. Economist, Mobil Oil, 1959–61; Pres., Overseas Equity Inc., 1961–68, and Bailey Tondu Warwick & Co. Inc., 1968–74. *Publs:* (with R. Linney and D. Cascio) Ten Plays for Radio, 1954; Harlequinade: A Musical Fantasy, 1955; (with R. Linney and D. Cascio) Radio Classics, 1956; Frustration, 1959; Latin America: Politics, Economics and Hemispheric Security, 1965; Latin America in World Politics, 1967; Operational Conflict Analysis, 1973; The Patch Unit, 1986; (with Richard Cohen) The Mexican Time Bomb, 1987. Add: 149 Wellington Rd., Garden City, N.Y.

BAILEY, Norman Thomas John. British, b. 1923. Mathematics/Statistics. Reader in Biometry, Univ. of Oxford, 1955–65; Prof. of Biomathematics, Cornell Univ., Medical Sch., NYC, and member, Sloan-Kettering Inst. for Cancer Research, 1966–67; scientist, 1967–73, and Chief, 1974–83, Health Statistical Methodology, W.H.O. Geneva; Prof., Div. of Medical Informatics, Univ. of Geneva, 1981–88. *Publs:* The Mathematical Theory of Epidemics, 1957; Statistical Methods in Biology, 1959; The Mathematical Theory of Genetic Linkage, 1961; Introduction to Stochastic Processes, 1964; The Mathematical Approach to Biology and Medicine, 1966; The Mathematical Theory of Infectious Diseases and Its Application, 1975; Mathematics, Statistics and Systems for Health, 1977; Biomathematics of Malaria, 1982. Add: Div. of Medical Informatics, Univ. Cantonal Hospital, 1211 Geneva, Switzerland.

BAILEY, Paul. British, b. 1937. Novels/Short stories, Plays/Screenplays, Biography. Freelance writer since 1967. Actor, 1953–63. *Publs:* At the Jerusalem, 1967, Trespasses, 1971; A Worthy Guest (play), 1973; A Distant Likeness, 1973; Peter Smart's Confessions, 1977; Old Soldiers, 1980; An English Madam: The Life and Work of Cynthia Payne, 1982; Gabriel's Lament, 1986. Add: 79 Davisville Rd., London W12 9SH, England.

BAILEY, Pearl (Mae). American, b. 1918. Cookery/Gastronomy/Wine, Autobiography/Memoirs/Personal. Singer and entertainer. *Publs:* The Raw Pearl, 1968; Pearlie Mae, Talking to Myself, 1971; Pearl's Kitchen: An Extraordinary Cookbook, 1973; Duey's Tale, 1975; Hurry Up, America, and Spit (essays and poetry), 1976. Add: c/o Tony Santozzi, William Morris Agency, 151 El Camino, Beverley Hills, Calif. 90212, U.S.A.

BAILY, Nathan, A. American, b. 1920. Business/Trade/Industry, Marketing. Prof. of Business Admin., since 1953, and Founding Dean, 1955–70, Sch. of Business Admin., The American Univ., Washington, D.C.. Sr. Staff Vice-Pres., Mortgage Bankers Assn. of America; Dir. of Education, Inst. of Industrial Launderers; Commnr. and Chief Economist, U.S. Postal Rate Commn.; Dir., Washington Mutual Investors Fund, A.W. Industries, General Business and Carl M. Freeman Assocs. Former Member, Bd. of Dirs., U.S. Chamber of Commerce, Washington, and National Selection Bd., U.S. Post Office. Pres., Seminars, Speakers, Travel, 1975–82, and Utility Shareholders Assoc., 1976–79. *Publs:* (ed.) Marketing Profitability Under the Robinson-Patman Act, 1964; A Charter for Business-Government Relations, 1965; Marketing Handbook, 2 vols.,

1970–71; Guide to Establishing a Company Marketing Program, 1972. Add: 5516 Greystone St., Chevy Chase, Md. 20815, U.S.A.

BAILYN, Bernard. American, b. 1922. History. Adams University Prof., Harvard Univ., since 1981 (joined faculty, 1949; Asst. Prof., 1954–58; Assoc. Prof., 1958–61; Prof., 1961–66; Winthrop Prof. of History, 1966–81; Ed.-in-Chief, John Harvard Library, 1962–70); Dir., Charles Warren Center for Studies in American History, since 1984. Co.-Ed., Perspectives in American History journal, 1967–77, and since 1984. *Publs:* The New England Merchants in the Seventeenth Century, 1955; Massachusetts Shipping, 1697-1714, 1959; Education in the Forming of American Society, 1960; (ed.) Pamphlets of the American Revolution, 1965; (ed.) The Apologia of Robert Keane: The Self-Portrait of a Puritan Merchant, 1965; The Ideological Origin of the American Revolution, 1967; The Origins of American Politics, 1968; (co-ed.) The Intellectual Migration, Europe and America 1930–1960, 1969; (co-ed.) Law in American History, 1972; The Ordeal of Thomas Hutchinson, 1974; (co-author) The Great Republic, 1977; (co-ed.) The Press and the American Revolution, 1980; The Peopling of British North America: An Introduction, 1986; Voyagers to the West, 1986. Add: 170 Clifton St., Belmont, Mass., 02178, U.S.A.

BAINBRIDGE, Beryl (Margaret). British, b. 1934. Novels/Short stories. Actress in repertory theatres in U.K., 1949–60; Clerk, Gerald Duckworth & Co. Ltd., publrs., London, 1971–73. *Publs:* A Weekend with Claude, 1967, 1981; Another Part of the Wood, 1968, 1979; Harriet Said, 1972; The Dressmaker (in U.S. as The Secret Glass), 1973; The Bottle Factory Outing, 1974; Sweet William, 1975; A Quiet Life, 1976; Injury Time, 1976; Young Adolf, 1978; Winter Garden, 1980; English Journey; or, The Road to Milton Keynes, 1984; Watson's Apology, 1984; Mum and Mr. Armitage, 1985; Forever England, 1986; Filthy Lucre, 1986. Add: 42 Albert St., London NW1 7NU, England.

BAINBRIDGE, John. American, b. 1913. Social commentary/phenomena, Biography. Member of Editorial Staff, The New Yorker mag. since 1938. Contributor, Gourmet mag., since 1972. *Publs:* Little Wonder, or The Reader's Digest and How It Grew, 1946; The Wonderful World of Toots Shor, 1951; Biography of an Idea, 1952; Garbo, 1955; The Super-Americans, 1961; Like a Homesick Angel, 1964; Another Way of Living, 1968; English Impressions, 1981. Add: c/o The New Yorker 25 W. 43rd St., New York, N.Y. 10036, U.S.A.

BAIRD, David McCurdy. Canadian, b. 1920. Earth sciences, Natural history. Dir., Rideau Canal Museum, Alta., since 1986. Hon. Treas., Royal Soc. of Canada, since 1972. Teaching Asst., Univ. of Rochester, N.Y., 1941–43; Demonstrator, McGill Univ., Montreal, 1943–46; Asst. Prof. of Geology, Mt. Allison Univ., Sackville, N.B., 1946–47; Asst. Prof., 1947–50, and Assoc. Prof. of Geology, 1950–52, Univ. of New Brunswick, Fredericton; Provincial Geologist for Newfoundland, 1952–58; Prof. of Geology, 1953–58, and Head of the Dept. and Member of the Univ. Senate, 1954–58, Memorial Univ. of Newfoundland, St. John's; Prof. and Chmn. of the Dept. of Geology, Univ. of Ottawa, 1958–66; Dir., National Museum of Science and Technology, Ottawa, 1966–81; Dir., Tyrrel Museum of Palaeontology, Drumheller, Alta., 1981–86. Chmn. Newfoundland Branch, 1954–55, and Councillor, 1955–57, Canadian Inst. of Mining and Metallurgy; Councillor, Geological Assn. of Can., 1956–58; National Advisory Cttee. on Research in the Geological Sciences, 1953–58; Secty., Geology Section, Royal Soc. of Can. 1960–63; Pres., Youth Science Foundn., 1968–71; Member, Exec. Cttee., XXIV Intnl. Geological Congress, Canada 1968–72; Hon. Treas., Royal Soc. of Canada, 1972–75; Vice-Pres., Intnl. Assn. of Transport Museums, 1981–83. *Publs:* An Introduction to Geology, 1959; Guide to Geology for Visitors in Canada's National Parks, 1960, 3rd Ed. 1974; Jasper National Park, 1977; Glacier and Mount Revelstoke National Parks, 1965, Banff National Park, 1977; Nature's Heritage, 1967–1971; Guide to Geology and Scenery of the National Capital Area, 1968; Our Earth in Continuous Change, 1971. Add: Box 7500, Drumheller, Alta. T0J 0YO, Canada.

BAIRD, Russell N(orman). American, b. 1922. Communications media, Writing/Journalism. Prof. of Journalism, Ohio Univ., Athens, since 1952. Combat Corresp., U.S. Army, 1942–46; Asst. Prof. of Journalism, Bowling Green State Univ., Ky., 1947–52. *Publs:* (with A.T. Turnbull) Industrial and Business Journalism, 1961; (with A.T. Turnbull) Graphics of Communication, 1964; Penal Press, 1967; (with J.W. Click) Magazine Editing and Production, 1974, 4th ed., 1986. Add: 49 Madison Ave., Athens, Ohio, U.S.A.

BAIRD, Thomas. American, b. 1923. Novels/Short stories. Prof., History of Art, Trinity Coll., Hartford, Conn. *Publs:* Triumphal Entry,

1962; The Old Masters, 1963; Sheba's Landing, 1964; Nice Try, 1965; Finding Out, 1967; People Who Pull You Down, 1970; Losing People, 1974; The Way to the Old Sailor's Home, 1977; Poor Millie, 1978; Finding Fever, 1982; Walk Out a Brother, 1983; Villa Aphrodite, 1984; Where Time Ends, 1988. Add: 70 Lorraine St., Hartford, Conn., U.S.A.

BAKER, Alan. British, b. 1939. Mathematics/Statistics. Fellow of Trinity Coll., Cambridge, since 1964, and Prof. of Pure Mathematics, Cambridge Univ., since 1974. *Publs:* Transcendental Number Theory, 1975; (ed., with D.W. Masser) Transcendence Theory: Advances and Applications, 1977; A Concise Introduction to the Theory of Numbers, 1984; (ed.) New Advances in Transcendence Theory, 1988. Add: Trinity Coll., Cambridge CB2 1TQ, England.

BAKER, Christopher John. British, b. 1948. Economics, History. Chief Exec., Lintas: Singapore, since 1987. Fellow, Tutor, and Dir. of Studies in History, Queens' Coll., Cambridge, 1975–81; Consultant, RDR, Bangkok, 1981–84. *Publs:* (with D.A. Washbrook) South India: Political Institutions and Political Change 1880-1940, 1975; The Politics of South India 1920–1937, 1976; (ghostwriter) The Palaces of India, by the Maharaja of Baroda, 1980; (co-ed.) Power, Profit, and Politics, 1981; An Indian Rural Economy, 1880-1955: The Tamilnad Countryside, 1984. Add: 5 Malcolm Rd., Singapore 1130.

BAKER, (John) Clifford Yorke. British, b. 1905. Engineering/Technology, Writing/Journalism. Member of the Council, Instn. of Scientific and Technical Communication. Repairs and Publs. Mgr., Handley Page Ltd., St. Albans, Herts., 1934–69, now retired; Ed., General Engineer, 1972–88. *Publs:* Metropolitan Railway, 1951; Technical Publications, 1957; Guide to Technical Writing, 1961; Guide to Technical Illustration, 1963; (with B.M. Cooper) Writing Technical Reports, 1964; Models in Cardboard; Models in Wood. Add: 80 Church Ave., Pinner, Middx. HA5 5JF, England.

BAKER, Elizabeth. American, b. 1923. Children's fiction. *Publs:* Tammy Camps Out, 1958; Treasures of Rattlesnake Hill, 1959; Fire in the Wind, 1961; Tammy Climbs Pyramid Mountain, 1962; Tammy Goes Canoeing, 1966; Stronger Than Hate, 1969; Tammy Camps in the Rocky Mountains, 1970; This Stranger My Son, 1971. Add: 100 Keyes Rd., Concord, Mass. 01742, U.S.A.

BAKER, Elliott. American, b. 1922. Novels/Short stories, Plays/Screenplays. *Publs:* A Fine Madness, 1964 (Putnam Award), screenplay, 1966; (adaptor) Luv (screenplay), 1967; The Penny Wars, 1968, play, 1969; Pocock and Pitt, 1971; Unrequited Loves, 1974; Klynt's Law, 1976; And We Were Young, 1979; Unhealthful Air, 1988. Add: c/o Times Books, 201 East 50th St., New York, N.Y. 10020, U.S.A.

BAKER, Frank. British, b. 1910. Theology/Religion. Prof. Emeritus of English Church History, Duke Univ., Durham, N.C. since 1960. Minister of British Methodist Church in various English Circuits, 1934–59. *Publs:* Treasure in Earthen Vessels, 1937; Sidelights on Sixty Years, 1941; A Charge to Keep: An Introduction to the People Called Methodists, 1947; Charles Wesley as Revealed by His Letters, 1948; Methodist Pilgrim in England, 1951; The Story of Cleethorpes, 1953; The Story of Methodism in Newland, 1958; Methodism and the Love-Feast, 1957; John Cennick: A Handlist of his Writings, 1718-55; Representative Verse of Charles Wesley, 1962; William Grimshaw, 1708-63, 1963; Charles Wesley's Verse: An Introduction, 1964, 2nd ed., 1988; (ed. with G. Walton Williams) John Wesley's First Hymn Book, 1964; A Union Catalogue of the Publications of John and Charles Wesley, 1966; John Wesley and the Church of England, 1970; From Wesley to Asbury: Studies in Early American Methodism, 1976; (ed.) The Works of John Wesley, vols. 25-26, Letters 1721-39, 1740-55, 1980–82; John Wesley's Own Choice: 1. Selections from William Law, 1985. John Wesley's Own Choice: 2. Selections from Thomas a Kempis, Pierre Poiret, Jean Duvergier de Hauranne, and Jacques Joseph Duguet, 1985; Milton for the Methodists, 1988. Add: 1505 Pinecrest Road, Durham, N.C. 27705, U.S.A.

BAKER, Houston Alfred, Jr. American, b. 1943. Poetry, Literature. Albert M. Greenfield Prof. of Human Relations, Univ. of Pennsylvania, Philadelphia, since 1982 (Dir. of Afro-American Studies, 1974–77; Prof. of English, 1974–82). Instr., Howard Univ., Washington, D.C., 1966; Instr., 1968–69, and Asst. Prof., 1969, Yale Univ., New Haven, Conn.; Assoc. Prof., 1970–73, and Prof. of English, 1973, Univ. of Virginia, Charlottesville. *Publs:* (ed.) Black Literature in America, 1971; Long Black Song: Essays in Black American Literature and Culture, 1972; (ed.) Twentieth-Century Interpretations of Native Son, 1972; A Many-Colored Coat of Dreams: The Poetry of Countee Cullen, 1974; Singers of Daybreak:

Studies in Black American Literature, 1974; (ed.) Reading Black: Essays in the Criticism of African, Caribbean and Black American Literature, 1976; No Matter Where You Travel, You Still Be Black (poems), 1979; The Journey Back: Issues in Black Literature and Criticism, 1980; Spirit Run (poems), 1982; (ed.) Three American Literatures: Essays in Chicano, Native American and Asian-American Literature for Teachers of American Literature, 1982; Blue, Ideology, and Afro-American Literature: A Vernacular Theory, 1984; Blues Journeys Home (poems), 1985; Modernism and the Harlem Renaissance, 1987; Afro-American Poetics: Revisions of Harlem and the Black Aesthetic, 1988. Add: Dept. of English, Univ. of Pennsylvania, Philadelphia, Pa. 19104, U.S.A.

BAKER, Howard (Wilson). American, b. 1905. Novels/Short stories, Plays/Screenplays, Poetry, Literature. Briggs-Copeland Instr., Harvard Univ., Cambridge, Mass., 1937–43; Founding Member, The Barn Theatre, Porterville, Calif.; Dir., Lindsay Ripe Olive Co., Lindsay, Calif., 1956–57; Pres., Bd. of Dirs., Grand View Heights Citrus Assn., 1962–73, and Tulare- Kern Citrus Exchange, 1969–73. *Publs:* Orange Valley (novel), 1931; Induction to Tragedy: A Study in the Development of Dramatic Form, 1939; A Letter from the Country and Other Poems, 1941; (with Dorothy Baker) Trio (play), 1944; (with D. Baker) The Ninth Day (play), 1957; Ode to the Sea and Other Poems, 1966; Persephone's Cave: Cultural Accumulations of the Early Greeks, 1979. Add: 24292 Ave. 108, Terra Bella, Calif. 93270, U.S.A.

BAKER, James Rupert. American, b. 1925. Literature. Prof. of English, San Diego State Univ. (Asst. Prof., 1956–61; Assoc. Prof., 1962–67). Co-Founder and member of Editorial Bd., Twentieth Century Literature, since 1955 (Founder and Ed., Current Bibliography Section, 1955–57); Advisory Ed., James Joyce Quarterly, 1966–85. *Publs:* (ed.) Poems of Bishop Henry King, 1960; (ed.) Casebook Edition of William Golding's Lord of the Flies, 1964; William Golding: A Critical Study, 1965; (ed.) James Joyce's Dubliners: A Critical Handbook, 1968; Critical Essays on William Golding, 1988. Add: Dept. of English, San Diego State Univ., San Diego, Calif. 92182, U.S.A.

BAKER, Jeannie. British, b. 1950. Children's fiction. Illustrator for Phoebus Books, 1974, I.P.C. mag., and The Times, London, 1974–75, H.M.S.O. and Transworld Publications, London, 1975, Craft Australia, Cleo, and Pol, Sydney, 1976, and The Observer and New Scientist, London, 1979. *Publs:* Grandfather, 1977; Grandmother, 1978; Millicent, 1980; One Hungry Spider, 1981; Home in the Sky, 1984. Add: 56 Denning Ave., Waddon, Croydon, Surrey, England.

BAKER, Lucinda. American, b. 1916. Novels/Short stories. *Publs:* (contrib.) The Kid Who Fractioned (textbook), 1969; The Place of Devils, 1976; Walk the Night Unseen, 1977; The Memoirs of the First Baroness, 1978. Add: 180 Pony Soldier Rd., Sedona, Ariz. 86336, U.S.A.

BAKER, Margaret J(oyce). British, b. 1918. Children's fiction, Biography. *Publs:* The Fighting Cocks, 1949; Nonsense Said the Tortoise (in U.S. as Homer the Tortoise), 1949; Four Farthings and a Thimble, 1950; A Castle and Sixpence, 1951; Benbow and the Angels, 1952; The Family That Grew and Grew, 1952; Treasure Trove, 1952; Homer Sees the Queen, 1953; The Young Magicians, 1954; Lions in the Potting Shed (in U.S. as Lions in the Woodshed), 1954; The Wonderful Wellington Boots, 1955; Anna Sewell and Black Beauty, 1956; Acorns and Aerials, 1956; The Bright High Flyer, 1957; Tip and Run, 1958; Homer Goes to Stratford, 1958; The Magic Seashell, 1959; The Birds of Thimblepins, 1960; Homer in Orbit, 1961; Into the Castle, 1962; The Cats of Honeytown, 1962; Away Went Galloper, 1962; Castaway Christmas, 1963; Cut Off from Crumpets, 1964; The Shoe Shop Bears, 1964; Homer Goes West, 1965; Hannibal and the Bears, 1965; Bears Back in Business, 1967; Porterhouse Major, 1967; Hi-Jinks Joins the Bears, 1970; Snails' Place, 1970; The Last Straw, 1971; Boots and the Ginger Bears, 1972; The Sand Bird, 1973; Prickets Way, 1973; Lock Stock and Barrel, 1974; Home from the Hill, 1968; Sand in Our Shoes, 1976; The Gift Horse, 1982; Catch as Catch Can, 1983; Beware of the Gnomes, 1985; The Waiting Room Doll, 1986; Fresh Fields for Daisy, 1987. Add: Prickets, Old Cleeve, nr. Minehead, Somerset TA24 6HW, England.

BAKER, Michael. British, b. 1938. Children's fiction. Head of Litigation and Prosecution Division, British Telecom Solicitor's Office, since 1981. Head of Branch (Legal) Post Office Solicitor's Office, 1971–81 (Legal Asst., 1965–71). *Publs:* The Mountain and the Summer Stars, 1968. Add: 22 Moor Lane, Rickmansworth, Herts. WD3 1LG, England.

BAKER, Paul R(aymond). American, b. 1927. Architecture, History,

Area Studies. Prof. of History and Dir. of American Civilization Program, New York Univ. (joined faculty, 1965). *Publs:* (ed.) Views of Society and Manners in America, by Frances Wright D'Arusmont, 1963; The Fortunate Pilgrims: Americans in Italy, 1800-1860, 1964; (ed.) The Atomic Bomb: The Great Decision, 1968, 1976; (with William Hall) The American Experience, vol. I, The American People, 1976; vol. II, Growth of a Nation, 1976; vol. III, Organizing a Democracy, 1979; vol. IV, The American Economy, 1979, vol. V, The United States in World Affairs, 1979; Richard Morris Hunt, 1980, 1986; (contributor) Around the Square, 1982; Master Builders, 1985; The Architecture of Richard Morris Hunt, 1986. Add: c/o Dept. of History, New York Univ., 19 University Pl., Room 523, New York, N.Y. 10003, U.S.A.

BAKER, Peter. British, b. 1926. Novels/Short stories, Plays/Screenplays. Ed., Films and Filming mag., London, 1955–68. *Publs:* To Win a Prize on Sunday, 1966; Cruise, 1968; Casino, 1968; The Antibodies, 1969; The Bedroom Sailors, 1970; Babel Beach, 1973; Clinic, 1982. Add: c/o Hilary Rubinstein, A.P. Watt & Son, Literary Agency, 26-28 Bedford Row, London WC1, England.

BAKER, Russell (Wayne). American, b. 1925. Humor/Satire, Autobiography. Writer of the "Observer" column, The New York Times, since 1962 (Member, Washington Bureau, 1954–62). With the Baltimore Sun, 1947–54. Recipient, Pulitzer Prize, 1979, 1983. *Publs:* An American in Washington, 1961; No Cause for Panic, 1964; All Things Considered, 1965; Our Next President, 1968; Poor Russell's Almanac, 1972; The Upside Down Man, 1977; So This Is Depravity, 1980; (with others) Home Again, Home Again, 1979; Growing Up, 1982; The Rescue of Miss Yaskell and Other Pipe Dreams, 1983; (ed.) The Norton Book of Light Verse, 1986. Add: Observer, New York Times, 229 W. 43rd St., New York, N.Y. 10036, U.S.A.

BAKER, Sheridan (Warner, Jr.). American, b. 1918. Literature. Prof. Emeritus, Univ. of Michigan, Ann Arbor, since 1984 (joined faculty, 1950). Lectr. in English, Univ. of California, Berkeley, 1949–50. *Publs:* The Practical Stylist, 1962, 5th ed., 1981; Ernest Hemingway: An Introduction and Interpretation, 1966; The Complete Stylist, 1966, 3rd ed. as The Complete Stylist and Handbook, 1984; (with I.A. Richards and Jacques Barzun) The Written Word, 1971; (with Northrop Frye and George Perkins) The Practical Imagination, 1980; (with Northrop Frye and George Perkins) The Harper Handbook to Literature, 1985. Add: 2866 Provincial Dr., Ann Arbor, Mich., U.S.A.

BAKER, Stephen. American, b. 1921. Advertising, Humor. Pres., Stephen Baker Assocs., Inc., New York. *Publs:* Advertising Layout and Art Direction, 1959; How to Live with a Neurotic Dog, 1960; Visual Persuasion, 1961; How to Play Golf in the Low 120's, 1962; How to Look Like Somebody in Business without Being Anybody, 1963; How to Live with a Neurotic Wife, 1970; How to Live with a Neurotic Husband, 1970; How to be Analyzed by a Neurotic Psychoanalyst, 1971; Systematic Approach to Advertising Creativity, 1979; Games Dogs Play, 1979; Motorist Guide to New York, 1981; I Hate Meetings, 1983; Executive Mother Goose, 1984; How to Live with a Neurotic Cat, 1985; My Cat: The First Twenty Years, 1986; The Advertiser's Manual, 1987. Add: Tudor City Pl., New York, N.Y. 10017, U.S.A.

BAKER, Thomas Francis Timothy. British, b. 1935. History. Ed., Victoria County History of Middlesex, Inst. of Historical Research, London, since 1967. Research Asst., History of Parliament, 1963–67. *Publs:* (abridger) Churchill's History of the English Speaking Peoples: as The Island Race, 1965; The Normans, 1966; Medieval London, 1970; (with J.S. Cockburn) Victoria County History of Middlesex, vol. IV, 1971, (sole ed.) vols. V-XI, 1976–88. Add: 50 Hastings Rd., Pembury, Kent, England.

BAKER, Thomas Harrison. American, b. 1933. Media. Prof. of History, Univ. of Arkansas at Little Rock (joined faculty, 1969). Asst. Prof., Mississippi State Coll. for Women, Columbus, 1963–68. *Publs:* The Memphis Commercial Appeal: History of a Southern Newspaper, 1971. Add: 33rd and University, Little Rock, Ark. 72204, U.S.A.

BAKEWELL, Kenneth (Graham Bartlett). British, b. 1931. Administration/Management, Information science/Computers, Librarianship. Reader, Liverpool Polytechnic, since 1987 (Lectr., 1966–68; Sr. Lectr., 1968–78; Principal Lectr., 1978–87). Librarian, British Inst. of Mgmt., 1961–64; Technical Documentation Officer and Librarian, Liverpool City Libraries, 1964–66. Pres., Soc. of Indexers, 1987. *Publs:* (compiler) Productivity in British Industry, 1963; (ed.) Classification for Information Retrieval, 1968; (ed.) Library and Information Services for Management,

1968; Industrial Libraries Throughout the World, 1969; How to Find Out: Management and Productivity, 2nd ed. 1970; A Manual of Cataloguing Practice, 1972; Management Principles and Practice: A Guide to Information Sources, 1977; Classification and Indexing Practice, 1978; (with E.J. Hunter) Cataloguing, 1979, 1983; (with K.D.C. Vernon and others) The London Classification of Business Studies, 2nd ed., 1979; (with G.A. Dare) The Manager's Guide to Getting the Answers, 1980, 1983; How to Organise Information, 1984; Business Information and the Public Library, 1987. Add: 9 Greenacre Rd., Liverpool L25 0LD, England.

BALAAM. *See* **LAMB,** Geoffrey Frederick.

BALASKAS, Arthur. South African, b. 1940. Sports/Physical education/Keeping fit. Assoc. Member, The Philadelphia Assn., since 1973. *Publs:* Bodylife, 1977; New Life, 1979; (with John L. Stirk) Soft Exercise, 1982; Active Birth, 1982. Add: 32 Cholmeley Crescent, London N6, England.

BALASSA, Bela. American, b. 1928. Economics. Prof. of Political Economy, Johns Hopkins Univ., Baltimore, Md., since 1967; Consultant, Intnl. Bank for Reconstruction and Development, since 1966; Consultant in economics to government, intnl. orgs., and industry. Asst. to Assoc. Prof. of Economics, Yale Univ., New Haven, Conn., 1959–67. Pres., Assn. of Comparative Economic Studies, 1979–80. *Publs:* The Hungarian Experience in Economic Planning, 1959; The Theory of Economic Integration, 1961; Trade Prospects for Developing Countries, 1964; Economic Development and Integration, 1965; Trade Liberalization among Industrial Countries: Objectives and Alternatives, 1967; Studies in Trade Liberalization, 1967; The Structure of Protection in Developing Countries, 1971; European Economic Integration, 1975; Policy Reform in Developing Countries, 1977; The Newly-Industrialized Countries in the World Economy, 1981; Turkey: Industrialisation and Trade Strategy, 1982; Morocco: Industrial Incentives and Export Promotion, 1984; Change and Challenge in the World Economy, 1985; Toward Renewed Economic Growth in Latin America, 1986; Adjusting to Success: Balance-of-Payments Policy in the East Asian NICs, 1987; Changing Trade Patterns in Manufactured Goods: An Econometric Investigation, 1988; Japan in the World Economy, 1988; New Directions in the World Economy, 1989. Add: 1818 H. St. N.W., Washington, D.C. 20433, U.S.A.

BALCHIN, William George Victor. British, 1916. Geography. Lectr. in Geography, King's Coll., Univ. of London, 1945–54; Prof. of Geography, 1954–78, now Emeritus, and Vice-Principal, 1964–66, and 1970–73, University Coll. of Swansea; Fellow, King's Coll., London, 1984. *Publs:* (ed.) Geography and Man, 1947, 1955; (ed. with A.W. Richards) Climate and Weather Exercises; 1949; (ed. with A.W. Richards) Practical and Experimental Geography, 1952; Cornwall: The Making of the Landscape, 1954; Cornwall: The Landscape Through Maps, 1967; (ed.) Geography for the Intending Student, 1970; (ed.) Swansea and Its Region, 1971; Concern for Geography, 1981; (ed.) The Living History of Britain, 1981; The Cornish Landscape, 1983. Add: 10 Low Wood Rise, Ben Rhydding, Ilkley, W. Yorks, England.

BALDERSON, Margaret. Australian, b. 1935. Children's fiction. Worked as Librarian in Sydney. Recipient: Australian Children's Book Council Book of the Year Award, 1969. *Publs:* When Jays Fly to Barbmo, 1969; A Dog Called George, 1975; Blue and Gold Day, 1979. Add: c/o Oxford Univ. Press, 253 Normanby Rd., South Melbourne, Vic. 3205, Australia.

BALDRY, Harold Caparne. British, b. 1907. Classics. Prof. Emeritus, Univ. of Southampton, since 1972 (Prof. of Classics, 1954–72; Deputy Vice-Chancellor, 1963–66). Prof. of Classics, Univ. of Cape Town, 1948–54; Chmn., Southern Arts Assn., 1972–74; Member, Arts Council of Great Britain, 1973–78. *Publs:* The Classics in the Modern World, 1949; Greek Literature for the Modern Reader, 1951; Ancient Utopias, 1956; (with others) Grecs et Barbares, 1962; (with others) The Birth of Western Civilization, 1964; The Unity of Mankind in Greek Thought, 1965; Ancient Greek Literature in Its Living Context 1968; The Greek Tragic Theatre, 1971; The Case for the Arts, 1981. Add: 19 Uplands Way, Southampton, SO2 1QW, England.

BALDWIN, Anne Norris. American, b. 1938. Children's fiction. *Publs:* The Sometimes Island, 1969; Sunflowers for Tina, 1970; Sunlight Valley, 1971; A Friend in the Park, 1973, Jenny's Revenge, 1974; A Little Time, 1978. Add: 1243 Los Trancos Rd., Portola Valley, Calif. 94025, U.S.A.

BALDWIN, Gordon C(ortis). Also writes as Gordo Baldwin and Lew

Gordon. American, b. 1908. Westerns/Adventure, Anthropology/Ethnology, Children's non-fiction. Instr. in Dendrochronology, 1934–36, and in Archaeology, 1936–37, Univ. of Arizona; Asst. Curator, Arizona State Museum, Tucson, 1937–40; Archaeologist for the National Park Service, in Boulder City, Nev., 1940–48, and in Omaha, Nebr., 1948–53; Instr. in Anthropology, Univ. of Omaha, 1953–54; freelance writer, 1954–74. Pres., 1968–69, and Ed. of the Roundup, 1962–65, Western Writers of America. *Publs:* western novels—Trouble Range, 1956; Trail North, 1956; Range War at Sundown, 1957, in U.S. as Sundown Country, 1959; Powdersmoke Justice, 1957, in U.S as Lew Gordon, 1961; Roundup at Wagonmound, 1960; (as Gordo Baldwin) Ambush Basin, 1960, in U.K. as Lew Gordon, 1965; Brand of Yuma, 1960; (as Gordo Baldwin) Wyoming Rawhide, 1961, in U.K. as Gordon C. Baldwin, 1965; juvenile nonfiction—America's Buried Past: The Story of North American Archaeology, 1962; The Ancient Ones: Basketmakers and Cliff Dwellers of the Southwest, 1963; The World of Prehistory: The Story of Man's Beginnings, 1963; Stone Age Peoples Today, 1964; The Riddle of the Past: How Archaeological Detectives Solve Prehistoric Riddles, 1965; The Warrior Apaches: A Story of the Chiricahua and Western Apache (for adults), 1965; Race Against Time: The Story of Salvage Archaeology, 1966; Strange People and Stranger Customs, 1967; Calendars of the Past: How Science Dates Archaeological Ruins, 1967; How Indians Really Lived, 1967; Games of the American Indian, 1969; Talking Drums to Written Word: How Early Man Learned to Communicate, 1970; Indians of the Southwest, 1970; Schemers, Dreamers, and Medicine Men: Witchcraft and Magic among Primitive People, 1971; Pyramids of the New World, 1971; Inventors and Inventions of the Ancient Worlds, 1973; The Apache Indians, Raiders of the Southwest, 1978. Add: 426 Poppy Pl., Mountain View, Calif. 94043, U.S.A.

BALE, Don. American, b. 1937. Recreation/Leisure/Hobbies. Pres., Bale Books and Bale Publs. *Publs:* Complete Guide for Profitable Coin Investing and Collecting, 1969. How to Invest in Singles, 1970, 1978; Fabulous Investment Potential of Singles, 1970, 1978; Fabulous Investment Potential of Uncirculated Singles, 1970, 1978; Fabulous Investment Potential of Liberty Walking Halves, 1971, 1978; A Gold Mine in Your Pocket, 1971, 1978; A Gold Mine in Gold, 1972, 1978; How to Invest in Uncirculated Singles, 1972, 1978; Out of Little Coins, Big Fortunes Grow, 1973, 3rd. 1982; (ed.) How to Find Valuable Old and Scarce Coins, 1984. Add: Box 2727, New Orleans, La. 70176, U.S.A.

BALFOUR, Michael (Leonard Graham). British, b. 1908. History, International relations/Current affairs. Lectr. in politics, Magdalen Coll., Oxford, 1932–36; Study Group Secty., Royal Inst. of Intnl. Affairs, 1936–39; Principal, Ministry of Information, 1939–42; Deputy Dir. of Intelligence, Political Warfare Exec., 1942–44; Deputy Chief, Intelligence Section, Psychological Warfare Div., SHAEF, 1944–45; Dir. of Information Services Control, British Control Commn. for Germany, 1945–47; Chief Information Officer, Bd. of Trade, 1947–64; Prof. of European History, Univ. of East Anglia, Norwich, 1966–74. *Publs:* Nationalism, 1939; States and Mind, 1952; Four-Power Control in Germany 1945–6, 1956; The Kaiser and His Times, 1964; West Germany, 1968; Helmuth von Moltke: A Leader Against Hitler, 1972; Propaganda in War 1939–45, 1979; The Adversaries: America, Russia, and the Open World 1941–62, 1981; West Germany: A Contemporary History, 1982; Britain and Joseph Chamberlain, 1985; Withstanding Hitler, 1988. Add: Waine's Cottage, Swan Lane, Burford OX8 4SH, England.

BALIAN, Lorna. American, b. 1929. Children's fiction. *Publs:* author and illustrator—Humbug Witch, 1965; I Love You, Mary Jane, 1967; The Animal, 1972; Where in the World is Henry?, 1972; Sometimes It's Turkey—Sometimes It's Feathers, 1973; Humbug Rabbit, 1974; The Sweet Touch, 1976; Bah! Humbug?, 1977; A Sweetheart for Valentine, 1979; Leprechauns Never Lie, 1980; Mother's Mother's Day, 1982; Humbug Potion, 1984; A Garden for a Groundhog, 1985; Amelia's Nine Lives, 1986; The Socksnatchers, 1988. Add: 6698 Highway 83 South, Hartford, Wisc. 53027, U.S.A.

BALINT, Enid. British. Medicine/Health. Consultant, Inst. of Marital Studies-Tavistock Inst. of Human Relations, since 1954; Leader of Balint Group, St. Thomas Hosp. Group Practice since 1975. Organiser, Family Welfare Assn., 1944–52; Visiting Assoc. Prof. of Research in Behavioral Sciences, Dept. of Psychiatry, 1957–71, and Visiting Prof. of Psychoanalysis, 1971–73, Univ. of Cincinnati, Ohio; Dir., British Inst. of Psychoanalysis, 1970–74; Hon. Clinical Asst., University Coll. Hosp., London, 1971–75. Leader, General Practitioner Training/Research Seminars, Tavistock Clinic, 1962–65, and University Coll. Hosp., London, 1965–75. *Publs:* (with Michael Balint) The Doctor, His Patient and the Illness, 1957; (with Michael Balint) Psychotherapeutic Techniques in

Medicine, 1961; (with others) A Study of Doctors, 1966; (contrib.) What Is Psycho-analysis, 1968; (with Michael Balint and Paul H. Ornstein) Focal Psychotherapy: An Example of Applied Psychoanalysis, 1971; (ed. and contrib., with J.S. Norell) Six Minutes for the Patient, 1973; The Basic Fault. Add: Raven House, Ramsbury, Wilts. SN8 2PA, England.

BALL, B.N. *See* **BALL,** Brian N(eville).

BALL, Brian N(eville). Also writes as B.N. Ball and as Brian Kinsey Jones. British, b. 1932. Novels/Short stories, Science fiction, Children's fiction. Staff Member, subsequently Sr. Lectr. in English, Doncaster Coll. of Education, since 1956. Chmn., Doncaster Prose and Poetry Soc., 1968–70. *Publs:* novels—(as Brian Kinsey Jones) Lay Down Your Wife for Another, 1971; Death of a Low Handicap Man, 1974; Montenegrin Gold, 1974; science-fiction novels—Sundog, 1965; Timepiece, Timepivot, and Timepit (trilogy), 1968–71; Lesson for the Damned, 1971; Night of the Robots (in U.S. as The Regiments of Night), 1972; Devil's Peak, 1972; The Probability Man, 1972; Planet Probability, 1973; Singularity Station, 1973; The Venomous Serpent (in U.S. as The Night Creature), 1974; The Space Guardians, 1975; Keegan: The No-Option Contract, 1975; Keegan: The One-Way Deal, 1976; Witchfinder: The Mark of the Beast, 1976; Witchfinder: The Evil at Monteine, 1977; children's books, as B.N. Ball—Mr. Tofat's Term, 1964; Paris Adventures, 1967; Princess Priscilla, 1975; Jackson's Friend, Jackson's House, Jackson's Holiday, 3 vols., 1975–77; Jackson and the Magpies, 1978; The Witch in Our Attic, 1979; Young Person's Guide to UFO's, 1979; Dennis and the Flying Saucer, 1980; The Baker Street Boys, 1983; The Starbuggy, 1983; The Doomship of Drax, 1985; other—(ed.) Tales of Science Fiction, 1964; Basic Linguistics for Secondary Schools, 3 vols., 1966–67. Add: c/o William Heinemann Ltd., 81 Fulham Rd., London SW3 6RB, England.

BALL, (Frederick) Clive. British, b. 1941. Travel/Exploration/Adventure. Lab. Mgr., Govt. of Western Australia, Technical Education Dept., since 1973. Development Engineer, S.T.C., 1964–65; Electronics Technician, Hills Electronics, Aust., 1966–70, and Philips, Canada, 1970–71; Technical Officer, ABC, 1972–73. *Publs:* Seven Years with Samantha: Around the World in a Vintage Austin Seven, 1974. Add: No. 18, Moefflin Ave., Darlington, W.A., Australia 6070.

BALL, George (Wildman). American, b. 1909. International relations, Autobiography. Law Practice, Chicago, 1935–42 and in Washington, D.C., 1946–61; Dir., U.S. Strategic Bombing Survey, London, 1944–45; Under-Secty. of State for Economic Affairs, 1961; Under-Secty. of State, 1961–66; Pres., 1966–68, and Sr. Partner, 1969–82, Lehmann Bros. Intnl., Ltd.; Permanent U.S. Rep. to United Nations, June-Sept. 1968. Add: The Discipline of Power: Essentials of Modern World Structure, 1968; Diplomacy for a Crowded World: An American Foreign Policy, 1976; The Past Has Another Pattern (memoirs), 1982; Error and Betrayal in Lebanon and the Implications for U.S.-Israel Relations, 1984. Add: 107 Library Pl., Princeton, N.J. 08540, U.S.A.

BALLANTYNE, John (Chalmers). British, b. 1917. Medicine/Health. Consulting Ear, Nose and Throat Surgeon, Royal Free Hosp., London, since 1958. Former Consultant, Royal Northern Hosp., London, and Consultant Otologist, L.C.C. *Publs:* (co-author) Synopsis of Otolaryology, 2nd ed. 1967, 3rd ed., 1978; Deafness, 2nd ed. 1970, 4th ed., 1983; (co-ed. and author) Diseases of the Ear, Nose and Throat, 4 vols., 4th ed. 1979; (co-ed.) Ultrastructural of the Inner Ear, 1984. Add: 11 Holland Park Rd., London W14 8NA, England.

BALLARD, J(ames) G(raham). British, b. 1930. Science fiction/Fantasy. *Publs:* The Wind from Nowhere, 1962; The Voices of Time and Other Stories, 1962; The Drowned World, 1962; Billenium and Other Stories, 1962; The 4-Dimensional Nightmare, 1963; Passport to Eternity and Other Stories, 1963; Terminal Beach, 1964; The Drought, 1965; The Crystal World, 1966; The Disaster Area, 1967; The Day of Forever, 1968; The Overloaded Man, 1968; The Atrocity Exhibition (in U.S. as Love and Napalm: Export USA), 1970; Vermilion Sands, 1971; Crash!, 1972; The Concrete Island, 1974; High-Rise, 1975; Low-Flying Aircraft (stories), 1976; The Best of J.G. Ballard, 1977; The Best Short Stories, 1978; The Unlimited Dream Company, 1979; Hello America, 1981; Myths of the Near Future (stories), 1982; Empire of the Sun, 1984; The Venus Hunters, 1986; The Day of Forever, 1986; The Day of Creation, 1987; Memories of the Space Age, 1988; Running Wild, 1988. Add: 36 Charlton Rd., Shepperton, Middx. TW17 8AT, England.

BALLARD, Martin. British, b. 1929. Children's non-fiction, Education, History, Technology. Intnl. Development Dir., Macmillan SA, since 1979. Served in the British Army, 1948–49; Asst. District Officer,

Colonial Service, Northern Nigeria, 1953–56; Clerk in Holy Orders, Church of England Sheffield Diocese, 1958–62 (resigned orders); History teacher, Bristol Education Authority, 1962–69; Dir., Educational Publishers Council, 1970–72, and Book Development Council, 1972–78, Publishers Assn., London. *Publs:* Bristol: Seaport City, 1966; The Emir's Son, 1967; The Monarch of Juan Fernandez, 1968; Genjie's Portion, 1969; The Story of Teaching, 1969; The Speaking Drums of Ashamti, 1970; Rome and Empire, A.D. 41-122, 1970; Faith and Violence: The Birth of Medieval Europe, A.D. 800-900, 1970; The Cross and the Sword: The Middle Ages 1270-1350, 1970; Sails and Guns: The Era of Discovery 1491-1534, 1970; Europe Reaches Round the World 1584-1632, 1970; Kings and Courtiers: The Era of Elegance, 1684-1716, 1970; (ed.) New Movements in the Study and Teaching of History, 1970; Revolutions and Steam Engines 1775-1815, 1971; The Age of Progress 1848-1866, 1971; The World at War 1900–1918, 1971; Who Am I? A Book of World Religions, 1971; Scholars and Ancestors: China under the Sung Dynasty, 1973; Dockie, 1972; Land of the Great Moguls: Akbar's India, 1973; Uthman dan Fodio, 1977. Add: c/o Heineman Educational, Halley Court, Jordan Hill, Oxford OX2 8EJ, England.

BALLIETT, Whitney. American, b. 1926. Music. Member of staff, New Yorker mag., since 1951. *Publs:* The Sound of Surprise, 1959, 1978; Dinosaurs in the Morning, 1962, 1978; Such Sweet Thunder, 1966; Super Drummer: A Profile of Buddy Rich, 1968; Ecstasy at the Onion, 1971; Alec Wilder and His Friends, 1974, 1983; New York Notes, 1976; Improvising, 1977; American Singers, 1979; Night Creature, 1981; Duke Ellington Remembered, 1981; Jelly Roll, Jabbo and Fats, 1982; American Musicians: 56 Portraits in Jazz, 1986. Add: The New Yorker, 25 West 43rd St., New York, N.Y. 10036, U.S.A.

BALODIS, Janis (Maris). Australian, b. 1950. Plays/Screenplays. Freelance writer since 1979; Assoc. Dir., Melbourne Theatre Co., since 1988. Primary teacher, Tully, Qld., 1971, and Bambaroo, Qld., 1972; Asst. Stage Manager, Queensland Theatre Co., Brisbane, 1974; Student and Director, E15 Acting School, Loughton, Essex, 1976–79. *Publs:* Too Young for Ghosts, 1985. Add: Suite 302, 9-13 Bronte Rd., Bondi Junction, N.S.W. 2022, Australia.

BALTAZAR, Eulalio. American. Philosophy. Prof. of Philosophy, Univ. of the District of Columbia, Washington, D.C., since 1969. Prof. of Philosophy, Univ. of Dayton, Ohio, 1962–69. *Publs:* Teilhard and the Supernatural, 1966; God Within Process, 1970; The Dark Center, 1973; (co-author) Logic for Black Under-Graduates, 1974. Add: 11501 Rokeby Ave., Kensington, Md. 20895, U.S.A.

BALY, Monica Eileen. British, b. 1914. Medicine. Chief Nursing Officer, Displaced Person's Div., Foreign Office, Germany, 1949–51; Area Officer, Royal Coll. of Nursing, 1951–74; Lectr., Bath Technical Coll. *Publs:* Nursing and Social Change, 1973, 1980; Professional Responsibility, 1975; Nursing, Past-into Present, 1977; A New Approach to District Nursing, 1981; Florence Nightingale and the Nursing Legacy, 1986; A History of the Queen's Nursing Institute, 1987. Add: 19 Royal Cres., Bath, England.

BAMFORD, Brian Reginald. South African, b. 1932. Law, Autobiography. Advocate, Cape Town Bar, 1956–83. Sr. Counsellor, 1973, Senator, 1974–77, and M.P., 1977–87. *Publs:* (with W.E. Cooper) Handbook on Criminal Procedure Act, 1956; The Law of Partnership and Voluntary Association in South Africa, 1958, 3rd ed. 1983; The Substance: The Story of a Rhodes Scholar at Oxford, 1959; The Law of Shipping and Carriage in South Africa, 1961, 3rd ed. 1982; (with L. Blackwell) Newspaper Law, 1962; Handbook on Electoral Law, 1963; Add: 47 Sandown Rd., Rondebosch 7700, South Africa.

BAN, Thomas Arthur. Canadian, b. 1929. Psychiatry. Prof. of Psychiatry, Vanderbilt Univ., Nashville, Tenn., since 1976; Assoc. Member of Psychiatry, McGill Univ., Montreal, since 1977 (Demonstrator, 1960–63; Lectr., 1964–65; Asst. Prof., 1965–70; Assoc. Prof., and Dir., Div. of Psychopharmacology, 1970–76). Sr. Research Psychiatrist, 1961–66, Assoc. Dir. of Research, 1966–70 and Chief of Research Services, 1970–72, Douglas Hosp., Verdun. *Publs:* Conditioning and Psychiatry, 1964; Psychopharmacology, 1969; (with H.E. Lehmann) Nicotinic Acid in the Treatment of Schizophrenias: Progress Report I, 1970; (with H.E. Lehmann) Pharmacotherapy of Tension and Anxiety, 1970; (with H.E. Lehmann) Experimental Approaches to Psychiatric Diagnosis, 1971; Nicotinic Acid in the treatment of Schizophrenias: Introduction, 1971; Nicotinic Acid in the Treatment of Schizophrenias: Complementary Report A, 1971; Schizophrenia: A Psychopharmacological Approach, 1972; Recent Advances in the Biology of Schizophrenia,

1973; Depression and the Tricyclic Antidepressants, 1974; Introduction to the Psychopharmacology of Doexpin, 1977; Psychopharmacology of Thiothixene, 1978; Psychopharmacology of Depression, 1981; Psychopharmacology for the Aged, 1980; (with M. Hollender) Psychopharmacology for Everyday Practice, 1981. Add: 2304 Valley Brook Rd., Nashville, Tenn., U.S.A.

BANBURY, Philip. British, b. 1914. Transportation. Draughtsman, Admiralty Signal Establishment, 1943–46; Cartographical Draughtsman, British European Airways, 1946–48; Aeronautical Chart Compiler, Intnl. Aeradio Ltd., 1948–76. *Publs:* Shipbuilders of the Thames and Medway from 1500-1914, 1971; Man and the Sea, 1975. Add: Great Circle, 19 High Ridge, Seabrook, Hythe, Kent CT21 5TE, England.

BANCROFT, Anne. British, b. 1923. Theology/Religion. *Publs:* Religions of the East, 1974; Twentieth Century Mystics and Sages, 1976; Zen: Direct Pointing to Reality, 1980; The Luminous Vision: Six Medieval Mystics, 1982; Chinese New Year, 1984; Festivals of the Buddha, 1984; The Buddhist World, 1984; The New Religious World, 1985; Origins of the Sacred, 1987. Add: 7 Dagmar Rd., Exmouth, Devon EX8 2AN, England.

BANCROFT, Iris. American, b. 1922. Also writes as Julia Barnright, Iris Brent, and Andrea Layton. Romance fiction, Sex. Full-time writer. Violist and trombonist with California orchestras. Bookkeeper, then Garment union organizer, Chicago, 1945–50; teacher, Chicago area, 1957–62; worked in publishing, California, 1962–77. *Publs:* Romance—(as Andrea Layton) Life's Gentle Fugitive, 1978; (as Andrea Layton) So Wild a Rapture, 1978; (as Andrea Layton) Midnight Fires, 1979; Love's Burning Flame, 1979; Rapture's Rebel, 1980; Rebel's Passion, 1981; Dawn of Desire, 1981; other—(as Julia Barnright) The Sexually Exciting Female, 1971; (as Julia Barnright) The Sexually Superior Male, 1971; (as Iris Brent) Swinger's Diary, 1973; Whispering Hope (fictionalized biography), 1981; (with Roger Callahan) The Five Minute Phobia Cure, 1984; (with William Hartman and Marilyn Fithian) Any Man Can, 1984; (with Mary Mattis) Sex and the Single Parent, 1986; (with Jerry DeHaan) Reaching Intimacy, 1986. Add: c/o Teal & Watt Literary Agency, 8033 Sunset Blvd., Los Angeles, Calif. 90046, U.S.A.

BANDURA, Albert. American, b. 1925. Psychology. Jordan Prof. of Social Science in Psychology, Stanford Univ., since 1964 (Instr., to Prof., 1953–64). Fellow, Center for Advanced Study in the Behavioural Sciences, 1969–70. Pres., American Psychological Assn., 1974, and Western Psychological Assn. 1980. *Publs:* (with W.H. Walters) Adolescent Aggression, 1959; (with W.H. Walters) Social Learning and Personality Development, 1963; Principles of Behavior Modification, 1969; (ed.) Psychological Modeling: Conflicting Theories, 1971; Aggression: A Social Learning Analysis, 1973; Social Learning Theory, 1977; Social Foundations of Thought and Action, 1986. Add: Dept. of Psychology, Stanford Univ., Stanford, Calif. 94305, U.S.A.

BANFIELD, A(lexander) W(illiam) Frank. Canadian, b. 1918. Environmental science/Ecology, Natural history, Zoology. Prof. Emeritus, Brock Univ., St. Catherines, Ont., since 1980 (Prof. of Biological Sciences, 1969–73, and Dir. of Inst. of Urban and Environmental Studies, 1974–78). Chief Mammalogist, Canadian Wildlife Service, 1947–57; Dir., National Museum of Natural Sciences, 1946–69. *Publs:* The Mammals of Banff National Park, Alberta, 1958; A Revision of the Genus Rangifer: Caribou-Reindeer, 1961; (co-author) Alive in the Wild, 1970; The Mammals of Canada, 1974. Add: 37 Yates St., St. Catharines, Ont. L2R 5R3, Canada.

BANGS, Robert B(abbitt). Also writes as Robert Babbitt. American, b. 1914. Children's fiction, Economics. Economist, U.S. Dept. of Commerce, Washington, D.C., 1941–53, 1951–53, and since 1962. Economist, National Housing Agency, 1946–47, and U.S. Treasury Dept., 1947–51; Member, Bd. of Govs., Federal Reserve System, Washington, D.C., 1956–62. *Publs:* Financing Economic Development, 1968; Men, Money and Markets, 1972; (as Robert Babbitt) The Adventures of Bumper (children), 1973. Add: 8514 Rosewood Dr., Bethesda, Md. 20014, U.S.A.

BANKS, James Albert. American, b. 1941. Cultural/Ethnic topics, Education, Race relations. Prof. of Education since 1973, Univ. of Washington, Seattle (Asst. Prof., 1969–71; Assoc. Prof., 1971–73; Chmn. of the Dept. of Curriculum and Instruction, 1982–88). Pres., National Council for the Social Studies, 1982. *Publs:* Teaching the Black Experience: Methods and Materials, 1970; March Toward Freedom: A History of Black Americans, 1970, 2nd ed. with Cherry A. Banks, 1978;

(ed. with William W. Joyce) Teaching Social Studies to Culturally Different Children, 1971; (ed. with Joyce) Teaching the Language Arts to Culturally Different Children, 1971; (ed. with Jean D. Grambs) Black Self-Concept (social science), 1972; (ed.) Teaching Ethnic Studies, 1973; Teaching Strategies for the Social Studies, 1973, 3rd ed. 1985; Teaching Strategies for Ethnic Studies, 1975, 4th ed. 1987; (with others) Curriculum Guidelines for Multiethnic Education, 1976; Multiethnic Education: Practices and Promises, 1977; Multiethnic Education: Theory and Practice, 1981, 1988; (ed.) Education in the 80's: Multiethnic Education, 1981; (with Sebesta) We Americans: Our History and People, 2 vols., 1982; (with James Lynch) Multicultural Education in Western Societies, 1986; (ed. with Cherry A. McGee Banks) Multicultural Education: Issues and Perspectives, 1989. Add: 115 Miller Hall-DQ-12, Univ. of Washington, Seattle, Wash. 98195, U.S.A.

BANKS, Russell (Earl). American, b. 1940. Novels/Short stories, Poetry. Teacher at New York Univ. and Princeton Univ., New Jersey, since 1981. Plumber in New Hampshire, 1959–64; Publisher and Ed., Lillabulero Press, and Co-Ed., Lillabulero mag., Chapel Hill, N.C., and Northwood Narrows, N.H., 1966–75; taught at Emerson Coll., Boston, 1968–71, Univ. of New Hampshire, Durham, 1968–75, and New England Coll., Henniker, N.H., 1975, 1977–81. *Publs:* (with William Matthews and Newton Smith) 15 Poems, 1967; 30/6 (poetry), 1969; Waiting to Freeze (poetry), 1969; Snow: Meditations of a Cautious Man in Winter (poetry), 1974; Searching for Survivors (short stories), 1975; Family Life (novel), 1975; The New World (short stories, 1978; Hamilton Stark (novel), 1978; The Book of Jamaica (novel), 1980; Trailerpark (short stories), 1981; The Relation of My Imprisonment (novel), 1983; Continental Drift (novel), 1985; Success Stories (short stories), 1986. Add: c/o Harper and Row, 10 E. 53rd St., New York, N.Y. 10022, U.S.A.

BANNATYNE, Jack. *See* **GASTON,** William James.

BANNER, Angela. Pseud. for Angela Mary Maddison. British, b. 1923. Children's fiction. *Publs:* Ant and Bee, 1950; More Ant and Bee, 1955; One Two Three with Ant and Bee, 1958; Around the World with Ant and Bee, 1960; More and More Ant and Bee, 1961; Ant and Bee and the Rainbow, 1962; Ant and Bee and King Dog, 1963; Happy Birthday with Ant and Bee, 1964; Ant and Bee and the ABC, 1966; Ant and Bee Time, 1969; Ant and Bee and the Secret, 1970; Ant and Bee and the Doctor, 1971; Ant and Bee Big Buy Bag, 1971; Ant and Bee Go Shopping, 1972; Which Two Will Meet?, 1972; King Dog on Monday, 1972; King Dog Up and Down the Hill, 1972; Dear Father Christmas, 1984. Add: The Ant and Bee Partnership, c/o Grindlays Bank Ltd., 13 St. James's Sq., London SW1Y 4LF, England.

BANNISTER, (Sir) Roger (Gilbert). British, b. 1929. Medicine, Sports. Chmn., The Sports Council, London, 1971–74. Consultant Neurologist, since 1963; Master, Pembroke Coll., Oxford, since 1985. Athletic achievements include: world record for one mile (first four minute mile), 1954; European 1500 metres title and record, 1954. *Publs:* The First Four Minutes, 1955; (ed.) Brain's Chemical Neurology, 1969, 5th ed. 1978; (ed.) Autonomic Failure, 1983. Add: Pembroke Coll., Oxford OX1 1DW, England.

BANNOCK, Graham. British, b. 1932. Business, Economics. Market Research Mgr., Rover Co., Solihull, 1958–60 and 1962–67; Sr. Admin., Economics Div., Org. for Economic Co-operation and Development, Paris, 1960–62; Mgr., Advanced Planning, Ford of Europe Inc., Dunton, 1967–69; Dir., Research Cttee. of Inquiry on Small Firms, Dept. of Trade, London, 1969–71; Managing Dir., Economists Advisory Group Ltd., London, 1971–81, and Economist Intelligence Unit Ltd., 1981–84. *Publs:* (with A.J. Merrett) Business Economics and Statistics, 1962; The Juggernauts: The Age of the Giant Corporation, 1971, 1973; (with R.E. Baxter and R. Rees) Dictionary of Economics, 1972, 4th ed., 1987; How to Survive the Slump, 1975; The Smaller Business in Britain and Germany, 1976; The Economics of Small Firms, 1981; (with A. Doran) Going Public, 1987; (with Alan Peacock) Governments and Small Business, 1989; (with W.A.P. Manser) A Dictionary of International Finance, 1989. Add: Graham Bannock and Partners, 53 Clarewood Ct., Crawford St., London WIH 5DF, England.

BANNON, Peter. *See* **DURST,** Paul.

BANTOCK, Gavin (Marcus August). British, b. 1939. Plays, Poetry. Prof. of English, Reitaku Univ., Japan, since 1969. *Publs:* Christ: A Poem in Twenty-Six Parts, 1965; Juggernaut, 1968; The Last of the Kings: Frederick the Great (play), 1968; A New Thing Breathing, 1969; Anhaga, 1970; Gleeman, 1972; Eirenikon, 1973; Isles, 1974; Dragons, 1979.

Add: c/o Peter Jay, 69 King George St., London SE10 8PX, England.

BANTOCK, Geoffrey Herman. British, b. 1914. Education, Literature. Emeritus Prof. of Education, Univ. of Leicester, since 1975. *Publs:* Freedom and Authority in Education, 1952; L.H. Myers: A Critical Study, 1956; Education in an Industrial Society, 1963; Education and Values, 1965; Education, Culture and the Emotions, 1967; Culture, Industrialisation and Education, 1968; T.S. Eliot and Education, 1969; Studies in the History of Educational Theory, 2 vols., 1980–84; Dilemmas of the Curriculum, 1980; The Parochialism of the Present, 1981. Add:c/o The Univ., Leicester, England.

BANVILLE, John. Irish, b. 1945. Novels/Short stories. Literary Ed., Irish Times, Dublin. *Publs:* Long Lankin (short stories), 1970; Nightspawn (novel), 1971; Birchwood (novel), 1973; Doctoer Copernicus (novel), 1976; Kepler (novel), 1981; The Newton Letter (novel), 1982; Mefisto (novel), 1986. Add: 6 Church St., Howth, Co. Dublin, Ireland.

BARACK, Nathan A. American, b. 1913. Philosophy, Theology/Religion. Rabbi, Congregation Beth El, Sheboygan, Wisc., since 1949. Rabbi, Congregation Beth El, Phoenix, Ariz., 1939–49. *Publs:* Tale of a Wonderful Ladder, 1943; Faith for Fallibles, 1952; Mt. Moriah View, 1956; History of the Sabbath, 1965; Jewish Way of Life, 1975; God Speaks Naturally, 1983. Add: 225 Mill St., Newton, Mass. 02160, U.S.A.

BARAKA, Imamu Amiri. *See* **JONES,** LeRoi.

BARASCH, Frances K. American, b. 1928. Literature. Prof. of English, Baruch Coll. Univ. of New York, since 1977 (Asst. Prof., 1965–72; Assoc. Prof., 1972–77). Consultant, Choice, since 1968; Publr., Release: A Newsletter for Adult and Continuing Educators, since 1979. Asst. to Dir. and Instr. of English, New York Univ., 1959–61; Adjunct Assoc. Prof. of English, Pace Coll., N.Y., 1961–69; Asst. Prof of English, Long Island Univ., 1964–65. *Publs:* Shakespeare's Second Part of Henry IV, 1964; (ed.) Study Guide Series: Julius Caesar, Merchant of Venice, Othello, Romantic Poets, 1964–66; (co-ed.) Modern British Authors, vol. III, 1966; Wright's History of Caricature and the Grotesque, 1968; The Critical Temper, vol. II, 1969; The Grotesque: A Study of Meanings, 1971. Add: Baruch Coll., 17 Lexington Ave., New York, N.Y. 10010, U.S.A.

BARASH, Samuel T. American, b. 1921. Money/Finance. Self-employed real estate appraiser. Pres., Newark, N.J. Chapter, Assn. of Federal Appraisers, 1971. *Publs:* Standard Real Estate Appraising Manual, 1979; How to Reduce Your Real Estate Taxes, 1979; How to Cash in on Little-Known Local Real Estate Investment Opportunities, 1980; Complete Guide to Condominium and Cooperative Appraising, 1981; Encyclopedia of Real Estate Appraisal Forms and Model Reports, 1983. Add: R.D.1, P.O. Box 130, Lakes Rd., Monroe, N.Y. 10950, U.S.A.

BARBA, Harry. Also writes as Ohan and Baron Mikan. American, b.1922. Novels/Short stories, Education, Writing. Publisher and Conference Dir., Harian Creative Books, since 1967; Ed., Harian Creative Awards series, since 1981. Instr., Wilkes Coll., Wilkes-Barre, Pa., 1947; Instr., Univ of Connecticut, Hartford Campus, 1947–49; Teacher, Seward Park High Sch., New York, 1955–59; Instr., Univ. of Iowa, 1959–63; Fulbright Prof.—American Specialist, Univ. of Damascus, Syria, 1963–64; Reader and Lectr., U.S.I.S. Library, Damascus, 1963–64; Asst. Prof. and Assoc. Prof., Skidmore Coll., Saratoga Springs, N.Y., 1964–68; Prof. of English and Dir. of Writing, Marshall Univ., Huntington, W. Va., 1968–70; Dir. of Writing Arts in West Virginia, 1969–70; Distinguished Visiting Lectr. in Contemporary Literature and Consultant to the Writing Cttee., S.U.N.Y., 1976–77. *Publs:* For the Grape Season, 1960; The Bulbul Bird, 1963, 3 by Harry Barba, 1967; How to Teach Writing. 1969; Teaching in Your Own Write, 1970; The Case for Socially Functional Education, 1973; Two Connecticut Yankees Teaching in Appalachia, 1974; One of a Kind: The Many Faces and Voices of America, 1976; The Day the World Went Sane, 1979; (with Marian Barba) What's Cooking in Congress?, 2 vols., 1979–82; (as Baron Mikan) The Gospel According to Everyman, 1981; Round Trip to Byzantium, 1985. Add: 47 Hyde Blvd., Ballston Spa, N.Y. 12020, U.S.A.

BARBER, Benjamin R(eynolds). American, b. 1939. Plays, Novels, Politics/Government. Walt Whitman Prof. of Political Science, Rutgers Univ. (member of faculty since 1969). Lectr. in Ethics and Politics, Albert Schweitzer Coll., Churwalden, Switzerland, 1962–64; Asst. Prof. of

Political Science, Univ. of Pennsylvania. Philadelphia, 1966–69. Ed-in-Chief, Political Theory, 1972–84. *Publs:* (with C.J. Friedrich and M. Curtis) Totalitarianism in Perspective: Three Views, 1969; Superman and Commen Men: Freedom, Anarchy and the Revolution, 1971; The Death of Communal Liberty: A History of Freedom in a Swiss Mountain Canton, 1974; Liberating Feminism, 1976; Marriage Voices: A Novel, 1981; The Artist and Political Vision, 1982; Strong Democracy, 1984; The Conquest of Politics, 1988. Plays Produced: The People's Heart, 1969; Delly's Oracle, 1970; The Bust, 1971; (with Martin Best) From Our Dissension, 1971; Doors, 1972; (with John Duffy and Robert Lamb) Fightsong (musical), 1975 (with George Quincy) Home and the River (opera), 1982; Making Kaspar, 1984; (with Patrick Watson) The Struggle for Democracy (television series and companion book), 1989. Add: Dept. of Political Science, Rutgers Univ., New Brunswick, N.J. 08903, U.S.A.

BARBER, Charles Laurence. British, b. 1915. Language/Linguistics, Literature. Lectr. in English, Univ. of Gothenburg, 1947–56; Lectr., 1959–62, Sr. Lectr., 1962–69, and Reader in English Language and Literature, 1969–80, Univ. of Leeds. *Publs:* The Idea of Honour in the English Drama 1591-1700, 1957; The Story of Language, 1964; Linguistic Change in Present-Day English, 1964; (ed.) Hamlet, 1964; (ed.) A Trick to Catch the Old One, by Middleton, 1969; (ed.) Women Beware Women, by Middleton, 1969; (ed.) A Chaste Maid in Cheapside, by Middleton, 1969; Early Modern English, 1976; Shakespeare's Henry V, 1980; Shakespeare's Richard III, 1980; Shakespeare's As You Like It, 1981; Poetry in English, 1983; The Theme of Honour's Tongue, 1985; Shakespeare's Richard II, 1987. Add: North Parade, Leeds LS16 5AY, England.

BARBER, James David. American, b. 1930. Politics/Government. James B. Duke Prof. of Political Science, Duke Univ., Durham, N.C. since 1978 (Prof. and Chmn., Dept. of Political Science, 1972–77). Research Staff, Industrial Relations Center, Univ. of Chicago, 1951–53, 1955; Asst. Prof. of Political Science, Stetson Univ., 1955–57; Instr., 1960–61, Assoc. Dir., Political Science Research Library, 1960–62, Asst. Prof., 1961–65, Dir. of Grad. Studies, 1965–67, Assoc. Prof., 1965–68, Dir., Office for Advanced Political Studies, 1967–68, and Prof., 1968–72, Yale Univ. Chmn., Bd. of Dirs., Amnesty Intnl., U.S.A., 1984–86. *Publs:* (ed.) Political Leadership in American Government, 1964; (ed.) Part II Heritage of Liberty, 1964; The Lawmakers: Recruitment and Adaptation to Legislative Life, 1965; Power in Committees: An Experiment in the Governmental Process, 1966; (ed. with R.E. Lane and F.I. Greenstein) An Introduction to Political Analysis, 1967; Citizen Politics, 1968; (ed.) Power to the Citizen, 1971; The Presidential Character: Predicting Performance in the White House, 1972, 1977, 1985; (ed.) Choosing the President, 1974; Race for the Presidency, 1978; The Pulse of Politics: Electing Presidents in the Media Age, 1980; Erasmus: A Play on Words, 1982; (with others) Women Leaders in American Politics, 1985; Politics by Humans: Research in American Leadership, 1988. Add: Dept. of Political Science, Duke Univ., Durham, N.C. 27706, U.S.A.

BARBER, John (Douglass). British, b. 1944. History, Literature, Politics/Government. Fellow of King's Coll., and Lectr. in Politics, Cambridge Univ. (former Asst. Lectr. in History, and Dir. of Studies in History); Hon. Research Fellow, Centre for Russian and East European Studies, Univ. of Birmingham, since 1980. *Publs:* Soviet Historians in Crisis 1928–1932, 1981. Add: King's College, Cambridge CB2 1ST, England.

BARBER, Richard (William). British, b. 1941. Gastronomy/Wine, History, Literature, Mythology/Folklore, Travel. Chairman, Boydell and Brewer Ltd. Ed., Arthurian Literature, since 1981. *Publs:* Arthur of Albion, 1961, rev. ed. as King Arthur: Hero and Legend, 1986; Henry Plantagenet, 1963; (with Francis Camps) The Investigation of Murder, 1965; The Knight and Chivalry, 1970; Samuel Pepys Esq., 1970; (with Anne Riches) A Dictionary of Fabulous Beasts, 1971; The Figure of Arthur, 1972; Cooking and Recipes from Rome to the Renaissance, 1974; Aubrey's Brief Lives, 1975; A Strong Land and a Sturdy, 1976; Companion Guide to South West France, 1977; The Devil's Crown, 1978; Tournaments, 1978; Edward Prince of Wales and Aquitaine, 1978; The Arthurian Legends, 1979; A Companion to World Mythology, 1979; The Reign of Chivalry, 1980; Living Legends, 1981; The Pastons, 1981; Penguin Guide to Medieval Europe, 1984. Add: Stangrove Hall. Alderton nr. Woodbridge, Suffolk IP12 3BL, England.

BARBETTE, Jay. *See* **SPICER**, Bart.

BARBOUR, Douglas. Canadian, b. 1940. Poetry. Prof., Univ. of Alberta, Edmonton, since 1982 (Asst. Prof., 1969–77; Assoc. Prof., 1977–81). Poetry Ed., Canadian Forum, 1978–80; Former Ed., Quarry mag.,

Kingston, Ont. *Publs:* Land Fall, 1971; A Poem as Long as the Highway, 1971; White, 1972; Songbook, 1973; He & She &, 1974; Visions of My Grandmother, 1977; Shore Lines, 1979; Vision/Sounding, 1980; (with Stephen Scobie) The Pirates of Pen's Chance, 1981; (co-ed.) The Maple Laugh Forever: An Anthology of Canadian Comic Poetry, 1981; (co-ed.) Writing Right: Poetry by Canadian Women, 1982; (ed.) Three Times Five: Short Stories by Harris, Sawai, Stenson, 1983; (ed.) Selected and New Poems, by Richard Sommer, 1984; The Harbingers, 1984; Visible Visions: The Selected Poems of Douglas Barbour, 1984; (co-ed.) Tesseracts II, 1987; Story for a Saskatchewan Night, 1989. Add: 11655-72 Ave., Edmonton, Alta. T6G 0B9, Canada.

BARBOUR, Hugh (Stewart). American (b. British), b. 1921. Theology/Religion. Prof. of Religion, Earlham Coll., since 1953, and Earlham Sch. of Religion, since 1960, Richmond, Ind. Pastor, First Congregational Church of Coventry, Conn., 1945–47; Instr., Dept. of Bible and Religion, Syracuse Univ., N.Y., 1947–49; Instr., to Asst. Prof., Wellesley Coll., Mass., 1950–53. *Publs:* The Quakers in Puritan England, 1964, 1986; Reading and Understanding the Old Testament, 1965; (ed. with A. Roberts) Early Quaker Writings, 1973; Margaret Fell Speaks, 1976; (with William J. Frost) The Quakers, 1988. Add: Pine Lane, 1840 South-West "E" St., Richmond, Ind. 47374, U.S.A.

BARCLAY, Tessa. *See* **BOWDEN**, Jean.

BARDIS, Panos D. American, b. 1924. Novels/Short stories, Poetry, History, Human relations, Language/Linguistics. Univ. Prof. of Sociology, Univ. of Toledo, Ohio, since 1959. Ed., and Book Review Ed. Intnl. Social Science Review; Ed.-in-Chief and Book Review Ed., Intnl. Journal on World Peace. *Publs:* Ivan and Artemis (novel), 1957; The Family in Changing Civilizations, 1967, 1969; Encyclopedia of Campus Unrest, 1971; History of the Family, 1975; Studies in Marriage and the Family, 1975, 1978; The Future of the Greek Language in the United States, 1976; (co-ed.) The Family in Asia, 1978, 1979; History of Thanatology, 1981; (co-ed.) Poetry Americas, 1982; Atlas of Human Reproductive Anatomy, 1983; Evolution of the Family in the West, 1983; Global Marriage and Family Customs, 1983; Nine Oriental Muses (poetry), 1983; Dictionary of Quotations in Sociology, 1985; A Cosmic Whirl of Melodies (poetry), 1985; Marriage and Family: Continuity, Change, and Adjustment, 1988. Add: 2533 Orkney, Ottawa Hills, Toledo, Ohio 43606, U.S.A.

BARDWICK, Judith M(arcia). American, b. 1933. Psychology, Women. Partner, Kielty Goldsmith & Boone, management consultants, La Jolla, Calif., since 1986. Clinical Prof. of Psychology, Univ. of California, San Diego, since 1984. Pres., In Transition, management consultants, La Jolla, Calif., 1983–86. *Publs:* (with others) Feminine Personality and Conflict, 1970, 1981; Psychology of Women, 1971; (ed. and contributor) Readings in the Psychology of Women, 1972; In Transition, 1979; Essays on the Psychology of Women, 1981; The Plateauing Trap, 1986; In Transition: How Feminism, Sexual Liberation, and The Search For Self-Fulfillment Have Altered America, 1989. Add: c/o Kielty Goldsmith & Boone, 1298 Prospect, La Jolla, Calif. 92037, U.S.A.

BAREHAM, Terence. British, b. 1937. Literature. Sr. Lectr. in English, The New Univ. of Ulster, Coleraine, since 1968. Lectr. in English, Univ. of Rhodesia, 1963–67, and Univ. of York, 1967–68. *Publs:* George Crabbe: A Critical Study, 1977; (co-author) A Bibliography of George Crabbe, 1978; (ed.) Anthony Trollope, 1980; Robert Bolt's "A Man for All Seasons," 1980; T.S. Eliot: Murder in the Cathedral, 1981; Shakespeare's Two Gentlemen of Verona, 1982; (ed.) Anthony Trollope's Barsetshire Novels, 1982; (ed.) Tom Stoppard: A Casebook, 1987; Malcolm Lowry, 1987. Add: c/o Dept. of English, The New Univ., Coleraine, Northern Ireland.

BARFIELD, Owen. British, b. 1898. History, Language/Linguistics, Literature, Philosophy. Former solicitor in private practice, and visiting prof. at various U.S. univs., 1964–74. *Publs:* History in English Words, 1926; Poetic Diction, 1928, 1952; Romanticism Comes of Age, 1944, 1966; Saving the Appearances, 1957; Worlds Apart, 1963; Unancestral Voice, 1965; Speaker's Meaning, 1967; What Coleridge Thought, 1971; (ed.) The Case for Anthroposophy, by Rudolf Steiner, 1976; the Rediscovery of Meaning (collected essays), 1977; History, Guilt and Habit, 1979; Orpheus, 1983; The Year Participated, 1985. Add: The Walhatch, Forest Row, East Sussex RH18 5AW, England.

BARGHOORN, Frederick C. American, b. 1911. International relations/Current Affairs, Politics/Government. Prof. of Political Science, Yale Univ., New Haven, since 1956 (member of faculty since 1947). Member, Editorial Bd., Slavic Review, and Studies on Comparative Communism; Member, Council on Foreign Relations. With U.S. Dept. of State, 1941–57, 1959–61; Press Attache, U.S. Embassy, Moscow, 1943–47. Member, Science Information Council, Washington, 1966–70. *Publs:* The Soviet Image of the United States, 1950; Soviet Russian Nationalism, 1956; The Soviet Cultural Offensive, 1960; Soviet Foreign Propaganda, 1964; Politics in the USSR, 1966, 3rd ed., 1986; Detente and the Democratic Movement in the USSR, 1976. Add: Dept. of Political Science, Yale Univ., New Haven, Conn. 06520, U.S.A.

BARICH, Bill. American, b. 1943. Travel/Exploration/Adventure, Autobiography, Essays, Fiction. Staff Writer, The New Yorker mag., NYC. *Publs:* Laughing in the Hills, 1981; Traveling Light, 1985; Hard to Be Good (short stories), 1987. Add: c/o The New Yorker, 25 W. 43rd St., New York, N.Y. 10036, U.S.A.

BARISH, Jonas A. American, b. 1922. Literature. Prof. of English, Univ. of California, Berkeley, since 1966 (Asst. Prof., 1954–60; Assoc. Prof., 1960–66). *Publs:* Milton's Schoolmasters, 1937, 1982; (ed.) Volpone, by Ben Jonson, 1958; Ben Jonson and the Language of Prose Comedy, 1960; (ed.) Ben Jonson: A Collection of Critical Essays, 1963; (ed.) All's Well that Ends Well, by William Shakespeare, 1964; (ed.) Sejanus, by Ben Jonson, 1965; (ed.) Volpone: A Casebook, 1972; The Antitheatrical Prejudice, 1981. Add: c/o Dept. of English, Univ. of California, Berkeley, Calif. 94720, U.S.A.

BARKER, Arthur E(dward). Canadian, b. 1911. Literature. Prof. Emeritus of Renaissance Literature, Univ. of Western Ontario, London, since 1980 (Prof., 1970–80). Prof. of English, Trinity Coll., Univ. of Toronto, 1942–61, and Univ. of Illinois, Urbana, 1961–69. *Publs:* Milton and the Puritan Dilemma, 1942; John Milton: Samson Agonistes and Early Poems, 2nd ed., 1965; John Milton: Modern Essays in Criticism, 1965; (ed.) The Seventeenth Century: Bacon Through Marvell, 1979. Add: 1109 Sunset Ave., London, Ont. N6A 2Y5, Canada.

BARKER, A(udrey) L(illian). British, b. 1918. Novels/Short stories, Plays/Screenplays. *Publs:* Innocents, 1947; Apology for a Hero, 1950; Novelette and Other Stories, 1951; The Joy Ride, 1963; Lost Upon the Roundabouts, 1964; A Case Examined, 1965; The Middling: Chapters in the Life of Ellie Toms, 1967; John Brown's Body, 1969; Femina Real, 1971; Source of Embarrassment, 1974; A Heavy Feather, 1978; Life Stories, 1981; Relative Successes, 1984; No Word of Love, 1985; The Gooseboy, 1987. Add: 103 Harrow Rd., Carshalton, Surrey, England.

BARKER, David J.P. British, b. 1938. Medicine/Health. Prof. of Clinical Epidemiology and Dir. of the Medical Research Council Environmental Epidemiology Unit, Univ. of Southampton, and Hon. Consultant Physician, Royal South Hampshire Hosp. Research Fellow, Dept. of Social Medicine, 1963–66, and Lectr., Dept. of Medicine, 1966–69, Univ. of Birmingham; Hon. Lectr. in Epidemiology, Makerere Univ., Uganda, 1969–72. *Publs:* Practical Epidemiology, 1973, 3rd ed. 1982; (with G. Rose) Epidemiology in Medical Practice, 1976, 1979. Add: M.R.C. Environmental Epidemiology Unit, South Block, General Hosp., Southampton SO9 4XY, England.

BARKER, Dennis (Malcolm). British, b. 1929. Novels/Short stories, Plays/Screenplays, Crafts, Military/Defence. Reporter, Feature Writer and Columnist, The Guardian, London, since 1967 (Midlands Corresp., Birmingham, 1963–67). Reporter, Suffolk Chronicle and Mercury, Ipswich, 1947–48; Reporter, Feature Writer, Theatre and Film Critic, East Anglian Daily Times, Ipswich, 1948–58; Estates and Property Ed., Feature Writer, Theatre Critic and Columnist, Express and Star, Wolverhampton, 1958–63. *Publs:* Candidate of Promise, 1969; Candidate of Promise (screenplay); The Scandalisers, 1974; Soldiering On: An Unofficial Portrait of the British Army, 1981; One Man's Estate, 1983; Parian Ware, 1985; Ruling the Waves: An Unofficial Portrait of the Royal Navy, 1986; Winston Three Three Three, 1987; Guarding the Skies: An Unofficial Portrait of the Royal Air Force, 1989; Fresh Start, 1989. Add: The Guardian, 119 Farringdon Rd., London EC1, England.

BARKER, E(lsa) M. Also writes as Nell Jordan. American, b. 1906. Westerns/Adventure. Teacher, city schs. in Las Vegas, N.M., 1930–71; Chmn. of English, Las Vegas Jr. High Sch., N.M., 1959–71; Pres., Western Writers of America, 1972–73. *Publs:* Riders of the Ramhorn, 1956; Clouds Over the Chupaderos, 1957; Cowboys Can't Quit, 1958; Showdown at Penasco Pass, 1958; War on the Big Hat, 1959; Secret of the Badlands, 1960. Add: 714 Myrtle Ave., Las Vegas, N.M. 87701, U.S.A.

BARKER, Garry. American, b. 1943. Short stories. Asst. Dir., Southern Highland Handicraft Guild, Asheville, N.C., 1965–71, and Kentucky Guild of Artists and Craftsmen, 1971–80; Communications Coordinator, Morehead State Univ., Kentucky, 1984–85. *Publs:* Fire on the Mountain, 1983; Copperhead Summer, 1985; Mountain Passage and Other Stories, 1986. Add: 110 Holly St., Berea, Ky. 40403, U.S.A.

BARKER, George (Granville). British, b. 1913. Novels, Plays, Poetry. Prof. of English Literature, Imperial Tohoku Univ., Sendai, Japan, 1939–41; Visiting Prof., New York State Univ., Buffalo, 1965–66; Arts Fellow, York Univ., 1966–67; Visiting Prof., Univ. of Wisconsin, Madison, 1971–72, Florida Intnl. Univ., Miami, 1974. *Publs:* Alanna Autumnal (novel), 1933; Thirty Preliminary Poems, 1933; Poems, 1935; Janus (novellena), 1935; Calamiterror, 1937; Elegy on Spain, 1939; Lament and Triumph, 1940; Selected Poems, 1941; Sacred and Secular Elegies, 1943; Eros in Dogma, 1944; Love Poems, 1947; The True Confessions of George Barker, 1950, augmented ed. 1964; The Dead Seagull (novel), 1950; News of the World, 1950; A Vision of Beasts and Gods, 1954; Collected Poems, 1930–1955, 1957; Two Plays, 1958; (ed.) Idylls of the King and a Selection of Poems, by Alfred, Lord Tennyson, 1961; The View from a Blind I, 1962; (with Charles Causley and Martin Bell) Penguin Modern Poets 3, 1962; Collected Poems, 1930–1965, 1965 (Levenson Prize); Dreams of a Summer Night, 1966; The Golden Chains, 1968; At Thurgarton Church, 1969; Runes and Rhymes and Tunes and Chimes, 1969; What is Mercy and a Voice, 1970; To Aylsham Fair, 1970; The Alphabetical Zoo, 1970; Essays, 1970; Poems of Places and People, 1971; III Hallucination Poems, 1972; In Memory of David Archer, 1973; Dialogues etc., 1976; Seven Poems, 1977; Villa Stellar, 1978; Anno Domini, 1983; Collected Poems, 1987; Seventeen, 1988. Add: Bintry House, Itteringham, Aylsham, Norfolk, England.

BARKER, Howard. British, b. 1946. Plays/Screenplays. Resident Dramatist, Open Space Theatre, London, 1974–75. *Publs:* Stripwell, with Claw, 1977; Fair Slaughter, 1978; That Good Between Us, with Credentials a Sympathiser, 1980; The Love of a Good Man, with All Bleeding, 1980; The Hang of the Gaol, with Heaven, 1981; Two Plays for the Right: Birth on a Hard Shoulder, and The Loud Boy's Life, 1981; No End of Blame: Scenes of Overcoming, 1981; The Castle/Scenes from an Execution (plays), 1984; Victory, 1984; Crimes in Hot Countries/Fair Slaughter, 1985; The Power of the Dog: Moments in History and Anti-History (play), 1985; A Passion in Six Days/Downchild (plays), 1985; Don't Exaggerate, 1986. Add: c/o Judy Daish Assocs., 83 Eastbourne Mews, London W2 6LQ, England.

BARKER, Pat(ricia). British, b. 1943. Novels. *Publs:* Union Street, 1982; Blow Your House Down, 1984; The Century's Daughter, 1986; The Man Who Wasn't There, 1989. Add: c/o Curtis Brown Associates, 162-168 Regent St., London W1R 5TA, England.

BARKER, Philip. British, b. 1929. Psychiatry. Prof. of Psychiatry and Paediatrics, Univ. of Calgary, and Psychiatrist, Albert Children's Hospital, Calgary, since 1980. Consultant, Dundee Child Psychiatry Service, 1962–67; Lectr. Univ. of St. Andrews, 1962–69; Consultant, Burns Clinic, Birmingham, and Lectr., Univ. of Birmingham, 1967–75; Dir. of Inpatient Services, 1975–79, and Dir. of Psychiatric Education, 1979–80, Thistletoun Regional Centre, Toronto; Prof. of Psychiatry, Univ of Toronto, 1975–80. Ed., Journal of the Assoc. of Workers for Maladjusted Children, 1978–80. *Publs:* Basic Child Psychiatry, 1971, 4th ed. 1983; Care Can Prevent, 1973; (ed.) The Residential Psychiatric Treatment of Children, 1974; Basic Family Therapy, 1981; Behaviour Therapy Nursing, 1982; Using Metaphors in Psychotherapy, 1985; Patient Assessment in Psychiatric Nursing, 1985; (ed., with Douglas Fraser) The Nurse as Therapist: A Behavioural Model, 1985; (ed.) Multimedia Computer Assisted Learning, 1988. Add: 1820 Richmond Rd. S.W., Calgary, Alta, Canada.

BARKER, S(quire) Omar. Has also written as Dan Scott. American, b. 1894. Westerns/Adventure, Children's fiction, Poetry, Cookery/Gastronomy/Wine. Pres., Western Writers of America, 1958–59. *Publs:* Winds the Mountains, 1924; Buckaroo Ballads, 1929; Born to Battle, 1951; Sunlight Through the Trees, 1954; Songs of the Saddlemen, 1954; Mystery of Ghost Canyon, 1960; (ed.) Legends and Tales of the Old West, 1960; Mystery of Rawhide Gap, 1960; Range Rodeo Mystery, 1960; Secret of Ft. Pioneer, 1961; (ed.) Frontiers West, 1961; Mystery at Blizzard Mesa, 1961; Mystery of the Comanche Caves, 1962; (ed.) Spurs West, 1962; Phantom of Wolf Creek, 1963; Mystery of Bandit Gulch, 1964; Little World Apart, 1966; (with C. Truax) The Cattleman's Steak Book, 1967; Rawhide Rhymes, 1968. Add: 714 Myrtle Ave., Las Vegas, N.M. 87701, U.S.A.

BARKER, Theodore Cardwell. British, b. 1923. Crafts, Economic history, Transportation. Prof. of Economic History, Univ. of London (Emeritus, but still teaching). Prof. of Economic and Social History, Univ. of Kent at Canterbury, 1964–76. *Publs:* (with J.R. Harris) A Merseyside Town in the Industrial Revolution, 1954; A History of the Girdlers Company, 1957; Pilkington Brothers and the Glass Industry, 1960; (with R.H. Campbell and P. Mathias) Business History, 1960; (with M. Robbins) A History of London Transport, vol. 1, 1963, vol. II, 1974; (with M.J. Hatcher) A History of British Pewter, 1974; (with C.I. Savage) An Economic History of Transport in Britain, 1974; (ed.) The Long March of Everyman, 1975; The Glassmakers, 1977; The Transport Contractors of Rye, 1982; (co-ed.) The Population Factor, 1982; (ed. and contributor) The Economic and Socialffects of the Spread of Motor Vehicles, 1987. Add: Minsen Dane, Faversham, Kent, England.

BARKIN, Carol. Also writes with Elizabeth James under joint pseudonyms Elizabeth Carroll and Beverly Hastings. American, b. 1944. Novels/Short stories, Children's fiction, Children's non-fiction, Money/Finance, Women's studies. Author, since 1975; free-lance ed., since 1976. Ed., Abelard–Schuman, London, 1965–67; Ed., Follett Publishing Co., Chicago, 1967–69; Ed., Elk Grove Press, Los Angeles, 1969–70; Ed., Sullivan Educational Systems, Los Angeles, 1970–72; Ed., Lothrop, Lee and Shepard Co., NYC, 1973–76. *Publs:* (all with Elizabeth James): The Simple Facts of Simple Machines, 1975; Slapdash Sewing, 1975; Are We Still Best Friends?, 1975; Doing Things Together, 1975; I'd Rather Stay Home, 1975; Sometimes I Hate School, 1975; Slapdash Cooking, 1976; Slapdash Alterations: How to Recycle Your Wardrobe, 1977; Slapdash Decorating, 1977; Managing Your Money, 1977; Understanding Money, 1977; What Is Money, 1977; How to Keep a Secret: Writing and Talking in Code, 1978; What Do You Mean by "Average"?: Means, Medians and Modes, 1978; How to Grow a Hundred Dollars, 1979; How to Write a Term Paper, 1980; The Complete Babysitter's Handbook, 1980; (as Beverly Hastings) Don't Talk to Strangers, 1980; A Place of Your Own, 1981; How to Write a Great School Report, 1983; The Scary Halloween Costume Book, 1983; (as Elizabeth Carroll) Summer Love, 1983; Helpful Hints for Your Pregnancy, 1984; (as Beverly Hastings) Don't Walk Home Alone, 1985 (as Beverly Hastings) Watcher in the Dark, 1986; How to Write Your Best Book Report, 1986; Happy Thanksgiving!, 1987; (as Beverly Hastings) Don't Cry, Little Girl, 1987; School Smarts: How to Succeed at Schoolwork, 1988; Happy Valentine's Day, 1988. Add: c/o Lothrop, Lee and Shepard Books, 105 Madison Ave., New York, NY 10016, U.S.A.

BARKOW, Al. American, b. 1932. History, Sports. Ed.-in-Chief, Golf Illustrated Mag., since 1985 Chief Writer, Shell's Wonderful World of Golf television series, 1962–68; Ed.-in-Chief, Golf Mag., 1969–71. *Publs:* Golf's Golden Grind. 1974; (with B. Casper) The Good Sense of Golf, 1978 (with Ken Venturi) The Venturi Analysis, 1981; (with George Low) The Master of Putting, 1983; (with Phil Rogers) Play Lower Handicap Golf, 1986; Gettin' to the Dance Floor: An Oral History of Golf, 1986. Add: 42-25 64th St., Woodside, N.Y. 11377, U.S.A.

BARKS, Coleman Bryan. American, b. 1937. Poetry. Assoc. Prof. of English, Univ. of Georgia, Athens, since 1972 (Asst. Prof., 1967–72). Instr. of English, Univ. of Southern California, Los Angeles, 1965–67. *Publs:* The Juice, 1972; New Words, 1976; We're Laughing at the Damage, 1977; (trans. with Robert Bly) Night and Sleep, Versions of Rumi, 1981; (trans. with John Moyne) Open Secret, by Rumi, 1984; (trans. with John Moyne) Unseen Rain, by Rumi, 1986; (trans. with John Moyne) We Are Three, by Rumi, 1987; (trans. with John Moyne) These Branching Moments, by Rumi, 1988; (trans. with John Moyne) This Longing, by Rumi, 1988. Add: 196 Westview Dr., Athens, Ga. 30606, U.S.A.

BARLAY, Stephen. British, b. 1930. Novels, Plays, Documentaries. *Publs:* (with P. Sasdy) Four Black Cars, 1958; Sex Slavery (in U.S. as Bondage), 1968; Aircrash Detective (in U.S. as The Search for Air Safety), 1969; Fire, 1972; Double Cross (in U.S. as The Secrets Business), 1973; (creator with J. Elliot) The Double Dealers (radio and TV series), 1972, 1974; Blockbuster (novel), 1976; That Thin Red Line (documentary), 1976; Point of No Return (radio play), 1977; Crash Course, (novel), 1979; Cuban Confetti (novel; in U.S. as In the Company of Spies), 1981; The Ruling Passion (novel), 1982; The Price of Silence (novel), 1983; radio serial 1983; Tsunami (novel), 1986. Add: c/o Hamish Hamilton, 27 Wright's Lane, London W8 5TZ, England.

BARLOW, Frank. British, b. 1911. History, Biography. Emeritus Prof., Univ. of Exeter, since 1976 (Lectr., 1946–69; Reader 1949–53; Prof. of History, 1953–76; Deputy Vice-Chancellor, 1961–63; Public Orator, 1974–76). Fereday Fellow, St. John's Coll., Oxford, 1934–38; Asst. Lectr., Univ. Coll., London., 1936–40. *Publs:* (ed.) The Letters of Arnulf

of Lisieux, 1939; (ed.) Durham Annals and Documents of the Thirteenth Century, 1945; Durham Jurisdictional Peculiars, 1950; The Feudal Kingdom of England, 1955; (ed. and trans.) The Life of King Edward the Confessor, The English Church 1000-1066, 1963; William I and the Norman Conquest, 1965; Edward the Confessor, 1970; (with Martin Biddle, Olof von Feilitzen and D.J. Keene) Winchester in the Early Middle Ages, 1976; The English Church 1066-1154, 1979; William Rufus, 1983; The Norman Conquest and Beyond, 1983; Thomas Becket, 1986. Add: Middle Court Hall, Kenton, Exeter EX6 8NA, England.

BARLOW, John (Alfred). American, b. 1924. Psychology. Prof. of Psychology, Kingsborough Community Coll., City Univ. of New York, since 1970 (Chmn., Dept. of Behavioral Sciences, 1970–72). *Publs:* Programmed Book in General Psychology, 1965; Stimulus and Response, 1968; Stimulus, Response and Contiguity, 1976. Add: 216 Maple St., Brooklyn, N.Y. 11225, U.S.A.

BARLOW, Wilfred. British, b. 1915. Medicine/Health. Medical Consultant, Wembley Hosp. and Alexander Inst., since 1953; Ed., The Alexander Journal. Sr. Registrar, Middlesex Hosp., 1947–49. *Publs:* The Alexander Technique, 1973; More Talk of Alexander, 1978. Add: 4B Wadham Gardens, London NW3 3DP, England.

BARLOWE, Raleigh. American, b. 1914. Economics. Prof., Michigan State Univ., East Lansing, since 1952 (Lectr., 1948–50; Assoc. Prof., 1950–52; Chmn., Dept. of Resource Development, 1959–71, 1980; Adjunct Prof., 1981–84). Agricultural Economist, U.S. Dept. of Agriculture, 1943–57. *Publs:* (with V.W. Johnson) Land Problems and Policies, 1954; Land Resource Economics, 1958, 4th ed. 1986. Add: 907 Southlawn, East Lansing, Mich. 48823, U.S.A.

BARLTROP, Robert. British, b. 1922. History, Literature. Ed., Socialist Standard, 1972–77, Cockney Ancestor, 1983–86. *Publs:* The Monument: Story of the Socialist Party of Great Britain, 1975; Jack London: The Man, the Writer, the Rebel, 1977; (ed.) Revolution: and Essays, 1978; (with Jim Wolveridge) The Muvver Tongue, 1981; My Mother's Calling Me, 1984; A Funny Age, 1985; Bright Summer Dark Autumn, 1986; A Cockney Dictionary, 1988. Add: 77 Idmiston Rd., Stratford, London E15 1RG, England.

BARMANN, Lawrence (Francis). American, b. 1932. Theology/Religion, History. Prof. of History since 1978, and Prof. of American Studies since 1983, St. Louis Univ. (Asst. Prof., 1970–73; Assoc. Prof., 1973–78). *Publs:* (ed.) Newman at St. Mary's 1962; (ed.) Newman on God and Self, 1965; Baron Friedrich von Hugel and the Modernist Crisis in England, 1972; The Letters of Baron Friedrich von Hugel and Professor Norman Kemp Smith, 1981. Add: 130 Stoneleigh Towers, St. Louis, Mo. 63132, U.S.A.

BARNABY, Charles Frank. British, b. 1927. International relations/Current affairs, Military/Defence. Scientist, U.K. Atomic Energy Authority, Aldermaston, 1951–57; Member of Scientific Staff, Medical Research Council, Univ. Coll., London, 1957–69; Exec. Secty., Pugwash Conferences on Science and World Affairs, London, 1969–71; Defence Consultant, New Scientist Mag., London, 1970–71; Dir., Stockholm Intnl. Peace Research Inst., 1971–81. *Publs:* The Nuclear Future, 1969; (ed. with A. Boserup) Anti-Ballistic Missile Systems, 1970; Radionuclides in Medicine, 1970; (ed.) Preventing the Spread of Nuclear Weapons, 1971; Man and the Atom, 1971; (ed. with C. Shaerf) Arms Control and Disarmament, 1972; (with R. Huiskens) Arms Uncontrolled, 1975; The Nuclear Age, 1976; Prospects for Peace, 1981; (ed.) Future Warfare, 1984; The Automated Battlefield, 1986; Star Wars Brought Down to Earth, 1986; (ed.) The Gaia Peace Atlas, 1988; The Invisible Bomb, 1989. Add: Brandreth, Station Rd., Chilbolton, Stockbridge, Hants. SO20 6AW, England.

BARNARD, Christaan (Neethling). South African, b. 1922. Medicine, Politics, Autobiography. Prof. Emeritus, Univ. of Cape Town (Head of Cardiac Research and Surgery, 1968–83). Developed the Barnard Valve used in open heart surgery; performed first successful heart transplant, and first double heart transplant, 1974. *Publs:* (with C.B. Pepper) One Life (autobiography), 1970; Heart Attack: All You Have to Know About It, 1971; (with S. Stander) The Unwanted, 1974; South Africa: Sharp Dissection, 1977; (with S. Stander) In the Night Season, 1977; Best Medicine, 1979; Good Life—Good Death, 1980; The Body Machine, 1981; (with Karl Sabbagh) The Living Body, 1984. Add: P.O. Box 988, Cape Town 8000, South Africa.

BARNARD, Frederick Mechner. British, b. 1921. Intellectual history,

Philosophy, Politics/Government, Sociology. Prof. of Political Science, Univ. of Western Ontario, since 1970. Member, Intnl. Political Science Assn. Head of Economics Dept., Wyggeston Grammar Sch., Leicester, 1948–59; Extra-Mural Lectr., Leicester Univ. and Leicester Coll. of Technology, 1948–59; St. Lectr. and Dir. of Social Studies, Univ of Salford, 1959–64; Assoc. Prof., 1964–67, and Prof. of Political Science, 1967–70, Univ. of Saskatchewan. *Publs:* Between Enlightenment and Political Romanticism, 1964; J.G. Herder's Social and Political Thought, 1965; (ed.) Herder on Social and Political Culture, 1969; Socialism with a Human Face: Slogan and Substance, 1973; Self-Direction and Political Legitimacy, 1988; Pluralism, Socialism, and Politics, 1988. Add: Dept. of Political Science, Univ. of Western Ontario, London, Ont., N6A 5C2, Canada.

BARNARD, Robert. British, b. 1936. Mystery/Crime/Suspense, Literature. Full-time writer since 1983. Lectr. in English Literature, Univ. of New England, New South Wales, 1961–66; Lectr. and Sr. Lectr., Bergen Univ., Norway, 1966–76; Prof. of English Literature, Tromso Univ., Norway, 1976–83. *Publs:* mystery novels—Death of an Old Goat, 1974; A Little Local Murder, 1976; Death on the High C's, 1977; Blood Brotherhood, 1977; Unruly son, 1978; Posthumous Papers, 1979; Death in a Cold Climate, 1980; Mother's Boys, 1981; Sheer Torture, 1981; Death and the Princess, 1982; The Missing Bronte, 1983; Little Victims, 1983; A Corpse in Gilded Cage, 1984; Out of the Blackout, 1985; The Disposal of the Living, 1985; Political Suicide, 1986; Bodies, 1986; Death in Purple Prose, 1987; The Skeleton in the Grass, 1987; At Death's Door, 1988; literary criticism — Imagery and Theme in the Novels of Dickens, 1974; A Talent to Deceive: An Appreciation of Agatha Christie, 1980; A Short History of English Literature, 1984. Add: Hazeldene, Houghley Lane, Leeds LS13 2DT, England.

BARNES, C.V. *See* **YOUNG**, Chesley Virginia.

BARNES, Clive (Alexander). British, b. 1927. Dance/Ballet. Assoc. Ed. and Chief Drama and Dance Critic, New York Post, since 1977. New York Corresp., The Times, London, since 1970. Admin. Officer, Town Planning Dept., London County Council, 1952–61; Exec. Ed., Dance and Dancers, Music and Musicians, and Plays and Players, London, 1961–65; Dance Critic, 1965–77, and Drama Critic, 1967–77, New York Times. *Publs:* Ballet in Britain Since the War, 1953; Frederick Ashton and His Ballet, 1961; (co-author) Ballet Here and Now, 1961; The Ballet Scene: U.S.A., 1967; (co-ed.) Best American Plays, 6th–8th series, 1971–81; Contemporary Dance, 1978; Nureyev, 1982; Inside American Ballet Theatre, 1983. Add: 45 W. 60th St., Apt 8A, New York, N.Y. 10023, U.S.A.

BARNES, Douglas. British, b. 1927. Education. English teacher in Secondary Schs., 1950–66; Reader in Education, Univ. of Leeds, 1966–89. Chmn., National Assn. for the Teaching of English, 1967–69. *Publs:* (ed. with R. Egford) Twentieth Century Short Stories, 1958; (ed.) Short Stories of Our Time, 1963; (ed. and contrib.) Drama in the English Classroom, 1968; (with J. Britton and H. Rosen) Language, The Learner and the School, 1969, 3rd ed. (with J. Britton and M. Torbe), 1986; Language in the Classroom, 1973; From Communication to Curriculum, 1976; (with F. Todd) Communication and Learning in Small Groups, 1977; Practical Curriculum Study, 1982; (with D. Barnes and S.R. Clarke) Versions of English, 1984. Add: 4 Harrowby Rd., Leeds LS16 5HN, England.

BARNES, James J. American, b. 1931. History. Prof. of History since 1976, and Hadley Prof. and Chmn. of the Dept. since 1979, Wabash Coll., Crawfordsville, Ind. (Asst. Prof., 1962–66; Assoc. Prof., 1966–76). Instr. in History, Amherst Coll., Mass., 1959–62. *Publs:* Free Trade in Books: A Study of the London Book Trade Since 1800, 1964; Authors, Publishers and Politicians: The Quest for an Anglo-American Copyright Agreement, 1815-54, 1974; (with Patience P. Barnes) Hitler's Mein Kampf in Britain and America 1930–39, 1980; (with Patience P. Barnes) James Vincent Murphy: Translator and Interpreter of Fascist Europe, 1880-1946, 1987. Add: Dept. of History, Wabash Coll., Crawfordsville, Ind. 47933, U.S.A.

BARNES, John Arundel. Australian, b. 1918. Anthropology, Sociology. Fellow, Churchill Coll., Cambridge, since 1969; Prof. of Sociology, Cambridge Univ., 1969–82; now retired. Prof. of Anthropology, Univ. of Sydney, 1956–58; Prof. of Anthropology, Australian National Univ., Canberra, 1958–69. *Publs:* Marriage in a Changing Society, 1951; Politics in a Changing Society, 1954; Inquest on the Murngin, 1967; Sociology in Cambridge, 1970; Three Styles in the Study of Kinship, 1971; Social Networks, 1972; The Ethics of Inquiry in Social Science, 1977; Who Should Know What?, 1979. Add: Sociology RSSS,

Australian National Univ., G.P.O. Box 4, Canberra, A.C.T. 2601, Australia.

BARNES, Jonathan. British, b. 1942. Philosophy. Fellow and Tutor, Balliol Coll., and Lectr. in Philosophy, Oxford Univ. (Fellow of Oriel Coll., 1968–78). Lectr. in Philosophy, Univ. of Chicago, 1972; Visiting Prof., Univ. of Massachusetts at Amherst, 1973, and Univ. of Texas, Austin, 1981. *Publs:* (trans.) Aristotle's Theory of the Syllogism, by G. Patzig, 1969; The Ontological Argument, 1972; (ed.) Articles on Aristotle, 1975; Aristotle's Posterior Analytics, 1976; The Presocratic Philosophers, 1979; (ed.) Doubt and Dogmatism, 1980; Terms and Sentences: Theophrastus on Hypothetical Syllogisms, 1985; The Modes of Scepticism, 1985; Early Greek Philosophy, 1987. Add: Balliol Coll., Oxford, England.

BARNES, (Dame Alice) Josephine (Mary Taylor). British, b. 1912. Medicine/Health. Consulting Obstetrician and Gynaecologist, Charing Cross Hosp., London, since 1954. With Obstetric Unit, Univ. Coll. Hosp., London, 1942–53. *Publs:* Gynaecological Histology, 1948; The Care of the Expectant Mother, 1954; Lecture Notes on Gynaecology; (co-ed.) Scientific Foundations of Obstetrics and Gynaecology. Add: 8 Aubrey Walk, London W8 7JG, England.

BARNES, Julian (Patrick). Also writes as Dan Kavanagh. British, b. 1946. Novels, Mystery. Lexicographer, Oxford English Dictionary Supplement, London, 1969–72; TV Critic, 1977–81, and Asst. Literary Ed., 1977–79, New Statesman, London; Contributing Ed., New Review, London, 1977–78; Deputy Literary Ed., Sunday Times, London, 1979–81; TV Critic, The Observer, London, 1982–1986. *Publs:* (novels): Metroland; (as Dan Kavanagh) Duffy (crime), 1980; (as Dan Kavanagh) Fiddle City (crime), 1981; Before She Met Me, 1982; Flaubert's Parrot, 1984; (as Dan Kavanagh) Putting the Boot In (crime), 1985; Staring at the Sun, 1986; (as Dan Kavanagh) Going to the Dogs (crime), 1987. Add: c/o A.D. Peters & Co., Ltd., The Chambers, Chelsea Harbour, Lots Rd., London SW10 0XF, England.

BARNES, Peter. British, b. 1931. Plays/Screenplays. *Publs:* The Ruling Class, 1969; Leonardo's Last Supper and Noonday Demons, 1970; Lulu, 1971; The Bewitched, 1974; Frontiers of Farce, 1977; Laughter, 1978; Collected Plays, 1981; Barnes People II: Seven Dialogues, 1983; Red Noses, 1985; The Real Long John Silver and Other Plays (Barnes' People III), 1986. Add: 7 Archery Close, London W2 2BE, England.

BARNES, Samuel Henry. American, b. 1931. Politics/Government. Prof. of Political Science, and Prog. Dir., Center for Political Studies, Univ. of Michigan, Ann Arbor, since 1970 (Instr. in Political Science, 1957–60; Asst. Prof., 1960–64; Assoc. Prof., 1965–68; Prof. and Acting Chmn., 1968–69; Prof. and Research Assoc., Survey Research Center, 1969–70). *Publs:* Party Democracy: Politics in an Italian Socialist Federation, 1967; Representation in Italy, 1977; (with others) Political Action, 1979. Add: Dept. of Political Science, Univ. of Michigan, 5607 Haven Hall, Ann Arbor, Mich. 48109, U.S.A.

BARNES, Steven (Emory). American, b. 1952. Science fiction. Tour guide, Columbia Broadcasting System, Hollywood, 1974–76; Mgr., Audio-Visual and Multi-Media Dept., Pepperdine Univ., Los Angeles, 1978–80; Creative Consultant, Don Bluth Productions, Los Angeles, 1980. *Publs:* (with Larry Niven) Dream Park, 1981; (with Larry Niven) The Descent of Anansi, 1982; Streetlethal, 1983; The Kundalini Equation, 1986; (with Larry Niven and Jerry Pournelle) The Legacy of Heorot, 1987; Gorgon Child, 1989; (with Larry Niven) The Barsoom Project, 1989. Add: c/o Ace Books, 200 Madison Ave., New York, N.Y. 10016, U.S.A.

BARNETT, Arthur Doak. American, b. 1921. International relations/Current affairs, Politics/Government. Prof., Johns Hopkins Univ. Sch. of Advanced Intnl. Studies, since 1982. Fellow, Inst. of Current Worldffairs in China and Southeast Asia, 1947–50 and 1952–53; Corresp., Chicago Daily News Foreign Service in China and Southeast Asia, 1947–50, 1952–53 and 1953–55; Assoc., American Univs. Field Staff, Hong Kong and other Asian Areas, 1953–55; Prof. Assoc., Intnl. Training and Research Prog., The Ford Foundn., NYC, and Asia, 1959–61; Assoc. Prof., 1960–64, and Prof., 1964–69, Columbia Univ., NYC; Sr. Fellow, The Brookings Instn., 1969–82. *Publs:* Turn East Towards Asia, 1958; Communist Economic Strategy: The Rise of Mainland China, 1959; Communist China and Asia: Challenge to American Policy, 1960; Communist China in Perspective, 1962; (ed.) Communist Strategies in Asia: A Comparative Analysis of Governments and Parties, 1963; China on the Eve of Communist Takeover, 1963; Communist China: The Early Years, 1959–1955, 1964; (ed.) The United States and China in World Affairs, by Robert

Blum, 1966; China after Mao, 1967; Cadres, Bureaucracy, and Political Power in Communist China, 1967; (ed.) Chinese Communist Politics in Action, 1969; (ed. with E.O. Reischauer) The United States and China: The Next Decade, 1970; A New United States Policy Toward China, 1971; Uncertain Passage: China's Transition to the Post-Mao Era, 1974; China Policy: Old Problems and New Challenges, 1977; China and the Major Powers in East Asia, 1977; China's Economy in Global Perspective, 1981; The FX Decision, 1981; U.S. Arms Sales: The China-Taiwan Tangle, 1982; The Making of Foreign Policy in China: Structure and Process, 1985; (ed. with Ralph N. Clough) Modernizing China: Post-Mao Reform and Development, 1986. Add: Johns Hopkins Univ., SAIS, Massachusetts Ave., N.W., Washington, D.C. 20036, U.S.A.

BARNETT, Correlli (Douglas). British, b. 1927. Social history, Military/Defence, Biography. Pres., East Anglian Writers, since 1971; Fellow, Churchill Coll., Cambridge, since 1977. Defence Lectr., Cambridge Univ., 1980–83. *Publs:* The Hump Organisation (novel), 1957; (co-author) The Channel Tunnel, 1958; The Desert Generals, 1960; The Swordbearers, 1963; (co-author) The Great War (television series), 1964 (Best Television Documentary Script Award, Screenwriter's Guild); (co-author) The Lost Peace (television series), 1966; Britain and Her Army, 1970 (Royal Soc. of Literature Award); The Collapse of British Power, 1972; The Commanders (television series), 1973; Marlborough, 1974; Strategy and Society, 1975; Bonaparte, 1978; The Great War, 1979; The Audit of War, 1986. Add: Catbridge House, East Carleton, Norwich, England.

BARNETT, George Leonard. American, b. 1915. Literature. Prof. Emeritus of English, Indiana Univ., Bloomington, (Supvr. of English and Correspondence, U.S. Naval Training Sch., 1942–55; Instr. in English, 1944–46; Asst. Prof., 1946–56; Assoc. Prof., 1956–63; Prof., 1963–81). Instr. in English, French and Latin, Randolph-Macon Coll., Ashland, Va., 1939–41. *Publs:* (with others) The English Romantic Poets and Essayists: A Review of Research and Criticism, 1957, 1966; Charles Lamb: The Evolution of Elia, 1964; (ed.) Eighteenth-Century British Novelists on the Novel, 1968; (ed.) Nineteenth-Century British Novelists on the Novel, 1971; Charles Lamb, 1976. Add: 1802 Weather Vane Ct., Richmond, Va. 23233, U.S.A.

BARNETT, Leonard (Palin). British, b. 1919. Sex, Theology/Religion. Methodist minister since 1942. National Secty., Methodist Assn. of Youth Clubs, 1949–58. *Publs:* Prayer Diary for Youth, 1953; Boy's Prayer Diary, 1954; Adventure with Youth; For Christian Beginners; Live for Kicks; Star Quality; Talking to Youth; Talking to Youth Again; Getting It Over; This I Can Believe!; Sex and Teenages in Love; Girl's Prayer Diary, 1955; Boy on the Corner, 1960; Pop! Goes the Patient, 1960; Windswept Weekend, 1960; The High Cost of Loving, 1970; The Way to the Stars, 1971; New Prayer Diary for Youth, 1975; Good Times with God, 1975; Homosexuality: Time to Tell the Truth, 1975; Sex and Young Lovers, 1979; What is Methodism, 1980. Add: c/o National Christian Education Council, Denholm House, Nutfield, Redhill RH1 4HW, England.

BARNETT, S(amuel) Anthony. Australian, b. 1915. Anthropology/Ethnology, Biology, Psychology, Zoology. Emeritus Prof., Australian National Univ., Canberra, since 1980 (Prof. and Head, Dept. of Zoology, 1971–80). Scientific Officer, 1943–46 and Principal Scientific Officer and Head of Research Unit on Mammalian Pests, 1946–51, Ministry of Food; Sr. Lectr. in Zoology, Glasgow Univ., 1951–71; Part-time Consultant, Ford Foundn., India, 1968–75. *Publs:* The Human Species, 1950, 1971; (ed.) A Century of Darwin, 1958; The Rat: A Study in Behavior, 1963, 1981; 'Instinct' and 'Intelligence', 1967, 1970; (ed.) Ethology and Development, 1973; (with I Prakash) Rodents of Economic Importance in India, 1975; Modern Ethology, 1981; Biology and Freedom, 1988. Add: ORAM, Australian National Univ., Canberra, A.C.T. 2601, Australia.

BARNIE, John. British, b.1941. Poetry, History. Asst. Ed., Planet, since 1985. Lectr. in English Literature, Copenhagen Univ., 1969–82. *Publs:* War in Medieval Society: Social Values and the Hundred Years War 1337-99, 1974; Borderland, 1984; Lightning Country, 1987. Add: Greenfields, Comins Coch, Aberystwyth, Dyfed, Wales.

BARNOUW, Erik. American, b. 1908. Plays/Screenplays, Film, History, Media. Emeritus Prof. of Dramatic Arts, Columbia Univ., NYC, since 1973 (Instr. to Prof., 1946–73). Script Ed., NBC, NYC, 1942–44; Supvr., Education Unit, Armed Forces Radio Service, War Dept., Washington, D.C., 1944–45; Chief, Motion Picture, Broadcasting and Recorded Sound Div., Library of Congress, Washington, D.C., 1978–81.

Secty., Authors League of America, NYC, 1949–53; Chmn., Writers Guild of America, NYC and Los Angeles, 1957–59; Pres., Intnl. Film Seminars, NYC, 1960–68. *Publs:* Open Collars (play), 1928; Handbook of Radio Writing, 1939; (ed.) Radio Drama in Action (anthology), 1945; Handbook of Radio Production, 1946; Mass Communication: Television, Radio, Film, Press, 1956; (with S. Krishnaswamy) Indian Film, 1963, 1980; A History of Broadcasting in the U.S.: vol. I: A Tower of Babel (to 1933), 1966, vol. II: The Golden Web (1933–53), 1968, vol. III: The Image Empire (from 1953), 1970; Documentary: A History of the Non-Fiction Film, 1974; Tube of Plenty: The Evolution of American Television, 1975, 1982; The Sponsor: Notes on a Modern Potentate, 1978; The Magician and the Cinema (early film history), 1981; (ed.) Intnl. Encyclopedia of Communications, 1989. Add: 39 Claremont Ave., New York, N.Y. 10027, U.S.A.

BARNRIGHT, Julia. *See* BANCROFT, Iris.

BARNWELL, William (Curtis). American, b. 1943. Science fiction, Writing. Writer-in-Residence, Columbia Coll., S.C., since 1977. Asst. Prof. of English, Univ. of South Carolina, Columbia, 1971–77. *Publs:* The Blessing Papers, 1980; Curve of the Sigmord, 1981; Imram, 1981; Writing for a Reason (non-fiction), 1983. Add: c/o Curtis Brown Ltd., 10 Astor Pl., New York, NY 10003, U.S.A.

BARON, Denis Neville. British, b. 1924. Medicine/Health. Prof of Chemical Pathology, Royal Free Hosp. Sch. of Medicine, Univ. of London, 1963–88. *Publs:* (with K. Lee and J.T. Whicher) A New Short Textbook of Chemical Pathology, 5th ed. 1989; (ed. with N.D. Compston and A.M. Dawson) Recent Advances in Medicine, 17th ed., 1977; (ed.) Units, Symbols and Abbreviations, 4th. ed. 1988. Add: 47 Holme Close, London N2 0QG, England.

BARON, Wendy. British, b. 1937. Art. Curator, Govt. Art Collection, Office of Arts and Libraries, London, since 1978. *Publs:* Sickert, 1973; Miss Ethel Sands and Her Circle, 1977; The Camden Town Group, 1979. Add: 139 Albert St., London NW1 7NB, England.

BARR, Alwyn. American, b. 1938. History, Race relations. Prof. of History, Texas Tech. Univ. (Chmn of the Dept., 1978–85; member of the faculty since 1975). Editorial Asst., South-western Historical Quarterly, Austin, Tex., 1961–66; Asst. Prof., Purdue Univ., Lafayette, Ind., 1966–69; Assoc. Prof. of History, 1969–75. *Publs:* (ed.) Charles Porter's Account of the Confederate Attempt to Seize Arizona and New Mexico, 1964; Polignac's Texas Brigade, 1964; Reconstruction to Reform: Texas Politics, 1876-1906, 1971; Black Texans: A History of Negroes in Texas, 1528-1971, 1974; (ed. with Calvert) Black Leaders: Texans for Their Times, 1981. Add: Dept. of History, Texas Tech Univ., Lubbock, Tex. 79409, U.S.A.

BARR, Densil. British. Novels/Short stories, Plays. *Publs:* The Man with Only One Head, 1955; radio plays—The Clapham Lamp-Post Saga, 1967; Gladys on the Wardrobe, 1970; But Petrovsky Goes on For Ever, 1971; The Last Tramp, 1972; The Square at Bastogne, 1973; The Battle of Brighton Beach, 1974; To a Green Land Far Away, 1974; With Puffins for Pawns, 1976; Anatomy of an Alibi, 1978; The Speech, 1979; Two Gaps in the Curtain, 1979; Klemp's Diary, 1980; Who Was Karl Raeder? 1980; The Boy in the Cellar, 1981; The Glory Hallelujah Micro-ship, 1982; The Dog That Was Only a Prophet, 1982; St. Paul Transferred, 1983. Add: 15 Churchfields, Broxbourne, Herts., England.

BARR, James. British, b. 1924. Language/Linguistics, Theology/Religion. Regius Prof. of Hebrew, Oxford Univ., since 1978. Prof. of New Testament, Presbyterian Coll., Montreal, 1953–55; Prof. of Old Testament, Univ. of Edinburgh, 1955–61; Prof., Princeton Theological Seminary, N.J., 1961–65; Prof. of Semitic Languages and Literatures, Univ. of Manchester, 1965–76; Oriel Prof. of the Interpretation of Holy Scripture, Oxford Univ., 1976–78. *Publs:* The Semantics of Biblical Language, 1961; Biblical Words for Time, 1962, 1969; Old and New in Interpretation, 1965; Comparative Philology and the Text of the Old Testament, 1968; The Bible and the Modern World, 1973; Fundamentalism, 1977; Explorations in Theology 7, 1980; Holy Scripture: Canon, Authority, Criticism, 1983; Escaping from Fundamentalism, 1984; The Variable Spellings of the Hebrew Bible, 1988. Add: 6 Fitzherbert Close, Iffley, Oxford OX4 4EN, England.

BARR, Patricia (Miriam). British, b. 1934. Historical Novels, History, Women, Biography, Medicine/Health. Full-time writer, Norwich. *Publs:* The Coming of the Barbarians (non-fiction), 1967; The Dear Cry Pavilion (non-fiction), 1968; The Elderly: Handbook on Care and Services, 1968;

Foreign Devils: Westerners in the Far East, 1970; Curious Life for a Lady (biography), 1970; (with Isabella Lucy Bishop) Unbeaten Tracks in Japan, 1971; To China with Love (non-fiction), 1972; The Memsahibs: Women of Victorian India, (non-fiction), 1976; Taming the Jungle (non-fiction), 1977; The Framing of the Female (non-fiction), 1978; (with Roy Desmond) Simla: A Hill Station in British India, 1978; Japan (guidebook), 1980; Chinese Alice (novel), 1981; The New Sourcebook for the Disabled, 1981; Jade (novel), 1982; Kenjiro (novel), 1985; Coromandel (novel), 1988. Add: 25 Montpelier Row, Blackheath, London SE3, England.

BARRAL, Mary-Rose. American, b. 1925. Philosophy, Psychology, Prof. of Philosophy, Seton Hall Univ., South Orange, N.J., since 1967 (Instr., 1960–62; Asst. Prof., 1962–64; Assoc. Prof. 1964–67). *Publs:* Merleau-Ponty: The Role of the Body-subject in Interpersonal Relations, 1965; Progressive Neutralism, 1970; Continuity of Perceptual Process—Husserliana III, 1974 Add: Dept. of Philosophy, Seton Hall Univ., South Orange, N.J. 07079, U.S.A.

BARRANGER, M(illy Hilliard) S(later). American, b. 1937. Literature, Theatre. Prof. and Chmn., Dept. of Dramatic Art, Univ. of North Carolina, Chapel Hill, since 1982; Producer, Play Makers Repertory Co., since 1982. Special Lectr. in English, Louisiana State Univ. in New Orleans, 1964–69; Assoc. Prof. and Chmn., Dept. of Theatre and Speech, Tulane Univ., New Orleans, 1971–82. Pres., American Theatre Assn., 1978–79. *Publs:* Henrik Ibsen: Peer Gynt, Doll's House, Enemy of the People, 1969; (co-ed.) Generations: An Introduction to Drama, 1971; Theatre: A Way of Seeing, 1980, 1986; Theatre: Past and Present, 1984; (co-ed.) Notable Women in the American Theatre, 1989; Understanding Plays, 1989. Add: Dept. of Dramatic Art, Univ. of North Carolina, Chapel Hill, N.C. 27599, U.S.A.

BARRATT BROWN, Michael. British, b. 1918. Economics, Environmental science/Ecology, History. Special Asst., to Chief of Balkan Mission, U.N. Relief and Rehabilitation Admin., 1944–47; Lectr., 1961–66, and Sr. Lectr., 1966–78, Dept. of Extra-Mural Studies, Univ. of Sheffield; Principal, Northern Coll., 1978–83. *Publs:* After Imperialism, 1963, 2nd rev. ed. 1970; What Economics is About, 1970; Essays on Imperialism, 1972; From Labourism to Socialism, 1972; The Economics of Imperialism, 1974; Resources and the Environment, 1976; Information at Work, 1978; Models in Political Economy, 1984. Add: Robin Hood Farm, Baslow, nr. Bakewell, Derbyshire, England.

BARRETT, Charles Kingsley. British, b. 1917. Theology/Religion. Prof. of Divinity, Univ. of Durham, 1958–82, now retired (Lectr., 1945–54; Sr. Lectr., 1954–58). *Publs:* The Holy Spirit and the Gospel Tradition, The Gospel According to St. John, 1955, 1978; (ed.) The New Testament Background: Selected Documents, 1956, 1987; The Epistle to the Romans, 1957; Luke the Historian in Recent Study, 1961; From First Adam to Last, 1962; The Pastoral Epistles, 1963; Jesus and the Gospel Tradition, 1967; The First Epistle to the Corinthians, 1968; The Signs of an Apostle, 1970; Das Johannesevangelium und das Judentum, 1970; New Testament Essays, 1972; The Second Epistle to the Corinthians, 1973; The Gospel of John and Judaism, 1975; (ed.) Donum Gentilicium: New Testament Studies in Honour of David Daube, 1978; Essays on Paul, 1982; Essays on John, 1982; Freedom and Obligation, 1985; Church, Ministry, and Sacraments in the New Testament, 1985. Add: 8 Prince's St., Durham DH1 4RP, England.

BARRETT, John G(ilchrist). American, b. 1921. History. Prof. Emeritus of History, Virginia Military Inst., Lexington. *Publs:* Sherman's March Through the Carolinas, 1956; North Carolina as a Civil War Battleground, 1960; (ed. with R.K. Turner) Letters of a New Market Cadet, 1961; The Civil War in North Carolina, 1963; (ed.) Yankee Rebel: The Civil War Journal of Edmund Dewitt Patterson, 1966; (ed. with W.B. Yearns) North Carolina Civil War Documentary, 1980. Add: 6 Junkin Pl., Lexington, Va. 24450, U.S.A.

BARRETT, John Henry. British, b. 1913. Geography, Natural history. Warden, Dale Fort Field Centre, Haverfordwest, Pembrokeshire, 1947–68; Dir., Pembrokeshire Countryside Unit, 1968–73. *Publs:* (with C.M. Yonge) Pocket Guide to the Seashore, 1958; Life on the Seashore, 1974; The Pembrokeshire Coast Park, 1974; Collins Handguide to the Seacoast, 1981. Add: Anchor Cottage, Dale, Haverfordwest, Pembrokeshire, Wales.

BARRETT, Judi. American, b. 1941. Children's fiction. Children's Book Reviewer, The New York Times, since 1974. Part-time children's teacher, and freelance designer. *Publs:* Old MacDonald had an Apartment House, 1969; Animals Should Definitely Not Wear Clothing, 1970;

An Apple a Day, 1973; Benjamin's 365 Birthdays, 1974; Peter's Pocket, 1974; I Hate to Take a Bath, 1975; I Hate to Go to Bed, 1977; The Wind Thief, 1977; Cloudy with a Chance of Meatballs, 1978; I'm Too Small, You're Too Big. 1981; Animals Should Definitely Not Act Like People, 1981; What's Left?, 1983; A Snake is Totally Tail, 1983; Pickles Have Pimples, 1986. Add: 230 Garfield Pl., Brooklyn, N.Y. 11215, U.S.A.

BARRETT, Nancy Smith. American, b. 1942. Economics. Prof., Dept. of Economics, The American Univ., Washington, D.C., since 1974 (joined faculty as Asst. Prof., 1966). *Publs:* The Theory of Macroeconomic Policy, 1972, 1975; (with G. Gerhardi and T. Hart) Prices and Wages in U.S. Manufacturing, 1973; The Theory of Microeconomic Policy, 1973. Add: Dept. of Economics, The American Univ., Washington, D.C., 20016, U.S.A.

BARRETT, Neal, Jr. American. Science fiction/Fantasy. *Publs:* Kelwin, 1970; The Leaves of Time, 1971; The Gates of Time, 1972; Highwood, 1972; Stress Patterns, 1974; Aldair in Albion, 1976; Aldair, Master of Ships, 1977; Aldair, Across The Misty Sea, 1980; Aldair: The Legion of Beasts, 1982; Karma Corps, 1984; Through Darkest America, 1987. Add: 2032 Kipling, Houston, Tex. 77098, U.S.A.

BARRIE, Alexander. British, b. 1923. Children's fiction, History. Principal, Alexander Barrie Assocs. (PR), London, since 1986. Ed., Business Papers, MacLean Hunter, 1952–56; Managing Dir., House Information Services Ltd., 1970–86. *Publs:* War Underground, 1961, 3rd ed. 1988; Fly for Three Lives, 1974; Operation Midnight, 1974; Let Them All Starve, 1974; Jonathan Kane's Jungle Run, 1977; Jonathan Kane Climbs High, 1978. Add: 33 Manor Way, London SE3, England.

BARRIE, Jane. *See* **WOODFORD,** Cecile.

BARRIE, Susan. Also writes as Anita Charles, and Pamela Kent. Historical/Romance/Gothic. *Publs:* Mistress of Brown Furrows, 1952; The Gates of Dawn, 1954; Marry a Stranger, 1954; Carpet of Dreams, 1955; Hotel Stardust, 1955; (as Pamela Kent) Moon over Africa, 1955; (as Pamela Kent) Desert Doorway, 1956; Dear Tiberius, 1956; The House of the Laird, 1956; So Dear to My Heart, 1956; (as Anita Charles) The Black Benedicts, 1956; (as Anita Charles) My Heart at Your Feet, 1957; (as Anita Charles) One Coin in the Fountain, 1957; Air Ticket, 1957; Four Roads to Windrush, 1957; (as Pamela Kent) City of Palms, 1957; (as Pamela Kent) Sweet Barbary, 1957; (as Pamela Kent) Meet Me in Istanbul, 1958; (as Anita Charles) Interlude for Love, 1958; (as Anita Charles) The Moon and Bride's Hill, 1958; Heart Specialist, 1958; The Stars of San Cecilio, 1958; (as Pamela Kent) Flight to the Stars, 1959; The Wings of the Morning, 1960; Nurse Nolan, 1961; Bride in Waiting, 1961; Moon at the Full, 1961; (as Pamela Kent) The Chateau of Fire, 1961; (as Pamela Kent) Dawn on the High Mountain, 1961; (as Pamela Kent) Journey in the Dark, 1962; Royal Purple, 1962; A Case of Heart Trouble, 1963; (as Pamela Kent) Bladon's Rock, 1963; (as Pamela Kent) The Dawning Splendour, 1963; (as Anita Charles) Autumn Wedding, 1963; (as Anita Charles) The King of the Castle, 1963; (as Anita Charles) White Rose of Love, 1963; Mountain Magic, 1964; Hotel at Treloan, 1964; (as Pamela Kent) Enemy Lover, 1964; (as Pamela Kent) The Gardenia Tree, 1965; (as Pamela Kent) Gideon Faber's Choice, 1965; (as Pamela Kent) Star Creek, 1965; Castle Thunderbird, 1965; No Just Cause, 1965; Master of Melincourt, 1966; The Quiet Heart, 1966; Rose in the Bud, 1966; (as Pamela Kent) Cuckoo in the Night, 1966; (as Pamela Kent) White Heat, 1966; Accidental Bride, 1967; Victoria and the Nightingale, 1967; (as Pamela Kent) Beloved Enemies, 1967; (as Pamela Kent) The Man Who Came Back, 1967; (as Pamela Kent) Desert Gold, 1968; The Marriage Wheel, 1968; Wild Sonata, 1968; Return to Tremarth, 1969; (as Pamela Kent) Man from the Sea, 1969; Night of the Singing Birds. 1970; (as Pamela Kent) Nile Dusk, 1972; (as Pamela Kent) Flight to the Stars, 1977. Add: c/o Mills and Boon Ltd., Eton House, 18-24 Paradise Rd., Richmond, Surrey TW9 1SR, England.

BARRINGTON, Thomas Joseph. Irish, b. 1916. Administration/Management, Travel, Topography. Civil Servant, Dept. of Local Government, 1944–60, Dublin; Dir., Inst. of Public Admin., Dublin 1960–77. Ed., Administration, 1953–63. *Publs:* Notes for Interview Boards; From Big Government to Local Government, 1975; Discovering Kerry, 1976; The Irish Administrative System, 1980; (gen. ed.) Irish County Guides series, 1985. Add: Dargleside, Enniskerry, Co. Wicklow, Ireland.

BARRIO, Raymond. American, b. 1921. Novels/Short stories, Art. Art Instr., Foothill Coll., Sunnyvale, Calif. *Publs:* The Big Picture, 1967; Experiments in Modern Art, 1968; The Plum Plum Pickers, 1969; Selections from Walden, 1970; Prism/67, 1970; Fisherman's Dwarf, 1970;

Mexico's Art and Chicano Artists, 1975; The Devil's Apple Corps, 1976; Political Portfolio, 1985. Add: c/o Ventura Press, P.O. Box 1076, Guerneville, Calif. 95446, U.S.A.

BARRIS, Chuck. American. Novels/Short stories. Television producer. *Publs:* You and Me, Babe, 1974; Confessions of a Dangerous Mind: An Unauthorized Autobiography, 1984. Add: c/o Harper's Mag. Press, 2 Park Ave., New York, N.Y. 10016, U.S.A.

BARRON, Milton L(eon). American, b. 1918. Sociology. Member of faculty, St. Lawrence Univ., Canton, N.Y., 1943–44, Syracuse Univ., N.Y., 1944–48, Cornell Univ., Ithaca, N.Y., 1948–54, and City Coll., City Univ. of New York, 1954–74. Prof. of Sociology, California State Univ., Fresno, 1974–85 (Visiting Lectr., 1969–70). *Publs:* People Who Intermarry, 1946; The Juvenile in Delinquent Society, 1954; (ed.) American Minorities, 1957; (co-author) Delinquent Behavior, 1959; The Aging American, 1961; (ed.) Contemporary Sociology, 1964; (ed.) Minorities in a Changing World, 1967; (ed.) The Blending American: Patterns of Intermarriage, 1972. Add: 3A Rehov Kashani, P.O. Box 67002, Ramat Aviv Gimel, Tel Aviv 69499, Israel.

BARROW, John D(avid). British, b. 1952. Astronomy. Lectr. in Astronomy, Univ. of Sussex, Brighton, since 1981. *Publs:* (with Joseph Silk) The Left Hand of Creation: The Origin and Evolution of the Expanding Universe, 1983; (with Frank Tipler) L'Homme et le Cosmos, 1984; (with Frank Tipler) The Anthropic Cosmological Principle, 1985; The World Within the World, 1988. Add: Astronomy Centre, Univ. of Sussex, Falmer, Brighton BN1 9QH, England.

BARROW, Pamela. *See* HOWARTH, Pamela.

BARROW, Robin (St. Clair). British, b. 1944. Classics, Education, History, Philosophy. Prof. of Curriculum Theory, Simon Fraser Univ., Burnaby, B.C., since 1982. Asst. Master, City of London School for Boys, 1968–72; Lectr., 1972–80, and Reader in Education, 1980–85, Univ. of Leicester. *Publs:* Athenian Democracy, 1973; Moral Philosophy for Education, 1975; (with R.G. Woods), Introduction to Philosophy of Education, 1975; Plato, Utilitarianism, and Education, 1975; Sparta, 1975; Common Sense and the Curriculum, 1976; Greek and Roman Education, 1976; Plato and Education, 1976; Plato: The Apology of Socrates, 1977; Radical Education, 1978; The Canadian Curriculum, 1979; Happiness, 1980; The Philosophy of Schooling, 1981; Injustice, Inequality, and Ethics, 1982; Language and Thought, 1982; Giving Teaching Back to Teachers, 1984; (with Geoffrey Milburn) Critical Dictionary of Educational Concepts, 1986. Add: Faculty of Education, Simon Fraser Univ., Burnaby, B.C. V5A 1S6, Canada.

BARRY, Clive. Australian, b. 1922. Novels/Short stories. U.N. Rep. in the Congo since 1961. *Publs:* The Spear Grinner, 1963; Crumb Borne, 1965; Fly Jamskoni, 1969. Add: c/o Faber and Faber Ltd., 3 Queen Sq., London WC1N 3AU, England.

BARRY, Hugh Collis. Australian, b. 1912. History, Medicine/Health. Consultant Orthopaedic Surgeon, Sydney, since 1958. Hon. Consultant Orthopaedic Surgeon to Royal Prince Alfred Hosp., Sydney, since 1970. Pres., Australian Orthopaedic Assn., 1969–70. *Publs:* Paget's Disease of Bone, 1969; A History of the Elanora Country Club, 1977; Orthopaedics in Australia, 1983. Add: 135 Macquarie St., Sydney, N.S.W. 2000, Australia.

BARRY, James P. American, b. 1918. Environmental science/Ecology, History. With U.S. Army Artillery, 1940 until retirement with rank of Col. in 1966; Admin., Capital Univ., Columbus, Ohio, 1967–71; freelance writer and ed., 1971–77. Dir., Ohioana Library Assn., and Ed., Ohioana Quarterly, 1977–88. *Publs:* Georgian Bay: The Sixth Great Lake, 1968, 1978; The Battle of Lake Erie, 1970; Bloody Kansas, 1972; The Noble Experiment, 1972; (author and photographer) The Fate of the Lakes: A Portrait of the Great Lakes, 1972; The Louisiana Purchase, 1973; Henry Ford and Mass Production, 1973; Ships of the Great Lakes: 200 Years of Navigation, 1973; 1936 Olympics—Berlin, 1975; The Great Lakes, 1976; Lake Erie, 1980; Wrecks and Rescues of the Great Lakes, 1981. Add: 353 Fairway Blvd., Columbus, Ohio 43213, U.S.A.

BARRY, Jane. American, b. 1925. Novels/Short stories. *Publs:* The Long March, 1956; The Carolinians, 1959; A Time in the Sun, 1962; A Shadow of Eagles, 1964; Maximilian's Gold, 1966; Grass Roots, 1968. Add: RD 3, Box 493, Lotus Point, Catskill, N.Y. 12414, U.S.A.

BARRY, Margaret Stuart. British, b. 1927. Children's fiction. Full-

time writer. *Publs:* Boffy and the Teacher Eater and Boffy and the Mumford Ghosts, 2 vols., 1971, 1974; Tommy Mac, 1972; Woozy, 1973; The Woozies Go to School, 1973; Bill Books (readers), 1973; The Woozies on Television, 1974; Tommy Mac Battles On, 1974; Tommy Mac on Safari, 1975; Simon and the Witch, 1976; Woozy and the Weight Watchers, 1977; The Woozies Go Visiting, 1977; Woozies Hold a Frubard Week, 1977; The Monster in a Woozy Garden, 1977; The Return of the Witch, 1978; Maggy Gumption and Maggy Gumption Flies High, 2 vols., 1979, 1981; The Witch of Monopology Manor, 1980; The Witch on Holiday, 1983; The Witch V.I.P., 1987; Diz and the Big Fat Burglar, 1987. Add: 5 Belvidere Rd., Liverpool L8 3TF, England.

BARRY, Mike. *See* MALZBERG, Barry Norman.

BARRY, Robert Everett. American, b. 1931. Children's fiction. Prof. Southeastern Massachusetts Univ., since 1969. Partner, Pava Prints, San Juan, Puerto Rico, 1957–63; member of faculty, Averett Coll., Danville, Va., 1967–68, and Texas Woman's Univ., Denton, 1968–69. *Publs:* Faint George, 1957; Just Pepper, 1957; Boo's, 1957; Next Please, 1962; Mr. Willowby's Christmas Tree, 1964; The Musical Palm Tree, 1964; Animals Around the World, 1964; The Riddle of Castle Hill, 1964; Ramon and the Pirate Gull, 1973; Snowman's Secret, 1975. Add: Driftwood, Cliff Ave., Newport, R.I. 02840, U.S.A.

BARSTOW, Stan(ley). British, b. 1928. Novels/Short stories, Plays/Screenplays. Draftsman and sales exec. in the engineering industry, 1945–62. *Publs:* A Kind of Loving, 1960; The Desperadoes, 1961; Ask Me Tomorrow, 1962; Joby, 1964; The Watchers on the Shore, 1966; (with A. Bradley) Ask Me Tomorrow (play), 1966; A Raging Calm (in U.S. as The Hidden Part), 1968; (ed.) Through the Green Woods: An Anthology of Contemporary Writing about Youth and Children, 1968; (with A. Bradley) Kind of Loving (play), 1970; Listen for the Trains, Love (play), 1970; A Season with Eros, 1971; (with A. Bradley) Stringer's Last Stand (play), 1971; The Right True End, 1976; An Enemy of the People (play), 1977; A Brother's Tale, 1980; A Kind of Loving: The Vic Brown Trilogy, 1982; The Glad Eye, 1984; Just You Wait and See, 1986; 'B'-Movie, 1987; Give Us This Day, 1989. Add: c/o Harvey Unna and Stephen Durbridge Ltd., 24 Pottery Lane, London W11 4LZ, _____

BART, Lionel. British, b. 1930. Plays/Screenplays, Songs, lyrics and libretti. *Works:* Lock Up Your Daughters, 1959; Fings Ain't Wot They Used T'be, 1959; Oliver, 1960 (Antoinette Perry Award as best composer and lyricist, 1962); Blitz, 1962; Maggie May, 1964; has also written for many films. Add: 8-10 Bulstrode St., London W1M 6AH, England.

BART, Peter. American, b. 1932. Novels. Reporter for Wall Street Journal, 1955–57, and for New York Times, 1957–67; Vice Pres. of production, Paramount Pictures, Hollywood, Calif., 1968–75; Pres., Lorimar Films Co., 1983–85; Senior Vice Pres., MGM, 1985–87. *Publs:* (with Denne Bart Petitclerc) Destinies, 1979; Thy Kingdom Come, 1981; Fade Out, 1989. Add: 1338 N. Beverly Dr., Beverly Hills, Calif. 90201, U.S.A.

BARTEK, Edward J. American, b. 1921. Philosophy, Psychology. Instr. of Philosophy and Psychology, Manchester, Middlesex, and Tunxis Community Colleges, Connecticut; lectr. at various colls. Instr. in Philosophy, Univ. of Connecticut Experimental Coll., Storrs, and Instr. in Labor Union Philosophy, Univ. of Connecticut Extension Service. *Publs:* Treasury of Parables (philosophy), 1959; To Relax Tensions, 1965; Truth and Wisdom I, II, III, IV (philosophical-poetry), 1965; The Mind of Future Man 1965; The Ultimate Philosophy—Trinityism, 1968; Unifying Principles of the Mind, 1969; Trinitarian Philosophical Psychology, vol. I, 1973, vol. II, 1978; The Philosophy of Trinityism, vol. I, 1973, vol. II, 1975; Trinitarian Philosophical-Psychological Poems, 1978; Ultimate Principles in Theology, 1983; G.U.T. Pending, 1984; Truth and Wisdom Poems I, 1987; Ultimate Principles, I, II, III, 1987; Truth and Wisdom poems II, III, 1988; Trinitarian Philosophy of History, 1988; Dream-Analysis for Self-Analysis, 1988; Universal Trinitarian Ethics, 1988. Add: 68 Walnut St., East Hartford, Conn. 06108, U.S.A.

BARTELS, Robert. American, b. 1913. Administration/Management, Business/Trade/Industry. Emeritus Prof., Ohio State Univ., Columbus, since 1978 (Prof. of Business Admin., 1946–78). Member of faculty, Univ. of Washington, 1938–41, and Univ. of California, 1941. *Publs:* Development of Marketing Thought, 1963; (ed.) Comparative Marketing: Wholesaling in Fifteen Countries, 1963; (ed.) Ethics in Business, 1963; Credit Management, 1967; Marketing Theory and Metatheory, 1970; History of Marketing Thought, 1974; Global Development and Marketing, 1981. Add: 1631 Roxbury Rd., Apt. F-2, Columbus, Ohio 43212, U.S.A.

BARTH, J(ohn) Robert. American, b. 1931. Literature. Dean, Coll. of Arts and Sciences, Boston Coll., since 1988. Entered Soc. of Jesus, 1948; ordained Roman Catholic Priest, 1961; Asst. Prof. of English, Canisius Coll., Buffalo, N.Y., 1967–70; Asst. Prof. of English, Harvard Univ., Cambridge, Mass., 1970–74; Prof. of English, Univ. of Missouri at Columbia, 1974–88. *Publs:* Coleridge and Christian Doctrine, 1969; (ed.) Religious Perspectives in Faulkner's Fiction: Yoknapatawpha and Beyond, 1972; The Symbolic Imagination: Coleridge and the Romantic Tradition, 1977; (co-ed.) Adam's Dream: Coleridge, Keats, and the Romantic Imagination, 1988; Coleridge and the Power of Love, 1988 . Add: Gasson 103, Boston College, Chestnut Hill, Mass. 02167, U.S.A.

BARTH, John (Simmons). American, b. 1930. Novels/Short stories, Essays. Alumni Centennial Prof. of English, Johns Hopkins Univ., Baltimore, since 1973. Jr. Instr. in English, Johns Hopkins Univ., Baltimore, Md., 1951–53; Instr., to Assoc. Prof. of English, Pennsylvania State Univ., University Park, 1953–65; Prof. of English, State Univ. of New York, Buffalo, 1965–73. *Publs:* The Floating Opera, 1956, 1967; The End of the Road, 1958, 1967; The Sot-Weed Factor, 1960, 1967; Giles Goat-Boy: or The Revised New Syllabus, 1966; Lost in the Funhouse: Fiction for Print, Tape, Live Voice, 1968; Chimera, 1972 (National Book Award); Letters, 1979; Sabbatical: A Romance, 1982; The Literature of Exhaustion, 1982; The Friday Book, 1984; Don't Count on It, 1984; The Tidewater Tales: A Novel, 1987. Add: c/o Writing Seminars, Johns Hopkins Univ., Baltimore, Md. 21218, U.S.A.

BARTH, Markus. Swiss, b. 1915. Theology/Religion. Minister, Evangelical Reformed Church, Bubendorf, Basel-Land, 1940–53; Visiting Prof. of New Testament, Univ. of Dubuque, Iowa, 1953–55; Assoc. Prof., Univ. of Chicago, 1956–65; Prof., Pittsburgh Theological Seminary, Pa., 1963–72; Prof. of New Testament, Univ. of Basel, 1973. *Publs:* Die Taufe—ein Sakrament? 1951; The Broken Wall: A Study in Ephesians, 1959; Was Christ's Death a Sacrifice?, 1961; (with V. Fletcher) Acquittal by Resurrection, 1964; Conversation with the Bible, 1964; Israel and the Church, 1969; Justification, 1971; Ephesians Commentary, Anchor Bible (2 vols.), 1974; The Jew Jesus, Israel, and the Palestinians, 1978; The People of God, 1983; Das Mahl des Herrn, 1987. Add: Inzlinger-Str. 275, 4125 Riehen BS, Switzerland.

BARTHELME, Donald. American, b. 1931. Novels/Short stories, Children's fiction. Former museum dir., Houston, Tex., and Managing Ed., Location mag., NYC. *Publs:* Come Back, Dr. Caligari, 1964; Snow White, 1967; Unspeakable Practices, Unnatural Acts, 1968; City Life, 1971; Sadness, 1972; The Slightly Irregular Fire Engine: or, The Hithering Dithering Djinn, 1972; Guilty Pleasures, 1974; The Dead Father, 1975; Amateurs, 1976; Great Days, 1979; Presents, 1981; Sixty Stories, 1982; Overnight to Many Distant Cities, 1983; Forty Stories, 1987; Sam's Bar, 1987. *Deceased, 1989.*

BARTHELME, Frederick. American, b. 1943. Novels/Short stories. Prof. of English, Dir. of the Center for Writers, and Ed. of Mississippi Review, Univ. of Southern Mississippi, Hattiesburg, since 1977. Also, an artist: has had exhibitions at galleries in Houston, New York City, Seattle, Vancouver, Buenos Aires, etc., since 1965. Architectural draftsman, Jerome Oddo and Assocs. and Kenneth E. Bentsen Assocs., Houston, 1965–66; Exhibition Organizer, St. Thomas Univ., Houston, 1966–67; Asst. to the Dir., Kornblee Gallery, NYC, 1967–68; Creative Dir., BMA Advertising, Houston, 1971–73; Sr. Writer, GDL & W Advertising, Houston, 1973–76. *Publs:* Rangoon (short stories), 1970; War and War (novel), 1971; Moon Deluxe (short stories), 1983; Second Marriage (novel), 1984; Tracer (novel), 1985; Chroma and Other Stories, 1987; Two Against One (novel), 1988. Add: 203 Sherwood Dr., Hattiesburg, Miss. 39401, U.S.A.

BARTHOLOMEW, Jean. *See* **BEATTY,** Patricia.

BARTLETT, Bruce R(eeves). American, b. 1951. Economics, Politics. Deputy Assistant Secretary, Treasury Department, Washington D.C., since 1988. Economist and Legislative Asst. for politicians, U.S. Congress, Washington, D.C., 1976–80; Deputy Dir. and Exec. Dir., Joint Economic Cttee. of Congress, Washington, D.C., 1981–84; Vice Pres., Polyconomics, Inc., Morristown, N.J., 1984–85; Senior Fellow, Heritage Foundation, Washington, D.C., 1985–87; Senior Policy Analyst, The White House, Washington, D.C., 1987–1988. *Publs:* Coverup: The Politics of Pearl Harbour, 1941–1946, 1979; Reaganomics: Supply-Side Economics in Action, 1981; (with Timothy Roth) The Supply-Side Solution, 1983. Add: 203 Yoakum Parkway, Apt. 1822, Alexandria, Va. 22304, U.S.A.

BARTLETT, Christopher John. British b. 1931. History, Biography. Prof. of International History, Univ. of Dundee, since 1978 (Lectr. in Modern History, 1962–68; Reader in Intnl. History, 1968–78). Lectr. in Modern History, Univ. of the West Indies, Jamaica, 1959–62. *Publs:* Great Britain and Sea Power 1815-53, 1963; Castlereagh, 1966; (ed.) Britain Pre-Eminent: Studies in British World Influence in the Nineteenth Century, 1969; The Long Retreat: A Short History of British Defence Policy 1945-70, 1972; The Rise and Fall of the Pax Americana, 1974; A History of Postwar Britain 1945-1974, 1977; The Global Conflict 1880-1970, 1984; British Foreign Policy in the Twentieth Century, 1989. Add: Dept. of History, Univ. of Dundee, Dundee DD1 4HN, Scotland.

BARTLETT, Eric George. British, b. 1920. Novels/Short stories, Sports/Physical education/Keeping fit. Instr., Yudachi Sch. of Judo, Cardiff, since 1976; Instr., Sakura Academy of Judo, New Tredegar, 1953–74. *Publs:* The Case of the Thirteenth Coach, 1958; The Complete Body Builder, 1961; Judo and Self Defence, 1962; Self Defence in the Home (in U.S. as New Ways of Self Defense), 1967; Basic Judo, 1974; Basic Fitness, 1976; Smoking Flax, 1977; Summer Day at Ajaccio, 1979; Basic Karate, 1980; Weight Training, 1984; Healing without Harm, 1985; (with Mary Southall) Weight Training for Women, 1986; (with Mary Southall) Weight Training for the Over-35's, 1987; World of Sport—Judo, 1988. Add: 5 Bryngwyn Rd., Cardiff CF2 6PQ, Wales.

BARTLEY, William Warren III. American, b. 1934. Philosophy, Biography. Prof. of Philosophy, California State Univ., Hayward, since 1970; Visiting Scholar, 1984, and Sr. Research Fellow, since 1985, Hoover Instn., Stanford Univ. Lectr., Univ. of London, 1960–63; Assoc. Prof., Univ. of California, 1963–67; Fellow, Gonville and Caius Coll., Cambridge, England, 1966–67; Prof. of Philosophy and of History and Philosophy of Science, and Assoc. Dir. and Sr. Research Assoc. of the Center for Philosophy and Science, Univ. of Pittsburgh, Pa., 1967–73. *Publs:* The Retreat to Commitment, 1962; Morality and Religion, 1971; Wittgenstein, 1973; Die Notwendigkeit des Engagements, 1974; (author and ed.) Lewis Carroll's Symbolic Logic, 1977; Werner Erhard: The Transformation of a Man: The Founding of Est, 1978; Karl Popper's Postscript to the Logic of Scientific Discovery, 1982; Evolutionary Epistemology, Rationality, and the Sociology of Knowledge, 1987. Add: c/o Hoover Instn., Stanford Univ., Stanford, Calif. 94305, U.S.A.

BARTON, Erle. *See* **FANTHORPE,** R. Lionel.

BARTON, Jon. *See* **HARVEY,** John B.

BARTON, Lee. *See* **FANTHORPE,** R. Lionel.

BARTZ, Albert. American, b. 1933. Mathematics/Statistics. Prof. of Psychology, Concordia Coll., Moorhead, Minn., since 1970 (Asst. Prof., Assoc. Prof., 1965–70; Chmn., Dept., of Psychology, 1972). *Publs:* Descriptive Statistics, 1979; Basic Statistical Concepts, 1988. Add: Dept. of Psychology, Concordia Coll., Moorhead, Minn. 56560, U.S.A.

BARZELAY, Walter Moshe. Israeli, b. 1914. Poetry, Translations. National Dir., Israeli Chapter, World Poetry Soc., since 1969. *Publs:* (trans.) Nicolas Guillen's Selected Verse, 1962; Tinge of Purple, 1967; Variations on a Theme, 1970; Semantics of the Heart, 1971; (ed.) Israeli Poets Anthology, 1971; From Past Nights' Shores, 1973; (ed.) Sandra Fowler: In the Shape of the Sun, 1973; (trans.) Bridge Between Shores, 1974; Song of the Sea, 1976; (trans.) Twenty-Two Poets, 1977; Man Flies Towards the Light, 1977; Beyond This I, 1978; Castle of Beauty, 1980; Stories from Palestine and Israel, 1981; Spanish Romances, 1986; (translator) Quicksand Generation, 1987. Add: P.O. Box 26464, Tel-Aviv 61263, Israel.

BARZUN, Jacques. American, b. 1907. History, Literature, Music, Philosophy. Univ. Prof. of History, Columbia Univ., 1967–75, now Emeritus (faculty member since 1927; Asst. Prof., 1938–42; Assoc. Prof., 1942–45; Prof., 1945–55; Dean of Grad. Faculties, 1955–58; Dean of Faculties and Provost, 1958–67; Seth Low Prof. of History, 1960); Extraordinary Fellow, Churchill Coll., Cambridge, since 1961; member, Bd. of Editors, Encyclopedia Britannica, since 1962; Literary Consultant to Charles Scribner's Sons, publrs., since 1975. *Publs:* The French Race: Theories of Its Origin, 1932, 1966; Race: A Study in Modern Superstition, 1937, 1965; Of Human Freedom, 1939, 1964; Darwin, Marx, Wagner, 1941, 1958; Teacher in America, 1945, 4th ed. 1981; Berlioz and the Romantic Century, 1950, 3rd ed. 1969; Pleasures of Music, 1951, 3rd ed. 1977; (trans.) Diderot: Rameau's Nephew, 1952; (ed.) Selected Letters of Lord Byron, 1953, 1957; God's Country and Mine, 1954, 1959; (trans.) Flaubert: Dictionary of Accepted Ideas, 1954, 3rd ed. 1968; (ed. and trans.) New Letters of Berlioz, 1954, 1974; The Energies of Art, 1956, 1962; Music in American Life, 1956, 1962; (with H. Graff) The Modern Researcher, 1957, 3rd ed. 1977; (ed.) Selected of John Jay Chapman, 1957, 1959; The House of Intellect, 1959, 1961; (trans.) Courteline: A Rule is a Rule, 1960; (trans.) Beaumarchais: The Marriage of Figaro, 1961; Classic Romantic and Modern, 1961; Science: The Glorious Entertainment, 1964; (ed. with others) Follett's Modern American Usage, 1966; The American University, 1968, 1970; (with W.H. Taylor) A Catalogue of Crime, 1971; On Writing, Editing and Publishing, 1971; Clio and the Doctors, 1974; The Use and Abuse of Art, 1974; Simple and Direct: A Rhetoric for Writers, 1975; Critical Questions, 1982; A Stroll with William James, 1983; A Word or Two Before You Go, 1986. Add: 1170 Fifth Ave., New York, NY 10029, U.S.A.

BASCOM, William Russel. American, b. 1912. Anthropology/Ethnology, Art, Mythology/Folklore. Prof. of Anthropology Emeritus, Univ. of California, Berkeley, since 1979 (Prof., 1957–79). Instr., to Prof. of Anthropology, Northwestern Univ., Evanston, Ill., 1939–57. *Publs:* (with P. Gebauer) Handbook of West African Art, 1953, 1964; (consulting ed.) New Century Cyclopedia of Names (3 vols.), 1954; Life of a Primitive People, 1957; (co-ed. and contrib.) Continuity and Change in African Cultures, 1959; (ed. with M.J. Herskovits) Continuity and Change in African Cultures, 1962; Ponape: A Pacific Economy in Transition, 1965; (ed. with M.J. Herskovits) Al Thaqafah a Afreeqiyyah, 1966; Ifa Divination, Communication Between Gods and Men in West Africa, 1969 (Pitre Intnl. Folklore Prize); The Yoruba of Southwestern Nigeria, 1969; The Sociological Role of the Yoruba Cult-Group, 1969; (ed. with M.J. Herskovits) Continuity and Change in African Cultures, 1970; Shango in the New World, 1972; African Art in Cultural Perspective, 1973; African Dilemma Tales, 1975; (ed.) Frontiers of Folklore, 1977; Sixteen Cowries: Yoruba Divination from Africa to the New World, 1980. Add: 624 Beloit Ave., Berkeley, Calif. 94708, U.S.A.

BASELEY, Godfrey. British, b. 1904. Agriculture. Country life/Rural societies. Free-lance actor, 1926–40; Staff Speaker, Ministry of Information, London, 1940–43; BBC Outside Broadcast Producer and and Countryside Prog. Producer, Sound Radio, Birmingham, 1943–53; Rural prog. organiser for television, BBC, 1953–56; Creator, Producer, and Ed., The Archers, BBC, 1950–72; Script Writer and Dir., BMT Visuals (Film Makers), Birmingham, 1960–65; Chmn., Godfrey Baseley Ltd. (Consultants in Agricultural Information), 1962–74; Bailiff of Bromsgrove, 1963–64. *Publs:* The Archers: A Slice of My Life, 1971; A Village Portrait, 1972; Country Calendar, 1975; A Country Compendium, 1977; Agricultural Education for Third World Countries Through Entertainment on Radio, 1985. Add: Ambridge, Corse Lawn, nr. Gloucester, England.

BASH, Frank N(ess). American, b. 1937. Astronomy. Prof. since 1981, and Edmonds Regents' Prof., since 1986, Dept of Astronomy, Univ of Texas, Austin (Assoc. Prof., 1975–81; Chmn., 1982–87). *Publs:* (with D. Schiller and Dilip Balamore) Astronomy, 1977. Add: Astronomy Dept., Univ of Texas, Austin, Tex. 78712, U.S.A.

BASHAM, Richard (Dalton). American, b. 1945. Anthropology/Ethnology, Cultural/Ethnic topics. Sr. Lectr. in Anthropology, Univ. of Sydney, since 1978. Asst Prof., State Univ. of New York, 1971–72, and Univ. of Colorado, Boulder, 1972–77. *Publs:* Urban Anthropology: The Cross-Cultural Study of Complex Societies, 1978; Crisis in Blanc and White: Urbanization and Ethnic Identity in French Canada, 1978. Add: Dept. of Anthropology, Univ. of Sydney, Sydney, N.S.W. 2006, Australia.

BASINGER, Jeanine (Deyling). American, b. 1936. Film. Corwin-Fuller Prof. of Film, Wesleyan Univ., Middletown, Conn. (Prof. since 1984; joined faculty, 1971). Trustee, American Film Institute, National Center for Film and Video Preservation. *Publs:* (ed., with John Frazer and Joseph W. Reed) Working with Kazan, 1973; Shirley Temple, 1975; Gene Kelly, 1976; Lana Turner, 1977; Anthony Mann: A Critical Analysis, 1979; World War II Combat Films: Anatomy of a Genre, 1985; (ed.) The "It's a Wonderful Life" Book, 1986. Add: c/o Wesleyan Cinema Archives, 301 Washington Terrace, Wesleyan Univ., Middletown, Conn. 06457, U.S.A.

BASS, Bernard M(orris). American, b. 1925. Business. Distinguished Prof. of Management and Dir., Center for Leadership Studies, Sch. of Management, State Univ. of New York at Binghamton, since 1977. Prof., Univ. of Rochester, N.Y. 1968–77. Exec. Ed., Leadership Quarterly. *Publs:* Objective Approach to Personality Assessment, 1959; Leadership, Psychology and Organizational Behavior, 1960; Conformity and Deviation, 1961; Leadership and Interpersonal Behavior, 1961; Organizational

Psychology, 1965, 2nd ed. (with E.C. Ryterband), 1979; Psychology of Learning for Managers, 1965; Training in Industry, 1967; Man, Work and Organizations, 1972; Assessment of Managers, 1979; People, Work, and Organizations, 1981; Stogdill's Handbook of Leadership, 1981; Interpersonal Communications in Organizations, 1982; Organizational Decision-making, 1983; Leadership and Performance beyond Expectations, 1985; Bass and Stogdill Handbook of Leadership, 1989. Add: c/o Sch. of Management, State Univ. of New York, Binghamton, N.Y. 13901, U.S.A.

BASS, Howard. British, b. 1923. Sports/Physical education/Keeping fit. Winter Sports Corresp., Telegraph, London, since 1960, Evening Standard, London, since 1973, and Mail, London, since 1987. Text Authority, Encyclopaedia Britannica, and Guinness Book of Records, since 1963. Ed., Winter Sports, 1948–68; Managing Dir., Howard Bass Publs. Ltd., 1948–70. *Publs:* The Sense in Sport, 1943; This Skating Age, 1958; The Magic of Skiing, 1959; Winter Sports, 1966; Success in Ice Skating, 1970; International Encyclopaedia of Winter Sports, 1971; Let's Go Skating, 1970; Tackle Skating, 1978; Ice Skating for Pleasure, 1979; Ice Skating, 1980; The Love of Skating, 1980; Elegance on Ice, 1980; (with Robin Cousins) Skating for Gold, 1980; Glorious Wembley, 1982; Super Book of Ice Skating, 1988; Ski Sunday, 1988. Add: 256 Willow Rd., Enfield, Middx., England.

BASS, Jack. American, b. 1934. Politics/Government, Social commentary/phenomena. Prof. of Journalism, Univ. of Mississippi, Oxford, since 1987. Bureau Chief, Knight Newspapers, Columbia, 1966–73; Visiting Research Fellow, Inst, of Policy Sciences and Public Affairs, Duke Univ., Durham, N.C., 1973–75; Writer-in-Residence, South Carolina State Coll., Orangeburg, 1975–78; Research Fellow and Dir. of American South Special Projects, Univ. of South Carolina, Columbia, 1979–85. *Publs:* (with Jack Nelson) The Orangeburg Massacre, 1970; (co-author) You Can't Eat Magnolias, 1972; Porgy Comes Home, 1972; (with Walter DeVires) The Transformation of Southern Politics, 1976; Unlikely Heroes, 1981; (ed. with Thomas E. Terrill) The American South Comes of Age, 1985. Add: 607 S. 8th St., Oxford, Miss. 38655, U.S.A.

BASS, T.J. Pseud. for Thomas J. Bassler. American, b. 1932. Science fiction/Fantasy. In private practice as a pathologist, since 1964. Deputy Medical Examiner, Los Angeles, 1961–64. Ed. American Medical Joggers Newsletter. *Publs:* Half Past Human, 1971; The Godwhale, 1974. Add: 27558 Sunnyridge Rd., Palos Verdes, Calif. 90274, U.S.A.

BASSETT, Ronald Leslie. Also writes as William Clive. British, b. 1924. Novels/Short stories, Historical/Romance/Gothic, Military/Defence. Full-time Author, documentary and medical film scriptwriter since 1958. Served with King's Royal Rifle Corps. 1938–39, and the Royal Navy 1940–54. *Publs:* The Carthaginian, 1963; The Pompeians, 1965; Witchfinder General, 1966; Amorous Trooper, 1968; Rebecca's Brat, 1969; Kill the Stuart, 1970; Tinfish Run, 1977; Pierhead Jump, 1978; Neptune Landing, 1979; Guns of Evening, 1980; Battle-Cruisers, 1982; H.M.S. Sheffield: The Life and Times of Old Shiny, 1988; as William Clive—Dando on Delhi Ridge, 1971; Dando and the Summer Palace, 1972; Dando and the Mad Emperor, 1973; The Tune That They Play, 1974; Blood of an Englishman, 1975; Fighting Mac, 1976. Add: 19 Binstead Dr., Blackwater, Camberley, Surrey, England.

BATCHELOR, David. British, b. 1943. Novels/Short stories. *Publs:* Brogan and Sons, 1976; A Dislocated Man, 1978; Children in the Dark, 1982; Why Tilbury?, 1985. Add: 52 Onslow Sq., London SW7, England.

BATCHELOR, George Keith. British, b. 1920. Technology, Physics. Head, Dept. of Applied Mathematics and Theoretical Physics, 1959–83, and Prof. of Applied Mathematics, 1964–83, now Emeritus, Univ. of Cambridge (Lectr. in Mathematics, 1948–59; Reader in Fluid Dynamics, 1959–64). Ed., Journal of Fluid Mechanics, Cambridge Univ. Press, since 1956. *Publs:* The Theory of Homogeneous Turbulence, 1953; (co-ed.) Surveys in Mechanics, 1956; (ed.) The Scientific Papers of G.I. Taylor, vol. 1, 1958, vol. 2, 1960, vol. 3, 1963, vol. 4, 1971; An Introduction to Fluid Dynamics, 1967. Add: Cobbers, Conduit Head Rd., Cambridge, England.

BATCHELOR, John. British, b. 1942. Novels, Biography, Literature. Fellow, New Coll., Oxford, since 1976 (Sr. Tutor, 1985–87). Lectr. in English, Birmingham Univ., 1968–76. *Publs:* Breathless Hush, 1974; Mervyn Peake, 1974; The Edwardian Novelists, 1982; (ed.) Lord Jim, by Conrad, 1983; H.G. Wells, 1985; (ed.) Victory, by Conrad, 1986; Lord Jim (Unwin Critical Library), 1988. Add: New Coll., Oxford, England.

BATCHELOR, John Calvin. American, b. 1948. Novels/Short stories, Science Fiction. Editor and Book Reviewer, SoHo Weekley News, New York, 1975–77; Book Reviewer, Village Voice, New York, 1977–80. *Publs:* The Further Adventures of Halley's Comet, 1981; The Birth of the People's Republic of Antarctica, 1983; American Falls, 1985; (with John R. Hamilton) Thunder in the Dust: Great Shots from the Western Movies, 1987. Add: c/o Barney Karpfinger, 18 East 48th St., Suite 1601, New York, N.Y. 10017, U.S.A.

BATE, Walter Jackson. American, b. 1918. Literature. Abbott Lawrnce Lowell Prof. of Humanities, Harvard Univ., Cambridge, Mass., since 1962 (Asst. Prof., 1946–49, Assoc. Prof., 1949–56, Chmn. of the Dept. of English, 1955–62, and Prof. of English, 1956–62). *Publs:* Negative Capability: The Intuitive Approach in Keats, 1939; The Stylistic Development of Keats, 1958; From Classic to Romantic: Premises of Taste in the Eighteenth Century, 1946; (ed.) Criticism: The Major Texts, 1952, 1972; The Achievement of Samuel Johnson, 1955; Prefaces to Criticism, 1959; (ed.) Selected Writings, by Edmund Burke, 1960; John Keats, 1963 (Pulitzer Prize for Biography); (ed.) Keats: A Collection of Critical Essays, 1964; (co-ed.) The Yale Edition of the Works of Samuel Johnson, vols. 2-5, 1963, 1969; (ed.) Essays from the Rambler, Adventurer, and Idler, by Samuel Johnson, 1968; Coleridge, 1968; The Burden of the Past and the English Poet, 1970, Samuel Johnson, 1978 (Pulitzer Prize for Biography); (ed.) Coleridge, Biographia Literaria, 1983; (ed.) British and American Poets, 1985. Add: 3 Warren House, Harvard Univ., Cambridge, Mass. 02138, U.S.A.

BATES, (Sir) (Julian) Darrell. British, b. 1913. Novels/Short stories, History, Travel/Exploration/Adventure, Autobiography/Memoirs/Personal, Biography. With H.M. Overseas Service: Colonial Secty., Gibraltar, 1953–64; Permanent Secty., 1964 until retirement, 1968. *Publs:* A Flyswitch from the Sultan, 1961; The Shell at My Ear, 1961; The Mango and the Palm, 1962; A Longing for Quails, 1963; Susie, 1964; A Gust of Plumes, 1972; A Comparison Guide to Devon and Cornwall, 1975; The Abyssinian Difficulty, 1979; The Fashoda Incident of 1898, 1984. Add: 21 Carrallack Terrace, St. Just, Penzance, Cornwall TR19 7LP, England.

BATES, James. British, b. 1926. Administration/Management, Business/Trade/Industry, Economics. Rothmans Prof. of Business Economics, and Head, Dept. of Business Studies, Queen's Univ., Belfast, since 1965. Asst. Lectr. in Applied Economics, Univ. of Nottingham, 1953–55; Research Officer, Univ. of Oxford, Inst. of Statistics, 1955–59; Lectr. in Economics, Dept. of Economic and Social Research, Univ. of Glasgow, 1959–61; Lectr. in Economics, Univ. of Bristol, 1961–65. *Publs:* (with J.R. Parkinson) Business Economics, 1963, 3rd ed. 1983; The Financing of Small Business, 1964, 3rd ed. 1983; (with M. Bell) The Management of Northern Ireland Industry, 1971; (with M. Bell) Small Manufacturing Business in Northern Ireland, 1973; The Management of Small Business, 1988. Add: Dept . of Business Studies, Queen's Univ., Belfast, Northern Ireland.

BATES, Peter Watson. New Zealander, b. 1920. Novels/Short stories, History. Managing-Ed., Church and People mag., 1958–68; Ed., Hutt News, 1968–80; Special Publs. Ed., INL Print, 1980–83; Speechwriter for the Prime Minister of New Zealand, 1984; Ed.-Mgr., Upper Hutt Leader, 1984–86. *Publs:* Supply Company, 1955; The Red Mountain, 1966; Man Out of Mind, 1968; Old Men are Fools, 1970; A Kind of Treason. Add: 43 Raukawa St., Stokes Valley, Lower Hutt, New Zealand.

BATEY, Tom. *See* **TOMKINS,** Jasper.

BATSON, (Harold) Edward. South African, b. 1906. Economics, Sociology. Dir., Social Survey of Cape Town, since 1936. Lectr., London Sch. of Economics, 1931–35; Prof., 1935–71, and Dean of Faculty of Social Science, 1945–71, Univ. of Cape Town; Prof. and Head of the Dept. of Sociology and Criminology, Univ. of Fort Hare, Cape Province, 1972–78. *Publs:* Practical Economics, 1929; Select Bibliography of Modern Economic Theory, 1930; Price Policies of German Public Utility Undertakings, 1933; (trans.) The Theory of Money and Credit, by Ludwig von Mises, 1934; Towards Social Security, 1943; Contemporary Dimensions of Africa, 1962. Add: P.O. Box 75, Rondebosch 7700, South Africa.

BATTEN, James William. American, b. 1919. Astronomy, Earth sciences. Prof. Emeritus, East Carolina Univ., Greenville, N.C. (Prof. 1960–86; Prof. of Research and Chmn., Dept. of Secondary Education, 1968–86) Narrator, Morehead Planetarium, Chapel Hill, N.C., 1958–60. *Publs:* Our Neighbors in Space, 1962, rev. ed. 1969; Stars, Atoms, and God,

1968; (with J. Sullivan Gibson) Soils: Their Nature, Classification and Uses, 1970, 1977; Understanding Research, 1970; Rumblings of a Rolling Stone, 1974; Human Procedures in Educational Research, 1978; Developing Competencies in Educational Research, 1980; Research in Education, 1984, 1986; The Batten Clan in Johnston Co., N.C., 1988. Add: 1014 East Wright Rd., Greenville, N.C. 27858, U.S.A.

BATTEN, T(homas) R(eginald). British, b. 1904. History, Sociology. Freelance community development consultant. With Colonial Education Service, Nigeria, 1927–43; Vice-Principal, Makerere Coll., Uganda, 1943–49; Sr. Lectr. in Community Development Studies, 1949–63, and Reader, 1963–72, Univ. of London. *Publs:* Handbook on the Teaching of History and Geography in Nigeria, 1933; Tropical Africa in World History, Books I-IV, 1939–40; The British Empire and the Modern World, 1941; Africa Past and Present, 1943; Thoughts on African Citizenship, 1944; Problems of African Development: vol. I, Land and Labour, 1947, vol. II, Government and People, 1948; (with G.A. Goodban and Chien Ching-Lien) China in World History, Books I-IV, 1958–61; Communities and Their Development, 1957; School and Community in the Tropics, 1959; Training for Community Development, 1962; (with M. Batten) The Human Factor in Community Work, 1965; (with M. Batten) The Non-Directive Approach in Group and Community Work, 1967; (with M. Batten) The Human Factor in Youth Work, 1970. Add: Tawh Cottage, Windyridge Close, Wimbledon Common, London SW19 5HB, England.

BATTENHOUSE, Roy W(esley). American, b. 1912. History, Theology, Literature. Prof. Emeritus of English, Indiana Univ., Bloomington, since 1982 (Prof., 1956–82, Assoc. Prof., 1950–56). Member, Editorial Bd., Shakespeare Studies since 1965. Instr. in English, Ohio State Univ., Columbus, 1938–40; Asst. Prof., and Assoc. Prof. of Church History, Vanderbilt Univ., Nashville, Tenn., 1940–46; Assoc. Prof. of Church History, Episcopal Theological Sch., 1946–49. Pres., Conference on Christianity and Literature, 1977–82. *Publs:* Marlowe's 'Tamburlaine': A Study in Renaissance Moral Philosophy, 1942; (ed. and contrib.) A Companion to the Study of St. Augustine, 1955; Shakespearean Tragedy: Its Art and Its Christian Premises, 1969. Add: 2455 Tamarack Trail, No. 230, Bloomington, Ind. 47401, U.S.A.

BATTESTIN, Martin Carey. American, b. 1930. Literature. Kenan Prof. of English Literature, Univ. of Virginia, Charlottesville, since 1975; (Asst. Prof., 1961–63; Assoc. Prof., 1963–67; Prof., 1967–75; Chmn. of Dept., 1983–86). Instr., 1956–58, and Asst. Prof., 1958–61, Wesleyan Univ., Middletown, Conn. *Publs:* The Moral Basis of Fielding's Art, 1959; (ed.) Fielding's Joseph Andrews and Shamela, 1961; (ed.) Fielding's Joseph Andrews, 1967; (ed.) Twentieth Century Interpretations of Tom Jones, 1968; The Providence of Wit: Aspects of Form in Augustan Literature and the Arts, 1974; (co-ed.) Fielding's Tom Jones, 1975; (ed.) Fielding's Amelia, 1983; British Novelists 1660-1800, 1985; New Essays by Henry Fielding: His Contributions to the Craftsman (1734-1739) and Other Early Journalism, 1989; Henry Fielding: A Life, 1989. Add: 1832 Westview Rd., Charlottesville, Va 22903, U.S.A.

BATTISCOMBE, Georgina. British, b. 1905. Biography. *Publs:* Charlotte Mary Yonge, 1943; Two on Safari, 1946; English Picnics, 1949; Mrs. Gladstone, 1956; John Keble, 1963; Queen Alexandra, 1969; Lord Shaftesbury, 1974; Reluctant Pioneer: The Life of Elizabeth Wordsworth, 1978; Christina Rossetti, 1981; The Spencers of Althorp, 1985. Add: 40 Phyllis Ct. Dr., Henley on Thames RG9 2HU, England.

BAUER, Caroline Feller. American, b. 1935. Children's fiction, Children's non-fiction, Literary Criticism/History. Lectr. and educational consultant. Children's librarian, New York Public Library, NYC, 1958–59, 1961; Librarian, Colorado Rocky Mountain Sch., Carbondale, 1963–66; Assoc. Prof. of Library Science, Univ. of Oregon, Eugene, 1966–79. Producer, "Caroline's Corner", KOAP-TV, 1973–74. *Publs:* Children's Literature: A Teletext, 1973; Getting It Together with Books, 1984; Storytelling, 1974; Caroline's Corner, 1974; Handbook for Storytellers, 1977; Children's Literature, 1978; My Mom Travels a Lot, 1981; This Way to Books, 1983; Too Many Books, 1974; Celebrations: Read-Aloud Holiday and Theme Book Program, 1985; (ed.) Rainy Day: Stories and Poems, 1986; (ed.) Snowy Day: Stories and Poems, 1986; Presenting Reader's Theater Plays and Poems to Read Aloud, 1987; Midnight Snowman, 1987; Halloween: Stories and Poems, 1988; Windy Day: Stories and Poems, 1988. Add: 6892 Seaway Circle, Huntington Beach, Calif. 92648, U.S.A.

BAUER, Peter Thomas (Baron Bauer of Market Ward in the City of Cambridge). British, b. 1915. Business/Trade/Industry, Economics, Marketing. Prof. Emeritus, Univ. of London (former Prof. of Economics,

London Sch. of Economics, 1960–83). Reader in Agricultural Economics, Univ. of London, 1947–48; Fellow, Gonville and Caius Coll., 1946–60, and since 1968; Lectr. in Economics, 1948–56, and Smuts Reader in Commonwealth Studies, 1956–60, Cambridge Univ. *Publs:* The Rubber Industry, 1948; West African Trade, 1954; (with B.S. Yamey) The Economics of Under-Developed Countries, 1957; Economic Analysis and Policy in Under-Developed Countries, 1958; Indian Economic Policy and Development, 1961; (with B.S. Yamey) Markets, Market Control and Marketing Reform, 1969; Dissent on Development, 1972; Aspects of Nigerian Development, a1974; Equality, The Third World, and Economic Delusion, 1981; Reality and Rhetoric: Studies in the Economics of Development, 1984. Add: c/o House of Lords, Westminster, London SW1, England.

BAUER, Yehuda. Israeli, b. 1926. History. Prof., and Head, Dept. of Holocaust Studies, since 1968, and Intnl. Center for the Study of Antisemitism, since 1983, Hebrew Univ., Jerusalem. Member, Advisory Scientific Cttee., Yad Vashem, Jerusalem, Editorial Bd., Yad Vashem Studies, and Yalkut Moreshet. *Publs:* From Diplomacy to Resistance, 1970; Flight and Rescue, 1970; They Chose Life, 1973; My Brother's Keeper, 1974; The Holocaust in Historical Perspective, 1978; The Jewish Emergence from Powerlessness, 1978; American Jewry and the Holocaust, 1981; A History of the Holocaust, 1982; Out of the Ashes, 1989. Add: Kibbutz Shoval, Negev, Israel.

BAUGHAN, Peter Edward. British, b. 1934. Industrial archaeology, Transportation. Technical Asst., Parliamentary Office, Chief Civil Engineer's Dept., British Railways, London, 1960–66; Technical Officer, Dept. of Transportation Development, GLC, 1966–86. *Publs:* North of Leeds, 1966; The Railways of Wharfedale, 1969; The Chester of Holyhead Railway, vol. I, 1972; A Regional History of the Railways of Great Britain, vol. XI, North and Mid Wales, 1980; Midland Railway North of Leeds, 1987; The North Wales Coast Railway, 1988. Add: 97 Royal George Rd., Burgess Hill, Sussex RH15 9SJ, England.

BAUM, Bernard H. American (born German), b. 1926. Administration/Management, Business/Trade/Industry. Prof. of Mgmt. and Sociology since 1969, and Dir. and Prof., Health Resources Mgmt. since 1973, Univ. of Illinois at Chicago. *Publs:* Decentralization of Authority in Bureaucracy, 1961; (with Robert W. French) Basics for Business, 1968; (ed. with Peter F. Sorensen, Jr.) Perspectives on Organizational Behavior, 1973; (ed. with others) Dimensions in Organization Behavior: Influence, Authority and Power, 1975; (ed. with R. Babcock and P. Sorensen) Intervention: The Management Use of Organizational Research, 1975. Add: Univ. of Illinois at Chicago Health Sciences Center, Chicago. Ill. 60680, U.S.A.

BAUM, Louis. South African, b. 1948. Children's fiction. Ed., Bookseller, London, since 1980. *Publs:* Juju and the Pirate, 1983; I Want to See the Moon, 1984; After Dark, 1984; Are We Nearly There Yet?, 1986. Add: c/o Bodley Head Ltd., 32 Bedford Sq., London WC1B 3EL, England.

BAUMANN, Carol Edler. American, b. 1932. International relations/Current affairs. Prof. of Political Science since 1972, and Dir., Inst. of World Affairs since 1964, Univ. of Wisconsin-Milwaukee (Lectr., 1961–62; Asst. Prof., 1962–67; Assoc. Prof., 1967–72; Dir., Office of Intl. Studies and Programs, 1982–88). Instr. Dept. of Political Science, 1957–61, and Project Assoc., National Security Studies Group, 1958–61, Univ. of Wisconsin, Madison; Deputy Asst. Secty. for Assessments and Research, Dept. of State, 1979–81. *Publs:* Political Cooperation in NATO, 1960; Western Europe: What Path to Integration?, 1967; (with Kay Wahner) Great Decisions—1968, 1969; The Diplomatic Kidnappings, 1973; Europe in NATO, 1987. Add: Inst. of World Affairs, Univ. of Wisconsin-Milwaukee, P.O. Box 413, Milwaukee, Wisc. 53201, U.S.A.

BAUMBACH, Jonathan. American, b. 1933. Novels/Short stories, Literature. Prof. of English, Brooklyn Coll., City Univ. of New York, since 1972 (Assoc. Prof., 1966–70, 1971–72). Film Critic, Partisan Review, since 1974. Instr., Stanford Univ., California, 1958–60; Instr., 1961–62, and Asst. Prof., 1962–64, Ohio State Univ., Columbus; Asst. Prof., New York Univ., NYC, 1964–66. *Publs:* The Landscape of Nightmare: Studies in the Contemporary American Novel, 1965; A Man to Conjure With (novel), 1965; What Comes Next (novel), 1968; (ed with A. Edelstein) Moderns and Contemporaries (anthology), 1968; (ed.) Writers as Teachers, Teachers as Writers, 1970; Reruns (novel), 1974; Statements: New Fiction from the Fiction Collective, 1974; Babble (novel), 1976; (ed. with Peter Spielberg) Statements 2: New Fiction, 1977; Chez Charlotte and Emily (novel), 1979; The Return of Service (short stories), 1980; My Father More or Less (novel), 1982; The Life and Times

of Major Fiction, 1987. Add: 320 Statford Rd., Brooklyn, N.Y. 11218, U.S.A.

BAUMOL, William J. American, b. 1922. Economics. Prof. of Economics, Princeton Univ., since 1954 (joined staff, 1949); Prof. of Economics, New York Univ., NYC, since 1971. Pres., Assn. of Environmental and Resource Economists, and Eastern Economic Assn., 1978–79, American Economic Assn., 1981, and Atlantic Economic Society, 1985. *Publs:* Economic Dynamics, 1951, 1959; Welfare Economics and the Theory of the State, 1952, 1965; (with L.V. Chandler) Economic Processes and Policies, 1954; Business Behavior, Value and Growth, 1959, rev. ed. 1966; Economic Theory and Operations Analysis, 1961, 4th ed. 1976; The Stock Market and Economic Efficiency, 1965; (with W.G. Bowen) Performing Arts: The Economic Dilemma, 1966; (ed. with S.M. Goldfeld) Precursors in Mathematical Economics: An Anthology, 1968; Portfolio Theory: The Selection of Asset Combinations, 1970; (with M. Marcus) Economics of Academic Libraries, 1973; (with W.E. Oates) The Theory of Environmental Policy, 1974, 1988; (with W.E. Oates and S.A. Batey-Blackman) Economics, Environmental Policy, and the Quality of Life, 1978; (with A.S. Blinder) Economics: Principles and Policy, 1979, 1987; (with John C. Panzar and Robert D. Willig) Contestable Markets and the Theory of Industry Structure, 1982; (with Hilda Baumol) Inflation and the Performing Arts, 1984; (ed. with K. McLennan) Productivity Growth and U.S. Competitiveness, 1985; Superfairness: Application and Theory, 1986; Microtheory: Applications and Origins, 1986; (with S.A. Batey Blackman and E.N. Wolff) Productivity and American Leadership: The Long View, 1989. Add: Dept. of Economics, Princeton Univ., Princeton, N.J. 08544, U.S.A.

BAUR, John Edward. American, b. 1922. History. Prof. of History, California State Univ., Northridge, since 1971 (Asst. Prof., 1964–68; Assoc. Prof., 1968–71). Member of Bd. of Eds., Southern California Quarterly, and San Diego History Journal. Editorial Assoc., Pacific Historical Review, 1949–53; History Instr., Los Angeles County Museum, 1954–64. *Publs:* Health Seekers of Southern California, 1870-1900, 1959; Christmas on the American Frontier, 1961; Dogs on the Frontier, 1964; Growing Up with California, 1978. Add: 8851 Hayvenhurst Ave., Sepulveda, Calif. 91343, U.S.A.

BAUS, Herbert Michael. American, b. 1914. Advertising/Public relations, Cookery/Gastronomy/Wine, Language/Linguistics, Politics/Government. Restaurant Ed. and Columnist, Orange County Register, California. Founding partner, Baus and Ross Co., political campaign firm, 1948–68. *Publs:* Public Relations at Work, 1948; Publicity in Action, 1954; (with W.B. Ross) Politics Battle Plan, 1968; Expert's Crossword Puzzle Dictionary, 1973; How to Wine Your Way to Good Health, 1973; Master Unabridged Crossword Puzzle Dictionary, 1981; Best Restaurants of Orange County, 1982; 1984. Add: c/o The Register, P.O. Box 11626, Santa Ana, Calif. 92711, U.S.A.

BAWDEN, Nina (Mary). British, b. 1925. Novels/Short stories, Mystery/Crime/Suspense, Chidren's fiction. *Publs:* Who Calls the Tune (in U.S. as Eyes of Green), 1953; The Odd Flamingo, 1954; Change Here for Babylon, 1955; The Solitary Child, 1956; Devil by the Sea, 1957; Just Like a Lady (in U.S. as Glass Slippers Always Pinch), 1960; In Honour Bound, 1961; Tortoise by Candlelight, 1963; The Secret Passage (in U.S. as The House of Secrets), 1963; On the Run (in U.S. as Three on the Run), 1964; Under the Skin, 1964; A Little Love, A Little Learning, 1966; The White Horse Gang, 1966; The Witch's Daughter, 1966; A Handful of Thieves, 1967; A Woman of My Age, 1967; The Grain of Truth, 1968; The Runaway Summer, 1969; The Birds on the Trees, 1970; Squib, 1971; Anna Apparent, 1972; Carrie's War; George Beneath a Paper Moon, 1974; The Peppermint Pig, 1975; Afternoon of a Good Woman, 1976; Rebel On A Rock, 1978; Familiar Passions, 1979; Walking Naked, 1981; Kept in the Dark, 1982; The Ice House, 1983; The Finding, 1985; Circles of Deceit, 1987; Keeping Henry, 1988; The Outside Child, 1989. Add: 22 Noel Rd., London N1 8HA, England.

BAX, Martin (Charles Owen). British, b. 1933. Novels/Short stories, Medicine/Health. Research Community Paediatrician, Charing Cross/Westminster Medical Sch., London, since 1974. Ed., Ambit Mag., since 1959. *Publs:* (with Judy Bernal) Your Child's First Five Years, 1974; The Hospital Ship, 1976. Add: 17 Priory Gardens, London N6, England.

BAX, Roger. *See* **GARVE,** Andrew.

BAXT, George. American, b. 1923. Mystery/Crime/Suspense, Plays/Screenplays. *Publs:* novels—A Queer Kind of Death, 1966; Swing

Low, Sweet Harriet, 1967; A Parade of Cockeyed Creatures; or, Did Some-one Murder Our Wandering Boy?, 1967; Topsy and Evil, 1968; "I!" Said the Demon, 1969; The Affair at Royalties, 1971; Burning Sappho, 1972; Process of Elimination; 1984; The Dorothy Parker Murder Case, 1984; The Alfred Hitchcock Murder Case: An Unauthorized Novel, 1986; The Tallulah Bankhead Murder Case, 1987; Who's Next?, 1988; screenplays—Circus of Horrors, 1960; The City of the Dead (Horror Hotel), 1960; The Shadow of the Cat, 1961; Payroll, 1961; Night of the Eagle (Burn Witch Burn), 1962; Strangler's Web, 1965; Thunder in Dixie, 1965. Add: c/o Macmillan Inc., 866 Third Ave., New York, N.Y. 10022, U.S.A.

BAXTER, Brian. British. Naval architecture and technology. Visit-ing Prof., Univ. of Strathclyde, since 1980. Royal Naval Scientific Ser-vice, 1948–50; Lectr. in Naval Architecture, King's Coll., Newcastle, 1950–57; Bureau Veritas, London, 1957–62; Dir., Yarrow Shipbuilders, 1962–82. *Publs:* Teach Yourself Naval Architecture, 1959, 1975; Naval Architecture: Examples and Theory, 1967; (reviser) Know Your Own Ship, 1969; A History of Technology: Ships and Shipbuilding, 1978; Get to Know Marine Technology, 1982. Add: Dunelm, Kilmacolm, Renfrew-shire, Scotland.

BAXTER, Craig. American, b. 1929. History, Politics/Government. Prof. of Politics and History, Juniata Coll., Huntingdon, Pa., since 1981. Member, Pakistan Studies Development Cttee., Assn. for Asian Studies, and National Seminar on Pakistan, Columbia Univ., NYC. Pres., American Inst. of Bangladesh Studies; Secty., American Inst. of Pakistan Studies. Instr. in History, Univ. of Pennsylvania, Philadelphia, 1955–56; Foreign Service Officer, U.S. Dept. of State, 1956–80. *Publs:* The Jana Sangh: A Biography of an Indian Political Party, 1969; District Voting Trends in A Research Tool, 1969; Bangladesh: A New Nation in a New Setting. 1984; From Martial Law to Martial Law: Politics in the Punjab 1919–1958, 1985; Zia's Pakistan: Politics and Stability in a Frontline State, 1985; Government and Politics in South Asia, 1987; Historical Dic-tionary of Bangladesh, 1989. Add: Dept. of Political Science, Juniata Coll., Huntingdon, Pa. 16652, U.S.A.

BAXTER, John. Australian, b. 1939. Novels/Short stories, Science fiction/Fantasy, Film, Biography. Dir. of Publicity, Australian Common-wealth Film Unit., Sydney, 1968–70; Lectr. in Film and Theatre, Hollins Coll, 1974–78; freelance TV producer and screenwriter, 1978–87; Visiting Lectr., Mitchell Coll., Australia, 1987. *Publs:* The Off Worlders, 1966, in Australia as The God Killers, 1968; (adaptor) Adam's Woman, 1968; Hollywood in the Thirties, 1968; (ed.) The Pacific Book of Australian Science Fiction, 1970; The Australian Cinema, 1970; Science Fiction in the Cinema, 1970; The Gangster Film, 1970; The Cinema of Josef von Sternberg, 1971; The Cinema of John Ford, 1971; (ed.) The Second Pacific Book of Australian Science Fiction, 1971; Hollywood in the Six-ties, 1972; Sixty Years of Hollywood, 1973; An Appalling Talent: Ken Russell, 1973; Stunt: The Story of the Great Movie Stunt Men, 1974; The Hollywood Exiles, 1976; (with Thomas R. Atkins) The Fire Came By, 1976; King Vidor, 1976; The Hermes Fall, 1978; The Bidders (in U.K. as Bidding), 1979; The Kid, 1981; (with Brian Norris) The Video Handbook, 1982; The Black Yacht, 1982; Who Burned Australia? The Ash Wednesday Fires, 1984; Filmstruck, 1987; The Time Guardian (screenplay), 1988. Add: c/o Curtis Brown Ltd., 27 Union St., Pad-dington, N.S.W. 2010, Australia.

BAXTER, William T(hreipland). British, b. 1906. Money/Finance. Prof. of Accounting, Univ. of Cape Town, 1937–47, and London Sch. of Economics, 1947–73. *Publs:* The House of Hancock: Business in Bos-ton 1724-1775, 1945; (ed. with Sydney Davidson) Studies in Accounting Theory, 1962; Depreciation, 1971; Accounting Values and Inflation, 1975; Collected Papers on Accounting, 1979; Depreciating Assets, 1981; In-flation Accounting, 1984. Add: 1 The Ridgeway, London NW11 8TD, England.

BAYBARS, Taner. Also writes as Timothy Bayliss. British, b. 1936. Novels/Short stories, Poetry, Autobiography/Memoirs/Personal, Transla-tions. Book Promotion Officer, British Council, London, since 1983, (joined Council, 1956). *Publs:* To Catch a Falling Man, 1963; A Trap for the Burglar (novel), 1965; (trans.) Selected Poems of Nazim Hikmet, 1967; Plucked in a Far-Off Land, 1970; (trans.) Moscow Symphony, 1970; (ed. with Osman Turkay) Modern Poetry in Translation: Turkey, 1971; (trans.) Day Before Tomorrow, 1972; Susila in the Autumn Woods, 1974; Narcissus in a Dry Pool, 1978; (trans.) The Snowy Day, by Ezra Jack Keats, 1980; (trans.) Peter's Chair, by Ezra Jack Keats, 1980; Pregnant Shadows, 1981. Add: Les Espardeaux, St. Amant de Bonnieure, 16230

Mansle, France.

BAYER, Cary Stuart. American, b. 1953. Social commentary. Pres., Bayer Communications, NYC, since 1983. Worked for Doyle Dane Bernbach, NYC, 1980–83; Ed. and Publisher, Fire Island Snooze, New York, 1984–85. *Publs:* (with Bob Levine) The Short Report: Good News for Guys 5' 7" and Under, 1983; (with Robert Romagnoli) Fire Island Fried, 1985. Add: 59 W. 12th St., New York, N.Y. 10011, U.S.A.

BAYER, William. Has also written as Leonie St. John. American, b. 1939. Novels/Short stories, Mystery/Crime/Suspense, Plays/Screenplays, Film. With U.S. Foreign Service, Washington, D.C., 1963–68. *Publs:* (as Leonie St. John: with Nancy Harmon) Love with a Harvard Accent, 1962; In Search of a Hero (novel), 1966; Breaking Through, Selling Out, Dropping Dead and Other Notes on Filmmaking, 1971; The Great Movies, 1973; Stardust (novel), 1974; Visions of Isabelle (novel), 1976; Tangier (novel), 1978; Punish Me with Kisses (novel) 1980; Peregrine (novel), 1981, (Edgar Allan Poe Award); Switch (novel), 1984; Pattern Crimes (novel), 1987; Blind Side (novel), 1989. Add: c/o Arlene Donovan, Intnl. Creative Mgmt. 40 W. 57th St., New York, N.Y. 10019, U.S.A.

BAYLEN, Joseph O. American, b. 1920. History, International rela-tions/Current affairs, Biography. Emeritus Regents' Prof. of History, Georgia State Univ., Atlanta, since 1982 (Prof. and Chmn., Dept. of His-tory 1966–69; Regents' Prof. from 1969). Asst. Prof., to Assoc. Prof. of History, New Mexico Highlands Univ., Las Vegas, 1950–54; Prof. and Chmn., Div. of Social Science, Delta State Teachers Coll., Miss., 1954–57; Prof. of History, Mississippi State Univ., State College, 1957–61; Prof. of History, 1961–66, and Chmn., Dept. of History, 1964–66, Univ. of Mississippi, University. *Publs:* Madame Juliette Adam, Gambetta, and the Idea of a Franco-Russian Alliance, 1960; Lord Kitchener and the Viceroyalty of India 1910, 1965; (with A. Conway) Soldier-Surgeon: The Crimean War Letters of Dr. Douglas A. Reid, 1855-1856, 1968; The Tsar's Lecturer-General: W.T. Stead and the Russian Revolution of 1905, 1969; (ed. with O.S. Pidhainy) East European and Russian Studies in the American South, 1972; (ed. with N.J. Gossman) Biographical Dic-tionary of Modern British Radicals, vol. I, 1770-1830, 1979, vol. II, 1830-1870, 1984, vol III, 1870-1914, 1988. Add: 45 Saffrons Ct., Compton Pl. Rd., Eastbourne BN21 1DY, England.

BAYLEY, Barrington John. British, b. 1937. Science fiction. Former civil servant, and coal miner. *Publs:* The Star Virus, 1970; Annihilation Factor, 1972; Empire of Two Worlds, 1972; Collision Course, 1973; The Fall of Chronopolis, 1974; The Soul of the Robot, 1974; The Garments of Caean, 1976; The Grand Wheel, 1977; Star Winds, 1978; The Knights of the Limits (anthology), 1978; The Seed of Evil (anthology), 1979; The Pillars of Eternity, 1982; The Zen Gun, 1983; The Forest of Peldain, 1985; The Rod of Light, 1985. Add: 48 Turrett Ave., Donnington, Telford, Salop TF2 8HE, England.

BAYLEY, Charles Calvert. Canadian, b. 1907. History, International relations/Current affairs. Prof. of History, McGill Univ., Montreal, since 1959 (Lectr., 1935–39; Asst. Prof., 1939–50; Assoc. Prof., 1950–59). *Publs:* The German College of Electors in the Mid-13th Century, 1949 (Prix Davis, Province of Quebec); (with F.P. Chambers and C.P. Grant) This Age of Conflict: A Contemporary World History, 1914–43, 1950; War and Society in Renaissance Florence, 1961; Mercenaries for the Crimea, 1979. Add: Dept. of History, McGill Univ., Montreal, Que. H3A 2T7, Canada.

BAYLEY, John (Oliver). British, b. 1925. Novels/Short stories, Poetry, Literature. Warton Prof. of English Literature, and Fellow, St. Catherine's Coll., Oxford Univ., since 1974 (Lectr. and Fellow, New Coll., Oxford, 1955–74). Member, St. Anthony's and Magdalen Colls., Oxford, 1951–55. *Publs:* El Dorado: The Newdigate Prize Poem, 1950; In Another Country (novel), 1955; The Romantic Survival: A Study in Poetic Evolution, 1957; The Characters of Love: A Study in the Literature of Personality, 1960; Tolstoy and the Novel, 1966; Pushkin: A Comparative Commentary, 1971; The Uses of Division: Unity and Disharmony in Literature, 1976; An Essay on Hardy, 1978; Selected Essays, 1980; Shakespeare and Tragedy, 1981; The Line of Battle at Trafalgar, 1985; The Short Story: Henry James to Elizabeth Bowen, 1987. Add: c/o Har-vester Press, 16 Ship St., Brighton BN1 1AD, England.

BAYLEY, Peter (Charles). British, b. 1921. Literature. Berry Prof. Emeritus, Univ. of St. Andrews, Fife, since 1985 (Berry Prof. and Head of English Dept., 1978–85). Fellow, University Coll., 1947–72, Praelec-tor in English, 1949–72, and Univ. Lectr., 1952–72, Oxford Univ.; Master,

Collingwood Coll., Univ. of Durham, 1972–78. *Publs:* (ed.) The Faerie Queene, by Spenser, Book II, 1965, Book I, 1966, 1970; Edmund Spenser, Prince of Poets, 1971; (ed.) Loves and Deaths, 1972; (ed.) A Casebook on Spenser's Faerie Queen, 1977; Poems of Milton, 1982; An ABC of Shakespeare, 1985. Add: 63 Oxford St., Woodstock, Oxon., England.

BAYLEY, Stephen. British, b. 1951. Architecture, Art, Design. Dir. of the Conran Foundn. (which created Boilerhouse Project, and the Design Museum). Lectr. in Art History, Liverpool Polytechnic, 1972–74, Open Univ., 1974–76 and Univ. of Kent, 1977–80. *Publs:* In Good Shape: Style in Industrial Products 1900–1960, 1979; The Albert Memorial, 1981; Harley Earl and the Dream Machine, 1983; The Conran Directory of Design, 1985; Twentieth Century Style and Design, 1986; Sex, Drink and Fast Cars, 1986. Add: Design Museum, 28 Shad Thames, London SE1 2YD, England.

BAYLIS, John. British, b. 1946. International relations/Current affairs, Military/Defence. Lectr., 1971–83, and since 1983 Sr. Lectr., Dept. of Intnl. Politics, Univ. of Wales, Aberystwth. Lectr., Univ. of Liverpool, 1969–71; Academic Adviser, National Defence Coll., Latimer, 1975–82. *Publs:* (co-author) Contemporary Strategy: Theories and Policies, 1975; (ed.) British Defence Policy in Changing World, 1977; Anglo-American Defence Relations 1939–80, 1980, 1984; (ed.) Soviet Strategy, 1980; (co-author) Nuclear War, Nuclear Peace, 1983, 1988; (ed.) Alternative Approaches to British Defence Policy, 1984; (co-author) Contemporary Strategy: Theories and Concepts, vol. I, 1987; (co-author) Contemporary Strategy: The Nuclear Powers, vol. II, 1987; (with others) Britain, NATO and Nuclear Weapons, 1989; British Defence Policy: Striking the Right Balance, 1989. Add: Dept. of Intnl. Politics, Univ. of Wales, Aberystwyth, Dyfed, Wales.

BAYLISS, Timothy *See* **BAYBARS,** Taner.

BAYNES, (Sir) John (Christopher Malcolm). British, b. 1928. History, Military/Defence. Former Lt. Col., H.M. Forces. *Publs:* Morale: A Study of Men and Courage, 1968, 1987; The Jacobite Rising of 1715, 1970; The History of the Cameronians: The End of Empire 1948–1968, vol. IV, 1971; The Soldier in Modern Society, 1971; Soldier of Scotland, 1988; The Forgotten Victor: The Life of General Sir Richard O'Connor, 1989. Add: Talwrn Bach, Llanfyllin, Powys, Wales.

BAYNHAM, Henry Wellesley Forster. British, b. 1933. History. Dir. of Studies and Head, Dept. of History and Politics, Canford Sch., Wimborne, Dorset (Asst. Master, 1958–65). Schoolmaster Fellow, Balliol Coll., Oxford, 1966. *Publs:* From the Lower Deck 1969; Before the Mast, 1971; Men from the Dreadnoughts, 1976. Add: New Rusko, Gatehouse-of-Fleet, Kirkcudbrightshire, Scotland.

BEACH, Edward L. American, b. 1918. Novels/Short stories, History, Military/Defence. With U.S. Navy, 1935 until retirement with rank of Capt., 1966; Naval Aide to Pres. of U.S., 1953–57; Comdr., U.S.S. Triton (SSN 586) during submerged world circumnavigation, 1960; Steven B. Luce Chair of Naval Science, U.S. Naval War Coll., Newport, R.I., 1967–69; Staff Dir., U.S. Senate Republican Policy Cttee., Washington, D.C., 1969–77. *Publs:* Submarine!, 1952; Run Silent, Run Deep (novel), 1955; Around the World Submerged, 1962; The Wreck of the Memphis, 1966; (co-author) Naval Terms Dictionary, 3rd ed. 1971, 4th ed. 1979; Dust on the Sea (novel), 1972; Cold Is the Sea (novel), 1978; (co-author) Keepers of the Sea, 1983; The United States Navy: 200 Years, 1986. Add: 1622 29th St. N.W., Washington, D.C. 20007, U.S.A.

BEACHCROFT, Nina. British, b. 1931. Children's fiction. Sub-Ed., Argosy, London, 1953–55, and Radio Times, London, 1955–57. *Publs:* Well Met by Witchlight, 1972; Under the Enchanter, 1974; Cold Christmas: Ghost Story, 1974; A Spell of Sleep, 1976; A Visit to Folly Castle, 1977: A Farthing for the Fair, 1978; The Wishing People, 1980; The Genie and Her Bottle, 1983; Beyond World's End, 1985. Add: The Cottage, Datchworth Green, Knebworth, Hertfordshire, England.

BEADELL, Len. Australian, b. 1923. Travel/Exploration/Adventure. Range Reconnaissance Officer, Weapons Research Establishment, since 1950. *Publs:* Too Long in the Bush, 1965; Blast the Bush, 1967; Bush Bashers, 1971; Still in the Bush, 1975; Beating About the Bush, 1976; Outback Highways, 1979; End of an Era, 1983. Add: 15 Fleet St., Salisbury, S.A. 5108, Australia.

BEADLE, George W(ells). American, b. 1903. Biology, Chemistry, Medicine/Health. President Emeritus since 1968, and Prof. Emeritus since 1975, Univ. of Chicago (President, 1961–68; William E. Wrather

Distinguished Service Prof., 1969–75). Teaching Asst. and Experimentalist, Cornell Univ., Ithaca, N.Y., 1926–31; National Research Council Fellow, 1931–33; Instr. California Inst. of Technology, Pasadena, 1933–35; Guest Investigator, Institut de Biologie, Paris, 1935; Asst. Prof. of Genetics, Harvard Univ., Cambridge, Mass., 1936–37; Assoc. Prof., Stamford Univ., Calif., 1937–46. Prof. of Biology and Chmn. of the Div. of Biology, California Inst. of Technology, Pasadena, 1946–60. President, American Assn. for the Advancement of Science, 1946. Recipient, Nobel Prize in Medicine and Physiology, with E.L. Tatum and J. Lederberg, 1958. *Publs:* (with A.H. Sturtevant) An Introduction to Genetics, 1939; The Place of Genetics in Modern Biology, 1959; (with others) Science and Resources: Prospects and Implications of Technological Advance, 1959; Genetics and Modern Biology, 1963; (with Muriel Beadle) The Language of Life: An Introduction to the Science of Genetics, 1966. Add: 900 E. Harrison St., Apt. D-33, Pomona, Calif. 91767, U.S.A.

BEAGLE, Peter S(oyer). American, b. 1939. Novels/Short stories, Plays/Screenplays. *Publs:* A Fine and Private Place, 1960; I See by My Outfit, 1965; The Last Unicorn, 1968; The California Feeling, 1969; The Lady and Her Tiger, 1976; The Dove (screenplay), 1977; The Lord of the Rings (screenplay), 1978; The Fantasy Worlds of Peter S. Beagle, 1978; The Last Unicorn (screenplay), 1982; The Garden of Earthly Delights, 1982; The Folk of the Air (novel), 1987. Add: 5517 Crystal Springs Drive, N.E., Bainbridge Island, Wash. 98110, U.S.A.

BEALES, D(erek) E(dward) D(awson). British, b. 1931. History. Fellow, Sidney Sussex Coll., since 1958, Prof. of Modern History, since 1980, and Chmn. of the Gen. Bd. of Faculties since 1987, Cambridge Univ. (Research Fellow, 1955–58, Tutor, 1961–70, and Vice-Master, 1973–75, Sidney Sussex Coll.; Asst. Lecturer, 1962–65, Lectr., 1965–80, and Chmn., Faculty Bd. of History, 1979–81, Cambridge Univ.). Ed., Historical Journal, 1971–75; Member of the Council, Royal Historical Soc., 1984–88. *Publs:* England and Italy 1859-60, 1961; From Castlereagh to Gladstone, 1969; The Risorgimento and the Unification of Italy, 1971; History and Biography, 1981; (ed. with G.F.A. Best) History, Society and the Churches, 1985; Joseph II: In the Shadow of Maria Theresa, 1741-1780, 1987. Add: Sidney Sussex College, Cambridge, England.

BEALEY, Frank (William). British, b. 1922. Industrial relations, Politics/Government. Prof. of Politics, Univ. of Aberdeen, since 1964. Lectr. on Political Institutions, Univ. of Keele, 1952–64. *Publs:* (with H. Pelling) Labour and Politics, 1958; (co-author) Constituency Politics, 1965; The Social and Political Thought of the British Labour Party, 1970; The Post Office Engineering Union, 1976; The Politics of Independence, 1981; Democracy in the Contemporary State, 1988. Add: 355 Clifton Rd., Aberdeen, Scotland.

BEAMAN, Joyce Proctor. American, b. 1931. Children's fiction. English and French Teacher, Snow Hill High Sch., N.C., 1953–59; Saratoga Central High Sch., 1959–78; Librarian, Elm City Middle Sch., N.C., 1978–82: now retired. *Publs:* Broken Acres, 1971; All for the Love of Cassie, 1973; Bloom Where You Are Planted, 1975; You Are Beautiful: You Really Are, 1981. Add: Rt. 2, Box 424, Walstonburg, N.C. 27888, U.S.A.

BEAR, Greg(ory Dale). American, b. 1951. Science fiction/Fantasy. Freelance writer since 1975. Lectr., San Diego Aerospace Museum, 1969–72; writer and planetarium operator, Fleet Space Theatre, San Diego, 1973. *Publs:* Hegira, 1979; Psychlone, 1979; Beyond Heaven's River, 1980; Strength of Stones, 1981; The Wind from a Burning Woman, 1983; Corona, 1984; The Infinity Concerto, 1984; Blood Music, 1985; Eon, 1985; The Serpent Mage, 1986; The Forge of God, 1987; Eternity, 1988; Tangents, 1989. Add: Lakeview Rd., Alderwood Manor, Wash. 98036, U.S.A.

BEARD, Geoffrey. British, b. 1929. Architecture, Art, Crafts. Dir.'s Asst., Leeds City Art Gallery, 1957–61; Dir., Cannon Hall Art Gallery, Barnsley, 1961–66; Sr. Lectr., Manchester Polytechnic, 1966–72; Dir., Visual Arts Centre, Univ. of Lancaster, 1972–82. *Publs:* XIXth Century Cameo Glass, 1956; Collecting Antiques on a Small Income, 1957; Georgian Craftsmen and Their Work, 1966; Modern Glass, 1968; Modern Ceramics, 1969; Decorative Plasterwork in Great Britain, 1975; International Modern Glass, 1976; The Work of Robert Adam, 1978; The Greater House in Cumbria, 1978; (with G. Berry) The Lake District: A Century of Conservation, 1980; Robert Adam's Country Houses, 1981; Craftsmen and Interior Decoration 1660-1820, 1981; The Work of Christopher Wren, 1981; Stucco and Decorative Plasterwork in Europe, 1982; The National Trust Book of English Furniture, 1985; The Work of John Vanbrugh, 1986; (ed., with C.G. Gilbert) Dictionary of English Furniture Makers 1660-

1840, 1986; (with Lady Goodison) English Furniture 1500-1840, 1987. Add: Earlsmere, Weston Lane, Bath BA1 4AA, England.

BEARDSLEY, Theodore S., Jr. American, b. 1930. Plays/Screenplays, Literature. Dir., The Hispanic Soc. of America, since 1965. Member of Faculty, Univ. of Wisconsin, Madison, 1962–65; Adjunct Prof., New York Univ., NYC, 1967–69, 1980. *Publs:* Hispano-Classical Translations, 1482-1699, 1970; Tomás Navarro Tomás: A Tentative Bibliography 1908–1970, 1971; (trans.) Marí Sabina (libretto), 1973; Ponce de Leon (libretto), 1973; (as El Bibliomaníaco gringüense) Elogio de la Bibliofilia; An Introduction to Hispanic Bibliography. Add: 613 West 155th St., New York, N.Y. 10032, U.S.A.

BEARDSWORTH, Millicent Monica. British, b. 1915. Historical/Romance/Gothic. Asst. Speech and Drama Teacher, 1934–47, Head, Speech and Drama Dept., 1947–68, and Deputy Head Mistress, 1968–76, Penrhos Coll., Colwyn Bay. *Publs:* King's Servant, 1966; King's Friend, 1968; King's Endeavour, 1969; King's Adversary, 1972; King's Contest, 1975; King's Victory, 1978. Add: 14 St. George's Rd., Rhos-on-Sea, Clwyd LL28 4HF, Wales.

BEASLEY, William Gerald. British, b. 1919. History, International relations/Current affairs. Prof. of— History of the Far East, Sch. of Oriental and African Studies, Univ. of London, 1954–83, now Emeritus. *Publs:* Great Britain and the Opening of Japan 1833-1858, 1951; (ed. and trans.) Select Documents on Japanese Foreign Policy 1853-1868, 1955; (ed. with E.G. Pulleyblank) Historians of China and Japan, 1961; The Modern History of Japan, 1963, 3rd ed. 1981; The Meiji Restoration, 1972; (ed.) Modern Japan: Aspects of History, Literature and Society, 1975; Japanese Imperialism 1894-1945, 1987. Add: 172 Hampton Rd., Twickenham TW2 5NJ, England.

BEASLEY-MURRAY, George Raymond. British, b. 1916. Theology/Religion. Lectr. in New Testament Language and Literature, Spurgeon's Coll., London, 1950–56; Prof. of Greek New Testament, Intnl. Seminary, Ruschlikon and Zurich, 1956–58; Principal, Spurgeon's Coll., London, 1958–73; Prof. of New Testament Interpretation, Southern Baptist Theological Seminary, Louisville, Ky., 1973–80. *Publs:* Christ Is Alive, 1947; Jesus and the Future, 1954; Preaching the Gospel from the Gospels, 1956; A Commentary on Mark Thirteen, 1957; Baptism in the New Testament, 1962; (trans.) Did the Early Church Baptize Infants? by Kurt Aland, 1963; (trans.) Baptism in the Thought of St. Paul, by R. Schnackenburg, 1964; The Resurrection of Jesus Christ, 1964; The General Epistles, 1965; Baptism Today and Tomorrow, 1966; (trans. and ed. with R.W.N. Hoare and J.K. Riches) The Gospel of John: A Commentary, by R. Bultmann, 1971; Commentary on Second Corinthians, 1971; Highlights in the Book of Revelation, 1972; Commentary on the Book of Revelation, 1974; The Coming of God, 1982; Jesus and the Kingdom of God, 1985; Gospel of John, 1987; World Biblical Themes: John, 1989. Add: 4 Holland Rd., Hove, East Sussex BN3 1JJ, England.

BEATTIE, Ann. American, b. 1947. Novels/Short stories. Visting Lectr., Univ. of Virginia, Charlottesville, 1976–77, 1980; Briggs Copeland Lectr. in English, Harvard Univ., Cambridge, Mass., 1977–78. *Publs:* Chilly Scenes of Winter (novel), 1976; Distortions (short stories), 1976; Secrets and Surprises (short stories), 1978; Falling in Place (novel), 1980; Jacklighting (short sotires), 1981; The Burning House (short stories), 1982; Love Always (novel), 1985; Where You'll Find Me and Other Stories, 1986; Alex Katz (art criticism), 1987. Add: c/o Random House, 201 E. 50th St., New York, N.Y. 10022, U.S.A.

BEATTIE, John Hugh Marshall. British, b. 1915. Anthropology/Ethnology, Sociology. Fellow of Linacre Coll., Oxford. Admin. Officer, Territory (now Tanzania), 1940–49; Lectr., and subsequently Sr. Lectr. in Social Anthropology, Univ. of Oxford, 1953–71; Prof. of African Studies, Univ. of Leiden, Netherlands, 1971–75. *Publs:* Bunyoro: An African Kingdom, 1960; Other Cultures: Aims, Methods and Achievements in Social Anthropology, 1964; Understanding an African Kingdom: Bunyoro, 1965; (ed. with John Middleton) Spirit Mediumship and Society in Africa, 1969; The Nyoro State, 1971; (ed. with R.G. Lienhardt) Studies in Social Anthropology: Essays in Memory of E.E. Evans-Pritchard by His Former Oxford Colleagues, 1975. Add: The Cottage, Headington Hill, Oxford, England.

BEATTY, Patricia. Also writes as Jean Bartholomew. American, b. 1922. Novels/Short stories, Children's fiction. English and History Teacher, Coeur d' Alene High Sch., Idaho, 1947–50; Librarian, E.I. du Pont Co., Wilmington, Del., 1952–53, and Riverside Public Library, Calif., 1953–57; Instr. in Creative Writing, Univ. of California Riverside,

1967–68, and Los Angeles, 1968–69. *Publs:* Indian Canoe-Maker, 1960; Bonanza Girl, 1962; (with John Beatty) At the Seven Stars, 1963; The Nickel-Plated Beauty, 1964; (with John Beatty) Campion Towers, 1965; Squaw Dog, 1965; (with John Beatty) A Donkey for the King, 1966; (with John Beatty) The Royal Dirk, 1966; The Queen's Own Grove, 1966; (with John Beatty) The Queen's Wizard, 1967; The Lady from Black Hawk, 1967; (with John Beatty) Witch Dog, 1968; Me, California Perkins, 1968; (with John Beatty) Pirate Royal, 1969; Blue Stars Watching, 1969; Station Four, 1969; Hail Columbia, 1970; The Sea Pair, 1970; (with John Beatty) King's Knight's Pawn, 1971; A Long Way to Whiskey Creek, 1971; (with John Beatty) Holdfast, 1972; O the Red Rose Tree, 1972; The Bad Bell of San Salvador, 1973; Red Rock over the River, 1973; (with John Beatty) Master Rosalind, 1974; How Many Miles to Sundown, 1974; (with John Beatty) Who Comes to King's Mountain?, 1975; Rufus, Red Rufus, 1975; (as Jean Bartholomew) The Englishman's Mistress (novel), 1975; By Crumbs, It's Mine!, 1976; Something to Shout About, 1976; Billy Bedamned, Long Gone By, I Want My Sunday, Stranger, 1977; Just Some Weeds from the Wilderness, 1978; Wait for Me, Watch for Me, Eula Bea, 1978; Lacy Makes Match, 1979; The Staffordshire Terror, 1979; That's One Ornery Orphan, 1980; Lupita Manana, 1981; Eight Mules from Monterey, 1982; Jonathan Down-Under, ·1982; Melinda Takes a Hand, 1983; Turn Homeward, Hannalee, 1984; The Coach That Never Came, 1985; Behave Yourself, Bethany Brant, 1986; Charley Skedaddle, 1987; Be Ever Hopeful, Hannalee, 1988; Sarah and Me and the Lady from the Sea, 1989. Add: 5085 Rockledge Dr., Riverside, Calif. 92506. U.S.A.

BEATY, Betty (Smith). Also writes as Karen Campbell and Catherine Ross. British. Historical/Romance/Gothic. Former WAAF Officer, airline hostess and medical social worker, London. *Publs:* Maiden Flight, 1956; South to the Sun, 1956; Amber Five, 1958; The Butternut Tree, 1958; Top of the Climb, 1958; The Atlantic Sky, 1958; (as Catherine Ross) From This Day Forward, 1959; (as Catherine Ross) The Colours of the Night, 1962; The Path of the Moonfish, 1964; (as Catherine Ross) The Trysting Tower, 1964; Miss Miranda's Walk, 1967; (as Karen Campbell) Suddenly, In the Air, 1969; (as Karen Campbell) Thunder on Sunday, 1971; (as Karen Campbell) Wheel Fortune, 1973; The Swallows of San Fedora, 1973; Love and the Kentish Maid, 1973; Head of Chancery, 1974; Master at Arms, 1975; Fly Away, Love, 1976; (as Karen Campbell) Death Descending, 1976; Exchange of Hearts, 1977; (as Karen Campbell) The Bells of St. Martin, 1979; (as Catherine Ross) Battle Dress, 1979; (with David Beaty) Wings of the Morning, 1982; The Missionary's Daughter, 1983; Matchmaker Nurse, 1983; (as Catherine Ross) The Shadow of the Peak, 1984; Airport Nurse, 1986; Wings of Love, 1988. Add: Manchester House, Church Rd., Slindon, near Arundel, West Sussex, England.

BEATY, (Arthur) David. Also writes as Paul Stanton. British, b. 1919. Novels/Short stories, Plays/Screenplays. Served in the Royal Air Force, 1940–46; Sr. Capt., B.O.A.C., 1946–53; Principal, Administrative Civil Service, 1966–70, 1972–74; Admin., Centre for Educational Development Overseas, 1970–72. *Publs:* The Takeoff (in U.S. as The Donnington Legend), 1948; The Heart of the Storm (in U.S. as The Four Winds), 1954; The Proving Flight, 1956; Cone of 1959; (as Paul Stanton) Call Me Captain, 1960; The Wind Off the Sea, 1962; (as Paul Stanton) Village of Stars, 1962; Milk and Honey, 1964; The Siren Song, 1964; (as Paul Stanton) The Gun Garden, 1965; Sword of Honour, 1965; The Human Factor in Aircraft Accidents, 1969; The Temple Tree, 1971; Electric Train, 1975; The Water Jump: The Story of Transatlantic Flight, 1976; Excellency, 1977; The Complete Skytraveller, 1978, 1986; The White Sea-Bird, 1979; (with Betty Beaty) Wings of the Morning, 1982; Strange Encounters, 1982; The Stick, 1984; The Blood Brothers, 1987. Add: Manchester House, Church Rd., Slindon, near Arundel, West Sussex, England.

BEAUCHAMP, Kenneth. American, b. 1939. Psychology. Prof. of Psychology, Coll. of the Pacific, Univ. of the Pacific, since 1978 (Assoc. Prof. of Psychology, 1969–78). Asst. Prof., California State Polytechnic Univ., Pomona, 1965–69. *Publs:* (with D.W. Matheson and R.L. Bruce) Experimental Psychology, 1970, 3rd ed. 1978; (ed. with Matheson & Bruce) Contemporary Topics in Experimental Psychology, 1970. Add: Psychology Dept., Coll. of the Pacific, Univ. of the Pacific, Stockton, Calif. 95211.

BEAUMAN, Katharine (Burgoyne) Bentley. British. Military/Defence, Women. Chmn., Crosby Hall Library Cttee., British Redn. of Univ. Women, since 1980; a Gov., Grey Coat Hosp. Women's Ed., Yorkshire Post, 1929–31; Public Relations Officer, WAAF Directorate, 1940–41; Gov. and Historian, St. Michael's Secondary Sch., Westminster, 1950–77; Member, Headquarters Staff, Women's Royal

Voluntary Service, 1957–67; Ed., Women's R.A.F. Officers Assn. Gazette, 1967–70; Vice Pres. and Chmn., Lady Margaret Hall Settlement, Lambeth, London, 1969–73. *Publs:* Wings on Her Shoulders, 1943; Partners in Blue: The Story of Women's Service with the Royal Air Force, 1971; Green Sleeves: The Story of Women's Voluntary Service/Women's Royal Voluntary Service, 1978; Sybil Campbell OBE, First Woman Stipendiary Magistrate, 1987. Add: 59 Chester Row, London SW1, England.

BEAUSAY, Florence E. American, b. 1911. Novels/Short stories, Children's fiction, Genealogy/Heraldry. Teacher and Leader of Mail Box Bible Club, Bible Club Movement, since 1973 (teacher, 1948–67). Dir., Child Evangelism Fellowship, 1959–61. *Publs:* Bold White Stranger, 1958; Moccasin Steps, 1960; Exceedingly Abundant, 1960; Retrospection, 1961; Clouded Sky, 1962; (with Phyllis A. Ryerse) Bosse: Beausay, 1963; (with P.A. Ryerse) Bosse: Vent, 1963: (with P.A. Ryerse) Bosse: Kramer, 1963; (with P.A. Ryerse) Bosse: Geckle, 1963; (with P.A. Ryerse) Frey: Smith, 1964; Styles n' Stuff, 1976; Mary Magdalene, 1982; Queen Esther, 1983; Naomi, 1984. Add: Box 1, Upper Sandusky, Ohio 43371, U.S.A.

BEAVER, Bruce (Victor). Australian, b. 1928. Novels/Short stories, Poetry. Freelance journalist. · *Publs:* Under the Bridge: Poems, 1961; Seawall and Shoreline: Poems, 1964; The Hot Spring (novel), 1965; You Can't Come Back (novel), 1966; Open at Random; Poems, 1967; Letters to Live Poets: Poems, 1969 (Captain Cook Bi-Centenary Prize: Grace Leven Prize; Poetry Soc. of Australia Award); Lauds and Plaints: Poems (1968–1972), 1974; Odes and Days, 1975; Death's Directives, 1978; As It Was, 1979; Selected Poems, 1979; Prose Sketches, 1986; Charmed Lives: Poems, 1988. Add: 14 Malvern Ave., Manly, N.S.W. 2095, Australia.

BEAVER, (Jack) Patrick. British, b. 1923. Business, Media, Social commentary/phenomena. Former merchant-seaman, orchestral composer, producer and dir. of documentary films. *Publs:* Leviathan (documentary film); Man in the Clouds (documentary film); The Big Ship: Brunel's Great Eastern, 1969; The Crystal Palace, 1970; History of Lighthouses, 1971; History of Tunnels, 1972; (ed.) The Wipers Times (World War I trench newspaper), 1973; Victorian Parlour Games, 1974; Yes! We Have Some, 1976; I.N.I.T.I.A.L., 1978; The Spice of Life (Victorian Entertainments), 1979; All About the Home, 1980; A Pedlar's Legacy, 1981; Sunderland Marine, 1982; Readson Textiles, 1982; The Alsford Tradition, 1982; The Matchmakers, 1985; Helix, 1987. Add: 50 Great Russell St., London 3BA, England.

BEAVER, Paul. British, b. 1953. Aerospace, History, Military/Defence, Transportation, Travel. Journalist and broadcaster: Managing Ed., Jane's Information Group, since 1988 (Naval Ed., Jane's Defence Weekly, 1987–88). Ed., Defence Helicopter World, 1982–86. *Publs:* Ark Royal: A Pictorial History, 1979; U-Boats in the Atlantic, 1979; German Capital Ships, 1980; E-Boats and Coastal Craft, 1980; German Destroyers, 1981; The British Aircraft Carrier, 1982, 3rd ed., 1987; Encyclopaedia of the Modern Royal Navy, 1982, 3rd ed., 1987; Carrier Air Operations since 1945, 1983; Fleet Command, 1984; "Invincible" Class, 1984; British Naval Air Power, 1985; (with P. Birtles) Missile Systems, 1985; Royal Navy of the 1980s, 1985; NATO Navies of the 1980s, 1985; Nuclear-Powered Submarines, 1986; Modern British Missiles, 1986; Encyclopedia of Aviation, 1986; Modern Royal Naval Warships, 1987; Modern Military Helicopters, 1987; Battlefield Helicopters, 1987; Attack Helicopters, 1987; Encyclopedia of the Fleet Air Arm Since 1945, 1987; Army Air Corps, 1988; The Modern Royal Navy, 1988; Today's Royal Marines, 1988; Jane's World Naval Aviation, 1989. Add: 19 Bexmoor Way, Old Basing, nr. Basingstoke RG24 0BL, England.

BECHERVAISE, John Mayston. Australian, b. 1910. Short stories, Poetry, History, Natural history, Recreation/Leisure/Hobbies, Travel/Exploration/Adventure. Warden, House of Guilds, Geelong Coll., 1934–36 and 1945–49; Co-Ed., Walkabout Travel Mag., Melbourne, 1949–53; Leader, Australian Antarctic Research Expeditions (ANARE), 1953–54, 1955–56, and 1959–60; Dir. of Studies, Geelong Grammar Sch., Vic., 1962–72. *Publs:* Barwon and Barrabools (poetry), 1947; (with Phillip Law) ANARE: Australia's Antarctic Outposts, 1957; Men on Ice, 1958; The Last Continent, 1958; Antarctica, 1959; The Far South, 1961; Blizzard and Fire, 1963; Antarctica, 1967; Australia: World of Difference, 1967; Australia and Antarctica, 1968; Ballarat and Western Goldfields, 1970; Bendigo and Eastern Goldfields, 1970; Blue Mountains, 1971; The Grampians, 1971; Mountaineering, 1971; Old Melbourne Hotels, 1973; Wilson's Promontory, 1976; The University of Melbourne, 1977; Science, and Men on Ice in Antarctica, 1978; Antarctica: The Last Horizon, 1979; Castlemaine Sketchbook, 1979; Rediscovering Victoria's Goldfields, 1980; The Bendigo Book, 1982; University of Melbourne: An Illustrated

Perspective, 1985. Add: 185 Roslyn Rd., Belmont, Vic. 3216, Australia.

BECHKO, P(eggy) A(nne). Also writes as Bill Haller. American, b. 1950. Westerns/Adventure. Former artist's model, legal secty., delivery person, and gift wrapper. *Publs:* Night of the Flaming Guns, 1974; Gunman's Justice, 1974; Blown to Hell, 1976; (as Bill Haller) Sidewinder's Trail, 1976; Dead Man's Feud, 1976; The Winged Warrior, 1977, in U.K. as Omaha Jones, 1979; Hawke's Indians, 1979; Dark Side of Love, 1983; Harmonie Mexicaine, 1984. Add: c/o Doubleday, 666 Fifth Ave., New York, NY 10103, U.S.A.

BECK, Earl Ray. American, b. 1916. Education, History, Biography. Prof. of History, Florida State Univ., Tallahassee, since 1960 (Asst. Prof., 1949–52; Assoc. Prof., 1952–60; Dept. Chmn., 1967–72). *Publs:* Verdict on Schacht, 1955; Death of Prussian Republic, 1959; On Teaching History in Colleges and Universities, 1966; Germany Rediscovers America, 1968; A Time of Triumph and of Sorrow: Spanish Politics During the Reign of Alfonso XII 1874-1885, 1979; Under the Bombs: The German Home Front 1942–1945, 1986. Add: 2514 Killarney Way, Tallahassee, Fla. 32308, U.S.A.

BECK, Evelyn Torton. American, b. 1933. Literature. Assoc. Prof. of Comparative Literature, German and Women's Studies, Univ. of Wisconsin, Madison, since 1972. Lectr., Univ. of Maryland, Baltimore, 1971–72. *Publs:* Kafka and the Yiddish Theater: Its Impact on his Work, 1971; (with J. Hermand) Interpretive Synthesis: The Task of Literary Scholarship, 1976; (ed. with J. Sherman) The Prism of Sex, 1979; Nice Jewish Girls: Lesbian Anthology, 1982. Add: Comparative Literature Dept., Univ. of Wisconsin, Madison, Wisc. 53706. U.S.A.

BECK, Hubert Frederick. American, b. 1931. Theology/Religion. Campus Pastor, Texas A & M Univ., College Station, since 1968. Pastor, St. John's, Topeka, 1956–58, Immanuel Lutheran Church, Charleston, 1958–65, and Immanuel Lutheran Church, Des Plaines, 1965–67, all in Illinois. *Publs:* The Christian Encounters the Age of Technology, 1970; Thoughts For Today, 1972; The Way of God and the Ways of Men (sermons), 1972; Why Can't the Church Be Like This?, 1973; (with Robert Otterstad) Into the Wilderness, 1975; Fantasies for Fantastic Christians, 1977; What Should I Believe?, 1980; Stay in the Sun-Shine, 1980. Add: 1405 Francis, College Station, Tex. 77840, U.S.A.

BECK, James. American, b. 1930. Art. Prof. of Art History, Columbia Univ., NYC, since 1972 (joined faculty, 1964). *Publs:* Michelangelo: A Lesson in Anatomy, 1975; Raphael, 1976; (co-author) Masaccio: The Documents, 1978; Leonardo's Rules of Painting, 1979; Italian Renaissance Painting, 1981; The Doors of the Florentine Baptistry, 1985; (ed.) Raphael Before Rome, 1986. Add: Dept. of Art History, Columbia Univ., New York, N.Y. 10027, U.S.A.

BECK, Lewis White. American, b. 1913. Philosophy. Emeritus Prof. of Philosophy, Univ. of Rochester (Prof. since 1949). *Publs:* (trans.) Kant's Critique of Practical Reason and Other Writings in Moral Philosophy, 1949; Philosophic Inquiry, 1952; A Commentary on Kant's Critique of Practical Reason, 1960; Six Secular Philosophers, 1960; (ed.) Kant on History, 1963; Studies in the Philosophy of Kant, 1965; (ed.) Eighteenth Century Philosophy, 1965; (co-author) Philosophic Inquiry, 2nd ed., 1968; Early German Philosophy, 1968; Kant Studies Today, 1969; (ed.) Proceedings of the Third International Kant Congress, 1972; The Actor and the Spectator, 1975; Essays on Kant and Hume, 1978; (ed.) Kant Selections, 1988. Add: Univ. of Rochester, Rochester, N.Y. 14627, U.S.A.

BECK, Warren Albert. American, b. 1918. History. Prof. of History, California State Univ., Fullerton, since 1961. Prof. of History, Augustana Coll., Sioux Falls, S.D., 1948–50, Capital Univ., Columbus, Ohio, 1950–55, Eastern New Mexico Univ., Portales, 1955–58, and Santa Ana Coll., Calif., 1958–61. *Publs:* A History of New Mexico, 1962; (co-author) Historical Atlas of New Mexico, 1968; (co-author) California: A History of the Golden State, 1972; (co-author) Understanding American History Through Fiction, 1975; (co-author) Historical Atlas of California, 1975; The California Experience, 1976; (co-author) Historical Atlas of the American West, 1989. Add: 537 Lee Pl., Placentia, Calif. 92670, U.S.A.

BECKELHYMER, (Paul) Hunter. American, b. 1919. Theology/Religion, Biography. Minister, North Shore Christian Church, Chicago, 1944–46, Kenton Christian Church, Ohio, 1946–53, and Hiram Christian Church, Ohio, 1953–66; Assoc. Prof. of Homiletics, Brite Divinity Sch., Texas Christian Univ., Fort Worth, 1966–85. *Publs:* Meeting Life on Higher Levels, 1956; Questions God Asks, 1961; Hocking Valley Iron Man, 1962; Dear Connie, 1967; (ed.) The Vital Pulpit of the Christian Church, 1969; (ed.) The Word We Preach, 1970. Add: 5725 Whitman Ave., Ft. Worth, Tex. 76133, U.S.A.

BECKER, Gary S. American, b. 1930. Economics. Prof., Dept. of Economics and Sociology, Univ. of Chicago, since 1983 (Asst. Prof., 1954–57; Visiting Prof., 1969–70; Prof., Dept. of Economics, 1970–83). Research Assoc., Economics Research Center, National Opinion Research Center, since 1980; Asst. to Assoc. Prof. of Economics, 1957–60, Prof., 1960–68, and Arthur Lehman Prof. of Economics, 1968–69, Columbia Univ., New York. *Publs:* The Economics of Discrimination, 1957, 1971; Human Capital, 1964, 1975; Human Capital and the Personal Distribution of Income: An Analytical Approach, 1967; Economic Theory, 1971; (ed. with W.M. Landes) Essays in the Economics of Crime and Punishment, 1974; (with G. Ghez) The Allocation of Time and Goods over the Life Cycle, 1975; (ed.) Essays in Labor Economics in Honor of H. Gregg Lewis, 1976; The Economic Approach to Human Behaviour, 1976; A Treatise on the Family, 1981. Add: Univ. of Chicago, Dept. of Economics, 1126 East 59th St., Chicago, Ill. 60637, U.S.A.

BECKER, George Joseph. American, b. 1908. Literature. Prof. of English, Swarthmore Coll., Pennsylvania, 1945–70, and Western Washington Univ., Bellingham, 1970–74. *Publs:* (trans.) Jean-Paul Sartre: Anti-Semite and Jew, 1948; (trans. and ed.) Documents of Modern Literary Realism, 1963; Paris under Siege 1870-1871, from the Goncourt Journal, 1969; Paris and the Arts 1851-1896, from the Goncourt Journal, 1971; John Dos Passos, 1974; Shakespeare's Histories, 1977; Realism in Modern Literature, 1980; D.H. Lawrence, 1980; Master European Realists of the Nineteenth Century, 1982; James A. Michener, 1983. Add: 3115 Squalicum Parkway, Bellingham, Wash. 98225, U.S.A.

BECKER, Jillian. British, b. 1932. Novels/Short stories, International relations/Current affairs. *Publs:* The Keep, 1967; The Union, 1971; The Virgins, 1976; Hitler's Children, 1977; The PLO: The Rise and Fall of the Palestine Liberation Organization, 1984. Add: c/o Weidenfeld & Nicolson, 91 Clapham High St., London SW4 7TA, England.

BECKER, Lucille Frackman. American, b. 1929. Literature, Biography. Prof. of French, Drew Univ., Madison, N.J., since 1969. Lectr. in French, Columbia Univ., NYC, 1954–58; Instr. in French, Rutgers Univ., Newark, N.J., 1959–69. *Publs:* (ed. with A. della Fazia) Le Maitre de Santiago, by Henry de Montherlant, 1965; Henry de Montherlant, 1970; Louis Aragon, 1971; Georges Simenon, 1978; Francoise Mallet-Joris, 1985; Twentieth Century French Women Novelists, 1989. Add: Drew Univ., Madison, N.J. 07940, U.S.A.

BECKER, Stephen (David). American, b. 1927. Novels/Short stories, Art, Biography, Translations. Prof. of English, Univ. of Central Florida, Orlando, since 1987. Faculty member, Tsing Hua Univ., Peking, China, 1947–48, Brandeis Univ., Waltham, Mass., 1951–52, Bennington Coll., Vermont, 1977–78, Hollins Coll., Va., 1986, Univ. of Central Florida, Orlando, 1986, Pacific Lutheran Univ., Tacoma, Wash., 1987. *Publs:* The Season of the Stranger, 1951; (trans.) The Colors of the Day, 1953; (trans.) Mountains in the Desert, 1954; (trans.) The Sacred Forest, 1954; Shanghai Incident, 1955; (trans.) Faraway, 1957; (trans.) Someone Will Die Tonight in the Caribbean, 1958; Juice, 1959; Comic Art in America, 1959; (trans.) The Last of the Just, 1961; (trans.) The Town Beyond the Wall, 1964; Marshall Field III, 1964; A Covenant with Death, 1965; The Outcasts, 1967; When the War Is over, 1969; Dog Tags, 1973; The Chinese Bandit. 1975; (trans.) The Conquerors, 1976; (trans.) Louis-Philippe's American Journal, 1977; The Last Mandarin, 1979; (trans.) Ana No. 1980; Blue-Eyed Shan, 1982 (trans.) The Aristotle System, 1985; A Rendezvous in Haiti, 1987. Add: English Dept., Univ. of Central Florida, Orlando, Fla., U.S.A.

BECKERMAN, Wilfred. British, b. 1925. Economics. Fellow, Balliol Coll., Oxford, since 1975. Gov., and Member of Exec. Cttee., National Inst., of Economic and Social Research, London, since 1972 (Member of Staff, 1962–64). Lectr. in Economics, Univ. of Nottingham, 1950–52; with OEEC (later OECD), Paris, 1952–62; with N.I.E.S.R., London, 1962–64; Fellow and Tutor in Economics, Balliol Coll., Oxford, 1964–69; Economic Advisor to Pres. of Bd. of Trade (on leave from Oxford), 1967–69; Prof. of Political Economy, University Coll., London, 1969–75. Member, Royal Commn. on Environmental Pollution. 1970–73. *Publs:* (co-author) The British Economy, in 1975, 1965; International Comparisons of Real Income, 1966; An Introduction to National Income Analysis, 1968; (ed.) Labour Government's Economic Record, 1964–70, 1972; In Defence of Economic Growth (in U.S. as Two Cheers for the

Affluent Society), 1974; Measures of Equality, Leisure and Welfare, 1979; Poverty and the Impact of Income Maintenance Payments, 1979; (ed.) Slow Growth In Britain: Causes and Consequences, 1979; (with S. Clark) Poverty and Social Security in Britain since 1961, 1982. Add: Balliol Coll., Oxford OX1 3BJ, England.

BECKETT, Samuel (Barclay). Irish, b. 1906. Novels/Short stories, Plays/Screenplays, Poetry, Translations. Lectr. in English, Ecole Normale Superieure, Paris, 1928–30; Lectr. in French, Trinity Coll., Dublin, 1930–31; closely associated with James Joyce in Paris in the late 1920's and 1930's; settled in Paris, 1938, and has written chiefly in French since 1945; translates his own work into English. *Publs:* plays—En Attendant Godot, 1952, trans. as Waiting for Godot, 1954; Fin de Partie: Suivi de Acte sans Paroles, 1957, trans. as Endgame: A Play in One Act; Followed by Act Without Words: A Mime for One Player, 1958; All That Fall, 1957; Krapp's Last Tape and Embers, 1959; Krapp's Last Tape and Other Dramatic Pieces, 1960; Happy Days, 1961; Cascando, 1963; Play and Two Short Pieces for Radio, 1964; Eh Joe and Other Writings, 1967; Cascando and Other Short Dramatic Pieces, 1968; Film, 1969; Breath and Other Shorts, 1971; Not I, 1973; That Time, 1976; Footfalls, 1976; Ends and Odds: Dramatic Pieces, 1976; Rockaby and Other Works, 1981; Three Occasional Pieces, 1982; Collected Shorter Plays, 1984; The Complete Dramatic Works, 1986; novels—Murphy, 1938; Molloy, 1951, trans. 1955; Malone meurt, 1951, trans. as Malone Dies, 1956; L'Innommable, 1953, trans. as the Unnamable, 1958; Watt, 1953; Comment C'est, 1961, trans. as How It Is, 1964; Mercier et Camier, 1970, trans. as Mercier and Camier, 1974; Company, 1980; short stories—More Pricks Than Kicks, 1934; Nouvelles et Textes pour Rien, 1955, trans. as Stories and Texts for Nothing, 1967; From an Abandoned Work, 1958; Imagination morte imaginez, 1965, trans. as Imagination Dead Imagine, 1965; Assez, 1966, trans. as Enough, 1967; Bing, 1966, trans. as Ping, 1967; Têtes-Mortes, 1967; No's Knife: Selected Shorter Prose 1945–1966, 1967; L'-Issue, 1968; Sans, 1969, trans. as Lessness, 1971; Séjour, 1970; Premier Amour, 1970, trans. as First Love, 1973; Le Dépeupleur, 1971, trans. as The Lost Ones, 1972; The North, 1972; First Love and Other Shorts, 1974; Fizzles, 1976; For to End Yet Again and Other Fizzles, 1976; All Strange Away, 1976; Four Novellas, 1977; Six Residua, 1978; Mal Vu Mal Dit, 1981, trans. as Ill Seen Ill Said, 1981; Worstward Ho, 1983; verse—Whoroscope, 1930; Echo's Bones and Other Precipitates, 1935; Gedichte, 1959; Poems in English, 1961; Collected Poems in English and French, 1977, rev. ed. as Collected Poems 1930–1978, 1984; other—Proust, 1931; (with others) Bram van Welde, 1958, trans. 1960; A Samuel Beckett Reader, 1967; I Can't Go On: A Selection from the Work of Samuel Beckett, 1976; Disjecta: Miscellaneous Writings and a Dramatic Fragment, 1983; Collected Shorter Prose 1945–1980, 1984. Translations—Anthology of Mexican Poetry, 1958; The Old Tune, by Robert Pinget, 1960; Zone, by Guillaume Apollinaire, 1960; Drunken Boat, by Arthur Rimbaud, 1977. Add: c/o Editions de Minuit, 7 rue Bernard-Palissy, Paris 6, France.

BECKHAM, Barry (Earl). American, b. 1944. Novels/Short stories. Education. Pres., Beckham House Publishers Inc. Assoc. Prof. in English, Hampton Univ., Hampton, Va. Public Relations Consultant, 1966–67, and Urban Affairs Assoc., Chase Manhattan Bank, NYC: Public Relations Assoc., YMCA National Council, NYC, 1967–68, and Western Electric Co., NYC, 1968–69. *Publs:* My Main Mother (in U.K. as Blues in the Night), 1969; Runner Mack, 1972; Double Dunk, 1981; (ed.) Black Student's Guide to the Colleges, 1982, 1984. Add: 140 Lancaster St., Providence, R.I. 02906, U.S.A.

BECKINGHAM, Charles Fraser. British, b. 1914. History, Translations. Intal. Dir., Fontes Historice Africannae Project, Union Académique Internationale, since 1986. Prof. of Islamic Studies, Univ. of London, 1965–81, now Emeritus. Vice-Pres. Hakluyt Soc., since 1972 (Pres., Prof. of Islamic Studies, Manchester Univ., 1958–65). Pres., Royal Asiatic Soc., 1967–70, 1976–79, and ed. of its journal, since 1984; Fellow, British Acad., since 1983. Vice-Pres., Royal Soc. for Asianffairs, 1973–77, 1980–85. *Publs:* (ed. and trans. with G.W.B. Huntingford) Some Records of Ethiopia, 1954; (ed. and trans. with G.W.B. Huntingford) A True Relation of the Prester John of the Indies, by F. Alvares, 1961; (ed.) Travels of James Bruce, 1964; The Achievements of Prester John, 1966; (ed. with A.J. Arberry and others) Religion in the Middle East, 1969; (with E. Ullendorff) The Hebrew Letters of Prester John, 1982; Between Islam and Christendom, 1983; (ed.) The Itinerário of Jerónimo Lobo, 1984. Add: 56 Queen Anne St., London W1M 9LA, England.

BECKINSALE, Robert Percy. British, b. 1908. Business/Trade/Industry, Natural history, Travel/Exploration/Adventure, Urban studies,

Biography. Fellow of Univ. Coll. since 1965, Oxford Univ. (Sr. Lectr. in Geography, 1945–75). *Publs:* Companion into Gloucestershire, 1939; (co-author) The Iberian Peninsula, 1941; (co-author) Portugal, 1942; (co-author) Spain, 1943; Land, Air and Ocean, 1943, 6th ed. 1966; (co-author) The Atlantic Islands, 1944; Trowbridge Woolen Industry, 1951; Companion into Berkshire, 1951; (co-author) History of Study of Land Forms, 1964; (co-ed. and author) Urbanisation and Its Problems, 1968; Berkshire, 1972; Gloucestershire and the Cotswolds, 1973; (co-author) Life and Work of W.M. Davis. 1973; (co-author) Southern Europe, 1974; The English Heartland, 1980; History of Study of Land Forms, vol. III, 1989. Add: 8 Park Rd., Abingdon, Oxon OX14 1DS, England.

BECKLES WILLSON, Robina Elizabeth. British, b. 1930. Children's fiction, Children's non-fiction. Teacher, Liverpool Sch. of Art, 1952–56, and Ballet Rambert Educational Sch., London, 1956–58. *Publs:* Leopards on the Loire, 1961; A Time to Dance, 1962; Musical Instruments, 1964; A Reflection of Rachel, 1967; The Leader of the Band, 1967; Roundabout Ride, 1968; Dancing Day, 1971; The Last Harper, 1972; The Shell on Your 1972; What a Noise, 1974; The Voice of Music, 1975; Musical Merry-go-Round, 1977; The Beaver Book of Ballet, 1979; Eyes Wide Open, 1981; Anna Pavlova; A Legend among Dancers, 1981; Pocket Book of Ballet, 1982; Secret Witch, 1982; Square Bear, 1983; Merry Christmas, 1983, Holiday Witch, 1983; Sophie and Nicky series, 2 vols., 1984; Hungry Witch, 1984; Music Maker, 1986; Sporty Witch, 1986. Add: 44 Popes Ave., Twickenham, Middx. TW2 5TL, England.

BECKMAN, Gail M(cKnight). American, b. 1938. Law. Prof., Georgia State Univ., Atlanta, since 1976 (Assoc. Prof., 1971–76). Lawyer, Morgan Lewis & Bockius, Philadelphia, 1963–66; Research Assoc., American Philosophical Assn., 1966–70' Lectr., Faculty of Law, Univ. of Glasgow, 1967–71. *Publs:* Estate Planning Considerations for U.S. Citizens Abroad, 1974; (co-author) Law for Business and Management, 1974; (ed.) Statutes at Large of Pennsylvania 1680-1700, 1976. Add: Box 404, Georgia State Univ., Univ. Plaza, Atlanta, Ga. 30303, U.S.A.

BECKWITH, Burnham Putnam. Also writes as John Putnam. American, b. 1904. Economics. History, Politics/Government. Assoc. Prof. of Economics, Univ. of Georgia, Athens, 1938–40; Economist, WPB, Washington, D.C. 1941–45, and OMGUS, Berlin 1946–48. *Publs:* (as John Putnam) Modern Case for Socialism, 1943; Economic Theory of a Socialist Economy, 1948; Marginal-Cost Price-Output Control, 1955; Religion, Philosophy and Science, 1957; The Next 500 Years, 1967; Government by Experts, 1972; Liberal Socialism, 1974; The Case for Liberal Socialism, 1976; Liberal Socialism Applied, 1978; Radical Essays, 1981; Ideas About the Future; A History of Futurism 1794-1982, 1984; The Deadline of U.S. Religious Faith, 1912–1984, and the Effect of Education and Intelligence on Such Faith, 1985; Beyond Tomorrow: A Rational Utopia, 1986; The Future of Money and Banking, 1987. Add: 19 Coleman Place, No. 38, Menlo Park, Calif. 94025, U.S.A.

BECKWITH, John Gordon. British. b. 1918. Art, Crafts. Keeper, Dept. of Architecture and Sculpture, Victoria and Albert Museum, London, 1974–79. Slade Prof. for the Fine Arts, Oxford, 1978–79. *Publs:* The Art of Constantinople, 1961, 1968; Coptic Sculpture, 1963; Early Medieval Art, 1964, 3rd ed. 1985. Early Christian and Byzantine Art. 1970, 1979; Ivory Carvings in Early Medieval England, 1972; Ivory Carvings in Early Medieval England 700-1200 (exhibition catalogue). 1974. Add: Flat 12, 77 Ladbroke Grove, London W11, England.

BECKWITH, Lillian. British, b. 1916. Novels/Short stories, Children's fiction, Cookery/Gastronomy/Wine, Autobiography/Memoirs/Personal. *Publs:* The Hills Is Lonely, 1959; The Sea for Breakfast, 1961; The Loud Halo, 1964; Green Hand, 1967; A Rope in Case, 1968; About My Father's Business, 1971; Lightly Poached, 1973; The Spuddy, 1974; Beautiful Just!; The Lillian Beckwith Omnibus, 1976; The Lillian Beckwith Hebridean Cookbook, 1976; Bruach Blend, 1978; A Shine of Rainbows, 1984; A Proper Woman, 1986; A Hebridean Omnibus, 1987; The Bay of Strangers, 1988; The Small Party, 1989. Add: c/o Century Hutchinson Publishing Group, 62-65 Chandos Pl., London WC2N 4NW, England.

BEDAU, Hugo Adam. American, b. 1926. Law, Philosophy, Politics. Prof. of Philosophy, Tufts Univ., Medford, Mass., since 1966. Assoc. Prof. of Philosophy, Reed Coll., Portland, Ore., 1962–66. *Publs:* The Courts, the Constitution, and Capital Punishment, 1977; Death Is Different, 1987; co-author—Nomos VI: Justice, 1963; Nomos IX: Equality, 1967; The Concept of Academic Freedom, 1972; Philosophy and Political Action, 1972; Philosophy, Morality, and International Affairs, 1974; Vic-

timless Crimes: Two Views, 1974; Justice and Punishment, 1977; Human Rights and U.S. Foreign Policy, 1979; Making Decisions, 1979; The Imposition of Law, 1979; Matters of Life and Death, 1980; Ethical Issues in Government, 1981; And Justice for All, 1982; Social Justice, 1982; Group Decision Making, 1984; Human Rights, 1984; Nomos XXVII: Criminal Justice, 1985; Current Issues and Enduring Questions, 1987; editor—The Death Penalty in America, 1964, 1981; Civil Disobedience: Theory and Practice, 1969; Justice and Equality, 1971. Add: c/o Dept. of Philosophy, Tufts Univ., Medford, Mass. 02155, U.S.A.

BEDDINGTON, Roy. British, b. 1910. Novels, Children's fiction, Poetry, Country life, Natural history, Angling. Writer and illustrator. Former Fishing Corresp., Country Life mag. *Publs:* Adventures of Thomas Trout, 1939; To Be a Fisherman, 1955; The Pigeon and the Boy, 1957; Pindar, A Dog to Remember, 1975; A Countryman's Verse, 1981. Add: Home Farm, Chute Cadley, nr. Andover, Hants, England.

BEDFORD, Henry Frederick. American, b. 1931. History, Industrial Relations. History teacher, Albuquerque Acad., N.M., since 1988. At Phillips Exeter Academy, New Hampshire: Instr. in History, 1957–66; Chmn. of the History Dept., 1966–69; Dean of the Faculty, 1969–73; Cowles Prof. in the Humanities, 1973–82; Librarian, 1973–77; Vice-Principal, 1979–82. Dean of Admissions, Amherst Coll., Mass., 1982–87. *Publs:* The Union Divides, 1963; Socialism and the Workers in Massachusetts, 1966; From Versailles to Nuremburg, 1969; (co-author) The Americans: A Brief History, 1972, 4th ed. 1985; Trouble Downtown, 1977. Add: Dept. of History, Albuquerque Acad., 6400 Wyoming Blvd. N.E., Albuquerque, N.M. 87109, U.S.A.

BEDFORD, Sybille. British, b. 1911. Novels, Law, Travel/Exploration/Adventure, Wine, Biography. *Publs:* A Sudden View: A Mexican Journey, 1953; A Legacy (novel), 1956; The Best We Can Do: The Trial of Doctor Bodkin Adams (in U.S. as The Trial of Dr. Adams), 1958; The Faces of Justice, 1961; A Favourite of the Gods (novel), 1962; A Compass Error (novel), 1968; Aldous Huxley: A Biography, vol I, 1894-1939, 1973, vol. II, 1939–63, 1974. Add: c/o Messrs. Coutts & Co., 1 Old Park Lane, London W1Y 4BS, England.

BEDINI, Silvio A. American, b. 1917. History, Sciences, Biography. Emeritus Keeper of the Rare Books, Smithsonian Instn., Washington. *Publs:* Early American Scientific Instruments and Their Makers, 1964; (with W. Van Braun and F. Whipple) Moon: Man's Greatest Adventure, 1970; The Life of Benjamin Banneker, 1972; Thinkers and Tinkers: The Early American Men of Science, 1975; The Spotted Stones, 1978; Declaration of Independence Desk: Relic of Revolution, 1981; Thomas Jefferson and His Copying Machines, 1984; Clockwork Cosmos, 1986. Add: 4303 47th St. N.W., Washington, D.C. 20016, U.S.A.

BEEBE, B(urdetta) F(aye). American, b. 1920. Children's fiction, Children's non-fiction, Natural history. Convention Mgr., National Food Brokers Assn., Washington, D.C., 1957–64. *Publs:* Run, Light Buck, Run, 1962; Appalachian Elk, 1962; Coyote, Come Home, 1963; Chestnut Cub, 1963; American Lions and Cats, 1963; American Wolves, Coyotes and Foxes, 1964; (with J.R. Johnson) American Wild Horses, 1964; Coyote for Keeps, 1965; Assateague Deer, 1965; (with J.R. Johnson) American Bears, 1965; American Desert Animals, 1966; Ocelot, 1966; Little Red, 1966; Yucatan Monkey, 1967, screenplay 1968; Animals South of the Border, 1968; African Elephants, 1968; African Lions and Cats, 1969; African Apes, 1969; Little Dickens, Jaguar Cub, 1970. Add: Box 5295, Santa Fe, N.M. 87501, U.S.A.

BEEBE, Ralph K. American, b. 1932. History, Industrial relations, Theology/Religion. Prof., George Fox Coll., Newberg, Ore., since 1974 (Dean of Men, and Dir. of Athletics, 1955–57). History Teacher, Willamette High Sch., Eugene, Ore., 1957–66, and Churchill High Sch., Eugene, 1966–74. *Publs:* A Garden of the Lord: A History of Oregon Yearly Meeting of Friends Church, 1968; The Worker and Social Change: The Pullman Strike of 1894, 1970; Thomas Jefferson, the Embargo and the Decision for Peace, 1972; (with John Lamoreau) Waging Peace: A Study in Biblical Pacifism, 1980. Add: 212 Carlton Way, Newberg, Ore. 97132, U.S.A.

BEEBY, Clarence Edward. New Zealander, b. 1902. Education (not textbooks on other subjects). Consultant, New Zealand Council for Educational Research, since 1975. Gen. Ed., Fundamentals of Educational Planning, Intnl. Inst. for Educational Planning, Paris, 1965–72; Ford Found. Consultant to the Ministry of Education, Indonesia, 1970–76. *Publs:* The Intermediate Schools of New Zealand, 1938; (with W. Thomas and M. H. Oram) Entrance to the University, 1939; Report on

Education in Western Samoa, 1954; The Quality of Education in Developing Countries, 1966; Planning and the Educational Administrator, 1967; (ed.) Qualitative Aspects of Educational Planning, 1969; Assessment of Indonesian Education: A Guide in Planning, 1979. Add: New Zealand Council for Educational Research, Education House, 178-182 Willis St., Wellington, New Zealand.

BEECH, H. R(eginald). British, b. 1925. Psychology. Consultant Psychologist, North West Regional Health Authority; Prof. of Clinical Psychology, Univ. of Manchester. Sr. Lectr., Inst. of Psychiatry, London, 1963–69; Consultant Psychologist, S.W. Metropolitan Region, 1969–72. Former Ed., British Journal of Social & Clinical Psychology. *Publs:* (with F. Fransella) Research and Experiment in Stuttering, 1968; Changing Man's Behaviour, 1969; (ed.) Obsessional States, 1974; (with M. Vaughan) Behavioural Treatment of Obsessional States, 1978; (with L.E. Burns and B.F. Sheffield) Behavioural Approaches to the Management of Stress; Staying Together, 1986. Add: 25 Park Lane, Congleton, Cheshire, England.

BEEKMAN, Allan. American, b. 1913. Novels/Short stories, History. Contrib., Pacific Citizen, Los Angeles, since 1949. *Publs:* (with Take Beekman) Hawaii's Great Japanese Strike (history), 1960; Such Stuff as Dreams (novelette), 1963; Hawaiian Tales (short stories), 1970; Niihau Incident (history), 1982; Crisis: The Japanese Attack on Pearl Harbor and Southeast Asia (history), 1989. Add: 1279-203 Ala (Kapuna) St., Honolulu, Hawaii 96819, U.S.A.

BEER, Patricia. British, b. 1924. Novels/Short stories, Poetry, Literature, Autobiography/Memoirs/Personal. Lectr. in English, Univ. of Padua, Italy, 1946–48, and Ministero Aeronautica, Rome, 1950–53; Sr. Lectr. in English, Goldsmiths' Coll., Univ. of London, 1962–68. *Publs:* Loss of the Magyar and Other Poems, 1959; (ed. with Ted Hughes and Vernon Scannell) New Poems 1962, 1962; The Survivors, 1963 (poetry), Just Like the Resurrection, 1967 (poetry), Mrs. Beer's House (autobiog.), 1968; The Estuary, 1971 (poetry), An Introduction to the Metaphysical Poets, 1972; Spanish Balcony, 1973; Reader, I Married Him (essays), 1974; Driving West, 1975 (poetry), Moon's Ottery (novel), 1978; Poems 1967–1979, 1979; Selected Poems, 1979; The Lie of the Land (poetry), 1983; Wessex, 1985; Collected Poems, 1988. Add: Tiphayes, Up Ottery, near Honiton, Devon, England.

BEER, Samuel (Hutchinson). American, b. 1911. Economics, Politics/Government. Prof. of Govt., Harvard Univ., Cambridge, since 1953 (Instr. in Govt., 1938–42; Asst. Prof., 1946–48; Assoc. Prof., 1948–53; and Chmn., Dept. of Govt., 1954–58). National Chmn., Americans for Democratic Action. *Publs:* The City of Reason, 1949; Treasury Control: The Coordination of Financial and Economic Policy in Great Britain, 1956, 1982; (co-author) Patterns of Government: The Major Political Systems of Europe, 1958, 3rd ed. 1972; Modern British Politics, 1965; Modern Political Development, 1974; British Political System, 1974; Britain Against Itself, 1982. Add: 87 Lakeview Ave., Cambridge, Mass. 02138, U.S.A.

BEER, Stafford. British, b. 1926. Poetry, Administration/Management, Business/Trade/Industry, Information science/Computers. Visiting Prof. of Cybernetics, Manchester Business Sch., since 1969; Adjunct Prof. of Social Science Systems, Wharton Sch., Philadelphia, since 1981 (Prof. of Statistics and Operations Research, 1972–81); Dir., Metapraxis, since 1984. Head of Operational Research and Cybernetics, United Steel, 1949–61; Managing Dir., Science in General Mgmt., 1961–66; Development Dir., Intnl. Publishing Corp. Ltd., 1966–69. Member, U.K. Automation Council, 1957–69, and Gen. Advisory Council, B.B.C., 1961–69; Pres., Operational Research Soc. (U.K.), 1970–71, and Soc. for General Systems Research (U.S.A.), 1971–72. *Publs:* Cybernetics and Management, 1959, 1967; Decision and Control, 1966; Management Science, 1967; Brain of the Firm, 1972, 1981; Designing Freedom, 1974; Platform for Change, 1975; Transit (verse), 1977; The Heart of Enterprise, 1979; Diagnosing the System for Organizations, 1985; Pebbles to Computers: The Thread, 1986; To Someone or Other, 1988. Add: Cwarel Isaf, Pont Creuddyn, Lampeter, Dyfed SA48 8PG, Wales.

BEERS, Burton Floyd. American, b. 1927. History, International relations/Current affairs. Prof. of History, since 1966, and Alumni Distinguished Prof., since 1970, North Carolina State Univ., Raleigh (Instr., 1955–57; Asst. Prof., 1957–61; Assoc. Prof., 1961–66). *Publs:* Vain Endeavour: Robert Lansing's Attempts to End the American–Japanese Rivalry. 1962; (with P.H. Clyde) The Far East: A History of Western Impacts and Eastern Responses, 6th ed. 1976; China in Old Photographs, 1978; (sr. writer) World History: Patterns of Civilization, 1983 (with Murray

S. Downs) N.C. Stake: A Pictorial History, 1986. Add: 629 South Lakeside Dr., Raleigh, N.C. 27607, U.S.A.

BEERY, Mary. American. Children's non-fiction. Instr., Continuing Education Div., Ohio State Univ., Lima, since 1978. Teacher, Lima South High Sch., 1929–53, Producer and Moderator, Teenpan Alley, Station WIMA, 1952–54, and Teacher, St. Rita's Hosp. Sch. of Nursing, 1954–67, all Lima, Ohio; French Instr., Ohio State Univ., Lima, 1960–78. *Publs:* Manners Made Easy, 1949, 3rd ed. 1966; Guide to Good Manners, 1952; Young Teens Talk It Over, 1957; Young Teens Plan Dates and Proms, 1962; Young Teens Away from Home, 1966; Young Teens and Money, 1971. Add: Galvin Hall, 4300 Campus Dr., Lima, Ohio 45804, U.S.A.

BEESON, Trevor Randall. British, b. 1926. Theology/Religion. Dean of Winchester, since 1987. Vicar, St. Chad's, Stockton-on-Tees, Curate, St. Martin-in-the-Fields, London, 1964–71; Vicar of Ware, Herts., 1971–76; Canon of Westminster Abbey, 1976–87, and Chaplain to Speaker of the House of Commons, 1982–87. Ed., New Christian, 1965–70; European Corresp., Christian Century, 1970–82. *Publs:* New Area Mission, 1963; (with R. Sharp) Worship in a United Church, 1964; (ed.) Partnership in Ministry, 1964; An Eye for an Ear, 1972; The Church of England in Crisis, 1973; Discretion and Valour: Religious Conditions in Eastern Europe, 1974; Britain Today and Tomorrow, 1978; (with J. Pearce). A Vision of Hope: Churches and Change in Latin America, 1984. Add: The Deanery, Winchester SO23 9LS, England.

BEGG, Alexander Charles. New Zealander, b. 1912. Travel/Exploration/Adventure. Specialist in Diagnostic Radiology, 1941–55, and Dir. of Diagnostic Radiology, 1956–77, Otago Hosp. Bd., Dunedin: Lectr., 1946–71, and Assoc. Prof. of Diagnostic Radiology, 1972–77, Otago Medical Sch. *Publs:* all with Neil C. Begg—Dusky Bay, 1966 (Hubert Church Award), 1968; James Cook and New Zealand, 1969; Port Preservation, 1973 (J.M. Sherrand Award); The World of John Boultbee, 1979. Add: 107 Braeview Cres., Maori Hill, Dunedin, New Zealand.

BEGG, (Sir) Neil (Colquhoun). New Zealander, b. 1915. Medicine/Health, Travel/Exploration/Adventure. Dir. of Medical Services, Plunket Soc., Royal Soc. for the Health of Women and Children, since 1956–77. Chmn., New Zealand Historic Places Trust, 1978–86. *Publs:* (with A.C. Begg) Dusky Bay, 1966, 1968; (with A.C. Begg) James Cook and New Zealand, 1969; Child and his Family, 1970, 1974; (with A.C. Begg) Port Preservation, 1973; (with A.C. Begg) The World of John Boultbee, 1979. Add: 86 Newington Ave., Dunedin, New Zealand.

BEGGS, David. New Zealander, b. 1909. Natural history. Writer, Radio Science Talks, Christchurch Recording Centre. Former Principal Lectr., Christchurch Teachers Coll., 1945–67 (Ed. Nature Study Bulletin, *Publs:* Nature Study: A Handbook for Teachers, 1954; Nature Tables and Team Discovery (6 vols.). 1962, rev. ed. 1966. Add: 17 Cron Ave., Te Atatu S., Auckland, New Zealand.

BEHLE, William Harroun. American, b. 1909. Zoology, Biography. Prof. Emeritus of Biology, Univ of Utah, Salt Lake City (Prof. since 1937). *Publs:* Biography of Augustus C. Behle, M.D., 1948; The Bird Life of Great Salt Lake, 1958; (with M.L. Perry) Utah Birds: Check-List, Seasonal and Ecological Occurrence Charts and Guides to Bird Finding, 1975; The Birds of Northeastern Utah, 1981; (with E.D. Sorenson and C.M. White) Utah Birds: A Revised Checklist, 1985; Utah Birds: Geographic Distribution and Systematics, 1985; Utah Birds: Historical Perspectives and Bibliography, 1989. Add: 1233 East 800 South St., Salt Lake City, Utah 84102, U.S.A.

BEHN, Noel. American, b. 1928. Mystery/Crime/Suspense. Producer/Operator, Cherry Lane Theatre, NYC, 1956–61; Producer, Edgewater Beach Playhouse, Chicago, summers 1957–60. *Publs:* The Kremlin Letter, 1966; The Shadowboxer, 1969; Big Stick-Up at Brink's (non-fiction), 1977; Seven Silent Men, 1984. Add: 73 Horatio St., New York, N.Y. 10014, U.S.A.

BEHR, Edward. British, b. 1926. Novels/Short stories, International relations/Current affairs, Autobiography/Memoirs/Personal Cultural Ed., Newsweek Intnl., Paris, since 1984 (Newsweek Bureau Chief, S.E. Asia, 1966–68, and Paris Bureau, 1968–73; European Ed., 1973–83). Reuters Correspondent, 1951–54; Correspondent, Time Mag., 1957–63; Contributing Ed., Saturday Evening Post, 1963–65. *Publs:* The Algerian Problem, 1961; (with Sydney Liu) The Thirty Sixth Way, 1969; Bearings, 1978 (in U.K. as Anyone Here Been Raped—and Speaks English? 1981); Getting Even (novel), 1980; The Last Emperor, 1987; Hirohito: Behind the

Myth, 1989; The Making of "Les Miserables", 1989. Add: c/o Newsweek, 162 Faubourg Saint Honoré, 75008 Paris, France.

BEHREND, George (Henry Sandham). British, b. 1922. Transportation, Travel. European Ed., Intnl. Railway Traveler, Louisville, since 1987. *Publs:* Grand European Expresses: The Story of Wagons-Lits, 1962; Pullman in Europe, 1962; Railway Holiday in France, 1963; Railway Holiday in Switzerland, 1965; Stanley Spencer at Burghclere, 1965; Jersey Airlines, 1968; Gone with Regret: Recollections of the Great Western Railway 1922–1947, 3rd ed. 1969; (with Vincent Kelly) Yatakli-Vagon: Turkish Steam Travel, 1969; (with Ian Scott-Hill) Channel Silver Wings, 1972; Steam over Switzerland, 1974; History of Trains de Luxe, 1982; Luxury Trains, 1982; (with G.C. Buchanan) Night Ferry: Britain's Only International Train, 1985; (trans.) The Orient Express: A Century of Railway Adventures, 1988; (with Gary Buchanan) Luxury Train Cruises, 1989. Add: Fliquet, St. Martin, Jersey, Channel Islands.

BEHRENS, John C. American, b. 1933. Business, Travel, Writing/Journalism. Prof. of Journalism, since 1965, Curator, Student Press Archives, since 1967, and Dir., PR/J Programs, since 1986, Utica Coll. of Syracuse Univ., N.Y. Ed., Commentary, since 1967. Editorial Bd., College Media Advisers' Review, since 1971; Columnist, American Printer, since 1978; Business Columnist, The Elks, since 1976; Staff Writer, N.Y. Business Journal, since 1987; Writer, McGraw-Hill's Physician's Financial News, since 1988. Newspaper ed. in Ohio, 1958–62; Chmn., Journalism Dept., Ohio Wesleyan Univ., Delaware, 1962–63; Asst. Prof. of Journalism, Marshall Univ., Huntington, W. Va., 1964–65; Ed., Laubach's Literary Advance, 1984–86. *Publs:* Magazine Writers' Workbook, 1968, 3rd ed. 1983; (ed.) Wood and Stone: Landmarks of Mohawk Valley, 1972; Reporting Worktext, 1974; Typewriter Guerrillas: Closeups of 20 Top Investigative Reporters, 1977, 2nd ed., 1979; Student Press Archives Directory, 1987. Add: 57 Stebbins Dr., Clinton, N.Y. 13323, U.S.A.

BEHRMAN, Jack Newton. American, b. 1922. Business/Trade/Industry, Engineering/Technology. Luther Hodges Distinguished Prof., Sch. of Business, Univ. of North Carolina, Chapel Hill, since 1965. Consultant, U.S. Dept. of State, Cttee. for Economic Development, Org. of AmericanaStates, U.S. Dept of the Treasury, United Nations, and private corporations. usU.S. Asst. Secty. of Commerce, Washington, D.C., 1961–64. Pres., Assn. for Education in Intnl. Business, 1966–68. *Publs:* (with Roy Blough) Regional Integration and the Trade of Latin America, 1968; Some Patterns in the Rise of the Multinational Enterprises, 1969; National Interest and the Multinational Enterprise, 1970; International Business and Governments, 1971; Multinational Production Consortia, 1971, The Role of International Companies, in Latin American Integration, 1972; Toward a New International Economic Order, 1974; International Business Government Communications: U.S. Structure, Actors and Issues, 1975; (with Harvey Wallender) Transfers of Manufacturing Technology Within Multinational Enterprises, 1976; (with W.A. Fischer) Science and Technology for Development, 1980; Overseas Research and Development Activities of Transnational Companies, 1980; Industry Ties with Science and Technology Policies in Developing Countries, 1980; Tropical Diseases: Responses of Pharmaceutical Companies, 1980; (with Raymond Mikesell) The Impact of U.S. Foreign Direct Investment on U.S. Export Competitiveness in Third World Markets, vol. II, 1980; Discourses on Ethics and Business, 1981; (with Robert E. Driscoll) National Industrial Policies, 1984; Industrial Policies: Intnl. Restructuring and Transnationals, 1984; China's Open Policy and Transnationals, 1987; The Rise of the Phoenix; The U.S. in a Restructured World Economy, 1987; Essays on Ethics in Business and the Professions, 1987. Add: 1702 Audubon Rd., Chapel Hill, N.C. 27514, U.S.A.

BEIER, Ulli. German, b. 1922. Art, Cultural/Ethnic topics, Autobiography/Memoirs/Personal. Dir., and Research Prof., Inst. of African Studies, Univ. of Ife, Nigeria, since 1971. Pres., and Tutor, 1961–64, and Assoc. Prof., 1965–66, Extra-Mural Dept., Univ. of Ibadan, Nigeria; Sr. Lectr., in Literature, Univ. of Papua New Guinea, 1967–71. *Publs:* Art in Nigeria, 1960; African Mud Sculpture, 1963; Contemporary Art in Africa, 1968; (with A.M. Kiki) Ten Thousand Years in a Lifetime: A New Guinea 1968; (with A.M. Kiki) Hohao, 1970; (with P. Cox) Home of Man, 1971; When the Moon Was Big, 1973; Words of Paradise, 1973; The Return of the Gods, 1975; Stolen Images, 1976; (ed.) Introduction to African Literature, 1980; Yoruba Myths, 1980. Add: Inst. of African Studies, Univ. of Ife, Ife, Nigeria.

BEISNER, Robert L. American, b. 1936. History. Prof. of History, since 1971, and Chmn. of Dept., since 1981, American Univ., Washington, D.C. (Asst. Prof., 1965–67; Assoc. Prof., 1967–71). Instr. in the Social Science, Univ. of Chicago, 1962–63; Instr. of History, Colgate Univ., Hamilton, N.Y. 1963–65. *Publs:* Twelve Against Empire: The Anti-Imperialists, 1898-1900, 1968, 1985; From the Old Diplomacy to the New, 1865-1900, 1975, 1986; (co-ed.) Arms at Rest: Peacemaking and Peacekeeping in American History, 1987. Add: Dept. of History, 4400 Massachusetts Ave., N.W., Washington, D.C. 20016, U.S.A.

BEISSEL, Henry (Eric). Canadian, b. 1929. Poetry, Plays/Screenplays, Travel/Exploration/Adventure, Translations. Prof. of English, Concordia Univ., Montreal, since 1976 (Asst. Prof., 1966–68; Assoc. Prof., 1968–76). Freelance writer and film-maker, CBC, 1954–58; Lectr., Univ. of Munich, 1960–62, Univ. of Alberta, Edmonton, 1962–64, and Univ. of the West Indies, Trinidad, 1964–66. *Publs:* Introduction to Spain, 1955; Witness the Heart, 1963; The Curve (play), 1963; New Wings for Icarus: A Poem in Four Parts, 1966; (trans.) The Price of Morning: Selected Poems, by Walter Bauer, 1969; The World is a Rainbow, 1969; Mister Skinflint: A Marionette Play, 1969; Face on the Dark: Poems, 1970; A Trumpet for Nap, 1973; Quays of Sadness, 1973; Inook and the Sun (play), 1973; The Salt I Taste, 1975; (trans.) A Different Sun, 1976; (trans.) Three Plays by Tankred Dorst, 1976; For Crying Out Loud (play), 1977; (ed.) Cues and Entrances (plays), 1977; Goya (play), 1978; Under Coyote's Eye (play), 1980; Improvisations for Mr. X (play), 1980; Cantos North (epic poem), 1980; (adaptation) The Emigrants (play), 1981; Season of Blood (poetry), 1984; Poems New and Selected, 1987; Ammonite (poetry), 1987. Add: P.O. Box 339, Alexandria, Ont. KOC 1AO, Canada.

BEJA, Morris. American, b. 1935. Film, Literature. Prof. and Chmn. of English, Ohio State Univ. (joined faculty as Instr., 1961). *Publs:* (ed.) Virginia Woolf's To The Lighthouse: A Selection of Critical Essays, 1970; Epiphany in the Modern Novel, 1971; (ed.) Psychological Fiction, 1971; (ed.) James Joyce's Dubliners and A Portrait of the Artist as a Young Man: Selection of Critical Essays, 1973; Film and Literature, 1979; (ed. with S.E. Gontarski and Pierre Astier) Samuel Beckett: Humanistic Perspectives, 1982; Critical Essays on Virginia Woolf, 1985; (co-ed.) James Joyce: The Centennial Symposium, 1987; (co-ed.) Coping with Joyce, 1989. Add: Dept. of English, Ohio State Univ., 164 West 17th Ave., Columbus, Ohio 43210, U.S.A.

BELFRAGE, Cedric. British, b. 1904. Historical/Romance/Gothic, History, Travel/Exploration/Adventure, Translations. Consulting Ed., Third World, Mexico City, since 1979. Film and Theatre Critic and Traveling Corresp., Daily Express and Sunday Express, London, 1930–36; Ed., National Guardian, NYC, 1948–55. *Publs:* Away From It All, 1937; Promised Land, 1938; Let My People Go, 1939 (reissued as South of God, 1941, and Faith to Free the People, 1944); They All Hold Swords, 1941; Abide With Me, 1948; Seeds of Destruction, 1954; The Frightened Giant, 1957; My Master Columbus, 1961; Man at the Door with the Gun, 1963; (trans.) Guatemala, Occupied Country, 1969; (trans.) We the Puerto Rican People, 1971; (trans.) Open Veins of Latin America, 1973; The American Inquisition, 1973; Something to Guard, 1978; (trans.) Memory of Fire, 1985. Add: Apdo 630, Cuernavaca, Mor., Mexico.

BELITT, Ben. American, b. 1911. Poetry, Translations. Prof., Dept. of Literature and Languages, Bennington Coll., Vt., since 1938. Asst. Literary Ed., The Nation, 1936–37. *Publs:* The Five-Fold Mesh, 1938; (ed. and trans.) Four Poems by Rimbaud: The Problem of Translation, 1947; Wilderness Stair, 1955; (ed. and trans.) Poet in New York: Lorca, 1955; (ed. and trans.) Pablo Neruda: Selected Poems, 1961; (ed. and trans.) Machado: Juan de Mairena, 1963; The Enemy Joy, 1964; (ed. and trans.) Selected Poems: Rafael Alberti, 1965; (trans.) Neruda: Poems from Canto General, 1968; (ed. and trans.) Neruda: A New Decade, 1969; Nowhere But Light, 1970; (ed. and trans.) Neruda: Splendor and Death of Joaquin Murieta, 1972; (trans.) Rafael Alberti: A La Pintura, 1972; (ed. and trans.) Pablo Neruda: New Poems, 1972; (ed. and trans.) Pablo Neruda: Five Decades, 1974; Adam's Dream: A Preface to Translation, 1978; The Double Witness: Poems 1970–1976, 1978; (ed. and trans.) Pablo Neruda: Skystones, 1981; Possessions: New and Selected Poems, 1985; (ed. and trans.) Late and Posthumous Poems by Pablo Neruda, 1988. Add: Bennington Coll., Bennington, Vt. 05201, U.S.A.

BELKNAP, Robert L. American, b. 1929. Education, Literature. Prof. of Russian, Columbia Univ., NYC, since 1970 (joined faculty as Instr., 1957). *Publs:* The Structure of The Brothers Karamazov, 1966; (with Richard Kuhns) Tradition and Innovation, General Education and the Reintegration of the University. Add: 718 Hamilton Hall, Columbia Univ., New York, N.Y. 10027, U.S.A.

BELL, Carolyn. *See* **RIGONI,** Orlando.

BELL, Catherine. *See* WEIR, Rosemary.

BELL, Charles G(reenleaf). American, b. 1916. History, Novels/Short stories, Philosophy, Poetry, Science. Tutor, St. John's Coll., Santa Fe, N.M., since 1967. Instr. in English, Blackburn Coll., Carlinville, Ill., 1929–40; Instr. and Asst. Prof. of English, then of Physics, Iowa State Coll., Ames, 1940–45; Research Asst. Electronics, then Asst. Prof. of English, Princeton Univ., N.J., 1945–49; Asst. Prof. of Humanities, Univ. of Chicago, 1949–56; Guest Prof. and Dir. of Honors Prog., Univ. of Puerto Rico, Mayaguez, 1955–56; Tutor, St. John's Coll., Annapolis, Md., 1956–67; Fulbright Prof. in art and philosophy, Technische Hochschule, Munich, 1958–59. *Publs:* Songs for a New America, 1953, rev. ed. 1966; Delta Return, 1956, rev. ed. 1969; The Married Land (novel), 1962; The Half Gods (novel), 1968; Symbolic History (39 slide–tape studies now available on video cassettes), 1975, 1988; Five Chambered Heart, 1985. Add: 1260 Canyon Rd., Santa Fe, N.M. 87501, U.S.A.

BELL, Daniel. American, b. 1919. Politics/Government, Sociology. Prof. of Sociology, Harvard Univ., Cambridge, Mass., since 1969. Member, President's Commn. on Technical Automation and Economic Progress. Staff Writer, 1939–41, and Managing Ed., 1941–44, The New Leader; Managing Ed., Common Sense, 1945; Instr., then Asst. Prof. of Social Sciences, Univ. of Chicago, 1945–58; Lectr. in Sociology, 1952–58, and Prof. of Sociology, 1958–59, Columbia Univ., NYC. *Publs:* History of Marxian Socialism in the United States, 1952; The New American Right, 1955; The End of Ideology, 1960; The Radical Right, 1963; The Reforming of General Education, 1966; Towards the Year 2000, 1968; Confrontation, 1969; Capitalism Today, 1971; The Coming of Post-Industrial Society, 1973; The Cultural Contradiction of Capitalism, 1976; The Winding Passage, 1980; (ed. with Irving Kristol) The Crisis in Economic Theory, 1981; The Social Sciences Since the Second World War, 1981; (with Lester Thurow) The Deficits: How Big? How Long: *How Dangerous?*, 1985. Add: 65 Francis Ave., Cambridge, Mass. 02138, U.S.A.

BELL, James Edward. American, b. 1941. Psychology. Prof. of Psychology, Howard Community Coll., Columbia, Md., since 1971. Instr., Univ. of Minnesota, Minneapolis, 1965–66; Asst. Prof. of Psychology, Hanover Coll., Ind., 1966–68; Asst. Prof. of Psychology, Elmira, Coll., N.Y., 1968–71. *Publs:* A Guide to Library Research in Psychology, 1971; (ed.) Ideas and Issues in Psychology, 6th ed. 1987. Add: Howard Community Coll., Columbia, Md. 21044, U.S.A.

BELL, James Kenton. American, b. 1937. Speech/Rhetoric, Writing/Journalism. Prof. of English, Coll. of San Mateo, Calif., since 1963. *Publs:* (ed. with A.A. Cohn) Toward the New America, 1970; (with A.A. Cohn) Rhetoric in a Modern Mode, 1968, 3rd ed. 1976; Rhetoric 2, 1972; Bell and Cohn's Handbook of Grammar, Style, and Usage, 1972, 3rd ed. 1981; Rhetoric 3, 1976. Add: 264 Highland Ave., San Carlos, Calif. 94070, U.S.A.

BELL, Madison Smartt. American, b. 1957. Novels/Short stories. Freelance writer. Lectr. in Fiction, Goucher Coll., Baltimore, 1984–86. *Publs:* The Washington Square Ensemble, 1983; Waiting for the End of the World (novel), 1985; Straight Cut (novel), 1986; Zero DB (short stories), 1987; The Year of Silence (novel), 1987. Add: 3005 Cresmont Ave., Baltimore, Md. 21211, U.S.A.

BELL, Marvin (Hartley). American, b. 1937. Poetry, Literature. Flannery O'Connor Prof. of Letters, Univ. of Iowa, Iowa City, since 1986 (Visiting Lectr., 1965; Asst. Prof., 1966–69, Assoc. Prof., 1970–74; Prof., 1975–85). Ed., Statements mag., 1959–64; Poetry Ed., North American Review, Mount Vernon, Iowa, 1964–69, and Iowa Review, 1969–71. *Publs:* (ed.) Iowa Workshop Poets 1963, 1963; Things We Dreamt We Died For, 1966; Poems for Nathan and Saul, 1966; A Probable Volume of Dreams: Poems, 1969; The Escape into You: A Sequence, 1971; Woo Havoc, 1971; Residue of Song, 1974; Stars Which See, Stars Which do Not See, 1977; These Green-Going-to-Yellow, 1981; William Stafford and Marvin Bell: Segues: A Correspondence in Poetry, 1983; Old Snow Just Melting: Essays and Interviews, 1983; Drawn by Stones, by Earth, by Things that Have Been in the Fire, 1984; New and Selected Poems, 1987; William Stafford and Marvin Bell: Annie-Over, 1988. Add: Writers Workshop, Univ. of Iowa, Iowa City, Iowa 52242, U.S.A.

BELL, Quentin (Claudian Stephen). British, b. 1910. Novels, Art, Biography. Emeritus Prof. of History and Theory of Art, Univ. of Sussex, Brighton. Slade Prof. of Fine Art, Oxford Univ., 1964–65; Ferens Prof. of Fine Art, Univ. of Hull, Yorks., 1965–66. *Publs:* On Human Finery, 1947, rev. ed. 1976; (with H. Gersheim) Those Impossible English, 1951;

Roger Montane, 1961; The Schools of Design, 1963; Ruskin, 1963; Victorian Artists, 1967; Bloomsbury, 1968; Virginia Woolf (2 vols.), 1972 (James Tait Black Memorial Prize); A New and Noble School, 1982; Techniques of Terracotta, 1983; The Brandon Papers (novel), 1985. Add: 81 Heighton St., Firle, Sussex BN8 6NZ, England.

BELL, Raymond M(artin). American, b. 1907. Communications Media, Genealogy/Heraldry, History, Physics. Emeritus Prof. of Physics, Washington and Jefferson Coll., Washington, Pa., since 1975 (Instr., 1937–39; Asst. Prof., 1939–45; Assoc. Prof., 1945–46; Prof., 1946–75). *Publs:* Your Future in Physics, 1967; Your Future in Astronomy, 1970; The Ancestry of Richard Milhous Nixon, 1970; (with O.H. Blackwood and W.C. Kelly) General Physics, 4th ed. 1973; Television in the Thirties, 1974; The Baskin Family, 1975; Seventy Years on the Planet Earth, 1977; Early Methodist Circuits on the Upper Ohio, 1978; Some Pennsylvania Families, 1978; Radio Reception in the Twenties, 1979; Some Pennsylvania Families II, 1979; The Dutch Fork Settlement of Donegal Township, Washington County, Pa., 1980; The Ancestry of Samuel Clemens, Grandfather of Mark Twain, 1980; The Seiberts of Saarland, Pennsylvania and West Virginia, 1982; The Vollenweider-Fullenwider Family in America, 1983; The Wolf Family, 1984; The Williamson Family, 1986; A Study of the Clayton Family, 1988. Add: 413 Burton Ave., Washington, Pa. 15301, U.S.A.

BELL, Robert Charles. Canadian, b. 1917. Crafts, Medicine/Health, Recreation/Leisure/Hobbies. Consultant Plastic Surgeon, Newcastle Health Authority, Newcastle upon Tyne, 1952–82. *Publs:* Board and Table Games from Many Civilisations (2 vols.), 1960, 1970; Commercial Coins, 1963; Copper Commercial Coins, 1964; Tradesman's Tickets and Private Tokens, 1966; Specious Tokens, 1968; Tyneside Pottery, 1971; (with M.R.Y. Gill) Potteries of Tyneside, 1973; The Use of Skin Grafts, 1973; Discovering Old Board Games (Backgammon, Mah-Jong, Chess, Dice and Dominoes), 5 vols., 1973–80; Unofficial Farthings 1820–1870, 1975; The Building Medalets of Kempson and Skidmore 1796–1797, 1978; The Board Game Book, 1979; Board and Table Game Antiques, 1981; Political and Commemorative Pieces Simulating Tradesmen's Tokens 1770–1802, 1987; (with M. Cornelius) Board Games Round the World, 1988; Games to Play, 1988. Add: 20 Linden Rd., Gosforth, Newcastle upon Tyne NE3 4EY, England.

BELL, Robert Eugene. American, b. 1914. Archaeology/Antiquities. Emeritus Research Prof. of Anthropology since 1980, Univ. of Oklahoma, Norman (Asst. Prof., 1947–51; Assoc. Prof., 1951–55; Prof., 1955–68; Research Prof., 1968–80; and Curator of Anthropology, Stovall Museum, 1955–80). *Publs:* Archaeological Investigations at the Site of El Inga, Ecuador, 1965; Oklahoma Archaeology: An Annotated Bibliography, 1969, 1978; The Harlan Site, Ck-6: A Prehistoric Mound Center in Cherokee County, Eastern Oklahoma, 1972; Oklahoma Indian Artifacts, 1980; (ed.) Prehistory of Oklahoma, 1984. Add: 1120 Berry Circle, Norman, Okla. 73072, U.S.A.

BELL, Robin. British, b. 1945. Poetry, Radio plays. Secty., Poetry Assn. of Scotland, since 1983. Worked as an editor, 1973–82. *Publs:* (with Alastair Robertson and Stephen Scobie) The Invisible Mirror (poetry), 1965; Culdee, Culdee (poetry), 1966; (ed.) Collected Poems of James Graham, Marquis of Montrose, 1970; (ed.) Guide book series to Scottish Ancient Monuments, 1978; Sawing Logs (poetry), 1980; Strathinver: A Portrait Album 1943–1953 (poetry), 1980; Strathinver (radio verse play), 1986; The Other Thief (radio verse play), 1986; Attic Archives (TV documentary), 1987; Melville Bay (radio verse play), 1987; Radio Poems, 1989; (ed.) Best of Scottish Poetry: An Anthology of Living Scottish Poets, 1989. Add: 38 Dovecot Rd., Edinburgh EH12 7LE, Scotland.

BELL, Roger. Australian, b. 1947. International relations/Current affairs, Politics/Government, Sociology. Assoc. Prof. of History, Univ. of New South Wales, Sydney, since 1985 (Lectr., 1975–80; Sr. Lectr., 1980–85). *Publs:* Unequal Allies: Australian–American Relations and the Pacific War, 1977; (ed. with Ian Bickerton) American Studies: New Essays from Australia and New Zealand, 1981; Last among Equals: Hawaiian Statehood and American Politics, 1984; Multicultural Societies: A Comparative Reader, 1987. Add: 7 Gardyne St., Bronte, Sydney, N.S.W. 2024, Australia.

BELL, Thornton. *See* FANTHORPE, R. Lionel.

BELLAIRS, Angus d'Albini. British, b. 1918. Natural history, Zoology. Prof. of Vertebrate Morphology, St. Mary's Hosp. Medical Sch., London, 1970–82, now Emeritus (Reader in Anatomy and Embryology, 1953–70). Hon. Consulting Herpetologist, Zoological Soc. of London, since 1957. Lectr. in Anatomy and Zoology, London Hosp. Medical Coll., 1946–51, and Cambridge Univ., 1951–53. *Publs:* Reptiles, 1957, 4th ed. (with J. Attridge), 1975; (with R. Carrington) The World of Reptiles, 1966; The Life of Reptiles (2 vols.), 1969; (ed. with C. Gans and T.S. Parsons) Biology of the Reptilia, vol. I, 1969; The Isle of Sea Lizards, 1989. Add: 7 Champion Grove, London SE5, England.

BELLAIRS, John. American, b. 1938. Children's fiction, Humor/Satire. *Publs:* St. Fidgeta and Other Parodies, 1966; The Pedant and the Shuffly, 1968; The Face in the Frost, 1969; The House with a Clock in Its Walls, 1973; The Figure in the Shadows, 1975; The Letter, the Witch, and the Ring, 1976; The Treasure of Alpheus Winterborn, 1978; The Curse of the Blue Figurine, 1983; The Mummy, the Will, and the Crypt, 1983; The Dark Secret of Weatherend, 1984; The Spell of the Sorcerer's Skull, 1984; The Revenge of the Wizard's Ghost, 1985; The Eyes of the Killer Robot, 1986; The Lamp from the Warlock's Tomb, 1987; The Trolley To Yesterday, 1989. Add: 28 Hamilton Ave., Haverhill, Mass. 01830, U.S.A.

BELLAMY, David James. British, b. 1933. Botany, Natural History. TV and Radio writer and presenter: series include Life in Our Sea, 1970; Bellamy on Botany, 1973; Bellamy's Britain, 1975; Bellamy's Europe, 1977; Botanic Man, 1978; Up a Gum Tree, 1980; Backyard Safari, 1981; The Great Seasons, 1982; Bellamy's New World, 1983. Founding Dir., Conservation Foundn.; Pres., WATCH, 1982–83; Pres., Youth Hostels Assn., 1983. *Publs:* books connected with TV series; also: Peatlands, 1974; Life Giving Sea., 1977; Half of Paradise, 1979; The Great Seasons, 1981; Discovering the Countryside with David Bellamy, 4 vols., 1982–83; The Mouse Book, 1983; The Queen's Hidden Garden, 1984; Turning the Tide, 1986; The Vanishing Bogs of Ireland, 1986. Add: Mill House, Bedburn, Bishop Auckland, Co. Durham, England.

BELLAN, Ruben Carl. Canadian, b. 1918. Economics, Urban studies. Prof. of Economics, St. Johns Coll., Univ. of Manitoba, Winnipeg. *Publs:* Principles of Economics and the Canadian Economy, 1960, 7th ed. 1985; The Evolving City, 1975; Winnipeg: First Century, 1978; (co-ed.) The Canadian Economy, 1981; The Unnecessary Evil, 1986. Add: 628 Niagara St., Winnipeg, Man. R3N 0W1, Canada.

BELLE, Pamela. British, b. 1952. Historical/Romance. Library Asst., Hemel Hempstead, Herts., 1976–77; primary sch. teacher, Hemel Hempstead, Tring and Berkhampstead, Herts., 1977–78, and Northchurch St. Mary's Sch., Berkhampstead, 1978–85. *Publs:* The Moon in the Water, 1983; The Chains of Fate, 1984; Alathea, 1985; The Lodestar, 1987; Wintercombe, 1988. Add: 184 Melksham Lane, Broughton Gifford, Melksham, Wilts. SN12 8LN, England.

BELLMAN, Samuel I. American, b. 1926. Education, Literature. Prof. of English, California State Polytechnic Univ., Pomona (joined faculty, 1959). Taught at Fresno State Coll., California, 1955–57, California State Polytechnic Coll., San Luis Obispo, 1957–59; and Portsmouth Polytechnic, Hampshire, England, 1975–76. *Publs:* (ed.) The College Experience (essays), 1962; (ed.) Survey and Forecast (essays), 1966; Marjorie Kinnan Rawlings, 1974; Constance Mayfield Rourke, 1981. Add: Dept. of English, California State Polytechnic Univ., Pomona, Calif., 91768, U.S.A.

BELLOW, Saul. American, b. 1915. Novels/Short stories, Plays/Screenplays, Literature. Prof., Cttee. on Social Thought, Univ. of Chicago, since 1962. Teacher, Pestalozzi-Froebel Teachers Coll., Chicago, 1938–42; Member, Editorial Dept., Encyclopedia Britannica, Chicago, 1943–46; Instr., 1946, Asst. Prof. of English, 1948–49, and Assoc. Prof., 1954–59, Univ. of Minnesota, Minneapolis; Visiting Lectr., New York Univ., NYC, 1950–52; Creative Writing Fellow, Princeton Univ., N.J., 1952–53; Member of English faculty, Bard Coll., Annandale-on-Hudson, N.Y., 1953–54; Founding Ed., Nobel Savage mag., Chicago, 1960–62. *Publs:* Dangling Man, 1944; The Victim, 1945; The Adventures of Augie March, 1953; Seize the Day, with Three Short Stories and a One-Act Play, 1956; Henderson the Rain King, 1959; (with C. Zervos) Dessins, 1960; Recent American Fiction; A Lecture, 1963; (ed.) Great Jewish Short Stories, 1963; The Last Analysis (play), 1964; Herzog, 1964; Like You're Nobody: The Letters of Louis Gallo to Saul Bellow, 1961–62, plus Oedipus Schmoedipus, the Story that Started It All, 1966; Under the Weather (in U.K. as The Bellow Plays), 1966; Mosby's Memoirs and Other Stories, 1968; Mr. Sammler's Planet, 1970; The Future of the Moon, 1970; The Portable Saul Bellow, 1974; Technology and the Frontiers of Knowledge, 1974; Humboldt's Gift, 1975; To Jerusalem and Back, 1976; The Dean's December, 1982; Him with His Foot in His Mouth (short stories), 1984; More Die of Heartbreak, 1987. Add: Cttee. on Social

Thought, Univ. of Chicago, 1126 East 59th St., Chicago, Ill. 60637, U.S.A.

BELOFF, Lord (formerly Sir Max). British, b. 1913. History, International relations/Current affairs, Politics/Government. Emeritus Prof., Oxford Univ. (Gladstone Prof. of Govt. and Public Admin., 1957–74); Emeritus Fellow, All Souls Coll., Oxford (Fellow, St. Anthony's Coll., 1975–83). Nuffield Reader in the Comparative Study of Instns., 1946–56, Fellow of Nuffield Coll., 1947–57, Fellow of All Souls Coll., 1957–74, Oxford Univ.; Principal, University Coll. at Buckingham, 1974–79. *Publs:* Public Order and Popular Disturbances 1660-1714, 1938; The Foreign Policy of Soviet Russia, vol. I, 1947, vol. II, 1949; Thomas Jefferson and American Democracy, 1948; (ed.) The Federalist, 1948, 1987; (ed.) Mankind and His Story, 1948; (ed.) The Debate on the American Revolution, 1949; Soviet Policy and the Far East, 1953; The Age of Absolutism 1660-1815, 1954; Foreign Policy and the Democratic Process, 1953; Europe and the Europeans, 1957; The Great Powers, 1959; The American Federal Government, 1959, 1969; (ed.) On the Track of Tyranny, 1960; (ed. with F. Schnabel, P. Renouvin and F. Valsecchi) L'Europe du XIXe et XX siècle, 1961–68; New Dimensions in Foreign Policy, 1961; The United States and the Unity of Europe, 1963; The Balance of Power, 1968; The Future of British Foreign Policy, 1969; Imperial Sunset, vol. I, 1969, 1987, vol. II, 1989; The Intellectual in Politics and Other Essays, 1970; (with Gillian Peele) The Government of the United Kingdom, 1980, 1985; Wars and Welfare 1914–1945, 1984. Add: Flat 9, 22 Lewes Cres., Brighton, Sussex, England.

BELOFF, Nora. British, b. 1919. Politics/Government, Social commentary/phenomena. Paris, Washington, Moscow, etc. corresp., Observer, London, 1948–78. Europe, and roving reporter. *Publs:* The General Says No, 1963; Transit of Britain, 1973; Freedom under Foot: The Battle over the Closed Shop in British Journalism, 1976; No Travel like Russian Travel (in U.S. as Inside the Soviet Empire), 1979; Tito's Flawed Legacy: Yugoslavia and the West, 1985. Add: 11 Belsize Rd., London NW6 4RX, England.

BELOOF, Robert Lawrence. American, b. 1923. Poetry, Literature. Prof of Rhetoric, Univ. of California, Berkeley. *Publs:* The One-Eyed Gunner (poems), 1956; The Performing Voice in Literature, 1966; (co-author) The Oral Study of Literature, 1967; (co-author) The Craft of Writing, 1969; Good Poems, 1973; The Children of Venus and Mars, 1974. Add: Dept. of Rhetoric, Univ. of California, Berkeley, Calif. 94720, U.S.A.

BEMMY, Karen (Amy). American, b. 1955. Novels/Short stories, Children's fiction. Intl. correspondent and asst. dir. of an intl. studies organization, Detroit, since 1982. Peace Corps Volunteer in West Africa, 1976–78; with the Afro-American Cultural Center, Ann Arbor, MI, 1979–82. *Publs:* Too Much of Anything Is Bad, 1981; Escape from Abidjan, 1982; Midnight Riders, 1984; When the Rains Come, 1985; Flames and Shadows: African Folklore, 1987. Add: 8330 Lochdale, Dearborn Heights, MI 48127, U.S.A.

BENARDE, Melvin Albert. American, b. 1924. Environmental science/Ecology, Medicine/Health, Travel/Exploration/Adventure. Prof. and Assoc. Dir., Asbestos Abatememt Center, Coll. of Engineering, Temple Univ., Philadelphia, since 1987. Member of faculty, Rutgers Univ., New Brunswick, N.J., 1962–67; Prof. and Chmn., Dept. of Community Medicine and Environmental Health, Hahnemann Medical Coll. and Hosp., Philadelphia, 1967–83. Assoc. Dir., Environmental Studies Inst., Drexel Univ., Philadelphia, 1983–87. *Publs:* Race Against Famine, 1968; (ed. and contrib.) Disinfection, 1970; Our Precious Habitat, 1970, rev. ed. 1989; The Chemicals We Eat, 1973, rev. ed. 1975; Beach Holidays: Portugal to Israel, 1974; The Food Additives Dictionary, 1981; (ed. and contrib.) Asbestos: The Hazardous Fiber, 1989. Add: 45 Cuyler Rd., Princeton, N.J. 08540, U.S.A.

BENASUTTI, Marion. American, b. 1908. Novels/Short stories. Women's Ed., Italian-American Herald, Philadelphia, Pa., 1960–62; Ed., Pen Woman, National League of Pen Women, Washington, D.C., 1964–68; Former columnist, Catholic Star Herald. *Publs:* No Steadyjob for Papa, 1966. Add: Mt. Vernon—6A3, 885 N. Easton Rd., Glenside, Pa. 19038, U.S.A.

BENAUD, Richie. Australian, b. 1930. Cricket. Sports consultant, and TV commentator, BBC, since 1960, and for Channel 9, since 1977. *Publs:* Way of Cricket, 1960; Tale of Two Tests, 1962; Spin Me A Spinner, 1963; The New Champions, 1965; Willow Patterns, 1972; Young Cricketer, 1976; Benaud on Reflection, 1984; Wide World of Sports: Cricket

Yearbook, 1985, 1986, 1987. Add: 19/178 Beach St., Coogee, N.S.W. 2034, Australia.

BENCE-JONES, Mark. Irish, b. 1930. Novels/Short stories, Architecture, History, Travel/Exploration/Adventure. Consultant Ed., Burke's Irish Family Records, 1973–76. *Publs:* All a Nonsense: Paradise Escaped; Nothing in the City; The Remarkable Irish; Palaces of the Raj; Clive of India; The Cavaliers; Burke's Guide to Irish Country Houses; (with Hugh Montgomery-Massingberd) The British Aristocracy; The Viceroys of India, 1982; Ancestral Houses, 1984; Twilight of the Ascendancy, 1987; Guide to Irish Country Houses, 1989. Add: Glenville Park, Glenville, Co. Cork, Ireland.

BENCHLEY, Peter (Bradford). American, b. 1940. Novels/Short stories, Children's fiction, Plays/Screenplays. Reporter, Washington Post, 1963; Assoc. Ed., Newsweek, NYC, 1964–67; Staff Asst. to the President, White House, Washington, D.C., 1967–69; freelance television news corresp., 1969–72. *Publs:* Time and A Ticket, 1964; Jonathan Visits the White House (children's novel), 1964; Jaws, 1974, screenplay (with Carl Gottlieb) 1975; The Deep, 1976, screenplay (with Tracy Keenan Wynn), 1977; The Island, 1979, screenplay, 1980; The Girl of the Sea of Cortez, 1982; Q Clearance (novel), 1986. Add: c/o Lyn Nesbit, Intnl. Creative Mgmt., 40 W. 57th St., New York, N.Y. 10019, U.S.A.

BENDER, Arnold. British, b. 1918. Health. Prof. of Nutrition and Dietetics, 1971–78, and Head of Dept. of Food Science and Nutrition, 1978–83, Queen Elizabeth Coll., Univ. of London. Vice Pres., Intnl. Union of Food Science & Technology, 1983–87; Chmn. of the Council, Royal Soc. of Health, 1987–88; Pres., Inst. of Food Science and Technology, 1988–90. *Publs:* Dictionary of Nutrition and Food Technology, 1960; Nutrition and Dietetic Foods, 1967; Value of Food, 1970; Facts of Food, 1970; Food Processing and Nutrition, 1978; Pocket Guide to Calories and Nutrition, 1979; (with D.A. Bender) Nutrition for Medical Students, 1982; Health or Hoax, 1985; (with D.A. Bender) Food Tables, 1986. Add: 2 Willow Vale, Fetcham, Leatherhead, Surrey KT22 9TE, England.

BENDER, Coleman. American, b. 1921. Language/Linguistics, Speech/Rhetoric. Prof. of Speech, Emerson Coll., Boston, Mass., since 1951. Lectr., New England Law Enforcement Mgmt. Inst. Instr. in Speech, Pennsylvania State Univ., 1946–48; Instr. in Speech, Univ. of Illinois, Urbana, 1948–50. *Publs:* (with B.P. McCabe) Speaking is a Practical Matter, 1968; Guidebook to Speech Communication, 1969; (with J. Zorn) Problems and Issues in Relevance, 1970; (with J. Zorn) Words in Context, 1970; (with J.C. Zacharis) Speech Communication, 1976. Add: 81 Bromfield St., Watertown, Mass. 02172, U.S.A.

BENDER, Thomas. American, b. 1944. History, Urban topics. Prof. of History since 1977, and Univ. Prof. of Humanities since 1982, New York Univ. (Asst. Prof., 1974–76; Assoc. Prof. of History, 1976–77; Samuel Rudin Prof. of Humanities, 1977–82). Asst. Prof. of History and Urban Studies, Univ. of Wisconsin at Green Bay, 1971–74. Ed., Intellectual History Group Newsletter, 1978–85. *Publs:* Toward Urban Vision, 1975; Community and Social Change in America, 1978; (with Edwin Rozwenc) The Making of American Society, 1978; (ed.) Democracy in America, 1981; New York Intellect: A History of Intellectual Life in New York City from 1750 to the Beginnings of Our Own Time, 1987. Add: 54 Washington Mews, New York, N.Y. 10003, U.S.A.

BENDER, Todd, K. American, b. 1936. Literature. Prof. of English, Univ, of Winsconsin, Madison, since 1973 (Assoc. Prof., 1966–73). Instr. Stanford Univ., Calif., 1961–62, and Dartmouth Coll., Hanover, N.H., 1962–63; Asst. Prof. Univ. of Virginia, Charlottesville, 1963–66. *Publs:* Gerard Manley Hopkins: The Classical Background and Critical Reception of His Work, 1966; (co-ed.) A Concordance to Hopkins, 1970; (co-ed.) Concordances to Complete Works of Conrad, 1973–; (co-ed.) Backgrounds to Modernism, 1974; Modernism in Literature, 1977. Add: Dept. of Univ. of Wisconsin, Madison, Wisc. 53706, U.S.A.

BENDINER, Robert. American, b. 1909. Environmental science/Ecology, Politics/Government, Travel/Exploration/Adventure, Humor/Satire. Managing Ed., The Nation, NYC 1938–44; Contrib. Ed., The Reporter, NYC, 1956–60; American Correspondent, New Statesman, London, 1959–61; Member, Ed. Bd., New York Times, 1968–77. *Publs:* The Riddle of the State Department, 1942; White House Fever, 1960; Obstacle Course on Capitol Hill, 1964; Just Around the Corner, 1967; The Politics of Schools, 1969; (co-ed.) The Strenuous Decade, 1970; The Fall of the Wild, the Rise of the Zoo, 1981. Add: 45 Central Parkway, Huntington, N.Y. 11743, U.S.A.

BENDIX, Reinhard. American (born German), b. 1916. Sociology. Research Sociologist, Inst. of Industrial Relations, since 1948, and Prof. of Political Science and Lectr. in Sociology, since 1972, Univ. of California, Berkeley (Asst. Prof., 1947–51; Assoc. Prof. of Sociology, 1951–56; Prof. of Sociology, 1956–71; Chmn., Dept. of Sociology, 1958–61). Vice-Pres., 1963–64, and Pres., 1969–70, American Sociological Assn.; Vice-Pres., Intnl. Sociological Assn., 1966–70; Fellow, Inst. for Advanced Study, Princeton, N.J., 1971–72, Woodrow Wilson Intnl. Center of Scholars, Washington, D.C., 1975–76, and Wissenschaftskolleg, Berlin, 1987–88. *Publs:* Higher Civil Servants in American Society, 1949, 1974; Social Science and the Distrust of Reason, 1951; (ed. with S.M. Lipset) Class, Status and Power, 1953; 1966; Work and Authority in Industry, 1956, 1974; (with S.M. Lipset) Social Mobility in Industrial Society, 1959; Max Weber: An Intellectual Portrait, 1960, 1977; Nation Building and Citizenship: Studies in Our Changing Social Order, 1964, 1977; (co-ed.) State and Society: A Reader in Comparative Political Sociology, 1968; Embattled Reason: Essays in Social Knowledge, 1970; (with G. Roth) Scholarship and Partisanship: Essays on Max Weber, 1971; Kings or People: Power and the Mandate to Rule, 1978; Force, Fate and Freedom, 1984; From Berlin to Berkeley, 1986; Embattled Reason, 2nd. 1987–88. Add: Dept. of Political Science, Univ. of California, Berkeley, Calif. 94720, U.S.A.

BENDIXSON, Terence. British, b. 1934. Transportation, Urban Affairs. Freelance writer, broadcaster, and consultant. Planning Corresp., The Guardian, London, 1963–69; Member, Environment Bureau of The Observer, London, 1970–71. *Publs:* Instead of Cars, 1974; The Peterborough Effect, 1988. Add: 9A Gunter Grove, London SW10 0UN, England.

BENEDICT, Rex (Arthur). American, b. 1920. Novels/Short stories, Children's fiction, Poetry, Translations. *Publs:* (trans.) The Prayers of Man, 1961; O...Brother Juniper, 1963; (trans.) Tales from the Decameron, 1963; (trans.) Those Cursed Tuscans, 1964; Fantasano, 1967; Moonwash, 1969; In the Green Grass Time, 1969; Nights in the Gardens of Glebe, 1970; Epitaph for a Lady, 1970; Haloes for Heroes, 1971; Good Luck Arizona Man, 1972; Goodbye to the Purple Sage, 1973; Last Stand at Good Bye Gulch, 1974; The Ballad of Cactus Jack, 1975; Run For Your Sweet Life, 1986. Add: Box 176, Jet, Okla. 73749, U.S.A.

BENEDICTUS, David (Henry). British, b. 1938. Novels/Short stories, Plays/Screenplays, Antiques, Biography. Book reviewer, and theatre dir. Drama Dir., 1964–65, and Story Ed., 1967, BBC Television, London; Asst. Dir., Royal Shakespeare Co., London, 1970–71; Visiting Fellow, Churchill Coll., Cambridge, 1981–82; Commissioning Ed., Channel 4 Drama Series, 1984–86. *Publs:* The Fourth of June, 1963; You're a Big Boy Now, 1964; This Animal is Mischievous, 1966; Hump: or, Bone by Bone, Alive, 1968; Angels (Over Your Grave) and Geese (Over Mine) (play), 1967; Dromedary (play), 1969; The Guru and the Golf Club, 1970; A World of Windows, 1972; What a Way to Run a Revolution! (play), 1972; The Rabbi's Wife, 1976; Junk, 1976; Betjemania, 1977; A Twentieth Century Man, 1978; The Antique Collector's Guide, 1980; Lloyd George, 1981; Whose Life Is It Anyway?, 1982; The Golden Key (play), 1982; Who the Prince Consort?, 1982; Floating Down to Camelot, 1985; The Streets of London, 1986; The Absolutely Essential London Guide, 1986. Add: 19 Oxford Rd., Teddington, Middx. TW11 0QA, England.

BENEDIKT, Michael. American, b. 1935. Poetry, Plays/Screenplays, Literary criticism/History. Contributing Ed., The American Poetry Review, since 1973. Assoc. Ed., Horizon Press, NYC, 1959–61, and Art News mag., NYC, 1963–72; New York Corresp., Art Intnl., Lugano, Switzerland, 1965–67; Instr. in Language and Literature, Bennington Coll., Vt., 1968–69; Poet-in-Residence, Sarah Lawrence Coll. Bronxville, N.Y., 1969–73; Assoc. Prof. of Arts and Humanities, Hampshire Coll., Amherst, Mass., 1973–75; Poetry Ed., Paris Review, Paris and NYC, 1973–78; Assoc. Prof. of English, Vassar Coll., Poughkeepsie, N.Y., 1976–77; Assoc. Prof. of English and Creative Writing, 1975, and Prof., 1977–79, Boston Univ., Mass. *Publs:* Serenade in Six Pieces (poetry), 1958; Changes (poetry), 1961; (ed. with G.E. Wellwarth) Modern French Theatre: The Avant-Garde, Dada, and Surrealism (in U.K. as Modern French Plays: An Anthology from Jarry to Ionesco), 1964; The Vaseline Photographer (play), 1965; 8 Poems, 1966; (ed. with G.E. Wellwarth) Postwar German Theatre: An Anthology of Plays, 1967; (ed. and trans.) Ring Around the World: The Selected Poems of Jean L'Anselme, 1967; (ed.) Theatre Experiment: New American Plays, 1967; (ed. with G.E. Wellwarth) Modern Spanish Theatre: An Anthology of Plays, 1968; The Body, 1968; The Orgy Bureau (play), 1968; Sky, 1970; (ed.) 22 Poems of Robert Desnos, 1971; Mole Notes, 1971; (ed.) The Poetry of Surrealism, 1975; Night Cries, 1976; (ed.) The Prose Poem: An International Anthology, 1976; Box (play), 1977; Benedikt: A Profile (critical anthology of author's work), 1978; The Badminton at Great Barrington; or, Gustave Mahler and the Chattanooga Choo-Choo, 1980; Benedikt: Retrospective at Library of Congress (video tape), 1986. Add: 315 W. 98th St., New York, N.Y. 10025, U.S.A.

BENFORD, Gregory (Albert). American, b. 1941. Science fiction/Fantasy. Prof. of Physics, Univ of California at Irvine, since 1973 (Asst. Prof., 1971–73). Fellow, 1967–69, and Research Physicist, 1969–72, Lawrence Radiation Lab., Livermore, Calif. *Publs:* Deeper Than the Darkness, 1970, as The Stars in Shroud, 1978; Jupiter Project, 1974; (with Gordon Eklund) If the Stars Are Gods, 1977; In the Ocean of Night, 1977; (with Gordon Eklund) Find the Changeling, 1980; Timescape, 1980; (with William Rotsler) Shiva Descending, 1980; Against Infinity, 1983; Across the Sea of Suns, 1984; Of Space-Time and the River, 1985; Artifact, 1985; Heart of the Comet, 1986; Great Sky River, 1987; Tides of Light, 1989. Add: Dept of Physics, Univ. of California, Irvine, Calif. 92717, U.S.A.

BENGTSON, Vern L. American, b. 1941. Sociology. Prof. of Sociology, since 1977, Chief, Lab. of Social Org. and Behavior, Preceptor in Sociology, since 1971, and Principal Investigator, Socio-Cultural Contexts of Aging, since 1972, Univ. of Southern California, Los Angeles (Asst. Prof., 1967–70). Member of Exec. Bd., Sociology of Education, since 1967; Member of Ed. Bd., Journal of Marriage and the Family, Los Angeles, since 1973. Fellow in Adult Development and Aging, 1963–67, and Research Coordinator of the Cross-National Study of Patterns of Aging, 1965–67, Univ. of Chicago. Member, Finance Cttee., Gerontological Soc., Washington, 1973–75. *Publs:* The Social Psychology of Aging, 1973; (ed., with Joan Robertson) Grandparenthood, 1985. Add: Univ. of Southern California, Andrus Gerontology Center, University Park, Los Angeles, Calif. 90007, U.S.A.

BENKOVITZ, Miriam J(eanette). American, b. 1911. Literature, Biography. Emeritus Prof. of English, Skidmore Coll., Saratoga Springs, N.Y. *Publs:* (ed.) Edwy and Elgiva, by Fanny Burney; A Bibliography of Ronald Firbank, 1963, 1982; Ronald Firbank: A Biography, 1969; (ed.) A Passionate Prodigality: Letters to Alan Bird from Richard Aldington, 1976; Frederick Rolfe, Baron Corvo: A Biography, 1977; (ed.) Frederick Rolfe: Letters to Harry Bainbridge, 1977; Aubrey Beardsley: An Account of His Life, 1981; (ed.) Frederick Rolfe, Baron Corvo, Writes to Wilfred Meynell, 1985. Add: 17 Ten Springs Dr., Saratoga Springs, N.Y. 12866, U.S.A.

BENN, Matthew. *See* SIEGEL, Benjamin.

BENN, Tony. (Anthony Wedgwood Benn). British, b. 1925. Politics/Government. Labour M.P. for Bristol South-East, 1950–60, 1963–83, and for Chesterfield, since 1984 (Chmn., Labour Party's Broadcasting Advisory Cttee., 1957–64; Member, Select Cttee. on Procedure, 1958; Principal Labour Spokesman on Transport Policies, 1959; Postmaster-Gen., 1964–66; Minister of Technology, 1966–70; Minister of Power, 1969–70; Chmn. of the Labour Party, 1971–72; Secty. of State for Industry, 1974–75, for Energy, 1975–79; Chmn. EEC Council of Energy Ministers, 1977). Producer, B.B.C. North American Service, 1949–50. Member, Exec. Cttee., British-American Parliamentary Group, 1953; Founder Member, Movement for Colonial Freedom, 1954; Member of the Exec., H-Bomb National Campaign, 1954; Chmn., Fabian Soc., 1964–65. *Publs:* The Privy Council as a Second Chamber, 1957; The Regeneration of Britain, 1964; The New Politics, 1970; Speeches, 1974; Arguments for Socialism, 1979; Arguments for Democracy, 1981; Sizewell Syndrome, 1984; (ed.) Writings on the Wall, 1984; Out of the Wilderness: Diaries 1963–67, 1987; Office Without Power: Diaries 1968–72, 1988; Fighting Back: Speaking Out for Socialism in the Eighties, 1988. Add: House of Commons, London SW1A 0AA, England.

BENNE, Kenneth Dean. American, b. 1908. Education. Prof. Emeritus of Human Relations, Boston Univ. (joined Faculty, 1953). *Publs:* A Conception of Authority, 1943, 1971; Education for Tragedy, 1967; From Pedagogy to Anthropogogy, 1981; (co-author) The Social Self, 1983; Society as Educator, 1987; Teach Me To Sing of Winter, 1988. Add: 4000 Cathedral Ave. N.W., Washington, D.C. 20016, U.S.A.

BENNET, Glin. British, b. 1927. Medicine/Health. Psychotherapist and Consultant Sr. Lectr. in Mental Health, Univ. of Bristol, since 1970. Surgeon, 1952–61. *Publs:* Patients and Their Doctors: The Journey Through Medical Care, 1979; Beyond Endurance: Survival at the Extremes, 1983; The Wound and the Doctor: Healing, Technology, and Power in Modern Medicine, 1987. Add: c/o A.M. Heath, 79 St. Martin's Lane, London WC2N 4AA, England.

BENNETT, Alan. British, b. 1934. Plays/Screenplays. *Publs:* (with Peter Cook, Jonathan Miller and Dudley Moore) Beyond the Fringe (revue), 1963; Forty Years On, 1969; Getting On, 1972; Habeas Corpus, 1973; The Old Country, 1977; Enjoy, 1980; Office Suite (2 plays), 1981; Objects of Affection, 1983; A Private Function, 1984; The Writer in Disguise, 1985; Prick Up Your Ears, 1987; Two Kafka Plays, 1987; Talking Heads, 1988; Single Spies, 1989. Add: c/o A.D. Peters, The Chambers, Chelsea Harbour, Lots Rd., London SW10 0XF, England.

BENNETT, Dwight. *See* NEWTON, D.B.

BENNETT, Edward M. American, b. 1927. History, International relations/Current affairs. Prof., Washington State Univ., Pullman, since 1971 (Asst. Prof., 1961–66; Assoc. Prof., 1966–71). Instr., Texas Agricultural and Mechanical Univ., College Station, 1960–61. *Publs:* (ed.) Polycentrism: Growing Dissidence in the Communist Bloc?, 1967; Recognition of Russia: An American Foreign Policy Dilemma, 1970; (co-ed.) Diplomats in Crisis: U.S.-Sino-Japanese Relations, 1919–1941, 1974; As the Storm Clouds Gathered: European Perceptions of American Foreign Policy in the Nineteen Thirties, 1979; Franklin D. Roosevelt and the Search for Security: American-Soviet Relations, 1933–39, 1985. Add: 323 Wilson Hall, Washington State Univ., Pullman, Wash. 99164, U.S.A.

BENNETT, Elizabeth Deare. *See* MERWIN, Sam, Jr.

BENNETT, Ernest Walter. British, b. 1921. Engineering/Technology. Hon. Lect., Dept. of Civil Engineering, Univ. of Leeds, since 1976 (Reader, 1970–86). *Publs:* (with R.H. Evans) Prestressed Concrete Theory and Design, 1958; Structural Concrete Elements, 1973; (with S.C.C. Bate) Design of Prestressed Concrete, 1976. Add: 98 Becketts Park Dr., Leeds, Yorks, LS6 3PL, England.

BENNETT, Hal (Zina). American, b. 1936. Novels/Short stories, Children's fiction, Recreation/Leisure/Hobbies. *Publs:* Behind the Scenes, 1967; The Vanishing Pirate (children's novel), 1967; Battle of Wits, 1968; Brave the Dragon (children's novel), 1969; No More Public School, 1972; (ed.) The Tooth Trip, 1972; The Well Body Book, 1973; Be Well, 1974; Spirit Guides, 1975; The Yellow Journal, 1978; Cold Comfort, 1979; Sewing for the Outdoors, 1980; The Doctor Within, 1981; (co-author) John Marino's Bicycling Book, 1981; The Complete Bicycle Commuter, 1982; (with Chas. A. Garfield) Peak Performance, 1984; A Wilderness of Vines, 1985; Mind Jogger, 1986; Inner Guides, Visions, Dreams and Dr. Einstein, 1986; The Lens of Perception, 1987; (with Michael Larsen) How to Write with a Collaborator, 1988. Add: Kensington, Calif., U.S.A.

BENNETT, H.O. *See* HARDISON, Osborne B.

BENNETT, James Richard. American, b. 1932. Literature. Prof., Univ. of Arkansas, since 1971 (Asst. Prof., 1965–66; Assoc. Prof., 1966–71); Dir., Myers Center for the Study of Human Rights. Ed., Style, 1966–82. *Publs:* Prose Style: A Historical Approach Through Studies, 1972; Bibliography of Stylistics and Related Criticism, 1986; Control of Information in the United States, 1987. Add: English Dept., Univ. of Arkansas, Fayetteville, Ark. 72701, U.S.A.

BENNETT, John (Frederic). American, b. 1920. Poetry, Literature. Bernard H. Pennings Distinguished Prof. of English since 1970, and Poet-in-Residence since 1979, St. Norbert Coll., De Pere, Wisc. (Prof., 1968–70). Instr., Indiana Univ., Jefferson, 1953–58; Asst. Prof., Beloit Coll., Wisc., 1958–59; Co-Ed., The Beloit Poetry Journal, 1958–72; Assoc. Prof., 1959–62, Prof., 1962–68, and Chmn., 1966–68, Rockford Coll., Ill. *Publs:* (ed.) Once We Thought: An Anthology of Oberlin Verse, 1941; Melville's Humanitarian Thought: A Study in Moral Idealism, 1956; The Zoo Manuscript (poetry), 1968; Griefs and Exultations (poetry), 1970; The Struck Leviathan: Poems on Moby Dick, 1970; Knights and Squires: More Poems on Moby Dick, 1972; Echoes from the Peaceable Kingdom (poetry), 1978; Seeds of Mustard, Seeds of Tare (aphorisms), 1979; Fire in the Dust (poetry), 1980; Beyond the Compass Rose: Last Poems on Moby Dick, 1983; The Nixon Rubaiyat (poetry), 1984; The Holy Unicorn (poetry), 1985; A Book of Trousered Apes (poetry), 1987; Beyond These Creatures Dragons Wait (poetry), 1988. Add: 526 Karen Lane, Green Bay, Wisc. 54301, U.S.A.

BENNETT, John M(ichael). American, b. 1942. Poetry. Publisher, Luna Bisonte Prods, Columbus, Ohio, since 1974. Asst. Prof. of Hispanic Literature, Ohio State Univ., Columbus, 1969–76. *Publs:*

Works, 1973; (with Pablo Virumbrales) La Revolucion: A Reader in Spanish American Revolutionary Thought, 1976; White Screen, 1976; Meat Dip, 1976; Do Not Cough, 1976; Meat Watch, 1977; Contents, 1978; Time Release, 1978; Nips Poems, 1980; (with C. Mehrl Bennett) Pumped Gravel, 1980; Main road, 1980; Motel Moods, 1980; (with Robin Crozier) Meat Click, 1980; Puking Horse, 1980; Jerks, 1980; (with C. Mehrl Bennett) Applied Appliances, 1981; (with C. Mehrl Bennett) Some Blood, 1982; Blender, 1983; Burning Dog, 1983; Antpath, 1984; Nose Death, 1984; No Boy, 1985; 13 Spits, 1986; (with Byron Smith) Ax Tongue, 1986; (with Byron Smith) The Blur, 1987; The The Poems, 1987; Cascade, 1987; Stones in the Lake, 1987; Twitch, 1988; Swelling, 1988; Regression, 1988.   Add: Luna Bisonte Prods, 137 Leland Ave., Columbus, Ohio 43214, U.S.A.

BENNETT, Louise.   Jamaican, b.1919.   Poetry, Mythology/Folklore. With BBC West Indies Section as resident actress, 1945–46 and 1950–53; Drama Specialist, Jamaica Social Welfare Commn., 1955–60; Lectr. in Drama and Jamaican folklore, Extra-Mural Dept., Univ. of the West Indies, Kingston, 1959–61.   Publs: Dialect Verses, 1940; Jamaican Dialect Verses, 1942, expanded version, 1951; Jamaican Humour in Dialect, 1943; Miss Lulu Sez, 1958; (with others) Anancy Stories and Dialect Verse, 1950; Laugh with Louise: A Potpourri of Jamaican Folklore, Stories, Songs, Verses, 1960; Jamaica Labrish, 1966; Anancy and Miss Lou, 1979; Selected Poems, 1982.   Add: Enfield House, Gordon Town, St. Andrew, Jamaica.

BENNETT, Neville.   British, b. 1937.   Education.   Prof. of Primary Education, Univ. of Exeter.   Former Prof. of Educational Research, Univ. of Lancaster.   Publs: Teaching Styles and Pupil Progress, 1976; Focus on Teaching, 1979; Open Plan Schools, 1980; The Quality of Pupil Learning Experiences, 1984; Recent Advances in Classroom Research, 1985; A Good Start: Four Year Olds in Infant Schools, 1989; Special to Ordinary: Case Studies in Integration, 1989; Learning and Instruction, vols. II and III, 1989.   Add: Sch. of Education, Univ. of Exeter, Exeter, England.

BENNETT-ENGLAND, Rodney (Charles).   British, b. 1936.   Journalism, Fashion, Cookery.   Secty., The Media Soc., since 1984. Reporter and Columnist, Sunday Express, 1961–68; Contrib. Ed., Penthouse, 1967–70, and Men Only, 1970–73; Chmn. and Managing Dir., R.B.E. Assocs., 1968–81; London Ed., B. & E. Intnl., 1977–79. Dir., 1982, and Chmn., 1985–87, Connections (Press and PR) Ltd.   Pres., Inst. of Journalists, 1985–86.   Publs: (ed.) Inside Journalism, 1967; Dress Optional—The Revolution in Menswear, 1967; As Young as You Look, 1970; The Dale Cottage Cookbook, 1980.   Add: Church Cottage, E. Rudham, Norfolk PE31 8QZ, England.

BENNION, (Barbara) Elisabeth.   British, b. 1930.   Antiques.   Publs: Antique Medical Instruments, 1979; Antique Dental Instruments, 1986. Add: 96 Pelham Rd., London SW19, England.

BENNIS, Warren   American, b. 1925.   Administration/Management. Social commentary/phenomena.   Distinguished Prof., of School Business, Univ. of Southern California, Los Angeles, since 1980.   Provost, Faculty of Social Sciences and Admin., State Univ. of New York, 1967–68; Vice-Pres. for Academic Development, State Univ. of New York at Buffalo, 1968–71; Pres., Univ. of Cincinnati, 1971–77.   Publs: (ed. with K.D. Benne R. Chin) The Planning of Change: Readings in Behavioral Sciences, 1961, 4th ed. 1985; The Role of the Nurse in the Out-Patient Department, 1961; The Marked Deck: A Non-Objective Playlet for Four Characters, 1963; (ed. with others) Interpersonal Dynamics: Essays and Readings on Human Interaction, 1964, 3rd ed. 1973; Changing Organizations: Essays on the Development and Evolution of Human Organization, 1966; (with E.H. Schein) Personal and Organizational Change through Group Methods: The Laboratory Approach, 1965; (ed. with E.H. Schein and C. McGregor) Leadership and Motivation: Essays by Douglas McGregor, 1966; (ed. with C. McGregor) The Professional Manager, by Douglas McGregor, 1967; (ed. with others) Readings in Group Development for Managers and Trainers, 1967; (with P.E. Slater) The Temporary Society, 1968; Organization Development: Its Nature, Origins, and Prospects, 1969; American Bureaucracy, 1970; Today, Tomorrow, and the Day After, 1972;(with J. Thomas) Management of Change and Conflict, 1973; The Leaning Ivory Tower, 1973; Leadership, 1974; The Unconscious Conspiracy: Why Leaders Can't Lead, 1976; Leaders: Strategies for Taking Charge, 1985.   Add: School of Business, University of Southern California, Los Angeles, Calif. 90089, U.S.A.

BENSEN, Alice R(hodus).   American, b. 1911.   Literature.   Prof. of English, Eastern Michigan Univ., Ypsilanti, now retired.   Publs:Rose Macaulay, 1969.   Add: 3416 Edgewood, Ann Arbor, Mich. 48104, U.S.A.

BEN SHIMON HALEVI, Zev.   See KENTON, Warren.

BENSON, Daniel.   See COOPER, Colin.

BENSON, Frank Atkinson.   British, b. 1921.   Technology.   Prof. of Electronic and Electrical Engineering, from 1967, now retired.   Univ. of Sheffield (Lectr., 1949–59; Sr. Lectr., 1959–61; Reader in Electronics, 1961–67; Pro-Vice-chancellor, 1972–76).   Publs:Electrical Engineering Problems with Solutions, 1954; Voltage Stabilized Supplies, 1957; Problems in Electronics with Solutions, 1958; (with D. Harrison) Electric Circuit Theory, 1959; Voltage Stabilization, 1965; Electric Circuit Problems with Solutions, 1967; (ed. and contrib) Millimetre and Submillimetre Waves, 1969.   Add: 64 Grove Rd., Sheffield S7 2GZ, England.

BENSON, Jackson J.   American, b. 1930.   Literature.   Prof. of American Literature, San Diego State Univ., Calif., since 1966.   Publs: Hemingway: The Writer's Art of Self-Defense, 1969; (co-ed.) Hemingway In Our Time, 1974; (ed.) The Short Stories of Ernest Hemingway: Critical Essays, 1974; (co-ed.) The Fiction of Bernard Malamud, 1977; The True Adventures of John Steinbeck, Writer, 1984; Looking for Steinbeck's Ghost, 1988; (ed.) The Short Novels of John Steinbeck: Critical Essays, 1989; (ed.) The Short Stories of Ernest Hemingway: New Critical Essays, 1990.   Add: Dept. of English, San Diego State Univ., San Diego, Calif. 92182, U.S.A.

BENSON, Lyman (David).   American, b. 1909.   Botany, Environmental science/Ecology.   Emeritus Prof. of Botany, Pomona Coll., Claremont, Calif., since 1974 (Assoc. Prof. and Chmn., Dept. of Botany, 1944–49; Prof., 1949–74).   Instr. in Botany and Zoology, Bakersfield Coll., Calif., 1931–38; Instr., to Asst. Prof. of Botany, Univ. of Arizona, Tucson, 1938–44.   Publs: The Cacti of Arizona, 1940, 3rd ed. 1969; The Native Cacti of California, 1940, 3rd ed. 1969; (with R.A. Darrow) The Trees and Shrubs of the Southwestern Deserts, 1955, 3rd ed. 1980; Plant Classification, 1957, 1979; Plant Taxonomy: Methods and Principles, 1962; The Cacti of the United States and Canada, 1982.   Add: The Sequoias, 501 Portola Rd., Box 8011, Portola Valley, Calif. 94025, U.S.A.

BENSON, (C.) Randolph.   American, b. 1923.   Social Sciences (general).   Prof. and Chmn., Dept. of Sociology, Roanoke Coll., Salem, Va., since 1969 (Asst. Prof., 1968–69).   Asst. Prof., Northwestern State Univ., Natchitoches, La. 1963–64; Special Lectr., Louisiana State Univ., Baton Rouge, 1964–65; Asst. Prof., New Mexico State Univ., Las Cruces, 1965–66 Trinity Univ., San Antonio, Tex., 1966–68.   Publs: Thomas Jefferson as Social Scientist, 1971.   Add: P.O. Box 4130, Roanoke, Va. 24015, U.S.A.

BENSTOCK, Bernard.   American, b. 1930 Literature.   Prof. of English, Univ. of Miami, Coral Gables, since 1986.   Instr. of English. 1957–61, and Asst. Prof., 1961–65, Louisianna State Univ., Baton Rouge; Assoc. Prof., 1965–67, and Prof., 1967–74, Kent State Univ., Ohio; Prof. of English and Comparative Literature, Univ. of Illinois, Urbana, 1974–82; Prof. of English and Comparative Literature, Univ. of Tulsa, Okla., 1982–86.   Publs: Joyce-again's Wake: An Analysis of Finnegans Wake, 1965; Sean O'Casey, 1970; (ed. with T.F. Stanley) Approaches to Ulysses: Ten Essays, 1970; Paycocks and Others: Sean O'Casey's World, 1976; (ed. with T.F. Stanley) Approaches to Joyce's Portrait, 1977; James Joyce: The Undiscover'd Country, 1977; (with Shari Benstock) Who's He When He's at Home: A James Joyce Directory, 1980; (ed.) Pomes for James Joyce, 1982; (co-ed.) James Joyce: An International Perspective, 1982; (ed.) James Joyce and His Contemporaries, 1982; (ed.) The Seventh of Joyce, 1982; (ed.) Essays in Detective Fiction, 1983; James Joyce, 1985; (ed.) Essays on James Joyce, 1985; (ed.) James Joyce: The Augmented Ninth, 1988; (ed. with T.F. Stanley) British Mystery Writers 1860-1919, 1988; (ed. with T.F. Stanley) British Mystery Writers 1920–1939, 1988. Add: Dept. of English, Univ. of Miami, Coral Gables, Fla. 33124, U.S.A.

BENSTOCK, Shari.   American, b. 1944.   Literary criticism, History. Member of the Dept. of Clinical Medicine, Univ. of Illinois, Urbana, since 1979 (with the Dept. of Political Science, 1975–77).   Publs: Who's He When He's at Home, 1980; Women of the Left Bank: Paris 1900–1940, 1986; Feminist Issues in Literary Scholarship, 1987; The Private Self, 1988.   Add: 615 W. University, Champaign, IL 61801, U.S.A.

BENTINE, Michael.   British.   Humour/Satire.Television and radio personality.   One of the original Goon Show members, BBC Radio.   Publs: Fifty Years in the Street, 1964; (with J. Ennis) Book of Square Games, 1966; Potty Khyber Pass, 1974; Big Potty Fun Book, 1974; The Long

Banana Skin, 1975; Potty Adventure Book, 1976; Madame's Girls, 1980; Smith and Son, Removers, 1981; The Door Marked Summer, 1981; Best of Bentine, 1982; Doors to the Mind, 1983; The Shy Person's Guide to Life, 1984; Lords of the Level, 1985; Condor and the Cross, 1987; The Templar, 1988. Add: c/o Transworld, 61-63 Uxbridge Rd., London W5 5SA, England.

BENTLEY, Beth. American, b. 1928. Poetry. Freelance teacher, Poetry-in-the-Schs. prog. *Publs:* Phone Calls from the Dead, 1971; Field Snow, 1973; Country of Resemblances, 1975; Philosophical Investigations, 1977; The Purely Visible, 1980; (ed.) Selected Poems of Hazel Hall, 1980. Add: 8762 25th Pl. N.E., Seattle, Wash. 98115, U.S.A.

BENTLEY, Eric (Russell). American (b. British), b. 1916. Plays/Screenplays, Literature, Theatre, Translations. Matthews Prof. of Dramatic Literature, Columbia Univ., NYC, 1953–69; Katharine Cornell Prof. of Theatre, State Univ. of New York, 1975–82. *Publs:* dramatic works—Orpheus in the Underworld; A Time to Die and A Time to Live; The Red, White and Black; Are You Or Have You Ever Been; The Recantation of Galileo Galilei; From the Memoirs of Pontius Pilate; Lord Alfred's Lover; Wannsee; Fall of the Amazons; Concord; German Requiem; Round Two; critical works—A Century of Hero Worship; The Playwright as Thinker; Bernard Shaw; In Search of Theatre; The Dramatic Event; What Is Theatre?; The Life of the Drama; The Theatre of Commitment; Theatre of War; Thinking about the Playwright; (ed. & trans.) Seven Plays by Brecht and other volumes in the Grove Press edition of Brecht; (ed. and trans.) Naked Masks, by Pirandello (five plays); (ed. and trans.) The Wire Harp, by Wolf Biermann; (trans.) Gogol's Inspector & Other Plays; The Brecht Commentaries; The Pirandello Commentaries, 1985; The Brecht Memoir, 1985. Add: 194 Riverside Dr., New York, N.Y. 10025, U.S.A.

BENTLEY, Gerald Eades. American, b. 1901. Literature, Theatre, Biography. Murray Prof. of English Emeritus, Princeton Univ., N.J., since 1970 (Prof., 1945–52; Murray Prof., 1952–70; Librarian for Rare Books and Special Collections, 1971–73; Bibliographer and Consultant, 1973–74). Pres., Malone Soc., since 1972. Instr., to Prof., Univ. of Chicago, 1929–45. Pres., Shakespeare Assn. of America, 1972–74. *Publs:* (with F.B. Millett) The Art of the Drama, 1935; (ed. with F.B. Millett) The Play's the Thing, 1936; The Jacobean and Caroline State (7 vols.), 1941–68; Shakespeare and Jonson (2 vols.) 1945, 1965; (ed.) The Alchemist, by Ben Jonson, 1947; The Swan of Avon and the Bricklayer of Westminster, 1948; The Development of English Drama, 1950; (ed.) The Arte of Angling, 1577, 1956; (ed.) William Shakespeare's Othello, 1957; Shakespeare: A Biographical Handbook, 1961, 1985; Shakespeare and His Theatre, 1964; The Seventeenth Century Theatre, 1968; The Profession of Dramatist in Shakespeare's Time, 1971, 1985; (with others) The Revels History of Drama in English (vol. IV), 1981; The Profession of Player in Shakespeare's Time, 1984, 1985; The Legacy of R.P. Blackmour, 1987. Add: Apt. 13-01U, Meadow Lakes, Hightstown, N.J. 08520, U.S.A.

BENTON, Kenneth (Carter). Also writes as James Kirton. British, b. 1909. Mystery/Crime/Suspense, International relations/Current affairs. With U.K. Diplomatic Service, 1937–68: served Vienna, 1937–38; Riga, 1938–40; Madrid, 1941–43; Rome, 1944–48, 1950–53; Madrid, 1953–56; Lima, 1962–63; Rio de Janeiro, 1966–68. *Publs:* Twenty-Fourth Level, 1969; Peru's Revolution from Above, 1970; Sole Agent, 1970; Spy in Chancery, 1972; Craig and the Jaguar, 1973; Death on the Appian Way, 1974; Craig and the Tunisan Tangle, 1974; Craig and the Midas Touch, 1975; A Single Monstrous Act, 1976; The Red Hen Conspiracy, 1977; Ward of Caesar, 1986; as James Kirton—Time for Murder, 1985; Greek Fire, 1985. Add: 2 Jubilee Terr., Chichester PO19 1XL, England.

BENTON, Patricia. American, b. 1907. Novels/Short stories, Children's fiction, Plays/Screenplays. Poetry Consultant, Arizona Dept. of Public Instruction, 1953–70; Arizona State Chmn., 1954–64, and New York Chmn., 1973, National Poetry Day Cttee.; Arizona State Pres., Composers Authors and Artists of America, 1970–74; Founder and Pres. of New York and Arizona Chapters, and National Literature Chmn., National Soc. of Arts and Letters, Washington, D.C., 1972–74. *Publs:* Pebbles, 1939; Voices in the Willows, 1947; The Whispering Earth, 1950; Signature in Sand, 1952; The Young Corn Rises, 1953; Medallion Southwest, 1954; Cradle of the Sun, 1958; Arizona: The Turquoise Land, 1959; Merry Go Sounds at the Zoo, 1960; Your Baby's First Horoscope, 1961; Gift of Christmas, 1962; Love Is, 1962; A Friend for Always, 1962; Magic of 1963; Love Has Many Faces, 1964; Manhattan Mosaic, 1964; Barkie the Dog, 1965; Of the Heart's Own Telling, 1965; The Miracle of Roses (play), 1965; Life Has Many Windows (film), 1965. Add: c/o Frederick

Fell Publishers Inc., 2131 Hollywood Blvd., Hollywood, Fl 33020, U.S.A.

BENTON, Peggie. Has also written as Shifty Burke. British, b. 1909. Cookery/Gastronomy/Wine, Sociology, Translations. With British Foreign Service, 1936–48. *Publs:* (trans.) Cooking in Ten Minutes, 1948, 1956; Finnish Food for Your Table, 1960; (adaptor) Cooking with Pomiane, 1961; (adaptor) Meat at Any Price, 1963; (co-author) Chicken and Game, 1964; (co-author) Fish for All Seasons, 1966; (trans.) Brick as an Element in Design, 1966; (as Shifty Burke) Peterman, 1966; (co-author) Eggs, Milk and Cheese, 1971; One Man Against the Drylands, 1972; Fight for the Drylands, 1977; Baltic Countdown, 1984. Add: 2 Jubilee Terr., Chichester PO19 1XL, England.

BENVENISTE, Asa. British (born American), b. 1925. Poetry, Plays/Screenplays, Design. Exec. Ed., Trigram Press Ltd., London (joined staff, 1965). Co-Ed., Zero-Quarterly, Paris, Tangier and London, 1948–56; Corresp., Nugget Mag., London, 1956–57; Copy Ed., Doubleday & Co., publrs., NYC, 1957–58; Sr. Art Ed., Paul Hamlyn Ltd., publrs., London, 1959–61; Sr. Ed., Studio Vista Ltd., publrs., London, 1961–63. *Publs:* Tangier for the Traveller (radio play), 1956; Piano Forte (radio play), 1957; Poems of the Month, 1966; (with Jack Hirschman) A Work in Your Season: Portfolio of Six Seriagraphs, 1967; Count Three, 1969; The Atoz Formula, 1969; Free Semantic No. 2, 1970; Umbrella, 1972; (with Ray Di Palma and Tom Raworth) Time Being, 1972; Blockmakers Black, 1973; Certainly Metaphysics, 1973; It's the Same Old Feeling Again, 1973; Autotypography: A Book of Design Priorities, 1974; Edge, 1975; Poems, 1976; Loose End, 1977; Colour Theory, 1977; Throw Out the Life Line, Lay Out the Corse: Poems 1965–1985, 1983; Pommes Poems, 1988. Add: 22 Leverton St., London NW5, England.

BEN-YOSEF, Avraham Chaim. *See* **MATSUBA**, Moshe.

BENZIE, William. British, b. 1930. Literature. Prof. of English, Victoria Univ., B.C. (joined faculty as Lectr., 1958). *Publs:* The Dublin Orator, 1972; Dr. F.J. Furnivall, A Victorian Scholar Adventurer, 1983. Add: English Dept., Victoria Univ., Victoria, B.C., Canada.

BERBRICH, Joan D. American, b. 1925. Literature, Women, Writing/Journalism. *Publs:* Three Voices from Paumanok: The Influence of Long Island on Cooper, Bryant and Whitman, 1969; Sounds and Sweet Airs: Poetry of Long Island (critical anthology), 1970; (ed.) Heritage of Long Island, by W. Oakley Cagney, 1970; 101 Ways to Learn Vocabulary (textbook), 1971; (ed.) Stories of Crime and Detection (textbook), 1973; (with Marie Hecht, Clare Cooper and Sally Healey) The Women, Yes!, 1973; (ed.) Heaven and Hell, 1974; Wide World of Words, 1975; Writing Practically, 1976; Writing Creatively, 1977; Writing Logically, 1978; Writing about People and Yourself, 1979; Writing about Fascinating Things, 1980; Writing about Curious Things, 1981; Writing about Amusing Things, 1981; Reading Today, 1983; Reading Around the World, 1986; Thirteen Steps to Better Writing, 1987; Fifteen Steps to Better Writing, 1987; Macbeth: A Resource Book, 1988. Add: 5 Owen Ave., Queensburg, N.Y. 12804, U.S.A.

BERE, Rennie Montague. British, b. 1907. Children's non-fiction, Natural history. Colonial Service, Uganda, 1930–55; Dir. and Chief Warden, Uganda National Parks, 1955–60, now retired. *Publs:* The Wild Mammals of Uganda, 1962; The Way to the Mountains of the Moon, 1966; Animals in an African National Park, 1966; The African Elephant, 1966; Birds in an African National Park, 1969; Antelopes, 1970; The Life of Antelopes, 1970; Wildlife in Cornwall, 1970; Crocodile's Eggs for Supper, 1973; Mammals of East and Central Africa, 1974; (with B.D. Stamp) The Book of Bude and Stratton, 1980; The Nature of Cornwall, 1982; Bude in Old Picture Postcards, 1985. Add: West Cottage, Bude Haven, Bude, Cornwall EX23 8LH, England.

BERESFORD, Anne. British, b. 1929. Plays/Screenplays, Poetry. Drama teacher, Wimbledon Girls High Sch., London, 1969–73, and Arts Educational Sch., 1973–76. *Publs:* (with Michael Hamburger) Struck by Appollo (radio play), 1965; Walking Without Moving, 1967; The Lair, 1968; The Villa (radio play), 1968; Footsteps in the Snow, 1972; The Courtship, 1972; The Curving Shore, 1975; (with Michael Hamburger) Words, 1977; Unholy Giving, 1977; Songs a Thracian Taught Me, 1980; The Songs of Almut from God's Country, 1980; Duet for Three Voices, 1983; The Sele of the Morning, 1988. Add: Marsh Acres, Middleton, Saxmundham, Suffolk IP17 3NH, England.

BERESFORD, Elisabeth. British. Historical/Romance/Gothic, Children's fiction. Freelance journalist, and screen and TV writer, since 1948. *Publs:* The Television Mystery, 1957; The Flying Docter Mystery,

1958; Trouble at Tullington Castle, 1958; Cocky and the Missing Castle, 1959; Gappy Goes West, 1959; The Tullington Film-Makers, 1960; Two Gold Dolphins, 1961; Danger on the Old Pull 'n Push, 1962; Strange Hiding Place, 1962; Diana in Television, 1963; The Missing Formula Mystery, 1963; The Mulberry Street Team, 1963; Paradise Island (romance), 1963; Awkward Magic, 1964, in U.S. as The Magic World, 1965; Escape to Happiness (romance), 1964; The Flying Docter to the Rescue, 1964; Holiday for Slippy, 1964; Game, Set, and Match, 1965; Knights of the Cardboard Castle, 1965; Travelling Magic, 1965, in U.S. as The Vanishing Garden, 1967; The Hidden Mill, 1965; Roses round the Door (romance), 1965; Peter Climbs a Tree, 1966; Island of Shadows (romance), 1966; Fashion Girl, 1967; The Black Mountain Mystery, 1967; Looking for a Friend, 1967; Veronica (romance), 1967; A Tropical Affair in U.S. as Tropical Affairs, 1978; The Island Bus, 1968; Sea-Green Magic, 1968; The Wombles, 1968; Saturday's Child (romance), 1968, in U.S. as Echoes of Love, 1979; David Goes Fishing, 1969; Gordon's Go-Kart, 1970; Stephen and the Shaggy Dog, 1970; Vanishing Magic, 1970; The Wandering Wombles, 1970; Love Remembered, 1970; Dangerous Magic, 1972; Love and the S.S. Beatrice (romance), 1972, in U.S. as Thunder of Her Heart, 1978; The Invisible Womble and Other Stories, 1973; The Secret Railway, 1973; The Wombles in Danger, 1973; The Wombles at Work, 1973; Invisible Magic, 1974; The Wombles Go to the Seaside, 1974; Pandora (romance), 1974; The Wombles Annual 1975–1978, 4 vols., 1974–77; The Wombles Gift Book, 1975; The Snow Womble, 1975; Snuffle to the Rescue, 1975; Tomsk and the Tired Tree, 1975; Wellington and the Blue Balloon, 1975; Orinoco Runs Away, 1975; The Wombles Make a Clean Sweep, 1975; The Wombles to the Rescue, 1975; The Mac Wombles's Pipe Band, 1976; Madame Cholet's Picnic Party, 1976; Bungo Knows Best, 1976; Tobermory's Big Surprise, 1976; The Wombles Go round the World, 1976; The World of the Wombles, 1976; Wombling Free, 1978; Toby's Luck, 1978; Secret Magic, 1978; The Happy Ghost, 1979; The Treasure Hunters, 1980; Curious Magic, 1980; The Steadfast Lover (romance), 1980; The Silver Chain (romance), 1980; The Four of Us, 1981; The Animals Nobody Wanted, 1982; The Restless Heart (romance), 1982; The Tovers, 1982; Jack and the Magic Stove, 1983; The Passionate Adventure (romance), 1983; The Adventures of Poon, 1984; The Mysterious Island, 1984; One of the Family, 1985; The Ghosts of Lupus Street School, 1986; Emily and the Haunted Castle, 1987; Once Upon a Time Stories, 1987; The Oscar Puffin Book, 1987; The Secret Room, 1987; The Armada Adventue, 1988; The Island Railway, 1988; Rose, 1989; The Wooden Gun, 1989. Add: c/o David Higham Assocs., 5–8 Lower John St., London WIR 4HA, England.

BERESFORD, Maurice (Warwick). British, b. 1920. Economics, History. Visiting Prof. of History, Univ. of Strathclyde, since 1987. Member, Leeds Prison Parole Bd., and Leeds Probation Cttee.; Member, Royal Commn. on Historical Monuments, since 1979. Lectr., 1948–55, Reader, 1955–59, and Prof. of Economic History, 1959–85, Univ. of Leeds. Member, Yorkshire Dales National Park Cttee., 1964–72; Chmn., Yorkshire Citizens Advice Bureaux Cttee., 1965–70; Member, Consumer Council, 1965–71, and Hearing Aid Council, 1967–71. *Publs:* The Leeds Chambers of Commerce, 1951; The Lost Villages of England, 1954; History on the Ground, 1957, 1971; (with J.K. St. Joseph) Medieval England: An Aerial Survey, 1958, 1979; Time and Place, 1962; New Towns of the Middle Ages, 1967, 1988; (ed. with G. Jones) Leeds and Its Region, 1967; Deserted Medieval Villages, 1971; (with H.P.R. Finberg) English Medieval Boroughs, 1973; (with B.J. Barber) The West Riding County Council 1889-1974), 1979; Walks round Red Brick, 1980; Time and Place: Collected Papers, 1985; East End, West End, 1988. Add: 6 Claremont Ave., Leeds 3, Yorks., England.

BERESFORD-HOWE, Constance (Elizabeth). Canadian, b. 1922. Novels/Short stories. Prof. of English, McGill Univ., Montreal, 1948–69, and Ryerson Polytechnic Inst., since 1972. *Publs:* The Unreasoning Heart, 1946; Of This Day's Journey, 1948; The Invisible Gate, 1949; My Lady Greensleeves, 1955; The Book of Eve, 1973; A Population of One, 1976; The Marriage Bed, 1981; Night Studies (novel), 1984; Prospero's Daughter, 1988. Add: 16 Cameron Cres., Toronto, Ont. M4G 1Z8, Canada.

BERG, A. Scott. American, b. 1949. Biography. Full-time writer. *Publs:* Max Perkins: Editor of Genius, 1978; Goldwyn, 1989. Add: c/o Russell and Volkening, 551 Fifth Ave., New York, N.Y. 10017, U.S.A.

BERG, Dave. (David Berg). American, b. 1920. Humor/Satire. Writer and Artist, Mad Mag., NYC, since 1955. *Publs:* Mad's Dave Berg Looks at the U.S.A., 1964; Mad's Dave Berg Looks at People, 1966; Mad's Dave Berg Looks at Things, 1967; Mad's Dave Berg Looks at Modern Thinking, 1969; Mad's Dave Berg Looks at Our Sick World,

1971; My Friend GOD, 1972; Mad's Dave Berg Looks at Living, 1973; Roger Kaputnik and GOD, 1974; Mad's Dave Berg Looks Around, 1975; Dave Berg's Mad Trash, 1977; Mad's Dave Berg Takes a Loving Look, 1977; Mad's Dave Berg Looks, Listens and Laughs, 1979; Mad's Dave Berg Looks at You, 1981; Mad's Dave Berg Looks at the Neighborhood, 1984; Mad's Dave Berg Looks at Our Planet, 1986; Mad's Dave Berg Looks At Today, 1989. Add: c/o Mad Magazine, 485 Madison Ave., New York, N.Y. 10022, U.S.A.

BERG, Leila. British, b. 1917. Children's fiction, Children's non-fiction, Education. *Publs:* fiction for children—Little Pete Stories, 1952; The Story of the Little Car, 1955, as The Little Car Has a Day Out, 1970, as The Little Car, 1972; A Box for Benny, 1958; My Dog Sunday, 1968; Folk Tales for Reading and Telling, 1966; The Nippers and Little Nippers series, 24 titles, 1968–76; Chatterbooks, 4 titles: A Tickle, 1981; The Hot, Hot Day, 1981; Our Walk, 1981; In a House I Know, 1981; Small World, 8 titles: Worms, 1983; Bees, 1983; Dogs, 1983; Blood and Plasters, 1983; Cars, 1985; Rainbows, 1985; Ducks, 1985; Vacuum Cleaners, 1985; Tales for Telling, 1983; Topsy Turvy Tales, 1984; Hanukka, 1985; Christmas, 1985; Time for One More, 1986; Steep Street Stories: Rosie and Mr. Brown, 1987; Having Friends, 1987; Call That a Hat, 1987; Loving Jonathan Jones, 1987; other—Risinghill: Death of a Comprehensive School, 1968, 1976; Children's Rights, 1971; (with Pat Chapman) The Train Back: A Search for Parents, 1972; Look at Kids, 1972, 1978; Reading and Loving, 1977. Add: Alice's Cottage, Brook St., Wivenhoe, Nr. Colchester, Essex C07 9DS, England.

BERG, Stephen. American, b. 1934. Poetry, Translations. Asst. Prof., Philadelphia Coll. of Art, Pa. Former Instr. in English, Temple Univ., Philadelphia, Pa.; Poetry Ed., Saturday Evening Post, Philadelphia, 1961–62; Founder and Co-Ed., The American Poetry Review, Philadelphia. *Publs:* Berg Goodman Mezey: Poems, 1957; Bearing Weapons: Poems, 1963; (co-trans.) Cantico: Selections, by Jorge Guillen, 1965; (ed. with Robert Mezey) Naked Poetry: Recent American Poetry in Open Forms, and Naked Poetry 2, 1969, 1974; The Queen's Triangle: A Romance, 1970 (Frank O'Hara Prize); The Daughters: Poems, 1971; (ed. with S.J. Marks) Between People, 1972; (trans.) Nothing in the Word, 1972; (co-trans.) Clouded Sky, by Miklos Radnoti, 1973; (ed. with S.J. Marks) Doing the Unknown, 1974; Grieve Like This, 1974; Grief: Poems and Versions of Poems, 1975; (ed., with Robert Mezey) The New Naked Poetry, 1976; (trans., with Diskin Clay) Oedipus the King, by Sophocles, 1978; With Akhmatova at the Black Gates, 1981; (ed.) In Praise of What Persists, 1983; Singular Voices: American Poetry Today, 1985; In It: Poems, 1986. Add: 1616 Walnut St., Philadelphia, Pa. 19103, U.S.A.

BERGÉ Carol. American, b. 1928. Novels/Short stories, Poetry. Contrib. Ed., The Woodstock Review, since 1978; Ed. and Publr., Center Mag., 1971–81. *Publs:* (with others) Four Young Lady Poets, 1962; The Vulnerable Island, 1964; The Vancouver Report (reportage), 1965; Lumina, 1965; Poems Made of Skin, 1968; The Chambers, 1969; Circles, as in the Eye, 1969; An American Romance, 1969; The Unfolding (fiction), 1969; From A Soft Angle, 1971; A Couple Called Moebius (fiction), 1972; Acts of Love: An American Novel, 1973; The Unexpected, 1976; Rituals and Gargoyles, 1976; Timepieces (fiction), 1977; A Song, a Chant, 1978; Alba Genesis, 1979; Alba Nemesis (The China Poems), 1979; The Doppler Effect (fiction), 1979; Fierce Metronome (fiction), 1981; (ed. with Dale Boyer) The Clock of Moss, 1983; Secrets, Gossip and Slander, 1984. Add: c/o William Morris Agency, 1350 Ave. of the Americas, New York, NY 10019, U.S.A.

BERGEN, Candice. American, b. 1946. Plays, Autobiography. Actress. Films include: The Group, 1966; The Sand Pebbles, 1966; Vivre Pour Vivre, 1967; The Magus, 1968; Getting Straight, 1970; Soldier Blue, 1970; The Adventurers, 1970; Carnal Knowledge, 1971; The Hunting Party, 1971; Bite the Bullet, 1975; The Wind and the Lion, 1976; The Domino Principle, 1977; A Night of Full Rain, 1977; Oliver's Story, 1978; Starting Over, 1979; Rich and Famous, 1981; Gandhi, 1982. Contributor, photojournalism, numerous mags. *Publs:* (contributor) "The Freezer" in Best Short Plays of 1968, 1969; Knock Wood (autobiography), 1984. Add: c/o William Morris Agency, 1350 Ave. of the Americas, New York, N.Y. 10019, U.S.A.

BERGER, Arthur A(sa). American, b. 1933. Anthropology/Ethnology, Film, Literature. Prof., Broadcast Communication Arts Dept., San Francisco State Univ. Fulbright Scholar, Univ. of Milan, Italy, 1963–64; Visiting Prof., Annenberg Sch. of Communications, Univ. of Southern California, Los Angeles, 1984–85. *Publs:* Li'l Abner: A Study in American Satire, 1970; The Evangelical Hamburger, 1970; (collaborator) Language in Thought and Action, 3rd ed. 1972, 4th ed. 1978; Pop Culture,

1973; The Comic-Stripped American, 1974; (ed.) About Man: An Introduction to Anthropology, 1974; The TV-Guided American, 1976; Television as an Instrument of Terror, 1980; (ed.) Film in Society, 1980; Media Analysis Techniques, 1982; Signs in Contemporary Culture: An Introduction to Semiotics, 1984; (ed.) Television in Society, 1987; (ed.) Humor, The Psyche and Society, 1987; (ed.) Visual Sociology and Semiotics, 1987; (ed.) Political Culture and Public Opinion, 1988; Seeing Is Believing: An Introduction to Visual Communication, 1989. Add: 118 Peralta Ave., Mill Valley, Calif. 94941, U.S.A.

BERGER, Evelyn Miller. Also writes as Evelyn Berger Brown. American, b. 1896. Psychology. Admin. Dir., Evelyn Berger Center for Counseling and Psychotherapy, Oakland, Calif., since 1941. Assoc. Prof. of Spanish and Dean of Women, Allegheny Coll., Meadville, Pa., 1932–36; Dean of Women, Univ. of Idaho, Moscow, 1936–37, and San Diego State Coll., Calif., 1937–38. *Publs:* Triangle, 1961; Extracurricular Activities; La Joven; Writing a Religious Play; This One Thing I Do. Add: 1850 Alice St., Apt. 214, Oakland, Calif. 94612, U.S.A.

BERGER, John (Peter). British, b. 1926. Novels/Short stories, Art, Literature, Sociology. Began career as a printer and art teacher; subsequently art critic for Tribune and New Statesman, London; now full-time writer. *Publs:* A Painter of Our Time, 1958; Permanent Red: Essays in Seeing (in U.S. as Towards Reality: Essays in Seeing), 1960; The Foot of Clive, 1962; Corker's Freedom, 1964; The Success and Failure of Picasso, 1965; A Fortunate Man: The Story of a Country Doctor, 1967; Art and Revolution: Ernst Niezvestny and the Role of the Artist in the U.S.S.R., 1969; The Moment of Cubism and Other Essays, 1969; The Look of Things (essays), 1971; G, 1972; Ways of Seeing, 1972; (with Jean Mohr) A Seventh Man: Migrant Workers in Europe, 1975; Pig Earth, 1979; About Looking, 1980; (with Jean Mohr) Another Way of Telling, 1982; And Our Faces, My Heart, Brief as Photos, 1984; (with Nella Bielski) Question of Geography (play), 1984; The White Bird, 1985, in U.S. as The Sense of Sight: Writings, ed. by Lloyd Spencer, 1986; Once in Europe (short stories), 1987. Add: Quincy, Mieussy 74440, France.

BERGER, Nan. British, b. 1914. Civil liberties/Human rights, Women. Govt. Statistician, 1947–50; Ed., Commentary, 1957–59; Ed., Hospitality, 1959–83. *Publs:* Women's Rights, 1960; (with Joan Maizels) Women: Fancy or Free?, 1962; Rights of Children and Young Persons, 1969; (co-author) Children's Rights, 1971; Rights, 1974. Add: 82 Hungerford Rd., London N7X 9LP, England.

BERGER, Terry. American, b. 1933. Children's fiction, Children's non-fiction, Psychology. *Publs:* Black Fairy Tales (adaptations), 1969; I Have Feelings (psychology), 1971; Lucky, 1974; Being Alone, Being Together, 1974; Big Sister, Little Brother, 1974; A Friend Can Help, 1974; A New Baby, 1974; Not Everything Changes, 1975; The Turtles' Picnic, 1977; How Does It Feel When Your Parents Get Divorced?, 1977; Special Friends, 1979; Stepchild, 1980; Friends, 1981; (co-author) The Haunted Dollhouse, 1982; Ben's ABC Day, 1982; Country Inns: The Rocky Mountains, 1983; (with Robert Reid) Great American Scenic Railroads, 1985. Add: 130 Hill Park Ave., Great Neck, N.Y. 11021, U.S.A.

BERGER, Thomas (Louis). American, b. 1924. Novels/Short stories, Westerns/Adventure, Plays. Librarian, Rand Sch. of Social Science, NYC, 1948–51; staff member, New York Times Index, 1951–52; Assoc. Ed., Popular Science Monthly, NYC, 1952–54; Distinguished Visiting Prof., Southampton Coll., 1975–76; Visiting Lectr., Yale Univ., New Haven, Conn., 1981–82. *Publs:* Crazy in Berlin, 1958; Reinhart in Love, 1962; Little Big Man, 1964; Killing Time, 1967; Other People (play), 1970; Vital Parts, 1970; Regiment of Women, 1973; Sneaky People, 1975; Who Is Teddy Villanova?, 1977; Arthur Rex, 1978; Neighbors, 1980; Reinhart's Women, 1981; The Feud, 1983; Nowhere, 1985; Being Invisible, 1987; The Houseguest, 1988. Add: c/o Don Congdon Assocs., 156 Fifth Ave., New York, N.Y. 10010, U.S.A.

BERGHAHN, Volker R. German, b. 1938. History, Politics/Government. Prof. of History, Brown Univ., Providence, since 1988. Reader in European History, Univ. of East Anglia, Norwich, 1971–75; Prof. of History, Univ. of Warwick, Coventry, 1975–88. *Publs:* Der Stahlhelm, S.D.F. 1918–1935, 1966; Der Tirpitz-Plan, 1971; Rüstung und Machtpolitik, 1973; Germany and the Approach of War in 1914, 1973; Militarism, 1981; Modern Germany, 1982; Westdeutsche Unternehmer und Politik 1945–1973, 1985. Add: Dept. of History, Brown Univ., Providence, RI 02912, U.S.A.

BERGMAN, Andrew. American. Mystery/Crime/Suspense. Film. *Publs:* mystery novels—The Big Kiss-Off of 1944, 1974; Hollywood and

LeVine, 1975; other—We're in the Money, 1971; James Cagney, 1975. Add: c/o Holt Rinehart, 6277 Sea Harbor Dr., Orlando, FL 32821, U.S.A.

BERGONZI, Bernard. British, b. 1929. Novels, Poetry, Literature. Prof. of English, Univ. of Warwick, Coventry, since 1971 (Sr. Lectr., 1966–71). *Publs:* The Early H.G. Wells, 1961; Heroes' Twilight, 1965, 1980; (ed.) Innovations: Essays on Art and Ideas, 1968; (ed.) T.S. Eliot: Four Quartets: A Casebook, 1969; The Situation of the Novel, 1970, 1979; T.S. Eliot, 1972, 1978; The Turn of a Century, 1973; (ed.) H.G. Wells: Collection of Critical Essays, 1975; Gerard Manley Hopkins, 1977; Reading the Thirties, 1978; Years: Sixteen Poems, 1979; (ed.) Poetry 1870-1914, 1980; The Roman Persuasion (novel), 1981; The Myth of Modernism and Twentieth Century Literature, 1986. Add: 19 St. Mary's Crescent, Leamington Spa CV31 1JL, England.

BERGREEN, Laurence. American, b. 1950. Communications Media, Biography. Asst. to the Pres., Museum of Broadcasting, NYC, 1977–78; Member of the faculty, New Sch. for Social Research, NYC, 1981–82. *Publs:* Look Now, Pay Later: The Rise of Network Broadcasting, 1980; James Agee: A Life, 1984. Add: The Wendy Weil Agency, Inc., 747 Third Ave., New York, N.Y. 10017, U.S.A.

BERGSON, Abram. American, b. 1914. Economics. George F. Baker Prof. of Economics Emeritus, Harvard Univ., Cambridge, Mass., since 1984 (Prof. of Economics, 1956–71; Dir., Regional Studies—Soviet Union, 1961–64; Dir., 1964–68, 1977–80, and Acting Dir., 1969–70, Russian Research Center; Frank W. Taussig Research Prof., 1970–71; George F. Baker Prof. of Economics, 1971–84). Asst. Prof. of Economics, Univ. of Texas, Austin, 1940–42; member of faculty, Columbia Univ., NYC, 1946–56. *Publs:* The Structure of Soviet Wages: A Study in Socialist Economics, 1944; Soviet National Income and Product in 1937, 1953; (ed. and contrib.) Soviet Economic Growth: Conditions and Perspectives, 1953; (with H. Heymann, Jr.) Soviet National Income and Product, 1940–58, 1954; Real National Income of Soviet Russia, 1961; (co-ed. and contrib.) Economic Trends in the Soviet Union, 1963; The Economics of Soviet Planning, 1964; Essays in Normative Economics, 1966; Planning and Productivity under Soviet Socialism, 1968; Productivity and the Social System, 1978; Welfare, Planning, and Employment: Selected Essays in Economic Theory, 1982; (co-ed. and contrib.) The Soviet Economy: Toward the Year 2000, 1983; Planning and Performance in Socialist Economies: The U.S.S.R. and Eastern Europe, 1988. Add: 334 Marsh St., Belmont, Mass. 02178, U.S.A.

BERKOFF, Steven. British, b. 1939. Novels/Short stories, Plays/Screenplays. Founding Dir., London Theatre Group, since 1973. Formerly worked in repertory in Nottingham, Liverpool, Coventry, and at the Citizens' Theatre, Glasgow. *Publs:* East, Agamemnon, The Fall of the House of Usher, 1977; Gross Intrusions and Other Stories, 1979; Decadence and Greek, 1980; The Trial and Metamorphosis, 1981; West, Lunch, and Harry's Christmas, 1985; Kvetch, and Acapulco, 1986; Sink the Belgrano, 1987; Massage, 1987; America, 1988. Add: c/o Rosica Colin Ltd., 1 Clareville Grove Mews, London SW7 5AH, England.

BERKSON, Bill. American, b. 1939. Art, Poetry. Instr., San Francisco Art Inst., since 1984. Editorial Assoc., Portfolio and Art News Annual, NYC, 1960–63; Assoc. Producer, Art-New York series, WNDT-TV, NYC, 1964–65; taught at New Sch. for Social Research, NYC, 1964–69; Guest Ed., Museum of Modern Art, NYC, 1965–69; Poet-teacher, Poets in the Schools, 1968–84; Ed., Best and Company mag., 1969; Teaching Fellow, Ezra Stiles Coll., Yale Univ., New Haven, Conn., 1969–70; Adjunct Prof., Southampton Coll., 1979–80; Ed., Big Sky mag. and Big Sky Books, Bolinas, Calif., 1971–78. *Publs:* Saturday Night: Poems 1960–61; (ed.) In Memory of My Feelings, by Frank O'Hara, 1967; Shining Leaves, 1969; (ed. with Irving Sandler) Alex Katz, 1971; (with Larry Fagin) Two Serious Poems and One Other, 1972; Recent Visitors, 1973; Ants, 1974; (with Frank O'Hara) Hymns of St.Bridget, 1974; Enigma Variations, 1975; Blue Is the Hero, 1977; (ed. with Joe LeSueur) Homage to Frank O'Hara, 1978; Start Over, 1983; Red Devil, 1983; Lush Life, 1984. Add: Box 389, Bolinas, Calif. 94924, U.S.A.

BERKSON, William Koller. American, b. 1944. Philosophy. Asst. Prof. of Philosophy, Bridgewater State Coll., Mass., 1973–76. *Publs:* Fields of Force: Development of a World View from Faraday to Einstein, 1974; (with J. Wettersten) Learning from Error: The Significance of Karl Popper's Psychology of Learning, 1984. Add: c/o Open Court, Box 599, La Salle, Ill. 61301, U.S.A.

BERLIN, (Sir) Isaiah. British, b. 1909. History, Philosophy, Biography. Fellow, All Souls Coll., Oxford, 1932–38, 1950–66, and since

1975 (Chichele Prof. of Social and Political Theory, 1957–67; and Pres., Wolfson Coll., 1966–75). Pres., Aristotelian Soc., 1963–64, and British Academy, 1974–78. *Publs:* Karl Marx, 1939, 3rd ed. 1978; (trans.) First Love, by Turgenev, 1950; The :Hedgehog and the Fox, 1953; Historical Inevitability, 1954; The Age of Enlightenment, 1956; Moses Hess, 1958; Two Concepts of Liberty, 1959; Mr. Churchill in 1940, 1964; Four Essays on Liberty, 1969; Fathers and Children, 1972; Vico and Herder, 1976; Russian Thinkers, 1978; Concepts and Categories, 1978; Against the Current, 1979; Personal Impressions, 1980; (trans.) A Month in the Country, by Turgenev, 1980. Add: All Souls Coll., Oxford, England.

BERMAN, Arthur I(rwin). American, b. 1925. Air/Space topics, Politics. English language ed., Ris Natl. Laboratory, Roskilde, since 1979. Consultant, NASA, Unesco, and OECD. Prof. of Physics, Rensselaer Polytechnic Inst., Troy, N.Y., 1956–69; Sr Research Fellow, Inst. for Studies in Higher Education, Univ. of Copenhagen, 1970–74; Visiting Prof., Technical Univ. of Denmark, 1974–78. *Publs:* The Physical Principles of Astronautics, 1961; Learning Media, 1974; Space Flight, 1979; Notes from Lonely Planet, 1988. Add: Gasvaerksvej 13, DK-2970 Hrsholm, Denmark.

BERMAN, Claire. Also writes as Noelle Gallant. American, b. 1936. Human Relations, Psychology. Chmn., Editorial Liaison Cttee., American Society of Journalists and Authors. Sr. Ed., Cosmopolitan, 1958–63; Contrib. Ed., New York mag., 1972–78; former Dir. of Public Education, Permanent Families for Children, Child Welfare League of America. *Publs:* A Great City for Kids: A Parent's Guide to a Child's New York, 1969; We Take This Child: A Candid Look at Modern Adoption, 1974; Making It as a Stepparent, 1980, 1986; "What Am I Doing in a Stepfamily?", 1982. Add: 52 Riverside Dr., New York, N.Y. 10024, U.S.A.

BERMAN, Sanford. American, b. 1933. Librarianship. Head Cataloguer, Hennepin County Library, Minnetonka, Minn., since 1973. Contrib. and Consulting Ed., New Pages; Reference Librarian, Collection Building. Asst. Chief, Acquisitions Dept., Public Library, Washington, D.C., 1957–62; Librarian (Admin.), U.S. Army Special Services Libraries in Karlsruhe, Worms and Germany 1962–66; Librarian, Schiller Coll., Kleiningersheim, Germany, 1966–67; Periodicals Librarian, Research Library, Univ. of California, Los Angeles, 1967–68; Asst. Librarian, Univ. of Zambia, Lusaka, 1968–70; Librarian, Makerere Inst. of Social Research, Kampala, Uganda, 1971–72. Ed., ALA/SRRT Newsletter, 1973–75; Ed., HCL Cataloging Bulletin, 1973–79. *Publs:* Spanish Guinea: An Annotated Bibliography, 1961; Prejudices and Antipathies: A Tract on the LC Subject Heads Concerning People, 1971; (compiler) African Liberation Movements and Support Groups: A Directory, 1972; (compiler) Subject Headings Employed at the Makerere Institute of Social Research Library, 1972; Joy of Cataloging, 1981; (co-ed.) Alternative Library Literature 1982–83, 1984; (ed.) Subject Cataloging: Critiques and Innovations, 1984; (ed.) Cataloging Special Materials: Critiques and Innovations, 1986; (co-ed.) Alternative Library Literature 1984–85, 1987; (co-ed.) Alternative Library Literature 1986–87, 1988; Worth Noting: Editorials, Letters, Essays, an Interview and Bibliography, 1988. Add: 4400 Morningside Rd., Edina, Minn. 55416, U.S.A.

BERMANGE, Barry. British, b. 1933. Plays/Screenplays. *Publs:* Nathan and Tabileth, and Oldenberg, 1967; No Quarter, and the Interview, 1969. Add: 35 Alexandra Park Rd., London N10 2DD, England.

BERMANT, Chaim (Icyk). British, b. 1929. Novels/Short stories, Cultural/Ethnic topics. Staff Writer, Scottish Television, 1958–60, and Granada Television, 1960–61; Features Ed., Jewish Chronicle, London, 1963–65. *Publs:* Jericho Sleeps Alone, 1963; Beryl, 1966; Troubled Eden, 1967; Israel, 1967; Swinging in the Rain, 1968; Here Endeth the Lesson, 1969; The Cousinhood, 1970; Now Dowager, 1971; Roses Are Blooming in Picardy, 1973; The Last Supper, 1974; Point of Arrival, 1974; The Walled Garden: The Saga of Jewish Family and Tradition, 1975; Coming Home, 1976; The Second Mrs. Whitberg, 1976; The Squire of Bor Shachor, 1977; The Jews, 1978; Now Newman Was Old, 1978; (with M. Weitzman) Ebla, 1979; Belshazzar, 1979; The Patriarch, 1981; On the Other Hand, 1982; House of 1983; Dancing Bear, 1984; What's the Joke?, 1986; Titch, 1987; The Companions. Add: 18 Hill Rise, London NW11 6NA, England.

BERNARD, Kenneth. American, b. 1930. Novels/Short stories, Plays/Screenplays. Member, English Dept., Long Island Univ., Brooklyn, N.Y., since 1959. Vice-Pres., New York Theatre Strategy, 1974–80. Asst. Ed., Confrontation, 1975–85. *Publs:* The Maldive Chronicles (novel and short fiction), 1970, 1987; Night Club and Other Plays, 1971;

Two Stories, 1973. Add: 800 Riverside Dr., New York, N.Y. 10032, U.S.A.

BERNARD, Oliver. British, b. 1925. Poetry, Translations. English and Drama Teacher, West Suffolk, 1965–73; West Norfolk Area Drama Specialist, Norfolk Education Cttee., 1974–81. Co-Chmn., Christian CND, 1986. *Publs:* (with others) Country Matters, 1960; (ed. and trans.) Rimbaud: Collected Poems, 1961; (ed. and trans.) Apollinaire: Selections, 1965; Moons and Tides, 1978; Poems, 1983; Five Peace Poems, 1985; The Finger Points at the Moon, 1989. Add: 1 East Church St., Kenninghall, Norwich NR16 2EP, England.

BERNARD, Robert. *See* **MARTIN,** Robert Bernard.

BERNARD, Sidney. American, b. 1918. Poetry, Social commentary/phenomena. Roving Ed., The Smith, and the Newsletter, NYC, since 1967. New York Ed., Literary Times, Chicago, 1963–67. *Publs:* This Way to the Apocalypse: The 1960s, 1969; Witnessing the Seventies, 1977; Metamorphosis of Peace: Essays and Poems, 1984. Add: 5 Beekman St., New York, N.Y. 10038, U.S.A.

BERNAYS, Edward L. American, b. 1891. Advertising/Public relations, Autobiography/Memoirs/Personal. Partner, Edward L. Bernays, Counsel on Public Relations, since 1919. *Publs:* (with others) Broadway Anthology, 1917; Crystallizing Public Opinion, 1923; (ed. and contrib.) An Outline of Careers, 1927; Propaganda, 1928; Speak Up for Democracy, Public Relations—A Growing Profession, 1945; Take Your Place at the Peace Table, 1945; Your Future in Public Relations, 1951; Public Relations, 1952; (ed.) The Engineering of Consent, 1955; Biography of an Idea (autobiography), 1965; (ed. with B. Hershey and contrib.) The Case for Reappraisal of U.S. Overseas Information Policies and Programs, 1970; Your Future in a Public Relations Career, 1979; The Later Years, 1987. Add: 7 Lowell St., Cambridge, Mass. 02138, U.S.A.

BERNDT, Ronald Murray. Australian, b. 1916. Anthropology. Emeritus Prof. since 1981, and Honorary Research Fellow, since 1982, Univ. of Western Australia, Nedlands (Sr. Lectr., 1956–58; Reader, 1958–63; Foundation Prof. of Anthropology, 1963–81). Foundn. Member, Australian Inst. of Aboriginal Studies. Pres., Anthropology Section, Australian and New Zealand Assn. for the Advancement of Science, 1962. *Publs:* Preliminary Report of Field Work in the Ooldea Region, Western South Australia, 1945; (with Catherine C.H. Berndt and A.P. Elkin) Art in Arnhem Land, 1950; (with C.H. Berndt) From Black to White in South Australia, 1951; (with C.H. Berndt) Sexual Behavior in Western Arnhem Land, 1951; Kunapipi: A Study of an Australian Aboriginal Religious Cult, 1951; Djanggawul: An Aboriginal Cult of North-Eastern Arnhem Land, 1952; (with C.H. Berndt) The First Australians, 1952; (with C.H. Berndt) Arnhem Land: Its History and Its People, 1954; Excess and Restraint: Social Control Among a New Guinea Mountain People, 1962; An Adjustment Movement in Arnhem Land, 1962; (with C.H. Berndt) The World of the First Australians, 1964; (with C.H. Berndt) Man, Land, and Myth in North Australia: The Gunwinggu People, 1970; A Question of Choice: An Australian Aboriginal Dilemma, 1971; (with C.H. Berndt) The Barbarians: An Anthropological View, 1971, 1973; Australian Aboriginal Religion, 1974; Love Songs of Arnhem Land, 1976, 1978; Three Faces of Love, 1976; (with C.H. Berndt) Pioneers and Settlers: The Aboriginal Australians, 1978, 2nd ed. as The Aboriginal Australians: The First Pioneers, 1983; (with J.E. Stanton) Australian Aboriginal Art: A Visual Perspective, 1982; (with C.H. Brandt) Aborigines in Australian Society, 1985; End of an Era: Aboriginal Labour in the Northern Territory, 1987; (with C.H. Berndt) The Speaking Land: Myth and Story in Aboriginal Australia, 1989. Add: c/o Dept. of Anthropology, Univ. of Western Australia, Nedlands, W.A. 6009, Australia.

BERNSTEIN, Barton Jannen. American, b. 1936. History, Politics/Government. Prof., since 1982, and Mellon Prof. of Interdisciplinary Studies, since 1987, Stanford Univ., Calif. (Asst. Prof., 1965–68; Assoc. Prof., 1968–82; Courtesy Prof. at the Medical Sch., 1984–86). Faculty member, Bennington Coll., Vt., 1963–65. *Publs:* (co-ed.) The Truman Administration: a Documentary History, 1966; (ed.) Towards A New Past: Dissenting Essays in American History, 1968; (co-ed.) Twentieth-Century America: Recent Interpretations, 1969, 1972; (ed.) Politics and Policies of the Truman Administration, 1970; (co-ed.) Understanding the American Experience: Recent Interpretations (2 vols.), 1973; Hiroshima Reconsidered: The Atomic Bombing of Japan and the Origins of the Cold War, 1941–1945, 1975; (ed.) The Atomic Bomb: The Critical Issues, 1975. Add: Dept. of History, Stanford Univ., Stanford, Calif. 94305, U.S.A.

BERNSTEIN, Basil (Bernard). British, b. 1924. Sociology. Head of Sociological Research Unit since 1963, and Karl Mannheim Prof. of Sociology since 1979, Univ. of London (Senior Lecturer in Sociology of Education, 1963–65; Reader, 1965–67; Prof., 1967–69). *Publs:* Class, Codes and Control: vol. 1, Theoretical Studies Towards a Sociology of Language, vol. 2, Applied Studies Towards a Sociology of Language, and vol. 3, Towards a Theory of Educational Transmission, 1971–75; (with Walter Brandis) Selection and Control: Teachers' Ratings of Children in Infant School, 1974; (with U. Lundgren) Macht und Control, 1985; (with M. Diaz) Towards a Theory of Pedagogic Discourse, 1987. Add: 90 Farquhar Road, Dulwich, London SE19 1LT, England.

BERNSTEIN, Burton. American, b. 1932. Novels/Short stories, Biography, Documentation/Reportage. Staff Writer, The New Yorker, NYC, since 1957. *Publs:* The Grove, 1961; The Lost Art, 1964; The Sticks, 1972; Thurber, 1975; Look I Am Kool! and Other Casuals, 1977; Sinai: The Great and Terrible Wilderness, 1979; Family Matters, 1982; Plane Crazy, 1986. Add: c/o The New Yorker, 25 West 43rd St., New York, N.Y. 10036, U.S.A.

BERNSTEIN, Carl. American, b. 1944. Politics/Government. Principal Corresp., ABC News, since 1981 (Washington Bureau Chief, 1979–81). From copyboy to reporter, Washington Star, 1960–65; Reporter, Elizabeth Journal, New Jersey, 1965–66, and Washington Post, 1966–76. *Publs:* (with Bob Woodward) All the President's Men, 1974; (with Bob Woodward) The Final Days, 1976; The Sophist, 1987; Artifice of Absorption, 1987; Pockets of Lime, 1987; Disloyal, 1988; Loyalties: A Son's Memoirs, 1989. Add: Lynn Nesbitt ICM, 40 W. 57th S, New York, N.Y., 10019, U.S.A.

BERNSTEIN, Charles. American, b. 1950. Poetry, Essays. Writer on medical and health topics. Ed., with Bruce Andrews, L=A=N=G=U=A=G=E, NYC, 1978–81. *Publs:* Parsing, 1976; Shade, 1978; Poetic Justice, 1979; Senses of Responsibility, 1979; (with others) Legend, 1980; Controlling Interests, 1980; Disfrutes, 1981; The Occurrence of Time, 1981; Stigma, 1981; Islets/Irritations, 1983; Resistance, 1983; (ed. with Bruce Andrews) The L=A=N=G=U=A=G=E Book, 1984; Content's Dream: Essays 1975–1984, 1985; The Sophist, 1987; Artiface of Absorption, 1987; Rough Trades, 1989; (ed.) The Politics of Poetic Form: Poetry and Public Policy, 1989. Add: 464 Amsterdam Ave., New York, N.Y. 10024, U.S.A.

BERNSTEIN, Leonard. American, b. 1918. Music. Laureate Conductor, N.Y. Philharmonic Orch. (Asst. Conductor, 1943; Conductor, various times, 1943–58; a Principal Conductor, 1957–58; Music Dir., 1958–69). Dir. NYC Symphony, 1945–48; Head of the Orch. and Conducting Dept., Berkshire Music Center, Tanglewood, Mass., 1951–55; Prof. of Music, Brandeis Univ., Waltham, Mass., 1951–56. Presented concert series on 'Omnibus' TV prog., and CBS series 'Leonard Bernstein and the N.Y. Philharmonic'; directed and conducted N.Y. Philharmonic's Young People's Concerts, nationwide television. *Publs:* The Joy of Music, 1959; Leonard Bernstein's Young People's Concerts, 1962; The Infinite Variety of music, 1966; The Unanswered Question, 1976; Findings, 1982. Add: c/o Amberson Enterprises, 24 W. 57th St., New York, N.Y. 10019, U.S.A.

BERRIGAN, Daniel J. American, b. 1921. Plays/Screenplay, Poetry, Social commentary/phenomena, Theology/Religion, Autobiography/Memoirs/Personal. Ordained Roman Catholic priest, 1952; member, Soc. of Jesus. Taught French and philosophy, Brooklyn Preparatory Sch., N.Y., 1954–57; Prof. of New Testament Studies, LeMoyne Coll., Syracuse, N.Y., 1957–63; Dir. of United Christian Work, Cornell Univ., Ithaca, N.Y., 1967–68; jailed for anti-war activities, 1968. *Publs:* Time Without Numbers, 1957 (Lamont Poetry Selection Award); The Bride: Essays in the Church, 1959; Encounters 1960; The Bow in the Clouds: Man's Covenant with God, 1961; The World for Wedding Ring: Poems, 1962; No One Walks Waters, 1966; False Gods, Real Men: New Poems, 1966; They Call Us Dead Men: Reflections on Life and Conscience, 1966; Consequences: Truth and . . . 1967; Go from Here: A Prison Diary, 1968; Love, Love at the End: Parables, Prayers and Meditations, 1968; Night Flight to Hanoi: War Diary with 11 Poems, 1968; Crime Trial, 1970; (with Thomas Lewis) Trial Poems, 1970; The Trial of the Catonsville Nine (play), 1970; No Bars to Manhood, 1970; The Dark Night of Resistance, 1971: The Geography of Faith: Conversations Between Daniel Berrigan, when Underground, and Robert Coles, 1971; Absurd Convictions, Modest Hopes: Conversations after Prison with Lee Lockwood, 1972; American is Hard to Find, 1972; Jesus Christ, 1973; Selected and New Poems, 1973; Prison Poems, 1973; Prison Poems, 1974; Lights on in the House of the Dead: A Prison Diary, 1974; (with Thich

Nhat Hanh) The Raft is Not the Shore: Conversations Toward Buddhist/Christian Awareness, 1975; Uncommon Prayer, 1978; Beside the Sea of Glass, 1978; The Discipline of the Mountain, 1979; We Die Before We Live, 1980; Ten Commandments for the Long Haul, 1981; Portraits: Of Those I Love, 1982; The Nightmare of God, 1983; Journey to Black Island, 1984; The Mission: A Film Journal, 1986; To Dwell in Peace: An Autobiography, 1987; (with Margaret Parker) Stations, 1988; Daniel Berrigan: Poetry, Drama, Prose, 1988. Add: 220 W. 98th St., New York, N.Y. 10025, U.S.A.

BERRILL, Norman John. Canadian, b. 1903. Biology, Environmental science/Ecology, Zoology. Lectr. in Biology, Swarthmore Coll., Pennsylvania. Lectr. in Zoology, Univ. of London, 1925–27; Lectr. in Physiology, Univ. of Leeds, 1927–28; Asst. Prof. of Zoology, 1928–31, Assoc. Prof., 1931–46, Chmn., Dept. of Zoology, 1937–47, and Strathcona Prof. of Zoology, 1946–65, McGill Univ., Montreal. *Publs:* The Living Tide, 1951; Journey into Wonder, 1952; Sex and the Nature of Things, 1953; The Origin of Vertebrates, 1955; Man's Emerging Mind, 1955; Growth, Development and Pattern, 1961; Worlds Without End, 1964; Biology in Action, 1966; The Person in the Womb, 1968; Developmental Biology, 1971; Development, 1976. Add: 410 Swarthmore Ave., Swarthmore, Pa. 19081, U.S.A.

BERRINGTON, Hugh Bayard. British, b. 1928. Politics/Government. Prof. of Politics, Univ. of Newcastle upon Tyne, since 1970 (Reader, 1965–70). Asst. Lectr., and subsequently Lectr., Univ. of Keele, Staffs., 1956–65. *Publs:* (with S.E. Finer and D.J. Bartholomew) Backbench Opinion in the House of Commons, 1955–59, 1961; How Nations are Governed (textbook); Backbench Opinion in the House of Commons, 1945–55, 1973. Add: 4 Fenwick Terr., Newcastle upon Tyne, Tyne and Wear NE2 2JQ, England.

BERRISFORD, Judith. *See* **LEWIS,** Judith Mary.

BERRY, Adrian M. British, b. 1937. Science fiction, Astronomy, Sciences. Fellow, Royal Astronomical Soc., London, since 1973; Sr. Fellow, British Interplanetary Soc., since 1986; Science Corresp., Daily Telegraph, since 1977. Former member of science staff, Daily Telegraph, London; Corresp., Time mag., NYC, 1965–67. *Publs:* The Next Ten Thousand Years: A Vision of Man's Future in the Univese, 1974; The Iron Sun: Crossing the Universe through Black Holes, 1977; From Apes to Astronauts, 1981; The Super Intelligent Machine, 1983; High Skies and Yellow Rain, 1983; Koyama's Diamond (fiction), 1984; Labyrinth of Lies, 1985; Ice with Your Evolution, 1986. Add: 11 Cottesmore Gardens, Kensington, London W8, England.

BERRY, Barbara. American, b. 1937. Children's fiction, Animals, Pets. *Publs:* Shannon (novel), 1968; Just Don't Bug Me (novel), 1971; Let'er Buck!—The Rodeo, 1971; A Look of Eagles (novel), 1973; The Thoroughbreds, 1974; His Majesty's Mark (novel), 1976; Horse Happy: A Complete Guide to Owning Your First Horse, 1978; The Standardbreds, 1979. Add: Box 231, Ashville, N.Y. 14710, U.S.A.

BERRY, Brian Joe Lobley. American, b. 1934. Geography, Planning. Founders Prof., Prof. of Political Economy, Univ. of Texas, Dallas, since 1986. Member of faculty, Brookings Instn., Washington, D.C., 1966–76; Prof., Harvard Univ., Cambridge, Mass., 1976–81. Prof. and Dean, Sch. of Urban and Public Affairs, Carnegie Mellon Univ., Pittsburgh, 1981–86. *Publs:* Growth Centers in the American Urban System, 1960–1970, 1973; The Human Consequences of Urbanization: Divergent Paths in the Urban Experience of the Twentieth Century, 1973; (with others) Land Use, Urban Form, and Environmental Quality, 1974; (with Frank E. Horton) Urban Environmental Management: Planning for Pollution Control, 1974; The Open Housing Question: Race and Housing in Chicago 1966–76, 1979; Comparative Urbanization, 2nd ed., 1983; (with others) Economic Geography, 1987; (with others) Market Centers and Retail Location, 1988; editor, numerous books. Add: School of Social Science, Univ. of Texas-Dallas, Richardson, Tx. 75083, U.S.A.

BERRY, Cicely. British, b. 1926. Speech/Rhetoric. Voice Dir., Royal Shakespeare Company, Stratford and London, since 1969. Teacher of Voice and Speech, Central Sch. of Speech and Drama, London, 1948–65. *Publs:* Voice and the Actor, 1973; Your Voice and How to Use It Successfully, 1975; The Actor and His Text, 1987. Add: The Old School House, Walton, Warwick CV35 9HX, England.

BERRY, Don. American, b. 1932. Westerns/Adventure, History. Freelance writer. *Publs:* Trask (novel), 1960; A Majority of Scoundrels: An Informal History of the Rocky Mountain Fur Company, 1961;

Moontrap (novel), 1962; To Build a Ship (novel), 1963; Mountain Men: The Trappers of the Great Fur-Trading Era 1822-1843 (juvenile), 1966. Add: c/o Viking Penguin, 40 W. 23rd St., New York, N.Y. 10010, U.S.A.

BERRY, Francis. British, b. 1915. Novels/Short stories, Poetry, Literature. Prof. of English, Royal Holloway Coll., Univ. of London, 1970–80, now Emeritus. Asst. Lectr., subsequently Lectr., Sr. Lectr., Reader and Prof., Univ. of Sheffield, 1947–70. *Publs:* Gospel of Fire, 1933; Snake in the Moon, 1936; The Iron Christ: A Poem, 1938; Fall of a Tower and Other Poems, 1943; Murdock and Other Poems; The Galloping Centaur: Poems 1933–1951, 1952; Herbert Read, 1953; (ed.) An Anthology of Medieval Poems, 1954; Poets' Grammar: Person, Time and Mood in Poetry, 1958; Morant Bay and Other Poems, 1961; Poetry and the Physical Voice, 1962; The Shakespeare Inset: Word and Picture, 1965; Ghosts of Greenland, 1966; (ed.) Essays and Studies 1969; Thoughts on Poetic Time, 1972; I Tell of Greenland (novel), 1977; From the Red Fort (poetry), 1984. Add: 4 Eastgate St., Winchester SO23 8EB, England.

BERRY, James. British, b. 1925. Short stories, Poetry, Children's fiction. Overseas telegraphist, Post Office, London, 1951–77. *Publs:* for adults—Fractured Circles (poetry), 1979; Cut-Way Feelings, Loving, Lucy's Letters (poetry), 1981; Chain of Days (poetry), 1985; The Girls and Yanga Marshall (short stories), 1987; for children—A Thief in the Village and Other Stories, 1987; When I Dance (poetry), 1988. Add: c/o Hamish Hamilton, 27 Wrights Lane, London W8 5TZ, England.

BERRY, Paul. British, b. 1919. Biography. Sr. Lectr., Kingsway-Princeton Coll. for Further Education, 1973–81 (Lectr., 1956–73). Literary Executor for Winifred Holtby and for Vera Brittain. *Publs:* (with Renee Huggett) Daughters of Cain, 1956; By Royal Appointment: A Biography of Mary Ann Clarke, Mistress of the Duke of York 1803-7, 1970; (co-ed.) The Selected Journalism of Winifred Holtby and Vera Brittain, 1985. Add: 1 Bridgefoot Cottages, Stedham, Midhurst, Sussex, England.

BERRY, Ron. British, b. 1920. Novels/Short stories, Plays/Screenplays. *Publs:* Hunters and Hunted, 1960; Travelling Loaded, 1962; Everybody Loves Saturday Night (radio play), 1963; The Full-time Amateur, 1964; Flame and Slag, 1966; Death of a Dog (television play), 1968; But Now They Have Fled (television play), 1969; So-long, Hector Bebb, 1970; Uncle Rollo (television play), 1971; Where Darts the Gar, Where Floats the Wrack (television play), 1974; Peregrine Watching, 1987. Add: 1 Ael-y-Bryn, Treherbert, Rhondda, Wales.

BERRY, Thomas. American, b. 1914. Philosophy, Theology/Religion. Assoc. Prof., Dept. of History of Religions, Fordham Univ., Bronx, N.Y., since 1966. Dir., Riverdale Center for Religious Research, Bronx., N.Y., since 1970. Assoc. Prof. of Asian History, Inst. for Asian Studies, Seton Hall Univ., South Orange, N.Y., 1957–61; Assoc. Prof. of Asian History, Center for Asian Studies, St. John's Univ., Jamaica, N.Y., 1961–65. *Publs:* Historical Theory of John Battista Vico, 1949; Buddhism, 1966; Religions of India: Hinduism, Yoga, Buddhism, 1971. Add: 5801 Palisade Ave., Bronx, N.Y. 10471, U.S.A.

BERRY, Wallace Taft. American, b. 1928. Music. Prof. of Music Theory, Univ. of British Columbia, Vancouver, since 1977. Lectr. in Opera and Composition, Univ. of Southern California, Los Angeles, 1956–57; Prof. of Music Theory, Univ. of Michigan, Ann Arbor, 1957–77. *Publs:* Form in Music, 1966; (with E. Chudacoff) Eighteenth-Century Imitative Counterpoint: Music for Analysis, 1969; Structural Functions in Music, 1975. Add: Dept. of Music, Univ. of British Columbia, 6361 Memorial Rd., Vancouver, B.C. V6T 1W5, Canada.

BERRY, Wendell (Erdman). American, b. 1934. Novels/Short stories. Poetry, Agriculture/Forestry, Environmental science/Ecology. Member of English Dept., Univ. of Kentucky, Lexington, 1964–77. *Publs:* Nathan Coulter (novel), 1960; November Twenty-Six, Nineteen Hundred Sixty-Three, 1964; The Broken Ground: Poems, 1964; A Place on Earth (novel), 1967; The Long-Legged House (essays), 1969; Openings: Poems, 1969; Findings, 1969; The Hidden Wound, 1970; Farming: A Hand Book, 1970; The Unforeseen Wilderness: An Essay on Kentucky's Red River Gorge, 1971; A Continuous Harmony: Essays Cultural and Agricultural, 1972; The Country of Marriage, 1973, 1985; The Memory of Old Jack (novel), 1974; An Eastward Look (verse), 1974; To What Listens (verse), 1975; Horses (verse), 1975; Sayings and Doings, 1975; The Kentucky River: Two Poems, 1976; Three Memorial Poems, 1977; The Unsettling of America, 1977; Clearing (verse), 1977; Recollected Essays, 1981; The Gift of Good Land, 1981; The Wheel (verse), 1982; Collected Poems, 1985; Standing by Words, 1985; Sabbaths (verse), 1987. Add: Port Royal, Ky. 40058, U.S.A.

BERTIN, Jack. *See* **CORD, Barry.**

BERTOLINO, James. American, b. 1942. Poetry. Ed., Abraxas mag. and Abraxas Press, Madison, Wisc., and Ithaca, N.Y., 1968–72; Teaching Asst., Washington State Univ., Pullman; Ed., Stone Marrow Press, Ithaca, N.Y., and Cincinnati, Ohio, 1970–76; Asst. Ed., Epoch mag., Ithaca, N.Y., 1971–73; Teaching Asst., 1971–73, and Lectr. in Creative Writing, 1973–74, Cornell Univ., Ithaca, N.Y.; Asst. Prof., 1974–77, Assoc. Prof. of English, 1977–84, Univ. of Cincinnati; Co-Ed., Cincinnati Poetry Review, 1975–82; Poetry Ed., Eureka Review, Cincinnati, 1975–81; Instructor, Skagit Valley College, 1984–89. *Publs:* Day of Change, 1968; Drool, 1968; (ed.) Quixote: Northwest Poets, 1968; Mr Nobody, 1969; Ceremony: A Poem, 1969; Maize: A Poem, 1969; Stone Marrow, 1969; Becoming Human: Poems, 1970; (ed.) The Abraxas/Five Anthology, 1972; The Interim Handout, 1972; Employed, 1972; Edging Through, 1972; Soft Rock, 1973; Making Space for Our Living, 1975; Terminal Placebos, 1975; The Gestures, 1975; The Alleged Conception, 1976; New and Selected Poems, 1978; Are You Tough Enough for the Eighties?, 1979; Precinct Kali and the Gertrude Spicer Story, 1981; First Credo, 1986. Add: P.O. Box 1157, Anacortes, Wash. U.S.A.

BERTON, Pierre. Canadian, b. 1920. Children's fiction, History, Social commentary/phenomena, Biography, Humor/Satire. Dir., McClelland & Stewart Ltd.; Editorial Dir., Natural Science of Canada Ltd. City Ed., Vancouver News Herald, 1940–41; Managing Ed., Maclean's, 1947–58; Assoc. Ed. and Columnist, The Toronto Star, 1948–62; Editorial Dir., Canadian Centennial Library, 1965–70. *Publs:* The Royal Family, 1954; The Golden Trail Stampede for Gold, 1955; The Mysterious North, 1956; Klondike, 1958; Klondike Fever, 1958; Just Add Water and Stir, 1959; Adventures of a Columnist, 1960; The New City, 1961; The Secret World of Og, 1961; Fast, Fast, Fast Relief, 1962; The Big Sell, 1963; The Comfortable Pew, 1965; My War with the Twentieth Century, 1965; Remember Yesterday, 1966; The Centennial Food Guide, 1966; The Cool, Crazy, Committed World of the Sixties, 1966; (ed. and contrib.) Voices from the Sixties: Historic Headlines, 1967; The Smug Minority, 1968; The National Dream, 1970; The Last Spike, 1971; The Great Railway Illustrated, 1972; The Impossible Railway, 1972; Drifting Home, 1973; Hollywood's Canada, 1974; My Country, 1976; The Dionne Years, 1977; The Wild Frontier, 1978; The Invasion of Canada, 1980; Flames Across the Border, 1981; Why We Act Like Canadians, 1982; Klondike Quest, 1983; The Promised Land, 1984; Masquerade, 1985; Vimy, 1986; Starting Out, 1987; The Arctic Grail, 1988. Add: 21 Sackville St., Toronto, Ont. M5A 3E1, Canada.

BERTRAM, James. New Zealander, b. 1910. Poetry, Literature, Travel/Exploration/Adventure. Emeritus Prof. of English, Victoria Univ. of Wellington, since 1975 (Sr. Lectr., 1947–65; Assoc. Prof., 1965–70; Prof., 1970–75). Press Attaché, British Embassy, Chungking, China, 1941; Advisor to Far Eastern Commn., Tokyo, 1946–47. *Publs:* Crisis in China (in U.S. as First Act in China), 1937; North China Front (in U.S. as Unconquered), 1938; The Shadow of a War (in U.S. as Beneath the Shadow), 1957; Return to China, 1957; The Young Traveller in China Today, 1961; (ed.) The New Zealand Letters of Thomas Arnold the Younger, 1966; Occasional Verses, 1971; Charles Brasch, 1976; (ed.) New Zealand Love Poems, 1977; (ed.) Letters of Thomas Arnold 1850-1900, 1980; Dan Davin, 1982; Flight of the Phoenix: Critical Notes on New Zealand Writers, 1985. Add: 30 Park Rd., Belmont, Lower Hutt, New Zealand.

BESTOR, Arthur E. American, b. 1908. Education, History. Emeritus Prof. of History, Univ. of Washington, Seattle, since 1976 (Prof., 1962–76). Instr., Yale Univ., New Haven, Conn., 1930–31 and 1934–36; Asst. Prof., Columbia Univ., NYC, 1937–42; Asst. Prof. of Humanities, 1942–45, and Assoc. Prof. of History, 1945–46, Stanford Univ., Calif.; Assoc. Prof. of History, 1947–51, and Prof., 1951–62, Univ. of Illinois, Urbana; Harmsworth Prof. of American History, Oxford Univ., 1956–57. *Publs:* David Jacks of Montery, and Lee L. Jacks, His Daughter, 1945; (ed. and author) Education and Reform at New Harmony: Correspondence of William Maclure and Marie D. Fretageot, 1948; Backwoods Utopias: The Sectarian and Owenite Phases of Communitarian Socialism in America 1663-1829, 1950, rev. ed. 1970; Educational Wastelands: The Retreat from Learning in Our Public Schools, 1953, 1985; The Restoration of Learning: A Program for Redeeming the Unfulfilled Promise of American Education, 1955; (with D.C. Mearns and J. Daniels) Three Presidents and Their Books, 1955; (with others) The Heritage of the Middle West, 1958; (with others) Education in the Age of Science, 1959; (with others) Interpreting and Teaching American History, 1961; (with others) The American Territorial System, 1973. Add: 55th Ave. N.E., Seattle, Wash. 98105, U.S.A.

BETHEL, Dell. American, b. 1929. Sports/Fitness. Professional baseball player, New York Giants, 1943–53; coach and teacher, Minnesota, Washington, and California, 1953–66; Assoc. Prof. of Physical Education, Dept. Head and Head Baseball Coach, Olivet Coll., Michigan, 1966–71; Asst. Prof. of Physical Education and Head Baseball Coach, City Coll. of the City Univ. of New York, 1971–73; Technical Dir., Bang the Drum Slowly (film), 1972–73; Coach, North Ridgeville, Ohio, 1973–77. *Publs:* Inside Baseball: Tips and Techniques for Coaches and Players, 1969; (with others) The Best in Baseball, 1970; The Complete Book of Baseball Instruction, 1978; Coaching Winning Baseball, 1979; The Men of Old Baldy, 1987. Add: c/o Spectrum Books, Prentice Hall, Englewood Cliffs, NJ 07632, U.S.A.

BETHELL, Nicholas (William). (Lord Bethell of Romford). British, b. 1938. History, International relations/Current affairs, Translations, Member of the House of Lords (Govt. Whip, 1970–71); Member of the European Parliament, since 1975. Sub-Ed., Times Literary Supplement, London, 1962–64; Script Ed., BBC, London, 1964–67. *Publs:* (ed. and trans.) Elegy to John Donne and Other Poems, by Joseph Brodsky, 1967; (trans.) Six Plays, by Slawomir Mrozek, 1967; Gomulka: His Poland and His Communism, 1969; (trans. with David Burg) Cancer Ward and The Love-Girl and the Innocent, by Alexander Solzhenitsyn, (play), 1969; The War Hitler Won, 1973; The Last Secret: Forcible Repatriation to Russia 1944–1947, 1974; Russia Besieged, 1977; The Palestine Triangle, 1979; The Great Betrayal, 1984. Add: 73 Sussex Sq., London W2 2SS, England.

BETHMANN, Erich (Waldemar). American b. 1904. Theology/Religion. Member of Seventh Day Adventist educational mission in Egypt, 1928–32; Dir. of Missions in Transjordan, 1933–37, Iraq, 1937–39, and India, 1939–46; writer and lectr. in U.S., 1946–50; Dir. of Research Publications, American Friends of the Middle East, Washington, D.C., 1951–69. *Publs:* Bridge of Islam, 1950; Decisive Years in Palestine, 1954; (ed.) The Proceedings of the First Muslim-Christian Convocation, 1955; The Fate of Muslims Under Soviet Rule, 1955; Yemen on the Threshold, 1960; Steps Toward Understanding Islam, 1966; (ed.) Basic Fact Series on Middle East; (ed.) Continuing Committee of Muslim-Christian Cooperation. Add: 1830 R St., N.W., Washington, D.C. 20009, U.S.A.

BETTELHEIM, Bruno. American, b. 1903. Psychology. Dir., Sonia Shankman Orthogenic Sch.; Stella Rowley Distinguished Prof. of Education, and Prof. of Psychology and Psychiatry, Univ. of Chicago, 1963–73, now retired (Research Assoc., Progressive Education Assn., 1939–41, Asst. Prof. of Educational Psychology, 1944–47, Assoc. Prof., 1947–52, and Prof., 1952–63). Assoc. Prof. of Psychology, Rockford Coll., Ill., 1942–44. *Publs:* (with M. Janowitz) Dynamics of Prejudice, 1950; Love Is Not Enough: The Treatment of Emotionally Disturbed Children, 1950; Symbolic Wounds, 1954; Truants from Life, 1955; The Informed Heart, 1960; Dialogues with Mothers, 1962; The Empty Fortress, 1967; The Children of the Dream, 1969; A Home for the Heart, 1974; The Uses of Enchantment: The Meaning and Importance of Fairy Tales, 1976; Surviving and Other Essays, 1979; (with Karen Zelan) On Learning to Read, 1982; Freud and Man's Soul, 1983; (with Anne Freedgood) A Good Enough Parent, 1987. Add: 718 Adelaide Pl., Santa Monica, Calif. 90402, U.S.A.

BETTERIDGE, Anne. *See* **POTTER**, Margaret.

BETTINA. Pseudonym for Bettina Ehrlich, née Bauer. British (born Austrian), b. 1903. Children's Fiction. Freelance writer and artist. *Publs:* Show Me Yours: A Little Paintbook, 1943; Poo-Tsee, The Water-Tortoise, 1943; Cocolo, 1945; Carmello, 1945; Cocolo Comes to America, 1949; Cocolo's Home, 1950; Castle in the Sand, 1951; A Horse for the Island, 1952; Piccolo, 1954; Pantaloni, 1957; Angelo and Rosaline, 1957; Trovato, 1959; Paolo and Panetto, 1960; For the Leg of a Chicken, 1960; Francesco and Francesca, 1962; Dolls (non-fiction), 1962; Of Uncles and Aunts, 1963; The Goat Boy, 1965; Sardines and the Angel, 1967; Neretto, 1969; A Day in Venice, 1973. Add: 22 Palace Gardens Terr., London W8 4RP, England.

BETTS, Charles L. American, b. 1908. Sports/Physical education/Keeping fit. Former Vice Pres., Soc. of Automotive Historians; former Assoc. Ed., Antique Automobile. Former Design Engineer, United Engineers and Constructors Inc., Philadelphia, Pa. *Publs:* American Vintage Cars, 1963; (with A. Bochroch) American Automobile Racing, 1974. Add: 2105 Stackhouse Dr., Yardley, Pa. 19067, U.S.A.

BETTS, John (Edward). Canadian, b. 1939. Technology, Physics.

Coordinator of Physics, Camosun Coll., Victoria, B.C., since 1978 (Instr. in Physics, 1971–78). Officer, Royal Canadian Air Force, 1957–64; student, 1964–69; Instr. in Physics, Mohawk Coll., Hamilton, Ont., 1969–71. *Publs:* Physics for Technology, 1976, 1981; (with N. Preston) Foundations of Elementary Physics, 1978. Add: 4886 W. Saanich Rd., Victoria, B.C. V8Z 3H7, Canada.

BETTS, Raymond Frederick. American, b. 1925. History, International relations/Current affairs. Prof. of History, Univ. of Kentucky, Lexington, since 1971. Columnist, Lexington Herald. Asst. Prof. of History, Bryn Mawr Coll., Pa., 1956–61; Prof. of History, Grinnell Coll., Iowa, 1961–71. *Publs:* Assimilation and Association in French Colonial Theory 1890-1914, 1961; (ed.) The Scramble of Africa, 1966; Europe Overseas: Phases of Imperialism, 1968; (ed.) The Ideology of Blackness, 1971; The False Dawn: European Imperialism in the Nineteenth Century, 1975; Tricouleur: The French Colonial Empire, 1978; Europe in Retrospect: A Brief History of the Past Two Hundred Years, 1979; Uncertain Dimensions: Western Overseas Empires in the Twentieth Century, 1985. Add: 311 Mariemont Dr., Lexington, Ky. 40505, U.S.A.

BETTS, Victoria Bedford. American, b. 1913. Crafts. Art Consultant, Biney & Smith Inc., NYC, 1936–58. *Publs:* Exploring Papier Maché 1955; Exploring Finger Paint, 1963. Add: 2105 Stackhouse Dr., Yardley, 19067, U.S.A.

BETTS, William Wilson, Jr. American, b. 1926. Literature, Humor/Satire. Prof. of English, Indiana Univ. of Pennsylvania, since 1957 (Assoc. Prof., 1955–57; Asst. Dean of Grad. Sch., 1968–71). Instr., Ohio Univ., Athens, 1954–55. Outdoors Ed., Indiana Evening Gazette, 1973–80. *Publs:* (ed. with Philip A. Shelley and Arthur O. Lewis) Anglo-German and American-German Crosscurrents, vol. I, 1957; Lincoln and the Poets, 1965; A Docketful of Wry (humor), 1970. Add: R.D.6, Indiana, Pa. 15701, U.S.A.

BEVAN, Gloria. New Zealander. Historical/Romance/Gothic. *Publs:* The Distant Trap, 1969; The Hills of Maketu, 1969; Beyond the Ranges, 1970; Make Way for Tomorrow, 1971; It Began in Te Rangi, 1971; Vineyard in a Valley, 1972; Flame in Fiji, 1973; The Frost and the Fire, 1973; Connelly's Castle, 1974; High-Country Wife, 1974; Always a Rainbow, 1975; Dolphin Bay, 1976; Bachelor Territory, 1977; Plantation Moon, 1977; Fringe of Heaven, 1978; Kowhai Country, 1979; Half a World Away, 1980; Master of Mahia, 1981; Emerald Cave, 1981; The Rouseabout Girl, 1983; Southern Sunshine, 1985; Golden Bay, 1986; Pacific Paradise, 1989. Lives in Onehunga, Auckland. Add: c/o Mills and Boon Ltd., Eton House, 18-24 Paradise Rd., Richmond, Surrey TW9 1SR, England.

BEVAN, James (Stuart). British, b. 1930. Medicine/Health. Physician: partner in a medical general practice, London. Medical Adviser, London Coll. of Music. *Publs:* State Final Questions and Answers for Nurses, 1962; Preliminary Questions and Answers for Nurses, 1963; Sex: The Plain Facts, 1966; A Pictorial Handbook of Anatomy and Physiology, 1979; The Pocket Medical and First Aid Guide, 1979; Your Family Doctor, 1980; The Family First Aid and Medical Guide, 1984. Add: 9 Hill Rd., London NW8 9QE, England.

BEVERIDGE, William (Ian Beardmore). Australian, b. 1908. Medicine/Health. Prof. of Animal Pathology, Cambridge Univ., 1947–75. Consultant, World Health Org., 1965–78, and Bureau of Animal Health, Canberra, 1979–85. *Publs:* The Art of Scientific Investigation, 1950; Frontiers in Comparative Medicine, 1972; Influenza: The Last Great Plague, 1977; Seeds of Discovery, 1980; Viral Diseases of Farm Livestock, 1981; Bacterial Diseases of Ruminants, 1982. Add: 5 Bellevue Rd., Wentworth Falls, N.S.W. 2782, Australia.

BEWES, Richard. British, b. 1934. Theology/Religion. Church of England Clergyman: Rector of All Souls, Langham Pl., London, since 1983. Vicar, St. Peter's, Harold Wood, Essex, 1965–74, and Emmanuel Church, Northwood, Middx., 1974–83. *Publs:* God in Ward 12, 1974; Advantage Mr. Christian, 1975; Talking about Prayer, 1979; John Wesley's England, 1981; The Church Reaches Out, 1981; The Pocket Handbook of Christian Truth, 1981; The Church Overcomes, 1984; On the Way, 1984; Quest for Truth, 1985; Quest for Life, 1985; The Church Marches On, 1986; When God Surprises, 1986. Add: 2 All Soul's Pl., London W1N 3DB, England.

BEYER, Werner W(illiam). American, b. 1911. Literature. Emeritus Rebecca Clifton Reade Prof. of English and Head of English Dept., Butler Univ., Indianapolis (Assoc. Prof., 1948–51; Prof., since 1951). Jr.

League Lectr., since 1963. Instr. in English, Drew Univ., Madison, N.J., 1943–45; Asst. Prof., Rutgers Univ., N.J., 1945–48. *Publs:* The Prestige of C.M. Wieland in England, 1936; Keats and the Daemon King, 1947; The Enchanted Forest, 1963; (bibliographer) The World in Literature, 2 vols., 1967. Add: 6455 East 96th St., Indianapolis, Ind. 46250, U.S.A.

BEYFUS, Drusilla. British. Human relations, Social commentary/phenomena. Contributing Ed., Vogue mag., London, since 1980 (Assoc. Ed., 1979–86). Assoc. Ed., Queen Mag., London, 1959–63; Home Ed., The Observer, London, 1962–64; Assoc. Ed., Weekend Telegraph mag., London, 1963–71; Ed., Brides and Setting Up Home mag., London 1971–79. *Publs:* (with Anne Edwards) Lady Behave, 1956, 1969; The English Marriage, 1968; The Brides Book, 1981. Add: 51g Eaton Sq., London SW1, England.

BEYNON, Huw. British, b. 1942. Industrial relations, Sociology. Prof. in Sociology, Univ of Manchester. Former Lectr. in Sociology, Univ. of Bristol; Research Fellow, Univ. of Manchester, 1973–74; former Reader in Sociology, Univ. of Durham. *Publs:* (with R.M. Blackburn) Perceptions of Work, 1972; Working for Ford, 1973, 1984; (with Theo Nichols) Living with Capitalism, 1977; What Happened at Speke?, 1978; (with Hilary Wainwright) The Workers Report on Vickers Ltd., 1979; (with Nick Hedges) Born to Work, 1982; (ed.) Digging Deeper: Issues in the Miners Strike, 1985. Add: Dept. of Sociology, Univ. of Manchester, Manchester M13 9PL, England.

BHAGAT, Goberdhan. Indian, b. 1928. History. Prof. of Political Science, Univ. of Mississippi, since 1969 (Asst. Prof., 1964–66; Assoc. Prof., 1966–69). Advisor, Permanent Mission of India to the U.N., NYC, 1956–64. *Publs:* Americans in India, 1784-1860, 1970. Add: Dept. of Political Science, Univ. of Mississippi, University, Miss. 38677, U.S.A.

BHARATI, Agehananda. American, b. 1923. Anthropology/Ethnology, Philosophy, Theology/Religion. Prof. and Chmn., Dept. of Anthropology, Syracuse Univ., N.Y. (joined faculty, 1961). Ed., Tibet Soc. Bulletin, Bloomington, Ind., since 1974. Fulbright Prof., Univ. of Marburg, West Germany, 1987. *Publs:* The Ochre Robe, 1962; A Functional Analysis of Indian Thought and Its Social Margins, 1964; The Tantric Tradition, 1969; The Asians in East Africa: Jayhind and Uhuru, 1973; The Light at the Center: Context and Pretext of Modern Mysticism, 1976; (ed.) Realm of the Extrahuman, 2 vols., 1976; Great Tradition and Little Traditions: Indological Investigations in Cultural Anthropology, 1978; Hindu Views and Ways: An Anthropological Assessment, 1980; India: South Asian Perspectives on Aggression, 1983. Add: 500 University Pl., Syracuse, N.Y. 13244, U.S.A.

BHATIA, Jamunadevi. Writes as June Bhatia, June Edwards, Helen Forrester, and J. Rana. British, b. 1919. Novels/Short stories, Autobiography/Memoirs/Personal. *Publs:* (as J. Rana) Alien There is None, 1959; (as June Bhatia) The Latchkey Kid, 1970; republished as by Helen Forrester, 1985; (as Helen Forrester) Twopence to Cross the Mersey, 1974; (as June Edwards) Most Precious Employee, 1974; (as Helen Forrester) Minerva's Stepchild, 1979; (as June Bhatia) Liverpool Daisy, 1979; (as Helen Forrester) By the Waters of Liverpool, 1981; (as Helen Forrester) Three Women of Liverpool, 1984. Add: 8734 117th St., Edmonton T6G 1R5, Canada.

BHATIA, June. *See* **BHATIA,** Jamunadevi.

BHATT, Jagdish J(eyshanker). American, b. 1939. Poetry, Earth sciences, Environmental science/Ecology, Marine science/Oceanography. Prof. of Geology and Oceanography since 1974, and Advisor to the Geological Club since 1974, Community Coll. of Rhode Island, Warwick, R.I. (Member, Curriculum Cttee., Arts and Science Div., 1977–78). Instr. in Physical Science and Chemistry, and Advisor to the Intnl. Club, Jackson Jr. Coll., Jackson Mich., 1964–65; Instr. in Physical Science and Geology, and Faculty Advisor to the Geological Soc., Panhandle State Univ., Goodwell, Okla., 1965–66; Post Doctoral Research Scholar, Stanford Univ., Calif., 1971–72; Asst. Prof., State Univ. of New York, Buffalo, 1972–74. Project Dir., Applied Oceanography Student Workshop, Community Coll. of Rhode Island, 1976–81. *Publs:* Lab. Manual on Physical Geology, 1966; Lab. Manual on Physical Science, 1966; Cretaceous History of Himalayan Geosyncline, 1966; Environmentology: Earth's Environment and Energy Resources, 1975; Geochemistry and Geology of South Wales Main Limestone, 1976; Geologic Exploration of Earth, 1976; Oceanography: Exploring the Planet Ocean, 1978; Applied Oceanography: Mining Energy and Management, 1979; Ocean Enterprise: Domain of Resources, Policies and Conflicts (textbook), 1984. Add: 11 Midlands Dr., E. Greenwich, R.I. 02818, U.S.A.

BIANCHI, Eugene Carl. American, b. 1930. Theology/Religion. Prof. of Religion, Emory Univ., Atlanta, Ga., since 1968. Asst. Ed., American mag., NYC, 1963–66; Asst. Prof. of Religion, 1966–68, and Dir., Center for Study of Contemporary Values, 1967–68, Univ. of Santa Clara, Calif.; Distinguished Visiting Prof., California State Univ., Sacramento, 1974–75. *Publs:* John XXIII and American Protestants, 1968; Reconciliation: The Function of the Church, 1969; The Religious Experience of Revolutionaries, 1972; (with Rosemary P. Ruether) From Machismo to Mutuality, 1975; Aging As a Spiritual Journey, 1982; On Growing Older, 1985. Add: Dept. of Religion, Emory Univ., Atlanta, Ga. 30322, U.S.A.

BIASIN, Gian-Polo. Italian, b. 1933. Literature. Prof., Univ. of Texas, Austin, since 1973. Asst. Prof., 1964–67, and Assoc. Prof. of Romance Studies, 1967–73, Cornell Univ., Ithaca, N.Y. *Publs:* The Smile of the Gods: A Thematic Analysis of C. Pavese's Works, 1968; Literary Diseases: Theme and Metaphor in the Italian Novel, 1975; Italian Literary Icons, 1985. Add: French and Italian Dept., Sutton Hall 105, Univ. of Texas, Austin, Tex. 78712, U.S.A.

BIBBY, Violet. British, b. 1908. Children's fiction. Worked as an English and Arts and Crafts teacher. *Publs:* Saranne, 1969; The Mirrored Shield, 1970; The Wilding, 1971; Many Waters (in U.S. as Many Waters Cannot Quench Love) 1974; Tinner's Quest, 1977; The Phantom Horse, 1979. Add: 1 Cumberland Rd., Angmering, Sussex BN16 4BG, England.

BIBOLET, R.H. *See* **KELLY,** Tim.

BICKEL, Lennard. Australian, b. 1923. Sciences, Biography. Member, Management Cttee. and Council, Australian Soc. of Authors. Science Coordinator, The Murdoch Chain, 1960–69. *Publs:* Rise Up to Life, 1970; Facing Starvation, 1972; The Southern Universe, 1974; This Accursed Land, 1976; Mawson's Will, 1976; The Deadly Element, 1979; In Search of Frank Hurley, 1980; Florey, The Man Who Made Penicillin, 1983; Shackleton's Forgotten Argonauts, 1984; Triumph Over Darkness, 1988. Add: Allen and Unwin, 8 Napier St., North Sydney, N.S.W. 2059, Australia.

BICKERSTAFF, Edwin Robert. British, b. 1920. Medicine/Health. Sr. Consultant Neurologist, Midland Center for Neurosurgery and Neurology, Birmingham, 1954–83. Hon. Consultant Neurologist, United Birmingham Hosps.; Consultant Neurologist, Hereford Hosps., and Shrewsbury Hosps. *Publs:* Neurological Examination in Clinical Practice, 1963, 5th ed. 1989; Neurology for Nurses, 1965, 4th ed. 1987; Neurological Complication of the Oral Contraceptives, 1974. Add: St. Helens, The Close, Trevone, Padstow, Cornwall, England.

BICKHAM, Jack M. Also writes as Jeff Clinton and John Miles. American, b. 1930. Novels/Short stories, Mystery/Crime/Suspense, Westerns/Adventure. Prof. of Journalism, Univ. of Oklahoma, Norman, since 1969. Managing Ed., The Oklahoma Courier, 1966–69. *Publs:* Gunman's Gamble, 1958; Feud Fury, 1959; Killer's Paradise, 1960; the Useless Gun, 1960; Dally with Deadly Doll, 1961; Hangman's Territory, 1961; Gunmen Can't Hide, 1961; (as Jeff Clinton) The Fighting Buckaroo, 1961; (as Jeff Clinton) Wildcat's Rampage, 1962; Range Killer, 1962; (as Jeff Clinton) Wildcat Against the House, 1963; (as John Miles) Troubled Trails, 1965; (as Jeff Clinton) Wildcat's Revenge, 1964; Trip Home to Hell, 1965; Killer's Choice, 1965; (as Jeff Clinton) Wildcat Takes His Medicine, 1966; (as Jeff Clinton) Wanted: Wildcat O'Shea, 1966; The Padre Must Die, 1967; (as Jeff Clinton) Wildcat's Witch Hunt, 1967; The War on Charity Ross, 1967; (as Jeff Clinton) Watch out for Wildcat, 1968; The Shadowed Faith, 1968; (as Jeff Clinton) Wildcat Meets Miss Melody, 1968; Target: Charity Ross, 1968; (as Jeff Clinton) Build a Box for Wildcat, 1969; Decker's Campaign (in U.K. as the Sheriff's Campaign), 1970; (as Jeff Clinton) Wildcat's Claim to Fame, 1970; (as Jeff Clinton) A Stranger Named O'Shea, 1970; Goin', 1971; (as Jeff Clinton) Bounty on Wildcat, 1971; The Apple Dumpling Gang, 1971; Fletcher, 1972; Jilly's Canal, 1972; Dopey Dan, 1972; (as Jeff Clinton) Hang High, O'Shea, 1972; Katie, Kelly and Heck, 1973; (as John Miles) The Night Hunters, 1973; Baker's Hawk, 1974; (as John Miles) The Silver Bullet Gang, 1974; (as John Miles) The Blackmailer, 1974; (as Jeff Clinton) Emerald Canyon, 1974; Hurry Home, Davey Clock, 1974; A Boat Named Death, 1975; (as John Miles with T. Morris) Operation Nightfall, 1974; (as Jeff Clinton) Showdown at Emerald Canyon, 1975; (as Jeff Clinton) Kane's Odyssey, 1975; Twister, 1976; The Winemakers, 1977; The Excalibur Disaster, 1978; Dinah, Blow Your Horn, 1979; A Question of Ethics, 1980; The Regensburg Legacy, 1980; All the Days Were Summer, 1981; I Still Dream About Columbus, 1982; Ariel, 1984; Miracleworker, 1987; Day Seven, 1988; Tiebreaker, 1989.

Add: Sch. of Journalism, Univ. of Oklahoma, Norman, Okla. 73019, U.S.A.

BIDDISS, Michael Denis. British, b. 1942. History, International relations/Current affairs. Prof. of History, Univ. of Reading, since 1979 (Dean, Faculty of Letters and Social Sciences, 1982–85). Fellow, 1966–73, and Dir. of Studies in History, 1970–73, Downing Coll., Cambridge; Lectr., 1973–78, and Reader in History, 1978–79, Univ. of Leicester. *Publs:* Father of Racist Ideology: The Social and Political Thought of Count Gobineau, 1970; (ed.) Gobineau: Selected Political Writings, 1970; (with F.F. Cartwright) Disease and History, 1972; The Age of the Masses: Ideas and Society in Europe since 1870, 1977; (ed.) Images of Race, 1979; (ed. with K. Minogue) Thatcherism: Politics and Personality, 1987. Add: Dept. of History, Univ. of Reading, Reading RG6 2AA, England.

BIDDLE, Bruce Jesse. American, b. 1928. Education, Psychology, Sociology. Prof. of Psychology and Sociology, and Dir., Center for Research in Social Behavior, Univ. of Missouri, Columbia, since 1966 (Assoc. Prof., 1960–66). Part-time teacher in primary and secondary sch., 1945–50; Instr. and Academic Asst. in Mathematics, Antioch Coll., Ohio; Instr. in Sociology, Michigan Univ., Ann Arbor; Instr. in Psychological Warfare, Fort Bragg Army Service; and Instr. in Sociology and Psychology, Univ. of Georgia, Columbus, all 1948–56; Asst. Prof. of Sociology, Univ. of Kentucky, 1957–58; Assoc. Prof. of Education, Univ. of Kansas City, 1958–60. *Publs:* (with J.R.P. French and J.V. Moore) Some Aspects of Leadership in the Small Work Group, 1954; (with H.A. Rosencranz and E.F. Rankin) Studies in the Role of the Public School Teacher (5 vols.), 1961; The Present Status of Role Theory, 1961; (with S. Eveloff, E.F. Rankin, J.P. Twyman and D. Warshay) Bibliographies on Role Terms, Role Conflict and the Role of the Teacher, 1961; (with A.M. Simpson) A Program for the Processing of Ordinal Data and Computation of Significance for Selected Central Tendency Differences, 1961; (with G. Barger, W.S. Gennett, D. Hays, R. Miller and S. Titus) Bibliographies on Role Methodology and Propositions, 1961; (ed. with W.J. Ellena) Contemporary Research on Teacher Effectiveness, 1964; (with P.F. Green) Role Accuracy and Conformity in Teachers, 1964; (with J.P. Twyman) The Uses of Role Conflict, 1964; The Social Systems of the School, 1965; (ed. with E.J. Thomas) Role Theory: Concepts and Research, 1966, 1979; (ed. with P.H. Rossi) The New Media: Their Impact on Education and Society, 1966; (with R.S. Adams) An Analysis of Classroom Activities, 1967; (with R.S. Adams) Realities of Teaching: Explorations with Videotape, 1970; (with B.J. Bank and others) A Propositional Coding System for Role Theory, 1973; Roles: Expectations, Identities, and Behaviors, 1974; (with M.J. Dunkin) The Study of Teaching, 1974; (with B.J. Bank) Role Theory: A Brief Introduction, 1974; (with T. Good and J. Brophy) Teachers Make a Difference, Add: Univ. of Missouri Center for Research in Social Behavior, 111 East Stewart Rd., Columbia, Mo. 65211, U.S.A.

BIEBUYCK, Daniel P. Belgian, b. 1925. Anthropology/Ethnology, Art, Cultural/Ethnic topics. H. Rodney Sharp Prof. of Anthropology and Humanities, Univ. of Delaware, Newark, since 1966 (Visiting Prof., 1961–62; Prof., 1962–63; H. Rodney Sharp Prof., 1963–65; Interim Dir. of Black Studies, 1970–71). Research Fellow, Inst. pour la Recherche scientifique en Afrique Centrale, 1949–57; Lovanium Univ., Kinshasa, 1957–61; Prof. of Curator of African Collections, Univ. of California, Los Angeles, 1964–66. *Publs:* (ed.) African Agrarian Systems, 1963; (ed. and trans. with K. Mateene) The Mwindo Epic from the Banyanga, 1969; (ed.) Tradition and Creativity in Tribal Art, 1969; (with K. Mateene) Anthologie de la Litterature orale Nyanga, 1970; Lega Culture: Art, Initiation and Moral Philosophy among a Central African People, 1973; Hero and Chief: Epic Literature from the Banyanga, 1978; Statuary from the Pre-Bembe Hunters, 1981; (with Nelly Van Den Abbeele) The Power of Headdresses: A Cross-Cultural Study of Forms and Functions, 1984; Southwestern Zaire, vol. I of The Arts of Zaire, 1985; Eastern Zaire, vol. II of The Arts of Zaire, 1986; The Arts of Central Africa: An Annotated Bibliography, 1987; (with B. Biebuyck) We Test Those Whom We Marry, 1987. Add: 271 W. Main St, Newark, Del. 19711, U.S.A.

BIELSKI, Alison (Joy Prosser). British, b. 1925. Poetry, Mythology/Folklore. Self-employed writer and retired lectr. Hon. Joint Secty., Yr Academi Gymreig, English Language Section. *Publs:* Twentieth-Century Flood, 1964; Across the Burning Sand; The Story of the Welsh Dragon, 1969; Flower Legends of Wales, 1972; Chwedlau'r Cymry am Flodau, 1973; Eve, 1973; Shapes and Colours, 1973; Zodiac Poems, 1973; Mermaid Poems, 1974; Flower Legends of the Wye Valley, 1974; The Lovetree, 1974; Seth, 1980; Tales and Traditions of Tenby, 1981; Eagles, 1983. Add: 24 Kingfisher Close, St. Mellons, Cardiff CF3 0DD, Wales.

BIEN, Peter A. American, b. 1930. Literature, Translations. Prof. of English, Dartmouth Coll., Hanover, N.H., since 1969. Teacher of English, American Language Center, Columbia Univ., NYC, 1957–61. *Publs:* (trans.) The Last Temptations of Christ, by Nikos Kazantzakis, 1960; L.P. Hartley, 1963; Constantine Cavafy, 1964; (trans.) Saint Francis, by Nikos Kazantzakis, 1962; (trans.) Report to Greco, by Kazantzakis, 1965; Kazantzakis and the Linguistic Revolution in Greek Literature, 1972; (ed. with E. Keeley) Modern Greek Writers, 1972; (with J. Rassias and C. Bien) Demotic Greek, 1972; Nikos Kazantzakis, 1972; (with N. Stangos) Yannis Ritsos: Selected Poems, 1974; (trans.) Life in the Tomb, by Stratis Myrivilis, 1977; Antithesi kai synthesi sti poiisi tou Yanni Ritsou, 1980; (with J. Rassias, C. Bien and C. Alexiou) Demotic Greek II: O Iptamenus Thalamos, 1982; Three Generations of Greek Writers: Introductions to Cavafy, Kazantzakis, Ritsos, 1983; Tempted by Happiness: Kazantzakis' Post-Christian Christ, 1984; Kazantzakis and Politics, 1989. Add: Dept. of English, Dartmouth Coll., Hanover, N.H. 03755, U.S.A.

BIERHORST, John. American, b. 1936. Cultural/Ethnic topics, Language/Linguistics, Mythology/Folklore. *Publs:* The Fire Plume: Legends of the American Indians, 1969; The Ring in the Prairie: A Shawnee Legend, 1970; In the Trail of the Wind: American Indian Poems and Ritual Orations, 1971; Four Masterworks of American Indian Literature, 1974; Songs of the Chippewa, 1974; Black Rainbow: Legends of the Incas and Myths of Ancient Peru, 1976; The Red Swan: Myths and Tales of the American Indians, 1976; The Girl Who Married a Ghost and Other Tales from the North American Indian, 1978; A Cry from the Earth: Music of the North American Indians, 1979; The Whistling Skeleton: American Indian Tales of the Supernatural, 1982; The Sacred Path: Spells, Prayers and Power Songs of the American Indians, 1983; The Hungry Woman: Myths and Legends of the Aztecs, 1984; Spirit Child: A Story of the Nativity, 1984; The Mythology of North America, 1985; Cantares Mexicanos: Songs of the Aztecs, 1985; A Nahuatl-English Dictionary with a Concordance to the Cantares Mexicanos, 1985; The Monkey's Haircut and Other Stories Told by the Maya, 1986; Doctor Coyote: A Native American Aesop's Fables, 1987; The Naked Bear: Folktales of the Iroquois, 1987; The Mythology of South America, 1988; The Mythology of Mexico and Central America, 1990. Add: Box 566, West Shokan, N.Y. 12494, U.S.A.

BIERMANN, Barrie. South African, b. 1924. Architecture, Cookery/Gastronomy/Wine. Assoc. Prof. in Architecture. Univ. of Natal, Durban, since 1971 (Lectr., 1952–63; Sr. Lectr., 1963–71). Member, Council for Heraldry, since 1963; Member, Commn. for Fine Arts, 1971; Member, Advisory Cttee. for Art in Public Buildings, since 1979—all South Africa. Member of the Council, South African National Soc., 1947–57; Adviser on Aesthetics, South African National Monuments Commn., 1956–66; Co-Founder, South African Vernacular Architecture Soc., 1964. *Publs:* Boukuns in Suid-Africa, 1964; Red Wine in South Africa, 1971. Add: Dept. of Architecture, Univ. of Natal, King George V Ave., Durban 4001, South Africa.

BIGELOW, Robert Sydney. Canadian, b. 1918. Children's fiction, Biology, Zoology. Reader in Zoology, Univ. of Canterbury, Christchurch, since 1962. Asst. Prof., 1953–59, and Assoc. Prof., 1959–62, McGill Univ., Montreal. *Publs:* The Grasshoppers of New Zealand, 1967; The Dawn Warriors, 1969; Stubborn Bear, 1970; A New Approach to Human Evolution, 1972. Add: Dept of Zoology, Univ. of Canterbury, Christchurch, New Zealand.

BIGGE, Morris L(ee). American, b. 1908. Education. Prof. Emeritus of Educational Foundns., California State Univ., Fresno, since 1977 (Prof., 1950–77; Chmn. of Dept. of Advanced Studies, 1950–63). Social Science Teacher, Washburn Rural High Sch., Topeka, Kans., 1931–41; Teacher of Social Studies and Mathematics, Roosevelt Jr. High Sch., Topeka, Kans., 1941–44; Psychological Asst. and Occupational Counselor in U.S. Army personnel centers, and Chief of Personnel Consultant Section, Army and Service Forces Redistribution Station, Hot Springs, Ark., 1944–46; Asst. Prof. of Education and Psychology, Dir. of Veterans Service Bureau, and Dean of Students, Washburn Municipal Univ., Topeka, Kans., 1946–50; Consultant and Lectr. in Secondary Education, Kansas State Teachers Coll., Emporia, 1964–71; Consultant, Mid-Continent Regional Educational Lab., Kansas City, Mo., 1971–72. *Publs:* (with M.P. Hunt) Psychological Foundations of Education, 1962; 3rd ed. 1980; Learning Theories for Teachers, 1964, 4th ed. 1982; Positive Relativism: An Emergent Educational Philosophy, 1971; Educational Philosophies for Teachers, 1982. Add: 3367 Punta Alta No. 1G, Laguna Hills, Calif. 92653, U.S.A.

BIGGLE, Lloyd, Jr. American, b. 1923. Mystery, Science fiction/

Fantasy. Secty.-Treas., and Chmn., Bd. of Trustees, 1965–73, Science Fiction Writers of America. Founder and Pres., Science Fiction Oral History Assn., 1977–87. *Publs:* The Angry Espers, 1961; All the Colors of Darkness, 1963; The Fury Out of Time, 1965; Watchers of the Dark, 1966; The Rule of the Door and Other Fanciful Regulations, (short stories), 1967, in U.K. as The Silent Sky, 1979; The Still Small Voice of Trumpets, 1968; The World Menders, 1971; The Light That Never Was, 1972; (ed.) Nebula Award Stories 7, 1972; The Metallic Muse (short stories), 1972; Monument, 1974; This Darkening Universe, 1975; A Galaxy of Strangers (short stories), 1976; Silence is Deadly, 1977; The Whirligig of Time, 1979; (with T.L. Sherred) Alien Main, 1985; The Quallsford Inheritance, A Memoir of Sherlock Holmes, 1986; Interface for Murder, 1987. Add: 569 Dubie Ave., Ypsilanti, Mich. 48198, U.S.A.

BIGGS, John Burville. Australian, b. 1934. Education, Mathematics/Statistics, Psychology. Prof. of Education, Univ. of Newcastle, Shortland, since 1973. Research Officer, National Foundn. for Education Research, U.K., 1958–62; Lectr. in Psychology, Univ. of New England, 1962–66; Education Research Officer, Monash Univ., 1966–69; Prof. of Educational Psychology, Univ. of Alberta, 1969–73. *Publs:* Anxiety and Primary Mathematics, 1963; Mathematics and the Conditions of Learning, 1967; Information and Human Learning, 1972; (with K. Collis) Evaluating the Quality of Learning, 1982; Student Approaches to Learning and Studying, 1987; (with R. Telfer) The Process of Learning, 1987. Add: Dept. of Education, Univ. of Newcastle, Shortland, Australia 2308.

BIGNELL, Alan. British, b. 1928. Travel. Journalist, Kent Messenger Group, since 1957. *Publs:* Kent Villages, 1975; Hopping Down in Kent, 1977; Kent Lore, 1983; The Kent Village Book, 1986; Tales of Old Kent, 1986; Kent, Surrey and Sussex, 1988. Add: 8 Woodleas, Barming, Maidstone, Kent, England.

BIGSBY, C(hristopher) W(illiam) E(dgar). British, b. 1941. Literature, Theatre. Prof. of American Studies, Univ. of East Anglia, Norwich, since 1984 (Reader, 1969–84). Lectr. in English and American Literature, Univ. of Wales, Aberystwyth, 1966–69. *Publs:* Confrontation and Commitment: Study of Contemporary American Drama, 1967; Albee, 1969; (ed.) Three Negro Plays, 1969; (ed.) The Black American Writer, 2 vols., 1969; Dada and Surrealism, 1972; (ed.) Superculture: The Impact of American Popular Culture on Europe, 1974; (ed.) Edward Albee, 1975; Approaches to Popular Culture, 1976; Tom Stoppard, 1976; The Second Black Renaissance: Essays in Black Literature, 1980; (ed.) Contemporary English Drama, 1981; (ed.) The Radical Imagination and the Liberal Tradition, 1982; Joe Orton, 1982; Critical Introduction to Twentieth Century American Drama, 3 vols., 1982–85; David Mamet, 1985; (ed.) Cultural Change in the United States Since World War II, 1986. Add: 3 Church Farm, Colney, Norwich, England.

BILLIAS, George Athan. American, b. 1919. History. Prof. of American History, since 1962, and Jacob & Frances Hiatt Prof. of History, since 1983, Clark Univ., Worcester, Mass. Prof. of American History, Univ. of Maine, Orono, 1954–61. *Publs:* Massachusetts Land Bankers of 1740, 1959; General John Glover and His Marblehead Mariners, 1960; (ed. and contrib.) George Washington's Generals, 1964; (ed. and contrib.) The American Revolution: How Revolutionary Was It?, 1965, 3rd ed. 1980; (ed.) Law and Authority in Colonial America, 1965; (ed. with G.N. Grob) Interpretations of American History, 1967; (ed. and contrib.) George Washington's Opponents, 1969; (ed.) The Federalists: Realists or Idealogues?, 1970; (ed. with G.N. Grob) American History: Retrospect and Prospect, 1971; (ed. with A. Vaughan) Perspectives on Early American History, 1973; Elbridge Gerry: Founding Father and Republican Statesman, 1976. Add: History Dept., Clark Univ., Worcester, Mass. 01610, U.S.A.

BILLING, Graham (John). New Zealander, b. 1936. Novels, Poetry, Travel/Exploration/Adventure. Freelance writer since 1978. Cadetfficer, Shaw Saville Line, 1953–54; able seaman, Union Steam Ship Co., 1956; construction worker, 1956–58; jr. reporter, later sr. reporter, Dunedin Evening Star, 1958–62; Information Officer, New Zealand Antarctic Research Programme, Wellington and Ross Dependency, Antarctica, 1962–64; Chief Reporter, Radio New Zealand News, Christchurch, 1964–65; freelance writer, 1965–67; Broadcast Media Ed. and Columnist, New Zealand Sunday Times, Wellington, 1967–68; Parliamentary Correspondent, New Zealand Truth, 1968–69; freelance writer, 1969–73; Lectr. in English, Mitchell Coll. of Advanced Education, Bathurst, N.S.W., 1974–75; freelance writer, 1975–76; Current Affairs Producer, Radio New Zealand, 1977. *Publs:* South: Man and Nature in Antarctica, 1964, 1969; Forbush and the Penguins (novel), 1965; New Zealand: The Sunlit Land, 1966; The Alpha Trip (novel), 1969; Statues

(novel), 1971; The Slipway (novel), 1973; The New Zealanders, 1975; The Primal Therapy of Tom Purslane (novel), Changing Countries (poetry), 1980. Add: 89 Mersey St., St. Albans, Christchurch 1, New Zealand.

BILLINGTON, Michael. British, b. 1939. Theatre. Drama Critic, The Guardian, London, since 1971; London Arts Correspondent, New York Times, since 1978. Deputy Drama and Film Critic, 1965–71, and Television Critic, 1968–70, The Times, London; Film Critic, Illustrated London News, and Birmingham Post, 1968–82. *Publs:* The Modern Actor, 1973; How Tickled I Am, 1977; (ed.) The Performing Arts, 1980; The Guinness Book of Theatre Facts and Feats, 1982; Alan Ayckbourn, 1983; Tom Stoppard: Playwright, 1987; Peggy Ashcroft, 1988. Add: 15 Hearne Rd., London W4 3NJ, England.

BILLINGTON, Rachel. British, b. 1942. Novels/Short stories, Children's fiction. *Publs:* All Things Nice, 1969; The Big Dipper, 1970; Lilacs Out of the Dead Land, 1971; Cock Robin, 1973; Beautiful, 1974; A Painted Devil, 1975; A Woman's Age, 1979; Rosanna and the Wizard-Robot (for children), 1981; Occasion of Sin, 1982; The First Christmas (for children), 1983; Star-Time (for children), 1984; The Garish Day, 1985; The First Easter (for children), 1987; Loving Attitudes, 1988. Add: c/o David Higham, 5-8 Lower John St., London W1, England.

BILLINGTON, Ray(mond John). British, b. 1930. Theology/Religion. Principal Lectr. in Humanities, Bristol Polytechnic since 1972 (Lectr., 1968–70; Sr. lectr., 1970–72). Open Univ. Lectr. in Philosophy, since 1972. Methodist Minister, 1952–68. *Publs:* The Basis of Pacifist Conviction, 1961; The Teaching of Worship, 1962; Concerning Worship, 1963; (with S. Hopkinson and J. Foster) Rev., 1967; (with T.M. Morrow) Worship and Preaching, 1967; The Liturgical Movement and Methodism, 1969; The Christian Outsider, 1971; A New Christian Reader, 1974; Living Philosophy, 1988. Add: 5 The Park, Frenchay, Bristol BS16 1PL, England.

BILLMEYER, Fred W., Jr. American, b. 1919. Business/Trade/Industry, Chemistry, Physics. Prof. Emeritus of Chemistry, Rensselaer Polytechnic Inst., Troy, N.Y., since 1984 (Prof. 1964–84). Sr. Research Chemist, E.I. du Pont de Nemours & Co., Wilmington, Del., 1945–64. *Publs:* Textbook of Polymer Chemistry, 1957; Textbook of Polymer Science, 1962, 3rd ed. 1984; (with M. Saltzman) Principles of Color Technology, 1966, 1981; Synthetic Polymers, 1972; (with J. Bares and E.A. Collins) Experiments in Polymer Science, 1973; (with R.N. Kelley) Entering Industry: A Guide for Young Professionals, 1975. Add: 2121 Union St., Schenectady, N.Y. 12309, U.S.A.

BINCHY, Maeve. Irish, b. 1940. Historical/Romance. Columnist, Irish Times, Dublin, since 1968. History and French teacher, Pembroke Sch., Dublin, 1961–68. *Publs:* Central Line (short stories), 1978; Victoria Line (short stories), 1980; Dublin Four (short stories), 1982; Light a Penny Candle, 1982; London Transports (non-fiction), 1983; The Lilac Bus (short stories), 1984; Echoes, 1985; Firefly Summer, 1987. Add: 28 Holland Rd., London W14 0LN, England.

BINFORD, Laurence C. American, b. 1935. Zoology. Teaching Asst., 1962–65, Instr., Dept. of Zoology and Physiology, 1965–66, and Research Asst., Museum of Zoology, 1966–67, Louisiana State Univ., Baton Rouge; Asst. Curator, 1968–73, and Assoc. Curator, 1973–80, California Academy of Sciences, San Francisco. *Publs:* Birds of Western North America, 1974; A Distributional Survey of the Birds of the Mexican State of Oaxaca, 1989. Add: 330 Grove St., Glencoe, Ill. 60022, U.S.A.

BINGHAM, Caroline. British, b. 1938. History, Biography. *Publs:* The Making of a King: The Early Years of James VI and I, 1969; James V, King of Scots, 1971; The Life and Times of Edward II, 1973; The Stewart Kingdom of Scotland, 1371-1603, 1974; The Kings and Queens of Scotland, 1975; The Crowned Lions: The Early Plantagenet Kings, 1978; James VI of Scotland, 1979; (ed.) The Voice of the Lion (Scottish historical verse), 1980; James I of England, 1981; Land of the Scots: A Short History, 1983; History of Royal Holloway College, 1886-1986, 1987. Add: 164 Regent's Park Rd., London NW1 8XN, England.

BINGHAM, Charlotte. British, b. 1942. Novels/Short stories, Autobiography/Memoirs/Personal, Biography. Television writer. *Publs:* Coronet Among the Weeds (biography), 1963; Lucinda (novel), 1965; Coronet Among the Grass (autobiography), 1972; Belgravia (novel), 1984; Country Life (novel), 1985; At Home (novel), 1986; with Terence Brady—Victoria (novel), 1972; Rose's Story (novel), 1972; Victoria and Company 1974; No Honestly (biography), 1975; I Wish, I Wish (play), 1987; To Hear a Nightingale, 1988; The Business, 1989. Add: c/o A.D. Peters Literary Agents, The Chambers, Lots Rd., Chelsea Harbour, London SW10 0XF, England.

BINGHAM, June Rossbach. American, b. 1919. Medicine/Health, Biography, Plays. Member of the Bd., African-American Inst.; Member, Riverdale Mental Health Assn.; Ittleson Center for Childhood Research; Woodrow Wilson Foundn. *Publs:* (with F. Redlich) The Inside Story: Psychiatry in Everyday Life, 1953; Courage to Change: An Introduction to the Life and Thought of Reinhold Niebuhr, 1961; U Thant: The Search for Peace, 1966; (with N. Tamarkin) The Pursuit of Health, 1985; Triangles (play), 1986. Add: 5000 Independence Ave., Bronx, N.Y. 10471, U.S.A.

BINGHAM, Sallie (Ellsworth). American, b. 1937. Novels/Short stories, Autobiography. Teacher of English and Creative Writing, Univ. of Louisville. Founder, Kentucky Foundation for Women. *Publs:* After Such Knowledge, 1960; The Touching Hand, and Six Short Stories, 1967; The Way It Is Now: Stories, 1972; Passion and Prejudice, 1989. Add: 3715 Glen Bluff Rd., Louisville, KY 40222, U.S.A.

BINGLEY, Clive (Hamilton). British, b. 1936. Writing/Journalism. Dir., Bingley Publishing Consultants. Managing Dir., Clive Bingley Ltd., Publishers, London 1965–78. *Publs:* Book Publishing Practice, 1966; The Business of Book Publishing, 1972. Add: 16 Pembridge Rd., London W11, England.

BINGLEY, David Ernest. Also writes as Bart Adams, Adam Bridger, Andrew Camber, Abe Canuck, Dave Carver, Larry Chatham, Henry Cheshan, Will Coltman, Ed Coniston, Luke Dorman, George Fallon, Horsley, Bat Jefford, Syd Kingston, Eric Lynch, James Martell, Colin North, Ben Plummer, Caleb Prescott, Mark Remington, John Roberts, Steve Romney, Frank Silvester, Henry Starr, Link Tucker, Christopher Wigan, and Roger Yorke. British, b. 1920. Novels, Western/Adventure. Teacher, since 1948; at New Romney Church of England Primary Sch., Romney Marsh, Kent, since 1966. *Publs:* Malayan Adventure, 1962; Famous Storybook Heroes, 1964; Gunsmoke at Nester Creek, 1964; Elusive Witness, 1966; Caribbean Crisis, 1967; Bridges, 1969; Rustlers' Moon, 1972; Hellions' Hideaway, 1974; The Man from Abilene, 1975; as Bart Adams—Owlhoot Raiders, 1966; Renegades' Rampage, 1967; as Dave Carver—The Bar T Brand, 1964; Gunsmoke Gambler, 1966; Renegade River, 1973; as Henry Chesham—Naples, or Die!, 1965; Skyborne Sapper, 1966; The Place of the Chins, 1975; A Surfeit of Soldiers, 1978; The Angry Atoll, 1981; A Tide of Chariots, 1983; Saboteurs from the Sea, 1985; as Will Coltman—The Torrington Trail, 1966; Killer's Creek, 1969; Ghost Town Killer, 1970; as Ed Coniston—Bar X Bandit, 1965; as George Fallon—Rendezvous in Rio, 1966; as David Horsley—Operation Pedestal, 1957; Tinfish Running, 1958; The Ocean, Their Grave, 1958; Torpedoes in the Wake, 1958; Vinegar Johnnie, 1958; The Decoys, 1959; Living Death, 1959; Dive, Dive—Dive!, 1960; The Time of the Locust: The Terrible Aftermath of the Fall of Singapore, 1960; Johnny Pronto, 1964; The Reluctant Renegade, 1965; Flying Horseshoe Trail, 1966; Sunset Showdown, 1977; Brigand's Blade, 1978; The Beauclerc Brand, 1979; Troubleshooter on Trial, 1980; Salt Creek Killing, 1981; Badlands Bonanza, 1982; The Long Siesta, 1983; Stolen Star, 1984; as Bat Jefford—Brigand's Bounty, 1969; Silver Creek Trail, 1971; as Syd Kingston—Railtown Roundup, 1964; The Necktie Trail, 1965; The Kid from Cougar, 1972; Alias Jake Dollar, 1974; Hideaway Heist, 1975; Boot Hill Bandit, 1982; Renegade Preacher, 1985; as Eric Lynch—Renegade's Retreat, 1971; as Caleb Prescott—Pecos River Posse, 1968; as John Roberts—Showdown at the Lazy T, 1964; Colorado Gun Law, 1966; Trailman's Truce, 1973; as Link Tucker—Renegade Valley, 1965; as Christopher Wigan—Mossyhorn 1957; The Man from Casagrande, 1964; The Trail Blazer, 1964; Buckboard Barber, 1981; El Yanqui's Woman, 1983; as Roger Yorke—The Iron Trail, 1966; Guadalupe Bandit, 1967; also many books under numerous other pen-names. Add: 9 Millfields Rd., Hythe, Kent CT21 4DH, England.

BINHAM, Philip Frank. British, b. 1924. Language/Linguistics, Translations. Lectr. in English, Helsinki Sch. of Economics, 1953–87. *Publs:* How to Say It, 1965; Executive English (3 vols.), 1968–70; (with James Murray) Speak Up, 1976; (ed., with Richard Dauenhauer) Snow in May: An Anthology of Finnish Writing 1945–1972, 1978; (trans.) Tamara, 1978; (with James Murray and Riitta Sinivaara) Service with a Smile, 1979; Hotel English, 1982; Restaurant English, 1982. Add: Seunalantie 34A2, 04200 Kerava, Finland.

BINION, Rudolph. American, b. 1927. History, Biography. Leff Prof. of History, Brandeis Univ., Waltham, Mass., since 1967. Instr. in History, Rutgers Univ., N.J., 1966–56; Instr. in Humanities, Massachusetts Inst. of Technology, Cambridge, 1956–59; Asst. Prof. of History 1959–63, and Assoc. Prof. of History 1963–67, Columbia Univ., NYC. *Publs:* Defeated Leaders, 1960; Frau Lou, 1968; Hitler Among the Germans, 1976; 1981; Introduction à la Psychohistoire, 1982; After Christianity, 1986. Add: P.O. Box 40, Humarock, Mass. 02047, U.S.A.

BINKLEY, Luther John. American, b. 1925. Philosophy, Theology/Religion. Prof. of Philosophy, Franklin and Marshall Coll., Lancaster, Pa., since 1962 (Instr., 1949–51; Asst. Prof., 1951–56; Assoc. Prof., 1956–62). Lectr., Temple Univ. Grad. Education Prog. for Teachers, Philadelphia, since 1965, and Pennsylvania State Univ., Capitol Campus, since 1975. Member, Public Committee for the Humanities in Pa., 1974–78; Pres., Philosophic Society for the Study of Sport, 1976–77. *Publs:* The Mercersburg Theology, 1953; Contemporary Ethical Theories, 1961; Conflict of Ideals: Changing Values in Western Society, 1969. Add: Franklin & Marshall Coll., Box 3003, Lancaster, Pa. 17604, U.S.A.

BIRCH, Anthony Harold. British and Canadian, b. 1924. Politics/Government. Prof. of Political Science, Univ. of Victoria, B.C., since 1977. Vice-Pres., Political Studies Assn. (U.K.). Lectr., and Sr. Lectr. in Govt., Manchester Univ., 1947–61; Prof. of Political Studies, Univ. of Hull, 1961–70; Prof. of Political Science, Univ. of Exeter, 1970–77. *Publs:* Federalism. Finance and Social Legislation, 1955; Small-Town Politics, 1959; Representative and Responsible Government, 1964; The British System of Government, 1967, 7th ed. 1986; Representation, 1971; Political Integration and Disintegration in the British Isles, 1977; Nationalism and National Integration, 1989. Add: 1901 Fairfield Rd., Victoria, B.C. V8S142, Canada.

BIRCHAM, Deric (Neale). New Zealander, b. 1934. International relations/Current affairs, Sports/Physical education/Keeping fit, Travel/Exploration/Adventure. Photographer. Head of Photography, Univ. of Otago, Dunedin, since 1980. Jr. Photographer, 1956–59, Photographer, 1959–68, and Chief Photographer, 1968–76, New Zealand Ministry of Works; Pres., Deric Bircham Crafts, since 1977. *Publs:* Seeing New 1971, 5th ed. 1973; (co-author) Towards a More Just World, 1973; Waitomo Tourist Caves, 1973; (co-author) Table Tennis, 1976; New Zealanders of Destiny, 1978; Old St. Paul's Cathedral, 1982; I Shall Pass This Way But Once, 1982; Rhapsody, 1984; major contributor—Thirteen Facets, 1977; A Day in the Life of New Zealand, 1983; Dunedin—New Zealand's Best Kept Secret, 1984; St. Joseph's Cathedral, 1986; Works of Gottfried Lindauer, 1986. Add: 130 Easter Crescent, Kew, Dunedin, New Zealand.

BIRD, Caroline. American, b. 1915. Social commentary/phenomena, Women. Researcher, Newsweek mag., 1941–42; Researcher, Fortune mag., 1943–46. *Publs:* The Invisible Scar, 1966; (with S. Briller) Born Female, 1968; Everything a Woman Needs to Know to Get Paid What She's Worth, 1974; The Case Against College, 1975; Enterprising Women: Their Contribution to the American Economy 1776-1976; What Women Want, 1979; The Two-Paycheck Marriage, 1979; The Good Years, 1983. Add: 31 Sunrise Lane, Poughkeepsie, N.Y. 12603, U.S.A.

BIRD, Dennis Leslie. Has also written as John Noel. British, b. 1930. Sports/Physical education/Keeping fit. Course Dir., Civil Service Coll., since 1973. Contrib., Ice and Roller Skate monthly, London, since 1973; Historian, National Skating Assn. of Great Britain, since 1977. Monthly columnist as John Noel, Skating World, London, 1948–73; Joined R.A.F. 1949, retired as squadron leader in 1968; reviewer of skating events, The Observer, London, 1959–63, and The Times, London, 1959–78; Principal, Urban Prog. Div., Home Office, London, 1968–73. *Publs:* (as John Noel) Figure Skating for Beginners, 1964; Artistry on Ice, 1968; Our Skating Heritage, 1979; Know the Game: Ice Skating, 1985. Add: 37 The Avenue, Shoreham-by-Sea, Sussex BN4 5GJ, England.

BIRD, James Harold. British, b. 1923. Geography. Prof. of Geography, Univ. of Southampton, 1967–88 (Deputy Vice-Chancellor, 1978–82). *Publs:* The Geography of the Port of London, 1957; The Major Seaports of the United Kingdom, 1963; Seaport Gateways of Australia, 1968; Seaports and Seaport Terminals, 1971; Centrality and Cities, 1977; The Changing Worlds of Geography, 1989. Add: 95 Lakewood Rd., Eastleigh SO5 1AD, England.

BIRD, Richard. Canadian, b. 1938. Economics. Prof. of Economics, Univ. of Toronto (Assoc. Prof., 1968–70; Dir., Inst. of Policy Analysis, 1980–85). With Harvard Univ., Cambridge, Mass., 1961–68; Chief of tax policy div., Intnl. Monetary Fund, 1972–74. *Publs:* Sales Tax and the Carter Report, 1967; (co-author) Financing Urban Development in

Mexico City, 1967; Taxation and Development: Lessons from Colombian Experience, 1970; The Growth of Government Spending in Canada, 1970; Taxing Agricultural Land in Developing Countries, 1974; Charging for Public Services: A New Look at an Old Idea, 1976; (with Enid Slack) Residential Property Tax Relief in Ontario, 1978; Financing Canadian Government: A Quantitative Overview, 1979; (with M.W. Bucovetsky and D.K. Foot) The Growth of Public Employment in Canada, 1979; Taxing Corporations, 1980; Tax Incentives for Investment: The State of the Art, 1980; (with Enid Slack) Urban Public Finance in Canada, 1983; (with others) Industrial Policy in Ontario, 1985; Federal Finance in Comparative Perspective, 1986; (with R.A. and P.B. Musgrave) Public Finance in Theory and Practice, 1987; (with Susan Horton) Government Policy and the Poor in Developing Countries, 1988. Add: c/o Dept. of Economics, Univ. of Toronto, Toronto, Ont. M5S 1A1, Canada.

BIRD, Vivian. British, b. 1910. History, Travel/Exploration/Adventure. Special Feature Writer, Birmingham Post and Mail Ltd., 1951–75. Former political organiser and teacher. *Publs:* Bird's Eye View: The Midlands, 1969; The Sunset Coasts, 1970; Portrait of Birmingham; Warwickshire, 1973; Staffordshire, 1974; Short History of Warwickshire, 1977; Exploring the West Midlands, 1977; The Shakespeare Country and Cotswolds, 1982; By Lock and Pond, 1988. Add: 486 Shirley Rd., Hall Green, Birmingham 28, England.

BIRDWOOD, George F(ortune) B(rodrick). British, b. 1929. Medicine/Health, Sociology. Medical Ed., Documenta Geigy, London, since 1966. Medical Corresp., World Medicine, London. *Publs:* The Willing Victim—A Parents' Guide to Drug Abuse, 1969, 1971; (ed. with S.S.B. Gilder and C.A.S. Wink) Parkinson's Disease—A New Approach to Treatment, 1971; (ed. and co-author) Steig Aus—Nur der Dealer uberlebt, 1972; (with J.V. Gantmacher) Further Experiences with Voltaven, 1985. Add: Westmeon, Kings Langley, Herts., England.

BIRENBAUM, William M. American, b. 1923. Social commentary/phenomena. Dir. of Student Affairs, 1949–54, and Dean of Students, University Coll., 1955–57, Univ. of Chicago; Asst. Vice Pres., Wayne State Univ., Detroit, 1957–61; Dean, New Sch. for Social Researc h, NYC, 1961–64; Vice Pres. and Provost, Brooklyn Center, Long Island Univ., 1964–67; Pres., Education Affiliate, Bedford-Stuyvesant Development Corp., Brooklyn, 1967–68; Pres., Staten Island Coll., City Univ. of New York, 1968–76; Member of Faculty, New York Univ. Grad. Sch. of Education, 1969–70; Pres., Antioch Coll., Yellow Springs, Ohio, 1976–85. Pres., Assn. of Community Councils of Metropolitan Chicago, 1955–57 *Publs:* Overlive: Power, Poverty and the University, 1968; Something for Everybody Is Not Enough, 1972. Add: 108 Willow St., Brooklyn, N.Y. 11201, U.S.A.

BIRKHOFF, Garrett. American, b. 1911. Mathematics. Prof. Emeritus, Harvard Univ., Cambridge, Mass., since 1983 (joined faculty 1936; George Putnam Prof. of Pure and Applied Mathematics, 1969–81). *Publs:* Hydrodynamics, 1960; Lattice Theory, 1967; co-author—Jets Wakes and Cavities, 1957; Modern Applied Algebra, 1970; Source Book on Classical Analysis, 1973; Ordinary Differential Equations, 1978; Algebra, 1979; Numerical Solution of Elliptical Problems, 1983; Dynamical Systems, 1983. Add: Harvard Univ., Dept. of Mathematics, Cambridge, Mass. 02138, U.S.A.

BIRMINGHAM, Maisie. British. Mystery/Crime/Suspense. Lectr. in Social Science, Univ. Coll. of South Wales, 1945–49; member, Cwmbran New Town Development Corp., 1949–51; Lectr. in Social Studies, Univ. of Ghana, 1958–60. *Publs:* You Can Help Me, 1974; The Heat of the Sun, 1976; Sleep in a Ditch, 1978. Add: 7 Gold Hill, Shaftesbury, Dorset, England.

BIRMINGHAM, Stephen. American, b. 1931. Novels/Short stories, Social commentary/phenomena, Biography. *Publs:* Young Mr. Keefe, 1958; Barbara Greer, 1959; The Towers of Love, 1961; Those Harper Women, 1963; Fast Start Fast Finish, 1966; Our Crowd: The Great Jewish Families of New York, 1967; The Right People, 1968; Heart Troubles, 1968; The Grandees, 1971; The Late John Marquand, 1972; The Right Places, 1973; Real Lace, 1973; Certain People, 1977; The Golden Dream: Suburbia in the 1970s, 1978; Jacqueline Bouvier Kennedy Onassis, 1978; Life at the Dakota, 1979; California Rich, 1980; Duchess, 1981; The Grandes Dames, 1982; The Auerbach Will, 1983; The Rest of Us, 1984; The LeBaron Secret, 1986; America: Secret Aristocracy, 1987. Add: c/o Brandt and Brandt, 1501 Broadway, New York, N.Y. 10036, U.S.A.

BIRMINGHAM, Walter (Barr). British, b. 1913. Economics, Third World problems. Warden of Toynbee Hall, London, 1964–72; Prof. of

Economics, Univ. of Cape Coast, 1972–75; Prof. of Economics, National Univ. of Lesotho, 1975–78. *Publs:* Introduction to Economics, 1955, 1966; (ed. and contrib. with A.G. Ford) Planning and Growth in Rich and Poor Countries, 1966; (ed. with I. Neustadt and E.N. Omaboe) A Study of Contemporary Ghana (2 vols.), 1966–67; Poverty and Development, 1974. Add: 7 Gold Hill, Shaftesbury, Dorset, England.

BIRN, Raymond Francis. American, b. 1935. History, Intellectual history. Prof. of History, Univ. of Oregon, Eugene, since 1972 (Instr., Asst. Prof., 1963–66; Assoc. Prof., 1966–72; Head, Dept. of History, 1971–78). Advisory Ed., Eighteenth-Century Studies, since 1974. Member, Bd. of Editors, French Historical Studies, 1977–80. *Publs:* Pierre Rousseau and the Philosophes of Bouillon, 1964; Crisis, Absolutism, Revolution: Europe 1648-1789/91, 1977; (ed.) The Printed Word in the Eighteenth Century, 1984. Add: Dept. of History, Univ. of Oregon, Eugene, Ore. 97403, U.S.A.

BIRNBACH, Martin. American, b. 1929. Politics/Government, Psychology. Prof. of Political Science, San Jose State Univ., Calif., since 1962. Visiting Lectr., Univ. of Puerto Rico, Rio Piedras, 1958–61; Instr., Univ. of Nebraska, Lincoln, 1961–62; Prof., Albion Coll., Mich., 1968–69. *Publs:* Neo-Freudian Social Philosophy, 1961; American Political Life, 1971. Add: Dept. of Political Science, San Jose State Univ., San Jose, Calif, 95192, U.S.A.

BIRNEY, Alice Lotvin. American, b. 1938. Literary Criticism/History. Subject Cataloguer (Performing Arts Specialist), Library of Congress, Washington, D.C., since 1973. Assoc. Prof., Dept. of English, Mansfield State Coll., Pa., 1968–69; Lectr. in Literature, Univ. of California, San Diego, 1970–72. *Publs:* Satiric Catharsis in Shakespeare: A Theory of Dramatic Structure, 1973; The Literary Lives of Jesus: An International Bibliography, 1989. Add: 112 Fifth St., N.E., Washington, D.C. 20002, U.S.A.

BIRNEY, Earle. Canadian, b. 1904. Novels/Short stories, Poetry, Literature, Autobiography/Memoirs/Personal. Instr. in English, Univ. of Utah, Salt Lake City, 1930–34; Lectr., later Asst. Prof. of English, Univ. of Toronto, 1936–42; Literary Ed., Canadian Forum, Toronto, 1936–40; Supvr., European Foreign Language Broadcasts, Radio Canada, Montreal, 1945–46; Ed., Canadian Poetry mag., Vancouver, 1946–48, and Prism Intnl., Vancouver, 1963–65; Prof. of Medieval English Literature, 1946–53; and Prof. and Chmn., Dept. of Creative Writing 1963–65, Univ. of British Columbia, Vancouver; Founding Ed., Prism International (magazine), Univ. of British Columbia, 1964–65; Advisory Ed., New American and Canadian Poetry, Trumansburg, N.Y., 1966–70. *Publs:* David (poetry), 1942; Now Is Time (poetry), 1945; Strait of Anian (poetry), 1948; Turvey, 1949; Trial of a City (verse drama), 1952; (ed.) Twentieth Century Canadian Poetry, 1953; Down the Long Table (novel), 1955; (ed.) Record of Service in the Second World War, 1955; (co-ed.) New Voices, 1956; (ed. with M. Lowry) Selected Poems of Malcolm Lowry, 1962; Ice Cod Bell or Stone (poetry), 1962; (ed. with M. Lowry) Lunar Caustic, by Malcolm Lowry, 1963; Near False Creek Mouth (poetry), 1964; Selected Poems, 1966; The Creative Writer, 1966; Memory No Servant (poetry), 1968; Pnomes, Jukollages and Other Stunzas, 1969; Rag and Bone Shop (poetry), 1971; The Cow Jumped Over the Moon, 1972; (with J. Copithorne, B. Bissett and A. Suknaski) Four Parts Sand, 1972; The Bear on the Delhi Road (poetry), 1973; What's So Big About Green? (poetry), 1973; Collected Poems, 1920–1974 (2 vols.), 1974; The Rugging and the Moving Times (poetry), 1975; Alphabeings and Other Seasyours (visual poems), 1976; Ghost in the Wheels (poetry), 1977; Fall by Fury (poetry), 1978; Big Bird in the Bush (stories), 1979; The Mammoth Corridors (poetry), 1980; Spreading Time (autobiography), 1980; Words on Waves (plays), 1985; Essays on Chancerian Irony, 1985; Copernican Fix (poetry), 1985. Add: c/o McClelland Stewart Publrs., 481 University Ave., Toronot, Ont. M5G 2E9, Canada.

BIRO, Val. (Balint Stephen Biro). British, b. 1921. Children's fiction. Studio Mgr., Sylvan Press, London, 1944–46; Production Mgr., C. and J. Temple, London, 1946–48; Art Dir., John Lehmann publishers, London, 1948–51; Urban District Councillor, 1966–70. *Publs:* writer and illustrator: Bumpy's Holiday, 1943; Gumdrop: The Adventures of a Vintage Car, and series, 32 vols., 1966–; The Honest Thief: A Hungarian Folktale, 1972; A Dog and His Bone (reader), 1975; Hungarian Folk-Tales, 1981; The Magic Doctor, 1982; The Pied Piper, 1985; The Hobyahs, 1986; The Donkey That Sneezed, 1986; Tobias and the Dragon, 1989; Drango Dragon, 1989; Peter Cheater, 1989; Tales from Hans Andersen, 1989; Miranda's Umbrellas, 1990. Add: Bridge Cottage, Brook Ave., Bosham, W. Sussex, England.

BIRRELL, James Peter. Australian, b. 1928. Biography. Principal, James Birrell & Partners, Architects and Town Planners, Maroochydore, Qld., since 1965. *Publs:* Walter Burley Griffin, 1964; (with Rory Barnes) Water from the Moon, 1989. Add: 94 Memorial Ave., Maroochydore, Qld., Australia.

BIRSTEIN, Ann. American, b. 1927. Novels/Short stories. *Publs:* Star of Glass, 1950; The Troublemaker, 1955; (ed. with A. Kazin) The Works of Anne Frank, 1959; The Sweet Birds of Gorham, 1967; Summer Situations, 1972; Dickie's List, 1973; American Children, 1980; The Rabbi on Forty-Seventh Street, 1982; The Last of the True Believers, 1988. Add: c/o Elaine Markson, 44 Greenwich Ave., New York, N.Y. 10011, U.S.A.

BISCHOFF, David F(rederick). American, b. 1951. Science fiction/Fantasy, Children's fiction. Staff member, NBC-TV, Washington, D.C., since 1974. Assoc. Ed., Amazing mag. Ed., Star Date Mag., 1985–86. *Publs:* (with Christopher Lampton) The Seeker, 1976; Quest (juvenile), 1977; Strange Encounters (juvenile), 1977; The Phantom of the Opera (juvenile), 1977; (with Dennis R. Bailey) The Woodman, 1979; Nightworld, 1979; Star Fall, 1980; The Vampires of the Nightworld, 1981; (with Dennis Bailey) Tin Woodman, 1982; Star Spring, 1982; War Games, 1983; Mandala, 1983; (with Thomas F. Monteleone) Day of the Dragonstar, 1983;(with Charles Sheffield) The Selkie, 1983; The Crunch Bunch, 1985; Destiny Dice, 1985; Galactic Warriors, 1985; The Infinite Battle, 1985; Wraith Board, 1985; The Macrocosmic Conflict, 1986; Manhattan Project, 1986; The Unicorn Gambit, 1986; Some Kind of Wonderful, 1987; The Blob, 1988. Add: c/o Henry Morrison Inc., 320 McLain St., Bedford Hill, N.Y. 10507, U.S.A.

BISHOP, Claire Huchet. American/French. Novels/Short stories, Children's fiction, Children's non-fiction. *Publs:* The Five Chinese Brothers, 1938; The King's Day, 1940; The Ferryman, 1941; The Man Who Lost His Head, 1942; Augustus, 1945; Pancakes-Paris, 1947; France Alive, 1947; Blue Spring Farm, 1948; Christopher the Giant, 1950; All Things Common, 1950; Bernard and His Dogs, 1952; Twenty and Ten, 1952; All Alone, 1953; Martin de Porres, Hero, 1954; The Big Loop, 1955; (ed.) Happy Christmas: Tales for Boys and Girls, 1956; Toto's Triumph, 1957; Lafayette: French-American Hero, 1960; French Roundabout, 1960; A Present from Petros, 1961; Yeshu, Called Jesus, 1966; Mozart: Music Magician, 1968; Here Is France, 1969; The Truffle Pig, 1971; Johann Sebastian Bach: Music Giant, 1972; Georgette, 1973; How Catholics Look at Jews: Inquiries into Italian, French and Spanish Teaching Methods, 1974; Miracle at Moreaux (TV film story), 1985. Add: 107 Rue de Vaugirard, 75006 Paris, France.

BISHOP, Donald G. American, b. 1907. International relations/Current affairs, Politics/Government. Prof. Emeritus of Political Science, Syracuse Univ., N.Y., since 1972 (Chmn, Intnl. Relations Prof, 1950–65; Dept. of Political Science, 1965–66; Prof., 1952–72). Prof. of Political Science, Slippery Rock State Coll., Pa., 1972–74. *Publs:* (ed.) Nations United for Peace, 1945; (co-author) Municipal and Other Local Governments, 1950; (ed.) Soviet Foreign Relations, 1952; The Future of the New Political System in France, 1959; The Administration of British Foreign Relations, 1961, 1974; The Roosevelt-Litvinof Agreements: An American View, 1965; The Administration of United States Foreign Policy Through the United Nations, 1967. Add: 1206 Fordham Dr., Sun City Center, Fla. 33570, U.S.A.

BISHOP, Ferman. American, b. 1922. Literature. Prof. of English, Illinois State Univ., Normal, since 1964 (Assoc. Prof., 1960–64). Instr. in English, Univ. of Wisconsin-Milwaukee, 1946–47, and Univ. of Colorado, Boulder, 1951–55; Assoc. Prof., Univ. of Wichita, Nebr., 1955–60. *Publs:* Allen Tate, 1967; Henry Adams, 1979. Add: R.R.2, Bloomington, Ill. 61701, U.S.A.

BISHOP, Ian Benjamin. British, b. 1927. Literature. Reader in English, Bristol Univ. (joined faculty, 1953). *Publs:* Pearl in its Setting: A Critical Study of the Middle English Poem, 1968; Chaucer's Troilus and Criseyde, 1981; The Narrative Art of the Canterbury Tales, 1987. Add: Dept. of English, Bristol Univ., Bristol BS8 1TB, England.

BISHOP, James Drew. British, b. 1929. History. Ed., Illustrated London News, since 1971, and Newsweek Intnl. Diary, since 1977; Dir., Intnl. Thomson Publishing Co., since 1980. Reporter, later Correspondent, The Times, London, 1954–70. *Publs:* A Social History of Edwardian Britain, 1977; Social History of the First World War, 1982; (with O. Woods) The Story of the Times, 1983; (ed.) Illustrated Counties of England, 1985. Add: Illustrated London News, 20 Upper Ground, London SE1 9PF, England.

England.

BISHOP, Michael. American, b. 1945. Science fiction/Fantasy, Poetry. Freelance writer, since 1974. Instr. of English, Univ. of Georgia, Athens, 1972–74. *Publs:* A Funeral for the Eyes of Fire, 1975; And Strange at Ecbatan the Trees, 1976, as Beneath the Shattered Moon, 1977; Stolen Faces, 1977; A Little Knowledge, 1977; Windows and Mirrors (Poetry), 1977; Catacomb Years, 1979; Blooded on Arachne (short stories) 1980; (with Ian Watson) Under Heaven's Bridge (novel), 1981; No Enemy But Time (novel), 1982; (ed.) Changes (anthology), 1983; One Winter in Eden (collection), 1984; Who Made Stevie Crye? (novel),1984; (ed.) Light Years and Dark (anthology), 1984; Ancient of Days (novel), 1985; Close Encounters with the Deity (short stories), 1986; Philip K. Dick Is Dead, Alas (novel), 1987; Unicorn Mountain (novel), 1988. Add: Box 646, Pine Mountain, Ga. 31822, U.S.A.

BISHOP, Robert. American, b. 1938. Antiques/Furnishings, Art, Crafts. Dir., Museum of American Folk Art, New York, since 1976; Adjunct Prof., Dept. of Art and Art Education, New York Univ., NYC, since 1980. Assoc. Ed., The Gray Letter, and Antique. Chmn., Museums and Council of New York City, 1978–81. *Publs:* (ed.) Greenfield Village and Henry Ford Museum: Preserving America's Heritage, 1972; (with C. Safford) America's Quilts and Coverlets, 1972; Centuries and Styles of the American Chair, 1640-1970, 1972; (with D.A. Fales) American Painted and Decorated Furniture, 1660-1880, 1972; How to Know American Antique Furniture, 1973; Guide to American Antique Furniture, 1973; (ed.) Mechanical Arts at the Henry Ford Museum, 1974; American Folk Sculpture, 1974; New Discoveries in American Quilts, 1975; (with E. Safanda) A Gallery of Amish Quilts, 1976; (with W. Distin) The American Clock, 1976; The Borden Limner and His Contemporaries, 1976; (with P. Coblentz) World Furniture, 1979; Treasures of American Folk Art, 1979; (with P. Coblentz) Folk Painters of America, 1979; (with P. Coblentz) The World of Antiques, Art, and Architecture in Victorian America, 1979; (with P. Coblentz) A Gallery of American Weathervanes and Whirligigs, 1980; American Decorative Arts, 1620-1980, 1982; (ed.) Collectors' Guide to Glass, Tableware, Bowls and Vases, 1982; (ed.) Collectors' Guide to Chests, Cupboards, Desks & Other Pieces, 1982; (ed.) Collectors' Guide to Chairs, Tables, Sofas & Beds, 1982; (with W. Secord and J.R. Weissman) Collectors' Guide to Quilts, Coverlets, Rugs and Samplers, 1982; (with W. Ketchum) Collectors' Guide to Folk Art, 1983; (ed.) Collectors' Guide to Toys, 1984; (ed.) Collectors' Guide to Silver and Pewter, 1984; (with C. Houck) All Flags Flying, 1986; (with J. Lipman and E. V. Warren) Young American, A Folk Art History, 1986; Hands All Around, 1986; American Quilts: Giftwraps by Artists, 1986. Add: 213 W. 22nd St., New York, N.Y. 10011, U.S.A.

BISSET, Donald. British, b. 1910. Children's fiction. Radio, television, and stage actor. *Publs:* Anytime Stories, 1954; Sometime Stories, 1957; Next Time Stories, 1959; This Time Stories, 1961; Another Time Stories, 1963; Little Bear's Pony, 1966; Hullo Lucy, 1967; Talks with a Tiger, 1967; Kangaroo Tennis, 1968; Nothing, 1969; Upside Down Land, 1969; Benjie the Circus Dog, 1969; Time and Again Stories, 1970; Barcha the Tiger, 1971; Tiger Wants More, 1971; Yak series, 6 vols., 1971–78; Father Tingtang's Journey, 1973; Jenny Hopalong, 1973; The Happy Horse, 1974; The Adventures of Mandy Duck, 1974; Hazy Mountain, 1974; "Oh Dear," Said the Tiger, 1975; Paws with Shapes, 1976; (with Michael Morris) Paws with Numbers, 1976; The Lost Birthday, 1976; The Story of Smokey Horse, 1977; This Is Ridiculous, 1977; Jungle Journey, 1977; What Time Is It, When It Isn't, 1980; Cornelia and Other Stories, 1980; Johnny Here and There, 1981; The Hedgehog Who Rolled Uphill, 1982; Snakey Boo series, 2 vols., 1982–85; Just a Moment, 1988. Add: 43 Andrewes House, Barbican, London EC2Y 8AX, England.

BISSETT, Bill. Canadian, b. 1939. Poetry, Songs/Lyrics and libretti. Ed. and Printer, Blewointmentpress, Vancouver, since 1962. Artist and musician. *Publs:* Th jinx ship nd othr trips: pomes-drawings-collage, 1966; we sleep inside each other all, 1966; Fires in the Tempul, 1967; where is Miss Florence riddle, 1967; what poetiks, 1967; (th) Gossamer Bed Pan, 1967; Lebanon Voices, 1967; Of th Land/Divine Service Poems, 1968; Awake in the Red Deaert!, 1968; Killer Whale, 1969; Sunday Work?, 1969; Liberating Skies, 1969; The Lost Angel Mining Co., 1969; S th Story I to, 1970; Th Outlaw, 1970; blew trewz, 1970; Nobody Owns th Earth, 1971; air 6, 1971; Tuff Shit Love Pomes, 1971; dragon fly, 1971; Rush what fukin thery, 1971; (with others) Four Parts Sand: Concrete Poems, 1972; th Ice bag, 1972; pomes for yoshi, 1972, 1977; drifting into war, 1972; air 10-11-12, 1972; Pass th Food, Release th Spirit Book, 1973; th first sufi line, 1973; Vancouver Mainland Ice & Cold Storage, 1973; Living with th vishyan, 1974; what, 1974; drawings, 1974; Medicine my mouths on fire, 1974; space travl, 1974; yu can eat it at th opening, 1974; th fifth sun, 1975; th wind up tongue, 1975; Stardust, 1975; an allusyun to macbeth, 1976; plutonium missing, 1976; sailor, 1978; Beyond Even Faithful Legends, 1979; soul arrow, 1980; sa/n th monkey, 1980; northern birds in color, 1981; sa n his crystal ball, 1981; parlant, 1982; seagull on yonge street, 1983; canada gees mate for life, 1985; Animal Uproar, 1987; what we have, 1988; luddites (cassett n lp), 1988. Add: Box 273, 1755 Robson St., Vancouver, B.C., V6G 387, Canada.

BISSOONDOYAL, Basdeo. Writes in Hindi and Sanskrit as Vishnudayal Vasudeva. Mauritian, b. 1906. History, Language/Linguistics, Literature, Theology/Religion/Biography. Primary sch. teacher, Mauritius, 1922–32; Lectr., Gurukula Univ., Hardwar, India, 1935. *Publs:* Geeta S'ar, 1944; Laghu Vyakaran, 1944; Hindi Pathya Pustak, 1945; Meri Kothariyan, 1949; Kavita-Kali, 1949; My Fourth Imprisonment, 1949; L'Histoire de l'Inde, 1950; L'Inde Eternelle, 1953; Gita Ka Adbhut Gyan, 1953; Mauritius Ka Parichay, 1954; Kutch Mahatwapuran Granth, 1956; (trans.) Paul aur Virginia, 1956; Paul aur Virginia Me kia he, 1956; Vyavahar Prakash, 1957; (trans.) Bhartiya Kutiya, 1959; Ala Bhagavadgita!, 1959; Amar Bharat, 1959; Vishnudayal Rachnavali, 1959; Hindu Scriptures, 1960; Sanskrit Without Tears, 1960; Meri Bengali Kothariyan, 1961; Struggles of a Missionary in Mauritius, 1961; French-Hindi Dictionary, 1962; Roopkishore aur Sujata, 1963; Vishnudayal Lekhavli, 1964; Paradis et Maria, 1964; Les Hindous et leurs Ecritures Sacrées, 1965; The Essence of the Vedas, 1966; Vishnudayal Granthavali, 1966; The Arya Samaj Introduced, 1966; France Looks at Modern India, 1966; Bissoondoyal's Speeches and Writings, 1967; The Truth About Mauritius, 1967; India in French Literature, 1967; Vishnudayal Nibandhavali, 1968; They Loved Mother India, 1968; Deux Indiens Illustrés, 1968; (trans.) Surat Ka Kahua Ghar, 1968; Mahatma Ka Satya Swaroop, 1969; La Litterature Hindoue, 1972; The Message of the Four Vedas, 1972; Ved Bhagwan Bole, 1972; Rishi ka Satya Swaroop, 1974; Le Rig Ve'da, 1974; India in World Literature, 1976; Mahatma Gandhi: A New Approach, 1976; Vedon ke Anupam Vichar, 1980; A Concise Study of the Hindu Scriptures, 1981; Life in Greater India, 1984; Katipaya Lekh, 1984; Maharshi ka Saccha Swaroop, 1984; The Vedas Introduced, 1987. Add: Sookdeo Bissoondoyal St., Port Louis, Mauritius.

BIXBY, Jerome (Lewis). American, b. 1923. Science fiction/Fantasy. Mag. Ed., Fiction House, 1949–51, Standard Publs., 1951–53, and Galaxy Publs., 1953–54; Owner, Exoterica mail-order business, 1963–64, and Walden Realty Co., 1964–65, both in Bullhead City, Ariz. *Publs:* The Devil's Scrapbook (short stories), 1964; Space by the Tale (short stories), 1964; Star Trek: Day of the Dove, 1978. Add: c/o Bantam, 666 Fifth Ave., New York, N.Y. 10009, U.S.A.

BIXBY, Ray Z. *See* **TRALINS,** S. Robert.

BLACK, Charles Lund, Jr. American, b. 1915. Poetry, Law. Sterling Prof. of Law, Emeritus, Yale University, New Haven, Conn., since 1987 (Luce Prof. of Jurisprudence, 1956–75; Sterling Prof., 1975–87); Adjunct Prof. of Law, Columbia Univ., NYC, since 1987. Member of faculty, Columbia Univ., NYC, 1947–56. *Publs:* (with G. Gilmore) Law of Admiralty, 1957, 1975; The People and the Court, 1960; The Occasions of Justice, 1963; Telescopes and Islands (poetry), 1963; Perspectives in Constitutional Law, 1963, rev. ed. 1970; Structure and Relationship in Constitutional Law, 1969; Capital Punishment: The Inevitability of Caprice and Mistake, 1974, 1981; Impeachment: A Handbook, 1974; (with B. Eckhardt) The Tides of Power, 1976; Owls Bay in Babylon (poetry), 1980; Decision According to Law, 1981; The Waking Passenger (poetry), 1983; The Humane Imagination, 1986. Add: Columbia Univ. Law Sch., 435 W. 116th St., New York, N.Y. 10027, U.S.A.

BLACK, Clinton V(ane De Brosse). Jamaican, b. 1918. History, Librarianship. Archivist of Jamaica, since 1955. Fellow, Soc. of Antiquaries of London, since 1972; Exec. Cttee. Member, Intnl. P.E.N. Club, Jamaica (former Pres.); Member, Jamaica History Soc. (former Secty.). *Publs:* Living Names in Jamaica's History, 1946; (with Bryce, Yates and Roberts) Historic Port Royal, 1952; Report on the Archives of British Guyana, 1955; (with Schellenberg) Report on the Archives of Trinidad and Tobago, 1958; The History of Jamaica, 1958; Spanish Town—The Old Capital, 1960; Our Archives, 1962; The Story of Jamaica, 1965; Port Royal—A History and Guide, 1970; A New History of Jamaica, 1973; Jamaica Guide, 1973; The History of Montego Bay, 1984; (ed.) Jamaica's Banana Industry, 1984. Add: 5 Avesbury Ave., Kingston 6, Jamaica.

BLACK, David (Macleod). British, b. 1941. Poetry. *Publs:* Theory of Diet, 1966; With Decorum, 1967; A Dozen Short Poems, 1968; (with D.M. Thomas and Peter Redgrove) Penguin Modern Poets 11, 1968; The

Educators, 1969; The Old Hag, 1972; The Happy Crow, 1974; Gravitations, 1979. Add: 30 Cholmley Gardens, London NW6 1AG, England.

BLACK, (Sir) Douglas (Andrew Kilgour). British, b. 1913. Medicine/Health. Physician, Manchester Royal Infirmary, since 1959. Lectr. and Reader in Medicine, 1946–58, and Prof. of Medicine, 1959–78, Univ. of Manchester. Pres., Royal Coll. of Physicians, 1977–83. *Publs:* Essentials of Fluid Balance, 1957, 4th ed., 1967; (ed.) Renal Disease, 1962, 4th ed. 1979; The Logic of Medicine, 1968; (ed.) Notes on Clinical Medicine, 1971; An Anthology of False Antitheses, 1984; Invitation to Medicine, 1987; Recollections and Reflections, 1987. Add: The Old Forge, Whitchurch-on-Thames RG8 7EN, England.

BLACK, Gavin. *See* **WYND,** Oswald.

BLACK, Laura. Historical/Romance/Gothic. *Publs:* Glendraco, 1977; Ravenburn (in U.K. as Castle Raven), 1978; Wild Cat, 1979; Strathgallant, 1981; Albany, 1984; Falls of Gard, 1986. Add: c/o St. Martin's Press, 175 Fifth Ave., New York, N.Y. 10010, U.S.A.

BLACK, Mansell. *See* **TREVOR,** Elleston.

BLACK, Max. American, b. 1909. Philosophy. Prof. Emeritus, Cornell Univ., Ithaca, N.Y., since 1977 (Prof. of Philosophy, 1946–54; Susan Linn Sage Prof. of Philosophy, 1954–77). Ed., Philosophical Review, since 1946. Prof. of Philosophy, Univ. of Illinois, Urbana, 1940–46. Co-Ed., Journal of Symbolic Logic, 1945–51; President, American Philosophical Assn., 1958. *Publs:* The Nature of Mathematics: A Critical Survey, 1933; The Teaching of Mathematics: A Bibliography, 1938; Critical Thinking: An Introduction to Logic and Scientific Method, 1946; (with others) Philosophical Studies: Essays in Memory of L. Susan Strebbing, 1948; Language and Philosophy: Studies in Method, 1949; (ed.) Philosophical Analysis: A Collection of Essays, 1950; Problems of Analysis: Philosophical Papers, 1954; (ed. with Peter Geach) Translations from the Philosophical Writings of Gottlob Frege, 1952, 1960; Problems of Analysis: Philosophical Papers, 1954; (ed.) The Sociological Papers of Talcott Parsons: A Critical Examination, 1961; Models and Metaphors: Studies in Language and Philosophy, 1962; A Companion to Wittgenstein's Tractatus, 1964; The Raison d'Etre of Inductive Argument, 1965; (ed.) Philosophy in America: Essays by William P. Alston and Others, 1965; (ed. with others) The Morality of Scholarship, 1967; The Labyrinth of Language, 1968; Margins of Precision: Essays in Logic and Language, 1970; (with others) Art, Perception and Reality, 1972; (ed. with Morton Bloomfield) In Search of Literary Theory, 1972; (ed.) Problems of Choice and Decision, 1975; Caveats and Critiques: Philosophical Essays on Language, Logic and Art, 1975; Prevalence of Humbug and Other Essays, 1983. Add: 408 Highland Road, Ithaca, N.Y. 14850, U.S.A.

BLACK, Percy. Canadian, b. 1922. Psychology. Prof. of Psychology, Pace Univ., Pleasantville, N.Y., since 1967. Asst. Prof. of Psychology, Univ. of New Brunswick, 1951–53; Principal in Motivational Research, Social Attitude Survey, Yonkers, N.Y., 1955–67. *Publs:* The Mystique of Modern Monarchy, 1953. Add: Pace Univ., Pleasantville, N.Y. 10570, U.S.A.

BLACK, Robert Perry. American, b. 1927. Economics, Money/Finance. Pres., Federal Reserve Bank of Richmond, since 1973 (Research Assoc., 1954–55; Assoc. Economist, 1956–58; Economist, 1958–60; Asst. Vice Pres., 1960–62; Vice Pres., 1962–68; First Vice Pres., 1968–73). Asst. Prof. of Finance, Univ. of Tennessee, Knoxville, 1955–56. *Publs:* (with B.U. Ratchford) The Federal Reserve at Work, 1961, 5th ed. 1973; The Federal Reserve Today, 1964, 5th ed. 1971; (with Doris E. Harless) Non-Bank Financial Institutions, 1965, 3rd ed. 1969. Add: Federal Reserve Bank, 701 East Byrd St., Richmond, Va. 23219, U.S.A.

BLACK, Veronica. *See* **PETERS,** Maureen.

BLACKBURN, John (Fenwick). British, b. 1923. Mystery/Crime/Suspense. *Publs:* A Scent of New Mown Hay, 1958; A Sour Apple Tree, 1958; Boy, 1959; Dead Man Running, 1960; The Gaunt Woman, 1962; Blue Octavo, 1963; The Winds of Midnight, 1964; Colonel Bogus, 1964; A Ring of Roses, 1964; Children of the Night, 1966; Nothing but the Night, 1968; Bury Him Darkly, 1969; Blow the House Down, 1970; Devil Daddy, 1972; Household Traitors, 1971; For Fear of Little Men, 1971; Deep Among the Dead Men, 1973; Our Lady of Pain, 1974; Mister Brown's Bodies, 1975; Face of the Lion, 1976; Cyclops Goblet, 1977; Dead Man's Handle, 1978; The Sins of the Father, 1978; A Beastly Business, 1982; The Book of the Dead, 1984; The Bad Penny, 1985.

Add: c/o A.M. Heath, 40-42 William IV St., London WC2N 4DD, England.

BLACKBURNE, Neville. British, b. 1913. Biography. Headmaster, Nowton Court Preparatory Sch., Bury St. Edmunds, Suffolk, now retired. *Publs:* Ladies' Chain, 1952; The Restless Ocean: Biography of George Crabbe, 1972. Add: The Small House, Nowton Court, Bury St. Edmonds, Suffolk, England.

BLACKHAM, Garth. American, b. 1926. Psychology. Prof., Arizona State Univ., Tempe, since 1965 (Assoc. Prof. of Elementary Education, 1962–65). Consultant, Devereux Center, Scottsdale, Ariz. Staff Psychologist, Child Study and Consultation, Phoenix, Ariz., 1954–62. *Publs:* The Deviant Child in the Classroom, 1967; (with A. Silberman) Modification of Child and Adolescent Behavior, 1971, 1975; Personality Assessment Manual, 1971; (with others) Counseling: Theory and Practice, 1977. Add: Arizona State Univ., Dept. of Counseling, Tempe, Ariz. 85281, U.S.A.

BLACKMER, Donald L.M. American, b. 1929. International relations/Current affairs, Social sciences. Prof. of Political Science, Massachusetts Inst. of Technology, since 1973 (Lectr., 1960–61; Asst. Prof., 1961–67; Asst. Dir., Center for Intnl. Studies, 1961–68; Assoc. Prof., 1967–73; Assoc. Dean, Sch. of Humanities and Social Sciences, 1973–81; Dir., Science, Technology, and Society Prog., 1978–81; Head, Political Science Dept., 1981–88). Research Assoc. in West European Studies, Harvard Univ. *Publs:* (ed. with M.F. Millikan & contrib.) The Emerging Nations: Their Growth and United States Policy, 1961; Unity in Diversity: Italian Communism and the Communist World, 1967; (ed. S. Tarrow & contrib.) Communism in Italy and France, 1974; (with A. Kriegel) The International Role of the Communist Parties of Italy and France, 1975. Add: Massachusetts Inst. of Technology, E53-449, Cambridge, Mass. 02139, U.S.A.

BLACKMORE, June. British. Historical/Romance/Gothic. *Publs:* Towards Tomorrow, 1941; They Carry a Torch, 1943; It Happened to Susan, 1944; Snow in June, 1947; The Square of Many Colours, 1948; So Dark the Mirror, 1949; The Nine Commandments, 1950; The Bridge of Strange Music, 1952; Beloved Stranger, 1953; Perilous Waters, 1954; Three Letters to Pan, 1955; The Closing Door, 1955; Bitter Love, 1956; Storm in the Family, 1956; A Woman on Her Own, 1957; The Lonely House, 1957; Beware the Night, 1958; Dangerous Love, 1958; Tears in Paradise, 1959; The Missing Hour, 1959; Bitter Honey, 1960; A Trap for Lovers, 1960; The Night of the Stranger, 1961; The Dark Between the Stars, 1961; Two in Shadow, 1962; It Couldn't Happen to Me, 1962; Joanna, 1963; That Night, 1963; Flight into Love, 1964; Return to Love, 1964, in U.S. paperback as Stephanie, 1972; Girl Alone, 1965; Man of Power, 1966; Miranda, 1966; Gold for My Girl, 1967, in U.S. paperback as Deed of Innocence, 1969; Raw Summer, 1967; The Other Room, 1968, in U.S. paperback as A Love Forbidden, 1974; The Velvet Trap, 1969; The Lilac Is for Sharing, 1969; Lonely Night, 1969; Broomstick in the Hall, 1970; Dance on a Hornet's Nest, 1970; Hunter's Mate, 1971; The Room in the Tower, 1972; The Deep Pool, 1972; My Sister Erica, 1973; The Cresselly Inheritance, 1973; Angel's Tear, 1974; Night of the Bonfire, 1974; And Then There Was Georgia, 1975; Lord of the Manor, 1975; Ravenden, 1976; Hawkridge, 1976; Silver Unicorn, 1977; Of Wind and Fire, 1980; Wildfire Love, 1980. Add: c/o Piatkus Books, 5 Windmill St., London W1P 1HF, England.

BLACKSTOCK, Charity. Pseud. for Ursula Torday; also writes as Paula Allardyce, Lee Blackstock, and Charlotte Keppel. British. Mystery/Crime/Suspense, Historical/Romance/Gothic. *Publs:* (as Ursula Torday) The Ballad-Maker of Paris, 1935; (as Ursula Torday) No Peace for the Wicked, 1937; (as Ursula Torday) The Mirror of the Sun, 1938; (as Paula Allardyce) After the Lady, 1954; (as Paula Allardyce) The Doctor's Daughter, 1955; (as Paula Allardyce) A Game of Hazard, 1955; (as Paula Allardyce) Adam and Evelina, 1956; (as Paula Allardyce) The Man of Wrath, 1956; Dewey Death, 1956, in U.S. as Dewey Death, and The Foggy, Foggy Dew, 1959; Miss Fenny, 1957, in U.S. (as Lee Blackstock) as The Woman in the Woods, 1958; (as Paula Allardyce) The Lady and the Pirate, 1957; (as Paula Allardyce) Southarn Folly, 1957; The Foggy, Foggy Dew, 1958, in U.S. as Dewey Death, and The Foggy, Foggy Dew, 1959; All Men Are Murderers, 1958, in U.K. as The Shadow of Murder, 1959; Beloved Enemy, 1958; (as Paula Allardyce) My Dear Miss Emma, 1958; The Bitter Conquest, 1959; Death My Lover, 1959; (as Paula Allardyce) A Marriage Has Been Arranged, 1959; The Briar Patch (in U.S. as Young Lucifer), 1960; Johnny Danger, 1960, in U.S. as The Rebel Lover, 1979; The Exorcism, 1961, in U.S. as A House Possessed, 1962; (as Paula Allardyce) Witches' Sabbath, 1961; (as Paula Allardyce) The

Gentle Highwayman, 1961; The Gallant, 1962; Mr. Christopoulos, 1963; Adam's Rib, 1963, in U.S. as Legacy of Pride, 1975; The Factor's Wife (in U.S. as The English Wife), 1964; The Respectable Miss Parkington-Smith, 1964, in U.S. as Paradise Row, 1976; When the Sun Goes Down (in U.S. as Monkey on a Chain), 1965; Octavia, or, The Trials of a Romantic Novelist, 1965; The Children, 1966, in U.K. as Wednesday's Children, 1967; The Knock at Midnight, 1966; The Moonlighters, 1966, in U.S. as Gentleman Rogue, 1975; Party in Dolly Creek (in U.S. as The Widow), 1967; Six Passengers for the "Sweet Bird," 1967; (as Paula Allardyce) Waiting at the Church, 1968, in U.S. as Emily, 1976; The Melon in the Cornfield (in U.S. as Lemmings), 1969; (as Paula Allardyce) The Ghost of Archie Gilroy, 1970, in U.S. as Shadowed Love, 1977; The Daughter, 1970; The Encounter, 1971; The Jungle, 1972; The Lonely Strangers, 1972; (as Paula Allardyce) Miss Jonas's Boy, 1972, in U.S. as Eliza, 1975; (as Paula Allardyce) The Gentle Sex, 1974, in U.S. as The Carradine Affair, 1976; (as Charlotte Keppel) Madam You Must Die, 1974, in U.S. as Loving Sands, Deadly Sands, 1975; People in Glass Houses, 1975; Ghost Town, 1976; (as Charlotte Keppel) My Name Is Clary Brown, 1976, in U.S. as When I Say Goodbye, I'm Clary Brown, 1977; I Met Murder on the Way (in U.S. as The Shirt Front), 1977; Miss Philadelphia Smith, 1977; (as Paula Allardyce) Haunting Me, 1978; Miss Charley, 1979; (as Paula Allardyce) The Rogue's Lady, 1979; With Fondest Thoughts, 1980; (as Paula Allardyce) The Vixen's Revenge, 1980; (as Charlotte Keppel) I Could Be Good to You, 1980; (as Charlotte Keppel) The Villains, 1980; Dream Towers, 1981; (as Charlotte Keppel) The Ghosts of Fontenoy, 1981. Add: 23 Montagu Mansions, London W1H 1LD, England.

BLACKSTOCK, Lee. *See* **BLACKSTOCK,** Charity.

BLACKSTONE, Baroness (of Stoke Newington in Greater London); Tessa Blackstone. British, b. 1942. Education. Master, Birbeck Coll., Univ. of London, since 1987. Asst. Lectr., 1966–69, and Lectr. in Social Admin., 1969–75, London Sch. of Economics; Adviser, Central Policy Review Staff, Cabinet Office, 1975–78; Prof. of Educational Admin., Univ. of London, 1978–83; Deputy Education Officer, Inner London Education Authority, 1983–86. Fellow, Centre for Studies in Social Policy, London, 1972–74. *Publs:* (with K. Gales, R. Hadley and W. Lewis) Students in Conflict: L.S.E. in 1967, 1970; A Fair Start: The Provision of Pre-School Education, 1971; Education and Day Care for Young Children in Need: The American Experience, 1973; (with G. Williams and D. Metcalf) The Academic Labour Market: Economic and Social Aspects of a Profession, 1974; (with Paul Lodge) Educational Policy and Educational Inequality, 1982; (with J. Mortimore) Disadvantage and 1982; (with G. Williams) Response and Adversity, 1983; (with others) Testing Children, 1983; (with William Plowden) Inside the Think Tank: Advising the Cabinet 1971-83, 1988. Add: 2 Gower St., London WC1, England.

BLACKWELL, Richard J. American, b. 1929. Sciences (general), Translations. Prof. of Philosophy, since 1966, and Danforth Chair in the Humanities, since 1986, Saint Louis Univ. (Assoc. Prof., 1961–66). Assoc. Ed., The Modern Schoolman, since 1961. Instr., 1954–57, and Asst. Prof., 1957–61, John Carroll Univ., Cleveland, Ohio. *Publs:* (trans. with R. Spath and W.E. Thirlkel) Commentary on Aristotle's Physics, by St. Thomas Aquinas, 1963; (trans.) Preliminary Discourse on Philosophy in General, by Christian Wolff, 1963; Discovery in the Physical Sciences, 1969; Bibliography of the Philosophy of Science 1945–1981, 1983; (trans.) the Pendulum Clock, by C. Huygens, 1986. Add: Dept. of Philosophy, Saint Louis Univ., 221 North Grand Blvd., St. Louis, Mo. 63103, U.S.A.

BLACKWOOD, Andrew W. American, b. 1915. Theology/Religion. Pastor, First Presbyterian Church, Newton, N.J., 1940–50; Northminster Presbyterian Church, Columbus, Ohio, 1950–56, First Presbyterian Church, West Palm Beach, Fla., 1956–67, and Covenant Presbyterian Church, Atlanta, 1967–80; Pastor Seroe Colorado Union Church, Aruba, Netherlands Antilles, 1980–83; Second Union Church, San Juan, Puerto Rico, 1984. *Publs:* The Voice from the Cross, 1955; When God Came Down, 1955; Devotional Introduction to Job, 1959; The Holy Spirit in Your Life, 1961; Ezekiel, Prophecy of Hope, 1965; The Other Son of Man, 1966; From the Rock to the Gates of Hell, 1968; We Need You Here, Lord, 1969; Commentary on Jeremiah: The Word, The Words, and the World, 1977; In All Your Ways: A Study in Proverbs, 1979. Add: 3069 Rhodenhaven Dr. N.W. Atlanta, Ga. 30327, U.S.A.

BLACKWOOD, Caroline. British, b. 1931. Novels/Short stories, Cookery/Gastronomy/Wine. *Publs:* For All That I Found There (short stories and essays), 1973; The Stepdaughter, 1976; Great Granny Webster, (with Anna Haycraft) Darling, You Shouldn't Have Gone to So Much

Trouble (cookbook), 1980; The Fate of Mary Rose, 1981; Goodnight Sweet Ladies (stories), 1983; On the Perimeter, 1984; Corrigan, 1984; In the Pink: Caroline Blackwood on Hunting, 1987.   Add: c/o Heinemann Ltd., 81 Fulham Rd., London SW3 6RB, England.

BLADES, Ann (Sager).   Canadian, b. 1947.   Children's fiction. Elementary sch. teacher, Peace River North Sch. District, Mile 18, B.C., 1967–68, Dept. of Indian Affairs and Northern Development, Taché, B.C., 1969, and Surrey Sch. District, B.C., 1969–71; Clerk, London, Ont., 1972; Registered Nurse, Vancouver Gen. Hosp., 1974–75, and Mt. St. Joseph Hosp., Vancouver, part-time, 1975–80.   Publs: Mary of Mile 18, 1971; A Boy of Taché, 1973; The Cottage at Crescent Beach, 1977; By the Sea: An Alphabet Book, 1985.   Add: 2701 Crescent Dr., Surrey, B.C. V4A 3J9, Canada.

BLADES, James.   British, b. 1901.   Music, Autobiography/Memoirs/Personal.   Professional timpanist with English Chamber Orchestra, English Opera Group, Melos Ensemble, and others, since 1919. Consultant Prof. of Timpani and Percussion, Royal Academy of Music, London, and Univ. of Surrey.   Publs: Orchestral Percussion Technique, 1961–73; Percussion Instruments and Their History, 1970–74; Drum Roll (autobiography), 1977.   Add: 191 Sandy Lane, Cheam, Surrey, England.

BLAINEY, Geoffrey Norman.   Australian, b. 1930.   History, Biography. Ernest Scott Prof. of History, Univ. of Melbourne, since 1977 (Prof. of Economic History, 1968–77).   Chmn., Commonwealth Literary Fund, 1971–73 and Australia Council, 1977–81.   Publs: The Peaks of Lyell, 1954; A Centenary History of the University of Melbourne, 1957; Gold and Paper, 1958; Mines in the Spinifex, 1960; The Rush That Never Ended, 1963; A History of Camberwell, 1964; (ed.) If I Remember Rightly: The Memoirs of W.S. Robinson, 1966; (co-author and ed.) Wesley College: The Hundred Years, 1967; The Tyranny of Distance, 1966; Across a Red World, 1968; The Rise of Broken Hill, 1968; The Steel Master, 1971; The Causes of War, 1973; Triumph of the Nomads, 1975; A Land Half Won, 1980; The Blainey View, 1982; Our Side of the Country, 1984; All for Australia, 1984; The Great Seesaw, 1988.   Add: Univ. of Melbourne, Parkville, Vic. 3052, Australia.

BLAIR, Claude.   British, b. 1922.   Crafts.   Consultant, Christie's, London, since 1982.   Asst., Tower of London Armouries, 1951–56; Hon. Ed., Journal of Arms and Armour Soc., 1953–77.   Keeper of Metalwork, Victorian and Albert Museum, London, 1972–82 (Asst. Keeper of Metalwork, 1966–72; Deputy Keeper, 1966–72).   Publs: European Armour, 1958; European and American Arms, 1962; Pistols of the World, 1968; Three Presentation Swords in the Victoria and Albert Museum, 1972; The James A. de Rothschild Collection at Waddesdon Manor: Arms, Armour and Base-Metalwork, 1974; (ed.) Pollard's History of Firearms, 1983.   Add: 90 Links Rd., Ashtead, Surrey KT21 2HW, England.

BLAIR, Clay Drewry.   American, b. 1925.   Military/Defence, Recreation, Social Commentary.   Correspondent, Time mag., 1949–55; Military Correspondent, Life mag., 1955–57; Assoc. Ed.,1957–61, Asst. Managing Ed., 1962–63, Managing Ed., 1962, and Ed., 1963–64, Saturday Evening Post.   Publs: The Atomic Submarine and Admiral Rickover, 1954; (with James R. Shepley) The Hydrogen Bomb, 1954; Beyond Courage, 1965; Valley of the Shadow, 1965; (with William R. Anderson) Nautilus 90 North, 1959; Diving for Pleasure and Treasure, 1960; (with A. Scott Crosfield) Always Another Dawn, 1960; The Board Room, 1969; The Strange Case of James Earl Ray, 1969; The Archbishop, 1970; Pentagon Country, 1971; Survive, 1973; Silent Victory: The U.S. Submarine War Against Japan, 1975; (with Joan Blair) The Search for J.F.K., 1976; MacArthur, 1977; Scuba, 1977; Combat Patrol, 1978; Return from the River Kwai, 1979; Mission Tokyo Bay, 1980; Swordray's First Three Patrols, 1980; (with Omar N. Bradley) A General's Life, 1983; Ridgeway's Paratroopers, 1985.   Add: c/o Meredith, 845 Third Ave., New York, N.Y. 10022, U.S.A.

BLAIR, Dorothy S(ara).   British, b. 1913.   Literature, Translations. Prof. of French Literature and Lanuguage, Univ. of Witwatersrand, Johannesburg, since 1970 (Lectr., 1954–64; Sr. Lectr., 1964–70).   Vice-Pres., Assn. for French Studies in Southern Africa, since 1974 (Founder and First Pres., 1970–74).   Publs: (ed. and trans.) Darkness and Light: An Anthology of African Writing, 1958; Jules Superveille: A Modern Fabulist, 1960; (trans.) The Tales of Amadou Koumba, by Birago Diop. 1966; African Literature in French, 1976; Sengalese Literature: A Critical History, 1984.   Add: 3 Gale Rd., Parktown, Johannesburg, 2001, South Africa.

BLAIR, George S.   American, b. 1924.   Politics/Government. Elisabeth Helm Rosecrans Prof. of Social Science, Claremont Grad. Sch., Calif. (Assoc. Prof. of Govt., 1960–64; Prof. of Govt., 1964–72).   Member faculty, Univ. of Tennessee, 1951–53, and Univ. of Pennsylvania, Philadelphia, 1953–60.   Publs: (with S.B. Sweeney) Metropolitan Analysis, 1958; Cumulative Voting in Illinois, 1960; American Local Government, 1964; (with H.I. Flournoy) Legislative Bodies in California, 1967; American Legislatures, 1967; Cumulative Voting, 1976; Government at the Grass-Roots, 1977, 1981, 1986.   Add: McManus Hall, Claremont Grad. Sch., Claremont, Calif. 91711, U.S.A.

BLAIR, Glenn Myers.   American, b. 1908.   Education, Psychology. Prof. Emeritus of Educational Psychology, Univ. of Illinois, Urbana, since 1973; (Prof., 1938–73; Co-Dir. of Reading Clinic, 1938–48; Head, Dept. of Educational Psychology, 1948–52).   Publs: Mentally Superior and Inferior Children, 1938; Diagnostic and Remedial Teaching, 1946, 1956; Development of Educational Psychology, 1948; (with R.S. Jones and R.H. Simpson) Educational Psychology, 1954; 4th ed. 1975; (ed.) The Words You Use, 1958; (with R.S. Jones) Psychology of Adolescence for Teachers, 1964.   Add: 51 Island Way, Apt. 510, Clearwater, Fla. 34630, U.S.A.

BLAIR, Kathryn.   Also writes as Rosalind Brett and Celine Conway. Historical/Romance/Gothic.   Publs: (as Rosalind Brett) Green Leaves, 1947; (as Rosalind Brett) Pagan Interlude, 1947; (as Rosalind Brett) Secret Marriage, 1947; (as Rosalind Brett) And No Regrets, 1948; (as Rosalind Brett) Winds of Enchantment, 1949; (as Rosalind Brett) They Came to Valeira, 1950; Bewildered Heart, 1950; The House at Tegwani, 1950; No Other Haven, 1950; Dearest Enemy, 1951; Flowering Wilderness, 1951; Mayenga Farm, 1951; (as Rosalind Brett) Brittle Bondage, 1951; (as Rosalind Brett) Love This Stranger, 1951; (as Rosalind Brett) Stormy Haven, 1952; (as Rosalind Brett) Fair Horizon, 1952; The Enchanting Island, 1952; The Fair Invader, 1952, in Can. as Plantation Doctor, 1962; The White Oleander, 1953, in Can. as Nurse Laurie, 1962; Dear Adversary, 1953; (as Rosalind Brett) Towards the Sun, 1953; (as Celine Conway) Return of Simon, 1953; (as Celine Conway) The Blue Caribbean, 1954; (as Conway) Flowers in the Wind, 1954, in Can. as Doctor's Assistant, 1964; (as Celine Conway) Full Tide, 1954; Barbary Moon, 1954; (as Rosalind Brett) Whispering Palms, 1954; (as Rosalind Brett) Winds in the Wilderness, 1954; Sweet Deceiver, 1955; (as Rosalind Brett) Sweet Waters, 1955; (as Rosalind Brett) A Cottage in Spain, 1955; (as Celine Conway) Three Women, 1955; Tamarisk Bay, 1956; Wild Crocus, 1956; (as Rosalind Brett) Portrait of Susan, 1956; (as Celine Conway) The Tall Pines, 1956; Valley of Flowers, 1957; (as Rosalind Brett) Quiet Holiday, 1957; in Can. as Nurse on Holiday, 1963; (as Rosalind Brett) Tangle in Sunshine, 1957; (as Celine Conway) The Rustle of Bamboo, 1957; (as Celine Conway) Wide Pastures, 1957; The Tulip Tree, 1958; Love This Enemy, 1958; (as Rosalind Brett) Young Tracy, 1958; (as Rosalind Brett) Too Young to Marry, 1958; (as Celine Conway) At the Villa Massina, 1958; The Golden Rose, 1959; The Man at Mulera, 1959; (as Rosalind Brett) The Reluctant Guest, 1959; (as Rosalind Brett) Hotel Mirador, 1959; (as Celine Conway) My Dear Cousin, 1959; A Summer at Barbazon, 1960, in. Can. as A Nurse at Barbazon, 1964; (as Rosalind Brett) Dangerous Waters, 1960; (as Celine Conway) Came a Stranger, 1960; (as Celine Conway) Flower of the Morning, 1960; The Primrose Bride, 1961; Children's Nurse, 1961; Battle of Love, 1961; (as Rosalind Brett) The Bolambo Affair, 1961; (as Rosalind Brett) Spring at the Villa, 1961, in Can. at Elizabeth Browne, Children's Nurse, 1965; (as Celine Conway) Perchance to Marry, 1961; (as Celine Conway) White Doctor, 1961; The Affair in Tangier, 1962; They Met in Zanzibar, 1962; (as Rosalind Brett) The Girl at White Drift, 1962; (as Celine Conway) The Rancher Needs a Wife, 1962; (as Celine Conway) Ship's Surgeon, 1962; The Surgeon's Marriage, 1963; The Dangerous Kind of Love, 1964; This Kind of Love, 1964; Doctor Westland, 1965; (as Rosalind Brett) For My Sins, 1966.   Add: c/o Mills and Boon Ltd., Eton House, 18-24 Paradise Rd., Richmond, Surrey TW9 1SR, England.

BLAIR, Kay Kimery Reynolds.   American, b. 1942.   History, Literature.   Curator, Healy House, State Historical Soc. of Colorado, 1974. Publs: E. Richard, L. Churchill and E. Blair) Fun with American Literature, 1968; Ladies of the Lamplight, 1971.   Add: 15036 6125 Rd., Montrose, Colo. 81401, U.S.A.

BLAIR, Ruth Van Ness.   American, b. 1912.   Children's fiction, Children's non-fiction.   Ed., Florida State NLAPW Newsletter, 1982–84. Poet.   Publs: Puddle Duck, 1966; A Bear Can Hibernate! Why Can't I, 1972; Willa-Willa, The Wishful Witch, 1972; The Talking Jack-o-Lantern, 1974; Mary's Monster, 1974, Condensed in Readers, 1977–83; (contrib.) The Study and Writing of Poetry: American Women Poets Discuss Their Craft, 1983.   Add: 51 Island Way, Apt. 510, Clearwater, Fla. 34630, U.S.A.

BLAIR, Thomas (Lucien Vincent). American, b. 1926. Regional/Urban planning, Sociology. Prof. and Assoc., Martin Centre for Architectural and Urban Studies, Dept. of Architecture, Univ. of Cambridge, since 1985. Prof. of Social and Environmental Planning, Polytechnic of Central London, and Dir., PCL-Habitat Forum Prog., 1967–75. *Publs:* Africa: A Market Profile, 1965; The Land To Those Who Work It: Algeria's Experiment in Workers' Management, 1969; The Poverty of Planning, 1973; The International Urban Crisis, 1974; Retreat to the Ghetto: The End of a Dream?, 1977; (ed.) Urban Innovation Abroad: Problem Cities in Search of Solutions, 1984; (ed.) Strengthening Urban Management: International Perspectives and Issues, 1985. Add: c/o Hilary Rubinstein, A.P. Watt & Son, 26-28 Bedford Row, London WC1R 4HL, England.

BLAIR, Walter. Has also written as Mortimer Post. American, b. 1900. Mystery/Crime/Suspense, Literature, Mythology/Folklore, Humor, Biography. Prof. Emeritus of English, Univ. of Chicago, since 1968 (Instr., 1926–30; Asst. Prof., 1930–39; Assoc. Prof., 1939–44; Prof., 1944–68; Chmn. of Dept., 1951–60). Departmental Ed., Encyclopedia Britannica, since 1951; member, Editorial Bd., Mark Twain Papers, since 1967, and Collected Works of Mark Twain, since 1970. *Publs:* (ed.) The Sweet Singer of Michigan: The Collected Poems of Julia A. Moore, 1928; (with F.J. Meine) Mike Fink, King of Mississippi Keelboatmen, 1933; (ed. with W.K. Chandler) Approaches to Poetry, 1935, 1953; (as Mortimer Post with C. Kerby-Miller) Candidate for Murder (novel), 1936; (ed.) Native American Humor, 1937, 1960; Horse Sense in American Humor, 1942, 1962; Tall Tale America, 1944; (ed.) Manual of Reading, 1943; (ed. with J. Gerber) Better Reading: Factual Prose, 1945, 4th ed. 1959; (ed. with T. Hornberger and R. Stewart) Literature of the United States (2 vols.), 1947, 6th ed. 1970; (ed. with J. Gerber) Better Reading: Literature, 1948, 3rd ed. 1959; Davy Crockett: Truth and Legend, 1955; (ed. with F.J. Meine) Half Horse Half Alligator: Growth of the Mike Fink Legend, 1956, 3rd ed. 1981; Mark Twain and Huck Finn, 1960, 1973 (Thurmod Monsen Award); (ed.) Selected Shorter Writings of Mark Twain, 1962; (ed. with H. Hill) The Art of Huckleberry Finn, 1962, 1969; (with Hornberger, Stewart and Miller) American Literature: A Brief History, 1964, 1975; (ed.) Hannibal, Huck and Tom, 1969; (ed. with H. Hayford) H. Melville: Omoo, 1972; (with H. Hill) America's Humor from Poor Richard to Doonesbury, 1978 (Soc. of Midland Authors Award); James Russell Lowell, 1979; (ed. with R.I. McDavid) The Mirth of a Nation: America's Great Dialect Humor, 1983; (ed.) Mark Twain's West, 1983; (ed., with Victor Fischer) Adventures of Huckleberry Finn, by Mark Twain, 1985. Add: Univ. of Chicago, Chicago, Ill. 60637, U.S.A.

BLAIRMAN, Jacqueline. *See* **PINTO,** Jacqueline.

BLAISE, Clark. Canadian, b. 1940. Novels/Short stories, Travel/Exploration/Adventure. Prof. of English, Skidmore Coll., Saratoga Springs, N.Y., since 1981. Instr., Univ. of Wisconsin, Milwaukee, 1964–65; Lectr., 1966–67, Asst. Prof., 1968–71, Assoc. Prof., 1971–75, and Prof. of English, 1976–78, Concordia Univ., previously Sir George Williams Univ., Montreal; Prof. of Humanities, York Univ., Toronto, 1978–81. *Publs:* A North American Education (short stories), 1973; Tribal Justice (short stories), 1974; (with Bharati Mukherjee) Days and Nights in Calcutta (travel memoir), 1977; Lunar Attractions (novel), 1979; Lusts, 1983. Add: c/o Tim Seldes, Russell and Volkening, 50 West 29th St., New York, N.Y. 10001, U.S.A.

BLAKE, Lord. *See* **BLAKE,** Robert.

BLAKE, Alfred. *See* **JANIFER,** Laurence M.

BLAKE, Andrew. *See* **JANIFER,** Laurence M.

BLAKE, Brian. British, b. 1918. History, Social commentary/phenomena. Talks Producer and Broadcaster, BBC, London, 1960–67; mgmt. consultant, 1967–70; Lectr., 1970–76, and Dir. of Media Services, 1976–81, Lancaster Univ. *Publs:* The Solway Firth, 1955, 3rd ed. 1982; (with J. Blake) The Story of Carlisle, 1958; People in the Electronic Age, 1973. Add: Silver Beck, Silverhowe, Grasmere, Cumbria, England.

BLAKE, Jennifer. *See* **MAXWELL,** Patricia Anne.

BLAKE, John Ballard. American, b. 1922. Medicine. Fellow in the History of Medicine, Johns Hopkins Univ., Baltimore, 1951–52; Research Fellow, History of Medicine, Yale Univ., New Haven, Conn., 1952–55. *Publs:* Benjamin Waterhouse and the Introduction of Vaccination, 1957; Public Health in the Town of Boston 1630–1822, 1959; (ed.) Medical

Reference Works, 1967; Education in the History of Medicine, 1968; Safeguarding the Public, 1970; Centenary of Index Medicus 1879–1979, 1980. Add: 3038 Newark St. N.W., Washington, D.C. 20008, U.S.A.

BLAKE, Justin. *See* **BOWEN,** John.

BLAKE, Ken. *See* **BULMER,** Kenneth.

BLAKE, Les(lie James). Australian, b. 1913. Education, History, Literature, Biography. Teacher, Geelong, Vic., 1946–52; Lectr. Teachers Coll., Geelong, 1953–58; Inspector of Schs., Horsham, Vic., 1958–64, and Ferntree Gully, Melbourne, 1964–67; Lectr., Sch. of Education, Univ. of Melbourne, 1965; Inspector of Schs., Doncaster, 1967–70; State Historian for Victoria, 1974–76. Foundn. Pres., Western Victorian Assn. of Historical Societies, 1963–64; Chmn., State Education History Cttee., Education Dept., 1966–70; Pres., Royal Historical Soc. of Victoria, 1966–71; Vice Pres., Australian Intnl. P.E.N., Melbourne Centre, 1971–72; Chmn., State Education Dept. Centenary Celebration Cttee., 1972–73. *Publs:* Teaching Social Studies, 1957, 3rd ed., 1964; Shaw Neilson in the Wimmera, 1961; (with J. Cole) Principles and Techniques of Teaching, 1962, 3rd ed. 1965; (ed.) Patterns in Poetry, 1962; (with K. Lovett) Wimmera Shire Centenary, 1962, 4th ed., 1970; Lost in the Bush, 1964; Richard Hale Budd, 1968; Australian Writers, 1968; Geelong Sketchbook, 1970; Gold Escort, 1971; (co-author) John Shaw Neilson, 1972; (gen. ed. and co-author) Vision and Realisation: A Centenary History of State Education in Victoria, 3 vols., 1973; Wimmera, 1973; (gen. ed. and co-author) Werribee Park, 1974; Letters of Charles Joseph LaTrobe, 1975; Place Names of Victoria, 1976; Pioneer Schools of Australia, 1976; Gold Escorts in Australia, 1978; Covered Wagons in Australia, 1979; Tales from Old Geelong, 1979; Peter Lalor, The Man from Eureka, 1979; (ed. and co-author) A Gold Digger's Diaries, 1980; (ed.) Aunt Spencer's Diaries by Mary Read and Mary Spencer, 1981; Tattyara: A History of the Kaniva District, Kaniva Shire, 1981; Schools of the Tattyara, Kaniva Shire, 1981; Captain Dana and the Native Police, 1982. Add: 4 Anton Ct., Karingal, Vic. 3199, Australia.

BLAKE, Norman Francis. British, b. 1934. Language/Linguistics, Literature, Biography, Translations. Prof. of English Language, Univ. of Sheffield, since 1973. Lectr., to Sr. Lectr., Univ. of Liverpool, 1959–73. *Publs:* (ed. and trans.) The Saga of the Jomsvikings, 1962; (ed.) The Phoenix, 1964; Caxton and His World, 1969; (ed.) William Caxton's Reynard the Fox, 1970; (ed.) Middle English Religious Prose, 1972; (ed.) Selections from William Caxton, 1973; (ed.) Caxton's Own Prose, 1973; Caxton's Quattros Sermones, 1973; (ed.) Caxton: England's First Publisher, 1976; The English Language in Medieval Literature, 1977; Non-Standard Language in English Literature, 1981; Shakespeare's Language, 1983; Textual Tradition of the Canterbury Tales, 1985; (ed.) William Caxton: A Bibliographical Guide, 1985; (ed.) The Index of Printed Middle English Prose, 1985; Traditional English Grammar and Beyond, 1988. Add: c/o Edward Arnold, 41-42 Bedford Sq., London WC1B 3DQ, England.

BLAKE, Patrick. *See* **EGLETON,** Clive.

BLAKE, Peter. American (b. German), b. 1920. Architecture. Prof., Dept. of Architecture, Catholic Univ., Washington, D.C., since 1979 (Chmn., 1979–86); a practicing architect. Curator, Dept. of Architecture and Industrial Design, Museum of Modern Art, NYC, 1948–50; Assoc. Ed., 1950–61, Managing Ed., 1961–64, and Ed.-in-Chief, 1964–72, Architectural Forum, NYC: Partner, Peter Blake and Julian Neski, architects, NYC, 1956–60, and James Baker and Peter Blake, architects, NYC, 1964–71; Contrib. Ed., New York Magazine, 1968–76; Ed.-in-Chief, Architecture Plus, NYC, 1972–75; Chmn., Sch. of Architecture, Boston Architectural Center, 1975–79. *Publs:* The Master Builders: Le Corbusier, Mies van der Rohe, Frank Lloyd Wright, 1960, 1976; God's Own Junkyard: The Planned Deterioration of America's Landscape, 1964; Form Follows Fiasco: Why Modern Architecture Hasn't Worked,1977; Harry Seidler: Australian Embassy, 1979. Add: Dept. of Architecture and Planning, The Catholic Univ. of America, Washington, D.C. 20064, U.S.A.

BLAKE, Quentin. British, b. 1932. Children's fiction. Illustrator for various British magazines, including Punch and Spectator, and for children's and educational books, since 1948; Visiting Tutor, Royal Coll. of Art, London, since 1986 (Tutor, Sch. of Graphic Design, 1965–78; Head of the Illustration Dept., 1978–86). *Publs:* (all self-illustrated) — Patrick, 1968; Jack and Nancy, 1969; A Band of Angels, 1969; Angele, 1970; Snuff, 1973; Lester at the Seaside, 1975; Lester and the Unusual Pet, 1975; (with John Yeoman) The Puffin Book of Improbable Records, 1975, in U.S. as The Improbable Book of Records, 1976; The Adventures of Lester, 1978; (ed.) Custard and Company: Poems by Ogden Nash, 1979; Mister Magnolia, 1980; (with John Yeoman) Rumbelow's Dance, 1982; Quentin Blake's Nursery Rhyme Book, 1983; The Story of the Dancing Frog, 1984; Mrs. Armitage on Wheels, 1987. Add: Flat 8, 30 Bramham Gardens, London SW5 0HF, England.

BLAKE, Robert (Norman William). (Lord Blake of Braydeston, Norfolk). British, b. 1916. History, Politics/Government, Biography. Lectr. 1946–47, and Student and Tutor in Politics 1947–68, Christ Church, Oxford; Ford's Lectr. in English History, Oxford Univ., 1967–68; Provost of Queen's Coll., Oxford, 1968–87. Conservative Member, Oxford City Council, 1957–64. *Publs:* (ed.) The Private Papers of Douglas Haig, 1952; The Unknown Prime Minister, The Life and Times of Andrew Bonar Law, 1955; Disraeli, 1966; The Conservative Party from Peel to Churchill, 1970, 2nd ed. as The Conservative Party from Peel to Thatcher, 1985; The Office of the Prime Minister, 1975; (ed. with John Patten) The Conservative Opportunity, 1976; A History of Rhodesia, 1977; Disraeli's Grand Tour, 1982; (ed.) The English World, 1982; The Decline of Power, 1985. Add: Riverview House, Brundall, Norwich, England.

BLAKE, Sally. *See* **SAUNDERS,** Jean.

BLAKE, Stephanie. American. Historical/Romance/Gothic. *Publs:* Flowers of Fire, 1977; Daughter of Destiny, 1977; Blazon of Passion, 1978; So Wicked My Desire, 1979; Secret Sins, 1980; Wicked Is My Flesh, 1980; Scarlet Kisses, 1981; Unholy Desires, 1981; Callie Knight, 1982; Bride of the Wind, 1984; A Glorious Passion, 1984; The World is Mine, 1988. Add: c/o Playboy Press, 200 Madison Ave., New York, NY 10019, U.S.A.

BLAKEMORE, Colin (Brian). British, b. 1944. Biology, Medicine. Waynflete Prof. of Physiology, Oxford Univ., since 1979; Professorial Fellow, Magdalen Coll., Oxford, since 1979. Member, editorial bd., Perception, since 1971, Behavioral and Brain Sciences, since 1977, Experimental Brain Research, since 1979, Language and Communication, since 1979, Reviews in the Neurosciences, since 1984, News in Physiological Sciences, since 1985, and Clinical Vision Sciences, since 1986. Univ. Demonstrator, Physiological Lab., Cambridge Univ., 1968–72; Fellow and Dir. of Medical Studies, Downing Coll., and Lectr. in Physiology, Cambridge Univ., 1977–79. *Publs:* (ed.) Handbook of Psychobiology, 1975; Mechanics of the Mind, 1977; (ed.) Mindwaves, 1987; The Mind Machine, 1988; (ed.) Images and Understanding, 1989. Add: Univ. Lab. of Physiology, Parks Rd., Oxford OX1 3PT, England.

BLAMIRES, David (Malcolm). British, b. 1936. Poetry, Literature, Sex, Sociology. Reader in German, Univ. of Manchester, since 1973 (Asst. Lectr., 1960–63; Lectr., 1963–69; Sr. Lectr., 1969–73). Ed., David Jones Soc. Newsletter, since 1976. *Publs:* An Echoing Death (verse), 1965; Characterization and Individuality in Wolfram's "Parzival," 1966; The Bible Half Hour, 1968; David Jones: Artist and Writer, 1971, 1978; (trans. with Peter Rickard and others) Medieval Comic Tales, 1973; Homosexuality from the Inside, 1973; A History of Quakerism in Liversedge and Scholes, 1973; Schöpferisches Zuhören, 1974; (co-author) David Jones: Eight Essays on His Work as Writer and Artist, 1976; (co-author) Towards a Theology of Gay Liberation, 1977; Herzog Ernst and the Otherworld Voyage, 1979. Add: 136 Wellington Rd., Manchester M14 6AR, England.

BLAMIRES, Harry. British, b. 1916. Novels/Short stories, Literature. Head of English Dept., 1948–72, Dean of Degrees, 1972–74, and Dean of Arts, 1974–76, King Alfred's Coll., Winchester. *Publs:* Repair the Ruins, 1950; English in Education, 1951; The Devil's Hunting Grounds, 1954; Cold War in Hell, 1955; Blessing Unbounded, 1955, as Highway to Heaven, 1984; The Faith and Modern Error, 1956, as The Secularist Heresy, 1980; The Will and the Way, 1957, as A God Who Acts, 1981; The Kirkbride Conversations, 1958; Kirkbride & Company, 1959; The Offering of Man, 1959; The Christian Mind, 1963; A Defence of Dogmatism (in U.S. as The Tyranny of Time), 1965; The Bloomsday Book: Guide Through Joyce's Ulysses, 1966; Word Unheard: A Guide Through Eliot's Four Quartets, 1969; Milton's Creation: A Guide Through Paradise Lost, 1971; A Short History of English Literature, 1974, 1984; Where Do We Stand?, 1980; Twentieth-Century English Literature, 1982, 1986; (ed.) Guide to Twentieth-Century Literature in English, 1983; On Christian Truth, 1983; Notes on "A Portrait of the Artist as a Young Man," 1984; Words Made Flesh, 1985, in U.K. as The Marks of the Maker, 1987; Studying James Joyce, 1987; Meat Not Milk (in U.S. as Recovering the Christian Mind), 1988; The Victorian Age of Literature, 1988. Add: Rough Close, Braithwaite, Keswick, Cumbria CA12 5RY, England.

BLANC, Suzanne. American. Mystery/Crime/Suspense. *Publs:* The Green Stone, 1961; The Yellow Villa, 1964; The Rose Window, 1967; The Sea Troll, 1969. Add: c/o Doubleday, 245 Park Ave., New York, N.Y. 10017, U.S.A.

BLANCH, Lesley (Madame Gary). British, b. 1907. Travel/Exploration/Adventure, Autobiography/Memoirs/Personal, Biography. *Publs:* The Wilder Shores of Love, 1954; Round the World in Eighty Dishes, 1955; The Game of Hearts, 1958; The Sabres of Paradise, 1960; Under a Lilac-Bleeding Star, 1964; The Nine Tiger Man, 1965; Journey into the Minds Eye, 1968; Pavillions of the Heart, 1974; Pierre Loti: A Biography, 1983. Add: c/o Collins, 8 Grafton St., London W1X 3LA, England.

BLANCH, Stuart Yarworth. (Baron of Bishopthorpe in the County of Yorkshire). British, b. 1918. Religion. Vicar of Eynsham, Oxford, 1952–57; Tutor and Vice Principal, Wycliffe Hall, Oxford, 1957–60; Oriel Canon of Rochester and Warden of Rochester Theological Coll., 1960–66; Bishop of Liverpool, 1966–75; Archibishop of York, 1975–83. *Publs:* The World Our Orphanage, 1972; For All Mankind, 1976; The Christian Militant, 1978; The Burning Bush, 1978; The Trumpet in the Morning, 1979; The Ten Commandments, 1981; Living By Faith, 1983; Way of Blessedness, 1985; Encounters with Jesus, 1988. Add: Bryn Celyn, The Level, Shenington, near Banbury, Oxon OX15 6NA, England.

BLANCHARD, William (Henry). American, b. 1922. Social commentary/phenomena, Biography. Dir. of Research, California Youth Authority, 1955–57; Scientist, Rand Corp., 1957–60; Scientist, System Development Corp., 1960–70; Lectr., Univ. of Southern California, Los Angeles, 1970–75; Sr. Research Fellow, Planning Analysis and Research Inst., Los Angeles, 1976–87. *Publs:* Rousseau and the Spirit of Revolt, 1967; Aggression American Style, 1978; Revolutionary Morality, 1984. Add: 4307 Rosario Rd., Woodland Hills, Calif. 91364, U.S.A.

BLAND, Jennifer. *See* **BOWDEN,** Jean.

BLANDFORD, Percy (William). British, b. 1912. Crafts, Recreation/Leisure/Hobbies. *Publs:* Netmaking, 1940; Workshop Practice Simplified, 1942; Rope Splicing, 1950; Tackle Canoeing This Way, 1961; Your Book of Knots, 1962; Canoes and Canoeing, 1962; Tackle Trailer Boating This Way, 1963; Working in Canvas, 1963; Camping, 1965; The Art of Sailing, 1965; Build Your Own Boat, 1966; Sailing Boat Recognition, 1970; Sailing Dinghies of the World, 1972; Practical Boatman, 1972; Country Craft Tools, 1974; Illustrated History of Small Boats, 1974; Boat Repairs Made Easy, 1975; Farm Implements, 1976; Scouts on the Water, 1976; Woodworkers Bible, 1976, 1986; Built-in-Furniture, 1976; Furniture Finishing, 1977; Sails and Sailmaking, 1978; Encyclopedia of Small Craft 1978; Upholstery, 1978; Woodturning, 1978; Small Boatsailing, 1978; Knots and Ropework, 1980; Blacksmithing and Metal Working, 1980; Sheet Metalwork, 1981; Rigging Sail and Other Boats, 1981; Drafting, 1981; Outdoor Furniture Projects, 1982; Built-In Furniture Projects, 1982; Giant Book of Wooden Toys, 1982; Rigging Sail, 1983; Building Better Beds, 1984; The Illustrated Handbook of Woodworking Joints, 1984; Maps and Compasses: A User's Handbook, 1984; 58 Home Shelving and Storage Projects, 1985; Making Knives and tools, 1985; 111 Garden Projects, 1986; Master Handbook of Woodworking Techniques, 1987; Do it Yourself Guide to Furniture Repair and Refinishing, 1988; Country Furniture, 1988; Designing and Building Children's Furniture, 1988; Designing and Building Outdoor Furniture, 1988; Designing and Building Space-Saving Furniture, 1989. Add: Quinton House, Newbold-on-Stour, Stratford-on-Avon, Warwicks, CV37 8UA, England.

BLANK, Robert H. American, b. 1943. Medicine/Health, Politics/Government. Prof. of Political Science and Assoc. Dir., The Prog. for Biosocial Research, Northern Illinois Univ., since 1986. Member of the Bd., Assn. of Politics and the Life Sciences, since 1983. Prof. of Political Science, Univ. of Idaho, 1971–86; Fulbright Lectr., Univ. of Canterbury, Christchurch, 1985. Fulbright Lectr., Republic of China, 1986–87. Member of the Exec. Council, 1974–77, and Pres., 1983–84, Pacific Northwest Political Science Assn.; Member of the Exec. Council, Western Political Science Assn., 1980–83. *Publs:* Regional Diversity of Political Values: Idaho Political Culture, 1978; Political Parties: An Introduction, 1980; The Political Implications of Human Genetic Technology, 1981; (co-ed.) Biological Differences and Social Equality, 1983; Redefining Human Life: Reproductive Technologies and Social Policy, 1984; Rationing Medicine, 1988; Life, Death, and Public Policy, 1988; Individualism in Idaho: The Territorial Foundations, 1988; Maternal Responsibility for Fetal Development, 1989. Add: R2 Box 49, Sycamore, Ill. 60178, U.S.A.

BLANKENSHIP, A.B. American, b. 1914. Marketing. Prof. Emeritus of Marketing, Bowling Green Univ., Ohio, since 1979 (Prof., 1971–79). Vice-Pres. and Dir., Canadian Facts Ltd., 1961–62 and 1968–71; Dir. of Market Research, Carter-Wallace Inc., 1962–68.; Member, Bd. of Dirs., Service Corps of Retired Execs. (SCORE), 1985–87. *Publs:* Consumer and Opinion Research, 1943; (ed.) How to Conduct Consumer and Opinion Research, 1946; (with M.S. Heidingsfield) Market and Marketing Research, 1953; (with J.B. Doyle) Marketing Research Management, 1965; (with M.S. Heidingsfield) Marketing: An Introduction, rev. ed. 1974; Professional Telephone Surveys, 1977; (with George E. Breen) Do-It-Yourself Marketing Research, 1982, rev. ed. 1989; (with Chuck Chaprapani and W. Harold Paole) A History of Marketing Research in Canada, 1985. Add: 101 N. Riverside Dr., New Smyrna Beach, Fla. 32069, U.S.A.

BLASE, Melvin G. American, b. 1933. Economics. Prof. of Agricultural Economics, Univ. of Missouri, Columbia, since 1965. Asst. to Dean, Sch. of Systems and Logistics, 1960–61, and Asst. Prof., 1961–63, Air Force Inst. of Technology, Wright-Patterson Air Force Base, Ohio; Asst. Prof., and member of Iowa Technical Assistance Team as advisor to Peruvian Govt., Lima, Iowa State Univ., Ames, 1963–65. *Publs:* Institution Building: A Source Book, 1973, 1986. Add: Mumford Hall, Univ. of Missouri, Columbia, Mo. 65201, U.S.A.

BLASER, Robin (Francis). Canadian, b. 1925. Poetry, Translations. Prof. of English, Simon Fraser Univ., B.C., since 1970 (Lectr. in Poetry, Librarian, Harvard Coll. Library, Cambridge, Mass., 1955–59; Asst. Curator, Calif. Historical Soc., 1960–61; Librarian, San Francisco State Coll., 1962–66. *Publs:* The Moth Poem, 1964; (trans.) Les Chimenes, by Nerval, 1965; Cups, 1968; The Holy Forest Section, 1970; Image-nations 1-12, 1974; (ed.) The Collected Books of Jack Spicer, 1975; (ed.) Troilus, by Jack Spicer, 1975; Image-nations 13-14, 1975; Suddenly, 1976; Syntax, 1983. Add: 2247 Bellevue Ave., West Vancouver, B.C. V7V 1C5, Canada.

BLASHFORD-SNELL, John Nicholas. British, b. 1936. Travel/Exploration/Adventure, Autobiography/Memoirs/Personal. Regular Army Officer; Chmn., Scientific Exploration Soc. Leader of: Great Abbai (Blue Nile) Expedition, 1968, Dahlak Quest Expedition, 1969–70, British Trans-Americas Expedition, 1971–72, Zaire River Expedition, 1974–75, and Operation Drake, 1978–80; Comdr., Operation Raleigh, 1984–89. *Publs:* (with G.R. Snailham) The Expedition Organisers Guide, 1969; (with T. Wintringham) Weapons and Tactics, 1974; Where the Trails Run Out, 1974; In the Steps of Stanley, 1975; (with A. Ballantine) Expeditions: The Experts' Way, 1977; A Taste for Adventure, 1978; (with M. Cable) In the Wake of Drake, 1980; (with M. Cable) Operation Drake, 1981; Mysteries: Encounters with the Unexplained, 1984; Operation Raleigh: The Start of an Adventure, 1987; (with Ann Tweedy) Operation Raleigh: Adventure Challenge, 1988. Add: c/o Lloyds Bank, 9 Broad St., St. Helier, Jersey, Channel Islands, United Kingdom.

BLATHWAYT, Jean. British, b. 1918. Children's fiction. Worked at nursery schs., 1939–70. *Publs:* Uncle Paul's House, 1957; The Well Cabin, 1957; Jenny Leads the Way, 1958; Jo's Neighbours, 1958; The Beach People, 1960; The Mushroom Girl, 1960; On the Run for Home, 1965; House of Shadows, 1967; Lucy's Brownie Road, 1970; River in the Hills, 1971; Lucy's Last Brownie Challenge, 1972; Brownie Discoverers, 1977; Laurie, 1982. Add: Sunbank, 9 East Terr., Budleigh Salterton, Devon, England.

BLATT, John Markus. Israeli, b. 1921. Economics, Information Physics. Asst. and Assoc. Prof., Univ. of Illinois, Urbana, 1950–53; Reader, Sydney Univ., 1953–58; Prof. of Applied Mathematics, Univ. of New South Wales, Kensington, 1959–84. *Publs:* (with V.F. Weisskopf) Theoretical Nuclear Physics, 1953; Theory of Superconductivity, 1964; Introduction to Fortran IV Programming, 1968; Basic Fortran IV Programming, 1969; Introduction to Optimal Control, 1981; Dynamic Economic Systems, 1983; (with Ian Boyd) Investment Confidence and Business Cycles, 1988. Add: 7 Nahshon St., Haifa, Israel 34612.

BLATTY, William (Peter). American, b. 1928. Novels/Short stories. Ed., U.S. Information Service, 1955–57; Publicity Dir., Univ. of Southern California, Los Angeles, 1957–58, and Loyola Univ. of Los Angeles, Calif., 1959–60. *Publs:* Which Way to Mecca, Jack?, 1960; John Goldfarb, Please Come Home!, 1963; I, Billy Shakespeare!, 1965; Twinkle Twinkle, Killer Kane, 1967; The Exorcist, 1973; The Making of The Exorcist, 1974; I'll Tell Them I Remember You, 1975; The Ninth Configuration, 1978; Legion, 1983. Add: c/o William Morris Agency, 1350 Ave. of the Americas, New York, N.Y. 10019, U.S.A.

BLAU, Francine D. American, b. 1946. Economics, Women. Prof. of Economics and Labor and Industrial Relations, Univ. of Illinois, Urbana, since 1983 (Asst. Prof., 1975–78; Assoc. Prof., 1978–83). Research Assoc., National Bureau of Economic Research, Cambridge, Mass., since 1988. Instr. in Economics, Trinity Coll., Hartford Conn., 1971–74; Research Assoc., Centre for Human Resource Research, Ohio State Univ., Columbus, 1974–75. *Publs:* (with A. Simmons, A. Freedman, and M. Dunkle) Exploitation from 9 to 5: Report of the Twentieth Century Fund Task Force on Women and Employment, 1975; Equal Pay in the Office, 1977; (with Marianne A. Ferber) The Economics of Women, Men and Work, 1985. Add: Dept. of Economics, Univ. of Illinois, Box 111, Commerce West, Urbana, Ill, 61801, U.S.A.

BLAU, Peter M(ichael). American, b. 1918. Institutions/Organizations, Sociology. Robert Broughton Distinguished Prof. of Sociology, Univ. of North Carolina, Chapel Hill, N.C. (Prof., 1970–77). Fellow, American Academy of Arts and Sciences, since 1975. Member, National Academy of Sciences, since 1980. Instr., Wayne State Univ., Detroit, Mich., 1949–51, and Cornell Univ., Ithaca, N.Y., 1951–53; Asst. Prof., 1953–58, Assoc. Prof., 1958–63, and Prof. of Sociology, 1963–69, Univ. of Chicago; Pitt Prof. of American History and Inst., Cambridge Univ., 1966–67; Pres., American Sociological Assn., 1973–74; Quetelet Prof., Columbia Univ., NYC, 1977–88. *Publs:* The Dynamics of Bureaucracy: A Study of Interpersonal Relations in Two Government Agencies, 1955; Bureaucracy in Modern Society, 1956, rev. ed. with M.Y. Meyer, 1971, 3rd ed., 1987; (with W.R. Scott) Formal Organizations: A Comparative Approach, 1962; Exchange and Power in Social Life, 1964; (with O.D. Duncan) The American Occupational Structure, 1967 (Sorokin Award); (with R.A. Schoenherr) The Structure of Organizations, 1971; The Organization of Academic Work, 1973; On the Nature of Organizations, 1974; (ed.) Approaches to the Study of Social Structure, 1975; Inequality and Heterogeneity, 1977; (ed. with R.K. Merton) Continuities in Structural Inquiry, 1981; (with J.E. Schwartz) Crosscutting Social Circles, 1984. Add: 12 Cobb Terrace, Chapel Hill, N.C. 27514, U.S.A.

BLAUSTEIN, Albert P(aul). Also edits as Allen De Graff. American, b. 1921. Civil liberties/Human rights, Law. Prof. of Law, Rutgers Univ., Camden, N.J., since 1955. *Publs:* (ed. with R.P. Tinkham and C.O. Porter) Public Relations for Bar Associations, 1952, 1953; (with C.O. Porter) The American Lawyer, 1954; (ed.) Fiction Goes to Court, 1954; (ed. with E.L. Fisch and M. Foner) Lawyers in Industry, 1956; (with C.C. Ferguson) Desegregation and the Law, 1957, 1961; (ed. with P. Blaustein) Doctors' Choice, 1957; (ed. with B. Davenport) Deals with the Devil, 1958; (ed. with B. Davenport) Invisible Men, 1960; (ed. with H. Cunningham and J. Kelly) Civil Affairs Legislation: Cases and Materials, 1960; (ed.) Fundamental Legal Documents of Communist China, 1962; Manual on Foreign Legal Periodicals and Their Index, 1962; Civil Rights U.S.A.: Public Schools in the North and West Philadelphia, 1962; (ed. as Allen De Graff) Human and Other Beings, 1963; Civil Rights U.S.A.: Public Schools in Camden and Environs, 1964; (ed. with R.L. Zangrando) Civil Rights and the American Negro, 1968, retitled Civil Rights and the Black American, 1968, 3rd ed. 1970; (ed. with A.R. Kortzinsky) Law and the Military Establishment, 1970, 1972; (with I. Wildman) Cataloging Manual for Use in Vietnamese Law Libraries, 1971; (ed. with R.A. Gorman) Intellectual Property: Cases and Materials, 3 vols., 1971–73; (ed. with G.H. Flanz) Constitutions of the Countries of the World, 18 vols., 1971 (updated quarterly); Housing Discrimination in New Jersey, 1972; (with J. Paust) Human Rights and the Bangladesh Trials, 1973, 1976; (ed. with J.L. Matthews and A. De Vergie) A Bibliography on the Common Law in French, 1974; (ed. with Phyllis Blaustein) Constitutions of Dependencies and Special Sovereignties, 6 vols., 1975; (ed. with J. Sigler and B. Beede) Independence Documents of the World, 2 vols., 1977; (with J. Paust) The Arab Oil Weapon, 1977; (with R. Mersky) The First 100 Justices: Statistical Studies on the Supreme Court of the United States, 1977; (with E.F. Sherman and D.N. Zillman) Cases and Materials: The Military and American Society, 1978, 1983; Disinvestment, 1985; (with D. Epstein) Resolving Language Conflicts: A Study of The World's Constitutions, 1985; Influence of the U.S. Constitution Abroad, 1986; (with R. Clark and J. Sigler) Human Rights Sourcebook, 1987; Bicentennial Concordance, 1987; (with J. Sigler) Constitutions That Made History, 1988; The Role of the Military in Modern Government: A Constitutional Analysis, 1989. Add: 415 Barby Lane, Cherry Hill, N.J. 08003, U.S.A.

BLAZYNSKI, Tadeusz (Zdzislaw). British, b. 1924. Engineering. Reader in Applied Plasticity, Univ. of Leeds, since 1980 (Lectr., 1963–70, Sr. Lectr., 1970–80). Research Engineer, Birmingham, 1954–59, and Walsall, 1959–62, Tube Investments Ltd. *Publs:* Use of High Energy-Rate Methods for Forming, Welding and Compaction, 1973; Metal Forming: Tool Profiles and Flow, 1976; High Energy Rate Fabrications, 1981; Explosive Welding, Forming and Compaction, 1982; Applied Elasto-Plasticity of Solids, 1983; Design of Tools for Deformation Processes, 1986; Materials at High Strain Rates, 1987. Add: Dept. of Mechanical Engineering, Univ. of Leeds, Leeds LS2 9JT, England.

BLEAKLEY, David Wylie. British, b. 1925. Economics, History, Biography. Gen. Secty., Irish Council of Churches, since 1980; Member Press Council, since 1988. Lectr. in Industrial Relations, Kivukoni Coll., Dar es Salaam, Tanzania, 1967–69; Head, Dept. of Economics, Methodist Coll., Belfast, 1969–79. *Publs:* (co-author) Ulster since 1800, 1955; Young Ulster and Religion in the Sixties, 1964; Peace in Ulster, 1972; Faulkner: A Biography, 1974; Saidie Patterson, An Irish Peacemaker, 1980; In Place of Work: The Sufficient Society, 1981; The Shadow and Substance, 1983; Beyond Work—Free to Be, 1985; (co-author) Will the Future Work?, 1986; (co-author) Peace Together, 1987. Add: 8 Thorn Hill, Bangor, Co. Down, Northern Ireland.

BLEASDALE, Alan. British, b. 1946. Novels/Short stories, Plays/Screenplays. Schoolteacher, 1967–75; resident playwright, Playhouse Theatre, Liverpool, 1975–76, and Contact Theatre, Manchester, 1976–78; joint artistic dir., 1981–84, and assoc. dir., 1984–86, Playhouse Theatre. *Publs:* Scully (novel), 1975, play version, 1985; Who's Been Sleeping in My Bed? (novel), 1977, rev. ed. as Scully and Mooey, 1984; No More Sitting on the Old School Bench (play), 1979; Boys from the Blackstuff (television series), 1985; Are You Lonesome Tonight? (play), 1985; The Monocled Mutineer, adaptation of a book by William Allison and John Fairley, 1986; No Surrender (play), 1986; Having a Ball, and It's a Madhouse (plays), 1986. Add: c/o Harvey Unna and Stephen Durbridge Ltd., 24-32 Pottery Lane, London W11 4LZ, England.

BLECHMAN, Burt. American, b. 1927. Novels/Short stories. Instr., New York Univ. Medical Sch., NYC, since 1973. *Publs:* How Much?, 1961; The War of Camp Omongo, 1963; Stations, 1963; The Octopus Papers, 1965; Maybe, 1967. Add: 200 Waverly Pl., New York, N.Y. 10014, U.S.A.

BLEECK, Oliver. *See* **THOMAS,** Ross.

BLENKINSOPP, Joseph. British, b. 1927. Theology/Religion. Prof., Univ. of Notre Dame, Ind., since 1970. Teacher of Biblical Studies, Chicago Theological Seminary, Ill., 1968–69; Assoc. Prof., Hartford Seminary Foundn., Conn., 1969–70. *Publs:* The Corinthian Mirror, 1964; The Promise to David, 1964; From Adam to Abraham, 1965; Jesus is Lord, 1967; Celibacy, Ministry, Church, 1969; Sexuality and the Christian Tradition, 1969; (with J. Challoner) Pentateuch, 1971; Gibeon and Israel, 1972; Prophecy and Canon: A Contribution to the Study of Jewish Origins, 1978; Wisdom and Law in the Old Testament, 1983; A History of Prophecy in Israel, 1984; Ezra-Nehemiah: A Commentary, 1988. Add: 1614 East Wayne, South Bend, Ind. 46615, U.S.A.

BLIGHT, John. Australian, b. 1913. Poetry. Worked as a clerk, orchardist, swagman, and public servant, retiring as secty. of sawmilling co. *Publs:* The Old Pianist, 1945; The Two Suns Met: Poems, 1954; A Beachcomber's Diary: Ninety Sea Sonnets, 1964; My Beachcombing Days: Ninety Sea Sonnets, 1968; Hart—Poems, 1975; Selected Poems, 1939–1975, 1976; Pageantry for a Lost Empire, 1977; The New City Poems, 1979; Holiday Sea Sonnets, 1985. Add: 34 Greenway St., The Grange, Brisbane, Qld. 4051, Australia.

BLISHEN, Edward. British, b. 1920. Novels/Short stories, Children's fiction, Education, Autobiography/Memoirs/Personal. Ed., Junior Pears Encyclopaedia, Pelham Books, London, since 1961. Ed. Miscellany I-VI, Oxford Univ. Press, London, 1964–69. *Publs:* Roaring Boys, 1955; (compiler) Oxford Book of Poetry for Children, 1963; Town Story, 1965; (compiler) Come Reading, 1967; This Right Soft Lot, 1969; (ed.) The School That I'd Like, 1969; (ed.) The Blond Encylcopaedia of Education, 1969; (with L. Garfield) The God Beneath The Sea, 1970; A Cackhanded War, 1972; (with L. Garfield) The Golden Shadow, 1973; Uncommon Entrance, 1974; (ed.) The Thorny Paradise, 1975; Sorry, Dad, 1978; A Nest of Teachers, 1980; Shaky Relations, 1981; Lizzie Pye, 1982; Donkey Work, 1983; A Second Skin, 1984; The Outside Contributor, 1986; The Disturbance Fee, 1988. Add: 12 Bartrams Lane, Hadley Wood, Barnet, Herts., England.

BLOCH, Marie Halun. American, b. 1910. Children's fiction, Children's non-fiction, Translations. Jr. Economist, U.S. Dept. of Labor, Washington D.C., 1938–38 and 1943–44; Children's Book Reviewer, Denver Post, 1950–60. *Publs:* Danny Doffer, 1946; Big Steve, 1952; Tun-

nels, 1954; Dinosaurs, 1955; Tony of the Ghost Towns, 1956; Marya of Clark Avenue, 1957; Mountains on the Move, 1960; The Dollhouse Story, 1961; Look at Dinosaurs, 1962; The House on Third High, 1962; Aunt America, 1963; (trans.) Ukrainian Folk Tales, 1964; The Two Worlds of Damyan, 1966; (trans.) Ivanko and the Dragon, 1969; Bern, Son of Mikula, 1972; Displaced Person, 1978; (trans.) Pilgrims of the Prairie, 1980; Footprints in the Swamp, 1984. Add: 654 Emerson St., Denver, Colo. 80218, U.S.A.

BLOCH, Robert. American, b. 1917. Novels/Short stories, Science fiction/Fantasy, Screenplays. National Pres., Mystery Writers of America, 1970. *Publs:* Opener of the Way, 1945; The Scarf, 1947; Spiderweb, 1954; The Kidnapper, 1954; The Will to Kill, 1954; Shooting Star, 1958; Terror in the Night, 1958; Psycho, 1959; Pleasant Dreams, 1959; The Dead Beat, 1960; Firebug, 1961; More Nightmares, 1962; Yours Truly, Jack the Ripper, 1962; The Couch, 1962, also screenplay; Terror, 1962; Atoms and Evil, 1962; Blood Runs Cold, 1962; Eighth Stage of Fandom, 1962; Horror Seven, 1963; The Bogey Men, 1963; Tales in a Jugular Vein, 1965; The Skull of Marquis de Sade, 1965, also screenplay; Chamber of Horrors, 1966; The Living Demons, 1967; Dragons and Nightmares, 1968; Fear Today, Gone Tomorrow, 1969; The Star-Stalker, 1969; The Todd Dossier, 1969; Sneak Preview, 1971; It's All In Your Mind, 1971; House of the Hatchet, 1971; American Gothic, 1974; Nightworld, 1974; Cold Chills, 1977; The King of Terrors, 1977; Out of the Mouths of Graves, 1978; There Is a Serpent in Eden, 1979; Strange Eons, 1979; Mysteries of the Worm, 1981; Psycho 2, 1982; The Twilight Zone: The Movie, 1983; Dr. Holmes Murder Castle, 1983; The Night of the Ripper, 1984; Out of My Head, 1986; Unholy Trinity, 1986; Midnight Pleasures, 1987; Through Time and Space With Lefty Feep, 1987; Selected Short Stories of Robert Bloch, 1988; Fear and Trembling, 1989; Lori, 1989; screenplays—Torture Garden, The Deadly Bees, Psychopath, The Night Walker, Straight-Jacket, The Cabinet of Doctor Caligari, The Couch, Asylum, The House That Dripped Blood. Add: Shapiro-Lichtman Talent Agency, 8827 Beverly Blvd., Los Angeles, Calif. 90067, U.S.A.

BLOCK, Lawrence. Also writes as Chip Harrison and Paul Kavanagh. American, b. 1938. Novels/Short stories, Mystery/Crime/Suspense, Recreation/Leisure/Hobbies, Writing/Journalism. *Publs:* mystery novels—Death Pulls a Double Cross, 1961; Mona, 1961; The Case of the Pornographic Photos, 1961 (in U.K. as Markham: The Case of the Pornographic Photos, 1965); The Girl with the Long Green Heart, 1965; The Cancelled Czech, 1966; The Thief Who Couldn't Sleep, 1966; Deadly 1967; Tanner's Twelve Swingers, 1967; Two for Tanner, 1967; Here Comes a Hero, 1968; Tanner's Tiger, 1968; After the First Death, 1969; The Specialists, 1969; (as Paul Kavanagh) Such Men Are Dangerous, 1969; Me Tanner, You Jane, 1970; (as Paul Kavanagh) The Triumph of Evil, 1971; (as Paul Kavanagh) Not Comin' Home to You, 1974; (as Chip Harrison) Make Out with Murder, 1974; (as Chip Harrison) The Topless Tulip Caper, 1975; In the Midst of Death, 1976; Sin of the Fathers, 1977; Time to Murder and Create, 1977; Burglars Can't Be Choosers, 1977; The Burglar in the Closet, 1978; The Burglar Who Liked to Quote Kipling, 1979; Aniel, 1980; The Burglar Who Studied Spinoza, 1981; A Stab in the Dark, 1981; Eight Million Ways to Die, 1982; The Burglar Who Painted Like Mondrian, 1983; Like a Lamb to Slaughter (in U.K. as Five Little Rich Girls), 1984; When the Sacred Ginmill Closes, 1986; Into the Night (completion of Cornell Woolrich novel), 1987; Coward's Kiss, 1987; You Could Call It Murder, 1987; Random Walk, 1988; other novels—(as Chip Harrison) No Score, 1970; Ronald Rabbit Is a Dirty Old Man, 1971; (as Chip Harrison) Chip Harrison Scores Again, 1971; Introducing Chip Harrison (omnibus), 1984; other—A Guide Book to Australian Coins, 1964; (with Delbert Ray Krause) Swiss Shooting Talers and Medals, 1965; Writing the Novel: From Plot to Print, 1979; Sometimes They Bite (short stories), 1984. Add: 3750 Estero Blvd., Fort Myers Beach, Fla. 33931, U.S.A.

BLOCK, Thomas H(arris). American, b. 1945. Novels. Airline Pilot (Captain), U.S. Air, Daytona Beach, Florida. Columnist, Plane and Pilot, since 1985. *Publs:* Mayday, 1980; Orbit, 1982; Forced Landing, 1983; Airship Nine, 1984; Sky Fall, 1987. Add: c/o Joseph Elder Agency, 150 West 87th St., New York, N.Y. 10024, U.S.A.

BLOEMBERGEN, Nicolaas. American, b. 1920. Physics. Gerhard Gade Univ. Prof., since 1980. Gordon McKay Prof. of Applied Physics, Harvard Univ., 1957–80 (Jr. Fellow, 1959–61; Assoc. Prof., 1951–57). *Publs:* Nuclear Magnetic Relaxation, 1961; (co-ed.) Proceedings of 3rd International Conference on Quantum Electronics, 1964; Nonlinear Optics, 1965. Add: Pierce Hall, Harvard Univ., Cambridge, Mass. 02138,

BLOESCH, Donald George. American, b. 1928. Theology/Religion. Prof. of Theology, Dubuque Theological Seminary, Iowa, since 1957. Past Pres., American Theological Soc., Midwest Division. *Publs:* Centers of Christian Renewal, 1964; The Christian Life and Salvation, 1967; The Crisis of Piety, 1968; The Christian Witness in a Secular Age, 1968; (co-author) Christian Spirtuality East and West, 1968; The Reform of the Church, 1970; (ed.) Servants of Christ, 1971; The Ground of Certainty, 1971; The Evangelical Renaissance, 1973; Wellsprings of Renewal, 1974; The Invaded Church, 1975; Jesus Is Victor!, 1976; Essentials of Evangelical Theology, 2 vols., 1978–79; The Struggle of Prayer, 1980; Faith and Its Counterfeits, 1981; Is the Bible Sexist?, 1982; The Future of Evangelical Christianity, 1983; Crumbling Foundations, 1984; Battle for the Trinity: The Debate Over Inclusive God-Language, 1985; Freedom for Obedience, 1987. Add: Dubuque Theological Seminary, 2000 University Ave., Dubuque, Iowa 52001, U.S.A.

BLOND, Anthony. British, b. 1928. Novels, Publishing. Dir., Pressdram Ltd. (Private Eye), and Piccadilly Radio. Sponsor and Trustee, Cobden Trust (civil liberties). Contributor to Spectator, Independent, Sunday Telegraph, Vogue, etc. Formerly Dir., Blond & Briggs Ltd., Publishers, London. *Publs:* The Publishing Game, 1971; Family Business, 1978; The Book Book, 1985. Add: 42 New Concordia Wharf, Mill St., London S.E.1, England.

BLONDEL, Jean (Fernand Pierre). French, b. 1929. Politics/Government. Prof. of Political Science, European Univ. Inst., Florence, since 1985. Chmn., Society and Politics Research Development Group, ESRC, since 1988. Asst. Lectr., and Lectr. in Politics, Univ. of Keele, Staffs., 1958–63; American Council of Learned Societies Fellow, Yale Univ., 1963–64; Prof. of Govt., Univ of Essex, Colchester, 1964–84; Visiting Prof. of Political Science, Carleton Ottawa, 1969–70; Visiting Scholars, Russel Sage Foundn., New York, 1984–85. Member, Political Science Cttee., Social Science Research Council, London, 1965–69; Member of Exec. Cttee., Political Studies Assn., 1968–69; Member of Cttee. on Western Europe, Foreign Area Fellowship Prog., New York, 1970–74. *Publs:* Voters, Parties and Leaders, 1963; (with F. Ridley) Public Administration in France, 1964, 1968; (with F. Bealey and P. McCann) Constituency Politics, 1965; An Introduction to Comparative Government, 1969; (ed.) Comparative Government, 1971; Comparing Political Systems, 1972; (with V. Herman) A Workbook for Comparative Government, 1972; Comparative Legislatures, 1973; The Government of France, 1974; Thinking Politically, 1976; Political Parties, 1979; World Leaders, 1980; The Discipline of Politics, 1981; The Organisation of Governments, 1982; Government Ministers in the Contemporary World, 1985; Political Leadership, 1987; (ed. with F. Muller Rommel) Cabinets in Western Europe, 1988. Add: 308 Fulham Rd., London SW10, England.

BLOOD, Marje. Also writes as Paige McKenzie. American. Novels/Short stories, Travel. Owner and Dir., Editorial Services Office, since 1973; Publisher, Image Imprints, since 1985. Admin. Secty., Co. Sch. District, Lowell, Ore., 1953–63, and Lane Community Coll., Eugene, Ore., 1964–68; Instr. in Creative Writing, Adult Education Class, Willamalane Park District, Springfield, Ore., 1970–72, and Linn-Benton Community Coll., Albany, Ore., 1973; Weekly Book Review Columnist, Eugene Register-Guard and Salem Statesman Journal, 1981–85. *Publs:* (as Page McKenzie) Heavens Help the Working Girl, 1972; (as Paige McKenzie) Astrology for the Working Girl, 1980; (as Paige McKenzie) Circle of the Suns, 1980; Exploring the Oregon Coast, 1981; A Song Heard in a Strange Land, 1985; Morning Song/Mourning Song, 1987. Add: P.O. Box 2764, Eugene, Ore., 97401, U.S.A.

BLOOM, Edward A. American, b. 1914. Literature. Prof. of English, Brown Univ., Providence, since 1947 (Nicholas Brown Prof. of Oratory and Belles Lettres, and Chmn. of the Dept. of English, 1960–67). Ed., Novel: A on Fiction, since 1967. *Publs:* Samuel Johnson in Grub Street, 1957; (with C.H. Philbrick and E.M. Blistein) The Order of Poetry, 1961; (with L.D. Bloom) Willa Cather's Gift of Sympathy, 1962; The Order of Fiction, 1964; (ed.) Shakespeare 1564-1964 (essays), 1964; (ed. with C.H. Philbrick and E.M. Blistein) The Variety of Poetry, 1964; (ed.) Evelina, by Frances Burney, 1968; (ed. with L.D. Bloom) The Variety of Fiction, 1969; (ed. with L.D. Bloom) A Discourse Concerning Ridicule and Irony, by Anthony Collins, 1970; (ed. with L.D. Bloom) Camilla, by Frances Burney, 1972; (with L.D. Bloom) Addison's Sociable Animal, 1971; (ed. with L.D. Bloom) Journals and Letters 1812-1814, by Frances Burney, 1978; (with L.D. Bloom) Satire's Persuasive Voice, 1979; (ed. with L.D. Bloom) Addison and Steele: Critical Heritage Series, 1980; (with L.D. Bloom) Joseph Addison: The Artist in the Mirror, 1984; (ed. with L.D. Bloom) The Piozzi Letters (6 vols.), vol. 1, 1989. Add: Huntingdon Library, San Marino, Calif. 91108, U.S.A.

BLOOM, Harold. American, b. 1930. Novels/Short stories, Literature. Prof. of English since 1964, and Sterling Prof. of Humanities, since 1983, Univ., New Haven (joined Dept. of English, 1955; William Clyde De Vane Prof. of Humanities, 1974–77). *Publs:* Shelley's Mythmaking, 1959; The Visionary Company, 1961; (ed.) English Romantic Poetry (anthology), 1961; Blake's Apocalypse, 1963; Commentary to Blake's Poetry and Prose, 1965; Yeats, 1970; (ed.) Romanticism and Consciousness, 1970; The Ringers in the Tower, 1971; (ed. with Kermode, Hollander, Price, Trilling and Trapp) Oxford Anthology of English Literature, 2 vols., 1972; (ed.) The Romantic Tradition in American Literature, 1972; (ed. with Lionel Trilling) Romantic Prose and Poetry, 1973; The Anxiety of Influence, 1973; Kabbalah and Criticism, 1975; A Map of Misreading, 1975; Figures of Capable Imagination, 1976; Poetry and Repression, 1976; Wallace Stevens: The Poems of Our Climate, 1977; The Flight to Lucifer: A Fantasy of the Gnosis, 1978; (ed.) Selected Poetry and Prose of Shelley, 1978; (with Adrienne Munich) Robert Browning, 1979; (co-author) Deconstruction and Criticism, 1979; Agon: Towards a Theory of Revisionism, 1981; The Breaking of the Vessels, 1982; (ed.) Selected Writings of Walter Pater, 1982; Freud: Transference and Authority, 1984; Poetics of Influence: New and Selected Criticism, 1984. Add: 179 Linden St., New Haven, Conn. 06511, U.S.A.

BLOOM, Harry. Australian, b. 1921. Chemistry. Emeritus Prof. of Chemistry, Univ. of Tasmania, Hobart, since 1982 (Prof., 1960–81). Lectr., Sr. Lectr., and Assoc., Prof. Univ. of Auckland, 1947–60. *Publs:* The Chemistry of Molten Salts, 1967; (co-ed.) Electrochemistry: The Past Thirty Years and the Next Thirty Years, 1977. Add: Dept. of Chemistry, Univ. of Tasmania, G.P.O. Box 252C, Hobart, Tas., Australia 7001.

BLOOM, Lynn (Marie Zimmerman). American, b. 1934. Literature, Biography. Prof. of English and Holder, Aetna Chair of Writing, Univ. of Connecticut, Storrs, since 1988. Lectr. in English, 1962–63, Instr., 1963–65, and Assoc., 1965–67, Western Reserve Univ., Cleveland, Ohio; Asst. Prof., 1970–73, and Prof., 1973–74, Butler Univ., Indianapolis, Ind.; Assoc. Prof., Univ. of New Mexico, Albuquerque, 1975–78; Assoc. Prof. of English, College of William and Mary, Williamsburg, 1978–82. Co-Dir., Eastern Va. Writing Project, 1979–81; Prof. of English, Virginia Commonwealth Univ., Richmond, 1982–88. *Publs:* (co-ed.) Bear, Man, and God: Seven Approaches to Faulkner's The Bear, 1964; (co-ed.) Symposium, 1969; (co-ed.) Symposium on Love, 1970; (co-ed.) Bear, Man, and God: Eight Approaches to Faulkner's The Bear, 1971; Dr. Spock: Biography of a Conservative Radical, 1972; (co-author) The New Assertive Woman, 1975; (ed.) Forbidden Diary: A Record of Wartime Internment 1941–45, 1980; (co-author) American Autobiography: A Bibliography, 1945–1980, 1982; Strategic Writing, 1983; (ed.) The Essay Connection, 1984, 1988; Fact and Artifact: Writing Non-Fiction, 1985; (ed.) The Lexington Reader, 1987; (ed.) Forbidden Family: Margaret Sams's Memoir of Wartime Internment, 1989. Add: English Dept., Box 25, Univ. of Connecticut, Storrs, Conn. 06269, U.S.A.

BLOOM, Murray Teigh. American, b. 1916. Plays/Screenplays, Law, Money/Finance. Founder and former Pres., American Soc. of Journalists and Authors. Chmn., Bd. of Trustees of the Llewellyn Miller Fund. *Publs:* Money of Their Own, 1957; The Man Who Stole Portugal, 1966; Leonora (play), 1966; The Trouble with Lawyers, 1969; Rogues to Riches, 1972; Lawyers, Clients and Ethics, 1974; The Thirteenth Man, 1978; The Brotherhood of Money, 1984; The White Crow (play), 1984. Add: 40 Hemlock Dr., Great Neck, N.Y. 11024, U.S.A.

BLOOM, Samuel W. American, b. 1921. Medicine/Health, Sociology. Prof. of Sociology and Community Medicine, Mount Sinai Sch. of Medicine, Dir., Div. of Behavioral Sciences, Dept. of Community Medicine, and Dir., Training Prog. in Medical Sociology, City Univ. of New York, since 1968. Research Assoc., Bureau of Applied Social Research, Columbia Univ., NYC, 1953–56; Asst. Prof. of Sociology, Baylor Univ. Coll. of Medicine, Waco, Tex., 1956–62; Visiting Assoc., Prof. in Sociology, Bryn Mawr Coll., Pa., 1961–62; Assoc. Prof. of Sociology in Admin., 1962–65, and Prof. of Sociology in Psychiatry, 1965–68, State Univ. of New York Coll. of Medicine, Downstate Medical Center; Visiting Prof. of Sociology, Medical Sch., Hebrew Univ., Jerusalem, 1973–74, 1985. *Publs:* The Doctor and His Patient: A Sociological Interpretation, 1963, 1965; Power and Dissent in the Medical School, 1973. Add: Mount Sinai Sch. of Medicine, Box 1043, New York, N.Y. 10029, U.S.A.

BLOOMFIELD, Anthony John Westgate. Also writes as John Westgate. British, b. 1922. Novels/Short stories, Plays/Screenplays. Sr. Ed., Television News, BBC, London. *Publs:* Russian Roulette, 1955; The Delinquents, 1958; The Tempter, 1961; Throw, 1965; Turn Off If You Know The Ending (TV play), 1966; One Day It Could Be Different (TV play), 1966; (as John Westgate) Victor, Victor (TV play), 1967; (as John Westgate) Life for a Life (TV play), 1967; (as John Westgate) Inventory for the Summer (TV play), 1967; (as John Westgate) Hands with the Magic Touch (TV play), 1970; (as John Westgate) Beneath the Tide (TV play), 1971; Life for a Life (novel), 1971, screenplay, 1973; Reilly's Fire (novel), 1980. Add: 22 Montpelier Ct., Montpelier Rd., Ealing, London W5 2QN, England.

BLOOMFIELD, Barry (Cambray). British, b. 1931. Librarianship, Literature. Dir., Collection Development, Humanities and Social Sciences, British Library, London, since 1985 (Dir., India Office Library and Records, 1978-85; Keeper, Oriental Manuscripts and Printed Books, 1983-85). Vice-Pres., Bibliographical Soc., since 1979; Trustee, Shakespeare Birthplace Trust, since 1987. Librarian, Coll. of St. Mark and St. John, 1956-61; Asst. Librarian, London Sch. of Economics, 1961-63; Deputy Librarian, 1963-71, and Librarian, 1972-78, Sch. of Oriental and African Studies, Univ. of London. Secty., Standing Conference on Library Materials on Africa, 1969-71; Chmn., Advisory Bd. of Librarians, Univ. of London, 1974-76. *Publs:* New Verse In The 1930s, 1960; W.H. Auden: A Bibliography, 1964; (ed.) The Autobiography of Sir James Phillips Kay Shuttleworth, 1964; (with J.D. Pearson and V.J. Bloomfield) Theses on Africa, 1964; (with M.D. McKee) Africa In The Contemporary World, 1967; Theses on Asia 1877-1964, 1967; (with E. W.H. Auden: A Bibliography, 1972; An Author Index to Selected British "Little Magazines" 1933-1976, 1976; Philip Larkin: A Bibliography, 1933-1976, 1979; (ed.) Middle East Studies and Libraries, 1980 Add: Brambling, 24 Oxenturn Rd., Wye, Kent TN25 5BE, England.

BLOOMFIELD, Lincoln P(almer). American, b. 1920. International relations/Current affairs, Military/Defence. Prof. of Political Science, Massachusetts Inst. of Technology, Cambridge, since 1963. With U.S. Dept. of State, 1946-57, and Natl. Security Council, 1979-80. *Publs:* Evolution or Revolution?, 1957; The United Nations and U.S. Foreign Policy, 1960, 1967; (co-author and ed.) Outer Space: Prospects for Man and Society, 1961, rev. ed. 1968; (co-author and ed.) International Military Forces, 1965, rev. ed. as The Power to Keep Peace, 1971; (co-author and ed.) Khrushchev and the Arms Race, 1966; (co-author) Controlling Small Wars, 1967; In Search of American Foreign Policy, 1974; What Future for the U.N.?, 1977; The Foreign Policy Process, 1982; (co-author and ed.) Prospects for Peacemaking, 1987; The Management of Global Disorder, 1987. Add: Dept. of Political Science, Massachusetts Inst. of Technology, Cambridge, Mass. 02139, U.S.A.

BLOS, Joan. American, b. 1928. Children's fiction. Research Asst., Jewish Bd. of Guardians, New York, 1949-50; teacher asst., City Coll., New York, 1950-51; research asst., Child Study Center, Yale Univ., New Haven, Conn., 1951-53; ed. and instructor, Bank St. Coll. of Education, New York, 1956-70; Medical Center research asst., 1970-72, and Lectr. in Education, 1972-80, Univ. of Michigan, Ann Arbor; U.S. Ed., Children's Literature in Education, 1976-81. *Publs:* "It's Spring," She Said, 1967; (with Betty Miles) Joe Finds a Way, 1967; (with Betty Miles) Just Think!, 1971; A Gathering of Days, 1979; Martin's Hats, 1984; Brothers of the Heart, 1985; Old Henry, 1987. Add: c/o Curtis Brown, Ltd., 10 Astor Pl., New York, N.Y. 10003, U.S.A.

BLOTNER, Joseph. American, b. 1923. Literature, Biography. Prof. of English, Univ. of Michigan, Ann Arbor, since 1971. Asst, Prof., 1955-61, Assoc. Prof., 1961-68, and Exec. Secty., Dept. of English, 1961-63, Univ. of Virginia, Charlottesville; Prof. of English, Univ. of North Carolina, Chapel Hill, 1968-71. *Publs:* The Political Novel, 1955; (with F.L. Gwynn) The Fiction of J.D. Salinger, 1959; (ed. with F.L. Gwynn) Faulkner in the University, 1959; (ed.) William Faulkner's Library: A Catalogue, 1964; The Modern American Political Novel: 1900-1960, 1966; Faulkner: A Biography, 2 vols., 1974, 1984, 1-vol. ed., 1984; (ed.) Selected Letters of William Faulkner, 1977; (ed.) Uncollected Stories of William Faulkner, 1979; (ed.) William Faulkner Novels: 1930-1935, 1986; (ed.) William Faulkner Manuscripts, 1987. Add: 1031 Belmont Rd., Ann Arbor, Mich. 48104, U.S.A.

BLOTNICK, Srully (D.). American, b. 1941. Business/Trade/Industry, Information science/Computers. Research Consultant. Former Columnist, Forbes mag. *Publs:* The Psychology of Successful Investing, 1979; Getting Rich Your Own Way, 1980; The Corporate Steeplechase: Predictable Crises in a Business Career, 1984; Computers Made Ridiculously Easy, 1984; Otherwise Engaged: The Private Lives of Successful Career Women, 1985; Ambitious Men: Their Drives, Dreams, and Delusions, 1987. Add: c/o Viking Penguin Inc., 40 W. 23rd St., New York, NY 10010, U.S.A.

BLUHM, Heinz. American, b. 1907. History, Literature. Prof. of German, Boston Coll., Chestnut Hill, Mass., since 1967. Member of faculty, Univ. of Wisconsin, Madison, 1931-37, Yale Univ., New Haven, Conn., 1937-67, and Univ, of California, Berkeley, 1968. *Publs:* (ed.) August von Goethe; (ed.) Ottilie von Goethes Tagebücher, 6 vols., 1962-79; (ed.) Essays in History and Literature, 1965; Martin Luther: Creative Translator, 1965; (ed.) Martin Luther: Von christlicher Religion und christlicher Bildung, 1968; Luther, Translator of Paul, 1985; Studies in Luther, 1987. Add: Carney Hall, Boston Coll., Chestnut Hill, Mass. 02167, U.S.A.

BLUM, Albert A. American, b. 1924. Administration/Management, Industrial relations. Prof. and Chmn., Intl. Business Dept., American Univ. of Paris, and Prof. of Management, New Mexico State Univ., since 1984. Prof. of Labor History, Michigan State Univ., East Lansing, 1960-74; Prof., Lyndon B. Johnson Sch. of Public Affairs, Univ. of Texas, Austin, 1974-78; Dean, Stuart Coll. of Management, Illinois Inst. of Technology, Chicago, 1978-82; Wilson Prof. of Intl. Management, Univ. of the Pacific, Stockton, Calif., 1982-84. *Publs:* The Army and Industrial Deferment During World War II, 1955; (with J. Bambrick) Unionization among American Engineers, 1956; (with J. Bambrick) Labor Relations in the Atomic Energy Field, 1957; An Annotated Bibliography of Industrial Relations and the Small Firm, 1960; Company Organization of Insurance Management, 1961; (co-author) Cases in Research Administration, 1961; (co-ed.) Problems of Competition and Economic Organization and Finding a Place in Contemporary Mass Society: A Problem of Roles, 1962; (ed.) The Proper Climate for Labor Relations, 1962; The Development of American Labor, 1962; (with J. Bambrick) Preparing for Collective Bargaining, 1963; (ed. with S. Barkin) The Crisis in the American Trade-Union Movement; (with D. Georgakas) Michigan Labor and the Civil War, 1964; Management and the White Collar Union, 1964; (ed. with W. Form) Industrial Relations and Social Change in Latin America, 1965; (co-ed.) Readings in Social Science: Problem of Power in American Society, 1967; (coordinating ed.) Manpower Adjustment Programmes, 1967-68; Drafted or Deferred Practices Past and Present, 1967; (gen. ed.) Masterworks in Industrial Relations, 4 vols., 1969-72; (ed.) Teachers Unions and Associations: A Comparative Study, 1969; (co-author) White Collar Workers, 1971; A Brief History of American Labor, 1970; A History of the American Labor Movement, 1972; International Handbook of Industrial Relations, 1981. Add: Intl. Business Dept., American Univ. of Paris, 31 Ave. Bosquet, 75007 Paris, France.

BLUM, Jerome. American, b. 1913. History. Prof. Emeritus of History, Princeton Univ., N.J. (joined faculty, 1947). *Publs:* Noble Landowners and Agriculture in Austria 1815-1848, 1948; Lord and Peasant in Russia from the Ninth to the Nineteenth Century, 1961; (with R. Cameron and T.G. Barnes) The European World, 1966; (with R.S. Lopez, R. Cameron and T.G. Barnes) Civilizations: Western and World, 2 vols., 1975; The End of the Old Order in Rural Europe, 1978; Our Forgotten Past, 1982. Add: 67 South Stanworth Dr., Princeton, N.J. 08540, U.S.A.

BLUMBERG, Arnold. American, b. 1925. History, International Relations. Prof. of History, Towson State Univ., Baltimore (joined faculty, 1958). Abstractor, Historical Abstracts, and America, History and Life, publs.; Critical Reader, The Historian journal; Book Reviewer for Choice mag., The Sunday Sun, Baltimore, etc. *Publs:* The Diplomacy of the Austro-Sardinian War of 1859, 1952; A History of Congregation Shearith Israel of Baltimore, 1970; A Manual for Under-graduate Term Papers, 1970; The Diplomacy of the Mexican Empire: 1863-1867, 1971, 1987; A View from Jerusalem 1849-1858: The Consular Diary of James and Elizabeth Ann Finn, 1980; Zion Before Zionism 1838-1880, 1985; A Carefully Planned Surprise: The Italian War of 1859, 1989. Add: Dept. of History, Linthicum Hall 119C, Towson State Univ., Baltimore, Md. 21204, U.S.A.

BLUMBERG, Phillip Irvin. American, b. 1919. Business/Trade/Industry. Prof. of Law and Business and former Dean, Univ. of Connecticut Sch. of Law. Member, Legal Advisory Cttee. to Bd. of Dirs., N.Y. Stock Exchange; Advisor, American Law Inst., Corporate Governance Project; Member, Connecticut Gov.'s Cttee. to Review Judicial Nominations, State Dept. Advisory Cttee. on Transnational Corporations, and American Law Inst.; Pres., Edward A. Filene Good Will Fund; Trustee, Connecticut Bar Foundn. Formerly, Prof. of Law, Boston Univ. Sch. of Law; Chmn., Finance Cttee., Federated Development Co. (formerly Federated Mortgage Investors), NYC: Chmn., Exec. Cttee., Excess and Treaty Reinsurance Corp. *Publs:* Corporate Responsibility in a Changing Society, 1972; The Megacorporation in American Society: The Scope of Corporate Power, 1975; The Law of Corporate Groups: Procedure, 1983; The Law of Corporate Groups: Bankruptcy, 1985; The Law of Corporate

Groups: Substantive Common Law, 1987; The Law of Corporate Groups: General Statutory Law, 1989. Add: 791 Prospect Ave., West Hartford, Conn. 06105, U.S.A.

BLUME, Judy. American, b. 1938. Novels, Children's fiction. *Publs:* Iggie's House, 1970; Are You There God? It's Me, Margaret, 1970; Freckle Juice, 1971; Then Again, Maybe I Won't, 1971; Tales of a Fourth Grade Nothing, 1972; It's Not the End of the World, 1972; Otherwise Known as Sheila the Great, 1972; Deenie, 1973; Blubber, 1974; Forever, 1976; Starring Sally J. Freedman as Herself, 1977; Wifey, 1978; Superfudge, 1980; Tiger Eyes, 1981; Judy Blume Diary, 1981; The One in the Middle is the Green Kangaroo, 1981; Smart Women, 1984; The Pain and the Great One, 1984; Letters to Judy: What Kids Wish They Could Tell You, 1986; Just As Long As We're Together, 1987. Add: c/o Harold Ober Assocs., 40 East 49th St., New York, N.Y. 10017, U.S.A.

BLUMENFELD, Hans. Canadian, b. 1892. Regional/Urban planning. Emeritus Prof. of Urban and Regional Planning, Univ. of Toronto, Ont., (joined faculty, 1961). Deputy Commnr., Metropolitan Toronto Planning Bd., 1955–61. *Publs:* The Modern Metropolis, 1967; (with Paul D. Spreiregen) Metropolis and Beyond, 1978; Life Begins at 65, 1987. Add: 123 Spadina Rd., Toronto, Ont. M5R 2T1, Canada.

BLUMENSON, Martin. American, b. 1918. Military/Defence, Biography. With U.S. Army, 1942–46 and 1950–57, retiring as Lt. Col.; Instr. in History, U.S. Merchant Academy, Kingspoint, N.Y., 1948–50; Sr. Historian, Office of Chief of Military History, Dept. of the Army, 1957–67; Visiting Prof. of Military and Strategic Studies, Acadia Univ., Wolfville, N.S., 1969–71; Ernest J. King Chair of History, U.S. Naval War Coll., 1971–73; Mark W. Clark Visiting Prof. of History, The Citadel, Charleston, S.C., 1974–75; Harold Keith Johnson Chair of Military History, Army War Coll., 1975–76; Adjunct Prof., Army War Coll., 1977–81; Professorial Lectr. in Intnl. Affairs, George Washington Univ., Washington, D.C., 1979–83; Visting Prof. Bucknell Univ., Lewisburg, Pa., 1982; Adjunct Prof., National War Coll., 1983–84. Marie Fisher Distinguished Prof., Univ. of North Texas, Denton, Tex. *Publs:* Breakout and Pursuit, 1961; The Duel for France, 1963; Anzio: The Gamble That Failed, 1963; Kasserine Pass (in U.K. as Rommel's Last Victory), 1967; Sicily: Whose Victory?, 1969; Salerno to Cassino, 1969; Bloody River: The Real Tragedy of the Rapido (in U.K. as Prelude to Mont Cassino), 1970; Eisenhower, 1972; The Patton Papers: vol. 1, 1885-1940, 1972, vol. 11, 1940–45, 1974; (co-author) Masters of the Art of Command, 1975; The Vildé Affair: Beginnings of the French Resistance, 1977; (co-author) Liberation, 1978; Mark Clark, 1984; Patton: The Man Behind the Legend, 1985. Add: 3900 Watson Pl. N.W., Washington, D.C. 20016, U.S.A.

BLUMENTHAL, Gerda Renée. American, b. 1923. Literature. Prof. Emeritus of French and Comparative Literature, Catholic Univ. of America, Washington, D.C.. Prof. of French, and Chmn., Dept. of Modern Languages, Washington Coll., 1955–68. *Publs:* André Malraux: The Conquest of Dread, 1960; The Poetic Imagination of Georges Bernanos, 1965; Thresholds: A Study of Proust, 1984. Add: 4530 Connecticut Ave. N.W., Washington, D.C. 20008, U.S.A.

BLUNT, Don. *See* **BOOTH,** Edwin.

BLY, Robert (Elwood). American, b. 1926. Poetry, Translations. Founder and Ed., The Fifties mag (later the Sixties and the Seventies mags.), and the Fifties Press (later The Sixties Press and The Seventies Press), Madison, Minn, since 1958. *Publs:* (trans.) Reptiles and Amphibians of the World, by Hans Hvass, 1960; (trans. with J. Wright) Twenty Poems of Georg Trakl, 1961; A Broadsheet Against the New York Times Book Review, 1961; (trans.) The Story of Gosta Berling, by Selma Lagerlof, 1962; (trans. with J. Wright and J. Knoepfle) Twenty Poems of Cesar Vallejo, 1962; (with J. Wright and W. Duffy) The Lion's Tail and Eyes; Poems Written Out of Laziness and Silence, 1962; Silence in the Snowy Fields: Poems, 1962; (trans. with E. Sellin and T. Buckman) Three Poems by Thomas Transtromer, 1966; (ed. with D. Ray) A Poetry Reading Against the Vietnam War, 1966; (ed.) The Sea and the Honeycomb: A Book of Poems, 1966; (trans.) Hunger, by Knut Hamsun, 1967; The Light Around the Body: Poems, 1967; Chrysanthemums, 1967; (trans. with C. Paulston) I Do Best Alone at Night, by Gunnar Ekelof, 1967; (trans. with C. Paulston) Late Arrival On Earth: Selected Poems of Gunnar Ekelof, 1967; (co-trans.) Selected Poems, by Ivan Goll, 1968; Ducks, 1968; (trans. with J. Wright) Twenty Poems of Pablo Neruda, 1968; (trans.) Forty Poems of Juan Ramon Jimenez, 1969; (trans.) Ten Poems, by Issa Kobayashi, 1969; The Morning Glory: Another Thing That Will Never Be My Friend: Twelve Prose Poems, 1969; rev. ed. 1970, 1973; (ed.) Forty Poems Touching on Recent American History, 1970; The Teeth

Mother Naked at Last, 1970; (with W.E. Stafford and W. Matthews) Poems for Tennessee, 1971; (trans. with J. Wright and J. Knoepfle) Neruda and Vallejo: Selected Poems, 1971; (trans.) Twenty Poems of Thomas Transtromer, 1971; (trans.) The Fish in the Sea Is Not Thirsty: Versions of Kabir, 1971; (trans.) Night Vision, by Thomas Transtromer, 1972; (trans.) The First Ten Sonnets of Orpheus, by Rainer Maria Rilke, 1972; Water under the Earth, 1972; Leaping Poetry, 1973; Jumping Out of Bed, 1973; Sleepers Joining Hands, 1973; (trans.) Lorca and Jimenez: Selected Poems, 1973; (trans.) Martinson, Ekelof, Transtromer: Selected Poems, 1973; (trans.) Basho, 1974; Old Man His Eyes, 1974; Point Reyes Poems, 1974; (ed.) Leaping Poetry: An Idea with Poems and Translations, 1975; (ed.) Selected Poems, by David Ignatow, 1975; This Body Is Made of Camphor and Gopherwood: Prose Poems, 1977; (ed.) News of the Universe: Poems of Twofold Consciousness, 1979; This Tree Will Be Here for a Thousand Years, 1979; Talking All Morning (interviews), 1980; (trans.) Selected Poems of Rainer Maria Rilke, 1981; The Man in the Black Coat Turns, 1981; (trans.) Time Alone: Selected Poems of Antonio Machado, 1983; Loving a Woman in Two Worlds, 1985; Love of Minute Particulars 1985; A Little Book on the Human Shadow, 1986; Selected Poems, 1986. Add: 308 1st St., Moose Lake, Minn, 55767, U.S.A.

BLYTH, Alan Geoffrey. British, b. 1929. Music, Biography. Music critic, Daily Telegraph, London; Board Member, Opera mag., London. Critic for Gramophone, Musical Times, and others. *Publs:* Enjoyment of Opera; Colin Davis; Janet Baker; Opera on Record; Remembering Britten; Wagner's Ring: An Introduction; Cinderella, 1981; Lohengin, 1981; Opera on Record 2, 1983; Opera on Record 3, 1984; Development, Experience and Curriculum in Primary Education, 1984; Song on Record, vol. I, 1986; Informal Primary Education Today, 1988. Add: 11 Boundary Rd., London NW8 0HE, England.

BLYTH, Chay. British, b. 1940. Travel/Exploration/Adventure, Autobiography/Memoirs/Personal. Co. Dir. and Managing Dir., Sailing Ventures, Ltd., Hants, England, since 1969. Holds various records for sailing. *Publs:* A Fighting Chance, 1967; Innocent Abroad, 1969; The Impossible Voyage, 1971; Theirs Is the Glory, 1974. Add: Penquite Farm, Rosecraddock, Liskeard, Cornwall PL14 5AQ, England.

BLYTH, John. *See* **HIBBS,** John.

BLYTHE, Ronald (George). British, b. 1922. Novels/Short stories, Country life/Rural societies, Literature. *Publs:* A Treasonable Growth (novel), 1960; Immediate Possession (short stories), 1961; The Age of 1963; (ed.) Emma, by Jane Austen, 1966; (ed.) Components of the Scene: An Anthology of the Prose and Poetry of the Second World War, 1966; Akenfield: Portrait of an English Village, 1969; (ed.) William Hazlitt: Selected Writings, 1970; (ed.) Aldeburgh Anthology, 1972; (ed.) A Pair of Blue Eyes by Thomas Hardy, 1976; (ed.) The Death of Ivan Ilyich, by Leo Tolstoy, 1977; (ed.) Far From The Madding Crowd, by Thomas Hardy, 1978; The View in Winter, 1979; Places, 1981; From the Headlands, 1982; The Stories of Ronald Blythe, 1985; Divine Landscapes, 1986. Add: Bottengom's Farm, Wormingford, Colchester, Essex, England.

BOALCH, Donald Howard. Also writes as Howard a'Bear. British, b. 1914. Poetry, Art, History, Music. Asst. in charge of Far Eastern section, Sch. of Oriental Studies, Univ. of London, 1940–47; Asst. Keeper, Dept. of Oriental Antiquities, British Museum, London, 1947–48; Librarian and Archivist, Rothamsted Experimental Station, Harpenden, Herts., 1950–62; Sublibrarian in charge of scientific books, Bodleian Library, Oxford, 1962–75; Fellow, Corpus Christi Coll., Oxford, 1965–75. *Publs:* The Manor of Rothamsted, 1953; Prints and Paintings of British Farm Livestock 1780-1910, 1953; Makers of the Harpsichord and Clavichord, 1440-1840, 1956, rev. ed. 1974; Caterwauls (verse), 2nd ed., 1984; (as Howard a'Bear) That Brave Vibration (verse), 2nd ed., 1984; (as Howard a'Bear) Each Way Free (verse), 1985. Add: 4 Hill Top Rd., Oxford, England.

BOARDMAN, Arthur. American, b. 1927. Novels/Short stories. Assoc. Prof. of English, Univ. of Colorado, Boulder, since 1970. Fulbright-Hays Lectr., Univ. of Mohammed V, Rabat, Morocco, 1975–77. *Publs:* Captives, 1975. Add: c/o John Johnson, 45/47 Clerkenwell Green, London EC1R 0HT, England.

BOARDMAN, Fon W(yman), Jr. American, b. 1911. Children's nonfiction, Reference. With Columbia Univ. Press, NYC 1934–51; Vice Pres. and Marketing Dir., Oxford Univ., Press, NYC, 1951–72. *Publs:* Castles, 1957; Roads, 1958; Canals, 1959; Tunnels, 1960; History and Historians, 1965; Economics: Ideas and Men, 1966; The Thirties: America and the Great Depression, 1967; America and the Jazz Age, 1968; America and the Progressive Era, 1970; America and the Gilded Age, 1972; America and the Virginia Dynasty, 1974; America and the Jacksonian Era, 1825-1850, 1975; Around the World in 1776, 1975; America and the Civil War Era, 1976; Tyrants and Conquerors, 1977; Against the Iroquois, 1978; America and the Robber Barons, 1979; (contrib. ed.) Encyclopedia of American Facts and Dates, 1987; Volume Library, 1988; Facts and Dates of American Sports, 1988. Add: 16 West 16th St., New York, N.Y. 10011, U.S.A.

BOARDMAN, John. British, b. 1927. Archaeology/Antiquities, Art, Classics. Lincoln Prof. of Classical Art and Archaeology, Univ. of Oxford, since 1978 (Asst. Keeper, Ashmolean Museum, 1955–59; Reader in Classical Archaeology, 1959–78). Fellow, British Academy, since 1969; Co-Ed., Oxford Monographs in Classical Archaeology. Asst. Dir., British Sch. at Athens, 1952–55; Ed., Journal of Hellenic Studies, 1958–65. *Publs:* (trans.) S. Marinatos and M. Hirmer: Crete and Mycenae, 1960; The Cretan Collection in Oxford, 1961; The Greeks Overseas, 1964, 1974, 1980; Island Gems, 1963; Greek Art, 1964, 1973; The Date of the Knossos Tablets, 1963; (with J. Hayes) Excavations at Tocra, 2 vols., 1966–73; (with J. Dorig, W. Fuchs and M. Hirmer) Die Griechische Kunst, 1966; Greek Emporio, 1967; Pre-Classical Style and Civilisation, 1967; Engraved Gems, the Ionides Collection, 1968; Archaic Greek Gems, 1968; Greek Gems and Finger Rings, 1970; (ed. with M. Brown and T. Powell) The European Community in Prehistory, 1971; (with D.C. Kurtz) Greek Burial Customs, 1971; Athenian Black Figure Vases, 1974; Athenian Red Figure Vases: The Archaic Period: A Handbook, 1975; (with D. Scarisbrick) The Ralph Harari Collection of Finger Rings, 1978; (with E. la Rocca) Eros in Greece, 1978; Greek Sculpture, Archaic Period, 1978; (with M.L. Vollenweider) Catalogue of Gems and Finger Rings, vol. I, 1978; (with M. Robertson) Castle Ashby Corpus Vasorum, 1979; Greek Sculpture, Classical Period, 1985; The Parthenon and its Sculptures, 1985; Athenian Red Figure Vases, Classical Period, 1989. Add: 11 Park St., Woodstock, Oxford England.

BOBINSKI, George S. American, b. 1929. Librarianship. Dean and Prof., Sch. of Information and Library Studies, State Univ. of New York at Buffalo, since 1970. Exec. Ed., Dictionary of American Library Biography, 1978. Dir. of Libraries, State Univ. Coll.,Cortland, N.Y., 1960–67; Prof. and Assoc. Dean, Coll. of Library Science, Univ. of Kentucky, Lexington, 1967–70. *Publs:* Carnegie Libraries: Their History and Impact on American Public Library Development, 1969. Add: 69 Little Robin Rd., W. Amherst, N.Y., 14228, U.S.A.

BOCHNER, Salomon. American, b. 1899. Mathematics/Statistics. Edgar Odell Lovett Prof. of Mathematics, Rice Univ., Houston, since 1968. Lectr., Univ. of Munich, 1926–33; Faculty Member, 1933–68, and Henry Burchard Fine Prof. of Mathematics, 1959–68, Princeton Univ., N.J. *Publs:* Fouriersche Integrale, 1932; Several Complex Variables, 1948; Fourier Transforms, 1949; Curvature and Betti Numbers, 1953; Harmonic Analysis and the Theory of Probability, 1955; Fourier Integrals, 1959; The Role of Mathematics in the Rise of Science, 1966; Eclosion and Synthesis: Perspectives on the History of Knowledge, 1969; Einstein Between Centuries, 1979; (co-author) History of Analysis, 1979. Add: Dept. of Mathematics, Rice Univ., P.O. Box 1892, Houston, Tex. 77001, U.S.A.

BOCK, Philip Karl. American, b. 1934. Anthropology/Ethnology. Prof. of Anthropology, Univ. of New Mexico, since 1962 (Dept. Chmn., 1977–80). Ed., Journal of Anthropological Research, since 1982. *Publs:* The Micmac Indians of Restigouche, 1966; Modern Cultural Anthropology, 1969, 3rd ed. 1978; (ed.) Peasants in the Modern World, 1969; (ed.) Culture Shock, 1970; Continuities in Psychological Anthropology, 1980; Shakespeare and Elizabethan Culture, 1984; The Formal Content of Ethnography, 1986; Rethinking Psychological Anthropology, 1988. Add: Dept. of Anthropology, Univ. of New Mexico, Albuquerque, N.M. 87131, U.S.A.

BOCOCK, Robert James. British, b. 1940. Sociology, Biography. Lectr., Richmond Fellowship, London, since 1967; Lectr. in Sociology, Open Univ., since 1978. Lectr. in Sociology, Brunel Univ., 1966–78. *Publs:* Ritual in Industrial Society, 1974; Freud and Modern Society, 1976; (ed.) Introduction to Sociology, 1980; Sigmund Freud, 1983; (ed.) Religion and Ideology, 1985; Hegemony, 1986; (ed.) The State or the Market, 1987. Add: Dept. of Sociology, The Open Univ., Walton Hall, Milton Keynes, Bucks., England.

BODDY, Frederick Arthur. British, b. 1914. Horticulture. Horticultural consultant in private practice, now retired. Supt. of Parks, Sale, Cheshire, 1946–50, and Dudley, Worcs., 1950–55; Dir. of Parks, London Borough of Ealing, 1955–69. *Publs:* Simple Gardening, 1964; Highway Trees, 1968; Some Practical Aspects of Parks Design, 1970; Foliage Plants, 1973; Ground Cover and Other Ways to Weed-Free Gardens, 1974; Garden Flowers, 1977. Add: Rannoch, Chiltern Rd., Great Missenden, Bucks., England.

BODE, Carl. American, b. 1911. Poetry, History, Literature, Biography. Prof. of American Literature, Univ. of Maryland, College Park, since 1947. Cultural Attaché, American Embassy to Great Britain, 1957–59. Chmn., Maryland State Arts Council, 1972–76, and Maryland Humanities Council, 1984–86. *Publs:* (ed.) Collected Poems of Henry Thoreau, 1943, rev. ed. 1964; (ed.) The Portable Thoreau, 1947, 1964, 1983; The Sacred Seasons, 1953; (ed. with L. Howard and L. Wright) American Heritage, rev. ed. as American Literature, 1966; The American Lyceum, 1956, 1968; (ed. with W. Harding) The Correspondence of Henry David Thoreau, 1958; The Anatomy of American Popular Culture 1840-1861, 1959, reissued as Antebellum Culture, 1970; The Man Behind You, 1959; (ed.) The Young Rebel in American Literature, 1959; (ed.) The Great Experiment in American Literature, 1961; The Half-World of American Culture, 1965; 1967; (ed.) American Life in the 1840s, 1967; (ed.) The Selected Journals of Henry David Thoreau, 1967, reissued as the Best of Thoreau's Journals, 1971; Mencken, 1969, 1986; (ed.) Ralph Waldo Emerson: A Profile, 1969; (ed.) Midcentury America: Life in the 1850s, 1972; (ed.) The Young Mencken, 1973; Highly Irregular, 1974; (ed.) The New Mencken Letters, 1977; Maryland: A Bicentennial History, 1978; Practical Magic, 1981; (ed. with Malcolm Cowley) The Portable Emerson, 1981; (ed.) P.T. Barnum, Struggles and Triumphs, 1982; (ed.) H. Alger, Struggling Upward, 1984; (ed.) The Editor, the Bluenose, and the Prostitute: H.L. Mencken's History of the "Hatrack" Censorship Case, 1988. Add: Dept. of English, Univ. of Maryland, College Park, Md. 20742, U.S.A.

BODEN, Margaret A(nn). British, b. 1936. Information science/Computers, Philosophy, Psychology. Prof. of Philosophy and Psychology, Univ. of Sussex, Brighton, since 1980 (Lectr. and Reader, 1965–80). Lectr. in Philosophy, Univ. of Birmingham, 1959–65. *Publs:* Purposive Explanation in Psychology, 1972; Artificial Intelligence and Natural Man, 1977, 1987; Piaget, 1979; Minds and Mechanisms, 1981; Computer Models of Mind, 1988; Artificial Intelligence in Psychology, 1989; (ed.) The Philosophy of Artificial Intelligence, 1989. Add: School of Cognitive and Computing Sciences, Univ. of Sussex, Brighton, England.

BODETT, Tom. (Thomas Edward Bodett). American, b. 1955. Novels/Short stories, Essays. Writer and broadcaster: Commentator, "Alaska News Nightly," Alaska Public Radio, since 1984; Pres., Kachemak Bay Broadcasting Inc., since 1985; Columnist, "We Alaskans," Anchorage Daily News, since 1985. Logger and commercial fisherman, 1975–77; Owner, Bodett Construction Inc., Homer and Petersburg, AK, 1977–85; Commentator, "All Things Considered," National Public Radio, 1984–86; Columnist, Cabin mag., 1986–87. *Publs:* As Far as You can Go Without a Passport: The View from the End of The Road, 1985; Small Comforts, 1987. Add: c/o Raphael Sagalyn, 2813 Bellevue Terr. N.W., Washington, D.C. 20007, U.S.A.

BODEY, Hugh. British, b. 1939. Archaeology/Antiquities, Business/Trade/Industry, Children's non-fiction. Lectr., South Devon Technical Coll., since 1974. Founding Dir., Colne Valley Museum, Yorks. *Publs:* Roads, 1971; Industrial History in Huddersfield, 1972; Religion, 1973; British Industry, 43-1970, 1975; Discovering Industrial History and Aechaeology, 1975; Factories, 1975; Textiles, 1976; Mining, 1976; (with M. Hallas) Elementary Surveying for Industrial Aechaeologists, 1978; Roman People, 1981; Immigrants and Emigrants, 1982. Add: Tracey Cottage, Bow, Crediton, Devon EX17 6EP, England.

BODMER, (Sir) Walter (Fred). British, b. 1936. Biology, Medicine/Health. Res. Dir., Imperial Cancer Research Fund Labs., London, since 1979. Research Fellow, 1958–60, and Official Fellow, 1961, Clare Coll., Cambridge, and Demonstrator, Dept. of Genetics, Cambridge Univ., 1960–61; Fellow and Visiting Asst. Prof., 1961–62, Asst. Prof., 1962–66, Assoc. Prof., 1966–68, and Prof. of Genetics,1968–70, Stanford Univ. Sch. of Medicine, California; Prof. of Genetics, Oxford Univ., 1970–79. Vice-Pres., Royal Instn., 1981–82; Pres., Royal Statistical Soc., 1984–85, British Assn. for Advancement of Science, 1987–88, and Assn. for Science Education, 1989. Assoc. Ed., American Journal of Human Genetics, 1968–70; Member, Ed. Bd., American Naturalist, 1969–71. *Publs:* (with L. Cavalli-Sporza) The Genetics of Human Population, 1971; (with A. Jones) Our Future Inheritance: Choice or Chance?, 1974; (with L. Cavalli-Sporza) Genetics, Evolution, and Man, 1976; (ed.) Inherited Susceptibility to Cancer in Man, 1982. Add: P.O. Box 123, Lincoln's Inn Fields, London WC2A 3PX, England.

BODSWORTH, (Charles) Fred(erick). Canadian, b. 1918. Novels/Short stories, Natural history. Reporter, Times-Journal, St. Thomas, Ont., 1940–43; Reporter and Ed., Daily Star and Weekly Star, Toronto, Ont., 1943–46; Staff Writer and Ed., Maclean's Mag., Toronto, Ont., 1947–55. *Publs:* Last of the Curlews, 1955; The Strange One, 1959; The Atonement of Ashley Morden (in U.K. as Ashley Morden), 1964; The Sparrow's Fall, 1967; The Pacific Coast, 1970; Wilderness Canada, 1970. Add: 294 Beech Ave., Toronto M4E 3J2, Canada.

BODY, Geoffrey. British, b. 1929. Transportation. Principal, Avon-Anglia Publs. and Services, since 1976. *Publs:* British Paddle Steamers, 1971; Railways for Pleasure, 1976; Clifton Suspension Bridge, 1976; Rocket 150: The Liverpool and Manchester Railway 1830-1980, 1980; Illustrated History of Preserved Railways, 1981; The Railway Era, 1982; Railways of the Western and Southern, Eastern Region, 3 vols., 1983–85. Add: Annesley House, 21 Southside, Weston-super-Mare B523 2QU, England.

BOER, Charles. American, b. 1939. Poetry, Literature, Translations. Prof. of English and Comparative Literature, Univ. of Connecticut, Storrs, since 1975 (Asst. Prof., 1966–70; Assoc. Prof., 1970–75). *Publs:* The Odes, 1969; (trans.) The Homeric Hymns, 1971; (trans.) The Bacchae of Euripides, 1972; Varmint Q: An Epic Poem on the Life of William Clarke Quantrill, 1972; (ed. with G. Butterick) The Maximus Poems of Charles Olson, vol. III, 1974; Charles Olson in Connecticut, 1975; (trans.) Marsilio Ficino: The Book of Life, 1980; (with James Hillman) Freud's Own Cookbook, 1985; (trans.) Metamorphosis, by Ovid, 1989. Add: Box 69, Pomfret Center, Conn. 06259, U.S.A.

BOGARD, Travis (Miller). American, b. 1918. Literary criticism, History. Prof. of Dramatic Art, Univ. of California, Berkeley, since 1960 (Instr., 1947–49; Asst. Prof., 1949–55; Assoc. Prof., 1955–59; Chmn. of the Dept., 1960–66). *Publs:* The Tragic Satire of John Webster, 1957; Modern Drama: Essays in Criticism, 1965; (ed.) The Later Plays of Eugene O'Neill, 1967; Contour in Time: The Plays of Eugene O'Neill, 1972, 1988; (ed.) The Actor from Point Arena, 1977; (with others) Revels History of Drama in English, vol. 8: American Drama, 1978; (with Jackson R. Bryer) Selected Letters of Eugene O'Neill, 1988. Add: c/o Yale Univ. Press, 302 Temple St., New Haven, CT 06520, U.S.A.

BOGARDE, Dirk. British, b. 1921. Novels/Short stories, Autobiography/Memoirs/Personal. Motion picture actor since 1947; films include: Victim; The Servant; King and Country; Darling; Accident; Death in Venice; Providence; etc. *Publs:* A Postillion Struck by Lightning (autobiography), 1977; Snakes and Ladders (autobiography), 1978; A Gentle Occupation (novel), 1980; Voices in the Garden (novel), 1981; An Orderly Man (autobiography), 1983; West of Sunset (novel), 1984; Backcloth (autobiography), 1986. Add: c/o Duncan Heath Assocs., 162 Wardour St., London W1, England.

BOGDANOR, Vernon. British, b. 1943. Politics/Government. Fellow and Tutor in Politics, Brasenose Coll., Oxford, since 1966. *Publs:* (ed., with Robert Skidelsky) The Age of Affluence 1951-1964, 1970; (ed.) Lothair, by Disraeli, 1975; Devolution, 1979; The People and the Party System, 1981; (ed.) Liberal Party Politics, 1983; Multi-Party Politics and the Constitution, 1983; (co-ed.) Democracy and Elections, 1983; (ed.) Coalition Government in Western Europe, 1983; What Is Proportional Representation?, 1984; (ed.) Parties and Democracy in Britain and America, 1984; (ed.) Science and Politics, 1984; (ed.) Representatives of the People?, 1985; (ed.) Blackwell's Encyclopaedia of Political Institutions, 1987; (ed.) Constitutions in Democratic Politics, 1988. Add: Brasenose Coll., Oxford, England.

BOGDANOVICH, Peter. American, b. 1939. Plays/Screenplays, Film. Film director, writer and actor; Film feature-writer, Esquire, NY Times and others, since 1961; Owner, Saticoy Productions, Inc., Los Angeles, since 1968; Co-founder and Member, Copa de Oro Productions, Los Angeles, since 1972; Owner, Moon Pictures, since 1984; Member, Dirs. Guild of America, Writers' Guild of America, Acad. of Motion Picture Arts and Sciences. Actor, American Shakespeare Festival, Stratford, Conn., 1956 and NY Shakespeare Festival, 1958; Dir. Producer, Off-Broadway plays, 1959–64; Gen. Partner, Bogdanovich Film Partners, 1982. *Publs:* The Cinema of Orson Welles, 1961; The Cinema of Howard Hawks, 1962; The Cinema of Alfred Hitchcock, 1963; John Ford, 1968; Fritz Lang in America, 1969; Allan Dwan: The Last Pioneer, 1971, 1981; Pieces of Time, The Killing of the Unicorn: Dorothy Stratten 1960–80,

1984. Add: c/o Camp and Peiffer, 2040 Ave. of the Stars, Century City, Calif. 90067, U.S.A.

BOGGS, Jean Sutherland. Canadian, b. 1922. Art. Chmn. and Chief Exec. Officer, Canadian Museums Construction Corp., Ottawa, since 1982. Asst. Prof., Mount Holyoke Coll., Massachusetts 1949–52; Asst. and Assoc. Prof., Univ. of California, Berkeley, 1954–62; Curator, Art Gallery of Toronto, 1962–64; Steinberg Prof. of Art History, Washington Univ., St. Louis, 1964–66; Dir., National Art Gallery of Canada, 1966–76; Prof. of Fine Arts, Harvard Univ., Cambridge, Mass., 1976–79; Dir., Philadelphia Museum of Art, 1978–82. *Publs:* Portraits by Degas, 1962; The National Gallery of Canada, 1971. Add: P.O. Box 395, Station A, Ottawa, Ont. K1N 8V4, Canada.

BOGNER, Norman. American. b. 1935. Novels/Short stories, Plays/Screenplays. Ed., 1960–61, and Editorial Mgr., 1962–63, Jonathan Cape Ltd., publrs., London; Story Ed., Armchair Theatre, ABC TV, Teddington, Surrey, 1963–65. *Publs:* In Spells No Longer Bound, 1961; Spanish Fever, 1963; Divorce, 1966; Seventh Avenue, 1967; Madonna Complex, 1968; Making Love, 1971; The Hunting Animal, 1975; Snowman, 1978; Arena, 1979; California Dreamers, 1981; plays—Boys and Girls Come Out to Play, The Waiters, The Man from Esher, The Match; Privilege (screenplay). Add: 9601 Charleville Blvd., Beverly Hills, Calif. 90212, U.S.A.

BOGUE, Lucile Maxfield. American, b. 1911. Novels/Short stories. Poetry, Biography. English Instr., Colegio Americano of Guayaquil, Ecuador, 1974–75. English Instr., Whiteman Sch., 1957–59; Founder and Pres., Yampa Valley Coll., Colo., 1962–66; Dir. of Guidance, American Sch., in Japan, Tokyo, 1966–68; Dean, Anna Head Sch., Calif., 1968–71; Lectr., Comparative Literature, Foreign Study League, London, Versailles, Vienna, and Rome, 1969. *Publs:* Typhoon! Typhoon!, 1970; Eye of the Condor, 1974; Bloodstones: Lines from a Marriage, 1980; Salt Lake (novel), 1982; Dancers on Horseback (biography), 1984; Miracle on the Mountain: The Story of a College, 1987. Add: 2611 Brooks, El Cerrito, Calif. 94530, U.S.A.

BOHANNAN, Paul (James). American, b. 1920. Anthropology/Ethnology, Human relations. Dean of Soc. Sciences, Univ. of Southern California, Los Angeles, since 1982. Lectr. in Social Anthropology, Oxford Univ., 1951–56; Assoc. Prof. of Anthropology, Princeton Univ., N.J., 1956–59; Stanley G. Harris Prof. of Social Sciences, Northwestern Univ., Evanston, Ill., 1959–75; Prof. of Anthropology, Univ. of Calfornia at Santa Barbara, 1976–82. *Publs:* (with L. Bohannan) The Tiv of Central Nigeria, 1953; Justice and Judgment among the Tiv, 1957; (ed. and contrib.) African Homicide and Suicide, 1960; (ed. with G. Dalton) Markets in Africa, 1962; Social Anthropology, 1963; Africa and Africans (in U.K. as African Outline), 1964, 3rd ed. 1988; (with L. Bohannan) Tiv Economy, 1968; (ed. and contrib.) Divorce and After, 1970; (ed. with M. Glazer) High Points in Anthropology, 1973; All the Happy Families, 1984. Add: Social Sciences, ADM 200, Univ. of Southern California, Los Angeles, Calif. 90089, U.S.A.

BOICE, James Montgomery. American, b. 1938. Theology/Religion. Pastor, Tenth Presbyterian Church, Philadelphia, since 1968. Asst. Ed., Christianity Today, Washington, D.C., 1966–68. *Publs:* Witness and Revelation in the Gospel of John, 1970; Philippians: An Expositional Commentary, 1971; The Sermon on the Mount, 1972; How to Really Live It Up, 1973; The Last and Future World, 1974; How God Can Use Nobodies, 1974; The Gospel of John, 5 vols., 1975–79; Can You Run Away from God?, 1977; (ed.) Our Sovereign God, 1977; (ed.) The Foundation of Biblical Authority, 1978; God the Redeemer, 1978; The Sovereign God, 1978; Awakening to God, 1979; Making God's Word Plain, 1979; The Epistles of John, 1979; Does Inerrancy Matter?, 1979; God and History, 1980; (ed.) Our Savior God, 1980; Genesis, 3 vols., 1982–87; Parables of Jesus, 1983; Minor Prophets, 2 vols., 1983–86; The Christ of Christmas, 1983; Standing on the Rock, 1984; The Christ of the Empty Tomb, 1985; Foundations of the Christian Faith, 1986; Christ's Call to Discipleship, 1986; (ed.) Transforming Our World: A Call to Action, 1988; Daniel: An Expositional Commentary, 1989; Ephesians: An Expositional Commentary, 1989; Joshua: We Will Serve the Lord, 1989. Add: 1935 Pine St., Philadelphia, PA. 19103, U.S.A.

BOISSEVAIN, Jeremy (Fergus). British, b. 1928. Anthropology/Ethnology, Politics/Government, Sociology. Prof. of Social Anthropology, Univ. of Amsterdam, since 1966. Chief of CARE Mission, Philippines, Japan, India and Malta, 1953–58; Asst. Prof. of Anthropology, Univ. of Montreal, 1963–65; Lectr. in Sociology, Univ. of Sussex, Brighton, 1965–66. *Publs:* Saints and Fireworks: Religion and Politics in Rural Malta,

1965, 1969; Hal-Farrug: A Village in Malta, 1969; The Italians of Montreal: Social Adjustment in a Plural Society, 1970; (ed. with J.C. Mitchell) Network Analysis: Studies in Human Interaction, 1973; Friends of Friends: Networks, Manipulators and Coalitions, 1974; (ed., with J. Friedl) Beyond the Community: Social Process in Europe, 1975. Add: Sarphatiestraat 105A, 1018 6V Amsterdam, The Netherlands.

BOK, Derek. American, b. 1930. Law. Prof. of Law since 1961, and President since 1971, Harvard Univ. (Asst. Prof., 1958–61; Dean of the Law Sch., 1968–71). *Publs:* The First Three Years of the Schuman Plan, 1955; (ed. with Archibald Cox) Cases and Materials on Labor Law, 8th ed. 1977; (with John Dunlop) Labor and the American Community, 1970; Beyond the Ivory Tower, 1982; Higher Learning, 1986. Add: Office of the Pres., Harvard Univ., Cambridge, Mass. 02138, U.S.A.

BOK, Sissela. Swedish, b. 1934. Philosophy. Assoc. Prof. of Philosophy, Brandeis Univ., Waltham, MA, since 1985. *Publs:* (ed. with John A. Behnke) The Dilemma of Euthanasia, 1975; Lying: Moral Choice in Public and Private Life, 1978; (ed. with Daniel Callahan) Ethics Teaching in Higher Education, 1980; Secrets: On the Ethics of Concealment and Revelation, 1983; A Strategy for Peace: Human Values and the Threat of War, 1989. Add: Dept of Philosophy, Brandeis Univ., Waltham, MA 02254, U.S.A.

BOLD, Alan. British, b. 1943. Poetry, Literature. Member, editorial staff, Times Educational Supplement, 1965–66. *Publs:* poetry—Society Inebrious, 1965; To Find the New, 1967; A Perpetual Motion Machine, 1969; (with Edward Brathwaite and Edwin Morgan) Penguin Modern Poets, 15, 1969; The State of the Nation, 1969; The Auld Symie, 1971; He Will Be Greatly Missed, 1971; A Century of People, 1971; A Pint of Bitter, 1971; A Lunar Event, 1973; Scotland, Yes, 1978; This Fine Day, 1979; (with John Bellany) A Celtic Quintet, 1983; In This Corner: Selected Poems 1963–83, 1983; (with John Bellany) Haven, 1984; Summoned by Knox, 1985; (with John Bellany) Homage to MacDiarmid, 1985; (with Gareth Owen and Julie O'Callaghan) Bright Lights Blaze Out, 1986; Scottish Satirical Sonnets, 1989; stories—(with David Morrison) Hammer and Thistle, 1975; The Edge of the Wood, 1984; other—Thom Gunn and Ted Hughes, 1976; George Mackay Brown, 1978; The Ballad, 1979; The Sensual Scot, 1982; Modern Scottish Literature, 1983; MacDiarmid: The Terrible Crystal, 1983; (with Robert Giddings) The Book of Rotters, 1985; Longman Dictionary of Poets, 1985; Muriel Spark, 1986; (with Robert Giddings) Who Was Really Who in Fiction, 1987; MacDiarmid: A Critical Biography, 1988; Scotland: A Literary Guide, 1989; editor—Penguin Book of Socialist Verse, 1970; The Martial Muse: Seven Centuries of War Poetry, 1976; Cambridge Book of English Verse 1939–75, 1976; Making Love: The Picador Book of Erotic Verse, 1978; The Bawdy Beautiful: The Sphere Book of Improper Verse, 1979; Mounts of Venus: The Picador Book of Erotic Prose, 1980; Drink to Me Only: The Prose (and Cons) of Drinking, 1982; Smollet: Author of the First Distinction, 1982; The Sexual Dimension in Literature, 1983; A Scottish Poetry Book, 1983; Scott: The Long-Forgotten Melody, 1983; Byron: Wrath and Rhyme, 1983; The Thistle Rises: A MacDiarmid Miscellany, 1984; MacDiarmid: Aesthetics in Scotland, 1984; The Letters of Hugh MacDiarmid, 1984; The Poetry of Motion, 1984; Muriel Spark: An Odd Capacity for Vision, 1984; Harold Pinter: You Never Heard Such Silence, 1984; A Second Scottish Poetry Book, 1985; Scottish Quotations, 1985; Auden: The Far Interior, 1985; The Quest for le Carré, 1988. Add: Balbirnie Burns East Cottage, near Markinch, Fife KY7 6NE, Scotland.

BOLDING, Amy (Agnes). American, b. 1910. Speech/Rhetoric, Theology/Religion. Public sch. teacher, Wake, Tex., 1928–29. *Publs:* Please Give a Devotion, 1963; Please Give Another Devotion, 1964; Words of Welcome, 1965; Please Give a Devotion of Gladness, 1965; Please Give a Devotion For Young People, 1966; Kind Words for Sad Hearts, 1967; Please Give a Devotion for All Occasions, 1967; Handy Introductions and Replies, 1968; Day By Day with Amy Bolding, 1968; Please Give a Devotion for Juniors, 1969; Installation Services for All Groups, 1969; Finger Tip Devotions, 1970; New Welcome Speeches, 1971; Inspiring Finger Tip Devotions, 1971; Please Plan a Program, 1971; Women's Devotional Discussion Guide, 1973; Dynamic Fingertip Devotions, 1973; Please Give a Devotion for Church Groups, 1974; Please Give a Devotion for Active Teens, 1974; I'll Be Glad to Give a Devotion, 1976; Easy Devotions to Give, 1981; Cheerful Devotions to Give, 1984. Add: 4802 10th St., Lubbock, Tex. 79416, U.S.A.

BOLES, Hal. *See* **BOLES,** Harold Wilson.

BOLES, Harold Wilson. Also writes as Hal Boles. American, b. 1915. Education, Genealogy. With Western Michigan Univ., Kalamazoo from

1961, retired as Prof. of Educational Leadership, 1984. *Publs:* Step by Step to Better School Facilities, 1965; (with D.B. Boles) Some Earlier Americans, 1970; (as Hal Boles) The 3Rs and the New Religion, 1973; (with J.A. Davenport) Introduction to Educational Leadership, 1974; (ed.) Multidisciplinary Readings in Educational Leadership, 1976; Speece Genealogy, 1980; Interdisciplinary Readings in Leadership, 1980; Leaders, Leading and Leadership, 1980; Boles-Linton Ancestors, 1986. Add: 5123 Ridgebrook Dr., Kalamazoo, Mich, 49001, U.S.A.

BOLINGER, Dwight LeMerton. American, b. 1907. Language/Linguistics. Visiting Prof. of Linguistics Emeritus, Stanford University, California, since 1978. Asst. Prof., then Prof. of Spanish, Univ. of Southern California, Los Angeles, 1944–60; Prof. of Spanish, Univ. of Colorado, Boulder, 1960–63; Prof. of Romance Languages and Literatures, Harvard Univ., Cambridge, Mass., 1963–73. *Publs:* What is Freedom?, 1941; The Symbolism of Music, 1941; Intensive Spanish, 1948; Spanish Review Grammar, 1956; (co-author) Modern Spanish, 1960, 1965; Generality, Gradience, and the All-or-None, 1961; Forms of English, 1965; Aspects of Language, 1968; 3rd ed. 1981; The Phrasal Verb in English, 1971; (ed.) Intonation, 1972; Degree Words, 1972; That's That, 1972; Meaning and Form, 1977; Language—The Loaded Weapon, 1980; Intonation and Its Parts, 1985; Intonation and Its Uses, 1989. Add: 2718 Ramona St., Palo Alto, Calif. 94306, U.S.A.

BOLINO, August C. American, b. 1922. Economics. Prof. of Economics, Catholic Univ. of America, Washington D.C., since 1966. Instr., Idaho State Univ., Pocatello, 1952–55; Assoc. Prof. of Economics, Saint Louis Univ., Mo., 1955–62; Dir., Economic Studies, Office of Manpower, Automation, and Training, 1962–64, and Evaluation of Manpower Branch, U.S. Office of Education, 1964–66. *Publs:* The Development of the American Economy, 1961, 1966; Manpower and the City, 1969; Career Education: Contributions to Economic Growth, 1973; The Ellis Island Source Book, 1985; The Watchmakers of Massachusetts, 1987. Add: 18 Yeatman Ct., Silver Spring, Md. 20902, U.S.A.

BOLL, Theophilus E.M. American, b. 1902. Literature, Biography. of English Emeritus, Univ. of Pennsylvania, Philadelphia, since 1972 (joined faculty as Instr., 1922). *Publs:* The Works of Edwin Pugh (1874-1930): A Chapter in the Novel of Humble London Life, 1934; Biographical Note and Critical Essay on Stephen Hudson, 1962; Miss May Sinclair: Novelist. A Biographical and Critical Introduction, 1973. Add: 16565 Chattanooga Place, Pacific Palisades, Calif. 90272, U.S.A.

BOLLER, Paul F., Jr. American, b. 1916. History, Intellectual history. Emeritus Prof. of History, Texas Christian Univ., Fort Worth, since 1983 (Prof., 1976–83). Member of the faculty, Southern Methodist Univ., 1948–66, Univ. of Massachusetts, 1966–76. *Publs:* (with Jean Tilford) This Is Our Nation, 1961; George Washington and Religion, 1963; Quotemanship: The Use and Abuse of Quotations for Polemical and Other Purposes, 1967; American Thought in Transition 1865-1900, 1967; American Transcendentalism 1830-1860, 1974; Freedom and Fate in American Thought: From Edwards to Dewey, 1978; Presidential Anecdotes, 1981; Presidential Campaigns, 1984; (with Ronald Story) A More Perfect Union: Documents in American History, 1984; (with Ronald Davis) Hollywood Anecdotes, 1987; Presidential Wives, 1988. Add: History Dept., Texas Christian Univ., Fort Worth, Tex. 76129, U.S.A.

BOLLES, (Edmund) Blair. American, b. 1911. Politics/Government. Reporter for Diplomatic Corresp., Washington Star, Washington, D.C., 1934–44; Dir., Washington Bureau, 1944–51, and Washington Corresp., 1951–53, Foreign Policy Assn., Washington, D.C.; U.S. Ed., France Actuelle, 1952–53; European Corresp., 1953–56, and Assoc. Ed., 1957–59, Toledo Blade, Toledo, Ohio; Vice-Pres. for Govt. Relations, Fairbanks Morse & Co., Chicago and Washington, D.C., 1959; Exec., Colt Industries, 1959–86. *Publs:* (with Duncan Aikman) America's Chance of Peace, 1939; Arctic Diplomacy, 1958; Military Establishment of the U.S., 1949; U.S. Military Policy, 1950; Tyrant from Illinois, 1951, 1974; Who Makes U.S. Foreign Policy?, 1951; How to Get Rich in Washington, 1952; Armed Road Peace (NATO), 1952; Big Change in Europe, 1958; Men of Good Intentions, 1960; Corruption in Washington, 1961. Add: 9201 Chanute Dr., Bethesda, Md. 20814, U.S.A.

BOLLES, Edmund Blair. American, b. 1942. Language/Lingusitics, Natural history, Travel/Exploration/Adventure. Member, U.S. Peace Corps, Kidodi, Tanzania, 1966–68. *Publs:* (with P. Rosenthal) Readings in Psychology 1973/74 (college text), 1973; (with J. Sommer and J.F. Hoy) The Language Experience (essays), 1974; (with R. Fisher) Fodor's Old West (travel guide), 1976; (ed. with J. Fireman) Cat Catalog (essays), 1976; (with J. Fireman) TV book (essays), 1977; Animal Parks of Africa,

1978; The Beauty of America, 1979; So Much to Say! A Parent's Guide to Baby Talk from Birth to Five, 1982; The Penguin Adoption Handbook, 1984; Who Owns America?, 1984; (with D. Papalia) A Child's World (coll. text), 4th ed., 1987; Remembering and Forgetting, 1987; When Acting Out Isn't Acting, 1988. Add: 414 Amsterdam Ave., Apt. 4N, New York, N.Y. 10024, U.S.A.

BOLLES, Richard Nelson. American, b. 1927. Business/Trade/Industry (career and vocational guidance). Western Regional Secretary, United Ministries in Education, San Fransisco, since 1978: Dir., National Career Development Project, since 1974. Rector of an episcopalian church in Passaic, NJ, 1958–66; Canon Pastor, Grace Cathedral, San Francisco, 1966–68. *Publs:* What Color Is Your Parachute?: A Practical Manual for Job-Hunters and Career-Changers, 1972– (revised annually); (with John Crystal) Where Do I Go from Here with My Life?, 1974, 1980; Quick Job-Hunting Map, 1975; Tea Leaves: A New Look at Resumés, 1977; The Three Boxes of Life and How to Get Out of Them, 1978, 1981; The New Quick Job-Hunting Map, 1985; The New Beginners Quick Job-Hunting Map, 1986. Add: National Career Development Project, United Ministries in Education, P.O. Box 379, Walnut Creek, CA 94596, U.S.A.

BOLLING, Richard (Walker). American, b. 1916. Politics/Government. Rep. from 5th District, Missouri 1949–82, and member, Joint Economic Cttee, 1951–82 (Chmn., 1977–78), and House Rules Cttee, 1955–82 (Chmn., 1979–82), U.S. Congress, Washington, D.C. (Chmn., Select Cttees. on Cttee., 1973–74). *Publs:* House Out of Order, 1965; Power in the House, 1968, 1974; America's Competitive Edge, 1981. Add: P.O. Box 277, Crumpton, Md. 21628, U.S.A.

BOLT, Bruce (Alan). American, b. 1930. Earth sciences, Engineering, Mathematics/Statistics. Prof. of Seismology, and Dir. of the Seismographic Stations, Univ. of California, Berkelely, since 1963. Lectr., then Sr. Lectr., Dept. of Applied Mathematics, Univ. of Sydney, 1954–62. Assoc. Ed., Journal of Computational Physics, 1973–79; Chmn., Geophysical Monograph Bd., American Geophysical Union, 1976–78; Chmn., Panel on National Seismograph Networks, National Academy of Sciences, 1977–80. *Publs:* (ed. with B. Alder and S. Fernbach) Methods in Computational Physics: Seismology: Surface Waves and Earth Oscillations, vol. XI, 1972; (ed., with B. Alder and S. Fernbach) Methods in Computational Physics: Seismology, Body Waves and Sources, vol. XII, 1972; (ed., with B. Alder and S. Fernbach) Methods in Computational Physics: Geophysics, vol. XIII, 1973; (ed.) Cumulative Index 1963–72, Bulletin of the Seismological Society of America, 1973; (with others) Geological Hazards, 1975; Nuclear Explosions and Earthquakes: The Parted Veil, 1976; Earthquakes: A Primer, 1978, 1987; (ed., with O. Anderson) Theory and Experiment Relevant to Geodynamic Processes: Tectonophysics, vol. XXX5, 1976; (ed., with D. Loewenthal) Journal of Computational Physics: Z. Alterman Memorial Volume 29, 1978: (ed.) Earthquakes and Volcanoes: Readings from "Scientific American," 1980; Inside the Earth, 1982; (with K.E. Bullen) Introduction to the Theory of Seismology, 4th ed., 1985; (ed.) Seismic Strong Motion Synthetics, 1987. Add: Seismographic Station, Univ. of California, Berkeley, Calif. 94720, U.S.A.

BOLT, Carol. Canadian, b. 1941. Plays/Screenplays. Dramaturge, 1972–73, Chairwoman, and Mgmt. Cttee., 1973–74, Playwrights Co-op, Toronto. Dramaturge, Toronto Free Theatre, 1973. Writer-in-Residence, Univ. of Toronto, 1977–78. *Publs:* Buffalo Jump, 1972; My Best Friend Is Twelve Feet High, 1972; Cyclone Jack, 1972; Gabe, 1973; Tangleflags, 1973; Red Emma: Queen of the Anarchists, 1974; Maurice, 1975; Shelter, 1975; Carol Bolt: Buffalo Jump, Gabe, Red Emma (3 plays), 1976; One Night Stand, 1977. Add: c/o Great North Agency, 345 Adelaide St. W., Toronto, Ont. M5V 1R5, Canada.

BOLT, Robert (Oxton). British, b. 1924. Plays/Screenplays. Schoolmaster, Bishopsteignton, Devon, 1950–51, and Millfield Sch., Street, Somerset, 1952–58. *Publs:* Flowering Cherry, 1958; A Man for All Seasons, 1960; The Tiger and the Horse, 1961; Lawrence of Arabia (screenplay), 1962; Gentle Jack, 1965; The Thwarting of Baron Bolligrew, 1966; Doctor Zhivago: The Screenplay Based on the Novel by Boris Pasternak, 1966; Three Plays, 1967; Ryan's Daughter (screenplay), 1970; Vivat! Vivat Regina!, 1971; State of Revolution, 1977; The Bounty (screenplay), 1984; The Mission (screenplay), 1986. Add: c/o Margaret Ramsay Ltd., 14a Goodwin's Ct., London WC2, England.

BOLTHO, Andrea. German, b. 1939. Economics. Fellow and Tutor in Economics, Magdalen Coll., Oxford since 1977. Head of Div., Economics Dept., Organisation for Economic Co-operation and Develop-

ment (OECD), Paris, 1966–77. *Publs:* Foreign Trade Criteria in Socialist Economies, 1971; Japan: An Economic Survey, 1975; (ed.) The European Economy, 1982. Add: Magdalen Coll., Oxford OX1 4AU, England.

BOLTON, Evelyn. *See* **BUNTING**, Eve.

BOMBECK, Erma. American, b. 1927. Humor/Satire. Author of syndicated newspaper column "At Wit's End," since 1965; author of column "Up the Wall," Good Housekeeping, 1969–76. Writer, Dayton Journal Herald, 1949–53. *Publs:* At Wit's End (collection of columns), 1967; (with Bil Keane) Just Wait Till You Have Children of Your Own!, 1971; I Lost Everything in the Post-Natal Depression, 1974; The Grass Is Always Greener over the Septic Tank, 1976; If Life Is a Bowl of Cherries, What Am I Doing in the Pits, 1978; Aunt Erma's Cope Book, 1979; Erma Bombeck Giant Economy Size, 1983; Motherhood: The Second Oldest Profession, 1983; Four of a Kind, 1985; Family: The Ties that Bind... and Gag!, 1987. Add: c/o Universal Press Syndicate, 4900 Main Street, Kansas City, Mo. 64112, U.S.A.

BOND, C(hristopher Godfrey). British, b. 1945. Novels/Short stories, Plays/Screenplays. Artistic Dir., Half Moon Theatre, London, Liverpool Playhouse, and Everyman Theatre, Liverpool, since 1976. Actor, 1968–70, and Resident Dramatist, 1970–71, Victoria Theatre, Stoke on Trent. *Publs:* You Want Drink Something Cold (novel), 1969; Sweeney Todd: The Demon Barber of Fleet Street, 1974. Add: c/o Blanche Marvin, 21a St. John's Wood High St., London NW8, England.

BOND, Edward. British, b. 1934. Plays/Screenplays, Songs/lyrics/libretti. *Publs:* Saved, 1966; Narrow Road to the Deep North, 1968; Early Morning, 1968; The Pope's Wedding and Other Plays, 1971; Lear, 1972; The Sea, 1973; Bingo: Scenes of Money and Death, 1974; (adaptor) Spring's Awakening, 1974; The Fool, 1975; We Come to the River (libretto), 1976; A-A-America!—The Swing and Grandma Faust, 1976; A-A-America, and Stone, 1976; Plays, 3 vols., 1977–87; The Woman, 1978; The Bundle, 1978; Theatre Poems and Songs, 1978; The Worlds; 1980; The Cat (libretto), 1980; The Restoration, 1981; Summer, 1982; Human Cannon, 1985; War Plays (Red, Black and Ignorant; The Tin Can Riots; Great Peace), 1985; Jackets, 1989; The Company of Men, 1989. Add: c/o Margaret Ramsay Ltd., 14a Goodwin's Ct., London WC2N 4LL, England.

BOND, Harold. American, b. 1939. Poetry. Instr., Cambridge, Mass. Center for Adult Education, since 1968; Founder and Dir., Seminars in Poetry Writing, Belmont, Mass., since 1978. Inst., Poets-in-the-Schools prog., Massachusetts, since 1983 (1971–74, 1977–79). Member, Editorial Bd., Ararat mag. (ed., 1969–70). Instr., Model Cities Higher Education Prog., Boston, 1972; Instr., Poets-in-the-Schools prog., New Hampshire, 1973–76; Instr., New England Poets' Conference, Cambridge, Mass., 1985. *Publs:* The Northern Wall, 1969; Dancing on Water, 1970; The Way It Happens to You, 1979. Add: 11 Chestnut St., Melrose, Mass. 02176, U.S.A.

BOND, (Thomas) Michael. British. Novels, Children's fiction. *Publs:* A Bear Called Paddington, and series, 30 vols., 1958–87; Thursday series, 4 vols., 1966–71; Olga de Polga series, 12 vols., 1971–87; The Day the Animals Went on Strike, 1972; Book of Bears, 1973; How to Make Flying Things, 1975; J.D. Polson, 2 vols, 1980; Monsieur Pamplemousse series (novels), 5 vols., 1983–87; The Pleasures of Paris (guidebook), 1987. Add: 22 Maida Ave., London W2 1SR, England.

BOND, Nancy. American, b. 1945. Children's fiction. Instr. in Children's Literature, Simmons Coll., Boston, since 1979. Head of Overseas Sales Publicity, Tutorial Books, Oxford Univ. Press, London, 1967–68; Asst. Children's Librarian, Lincoln Public Library, Massachusetts, 1969–71; Head Librarian, Levi Heywood Memorial Library, Gardner, Mass., 1973–75; Sr. Secty., Massachusetts Audubon Soc., Lincoln, 1976–77. *Publs:* A String in the Harp, 1976; The Best of Enemies, 1978; Country of Broken Stone, 1980; The Voyage Begun, 1981; A Place to Come Back To, 1984; Another Shore, 1988. Add: 109 The Valley Rd., Concord, Mass. 01742, U.S.A.

BOND, Nelson S(lade). American, b. 1908. Science fiction/Fantasy, Plays/Screenplays, Recreation/Leisure/Hobbies. Freelance writer and book dealer. Public Relations Field Dir., Govt. of Nova Scotia, 1934–35. *Publs:* Mr. Mergenthwirker's Lobblies and Other Fantastic Tales (short stories), 1946, title story as play, 1957; Exiles of Time, 1949; The Thirty-First of February (short stories), 1949; The Remarkable Exploits of Lancelot Biggs, Spaceman (short stories), 1950; The Postal Stationery of Canada: A Reference Catalogue, 1953; No Time Like the Future (short stories), 1954; State of Mind (play), 1958; Animal Farm (play), 1964; Nightmares and Daydreams (short stories), 1968.　Add: 4724 Easthill Dr., Sugarloaf Farms, Roanoke, Va. 24018, U.S.A.

BOND, Ruskin. Indian, b. 1934. Novels/Short stories, Children's fiction, Children's non-fiction. Managing Ed., Imprint, Bombay, 1975–79. *Publs:* The Room on the Roof, 1956; Grandfather's Private Zoo, 1967; The Last Tiger, 1971; Angry River, 1972; The Blue Umbrella, 1974; Once upon a Monsoon Time (memoirs), 1974; Man of Destiny: A Biography of Jawaharlal Nehru, 1976; Night of the Leopard, 1979; Big Business, 1979; The Cherry Tree, 1980; The Road to the Bazaar, 1980; A Flight of Pigeons, 1980; The Young Vagrants, 1981; Flames in the Forest, 1981; The Adventures of Rusty, 1981; Tales and Legends of India, 1982; A Garland of Memories, 1982; To Live in Magic, 1982; Tigers Forever, 1983; Earthquakes, 1984; Getting Granny's Glasses, 1985; Cricket for the Crocodile, 1986; The Eyes of the Eagle, 1987.　Add: Ivy Cottage, Landour, Mussouri, U.P. 248179, India.

BONE, Hugh A. American, b. 1909. Politics/Government. Prof. of Political Science, Univ. of Washington, Seattle, since 1948. Instr., to Asst. Prof., Univ. of Maryland, College Park, 1937–42, and Queens Coll., NYC, 1942–48. *Publs:* Smear Politics, 1941; (co-author) Current American Government, 1943; American Politics and the Party System, 1949, 3rd ed. 1971; Grass Roots Party Leadership, 1952; Party Committees and National Politics, 1958; (co-author) Washington Politics, 1960; (co-author) Politics and Voters, 1963, 1980; Political Party Management, 1973; (co-author) American Democracy: Democracy and Liberty in Balance, 1976; The People's Right to Know, 1979; Public Policy Making, Washington Style, 1980.　Add: 6001 51st St., N.E., Seattle, Wash. 98115, U.S.A.

BONE, J(esse) F(ranklin). American, b. 1916. Science fiction/Fantasy, Animals/Pets. Instr. of Veterinary Medicine, 1950–52, Asst. Prof., 1953–57, Assoc. Prof., 1958–65, and Prof., 1965–79, Oregon State Univ., Corvallis. *Publs:* Observations of the Ovaries of Infertile and Reportedly Infertile Dairy Cattle, 1954; Animal Anatomy, 1958, rev. ed. as Animal Anatomy and Physiology, 1975, 1982; (ed.) Canine Medicine, 1959, 1962; The Lani People, 1962; (co-ed.) Equine Medicine and Surgery, 1963, 1972; Legacy, 1976; The Meddlers, 1976; (with R. Myers) Gift of the Manti, 1977; Confederation Matador, 1978; Animal Anatomy and Physiology, 1979, 3rd ed. 1988.　Add: 3329 S.W. Cascade Ave., Corvallis, Ore. 97333, U.S.A.

BONETT, Emery. *See* **CARTER,** Felicity Winifred.

BONETT, John. *See* **COULSON,** John.

BONHAM, Barbara. American, b. 1926. Mystery/Crime/Suspense, Historical/Romance/Gothic, Children's fiction, Children's non-fiction. *Publs:* Diagnosis: Love, 1964; Challenge of the Prairie, 1965; Army Nurse, 1965; Nine Stewart, R.N., 1966; Crisis at Fort Laramie, 1967; To Secure the Blessings of Liberty, 1970; Willa Cather, 1970; Heroes of the Wild West, 1970; Proud Passion, 1976; Sweet and Bitter Fancy, 1976; Passion's Price, 1977; Dance of Desire, 1978; (as Sara North; later pub. under Bonham) Jasmine for My Grave, 1978; The Dark Side of Passion, 1980; Green Willow, 1982; Bittersweet, 1984.　Add: Rural Route 2, Box 123, Franklin, Nebr. 68939, U.S.A.

BONHAM-CARTER, Victor. British, b. 1913. Agriculture/Forestry, Architecture, History, Biography. Historian and Records Officer, Dartington Hall Estate, Devon, 1951–65; Secty., Royal Literary Fund, 1966–82; Joint Secty., Soc. of Authors, London, 1971–78. *Publs:* The English Village, 1952; (with W.B. Curry) Dartington Hall, 1958; Exploring Parish Churches, 1959; Farming the Land, 1959; In a Liberal Tradition, 1960; Soldier True (in U.S. as The Strategy of Victory), 1965; (ed.) Surgeon in the Crimea 1968; The Survival of the English Countryside (in U.S. as Land and Environment), 1971; Authors by Profession, 2 vols., 1978–84. Add: The Mount, Milverton, Taunton, Somerset TA4 1QZ, England.

BONICA, John Joseph. American, b. 1917. Medicine/Health. Prof. of Anesthesiology, Univ. of Washington Sch. of Medicine, Seattle, since 1960 (Assoc., Dept. of Anatomy, 1949–60, Sr. Consultant, Div. of Anesthesiology, 1955–60, Dir., Anesthesia Research Center, 1968); Dir. of the Pain Center, Univ. of Washington Medical Center and affiliated hospitals, 1961–79; Sr. Consultant in Anesthesiology, Veterans Admin. Hosp., Seattle, since 1960. Dir., Dept. of Anesthesiology, Tacoma General Hosp., 1947–63, and Pierce County Hosp., Wash., 1947–63; Attending Anesthesiologist, St. Joseph's Hosp., and Medical Arts Hosp., Tacoma, 1947–60. Pres., American Soc. of Anesthesiologists, 1966; Pres., Assn. of

Univ. Anesthetists, 1969. *Publs:* Manual of Anesthesiology for Medical Students, Interns and Residents, 1947; Management of Pain, 1953; Il Dolore, 1959; Tratemiento del Dolor, 1959; Clinical Applications of Diagnostic and Therapeutic Nerve Blocks, 1959; Principles and Practice of Obstetric Analgesia and Anesthesia, vol. I, 1967, vol. II, 1969; (ed.) Regional Anesthesia: Recent Advances and Current Status, 1971; (with P. Procacci and C. Pagni) Recent Advances on Pain, 1974; Advances in Neurology, vol. IV, 1974; Obstetric Analgesia-Anesthesia: Recent Advances and Current Status, 1974; (with others) Advances in Pain Research and Therapy, 3 vols., 1976–79; Pain, 1980; Pain, Discomfort, and Humanitarian Care, 1981; (ed. with others) Management of Superior Pulmonary Sukus Syndrome, Pancoast Syndrome, 1982; Management of Pain in Clinical Practice, (2 vols) 2nd ed. 1989.　Add: Dept. of Anesthesiology RN-10, Univ. of Wash., Seattle, Wash. 98195, U.S.A.

BONINGTON, Chris(tian). British, b. 1934. Travel/Exploration/Adventure, Autobiography/Memoirs/Personal. Mountaineer, writer and photographer. Leader, successful British climb of Everest Southwest Face, 1975. *Publs:* I Chose to Climb, 1966; Annapurna South Face, 1971; Next Horizon, 1973; Everest Southwest Face: Ultimate Challenge, 1973; (with others) Changabang, 1975; Everest the Hard Way, 1976; Quest for Adventure, 1981; Kongur: China's Elusive Summit, 1982; (co-author) Everest: The Unclimbed Ridge, 1983; The Everest Years, 1986.　Add: Badger Hill, Nether Row, Heskett Newmarket, Wigton, Cumbria, England.

BONNER, Brian. Irish, b. 1917. History. Accountant. *Publs:* Our Inis Eoghain Heritage, 1972; Where Aileach Guards, 1974; That Audacious Traitor, 1975; Derry: An Outline History of the Diocese, 1982; The Homeland of O Dochartaigh: An Historical Conspectus of Inis Eoghain, 1985.　Add: Dunaghrianain, Culdaff, Lifford, Co. Donegal, Ireland.

BONNER, James. American, b. 1910. Biology. Prof. of Biology, California Inst. of Technology, Pasadena since 1946 (member of faculty since 1936). Eastman Prof., Oxford Univ., 1963–64. *Publs:* Plant Biochemistry, 1950, 3rd ed. 1975; Principles of Plant Physiology, 1952; The Next 100 Years, 1957; The Nucleohistones, 1964; The Molecular Biology of Development, 1965; The Next 90 Years, 1967; The Next 80 Years, 1977.　Add: 1914 Edgewood Dr., South Pasadena, Calif. 91030, U.S.A.

BONNER, John Tyler. American, b. 1920. Biology. George M. Moffett Prof., Princeton Univ., N.J., since 1966 (joined faculty, 1947; Chmn., Dept. of Biology, 1965–77, 1983–84, and 1987–88). Member, editorial bds., Growth, 1955, Differentiation, since 1976, and Oxford Surveys in Evolutionary Biology, since 1982. *Publs:* Morphogenesis: An Essay on Development, 1952; Cells and Societies, 1955; The Evolution of Development, 1958; The Cellular Slime Molds, 1959; (ed.) On Growth and Form, by D'Arcy Thompson, abridged ed., 1961; The Ideas of Biology, 1962; Size and Cycle, 1965; The Scale of Nature, 1969; On Development: The Biology of Form, 1974; The Evolution of Culture in Animals, 1980; (with T.A. McMahon) On Size and Life, 1983; The Evolution of Complexity, 1988.　Add: Dept. of Biology, Princeton Univ., Princeton, N.J. 08544, U.S.A.

BONNER, Michael. Pseud. for Anne (Bonner) Glasscock. American, b. 1924. Westerns/Adventure. *Publs:* Kennedy's Gold, 1960; The Iron Noose, 1961; Shadow of a Hawk, 1963; The Disturbing Death of Jenkin Delaney, 1966.　Add: c/o Doubleday, 666 Fifth Ave., New York, NY 10103, U.S.A.

BONNOR, William Bowen. British, b. 1920. Astronomy, Mathematics/Statistics, Physics. Visiting Professorial Research Fellow, Queen Mary Coll., Univ. of London, since 1987. Lectr., Univ. of Liverpool, 1949–57; Reader, 1957–61, and Prof. of Mathematics, 1962–84, Queen Elizabeth Coll., Univ. of London; Sr. Research Officer, Univ. of Cape Town, 1984–87. *Publs:* (with H. Bondi, R.A. Lyttleton and G.J. Whitrow) Rival Theories of Cosmology, 1960; The Mystery of the Expanding Universe, 1964; Status of General Relativity, 1969; (co-ed.) Classical General Relativity, 1983.　Add: Sch. of Mathematics, Queen Mary Coll., Mile End Rd., London E1 4NS, England.

BONSALL, Crosby (Newell). Has also written as Crosby Newell. American, b. 1921. Children's fiction. Worked in advertising agencies. *Publs:* The Surprise Party, 1955; Captain Kangaroo's Book, 1958; (as Crosby Newell) Polar Bear Brothers, 1960; (as Crosby Newell) Kippy the Koala, 1960; Tell Me Some More, 1961; Listen, Listen!, 1961; Hurry Up, Slowpoke, 1961; Who's a Pest?, 1962; Look Who's Talking, 1962; The of the Hungry Stranger, 1963; What Spot?, 1963; Let Papa Sleep (reader), 1963; It's Mine, 1964; I'll Show you Cats, 1964; The Case of the Cat's Meow, 1965; The Case of the Dumb Bells, 1966; Here's Jellybean Reilly, 1966; Whose Eye Am I?, 1968; The Case of the Scaredy Cats, 1971; The Day I Had to Play with My Sister, 1972; Mine's the Best, 1973; Piggle, 1973; And I Mean It, Stanley, 1974; Twelve Bells for Santa, 1977; The Goodbye Summer, 1979; Who's Afraid of the Dark?, 1980; The Case of the Double Cross, 1980; The Amazing, the Incredible Super Dog, 1986. Add: c/o Harper & Row Inc., 10 E. 53rd St., New York, N.Y. 10022. U.S.A.

BONYTHON, Hugh (Reskymer). Australian, b. 1920. Art. Dir., Bonython Art Gallery, Sydney, since 1965. Broadcaster on Jazz, Australian Broadcasting Commn., since 1937. Dir., Speedways Pty. Ltd., Adelaide, 1953–73; Dir., Bonython Art Gallery, Adelaide, 1960–72. Member of Council, Australian Sch. of Art, 1960–73; Chmn., Experimental Film and Television Cttee., 1970–71; Member Australian Council for the Arts, 1970–74; Chmn., Govt. Enquiry into the Crafts, 1972–74. Australian National Hydroplane Champion, 1956, 1957, and Australian National Speedway Champion, 1956, 1959. *Publs:* (ed.) Modern Australian Painting and Sculpture, 1960; Modern Australian Painting 1960–70, 1970; Modern Australian Painting 1970–75, 1977. Add: Bonython Art Gallery, 52 Victoria St., Paddington, Sydney, N.S.W., Australia.

BOONE, Daniel R. American, b. 1927. Medicine/Health, Speech/Rhetoric. Consultant, BEH, U.S. Office of Education, since 1968. Prof., Univ. of Arizona Coll. of Medicine, since 1973; Prof. and Dir. of Speech Pathology, Univ. of Arizona, Tucson, since 1973. Asst. Prof., Case Western Reserve Univ., Cleveland, Ohio, 1960–63; Assoc. Prof., Univ. of Kansas Medical Sch., Kansas City, 1963–66; Prof., Univ. of Denver, Colo., 1966–73. *Publs:* An Adult Has Aphasia, 1965; The Voice and Voice Therapy, 1971, 3rd ed. 1983; Cerebral Palsy, 1973; Human Communication and Its Disorders, 1987. Add: Dept. of Speech and Hearing Sciences, of Arizona, Tucson, Ariz. 85721, U.S.A.

BOONE, Pat. (Charles Eugene Boone). American, b. 1934. Social commentary/phenomena, Theology/Religion, Autobiography/Memoirs/Personal. Singer and actor. Pres., Cooga Mooga Film Productions Corp., Beverly Hills, Calif. *Publs:* Twixt Twelve and Twenty, 1958; Between You, Me and the Gatepost, 1960; The Real Christmas, 1961; Care and Feeding of Parents, 1967; A New Song, 1971; Joy, 1973; A Miracle A Day Keeps the Devil Away, 1974; A New Song, 1975; Put Your Life Together, 1976; (with Shirley Boone) The Honeymoon Is Over, 1977; Together: 25 Years with the Boone Family, 1979; Pray to Win, 1980; Pat Boone's Favorite Bible Stories for Children, 1984; (with Shirley Boone) The Marriage Game, 1984. Add: c/o Jim Halsey Co., Inc., 3225 S. Norwood, Tulsa, Okla. 74135, U.S.A.

BOORE, Walter Hugh. British, b. 1904. Novels/Short stories, Poetry, Philosophy, Travel/Exploration/Adventure. *Publs:* Winter Seas (poetry), 1953; Eternity is Swift, 1958; The Valley and the Shadow, 1963; Flower after Rain, 1964; A Window in High Terrace, 1966; The Old Hand, 1966; Cry on the Wind, 1967; Riot of Riches, 1968, Ship to Shore, 1969; First Light: A Study in Belief, 1973; Dale Street: A Tale of Two Worlds, 1976; Odyssey of Dai Lews and Other Short Stories, 1984. Add: 12 Francis St., New Quay, Dyfed SA45 9QL, Wales.

BOORSTIN, Daniel J. American, b. 1914. Engineering/Technology, History, Politics/Government, Social commentary/phenomena. Librarian of Congress, Washington, D.C., 1975–87, now Emeritus; Contributing Ed., U.S. News and World Report mag., since 1987. Member, Commn. on Critical Choices for Americans, since 1973, Bd., Thomas Gilcrease Museum, since 1974, and State Dept., Indo-American Joint Subcomm. for Education and Culture, since 1974; Member, Advisory Bd., Cafritz Foundn., since 1976; Founding Member, Albert Congressional Research and Studies Center, since 1979. Member, Presidential Task Force on the Arts and Humanities, since 1981; Member, Board of Editors, Encyclopedia Britannica, since 1981; Member, Research Advisory Comm., National Air and Space Museum, since 1984. Asst. Prof., Swarthmore Coll., Pa., 1942–44; Prof. of American History, and Preston and Sterling Morton Distinguished Service Prof. of History, Univ. of Chicago, 1944–69; Dir., National Museum of History and Technology, Washington, D.C., 1969–73; Sr. Historian, Smithsonian Instn., Washington, 1973–75. Trustee, Colonial Williamsburg, 1969–84, and American Film Inst., 1972–77; Member, Japan-U.S. Friendship Commn., 1978–84. *Publs:* The Mysterious Science of the Law, 1941; The Lost World of Thomas Jefferson, 1948; The Genius of American Politics, 1953; The Americans: The Colonial Experience, 1958; America and the Image of Europe, 1960; (ed.) A Lady's Life in the Rocky Mountains, 1960; The Image, 1962;

The Americans: The National Experience, 1965; (ed.) An American Primer, 2 vols., 1966; The Landmark History of the American People: From Plymouth to Appomattox, 1968; The Decline of Radicalism, 1969; The Landmark History of the American People: From Appomattox to the Moon, 1970; The Sociology of the Absurd, 1970; (ed.) American Civilization, 1972; The Americans: The Democratic Experience, 1973; Democracy and its Discontents, 1974; Portraits from the Americans: The Democratic Experience, 1976; The Exploring Spirit, 1977; The Republic of Technology, 1978; (with Brooks M. Kelley) A History of the United States, 1980; The Discoverers, 1983; Hidden History, 1987. Add: 3541 Ordway St. N.W., Washington, D.C. 20016, U.S.A.

BOOT, John C.G. Dutch, b. 1936. Economics, Mathematics/Statistics. Prof. of Mgmt. Science, State Univ. of New York, Buffalo, since 1965. *Publs:* Quadratic Programming, 1964; (co-author) Introduction to Operations Research and Management Science, 1964; Mathematical Reasoning in Economics and Management Science, 1967; (co-author) Statistical Analysis for Managerial Decisions, 1970, 1974; Common Globe or Global Commons, 1974. Add: Jacobs Center, State Univ. of N.Y., Buffalo, N.Y. 14260, U.S.A.

BOOTH, Edwin. Also writes as Don Blunt and Jack Hazard. American. Westerns/Adventure, Biography. Former post office clerk, guide, grocery store mgr., and accountant. Secty.-Treas., 1963–67, and Vice-Pres., 1970, Western Writers of America. *Publs:* Showdown at Warbird, 1957; Jinx Rider, 1957; Boot Heel Range, 1958; The Man Who Killed Tex, 1958; The Trail to Tomahawk, 1958; Wyoming Welcome, 1959; Danger Trail, 1959, in U.K. as Danger on the Trail, 1960; Lost Valley, 1960; The Broken Window, 1960; The Desperate Dude, 1960; Return to Apache Springs, 1960; (as Jack Hazard) Crooked Spur, 1960; Reluctant Lawman, 1961; Outlaw Town, 1961; The Troublemaker, 1961; (as Don Blunt) Short Cut, 1962; Valley of Violence, 1962; Sidewinder, 1962; Hardcase Hotel, 1963; John Sutter, Californian (biography), 1963; (as Don Blunt) Dead Giveaway, 1963; Devil's Canyon, 1964; The Dry Gulchers, 1964; The Stolen Saddle, 1964; Renegade Guns, 1965; Trouble at Tragedy Springs, 1966; Triple Cross Trail, 1967; Shoot-Out at Twin Buttes, 1967; No Spurs for Johnny Loop, 1967; One Man Posse, 1967; The Man from Dakota, 1968; Stranger in Buffalo Springs, 1969; The Backshooters, 1969; The Prodigal Gun, 1971; Grudge Killer, 1971; Hardesty, 1971; Stage to San Felipe, 1972; Bushwack, 1974; Small Spread, 1974; The Colt-Packin' Parson, 1975; Ambush at Adams Crossing, 1976; Crossfire, 1977; The Colorado Gun, 1980; Leadville, 1980; Rebel's Return, 1980. Add: 1850 Alice St., No. 712, Oakland, Calif. 94612, U.S.A.

BOOTH, Geoffrey. *See* **TANN,** Jennifer.

BOOTH, Ken. British, b. 1943. International relations/Current affairs, Military/Defence, Politics/Government. Reader, Dept. of Intnl. Politics, University Coll. of Wales, Aberystwyth, since 1985 (Lectr., 1967–69; Sr. Lectr., 1979–85). Sr. Research Fellow, Centre for Foreign Policy Studies, Dalhousie Univ., Halifax, N.S., 1979–81. *Publs:* The Military Instrument in Soviet Foreign Policy 1917–1972, 1974; (ed. with Michael MacGwire and John McDonnell) Soviet Naval Policy: Objectives and Constraints, 1974; (with others) Contemporary Strategy: Theories and Policies, 1975, 2nd ed., vols., 1987; Navies and Foreign Policy, 1977; (joint ed. and contrib. with Moorhead Wright) American Thinking about Peace and War: Reflections 200 Years On, 1978; Strategy and Ethnocentrism, 1979; Law, Force, and Diplomacy at Sea, 1985. Add: Dept. of Intnl. Politics, University Coll. of Wales, Aberystwyth, Dyfed SY23 3DB, Wales.

BOOTH, Martin. British, b. 1944. Novels, Poetry, Literature, Biography. Poetry Critic, Tribune, since 1970; Literary Critic for The Tablet, and British Book News; also travel journalist. *Publs:* fiction—The Carrier, 1978; The Bad Track, 1980; Hiroshima Joe, 1985; The Jade Pavilion, 1987; Black Chameleon, 1988; Dreaming of Samarkand, 1989; poetry—The Crying Embers, 1971; Coronis, 1973; Snath, 1975 The Brevities, 1975; The Knotting Sequence, 1977; Extending Upon the Kingdom, 1978; Devil's Wine, 1980; The Cnot Dialogues, 1981; Meeting the Snowy North Again, 1982; Killing the Moscs, 1985; (trans) Stalks of Jade; other—Travelling Through the Senses: The Poetry of George MacBeth, 1984; British Poetry 1964–84: Driving Through the Barricades, 1985; Carpet Sahib: A Life of Jim Corbett, 1986; A History of the Triads: Chinese Secret Societies, 1989; editor—(with George Macbeth) The Book of Cats, 14 vols. since 1976; Contemporary British and North American Verse, 1981; A Love of Minute Particulars: The Selected Poems of Robert Bly, 1986; The Selected Poems of Aleister Crowley, 1986. Add: c/o A.M. Heath and Co., 79 St. Martin's Lane, London WC2N 4AA, England.

BOOTH, Philip. American, b. 1925. Poetry. Prof. of English and Poet-in-Residence, Syracuse Univ., N.Y., 1965–86 (Assoc. Prof., 1961–65). Member of faculty, Wellesley Coll., Mass., 1954–61. *Publs:* Letter from a Distant Land, 1957; (ed.) The Dark Island, 1960; The Islanders, 1961; (ed.) Syracuse Poems, 1965, 1970, 1973, 1978; Weathers and Edges, 1966; Margins, 1970; Available Light, 1976; Before Sleep, 1980; Relations: Selected Poems 1950–85, 1986. Add: Main St., Castine, Me. 04421, U.S.A.

BOOTH, Wayne Clayson. American, b. 1921. Literature, Speech/Rhetoric. George M. Pullman Distinguished Service Prof. of English, Univ. of Chicago, since 1962 (Dean of Coll., 1964–69; Chmn., Cttee. on Ideas and Methods, 1972–75). Co-Ed., Critical Inquiry; Member, Editorial Bd., Novel, Philosophy and Rhetoric, and Scholia Satyrica. Asst. Instr. of English, Univ. of Chicago, 1947–50; Lectr., Brigham Young Univ., Provo, Utah, 1950; Asst. Prof., Haverford Coll., Pa., 1950–53; Prof. of English and Chmn. of Dept., 1953–62, and Trustee, 1965–75, Earlham Coll., Richmond, Ind. Member, Exec. Council, 1971–75, and Pres., 1980–82, Modern Language Assn. *Publs:* The Rhetoric of Fiction, 1961; (ed.) The Knowledge Most Worth Having, 1967; Now Don't Try to Reason with Me: Essays and Ironies for a Credulous Age, 1970; A Rhetoric of Irony, 1974; Modern Dogma and the Rhetoric of Assent, 1974; Critical Understanding: The Powers and Limits of Pluralism, 1979; (with Marshall Gregory) The Harper and Row Reader, 1984; (with Marshall Gregory) The Harper and Row Rhetoric, 1987; The Company We Keep: Ethical Criticism and the Ethics of Reading, 1988; The Vocation of a Teacher: Occasions for Rhetoric 1967–88, 1989. Add: Dept. of English, 1050 E. 59th St., Univ. of Chicago, Chicago, Ill. 60637, U.S.A.

BORCHARDT, Frank L. American, b. 1938. Literature. Assoc. Prof. of German, Duke Univ., Durham, N.C., since 1971. Asst. Prof. of German, Northwestern Univ., Evanston, Ill., 1965–68; Asst. Prof. of German and Comparative Literature, Queens Coll., City Univ. of New York, Flushing, 1968–71; Fulbright Research Fellow, Univ. of Wurzburg, W. Germany, 1971–72. *Publs:* German Antiquity in Renaissance Myth, 1971. Add: 1531 Hermitage Ct., Durham, N.C. 27707, U.S.A.

BORENSTEIN, Emily. American, b. 1923. Poetry. Psychiatric Social Work Therapist. *Publs:* Woman Chopping, 1978; Finding My Face, 1979; Cancer Queen, 1979; Night of the Broken Glass, 1981. Add: 189 Highland Ave., Middletown, N.Y. 10940, U.S.A.

BORER, Mary Cathcart. British, b. 1906. Children's fiction, Archaeology/Antiquities, Children's non-fiction, History, Travel/Exploration/Adventure. Research Asst., Ethnographical Dept., Wellcome Historical Medical Museum, 1928–35; Film scriptwriter, 1939–51; Story Ed., Children's Entertainment Films, Rank Org., 1944–51. *Publs:* Kilango, 1936; Taha, the Egyptian, 1937; The House with the Blue Door, 1939; The Highcroft Mystery, 1939; The Valley of the White Lake, 1948; Distant Hills, 1951; The Birthday Present, 1954; The Baobab Tree, 1955; The Dragons Remembered, 1956; Sophie and the Countess, 1960; People Like Us, 1960; Mankind in the Making, 1962; The City of London, 1962; Citizenship, 1962; Women Who Made History, 1963; Africa: A History, 1963; Britain 20th Century, 1966; Famous Rogues, 1966; People of Medieval England, 1966; People of Tudor England, 1966; Covent Garden, 1967; England's Markets, 1968; People of Stuart England, 1968; People of Georgian England, 1969; People of Victorian England, 1969; What Became of the Mamelukes?, 1969; Agincourt, 1970; The First World War, 1970; Liverpool, 1971; The Boer War, 1971; A Visitor's Guide to Britain, 1971; The British Hotel Through the Ages, 1972; Two Villages: History of Chelsea and Kensington, 1973; A Week in London, 1973; The American Civil War, 1974; Background to Archaeology, 1975; Mayfair: The Years of Grandeur, 1975; Willingly to School: A History of Women's Education, 1976; Hampstead and Highgate: The Story of Two Hilltop Villages, 1976; The City of London, 1977; London Walks and Legends, 1981; The Story of Covent Garden, 1984; An Illustrated Guide to London 1800, 1988. Add: Robin Hill, Station Rd., Tring, Herts. HP23 5NG, England.

BORGENICHT, Miriam. American, b. 1915. Mystery/Crime/Suspense. *Publs:* A Corpse in Diplomacy, 1949; Ring and Walk In, 1952; Don't Look Back, 1956; To Borrow Trouble, 1964; Extreme Remedies, 1967; Margin for Doubt, 1968; The Tomorrow Trap, 1969; A Very Thin Line, 1970; Roadblock, 1972; No Bail for Dalton, 1974; True or False?, 1982; Fall From Grace, 1984; False Colors, 1985; Still Life, 1986; Booked for Death, 1987. Add: c/o Bobbs Merrill, 4300 W. 62nd St., Indianapolis, Ind. 46268, U.S.A.

BORKO, Harold. American, b. 1922. Information science/Computers, Librarianship. Prof. of Library and Information Science, Univ. of California, Los Angeles. *Publs:* Computer Applications in the Behavioral Sciences, 1962; Automated Language Processing, 1967; (with H. Sackman) Computers and the Problems of Society, 1972; Targets for Research in Library Education, 1973; (with C.L. Bernier) Abstracting Concepts and Methods, 1975; (with C.L. Bernier) Indexing Concepts and Methods, 1978. Add: Univ. of California, Sch. of Library and Information Science, 405 Hilgard Ave., Los Angeles, Calif. 90024, U.S.A.

BORLAND, Kathryn. Writes with Helen Ross Speicher under joint pseuds. Alice Abbott, Jane Land, and Jane and Ross Land. American, b. 1916. Novels/Short stories, Historical/Romance/Gothic, Children's fiction, Children's non-fiction. Ed., North Side Topics weekly newspaper, Indianapolis, 1939–42. *Publs:* all with Helen Ross Speicher—(as Alice Abbott) Southern Yankees, 1960; (as Alice Abbott) Allan Pinkerton, Young Detective , 1962; (as Jane and Ross Land) Miles and the Big Black Hat, 1963; (as Alice Abbott) Everybody Laughed and Laughed, 1964; (as Alice Abbott) Eugene Field, Young Poet, 1964; (as Alice Abbott) Phillis Wheatley, Young Colonial Poet, 1968; (as Alice Abbott) Harry Houdini, Young Magician, 1969; (as Alice Abbott) Clocks, From Shadow to Atom, 1969; (as Alice Abbott) Good-by to Stony Crick, 1974; (as Alice Abbott) The Third Tower (romance novel), 1974; (as Jane Land) Stranger in the Land (novel), 1974; (as Alice Abbott) Good-bye, Julie Scott (romance novel), 1975. Add: 1050 S. Maish Rd., Frankfurt, Ind. 46041, U.S.A.

BORNSTEIN, George. American, b. 1941. Literature. Prof. of English, Univ. of Michigan, Ann Arbor, since 1975 (Assoc. Prof., 1970–75). Asst. Prof. of Humanities, Massachusetts Inst. of Technology, Cambridge, 1966–69; Asst. Prof. of English, Rutgers Univ., New Brunswick, N.J., 1969–70. *Publs:* Yeats and Shelley, 1970; (with Daniel Fader) British Periodicals of the 18th and 19th Centuries, 1972; (with Daniel Fader) Two Centuries of British Periodicals, 1974; Transformations of Romanticism in Yeats, Eliot, and Stevens, 1976; The Post-Romantic Consciousness of Ezra Pound, 1977; (ed.) Romantic and Modern; Revaluations of Literary Tradition, 1977; (ed.) Ezra Pound Among the Poets, 1985; (ed.) W.B. Yeats: The Early Poetry, 1987; Poetic Remaking: The Art of Browning, Yeats, and Pound, 1988. Add: 2020 Vinewood, Ann Arbor, Mich. 48104, U.S.A.

BORRIE, John, New Zealander, b. 1915. Art, History, Medicine/Health. Surgeon in Charge, Southern Thoracic Surgical Unit., Otago Hosp. Bd. and Univ. of Otago, 1952–80, now retired. *Publs:* Graduates Travel Guide, 1957, 18th ed. 1980; Management of Emergencies in Thoracic Surgery, 1958, 3rd ed. 1980; Dunedin Public Art Gallery, 1964; Lung Cancer: Surgery and Survival, 1965; Olveston, 1968, 15th ed., 1982; Despite Captivity, 1974; Art and Observables in the Otago Medical School, 1974; (ed.) In Durance Vile, by John Brown, 1980. Add: Otago Medical School, P.O. Box 913, Dunedin, New Zealand.

BORRIE, Wilfred (David). Australian, b. 1913. Demography. Emeritus Prof. of Demography, Australian National Univ., Canberra, since 1978 (Sr. Research Fellow, 1948–51; Reader in charge of Dept. of Demography, 1952–57; Prof., 1957–78; Dir., Research Sch. of Social Sciences, 1968–73). Exec. Dir., Acad. of the Social Sciences in Australia, 1978–85. Hon. Secty., 1953–58, Chmn., 1962–64, Social Science Research Council of Australia; Chmn., U.N. Population Commn., 1966–69. *Publs:* Population Trends and Policies, 1948; Italians and Germans in Australia, 1954; The Cultural Integration of Immigrants, 1959; Australia's Population Structure and Growth, 1965; The Growth and Control of World Population. 1970; Population, Environment and Society, 1973; Population and Australia, 2 vols, 1975; Supplementary Report, 1978; (contrib. and ed.) Implications of Australian Population Trends, 1981. Add: 29 Norman St., Deakin, A.C.T. 2600, Australia.

BORTEN, Helen. American, b. 1930. Children's fiction, Children's non-fiction. *Publs:* Do You See What I See?, 1959; Do You Hear What I hear?, 1960; A Picture Has a Special Look, 1961; Copycat, 1962; Do You Move as I Do?. 1963; Halloween, 1965; The Jungle, 1968; Do You Know What I Know?, 1970; Do You Go Where I Go?, 1972. Add: c/o Harper and Row, 10 E. 53rd St., New York, NY 10022, U.S.A.

BOSKIN, Joseph. American, b. 1929. History, Race relations, Social commentary. Prof. of History and Afro-American Studies, and Dir. of Urban Studies and Public Policy Prog., Boston Univ., Mass., since 1969. Member, Advisory Bd., Humor in Life & Letters Series. Faculty member, State Univ. of Iowa, 1959–60, and Univ. of Southern California, Los Angeles, 1960–69. Exec. Member and Consultant, Riots & Disorder Task Force, California Council on Criminal Justice, 1968–70; Exec. Member, Coordinating Council of Higher Education, Title I, State of California,

1970–71. *Publs:* (with Fred Krinsky) The Oppenheimer Affair: A Political Play in Three Acts, 1968; (ed.) Opposition Politics: The Anti-New Deal Tradition, 1968; Urban Racial Violence in the 20th Century, 1969, 1976; (with Robert R. Rosenstone) Seasons of Rebellion: Protest and Radicalism in Recent America, 1971, 1980; Into Slavery: Racial Decisions in the Virginia Colony, 1976; Issues in American Society, 1978; Humor and Social Change in 20th Century America, 1979; Sambo: The Rise & Demise of an American Jester, 1986. Add: Dept. of History, Boston Univ., 226 Bay State Rd., Boston, Mass. 02215, U.S.A.

BOSKOFF, Alvin. American, b. 1924. Politics/Government, Sociology, Urban studies. Prof. of Sociology, Emory Univ., Atlanta, Ga., since 1958. *Publs:* (with H. Becker) Modern Sociological Theory, 1957; The Sociology of Urban Regions, 1962, rev. ed. 1970; (with W. Cahnman) Sociology and History, 1964; Theory in American Sociology, 1969; The Mosaic of Sociological Theory, 1972; (with J. Doby and W. Pendleton) Sociology: The Study of Man in Adaptation, 1973. Add: Dept. of Sociology, Emory Univ., Atlanta, Ga. 30322, U.S.A.

BOSLAND, Chelcie Clayton. American, b. 1901. Economics, Money/Finance. Prof. Emeritus, Brown Univ., Providence, R.I., since 1968 (Asst. Prof., 1929–36; Assoc. Prof., 1936–45; Eastman Prof. of Political Economy, 1947–68). Instr. of Economics, Univ of Michigan, Ann Arbor, 1924–26; Instr. in Finance, Univ. of Minnesota, Minneapolis, 1926–29. Pres., American Finance Assn., 1941. *Publs:* Common Stock Theory of Investment, 1937; Corporate Finance and Regulation, 1949; Estate Tax Valuation in the Sale or Merger of Small Firms, 1963; Valuation Theories and Decisions of the S.E.C., 1964. Add: Jerry Brown Farm, Wakefield, R.I. 02879, U.S.A.

BOSLEY, Keith. British, b. 1937. Poetry, Translations. *Publs:* Tales from the Long Lakes: Finnish Legends from the Kalevala (in U.S. as The Devil's Horse: Tales from the Kalevala), 1966; Russia's Other Poets (in U.S. as Russia's Underground Poets), 1968; An Idiom of Night, translations from Pierre Jean Jouve, 1968; The Possibility of Angels: Poems, 1969; The War Wife: Vietnamese Poetry (trans.), 1972; And I Dance: Poems Original and Translated, 1972; The Song of Aino, 1973; Dark Summer, 1976; (trans.) The Song of Songs, 1976; (trans.) Finnish Folk Poetry: Epic, 1977; (trans.) Mallarmé: The Poems, 1977; A Round O, translations from Frénaud, 1977; Whitsongs, translations from Leino, 1978; Stations, 1979; (ed.) The Elek Book of Oriental Verse (in U.S. as Poetry of Asia), 1979; (trans.) A Reading of Ashes, by Jerzy Ficowski, 1981; (trans.) From the Theorems of Master Jean de la Ceppède, 1983; (trans.) Wanton Loverboy, 1985; A Chiltern Hundred, 1987; (trans.) The Kalevala, 1989; (trans.) Camões: Selected Poems, 1989. Add: 108 Upton Rd., Slough SL1 2AW, England.

BOSMAJIAN, Haig. American, b. 1928. Civil liberties/Human rights, Language/Linguistics, Speech/Rhetoric. Prof., Dept. of Speech, Univ. of Washington, Seattle, since 1964. Asst. Prof., Univ. of Connecticut, Storrs, 1960–64. *Publs:* (ed.) Readings in Speech, 1965; (ed.) The Rhetoric of the Speaker, 1967; (ed.) Readings in Parliamentary Procedure, 1968; (ed. with H. Bosmajian) The Rhetoric of the Civil Rights Movement, 1969; (ed.) The Principles and Practice of Freedom of Speech, 1971; (ed.) The Rhetoric of Nonverbal Communication, 1971; (ed.) Dissent: Symbolic Behavior and Rhetorical Strategies, 1972; (ed. with H. Bosmajian) This Great Argument: The Rights of Women, 1972; The Language of Oppression, 1974; (ed.) Obscenity and Freedom of Expression, 1975; (ed.) Justice Douglas and Freedom of Speech, 1980; (ed.) Censorship, Libraries, and the law, 1982; (ed.) First Amendment in the Classroom Series: vol. I, The Freedom to Read, 1987; vol. II, Freedom of Religion, 1987; vol. III, Freedom of Expression, 1988; vol. IV, Academic Freedom, 1988; vol. V, Freedom to Publish, 1989. Add: Dept. of Speech, Univ. of Washington, Seattle, Wash. 98195, U.S.A.

BOSSONE, Richard M. American, b. 1924. Education, Language/Linguistics. Univ. Dean for Instructional Research and Prof. of English, Grad. Sch. of City Univ. of New York, since 1974 (prof. of English, Baruch Coll., 1970–74; Assoc. Prof. of English Education, Richmond Coll., 1967–71). Assoc. Prof. of English Education, Univ. of California, Riverside, 1961–67. *Publs:* (ed.) Talks to Secondary English Teachers, 1963; Remedial English Instruction in California Public Junior Colleges: An Analysis and Evaluation of Current Practices, 1966; The Writing Problems of Remedial English Students in Community Colleges of the City University of New York, 1969; Reading Problems of Community College Students, 1970; (co-author) Basic English: Computer Assisted Instruction, 1970; Teaching Basic English Courses: Readings and Comments, 1971; (co-author) Handbook of Basic English Skills, 1971; (co-author) Three Modes of Teaching Remedial English: A Comparative

Analysis, 1973; English Proficiency, 1979; The Writing Proficiency Program, 1982; (co-author) Writing: Process and Skills, 1986. Add: 300 E, 34th St., New York, N.Y. 10016, U.S.A.

BOSTICCO, (Isabel Lucy) Mary. British. Administration/Management, Business/Trade/Industry. Writer and Ed., Cement and Concrete Assn., Wexham Springs, Bucks., 1968–71; Assoc. Ed., Intnl. Mgmt., 1973–74; Press Officer, Bracknell Development, 1974–82. *Publs:* Modern Personnel Management, 1964; Personal Letters for Businessmen, 1965; Etiquette for the Businessman, at Home and Abroad, 1967; Instant Business Letters, 1968; Top Secretary, 1970; (trans.) Modern Filing Methods and Equipment, 1970; Creative Techniques for Management, 1971; The Businessman's Wife, 1972; Teach Yourself Secretarial Practice, 1984. Add: The Oasis, 7A Telston Close, Bourne End, Bucks., England.

BOSTOCK, David. British, b. 1936. Philosophy. Fellow and Tutor in Philosophy. Merton Coll., Oxford, and Lectr. in Philosophy, Oxford Univ., since 1968. Temporary Lectr. in Philosophy, Univ. of Leicester, 1963; Lectr. in Philosophy, Aust. Natl. Univ., Canberra, 1964–67; Loeb Research Fellow, Harvard Univ., Cambridge, Mass., 1967–68. *Publs:* Logic and Arithmetic, 2 vols., 1974–79; Plato's Phaedo, 1986; Plato's Theaetetus, 1988. Add: Merton Coll., Oxford, England.

BOSTOCK, Donald Ivan. British, b. 1924. Music. Musical Dir., Ashford Methodist Church, Middx., since 1947. Asst. Conductor, The Echelforde Singers, 1950–53, and Ashford and District Choral Soc., 1954–58. *Publs:* Choirmastery, 1966. Add: Kerridge, Gorse Hill Lane, Virginia Water, Surrey, England.

BOSTON, L(ucy) M(aria). British, b. 1892. Novels/Short stories, Children's fiction. Autobiography/Memoirs/Personal. *Publs:* Yew Hall, 1954; The Children of Green Knowe, 1957; The River at Green Knowe, 1959; A Stranger at Green Knowe, 1961; The Castle of Yew, 1965; The Sea Egg, 1967; Persephone, 1969; The House that Grew, 1969; The Horned Man, 1970; Memory in a House, 1973; The Guardians of the House, 1974; The Fossil Snake, 1975; The Stones of Green Knowe, 1976; Perverse and Foolish: A Memoir of Childhood and Youth, 1979. Add: The Manor, Hemingford Grey, Huntingdon PE18 9BN, England.

BOSWELL, John (Eastburn). American, b. 1947. History, Theology/Religion, Social commentary. Prof. of History, Yale Univ., New Haven, since 1982 (Asst. Prof., 1975–81; Assoc. Prof., 1981–82; Dir. of Graduate Studies, 1984–86). *Publs:* The Royal Treasure: Muslim Communities under the Crown of Aragon in the Fourteenth Century, 1977; Christianity, Social Tolerance, and Homosexuality: Gay People in Western Europe from the Beginning of the Christian Era to the Fourteenth Century, 1980; The Awful Truth about Publishing, 1986; The Kindness of Strangers: The Abandonment of Children in Western Europe, 1989. Add: 100 York Str., New Haven, CT 06520, U.S.A.

BOSWORTH, Allan R(ucker). Also writes as Alamo Boyd. American, b. 1909. Westerns/Adventure, Children's fiction, History, Autobiography/Memoirs/Personal. Apprentice seaman in the United States Navy, 1922–25, commissioned Ensign in Naval Reserve 1927, active duty, 1940–45, recalled, 1948–60, retired as Capt., 1960; Reporter, San Diego Sun, 1925–26, and San Diego Union, 1926–28; Copyreader, Los Angeles Examiner, 1928–30; Copyreader and News Ed., San Francisco Chronicle, 1930–36; Picture Ed., San Francisco Examiner, 1937. *Publs:* Wherever the Grass Grows, 1941; (as Alamo Boyd) Steel to the Sunset, 1941; Full Crash Dive, 1942, in U.K. as Murder Goes to Sea, 1948; Border Roundup, 1947; Hang and Rattle, 1947; A Cabin in the Hills (non-fiction), 1947; Sancho of the Long, Long Horns (juvenile), 1952; Double Deal, 1947; Bury Me Not, 1948; Ladd of the Lone Star (juvenile), 1952; Ginza Go, Papa-san (non-fiction), 1955; Only the Brave, 1955; The Drifters, 1956; The Lovely World of Richi-san (non-fiction), 1960; The Crows of Edwina Hill, 1961; New Country (non-fiction), 1962; Ozona Country, (non-fiction), 1964; Storm Tide, 1965; America's Concentration Camps (non-fiction), 1967; My Love Affair with the Navy (autobiography), 1969. Add: c/o Marie Rodell–Frances Collin Literary Agency, 110 W. 40th St., New York, NY 10018, U.S.A.

BOSWORTH, R(ichard) J(ames) B(oon). Australian, b. 1943. History, International relations/Current affairs. Assoc. Prof. of History, Univ. of Sydney, since 1981 (Lectr., 1969–73, Sr. Lectr., 1974–80). Deputy Dir., May Foundn. for Italian Studies, since 1981. *Publs:* Benito Mussolini and the Fascist Destruction of Liberal Italy, 1973; (ed. with G. Cresciani) Altro Polo: A Volume of Italian Studies, 1979; Italy, The Least of the Great Powers: Italian Foreign Policy Before the First World War, 1979; Italy and the Approach of the First World War, 1983; (ed. with G. Rizzo)

Altro Polo: Study of Ideas and Intellectuals in Contemporary Italy, 1983; (with J. Witton) Old Worlds and New Australia: A History of Non-British Migration to Australia since the Second World War, 1984; La Politica estera dell'Italia giolittiana, 1985. Add: History Dept., Univ. of Western Australia, Nedlands, W.A. 6009, Australia.

BOTT, George. British, b. 1920. History, Literature. Formerly Sr. English Master and Librarian, Cockermouth Grammar Sch. Book Ed., Scholastic Publs., 1960–68. *Publs:* (ed.) George Orwell: Selected Writings, 1958; (ed.) Read and Relate, 1960; (ed.) Shakespeare: Man and Boy, 1961; Sponsored Talk, 1971; Read and Respond, 1984; Read, Relate, Communicate, 1984. Add: 16 Penrith Rd., Keswick, Cumbria CA12 4HF, England.

BOTTEL, Helen. American, b. 1914. Human relations. Freelance mag. writer and lectr., since 1958; Contrib. Ed., Real World, since 1977. Ed., Illinois Valley News, Cave Junction, Ore., and reporter for Oregon newspapers, 1954–58. *Publs:* To Teens With Love, 1968; Helen Help Us, 1970; Parents' Survival Kit, 1979. Add: 2060 56th Ave., Sacramento, Calif. 95822, U.S.A.

BOTTING, Douglas. British, b. 1934. History, Natural history, Travel/Exploration, Biography. Freelance writer, photographer, and television film-maker, since 1958. *Publs:* Island of the Dragon's Blood (exploration), 1958; The Knights of Bornu (travel), 1961; One Chilly Siberian Morning (travel), 1965; Humboldt and the Cosmos (biography), 1973; Wilderness Europe, 1977; Rio de Janeiro (reportage), 1977; The Pirates (history), 1978; The Second Front (war), 1978; The U-Boats (war), 1979; The Great Airships (history), 1980; Aftermath Europe, 1982; Nazi Gold, 1984; In the Ruins of the Reich, 1985; Wild Britain, 1988; Hitler's Last General, 1989; America's Secret Army, 1989. Add: 44 Worcester Rd., London SW19 7QG, England.

BOTTOMORE, Thomas (Burton). British, b. 1920. Politics/Government, Sociology. Prof. of Sociology, Univ. of Sussex, Brighton, since 1968, Emeritus since 1985. Reader in Sociology, London Sch. of Economics, 1952–64; Prof. of Sociology, Simon Fraser Univ., Vancouver, B.C., 1965–67. *Publs:* (with M. Rubel) Karl Marx: Selected Writings in Sociology and Social Philosophy, 1956; Sociology: A Guide to Problems and Literature, 1962, 3rd ed., 1987; Karl Marx: Early Writings, 1963; Elites and Society, 1964; Classes in Modern Society, 1965; Critics of Society, 1967, 1969; Karl Marx, 1973; Sociology as Social Criticism, 1974; Marxist Sociology, 1974; (with P. Goode) Austro-Marxism, 1978; (with R. Nisbet) A History of Sociological Analysis, 1978; Political Sociology, 1979; A Dictionary of Marxist Thought, 1983; Sociology and Socialism, 1984; The Frankfurt School, 1984; Theories of Modern Capitalism, 1985. Add: Cherry Tree Cottage, East End Lane, Ditchling, Sussex BN6 8UP, England.

BOTTRALL, Margaret (Florence Saumarez). British, b. 1909. Literature, Biography. Univ. Lectr., Dept. of Education, and Sr. Tutor, Hughes Hall, Univ. of Cambridge, until 1972. Hon. Fellow, Lucy Cavendish Coll., Cambridge, since 1980. *Publs:* George Herbert, 1954; Izaak Walton, 1955; Every Man a Phoenix: Studies in 17th Century Autobiography, 1958; (ed.) Personal Records, 1961; (ed.) William Blake: Songs of Innocence and Experience, 1970 (Casebook series); (ed.) Gerard Manley Hopkins: Poems, 1974; Hughes Hall 1885–1985, 1985. Add: 72 Cavendish Ave., Cambridge, England.

BOTTRALL, (Francis James) Ronald. British, b. 1906. Poetry, Travel/Exploration/Adventure. Lector in English, Univ. of Helsingfors, Finland, 1928–31 Commonwealth Fellow, Princeton Univ., N.J., 1931–33; Johore Prof. of English Language and Literature, Raffles Coll., Singapore, 1933–37; Asst. Dir. and Prof. of English, British Inst. Florence, 1937–38; Secty., Sch. of Oriental and African Studies, London, 1939–45; with Air Ministry, 1940–41; British Council Rep. in Sweden, 1941, Italy, 1945, Brazil, 1954, Greece, 1957, and Cultural Counsellor, Tokyo, 1959–61; Chief, Fellowships and Training Branch, Food and Agricultural Org. of U.N., Rome, 1963–65; Reviewer Times Literary Supplement, 1965–74. *Publs:* The Loosening and Other Poems, 1931; Festivals of Fire, 1934; The Turning Path, 1939; (ed. with G. Ekelof) Dikter, by T.S. Eliot, 1942; (ed. with M. Bottrall) The Zephyr Book of English Verse, 1945; Farewell and Welcome: Poems, 1945: (ed. with M. Bottrall) Collected English Verse, 1946; Selected Poems, 1946; The Palisades of Fear: Poems, 1949; Adam Unparadised, 1954; The Collected Poems of Ronald Bottrall, 1961; Rome, 1968; Day and Night, 1973; Poems 1955–1973, 1974; Reflections on the Nile, 1980; Against a Setting Sun: Poems 1974–1983, 1984. Lives in Alicante, Spain. Add: c/o 39 New Cavendish St., London W1M 7RJ, England.

BOULDING, Kenneth Ewart. American, b. 1910. Poetry, Economics, Social sciences. Prof. Emeritus, since 1980, and Research Assoc. & Project Dir., Inst. of Behavioral Science, Univ. of Colorado, Boulder (Prof. of Economics and a prog. dir., Inst. of Behavioral Science, 1968–81). Prof. of Economics, Univ. of Michigan, Ann Arbor, 1949–68. Pres., American Economics Assn., 1968, and American Assn. for the Advancement of Science, 1979. *Publs:* Economic Analysis, 1941, 4th ed., 1966; The Economics of Peace, 1945; The Naylor Sonnets, 1945; A Reconstruction of Economics, 1950; The Organizational Revolution, 1953; The Image, 1956; Principles of Economic Policy, 1958; The Skills of the Economist, 1958; Conflict and Defense, 1962; The Meaning of the Twentieth Century, 1964; The Impact of the Social Sciences, 1966; Beyond Economics, 1968; Economics as a Science, 1970; A Primer on Social Dynamics, 1970; The Prosperity of Truth, 1970; The Economy of Love and Fear: A Preface to Grants Economics, 1973, 1981; Sonnets from the Interior Life and Other Autobiographical Verse, 1975; Stable Peace, 1978; Ecodynamics: A New Theory of Social Evolution, 1978; (co-author) The Social System of the Planet Earth, 1980; Evolutionary Economics, 1981; Human Betterment, 1985; The World as a Total System, 1985; Conflict and Defense: A General Theory, 1988. Add: Inst. of Behavioral Science, Univ. of Colorado, Campus Box 484, Boulder, Colo. 80309, U.S.A.

BOULTON, David. British, b. 1935. History, Politics. Head, News, Current Affairs and Regional Progs., Granada TV, Bolton, Lancs., since 1985 (joined co., 1965; edited and produced What the Papers Say, and World in Action progs.). *Publs:* Objection Overruled, 1968; The UVF: Protestant Paramilitaries in Ulster, 1973; The Lockheed Papers, 1978; The Grease Machine, 1978; Adam Sedgwick's Dent, 1984. Add: Hobson's Farm, Dent, Sedburgh, Cumbria, England.

BOULTON, James T(hompson). British, b. 1924. Literature. Dir., Inst. for Advanced Research in the Humanities, Univ. of Birmingham, since 1987 (Prof. of English Studies, and Head of Dept., 1975–88). Prof. of English Literature, Univ. of Nottingham, 1964–75. *Publs:* (ed.) Edmund Burke: Philosophical Enquiry into . . . Sublime and Beautiful, 1958, 1987; (ed.) C.F.G. Masterman's The Condition of England, 1960; The Language of Politics in the Age of Wilkes and Burke, 1963; (ed.) Dryden's Essay of Dramatick Poesie, etc., 1964; (ed.) Defoe: Prose and Verse, 1965; (ed.) English Satiric Poetry: Dryden to Byron, 1966; (ed.) Lawrence in Love: Letters from D.H. Lawrence to Louie Burrows, 1968; (ed. with S.T. Bindoff) Research in Progress in English and Historical Studies, 2 vols., 1971–75; (ed.) Samuel Johnson: The Critical Heritage, 1971; (ed.) Defoe's Memoirs of a Cavalier, 1972; (ed.) The Letters of D.H. Lawrence, vol. 1, 1979, vol. 2, 1982, vol. 3, 1984, vol. 4, 1987, vol. 5, 1989. Add: 6 Pebble Mill Rd., Birmingham B5 7SA, England.

BOUMA, J(ohanas) L. Also writes as Steve Shannon. Westerns/Adventure. *Publs:* Danger Trail, 1954; Texas Spurs, 1955; Border Vengeance, 1956; (as Steven Shannon) The Hell-Fire Kid, 1957; Burning Valley, 1957; Avenging Gun, 1958; Outlaw Frenzy, 1967; Bitter Guns, 1972; Slaughter at Crucifix Canyon, 1975; Vengeance, 1976; Six-Gun Mule-Skinner, 1976; Ride to Violence, 1978; Longrider, 1978; Beyond Vengeance, 1979; Hell on Horseback, 1981; Mediterranean Caper, 1981. Add: c/o Dorchester Publishing Co., 6 E. 39th St., New York, N.Y. 10016, U.S.A.

BOUNDS, Sydney J(ames). Has also written as Wes Saunders. British, b. 1920. Westerns/Adventure, Science fiction/Fantasy. Freelance writer since 1951. Worked for London Transport until 1951. *Publs:* Dimension of Horror, 1953; (as Wes Saunders) Vengeance Valley, 1953; The Moon Raiders, 1955; The World Wrecker, 1956; The Robot Brains, 1957; The Yaqui Trail, 1964; Gun Brothers, 1966; Lynching at Noon City, 1967; The Predators, 1977; Star Trail, 1978. Add: 27 Borough Rd., Kingston-upon-Thames, Surrey KT2 6BD, England.

BOURDEAUX, Michael Alan. British, b. 1934. History, Theology/Religion. Dir., Keston Coll., Kent, since 1970. Research Fellow, Centre for Intnl. Studies, London Sch. of Economics, 1968–71; Research Staff Member, Royal Inst. of Intnl. Affairs, 1971–73. *Publs:* Opium of the People, 1965; Religious Ferment in Russia, 1968; Patriarch and Prophets, 1969; Faith on Trial in Russia, 1971; (ed. with X. Howard-Johnston) Aida of Leningrad, 1972; Land of Crosses: The Struggle for Religious Freedom in Lithuania 1939–78, 1979; Risen Indeed: Lessons in Faith from the U.S.S.R., 1983; (with Lorna Bourdeaux) Ten Growing Soviet Churches, 1987. Add: 34 Lubbock Rd., Chislehurst, Kent BR7 5JJ, England.

BOURDON, David. American, b. 1934. Art. Asst. Ed., Life mag.,

NYC, 1966–71; Assoc. Ed., Smithsonian mag., Washington, 1972–74; Art Critic, The Village Voice, NYC, 1964–66, 1974–77; Sr. Ed., Geo, 1981–83, Vogue mag., NYC, 1983–86. *Publs:* Christo, 1972; Carl Andre: Sculpture 1959–77, 1978; Calder, 1980. Add: 315 W. 23rd St., Apt. 3C, New York, N.Y. 10011, U.S.A.

BOURJAILY, Vance (Nye). American, b. 1922. Novels/Short stories. Dir., MFA Prog., Louisiana State Univ., Baton Rouge, since 1985. Teacher, Writers Workshop, 1957–58, and Assoc. Prof., 1960–64, 1966–67 and 1971–72, and Prof., 1972–80, Univ. of Iowa, Iowa City; Prof. Univ. of Arizona, Tucson, 1980–85. *Publs:* The End of My Life, 1947; (ed.) Discovery 1-6, 1953–55; The Girl in the Abstract Bed (cartoon text), 1954; The Hound of Earth, 1955; Confessions of a Spent Youth, 1960, play, 1971; The Unnatural Enemy, 1963; The Man Who Knew Kennedy, 1967; Brill among the Ruins, 1970; Country Matters: Collected Reports from the Fields and Streams of Iowa and Other Places, 1973; Now Playing at Canterbury, 1976; A Game Men Play, 1980; The Great Fake Book, 1987. Add: c/o William Morris Agency, 1350 Ave. of the Americas, New York, N.Y. 10019, U.S.A.

BOURKE, Vernon J(oseph). American, b. 1907. Philosophy, Theology/Religion, Biography, Translations. Emeritus Prof. of Philosophy, St. Louis Univ., Mo., since 1976 (Prof., 1931–75); Research Prof., Center for Thomistic Studies, Univ. of St. Thomas, Houston, since 1979. Assoc. Ed., The Modern Schoolman, since 1935, American Journal of Jurisprudence, since 1954 and Augustinian Studies, since 1969. Lectr. in Ancient Philosophy, Univ. of Toronto, Canada, 1928–31; Assoc. Ed., Speculum, 1948–68. *Publs:* Augustine's Quest of Wisdom, 1945; St. Thomas and the Greek Moralists, 1947; Ethics, 1951, rev. ed. 1966; (trans.) St. Augustine's Confessions, 1953; (trans.) On the Truth of the Catholic Faith, Book Three: Providence, by St. Thomas Aquinas, (2 vols.), 1956; (ed.) St. Augustine's City of God, 1958; (ed.) The Pocket Aquinas, 1960; Will in Western Thought, 1964; (ed.) The Essential Augustine, 1964, rev. ed. 1974; Augustine's View of Reality, 1964; Aquinas' Search for Wisdom, 1965; History of Ethics, 1968; Joy in Augustine's Ethics, 1978; Wisdom from St. Augustine, 1984. Add: Dept. of Philosophy, St. Louis Univ., 221 N. Grand, St. Louis, Mo. 63103, U.S.A.

BOURNE, Kenneth. British, b. 1930. History. Prof. of Intnl. History, London Sch. of Economics, Univ. of London, since 1976 (Lectr., 1957–69; Reader, 1969–76). *Publs:* (contrib. and ed. with D.C. Watt) Studies in International History, 1967; Britain and the Balance of Power in North America, 1815-1908, 1967; The Foreign Policy of Victorian England 1830-1902, 1970; The Blackmailing of the Chancellor, 1975; The Letters of the Third Viscount Palmerston to Lawrence and Elizabeth Sulivan 1804-1863, 1979; Palmerston: The Early Years 1784-1841, 1982; (ed. with D.C. Watt) British Documents on Foreign Affairs, 1984–. Add: 15 Oakcroft Rd., London SE13 7ED, England.

BOURNE, Larry Stuart. Canadian, b. 1939. Regional/Urban planning, Urban studies. Prof. of Geography, Univ. of Toronto, since 1973 (Asst. Prof., 1966–69; Assoc. Prof. 1969–73; Dir., Centre for Urban and Community Studies, 1972–84). *Publs:* The Urban and Regional Economy of Yellowknife, N.W.T., 1964; Private Redevelopment of the Central City, 1967; (ed. and contrib.) Internal Structure of the City: Readings on Space and Environment, 1971, 1982; (ed. with R. Mackinnon, and contrib.) Urban Systems in Central Canada: Selected Papers, 1972; (contrib. and ed. with Mackinnon and J. Simmons) The Form of Cities in Central Canada: Selected Papers, 1973; (contrib. and ed. with Mackinnon, Simmons, and J. Siegel) Urban Futures for Central Canada: Perspectives on Forecasting Growth and Form, 1974; Urban Systems: Strategies for Regulation, 1976; (ed. with J. Simmons) Systems of Cities: Readings on Structure, Growth and Policy, 1978; (ed. with J. Hitchcock) Urban Housing Markets: Recent Directions in Research and Policy, 1980; The Geography of Housing, 1981; (ed. with R. Sinclair and contrib.) Urbanization and Settlement Systems, 1984; Progress in Settlement Systems Geography, 1986; (ed.) Urban Systems in Transition, 1986. Add: 26 Anderson Ave., Toronto, Ont. M5P 1H4, Canada.

BOURNE, Lesley. *See* **MARSH,** Jean.

BOURQUIN, Paul Henry James. Also writes as Richard Amberley, British, b. 1916. Mystery/Crime/Suspense, Historical/Romance/Gothic. Schoolmaster, London Borough of Bromley, 1970–80, now retired. With UK Foreign Office, 1947–50, and H.M.S.O., 1950–67. *Publs:* The Lord of the Ravens, 1961; Beltane Fires, 1964; The Cockpit, 1965; The Seven Reductions, 1966; The Land of Delight, 1967; (as Richard Amberley) Incitement to Murder, 1968; Phocas the Gardener, 1969; (as Richard Amberley) Death on the Stone, 1969; (as Richard Amberley) An Ordinary

Accident, 1970. Add: 9 Broughton Rd., Otford, Kent, England.

BOVA, Ben(jamin William). American, b. 1932. Science fiction, Sciences (general). Social commentary/phenomena. Former Technical Ed., Project Vanguard, Martin Co., Baltimore, Md., and with Physics Dept., Massachusetts Inst. of Technology, Cambridge; Marketing Mgr., Avco Everett Research Lab., Mass., 1960–71; Former Ed., Analog science fiction mag.; Ed. Dir., Omni. *Publs:* The Star Conquerors, 1959; The Milky Way Galaxy, 1961; Giants of the Animal World, 1962; Reptiles since the World Began, 1964; Star Watchman, 1964; The Uses of Space, 1965; The Weathermakers, 1967; Out of the Sun, 1968; The Dueling Machine, 1969; In Quest of Quasars, 1970; Planets, Life and LGM, 1970; Escape!, 1970; (ed.) The Many Worlds of SF, 1971; The Fourth State of Matter, 1971; Exiled from Earth, 1971; (with G. Lucas) THX 1138, 1971; The Amazing Laser, 1972; The New Astronomies, 1972; Flight of Exiles, 1972; As on a Darkling Plain, 1972; Starflight and Other Improbabilities, 1973; Man Changes the Weather, 1973; The Winds of Altair, 1973; (ed.) Analog 9, 1973; (ed.) SFWA Hall of Fame, vol. II, 1973; When the Sky Burned, 1973; Forward in Time, 1973; (ed.) The Analog Science Fact Reader, 1974; (with B. Berson) Survival Guide for the Suddenly Single, 1974; The Weather Changes Man, 1974; Workshops in Space, 1974; (with G.R. Dickson) Gremlins, Go Home!, 1974; End of Exile, 1975; Notes to a Science Fiction Writer, 1975; Through Eyes of Wonder, 1975; Science—Who Needs It?, 1975; The Starcrossed, 1975; Millenium, 1976; (ed.) Analog Annual, 1976; Multiple Man, 1976; City of Darkness, 1976; The Seeds of Tomorrow, 1977; (with Trudy E. Bell) Closeup: New Worlds, 1977; Viewpoint, 1977; Colony, 1978; (ed.) Analog Yearbook, 1978; Maxwell's Demons, 1978; Kinsman, 1979; The Weathermakers, 1979; The Exiles Trilogy, 1980; (ed.) Best of Omni Science Fiction, 1980–82; Voyagers, 1981; The High Road, 1981; Test of Fire, 1982; Vision of Tomorrow, 1982; Escape Plus Ten, 1984; Assured Survival: How to Stop the Nuclear Arms Race, 1984; The Astral Mirror, 1985; Privateers, 1985; Prometheus, 1986; Voyager Two: The Alien Within, 1987; The Kinsman Saga, 1987; Welcome to Moonbase, 1987; Vengeance of Orion, 1988; The Beauty of Light, 1988. Add: 350 Madison Ave., New York, N.Y. 10017, U.S.A.

BOVASSO, Julie. American, b. 1930. Plays/Screenplays. Stage dir. and actress. Assoc., Theatre Dept., Sarah Lawrence Coll., Bronxville, N.Y., since 1969. Founder, Dir., Producer, and actress, Tempo Playhouse, NYC, 1953–56; faculty member, New Sch. for Social Research, NYC, 1965–71, and Brooklyn Coll., N.Y., 1968–69. *Publs:* The Moon Dreamers, 1972; Gloria and Esperanza, 1973; Standard Safety, 1976. Add: c/o Helen Harvey Assocs., 4110W. 24th St., New York, NY 10011, U.S.A.

BOWD, Douglas Gordon. Australian, b. 1918. History, Institutions/Organizations. Deputy Principal, Windsor Sch., N.S.W., 1960–78. *Publs:* Hawkesbury Benevolent Society and Hospital 1818-1947, 1947; Short History of Wilberforce, 1960; Lucy Osburn—Founder of Nightingale System of Nursing at Sydney Hospital, 1968; Macquarie Country—History of the Hawkesbury, 1969, 4th ed. 1982; Windsor Primary School 1869-1969, 1969; Historic Hawkesbury, 3rd ed. 1970; Wilberforce Public School 1880-1980. 1980; Windsor Bowling Club Golden Anniversary 1931–1981, 1981; Hawkesbury Journey, 1986. Add: 90 The Terrace, Windsor, N.S.W., Australia 2756.

BOWDEN, Jean. Also writes as Barbara Annandale, Belinda Dell, Jocelyn Barry, Avon Curry, Lee Mackenzie, Tessa Barclay and Jennifer Bland. British, b. 1928. Historical/Romance/Gothic, Dance/Ballet. Editorial Consultant, Mills & Boon Ltd., London, since 1971. Editorial Asst., Panther Books, 1957–59, Four Sq. Books, 1959–61, and Armada Books, 1961–62; Feature Writer, Woman's Mirror mag., London, 1962–64; Asst. Fiction Ed., Woman's Own mag., London, 1964–71. *Publs:* (as Belinda Dell) Island of Love; Grey Touched with Scarlet; (as Belinda Dell) The Heights of Love; (as Belinda Dell) Who Claims My Heart; (as Belinda Dell) See If I Care; (as Avon Curry) Derry Down Death; (as Belinda Dell) Dearest Enemy; (as Belinda Dell) Fateful Enchantress: In a Winged World; (as Avon Curry) Dying High; (as Belinda Dell) There's No Turning Back: Call an Ambulance; (with F. and P. Spencer) Come Dancing: The Ceaseless Challenge; (as Jocelyn Barry) Summer in the City; (as Belinda Dell) Where the Rata Blossoms; (as Belinda Dell) The Cruise to Curacao; (as Avon Curry) A Place of Execution; (as Belinda Dell) Dancing on My Heart; (with B. Irvine) The Dancing Years; (as Belinda Dell) The Vermilion Gateway; (as Belinda Dell) Next Stop Gretna: (as Avon Curry) Shack Up (in U.S. as The Girl in the Killer's Bed; (as Belinda Dell) Change Partners; (as Belinda Dell) Flowers for the Festival; (as Belinda Dell) The Darling Pirate; (as Belinda Dell) Lake of Silver; (as Avon Curry) Hunt for Danger; (as Jennifer Bland) Accomplice;

(as Jean Bowden) Nanny, 1981; (as Lee Mackenzie) Emmerdale Farm series, 22 vols.; (as Tessa Barclay) The Craigallan Saga, 4 vols.; (as Tessa Barclay) The Tramont Saga, 3 vols; (as Barbara Annandale) The Bonnet Laird's Daughter; (as Barbara Annandale) High Banbaree; (as Tessa Barclay) Garland of War; (as Tessa Barclay) The Weaving Saga, 3 vols. Add: 138 Himley Rd., London SW17, England.

BOWDEN, Jim. *See* **SPENCE**, William John Duncan.

BOWDEN, Mary W(eatherspoon). American, b. 1941. Literature. Member. Bd. of Review, Public Programs Div., National Endowment for the Humanities. Instr., Drake Univ., Des Moines, Iowa, 1965–66; Asst. Prof., Indiana Univ., Fort Wayne, 1968–70; Asst. Instr., 1970–71, and Instr., 1971–82, Univ. of Texas at Austin. *Publs:* Philip Freneau, 1976; Washington Irving, 1981. Add: 3402 Hillview, Austin, Tex. 78703, U.S.A.

BOWDEN, Roland Heywood. British, b. 1916. Plays/Screenplays, Poetry. Head of Art Dept., Manhood High Sch., Selsey, Sussex, since 1956. Former Head of Art Dept., Blackwell Sch., Harrow, Middx. *Publs:* Poems from Italy, 1970; And (play), 1972; The Last Analysis (play), 1974; The Death of Pasolini (play), 1980; After Neruda (play), 1984; The Fence, 1985; Every Season is Another (verse) 1986; The Sea of Azov (play), 1987. Add: 2 Roughmere Cottage, Lavant, Chichester, Sussex, England.

BOWEN, Barbara C(herry). British, b. 1937. Intellectual history, Literature. Prof. of French, Vanderbilt Univ., Nashville, since 1987. Instr. to Prof., Univ. of Illinois, Urbana, 1962–87. Univ. of Illinois, since 1973 (Instr., 1962–63; Asst. Prof., 1963–66; Assoc. Prof., 1966–73). *Publs:* Les Caracteristiques essentielles de la farce francaise, et leur survivance dans les années 1550-1620, 1964; (ed.) Four Farces, 1967; The Age of Bluff: Paradox and Ambiguity in Rabelais and Montaigne, 1972; (ed.) The French Renaissance Mind, 1976; Words and the Man in French Renaissance Literature, 1983. Add: Dept. of French, Vanderbilt Univ., Nashville, Tenn. 37235, U.S.A.

BOWEN, Howard R(othmann). American, b. 1908. Economics, Education. Prof. of Economics, Claremont Grad. Sch. (Chancellor, 1969–74). Dean. Coll. of Commerce, Univ. of Illinois, Urbana, 1947–52; Prof. of Economics, Williams Coll., Williamstown, Mass. 1952–55; Pres., Grinnell Coll., Iowa, 1955–64, and Univ. of Iowa, Iowa City, 1964–69. *Publs:* English Grants-in-Aid, 1939; Toward Social Economy, 1948; Social Responsibilities of the Businessman, 1953; Graduate Education in Economics, 1954; (with Garth Mangum) Automation and Economic Progress, 1966; Finance of Higher Education, 1969; (with Gordon Douglass) Efficiency in Liberal Education, 1971; Investment in Learning, 1977; The Costs of Higher Education, 1980; The State of the Nation and the Agenda for Higher Education, 1981; (with Jack Schuster) American Professors: A National Resource Imperiled, 1986. Add: 900 E. Harrison, D29, Pomona, Calif. 91767, U.S.A.

BOWEN, Humphry J.M. British, b. 1929. Botany, Chemistry. Reader in Chemistry, Univ. of Reading, since 1974 (Lectr., 1964–74). Sr. Scientific Officer, Atomic Energy Research Establishment, Harwell, 1956–64. *Publs:* (with L.E. Sutton and others) Tables of Interatomic Distances, 1958; (with D. Gibbons) Radioactivation Analysis, 1963; Introduction to Botany, 1965; Trace Elements in Biochemistry, 1966; Properties of Solids and Their Atomic Structures, 1967; The Flora of Berkshire, 1968; Chemical Applications of Radioisotopes, 1969; (with G.V. Iyengar and W.E. Kollmer) The Elemental Composition of Human Tissues and Body Fluids, 1978; Environmental Chemistry of the Elements, 1979. Add: Dept. of Chemistry, Univ. of Reading, Reading, Berks., England.

BOWEN, John (Griffith). With Jeremy Bullmore writes as Justin Blake. British, b. 1924. Novels/Short stories, Children's fiction, Plays/Screenplays. *Publs:* The Truth Will Not Help Us; Embroidery on an Historical Theme, 1956; Pegasus, 1957; The Mermaid and the Boy, 1958; After the Rain,1958; The Centre of the Green, 1959; Storyboard, 1960; (with J. Bullmore as Justin Blake) Garry Halliday series 5 vols., 1960–64; The Birdcage, 1962; The Essay Prize, with A Holiday Abroad and The Candidate: Plays for Television, 1962; I Love You, Mrs. Patterson, 1964; A World Elsewhere, 1964; After the Rain, 1967; The Fall and Redemption of Man, 1968; Little Boxes, 1968; The Disorderly Women, 1969; The Waiting Room, 1970; The Corsican Brothers, 1970; Heil Caesar!, 1974; Florence Nightingale, 1976, Squeak, 1983; The McGuffin, 1984; The Girls, 1986; Fighting Back, 1989. Add: Old Lodge Farm, Sugarswell Lane, Edgehill, Banbury, Oxon. OX15 6HP, England.

BOWEN, Robert O. American, b. 1920. Novels/Short stories,

Plays/Screenplays, Writing/Journalism. Instr., Cornell Univ., Ithaca, N.Y., 1953–55; Visiting Lectr., Univ. of Iowa, Iowa City, 1955–56; Asst. Prof. of English, Montana State Univ., Missoula, 1956–58, and Univ. of Washington, Seattle, 1958–60; Assoc. Prof. of English, Univ. of Santa Clara, Calif., 1960–61, Univ. of Dallas, Tex., 1961–63, and Alaska Methodist Univ., Anchorage, 1963–65; Ed., Dallas Review, Tex., 1962–63, Alaska Review, Anchorage, 1963–65, and Fur Rendezvous Mag., Anchorage, 1964. *Publs:* The Weight of the Cross, 1951; Bamboo, 1953; Sidestreet, 1954; (ed.) Practical Prose Studies: A Critical Anthology of Contemporary American Prose Readings for the College Freshman, 1956; (ed.) The New Professors, 1960; The Christmas Child (libretto), 1960; The Truth about Communism, 1962; Marlow the Master and Other Stories, 1963; College Style Manual, 1963; (ed. with R.A. Charles) Alaska Literary Directory, 1964; An Alaskan Dictionary, 1965. Add: P.O. Box 1862, Anchorage, Alaska 99510, U.S.A.

BOWEN, William (Gordon). American, b. 1933. Economics. Pres., The Andrew W. Mellon Foundation, since 1988. Prof. of Economics, 1958–88, and Pres., 1972–88, Princeton Univ., New Jersey. *Publs:* The Wage-Price Issue: A Theoretical Analysis, 1960; Wage Behaviour in the Postwar Period: An Empirical Analysis, 1960; Economic Aspects of Education: Three Essays, 1964; (with W.J. Baumol) Performing Arts: The Economic Dilemma, 1966; (with T.A. Finegan) The Economics of Labor Force Participation, 1969; Ever the Teacher, 1987. Add: 140 E. 62nd St., New York, N.Y. 10021, U.S.A.

BOWEN, Zack. American, b. 1934. Literature, Biography. Prof. and Chmn. of the English Dept., Univ. of Miami, since 1986. Gen. Ed., Irish Renaissance Annual, since 1980. Asst. Prof. of English, State Univ. Coll., Fredonia, N.Y., 1960–64; Asst. Prof., Prof., Distinguished Prof., and Chmn. of the English Dept., State Univ. of New York at Binghamton, 1964–76; Prof. and Chmn. of the English Dept., Univ. of Delaware, Newark, 1976–86. *Publs:* Padraic Colum: A Biographical-Critical Introduction, 1970; Musical Allusions in the Works of James Joyce, 1974; Mary Lavin, 1975; A Companion to Joyce Studies, 1984. Add: Dept. of English, Univ. of Miami, Coral Gables, Fla. 33124, U.S.A.

BOWEN-JUDD, Sara. *See* **WOODS**, Sara.

BOWERING, George. Canadian, b. 1938. Novels/Short stories, Plays/Screenplays, Poetry. Prof. of English, Simon Fraser Univ., Burnaby, B.C., since 1972. Ed., Imago mag., Vancouver. Prof., Univ. of Calgary Alta., 1963–66; Writer-in-Residence, 1967–68, and Asst. Prof. of English, 1968–72; Sir George Williams Univ., Montreal. *Publs:* A Home for Heroes (play), 1962; Sticks and Stones, 1963; Points on the Grid, 1964; The Man in the Yellow Boots, 1965; The Silver Wire, 1966; Mirror on the Floor (novel), 1967, screenplay, 1971; Baseball, 1967; Two Police Poems, 1968; Rocky Mountain Foot, 1969; The Gangs of Kosmos, 1969; Al Purdy, 1970; (ed.) Vibrations, 1970; George, Vancouver, 1970; Sitting in Mexico, 1970; Geneve, 1971; Selected Poems, 1971; Autobiology, 1971; (ed.) The Story So Far, 1971; Touch: Selected Poems 1960-1970, 1971; The Sensible, 1972; Layers 1-13, 1973; Curious, 1973; In the Flesh, 1974; Flycatcher (short stories), 1974; At War with the U.S., 1974; Allophanes, 1976; Poem and Other Baseballs, 1976; The Catch, 1976; The Concrete Island, 1977; A Short Sad Book, 1977; Concentric Circles, 1977; Protective Footwear, 1978; Another Mouth, 1979; Burning Water, 1980; Particular Accidents: Selected Poems, 1981; West Window, 1982; Smoking Mirror, 1982; A Way with Words (Essays), 1982; The Mask in Place (essays), 1983; Kerrisdale Elegies (poetry), 1984; A Place to Die (stories), 1984; Craft Slices (essays), 1985; 71 Poems for People, 1985; Delayed Mercy (poems), 1986; Caprice (novel), 1987; Errata (literary theory), 1987; Imaginary Hand (essays), 1988. Add: 2499 W. 37th Ave., Vancouver 13, B.C., Canada.

BOWERING, Marilyn (Ruthe). Canadian, b. 1949. Novels/Short Stories, Poetry. Editor and Writer, Gregson Graham Marketing, Victoria, 1978–82; Sessional Lectr., 1982–86, and Visiting Lectr., Univ of Victoria. *Publs:* The Liberation of Newfoundland (verse), 1973; One Who Became Lost (verse), 1976; The Killing Room (verse), 1977; (ed. with David A. Day) Many Voices: An Anthology of Contemporary Canadian Indian Poetry, 1977; Third Child; Zian (verse), 1978; The Book of Glass (verse), 1978; The Visitors Have All Returned (novel), 1979; (ed.) Guide to the Labour Code of British Columbia, 1980; Sleeping with Lambs (verse), 1980; Giving Back Diamonds (verse), 1982; The Sunday Before Winter (verse), 1984; Anyone Can See I Love You (verse), 1987; Grandfather was a Soldier (verse), 1987. Add: Manzer Rd., R.R.1, Sooke, B.C. V0S 1N0, Canada.

BOWERS, Edgar. American, b. 1924. Poetry. Prof. of English, Univ.

of California, Santa Barbara, since 1967 (Asst. Prof., 1958–61; Assoc. Prof., 1961–67). *Publs:* The Form of Loss, 1956; The Astronomers, 1965; Living Together, 1973; Witnesses, 1981; For Louis Pasteur, 1989. Add: 1502 Miramar Beach, Santa Barbara, Calif. 93108, U.S.A.

BOWERS, Fredson (Thayer). American, b. 1905. Literature. Emeritus Linden Kent Prof. of English, Univ. of Virginia, Charlottesville (Asst. Prof. of English, 1938–45. Assoc. Prof., 1945–49, Prof., 1959–75, Chmn., Dept. of English, 1961–68, and Dean of Faculty, 1968–69). Ed., Studies in Bibliography, since 1948. *Publs:* Elizabethan Revenge Tragedy, 1940; Principles of Bibliographical Description, 1949; (ed.) Dramatic Works of Thomas Dekker, 4 vols., 1953–61; On Editing Shakespeare and Elizabethan Dramatists, 1955; Whitman's Manuscripts for 1860 Leaves of Grass, 1955; Textual and Literary Criticism, 1959; (ed.) Works of Nathaniel Hawthorne, 10 vols., 1962–75; Bibliography and Textual Criticism, 1964; (gen. ed.) The Dramatic Works in the Beaumont and Fletcher Canon, 1966–; (ed.) Works of Stephen Crane, 10 vols., 1969–75; (ed.) Works of Christopher Marlowe, 2 vols., 1973; Stephen Crane: The Red Badge of Courage, A Facsimile Edition of the Manuscript, 1973; (ed.) Tom Jones by Fielding, 1974; Essays in Bibliography, Text and Editing, 1975; (ed.) Works of William James, 1975–88; (ed.) Lectures in Literature and Russian Literature by Vladimir Nabokov, 2 vols., 1980–81. Add: Woodburn, Route 14, Box 7, Charlottesville, Va. 22901, U.S.A.

BOWERS, John. American, b. 1928. Novels/Short stories, Autobiography/Memoirs/Personal. *Publs:* The Colony (autobiography), 1971; The Golden Bowers, 1971; No More Reunions (novel), 1973; Helene, 1979. Add: c/o Georges Borchardt Inc., 136 E. 57th St., New York, N.Y. 10022, U.S.A.

BOWETT, Derek W(illiam). British, b. 1927. Law. Professorial Fellow, Queens' Coll., and Whewell Prof. of International Law, Cambridge Univ., since 1981 (Fellow, 1960–69, and Pres., 1969–82, Queens' Coll.; Lectr., 1960–76, and Reader, 1976–81, Cambridge Univ.). Lectr., Manchester Univ., 1951–59; Legal Officer, U.N., New York, 1957–59; Gen. Counsel, U.N. Relief and Works Admin., Beirut, 1966–68. *Publs:* Self-Defence in International Law, 1958; Law of International Institutions, 1964; United Nations Forces, 1964; Law of the Sea, 1967; Search for Peace, 1972; Legal Regime of Islands in International Law, 1978. Add: Queens' College, Cambridge, England.

BOWIE, Norman E. American, b. 1942. Philosophy. Dir. of the Center for the Study of Values, and Prof., Univ. of Delaware, Newark, since 1980 (Assoc. Prof., 1975–80). Asst. Prof., Lycoming Coll., Williamsport, Pa., 1968–69; Assoc. Prof. of Philosophy, Hamilton Coll., Clinton, N.Y., 1969–75. Exec. Secty., American Philosophical Assn., 1972–77. *Publs:* Toward a New Theory of Distributive Justice, 1971; (co-author) The Individual and Political Order, 1977, 1985; (ed. with Thomas Beauchamp) Ethical Theory and Business, 1979, 3rd ed. 1988; (ed.) Ethical Issues in Government, 1981; Business Ethics, 1982; (ed. with Frederick Elliston) Ethics, Public Policy and Criminal Justice, 1982; (ed.) Ethical Theory in the Last Quarter of the 20th Century, 1983; (ed.) Making Ethical Decisions, 1984; (ed. with Harrison Hall) The Tradition of Philosophy, 1986; (ed.) Equal Opportunity, 1988. Add: 13 Woodshaw Rd., Newark, Del. 19711, U.S.A.

BOWKER, John Westerdale. British, 1935. Children's fiction, Theology/Religion. Fellow and Dean, Trinity Coll., Cambridge since 1984; Adjunct Prof. of Religion, North Carolina State Univ., since 1986. Hon. Canon of Canterbury Cathedral, since 1985. Fellow, Corpus Christi Coll., 1962–74, and 1965–74, Univ. of Cambridge; Prof. of Religious Studies, Univ. of Lancaster, 1974–85. *Publs:* The Targums and Rabbinic Literature, 1969; Problems of Suffering in Religions of the World, 1970; Jesus and the Pharisees, 1973; The Sense of God: Sociological Anthropological and Psychological Approaches to the Origin of the Sense of God, 1973; Uncle Bolpenny Tries Things Out, 1973; The Religious Imagination and the Sense of God, 1978; Worlds of Faith, 1983; (ed.) Violence and Aggression, 1984; Licensed Insanities: Religions and Belief in God in the Contemporary World, 1987. Add: 14 Bowers Croft, Cambridge CB1 4RP, England.

BOWKER, Margaret. British, b. 1936. Theology/Religion. Emeritus Reader in History, Lancaster Univ. (Reader, 1977–85). Lectr., Girton Coll., 1960–77, and Univ. Lectr., 1963–77, Cambridge Univ. *Publs:* (ed.) An Episcopal Court Book 1514-20, 1967; Secular Clergy in the Diocese of Lincoln 1495-1520, 1968; The Henrician Reformation, 1981. Add: 14 Bowers Croft, Cambridge CB1 4RP, England.

BOWKER, Robin Marsland. British. Recreation/Leisure/Hobbies. Managing Dir., Bowker & Budd, 1952–73. *Publs:* (with S.A. Budd) Make Your Own Sails, 1957; A Boat of Your Own, 1959; The Channel Handbook, 3 vols., 1977–80; Mutiny, 1979; Historical Postscript to Erskine Childer's Riddle of the Sands, 1988. Add: Whitewalls, Harbour Way, Old Bosham, Sussex, England.

BOWLBY, John. British, b. 1907. Human relations, Psychology. Hon. Consultant Psychiatrist, Tavistock Clinic, London, since 1972 (Consultant Psychiatrist, 1946–72; Dir., Dept. for Children and Parents, 1946–68). Psychiatrist, London Child Guidance Clinic, 1937–40; Part-time Member, External Staff, Medical Research Council, 1963–72. Consultant in Mental Health, World Health Org., Geneva, 1950–72. *Publs:* (with E.F.M. Durbin) Personal Aggressiveness and War, 1938; Maternal Care and Mental Health, 1951; Child Care and the Growth of Love, 1953, 1963; Attachment and Loss, vol. I, Attachment, 1969, vol. II, Separation, 1973, and vol. III, Loss, 1980; The Making and Breaking of Affectional Bonds, 1979; A Secure Base, 1988. Add: Tavistock Clinic, Belsize Lane, London NW3 5BA, England.

BOWLES, Paul. American, b. 1910. Novels/Short stories, Poetry, Travel/Exploration/Adventure, Autobiography/Memoirs/Personal, Translations. *Publs:* (trans.) J.P. Sartre: No Exit, 1946; The Sheltering Sky, 1949; A Little Stone, 1950; The Delicate Prey, 1950; (trans.) Frison-Roche: The Lost Trail of the Sahara, 1952; Let It Come Down, 1952; The Spider's House, 1955; Yallah!, 1957; The Hours After Noon, 1959; A Hundred Camels in the Courtyard, 1962; Their Heads Are Green, 1963; (trans.) Charhadi: A Life Full of Holes, 1964; (trans.) Mrabet: Love with a Few Hairs, 1967; Up Above the World, 1967; The Time of Friendship, 1967; Pages From Cold Point, 1968; Scenes, 1968; (trans.) Mrabet: M'-Hashish, 1969; (trans.) Mrabet: The Lemon, 1969; The Thicket of Spring, 1972; Without Stopping, 1972; (trans.) Choukri: For Bread Alone, 1973; (trans.) Mrabet: The Boy Who Set the Fire, 1974; (trans.) Choukri: Jean Genet in Tangier, 1974; (trans.) The Oblivion Seekers, by Isabelle Eberhardt, 1975; (trans.) Look and Move On, by Mrabet, 1976; (trans.) Harmless Poisons, Blameless Sins, by Mrabet, 1976; Next to Nothing (poems), 1976; Things Gone and Things Still Here (stories), 1977; (trans.) The Big Mirror, by Mrabet, 1977; Collected Stories, 1979; (trans.) Five Eyes, 1979; (trans.) Tennessee Williams in Tangiers, by Choukri, 1979; (trans.) The Beach Cafe and The Voice, by Mrabet, 1980; Points in Time, 1981; (trans.) The Chest, by Mrabet, 1983; (trans.) She Woke Me Up So I Killed Her, by various authors, 1985; Midnight Mass, 1985; (trans.) Marriage with Papers, by Mrabet, 1986; Welcome Words, 1988. Add: 2117, Tanger Socco, Tangier, Morocco.

BOWLEY, Marian E.A. British, b. 1911. Economics, Technology. Emeritus Prof., Univ. of London, since 1975 (former Prof. of Political Economy). *Publs:* Nassau Senior and Classical Economics, 1937; Housing and the State, 1919-1944, 1945; Innovations in Building Materials: An Economic Study, 1960; The British Building Industry, 1966; Studies in the History of Economic Theory before 1870, 1973; Housing and the State, 1985. Add: Graffham, Sussex, England.

BOWLEY, Rex Lyon. British, b. 1925. Education, Religion, History, Travel. Boarding Housemaster, Reading Sch., 1960–70; Sr. History Master and Housemaster, Bancroft's Sch., Essex, 1970–85. *Publs:* The Fortunate Islands: The Story of the Isles of Scilly, 7th ed. 1980; Tresco: The Standard Guidebook to the Isle of Tresco, 1970; Teaching Without Tears: Guide to Teaching Technique, 4th ed. 1973; Scillonian Quiz-Book, 1974; Readings for Assembly, 1976. The Isles of Scilly Standard Guidebook, 46th ed. 1986, 47th ed. 1988. Add: White Cottage, 44 Tredarvah Rd., Penzance, Cornwall, England.

BOWLT, John Ellis. American, b. 1943. Art, Translations. Prof., Dept. of Slavic Languages, and Dept. of Art, Univ. of Texas, Austin, since 1972; Dir., Inst. of Modern Russian Culture at Blue Lagoon, Tex., and N.Y.C., since 1979. Lectr., Univ. of St. Andrews, Scotland, 1968–69; Lectr., Univ. of Birmingham, England, 1970; Asst. Prof., Univ. of Kansas, Lawrence, 1970–71. *Publs:* (ed., with Stephen Bann) Russian Formalism, 1973; (ed.) The Archer, by Bennedikt Livshits (memoirs), 1977; The Silver Age: Russian Art of the Early 20th Century, 1979; (trans.) Nijinsky, by Vera Krasovskaya, 1979; (with Rose-Carol Washton Long) The Life of Vasili Kandinsky in Russian Art, 1980; Journey into Non-Objectivity, 1980; Russian Stage Design; Scenic Innovation 1900-1930, 1982; with Nicoletta Misler) Pavel Filonov, 1983; (with Szymon Bojko) Russian Samizdat Art, 1986; (ed.) A Slap in the Face of Public Taste, 1986; (with Alfred Senn) Mikalojus Konstantinas Ciurlionis, 1986; Russian Avant-Garde: Theory and Criticism, 1988; (ed.) Varvara Stepanova, 1988. Add: c/o Slavic Dept., Univ. of Texas, Austin, Tex. 78712, U.S.A.

BOWNESS, Alan. British, b. 1928. Art. Dir., Tate Gallery, London. Formerly, Prof. of History of Art, and Deputy Dir., Courtauld Inst., London. *Publs:* William Scott: Paintings, 1964; Modern Sculpture, 1965; Henry Moore: Complete Sculpture, 1965–83; Alan Davie, 1968; Gauguin, 1971; Complete Sculpture of Barbara Hepworth 1960–69, 1972; Modern European Art, 1972; Ivon Hitchins, 1973. Add: 91 Castelnau, London SW13, England.

BOWYER, Mathew Justice. American, b. 1926. Business/Trade/Industry, Recreation/Leisure/Hobbies, Theology/Religion. *Publs:* They Carried the Mail: A Survey of Postal History and Hobbies, 1972; Collecting Americana, 1977; Encyclopedia of Mystical Terminology, 1979; Real Estate Investor's Desk Encyclopedia, 1982. Add: 5397 Summit Dr., Fairfax, Va. 22030, U.S.A.

BOX, Edgar. *See* VIDAL, Gore.

BOX, Muriel (Lady Gardiner). British, b. 1905. Plays/Screenplays, Autobiography/Memoirs/Personal, Biography. Founder and Dir., Femina Books Ltd., London. *Publs:* plays, with Sydney Box—Ladies Only, 1934; No Man's Land, 1934; Petticoat Plays, 1935; Angels of War, 1935; Home from Home, 1941; The Seventh Veil, 1951; Stranger in My Bed, 1965; screenplays, with Sydney Box—14, including The Seventh Veil, 1946; books—(ed.) Vigil, 1939; Forbidden Cargo, 1956; The Big Switch, 1964; The Trial of Marie Stopes, 1967; Odd Woman Out (autobiography), 1974; Rebel Advocate (biography of Gerald Gardiner), 1983. Add: Mote End, Nan Clark's Lane, Mill Hill, London NW7, England.

BOXER, Arabella. British. Cookery/Gastronomy, Travel. Food Corresp., Vogue mag., London, 1965–67, and since 1975. Contrib., Sunday Times Mag., London. *Publs:* First Slice Your Cookbook, 1964; A Second Slice, 1966; Garden Cookbook, 1974; The Vogue Summer and Winter Cookbook, 1980; Mediterranean Cookbook, 1981; Wind in the Willows Country Cookbook, 1983; Sunday Times Complete Cookbook, 1983. Add: c/o Vogue, Vogue House, Hanover Sq., London W1R 0AD, England.

BOYCOTT, Geoff(rey). British, b. 1940. Cricket, Cricketer for Yorkshire, 1962–83, and since 1984; played for England, 1964–74, 1977–82. *Publs:* Geoff Boycott's Book for Young Cricketers, 1976; Put to the Test: Ashes Series in Australia 1978/79, 1979; Geoff Boycott's Cricket Quiz, 1970; Boycott on Batting, 1980; Opening Up, 1980; In the Fast Lane, 1981; Master Class, 1982; Boycott: The Autobiography, 1987. Add: c/o Yorkshire County Cricket Club, Headingly Cricket Ground, Leeds LS6 3BV, England.

BOYD, Alamo. *See* BOSWORTH, Allan R.

BOYD, Elizabeth French. American, b. 1905. History, Literature, Biography. Prof. Emeritus, Douglass Coll., Rutgers Univ., since 1970 (Instr. in English, 1936–39, Asst. Prof., 1944–50, Assoc. Prof., 1950–57, Prof., 1957–70, and Chmn., Dept. of English, 1962–68). Elder-Trustee, Presbyterian Church, New Brunswick, N.J., since 1958. Instr. in English, Briarcliff Jr. Coll., New York, 1935–36, and Lawrence Coll., Appleton, Wisc., 1943–44. Pres., New Brunswick Branch, English Speaking Union, 1973–75. *Publs:* Byron's Don Juan, 1945; Bloomsbury Heritage: Their Mothers and Their Aunts, 1976; The First Quarter-Millenium: A History of the Presbyterian Church in New Brunswick, N.J. 1726-1976, 1976. Add: c/o Cenedella, 317 W. 83 St., New York, N.Y. 10024, U.S.A.

BOYD, John. Pseud. for Boyd Bradfield Upchurch. American, b. 1919. Novels/Short stories, Science fiction/Fantasy. Production Mgr. Star Engraving Co., Los Angeles, 1947–71; freelance writer, 1971–79. *Publs:* The Last Starship from Earth, 1968; The Slave Stealer (novel), 1968; The Pollinators of Eden, 1969; The Rakehells of Heaven, 1969; Sex and the High Command, 1970; The Organ Bank Farm, 1970; The Gorgon Festival, 1972; The I.Q. Merchant, 1972; The Doomsday Gene, 1972; The Andromeda Gun, 1974; Barnard's Planet, 1975; Scarborough Hall (novel), 1975; The Girl with the Jade Green Eyes, 1978. Add: 1151 Aviemore Terr., Costa Mesa, Calif., 92627, U.S.A.

BOYD, Malcolm. American, b. 1923. Sex, Theology/Religion, Autobiography/Memoirs/Personal. Episcopal Priest, since 1955; Assoc. Fellow, Calhoun Coll., Yale Univ., New Haven, Conn., since 1971; Writer-Priest-in-Residence, St. Augustine-by-the-Sea Episcopal Church, Santa Monica, Calif.; Dir., Inst. of Gay Spirituality and Theology, Los Angeles. Book Reviewer, Los Angeles Times. Pres., Los Angeles Center, P.E.N. Intnl., 1984–87. *Publs:* Crisis in Communication, 1957; Christ and Celebrity Gods, 1958; Focus, 1960; If I Go Down to Hell, 1962; The Hunger, The Thirst, 1964; (ed.) On the Battle Lines, 1964; Are You Running with Me Jesus?, 1965; Free to Live, Free to Die, 1967; Malcolm Boyd's Book of Days, 1968; (ed.) The Underground Church, 1968; The Fantasy Worlds of Peter Stone, 1969; As I Live and Breathe, 1969; My Fellow Americans, 1970; Human Like Me, Jesus, 1971; The Lover, 1972; (with P. Conrad) When in the Course of Human Events, 1973; The Runner, 1974; The Alleluia Affair, 1975; Christian: Its Meaning in an Age of Future Shock, 1975; Am I Running with You, God?, 1977; Take Off the Masks, 1978; Look Back in Joy: Celebration of Gay Lovers, 1981; Half Laughing, Half Crying, 1986; Gay Priest: An Inner Journey, 1986. Add: 2517 Hyperion Ave., Los Angeles, Calif. 90027, U.S.A.

BOYD, Waldo T. Also writes as Karl Andreassen. American, b. 1918. Sciences. With U.S. Navy, 1936–40 and on assignment to CSIR, Univ. of Sydney, Australia, 1941–45; teacher of electronics, Des Moines, Iowa, 1945–47; Field Electronics Engineer, Philco Corp., Germany, 1948–50; Dir. of Public Relations and Publs., Dianetic Foundn., Wichita, Kans., 1950–53; Mgr. of Technical Manuals Dept., Aerojet-Gen. Corp., Sacramento, Calif., 1956–65; Mgr., Geyserville Baha'i Sch., 1967–73, and Instr. in Industrial Arts, Geyserville Educational Park, 1973–74, California; Electronics Instr., Goodwill Industries, Santa Rosa, Calif., 1976–81. *Publs:* Your Career in the Aerospace Industry, 1966; Your Career in Oceanology, 1968; The World of Cryogenics, 1969; Oceanologia, 1975; The World of Energy Storage, 1977; Fiber Optics, 1982; (as Karl Andreassen) Computer Cryptology: Beyond Decoder Rings, 1987. Add: P.O. Box 86, Geyserville, Calif. 95441, U.S.A.

BOYD, William. British, b. 1952. Novels/Short stories, Full-time writer. Lectr. in English Literature, St. Hilda's Coll., Oxford, 1980–83; Television Critic, New Statesman, London, 1981–83. *Publs:* A Good Man in Africa (novel), 1981; On the Yankee Station (short stories), 1981; An Ice-Cream War (novel), 1982; Stars and Bars (novel), 1984; School Ties (screenplay), 1985; The New Confessions (novel), 1987. Add: c/o Richard Scott Simon, 32 College Cross, London N1 1PR, England.

BOYD, W(illiam) Harland. American, b. 1912. History, Transportation, Biography. Prof. Emeritus, Bakersfield Coll., California, since 1973 (Prof., 1946–73). *Publs:* Land of Havilah, 1952; (ed. with Glendon J. Rodgers) San Joaquin Vignettes, 1955; (ed. with Jesse D. Stockton and Glendon J. Rodgers) Spanish Trailblazers in the South San Joaquin Valley, 1957; A Centennial Bibliography on the History of Kern County, California, 1966; A California Middle Border, 1972; (ed.) A Climb Through History, 1973; Bakersfield's First Baptist Church, 1975; (ed.) Kern County Wayfarers, 1977; Kern County Tall Tales, 1980; The Shasta Route, 1981; Stagecoach Heyday in the San Joaquin Valley, 1983; (ed. with Jane A. Watts) Lawrence Weill's Bakersfield, 1984. Add: 339 Cypress St., Bakersfield, Calif. 93304, U.S.A.

BOYERS, Robert. American, b. 1942. Literature. Prof. of English, and Ed. of Salmagundi mag., Skidmore Coll., Saratoga Springs, since 1969 (founded Salmagundi, Flushing, N.Y., 1965). Taught at the New Sch. for Social Research, NYC, Fall 1967; Baruch Sch. of the City Univ. of New York, 1967–68; Sullivan County Community Coll., 1968–69. *Publs:* (ed., with M. London) Robert Lowell: A Portrait of the Artist in His Time, 1970; (ed., with Robert Orrill) R.D. Laing and Anti-Psychiatry, 1971; (ed.) The Legacy of the German Refugee Intellectuals, 1972; (ed., with Robert Orrill) Psychological Man: Approaches to an Emergent Social Type, 1975; (ed.) Contemporary Poetry in America, 1975; Excursions: Selected Literary Essays of Robert Boyers, 1976; Lionel Trilling: Negative Capability and the Wisdom of Avoidance, 1977; F.R. Leavis: Judgment and The Discipline of Thought, 1978; R.P. Blackmur: Poet-Critic, 1980; Atrocity and Amnesia: The Political Novel since 1945, 1985; After the Avant-Garde: Essays on Art and Culture, 1987. Add: English Dept., Skidmore Coll., Saratoga Springs, N.Y. 12866, U.S.A.

BOYES, Megan. British, b. 1923. Children's fiction, Biography. *Publs:* Auntie Blodwen and the Pageant, 1967; Bess of Holme Pierrepont (radio series), 1973; Mary of Annesley (radio series), 1974; Margaret of Welbeck (radio series), 1976; Mary of Thoresby (radio series), 1977; Allestree Hall, 1983; Queen of a Fantastic Realm, 1986; Love Without Wings, 1988. Add: The Glade, 49 Evans Ave., Allestree, Derby DE3 2EP, England.

BOYLAN, Clare. Irish, b. 1948. Novels/Short stories. Presenter, Radio Telefis Eireann; book reviewer, Cosmopolitan, London; and contributor, Good Housekeeping, London, and Vogue, New York.Reporter, 1968–69, and Staff Feature Writer, 1973–78, Dublin Evening Press; Ed., Young Woman mag., Dublin, 1969–71, and Image mag., Dublin, 1978–81. *Publs:* Holy Pictures (novel), 1983; A Nail on the Head (short stories),

1983; Last Resorts (novel), 1984. Add: c/o Gill Coleridge, Rogers Coleridge and White Ltd., 20 Powis Mews, London W11 1JN, England.

BOYLAND, Eric. British, b. 1905. Chemistry, Medicine/Health. Visiting Prof. in Environmental Toxicology, TUC Centenary Inst. of Occupational Health, London. Reader in Biochemistry, 1935–47, Prof. of Biochemistry, 1948–70, now Prof. of Biochemistry Emeritus, Univ. of London; Visiting Prof., Univ. of London, 1972–77. *Publs:* The Biochemistry of Bladder Cancer, 1963; (co-ed.) Modern Trends in Toxicology, vol. I, 1962, vol. II, 1974. Add: TUC Centenary Inst. of Occupational Health, London Sch. of Hygiene and Tropical Medicine, Keppel St., London WC1E 7HT, England.

BOYLE, Andrew (Philip More). British, b. 1919. International relations/Current affairs, Biography. Producer, Radio Newsreel, etc., 1947–65; Ed., The World at One, PM, and The World This Weekend, all BBC Radio, London, 1965–75; Head, News and Current Affairs, B.B.C., Scotland, 1976. *Publs:* No Passing Glory: The Life of Cheshire V.C., 1955; Trenchard: Man of Vision, 1962; Montagu Norman, 1967; The God I Want, 1967; Only the Wind Will Listen: John Reith of the BBC, 1972; Poor, Dear Brendan: The Quest for Brendan Bracken, 1974; The Riddle of Erskine Childers, 1977; The Climate of Treason, 1979 (in U.S. as The Fourth Man), 1980, 1981. Add: 39 Lansdowne Rd., London W11 2LQ, England.

BOYLE, Ann (Peters). American, b. 1916. Mystery/Crime/Suspense, Historical/Romance/Gothic, Children's fiction. *Publs:* (with others) The Jack and Jill Mystery Book, 1959; Stormy Slopes, 1971; Sundown Girl, 1972; The Well of Three Echoes, 1972; Rim of Forever, 1973; One Golden Earring, 1974; Dark Mountain, 1975; Beyond the Wall, 1976; The Snowy Hills of Innocence, 1977; Veil of Sand, 1977; Moon Shadows, 1978; Never Say Never, 1984. Add: 15991 Bliss Lane, Apt. A, Tustin, Calif. 92680, U.S.A.

BOYLE, Kay. American, b. 1902. Novels/Short stories, Children's fiction, Poetry, Biography, Translations. Prof. of English, San Francisco State Univ., since 1963, now Emeritus. Foreign Corresp., The New Yorker mag., 1946–53. *Publs:* Short Stories, 1929; Wedding Day and Other Stories, 1930; Plagued by the Nightingale, 1931; (trans.) Don Juan, by Joseph Delteil, 1931; (trans.) Mr. Knife, Miss Fork, by R. Crevel, 1931; (trans.) Devil in the Flesh, by Raymond Radiguet, 1932; Year Before Last, 1932; Gentlemen, I Address You Privately, 1933; The First Lover and Other Stories, 1933; My Next Bride, 1934; Death of a Man, 1936; The White Horses of Vienna and Other Stories, 1936; Monday Night, 1938, 3rd ed. 1977; A Glad Day (poetry), 1938; The Youngest Camel, 1939, rev. ed. 1959; The Crazy Hunter: Three Short Novels (in U.K. as The Crazy Hunter and Other Stories), 1940; Primer for Combat, 1942; Avalanche, 1944; American Citizen: Naturalized in Leadville, Colorado (poetry), 1944; A Frenchman Must Die, 1946; Thirty Stories, 1946; 1939,1948; His Human Majesty, 1949; The Smoking Mountain: Stories of Post War Germany, 1951; The Seagull on the Step, 1955; Three Short Novels, 1958; Generation Without Farewell, 1960; Collected Poems, 1962; Breaking the Silence: Why a Mother Tells Her Son about the Nazi Era, 1962; Pinky: The Cat Who Liked to Sleep, 1966; Nothing Ever Breaks Except the Heart (short stories), 1966; (ed.) The Autobiography of Emanuel Carnevali, 1967; Pinky in Persia, 1968; (with R. McAlmon) Being Geniuses Together, 1968; The Long Walk at San Francisco State and Other Essays, 1970; Testament for My Students (poetry), 1970; (ed.) Enough of Dying! An Anthology of Peace Writings, 1972; Underground Woman, 1975; (with others) Four Visions of America, 1977; Fifty Stories, 1980; Three Short Novels, 1982; (with Robert McAlmon) Being Geniuses Together: 1920–1930, 1984; This Is Not a Letter and Other Poems, 1985; Words That Must Somehow Be Said: Selected Essays, 1985; (trans.) Babylon, by R. Crevel, 1987; Life Being The Best and Other Stories, 1988. Add: c/o A. Watkins/Loomis Inc., 150 E. 35th St., New York, N.Y. 10016, U.S.A.

BOZEMAN, Adda (von Bruemmer). American, b. 1908. Civil liberties/Human rights, International relations/Current affairs, Law. Emeritus Prof. of Intnl. Relations, Sarah Lawrence Coll., Bronxville, N.Y., since 1977 (Prof., 1947–77). Member, Bd. of Eds., Comparative Strategy, Conflict, and Orbis: A Journal of World Affairs; Member, Bd. of Dirs., Chinese Cultural Center. Assoc., Intl. Law Offices, Charles Henry Huberich, London and The Hague, 1933–36; Assoc. Prof. of History, Augustana Coll., Rock Island, Ill., 1943–47. *Publs:* Regional Conflicts Around Geneva: Study of Neutralized Zones, 1948; Politics and Culture in International History, 1960; The Future of Law in a Multicultural World, 1971; Conflict in Africa: Concepts and Realities, 1976; How to Think about Human Rights, 1978; The Roots of the American Commit-

ment to the Rights of Man, 1980; On the Relevance of Hugo Grotius and De Jure Belli ac Pacis for Our Times, 1980; Covert Action and Foreign Policy, 1981; Human Rights and National Security, 1983; The Future of International Law, 1984; Intelligence and Statecraft, 1984. Add: 24 Beall Circle, Bronxville, N.Y. 10708, U.S.A.

BRABAZON, James. Pseud. for Leslie James Seth-Smith. British, b. 1923. Plays/Screenplays, Biography. Freelance television writer and producer. Actor, 1946–54; advertising copywriter, 1954–58; Story Ed., 1963–68, and Drama Dir., 1969, BBC Television; Drama Producer, Granada Television Ltd., 1970–74, 1978–82, and London Week-end Television Ltd., 1976–77. *Publs:* People of Nowhere (play), 1959; Albert Schweitzer, 1975; Dorothy L. Sayers, 1981. Add: 36 Kingswood Rd., Chiswick, London W4 5ET, England.

BRACEGIRDLE, Brian. British, b. 1933. Archaeology/Antiquities, Biology, Photography. Asst. Dir. and Head of Collections Management, Science Museum, London, since 1987 (Keeper, Wellcome Museum of the History of Medicine, 1977–87). Technician in industry, 1950–57; Biology Master, Erith Grammar Sch., 1958–61; Sr. Lectr. in Biology, St. Katharine's Coll., London, 1961–64; Head, Depts. of National Science and Learning Resources, Coll. of All Saints, London, 1964–77. Secty., then Chmn., Inst. of Medicine and Biological Illustration, 1971–75. Former Chmn., Fellowship and Associateship Panel, Royal Photographic Soc. *Publs:* (with W.H. Freeman) An Atlas of Embryology, 1963; (with W.H. Freeman) An Atlas of Histology, 1966; Photography for Books and Reports, 1970; (with W.H. Freeman) An Atlas of Invertebrate Structure, 1971; (with P.H. Miles) An Atlas of Plant Structure, vol. I, 1971, vol. II, 1973; The Archaeology of the Industrial Revolution, 1973; (with P.H. Miles) Thomas Telford, 1973; (with P.H. Miles) The Darbys and the Ironbridge Gorge, 1974; (with W.H. Freeman) An Advanced Atlas of Histology, 1976; (with P.H. Miles) An Atlas of Chordate Structure, 1977; The Evolution of Microtechnique, 1978; (ed.) Beads of Glass: Leeuwenhoek and the Early Microscope, 1983. Add: 67 Limerston St., London SW10 OBL. England.

BRACEWELL-MILNES, (John) Barry. British, b. 1931. Economics. Freelance writer and economic consultant. Economic Adviser, Inst. of Directors, London, since 1973. Economist, Iron and Steel Bd., London, 1960–63, and Fedn. of British Industries, London, 1964–65; Asst. Economic Dir., 1965–67, Deputy Economic Dir., 1967–68, and Economic Dir., 1968–73, Confedn. of British Industry, London. *Publs:* (contrib.) Taxation: A Radical Approach, 1970; (contrib.) Private Foreign Investment and the Developing World, 1971; The Measurement of Fiscal Policy, 1971; Saving and Switching, 1971; Pay and Price Control Guide, 1973; (contrib.) Government and the Land, 1974; Is Capital Taxation Fair?, 1974; Economic Integration in East and West, 1976; The Camel's Back: An International Comparison of Tax Burdens, 1976; (with J.C.L. Huiskamp) Investment Incentives: A Comparative Analysis of the Systems in the EEC, the USA and Sweden, 1977; (with others) International Tax Avoidance, vols A and B, 1978–79; Tax Avoidance and Evasion: The Individual and Society, 1979; The Economics of International Tax Avoidance, 1980; The Taxation of Industry, 1981; Land and Heritage: The Public Interest in Personal Ownership, 1982; A Market in Corporation Tax Losses, 1983; Smoking and Personal Choice: The Problem of Tobacco Taxation, 1985; The Public Sector Borrowing Requirement, 1985; Are Equity Markets Short-Sighted?: "Short-Termism" and Its Critics, 1987. Add: 26 Lancaster Ct., Banstead, Surrey, England.

BRADBROOK, Muriel Clara. British, b. 1909. History, Literature. Fellow, Girton Coll., Cambridge, 1932–35 and since 1936 and Prof. Emeritus, Cambridge Univ., since 1976 (Lectr. in English 1945–62; Reader 1962–65; Prof. of English Literature, 1965–76; Mistress of Girton Coll., 1968–76). *Publs:* Elizabethan Stage Conditions, 1932; Themes and Conventions of Elizabethan Tragedy, 1934; The School of Night, 1936; (with M.G. Lloyd Thomas) Andrew Marvell, 1940; Joseph Conrad, 1941; Ibsen the Norwegian, 1946; T.S. Eliot, 1950; Shakespeare and Elizabethan Poetry, 1951; (compiler) The Queen's Garland, 1953; The Growth and Structure of Elizabethan Comedy, 1955; Sir Thomas Malory, 1957; The Rise of the Common Player, 1962; English Dramatic Form, 1965; That Infidel Place: History of Girton College, 1969; Shakespeare the Craftsman, 1969; Literature in Action, 1972; T.S. Eliot: The Making of the Waste Land, 1972; Malcolm Lowry: His Art and Early Life, 1974; Shakespeare, 1978; George Chapman, 1978; John Webster, 1980; Collected Papers, 4 vols., 1982–84; Muriel Bradbrook on Shakespeare, 1984. Add: Girton Coll., Cambridge CB3 OJG, England.

BRADBURY, Malcolm (Stanley). British, b. 1932. Novels/Short stories, Plays/Screenplays, Poetry, Literature. Prof. of American Studies,

Univ. of East Anglia, Norwich, since 1970 (Lectr., Sr. Lectr., then Reader, 1965–70). Lectr. in English, Univ. of Birmingham, 1961–65. *Publs:* Eating People is Wrong, 1959; Phogey! How to Have Class in a Classless Society, 1960; All Dressed Up and Nowhere to Go, 1962, 1982; (with D. Lodge and J. Duckett) Between These Four walls (play), 1963; Evelyn Waugh, 1964; (with D. Lodge, D. Turner and J. Duckett) Slap in the Middle (play), 1965; (with A. Rodway) Two Poets, 1966; Stepping Westward, 1965; What is a Novel?, 1969; The Social Context of Modern English Literature, 1971; Possibilities; Essays on the State of the Novel, 1972; The History Man, 1975; (with J. McFarlane) Modernism, 1976; Who Do You Think You Are? Stories and Parodies, 1976; The Novel Today, 1977; (with H. Temperley) An Introduction to American Studies, 1981; The After Dinner Game: Stories and Parodies, 1982; Saul Bellow, 1982; The Modern American Novel, 1983; Rates of Exchange, 1983; Cuts: A Novella, 1987; No, Not Bloomsbury (essays), 1987; My Strange Quest for Mensonge (humour), 1987; (ed.) Penguin Book of Modern British Short Stories, 1987; The Modern World: Ten Great Writers, 1988. Add: University of East Anglia, Norwich, England.

BRADBURY, Ray (Douglas). American, b. 1920. Novels/Short stories, Science fiction/fantasy, Children's fiction, Plays/Screenplays, Poetry. Pres., Science-Fantasy Writers of America, 1951–53; Member, Bd. of Dirs., Screen Workers Guild of America, 1957–61. *Publs:* Dark Carnival, 1947; The Meadow (play), 1948; The Martian Chronicles, 1950; The Illustrated Man, 1951; It came from Outer Space (screenplay), 1952; (ed.) Timeless Stories for Today and Tomorrow, 1952; Fahrenheit 451, 1953; The Golden Apples of the Sun, 1953; Moby Dick (screenplay), 1954; The October Country, 1955; Switch on the Night, 1955; (ed.) The Circus of Dr. Lao, 1956; Dandelion Wine, 1957; A Medicine for Melancholy (in U.K. as The Day It Rained Forever), 1959, play as The Day It Rained Forever, 1966; Icarus Montgolfier Wright (screenplay), 1961; R is for Rocket, 1962; Something Wicked This Way Comes, 1962; The Anthem Sprinters and Other Antics (play), 1963; The World of Ray Bradbury (play), 1964; The Machineries of Joy: Short Stories, 1964; The Vintage Bradbury, 1965; The Wonderful Ice-Cream Suit (play), 1965; The Autumn People, 1965; Tomorrow Midnight, 1966; The Pedestrian (play), 1966; S is for Space, 1966; The Picasso Summer (screenplay), 1968; I Sing the Body Electric!, 1969; Christus Apollo (play), 1969; Old Ahab's Friend, and Friend to Nosh, Speaks His Piece: A Celebration, 1971; The Halloween Tree, 1972; The Wonderful Ice Cream Suit and Other Plays: For Today, Tomorrow, and Beyond Tomorrow, 1972; When Elephants Last in the Dooryard Bloomed (poetry), 1972; The Small Assassin, 1973; Zen and the Art of Writing, 1973; Mars and the Mind of Man, 1973; The Son of Richard III, 1974; Long after Midnight (stories), 1976; Pillar of Fire and Other Plays, 1976; Where Robot Mice and Robot Men Run Round in Robot Towns: New Poems Both Light and Dark, 1977; Beyond 1984, 1979; The Stories of Ray Bradbury, 1980; The Ghosts of Forever, 1981; The Haunted Computer and the Android Pope, 1981; The Last Circus, 1981; The Complete Poems of Ray Bradbury, 1982; The Love Affair, 1983; Dinosaur Tales, 1983; A Memory for Murder, 1984; Forever and the Earth, 1984; Death Is a Lonely Business, 1986; The Toynbee Convector, 1988. Add: 10265 Cheviot Dr., Los Angeles, Calif. 90064, U.S.A.

BRADDON, Russell. Australian, b. 1921. Novels/Short stories, History, Biography. *Publs:* The Piddingtons, 1950; The Naked Island, 1951; Those in Peril, 1954; Cheshire V.C., 1954; Out of the Storm, 1956; Nancy Wake, 1956; End of a Hate, 1958; Gabriel Comes to 24, 1958; Proud American Boy, 1960; Joan Sutherland, 1962; The Year of the Angry Rabbit, 1964; Roy Thompson of Fleet Street, 1965; Committal Chamber, 1966; When the Enemy is Tired, 1968; The Inseparables, 1968; Will You Walk a Little Faster, 1969; The Seige, 1969; Prelude and Fugue for Lovers, 1971; The Progress of Private Lilyworth, 1971; End Play, 1972; Suez: Splitting of a Nation. 1973; A Hundred Days in Darien, 1974; All the Queen's Men, 1977; The Finalists, 1977; The Predator, 1980; The Other Hundred Years War, 1983; Thomas Baines, 1986; Images of Australia, 1988. Add: c/o John Farquharson Ltd., 162-168 Regent St., London W1R 5TB, England.

BRADEN, Waldo W. American, b. 1911. Speech/Rhetoric. Boyd Prof. Emeritus, Louisiana State Univ. *Publs:* (with G. W. Gray) Public Speaking, Principles and Practices, 1951, 1963; (with Ernest Brandenburg) Oral Decision-Making, 1955; (with Mary Louise Gehring) Speech Practices, a Resource Book for the Student of Public Speaking, 1958; (ed.) Speech Methods and Resources, A Textbook for the Teaching of Speech, 1961, 1972; Public Speaking: The Essentials, 1966; (ed. with Dorothy I. Anderson) Lectures Read to the Seniors in Harvard College, 1968; (with John H. Pennybacker) Broadcasting and the Public Interest, 1969; (with Lester Thonssen and A. Craig Baird) Speech Criticism, 1970;

(ed.) Oratory in the Old South, 1970; (ed.) Representative American Speeches, 10 vols., 1970–80; (ed.) Oratory in the New South, 1979; Oral Tradition in the South, 1983; Abraham Lincoln: Public Speaker, 1988. Add: Terrace Apts., W201, 1408 Business 70W., Box 21, Columbia, Mo. 65202, U.S.A.

BRADFIELD, Nancy. Pseud. for Nancy Margetts Sayer. British, b. 1913. Fashion/Costume. Adviser, National Trust on the Costume Collection, Snowshill Manor, Worcestershire; illustrator; lecturer on the history of costume, now retired. Formerly, Sr. Visiting Lectr. on the History of Costume, Textile and Fashion Dept., Gloucestershire Coll. of Art, Cheltenham. *Publs:* Historical Costumes of England 1066-1968, 1938, 3rd ed. 1970; Costume in Detail 1730-1930, 1968, 1981. Add: Elm Cottage, Far End, Sheepscombe, Stroud, Glos. GL6 7RL, England.

BRADFORD, Barbara Taylor. British, b. 1933. Historical/Romance. Reporter, 1949–51, and Women's Ed., 1951–53, Yorkshire Evening Post, Leeds; Fashion Ed., Woman's Own, London, 1953–54; Columnist, Evening News, London, 1955–57; freelance ed., London, 1959–62; Features Ed., Woman, London, 1962–64; Ed., National Design Center, NYC, 1964–65; syndicated columnist, Newsday, Long Island, NY, 1966. *Publs:* novels—A Woman of Substance, 1979; Voice of the Heart, 1983; Hold the Dream, 1985; Act of Will, 1986; To Be the Best, 1988; other—How to Be the Perfect Wife: Entertaining to Please Him, Etiquette to Please Him, and Fashions That Please Him, 3 vols., 1969–71; Easy Steps to Successful Decorating, 1971; How to Solve Your Decorating Problems, 1976; Decorating Ideas for Casual Living, 1977; Making Space Grow, 1979; Luxury Designs for Apartment Living, 1981. Add: 450 Park Ave. South, New York, NY 10003, U.S.A.

BRADFORD, Leland Powers. American, b. 1905. Psychology. Writer-consultant in org. development. Instr., Univ. of Illinois, Urbana, 1936–41; Dir., Service Projects, Illinois Works Projects Admin., 1940–43; Chief of Training, U.S. Immigration and Naturalization Service, 1943–44; Chief of Training, Federal Security Agency, 1944–45; Dir., Div. of Adult Education, National Educational Assn., 1945–63; Dir., National Inst. of Applied Behavioral Science, 1947–70. *Publs:* (ed. with J.R. Gibb and K.D. Benne) T-Group Theory and Laboratory Method, 1964; (ed. with K.D. Benne, J.R. Gibb and R. Lippitt) The Laboratory Method of Learning and Changing, 1975; The History of the National Training Laboratories 1947–70, 1975; Making Meetings Work, 1976; Group Development, 1978; (with M. Bradford) Retirement: Coping with Emotional Upheavals, 1979; Preparing for Retirement: A Program For Survival, 1981. Add: Box 548, Pinehurst, N.C. 28374, U.S.A.

BRADFORD, M(elvin) E(ustace). American, b. 1934. History, Literature, Biography. Prof. of English, Univ. of Dallas, since 1967 (Chmn. of the Dept., 1970–73). Instr. in English, U.S. Naval Academy, Annapolis, 1957–59, and Vanderbilt Univ., Nashville, 1959–62; Assoc. Prof. of English, Hardin-Simmons Univ., Abilene, Tex., 1962–64; Asst. Prof. of English, Northwestern State Coll., Natchitoches, La., 1964–67. Pres., Southwestern American Literature Assn., 1975–79. *Publs:* Rumors of Mortality: An Introduction to Allen Tate, 1969; (ed.) The Form Discovered: Essays on the Achievement of Andrew Lytle, 1973; (ed.) Arator, by John Taylor of Caroline, 1977; (ed.) A Better Guide Than Reason: Studies in the American Revolution, 1978; (ed., with James McClellan) Debates in the Several States on the Ratification of the Constitution of the United States, by Jonathan Elliot, 6 vols., 1980–88; A Worthy Company; Brief Lives of the Framers of the U.S. Constitution, 1982; Generations of the Faithful Heart: On the Literature of the South, 1982; Remembering Who We Are: Observations of a Southern Conservative, 1985; The Reactionary Imperative: Essays Literary and Political, 1989; Original Intentions: On the Making and Ratification of the U.S. Constitution, 1990. Add: English Dept., Univ. of Dallas Station, Irving, Tex. 75062, U.S.A.

BRADFORD, Peter Amory. American, b. 1942. Environmental Science/Ecology. Politics/Government. Cabinet Member, State of Maine, since 1982. Federal-State Coordinator, State of Maine, 1969–71; Commissioner, 1972–74, 1975–77, and Chmn., 1974–75, State of Maine Public Utilities Commn.; Commissioner, U.S. Nuclear Regulatory Commn., 1977–82. *Publs:* Fragile Structures: A Story of Oil Refineries, National Security, and the Coast of Maine, 1975. Add: N.Y. State Public Services, Commn. 3 Empire State Plaza, Albany, N.Y. 12210, U.S.A.

BRADFORD, Richard (Roark). American, b. 1932. Westerns/Adventure. Staff writer, New Mexico State Tourist Bureau, Santa Fe, 1956–59; Technical Writer and Ed., New Orleans Chamber of Commerce, 1959–61; Research Analyst, New Mexico Dept. of Development in the 1960's;

Screenwriter, Universal Pictures, 1968–71. *Publs:* Red Sky at Morning, 1968; So Far from Heaven, 1973. Add: P.O. Box 1395, Santa Fe, N.M. 87501, U.S.A.

BRADLEE, Ben(jamin Crowninshield). American, b. 1921. International relations/Current affairs. Vice Pres. and Exec. Ed., Washington Post, since 1968 (Managing Ed., 1965–68). Reporter, New Hampshire Sunday News, Manchester, 1946–48, and Washington Post, 1958–51; Press Attaché American Embassy, Paris, 1951–53; European Corresp., 1953–57, Reporter, Washington Bureau, 1957–61, and Sr. Ed. and Chief of Bureau, 1961–65, Newsweek mag. *Publs:* The Special Grace, 1964; Conversations with Kennedy, 1976. Add: Washington Post, 1150 15th St. N.W., Washington, D.C. 20071, U.S.A.

BRADLEY, David (Henry, Jr.). American, b. 1950. Novels. Assoc. Prof. of English, Temple Univ., Philadelphia, since 1982 (Asst. Prof., 1977–82). Reader and Asst. Ed., Lippincott, publishers, Philadelphia, 1974–76; Visiting Lectr., Univ. of Pennsylvania, Philadelphia, 1975; Editorial Consultant, Lippincott, 1977–78, and Ace Science Fiction, NYC, 1979. Member, Exec. Bd., PEN American Center, 1982–84. *Publs:* South Street, 1975; The Chaneysville Incident, 1981, in U.K. as Serpent's Tail, 1986. Add: Dept. of English, Temple Univ., Philadelphia, Pa. 191122, U.S.A.

BRADLEY, Ian (Roberts Ambrose). With N.F. Hallows, writes as Duplex. British, b. 1900. Engineering/Technology. In charge of research and development workshops, South Marston Works, Vickers Ltd., Swindon, 1955–65. *Publs:* (with N.F. Hallows) Lathe Devices, 1947; (with N.F. Hallows as Duplex) Sharpening Small Tools, 1948, 4th ed. 1976; Screw Threads and Twist Drills, 1949, 5th ed. 1977; (with N.F. Hallows as Duplex) In the Workshop, 3 vols., 1949–51; (with N.F. Hallows as Duplex) Lathe and Shaping Machine Tools, 1949, 5th ed. 1976; (with N.F. Hallows as Duplex) Electricity in the Small Workshop, 1949; (with N.F. Hallows) Workshop Equipment, 1949; (with N.F. Hallows as Duplex) Belt Drives in the Workshop, 1950, 4th ed. 1967; (with N.F. Hallows as Duplex) Fitting Bearings, 1950; (with N.F. Hallows as Duplex) The Novice's Workshop, 1967, rev. ed. as the Beginner's Workshop, 1975; The Drilling Machine, 1973; The Shaping Machine, 1973; The Grinding Machine, 1973; The Amateur's Workshop, 1973; A History of Machine Tools, 1974; Shaping Machine and Lathe Tools, 1976; Metal Working Tools and Their Uses, 1978. Add: Rossmore, Park St., Hungerford, Berks., England.

BRADLEY, James Vandiver. American, b. 1924. Mathematics/Statistics. Prof. of Psychology, New Mexico State Univ., since 1973 (Assoc. Prof. of Mathematics, 1968–70; Assoc. Prof of Psychology, 1968–73). Research Psychologist, Aerospace Medical Research Lab., Wright-Patterson Air Force Base, Ohio, 1952–66; Mathematical Statistician, Dept. of Health, Education and Welfare, Washington, D.C., 1966–67; Research Assoc., Behavior Research Lab., Antioch Coll., Yellow Springs, Ohio, 1967–68. *Publs:* Distribution-Free Statistical Tests, 1968; Probability, Decision, Statistics, 1976; File and Data-Base Techniques, 1982; Introduction to Data-Base Management in Business, 1983, 2nd ed., 1987. Add: Dept. of Psychology, New Mexico State Univ., Las Cruces, N.M. 88003, U.S.A.

BRADLEY, John Lewis. British, b. 1917. Literature. Instr., Wellesley Coll., Mass., 1948–51, and Univ. of Maryland, College Park, 1952–53; Asst. Prof., Clark Univ., Worcester, Mass., 1953–55; Asst. Prof., 1955–58, and Assoc. Prof., 1958–64, Mount Holyoke Coll., South Hadley, Mass.; Prof., Ohio State Univ., Columbus, 1964–66, Grad. Div., Univ. of South Carolina, Columbia, 1966–69, Univ. of Durham, England, 1969–78, and Univ. of Maryland, College Park, 1978–82. *Publs:* (ed.) Ruskin's Letters from Venice 1851-1852, 1955; (ed.) Ruskin's Letters to Lord and Lady Mount-Temple, 1964; (ed.) Selections From Mayhew's London Labour and the London Poor, 1966; (ed. with M. Stevens) Masterworks of English Prose, 1968; An Introduction to Ruskin, 1971; (ed.) Ruskin: The Critical Heritage, 1984; Lady Curzon's India, 1985; (co-ed.) The Correspondence of John Ruskin and Charles Eliot Norton, 1987. Add: Church Cottage, Hinton St. George, Somerset TA17 8SA, England.

BRADLEY, Marion Zimmer. Has also written as Lee Chapman, John Dexter, Miriam Gardner, Valerie Graves and Morgan Ives. American, b. 1930. Novels/Short stories, Historical/Romance/Gothic, Science fiction/Fantasy, Literature, Translations. *Publs:* Songs from Rivendell, 1959; A Complete, Cumulative Checklist of Lesbian, Variant, and Homosexual Fiction, 1960; The Door Through Space, 1961; Seven from the Stars, 1962; The Planet Savers, The Sword of Aldones, 1962; (as Lee Chapman) I Am a Lesbian (novel), 1962; (as Miriam Gardner) The

Strange Woman (novel), 1962; The Colours of Space (juvenile), 1963; (as Morgan Ives) Spare Her Heaven (novel), 1963, in Aust. as Anything Goes, 1964; (as Miriam Gardner) My Sister, My Love (novel), 1963; The Bloody Sun, 1964; Falcons of Narabedla, 1964; The Dark Intruders and Other Stories, 1964; (as Miriam Gardner) Twilight Lovers (novel), 1964; Star of Danger, 1965; (as Morgan Ives) Knives of Desire (novel), 1966; (as John Dexter) No Adam for Eve (novel), 1966; Castle Terror (novel), 1966; Souvenir of Monique (novel), 1967; Bluebeard's Daughter (novel), 1968; The Brass Dragon, 1969; The Winds of Darkover, 1970; The World Wreckers, 1971; (trans.) E. Villano in su Rincon, by Lope de Vega, 1971; Darkover Landfall, 1972; (as Valerie Graves) Witch Hill (novel), 1972; Dark Satanic (novel), 1972; Hunters of the Red Moon, 1973; In the Steps of the Master (novel), 1973; Men, Halflings, and Hero-Worship (criticism), 1973; The Spell Sword, 1974; the Necessity of Beauty: Robert W. Chambers and the Romantic Tradition (criticism), 1974; The Jewel of Arwen, 1974; Endless Voyage, 1975, as Endless Universe, 1979; The Heritage of Hastur, 1975; Can Ellen Be Saved? (novel), 1975; The Parting of Arwen, 1975; The Shattered Chain, 1976; Drums of Darkness (novel), 1976; The Forbidden Tower, 1977; The Storm Queen, 1978; The Ruins of Isis, 1978; The Catch Trap (novel), 1979; (with Paul E. Zimmer) The Survivors, 1979; The House Between the Worlds, 1980; Two to Conquer, 1980; Survey Ship, 1980; (ed.) Elbow Room, 1980; The Keeper's Price (short stories), 1980; Sharra's Exile, 1981; Sword of Chaos, 1982; Hawkmistress, 1982; The Mists of Avalon, 1983; Thendara House, 1983; City of Sorcery, 1984; Sword and Sorceress, 1984; The Inheritor, 1984; Night's Daughter, 1985; Free Amazons of Darkover, 1985; Warrior Woman, 1985; Sword and Sorceress, 3 vols, 1985–87; Other Side of the Mirror, 1987; Red Sun of Darkover, 1987; The Firebrand, 1987. Add: Box 245-A, Berkeley, Calif. 94701, U.S.A.

BRADLEY, R.C. American, b. 1929. Education. Prof. of Education, North Texas State Univ., Denton, since 1963. Ed., The TEPSA Journal, Austin, Tex. Instr., Univ. of Missouri, Columbia, 1959–63. *Publs:* (with N. Wesley Earp) Exemplars of the Teacher's Cognitive Domain, 1967; (with Earp) Circus Fun for More than One, 1969; The Education of Exceptional Children, 1970; The Emergency Exceptionality Teachers Manual, 1970; Parent Teacher Interviews: A Modern Concept of Oral Reporting, 1971; Improving Instruction of Experienced Teachers, 1974; (with Frank E. Halstead) The Beginning Elementary School Teacher in Action, 1974; Driving Little Boys Sane, 1976; Teaching Power, 1977; Motivating Secondary School Students: How to Perform the Miracle, 1978; Schools as Joyous Places, 1979; Teen-Ager! How Would You Like to Make Tomorrow the Greatest Day in Your Life, 1979; Sugar and Spice plus Little Girls' Rights, 1980; Smile! Increase Your Face Value, 1980; How to Handle Stress Before Distress Mis-Handles You, 1981; You Can Make a Difference, 1983. Add: 2032 Houston Pl., Denton, Tex. 76201, U.S.A.

BRADLEY, Ramona K(aiser). American, b. 1909. Plays/Screenplays, Mythology/Folklore. Curator, Sherman Museum, Sherman Indian High Sch., Riverside, Calif., since 1970 (Secty., Patent Attorney, 1939–54). Former Pres., Riverside Branch, National League of American Pen Women Inc.; Trustee, Riverside Public Library, 1968–74; Member, Riverside Cultural Heritage Bd., Calif., 1974–80. *Publs:* Glimpses Into the Past, 1940; Spirits of Hetuck (play), 1941; Mahaskah (play), 1944; Weavers of Tales. Add: 9130 Andrew St., Riverside, Calif. 92503, U.S.A.

BRADLOW, Frank Rosslyn. South African, b. 1913. History, Autobiography/Memoirs/Personal, Biography. Pres., Friends of South African Library, since 1966, and Van Riebeeck Soc., since 1970; Trustee, South African Library, and William Fehr Art Collection; Member, Council of Univ. of Cape Town. Past Pres., South African P.E.N. Centre, Cape. *Publs:* (with Edna Bradlow) Thomas Bowler of the Cape of Good Hope, 1955; (with Edna Bradlow) Here Comes the Alabama, 1958; Baron von Ludwig and the Ludwigsburg Garden, 1965; Thomas Bowler: His Life and Work, 1967; C.I. Latrobe: Missionary, 1970; Thomas Bowler in Mauritius, 1970; Art and Africana, 1975; Tales of a Trout Fishing Duffer, 1975; Thomas Baines: His Art and Work, 1976; Printing for Africa, 1988. Add: Sha-anan, 5 Shetland St., Rondebosch 7700, Cape, South Africa.

BRADMAN, (Sir) Donald (George). Australian, b. 1908. Cricket. Company dir. Played cricket for New South Wales, 1927–34, for South Australia, 1935–49, and for Australia, 1928–48, Captain 1936–48; Chmn., Australian Cricket Bd., 1960–63, 1969–72. *Publs:* Don Bradman's Book, 1930; How to Play Cricket, 1935; My Cricketing Life, 1938; Farewell to Cricket, 1950, 1988; The Art of Cricket, 1958; The Bradman Albums, 1988. Add: 2 Holden St., Kensington Park, S.A. 5068, Australia.

BRADSHAW, Gillian. American, b. 1956. Historical/Romance. *Pubs:* Down the Long Wind: The Magical Trilogy of Arthurian Britain, 1984, comprising Hawk of May, 1980, Kingdom of Summer, 1981, and In Winter's Shadow, 1982; The Beacon at Alexandria, 1986; The Bearkeeper's Daughter, 1987; Imperial Purple, 1989. Add: c/o Houghton Mifflin Co., 2 Park St., Boston, MA 02108, U.S.A.

BRADWELL, James. *See* KENT, Arthur.

BRADY, William S. *See* HARVEY, John B.

BRAGG, Melvyn. British, b. 1939. Novels/Short stories, Plays/Screenplays, Biography. Head of Arts, and Ed. and Presenter, ITV Arts Prog., London Weekend T.V., The South Bank Show, since 1978. Presenter and Producer, BBC Television, 1961–67 and 1974–77. Chmn., Arts Council Literature panel, 1977–78. *Pubs:* For Want of a Nail, 1965; The Second Inheritance, 1966; Without a City Wall, 1968; The Hired Man, 1969; Play Dirty (screenplay), 1969; Isadora (screenplay), 1969; A Place in England, 1970; The Music Lovers (screenplay), 1971; The Nerve, 1971; The Hunt, 1972; Josh Lawton, 1972; The Silken Net, 1974; Speak for England, 1976; A Christmas Child, 1977; Autumn Manouvers, 1978; Kingdom Come, 1980; Love and Glory, 1983; Land of the Lakes, 1983; Laurence Olivier, 1984; (ed.) Cumbria in Verse, 1984; The Maid of Buttermere, 1987; Rich: The Life of Richard Burton, 1988. Add: 12 Hampstead Hill Gardens, London NW3, England.

BRAHAM, Allan (John Witney). British, b. 1937. Architecture, Art. Keeper and Deputy Dir., National Gallery, London, since 1978 (Asst. Keeper, 1962–73; Deputy Keeper, 1973–78). *Pubs:* exhibition catalogues and National Gallery booklets; and, Dürer, 1965; Murillo, 1966; The National Gallery Italian Painting of the High Renaissance, 1971; (with Peter Smith) François Mansart, 1971, 1973; Funeral Decorations in Early Eighteenth Century Rome, 1975; (with Hellmut Hager) Carlo Fontana: The Drawings at Windsor Castle, 1977; The Architecture of the French Enlightenment, 1980; National Gallery: Italian Paintings of the 16th Century, 1985. Add: 15A Acol Rd., London NW6 3AA, England.

BRAHMANANDA, Palahally Ramaiya. Indian, b. 1926. Economics. Prof., since 1963, and Dir., Dept. of Economics, since 1976, Univ. of Bombay (joined faculty, 1950). Ed., Indian Economic Journal, since 1956. *Pubs:* (with C.N. Vakil) Planning for a Shortage Economy, 1952; (with C.N. Vakil) Economics of Electricity Planning, 1952; (with C.N. Vakil) Planning for an Expanding Economy, 1956; Studies in Welfare Maximization, 1959; The New Classical vs. the Neo-Classical Economics, 1967; The Gold-Money Rift—A Classical Theory of International Liquidity, 1969; Explorations in the New Classical Theory of Political Economy and a Connected Critique of Economic Theory, 1974; Determinants of Real National Income and of Price Level, 1976; The Falling Economy and How to Revive It, 1977; Planning for a Futureless Economy—A Critique of the Sixth Plan, 1978; Growthless Inflation by Means of Stockless Money, 1980; The I.M.F. Loan and India's Economic Future, 1982; Productivity in the Indian Economy: Rising Inputs for Falling Outputs, 1982; New Models for the American Ecomomy, 1985; Keynes' "General Theory:" A New-Classical Critique, 1986; Monetary Theory—A Real Angle, 1986. Add: Dept. of Economics, Univ. of Bombay, Vidyanagari P.O., Vidyanagari Marg, Bombay 400098, India

BRAITHWAITE, E(dward) R(ichard). Guyanan, b. 1922. Novels/Short stories, Autobiography/Memoirs/Personal. Sch. teacher, London, 1950–57; Welfare Officer, L.C.C., 1958–60; Human Rights Officer, World Veterans Foundn., Paris, 1960–63; Lectr. and Educational Consultant, Unesco, Paris, 1963–66; Permanent Rep. of Guyana to the U.N., NYC, 1967–68; Ambassador of Guyana to Venezuela, 1968–69. *Pubs:* To Sir, With Love, 1959; Paid Servant, 1962; A Kind of Homecoming, 1962; Choice of Straws (novel), 1965; Reluctant Neighbours, 1972; Honorary White, 1975. Add: The Parker 40, Apt. 16K, 305 E. 40th St., New York, N.Y. 10017, U.S.A.

BRAKHAGE, (James) Stan(ley). American, b. 1933. Film, Autobiography/Memoirs/Personal. Freelance film-maker since 1952. Prof., Univ. of Colorado, Boulder, since 1981. Lectr., Chicago Art Inst., 1969–1981. *Pubs:* Metaphors on Vision, 1963; A Moving Picture Giving and Taking Book, 1971; The Brakhage Lectures, 1972; Seen, 1975; Film Biographies, 1977; Brakhage Scrapbook, 1982; I...Sleeping (Being a Dream Journal and Parenthetical Explication), 1989; Film at Wit's End, 1989. Add: 1405 Broadway #304, Boulder, Colo. 80302, U.S.A.

BRAMBLE, Forbes. British, b. 1939. Novels/Short stories. Plays/Screenplays. Partner, Bickerdike, Allen, Bramble, architects, London. Theatre Architecture Critic, Theatre Quarterly, London, 1971–73. *Pubs:* The Dice (play), 1962; The Two-Timers (play), 1963; (contrib.) Essays on Local Government Enterprise, 1964; Stone (novel), 1973; The Strange Case of Deacon Brodie, 1975; Prevailing Spirits, 1976; Regent Square, 1977. Add: 59 Mercers Rd., London., N19, England.

BRAMSON, Leon. American, b. 1930. Sociology. Asst. Dir. and Prog. Officer, National Endowment for the Humanities, Washington, D.C., since 1982. Prof. of Sociology, Swarthmore Coll., Pa., since 1970 (Assoc. Prof., 1965–70). Instr., 1959–61, and Asst. Prof., 1961–65, Dept. of Social Relations, Harvard Univ., Cambridge, Mass.; Program Officer, Exxon Education Foundn, NYC, 1978–80; Coordinator for Social Analysis, Corporate Planning Dept., Exxon Corp., 1980–82. *Pubs:* The Political Context of Sociology, 1961; (ed.) Examining in Harvard College: A Collection of Essays by Members of the Harvard Faculty, 1963; (ed. with G.W. Goethals) War: Studies from Psychology, Sociology, Anthropology, 1964; (ed.) Robert MacIver: On Community, Society and Power, 1970. Add: National Endowment for the Humanities, 1100 Pennsylvania Ave. N.W., Washington, D.C. 20506, U.S.A.

BRANCH, Alan E(dward). British, b. 1933. Business, Marketing. Sr. Lectr., Basingstoke Technical Coll. Marketing, shipping and export consultant. *Pubs:* Elements of Shipping, 1964, 6th ed., 1989; Elements of Export Practice, 1979, 1985; Economics of Shipping Practice and Management, 1982, 1988; Dictionary of Shipping International Trade Terms and Abbreviations, 3rd ed., 1987; Elements of Export Marketing and Management, 1984, 1990; Dictionary of Commercial Terms and Abbreviations, 1984; Elements of Port Operation and Management, 1986; Dictionary of English-Arabic Commercial, International Trade and Shipping Terms, 1988; Export-Import Shipping Documentation, 1989; Elements of Import Practice, 1990. Add: 19 The Ridings, Emmer Green, Reading, Berkshire, England.

BRANCH, Edgar Marquess. American, b. 1913. Literature, Biography. Research Prof. of English Emeritus and Research Assoc. in American Literature, Miami Univ., Oxford, Ohio, since 1978 (Prof. of English, 1941–64; Chmn. of Dept., 1959–64; Research Prof. of English. 1964–78). Sr. Fellow, National Endowment for the Humanities, 1971–72. *Pubs:* The Literary Apprenticeship of Mark Twain, 1950; A Bibliography of the Writings of James T. Farrell, 1921–1957, 1959; Clemens of the "Call", 1969, James T. Farrell, 1971; (with F. Anderson) The Great Landslide Case, 1972; (ed.) Mark Twain's Early Tales and Sketches, vol. I, 1851-64, 1979, vol. II, 1864-65, 1981; "Men Call Me 'Lucky'": Mark Twain and the Pennsylvania, 1985; (with Robert H. Hirst) Life and Death at Compromise, 1985. Add: English Dept., Miami Univ., Oxford, Ohio 45056, U.S.A.

BRAND, Mona. Pseud. for Mona Alexis Fox. Australian, b. 1915. Novels/Short stories, Plays/Screenplays, Children's non-fiction. Advertising copywriter, 1935–43; Industrial Welfare Research Officer, Australian Dept. of Labour and National Service, 1943–48. *Pubs:* Wheel and Bobbin, 1936; Silver Singing, 1938; Lass in Love, 1946; Daughters of Vietnam, 1958; Three Plays, 1965; Here Under Heaven, 1970; How Our Country Is Governed, 1976; (with others) Australian political Milestones, 1976; The Chinese in Australia, 1978; Australiana, 1979; Australian Transport, 1980; Flying Saucery (plays for children), 1981; Here Comes Kisch! (play), 1983. Add: 10 Little Surrey St., Potts Point, N.S.W., Australia.

BRAND, Oscar. Canadian/American, b. 1920. Children's fiction, Plays/Screenplays, Songs, lyrics and libretti. Freelance writer, composer and folk-singer. Pres., Harlequin Productions, and Gypsy Hill Music; Lectr. on Dramatic Writing, Hofstra Univ., Hempstead, N.Y.; Co-ordinator of Folk Music, WNYC; host of numerous television folk-song progs.; Curator, Songwriters Hall of Fame, N.Y.C. *Pubs:* Courting Songs. 1952; Folksongs for Fun, 1957; The Ballad Mongers (autobiography), 1957; Bawdy Songs, 1958; (writer-composer) The Gold Rush (ballet), 1961; (co-writer-composer) In White America (play), 1962; (co-writer-composer) A Joyful Noise (musical play), 1966; (co-writer-composer) The Education of Hyman Kaplan (musical play), 1967; (writer-composer) Celebrate (religious songs), 1968; (co-writer-composer) How to Steal an Election (musical play), 1969; Songs of '76 (music history), 1973; When I First Came To This Land (children), 1974; (writer-composer) Thunder Rock (musical play), 1974, Party Songs, 1985. Add: 141 Baker Hill, Great Neck, N.Y. 11023, U.S.A.

BRANDEN, Nathaniel. American, b. 1930. Literature, Psychology. Psychotherapist in private practice and author, since 1956; Owner and Dir., The Biocentric Inst. (now the Branden Inst. for Self-Esteem), Los Angeles, since 1968. Contrib., Co-Founder and Co-Ed. with Ayn Rand, the Objectivist Newsletter, 1962–65, and under new title The Objectivist, 1966–68. *Publs:* Who is Ayn Rand?: An Analysis of the Novels of Ayn Rand, 1962; The Psychology of Self-Esteem, 1969; Breaking Free, 1970; The Disowned Self, 1971; The Psychology of Romantic Love, 1980; (with E. Devers Branden) The Romantic Love Question and Answer Book, 1982, revised ed. as What Loves Asks of Us, 1987; If You Could Hear What I Cannot Say, 1983; Honoring the Self, 1984; To See What I See and Know What I Know, 1986; How to Raise Your Self-Esteem, 1987; Judgement Day: My Years with Ayn Rand, 1989. Add: P.O. Box 2609, Beverly Hills, Calif. 90213, U.S.A.

BRANDENBERG, Aliki. Writes as Aliki. American, b. 1929. Children's fiction, Children's non-fiction. *Publs:* The Story of William Tell, 1961; The Wish Workers, 1962; My Five Senses, 1962; My Hands, 1962; The Story of Johnny Appleseed, 1963; The Story of William Penn, 1964; George and the Cherry Tree, 1964; A Weed is a Flower, 1965; Keep Your Mouth Closed, Dear, 1966; Three Gold Pieces, 1967, Hush Little Baby, 1968; Diogenes, 1969; The Eggs, 1969; My Visit to the Dinosaurs, 1969; Fossils Tell of Long Ago, 1972; June 7, 1972; The Long Lost Coelacanth and Other Living Fossils, 1973; Go Tell Aunt Rhody, 1974; Green Grass and White Milk, 1974; At Mary Bloom's 1976; Corn Is Maize, 1976; The Many Lives of Benjamin Franklin, 1977; Wild and Wooly Mammoths, 1977; The Twelve Months, 1978; Mummies, 1979; The Two of Them, 1979; Digging Up Dinosaurs, 1981; We Are Best Friends, 1982; Use Your Head, Dear, 1983; A Medieval Feast, 1983; Feelings, 1984; Dinosaurs Are Different, 1985; Jack and Jake, 1986; How a Break is Made, 1986; Overnight at Mary Bloom's, 1987; Welcome Little Baby, 1987; Dinosaur Bones, 1988. Add: 17 Regent's Park Terrace, London NW1 7ED, England.

BRANDENBERG, Franz. Swiss, b. 1932. Children's fiction. *Publs:* I Once Knew a Man, 1970; Fresh Cider and Pie, 1973; A Secret for Grandmother's Birthday, 1975; No School Today, 1975; A Robber! A Robber!, 1976; I Wish I Was Sick Too!, 1976; Nice New Neighbors, 1977; What Can You Make of It?, 1977; A Picnic, Hurrah!, 1978; Six New Students, 1978; Everyone Ready?, 1979; It's Not My Fault, 1980; Leo and Emily series, 3 vols., 1981–84; Aunt Nina series, 2 vols., 1983; Otto Is Different, 1985; The Hit of the Party, 1985; Cock-a-Doodle-Doo, 1980; What's Wrong with a Van?, 1987; Leo and Emily's Zoo, 1988; Aunt Nina, Good Night, 1988. Add: 17 Regent's Park Terrace, London NW1 7ED, England.

BRANDES, Joseph. American, b. 1928. History. Prof. of History, William Paterson Coll., Wayne, N.J., since 1958. Research Assoc., American Jewish History Center, since 1965; member, Academic Council and Publication Cttee., American Jewish Historical Society, since 1971. Consulting Economist, U.S. Dept. of Commerce, Washington, D.C., 1958–60. *Publs:* (contrib. ed.) Pictorial History of the World, 1956; Herbert Hoover and Economic Diplomacy, 1962; Immigrants to Freedom, 1971. Add: 16-36 Raymond St., Fair Lawn, N.J. 07410, U.S.A.

BRANDEWYNE, Rebecca. American, b. 1955. Historical/Romance/Gothic, Science fiction/Fantasy. Full-time writer. *Publs:* No Gentle Love, 1980; Forever My Love, 1982; Love, Cherish Me, 1983; Rose of Rapture, 1984; And Gold Was Ours, 1984; The Outlaw Hearts, 1986; Desire in Disguise, 1987; Passion Moon Rising, 1988; Upon a Moon-Dark Moor, 1988; Across A Starlit Sea, 1989. Add: 8928 Crestwood Court, Country Place, Wichita, Kans. 67206, U.S.A.

BRANDI, John. American, b. 1943. Short stories, Poetry. Artist. Member, Peace Corps, South America, 1965–68. *Publs:* Poem Afternoon in a Square of Guadalajara, 1970; Emptylots: Poems of Venice and L.A., 1971; Field Notes from Alaska, 1971; Desde Alla (short stories), 1971; One Week of Mornings at Dry Creek (short stories), 1971; Y Aun Hay Mas, Dreams and Exploration: New and Old Mexico, 1972; Narrowgauge to Riobamba (short stories), 1973; San Francisco Lastday Homebound Hangover Highway Blues, 1973; A Partial Exploration of Palo Flechado Canyon, 1973; Firebook, 1974; The Phoenix Gas Slam, 1974; In a December Storm, 1975; Looking for Minerals, 1975; Chimborazo: Life on the Haciendas of Highland Ecuador, 1976; Memorandum from a Caribbean Isle, 1977; Diary from Baja, California, 1978; Poems from Four Corners, 1978; Andrean Town Circa 1980, 1978; Diary from a Journey to the Middle of the World, 1979; Rite for the Beautification of All Beings, 1983;

The Cowboy from Phantom Banks (short stories), 1983; That Crow That Visited Was Flying Backwards, 1984; That Back Road In, 1985; Poems at the Edge of Day, 1984; Zuleikha's Book, 1985; Hymn for a Night Feast, 1988. Add: P.O. Box 2553, Corrales, N. Mex. 87048, U.S.A.

BRANDON, (Oscar) Henry. British, b. 1916. Politics/Government, Social commentary/phenomena. Assoc. Ed. and Chief American Correspondent, The Sunday Times newspaper, London, retired 1983 (joined paper, 1939, War Correspondent, North Africa and Western Europe, 1943–45, Paris Correspondent, 1945–46, Roving Diplomatic Correspondent, 1947–49, Washington Correspondent, since 1950); syndicated columnist for the New York Times News Service, since 1983. Syndicated columnist for the Washington Star 1979–81. *Publs:* As We Are, 1961; In the Red, 1966; Conversations with Henry Brandon, 1966; The Anatomy of Error, 1970; Retreat of American Power, 1973. Add: 3604 Winfield Lane N.W., Washington, D.C. 20007, U.S.A.

BRANDON, Joe. *See* DAVIS, Robert Prunier.

BRANDON, Sheila. *See* RAYNER, Claire.

BRANDRETH, Gyles (Daubeney). British, b. 1948. Children's non-fiction, Criminology/Law enforcement/Prisons, Recreation/Leisure/Hobbies. Chmn., Victorama Ltd., London, since 1974; Deputy Chmn., Unicorn Heritage, since 1987. Organiser, National Scrabble Championships, and Dir., British Pantomime Assn., since 1971; Dir., European Movement's People for Europe campaign, since 1975; broadcaster, Countdown and TV-AM, both since 1983. *Publs:* Created in Captivity, 1972; Party Games, 1972; Bedroom Book, 1973; I Scream for Ice Cream, 1974; Games for Trains, Planes and Wet Days, 1974; Complete Book of Home Entertainment, 1974; Christmas Book, 1975; Waiting Games, 1975; Hospital Fun and Games, 1975; (with Cyril Fletcher) Generation Quiz Book, 1975; Domino Games and Puzzles, 1975; Games and Puzzles with Coins and Matches, 1976; Hotchpotch, 1976; Fun and Games for a Rainy Day, 1976; Edward Lear's Book of Mazes, 1977; The Funniest Man on Earth: The Story of Dan Leno, 1977; Indoor Games, 1977; Be Kind to Mum and Dad, 1977; Big Book of Secrets, 1977; Book of Tongue Twisters, 1977; Brain-Teasers and Mind-Benders, 1977; Bumper Wonder Book, 1977; Castles and Historic Houses, 1977; The Magic of Houdini, 1978; The Complete Husband, 1978; The Last Word, 1979; The Joy of Lex, 1980; More Joy of Lex, 1982; Great Theatrical Disasters, 1982; The Books of Mistaikes, 1982; The Complete Public Speaker, 1983; The Christmas Book, 1984; Everyman's Classic Puzzles, 1984; Everyman's Children's Games, 1984; John Gielgud: A Celebration, 1984; Great Sexual Disasters, 1984; (with George Hostler) Wit Knits, 1985; Cats' Tales, 1986; (with Linda O'Brien) Knitability, 1987; Even Greater Sexual Disasters, 1987. Add: Victorama Ltd., Britannia House, Glenthorpe Rd., London W6 0LF, England.

BRANDT, Leslie F. American, b. 1919. Theology/Religion. Lutheran Clergyman, since 1945: missionary service, China, Taiwan, and Japan; parishes in S.D., Minn., N.D., and Calif. *Publs:* Good Lord, Where Are You?, 1967; Great God, Here I Am, 1968; Can I Forgive God?, 1969; God is Here, Let's Celebrate!, 1970; The Lord Rules, Let's Serve Him, 1972; What the Devil, 1972; Contemporary Introits and Collects, 1972; Meditations of a Radical Christian, 1973; Psalms/Now, 1974; Book of Christian Prayer, 1974; Living Through Loving, 1974; Growing Together, 1975; Epistles/Now, 1976; Jesus/Now, 1978; Prophets/Now, 1979; Book of Christian Prayer, 1980; Christ in Your Life, 1980; Battle Manual for Christian Survival, 1980; Meditations on a Loving God, 1983; Bible Readings for the Retired, Bible Readings for Troubled Times, 1984; Meditations on the Journey of Faith, 1986; Two Minutes for God, 1988. Add: 2255 Cottage Way, Vista, Calif. 92083, U.S.A.

BRANDT, Richard M. American, b. 1922. Education, Psychology. Curry Prof. of Education, Univ. of Virginia, Charlottesville, since 1984 (Assoc. Prof., 1965–68; Prof. and Chmn., Dept. of Foundns. of Education, 1968–74; Dean, Sch. of Education, 1974–84). Instr., 1953–54, Asst. Prof., 1954–57, and Assoc. Prof., 1957–65, Univ. of Maryland, College Park. *Publs:* Studying Behavior in Natural Settings, 1972, 1981; (ed.) Observational Methods in the Classroom, 1973; Public Education under Scrutiny, 1981. Add: Rt. 1, Box 619, Crozet, Va. 22932, U.S.A.

BRANDT, Tom. *See* DEWEY, Thomas B.

BRANFIELD, John (Charles). British, b. 1931. Novels/Short stories, Children's Fiction. English Teacher, 1961–64, Head of English, 1964–75, and Sixth Form Tutor, 1975–81, Camborne Grammar School, later Camborne Comprehensive Sch., Cornwall. *Publs:* A Flag in the Map (adult novel), 1960; Look the Other Way (adult novel), 1963; In the Country (adult novel), 1966; Nancekuke (in U.S. as The Poison Factory; children's fiction), 1972; Sugar Mouse (in U.S. as Why Me?; children's fiction), 1973; The Scillies Trip (children's fiction), 1975; Castle Minalto, or, The Entertainment of Dr. Trevail (children's fiction), 1979; The Fox in Winter (children's fiction), 1980; Brown Cow (children's fiction), 1983; Thin Ice (children's fiction), 1983; The Falkland's Summer (children's fiction), 1987; The Day I Shot My Dad and Other Stories (children's fiction), 1989. Add: Mingoose Villa, Mingoose, Mount Hawke, Truro, Cornwall, England.

BRANIGAN, Keith. British, b. 1940. Archaeology/Antiquities, History. Prof. of Prehistory and Archaeology, Univ. of Sheffield, since 1976. General Ed., Peoples of Roman Britain, Duckworth, London, since 1973. Research Fellow, Univ. of Birmingham, 1965–66; Lectr. in Archaeology, Univ. of Bristol, 1966–76. *Publs:* Copper and Bronze Working in Early Bronze Age Crete, 1968; Foundations of Palatial Crete, 1970; The Tombs of Mesara, 1970; Latimer, 1971; Town and Country, 1973; Reconstructing the Past, 1974; Aegean Metalwork of the Early and Middle Bronze Ages, 1974; Atlas of Ancient Civilisations, 1976; Prehistoric Britain, 1976; The Roman Villa in S.W. England, 1977; Gatcombe: A Roman-British Villa and Its Estate, 1978; (ed.) Rome and the Brigantes, 1980; Roman Britain: Life in an Imperial Province, 1980; (with M. Vickers) Hellas, 1980; Atlas of Archaeology, 1982; Prehistory, 1984; The Catuvellauni, 1985; Archaeology Explained, 1987; (co-ed.) The Economy of Romano-British Villas, 1988. Add: Dept. of Prehistory and Archaeology, Univ. of Sheffield, Sheffield S10 2TN, England.

BRANSON, H(enry) C(lay). American. Mystery/Crime/Suspense. *Publs:* mystery novels—I'll Eat You Last, 1941 (as I'll Kill You Last, 1942); The Pricking Thumb, 1942; Case of the Giant Killer, 1944; The Fearful Passage, 1945; Last Year's Blood, 1947; The Leaden Bubble, 1949; Beggar's Choice, 1953; other novel—Salisbury Plain, 1965. Add: c/o Simon and Schuster, 1230 Sixth Ave., New York, N.Y. 10020, U.S.A.

BRASCH, Rudolph. Australian, b. 1912. Theology/Religion, Travel/Exploration/Adventure, Biography. Minister, North London Progressive Synagogue, and Southgate & Enfield Liberal Synagogue, 1938–48; Founder and Minister, Dublin Progressive Synagogue, 1946–47; Minister and Dir. of Public Relations, Springs & District Reform Synagogues, South Africa, 1948–49; Chief Minister, Temple Emanuel, Sydney, 1949–79; founder, North Shore Temple Emanuel, Sydney, 1960; Rabbi, Temple Etz Ahayem, Montgomery, Ala., 1980. *Publs:* (with Lily H. Montagu) A Little Book of Comfort, 1948; Symbolism of King Solomon's Temple, 1954; General Sir John Monash, 1959; The Star of David, 1955; The Eternal Flame, 1958; How Did it Begin?, 1965, 7th ed. 1973; Mexico—A Country of Contrasts, 1967; The Judaic Heritage, 1969; The Unknown Sanctuary, 1969; How Did Sports Begin?, 1970, 5th ed. 1973; How Did Sex Begin?, 1973, 1974; The Supernatural and You!, 1976; Strange Customs, 1976, 1984; Australian Jews of Today, 1977; There's a Reason for Everything, 1982; Mistakes, Misnomers, and Misconceptions, 1983; Thank God I'm an Atheist, 1987; Permanent Addresses, 1987; Even More Permanent Addresses, 1989. Add: 14 Derby St., Vaucluse, N.S.W., 2030, Australia.

BRASHER, Christopher (William). British, b. 1928. Sports/Physical education/Keeping fit, Travel/Exploration/Adventure. Corresp., The Observer (Sports Ed.), 1957–61. Organizer of the London Marathon. Head of General Features, BBC Television, 1969–72. Ed. Mountain Life, British Mountaineering Council, 1973–75. *Publs:* (with J. Hunt) the Red Snows, 1960; Sportsmen of Our Time, 1962; Tokyo 1964; A Diary of the XVIIIth Olympiad, 1964; Mexico 1968: A Diary of the XIXth Olympics, 1968; Munich 72, 1972. Add: The Navigator's House, River Lane, Richmond, Surrey TW10 7AG, England.

BRASHER, Norman Henry. British, b. 1922. History, Politics/Government. Dir. of Studies, Bexley Grammar Sch., 1973–82. Vice-Chmn., Teaching of History Cttee., Asst. Masters Assn., 1972–75. *Publs:* Studies in British Government, 1965, 1971; (with E.E. Reynolds) Britain in the Twentieth Century 1900–1964, 1966; Arguments in History: Britain in the 19th Century, 1968; The Young Historian, 1970. Add: 17 Willingdon Park Dr., Eastbourne, E. Sussex BN22 0BS, England.

BRASHLER, William. American, b. 1947. Novels/Short stories, Biography. Full-time writer since 1973. Reporter, Lerner Newspapers, Chicago, 1971–73. *Publs:* The Bingo Long Traveling All-Stars and Motor Kings (novels), 1973; (with Christopher Janus) The Search for Peking Man, 1975; City Dogs (novel), 1976; The Don: The Life and Death of Sam Giancana, 1977; Josh Gibson: A Life in the Negro Leagues, 1978;

(with Johnny Bench) Catch You Later: The Autobiography of Johnny Bench, 1979; The Chosen Prey, 1983; Traders, 1989. Add: 3802 N. Hoyne, Chicago, Ill. 60618, U.S.A.

BRATA, Sasthi (Sasthibrata Chakravarti). British (b. Indian), b. 1939. Novels/Short stories, Poetry, Autobiography/Memoirs/Personal, Documentaries/Reportage. London Columnist, Statesman, 1977–80. *Publs:* Eleven Poems, 1960; My God Died Young (autobiography), 1968; Confessions of an Indian Woman Eater, 1971, in India as Confessions of an Indian Lover, 1973; She and He, 1973; Astride Two Worlds: Traitor to India (autobiography; in U.K. as Traitor to India: A Search for Home), 1976; Encounter (short stories), 1978; The Sensuous Guru: The Making of a Mystic President, 1980; India: Labyrinths in the Lotus Land, 1985; India: The Perpetual Paradox, 1986. Add: 33 Savernake Rd., London NW3, England.

BRATBY, John Randall. British, b. 1928. Novels/Short stories, Art. Artist and writer. Member, The London Group, and Ed.-in-Chief, Art Quarterly. One-man exhibitions, Beaux Arts Gallery, since 1954, and Zwemmer Gallery, since 1959, both London. *Publs:* Breakdown, 1960; Breakfast and Elevenses, 1961; Break-Pedal Down (play and novel), 1962; Break-50 Kill, 1963; Stanley Spencer, 1969. Add: The Cupola and Tower of the Winds, Belmont Rd., Hastings, E. Sussex, England.

BRATHWAITE, Edward Kamau. Barbadian, b. 1930. Plays/Screenplays, Poetry, History. Reader in History, Univ. of the West Indies, Mona, since 1972 (Lectr., 1962–72; Sr. Lectr., 1972–76). Ed., Savacou mag., Mona, since 1970. Education Officer, Ministry of Education, Ghana, 1954–62; Plebiscite Officer, Trans-Volta Togoland, U.N., 1956–57; Tutor, Univ. of the West Indies Extra Mural Dept., St. Lucia, 1962–63. *Publs:* Four Plays for Primary Schools, 1961; Odale's Choice (play), 1962; Iounaloa: Recent Writing from St. Lucia, 1963; Rights of Passage, 1967; Masks, 1968; The People Who Came, 1-3, 1968–72; Islands, 1969; (with Alan Bold and Edwin Morgan) Penguin Modern Poets 15, 1969; Panda No. 349, 1969; Folk Culture of the Slaves in Jamaica, 1970; The Development of Creole Society in Jamaica, 1971; The Arrivants: A New World Trilogy, 1973; Caribbean Man in Space and Time, 1974; Contradictory Omens: Cultural Diversity and Integration in the Caribbean, 1974; Other Exiles, 1975; Our Ancestral Heritage, 1976; Black and Blues, 1976; Mother Poem, 1977; Wars of Respect, 1977; Jamaica Poetry, 1979; Sun Poem, 1982; Third World Poems, 1982; X-Self, 1986; Mother Poem (play), 1989. Add: Dept. of History, Univ. of the West Indies, Mona, Kingston 7, Jamaica.

BRATHWAITE, Errol (Freeman). New Zealander, b. 1924. Novels/Short stories, History, Travel/Exploration/Adventure. Copywriter since 1969, and Mgr. since 1971, Carlton Caruthers du Chateau, Christchurch. Creative Dir., Dobbs-Wiggins McCann Erickson, Christchurch, 1956–67. *Publs:* Fear in the Night, 1959; An Affair of Men, 1961; Long Way Home, 1962; The Flying Fish, 1963; The Needle's Eye, 1965; The Evil Day, 1967; The Companion Guide to the North Island of New Zealand (South Island; Westland; Otago, Southland, and Stewart Island), 4 vols., 1969–82; New Zealand and Its People, 1974; The Beauty of New Zealand, (Waikato-Bay of Plenty, North Island, South Island), 4 vols., 1974–82; The Flame Box, 1979; Historic New Zealand, 1980; Sixty Red Nightcaps, 1980; The Companion Guide to Westland, 1981; Dunedin, 1981; Just Looking: A View of New Zealand, 1982; Beautiful New Zealand, 1985. Add: 12 Fulton Ave., Fendalton, Christchurch 1, New Zealand.

BRATTON, J(acqueline) S(usan). British, b. 1945. Literature, Theatre. Reader in Theatre and Cultural Studies, Royal Holloway and Bedford New Coll., Univ. of London, since 1985. *Publs:* The Victorian Popular Ballad, 1975; Wilton's Music Hall, 1975, 1980; (with Jane Traies) Astley's Amphitheatre, 1980; The Impact of Victorian Children's Fiction, 1981; (ed.) Music Hall: Performance and Style, 1986; King Lear: A Stage History Edition, 1987. Add: Royal Holloway and Bedford New Coll., Egham, Surrey TW20 0EX, England.

BRAUDY, Leo. American, b. 1941. Film, Literature. Leo S. Bing Prof. of English, Univ. of Southern California, Los Angeles, since 1983. Taught at Yale Univ., New Haven, Conn., 1966–68, Columbia Univ., NYC, 1968–76, and Johns Hopkins, Baltimore, 1976–83. *Publs:* Narrative Form in History and Fiction: Hume, Fielding, and Gibbon, 1970; Jean Renoir: The World of His Film, 1972; (ed.) Norman Mailer: A Collection of Critical Essays, 1972; (ed.) Focus on Shoot the Piano Player (film), 1972; World in a Frame: What We See in Films, 1977; (ed. with Morris Dickstein) Great Film Director, 1978; The Frenzy of Renown: Fame and Its History, 1986. Add: Dept. of English, Univ. of Southern

California, Los Angeles, Calif. 90089, U.S.A.

BRAUER, Jerald C(arl). American, b. 1921. Theology/Religion. Prof. of the History of Christianity since 1959, and Naomi Shenstone Donnelley Prof., Divinity Sch. since 1969, Univ. of Chicago (Asst. Prof., 1950–54; Assoc. Prof., 1954–59; Dean, Federated Theological Faculty, 1955–60, and the Divinity Sch., 1960–70). Co-Ed. with R. Grant and M. Marty, Church History mag., since 1962; Pres. since 1973 and member, Bd. of Govs., Intnl. House of the Univ. of Chicago; Consultant, State of New York Education Dept., since 1969; Instr. in Church History and History of Christian Thought, Union Theological Seminary, NYC, 1948–50. Ordained, 1951, and Member, Bd. of Social Missions 1954–60, United Lutheran Church of America. Chmn. of the Bd., Council on Religion and Intnl. Affairs, NYC, 1979–83. *Publs:* Protestantism in America, 1953, rev. ed. 1965; (with Jaroslav Pelikan) Luther and the Reformation, 1953; Basic Questions for the Christian Scholar, 1954, 1963; Images of Religion in America, 1967; (gen. ed.) Essays in Divinity (7 vols.), 1967–69; (ed.) The Future of Religions, by Paul Tillich, 1966; (ed.) My Travel Diary: 1936, by P. Tillich, 1970; (ed.) Westminster Dictionary of Church History, 1971; (ed.) Religion and the American Revolution, 1976; (ed.) The Lively Experiment Continued, 1987. Add: 5620 South Blackstone Ave., Chicago, Ill. 60637, U.S.A.

BRAUN, Matt(hew). American, b. 1932. Westerns/Adventure. Journalist, 1956–69, then freelance writer. Member, Bd. of Dirs., Western Writers of America. *Publs:* Mattie Silks, 1972; Black Fox, 1972; The Savage Land, 1973; El Paso, 1973; Noble Outlaw, 1975; Bloody Hand, 1975; Cimarron Jordan, 1975; Kinch, 1975; Buck Colter, 1975; The Kincaids, 1976; The Second Coming of Lucas Brokaw, 1977; The Save-Your-Life Defense Handbook (non-fiction), 1977; Hangman's Creek, 1979; Lords of the Land, 1979; The Stuart Women, 1980; Jury of Six, 1980; Tombstone, 1981; The Spoilers, 1981; The Manhunter, 1981; Deadwood, 1981; The Judas Tree, No. 7, 1982; Deadwood, No. 6, 1981; This Loving Promise, 1984; Sante Fe, 1985; Rio Hondo, 1987; Winward West, 1987; A Distant Land, 1988; Matt Braun's Western Cooking, 1988. Add: c/o Robert Hale, 45-47 Clerkenwell Green, London EC1R 0HT, England.

BRAUN, Richard Emil. American, b. 1934. Poetry, Translations. Prof., Dept. of Classics, Univ. of Alberta, since 1976 (Lectr., 1962–64; Asst. Prof., 1964–69; Assoc. Prof., 1969–76). Poetry Ed., Modern Poetry Studies, 1970–77. *Publs:* Companions to Your Doom, 1961; Children Passing, 1962; Bad Land, 1971; The Foreclosure, 1972; (trans.) Sophocles: Antigone, 1973; (trans.) Euripides: Rhesos, 1978; (trans. and commentary) Persius: Satires, 1984. Add: Dept. of Classics, Univ. of Alberta, Edmonton, Alta. T6G 2E5, Canada.

BRAUNTHAL, Gerard. American, b. 1923. International relations/Current affairs, Politics/Government. Prof. Emeritus of Political Science, Univ. of Massachusetts, Amherst, since 1988 (Instr., 1954–57; Asst. Prof., 1957–62; Assoc. Prof., 1962–67; Prof., 1967–88). *Publs:* The Federation of German Industry in Politics, 1965; The West German Legislative Process: A Case Study of Two Transportation Bills, 1972; Socialist Labor and Politics in Weimar Germany: The General Federation of German Trade Unions, 1978; The West German Social Democrats 1969–1982: Profile of a Party in Power, 1983. Add: 161 Red Gate Lane, Amherst, Mass. 01002, U.S.A.

BRAWLEY, Ernest. American, b. 1937. Novels/Short stories. Railroad brakeman, 1956–59; prison guard, 1962; English teacher, 1963–64, and 1969–70; barman, 1965; janitor, 1967–68. *Publs:* The Rap, 1974; Selena, 1979; The Alamo Tree, 1984. Add: c/o Paul Reynolds, Inc., 599 Fifth Ave., New York, N.Y. 10017, U.S.A.

BRAWNE, Michael. British, b. 1925. Architecture. Principal, Michael Brawne and Assocs., London, since 1964; Prof. of Architecture, Univ. of Bath, since 1978. Worked for the Soullee Steel Co., San Francisco, 1954–56, Architects Co-Partnership, London, 1956–59, British Transport Commn., 1959–61, and Denys Lasdun and Partners, London, 1961–64; Instr. in Architecture, Cambridge Univ., 1964–78. *Publs:* The New Museum: Architecture and Display, 1965; (ed.) University Planning and Design: A Symposium, 1967; Libraries: Architecture and Equipment, 1970; The Museum Interior: Temporary and Permanent Display Techniques, 1982; Arup Associates: The Biography of an Architectural Practice, 1983. Add: Michael Brawne and Assocs., 28 College Rd., Bath BA1 5RR, England.

BRAY, Jeremy (William). British, b. 1930. Politics/Government. Labour M.P. for Motherwell S., and Opposition Spokesman on Science and Technology, since 1983. Researcher in pure mathematics,

Cambridge Univ., 1953–55; Choate Fellow, Harvard Univ., Cambridge, Mass., 1955–56; Technical Officer, ICI Ltd., Wilton Works, 1956–62; Labour M.P. for Middlesbrough West, 1962–70: Member, Select Cttee. on Nationalised Industries, 1962–64; Chmn. Estimates Cttee. Enquiries into Civil Service Recruitment, and into Govt. Statistical Services. 1964–66; Parliamentary Secty., Ministry of Power, 1966–67; and Ministry of Technology, 1967–69; Dir. of Personnel, Mullard Ltd., London, 1970–73; Labour M.P. for Motherwell and Wishaw, 1979–83: Member, Treasury and Civil Service Select Cttee., 1979–83. Chmn., Fabian Soc., 1971–72. *Publs:* The New Economy, 1965; Decision in Government, 1970; Politics of the Environment, 1972; Production Purpose and Structure, 1982. Add: House of Commons, London SWI, England.

BRAY, John Jefferson. Australian, b. 1912. Poetry. Admitted to South Australia Bar in 1933: Queen's Counsel, since 1957. Acting Lectr. in Legal History 1957–58, Lectr. in Roman Law 1959–66, and Chancellor, 1968–83, Univ. of Adelaide; Chief Justice of the Supreme Court of South Australia, 1967–78. *Publs:* Poems, 1962; Poems 1961–71, 1972; Poems 1972–79, 1979; The Bay of Salamis and Other Poems, 1986; Satura (selected poetry and prose), 1988; The Emperor's Doorkeeper (occasional addresses 1955–87), 1988. Add: 39 Hurtle Sq., Adelaide, S.A. 5000, Australia.

BRAYBROOKE, Neville (Patrick Bellairs). British, b. 1928. Novels/Short stories, Plays/Screenplays, Poetry, Literature, Travel/Exploration/Adventure. *Publs:* This Is London, 1953; (ed.) T.S. Eliot: Symposium for His 70th Birthday, 1958; London Green: History of the Royal Parks, 1959; Batsford Colour Book of London, 1960; The Idler (novel), 1960; (ed.) Pilgrim of the Future: Teilhard de Chardin Symposium, 1964; The Delicate Investigation (play), 1968; (ed.) Letters of J.R. Ackerley, 1975; Four Poems for Christmas, 1986; (ed.) Seeds in the Wind: 20th Century Juvenilia, 1989. Add: Grove House, Castle Rd., Cowes, Isle of Wight PO31 7QZ, England.

BREAKWELL, Glynis M(arie). British, b. 1952. Psychology, Social sciences, Sociology. Lectr. in Social Psychology, Univ. of Surrey, Guildford, since 1981 (Warden, Manor Hall, 1981–83). Lectr. in Social Psychology, Univ. of Bradford, 1976–78; Tutor in Social Psychology, Nuffield Coll., 1978–81, and Tutor in External Studies, 1978–85, Oxford Univ. *Publs:* (with Colin Rowett) Social Work: The Social Psychological Approach, 1982; (ed. with Hugh Foot and Robin Gilmour) Social Psychology: A Practical Manual, 1982; (ed.) Threatened Identities, 1983; The Quiet Rebel: Women at Work in a Man's World, 1985; Coping with Threatened Identities, 1986; (ed. with Hugh Foot and Robin Gilmour) Doing Social Psychology, 1987. Add: Dept. of Psychology, Univ. of Surrey, Guildford, Surrey, GU2 5HX, England.

BREARLEY, Mike (John Michael). British, b. 1942. Cricket. Played cricket for Cambridge Univ., 1961–64, Captain 1964; joined Marylebone Cricket Club (M.C.C.), 1964, Captain 1971–82; first Test, 1976, and Captain of England team, 1977–80, 1981. Lectr. in Philosophy, Univ. of Newcastle upon Tyne, 1968–71. *Publs:* (with Dudley Doust) The Return of the Ashes, 1978; (with Dudley Doust) The Ashes Retained, 1979; Phoenix: The Series that Rose from the Ashes, 1982; The Art of Captaincy, 1985. Add: c/o M.C.C., Lord's Cricket Ground, St. John's Wood Rd., London NW8 8QN, England.

BREARS, Peter C.D. British, b. 1944. Crafts, History. Dir., Leeds City Museums, since 1979. Curator, Curtis Museum, Alton, Hants, 1967–69; Keeper, Shibden Hall, Halifax, 1969–72; Curator, Clarke Hall, Wakefield, 1972–75; Curator, The Castle Museum, York, 1975–79. *Publs:* The English Country Pottery: Its History and Techniques, 1971; The Collector's Book of English Country Pottery, 1971; Yorkshire Probate Inventories 1542-1685, 1972; St. Mary's Heritage Centre, York, 1976; York Castle Museum, 1978, Yorkshire Farmhouse Fare, 1978; The Castle Museum, York, Guidebook, 1978; The Kitchen Catalogue, 1979; The Dairy Catalogue, 1979; Horse Brasses, 1981; The Gentlewoman's Kitchen, 1984; Food and Cooking in Britain, 1985; Traditional Food in Yorkshire, 1987. Add: The City Museum, Municipal Bldgs., Leeds 1, England.

BREATHNACH, Aodán S. British, b. 1922. Medicine/Health. Prof. of Anatomy, St. Mary's Hosp. Medical Sch., London, since 1967, retired 1988. Formerly, Consultant in Electron Microscopy, S. Gallicano Dermatological Inst., Rome. *Publs:* (ed.) Frazer's Anatomy of the Human Skeleton, 5th ed. 1958, 6th ed. 1965; An Atlas of the Ultrastructure of Human Skin, 1971; (with C. Stolinski) Freeze-Fracture Replication of Biological Tissues, 1976. Add: 4 Pelhams Close, Pelhams Walk, Esher, Surrey KT10 8QB, England.

BRECHER, Michael. Canadian, b. 1925. International relations/Current affairs, Politics/Government. Prof. of Political Science, McGill Univ., Montreal, since 1963 (Lectr., 1952–54; Asst. Prof., 1954–58; Assoc. Prof., 1958–63). *Publs:* The Struggle for Kashmir, 1953; Nehru: A Political Biography, 1959, abridged ed. 1961; The New States of Asia, 1963; Succession in India: A Study in Decision-Making, 1966; India and World Politics: Krishna Menon's View of the World, 1968; Political Leadership in India: An Analysis of Elite Attitudes, 1969; The Foreign Policy System of Israel: Setting, Images, Process, 1972; Israel, the Korean War and China, 1974; Decisions in Israel's Foreign Policy, 1974; Studies in Crisis Behavior, 1979; Decisions in Crisis: Israel 1967 and 1973, 1980; Crisis and Change in World Politics, 1986; Crises in the Twentieth Century, 2 vols., 1987; Crises, Conflict, and Instability, 1989. Add: 5 Dubnov St., Talbieh, Jerusalem, Israel.

BRECKENRIDGE, Adam (Carlyle). American, b. 1916. Civil liberties/Human rights, Law, Politics/Government. Prof. of Political Science, Univ. of Nebraska, since 1955 (Instr., 1946–48; Asst. Prof., 1948–50; Assoc. Prof., 1950–55; Dept. Chmn., 1953–55; Dean of Faculties, 1955–66; Vice Chancellor, 1962–68; Acting Dir. of Libraries, 1973–74; Vice-Chancellor for Academic Affairs, 1974–77; Acting Chancellor, 1975–76). *Publs:* (with J.G. Heinberg) Law Enforcement in Missouri, 1942; (ed. with L.W. Lancaster) Readings in American State Government, 1950; One House for Two— The Nebraska Unicameral Legislature, 1957; The Right to Privacy, 1970; Congress Against the Court, 1970; The Executive Privilege—Presidential Control over Information, 1974; Electing the President, 1982. Add: 511 Oldfather Hall, Univ. of Nebraska, Lincoln, Nebr, 68588, U.S.A.

BREDSDORFF, Elias Lunn. Danish, b. 1912. Mystery/Crime/Suspense, Language/Linguistics, Literature, Biography. Univ. Lectr. in Danish. 1949–62, and Reader in Scandinavian Studies, 1962–79, Cambridge Univ. Ed., Scandinavica: An International Journal of Scandinavian Studies, 1962–74. *Publs:* D.H. Lawrence, 1937; John Steinbeck, 1943; A Bibliography of Danish Literature in English Translation, 1950; (with B. Mortensen and R.G. Popperwell) An Introduction to Scandinavian Literature, 1951; Hans Christian Andersen and Charles Dickens, 1951; H.C. Andersen og England, 1954; Danish: An Elementary Grammar and Reader, 1956; Drama i Syrakus, 1956; Kinas Vej, 1957; (ed.) Sir Edmund Gosse's Correspondence with Scandinavian Writers, 1960; Bag Ibsens maske, 1962; Goldschmidt's Corsaren, 1962; Henrik Pontoppidan og Georg Brandes I-II, 1964; Literatura i obschestvo Skandinavii, 1971; Kommer det os ved?, 1971; Den store nordiske krig om seksualmoralen, 1973; Hans Christian Andersen, 1975; Fra Andersen til Scherfig, 1978; Nonsens og bonsens, 1978; Kjeld Abells billed kunst, 1979; Revolutionaer humanisme, 1982; Min egen Kurs, 1983; Mit engelske liv, 1984; H.C Andersen: Mennesket og Digteren, 1985. Add: Kronprinsesse Sofies vej 28, 2000 Copenhagen F, Denmark.

BREE, Germaine. American (born French), b. 1907. Literature, Biography. Kenan Prof. Emeritus, Wake Forest Univ., Winston-Salem, N.C., since 1985. (Kenan Prof., 1973–85). Teacher in Algeria, 1932–36; Lectr., to Prof., Bryn Mawr Coll., Pa., 1936–53; Chmn., Dept. of French, Washington Sq. Coll., 1953–60, and Head, Romance Language Dept., Grad. Sch. of Arts and Sciences, 1954–60, New York Univ., NYC; Vilas Prof. of French, Inst. for Research in the Humanities, Univ. of Wisconsin, Madison, 1960–73. *Publs:* L'Etranger; France de nos Jours; (trans.) Jules Romains: Seven Mysteries of Europe, 1940; Du temps perdu au Temps retrouvé: Introduction a l'oeuvre de Marcel Proust, 1950, 1969; (ed. with C. Lynes) Marcel Proust; Combray, 1952; André Gide: L'insaississable Proteè: Etude critique de l'oeuvre d'André Gide, 1953, English rev. ed. 1963; Marcel Proust and Deliverance from Time, 1955, rev. ed. 1969; (with M. Guiton) An Age of Fiction, 1957; (with A.P. Jones) Hier et Aujourd'hui, 1958; Camus, 1959, rev. English ed. 1961; Contes en Nouvelles 1950–1960, 1961; (ed.) Camus: A Collection of Critical Essays, 1962; Twentieth Century French Literature, 1962; (with M. Dufau) Voix d'aujourd'hui, 1963; The World of Marcel Proust, 1966; (with A. Kroff) Twentieth Century French Drama, 1969; (with P. Solomon) Choix d'-Essais du vingtième siècle, 1969; (with G. Bernauer) Defeat and Beyond: An Anthology of French Wartime Writing (1940–1945), 1970; Camus and Sartre: Crisis and Commitment, 1972; Women Writers in France, 1973; Le XXe Siècle 1920–1970, 1978, English ed., 1983. Add: 2135 Royall Dr., Winston-Salem, N.C. 27106, U.S.A.

BREEDEN, Stanley. Australian, b. 1938. Environmental science/Ecology, Natural history. Freelance photographer, since 1967. Photographer, Queensland Museum, Fortitude Valley, 1958–66. *Publs:* all with Kay Breeden—The Life of the Kangaroo, 1966; (with Peter Slater) Birds of Australia, 1968; Tropical Queensland, 1970; Living Marsupials, 1970; Australia's Southeast, 1972; Wildlife of Eastern Australia, 1973; Australia's North, 1977. Add: 35 Stoneleigh St., Albion, Brisbane, Qld., 4010, Australia.

BREEN, Dana. American, b. 1946. Psychology. In private practice as psychoanalyst. Research Fellow, 1970–72, and Psychotherapist, 1972–74, Student Health Centre, Univ. of Sussex. *Publs:* The Birth of a First Child, 1975; The Mother and the Hospital in Tearing the Veil, 1978; Talking with Mothers, 1981. Add: 57 Wood Lane, London N6, England.

BREEN, Jon L(inn). American, b. 1943. Mystery/Crime/Suspense, Literature. Librarian, Rio Hondo Coll., Whittier, Calif., since 1975. Sports broadcaster, Radio KWAV, Los Angeles, 1963–65; Librarian, California State Univ., Long Beach, 1966–67, and Dominguez Hills, 1969–75. *Publs:* A Little Fleshed Up Around the Crook of the Elbow: A Selected Bibliography of Some Literary Parodies, 1970; The Girl in the Pictorial Wrapper: An Index to Reviews of Paperback Original Novels in the New York Times' "Criminals at Large" Column 1953–1970, 1972, 1973; What About Murder? A Guide to Books about Mystery and Detective Fiction, 1981; Hair of the Sleuthhound: Parodies of Mystery Fiction (short stories), 1982; Listen for the Click (novel), 1983, in U.K. as Vicar's Roses, 1984; The Gathering Place (novel), 1984; Triple Crown (novel), 1985; Novel Verdicts: A Critical Guide to Courtroom Fiction, 1985; (ed. with Rita A. Breen) American Murders (anthology), 1986; (ed. with John Ball) Murder California Style, 1987; Touch of the Past (novel), 1988; (ed. with Martin H. Greenberg) Murder Off the Rack: Critical Studies of 10 Paperback Masters, 1989. Add: 10642 La Bahia Ave., Fountain Valley, Calif. 92708, U.S.A.

BREESE, Gerald (William). American, b. 1912. Regional/Urban planning, Urban studies. Prof. of Sociology Emeritus, Princeton Univ., since 1977 (Asst. Prof., 1949–51, Assoc. Prof., 1951–59, Prof., 1959–77, Dir., Bureau of Urban Research, 1950–66); Licensed Urban Planner, N.J. since 1967. *Publs:* Daytime Population of Central Business District of Chicago, 1949; Industrial Land Use in Burlington County, N.J., 1951; An Approach to Urban Planning, 1953; Regional Analysis Trenton-Camden Area, 1954; Industrial Site Selection, 1954; Accelerated Urban Growth in a Metropolitan Fringe Area, 1954; Unrbanization in Old and New Countries, 1964; Urbanization in Newly Developing Countries, 1966; (ed. contrib.) The City in Newly Developing Countries: Reading on Urbanism and Urbanization, 1969; (co-author) The Impact of Large Installations on Nearby Areas: Accelerated Urban Growth, 1969; Urban South East Asia, 1973; Urban and Regional Planning in the Delhi-New Delhi Area, 1974; From Woodlots to Campus: The First 232 Years of Land for Princeton University, 1985. Add: 65 Cleveland Lane, Princeton, N.J. 08540, U.S.A.

BREIMYER, Harold F. American, b. 1914. Agriculture/Forestry. Prof. of Agricultural Economics, Univ. of Missouri, Columbia, 1966–84 (Prof. Emeritus, since 1984). Economist, U.S. Agricultural Adjustment Admin., 1936–39, U.S. Bureau of Agricultural Economics, 1939–59, U.S. Council of Economic Advisers, 1959–61, and U.S. Agricultural Marketing Service, 1961–66. *Publs:* Individual Freedom and the Economic Organization of Agriculture 1965; Economics of the Product Markets of Agriculture, 1976; Farm Policy: 13 Essays, 1977. Add: Dept. of Agricultural Economics, Univ. of Missouri, 200 Mumford Hall, Columbia, Mo. 65211, U.S.A.

BREINBURG, Petronella (Alexandrina). Dutch, b. 1927. Children's fiction. Part-time English Teacher, Bexley Education Authority, since 1974. Storyteller and lectr. at various libraries in London. *Publs:* Legends of Surinam, 1971; Ballad of a Swan (poetry), 1972; Shawn Goes to School, 1973; Doctor Sean, 1973; My Brother Sean, 1974; Paleface and Me, 1974; Tinker and Me, 1975; Sean's Red Bike, 1975; Us Boys of Westcroft, 1975; Sally-Ann's Umbrella, 1975; What Happened at Rita's Party, 1976; Tiger, Paleface and Me, 1976; Sally-Ann in the Snow, 1977; A Girl, A Frog, and a Petticoat, 1978; Sally-Ann's Skateboard, 1979. Add: 7 Tuam Rd., Plumstead Common, London SE18 2QX, England.

BREMS, Hans J. American, b. 1915. Economics. Prof. of Economics, Univ. of Illinois, Urbana, since 1954. Lectr., 1943–51, and Visiting Prof., 1975, Univ. of Copenhagen; Lectr., Univ. of California at Berkeley, 1951–54. *Publs:* Product Equilibrium under Monopolistic Competition, 1951; Output, Employment, Capital and Growth, 1959; Quantitative Economic Theory, 1968; Labor, Capital and Growth, 1973; A Wage Earners' Investment Fund: Forms and Economic Effects, 1975; Inflation, Interest, and Growth, 1980; Dynamische Makrotheorie, 1980; Fiscal Theory, 1983; Pioneering Economic Theory 1630-1980, A Mathematical Restatement, 1986. Add: 1103 S. Douglas Ave., Urbana, Ill. 61801, U.S.A.

BREMSER, Ray. American, b. 1934. Poetry. Served prison sentence for armed robbery, parole violation, and bail jumping. *Publs:* Poems of Madness, 1965; Angel: The Work of One Night in the Dark, Solitary Confinement, New Jersey State Prison, Trenton, 1967; Drive Suite: An Essay on Composition, Materials, Reference, Etc., 1968; Black is Black Blues, 1972; Blowing Mouth: The Jazz Poems, 1958–1970, 1978. Add: c/o Cherry Valley Editions, 2314 Georgian Woods Pl., Wheaton, Md. 20902, U.S.A.

BRENDON, Piers. British, b. 1940. Biography. Freelance writer. Lectr., 1971–76, and Head of the History Dept., 1977–80, Cambridgeshire Coll. of Arts and Technology. *Publs:* (ed. with W. Shaw) Reading They've Liked, 1967; (ed. with W. Shaw) Reading Matters, 1969; (ed. with W. Shaw) By What Authority?, 1972; Hurrell Froude and the Oxford Movement, 1974; Hawker of Morwenstow: Portrait of a Victorian Eccentric, 1975; Eminent Edwardians, 1979; The Life and Death of the Press Barons, 1982; Winston Churchill, 1984; Our Own Dear Queen, 1986; Ike: The Life and Times of Dwight D. Eisenhower, 1987. Add: 4b Millington Rd., Cambridge, England.

BRENNAN, Joseph Payne. American, b. 1918. Novels/Short stories, Mystery/Crime/Suspense, Poetry. Library Asst., Yale Univ. Library, New Haven, Conn., 1941–85. Ed. and Publr., Essence, 1950–77, and Macabre, 1957–76. *Publs:* Heart of Earth (poetry), 1950; The Humming Stair (poetry), 1953; Nine Horrors and a Dream, 1958; The Dark Returners, 1959; The Wind of Time (poetry), 1962; Scream at Midnight, 1963; Nightmare Need (poetry), 1964; Stories of Darkness and Dread, 1973; The Casebook of Lucius Leffing, 1973; Edges of Night (poetry), 1974; The Chronicles of Lucius Leffing, 1977; As Evening Advances (poetry), 1978; Webs of Time (poetry), 1980; The Shapes of Midnight, 1980; Creep to Death (poetry), 1981; Evil Always Ends, 1982; Sixty Selected Poems, 1985; The Borders Just Beyond, 1986. Add: 26 Fowler St., New Haven, Conn. 06515, U.S.A.

BRENNAN, Neil F. American, b. 1923. Literature. Prof. of English Literature, Villanova Univ., Pa. (joined faculty, 1960). *Publs:* (coauthor) Graham Greene: Some Critical Considerations, 1963; Anthony Powell, 1974; (with A.R. Redway) A Bibliography of Graham Greene, 1985. Add: 122 Buckingham Dr., Rosemont, Pa. 19010, U.S.A.

BRENNEMAN, Helen Good. American, b. 1925. Novels/Short stories, Theology/Religion. *Publs:* Meditation for the New Mother, 1953; But Not Forsaken, 1954; (co-author) Breaking Bread Together, 1958; My Comforters, 1966; Meditations for the Expectant Mother, 1968; House By the Side of the Road, 1971; Ring a Dozen Doorbells, 1973; Marriage: Agony and Ecstacy, 1975; Learning to Cope, 1976; Morning Joy, 1981. Add: 516 E. Waverly Ave., Goshen, Ind. 46526, U.S.A.

BRENNER, Yehojachin Simon. Dutch, b. 1926. Economics. Prof. of Economics, Univ. of Utrecht, since 1972. Head of Economics Dept., Univ. of Cape Coast, Ghana, 1962–67; Deputy Chmn. of Economic Planning Courses, Inst. of Social Studies, The Hague, 1967–69; Prof. of Economics, Middle East Technical Univ., Ankara, 1969–72. *Publs:* Theories of Economic Development and Growth, 1966, 1969; A Short History of Economic Progress, 1969; Agriculture and the Economic Development of Low Income Countries, 1971; Introduction to Economics, 1972; A Short History of Economic Progress, 1973; Looking into the Seeds of Time, 1979; (co-author) Bezuinigen is geen Werk, 1981; Capitalism, Competition, and Economic Crisis, 1984; (co-author) Visies op Verdelng, 1986; The Theory of Income and Wealth Distribution, 1988. Add: Rijksuniversiteit te Utrecht, Heidelberglaan 1, De Uithof, Utrecht, Netherlands.

BRENT, Iris. *See* **BANCROFT,** Iris.

BRENT, Madeleine (pseud). British. Historical/Romance/Gothic. *Publs:* Tregaron's Daughter, 1971; Moonraker's Bride, 1973; Kirby's Changeling, 1975; in U.S. as Stranger at Wildings, 1976; Merlin's Keep, 1977; The Capricorn Stone, 1979; The Long Masquerade, 1981; A Heritage of Shadows, 1983; Stormswift, 1984; Golden Urchin, 1986. Add: c/o Doubleday, 245 Park Ave., New York, N.Y. 10167, U.S.A.

BRENTON, Howard. British, b. 1942. Plays/Screenplays, Poetry. Resident Dramatist, Royal Court Theatre, London, 1972–73; Resident Writer, Univ. of Warwick, 1978–79. *Publs:* Notes from a Psychotic Journal and Other Poems, 1969; Revenge, 1970; Christie in Love and Other

Plays, 1970; (co-author) Lay By, 1972; Plays for Public Places, 1972; (with David Hare) Brassneck, 1973; Magnificence, 1973; Weapons of Happiness, 1976; Epsom Downs, 1977; Sore Throats, with Sonnets of Love and Opposition, 1979; (adaptor) The Life of Galileo, 1980; The Romans in Britain, 1980; Plays for the Poor Theatre, 1980; Thirteenth Night, and A Short Sharp Shock, 1981; (adaptor) Danton's Death, 1982; Hitler Diaries, 1982; (trans.) Bertolt Brecht: Conversations in Exile, 1982; The Genius, 1983; (with Tunde Ikoli) Sleeping Policemen, 1984; Bloody Poetry, 1985; (with David Hare) Pravda, 1985; Dead Head (TV series), 1987; Greenland, 1988. Add: c/o Margaret Ramsey Ltd., 14a Godwin's Ct., London WC2N 4LL, England.

BRESLIN, Jimmy. American, b. 1930. Novels/Short stories, Documentaries/Reportage. Former reporter, WNBC-TV, and syndicated columnist, New York Herald Tribune, Paris Tribune, etc. *Publs:* Can't Anybody Here Play this Game?, 1963; The Gang that Couldn't Shoot Straight, 1969; How the Good Guys Finally Won: Notes from an Impeachment Summer, 1975; The World of Jimmy Breslin. 1976; World Without End, Amen, 1976; (with Dick Schaap) Forty-Four Caliber, 1978; Forsaking All Others, 1983; Queens: People and Places, 1984; The World According to Breslin, 1984; Table Money, 1986; He Got Hungry and Forgot His Manners, 1987; World Without End, Amen, 1987; The Queen of the Leaky-Roof Circuit (play), 1988. Add: c/o New York Daily News, 220 E. 42nd St., New York, N.Y. 10017, U.S.A.

BRETNOR, Reginald. Also writes as Grendel Briarton. American, b. 1911. Novels/Short stories, Science fiction/Fantasy, Military/Defence, Translations. *Publs:* (ed.) Modern Science Fiction, 1953; (trans.) Moncrif's Cats, by François-Augustin Paradis de Moncrif, 1961; (as Grendel Briarton) Through Space and Time with Ferdinand Feghoot (short stories), 1962, as The Compleat Feghoot, 1975; Decisive Warfare: A Study in Military Theory, 1969, 1986; (ed.) Science Fiction Today and Tomorrow, 1974; (ed.) The Craft of Science Fiction, 1976; A Killing in Swords (novel), 1978; The Schimmelhorn File (short stories), 1979; (ed.) The Future at War, vols., 1979–80; Schimmelhorn's Gold (novel), 1985. Add: Box 1481, Medford, Ore. 97501, U.S.A.

BRETON, Albert. Canadian, b. 1929. Economics. Prof. of Economics, Univ. of Toronto, since 1970. Member, Canadian Economic Policy Cttee. of the C.D. Howe Research Inst., since 1974. Guest, Massachusetts Inst. of Technology, 1959–60; Dir of Research, The Social Research Group, 1956–65; Asst. Prof. of Economics, Univ. of Montreal, 1957–65; Visiting Assoc. Prof., Carleton Univ., 1964–65; Lectr., 1966–67, and Reader in Economics, 1967–69, London Sch. of Economics; Visiting Prof., Catholic Univ., of Louvain, 1968–69; Visiting Prof. of Canadian Studies, Harvard Univ., 1969–70. *Publs:* (contrib.) Social Purpose for Canada, 1961; (contrib.) Le Role de L' Etat, 1962; (contrib.) Canada: An Appraisal of Its Needs and Resources, 1965; Discriminatory Government Policies in Federal Countries, 1967; (contrib.) Canadian Economic Problems and Policies, 1970; (contrib.) A Challenge to Social Scientists, 1970; (contrib.) Canadian Perspectives in Economics, 1972; A Conceptual Basis for an Industrial Strategy, 1974; (contrib.) Issues in Canadian Economics, 1974; The Economic Theory of Representative Government, 1974; (with A.D. Scott) The Economic Constitution of Federal Studies, 1978; (with R. Wintnobe) The Logic of Bureaucratic Conduct, 1982. Add: 160 Rosedale Heights Dr., Toronto, Ont. M4T 1C8, Canada.

BRETT, Leo. *See* **FANTHORPE,** R. Lionel.

BRETT, Michael. *See* **TRIPP,** Miles.

BRETT, Michael. American, b. 1928. Novels/Short stories, Mystery/Crime/Suspense. *Publs:* Kill Him Quickly, It's Raining, 1966; Another Day, Another Stiff, 1967; Dead, Upstairs in a Tub, 1967; An Ear for Murder, 1967; The Flight of the Stiff, 1967; Turn Blue, You Murderers, 1967; We, The Killers, 1967; Death of a Hippie, 1968; Lie a Little, Die a Little, 1968, as Cry Uncle, 1971; Slit My Throat, Gently, 1968; Jungle (non-mystery novel), 1976; Diamond Kill, 1977. Add: c/o Berkley Publishing Corp., 200 Madison Ave., New York, N.Y. 10016, U.S.A.

BRETT, Molly. (Mary Elizabeth Brett). British. Children's fiction. Freelance artist and writer. *Publs:* The Japanese Garden; Story of a Toy Car; Drummer Boy; Duckling; Mr. Turkey Runs Away; Puppy Schooldays; Tom Tit Moves House; Follow Me Round the Farm; Master Bunny the Baker's Boy; Adventures of Plush and Tatty; A Surprise for Dumpy; The Untidy Little Hedgehog; Robin Finds Christmas; The Forgotten Bear; Two in a Tent; Flip Flop's Secret; Paddy Gets into Mischief; Teddy Flies Away; Midget and the Pet Shop, 1969; Jiggy's Treasure Hunt, 1973; The

Party That Grew, 1976; Jumble Bears, 1977; The Molly Brett Picture Book, 1978; An Alphabet by Molly Brett, 1980; The Runaway Fairy, 1982; Good-Night Time Tales, 1982; Plush and Tatty on the Beach, 1987; The Magic Spectacles, 1987. Add: Chimes Cottage, Horsell Vale, Woking, Surrey, England.

BRETT, Raymond Laurence. British, b. 1917. Literature. G.F. Grant Prof. of English, Univ of Hull, 1952–82, now Emeritus (Dean of Faculty of Arts, 1960–62). Gen. Ed., Writers and Their Backgrounds Series. Lectr. in English, Univ. of Bristol, 1946–52. *Publs:* The Third Earl of Shaftesbury, 1952; George Crabbe, 1956, rev. ed. 1968; Reason and Imagination, 1960; (ed. with A.R. Jones) Lyrical Ballads by Wordsworth and Coleridge, 1798-1805, 3rd ed. 1968; An Introduction to English Studies, 1965; (ed.) Poems of Faith and Doubt, 1965; Fancy and Imagination, 1969; (ed.) S.T. Coleridge, 1971; William Hazlitt, 1977; (ed.) Andrew Marvell Tercentenary Essays, 1979; (ed.) Barclay Fox's Journal, 1979; Coleridge (Writers and Their Work series), 1980. Add: 19 Mill Walk, Cottingham, North Humberside HU16 4RP, England.

BRETT, Rosalind. *See* BLAIR, Kathryn.

BRETT, Simon (Anthony Lee). British, b. 1945. Mystery/Crime/-Suspense, Plays/Screenplays. Producer, BBC Radio, London, 1967–77, and London Weekend Television, 1977–79. *Publs:* Mrs. Gladys Moxon (play), 1970; Did You Sleep Well, and A Good Day at the Office (plays), 1971; Third Person (play), 1972; Cast, In Order of Disappearance (novel), 1975; So Much Blood (novel), 1976; Drake's Dream (play), 1977; Star Trap (novel), 1977; An Amateur Corpse (novel), 1978; Frank Muir Goes into . . ., vols., 1978–81; A Comedian Dies (novel), 1979; The Dead Side of Mike (novel), 1980; Frank Muir on Children, 1980; Situation Tragedy (novel), 1981; (ed.) The Faber Book of Useful Verse, 1981; Murder Unprompted (novel), 1982; Molesworth Rites Again, 1983; Murder in the Title (novel), 1983; The Childowner's Handbook, 1983; Not Dead, Only Resting (novel), 1984; Bad Form, 1984; A Shock to the System (novel), 1984; (ed.) The Faber Book of Parodies, 1984; A Box of Tricks (novel), 1985; Dead Romantic, 1985; A Nice Class of Corpse, 1986; The Three Detectives and the Missing Superstar, 1986; Dead Giveaway, 1986; What Bloody Man Is That?, 1987; The Three Detectives and the Knight-in-Armour, 1987; (ed.) The Faber Book of Diaries, 1987; Mrs., Presumed Dead, 1988; A Series of Murders, 1989. Add: Frith House, Burpham, Arundel, W. Sussex BN18 9RR, England.

BREUER, Lee. American, b. 1937. Plays. Co-Artistic Dir., Mabou Mines theatre company, N.Y., since 1970, and N.Y. Shakespeare Festival, since 1982. Dir., San Francisco Actors Workshop, 1963–65; worked in Europe, 1965–70; taught at Yale Drama School, New Haven, Conn., 1978–80, Harvard Univ., Cambridge, Mass., 1981–82, and New York Univ., 1981–82. *Publs:* The Red Horse Animation (in The Theatre of Images), 1977; A Prelude to Death in Venice (in New Plays USA 1), 1982; Hajj (in Workplays 3), 1983; Sister Suzie Cinema, 1986; Animations: A Trilogy for Mabou Mines, 1986. Add: c/o Mabou Mines, Performing Arts Journal, 325 Spring St., New York, NY 10013, U.S.A.

BREW, O.H. Kwesi. Ghanaian, b. 1928. Plays/Screenplays, Poetry. With Ghana Foreign Service (has been Ambassador for Ghana to England, France, India, Germany, the U.S.S.R., and Mexico), *Publs:* The Shadows of Laughter: Poems, 1968; (with others) Pergamon Poets 2: Poetry from Africa, 1968; The Harvest (screenplay); African Panorama, 1981. Add: c/o Foreign Office, Accra, Ghana.

BREWARD, Ian. New Zealander, b. 1934. Theology/Religion. Prof. of Church History, Ormond Coll., Melbourne, since 1982. Prof. of Church History, Knox Coll., Dunedin, 1965–82. Moderator, Presbyterian Church of N.Z., 1975; Deputy Chmn., Radio N.Z., 1976–77. *Publs:* Godless Schools?, 1967; Authority and Freedom, 1969; (ed.) The Work of William Perkins, 1970; Grace and Truth, 1975; The Future of Our Heritage, 1984; Australia: "The Most Godless Place Under Heaven"?, 1988; (ed.) John Bunyan, 1988. Add: Ormond Coll., Melbourne, Vict. 3052, Australia.

BREWER, Garry D(wight). American, b. 1941. Politics/Government, Sociology. Prof. Sch. of Organization and Mgmt., Sch. of Forestry and Environmental Studies, and Dept. of Political Science, Yale Univ., New Haven since 1978 (Assoc. Prof., 1975–78). Member, Sr. Staff, The Rand Corp., Santa Monica Calif., 1970–74; Center for Advanced Studies in the Behavioral Sciences, Stanford, Calif., 1974–75 *Publs:* (with Ronald D. Brunner) Organized Complexity: Empirical Theories of Political Development, 1971; Politicians, Bureaucrats and the Consultant: A Critique of Urban Problem-Solving, 1973; (ed. with Brunner and contrib.)

Political Development and Change: A Policy Approach, 1974; (with J. Kakalik) Mental Health and Mental Retardation Services, 1976; (with M. Shubik) The War Game: A Critique of Military Problem Solving, 1979 (with J. Kakalik) Handicapped Children: Strategies for Improving Services, 1979; (with P. de Leon) The Foundations of Policy Analysis, 1983; (with M. Greenberger and others) Caught Unawares: The Energy Decade in Retrospect, 1983. Add: SOM Box 1A, Yale Station, New Haven, Conn. 06520, U.S.A.

BREWER, Wilmon. American, b. 1895. Poetry, Literature. Instr. in English, Harvard Univ., Cambridge, Mass., 1923–24; Pres., American Poetry Assn., 1939–41, and Boston Authors Club, 1944–46; Lectr. on Poetry, Cooper's Hill Writers' Conference, East Dover, Vt., 1968–70. *Publs:* Dante's Eclogues, 1927, 1961; Ovid's Metamorphoses in European Culture, vol. I, 1933, vol. II, 1941, vol. III, 1957, new ed. 1978; Sonnets and Sestinas, 1937; (ed.) The Twentieth Anniversary Volume of the American Poetry Association, 1942; About Poetry and Other Matters, 1943; Adventures in Verse, 1945, 1963; Talks About Poetry, 1948; New Adventures, 1950; Life of Maurice Parker, 1954; Adventures Further, 1958; Still More Adventures, 1966; Concerning the Art of Poetry, 1979; Life and Poems of Brookes More, 1980; Latest Adventures, 1981. Add: Great Hill, Hingham, Mass. 01043, U.S.A.

BREWSTER, Benjamin. *See* FOLSOM, Franklin Brewster.

BREWSTER, Elizabeth (Winifred). Canadian, b. 1922. Novels/Short stories, Poetry. Prof. of English, Univ. of Saskatchewan, Saskatoon, since 1980 (Asst. Prof., 1972–75; Assoc. Prof., 1975–80). Cataloguer, Carleton Univ. Library, Ottawa, 1953–57, and Indiana Univ. Library, Bloomington, 1957–58; Member of English Dept., Victoria Univ., B.C., 1960–61; Reference Librarian, Mount Allison Univ. Library, Sackville, N.B., 1961–65; Cataloguer, New Brunswick Legislative Library, Fredericton, 1965–68, and Univ. of Alberta Library, Edmonton, 1968–70. *Publs:* East Coast, 1951; Lillooet, 1954; Roads and Other Poems, 1957; Passage of Summer: Selected Poems, 1969; Sunrise North, 1972; In Search of Eros, 1974; The Sisters (novel), 1974; Sometimes I Think of Moving, 1977; It's Easy to Fall on the Ice (stories), 1977; The Way Home, 1982; Digging In, 1982; Junction (novel), 1982; A House Full of Women (short stories), 1983; Selected Poems 1944–1984, 2 vols., 1985; Visitations (short stories), 1987. Add: Dept. of English, Univ. of Saskatchewan, Saskatoon, Sask., S7N 0W0, Canada.

BRIARTON, Grendel. *See* BRETNOR, Reginald.

BRIDGER, Adam. *See* BINGLEY, David Ernest.

BRIDGERS, Sue Ellen (née Hunsucker). American, b. 1942. Novels, Children's fiction. *Publs:* children's fiction—Home Before Dark, 1976; All Together Now, 1979; Notes for Another Life, 1981; Permanent Connections, 1987; adult fiction—Sara Will, 1985. Add: P.O. Box 248, Sylva, N.C. 28779, U.S.A.

BRIDGES, William. American, b. 1901. Animals/Pets. Curator of Publs., New York Zoological Soc., NYC, 1935 until retirement in 1966. *Publs:* (with Raymond L. Ditmars) Snake-Hunters' Holiday, 1936; (with Ditmars) Wild Animal World, 1938; (with Roger Conant) What Snake is That?, 1939; Toco Toucan (children), 1940; Big Zoo, 1941; True Zoo Stories, 1948; The Illustrated Book of Wild Animals of the World, 1948; Zoo Babies, 1953; Zoo Expeditions, 1954; Zoo Pets, 1955; Zoo Doctor, 1957; Zoo Celebrities, 1959; The Golden Book of Zoo Animals, 1962; Ookie, 1962; Walt Disney's Animal Adventures in Lands of Ice and Snow, 1963; Lion Island, 1964; (with Lee Saunders Crandall) A Zoo Man's Notebook, 1966; The Bronx Zoo Book of Wild Animals, 1968; The New York Aquarium Book of Water World, 1970; Zoo Careers, 1971; Gathering of Animals: An Unconventional History of the New York Zoological Society, 1974; Transitions: Making Sense of Life's Changes, 1980; Surviving Transition: Rational Management in a World of Mergers, Layoffs, Start-Ups, Takeovers, Divestitures, Deregulation and New Technologies, 1988. Add: 85 Brook Manor, Pleasantville, N.Y. 10570, U.S.A.

BRIDWELL, Norman Ray. American, b. 1928. Children's fiction. Freelance artist since 1962. *Publs:* Clifford the Big Red Dog, 1962; Zany Zoo, 1963; Bird in the Hat, 1964; Clifford Gets a Job, 1965; The Witch Next Door, 1965; Clifford Takes a Trip, 1966; Clifford's Halloween, 1966; A Tiny Family, 1968; The Country Cat, 1969; What Do They Do When It Rains?, 1969; Clifford's Tricks, 1969; How To Care for Your Monster, 1970; The Witch's Christmas, 1970; Monster Jokes and Riddles, 1972; Clifford the Small Red Puppy, 1972; The Witch's Vacation, 1973; Merton, the Monkey Mouse, 1973; The Dog Frog Book, 1973; Clifford's Riddles,

1974; Monster Holidays, 1974; Clifford's Good Deeds, 1974; Ghost Charlie, 1974; Boy on the Ceiling, 1976; The Witch's Catalog, 1976; The Big Water Fight, 1977; Clifford at the Circus, 1977; Kangaroo Stew, 1978; The Witch Grows Up, 1979; Clifford Goes to Hollywood, 1980; Clifford's ABC's, 1983; Clifford's Story Hour, 1983; Clifford's Family, 1984; Clifford's Kitten, 1984; Clifford's Christmas, 1984; Clifford's Grouchy Neighbors, 1985; Clifford's Pals, 1985; Count on Clifford, 1985; Clifford's Manners, 1987; Clifford's Birthday Party, 1988. Add: Box 869, Edgartown, Mass. 02539, U.S.A.

BRIGGS, Asa. (Baron Briggs of Lewes). British, b. 1921. Economics, History. Provost, Worcester Coll., Oxford, since 1976 (Fellow, 1945–55). Reader in Recent Social and Economic History, Oxford Univ., 1950–55; Prof. of Modern History, Leeds Univ., 1955–61; Dean of Social Studies, 1961–65; Pro-Vice-Chancellor, 1961–67; Prof. of History, 1961–76; and Vice-Chancellor, 1967–76, Univ. of Sussex, Brighton. *Publs:* (with D. Thomson and E. Meyer) Patterns of Peacemaking, 1945; History of Birmingham, 1952; Victorian People, 1954; Friends of the People, 1956; The Age of Improvement, 1959; (ed.) Chartist Studies, 1959; (ed. with J. Saville) Essays in Labour History, 2 vols., 1960, 1971; (ed.) They Saw It Happen 1897-1940, 1961; A Study of the Work of Seebohm Rowntree, 1961; History of Broadcasting in the United Kingdom, 4 vols., 1961–79; Victorian 1815, 1969; (ed.) The Nineteenth Century, 1970; (ed. with Susan Briggs) Cap and Bell: Punch's Chronicle of English History in the Making, 1972; (gen. ed.) Essays in the History of Publishing, 1974; From Ironbridge to the Crystal Palace, 1979; The Power of Steam, 1982; A Social History of England, 1984; Victorian Things, 1988. Add: Worcester Coll., Oxford, England.

BRIGGS, Jean. British, b. 1925. Historical/Romance/Gothic, Children's non-fiction, Education. Dir., Educational Closed Circuit Television, Essex Co. Council, since 1967; Sr. Adviser for English, London Borough of Redbridge, since 1977. Lectr. in English literature, 1962–67. *Publs:* Jewels and Jewelery, 1967; (with S. Bridges, A. Kinsey and P. Meldon) Gifted Children and the Brentwood Experiment, 1969; Flame of the Borgias, 1974. Add: 5 Denham Dr., Gants Hill, Ilford, Essex IG2 6QU, England.

BRIGGS, Kenneth. American, b. 1934. Education. Regents Prof. of Curriculum and Instruction, Lamar Univ. (joined faculty as Asst. Prof., 1966). *Publs:* Teaching in the 70s, 1971. Add: Lamar Univ. Station, Box 10034, Beaumont, Tex. 77710, U.S.A.

BRIGGS, Raymond (Redvers). British, b. 1934. Children's fiction. Part-time Lectr. in Illustration, Faculty of Art, Brighton Polytechnic. *Publs:* author—The Strange House, 1961; Midnight Adventure, 1961; Sledges to the Rescue, 1963; author and illustrator—Jim and the Beanstalk, 1970; Father Christmas, 1973; Father Christmas Goes on Holiday, 1975; Fungus the Bogeyman, 1977; The Snowman, 1978; Gentleman Jim, 1980; When the Wind Blows, 1982; The Tin-Pot Foreign General and the Old Iron Woman, 1984. Unlucky Wally, 1987. Add: Weston, Underhill Lane, Westmeston, Hassocks, Sussex, England.

BRILEY, John. American, b. 1925. Novels/Short stories, Plays/Screenplays. Freelance screenwriter, Trevone Productions Inc., Los Angeles, since 1965. Member, Exec. Cttee., Writers Guild of Great Britain, since 1978. Staff Writer, M.G.M. 1960–64. *Publs:* (with J.T. Storey) Invasion Quartet (screenplay)s; (with J.T. Storey) Postman's Knock (screenplay); Children of the Damned (screenplay); Seven Bob a Buck (play); Pope Joan (screenplay); The Traitors (novel; in U.K. as How Sleep the Brave), 1969; So Who Needs Men (play); The Last Dance (novel), 1978; That Lucky Touch (screenplay); The Medusa Touch (screenplay); Eagle's Wing (screenplay); Enigma (screenplay); Gandhi (screenplay); Marie (screenplay); Cry Freedom (novel and screenplay). Add: c/o Douglas Rae Management, 28 Charing Cross Rd., London WC2, England.

BRILLIANT, Alan. American, b. 1936. Poetry, Translations. Co-Founding Dir., Unicorn Press, Santa Barbara, Calif., later Greensboro, N.C., since 1966. *Publs:* At Trail, 1969; Searching for Signs, 1969; (trans.) Nine Poems, by Belkis Cuza Male, 1969; (trans.) Selected Poems of Garcia Lorca, 1969, Journeyman, 1970; (trans.) Selected Poems of Vicente Aleixandre, 1978; Five Prose Poems of Escape, 1980. Add:Unicorn Press, P.O. Box 3307, Greensboro, N.C. 27402, U.S.A.

BRILLIANT, Richard. American, b. 1929. Archaeology/Antiquities, Art. Prof. of Art History, Columbia Univ., since 1970. Asst. Prof., 1962–64, Assoc. Prof., 1964–69, and Prof., 1969–70. Univ. of Pennsylvania, Philadelphia. *Publs:* Gesture and Rank in Roman Art, 1963; The

Arch of Septimus Severus in the Roman Forum, 1967; Arts of the Ancient Greeks, 1973; Roman Art, 1974; Pompeii AD 79, 1979; Visual Narratives, 1984. Add: Dept of Art History and Archaeology, Columbia Univ., New York, N.Y. 10027, U.S.A.

BRIN, David. American, b. 1950. Science fiction. Member of the Technical Staff, Hughes Research Lab., Newport Beach, Calif., 1973–75, and Carlsbad, Calif., 1975–77; taught at San Diego State Univ., 1982–83, and San Diego community colleges, 1983–84. Secty., Science Fiction Writers of American. *Publs:* Sundiver, 1980; Startide Rising, 1983; The Practice Effect, 1984; The Postman, 1985; (with Gregory Ben Ford) Heart of the Comet, 1986; The River of Time, 1986; The Uplift War 1987; Dr. Pak's Pre-School, 1988. Add: c/o Richard Curtis, 164 E. 64th St., New York, NY 10021, U.S.A.

BRINDLE, Reginald Smith. British, b. 1917. Music. Prof. of Music, Univ. Coll., Bangor, 1967–70, and Univ. of Surrey, Guildford, 1970–83. *Publs:* Serial Composition, 1966; (ed.) New Sounds for Woodwind, by Bruno Bartolozzi, 1967; Contemporary Percussion, 1970; (co-author) Encyclopedia des Musiques Sacrées, 1970; The New Music, 1975; Musical Composition, 1986. Add: 219 Farleigh Rd., Warlingham, Surrey CR3 9EL, England.

BRINGHURST, Robert. Canadian, b. 1946. Poetry. Visiting Lectr. in Creative Writing, 1975–77, and Lectr. in English, 1979–80, Univ. of British Columbia; Lectr. in Typographical History, Simon Fraser Univ., Burnaby, B.C., 1983–84; Poet-in-Residence, Banff Centre Sch. of Fine Arts, Alberta, 1983. *Publs:* verse—The Shipwright's Log, 1972; Cadastre, 1973; Deuteronomy, 1974; Pythagoras, 1974; Eight Objects, 1975; Bergschrund, 1975; Jacob Singing, 1977; Death by Water, 1977; The Stonecutter's Horses, 1979; The Knife in the Measure, 1980; Song of the Summit, 1982; The Salute by Tasting, 1982; Tzuhalem's Mountain, 1982; The Beauty of the Weapons: Selected Poems 1972-82, 1982; Saraha, 1984; Pieces of Map, Pieces of Music, 1987; other—(ed., with others) Visions: Contemporary Art in Canada, 1983; (with Bill Reid) The Raven Steals the Light: Stories, 1984; Ocean/Paper/Stone, 1984. Add: c/o Writers Union, 24 Ryerson Ave., Toronto, Ont. M5T 2P3, Canada.

BRINK, André South African, b. 1935. Novels. Prof. of Afrikaans and Dutch Literature, Rhodes Univ., Grahamstown, S. Africa (Member of Staff, since 1961). *Publs:* File on a Diplomat, 1966; Looking on Darkness, 1974; An Instant in the Wind, 1976; Rumours of Rain, 1978; Dry White Season, 1979; A Chain of Voices, 1981; Mapmakers, 1983; The Wall of the Plague, 1984; The Ambassador, 1985; States of Emergency, 1988. Add: Rhodes Univ., Dept. of Afrikaans and Dutch Literature, Grahamstown, South Africa.

BRINKLEY, Alan. American, b. 1949. History. Dunwalke Assoc. Prof. of American History, Harvard Univ., Cambridge, Mass., since 1982. Asst. Prof. of History, Massachusetts Inst. of Technology, Cambridge, 1978–82. *Publs:* Voices of Protest: Huey Long, Father Coughlin, and the Great Depression, 1982 (American Book Award); (with Frank Freidel) America in the Twentieth Century, 1982; (with Richard N. Current, T. Harry Williams, and Frank Freidel) American History: A Survey, 1983, 1987. Add: Dept. of History, Harvard Univ., Cambridge, Mass. 02138, U.S.A.

BRINNIN, John Malcolm. American, b. 1916. Children's fiction, Poetry, Literature, Social commentary/phenomena, Biography. Prof. of English, Boston Univ., Mass., 1961–81, now Emeritus. Assoc. Ed., Dodd Mead, publrs., NYC, 1948–50; Member of faculty, Vassar Coll., Poughkeepsie, N.Y., 1942–47, and Univ. of Connecticut, Storrs, 1951–62; Dir., YM-YWHA Poetry Center, NYC, 1949–65. *Publs:* The Garden Is Political, 1942; The Lincoln Lyrics, 1942; No Triumph, 1945; The Sorrows of Cold Stone: Poems 1940–1950, 1951; (ed. with K. Friar) Modern Poetry: American and British, 1951; Dylan Thomas in America: An Intimate Journal, 1955; The Third Rose: Gertrude Stein and Her World, 1959; (ed.) Casebook on Dylan Thomas, 1960; (ed.) Poems, by Emily Dickinson, 1960; William Carlos Williams: A Critical Study, 1961; Arthur: The Dolphin Who Didn't See Venice, 1961; The Selected Poems of John Malcolm Brinnin, 1963; William Carlos Williams, 1963; (with Bill Read) The Modern Poets: An American-British Anthology, 1963, rev. ed. 1970; Dylan, 1964; Skin Diving in the Virgins and Other Poems, 1970; (ed.) Selected Operas and Plays of Gertrude Stein, 1970; (ed. with Bill Read) Twentieth Century Poetry, American and British (1900–1970): An American-British Anthology, 1971; The Sway of the Grand Saloon: A Social History of the North Atlantic, 1971; Beau Voyage: Life Aboard the Last Great Ships, 1981; Sextet: T.S. Eliot, Truman Capote and Others, 1982; Truman Capote: A Memoir, 1986; (with Kenneth Gaulin) Grand

Luxe: The Transatlantic Style, 1988. Add: King Caesar Rd., Duxbury, Mass. 02332, U.S.A.

BRINSMEAD, H(esba) F(ay). Australian, b. 1922. Children's fiction. *Publs:* Pastures of the Blue Crane, 1964; Season of the Briar, 1965; Beat of the City, 1966; A Sapphire for September, 1967; Isle of the Sea Horse, 1969; Listen to the Wind, 1970; Who Calls from Afar?, 1971; Long time Passing, 1972; Echo in the Wildnerness, 1973; Under the Silkwood, 1975; The Wind Harp, 1977; The Ballad of Benny Perhaps, 1978; Once There Was A Swagmen, 1978; The Honey Forest, 1978; Time for Tarquinia, 1982; Longtime Dreaming, 1982; Christmas at Longtime, 1984; The Sand Forest, 1985; Someplace Beautiful, 1986. Add: Shamara Rd., Terranora, N.S.W. 2485, Australia.

BRISCO, P.A. *See* **MATTHEWS,** Patricia.

BRISCO, Patty. *See* **MATTHEWS,** Patricia.

BRISKIN, Jacqueline. American, b. 1927. Novels/Short stories. *Publs:* California Generation, 1970; Afterlove, 1974; Rich Friends, 1976; Paloverde, 1978; The Onyx, 1982; Everything and More, 1983; Too Much Too Soon, 1985; Dreams Are Not Enough, 1987. Add: 984 Casiano Rd., Los Angeles, Calif. 90049, U.S.A.

BRISSENDEN, Alan (Theo). Australian, b. 1932. Literature, Theatre. Reader, Dept. of English, Univ. of Adelaide, since 1983 (Lectr., 1963; Sr. Lectr., 1968; Chmn. of the Dept., 1985–86). Dance Critic, Dance Australia, since 1980. Joint Gen. Ed., with F.H. Mares, Studies in Tudor and Stuart Literature, since 1973; Gov., Adelaide Festival of Arts, since 1981. Dance Critic, Dance Mag., 1979–84. Pres., Bibliographical Soc. of Australia and New Zealand, 1983–85. *Publs:* (ed. with Charles Higham) They Came to Australia (prose anthology), 1961, 1962; (ed.) A Chaste Maid in Cheapside, by T. Middleton, 1968, 4th ed. 1988; Rolf Boldrewood, 1972; (ed.) Lawson's Australia (prose/verse anthology), 1973, 1979; (ed.) The Drover's Wife and Other Stories by Henry Lawson (prose anthology), 1974; (contrib. ed.) Shakespeare and Some Others (critical essays), 1976; (ed.) Rolf Boldrewood (prose anthology), 1979; Shakespeare and the Dance, 1981. Add: Dept. of English, Univ. of Adelaide, P.O. Box 498, Adelaide, S.A. 5001, Australia.

BRISTER, Richard. American, b. 1915. Westerns/Adventure. Professional cartoonist since 1989. Former Mgr., Pennsylvania State Store. *Publs:* The Kansan, 1954; Renegade Brand, 1955; The Wolf Streak, 1958; Law Killer, 1959; Shoot-Out at Sentinel Peak, 1965; Cat Eyes, 1973. Add: 2122 Wayne Ave., Abington, Pa. 19001, U.S.A.

BRISTOW, Robert O'Neil. American, b. 1926. Novels/Short stories. Prof. Emeritus of English and Communications, Winthrop Coll., Rock Hill, S.C., since 1988 (Asst. Prof., 1961–65; Assoc. Prof., 1966–74; Prof., 1974–88). *Publs:* Time for Glory, 1968; Night Season, 1970; A Faraway Drummer, 1973; Laughter in Darkness, 1974. Add: 613½ Charlotte Ave., Rock Hill, S.C. 29730, U.S.A.

BRITAIN, Dan. *See* **PENDLETON,** Don.

BRITT, Katrina. British. Historical/Romance/Gothic. *Publs:* A Kiss in a Gondola, 1968; Healer of Hearts, 1969; A Fine Romance, 1969; The Fabulous Island, 1970; The Masculine Touch, 1970; The Unknown Quest, 1971; The Gentle Flame, 1971; A Spray of Edelweiss, 1972; Strange Bewilderment, 1973; Reluctant Voyager, 1973; The Guarded Gates, 1973; Famous Island; The Greater Happiness, 1974; The House Called Sakura, 1974; The King of Spades, 1974; The Cruiser in the Bay, 1975; Take Back Your Love, 1975; The Spanish Grandee, 1975; The Emerald Garden 1976; Girl in Blue, 1976; If Today Be Sweet, 1976; The Villa Faustina, 1977; The Faithful Heart, 1977; The Silver Tree, 1977; The Enchanted Woods, 1978; The Hills Beyond, 1978; Open Not the Door, 1978; The Man on the Peak, 1979; Flowers for My Love, 1979; The Midnight Sun, 1979; The Wrong Man, 1980; A Girl Called Tegi, 1980; Island for Dreams, 1980; Hotel Jacarandas, 1980; Another Time, Another Place, 1981; Conflict of Love, 1981; Man at Key West, 1982. Add: c/o Mills and Boon Ltd., Eton House, 18-24 Paradise Rd., Richmond, Surrey TW9 1SR, England.

BRITTAIN, Bill. *See* **BRITTAIN,** William.

BRITTAIN, William. Writes as Bill Brittain. American, b. 1930. Children's fiction. Teacher, Union Free School District 15, Lawrence, N.Y., 1954 until retirement, 1986. *Publs:* Survival Outdoors, 1977; All the Money in the World (children's novel), 1979; Devil's Donkey (children's novel), 1981; Sherlock Holmes, Master Detective (text), 1982; The Wish Giver (children's novel), 1983; Who Knew There'd Be Ghosts (children's novel), 1985; Dr. Dredd's Wagon of Wonders (children's novel), 1987; The Fantastic Freshman (children's novel), 1988; My Buddy, The King, 1989. Add: 17 Wisteria Dr., Ashville, N.C. 28804, U.S.A.

BRITTAN, Samuel. British, b. 1933. Economics, Politics/Government. Economics writer since 1966, and Asst. Ed. since 1978, Financial Times, London (Member, Editorial staff, 1955–61). Economics Ed., Observer, London, 1961–64; Economic Adviser, Dept. of Economic Affairs, London, 1965. Research and Visiting Fellow, Nuffield Coll., Oxford, 1973–82; Visiting Prof., Univ. of Chicago Law Sch., 1978. Member, Peacock Cttee. on Finance of the BBC, 1985–86. *Publs:* The Treasury Under the Tories, 1964, as Steering the Economy: The Role of the Treasury, 1969, 1971; Left or Right: The Bogus Dilemma, 1968; The Price of Economic Freedom: A Guide to Flexible Rates, 1970; Capitalism and the Permissive Society, 1973, as A Restatement of Economic Liberalism, 1988; Is There An Economic Consensus? An Attitude Survey, 1973; Second Thoughts on Full Employment Policy, 1975; (with P. Lilley) The Delusion of Incomes Policy, 1977; The Economic Consequences Of Democracy, 1977; How to End the "Monetarist" Controversy, 1981; The Role and Limit of Government, 1983. Add: Flat 10, The Lodge, Kensington Park Gardens, London W11 3HA, England.

BRITTIN, Norman Aylsworth. American, b. 1906. Literature, Writing/Journalism. Hollifield Prof. of English Literature Emeritus, Auburn Univ. Ala. (Assoc. Prof. and Prof. of English, 1948–62). Instr. in English, 1937–45, and Asst. Prof. of English, 1946, Univ. of Utah, Salt Lake City; Lectr. and Prof. of English, Univ. of Puerto Rico, 1962–66; Fulbright Lectr., Univ. of La Laguna, Tenerife, Spain, 1968–69. Co-Ed., Southern Humanities Review, 1967–77. *Publs:* A Writing Apprenticeship, 1963, 5th ed. 1981; Edna St. Vincent Millay, 1967, 1982; Writing Description and Narration, 1969; A Reading Apprenticeship: Literature, 1971; Thomas Middleton, 1972. Add: Dept. of English, Auburn Univ., Auburn, Ala. 36830, U.S.A.

BRITTON, Denis (King) British, b. 1920. Agriculture/Forestry. Lectr., Agricultural Economics Research Inst., Oxford Univ., 1947–52; Economist, U.N. Food and Agriculture Org., Geneva, 1952–59; Gen. Mgr., Marketing and Economic Research, Massey-Ferguson (U.K.) Ltd., Coventry, 1959–61; Prof. of Agricultural Economics, Nottingham Univ., 1961–70, and Wye Coll., Univ. of London, 1970–82. Member, Home Grown Cereals Authority, since 1969. Pres., Intnl. Assn. of Agricultural Economists, 1976–79. *Publs:* Cereals in the United Kingdom, 1969; (with N.B. Hill) Size and Efficiency in Farming, 1975; (with J.C. Dunning and R.M. Harley) Report on Research on the Integration of Farming and Forestry in Lowland Britain, 1984; (co-ed) A Hundred Years of British Food and Farming: A Statistical Survey, 1988. Add: 29 Chequers Park, Wye, Ashford, Kent TN25 5BB, England.

BROADBENT, Donald (Eric). British, b. 1926. Psychology. Member, External Staff, Medical Research Council, since 1974 (Member of Staff, 1949–58, and Dir., 1958–74, M.R.C. Applied Psychology Unit); Fellow of Wolfson Coll. Oxford, since 1974 (Fellow, Pembroke Coll., 1965–74). Pres., British Psychological Soc., 1965, and Psychology Section, British Assn. for the Advancement of Science, 1967. *Publs:* Perception and Communication, 1958; Behaviour, 1961; Decision and Stress, 1971; In Defence of Empirical Psychology, 1973. Add: Dept. of Experimental Psychology, South Parks Rd., Oxford OX1 3UD, England.

BROADFIELD, Aubrey Alfred (Alan). British, b. 1910. History, Librarianship. Local History Librarian, Leics. Libraries, 1963–75. *Publs:* Philosophy of Classification, 1946; Philosophy of Librarianship, 1949; Leicester as It Was, 1972; The Chapel of William Wyggeston's Hospital, 1974. Add: 99 Station Rd., Glenfield, Leicester LE3 8GS, England.

BROCK, Betty (Carter). American, b. 1923. Children's fiction. *Publs:* No Flying in the House, 1970; The Shades, 1971. Add: 1010 Collingwood Rd., Alexandria, Va. 22308, U.S.A.

BROCK, Edwin. British, b. 1927. Novels/Short stories, Plays/Screenplays, Poetry, Autobiography/Memoirs/Personal. Freelance writer, Ogilvy Benson & Mather, London, since 1972. Poetry Ed., Ambit mag., London, since 1960. Editorial Asst., Stonhill & Gillis, London, 1947–51; Police Constable, Metropolitan Police, London, 1951–59; Advertising Writer, Mather & Crowther, 1959–63, J. Walter Thompson, 1963–64, and Masius Wynne-Williams, 1964, all London; Creative Group

Head, S.H. Benson, London, 1964–72. *Publs:* An Attempt at Exorcism, 1959; Night Duty on Eleven Beat (radio play), 1960; A Family Affair; Two Sonnet Sequences, 1960; The Little White God (novel), 1962; televised 1964; With Love from Judas, 1963; (with Geoffrey Hill and Stevie Smith) Penguin Modern Poets 8, 1966; Fred's Primer: A Little Girl's Guide to the World Around Her, 1969; A Cold Day at the Zoo, 1970; Invisibility is the Art of Survival: Selected Poems, 1972; The Portraits and the Poses, 1973; Paroxisms, 1974; I Never Saw it Lit, 1974; The Blocked Heart, 1975; Song of Battery Hen (Selected Poems 1959–75), 1977; Here, Now, Always (autobiography), 1977; The River and the Train, 1979. Add: The Granary, Lower Tharston, Norfolk NR15 2YN, England.

BROCK, Michael (George). British, b. 1920. History. Warden, St. George's House, Windsor Castle, since 1988. Fellow and Tutor in Modern History and Politics, Corpus Christi Coll., Oxford, 1950–66; Vice Pres. and Bursar, Wolfson Coll., Oxford, 1967–76; Prof. of Education and Dir. of Sch. of Education, Exeter Univ., 1977–78; Warden, Nuffield Coll., Oxford, 1978–88. *Publs:* The Great Reform Act, 1973; (co-ed.) H.H. Asquith: Letters to Venetia Stanley, 1982, 1985. Add: 24 The Cloisters, Windsor Castle, Berks. SL4 1NJ, England.

BROCK, Peter de Beauvoir. Canadian, b. 1920. History. Prof. Emeritus of History, Univ. of Toronto, Ont., since 1985 (Lectr., 1957–58; Prof., 1966–85). Asst. Prof. of History, Univ. of Alberta, Edmonton, 1958–61; Assoc. Prof., Columbia Univ., NYC, 1961–65. *Publs:* The Political and Social Doctrines of the Unity of Czech Brethren in the 15th and Early 16th Centuries, 1957; Pacifism in the United States: From the Colonial Era to the First World War, 1968; Twentieth-Century Pacifism, 1970; (ed. with H.G. Skilling) The Czech Renascence of the Nineteenth Century, 1970; Pacifism in Europe to 1914, 1972; Nationalism and Populism in Partitioned Poland, 1973; The Slovak National Awakening, 1976; Polish Revolutionary Populism, 1977; The Roots of War Resistance: Pacifism from the Early Church to Tolstoy, 1981; The Mahatma and Mother India: Essays on Gandhi's Non-Violence and Nationalism, 1983. Add: Dept. of History, Univ. of Toronto, Toronto, Ont. M5S 1A1, Canada.

BROCK, Rose. *See* **HANSEN,** Joseph.

BROCK, William Hodson. British, b. 1936. History, Sciences. Reader in the History of Science and Dir. of the Victorian Studies Centre, Univ. of Leicester, since 1974 (Lectr., 1960–74). Chmn., Steering Cttee., Royal Instn. Centre for History of Science and Technology, since 1984. Ed., AMBIX, 1968–83; Member, Royal Soc. British National Cttee for History of Science, 1970–75, 1978–84; Pres., British Soc. for History of Science, 1978–80. *Publs:* (ed.) The Atomic Debates, 1967; (ed.) Science Case Histories, 1972; (ed.) H.E. Armstrong and the Teaching of Science 1880-1930, 1973; (with R.M. MacLeod) Natural Knowledge in Social Context: The Journals of Thomas Archer Hirst, 1980; (ed. with N.D. McMillan and R.C. Mollan) John Tyndall: Essays on a Natural Philosopher, 1981; (with A.J. Meadows) The Lamp of Learning, 1984; (ed.) Liebig und Hofmann in ihren Briefen, 1984; From Protyle to Proton, 1985. Add: Victorian Studies Centre, Univ. of Leicester, Leicester, England.

BROCK, William Ranulf. British, b. 1916. History. Fellow, Selwyn Coll., Cambridge, 1947 (Life Fellow, since 1967); Lectr. in History, Cambridge Univ., 1949–67; Prof. of History, Univ. of Glasgow, 1967–81. *Publs:* Lord Liverpool and Liberal Toryism, 1941; Britain and the Dominions, 1950; The Character of American History, 1960; An American Crisis, 1963; The Evolution of American Democracy, 1970; Conflict and Transformation in the U.S., 1844-1877, 1973; The United States, 1789-1890: Sources of History, 1975; Politics and Political Conscience, 1979; Scotus Americanus, 1981; Investigation and Responsibility, 1984; Welfare Democracy, and the New Deal, 1988. Add: 49 Barton Rd., Cambridge CB3 9LG, England.

BROCKETT, Oscar Gross. American, b. 1923. Theatre. Holder, Z.T. Scott Family Chair in Drama, Univ. of Texas at Austin, since 1981. Instr. in English, Univ. of Kentucky, Lexington, 1949–50; Asst. Prof. of Drama, Stetson Univ., DeLand, Fla., 1952–56; Asst. Prof., then Assoc. Prof. of Drama, Univ. of Iowa, Iowa City, 1956–63; Prof. of Theatre, Indiana Univ., Bloomington, 1963–78; Dean, Coll. of Fine Arts, Univ. of Texas at Austin, 1978–80; DeMille Prof. of Drama, Univ. of Southern California, Los Angeles, 1980–81. *Publs:* (ed. with S. Becker and D. Bryant) A Bibliographical Guide to Research in Speech and Dramatic Art, 1963; The Theatre: An Introduction, 1964, 4th ed., 1979; (ed. with L. Brockett) Plays for the Theatre, 1967, 5th ed., 1988; History of the Theatre, 1968, 5th ed. 1987; Perspectives on Contemporary Theatre, 1971; (ed.) Studies

in Theatre and Drama, 1972; (with R. Findlay) Century of Innovation: A History of European and American Theatre and Drama since 1870, 1973; The Essential Theatre, 1976, 4th ed., 1988; (with M. Pape) World Drama, 1984. Add: Dept. of Drama, Univ. of Texas, Austin, Tex. 78712, U.S.A.

BROCKINGTON, Raymond Bernard. British, b. 1937. Money/Finance. Lectr., in Finance and Accounting, Univ. of Bath, since 1974. Lectr., Bromsgrove Coll. of Further Education, 1963–68; Sr. Lectr., The Polytechnic, Wolverhampton, 1968–71; Principal Lectr., North Staffordshire Polytechnic, 1971–74. *Publs:* Statistics for Accountants, 1965; Accounting, 1969; Statistics for Accountants and Administrators, 1974; Financial Management, 1978; Financial Accounting, 1982. Add: Sch. of Management, Univ. of Bath, Claverton Down, Bath BA2 7AY, England.

BRODERICK, Damien. Australian, b. 1944. Science fiction/Fantasy. *Publs:* A Man Returned (short stories), 1965; Sorcerer's World, 1970; (ed.) The Zeitgeist Machine: A New Anthology of Science Fiction, 1977; The Dreaming Dragons, 1980; The Judas Mandala, 1982; (with Rory Barnes) Valencies, 1983; Transmitters, 1984; (ed.) Strange Attractors, 1985; The Black Grail, 1986; (ed.) Matilda at the Speed of Light, 1988; Striped Holes, 1988. Add: 23 Hutchinson St., Brunswick, Vic. 3056, Australia.

BRODERICK, John. Irish, b. 1927. Novels. *Publs:* The Pilgrimage (in U.S. as The Chameleons), 1961; The Fugitives, 1962; Don Juaneen, 1963; The Waking of Willie Ryan, 1965; An Apology for Roses, 1973; The Pride of Summer, 1976; London Irish, 1979; The Trial of Father Dillingham, 1982; A Prayer for Fair Weather, 1984; The Rose Tree, 1985; The Flood, 1987. *Deceased, 1989.*

BRODEUR, Paul (Adrian, Jr.). American, b. 1931. Novels/Short stories, Environment. Staff Writer, The New Yorker mag., since 1958. *Publs:* The Sick Fox, 1963; The Stunt Man, 1970; Downstream (short stories), 1972; Expendable Americans, 1974; The Zapping of America, 1977; Restitution: The Land Claims of the Mashpee, Paasamaguoddy, and Penobscot Indians of New England, 1985; Outrageous Misconduct: The Asbestos Industry on Trial, 1985. Add: c/o The New Yorker, 25 West 43rd St., New York, N.Y. 10036, U.S.A.

BRODINE, Karen. American, b. 1947. Poetry. Asst. Ed., American Journal of Human Genetics, Univ. of California, San Francisco, since 1987. Instr. of Creative Writing, San Francisco State Univ., 1975–81; typesetter and writer, 1981–7. *Publs:* Slow Juggling, 1975; Workweek, 1978; Illegal Assembly, 1980; Woman Sitting at the Machine, Thinking, 1987. Add: 2661 21st St., San Francisco, CA 94110, U.S.A.

BRODKEY, Harold. American, b. 1930. Short stories. Assoc. Prof. of English, Cornell Univ., Ithaca, N.Y., 1977–78, 1979, 1981. Visiting Prof. of English, City Coll. of City Univ. of New York, 1987. *Publs:* First Love and Other Sorrows, 1957; Women and Angels, 1985; Stories in an Almost Classical Mode, 1988. Add: 255 W. 88th St., New York, N.Y. 10024, U.S.A.

BRODRIBB, (Arthur) Gerald (Norcott). British, b. 1915. Poetry, Archaeology, Cricket. Schoolmaster, Canford Sch., 1944–54; Headmaster, Hydneye House Sch., 1954–72. *Publs:* (ed.) The English Game, 1948; Cricket in Fiction, 1950; All Round the Wicket, 1951; Next Man In, 1952, 1985; (ed.) Book of Cricket Verse, 1953; The Bay and Other Poems, 1953; Hastings and Men of Letters, 1954; (with H. Sayen) A Yankee Looks at Cricket, 1956; Hit for Six, 1960; Felix on the Bat, 1962; Stamped Tiles of Classis Britannica, 1969; The Croucher: Gilbert Jessop, 1974; Maurice Tate, 1976; The Art of Nicholas Felix, 1985; Roman Brick and Tile, 1987. Add: Stubbles, Ewhurst Green, Robertsbridge, East Sussex, England.

BRODSKY, Joseph (Iosif Alexandrovich). Russian, b. 1940. Essays. Poet. Andrew W. Mellon Prof. of Literature, Mount Holyoke Coll., South Hadley, Mass., since 1986. Poet in Residence, Univ. of Mich., Ann Arbor, 1972–73, 1974–79. Visiting Prof., Smith Coll., Amherst Coll., Queens Coll., Hamshire Coll., 1981–86. MacArthur Foundation fellow, 1981. Nobel Prize for Literature, 1987. *Publs:* Less Than One: Selected Essays, 1986; Numerous other books in Russian (see Alan Myers, transl.). Add: Mount Holyoke Coll., Dept. of Literature, South Hadley, Mass. 01075, U.S.A.

BRODY, Jane E(llen). American, b. 1941. Medicine/Health. Writer, Personal Health column, New York Times, since 1976 (science writer, 1965–76); Columnist, Family Circle mag. Reporter, Minneapolis Tribune, 1962–65. *Publs:* (with Richard Engquist) Secrets of Good Health, 1970; (with Arthur I. Holleb) You Can Fight Cancer and Win,

1977; Jane Brody's Nutrition Book, 1981; Jane Brody's The New York Times Guide to Personal Health, 1982; Jane Brody's Good Food Book: Living the High Carbohydrate Way, 1985. Add: c/o New York Times, 229 West 43rd St., New York, N.Y. 10036, U.S.A.

BROER, Lawrence R(ichard). American, b. 1938. Literature. Prof. of English, Coll. of Arts and Letters, Univ. of South Florida, Tampa, since 1979 (Instr., 1965–68; Asst. Prof., 1968–73; Assoc. Prof., 1973–79). *Publs:* Hemingway's Spanish Tragedy, 1973; Counter Currents, 1973; (with Herb Karl and Charles Weingartner) The First Time, 1974; (with Richard Dietrich) The Realities of Literature, 1980; with Jack Walther) Thirteen on the Twenties: Cultural Essays, 1980; Sanity Plea: Schizophrenia in the Novels of Kurt Vonnegut, 1988. Add: Dept of English, Univ. of South Florida, Tampa, FL, U.S.A.

BROGAN, Elise. *See* URCH, Elizabeth.

BROGAN, James. *See* HODDER-WILLIAMS, Christopher.

BROMBERT, Victor (Henri). American, b. 1923. Literature. Henry Putnam Univ. Prof. of Romance and Comparative Literature, Princeton Univ., since 1975. Formerly, Prof. and Chmn., Dept of Romance Literatures, Yale Univ., New Haven. *Publs:* The Criticism of T.S. Eliot, 1949; Stendhal et la Voie oblique, 1954; The Intellectual Hero, 1961; (ed.) Stendhal: A Collection of Critical Essays, 1962; The Novels of Flaubert, 1966; Stendhal: Fiction and the Themes of Freedom, 1968; (ed.) The Hero in Literature, 1969; Flaubert par lui-meme, 1971; The Romantic Prison, 1978; Victor Hugo and the Visionary Novel, 1984; The Hidden Reader, 1988. Add: 187 Library Place, Princeton, N.J. 08540, U.S.A.

BROME, Vincent. British. History, Literature, Biography. Member, British Library Advisory Cttee., 1975–83. Former Feature Writer, News-Chronicle; Ed., Menu Mags.; Member of staff, Ministry of Information; Asst. Ed., Medical World. *Publs:* Anthology, 1936; Clement Attlee, 1947; H.G. Wells, 1951; Aneurin Bevin, 1953; The Last Surrender, 1954; The Way Back, 1956; Six Studies in Quarrelling, 1958; Sometimes at Night, 1959; Frank Harris, 1959; Acquaintance With Grief, 1961; We Have Come Long Way, 1963; The Problem of Progress, 1963; Love in Our Time, 1964; Four Realist Novelists, 1964; The International Brigades, 1965; The World of Luke Jympson, 1966; Freud and His Early Circle, 1967; The Surgeon, 1967; Diary of a Revolution, 1968; The Revolution, 1969; The Imaginary Crime, 1969; Confessions of a Writer, 1970; The Brain Operators, 1970; Private Prosecutions, 1971; Reverse Your Verdict, 1971; London Consequences, 1972; The Embassy, 1972; The Day of Destruction, 1974; The Happy Hostage, 1976; C.G. Jung, 1978; Havelock Ellis, 1979; Ernest Jones, Freud's Alter Ego, 1982; The Day of the Fifth Moon, 1984; J.B. Priestley, 1988. Add: 45 Great Ormond St., London WC1, England.

BROMELL, Henry. American, b. 1947. Novels/Short stories. Visiting Lectr., Iowa Writers Workshop, Univ. of Iowa, Iowa City, 1975–76; Writer-in-Residence, Amherst Coll., Mass., 1976–77. *Publs:* The Slightest Distance, 1974; I Know Your Heart, Marco Polo, 1979; The Follower, 1983. Add: c/o Nan Blitman, Phil Gersh Agency, 222 N. Canon, Beverly Hills, Calif. 90201, U.S.A.

BROMHEAD, Peter Alexander. British, b. 1919. History, Politics/Government. Lectr., and Tutor, Wilton Park, 1946–47; Lectr. in Politics, Univ. of Durham, 1947–62; Visiting Prof. of Social Sciences, Univ. of Florida, 1959–60; Prof. of Politics, Univ. of Wales, 1963–64. Prof. of Politics, Univ. of Bristol, 1964–80. *Publs:* Private Members' Bills in the British Parliament, 1956; The House of Lords and Contemporary Politics, 1958; Life in Modern Britain, 1962, 6th ed. 1985; Life in Modern America, 1970, 3rd ed. 1988; The Great White Elephant of Maplin Sands, 1973; Britain's Developing Constitution, 1974; Politics in Britain, 1979. Add: Glebe House, Abbots Leigh, Bristol BS8 3QU, England.

BROMIGE, David (Mansfield). Canadian (b. British), b. 1933. Short stories, Plays/Screenplays, Poetry. Asst. Prof. to Prof. of English, California State Univ., Sonoma, since 1970. Dairy farm worker, 1950–53; Mental hosp. attendant, 1954–55; Elementary Sch. Teacher, England, 1957–58, and B.C., 1959–62; Freelance Reviewer, CBC, 1960–62; Ed., Raven mag., 1960–62; Poetry Ed., Northwest Review, Eugene, Ore., 1963–64; Teaching Asst., 1966–69, and Instr. in English, 1969–70, Univ. of California, Berkeley; Lectr., California Coll. of Arts and Crafts, 1970. Ed., R.C. Lion, Berkeley, 1966–67; Ed., Open Reading Cotat:. 1971–76. *Publs:* Palace of Laments (play), 1957; The Medals (play), 1959; The Cobalt Poet (play), 1960; Save What You Can (play), 1961; The Gather-

ing, 1965; Please Like Me, 1968; The Ends of the Earth, 1968; The Quivering Roadway, 1969; In His Image, 1970; Threads, 1971; The Fact So of Itself, 1971; They are Eyes, 1972; Birds of the West, 1973; Three Stories, 1973; Tight Corners and What's Around Them, 1974; Ten Years in the Making, 1974; Spells and Blessing, 1974; Out of My Hands, 1974; Credences of Winter, 1976; Living in Advance, 1976; Six of One, Half a Dozen of the Other, 1977; My Poetry, 1980; P-E-A-C-E, 1981; In the Uneven Steps of Hung-Chow, 1982. Add: Dept. of English, Sonoma State Univ., Rohnert Park, Calif. 94928, U.S.A.

BROMIGE, Iris (Amy Edna). British, b. 1910. Romance. *Publs:* The Traceys, 1946; Stay But till Tomorrow, 1946; Chequered Pattern, 1947; in U.S. as A Chance for Love, 1975; Tangled Roots, 1948; Marchwood, 1949; The Golden Cage, 1950; April Wooing, 1951; Laurian Vale, 1952; The House of Conflict, 1953; in U.S. as Shall Love Be Lost?, 1974; Gay Intruder, 1954; Diana Comes Home, 1955; The New Owner, 1956; The Enchanted Garden, 1956; A New Life for Joanna, 1957; Family Group, 1958; The Conway Touch, 1958; The Flowering Year, 1959; The Second Mrs. Rivers, 1960; Fair Prisoner, 1960; Alex and the Raynhams, 1961; Come Love, Come Hope, 1962; Rosevean, 1962; The Family Web, 1963; A House Without Love, 1964; The Young Romantic, 1964; The Challenge of Spring, 1965; The Lydian Inheritance, 1966; The Stepdaughter, 1966; The Quiet Hills, 1967; An April Girl, 1967; Only Our Love, 1968; The Master of Heronsbridge, 1969; The Tangled Wood, 1969; Encounter at Alpenrose, 1970; A Sheltering Tree, 1970; A Magic Place, 1971; Rough Weather, 1972; Golden Summer, 1972; The Broken Bough, 1973; The Night of the Party, 1974; The Bend in the River, 1975; A Haunted Landscape, 1976; A Distant Song, 1977; The Happy Fortress, 1978; The Paths of Summer, 1979; One Day, My Love, 1980; Old Love's Domain, 1982; A Slender Thread, 1985; Farewell to Winter, 1986; The Changing Tide, 1987. Add: c/o Hodder and Stoughton Ltd., Mill Rd., Dunton Green, Sevenoaks, Kent TN13 2YA, England.

BROMILEY, Geoffrey William. British, b. 1915. Theology/Religion, Translations. Prof. of Church History and Historical Theology, Fuller Theological Seminary, Pasadena, Calif., 1958–86, now Emeritus. Vice Principal, Trinity Theological Coll., Bristol, England, 1946–51; Rector, St. Thomas's Church, Edinburgh, 1951–58. *Publs:* Reasonable Service, 1949; Baptism and the Anglican Reformers, 1953; (ed. and trans.) Zwingli and Bullinger Classics, 1953; Thomas Cranmer, Theologian, 1956; (co-ed. and co-trans.) Karl Barth's Church Dogmatics, vols. I-IV, 1956–74; Sacramental Teaching, 1957; Unity and Disunity, 1958; Christian Ministry, 1959; (ed. and trans.) DeSenarclens' Heirs of the Reformation, 1963; (ed. and trans.) Theological Dictionary of the New Testament, vols. I-IX, 1964–74; (ed. and trans.) Helmut Thielicke's Evangelical Faith, 3 vols., 1974–82; Ellul's Ethics of Freedom, 1974; Thomas Cranmer, 1977; Historical Theology, 1978; Theology of Karl Barth, 1979; Children of Promise, 1979; (ed.) International Standard Bible Encyclopedia, 1979–; God and Marriage, 1980; (trans.) Kasemann's Romans, 1980; Karl Barth's Letters, Ethics, Christian Life, 1981; Karl Barth's Theology of Schleiermacher, 1982; Helmut Thielicke's Being Human—Becoming Human, 1984. Add: 2261 Queensberry Rd., Pasadena, Calif. 91104, U.S.A.

BROMKE, Adam. Canadian, b. 1928. International relations/Current Affairs, Politics/Government. Prof. of Political Science, McMaster Univ., Hamilton, Ont., since 1973. Lectr., Dept. of Economics and Political Science, McGill Univ., Montreal, 1957–60; Research Fellow, Russian Research Centre, Harvard Univ., Cambridge, Mass., 1960–62; Prof. Dept. of Political Science, Carleton Univ., Ottawa, 1962–73. *Publs:* (ed.) The Communist States at the Crossroads, 1965; Poland's Politics, Idealism vs. Realism, 1967; (ed. with P.E. Uren) The Communist States and the West, 1967; (ed. with T.H. Rakowski-Harmstone) The Communist States in Disarray, 1965–1973; (ed. with J.W. Strong) Gierek's Poland, 1973; (ed. with D. Novak) The Communist States in the Era of Détente: 1971–77, 1978; Poland: The Last Decade; Poland: The Protracted Crisis, 1983; Eastern Europe in the Aftermath of Solidarity, 1985; The Meanings and Uses of Polish History, 1987. Add: Vista Communications, Inc., Pheasant Run Newtown Indsl. Commons, Newtown, Pa. 18940, U.S.A.

BRONER, E(sther) M(asserman). American, b. 1930. Novels/Short stories, Plays/Screenplays, Literature. Assoc. Prof. of English and Writer-in-Residence, Wayne State Univ., Detroit, Mich., since 1964. *Publs:* Summer is a Foreign Land (verse-drama), 1966; Journal/Nocturnal and Seven Stories, 1968; (with M. Zieve) Colonel Higginson (musical drama), 1968; Her Mothers (novel) 1975; A Weave of Women (novel), 1978; The Body Parts of Margaret Fuller (play), 1978; (with Cathy N. Davidson) The Last Tradition: Mothers and Daughters in Literature, 1980. Add: English Dept., Wayne State Univ., Detroit, Mich. 48202, U.S.A.

BRONK, William. American, b. 1918. Poetry. *Publs:* Light and Dark, 1956; The World, The Worldless, 1964; The Empty Hands, 1969; That Tantalus, 1971; To Praise the Music, 1972; Utterances, 1972; Looking at It, 1973; The New World (essays), 1974; A Partial Glossary: Two Essays, 1974; Silence and Metaphor, 1975; The Stance, 1975; My Father Photographed with Friends and Other Pictures, 1976; The Meantime, 1976; Finding Losses, 1976; Twelve Losses Found, 1976; That Beauty Still, 1978; The Force of Desire, 1979; Life Supports: New and Collected Poems, 1981; Six Duplicities, 1980; The Brother in Elysium (essays), 1980; Light in a Dark Sky, 1982; Vectors and Smoothable Curves (collected essays), 1983; Careless Love and Its Apostrophes, 1985; Manifest; and Furthermore, 1987. Add: 57 Pearl St., Hudson Falls, N.Y. 12839, U.S.A.

BRONNER, Edwin Blaine. American, b. 1920. History, Biography. Curator of Quaker Collection and Prof. of History since 1962, and Librarian, 1969–86, Haverford Coll., Pa. Book Review Ed., Quaker History, since 1974. Pres., Friends Historical Assn., 1970–72 and 1974–77; Pres., Friends Historical Society (London), 1970. *Publs:* Thomas Earle as Reformer, 1948; William Penn's Holy Experiment, 1962; (ed.) American Quakers Today, 1966; (ed.) Walter Robson's Journal, 1970; The Other Branch, 1974; William Penn, 1975; (co-author) The Papers of William Penn, V, Bibliography, 1985; (ed.) The Quakers, by W.W. Comfort, 1986. Add: Magill Library, Haverford Coll., Haverford, Pa. 19041, U.S.A.

BRONSTEIN, Arthur J. American, b. 1914. Language/Linguistics, Speech/Rhetoric. Prof. Emeritus of Speech and Linguistics, Herbert H. Lehman Coll., City Univ. of New York, since 1983 (Acting Dean of Faculties, 1972; Acting Dean of Humanities, 1974–75; Prof., 1968–83). Faculty member, Ohio Univ., Athens, 1936–37, The City Coll., NYC, 1937–38, and Queens Coll., Flushing, N.Y., 1938–68; The Graduate School, City Univ. of New York, since 1963; Fulbright Prof., English Linguistics, Univ. of Tel Aviv, Israel, 1967–68; Univ. of Trondheim, Norway, 1979. *Publs:* The Pronunciation of American English, 1960; (with B.F. Jacoby) Your Speech and Voice, 1967; (ed. with C. Chaver and C. Stevens) Essays in Honor of Claude M. Wise, 1970; (ed. with Raphael and Stevens) Biographical Dictionary of Phonetic Sciences, 1977. Add: Box 236, Monterey, Mass. 01245, U.S.A.

BRONTE, Louisa. *See* **ROBERTS**, Janet Louise.

BROOK, David. American, b. 1932. International relations/Current Affairs. Prof. of Political Science since 1972, Jersey City State Coll. N.J., (Asst. Prof. 1967–69; Assoc. Prof., 1969–70): Rep. of Intnl. Studies Assoc. to the UN, since 1981; Chairman, UN Non-Governmental Organ. Sub-Comm. on Global Ed. of the Comm. on Youth, since 1984. Consultant, Dodd Mead & Co., publrs. Instr., St. John Univ., NYC, 1961–63; Asst. Prof., City Univ. of New York, 1964–67; Lectr. in Political Science, Rutgers Univ., New Brunswick, N.J., 1964–67. *Publs:* The United Nations and the China Dilemma, 1956; Preface to Peace: The United Nations and the Arab-Israel Armistice System, 1964; (ed.) Search for Peace: Readings in International Relations, 1970. Add: 135 Hawthorne St., Apt. 6-H, Brooklyn, N.Y. 11225, U.S.A.

BROOK, Judy. (Judith Penelope Brook). British, b. 1926. Children's fiction. Fulltime artist and illustrator. *Publs:* (self-illustrated)—Tim Mouse, 1966; Tim Mouse and the Major, 1967; Tim Mouse Visits the Farm, 1968; Tim Mouse Goes Down the Stream, 1970; Tim and Helen Mouse, 1970; Tim Mouse and Father Christmas, 1971; Noah's Ark, 1972; This Little Pig, 1973; Alfred the Helpful Donkey, 1974; The Friendly Letter Box, 1975; Belinda, 1976; Mrs. Noah and the Animals, 1977; Belinda and Father Christmas, 1978; Mrs. Noah's ABC 123, 1979; Around the Clock, 1980; Dicky and Geoff, The Jaunting Gerbils, 1984; Hector and Harriet, The Night Hamsters, 1985; (with Pam Royde) The Wind in the Willows Activity Book, 1984; Charlie Clown at the Seaside, 1986; Charlie Clown at the Circus, 1986. Add: 27 Short Rd., Chiswick, London W4 2QU, England.

BROOKE, Bryan Nicholas. British, b. 1915. Medicine/Health. Emeritus Prof. of Surgery, St. George's Hosp., London, since 1980 (Prof., 1963–80). Sr. Lectr. in Surgery, Univ. of Aberdeen, 1946–47; Reader in Surgery, Univ. of Birmingham, 1947–63; Consultant Ed., World Medicine, 1980–82. *Publs:* Ulcerative Colitis and Its Surgical Treatment, 1954; You and Your Operation, 1955; (with G. Slaney) Metabolic Derangements in Gastro-Intestinal Surgery, 1967; Understanding Cancer, 1971; Crohn's Disease, 1977; Inflammatory Disease of the Bowel, 1980; The Troubled Gut, 1986; (with Grahame Stuart Thomas) A Garden of Roses, 1987. Add: 112 Balham Park Rd., London SW12 8EA, England.

BROOKE, Christopher N.L. British, b. 1927. History. Dixie Prof. of Ecclesiastical History, Univ. of Cambridge, and Fellow, Gonville and Caius Coll., Cambridge, since 1977. General Ed., Oxford (formerly Nelson's) Medieval Texts, since 1959. Fellow of Gonville and Caius Coll., Cambridge, 1949–56; Lectr. in History, Cambridge Univ., 1954–56; Prof. of Mediaeval History, Univ. of Liverpool, 1956–67; Prof. of History, Westfield Coll., Univ. of London, 1967–77. *Publs:* (with W.J. Millor and H.E. Butler) The Letters of John of Salisbury, 2 vols., 1955–79; (with M. Postan) Carte Nativorum: A Peterborough Abbey Cartulary of the Fourteenth Century, 1960; From Alfred to Henry III, 871-1272, 1961; The Saxon and Norman Kings, 1963; Europe in the Central Middle Ages, 1964, 1987; (with A. Morey) Gilbert Foliot and His Letters, 1965; (with A. Morey) The Letters and Charters of Gilbert Foliot: . . . Bishop of London (1163-87), 1967; The Twelfth Century Renaissance, 1969; The Structure of Medieval Society, 1971; (with D. Knowles and V.C.M. London) The Heads of Religious Houses, England and Wales, 940-1216, 1972; (with W. Swaan) The Monastic World, 1000-1300, 1974; (with G. Keir) London, 800-1216: The Shaping of a City, 1975; (with D. Whitelock and M. Brett) Councils and Synods, I, 871-1204, 1981; (with R.B. Brooke) Popular Religion in the Middle Ages, 1984; A History of Gonville and Caius College, 1985; (with D.N. Dumville) The Church and the Welsh Border in the Central Middle Ages, 1986; (with R. Highfield and W. Swann) Oxford and Cambridge, 1988. Add: Faculty of History, West Rd., Cambridge CB3 9EF, England.

BROOKE, Dinah. British, b. 1936. Novels/Short stories, Plays/Screenplays, Translations. *Publs:* (trans.) Children of the Gods, 1967; (trans.) Daybreak, 1968; Love Life of a Cheltenham Lady, 1970; Lord Jim at Home, 1973; The Miserable Child and Her Father in the Desert, 1974; Sinksongs (play), 1975; Don't Worry Dad (play), 1976; Games of Love and War, 1976. Add: c/o Andre Deutsch Ltd., 105 Great Russell St., London WC1B 3IJ, England.

BROOKE-LITTLE, John (Philip Brooke). British, b. 1927. Genealogy/Heraldry, History. Norroy and Ulster King of Arms, since 1980 (Bluemantle Pursuivant of Arms, 1956–67; Richmond Herald of Arms, 1967–80); Officer of Arms, Royal Household, since 1956. Hon. Ed., The Coat of Arms, since 1950; Chmn., Tabard Publs, Ltd. Ed., Dod's Peerage, and Dod's Parliamentary Companion, 1955–58. *Publs:* Royal London, 1953; Pictorial History of Oxford, 1954; (ed. with C.W. Scott-Giles) Boutell's Heraldry, 1963, (sole ed.) 9th ed., 1983; Knights of the Middle Ages, 1966; (ed.) Complete Guide to Heraldry, 1969; The Prince of Wales,1969; (with A. Tauté and D. Pottinger) The Kings and Queens of Great Britain, 1970; An Heraldic Alphabet, 3rd ed. 1985; (with M. Angel) Beasts in Heraldry, 1974; Royal Arms, Beasts and Badges, 1977; The British Monarchy in Colour, 1977; Royal Ceremonies of State, 1980. Add: Coll. of Arms, Queen Victoria St., London EC4V 4BT, England.

BROOKE-ROSE, Christine. British. Novels/Short stories, Literature. Freelance journalist, London, 1956–68; Lectr., 1969–75, and Prof., 1975–88, Dept. of English and American Literature, Univ. of Paris. *Publs:* The Languages of Love, 1957; A Grammar of Metaphor, 1958; The Sycamore Tree, 1958; The Dear Deceit, 1960; The Middlemen: A Satire, 1961; Out, 1964; Such, 1966; Between, 1968; Go When You See the Green Man Walking (short stories), 1970; A ZBC of Ezra Pound, 1971; Thru, 1975; A Rhetoric of the Unreal, 1981; Amalgamemnon, 1984; Xorandor, 1986; The Christine Brooke-Rose Omnibus, 1986; Verbivore (novel), 1989. Add: c/o Carcanet Press, 208 Corn Exchange Bldgs., Manchester M4 3BQ, England.

BROOKES, Murray. British, b. 1926. Medicine/Health. Prof. of Orthopaedic Anatomy, Univ. of London, since 1983; Dir., Orthopaedic Research Unit, United Medical Schs., Guy's Hosp., London, since 1985 (Sr. Lectr., 1962–67; Reader, 1967–83; Dir., Arthritis Research Unit, 1966–74). UK Secty., Symposium sur la Circulation Osseuse, Toulouse, France, since 1977; Convenor, Nomina Embryologica Intnl. Anatomical Nomenclature Cttee., since 1986. *Publs:* The Blood Supply of Bone, 1971; Nomina Anatomica, 6th ed., 1989. Add: Dept. of Anatomy, Guy's Hosp. Medical Sch., London SE1 9RT, England.

BROOKES, Pamela. British, b. 1922. History, Politics/Government. Freelance corresp. *Publs:* Women at Westminster: History of Women MP's 1918–1966, 1967; The Consul and The Queen of Geneva, 1977. Add: Esterella, 83440 Seillans, France.

BROOKNER, Anita. British, b. 1928. Novels, Art. Reader, Courtauld Int. of Art, London, since 1977 (Lectr., 1964). Lectr., Univ. of Reading, 1959–64; Slade Prof., Cambridge Univ., 1967–68. *Publs:* Watteau, 1968; The Genius of the Future, 1971; Greuze, 1972; Jacques-Louis

David, 1980; A Start in Life (novel), 1981; Providence (novel), 1982; Look at Me (novel), 1983; Hotel du Lac, 1984 (Booker Prize); Family and Friends, 1985; A Misalliance, 1986, in U.S. as The Misalliance, 1987; A Friend from England, 1987; Latecomers, 1988; (ed.) The Stories of Edith Wharton, 1988. Add: 68 Elm Park Gdns., London SW10, England.

BROOKOVER, Wilbur. American, b. 1911. Education, Sociology. Prof. of Social Science, Sociology and Anthropology since 1953, and Chmn., Dept. of Urban and Metropolitan Studies since 1973, Michigan State Univ., East Lansing, now Emeritus. (Asst. Prof., 1946–48; Assoc. Prof., 1948–53; Dir., Bureau of Educational Research and Coordinator, Ford Foundn. Pakistan Project, 1957–60; Asst. Dean, Research and Publs., Coll. of Education, 1960–63; Chmn., Foundn. of Education, Coll. of Education, 1963; Dir., Social Science Teaching Inst., 1964–67; Assoc. Dir., Center for Urban Affairs, 1970–73). High sch. teacher of social studies and athletic coach. Indiana, 1933–38; Instr. of Sociology, Butler Univ., Indianapolis, Ind., 1940–41; Instr. of Social Science, Indiana State Teachers Coll., Terre Haute, 1941–43; Educational Service Officer, U.S. Navy, 1943–46; Lectr. of Sociology, Univ. of Wisconsin, Madison, 1946. *Publs:* (co-author) Youth and the World at Work, 1949; (co-ed.) Readings in Sociology, 1952, 5th ed. 1974; Sociology of Education, 1955, (with D. Gottlieb) 1964; (co-ed.) Readings in Social Science, 3 vols., 1955; (with E. Erickson) Society, Schools, and Learning, 1969, 1973; (with E. Erickson) Sociology of Education, 1974; Schools Can Make a Difference, 1977; School Systems and Student Achievement, 1979; (with others) Creating Effective Schools, 1982. Add: 138 West Owen Grad. Hall, Michigan State Univ., East Lansing, Mich. 48824, U.S.A.

BROOKS, A. Russell. American, b. 1906. Literature. Chmn., Dept. of English, North Carolina M. and T. Coll., Greensboro, 1934–44; Assoc. Prof. of English, Morehouse Coll., Atlanta, Ga., 1946–60; Chmn., Dept of English, Kentucky State Univ., Frankfort, 1960–72; now retired. Advisory Ed., CLA Journal. *Publs:* James Boswell, 1971. Add: 415 College Park Dr., Frankfort, Ky. 40601, U.S.A.

BROOKS, Cleanth. American, b. 1906. Literature. Gray Prof. of Rhetoric Emeritus, Yale Univ., New Haven, Conn. (joined faculty, 1947). Prof. of English. Louisiana State Univ., Baton Rouge, 1932–47; Managing Ed., 1935–41, and Co-Ed., 1941–42, Southern Review, Baton Rouge, La.; Cultural Attaché U.S. Embassy, London, 1964–66. *Publs:* (with Robert Penn Warren) Understanding Poetry, 1938; Modern Poetry and the Tradition, 1939; (ed. with D.N. Smith and A.F. Falconer) The Percy Letters, 8 vols., 1942; (with R.P Warren) Understanding Fiction, 1943; (ed.) The Correspondence of Thomas Percy and Richard Farmer, 1946; The Well-Wrought Urn, 1947; (with R.P. Warren) Modern Rhetoric, 1956; (with W.K. Wimsatt) Literary Criticism: A Short History, 1957; The Hidden God, 1963; William Faulkner: The Yoknapatawpha Country, 1963; A Shaping Joy, 1972; (with others) American Literature: The Makers and the Making, 1973; The Correspondence of Thomas Percy and William Shenstone, 1977; William Faulkner: Toward Yoknapatawpha and Beyond, 1978; William Faulkner; First Encounters, 1983; The Language of the American South, 1985; On the Prejudices, Predilections, and Firm Beliefs of William Faulkner, 1987. Add: 70 Ogden St., New Haven, Conn. 06511, U.S.A

BROOKS, Edwin. British, b. 1929. Geography. Deputy Principal, Riverina-Murray Inst. of Higher Education, Wagga Wagga, N.S.W., since 1988 (Dean of Commerce, 1977–88). Lectr., 1954–66, 1970–72, Sr. Lectr. in Geography 1972–77, and Dean of College Studies, 1975–77, Univ. of Liverpool. Councillor, Birkenhead, Cheshire, 1958–67; Labour M.P. for Bebington, 1966–70. *Publs:* This Crowded Kingdom, 1973; (ed.) Tribes of the Amazon Basin in Brazil, 1973. Add: P.O. Box 588, Wagga Wagga, N.S.W. 2650, Australia.

BROOKS, George E., Jr. American, b. 1933. History. Prof. Indiana Univ., Bloomington, since 1975 (Asst Prof., 1962–68; Assoc. Prof., 1968–75). Research Asst., Training Prog. for Africa, 1959–60, and Instr. in History, 1960, 1962, Boston Univ., Mass. Member. Editorial Advisory Bd., Intnl. Journal of African Historical Studies, and Liberian Studies Journal, 1968–77. *Publs:* (ed. with N.R. Bennett) New England Merchants in Africa: A History Through Documents, 1802-1865, 1965; Yankee Traders, Old Coasters and Africa Middlemen: A History of American Legitimate Trade with West Africa in the Nineteenth Century, 1970; The Kru Mariner in the Nineteenth Century: An Historical Compendium, 1972; Themes in African and World History, 1973. Add: Dept. of History, Indiana Univ., Bloomington, Ind. 47405, U.S.A.

BROOKS, Gwendolyn. American, b. 1917. Novels/Short stories, Poetry, Autobiography/Memoirs/Personal. Ed., The Black Position Mag.

Poet Laureate of Illinois. Former Publicity Dir., NAACP Youth Council, Chicago; former member of faculty: Northeastern Illinois State Coll., Chicago, Columbia Coll., Chicago, Elmhurst Coll., Ill., City Coll. of New York, and Univ. of Wisconsin, Madison. *Publs:* A Street in Bronzeville, 1945; Annie Allen, 1949; Maud Martha (novel), 1953; Bronzeville Boys and Girls, 1956; The Bean Eaters, 1960; Selected Poems, 1963; In the Mecca: Poems, 1968; For Illinois 1968; A Sesquecentennial Poem, 1968; Riot, 1969; The Wall; Family Pictures, 1970; The World of Gwendolyn Brooks, 1971; (ed.) A Broadside Treasury, 1971; (ed.) Jump Bad: A New Chicago Anthology, 1971; Aloneness, 1971; Beckonings, 1972; Report from Part One: An Autobiography, 1972; Aurora, 1972; The Tiger Who Wore White Gloves (juvenile), 1974; Primer for Blacks, 1980; To Disembark, 1981; Young Poets' Primer, 1981; Very Young Poets, 1983; The Near-Johannesburg Boy, 1987; Blacks, 1987; Gottschalk and the Grand Tarantelle, 1988; Winnie, 1988. Add: 7428 S. Evans Ave., Chicago, Ill. 60619, U.S.A.

BROOKS, H(arold) Allen. American, b. 1925. Architecture. Prof., Emeritus, Dept. of Fine Art, Univ. of Toronto (joined faculty, 1958). Dir., 1961–64, 1967–70, 1971–74, and Pres., 1964–66, Soc. of Architectural Historians (U.S.A.). *Publs:* The Prairie School: Frank Lloyd Wright and His Midwest Contemporaries, 1972, 1976; (ed.) Prairie School Architecture: Studies from the "Western Architect," 1975; (ed. and contrib.) Writings on Wright: Selected Comment on Frank Lloyd Wright, 1981; (gen. ed. and contrib.) The Le Corbusier Archive: The Drawings, 32 vols., 1982–85; Frank Lloyd Wright and the Prairie School, 1984; (ed.) Le Corbusier, 1987. Add: 9 River Ridge Rd., Hanover, N.H. 03755, U.S.A.

BROOKS, Jeremy. British, b. 1926. Novels/Short stories, Plays/Screenplays. Reviewer, Sunday Times, since 1962. Play Adviser, Royal Shakespeare Co., Stratford-upon-Avon and London, since 1969 (Literary Mgr., 1962–69). Feature Writer, Pictorial Press, London, 1950–52; Literary Agent, Christy & Moore, London, 1952–53; Fiction and Gen. Reviewer, The Guardian, 1958–60; Play Reader, BBC Television, London, 1959–60; Drama Critic, New Statesman, 1961–62. *Publs:* The Water Carnival, 1957; Jampot Smith, 1960; Henry's War, 1962; Smith, As Hero, 1965; The Magic Perambulator, 1965; I'll Fight You, 1966; A Value, 1976; Doing The Voices, 1985. Add: 12 Bartholomew Rd., London NW5, England.

BROOKS, John. American, b. 1920. History, Social commentary. Staff writer, The New Yorker, since 1949. Contributing Ed., Time mag., NYC, 1945–47. Trustee, New York Public Library, 1978–84; Pres., Soc. of American Historians, 1987. *Publs:* The Big Wheel, 1949; A Pride of Lions, 1954; The Man Who Broke Things, 1948; The Seven Fat Years, 1958; The Fate of the Edsel, 1963; The Great Leap, 1966; Business Adventures, 1969; Once in Golconda, 1969; The Go-Go Years, 1973; (ed.) The Autobiography of American Business, 1974; Telephone, 1976; The Games Players, 1980; Showing Off in America, 1981; The Takeover Game, 1987. Add: 41 Barrow St., New York, N.Y. 10014, U.S.A.

BROOKS, Paul. American, b. 1909. Environmental science/Ecology, Biography. Editorial Adviser, Houghton Mifflin Co., Boston, since 1969 (Ed., Reader, Asst. Ed., Managing Ed., Ed.-in-Chief of General Books Dept., and Dir., 1943–69; Vice Pres., 1968–69). Chief, Book Section, European Theater of Operations, Office of War Information, 1945. *Publs:* Roadless Area, 1964; The Pursuit of Wilderness, 1971; The House of Life: Rachel Carson at Work, 1972; The View from Lincoln Hill: Man and the Land in a New England Town, 1976; Speaking for Nature, 1980; Two Park Street, 1986. Add: c/o Houghton Mifflin Co., 1 Beacon St., Boston, Mass. 02107, U.S.A.

BROOKS, Peter Wright. British, b. 1920. Air/Space topics, Transportation. Intnl. Fellow, National Air and Space Museum, Washington, D.C., 1985–86. Operations Officer, Ministry of Civil Aviation, 1947–51; Asst. to Chief Exec., Asst. to Chmn., and Fleet Planning Mgr., British European Airways, London, 1951–61; Deputy/Joint Managing Dir., Beagle Aircraft Ltd., 1961–69; Mgr., Intnl. Collaboration, British Aircraft Corp., 1969–77; with British Aerospace, 1977–79, Regional Exec., 1979–85. *Publs:* (with K.G. Wilkinson and B.S. Shenstone) World's Sailplanes, 1958; The Modern Airliner: Its Origins and Development, 1960; The World's Airliners, 1961; Historic Airships, 1973; (with C.H. Gibbs-Smith) Flight Through the Ages, 1974; Cierva Autogiros: The Development of Rotary Wing Flight, 1988. Add: The Pightle, Ford, nr. Aylesbury, Bucks., England.

BROOKS, Richard. American, b. 1912. Novels, Screenplays. Film writer and director since 1940's. *Films:* Co-scriptwriter—Sin Town,

Men of Texas, 1942; The White Savage, Cobra Women, My Best Gal, Don Winslow of the Coast Guard, 1943; Swell Guy, The Killers, 1946; Brute Force, 1947; To the Victor, Key Largo, The Naked City, 1948; Storm Warning, Any Number Can Play, 1949; Mystery Street, 1950; scriptwriter and director—Crisis, 1950; The Light Touch, 1951; Deadline USA, 1952; Battle Circus, Take the High Ground (dir. only), 1953; The Flame and the Flesh (dir. only), The Last Time I Saw Paris (co-screenwriter), 1954; The Blackboard Jungle, 1955; The Last Hunt, The Catered Affair (dir. only), 1956; Something of Value, 1957; The Brothers Karamazov (co-screenwriter), Cat on a Hot Tin Roof (co-screenwriter), 1958; Elmer Gantry (Academy Award for screenplay), 1960; Sweet Bird of Youth, 1961; Lord Jim, 1965; The Professionals, 1966; In Cold Blood, 1967; The Happy Ending, 1969; Dollars (co-screenwriter; as The Heist in UK), 1971; Bite the Bullet, 1975; Looking for Mr. Goodbar, 1977; Wrong Is Right (also producer), 1982; The Man with the Deadly Lens; Fever Pitch, 1985. *Publs:* Brick Foxhole (novel), 1946; Boiling Point (novel), 1948; The Producer (novel), 1951. Add: c/o Geald Lipsky, 190 N. Canon Dr., Beverly Hills, Calif. 90210, U.S.A.

BROPHY, Brigid. British, b. 1929. Novels/Short stories, Plays/Screenplays, Literature, Biography. Co-Dir., Writers Action Group, London, 1972–78; Member, Exec. Council, Writers' Guild of Great Britain, 1976–78; Vice-Chmn., British Copyright Council, 1977–78. *Publs:* Hackenfeller's Ape, 1953; The Crown Princess and Other Stories, 1953; The King of a Rainy Country, 1956; Flesh, 1962; Black Ship to Hell, 1962; The Finishing Touch, 1963; Mozart the Dramatist, 1964, 1988; The Snow Ball, 1964; Don't Never Forget: Collected Views and Reviews, 1966; Religious Education in State Schools, 1967; The Burglar (play), 1967; (with M. Levey and C. Osborne) Fifty Works of English and American Literature We Could Do Without, 1967; Black and White: A Portrait of Aubrey Beardsley, 1968; In Transit, 1969; Prancing Novelist: A Defence of Fiction in the Form of a Critical Biography in Praise of Ronald Firbank, 1972; The Adventures of God in His Search for the Black Girl: A Novel and Some Fables, 1973; Beardsley and His World, 1976; Pussy Owl, 1976; Palace Without Chairs, 1978; A Guide to Public Lending Right, 1983; The Prince and the Wild Geese, 1983; Baroque-'n'-Roll, 1987; Reads, 1989. Add: Flat 3, 185 Old Brompton Rd., London SW5 0AN, England.

BROSNAHAN, L(eonard) F(rancis). New Zealander, b. 1922. Language/Linguistics. Prof. of English, Univ. of South Pacific, Suva, Fiji, 1969–82, Vice-Chancellor, 1982–83, now retired (Deputy Vice-Chancellor, 1972–79). Former Lectr., and Sr. Lectr., Univ. of Ibadan, Nigeria, and Prof., Victoria Univ. of Wellington, New Zealand. *Publs:* Some Old English Sound Changes, 1953; Genes and Phonemes, 1957; The Sounds of Language, 1961; The English Language in the World, 1963; (with B. Malmberg) Introduction to Phonetics, 1970, 1975; Grammar Usage and the Teacher, 1971. Add: Lake Okareka, Rotorua, New Zealand.

BROSS, Irwin D.J. American, b. 1921. Medicine/Health. Pres., Biomedical Metatechnology, Inc., Eggertsville, N.Y., since 1983. Dir. of Biostatistics, Roswell Park Memorial Inst., Eggertsville, N.Y., 1959–83, (Acting Chief of Epidemiology, 1966–73); Research Prof. of Biostatistics, State Univ. of New York at Buffalo 1961–83; Assoc., Dept. of Epidemiology, Johns Hopkins Univ., Baltimore, Md., since 1971 (Research Assoc., Dept. of Biostatistics, 1949–52). *Publs:* Design for Decision, 1953; Scientific Strategies in Human Affairs: To Tell the Truth, 1975; Scientific Strategies to Save Your Life, 1981; Crimes of Official Science: A Casebook, 1988. Add: 109 Maynard Dr., Eggertsville, N.Y. 14226, U.S.A.

BROSSARD, Chandler. Also writes as Daniel Harper. American, b. 1922. Novels/Short stories, Plays/Screenplays, Social commentary/phenomena. Reporter, Washington Post, Washington, D.C., 1940–42; Writer, The New Yorker, NYC, 1942–43; Sr. Ed., Time mag., NYC, 1944; Exec. Ed., American Mercury, NYC, 1950–51; Sr. Ed., Look mag., NYC, 1956–67; Assoc. Prof., Old Westbury Coll., Oyster Bay, L.I., N.Y., 1968–70. *Publs:* Who Walk in Darkness, 1952; The Bold Saboteurs, 1953; (as Daniel Harper) The Wrong Turn, 1954; All Passion Spent (also as Episode with Erika), 1954; (ed.) The Scene Before You: A New Approach to American Culture, 1955; Harry the Magician (play), 1961; The Double View, 1961; Some Dreams Aren't Real (play), 1962; The Man with Ideas (play), 1962; The Insane World of Adolf Hitler, 1967; The Spanish Scene, 1968; Wake Up, We're Almost There, 1971; Did Christ Make Love?, 1973; Raging Joys, Sublime Violations, 1981. Add: 251 West 89th St., New York, N.Y. 10024, U.S.A.

BROTHERS, Joyce (Diane). American. Psychology. Columnist, Good Housekeeping mag., and King Features Syndicate. Independent

psychologist, writer since 1952. *TV programs:* Dr. Joyce Brothers, 1958–63; Consult Dr. Brothers, 1960–66; Ask Dr. Brothers, 1965–75; Living Easy with Dr. Joyce Brothers, 1972–75. *Publs:* Ten Days to a Successful Memory, 1959; Woman, 1961; The Brothers System for Liberated Love and Marriage, 1973; Better Than Ever, 1976; How to Get What You Want Out of Life, 1978; What Every Woman Should Know About Men, 1982; What Every Woman Ought to Know About Love and Marriage, 1984; Dr. Joyce Brothers' The Successful Woman: How You Can Have a Career, a Husband, a Family - And Not Feel Guilty About It, 1988. Add: c/o NBC, 30 Rockefeller Plaza, New York, N.Y. 10020, U.S.A.

BROTHERSTON, Gordon. British, b. 1939. Literature, Translations. Prof., Dept. of Literature, Univ. of Essex, since 1978 (Lectr., 1965–68; Sr. Lectr., 1968–73; Reader, 1973–78). Ed., Latin American Series, Pergamon Press, Oxford, since 1965. *Publs:* (ed.) José Enrique Rodo: Ariel, 1967; (ed. with M. Vargas Llosa) Seven Stories from Spanish America, 1968, 1973; Manuel Machado: A Revaluation, 1968; Spanish American Modernista Poets: A Critical Anthology, 1968; (ed. and trans. with E. Dorn) Our Word, 1968; (ed. and co-trans. with E. Dorn) César Vallejo: Selected Poems, 1976; Origins and Presence of Latin American Poetry, 1976; (ed. with P. Hulme) Borges: Ficciones, 1976; The Emergence of the Latin American Novel, 1977; Image of the New World, 1979; A Key to the Mesoamerican Reckoning of Time, 1982; Voices of the First America, 1985; Aesop in Mexico, 1987. Add: 2 The Dale, Wivenhoe, Essex, England.

BROUGHTON, Geoffrey. British, b. 1927. Language/Linguistics. Lectr., Malayan Teachers' Training Coll., Kirkby, 1955–60; Head of English as a Foreign Language Dept., Univ. of London, 1960–80, Dir., Eaton Hall Intnl., 1980–84. *Publs:* (ed.) Bandoola, 1960; (ed.) Climbing Everest, 1960; English Through Activity, 1960; (ed.) Vanity Fair, 1960; (ed.) The Splendid Tasks, 1961; (gen. ed.) Pattern Readers, 1964–66; (ed.) A Technical Reader, 1965; Peter and Molly (radio series), 1965; (gen. ed.) Success with English, 1968–70; Let's Go, 1976; Know Your English, 1976; Know the British, 1977; Teaching English as a Foreign Language, 1978; Express, 1985; Expressions, 1987. Add: Harrowby Hall, Grantham, Lincs., England.

BROUGHTON, James (Richard). American, b. 1913. Plays/Screenplays, Poetry. Dir., Farallone Films, since 1948. Resident Playwright, Playhouse Repertory Theater, San Francisco, Calif., 1958–64; Prof. of Creative Arts, San Francisco State Univ., 1966–76; Lectr., San Francisco Art Inst., 1968–81. *Publs:* Songs for Certain Children, 1947; The Playground, 1949; The Ballad of Mad Jenny, 1949; Musical Chairs, 1950; The Right Playmate, 1952; An Almanac for Amorists, 1955; True and False Unicorn, 1957; The Water Circle, 1965; Tidings, 1966; Look In Look Out, 1968; High Kukus, 1968; A Long Undressing, 1971; The Androgyne Journal, 1977; Odes for Odd Occasions, 1977; Seeing the Light, 1977; Song of the Godbody, 1978; Hymns to Hermes, 1979; Shaman Psalm, 1981; Graffiti for the Johns of Heaven, 1982; Ecstasies (poetry), 1983; A to Z, 1986; Hooplas, 1988; 75 Life Lines, 1988; Keys to the Compass, 1988. Add: P.O. Box 1330, Port Townsend, Wash., U.S.A.

BROUGHTON, T. Alan. American, b. 1936. Novels/Short stories, Poetry. Prof. of English and Dir. of Writers' Workshop Prog., Univ. of Vermont, since 1966. Has held teaching positions at Univ. of Washington, 1962–64, the Sweet Briar Coll., 1964–66. *Publs:* In the Face of Descent, 1975; Adam's Dream, 1975; A Family Gathering (novel), 1977; The Man on the Moon, 1979; Far from Home, 1979; The Others We Are, 1979; Winter Journey (novel), 1980; The Horsemaster (novel), 1981; Dreams Before Sleep, 1982; Hobs Daughter (novel), 1984; Preparing to Be Happy, 1988; The Jesse Tree (stories), 1988. Add: English Dept., 315 Old Mill, Univ. of Vermont, Burlington, Vt. 05401, U.S.A.

BROUMAS, Olga. American, b. 1949. Poetry, Translations. Visiting Faculty, Boston Univ., since 1989. Founder and Assoc. Faculty Member, Freehand community of women writers and photographers, Provincetown, Mass., since 1982. Poet-in-Residence, Goddard Coll., Plainfield, Vt., 1979–81. *Publs:* Caritas, 1976; Beginning with O, 1977; Namaste, 1978; Soie Sauvage, 1980; Pastoral Jazz, 1983; Black Holes, Black Stockings, 1985; What I Love: Selected Translations of Odysseas Elytis, 1986; (trans.) The Little Mariner, by Odysseas Elytis, 1988; Perpetua, 1989. Add: c/o Freehand, Provincetown, Mass., U.S.A.

BROWN, Archibald Haworth. British, b. 1938. Politics/Government. Fellow, St. Antony's Coll., and Lectr. in Soviet Instns., Univ. of Oxford, since 1971. British Council Exchange Scholar, Moscow Univ., 1967–68;

Lectr. in Politics, Glasgow Univ., 1964–71; Visiting Prof., Yale Univ., New Haven, Conn., 1980, and Columbia Univ., NYC, 1985. *Publs:* Soviet Politics and Political Science, 1974; (ed. with M. Kaser) The Soviet Union since the Fall of Khrushchev, 1975, 1978; (ed., with Jack Gray) Political Culture and Political Change in Communist States, 1977, 2nd ed., 1979; (ed. with T.H. Rigby and P. Reddaway) Authority, Power and Policy in the USSR, 1980; (co-ed.) The Cambridge Encyclopedia of Russia and the Soviet Union, 1982; (ed., with M. Kaser) Soviet Policy for the 1980s, 1982; (ed.) Political Culture and Communist Studies, 1984; (ed.) Political Leadership in the Soviet Union, 1989. Add: St. Antony's Coll., Oxford OX2 6JF, England.

BROWN Bernard E(dward). American, b. 1925. Politics/Government. Prof. of Political Science, Graduate Sch. and University Center and Herbert H. Lehmann Coll., City Univ. of New York, since 1974 (Prof. of Political Science, Brooklyn Coll., 1965–74). Instr. in Govt., City Coll. of New York, 1951–53; Asst. Prof. of Political Science, Michigan State Univ., East Lansing, 1954–56; Asst. Prof., then Assoc. Prof. of Political Science, Vanderbilt Univ., Nashville, 1959–65. *Publs:* American Conservatives: The Political Thought of Francis Lieber and John W. Burgess, 1951; (with Roy C. Macridis) The DeGaulle Republic: Quest for Unity, 1960; (ed. with Macridis) Comparative Politics, Notes and Readings, 1971, 6th ed. 1986; New Directions in Comparative Politics, 1962; (with others) Government and Politics: An Introduction to Political Science, 1966; (ed. with Wahlke) The American Political System: Notes and Readings, 1967, 1971; Protest in Paris: Anatomy of a Revolt, 1974; (ed.) Eurocommunism and Eurosocialism: The Left Confronts Modernity, 1978; Intellectuals and Others Traitors, 1980; Socialism of a Different Kind: Reshaping the Left in France, 1982; (ed.) Great American Political Thinkers, 2 vols., 1983. Add: Dept. of Political Science, CUNY, 33 W. 42nd St., New York, N.Y. 10036, U.S.A.

BROWN, Blanche R. American, b. 1915. Art. Prof. of Fine Arts, New York Univ., NYC, since 1973 (Assoc. Prof., 1966–73). Staff Lectr., Metropolitan Museum of Art, NYC, 1942–65. *Publs:* Ptolemaic Paintings and Mosaics and the Alexandrian Style, 1957; Five Cities: An Art Guide to Athens, Rome, Florence, Paris, London, 1964; Anticlassicism in Greek Sculpture of the Fourth Century, B.C., 1973. Add: 15 West 70th St., New York, N.Y. 10023, U.S.A.

BROWN, Dale W. American, b. 1926. Theology/Religion. Prof. of Christian Theology, Bethany Theological Seminary, Oak Brook, Ill., since 1963. Dir. of Religious Life, and Asst. Prof. of Philosophy and Religion, McPherson Coll., 1958–62. *Publs:* In Christ Jesus: The Significance of Jesus as the Christ, 1965; Four Words for the World, 1968; So Send I You, 1969; Brethren and Pacifism, 1970; The Christian Revolutionary, 1971; Flamed by the Spirit, 1978; Understanding Pietism, 1978; What About the Russians?, 1984; Biblical Pacifism, 1986. Add: Bethany Theological Seminary, Butterfield and Meyers Road, Oak Brook, Ill; 60521, U.S.A.

BROWN, Dee (Alexander). American, b. 1908. Western/Adventure, Cultural/Ethnic topics, History. Prof. of Library Science. Univ. of Illinois, Urbana, since 1962 (Agricultural Librarian, 1948–72). Librarian, Dept. of Agriculture, Washington, D.C., 1934–42, and Aberdeen Proving Ground, Md., 1945–48; Ed., Agricultural History mag., 1956–58. *Publs:* Wave High the Banner, 1942; (with M. Schmitt) Fighting Indians of the West, 1948; Trail Driving Days, 1952; Grierson's Raid, 1954; The Settler's West, 1955; Yellowhorse, 1956; Cavalry Scout, 1957; The Gentle Tamers: Women of the Old Wild West, 1958; The Bold Cavaliers, 1959; They Went Thataway, 1960; Pawnee, Blackfoot and Cheyenne, 1961; Fort Phil Kearny, 1962; The Galvanized Yankees, 1963; Showdown at Little Big Horn, 1964; The Girl from Fort Wicked, 1964; The Year of the Century, 1966; Bury My Heart at Wounded Knee, 1971, adapted for children as Wounded Knee: An Indian History of the American West, 1975; The Westerners, 1974; Hear That Lonesome Whistle Blow, 1977, adapted for children as Lonesome Whistle, 1980; Tepee Tales of the American Indian, 1979; Creek Mary's Blood, 1980; The American Spa, 1982; Killdeer Mountain, 1983; Conspiracy of Knaves, 1987. Add: 7 Overlook Dr., Little Rock, Ark. 72207, U.S.A.

BROWN, Evelyn Berger. *See* **BERGER,** Evelyn Miller.

BROWN, Frederick G. American, b. 1932. Education, Psychology. Prof., Psychology and Education, Iowa State Univ., Ames, since 1968 (Asst. Prof., and Assoc. Prof. 1961–68). Asst. Prof., Univ. of Missouri, Columbia, 1958–61; Fellow, Center for Advanced Study in the Behavioural Sciences, Stanford, Calif., 1967–68: Visiting Scholar, Educational Testing Service, Princeton, N.J., 1985–86. *Publs:* Principles of

Educational and Psychological Testing, 1970, 3rd ed., 1983; Measurement and Evaluation, 1971; Guidelines for Test Use: A Commentary on the Standards for Educational and Psychological Tests, 1980; Measuring Classroom Achievement, 1981. Add: Dept. of Psychology, Iowa State Univ., Ames, Iowa 50011, U.S.A.

BROWN, George Mackay. British, b. 1921. Novels/Short stories, Children's fiction, Plays/Screenplays, Poetry. *Publs:* The Storm, 1954; Loaves and Fishes, 1959; The Year of the Whale, 1965; The Five Voyages of Arnor, 1966; A Spell for Green Corn (play), 1967; A Calendar of Love, 1967; Twelve Poems, 1968; An Orkney Tapestry, 1969; Witch (play), 1969; A Time to Keep, 1969; Fishermen with Ploughs: A Poem Cycle, 1971; New and Selected Poems, 1971; Loom of Light (play), 1971; Greenvoe (novel), 1972; Hawkfall and Other Stories, 1974; The Two Fiddlers: Legends for Children, 1974; Magnus (novel), 1973; Letters from Hamnavoe, 1975; The Sun's Net (short stories), 1976; Winterfold, 1976; Witch and Other Stories, 1977; Pictures in the Cave (juvenile), 1977; Selected Poems, 1977; Under Brinkie's Brae, 1979; Six Lives of Fankle the Cat (for children), 1980; Portrait of Orkney, 1981; Voyages, 1983; Three Plays, 1984; Christmas Poems, 1984; Christmas Stories, 1985; Time in a Red Coat (novel), 1985; The Loom of Light (play), 1986; The Golden Bird (2 novellas), 1987; (ed.) Edwin Muir: Selected Prose, 1987; The Masked Fisherman (stories), 1989; The Wreck of the Archangel (poetry), 1989. Add: 3 Mayburn Ct., Stromness, Orkney, Scotland.

BROWN, Helen Gurley. American, b. 1922. Human relations, Sex, Women. Ed.-in-Chief since 1965, and Editorial Dir. of foreign eds. since 1972, Cosmopolitan mag., NYC. Exec. Secty., Music Corp. of America, 1942–45, and William Morris Agency, 1956–47; Copywriter, Foote Cone and Belding Advertising Agency, Los Angeles, Calif., 1948–58; Advertising Writer and Account Exec., Kenyon and Eckhardt Advertising Agency, Hollywood, Calif., 1958–62. *Publs:* Sex and the Single Girl, 1962; Sex and the Office, 1965; The Outrageous Opinions of Helen Gurley Brown, 1967; Helen Gurley Brown's Single Girl's Cookbook, 1969; Sex and the New Single Girl, 1970; Cosmopolitan's Love Book, 1978; Having It All, 1982. Add: Cosmopolitan, 224 W. 57th St., New York, N.Y. 10019, U.S.A.

BROWN, (Sir) (Ernest) Henry Phelps. British, b. 1906. Economics. Fellow of New Coll., Oxford, 1930–47; Prof. of the Economics of Labour, London Sch. of Economics, 1947–68. Member, U.K. Council on Prices, Productivity and Incomes, 1959–61, U.K. National Economic Development Council, 1962–66, and Royal Commn. on the Distribution of Income and Wealth, 1974–78; Chmn., Tavistock Inst. of Human Relations, London, 1966–68; Pres., Royal Economic Soc., 1970–72. *Publs:* The Framework of the Pricing System, 1936; A Course in Applied Economics, 1951, 2nd ed., with J. Wiseman, 1964; Economic Growth and Human Welfare, 1953; The Balloon (fiction), 1953; The Growth of British Industrial Relations, 1959; The Economics of Labour, 1962; Pay and Profits, 1968; (with M.H. Browne) A Century of Pay, 1968; The Inequality of Pay, 1977; The Origins of Trade Union Power, 1983; Egalitarianism and the Generation of Inequality, 1988. Add: 16 Bradmore Rd., Oxford OX2 6QP, England.

BROWN, Herbert C. American, b. 1912. Chemistry. Wetherill Research Prof., Purdue Univ., West Lafayette, Ind., since 1959, now Emeritus (Prof. of Chemistry, 1947–59). Instr., Univ. of Chicago, 1939–43; Asst. Prof., 1943–46, and Assoc. Prof., 1946–47, Wayne State Univ., Detroit. Recipient, Nobel Prize in chemistry, 1979. *Publs:* Hydroboration, 1962; Boranes in Organic Chemistry, 1972; Organic Syntheses via Boranes, 1975; The Non-classical Ion Problem, 1977; (with A. Pelter and K. Smith) Borane Reagents, 1988. Add: 1840 Garden St., West Lafayette, Ind. 47906, U.S.A.

BROWN, Howard Mayer. American, b. 1930. Music. Ferdinand Schevill Distinguished Service Prof. of Music, Univ. of Chicago, since 1976 (Asst. Prof., Assoc. Prof., and Prof., 1960–76). King Edward Prof. of Music, Univ. of London, King's Coll., 1972–74. Pres., American Musicological Soc., 1978–80; V. Pres., International Musicological Society, 1982–87. *Publs:* Music in the French Secular Theatre, 1400-1550, 1963; (ed.) Theatrical Chansons of the 15th and Early 16th Centuries, 1963; Instrumental Music Printed Before 1600, 1965; (with Joan Lascelle) Musical Iconography, 1973; Sixteenth Century Instrumentation, 1973; (ed. with H.T. David and E.E. Lowinsky) Eustachio Romano, Music for Two, 1974; Music in the Renaissance, 1977; A Florentine Chansonnier from the Time of Lorenzo the Magnificent, 2 vols., 1983. Add: 1415 East 54th St., Chicago, Ill. 60615, U.S.A.

BROWN, James I. American, b. 1908. Language/Linguistics,

Speech/Rhetoric. Prof. Emeritus of Rhetoric, Univ. of Minnesota, Minneapolis, since 1977, (Instr., 1934–46; Asst. Prof., 1946–49; Assoc. Prof., 1949–54; Prof., 1954–77). *Publs:* Efficient Reading, 1952, 6th ed. 1984; (with Carlsen) Listening Comprehension Test, 1953; (with Nelson and Denny) Nelson-Denny Reading Test, 1958; Explorations in College Reading, 1959; Exercise Manual for Explorations, 1959; (with Salisbury) Building a Better Vocabulary, 1959; (with Sanderlin) Effective Writing and Reading, 1962; Programmed Vocabulary, 1964, 3rd ed. 1980; Guide to Effective Reading, 1966; Alphy's Show and Tell Book, 1966; (coauthor) Visual-Linguistic Reading Series, 6 vols., 1966–67; Putting Words to Work (TV series), 1966; (with Haugh) College English Placement Test, 1969; (with Pearsall) Better Spelling, 1971, 3rd ed. (with Thomas E. Pearsall) 1985; (with Nelson and Denny) Nelson-Denny Reading-Test: Forms C and D, 1973, Forms E and F, 1980; Reading Power, 1975, 3rd ed. 1987; Success Through Word Power (TV series), 1981. Add: 1395 Solar Heights Dr., Prescott, Ariz. 86303. U.S.A.

BROWN, Jamie. Canadian, b. 1945. Fiction, Children's fiction, Screenplays. Film producer. Consultant, National Film Bd. of Canada, 1974–77; Lectr. in Creative Writing, Concordia Univ., Montreal, 1979–85. *Publs:* The Lively Spirits of Provence (non-fiction), 1974; Stepping Stones (fiction), 1975; So Free We Seem (fiction), 1976; Shrewsbury (fiction), 1977; The War Is Over (screenplay), 1979; Superbike (for children), 1980; Toby McTeague (screenplay), 1986; Keeping Track (screenplay; also co-prod.), 1986. Add: 174 Beacon Hill Rd., Beaconsfield, Que. H9W 1T6, Canada.

BROWN, John Russell. British, b. 1923. Literature, Theatre. Prof. of Theatre, and Dir. of Project Theatre, Univ. of Michigan, Ann Arbor, since 1985. Gen. Ed., Theatre Production Series, Routledge, since 1970. Gen. Ed., Stratford-upon-Avon Studies, 1960–67; Prof. and Head of the Dept. of Drama and Theatre Arts, Univ. of Birmingham, 1964–71; Gen Ed., Stratford-upon-Avon Library, 1964–71; Prof. of English, Univ. of Sussex, Brighton, 1971–82; Assoc. Dir., National Theatre, London, 1973–88; Chmn., Drama Advisory Panel, Arts Council, 1979–82; Prof. of Theatre Arts, State Univ. of New York at Stony Brook, 1982–85. *Publs:* (ed.) The Merchant of Venice, 1955; Shakespeare and His Comedies, 1957; (ed.) The White Devil, by John Webster, 1960; Shakespeare's "Macbeth," 1963; (ed.) Henry V, 1965; (ed.) The Duchess of Malfi, by John Webster, 1965; Shakespeare's Plays in Performance, 1966; Effective Theatre, 1969; Shakespeare's "The Tempest," 1969; Shakespeare's Dramatic Style, 1970; Theatre Language: A Study of Arden, Osborne, Pinter, Wesker, 1972; Free Shakespeare, 1974; Shakespeare in Performance, 1976; Discovering Shakespeare, 1981; Shakespeare and His Theatre, 1982; A Short Guide to Modern British Theatre, 1982. Add: Court Lodge, Hooe, Battle, E. Sussex, England.

BROWN, Jonathan. American, b. 1939. Art. Carroll and Milton Petrie Prof., Inst. of Fine Arts, New York Univ., since 1984 (joined faculty, 1973). Taught at Princeton Univ., New Jersey, 1965–73; Slade Prof. of Fine Art, Oxford Univ., 1981–82. *Publs:* Prints and Drawings by Jusepe de Ribera, Zurburan, 1973; Murillo and His Drawings, 1976; Images and Ideas in Seventeenth–Century Spanish Painting, 1978; (with J.H. Elliott) A Palace for a King: The Buen Retiro and the Court of Philip IV, 1980; Velazquez, Painter and Courtier, 1986. Add: 1 E. 78th St., New York, N.Y. 10021, U.S.A.

BROWN, J(oseph) P(aul) S(ummers). American, b. 1930. Westerns/Adventure. Boxer, motion picture stuntman and actor, and cattleman. Reporter, El Paso Herald Post, Tex., 1953–54. *Publs:* Jim Kane, 1970; in U.K. as Pocket Money, 1972; The Outfit: A Cowboy's Primer, 1971; The Forests of the Night, 1974; Steeldust, 1986; Steeldust II: The Flight, 1987. Add: 1020 Avenida Agula, Tucson, Ariz. 85748, U.S.A.

BROWN, Kenneth H. American, b. 1936. Novels/Short stories, Plays/Screenplays. Resident Playwright, Living Theatre, NYC, 1963–67; Private Tutor, 1966–69, and Resident Playwright, 1968–69, Yale Grad. Sch. of Drama, New Haven, Conn.; Visiting Lectr. in the History of the Theatre, Hunter Coll., NYC, 1969–70. *Publs:* The Brig (Obie Award-winning play), 1964; The Narrows (novel), 1970; Nightlight (play), 1973. Add: 150 74th St., Brooklyn, N.Y. 11209, U.S.A.

BROWN, Leland. American, b. 1914. Writing/Journalism, Business/Trade/Industry. Prof. of Business Communication, Eastern Michigan Univ., Ypsilanti, 1964–83, now Emeritus. Instr., Univ. of Illinois, Urbana, 1946–49; Assoc. Prof., Tulane Univ., New Orleans, La., 1949–64. *Publs:* ffective Business Report Writing, 1955, 4th ed. 1985; Communicating Facts and Ideas in Business, 1960, 3rd ed. 1982; Discussion Leaders Guide, 1982. Add: 1929 Witmire St., Ypsilanti, Mich.

48197, U.S.A.

BROWN, Marc (Tolon). American, b. 1946. Children's fiction, Children's non-fiction. Writer and artist. Art Dir., WICU-TV, Erie, PA, 1968–69; Asst. Prof. of Art, Garland Jr. Coll., Boston, 1969–76. *Publs:* children's fiction—Arthur's Nose, 1976; Full House, 1977; Lenny and Lola, 1978; Moose and Goose, 1978; Arthur's Eyes, 1979; The Cloud over Clarence, 1979; Arthur's Valentine, 1980; Pickle Things, 1980; Witches Four, 1981; The True Francine, 1981; Arthur Goes to Camp, 1982; Arthur's Halloween, 1982; Arthur's April Fool, 1983; Arthur's Thanksgiving, 1983; The Silly Tail Book, 1983; Arthur's Christmas, 1985; The Bionic Bunny Show, 1984; There's No Place Like Home, 1986; Arthur's Tooth, 1985; Arthur's Teacher Trouble, 1986; Arthur's Baby, 1987; D.W. Flips!, 1987, in U.K. as Roll Over, D.W., 1988; D.W. All Wet, 1988; Arthur's Birthday, 1989; children's non-fiction—One, Two, Three: An Animal Counting Book, 1976; Your First Garden Book, 1981; Boat Book, 1982; Count to Ten, 1982; (with Stephen Krensky) Dinosaurs, Beware!: A Safety Guide, 1982; Wings on Things, 1982; (with Stephen Krensky) Perfect Pigs: An Introduction to Manners, 1983; Spooky Riddles, 1983; What Do You Call a Dumb Bunny? and Other Rabbit Riddles, Games, Jokes, and Cartoons, 1983; Dinosaurs Divorce: A Guide for Changing Families, 1986; (with Laurene Kransy Brown) Visiting the Art Museum (in U.K. as Visiting an Exhibition), 1986; (with Laurene Kransy Brown) Dinosaurs Travel: A Guide for Families on the Go, 1988; (with Laurene Kransy Brown) Baby Time, 1989; (ed.) One, Two, Buckle My Shoe, 1989. Add: 562 Main St., Hingham, MA 02043, U.S.A.

BROWN, Marcia. American, b. 1918. Children's fiction, Children's non-fiction, Education. Fulltime writer. Drama teacher in a high sch. in Cornwall, NY, 1940–43; teacher of puppetry, Univ. of the West Indies, Jamaica, 1953. *Publs:* children's fiction—The Little Carousel, 1946; Henry, Fisherman: A Story of the Virgin Islands, 1949; Skipper John's Cook, 1951; Felice, 1958; Taramindo!, 1960; Backbone of the King, 1966; The Neighbors, 1967; How, Hippo!, 1969; The Blue Jackal, 1977; children's non-fiction—Stone Soup (retelling), 1947; Dick Whittington and His Cat (retelling), 1950; Puss in Boots (retelling), 1952; Cinderella (retelling), 1954; The Flying Carpet (retelling), 1956; Peter Piper's Alphabet, 1959; Once a Mouse (retelling), 1961; The Bun: A Tale from Russia, 1972; All Butterflies: An ABC, 1974; Listen to a Shape, 1979; Touch Will Tell, 1979; Walk with Your Eyes, 1979; Shadow (retelling), 1982; other—Lotus Seeds: Children, Pictures, and Books, 1986. Add: c/o Scribner's, 866 Third Ave., New York, NY 10022, U.S.A.

BROWN, Marel. American, b. 1899. Children's fiction, Poetry. Secty. to Ed., The Christian Index, 1924–30; Secty. to Pastor, Druid Hills Baptist Church, Atlanta, 1930–37. *Publs:* Red Hills Poetry and Essays, 1941; Hearth-Fire (poetry), 1943; Lilly May and Dan, 1946; Fence Corners: Poetry and Essays, 1952; The Greshams of Greenway, 1950; The Cherry Children, 1956; The Shape of a Song: Poetry and Essays, 1968; Three Wise Women of the East (fiction), 1970; Presenting Georgia Poets, 1979. Add: 1938 N. Decatur Rd., N.E., Atlanta, Ga. 30307, U.S.A.

BROWN, Mark H(erbert). American, b. 1900. Cultural/Ethnic topics, History. Former Soil Scientist, U.S. Dept. of Agriculture; Lieut. Col. U.S. Air Force, Ret. *Publs:* (with others) The Frontier Years, 1955; (with others) Before Barbed Wire, 1956; The Plainsmen of the Yellowstone, 1961; The Flight of the Nez Perce, 1967. Add: 815 Russell St., Storm Lake, UT, 50588, U.S.A.

BROWN, Michael Douglas. New Zealander, b. 1948. Novels, Autobiography. Assoc. Dir., Management Inter-Personnel Ltd., Christchurch, since 1986; Journalist, Television New Zealand, since 1988. Teacher of Physics, Christchurch, 1972–75; Reporter, Dir., and Presenter for Television New Zealand, 1977–78, 1979–80, and 1982–86; actor, feature films and amateur theatre, 1986–87. *Publs:* The Weaver and the Abbey (autobiography), 1982; The Weaver's Apprentice (novel), 1986; The Idiot Played Rachmaninov (novel), 1989. Add: 146 Rutland St., Papanui, Christchurch, New Zealand.

BROWN, Muriel. British, b. 1938. Public/Social administration, Sociology. Lectr. in Social Admin., London Sch. of Economics, 1970–72, and since 1974. Lectr. in Social Admin., Univ. of Manchester, 1962–70, and Univ. of Bristol, 1973–74. *Publs:* Introduction to Social Administration in Britain, 1969, 6th ed. 1985; (ed. with Sally Baldwin) Year Book of Social Policy in Britain, 1977, 1978, 1979; (with Nicola Madge) Despite the Welfare State, 1982; The Structure of Disadvantage, 1983. Add: Dept. of Social Science and Admin., London Sch. of Economics, Houghton St., London WC2A 2AE, England.

BROWN, Murray. American, b. 1929. Economics. Goodyear Prof. of Economics, State Univ. of New York at Buffalo, since 1972 (Prof., 1967–72); Research Assoc., Center of Economic Studies and Plans, Rome, N.Y., since 1966. Asst. Prof., Dept. of Economics, The Wharton Sch., Univ. of Pennsylvania, Philadelphia, 1956–62; Consultant, Patent & Trademark Foundn., The George Washington Univ. 1958–60, and Office of Business Economics, U.S. Dept. of Commerce 1962–65, Washington, D.C. *Publs:* On the Theory and Measurement of Technological Change, 1966; (ed.) The Theory and Empirical Analysis of Production, 1967; (co-ed.) Regional National Econometric Modeling, 1978. Add: Dept. of Economics, John Lord O'Brian Hall, North Campus, State Univ. of New York, Buffalo, N.Y. 14260, U.S.A.

BROWN, Palmer. American, b. 1919. Children's fiction. Freelance writer. *Publs:* Beyond the Pawpaw Trees, 1954; The Silver Nutmeg, 1956; Cheerful, 1957; Something for Christmas, 1958; Hickory, 1978. Add: c/o Harper and Row 10, E. 53rd St., New York, NY 10022, U.S.A.

BROWN, Peter Douglas. British, b. 1925. History. *Publs:* The Chathamites, 1967; William Pitt, Earl of Chatham, 1978; (co-ed.) The Devonshire Diary, 1982. Add: 18 Davenant Rd., Oxford OX2 8BX, England.

BROWN, Ralph Adams. American, b. 1908. History. Distinguished Teaching Prof. of American History, State Univ. of New York, Coll. at Cortland, since 1973 (Chmn., Social Studies Dept., 1947–58; Dean of Coll., 1958–61; Prof. of American History, 1961–73). Sr. Ed., Kennikat Press, Port Washington, N.Y. 1969–75. *Publs:* (co-ed.) Impressions of America, 2 vols., 1965; Exploring with American Heroes, 1966; (co-author) The United States: A History, 1967; (co-author) American History For High Schools: An Annotated List, 1969; The Presidency of John Adams, 1975; Europeans Observe the American Revolution, 1976. Add: 44 West Court, Cortland, N.Y. 13045, U.S.A.

BROWN, Raymond George. Australian, b. 1924. Medicine/Health, Social Sciences. Prof. of Social Admin., Flinders Univ. of South Australia, Bedford Park, since 1965, retired 1989. Lectr. in Social Medicine, Univ. of Birmingham, England, 1954–57; Lectr. in Social Studies, Univ. of Melbourne, 1958; Reader-in-Charge of Social Studies, Univ. of Adelaide, 1959–64. *Publs:* Medical Evidence Related to English Population Changes, 1955; Medicine and the Community, 1970; Children in Australia, 1980. Add: Sch. of Social Sciences, Flinders Univ., Bedford Park, S.A. Australia, 5042.

BROWN, R(ichard) H(arvey). American, b. 1940. Sociology. Assoc. Prof. of Sociology, Univ. of Maryland, College Park, since 1975. *Publs:* A Poetic for Sociology: Toward a Logic of Discovery for the Human Sciences, 1977; (with Stanford M. Lyman) Structure, Consciousness and History, 1978; Society as Text: Essays on Reason, Rhetoric, and Reality, 1987. Add: Dept. of Sociology, Univ. of Maryland, College Park, Md. 20742, U.S.A.

BROWN, Rita Mae. American, b. 1944. Novels, Poetry, Translations. Photo Editor, Sterling Publishing Co., New York, 1969–70; co-founded Radicalesbians, New York; Lectr. in Sociology, Federal City Coll., Washington, D.C., 1970–71; Research Fellow, Inst. for Policy Studies, Washington, D.C., 1971–73; an exec. officer with National Org. for Women (NOW), resigned 1970; a founder of Redstockings radical feminist group, New York; involved with lesbian separatist movement, early 1970's; active with National Gay Task Force, and National Women's Political Caucus, from mid-1970's. *Publs:* (trans.) Hrotsvitha: Six Medieval Latin Plays, 1971; The Hand That Cradles the Rock (poetry), 1971; A Plain Brown Rapper (essays), 1976; Rubyfruit Jungle (novel), 1973, 1977; Songs to a Handsome Woman (poetry), 1973; In Her Day (novel), 1976; Six of One (novel), 1978; I Love Liberty (screenplay), 1981; Southern Discomfort (novel), 1982; Sudden Death (novel), 1983; The Long Hot Summer (screenplay), 1983; My Two Loves (screenplay), 1985; Table Dancing (screenplay), 1986; High Hearts (novel), 1986; Starting from Scratch (writer's manual), 1988; Bingo (novel), 1988; Girls of Summer (screenplay), 1989; Rich Men, Single Women (screenplay), 1989; Sweet Surrender (screenplay), 1989. Add: c/o Julian Bach Literary Agency, 747 Third Ave., New York, N.Y. 10017, U.S.A.

BROWN, Robert G(oodell). American, b. 1923. Administration/Management, Information science/Computers. Pres., Materials Mgmt. Systems Inc., Thetford Center, VT., since 1970. Visiting Prof., Northeastern Univ., Boston, 1960, Dartmouth Coll., 1963, Boston Univ., 1967, and Lehigh Univ., Bethlehem, Pa., 1971. *Publs:* Statistical Forecasting for Inventory Control, 1959; Smoothing, Forecasting and

Prediction of Discrete Time Series, 1963; Decision Rules for Inventory Management, 1967; Management Decisions for Production Operations, 1971; (compiler) Source Book in Production Management, 1971; APL-Plus 747 Forecasting Users Guide, 1973; Materials Management Systems, 1977; Advanced Service Parts Inventory Control, 1982; Shirley He Hath Born, 1984; LOGOL Systems Manual, 1985; Twigs Systems Manual, 1988. Add: P.O. Box 239, Thetford Center, VT., 05075, U.S.A.

BROWN, Robert L. American, b. 1921. History. Teacher, Denver Public Schs., and Univ. of Colorado. Staff member, Univ. of Denver, 1948–51; Staff member, Regis Coll., Denver, 1956–66. *Publs:* Jeep Trails to Colorado Ghost Towns, 1963; An Empire of Silver, 1965; Holy Cross: The Mountain and the City, 1968; Ghost Towns of the Colorado Rockies, 1968; Colorado Ghost Towns: Past and Present, 1972; Uphill Both Ways: Hiking Colorado's High Country, 1976; (with Ed Collman) Saloons of the American West: An Illustrated Chronicle, 1978; The Great Pike's Peak Gold Rush, 1985. Add: 3100 S. Lowell Blvd., Denver, Colo. 80236, U.S.A.

BROWN, Robert McAfee. American, b. 1920. Theology/Religion, Autobiography/Memoirs/Personal. Asst. Chaplain, Amherst Coll., Mass., 1946–48; Prof. of Religion and Chmn. of Dept., Macalester Coll., St. Paul, Minn., 1951–53; Prof. of Systematic Theology, Union Theological Seminary, NYC, 1953–62; Prof. of Religious Studies, Stanford Univ., California, 1962–76; Prof. of Ecumenism and Christianity, Univ. Theological Seminary, NYC., 1976–79; Prof. of Theology and Ethics, Pacific Sch. of Religion, Berkeley, Calif., 1979–86. Member, President's Council on the Holocaust, 1980–87. *Publs:* P.T. Forsyth: Prophet for Today, 1952; The Bible Speaks to You, 1955; The Significance of the Church, 1956; (with G. Weigel) An American Dialogue, 1960; The Spirit of Protestantism, 1961; Observer in Rome: A Protestant Report on the Vatican Council, 1964; The Collected Writings of St. Hereticus, 1964; (with A. Heschel and M. Novak) Vietnam: Crisis of Conscience, 1967; The Ecumenical Revolution, 1967, rev. ed. 1969; The Pseudonyms of God, 1972; Religion and Violence, 1973; Frontiers for the Church Today, 1973; Is Faith Obsolete?, 1974; Theology in a New Key: Responding to Liberation Themes, 1978; The Hereticus Papers, 1979; Creative Dislocation: The Movement of Grace, 1980; Gustavo Gutierrez, 1980; Making Peace in the Global Village, 1981; Elie Wiesel: Messenger to All Humanity, 1983; Unexpected News: Reading the Bible with Third World Eyes, 1984; Saying Yes and Saying No: On Rendering to God and Caesar, 1986; (ed.) The Essential Reinhold Niebuhr, 1986; Spirituality and Liberation: Overcoming the Great Fallacy, 1988. Add: 2090 Columbia Ave., Palo Alto, Calif. 94306, U.S.A.

BROWN, Roger William. American, b. 1925. Language/Linguistics, Psychology. Prof. of Social Psychology, Harvard Univ., Cambridge, since 1962, and John Lindsley Prof. of Psychology in Memory of William James, since 1974. *Publs:* Words and Things, 1958; (with others) New Directions in Psychology, 1962; The Acquisition of Language, 1964; Social Psychology, 1965, 1986; Psycholinguistics, 1970; A First Language, 1973; Psychology, 1975; Innocence Is Not Enough: The Life and Death of Herbert Norman, 1987. Add: 270 William James Hall, Harvard Univ., Cambridge, Mass. 02138, U.S.A.

BROWN, Sandra. Also writes as Rachel Ryan, Erin St. Claire, and Laura Jordan. American, b. 1948. Historical/Romance. Mgr. Merle Norman Cosmetics Studios, Tyler, Texas, 1971–73; weather reporter, KLTV-TV, Tyler, 1972–75, and WFAA-TV, Dallas, 1976–79; model, Dallas Apparel Mart, 1976–87. *Publs:* (as Rachel Ryan) Love Beyond Reason, 1981; (as Rachel Ryan) Love's Encore, 1981; (as Rachel Ryan) Eloquent Silence, 1982; (as Rachel Ryan) A Treasure Worth Seeking, 1982; (As Laura Jordan) Hidden Fires, 1982; (As Laura Jordan) The Silken Web, 1982; (as Erin St. Claire) Not Even for Love, 1982; (as Rachel Ryan) Prime Time, 1983; (as Erin St. Claire) A Kiss Remembered, 1983; (as Erin St. Claire) A Secret Splendor, 1983; (as Erin St. Claire) Seduction by Design, 1983; Breakfast in Bed, 1983; Heaven's Price, 1983; Relentless Desire, 1983; Tempest in Eden, 1983; Temptation's Kiss, 1983; Tomorrow's Promise, 1983; in a Class by Itself, 1984; Send No Flowers, 1984; Bittersweet Rain, 1984; Words of Silk, 1984; Sunset Embrace, 1984; (as Erin St. Claire) Led Astray, 1985; (as Erin St. Claire) A Sweet Anger, 1985; (as Erin St. Claire) Tiger Prince, 1985; Riley in the Morning, 1985; Thursday's Child, 1985; Another Dawn, 1985; (as Erin St. Claire) Above and Beyond, 1986; (as Erin St. Claire) Honor Bound, 1986; 22 Indigo Place, 1986; The Rana Look, 1986; Demon Rumm, 1987; Fanta C, 1987; Sunny Chandler's Return, 1987; Tidings of Great Joy, 1987; (as Erin St. Claire) The Devil's Own, 1987 (as Erin St. Claire) Two Alone, 1987; Adam's Fall, 1988; Hawk O'Toole's Hostage, 1988; Slow Heat in Heaven, 1988; (as Erin St. Claire) Thrill of Victory, 1989; Long Time

Coming, 1989; Temperatures Rising, 1989; Best Kept Secrets, 1989. Add: 1000 N. Bowen, Arlington, Tex. 76012, U.S.A.

BROWN, Terence. Irish, b. 1944. History, Literature. Fellow since 1976, and Assoc. Prof. of English since 1981, Trinity Coll., Dublin (Lectr., 1968–81). Secty., Intnl. Assn. for the Study of Anglo-Irish Literature, since 1976; Chmn. of Sub-Cttee. for Anglo-Irish Literature, Royal Irish Academy, Dublin. *Publs:* (ed. with Alec Reid) Time Was Away: The World of Louis MacNeice, 1974; Louis MacNeice: Sceptical Vision, 1975; Northern Voices: Poets from Northern Ulster, 1975; (ed. with Patrick Rafroidi) The Irish Short Story; Ireland: A Social and Cultural History 1922–79, 1981; Impressions of Dublin, 1986. Add: Dept. of English, Trinity Coll., Dublin 2, Ireland.

BROWN, Theodore M. American, b. 1925. Architecture, Photography. Prof. Emeritus of History of Art, Cornell Univ., Ithaca, N.Y. (Assoc. Prof., 1967–71; Prof., 1971–88). Asst. and Assoc. Prof. of History of Art, Univ. of Louisville, Ky., 1958–67. *Publs:* The Work of G. Rietveld, Architect, 1958; Introduction to Louisville Architecture, 1960; (with M.M. Bridwell) Old Louisville, 1961; Margaret Bourke-White, Photojournalist, 1972. Add: 92 Ithaca Rd., Ithaca, N.Y. 14850, U.S.A.

BROWN, Vinson. American, b. 1912. Natural history. Pres., Naturegraph Publishers, Happy Camp, Calif., since 1946. *Publs:* The Amateur Naturalist's Handbook, 1948; rev. ed. 1980; John Paul Jones (remedial reader), 1949; Black Treasure (novel), 1950; How to Make a Home Nature Museum, 1954; The Sierra Nevadan Wildlife Region, 1954, 3rd ed. 1987; How to Make a Miniature Zoo, 1956; (with George Lawrence) The Californian Wildlife Region, 1957, 1987; (with David Allan III) Rocks and Minerals of California, 1957, 3rd ed. 1972; How to Understand Animal Talk, 1958, rev. ed. as The Secret Languages of Animals, 1987; Exploring Ancient Life, 1958; (with Yocom and Starbuck) Wildlife of the Intermountain West, 1958; (with Henry Weston Jr.) Handbook of California Birds, 1961; (with William Willoya) Warriors of the Rainbow, 1962; How to Explore the Secret Worlds of Nature, 1962; Backyard Wild Birds of California and the Pacific North West, 1965; (with Ernest Braun) Exploring Pacific Coast Tide Pools, 1966; How to Follow the Adventures of Insects, 1968; The Pomo Indians of California, 1969; Reading the Woods, 1969; Backyard Wild Birds of the East and Midwest, 1970; (with Charles Yocom) Wildlife and Plants of the Cascades, 1971; Great Upon the Mountain, 1971; Knowing the Outdoors in the Dark, 1972; Reptiles and Amphibians of the West, 1974; Voices of Earth and Sky, 1974; (with David Allan III) Illustrated Guide to Common Rocks and Their Minerals, 1975; Sea Mammals and Reptiles of the Pacific Coast, 1976; Peoples of the Sea Wind, 1977; Amateur Naturalist's Diary, 1983; Field Guide to the Golden Sunbelt, 1983; Return of the Indian Spirit, 1983; Investigating Nature Through Outdoor Projects, 1983; (with others) Prevent Doomsday! An Anti-Nuclear Anthology, 1983; Building Your Own Nature Museum, 1984; Native Americans of the Pacific Coast, 1984; Tracking the Glorious Lord, 1987. Add: c/o Naturegraph Publishers, P.O. Box 1075, Happy Camp, Calif. 96039, U.S.A.

BROWNE, Anthony (Edward Tudor). British, b. 1946. Children's fiction. Medical artist, Royal Infirmary, Univ. of Manchester, 1968–70; Designer, Gordon Fraser Greeting Cards, London, 1971–87. *Publs:* Through the Magic Mirror, 1976; A Walk in the Park, 1977; Bear Hunt, 1979; Look What I've Got!, 1980; Hansel and Gretel (retelling), 1981; Bear Goes to Town, 1982; Gorilla, 1983; Willy the Wimp, 1984; Willy the Champ, 1985; Piggybook, 1986; The Little Bear Book, 1988; I Like Books, 1989; A Bear-y Tale, 1989; The Tunnel, 1989. Add: The Chalk Garden, The Length, St. Nicholas-at-Wade, Birchington, Kent CT7 0PJ, England.

BROWNE, Harry. *See* **BROWNE,** Henry.

BROWNE, Harry. American, b. 1933. Money/Finance. Account Exec. and Salesman, James E. Munford Co., Los Angeles., 1958–61; Area Mgr., John Birch Soc., Los Angeles, 1961–62; Ed., Freedom mag., 1962–66; author of weekly newspaper columns, "The American Way" and "Between the Bookends," 1962–67; Owner, Writer and Ed., American Way Features Inc., Los Angeles, 1962–67; Marketing Mgr., Evelyn Woods Reading Dynamics, Los Angeles, 1967; Member, Sales and Service Staff, Economic Research Counselors, Los Angeles, 1967–70. *Publs:* How You Can Profit from the Coming Devaluation, 1970; How I Found Freedom in an Unfree World, 1973; You Can Profit from a Monetary Crisis, 1974, 1975; Complete Guide to Swiss Banks, 1976; New Profits from the Monetary Crisis, 1978; (with Terry Coxon) Inflation-Proofing Your Investments, 1981; Why the Best Laid Business Plans Usually Go Wrong,

1989. Add: c/o Collier Associates, 280 Madison Ave., New York, N.Y. 10016, U.S.A.

BROWNE, Henry. Writes as Harry Browne. British, b. 1918. History. Gen. Ed., Flashpoints, Longman, since 1970. Lectr. in History, 1949–60, and Head, Faculty of Arts and Languages, 1969–82, Cambridgeshire Coll. of Arts and Technology. *Publs:* Struggle in the Deserts, 1968; (ed.) A. Koestler's Darkness at Noon, 1968; Hitler and the Rise of Nazism, 1969; World History 2, 1970; Suez and Sinai, 1971; Joseph Chamberlain: Radical and Imperialist, 1974; World History 1, 1974; Rise of British Trade Unions, 1978; Spain's Civil War, 1981. Add: 4 Kentings, Comberton, Cambridge CB3 7DT, England.

BROWNE, Howard. Has also written as John Evans. American, b. 1908. Novels/Short stories, Mystery/Crime/Suspense, Plays/-Screenplays. Ed., Ziff-Davis, publishers, Chicago and NYC, 1941–56, thereafter Executive Story Consultant, 20th Century Fox Television Studios, and Story Ed. for Kraft Mystery Theatre, The Virginian, and Longstreet television series, all Hollywood; Instr., Univ. of California at San Diego, from 1973. *Publs:* novels—Warrior of the Dawn, 1943; Pork City, 1988; mystery novels—(as John Evans) Halo in Blood, 1946; (as John Evans) If You Have Tears, 1947, as Lona, 1952; (as John Evans) Halo for Satan, 1949; (as John Evans) Halo in Brass, 1949; Thin Air, 1954; The Taste of Ashes, 1957; The Paper Gun, 1985; screenplays—Portrait of a Mobster, 1961; The St. Valentine's Day Massacre, 1967; A Bowl of Cherries, 1969; Capone, 1975; also numerous plays for television. Add: 3303 La Costa Ave., Carlsbad, Calif. 92009, U.S.A.

BROWNE, Michael Dennis. American (b. British), b. 1940. Poetry, Songs, lyrics and libretti. Prof. of English, Univ.. of Minnesota, Minneapolis, since (joined faculty, 1971). Visiting Lectr. in Creative Writing, Univ. of Iowa, Iowa City, 1967–68; Adjunct Asst. Prof., Columbia Univ., NYC, 1968–69; Member of English Dept., Bennington Coll., Vt., 1969–71. *Publs:* How the Stars Were Made (cantata for children), 1967; The Wife of Winter, 1968 (song cycle), as poetry, 1970; The Sea Journey (cantata for children), 1969; Non-songs, 1973; Sun Exercises (poetry), 1976; The Sun Fetcher (poetry), 1978; Smoke from the Fires (poetry), 1984. Add: Dept. of English, Univ. of Minnesota, Minneapolis, Minn. 55455, U.S.A.

BROWNING, Dixie Burrus. Also writes as Zoe Dozier and Bronwyn Williams. American, b. 1930. Romance/Historical fiction. Pres. and Co-Owner, Browning Artworks, Frisco, NC, since 1984. Founder and Co-Dir., Art Gallery Originals, Winston-Salem, NC, 1968–73; Co-Dir., Art V Galley, Clemmons, NC, 1974–75. *Publs:* (as Zoe Dozier) Home Again My Love, 1977; (as Zoe Dozier) Warm Side of the Island, 1977; Tumbled Wall, 1980; Unreasonable Summer, 1980; Chance Tomorrow, 1981; East of Today, 1981; Winter Blossom, 1981; Wren of Paradise 1981; Finders Keepers, 1982; Island on the Hill, 1982; Logic of the Heart, 1982; The Loving Rescue, 1982; Renegade Player, 1982; Practical Dreamer, 1983; Reach Out to Cherish, 1983; A Secret Valentine, 1983; Shadow of Yesterday, 1983; First Things Last, 1984; The Hawk and the Honey, 1984; Image of Love, 1984; Journey to Quiet Waters, 1984; Just Desserts, 1984; Late Rising Moon, 1984; The Love Thing, 1984; Stormwatch, 1984; Time and Tide, 1984; Visible Heart, 1984; A Bird in Hand, 1985; By Any Other Name, 1985; Matchmaker's Moon, 1985; Something for Herself, 1985; The Tender Barbarian, 1985; Reluctant Dreamer, 1986; The Security Man, 1986; In the Palm of Her Hand, 1986; A Winter Woman, 1986; Belonging, 1987; Henry the Ninth, 1987; A Matter of Timing, 1987; There Once Was a Lover, 1987; Along Came Jones, 1988; Fate Takes a Holiday, 1988; (with Mary Williams, as Bronwyn Williams) White Witch, 1988; Thin Ice, 1989. Add: 5316 Robinhood Rd., Winston-Salem, N.C. 27106, U.S.A.

BROWNING, Don. American, b. 1934. Psychiatry, Psychology, Theology/Religion. Alexander Campbell Prof. of Religion and Psychological Studies, Divinity Sch., Univ. of Chicago, Ill, since 1980 (Instr., 1965–66; Asst. Prof., 1967–68; Assoc. Prof., 1968–77; Prof. of Religion and Psychological Studies, 1977–80). Dean, Disciples Divinity House of the Univ. of Chicago, 1977–83; Consultant, Center for Religion and Psycho-therapy, since 1970. Counselor, William Healy Sch., 1962–63; Asst. Prof. of Theology and Pastoral Care, Grad. Seminary, Phillips Univ., Enid, Okla., 1963–65. *Publs:* Atonement and Psycho-therapy, 1966; Generative Man: Society and Good Man in Philip Riff, Norman Brown, Erich Fromm, and Erik Erikson, 1973; The Moral Context of Pastoral Care, 1976; Pluralism and Personality: William James and Some Contemporary Cultures of Psychology, 1980; (ed.) Practical Theology, 1983; Religious Ethics and Pastoral Care, 1983; Religious Thought and the Modern Psychologies, 1986. Add: The Divinity Sch., Univ. of

Chicago, 1025 East 58th St., Chicago, Ill. 60637, U.S.A.

BROWNING, Robert. British, b. 1914. History, Language/Linguistics. Prof. of Classics, Univ. of London, 1965–81, now retired (Lectr., 1947–55; Reader, 1955–65). Fellow of Dumbarton Oaks, Washington, D.C., since 1983. *Publs:* Notes on Byzantine Prooemia, 1966; Medieval and Modern Greek, 1969, 1983; Justinian and Theodora, 1971, 1987; Byzantium and Bulgaria, 1975; The Emperor Julian, 1976; Studies in Byzantine History, Literature and Education, 1977; The Byzantine Empire, 1980; (ed.) The Greek World: Classical, Byzantine, and Modern, 1985. Add: 17 Belsize Park Gardens, London NW3, England.

BROWNING, Sterry. *See* **GRIBBLE,** Leonard.

BROWNING, Wilfrid (Robert Francis). British, b. 1918. Theology/Religion. Canon of Christ Church Cathedral, Oxford, since 1965, and Lectr. in New Testament Studies, Oxford Univ. *Publs:* (co-trans.) Vocabulary of the Bible; (ed.) The Anglican Synthesis, 1964; Meet the New Testament, 1964; Saint Luke's Gospel, 6th ed. 1981; Handbook of the Ministry, 1985. Add: Christ Church Cathedral, Oxford, England.

BROWNJOHN, Alan (Charles). British, b. 1931. Poetry, Literature. Deputy Pres., Poetry Soc., London, since 1988 (Chmn., 1982–88). Wandsworth Borough Councillor, London, 1962–65; Sr. Lectr. in English, Battersea Coll. of Education, now Polytechnic of the South Bank, London, 1965–79; Member Arts Council Literature Panel, 1968–72; Poetry Critic, New Statesman, London, 1968–76, and Encounter, 1978–80; Chmn., Literature Panel, Greater London Arts Assn., 1973–77. *Publs:* verse— Travellers Alone, 1954; The Railings, 1961; The Lions' Mouths, 1967; Oswin's Word (libretto for children), 1967; Woman Reading Aloud, 1969; Being a Garoon, 1969; Sandgrains on a Tray, 1969; (with Michael Hamburger and Charles Tomlinson) Penguin Modern Poets 14, 1969; A Day by Indirections, 1969; Brownjohn's Beasts, 1970; Synopsis, 1970; Frateretto Calling, 1970; Transformation Scene, 1971; An Equivalent, 1971; Warrior's Career, 1972; She Made of It, 1974; A Song of Good Life, 1975; A Night in the Gazebo, 1980; Collected Poems 1952–1983, 1983; The Old Flea-Pit, 1987; Collected Poems 1952–88, 1988; other— (as John Berrington) To Clear the River, 1964; (ed.) First I Say This: A Selection of Poems for Reading Aloud, 1969; (ed. with Seamus Heaney and Jon Stallworthy) New Poems 1970–71, 1971; The Little Red Bus Book, 1972; Philip Larkin, 1975; (ed. with Maureen Duffy) New Poetry 3, 1977; (ed.) New Year Poetry Supplement, 1982; (trans.) Torquato Tasso, by Goethe, 1985; (ed. with Sandy Brownjohn) Meet and Write, I, II and III, 1985–87. Add: 2 Belsize Park, London NW3, England.

BROWNLIE, Ian. British, b. 1932. Law. Member of the Bar, since 1958; in practice since 1967; Fellow, All Souls Coll., and Chichele Prof. of Public International Law, Oxford Univ., since 1980; Dir. of Studies, Intnl. Law Assoc., since 1982. Q.C., since 1979. Lectr., Nottingham Univ., 1957–63; Fellow and Tutor, Wadham Coll., 1963–76, and Lectr., 1964–76, Oxford Univ.; Reader, Inns of Court School of Law, London, 1973–76; Prof. of Intnl. Law, London School of Economics, 1976–80. Ed., British Year Book of Intnl. Law, since 1974. *Publs:* International Law and the Use of Force by States, 1963; Principles of Public International Law, 1966, 3rd ed., 1979; Basic Documents in International Law, 1967, rev. ed., 1972; The Law Relating to Public Order, 1968; Basic Documents on Human Rights, 1971, rev. ed., 1981; Basic Documents on African Affairs, 1971; African Boundaries: A Legal and Diplomatic Encyclopedia, 1979. Add: 2 Hare Court, Temple, London EC4Y 7BH, England.

BROWNLOW, Kevin. British, b. 1938. Film. Former film editor. *Publs:* The Parade's Gone By . . ., 1968; How It Happened Here, 1968; (ed.) Adventures with D.W. Griffith, by Karl Brown, 1973; Hollywood: The Pioneers, 1979; The War, The West, and the Wilderness, 1979; Napoleon: Abel Gance's Classic Film, 1983. Add: c/o Thames TV, 306 Euston Rd., London NW1, England.

BROWNLOW, (David) Timothy. Irish, b. 1941. Poetry. Asst. Prof. of English, St. Mary's Univ., Halifax, N.S., since 1978. Co-Ed., The Dublin Mag., 1963–69; Fellow, Dalhousie Univ., Halifax, 1975–78. *Publs:* The Hurdle Ford, 1964; (with R. Carew) Figures Out of Mist, 1966; John Clare and Picturesque Landscape, 1983. Add: Byfield House, R.R.2, Porters Lake, Halifax Cty., N.S. B0J 2S0, Canada.

BROWNMILLER, Susan. American, b. 1935. Human Relations, Women. Freelance writer. Formerly: Reporter, NBC-TV, Philadelphia, 1965; network newswriter, ABC-TV, NYC, 1965–67; researcher, Newsweek mag., NYC, and staff writer, Village Voice newspaper, NYC.

Publs: Shirley Chisholm, 1970; Against Our Will: Men, Women and Rape, 1975. Add: c/o Simon and Schuster, 1230 Sixth Ave., New York, N.Y. 10020, U.S.A.

BROWNSTEIN, Michael. American, b. 1943. Novels/Short stories, Poetry. *Publs:* Behind the Wheel (poetry), 1967; Highway to the Sky (poetry), 1969; Three American Tantrums (poetry), 1970; Brainstorms: Stories, 1971; 30 Pictures (poetry), 1972; Country Cousins (novel), 1974; Strange Days Ahead (poetry), 1975; (ed.) The Dice Cup: Selected Prose Poems of Max Jacob, 1979; When Nobody's Looking (poetry), 1981; Oracle Night (poetry), 1982; Music from the Evening of the World (short stories), 1989. Add: c/o Sun and Moon Press, 4330 Hartwick Rd., College Park, MD 20740, U.S.A.

BROXON, Mildred Downey. Has also written as Sigfridur Skaldaspillir. American, b. 1944. Science fiction/Fantasy. Self-employed freelance writer. Staff nurse, Harborview Medical Center psychiatric unit, 1970–71. Vice-Pres., Science Fiction Writers of America, 1976–78. *Publs:* (as Sigfridur Skaldaspillir) A Witch's Welcome, 1979; (with Poul Anderson) The Demon of Scattery, 1979; Too Long a Sacrifice, 1981; Too Long a Sacrifice, 1984. Add: c/o Sharon Jarvis and Co., 260 Willard Ave., Staten Island, N.Y. 10314, U.S.A.

BRUBACHER, John Seiler. American, b. 1898. Education. Prof. of History and Philosophy of Education, Yale Univ., New Haven, Conn., 1928–58; Prof. of Higher Education, Univ. of Michigan, Ann Arbor, 1959–69. *Publs:* Judicial Power of the New York State Commissioner of Education, 1927; (ed.) Henry Barnard on Education, 1931; Modern Philosophies of Education, 1939; (ed.) Public School and Spiritual Values, 1944; History of the Problems of Education, 1947; (ed.) Eclectic Philosophy of Education, 1952; (with W. Rudy) Higher Education in Transition, 1958, 3rd rev. ed., 1976; The Courts and Higher Education, 1971; (ed.) Case Book in the Law of Higher Education, 1971; On the Philosophy of Higher Education, 1977, rev. ed., 1982. Add: 3030 Park Ave., 8-W-1, Bridgeport, Conn. 06604, U.S.A.

BRUCCOLI, Matthew J. American, b. 1931. Literature. Partner, Bruccoli Clark Publrs., Columbia, S.C., and Bloomfield Hills, Michigan, since 1972. Prof. of English and Dir. of the Center for Editions of American Authors, Univ. of South Carolina, Columbia, 1969–76, and Jefferies Prof. of English, since 1976. Ed., Fitzgerald/Hemingway Annual, 1969–79. *Publs:* Notes on the Cabell Collection at the University of Virginia, 1957; The Composition of "Tender Is the Night": A Study of the Manuscripts, 1963; (ed.) Zelda Fitzgerald: Save Me the Waltz, 1967; Raymond Chandler: A Checklist, 1968; (ed.) The Profession of Authorship in America 1800-1970: The Papers of William Charvat, 1968; (ed.) Fitzgerald/Hemingway Annual, 1969; Profile of F. Scott Fitzgerald, 1971; (ed. with J.R. Bryer) F. Scott Fitzgerald in His Own Time: A Miscellany, 1971; Kenneth Millar/Ross Macdonald: A Checklist, 1971; John O'Hara: A Checklist, 1972; (ed. with J.M. Atkinson) As Ever, Scott Fitz: Letters Between F. Scott Fitzgerald and His Literary Agent Harold Ober 1919–1940, 1972; (ed.) F. Scott Fitzgerald: A Descriptive Bibliography, 1972, 1987; (ed. with C.F. Clark, Jr.) Hemingway at Auction, 1972; (with Scottie Fitzgerald Smith and Joan Kerr) The Romantic Egoists, 1974; The O'Hara Concern: Biography of John O'Hara, 1975; (ed.) "An Artist Is His Own Fault:" John O'Hara on Writers and Writing, 1976; (with R. Layman) Ring Lardner: A Descriptive Bibliography, 1976; (with R. Layman) Some Champions, 1976; "The Last of the Novelists": F. Scott Fitzgerald and the Last Tycoon, 1977; The Notebooks of F. Scott Fitzgerald, 1978; Selected Letters of John O'Hara, 1978; Scott and Ernest, 1978; John O'-Hara: A Descriptive Bibliography, 1978; Raymond Chandler: A Descriptive Bibliography, 1979; (ed. with M. Duggan) Correspondence of F. Scott Fitzgerald, 1980; Some Sort of Epic Grandeur, 1981; Ross Macdonald: A Descriptive Bibliography, 1983; James Gould Cozzens, 1983; Ross Macdonald, 1984; The Fortunes of Mitchell Kennerley, Bookman, 1986. Add: Dept. of English, Univ. of South Carolina, Columbia, S.C. 29208, U.S.A.

BRUCE, David. *See* **PATCHETT,** Mary Elwyn.

BRUCE, Dickson Davies, Jr. American, b. 1946. History. Prof., Univ. of California, Irvine, since 1971. *Publs:* And They All Sang Hallelujah: Plain-Folk Camp-Meeting Religion, 1800-1845, 1974; Violence and Culture in the Antebellum South, 1979; The Rhetoric of Conservatism: The Virginian Convention of 1829-30 and the Conservative Tradition in the South, 1982; Black American Writing from the Nadir: The Evolution of a Literary Tradition 1877–1915, 1989. Add: Sch. of Social Sciences, Univ. of California, Irvine, Calif. 92717, U.S.A.

BRUCE, Frederick (Fyvie). British, b. 1910. Theology/Religion. Prof. Emeritus, Univ. of Manchester, since 1978 (Rylands Prof. of Biblical Criticism and Exegesis, 1959–78; Dean, Faculty of Theology, 1963–64). Asst. in Greek, Edinburgh Univ., 1935–38; Lectr. in Greek, Leeds Univ., 1938–47; Member of the Faculty, Univ. of Sheffield, 1947–59: Prof. of Biblical History and Literature, 1955–59. Ed. Evangelical Quarterly, 1949–80. *Publs:* Are the New Testament Documents Reliable?, 1943; The Hittites and the Old Testament, 1948; The Books and the Parchments, 1950; The Acts of the Apostles, 1951; The Book of the Acts, 1954; Second Thoughts on the Dead Sea Scrolls, 1956; The Teacher of Righteousness in the Qumran Texts, 1957; The Spreading Flame, 1958; Commentary on the Epistle to the Colossians, 1958; Biblical Exegesis in the Qumran Texts, 1959; The Defence of the Gospel in the New Testament, 1959; The English Bible, 1961; The Epistle to the Ephesians, 1961; Paul and His Converts, 1961; The Epistle of Paul to the Romans, 1963; Israel and the Nations, 1963; Commentary on the Epistle to the Hebrews,1964; Expanded Paraphrase of the Epistles of Paul, 1965; This Is That, 1968; New Testament History, 1969; Tradition Old and New, 1970; The Epistles of John, 1970; St. Matthew, 1970; 1 and 2 Corinthians, 1971; The Message of the New Testament, 1972; Jesus and Christian Origins Outside the New Testament, 1974; Paul and Jesus, 1974; Paul: Apostle of the Free Spirit, 1977; First-Century Faith, 1977; The Time Is Fulfilled, 1978; The Work of Jesus, 1979; Men and Movements in the Primitive Church, 1980; In Retrospect, 1980; Bible History Atlas, 1982; The Epistle to the Galatians, 1982; 1 and 2 Thessalonians, 1982; The Hard Sayings of Jesus, 1983; Paul's Letter to the Philippians, 1983; The Gospel of John, 1983; The Pauline Circle, 1985; The Real Jesus, 1985; The Canon of Scripture, 1988. Add: 2 Temple Rd., Buxton, Derbys., England.

BRUCE, George. British, b. 1909. Plays/Screenplays, Poetry, Literature. Teacher of English and History, Dundee High Sch., 1933–46; General Progs. Producer, Aberdeen, 1946–56, and Documentary Talks Producer, Edinburgh, 1956–70, B.B.C.; Fellow in Creative Writing, Glasgow Univ., 1971–73; Visiting Prof., Union Theological Seminary, Richmond, Va., 1974; Writer-in-Residence, Prescott Coll., Arizona, 1974; Visiting Prof. of English, Coll. of Wooster, Ohio, 1976–77; Scottish Australian Writing Fellow, 1982; Visiting Prof., St. Andrews Presbyterian Coll., Laurinburg, N.C., 1985. *Publs:* Sea Talk, 1944; (with T.S. Halliday) Scottish Sculpture, 1946; Selected Poems, 1947; (ed.) The Exiled Heart: Poems 1941–46, by Maurice Lindsay, 1957; To Scotland, with Rhubarb (play), 1965; (ed. with Edwin Morgan and Maurice Lindsay) Scottish Poetry, 6 vols., 1966–72; Landscapes and Figures: A Selection of Poems, 1967; (ed.) The Scottish Literary Revival: An Anthology of Twentieth Century Poetry, 1968; The Collected Poems of George Bruce, 1970; Anne Redpath: A Monograph of the Scottish Artist, 1974; Festival in the North: The Story of the Edinburgh Festival, 1975; Some Practical Good: The Cockburn Association 1875-1975, 1975; William Soutar: The Man and the Poet, 1978; The Red Sky (poetry), 1985; To Foster and Enrich: The First Fifty Years of the Saltire Society, 1986; Perspectives, 1970–1986 (poetry), 1987. Add: 25 Warriston Cres., Edinburgh 3, Scotland.

BRUCE, Lennart. Swedish, b. 1919. Poetry, Translations. *Publs:* Making the Rounds, 1967; (trans. with M. Zion) Instructions for Undressing of the Human Race, by Fernando Alegria, 1968; Observations, 1968; Moments of Doubt, 1969; The Mullioned Window, 1970; The Robot Failure (novella), 1971; Letter of Credit, 1973; Subpoemas, 1974; Exposure, 1975; (trans.) Agenda, by Vilhelm Ekelund, 1976; En Sannsaga (A True Fairytale), autobiography in Swedish, 1982; The Broker, 1984; (trans.) The Second Light, by Vilhelm Ekelund, 1986; Utan synbar anledning (For No Apparent Reason), Poems in Swedish, 1988. Add: 31 Los Cerros Pl., Walnut Creek, Calif. 94598, U.S.A.

BRUCE LOCKHART, Robin. British, b. 1920. Biography. Member, Stock Exchange, London, since 1960. Foreign Mgr., Financial Times, London, 1946–52; with Beaverbrook Newspapers Ltd., London, 1953–59. *Publs:* Ace of Spies: Biography of Sidney Reilly, 1967; Halfway to Heaven: The Hidden Life of the Sublime Carthusians, 1985; Reilly: The First Man, 1987. Add: 37 Adelaide Cres., Hove, Sussex, England.

BRUCHAC, Joseph. American, b. 1942. Novels/Short stories, Children's fiction, Poetry, Literature, Writing/Journalism. Ed., Greenfield Review, since 1970; Dir., Greenfield Review Literary Center, since 1981. Teacher, Ghana, 1966–69; Teacher and Coordinator, Univ. Without Walls, College Program for Skidmore Coll., Saratoga Springs, N.Y., 1969–81. *Publs:* Indian Mountain & Other Poems, 1971; (co-ed.) Words from the House of the Dead: Prison Writings from Soledad, 1972; The Poetry of Pop, 1973; (ed.) The Last Stop, 1974; Flow, 1975; The Road to Black Mountain, 1976; (co-ed.) Aftermath: Poems in English

from Africa, Asia and the Caribbean, 1977; The Earth Is a Drum, 1977; Entering Onondaga, 1978; The Dreams of Jesse Brown, 1978; (ed.) The Next World: Poems by 32 Third World Americans, 1978; There Are No Trees in the Prison, 1978; Stone Giants and Flying Heads: More Iroquois Folk Tales, 1978; Mu'ndu Wi Go: Mohegan Poems, 1978; The Good Message of Handsome Lake, 1979; Ancestry, 1980; How to Start and Sustain a Literary Magazine, 1980; Translator's Son, 1981; (ed.) Songs from this Earth on Turtle's Back (verse), 1983; (ed.) The Light From Another Country (verse), 1984; (ed.) Breaking Silence (verse), 1984; Remembering the Dawn and Other Poems (verse), 1983; The Wind Eagle and other Abenaki Stories, 1985; Iroquois Stories, 1985; No Telephone to Heaven (novel), 1985; Walking with my Sons and Other Poems, 1985. Tracking, 1986; Near the Mountains: Selected Poems, 1987; Survival This Way: Interviews with American Indian Poets, 1987; The Faithful Hunter: More Abenaki Stories, 1988; (with Michael Catudo) Keepers of the Earth: American Stories and Environmental Activities for Children, 1988. Add: c/o The Greenfield Review, Greenfield Center, N.Y. 12833, U.S.A.

BRUEMMER, Fred. Canadian, b. 1929. Anthropology/Ethnology, Natural history. Freelance photographer. *Publs:* The Long Hunt, 1969; Seasons of the Eskimo, 1971; Encounters with Arctic Animals, 1972; The Arctic, 1974; The Life of the Harp Seal, 1977; Children of the North, 1979; Summer at Bear River, 1980; The Arctic World, 1985; Arctic Animals, 1986; Seasons of the Seal, 1988. Recipient of Order of Canada award, 1983. Add: 5170 Cumberland Ave., Montreal, Que. H4V 2N8, Canada.

BRUFF, Nancy. Also writes as Nancy Bruff Gardner. American, b. 1909. Novels/Short stories, Poetry. *Publs:* The Manatee, 1946; Cider from Eden, 1947; My Talon in Your Heart, 1948; Beloved Woman, 1949; Love Is Not Love, 1950; (as Nancy Bruff Gardner) The Fig Tree, 1965; The Country Club, 1969; Mist Maiden, 1974; Desire on the Dunes, 1984. Add: 150 East 72nd St., New York, N.Y., U.S.A.

BRUIN, John. *See* **BRUTUS,** Dennis.

BRUMBAUGH, Robert S(herrick). American, b. 1918. Classics, Philosophy. Prof. of Philosophy, Yale Univ., since 1961 (Asst. Prof., and Assoc. Prof., 1952–61). *Publs:* (with N.P. Stallknecht) Spirit of Western Philosophy, 1950; (with N.P. Stallknecht) The Compass of Philosophy, 1952; Plato's Mathematical Imagination, 1952; Plato on the One, 1961; (with N.M. Lawrence) Philosophers on Education, 1962; Ancient Greek Gadgets and Machines, 1964; (ed.) Six Trials, 1964; The Philosophers of Greece, 1964; Plato for the Modern Age, 1967; (with R. Wells) The Plato Manuscripts: A New Index, 1968; (with N.M. Lawrence) Philosophic Themes in Modern Education, 1973; (ed.) The Most Mysterious Manuscript: The Voynich "Roger Bacon" Cipher Manuscript, 1978; Whitehead, Process Philosophy, and Education, 1982; Unreality and Time, 1984. Add: 150 Ridgewood Ave., North Haven, Conn. 06473, U.S.A.

BRUNDAGE, James A. American, b. 1929. History. Prof. of History, Univ. of Wisconsin-Milwaukee, since 1964 (Asst. Prof., 1957–60; Assoc. Prof., 1960–64; Chmn. of the Dept., 1972–76). Assoc. Ed., Journal of Medieval History, since 1974. Pres., American Catholic Historical Association, 1985; Instr., Fordham Univ., NYC, 1953–57. *Publs:* The Chronicle of Henry of Livonia, 1961; The Crusades: A Documentary History, 1962; (ed.) The Crusades: Motives and Achievements, 1964; (with J. Donnelly) Old World Heritage, 1965; Medieval Canon Law and the Crusader, 1969; Richard Lion-Heart: A Biography, 1974; (V.L. Bullough) Sexual Practices and the Medieval Church, 1982; Law, Sex, and Christian Society in Medieval Europe, 1988. Add: Dept. of History, Univ. of Wisconsin-Milwaukee, Milwaukee, Wisc. 53201, U.S.A

BRUNER, Jerome S(eymour). American, b. 1915. Education, Psychology. G. H. Mead University Prof., New Sch. for Social Research, NYC. Watts Prof. of Psychology, Oxford Univ., since 1972. Assoc. Dir., Office of Public Opinion Research, Princeton, N.J., 1942–44; Lectr., 1945–48, Assoc. Prof., 1948–52, Prof. of Cognitive Studies, 1957–72, and Dir. of the Center for Cognitive Studies, 1961–72, Harvard Univ., Cambridge, Mass.; Watts Prof. of Psychology, Oxford Univ., 1972–80. Ed., Public Opinion Quarterly, 1943–44; Pres., American Psychological Assn., 1964–65. *Publs:* Public Thinking and Post-War Problems, 1943; Mandate from the People, 1944; (ed.) Perception and Personality: A Symposium, 1950; (with Jacqueline J. Goodnow and George A. Austin) A Study of Thinking, 1956; (with others) Opinions and Personality, 1956; (with others) Contemporary Approaches to Cognition, 1957; Logique et perception, 1958; On Knowing: Essays for the Left Hand, 1962; Man: A Course of Study, 1965; (with others) Studies in Cognitive Growth, 1966; Learning About

Learning: A Conference Report, 1966; The Growth of the Mind, 1966; A Look at Incongruity, 1966; Processes of Cognitive Growth: Infancy, 1968; (with others) Education of the Infant and Young Child, 1970; Dare to Care/Dare to Act: Racism and Education, 1971; (with others) The Application of Learning Principles to Classroom Instruction, 1971; (ed. by Anita Gil) The Relevance of Education, 1971, 1974; Beyond the Information Given: Studies in the Psychology of Knowing, 1973; Patterns of Growth, 1974; (ed.) The Growth of Competence, 1974; Entry into Early Language: A Spiral Curriculum, 1975; (ed.) Play: Its Role in Development and Evolution, 1976; (ed., with Alison Garton) Human Growth and Development, 1978; Under Five in Britain, 1980; Communication as Language, 1982; In Search of Mind: Essays in Autobiography, 1983; Child's Talk, 1983; Actual Minds, Possible Worlds, 1986. Add: 200 Mercer St., New York, NY 10012, U.S.A..

BRUNNER, John (K.H.). Also writes as John Loxmith and Keith Woodcott. British, b. 1934. Novels/Short stories, Science fiction, Plays/Screenplays, Poetry, Songs, lyrics and libretti. Owner and Dir., Brunner Fact and Fiction Ltd., since 1966. Contributing Ed., Sanity (CND journal), 1965–73. Publs: Echo in the Skull, 1959; Threshold of Eternity, 1959; The World Swappers, 1959; The Hundredth Millennium, 1959; The Brink, 1959; The Atlantic Abomination, 1960; Sanctuary in the Sky, 1960; The Skynappers, 1960; Slavers of Space, 1960; (as Keith Woodcott) I Speak for Earth, 1961; Meeting at Infinity, 1961; (as Keith Woodcott) The Ladder in the Sky, 1962; Secret Agent of Terra, 1962; The Super Barbarians, 1962; Times Without Number, 1962, 1969; No Future in It, 1962; The Astronauts Must Not Land, 1963; Castaways' World, 1963; The Dreaming Earth, 1963; Listen! The Stars!, 1963; (as Keith Woodcott) The Psionic Menace, 1963; The Rites of Ohe, 1963; The Space Time Juggler, 1963; Endless Shadow, 1964; To Conquer Chaos, 1964; The Whole Man (in U.K. as Telepathist), 1964; The Crutch of Memory, 1964; The Altar on Asconel, 1965; Day of the Star Cities, 1965; Enigma from Tantalus, 1965; The Long Result, 1965; (as Keith Woodcott) The Martian Sphinx, 1965; The Repairmen of Cyclops, 1965; The Squares of the City, 1965; Wear the Butchers' Medal, 1965; Now Then, 1965; A Planet of Your Own, 1966; No Other Gods But Me, 1966; Born under Mars, 1967; The Productions of Time, 1967; Quicksand, 1967; Out of My Mind, 1967; Bedlam Planet, 1968; Into the Slave Nebula, 1968; Stand on Zanzibar, 1968; Catch a Falling Star, 1968; Father of Lies, 1968; Not Before Time, 1968; The Avengers of Carrig, 1969; Double, Double, 1969; The Jagged Orbit, 1969; Timescoop, 1969; The Evil That Men Do, 1969; Black Is the Colour, 1969; A Plague on Both Your Causes (in U.S. as Blacklash), 1969; The Gaudy Shadows , 1970; Good Men Do Nothing, 1970; The Devil's Work, 1970; Life in an Explosive Forming Press (poetry), 1970; The Dramaturges of Yan, 1971; The Wrong End of Time, 1971; The Traveler in Black, 1971; Honky in the Woodpile, 1971; Trip (poetry), 1971; The Sheep Look Up, 1972; The Stardroppers, 1972; Entry to Elsewhen,. 1972; From This Day Forward, 1972; Age of Miracles, 1973; More Things in Heaven, 1973; The Stone That Never Came Down, 1973; Time-jump, 1973; Total Eclipse, 1974; Web of Everywhere, 1974; The Shockwave Rider, 1975; The Book of John Brunner, 1976; Interstellar Empire, 1976; Tomorrow May Be Even Worse (verse), 1978; Foreign Constellations, 1980; The Infinitive of Go, 1980; Players at the Game of People, 1981; The Crucible of Time, 1983; The Great Steamboat Race, 1983; A New Settlement of Old Scores (songs), 1983; The Tides of Time, 1984; The Compleat Traveller in Black, 1986; The Shift Key, 1987; The Best of John Brunner (stories), 1988; Children of the Thunder, 1989. Add: c/o Nat West Bank, 7 Fore St., Chard, Somerset TA20 1PJ, England.

BRUNNER, Marguerite Ashworth. American, b. 1913. Antiques/Furnishings, Crafts. Founder, Washington, D.C. Area Writer's Club, 1972. Publs: Antiques for Amateurs on a Shoestring Budget, 1976; How to Sell Your Collectibles, Antiques and Crafts at a Profit; Goldmine of Money Making Ideas, 1977; Pass it On: How to Make Your Own Family Keepsakes, 1979. Add: 1884 Columbia Rd. N.W., Washington D.C. 20009, U.S.A.

BRUNS, William John, Jr. American, b. 1935. Administration/Management, Economics. Prof. of Business Admin., Harvard Univ., Cambridge, Mass., since 1972 (Visiting Assoc. Prof., 1969–70). Advisory Ed., Addison-Wesley Publishing Co. Asst. Prof. of Economics and Industrial Admin., 1962–66, Yale Univ., New Haven, Conn., and Prof. of Accounting, 1966–72, Univ. of Washington, Seattle. Publs: Accounting for Decisions: Business Game, 1966; (ed. with Don T. DeCoster) Accounting and Its Behavioral Implications, 1969; Introduction to Accounting: Economic Measurement for Decisions, 1971; (with R. Vancil) A Primer on Replacement Cost Accounting, 1976; (with M.E. Barrett) Case Problems in Management Accounting, 1982, 2nd ed. 1985; (ed. with Robert S. Kaplan) Accounting and Management: Field Study Perspec-

tives, 1987. Add: Harvard Business Sch., Soldiers Field, Boston, Mass. 02163, U.S.A.

BRUNSKILL, Ronald William. British, b. 1929. Architecture. Reader in Architecture, Univ. of Manchester, since 1984 (Lectr., 1960–73; Sr. Lectr., 1973–83). Member, Cathedrals Advisory Commn. for England, since 1981; Member, Royal Commn. on Ancient and Historical Monuments of Wales, since 1983; Member, Historic Bldgs. and Ancient Monuments Advisory Cttees. of Historic Bldgs. and Monuments Commn., since 1984. Pres., Vernacular Architecture Group, 1974–77; member Historic Bldgs. Council for England, 1978–83. Publs: Illustrated Handbook of Vernacular Architecture, 1970, 3rd ed. 1987; Vernacular Architecture of the Lake Counties, 1974; (with Alec Clifton-Taylor) English Brickwork, 1978; Traditional Buildings of Britain, 1981; Houses, 1982; Traditional Farm Buildings of Britain, 1982, 1987; Timber Buildings of Britain, 1985. Add: Sch. of Architecture, Univ. of Manchester, Manchester M13 9PL, England.

BRUSTEIN, Robert. American, b. 1927. Theatre. Prof. of English, Harvard Univ., Cambridge, Mass., since 1979. Drama Critic, New Republic, Washington, D.C. 1959–67 and since 1979; Host and writer, Opposition Theatre, network TV, since 1966; Contributor, New York Times, since 1967; Founder and Publisher, Yale/Theatre, since 1967; Advisory Ed., Theatre Quarterly, since 1967. Lectr. to Prof., Columbia Univ., New York, 1957–66; Prof. of English, Dean of Drama Sch., and Artistic Dir., Yale Repertory Theatre, Yale Univ., New Haven, Conn., 1966–79. Publs: Introduction to the Plays of Chekhov, 1964; (ed.) The Plays of Strindberg, 1964; The Theatre of Revolt, 1964; Season of Discontent, 1965; The Third Theatre, 1969; Revolution as Theatre, 1971; The Culture Watch, 1975; Making Scenes, 1981; Who Needs Theatre, 1987. Add: Loeb Drama Centre, 64 Brattle St., Cambridge, Mass. 02138, U.S.A.

BRUTEAU, Beatrice. American, b. 1930. Philosophy, Theology/Religion. Dir., Philosophers' Exchange, since 1972; Assoc., Ed., Anima, since 1976. Managing Ed., Intnl. Philosophical Quarterly, 1960–66. Coordinator, Teilhard Research Inst., Fordham Univ., Bronx, N.Y., 1964–66; Asst. Dir., Cardinal Bea Inst. of Spirituality, Fordham Univ., 1965–66; Exec. Dir., Foundn. for Integrative Education, NYC, 1967. Publs: Worthy Is the World: The Hindu Philosophy of Sri Aurobindo, 1972; Evolution toward Divinity: Teilhard de Chardin and the Hindu Traditions, 1974; The Psychic Grid: How We Create the World We Know, 1979; Neo-Feminism and Communion Consciousness, 1981. Add: P.O. Box 11144, Bethabara Station, Winston-Salem, N.C. 27106, U.S.A.

BRUTON, Eric (Moore). British, b. 1915. Mystery/Crime/Suspense, Antiques. Dir., since 1963, and Managing Dir. since 1983, NAG Press Ltd., London. Member, Council Gemmological Assn. of Great Britain, since 1972; Member, Council, British Horological Inst., 1955–62, and since 1977. Managing Dir., Diamond Boutique Ltd., 1965–80; Chmn., Things and Ideas Ltd., 1970–80. Member, Cttee., Crime Writers Assn., 1959–62. Publs: True Book about Clocks, 1957; Death in Ten Point Bold, 1957; Die, Darling, Die, 1959; Violent Brothers, 1960; True Book about Diamonds, 1961; The Hold Out, 1961; King Diamond, 1961; The Devil's Pawn, 1962; Automation, 1962; Dictionary of Clocks and Watches, 1962; The Laughing Policeman, 1963; The Longcase Clock, 1964, 1978; The Finsbury Mob, 1964; The Smithfield Slayer, 1964; The Wicked Saint, 1965; The Fire Bug, 1967; Clocks and Watches 1400-1900, 1967; Clocks and Watches, 1968; Diamonds, 1970, 1977; Antique Clocks and Clock Collecting, 1974; The History of Clocks, 1978; The Wetherfield Collection of Clocks, 1980; Legendary Gems, 1986; Clock and Watch Compendium, 1989. Add: The House by the Pond, The Green, Great Bentley, Essex CO7 8QG, England.

BRUTUS, Dennis (Vincent). Has also written as John Bruin. South African, b. 1924. Poetry. Prof. of Black Studies and English, and Chmn., Dept. of Black Community Education Research and Development, Univ. of Pittsburgh, since 1986. Secty., South African Sports Assn., since 1959; Pres., South African Non-Racial Olympic Cttee., since 1963; Chmn., Intnl. Campaign Against Racism in Sport, since 1972; Member of the Editorial Bd., Africa Today, Denver, since 1976; Chmn., Africa Network, since 1984. Served 18 months in Robben Island Prison, South Africa, for opposition to apartheid, 1964–65; Dir., Campaign for Release of South African Political Prisoners, London, and staff member, Intnl. Defence and Aid Fund, London, 1966–71; Visiting Prof., Univ. of Texas, Austin, 1974–75; Visiting Writer, Amherst Coll., Mass., 1981–82. Prof. of English, Northwestern Univ., Evanston, Ill., 1971–85; Cornell Prof. of English Literature, Swarthmore Coll., Pa., 1985–86. Publs: Sirens, Knuckles, Boots: Poems, 1963; Letters to Martha and Other Poems from a South African Prison, 1968; The Denver Poems, 1969; Poems from Algiers, 1970; (as John Bruin) Thoughts Abroad, 1971; A Simple Lust: Collected Poems of South African Jail and Exile, 1973; China Poems, 1975; Strains, 1975; Stubborn Hope (poems), 1978; Salutes and Censures, 1982. Add: Univ. of Pittsburgh English Dept., Pittsburgh, Pa. 15260, U.S.A.

BRYAN, Harrison. Australian, b. 1923. Librarianship. Librarian, Univ. of Queensland, Brisbane, 1950–63, and Univ. of Sydney, 1963–80; Dir.-Gen., National Library of Australia, 1980–85. Pres., Library Assn. of Australia, 1973–74. *Publs:* John Murtagh Macrossan, His Life and Career, 1958; Australian University Libraries Today and Tomorrow, 1965; Critical Survey of University Libraries and Librarianship in Great Britain, 1967; (with E.L. Hean) The Function of the Library in a College of Advanced Education, 1970; (with R.M. McGreal) The Pattern of Library Services in Australia, 1972; The Vision Splendid: An Essay on Libraries and Education, 1972; Report on the Development of National Documentation Information Services in Indonesia, 1972; University Libraries in Britain: A New Look, 1976; (co-ed.) Design for Diversity: Library Services for Higher Education and Research in Australia, 1977; (co-ed.) Australian Academic Libraries in the Seventies, 1984. Add: 16 Asquith St., Oatley, N.S.W. 2223, Australia.

BRYANS, Robin. (Robert Harbinson Bryans). Also writes as Robert Harbinson and Donald Cameron. British, b. 1928. Novels/Short stories, Poetry, Travel/Exploration/Adventure, Autobiography/Memoirs/Personal. Schoolmaster, 1948–52; Lectr., British Council, 1954–55. *Publs:* Gateway to the Khyber, 1959; Madeira, 1959; Summer Saga, 1960 (as Robert Harbinson) No Surrender, 1960; (as R. Harbinson) Song of Erne, 1960; (as R. Harbinson) Up Spake the Cabin Boy, 1961; Danish Episode, 1961; (as R. Harbinson) Tattoo Lily, 1962; Fanfare for Brazil, 1962; (as R. Harbinson) The Protugé, 1963; (as R. Harbinson) The Far World, 1963; The Azores, 1963; Ulster, 1964; Lucio, 1964; Malta and Gozo, 1966; (as Donald Cameron) The Field of Sighing, 1966; Trinidad and Tobago, 1967; (ed.) Faber Best True Adventure Stories, 1967; Sons of El Dorado, 1968; Crete, 1969; (as R. Harbinson) Songs out of Oriel, 1975. Add: 58 Argyle Rd., London W13 8AA, England.

BRYANT, Dorothy (Mae). American, b. 1930. Novels/Short stories, Speech/Rhetoric. Publisher, Ata Books, since 1978. English Teacher, San Francisco Public Schs., 1953–56, and Lick-Wilmerding High Sch., 1956–61; Instr. in English, San Francisco State Univ., 1962, and Golden Gate Coll., San Francisco, 1963; Instr. in English and Creative Writing, Contra Coll., San Pablo, Calif., 1964–76. *Publs:* The Comforter, 1971, retitled The Kin of Ata Are Waiting For You, 1976; Ella Prince's Journal, 1972; Miss Giardino, 1978; Writing a Novel (non-fiction), 1979; The Garden of Eros, 1979; Prisoners, 1980; Killing Wonder, 1981; A Day in San Francisco, 1983; Myths to Lie By, 1984; Confessions of Madame Psyche, 1986. Add: 1928 Stuart St., Berkeley, Calif. 94703, U.S.A.

BRYANT, Edward (Winslow, Jr.). American, b. 1945. Science fiction/Fantasy, Plays/Screenplays. Broadcaster, Disc-Jockey, and News Dir., KOWB-Radio, 1965–66; High Sch. and Coll. Teacher in Science Fiction and Writing. *Publs:* Among the Dead: And Other Events Leading up to the Apocalypse, 1973; The Synar Calculation (screenplay), 1973; Cinnabar, 1976; (with H. Ellison) Phoenix Without Ashes, 1978; Particle Theory, 1980; Wyoming Sun, 1980. Add: c/o Jelm Mountain Publications, 209 Park, Laramie, Wyo. 82070, U.S.A.

BRYANT, Gay. American (born British), b. 1945. Social commentary. Ed., Family Circle mag., NYC, since 1984. Sr. Ed., Penthouse mag., NYC, 1968–74; Assoc. Ed., Oui mag., NYC, 1974–75; Founding Ed., New Dawn mag., NYC, 1975–79; Exec. Ed., 1979–81, and Ed., 1981–84, Working Woman mag., NYC. *Publs:* The Underground Travel Guide, 1973; How I Learned to Like Myself, 1975; The Working Woman Report, 1984. Add: 34 Horatio St., New York, N.Y. 10014, U.S.A.

BRYANT, Joseph Allen, Jr. American, b. 1919. Literature. Prof. of English, Univ. of Kentucky, Lexington, since 1973. Prof. and Chmn. of English, Univ. of North Carolina at Greensboro, 1961–68, and Syracuse Univ., N.Y., 1968–71. *Publs:* Hippolyta's View: Some Christian Aspects of Shakespeare's Plays, 1961; (ed.) Shakespeare: Romeo and Juliet, 1964; Eudora Welty, 1968; The Compassionate Satirist: Ben Jonson and His Imperfect World, 1972; Understanding Randall Jarrell, 1986; Shakespeare and the Uses of Comedy, 1986. Add: 713 Old Dobbin Rd., Lexington, Ky. 40502, U.S.A.

BRYANT, Robert Harry. American, b. 1925. Theology/Religion. Prof. of Constructive Theology, United Theological Seminary of the Twin Cities, New Brighton, Minn., since 1971 (Prof. of Systematic Theology,

1961–71). Asst. Prof. of Religion, Mt. Holyoke Coll., South Hadley, Mass., 1956–58; Assoc. Prof. of Philosophy and Religion, Centre Coll. of Kentucky, Danville, 1958–61; Visiting Prof., St. John's Univ., Collegeville, Minn., 1971–72; and Adams United Coll., Federal Theological Seminary, S. Africa, 1973–74. *Publs:* The Bible's Authority Today, 1968. Add: United Theological Seminary of the Twin Cities, 3000 Fifth St., N.W., New Brighton, Minn. 55112, U.S.A.

BRZEZINSKI, Zbigniew. American (born Polish), b. 1928. International relations/Current affairs, Politics/Government. Herbert Lehman Prof. of Govt., and Dir., Research Inst. on Intnl. Change (formerly, Research Inst. on Communist Affairs), Columbia Univ., New York City, since 1960. Dir., Trilateral Commn., New York City; Member, Bd. of Trustees, Council on Foreign Relations, Teacher and Researcher, Harvard Univ., Cambridge, Mass., 1953–60. Member, Policy Planning Council, of Dept. of State, Washington, D.C., 1966–68; Dir., Foreign Policy Task Forces, 1968; White House National Security Adviser, 1977–81. *Publs:* Political Controls in the Soviet Army, 1954; The Permanent Purge: Politics in Soviet Totalitarianism, 1956; (co-author) Totalitarian Dictatorship and Autocracy, 1957; The Soviet Bloc: Unity and Conflict, 1960; Ideology and Power in Soviet Politics, 1962; (ed. and contrib.) Africa and the Communist World, 1963; (co-author) Political Power: USA/USSR, 1964; Alternative to Partition: For A Broader Conception of America's Role in Europe, 1965; Dilemmi Internazionali in Un'Epoca Tecnetronica, 1969; (ed. and contrib.) Dilemmas of Change in Soviet Politics, 1969; Between Two Ages: America's Role in the Technetronic Era, 1970; The Fragile Blossom: Crisis and Change in Japan, 1972; Power and Principle: Memoirs of the National Security Adviser 1977–1981, 1983; Game Plan: How to Conduct the U.S.–Soviet Contest, 1986; Promise or Peril: The Strategic Defense Initiative, 1986; The Grand Failure: The Birth and Death of Communism in the 20th Century, 1989. Add: Center for Strategic and International Studies, 1800 K St. N.W., Washington, D.C. 20006, U.S.A.

BUBE, Richard H. American, b. 1927. Physics, Theology/Religion. Prof., since 1962, and Chmn. of Materials Science and Engineering, 1975–86, Stanford Univ., Calif. Ed., Journal of the American Scientific Affiliation, 1969–83; Assoc. Ed., Annual Review of Materials Science, 1969–83; Member, Ed. Bd., Solid-State Electronics, since 1975; Assoc. Ed., Materials Letters, since 1981. Sr. Research Staff, RCA Labs., Princeton, N.J., 1948–62. *Publs:* A Textbook of Christian Doctrine, 1955; Photoconductivity of Solids, 1960; The Encounter Between Christianity and Science, 1968; The Human Quest: A New Look at Science and Christian Faith, 1971; Electronic Properties of Crystalline Solids, 1974; Electrons in Solids, 1981; Fundamentals of Solar Cells, 1983; Science and the Whole Person, 1985. Add: Dept. of Materials Science and Engineering, Stanford Univ., Stanford, Calif. 94305, U.S.A.

BUCHAN, Tom. (Thomas Buchanan Buchan). British, b. 1931. Novels/Short stories, Poetry. Partner, Poni Press, Offshore Theatre Co., and Arts Projects, all Edinburgh. Teacher, Denny High Sch., Stirlingshire, 1953–56; Lectr. in English, Univ. of Madras, India, 1957–58; Warden, Community House, Glasgow, 1958–59; Teacher, Irvine Royal Academy, 1963–65; Sr. Lectr. in English and Drama, Clydebank Technical Coll., Glasgow, 1967–70. *Publs:* Ikons, 1958; Dolphins at Cochin, 1969; Makes You Feel Great (novel), 1971; Exorcism, 1972; Poems 1969–1972, 1972; Forwards, 1978. Add: Scoraig, Dundonnell, Wester Ross IV23 2RE, Scotland.

BUCHANAN, Colin (Ogilvie). British, 1934. Theology/Religion. Bishop Suffragan of Aston, since 1985. Member, Church of England Doctrinal Commn., since 1986. Asst. Curate, Cheadle Parish Church, Cheshire, 1961–64; Librarian, 1964–69, Registrar, 1969–74, Dir. of Studies, 1974–75, Vice Principal, 1975–78, and Principal, 1979–85, St. John's Coll., Bramcote, Notts. *Publs:* New Communion Service—Reasons for Dissent, 1966; A Guide to the New Communion Service, 1966; (ed.) Prospects for Reconciliation, 1967; (ed.) Modern Anglican Liturgies 1958–68, 1968; A Guide to Second Series Communion Service, 1968; (with P.S. Dawes) Proportional Representation in Church Elections, 1969, republished as Election by Preference, 1970; Evangelical Structures for the Seventies, 1969; (co-author) Growing into Union, 1970; (co-author) Growing into Union and Six Methodist Leaders, 1970; The Clarified Scheme Examined, 1971; (ed.) Evangelical Essays on Church and Sacraments, 1972; (ed.) Unity on the Ground, 1972; Baptismal Discipline, 1972; The Job Prospects of the Anglican Clergy, 1972; Patterns of Sunday Worship, 1972; Recent Liturgical Revision in the Church of England, 1973; A Case for Infant Baptism, 1973; (with J.D. Pawson) Infant Baptism under Cross-Examination, 1974; Supplement for 1973–74 to Recent Liturgical Revision in the Church of England, 1974; (ed.) Further Anglican Liturgies 1968–1975, 1975; Liturgy for Infant Baptism: Series 3, 1975; Supplement for 1974–76 to Recent Liturgical Revision in the Church of England, 1976; What Did Cranmer Think He Was Doing?, 1976; Inflation, Deployment and the Job Prospects of the Clergy, 1976; Encountering Charismatic Worship, 1977; The End of the Offertory, 1978; Supplement for 1976–78 to Recent Liturgical Revision in the Church of England, 1978; One Baptism Once, 1978; Liturgy for Initiation: The Series 3 Services, 1979; Liturgy for Communion: The Revised Series 3 Service, 1979; (compiler) The Development of the New Eucharistic Prayers of the Church of England, 1979; The Role and Calling of an Evangelical Theological College in the 1980's, 1980; (jt. ed.) Anglican Worship Today: Collins' Illustrated Guide to the Alternative Service Book 1980, 1980; Leading Worship, 1981; The Kiss of Peace, 1982; (jt. ed., Liturgy for the Sick: The New Church of England Services, 1983; (ed.) Eucharistic Liturgies of Edward VI, 1983; (ed.) Background Documents to Liturgical Revision 1547-1549, 1983; ACIC and Lima on Baptism and Eucharist, 1983; The Christian Conscience and Justice in Representation, 1983; Latest Liturgical Revision in the Church of England 1978–1984, 1984; Evangelical Anglicans and Liturgy, 1984; (ed.) Essays on Eucharistic Sacrifice in the Early Church, 1984; Adult Baptisms, 1985; Anglican Eucharistic Liturgy 1975–1985, 1985; (ed.) Latest Anglican Liturgies 1976–1984, 1985; (ed.) Liturgies of the Spanish and Portuguese Reformed Episcopal Churches, 1985; (ed.) Nurturing Children in Communion: Essays from the Boston Consultation, 1985; Anglican Confirmation, 1986; Policies for Infant Baptism, 1987; (ed.) Bishop Hugh—With Affection, 1987; Anglicans and Worship in Local Ecumenical Projects, 1987; (ed.) Modern Anglican Ordination Rites, 1987; (ed.) The Bishop in Liturgy, 1988; Lambeth and Liturgy 1988, 1989. Add: 60 Handsworth Wood Rd., Birmingham B20 2DT, England.

BUCHANAN, George (Henry Perrott). British, b. 1904. Novels/Short stories, Plays/Screenplays, Poetry, Social commentary/Phenomena, Autobiography/Memoirs/Personal. Member, Exec. Council, European Soc. of Culture, since 1954. Book Reviewer, Times Literary Supplement, London, 1928–40; Member, Editorial Staff, The Times, London, 1930–35; Columnist and Drama Critic, News Chronicle, London, 1935–38; Operations Officer, R.A.F. Coastal Command, 1940–45; Chmn., Town and Country Development Cttee., N. Ire., 1959–53. *Publs:* Passage Through the Present: Chiefly Notes from a Journal, 1932; Dance Night (play), 1934; London Story, 1935; Words for Tonight: A Notebook, 1936; Rose Forbes: The Biography of an Unknown Woman (part 1), 1937; Entanglement, 1938; The Soldier and the Girl, 1940; Rose Forbes (parts 1 and 2), 1950; A Place to Live, 1952; Bodily Responses (poetry), 1958; Green Seacoast (autobiography), 1959; A Trip to the Castle (play), 1960; Conversation with Strangers (poetry), 1961; Tresper Revolution (play), 1961; Morning Papers (autobiography), 1965; War Song (play), 1965; Annotations (poetry), 1970; Naked Reason, 1971; Minute-Book of a City, 1972; Inside Traffic, 1976; The Politics of Culture, 1977; Possible Being (poetry), 1980; Adjacent Columns (poetry), 1984. Add: c/o Carcanet Press, 208 Corn Exchange Bldgs., Manchester M4 3BQ, England.

BUCHANAN, James J. American, b. 1925. Classics. Prof. of Classical Languages, Tulane Univ., New Orleans, La., since 1964. Asst. Prof. of Classics, Princeton Univ., N.J., 1953–60; Dean of Arts and Sciences Coll., and Chmn., Dept. of Classics, Southern Methodist Univ., Dallas, Texas, 1960–64. *Publs:* (ed. and trans.) Boethius: The Consolation of Philosophy, 1957; Theorika: A Study of Monetary Distributions to the Athenian Citizenry during the Fifth and Fourth Centuries B.C., 1962; (trans. with Harold T. Davis) Zosimus: Historia Nova, 1967. Add: 1721 Joseph St., New Orleans, La. 70115, U.S.A.

BUCHANAN, James M. American, b. 1919. Economics, Philosophy, Politics/Government. Univ. Distinguished Prof. of Economics, George Mason Univ., since 1983. Prof., Univ. of Virginia, Charlottesville, 1958–68; Prof., Univ. of California, 1968–69; University Distinguished Prof. of Economics, Virginia Polytechnic Inst., Blacksburg, 1969–83. *Publs:* (with C.L. Allen and M.C. Colberg) Prices, Income, and Policy, 1954; Public Principles of Public Debt. 1958; The Public Finances, 1960, 5th ed. 1980; Fiscal Theory and Political Economy, 1960; (with G. Tullock) The Calculus of Consent, 1962; Public Finance in Democratic Process, 1967; Demand and Supply of Public Goods, 1968; (with N. Devletoglov) Academia in Anarchy, 1969; Cost and Choice, 1970; (ed. with R. Tollison) Theory of Public Choice, 1972, vol. II, 1984; (ed. with G.F. Thurlby) LSE Essays on Cost, 1973; The Limits of Liberty, 1975; (with R. Wagner) Democracy in Deficit, 1977; Freedom in Constitutional Contract, 1978; What Should Economists Do?, 1979; (with G. Brennan) The Power to Tax,1980; (with others) Toward a Theory of the Rent-Seeking Society, 1981; (with G. Brennan) The Power to Tax, 1985; (ed. with G. Brennan) The Reason of Rules, 1985; Liberty, Market and State, 1986; (ed. with

others) Deficits, 1987; Economics: Between Predictive State and Moral Philosophy, 1987. Add: George Mason Univ., Dept. of Economics, 4400 University Dr., Fairfax, Va., 22030.

BUCHANAN, (Eileen) Marie (Duell). Writes mystery novels as Rhona Petrie and Clare Curzon. British, b. 1922. Novels/Short stories, Mystery/Crime/Suspense. Worked as a teacher, probation officer, interpreter, translator, and social secretary; now full-time writer. *Publs:* mystery novels, as Rhona Petrie—Death in Deakins Wood, 1963; Murder by Precedent, 1964; Running Deep, 1964; Dead Loss, 1966; Foreign Bodies, 1967; MacLurg Goes West, 1968; Despatch of a Dove, 1969; Come Hell and High Water: Eleven Short Stories, 1970; Thorne in the Flesh, 1971; novels, as Marie Buchanan—Greenshards (in U.S. as Anima), 1972; An Unofficial Death, 1973; The Dark Backward, 1975; Morgana, 1977; The Countess of Sedgwick, 1980; crime detection novels as Clare Curzon—A Leaven of Malice, 1979; Special Occasion, 1981; I Give You Five Days, 1983; Masks and Faces, 1984; The Trojan Hearse, 1985; The Quest for K, 1986; Trail of Fire, 1987; Shot Bolt, 1988; Three-Core Lead, 1988; The Face in the Stone, 1989. Add: c/o David Grossman Literary Agency, 110-114 Clerkenwell Rd., London EC1M 5S, England.

BUCHANAN, Robert Angus. British, b. 1930. Archaeology/Antiquities, History. Reader in Social History, and Dir., Centre for the History of Technology, Science and Society, Univ. of Bath, since 1960. Ed., Annual Journal of the Bristol Industrial Archaeological Soc., 1968–74; Ed., Technology and Society, 1971–74. *Publs:* Technology and Social Progress, 1965; (with N. Cossons) Industrial Archaeology of the Bristol Region, 1969; (with N. Cossons) Industrial History in Pictures: Bristol, 1969; The Industrial Archaeology of Bath, 1969; Industrial Archaeology in Britain, 1972; (with George Watkins) Industrial Archaeology of the Stationary Steam Engine, 1976; History and Industrial Civilisation, 1979; (with C.A. Buchanan) Industrial Archaeology of Central Southern England, 1980; (with M. Williams) Brunel's Bristol, 1982. Add: Univ. of Bath, Claverton Down, Bath BA2 7AY, England.

BUCHDAHL, Gerd. British, b. 1914. Philosophy, Sciences (general). Reader in History and Philosophy of Science, Univ. of Cambridge, 1966–81, now Emeritus (Lectr., 1958–66). Sr. Consultant Ed., Studies in History and Philosophy of Science, since 1970. Asst. Design Engineer, Mouchel & Partners, London, 1938–40, and Moore & Co., Melbourne, 1941–47; Sr. Lectr. and Head of Dept. of History and Philosophy of Science, Melbourne Univ., 1947–57. *Publs:* The Image of Newton and Locke in the Age of Reason, 1961; Metaphysics and the Philosophy of Science, The Classical Origins; Descartes to Kant, 1969. Add: Dept. of History and Philosophy of Science, Univ. of Cambridge, Free Sch. Lane, Cambridge CB2 3RH, England.

BUCHEISTER, Patt. Also writes as Patt Parrish. American, b. 1942. Novels/Short stories, Historical/Romance. Writer and artist; editor of the newsletter Brushstrokes. *Publs:* (as Patt Parrish) Make the Angel Weep, 1979, published as His Fierce Angel, 1983; (as Patt Parrish) Summer of Silence, 1980, as A Gift to Cherish, 1985; (as Patt Parrish) Feather in the Wind, 1981; (as Patt Parrish) The Sheltered Haven, 1981; (as Patt Parrish) The Amberley Affair, 1983; (as Patt Parrish) Lifetime Affair, 1985; (as Patt Parrish) Escape the Past, 1985; Night and Day, 1986; The Dragon Slayer, 1987; Touch the Stars, 1987; Two Roads, 1988; The Luck o' the Irish, 1988; Flynn's Fate, 1988. Add: 901 Shady Hollow Lane, Virginia Beach, VA 23452, U.S.A.

BUCHER, Fran#ois. American, b. 1927. Architecture, Art. Prof., State Univ. of New York, Binghamton, since 1969. Dir., Soc. of Architectural Historians. Prof., Yale Univ., New Haven, Conn., 1954–60, Brown Univ., Providence, R.I., 1960–62, and Princeton Univ., N.J., 1962–69; Ed., Gesta, 1960–67; Pres., Intnl. Center of Medieval Art, 1966–71. *Publs:* Notre Dame de Bonmont and the Earliest Cistercian Monasteries of Switzerland, 1957; Josef Albers: Despite Straight Lines, 1961, 1977; The Pamplona Bibles, 2 vols., 1970; Architector, 2 vols., 1978. Add: Art and Art History, S.U.N.Y., Binghamton, N.Y. 13901, U.S.A.

BUCHWALD, Art. American, b. 1925. Humor/Satire. Journalist: syndicated Washington columnist, since 1962. Paris columnist, New York Herald Tribune, 1949–62. *Publs:* Paris After Dark, 1950; Art Buchwald's Paris, 1954; The Brave Coward, 1957; I Chose Caviar, 1957; More Caviar, 1958; A Gift from the Boys, 1958; Don't Forget to Write, 1960; Art Buchwald's Secret List to Paris, 1961; How Much Is That In Dollars, 1961; Is it Safe to Drink the Water, 1962; I Chose Capitol Punishment, 1963; And Then I Told the President, 1965; Son of the Great Society, 1966; Have I Ever Lied To You, 1968; The Establishment Is Alive and Well in Washington, 1969; Sheep on the Runway (play), 1970;

Getting High in Government Circles, 1971; I Never Danced at the White House, 1973; Irving's Delight, 1975; Washington Is Leaking, 1976; Down the Seine and Up the Potomac: 25 Years of Art Buchwald's Best Humor, 1977; The Buchwald Stops Here, 1978; (with Ann Buchwald) Seems Like Yesterday, 1980; While Reagan Slept, 1983; You *Can* Fool All of the People All The Time, 1985; I Think I Don't Remember, 1987. Add: 2000 Pennsylvania Ave. N.W., Washington, D.C. 20006, U.S.A.

BUCK, Harry M. American, b. 1921. Theology/Religion. Prof. of Religion Studies, Wilson Coll., Chambersburg, since 1959. Ed., ANIMA: An Experiential Journal. Asst. Prof. of Biblical History, Literature and Interpretation, Wellesley Coll., Mass., 1951–59; Exec. Dir., American Academy of Religion, 1958–72; Managing Ed., Journal of the American Academy of Religion, 1961–73. *Publs:* Johannine Lessons in the Greek Gospel Lectionary, 1958; People of the Lord: The History, Scripture and Faith of Ancient Israel, 1966; (ed. with Glenn Yocum) Structural Approaches to South India Studies, 1974; Spiritual Discipline in Hinduism, Buddhism, and the West, 1981; (ed. with Louis Hammann) Religious Traditions and the Limits of Tolerance, 1988. Add: 1053 Wilson Ave., Chambersburg, Pa. 17201, U.S.A.

BUCK, Margaret Waring. American, b. 1910. Children's non-fiction, Psychology. Freelance illustrator. *Publs:* Animals Through the Year, 1941; Country Boy, 1947; In Woods and Fields, 1950; In Yards and Gardens, 1952; In Ponds and Streams, 1955; Pets from the Pond, 1958; Small Pets from Woods and Fields, 1960; Along the Seashore, 1964; Where They Go in Winter, 1968; How They Grow, 1972; The Face—What It Means, 1979. Add: 38 Ocean View Ave., Mystic, Conn. 06355, U.S.A.

BUCKERIDGE, Anthony. British, b. 1912. Children's fiction, Plays/Screenplays. Has worked as a teacher, actor, and broadcaster. *Publs:* Draw the Line Somewhere (play), 1948; Jennings at School (radio series), 1948–74; Jennings series, 23 vols., 1950–77; A Funny Thing Happened!, 1953; Rex Milligan series, 4 vols., 1953–61; Rex Milligan (television series), 1954–55; (ed.) Stories for Boys 1 and 2, 1957; (ed.) In and Out of School: Stories, 1958; Jennings (television series), 1958; A Funny Thing Happened! (radio play), 1963; Happy Christmas, Jennings (play), 1969; Liz (radio play), 1974; Jennings Abounding (play), 1979; It Happened in Hamelin (musical), 1980; (with Corin Buckeridge) The Cardboard Conspiracy (musical), 1985. Add: East Crink, Barcombe Mills, Lewes, Sussex BN8 5BL, England.

BUCKINGHAM, Nancy. *See* **SAWYER,** John and **SAWYER,** Nancy.

BUCKLE, (Christopher) Richard (Sandford). British, b. 1916. Art, Dance/Ballet, Autobiography/Memoirs/Personal, Biography. Member, Advisory Council, Theatre Museum, London. Founder, Ballet mag., 1939; Ballet Critic, Observer newspaper, London, 1948–55, and The Sunday Times, London, 1959–75. *Publs:* John Innocent at Oxford (novel), 1939; The Adventures of a Ballet Critic, 1953; In Search of Diaghilev, 1955; Modern Ballet Design, 1955; The Prettiest Girl in England, 1958; Harewood (guidebook), 1959, 1966; (with L. Sokolova) Dancing for Diagilev: The Memoirs of Lydia Sokolova, 1960; Jacob Epstein: Sculptor, 1963; Monsters at Midnight: The French Romantic Movement as a Background to the Ballet Giselle, 1966; The Message: A Gothic Tale of the A1, 1969; Nijinsky, 1971; Nijinsky on Stage (commentary on drawings of Valentine Gross), 1971; (ed.) U and Non-U Revisited, 1978, Diaghilev, 1979; (ed.) Self-Portrait with Friends: Selected Diaries of Cecil Beaton, 1979; Buckle at the Ballet, 1980; The Most Upsetting Woman (autobiography), 1981; (with others) Designing for the Dancer, 1981; In the Wake of Diaghilev (autobiography), 1982. Add: Roman Rd., Gutch Common, Semley, Shaftesbury, Dorset, England.

BUCKLER, William Earl. American, b. 1924. Literature. Prof. of English, New York Univ., since 1961 (joined faculty 1953; Assoc. Dean, 1959–61, and Dean, 1961–70, Washington Square Coll.; Vice-Chancellor of the Univ., 1970–71). Instr., Univ. of Illinois, Urbana, 1950–53. *Publs:* Matthew Arnold's Books: Toward a Publishing Diary, 1958; Prose of the Victorian Period, 1958; Novels in the Making, 1961; The Major Victorian Poets: Tennyson, Browning, Arnold, 1973; The Victorian Imagination: Essays in Aesthetic Exploration, 1980; On the Poetry of Matthew Arnold, 1982; Matthew Arnold's Prose, 1983; The Poetry of Thomas Hardy, 1983; Man and His Myths: Tennyson's "Idylls of the King" in Critical Context, 1984; Poetry and Truth in Robert Browning's "The Ring and the Book", 1985; Walter Pater: Three Major Tests, 1986; Walter Pater: The Critic as Artist of Ideas, 1987. Add: Dept. of English, New York Univ., New York, N.Y. 10003, U.S.A.

BUCKLEY, Francis Joseph. American, b. 1928. Theology/Religion.

Prof. of Dogmatic and Pastoral Theology, Univ. of San Francisco, Calif., since 1972, and Chmn., Dept. of Theology, since 1988 (Instr., 1960–63; Asst. Prof., 1963–68; Chmn., Dept. of Theology, 1971–73, 1978–79; Chmn., Dept. of Religious Education and Pastoral Ministries, 1979–82). Pres., Coll. Theology Soc. of the U.S. and Canada, 1972–74. *Publs:* Christ and the Church according to Gregory of Elvira, 1964; (with Maria de la Cruz Aymes) On Our Way (series), 1966–70; (with Maria de la Cruz Aymes) New Life (series), 1971–74; (with Johannes Hofinger) The Good News and its Proclamation, 1968; (ed. with Cyr Miller) Faith and Life (series), 1971–72; Children and God: Communion, Confession, Confirmation, 1970, rev. ed. 1973; "I Confess"—The Sacrament of Penance Today, 1972; (with Maria de la Cruz Aymes) Jesus Forgives, 1974; (with Maria de la Cruz Aymes) Lord of Life (series), 1978–80; Reconciling, 1981; (with Maria de la Cruz Aymes) We Share Forgiveness, 1981; (with Maria de la Cruz Aymes) We Share Reconciliation, 1981; (with Maria de la Cruz Aymes and Thomas H. Groome) God with Us (series), 1982–85; (with Maria de la Cruz Aymes) Fe y Cultura, 1985; Come Worship with Us, 1987; (with Donald B. Sharp) Deepening Cristian Life: Integrating Faith and Maturity, 1987. Add: Univ. of San Francisco, San Francisco, Calif. 94117, U.S.A.

BUCKLEY, Ruth (Victoria). British, b. 1924. Engineering. Principal Lectr., Leeds Polytechnic, since 1972 (Sr. Lectr. in predecessor instn., Leeds Coll. of Technology, 1958–72), and Chmn. of the Control Engineering Faculty since 1978. Commercial/Control Engineer, Yorkshire Electricity Bd., 1949–56. *Publs:* A Guide to Advanced Electrical Engineering, 1964; Fundamentals of Servomechanisms, 1970; Control Engineering, 1976; Transmission Network and Circuits, 1979; Electromagnetic Fields, 1981. Add: Sch. of Electrical Engineering, The Polytechnic, Calverley St., Leeds, Yorks., England.

BUCKLEY, Thomas. American, b. 1932. History, Biography. Jay P. Walker Research Prof. of American History, Univ. of Tulsa, Okla., since 1981 (Chmn., Dept. of History, 1971–81). Member of faculty, Univ. of South Dakota, Vermillion, 1960–69, and Indiana Univ., Bloomington, 1969–71. *Publs:* The United States and the Washington Conference, 1921–1922, 1970; Challenge Was My Master, 1979; Walter H. Helmerich, Independent Oilman, 1980; (with Edwin Strong) American Foreign and National Security Policies 1914–1945, 1987. Add: Dept. of History, Univ. of Tulsa, 600 S. College Ave., Tulsa, Okla. 74104, U.S.A.

BUCKLEY, Vincent (Thomas). Australian, b. 1925. Poetry, Literature. Prof. of English, Univ. of Melbourne, since 1967 (Lockie Fellow, 1958–60; Reader, 1960–67). Former member of the Editorial Bd., Prospect mag. *Publs:* The World's Flesh, 1954; (ed.) The Incarnation in the University: Studies in the University Apostolate, 1955; Essays in Poetry, Mainly Australian, 1957; (ed.) Australian Poetry 1958, 1958; Poetry and Morality: Studies in the Criticism of Matthew Arnold, T.S. Eliot, and F.R. Leavis, 1959; Masters in Israel: Poems, 1961; Henry Handel Richardson, 1961; (ed.) The Campion Paintings, by Leonard French, 1962; (ed.) Eight by Eight, 1963; Arcady and Other Places: Poems, 1966; Poetry and the Sacred, 1968; Golden Builders and Other Poems, 1976; Late-Winter Child, 1979; The Pattern, 1979; Between Two Worlds: "Loss of Faith" and Late Nineteenth Century Australian Literature, 1979; Selected Poems, 1981. Add: Dept. of English, Univ. of Melbourne, Pankville, Vic. 3052, Australia.

BUCKLEY, William F(rank), Jr. American, b. 1925. Mystery/Crime/Suspense, Politics/Government, Essays. Founder and Ed., National Review, NYC, since 1955; Syndicated Columnist, On the Right, since 1962; Host, weekly TV show, Firing Line, since 1966. Member, USIA Advisory Commn., 1969–72; Public Member, U.S. Delegation to 28th U.N. Gen. Assembly, 1973. *Publs:* God and Man at Yale, 1951; (co-author) McCarthy and His Enemies, 1954; Up from Liberalism, 1959; The Committee and Its Critics, 1962; Rumbles Left and Right, 1963; The Unmaking of a Mayor, 1966; The Jeweler's Eye, 1968; The Governor Listeth, 1970; (ed.) Odyssey of Friend, 1970; Cruising Speed, 1971; Inveighing We Will Go, 1972; Four Reforms, 1973; The United Nations Journal, 1974; Execution Eve, 1975; Airborne, 1976; Saving the Queen (novel), 1976; Stained Glass (novel), 1978; A Hymnal, 1978; Who's On First (novel), 1980; Marco Polo, If You Can (novel), 1982; Atlantic High, 1982; Overdrive, 1983; The Story of Henri Tod (novel), 1984; Right Reason, 1985; See You Later, Alligator (novel), 1985; High Jinx (novel), 1986; Racing Through Paradise, 1987; Mongoose, R.P.I. (novel), 1988; On the Firing Line: The Public Life of Our Public Figures, 1989. Add: National Review, 150 East 35th St., New York, N.Y. 10016, U.S.A.

BUCKMAN, Peter (Michael Amiel). British, b. 1941. Novels, Plays,

History, Politics, Social commentary. Editorial Bd. Member, Penguin Books, 1962–64, and New American Library, 1964–65; European Ed., McGraw-Hill, 1966–67; Advisory Ed., Paris Review, 1966–70; London Ed., Ramparts mag., 1968–70. *Publs:* The Limits of Protest, 1970; Playground, 1971; (ed.) Education Without Schools, 1973; Lafayette, 1975; Let's Dance, 1978; The Rothschild Conversion, 1979; All for Love: A Study in Soap Opera, 1984. Add: c/o Peters Fraser and Dunlop, The Chambers, Chelsea Harbour, Lots Rd., London SW10 0XF, England.

BUCKNALL, Barbara Jane. British, b. 1933. Literature. Assoc. Prof., Dept. of French, Italian and Spanish, Brock Univ., since 1971 (Asst. Prof., 1969–71). Instr., 1962–66, and Asst. Prof., 1966–69, Dept. of French, Univ. of Illinois, Champaign-Urbana. *Publs:* The Religion of Art in Proust, 1969; Ursula K. Le Guin, 1981; (ed.) Critical Essays on Marcel Proust, 1987. Add: Dept. of Romance Languages, Brock Univ., St. Catharines, Ont. L2S 3A1, Canada.

BUDAY, George. Hungarian, b. 1907. Cultural/Ethnic topics, Dance/Ballet, Design, Mythology/Folklore. Lectr. in Graphic Arts, Royal Franz Josef Univ., Szeged, Hungary, 1935–41; Dir., Hungarian Cultural Inst., London, 1947 until resignation in 1949. *Publs:* (trans.) Hungarian Folk Tales, 1943–48; A Christmas Keepsake, 1945; The Hearth, 1947; The Sentiment: The Greeting Rhymes of Old Christmas Cards, 1949; Dances of Hungary, 1950; Old Charms and Spells, Superstitions and Other Credulities, 1950; The Story of the Christmas Card, 1951; The Language of Flowers, 1951; (ed.) Graven Adages or Proverbs Illustrated, 1952; Cries of London, Ancient and Modern, 1953; The History of the Christmas Card, 1954, 1964; (ed.) The Rules of Etiquette for Ladies and Gentlemen, 1954; (ed.) Proverbial Cats and Kittens with Curious Old and New Cuts, 1955; Artist's Recollections, 1970; Illustrating a Poetical Anthology: Multiple Portraiture, 1980. Add: P.O. Box 150, Coulsdon, Surrey CR3 1YE, England.

BUDBILL, David. American, b. 1940. Novels/Short Stories, Poetry, Plays. Full-time writer. *Publs:* Mannequins Demise (play), 1964; Barking Dog (verse), 1968; Christmas Tree Farm (for children), 1974; Snowshoe Trek to Otter River (for children), 1976; The Chain Saw Dance (verse), 1977; The Bones on Black Spruce Mountain (novel), 1978; Pulp Cutters Nativity (verse), 1981; From Down to the Village (verse), 1981. Add: c/o Countryman Press, Box 175, Woodstock, Vt. 05091, U.S.A.

BUDD, Lillian. American, b. 1897. Novels/Short stories, Children's fiction, History. *Publs:* April Snow, 1951; Land of Strangers, 1953; April Harvest, 1959; The Pie Wagon, 1960; The Bell of Kamela, 1960; Tekla's Easter, 1962; The People on Long Ago Street, 1964; One Heart, One Way, 1964; Calico Row, 1965; Larry, 1966; Full Moons, 1971; Footsteps on the Tall Grass Prairie: A History of Lombard, Illinois, 1976. Add: 2535 Orella St., Santa Barbara, Calif. 93105, U.S.A.

BUDD, Mavis. British. Autobiography/Memoirs/Personal. Freelance writer and painter. *Publs:* Dust to Dust, 1966; A Prospect of Love, 1968; Fit for a Duchess, 1970; So Beautiful, 1981; The Little Apple Honey Book, 2 vols., 1983–84; Weather Wisdom, 1986. Add: Mill Cottage, Hawkley, Liss, Hants GU33 6NU, England.

BUDDEE, Paul Edgar. Australian, b. 1913. Children's fiction, Poetry. Principal, Education Dept. of Western Australia (began teaching, 1932). Pres., Fellowship of Writers, W.A., 1947–49. *Publs:* Stand To and Other War Poems, 1943; Osca and Olga Trilogy, 1943–47; The Unwilling Adventurers, 1967; Mystery of Moma Island, 1969; Escape of the Fenians, 1971; The Escape of John O'Reilly, 1972; Air Patrol Series (4 books), 1973; Ann Rankin Series (4 books), 1973; Peter Devlin Series (4 books), 1973; Jim Meredith Series (4 books), 1974; Call of the Sky, 1978; Fate of the Artful Dodger, 1984. Add: 11 The Parapet, Burrendah-Willetton, W.A. 6155, Australia.

BUDGE, Ian. British, b. 1936. Politics/Government. Prof., Univ. of Essex, Colchester, since 1976 (on faculty since 1966). Asst. Lectr., Univ. of Edinburgh, 1962–64; Asst. Lectr., 1963–64, and Lectr., 1964–66, Univ. of Strathclyde, Glasgow. *Publs:* (with D.W. Urwin) Scottish Political Behaviour, 1966; Agreement and the Stability of Democracy, 1970; (with others) Political Stratification and the Functioning of Democracy, 1972; (with Cornelius O'Leary) Belfast: Approach to Crisis: A Study of Belfast Politics 1613-1970, 1973; (with D. Farlie) Party Identification and Beyond, 1976; Voting and Party Competition, 1977; Explaining and Predicting Elections, 1983; (with others) The New British Political System, 1983, 1986; Ideology, Strategy and Party Movement: Election Programmes in 19 Democracies, 1987. Add: 4 Oxford Rd., Colchester, Essex, England.

BUDRYS, Algis. Lithuanian, b. 1931. Science fiction/Fantasy. Pres., Unifont Co., Evanston, since 1974. Asst. Ed., Gnome Press, NYC, 1952, and Galaxy mag., NYC, 1953; on staff, Royal Publs., NYC, 1958–61; Ed.-in-Chief, Regency Books, Evanston, Ill., 1961–63; Editorial Dir., Playboy Press, Chicago, 1963–65; magazine manager, Woodall Publrs., 1973–74. *Publs:* False Night, 1953, as Some Will Not Die, 1961; Man of Earth, 1955; Who?, 1958; The Falling Torch, 1959; The Unexpected Dimension, 1960; Rogue Moon, 1960; The Furious Future, 1964; The Iron Thorn, 1968; Michaelmas, 1977; Blood and Burning, 1978; The Life Machine, 1979; Benchmarks: Galaxy Bookshelf, 1985. Add: 824 Seward St., Evanston, Ill. 60202, U.S.A.

BUECHE, Frederick J. American, b. 1923. Physics. Prof. of Physics, Univ. of Dayton, since 1962. Research Assoc., Cornell Univ., Ithaca, N.Y., 1949–52; Prof. of Physics, Univ. of Wyoming, Laramie, 1952–59, Univ. of Akron, 1959–62, and Middle East Technical Univ., Ankara, 1964–66. *Publs:* Physical Properties of Polymers, 1962; Principles of Physics, 1965, 5th ed. 1987; Introduction to Physics for Scientists and Engineers, 1969, 4th ed. 1986; Physical Science, 1972; Technical Physics, 1977, 1984; (ed.) Schaum's Outline on College Physics, 8th ed., 1988; Understanding the World of Physics, 1981. Add: 7323 W. Coldwater Rd., Flushing, Mich. 48433, U.S.A.

BUECHNER, (Carl) Frederick. American, b. 1926. Novels/Short stories, Theology/Religion, Autobiography/Memoirs/Personal. Clergyman, English Master, Lawrenceville Sch., N.J., 1948–53; Head of Employment Clinic, East Harlem Protestant Parish, NYC, 1954–58; Chmn. of Religion Dept., 1958–67, and Sch. Minister, Phillips Exeter Academy, Exeter, N.H. *Publs:* A Long Day's Dying, 1950; The Season's Difference, 1952; The Return of Ansel Gibbs, 1958; The Final Beast, 1965; The Magnificent Defeat (meditations), 1966; The Hungering Dark (meditations), 1969; The Entrance to Porlock, 1970; The Alphabet of Grace (autobiography), 1970; Lion Country, 1971; Open Heart, 1972; Wishful Thinking: A Theological ABC, 1973; Love Feast, 1974; The Faces of Jesus, 1974; Telling the Truth, 1977; Treasure Hunt, 1977; Peculiar Treasures: A Biblical Who's Who, 1979; The Book of Bebb, 1979; Godric, 1980; The Sacred Journey (autobiography), 1982; Now and Then (autobiography), 1983; A Room Called Remember (essays and sermons), 1984; Brendan, 1987; Whistling in the Dark, 1988. Add: Box 1160, Pawlet, Vt. 05761, U.S.A.

BUELER, William Merwin. American, b. 1934. History, International relations/Current affairs, Travel/Exploration/Adventure. Instr. of Chinese, Defense Language Inst., Monterey, Calif. *Publs:* Mountains of the World: A Handbook for Climbers and Hikers, 1970, 1978; U.S. China Policy and the Problem of Taiwan, 1971, 1980; (compiler-trans.) Chinese Sayings, 1972; Roof of the Rockies: A History of Mountaineering in Colorado, 1974, 1986; The Teton Controversy: Who Climbed the Grand?, 1980. Add: 648 Lottie St., Monterey, Calif. 93940, U.S.A.

BUELL, Frederick (Henderson). American, b. 1942. Poetry, Literature. Prof. of English, Queens Coll., Flushing, N.Y., since 1980 (Instr., 1971–72; Asst. Prof., 1972–74; Assoc. Prof., 1974–79). *Publs:* Theseus and Other Poems, 1971; W.H. Auden as a Social Poet, 1973; Full Summer, 1979. Add: Dept. of English, Queens Coll., Flushing, N.Y. 11367, U.S.A.

BUELL, Victor P. American, b. 1914. Administration/Management, Advertising/Public relations, Marketing. Prof. Emeritus of Marketing, Sch. of Management, Univ. of Massachusetts, Amherst, since 1983 (Prof., 1970–83). Marketing Consultant, McKinsey & Co., 1951–55; Mgr., Marketing Div., Hoover Co., 1955–59; Vice-Pres., and Dir. of Marketing, Archer Daniels Midland Co., 1959–64; Corporate Vice-Pres., Marketing, American Standard Inc., 1964–70. *Publs:* Marketing Management in Action, 1966; (co-ed.) Handbook of Modern Marketing, 1970, (ed.) 1986; Changing Patterns in Advertising Decision-making and Control, 1973; British Approach to Improving Advertising Standards and Practices, 1977; Organizing for Marketing/Advertising Success in a Changing Business Environment, 1982; Marketing Management: A Strategic Planning Approach, 1984; (co-author) Marketing Definitions: A Glossary of Marketing Terms, 1989. Add: 9 Bridle Path, Amherst, Mass. 01002, U.S.A.

BUESCHEL, Richard (Martin). American, b. 1926. Air/Space topics, Engineering/Technology, Recreation/Leisure/Hobbies. Affiliate, Zylke and Associates, Industrial Marketing Services. Historical Ed., The Coin Slot, since 1973. *Publs:* Japanese Fighters, 8 vols.; Japanese Bombers, 6 vols.; Communist Chinese Airpower, 1968; An Illustrated Price Guide to 100 Collectible Slot Machines, 5 vols., 1978–91; An Illustrated Price Guide to 100 Collectible Trade Stimulators, 3 vols., 1978–91; Pinball 1,

Illustrated Historical Guide to Pinball Machines 1775–1931, 1988; Arcade 1, Illustrated Historical Guide to Arcade Machines 1872–1989; Jennings Slot Machines, 1989; Slots 1, 10th Anniversary Ed., 1989; Juke Box 1, Illustrated Historical Guide to Automatic Phonographs 1889–1934, 1990; Electric Consoles, 1990; International Slot Machines, 1991. Add: 414 N. Prospect Manor, Mt. Prospect, Ill. 60056, U.S.A.

BUGENTAL, James F(rederick) T(homas). American, b. 1915. Psychology. Self-employed psychotherapist, since 1950. Member, Adjunct Faculty, Saybrook Inst., San Francisco; Lectr., Stanford Medical Sch., Calif. (Consultant, Stanford Research Inst., 1968–71). Asst. Prof. of Psychology, Univ. of California, Los Angeles, 1948–54; Partner, Psychological Service Assocs., Los Angeles, 1953–68. *Publs:* Psychological Interviewing, 1951, 3rd ed. 1966; The Search for Authenticity: An Existential Approach to Psychotherapy, 1965, 1988; (ed.) Challenges of Humanistic Psychology, 1967; The Human Possibility, 1971; The Search for Existential Identity: Patient–Therapist Dialogues in Existential–Humanistic Psychotherapy, 1976; Psychotherapy and Process: The Fundamentals of an Existential–Humanistic Approach, 1978; Talking: The Fundamentals of Humanistic Professional Communication, 1981; The Art of the Psychotherapist, 1987. Add: 866 Green Way, Santa Rosa, Calif. 95404, U.S.A.

BUITENHUIS, Peter M. Canadian, b. 1925. Literature. Prof., Dept. of English, Simon Fraser Univ., Burnaby, B.C., since 1975 (Chmn., 1975–81). Member of faculty, Yale Univ., New Haven, Conn., 1955–59, and Univ. of Toronto, 1959–66; Prof. of English, McGill Univ., Montreal, 1967–75. *Publs:* (ed.) French Writers and American Women: Essays by Henry James, 1960; Five American Moderns, 1965; (ed.) Selected Poems by E.J. Pratt, 1968; (ed.) Twentieth Century Interpretations of The Portrait of a Lady, 1968; Hugh MacLennan, 1969; The Grasping Imagination: The American Writings of Henry James, 1970; The Restless Analyst: Essays by Henry James, 1980; The Great War of Words: British, American and Canadian Fiction and Propaganda 1914–1933, 1987; (ed.) George Orwell: A Reassessment, 1988. Add: 7019 Marine Dr., W. Vancouver, B.C. V5A 1S6, Canada.

BUKOWSKI, Charles. American, b. 1920. Novels/Short stories, Poetry, Autobiography/Memoirs/Personal. Former Ed., Harlequin, Wheeler, Tex., later Los Angeles, Calif., and Laugh Literary, and Man the Humping Guns, both Los Angeles; Former Columnist, "Notes of a Dirty Old Man", Open City, Los Angeles, later Los Angeles Free Press. *Publs:* Flower, Fist and Bestial Wail, 1959; Longshot Poems for Broke Players, 1961; Run with the Hunted, 1962; Poems and Drawings, 1962; It Catches My Heart in Its Hand: New and Selected Poems, 1955–1963, 1963; Cold Dogs in the Courtyard, 1965; Crucifix in a Deathhand: New Poems, 1963–65, 1965; Confessions of a Man Insane Enough to Live with Beasts, 1965; The Genius of the Crowd, 1966; True Story, 1966; On Going Out to Get the Mail, 1966; To Kiss the Worms Goodnight, 1966; The Girls, 1966; The Flower Lover, 1966; All the Assholes in the World and Mine, 1966; 2 by Bukowski, 1967; The Curtains are Waving, 1967; At Terror Street and Agony Way, 1968; Notes of a Dirty Old Man, 1969; If We Take . . ., 1969; The Days Run Away Like Wild Horses over the Hills,1969; (with Philip Lamantia and Harold Norse) Penguin Modern Poets 13, 1969; Another Academy, 1970; Fire Station, 1970; Post Office (novel), 1971; Erections, Ejaculations, Exhibitions and General Tales of Ordinary Madness, 1972; Mockingbird Wish Me Luck, 1972; Me and Your Sometimes Love Poems, 1972; South of No North (short stories), 1973; While the Music Played, 1973; Life and Death in the Charity Ward (short stories), 1974; Factotum: A Novel, 1975; Burning in Water, Drowning in Flames: Poems, 1977; Love Is a Dog from Hell (poetry), 1977; Women (novel), 1978; You Kissed Lilly, 1978; Shakespeare Never Did This, 1979; Dangling in the Tournefortia, 1981; Ham on Rye, 1982; Play the Piano Drunk like a Percussion Instrument until the Fingers Begin to Bleed a Bit, 1982; The Most Beautiful Woman in Town, 1983; Bring Me Your Love, 1983; Hot Water Music, 1983; There's No Business, 1984; War All the Time: Poems 1981–84, 1984; You Get So Alone at Times That It Just Makes Sense, 1986; The Day It Snowed in L.A. (stories), 1987. Add: P.O. Box 132, San Pedro, Calif. 90731 U.S.A.

BULL, Angela (Mary). British, b. 1936. Children's fiction, Literature. Teacher, Casterton Sch., Kirkby Lonsdale, Westmorland, 1961–62; Asst., Medieval Manuscript Room, Bodleian Library, Oxford, 1962–63. *Publs:* The Friend with a Secret, 1965; (with Gillian Avery) Nineteenth Century Children: Heroes and Heroines in English Children's Stories, 1780-1900, 1965; Wayland's Keep, 1966; Child of Ebenezer, 1974; Treasure in the Fog, 1976; Griselda, 1977; The Doll in the Wall, 1978; The Machine Breakers, 1980; The Bicycle Parcel, 1980; The Accidental Twins, 1982;

Noel Streatfeild, 1984; Anne Frank, 1984; Florence Nightingale, 1985; Marie Curie, 1986; The Visitors, 1986; A Hat for Emily, 1986; Elizabeth Fry, 1987; A Wish at the Baby's Grave, 1988; Up the Attic Stairs, 1989. Add: The Vicarage, Hall Bank Dr., Bingley, W. Yorks., England.

BULL, Norman John. British, b. 1916. Education, Theology/Religion. Principal Lectr. and Head of Dept., St. Luke's Coll. of Education, Exeter, 1948–75. *Publs:* The Bible Story and Its Background, 8 vols., 1965–70; The Symbols Series, 4 vols., 1967; The Rise of the Church, 1967; Moral Judgement from Childhood to Adolescence, 1969; Moral Education, 1969; Way of Wisdom Series, 5 vols., 1970–76; Colours, 1973; Stories Jesus Told, 1973; Food and Drink, 1979; Light and Darkness, 1979; You and Me, 1979; Festivals and Customs, 1979; The Story of Jesus, 1980; 100 Bible Stories, 1980; My Little Book of Prayers, 1980; One Hundred New Testament Stories, 1981; (with R.J. Ferris) Stories from World Religions series, 4 vols., 1982–83. Add: 21 Wonford Rd., Exeter, Devon EX2 4LH, England.

BULLA, Clyde Robert. American. b. 1914. Novels/Short stories, Children's fiction, Translations. Farmer until 1943; Linotype Operator and Columnist, Tri-County News, King City, Mo., 1943–49. *Publs:* These Bright Young Dreams, 1941; The Donkey Cart, 1946; Riding the Pony Express, 1948; The Secret Valley, 1949; Surprise for a Cowboy, 1950; A Ranch for Danny, 1951; Johnny Hong of Chinatown, 1952; Song of St. Francis, 1952; Star of Wild Horse Canyon, 1953; Eagle Feather, 1953; Squanto, Friend of the White Men, 1954, as Squanto, Friend of the Pilgrims, 1969; Down the Mississippi, 1954; White Sails to China, 1955; A Dog Named Penny (reader), 1955; John Billington, Friend of Squanto, 1956; The Sword in the Tree, 1956; Old Charlie, 1957; Ghost Town Treasure, 1957; Pirate's Promise, 1958; The Valentine Cat, 1959; Stories of Favorite Operas, 1959; A Tree Is a Plant, 1960; Three-Dollar Mule, 1960; The Sugar Pear Tree, 1961; Benito, 1961; What Makes a Shadow?, 1962; The Ring and the Fire: Stories from Wagner's Niebelung Operas, 1962; Viking Adventure, 1963; Indian Hill, 1963; St. Valentine's Day, 1965; More Stories of Favorite Operas, 1965; Lincoln's Birthday, 1966; White Bird, 1966; Washington's Birthday, 1967; Flowerpot Gardens, 1967; Stories of Gilbert and Sullivan Operas, 1968; The Ghost of Windy Hill, 1968; Mika's Apple Tree; A Story of Finland, 1968; The Moon Singer, 1969; New Boy in Dublin: A Story of Ireland, 1969; Jonah and the Great Fish, 1970; Joseph the Dreamer, 1971; Pocahontas and the Strangers, 1971; (trans.) Noah and the Rainbow, by Max Bollinger, 1972; Open the Door and See All the People, 1972; Dexter, 1973; The Wish at the Top, 1974; Shoeshine Girl, 1975; Marco Moonlight, 1976; The Beast of Lor, 1977; (with Michael Syson) Conquista!, 1978; Last Look, 1979; The Stubborn Old Woman, 1980; My Friend the Monster, 1980; Daniel's Duck, 1980; A Lion to Guard Us, 1981; Almost a Hero, 1981; Dandelion Hill, 1982; Poor Boy, Rich Boy, 1982; Charlie's House, 1983; The Cardboard Crown, 1984; A Grain of Wheat, 1985; The Chalk Box Kid, 1987; Singing Sam, 1989. Add: 1230 Las Flores Dr., Los Angeles, Calif. 90041, U.S.A.

BULLARD, Helen. American, b. 1902. Crafts, History. Founder, 1963, and Pres., 1963–67, 1969–71, National Inst. of American Doll Artists; Vice-Pres., United Fedn. of Doll Clubs, 1967–69. *Publs:* (ghost writer) Doctor Woman of the Cumberlands, 1953; (with J. Krechniak) Cumberland County's First Hundred Years, 1956; The American Doll Artist, vol. I, 1965, vol. II, 1975; Dorothy Heizer: The Artist and Her Dolls, 1972; Craftsmen of the Tennessee Mountains, 1976; My People in Wood, 1982, 1985; Faith Wrick: The Artist and Her Dolls, 1985; Faith Wrick: Doll Maker Extraordinaire, 1986. Add: P.O. Box 545, Pleasant Hill, Tenn. 38578, U.S.A.

BULLEN BEAR. *See* **DONNELLY**, Austin S.

BULLER, Herman. Canadian, b. 1927. Novels/Short stories, Plays/Screenplays. Teacher, Toronto Bd. of Education. *Publs:* One Man Alone, 1968; Quebec in Revolt, 1970; Days of Rage, 1974; Tania: The Liberation of Patty Hearst (play), 1974; Barricades, 1974–75. Add: 9 Kingsbridge Ct., Suite 401, Willowdale, Ont., Canada.

BULLINS, Ed. American, b. 1935. Novels/Short stories, Plays/Screenplays. Producing Dir., The Surviving Theatre, NYC, since 1974, English Writing Instr., Elmcor Youth Rehabilitation Agency, Queens, N.Y., since 1973. Resident Playwright and Assoc. Dir., The New Lafayette Theatre, Harlem, NYC, 1968–73. *Publs:* Five Plays by Ed Bullins, 1968; (ed.) New Plays from the Black Theatre, 1969; The Duplex, 1971; The Hungered One (short stories), 1971; Four Dynamite Plays, 1972; The Theme Is Blackness, 1973; The Reluctant Rapist (novel), 1973; (ed.) The New Lafayette Theatre Presents, 1974. Add: 932 East 212th

St., Bronx, N.Y. 10469, U.S.A.

BULLOCK, Lord; Alan (Louis Charles) Bullock. British, b. 1914. History, Biography. Hon. Fellow, Wadham Coll., Merton Coll., and Linacre Coll., Oxford; Ed. (with F. Deakin), Oxford History of Modern Europe (Vice-Chancellor, Oxford Univ., 1969–73). Member, Advisory Council on Public Records; Chmn., Research Cttee., Royal Inst. of Intnl.ffairs, and Bd. of Intnl. Assn. for Cultural Freedom; Trustee and Fellow, Aspen Inst. of Humanities Studies. Founding Master of St. Catherine's Coll., Oxford, 1960–80. Member, Arts Council of Great Britain, 1961–64; Chmn., National Advisory Council on Training and Supply of Teachers, 1963–65; Member, Social Science Research Council, 1966; Chmn., The Schools Council, 1966–69; Member, Cttee. of Vice-Chancellors and Principals, 1969–73; Chmn., Cttee. on Reading and Other Uses of the English Language, 1972–74; Chmn. of the Trustees, Tate Gallery, London, 1973–80; Chmn., Cttee. of Enquiry on Industrial Democracy, 1976; Dir., The Observer newspaper, London, 1977–81. *Publs:* Hitler: A Study in Tyranny, 1952, 1964; (with M. Shock) The Liberal Tradition, 1956; The Life and Times of Ernest Bevin, 3 vols., 1967–83; Hitler and the Origins of the Second World War, 1967; (ed.) The Twentieth Century, 1971 (ed. with O. Stallybrass) The Fontana Dictionary of Modern Thought, 1977; (ed. with R.B. Woodings) The Fontana Dictionary of Modern Thinkers, 1983. Add: St. Catherine's Coll., Oxford, England.

BULLOCK, Michael (Hale). Has also written as Michael Hale. British/Canadian, b. 1918. Novels/Short stories, Plays, Poetry, Translations. Prof. Emeritus of Creative Writing, Univ. of British Columbia, Vancouver, since 1983 (Prof., 1969–83). Chmn., Translators Assn., London, 1964–67. *Publs:* (as Michael Hale) Transmutations, 1938; Sunday is a Day of Incest: Poems, 1961; (trans. with Jerome Ch'en) Poems of Solitude, 1961; (trans.) The Tales of Hoffmann, 1962; World Without Beginning, Amen!, 1963; Zwei Stimmen in Meinem Mund, 1967; A Savage Darkness, 1969; Sixteen Stories as They Happened, 1960; (trans.) The Stage and Creative Arts, 1969; (trans.) Foreign Bodies, by Karl Krolow, 1969; (trans.) Invisible Hands, by Karl Krolow, 1969; Green Beginning Black Ending (short stories), 1971; Not to Hong Kong (play), 1972; The Island Abode of Bliss (play), 1973; Randolph Cranstone and the Pursuing River (short stories), 1975; Randolph Cranstone and the Glass Thimble (novel), 1977; Black Wings White Dead (poetry), 1978; (trans.) Stories for Late Night Drinkers, by Michel Tremblay, 1978; Lines in the Dark Wood (poetry), 1981; Quadriga for Judy (poetry), 1982; Prisoner of the Rain (poetry), 1983; The Man with Flowers Through His Hands (fables), 1985; The Double Ego: An Autocollage (novella), 1985; Randolph Cranstone and the Veil of Maya (novel), 1986; The Story of Noire (novel), 1987; Poems on Green Paper (poetry), 1988; (trans.) The Persian Mirror by Thomas Pavel, 1988; Vancouver Moods (poetry), 1989; Randolph Cranstone Takes the Inward Path (novel), 1989. Add: 3836 West 18th Ave., Vancouver, B.C. V6S 1B5, Canada.

BULLOUGH, Vern L. American, b. 1928. Medicine/Health, Sex, Women. Prof. of History, California State Univ., Northridge, 1959–84; Dean of the Faculty of Natural and Social Sciences, State University of New York College at Buffalo, since 1980, and SUNY Distinguished Prof., since 1987. *Publs:* (with B. Bullough) Emergence of Modern Nursing, 1964, 1969; History of Prostitution, 1964; (ed. with B. Bullough) Issues in Nursing, 1966; Development of Medicine as a Profession, 1966; Man in Western Civilization, 1970; (ed.) The Scientific Revolution, 1971; (ed. with B. Bullough) New Directions in Nursing, 1971; (with B. Bullough) Poverty, Ethnic Identity and Health Care, 1972; The Subordinate Sex: A History of Attitudes Towards Women, 1973; (with R. and F. Naroll) Military Deference in History, 1974; Sex, History, and Society, 1976; Sexual Variance in Society and History, 1976, 1981; (with others) An Annotated Bibliography of Homosexuality, 1976; (with B. Bullough and B. Elcano) A Bibliography of Prostitution, 1977; (with B. Bullough) Sin, Sickness, and Sanity, 1977; (with B. Bullough) Prostitution, 1977; (with B. Bullough) Expanding Horizons in Nursing, 1977; (with B. Bullough) The Care of the Sick, 1978; Homosexuality: A History, 1979; (ed.) The Frontiers of Sex Research, 1979; (with B. Elcano and B. Bullough) A Bibliography of the History of Nursing, 1980; (with J. Brundage) Sexual Practices and the Medieval Catholic Church, 1982; (with B. Bullough) Health Care for the Other Americans, 1982; (with B. Bullough and M.C. Soukup) Nursing Issues and Strategies for the Eighties, 1983; (with B. Bullough) History, Trends and Politics of Nursing, 1984; (with B. Bullough, J. Garvey and K. Allen) Issues in Nursing, 1985; (with B. Bullough) Women and Prostitution, 1987; (with O. Church and A. Stein) American Nursing: A Biographical Dictionary, 1988; (with B. Shelton and S. Slavin) The Subordinated Sex, 1988. Add: 590 LeBrun Rd., Amherst, N.Y. 14226, U.S.A.

BULLUS, (Sir) Eric E(dward). British, b. 1906. History, Sports. Journalist, Yorkshire Post, Leeds and London, 1923–46; Conservative M.P. (U.K.) for Wembley North, 1950–74; Parliamentary Private Secty. to the Secty. for Overseas Trade, 1953–56, to the Minister of Aviation, 1960–62, and to the Secty. of State for Defence, 1962–64. *Publs:* History of Parish of Meanwood; History of Leeds Modern School, 1931; History of the Church in Delhi, 1944; History of Lords and Commons Cricket, 1959. Add: Westway, Herne Bay, Kent, England.

BULMER, (Henry) Kenneth. Also writes as Alan Burt Akers, Ken Blake, Ernest Corley, Arthur Frazier, Adam Hardy, Bruno Krauss, Neil Langholm, Charles R. Pike, Dray Prescott, Andrew Quiller, and Richard Silver. British. Novels/Short stories, Science fiction/Fantasy. Ed., New Writing in Science Fiction, London, since 1972. Former Ed., Sword and Sorcery mag., Newcastle. *Publs:* as Henry Kenneth Bulmer—(with A.V. Clarke) Space Treason, 1952; (with A.V. Clarke) Cybernetic Controller, 1952; Encounter in Space, 1952; Space Salvage, 1953; The Stars Are Ours, 1952; Galactic Intrigue, 1953; Empire of Chaos, 1953; World Aflame, 1954; Challenge, 1954; City under the Sea, 1957; The Secret of ZI (in U.K. as The Patient Dark), 1958; The Changeling Worlds, 1959; (with J. Newman) The True Book about Space Travel, 1960, 1965; The Earth Gods Are Coming (in U.K. as Of Earth Foretold), 1960; No Man's World (in U.K. as Earth's Long Shadow), 1961; Beyond the Silver Sky, 1961; New Writings in SF No. 26, (29), 1975; The Diamond Contessa, 1983; as Alan Burt Akers—The Dray Prescot Saga 1972–83; New Writings in SF No. 30, 1978; Allies of Antares, 1981; Mazes of Scorpio, 1982; Delia of Vallia, 1982; Fires of Scorpio, 1983; Talons of Scorpio, 1983; Masks of Scorpio, 1984; Seg the Bowman, 1984; Werewolves of Kregen, 1985; Witch of Kregen, 1985; as Ken Blake—Where the Jungle Ends, 1978; Long Shot, 1978; Stake-Out, 1978; Hunter Hunted, 1978; Blind Run, 1979; Fall Girl, 1979; Dead Reckoning, 1980; No Stone, 1981; Spy Probe, 1981; Foxhole, 1981; as Ernest Corley—White-Out, 1960, 1969; The Fatal Fire, 1962; Wind of Liberty, 1962; Defiance, 1963; The Wizard of Starship, 1963; The Million Year Hunt, 1964; Demon's World (in U.K. as The Demons), 1964; Land Beyond the Map, 1965; Behold the Stars, 1965; Worlds for the Taking, 1966; To Outrun Doomsday, 1967; The Key to Irunium, 1967; The Key to Venudine, 1968; The Doomsday Men, 1968; Cycle of Nemesis, 1968; The Star Venturers, 1969; The Wizards of Senchuria, 1969; Kandar, 1969; The Ships of Durostorum, 1970; Blazon (in U.K. as Quench the Burning Stars), 1970; The Ulcer Culture, 1970; Star Trove, 1970; Swords of the Barbarians, 1970; The Hunters of Jundagai, 1971; The Chariots of Ra, 1971; On the Symb Socket Circuit, 1972; Pretenders, 1972; Roller Coaster World, 1972; as Arthur Frazier—Wolfshead series, 6 vols., 1973–75; (ed.) New Writings in SF No. 22, (24, 25) 3 vols., 1973–74; as Adam Hardy—Fox series, 14 vols., 1972–77; New Writings in SF No. 28, 1976; Strike Force Falklands, 6 vols., 1984–85; as Bruno Krauss—Shark series, 8 vols., 1978–82; as Neil Langholm—The Dark Return, 1975; Trail of Blood, 1976; as Andrew Quiller—The Land of Mist, 1976; Sea of Swords, 1977; New Writings in SF No. 29, 1976; as Richard Silver—Captain Shark: By Pirate's Blood, 1975; Captain Shark: Jaws of Dark, 1976; as Charles R. Pike—Brand of Vengeance, 1978; as Dray Prescott—Warlord of Antares, 1988. Add: 5/20 Frant Rd., Tunbridge Wells, Kent, England.

BULMER-THOMAS, Ivor. Also writes as Ivor Thomas. British, b. 1905. Mathematics/Statistics, Politics/Government, Theology/Religion. Hon. Dir., Friends of Friendless Churches, since 1957; Secty. Chmn., Ancient Monuments Soc., since 1958. Labour M.P. (U.K.) for Keighley, 1942–48, and Conservative M.P. for Keighley, 1948–50: Parliamentary Secty., Ministry of Civil Aviation, 1945–46; Parliamentary Under-Secty. of State, Colonial Office, 1946–47. Chmn., Redundant Churches Fund, 1969–76. *Publs:* Coal in the New Era, 1934; Gladstone of Hawarden, 1936; Top Sawyer: A Biography of David Davies of Llandinam, 1938; (ed. and trans.) Selections Illustrating the History of Greek Mathematics; The Party System in Great Britain, 1953; The Growth of the British Party System, 1965; (ed.) St. Paul: Teacher and Traveller, 1976; Dilysia: A Threnody, 1987. Add: 12 Edwardes Sq., London W8 8HG, England.

BULPIN, Thomas Victor. South African, b. 1918. History, Travel/Exploration/Adventure, Biography. Writer and Publr., Books of Africa (Pty.) Ltd., and T.V. Bulpin Ltd., Cape Town, since 1946. *Publs:* Lost Trails on the Low Veld, 1950; Shaka's Country, 1952; To the Shores of Natal, 1953; The Golden Republic, 1953; The Ivory Trail, 1954; Storm Over the Transvaal, 1955; Lost Trails of the Transvaal, 1956; Islands in a Forgotten Sea, 1958; Trail of the Copper King, 1959; The White Whirlwind, 1961; The Hunter is Death, 1962; To the Banks of the Zambezi, 1965; Natal and the Zulu Country, 1966; Low Veld Trails, 1968; The Great Trek, 1969; Discovering Southern Africa, 1970; Treasury of Travel Series, 1973–74; Southern Africa Land of Beauty and Splendour,

1976; Illustrated Guide to Southern Africa, 1978; Scenic Wonders of Southern Africa, 1985. Add: P.O. Box 1516, Cape Town, South Africa.

BUMSTED, J(ohn) M(ichael). Canadian, b. 1938. History. Fellow of St. John's Coll., and Prof. of History, Univ. of Manitoba, Winnipeg, since 1980. Instr., Tufts Univ., Medford, Mass., 1965–67; Asst. Prof., McMaster Univ., Hamilton, Ont., 1967–69; Assoc. Prof., 1969–75, and Prof. of History, 1975–80, Simon Fraser Univ., Burnaby, B.C. *Publs:* (ed.) Documentary Problems in Canadian History, 2 vols., 1969; (ed.) The Great Awakening in Colonial America: The Beginnings of Evangelical Pietism, 1970; Henry Alline 1748-1784, 1971; (ed.) Canada before Confederation: Readings and Interpretations, 1972, 1979; (with J. Van de Wetering) "What Must I Do to be Saved?": The Great Awakening in Colonial America, 1976; The People's Clearance, 1982; (ed. with R. Fisher) The Journal of Alexander Walker, 1982; (ed.) The Collected Writings of Lord Selkirk 1799-1809, 1984; (ed.) Interpreting Canada's Past, 2 vols., 1986; Understanding the Loyalists, 1986; Land, Settlement and Politics in 18th Century Prince Edward Island, 1987; The Collected Writings of Lord Selkirk 1810–1820, 1988. Add: Dept. of History, Univ. of Manitoba, Winnipeg, Man. R3T 2N2, Canada.

BUNCH, David R(oosevelt). American. Science fiction/Fantasy. Cartographer, Air Force Aeronautical Chart and Information Center, St. Louis, 1954–73. *Publs:* Moderan, 1971; We Have a Nervous Job (poetry), 1983. Add: P.O. Box 12233, Soulard Station, St. Louis, Mo. 63517, U.S.A.

BUNGEY, John Henry. British, b. 1944. Engineering. Sr. Lectr. in Civil Engineering, Univ. of Liverpool, since 1981 (Lectr., 1971–81). Asst. (under agreement), Scott, Wilson, Kirkpatrick and Partners, London, 1966–68; Asst. Engineer, North West Rd. Construction Unit, Cheshire Sub-Unit, 1969–71. *Publs:* (with W.H. Mosley) Reinforced Concrete Design, 1976, 3rd ed. 1987; The Testing of Concrete in Structures, 1982, 1989. Add: Dept. of Civil Engineering, Univ. of Liverpool, P.O. Box 147, Brownlow St., Liverpool L69 3BX, England.

BUNTING, A.E. *See* **BUNTING,** Eve.

BUNTING, (Anne) Eve(lyn, née Bolton). Also writes as Evelyn Bolton and A.E. Bunting. American (born Irish), b. 1928. Children's Fiction. Freelance writer. *Publs:* children's fiction, as Eve Bunting—A Gift for Lonny, 1973; Box, Fox, Ox, and the Peacock, 1974; The Wild One, 1974; We Need a Bigger Zoo, 1974; The Once-a-Year Day, 1974; Barney the Beard, 1975; The Dinosaur Machines, 4 vols., 1975; No Such Things . . .?, 4 vols., 1976; Josefina Finds the Prince, 1976; Blacksmith at Blueridge, 1976; Skateboard Saturday, 1976; One More Flight, 1976; Skateboard Four, 1976; Winter's Coming, 1977; The Big Cheese, 1977; Cop Camp, 1977; Ghost of Summer, 1977; Creative Science Fiction, 8 vols., 1978; Creative Romance, 10 vols., 1978; The Big Find, 1978; Magic and the Night River, 1978; Going Against Cool Calvin, 1978; The Haunting of Kildoran Abbey, 1978; The Big Red Barn, 1979; The Cloverdale Switch, 1979; Yesterday's Island, 1979; Mr. Pride's Umbrella, 1980; The Robot Birthday, 1980; Demetrius and the Golden Goblet, 1980; Terrible Things, 1980; St. Patrick's Day in the Morning, 1980; Blackbird Singing, 1980; The Empty Window, 1980; The Skate Patrol, The Skate Patrol Rides Again, and the Skate Patrol and the Mystery Writer, 3 vols., 1980–82; Goose Dinner, 1981; The Waiting Game, 1981; The Spook Birds, 1981; The Happy Funeral, 1982; The Ghosts of Departure Point, 1982; The Travelling Men of Ballycoo, 1983; The Valentine Bears, 1983; Someone Is Hiding on Alcatraz Island, 1984; Mohammed's Monkey, 1984; Jane Martin, Dog Detective, 1984; Sixth Grade Sleepover, 1986; Scary, Scary, Halloween, 1986; children's fiction as Evelyn Bolton—Stable of Fear, 1974; Lady's Girl, 1974; Goodbye, Charlie, 1974; Ride When You're Ready, 1974; The Wild Horses, 1974; Dream Dancer, 1974; children's fiction as A.E. Bunting—Pitcher to Center Field, 1974; Surfing Country, 1974; High Tide for Labrador, 1975; Springboard to Summer, 1975; other children's books, as Eve Bunting—The Two Giants (Irish folktale), 1972; Say It Fast (tongue twisters), 1974; Skateboards: How to Make Them, How to Ride Them, 1977; The Sea World Book of Sharks, 1979; The Sea World Book of Whales, 1980; The Giant Squid, 1981; Ghost's Hour, Spook's Hour, 1987; Happy Birthday, Dean Duck, 1988; How Many Days to America, 1988; Is Anybody There, 1988; A Sudden Silence, 1988; The Wednesday Surprise, 1989. Add: 1512 Rose Villa St., Pasadena, Calif. 91106, U.S.A.

BURACK, Elmer H(oward). American, b. 1927. Administration/Management. Consultant, Booz, Allen and Hamilton, 1959–60; Lectr., 1960–64, Assoc. Prof., 1964–66, and Prof. of Management, 1966–77, Illinois Inst. of Technology, Chicago. Chmn., Personnel and Human

Resource Div., 1975, and Health Care Div., 1977, National Academy of Mgmt.; Prof. and Head of the Dept. of Management, Univ. of Illinois at Chicago Circle, 1977–82. Member of the Bd., Personnel Accreditation Inst., 1975–87; Assoc. Chmn., Illinois Governor's Advisory Council on Employment/Training, 1978–86. *Publs:* Strategies for Manpower Planning and Programming, 1972; (co-author) Human Resource Planning: Technology, Policy, Change, 1973; Organization Design, 1973; Organizational Analysis, 1975; Personnel Management, 1977; The Manager's Guide to Change, 1979; Human Resource Planning, 1980, 1987; Career Management in Organizations, 1980; Growing: Women's Career Guide, 1980; Personnel Management, 1982; Introduction to Management, 1983; Creative Human Resource Planning, 1988. Add: Coll. of Business, Univ. of Illinois, Box 4348, Chicago, Ill. 60680, U.S.A.

BURANELLI, Vincent. American, b. 1919. History, Literature, Biography. Freelance writer and ed., since 1968. Staff Writer, Lowell Thomas Newscasting, 1952–64, and American Heritage, NYC, 1966–67; Sr. Ed., Silver Burdett Co., Morristown, N.J. 1967–68; Book Reviewer, New York Historical Soc. 1967; Feature Writer, National Star and National Enquirer, 1974–75. *Publs:* (ed.) The Trial of Peter Zenger, 1957; Edgar Allan Poe, 1961, 1977; The King and the Quaker: A Study of William Penn and James II, 1962; Josiah Royce, 1964; Louis XIV, 1966; (contrib. ed.) Encyclopedia of World Drama, 1972; The Wizard from Vienna: Franz Anton Mesmer, 1975; Gold: An Illustrated History, 1979; (with N. Buranelli) Spy/Counterspy: An Encyclopedia of Espionage, 1982; (with Murray Wolfson) In Long Run We Are All Dead: A Macroeconomics Murder Mystery, 1984, 1989; Thomas Edison, 1989. Add: 217 W. Eden St., Edenton, N.C. 27932, U.S.A.

BURCH, Robert. American, b. 1925. Children's fiction. *Publs:* The Traveling Bird, 1959; (trans.) A Jungle in the Wheat Field, 1960; A Funny Place to Live, 1962; Tyler, Wilkin and Skee, 1963; Skinny, 1964; D.J.'s Worst Enemy, 1965; Queenie Peavy, 1966; Renfroe's Christmas; Joey's Cat; Simon and the Game of Chance; Doodle and the Go-Cart; The Hunting Trip, Hut School and the War-time Home-Front Heroes; The Jolly Witch; Two that Were Tough; The Whitman Kick; Wilkin's Ghost, 1978; Ida Early Comes over the Mountain, 1980; Christmas with Ida Early, 1983; King Kong and Other Poets, 1986. Add: 2021 Forest Dr., Fayetteville, Ga., 30214, U.S.A.

BURCHAM, William Ernest. British, b. 1913. Physics. Fellow, Selwyn Coll., Cambridge, 1944–51; Univ. Lectr., Cambridge Univ., 1945–51; Prof. of Physics, Univ. of Birmingham, 1951–80, now Emeritus. *Publs:* Nuclear Physics: An Introduction, 1963, 1973; Elements of Nuclear Physics, 1979. Add: 95 Witherford Way, Birmingham B29 4AN, England.

BURCHARDT, Bill. (William Robert Burchardt). American, b. 1917. Westerns/Adventure, Travel/Exploration/Adventure. Adjunct Prof. of History, Univ. of Oklahoma, Norman, since 1982. High sch. music dir., Seminole and Oklahoma City Schs., 1938–42; former music and journalism teacher, Grove and Duncan High Schs., Okla. and Northern Oklahoma Jr. Coll., Tonkawa; Assoc. Ed., 1957–60, and Ed., 1960–80, Oklahoma Today, Oklahoma City. Writer-in-Residence, Central State Univ., 1955–60, 1972–75. Pres., Western Writers of America, 1960. *Publs:* The Wildcatters, 1963; Yankee Longstraw, 1965; Shotgun Bottom, 1966; The Birth of Logan Station, 1974; The Mexican, 1977; Oklahoma (non-fiction), 1979; Buck, 1978; Medicine Man, 1980; The Lighthorsemen, 1981; Black Marshal, 1981. Add:127 East Shore Dr., Lake Hinassee, Arcadia, Okla. 73007, U.S.A.

BURCHELL, R(obert) A(rthur). British, b. 1941. History. Sr. Lectr. in American History and Institutions, Univ. of Manchester, since 1980 (Asst. Lectr., 1965–68; Lectr., 1968–80). Secty., British Assn. for American Studies, since 1984; Member, Editorial Bd., Journal of American Studies, since 1979; Secty., European Assn. for American Studies, since 1988. *Publs:* Westward Expansion, 1974; The San Francisco Irish 1848-80, 1980. Add: Dept. of American Studies, The University, Manchester M13 9PL, England.

BURCHFIELD, Robert William. New Zealander, b. 1923. Language. Sr. Research Fellow, St. Peter's Coll., Oxford (Lectr., 1955–63; Tutorial Fellow, 1963–79). Jr. Lectr., Magdalen Coll., Oxford, 1952–53; Lectr. in English Language, Christ Church, Oxford, 1953–57; Chief Ed., The Oxford English Dictionaries, Oxford Univ. Press, 1971–84. Ed., Notes and Queries, 1959–62. Hon. Secty., Early English Text Soc., 1955–68; Pres., English Assn., 1978–79. *Publs:* (with C.T. Onions and G.W.D. Friedrichsen) The Oxford Dictionary of English Etymology, 1966; A Supplement to the Oxford English Dictionary, 4 vols., 1972–86; (with D.

Donoghue and A. Timothy) The Quality of Spoken English on BBC Radio, 1979; The Spoken Language as an Art Form, 1981; The Spoken Word, 1981; The English Language, 1985; The New Zealand Pocket Oxford Dictionary, 1986; (ed.) Studies in Lexicography, 1987; Unlocking the English Language, 1989. Add: The Barn, 14 The Green, Sutton Courtenay, Oxon. OX14 4AE, England.

BURDEN, Jean. Also writes as Felicia Ames. American, b. 1914. Poetry, Animals/Pets. Poetry Ed., Yankee mag., since 1955; Contrib. author to Atlantic, Family Weekly, Ladies Home Journal, Good Housekeeping, Mademoiselle, Poetry, and others. Pet Ed., Woman's Day, 1973–82. Public Relations Officer, Meals for Millions Foundn., 1956–65; owner, public relations agency, 1966–72. *Publs:* Naked as the Glass, 1963; Journey Toward Poetry, 1966; (as Felicia Ames) The Cat You Care For, 1968; (as Felicia Ames) The Dog You Care For, 1968; (as Felicia Ames) The Bird You Care For, 1970; (as Felicia Ames) The Fish You Care For, 1971; (ed.) A Celebration of Cats, 1974; The Classic Cats, 1975; The Woman's Day Book of Hints for Cat Owners, 1980, 1984. Add: 1129 Beverly Way, Altadena, Calif. 91001, U.S.A.

BURFORD, Eleanor. *See* **HOLT,** Victoria.

BURFORD, Lolah. American, b. 1931. Historical/Romance/Gothic. *Publs:* Vice Avenged: A Moral Tale, 1971; The Vision of Stephen: An Elegy, 1972; Edward, Edward, 1973; MacLyon, 1974; Alyx, 1977; Seacage, 1979. Add: c/o Macmillan Publishing Co., 866 Third Ave., New York, N.Y. 10022 U.S.A.

BURFORD, William (Skelly). American, b. 1927. Poetry, Translations. Fellow, Dallas Inst. of Humanities and Culture, since 1981. Asst. to the Pres., Richardson Refining Co., Texas City, 1949–50; Instr. in English, Southern Methodist Univ., Dallas, Tex., 1950–51, 1952–54, and Johns Hopkins Univ., Baltimore, Md., 1955–58; Asst. Prof., 1958–64, and Assoc. Prof. of English, 1964–65, Univ. of Texas, Austin; Assoc. Prof. of Humanities, Univ. of Montana, Missoula, 1966–68; Prof. of English, Texas Christian Univ., Fort Worth, 1968–72; Teacher in the National Endowment for the Arts Poetry-in-the-Schs. Prog., 1972–81. *Publs:* Man Now, 1954; Faccia della Terra/Face of the Earth, 1960; A World, 1962; A Beginning: Poems, 1966; (ed. and trans. with Christopher Middleton) The Poet's Vocation: Selections from the Letters of Holderlin, Rimbaud, and Hart Crane, 1967; (ed. and trans. with J. Autret) On Reading, by Marcel Proust, 1972; Gymnos, 1973; (ed. and trans.) On Reading Ruskin, by Proust, 1987. Add: 3000 W. Gambrell, Fort Worth, Tex. 76133, U.S.A.

BURGER, Robert (Eugene). American, b. 1931. Health, Social commentary. Freelance writer since 1968. *Publs:* Where They Go to Die, 1968: McCarthy: Words to Remember, 1969; Out from Under, 1970; Twilight Believers, 1971; Pietro on Wine, 1972; The Love Contract, 1972; Ego Speak, 1973; The Simplified Guide to Personal Bankruptcy, 1974; The Chess of Bobby Fischer, 1975; Inside Divorce, 1975; Forbidden Cures, 1976; Jogger's Catalog, 1978; The Polish Prince, 1978; The Jug Wine Book, 1979; The Whole Life Diet, 1979; Meganutrition, 1980; The Courage to Believe, 1980; Meganutrition for Women, 1982; The Healing Arts, 1986. Add: 802 Montgomery St., San Francisco, Calif. 94133, U.S.A.

BURGES, Norman Alan. British, b. 1911. Biology, Botany. Chmn., Scotch–Irish Trust, since 1973. Prof. of Botany, Univ. of Sydney, 1947–52; Holbrook Gaskell Prof. of Botany, 1952–66, Acting Vice-Chancellor, 1964–65, and Pro-Vice-Chancellor, 1965–66, Univ. of Liverpool. Pres., British Ecological Soc., 1958–59, and British Mycological Soc., 1962; Chmn., Northern Ireland Advisory Council for Education, 1966–73; Vice-Chancellor, New Univ. of Ulster, Coleraine, 1966–76. *Publs:* Micro-organisms in the Soil, 1958; (co-ed, and contrib.) Flora Europaea, 5 vols., 1964–78; (with F. Raw) Soil Biology, 1967. Add: Beechcroft, Aghadowey, Coleraine, Co. Londonderry, Northern Ireland.

BURGESS, Anthony. Also writes as Joseph Kell, and John Burgess Wilson. British, b. 1917. Novels/Short stories, Science fiction/Fantasy, Children's fiction, Literature, Autobiography, Translations. Literary Adviser, Guthrie Theatre, Minneapolis, Minn. since 1972. Master, Banbury Grammar Sch., Oxon, 1950–54; Education Officer, Colonial Service, Malaya and Brunei, 1954–59; Prof., Columbia Univ., NYC, 1970–71. *Publs:* Time for a Tiger, 1956; (as John Burgess Wilson) English Literature: A Survey for Students, 1958; The Enemy in the Blanket, 1958; Beds in the East, 1959; The Right to an Answer, 1960; The Doctor is Sick, 1960; The Worm and the Ring, 1961; Devil of a State, 1961; (as Joseph Kell) One Hand Clapping, 1961; A Clockwork Orange, 1962; The Wanting

Seed, 1962; Honey for the Bears, 1963; (as Joseph Kell) Inside Mr. Enderby, 1963; The Novel Today, 1963; Nothing Like the Sun: A Story of Shakespeare's Love-Life, 1964; The Eve of Saint Venus, 1964; Language Made Plain, 1964, in paperback as Language Made Plain: A Demystification of Linguistics, 1975; Here Comes Everybody: An Introduction to James Joyce for the Ordinary Reader (in U.S. as Re Joyce), 1965; The Long Day Wanes, 1965; A Vision of Battlements, 1965; Tremor of Intent, 1966; (ed.) Coaching Days of England, 1966; (ed.) A Journal of the Plague Year, by Daniel Defoe, 1966; (ed.) A Shorter Finnegans Wake by James Joyce, 1966; The Novel Now: A Student's Guide to Contemporary Fiction (in U.S. as The Novel Now: A Guide to Contemporary Fiction), 1967; (ed. with F. Haskell) The Age of the Grand Tour, 1967; Enderby Outside, 1968; Enderby, 1968; Urgent Copy: Literary Studies, 1968; Shakespeare, 1970; MF, 1971; (trans.) Oedipus the King, 1972; Joysprick: An Introduction to the Language of James Joyce, 1973; Napoleon Symphony, 1974; The Clockwork Testament: or, Enderby's End, 1974; Moses, 1975; Abba Abba, 1976; Beard's Roman Women, 1976; A Long Trip to Teatime (juvenile), 1976; 1985, 1978; Ernest Hemingway and His World, 1978; Man of Nazareth, 1979; The Land Where Ice Cream Grows (juvenile), 1979; Earthly Powers, 1980; On Going to Bed, 1981; This Man and Music, 1982; The End of the World News, 1982; Enderby's Dark Lady, 1983; The Kingdom of the Wicked, 1984; (trans.) Cyrano de Bergerac, 1984; Homage to Qwert Yuiop, 1985; Flame Into Being, 1986; The Pianoplayers, 1986; (trans.) Carmen (libretto), 1986; (trans.) Oberon (libretto), 1986; Little Wilson and Big God (autobiography), 1987; Any Old Iron, 1989. Add: c/o Hutchinson, 62-65 Chandos Pl., London WC2N 4NW, England.

BURGESS, Charles. American, b. 1932. Education, Biography. Chmn., Educational Policy Studies, and Prof. of History of Education, Univ. of Washington, Seattle, since 1970 (Asst. Prof., 1964–66; Assoc. Prof., 1966–70). National Post-Doctoral Fellow, Harvard Univ., Cambridge, Mas., 1967–68; Pres., History of Education Soc., 1971–72, and Div. F, American Educational Research Assn., 1977–79. Foreign Expert, People's Republic of China, 1984–85. *Publs:* Nettie Fowler McCormick: Profile of an American Philanthropist, 1962; (ed. with C. Strickland) Health, Growth, and Heredity: G. Stanley Hall on Natural Education, 1965; (with M.L. Borrowman) What Doctrines to Embrace: Studies in the History of American Education, 1969; Western Ideas and the Shaping of America, 1985. Add: Univ. of Washington, 309 Miller Hall, DQ-12, Seattle, Wash. 98195, U.S.A.

BURGESS, C(hester) F(rancis). American, b. 1922. Literature. Prof. Emeritus of English, The Virginia Military Inst., Lexington, since 1968 (Prof., 1962–68). Instr. in English, Yale Univ. New Haven, Conn., 1946–49, and Univ. of Notre Dame, Ind., 1960–62. *Publs:* (ed.) The Letters of John Gay; (ed.) The Beggar's Opera and Companion Pieces, 1966; The Fellowship of the Craft, 1976. Add: 800 Bowyer Lane, Lexington, Va. 24450, U.S.A.

BURGESS, Norman. British, b. 1923. Information science/Computers. Sr. Tutor-Librarian, Bolton Metropolitan Coll., 1959 until retirement, 1986. Deputy Librarian, Droylsden Area, Lancashire County Libraries, 1952–59. *Publs:* How to Find Out About Secretarial and Office Practice, 1967; How to Find Out about Banking and Investment, 1969; How to Find Out About Exporting, 1970. Add: 75 Heathside Rd., Manchester M20 9XH, England.

BURGESS, Robert Herrmann. American, b. 1913. History, Transportation. Curator of Exhibits, then Publications, 1941–78, and Consultant Ed., 1980, Mariners Museum, Newport News, Va. *Publs:* This Was Chesapeake Bay, 1963; Chesapeake Circle, 1965; (with H.G. Wood) Steamboats Out of Baltimore, 1968; (ed.) Coasting Captain, 1967; Sea, Sails and Shipwreck, 1970; Chesapeake Sailing Craft, 1975; (ed.) The Sea Serpent Journal: Hugh McCulloch Gregory's Voyage Around the World in a Clipper Ship 1854-55, 1975; Louis J. Feuchter, Chesapeake Bay Artist, 1976; Coasting Schooner: The Four-Masted Albert F. Paul, 1978; (ed.) The Big Ship: Story of the S.S. United States, 1981. Add: 1504 Gatewood Rd., Newport News, Va. 23601, U.S.A.

BURGESS, Warren E. American, b. 1932. Marine Science/Oceanography, Animals/Pets, Zoology. Sr. Ed., TFH Publs. Inc., since 1972. *Publs:* (with Axelrod) Pacific Marine Fishes, Book 1, 1972, Books 2 and 3, 1973, Books 4 and 5, 1974, Book 6, 1975, Book 7, 1976, Book 8, 1985; (with Axelrod) Saltwater Aquarium Fishes, 2nd ed. 1973, 3rd ed. 1987; (with Axelrod) Exotic Marine Fishes, 6th ed. 1982; (with others) Exotic Tropical Fishes, 25th ed. 1976, expanded ed. 1980; (with Axelrod) African Cichlids of Lakes Malawi and Tanganyika, 4th ed. 1976, 12th ed. 1987; Butterfly Fishes of the World, 1978; (with Axelrod) Freshwater Angelfishes, 1979; (with Axelrod) Marine Fishes, 1979; Corals, 1979;

Marine Aquaria, 1980; TFH Book of Marine Aquariums, 1982; (with Axelrod) Dr. Axelrod's Atlas of Freshwater Aquarium Fishes, 1985; (with Axelrod) Dr. Axelrod's Mini-Atlas of Freshwater Aquarium Fishes, 1987; Corydoras and Related Catfishes, 1987; (with Axelrod) Dr. Burgess's Atlas of Marine Aquarium Fishes, 1988; Atlas of Freshwater and Marine Catfishes, 1989. Add: TFH Publs, Inc., 211 W. Sylvania Ave., Neptune City, N.J. 07753, U.S.A.

BURGHLEY, Rose. Historical/Romance/Gothic. British. *Publs:* And Be My Love, 1958; Love in the Afternoon, 1959; The Sweet Surrender, 1959; Bride by Arrangement, 1960; A Moment in Paris, 1961; Highland Mist, 1962; The Garden of Don José, 1964; Man of Destiny, 1965; A Quality of Magic, 1966; The Afterglow, 1966, in Can. as Alpine Doctor, 1970; Bride of Alaine, 1966; Folly of the Heart, 1967; The Bay of Moonlight, 1968; Return to Tremarth, 1969. Add: c/o Mills and Boon Ltd., Eton House, 18-24 Paradise Rd., Richmond, Surrey TW9 1SR, England.

BURIAN, Jarka M. American, b. 1927. Theatre. Prof., Dept. of Theatre, State Univ. of New York, Albany, since 1963, (Asst. Prof., 1955–59; Assoc. Prof., 1959–63; Chmn., 1971–74, 1977–78). *Publs:* Americke Drama a Divadelnictvi, 1966; The Scenography of Josef Svoboda, 1971 (Special Award, U.S. Inst. of Theatre Technology, 1973); Josef Svoboda's Scenography for Richard Wagner's Operas, 1983. Add: 7 MacPherson Terr., Albany, N.Y. 12206, U.S.A.

BURKE, Arvid James. American, b. 1906. Education. Prof. Emeritus, State Univ. of New York, Albany, since 1971 (Prof. of Education Admin., 1966–71). Dir. of Studies, New York State Teachers Assn., Albany, 1936–66. *Publs:* (with Cyr and Mort) Paying for Our Public Schools, 1938; Defensible Spending for Public Schools, 1943; (with C. Alexander) How to Locate Educational Information and Data, 1952, 3rd ed. 1962; Financing Public Schools in the United States, 1951, 1957; (with W. Strevell) Administration of the School Buiding Program, 1959; (with C. Alexander) Metodos de Investigacion, 1962; (with M. Burke) Documentation in Education, 1967. Add: Bldg. 30, Apt. 6, Park Hill, Menands, N.Y. 12204, U.S.A.

BURKE, James. British, b. 1936. History, Sciences. Dir., English Sch., Bologna, 1961–63, and Rome, 1963–65. *Publs:* (with R. Baxter) Tomorrow's World, vol. I, 1970, vol. II, 1972; Connections, 1978; The Day the Universe Changed, 1985. Add: 22 Prince Albert Rd., London NW1 7ST, England.

BURKE, John (Frederick). Also writes as Jonathan Burke, Owen Burke, Harriet Esmond (in collaboration with his wife), Jonathan George, Joanna Jones, Sara Morris, and Martin Sands. British, b. 1922. Novels/Short stories, Mystery/Crime/Suspense, Science fiction/Fantasy. Free-lance writer since 1966. Assoc. Ed., 1953–56, and Production Mgr., 1956–57, Museum Press, London; Editorial Mgr., Books for Pleasure Group, London, 1957–58; Public Relations and Publications Executive, Shell Intnl., London, 1959–63; Story Ed., Twentieth Century Fox, London, 1963–65. *Publs:* Swift Summer (novel), 1949; Another Chorus (novel), 1949; These Haunted Streets (novel), 1950; The Outward Walls (novel), 1952; Chastity House (novel), 1952; Dark Gateway (science fiction novel), 1953; The Echoing Worlds (science fiction novel), 1954; Twilight of Reason (science fiction novel), 1954; Pattern of Shadows (science fiction novel), 1954; Hotel Cosmos (science fiction novel), 1954; Deep Freeze (science fiction novel), 1955; Revolt of the Humans (science fiction novel), 1955; Alien Landscapes: Science Fiction Stories, 1955; (trans.) The West Face, by Guido Magnone, 1955; Pursuit Through Time (science fiction novel), 1956; The Poison Cupboard (mystery novel), 1956; (with William Luscombe) The Happy Invaders: A Picture of Denmark in Springtime, 1956; (trans.) The Spark and the Flame, by F.B. Muus, 1957; (trans., with Eiler Hansen) The Moon of Beauty, by Jorgen Andersen-Rosendal, 1957; Corpse to Copenhagen (mystery novel), 1957; (as Joanna Jones) Nurse Is a Neighbour (novel), 1958; (as Joanna Jones) Nurse on the District (novel), 1959; Echo of Barbara (mystery novel), 1959; Fear by Instalments (mystery novel), 1960; The Entertainer (novelization of play), 1960; Look Back in Anger (novelization of play), 1960; (as Sara Morris) A Widow for the Winter (novel), 1961; The Lion of Sparta (in U.S. as The 300 Spartans) (novelization of screenplay), 1961; Flame in the Streets (novelization of screenplay), 1961; (trans., with Eiler Hansen) The Happy Lagoons: The World of Queen Salote, by Jorgen Andersen-Rosendal, 1961; The Angry Silence (novelization of screenplay), 1961; Teach Yourself Treachery (mystery novel), 1962; Deadly Downbeat (mystery novel), 1962; The Boys (novelization of screenplay), 1962; Private Potter (novelization of screenplay), 1962; The World Ten Times Over (novelization of screenplay), 1962; (as Joanna Jones) The Artless Flat-Hunter, 1963; The Man Who Finally Died (novelization of screenplay), 1963;

Guilty Party (novelization of stage play), 1963; The Twisted Tongues, 1964 (in U.S. as Echo of Treason, 1966) (mystery novel); The System (novelization of screenplay), 1964; A Hard Day's Night (novelization of screenplay), 1964; The Magnificent Air Race (in U.S. as Those Magnificent Men and Their Flying Machines), 1965 (novelization of screenplay); Dr. Terror's House of Horrors (adaptation of screenplay), 1965; (as Joanna Jones) The Artless Commuter, 1965; Only the Ruthless Can Play (mystery novel), 1965; The Hammer Horror Omnibus, 1966; The Power Game (adaptation of screenplays), 1966; (ed.) Tales of Unease, 1966; The Weekend Girls (mystery novel), 1966; The Trap (novelization of screenplay), 1966; Gossip to the Grave, 1967 (in U.S. as The Gossip Truth, 1968) (mystery novel); (as Martin Sands) The Jokers (novelization of screenplay), 1967; (as Martin Sands) Maroc 7 (novelization of screenplay), 1967; Privilege (novelization of screenplay), 1967; The Suburbs of Pleasure (novel), 1967; Till Death Us Do Part (novelization of tv series), 1967; The Second Hammer Horror Film Omnibus, 1967; Someone Lying, Someone Dying (mystery novel), 1968; Chitty Chitty Bang Bang: The Story of the Film, 1968; Smashing Time (novelization of screenplay), 1968; Rob the Lady (mystery novel), 1969; Moon Zero Two: The Story of the Film, 1969; The Smashing Bird I Used to Know (novelization of screenplay), 1960; (ed.) More Tales of Unease, 1969; Four Stars for Danger (mystery novel), 1970; Strange Report (novelization of tv play), 1970; (as Jonathan George with George Theiner) The Killdog (mystery novel), 1970; All the Right Noises (novelization of screenplay), 1970; Suffolk, 1971; (as Jonathan George) Dead Letters (mystery novel), 1972; Expo 80 (novel), 1972; England in Colour, 1972; (as Harriet Esmond) Darsham's Tower, 1973 (in U.K. as Darsham's Folly, 1974) (mystery novel); Sussex, 1974; An Illustrated History of England, 1974, rev. ed., 1985; English Villages, 1975; South East England (juvenile), 1975; (as Harriet Esmond) The Eye Stones (mystery novel), 1975; The Devil's Footsteps (mystery novel), 1976; Luke's Kingdom (novelization of tv play), 1976; Suffolk in Photographs, 1976; Beautiful Britain, 1976; Czechoslovakia, 1976; (ed.) New Tales of Unease, 1976; Historic Britain, 1977; The Black Charade (mystery novel), 1977; (as Harriet Esmond) The Florian Signet (mystery novel), 1977; Life in the Castle in Mediaeval England, 1978; Life in the Villa in Roman Britain, 1978; Ladygrove (mystery novel), 1978; The Prince Regent (novelization of tv play), 1979; (as Owen Burke) The Figurehead (novel), 1979; Look Back on England, 1980; The English Inn, 1981; Musical Landscapes, 1983; Roman England, 1983; The Bill (novelization of TV series), 1985; The Fourth Floor (novelization of TV series), 1986; King and Castle (novelization of TV series), 1986; The Bill II (novelization of TV series), 1987; Illustrated History of Music, 1988. Add: 8 North Parade, Southwold, Suffolk, England.

BURKE, Jonathan. *See* **BURKE,** John.

BURKE, Kenneth (Duva). American, b. 1897. Novels/Short stories, Poetry, Literature, Philosophy. Research Worker, Laura Spelman Rockefeller Memorial, NYC, 1926–27; Music Critic, Dial, NYC, 1927–29, and The Nation, NYC, 1934–35; Ed., Bureau of Social Hygiene, NYC, 1928–29; Lectr., Univ. of Chicago, 1938 and 1949–50, and Bennington Coll., Vt., 1943–61; Regents Prof., Univ. of California, Santa Barbara, 1964–65; Lectr., Harvard Univ., Cambridge, Mass., 1967–68, and Washington Univ., St. Louis, Mo., 1970–71. *Publs:* The White Oxen and Other Stories, 1924; (trans.) Death in Venice, by Thomas Mann, 1925; (trans.) Genius and Character, by Emil Ludwig, 1927; (trans.) Saint Paul, by Emile Baumann, 1929; Counter-Statement, 1931, rev. ed. 1968; Towards a Better Life: Being Series of Epistles or Declarations (novel), 1932, rev. ed. 1966; Permanence and Change: An Anatomy of Purpose, 1935, rev. ed. 1954; Attitudes Towards History, 2 vols., 1937, rev. ed. 1959; The Philosophy of Literary Forms: Studies in Symbolic Action, 1941, rev. ed. 1957, 3rd ed. 1974; A Grammar of Motives, 1945; A Rhetoric of Motives, 1950; Book of Moments: Poems 1915–1954, 1955; The Rhetoric of Religion: Studies in Logology, 1961; Perspective by Incongruity, 1964; Terms for Order, 1964; Language as Symbolic Action: Essays on Life, Literature and Method, 1966; The Complete White Oxen: Collected Shorter Fiction 1968; Collected Poems, 1915–1967, 1968; Dramatism and Development, 1972; (with others) Surrealism Pro and Con, 1973; (with others) Rhetoric in Change, 1982; The Selected Letters of Kenneth Burke and Malcolm Cowley 1915–1981, edited by Paul Jay, 1988. Add: R.D. 2, Andover, N.J. 07821, U.S.A.

BURKE, Owen. *See* **BURKE,** John.

BURKE, Shifty. *See* **BENTON,** Peggie.

BURKE, Ulick Peter. British, b. 1937. History, Intellectual history. Fellow, Emmanuel Coll., Cambridge, since 1979. Taught at the Univ.

of Sussex, Brighton, 1962–79. *Publs:* (ed.) The Renaissance, 1964; (ed. and trans.) Sarpi: Selections, 1967; The Renaissance Sense of the Past, 1969; Culture and Society in Renaissance Italy, 1972, in paperback as Tradition and Innovation in Renaissance Italy, 1974; (ed.) A New Kind of History: Selections from L. Febvre, 1973; (ed.) Economy and Society in Early Modern Europe, 1972; Venice and Amsterdam, 1974; Popular Culture in Early Modern Europe, 1978; (ed.) New Cambridge Modern History, vol. XIII, 1979; Sociology and History, 1980; Montaigne, 1981. Add: 19 Devonshire Pl., Brighton, Sussex BN2 1QA, England.

BURLAND, Brian (Berkeley). British. Novels/Short stories, Children's fiction. *Publs:* St. Nicholas and the Tub (children's fiction), 1964; A Fall From a Loft, 1968; A Few Flowers for St. George, 1969; Undertow, 1971; To Celebrate a Happiness that Is America (poetry), 1971; The Sailor and the Fox, 1973; Surprise, 1975; Stephen Decatur: The Devil and the Endymion, 1975; The Flight of the Cavalier, 1980; Love is a Durable Fire, 1985; What Wanderwith, 1988. Add: c/o Carol E. Rinzler, Rember & Curtis, 19 W. 44th St., New York, N.Y. 10036, U.S.A.

BURLEY, W(illiam) J(ohn). British, b. 1914. Novels/Short stories, Mystery/Crime/Suspense. Full-time writer since 1974. Engineer and Mgr. for South Western Gas and Water Corp. Ltd. in southwest England, 1936–50; Head of the Biology Dept., Richmond Grammar Sch., Surrey, 1953–55; Head of Biology, 1955–59, and Tutor, 1959–74, Newquay Sch., Cornwall. *Publs:* A Taste of Power, 1966; Three-Toed Pussy, 1968; Death in Willow Pattern, 1969; To Kill a Cat, 1970; Guilt Edged, 1971; Death in a Salubrious Place, 1973; Death in Stanley Street, 1974; Wycliffe and the Pea-Green Boat, 1975; Wycliffe and the Schoolgirls, 1976; The Schoolmaster, 1977; Centenary History of the City of Truro, 1977; The Sixth Day (non-mystery novel), 1978; Wycliffe and the Scapegoat, 1978; Charles and Elizabeth, 1979; Wycliffe in Paul's Court, 1979; The House of Care, 1981; Wycliffe's Wild Goose Chase, 1982; Wycliffe and the Beales, 1983; Wycliffe and the Four Jacks, 1985; Wycliffe and the Quiet Virgin, 1986; Wycliffe and the Windsor Blue, 1987; Wycliffe and the Tangled Web, 1988; Wycliffe and the Little Hut, 1989. Add: St. Patricks, Holywell, Newquay, Cornwall, England.

BURMAN, Jose Lionel. South African, b. 1917. History. Travel/Exploration/Adventure. Solicitor, since 1945. *Publs:* Safe to the Sea, 1962; Peninsula Profile, 1963; So High the Road, 1963; Garden Route, 1964; A Peak to Climb, 1965; Where to Walk in the Cape Peninsula, 1966; Great Shipwrecks off the Coast of South Africa, 1967; Strange Shipwrecks of the Southern Seas, 1968; Who Really Discovered South Africa?, 1969; Waters of the Western Cape, 1970; Cape of Good Intent, 1971; Disasters Struck South Africa, 1971; Guide to the Garden Route, 1973; 1652 and So Forth, 1973; The Saldanha Bay Story, 1974; Bay of Storms, 1976; False Bay Story, 1977; Wine of Constantia, 1979; Trails and Walks in the Southern Cape, 1980; The Little Karoo, 1981; Latest Walks in the Cape Peninsula, 1982; Early Railways at the Cape, 1984; Day Walks in the South Western Cape, 1984; Rediscovering the Garden Route, 1985; Shipwreck, 1986; Cape Trails and Wilderness Areas, 1987; Towards the Far Horizon, 1988. Add: P.O. Box, 500, Hermanus, South Africa.

BURMEISTER, Jon. South African, b. 1933. Novels/Short stories. Partner, law and notary public firm, East London, S. Africa, 1960–70. *Publs:* The Edge of the Coast, 1968; A Hot and Copper Sky, 1969; The Darkling Plain, 1970; Running Scared, 1972; The Weatherman Guy, 1975; The Protector Conclusion, 1977; Glory Hunters, 1979. Add: c/o John Farquharson Ltd., 162-168 Regent St., London W1R 5TB, England.

BURN, Andrew Robert. British, b. 1902. Classics, History. Rep., British Council, Greece, 1940–41; Officer, U.K. Intelligence Corps., Middle East Forces, 1941–44; Second Secty., British Embassy, Athens, 1944–46; Sr. Lectr. in Ancient History, 1946–65, and Reader, 1965–69, Univ. of Glasgow; Visiting Prof., Coll. of Wooster, Ohio, 1958–59; Member, Inst. of Advanced Studies, Princeton, N.J., 1961–62; Visiting Prof., A Coll. Year in Athens Inc., 1969–72. *Publs:* Minoans, Philistines and Greeks, 1400-900 B.C., 1930; The World of Hesiod, c.900-700 B.C., 1936; (compiler) This Scepter'd Isle (poetry) 1940; The Romans in Britain: An Anthology of Inscriptions, 1932, 1969; The Modern Greeks, 1942; Alexander the Great and the Hellenistic World, 1947, 1962, rev. ed. published as Alexander the Great and the Middle East, 1973; Pericles and Athens, 1948; Agricola and Roman Britain, 1953; The Lyric Age of Greece, 1960; Persia and the Greeks, 1962; Traveller's History of Greece, 1965, reprinted as The Pelican History of Greece, 1966, 1984; The Warring States of Greece, 1968; (with J.M.B. Edwards) Greece and Rome, 1971; (ed. and reviser of trans.) The Penguin Herodotus, 2nd rev. ed. 1972; (with Mary Burn) The Living Past of Greece, 1980. Add: Flat

23, 380 Banbury Rd., Oxford OX2 7PW, England.

BURNET, Alastair. (Sir James William Alexander Burnet). British, b. 1928. Social commentary, Biography. Journalist and Broadcaster: Dir. since 1981, and Assoc. Ed. since 1982, Independent Television News (ITN) (Political Ed., 1963–64). With Glasgow Herald, 1951–58; Leader Writer, 1958–62, and Ed., 1965–74, The Economist, London; Ed., The Daily Express, London, 1974–76. *Publs:* (with Willie Landels) The Times of Our Lives, 1981; The Queen Mother, 1985. Add: 43 Hornton Court, Campden Hill Rd., London W8, England.

BURNETT, Alfred David. British, b. 1937. Poetry, Librarianship. Asst. Librarian, Durham Univ. Library, since 1964. Library Asst., Glasgow Univ. Library, 1959–64. *Publs:* Mandala, 1967; Diversities, 1968; A Ballad Upon a Wedding, 1969; Columbaria, 1971; Shimabara, 1972; Thirty Snow Poems, 1973; Fescennines, 1973; (with S. Simsova and R.K. Gupta) Studies in Comparative Librarianship, 1973; The True Vine, 1974; The Abbott Collection of Literary Manuscripts, 1975; Hero and Leander, 1975; He and She, 1976; The Heart's Undesign, 1977; Figures and Spaces, 1978; (with E. Havard-Williams) International Library and Information Programmes, 1978; Jackdaw, 1980; (with H.A. Whatley) Language and Literacy: The Public Library Role, 1981; Thais, 1981; Romans, 1983; Vines, 1984; Arabic Resources: Acquisition and Management in British Libraries, 1986; Autolycus, 1987; (ed.) Technology for Information in Development, 1988; Kantharos, 1989; (trans. with J. Cayley) Mirror and Pool: Poems from the Chinese, 1989; Lesbos, 1989; Nine Poets, 1989; Marina Tsvetaeva, 1989. Add: 33 Hastings Ave., Merry Oaks, Durham DH1 3QG, England.

BURNETT, Hallie (Southgate). American. Novels/Short stories, Cookery/Gastronomy/Wine, Travel, Writing/Journalism. Ed., Story mag. and The Story Press 1942–70; Fiction Ed., Prentice-Hall, 1959–60; Fiction Ed., Yankee Mag., 1960–61; Assoc. Prof. of Literature, Sarah Lawrence Coll., Bronxville, N.Y., 1960–64. *Publs:* A Woman in Possession, 1952; This Heart, This Hunter, 1955; The Brain Pickers, 1958; Watch on the Wall, 1964; Boarders in the rue Madame (short stories), 1966; On Writing the Short Story, 1983; ed. with Whit Burnett of the following—Story: The Fiction of the Forties; Story: Nos. 1, 2, 3, 4; Sextet; The Best College Writing; Prize College Stories; The Modern Short Story in the Making; Story Jubilee; Story: The Yearbook of Discovery; Fiction of a Generation; The Tough Ones; Thirteen Tales of Terror; The Important Thing: The Daughter-in-Law Cookbook; The Millionaires Cookbook; Fiction Writers Handbook, 1975. Add: 6804 Greystone Dr., Raleigh, N.C. 27609, U.S.A.

BURNETT, John. British, b. 1925. Economics, History. Prof. of Social History, Brunel Univ., since 1972 (Head, Dept. of Gen. Studies, 1962–66; Reader in Social and Economic History, 1966–72). Chmn. Social History Soc. of the U.K., since 1985. Lectr. in Social History, London Univ., 1952–1972; Head, Div. of Liberal Studies, Borough Polytechnic (now Polytechnic of the South Bank), 1959–62. *Publs:* Plenty and Want: A Social History of Diet in England from 1815 to the Present Day, 1966; A History of Cost of Living, 1969; The Challenge of the 19th Century, 1970; (ed.) Useful Toil: Autobiographies of Working People from the 1820s to the 1920s, 1974; Housing: A Social History 1815-1970, 1978; Destiny Obscure: Autobiographies of Childhood, 1982; (co-ed.) The Autobiography of the Working Class: A Critical Annotated Bibliography, vol. I, 1984, vol. II, 1987. Add: Faculty of Social Sciences, Brunel Univ., Kingston Lane, Uxbridge, Middx., England.

BURNETTE, O. Lawrence, Jr. American, b. 1927. History. Dean of Faculty, and Research Prof. of History, Stratford Coll., Danville, Va., since 1972. Pres. and Chmn. of Bd., Timber Ridge Enterprises Ltd. Instr. in History, Virginia Military Inst., Lexington, 1951–53; Field Ed., Charles Scribner's Sons Inc., Charlottesville, Va., 1953–57; Book Ed., State Historical Soc. of Wisconsin, Madison, 1957–63; Research Prof. of History, Birmingham Southern Coll., Ala., 1963–65. *Publs:* A Syllabus of American History, 1960; (ed.) Wisconsin Witness to Frederick Jackson Turner: A Collection of Essays on the Historian and the Thesis; (co-author) Life in America, 1964; (ed. with Howard H. Creed) Readings in American Studies, 1969; Beneath the Footnote: A Guide to the Preservation and Use of American Historical Documentation, 1970. Add: Dept. of History, Stratford Coll., Danville, Va., U.S.A.

BURNINGHAM, John (Mackintosh). British, b. 1936. Children's fiction. *Publs:* Borka: The Adventures of a Goose with No Feathers, 1963; Trubloff: The Mouse Who Wanted to Play the Balalaika, 1964; ABC, 1964; Humbert, Mister Firkin and the Lord Mayor of London, 1965; Cannonball Simp, 1966; Birdland: Wall Frieze, 1966; Lionland: Wall Frieze,

1966; Storyland: Wall Frieze, 1966; Harquin: The Fox Who Went Down to the Valley, 1967; Jungleland: Wall Frieze, 1968; Wonderland: Wall Frieze, 1968; Seasons, 1969; Mr. Grumpy's Outing, 1970; Around the World: Two Wall Friezes, 1972; Around the World in Eighty Days, 1972; The Baby (reader), 1974; The Rabbit (reader), 1974; The School (reader), 1974; The Snow (reader), 1974; Mr. Grumpy's Motor Car, 1974; The Blanket (reader), 1975; The Cupboard (reader), 1975; The Dog (reader), 1975; The Friend (reader), 1975; Come Away from the Water, Shirley, 1977; Time to Get Out of the Bath, Shirley, 1978; Would You Rather, 1978; The Shopping Basket, 1980; Avocado Baby, 1982; Granpa, 1984; Opposites, Colours, 1985; John Patrick Norman McHennessy—The Boy Who Is Always Late, 1987. Add: c/o Jonathan Cape Ltd., 32 Bedford Sq., London WC1B 3EL, England.

BURNS, Alan. British, b. 1929. Novels/Short stories, Plays/Screenplays. Assoc. Prof., Univ. of Minnesota, Minneapolis. Barrister-at-Law, since 1977. *Publs:* Buster, 1961; Europe after the Rain, 1965; Celebrations, 1967; Babel, 1969; Palach (play), 1970; Dreamerika!, 1972; The Angry Brigade, 1974; The Day Daddy Died, 1981; (with Charles Sugnet) The Imagination on Trial (non-fiction), 1981; Revolutions of the Night, 1986. Add: English Dept., Univ. of Minnesota, Minneapolis, Minn. 55455, U.S.A.

BURNS, Carol. British, b. 1934. Novels/Short stories. Lectr. in Creative Writing, City Literary Inst., London, since 1972 (Lectr. in Art History, 1973). Ed., Matrix, City Literary Inst. Mag. Painter. *Publs:* Infatuation, 1967; The Narcissist, 1967. Add: 26a Ladbroke Gardens, London W11, England.

BURNS, George (Nathan Birnbaum). American, b. 1896. Humor. Comedian; appeared with spouse, Gracie Allen. TV shows: Burns & Allen Show, 1950–58; George Burns Show, 1959–60; Wendy and Me, 1964. Films include: The Big Broadcast, 1932; International House, 1932; Love In Bloom, 1933; Many Happy Returns, 1939; Honolulu, 1939; The Sunshine Boys (Acad. Award for Best Supporting Actor). 1975; Oh God!, 1977; Going in Style, 1979; Just You and Me, Kid, 1979; Oh God! You Devil, 1984; Eighteen Again, 1988. *Publs:* I Love Her, That's Why!, 1955; Living It Up, or They Still Love Me in Altoona, 1976; How to Live to Be One Hundred or More, 1983; Dear George: Advice & Answers from America's Leading Expert on Everything from A-B, 1985; Dear George; Dr. Burns' Prescription for Happiness, 1986; Gracie: A Love Story, 1988. Add: c/o Irving Fine, 1100 N. Alta Loma Rd., Los Angeles, Calif. 90069, U.S.A.

BURNS, James MacGregor. American, b. 1918. History, Politics/Government. Prof. of Political Science, Williams Coll., Williamstown, since 1953 (Asst. Prof., 1947–50; Assoc. Prof., 1950–53). Co-Chmn. Project 87, interdisciplinary study of constitution during bicentennial era, 1976–87. *Publs:* Congress on Trial: The Legislative Process and the Administrative State, 1949; (with Jack Walter Peltason) Government by the People: The Dynamics of American National Government, 1952; (with Peltason) Government by the People: The Dynamics of American State and Local Government, 1952; (with Peltason) Government by the People: The Dynamics of American National State and Local Government (revision of two previous books), 1954, (with Peltason and E. Cronin) 12th ed. 1984; Roosevelt: The Lion and the Fox, 1956; (ed. with Peltason) Functions and Policies of American Government, 1958, 3rd ed. 1967; John Kennedy: A Political Profile, 1960; The Deadlock of Democracy: Four-Party Politics in America, 1963; (with others) Dialogues in Americanism, 1964; Presidential Government: The Crucible of Leadership, 1966; (with others) Our American Government Today, 1966; (ed.) Lyndon Baines Johnson: To Heal and to Build, 1968; Roosevelt: The Soldier of Freedom, 1970; Uncommon Sense, 1973; Leadership, 1978; The Vineyard of Liberty, 1982; The Power to Lead, 1984; The Workshop of Democracy, 1985. Recipient of Pulitzer Prize and National Book Award. Add: Dept. of Political Science, Williams Coll., Williamstown, Mass. 01267, U.S.A.

BURNS, Jim. British, b. 1936. Poetry. Regular Contrib., Tribune, London, and Ambit, London, since 1964. Ed., Move mag., Preston, 1964–68, Palantir, Preston, 1976–83. *Publs:* Some Poems, 1965; Some More Poems, 1966; My Sad Story and Other Poems, 1967; Cells: Prose Pieces, 1967; Saloon Bar: 3 Jim Burns Stories, 1967; The Store of Things, 1969; Types: Prose Pieces and Poems, 1970; A Single Flower, 1972; Leben in Preston, 1973; Easter in Stockport, 1976; Fred Engels in Woolworths, 1975; Playing it Cool, 1976; The Goldfish Speaks from Beyond the Grave, 1976; Catullus in Preston, 1979; Aristotle's Grill, 1979; Notes from a Greasy Spoon, 1980; Internal Memorandum, 1982; The Real World, 1986; Out of the Past: Selected Poems 1961–1986, 1987; Poems

for Tribune, 1988. Add: 11 Gatley Green, Gatley, Cheadle, Cheshire, England.

BURNS, Joan Simpson. American, b. 1927. Novels/Short stories, Poetry, Biography. Managing Dir., Highgate Art Trust and Research Assoc., Williams Coll. Formerly Managing Ed., Readers' Subscription Book Club, Trade Ed., Harcourt Brace & Jovanovich, publrs., NYC, and Special Projects Ed., CBS/Columbia Records, 1960–67. *Publs:* (with G. Whitaker) Dinosaur Hunt, 1965; (ed.) John Fitzgerald Kennedy as We Remember Him, 1965; Poems and a Libretto, 1965; The Awkward Embrace, 1975. Add: High Mowing, Bee Hill Rd., Williamstown, Mass. 01267, U.S.A.

BURNS, Rex. American, b. 1935. Mystery/Crime/Suspense. Prof., Univ. of Colorado, Denver, since 1969. Asst. Prof., Central Missouri State Univ., Warrensburg, 1965–68. *Publs:* mystery novels—The Alvarez Journal, 1975; The Farnsworth Score, 1977; Speak for the Dead, 1978; Angle of Attack, 1979; The Avenging Angel, 1983; Strip Search, 1984; Ground Money, 1986; Suicide Season, 1987; other—Success in America: The Yeoman Dream and the Industrial Revolution, 1975; The Killing Zone, 1988; Parts Unknown, 1989. Add: 1017 Vivian Circle, Boulder, Colo. 80303, U.S.A.

BURNSHAW, Stanley. American, b. 1906. Novels/Short stories, Plays/Screenplays, Poetry, Literature. Founding Ed., Poetry Folio mag. and Folio Press, Pittsburgh, Pa., 1926–29; Contrib. Ed., Modern Quarterly, 1932–33, and Theatre Workshop mag., 1935–38; Co-Ed. and Drama Critic, The New Masses, NYC, 1934–36; Ed.-in-Chief, Cordon Co., publrs., NYC, 1937–39; Pres. and Ed.-in-Chief, Dryden Press, NYC, 1939–58; Vice-Pres., 1958–66, and Consultant to Pres., 1966–68, Holt Rinehart & Winston Inc., publrs., NYC. Lectr., New York Univ., NYC, 1958–62; Dir., American Inst. of Graphic Arts, 1960–61. Visiting Prof. in English Literature, Univ. of Miami, 1989–90. *Publs:* Poems, 1927; A Short History of the Wheel Age, 1928; The Great Dark Love, 1932; André Spire and His Poetry: Two Essays and Forty Translations, 1933; The Iron Land: A Narrative, 1936; (ed.) Two New Yorkers, 1938; The Revolt of the Cats in Paradise: A Children's Book for Adults, 1945; The Bridge (verse play), 1945; The Sunless Sea (novel), 1949; Early and Late Testament, 1952; (co-ed.) The Poem Itself: 45 Modern Poets in a New Presentation, 1960, 1989; (ed. with T. Carmi and E. Spicehandler) The Modern Hebrew Poem Itself: From the Beginnings to the Present: Sixty-Nine Poems in a New Presentation, 1960, 1989; (ed.) Varieties of Literary Experience: Eighteen Essays in World Literature, 1962; Caged in an Animal's Mind, 1963; The Hero of Silence, 1965; The Seamless Web: Language-Thinking, Creature-Knowledge, Art-Experience, 1970, 1989; In the Terrified Radiance, 1972; Mirages: Travel Notes in the Promised Land, 1977; The Refusers: An Epic of the Jews, 1981; Robert Frost Himself, 1986, 1989. Add: 250 W. 89th St., New York, N.Y. 10024, U.S.A.

BURR, Wesley R. American, b. 1936. Family science. Prof. of Family Science, Brigham Young Univ., Provo, since 1969. Asst. Prof., Portland State Univ., Ore., 1966–69. *Publs:* Love—Its Meaning and Recognition, 1960; (ed. with Richard Cantrell and Everett Pollard) Supplementary Readings for Family Relationships, 1970; The Family: Theory Building Assessment, 1970; Theory Construction and the Sociology of the Family, 1973; Successful Marriage, 1976; (co-ed.) Contemporary Theories about the Family, 2 vols., 1979; From Two To One, 1981; Marriage and Family Stewardships, 1982; From This Day Forth, 1982; Famology: A New Discipline, 1983; Introduction to Family Science, 1989. Add: 3290 Mohawk Circle, Provo, Utah 84601, U.S.A.

BURRELL, Thomas William. British, b. 1923. Education, Information science/Computers, Librarianship. Formerly, librarian in Yorkshire; Sr. Lectr., Information Systems Studies, Coll. of Librarianship Wales, Aberystwyth, 1970–80; Librarian, Royal Shrewsbury Hosp., from 1980. *Publs:* Learn to Use Books and Libraries, 1969; (with K.J. McGarry) Logic and Semantics in the Organization of Knowledge, 1972; (with K.J. McGarry) Communication Studies, 1973; Curriculum Design and Development for Nurse Educators, 1988. Add: 34 Norridge View, Warminster, Wilts. BA12 8TA, England.

BURROUGHS, William S(eward). Has also written as William Lee. American, b. 1914. Novels/Short stories, Science fiction/Fantasy, Plays/Screenplays, Poetry, Medicine/Health. Former journalist, private detective, and bartender. *Publs:* (as William Lee) Junk, 1953, reissued under real name as Junkie, 1964; The Naked Lunch (in U.S. and U.K. as Naked Lunch), 1959; The Exterminator (poetry), 1960, novel, 1973; The Soft Machine, 1961; The Ticket That Exploded, 1962; Dead Fingers Talk, 1963; (with Allen Ginsberg) The Yage Letters, 1963; Towers Open

Fire (screenplay), 1963; Nova Express, 1964; Time (poetry), 1965; APO-33: A Metabolic Regulator: A Report on the Synthesis of the Amorphine Formula, 1968; The Third Mind (poetry), 1970; The Job: Interviews with William Burroughs, by Daniel Odier, 1970; The Last Words of Dutch Schultz (play), 1970, novel, 1975; (with A. Bulch) Who's Who (screenplay), 1970; The Wild Boys: A Book of the Dead, 1971; White Subway, 1974; Port of Saints, 1975; Short Novels, 1978; Ah Pook is Here, 1979; City of the Red Night, 1980; Blade Runner (screenplay), 1980; Book of Breeething, 1980; The Place of Dead Roads, 1983; The Burroughs File, 1984; (with Francis S. Leighton) The Adding Machine, 1984; Queer, 1985; Mind Wars, 1985; The Western Lands, 1987. Add: Box 147, Lawrence, Kansas, 66044, U.S.A.

BURROW, J(ohn) A(nthony). British, b. 1932. Literature. Winterstoke Prof. of English, Univ. of Bristol, since 1976. Hon. Dir., Early English Text Soc., since 1983. Fellow, Jesus Coll., Oxford Univ., 1961–75. *Publs:* A Reading of Sir Gawain and the Green Knight, 1965; (ed.) Geoffrey Chaucer: A Critical Anthology, 1969; Ricardian Poetry: Chaucer, Gower, Langland, and the Gawain Poet, 1971; (ed.) Sir Gawain and the Green Knight, 1972; (ed.) English Verse 1300-1500, 1977; Medieval Writers and Their Work, 1982; Essays on Medieval Literature, 1984; The Ages of Man, 1986. Add: 9 The Polygon, Clifton, Bristol, England.

BURROWAY, Janet (Gay). American, b. 1936. Novels/Short stories, Children's fiction, Poetry. FSU Foundation Prof. of Literature and Writing, Florida State Univ., Tallahassee (member of faculty since 1975). Lectr. in English Literature, Univ. of Sussex, Brighton, 1965–70; Reviewer, New Statesman, London, 1970–75. *Publs:* Descend Again, 1960; But to the Season (poetry), 1961; The Dancer from the Dance, 1965; Eyes, 1966; The Buzzards, 1970; The Truck on the Track, 1971; (with J.V. Lord), The Giant Jam Sandwich, 1972; Raw Silk, 1977; Material Goods (poetry), 1981; Writing Fiction, 1982, 2nd ed. 1987; Opening Nights (novel), 1985. Add: English Dept., Florida State Univ., Tallahassee, Fla. 32306, U.S.A.

BURROWES, Mike. Pseudonym for Michael Anthony Bernard. British, b. 1937. Westerns/Adventure. Owner/Operator, Sunshine Cleaners. Formerly a postman. *Publs:* North of Paola, 1965; Chinook, 1965; Action at Las Animas, 1965; Blood Trail, 1966; Deadly Justice, 1967; Requiem for a Gunfighter, 1967; Wolf Creek Pass, 1968; Echoes of Shiloh, 1968; Hell in San Pedro, 1971. Add: 102 Moyne Close, Hove, Sussex BN3 7JX, England.

BURROWS, John. British, b. 1945. Plays/Screenplays. Actor and Dir. *Publs:* The Golden Pathway Annual, 1975; It's a Girl!, 1988. Add: Michael Imison Ltd., 28 Almeida St., London N1 1TD, England.

BURT, Nathaniel. American, b. 1913. Novels/Short stories, Poetry, Social commentary/phenomena. *Publs:* Rooms in a House, 1947; Question on a Kite, 1950; Scotland's Burning, 1954; Make My Bed, 1957; Leopards in the Garden, 1968; The Perennial Philadelphians, 1963; War Cry of the West, 1964; First Families, 1970; Palaces for the People, 1977; Jackson Hole Journal, 1983. Add: 13 Campbelton Circle, Princeton, N.J. 08540, U.S.A.

BURTCHAELL, James Tunstead. American, b. 1934. Theology/Religion. Prof. of Theology, Univ. of Notre Dame, Indiana, since 1966 (Chmn., Dept. of Theology, 1968–70; Provost, 1970–77). Pres., American Academy of Religion, 1970. *Publs:* Catholic Theories of Biblical Inspiration since 1810: A Review and Critique, 1969; Philemon's Problem: The Daily Dilemma of the Christian, 1973; (ed.) Marriage among Christians: A Curious Tradition, 1977; Bread and Salt, 1978; (ed.) Abortion Parley, 1980; Rachel Weeping, and Other Essays on Abortion, 1982; For Better For Worse: Sober Thoughts on Passionate Promises, 1985; There Is No More Just War: The Teaching and Trial of Don Lorenzo Milani, 1988; The Giving and Taking of Life: Essays Ethical, 1989. Add: Dept. of Theology, Univ. of Notre Dame, Notre Dame, Ind. 46556, U.S.A.

BURTON, Anthony. British, b. 1934. Novels/Short stories, History, Transportation, Travel. Self-employed writer since 1968. Ed., Weidenfeld and Nicolson, London, 1963–67; Publicity Mgr., Penguin Books, London, 1967–68. *Publs:* Programmed Guide to Office Warfare (humour), 1969; The Jones Report (humour), 1970; The Canal Builders, 1972, 1981; The Reluctant Musketeer (novel), 1973; Canals in Colour, 1974; Remains of a Revolution, 1975; The Master Idol (novel), 1975; The Navigators (novel), 1976; Canal, 1976; Josiah Wedgwood, 1976; The Miners, 1976; A Place to Stand (novel), 1977; Back Door Britain, 1977; Industrial Archaeological Sites of Britain, 1977; (with Pip Burton) The Green Bag Travellers, 1978; The Past at Work, 1980; The Rainhill Story, 1980; The Changing River, 1982; The Past Afloat, 1982; The Shell Book of Curious Britain, 1982; The National Trust Guide to Our Industrial Past, 1983; The Waterways of Britain, 1983; The Rise and Fall of King Cotton, 1984; (co-ed.) Canals: A New Look, 1984; Walking the Line, 1985; Wilderness Britain, 1985; (with John Morgan) Britain's Light Railways, 1985; The Shell Book of Undiscovered Britain & Ireland, 1986; (with John May) Landscape Detective, 1986; Britain Revisited, 1986; Opening Time, 1987; Steaming Through Britain, 1987; Walk the South Downs, 1988; Walking Through History, 1988. Add: c/o Murray Pollinger, 4 Garrick St., London WC2E 9BH, England.

BURTON, (Alice) Elizabeth. Also writes as Susan Kerby. British, b. 1908. Novels/Short stories, History. London Corresp., Windsor Star, Canada, 1945–65. *Publs:* Cling to Her Waiting, 1939; Fortnight in Frascati, 1940; (as Susan Alice Kerby) Many Strange Birds (in U.S. as Fortune's Gift), 1951; (as Susan Kerby) Gone to Grass (in U.S. as The Roaring Dove), 1947; (as Susan Kerby) Mr. Kronion, 1949; (as Susan Alice Kerby) Le Don de la Fortune, 1950; The Elizabethans (Jacobeans, Georgians, Early Victorias, Early Tudors) at Home (in U.S. as Pageant series), 5 vols., 1958–76; Here Is England, 1965. Add: c/o John Farquharson Ltd., 162-168 Regent St., London W1R 2TB, England.

BURTON, Hester. British, b. 1913. Children's fiction, History. *Publs:* Barbara Bodichon, 1949; Coleridge and the Wordsworths, 1953; Tennyson, 1954; (ed.) A Book of Modern Short Stories, 1959; (ed.) Her First Ball, 1960; The Great Gale (in U.S. as The Flood at Redesmere), 1960; Castors Away!, 1962; Time of Trial, 1963; No Beat of Drum, 1966; In Spite of All Terror, 1968; Otmoor Forever!, 1968; Through the Fire, 1969; Thomas (in U.S. as Beyond the Weir Bridge), 1969; The Henchmans at Home, 1970; The Rebel, 1971; Riders of the Storm, 1972; Kate Rider, 1974; To Ravensrigg, 1976; A Grenville Goes to Sea, 1977; Tim at the Fur Fort, 1977; When the Beacons Blazed, 1978; Five August Days, 1981. Add: Mill House, Kidlington, Oxford, England.

BURTON, Ivor (Flower). British, b. 1923. History, Politics/Government. Prof. of Social Policy, Royal Holloway and Bedford New Coll., Univ. of London, 1983–88 (joined faculty, 1950). *Publs:* The Captain General: The Career of John Churchill, 1st Duke of Marlborough, 1702-11, 1968; (with Gavin Drewry) Legislation and Public Policy: Public Bills in the 1970–4 Parliament, 1980. Add: 21 Downs View Lodge, Surbiton, Surrey KT6 6EG, England.

BURTON, John Andrew. British, b. 1944. Natural History, Zoology. Dir., Fauna and Flora Preservation Soc., U.S.A., since 1982, Natural History Book Service Ltd., since 1987, and The Nature Company Ltd., since 1988. Exhibition Sect., Natural History Museum, London, 1963–69; Asst. Ed., Birds of the World, 1969–71; Natural History Consultant, Friends of the Earth, London, 1971–75; Exec. Secty., Fauna and Flora Preservation Soc., 1975–88. Ed., Birds International, 1974–76. *Publs:* Extinct Animals, 1972; Birds of the Tropics, 1973; Fossils, 1974; (ed.) Owls of the World, 1974; The Naturalist in London, 1974; (with D.H.S. Risdon) Love of Birds, 1975; Nature in the City, 1976; (with E.N. Arnold) A Field Guide to the Reptiles and Amphibians of Europe, 1978; Rare Animals, 1978; Gem Guide to Wild Animals, 1980; The Guinness Book of Mammals, 1982; Gem Guide to Zoo Animals, 1984; (ed.) National Trust Book of Wild Animals, 1984; Collins' Guide to Rare Mammals of the World, 1987; Close to Extinction, 1988. Add: Old Mission Hall, Sibton Green, Saxmundham, Suffolk IP17 2JY, England.

BURTON, John (Wear). Australian, b. 1915. International relations/Current affairs. Teacher at the Univ. of Kent at Canterbury since 1978. Permanent Head, Australian Dept. of External Affairs, 1947–51; Australian High Commissioner in Ceylon, 1952; Research Fellow and Rockefeller Grantee, Australian National Univ., 1960–63; Reader in Intnl. Relations, 1963–78 and Dir. of the Centre for the Analysis of Conflict, 1965–78, University Coll., London; Prof. of Intl. Relations and Conflict Resolution, George Mason Univ., 1985. *Publs:* The Alternative: An Examination of Western Policies in S.E. Asia, 1954; Peace Theory, 1962; International Relations: A General Theory, 1965; (ed. and contrib.) Nonalignment, 1966; Systems, States, Diplomacy, Rules, 1968; conflict and Communication, 1969; World Society, 1972; Deviance, Terrorism and War, 1979; Dear Survivors, 1982; Global Conflict, 1984; Resolving Deep-Rooted Conflict, 1987. Add: c/o Wheatsheaf Books, 16 Ship St., Brighton BN1 1AD, England.

BURTON, Maurice. British, b. 1898. Natural history, Zoology. Nature Correspondent, Daily Telegraph newspaper, London, since 1949. Member of Staff, Zoology Dept., British Museum of Natural History, London, 1927–58; Science Ed., Illustrated London News mag., 1946–64. *Publs:* The Story of Animal Life, 1949; Animal Courtship, 1953; Living Fossils, 1954; Phoenix Reborn, 1959; Systematic Dictionary of Mammals, 1962; Sixth Sense of Animals, 1973; Animals of Europe, 1973; Daily Telegraph Nature Book, 1975; How Mammals Live, 1975; Guide to the Mammals of Britain and Europe, 1977; Cold-Blooded Animals, 1985; and others. Add: Weston House., Albury, Guildford, Surrey, England.

BURTON, Thomas. *See* **LONGSTREET,** Stephen.

BURTSCHI, Mary Pauline. American, b. 1911. History, Biography. Research Historian, since 1966, and Vice-Pres., since 1972, Vandalia Historical Soc., Ill.; Dir., James Hall Library, since 1966. Site Interpreter and Writer, Little Brick House, since 1961; Dir. and Poetry Consultant, Fayette County Cultural and Arts Assn., since 1974. Teacher of English, Carlyle High Sch., Ill., 1936–39, and Effingham High Sch., Ill., 1939–70. Dir., 1965–68, and Vice-Pres., 1969–77, Ill. State Historical Soc. *Publs:* Biographical Sketch of Joseph Charles Burtschi, 1962; Vandalia: Wilderness Capital of Lincoln's Land, 1963; A Portfolio for James Hall, 1968; A Guide Book of Historical Vandalia, 1974; (ed.) Seven Stories by James Hall, 1975; James Hall of Lincoln's Frontier World 1978; (ed.) Sesquicentennial Celebration of the Antiquarian and Historical Society of Illinois 1827-1977, 1981; European Journey, 1983; A Descriptive Sketch of the Little Brick House in Historic Vandalia, Illinois, 1987. Add: 307 N. Sixth St., Vandalia, Ill. 62471, U.S.A.

BURTT, Edwin Arthur. American, b. 1892. Philosophy, Theology/Religion. Susan Linn Sage Prof. Emeritus of Philosophy, Cornell Univ., Ithaca, N.Y., since 1960 (member of faculty since 1932). Teacher, Dept. of Philosophy, Univ. of Chicago, 1923–31. *Publs:* Metaphysical Foundations of Modern Physical Science, 1925, 2nd ed., 1967; The English Philosophers from Bacon to Mill, 1939; (ed.) The Teachings of the Compassionate Buddha, 1955; Man Seeks the Divine, 1957; In Search of Philosophic Understanding, 1966; Light, Love and Life, 1986; A Critical and Comparative Analysis of Copernicus, Kepler, Galileo and Descartes, repr. of 1924 ed., 1987. Died, 1989.

BURTT, Everett J(ohnson). American, b. 1914. Economics. Prof. Emeritus of Economics, Boston Univ., since 1980 (Asst. Prof., 1947–52; Assoc. Prof., 1952–57; Prof., 1957–80; and Chmn., 1952–68). Sr. Instr. in Economics, Univ. of Maine, 1939–41, and Denver Univ., 1941–42; Labor Market Analyst, War Manpower Commn., 1942–43; Employment Analyst, U.S. Bureau of Labor Statistics, Boston, 1946–47. Pres., Industrial Relations Research Assn., Boston, 1966–67. *Publs:* Labor Markets, Unions and Government Policies, 1963; Plant Relocation and the Core City Worker, 1967; Social Perspectives in the History of Economic Theory, 1972; Labor in the American Economy, 1979. Add: 9 Mary Dyer Lane, N. Easton, Mass. 02356, U.S.A.

BUSBEE, Shirlee. American, b. 1941. Historical/Romance/Gothic. *Publs:* Gypsy Lady, 1977; Lady Vixen, 1980; While Passion Sleeps, 1983; Deceive Not My Heart, 1984; The Tiger Lily, 1985; Spanish Rose, 1986; Midnight Masquerade, 1988. Add: c/o Avon Books, 105 Madison Ave., New York, N.Y. 10016, U.S.A.

BUSBY, F(rancis) M(arion). American, b. 1921. Science fiction/Fantasy. Freelance writer, since 1970. Project Supvr., Alaska Communication System, Seattle, 1947–53; telegraph engineer, 1953–70. Vice-Pres., Science Fiction Writers of America, 1974–76. *Publs:* Cage a Man, 1973; The Proud Enemy, 1975; Rissa Kerguelen, (and) The Long View, 1976, combined paperback as Rissa Kurguelen, 1977, reissued in 3 parts, Young Rissa, Rissa and Tregare, The Long View, 1984; All These Earths, 1978, 1985; Zelde M'tana, 1980, 1986; The Demo Trilogy, 1980; Star Rebel, 1984; The Alien Debt, 1984; Rebel's Quest, 1985, reissued (together with Star Rebel) as The Rebel Dynasty, vol. I, 1987; Rebels' Seed, 1986, reissued (together with The Alien Debt) as The Rebel Dynasty, vol. II, 1988; Getting Home (short stories), 1987; The Breeds of Man, 1988. Add: 2852 14th Ave. W., Seattle, Wash. 98119, U.S.A.

BUSBY, Roger (Charles). British, b. 1941. Mystery/Crime/Suspense. Public Relations Officer, Devon and Cornwall Constabulary, Exeter, since 1973. Journalist, Caters News Agency, Birmingham, 1959–66, and Birmingham Evening Mail, 1966–73. *Publs:* (with Gerald Holtham) Main Line Kill, 1968; Robbery Blue, 1969; The Frighteners, 1970; Deadlock, 1971; A Reasonable Man, 1972; Pattern of Violence, 1973; New Face in Hell, 1976; Garvey's Code, 1978; The Negotiator, 1984; The Hunter, 1986; Snow Man, 1987. Add: Sunnymoor, Bridford, nr. Exeter, Devon, England.

BUSCAGLIA, Leo F(elice). American, b. 1924. Human Relations, Social Commentary/Phenomena. Prof. of Education, Dept. of Counseling and Special Education, Univ. of Southern California, Los Angeles, since 1975 (Asst. Prof., 1965–68; Assoc. Prof., 1968–75). Fundraiser for various organizations, since 1980. Chmn. of the Bd., The Felice Foundn., South Pasadena, Calif., since 1984. Supervisor of Special Education, Pasadena, Calif. City Schools, 1960–65; Columnist, New York Times Syndicate, 1984–88. *Publs:* Because I Am Human, 1972; Love, 1972; The Way of the Bull, 1973; The Disabled and Their Parents: A Counseling Challenge, 1975, 1983; Personhood: The Art of Being Fully Human, 1978; Human Advocacy: P.L. 94-142 and Mainstreaming, 1979; Living, Loving and Learning, 1982; The Fall of Freddie the Leaf, 1982; Loving Each Other: The Challenge of Human Relationships, 1984; Bus 9 to Paradise, 1986; Seven Stories of Christmas Love, 1987; A Memory for Tino, 1988; PAPA, My Father, 1989. Add: P.O. Box 686, South Pasadena, Calif. 91031, U.S.A.

BUSCH, Briton Cooper. American, b. 1936. History, International relations/Current affairs. William R. Kenan Jr. Prof. of History since 1978, and Dir., Social Sciences Div., since 1985, Colgate Univ., Hamilton, N.Y. (Instr., 1962–63; Asst. Prof., 1963–65; Assoc. Prof., 1965–73; Prof., 1973–78; Chmn., 1980–85; Dir., Intnl. Relations, 1984–85). *Publs:* Britain and the Persian Gulf 1894-1914, 1967; Britain, India and the Arabs 1914–1921, 1971; Mudros to Lausanne: Britain's Frontier in West Asia 1918–1923, 1976; Hardinge of Penshurst: A Study in the Old Diplomacy, 1980; Master of Desolation: The Memoirs of Capt. Joseph Fuller, 1980; Alta California 1840-1842: The Journal and Observations of William Dane Phelps, Master of the Ship Alert, 1983; The War Against Seals: A History of the North American Seal Fishery, 1985; Fremont's Private Navy: The 1846 Journal of Captain William Dane Phelps, 1987. Add: Dept. of History, Colgate Univ., Hamilton, N.Y. 13346, U.S.A.

BUSCH, Frederick. American, b. 1941. Novels/Short stories, Literature. Prof. of English, Colgate Univ., Hamilton, N.Y., since 1976 (staff member since 1966). *Publs:* I Wanted a Year Without Fall, 1971; Hawkes: A Guide to His Fictions, 1973; Breathing Trouble (short stories), 1974; Manual Labor, 1974; Domestic Particulars (short stories), 1976; The Mutual Friend (novel), 1978; Hardwater Country (short stories), 1979; Rounds, 1980; Take This Man (novel), 1981; Invisible Mending (novel), 1984; Too Late American Boyhood Blues (short stories), 1984; Sometimes I Live in the Country (novel), 1986; When People Publish (essays), 1987; Absent Friends (short stories), 1989. Add: Dept. of English, Colgate Univ., Hamilton, N.Y. 13346, U.S.A.

BUSCH, Niven. American, b. 1903. Novels/Short stories, Westerns/Adventure, Biography. Staff writer, Time Mag., and Contrib. Ed., New Yorker mag., 1927–31, then freelance writer and film producer. *Publs:* Twenty-One Americans, Being Profiles of Some People Famous in Our Time, Together with Silly Pictures of Them Drawn by De Miskey, 1930; The Carrington Incident, 1941; The Dream of Home, 1944; Duel in the Sun, 1944; Day of the Conquerors, 1946; The Furies, 1948; The Hate Merchant, 1953; The Actor, 1955; California Street, 1959; The San Franciscans, 1962; The Gentleman from California, 1965; The Takeover, 1973; No Place for a Hero, 1976; Continent's Edge, 1980; The Titan Game, 1989. Add: c/o Frederick Hill, 2237 Union St., San Francisco, CA 94123, U.S.A.

BUSH, Barry (Michael). British, b. 1938. Animals/Pets, Medicine/Health. Veterinary surgeon since 1961. Lectr. and Course Adviser, Hounslow Borough Coll., since 1962; Sr. Lectr., Royal Veterinary Coll., Univ. of London, since 1980 (Lectr., 1964–80). Lectr., Coll. for the Distributive Trades, London, 1967–88. Member of Council, 1968–69, Hon. Secty., 1969–70, Jr. Vice Pres., 1970–73, Pres., 1973–74 and Sr. Vice Pres., 1974–75, Central Veterinary Soc.; Member, Small Animal Cttee., 1969–72, and Member of Council, 1969–72 and 1973–74, British Veterinary Assn. *Publs:* Veterinary Laboratory Manual, 1975; First Aid for Pet Animals, 1980, rev. ed. as First Aid for Pets, 1984; The Cat and Dog Care Question and Answer Book, 2 vols., 1981–82. Add: Dept. of Medicine, Royal Veterinary Coll., Hawkshead Lane, North Mymms, Herts. AL9 7TA, England.

BUSH, Martin H. American, b. 1930. Art, Social commentary/phenomena. Vice Pres. for Academic Resource Development, Wichita State Univ., Kans., since 1974 (Asst. Vice-Pres., 1971–74). Instr., Dept of History, 1963–65, and Asst. Dean, 1965–70, Syracuse Univ., N.Y. *Publs:* Ben Shahn: The Passion of Sacco and Vanzetti, 1968; Revolutionary Enigma, 1969; Doris Caesar, 1970; Goodnough, 1973, 1982; Duane Hanson, 1976; Ernest Trova, 1977; The Photographs of Gordon Parks, 1983; Philip Reisman: People Are His Passion, 1986. Add:

9201 E. Elm St., Wichita, Kans. 67206, U.S.A.

BUSHELL, Raymond. American, b. 1910. Art. Attorney, Bushell and Asahina, Tokyo, since 1950. *Publs:* The Netsuke Handbook, 1961; The Wonderful World of Netsuke, 1964; Collectors' Netsuke, 1971; An Introduction to Netsuke, 1971; Netsuke Familiar and Unfamiliar, 1975; The Inro Handbook, 1979; (with Masatoshi) The Art of Netsuke Carving, 1981; Netsuke Masks, 1985. Add: Sogo Building No. 10, 11-28 Nagata-cho 1-chome, Chiyoda-ku, Tokyo 100, Japan.

BUSHMAN, Richard Lyman. American, b. 1931. History. Prof. of History, Columbia Univ., NYC, since 1989. Asst. Prof., 1960–66, and Assoc, Prof., 1966–68, Brigham Young Univ., Provo, Utah; Prof. of History, Boston Univ., 1968–77; Prof. of History, Univ. of Delaware, 1977–89. *Publs:* (ed.) Religion at Harvard, 1957; From Puritan to Yankee: Character and the Social Order in Connecticut 1690-1765, 1967; (ed.) The Great Awakening, 1970; (co-ed.) Uprooted Americans, 1979; Joseph Smith and the Beginnings of Mormonism, 1984; King and People in Provincial Massachusetts, 1985. Add: Dept. of History, Columbia Univ., New York, N.Y. 10027, U.S.A.

BUSVINE, James Ronald. British, b. 1912. Medicine/Health. Member, WHO Panel of Experts on Insecticides, since 1960. Entomological Adviser to the Minister of Health, 1943–45; Lectr., 1946–54, Reader, 1954–64, and Prof. of Entomology as applied to Hygiene, 1964–76, London Sch. of Hygiene and Tropical Medicine. *Publs:* Insects and Hygiene, 1951, 3rd ed. 1980; Techniques for Testing Insecticides, 1957, 1971; Arthropod Vectors of Disease, 1975; Insects, Hygiene, and History, 1976; I Warmed Both Hands, 1986. Add: 26 Braywick Rd., Maidenhead, Berks., England.

BUTCHER, Thomas Kennedy. British, b. 1914. Children's non-fiction. Freelance writer and broadcaster since 1972. Producer, Schs. Radio, BBC, London, 1951–72; Tutor and Counsellor, Open Univ., 1973–77. *Publs:* The Great Explorations: Asia and Australia, 1955; The Great Explorations: Africa, 1959; Country Life, 1970; The Navy, 1973; The Firefighters, 1977. Add: Woodman Cottage, Pishill Bottom, Henley-on-Thames, Oxon, England.

BUTLAND, Gilbert J(ames). Australian, b. 1910. Education, Geography, International relations/Current affairs, Autobiography. With the Univ. of New England, Armidale, N.S.W.: Foundn. Prof. of Geography, 1959–72; Dean of Faculty of Arts, 1960–62; Chmn., Professorial Bd., 1964–66; Pro-Vice-Chancellor, 1972–75. Headmaster, The Whitney Inst. Sch., Bermuda, 1937–42, and The British Sch., Punta Arenas, Chile, 1943–47; Sr. Lectr. in Geography, Univ. of Birmingham, 1948–59; Honorary Consul for Chile, Birmingham, 1950–59. *Publs:* Chile: An Outline of its Geography, Economics and Politics, 1951, 3rd ed. 1956; The Human Geography of Southern Chile, 1957; Latin America: A Regional Geography, 1960, 3rd ed., 1972; Letters from Grenfell: from a New South Wales Goldminer in the 1870s, 1971; The Other Side of the Pacific: Problems of Latin America, 1972; (ed.) Australian Regional Geographies: Tasmania, 1972, Interior Queensland, 1972; Melbourne: An Urban Profile, 1973; Southern South Australia, 1975; Bermuda: A New Study, 1980; The Prof and Penny: An Autobiography, 1986. Add: 5 Poinciana Ave., North Sapphire, Coff's Habour, N.S.W. 2450, Australia.

BUTLER, Colin G(asking). British, b. 1913. Biology, Natural history. Formerly, Head of Entomology Dept., Rothamsted Experimental Station. *Publs:* The Honeybee: An Introduction to Her Sense-Physiology and Behaviour, 1949; The World of the Honeybee, 1954, rev. ed. 1975; (with J. Free) Bumblebees, 1959. Add: "Silver Birches", Porthpean, St. Austell, Cornwall PL26 6AU, England.

BUTLER, David (Edgeworth). British, b. 1924. Politics/Government. Fellow, Nuffield Coll., Oxford, since 1954. Personal Asst. to the British Ambassador, Washington, D.C., 1955–56. *Publs:* The British General Election of 1951, 1952; The Electoral System in Britain since 1918, 1953, 1962; The British General Election of 1955, 1955; The Study of Political Behaviour, 1958; (ed.) Elections Abroad, 1958; (with R. Rose) The British General Election of 1959, 1960; British Political Facts 1900–1979, 1963, 5th ed. 1980; (with A.S. King) The British General Election of 1964, 1965; (with A.S. King) The British General Election of 1966, 1966; (with M. Pinto-Duschinsky) The British General Election of 1970, 1971; (with D. Stokes) Political Change in Britain, 1969, 1973; The Canberra Model, 1973; (with D. Kavanagh) The British General Election of February 1974, 1974; (with D. Kavanagh) The British General Election of October 1974, 1975; (with U.W. Kitzinger) The 1975 Referendum, 1976; (with A.H. Halsey) Policy and Politics, 1978; (with A. Ranney) Referendums, 1978;

(with D. Kavanagh) The British General Election of 1979, 1980; (with D. Marquand) European Elections and British Politics, 1981; (with A. Ranney) Democracy at the Polls, 1981; (with V. Bogdanor) Democracy and Elections, 1983; Governing Without a Majority, 1983; (with D. Kavanagh) The British General Election of 1983, 1984; A Compendium of Indian Elections, 1984; (with P. Jowett) Party Strategies in Britain, 1985; (with G. Butler) British Political Facts 1900–85, 1986; (with D. Kavanagh) The British General Election of 1987, 1988. Add: Nuffield Coll., Oxford, England.

BUTLER, Dorothy. New Zealander, b. 1925. Children's non-fiction, Education, Literature. Managing Dir., Dorothy Butler Ltd. children's bookshop, since 1965. Principal, Dorothy Butler (remedial) Reading Centre, 1978–84. *Publs:* Cushla and Her Books, 1979; (with Marie Clay) Reading Begins at Home, 1979; Babies Need Books, 1980; (ed.) The Magpies Said: Stories and Poems from New Zealand, 1980; The Dorothy Butler Pre-Reading Kit, 1980; (ed.) For Me, Me, Me, 1983; (ed.) I Will Build You a House, 1984; Five to Eight, 1985; Come Back, Ginger, 1987; A Bundle of Birds, 1987; My Brown Bear Barney, 1988. Add: 132 Sunnybrae Rd., Takapuna, Auckland 10, New Zealand.

BUTLER, (Frederick) Guy. South African, b. 1918. Plays/Screenplays, Poetry, Literature, Autobiography/Memoirs/Personal. Member of faculty, Univ. of Witwatersrand, Johannesburg, 1948–50; Prof. of English, Rhodes Univ., Grahamstown, 1952–86, Research Fellow, 1987. Founded New Coin mag., Grahamstown. *Publs:* Stranger to Europe, 1952, augmented ed. 1960; The Dam (play), 1953; An Aspect of Tragedy, 1953; The Dove Returns (play), 1956; (ed.) A Book of South African Verse, 1959; The Republic of the Arts, 1964; South of the Zambezi: Poems from South Africa, 1966; Take Root or Die (play), 1966; On First Seeing Florence, 1968; Cape Charade (play), 1968; (ed.) When Boys Were Men, 1969; (ed.) The 1820 Settlers, 1974; Karoo Morning: An Autobiography 1918–35, 1977; Selected Poems, 1978, rev. and enlarged, 1989; Songs and Ballads, 1978; (ed. with Christopher Mann) A New Book of South African Verse, 1979; Richard Gush of Salem (play), 1982; Bursting World: An Autobiography 1936–45, 1983; (ed. with N. Visser) S.C. Cronwright Schreiner: My Diary 7-15 June and 8-29 August 1921; Pilgrimage to Dias Cross (poetry), 1987; (ed. with David Butler) Out of the African Dark (poetry), 1988; A Rackety Colt, or The Adventures of Thomas Stubbs (novel), 1989; Tales of the Old Karoo (short stories), 1989; (ed. with Jeff Opland) The Magic Tree (poetry), 1989. Add: Dept. of English, Rhodes Univ., Grahamstown 6140, South Africa.

BUTLER, Gwendoline (Williams). Also writes as Jenny Melville. British, b. 1922. Mystery/Crime/Suspense, Historical/Romance/Gothic. *Publs:* Receipt for Murder, 1956; Dead in a Row, 1957; The Dull Dead, 1958; The Murdering Kind, 1958; The Interloper, 1959; Death Lives Next Door (in U.S. as Dine and Be Dead), 1960; Make Me a Murderer, 1961; Coffin in Oxford, 1962; Coffin for Baby, 1963; Coffin Waiting, 1963; Coffin in Malta, 1964; A Nameless Coffin, 1966; Coffin Following, 1968; Coffin's Dark Number, 1969; A Coffin from the Past, 1970; A Coffin for Pandora, 1973, in U.S. as Olivia, 1974; A Coffin for the Canary (in U.S. as Sarsen Place), 1974; The Vesey Inheritance, 1975; Brides of Friedberg (in U.S. as Meadowsweet), 1977; The Red Staircase, 1979; Albion Walk, 1982, in U.K. paperback as Cavalcade, 1984; Coffin in the Water, 1986; Coffin Underground, 1988; Coffin in the Black Museum, 1989; A Cure for Dying, 1989; as Jenny Melville—Come Home and Be Killed, 1962; Burning Is a Substitute for Loving, 1963; Murderers' Houses, 1964; There Lies Your Love, 1965; Nell Alone, 1966; A Different Kind of Summer, 1967; The Hunter in the Shadows, 1969; A New Kind of Killer, An Old Kind of Death, 1970, in U.S. as A New Kind of Killer, 1971; Ironwood, 1972; Nun's Castle, 1973; Raven's Forge, 1975; Dragon's Eye, 1976; Axwater (in U.S. as Tarot's Tower), 1978; Murder Has a Pretty Face, 1981; The Painted Castle, 1982; The Hand of Glass, 1983; Listen to the Children, 1986; Windsor Red, 1988. Add: c/o John Farquharson Ltd., 162-168 Regent St., London W1R 5TB, England.

BUTLER, Iris Mary. British, b. 1905. Biography. *Publs:* Rule of Three (in U.S. as the Great Duchess), 1967; (ed.) The Viceroy's Wife: Letters of Alice Countess of Reading from India, 1970; The Eldest Brother: The Marquess Wellesley 1760-1845, 1973. Add: 50 Gretton Ct., Girton, Cambridge CB3 0QN, England.

BUTLER, Ivan. British, b. 1909. Plays/Screenplays, Criminology/Law enforcement/Prisons, Film, Theatre. Reviewer, Film Review Annual, since 1968 and Films and Filming, since 1981. Film Critic, What's On in London, 1970–76. *Publs:* plays—Crime Out of Mind, 1949; The Wise Children, 1953; (with F. Cary) The Paper Chain, 1953; Columbine in Camberwell, 1953; (with F. Cary) Danger Inside!, 1954; Tranquil House, 1954;

other—Producing Pantomime and Revue, 1962; The Horror Film, 1967; Religion in the Cinema, 1969; The Cinema of Roman Polanski, 1970; Horror in the Cinema, 1970; 1979; The Making of Feature Films, 1971; (ed.) 100 Best Full-Length Plays for Amateurs, 1972; To Encourage the Art of the Film: The History of the British Film Institute, 1972; Cinema in Britain, 1973; Murderers' London (and England), 2 vols., 1973; The War Film, 1974; (ed.) The Trials of Brian Donald Hume, 1976; Silent Magic: Reminiscenses of the Silent Cinema, 1987. Add: 9 Foxdell, off Dene Rd., Northwood HA6 2BU, England.

BUTLER, Joseph T(homas). American, b. 1932. Antiques/Furnishings, Architecture. Senior Dir., Museum Operations: Historic Hudson Valley, Tarrytown, N.Y., since 1957. Prof., Fashion Inst. of Technology, since 1987. Adjunct Assoc. Prof. of Architecture, Univ. of Columbia, NYC, 1970–80. American Ed., The Connoisseur, 1967–77; Member, Editorial Bd., Art and Antiques, 1978–83. *Publs:* Washington Irving's Sunnyside, 1962, rev. ed. 1974; American Antiques 1800-1900: A Collector's History and Guide, 1965; (co-author) World Furniture, 1965; Candleholders in America 1650-1900, 1967; The Family Collections at Van Cortlandt Manor, 1967; (co-author) The Arts in America: The 19th Century, 1969; American Furniture, 1973; (co-author) The Collectors' Encyclopedia of Antiques, 1973; The Story of Boscobel and Its Builder: States Morris Dyckman, 1974; Van Cortlandt Manor, 1978; Sleepy Hollow Restorations. A Cross Section of the Collection, 1983; A Field Guide to American Antique Furniture, 1985. Add: 222 Martling Ave., Tarrytown, N.Y. 10591, U.S.A.

BUTLER, Margaret (Gwendoline). British. Fashion/Costume. Principal Lectr., in Dress and Design, St. Osyth's Coll. of Education, Clacton-on-Sea, 1956–72. *Publs:* Clothers, 1958, 1975; (with B. Greves) Fabric Furnishings, 1972. Add: 83 Holland Rd., Clacton-on-Sea, Essex, England.

BUTLER, Marilyn (Speers). British, b. 1937. Literature. King Edward VII Prof. of English Literature, Cambridge Univ., since 1986. Current Affairs Producer, B.B.C., 1960–63; Research Fellow, St. Hilda's Coll., Oxford, 1970–73; Fellow and Tutor, St. Hugh's Coll., and Lectr. in English Literature, Oxford Univ., 1976–86. *Publs:* Maria Edgeworth: A Literary Biography, 1972; Jane Austen and the War of Ideas, 1975; Peacock Displayed: A Satirist in His Context, 1979; Romantics, Rebels, and Reactionaries: English Literature and Its Background 1760-1830, 1981; (ed.) Burke, Paine, Godwin and the Revolution Controversy, 1984. Add: King's Coll., Cambridge, England.

BUTLER, Nathan. *See* **SOHL**, Jerry

BUTLER, Octavia E. American, b. 1947. Science fiction/Fantasy. *Publs:* Pattermaster, 1976; Mind of My Mind, 1977; Survivor, 1978; Kindred, 1979; Wild Seed, 1980; Clay's Ark, 1984; Dawn, 1987; Adulthood Rites, 1988. Add: P.O. Box 6604, Los Angeles, Calif. 90055, U.S.A.

BUTLER, Patrick. *See* **DUNBOYNE**, Lord.

BUTLER, Richard. British, b. 1925. Novels/Short stories, Plays/Screen plays. Television actor, since 1972. Teacher and Lectr. in England and Australia, 1950–73. *Publs:* Fingernail Beach, 1964; South of Hell's Gates, 1967; More Dangerous Than the Moon, 1968; The Doll (teleplay), 1970; Sharkbait, 1970, Jakt I Morker, 1971; I Sista Sekunden, 1972; The Buffalo Hook, 1974; The Men that God Forgot, 1975; And Wretches Hang, 1977; Lift-Off at Satan, 1978. Add: c/o St. Martin's Press, 175 Fifth Ave., New York, N.Y. 10010, U.S.A.

BUTLER, Richard. *See* **ALLBEURY**, Ted.

BUTLIN, Martin (Richard Fletcher). British, b. 1929. Art. Keeper of the Historic British Collection, Tate Gallery, London, 1967–89 (Asst. Keeper, 1955–67). *Publs:* Catalogue of the Works of William Blake in the Tate Gallery, 1957, 3rd ed. 1979; Samuel Palmer's Sketch Book of 1824, 1962; Turner Watercolours, 1962; (with John Rothenstein) Turner, 1965; (co-author) Tate Gallery Catalogues: Modern British Paintings, Drawings and Sculpture, 1964; The Later Works of J.M.W. Turner, 1965; William Blake, 1966; The Blake-Varley Sketchbook of 1819, 1969; (with A. Wilton and John Gage) Turner 1775-1851 (exhibition catalogue), 1974; (with Evelyn Joll) The Paintings of J.M.W. Turner, 1977, 1984; William Blake (exhibition catalogue) 1978; The Paintings and Drawings of William Blake, 1981; Aspects of British Painting 1550-1800, 1988; (with Millie Luther and Ian Warrell) Turner and Petworth, 1989. Add: Tate Gallery, Millbank, London SW1, England.

BUTOW, Robert J.C. American, b. 1924. International relations, Area studies (diplomatic history). Prof., Jackson Sch. of Intnl. Studies, Univ. of Washington, Seattle, since 1966 (Assoc. Prof., 1960–66). Instr. in History, 1954–59, and Asst. Prof., 1959–60, Princeton Univ., N.J. *Publs:* Japan's Decision to Surrender, 1954; Tojo and the Coming of the War, 1961; The John Doe Associates: Backdoor Diplomacy for Peace 1941, 1974. Add: Jackson Sch. of Intnl. Studies, Thomson Hall, DR-05, Univ. of Washington, Seattle, Wash. 98195, U.S.A.

BUTRYM, Zofia T(eresa). Polish, b. 1927. Sociology. Sr. Lectr. in Social Work, London Sch. of Economics, since 1970 (Lectr., 1958–70). Medical Social Worker, 1950–55, and Sr. Medical Social Worker and Student Supervisor, 1956–58, Hammersmith Hosp. and Postgraduate Medical Sch., London. Chmn. of Education Ctte., Inst. of Medical Social Workers, 1966–70; Member of Council, British Assn. of Social Workers, 1970–71. *Publs:* Social Work in Medical Care (textbook), 1967; Medical Social Work in Action, 1968; The Nature of Social Work, 1976; (with J. Horner) Health Doctors and Social Workers, 1983. Add: London Sch. of Economics, Houghton St., London WC2A 2AE, England.

BUTTER, Peter Herbert. British, b. 1921. Literature, Biography. Lectr., Univ. of Edinburgh, 1948–58; Prof., Queen's Univ., of Belfast, 1958–65; Regius Prof. of English, Univ. of Glasgow, 1965–86. *Publs:* Shelley's Idols of the Cave, 1954; Francis Thompson, 1961; Edwin Muir, 1962; Edwin Muir: Man and Poet, 1966; (ed.) Shelley's Alastor, Prometheus Unbound and Other Poems, 1971; (ed.) Selected Letters of Edwin Muir, 1974; (ed.) Selected Poems of William Blake, 1982; (ed.) The Truth of Imagination: Uncollected Essays and Reviews by Edwin Muir, 1988. Add: Ashfield, Bridge of Weir, Renfrewshire PA11 3AW, Scotland.

BUTTERFIELD, (Sir) (William) John. British, b. 1920. Medicine/Health. Chmn., Health Promotion Research Trust, and Jardine Education Trust; Vice-Pres., Byron Soc. Member, Scientific Staff, Medical Research Council, London, 1946–58; Major, Royal Army Medical Corps Army Operational Research Group, 1947–50; Research Fellow, Medical Coll. of Virginia, 1950–52; seconded to the Ministry of Supply, 1952, and the Atomic Energy Authority, 1956; Prof. of Experimental Medicine, Guy's Hosp., London, 1958–63; Prof. of Medicine, Guy's Hosp. Medical Sch., London, 1963–71; Vice Chancellor, Univ. of Nottingham, 1971–75; Regius Prof. of Physic, Cambridge Univ., 1975–87, Master of Downing Coll., Cambridge, 1978–87, and Vice-Chancellor, Cambridge Univ., 1983–85. Chmn., South East Metropolitan Regional Hosp. Bd.'s Clinical Research Cttee., 1960–71; Chmn., British Diabetic Assn., 1967–74; Member of the Council, European Assn. for the Study of Diabetes, 1968–71; Member, Medical Research Council, 1974–78. *Publs:* On Burns, 1953; Tolbutamide after 10 Years, 1967; Priorities in Medicine, 1968; Health and Sickness: The Choice of Treatment, 1971; (co-ed.) The International Dictionary of Medicine and Biology, 1986. Add: Downing Coll., Cambridge CB2 1DQ, England.

BUTTERFIELD, William H(enry). American, b. 1910. Advertising/Public relations, Writing/Journalism. Self-employed correspondence consultant, since 1964. Fellow, American Business Communication Assn., since 1961 (Pres., 1943–45). Exec. Dir., Univ. Illinois Foundn., Urbana, 1948–58; Vic. Pres. for Development, Texas Technological Coll., Lubbock, 1959–64. *Publs:* The Business Letter in Modern Form, 1938, 1951; Goodwill Letters That Build Business, 1940; Successful Collection Letters, 1941; Twelve Ways to Write Better Letters, 1943; Credit Letters That Win Friends, 1944; How to Use Letters in College Public Relations, 1944; Building Hotel Business by Letter, 1945; Bank Letters—How To Use Them in Public Relations, 1946; How to Write Good Credit Letters, 1947; Effective Personal Letters, 1951; Letters That Build Bank Business, 1953; Common Sense in Letter Writing, 1963; Guides to Better Business Letters, 1985. Add: 54975 South Circle Dr., Idyllwild, Calif. 92349, U.S.A.

BUTTERS, Dorothy Gilman. *See* **GILMAN**, Dorothy.

BUTTERWORTH, Oliver. American, b. 1915. Children's Fiction. Instr. in English, Hartford Coll., Connecticut, since 1949. Teacher, Kent Sch., 1937–48, and The Jr. Sch., West Hartford, 1948–49. *Publs:* The Enormous Egg, 1956; The Trouble with Jenny's Ear, 1960; The Narrow Passage, 1973; The First Blueberry Pig, 1986; The Visit to the Big House, 1987. Add: 81 Sunset Farm Rd., West Hartford, Conn. 06107, U.S.A.

BUTTINGER, Joseph. American, b. 1906. Politics/Government. Active in rescue work for refugees from Fascism since 1939, and Iron Curtain countries since 1945. Member of the Bd., International Rescue

Cttee., since 1945 (European Dir., 1945–47). *Publs:* In the Twilight of Socialism, 1952; The Smaller: A Political History of Vietnam, 1958; Vietnam: A Dragon Embattled, 2 vols., 1967; A Dragon Defiant: A Short History of Vietnam, 1972; Vietnam: The Unforgettable Tragedy, 1976. Add: R.R. 1, Box 264, Pennington, N.J. 08534, U.S.A.

BUTTITTA, Tony. American, b. 1907. Plays/Screenplays, Theatre, Autobiography/Memoirs/Personal. Former theatrical press agent in New York and California; also United Press Corresp. for various U.S. newspapers. Ed., Contempo, 1931–34. *Publs:* Singing Piedmont (play), 1937; After the Good Gay Times: A Season with F. Scott Fitzgerald, 1974; Uncle Sam Presents: A Memoir of the Federal Theatre, 1935–39, 1982; The Lost Summer: A Memoir of F. Scott Fitzgerald, 1987. Add: 28 Jones St., New York, N.Y. 10014, U.S.A.

BUTTON, Kenneth J(ohn). British, b. 1948. Economics, Transportation. Reader in Economics, Loughborough Univ., Leicestershire. *Publs:* (with P.J. Barker) Case Studies in Cost Benefit Analysis, 1975; Urban Economics: Theory and Policy, 1976; (with D. Gillingwater) Case Studies in Regional Economics, 1976; The Economics of Urban Transport, 1977; (with A.D. Pearman) The Economics of Urban Freight Tranport, 1981; (with A.D. Pearman and A.S. Fowkes) Car Ownership Modelling and Forecasting, 1982; Transport Economics, 1982; (ed. with D. Gillingwater) Transport Location and Spatial Policy, 1983; (with A.D. Pearman) The Practice of Transport Investment Appraisal, 1983; Road Haulage Licensing and EC Transport Policy, 1984; (with A.D. Pearman) Applied Transport Economics, 1985; (ed. with D. Pitfield) International Railway Economics, 1985; (with D. Gillingwater) Future Transport Policy, 1986; (ed.) The Collected Essays of Harvey Leibenstein, 2 vols., 1989; (with A.J. Westaway) The Economic Impact of Aid Policy on Donor Country's Economies, 1989; (ed. with D. Swann) The Age of Regulatory Reform, 1989. Add: Dept. of Economics, Loughborough Univ., Loughborough, Leics., England.

BUTTREY, Douglas Norton. British. Chemistry, Technology. Member of the Technical Staff, Plastics Div., ICI Ltd., 1949–77. *Publs:* Cellulose Plastics, 1947; Plasticizers, 1950, 1957; Plastics in the Furniture Industry, 1964; Plastics in Furniture, 1976; ESPI Guides: Plastics in Furniture Agriculture and Horticulture, Building, 3 vols., 1982–84. Add: 15 Churchfields, Broxbourne, Herts., England.

BUTZER, Karl W. Canadian, b. 1934. Archaeology/Antiquities, Earth sciences, Environmental science/Ecology. Dickson Prof. of Liberal Arts, Univ. of Texas, Austin, since 1984. Henry Schultz Prof. of Anthropology and Geography, Univ. of Chicago, 1966–83. *Publs:* Environment and Archaeology, 1964, 1971; (with C.L. Hansen) Desert and River in Nubia, 1978; Recent History of an Ethiopian Delta, 1971; (ed. with G.L. Isaac) After the Australopithecines: Early Hydraulic Civilization in Egypt, 1976; Geomorphology from the Earth, 1976; (ed.) Dimensions of Human Geography, 1978; Archaeology as Human Ecology, 1982. Add: Dept. of Geography. University of Texas, Austin, Tex. 78712-1098, U.S.A.

BUXBAUM, Martin. American, b. 1912. Poetry. Autobiography/Memoirs/Personal, Humor/Satire. Ed. Table Talk, since 1953, Marriott Corp., Washington D.C. (Dir. of Communications, 1953–76); Ed., Milestones Mag., since 1980; Ed., Kee-Notes newsletter, since 1980. Contrib., Reader's Digest, since 1958; Counselor, Sunshine Mag., since 1965; Advisor, Praying Hands Mag., since 1975. *Publs:* Bux's Scrapbook, 1958; Rivers of Thought (poetry), 1958; The Underside of Heaven (poetry), 1963; Table Talk, 1964; (ed.) The Unsung, vol. I, 1964, vol. II, 1965; Around Our House (humor), 1966, Once Upon a Dream (poetry), 1970; Whispers in the Wind (poetry), 1970; 15 Years of Table Talk, 1973; The Warm World of Martin Buxbaum (poetry), 1974; The Bedside Book, 1987. Add: 7819 Custer Rd., Bethesda, Md. 20814, U.S.A.

BUXTON, David Roden. British, b. 1910. Architecture, Travel/Exploration/Adventure. With British Council Overseas Service, 1946–67; Research Fellow, Clare Hall, Cambridge Univ., 1967–73. *Publs:* Russian Mediaeval Architecture, 1934; Travels in Ethiopia 1949, 1957; (trans.) The Early Churches of Rome, by Emile Mâle, 1960; The Abyssinians, 1970; The Wooden Churches of Eastern Europe, 1981. Add: Old Ellwoods, 55 Bridleway, Grantchester, Cambs. CB3 9NY, England.

BUXTON, John. British, b. 1912. Poetry, Literature, Biography. Emeritus Fellow of New Coll., Oxford, since 1979 (Lectr., 1946–48; Fellow, since 1949); Reader Emeritus in English Literature, Oxford Univ., since 1979 (Reader, 1972–79). Gen. Ed., Oxford Paperback English Texts, since 1967, and Oxford History of English Literature, since 1973. *Publs:* Such Liberty (verse), 1944; (with Ronald Lockley) Island of

Skomer, 1950; The Redstart, 1950; (ed.) Poems of Michael Drayton, 1953; Sir Philip Sidney and the English Renaissance, 1954; (ed.) Poems of Charles Cotton, 1958; Elizabethan Taste, 1963; A Tradition of Poetry, 1967; Twelve Poems, 1967; Byron and Shelley, 1968; The Grecian Taste, 1978; (co-ed.) New College, Oxford 1379-1979, 1979; (ed.) Walton and Cotton: The Compleat Angler, 1982. Add: The Grove, East Tytherton, Chippenham, Wilts., England.

BUZO, Alexander. Australian b. 1944. Novels, Plays/Screenplays. Salesman, David Jones Ltd., Sydney, 1960; Messenger, E.L. Davis & Co., Sydney, 1961; Storeman-Packer, McGraw-Hill Book Co., Sydney, 1967; Clerk, N.S.W. Public Service, Sydney, 1967–68; Resident Playwright, Melbourne Theatre Co., 1972–73. *Publs:* Macquarie, 1971; Norm and Ahmed, Rooted, and The Roy Murphy Show: Three Plays, 1973; Coralie Lansdowne Says No, 1974; Tom, 1975; Martello Towers, 1976; Makassar Reef, 1978; Tautology (non-fiction), 1981; Meet the New Class, 1981; Big River, The Marginal Farm, 1985; The Search for Harry Allway (novel), 1985. Add: 14 Rawson Ave., Bondi Junction, Sydney, N.S.W. 2022, Australia.

BYARS, Betsy (Cromer).American, b. 1928. Children's fiction. *Publs:* Clementine, 1962; The Dancing Camel, 1965; Rama, The Gypsy Cat, 1966, The Groober, 1967; The Midnight Fox, 1968; Trouble River, 1969; The Summer of the Swans, 1970; Go and Hush the Baby, 1971; The House of Wings, 1972; The 18th Emergency, 1973; The Winged Colt of Casa Mia, 1973; After the Goat Man, 1974; The Lace Snail, 1975; The T.V. Kid, 1976; The Pinballs, 1977; The Cartoonist, 1978; Goodbye, Chicken Little, 1979; Night Swimmers, 1980; The Animal, The Vegetable, and John D. Jones, 1981; The Two Thousand Pound Goldfish, 1981; The Cybil War, 1982; The Glory Girl, 1983; The Computer Nut, 1984; Cracker Jackson, 1985; The Blossoms Meet the Vulture Lady, 1986; The Golly Sisters Go West, 1986; The Not-Just-Anybody Family, 1986; A Blossom Promise, 1987; The Blossoms And the Green Phantom, 1987; Sugar and Other Stories, 1987; The Burning Questions of Bingo Brown, 1988; Beans on the Roof, 1988; Bingo Brown and the Language of Love, 1989. Add: 4 Riverpoint, Clemson, S.C. 29631, U.S.A.

BYATT, A(ntonia) S(usan). British, b. 1936. Novels/Short stories, Literature. Extra-Mural Lectr., London Univ., 1965–72; Lectr., 1972–81, and Sr. Lectr., 1981–83, University Coll., London. *Publs:* Shadow of a Sun, 1964; Degrees of Freedom: The Novels of Iris Murdoch, 1965; The Game, 1967; Wordsworth and Coleridge in Their Time, 1970; Iris Murdoch, 1976; The Virgin in the Garden, 1978; (ed.) The Mill on the Floss, by George Eliot, 1979; Still Life, 1985; Sugar and Other Stories, 1987. Add: 37 Rusholme Rd., London SW15, England.

BYE, Beryl (Joyce Rayment). British, b. 1926. Children's fiction, Children's non-fiction, Theology/Religion. *Publs:* Three's Company, 1961; Wharf Street, 1962; Prayers at Breakfast, 1964; Teaching Our Children the Christian Faith, 1965; Please God, 1966; About God, 1967; Nobody's Pony, 1967; Looking into Life, 1967; Jesus Said, 1968; Pony for Sale, 1969; Learning from Life, 1969, Jesus at Work, 1969; Start the Day Well, 1970; Prayers for All Seasons, 1971; People Like Us, 1971; More People Like Us, 1972; To be Continued, 1972; Belles Bridle, 1973; Following Jesus, 1974; What about Lifestyle?, 1977; Time for Jesus, 1980. Add: The Old Coach House, Lye Lane, Cleeve Hill, Cheltenham, Glos., England.

BYERS, Horace (Robert). American, b. 1906. Meteorology/Atmospheric sciences. Research Meteorologist, U.S. National Weather Service, Washington, 1935–40; Assoc. Prof., 1940–44, Prof. of Meteorology, 1944–65, and Chmn., Dept. of Meteorology, 1948–60, Univ. of Chicago; Dean, Coll. of Geosciences, 1965–68, Academic Vice-Pres., 1968–71, and Distinguished Prof. of Meteorology, 1965–74, Texas A and M Univ. Pres., American Geophysical Union Section of Meteorology, 1947–49, American Meteorological Soc., 1952–54, and Intnl. Assn. of Meteorology and Atmospheric Physics of the Intnl. Union of Geodesy and Geophysics, 1960–63; Chmn., Section of Geophysics, U.S. National Academy of Sciences, 1966–69. *Publs:* Synoptic and Aeronautical Meteorology, 1937; General Meteorology, 1944, 4th ed. 1974; (with R. Braham, Jr.) The Thunderstorm, 1950; (ed.) Thunderstorm Electricity, 1953; Elements of Cloud Physics, 1965. Add: 300 Hot Springs Rd., Apt. 178, Santa Barbara, Calif. 93108, U.S.A.

BYERS, Irene. British, b. 1906. Children's fiction, Children's non-fiction. *Publs:* The Young Brevingtons, 1953; Tim of Tamberly Forest, 1954; The Strange Story of Pippin Wood, 1956; Sign of the Dolphin, 1956; The Missing Masterpiece, 1957; Flowers for Melissa, 1958; Kennel Maid Sally, 1960; Farm on the Fjord, 1961; Tim Returns to Tamberly,

1962; Jewel of the Jungle, 1962; Foresters of Fourways, 1963; Two on the Trail, 1963; Trouble at Tamberly, 1964; Joanna Joins the Zoo, 1964; The Merediths of Mappins, 1964; Mystery at Mappins, 1964; Out and About Tales, 1964; Magic in Her Fingers, 1965; Outdoor Friends, 1965; Foresters Afield, 1966; Danny Finds a Family, 1966; Half Day Thursday, 1966; House of the Speckled Browns, 1967; The Stage Under the Cedars, 1969; Cameras on Carolyn, 1971; Timothy and Tiptoes, 1975; Silka The Seal, 1976; Tiptoes Wins Through, 1977; Tiptoes the Big Race, 1979; Fox on the Pavement, 1984. Add: 69 Baldry Gardens, London SW16, England.

BYERS BROWN, (Dorothy) Betty. British, b. 1927. Speech/Rhetoric. Speech therapist, Borough of Reading, 1947–52, St. Thomas' Hospital, London, 1953–62, and Central Middlesex Hospital, London, 1954–59; Tutor, Central School of Speech and Drama, London, 1953–62; Supervisor, Dept. of Communication, Univ. of Wisconsin, Madison, 1963–67; Sr. Lectr. in Speech Therapy, Univ. of Manchester, 1968–82, retired; Adjunct Asst. Prof. of Pediatrics, Robert Wood Johnson Medical Sch., Princeton, N.J. *Publs:* Speak for Yourself: A Career in Speech Therapy, 1971; Speech Therapy: Principles and Practice, 1981. Add: c/o College of Speech Therapists, 6 Lechmere Rd., London NW12 5BU, England.

BYLINSKY, Gene (Michael). American, b. 1930. Sciences, Social commentary. Member, Bd. of Editors, Fortune mag., NYC, since 1966. Staff reporter, Wall Street Journal, in Dallas, 1957–59, San Francisco, 1959–61, and NYC, 1961; Science Writer, National Observer, Washington, 1961–62, and Newshouse newspapers, 1962–66. *Publs:* The Innovation Millionaires, 1976; Mood Control, 1978; Life in Darwin's Universe, 1981; High Tech Window on the Future, 1985. Add: Fortune, Time and Life Bldg., Rockefeller Center, New York, N.Y. 10020, U.S.A.

BYRNE, Donn E. American. Psychology. Prof. of Psychology, since 1979 and Chmn. of Dept., since 1984, State Univ. of New York, Albany. Instr., California State Univ., San Francisco, 1957–59; Asst., Assoc., then Prof., Univ. of Texas, 1959–69; Prof. of Psychological Sciences, Purdue Univ., West Lafayette, Ind., 1969–79. *Publs:* (ed. with P. Worchel) Personality Change, 1964; (ed. with M. Hamilton) Personality Research, 1966; The Attraction Paradigm, 1971; (with H. and G. Lindgren) Current Research in Personality, 1971; (with R. Baron) Social Psychology, 1974, 1977, 1981, 1984, 1987; An Introduction to Personality, 3rd. ed. 1981; (with H. Lindgren) Psychology, 4th ed. 1975; (ed. with L. Byrne) Exploring Human Sexuality, 1977; (with R. Baron and B. Kantowitz) Psychology, 1977, 1980; (with W. A. Fisher) Adolescents, Sex, and Contraception, 1983; (with K. Kelly) Alternative Approaches to the Study of Sexual Behavior, 1986; (with R. Baron and J. Suls) Exploring Social

Psychology, 1989. Add: 265 Indian Hill Rd., Feura Bush, N.Y. 12067, U.S.A.

BYRNE, John. British, b. 1940. Plays/Screenplays. Set and costume designer. Writer-in-Residence, Borderline Theatre, Irvine, Ayrshire, 1979, and Duncan of Jordanstone College, Dundee, 1981. *Publs:* The Slab Boys, 1981; Threads, 1980, rev. ed. as Cutting a Rug, 1982; The London Cuckolds, 1986; Tutti Frutti (novel), 1987. Add: 3 Castle Brae, Newport on Tay, Fife, Scotland.

BYRNE, Robert. American, b. 1930. Novels/Short stories, Language/Linguistics, Recreation/Leisure/Hobbies, Writing/Journalism. Former trade journal ed. *Publs:* Writing Rackets, 1969; Memories of a Non-Jewish Childhood (novel), 1971; McGoorty, 1972; (ed.) Mrs. Byrne's Dictionary of Unusual Words, 1974; The Tunnel (novel), 1977; Byrne's Standard Book of Pool and Billiards, 1978; The Dam (novel), 1981; Always Catholic (novel), 1981; Byrne's Treasury of Trick Shots in Pool and Billiards, 1982; The 637 Best Things Anybody Ever Said, 1982; Cat Scan, 1983, in England as The Quotable Cat, 1985; Skyscraper (novel), 1984; The Other 637 Best Things Anybody Ever Said, 1984; The Third 637 Best Things Anybody Ever Said, 1986; Mannequin (novel) (in England, as Death Train), 1988; Every Day is Father's Day, 1989. Add: 85 Ashford Ave., Mill Valley, CA 94941, U.S.A.

BYRNES, Robert Francis. American, b. 1917. History, International relations/Current affairs. Sr. Fellow, Columbia Univ., NYC, 1948–50; Fellow, Inst. for Advanced Study, Princeton, N.J., 1950, and Netherlands Inst. for Advanced Study, 1976–77; Fellow, Inst. of History, Soviet Academy, 1963, 1978; Fellow, History of Ideas Unit, Australian National Univ., 1987–88. *Publs:* Antisemitism in Modern France: The Prologue to the Dreyfus Affair, 1950, 1969; Bibliography of American Publications on East Central Europe 1945–57, 1959; The Non-Western Areas in Undergraduate Education in Indiana, 1969; (with others) The College and World Affairs, 1964; Pobedonostev: His Life and Thought, 1967; The United States and Eastern Europe, 1967; (ed.) Germany and the East: The Collected Essays of Fritz Epstein, 1973; Soviet-American Academic Exchanges 1958–75, 1976; Awakening American Education to the World, 1982; After Brezhnev: Sources of Soviet Conduct in the 1980's, 1983. Add: 402 Reisner Dr., Bloomington, Ind. 47401, U.S.A.

BYRT, Edwin Andrew. Australian, b. 1932. Mathematics/Statistics. Sr. Lectr., Victoria Coll., Rusden. Teacher, Education Dept. of Vic., 1954–66, and Suva Grammar Sch., Fiji, 1967–68; Lectr., Univ. of the South Pacific, Suva, Fiji, 1969. *Publs:* Contemporary Mathematics, 4 vols., 1969–72. Add: 13 Westley St., Ferntree Gully, Vic., Australia 3156.

C

CABECEIRAS, James. American, b. 1930. Information science/Computers, Librarianship. Prof., San Jose State Univ., California, since 1968. Supervisor of Libraries and Instructional Media, Syracuse, N.Y. School District, 1963–67; Instructor, Syracuse Univ., 1964–67. *Publs:* (with others) AV Instructional Technology Manual, 4th and 5th eds., 1973, 1977; Auto Instructional Audio Unit, 1974; The Multimedia Library Material Selection and Use, 1978, 1982. Add: Washington Sq., San Jose State Univ., San Jose, Calif. 95192, U.S.A.

CACCIATORE, Vera. Italian, b. 1911. Novels/Short stories, Literature. Former Curator of the Keats-Shelley Memorial House, Rome. *Publs:* La Vendita All'Asta, 1953; The Swing, 1959; La Palestra, 1961; Shelley and Byron at Pisa, 1961; La Forza Motrice,1968; A Room in Rome, 1970; La Scalinata, 1984; C'è una stanza a Roma, 1987. Add: Largo Cristina di Svezia 12, 00165 Rome, Italy.

CACHIA, Pierre (Jacques Elie). British, b. 1921. Language/Linguistics, Literature. Prof. of Arabic Language and Literature, Columbia Univ., NYC, since 1975 (Chmn., Dept. Middle Eastern Languages and Cultures, 1980–83). Joint Ed., Journal of Arabic Literature, Leiden, since 1970. Asst. Lectr., 1949–50, Lectr., 1950–65, Sr. Lectr., 1965–69, and Reader in Arabic, 1969–76, Edinburgh Univ. *Publs:* Taha Husayn: His Place in the Egyptian Literary Renaissance, 1956; (ed.) The Book of the Demonstration by Eutychius of Alexandria, vol. 1, 1960, vol. 2, 1961; (with W. Watt) A History of Islamic Spain, 1965; (compiler) The Monitor: A Dictionary of Arabic Grammatical Terms, 1973; Al-Arif: A Dictionary of Grammatical Terms, Arabic–English, English–Arabic, 1974; (joint ed.) Islam: Past Influence and Present Challenge, 1979. Popular Narrative Ballads of Modern Egypt, 1988. Add: 605 Kent Hall, Columbia Univ., New York, N.Y. 10027, U.S.A.

CADE, Robin. *See* **NICOLE,** Christopher.

CADE, Steven. *See* **WILLIAMSON,** Tony.

CADELL, (Violet) Elizabeth (Vandyke). Also writes for U.K. publr. as Harriet Ainsworth. British, b. 1903. Historical/Romance/Gothic, Children's fiction. *Publs:* My Dear Aunt Flora, 1946; Last Straw for Harriet, 1947, in U.K. as Fishy, Said the Admiral, 1948; River Lodge, 1948; Gay Pursuit, 1948, 2nd U.K. ed. as Family Gathering, 1979; Iris in Winter, 1951; Brimstone in the Garden, 1950; Sun in the Morning (juvenile), 1950; The Greenwood Shady, 1951; Enter Mrs. Belchamber, 1951, in U.K. as The Frenchman and the Lady, 1952; Men and Angels, 1952; Crystal Clear (in U.K. as Journey's Eve), 1953; Spring Green, 1953; The Cuckoo in Spring, 1954; Around the Rugged Rock (in U.K. as The Gentlemen Go By), 1954; Money to Burn, 1955; The Lark Shall Sing, 1955, 2nd U.S. ed., as The Singing Heart, 1959; The Blue Sky of Spring, 1956; I Love a Lass, 1956; (as Harriet Ainsworth) Consider the Lillies, 1956; Bridal Array, 1957; The Green Empress, 1958; Sugar Candy Cottage, 1958; (as Harriet Ainsworth; in U.S. as Elizabeth Cadell) Shadows on the Water, 1958; Alice, Where Art Thou?, 1959; The Yellow Brick Road, 1960; Honey for Tea, 1961; Six Impossible Things, 1961; Language of the Heart (in U.S. as The Toy Sword), 1962; Letter to My Love, 1963; Mixed Marriage: The Diary of a Portuguese Bride, 1963; Be My Guest (in U.S. as Come Be My Guest), 1964; (as Harriet Ainsworth) Death Among Friends, 1964; Canary Yellow, 1965; The Fox from His Lair, 1965; The Corner Shop, 1966; The Stratton Story, 1967; Mrs. Westerby Changes Course, 1968; The Golden Collar, 1969; The Friendly Air, 1970; The Past Tense of Love, 1970; Home for the Wedding, 1971; The Haymaker, 1972;

Royal Summons, 1973; Deck with Flowers, 1973; The Fledgling, 1975; Game in Diamonds, 1976; Parson's House, 1977; Round Dozen, 1978; Return Match, 1979; The Marrying Kind, 1980; Any Two Can Play, 1981; Lion in the Way, 1982; Remains to be Seen, 1983; The Waiting Game, 1984; The Empty Nest, 1985; Out of the Rain, 1987. Add: c/o Hodder and Stoughton, Mill Rd., Dunton Green, Sevenoaks, Kent TN13 2YA, England.

CADOGAN, Mary (Rose). British, b. 1928. Literature. Secty., The Krishnamurti Foundn., Beckenham, Kent, since 1968 (Secty. of Krishnamurti Writings Inc., London, 1958–68). Gov., Brockwood Park Educational Centre, Bramdean, Hants., since 1968. Worked at the BBC in the variety and school broadcasting depts., 1945–48, 1953–57; Secty., Welfare Cttee. of the Infantile Paralysis Fellowship, London, 1948–51; teacher, remedial movement and Margaret Morris movement, 1952–60. *Publs:* (with John Wernham) The Greyfriars Characters, 1976; (with Patricia Craig) You're a Brick, Angela: A New Look at Girls' Fiction from 1839 to 1975, 1976; (with Patricia Craig) Women and Children First: The Fiction of Two World Wars, 1978; (with John Wernham) Charles Hamilton Schoolgirls' Album, 1978; (with Patricia Craig) The Lady Investigates: Women Detectives and Spies in Fiction, 1981; (with Tommy Keen) The Morcove Companion, 1981; (with Tommy Keen) From Wharton Lodge to Linton Hall: The Charles Hamilton Christmas Companion, 1984; Richmal Crompton: The Woman Behind William, 1986; Frank Richards: The Chap Behind the Chums, 1988. Add: 46 Overbury Ave., Beckenham, Kent BR3 2PY, England.

CADY, Edwin H(arrison). American, b. 1917. Literature. Andrew W. Mellon Prof. of Humanities, and Prof. Emeritus of English, Duke Univ., Durham, N.C. Formerly, Rudy Prof. of English, Indiana Univ., Bloomington. Member, U.S. National Comm. for Unesco. *Publs:* The Gentleman in America, 1949; (ed. with Lester Wells) Stephen Crane's Love Letters to Nellie Crouse, 1954; W.D. Howells, Dean of American Letters, 1956; 1958; Stephen Crane, 1962, 1980; John Woolman, 1965; The Light of Common Day, 1971; W.D. Howells as Critic, 1973; The Big Game: College Sports and American Life, 1978; (with Norma H. Cady) Critical Essays on William Dean Howell 1866-1920, 1983; Young Howells and John Brown, 1985. Add: Route 4, Box 1056, Hillsborough, N.C. 27278, U.S.A.

CADY, John Frank. American, b. 1901. History, International relations/Current affairs. Distinguished Prof. Emeritus, Ohio Univ., Athens, since 1971 (Prof. of History, 1949–71). Prof., Univ. of Rangoon, Burma, 1935–38; Dean, Franklin Coll. of Indiana, 1938–43; with U.S. Dept. of State, Washington, D.C. and Rangoon, Burma, 1943–49; Lectr., Thammasat Univ., Bangkok, Thailand, 1967–68. *Publs:* Foreign Intervention in the Rio de la Plata, 1838-1850, 1929, 1969; Centennial History of Franklin College, 1934; Origins and Development of the Missionary Baptist Church of Indiana, 1942; The Development of Self-Rule and Independence in Burma, 1948; The Roots of French Imperialism in Eastern Asia, 1954, 1967; A History of Modern Burma, 1958, 5th ed. 1967; Southeast Asia: Its Historical Development, 1964; Thailand, Burma, Laos and Cambodia, 1966; A History of Post-War Southeast Asia, 1974; The United States and Burma, 1975; The Southeast Asian World, 1977; Contacts with Burma 1935–1949: A Personal Account, 1983. Add: 9 Harris Dr., Athens, Ohio 45701, U.S.A.

CAGAN, Phillip. American, b. 1927. Economics. Prof. of Economics, Columbia Univ., NYC, since 1966. Adjunct Scholar,

American Enterprise Inst., since 1972. Member, Research Staff, National Bureau of Economic Research, NYC, 1959–80; Prof. of Economics, Brown Univ., Providence, R.I., 1962–65; member, Sr. Staff, Council of Economic Advisers, 1969–70. *Publs:* Determinants and Effects of Changes in the Stock of Money, 1875-1960, 1965; (ed. with J. Guttentag) Essays on Interest Rates, vol. I, 1969; The Channels of Monetary Effects on Interest Rates, 1972; (with R.E. Lipsey) The Financial Effects of Inflation, 1978; Persistent Inflation, 1979. Add: Dept. of Economics, Columbia Univ., New York, N.Y. 10027, U.S.A.

CAGE, John. American, b. 1912. Poetry, Music. Musician, Merce Cunningham Dance Company, NYC (Musical Dir., 1943–67); Assoc., Center for Advanced Study, Univ. of Illinois (Visiting Prof., Sch. of Music, 1967–69). *Publs:* (with K. Hoover) The Life and Works of Virgil Thomson, 1958; Silence, 1961; A Year from Monday, 1967; Diary: Part III, 1967, Diary: Part IV, 1968; (with A. Knowles) Notations, 1969; (with others) Liberations: New Essays on the Humanities in Revolution, 1971; (with L. Long and A.H.Smith) Mushroom Book, 1972; M: Writings '67-'72, 1973; Writings Through Finnegans Wake, 1978; Empty Words, 1979; (with S. Barron) Another Song, 1981; Themes and Variations, 1982; (with Daniel Charles) For the Birds, 1980; A. John Cage Reader, 1982; X: Writings '79-82, 1983. Add: 101 W. 18th St., New York, N.Y. 10011, U.S.A.

CAIDIN, Martin. American, b. 1927. Novels/Short stories, Science fiction/Fantasy, Air/Space topics, Children's non-fiction, Military/Defence. Assoc. Ed., Air News and Air Tech mags. Consultant to N.Y. State Civil Defense Commn., 1950–62, Air Force Missile Test Center, Cape Canaveral, 1955, and Federal Aviation Agency, 1961–64; Corresp., Metropolitan Broadcasting (radio and TV), 1961–62. *Publs:* science fiction novels—The Long Night, 1956; Marooned, 1964; The Last Fathom, 1967; No Man's World, 1967; Aquarius Mission, 1968; Four Came Back, 1968; The God Machine, 1969; The Mendelov Conspiracy, 1969, as Encounter Three, 1978; The Cape, 1971; Cyborg, 1972; Operation Nuke, 1973; High Crystal (novelization), 1974; Cyborg IV, 1975; other—(with David C. Crooke) Jets, Rockets, and Guided Missiles, 1951, as Rockets and Missiles, Past and Present, 1954; Rockets Beyond the Earth, 1952; Worlds in Space, 1954; (with M. Okumiya and J. Horikoshi) Zero!, 1956; Vanguard, 1957; (with Saburo Sakai and Fred Saito) Samurai!, 1957; Air Force: A Pictorial History of American Airpower, 1957; Countdown for Tomorrow, 1958; (with Robert S. Johnson) Thunderbolt!, 1958; (with M. Okumiya and J. Horikoshi) The Zero Fighter, 1958; Spaceport, U.S.A., 1959; War for the Moon, 1959, in U.K. as Race for the Moon, 1960; Let's Go Flying!, 1959; Boeing 707, 1959; X-15: Man's First Flight into Space, 1959; Black Thursday, 1960; Golden Wings: A Pictorial History of the United States Navy and Marine Corps in the Air, 1960; The Astronauts, 1960, 1961; The Night Hamburg Died, 1960; A Torch to the Enemy: The Fire Raid of Tokyo, 1960; Man into Space, 1961; Thunderbirds!, 1961; (with Joseph W. Kittinger) The Long, Lonely Leap, 1961; Cross-Country Flying, 1961; Test Pilot (juvenile), 1961; This Is My Land, 1962; (with G.S. Titov) I Am Eagle, 1962; Rendezvous in Space, 1962; (with Grace Caidin) Aviation and Space Medicine, 1962; The Man-in-Space Dictionary, 1963; The Moon: New World for Men, 1963; Red Star in Space, 1963; The Power of Decision, 1963; Overture to Space, 1963; The Long Arm of America, 1963; By Apollo to the Moon (juvenile), 1963; The Silken Angela: A History of Parachuting, 1964; The Winged Armada, 1964; Hydrospace, 1964; Everything but the Flak, 1964; (with Edward Hymoff) The Mission, 1964; Wings into Space, 1964; The Mighty Hercules (juvenile), 1964; Why Space?, 1965; Barnstorming, 1965; The Greatest Challenge, 1965; The Ragged, Rugged Warriors, 1966; Devil Takes All (novel), 1966; (ed.) The DC-3: The Story of the Dakota, by Carroll V. Glines and Wendell F. Moseley, 1967; Flying Forts, 1968; Me 109: Willy Messerschmitt's Peerless Fighters, 1968; Anytime, Anywhere (novel), 1969; Almost Midnight (novel), 1971; Fork-Tailed Devil: The P-38, 1971; Destination Mars, 1972; Maryjane Tonight at Angels Twelve (novel), 1972; When War Comes, 1972; (with Jay Barbree) Bicycles in War, 1974; Planetfall, 1974; The Tigers Are Burning, 1974; The Last Dogfight (novel), 1974; Three Corners to Nowhere (novel), 1975; Whip (novel), 1976; Wingborn, 1979; The Saga of Iron Annie, 1979; Sun Bright, 1979; (with Harvey B. Combs) Kill Devil Hill: Discovering the Secret of the Wright Brothers, 1979; Manfrac (novel), 1981; Ragwings and Heavy Iron: The Agony and Ecstasy of Flying History's Greatest Warbirds, 1984; Killer Station, 1985; Zaboa, 1986. Add: c/o Houghton Mifflin, 2 Park St., Boston, Mass. 02108, U.S.A.

CAILLOU, Alan. Pseudonym for Alan Lyle-Smythe. American (born British), b. 1914. Novels/Short stories, Mystery/Crime/Suspense, Plays/Screenplays, Autobiography/Memoirs/Personal. Actor and writer in California since 1957 (in Canada, 1952–57). Commissioner for the Reserved Areas Police in Ethiopia and Somalia, 1945–47; guide/inter-preter, hunter, and trapper in Africa, 1947–52. *Publs:* (with Arnold M. Walter and Frank Chappell) The Shakespeare Festival: A Short History of Canada's First Shakespeare Festival 1949–54, 1954; The World Is Six Feet Square (autobiography), 1954; Rogue's Gambit (mystery novel), 1955; Alien Virus (mystery novel), 1957 (in U.S. as Cairo Cabal, 1974); The Mindanao Pearl (mystery novel), 1959; The Plotters (mystery novel), 1960; The Walls of Jolo (novel), 1960; Rampage (novel), 1961; Field of Woman (novel), 1963; The Hot Sun of Africa (novel), 1964; Marseilles (mystery novel), 1964; A Journey to Orassia (mystery novel), 1965; Who'll Buy My Evil? (mystery novel), 1966; Khartoum (novelization of screenplay), 1966; Charge of the Light Brigade, 1968; Bichu the Jaguar (novel), 1969; Assault on Kolchak (mystery movel), 1969; Assault on Loveless (mystery novel), 1969; Assault on Ming (mystery novel), 1970; The Cheetahs (novel), 1970; The Dead Sea Submarine (mystery novel), 1971; Terror in Rio (mystery novel), 1971; Congo War-Cry (mystery novel), 1971; Afghan Onslaught (mystery novel), 1971; Assault on Fellawi (mystery novel), 1972; Assault on Agathon (mystery novel), 1972; Swamp War (mystery novel), 1973; Death Charge (mystery novel), 1973; The Garonsky Missile (mystery novel), 1973; Sheba Slept Here (autobiography), 1973; South from Khartoum: The Story of Emin Pasha, 1974; Assault on Aimata (mystery novel), 1975; Diamonds Wild (mystery novel), 1979; Joshua's People, 1982; The House on Curzon Street, 1983; The Prophetess, 1984; A Woman of Quality, 1984; The Swords of God, 1987. Add: 55 Grasshopper Lane, Sedona, Ariz. 86366, U.S.A.

CAIRD, Janet (Hinshaw). British, b. 1913. Mystery/Crime/Suspense, Historical/Romance/Gothic, Children's fiction, Poetry. Teacher of English, Park Sch., Glasgow, 1937–38, Royal High Sch., Edinburgh, 1940–41, and Dollar Academy, 1941–43, 1959–63. *Publs:* Angus the Tartan Partan (juvenile), 1961; Murder Reflected, 1965, in U.S. as In a Glass Darkly, 1966; Perturbing Spirit, 1966; Murder Scholastic, 1967; The Loch, 1968; Murder Remote (in U.S. paperback as The Shrouded Way), 1973; Some Walk a Narrow Path (poems), 1977; The Umbrella-Maker's Daughter, 1980; A Distant Urn (poems), 1983; John Donne, You Were Wrong (poems), 1987. Add: 1 Drummond Cres., Inverness IV2 4QW, Scotland.

CAIRNCROSS, (Sir) Alexander (Kirkland). British, b. 1911. Administration/Management, Economics. Chancellor, Univ. of Glasgow, since 1972. Prof. of Applied Economics, Univ. of Glasgow, 1951–61; Dir., Economic Development Inst., Washington, D.C., 1955–56; Economic Adviser to British Govt., 1961–64; Head of Govt. Economic Service, 1964–69; Master, St. Peter's Coll., Oxford, 1969–78. *Publs:* Introduction to Economics, 1944, 6th ed. 1981; Home and Foreign Investment 1870-1913, 1953; (ed.) The Crofting Problem, 1953; (ed.) The Scottish Economy, 1954; Monetary Policy in a Mixed Economy, 1960; Economic Development and the Atlantic Provinces, 1961; Factors in Economic Development, 1962; (ed.) The Managed Economy, 1970; (ed.) Papers on Planning and Economic Management, 1971; (ed.) Britain's Economic Prospects Reconsidered, 1971; Essays in Economic Management, 1971; Learning to Learn, 1972; Control of Long-term International Capital Movements, 1973; (co-author) Economic Policy for the European Community, 1974; Inflation, Growth and International Finance, 1975; (ed.) Employment, Income Distribution and Development Strategy, 1976; (ed.) Public Expenditure, Management, and Control, 1978; Snatches, 1980; (ed.) Anglo-American Collaboration in War and Peace, 1982; (co-author) Sterling in Decline, 1983; Years of Recovery, 1985; The Price of War, 1986; Economics and Economic Policy, 1986; A Country To Play With, 1987; (ed.) The Diaries of Robert Hall, 1989; (co-author) The Economic Section 1939–61, 1989. Add: 14 Staverton Rd., Oxford, England.

CAIRNS, David. British, b. 1904. Theology/Religion. Prof. of Practical Theology, Univ. of Aberdeen, now retired. Former Consulting Ed., Scottish Journal of Theology; Member, Faith and Order Commn., World Council of Churches, 1957–67. *Publs:* The Image of God, 1953, rev. ed. 1973; A Gospel Without Myth?, 1960; In Remembrance of Me: Aspects of the Lord's Supper, 1967; God Up There?: A Study in Divine Transcendence; (joint compiler) Worship Now, 1972; (ed.) System of Christian Doctrine, 1980. Add: 29 Viewfield Gardens, Aberdeen AB1 7XN, Scotland.

CAIRNS, Earle E(dwin). American, b. 1910. History, Theology/Religion. Prof. of History, Wheaton Coll., Ill., 1943–79 (Chmn. 1948–73). Member of faculty, Presbyterian Theological Seminary, Omaha, Nebr., 1941–43. *Publs:* Christianity Through the Centuries, 1954; Christianity in the United States, 1964; V.R. Edman: In the Presence of the King, 1972; The Christian in Society, 1973; (consulting ed.) The New International Dictionary of Church History, 1974; God and Man in

Time, 1978; (ed.) Wycliffe Biographical Dictionary of the Church by Elgin Moyer (revised and enlarged by Cairns), 1982; An Endless Line of Splendor, 1986. Add: 265 E. Park Ave., Wheaton, Ill. 60187, U.S.A.

CALDER, Angus. British, b. 1942. History, Literature. Reader in Literature and Cultural Studies and Staff Tutor, Open University in Scotland, since 1979. Lectr., in Literature, Univ. of Nairobi, 1968–71. *Publs:* (ed.) Dickens: Great Expectations, 1965; (with J. Calder) Scott, 1969; The People's War: Britain 1939–1945, 1969; (ed. with A. Gurr) Writers in East Africa, 1974; (ed.) Scott: Old Mortality; Russia Discovered: Nineteenth Century Fiction from Pushkin to Chekhov, 1976; Revolutionary Empire, 1981; (co-ed.) Speak for Yourself, 1984; T.S. Eliot, 1987; Byron, 1987. Add: c/o A.D. Peters & Co., 10 Buckingham St., London WC2, England.

CALDER, Nigel (David Ritchie). British, b. 1931. Sciences. Physicist, Mullard Research Labs., 1954–56; Member, Editorial Staff, New Scientist, London, 1956–66; Science Ed., 1960–62, and Ed., 1962–66; Science Corresp., New Statesman, London, 1959–62, 1966–71; Chmn., Assn. of British Science Writers, 1962–64; Member, U.K. National Unesco Cttee., 1970–77. *Publs:* Electricity Grows Up; Robots; Radio Astronomy; The World in 1984, 1965; The Environment Game (in U.S. as Eden Was No Garden); Russia: Beneath the Sputniks (TV script), 1967; The World in a Box (TV script), 1968; Unless Peace Comes, 1968; Violent Universe: An Eyewitness Account of the New Astronomy, 1969; Technopolis, 1969; The Mind of Man, 1970; Living Tomorrow, 1970; Restless Earth: A Report on the New Geology, 1972; Nature in the Round, 1973; The Life Game: Evolution and the New Biology, 1973; The Weather Machine, 1974; The Human Conspiracy, 1975; The Key to the Universe, 1977; The Whole Universe Show (television script), 1977; Spaceships of the Mind, 1978; Einstein's Universe, 1979; Nuclear Nightmares, 1979; The Comet Is Coming!: The Feverish Legacy of Mr. Halley, 1980; 1984 and After, 1983; Timescale, 1983; The English Channel, 1986; The Green Machines, 1986; (ed.) Scientific Europe, 1987. Add: 8 The Chase, Furnace Green, Crawley, Sussex RH10 6HW, England.

CALDER-MARSHALL, Arthur. British, b. 1908. Novels/Short stories, Children's fiction, Literature, Autobiography/Memoirs/Personal, Biography. *Publs:* Two of a Kind, 1932; About Levy, 1933; At Sea, 1934; The Crime Against Cania, 1934; A Pink Doll, 1934; Challenge to Schools: A Pamphlet on Public School Education, 1935; Dead Centre, 1935; Pie in the Sky, 1937; Date with a Duchess and Other Stories, 1937; The Changing Scene, 1937; Glory Dead (travel), 1939; The Way to Santiago, 1940; The World is Rich (screenplay), 1946; The Watershed (travel), 1947; The Book Front, 1947; A Man Reprieved, 1949; The Magic of My Youth, 1951; Occasion of Glory, 1955; No Earthly Command, 1957; The Man from Devil's Island, 1958; The Fair to Middling, 1959; Havelock Ellis: A Biography (in U.S. as The Sage of Sex: Havelock Ellis), 1959; Lone Wolf: The Story of Jack London, 1961; The Scarlet Boy, 1961: The Enthusiast, 1962; The Innocent Eye, 1963; (ed.) The Bodley Head Jack London, 4 vols., 1963–66; Wish You Were Here: The Art of Donald McGill, 1966; Prepare to Shed Them Now: The Ballads of George R. Sims, 1968; Lewd, Blasphemous and Obscene: Beings the Trials and Tribulations of Sundry Founding Fathers of Today's Alternative Societies, 1972; The Grand Century of the Lady, 1976; The Two Duchesses, 1978. Add: c/o Elaine Greene Ltd., 31 Newington Green, London N16 9PU, England.

CALDERWOOD, James Lee. American, b. 1930. Literature. Prof. of English since 1966, and Assoc. Dean of Humanities since 1974, Univ. of California, Irvine (Asst. Prof., Los Angeles, 1963–66). Instr., Michigan State Univ., East Lansing, 1961–63. *Publs:* (co-ed.) Forms of Poetry, 1968; (co-ed.) Perspectives on Poetry, 1968; (co-ed.) Perspectives on Fiction, 1968; (co-ed.) Perspectives on Drama, 1968; (co-ed.) Forms of Drama, 1969; (co-ed.) Essays in Shakespearean Criticism, 1969; Love's Labour's Lost, by Shakespeare, 1970; Shakespearean Metadrama, 1971; (co-ed.) Forms of Prose Fiction, 1972; (co-ed.) Forms of Tragedy, 1972; Metadrama in Shakespeare's Henriad, 1979; To Be and Not to Be, 1983; If It Were Done: Tragic Action in Macbeth, 1986; Shakespeare and the Denial of Death, 1987; The Properties of Othello, 1989. Add: 1323 Terrace Way, Laguna Beach, Calif. 92651, U.S.A.

CALHOUN, Richard J(ames). American, b. 1926. History, Literature. Alumni Prof. of English, Clemson Univ., S.C., since 1969 (Asst. Prof., 1961–63; Assoc. Prof., 1963–67). Ed. Modern American Poetry Cassette Series, since 1969; Ed., South Carolina Review, since 1973. Fellow, Cooperative Prog. in Humanities, 1964–65; Fulbright Senior Lectures, Yugoslavia, 1969–70, Denmark, 1975–76. *Publs:* The Southern Renascence, 1925–45, 1969; (ed.) James Dickey: The Expansive Imagination,

1973; (co-ed.) A Tricentennial Anthology of South Carolina Literature, 1973; (co-ed.) Two Decades of Change: The South since Desegregation, 1975; James Dickey, 1983. Add: Dept. of English, Clemson Univ., Clemson, S.C. 29631, U.S.A.

CALIAN, Carnegie Samuel. American, b. 1933. Theology/Religion. Pres. and Prof. of Theology, Pittsburgh Theological Seminary, since 1981. Asst. Pastor, Calvary Presbyterian Church, Hawthorne, Calif., 1958–60; Visiting Prof. of Theology, 1963–67, Assoc. Prof., 1967–72, and Prof., 1972–81, Univ. of Dubuque Theological Seminary, Iowa. *Publs:* The Significance of Eschatology in the Thoughts of Nicolas Berdyaev, 1965, rev. ed. as Berdyaev's Philosophy of Hope: A Contribution to Marxist-Christian Dialogue, 1968; Icon and Pulpit: The Protestant-Orthodox Encounter, 1968; Grace, Guts and Goods: How to Stay Christian in an Affluent Society, 1971; The Gospel According to The Wall Street Journal, 1975; Today's Pastor In Tomorrow's World, 1977, rev. ed., 1982; For All Your Seasons, 1979; Where's the Passion for Excellence in the Church?, 1989. Add: Pittsburgh Theological Seminary, 616 N. Highland Ave., Pittsburgh, Pa. 15215, U.S.A.

CALIFANO, Joseph A., Jr. American, b. 1931. Communications Media, Medicine/Health, Politics/Government, Social commentary/phenomena. Partner, Dewey, Ballantine, Bushby, Palmer and Wood, Washington, D.C., since 1983. Admitted to New York Bar, 1955; U.S. Naval Reserve, 1955–58; With law firm of Dewey, Ballantine, Bushby, Palmer and Wood, NYC, 1958–61; Special Asst. to Gen. Counsel, Dept. of Defense, 1961–62; Gen. Counsel, Dept. of the Army, 1963–64; Special Asst. to the Secty. and Deputy Secty. of Defense, 1964–65, and to President Lyndon Johnson, 1965–69; Member of the firm of Arnold and Porter, Washington, 1969–71; Partner, Williams, Connolly, and Califano, Washington, 1971–76; United States Secty. of Health, Education and Welfare, 1977–79. *Publs:* The Student Revolution: A Global Confrontation, 1969; A Presidential Nation, 1975; (with H. Simons) Media and the Law, 1976; (with H. Simons) The Media and Business, 1978; Governing America: An Insider's Report from the White House and the Cabinet, 1981; Report on Drug Abuse and Alcoholism, 1982; America's Health Care Revolution: Who Lives? Who Dies? Who Pays?, 1986. Add: 1775 Pennsylvania Ave. N.W., Washington, D.C. 20006, U.S.A.

CALISHER, Hortense. American, b. 1911. Novels/Short stories, Autobiography/Memoirs/Personal. Distinguished Prof., Brown Univ., Providence, since 1986. Adjunct Prof. of English, Barnard Coll., NYC. 1956–60; Writer in residence, State Univ. of Iowa, 1959–60; Member, Literature Faculty, Sarah Lawrence Coll., Bronxville, N.Y., 1962; Visiting Prof. of Literature, Brandeis Univ., Waltham, Mass., 1963–64; Writer-in-Residence, 1965, and Visiting Lectr., 1968, Univ. of Pennsylvania, Philadelphia; Adjunct Prof. of English, Columbia Univ., NYC, 1968–70; Regents Prof., Univ. of California, Irvine, 1975. Pres., American P.E.N., 1986; Pres., American Academy/Inst. of Arts and Letters, 1987–90. *Publs:* In the Absence of Angels: Stories, 1951; False Entry, 1961; Tale for the Mirror, 1962; Textures of Life, 1963; Extreme Magic: A Novella and Other Stories, 1964; Journal from Ellipsia, 1965; The Railway Police and The Last Trolley Ride (2 novellas), 1966; The New Yorkers, 1969; Queenie, 1971; Standard Dreaming, 1972; Herself (autobiography), 1972; Eagle Eye, 1974; Collected Stories, 1975; On Keeping Women, 1977; Mysteries of Motion (novel), 1983; Saratoga, Hot (short stories), 1985; The Bobby-Soxer (novel), 1986; Age (novel), 1987; Kissing Cousins (memoir), 1988. Add: c/o Candida Donadio Inc., 231 W 22nd St., New York, N.Y. 10011, U.S.A.

CALLAGHAN, Morley (Edward). Canadian, b. 1903. Novels/Short stories, Children's fiction, Plays/Screenplays, Autobiography/Memoirs/Personal. *Publs:* Strange Fugitive, 1938; Native Argosy (short stories), 1929; It's Never Over, 1930; No Man's Meat, 1931; A Broken Journey, 1932; Such is My Beloved, 1934; They Shall Inherit the Earth, 1935; Now That April's Here (short stories), 1936; More Joy in Heaven, 1937; Turn Again George (play), 1940; Luke Baldwin's Vow (children's fiction), 1948; Varsity Story, 1948; The Loved and the Lost, 1951; Stories, 2 vols., 1959, 1967; The Many Colored Coat, 1960; A Passion in Rome, 1961; That Summer in Paris: Memories of Tangled Friendships with Hemingway, Fitzgerald and Some Others, 1963; An Autumn Penitent, 1973; Winter, 1974; A Fine and Private Place: A Footnote, 1975; Close to the Sun Again, 1978; No Man's Meat, and The Enchanted Pimp, 1978; A Time for Judas, 1984; Our Lady of the Snows, 1986; The Man with the Coat, 1987; The Wild Old Man on the Road, 1988. Add: 20 Dale Ave., Toronto, Ont. M4W 1K4, Canada.

CALLAHAN, John F. American, b. 1912. Philosophy. Emeritus Prof. of Classics and Philosophy, Georgetown Univ., Washington, D.C., since

1977 (Prof. 1950–77). Visiting Scholar and Fellow, Dumbarton Oaks, Washington, 1977–86. Member, Bd. of Editors, Journal of the History of Ideas, since 1970. *Publs:* Four Views of Time in Ancient Philosophy, 1948, 3rd ed. 1979; Augustine and the Greek Philosophers, 1967; (co-author) Interpretations of Plato, 1977. Add: 3 Pooks Hill Rd., Bethesda, Md. 20814, U.S.A.

CALLAHAN, Nelson J. American. Theology/Religion. Pastor, St. Raphael Parish, Bay Village, Ohio, since 1974. Prosynodal Judge, Diocesan Matrimonial Tribunal, Cleveland; Moderator, First Friday Club, Cleveland. Asst. Pastor of St. Patrick, and St. Agatha; and Dir. of Guidance, St. Peter High Sch., all Cleveland, 1953–67; Asst. Prof. of Theology, and Chaplain, St. John Coll., Cleveland, 1967–74. Archivist, Diocese of Cleveland, 1947–78. *Publs:* A Case for Due Process in the Church, 1971; The Role of an Ethnic Pastor in a Cleveland Parish, 1972; (ed.) A Catholic Journey Through Ohio, 1976; (co-author) The Irish and Their Communities of Cleveland, 1977; The Diary of Richard Burtsell Priest of New York: The First Three Years (1865-1868), 1978; St. Ignatius High School 1886-1986, 1986. Add: 525 Dover Rd., Bay Village, Ohio 44140, U.S.A.

CALLAHAN, North. American, b. 1908. History, Biography. Prof. Emeritus of History, New York Univ. (Assoc. Prof., 1957–62; Prof. 1962–75). Writer, syndicated column, So This is New York, 1943–68; Public relations consultant, NYC, 1945–55; Prof. of American History, Finch Coll., NYC, 1956–57. *Publs:* Armed Forces as a Career, 1947; Smoky Mountain Country, 1952; Henry Knox: General Washington's General, 1958; Daniel Morgan: Ranger of the Revolution, 1962; Tories of the American Revolution, 2 vols., 1963, 1967; Carl Sandburg: Lincoln of Our Literature, 1970; George Washington: Soldier and Man, 1972; TVA: Bridge over Troubled Waters, 1980; Peggy (novel), 1982; Daybreak (novel), 1985; Carl Sandburg: His Life and Work, 1987. Add: 25 South Germantown Rd., Chattanooga, Tenn. 37411, U.S.A.

CALLARD, Maurice (Frederic Thomas). British, b. 1912. Novels/Short stories, Plays/Screenplays. Lectr. in Creative Writing, W.E.A. and Southampton Univ. *Publs:* The City Called Holy, 1954; The Splendour and the Havoc, 1956; The World and the Flesh, 1960; The End of the Visit, 1961; Across the Frontier, 1964; Sweet Nelly (play), 1972; Will You Take This Woman?, 1974; A Night in October (play), 1980; Bound for Botany Bay (play), 1987. Add: 14 Ferrol Rd., Gosport, Hants, England.

CALLAS, Theo. *See* McCARTHY, Shaun.

CALLENBACH, Ernest. American, b. 1929. Science fiction, Film, Human relations, Social commentary. Ed., Film Quarterly, and Film Book Ed., Univ. of California Press, Berkeley, since 1958. Founder, Banyan Tree Books, 1975. *Publs:* science fiction—Ecotopia: A Novel about Ecology, People and Politics in 1999, 1975; Ecotopia Emerging, 1981; other—Our Modern Art: The Movies, 1955; Living Poor with Style, 1971; (with Christine Leefeldt) The Art of Friendship, 1979; The Ecotopian Encyclopedia for the 80's, 1981; (with Christine Leefeldt) Humphrey the Wayward Whale, 1985; (with Michael Phillips) A Citizen Legislature, 1985; Publisher's Lunch, 1989. Add: Univ. of California Press, 2120 Berkeley Way, Berkeley, Calif. 94720, U.S.A.

CALLIHAN, E. Lee. American, b. 1903. Writing/Journalism. Prof. and Chmn., Dept. of Journalism, Drake Univ., Des Moines, Iowa, 1940–45, Baylor Univ., Waco, Tex., 1945–46 and Southern Methodist Univ., Dallas, Tex., 1946–69. *Publs:* Grammar for Journalists, 1957, 3rd ed. 1979; (with L. Nelson and W. Danielson) Exercises and Tests for Journalists, 1970, 1981; Instructor's Manual of Corrected Exercises, 1970; (ed.) Drake Creative Awards Anthologies 1940-45. Add: Rt. 2, Box 1030, Sunnyvale, Tex. 75182, U.S.A.

CALLINAN, Bernard J(ames). Australian, b. 1913. Engineering, Military/Defence. Dir., Westgate Bridge Authority, since 1965 (Dept. Chmn., 1971–81; Chmn., 1981–82); Chmn., CCI Insurances Ltd., since 1984. Pres., Royal Humane Soc. of Australasia, since 1986 (Dir., since 1979). Sr. Partner, 1948–70, Chmn. and Managing Dir., 1971–78, and Consultant, 1978–83, Gutteridge Haskins and Davey Pty Ltd. Councillor, Univ. of Melbourne, 1976–81. *Publs:* Independent Company, 1953, 1984; Domestic and Industrial Use of Water, 1969; John Monash, 1981. Add: Belulic, 111 Sackville St., Kew, Melbourne, Vic., Australia 3101.

CALLISON, Brian (Richard). British, b. 1934. Novels/Short stories. Freelance writer since 1967. Deck Officer, British Merchant Navy, 1951–54; managing dir., construction co., 1956–63; gen. mgr., entertain-

ment centre, 1963–67. *Publs:* A Flock of Ships, 1970; A Plague of Sailors, 1971; Dawn Attack, 1972; A Web of Salvage, 1973; Trapp's War, 1974; A Ship is Dying, 1976; A Frenzy of Merchantmen, 1977; The Judas Ship, 1978; Trapp's Peace, 1979; The Auriga Madness, 1980; The Sextant, 1981; Spearfish, 1982; Bone Collectors, 1984; Thunder of Crude, 1986; Trapp and World War Three, 1988. Add: c/o Collins, 8 Grafton St., London W1X 3LA, England

CALLOW, Philip. British, b. 1924. Novels/Short stories, Plays/Screenplays, Poetry, Autobiography/Memoirs/Personal, Biography. *Publs:* The Hosanna Man, 1956; Common People, 1958; Native Ground, 1959; Pledge for the Earth, 1960; The Honeymooners (TV play), 1960; Turning Point (poetry), 1961; Clipped Wings, 1963; The Real Life (poetry), 1964; In My Own Land (autobiography), 1965; Going to the Moon, 1968; The Bliss Body, 1969; Flesh of Morning, 1971; The Lamb (radio play), 1971; Bare Wires (poetry), 1972; Yours, 1972; Son and Lover: The Young D.H. Lawrence (biography), 1975; The Story of My Desire (novel), 1976; Janine, 1977; The Subway to New York, 1979; Cave Light (poetry), 1981; Woman with a Poet (stories), 1983; New York Insomnia (poetry), 1984. Add: Little Thatch, Haselbury, nr. Crewkerne, Somerset, England.

CALLWOOD, June. Canadian, b. 1924. Social commentary, Women. Columnist, Toronto Globe & Mail, since 1983. Member of the Council, Amnesty Intnl. (Canada), since 1978. Founder and Pres., Nellie's Hostel for Women, 1974–78, Learnex Foundn., 1977–79, Justice for Children, 1979–80, Jessie's Centre for Teenagers, 1982–83, 1987–89, and Casey House Hospice, 1987–88; Chmn., The Writers' Union of Canada, 1979; Dir., Canadian Inst. for Admin. of Justice, 1983–84. *Publs:* (with Marion Hillard) A Woman Doctor Looks at Life and Love, 1957; Love, Hate, Fear, and Anger, 1964; (with Marvin Zuker) Canadian Women and the Law, 1971; (with Barbara Walters) How to Talk to Practically Anybody about Practically Anything, 1973; The Law Is Not for Women, 1973; (with Judianne Densen-Gerber) We Mainline Dreams, 1974; Naughty Nineties; Canada's Illustrated Heritage, 1978; Portrait of Canada, 1981; (with Helen Gahagan Douglas) A Full Life, 1982; Emma, 1984; Emotions, 1986; Twelve Works in Spring, 1986; Jim: A Life with AIDS, 1988. Add: 21 Hillcroft Dr., Islington, Ont. M9B 4X4, Canada.

CALVERT, Mary. *See* DANBY, Mary.

CALVERT Peter (Anthony Richard). British, b. 1936. History, International relations/Current affairs, Politics/Government. Prof. of Comparative and Intnl. Politics, Univ. of Southampton, since 1984 (Lectr., 1964–71; Sr. Lectr., 1971–74; Reader, 1974–83). Teaching Fellow, Univ. of Michigan, Ann Arbor, 1960–61. *Publs:* The Mexican Revolution 1910–1914: The Diplomacy of Anglo-American Conflict, 1968; Latin America: Internal Conflict and International Peace, 1969; Revolution, 1970; A Study of Revolution, 1970; Mexico, 1973; The Mexicans: How They Live and Work, 1975; Emiliano Zapata, 1979; The Concept of Class, 1982; The Falklands Crisis, 1982; Politics, Power, and Revolution, 1983; Boundary Disputes in Latin America, 1983; Revolution and International Politics, 1984; Guatemalan Insurgency and American Security, 1984; Guatemala, A Nation in Turmoil, 1985; Britain's Place in the World, 1986; The Foreign Policy of New States, 1986; (ed.) Political Succession, 1987; (ed.) The Central American Security System, 1988; (with Susan Calvert) Argentina: Political Culture and Instability, 1989. Add: Dept. of Politics, Univ. of Southampton, Highfield, Southampton, SO9 5NH, England.

CALVIN, Henry. *See* HANLEY, Clifford.

CALVIN, Melvin. American, b. 1911. Chemistry. Univ. Prof of Chemistry, Univ. of California, Berkeley, since 1971 (joined faculty, 1937; successively Instr. in Chemistry, Asst. Prof., Assoc. Prof., and Prof; Dir., Lab. of Chemical Biodynamics, 1960–80; Assoc. Dir., Lawrence Berkeley Lab., 1967–80). Pres., American Soc. of Plant Physiology, 1963–64, and American Chemical Soc., 1971. *Publs:* (with G.E.K. Branch) The Theory of Organic Chemistry, 1940; (with others) Isotopic Carbon, 1949; (with Martell) Chemistry of Metal Chelate Compounds, 1952; (with Bassham) Path of Carbon in Photosynthesis, 1957; Chemical Evolution, 1961; (with Bassham) Photosynthesis of Carbon Compounds, 1962; Chemical Evolution: Molecular Evolution Towards the Origins of Living Systems on Earth and Elsewhere, 1969; (ed. with W.A. Pryor) Organic Chemistry of Life, 1974. Add: Dept. of Chemistry, Univ. of California, Berkeley, Calif. 94720, U.S.A.

CALVIN, William H(oward). American, b. 1939. Medicine/Health, Sciences, Essays. Affiliate Assoc. Prof. of Biology, Univ. of Washington, Seattle, since 1986 (Instr., 1967–69; Asst. Prof., 1969–73;

Assoc. Prof. of Neurological Surgery, 1974–86). Member, Editorial Bd., Journal of Theoretical Neurobiology, since 1982. Visiting Prof. of Neurobiology, Hebrew Univ. of Jerusalem, 1978–79. *Publs:* (with George A. Ojemann) Inside the Brain, 1980; The Throwing Madonna: From Nervous Cells to Hominid Brains, 1983; The River That Flows Uphill: A Journey from the Big Bang to the Big Brain, 1986. Add: 1543 17th Ave. E., Seattle, Wash. 98112, U.S.A.

CALVOCORESSI, Peter (John Ambrose). British, b. 1912. History, International relations/Current affairs. Called to the Bar, 1934; Wing Comdr., trial of major war criminals, Nuremberg, 1945–46; Member of Staff, 1949–54, and of Council, 1955–72, Royal Inst. of Intnl. Affairs; Dir., Chatto and Windus Ltd. and The Hogarth Press Ltd., publishers, London 1954–65; Reader, part-time, in Intnl. Relations, Univ. of Sussex, Brighton, 1965–71; Editorial Dir., 1972–73, and Publisher and Chief Exec., 1973–76, Penguin Books Ltd., London; Chmn., Open University Educational Enterprises, 1979–88. Member of the Council, Inst. for Strategic Studies, 1961–71; Chmn, The Africa Bureau, 1963–71; Chmn, London Library, 1970–73. *Publs:* Nuremberg: The Facts, the Law and the Consequences, 1947; Survey of International Affairs, 5 vols., 1947–54; (with G. Wint) Middle East Crisis, 1957; South Africa and World Opinion, 1961; World Order and New States, 1962; World Politics since 1945, 1968, 1975; (with G. Wint) Total War, 1972, 1989; The British Experience 1945–1975, 1978; Top Secret Ultra, 1980; Independent Africa and the World, 1985; A Time for Peace, 1988; Who's Who in the Bible, 1988. Add: 1 Queen's Parade, Bath BA1 2NJ, England.

CAMBER, Andrew. *See* **BINGLEY,** David Ernest.

CAMERON, D.Y. *See* **COOK,** Dorothy Mary.

CAMERON, Donald. *See* **BRYANS,** Robin.

CAMERON, Eleanor (Butler). American, b. 1912. Children's fiction. Member of Editorial Bd., Cricket Mag., since 1975; Member of Editorial Bd., Children's Literature in Education, since 1982. Library Clerk, Los Angeles Public Library, 1930–36, and Los Angeles Schs. Library, 1936–42; Special Librarian, Foote Cone and Belding Advertising, Los Angeles, 1942–43; Research Librarian, Honig Cooper and Harrington Advertising, Los Angeles, 1956–58. *Publs:* The Wonderful Flight to the Mushroom Planet, 1954; Stowaway to the Mushroom Planet, 1956; Mr. Bass's Planetoid, 1958; The Terrible Churnadryne, 1959; A Mystery for Mr. Bass, 1960; The Mysterious Christmas Shell, 1961; The Beast with the Magical Horn, 1963; A Spell Is Cast, 1964; Time and Mr. Bass, 1967; The Green and Burning Tree: On the Writing and Enjoyment of Children's Books, 1969; Room Made of Windows, 1971; The Court of the Stone Children, 1973; To the Green Mountains, 1975; Julia and the Hand of God, 1977; Beyond Silence, 1980; That Julia Redfern, 1982; Julia's Magic, 1984; The Private Worlds of Julia Redfern, 1988. Add: c/o E.P. Dutton and Co. Inc., 2 Park Ave., New York, N.Y. 10016, U.S.A.

CAMERON, Ian. *See* **PAYNE,** Donald Gordon.

CAMERON, James Munro. British, b. 1910. Education, Philosophy, Biography. Emeritus Prof., St. Michael's, Coll., Univ. of Toronto, since 1978 (Prof., 1971–78). Staff Tutor, University Coll., Southampton, England, 1932–35, Vaughan Coll., Leicester, 1935–43; Staff Tutor, 1943–47, Lectr. in Philosophy, 1947–52, Sr. Lectr., 1952–60, Acting Head of Dept. of Philosophy, 1954–55, 1959–60, and Prof. of Philosophy, 1960–67, Univ. of Leeds; Prof. of Philosophy, and Master of Rutherford Coll., Univ. of Kent, Canterbury, 1967–71. *Publs:* Scrutiny of Marxism, 1948; (trans. with M. Kuschnitzky) The Flight from God, by Max Picard, 1951; John Henry Newman, 1956; Poetry and Dialectic, 1961; The Night Battle, 1962; Images of Authority, 1966; (ed.) Essay on Development (1845 ed.), by J.H. Newman, 1974; On the Idea of a University, 1978; The Music Is in the Sadness (poetry), 1988. Add: 360 Bloor St.E., Apt. 409, Toronto, Ont. M4W 3M3, Canada.

CAMERON, Julie. *See* **CAMERON,** Lou.

CAMERON, Lou. Also writes as Justin Adams and Julie Cameron. American, b. 1924. Mystery/Crime/Suspense, Westerns/Adventure. Writer since 1957: has also written books using the house names Tabor Evans, and Ramsey Thorne. Freelance artist for mags. and comic books, 1950–57. *Publs:* Angel's Fight, 1960; The Big Red Ball, 1961; The Sky Divers, 1962; The Empty Quarter, 1962; Not Even Your Mother, 1963; The Bastard's Name is War, 1963; The Black Camp, 1963; The Green Fields of Hell, 1964; The Block Busters, 1964; None But the Brave (novelization of screenplay), 1965; (ed.) Morituri, 1965; The Dirty War

of Sergeant Slade, 1966; Iron Men with Wooden Wings, 1967; The Dragon's Spine, 1968; File on a Missing Redhead, 1968; The Good Guy, 1968; The Outsider (novelization of TV series), 1969; Before It's Too Late, 1970; The Amphorae Pirates, 1970; Behind the Scarlet Door, 1971; Spurhead, 1971; Cybernia, 1972; The Girl with the Dynamite Bangs, 1973; The First Blood: Hannibal Brooks (novelization of screenplays); Mistress Bayou Labelle; Mud War; Tipping Point, Tunnel War; California Split (novelization of screenplay), 1974; Barca, 1974; The Closing Circle, 1974; (as Julie Cameron) Devil in the Pines, 1975; The Darklings, 1975; Tancredi, 1975; Doc Travels (western), 1975; North to Cheyenne (western), 1975; Dekker, 1976; Drop into Hell, 1976; The Guns of Durango (western), 1976; The Spirit Horses (western), 1976; (as Justin Adams) Chains, 1977; Code Seven, 1977; How the West Was Won (novelization of screenplay), 1977; The Big Lonely, 1978; The Cascade Ghost, 1978; The Subway Stalker, 1980; This Fever in My Blood, 1980; The Track Stalker, 1980; The Wilderness Seekers (western), 1980; The Hot Can, 1981; The Grass of Goodnight, 1987; Stringer, 1987; Stringer on Dead Man's Range, No. 2, 1987; Stringer on Assassin's Trail, 1987; Stringer and the Hangman's Rodeo, No. 4, 1988; Stringer and the Hanging Judge, No. 6, 1988; Stringer and the Deadly Flood, No. 8, 1988. Add: c/o Ace, Berkley Publishing Group, 200 Madison Ave., New York, N.Y. 10016, U.S.A.

CAMERON, Rondo. American, b. 1925. Economics, History. William Rand Kenan, Jr. Univ. Prof., Emory Univ., Altanta, Ga., since 1969. Member, Exec. Cttee., Intnl. Assn. of Economic History, since 1973 and Vice-Pres., 1986–90. Ed., Journal of Economic History, 1975–81. *Publs:* (co-ed.) Europe in Review, 1957, 1964; France and the Economic Development of Europe 1800-1914, 1961, 1966; (with J. Blum and T. Barnes) The European World: A History, 1966, 1970; (co-author) Banking in the Early Stages of Industrialization, 1967; (ed.) Essays in French Economic History, 1970; (ed.) Civilization Since Waterloo, 1971; (ed.) Banking and Economic Development: Some Lessons of History, 1972; (co-author) Civilizations, Western and World, 1975; A Concise Economic History of the World from Paleolithic Times to the Present, 1989. Add: 1088 Clifton Rd., Atlanta, Ga. 30307, U.S.A.

CAMERON, Silver Donald. Canadian, b. 1937. Novels/Short stories, Children's fiction, Literature. Writer-in-Residence, Coll. of Cape Breton, Sydney, N.S., 1978–80; Univ. of Prince Edward Island, 1985–86; Nova Scotia Coll. of Art and Design, 1987–88. Founding Ed., The Mysterious East, 1969–71; Contrib. Ed., Weekend mag., 1974–77. *Publs:* Faces of Leacock (criticism), 1967; Conservations with Canadian Novelists, 1973; The Education of Everett Richardson, 1977; Seasons in the Rain (essays), 1978; Dragon Lady (novel), 1980; The Baitchopper (children's novel), 1982; Schooner (non-fiction), 1984, The Prophet at Tanhamar (play), 1988. Add: D'Escousse, Nova Scotia, Canada.

CAMERON WATT, Donald. British, b. 1928. History, International relations/Current affairs. Stevenson Prof. of Intnl. History, Univ. of London, since 1981 (Asst. Lectr. in Political History, 1954–56; Lectr. in Intnl. History, 1956–62; Sr. Lectr., 1962–66; Reader, 1966–72; Prof. of Intnl. History, 1972–81). Chmn., Assn. of Contemporary Historians. Asst. Ed., Documents on German Foreign Policy 1918–1945, 1951–54, 1957–59; Ed., Survey of Intnl. Affairs, 1962–71; Chmn., Greenwich Forum, 1974–84. *Publs:* Britain and the Suez Canal, 1956; (ed.) Documents on the Suez Crisis, 1957; Britain Looks to Germany, 1965; Personalities and Policies: Studies in the Formulation of British Foreign Policy in the Twentieth Century, 1965; (ed.) Documents on International Affairs 1961, 1966; (ed. with K. Bourne) Studies in International History, 1967; (with F. Spencer and N. Brown) A History of the World in the Twentieth Century, 1967; (ed.) Contemporary History in Europe, 1969; (ed.) Hitler's Mein Kampf, 1970; (ed. with J.B. Mayall) Current British Foreign Policy in 1970, 1971; (ed. with J.B. Mayall) Current British Foreign Policy 1971, 1973; (ed. with J.B. Mayall) Documents on International Affairs 1963, 1973; Too Serious a Business: European Armies and the Approach of the Second World War, 1977; Succeeding John Bull: America in Britain's Place 1900–1975, 1983; 1939: How War Came, 1989. Add: c/o London Sch. of Economics, Aldwych, London WC2, England.

CAMP, John. British, b. 1915. Criminology/Law enforcement/Prisons, Medicine/Health. Justice of the Peace, Bucks., since 1964. Medical Writer, Wellcome Foundn., London, 1966–70. *Publs:* Oxfordshire and Buckinghamshire Pubs, 1965; Discovering Bellringing, 1968; Discovering London Railway Station, 1971; Portrait of Buckinghamshire, 1972; Magic, Myth and Medicine, 1973; Bellringing, 1974; Holloway Prison, 1974; The Healing Art, 1978; A Hundred Years of Medical Murder, 1982; The Folklore of Bells, 1988; In Praise of Bells, 1988. Add: Thurston House, Mill Close, Wingrave, Aylesbury, Bucks. HP22 4QE, England.

CAMPBELL, Alistair (Te Ariki). New Zealander, b. 1925. Novels, Children's fiction, Plays, Poetry, Mythology/Folklore. Ed., Dept. of Education Sch. Publs. Branch, Wellington, 1955–72; Sr. Ed., New Zealand Council for Educational Research, Wellington, 1972–87. Pres., P.E.N., New Zealand, 1976–79. *Publs:* Mine Eyes Dazzle: Poems 1947–49, 1951, 1956; The Fruit Farm, 1953; The Happy Summer, 1961; Wild Honey, 1964; Sanctuary of Spirits, 1967; Blue Rain: Poems, 1967; New Zealand: A Book for Children, 1967; Maori Legends, 1969; When the Bough Breaks (play), 1970; Drinking Horn, 1971; Walk the Black Path, 1971; Kapiti: Selected Poems, 1947–71, 1972; Dreams, Yellow Lions, 1975; The Dark Lord of Savaiki, 1980; Collected Poems, 1982; Island to Island (memoirs), 1984; Soul Traps: Lyric Sequence, 1985; The Frigate Bird (novel), 1989. Add: 4 Rawhiti Rd., Pukerua Bay, Wellington, New Zealand.

CAMPBELL, Bridget. *See* **SANCTUARY,** Brenda.

CAMPBELL, Donald. British, b. 1940. Plays/Screenplays, Poetry. Writer-in-Residence, Edinburgh Education Dept., 1974–77; Dir., Lothian Young Writers Project, 1978–79, Writer in Residence, Royal Lyceum Theatre, 1981–82. *Publs:* Poems, 1971; Rhymes 'n Reasons, 1972; Murals: Poems in Scots, 1974; The Jesuit (play), 1976; Somerville the Soldier (play), 1978; The Widows of Clyth (play), 1979; Blether, 1979; A Brighter Sunshine, 1983; Dr. Jekyll and Mr. Hyde (play; from Stevenson), 1985. Add: 85 Spottiswoode St., Edinburgh EH9 1BZ, Scotland.

CAMPBELL, Francis Stuart. *See* **KUEHNELT-LEDDIHN,** Erik.

CAMPBELL, G(aylon) S(anford). American, b. 1940. Environmental science/Ecology. Prof., Dept. of Agronomy and Soils, Washington State Univ., Pullman, since 1971. *Publs:* An Introduction to Environmental Biophysics, 1977; Soil Physics with BASIC, 1985. Add: Dept. of Agronomy and Soils, Washington State Univ., Pullman, Wash. 99164, U.S.A.

CAMPBELL, Ian. British, b. 1942. Literature, Biography. Reader in English Literature, Univ. of Edinburgh, since 1981 (Lectr., 1967–81). *Publs:* (ed. with R.D.S. Jack) Jamie the Saxt, by Robert McLellan, 1970; (co-ed.) The Duke-Edinburgh Edition of the Letters of Thomas and Jane Welsh Carlyle, vols. 1-17, 1970–89; (ed.) Reminiscences of Thomas Carlyle, 1972; Thomas Carlyle, 1974, 1981; Thomas Carlyle: Writers and their Work, 1978; (ed.) Critical Essays in Nineteenth Century Scottish Fiction, 1979; Billy Budd, 1980; Thomas and Jane, 1980; Kailyard, 1981; (ed.) Stevenson: Short Stories, 1981; Dr. Jekyll and Mr. Hyde, 1981; The Speak of the Mearns, 1982; Lewis Grassic Gibbon, 1986; Spartacus; George Douglas Browne, 1989. Add: Dept. of English, Univ. of Edinburgh, David Hume Tower, George Sq., Edinburgh EH8 9JX, Scotland.

CAMPBELL, Ian Barclay. New Zealander, b. 1916. Law. Teaching Fellow, Massey Univ.; Safety Dir., Accident Compensation Commn.; Secty., Workers' Compensation Bd. *Publs:* Hand Book to Workers' Compensation Act 1956, 1958; (with D.P. Neazor) Workers' Compensation Law in New Zealand, 1964; Safety Legislation and the Work Place, 1982; Legislating for Workplace Hazards in New Zealand, 1987. Add: 50 Field Way, Waikanae, New Zealand.

CAMPBELL, Judith. (Marion Staplyton Pares). Also writes as Anthony Grant. British, b. 1914. Animals/Pets, Biography. Journalist, and broadcaster. *Publs:* Family Pony, 1962; The Queen Rides, 1965; Horses in the Sun, 1966; Police Horse, 1967; Pony Events, 1969; World of Horses, 1969; Horses and Ponies, 1970; World of Ponies, 1970; Anne—Portrait of a Princess, 1970; (with N. Toyne) Family on Horseback, 1972; Princess Anne and Her Horses, 1972; Elizabeth and Philip, 1972; The Champions, 1973; Royalty on Horseback, 1974; The World of the Horse, 1975; Eventing, 1976; Anne and Mark, 1976; Your own Pony Club, 1979; Queen Elizabeth II, 1979; (as Anthony Grant) The Mutant, 1980; Charles, A Prince of His Time, 1980; The Royal Partners, 1982; Royal Horses, 1983; Ponies, People and Palaces, 1989. Add: c/o A.M. Heath Ltd., 79 St. Martin's Lane, London WC2N 4AA, England.

CAMPBELL, Karen. *See* **BEATY,** Betty.

CAMPBELL, Paul N(ewell). American, b. 1923. Literature, Theatre. Prof., Dept of Theatre and Media Arts, Univ. of Kansas, Lawrence, since 1974. Asst., then Assoc. Prof., California State Univ., Los Angeles, 1959–71; Assoc., then Prof., Queens Coll., City Univ. of New York, 1971–74. *Publs:* Oral Interpretation, 1966; The Speaking and the Speakers of Literature, 1967; Rhetoric Ritual: A Study of the Communicative and Aesthetic Dimensions of Language, 1972; Form and the Art of Theatre, 1984. Add: Dept. of Theatre and Media Arts, Univ. of Kansas, Lawrence, Kans. 66045, U.S.A.

CAMPBELL, Peter (Walter). British, b. 1926. Politics/Government. Prof. of Politics, Univ. of Reading, since 1964 (Prof. of Political Economy, 1960–64; Dean, Faculty of Letters, 1966–69; Chmn., Grad. Sch. of Contemporary European Studies, 1971–73). Lectr. in Govt., Univ. of Manchester, 1949–60. *Publs:* (with W. Theimer) Encyclopaedia of World Politics, 1950; French Electoral Systems and Elections 1789-1957, 1958; (with B. Chapman) The Constitution of the Fifth Republic, 1958; French Electoral Systems and Elections since 1789, 1965. Add: Dept. of Politics, Univ. of Reading, Reading, Berks. RG6 2AA, England.

CAMPBELL, Ramsey. British, b. 1946. Novels/Short stories. Film Critic, B.B.C., Liverpool. Pres., British Fantasy Soc., since 1976. Tax Officer, Liverpool, 1962–66; Library Asst., Liverpool Public Libraries, 1966–73. *Publs:* The Inhabitant of the Lake and Less Welcome Tenants, 1964; Demons by Daylight, 1973; The Height of the Scream, 1976; The Doll Who Ate His Mother, 1976; (ed.) Superhorror, 1976; The Face That Must Die, 1979; To Wake the Dead (in U.S. as the Parasite), 1980; (ed.) New Terrors, 2 vols., 1980; (ed.) New Tales of the Cthulhu Mythos, 1980; The Nameless, 1981; Dark Companions, 1982; Night of the Claw, 1983; Incarnate, 1983; (ed.) The Gruesome Book, 1983; Obsession, 1985; Cold Print, 1985; The Hungry Moon, 1986; (with Charles L. Grant) Black Wine, 1986; (with Lisa Tuttle and Clive Barker) Night Visions III, 1986; Scared Stiff, 1986; The Influence, 1987; Dark Feasts, 1987; (ed.) Stories That Scared Me, 1987; Ancient Images, 1989. Add: 31 Penkett Rd., Wallasey L45 7QF, Merseyside, England.

CAMPBELL, Robert. American, b. 1926. Economics. Distinguished Prof. of Economics, Indiana Univ., Bloomington, since 1961. Consultant to Rand Corp. amd Hudson Inst. Former Asst. Prof., Dept. of Economics, Univ. of Southern California, Los Angeles. *Publs:* Soviet Economic Power: Its Structure, Growth, and Prospects, 1960 (3rd ed. as The Soviet-type Economies); Accounting in Soviet Planning and Management, 1963; Economics of the Soviet Oil and Gas Industry, 1968; (with J.E. Elliott) Comparative Economic Systems, 1973. Add: Dept. of Economics, Indiana Univ., Bloomington, Ind. 47405, U.S.A.

CAMPLING, Christopher Russell. British, b. 1925. Theology/Religion. Dean of Ripon, since 1984. Asst. Curate, Basingstoke, 1951–55; Chaplain, King's Sch., Ely, 1955–60, and Lancing Coll., Sussex, 1961–67; Vicar and Rural Dean of Pershore, and Canon of Worcester Cathedral, 1968–76; Archdeacon of Dudley, 1976–84. *Publs:* (co-author) Guide to Divinity Teaching, 1960; The Way, the Truth and the Life (series), 1965; (co-ed.) Words for Worship, 1970; (ed.) The Fourth Lesson, Book 1, 1973, Book 2, 1974. Add: The Minster House, Ripon, Yorks. HG4 1PE, England.

CAMPLING, Elizabeth. British, b. 1948. Children's non-fiction, History, Biography. Full-time writer since 1985. Part-time Lectr., Chichester Coll. of Technology, 1974–85. *Publs:* Africa in the Twentieth Century, 1980; Kennedy, 1980; (with James Campling) Living Through History: The French Revolution, 1984; Living Through History: The Russian Revolution, 1985; How and Why: The Russian Revolution, 1986; Living Through History: The 1960's, 1987. Add: 17 Church Lane, Pagham, Bognor Regis, W. Sussex PO21 4NS, England.

CAMPTON, David. British, b. 1924. Plays/Screenplays, Children's non-fiction. Clerk, City of Leicester Education Dept., 1941–49, and East Midlands Gas Bd., Leicester, 1949–56. *Publs:* Going Home, 1951; Honeymoon Express, 1951; Change Partners, 1951; Sunshine on the Righteous, 1952; The Laboratory, 1955; The Cactus Garden, 1955; Doctor Alexander, 1956; Cuckoo Song, 1956; The Lunatic View: A Comedy of Menace, 1960; Roses Round the Door, 1958; Frankenstein: The Gift of Fire, 1959; Little Brother, Little Sister, 1960; Four Minute Warning, 1960; Funeral Dance, 1960; Passport to Florence, 1961; Silence on the Battlefield, 1961; Usher, 1962; Incident, 1962; On Stage: Containing Seventeen Sketches and One Monologue, 1964; Resting Place, 1964; The Manipulator, 1964; Split Down the Middle, 1965; Little Brother, Little Sister and Out of the Flying Pan, 1966; Two Leaves and a Stalk, 1967; Angel Unwilling, 1967; More Sketches, 1967; Ladies Night: Four Plays for Women, 1967; The Right Place, 1969; Laughter and Fear: 9 One-Act Plays, 1969; On Stage Again: Containing Fourteen Sketches and Two Monologues, 1969; The Life and Death of Almost Everybody, 1970; Now and Then, 1970; Timesneeze, 1970; Gulliver in Lilliput (reader), 1970; Gulliver in the Land of the Giants (reader), 1970; The Wooden Horse of Troy (reader), 1970; Jonah, 1971; The Cagebirds, 1971; Us and Them, 1972; Carmilla, 1972; Come Back Tomorrow, 1972; In Committee, 1972;

Three Gothic Plays, 1973; Modern Aesop (reader), 1976; One Possessed, 1977; The Do-It-Yourself Frankenstein Outfit, 1978; What are You Doing Here?, 1978; Zodiac, 1978; After Midnight: Before Dawn, 1978; Parcel, 1979; Everybody's Friend, 1979; Pieces of Campton, 1979; Who Calls?, 1980; Attitudes, 1980; Freedom Log, 1980; Dark Wings, 1981; Look—Sea, 1981; Great Whales, 1981; Who's a Hero?, 1981; But Not Here, 1984; Dead and Alive, 1983; Mrs. Meadowsweet, 1986; Singing in the Wilderness, 1986; Our Branch in Brussels, 1986; Cards, Cups and Crystal Ball, 1986; The Vampyre (children's book), 1986; Can You Hear the Music?, 1989. Add: 35 Liberty Rd., Glenfield, Leicester LE3 8JF, England.

CANDILIS, Wray O. American, b. 1927. Economics. Dir., Finance and Management Industries Div., Office of Service Industries, International Trade Admin., U.S. Dept. of Commerce, Washington, D.C., since 1971 (former Special Asst., for Financial Affairs, Office of Business Research and Analysis). Asst. Dir., Dept. of Research, National Assn. of Real Estate Bds., Washington, D.C., 1960–64; Sr. Economics Assoc., Div. of Statistics and Research, Inst. of Life Insurance, NYC, 1964–66; Research Project Dir., Dept. of Research and Planning, American Bankers Assn., Washington, D.C., 1966–71. *Publs:* The Economy of Greece 1944–66, 1968; Long-Range Planning in Banking, 1968; Financing America's States and Cities, 1970; Variable Rate Mortgage Plans, 1971; (ed. and co-author) The Future of Commercial Banking, 1975; Consumer Credit–Factors Influencing Its Availability and Costs, 1976; (ed.) Changing Minority Markets, 1978; (co-author and ed.) Franchising in the Economy 1976–1978, 1978; (ed.) Market Center Shifts, 1978; (ed.) The Motor Vehicle Leasing and Rental Industry: Trends and Prospects, 1979; (ed.) Measuring Markets: Guide to the Use of Federal and State Statistical Data, 1979; (ed.) United States Service Industries Handbook, 1987. Add: 4101 Cathedral Ave N.W., Washington, D.C. 20016, U.S.A.

CANDLAND, Douglas Keith. American, b. 1934. Psychology. Presidential Prof. of Animal Behavior, Bucknell Univ., Lewisburg, Pa., since 1973 (Asst. Prof., 1960–64; Assoc. Prof., 1964–67; Prof., 1967–73). Consulting Ed., Journal of Comparative Psychology, since 1988. Consulting Ed., Teaching of Psychology, 1976–84, and American Journal of Primatology, 1980–84. Assoc. Ed., Animal Learning and Behavior, 1976–84. *Publs:* (with J. Campbell) Exploring Behavior, 1960; (ed.) Emotion: Bodily Change, 1962; Psychology: The Experimental Approach, 1968; (with others) Emotion, 1977; (with R. Moyer) Psychology: The Experimental Approach, 1978. Add: 125 Stein Lane, Lewisburg, Pa. 17837, U.S.A.

CANDY, Edward. Pseudonym for Barbara Alison Neville. British, b. 1925. Novels/Short stories. Mystery/Crime/Suspense. Physician: worked in hospitals in Norwich, Sheffield, Northwood, and Liverpool. Reviewer, The Times and The Sunday Times, London, 1967–76. *Publs:* Which Doctor (mystery novel), 1953; Bones of Contention (mystery novel), 1954; The Graver Tribe (novel), 1958; A Lady's Hand (novel), 1959; A Season of Discord (novel), 1964; Stokes of Havoc (novel), 1966; Parents' Day (novel), 1967; Doctor Amadeus (novel), 1969; Words for Murder, Perhaps (mystery novel), 1971; Scene Changing (novel), 1977; Voices of Children (novel), 1980. Add: 2 Mile End Rd., Newmarket Rd., Norwich NR4 7QY, England.

CANNAN, Denis. British, b. 1919. Plays/Screenplays. *Publs:* Captain Carvallo, 1952; (adaptor) Colombe, by Anouilh, 1952; Misery Me! A Comedy of Woe, 1956; You and Your Wife, 1956; (adaptor with Pierre Bost) The Power and the Glory, by Graham Greene, 1959; Who's Your Father?, 1959; (with others) US (in U.S. as Tell Me Lies . . .), 1968; One at Night, 1971; (adaptor and collaborator) The IK, 1975; Dear Daddy, 1978. Add: 43 Osmond Rd., Hove, E. Sussx BN3 1TF, England.

CANNON, Garland. American, b. 1924. Language/Linguistics, Biography. Prof. of English and Linguistics, Texas A. and M. Univ., College Station, since 1966. Asst. Prof., Teachers Coll., Columbia Univ., N.Y.C., 1959–62; Assoc. Prof., City Univ. of New York, 1963–66. *Publs:* Sir William Jones: Orientalist, 1952; Oriental Jones, 1964; (ed.) The Letters of Sir William Jones, 2 vols., 1970; A History of the English Language, 1972; An Integrated Transformational Grammar of English, 1978; Sir William Jones: A Secondary and Primary Bibliography, 1979; Historical Change and English Word-Formation, 1987; Oriental Jones: The Life and Mind of Sir William Jones, 1989. Add: Dept. of English, Texas A. & M. Univ., College Station, Tex. 77843, U.S.A.

CANOVAN, Margaret Evelyn. British, b. 1939. Politics/Government, Biography. Lectr. in Politics, Keele Univ., since 1974. Lectr. in Politics, Univ. of Lancaster, 1965–71. *Publs:* The Political Thought of Hannah Arendt, 1974; G.K. Chesterton: Radical Populist, 1977; Populism, 1981. Add: Dept. of Politics, Keele Univ., Keele, Staffs., England.

CANUCK, Abe. *See* **BINGLEY**, David Ernest

CAPE, Judith. *See* **PAGE**, P.K.

CAPELLE, Russell B(eckett). American, b. 1917. International relations/Current affairs, Politics/Government, Autobiography/Memoirs/Personal. Prof. of History and Govt., Norwich Univ., Northfield, Vt., since 1954 (Chmn. of the Dept., 1972–78; Prof. Emeritus, since 1982). Instr., Bradford Jr. Coll., Mass., 1946–54. *Publs:* The M.R.P. and French Foreign Policy, 1963; (contrib. ed.) Dictionary of Political Science, 1964; Casablanca to the Neckar: Recollections of the Grand Tour, 1969. Add: RDF 1, Roxbury Rd., Northfield, Vt. 05663, U.S.A.

CAPITAN, William H(arry). American, b. 1933. Art, Philosophy, Theology/Religion. Pres., Georgia Southwestern Coll., Americus, since 1979. Instr. in Philosophy, Univ. of Minnesota, Minneapolis, 1959–60; Instr., Univ. of Maryland, College Park, 1960–62; Asst. Prof., 1962–65, Assoc. Prof., 1965–70, and Chmn., Dept. of Philosophy, 1968–70, Oberlin Coll., Ohio; Dean, 1970–72, Vice-Pres., 1972–74, and Acting Pres., 1974–79, Saginaw Valley Coll., Michigan. *Publs:* (ed. with D.D. Merrill) Metaphysics and Explanation, 1966; (ed. with Merrill) Art, Religion and Mind, 1967; Introduction to The Philosophy of Religion (textbook), 1972; Speak for Yourself, 1989. Add: Georgia Southwestern Coll., Americus, Ga. 31709, U.S.A.

CAPLAN, Arthur L(eonard). American, b. 1950. Humanities (general), Medicine/Health. Assoc. Dir., Assoc. for the Humanities, Hastings Center, Inst. of Society, Ethics and the Life Sciences, Hastings, N.Y., since 1985 (with Assoc. since 1976); Assoc. for Social Medicine, Columbia Univ., NYC, since 1978 (Instr., Sch. of Public Health, 1977–78). *Publs:* (ed.) The Sociobiology Debate, 1978; (ed., with H. Tristram Engelhardt, Jr.) Concepts of Health and Disease: Interdisciplinary Perspectives, 1980; (ed.with Daniel Callahan) Ethics in Hard Times, 1981; (ed.) In Search of Equity, 1983; (ed. with Bruce Jennings) Darwin, Marx and Freud: Their Influence on Moral Theory, 1983; (ed.) Scientific Controversies, 1985. Add: Hastings Center, 360 Broadway, Hastings-on-Hudson, N.Y. 10706, U.S.A.

CAPON, Edmund (George). British, b. 1940. Archaeology/Antiquities, Art. Dir., Art Gallery of New South Wales, Sydney, since 1978. Ed., Oriental Art Mag., London, since 1974; Dir., Intnl. Cultural Corp. of Australia. Mgr., Molton Gallery, London, 1964–65; Asst. Keeper, Far Eastern Section, Victoria and Albert Museum, London, 1966–78. Member of the Council, Oriental Ceramic Soc., London, 1976–78, and Royal Soc. for Asian Affairs, London, 1977–78. *Publs:* Princes of Jade, 1973; Art and Archaeology in China, 1977; Chinese Painting, 1979; (with M.A. Pang) Chinese Painting of the Ming and Qing Dynasties, 1981; Qin Shihuang: Terracotta Warriors and Horses, 1983; Tang China, 1989. Add: 3 Mansion Rd., Bellevue Hill, Sydney, N.S.W. 2023, Australia.

CAPPON, Daniel. Canadian, b. 1921. Human relations, Psychiatry, Psychology. Prof. of Environmental Studies, York Univ., Toronto, Ont., since 1969. Prof. of Psychiatry, Univ. of Toronto, 1949–68; Prof. of Psychiatry, Univ. of Maryland, Baltimore, 1968–69. *Publs:* Towards an Understanding of Homosexuality, 1966; Technology and Perception, 1971; Eating, Loving and Dying: A Psychology of Appetites, 1973; Coupling, 1981. Add: 32 York Valley Cres., Willowdale, Ont. M2P 1A7, Canada.

CAPPS, Ben(jamin F.). American, b. 1922. Westerns/Adventure, History. *Publs:* Hanging at Comanche Wells, 1962; The Trail to Ogallala, 1964; Sam Chance, 1965; A Woman of the People, 1966; The Brothers of Uterica, 1967; The White Man's Road, 1969; The True Memoirs of Charley Blankenship, 1972; The Indians, 1973; The Warren Wagontrain Raid, 1974; The Great Chiefs, 1975; (ed.) Duncan Robinson, Texas Teacher and Humanist, 1976; Woman Chief, 1979. Add: 366 Forrest Hill Lane, Grand Prairie, Tex. 75051, U.S.A.

CAPUTI, Anthony. American, b. 1924. Novels/Short stories, Literature, Theatre. Prof. of English, Cornell Univ., Ithaca, N.Y., since 1969 (Asst. Prof., 1960–63; Assoc. Prof., 1964–69). *Publs:* John Marston: Satirist, 1961; (ed.) Norton Anthology of Modern Drama, 1966; (ed.) Masterworks of World Drama, 6 vols., 1968; Loving Evie (novel), 1974; Buffo: The Genius of Vulgar Comedy, 1978; Storms and Son (novel), 1985; Pirandello and the Crisis of Modern Consciousness, 1988. Add: 1968 Gee Hill Rd., Dryden, N.Y. 13053, U.S.A.

CARAS, Roger A(ndrew). American, b. 1928. Humanities (general), Natural history, Travel/Exploration/Adventure. Commentator, ABC Radio, since 1981; Special Correspondent on Pets, Wildlife and the Environment, ABC-TV News, since 1974. Commentator, CBS Radio, 1969–80. *Publs* (partial list): Antarctica: Land of Frozen Time, 1962; Wings of Gold, 1965; The Throwbacks, 1965; Dangerous to Man: The Definitive Story of Wildlife's Reputed Dangers, 1966, rev. ed. 1976; The Custer Wolf, 1966; Last Chance on Earth, 1966; North American Mammals, 1967; Sarang, 1968; Monarch of Deadman Bay, 1969; Source of the Thunder, 1970; Panther!, 1970; Death as Way of Life, 1971; Vanishing Wildlife, 1971; Animal Children, 1971; Animal Architects, 1971; Birds and Flights, 1971; Protective Coloration, 1972; Animal Courtship, 1972; Boundary: Land and Sea, 1972; Creatures of the Night, 1972; Going to the Zoo with Roger Caras, 1973; The Wonderful World of Mammals: Adventuring with Stamps, 1973; The Bizarre Animals, 1974; Venomous Animals of the World, 1974; Roger Caras' Nature Quiz Book, 2 vols., 1974; The Private Lives of Animals, 1974; Sockeye: The Life of a Pacific Salmon, 1975; Skunk for a Day, 1976; The Roger Caras Pet Book, 1977; Coyote for a Day, 1977; (ed.) Dog Owner's Bible, 1978; (with P. Graham) Dogs, 1979; Mysteries of Nature, 1979; The Forest, 1979; Yankee, 1979; The Roger Caras Dog Book, 1980; A Celebration of Dogs, 1983; Mara Simba, 1985; The Endless Migration, 1985; A Celebration of Cats, 1985; (ed.) Harper's Illustrated Handbook of Cats [and Dogs], 2 vols., 1985; Roger Caras' Treasury of Great Cat [and Dog] Stories, 2 vols., 1987; Animals in Their Places, 1987. Add: Thistle Hill Farm, 21108 Slab Bridge Rd., Freeland, Md. 21053, U.S.A.

CARD, Orson Scott. American, b. 1951. Novels, Science fiction, Plays. Volunteer Mormon missionary in Brazil, 1971–73; operated repertory theatre, Provo, Utah, 1974–75; Proofreader, 1974, and Ed., 1974–76, Brigham Young Univ. Press, Provo.; Ed., Ensign Mag., Salt Lake City, 1976–78, and Compute Books, Greensboro, N.C., 1983. *Publs:* Listen, Mom and Dad, 1978; Hot Sleep (science fiction), 1978; Capitol (short stories), 1978; A Planet Called Treason (science fiction), 1979; Songmaster (science fiction), 1980; Unaccompanied Sonata and Other Stories, 1981; Saintspeak, 1981; (ed.) Dragons of Darkness, 1981; Ainge, 1982; Hart's Hope (science fiction), 1983; (ed.) Dragons of Light, 1983; The Worthing Chronicle (science fiction), 1983; Saints (A Woman of Destiny) (novel), 1984; Ender's Game (science fiction), 1985; Speaker for the Dead (science fiction), 1986; Seventh Son (novel), 1987; Wyrms (science fiction), 1987; Red Prophet (novel), 1988; Character and Viewpoint, 1988; Prentice Alvin (novel), 1989; Folk of the Fringe (science fiction), 1989. Add: 546 Lindley Rd., Greensboro, N.C. 27410, U.S.A.

CAREW, Jan (Rynveld). Guyanese, b. 1925. Novels/Short stories, Children's fiction, Plays/Screenplays, Poetry, History. Prof., Dept. of African-American Studies, Northwestern Univ., Evanston, Ill., 1972–87, now Emeritus. Co-Chmn., Third World Energy Inst., since 1978. Chmn., Caribbean Soc. for Culture and Science, since 1979. Lectr. in Race Relations, Univ. of London Extra-Mural Dept., 1953–57; Writer and Ed., BBC Overseas Service, London, 1954–65; Ed., African Review, Ghana, 1965–66; CBC Broadcaster, Toronto, 1966–69; Sr. Fellow, Council of Humanities, and Lectr., Dept. of Afro-American Studies, Princeton Univ., 1969–72. *Publs:* Streets of Eternity (poetry), 1952; Black Midas (in U.S. as A Touch of Midas), 1958; The Wild Coast, 1958; The Last Barbarian, 1961; Green Winter, 1964; University of Hunger (play), 1966; The Third Gift (children's fiction), 1975; Save the Last Dance for Me, 1976; The Origins of Racism and Resistance in the Americas, 1976; Rape of the Sun-people (history), 1976; Lost Love and Other Stories, 1978; Children of the Sun (children's fiction), 1980; Sea Drums in My Blood (poetry), 1981; Dark Night, Deep Water, 1981; Death Comes to the Circus, 1983; Time Loop, 1983; Grenada: The Hour Will Strike Again (history), 1985; Fulcrums of Change (essays), 1987. Add: Dept. of African-American Studies, Northwestern Univ., 2003 Sheridan Rd., Evanston, Ill. 60201, U.S.A.

CAREW, (Sir) Rivers (Verain). British, b. 1935. Poetry. Chief Sub-Ed., BBC World Service, since 1987. Asst. Ed., Ireland of the Welcomes mag, Dublin, 1964–67; Joint Ed., The Dublin Magazine, 1964–69; Sub-Ed., 1967–77, Deputy Chief Sub-Ed., 1977–82, and Chief Sub-Ed., 1982–87, Radio Telefis Eireann, Dublin. *Publs:* (with T. Brownlow) Figures out of Mist, 1966. Add: 148 Catharine St., Cambridge CB1 3AR, England.

CAREY, Ernestine Gilbreth. American. Novels/Short stories, Autobiography/Memoirs/Personal. *Publs:* (with F.B. Gilbreth) Cheaper by the Dozen, 1949; (with F.B. Gilbreth) Belles on Their Toes, 1951; Jumping Jupiter, 1952; Rings Around Us, 1956; Giddy Moment, 1958. Add: 6148 E. Lincoln Dr., Paradise Valley, Ariz. 85253, U.S.A.

CAREY, John. British, b. 1934. Literature. Merton Prof. of English Literature, Oxford Univ., since 1976 (Lectr., Christ Church, 1958–59; Tutorial Fellow, Keble Coll., 1960–64, and St. John's Coll., 1964–75). *Publs:* (ed. with Alastair Fowler) Poems of John Milton, 1968; Milton, 1969; The Violent Effigy: A Study of Dickens' Imagination, 1971; Thackeray: Prodigal Genius, 1977; John Donne: Life, Mind, and Art, 1981; (ed.) The Private Memoirs and Confessions of a Justified Sinner, by James Hogg, 1981; (ed.) William Golding: The Man and His Books, 1987; Original Copy: Selected Reviews and Journalism, 1987; (ed.) The Faber Book of Reportage, 1987. Add: 57 Stapleton Road, Headington, Oxford, England.

CAREY, Peter. Australian, b. 1943. Novels/Short stories. Worked part-time in advertising in Australia 1962–88 (Partner, McSpedden Carey Advertising Consultants, Sydney); currently full-time writer. *Publs:* The Fat Man in History (short stories), 1974, in U.K. as Exotic Pleasures, 1981; War Crimes (short stories), 1979; Bliss (novel), 1981, as film, 1985; Illywhacker (novel), 1985; Oscar and Lucinda (Booker Prize), 1988. Add: c/o Univ. of Queensland Press, P.O. Box 42, St. Lucia, Qld. 4067, Australia.

CARFAX, Catherine. *See* **FAIRBURN,** Eleanor.

CARKEET, David. American, b. 1946. Novels/Short stories. Prof., Dept. of English, Univ. of Missouri, St. Louis, since 1973. *Publs:* Double Negative, 1980; The Greatest Slump of All Times, 1984; I Been There Before, 1985; The Silent Treatment, 1988. Add: 435 Westgate, St. Louis, Mo. 63130, U.S.A.

CARLE, Eric. American, b. 1929. Children's fiction, Children's non-fiction. Freelance writer, illustrator and designer, since 1963. Poster designer, U.S. Information Ctr., Stuttgart, 1950–52; graphic designer, N.Y. Times, 1954–56; Art Dir., L.W. Frohlick and Co., NYC, 1956–63; Guest Instr., Pratt Inst., Brooklyn, 1964. *Publs:* children's fiction—1,2,3, to the Zoo, 1969; The Very Hungry Caterpillar, 1969; Pancakes, Pancakes!, 1970; Do You Want To Be My Friend?, 1971; The Rooster Who Set Out To See the World, 1972, in U.K. as Rooster's Off to See the World, 1988; The Secret Birthday Message, 1972; Have You Seen My Cat?, 1973; I See a Song, 1973; All About Arthur (An Absolutely Absurd Ape), 1975; My Very First Library, 1974; The Mixed-Up Chameleon, 1975, 1985; The Grouchy Ladybug, 1977, in the U.K. as The Bad-Tempered Ladybird, 1978; Watch Out! A Giant!, 1978; The Honeybee and The Robber, 1981; The Very Busy Spider, 1984; All Around Us, 1986; Papa, Please Get the Moon for Me, 1986; Have You Seen My Cat?, 1987; A House for Hermit Crab, 1987; (ed.) Treasury of Classic Stories for Children, 1988; children's non-fiction and retellings—The Say-with-Me ABC Book, 1967; The Tiny Seed, 1970, in U.K. as The Tiny Seed and the Giant Flower, 1970; The Very Long Tail, 1972; The Very Long Train, 1972; Walter the Baker (retelling), 1972; My Very First Book of Colors (Numbers, Shapes, Words, Food, Growth, Heads and Tails, Homes, Motion, Sounds, Tools, Touch), 12 vols., 1974–86; Storybook: Seven Tales by the Brothers Grimm, 1976; Seven Stories by Hans Christian Andersen, 1978; Twelve Tales from Aesop, 1980; Catch the Ball!, 1982; Let's Paint a Rainbow, 1982; What's for Lunch?, 1982. Add: 231 Crescent St., Northampton, Mass. 01060, U.S.A.

CARLEON, A. *See* **O'GRADY,** Rohan.

CARLETON, Mark Thomas. American, b. 1935. Criminology/Law enforcement/Prisons, History. Assoc. Prof. of History, Louisiana State Univ., Baton Rouge, since 1973 (Instr., 1965–68; Asst. Prof., 1968–73). Member, Governor's Council of Economic Advisers, Louisiana. *Publs:* Politics and Punishment—The History of the Louisiana State Penal System, 1971; (co-ed.) Readings in Louisiana Politics, 1975; River Capital: An Illustrated History of Baton Rouge, 1981; (co-author) Louisiana: A History, 1982. Add: Dept. of History, Louisiana State Univ., Baton Rouge, La. 70803, U.S.A.

CARLINO, Lewis John. American, b. 1932. Novels/Short stories, Plays/Screenplays. Member, Actors Studio Playwrights Unit, New York. *Publs:* The Brick and the Rose: A Collage for Voices, 1957; Junk Yard, 1959; Used Car for Sale, 1959; Objective Case, 1962; Mr. Flanner's Ocean, 1962; Piece and Precise, 1962; Two Short Plays: Sarah and the Sax, and High Sign, 1962; Cages: Snowangel and Epiphany, 1963; Telemachus Clay: Collage for Voices, 1963; Doubletalk: Sarah and the Sax, and The Dirty Old Man, 1964; The Exercise, 1968; The Brotherhood (screenplay and novel), 1968; The Mechanic (screenplay and novel), 1972. Add: c/o Gilbert Parker, William Morris, 1350 Ave. of the Americas, New York, NY 10019, U.S.A.

CARLISLE, D.M. *See* **COOK,** Dorothy Mary.

CARLSEN, G(eorge) Robert. American, b. 1917. Literature. Emeritus Prof. of English and Education, Univ. of Iowa, Iowa City, since 1982 (Prof., 1958–82). Instr. in Education, Univ. of Minnesota, Minneapolis, 1942–47; Asst. Prof. of Education and English, Univ. of Colorado, Boulder, 1947–52; Assoc. Prof. of Education, Univ. of Texas, Austin, 1952–58. *Publs:* (ed. with Ruth C. Carlsen) The Great Auto Race, 1965; (ed. with R.C. Carlsen) 52 Miles to Terror, 1965; Books and the Teen Age Reader, 1967, 3rd ed. 1980; (sr. ed. and author) Themes and Writers Series, 1967, 4th ed. 1985; American Literature, A Chronological Approach, and English Literature, A Chronological Approach, 1985; (with Anne Sherrill) Voices of Readers, 1988. Add: 817 N. Gilbert St., Iowa City, Iowa 52240, U.S.A.

CARLSON, Andrew R. American, b. 1934. Novels/Short stories, History. Archivist, Kalamazoo, Mich., since 1976. Member of faculty, Michigan State Univ., East Lansing, 1964–65, Prof. of Social Science, Eastern Kentucky Univ., Richmond, 1967–70, Ferris State Coll., 1970–73, and Western Michigan Univ., 1974–75. *Publs:* German Foreign Policy 1890-1914, and Colonial Policy to 1914, 1970; Anarchism in Germany: The Early Years, 1972; Bulow, Holstein, Wilhelm II and the Daily Telegraph Affair, 1974; Can Life Begin Again (novel), 1982. Add: 968 124th St., Shelbyville, Mich. 49344, U.S.A.

CARLSON, Bernice Wells. American, b. 1910. Children's fiction, Children's non-fiction. *Publs:* Junior Party Book, 1939, rev. ed. 1948; Make It Yourself, 1950; Do It Yourself, 1952; Fun for One or Two, 1954; Act It Out, 1956; Make It and Use It, 1958; The Right Play for You, 1960; (with K. Hunt) Masks and Mask Makers, 1962; (with D. Ginglend) Play Activities for the Retarded Child, 1963; The Party Book for Boys and Girls, 1963; Listen and Help Tell the Story, 1965; (with C.W. Carlson) Water Fit to Use, 1966, 1972; You Know What? I Like Animals, 1967; (with D. Ginglend) Recreation for Retarded Teenagers and Young Adults, 1968; Play a Part, 1970; (with R. Wigg) We Want Sunshine in Our Houses, 1973; Let's Pretend it Happened to You, 1973; Funny-Bone Dramatics, 1974; Picture That!, 1978; (with D. Ginglend) Ready to Work?, 1978; Quick Wits and Nimble Fingers, 1979; Let's Find the Big Idea, 1982. Add: Rt. 2. Box 332 D. Skillman Lane, Somerset, N.J. 08873, U.S.A.

CARLSON, Loraine. American, b. 1923. Travel/Exploration/Adventure. *Publs:* Mexico: An Extraordinary Guide, 1971; The Traveleer Guide to Mexico City, 1978, 1981; The Traveleer Guide to Yucatan and Guatamala, 1980; The Traveleer Guide to Yucatan, 1982. Add: 2021 W. Homer St., Chicago, Ill. 60647, U.S.A.

CARLSON, Natalie Savage. American, b. 1906. Children's fiction. *Publs:* The Talking Cat and Other French Canadian Stories, 1952; Alphonse, That Bearded One, 1954; Wings Against the Wind, 1955; Sashes Red and Blue, 1956; Hortense, the Cow for a Queen, 1957; Orpheline series, 4 vols., 1957–80; The Family Under the Bridge, 1958; Evangeline, Pigeon of Paris, 1960; The Tomahawk Family, 1960; The Song of the Lop-Eared Mule, 1961; Carnival in Paris, 1962; Jean-Claude's Island, 1963; The Empty Schoolhouse, 1965; Sailor's Choice, 1966; Chalou, 1967; Luigi of the Streets, 1967; Ann Aurelia and Dorothy, 1968; Befana's Gift, 1969; The Half Sisters, 1970; Luvvy and the Girls, 1971; Marie Louise series, 4 vols., 1974–81; Time for the White Egret, 1978; The Night the Scarecrow Walked, 1979; King of Cats, 1980; A Grandmother for the Orphelines, 1980; Marie Louise and Christopher at the Carnival, 1981; Spooky Night, 1982; The Surprise in the Mountains, 1983; The Ghost in the Lagoon, 1984; Spooky and the Ghost Cat, 1985; Spooky and the Wizard's Bats, 1986. Add: 17 Doral Mobile Home Villas, Clearwater, Fla. 33515, U.S.A.

CARLSON, Ron. American, b. 1934. Criminology/Law enforcement/Prisons, Law. John Byrd Martin Prof. of Law, Univ. of Georgia, since 1984. Prof. of Law, Univ. of Iowa, Iowa City, 1965–73; Prof. of Law, Washington Univ., St. Louis, Mo., 1973–84. *Publs:* Criminal Justice Procedure, 1978; Criminal Law Advocacy, 1982; Successful Techniques for Civil Trials, 1983; Adjudication of Criminal Justice, 1986; Materials for the Study of Evidence, 1986; Dynamics of Trial Practice, 1989. Add: Univ. of Georgia, School of Law, Athens, Georgia. 30602, U.S.A.

CARLSON, Ron. American, b. 1947. Novels/Short stories. Asst. Dir., Creative Writing Prog., Arizona State Univ., Tempe, since 1989 (Prof., 1986–88); participant, Artist in the Schools progs. for Utah, Idaho, and Alaska arts councils. English teacher, Hotchkiss Sch., Lakeville, Conn., 1971–81. *Publs:* Betrayed by F. Scott Fitzgerald (novel), 1977;

Truants (novel), 1981; The News of the World (stories), 1987. Add: c/o English Dept., Arizona State Univ., Tempe, Ariz. 85287, U.S.A.

CARLTON, David. British, b. 1938. International relations/Current Affairs. Lectr. in Intnl. Studies, Univ. of Warwick. Formerly, Sr. Lectr. in Diplomatic History, Polytechnic of North London. *Publs:* MacDonald Versus Henderson: The Foreign Policy of the Second Labour Government, 1970; (ed.) The Dynamics of the Arms Race, 1975; (ed.) International Terrorism and World Security, 1975; (ed.) Arms Control and Technological Innovation, 1977; (ed.) Terrorism: Theory and Practice, 1979; Anthony Eden: A Biography, 1981; (ed.) Contemporary Terror, 1981; (ed.) The Hazards of the International Energy Crisis, 1982; (ed.) The Arms Race in the 1980s, 1982; (ed.) South-Eastern Europe after Tito, 1983; (ed.) Reassessing Arms Control, 1984; (ed.) The Nuclear Arms Race Debated, 1986; (ed.) The Cold War Debated, 1988; (ed.) The Arms Race in the Era of Star Wars, 1988; Britain and the Suez Crisis, 1988. Add: Univ. of Warwick, Coventry CV4 7AL, England.

CARMAN, William Young. British, b. 1909. Military/Defence. Fellow, Soc. of Antiquaries, and Royal Historical Soc.; Vice-Pres., Military Historical Soc., Life Vice-Pres., British Model Soldiers Soc.; Council Member, Soc. for Army Historical Research; Pres., Military Historical Soc., and Military Heraldry Soc. With Imperial War Museum, London, 1950–65; Deputy Dir., National Army Museum, London, 1965–74. *Publs:* A History of Firearms, 1955; British Military Uniforms, 1957; British Military Uniforms, 1962; Indian Army Uniforms: vol. 1, Cavalry, 1961, vol. 2, Infantry, 1969; Louis Napoleon on Artillery, 1967; (ed.) Military Uniforms of the World, 1968; (ed.) Dress Regulations 1900, 1969; (ed.) Dress Regulations 1846. 1971; Headdress of the British Army: vol. 1, Cavalry, 1968, vol. 2, Yeomanry, 1970; (ed.) Regiments of Scotland, 1970; (co-author) History of the British Army, 1970; Model Soldiers for Collectors, 1972; Royal Artillery, 1973; Glengarry Badges pre 1881, 1973; (co-author) Badges and Insignia of Armed Forces, 1974; Dictionary of Military Uniform, 1977; (ed.) Richard Simkin's Uniforms of the British Army, 2 vols., 1982, 1985; Some English Yeomanry Sabretaches, 1987. Add: 94 Mulgrave Rd., Sutton, Surrey SM2 6LZ, England.

CARMICHAEL, Fred Walker. American, b. 1924. Plays/Screenplays. Producer, with Patricia Carmichael, of Caravan Theatre Inc., summer theatre, Dorset Playhouse, Vt., 1949–76. *Publs:* plays—More Than Meets the Eye, 1954; Inside Lester, 1955; The Night is My Enemy, 1956; Petey's Choice, 1958; The Pen is Deadlier, 1959; Luxury Cruise, 1960; Exit the Body, 1962; The Robin Hood Caper, 1963; Dream World, 1964; Any Number Can Die, 1965; The Best Laid Plans, 1966; Double in Diamonds, 1967; All The Better To Kill You With, 1968; Victoria's House, 1970; Ten Nights in a Bar Room (musical adaptation), 1970; Surprise!, 1971; Done to Death, 1972; Mixed Doubles, 1973; Who Needs a Waltz, 1974; Hey, Naked Lady, 1975; Last of the Class, 1976; Whatever Happened to Mrs. Kong, 1977; Don't Step on My Footprint, 1978; Exit Who?, 1982; Out of Sight . . . Out of Murder, 1983, one-act plays—Florence Unlimited, 1952; He's Having a Baby, 1953; She Sickness, 1954; Four For the Money, 1956; Divorce Granted, 1959; Green Room Blues, 1961; Dear Millie, 1965; So Nice Not to See You, 1968; Land of Promise, 1969; A Pack of Rascals, 1969; The Turning Point, 1969; There's a Fly in my Soap, 1973; Foiled by an Innocent Maid, 1977; The Three Million Dollar Lunch, 1982; P is for Perfect, 1983. Add: 307 W. 4th St., New York, N.Y. 10014, U.S.A.

CARMICHAEL, Joel. American, b. 1915. History, Biography, Translations. Ed., Weizmann Letters and Papers, 1968–71, and Midstream mag., NYC, 1975–87. *Publs:* (ed. and trans.) The Russian Revolution 1917: A Personal Record, 1955; (trans.) Anna Karenina by Tolstoy, 1962; The Death of Jesus, 1962; An Illustrated History of Russia, 1963; Karl Marx: The Passionate Logician, 1964; A Short History of the Russian Revolution, 1965; A Cultural History of Russia, 1966; The Shaping of the Arabs, 1967; Trotsky, 1975; Stalin's Masterpiece, 1976; Stehe auf und Rufe Deinen Herrn, 1982; The Birth of Christianity: Reality and Myth, 1989; What Is Anti-Semitism?, 1989. Add: 302 W. 86th St., New York, N.Y. 10024, U.S.A.

CARNALL, Geoffrey Douglas. British, b. 1927. Literature, Biography. Reader in English Literature, Univ. of Edinburgh, since 1969 (Lectr., 1960–65; Sr. Lectr., 1965–69). Lectr. in English, Queen's Univ., Belfast, 1952–60 *Publs:* Robert Southey and His Age: The Development of a Conservative Mind, 1960; Robert Southey, 1964. rev. ed. 1971; To Keep the Peace: The United Nations Peace Force, 1965; (ed.) Pope Dickens, and Others: Essays and Addresses by John Butt, 1969; (with John Butt) The Mid-Eighteenth Century, 1979; (ed. with Colin Nicholson) The Impeachment of Warren Hastings, 1989. Add: Dept. of English Literature, David Hume Tower, George Sq., Edinburgh EH8 9JX, Scotland.

CARNEGIE, Raymond Alexander. *See* **CARNEGIE,** Sacha.

CARNEGIE, Sacha. Pseud. for Raymond Alexander Carnegie. British, b. 1920. Romance/Historical fiction, Travel. Served in the Scots Guards, 1940–52: Major. *Publs:* novels—Noble Purpose, 1954; Sunset in the East, 1955; The Devil and the Deep, 1957; The Lion and Francis Conway, 1958; The Dark Night, 1960; The Deerslayers, 1961; The Guardian, 1966, as The Colonel, 1979; The Banners of Love (in U.S. as Scarlet Banners of Love), 1968; Banners of War, 1970; Banners of Power, 1976; Banners of Courage, 1976; Banners of Revolt, 1977; other—Holiday from Life, 1957; Pigs I Have Known, 1958; Red Dust of Africa, 1959; The Golden Years (memoirs), 1962; A Dash of Russia, 1966. Add: Crimongate, Lonmay, Aberdeenshire, Scotland.

CARNLEY, Peter Frederick. Australian, b. 1937. Theology/Religion. Anglican Archbishop of Perth and Metropolitan of the Province of Western Australia, since 1981. Deacon, 1962, and Priest, 1964, Diocese of Bath; Asst. Curate of Parkes, Diocese of Melbourne, 1966; with Diocese of Ely, England, 1966–69; Chaplain, Mitchell Coll. of Advanced Education, Bath, 1970–72; Research Fellow, St. John's Coll., Cambridge, 1971–72; Warden, St. John's Coll., St. Lucia, Queensland, 1978–81; Residentiary Canon, St. John's Cathedral, Brisbane, 1975–81; Examining Chaplain to Archbishop of Brisbane, 1975–81. *Publs:* The Poverty of Historical Scepticism, in Christ, Faith and History, 1972; The Structure of Resurrection Belief, 1985. Add: 52 Mount St., Perth, W.A. 6000, Australia.

CARNOCHAN, W.B. American, b. 1930. Literature. Prof. of English, Stanford Univ., California, since 1973 and Dir., Stanford Humanities Center, since 1985 (Instr., 1960–62; Asst. Prof., 1962–68; Assoc. Prof., 1968–73; Dean of Grad Studies, 1975–80; Vice-Provost, 1976–80). *Publs:* (ed.) The Man of Mode, by George Etherege, 1966; Lemuel Gulliver's Mirror for Man, 1968; Confinement and Flight: An Essay on English Literature of the Eighteenth Century, 1977; Gibbon's Solitude: The Inward World of the Historian, 1987. Add: English Dept., Stanford Univ., Stanford, Calif. 94305, U.S.A.

CARO, Robert A. American. Biography. Former staff memeber, Newsday newspaper, Long Island, N.Y. *Publs:* The Power Broker: Robert Moses and the Fall of New York, 1974; The Years of Lyndon Johnson: The Path to Power, 1982. Add: c/o Alfred A. Knopf Inc., 201 East 50th St. New York, N.Y. 10022, U.S.A.

CAROL, Bill J. *See* **KNOTT,** William C.

CARPENTER, Allan. American, b. 1917. Geography, History. Founder and Pres., Carpenter Publishing House, Chicago, since 1962. Founder and Chmn. of the Bd., Infordate Intnl. Inc., since 1973; Founder Ed., Issues in Education, since 1973, and Index to U.S. Govt. Periodicals, since 1974. Founder, 1940, and Ed. and Publr., 1940–48, Teacher's Digest mag.; Founder, Index to Reader's Digest, 1981. *Publs:* Between Two Rivers, 1939; (co-author) Hi Neighbor, 1943; The Twelve (verse), 1946; Enchantment of America, 52 vols., 1962–68, 1979; (ed.) Popular Mechanics Home Handyman Encyclopedia, 16 vols., 1966; Illinois: Land of Lincoln, 1968; (co-author) Enchantment of Central and South America, 20 vols., 1968–70; (co-author) Enchantment of Africa, 42 vols., 1970–75; All About the U.S.A., 7 vols., 1986; Mighty Warrior series, 4 vols., 1987. Add: Suite 4602, 175 E. Delaware Pl., Chicago, Ill. 60611, U.S.A.

CARPENTER, Frederic I(ves). American, b. 1903. Literature. Lectr. in English, Univ. of Chicago, 1925–27, Harvard Univ., Cambridge, Mass., 1929–35, and the Univ. of California, Berkeley, 1946–51. Ed., New England Quarterly, 1934–42. *Publs:* Emerson and Asia, 1930; Emerson Handbook, 1953; American Literature and the Dream, 1955; Robinson Jeffers, 1962; Eugene O'Neill, 1964; (ed.) Metaphor and Simile in Minor Elizabethan Drama, 1967; Laurens van der Post, 1969; (ed.) Arte or Crafte of Rhethoryke (1899), by Leonard Cox, 1973. Add: 2589 Pine Knoll Dr., No. 5, Walnut Creek, Calif. 94595, U.S.A.

CARPENTER, Humphrey (William Bouverie). British, b. 1946. Children's fiction, Biography. Freelance broadcaster and reviewer. Staff Producer, BBC, 1968–74. *Publs:* (with M. Prichard) A Thames Companion, 1975; J.R.R. Tolkien, 1977; The Joshers (children's fiction), 1977; The Inklings: C.S. Lewis, J.R.R. Tolkien, Charles Williams, and Their Friends, 1978; The Captain Hook Affair (children's fiction), 1979; Jesus, 1980; W.H. Auden, 1981; (ed. with C. Tolkien) The Letters of J.R.R. Tolkien, 1981; Mr. Majeika (children's fiction), 1984; (with M. Prichard)

The Oxford Companion to Children's Literature, 1984; O.U.D.S.: A Centenary History of the Oxford University Dramatic Society, 1985; Secret Gardens: A Study of the Golden Age of Children's Literature, 1985; Mr. Majeika and the Music Teacher (children's fiction), 1986; (with others) Founders of Faith: Past Masters of Religion, 1986; Geniuses Together: American Writers in Paris in the 1920's, 1987; Mr. Majeika and the Haunted Hotel (children's fiction), 1987; A Serious Character: The Life of Ezra Pound, 1988. Add: c/o Unwin Hyman Ltd., 40 Museum St., London WC1A 1LU, England.

CARPENTER, Nan Cooke. American, b. 1912. Literary History/Criticism, Music. Retired Prof., Dept. of Comparative Literature, Univ. of Georgia, Athens, since 1980 (Prof., 1967–79 and Head of the Dept., 1974–79). Prof. of English, Univ. of Montana, Missoula, 1948–64; Prof. of Fine Arts, Syracuse Univ., N.Y., 1965–66. *Publs:* Rabelais and Music, 1954; Music in the Medieval and Renaissance Universities, 1958; John Skelton, 1968; A Quiver of Quizzes for Quidnuncs, 1985. Add: Dept. of Comparative Literature, Park Hall, Univ. of Georgia, Athens, Ga. 30602, U.S.A.

CARR, Glyn. Pseudonym for Frank Showell Styles. British, b. 1908. Novels/Short stories, Mystery/Crime/Suspense, Children's non-fiction, Travel/Exploration/Adventure. Explorer. Full-time writer since 1946. *Publs:* mystery novels—(as Showell Styles) Traitor's Mountain, 1945; (as Showell Styles) Kidnap Castle, 1947; (as Showell Styles) Hammer Island, 1947; (as Showell Styles) Dark Hazard, 1948; Death on Milestone Buttress, 1951; Murder on the Matterhorn, 1951; The Youth Hostel Murders, 1952; The Corpse in the Crevasse, 1952; Death under Snowdon, 1952; A Corpse at Camp Two, 1954; Murder of an Owl, 1956; The Ice Axe Murders, 1958; Swing Away, Climber, 1959; Holiday with Murder, 1960; Death Finds a Foothold, 1961; Lewker in Norway, 1963; Death of a Weirdy, 1965; Lewker in Tirol, 1967; Fat Man's Agony, 1969; other novels—The Rising of the Lark, 1948; Sir Devil, 1949; Path to Glory, 1951; Land from the Sea, 1952; Mr. Nelson's Ladies, 1953; The Frigate Captain, 1954; His Was the Fire, 1956; Tiger Patrol, 1957; The Admiral's Fancy, 1958; Tiger Patrol Wins Through, 1958; The Tiger Patrol at Sea, 1959; Wolfe Commands You, 1959; Shadow Buttress, 1959; The Flying Ensign (in U.S. As Greencoats against Napoleon), 1960; The Sea Officer, 1961; Tiger Patrol Presses On, 1961; Gentleman Johnny, 1962; Byrd of the 95th (in U.S. as Thunder over Spain), 1962; H.M.S. Diamond Rock, 1963; A Necklace of Glaciers, 1963; Number Two-Ninety, 1966 (in U.S. as Confederate Raider, 1967); A Tent on Top, 1971; "Vincey Joe" at Quiberon, 1971; Admiral of England, 1973; A Sword for Mr. Fitton, 1975; Mr. Fitton's Commission, 1977; The Baltic Convoy, 1979; A Kiss for Captain Hardy, 1979; Centurion Comes Home, 1980; The Quarterdeck Ladder, 1982; Seven-Gun Broadside, 1982; The Malta Frigate, 1983; Mutiny in the Caribbean, 1984; The Lee Shore, 1985; Gun-brig Captain, 1987; HMS Cracker, 1988; other works—Two Longer Plays for Juniors, 1938; Walks and Climbs in Malta, 1944; A Climber in Wales, 1959; The Mountaineer's Week-End Book, 1951; Mountains of the Midnight Sun, 1954; Introduction to Mountaineering, 1955; The Moated Mountain, 1955; The Lost Glacier (juvenile), 1955; (trans.) White Fury, by Raymond Lambert and Claude Kogan, 1956; Kami the Sherpa (juvenile), 1957 (in U.S. as Sherpa Adventure, 1960) Midshipman Quinn (juvenile), 1957; The Camper's and Tramper's Weekend Book, 1957; How Mountains Are Climbed, 1958; Introduction to Caravanning, 1958; How Underground Britain is Explored, 1958; Getting to Know Mountains, 1958; Quinn of the "Fury" (juvenile), 1958; The Battle of Cotton (juvenile), 1959; The Battle of Steam (juvenile), 1960; The Lost Pothole (juvenile), 1961; The Shop in the Mountain (juvenile), 1961; Midshipman Quinn Wins Through (juvenile; in U.S. as Midshipman Quinn and Denise the Spy), 1961; The Ladder of Snow (juvenile), 1962; Look at Mountains, 1962; Greenhorn's Cruise (juvenile), 1964; The Camp in the Hills, 1964; Modern Mountaineering, 1964; Blue Remembered Hills, 1965; Quinn at Trafalgar (juvenile), 1965; Red for Adventure (juvenile), 1965; Mr Fiddle (juvenile), 1965; The Foundations of Climbing, 1966 (in U.K. paperback as The Arrow Book of Climbing, 1967); Wolf Club Island (juvenile), 1966; The Pass of Morning (juvenile), 1966; Mr. Fiddle's Pig (juvenile), 1966; Mallory of Evert, 1967; The Sea Club, 1967; On Top of the World: An Illustrated History of Mountaineering and Mountaineers, 1967; Mr. Fiddle's Band (juvenile), 1967; Rock and Rope, 1967; Indestructible Jones (juvenile), 1967; The Climber's Bedside Book, 1968; (ed.) Men and Mountaineering: An Anthology of Writings by Climbers, 1968; A Case for Mr. Fiddle (juvenile), 1969; Jones's Private Navy (juvenile), 1969; First on the Summits, 1970; First Up Everest, 1970; The Forbidden Frontiers: A Survey of India from 1765 to 1949, 1970; Welsh Walks and Legends, 1972; Snowdon Range, 1973; The Mountains of North Wales, 1973; Glyder Range, 1974; Backpacking: A Comprehensive Guide, 1976; Backpacking in Alps and Pyrenees, 1976; Backpacking in Wales, 1977;

Welsh Walks and Legends: South Wales, 1977. Add: Trwyn Cae Iago, Borth y Gest, Porthmadog, Gwynedd LL49 9TW, Wales.

CARR, J(ames Joseph) L(loyd). British, b. 1912. Novels/Short stories, Biography. Publr. of architectural/historical county maps. *Publs:* The Old Timers, 1957; A Day in Summer, 1964; A Season in Sinji, 1967; The Red Windcheater, 1969; The Dustman, 1971; The Harpole Report, 1972; The Old Farm Cart, 1973; Red Foals' Coat, 1973; How Steeple Sinderby Wanderers Won the F.A. Cup, 1974; An Ear-ring for Anma Beer, 1977; Dictionary of Extraordinary English Cricketers, 1977; Dictionary of English Queens, 1977; A Month in the Country, 1980; The Battle of Pollocks Crossing, 1985; What Hetty Did, 1988. Add: 27 Mill Dale Rd., Kettering, Northants, England.

CARR, Jayge. American, b. 1940. Science fiction. Nuclear physicist, National Aeronautics and Space Admin. (NASA), Cleveland, 1962–65. *Publs:* Leviathan's Deep, 1979; Navigator's Sindrome, 1983; The Treasure in the Heart of the Maze, 1985; Rabelaisian Reprise, 1988; Knight of a Thousand Eyes, 1990. Add: c/o Ralph Vicinanza (Agent), 432 Park Ave. S., Suite 1205, New York, N.Y. 10016, U.S.A.

CARR, Jess. American, b. 1930. Novels/Short stories, History, Social commentary/phenomena. *Publs:* A Creature Was Stirring and Other Stories, 1969; The Second Oldest Profession: An Informal History of Moonshining in America, 1972; The Falls of Rabbor (novel), 1973; Birth of Book, 1974; The Saint of the Wilderness (biographical novel), 1974; The Frost of Summer, 1975; The Moonshiners (novel), 1977; How a Book is Born, 1978; Shipride Down the Spring Branch and Other Stories, 1978; Millie and Cleve, 1979; A Star Rising, 1980; Murder on the Appalachian Trail, 1984; The Midas Touch, 1986; Intruder in the Wind, 1987; (as Kathleen Carrera) Nantahala Love Feast, 1987. Add: 1401 Madison St., Radford, Va. 24141, U.S.A.

CARR, (Bettye) Jo Crisler. American, b. 1926. Children's fiction, Theology/Religion. Pastor, United Methodist Church, since 1977. Instr., Texas Technological Univ., Lubbock, 1970–77. *Publs:* (with I. Sorley) Too Busy Not to Pray, 1966; (with I. Sorley) Bless This Mess, 1969; The Trouble with Tiki, 1970; (with I. Sorley) The Intention Family, 1971; Living on Tiptoe, 1972; (with I. Sorley) Plum Jelly and Stained Glass, 1973; Touch the Wind, 1975; (with I. Sorley) Mocking Bird and Angel Song, 1975; Beyond Fact: Nonfiction for Children and Young People, 1982. Add: 1708 College, Levelland, Tex. 79336, U.S.A.

CARR, Margaret. Also writes as Martin Carroll, Belle Jackson and Carole Kerr. British, b. 1935. Novels/Short stories, Mystery/Crime/Suspense, Historical/Romance/Gothic. Local government secretary. *Publs:* (as Martin Carroll) Begotten Murder (mystery novel), 1967; Spring into Love (novel), 1967; (as Martin Carroll) Blood Vengeance (mystery novel), 1968; (as Martin Carroll) Dead Trouble (mystery novel), 1968; (as Martin Carroll) Goodbye Is Forever (mystery novel), 1968; (as Martin Carroll) Too Beautiful to Die (mystery novel), 1969; (as Martin Carroll) Bait (mystery novel), 1970; (as Martin Carroll) Miranda Said Murder (mystery novel), 1970; (as Martin Carroll) Hear No Evil (mystery novel), 1971; Tread Warily at Midnight (mystery novel), 1971; Sitting Duck (mystery novel), 1972; Who's The Target (mystery novel), 1974; Wait for the Wake (mystery novel), 1974; Too Close for Comfort (mystery novel), 1974; (as Carole Kerr) Not for Sale (novel), 1975; (as Carole Kerr) Shadow of the Hunter (novel), 1975; (as Carole Kerr) A Time to Surrender (novel), 1975; Blood Will Out (mystery novel), 1975; Blindman's Bluff (mystery novel), 1976; Dare the Devil (mystery novel), 1976; Sharendel (mystery novel), 1976; Out of the Past (mystery novel), 1976; Twin Tragedy (mystery novel), 1977; (as Carole Kerr) Love All Start (novel), 1977; (as Carole Kerr) Lamb to the Slaughter (novel), 1978; The Witch of Wykham (mystery novel), 1978; (as Carole Kerr) An Innocent Abroad (novel), 1979; Daggers Drawn, 1980; (as Carole Kerr) When Dreams Come True, 1980; (as Carole Kerr) Stolen Heart, 1981; (as Belle Jackson) In the Dark of the Day, 1988; (as Belle Jackson) Valdez's Lady, 1989. Add: Waverley, Wavering Lane, Gillingham, Dorset, England.

CARR, Philippa. *See* **HOLT,** Victoria.

CARR, (Sir) Raymond. British, b. 1919. History, Sports/Physical education/Keeping fit. Warden, St. Antony's Coll., Oxford, 1968–88 (Fellow of All Souls Coll., 1946–53, and New Coll., 1953–64; Prof. of History of Latin America, 1976–78). Member of National Theatre Bd., 1971–76. *Publs:* Spain 1808-1939, 1966; (ed.) Republic and the Civil War In Spain, 1971; English Fox Hunting: A History, 1976; The Spanish Tragedy, 1977; (with J.P. Fusi) Spain: From Dictatorship to Democracy,

1979; Puerto Rico: A Colonial Experiment, 1984. Add: Burch, North Molton EX36 3JU, England.

CARR, Roberta. *See* **ROBERTS,** Irene.

CARR, Robyn. American, b. 1951. Historical/Romance/Gothic. *Publs:* Chelynne, 1980; The Blue Falcon, 1981; The Bellerose Bargain, 1982; The Braeswood Tapestry, 1984; The Troubadour's Romance, 1985; By Right of Arms, 1986; The Everlasting Covenant, 1987; Tempted, 1987; Rogue's Lady, 1988; Informed Risk, 1989. Add: c/o Little, Brown and Co., 34 Beacon St., Boston, Mass. 02106, U.S.A.

CARR, William George. American, b. 1901. Education, International relations, History, Area Studies (U.S. History). Pres., Sino-American Cultural Soc., since 1969. Teacher, Roosevelt Jr. High Sch., Glendale, Calif., 1924–25; Prof., Pacific Univ., Forest Grove, Ore., 1926–27; Dir. of Research, California Teachers' Assn., 1927–28; Asst. Dir. of Research, 1929–31, Dir. of Research, 1931–41, Secty., Educational Policies Commn., 1937–52, Assoc. Secty., 1940–52, and Exec. Secty., 1952–67, National Education Assn., Washington D.C.; Secty.-Gen., 1946–70, and Pres., 1970–72, World Confedn. of the Orgs. of the Teaching Profession. *Publs:* Education for World Citizenship, 1928; (ed.) County Unit of School Administration, 1931; (with J. Waage) The Lesson Assignment, 1931; John Swett: Biography of an Educational Pioneer, 1933; School Finance, 1933; (with H. Lutz) Essentials of Taxation, 1935; (with C. Beard) Schools in the Story of Culture, 1937; The Purposes of Education in American Democracy, 1938; (co-author) Learning the Ways of Democracy, 1940; Education and the People's Peace, 1943; One World in the Making, 1946; On the Waging of Peace, 1946; Discovery of the Citizen, 1955; The Words of William G. Carr, 1967; (ed.) Values and the Curriculum, 1970; White Revolution in Iranian Education, 1970; The Continuing Education of William Carr, 1978; Collecting My Thoughts, 1980; Life of Benjamin Franklin, 1987. Add: 3601 Connecticut Ave., Washington, D.C. 20008, U.S.A.

CARRELL, Norman Gerald. British, b. 1905. Music. Teacher of music, freelance writer and adjudicator, since 1969. Viola player, BBC Symphony Orchestra, 1930–41; Music Booking Mngr., BBC, 1948–69. *Publs:* Bach's Brandenburg Concertos, 1963; Bach the Borrower, 1967. Add: 57 Wimbledon Hill Rd., Wimbledon, London SW19, England.

CARRICK, Edward. *See* **CRAIG,** Edward Anthony.

CARRICK, Malcolm. British, b. 1945. Children's fiction. Owner, Malcolm Carrick Productions, advertising agency, since 1985. Freelance writer, illustrator, and songwriter; numerous scripts for children's television and radio light entertainment progs. *Publs:* Allsorts of Every Thing, 1973; The Wise Men of Gotham, 1973; The Extraordinary Hat-Maker, 1974; Mr. Pedagouge's Sneeze, 1974; Once There Was a Boy and Other Stories, 1974; The Little Pilgrim, 1975; Tramp, 1977; Today Is Shrew's Day, 1978; I Can Squash Elephants!, 1978; Happy Jack, 1979; Making Devil and Demon Masks, 1979; Mr. Tod's Trap, 1980; I'll Get You, 1981; Butterfingers!, 1985. Add: 4 Palace Grove, Fox Hill, Upper Norwood, London SE19 2XD, England.

CARRIER, Constance. American, b. 1908. Poetry, Translations. *Publs:* Middle Voice, 1955; (trans). Poems of Propertius, 1961; (trans.) Poems of Tibullus, 1967; The Angled Road, 1974; (with P. Bovie and D. Parker) The Complete Plays of Terence, 1974; (with D. MacLaren) Aesopus Hodie, 1985. Add: 225 West Main, New Britain, Conn. 06052, U.S.A.

CARRIER, Warren. American, b. 1918. Novels/Short stories, Poetry, Translations. Chancellor Emeritus, Univ. of Wisconsin, Platteville, since 1982 (Chancellor, 1975–82). Assoc. Dean, Rutgers Univ., New Brunswick, N.J., 1968–69; Dean, California State Univ., San Diego, 1969–72; Vice-Pres., Univ. of Bridgeport, Conn., 1972–75. Founder, and former Ed., Quarterly Review of Literature. *Publs:* (trans.) City Stopped in Time, 1949; The Hunt (novel), 1952; The Cost of Love (poetry), 1953; (ed. with Paul Engle) Reading Modern Poetry, 1955, rev. ed. 1968; Bay of the Damned (novel), 1957; Toward Montebello (poetry), 1966; Leave Your Sugar for the Cold Morning (poetry), 1978; (ed.) Guide to World Literature, 1980; (ed. with Bonnie Neumann) Literature from the World, 1981; The Diver (poetry), 1986; Death of a Chancellor (novel), 1986. Add: 69 Colony Park Circle, Galveston, Texas 77551, U.S.A.

CARRILLO, Lawrence W. American, b. 1920. Language/Linguistics. Emeritus Prof. of Education, San Francisco State Univ., since 1976 (Prof., 1957–76). Specialist in Elementary Curriculum and Materials, Liberia

Project, Liberia, 1964–66. *Publs:* (with W.D. Sheldon) College Reading Workbook, 1953; (with H. Campbell) Reader's Digest Reading Skill Builder, Grade 6, Part 3, 1960; Reading Institute Extension Service, Grades K-6, and Grades 7-12, 1960–68; (ed.) Lessons for Self-Instruction in Basic Skills, 1963–66, 1979; (ed.) Chandler Reading Program, 1964–71; Writing Book I, 1965; (ed.) Landon Phonics Program Kit, 1967; (with I. Curry and P. Shew) Reading Through the Subject-Matter Areas, K-12, 1968; (ed.) Handbook for Teaching Language Arts, 1969; (ed.) Language Art: An Ideabook, 1970; Teaching Reading: A Handbook, 1976, (ed.) Doctor Bird Reading Series, 1980. Add: 3955 Vine Hill Rd., Sebastopol, Calif., 95472, U.S.A.

CARRINGTON, Charles Edmund. Also writes as Charles Edmonds. British, b. 1897. History, Autobiography/Memoirs/Personal, Biography. With Cambridge Univ. Press, 1929–54; Prof. of British Commonwealth Relations, Royal Inst. of Intnl. Affairs, London, 1954–62. *Publs:* War Record of the Fifth Royal Warwickshire Regiment, 1922; (as Charles Edmonds) A Subaltern's War, 1929; (with J. Jackson) History of England, 1932; (as Charles Edmonds) T.E. Lawrence, 1935; An Exposition of Empire, 1947; The British Overseas, 1950; Godley of Canterbury, 1951; Life and Work of Rudyard Kipling, 1955, 1978; (co-ed.) An African Survey, by Lord Hailey, 1957; (co-ed.) Cambridge History of the British Empire, vol. III, 1959; Liquidation of the British Empire, 1962; Soldier from the Wars Returning, 1965; (ed.) The Complete Barrack Room Ballads of Rudyard Kipling, 1973; Kipling's Horace, 1978; Soldier at Bomber Command, 1987. Add: 31 Grange Road, London N1 2NP, England.

CARRINGTON, Paul Dewitt. American, b. 1931. Law. Prof., Duke Univ. Sch. of Law, Durham, N.C., since 1978 (Dean, 1978–88). Asst. Prof., Indiana Univ., Bloomington, 1960–62; Assoc. Prof., 1962–64, and Prof., 1964–65, Ohio State Univ., Columbus; Walter C. Meyer Research Prof., Columbia Univ., NYC,1972–73; Prof. of Law, Univ. of Michigan Law Sch., Ann Arbor, 1965–78. *Publs:* Accommodating the Workload of the United States Courts of Appeal, 1968; (ed.) Civil Procedure: Cases with Comment on the Process of Adjudication, 1969, 3rd ed. 1983; Manual for Civil Procedure Teachers, 1970; (with Meador and Rosenberg) Justice on Appeal, 1976. Add: Duke Univ. Sch. of Law, Durham, N.C. 27706, U.S.A.

CARROLL, C. Edward. American, b. 1923. Librarianship. Prof. of Library and Information Science, Univ. of Missouri-Columbia, since 1972 (Dir. of Libraries, 1970–72); also Episcopal Priest. Dir. of Libraries, Southern Oregon Coll., Ashland, 1965–67, and Wichita State Univ., Kans., 1967–70. *Publs:* The Professionalization of Education for Librarianship, 1969. Add: 2001 Country Club Dr., Columbia, Mo. 65201, U.S.A.

CARROLL, Elizabeth. *See* **BARKIN,** Carol and **JAMES,** Elizabeth.

CARROLL, Gladys Hasty. American, b. 1904. Novels/Short stories, Children's fiction, Autobiography/Memoirs/Personal. Founder, Donnybrook Historical Foundn. and speaker and writer on historical subjects at the Foundn., since 1984. *Publs:* Cockatoo, 1929; Land Spell, 1930; As the Earth Turns, 1933; A Few Foolish Ones, 1935; Neighbor to the Sky, 1937; Head of the Line (short stories), 1942; Dunnybrook, 1943, 1978; While the Angels Sing, 1947; West of the Hill, 1949; Christmas Without Johnny, 1950; One White Star, 1954; Sing Out the Glory, 1957; Come with Me Home, 1960; Only Fifty Years Ago, 1962; To Remember Forever, 1963; The Road Grows Strange, 1965; The Light Here Kindled, 1967; Christmas Through the Years, 1968; Man on the Mountain, 1969; Years Away from Home, 1972; Next of Kin, 1974; Unless You Die Young, 1977; The Book That Came Alive, 1979. Add: 8 Earls Rd., South Berwick, Me. 03908, U.S.A.

CARROLL, James. American, b. 1943. Novels/Short stories. *Publs:* The Winter Name of God, 1974; Madonna Red, 1976; (with Barbara Overton) Be Sure Your Child Learns to Read, 1976; Utopia Now, 1977; Mortal Friends, 1978; Fault Lines, 1980; Family Trade, 1982; Eleven Hundred Powerful Words, 1982; Nature's Basic Law of Economics, 1982; Prince of Peace, 1984; Seventeen Commandments not from Heaven but from Earth, 1985; A Supply of Heroes, 1986; Firebird, 1989. Add: c/o E.P. Dutton Co., 2 Park Ave., New York, N.Y. 10016, U.S.A.

CARROLL, Martin. *See* **CARR,** Margaret.

CARROLL, Paul. American, b. 1927. Poetry, Literature. Prof. of English, Univ. of Illinois, Chicago, since 1968. Poetry Ed., Chicago Review, 1957–59; Ed., Big Table Mag., Chicago, 1959–61, and Big Table Books, Follett Publishing Co., Chicago, 1966–71; Visiting Prof. of English, Univ. of Iowa, Iowa City, 1966–67. *Publs:* (ed.) Edward

Dahlberg Reader, 1966; Odes, 1968; The Poem in Its Skin (criticism), 1968; (ed.) The Young American Poets, 1968; The Luke Poems, 1971; New and Selected Poems, 1978; (ed.) The Earthquake on Ada Street: An Anthology of Poems from the "The Sculpture Factory", 1979; The Garden of Earthly Delights, 1986; Poems, 1987. Add: 1682 N. Ada St., Chicago, Ill. 60622, U.S.A.

CARROLL, Robert. *See* **ALPERT,** Hollis.

CARROTHERS, Alfred (William Rooke). Canadian, b. 1924. Industrial relations. Prof., Common Law Section, Faculty of Law, Univ. of Ottawa, Ont., since 1981. Dir., Inst. of Industrial Relations, Univ. of British Columbia, Vancouver, 1960–62; Dean, Faculty of Law, Univ. of Western Ontario, London, 1964–68; Pres., Univ. of Calgary, Alta., 1969–74; Pres., Inst. for Research on Public Policy, Montreal, 1974–77; practiced Labour Law, 1977–81; Dean, Common Law Section, Univ. of Ottawa, 1981–83. *Publs:* The Labour Injunction in British Columbia, 1956; (ed.) University of British Columbia Cases and Materials on Labour Law, 1958; (ed.) Univ. of British Columbia Manual of Legal and Commercial Forms, 1958; Labour Arbitration in Canada, 1961; Collective Bargaining Law in Canada, 1965, 1985. Add: Fauteux Hall, 57 Copernicus, Ottawa, Ont. K1N 6N8, Canada.

CARRUTH, Hayden. American, b. 1921. Poetry. Prof. of English, Syracuse Univ., New York, since 1979. Member of Editorial Bd., Hudson Review, NYC. Ed., Poetry, Chicago, 1949–50; Assoc. Ed., Univ. of Chicago Press, 1950–51, and Intercultural Publs. Inc., NYC, 1952–53; Poetry Ed., Harpers Mag., NYC, 1979–84. *Publs:* The Crow and the Heart, 1946–1959, 1959; Journey to a Known Place, 1961; The Norfolk Poems: 1 June to 1 September 1961, 1962; Appendix A, 1963, 1963; North Winter, 1964; (ed. with J. Laughlin) A New Directions Reader, 1964; Nothing for Tigers: Poems 1959–1964, 1965; After "The Stranger": Imaginary Dialogues with Camus, 1965; Contra Mortem, 1967; For You: Poems, 1970; The Clay Hill Anthology, 1970; (ed.) The Voice That Is Great Within Us: American Poetry of the Twentieth Century, 1970; (ed.) The Bird/Poem Book: Poems on the Wild Birds of North America, 1970; From Snow and Rock, From Chaos, 1973; Dark World, 1974; The Bloomingdale Papers, 1974; Loneliness, 1976; Aura, 1977; Brothers, I Loved You All, 1978; Working Papers, 1981; Sleeping Beauty, 1982; If You Call This Cry a Song, 1983; The Mythology of Dark and Light, 1983; Effluences From the Sacred Caves, 1984; Asphalt Georgies, 1985; The Oldest Killed Lake in North America, 1985; Mother, 1985; Lighter than Air Craft, 1985; The Selected Poetry of Hayden Carruth, 1986; Sitting In: Selected Writings on Jazz, Blues and Related Topics, 1986; Tell Me Again, 1989; Sonnets, 1989. Add: c/o Dept. of English, Syracuse Univ., Syracuse, N.Y. 13244, U.S.A.

CARRUTHERS, Malcolm (Euan). British, b. 1938. Medicine/Health. Consultant in Chemical Pathology, Bethlem Royal and Maudsley Hospital, London, since 1976. Former Lectr., Middlesex Hosp., London; Sr. Lectr. in Chemical Pathology, St. Mary's Hospital, London, 1972–76. *Publs:* Western Way of Death, 1974; (with Alistair Murray) Fitness for All, 1974; (with Alistair Murray) Fitness on Forty Minutes a Week, 1976; (ed. with R. Priest) Psychosomatic Approach to Prevention of Disease, 1977; (with A. Poteliakhoff) Real Health, 1981. Add: 101 Harley St., London W1N 1DF, England.

CARSON, Ciaran. British, b. 1948. Poetry, Music. Traditional Arts Officer, Northern Ireland Arts Council, Belfast, since 1975. Sch. Teacher, Belfast, 1974–75. *Publs:* The New Estate, 1976; The Lost Explorer, 1979; Pocket Guide to Irish Traditional Music, 1986; The Irish for No (poetry), 1987. Add: Arts Council of Northern Ireland, 181A Stranmills Rd., Belfast BT9 5DU, Northern Ireland.

CARSON, Herbert L. American, b. 1929. Literary Criticism/History, Philosophy. Prof. of Humanities and Philosophy, Ferris State Univ., Big Rapids, Mich., since 1960 (designated Distinguished Teacher, 1984). Book Reviewer, Grand Rapids Press, since 1973. Formerly, Originator and Dir., Workshop on Film, Ford Foundn. and National Endowment for the Humanities, and Chataugua Tonight, Michigan Council for the Humanities. *Publs:* Steps in Successful Speaking, 1967; (ed. with A. Carson) The Impact of Fiction, 1970; (with A. Carson) Royall Tyler, 1979; (with A. Carson) Domestic Tragedy in England, 1982; (with A. Carson) The Image of the West, 1989. Add: Dept. of Humanities, Ferris State Univ., Big Rapids, Mich. 49307, U.S.A.

CARSTEN, Francis Ludwig. British, b. 1911. History. Emeritus Prof. of Central European History, Univ. of London. *Publs:* The Origins of Prussia, 1954; Princes and Parliaments in Germany, 1959; The

Reichswehr and Politics, 1918–1933, 1966; The Rise of Fascism, 1967, 1980; Revolution in Central Europe, 1918–1919, 1973; Fascist Movements in Austria: From Schönerer to Hitler, 1977; War Against War: British and German Radical Movements in the First World War, 1982; Britain and the Weimar Republic, 1984; Essays in German History, 1985; The First Austrian Republic, 1986; A History of the Prussian Junkers, 1988. Add: 11 Redington Rd., London NW3, England.

CARSTENSEN, Roger (Norwood). American, b. 1920. Theology/Religion. Pres., Inst. for Biblical Literacy Inc., Athens, Ga., since 1978. Prof., Northwest Christian Coll., Eugene, Ore., 1941–49; Assoc. Prof., Prof., Phillips Univ., Enid, Okla., 1949–66; Dean, 1960–70, and Pres., 1970–78, Christian Coll. of Georgia, Athens. *Publs:* Job: Defense of Honor, 1963; Jonah, 1970; Help Stamp Out Biblical Illiteracy, 1984; Life Through the Lens of Scripture, 1987. Add: 67 Gail Dr., Athens, Ga. 30606, U.S.A.

CARSWELL, John Patrick. British, b. 1918. History, Biography. Served with Treasury, 1960–64; Asst. Under Secty. of State, Dept. of Education and Science, London, 1964–74; Secty., Univ. Grants Cttee., 1974–78; Secty., British Academy, London, 1978–83. *Publs:* (ed.) Marvellous Campaigns of Baron Munchausen, 1946; The Prospector: The Life of Rudolf Erich Raspe (in U.S. as The Romantic Rogue), 1950; The Old Cause: Four Biographical Studies in Whiggism, 1954; The South Sea Bubble, 1960; The Civil Servant and His World, 1966; The Descent on England, 1969; From Revolution to Revolution: English Society 1688-1776, 1973; Lives and Letters, 1978; The Exile, 1983; The State and the Universities in Britain 1966–1978, 1985; The Porcupine: The Life of Algernon Sidney, 1989. Add: 5 Prince Arthur Rd., London NW3, England.

CARTER, Angela (Olive Stalker). British, b. 1940. Science fiction, Children's fiction, Plays, Poetry, Translations. Journalist, Croydon, Surrey, 1958–61. *Publs:* Unicorn (poetry), 1966; Shadow Dance, 1966, in U.S. as Honeybuzzard, 1967; The Magic Toyshop, 1967; Several Perceptions, 1968; Heroes and Villains, 1969; Miss Z, The Dark Young Lady (juvenile), 1970; The Donkey Prince (juvenile), 1970; Love, 1971; The Infernal Desire Machines of Dr. Hoffman, 1972, in U.S. as The War of Dreams, 1974; Fireworks: Nine Profane Pieces, 1974; The Passion of New Eve, 1977; (trans.) The Fairy Tales of Charles Perrault, 1977; The Bloody Chamber and Other Stories, 1979; Martin Leman's Comic and Curious Cats (non-fiction), 1979; The Sadeian Woman: An Exercise in Cultural History (non-fiction) 1979, in U.S. as the Sadeian Woman and the Ideology of Pornography, 1979; (with Michael Foreman) Sleeping Beauty and Other Favourite Fairy Tales, 1982; (with others) Moonshadow (juvenile), 1982; Nothing Sacred: Selected Journalism, 1982; Nights at the Circus, 1984; Black Venus (short stories), 1985, in U.S. as Saints and Strangers, 1986; Come Unto These Yellow Sands and Other Plays for Radio, 1985; (ed.) Wayward Girls and Wicked Women, 1986. Add: c/o Virago Press Ltd., Centro House, 20-23 Mandela St., Camden Town, London NW1 0HQ, England.

CARTER, Ashley. *See* **WHITTINGTON,** Harry.

CARTER, Bruce. *See* **HOUGH,** Richard.

CARTER, (Sir) Charles (Frederick). British, b. 1919. Economics, Education. Pres., Policy Studies Inst., since 1989 (Chmn., Research Cttee., 1978–89). Hon. Fellow, Emmanuel Coll., Cambridge, since 1965 (Fellow, 1947–51). Lectr. in Statistics, Cambridge Univ., 1945–51; Prof. of Economics, Univ. of Belfast, 1952–59; Stanley Jevons Prof. of Political Economy, Univ. of Manchester, 1959–63; Vice Chancellor, Univ. of Lancaster, 1963–79. *Publs:* (co-author) The Measurement of Production Movements, 1948; (with A. Roy) British Economic Statistics, 1954; (with B. Williams) Industry and Technical Progress, 1957; (with B. Williams) Investment in Innovation, 1958; (with B. Williams) Science in Industry, 1959; The Science of Wealth, 1960, 3rd ed. 1973; (with D. Barritt) The Northern Ireland Problem, 1962, 1972; Wealth, 1968; (co-author) Patterns and Policies in Higher Education, 1971; On Having a Sense of All Conditions, 1971; Higher Education for the Future, 1980; (with J. Pinder) Policies for a Constrained Economy, 1982. Add: 1 Gosforth Rd., Seascale, Cumbria CA20 1PU, England.

CARTER, Everett. American, b. 1919. Literature. Prof. of English, Univ. of California, Davis, since 1961 (Vice-Chancellor, 1959–61; Dean of Research, 1961–66). Writer, Universal Studios, 1940–45; Asst. Prof., Claremont Men's Coll., Calif., 1946–49; Asst. Prof., Univ. of California, Berkeley, 1959–57. *Publs:* Howells and the Age of Realism, 1954; (ed.) The Rise of Silas Lapham, by W.D. Howells, 1958; (ed.) The Damnation

of Theron Ware, by Harold Frederic, 1960; (ed.) A Hazard of New Fortunes, by Howells, 1976; The American Idea: The Literary Response to American Optimism, 1977. Add: 734 Hawthorn Lane, Davis, Calif. 95616, U.S.A.

CARTER, Felicity (Winifred). Writes as Emery Bonett: collaborates with John H.A. Coulson (as John Bonett) on mystery novels. British, b. 1906. Novels/Short stories, Mystery/Crime/Suspense. *Publs:* mystery novels, with Coulson, as John and Emery Bonett—Dead Lion, 1949; A Banner for Pegasus (in U.S. as Not in the Script), 1951; No Grave for a Lady, 1959; Better Dead (in US as Better Off Dead), 1964: The Private Face of Murder, 1966; The Side Murder?, 1967 (in U.S. as Murder on the Costa Brava, 1968); The Sound of Murder, 1970; No Time to Kill, 1972; other mystery novels—(as Felicity Carter) Never Go Dark, 1940; Make Do with Spring, 1941; High Pavement (in U.S. as Old Mrs. Camelot), 1944; novel—A Girl Must Live, 1936. Add: c/o Curtis Brown Ltd., 162-168 Regent St., London W1, England.

CARTER, Frances Monet. Also writes as Frances Evans. American, b. 1923. Medicine/Health. Prof. of Psychiatric Nursing, Univ. of San Francisco, since 1970, Emerita since 1988 (Instr. to Assoc. Prof., 1957–70). Member, San Francisco Mental Health Advisory Bd., 1969–78 (Pres., 1976). *Publs:* The Role of the Nurse in Community Mental Health, 1968; Psychosocial Nursing: Theory and Practice in Hospital and Community Mental Health, 1971, 3rd ed. 1981. Add: 55 Conrad St., San Francisco, Calif., 94131, U.S.A.

CARTER, Frances Tunnell. American. Children's fiction, Children's non-fiction. Pres. of CarterCraft since 1985. National Exec. Dir., Kappa Delta Epsilon, since 1987. Prof. of Education and Home Economics, Samford Univ., Birmingham, Ala., 1956–85; Editor, Youth and Children Materials, National Office of Woman's Missionary Union, Birmingham, Alab. Teacher, Wood Jr. Coll., 1948, East Central Jr. Coll., 1948–49, and Clarke Coll., Miss., 1950–56. *Publs:* Sammy in the Country; 'Tween-Age Ambassadors; (with John T Carter) Sharing Times Seven, 1970; Ching Fu and Jim, 1978. Add: 2561 Rocky Ridge Rd., Birmingham, Ala., 35243, U.S.A.

CARTER, Gwendolen Margaret. American, b. 1906. History, International relations/Current affairs, Race relations. Adjunct Prof. of Political Science and African Studies, Univ. of Florida, Gainsville, since 1984; Prof. of Political Science, Indiana Univ. Bloomington, 1974–84. Ed., Cornell Univ. Press series, Africa in the Modern World, since 1968. Lectr., McMaster Univ., Hamilton, Canada, 1932–35; Instr., Wellesley Coll., Mass., 1938–41, and Tufts Coll., Medford, Mass., 1942–43; Asst. Prof., 1943–47, Assoc. Prof., 1947–51, Prof. of Govt., 1951–64, and Sophia Smith Prof., 1961–64, Smith Coll., Northampton, Mass.; Member, Grad. Council, Univ. of Massachusetts, Amherst, 1961–64; Visiting Lectr., Yale Univ., New Haven, Conn., 1962–64; Melville J. Herskovits Prof. of African Affairs, Dir., Prog. of African Studies, and Prof. of Political Science, Northwestern Univ., Evanston, Ill., 1964–74. *Publs:* British Commonwealth and International Security, 1919–1939, 1947; (with J. Herz) Major Foreign Powers, 1948, 6th ed. 1972; The Politics of Inequality: South Africa since 1949, 1958; (ed. with W.O. Brown) Transition in Africa, 1959; Independence for Africa, 1960; (co-author) Government and Politics in the Twentieth Century, 1961, 3rd ed. 1972; (ed.) African One-Party States, 1962; (ed.) Five African States: Responses to Diversity, 1963; The Government of the United Kingdom, 1964, 3rd ed. 1972; The Government of the Soviet Union, 1964, 3rd ed. 1972; (ed. with A. Westin) Politics in Europe, 1965; (ed.) National Unity and Regionalism in Eight African States, 1966; (ed.) Politics in Africa: Six Cases, 1966; (with T. Karis and N. Stultz) South Africa's Transkei: The Politics of Domestic Colonialism, 1967; The Government of France, 1968; 1972; (ed. with L.W. Holborn and J. Herz) Documents of Major Foreign Powers, 1968; (ed. with A. Paden) Expanding Horizons in African Studies, 1969; (ed. with L.W. Holborn and J. Herz) German Constitutional Documents since 1871, 1970; (ed. with T. Karis) From Protest to Challenge: A Documentary History of African Politics in South Africa, 1882-1964, 4 vols., 1972–77; (ed. with P.O'Meara) Southern Africa in Crisis, 1977; (ed. with P. O'-Meara) Southern Africa: The Continuing Crisis, 1979, 1982; Which Way Is South Africa Going?, 1980; International Politics in Southern Africa, 1982; (co-ed.) African Independence: The First Twenty-five Years, 1985. Add: 190 W. Fern Dr., Orange City, Flor. 32763, U.S.A.

CARTER, Harold. British, b. 1925. Geography, Urban studies. Emeritus Prof., Univ. Coll. of Wales, Aberystwyth, since 1986 (Lectr., 1952–68; Gregynog Prof. of Human Geography, 1968–86). *Publs:* Towns of Wales: A Study in Urban Geography, 1965; (ed.) Urban Essays: Studies in the Geography of Wales, 1970; The Study of Urban Geography,

1972, 3rd ed. 1981; An Introduction to Urban Historical Geography, 1983; The Welsh Language 1961–1981: An Interpretive Atlas, 1988. Add: Dept. of Geography, Llandinam Bldg., Penglais, Aberystwyth, SY23 3DB, Wales.

CARTER, Jimmy. (James Earl Carter, Jr.) Politics, Memoirs. Distinguished Prof., Emory Univ., Atlanta, since 1982; Chmn., Carter Center, Atlanta, since 1986. Businessman/Farmer (Carter Peanut Farms), 1953–77; Georgia State Senator, 1962–66; Gov. of Georgia, 1971–74; President of the United States, 1977–81. *Publs:* Why Not the Best?, 1975; A Government as Good as its People, 1977; Keeping Faith: Memoirs of a President, 1982; Negotiation: The Alternative to Hostility, 1984; The Blood of Abraham: Insights into the Middle East, 1985; (with Rosalynn Carter) Everything to Gain: Making the Most of the Rest of Your Life, 1987; An Outdoor Journal, 1988. Add: The Carter Center, One Copenhill, Atlanta, Ga. 30307, U.S.A.

CARTER, John T(homas). American, b. 1921. Children's fiction, Children's non-fiction. Dean of Education Emeritus, Samford Univ., Birmingham, Ala., since 1977 (Prof., 1956–77). *Publs:* Mike and His Four-Star Coal, 1960; East is West, 1964; Witness in Israel, 1966; (with Frances Carter) Sharing Times Seven, 1970. Add: 2561 Rocky Ridge Rd., Birmingham, Ala. 35243, U.S.A.

CARTER, Lin(wood Vrooman). American, b. 1930. Science fiction/Fantasy, Literature. Freelance writer; and Ed. Consultant, Ballantine Books Adult Fantasy, since 1969. Advertising and publrs. copywriter, 1957–69. *Publs:* The Wizard of Lemuria, 1965, as Thongor and the Wizard of Lemuria, 1969; Thongor of Lemuria, 1966, as Thongor and the Dragon City, 1970; The Star Magicians, 1966; The Man Without a Planet, 1966; (with David Grinnell) Destination: Saturn, 1967; (with Robert E. Howard) King Kull (short stories), 1967; The Flame of Iridar, 1967; Thongor Against the Gods, 1967; (with Robert E. Howard and L. Sprague de Camp) Conan (short stories), 1967; The Thief of Thoth, 1968; (with L. Sprague de Camp) Conan of the Isles, 1968; Tower at the Edge of Time, 1968; Thongor at the End of Time, 1968; Thongor in the City of Magicians, 1968; (with Robert E. Howard and L. Sprague de Camp) Conan the Wanderer, 1968; The Purloined Planet, 1969; Giant of World's End, 1969; (with Robert E. Howard and L. Sprague de Camp) Conan of Cimmeria, 1969; Lost World of Time, 1969; Tower of the Medusa, 1969; Beyond the Gates of Dream (short stories), 1969; Tolkien: A Look Behind "The Lord of the Rings", 1969; (ed.) Dragons, Elves and Heroes, 1969; (ed.) The Young Magicians, 1969; (ed.) The Magic of Atlantis, 1970; Star Rogue, 1970; Thongor Fights the Pirates of Tarakus, 1970, in U.K. as Thongor and the Pirates of Tarakus, 1971; (with L. Sprague de Camp) Conan the Buccaneer, 1971; Outworlder, 1971; (ed.) Golden Cities, Far, 1971; (ed.) The Spawn of Cthulhu, 1971; (ed.) New Worlds for Old, 1971; (ed.) Discoveries in Fantasy, 1972; (ed.) Great Short Novels of Adult Fantasy 1-2, 2 vols., 1972; Black Legion of Callisto, 1972; The Quest of Kadji, 1972; Under the Green Star, 1972; Lovecraft: A Look Behind the "Cthulhu Mythos", 1972; Imaginary World: The Art of Fantasy, 1973; The Black Star, 1973; Jandar of Callisto, 1973; The Man Who Loved Mars, 1973; Sky Pirates of Callisto, 1973; When the Green Star Calls, 1973; (ed.) Flashing Swords! 1-5, 3 vols., 1973–81; The Valley Where Time Stood Still, 1974; Time War, 1974; By the Light of the Green Star, 1974; The Warrior of World's End, 1974; The Nemesis of Evil, 1975; Invisible Death, 1975; Mad Empress of Callisto, 1975; Mind Wizard of Callisto, 1975; Lankar of Callisto, 1975; As the Green Star Rises, 1975; Dreams from R'lyeh (poetry), 1975; (ed.) The Year's Best Fantasy Stories 1-4, 4 vols., 1975–78; (ed.) Kingdoms of Sorcery, 1975; (ed.) Realms of Wizardry, 1976; The Volcano Ogre, 1976; The Immortal of World's End, 1976; In the Green Star's Glow, 1976; The Barbarian of World's End, 1977; Middle-Earth: The World of Tolkien, 1977; (with L. Sprague de Camp) Conan of Aquilonia (collection), 1977; Ylana of Callisto, 1977; The City Outside the World, 1977; Renegade of Callisto, 1978; The Wizard of Zao, 1978; The Pirate of World's End, 1978; (with L. Sprague de Camp) Conan the Swordsman, 1978; (with L. Sprague de Camp) Conan the Liberator, 1979; Journey to the Underground World, 1979; Tara of the Twilight, 1979; Lost Worlds, 1980; (ed.) Weird Tales, No. 1-4, 4 vols., 1981–83; Beyond The Gates of Dream, 1982; Eric of Zanthodon, 1982; Tower at the Edge of Time, 1982; Down to a Sunless Sea, 1984; Kellory the Warlock, 1984; Horror Wears Blue, 1987; Mandricardo, 1987. Add: c/o Henry Morrison Inc., 320 McLain St., Bedford Hills, N.Y. 10705, U.S.A.

CARTER, Martin (Wylde). Guyanan, b. 1927. Poetry. Former civil servant and diplomat, Guyana. *Publs:* The Hill of Fire Glows Red, 1951; To a Dead Slave, 1951; The Kind Eagle, 1952; The Hidden Man, 1952; Poems of Resistance from British Guiana, 1954; Poems of Succession,

1977; Poems of Affinity 1978–80, 1980. Add: c/o New Beacon Books, 76 Stroud Green Rd., London N4 3EN, England.

CARTER, Nick. *See* **AVALLONE,** Michael.

CARTER, Nick. *See* **CHASTAIN,** Thomas.

CARTER, Nick. *See* **LYNDS,** Dennis.

CARTER, Nick. *See* **RANDISI,** Robert J.

CARTER, Nick. *See* **SMITH,** Martin Cruz.

CARTER, Peter. British, b. 1929. Children's fiction. Apprentice in the building trade, 1942–49; Teacher in Birmingham. *Publs:* The Black Lamp, 1973; The Gates of Paradise, 1974; Madatan, 1975; Mao, 1976; Under Goliath, 1977; The Sentinels, 1980; Children of the Book, 1982; Bury the Dead, 1986; The Sea Green Man, 1986. Add: c/o Oxford Univ. Press., Walton St., Oxford OX2 6DP, England.

CARTER, Samuel, III. American, b. 1904. History. Radio and television scriptwriter, since 1955. Radio Commercial Writer, J. Walter Thompson Co., NYC, 1931–40; Radio Scriptwriter, Hollywood, 1940–48; Ed. of television scripts, NBC, NYC, 1950–55. Vice-Pres. in charge of TV, Stauffer, Colwell and Bayles, 1962–67. *Publs:* How to Sail, 1936; 1967; Kingdom of the Tides, 1966; Cyrus Field: Man of Two Worlds, 1968; Lightning Beneath the Sea: The Story of the Atlantic Cable, 1969; The Boat Builders of Bristol, 1970; The Gulf Stream Story, 1970; The Incredible Great White Fleet, 1971; The Happy Dolphins, 1971; Blaze of Glory: The Fight for New Orleans 1814-1815, 1971; Vikings Bold: The Voyages and Adventures, 1972; Dodge City: Cowboy Capital of the World, 1973; The Siege of Atlanta 1864, 1973; The Riddle of Dr. Mudd, 1974; Cherokee Sunset: A Nation Betrayed, 1976; The Last Cavaliers, 1979; The Final Fortress, 1980. Add: 57 Silver Hill Rd., Ridgefield, Conn. 06877, U.S.A.

CARTLAND, Barbara (Hamilton). Also writes for U.K. publr. as Barbara McCorquodale. British. Historical/Romance/Gothic, Cookery/Gastronomy/Wine, Human relations, Medicine/Health, Autobiography/Memoirs/Personal, Biography. Freelance writer since 1925; also lectr. and public speaker. Ed., Library of Love series. Vice-Pres., Romantic Novelists Assn. and Oxfam. *Publs:* romance—Jig-Saw, 1925; Sawdust, 1926; If the Tree is Saved, 1929; For What?, 1930; Sweet Punishment, 1931; A Virgin in Mayfair, 1932; Just Off Piccadilly, 1933; Not Love Alone, 1933; A Beggar Wished ..., 1934; Passionate Attachment, 1935; First Class, Lady?, 1935; Dangerous Experiment, 1936, in U.S. as Search for Love, 1937; Desperate Defiance, 1936; The Forgotten City, 1936; Saga at Forty, 1937; But Never Free, 1937, as The Adventurer, 1977; Broken Barriers, 1938; Bitter Winds, 1938; The Gods Forget, 1939; The Black Panther, 1939; Stolen Halo, 1940; Now Rough—Now Smooth, 1941; Open Wings, 1942; The Leaping Flame, 1942; (as Barbara McCorquodale) Sleeping Swords, 1942; The Dark Stream, 1944; After the Night, 1944, as Towards the Stars, 1971; Yet She Follows, 1944, as A Heart Is Broken, 1972; Escape from Passion, 1945; Armour Against Love, 1945; Out of Reach, 1945; The Hidden Heart, 1946; Against the Stream, 1946; The Dream Within, 1947; If We Will, 1947, as Where Is Love?, 1971; Against This Rapture, 1947; No Heart Is Free, 1948; A Hazard of Hearts, 1949; The Enchanted Moment, 1949; A Duel of Hearts, 1949; The Knave of Hearts, 1950; The Little Pretender, 1951; Love Is an Eagle, 1951; A Ghost in Monte Carlo, 1951; Love Is the Enemy, 1952; Cupid Rides Pillion, 1952; (as Barbara McCorquodale) Love Is Mine, 1952, in U.S. (as Barbara Cartland), 1972; (as Barbara McCorquodale) The Passionate Pilgrim, 1952; Elizabethan Lover, 1953; Love Me for Ever, 1953, in U.S. as Love Me Forever, 1970; (as Barbara McCorquodale) Blue Heather, 1953; Desire of the Heart, 1954; (as Barbara McCorquodale) Wings on My Heart, 1954; The Enchanted Waltz, 1955; The Kiss of the Devil, 1955; The Captive Heart, 1956; The Coin of Love, 1956; (as Barbara McCorquodale) The Kiss of Paris, 1956; Sweet Adventure, 1957; Stars in My Heart, 1957; (as Barbara McCorquodale) The Thief of Love, 1957; (as Barbara McCorquodale) Love Forbidden, 1957; The Golden Gondola, 1958; (as Barbara McCorquodale) Sweet Enchantress, 1958; (as Barbara McCorquodale) Lights of Love, 1958, in U.S. (as Barbara Cartland), 1973; Love in Hiding, 1959; The Smuggled Heart, 1959; (as Barbara McCorquodale) A Kiss of Silk, 1959; Love under Fire, 1960; (as Barbara McCorquodale) The Price Is Love, 1960; Messenger of Love, 1961; (as Barbara McCorquodale) The Runaway Heart, 1961; The Wings of Love, 1962; (as Barbara McCorquodale) A Light to the Heart, 1962; The Hidden Evil, 1963; (as Barbara McCorquodale)

Love Is Dangerous, 1963; The Fire of Love, 1964; The Unpredictable Bride, 1964; (as Barbara McCorquodale) Danger by the Nile, 1964; Love Holds the Cards, 1965; (as Barbara McCorquodale) Love on the Run, 1965, in U.S. (as Barbara Cartland), 1973; A Virgin in Paris, 1966; (as Barbara McCorquodale) Theft of the Heart, 1966; Love to the Rescue, 1967; Love Is Contraband, 1968; The Enchanting Evil, 1968; The Unknown Heart, 1969; Debt of Honor, 1970; Innocent Heiress, 1970; Lost Love, 1970; The Reluctant Bride, 1970; The Royal Pledge, 1970; The Secret Fear, 1970; The Secret Heart, 1970; The Pretty Horse-Breakers, 1971; The Queen's Messenger, 1971; Stars in Her Eyes, 1971; Innocent in Paris, 1971; The Audacious Adventuress, 1971; A Halo for the Dead, 1972; The Irresistible Buck, 1972; The Complacent Wife, 1972; Lost Enchantment, 1972; The Odious Duke, 1973; The Little Adventure, 1973; The Daring Deception, 1973; The Wicked Marquis, 1973; No Darkness for Love, 1974; The Ruthless Rake, 1974; The Glittering Lights, 1974; A Sword to the Heart, 1974; The Penniless Peer, 1974; The Magnificent Marriage, 1974; Lessons in Love, 1974; The Karma of Love, 1974; The Bored Bridegroom, 1974; The Castle of Fear, 1974; The Cruel Count, 1974; The Dangerous Dandy, 1974; Journey to Paradise, 1974; Call of the Heart, 1975; Love Is Innocent, 1975; Shadow of Sin, 1975; Bewitched, 1975; The Devil in Love, 1975; Fire on the Snow, 1975; The Flame Is Love, 1975; Food for Love, 1975; The Frightened Bride, 1975; The Impetuous Duchess, 1975; The Mask of Love, 1975; The Tears of Love, 1975; A Very Naughty Angel, 1975; An Arrow of Love, 1975; As Eagles Fly, 1975; A Frame of Dreams, 1975; A Gamble with Hearts, 1975; A Kiss for the King, 1975; Say Yes, Samantha, 1975; The Elusive Earl, 1976; the Blue-Eyed Witch, 1976; An Angel in Hell, 1976; The Bitter Winds of Love, 1976; A Dream from the Night, 1976; Fragrant Flower, 1976; The Golden Illusion, 1976; The Heart Triumphant, 1976; Hungry for Love, 1976; The Husband Hunters, 1976; The Incredible Honeymoon, 1976; Love and Linda, 1976; Moon over Eden, 1976; Never Laugh at Love, 1976; No Time for Love, 1976; Passions in the Sand, 1976; The Proud Princess, 1976; A Rainbow to Heaven, 1976; The Secret of the Glen, 1976; The Slaves of Love, 1976; The Wild Cry of Love, 1976; The Disgraceful Duke, 1976; The Mysterious Maid-Servant, 1977; The Dragon and the Pearl, 1977; Conquered by Love, 1977; The Curse of the Clan, 1977; Dance on My Heart, 1977; The Dream and the Glory, 1977; A Duel with Destiny, 1977; Kiss the Moonlight, 1977; Look, Listen, and Love, 1977; Love at Forty, 1977; Love in Pity, 1977; Love Locked In, 1977; The Magic of Love, 1977; The Marquis Who Hated Women, 1977; The Outrageous Lady, 1977; The Sign of Love, 1977; A Rhapsody of Love, 1977; The Taming of Lady Lorinda, 1977; This Time It's Love, 1977; Vote for Love, 1977; The Wild, Unwilling Wife, 1977; The Love Pirate, 1977; Punishment of a Vixen, 1977; A Touch of Love, 1977; The Temptation of Torilla, 1977; Love and the Loathsome Leopard, 1977; The Hell-Cat and the King, 1977; No Escape from Love, 1977; The Saint and the Sinner, 1977; The Naked Battle, 1977; Love Leaves at Midnight, 1978; The Passion and the Flower, 1978; Love, Lords, and Lady-Birds, 1978; A Fugitive from Love, 1978; The Problems of Love, 1978; The Twists and Turns of Love, 1978; Magic or Mirage, 1978; The Ghost Who Fell in Love, 1978; The Chieftain Without a Heart, 1978; Love Ravenscar's Revenge, 1978; A Runaway Star, 1978; A Princess in Distress, 1978; The Judgement of Love, 1978; Lovers in Paradise, 1978; The Race for Love, 1978; Flowers for the God of Love, 1978; The Irresistible Force, 1978; Alone in Paris, 1978; Love in the Dark, 1979; The Duke and the Preacher's Daughter, 1979; The Drums of Love, 1979; The Prince and the Pekingese, 1979; A Serpent of Satan, 1979; Love in the Clouds, 1979; The Treasure Is Love, 1979; Imperial Splendour, 1979; Light of the Moon, 1979; The Prisoner of Love, 1979; The Duchess Disappeared, 1979; Love Climbs In, 1979; A Nightingale Sang, 1979; Terror in the Sun, 1979; Who Can Deny Love?, 1979; Bride to the King, 1979; Only Love, 1979; The Dawn of Love, 1979; Love Has His Way, 1979; Gentleman in Love, 1979; Women Have Hearts, 1979; The Explosion of Love, 1980; A Heart Is Stolen, 1980; The Power and the Prince, 1980; Free from Fear, 1980; A Song of Love, 1980; Love for Sale, 1980; Little White Doves of Love, 1980; The Perfection of Love, 1980; Lost Laughter, 1980; Punished with Love, 1980; Lucifer and the Angel, 1980; Ola and the Sea Wolf, 1980; The Prude and the Prodigal, 1980; The Goddess and the Gaiety Girl, 1980; Signpost to Love, 1980; Money, Magic and Marriage, 1980; Love in the Moon, 1980; Pride and the Poor Princess, 1980; The Waltz of Hearts, 1980; From Hell to Heaven, 1981; The Kiss of Life, 1981; Afraid, 1981; Dreams Do Come True, 1981; In the Arms of Love, 1981; For All Eternity, 1981; Pure and Untouched, 1981; Count the Stars, 1981; Kneel for Mercy, 1982; Call of the Highlands, 1982; A Miracle in Music, 1982; From Hate to Love, 1983; Lights, Laughter and a Lady, 1983; Diona and a Dalmatian, 1983; Moonlight on the Sphinx, 1984; Bride to a Brigand, 1984; Love Comes West, 1984; A

Witch's Spell, 1984; White Lilac, 1984; Miracle for a Madonna, 1984; Royal Punishment, 1985; The Devilish Deception, 1985; Secrets of the Heart, 1985; A Caretaker of Love, 1985; The Devil Defeated, 1985; Riding to the Sky, 1986; Lovers in Lisbon, 1986; Love is Invincible, 1986; The Goddess of Love, 1986; An Adventure of Love, 1986; A Herb for Happiness, 1986; Only a Dream, 1986; Saved by Love, 1986; Little Tongues of Fire, 1986; A Chieftain Finds Love, 1986; The Lovely Liar, 1986; The Perfume of the Gods, 1986; A Knight in Paris, 1987; Revenge Is Sweet, 1987; The Passionate Princess, 1987; Solita and the Spies, 1987; The Perfect Pearl, 1987; Love Is a Maze, 1987; A Circus for Love, 1987; The Temple of Love, 1987; The Bargain Bride, 1987; The Haunted Heart, 1987; Real Love or Fake, 1987; A Kiss from a Stranger, 1987; A Very Special Love, 1987; A Necklace of Love, 1987; No Disguise for Love, 1987; A Revolution of Love, 1988; The Marquis Wins, 1988; Love Is the Key, 1988; Free as the Wind, 1988; Desire in the Desert, 1988; A Heart in the Highlands, 1988; The Music of Love, 1988; The Wrong Dutchess, 1988; The Taming of a Tigree, 1988; Love Comes to the Castle, 1988; The Magic of Paris, 1988; Stand and Deliver Your Heart, 1988; The Scent of Roses, 1988; Love at First Sight, 1988; The Secret Princess, 1988; Heaven in Hong Kong, 1988; Paradise in Penang, 1988; A Game of Love, 1988; The Sleeping Princess, 1988; A Wish Comes True, 1988; Loved for Himself, 1988; Two Hearts in Hungary, 1988; A Theatre of Love, 1988; A Dynasty of Love, 1988; Magic from the Heart, 1988; Windmill of Love, 1988; Love Strikes Satan, 1988; The Earl Rings a Belle, 1988; The Queen Saves the King, 1988; Love Lifts the Curse, 1988; Beauty of Brains, 1988; Too Precious to Lose, 1988; Hiding, 1988; A Tangled Webb, 1988; Just Fate, 1988; Year of Royal Days, 1988; Mission to Monte Carlo, 1989; Light of the Moon, 1989; other—Touch the Stars: A Clue to Happiness, 1935; Ronald Cartland, 1942, as My Brother, Ronald, 1980; The Isthmus Years 1919–1939 (autobiography), 1943; (ed.) The Common Problem, by Ronald Cartland, 1943; You—In the Home, 1946; The Years of Opportunity 1935–1945 (autobiography), 1948; The Fascinating Forties: A Book for the Over-Forties, 1954, 1973; Marriage for Moderns, 1955; Bewitching Women, 1955; The Outrageous Queen: A Biography of Christina of Sweden, 1956; Polly—My Wonderful Mother, 1956; Be Vivid, Be Vital, 1956; Love, Life, and Sex, 1957, 1973; The Scandalous Life of King Carol, 1957; The Private Life of Charles II: The Women He Loved, 1958; Look Lovely, Be Lovely, 1958; Vitamins for Vitality, 1959; The Private Life of Elizabeth, Empress of Austria, 1959; Husbands and Wives, 1961, as Love and Marriage, 1971; Josephine, Empress of France, 1961; Diane de Poitiers, 1962; Etiquette Handbook, 1963, as Book of Etiquette, 1972; The Many Facets of Love, 1963; Metternich, The Passionate Diplomat, 1964; Sex and the Teenager, 1964; Living Together, 1965; The Pan Book of Charm, 1965; Woman: The Enigma, 1965; I Search for the Rainbow 1946–1966 (autobiography), 1967; The Youth Secret, 1968; The Magic of Honey, 1970, 1976; We Danced All Night 1919–1929 (autobiography), 1970; Health Food Cookery Book, 1971; Book of Beauty and Health, 1972; Lines on Life and Love (poetry), 1972; Men Are Wonderful, 1973; Food for Love, 1975; The Magic of Honey Cookbook, 1976; (with Nigel Gordon) Recipes for Lovers, 1977; Book of Useless Information, 1977; I Seek the Miraculous, 1978; Book of Love and Lovers, 1978; (ed.) The Light of Love: A Thought for Every Day, 1979; Love at the Helm (Mountbatten Memorial Trust vol.), 1980; Romantic Royal Marriages, 1981; (with Elinor Glyn) Keep Young and Beautiful (selections), 1982; The Romance of Food, 1984; Barbara Cartland's Book of Health, 1985; Barbara Cartland's Book of Royal Days, 1988. Add: Camfield Pl., Hatfield, Herts., England.

CARUSO, John Anthony. American, b. 1907. History. Prof. Emeritus of History, West Virginia Univ., Morgantown, since 1974 (Asst. Prof., 1950–58; Assoc. Prof., 1958–62; Prof., 1962–74). Publs: Liberators of Mexico, 1954; Appalachian Frontier, 1959; (co-author) America's Historylands, 1961; Great Lakes Frontier, 1961; Southern Frontier, 1963; (co-author) Le Sud au Temps de Scarlett, 1966; Mississippi Valley Frontier, 1966; (co-author) Illustrated Bicentennial History of the United States, 2 vols., 1973; (with others) Reading in Louisiana History, 1978. Add: 888 Riverview Dr., Morgantown, W. Va., 26505 U.S.A.

CARVER, Dave. See BINGLEY, David Ernest.

CARVER, (Lord); (Richard) Michael (Power) Carver. British, b. 1915. History. Field Marshal, British Army (commissioned, 1935; Comdr.-in-Chief, Far East, 1967–69; Gen. Officer Comdr. in Chief, Southern Command, 1969–71; Chief of the Gen. Staff, 1971–73; Chief of the Defence Staff, 1973–76. Publs: Second to None, 1952; El Alamein, 1962; Tobruk, 1964; (ed.) The War Lords, 1976; Harding of Petherton, 1978;

The Apostles of Mobility, 1979; War since 1945, 1980; A Policy for Peace, 1982; The Seven Ages of the British Army, 1984; Dilemmas of the Desert War, 1986; Twentieth Century Warriors, 1987. Add: Wood End House, Wickham, Fareham, Hants. PO17 6JZ, England.

CARVER, Norman Francis, Jr. American, b. 1928. Architecture. Architect in private practice, Kalamazoo, Mich., since 1955. *Publs:* Form and Space of Japanese Architecture, 1955; Silent Cities: Mexico and the Maya, 1965, 1986; Italian Hilltowns, 1979; Iberian Villages, 1980; Japanese Folkhouses, 1984. Add: 3201 Lorraine Ave., Kalamazoo, Mich. 49008, U.S.A.

CARY, Jud. *See* **TUBB**, E.C.

CARY, Richard. American, b. 1909. Literature, Biography. Prof. of English, 1952–75, Curator of Rare Books and Manuscripts, 1958–75, Ed., Colby Library Quarterly, 1959–75, and Dir., Colby Coll. Press 1959–75, Colby Coll., Waterville, Me. *Publs:* The Genteel Circle: Bayard Taylor and His New York Friends, 1952; (ed.) Sarah Orne Jewett Letters, 1956, rev. ed. 1967; Sarah Orne Jewett, 1962; (ed.) Deephaven and Other Stories by Sarah Orne Jewett, 1966; Mary N. Murfree, 1967; (ed.) Edwin Arlington Robinson's Letters to Edith Brower, 1968; (ed.) Thomas Hardy: The Return of the Native, 1968; (ed.) Thomas Hardy: The Mayor of Casterbridge, 1969; (ed.) Appreciation of Edwin Arlington Robinson, 1969; (ed.) The Uncollected Short Stories of Sarah Orne Jewett, 1971; (ed.) Appreciation of Sarah Orne Jewett, 1973; (author and ed.) Early Reception of Edwin Arlington Robinson, 1974; (ed.) Uncollected Poems and Prose of Edwin Arlington Robinson, 1975. Add: 31 Highland Ave., Waterville, Me. 04901, U.S.A.

CASE, David. American, b. 1937. Historical/Romance/Gothic, Westerns/Adventure. Full-time writer: has written over 300 works under various pseuds. *Publs:* The Cell: Three Tales of Horror (in U.K. as The Cell and Other Tales of Horror), 1969; Fengriffen: A Chilling Tale, 1970; Fengriffen and Other Stories, 1971, as And Now the Screaming Starts, 1973; Plumb Drilling (western), 1975, as Gold Fever, 1982; The Fighting Breed (western), 1980; Wolf Tracks (western), 1980; The Third Grave, 1981; Among the Wolves and Other Tales, 1982; Guns of Valentine (western), 1982; A Cross to Bear, 1982. Add: c/o Ackham House, Sauk City, Wisc. 53583, U.S.A.

CASEY, Kevin. Irish, b. 1940. Novels/Short stories, Plays/Screenplays. Former advertising copywriter. *Publs:* The Living and the Lost, 1962; Not With a Bang, 1965; The Sinner's Bell, 1968; A Sense of Survival, 1974; Dreams of Revenge, 1977; American Aussie: My Life as an Illegal Alien in Australia, 1987. Add: c/o Murray Pollinger, 4 Garrick St., London WC2 9B4, England.

CASEY, Michael. American, b. 1947. Poetry. Editorial Adviser, Alice James Press, Cambridge, Mass., since 1972. Research Asst., State Univ. of New York, Buffalo, 1972–73. *Publs:* Obscenities, 1972; On Scales, 1972; My Youngest That Tall, 1972; My Brother-in-Law and Me, 1974; The Company Pool, 1976. Add: c/o Yale Univ. Press, 92a Yale Station, New Haven, Conn. 06520, U.S.A.

CASH, Anthony. British, b. 1933. History. Producer and Dir., Granada TV's "Man and Music", since 1984. Asst. Master for Russian, Tottenham Grammar Sch., London, 1960–63; Prog. Asst., Russian Section, External Service, 1963–68, and Producer and Dir., 1968–77, B.B.C. Television, London; Producer and Dir., London Weekend Television, 1977–84. *Publs:* Great Neighbors: U.S.S.R., 1965; (co-trans.) Years of My Life, 1966; The Russian Revolution, 1967; Lenin, 1972. Add: Lilyville Rd., London SW6, England.

CASHIN, James A. American, b. 1911. Business/Trade/Industry, Money/Finance. Prof. of Accounting, Hofstra Univ., Hempstead, N.Y., since 1963. Chief Accountant and Gen. Auditor, St. Regis Paper Co., NYC, 1950–63; Teacher, Univ. of New York, 1954–58, and Baruch Sch., City Univ., NYC, 1959–63. *Publs:* (with Kamp) Internal Control Standards, 1947; (contrib.) Accountant's Encyclopedia, 1962; Internal Revision, 1962; (with Owens) Auditing, 1963, 1981; Careers and Opportunities in Accounting, 1965; Management Controls, 1967; Impact of Medicare on Hospital Costs, 1970; Handbook for Auditors, 1971; (with Brink and Witt) Internal Auditing, 1973; (with Lerner) Accounting, 2 vols., 1973–74, 1980–81; (with Feldman and Lerner) Intermediate Accounting, 1975; (with Polimeni) Cost Accounting, 1978; CPA Examination Review, 1979; Current Problems in the Accounting Profession, 1979; (with Moss) Tax Accounting, 1980; (with Polimeni) Cost Accounting Textbook, 1981; CPA Examination (Auditing), 1981; (with Wiseman) Advanced Accounting, 1982; (with Wiesner) Business Law, 1982; (co-author) Cost Accounting II, 1982. Add: 1830 Bridge St., Englewood, Fla. 33533, U.S.A.

CASPER, Leonard (Ralph). American, b. 1923. Novels/Short stories, Literature. Prof. of English, Boston Coll., Chestnut Hill, Mass., since 1956. Contrib. Ed., Solidarity, Manila, 1966–68, and Literature East and West, 1969–77. Visiting Prof., Univ. of the Philippines, Quezon City, 1953–56; Contrib. Ed., Panorama, Manila, 1954–61, and Drama Critique, 1959–62. *Publs:* (ed.) Six Filipino Poets, 1955; Robert Penn Warren: The Dark and Bloody Ground, 1960; Wayward Horizon: Essays on Modern Philippine Literature, 1961; (ed. with T.A. Gullason) The World of Short Fiction: An International Collection, 1962; (ed.) Modern Philippine Short Stories, 1962; The Wounded Diamond: Studies in Modern Philippine Literature, 1964; New Writing from the Philippines: A Critique and Anthology, 1966; A Lion Unannounced: 12 Stories and a Fable, 1971; Firewalkers, 1987. Add: 54 Simpson Dr., Saxonville, Mass. 01701, U.S.A.

CASS, Joan E(velyn). British. Children's fiction, Education. Former Lectr. in Child Development, Inst. of Education, Univ. of London. *Publs:* The Cat Thief, 1961; The Cat Show, 1962; Blossom Finds a Home, 1963; The Canal Trip, 1966; Literature and the Young Child, 1967; The Cats Go to Market, 1969; The Cats and the Cat Thieves, 1971; Aloysius the Redundant Engine, 1971; The Dragon Who Was Too Hot, 1971; The Significance of Children's Play (in U.S. as Helping Children Grow Through Play), 1971; Chang and the Robber, 1971; The Dragon Who Grew, 1973; The Witch of Witchery Wood, 1973; The Role of the Teacher in the Nursery School, 1975; Hubert Hippo, 1975; Milly Mouse, 1975; Baby Bear's Bath, 1976; Milly Mouse's Measles, 1976; The Witch and the Naughty Princesses, 1976; Alexander's Magic Quilt, 1978; The Witch's Lost Spell Book, 1980; The Four Surprises, 1981; Trouble Among the Witches, 1983; The Persistent Mouse, 1984; The Witches School, 1985; Six Mice Too Many, 1985; A Book of Dragons, 1985; The Dragon Who Grew, 1987. Add: c/o Abelard-Schuman Ltd., 14-18 High Holborn, London WC1V 6BX, England.

CASS, Zoe. *See* **LOW**, Dorothy Mackie.

CASSEDY, James H(iggins). American, b. 1919. Demography, History, Medicine/Health. Historian, National Library of Medicine, Bethesda, Md., and Ed., Bibliography of the History of Medicine, since 1968. Personnel Officer, U.S. Veterans Admin., 1946–48; Dir., Bi-national Centers, Haiti, Burma and Pakistan, for U.S. Information Service, 1951–55 and 1960–62; Science Admin., National Insts. of Health, 1962–68. *Publs:* Charles V. Chapin and the Public Health Movement, 1962; Demography in Early America: Beginnings of the Statistical Mind 1600-1800, 1969; American Medicine and Statistical Thinking 1800-1860, 1984; Medicine and American Growth 1800-1860, 1986. Add: c/o Univ. of Wisconsin Press, 114 N. Murray St., Madison, Wisc. 53715, U.S.A.

CASSEDY, Sylvia. American, b. 1930. Children's fiction, Poetry, Translations. Teacher of creative writing to children, Queen's Coll., City Univ. of New York, Flushing, 1973–74, Great Neck Public Library, New York, 1975–79, and Manhasset Public Schs., New York, 1977–84. Instr. in teaching creative writing to children, Nassau County Bd. of Cooperative Education, New York, 1978–79. *Publs:* children's fiction—Little Chameleon, 1966; Pierino and the Bell, 1966; Marzipan Day on Bridget Lane, 1967; Behind the Attic Wall, 1983; M.E. and Morton, 1987; Lucie Babbidge's House, 1989; other—(ed. and trans., with K. Suetake) Birds, Frogs, and Moonlight, 1967; (ed. and trans., with P. Thampi) Moon-Uncle, Moon-Uncle: Rhymes from India, 1973; In Your Own Words:A Beginner's Guide to Writing, 1979; Roomrimes (poetry), 1987. Add: 6 Hampshire Rd., Great Neck, N.Y. 11023, U.S.A.

CASSEL, Russell N. American, b. 1911. Education, Psychology. Dir., Cassel Psychology Center, Chula Vista, Calif., since 1974. Ed., Project Innovation. Research Psychologist, U.S. Air Force, 1951–57; Chief Psychologist, Phoenix High Schs. and Coll., Ariz., 1957–59; Dir. of Pupil Personnel Services, Lompoc Unified Schs., Calif., 1959–62; Research Consultant, Viet Nam, 1962–65, and Liberia, 1965–67; Prof. of Educational Psychology, Univ. of Wisconsin, Milwaukee, 1967–74. *Publs:* The Psychology of Instruction, 1957; Drug Abuse Education, 1971; UWM Fortran Measurements Programs, 1971; The Psychology of Decision Making, 1973; The Computerized Drug Abuse Education System, 1973; The Computerized Decision Development System, 1973; The Science of Psychical Activity, 1974; (ed. with R.L. Heichberger) Leadership Development: Theory and Practice, 1974. Add: 1362 Santa Cruz Court, Chula Vista, Calif. 92010, U.S.A.

CASSELS, Alan. British, b. 1929. History, International relations. Prof. of History, McMaster Univ., Hamilton, Ont., since 1971 (Assoc. Prof. of History, 1967–71). Vice-Pres., 1978–80, and Pres., 1980–82, Soc. for Italian Historical Studies. Instr. in History, Trinity Coll., Hartford, Conn., 1959–62; Asst. Prof. of History, Univ. of Pennsylvania, Philadelphia, 1962–67. *Publs:* Fascist Italy, 1968; Mussolini's Early Diplomacy, 1970; Fascism, 1974; Italian Foreign Policy 1918–1945; A Guide to Research and Research Materials, 1981. Add: Dept. of History, McMaster Univ., Hamilton, Ont., L8S 4L9, Canada.

CASSIDY, Frederic Gomes. American, b. 1907. Language/Linguistics. Prof. of English, Univ. of Wisconsin, Madison (joined faculty, 1939). Chief Ed., Dictionary of American Regional English, since 1965. Member of faculty, Univ. de Strasbourg, France, 1935–36, Univ. of Michigan, Ann Arbor, 1936–39, and Stanford Univ., Calif., 1963–64. *Publs:* Place Names of Dane County, Wisconsin, 1947; (co-author) A Method for Collecting Dialect, 1953; Jamaica Talk, 1961, 1971; (co-author) Dictionary of Jamaican English, 1967, 1980; (ed.) Dictionary of American Regional English, vol. 1, A-C, 1985. Add: Univ. of Wisconsin, 6125 Helen White Hall, Madison, Wisc. 53706, U.S.A.

CASSIDY, Michael. South African, b. 1936. Human relations, Theology/Religion. Pres. and Team Leader, African Enterprise, Pietermaritzburg, since 1964. Religious Columnist, The Natal Witness, since 1968. Religious Columnist, Johannesburg Star, and Natal Witness, 1968–73; Chmn., National Initiative for Reconciliation, 1985–88. *Publs:* Decade of Decisions (in U.S. as Where are You Taking the World Anyway?), 1970; Prisoners of Hope, 1974; (ed. with A. Blane and C. le Feuvre) The Relationship Tangle, 1974; (ed.) I Will Heal Their Land, 1974; Together in One Place, 1978; (co-ed.) Facing the New Challenges, 1978; Christianity for the Open Minded, 1978; Bursting the Wineskins, 1983; Chasing the Wind, 1985; The Passing Summer, 1989. Add: c/o African Enterprise, P.O. Box 647, Pietermaritzburg 3200, Natal, South Africa.

CASSILL, R(onald) V(erlin). American, b. 1919. Novels/Short stories, Writing/Journalism. Instr., Univ. of Iowa, Iowa City, 1948–52; Ed., Western Review, Iowa City, 1951–52; Lectr., Columbia Univ., and new Sch. for Social Research, both NYC, 1957–59; Lectr. Univ. of Iowa, 1960–65; Writer-in-Residence, Purdue Univ., Lafayette, Ind., 1965–66; Prof. of English, Brown Univ., Providence, R.I., 1966–82. *Publs:* The Eagle on the Coin, 1950; Dormitory Women, 1953; The Left Bank of Desire, 1954; A Taste of Sin, 1955; The Hungering Shame, 1956; The Wound of Love, 1956; Naked Morning, 1957; (with H. Gold and J. Hall) 15 x 3 (short stories), 1957; Lustful Summer, 1958; Nurses Quarters, 1958; The Wife Next Door, 1959; Clem Anderson, 1961; My Sister's Keeper, 1961; Night School, 1961; Pretty Leslie, 1963; Writing Fiction, 1963, 1975; The President, 1964; The Father and Other Stories, 1965; The Happy Marriage and Other Stories, 1967; In an Iron Time: Statements and Reiterations: Essays, 1967; (ed.) Intro 1, 2, and 3, 1968–70; Doctor Cobb's Game, 1970; The Goss Women, 1974; Hoyt's Child, 1976; (ed.) Norton Anthology of Short Fiction, 1977, 1981; Labors of Love, 1980; Flame, 1980; Three Stories, 1982; After Goliath, 1985. Add: 22 Boylston Ave., Providence, R.I. 02906, U.S.A.

CASSITY, (Allen) Turner. American, b. 1929. Poetry. Asst. Univ. Librarian, Emory Univ. Library, Atlanta, since 1962. Asst. Librarian, Jackson Municipal Library, South Africa, 1959–61. *Publs:* Watchboy, What of the Night?, 1966; Steeplejacks in Babel, 1973; Yellow for Peril, Black for Beautiful, 1975; The Defense of the Sugar Islands, 1979; Keys to Mayerling, 1983; The Book of Alma: A Narrative of the Mormon Wars, 1985; Hurricane Lamp, 1986. Add: 510-J East Ponce de Leon Ave., Decatur, Ga. 30030, U.S.A.

CASSON, (Sir) Hugh (Maxwell). British, b. 1910. Architecture, Autobiography/Memoirs/Personal. Partner, Casson, Conder and Partners, London (in practice as architect since 1937). Prof. of Environmental Design, Royal Coll. of Art, London, 1953–75. Dir. of Architecture, Festival of Britain, 1948–51. Pres., Royal Academy, 1976–84. *Publs:* New Sights of London, 1937; Bombed Churches, 1946; Homes by the Million, 1947; (with A. Chitty) Houses: Permanence and Prefabrication, 1947; An Introduction to Victorian Architecture, 1948; Inscape, 1967; (with Joyce Grenfell) Nanny Says, 1972; Sketchbook, 1975; Diary, 1981; Hugh Casson's London, 1983; Hugh Casson's Oxford, 1988. Add: 60 Elgin Cres., London W11 2JJ, England.

CASSTEVENS, Thomas William. American, b. 1937. Politics/Government. Prof. of Political Science, Oakland Univ., Rochester Hills, Mich., since 1972 (Asst. Prof., 1966–69; Assoc. Prof,

1969–72). Asst. Research Political Scientist, Inst. of Governmental Studies, Univ. of California at Berkeley, 1963–66. *Publs:* Politics, Housing and Race Relations: The Defeat of Berkeley's Fair Housing Ordinance, 1965; Politics, Housing and Race Relations: The Rumford Act and Proposition 14, 1967; (co-ed.) The Politics of Fair Housing Legislation, 1968; (co-ed.) American Government and Politics, 1980. Add: 560 McGill Dr., Rochester Hills, Mich., U.S.A.

CASTANEDA, Carlos. Brazilian, b. 1931. Anthropology/Ethnology, Philosophy. Anthropologist: spent five years in Mexico apprenticed to a Yaqui Indian sorcerer. *Publs:* The Teachings of Don Juan: A Yaqui Way of Knowledge, 1968; A Separate Reality: The Phenomenology of Special Consensus, 1971; Journey to Ixtlan, 1974; Tales of Power, 1975; The Second Ring of Power, 1977; The Eagle's Gift, 1982; The Fire From Within, 1984; The Power of Silence: Further Lessons of Don Juan, 1987. Add: c/o Univ. of California Press, 2223 Fulton St., Berkeley, Calif. 94720, U.S.A.

CASTLE, Charles. British, b. 1939. Plays/Screenplays, Autobiography/Memoirs/Personal, Biography. Producer, BBC Television (former Production Asst. and Film Instr.) Former Production Mgr., MGM Television. *Publs:* I Start Running (radio and television play); The Keys on the Street (radio play); This Was Richard Tauber (TV documentary), 1970, biography with D.N. Tauber, 1971, Noel, 1972; This is Noel Coward (TV documentary), 1973; Farewell to Woburn: The Duke and Duchess of Bedford Leave Home (TV documentary), 1974; Raging Star: Biography of Joan Crawford, 1977; Model Girl, 1977; Belle Otero: The Last Great Courtesan, 1981; The Folies Bergère, 1982; Oliver Messel, 1983. Add: Ewhurst Green, nr. Robertsbridge, Sussex, England.

CASTY, Alan Howard. American, b. 1929. Film, Media, Writing/Journalism. Prof., Dept. of English, Santa Monica Coll., Calif., since 1956. *Publs:* (co-author) Writers in Action, 1959; The Act of Reading, 1961; The Act of Writing and Reading, 1966, 1970; The Shape of Fiction, 1967, 1975; Robert Rossen, 1967; Mass Media and Mass Man, 1968, 1973; (co-author) Staircase to Writing and Reading, 1967, 5th ed. 1979; The Films of Robert Rossen, 1969; A Mixed Bag, 1970, 1975; Building Writing Skills, 1971; The Dramatic Art of the Film, 1971; Development of the Film: An Interpretive History, 1973; Let's Make It Clear, 1977; Improving Writing, 1981; The Writing Project, 1982. Add: 3646 Mandeville Canyon Rd., Los Angeles, Calif., 90049, U.S.A.

CATANESE, Anthony James. American, b. 1942, Transportation, Urban studies. Dir., Center for Planning and Development, Georgia Inst. of Tech., Atlanta. Instr., Univ. of Wisconsin, Madison, 1966–67; Assoc. Prof. of City Planning, Georgia Technological Inst., Atlanta, 1967–73; Dir. and Prof., Ryder Prog. in Transportation, Univ. of Miami, 1973–75; Dean, Sch. of Architecture and Urban Planning, Univ. of Wisconsin, Milwaukee, 1975–82; Provost, Pratt Inst., NYC, 1982–84. *Publs:* (with A.W. Steiss) Systemic Planning: Theory and Application, 1970; New Perspectives on Transportation Research, 1972; Scientific Methods of Urban Analysis, 1972; Planners and Local Politics; Impossible Dreams, 1974; Personality, Politics and Planning: How City Planners Work, 1978; Urban Planning: Guide to Information Sources, 1978, 2nd ed. with J. C. Snyder, 1988; (with J. C. Snyder) Introduction to Urban Planning, 1979; Introduction to Architecture, 1979; Politics of Planning and Development, 1984. Add: Center for Planning and Development, Georgia Inst. of Tech., Atlanta, Geor. 30332-0155, U.S.A.

CATE, Curtis (Wilson). American, b. 1924. Literature, Biography. European Ed., Atlantic Monthly, 1958–65. *Publs:* Antoine de Saint-Exupéry: His Life and Times, 1970; George Sand: A Biography, 1975; The Ides of August, 1978; (with Boris Goldovsky) My Road to Opera, 1979; The War of the Two Emperors: The Duel of Napoleon and Alexander of Russia 1812, 1985. Add: c/o Anthony Sheil Assocs., 43 Doughty St., London WC1N 2LF, England.

CATER, (Silas) Douglass (Jr.). American, b. 1923. Novels/Short stories, Politics/Government, Social commentary/phenomena. Pres., Washington Coll., Chestertown, Md., since 1982. Founding Fellow and Trustee, Aspen Inst. Prog. on Communications and Soc. Washington Ed., 1950–63, and National Affairs Ed., 1963–64, Reporter mag.; Special Asst. to Pres. Johnson, 1964–68; Pres., Observer Intnl., and Vice-Chmn., The Observer Ltd., London, 1977–82. *Publs:* (with Marquis Childs) Ethics in a Business Society, 1953; The Fourth Branch of Government, 1959; Power in Washington, 1964; Dana: The Irrelevent Man, 1970; (ed. with Phillip Lee) Politics of Health, 1973; (with Stephen Strickland) TV Violence and the Child: The Evolution and Fate of the Surgeon General's Report, 1975. Add: Office of the Pres., Washington Coll., Chestertown,

Md. 21620, U.S.A.

CATHCART, Helen. British. Biography. *Publs:* The Queen and the Turf, 1959; H.R.H. Prince Philip, Sportsman, 1961; Her Majesty, Biography of H.M. the Queen, 1962; Sandringham, 1964; The Queen Mother, 1965; Royal Lodge Windsor, 1966; Princess Alexandra, 1967; Lord Snowdon, 1968; The Royal Bedside Book, 1969; The Married Life of the Queen, 1970; The Duchess of Kent, 1971; Anne and the Princess Royal, 1973; Princess Margaret, 1974; Prince Charles, 1976; The Queen in Her Circle, 1977; The Queen Mother Herself, 1979; The Queen Herself, 1982; The Queen Mother: Fifty Years a Queen, 1986; The Queen and Prince Philip: Forty Years of Happiness, 1987. Add: c/o 1A King's Mews, Gray's Inn Rd., London WC1, England.

CATHERWOOD, (Sir) (Henry) Frederick (Ross). British, b. 1925. Social commentary/phenomena. Theology/Religion. Member of the European Parliament, since 1979. Chief Exec., Richard Costain Ltd., 1955–60; Asst. Managing Dir., 1960–62, and Managing Dir., 1962–64, British Aluminium Co. Ltd; Chief Industrial Adviser, Dept. of Economi Affairs, 1964–66; Dir. Gen., National Economic Development Council, 1966–71; Managing Dir., John Laing & Son Ltd., 1971–74; Chmn., British Overseas Trade Bd., 1975–79. *Publs:* The Christian in Industrial Society, 1964, 1980, in U.S. as Nine to Five, 1983; Britain with the Brakes Off, 1966; The Christian Citizen, 1969; A Better Way, 1976; First Things First, 1979; God's Time, God's Money, 1987. Add: Shire Hall, Castle Hill, Cambridge CB3 0AW, England.

CATO, Nancy. Australian, b. 1917. Romance/Historical fiction. Journalist, News, Adelaide, 1936–41; Art Critic, News, Adelaide, 1957–58. *Publs:* All the Rivers Run, 1958; Green Grows the Vine, 1960; Time, Flow Softly, 1960; But Still the Stream, 1960; The Sea Ants and Other Stories, 1964; North-West by South, 1965; Brown Sugar, 1974; (with Vivienne Rae Ellis) Queen Trucanini, 1976; Forefathers, 1982; A Distant (short stories), 1988. Add: c/o David Higham Assocs., 5-8 Lower John St., Golden Sq., London W1R 4HA, England.

CATTAN, Henry. Lebanese, b. 1906. International relations/Current affairs, Law. Lawyer since 1932. *Publs:* Law of Oil Concessions in the Middle East and North Africa, 1967; Evolution of Oil Concessions in the Middle East and North Africa, 1967; Palestine, the Arabs and Israel, 1969; Palestine, the Road to Peace, 1971; Palestine and International Law, 1973, 1976; The Garden of Joys, 1979; The Question of Jerusalem, 1980; Jerusalem, 1981; The Palestine Question, 1987. Add: 32 Ave. George V, 75008 Paris, France.

CATTELL, Raymond Bernard. American, b. 1905. Psychology. Lectr. in Psychology, Harvard Univ., Cambridge, Mass., since 1941; Distinguished Research Prof., Univ. of Illinois, Champaign, since 1945. Chief Consultant, Inst. for Personality and Ability Testing, Champaign. Lectr., Univ. of Exeter, 1927–32; Dir., City of Leicester Child Guidance Clinic, 1932–37; G. Stanley Hall Prof. of Genetic Psychology, Clark Univ., Worcester, Mass., 1938–41. *Publs:* Cattell Group Intelligence Scale, 1930; Psychology and Social Progress, 1933; (trans.) E. Kretschmer: The Psychology of Men of Genius, 1934; Your Mind and Mine: A Popular Introduction to Psychology, 1934; A Guide to Mental Testing, 1936, 3rd ed. 1950; (with R.B. Travers and J. Cohen) Human Affairs from the Standpoint of the Social Sciences, 1937; The Fight for Our National Intelligence, 1937; Under Sail Through Red Devon (travel), 1937; Crooked Personalities: An Introduction to Clinical Psychology, 1938; Psychology and the Religious Quest, 1938; General Psychology, 1941, 1947; The Description and Measurement of Personality, 1946; An Introduction to Clinical Psychology, 1938; Psychology and the Religious Quest, 1938; General Psychology, 1941, 1947; The Description and Measurement of Personality, 1946; An Introduction to Personality Study, 1949; Personality: A Systematic Theoretical and Factual Study, 1950; Factor Analysis, 1952; Personality and Motivation Structure and Measurement, 1957; (with G.F. Stice) The Dimensions of Groups and their Relations to the Behavior of Members, 1960; (with I.H. Schier) The Meaning and Measurement of Neuroticism and Anxiety, 1961; Personality and Social Psychology: Collected Papers, 1964; (with J.D. Hundleby and K. Pawlik) Personality Factors in Objective Test Devices, 1965; The Scientific Analysis of Personality, 1965; Handbook of Multivariate and Experimental Psychology, 1966; (with I.W. Warburton) Objective Personality and Motivation Tests: A Theoretical Introduction and Practical Compendium, 1967; (with H.J. Butcher) The Prediction of Achievement and Creativity, 1968; Abilities: Their Structure, Growth and Action, 1971; A New Morality from Science: Beyondism, 1972; Personality and Mood by Questionnaire, 1973; (with Child) Motivation and Dynamic Structure, 1975; (with Dreger) Handbook of Modern Personality Theory, 1977; Handbook

of the Objective-Analytic Personality Test Kit, 1978; The Scientific Use of Factor Analysis, 1978; Personality and Learning Theory, 2 vols., 1979–80; The Inheritance of Personality and Ability, 1982; Structured Personality Learning Theory, 1983; (with Johnson) Functional Psychological Testing, 1985; Human Motivation and the Dynamic Calculus, 1985; Psychotherapy by Structured Learning Theory, 1986. Add: 662 Kalanipuu St., Honolulu, Hawaii 96825, U.S.A.

CAUFFIELD, Margaret E. American, b. 1932. Children's fiction, Antiques/Furnishings. Homemaker and freelance writer since 1964; also teaches adult education classes on writing for children. High sch. English teacher, Fenton, Mich., 1954–56; Instr., Forest Hills Community Coll., Flint, Mich., 1956–64. *Publs:* The Dollhouses of Williamsburg, 1971; Early Twentieth-Century Christmas Tree Ornaments, 1972; Christmas Toys Through the Ages, 1975; Collectibles of the 1940's: Glassware, China, and Toys, 1975; Beth Ann's Marvelous Adventure, 1980; Victoria Visits Copenhagen, 1981; Lady Bru, Movie Star, 1983; Sasha and Eric at Cape Canaveral, 1984; Queen Anne's House, 1986. Add: 221 Lewiston Rd., Grosse Pointe Farms, Mich. 48236, U.S.A.

CATUDAL, Honoré (Marc), Jr. American, b. 1944. International relations/Current affairs, Politics/Government. Asst. Prof. of Intnl. Relations and Comparative Politics, St. John's Univ., Collegeville, Minn., since 1973. *Publs:* Steinstücken: A Study in Cold War Politics, 1971; The Diplomacy of the Quadripartite Agreement on Berlin; A Balance Sheet of the Quadripartite Agreement on Berlin, 1978; The Exclave Problem of Western Europe, 1979; Kennedy and the 1961 Berlin Wall Crisis: A Case Study in U.S. Decision Making, 1980; Nuclear Deterrence: Does It Deter?, 1985; Soviet Nuclear Strategy from Stalin to Gorbachev: A Revolution in Soviet Military and Political Thinking, 1988. Add: Dept. of Govt., St. John's Univ., Collegeville, Minn. 56321, U.S.A.

CAUDWELL, Sarah. Pseud. for Sarah Cockburn. British. Mystery/Crime/Suspense. Barrister. *Publs:* Thus Was Adonis Murdered, 1981; The Shortest Way to Hades, 1984; The Sirens Sang of Murder, 1989. Add: c/o William Collins Ltd., 8 Grafton St., London W1X 3LA, England.

CAULDWELL, Frank. *See* **KING,** Francis.

CAUSEY, Gilbert. British, b. 1907. Medicine/Health. Prof. of Anatomy Emeritus, Univ. of London (Prof., 1952–70). Sir William Collins Prof. of Human and Comparative Anatomy, Royal Coll. of Surgeons, London, 1952–70. *Publs:* The Cell of Schwann, 1960; Electron Microscopy, 1962; (with Aitken, Joseph and Young) A Manual of Human Anatomy; (with Frankis Evans) Anatomy for Anaesthetists. Add: Orchard Cottage, Bodinnick-by-Fowey, Cornwall, England.

CAUSLEY, Charles (Stanley). British, b. 1917. Short stories, Children's fiction, Plays, Poetry, Translations. Literary Ed., Apollo in the West, and Signature, BBC mags., 1953–56; Honorary Visiting Fellow in Poetry, Univ. of Exeter, 1973–74; Teacher in Cornwall, 1947–76. *Publs:* Runaway (play), 1936; The Conquering Hero (play), 1937; Benedict (play), 1938; Hands to Dance and Skylark (adult short stories), 1951, 1979; Farewell, Aggie Weston, 1951; Survivor's Leave, 1953; Union Street: Poems, 1957; (ed.) Peninsula: An Anthology of Verse from the West-Country, 1957; The Ballad of Charlotte Dymond, 1958; Johnny Alleluia: Poems, 1961; (with George Barker and Martin Bell) Penguin Modern Poets 3, 1962; (ed.) Dawn and Dusk: Poems of Our Time, 1962; (ed.) Rising Early: Story Poems and Ballads of the 20th Century (in U.S. as Modern Ballads and Story Poems), 1964; (ed.) Modern Folk Ballads, 1966; Ballad of the Bread Man, 1968; Underneath the Water: Poems, 1968; Figure of 8: Narrative Poems, 1969; Figgie Hobbin: Poems for Children, 1971; (with Laurie Lee) Pergamon Poets 10, 1970; Timothy Winters, 1970; (ed.) In the Music I Hear: Poems by Children, 1970; (ed.) Oats and Beans and Barley: Poems by Children, 1971; The Tail of the Trinosaur (in verse for children), 1973; (ed.) The Puffin Book of Magic Verse, 1974; Collected Poems, 1951–1975, 1975; When Dad Felt Bad, 1975; Dick Whittington (children's story) 1976; Here We Go Round The Round House (verse), 1976; The Hill of the Fairy Calf (verse), 1976; (ed.) The Puffin Book of Salt-Sea Verse, 1978; Three Heads Made of Gold (children's story), 1978; The Gift of a Lamb (verse-play), 1978; The Animals' Carol (verse), 1978; The Last King of Cornwall (children's story), 1978; St. Martha and the Dragon, 1978; (ed.) The Batsford Book of Stories in Verse, 1979;(trans.) 25 Poems by Hamdija Demirovic 1980; The Ballad of Aucassin and Nicolette, 1981; (ed.) The Sun, Dancing, 1982; Hymn., 1983; Secret Destinations, 1984; (trans.) King's Children (German ballads), 1986; 21 Poems, 1986; Early in the Morning: Poems for Children, 1986; Jack the Treacle Eater: Poems for Children, 1987;

A Field of Vision: Poems, 1988. Add: 2 Cyprus Well, Launceston, Cornwall, England.

CAUTE, (John) David. Also writes as John Salisbury. British, b. 1936. Novels/Short stories. Plays/Screenplays, History, Politics/Government. Fellow, All Souls Coll., Oxford, 1959–65; Reader in Social and Political Theory, Brunel Univ., Uxbridge, Middx., 1967–70; Regents Lectr., Univ. of Calif., 1974; Literary and Arts Ed., New Statesman, London, 1979–80. Co-Chmn., Writers Guild of Great Britain, 1981–82. *Publs:* At Fever Pitch (novel), 1959; Comrade Jacob (novel), 1961; Communism and the French Intellectuals 1914–1960, 1964; The Decline of the West (novel), 1966; The Left in Europe since 1789, 1966; (ed.) Essential Writings of Karl Marx, 1967; The Demonstration (play), 1969; Fanon, 1970; The Occupation (novel), 1971; The Fellow-Travellers, 1973, Collisions: Essays and Review, 1974; Cuba, Yes?, 1974; The Great Fear, 1978; The K-Factor (novel), 1983; Under the Skin: The Death of White Rhodesia, 1983; The Espionage of the Saints, 1986; News from Nowhere (novel), 1986; Sixty-Eight: The Year of the Barricades, 1988; Veronica or the Two Nations (novel), 1989; as John Salisbury—The Baby Sitters, 1978; Moscow Gold, 1980. Add: 41 Westcroft Sq., London W6 0TA, England.

CAUTHEN, Irby Bruce, Jr. American, b. 1919. Literature. Emeritus Prof. of English, Univ. of Virginia, Charlottesville, since 1987 (Asst. Prof., 1954–58; Assoc. Prof., 1958–62; Prof., 1962–87; Assoc. Dean, 1958–62; Dean, 1962–78; Assoc. Dir. of the Summer Session, 1958–71). Regional Chmn., Woodrow Wilson Fellowship Foundn.; Pres., Bibliographical Soc., Univ. of Virginia. Asst. Prof. of English, Hollins Coll., Va., 1951–54. *Publs:* (ed.) The Coxcomb in the Dramatic Works in the Beaumont and Fletcher Canon, 1966; (ed.) Gorboduc, by Thomas Sackville and Thomas Norton, 1970; Two Mementoes from the Poe-Ingram Collection, 1971; (with J.L. Dameron) Edgar Allan Poe: A Bibliography of Criticism, 1974. Add: 1824 Winston Rd., Charlottesville, Va. 22903, U.S.A.

CAUTHEN, (W.) Kenneth. American, b. 1930. Theology/Religion. Prof. of Theology, Colgate-Rochester/Bexley Hall/Crozer Theological Seminary, since 1970. Asst. Prof. of Christian Ethics, 1957–60, and Assoc. Prof. of Christian Ethics, 1960–61, Mercer Univ., Georgia; Assoc. Prof., 1961–63, and Prof. of Theology, 1963–70, Crozer Theological Seminary, Chester, Pa. *Publs:* The Impact of American Religious Liberalism, 1962; The Triumph of Suffering Love, 1966; Science, Secularization and God, 1969; (ed. and contrib.) Shailer Mathews: Jesus on Social Institutions, 1971; Christian Biopolitics, 1971; The Ethics of Enjoyment, 1975; Process Ethics, 1984; Systematic Theology, 1986; The Passion for Equality, 1987. Add: 1100 S. Goodman St., Rochester, New York 14620, U.S.A.

CAVALLO, Diana. American, b. 1931. Novels/Short stories, History. Lectr. in Creative Writing, Univ. of Pennsylvania, Philadelphia, since 1980. Fulbright Teaching Fellowship, 1961–63; Lectr. in Literature, Univ. of Pisa, Italy, 1961–63, and 1969–73; Lectr. in Literature Queen's Coll., Flushing, N.Y., 1966–69, and Bronx Community College and Mercy College, New York, 1974–80. *Publs:* A Bridge of Leaves, 1961; Certain Fathoms in the Earth, 1964; New York, Its Coexisting Past and Present, 1969; Lower East Side: A Portrait in Time, 1971. Add: Dept. of English, Univ. of Pennsylvania, Philadelphia, Pa. 19104, U.S.A.

CAVANNA, Betty. (Elizabeth Cavanna Harrison). American, b. 1909. Children's fiction. Former Art Dir., Westminster Press, Philadelphia. *Publs:* The Black Spaniel Mystery, 1945; Going on Sixteen, 1946; Spurs for Suzanna, 1947; Spring Comes Riding, 1950; Two's Company, 1951; Love Laurie, 1953; Passport to Romance, 1955; The Boy Next Door, 1956; Angel on Skis, 1957; Stars in Her Eyes, 1958; The Scarlet Sail, 1959; Accent on April, 1960; Fancy Free, 1961; A Touch of Magic, 1961; A Time for Tenderness, 1962; Almost Like Sisters, 1963; Jenny Kimura, 1964; Mystery at Love's Creek, 1965; A Breath of Fresh Air, 1966; The Country Cousin, 1967; Mystery in Marrakech, 1968; Spice Island Mystery, 1969; Mystery on Safari, 1970; The Ghost of Ballyhooly, 1971; Mystery in the Museum, 1972; Petey, 1973; Joyride, 1974; Ruffles and Drums, 1975; Catchpenny Street, 1975; Mystery of the Emerald Buddha, 1976; You Can't Take Twenty Dogs on a Date, 1977; Runaway Voyage, 1978; Ballet Fever, 1978; The Surfer and the City Girl, 1981; Stamp Twice for Murder, 1981; Storm in Her Heart, 1983; Wanted: A Girl for the Horses, 1984; Romance on Trial, 1984; Banner Year, 1987. Add: 45 Pasture Lane, Bryn Mawr, Pa. 19010, U.S.A.

CAVE, Emma. Pseud. for Caroline Lassalle. British. Novels. Ed., Picador Books, London, 1972–77. Lives in Cyprus. *Publs:* Little Angie, 1977; The Blood Bond, 1979; Cousin Henrietta, 1981; (as Caroline Lassalle) Breaking the Rules, 1986. Add: c/o Hamish Hamilton Ltd., 27 Wright's Lane, London W8 5TZ, England.

CAVENAGH, Winifred (Elizabeth). British. Law, Sociology. Prof. Emeritus of Criminology and Social Admin., Univ. of Birmingham, since 1976 (Lectr., Sr. Lectr. and Prof., 1946–76); Magistrate since 1949. Gov., Birmingham United Teaching Hosps., 1958–64; Member, Lord Chancellor's Advisory Cttee. on Legal Aid, 1960–71, and Advisory Council on Magistrates' Training, 1965–72; Member, Council of Magistrates' Assn., 1965–76; Member, Gen. Advisory Bd., BBC, 1977–80. *Publs:* The Child and the Court, 1959; Juvenile Courts, The Child, and the Law, 1967; Guide to Procedure in Juvenile Court, 1982. Add: 25 High Point, Richmond Hill Rd, Edgbaston, Birmingham B15 3RU, England.

CAVENDISH, Richard. British, b. 1930. Novels/Short stories, Mythology/Folklore, Supernatural/Occult topics. Ed., Out of Town mag., since 1983. Ed., Partworks Div., B.P.C. Publishing Ltd., London, 1967–72. *Publs:* Nymph and Shepherds, 1959; The Balancing Act, 1960; On the Rocks, 1963; The Black Arts, 1967; (ed. and co-author) Man, Myth, & Magic, 1970–72; (ed. and co-author) Encyclopedia of the Unexplained, 1974; The Powers of Evil, 1975; The Tarot, 1975; A History of Magic, 1977; Visions of Heaven and Hell, 1977; King Arthur and the Grail, 1978; (ed. and co-author) Mythology, 1980; Legends of the World, 1982; Prehistoric England, 1983; Red Cross: Then and Now, 1984; Unsolved Mysteries of the Universe, 1987. Add: 19 Campion Rd., London SW15, England.

CAVES, Richard Earl. American, b. 1931. Economics. Prof. of Economics, Harvard Univ., Cambridge, Mass., since 1962. Asst., and Assoc. Prof., Univ. of California, Berkeley, 1957–62. *Publs:* (with R.H. Holton) The Canadian Economy, 1959; Trade and Economic Structure, 1960; Air Transport and Its Regulators, 1962; American Industry, 1964; (ed. with H.G. Johnson and P.B. Kenen, and contrib.) Trade, Growth and the Balance of Payments, 1965; (with J.S. Bain and J. Margolis) Northern California's Water Industry, 1966; (ed. with H.G. Johnson) Readings in International Economics, 1967; (ed. and contrib.) Britain's Economic Prospects, 1968; (with G.L. Reuber) Canadian Economic Policy and the Impact of International Capital Flows, 1969; (with G.L. Reuber) Capital Transfers and Economic Policy, 1971; (with R.W. Jones) World Trade and Payments, 1973; Diversification, Foreign Investment, and Scale in North American Manufacturing Industries, 1975; (ed. with M.J. Roberts, and contrib.) Regulating the Product, 1975; (with M. Uekusa) Industrial Organization in Japan, 1976; (with others) Studies in Canadian Industrial Organization, 1977; (with M.E. Porter and A.M. Spence) Competition in the Open Economy, 1980; (ed. with L.B. Krause and contrib.) Britain's Economic Performance, 1980; Multinational Enterprise and Economic Analysis, 1982; (ed. with L.B. Krause and contrib.) The Australian Economy: A View from the North, 1984; (with S.W. Davies) Britain's Productivity Gap, 1987; (with D. R. Barton) Efficiency in U.S. Manufacturing Industries, 1989; Adjustment to International Competition, 1989. Add: Dept. of Economics, Harvard Univ., Cambridge, Mass. 02138, U.S.A.

CAWLEY, Winifred. British, b. 1915. Children's fiction. English teacher, English Sch., Cairo, 1941–44; Leeds Coll. of Technology, 1950–54, West Park Sch., Leeds, 1954–58, Leeds Girls' High Sch., 1958–59, and 1966–73, Lourdes Hill Convent, Brisbane, Qld., 1960–63, and Indooroopilly High Sch., Brisbane, 1964–65. *Publs:* Down the Long Stairs, 1964; Feast of the Serpent, 1969; Gran at Coalgate, 1974; Silver Everything, and many Mansions, 1976. Add: 2 Harrowby Rd., West Park, Leeds LS16 5HN, England.

CAWS, Mary Ann. American (b. British). b. 1933. Art, Literature, Translations. Distinguished Prof. of English, French and Comparative Literature, Grad. Center, City Univ. of New York, since 1986 (Asst. Prof., 1966–70; Assoc. Prof., 1970–72; Prof. since 1972); Co-Dir., Peyre Institute, since 1981. Ed., Dada/Surrealism, Univ. of Iowa; Dir., Le Siècle éclaté, Paris; Member, Editorial and Advisory Bds., French Review, Diacritics, and New York Literary Forum; Vice-Pres., 1982–83, and Pres., 1983–84, Modern Language Assn. Faculty member, Barnard Coll., Columbia Univ., NYC, 1962–63, and Sarah Lawrence Coll., Bronxville, N.Y., 1963. *Publs:* Surrealism and the Literary Imagination, 1966; The Poetry of Dada and Surrealism, 1970; André Breton, 1971; The Inner Theatre of Recent French Poetry, 1972; (ed. and trans.) Approximate Man and Other Writings of Tristan Tzara, 1974; (ed.) About French Poetry from Dada to Tel Quel, 1975; The Presence of René Char, 1976; (trans. and ed.) Selected Poems of René Char, 1976; The Surrealist Voice of Robert Desnos, 1977; René Char, 1977; La Main de Pierre Reverdy, 1979; (co-trans.-ed.) Roof Slates and Other Poems of Pierre Reverdy, 1981;

(ed.) Stephen Mallarmé: Selected Poetry and Prose, 1981; A Metapoetics of the Passage, 1981; (ed.) St. John Perse, Selected Poems, 1982; The Eye in the Text: Essays on Perception, 1982; L'Oeuvre Filante de René Char, 1983; (ed.) Writing in a Modern Temper, 1984; Reading Frames in Modern Fiction, 1985; (ed.) Textual Analysis: Some Readers Reading, 1986; (trans.) Mad Love, by André Breton, 1988; The Art of Interference, 1989. Add: 140 E. 81st St., Apt. 11D, New York, N.Y. 10028, U.S.A.

CAWS, Peter (James). British, b. 1931. Education, Philosophy, Sciences, Translations. Univ. Prof. of Philosophy, George Washington Univ., Washington, D.C., since 1982. Exec. Assoc. Carnegie Corp., NYC, 1962–65; Prof. of Philosophy, Hunter Coll., 1965–82. *Publs:* The Philosophy of Science: A Systematic Account, 1965; (trans.) The Methods of Contemporary Thought, by J.M. Bochenski, 1965; Science and the Theory of Value, 1967; (with S. Dillon Ripley) The Bankruptcy of Academic Policy, 1972; Sartre, 1979; (ed.) Two Centuries of Philosophy in America, 1980; Structuralism: The Art of the Intelligible, 1988; (ed.) The Causes of Quarrel: Essays on Peace, War, and Thomas Hobbes, 1989. Add: 637 S. Saint Asaph St., Alexandria, Va. 22314, U.S.A.

CAZET, Denys. American, b. 1938. Children's fiction. Teacher, Corcoran and St.Helena, Calif., 1960–75; Founder, Parhelion and Co., 1972–73; Elementary sch. librarian and media specialist, St. Helena, 1975–85; Faculty member and teacher of extension classes, Univ. of California at Davis, 1976–78; Dir., St. Helena Sch. District Media Centers, 1979–81; Instr., California Coll. of Arts and Crafts, Oakland, 1985–86. *Publs:* (all self-illustrated) Requiem for a Frog, 1971; The Non-Coloring Book: A Drawing Book for Mind Stretching and Fantasy Building, 1973; The Duck with Squeaky Feet, 1980; Mud Baths for Everyone, 1981; You Make the Angels Cry, 1983; Lucky Me, 1983; Big Shoe, Little Shoe, 1984; Christmas Moon, 1984; Saturday, 1985; December Twenty-Fourth, 1986; Frosted Glass, 1987; A Fish in His Pocket, 1987; Sunday, 1988; Great-Uncle Felix, 1988; Mother Night, 1988. Add: 1300 Ink Grade Rd., Pope Valley, Calif. 94567, U.S.A.

CEBULASH, Mel. Also writes as Ben Farrell, Glen Harlan and Jared Jansen. American, b. 1937. Children's fiction, Children's non-fiction. Teacher, New Jersey Public Schs., 1962–65; Assoc. Ed., 1966–68, Ed., Language Arts, 1969–72 Editorial Dir., Reading Skills, 1972–74, and Assoc. Ed.-in-Chief, 1974–76, Scholastic Mag. Inc., N.Y.C.; Ed.-in-Chief, Bowmar/Noble Publ. Inc., Los Angeles, 1976–80; V. Pres. and Publr., David S. Lake Publr., San Francisco, 1982–85. *Publs:*Through Basic Training with Walter Young, 1968; Man in a Green Beret and Other Medal of Honor Winners, 1969; (as Jared Jansen) Penny the Poodle, 1972; Benny's Nose, 1972; The See-Saw, 1972; (as Glen Harlan) Petey the Pup, 1972; Willie's Pet, 1972; The Ball That Wouldn't Bounce, 1972; (as Ben Farrell) Nancy and Jeff, 1972; Dictionary Skilz, 1973; Baseball Players Do Amazing Things, 1973; Herbie Rides Again, 1974; Football Players Do Amazing Things, 1975; Basketball Players Do Amazing Things, 1976; The Grossest Book Of World Records, 2 vols., 1977–78; The Champion's Jacket, 1978; Big League Reading Kit, 1979; Blackouts, 1979; A Horse to Remember, 1980; The Spring Street Boys series, 4 vols., 1981–82; I'm an Expert: Motivating Indepedent Study Projects for Grades 4-6, 1985; 1982; Ruth Marini of the Dodgers, 1982; Ruth Marini: Dodger Ace, 1983; Ruth Marini: World Series Star, 1985; Hot Like the Sun: A Terry Tyndale Mystery, 1986. Add: c/o Lerner Publications Co., 241 First Ave. N., Minneapolis, Minn. 55401, U.S.A.

CEGIELKA, Francis (Anthony). American, b. 1908. Theology/Religion, Biography. Roman Catholic priest: Retreat Master and Lectr.Instr. of Minor Seminary, 1932–34, and of Major Seminary, 1934–37, Soc. of the Catholic Apostolate in Poland; Rector, Polish Catholic Mission in France, 1937–47; Retreat Master and Lectr, in various American colls., 1948–67; Prof. of Theology, Felician Coll., Lodi, N.J., 1967–71; Chmn., Religious Studies Dept., Holy Family Coll., Philadelphia, 1971–76. *Publs:* The Pierced Heart (biography), 1955; Life on Rocks, Among the Natives of the U. of S.A., 1957; In the Service of Redemption, 1959; Spiritual Theology for Novices, 1961; Segregavit non Dominus, 1963; Three Hearts, vol. 1, 1963, vol. 2, 1964; Nazareth Spirituality, 1966; All Things New, 1969; Handbook of Ecclesiology and Christology, 1971; Toward a New Spring of Humankind, 1987. Add: 3452 Niagara Falls Blvd., North Tonawanda, N.Y. 14120, U.S.A.

CELL, Edward Charles. American, b. 1928. Theology/Religion. Prof. of Philosophy, Sangamon State Univ., Springfield, Ill., since 1974. Prof. of Philosophy and Chmn. of Div. of Comparative World Studies, U.S. Intnl. Univ., San Diego, Calif., 1972–74. *Publs:* (ed.) Religion and Contemporary Western Culture, 1967; Language, Existence and God, 1971; 1978; Learning to Learn from Experience, 1984; Daily Readings from Quaker Spirituality, 1987. Add: Sangamon State Univ., Springfield, Ill. 62708, U.S.A.

CERNEY, James V(incent). American, b. 1914. Medicine/Health, Sports/Physical education/Keeping fit. Pres., Professional Research, consultancy org., Dayton, Ohio, since 1944. Podiatrist since 1943. Mechanotherapist since 1948; chiropractor, since 1953. Publicity Dir., WING radio station 1939–40; Ed., Ohio Podiatry Journal, 1944; Dir. of Public Information, Civil Defense, 1957–58; Pres., Dayton Triangle Football Team, 1958–59, and Central States Coll. of Physiatrics, 1960–61. *Publs:* Encyclopedia of Athletic Injuries, 1963; How to Develop a Million Dollar Personality, 1964; Confidence and Power for Successful Living, 1966; Dynamic Laws of Thinking Rich, 1967; (co-author) Parker Prosperity Program, 1967; Stay Younger—Live Longer, 1968; (co-author) Principles and Practices of Podiatry, 1968; Talk Your Way to Success with People, 1968; Thirteen Steps to New Personal Power, 1969; Complete Book of Athletic Tapping Techniques, 1971; Flame Durrell (novel), 1971; Acupuncture Without Needles, 1974; Modern Magic of Natural Healing with Water Therapy, 1974; Handbook of Unusual and Unorthodox Healing Methods, 1975; Prevent System for Football Injuries, 1975; All-American Slimline, 1980; Sports Clinic Care, 1980. Add: 5235 N. Main St., Dayton, Ohio 45415, U.S.A.

CEVASCO, G(eorge) A(nthony). American, b. 1924. Art, Language/Linguistics, Literature. Prof. of English, St. John's Univ., N.Y., since 1955. Lectr., Fordham Univ., N.Y., 1954–63. *Publs:* J.K. Huysmans in England and America, 1962; (with J. Fee) Wordcraft, 1962; Grammar Self-Taught, 1963; (co-author) Functional English, 1963; Salvador Dali: Master of Surrealism and Modern Art, 1971; Oscar Wilde, 1972; The Population Problem, 1973; New Words for You, 1977; J.K. Huysmans: A Reference Guide, 1980; John Gray, 1982; The Sitwells: Edith, Osbert, Sacheverell, 1987; Three Decadent Poets: Ernest Dowson, John Gray and Lionel Johnson, 1989. Add: Dept. of English, St. John's Univ., Jamaica, N.Y. 11439, U.S.A.

CHACE, Isobel. Pseud. for Elizabeth (Mary Teresa) Hunter. British, b. 1934. Historical/Romance/Gothic. *Publs:* The African Mountain, 1960; The Japanese Lantern, 1960; Flamingoes on the Lake, 1961; (as Elizabeth Hunter) Cherry-Blossom Clinic, 1961; The Song and the Sea, 1962; (as Elizabeth Hunter) Spiced with Cloves, 1962; The Hospital of Fatima, 1963; The Wild Land, 1963; (as Elizabeth Hunter) Watch the Wall My Darling, 1963; A House for Sharing, 1964; (as Elizabeth Hunter) No Sooner Met, 1965; The Rhythm of Flamenco, 1966; The Spider's Web (in Can. as The Secret Marriage), 1966; The Land of the Lotus-Eaters, 1966; A Garland of Marigolds, 1967; Brittany Blue, 1967; Oranges and Lemons, 1967; (as Elizabeth Hunter) There Were Nine Castles, 1967; The Saffron Sky, 1968; The Damask Rose, 1968; A Handful of Silver, 1968; The Legend of Katmandu, 1969; Flower of Ethiopia, 1969; Sugar in the Morning, 1969; The Day That the Rain Came Down, 1970; The Flowering Cactus, 1970; To Marry a Tiger, 1971; The Wealth of the Islands, 1971; Home Is Goodbye, 1971; The Flamboyant Tree, 1972; The English Daughter, 1972; Cadence of Portugal, 1972; A Pride of Lions, 1972; The Tartan Touch, 1972; The House of Scissors, 1972; The Dragon's Cave, 1972; The Edge of Beyond, 1973; A Man of Kent, 1973; (as Elizabeth Hunter) The Crescent Moon, 1973; (as Elizabeth Hunter) The Tree of Idleness, 1973; (as Elizabeth Hunter) The Tower of the Winds, 1973; (as Elizabeth Hunter) The Beads of Nemesis, 1974; (as Elizabeth Hunter) The Bride Price, 1974; The Cornish Hearth, 1975; (as Elizabeth Hunter) The Bonds of Matrimony, 1975; (as Elizabeth Hunter) The Spanish Inheritance, 1975; (as Elizabeth Hunter) The Voice in the Thunder, 1975; (as Elizabeth Hunter) The Sycamore Song, 1975; A Canopy of Rose Leaves, 1976; The Clouded Veil, 1976; The Desert Castle, 1976; Singing in the Wilderness, 1976; (as Elizabeth Hunter) The Realms of Gold, 1976; The Whistling Thorn, 1977; The Mouth of Truth, 1977; (as Elizabeth Hunter) Pride of Madeira, 1977; Second Best Wife, 1978; (as Elizabeth Hunter) Bride in the Sun, 1980; (as Elizabeth Hunter) The Lion's Shadow, 1980; (as Elizabeth Hunter) A Touch of Magic, 1981; (as Elizabeth Hunter) A Silver Nutmeg, 1982; (as Elizabeth Hunter) Written in the Stars, 1982; (as Elizabeth Hunter) One More Time, 1982; (as Elizabeth Hunter) Fountains of Paradise, 1983; (as Elizabeth Hunter) A Tower of Strength, 1983; (as Elizabeth Hunter) London Pride, 1983; (as Elizabeth Hunter) Rain on the Wind, 1984; (as Elizabeth Hunter) Shared Destiny, 1984; (as Elizabeth Hunter) A Time to Wed, 1984. Add: c/o Mills and Boon Ltd., Eton House, 18-24 Paradise Rd., Richmond, Surrey TW9 1SR, England.

CHADWICK, Henry. British, b. 1920. Theology/Religion. Master of Peterhouse, Cambridge, since 1987, and Regius Prof. Emeritus of Divinity, Cambridge Univ., since 1983 (Regius Prof., 1979–83; Fellow of Magdalene Coll., 1979–87). Fellow, Queens Coll., Cambridge, 1946–58; Regius Prof. of Divinity, 1959–69 Canon, 1959–69, and Dean, 1969–79, Christ Church, and Pro-Vice Chancellor, 1974–75, Oxford Univ. Ed., Journal of Theological Studies, 1954–85; Member, Anglican-Roman Catholic Intnl. Commn., 1969–81, 1983–87. *Publs:* Origen: Contra Celsum, 1953; (with J.E.L. Oulton) Alexandrian Christianity, 1954; Lessing's Theological Writings, 1956; The Sentences of Sextus, 1959; Early Christian Thought and the Classical Tradition, 1966; The Early Church, 1967; (ed.) The Treatise on the Apostolic Tradition of St. Hippolytus of Rome, edited by G. Dix, 1968; Priscillian of Avila, 1976; Boethius, 1981; History and Thought of the Early Church, 1982; Augustine, 1986. Add: Peterhouse, Cambridge, England.

CHADWICK, John. British, b. 1920. Classics, Language/Linguistics. P.M. Laurence Reader in the Greek Language, Cambridge Univ., 1966–84 (Asst. Lectr., 1952–54; Lectr. in Classics, 1954–66). Ed. Asst., Oxford Latin Dictionary, Clarendon Press, Oxford, 1946–52. *Publs:* (trans. with W. Mann) The Medical Works of Hippocrates, 1950; (with M. Ventris) Documents in Mycenaean Greek, 1956, 2nd ed. as sole author, 1973; The Decipherment of Linear B, 1958, 1970; (ed.) The Mycenae Tablets III, 1962; (co-ed.) The Knossos Tablets, 3rd ed. 1964, 4th ed. 1971; The Mycenaean World, 1976; (co-ed.) Corpus of Mycenaean Inscriptions from Knossos, vol. 1, 1986; Linear B and Related Scripts, 1987. Add: Downing Coll., Cambridge CB2 1DQ, England.

CHADWICK, (Gerald William St.) John. British, b. 1915. Institutions/Organizations, International relations/Current affairs, Travel/Exploration/Adventure. Councillor, Royal Commonwealth Soc. Member, British Diplomatic Service, 1938–66; Counsellor, British High Commn. in Canada, British Embassy in Dublin, and British Delegation to NATO; former Under-Secty. of State, Foreign and Commonwealth Office, London; Dir., Commonwealth Foundn., London, 1966–80; Dir., London Science Centre, 1981. Gov., Commonwealth Inst., 1967–80. *Publs:* The Shining Plain, 1936; Newfoundland: Island into Province, 1967; International Organizations, 1970; (co-ed.) Professional Organisations in the Commonwealth, 1976; The Unofficial Commonwealth, 1982. Add: c/o The Athenaeum, London SW1, England.

CHADWICK, (Sir) Owen. British, b. 1916. History, Intellectual history. Regius Prof. of Modern History, Cambridge Univ., 1968–83 (Prof. of Ecclesiastical History, 1958–68; Vice-Chancellor, 1969–71). *Publs:* John Cassian, 1950, 1968; The Founding of Cuddesdon, 1954; From Bossuet to Newman, 1957; (trans. and ed.) Western Asceticism, 1958; Mackenzie's Grave, 1959; (ed.) The Mind of the Oxford Movement, 1960; Victorian Miniature, 1960; The Reformation, 1964, 15th ed. 1984; The Victorian Church, vol. 1, 1966, 3rd ed. 1972, vol. 2, 1970, 3rd ed. 1979; The Secularization of the European Mind, 1976; Catholicism and History, 1978; The Popes and European Revolution, 1981; Newman, 1983; Hensley Henson, 1983; Britain and the Vatican in the Second World War, 1986. Add: Selwyn Coll., Cambridge CB3 9DQ, England.

CHAFE, Wallace L. American, b. 1927. Anthropology/Ethnology, Language/Linguistics. Prof. of Linguistics, Univ. of California, Berkeley, since 1962, Univ. of California at Santa Barbara, since 1986. *Publs:* Seneca Thanksgiving Rituals, 1961; Seneca Morphology and Dictionary, 1967; Meaning and the Structure of Language, 1970; The Caddoan, Iroquoian and Siouan Languages, 1976; The Pear Stories, 1980; Evidentiality, 1986. Add: Dept. of Linguistics, Univ. of California, Santa Barbara, Calif. 93105, U.S.A.

CHAFFIN, James B. *See* **LUTZ,** Giles A.

CHAFFIN, Lillie D. American. Novels/Short stories, Children's fiction, Poetry. Writer-in-Residence, Pikeville Coll., Ky., and Ed., Twigs Mag., since 1973. Consultant, Writing Workshop, Univ. of Kentucky, Lexington; Consultant and Special Lectr., Right to Read Prog., Eastern Kentucky Univ., Richmond, since 1974, and Appalachian Studies Prog., Berea Coll., Ky. *Publs:* A Garden is Good, 1963; Tommy's Big Problem, 1965; Lines and Points (poetry), 1955; First Notes (poetry), 1969; Bear Weather (children's poetry), 1969; I Have a Tree (children's poetry), 1969; (with M. Butwin) America's First Ladies, 2 vols., 1969; (with R. Stenn) A World of Books, 1969; John Henry McCoy (novel), 1971; Freeman (novel), 1972; Coal: Energy and Crisis, 1974; 8th Day 13th (poetry), 1974; Star Following (poetry), 1976; Appalachian History and Other Poems, 1980; We Be Warm Till Springtime Comes, 1980; Up Hatfield Holler, 1982. Add: 644 Laura Dr., Winchester, Ky. 40391, U.S.A.

CHALFONT, Lord; Alun Arthur Gwynne Jones. British, b. 1919. History, Military/Defence, Biography. Chmn., All Party Defence Group,

House of Lords, since 1980; Chmn., VSEL Consortium, since 1987. Dir., IBM UK Ltd., and Lazard Bros. Ltd.; Pres., Nottingham Bldg. Soc. Served as regular officer in the British Army, 1939–61; Defence Corresp., The Times, London, 1961–64; Minister of State, Foreign and Commonwealth Office, 1964–70; Rep. to the Council of the Western European Union, 1969–70; Foreign Affairs Corresp., New Statesman, London, 1970–71. Chmn., U.N. Assn., 1972–73. *Publs:* The Sword and the Spirit, 1963; The Great Commanders, 1973; Montgomery of Alamein, 1976; (ed.) Waterloo, 1979; Star Wars: Suicide or Survival, 1985; Defence of the Realm, 1987. Add: House of Lords, London SW1, England.

CHALKER, Jack L(aurence). American, b. 1944. Science fiction/Fantasy, Literature. Founder-Dir., Mirage Press, Baltimore, since 1961. English, history and geography teacher, Baltimore public high schs., 1966–78. *Publs:* The New H.P. Lovecraft Bibliography, 1962, (with Mark Owings) as The Revised H.P. Lovecraft Bibliography, 1973; (ed.) In Memoriam Clark Ashton Smith, 1963; (ed.) Mirage on Lovecraft, 1964; (with Mark Owings) The Index to the Science-Fantasy Publishers, 1966, as Index to the SF Publishers, 1979; (with Mark Owings) The Necronomicon: A Study, 1967; An Informal Biography of Scrooge McDuck, 1974; A Jungle of Stars, 1976; Midnight in the Well of Souls, 1977; Dancers in the Afterglow, 1978; The Web of the Chozen, 1978; Exiles at the Well of Souls, 1978; Quest for the Well of Souls, 1978; A War of Shadows, 1979; And the Devil Will Drag You Under, 1979; Twilight at the Well of Souls, 1980; The Devil's Voyage, 1980; Dancers in the Afterglow, 1979; Lilith: A Snake in the Grass, 1981; Cerberus: A Wolf in the Fold, 1982; The Identity Matrix, 1982; Medusa: A Tiger by the Tail, 1983; Four Lords of the Diamond, 1983; The River of Dancing Gods, 1984; Spirits of Flux and Anchor, 1984; Empires of Flux and Anchor, 1984; Masters of Flux and Anchor, 1985; Downtiming the Night Side, 1985; Vengeance of the Dancing Gods, 1985; The Messiah Choice, 1985; The Birth of Flux and Anchor, 1985; Children of Flux and Anchor, 1986; Rings of the Masters series, 4 vols., 1987–88; When the Changewinds Blow, 1987; Riders of the Winds, 1988; War of the Maelstrom, 1988. Add: Box 28, Manchester, Md. 21102, U.S.A.

CHALLICE, Kenneth. *See* **HUTCHIN,** Kenneth Charles.

CHALMERS, Mary (Eileen). American, b. 1927. Children's fiction. Commercial artist in the 1950s; now a full-time writer. *Publs:* Come for a Walk with Me, 1955; Here Comes the Trolley Car, 1955; A Hat for Amy Jean, 1956; A Christmas Story, 1956; George Appleton, 1957; Kevin, 1957; Boats Finds a House, 1958; Throw a Kiss, Harry, 1958; The Cat Who Liked to Pretend, 1959; Mr. Cat's Wonderful Surprise, 1961; Take a Nap, Harry, 1964; Be Good, Harry, 1967; Merry Christmas, Harry, 1977; Come to the Doctor, Harry, 1981; Six Dogs, Twenty-Three Cats, Forty-Five Mice, and One Hundred Sixteen Spiders, 1986; Easter Parade, 1988. Add: 1644 Oak Ave., Haddon Heights, N.J. 08035, U.S.A.

CHALON, Jon. *See* **CHALONER,** John.

CHALONER, John. British. Also writes as Jon Chalon. Children's fiction. *Publs:* as Jon Chalon—The Flying Steamroller, 1967; The House Next Door, 1967; Sir Lance-a-little and the Knights of the Kitchen Table, 1971; The Voyage of the Floating Bedstead, 1972; The Green Bus, 1973; The Dustmen's Holiday, 1976; The Great Balloon Adventure, 1984; as John Chaloner—Three for the Road, 1954; Eager Beaver, 1965; Family Hold Back, 1975; To the Manner Born, 1978; Bottom Line, 1984. Add: 4 Warwick Sq., London SW1, England.

CHAMBERLAIN, Mary (Christina). British, b. 1947. Women. Research Officer, Arms Control and Disarmament Research Unit, Foreign and Commonwealth Office, London, 1970–71, and Richardson Inst. for Peace and Conflict Research, London, 1972; Administrative Officer, Social Science Research Council, London, 1972; Lectr. in Liberal Studies, Norfolk Coll. of Art and Technology, King's Lynn, 1973–74, London Coll. of Fashion, 1974–75, and Ipswich Civic Coll., 1977–87. Sr. Lectr. in Cultural Studies, London Coll. of Printing, 1977–87. *Publs:* Fenwomen, 1975, 1983; Old Wives' Tales, 1981; Writing Lives, 1988; Growing Up in Lambeth, 1989. Add: c/o Anne McDermid, Curtis Brown, 162-168 Regent St., London W1R 5TB, England.

CHAMBERLIN, Mary. American, b. 1914. Novels/Short stories, Travel/Exploration/Adventure. *Publs:* Dear Friends and Darling Romans, 1959; The Palazzo, 1971. Add: Via Numana 35, 00050 Fregene (Rome), Italy.

CHAMBERS, Aidan. British, b. 1934. Children's fiction, Plays/Screenplays, Children's non-fiction, Literature. Freelance writer and ed. Ed., Topliners, Club 75, and Rockets series, Macmillan; Proprietor, Thimble Press, since 1970. *Publs:* plays—Everyman's Everybody (for adults), 1957; Johnny Salter, 1966; The Car, 1967; The Chicken Run, 1968; The Dream Cage (for adults), 1982; mother works—Cycle Smash, 1967; Marle, 1968; The Reluctant Reader (for adults), 1969; Haunted Houses, 1971; Mac and Lugs, 1971; Don't Forget Charlie, and The Vase, 1971; Ghosts 2, 1972; More Haunted Houses, 1973; Introducing Books to Children, 1973; Great British Ghosts, 1974; Great Ghosts of the World, 1974; (ed.) The Tenth (and Eleventh) Ghost Book, 1974–75; Snake River, 1975; Funny Folk, 1976; Ghost Carnival, 1977; Breaktime, 1978; Fox Tricks, 1980; Seal Secret, 1980; Dance on My Grave, 1982; The Present Takers, 1983; Booktalk, 1985; Now Know, 1987; also ed. of several books for children. Add: Lockwood, Station Rd., S. Woodchester, Stroud, Glos. GL5 5EQ, England.

CHAMBERS, Catharine E. *See* **ST. JOHN,** Nicole.

CHAMBERS, Jim Bernard. New Zealander, b. 1919. Theology/-Religion. Minister, Cambridge Terrace Congregational Church, Wellington, 1963–82. Chmn., Congregational Union of N.Z., 1952–53, 1966–68, 1969–79 and 1982–86. *Publs:* The Karori Congregational Church 1842-1956, 1956; Hands Can Heal, 1958; Is Any Sick Among You, 1962; To God Be the Glory, 1965; The Cambridge Terrace Congregational Church, 1967; "A Peculiar People": History of Congregationalism in New Zealand 1840-1984, 1984. Add: 29 Alexander Rd., Raumati Beach, New Zealand.

CHAMBERS, Kate. *See* **ST. JOHN,** Nicole.

CHAMBERS, R(aymond John). Australian, b. 1917. Administration/Management, Economics, Money/Finance. Prof. of Accounting, Univ. of Sydney, 1960–82, now Emeritus (Sr. Lectr., 1953–55; Assoc. Prof., 1955–59). Ed. Abacus, 1964–74. *Publs:* Financial Management, 1947, 4th ed. 1986; Function and Design of Company Annual Reports, 1955; Accounting and Action, 1957, rev. ed. 1964; (ed. with L.Goldberg and R.L. Mathews) The Accounting Frontier, 1965; Accounting, Evaluation and Economic Behavior, 1966; Accounting Finance and Management, 1969; Securities and Obscurities, 1973; Price Variation and Inflation Accounting, 1980. Add: 18 Amy St., Blakehurst, N.S.W. 2221, Australia.

CHAMBERS, Robin (Bernard). British, b. 1942. Children's fiction. Head of Stoke Newington Sch., London, since 1979. Teacher of English, Dunraven Sch., 1967–68; English Teacher, Holloway Sch., 1969–71; Head of English, Hackney Downs Sch., 1971–76; Visiting Lectr. in English, Inst. of Education, Univ. of London, 1973–74; Deputy Head Teacher, Quintin Kynaston Sch., London, 1976–79. Member of the Exec. Cttee., National Assn. for the Teaching of English, 1973–76. *Publs:* The Ice Warrior and Other Stories, 1976; (co-author) Understanding Children's Writing, 1973; The Flight of Neither Century and Other Stories, 1980; Shadows in the Pit, 1980. Add: c/o Penguin Books, Harmondsworth, Middx. UB7 0DA, England.

CHAMPERNOWNE, David (Gawen). British, b. 1912. Economics. Fellow, Trinity Coll., Cambridge, since 1959, and Prof. of Economics and Statistics, Cambridge Univ., 1970–78, now Emeritus (Reader in Economics, Cambridge Univ., 1959–70). Asst. Lectr., London Sch. of Economics, 1936–38; Research Fellow, King's Coll., Cambridge, 1937–45; Member, Prime Minister's Statistical Section, 1940–41; Asst. Dir. of Progs., Ministry of Aircraft Production, 1941–45, Fellow of Nuffield Coll., Oxford, 1945–59, and Prof. of Statistics, Oxford Univ., 1949–59. Joint Ed., Economic Journal 1970–76. *Publs:* Uncertainty and Estimation in Economics, 3 vols., 1969; The Distribution of Income Between Persons, 1973. Add: Trinity Coll., Cambridge, England.

CHAMPION, Larry S. American, b. 1932. Literature. Prof. of English, North Carolina State Univ., Raleigh, since 1971 (joined Dept. as Instr., 1960; Assoc. Head, 1967–71; Head of Dept., 1971–84). Instr. in English, Davidson Coll., N.C., 1955–56; with U.S. Army, Panama, 1956–58; Teaching Fellow, Dept. of English, Univ. of North Carolina, Chapel Hill, 1958–60. *Publs:* Ben Jonson's Dotages, 1967; The Evolution of Shakespeare's Comedy, 1970; (ed.) Quick Springs of Sense: Studies in the 18th Century, 1974; Shakespeare's Tragic Perspective, 1976; Tragic Patterns in Jacobean and Caroline Drama, 1977; Perspective in Shakespeare's English Histories, 1980; (ed.) The Garland Shakespeare Bibliographies: King Lear, 2 vols., 1980; Thomas Dekker and the Traditions of English Drama, 1985; The Essential Shakespeare: An Annotated Bibliography of Major Modern Studies, 1986. Add: 5320 Sendero Dr., Raleigh, N.C. 27612, U.S.A.

CHAMPKIN, Peter. British, b. 1918. Poetry. Asst. Secty. and Admin. Officer, Secondary Sch. Exams., Univ. of London, 1951–78. *Publs:* In Another Room, 1959; The Enmity of Noon, 1960; Poems of Our Time, 1962; For the Employed, 1965; The Waking Life of Aspern Williams, 1970; The Sleeping Life of Aspern Williams, 1987. Add: Hemingfold Oast, Telham, Battle, Sussex, England.

CHAMPLIN, Joseph M(asson). American, b. 1930. Religion. Resident Weekend Assoc., St. Joseph Church, Camillus, N.Y. Ordained Roman Catholic priest, 1956; Asst. Pastor, Cathedral of the Immaculate Conception, Syracuse, 1956–68; Assoc. Dir. of Secretariat, Bishops' Cttee. on the Liturgy, Washington, D.C., 1968–71; Pastor, Holy Family Church, Fulton, N.Y., 1971–78; Vicar, Diocese of Syracuse, 1979–87. *Publs:* Don't You Really Love Me?, 1968; (ed.) The Priest Today and Tomorrow, 1969; Together for Life, 1970; Christ Present and Yet to Come, 1971; The Mass in a World of Change, 1973; The Sacraments in a World of Change, 1973; Together in Peace, 1975, and children's ed. (with Brian A. Haggerty), 1976; Preparing for the New Rite of Penance, 1975; The Living Parish, 1977; The New, Yet Old Mass, 1977; Alone No Longer, 1977; Preaching and Teaching about the Eucharist, 1977; Through Life to Death, 1979; Together by Your Side: A Book for Comforting the Sick and Dying, 1979; An Important Office of Immense Love, 1980; Sharing Treasure, Time, and Talent, 1982; Messengers of God's Word, 1982; Behind Closed Doors, 1984; Healing in the Catholic Church, 1985; Special Signs of Grace, 1987; What It Means to Be Catholic, 1987; Challenge, Don't Crush, 1989. Add: St. Joseph's Rectory, 5600 West Genesee St., Camillus, N.Y. 13031, U.S.A.

CHANAN, Michael. British, b. 1946. Film, Cultural/Ethnic topics, Translations. Independent film maker; Lectr. in Film, Sch. of Communication, Polytechnic of Central London, 1976–80. *Publs:* Labour Power in the British Film Industry, 1976; (ed.) Chilean Cinema, 1976; (trans.) Multinational Corporations and the Control of Culture, by Armand Mattelart, 1979; The Dream That Kicks: The Prehistory and Early Years of Cinema in Britain, 1980; (ed.) Santiago Alvarez, 1980; The Cuban Image, 1985. Add: 18 Cedar Ct., Birchington Rd., Windsor, Berks., England.

CHANCE, Stephen. *See* **TURNER,** Philip.

CHANDLER, David (Geoffrey). British, b. 1934. Military/Defence, Travel/Exploration/Adventure, Biography. Head, Dept. of War Studies, Royal Military Academy Sandhurst, Camberley, Surrey, since 1980 (Lectr., Dept. of Modern Subjects, 1960–64; Sr. Lectr., Dept. of Military History, 1964–69; Deputy-Head, Dept. of War Studies, 1969–80). Ed., David Chandler's Newsletter on the Age of Napoleon, since 1987. Pres., British Military History Commn., 1967–86, and Hon. Pres., since 1986; Vice-Pres., Intnl. Commn. of Military History, since 1975. British Army Officer, 1957–60; Mershon Visiting Prof., Ohio State Univ., Columbus, 1969–70. *Publs:* (ed.) A Traveller's Guide to the Battlefields of Europe, 2 vols., 1965; The Campaigns of Napoleon, 1966; (ed. and trans.) Two Soldiers of Marlborough's Wars: Capt. Robert Parker and the Count of Mérode Westerloo, 1968; Marlborough as Military Commander, 1973; The Art of Warfare on Land, 1974; Napoleon, 1974; The Art of Warfare in the Age of Marlborough, 1976; Dictionary of the Napoleonic Wars, 1979; Waterloo: The Hundred Days, 1980; Atlas of Military Strategy, 1980; (ed.) A Journal of Marlborough's Wars, by Private J.M. Deane, 1984; Sedgemoor: An Account on Anthology, 1985; (ed.) Napoleon's Marshals, 1987; Napoleaon: Military Maxims, 1987. Add: Hindford, Monteagle Lane, Yateley, Camberley, Surrey, England.

CHANDLER, Frank. *See* **GILMAN,** George G.

CHANDLER, George. Australian, b. 1915. History, Information science/Computers, Librarianship. Ed., Intnl. Library Review, since 1969, and Recent Advances in Library and Information Services, since 1981. City Librarian, Liverpool City Libraries, Lancs., 1952–74; Dir.-Gen., National Library of Australia, Canberra, 1974–80. *Publs:* Dudley, 1959; (with Hannah) William Roscoe of Liverpool, 1753-1831, 1953; Liverpool 1207-1957, 1960; Liverpool Shipping, 1960; (with Saxton) Liverpool under James, I, 1960; Four Centuries of Banking: Martins Bank, vol. I, 1964, vol. II, 1968; (with Wilson) Liverpool under Charles I, 1965; Libraries in the Modern World, 1965; How to Find Out About Literature, 1968, 5th ed. 1982; Libraries in the East, 1971; Libraries, Documentation and Bibliography in the USSR, 1972; An Illustrated History of Liverpool, 1972; International Librarianship, 1972; International Series of Monographs on Library and Information Science, 1972; Victorian and Edwardian Liverpool and the North West, 1973; Merchant Venturers, 1973; Victorian and Edwardian Manchester and North West, 1974; Liverpool in Literature, 1974; Recent Advances in International and National Library and Information Sources, 1982. Add: 43 Saxon Close, Stratford-upon-Avon, Warwicks, CV37 7DX, England.

CHANDLER, S(tanley) Bernard. Canadian, b. 1921. Literature. Prof., 1963–87, now Emeritus, and Chmn., Dept. of Italian, 1973–84, Univ. of Toronto (Assoc. Prof., 1957–63). Asst. Lectr. in Italian, Univ. Coll., London, 1948–50; Lectr. in Italian, Univ. of Aberdeen, 1950–57. *Publs:* (ed. with J.A. Molinaro) The World of Dante: Six Studies in Language and Thought, 1966; Alessandro Manzoni: The Story of a Spiritual Quest, 1974; (ed. with J.A. Molinaro) The Culture of Italy, Mediaeval to Modern, 1979. Add: Dept. of Italian Studies, Univ. of Toronto, Toronto, Ont. M5S 1A1, Canada.

CHANDLER, Tertius. American, b. 1915. Demography, History, Essays. Volunteer teacher, Sr. Center, Berkeley, Calif., 1980–87. Secty., Henry George Sch., San Francisco, 1979–81. *Publs:* Poems and Essays, 1952; Half-Encyclopedia, 1956, 2nd ed. 1983; (with Gerald Fox) 3000 Years of Urban Growth, 1974; Remote Kingdoms, 1976, 1981; Progress, 1976, 1981; Godly Kings and Early Ethics, 1976; The Tax We Need, 1980; Moses and the Golden Age, 1986; 4000 Years of Urban Growth, 1987. Add: 2500 Buena Vista, Berkeley, Calif. 94708, U.S.A.

CHANDOS, Fay. *See* **CHARLES,** Theresa.

CHANDRASEKHAR, Subrahmanyan. Naturalized American, b. 1910. Physics. Morton D. Hull Distinguished Service Prof. of Theoretical Astrophysics, Univ. of Chicago, since 1952 (Research Assoc., 1952–53; Prof., 1944–46; Distinguished Service Prof., 1947–52). Fellow, Trinity Coll., Cambridge, England, 1933–37. Managing Ed., Astrophysical Journal, 1952–71. *Publs:* Introduction to the Study of Stellar Structure, 1939; Principles of Stellar Dynamics, 1942; Radiative Transfer, 1950; Hydrodynamic and Hydromagnetic Stability, 1961, 1968; Ellipsoidal Figures of Equilibrium, 1969; The Mathematical Theory of Black Holes, 1983; Eddington: The Most Distinguished Astrophysicist of His Time, 1983; Truth and Beauty: Aesthetics and Motivations in Science, 1987. Add: Lab. for Astrophysics and Space Research, 933 E. 56th St., Chicago, Ill. 60637, U.S.A.

CHANEY, Jill. Pseud. for Jill Leeming. British, b. 1932. Children's fiction. *Publs:* On Primrose Hill, 1961; Half a Candle, 1968; A Penny for the Guy, 1970; Mottram Park, 1971; Christopher's Dig, 1972; Taking the Woffle to Pebblecombe on Sea, 1974; Return to Mottram Park, 1974; Woffle, R.A., 1976; Christopher's Find, 1976; The Buttercup Field, 1976; Canary Yellow, 1977; Angel Face, 1978; Vectis Diary, 1979. Add: Glen Rosa, Colleyland, Chorleywood, Herts., England.

CHANG, Isabelle C. American, b. 1925. Children's non-fiction, Cookery/Gastronomy/Wine. Librarian and Media Specialist, Shrewsbury Sch. System, Mass., since 1964. Freelance writer, Worcester Sunday Telegram, 1958–68; Library Dir., Shrewsbury Public Library, 1959–64. *Publs:* What's Cooking at Changs', 1959, rev. ed. 1971; Chinese Fairy Tales, 1965; Tales from Old China, 1969; Gourmet on the Go, 1971; The Magic Pole, 1978. Add: 15 Fiske St., Shrewsbury, Mass. 01545, U.S.A.

CHANNING, Steven A. American, b. 1940. History. Freelance video and film writer and producer (productions include This Other Eden, 1979, Upon This Rock, 1981, The Fulbright Experience, 1986, and The First Colony, 1987). Assoc. Prof. of History, Univ. of Kentucky, Lexington, 1968–82. *Publs:* Crisis of Fear: Secession in South Carolina, 1970; Kentucky: A History, 1977; The Confederate Ordeal, 1984; The Encyclopedia of Kentucky, 1985. Add: 47 N. Circle Dr., Chapel Hill, N.C. 27514, U.S.A.

CHANTLER, David T(homas). American, b. 1925. Novels/Short stories, Film. *Publs:* Fellow Creature, 1970; The Man Who Followed in Front, 1974; The Capablanca Opening, 1975. Add: 14001 Palawan Way, Apt. PH 18, Marina del Rey, Calif. 90292, U.S.A.

CHAPIN, F. Stuart, Jr. American, b. 1916. Regional/Urban planning. Emeritus Alumni Distinguished Prof. of Planning, Dept. of City and Regional Planning, Univ. of North Carolina, Chapel Hill, since 1978 (Assoc. Prof., 1949–54; Prof., 1954–78). Member, Bistall Columbia River Gorge Commission, since 1987. With Tennessee Valley Authority, 1940–42 and 1945–47; Dir. of Planning, City of Greensboro, N.C., 1947–49; Member, Cttee. on Urban Economics, Resources for the Future Inc., 1964–69; Member, President Johnson's Task Force on Cities, 1966–67; Member, Dept. of Urban Transportation, Highway Research Bd., National

Academy of Sciences, 1964–67; Member, State of Washington Columbia River Gorge Commission, 1985–87. *Publs:* Communications for Living, 1941; Urban Land Use Planning, 1957, 1965, 3rd ed. (co-author) 1979; (co-ed. and contrib.) Urban Growth Dynamics, 1962; (co-author) Across the City Line, 1974; Human Activity Patterns in the City, 1974; (contrib.) Human Activity and Time Geography, 1978. Add: 464 5W Eyrie Rd., White Salmon, Wash. 98672, U.S.A.

CHAPLIN, James Patrick. American, b. 1919. Psychology. Prof. Emeritus of Pyschology, and Chmn. of Dept., St. Michael's Coll., Winooski, Vt., since 1984 (Prof., 1970–84). Asst. Prof., 1947–50, Assoc. Prof., 1950–54, and Prof. of Psychology, 1956–69, Univ. of Vermont, Burlington. *Publs:* Rumor, Fear and the Madness of Crowds, 1959; The Unconscious, 1960; (with T.S. Krawiec) Systems and Theories of Pyschology, 1960, 4th ed. 1979; Dictionary of Psychology, 1969, 1985; Dictionary of the Occult and Paranormal, 1976; (with A. Demers) Primer of Neurology and Neurophysiology, 1978. Add: 1741 Spear St., South Burlington, Vt. 05403, U.S.A.

CHAPMAN, (Constance) Elizabeth. British, b. 1919. Children's fiction. *Publs:* Marmaduke the Lorry, 1953; Marmaduke and Joe, 1954; Riding with Marmaduke, 1955; Adventures with Marmaduke, 1956; Merry Marmaduke, 1957; Marmaduke and His Friends, 1958; Marmaduke and the Elephant, 1959; Marmaduke and the Lambs, 1960; Marmaduke Goes to France, 1962 ; Marmaduke Goes to Holland, 1963; Marmaduke Goes to America, 1965; Marmaduke Goes to Italy, 1970; Marmaduke and Joes, 1973; Marmaduke Goes to Switzerland, 1977; Marmaduke Goes to Spain, 1978; Marmaduke Goes to Morocco, 1979; Marmaduke Goes to Wales, 1982; Marmaduke Goes to Scotland, 1986; Marmaduke Goes to Ireland, 1987. Add: 88 Grange Gardens, Pinner, Middx., England.

CHAPMAN, J. Dudley. American, b. 1928. Psychology, Sex. Gynecologist, sex researcher, and writer. Ed.-in-Chief, Osteopathic Physician, since 1968; Clinical Prof., Ohio Univ. College of Osteopathic Medicine; Faculty and member of Academic Board, The Institute for the Advanced Study of Human Sexuality, San Francisco, since 1979; Member of Executive Council, The Academy of Psychosomatic Medicine, since 1983; Editorial Consultant, Penthouse FORUM, The J. Am. Osteopathic Assn. and others. Assoc. Prof. of Obstetrics and Gynecology, Coll. of Osteopathic Medicine and Surgery, Des Moines, Iowa, 1955–58; Pres., American Coll. of Osteopathic Obstetricians and Gynecologists, 1966–67; Former member, Editorial Consulting Bd., Inst. of Comprehensive Medicine, and Chronic Disease Mgmt. and Modern Medicine. *Publs:* The Feminine Mind and Body, 1967; The Sexual Equation, 1977. Add: P.O. Box 340, North Madison, Ohio 44057, U.S.A.

CHAPMAN, Lee. *See* **BRADLEY,** Marion Zimmer.

CHAPMAN, Robert (DeWitt). American, b. 1937. Astronomy. Sr. Policy Analyst, Office of Science and Technology Policy, Exec. Office of the President, Washington, D.C., since 1986. Asst. Prof. of Astronomy, Univ. of California at Los Angeles, 1964–67; joined NASA-Goddard Spaceflight Center, Greenbelt, Md., 1967: Assoc. Chief, Lab. for Astronomy and Solar Physics, 1978–86. Secty., Solar Physics Div., American Astronomical Soc., 1979–82. *Publs:* Comet Kohoutek 1973-74, 1973; Discovering Astronomy, (co-author) Introduction to Comets, 1980; Crimson Web of Terror, 1980; (with John C. Brandt) The Comet Book, 1984. Add: 10976 Swansfield Rd., Columbia, Md. 21044, U.S.A.

CHAPMAN, Ronald (George). British, b. 1917. Novels/Short stories, Poetry, Biography. Asst. Librarian, Bodleian Library, Oxford, 1941–72; Ed., Oxoniensia, 1960–64. *Publs:* The Laurel and the Thorn: A Study of G.F. Watts, 1945; Father Faber, 1961; The Education of Davey Porteous, 1968; (co-author) The Thought of George Tyrrell, 1970; This Is My Winter, 1973. Add: 25 Red Lion St., Aylsham, Norfolk, England.

CHAPMAN, Samuel Greeley. American, b. 1929. Criminology/Law enforcement/Prisons. Prof. of Political Science, Univ. of Oklahoma, Norman, since 1967. Member, Norman City Council, 1972–76; and since 1977 (Vice-Mayor, 1976, 1978, 1982–84). Patrolman, Dept. of Police, Berkeley, Calif., 1951–56; Police Consultant, Public Admin. Service, Chicago, 1956–59; Asst. Prof., Sch. of Police Admin. Michigan State Univ., East Lansing, 1959–63; Police Chief, Multnomah County Sheriff's Police Dept., Portland Ore., 1963–65; Asst. Dir., President's Commn. on Law Enforcement and Admin. of Justice, Washington, D.C., 1965–67. *Publs:* Dogs in Police Work, 1960; (with E. St. Johnston) The Police Heritage in England and America, 1962; Police Patrol Readings, 1964, rev. ed. 1970; (with D. Clark) Educational Backgrounds for Police, 1966; Perspectives on Police Assaults in the South Central United States, 1974;

(with G. Eastman) Short of Merger: Countywide Police Resource Pooling, 1976; Police Murders and Effective Countermeasures, 1976; Police Dogs in America, 1979; Cops, Killers, and Staying Alive, 1986. Add: Dept. of Political Science, Univ. of Oklahoma, Norman, Okla. 73019, U.S.A.

CHAPMAN, Stanley David. British, b. 1935. Business/Trade/-Industry, Economics. Pasold Reader in Business History, Univ. of Nottingham, since 1973 (Lectr., 1968–73); Ed., Textile History bi-annual *Publs:* The Early Factory Masters, 1967; (co-author) The Beginnings of Industrial Britain, 1970; (ed.) The History of Working Class Housing, 1971; The Cotton Industry in the Industrial Revolution, 1972, 1987; Jesse Boot of Boot's the Chemists, 1974; The Devon Cloth Industry in the Eighteenth Century, 1978; Stanton and Staveley: A Business History, 1981; (co-author) European Textile Printers in the 18th Century, 1981; The Rise of Merchant Banking, 1984. Add: 35 Park Lane, Sutton Bonington, Loughborough, Leics. LE12 5NQ, England.

CHAPMAN, Walter. *See* **SILVERBERG,** Robert.

CHAPMAN-MORTIMER, William Charles. Writes as Chapman Mortimer; has also written as Charles Mortimer. British, b. 1907. Novels/Short stories, Plays/Screenplays. *Publs:* (as Charles Mortimer) Some Queer Animals and Why, 1947; A Stranger on the Stair, 1950; Father Goose, 1951; Young Men Waiting, 1952; Mediterraneo, 1955; Here in Spain (biography), 1955; Madrigal, 1960; (with G. Hill) Reflections in a Golden Eye (screenplay), 1966; Amparo, 1971. Add: Asenvagen 12, Jonkoping 55258, Sweden.

CHAPPELL, Mollie. British. Historical/Romance/Gothic, Children's fiction. *Publs:* juvenile—Little Tom Sparrow, 1950; Tusker Tales, 1950; Rhodesian Adventure, 1950; The Gentle Giant, 1951; The House on the Kopje, 1951; The Sugar and Spice, 1952; St. Simon Square, 1952; The Fortunes of Frick, 1953; Cat with No Fiddle, 1954; The Mystery of the Silver Circle, 1955; Kit and the Mystery Man, 1955; romance—The Widow Jones, 1956; Endearing Young Charms, 1957; Bachelor Heaven, 1958; A Wreath of Holly, 1959; One Little Room, 1960; A Lesson in Loving, 1961; The Measure of Love, 1961; Caroline, 1962; Come by Chance, 1963; The Garden Room, 1964; The Ladies of Lark, 1965; Bright Promise, 1966; Bid Me Live, 1967; Since Summer, 1967; The Wind in the Green Trees, 1969; The Hasting Day, 1970; Summer Story, 1972; Valley of Lilacs, 1972; Family Portrait, 1973; Cressy, 1973; Five Farthings, 1974; A Letter from Lydia, 1974; Seton's Wife, 1975; In Search of Mr. Rochester, 1976; Loving Heart, 1977; Country Air, 1977; The Romantic Widow, 1978; Wintersweet, 1978; Serena, 1980; Dearest Neighbour, 1981; Cousin Amelia, 1982; Springtime for Sophie, 1983; The Yellow Straw Hat, 1983; Stepping Stones, 1985; The Family at Redburn, 1985. Add: c/o Curtis Brown Ltd., 162-168 Regent St., London W1R 5TB, England.

CHAPPLE, John Alfred Victor. British, b. 1928. History, Literature. Prof. of English, Hull Univ., since 1971. Asst. Univ. Coll., London, 1953–55; Research Asst., Yale Univ., New Haven, Conn., 1955–58; Asst. Lectr., Aberdeen Univ., 1958–59; Asst. Lectr., 1959–61, Lectr., 1961–67, and Sr. Lectr., 1967–71, Manchester Univ. *Publs:* (ed. with A. Pollard) The Letters of Mrs. Gaskell, 1966; Documentary and Imaginative Literature 1880-1920, 1970; Dryden's Earl of Shaftesbury, 1973; (with J.G. Sharps) Elizabeth Gaskell: A Portrait in Letters, 1980; Science and Literature in the Nineteenth Century, 1986. Add: 173 Newland Park, Hull, Yorks., England.

CHARBONNEAU, Louis (Henry). Also writes western adventure as Carter Travis Young. American, b. 1924. Mystery/Crime/Suspense, Westerns/Adventure, Science fiction/Fantasy. Instr. in English, Univ. of Detroit, 1948–52; Copywriter, Mercury Advertising Agency, Los Angeles, 1952–56; Staff Writer, Los Angeles Times, 1956–71; freelance writer, 1971–74; Ed. Security World Publishing Co., Los Angeles, 1974–79. *Publs:* No Place on Earth (science fiction), 1958; Night of Violence, 1959, in U.K. as The Time of Desire, 1960; Corpus Earthling (science fiction), 1960; (as Carter Travis Young) The Wild Breed (in U.K. as The Sudden Gun), 1960; (as Carter Travis Young) The Savage Plain, 1961; (as Carter Travis Young) Shadow of a Gun, 1962; The Sentinel Stars (science fiction), 1964; (as Carter Travis Young) The Bitter Iron, 1964; (as Carter Travis Young) Long Boots, Hard Boots, 1965; Psychedelic-40 (science fiction), 1965, in U.K. as the Specials, 1967; (as Carter Travis Young) Why Did They Kill Charley?, 1967; The Sensitives (science fiction), 1968; Down from the Mountain, 1969; And Hope to Die, 1970; (as Carter Travis Young) Winchester Quarantine, 1970; Barrier World (science fiction), 1970; (as Carter Travis Young) The Pocket Hunters, 1972; (as Carter Travis Young) Winter of the Coup, 1972; (as Carter Travis Young) The

Captive, 1973; (as Carter Travis Young) Guns of Darkness, 1974; (as Carter Travis Young) Blaine's Law, 1974; From a Dark Place, 1974; Embryo (novelization of S.F. screenplay), 1976; (as Carter Travis Young) Red Grass, 1976; Intruder, 1979; The Lair, 1979; (as Carter Travis Young) Winter Drift, 1980; The Brea File, 1983. Add: c/o Scott Meredith Lietrary Agency, 845 Third Ave., New York, N.Y. 10022, U.S.A.

CHARD, Judy (née Gordon). Also writes as Lyndon Chase. British, b. 1916. Romance/Historical fiction, Travel. Dir. of Studies, David and Charles Writing Coll., Newton Abbot, since 1989. Ed. Devon Life, Exeter, 1979–82. MIPubls: novels—Through the Green Woods, 1974; The Weeping and the Laughter, 1975; Encounter in Berlin, 1976; The Uncertain Heart, 1976; The Other Side of Sorrow, 1977; In the Heart of Love, 1978; Out of the Shadows, 1978; All Passion Spent, 1979; Seven Lonely Years, 1980; The Darkening Skies, 1981; When the Journey's Over, 1981; Haunted by the Past, 1982; Sweet Love Remembered, 1982; Where the Dream Begins, 1982; Rendezvous with Love, 1983; Hold Me in Your Heart, 1983; (as Lyndon Chase) Tormentil, 1984; To Live with Fear, 1985; Wings of the Morning, 1985; A Time to Love, 1987; Wild Justice, 1987; For Love's Sake Only, 1988; Person Unknown, 1988; To Be So loved, 1988; Enchantment, 1989; other—Along the Dart, 1979; About Widecombe, 1979; Devon Mysteries, 1979; The South Hams, 1980; Along the Teign, 1981; Tales of the Unexplained in Devon, 1986. Add: Morley farm, Morley Rd., Highweek, Newton Abbot, Devon TQ12 6NA, England.

CHARLES, Anita. *See* **BARRIE,** Susan.

CHARLES, Gerda. British. Novels/Short stories

CHARLES, Henry. *See* **HARRIS,** Marion Rose.

CHARLES, Nicholas. *See* **KUSKIN<D** Karia.

CHARLES, Theresa. Joint pseud. for Irene Maude (Mossop) Swatridge and her deceased husband, Charles Swatridge. Other joint pseuds.: Fay Chandos, Leslie Lance, Les Lincoln, Virginia Storm, and Jan Tempest (after 1965, publs. under these names solely written by Irene Swatridge). Prior to marriage, Irene Swatridge wrote children's fiction under maiden name, Irene Mossop. British. Mystery/Crime/Suspense, Historical/Romance/Gothic, Children's fiction. *Publs:* children's fiction as Irene Mossop—Well Played, Juliana!, 1928; Prunella Plays the Game, 1929; Freesia's Feud, 1930; The Luck of the Oakleighs, 1930; Chris in Command, 1930; Sylvia Sways the School, 1930; Theresa's First Term, 1930; Vivien of St. Val's, 1931; Charm's Last Chance, 1931; Nicky—New Girl, 1931; Rona's Rival, 1931; A Rebel at "Rowans," 1932; Barbara Black-Sheep, 1932; Una Wins Through, 1932; Feud in the Fifth, 1933; Hilary Leads the Way, 1933; The Taming of Pickles, 1933; The Fifth at Cliff House, 1934; The Four V's, 1934; The Fourth at St. Faith's, 1934; Play Up, Pine House!, 1934; Theresa on Trial, 1935; Theda Marsh, 1935; The Gay Adventure, 1937; romance and mystery novels—(as Jan Tempest) Step-mother of Five, 1936; (as Jan Tempest) Someone New to Love, 1936; (as Jan Tempest) Be Still, My Heart!, 1936; (as Jan Tempest) Kiss—and Forget, 1936; (as Jan Tempest) Believe Me, Beloved—, 1936; (as Jan Tempest) All This I Gave, 1937; (as Jan Tempest) If I Love Again, 1937; (as Jan Tempest) No Other Man—, 1937; (as Jan Tempest) Grow Up, Little Lady!, 1937; (as Jan Tempest) Carey, Come Back!, 1937; (as Fay Chandos) No Limit to Love, 1937; (as Fay Chandos) No Escape from Love, 1937; (as Fay Chandos) Man of My Dreams, 1937; (as Jan Tempest) Face the Music—for Love, 1938; (as Jan Tempest) Man—and Waif, 1938; (as Jan Tempest) Because My Love Is Come, 1938, 1958; (as Jan Tempest) When First I Loved . . ., 1938; (as Jan Tempest) Hilary in His Heart, 1938; (as Fay Chandos) Before I Make You Mine, 1938; (as Fay Chandos) Wife for a Wager, 1938; (as Fay Chandos) Gay Knight I Love, 1938; (as Jan Tempest) Say You're Sorry, 1939; (as Jan Tempest) My Only Love, 1939; (as Jan Tempest) Uninvited Guest, 1939; (as Jan Tempest) I'll Try Anything Once, 1939; (as Fay Chandos) All I Ask, 1939; (as Fay Chandos) When Three Walk Together, 1939; (as Fay Chandos) Another Woman's Shoes, 1939; (as Fay Chandos) The Man Who Wasn't Mac, 1939; (as Jan Tempest) Top of the Beanstalk, 1940; (as Jan Tempest) The Broken Gate, 1940; (as Jan Tempest) Why Wouldn't He Wait, 1940; (as Jan Tempest) Little Brown Girl, 1940; (as Fay Chandos) Husband for Hire, 1940; (as Fay Chandos) You Should Have Warned Me, 1940; (as Fay Chandos) When We Two Parted, 1940; (as Fay Chandos) Substitute for Sherry, 1940; The Distant Drum, 1940; (as Leslie Lance) Alice, Where Are You?, 1940; (as Leslie Lance) Take a Chance, 1940; My Enemy and I, 1941; (as Jan Tempest) Always Another Man, 1941; (as Jan Tempest) The Moment I Saw You, 1941;

(as Jan Tempest) The Unknown Joy, 1941; (as Jan Tempest) Ghost of June, 1941; (as Fay Chandos) Women Are So Simple, 1941; (as Fay Chandos) Only a Touch, 1941; (as Jan Tempest) No Time for a Man, 1942; (as Jan Tempest) Romance on Ice, 1942; (as Jan Tempest) If You'll Marry Me, 1942; (as Fay Chandos) Awake, My Love, 1942; (as Fay Chandos) A Letter to My Love, 1942; (as Jan Tempest) A Prince for Portia, 1943; (as Jan Tempest) Wife after Work, 1943; (as Jan Tempest) The Long Way Home, 1943; (as Fay Chandos) Eve and I, 1943; (as Fay Chandos) A Man to Follow, 1943; (as Jan Tempest) "Never Again!" Said Nicola, 1944; (as Jan Tempest) The One Thing I Wanted, 1944; (as Jan Tempest) Utility Husband, 1944; (as Jan Tempest) Westward to My Love, 1944; (as Jan Tempest) Love While You Wait, 1944; (as Fay Chandos) Away from Each Other, 1944; (as Fay Chandos) Just a Little Longer, 1944; (as Jan Tempest) Not for This Alone, 1945; (as Jan Tempest) To Be a Bride, 1945; (as Fay Chandos) Last Year's Roses, 1945; (as Fay Chandos) A Man for Margaret, 1945; (as Fay Chandos) Three Roads to Romance, 1945; To Save My Life, 1946; (as Jan Tempest) The Orange Blossom Shop, 1946; (as Jan Tempest) Happy with Either, 1946; (as Jan Tempest) House of the Pines, 1946, 2nd U.S. ed. as House of Pines, 1975; (as Jan Tempest) Bachelor's Bride, 1946; (as Jan Tempest) Lovely, Though Late, 1946; (as Fay Chandos) When Time Stands Still, 1946; (as Fay Chandos) Home Is the Hero, 1946; (as Leslie Lance) The Dark Stranger, 1946; Happy Now I Go, 1947, in U.S. as Dark Legacy, 1968; (as Jan Tempest) Close Your Eyes, 1947; (as Jan Tempest) Teach Me to Love, 1947; (as Fay Chandos) Because I Wear Your Ring, 1947; (as Fay Chandos) Cousins May Kiss, 1947; (as Jan Tempest) How Can I Forget?, 1948, in U.S. as Virginia Storm) First I Must Forget, 1951; (as Jan Tempest) Cinderella Had Two Sisters, 1948, in U.S. (as Virginia Storm), 1950; (as Fay Chandos) Lost Summer, 1948; (as Fay Chandos) Since First We Met, 1948; Man-Made Miracle, 1949; (as Jan Tempest) Short-Cut to the Stars, 1949; (as Jan Tempest) Never Another Love, 1949; (as Jan Tempest) Promise of Paradise, 1949; (as Fay Chandos) June in Her Eyes, 1949; (as Fay Chandos) For a Dream's Sake, 1949; (as Virginia Storm) The Ugly Prince, 1950; (as Jan Tempest) Nobody Else—Ever, 1950; (as Jan Tempest) Match Is Made, 1950; (as Jan Tempest) Now and Always, 1950; (as Jan Tempest) Until I Find Her, 1950; (as Fay Chandos) Fugitive from Love, 1950; (as Fay Chandos) There Is a Tide . . ., 1950; (as Jan Tempest) Two Loves for Tamara, 1951; (as Fay Chandos) This Time It's Love, 1951; At a Touch I Yield, 1952; (as Jan Tempest) Open the Door to Love, 1952; (as Jan Tempest) Without a Honeymoon, 1952; (as Jan Tempest) Happy Is the Wooing, 1952; (as Fay Chandos) First and Favourite Wife, 1952; (as Fay Chandos) Families Are Such Fun, 1952; (as Leslie Lance) Man of the Family, 1952; Fairer Than She, 1953; (as Jan Tempest) Meet Me by Moonlight, 1953; (as Jan Tempest) Give Her Gardenias, 1953; (as Fay Chandos) Leave It to Nancy, 1953; (as Fay Chandos) The Other One, 1953; (as Fay Chandos) Find Another Eden, 1953; (as Jan Tempest) Enchanted Valley, 1954; (as Jan Tempest) First-Time of Asking, 1954; (as Fay Chandos) Just Before the Wedding, 1954; (as Fay Chandos) Doctors Are Different, 1954; The Kinder Love, 1955; (as Jan Tempest) Ask Me Again, 1955; (as Jan Tempest) Where the Heart Is, 1955; (as Fay Chandos) Husbands at Home, 1955; (as Fay Chandos) Hibiscus House, 1955, in Can. as Nurse Incognito, 1964; The Burning Beacon, 1956; (as Jan Tempest) For Those in Love, 1956; (as Jan Tempest) Wedding Bells for Willow, 1956; (as Fay Chandos) So Nearly Married, 1956; (as Jan Tempest) Craddock's Kingdom, 1957; (as Jan Tempest) . . . Will Not Now Take Place, 1957; (as Fay Chandos) The Romantic Touch, 1957; (as Fay Chandos) Partners are a Problem, 1957; The Ultimate Surrender, 1958; (as Jan Tempest) The Younger Sister, 1958; (as Jan Tempest) Because There Is Hope, 1958; (as Fay Chandos) Model Girl's Farm, 1958; A Girl Called Evelyn, 1959; (as Jan Tempest) Romance for Rose, 1959; (as Fay Chandos) Nan—and the New Owner, 1959; (as Fay Chandos) Wild Violets, 1959; No Through Road, 1960; (as Jan Tempest) Stranger to Love, 1960; (as Leslie Lance) Spun by the Moon, 1960; (as Leslie Lance) Sisters in Love, 1960; (as Jan Tempest) Mistress of Castlemount, 1961; (as Jan Tempest) The Turning Point, 1961; (as Fay Chandos) When Four Ways Meet, 1961; (as Leslie Lance) A Summer's Grace, 1961; House on the Rocks, 1962; (as Fay Chandos) Sister Sylvan, 1962; (as Leslie Lance) Springtime for Sally, 1962; Widower's Wife, 1963, in U.S. as Return to Terror, 1966; Patient in Love, 1963; (as Jan Tempest) That Nice Nurse Nevin, 1963; (as Jan Tempest) The Madderleys Married, 1963; (as Leslie Lance) Spreading Sails, 1963; Nurse Alice in Love, 1964, in U.S. as Lady in the Mist, 1966; (as Jan Tempest) The Flower and the Fruit, 1964; (as Fay Chandos) Two Other People, 1964; (as Leslie Lance) The Young Curmudgeon, 1964; (as Les Lincoln) Une Curieuse Chasse aux Papillons, 1964; (as Les Lincoln) Le Talon a Aiguille, 1965; The Man for Me, 1965, in U.S. as The Shrouded Tower, 1966; (as Jan Tempest)

Nurse Willow's Ward, 1965; (as Jan Tempest) The Way We Used to Be, 1965; (as Leslie Lance) I'll Ride Beside You, 1965; (as Leslie Lance) Bright Winter, 1965; How Much You Mean to Me, 1966; (as Jan Tempest) Jubilee Hospital, 1966; (as Jan Tempest) The Lonesome Road, 1966; (as Fay Chandos) Don't Give Your Heart Away, 1966; (as Fay Chandos) Stranger in Love, 1966; Proud Citadel, 1967; The Way Men Love, 1967; (as Jan Tempest) Meant to Meet, 1967; (as Fay Chandos) Farm by the Sea, 1967; (as Leslie Lance) No Summer Beauty, 1967; (as Leslie Lance) Return to King's Mere, 1967; (as Leslie Lance) Bride of Emersham, 1967; The Shadowy Third, 1968; From Fairest Flowers, 1968; (as Jan Tempest) Lyra, My Love, 1969; (as Leslie Lance) Nurse in the Woods, 1969; (as Leslie Lance) The Summer People, 1969; Wayward as the Swallow, 1970; Second Honeymoon, 1970; (as Fay Chandos) The Three of Us, 1970; (as Leslie Lance) Nurse Verena at Weirwater, 1970; My True Love, 1971; (as Leslie Lance) No Laggard in Love, 1971; Therefore Must Be Loved, 1972; (as Fay Chandos) Sweet Rosemary, 1972; Castle Kelpiesloch, 1973; (as Leslie Lance) The New Lord Whinbridge, 1973; (as Leslie Lance) Now I Can Forget, 1973; Nurse by Accident, 1974; (as Leslie Lance) The Love That Lasts, 1974; The Flower and the Nettle, 1975; Trust Me, My Love, 1975; (as Leslie Lance) The Maverton Heiress, 1975; One Who Remembers, 1976; (as Leslie Lance) The Return of the Cuckoo, 1976; (as Leslie Lance) Romance at Wrecker's End, 1976; (as Leslie Lance) Island House, 1976; Rainbow After Rain, 1977; Crisis at St. Chad's, 1977; (as Leslie Lance) Cousins by Courtesy, 1977; Just for One Weekend, 1978; (as Leslie Lance) The Family at the Farm, 1978; (as Leslie Lance) Orchid Girl, 1978; Surgeon's Reputation, 1979; (as Leslie Lance) The Girl in the Mauve Mini, 1979; (as Leslie Lance) The Rose Princess, 1979; (as Leslie Lance) Doctor in the Snow, 1980; (as Leslie Lance) The House in the Woods, 1980; With Somebody Else, 1981; Surgeon's Sweetheart, 1981; (as Leslie Lance) Hawk's Head, 1981; (as Leslie Lance) Someone Who Cares, 1982; (as Leslie Lance) Dear Patience, 1983; No Easier Road to Love, 1983; Always in My Heart, 1985; Dr. Angel, 1985; Looking for Love, 1986; (as Leslie Lance) Heiress to the Isle, 1987. Add: Middlecombe, Beeson, Kingsbridge, Devon TQ7 2EW, England.

CHARLESTON, Robert Jesse. British, b. 1916. Antiques, Crafts. Asst., 1948–59, Deputy, 1959–63, and Keeper, 1963–76, Dept. of Ceramics, Victoria and Albert Museum, London. *Publs:* Roman Pottery, 1955; (ed. and co-author) English Porcelain 1745-1850, 1965; (ed. and co-author) World Ceramics, 1968; (with J.G. Ayers) The James A. de Rothschild Collection . . . Meissen and other European Porcelain: Oriental Porcelain, 1971; (with D.M. Archer and M. Marcheix) Glass, Stained Glass and Painted Enamels, 1978; Islamic Pottery, 1979; Masterpieces of Glass, 1980; English Glass, 1984. Add: Whittington Court, Whittington, Glos., England.

CHARLIER, Roger Henri. Also writes as Henri Rochard. American, b. 1921. Novels/Short stories, Poetry, Earth sciences. Prof. Emeritus of Geology, Geography and Oceanography, Northeastern Illinois Univ., Chicago, since 1961 (Dir., Bureau of Educational Travel, 1961–64; Coordinator, Earth Science Area, 1961–65; Research Scholar in Oceanography, 1962–64; Dir., Oceanography Prog., 1966–71; Vice-Chmn., Dept. of Geography, 1962–70); Prof. Emeritus in the Extraordinary, Univ. of Brussels, Belgium, since 1970; Visiting Prof., Univ. of Maryland (European Div.), since 1976. *Publs:* Analyse-mathématique, 1941; (as Henri Rochard) I Was a Male War Bride (novel), 1950; The Gifted: A National Resource, 1960; Introductory Earth Science, 1961; (as Henri Rochard) For the Love of Kate (novel), 1963; (as Henri Rochard) Pensées (poetry), 1964; The Physical Environment, 1966; Harnessing the Energies of the Ocean, 1970; The World Around Us, 1971; The Study of Rocks, 1971; The Study of Oceans, 1971; Ocean Resources, 1976, 1978; Marine Science and Technology, 1980; Our Physical Environment, 1980; Marine Geology, 1980; Tidal Energy, 1982; Handbook of Ocean Energies, 1987; Economic Oceanography, 1987; Ocean Energies, 1989. Add: 4055 North Keystone Ave., Chicago, Ill. 60641, U.S.A.

CHARLIP, Remy. American, b. 1929. Novels, Children's fiction. Dir., Intnl. All-Star Dance Co., New York, since 1977. Choreographer, London Contemporary Dance Theatre, 1972–76; Choreographer, Scottish Theatre Ballet, 1973, and Welsh Dance Theatre, 1974. *Publs:* Dress Up and Let's Have a Party, 1956; Where Is Everybody?, 1957; It Looks Like Snow, 1962, 1982; Fortunately, 1964; (with Burton Supree) Mother Mother I Feel Sick Send for the Doctor Quick Quick Quick, 1966; I Love You, 1967, 1981; Arm in Arm, 1973; (with Burton Supree) Harlequin and the Gift of Many Colors, 1973; (with Judith Martin) The Tree Angel; (with Judith Martin) Jumping Beans; (with Mary Beth) Handtalk: An ABC of Finger Spelling and Sign Language, 1974; (with Jenny Joyner) Thirteen, 1975; Hooray for Me, 1975; Arm in Arm, 1980; I Love You, 1981; It Looks Like Snow, 1982; First Remy Charlip Reader, 1986; (with Mary Beth) Handtalk Birthday: A Number and Storybook in Sign Language, 1987. Add: 60 E. 7th St., New York, N.Y. 10003, U.S.A.

CHARLTON, Bobby. British, b. 1937. Sports/Physical education/Keeping fit. Chmn., North West Council for Sport and Recreation, since 1982; Dir., Manchester United Football Club, since 1984. Professional Footballer with Manchester United, 1954–73; Mgr., Preston North End Football Club, 1973–75. Recipient: Footballers Assn. Championship Medals, 1956–57, 1964–65 and 1966–67; Footballers Assn. Cup Winners Medal, 1963; World Cup Winners Medal (Intnl.), 1966; European Cup Winners Medal, 1968; 100th England Cap, 1970. *Publs:* My Soccer Life, 1965; Forward for England, 1967; The Game of Soccer, 1967; Book of European Football, vols. 1-4, 1969–72. Add: Garthollerton, Chelford Rd., Ollerton, nr. Knutsford, Cheshire, England.

CHARLTON, John. *See* **WOODHOUSE,** Martin.

CHARLTON, Thomas Malcolm. British, b. 1923. Engineering. Emeritus Prof., Univ. of Aberdeen, since 1979 (Jackson Prof. of Engineering, 1970–79); Visiting Prof. of Civil Engineering, Univ. of Newcastle upon Tyne, since 1982. Jr. Scientific Officer, Ministry of Aircraft Production, 1943–46; Asst. Engineer, Merz and McLellan, Newcastle upon Tyne, 1946–54; Univ. Lectr. in Engineering, 1954–63, and Fellow of Sidney Sussex Coll., 1959–63, Cambridge Univ.; Prof. of Civil Engineering, Queen's Univ. of Belfast, 1963–70. *Publs:* Model Analysis of Structures, 1954, 1966; (with others) Hydroelectric Engineering Practice, 1957; Energy Principles in Applied Statics, 1959; Analysis of Statically-Indeterminate Frameworks, 1961; Principles of Structural Analysis, 1969, 1977; Energy Principles in the Theory of Structures, 1973; (with others) The Works of I.K. Brunel, 1976; History of Theory of Structures in the Nineteenth Century, 1982; (with others) Encyclopaedia of Building Technology, 1988. Add: 8 Lambourn Close, Trumpington, Cambridge CB2 2JX, England.

CHARLWOOD, D(onald) E(rnest Cameron). Australian, b. 1915. Novels/Short stories, History, Autobiography/Memoirs/Personal. Sr. Supvr., Air Traffic Control, Dept. of Aviation, 1945–75, now retired. *Publs:* No Moon Tonight (memoirs), 1956; All the Green Year (novel), 1965; An Afternoon of Time (short stories), 1966; Take-Off to Touchdown, 1967; The Wreck of the Loch Ard, 1971; Wrecks and Reputations, 1978; Settlers under Sail, 1978; Flight and Time (short stories), 1979; The Long Farewell, 1981. Add: Qualicum, Mount View Rd., Templestowe, Vic., Australia 3106.

CHARNAS, Suzy McKee. American, b. 1939. Science fiction/Fantasy. Freelance writer since 1969. Formerly English and history teacher for the Peace Corps in Nigeria; teacher, New Lincoln School, NYC; and worker for Community Mental Health org., NYC. *Publs:* Walk to the End of the World, 1974; Motherlines, 1979; The Vampire Tapestry, 1980; The Bronze King, 1985; Dorothea Dreams, 1986; The Silver Glove, 1988; The Golden Thread (juvenile), 1989. Add: 520 Cedar N.E., Albuquerque, N.M. 87106, U.S.A.

CHARNY, Israel. American, b. 1931. Human relations. Assoc. Prof. of Psychology, Bob Shapell Sch. of Social Work, Tel Aviv Univ., since 1973; Exec. Dir., Inst. of the Intnl. Conference on the Holocaust and Genocide, Jerusalem, since 1979. Dir., Guidance Consultants Psychological Group Practice, Paoli, Pa. 1962–73. *Publs:* Individual and Family Developmental Review, 1964; Marital Love and Hate, 1972; Strategies Against Violence, 1978; How Can We Commit the Unthinkable?, 1982; Toward the Understanding and Prevention of Genocide, 1984; Genocide: A Critical Bibliographical Review, 1988. Add: P.O. Box 10311, Jerusalem 93624, Israel.

CHARTERIS, Leslie. American, b. 1907. Novels/Short stories, Mystery/Crime/Suspense, Plays/Screenplays. Creator of "The Saint." Supervising Ed., The Saint Mag., 1953–67; Roving Corresp., Gourmet Mag., NYC, 1966–68. *Publs:* 20 books in The Saint series before 1939; The First Saint Omnibus, 1939; The Happy Highwayman, 1939; The Saint in Miami, 1940; The Saint Goes West, 1942; The Saint Steps In, 1943; The Saint on Guard, 1944; The Saint Sees It Through, 1946; Call for the Saint, 1948; Saint Errant, 1948; The Second Saint Omnibus, 1951; The Saint in Europe, 1943; The Saint on the Spanish Main, 1955; The Saint Around the World, 1956; Thanks to the Saint, 1957; Senor Saint, 1958; The Saint to the Rescue, 1959; Trust the Saint, 1962; The Saint in the Sun, 1963; Vendetta for the Saint, 1964; Spanish for Fun (linguistics), 1964; The Saint Returns, 1968; The Saint on TV, 1968; The

Saint and the People Importers, 1971; The Saint in Pursuit, 1971; Paleneo (linguistics), 1972; Saints Alive, 1974; Catch the Saint, 1975; The Saint and the Hapsburg Necklace, 1976; Send for the Saint, 1977; The Saint in Trouble, 1978; The Saint and the Templar Treasure, 1978; Count on the Saint, 1980; The Fantastic Saint, 1982; Salvage for the Saint, 1983. Add: c/o Thompson Levett & Co., 3-4 Great Marlborough St., London W1V 2AR, England.

CHARTERS, Ann. American, b. 1936. Literature, Biography. Assoc. Prof., then Prof. of English, Univ. of Connecticut, Storrs. *Publs:* A Bibliography of Jack Kerouac, 1968; Olson/Melville: A Study of Affinity, 1968; (ed.) The Special View of History: Charles Olson at Black Mountain College, 1970; Scenes Along the Road: Photographs of the Desolation Angels, 1970, 1985; Nobody: The Story of Bert Williams, 1970; Kerouac: A Biography, 1973, 1987; (with Samuel Charters) I Love, 1979; (ed.) The Dictionary of Literary Biography: vol. 16: Beat Writers, 1983; (ed.) The Story and Its Writer, 1983, 1986; Beats and Company: Portrait of a Literary Generation, 1986. Add: Dept. of English, Univ. of Connecticut, Storrs, Conn. 06268, U.S.A.

CHARTERS, Samuel. American, b. 1929. Novels/Short stories, Poetry, Music. Producer, Vanguard Recording Soc., NYC, 1965–70 and since 1984. Producer, Sonet Grammofon AB, Stockholm, 1970–84. *Publs:* Jazz: New Orleans, 1958; The Country Blues, 1959; (with Leonard Kunstadt) Jazz: The New York Scene, 1962; Heroes of the Prize Ring (poetry), 1963; The Poetry of the Blues, 1963; The Bluesmen, 1967; Days (poetry), 1967; To This Place (poetry), 1969; Some Poems/Poets (literary criticism), 1971; Sweet as the Showers of Rain (poetry), 1972; From a London Notebook (poetry), 1973; From a Swedish Notebook, 1973; Robert Johnson, 1973; (trans.) Baltics, by Tomas Tranströmer, 1975; The Legacy of the Blues, 1975; In Lagos (poetry), 1976; (trans.) We Women, by Edith Södergran, 1977; Spelmännen, 1979; Of Those Who Died (poetry), 1980; (with Ann Charters) I Love (biography), 1980; The Roots of the Blues, 1981; (trans.) The Courtyard, by Bo Carpelan, 1982; Mr. Jabi and Mr. Smythe (novel), 1983; Jelly Roll Morton's Last Night at the Jungle Inn (novel), 1984; Louisiana Black (novel), 1986. Add: c/o Marion Boyars Publishers, 24 Lacy Rd., London SW15 1NL, England.

CHARYN, Jerome. American, b. 1937. Novels/Short stories, Plays/Screenplays. Founding Ed., The Dutton Review, NYC, 1970. English teacher, High Sch. of Music and Art, and Sch. of Performing Arts, NYC, 1962–64; Asst. Prof. of English, Stanford Univ., Calif., 1965–68; Prof. of English, Herbert Lehman Coll., City Univ. of New York, 1968–80; Lectr. in Creative Writing, Princeton Univ., N.J., 1980–86; Visiting Distinguished Prof. of English, The City College of New York, 1988–89. *Publs:* Once Upon a Droshky, 1964; On the Darkening Green, 1965; The Man Who Grew Younger and Other Stories, 1967; Going to Jerusalem, 1967; American Scrapbook, 1969; (ed.) The Single Voice: An Anthology of Contemporary Fiction, 1969; (ed.) The Troubled Vision, 1970; Eisenhower, My Eisenhower, 1971; The Tar Baby, 1973; Blue Eyes, 1975; The Education of Patrick Silver, 1976; Marilyn the Wild, 1976; The Franklin Scare, 1977; Secret Isaac, 1978; The Seventh Babe, 1979; The Catfish Man, 1980; Darlin' Bill, 1980; Panna Maria, 1982; Pinocchio's Nose, 1983; The Isaac Quartet, 1984; War Cries Over Avenue C, 1985; Metropolis: New York as Myth, Marketplace and Magical Land, 1986; Paradise Man, 1987; The Magician's Wife (illustrated by François Boncq), 1987; Movieland, 1989. Add: 302 W. 12th St., Apt. 10-C, New York, N.Y. 10014, U.S.A.

CHASE, Alston Hurd. American, b. 1906. Classics, Translations. Instr., and Tutor in the Classics, Harvard Univ., Cambridge, Mass., 1928–34; Instr. in Latin and Greek, Phillips Academy, Andover, Mass., 1934–71. *Publs:* (with H. Phillips) A New Introduction to Greek, 1941; (trans. with W.G. Perry) Homer's Iliad, 1950; (with H. Phillips) A New Greek Reader, 1954; A New Introduction to Latin, 1959. Add: P.O. Box 12, Berwick, Me. 03901, U.S.A.

CHASE, Elaine Raco. American, b. 1949. Romance/Historical fiction. Full-time writer. Secty., Narcotic Addiction Control Commn., Albany, N.Y., 1967–68; Audio-Visual Librarian, WGY-WRGB-TV, Schenectady, N.Y., 1968–70; Copywriter, Beckman Advertising, Albany, 1970–71. *Publs:* Rules of the Game, 1980; Tender Yearnings, 1981; A Dream Come True, 1982; Double Occupancy, 1982; Designing Woman, 1982; Calculated Risk, 1983; No Easy Way Out, 1983; Video Vixen, 1983; Best Laid Plans, 1984; Lady Be Bad, 1984; Special Delivery, 1984; Dare the Devil, 1987; Dangerous Places, 1987; Dark Corners, 1988; Rough Edges, 1989. Add: 4451 Majestic Lane, Fairfax, Va. 22030, U.S.A.

CHASE, Lyndon. *See* **CHARD** Judy.

CHASTAIN, Thomas. Has also written as Nick Carter. American. Novels/Short stories, Mystery/Crime/Suspense. Has worked as a newspaper reporter and editor. *Publs:* non-mystery novel—Judgment Day, 1962; mystery novels—Death Stalk, 1971; (as Nick Carter) Assassination Brigade, 1973; Pandora's Box, 1974; 911 (in U.K. as The Christmas Bomber), 1976; Vital Statistics, 1977; High Voltage, 1979; The Diamond Exchange, 1981; Nightscape, 1982; Who Killed the Robins Family? And Where and When and Why and How Did They Die?, 1983; (with Bill Adler) The Revenge of the Robins Family, 1984; (with M. H. Clark) Murder in Manhattan, 1986; (with Bill Adler) The Picture Perfect Murders, 1987; (with Helen Hayes) Where the Truth Lies, 1988; The Case of Too Many Murders, 1989. Add: c/o William Morrow Inc., 105 Madison Ave., New York, N.Y. 10016, U.S.A.

CHATFIELD, E. Charles. American, b. 1934. History, Institutions/Organizations, International relations/Current affairs, Biography. Prof. of History, Wittenberg Univ., Springfield, Ohio, since 1974 (Instr., 1961–65; Asst. Prof., 1965–69; Assoc. Prof., 1969–74). Co-Ed., Peace and Change, 1980–83. Danforth Theological Year, Univ. of Chicago Divinity Sch., Ill., 1965–66. *Publs:* For Peace and Justice: Pacifism in America, 1914-1941, 1971; (ed.) Peace Movements in America, 1973; (co-ed. and contrib.) The Garland Library of War and Peace, 1974; The Radical "No": The Correspondence and Writings of Evan Thomas on War, 1974; International War Resistance Through 1945, 1975; The Life and Writings of Devere Allen, 1976; The Americanization of Gandhi: Images of the Mahatma, 1977; (with C. De Benedetti) Kirby Page and the Social Gospel, 1977; (co-ed.) Peace Movements and Political Cultures, 1988. Add: Dept. of History, Wittenberg Univ., Springfield, Ohio 45501, U.S.A.

CHATHAM, Larry. *See* BINGLEY, David Ernest.

CHATMAN, Seymour. American, b. 1928. Film, Literature. Prof. of Rhetoric, Univ. of California, Berkeley, since 1961. Asst. Prof. of English, Univ. of Pennsylvania, Philadelphia, 1956–60. *Publs:* A Theory of Meter, 1965; (ed. with S.R. Levin) Essays on the Language of Literature, 1967; (ed. and trans.) Literary Style: A Symposium, 1971; Later Style of Henry James, 1972; (ed.) Approaches to Poetics: English Institute Essays, 1973; Story and Discourse: Narrative Structure in Fiction and Film, 1978; (co-ed.) A Semiotic Landscape, 1979; Antonioni, or the Surface of the World, 1985. Add: Dept. of Rhetoric, Univ. of California, Berkeley, Calif. 94720, U.S.A.

CHAZANOF, William. American, b. 1915. Business/Trade/Industry, History. Prof. of History, State Univ. Coll. at Fredonia, N.Y. (joined faculty as Instr., 1948). *Publs:* Joseph Ellicott and the Holland Land Company, 1970; Welch's Grape Juice: From Corporation to Co-operative, 1977. Add: State Univ. Coll. at Fredonia, State Univ. of New York, Fredonia, N.Y. 14063, U.S.A.

CHEAVENS, Frank. American, b. 1905. Novels/Short stories, Poetry, Human relations. Prof., Dept. of Psychology, Univ. of Texas, Arlington, 1961–85, now Emeritus (Asst. Prof., 1957–59; Assoc. Prof., 1959–61). Psychologist, Austin State Sch., Tex., 1946–51; Counselor in public schs., Austin, Tex., 1951–54; Psychologist, Austin Child Guidance Clinic, Tex., 1954–57. *Publs:* Arrow Lie Still (novel), 1950; Leading Group Discussion, 1958; Developing Discussion Leaders in Brief Work Shops, 1963; How to Stop Feeling Blue, 1971; Creative Parenthood, 1972; They Were Better Parents After Group Discussion, 1974; Dandelion and Devil Horse (poetry), 1975; Child of the Sun, 1985. Add: 400 Jackson St., Diboll, Tex. 75941, U.S.A.

CHEEVER, Susan. American, b. 1943. Novels/Short stories, Biography. Teacher, Colorado Rocky Mountain School, Carbondale, Colo., 1965–67, The Scarborough Sch., Scarborough, N.Y., 1968–69; Reporter, Tarrytown Daily News, Tarrytown, N.Y., 1970–72, and Westchester Rockland Newspapers, White Plains, N.Y., 1972; General Ed. and Writer, Newsweek mag., NYC, 1974–79. *Publs:* Looking for Work (novel), 1980; A Handsome Man (novel), 1981; The Cage (novel), 1982; Home Before Dark: A Biographical Memoir of John Cheever, 1984; Doctors and Women (novel), 1987. Add: c/o Literistic, 264 Fifth Ave., New York, N.Y. 10001, U.S.A.

CHELF, Carl P. American, b. 1937. Politics/Government. Dean Public Service and Continuing Education, Western Kentucky Univ., since 1974 (Asst. Prof. of Government, 1964–68; Staff Asst. to Vice Pres., 1968–69; Asst. Dean of Faculties, 1970–71; Asst. Dean of Instruction, 1971–72; Assoc. Dean of Instruction, 1972–73). Congressional Fellow, American Political Science Assn., 1962–63; Academic Admin. Intern and Fellow, American Council on Education, 1969–70. *Publs:* (co-author)

100 Questions about a Constitutional Convention, 1960; (co-author) Planning and Zoning Law in Kentucky, 1961; A Manual for Members of the Kentucky General Assembly, 1973; (co-author) Political Parties in the United States: A Systems Analysis, 1974; Congress in the American System, 1977; Challenges and Decisions: The National Policymaking Process, 1980; Public Policymaking in America: Difficult Choices, Limited Options, 1981. Add: 498 Lansdale Ave., Bowling Green, Ky. 42100, U.S.A.

CHELTON, John. *See* DURST, Paul.

CHEN, Anthony. American, b. 1929. Children's fiction. Freelance artist and writer. Art Dir., Newsweek mag., 1960–71; Instr., Nassau Community Coll., 1972–74. *Publs:* Run, Zebra, Run, 1972; Little Koala, 1979; Family ABC Book, 1986. Add: 53-31 96th St., Corona, N.Y. 11368, U.S.A.

CHEN, Joseph T. American, b. 1925. History. Prof. of History, California State Univ., Northridge, since 1971 (Asst. Prof., 1964–68; Assoc. Prof., 1968–71). Head Librarian, Center for Chinese Studies, Univ. of California, Berkeley, 1963–64; Guest Lectr., Univ. of California, Santa Barbara, 1970–73. *Publs:* The May Fourth Movement in Shanghai, 1971; trans. into Chinese, 1981. Add: Dept. of History, California State Univ., Northridge, Calif. 91330, U.S.A.

CHENERY, Hollis (Burnley). American, b. 1918. Economics. Prof. of Economics, Harvard Univ., Cambridge. Mass. Formerly, Asst. Admin., U.S. AID, Washington, and Vice Pres., Development Policy, Intnl. Bank for Reconstruction and Development, Washington, D.C. *Publs:* (with P. Clark) Interindustry Economics, 1959; (ed.) Studies in Development Planning, 1971; Redistribution with Growth, 1974; (co-author) Patterns of Development 1950-1970, 1975; Structural Change and Development Policy, 1979; (co-author) Industrialization and Growth, 1986. Add: 5 Hemlock Rd., Cambridge, Mass. 02138, U.S.A.

CHENG, J(ames) Chester. American, b. 1926. History, Politics/Government. Prof. of History, California State Univ., San Francisco, since 1960. Consultant, Asia Foundn., since 1983. Research Assoc., Hoover Instn., Stanford, Calif., since 1964. Lectr. in History, Univ. of Hong Kong, 1952–59; Visiting Assoc. Prof. of Univ. of Oregon, Eugene, 1959–60; Consultant, U.S. Office of Education, 1960–61. *Publs:* Basic Principles Underlying Chinese Communist Approach to Education, 1961; Chinese Sources for the Taiping Rebellion in China 1850-1864, 1963; (ed.) The Politics of the Chinese Red Army, 1966; Documents of Dissent: Chinese Political Culture since Mao, 1980. Add: Dept. of History, San Francisco State Univ., San Francisco, Calif. 94132, U.S.A.

CHENG, James K. Also writes as Cheng Yi Kuo-Chiang. Canadian, b. 1936. Novels/Short stories. Translations. Corresp., Central News Agency, and Newsdom Weekly, since 1970, and Chmn. Bd. of Dirs., The New Republic Daily, since 1972—all Vancouver, B.C. Prof. and Chief Librarian, Warner Pacific Coll., Portland Ore., 1965–67, and Okanagan Coll., Kelowna, B.C., 1968–70. Secty.-Gen., Chinese Nationalist League of Canada, 1970–74. *Publs:* The Stranger, 1963; (as Cheng Yi Kuo-Chiang) Man Without a Country, 1964; (trans. into Chinese) Erich M. Remarque: Night in Lisbon, 1964; (as Cheng Yi Kuo-Chiang) Those Who Love, 1965; (as Cheng Yi Kuo-Chiang) Song of a Wanderer, 1966; (trans. into Chinese) M.E. Chaber: Wild Midnight Falls, 1968; (as Cheng Yi Kuo-Chiang) Cry Beloved People, 1969; The Dirty Group, 1973; The Collected Short Stories, 1973. Add: Box 33793, Station D. Vancouver 9, B.C., Canada.

CHENG, Yi Kuo-Chiang. *See* CHENG, James K.

CHERRY, Charles Conrad. American, b. 1937. Theology/Religion. Prof. of Religious Studies, Indiana Univ., Indianapolis, since 1988. Prof. of Religious Studies, Pennsylvania State Univ., University Park, 1964–81; Dir., Scholars Press, Atlanta, 1981–88. *Publs:* Theology of Jonathan Edwards, 1966; (ed.) God's New Israel, 1970; Nature and Religious Imagination, 1980; (ed.) Horace Bushnell, 1985. Add: c/o Project on Religion and American Culture, 425 Agnes St., Indianapolis, Ind. 46202, U.S.A.

CHERRY, Kelly. American. Novels/Short stories, Poetry, Philosophy. Prof. of English and Writer-in-Residence, Univ. of Wisconsin, Madison, since 1977. *Publs:* (assoc. ed. and co-author) Lessons From Our Living Past, 1972; Teacher's Guide to Lessons From Our Living Past, 1972; Sick and Full of Burning, 1974; Lovers and Agnostics, 1975; Relativity, 1977; Conversion, 1979; Augusta Played, 1979; Songs for a Soviet Composer,

1980; In the Wink of an Eye, 1983; The Lost Traveller's Dream, 1984; Natural Theology, 1988. Add: Dept. of English, University of Wisconsin, Madison, Wisc. 53706, U.S.A.

CHERRYH, C. J. Pseud. for Carolyn Janice Cherry. American, b. 1942. Science fiction/Fantasy. Teacher of Latin and ancient history, Oklahoma City public schs., 1965–76. *Publs:* Brothers of Earth, 1976; Hunter of Worlds, 1977; The Faded Sun: Kesrith, 1978; The Faded Sun: Shon'Jir, 1979; Serpent's Reach, 1979; Hestia, 1979; The Book of Morgaine, 1979 (trilogy: first published as Gates of Ivrel, 1976; Well of Shiuan, 1978; and Fires of Azeroth, 1979); The Faded Sun: Kutath, 1980; Serpent's Reach, 1980; Merchanter's Luck, 1982; The Port Eternity, 1982; The Pride of Chanur, 1982; Downbelow Station, 1983; The Dreamstone, 1983; Sunfall, 1983; The Tree of Swords and Jewels, 1983; Voyager in Night, 1984; Chanur's Venture, 1984; Cuckoo's Egg, 1985; The Kif Strikes Back, 1985; Angel with a Sword, 1985; Chanur's Homecoming, 1986; The Faded Sun Trilogy, 1987; Exile's Gate, 1988; Cyteen, 1988; Smuggler's Gold, 1988; Rimrunners, 1989. Add: 11217 N. McKinley, Oklahoma City, Okla. 73114, U.S.A.

CHESEN, Eli S. American, b. 1944. Psychiatry. Psychiatrist in private practice, 1974. Chief of Mental Health, Nellis A.F.B., Nevada, 1974. *Publs:* Religion May Be Hazardous to Your Health, 1972; President Nixon's Psychiatric Profile, 1973; The Fitness Compulsion, 1988. Add: 2132 The Knolls, Lincoln, Nebr. 68512, U.S.A.

CHESHAM, Henry. *See* **BINGLEY**, David Ernest.

CHESHAM, Sallie. American. Poetry, History, Sociology. Minister, colonel, and social worker, Salvation Army, NYC (Dir., Old Hat inner city prog., Chicago, 1967–71). *Publs:* Born to Battle (history), 1965; Walking With the Wind (poetry), 1969; Trouble Doesn't Happen Next Tuesday (social work), 1972; One Hand upon Another, 1978; Peace Like a River, 1981; Wind Chimes, 1983; Preaching Ladies, 1983; Catalogue Roses, 1987; The Brengle Book: A Samuel Logran Brengle Treasury, 1988. Add: c/o Salvation Army Supplies, Southern, 1424 NE Expressway, Atlanta, Ga. 30329, U.S.A.

CHESHER, Kim. British, b. 1955. Children's fiction. Free-lance writer, since 1981. Editorial trainee, Hamish Hamilton Children's Books, London, 1975–76. Plays Asst., Evans Bros., London, 1978–81. *Publs:* The Fifth Quarter, 1976; Cuthbert series, 5 vols., 1976–82; The Carnford Inheritance, 1977; The Finn Bequest, 1978. Add: c/o Hamish Hamilton Ltd., 27 Wrights Lane, London W8 5TZ, England.

CHESNEY, Marion. Also writes as Helen Crampton, Ann Fairfax, Jennie Tremaine and Charlotte Ward. Scottish, b. 1936. Historical/Romance, Novels/Short stories. Has worked as a fiction buyer for a bookseller; Women's Fashion Ed., Scottish Field mag., Glasgow; Theatre Critic and Reporter, Scottish Daily Express, Glasgow; Chief Reporter, Daily Express, London. *Publs:* (as Ann Fairfax) Henrietta, 1979; (as Jennie Tremaine) Kitty, 1979; Regency Gold, 1980; Lady Margery's Intrigue, 1980; The Constant Companion, 1980; (as Helen Crampton) The Marquis Takes a Bride, 1980; (as Jennie Tremaine) Daisy; (as Jennie Tremaine) Lucy, 1980; (as Jenny Tremaine) Polly, 1980; (as Jennie Tremaine) Molly, 1980; (as Jennie Tremaine) Ginny, 1980; Quadrille, 1981; My Lords, Ladies, and Marjorie, 1981; (as Helen Crampton) The Highland Countess, rev. ed. (as by Marion Chesney), 1987; (as Ann Fairfax) Annabelle, 1981; (as Ann Fairfax) Penelope, 1981; (as Jennie Tremaine) Tilly, 1981; (as Jennie Tremaine) Susie, 1981; Love and Lady Lovelace, 1982; (as Jennie Tremaine) Poppy, 1982; (as Jenny Tremaine) Sally, 1982; (as Charlotte Ward) The Westerby Inheritance, 1982; Duke's Diamonds, 1983; The Westerby Sisters, 1983; Minerva: Being the First of Six Sisters, 1983; The Taming of Annabelle, 1983; The Viscount's Revenge, 1983; Deidre and Desire, 1984; The Poor Relation, 1984; Daphne, 1984; The French Affair, 1984; The Miser of Mayfair, 1984; Diana the Huntress, 1985; The Flirt, 1985; Frederica in Fashion, 1985; Plain Jane, 1986; Miss Fiona's Fancy, 1987; My Dear Duchess, 1987; The Paper Princess, 1987; The Wicked Godmother, 1987; The Wicked Grandmother, 1987; Rake's Progress, 1987; Perfect Gentleman, 1988; Rainbird's Revenge, 1988; Refining Felicity: Being the First Volume of the School for Manners, 1988; The Savage Marquess, 1988. Add: 5 Clarges Mews, London W1, England.

CHESTERMAN, Charles W(esley). American, b. 1913. Earth sciences. Curator of Mineralogy, California Academy of Sciences, San Francisco, since 1954. Teacher of Mechanical and Civil Engineering, Geology and Mineralogy, San Francisco City Coll., 1941–42; Geologist with U.S. Geological Survey, in the United States and Japan, 1942–47;

Geologist, California Div. of Mines and Geology, San Francisco, 1947–58. *Publs:* The Audubon Society Field Guide to North American Rocks and Minerals, 1979; (with others) Familiar Rocks and Minerals of North America, 1990. Add: 721 Claret South, Calistoga, Calif. 94515, U.S.A.

CHESTERS, Graham. British, b. 1944. Literature. Prof. of French, Univ. of Hull, since 1988 (Sn. Lectr., 1980–88). Tutor in French, University Coll., Swansea, 1969–70; Lectr. in French, Queen's Univ., Belfast, 1970–72. *Publs:* Some Functions of Sound Repetition in "Les Fleurs du Mal", 1975; (ed., with P. Broome) An Anthology of Modern French Poetry 1850-1950, 1976; (with P. Broome) The Appreciation of Modern French Poetry 1850-1950, 1976; Baudelaire and the Poetics of Craft, 1988. Add: Dept. of French, Univ. of Hull, Hull HU6 7RX, England.

CHETWIN, Grace. British. Children's fiction, Science fiction/Fantasy. Full-time writer since 1983. High sch. English and French teacher, Auckland, New Zealand, 1958–62; High sch. English teacher and dept. head, Devon, England, 1962–63; Dir., Group '72–'76, Auckland, 1972–76. *Publs:* On All Hallow's Eve, 1984; Out of the Dark World, 1985; Gom on Windy Mountain, 1986; The Riddle and the Rune, 1987; The Crystal Stairs: From the Tales of Gom in the Legends of Ulm, 1988; The Atheling, 1988. Add: c/o Jean V. Naggar Literary Agency, 336 E. 73rd St., New York, N.Y. 10021, U.S.A.

CHEW, Allen F. American, b. 1924. History. Freelance writer. Assoc. Prof. of History, U.S. Air Force Academy, Colo., 1964–69; Prof. and Chmn., Dept. of History, Univ. of Wisconsin, Oshkosh, 1971–74; Research Fellow and Visiting Assoc. Prof., U.S. Army Command and Gen. Staff Coll., Ft. Leavenworth, KS., 1979–81. *Publs:* An Atlas of Russian History, 1967, 1970; The White Death: The Epic of the Soviet-Finnish Winter War, 1971; Fighting the Russians in Winter: Three Case Studies, 1981. Add: 2102 Essex Lane, Colorado Springs, Colo. 80909, U.S.A.

CHEYNEY-COKER, Syl. Sierra Leonean, b. 1945. Poetry. Sr. Lectr., Univ. of Maiduguri, Nigeria, since 1979 (Lectr., 1977–79). Former drummer, radio producer, factory worker, and dock worker; journalist, Eugene, Ore., 1968–69. *Publs:* Concerto for an Exile, 1972; The Graveyard Also Has Teeth, 1974. Add: Dept. of English, Univ. of Maiduguri, P.M.B. 1069, Maiduguri, Nigeria.

CHIBNALL, Marjorie McCallum. Before 1947 wrote as Marjorie Morgan. British, b. 1915. History, Theology/Religion. Fellow, Clare Hall, Cambridge, since 1975 (Research Fellow, 1969–75). Asst. Lectr., 1943–45 and Lectr. in History, 1945–47, Univ. of Aberdeen; Lectr. in History and Fellow, Girton Coll., Cambridge, 1947–65; Fellow, British Academy, 1978. *Publs:* The English Lands of the Abbey of Bec, 1946, 1968; (ed.) Select Documents of the English Lands of the Abbey of Bec, 1951; (ed. and trans.) The Historia Pontificalis of John Salisbury, 1956; (ed. and trans.) The Ecclesiastical History of Orderic Vitalis, 6 vols., 1969–80; (with A.T. Gaydon) Victoria County History of Shropshire, vol. II, 1973; The World of Orderic Vitalis, 1984; Anglo-Norman England 1066-1166, 1986. Add: 7 Croftgate, Fulbrooke Rd., Cambridge CB3 9EG, England.

CHILCOTE, Ronald H. American, b. 1935. Politics, International relations/Current affairs. Prof. of Political Science, Univ. of California at Riverside, since 1975 (joined faculty, 1963). *Publs:* (with Joel Edelstein) Latin America: The Struggle with Dependency and Beyond, 1974; Theories of Comparative Politics: The Search for a Paradigm, 1981; Theories of Development and Underdevelopment, 1984; (with Joel Edelstein) Latin America: Capitalist and Socialist Perspectives of Development and Underdevelopment, 1986. Add: Dept. of Political Science, Univ. of California at Riverside, Riverside, Calif. 92521, U.S.A.

CHILD, Julia. American, b. 1912. Cookery/Gastronomy/Wine. Presenter, The French Chef prog., WGBH-TV, Boston, since 1962; occasional weekly cooking segment, ABC TV-series, Good Morning America. Advertising Dept., W. & J. Sloane, NYC, 1939–40; with Office of Strategic Services, Washington, Ceylon, and China, 1941–45; monthly food Columnist, McCalls mag., 1975–82; Food Ed., Parade mag., 1982–86. *Publs:* (with Simone Beck and Louisette B25otholle) Mastering the Art of French Cooking, vol. I, 1961; The French Chef Cookbook, 1966; (with Simone Beck) Mastering the Art of French Cooking, Vol. II, 1971; From Julia Child's Kitchen, 1976; Julia Child and Company, 1978; Julia Child and More Company, 1979; The Way to Cook, 1989. Add: c/o French Chef Office, WGBH-TV, 125 Western Ave., Boston, Mass. 02134, U.S.A.

CHILDRESS, Alice. American, b. 1920. Novels/Short stories, Children's fiction, Plays/Screenplays. Actress; Dir., American Negro Theater, NYC, for twelve years. Scholar, Radcliffe Inst. for Independent

Study, Cambridge, Mass., 1966–68. *Publs:* Like One of the Family: Conversations from a Domestic's Life, 1956; Wedding Band, 1966; Wine in the Wilderness (television play), 1969; Mojo and Strings, 1971; (ed.) Black Scenes: Collections of Scenes from Plays Written by Black People about Black Experience, 1971; A Hero Ain't Nothin' But a Sandwich (juvenile fiction), 1973; When the Rattlesnake Sounds (juvenile), 1975; Let's Hear It for the Queen (juvenile), 1976; A Short Walk (novel), 1979; Sea Island Song, 1979; Rainbow Jordan (juvenile fiction), 1981; These Other People (juvenile), 1989. Add: Beacon Press, 25 Beacon St., Boston, Mass., 02108, U.S.A.

CHILDS, David (Haslam). British, b. 1933. History, Politics/Government. Reader in Politics, since 1976, and Dir. of Inst. of German, Austrian, and Swiss Affairs, since 1987, Univ. of Nottingham (Lectr., 1966–71; Sr. Lectr., 1971–76). *Publs:* From Schumacher to Brandt, 1966; East Germany, 1969; Germany since 1918, 1971, 1981; Marx and the Marxists, 1973; Britain since 1945, 1979, 1986; (ed.) The Changing Face of Western Communism, 1980; (with J. Johnson) West Germany: Politics and Society, 1981; The GDR: Moscow's German Ally, 1983; (ed.) Honecker's Germany, 1985; (co-ed) East Germany in Comparative Perspective, 1989. Add: Institute of German, Austrian, and Swiss Affairs, Univ. of Nottingham, University Park, Nottingham NG7 2RD, England.

CHILDS, Marquis (William). American, b. 1903. History, Politics/Government, Social commentary/phenomena. Chief Washington Corresp., St. Louis Post Dispatch, since 1962 (Corresp., 1926–44; Special Corresp., 1954–62). United Features Syndicated Columnist, 1944–79. *Publs:* Sweden: The Middle Way, 1936; They Hate Roosevelt, 1936; Washington Calling, 1937; This Is Democracy, 1938; This Is Your War, 1942; I Write from Washington, 1942; The Cabin, 1944; The Farmer Takes a Hand, 1952; (with D. Cater) Ethics in Business Society, 1954; The Ragged Edge, 1955; Eisenhower: Captive Hero, 1959; (co-ed.) Walter Lippmann and His Times, 1959; The Peacemakers, 1961; Taint of Innocence, 1967; Witness to Power, 1975; Sweden: The Middle Way on Trial, 1980; Mighty Mississippi: Biography of a River, 1983. Add: 1701 Pennsylvania Ave, NW, Washington D.C., 20036, U.S.A.

CHILSON, Robert. American, b. 1945. Science fiction/Fantasy. Freelance writer, since 1967. *Publs:* As the Curtain Falls, 1974; The Star-Crowned Kings, 1975; The Shores of Kansas, 1976. Add: c/o Richard Curtis Assocs., 164 E. 64th St., New York, N.Y. 10021, U.S.A.

CHILVER, Peter. British, b. 1933. Education, Theatre. Head of English Dept., Langdon Sch., London, since 1977. Teacher, I.L.E.A., 1964–68; Sr. Lectr. in Drama, Thomas Huxley Coll., London, 1968–77; Member of Faculty of Education, Univ. of London, 1974–77. *Publs:* Improvised Drama, 1967; Talking: Discussion, Improvisation and Debate in Schools, 1968; Stories for Improvisation, 1969; Producing the Play, 1974; Teaching Improvised Drama, 1978; (with G. Gould) Learning and Language in the Classroom, 1982; In the Picture series, 1985; English Coursework for GCSE, 1987. Add: 27 Cavendish Gardens, Barking, Essex, England.

CHINERY, Michael. British, b. 1938. Biology, Natural history, Zoology. *Publs:* Pictorial Dictionary of the Animal World, 1966; (with Michael Gabb) Human Kind, 1966; (with Michael Gabb) The World of Plants, 1966; (with David Larkin) Patterns of Living, 1966; (with Michael Gabb) The Life of Animals with Backbones, 1966; (with Michael Gabb) The Life of Animals without Backbones, 1966; Breeding and Growing, 1966; Pictorial Dictionary of the Plant World, 1967; Visual Biology, 1968; Purnell's Concise Encyclopedia of Nature, 1971; Animal Communities, 1972; Animals in the Zoo, 1973; Field Guide to the Insects of Britain and Northern Europe, 1973; Life in the Zoo, 1976; The Natural History of the Garden, 1977; The Family Naturalist, 1977; Nature All Around, 1978; Discovering Animals, 1978; Killers of the Wild, 1979; (with Maurice Pledger) Garden Birds, 1979; Collins Gem Guide to Butterflies and Moths, 1981; The Natural History of Britain and Europe, 1982; Collins Guide to the Insects of Britain and Western Europe, 1986; Garden Creepy Crawlies, 1986; The Living Garden, 1986; Collins Gem Guide to Insects, 1986; Exploring the Countryside, 1987. Add: Mousehole, Hundon, Suffolk CO10 8EG, England.

CHIPLIN, Brian. British, b. 1945. Economics. Prof., Dept. of Industrial Economics, Univ. of Nottingham, since 1984 (Research Fellow, 1966–67; Lectr., 1967–84); Assoc., Economists Advisory Group Ltd., since 1973. *Publs:* The Cotton and Allied Textiles Industry, 1973; (with D.S. Lees) Acquisition and Mergers: Government Policy in Europe, 1975; (with P.J. Sloane) Sex Discrimination in the Labour Market, 1976; Can

Workers Manage?, 1977; Economics of Advertising, 1981; (with P.J. Sloane) Tackling Discrimination at the Workplace, 1982. Add: Dept. of Industrial Economics, Univ. of Nottingham, University Park, Nottingham NG7 2RD, England.

CHIPMAN, Bruce Lewis. American, b. 1946. Film, Social commentary/phenomena. Head of English Dept. and Teacher of Literature and Writing, Tatnall Sch., Wilmington, Del., since 1973; Lectr. in English, Univ. of Delaware, since 1977. Fulbright Lectureship, Univ. of Khartoum, Sudan, Africa, 1983; Instr. of English, Tufts Univ., Medford, Mass., 1969–73. *Publs:* Hardening Rock, 1972; Hollywood: America's Dream Dump, 1981. Add: 39 Tenby Chase Dr., Newark, Del. 19711, U.S.A.

CHIPMAN, Donald. American, b. 1928. History. Prof. of History, North Texas State Univ., Denton, since 1967 (Assoc. Prof., 1964–67). Contrib. Ed. of History Gen. Section, Handbook of Latin American Studies. *Publs:* Nuño de Guzmán and the Province of Pánuco in New Spain 1518-1533, 1967; (contrib.) Reflections of Western Historians, 1969; (contrib.) Homenaje a Don José Maria de La Pena y Camera, 1969; (co-author) The Dallas Cowboys and the NFL, 1970; (with others) Struggle and Survival, 1981. Add: Dept. of History, North Texas State Univ., Denton, Tex. 76203, U.S.A.

CHISHOLM, Michael. British, b. 1931. Economics, Geography. Prof. of Geography, Univ. of Cambridge, since 1976. Member, Development Commn., since 1981. Departmental Demonstrator in Agricultural Economics, Oxford Univ., 1954–59; Asst. Lectr. and Lectr. in Geography, Bedford Coll., Univ. of London, 1960–64; Lectr. to Reader, 1965–72, and Prof. of Economic and Social Geography, Univ. of Bristol, 1972–76. Member, Social Science Research Council, 1967–72, and Local Govt. Boundary Commn. for England, 1971–78. *Publs:* Rural Settlement and Land Use: An Essay in Location, 1962, 3rd ed. 1979; Geography and Economics, 1966, rev. ed. 1970; (ed. with A.E. Frey and P. Haggett) Regional Forecasting, 1971; Research in Human Geography, 1971; (ed.) Resources for Britain's Future, 1972; (with P. O'Sullivan) Freight Flows and Spatial Aspects of the British Economy, 1973; (with J. Oeppen) The Changing Pattern of Employment: Regional Specialisation and Industrial Localisation in Britain, 1973; (ed. with B. Rodgers) Studies in Human Geography, 1973; (co-ed.) Processes in Physical and Human Geography, 1975; Human Geography: Evolution or Revolution?, 1975; Modern World Development: A Geographical Perspective, 1982. Add: Dept. of Geography, Downing Place, Cambridge CB2 3EN, England.

CHISSELL, Joan Olive. British. Music. Regular Broadcaster for BBC, and Reviewer for the Gramophone. Lectr., Extra-Mural Depts. of Oxford and London Univs., 1943–48; Piano Teacher, Jr. Special Talent Dept., Royal Coll. of Music, London, 1943–53; Asst. Music Critic, The Times, London, 1948–84. *Publs:* Schumann, 1948; (co-author) The Music of Britten, 1952; Chopin, 1965; Schumann's Piano Music, 1972; Brahms, 1977; Clara Schumann, "A Dedicated Spirit", 1983; (co-author) A Companion to the Concerts, 1988. Add: 7d Abbey Rd., London NW8, England.

CHITHAM, Edward. British, b. 1932. Children's fiction, History, Literature. Sr. Lectr., Faculty of Education, The Polytechnic, Wolverhampton, since 1977; Part-time Tutor, The Open Univ., since 1988. Master in charge of Latin, 1956–61, and Head of Library Dept., 1961–67, Rowley Regis Grammar Sch.; Sr. Lectr. in English, Dudley Coll. of Education, 1973–77. *Publs:* The Black Country, 1972; Ghost in the Water, 1973; The Poems of Anne Brontë, 1979; Brontë Facts and Brontë Problems, 1984; (with T. Winnifrith) The Brontës' Irish Background, 1985; A Life of Emily Brontë, 1987; (with T. Winnifrith) Literary Lives: Charlotte and Emily Brontë, 1989. Add: 11 Victoria Rd., Harborne, Birmingham B17 0AG, England.

CHITTUM, Ida. American, b. 1918. Children's fiction. *Publs:* Farmer Hoo and the Baboons, 1971; The Hermit Boy, 1972; Clabber Biscuits, 1972; Nutty Business, 1973; The Empty Grave, 1974; The Secrets of Madam Renee, 1975; Tales of Terror, 1975; The Ghost Boy of El Toro, 1977; The Buried Casket, 1979; The Cat's Pajamas, 1980; Thing Without a Name and Other Strange Tales, 1981. Add: c/o Independence Press, Div. of Herald House, P.O. Box HH, 3225 S. Noland Rd., Independence, Mo. 64055, U.S.A.

CHITTY, Susan. British, b. 1929. Novels, Travel/Exploration/Adventure, Biography. Freelance writer, lectr. and journalist. *Publs:* The Diary of a Fashion Model, 1958; (ed.) The Intelligent Woman's Guide to Good Taste, 1958; White Huntress, 1963; My Life and Horses, 1966; The Woman Who Wrote Black Beauty, 1971; The Beast and the Monk:

A Life of Charles Kingsley, 1975; (with Thomas Hinde) On Next to Nothing, 1975; Charles Kingsley's Landscape, 1976; (with Thomas Hinde) The Great Donkey Walk, 1977; The Young Rider, 1979; Gwen John, 1981; Now to My Mother, 1985; Edward Lear, 1988. Add: Bow Cottage, West Hoathly, East Grinstead, Sussex RH19 4QF, England.

CHITTY, (Sir) Thomas (Willes). *See* **HINDE,** Thomas.

CHIU, Hungdah. Chinese, b. 1936. History, International relations/Current affairs, Law. Prof. of Law, Univ. of Maryland Sch. of Law, Baltimore, since 1977 (Assoc. Prof., 1974–77); Ed.-in-chief, Chinese Yearbook of Intnl. Law and Affairs, vols. 1-7, 1981–89. Assoc. Prof. of Intnl. Law, National Taiwan Univ., 1965–66; Research Assoc. in Law, Harvard Law Sch., Cambridge, Mass., 1966–70, and 1972–74; Prof. of Law, National Chengchi Univ., Taipei, Taiwan, 1970–72. *Publs:* The Capacity of International Organization to Conclude Treaties, 1966; (ed. with D.M. Johnston) Agreements of the People's Republic of China, 1949–1967; A Calendar, 1968; The People's Republic of China and the Law of Treaties, 1972; (contrib., and ed. with S.C. Leng) Law in Chinese Foreign Policy, 1972; (ed. and contrib.) China and the Question of Taiwan: Documents and Analysis, 1973; (with Jerome Alan Cohen) People's China and International Law: A Documentary Study, 2 vols., 1974; (ed. with D. Simon) Legal Aspects of U.S.-Republic of China Trade and Investment, 1977; (ed.) Normalizing Relations with the People's Republic of China: Problems, Analysis and Documents, 1978; (ed. and contrib.) China and the Taiwan Issue, 1979; (ed. with K. Murphy) The Chinese Connection and Normalization, 1980; Agreements of the People's Republic of China: A Calendar of Events, 1966–80, 1981; (ed. with R. Downen) Multi-System Nations and International Law, 1981; (contrib., and ed. with S.C. Leng) China, 70 Years After the 1911 Hsin-hai Revolution, 1984; (with S.C. Leng) Criminal Justice in Post-Mao China, 1985; (co-ed.) The Future of Hong Kong: Toward 1997 and Beyond, 1987; (ed. and contrib.) The Draft Basic Law of Hong Kong: Analysis and Documents, 1988. Add: Univ. of Maryland Sch. of Law, 500 West Baltimore St., Baltimore, Md. 21201, U.S.A.

CHODOROV, Jerome. American, b. 1911. Plays/Screenplays, Libretti. *Publs:* (with J. Fields) Schoolhouse on the Lot, 1938; (with J. Fields) My Sister Eileen, 1940, screenplay, 1942; (with J. Fields) Junior Miss, 1941; (with J. Fields) Louisiana Purchase (screenplay), 1942; (with J. Fields) The French Touch, 1945; (with J. Fields) Wonderful Town, 1953; (with J. Fields) Girl in Pink Tights (musical), 1953; (with J. Fields) Anniversary Waltz, 1954; (with J. Fields) Happy Anniversary (screenplay), 1955; (with J. Fields) The Tunnel of Love, 1957; (with J. Fields) The Ponder Heart; 3 Bags Full, 1966; I Had a Ball (musical), 1967; The Great Waltz (musical), 1967; Dumas and Son (musical), 1968; A Community of Two, 1973; (with N. Panama) A Talent for Murder, 1981. Add: Dramatists Guild, 234 W. 44th St., New York, N.Y., U.S.A.

CHOMSKY, (Avram) Noam. American, b. 1928. International relations/Current affairs, Language/Linguistics, Philosophy, Politics/Government. Inst. Prof., Dept. of Linguistics and Philosophy, Massachusetts Inst. of Technology, Cambridge, since 1976 (Asst. Prof., 1955–58; Assoc. Prof., 1958–61; Prof., 1961–66; Ferrari P. Ward Prof., 1966–76). *Publs:* Syntactic Structures, 1957; Current Issues in Linguistic Theory, 1964; Aspects of the Theory of Syntax, 1965; Cartesian Linguistics, 1966; Topics in the Theory of Generative Grammar, 1966; (with M. Halle) Sound Pattern of English, 1968; Language and Mind, 1968; American Power and the New Mandarins, 1969; At War with Asia, 1970; Problems of Knowledge and Freedom, 1971; Studies on Semantics in Generative Grammar, 1972; (with E.S. Herman) Counter-revolutionary Violence, 1973; For Reasons of State, 1973; Peace in the Middle East?, 1974; (with E.S. Herman) Bains de sang, 1975; The Logical Structure of Linguistic Theory, 1975; Reflections on Language, 1975; Essays on Form and Interpretation, 1977; Human Rights and American Foreign Policy, 1978; (with E.S. Herman) Political Economy of Human Rights, 2 vols., 1979; Rules and Representations, 1980; Lectures on Government and Binding, 1981; Radical Priorities, 1981; Towards a New Cold War, 1982; Some Concepts and Consequences of the Theory of Government and Binding, 1982; Fateful Triangle: the U.S., Israel and the Palestinians, 1983; Turning the Tide, 1985; Knowledge of Language, 1986; Barriers, 1986; Pirates and Emperors, 1986; On Power and Ideology, 1987; Language in a Psychological Setting, 1987; Language and Problems of Knowledge, 1987; The Chomsky Reader, 1987; The Culture of Terrorism, 1988. Add: Massachusetts Inst. of Technology, 77, Massachusetts Ave., Cambridge, Mass. 02139, U.S.A.

CHORAFAS, Dimitris N. Greek, b. 1926. Administration/Management, Communications media, Engineering, Information science/Computers. Consultant in private practice; teacher. *Publs:* Operations Research for Industrial Management, 1958; Statistical Processes and Reliability Engineering, 1960; The Functions of Research in the Enterprise, 1960; Computer Theory, 1960; Computer Applications in Industry and Commerce, 1961; Programming Systems for Electronic Computers, 1962; Industrial Strategy, 1962; New Methods of Economic Analysis, 1963; The Influence of the Computer on the Organization, 1964; Systems and Simulation, 1965; Control Systems Functions and Programming Approaches, 2 vols., 1966; La Direction des Produits Nouveaux, 1967; An Introduction to Product Planning, 1967; Sales Engineering, 1967; Managing Industrial Research for Profits, 1967; Selecting the Computer System, 1967; Developing the International Executive, 1967; The Knowledge Revolution, 1968; How to Manage Computers for Results, 1969; The Communication Barrier in International Management, 1970; Management Development, 1971; Information Systems Design, 1972; Computers in Medicine, 1972; Warehousing, 1973; Management Planning, 1973; Die Kranke Gesellschaft, 1974; Microform and Computer Output to Microfilm, 1976; Computer Networks for Distributed Information Systems, 1980; Data Communication, 1980; Interactive Videotex, 1981; Office Automation, 1982; Money: The Banks of the 1980's, 1982; Information Systems in Financial Institutions, 1983; Microprocessors for Management, 1983; DBMS for Distributed Computers and Networks, 1983; Local Area Networks, 1984; Telephony, Today and Tomorrow, 1984; Software Handbook, 1985; Interactive Message Services, 1985; Handbook of Data Communications, 1986; Fourth and Fifth Generation Languages, 2 vols., 1986; Personal Workstations for Greater Productivity, 1986; Interactive Workstations, 1986; Engineering Productivity through CAD/CAM, 1987; The New Communications Disciplines, 1987; Applying Expert Systems in Business, 1987; Engineering Databases, 1988; Electronic Funds Transfer, 1988; (with H. Steinmann) High Technology at UBS, 1988; Implementing Networks for Banks and Financial Institutions, 1988. Add: Villa Romantic, Vitznau, Switzerland.

CHORLEY, Richard J(ohn). British, b. 1927. Geography. Prof. of Geography, Cambridge Univ., since 1974 (Demonstrator, 1958–62; Lectr., 1962–70; Reader, 1970–74). Instr. in Geography, Columbia Univ., NYC, 1952–54, and in Geology, Brown Univ., Providence, R.I., 1954–57. *Publs:* (co-author) The History of the Study of Landforms, 2 vols., 1964–73; (co-ed.) Frontiers in Geographical Teaching, 1965; (co-ed.) Models in Geography, 1967; (co-author) Atmosphere, Weather, and Climate, 1968, 1987; (co-author) Network Analysis in Geography, 1969; (ed.) Water, Earth, and Man, 1969; (co-author) Physical Geography, 1971; (ed.) Spatial Analysis in Geomorphology, 1972; (ed.) Directions in Geography, 1973; (co-author) Environmental Systems, 1978; (co-author) Geomorphology, 1985. Add: 76 Grantchester Meadows, Newnham, Cambridge CB3 9JL, England.

CHRIST, Henry I. American, b. 1915. Language/Linguistics, Literature, Sports/Physical education/Keeping fit, Biography. Teacher, 1936–46; Chmn. of English, Andrew Jackson High Sch., St. Albans, N.Y., 1947–70. *Publs:* Winning Words, 1948, 3rd ed. 1967; (adaptor) Odyssey of Homer, 1948, 1968; Myths and Folklore, 1952, 1968; Modern English in Action 7-12, 1965, 1968, 1975, 1978, 1982; Modern Short Biographies, 1970; Language and Literature, 1972; Short World Biographies, 1973; The World of Sports, 2 vols., 1975, 1977; The Challenge of Sports, 1978; Going Places, 1980; Globe American Biographies, 1987; Globe World Biographies, 1987; English for the College Boards, 1987; Myths and Folklore, 1989. Add: P.O. Box 361062, Melbourne, Fla. 32936, U.S.A.

CHRIST, Ronald. American, b. 1936. Literary criticism/History, Translations. Prof. of English, Rutgers Univ., New Brunswick, N.J., since 1969. Member, Exec. Bd., American P.E.N., 1978–83. Managing Ed., Sites, since 1980; Co-Publisher, Lumen Books, since 1983. Asst. Prof., Manhattan Coll., Riverdale, N.Y., 1961–68; Ed., Review, 1970–78. Dir., Literature Prog., Center for Inter-American Relations, 1973–78. *Publs:* The Narrow Act: Borges' Art of Allusion, 1969; (trans.) Capt. Pantoja and the Special Service, by Mario Vargas Llosa, 1978; (with Gregory Kolovakos) The Cubs and Other Stories, 1979; (trans.) Under a Mantle of Stars, by Manuel Puig, 1985; (trans.) Augusto Torres, by Guido Castillo, 1986; (trans. with Gloria Waldman) Borges in/and/on Film, by Edgardo Cozarinsky, 1988. Add: 446 West 20th St., New York, N.Y. 10011, U.S.A.

CHRISTENSEN, J(ack) A(rden). American, b. 1927. Poetry, Writing/Journalism. Teacher, Salt Lake City Bd. of Education, Utah, 1956–82, and Chmn., Depts. of English and Humanities, East High Sch., Salt Lake City, Utah, 1974–82. Assoc. Ed., Media and Methods mag., 1971–81. *Publs:* Impressions and Aftermaths, 1960; Whispers in the Wind, 1963; Deep Song, 1969; The Young Writer, 1970; (co-author) Building

English Skills, 1976, 1977; The Garden of the Moon's Embrace, 1977; St. Nichiren, 1981; Cut Art: An Introduction to Chinese and Japanese Papercuts, 1989. Add: 967 S. 13th St. E., Salt Lake City, Utah 84105, U.S.A.

CHRISTENSEN, Paul. American, b. 1943. Poetry, Literature. Prof., Dept. of English, Texas A and M Univ., College Station, since 1974. Ed. Publisher, Cedarshouse Press, Bryan, Tex., since 1979. Assoc. Ed., Eastern Publishing Co., Alexandria, Va., 1967–68; Poetry Ed., Quartet mag., College Station, Tex., 1975–77; Host, Poetry Southwest, KAMU-FM, Texas, 1976–86. *Publs:* Old and Lost Rivers (verse), 1977; Charles Olson: Call Him Ishmael (criticism), 1979; Signs of the Whelming, 1982; Gulfsongs, 1982; The Vectory (verse), 1983; Weights and Measures (verse), 1985; Minding the Underworld: Clayton Eshleman and Late Postmodernism, 1989; The Complete Correspondence of Charles Olson and Edward Dahlberg, 1989. Add: 206 S. Sims St., Bryan, Tex. 77803, U.S.A.

CHRISTESEN, C(lement) B(yrne). Australian, b. 1911. Novels/Short stories, Poetry, Literature. Founder and Ed., Meanjin Quarterly, Melbourne, 1940–75. *Publs:* North Coast, 1943; South Coast, 1944; Dirge and Lyrics, 1945; (ed.) Australian Heritage, 1949; (ed.) Coast to Coast: Australian Stories 1953–1954, 1955; (ed.) On Native Grounds: Australian Writing from Meanjin Quarterly, 1968; (ed.) Meanjin Quarterly Index 1940–1965, 1969; The Hand of Memory (stories and poems), 1970; The Gallery on Eastern Hill, 1971; Having Loved (poems), 1979. Add: Stanhope House, Eltham, Vic. 3095, Australia.

CHRISTIAN, Carol Cathay. American, b. 1923. Novels/Short stories, Biography. *Publs:* Into Strange Country, 1958; (with G. Plummer) God and One Redhead: Mary Slessor of Calabar, 1970; Tales of the Cross River, 1972; Great People of Our Time, 1973; Proverbs and Rhymes, 1974; Johnny Ring, 1975; More People of Our Time, 1978; (with D. Christian) Famous Women of the 20th Century, 1982; and other English language readers. Add: 22 Pitfold Ave., Shottermill, Haslemere, Surrey GU27 1PN, England.

CHRISTIAN, Frederick H. Pseud. for Frederick Nolan. Mystery/Crime/Suspense, Westerns/Adventure, Children's non-fiction, Translations. *Publs:* western novels—Sudden Strikes Back, 1966; Sudden: Apache Fighter, 1967; Sudden: Troubleshooter, 1967; Sudden at Bay, 1968; Sudden: Dead or Alive!, 1970; Find Angel, 1973; Kill Angel, 1973; Send Angel, 1973; Trap Angel, 1974; Take Angel, 1975, Frame Angel, 1975; Hang Angel, 1975; Warn Angel, 1975; Hunt Angel, 1975; Stop Angel!, 1976; Massacre in Madison, 1980; suspense novels, as Frederick Nolan—The Ritter Double-Cross, 1974; The Oshawa Project, 1974, in U.S. as the Algonquin Project, 1975; N.Y.P.D.: No Place to Be a Cop, 1974; Kill Petrosino!, 1975; The Mittenwald Syndicate, 1976; Carver's Kingdom, 1978; Brass Target, 1979; White Nights, Red Dawn, 1980; Wolf Trap, 1986; Red Center, 1987; other—(trans.) The Stage Coach, by Goscinny, 1972; (trans.) Dalton City, by Goscinny, 1973; Jay J. Ames, Investigator, as Told to Frederick Nolan, 1976; Battle of the Alamo (juvenile), 1978. Add: c/o Arthur Pine Assocs., 1780 Broadway, New York, N.Y. 10019, U.S.A.

CHRISTIAN, John. *See* DIXON, Roger.

CHRISTIAN, John Wyrill. British, b. 1926. Metallurgy and materials sciences. Fellow, St. Edmund Hall, Oxford, since 1963; (George Kelly Reader in Metallurgy, 1958–67, and Prof. of Physical Metallurgy, 1967–88, now Emeritus, Oxford Univ.). Co-ed., Progress in Material Science, since 1964; Trans. Ed., Physics of Metals and Metallurgy, since 1974. Assoc. Ed., AETA Metallurgica, 1967–74; Ed., Less Common Metals, 1976–85. *Publs:* (with W. Hume-Rothery and W.B. Pearson) Metallurgical Equilibrium Diagrams, 1952; Theory of Transformations in Metals and Alloys, 1965, 1975. Add: Dept. of Metallurgy and Science of Materials, Oxford Univ., Parks Rd., Oxford OX1 3PH, England.

CHRISTIAN, Mary Blount. American, b. 1933. Children's fiction. Instr., Creative Writing, Rice Univ., Continuing Studies; Lectr.; Cofounder, Associated Authors of Children's Literature, Houston, Tex.; correspondence sch. teacher; Book Reviewer, The Houston Chronicle; Creator and Moderator, Children's Bookshelf, PBS-TV. *Publs:* Scarabee, The Witch's Cat, 1973; The First Sign of Winter, 1973; Nothing Much Happened Today, 1973; Sebastian, Super Sleuth, 1974; Devin and Goliath, 1974; No Dogs Allowed, Jonathan, 1974; Rotten Old River Raft/Super Submarine, 1974; The Chocolate Cake Caper, 1976; The Disappearing Dues, 1976; Hats Are for Watering Horses, 1976; Jonah, Go to Nineveh, 1976; The Test Paper Thief, 1976; The Vanishing Sandwich, 1976; When

Time Began, 1976; The C.B. Convoy Caper, 1977; The Christmas Shoe Thief, 1977; Daniel, Who Dared, 1977; The Pocket Park Problem, 1977; The Riddle of the Runaway House, 1977; Felina, 1978; The Ghost in the Garage, 1978; The Goosehill Gang Cookbook, 1978; The Goosehill Gang Craft Book, 1978; His Brother's Keeper, 1978; J.J. Leggett, Secret Agent, 1978; The May Basket Mystery, 1978; The Sand Lot, 1978; The Shadow on the Shade, 1978; The Stitch in Time Solution, 1978; Il a du Flair, Babylas!, 1978; The Lucky Man, 1979; The Devil Take You, Barnabas Beane!, 1980; Christmas Reflections, 1980; Anna and the Strangers, 1981; Doggone Mystery, 1980; Two Ton Secret, 1981; The Ventriloquist, 1982; The Firebug Mystery, 1982; (co-author) Bible Heros, Kings and Prophets, 1982; The Green Thumb Thief, 1982; April Fool, 1982; The Double Double Cross, 1982; Sebastian Super Sleuth and the Hair of the Dog Mystery, 1982; Deadline for Danger, 1982; Grandfathers: God's Gift to Children, 1982; Grandmothers: God's Gift to Children, 1982; Just Once, 1982; Microcomputers, 1983; Sebastian (Super Sleuth) and the Hair of the Dog Mystery, 1982, 1984; Sebastian (Super Sleuth) and the Bone to Pick Mystery, 1983, 1986; Sebastian (Super Sleuth) and the Crummy Yummies Caper, 1983, 1985; Swamp Monsters, 1983; The Museum Mystery, 1983; Sebastian (Super Sleuth) and the Santa Claus Caper, 1984; Sebastian (Super Sleuth) and the Secret of the Skewered Skier, 1984; Deadman in Catfish Bay, 1985; Everybody Else Is, 1985; Go West, Swamp Monsters!, 1985; Growin' Pains, 1985; Mystery at Camp Triumph, 1985; The Mysterious Case Case, 1985; The Toady and Dr. Miracle, 1985; Sebastian (Super Sleuth) and the Clumsy Cowboy, 1985; Penrod's Pants, 1986; Sebastian (Super Sleuth) and Purloined Sirloin, 1986; Singin' Somebody Else's Song, 1986. Add: 1108 Danbury Rd., Houston, Tex. 77055, U.S.A.

CHRISTIAN, Roy Cloberry. British, b. 1914. History, Mythology/Folklore, Travel/Exploration/Adventure. Lectr.-in-Charge of Mature Students, Derby Coll. of Further Education, 1966–76 (joined faculty, 1955). *Publs:* Ships and the Sea, 1962; Old English Customs, 1966; Ghosts and Legends, 1972; (ed.) Nature-Lover's Companion, 1972; Nottinghamshire, 1974; Factories, Forges, and Foundries, 1974; Peak District, 1976; Vanishing Britain, 1977; Derbyshire, 1978; (with J.E. Heath) Derby, 1985. Add: 53 Littleover Lane, Littleover, Derby DE3 6JH, England.

CHRISTIE, A(ndrew) B(arnett). British, b. 1909. Medicine/Health, Travel/Exploration/Adventure. Head of the Dept. of Infectious Diseases, Univ. of Liverpool, and Physician Supt., Fazakerley Hospital, Liverpool, 1946–74; short-term consultancies, WHO, Geneva, 1975–79; Visiting Professorships, Nigeria, Middle East, etc., 1979–86. *Publs:* Infectious Diseases with Chapters on Venereal Diseases, 1947, 5th ed., 1968; Motoring and Camping in Greece, 1965; Infectious Diseases, Epidemiology and Clinical Practice, 1969, 4th ed., 1987; (with M.C. Christie) Food Hygiene and Food Hazards, 1971, 1977. Add: 2 Beach Lawn, Waterloo, Liverpool L22 8QA, England.

CHRISTIE, Ian (Ralph). British, b. 1919. History. Astor Prof. of British History, University Coll., Univ. of London, 1979–84, now Prof. Emeritus (Asst. Lectr. in History, 1948–51; Lectr., 1951–61; Reader, 1961–66; Prof., 1966–79; Dean of Arts, 1971–73; Chmn., Dept. of History, 1975–79); Member, Editorial Bd., History of Parliament Trust, since 1973. Joint Literary Dir., Royal Historical Soc., 1964–70. *Publs:* The End of North's Ministry 1780-1782, 1958; Wilkes, Wyvill and Reform, 1962; Crisis of Empire: Great Britain and the American Colonies 1754-83, 1966, 1974; (ed.) Essays in Modern History Selected from the Transactions of the Royal Historical Society, 1968; Myth and Reality in Late Eighteenth-Century British Politics, 1970; (ed.) The Correspondence of Jeremy Bentham, Vol. 3: January 1781-October 1788, 1971; (with B.W. Labaree) Empire or Independence 1760-1776, 1976; (with Lucy M. Brown) Bibliography of British History 1789-1851, 1977; Wars and Revolutions: Britain 1760-1815, 1982; Stress and Stability in Late Eighteenth-Century Britain, 1984. Add: 10 Green Lane, Croxley Green, Herts., England.

CHRISTIE-MURRAY, David (Hugh Arthur). British, b. 1913. Genealogy/Heraldry, Supernatural/Occult topics, Theology/Religion. Youth Organizer, Diocese of Rochester, 1942–46; Asst. Master, Harrow Sch., Harrow-on-the-Hill, 1946–73. *Publs:* Heraldry in the Churches of Beckenham, 1954; Armorial Bearings of British Schools, 1967 (originally published as School Heraldry); The Hamlyn Bible for Children, 1974; A History of Heresy, 1976; Voices From the Gods, 1978; Reincarnation, 1981; My First Prayer-Book, 1981. Add: Imber Court Cottage, Orchard Lane, East Molesey, Surrey KT8 OBN, England.

CHRISTMAS, Joyce. Also writes with Jon Peterson under joint pseudonym as Christmas Peterson. American, b. 1939. Mystery/

Crime/Suspense. Public Relations and Advertising Writer and Copy Ed., Writer mag., Boston, since 1976 (Editorial Asst., 1963–68; Assoc. Ed., 1973–76); Hotel computer consultant and Managing Ed. CKC Report: Hotel Technology Newsletter, NYC, since 1981. *Publs:* (as Christmas Peterson) Hidden Assets, 1981; Blood, 1982; Dark Tide, 1983; Suddenly, in Her Sorbet, 1988. Add: c/o Evan Marshall, 228 Watchung Ave., Upper Montclair, N.J., 07043, U.S.A.

CHRISTOPH, James B. American, b. 1928. Politics/Government. Prof. of Political Science and West European Studies, Indiana Univ. Bloomington, since 1967. (Chmn. of Dept., 1967–71; Dir., West European Studies, 1973–74). Instr., then Prof., Ohio State Univ., Columbus, 1955–66; Fulbright-Hays Prof. of Political Science, Bologna Center of Johns Hopkins Univ., Baltimore, Md., 1966–67. Member, Exec. Council, American Political Science Assn., 1975–77; Pres., British Politics Group, 1978–80. *Publs:* Capital Punishment and British Politics, 1962; Britain at the Crossroads, 1969; (ed. and author with B. Brown) Cases in Comparative Politics: Europe, 3rd ed. 1976. Add: 4875 Heritage Woods Rd., Bloomington, Ind. 47401, U.S.A.

CHRISTOPHER, John. Pseudonym for C.S. Youd; also writes as Hilary Ford. British, b. 1922. Novels/Short stories, Science fiction/Fantasy, Children's fiction. *Publs:* The Twenty-Second Century (stories), 1954; The Year of the Comet, 1955; The Death of Grass (in U.S. as No Blade of Grass), 1956; The Caves of Night, 1958; (as Hilary Ford) Felix Walking, 1958; (as Hilary Ford) Felix Running, 1959; A Scent of White Poppies, 1959; The Long Voyage (in U.S. as The White Voyage), 1960; The World in Winter (in U.S. as The Long Winter), 1962; Cloud on Silver (in U.S as Sweeney's Island), 1964; (as Hilary Ford) Bella on the Roof, 1965; The Possessors, 1965; A Wrinkle in the Skin (in U.S. as The Ragged Edge), 1965; The Little People, 1967; Pendulum, 1968; (as Hilary Ford) Sarnia, 1974; (as Hilary Ford) Castle Malindine, 1975; (as Hilary Ford) A Bride for Bedivere, 1977; for children—The White Mountains, 1967; The City of Gold and Lead, 1967; The Pool of Fire, 1968; The Lotus Caves, 1969; The Guardians, 1970; The Prince in Waiting, 1970; Beyond the Burning Lands, 1971; The Sword of the Spirits, 1972; In the Beginning, 1972; (as Hilary Ford) A Figure in Grey, 1973; Dom and Va, 1973; Wild Jack, 1974; Empty World, 1978; Fireball, 1981; New Found Land, 1984; Dragon Dance, 1986; When the Tripods Came, 1988. Add: c/o Soc. of Authors, 84 Drayton Gardens, London SW10, England.

CHRISTOPHER, Matt(hew) F. Also writes as Fredric Martin. American, b. 1917. Novels/Short stories, Children's fiction. Member, Soc. of Children's Book Writers. *Publs:* Look for the Body, 1952; The Lucky Baseball Bat, 1954; Baseball Pals, 1956; Basketball Sparkplug, 1957; Two Strikes on Johnny, 1958; Slide, Danny, Slide, 1958; Little Lefty, 1959; Touchdown for Tommy, 1959; Shadow Over the Back Court, 1959; Long Stretch at First Base, 1960; Break for the Basket, 1960; Wing T Fullback, 1960; Tall Man in the Pivot, 1961; Challenge at Second Base, 1962; Crackerback Halfback, 1962; Baseball Flyhawk, 1963; Sink It, Rusty, 1963; Catcher with a Glass Arm, 1964; Wingman on Ice, 1964; Too Hot to Handle, 1965; (as Fredric Martin) Mystery on Crabapple Hill, 1965; The Counterfeit Tackle, 1965; (as Fredric Martin) Mystery at Monkey Run, 1966; The Reluctant Pitcher, 1966; Long Shot for Paul, 1966; Miracle at the Plate, 1967; The Team that Couldn't Lose, 1967; The Year Mom Won the Pennant, 1968; (as Fredric Martin) Mystery under Fugitive House, 1968; The Basket Counts, 1968; Hard Drive to Short, 1969; Catch That Pass!, 1969; Shortstop from Tokyo, 1970; Lucky Seven, 1970; Johnny Long Legs, 1970; Look Who's Playing First Base, 1971; Tough to Tackle, 1971; The Kid Who Only Hit Homers, 1972; Face-off, 1972; Mystery Coach, 1973; Ice Magic, 1973; Front Court Hex, 1974; No Arm in Left Field, 1974; Jinx Glove, 1974; Stranded, 1974; The Team that Stopped Moving, 1975; Glue Fingers, 1975; The Pigeon with a Tennis Elbow, 1975; Earthquake, 1975; Football Fugitive, 1976; Power Play, 1976; The Submarine Pitch, 1976; Devil Pony, 1977; The Diamond Champs, 1977; Johnny No Hit, 1977; The Fox Steals Home, 1978; Jackrabbit Goalie, 1978; Soccer Halfback, 1978; Dirt Bike Racer, 1979; The Twenty-One Mile Swim, 1979; The Dog That Stole Football Plays, 1980; Wild Pitch, 1980; Run, Billy, Run, 1980; Tight End, 1981; Drag Strip Racer, 1982; The Return of the Headless Horseman, 1982; The Dog That Called the Signals, 1982; Dirt Bike Runaway, 1983; Favor for a Ghost, 1983; The Great Quarterback Switch, 1984; Supercharged Infield, 1985; The Hockey Machine, 1986; Red Hot Hightops, 1987; The Dog That Pitched a No-Hitter, 1988; The Hit-Away Kid, 1988; The Spy on Third Base, 1988; Tackle Without a Team, 1989. Add: 1830 Townes Court, Rock Hill, S.C. 29730, U.S.A.

CHRISTOPHERSEN, Paul (Hans). Danish, b. 1911. Language/Linguistics, Literature, Translations. Emeritus Prof., New Univ. of Ulster,

since 1977 (Reader in English, 1969–74; Prof., 1974–77). Research Asst., Royal Inst. of Intnl. Affairs, London, 1944–46; Prof. of English, Univ. of Copenhagen, 1946–48, Univ. of Ibadan, Nigeria, 1948–54, and Univ. of Oslo, 1954–68, and Univ. of Qatar, 1977–81. *Publs:* The Articles, 1939; (with O. Jespersen) A Modern English Grammar, vol. 6, 1942; (with H. Krabbe) To Start You Talking, 1948; Bilingualism, 1949; The Ballad of Sir Aldingar, 1952; An English Phonetics Course, 1956; Some Thoughts on the Study of English as a Foreign Language, 1957; (with A. Sandved) An Advanced English Grammar, 1969; Second-Language Learning, 1973; (trans.) Tina, by Herman Bang, 1984. Add: 1 Corfe Close, Cambridge CB2 2QA, England.

CHURCHILL, Caryl. British, b. 1938. Plays/Screenplays. Resident Writer, Royal Court Theatre, London, 1974. *Publs:* Owners, 1973; Vinegar Tom, 1978; Light Shining in Buckinghamshire, 1976; Traps, 1978; Cloud Nine, 1979; Top Girls, 1982; Fen, 1983; Softcops, 1984; Collected Plays, vol. I, 1985; (with David Lan) A Mouthful of Birds, 1987; Serious Money, 1987. Add: c/o Margaret Ramsay Ltd., 14a Goodwin's Ct., London WC2N 4LL, England.

CHURCHILL, Elizabeth. *See* **HOUGH,** Richard.

CHURCHILL, E. Richard. American, b. 1937. History, Recreation/Leisure/Hobbies. Freelance writer. Teacher, Park-Washington Elementary Sch., Sch. District No. 6, 1959–80. *Publs:* (co-author) Games and Puzzles for Family Leisure, 1965; (co-author) Fun with American History, 1966; (co-author) Fun with American Literature, 1968; (co-author) Short Lessons in World History, 1971; (co-author) How Our Nation Became Great, 1971; (co-author) Puzzle It Out, 1971; (co-author) Everybody Came to Leadville, 1971; The McCartys, 1972; Colorado Quiz Bag, 1973; (co-author) Community Civic Case Book, 1973; (co-author) Enriched Social Studies Teaching, 1973; (co-author) Puzzles and Quizzes, 1974; (co-author) American History Activity Reader, 1974; Doc Holliday, Bat Masterson and Wyatt Earp: Their Colorado Careers, 1974; (co-author) World History Activity Reader, 1974; Hidden Word Puzzles, 1975; Shaggy Dog Stories, 1975; Six-Million Dollar Cucumber, 1976; Hidden Word Puzzles 2, 1977; Holiday Hullabaloo!, 1977; Bionic Banana, 1979; New Puzzles, 1980; Classroom Activity Program, 1980; I Bet I Can!, 1981; Sneaky Tricks to Fool Your Friends, 1986; Instant Paper Toys, 1986; Quick and Easy Paper Toys, 1988; Instant Paper Airplanes, 1988. Add: 25890 Weld County Rd. 53, Kersey, Colo. 80644, U.S.A.

CHURCHWARD, L(loyd) G(ordon). Australian, b. 1919. History, Politics/Government. Sr. Assoc. in Political Science, Univ. of Melbourne, since 1981 (Lectr., 1945–56; Sr. Lectr., 1956–66; Reader, 1966–81). Former Sr. History Master, Knox Grammar Sch., Wahroonga, N.S.W. *Publs:* (ed.) The Australian Labor Movement 1850-1907: Extracts from Contemporary Documents by R.N. Ebbels, 1960; (with T.H. Rigby) Policy-Making in the USSR 1953–1961: Two Views, 1962; Contemporary Soviet Government, 1968, 1975; The Soviet Intelligentsia, 1973; Australia and America 1788-1972, 1979; Soviety Socialism: Social and Political Essays, 1987. Add: 18 Dalmor Ave., Mitcham, Vic. 3132, Australia.

CHUTE, Carolyn. American, b. 1947. Novels/Short stories. Full-time writer. Formerly worked as waitress, factory and farm worker, tutor, teacher, etc.; part-time Suburban Corresp., Portland Evening Express, Maine, 1976–81; Columnist, Courier Free Press, 1978–79; Creative Writing Instr., Univ. of Southern Maine, 1985. *Publs:* (with others) Inside Vacationland: New Fiction from the Real Maine, 1985; The Beans of Egypt, Maine, 1985; Metal Man, 1988. Add: c/o Jane Gelfman, John Farquharson Ltd., 250 W. 57th St., Suite 1914, New York, N.Y. 10107, U.S.A.

CHUTE, Marchette. American, b. 1909. Children's fiction, History, Biography. *Publs:* Rhymes about Ourselves, 1932; The Search for God, 1941; Rhymes about the Country, 1941; The Innocent Wayfaring, 1943; Geoffrey Chaucer of England, 1946; Rhymes about the City, 1946; The End of the Search, 1947; Shakespeare of London, 1950; An Introduction to Shakespeare (in U.K. as Shakespeare and His Stage), 1951; Ben Jonson of Westminster, 1953; The Wonderful Winter, 1954; Stories from Shakespeare, 1956; Around and About, 1957; Two Gentle Men: The Lives of George Herbert and Robert Herrick, 1959; Jesus of Israel, 1961; (with E. Perrie) The Worlds of Shakespeare, 1963; The First Liberty: A History of the Right to Vote in America, 1619-1850, 1969; The Green Tree of Democracy, 1971; Rhymes about Us, 1974. Add: c/o Elizabeth Roach, 66 Glenbrook Rd., Morris Plains, N.J. 07950, U.S.A.

CICELLIS, Kay. Greek, b. 1926. Novels/Short stories, Translations.

Publs: The Easy Way, 1950; No Name in the Street (novel), 1952; Death of a Town, 1954; Ten Seconds from Now (novel), 1957; The Way to Colonos: A Greek Triptych, 1960; (trans.) Their Most Serene Majesties, by Angel Vlachos, 1963; (trans.) Drifting Cities, by Stratis Tsirkas, 1974; (trans.) The Lost Center, by Zissimos Lorentzatos, 1980. Add: 6 Hatzikostas St., Mavili Sq., Athens 11521, Greece.

CIMINO, Michael. American, b. 1943. Screenplays. Film writer and director. *Publs:* Silent Running, 1972; Magnum Force, 1973; Thunderbolt and Lightfoot (also dir.), 1974; The Deer Hunter (also prod. and dir.) 1978; Heaven's Gate (also dir.), 1980; Year of the Dragon, 1985; The Sicilian, 1987. Add: William Morris Agency, 151 El Camino Blvd., Beverly Hills, Calif. 91212, U.S.A.

CIPOLLA, Carlo M. Italian, b. 1922. Demography, Economics, Medicine/Health. Prof. of Economic History, Univ. of California, Berkeley, and Scuola Normale Superiore, Pisa, Italy. *Publs:* Studi di Storia della moneta, 1948; Money, Prices and Civilization, 1956; (ed.) Storia dell'economia Italiana, 1959; The Economic History of World Population, 1962; Guns and Sails, 1965; Clocks and Culture, 1967; Literacy and Development, 1969; (ed.) The Economic Decline of Empires, 1970; (ed.) The Fontana Economic History of Europe, 1970; Cristofano and the Plague, 1973; Before the Industrial Revolution, 1976; Public Health and the Medical Profession in the Renaissance, 1976; Chi ruppe i rastelli a Monte Lupo, 1977; I pidocchi e il Granduca, 1979; Fighting the Plague in 17th Century Italy, 1981; The Monetary Policy of Fourteenth Century Florence, 1982; La moneta a Firenze nel Cinquecento, 1987; La moneta a Milano nel quattrocento, 1988; Tra due culture, 1988. Add: Via Montebello Battaglia 4, Pavia, Italy.

CLAIBORNE, Craig. American, b. 1920. Cooking/Gastronomy/Wine. With ABC, Chicago, 1946–49; Food Ed., New York Times, 1957–88. *Publs:* (ed.) New York Times Cook Book, 1961, 1979; New York Times Menu Cook Book, 1966; (with Pierre Franey) Time-Life Books' Classic French Cookery, 1970; Classic French Cuisine, 1970; Cooking with Herbs and Spices, rev. ed., 1970; New York Times International Cook Book, 1971; Craig Claiborne's Kitchen Primer, 1972; (with Virginia Lee) The Chinese Cook Book, 1972; Craig Claiborne's Favorites from The New York Times, vol. I, 1975, vol. II, 1976, vol. III, 1977, and vol. IV, 1978; Veal Cookery, 1978; The Gourmet Diet Cook Book, 1980; A Feast Made for Laughter: Memorable Meals: A Memoir with Recipes, 1982; Craig Claiborne's Southern Cooking, 1987. Add: 15 Clamshell Ave., Long Island, N.Y. 11937, U.S.A.

CLAMPITT, Amy. American, b. 1920. Poetry. Secty. and Promotion Dir., Oxford Univ. Press, NYC, 1943–51; Reference Librarian, National Audubon Soc., NYC, 1952–59; freelance editor and researcher, NYC, 1960–77; Editor, Dutton, publishers, NYC, 1977–82; Writer-in-Residence, Coll. of William and Mary, Williamsburg, Va., 1984–85; Visiting Writer, Amherst Coll., Massachusetts, 1986–87. *Publs:* Multitudes, Multitudes, 1974; The Isthmus, 1982; The Kingfisher, 1983; The Summer Solstice, 1983; Homage to John Keats, 1984; What the Light Was Like, 1985; Archaic Figure, 1987; (ed.) The Essential Donne, 1988. Add: c/o Alfred A. Knopf, Inc., 201 E. 50th St., New York, NY 10022, U.S.A.

CLANCY, Laurie. (Laurence James Clancy). Australian, b. 1942. Novels/Short stories. Sr. Lectr., Dept. of English, La Trobe Univ., Bundoora, Vic. (joined faculty, 1967). Tutor in English, Univ. of Melbourne, 1965–67. *Publs:* A Collapsible Man (novel), 1975; The Wife Specialist (short stories), 1979; Perfect Love (novel), 1983. Add: 647 Canning St., North Carlton, Vic. 3054, Australia.

CLANCY, Thomas H. American, b. 1923. Politics/Government, Vice-Pres. for Communications, Loyola Univ., New Orleans, since 1978. Prof., 1960–70, and Chmn., 1966–69, Dept. of Political Science, and Academic Vice-Pres., 1968–70, Loyola Univ., New Orleans, La.; Assoc. Ed., American weekly, 1970–71; Provincial Superior, New Orleans Province, Soc. of Jesus, 1971–77. *Publs:* Papist Pamphleteers, 1964; English Catholic Books 1641-1700, 1974; An Introduction to Jesuit Life, 1976; The Conversational Word of God, 1978. Add: WWL, 1024 N. Rampart St., New Orleans, La. 70176, U.S.A.

CLANCY, Tom. American, b. 1947. Novels/Short stories. *Publs:* The Hunt for Red October, 1984; Red Storm Rising, 1986; Patriot Games, 1987; The Cardinal in the Kremlin, 1988. Add: c/o Putnam, 200 Madison Ave., New York, N.Y. 10016, U.S.A.

CLAPHAM, Christopher. British, b. 1941. International relations/Current affairs. Sr. Lectr. in Politics, Univ. of Lancaster, since 1974. *Publs:* Haile-Selassie's Government, 1969; Liberia and Sierra Leone: An Essay in Comparative Politics, 1976; Foreign Policy Making in Developing States, 1977; Private Patronage and Public Power, 1982; (ed.) Political Dilemmas of Military Regimes, 1984; Third World Politics, 1985; Transformation and Continuity in Revolutionary Ethiopia, 1988. Add: Dept. of Politics, Univ. of Lancaster, LA1 4YF, England.

CLAPHAM, John. British, b. 1908. Music. Lectr., University Coll. of Wales, Aberystwyth, 1946–62; Sr. Lectr., 1962–69, and Reader, 1969–75, Univ. of Edinburgh. Examiner to Associated Bd. of Royal Schs. of Music, 1948–76. *Publs:* Antonin Dvořák: Musician and Craftsman, 1966; Smetana, 1972; Dvořák, 1979. Add: Dulas Court, Pontrilas, Herefordshire HR2 0HL, England.

CLAPP, Patricia. American, b. 1912. Children's fiction, Plays/Screenplays. *Publs:* Peggy's on the Phone, 1956; Smart Enough to be Dumb, 1956; Incompleted Pass, 1957; The Kissing Cousin, 1957; The Curley Tale, 1958; The Girl Out Front, 1958; The Ghost of a Chance, 1958; Inquire Within, 1959; Edie-Across-the-Street, 1960; The Honeysuckle Hedge, 1960; Never Keep Him Waiting, 1961; Red Heels and Roses, 1961; If a Body Meet Body, 1963; Now Hear This, 1963; Constance (novel), 1968; Jane-Emily (novel), 1969; The Invisible Dragon, 1971; Dr. Elizabeth, 1974; King of the Dollhouse, 1974; I'm Deborah Sampson (novel), 1977; The Mudcake Princess, 1978; The Truly Remarkable Puss-in-Boots, 1979; Witches' Children (novel), 1982; The Tamarack Tree (novel), 1986. Add: 83 Beverley Rd., Upper Montclair, N.J. 07043, U.S.A.

CLARE, Elizabeth. *See* **COOK,** Dorothy Mary.

CLARE, Ellen. *See* **SINCLAIR,** Olga Ellen.

CLARE, George (Peter). British, b. 1920. Autobiography/Memoirs/Personal, Documentaries/Reportage. Managing Dir., Axel Springer Publishing Group, London, 1963–83. *Publs:* Last Waltz in Vienna, 1981; Berlin Days 1946–1947, 1989. Add: 6-8 The Street, Dalham, Suffolk CB8 8TF, England.

CLARE, Helen. *See* **CLARKE,** Pauline.

CLARE, William. American, b. 1935. Poetry, Literature. Dir., Washington Office, State Univ. of New York, since 1971. Chief Legislative Asst., U.S. Representative Silvio O. Conte, House of Representatives, Washington, 1961–64; Dir. of Govt. Relations, American Paper Inst., Washington, 1964–68; Exec. Dir., World Federalists, Washington, D.C., 1968–71; Ed. and Pubr., Voyages: A National Literary Mag., Washington, 1967–73; Judge, D.C. Commn. on the Arts, 1975–76; Member of the Bd., Folger Shakespeare Library Coordinating Cttee., Washington, 1977–78. *Publs:* Strange Coherence of Our Dreams (verse), 1974; (ed.) Publishing in the West: Alan Swallow, 1975; From a Southern France Notebook (verse), 1975; To Break the Marble Shell: The Poetry of Michelangelo, 1977; (ed.) The Essays of Mark Van Doren 1924–1972, 1980. Add: Washington Office, SUNY, 1730 Rhode Island Ave. N.W., Suite 500, Washington, D.C. 20036, U.S.A.

CLARK, Ann Nolan. American, b. 1896. Novels/Short stories, Children's fiction. Education Supvr., Bureau of Indian Affairs, 1920–62; trained teachers in Latin America, 1945–50. *Publs:* Who Wants to Be a Prairie Dog? (reader), 1940; Little Herder in Spring [Autumn, Winter, Summer] (readers), 4 vols., 1940, 1942; Little Boy with Three Names: Stories of Taos Pueblo (reader) 1940; In My Mother's House (reader), 1941; The Pine Ridge Porcupine (reader), 1941; (with Frances Carey) A Child's Story of New Mexico, 1941; There Still Are Buffalo (reader), 1942; the Slim Butte Raccoon (reader), 1942; The Grass Mountain Mouse (reader), 1942; Buffalo Caller: The Story of a Young Sioux Boy of the Early 1700's Before the Coming of the Horse, 1942; Young Hunter of Picuris, 1943; Little Navajo Bluebird, 1943; The Hen of Wahpeton (reader), 1943; Bringer of the Mystery Dog (reader), 1943; Brave Against the Enemy: A Story of Three Generations—of the Day Before Yesterday, of Yesterday and of Tomorrow (reader), 1944; Sun Journey: A Story of the Zuni Pueblo (reader), 1945; Singing Sioux Cowboy Reader, 1947; Magic Money, 1950; Secret of the Andes, 1952; Looking-for-Something: The Story of a Stray Burro of Ecuador, 1952; Blue Canyon Horse, 1954; Santiago, 1955; Third Monkey (verse), 1956; Little Indian Pottery Maker, 1957; The Little Indian Basket Maker, 1957; A Santo for Pasqualita, 1959; World Song, 1960; Paco's Miracle, 1962; The Desert People, 1962; Father Kino: Priest to the Pimas, 1963; Tia Maria's Garden, 1963; Medicine Man's Daughter, 1963; This for That, 1965; Bear Cub (verse), 1965; Brother Andre of Montreal, 1967; Summer Is for Growing, 1968; Along

Sandy Trails, 1969; Journey to the People (for adults), 1969; These Were the Valiant: A Collection of New Mexico Profiles (for adults), 1969; Circle of Seasons, 1970; Hoofprint on the Wind, 1972; Year Walk, 1975; All This Wild Land, 1976; To Stand Against the Wind, 1978; In the Land of Small Dragon, 1979. Add: P.O. Box 164, Cortaro, Ariz. 95230, U.S.A.

CLARK of Herriotshall, Arthur Melville. British, b. 1895. Poetry, Language/Linguistics, Literature, Biography. Reader Emeritus in English Literature, Univ. of Edinburgh. Ed., Edinburgh Univ. Calendar, 1933–46. *Publs:* Realistic Revolt in Modern Poetry, 1922; Bibliography of Thomas Heywood, 1924; Thomas Heywood: Playwright and Miscellanist, 1931; Autobiography: Its Genesis and Phases, 1935; (ed. with John Purves) Seventeenth Century Studies, 1938; (ed. with A. Muir and J.W. Oliver) George Saintsbury: The Memorial Volume (in U.S. as A Saintsbury Miscellany), 1945; Studies in Literary Modes, 1946, 1958; Spoken English, 1946, 4th ed. 1965; (ed. with A. Muir and J.W. Oliver) A Last Vintage: Essays and Papers by George Saintsbury, 1950; Sonnets from the French and Other Verses, 1966; Sir Walter Scott: The Formative Years, 1969; Murder under Trust, 1982. Add: 3 Woodburn Terr., Edinburgh EH10 4SH, Scotland.

CLARK, Brian (Robert). British, b. 1932. Children's fiction, Plays/Screenplays, Theatre. Founder, Amber Lane Press. Former sch. teacher; Staff Tutor in Drama, Univ. of Hull, 1968–72. *Publs:* Group Theatre (non-fiction), 1972; (with others) Lay By, 1972; Whose Life Is It Anyway?, 1979; Can You Hear Me at the Back?, 1979; (with Jim Hawkins) Out of Bounds (juvenile; novelization of TV series), 1979; Post Mortem, 1979; The Petition, 1986. Add: c/o Judy Daish Assocs., 83 Eastbourne Mews, London W2 6LQ, England.

CLARK, Bruce (Budge). American, b. 1918. Literature. Prof. of English, and Dean, Emeritus, Coll. of the Humanities, Brigham Young Univ., Provo, Utah. *Publs:* The Longer Carmel Narrative Poems of Robinson Jeffers, 1947; The English Sonnet Sequence 1850 to 1900, 1951; The Spectrum of Faith in Victorian Literature, 1962; The Challenge of Teaching, 1964; Out of the Best Books: A Critical Anthology of Literature, 5 vols., 1964–69; Wisdom and Beauty Through Literature, 1966; Oscar Wilde: A Study in Genius and Tragedy, 1970; Romanticism Through Modern Eyes, 1970; Brigham Young on Education, 1970; Richard Evans' Quote Book, 1971; Idealists in Revolt: An Introduction to English Romanticism, 1975; Favorite Selections from Out of the Best Books, 1979; Great Short Stories for Discussion and Delight, 1980; The Brigham Young Univ., College of Humanities, 1965–1981, 3 vols., 1985; (ed.) My Brother Richard L., 1985. Add: 365 E. 1655 St., Orem, Utah 84058, U.S.A.

CLARK, Charles E. American, b. 1929. History. Prof. of History, Univ. of New Hampshire, Durham, since 1975 (Asst. Prof., 1967–70; Assoc. Prof., 1970–75; Chmn. of the Dept., 1977–80). Reporter, Providence Journal, and Evening Bulletin, R.I., 1956–61; Asst. Prof. of History, Southeastern Massachusetts Technological Inst., North Dartmouth, 1965–67. *Publs:* The Eastern Frontier: The Settlement of Northern New England, 1610-1763, 1970, 1983; Maine: A Bicentennial History, 1977; (ed. with James S. Leamon and Karen Bowden) Maine in the Early Republic: From Revolution to Statehood, 1988. Add: 2 Thompson Lane, Durham, N.H. 03824, U.S.A.

CLARK, Curt. *See* **WESTLAKE,** Donald E.

CLARK, David. *See* **HARDCASTLE,** Michael.

CLARK, David Ridgley. American, b. 1920. Poetry, Literature. Emeritus Prof. of English, Univ. of Massachusetts, Amherst, since 1985 (Instr., 1951–58; Asst. Prof., 1958; Assoc. Prof., 1958–65; Prof., 1965–85; Chmn., Dept. of English, 1975–76). *Publs:* (with G.S. Koehler, L.O. Barron and R.G. Tucker) A Curious Quire (poetry), 1962, 1967; W.B. Yeats and the Theatre of Desolate Reality, 1965; (ed. with R. Skelton) Irish Renaissance, 1965; Dry Tree (poetry), 1966; (with F.B. Millett and A.W. Hoffman) Reading Poetry, 1968; (ed.) Riders to the Sea, 1970; (ed.) Studies in "The Bridge", 1970; (ed. with G.P. Mayhew) A Tower of Polished Black Stones: Early Versions of "The Shadowy Waters", 1971; (ed. with M.J. Sidnell and G.P. Mayhew) Druid Craft: The Writing of "The Shadowy Waters", 1971; (ed.) Twentieth Century Interpretations of "Murder in the Cathedral", 1971; Lyric Resonance: Glosses on Some Poems of Yeats, Frost, Crane, Cummings and Others (essays), 1972; "That Black Day": The Manuscripts of "Crazy Jane on the Day of Judgment", 1980; (ed.) Critical Essays on Hart Crane, 1982; Yeats at Songs and Choruses, 1983; (ed. with James McGuire) W.B. Yeats: The Writing of "Sophocles' King Oedipus", 1989. Add: 330 Market Hill Rd., Amherst, Mass. 01002, U.S.A.

CLARK, Douglas (Malcolm Jackson). Has also written as James Ditton and Peter Hosier. British, b. 1919. Mystery/Crime/Suspense. Executive with a pharmaceutical company, now retired. *Publs:* (as D.M.J. Clark) Suez Touchdown: A Soldier's Tale, 1964; Nobody's Perfect, 1969; Death after Evensong, 1969; Deadly Pattern, 1970; Sweet Poison, 1970; Sick to Death, 1971; (as Peter Hosier) The Miracle Makers (non-mystery novel), 1971; (as James Ditton) You're Fairly Welcome, 1973; (as James Ditton) The Bigger They Are, 1973; (as James Ditton) Escapemanship, 1975; Premedicated Murder, 1975; Dread and Water, 1976; Table d'Hôte, 1977; The Gimmel Flask, 1977; The Libertines, 1978; Heberden's Seat, 1979; Poacher's Bag, 1980; Golden Rain, 1980; Roast Eggs, 1981; The Longest Pleasure, 1981; Shelf Life, 1982; Doone Walk, 1982; Vicious Circle, 1983; The Monday Theory, 1983; Bouquet Garni, 1984; Dead Letter, 1984; Performance, 1985; Jewelled Eye, 1985; Storm Centre, 1986; The Big Grouse, 1986; Bitter Water, 1988. Add: c/o John Farquharson Ltd., 162-168 Regent St., London W1R 5TB, England.

CLARK, Eleanor. American, b. 1913. Novels/Short stories, Travel/Exploration/Adventure, Translations. Editorial Staff Member, W.W. Norton & Co., publrs., NYC, 1936–39. *Publs:* (ed. with H. Gregory) New Letters in America, 1937; (trans.) Dark Wedding, by Ramón José Sender, 1943; The Bitter Box (novel), 1946; Rome and a Villa, 1952, rev. ed. 1974; Song of Roland, 1960; The Oysters of Locmariaquer, 1964; Baldur's Gate (novel), 1970; Dr. Heart: A Novella and Other Stories, 1974; Eyes, Etc.: A Memoir, 1977; Gloria Mundi (novel), 1979; Tamrart: Thirteen Days in the Sahara, 1984; Camping Out (novel), 1986. Add: 2495 Redding Rd., Fairfield, Conn. 06430, U.S.A.

CLARK, Eric. British, b. 1937. Novels, Current affairs. Reporter, Daily Mail, London, 1962–64; Writer, The Guardian, London, 1964–66, and The Observer, London, 1966–72. *Publs:* (co-author) Len Deighton's London Dossier, 1967; Everybody's Guide to Survival, 1969; Corps Diplomatique (in U.S. as Diplomat: The World of International Diplomacy), 1973; Black Gambit, 1978; The Sleeper, 1979; Send in the Lions, 1981; Chinese Burn (in U.S. as China Run), 1984; The Want Makers: Lifting the Lid Off the World Advertising Industry, 1988. Add: c/o Jonathan Clowes Agency, 22 Prince Albert Rd., London NW1 7ST, England.

CLARK, J(onathan) C(harles) D(ouglas). British, b. 1951. History. Fellow of All Souls Coll., Oxford, since 1986. Research Fellow, Peterhouse, Cambridge, 1977–81. *Publs:* The Dynamics of Change: The Crisis of the 1750s and English Party Systems, 1982; English Society 1688-1832: Ideology, Social Structure and Political Practice During the Ancien Regime, 1985; Revolution and Rebellion: State and Society in England in the Seventeenth and Eighteenth Centuries, 1986; (ed.) The Memoirs and Speeches of James, 2nd Earl Waldegrave, 1742-1988. Add: All Souls Coll., Oxford, England.

CLARK, J(ohn) Desmond. British, b. 1916. Anthropology/Ethnology. Prof. Emeritus of Anthropology, Univ. of California, Berkeley, since 1986 (member of Faculty since 1961). Dir., Rhodes-Livingstone Museum, Zambia, 1938–61; Secty., Northern Rhodesia National Monuments Commn., 1948–61, and Victoria Falls Trust, Zambia, 1950–61; Curator of Archaeology, Lowie Museum of Anthropology, 1963–87. *Publs:* The Stone Age Cultures of Northern Rhodesia, 1950; The Prehistoric Cultures of the Horn of Africa, 1954; (ed. with S. Cole) Proceedings of the Third Pan-African Congress, Livingstone 1955, 1957; The Prehistory of Southern Africa, 1959; (ed. and contrib.) The Victoria Falls and the Batoka Gorge, 1952; (with R.F. Summers, C.K. Cooke and E. Goodall) The Rock Art of the Federation of Rhodesia and Nyasaland, 1959; Prehistoric Cultures of North East Angola and Their Significance in Tropical Africa, 2 vols., 1963; (ed. with F.C. Howell, and contrib.) Recent Studies in Palaeoanthropology, 1966; The Distribution of Prehistoric Culture in Angola, 1966; (compiler and contrib.) Atlas of African Prehistory, 1967; (ed. with W.W. Bishop, and contrib.) Background to Evolution in Africa, 1967; Further Palaeoanthropological Studies in Northern Lunda, 1968; Kalambo Falls Prehistoric Site, vol. I, 1969, vol. II, 1974; Prehistory of Africa, 1970; (ed. and contrib.) Cambridge History of Africa (vol. I), 1981; (ed. with G.R. Sharma and contrib.) Palaeoenvironments and Prehistory in the Middle Son Valley, Northern Central India, 1983; (ed. with S.A. Brandt and contrib.) From Hunters to Farmers, 1984. Add: Dept. of Anthropology, Univ. of California, Berkeley, Calif. 94720, U.S.A.

CLARK, John Grahame Douglas. British, b. 1907. Anthropology/Ethnology, Archaeology/Antiquities. Master of Peterhouse, Cambridge, 1973–80 (Disney Prof. of Archaeology, Cambridge Univ., 1952–74). *Publs:* The Mesolithic Age in Britain, 1932; The Mesolithic Settlement of Northern Europe, 1936; Archaeology and Society, 1939, 3rd ed. 1957; Prehistoric England, 1940, 5th ed. 1962; From Savagery to Civilisation, 1946; Prehistoric Europe: The Economic Basis, 1952; Excavations at Star Carr, 1954; World Prehistory: An Outline, 1961; (with S. Piggott) Prehistoric Societies, 1965; The Stone Age Hunters, 1967; World Prehistory: A New Outline, 1969; Aspects of Prehistory, 1970; The Earlier Stone Age Settlements of Scandinavia, 1974; World Prehistory in New Perspective, 3rd ed. 1977; Sir Mortimer and Indian Archaeology, 1979; Mesolithic Prelude, 1980; The Identity of Man as Seen by an Archaeologist, 1982; Symbols of Excellence, 1986; Prehistory at Cambridge and Beyond, 1989; Economic Prehistory, 1989. Add: 36 Millington Rd., Cambridge, England.

CLARK, John Pepper. Nigerian, b. 1935. Plays/Screenplays, Poetry, Literature. Prof. of English, Univ. of Lagos, Nigeria. Nigerian Govt. Information Officer, 1960–61; Head of Features and Editorial Writer, Daily Express, Lagos, 1961–62; Founding Ed., The Horn mag., Ibadan. *Publs:* Song of a Goat, 1961; Poems, 1962; Three Plays: Song of a Goat, The Raft, The Masquerade, 1964; America, Their America, 1964; A Reed in the Tide: A Selection of Poems, 1964; Ozidi, 1966; Examples of Shakespeare: Critical Essays on African Literature, 1970; Casualties: Poems 1966–1968, 1970; The Ozidi Saga, 1975; The Hero as a Villain, 1978; Urhobo Poetry, 1980; A Decade of Tongues: Selected Poems 1958–1968, 1981. Add: Dept of English, Univ. of Lagos, Lagos, Nigeria.

CLARK, John R(ichard). American, b. 1930. Literature. Prof. of English, Univ. of South Florida, Tampa, since 1973. Contributing Ed., Freshman English News, since 1972. Member, Editorial Bd., Studies in Contemporary Satire, since 1977. Asst. Prof., Alfred Univ., Alfred, New York, 1958–65; Muhlenberg Coll., Allentown, Pa., 1965–66, and City Coll., NYC, 1966–68; Assoc. Prof., Fordham Univ., NYC, 1968–69, and New York Univ., 1969–73; Assoc. Ed., Seventeenth-Century News, 1974–82. *Publs:* Form and Frenzy in Swift's "Tale of a Tub", 1970; (co-author) Satire: That Blasted Art, 1973; Senecan Tragedy, 1988. Add: Dept. of English, Univ. of South Florida, Tampa, Fla. 33620, U.S.A.

CLARK, Kenneth Bancroft. American, b. 1914. Psychology, Race relations. Prof. Emeritus of Psychology of City Coll. of City Univ. of N.Y., since 1976 (Staff, 1942–75; Prof. 1960–70; Distinguished Univ. Prof., 1970–75). Pres., Kenneth B. Clark and Assocs. Inc., since 1986. Social Science Consultant, Legal and Educational Div., NAACP, since 1950; Consultant, Personnel Div., U.S. Dept. of State; Member Emeritus, Bd. of Regents, State of New York, and Bd. of Dirs., Harper and Row, Lincoln Savings Bank, Univ. of Chicago, Northside Center for Child Development and Woodrow Wilson Intnl. Center for Scholars. Pres., Metropolitan Applied Research Center, 1967–75; Member, Bd. of Dirs., Urban Development Corp. and Chmn., Affirmative Action Commn. of Urban Development Corp., 1971–75. Member, Commn. of Foreign Affairs Personnel, 1961–62; Pres., American Psychological Assn., 1970–71. *Publs:* Desegregation: An Appraisal of the Evidence, 1953; Prejudice and Your Child, 1955; Dark Ghetto, 1965; (with Talcott Parsons) The Negro American, 1966; (with Jeanette Hopkins) A Relevant War Against Poverty, 1968; (co-author) How Relevant is Education in America Today, 1970; A Possible Reality, 1972; Pathos of Power, 1974; (with John H. Franklin) The Nineteen Eighties: Prologue and Prospect, 1981. Add: Kenneth B. Clark and Assocs., Inc., 615 Broadway, Hastings-on-Hudson, N.Y. 10706, U.S.A.

CLARK, La Verne Harrell. American, b. 1929. Novels/Short stories, Cultural/Ethnic topics, Mythology/Folklore. Lecturer, freelance writer and photographer. Dir., Univ. of Arizona Poetry Center, Tucson, 1962–66. *Publs:* They Sang for Horses: The Impact of the Horse on the Folklore of the Navajo and Apache Indians, 1966, 1971, 1984; (ed.) The Face of Poetry: 101 Poets in Two Significant Decades: The Sixties and the Seventies, 1977, 1979; Re-visiting the Plains Indian Country of Mari Sandoz, 1977; Focus 101, 1979; The Deadly Swarm and Other stories, 1985, 1987. Add: 4690 N. Campbell Ave., Tucson, Ariz. 85718, U.S.A.

CLARK, Margaret Goff. American, b. 1913. Children's fiction. Taught in elementary schs., also creative writing in adult education progs. *Publs:* The Mystery of Seneca Hill, 1961; The Mystery of the Buried Indian Mask, 1962; Mystery of the Marble Zoo, 1964; Mystery at Star Lake, 1965; Adirondack Mountain Mystery, 1966; The Mystery of the Missing Stamps, 1967; Danger at Niagara, 1968; Freedom Crossing, 1971; Mystery Horse, 1972; Their Eyes on the Stars: Four Black Writers, 1973; John Muir, 1974; Death at Their Heels, 1975; Mystery of Sebastian Island, 1976; Mystery in the Flooded Museum, 1978; Barney and the UFO, 1979; Who Stole Kathy Young, 1980; Barney in Space, 1981; The Boy from the UFO, 1981; Barney on Mars, 1983; The Latchkey Mystery, 1985.

Add: 5749 Palm Beach Blvd., No. 334, Fort Myers, Fla. 33905, U.S.A.

CLARK, Mary Higgins. American, b. 1929. Mystery/Crime/Suspense. Creative Dir. and Chmn. of the Bd., D.J. Clark Enterprises, NYC, since 1980. Radio scriptwriter and producer for Robert G. Jennings, 1965–70; Partner and Vice-Pres., Aerial Communications, 1970–80. Pres., Mystery Writers of America, 1987. *Publs:* Where Are the Children?, 1975; A Stranger Is Watching, 1978; The Cradle Will Fall, 1980; A Cry in the Night, 1982; Stillwatch, 1984; Weep No More, My Lady, 1987; While My Pretty One Sleeps, 1989. Add: 210 Central Park S., New York, N.Y. 10019, U.S.A.

CLARK, Mary T. American. Philosophy. Prof. of Philosophy, Manhattanville Coll., Purchase, N.Y., since 1951; Exec. Cttee., Catholic Commn. on Intellectual and Cultural Affairs, since 1988. Visiting Prof., State Univ. of New York at Purchase, since 1989. N.E.H. Fellowship for College Teachers, 1984–85; Secretary-Treasurer, Society for Medieval and Renaissance Philosophy, since 1978; Executive Council, The Metaphysical Soc. of America, 1984–88. Editorial Adviser, Dionysius; Logos; The Personalist Forum. Pres., American Catholic Philosophical Assn., 1976–77; Visiting Prof., Univ. of San Francisco, 1967, Villanova Univ., 1980, Fordham Univ., 1981, and Univ. of Santa Clara, 1983. Exec. Cttee., American Philosophical Assn., 1988–91. *Publs:* Augustine, Philosopher of Freedom, 1959; (with Casey) Logic, A Practical Approach, 1963; Discrimination Today, 1966; Augustinian Personalism, 1970; (ed. and trans.) An Aquinas Reader, 1973; (ed.) Problem of Freedom, 1973; (trans.) Theological Treatises of Marius Victorinus, 1981; Augustine of Hippo, 1984. Add: Manhattanville Coll., Purchase, N.Y. 10577, U.S.A.

CLARK, Mavis Thorpe. Also writes as Mavis Latham. Australian. Children's fiction, Children's non-fiction, Biography. *Publs:* Hatherly's First Fifteen, 1930; Dark Pool Island, 1949; Missing Gold, 1949; The Twins from Timber Creek, 1949; Home Again at Timber Creek, 1950; Jingaroo, 1951; The Brown Land Was Green, 1956; Gully of Gold, 1958; Pony from Tarella, 1959; (as Mavis Latham) John Batman, 1962; (as Mavis Latham) Fishing, 1963; They Came South, 1963; Pastor Doug, 1965, 1972; The Min-Min, 1966; Blue Above the Trees, 1967; Spark of Opal, 1968; A Pack Tracker, 1968; Opal Mining, 1969; Nowhere to Hide, 1969; Iron Mountain, 1970; Strolling Players, 1972; New Golden Mountain (in U.S. as If the Earth Falls In), 1973; Wildlife, 1973; The Sky Is Free, 1974; The Hundred Islands, 1976; Spanish Queen, 1977; The Boy from Cumeroogunga, 1979; The Lilly-Pilly, 1979; A Stranger Came to the Mine, 1980; Solomon's Child, 1982; Young and Brave, 1984; No Mean Destiny: History of the War Widows' Guild, Australia, 1986; Soft-Shoe, 1988. Add: 1/22 Rochester Rd., Canterbury, Vic. 3126, Australia.

CLARK, Merle. *See* **GESSNER**, Lynne.

CLARK, Robert. Australian, b. 1911. Poetry. Co-Ed., Verse in Australia, Australian Letters, Adelaide, 1958–61. *Publs:* The Dogman and Other Poems, 1962; (ed.) A Window at Night: The Poems of Max Harris, 1967: Segments of the Bowl, 1968; Thrusting into Darkness, 1978; Walking to Bethongabel, 1986. Add: 42 Burlington St., Walkerville, S.A. 5081, Australia.

CLARK, Ronald Harry. British, b. 1904. Engineering, Transportation. Chartered mechanical engineer. *Publs:* Steam Engine Builders of Norfolk, 1948, 3rd ed. 1988; Steam Engine Builders of Suffolk, Essex, and Cambridgeshire, 1950; Chronicles of a Country Works, 1952; Steam Engine Builders of Lincolnshire, 1955; The Development of the English Traction Engine, 1962; Brough Superior: The Rolls-Royce of Motor Cycles, 1964, 3rd ed. 1984; Savages Limited 1850-1964, 1964; The Development of the English Steam Wagon, 1966: A Short History of the Midland and Great Northern Joint Railway, 1967; A Traction Engine Miscellany, 1975; Some Adventures of Samson Cogg, 1975; Scenes On the Midland and Great Northern Joint Railway, 1978. Add: Diamond Cottage, Shotesham All Saints, Norwich, Norfolk, England.

CLARK, Terry N(icholas). American, b. 1940. Sociology. Prof. of Sociology, since 1985, and Research Assoc. National Opinion Research Center, since 1974, Univ. of Chicago (Asst. Prof., 1966–71; Assoc. Prof., 1971–85). Member, Editorial Bds.: American Journal of Sociology, since 1966, Comparative Urban Research, since 1972, and Policy and Politics, since 1973; Dir., Comparative Study of Community Decision- Making, Univ. of Chicago, since 1967; Pres., Research Cttee. on Community Research, Intnl. Sociological Assn., since 1970. Member, Editorial Bd., Social Science Quarterly, 1967–70, and Administrative Science Quarterly, 1968–72; Chmn., Cttee. on Community Research and Development, Soc. for the Study of Social Problems, 1970–71. *Publs:* (ed. and co-author)

Community Structure and Decision-Making: Comparative Analyses, 1968; (ed.) Gabriel Tarde on Communication and Social Influence, 1969; (author and ed. with C.M. Bonjean and R.L. Lineberry) Community Politics: A Behavioral Approach, 1971; Prophets and Patrons: The French University and the Emergence of the Social Sciences, 1973; Community Power and Policy Outputs, 1973; (co-author and co-ed.) Comparative Community Politics, 1974; (with I. Leif) Community Power and Decision-Making: Trend Report and Bibliography, 1974; Leadership in American Cities: Resources, Interchanges and the Press, 1974; (co-author and ed.) Citizen Preferences and Urban Public Policy, 1976; (with Joseph Ben-David) Culture and Its Creators: Essays in Honor of Edward Shils, 1977; (with Schumaker and Getter) Policy Responsiveness and the Fiscal Strain in 51 American Communities, 1979; Urban Policy Analysis: Directions for Future Research, 1981; (co- author) City Money, 1983; (ed.) Research in Urban Policy (annual), 1985–; (with others) Financial Handbook for Mayors and City Managers, 1985. Add: Dept. of Sociology, Univ. of Chicago, 1126 E. 59th St., Chicago, Ill. 60637, U.S.A.

CLARK, Tom. American, b. 1941. Novels/Short stories, Plays/Screenplays, Poetry, Literature. Sr. Writer, Boulder Monthly, since 1978. Poetry Ed., Paris Review, NYC and Paris, 1963–73; Instr. in American Poetry, Univ. of Essex, Wivenhoe, 1966–67. *Publs:* Airplanes, 1966; The Sand Burg: Poems, 1966; The Emperor of the Animals (play), 1967; (with Ron Padgett) Bun, 1968; Stones, 1969; Air, 1970; Green, 1971; John's Heart, 1972; (with Ted Berrigan and R. Padgett) Back in Boston Again, 1972; Smack, 1972; Blue, 1974; Suite, 1974; Chicago, 1974; At Malibu, 1975; Baseball, 1976; Champagne and Baloney, 1976; Fan Poems, 1976; 35, 1977; (with Mark Fidrych) No Big Deal, 1977; How I Broke In Six Modern Masters, 1978; The World of Damon Runyon, 1978; When Things Get Tough on Easy Street: Selected Poems, 1978; One Last Round for the Shuffler, 1979; Who is Sylvia? (novel), 1979; The Master (novel), 1979; The Great Naropa Poetry Wars, 1980; The Last Gas Station and Other Stories, 1980; The End of the Line, 1980; A Short Guide to the High Plains, 1981; Nine Songs, 1981; Heartbreak Hotel, 1981; Under the Fortune Palms, 1982; Jack Kerouac, 1984; The Exile of Celine, 1987; Easter Sunday, 1987. Add: 822 Windsor Way, Santa Barbara, Calif. 93105, U.S.A.

CLARKE, Anna. British, b. 1919. Mystery/Crime/Suspense. Secty., Victor Gollancz, publishers, London, 1947–50, and Eyre and Spottiswoode, publishers, London, 1951–53; Admin. Secty., British Assn. for American Studies, London, 1956–63. *Publs:* The Darkened Room, 1968; A Mind to Murder, 1971; The End of a Shadow, 1972; Plot Counter-Plot, 1974; My Search for Ruth, 1975; Legacy of Evil, 1976; The Deathless and the Dead, 1976 (in U.S. as This Downhill Path, 1977); The Lady in Black, 1977; Letter from the Dead, 1977; One of Us Must Die, 1978; The Poisoned Web, 1979; Poison Parsley, 1979; Last Voyage, 1980; Game Set and Danger, 1981; Desire to Kill, 1982; We the Bereaved, 1982; Soon She Must Die, 1983; Last Judgement, 1985; Cabin 3033, 1986; The Mystery Lady, 1986; Last Seen in London, 1987; Murder in Writing, 1988; The Whitelands Affair, 1989. Add: 12 Franklin Rd., Brighton, Sussex, England.

CLARKE, Arthur C(harles). British, b. 1917. Science fiction/Fantasy, Air/Space topics, Astronomy, Marine science/Oceanography, Travel/Exploration/Adventure. Chancellor, Univ of Moratuwa, Sri Lanka, since 1979. Engaged in underwater exploration and photography of the Great Barrier Reef of Australia and the coast of Ceylon, since 1954. Asst. Auditor, Exchequer and Audit Dept., London, 1936–41; Asst. Ed., Physics Abstracts, London, 1949–50; has made numerous radio and T.V. appearances, and has lectured widely in Britain and the U.S.; Commentator, for CBS-T.V., on lunar landing flights of Apollo 11, 12 and 15. *Publs:* novels—Prelude to Space: The Sands of Mars, 1951; Islands in the Sky, 1952; Against the Fall of Night, 1953; Childhood's End, 1953; Earthlight, 1955; The City and the Stars, 1956; The Deep Range, 1957; Across the Sea of Stars, 1962; Dolphin Island: A Story of the People of the Sea, 1963; Glide Path, 1963; Prelude to Mars, 1965; An Arthur C. Clarke Omnibus, 1965; 2001: A Space Odyssey (novel and screenplay), 1968; An Arthur C. Clarke Second Omnibus, 1968; The Lion of Comarre, 1970; Rendezvous with Rama, 1972; Imperial Earth, 1975; The Fountains of Paradise, 1979; 2010: Odyssey Two, 1982; The Songs of Distant Earth, 1986; short stories—Expedition to Earth, 1953; Reach for Tomorrow, 1956; Tales of White Hart, 1957; The Other Side of the Sky, 1958; Tales of Ten Worlds, 1962; The Nine Billion Names of God: The Best Short Stories of Arthur C. Clarke, 1967; The Wind from the Sun: Stories of the Space Age, 1972; Of Time and Stars: The Worlds of Arthur C. Clarke, 1972; The Best of Arthur C. Clarke 1937–1971, 1973; The Sentinel, 1983; non-fiction—Interplanetary Flight: An Introduction to Astronautics, 1950, 1960; The Exploration of Space, 1951, 1959; The Young Traveler in Space

(in U.S. as Going into Space), 1954, rev. ed. as Into Space: A Young Person's Guide to Space, 1971; (with R.A. Smith) The Exploration of the Moon, 1954; The Coast of Coral, 1956; The Making of a Moon: The Story of the Earth Satellite Program, 1957, 1958; The Reefs of Taprobane: Underwater Adventures Around Ceylon, 1957; Voice Across the Sea, 1958, 1974; (with Mike Wilson) Boy Beneath the Sea, 1958; The Challenge of the Spaceship: Previews of Tomorrow's World, 1959; (with Mike Wilson) The First Five Fathoms: A Guide to Underwater Adventure, 1960; The Challenge of the Sea, 1960; (with Mike Wilson) Indian Ocean Adventure, 1961; Profiles of the Future: An Inquiry into the Limits of the Possible, 1962, 1973; The Treasure of the Great Reef, 1964, 1974; (with Mike Wilson) Indian Ocean Treasure, 1964; (with eds. of Life) Man and Space, 1964; Voices from the Sky: Previews of the Coming of Space Age, 1965; (ed.) Time Probe, 1966; (ed.) The Coming of the Space Age, 1967; The Promise of Space, 1968; (co-author) First on the Moon, 1970; Report on Planet Three and Other Speculations, 1972; The Lost Worlds of 2001, 1972; (with Chesley Bonestell) Beyond Jupiter: The Worlds of Tomorrow, 1972; (with Robert Silverberg) Into Space, 1972; (co-author) Technology and the Frontiers of Knowledge (lectures), 1975; The Best of Arthur C. Clarke, 2 vols., 1977; The View from Serendip, 1978; 1984: Spring: A Choice of Futures, 1984; Ascent to Orbit: A Scientific Autobiography: The Technical Writings of Arthur C. Clarke, 1984; (with Peter Hyams) The Odyssey File, 1985; July 20, 2019: Life in the 21st Century, 1986. Add: 25 Barnes Place, Colombo 7, Sri Lanka.

CLARKE, Austin (Ardinel) C(hesterfield). Barbadian, b. 1934. Novels/Short stories, Autobiography/Memoirs/Personal. Jacob Ziskind Visiting Lectr., Brandeis Univ., Waltham, Mass., since 1968; Producer and freelance broadcaster, CBC, Toronto. Visiting Prof. of Afro-American Literature and Creative Writing, Yale Univ., New Haven, Conn., 1968–71. *Publs:* The Survivors of the Crossing, 1964; Amongst Thistles and Thorns, 1965; The Meeting Point, 1967; When He Was Free and Young and He Used to Wear Silks: Stories, 1971; A Storm of Fortune, 1972; A Bigger Light, 1974; The Prime Minister, 1977; Growing Up Stupid Under the Union Jack (memoir), 1980; When Women Rule (stories), 1985; Nine Men Who Laughed (stories), 1986; Proud Empires, 1986. Add: 432 Brunswick Ave., Toronto 4, Ont., Canada.

CLARKE, Brenda (Margaret Lilian, née Honeyman). Has also written as Brenda Honeyman. British, b. 1926. Romance/Historical fiction. Full-time writer. Clerical officer in the Civil Service, Bristol, 1943–55. *Publs:* (as Brenda Honeyman) Richard by Grace of God, 1968; (as Brenda Honeyman) The Kingmaker, 1969; (as Brenda Honeyman) Richmond and Elizabeth, 1970; (as Brenda Honeyman) Harry the King, 1971, in U.S. as The Warrior King, 1972; (as Brenda Honeyman) Brother Bedford, 1972; (as Brenda Honeyman) Good Duke Humphrey, 1973; (as Brenda Honeyman) The King's Minions, 1974; (as Brenda Honeyman) The Queen and Mortimer, 1974; (as Brenda Honeyman) Edward the Warrior, 1975; (as Brenda Honeyman) All the King's Sons, 1976; (as Brenda Honeyman) The Golden Griffin, 1976; (as Brenda Honeyman) At the King's Court, 1977; (as Brenda Honeyman) The King's Tale, 1977; (as Brenda Honeyman) Macbeth, King of Scots, 1977; (as Brenda Honeyman) Emma the Queen, 1978; The Glass Island, 1978; (as Brenda Honeyman) Harold of the English, 1979; The Lofty Banners, 1979; The Far Morning, 1982; All Through the Day, 1983; A Rose in May, 1984; Three Women, 1985; Winter Landscape, 1986; Under Heaven, 1988; An Equal Chance, 1989. Add: 25 Torridge Rd., Keynsham, Bristol BS18 1QQ, England.

CLARKE, (Sir) Cyril (Astley). British, b. 1907. Biology, Medicine/Health. Emeritus Prof. of Medicine and Nuffield Research Fellow, Dept. of Genetics, Univ. of Liverpool, since 1972 (Clinical Lectr., 1946–58; Reader, 1958–65; Dir., Nuffield Unit of Medical Genetics, 1963–72; Prof. of Medicine, 1965–72). Pres., 1972–77, Dir., Medical Services Study Group, 1977–83, and Dir., Research Unit, 1983–88, Royal Coll. of Physicians. *Publs:* Genetics for the Clinician, 1962, 1964; (ed.) Selected Topics in Medical Genetics, 1969; Human Genetics and Medicine, 1970, 3rd ed. 1987; (with R.B. McConnell) Prevention of Rh Haemolytic Disease, 1972; (ed.) Rhesus Haemolytic Disease. Add: Dept. of Genetics, The University, P.O. Box 147, Liverpool L69 3BX, England.

CLARKE, Derrick Harry. British, b. 1919. Transportation, Travel/Exploration/Adventure, Autobiography/Memoirs/Personal. Listed by Guinness Book of Records as having most different paid jobs, total of 137. *Publs:* What Were They Like to Fly?, 1964; Trimarans—An Introduction, 1969, 3rd ed. 1974; The Lure of the Sea, 1970; East Coast Passage (autobiography), 1971; Trimaran Development, 1972; An Evolution of Singlehanders, 1976; The Multihull Primer, 1976; The Bluewater Dream, 1981. Add: Gables, Woolverstone, Ipswich, Suffolk IP9 1BA, England.

CLARKE, Dorothy Clotelle. American, b. 1908. Literature. Emerita Prof. of Spanish, Univ. of California, Berkeley, since 1976 (Lectr., 1945–48; Asst. Prof., 1948–55; Assoc. Prof., 1955–61; Asst. Dean, Coll. of Letters and Science, 1963–66; Prof., 1961–76). Prof. of Spanish, Dominican Coll. of San Rafael, 1935–37. *Publs:* Una Bibliografia de Versificación Española, 1937; A Chronological Sketch of Castilian Versification Together with a List of Its Metric Terms, 1952; Morphology of Fifteenth Century Castilian Verse, 1964; Early Spanish Lyric Poetry: Essays and Selections, 1967; Allegory, Decalogue and Deadly Sins in La Celestina, 1968; Agudiecism, Thematics and the Newest Novel: A Study of Juan Ventura Agudiez's Heuristic Novel Las Tardes de Thérèze Lamarck, 1969; Juan de Mena's Laberinto de Fortuna: Classic Epic and Mester de Clerecía, 1973; Garcilaso's "First Eclogue": Perspective, Geometric Figure, Epic Structure, 1977. Add: 944 Arlington Ave., El Cerrito, Calif. 94530, U.S.A.

CLARKE, Gillian. Welsh, b. 1937. Poetry. Lectr. in Art History, Gwent Coll. of Art and Design, Newport, 1975–84; Ed., Anglo-Welsh Review, Cardiff, 1976–84. *Publs:* Snow on the Mountain, 1971; The Sundial, 1978; Letter from a Far Country, 1982; Letting in the Rumour, 1989. Add: Blaen Cwrt, Talgarreg, Dyfed, Wales.

CLARKE, H(enry) Harrison. American, b. 1902. Sports/Physical education/Keeping fit. Research Prof. Emeritus, Univ. of Oregon, Eugene, since 1972 (Research Prof. of Physical Education, 1953–72). Dir. of Physical Education, Public Schs., Chautauqua, N.Y., 1925–30; Assoc. Prof. of Physical Education, Syracuse Univ., N.Y., 1930–46; Dir. of Grad. Studies, Springfield Coll., Mass., 1946–53; Editor and contributor, Physical Fitness Research Digest, President's Council on Physical Fitness and Sports, 1971–79. *Publs:* Application of Measurement to Health and Physical Education, 1945, 6th ed. 1987; (with D. Clarke) Developmental and Adapted Physical Education, 1963, 1978; (with F. Haar) Health and Physical Education for Elementary School Classroom Teachers, 1964; Muscular Strength and Endurance in Man, 1966; (with D. Clarke) Research Processes in Physical Education, Recreation and Health, 1970, 2nd ed. 1984; Physical and Motor Tests in the Medford Boys' Growth Study, 1971; (with D. Clarke) Advanced Statistics with Applications to Physical Education, 1972. Add: 2561 Pioneer Pike, Eugene, Ore. 97401, U.S.A.

CLARKE, Hugh Vincent. Australian, b. 1919. Novels/Short stories, Travel/Exploration/Adventure. Dir. of Information and Publicity, Dept. of External Territories, 1966–73, and Dir. of Information and Public Relations, Dept. of Aboriginal Affairs, 1973–77, Canberra. *Publs:* The Tub (novel), 1963; Break Out (documentary), 1965; (with T. Yamashata) To Sydney by Stealth, 1966; The Long Arm (biography), 1974; Fire One! (documentary), 1978; The Broke and the Broken: Life in the Great Depression (documentary), 1982; Last Stop Nagasaki (documentary), 1984; Twilight Liberation (documentary), 1985; A Life for Every Sleeper (documentary), 1986. Add: 14 Chermside St., Deakin, Canberra, A.C.T., Australia.

CLARKE, Joan L(orraine). Australian, b. 1920. Plays, Biography. Vice-Pres., Sydney Branch, Intl. P.E.N., since 1988. Treas., Australian Soc. of Authors, 1965–69, and the Sydney Branch, Intnl. P.E.N., 1972–77; Ed., The Australian Author, 1977–81. *Publs:* Home Brew (play), 1954; (with John Meredith) Wild Colonial Boy (play), 1956; (with Zoe O'Leary) Girl Fridays in Revolt, 1969; Dr. Max Herz, Surgeon Extraordinary, 1976; (ed.) Australia and New Zealand Writers' Handbook, 2nd ed. 1979; (with G. Weller) Gold!, 1981; The Doctor Who Dared, 1982; Just Us, 1988. Add: 42/114 Spit Rd., Mosman, N.S.W., Australia.

CLARKE, Martin Lowther. British, b. 1909. Classics, Education, Biography. Asst. Lectr., 1935–37, Lectr., 1946–47, and Reader, 1947–48, Univ. Coll., London; Prof. of Latin, Univ. Coll. of North Wales, Bangor, 1948–74. *Publs:* Richard Porson, 1937; Greek Studies in England 1700-1830, 1945; Rhetoric at Rome, 1953; Classical Education in Britain 1500-1900, 1959; George Crote, 1962; The Roman Mind, 1968; Bangor Cathedral, 1969; Higher Education in the Ancient World, 1971; Paley, 1974; The Noblest Roman, 1981. Add: Lollingdon House, Cholsey, Wallingford, Oxon OX10 9LS, England.

CLARKE, Mary. British, b. 1923. Dance/Ballet, Theatre. Ed., The Dancing Times, London, since 1963 (Asst. Ed., 1954–63). Asst. Ed., The Ballet Annual, 1952–63; London Ed., Dance News of New York, 1955–70. *Publs:* The Sadler's Wells Ballet, 1955; Six Great Dancers, 1957; Dancers of Mercury: The Story of Ballet Rambert, 1962; (with Clement Crisp) Ballet: An Illustrated History, 1973; (with Clement Crisp) Making a Ballet, 1974; (ed., with David Vaughan) An Encyclopedia of

Dance and Ballet, 1977; (with Clement Crisp) Design for Ballet, 1978; (with Clement Crisp) The History of Dance, 1980; (with Clement Crisp) Men in Dance, 1985; Ballerina, 1987. Add: 11 Danbury St., Islington, London N1 8LD, England.

CLARKE, Mary Stetson. American, b. 1911. Children's fiction, History, Biography. Dir., Experiment in Intnl. Living; Trustee, Melrose Public Library, since 1970; Dir., Melrose Historical Society, since 1976. Dir., Boston Authors Club, 1966–67; Dir., First Iron Works Assn., Saugus, Mass., 1967–69. *Publs:* Petticoat Rebel, 1964; The Iron Peacock, 1966; The Limner's Daughter, 1967; Pioneer Iron Works, 1968; The Glass Phoenix, 1969; Piper to the Clan, 1970; Guide to the Middlesex Canal, 1971; Bloomers and Ballots (biography), 1972; Emigration in Colonial Times, 1973; Women's Rights in the U.S., 1974; The Old Middlesex Canal, 1974; A Visit to the Iron Works, 1975; (ed.) Growing Up in Melrose, 1981; Iron in Colonial Times, 1981; (ed.) History of Trinity Parish, Melrose, 1982; The Russells in America, 1640-1988, 1988. Add: 333 W. Emerson St., Melrose, Mass. 02176, U.S.A.

CLARKE, Mary Whatley. American, b. 1899. History. Former owner and operator of Palo Pinto County Star, Tex., and the Norwood Press, Man., Canada, both weekly newspapers. *Publs:* The Palo Pinto Story, 1957; Life in the Saddle, 1963; David Burnet, 1969; Thomas J. Rusk: Soldier, Statesman, Jurist, 1971; Chief Bowles and the Texas Cherokees, 1971; The Swenson Saga and the SMS Ranches, 1976; A Century of Cow Business, 1976; Kentucky Quilts and Their Makers, 1976; The Slaughter Ranches and Their Makers, 1979. Add: c/o University Press of Kentucky, 663 S. Limestone St., Lexington, Ky. 40506, U.S.A.

CLARKE, Pauline. (Mrs. P. Hunter Blair) Also writes as Helen Clare. British, b. 1921. Children's fiction. *Publs:* The Pekinese Princess, 1948; The Great Can, 1952; The White Elephant, 1952; (as Helen Clare) Five Dolls series, 5 vols., 1953–63; (as Helen Clare) Merlin's Magic, 1953; Smith's Hoard (in U.S. as Hidden Gold), 1955, retitled in U.K. as The Golden Collar, 1967; Sandy the Sailor, 1956; The Boy with the Erpingham Hood, 1956; (as Helen Clare) Bel the Giant and Other Stories (in U.S. as The Cat and the Fiddle, and Other Stories), 1956; James the Policeman series, 4 vols., 1957–63; Torolv the Fatherless, 1959; (as Helen Clare) Seven White Pebbles, 1960; The Lord of the Castle, 1960; The Robin Hooders, 1960; Keep the Pot Boiling, 1961; The Twelve and the Genii (in U.S. as The Return of the Twelves), 1962; Silver Bells and Cockle Shells (verse), 1962; Crowds of Creatures, 1964; The Bonfire Party, 1966; The Two Faces of Silenus, 1972. Add: Church Farm House, 69 High St., Bottisham, Cambridge CB5 9BA, England.

CLARKE, Peter Frederick. British, b. 1942. Economics, Politics/Government. Fellow, St. John's Coll., Cambridge, since 1980; Reader in Modern History, Cambridge Univ., since 1987. Lectr. and Reader, University Coll., London, 1966–80. Review Ed. of History, 1967–73. *Publs:* Lancashire and the New Liberalism, 1971; (ed.) Democracy and Reaction by L.T. Hobhouse, 1972; (ed.) The Crisis of Liberalism by J.A. Hobson, 1974; Liberals and Social Democrats, 1978; The Keynesian Revolution in the Making, 1924–36, 1988. Add: St. John's College, Cambridge CB2 1TP, England.

CLARKSON, E. Margaret. Canadian, b. 1915. Poetry, Education, Music, Natural History, Theology/Religion. Public sch. teacher, Toronto, Ontario, Canada, 1935–73. *Publs:* Let's Listen to Music, 1944; The Creative Classroom. 1958; Susie's Babies, 1960; Our Father, 1961; Growing Up, 1962; Clear Shining After Rain (poetry), 1962; The Wondrous Cross, 1966; Rivers Among the Rocks (poetry), 1967; God's Hedge, 1968; Grace Grows Best in Winter, 1972, 1985; Conversations with a Barred Owl, 1975; Celebration of Discipleship, 1976; So You're Single!, 1978, Destined for Glory: The Meaning of Suffering, 1983; All Nature Sings: Nature Sketches, 1986; A Singing Heart: The Collected Hymns of Margaret Clarkson, 1987. Add: 72 Gwendolen Cres., Willowdale, Ont. M2N 2L7, Canada.

CLARKSON, Ewan. British, b. 1929. Novels, Children's fiction, Children's non-fiction. *Publs:* Break for Freedom (in U.S. as Syla the Mink), 1967; Halic, The Story of a Grey Seal, 1970; The Running of the Deer, 1972; In the Shadow of the Falcon, 1973; Wolf Country, a Wilderness Pilgrimage, 1975; The Badgers of Summercombe, 1977; The Many Forked Branch, 1980; Wolves, 1980; Reindeer, 1981; Eagles, 1981; Beavers, 1981; In the Wake of the Storm (novel), 1984; Ice Trek, 1986. Add: Moss Rose Cottage, Preston, Kingsteignton, Newton Abbot, Devon, England.

CLARKSON, G(eoffrey) P. Canadian, b. 1934. Money/Finance. Dean,

Coll. of Business Admin., since 1977, and Prof., since 1980, Northeastern Univ., Boston. Prof., 1967–69, and National Westminster Prof. of Business Finance, 1969–77, Univ. of Manchester. *Publs:* Portfolio Selection: A Simulation of Trust Investment, 1962; The Theory of Consumer Demand: A Critical Appraisal, 1963; (ed.) Managerial Economics, 1968; (with B.J. Elliott) Managing Money and Finance, 1969, 3rd ed. 1982; Jihad, 1981. Add: Coll. of Business Administration, Northeastern University, Boston, Mass. 02115, U.S.A.

CLARKSON, Helen. *See* **McCLOY,** Helen.

CLARKSON, J.F. *See* **TUBB,** E.C.

CLAUDE, Richard Pierre. American, b. 1934. Civil liberties/Human rights, Law. Prof., Dept. of Govt. and Politics, Univ. of Maryland, College Park, since 1978 (Assoc. Prof., 1965–78). Founding Ed., Human Rights Quarterly; Member, National Advisory Council, Amnesty Intnl. U.S.A., since 1978. Instr. in Political Science, Vassar Coll., Poughkeepsie, N.Y., 1962–64; Visiting Prof., Coll. of William and Mary, Williamsburg, Va., 1964–65. Dir., American Bar Assn. National Survey on Human Rights Teaching, 1979. Rockefeller Residency Fellow, Bellagio, Italy, 1985; Bd. of Dirs., Physicians for Human Rights, 1988; Vice-Pres., Survival International, U.S.A., 1988; Advisory Bd. of Pennsylvania Studies in Human Rights, 1989; Scientific Freedom and Responsibility Cttee., American Assn. for the Advancement of Science, 1989. *Publs:* The Supreme Court and the Electoral Process, 1970; (ed.) Comparative Human Rights, 1976; (co-ed.) Making Government Work, 1981; (co-author) Health Professionals and Human Rights in the Philippines, 1986; (co-ed.) Human Rights in the World Community, 1989. Add: 5107 Moorland Lane, Bethesda, Md. 20814, U.S.A.

CLAVELL, James. American (born British), b. 1924. Novels/Short stories, Plays/Screenplays. Film and television producer and director. *Publs:* King Rat, 1962; Taipan, 1966; Countdown at Armageddon (play), 1966; Shogun, 1975; Noble House, 1981; Children's Story, 1981; Thrump-O-moto (fantasy), 1985; Whirlwind, 1986; screenplays—The Fly, 1958; Watussi, 1959; Five Gates to Hell, 1959; Walk Like a Dragon, 1960; The Great Escape, 1963; 633 Squadron, 1964; The Satan Bug, 1965; Where's Jack, 1968; To Sir With Love, 1969; The Last Valley, 1969. Add: c/o Foreign Rights Inc., 200 W. 57th St., New York, N.Y. 10019, U.S.A.

CLAYTON, C. Guy. British, b. 1936. Novels. English teacher, Douglas, Isle of Man, since 1976. Teacher at schs. in Plymouth, England, 1963–76. *Publs:* Daughter of the Revolution, 1984; Such Mighty Rage, 1985; Bordeaux Red, 1986. Add: Davian, Main Rd, Foxdale, Isle of Man.

CLEALL, Charles. British, b. 1927. Literature, Music, Theology/Religion. H.M. Inspector of Schs., Scottish Education Dept., 1972–87. Ed., Journal of the Ernest George White Soc., 1983–88. *Publs:* Voice Production in Choral Techniques, 1955, 1970; The Selection and Training of Mixed Choirs in Churches, 1960; (ed.) Sixty Songs from Sankey, 1960, 1966; (ed.) John Merbeck's Music for the Congregation, 1963; Music and Holiness, 1964; Authentic Chanting, 1969; (ed.) Plainsong for Pleasure, 1969; Guide to Vanity Fair, 1982. Add: 10 Carronhall, Stonehaven, Kincardineshire AB3 2HF, Scotland.

CLEARE, John S. British, b. 1936. Photography, Travel/Exploration/Adventure. Proprietor, Mountain Camera Library and consultancy, since 1976. Photographer, Queen Mag., 1960–61; Dir., Gamma Group, Photography and Design, Sargent/Gamma Ltd., 1961–69. *Publs:* (with T. Smythe) Rock-Climbers in Action in Snowdonia, 1966, 1967; (with R. Collomb) Sea-Cliff Climbing in Britain, 1973; Mountains, 1974, 1975; World Guide to Mountains and Mountaineering, 1979; Mountaineering in Colour, 1980; (ed./illustrator) Whymper's Scrambles amongst the Alps, 7th ed. 1986; (with Ordnance Survey) John Cleare's Fifty Best 100 Hill Walks in Britain, 1988; Trekking: Great Walks of the World, 1988. Add: Hill Cottage, Fonthill Gifford, Salisbury, Wilts. SP3 6QW, England.

CLEARY, Beverly. American, b. 1916. Children's fiction. Children's Librarian, Yakima, Wash., 1939–40; Post Librarian, U.S. Army Hosp., Oakland, Calif., 1942–45. *Publs:* Henry Huggins series, 5 vols., 1950–62; Ellen Tebbits, 1951; Otis Spofford, 1953; Ramona series, 6 vols., 1955–84; Fifteen, 1956; The Luckiest Girl, 1958; Jean and Johnny, 1959; The Real Hole, 1960; Hullabaloo ABC, 1960; Two Dog Biscuits, 1961; Emily's Runaway Imagination, 1961; Sister of the Bride, 1963; Ribsy, 1964; The Mouse and the Motorcycle, 1964; Mitch and Amy, 1967; Runaway Ralph, 1970; Socks, 1973; Ralph S. Mouse, 1982; Dear Mr. Henshaw, 1983; Lucky Chuck, 1984; A Girl from Yamhill: A Memoir,

1988. Add: c/o William Morrow & Co. Inc., 105 Madison Ave., New York, N.Y. 10016, U.S.A.

CLEARY, Jon (Stephen). Australian, b. 1917. Novels/Short stories, Mystery/Crime/Suspense, Plays/Screenplays. Journalist, Australian News and Information Bureau, London, 1948–49, and NYC, 1949–51. *Publs:* The Small Glories (short stories), 1945; You Can't See Round Corners, 1947; The Long Shadow, 1949; Just Let Me Be, 1950; The Sundowners, 1952, screenplay, 1961; The Climate of Courage (in U.S. as Naked in the Night), 1954; Justin Bayard, 1955; The Green Helmet, 1957, screenplay, 1960; Back of Sunset, 1959; (with H. Watt) The Siege of Pinchgut (screenplay), 1959; North from Thursday, 1960; The Country of Marriage, 1961; Forest of the Night, 1962; Pillar of Salt (short stories). 1963; A Flight of Chariots, 1964; The Fall of an Eagle, 1965; The Pulse of Danger, 1966; The High Commissioner, 1967; The Long Pursuit, 1968; Season of Doubt, 1969; Remember Jack Hoxie, 1970; Helga's Web, 1971; The Liberators (in U.K. as Mask of the Andes), 1971; The Ninth Marquess (in U.K. as Man's Estate), 1972; Ransom, 1973; Peter's Pence, 1974; Sidecar Boys (screenplay), 1974; The Safe House, 1975; A Sound of Lightning, 1976; High Road to China, 1977; Vortex, 1977; The Beaufort Sisters, 1979; Very Private War, 1980; The Golden Sabre, 1981; The Faraway Drums, 1981; Spearfield's Daughter, 1982; The Phoenix Tree, 1984; The City of Fading Light, 1985; Dragons at the Party, 1987; Now and Then, Amen, 1988; Babylon South, 1989. Add: c/o Collins, 8 Grafton St., London W1X 3LA, England.

CLEAVER, Eldridge. American, b. 1935. Civil liberties/Human rights, Autobiography/Memoirs/Personal. Asst. Ed., and contrib., Ramparts mag. *Publs:* Soul on Ice, 1968; Post Prison Writings and Speeches, 1969; Eldridge Cleaver's Black Papers, 1969; Soul on Fire, 1978. Add: c/o Random House Inc., 201 East 50th St., New York, N.Y. 10022, U.S.A.

CLEAVER, Vera. American, b. 1919. Novels/Short stories, Children's fiction. *Publs:* The Nurse's Dilemma (for adults), 1966; with Bill Cleaver—Ellen Grae, 1967; Lady Ellen Grae, 1968; Where the Lilies Bloom, 1969; Grover, 1970; The Mimosa Tree, 1970; The Mock Revolt, 1971; I Would Rather Be a Turnip, 1971; Delpha Green and Company, 1972; Me Too, 1973; The Why's and Wherefore's of Littabelle Lee, 1973; Dust of the Earth, 1975; Trial Valley, 1977; Queen of Hearts, 1978; A Little Destiny, 1979; The Kissimee Kid, 1981; Hazel Rye, 1983; Sugar Blue, 1984; Sweetly Sings the Donkey, 1985; Belle Pruitt, 1988. Add: 600 E. Lake Elbert Dr., Winter Haven, Fla. 33881, U.S.A.

CLECAK, Peter. American, b. 1938. Politics/Government, Social commentary/phenomena, Nutrition. Prof. of Social Thought and Comparative Culture. Univ. of California at Irvine, since 1976 (Asst. Prof. of English and Comparative Literature, 1966–71; Assoc. Prof. of Social Thought, and Acting Dir. of Prog. in Comparative Culture, 1972–74; Assoc. Dean of Grad. Study and Research, 1981–83). Contrib. Ed., Book Forum; Member of Panel, Div. of Education Progs., and National Bd. of Consultants, National Endowment for the Humanities. Lectr. in English, Stanford Univ., 1963–64; Fellow, International College of Applied Nutrition. *Publs:* Radical Paradoxes: Dilemmas of the American Left 1945-1970, 1973; Crooked Paths: Reflections on Socialism, Conservatism, and the Welfare State, 1977; (with others) Investment in Learning, 1977; The Quest: Dissent and Fulfillment in America 1960-1980, 1982; America's Quest for the Ideal Self: Dissent and Fulfillment 1960-1980, 1983. Add: 1486 Morningside Circle, Laguna Beach, Calif. 92651, U.S.A.

CLEESE, John (Marwood). British, b. 1939. Humour. Owner, Video Arts Ltd., London, since 1976. Actor: Frequent appearances on stage, television, and in films. *Publs:* (contributor) Monty Python's Big Red Book, 1975; (contributor) The Strange Case of the End of Civilization As We Know It, 1977; (with Robin Skynner) Families and How to Survive Them, 1983; The Golden Skits of Wing Commander Muriel Volestrangler FRHS and Bar, 1984. Add: c/o David Wilkinson, 24 Denmark St., London WC2, England.

CLEEVE, Brian (Talbot). Irish, b. 1921. Novels/Short stories, Mystery/Crime/Suspense, Historical/Romance/Gothic, History, Theology/Religion. Freelance journalist since 1948: in S. Africa, 1948–54, and in Ireland, since 1954. Broadcaster, Radio Telefis Eireann, Dublin, 1962–72. *Publs:* The Far Hills, 1952; Portrait of My City, 1952; Birth of a Dark Soul, 1953, in U.S. as The Night Winds, 1954; Colonial Policies in Africa (non-fiction), 1954; Assignment to Vengeance (suspense), 1961; Death of a Painted Lady (crime), 1962; Death of a Wicked Servant (crime), 1963; Vote for Treason (suspense), 1964, 2nd U.S. ed. as Counterspy, 1966; Dark Blood, Dark Terror (suspense), 1965; The Judas

Goat (suspense) (in U.S. as Vice Isn't Private), 1966; The Horse Thieves of Ballysaggert and Other Stories, 1966; Violent Death of a Bitter Englishman (suspense), 1967; (ed.) Dictionary of Irish Writers, 3 vols., 1967-71, (ed. with Anne Brady) as Biographical Dictionary of Irish Writers, 1 vol., 1985; You Must Never Go Back (suspense), 1968; Exit from Prague (suspense), 1970, in U.S. as Escape from Prague, 1973; Cry of Morning, 1971, in U.S. as The Triumph of O'Rourke, 1972; Tread Softly in This Place (novel), 1972; A Question of Inheritance, 1974, in U.S. as For Love of Crannagh Castle, 1975; Sara (romance), 1976; Kate (romance), 1977; Judith (romance), 1978; Hester (romance), 1979; The House on the Rock (religion), 1980; The Seven Mansions (religion), 1980; The Fourth Mary (religion), 1982; 1983: A World Vanishing, 1982; A View of the Irish, 1983. Add: 60 Heytesbury Lane, Ballsbridge, Dublin 4, Ireland.

CLEGG, John. British, b. 1909. Natural history. Editorial Advisor, Frederick Warne & Co., Ltd. Publrs., London, since 1960. Curator, Haslemere Educational Museum, 1948–62, Torquay Museum, 1965–66, and Gilbert White Museum, Selborne, Hants, 1970–72; Education Officer, Royal Soc. for the Protection of Birds, 1962–64. Publs: Freshwater Life of the British Isles, 1952, 4th ed. as Freshwater Life, 1974; Observer's Book of Pond Life, 1956, 5th ed., 1989; Insects, 1957, 1969; (ed.) Pond and Stream Life of Europe, 1963, 3rd ed. 1973; Your Book of Freshwater Life, 1968; Guide to Ponds and Streams, 1985. Add: Windrush, Carter Rd., Kent's Bank, Grange-Over-Sands, Cumbria LA11 7AP, England.

CLEM, Alan L(eland). American, b. 1929. Politics/Government. Prof. of Political Science, Univ. of South Dakota, Vermillion, since 1964 (Asst. Prof., 1960–62; Assoc. Prof., 1962–64). Copywriter, Ayres Advertising Agency, Lincoln, Nebr., 1950–52; Press Secty., U.S. House of Reps., Washington, D.C., 1953–59; Information Specialist, Foreign Agricultural Service, Washington, D.C., 1959–60. Publs: The Nomination of Joe Bottum, 1963; South Dakota Political Almanac, 2nd ed. 1969; Prairie State Politics, 1967; (sr. author) The Making of Congressmen: Seven Campaigns of 1974, 1976; American Electoral Politics: Strategies for Renewal, 1981; (with James Rumbolz) Law Enforcement: The South Dakota Experience, 1982; The Government We Deserve, 1985; Congress: Powers, Processes, and Politics, 1989. Add: 902 Valley View, Vermillion, S.D. 57069, U.S.A.

CLEMEN, Wolfgang H. German, b. 1909. Literature. Head of the Shakespeare Library, Univ. of Munich (Prof. of English, 1946–74). Publs: Shakespeare's Bilder, 1936; Der junge Chaucer, 1938; The Development of Shakespeare's Imagery, 1951, 1977; Kommentar zu Shakespeare's Richard III, 1957; English Tragedy before Shakespeare, 1961; (ed.) Shakespeare's Midsummer Night's Dream, 1963; Chaucer's Early Poetry, 1963; Shakespeare's Soliloquies, 1964, 1987; Past and Future in Shakespeare's Drama, 1966; Das Problem des Stilwandels in der englischen Dichtung, 1968; Das Drama Shakespeares, 1969; (ed.) Gerard Manley Hopkins Gedichte, 1973; Shakespeare's Dramatic Art, 1973; The Pursuit of Influence, 1975; Originalita und Tradition in der englischen Dichtungsgeschichte, 1978; Some Aspects of Style in Shakespeare's Henry VI Plays, 1980; Shakespeares Monologe, 1985. Add: 8207 Endorf, Hofhamerweg 3, Germany.

CLEMENS, Walter C., Jr. American, b. 1933. International relations/Current affairs. Prof. of Political Science, Boston Univ., since 1966; Adjunct Research Fellow, Harvard Center for Science and International Affairs, since 1986. Chmn., Language Dept., Iolani Sch., Honolulu, Hawaii, 1960–61; Asst. Prof., Dept. of Political Science, Univ. of California, Santa Barbara, 1961–63, and Massachusetts Inst. of Technology, Cambridge, 1963–66; Assoc., Russian Research Center, Harvard Univ., Cambridge, Mass., 1963–78. Publs: (compiler) Soviet Disarmament Policy, 1917-1963, 1965; (ed.) World Perspectives on International Politics, 1965; (ed.) Toward a Strategy of Peace, 1965; (with L. Bloomfield and F. Griffiths) Khrushchev and the Arms Race, 1966; Outer Space and Arms Control, 1966; The Arms Race and Sino-Soviet Relations, 1968; Die Tschechoslowakei unter Husak, 1970; (with others) The Soviet Union and Arms Control: A Superpower Dilemma, 1970; The Superpowers and Arms Control, 1973; The U.S.S.R. and Global Interdependence, 1978; National Security and U.S.-Soviet Relations, 1981, 1982; Can Russia Change? 1989. Add: 232 Bay State Rd., Dept. of Political Science, Boston, Univ., Boston, Mass. 02215, U.S.A.

CLEMENT, Hal. Pseud. for Harry Clement Stubbs. American, b. 1922. Science fiction/Fantasy. Science teacher, Milton Academy, Mass., 1949–87. Publs: Needle, 1951, as From Outer Space, 1957; Iceworld, 1953; Mission of Gravity, 1954; The Ranger Boys in Space (juvenile), 1956; Cycle of Fire, 1957; Some Notes on Xi Bootis, 1959; Close to Critical, 1964; Natives of Space (short stories), 1965; Small Changes

(short stories), 1969, as Space Lash, 1969; (ed.) First Flights to the Moon, 1970; (ed.) The Moon, by George Gamow, 1971; Star Light, 1971; Ocean on Top, 1973; Left of Africa, 1976; Through the Eye of the Needle, 1978; The Best of Hal Clement (short stories), 1979; The Nitrogen Fix, 1982; Still River, 1987; Intuit, 1987. Add: 12 Thompson Lane, Milton, Mass. 02187, U.S.A.

CLEMENTS, Arthur L. American, b. 1932. Literature. Prof. of English, State Univ. of New York at Binghamton, since 1988 (Asst. Prof., 1964–69; Assoc. Prof., 1969–88). Lectr., Syracuse Univ., N.Y., 1962–64. Publs: (ed.) John Donne's Poetry, 1966; The Mystical Poetry of Thomas Traherne, 1969; Common Blessings, 1987; Poetry of Contemplation, 1989. Add: Dept. of English, State Univ. of New York at Binghamton, Binghamton, N.Y. 13901, U.S.A.

CLEMENTS, Bruce. American, b. 1931. Children's fiction. Member of the Dept. of English, Eastern Connecticut State Univ., Willimantic, since 1967. Pastor in Schenectady, N.Y., 1957–64; Instr., Union Coll., Schenectady, 1964–67. Publs: fiction—Two Against the Tide, 1967; The Face of Abraham Candle, 1969; I Tell a Lie Every So Often, 1974; Prison Window, Jerusalem Blue, 1977; Anywhere Else But Here, 1980; Coming About, 1984; The Treasure of Plunderell Manor, 1986; other—From Ice Set Free: The Story of Otto Kiep, 1972; Coming Home to a Place You've Never Been Before, 1975. Add: Eastern Connecticut State Univ., Willimantic, Conn. 06226, U.S.A.

CLEMENTS, Ellen Catherine. British, b. 1920. Animals/Pets. Manager of voluntary wild bird hospital, Leicester. Publs: Birds at My Door, 1963; Birds of Character; Birds' Diseases and Hand-Rearing: Dog's Early Warning System, 1970. Add: 12 The Chestnuts, Countesthorpe, Leicester LE8 3TL, England.

CLEMENTS, Robert (John). American, b. 1912. Literature. Chmn., Comparative Literature Dept., New York Univ., NYC (joined faculty as Prof. of Romance Languages and Literature, 1954). Columnist, European literary scene, Saturday Review, NYC; Pres., Intnl. Assn. for the Study of Italian Language and Literature. Instr., then Asst. Prof., Harvard Univ., Cambridge, Mass., 1940–47; Prof. and Chmn., Dept. of Romance Languages and Literature, Pennsylvania State Univ., University Park, 1947–54. Pres., American Assn. of Teachers of Italian, 1960–62; Member, Exec. Council, American Comparative Literature Assn., 1970–73. Publs: Critical Theory and Practice of the Pleiade, 1942; (with R.V. Merrill) Platonism in French Renaissance Poetry, 1957; The Peregrine Muse: Studies in Comparative Renaissance Literature, 1959; Picta Poesis: Humanistic and Literary Theory in Renaissance Books, 1960; Michelangelo's Theory of Art, 1961; Michelangelo: Self Portrait, 1963; (co-author) Michelangelo, Sculptor, 1963; The Poetry of Michelangelo, 1965; (ed.) American Critical Essays on the Divine Comedy, 1967; (with Lorna Clements) Renaissance Letters, 1976; (with J. Gibaldi) Anatomy of the Novella, 1977; Comparative Literature as Academic Discipline, 1978. Add: P.O. Box 826, Mahopac, N.Y. 10541, U.S.A.

CLEMO, Jack. (Reginald John Clemo). British, b. 1916. Novels/Short stories, Poetry, Theology/Religion, Autobiography/Memoirs/Personal. Publs: Wilding Graft (novel), 1948; Confession of a Rebel, 1949; The Clay Verge, 1951; The Invading Gospel, 1958; The Map of Clay, 1961; Cactus on Carmel, 1967; The Echoing Tip, 1971; Broad Autumn, 1975; The Marriage of a Rebel, 1980; The Bouncing Hills, 1983; The Shadowed Bed (novel), 1986; A Different Drummer, 1986; Selected Poems, 1988. Add: 24 Southlands Rd., Rodwell, Dorset DT4 9LQ, England.

CLEVELAND, (James) Harlan. American, b. 1918. Education, International relations/Current affairs, Politics/Government. Prof. Emeritus of Public Affairs and Former Dean of the Hubert H. Humphrey Inst. of Public Affairs, Univ. of Minnesota since 1980 (member of the faculty). Dean, Maxwell Grad. Sch. of Citizenship and Public Affairs, Syracuse Univ., N.Y., 1956–61; Asst. Secty. of State for Intnl. Org. Affairs, Washington, D.C., 1961–65; U.S. Ambassador, NATO, Paris, and Brussels, 1965–69; Pres., Univ. of Hawaii, Honolulu, 1969–74; Dir., Prog. in Intnl. Affairs, Aspen Inst., Princeton, N.J., 1974–80. Publs: (with others) The Overseas Americans, 1960; (ed.) The Promise of World Tensions, 1961; (co-ed.) Ethics and Bigness, 1962; (co-ed.) The Ethics of Power, 1962; The Obligations of Power, 1966; NATO: The Transatlantic Bargain, 1970; The Future Executive, 1972; Seven Everyday Collisions in American Higher Education, 1974; China Diary, 1976; The Third Try at World Order, 1977; Humangrowth: An Essay on Growth, Values and the Quality of Life, 1978; (with others) National Perceptions and Cultural Identities, 1978; Triple Collision of Modernization, 1979; (co-ed.) Bioresources for Development, 1980; (ed.) Energy Futures of Developing

Countries, 1980; (ed.) The Management of Sustainable Growth, 1981; Toward a Strategy for the Management of Peace, 1983; The Knowledge Executive, 1985; (co-ed.) Prospects for Peacemaking, 1987; (co-author) Rethinking International Cooperation, 1988; (co-ed.) The Global Commons, 1988. Add: Hubert H. Humphrey Inst. of Public Affairs, Univ. of Minnesota, Minneapolis, Minn. 55455, U.S.A.

CLEVELAND, John. *See* **McELFRESH,** Adeline.

CLEVELAND, Leslie. New Zealander, b. 1921. Poetry, Politics/Government, Sociology. Reader, Victoria Univ. of Wellington, 1966–87. Ed., Political Science journal, 1969–75; Sr. Fellow, Smithsonian Inst., Washington, D.C., 1988–89. *Publs:* The Songs We Sang, 1959; The Silent Land, 1966; The Anatomy of Influence, 1972; (with A.D. Robinson) Readings in New Zealand Government, 1972; The Iron Hand, 1979; The Politics of Utopia, 1979. Add: 38 Havelock St., Wellington, New Zealand.

CLEVELAND, Ray L. American, b. 1929. History. Prof. of History, Univ. of Regina, Sask., Canada, since 1974. Research Fellow, American Foundn. for the Study of Man, 1964–66; Assoc. Prof., 1966–72, and Prof., 1972–74, Univ. of Saskatchewan, Regina. *Publs:* An Ancient South Arabian Necropolis, 1965; The Middle East and South Asia, 1967, rev. annually 1967–88; Readings on the History of the Holy Land, 1979. Add: Dept. of History, Univ. of Regina, Regina, Sask. S4S 0A2, Canada.

CLEVERLY FORD, D.W. *See* **FORD,** Douglas.

CLEWES, Dorothy (Mary). British, b. 1907. Novels/Short stories, Children's fiction. Worked as a secty. and physician's dispenser, Nottingham, 1924–32. *Publs:* The Rivals of Maidenhurst, 1925; She Married a Doctor (novel) (in U.S. as Stormy Hearts), 1943; Shepherd's Hill (novel), 1945; To Man Alone (novel), 1945; The Cottage in the Wild Wood, 1945; The Stream in the Wild Wood, 1946; The Treasure in the Wild Wood, 1947; Stranger in the Valley, 1948; The Blossom on the Bough, 1949; Henry Hare's Boxing Match, 1950; Henry Hare's Earthquake, 1950; The Brown Burrows, Books, 1950; Summer Cloud, 1951; Henry Hare, Painter and Decorator, 1951; Henry Hare and the Kidnapping of Selina Squirrel, 1951; The Adventure of the Scarlet Daffodil (in U.S. as The Mystery of the Scarlet Daffodil), 1952; The Mystery of the Blue Admiral, 1954; Merry-Go-Round, 1954; Came to a Wood, 1956; The Secret, 1956; The Runaway, 1957; Adventure on Rainbow Island (in U.S. as Mystery on Rainbow Island), 1957; The Jade Green Cadillac (in U.S. as The Mystery of the Jade-Green Cadillac), 1958; The Happiest Day, 1958; The Old Pony, 1959; Hide and Seek, 1959; The Lost Tower Treasure (in U.S. as The Mystery of the Lost Tower Treasure), 1960; The Hidden Key, 1960; The Singing Strings (in U.S. as The Mystery of the Singing Strings), 1961; All the Fun of the Fair, 1961; Wilberforce and the Slaves, 1961; Skyraker and the Iron Imp, 1963; The Purple Mountain (in U.S. as The Golden Eagle), 1962; The Birthday, 1962; The Branch Line, 1963; Operation Smuggle (in U.S. as The Mystery of the Midnight Smugglers), 1964; Boys and Girls Come Out to Play, 1964; The Holiday, 1964; Guide Dog, 1965, as Dog for the Dark, 1974; Guide Dogs for the Blind, 1966; Red Ranger and the Combine Harvester, 1966; Roller Skates, Skooter and Bike, 1966; A Boy like Walt, 1967; A Bit of Magic, 1967; A Girl like Cathy, 1968; Adopted Daughter, 1968; Upside-down Willie, 1968; Peter and the Jumbie, 1969; Special Branch Willie, 1969; Library Lady (in U.S. as The Library), 1970; Fire-Brigade Willie, 1970; Two Bad Boys, 1971; The End of Summer, 1971; Storm Over Innish, 1972; Skein of Geese, 1972; (ed.) The Secret of the Sea: An Anthology of Underwater Exploration and Adventure, 1973; Ginny's Boy, 1973; Hooray for Me, 1971; Wanted—A Grand, 1974; Missing from Home, 1975; Nothing to Declare, 1976; The Testing Year, 1977. Add: Soleig, King's Ride, Alfriston, Sussex BN26 5XP, England.

CLIFFORD, Derek Plint. British, b. 1917. Novels/Short stories, Poetry, Art, Homes/Gardens, Horticulture. *Publs:* Mad Pelynt and the Bullet, 1940; The Perracotts, 1948; Geraniums, 1953; Pelargoniums Including the Popular Geranium, 1958, 1970; A History of Garden Design, 1962, 1966; Watercolours of the Norwich School, 1967; Art and Understanding, 1968; (co-author) John Crome, 1968; The Paintings of Philip de Laszlo, 1969; Collecting English Watercolours, 1970, 1976; To Catch a Fox, 1982; The Affair of the Forest, 1982; Anne Clifford's Antique Jewellery: The Story of a Collection, 1985. Add: c/o Springwood Books, The Avenue, Ascot SL5 7LY, England.

CLIFFORD, Mary Louise. American, b. 1926. Children's fiction, Children's non-fiction, Writing. With U.S. Foreign Service, Beirut, Lebanon, 1949–51; Staff Assoc., National Center for State Courts, 1977–

87. *Publs:* The Land and People of Afghanistan, 1962, 3rd ed. 1989; The Land and People of Malaysia, 1968; The Land and People of Liberia, 1971; (co-author) The Noble and Noble African Studies Program, 1971; Bisha of Burundi (children's fiction), 1973; The Land and People of Sierra Leone, 1974; Salah of Sierra Leone (children's fiction), 1975; The Land and People of the Arabian Peninsula, 1976; State Court Model Statistical Dictionary, 1980, Supplement, 1984, 1989; Computer-Aided Transcription in the Courts, 1981; Court Case Management Information Systems Manual, 1983; State Trial Court Jurisdiction Guide for Statistical Reporting, 1985. Add: 109 Shellbank Dr., Williamsburg, Va. 23185, U.S.A.

CLIFTON, Harold Dennis. British, b. 1927. Information science/Computers. Principal Lectr. in Business Information Systems, The Polytechnic, Wolverhampton, since 1967. Systems Analyst, Intnl. Computers Ltd., 1956–67. *Publs:* Data Processing Systems Design, 1971; Systems Analysis for Business Data Processing, 1972, 1978; Accounting and Computer Systems, 1973; (with T. Lucey) Business Data Systems, 1978, 1982. Add: The Polytechnic, Wolverhampton, England.

CLIFTON, Lucille. American, b. 1936. Novels/Short stories, Children's fiction, Poetry. Former Visiting Writer, Columbia Univ. Sch of Arts, NYC, and Coppin State Coll., 1971–74. *Publs:* Good Times (poetry), 1969; Everett Anderson series (poetry), 7 vols., 1970–83; The Black B C's, 1970; Good News About the Earth (poetry), 1972; All Us Come Cross the Water, 1973; Good, Says Jerome, 1983; The Boy Who Didn't Believe in Spring, 1973; Don't You Remember, 1974; The Times They Used to Be, 1974; An Ordinary Woman (poetry), 1974; Three Wishes, 1974; Generations, 1976; My Brother Fine with Me, 1976; Anifica, 1978; The Lucky Stone, 1979; My Friend Jacob, 1980; Two-Headed Woman (poetry), 1980; Sonora Beautiful, 1981. Add: c/o Curtis Brown, 10 Astor Pl., New YOrk, NY 10003, U.S.A.

CLINEBELL, Howard J., Jr. American, b. 1922. Psychology, Theology/Religion. Prof. of Pastoral Psychology and Counseling, Sch. of Theology at Claremont, Calif., since 1959; Dir., Inst. for Religion and Wholeness, since 1981. Sr. Ed., Creative Pastoral Care and Counseling Series. Member of faculty, Depts. of Psychology and Religion, Claremont Grad. Sch., since 1968. Dir., Pasadena Area Pastoral Counseling Center, Calif. 1959–63, and Claremont Area Pastoral Counseling and Growth Center, Calif. 1963–66, 1976–78, 1982–87. *Publs:* Understanding and Counseling the Alcoholic, 1956, 1968; Mental Health Through Christian Community, 1965; Basic Types of Pastoral Counseling, 1966; (with Harvey Seifert) Personal Growth and Social Change, 1969; (with Charlotte H. Clinebell) The Intimate Marriage, 1970; (ed.) Community Mental Health: The Role of Churches and Temples, 1970; (with Charlotte H. Clinebell) Crisis and Growth: Helping Your Troubled Child, 1971; The Mental Health Ministry of the Local Church, 1972; The People Dynamic: Changing Self and Society through Growth Groups, 1972; Growth Counseling: New Tools for Clergy and Laity, 1973; Growth Counseling for Marriage Enrichment: Pre-Marriage and the Early Years, 1975; (ed.) Crisis Counseling, by H.W. Stone, 1976; (ed. with H.W. Stone) Pastoral Care and Counseling in Grief and Separation, by W.E. Oates, 1976; Growth Counseling for Mid-Years Couples, 1977; Growth Groups, Marriage and Family Enrichment, Creative Singlehood, Human Liberation, Youth Work, Social Change, 1977; Growth Counseling: Hope-Centred Methods of Actualizing Human Wholeness, 1979; Contemporary Growth Therapies, 1981; Growing Through Loss, 1983; Growing Through Grief, 1984; Basic Types of Pastoral Care and Counseling, 1984. Add: Sch. of Theology, Foothill Blvd. at College Ave., Claremont, Calif. 91711, U.S.A.

CLINTON, Jeff. *See* **BICKHAM,** Jack M.

CLIVE, William. *See* **BASSETT,** Ronald Leslie.

CLOSE, Reginald Arthur. British, b. 1909. Language/Linguistics. Adviser, Longman Group Ltd., Publrs., Harlow, Essex, since 1968. Hon. Research Fellow, Univ. Coll., Univ. of London. Rep., Chile, 1944–45, and Czechoslovakia, 1946–50, and Rep. and Cultural Attaché, Tokyo, 1952–56 and Athens, 1959–68; British Council. *Publs:* The English We Use, 1961, 1971; English as a Foreign Language, 1962, 3rd ed. 1981; The New English Grammar, 2 vols., 1964, 1968; The English We Use for Science, 1965; (trans.) Girard: Linguistics and Foreign Language Teaching, 1972; The University Grammar of English Workbook, 1974; A Reference Grammar for Students of English, 1975; (co-author) English Grammatical Structure, 1975; (co-author) An English Grammar for Greek Students, 1982. Add: 5 Second Ave., Hove, Sussex BN3 2LH, England.

CLOSS, August. British, b. 1898. Literature. Prof. Emeritus of German Language and Literature, Univ. of Bristol (Dean of Faculty of Arts, 1962–64). Co-ed., Universitas, and German Studies. *Publs:* Medieval Exampla, 1934; The Genius of the German Lyric, 1938, rev. ed. 1962; (ed. with W. Mainland) German Lyrics of the 17th Century, 1940; Holderlin, 1942; Tristan and Isolt, 1944, 4th ed. 1974; Die Freien Rhythmen in der Deutschen Dichtung, 1947; Woge im Westen, 1954; Medusa's Mirror, Reality and Symbol: Essays in Literature, 1957; (ed. with T.P. Williams) The Harrap Anthology of German Poetry, 1957, rev. ed. 1969; Reality and Creative Vision, 1963; (ed.) Introduction to German Literature, 4 vols., 1967–69, 1971; The Sea in the Shell, 1978; Briefwechsel, 1979; The Love-Potion as a Poetic Symbol in Gottfried's Tristan, 1989. Add: 40 Stoke Hill, Bristol BS9 1EX, England.

CLOTFELTER, Beryl E. American, b. 1926. Astronomy, Physics. S.S. Williston Prof. of Physics, Grinnell Coll., since 1973 (joined faculty, 1963). Research Physicist, Phillips Petroleum Co., Bartlesville, Okla., 1953–55; Asst. Prof. of Physics, Univ. of Idaho, Moscow, 1955–56; Asst. Prof. to Prof. of Physics, Oklahoma Baptist Univ., Shawnee, 1956–63. *Publs:* Reference Systems and Inertia, 1970; The Universe and Its Structure, 1976. Add: Dept. of Physics, Grinnell Coll., Grinnell, Iowa 50112, U.S.A.

CLOUDSLEY-THOMPSON, John (Leonard). British, b. 1921. Children's non-fiction, Biology, Natural history, Zoology. Prof. of Zoology Emeritus, Birkbeck Coll., Univ. of London, since 1985 (Reader, 1971–72; Prof. of Zoology, 1972–85). Ed., Journal of Arid Environments. Lectr. in Zoology, King's Coll., Univ. of London, 1950–60; Prof. of Zoology, Univ. of Khartoum, and Keeper, Sudan Natural History Museum, 1960–71; took part in Cambridge Iceland Expedition, 1947, expedition to Southern Tunisia, 1954, and univ. expeditions to various parts of Africa, 1960–73, including Trans-Sahara crossing, 1967. Vice-Pres., Linnean Soc., 1975–76 and 1977–78; Pres., British Arachnological Soc., 1982–85. *Publs:* (ed.) Biology of Deserts, 1954; Spiders, Scorpions, Centipedes and Mites, 1958, 1968; Animal Behaviour, 1960; (with John Sankey) Land Invertebrates, 1961; Rhythmic Activity in Animal Physiology and Behaviour, 1961; (with M.J. Chadwick) Life in Deserts, 1964; Desert Life, 1965; Animal Conflict and Adaptation, 1965; Animal Twilight, 1967; Microecology, 1967; The Zoology of Tropical Africa, 1969; Animals of the Desert, 1969; (with Faysal T. Abushama) A Guide to the Physiology of Terrestrial Arthropods, 1970; The Temperature and Water Relations of Reptiles, 1971; Spiders and Scorpions, 1973; Bees and Wasps, 1974; The Ecology of Oases, 1974; Desert Life, 1974; Crocodiles and Alligators, 1974; Terrestrial Environments, 1975; Insects and History, 1976; Man and the Biology of Arid Zones, 1976; (ed., with J. Bligh and A.G. Macdonald) Environmental Physiology of Animals, 1976; The Size of Animals, 1976; Dietary Adaptations of Animals, 1976; Evolutionary Trends in the Mating of Arthropods. 1976; The Water and Temperature Relations of Woodlice, 1976; Tortoises and Turtles, 1976; The Desert, 1977; Form and Function in Animals, 1978; Animal Migration, 1978; Why the Dinosaurs Became Extinct, 1978; Wildlife of the Desert, 1979; Camels, 1980; Crocodiles and Alligators, 1980; Biological Clocks, 1980; Tooth and Claw: Defensive Strategies in the Animal World, 1980; Seals and Sea Lions, 1981; Vultures, 1981; (with D.G. Applin) Biological Periodicities, 1982; (ed.) Sahara Desert, 1984; Guide to Woodlands, 1985; Living in the Desert, 1985; Evolution and Adaptation of Terrestrial Arthropods, 1988. Add: Flat 9, 4 Craven Hill, London W2 3DS, England.

CLOUGH, Shepard. American, b. 1901. History, Autobiography/Memoirs/Personal. Prof. Emeritus of European History, Columbia Univ., NYC (faculty member, 1928–70). *Publs:* (with H. Schneider) Making Fascists, 1929; History of the Flemish Movement in Belgium, 1930; Visual Outline of Modern History, 1933; France: A Study in National Economics, 1939; (with C. Cole) An Economic History of Europe, 1939; A History of American Life Insurance, 1946; The Rise and Fall of Civilization, 1951; The American Way, 1953; Histoire Economique des Etats-Unis, 1954; The Economic Development of Western Civilization, 1959; Basic Values in Western Civilization, 1960; An Economic History of Modern Italy 1861-1963, 1964; (with P. Gay and C. Warner) The European Past: Reappraisals in History from the Renaissance, 1964; (co-author) A History of the Western World, 1964; (with C.G. Moodie) European Economic History, Documents and Readings, 1965; (with S. Saladino) A History of Modern Italy in Readings and Documents, 1968; (with T. and C. Moodie) European Economic History in the Twentieth Century in Documents; (co-author) The European Past, 1970; (with others) Columbia History of the World, 1972; (with L. deRosa) Storia dell'economia Italiana dal 1861 ad oggi, 1974; (with others) European History in a World Perspective, 1975; (with Richard T. Rapp) European Economic History, 1975; The Life I've Lived (autobiography), 1981.

Add: E. Hill Rd., East Peacham, Vt. 05862, U.S.A.

CLOUSE, Robert Gordon. American, b. 1931. History, Theology/Religion. Prof. of History, Indiana State Univ., Terre Haute, since 1963. Minister, First Brethren Church, Cedar Rapids, Iowa, 1957–60; Visiting Prof., Indiana Univ., Bloomington, 1965–66 and 1966–68. *Publs:* (with others) Puritans, the Millennium and the Future of Israel, 1970; (with Robert D. Linder and Richard V. Pierard) The Cross and the Flag (social criticism), 1972; (with others) Christ and the Modern Mind, 1972; The Meaning of the Millennium: Four Views, 1977; The Church in the Age of Orthodoxy and the Enlightenment, 1980; (with R.V. Pierard) Streams of Civilization: The Modern World to the Nuclear Age, 1980; War: Four Christian Views, 1981; Wealth & Poverty, Four Christian Views, 1984. Add: 2122 South 21st St., Terre Haute, Ind. 47802, U.S.A.

CLUBB, O. Edmund. American, b. 1901. History. With U.S. Foreign Service, 1928–52: Consul Gen., Vladivostok, 1944–46, Mukden, 1946, Changchun, 1946–47, and Peking, 1947–50; Dir., Office of Chinese Affairs, U.S. Dept. of State, Washington, D.C., 1950–52; Visiting Lectr., Columbia Univ., NYC, 1959–62, 1964–65, 1967–68, Brooklyn Coll., N.Y., 1959–61, New York Univ., 1960–63, and New Sch. for Social Research, NYC, 1960–63; Sr. Research Assoc., East Asian Inst., Columbia Univ, 1966–67 and 1968–70. *Publs:* 20th Century China, 1964, 3rd ed. 1978; Communism in China: As Reported From Hankow in 1932, 1968; China and Russia: The "Great Game", 1971; The Witness and I, 1974. Add: Bogart Rd., Palenville, N.Y. 12463, U.S.A.

CLUBBE, John L(ouis) E(dwin). American, b. 1938. Literature, Biography. Prof. of English, Univ. of Kentucky, Lexington, since 1976. Lektor, Univ. of Munster, Germany, 1965–66; Asst. Prof., 1966–70, and Assoc. Prof. of English, 1970–76, Duke Univ., Durham, N.C. *Publs:* Victorian Forerunner: The Later Career of Thomas Hood, 1968; (ed.) Selected Poems of Thomas Hood, 1970; (co-ed.) The Collected Letters of Thomas and Jane Welsh Carlyle, 9 vols., 1970, 1977, 1981; (ed.) Two Reminiscences of Thomas Carlyle, 1974; (co-ed.) Nineteenth-Century Literary Perspectives, 1974; (ed.) Carlyle and His Contemporaries, 1976; (ed.) Froude's Life of Carlyle, 1979; (co-author) English Romanticism: The Grounds of Belief, 1983; (with others) The English Romantic Poets: A Review of Research and Criticism, 1985; (co-ed.) Victorian Perspectives: Six Essays, 1989; Cincinnati: Portrait of a City, 1990. Add: 247 S. Hanover Ave., Lexington, Ky. 40502, U.S.A.

CLUTTERBUCK, Richard (Lewis). British, b. 1917. Novels/Short stories, International relations/Current affairs, Politics/Government. With British Army, 1937, until retirement as Maj. Gen., 1972; Lectr., Univ. of Exeter, 1972–83. *Publs:* Across the River, 1957; The Long Long War, 1966; Riot and Revolution in Singapore and Malaya, 1973; Protest and the Urban Guerrilla, 1973; Living with Terrorism, 1975; Guerrillas and Terrorists, 1977; Britain in Agony, 1978, 1980; Kidnap and Ransom, 1978; The Media and Political Violence, 1983; Industrial Conflict and Democracy, 1984; Conflict and Violence in Singapore and Malaysia, 1985; The Future of Political Violence, 1986; Kidnap, Hijack, and Extortion, 1987. Add: Lloyds Bank Ltd., R Section, 6 Pall Mall, London SW1Y 5NH, England.

CLUTTON, Cecil. British, b. 1909. Antiques/Furnishings, Music, Transportation. Sr. Partner, Cluttons, Chartered Surveyors, until 1972, now retired. Vice-Pres., Antiquarian Horological Soc. Pres., Vintage Sports Car Club, 1954–57; Master, Worshipful Co. of Clockmakers, 1973–74. *Publs:* (with George Dixon) The Organ: Its Tonal Structure and Registration, 1950; (with John Stanford) The Vintage Motor Car, 1954, 5th ed. 1961; (with Cyril Posthumus and Denis Jenkinson) The Racing Car Development and Design, 1956; (with G.H. Baille and C.A. Ilbert) Britten's Old Clocks and Watches and Their Makers, 7th ed. 1956, sole author 9th ed., 1982; (with P. Bird and A. Harding) The Vintage Motor Car Pocket Book, 1959, 1975; (with A. Niland) The British Organ, 1963, 1982; (with G. Daniels) Watches, 1965, 1971, 1978; Collector's Collection, 1975. Add: Old Vicarage, Lezayre, Ramsey, Isle of Man, United Kingdom.

CLUYSENAAR, Anne (Alice Andrée). Irish, b. 1936. Poetry, Literature. Taught at Manchester Univ., 1957–58, Trinity Coll., Dublin, 1961–62, King's Coll., Aberdeen, 1963–65, Lancaster Univ., 1965–67, Huddersfield Polytechnic, 1972–73, and Birmingham Univ., 1973,19676; taught at Sheffield Polytechnic, 1976–87. Dir., Verbal Arts Assn., 1983–86. *Publs:* A Fan of Shadows, 1967; Nodes, 1969; An Introduction to Literary Stylistics: A Discussion of Dominant Structure in Verse and Prose (in U.S. as Aspects of Literary Stylistics), 1976; (ed.) Selected Poems of James Burns Singer, 1977; Poetry Introduction 4, 1978; Double Helix,

1982; Verbal Arts: The Missing Subject, 1987. Add: Little Wentwood Farm, Llantrisant, Usk, Gwent NP5 1ND, South Wales.

CLYMER, Eleanor. Also writes as Elizabeth Kinsey. American, b. 1906. Children's fiction, Children's non-fiction. Member, Children's Book Cttee., The Authors Guild. *Publs:* A Yard for John, 1943; Here Comes Pete, 1944; The Grocery Mouse, 1945; Little Bear Island, 1945; The Country Kittens, 1947; Trolley Car Family, 1947; The Latch-Key Club, 1949; Treasure at First Base, 1950; Tommy's Wonderful Airplane, 1951; Thirty-three Bunn Street, 1952; (as Elizabeth Kinsey) Sea View Secret, 1952; (as Elizabeth Kinsey) Donny and Company, 1953; Make Way for Water, 1953; (with L.M. Gilbreth and O.M. Thomas) Management in the Home, 1954; Chester, 1955; (as Elizabeth Kinsey) This Cat Came to Stay, 1955; Not Too Small After All, 1955; Sociable Toby, 1956; (with L. Erlich) Modern American Career Women, 1959; Mr. Piper's Bus, 1961; Case of the Missing Link, 1962, 1968; Benjamin in the Woods, 1962; Now That You Are Seven, 1963; Search for a Living Fossil, 1963; Harry the Wild West Horse, 1963; Communities at Work, 1964, 1969; The Tiny Little House, 1964; Chipmunk in the Forest, 1965; Adventure of Walter, 1965; Wheels, 1965; My Brother Stevie, 1967; The Big Pile of Dirt, 1968; Horatio, 1968; Second Greatest Invention, 1969; Belinda's New Spring Hat, 1969; We Lived in the Almont, 1970; House on the Mountain, 1971; Spider, the Cave and the Pottery Bowl, 1971; Me and the Eggman, 1972; How I Went Shopping and What I Got, 1972; Santiago's Silvermine, 1973; Luke Was There, 1973; Take Tarts as Tarts Is Passing, 1974; Leave Horatio Alone, 1974; Engine Number Seven, 1975; Hamburgers—And Ice Cream for Dessert, 1975; Horatio's Birthday, 1976; The Get-Away Car, 1978; Horatio Goes to the Country, 1978; Horatio Solves a Mystery, 1980; A Search for Two Bad Mice, 1980; My Mother Is the Smartest Woman in the World, 1982; The Horse in the Attic, 1983. Add: 11 Nightingale Rd., Katonah, N.Y. 10536, U.S.A.

CLYNE, Douglas (George Wilson). Also writes as Alasdair Sinclair. British, b. 1912. Language/Linguistics, Medicine/Health, Travel/Exploration/Adventure, Autobiography/Memoirs/Personal. Consultant Obstetrician and Gynaecologist, East Ham Memorial Hosp., London, 1942–53, and King Edward VII Hosp., Windsor, 1946–53; Consultant Gynaecologist, Maidenhead Hosp., 1945–53, Royal London Homoeopathic Hosp., 1946–53, and Italian Hosp., 1947–53; Obstetrician, East End Maternity Hosp., London, 1946–53, now retired. *Publs:* (as Alasdair Sinclair) Ladies in Emergency, 1955; Anchorage on the Costa Brava, 1958; Handbook of Obstetrics and Gynaecology for Nurses, 1959; Your Guide to the Costa Brava, 1959, 1965; A Concise Textbook for Midwives, 1960, 5th ed. 1980; Preliminary Examination Questions for Nurses (England and Wales), 1960; Final Examination Questions for Nurses (England and Wales), 1960; Preliminary and Final Examination Questions for Nurses (Scotland), 1960; A Textbook of Gynaecology and Obstetrics, 1963; Your Guide to Portugal, 1965; Your Guide to the Costa del Sol, 1966; Gaelic Verbs and Their Prepositions, 1984; A Dictionary of English-Gaelic Expressions, Idioms and Phrases, 1985. Add: Blue Waters, Porthpean, St. Austell, Cornwall, England.

COAKLEY, Mary Lewis. American, b. 1907. Children's non-fiction, Women, Biography. *Publs:* Fitting God into the Picture, 1950, as A Woman's Way; Our Child—God's Child, 1953; Mister Music Maker: A Biography of Lawrence Welk, 1958; Never Date Women, 1964; Rated X: The Moral Case Against TV, 1978; Not Alone, 1982; How to Live Life to the Fullest: Handbook for Seasoned Citizens, 1984; Long Literated Ladies, 1988. Add: 110 Hewett Rd., Wyncote, Pa. 19095, U.S.A.

COAN, Richard W. American, b. 1928. Psychology. Prof. of Psychology, Univ. of Arizona, since 1964 (Asst. Prof., 1957–60; Assoc. Prof., 1960–64). Research Assoc. in Psychology, Univ. of Illinois, Urbana, 1955–57. *Publs:* The Optimal Personality: An Empirical and Theoretical Analysis, 1974; Hero, Artist, Sage, or Saint?: A Survey of Views on What Is Variously Called Mental Health, Normality, Maturity, Self-Actualization, and Human Fulfillment, 1977; Psychologists: Personal and Theoretical Pathways, 1979; Psychology of Adjustment: Personal Experience and Development, 1983; Human Consciousness and Its Evolution: A Multidimensional View, 1987. Add: Dept. of Pyschology, Univ. of Arizona, Tucson, Ariz. 85721, U.S.A.

COATES, Austin. British, b. 1922. Novels/Short stories, History, Travel/Exploration/Adventure, Autobiography/Memoirs/Personal, Biography. Asst. Colonial Secty., 1949–52, District Officer and Magistrate, New Territories, 1953–55, Secretariat, 1955–56, Govt. of Hong Kong; Chinese Affairs Officer and Magistrate, 1957, Chmn., Kuching Rural District Council, 1957–58, Secty. to Gov., 1958–59, Sarawak; First Secty., British High Commn., Malaya, 1959–62. *Publs:* Invitation to an Eastern

Feast, 1953; Personal and Oriental, 1957; The Road, 1959; Basutoland, 1966; Prelude to Hongkong, 1966, as Macao and the British, 1988; City of Broken Promises, 1967; Rizal: Philippine Nationalist and Martyr, 1968; Myself a Mandarin, 1968; Western Pacific Islands, 1970; China, India and the Ruins of Washington, 1972; Islands of the South, 1974; Numerology, 1974; A Mountain of Light, 1977; A Macao Narrative, 1978; Whampoa Ships on the Shore, 1980; China Races, 1983; The Commerce in Rubber, 1987; Quick Tidings of Hong Kong, 1990. Add: 80 Macdonnell Rd., Hong Kong.

COATES, Doreen (Frances). British, b. 1912. Children's fiction and non-fiction. Headmistress, Carlisle Infant Sch., Hampton, Middx., 1953–72. *Publs:* Yellow Door Stories, 6 books, 1966; Red Door Stories, 3 books, 1968; Blue Door Stories, 3 books, 1968; Methuen Number Cards 1-6, 1968, 7-10, 1974; Methuen Stories About Numbers, 4 books, 1972; Jacko and Delilah Stories, 4 books, 1978; Whatever Next Books, 6 books, 1980; (co-ed) Thunder the Dinosaur, 8 books, 1982. Add: c/o Ginn and Co. ltd., Prebendal House, Parson's Fee, Aylesbury, Bucks. HP20 2QZ, England.

COATES, Ken. British, b. 1930. Business/Trade/Industry, Industrial Relations, International relations/Current affairs, Money/Finance, Politics/Government, Social commentary. Reader in Adult Education, Univ. of Nottingham (member of the faculty since 1960). Member, Bertrand Russell Peace Foundn., since 1965; Joint Secty., European Nuclear Disarmament Liaison Cttee., since 1981. Coal miner, 1948–56. *Publs:* (with Richard Silburn) Poverty, Deprivation, and Morale in a Nottingham Community, 1967; (with Tony Topham) Industrial Democracy in Great Britain, 1967; (with Richard Silburn) Poverty: The Forgotten Englishman, 1970; The Crisis of British Socialism, 1971; Essays on Industrial Democracy, 1971; (with Tony Topham) The New Unionism:) The Case for Workers' Control, 1972; (ed.) Democracy in the Mines, 1974; Socialists and the Labour Party, 1975; New Worker Co-operatives, 1976; Beyond Wage Slavery, 1977; Democracy in the Labour Party, 1977; (with Tony Topham) The Shop Steward's Guide to the Bullock Report, 1977; Industrial Development and Economic Planning, 1978; The Case of Nikolai Bukharin, 1978; European Nuclear Disarmament, 1980; (with Tony Topham) Trade Unions in Britain, 1980; (with Richard Silburn) Beyond the Bulldozer, 1980; Eleventh Hour for Europe, 1981; Work-Ins, Sit-Ins, and Industrial Democracy, 1981; Deterrence: Why We Must Think Again, 1981; Heresies: Resist Much, Obey Little, 1982; An Alternative Economy Strategy, 1982; The Social Democrats, 1983; (with Richard Silburn) Poverty: The Forgotten Englishman, 1983; The Most Dangerous Decade: World Militarism and the New Non-Aligned Peace Movement, 1984; (with Tony Topham) Trade Unions and Politics, 1986; (ed.) China and the Bomb, 1986; (ed.) Civil and Academic Freedom in the U.S.S.R. and Eastern Europe, 1988. Add: 112 Church St., Matlock, Derbyshire DE4 3BZ, England.

COATES, Sheila. *See* HOLLAND, Sheila.

COATS, George W(esley). American, b. 1936. Theology/Religion. Prof. of Old Testament Theology, Lexington Theological Seminary, Ky., since 1971 (Assoc. Prof., 1968–71). Contrib. Member, Forms of Old Testament Literature, Eerdmans, Grand Rapids, Mich., since 1967. Asst. Prof. of Religion, McMurry Coll., Abilene, Tex., 1965–68. *Publs:* Rebellion in the Wilderness, 1968; From Canaan to Egypt: Structural and Theological Context for the Joseph Story, 1975; Genesis: With an Introduction to Narrative, 1984; Heroic Man and Man of God: Theological Expositions of the Moses Tradition, 1986. Add: 631 S. Limestone, Lexington, Ky. 40508, U.S.A.

COBB, Richard (Charles). British, b. 1917. History. Sr. Research Fellow, Worcester Coll., Oxford, from 1984, now Emeritus (Tutor in Modern History, Balliol Coll., 1962–72; Reader in French Revolutionary History, Oxford Univ., 1969–72; Prof. of Modern History, 1973–84). Engaged in research in Paris, 1946–55; Lectr. in History, University Coll. of Wales, Aberystwyth, 1955–61. *Publs:* L'armée révolutionnaire a Lyon, 1952; Les armées révolutionnaires du Midi, 1955; Les armées révolutionnaires, 2 vols., 1961–63; Terreur et Subsistances, 1965; A Second Identity: Essays on France and French History, 1969; The Police and the People: French Popular Protest 1789-1820, 1970; Reactions to the French Revolution, 1972; Paris and Its Provinces 1792-1802, 1975; A Sense of Place, 1975; Tour de France, 1976; Death in Paris 1795-1801, 1978; Promenades, 1980; Streets of Paris, 1980; French and Germans, Germans and French, 1983; Still Life: Sketches from Tunbridge Wells Childhood, 1983; A Classical Education, 1985; People and Places, 1985; Something to Hold Onto, 1988. Add: Worcester Coll., Oxford, England.

COBB, Vicki. American, b. 1938. Children's non-fiction. *Publs:* Logic, 1969; (ed.) Biology Study Prints, 1970; Cells, 1970; Gases, 1970; Making Sense of Money, 1971; Sense of Direction, 1972; Science Experiments You Can Eat, 1972; Heat, 1973; The Long and Short of Measurement, 1973; How the Doctor Knows You're Fine, 1973; Arts and Crafts You Can Eat, 1974; Supersuits, 1975; Magic . . . Naturally!, 1976; More Science Experiments You Can Eat, 1979; Truth on Trial: The Story of Galileo, 1979; (with Kathy Darling) Bet You Can't: Science Impossibilities to Fool You, 1980; How to Really Fool Yourself: Illusions for All Your Senses, 1980; Lots of Rot, 1981; The Secret Life of School Supplies, 1981; The Secret Life of Hardware, 1982; Fuzz Does It!, 1982; Gobs of Goo, 1983; The Monsters Who Died, 1983; (with Kathy Darling) Bet You Can! Science Possibilities to Fool You, 1983; Brave in the Attempt, 1983; Chemically Active, 1984; The Secret Life of Cosmetics, 1985; The Scoop on Ice Cream, 1986; Sneakers Meet Your Feet, 1986; More Power to You, 1986; The Trip of a Drip, 1986; Inspector Bodyguard Patrols the Land of U, 1986; Skyscraper Going Up!, 1987; Scraps of Wraps, 1988; Why Doesn't the Earth Fall Up?, 1988; This Place Is Cold, 1989; This Place Is Dry, 1989; This Place Is High, 1989; This Place Is Wet, 1989; Why Can't You Unscramble an Egg?, 1989. Add: c/o J.B. Lippincott Co., 10 E. 53rd St., New York, N.Y. 10022, U.S.A.

COBBETT, Richard. *See* **PLUCKROSE**, Henry.

COBBING, Bob. British, b. 1920. Poetry. Coordinator, Assn. of Little Presses, since 1987 (Chmn., 1970–86); Co-Ed, Poetry and Little Press Information, since 1980. Treas., The Poetry Soc., National Poetry Centre, London, 1972–74. *Publs:* (with J. Rowan) Massacre of the Innocents, 1963; Sound Poems: An ABC in Sound, 1965; Eyearun, 1966; Chamber Music, 1967; Kurrirrurriri, 1967; SO (Six Sound Poems), 1968; Octo, 1969; Whisper Piece, 1969; Why Shiva Has Ten Arms, 1969; Whississippi, 1969; Kwatz, 1970; Sonic Icons, 1970; Etcetera, 1970; Kris Kringles Kesmes Korals, 1970; Three Poems for Voice and Movement, 1971; Spearhead, 1971; Five Visual Poems, 1971; The Judith Poem, 1971; Konkrete Canticle, 1971; Beethoven Today, 1971; 15-Shakespeare Kaku, 1972; Trigram, 1972; Songsignals, 1972; Circa, 1973; (ed.) Gloup and Woup: A Folio of English Concrete Poetry, 1974; The Five Vowels, 1974; Five Performance Pieces, 1975; Poems for the North West Territories, 1976; Kyoto to Tokyo, 1975; Jade-Sound Poems, 1976; Tu to Ratu/Earth Best, 1977; (with Lawrence Upton) Furst Fruts, 1977; And Avocado, 1977; Bob Cob's Rag Bag Mark One, 1977; Scorch Scores, 1977; Bill Jubobe, 1976; Citycisms, 1977; Cygnet Ring (Collected Poems), 1977; ABC/Wan do Tree, 1978; A Movie Book, 1978; Two-Leaf Book, 1978; (with Peter Mayer) Concerning Concrete Poetry, 1978; Found: Sound, 1978; Principles of Movement, 1978; Meet Bournemouth, 1978; Fugitive Poem No. X, 1978; Game and Set, 1978; Ginetics, 1978; ABC/Wan do Tree: Collected Poems 2, 1978; Sensations of the Retina, 1978; A Peal in Air: Collected Poems 3, 1978; Fiveways, 1978; Niagara, 1978; Grin, 1979; (with Jeremy Adler) A Short History of London, 1979; The Kollekted Kris Kringle: Collected Poems 4, 1979; Pattern of Performance, 1979; The Sacred Mushroom, 1980; (with Jeremy Adler) Notes from the Correspondence, 1980; Voicings, 1980; (Soma) Light Song, 1981; Serial Ten (Portraits), 1981; Four Letter Poems, 2 series, 1981; Sound of Jade, 1982; In Line, 1982; Baker's Dozen, 1982; Lightsong Two, 1983; Bob Cobbing's Girlie Poems: Collected Poems 5, 1983; Sockless in Sandals: Collected Poems 6, 1985; Vowels and Consequences, Collected Poems 7, 1985; Lame, Limping, Mangled, Marred and Mutilated: Collected Poems 9, 1986; Metamorphosis, 1986; Variations on a Theme, 1986; Astound and Risible: Collected Poems 8, 1987; Processual, Collected Poems 10, 1987; Entitled: Entitled (Collected Poems 11), 1987; Six Computer Scores, 1987; (with Bruce Anderson) Both Both, 1987; Twelve, 1987; Computer Poems, 1988; Stracci (3 vols.), 1988; Changing Forms in English Visual Poetry, 1988; Serious Dissertations on Something or Other, 1989; Improvisation Is a Dirty Word (Collected Poems 12), 1989. Add: 89A Petherton Rd., London N5 2QT, England.

COBURN, Andrew. American, b. 1932. Mystery/Crime/Suspense. Full-time writer since 1978. Feature Writer, and later Police Reporter, Suburban Ed., and City Ed., Eagle-Tribune, Lawrence, Mass., 1963–73; Book Reviewer and Part-time Copy Ed., Boston Globe, 1973–78; political columnist for several Massachusetts newspapers, 1978–81. *Publs:* The Trespassers, 1974; The Babysitter, 1979; Off Duty, 1980; Company Secrets, 1982; Widow's Walk, 1984; Sweetheart, 1985; Love Nest, 1987; Goldilocks, 1989. Add: 3 Farrwood Dr., Andover, Mass. 01810, U.S.A.

COBURN, L.J. *See* **HARVEY**, John B.

COCHRAN, Jeff. *See* **DURST**, Paul.

COCHRAN, Thomas (Childs). American, b. 1902. Business/Trade/Industry, Economics, History. Benjamin Franklin Prof. of History Emeritus, Univ. of Pennsylvania, Philadelphia (joined faculty as Prof. of U.S. History, 1950; Grad. Chmn., Dept. of American Civilization, 1951; Chmn., Dept. of History, 1953–55). Instr. in History, 1927–36, Asst. Prof., 1936–43, Assoc. Prof., 1943–44, and Prof., 1944–50, New York Univ. Pres. and Chmn., National Records Management Council, 1948–51; Pres., Economic History Assn., 1958–60; Pres., Org. of American Historians, 1966–67; Pres., American Historical Assn., 1972; Pres., Business History Conference, 1979–80. *Publs:* New York in the Confederation, 1932; A History of the Pabst Brewing Company, 1948; (with others) History of the City of Greater New York; Railroad Leaders 1845-1890, 1953; (with others) The Social Sciences in Historical Studies, 1954; The American Business System, 1957; The Puerto Rican Businessman, 1959; A Basic History of American Business, 1959; The Age of Enterprise, 1961; (co-author) Entrepreneurship in Argentine Culture, 1962; The Inner Revolution, 1965; Social Change in Industrial Society, 1972; Business in American Life, 1972; American Business in the Twentieth Century, 1972; The Uses of History, 1973; Pennsylvania, 1977; 200 Years of American Business, 1978; Frontiers of Change: Early Industrialism in America, 1981; Challenges to American Values: Society, Business and Religion, 1985. Add: c/o Oxford Univ. Press, Inc., 200 Madison Ave., New York, N.Y. 10016, U.S.A.

COCHRANE, Peggy. American, b. 1926. Plays/Screenplays, Medicine/Health. Architect in private practice since 1960. Member of the Bd., L.A. Architect, since 1975. Pres., Assn. of Women in Architecture, 1970–72. *Publs:* Mayaland (musical), 1967; Best Friends (play), 1975; I Gave at the Office (play), 1978; Witch Doctor's Cookbook, 1980; Witch Doctor's Manual, 1980. Add: 14755 Ventura Blvd., Suite 1-626, Sherman Oaks, Calif. 91403, U.S.A.

COCKETT, Mary. British, b. 1915. Children's fiction, Children's non-fiction. Ed., National Inst. of Industrial Psychology, 1943–48, and Intnl. Congress of Mental Health, 1948–49. *Publs:* Jonathan on the Farm, 1954; Jonathan and Felicity, 1955; Fourteen Stories About Jonathan, 1956; More About Jonathan, 1957; Jan the Market Boy, 1957; Bouncing Ball, 1958; Jasper Club, 1959; When Felicity Was Small, 1959; Rolling On, 1960; Seven Days with Jan, 1960; Mary Ann Goes to Hospital, 1961; Out with Felicity and Jonathan, 1962; Cottage by the Lock, 1962; Roads and Travelling, 1964; Benny's Bazaar, 1964; Acrobat Hamster, 1965; Bridges, 1965; The Birthday Ride, 1965; Sunflower Giant, 1966; There for the Picking, 1966; Ash Dry, Ash Green, 1968; Strange Valley, 1967; Twelve Gold Chairs, 1967; Something Big, 1968; The Wild Place, 1968; Tufty (reader), 1968; Rosanna the Goat, 1969; Pelican Park, 1960; Another Home, Another Country, 1969; The Wedding Tea (reader), 1970; Magic and Gold: Tales from Northern Europe, 1970; Farthing Bundles, 1970; Towns, 1971; The Marvellous Stick (reader), 1972; The Joppy Stories (Joppy Crawling, and Joppy on His Feet; Joppy Steps Out, and Caught on a Tree Stump; Joppy in Bucket, and the Moving Cat), 3 vols., 1972; Boat Girl, 1972; Bells in Our Lives, 1973; Treasure, 1973; The Rainbow Walk (reader), 1973; An Armful of Sparrows (reader), 1973; As Big as the Ark, 1974; Look at the Little One, 1974; Dolls and Puppets, 1974; Walls, 1974; He Cannot Really Read (reader), 1974; Snake in the Camp, 1975; Tower Raven, 1975; Backyard Hospital, 1975; The Story of Cars, 1976; The Magician (reader), 1976; Fly High, Magpie (reader), 1976; Missing (reader), 1978; The Drowning Valley, 1978; The Birthday, 1979; Ladybird at the Zoo, Monster in the River, Pig at the Market, 3 picture books, 1979; The Christmas Tree, 1979; Money to Spend (reader), 1980; The Bell (reader), 1980; Witch of Candlewick, 1980; Enough Is Enough, 1980; Shadow at Applegarth, 1981; Hoo-Ming's Discovery, 1982; The Cat and the Castle, 1982; The School Donkey, 1982; At the Tower (reader), 1984; Crab Apples (reader), 1984; Strange Hill, 1984; Tracker, 1984; Paper Boys (reader), 1984; Better Than a Party, 1985; Zoo Ticket, 1985; Rescue at the Zoo, 1986; Winning All the Way, 1987; Kate of Candlewick, 1987; The Day of the Squirrels, 1987; A Place of His Own, 1987; Mystery on the Farm, 1988; Bridesmaids (picture book), 1989. Add: 24 Benville Ave., Bristol BS9 2RX, England.

COCKRELL, Marian (Brown). American, b. 1909. Historical/Romance/Gothic, Children's fiction. *Publs:* Yesterday's Madness, 1943; Lillian Harley, 1943; (with Frank Cockrell) Dark Waters, 1944; Shadow Castle (juvenile), 1945; Something Between, 1946; The Revolt of Sarah Perkins, 1965; Mixed Blessings, 1978; The Misadventures of Bethany Price, 1979; Mixed Company, 1979. Add: 6718 Circle Creek Dr., Boone's Mill, Virginia 24065, U.S.A.

COCKSHUT, A(nthony) O(liver) J(ohn). British, b. 1927. Literature, Theology/Religion. G.M. Young Lectr. in Nineteenth Century Literature,

Oxford Univ., since 1965 (Research Fellow, Balliol Coll., 1950–54). Fellow, Hertford Coll., Oxford, since 1966. Asst. Master, Manchester Grammar Sch., England, 1954–64. *Publs:* Anthony Trollope: A Critical Study, 1955; Anglican Attitudes: A Study of Victorian Religious Controversies, 1959; The Imagination of Charles Dickens, 1961; The Unbelievers: English Agnostic Thought, 1840-1890, 1964; (ed.) Religious Controversies of the 19th Century: Selected Documents, 1966; Achievement of Walter Scott, 1969; Truth to Life, 1974; Man and Women: Love in the Novel, 1977; The Art of Autobiography in 19th and 20th Century England, 1984. Add: Hertford Coll., Oxford, England.

CODDING, George A., Jr. American, b. 1923. Communications media, Institutions/Organizations, Politics/Government. Prof. of Political Science, Univ. of Colorado, Boulder, since 1961 (Dir., International Affairs Prog., since 1988). Asst. Prof., Univ. of Pennsylvania, Philadelphia, 1955–61. *Publs:* The International Telecommunication Union, An Experiment in International Cooperation, 1952; Broadcasting Without Barriers, 1959; The Federal Government of Switzerland, 1961; The Universal Postal Union: Coordinator of the International Mails, 1964; Governing the Commune of Veyrier: Politics in Swiss Local Government, 1967; (with William Safran) Politics and Ideology: The Socialist Party of France, 1979; (with Anthony Rutkowski) The ITU in a Changing World, 1982. Add: Dept. of Political Science, Univ. of Colorado, Boulder, Colo. 80309, U.S.A.

CODER, S. Maxwell. American, b. 1902. Theology/Religion, Biography. Dean of Education Emeritus, Moody Bible Inst. of Chicago, since 1969 (Ed.-in-Chief, Moody Press 1946–47; Vice Pres. and Dean of Education 1947–69). Co-Ed. with Wilbur M. Smith, Wycliffe Series of Christian Classics, Moody Press, since 1947. Presbyterian Minister, Camden, N.J., 1935–38, Atlantic City, N.J., 1938–43, and Philadelphia, 1944–45. *Publs:* Dobbie, Defender of Malta, 1946; Youth Triumphant, 3 vols., 1946; (ed.) Memoirs of M'Cheyne, 1947; God's Will for Your Life, 1950; (ed.) Our Lord Prays for His Own, 1950, (ed.) The World to Come, 1954; Jude: The Acts of the Apostates, 1955; (with William Evans) Great Doctrines of the Bible, 1974; (ed.) Nave's Topical Bible, 1975; Israel's Destiny, 1978; Christian Worker's New Testament, 1979; The Final Chapter, 1984. Add: 1860 Sherman Ave., Evanston, Ill. 60201, U.S.A.

CODRESCU, Andrei. American, b. 1946. Novels/Short stories, Poetry, Autobiography/Memoirs/Personal. Dir., Inst. for Paleo-Cybernetic Research, Palo Alto, Calif., 1967–73. *Publs:* License to Carry a Gun, 1970; The, Here, What, Where, 1971; Why I Can't Talk on the Telephone (short stories), 1972; Grammar and Money, 1972; A Serious Morning, 1973; Secret Training (essays), 1973; (with Aram Saroyan) San Francisco, 1973; The History of the Growth of Heaven, 1973; The Life and Times of an Involuntary Genius (autobiography), 1974; Travels of a Vigilante, 1975; For Max Jacob, 1975; Necrocorrida, 1980; (with Alice Notley) Three Zero, Turning Thirty, 1982; Selected Poems 1970-1980, 1983; In America's Shoes, 1983; A Craving for Swan, 1986; Comrade Past and Mister Present, 1986; Ectoplasm Is My Hobby: Blackouts and Dramatic Objects 1971 and 1986, 1987; Monsieur Teste in America and Other Instances of Realism, 1987; (ed.) American Poetry Since 1970: Up Late, 1987; (ed.) The Stiffest of the Corpse: An Exquisite Corpse Reader, 1988. Add: P.O. Box 341, Monte Rio, Calif. 95462, U.S.A.

CODY, James R. *See* **ROHRBACH**, Peter Thomas.

COE, Michael (Douglas). American, b. 1929. Anthropology/Ethnology. Prof. of Anthropology, Yale Univ., New Haven, Conn., since 1968 (Instr., 1960–62; Asst. Prof., 1962–63). *Publs:* La Victoria, 1961; Mexico, 1962; The Jaguar's Children: Preclassic Central Mexico, 1965; The Maya, 1966, 1971; (with K.V. Flannery) Early Cultures and Human Ecology in South Coastal Guatemala, 1967: America's First Civilization, 1968; The Maya Scribe and His World, 1973; Classic Maya Poetry at Dumbarton Oaks, 1975; The Lords of the Underworld: Masterpieces of Classic Maya Ceramics, 1978; (with Richard A. Diehl) In the Land of the Olmec, 1980; Old Gods and Young Heroes: The Pearlman Collection of Maya Ceramics, 1982; (with Gordon Whittaker) Aztec Sorcerers in Seventeenth Century Mexico: The Treatise on Superstitions by Hernando Ruiz de Alarcon, 1983; (with Dean Snow and Elizabeth Benson) Atlas of Ancient America, 1987. Add: 376 St. Ronan St., New Haven, Conn. 06511, U.S.A.

COE, Richard N(elson Caslon). British, b. 1923. Literature, Translations. Prof. of French and Comparative Literature, Univ. of California, Davis, since 1979. Member, Editorial Bd., Australian Journal of French Studies, since 1964; Fellow, Australian Academy of the Humanities, since 1970; Member, Editorial Bd., Comparison, 1975–83, New Comparison,

since 1985. Lectr., Univ. of Leeds, 1950–62; Sr. Lectr., Univ. of Queensland, 1962–63; Reader, 1963–66, and Personal Prof. of French, 1969–72, Univ. of Melbourne; Reader, 1966–69, and Prof. of French, 1972–79, Univ. of Warwick, Coventry. *Publs:* (trans.) Stendhal's Life of Rossini, 1956; (trans.) Stendhal's Rome, Naples and Florence in 1826, 1959; Morelly: Ein Rationalist auf dem Wege zum Sozialismus, 1961; Ionesco, 1961, ed. 1969; (trans.) Robert Pinget's No Answer, 1961; Beckett, 1964; (adaptor) Crocodile, by Kornyei Chukovsky, 1964; (adaptor) Doctor Concoctor, by Kornyei Chukovsky, 1967; The Vision of Jean Genet, 1968; (ed.) The Theater of Jean Genet: A Casebook, 1970; Eugène Ionesco: A Study of His Theatre, with (trans.) The Niece-Wife, by Ionesco, 1971; (trans. and ed.) Stendhal's Lives of Haydn, Mozart and Metastasio, 1972; When the Grass Was Taller: Autobiography and the Experience of Childhood, 1984. Add: 307 Balboa Ave., Davis, Calif. 95616, U.S.A.

COE, Tucker. *See* **WESTLAKE**, Donald E.

COE, William C. American, b. 1930. Psychology. Private practice, clinical psychology, since 1964. Prof. of Psychology, California State Univ., Fresno, since 1972; (Asst. Prof., 1966–68; Assoc. Prof., 1968–72). Asst. Clinical Prof. of Medical Psychology, Univ. of California, San Francisco, 1964–66; Asst. Prof. of Psychology, Fresno State Coll., 1966–68. Correspondence Instr., Univ. of California, Berkeley, 1967–76. *Publs:* (with T.R. Sarbin) The Student Psychologists' Handbook: A Guide to Sources, 1969; Challenges of Personal Adjustment, 1972; (with L. Gagnon and D. Swiercinsky) Instructor's Manual for Challenges of Personal Adjustment, 1972; (with T.R. Sarbin) Hypnosis: A Social Psychological Analysis of Influence Communication, 1972; Psychology X118: Psychological Adjustment, 1973; (with T.R. Sarbin) Mastering Psychology, 1984. Add: Dept. of Psychology, California State Univ., Fresno, Calif. 93740, U.S.A.

COEN, Rena Neumann. American, b. 1925. Art, Children's non-fiction. Prof. of Art History, St. Cloud State Univ., Minn., since 1978 (Asst. Prof., 1969–73; Assoc. Prof., 1973–78). Research Assoc. and Lectr., Minneapolis Inst. of Arts, Minn., 1961–66. *Publs:* Kings and Queens in Art (children's), 1965; American History in Art (children's), 1966; Medicine in Art (children's), 1970; The Old Testament in Art (children's), 1970; The Black Man in Art (children's), 1970; The Red Man in Art (children's), 1970; Painting and Sculpture in Minnesota 1820-1914, 1976; In the Mainstream, The Art of Alexis Jean Fournier, 1985; The Paynes, Edgar and Ellie, American Artists, 1988. Add: 1425 Flag Ave. S., Minneapolis, Minn. 55426, U.S.A.

COERR, Eleanor Beatrice. Also writes as Eleanor Hicks. American, b. 1922. Children's non-fiction. Lectr., Chapman Coll., Orange, Calif., and Monterey Peninsula Coll., Calif. Reporter and Ed., Edmonton Journal, Can., 1944–49; Ed. and Illustrator, syndicated weekly column in the Manila Times, Philippines, 1958–61; Contract Writer for USIS in Taiwan, 1960–62, and for Voice of America Special English Div., Washington, D.C., 1963–65; Librarian, Davis Library, Bethedsa, Md., 1971–72. *Publs:* (as Eleanor Hicks) Circus Day in Japan, 1953, 1968; The Mystery of the Golden Cat, 1968, 1973; Twenty-Five Dragons, 1971; Biography of a Giant Panda, 1975; The Mixed-Up Mystery Smell, 1975; The Biography of Jane Goodall, 1976; Biography of a Red Kangaroo, 1976; Sadako and the Thousand Paper Cranes, 1977; Waza at Windy Gulch, 1977; Gigi, A Whale Borrowed for Science and Returned to Sea, 1980; The Big Balloon Race, 1980; The Bell Ringer and the Pirates, 1983; The Josefina Story Quilt, 1986; Lady with a Torch, 1986; Chang's Paper Pony, 1988. Add: 1360 Josselyn Canyon Rd. 34, Monterey, Calif. 93940, U.S.A.

COETZEE, J(ohn) M(ichael). South African, b. 1940. Novels, Translations. Prof. of Gen. Literature, Univ. of Cape Town, since 1984 (Lectr., 1972–83). Applications programmer, IBM, London, 1962–63; Systems Programmer, International Computers, Bracknell, Berks., 1964–65; Asst. Prof., 1968–71, and Butler Prof. of English, 1984, State Univ. of New York, Buffalo; Hinkley Prof. of English, Johns Hopkins Univ., Baltimore, 1986, 1989. *Publs:* Dusklands (two novellas), 1974; (trans.) A Posthumous Confession, by Marcellus Emants, 1976; In the Heart of the Country (in U.S. as From the Heart of the Country), 1977; Waiting for the Barbarians, 1980; (trans.) The Expedition to the Baobab Tree, by Wilma Stockenstrom, 1983; Life and Times of Michael K, 1983; Foe, 1986; White Writing: On the Culture of Letters in South Africa, 1988. Add: P.O. Box 92, Rondebosch, Cape Province 7700, South Africa.

COFFEY, Brian. *See* **KOONTZ**, Dean R.

COFFIN, David R. American, b. 1918. Architecture, Homes/Gardens.

Howard Crosby Butler Prof., of the History of Architecture, Princeton Univ., N.J., since 1970 now Emeritus (Lectr., 1949–54, Asst. Prof., 1954–56, Assoc. Prof., 1956–60, Prof., 1960–70, and Chmn., 1964–70, Dept. of Art and Archaeology). Ed.-in-Chief, The Art Bulletin, 1959–63. *Publs:* The Villa d'Este at Tivoli, 1960; (ed.) The Italian Garden, 1972; The Villa in the Life of Renaissance Rome, 1979. Add: Dept. of Art and Archaeology, Princeton Univ., Princeton, N.J. 08544, U.S.A.

COFFIN, George Sturgis. American, b. 1903. Recreation/Leisure/Hobbies. Publr., Waltham, Mass., since 1947. *Publs:* Pocket Contract Bridge and Automatic Score Calculator, 1931; Self-Teaching Contract Cards: Culbertson System, 1931; End plays at Bridge Explained, 1932, 6th rev. ed. 1975; Winning Duplicate, 1943; Fortune in Poker, 1949, 3rd rev. ed. as The Poker Game Complete, 1955; Learn Bridge the Easy Way, 1950; Sure Tricks, 1952; Acol and the New Point Count, 1953, rev. ed. 1958; Bridge Play from A to Z, 1954, 4th ed. 1979; Contract Bridge for Three, 1955, 1956; Pocket Guide to Pinochle, 1956; Pocket Guide to Play of Poker, 1956; Pocket Guide to Cribbage, 1956; Pocket Guide to Laws of Poker, 1956; The Weak Notrump, 1956; Bridge on Deck, 1959; 6th ed. 1969; (with C.M. Hammond and M.M. Lewis) Twenty Common Mushrooms and How to Cook Them, 1965; Double Dummy Bridge, 1967; Natural Big Club: Coffin Bidding System, 1969; Canape Bidding; Bridge Writer's Manual; Contract Calculator for Duplicate Bridge; Honeymoon Bridge; Little Drill Book; The Poker Game Complete; Autowords; Instant Match Points for Pair Games; Bridge Play Four Classics; Compendium of Bridge Play A-Z; Sure Tricks; Double Dummy Bridge and End Plays, 1975; (with J. Andrews) The Hearts Game Complete, 1976; Design for Equity in Games and Sports, 1977. Add: 257 Trapelo Rd., Waltham, Mass. 02154, U.S.A.

COFFIN, Tristram. American, b. 1912. Novels/Short stories, History, Sex, Biography. Writer and Ed., Washington Spectator. *Publs:* Missouri Compromise, 1947; Your Washington, 1954; (ghost writer) Land, Wood and Water, 1960; Not to the Swift, 1961; Passion of the Hawks (in paperbacks as The Armed Society), 1964; Mine Eyes Have Seen the Glory, 1964; The Sex Kick, 1966; Senator Fulbright, 1966. Add: 5601 Warwick Pl., Chevy Chase, Md. 20815, U.S.A.

COFFIN, Tristram Potter. American, b. 1922. Mythology/Folklore. Prof. Emeritus of English, Univ. of Pennsylvania, Philadelphia, since 1984 (Asst. Instr. of English, 1946–49; Assoc. Prof. of English, 1958–64; Prof. of English, 1964–84; Vice-Dean, Grad. Sch. of Arts and Sciences, 1965–68). Instr., English, 1949–50, Asst. Prof. of English, 1950–56, Assoc. Prof. of English, 1956–58, Denison Univ., Granville, Ohio. *Publs:* The British Traditional Ballad in North America, 1950, 3rd ed. 1968; An Analytical Index to Journal Folklore, 1958; (with Helen H. Flanders and Bruno Nettl) Ancient Ballads Traditionally Sung in New England, 4 vols., 1960; (ed. with MacEdward Leach) The Critics and the Ballad, 1961; (ed.) Indian Tales of North America, 1961; (ed. with Hennig Cohen) Folklore in America, 1966; (ed.) Our Living Traditions, 1968; Uncertain Glory: Folklore and the American Revolution, 1971; The Old Ball Game: Baseball in Folklore and Fiction, 1971; (ed. with Hennig Cohen) Folklore from the Working Folk of America, 1972; The Book of Christmas Folklore, 1973; The Female Hero in Folklore and Legend, 1975; The Proper Book of Sexual Folklore, 1978; (ed. with H. Cohen) The Parade of Heroes, 1978; Great Game for a Girl, 1980; (ed. with H. Cohen) Folklore of the American Holidays, 1985, 1990. Add: Box 509, Wakefield, R.I. 02880, U.S.A.

COFFMAN, Barbara Frances. Canadian, b. 1907. History, Biography. Dir., Ontario Mennonite Historical Soc., 1965–81. Local Corresp., St. Catherines Standard and Hamilton Spectator, 1945–60; Piano teacher, Vineland, Ont., 1950–76; Dir., Pennsylvania German Folklore Soc., Ont., 1962–72; Dir., Niagara Peninsular Historical Council, 1965–66. *Publs:* (ed. with R. Powell) Lincoln County 1856-1956, 1956; His Name Was John, 1974; (ed. with Ivan Groh) Tales of the Twenty, 1979; Samuel Fry the Weaver and Mennonites of the Twenty, 1982. Add: P.O. Box 54, Vineland, Ont. LOR 2CO, Canada.

COFFMAN, Edward M. American, b. 1929. History. Prof. of History, Univ. of Wisconsin, Madison, since 1968 (Asst. Prof., 1961–66; Assoc. Prof., 1966–68). Member, Dept. of the Army Historical Advisory Cttee., since 1987 (and 1972–76); Instr., to Asst. Prof., Memphis State Univ., Tenn., 1957–60: Research Assoc., G.C. Marshall Research Foundn., Arlington, Va., 1960–61 (Guggenheim Fellow, 1973–74); Visiting Prof., Kansas State Univ., 1969–70; Visiting Prof., U.S. Military Acad., 1977–78; Visiting Prof., U.S. Air Force Acad., 1982–83. Visiting Prof., U.S. Army Military History Inst., 1986–87. Member, National Historical Publications and Records Commn., 1972–76. *Publs:* The Hilt of the Sword:

The Career of Peyton C. March, 1966; The War to End All Wars: The American Military Experience in World War I, 1968; The Old Army: A Portrait of the American Army in Peacetime 1784-1898, 1986. Add: Dept. of History, Univ. of Wisconsin, Madison, Wisc. 53706, U.S.A.

COFFMAN, Virginia (Edith). Also writes as Victor Cross, Jeanne Duval, Virginia C. DuVaul, and Anne Stanfield. American, b. 1914. Historical/Romance/Gothic. Film Reviewer, Oakland Tribune, Calif., 1933–40; Secty. and Writer, various film and TV studios, Hollywood, Calif., 1944–56; Secty. and Office Mgr., "Chick" Bennett Inc., realtors, Reno, Nev., 1956–66. *Publs:* Moura, 1959; The Affair at Alkali, 1960, in U.K. as Nevada Gunslinger, 1962; The Beckoning, 1965, as The Beckoning from Moura, 1977; Curse of the Island Pool, 1965; Castle Barra, 1966; The Secret of Shower Tree, 1966, as Strange Secrets, 1976; Black Heather, 1966; The High Terrace, 1966, in U.K. as To Love a Dark Stranger, 1969; Castle at Witches' Coven, 1966; A Haunted Place, 1966; The Demon Tower, 1966; The Devil Vicar, 1966, as Vicar of Moura, 1972; The Shadow Box, 1966; (as Victor Cross) Blood Sport, 1966; The Small Tawny Cat, 1967, as The Stalking Terror, 1977; Richest Girl in the World, 1967; The Chinese Door, 1967; The Rest Is Silence, 1967; A Few Friends to Tea, 1967; The Hounds of Hell, 1967; One Man Too Many, 1968; The Villa Fountains, 1968; The Mist at Darkness, 1968; Call of the Flesh, 1968; The Candidate's Wife, 1968; The Dark Gondola, 1968, as The Dark Beyond Moura, 1977; Of Love and Intrigue, 1969; Lucifer Cove: The Devil's Mistress, 1969; Priestess of the Damned, 1970; The Devil's Virgin, 1970; Masque of Satan, 1971; Chalet Diabolique, 1971; From Satan, with Love, 1972, 6 vols.; Isles of the Undead, 1969, in U.K. as Voodoo Widow, 1970; The Beach House, 1970; Masque by Gaslight, 1970, in U.K. (as Virginia C. DuVaul) The Vampire of Moura, 1970; The Master of Blue Mire, 1971; Night at Sea Abbey, 1972; The House on the Moat, 1972; Mistress Devon, 1972; The Cliffs of Dread, 1972; The Dark Palazzo, 1973; Garden of Shadows, 1973; Fear of Heights, 1973, as Legacy of Fear, 1979; The Evil at Queens Priory, 1973; Survivor of Darkness, 1973; The House at Sandalwood, 1974; Hyde Place, 1974; The Ice Forest, 1975; Veronique, 1975; Marsanne, 1976; The Alpine Coach, 1976; Careen, 1977; Enemy of Love, 1977; Fire Dawn, 1977; The Gaynor Women, 1978; Looking-Glass, 1979; Dinah Faire, 1979; (as Jeanne Duval) The Lady Serena, 1979; (as Jeanne Duval) The Ravishers, 1980; Pacific Cavalcade, 1980; (as Anne Stanfield) The Golden Marquerite, 1981; The Lombard Cavalcade, 1982; Dynasty of Desire, 1982; The Lombard Heiress, 1983; Dynasty of Dreams, 1984; The Orchid Tree, 1984; Dark Winds, 1985; Dark Desire, 1987; The Richest Girl in the World, 1988; One Man Too Many, 1988; The Jewelled Darkness, 1989. Add: c/o Jay Garon-Brooke Assocs., 415 Central Park W., New York, N.Y. 10025, U.S.A.

COGGAN, Lord; (Frederick) Donald Coggan. British, b. 1909. Theology/Religion. Anglican clergyman: Curate of St. Mary Islington, London 1934–37; Prof. of New Testament, Wycliffe Coll., Toronto, 1937–44; Principal, London Coll. of Divinity, 1944–56; Bishop of Bradford, 1956–61; Archbishop of York, 1961–74; Archbishop of Canterbury, 1974–80. Asst. Lectr. in Semitic Languages and Literature, Univ. of Manchester, 1931–34; Chmn. of Liturgical Commn., 1960–64; Pro- Chancellor, York Univ., 1962–74, and Univ. of Hull, 1968–74; Pres., Soc. for Old Testament Studies, 1967–68. *Publs:* A People's Heritage, 1944; The Ministry of the Word, 1945; The Glory of God, 1950; Stewards of Grace, 1958; Five Makers of the New Testament, 1962; Christian Priorities, 1963; The Prayers of the New Testament, 1967, 1974; Sinews of Faith, 1969; Word and World, 1971; Convictions, 1975; On Preaching, 1978; The Name Above All Names, 1981; Sure Foundation, 1981; Mission to the World, 1982; Paul: Portrait of a Revolutionary, 1984; The Sacrament of the Word, 1987; Cuthbert Bardsley: Bishop, Evangelist, Pastor, 1989. Add: 28 Lions Hall, St. Swithin St., Winchester S023 9HW, England.

COGGIN, Philip A(nnett). British, b. 1917. Education, Technology, Humanities, Theology/Religion. Teacher, St. Bees School, Cumberland, 1944–45, Royal Naval Coll., Dartmouth, 1945–49, Plymouth Coll., 1949–55, and Lycée Janson de Sailly, Paris, 1952–53; Headmaster, White House Grammar School, Brampton, Cumberland, 1955–60, Park Grammar School, Swindon, 1960–65, and Park Senior High School, 1965–80. *Publs:* Drama and Education, 1956; L'Examen oral, 1956, 1978; Art, Science, and Religion, 1962; (ed.) Birth of a Road, 1973; (ed. with E. Semper) Hidden Factors in Technological Change, 1976; Education for the Future, 1979; Technology and Man, 1980. Add: 18 Stone House, North Foreland Rd., Broadstairs, Kent CT10 3NT, England.

COGGINS, Jack B. American, b. 1914. Marine science/Oceanography, Military/Defence. *Publs:* The Illustrated Book of Knights, 1957; Arms and Equipment of the Civil War, 1962; Horsemen of the World,

1963; Flashes and Flags, 1963; Nets Overboard, 1965; Hydrospace, Frontier Beneath the Sea, 1966; The Horseman's Bible, 1966; The Fighting Man, 1966; By Star and Compass, 1967; Boys in the Revolution, 1967; Ships and Seamen of the American Revolution, 1969; Prepare to Dive, 1971; The Campaign for Guadalcanal, 1972; The Campaign for North Africa, 1980; The Marine Painter's Guide, 1983. Add: Box 57, Boyertown, Pa. 19512, U.S.A.

COGSWELL, Fred(erick William). Canadian, b. 1917. Poetry, Literature, Translations. Prof. of English, Univ. of New Brunswick, Fredericton, since 1961 (Asst. Prof., 1952–57; Assoc. Prof., 1957–61). Ed., Fiddlehead Poetry Books, Fredericton, since 1960. Ed., Fiddlehead mag., 1952–66, and Humanities Assn. Bulletin, 1967–72, both Fredericton. *Publs:* The Stunted Strong, 1955; The Haloed Tree, 1956; Testament of Cresseid, 1957; Descent from Eden, 1959; Lost Dimension, 1960; (ed.) A Canadian Anthology, 1960; (ed. and contrib.) Five New Brunswick Poets, 1962; (ed. with R. Tweedie and S.W. MacNutt, and contrib.) The Arts in New Brunswick, 1966; (ed. with T.R. Lower) The Enchanted Land: Canadian Poetry for Young Readers, 1967; Star-People, 1968; Immortal Plowman, 1969; In Praise of Chastity, 1970; (trans.) One Hundred Poems of Modern Quebec, 1970; (trans.) A Second Hundred Poems of Modern Quebec, 1971; The Chains of Liliput, 1971; The House Without a Door, 1973; (trans.) Confrontation, by G. Lapointe, 1973; Light Bird of Life, 1974; (ed.) The Poetry of Modern Quebec, 1977; Against Perspective, 1979; A Long Apprenticeship: Collected Poems, 1980; Selected Poems, 1983; Pearls, 1983; Meditations, 1986; The Edge to Life, 1987; The Best Notes Merge, 1988. Add: Conf. A6, Site 6, Fredericton, N.B. E3B 4X5, Canada.

COHEN, Barbara (née Kauder). American, b. 1932. Children's fiction. English teacher in New Jersey public high schools, Tenafly, 1955–57, Somerville, 1958–60, and Hillsborough, 1970–78. *Publs:* The Carp in the Bathtub, 1972; Thank You, Jackie Robinson, 1974; Bitter Herbs and Honey, 1976; Where's Florrie?, 1976; Benny, 1977; R, My Name Is Rosie, 1978; The Innkeeper's Daughter, 1979; Fat Jack, 1980; I Am Joseph, 1980; Unicorns in the Rain, 1980; Queen for a Day, 1981; Gooseberries to Oranges, 1982; King of the Seventh Grade, 1982; (with B. Lovejoy) Seven Daughters and Seven Sons, 1982; Lover's Games, 1983; Molly's Pilgrim, 1983; Here Come the Purim Players!, 1984; Roses, 1984; Coasting, 1985; The Secret Grove, 1985; The Christmas Revolution, 1987; First Fast, 1987; People Like Us, 1987; The Orphan Game, 1988; Tell Us Your Secret, 1989; other (retellings)—The Binding of Isaac, 1978, Lovely Vassilisa, 1980; Yussel's Prayer, 1981; The Demon Who Would Not Die, 1982; Even Higher, 1987; The Donkey's Story: A Bible Story, 1988; Canterbury Tales (from Chaucer), 1988. Add: 540 Foothill Rd., Bridgewater, N.J. 08807, U.S.A.

COHEN, Bernard (Cecil). American, b. 1926. International relations/Current affairs. Prof. of Political Science, Univ. of Wisconsin, Madison. *Publs:* The Political Process and Foreign Policy, 1957; The Press and Foreign Policy, 1963; The Public's Impact on Foreign Policy, 1973. Add: Dept. of Political Science, North Hall, Univ. of Wisconsin, Madison, Wisc. 53706, U.S.A.

COHEN, Bernard Lande. Canadian, b. 1902. Economics, Law, History. Former lawyer and insurance broker. *Publs:* Introduction to the New Economics, 1959; Law Without Order, 1970; Jews Among Nations, 1978; Economics Without Ideology, 1987. Add: 5160 Macdonald Ave., Montreal H3X 2V8, Canada.

COHEN, Daniel (E.). American, b. 1936. Children's non-fiction, Film, Supernatural/Occult. Writer for Science Digest mag., New York, since 1969 (Managing Ed., 1960–69). *Publs:* young adult non-fiction—Secrets from Ancient Graves, 1968; Vaccination and You, 1968; The Age of Giant Mammals, 1969; Animals of the City, 1969; Night Animals, 1970; Conquerors on Horseback, 1970; Talking with Animals, 1971; Superstition, 1971; A Natural History of Unnatural Things, 1971; Ancient Monuments and How They Were Built, 1971; Watchers in the Wild, 1972; In Search of Ghosts, 1972; The Magic Art of Foreseeing the Future, 1973; How Did Life Get There?, 1973; Magicians, Wizards and Sorcerers, 1973; How the World Will End, 1973, as Waiting for the Apocalypse, 1983; Shaka: King of the Zulus, 1973; ESP: The Search Beyond the Senses, 1973; The Black Death, 1974; The Magic of the Little People, 1974; Curses, Hexes, and Spells, 1974; Intelligence: What Is It?, 1974; Not of the World, 1974; Human Nature, Animal Nature, 1974; The Mysteries of Reincarnation, 1975; The Greatest Monsters in the World, 1975; The Body Snatchers, 1975; The Human Side of Computers, 1975; Monsters, Giants, and Little Men from Mars, 1975; The New Believers, 1975; The Spirit of the Lord, 1975; Animal Territories, 1975; Mysterious Disap-

pearances, 1976; The Ancient Visitors, 1976; Dreams, Visions, and Drugs, 1976; Gold, 1976; Supermonsters, 1977; Ghostly Animals, 1977; The Science of Spying, 1977; Real Ghosts, 1977; Meditation, 1977; What Really Happened to the Dinosaurs?, 1977; Creativity: What Is It?, 1977; Ceremonial Magic, 1978; The World of UFOs, 1978; The World's Most Famous Ghosts, 1978; Young Ghosts, 1978; Frauds, Hoaxes, and Swindles, 1979; Missing, 1979; Mysteries of the World, 1979; What's Happening to Our Weather, 1979; Dealing with the Devil, 1979; Famous Curses, 1979; Great Mistakes, 1979; The Monsters of "Star Trek", 1980; Monsters You Never Heard Of, 1980; The Tomb Robbers, 1980; Bigfoot: America's Number One Monster, 1980; Everything You Need to Know about Monsters and Still Be Able to Sleep, 1981; Ghostly Terrors, 1981; The Headless Roommate and Other Tales of Terror, 1981; The Last Hundred Years' Medicine, 1981; America's Very Own Monsters, 1982; How to Buy a Car, 1982; Horror in the Movies, 1982; How to Test your ESP, 1982; Real Magic, 1982; The Last Hundred Years' Household Technology, 1982; Monster Hunting Today, 1983; The Simon and Schuster Question and Answer Book on Computers, 1983; Southern Fried Rat and Other Gruesome Tales, 1983; Monster Dinosaur, 1983; The Restless Dead, 1983; (with Susan Cohen) The Kids' Guide to Home Computers, 1983; (with S. Cohen) Teenage Stress, 1984; Hiram Bingham and the Dream of Gold, 1984; Masters of Horror, 1984; (with S. Cohen) The Kids' Guide to Home Video, 1984; America's Very Own Ghosts, 1985; Henry Stanley and the Quest for the Source of the Nile, 1985; (with S. Cohen) Rock Video Superstars, 1985; (with S. Cohen) Wrestling Superstars, 1985; (with S. Cohen) Wrestling Superstars, 1985, vol. II, 1986; (with S. Cohen) Heroes of the Challenger, 1986; (with S. Cohen) A Six-Pack and a Fake ID, 1986; other—Myths of the Space Age, 1967; Mysterious Places, 1969; A Modern Look at Monsters, 1970; Masters of the Occult, 1971; Voodoo, Devils, and the New Invisible World, 1972; The Far Side of Consciousness, 1974; Biorhythms in Your Life, 1976; Close Encounters with God, 1979; The Great Airship Mystery, 1981; Re-Thinking, 1982; The Encyclopedia of Monsters, 1983; The Encyclopedia of Ghosts, 1984; Musicals, 1984; Horror Movies, 1984; (with S. Cohen) Screen Goddesses, 1984; The Encyclopedia of the Strange, 1985; (with S. Cohen) Hollywood Hunks and Heroes, 1985; (with S. Cohen) The Encyclopedia of Movie Stars, 1986; (with S. Cohen) A History of the Oscars, 1986. Add: 24 Elizabeth St., Port Jervis, N.Y. 12771, U.S.A.

COHEN, Henry. American, b. 1933. History, Criminology/Law enforcement, Economics, Psychology. Prof., Loyola Univ., Chicago, since 1980 (Asst. Prof., 1969–71; Assoc. Prof., 1971–80). *Publs:* Business and Politics in America from the Age of Jackson to the Civil War, 1971; Brutal Justice: Ordeal of an American City, 1980; (ed.) Criminal Justice History: An International Annual, 1980–83; (ed.) The Public Enemy, 1981. Add: History Dept., Loyola Univ., Chicago, Ill. 60611, U.S.A.

COHEN, Laurence Jonathan. British, b. 1923. Philosophy. Fellow and Praelector, Queen's Coll., Oxford, since 1957; Fellow, British Academy, since 1973. Asst. in Logic and Metaphysics, Edinburgh, 1947–50; Lectr. in Philosophy, Univ. of St. Andrews at Dundee, 1950–57. Pres., British Soc. of Philosophy of Science, 1977–79. *Publs:* The Principle of World Citizenship, 1954; The Diversity of Meaning, 1962, 1966; The Implications of Induction, 1970; The Probable and the Provable, 1977; (co-ed.) Applications of Inductive Logic, 1980; (ed.) Logic, Methodology, and Philosophy of Science, 1981; The Dialogue of Reason, 1986; An Introduction to the Philosophy of Induction and Probability, 1988. Add: Sturt House, East End, North Leigh, Oxon, England.

COHEN, Leonard. Canadian, b. 1934. Novels/Short stories, Plays/Screenplays, Poetry, Songs, lyrics and libretti. Professional composer and singer. *Publs:* Let Us Compare Mythologies, 1956; The Spice-Box of Earth, 1961; The Favorite Game (novel), 1963; Flowers for Hitler, 1964; Parasites of Heaven, 1966; Beautiful Losers (novel), 1966; Selected Poems, 1956-68, 1968; Leonard Cohen's Song Book, 1969; The Energy of Slaves, 1972; The Next Step (play), 1972; Sisters of Mercy: A Journey to the Words and Music of Leonard Cohen, 1973; Death of a Lady's Man, 1979; Two Views (poetry), 1980; Book of Mercy (poetry), 1984. Add: McClelland and Stewart Ltd., 25 Hollinger Rd., Toronto, Ont. M4B 3G2, Canada.

COHEN, Matt(hew). Canadian, b. 1942. Novels/Short stories, Poetry. Lectr. in Religion, McMaster Univ., Hamilton, Ont., 1967–68; Visiting Prof., Univ. of Victoria, British Columbia, 1979–80. *Publs:* Korsoniloff, 1969; Johnny Crackle Sings, 1971; Columbus and the Fat Lady and Other Stories, 1972; Too Bad Galahad (short stories), 1972; The Disinherited, 1974; Wooden Hunters, 1975; Peach Melba (poetry), 1975; The Colours of War, 1978; Night Flights: Stories New and Selected, 1978; The Sweet Second Summer of Kitty Malone, 1979; Flowers of Darkness, 1981; The

Expatriate: Collected Short Stories, 1982; Café Le Dog (short stories), 1983; The Spanish Doctor (novel), 1984; Nadine (novel), 1987; Living on Water (novel), 1989. Add: P.O. Box 401, Verona, Ont. K0H 2W0, Canada.

COHEN, Maxwell. Canadian, b. 1910. Law, Politics/Government. Judge ad hoc, Intnl. Court of Justice, since 1982. Emeritus Prof. of Law, McGill Univ., Montreal (Lectr., 1946–47; Assoc. Prof., 1947–52; Prof., 1952–78; Acting Dean, 1960–61; Dir., Inst. of Air and Space Law, 1962–66; Dean, 1964–69); Scholar in Residence, Univ. of Ottawa, since 1981. Chmn., Intnl. Joint Commn., Canadian Section, Ottawa, 1974–79. Chmn., Intnl. and Constitutional Law Section, Canadian Bar Assn., 1964–71; Pres., Quebec Advisory Council on the Admin. of Justice, 1972–74. Publs: Dominion and Provincial Relations, 1945; Law and Politics in Space, 1964; (ed.) Lawyers and the Nuclear Debate, 1988. Add: Suite 1404, 200 Rideau Terr., Ottawa, Ont. K1M 0Z3, Canada.

COHEN, Morton N(orton). Also writes fiction for children as John Moreton. American, b. 1921. Children's fiction, Literature, Biography. Prof. of English, City Coll. and Grad. Sch., City Univ. of New York, 1971–81, now Emeritus (Assoc. Prof., 1952–71). Visiting Prof., Syracuse Univ., N.Y., 1965–66, 1967–68. Publs: Rider Haggard: His Life and Works, 1960, 1968; (as John Moreton) Punky: Mouse for a Day, 1962; Rudyard Kipling to Rider Haggard: The Record of a Friendship, 1965; (reteller as John Moreton) The Love for Three Oranges, by Sergei Prokofiev, 1966; (ed.) The Letters of Lewis Carroll, 1979; (ed.) The Russian Journal-II: A Record Kept by Henry Parry Liddon of a Tour Taken with C.L. Dodgson in the Summer of 1867, 1979; Lewis Carroll, Photographer of Children: Four Nude Studies, 1979; Lewis Carroll and the Kitchins, 1980; Lewis Carroll and Alice 1832-1982, 1982; (ed.) Selected Letters of Lewis Carroll, 1982; (co-ed.) Lewis Carroll and the House of Macmillan, 1987; (ed.) Lewis Carroll: Interviews and Recollection, 1989. Add: 72 Barrow St., Apt. 3-N, New York, N.Y. 10014, U.S.A.

COHEN, Peter Zachary. American, b. 1931. Children's fiction, Plays/Screenplays. Assoc. Prof., Kansas State Univ., Manhattan (Instr. to Asst., 1961–1985). Secty., County Planning Commn., since 1969. Publs: The Muskie Hook, 1969; The Bull in the Forest, 1969; Morena, 1970; Foal Creek, 1972; Authorized Autumn Charts of the Upper Red Canoe River Country, 1972; Bee, 1975; The Cannon in the Park (play), 1975; Deadly Game at Stony Creek, 1978; Calm Horse, Wild Night, 1982; The Great Red River Raft, 1984; Brave Men in Wooden Boats, 1989. Add: Rt. 1, Alta Vista, Kans, 66834, U.S.A.

COHEN, Selma Jeanne. American, b. 1920. Dance/Ballet. Ed., International Encyclopedia of Dance; Dance Ed., World Encyclopaedia of Contemporary Theatre. Teacher of Dance History and Aesthetics, Sch. of Performing Arts, NYC, 1953–55, Connecticut Coll. Sch. of Dance, New London, 1963–72, and New York Univ., NYC, 1968–70 and 1974–75. Managing Ed., 1959–65, and Ed., 1965–76, Dance Perspectives, NYC. Publs: The Modern Dance: Seven Statements of Belief, 1966; Doris Humphrey: An Artist First, 1972; Dance as a Theatre Art: Source Readings in Dance History, 1974; Next Week, Swan Lake: Reflections on Dance and Dances, 1982. Add: 29 E. 9th St., New York, N.Y. 10003, U.S.A.

COHEN, Stanley I. American, b. 1928. Novels/Short stories. Publs: Taking Gary Feldman (in U.K. as The Abduction), 1970; Tell Us Jerry Silver, 1973; The Diane Game, 1973; 330 Park, 1977; Angel Face, 1982. Add: 322 Pine Tree Dr., Orange, Conn. 06477, U.S.A.

COHEN, Stephen F(rand). American, b. 1938. History, Politics/Government. Prof. of Politics since 1980, Princeton Univ., New Jersey (Asst. Prof., 1968–73; Assoc. Prof. and Dir. of Russian Studies, 1973–80). Assoc. Ed., World Politics; Member of Editorial Bd., Slavic Review, Instr. and Jr. Fellow, Research Inst. of Communist Affairs, 1965–68; Visiting Prof. of History, 1973–75, and Sr. Fellow, Russian Inst., 1970–71, 1972–73, and 1976–77, Columbia Univ., NYC. Publs: (ed. with Robert C. Tucker) The Great Purge Trial, 1965; Bukharin and the Bolshevik Revolution: A Political Biography 1888-1938, 1973; (with Alexander Rabinowitch and Robert Sharlet) The Soviet Union Since Stalin, 1980; (ed.) An End to Silence: Uncensored Opinion in the Soviet Union, 1982; Rethinking the Soviet Experience: Politics and History Since 1917, 1985; Sovieticus: American Perceptions and Soviet Realities, 1985. Add: Dept. of Politics, 204 Corwin Hall, Princeton Univ., Princeton, N.J. 08544, U.S.A.

COHEN, Susan. Writes novels as Elizabeth St. Clair. American, b. 1938. Mystery, Gothic, Children's non-fiction, Film, Human relations. Social worker in New York City, 1962–67. Publs: gothic novels as Elizabeth St. Clair—Stonehaven, 1974; The Singing Harp, 1975; Secret of the Locket, 1975; Provenance House, 1976; Mansion in Miniature, 1977; Dewitt Manor, 1977; The Jeweled Secret, 1978; mysteries as Elizabeth St. Clair—Murder in the Act, 1978; Sandcastle Murder, 1979; Trek or Treat, 1980; Sealed with a Kiss, 1981; with husband, Daniel Cohen—The Kids' Guide to Home Computers, 1983; The Kids' Guide to Home Video, 1984; Teenage Stress, 1984; Screen Goddesses, 1984; Rock Video Superstars, 1985; Wrestling Superstars, 1985, vol. II, 1986; Hollywood Hunks and Heroes, 1985; Heroes of the Challenger, 1986; A Six-Pack and a Fake ID, 1986; The Encyclopedia of Movie Stars, 1986; A History of the Oscars; 1986; other—(sole author) The Liberated Couple, 1971, as Liberated Marriage, 1973. Add: 24 Elizabeth St., Port Jervis, N.Y. 12771, U.S.A.

COHEN, William Benjamin. American, b. 1941. History. Prof. of History, Indiana Univ., Bloomington, since 1980 (Lectr., 1967–68; Asst. Prof., 1968–71; Assoc. Prof., 1971–79). Visiting Instr. of History, Northwestern Univ., Evanston, Ill., 1966–67. Pres., Soc. for French Historical Studies, 1980–81. Publs: Rulers of Empire: The French Colonial Service in Africa, 1971; (ed.) Robert Delavignette on the French Empire, 1977; (ed.) European Empire Building in the Nineteenth Century, 1980; The French Encounter with Africans: White Response to Black 1530-1880, 1980. Add: Dept. of History, Indiana Univ., Bloomington, Ind. 47405, U.S.A.

COHN, Jules. American, b. 1930. Business/Trade/Industry. Prof. of Urban Studies, City Univ. of New York, since 1969. Publs: The Conscience of the Corporations, 1972; The New Business of Business, 1972; Love and Work, 1984; Money and Mysticism, 1984. Add: 4 Washington Sq. Village, New York, N.Y. 10012, U.S.A.

COHN, Norman. British, b. 1915. History, Translations. Prof. of French, Univ. of Durham, 1960–63, Prof., Univ. of Sussex, Brighton, 1966–80. Publs: (trans.) Gold Khan and Other Siberian Legends, 1946; The Pursuit of the Millennium, 1957, 1970; Warrant for Genocide, 1967, 3rd ed. 1981; Europe's Inner Demons, 1975, 1976. Add: Orchard Cottage, Wood End, Ardeley, Herts. SG2 7AZ, England.

COHN, Ruby. American, b. 1922. Theatre. Prof. of Comparative Drama, Univ. of California at Davis. Publs: Samuel Beckett: The Comic Gamut, 1962; Currents in Contemporary Drama, 1969; Dialogue in American Drama, 1971; Back to Beckett, 1973; Modern Shakespeare Offshoots, 1976; Just Play: Beckett's Theatre, 1980; New American Dramatists, 1982; (ed.) Samuel Beckett Disjecta, 1983; From Desire to Godot, 1987. Add: Dept. of Dramatic Art, Univ. of California, Davis, Calif. 95616, U.S.A.

COJEEN, Robert Henry. American, b. 1920. Administration/Management, Business/Trade/Industry. Prof., Sch. of Mgmt., Univ. of Michigan, Flint, since 1964 (Assoc. Prof., 1956–61). Book Reviewer, Choice, since 1964. Instr., Univ. of Florida, Gainesville, 1947–48; Assoc. Prof., Univ. of Kentucky, Lexington, 1948–56; Prof., Univ. of Pittsburgh, 1965–66; Prof., Ahmadu Bello Univ., Zaria, Nigeria, 1965–66. Publs: Cases in Branch Plant Personnel Administration, 1955; (ed.) Case Studies in Nigerian Business, 1966; (ed.) Nigerian Business, 1966; (ed.) Personnel Management Cases in Developing Countries, 1968. Add: 6035 Greenwich Lane, Grand Blanc, Mich. 48439, U.S.A.

COLBECK, Maurice. British, b. 1925. Children's fiction, Children's non-fiction, Travel/Exploration/Adventure, Biography. Assoc. Ed. and Group Feature Writer, Yorkshire Life, since 1956. Publs: Jungle Rivals; White God's Fury; Four Against Crime, 1959; Mosquitoes!: A Biography of Ronald Ross, 1964; Sister Kenny of the Outback, 1965; How to Be a Family Man, 1970; Yorkshire, 1976; Yorkshire Historymakers, 1977; Queer Folk, 1977; Yorkshire Laughter, 1978; Queer Goings On, 1979; Yorkshire: The Dales, 1980; Yorkshire Moorlands, 1983; (ed.) The Calendar Year, 1983; Village Yorkshire, 1987. Add: 164 Soothill Lane, Batley, W. Yorks, WF17 6HP, England.

COLBERT, Edwin Harris. American, b. 1905. Natural history, Zoology. Curator of Vertebrate Paleontology, Museum of Northern Arizona, Flagstaff, since 1970. Prof. Emeritus, Columbia Univ., NYC, since 1969 (Prof., 1945–69); Curator Emeritus, American Museum of Natural History, NYC, since 1970 (Asst., Asst. Curator, and Curator, 1930–70). Publs: The Dinosaur Book, 1945, 1951; Evolution of the Vertebrates, 1955, 3rd ed. 1980; Millions of Years Ago, 1958; (with W.A. Burns) Digging for Dinosaurs, 1960; The World of Dinosaurs, 1961; Dinosaurs, 1961; (with M. Kay) Stratigraphy and Life History, 1965; The Age of Reptiles, 1965; Men and Dinosaurs, 1968; Wandering Lands and Animals, 1973;

The Year of the Dinosaur, 1977; A Fossil Hunter's Notebook, 1980; A Primitive Ornithischian Dinosaur from the Kayenta Formation of Arizona, 1981; An Outline of Vertebrate Evolution, 1983; Dinosaurs: An Illustrated History, 1983; The Great Dinosaur Hunters and Their Discoveries, 1984; Digging into the Past, 1989. Add: Rt. 4, Box 720, Flagstaff, Ariz. 86001, U.S.A.

COLBY, Jean Poindexter. American, b. 1909. Children's fiction, History, Sports. Ed., Houghton Mifflin publrs., Boston, 1945–50, Farrar Straus & Giroux, NYC, 1950–60, and Hastings House, NYC, 1960–70. *Publs:* Peter Paints the U.S.A.; Jim the Cat; Dixie of Dover; Jennie; Elegant Eleanor; Writing, Illustrating and Editing Children's Books; Building Wrecking; Mystic Seaport: Age of Sail; Plymouth Plantation; The Rebirth of an Ancient Area; Lexington and Concord; Your Game of Golf and How It Came to Be; Tiny Buildings of Old New England; Duxbury, An Old New England Town. Add: 73 Eagle's Nest Rd., Duxbury, Mass. 02332, U.S.A.

COLDSMITH, Don(ald C.). American, b. 1926. Westerns/Adventure. Former congregational Minister, gunsmith, YMCA youth dir., grain inspector; Intern, Bethany Hosp., Kansas City, 1958–59, then physician in family practice, Emporia, Kans. Adjunct Assoc. Prof. of English, Emporia State Univ., 1981; Pres., Western Writers of America, 1983–84. *Publs:* Horsin' Around, 1975; Trail of the Spanish Bit, 1980; Buffalo Medicine, 1981; Horsin' Around Again, 1981; The Elk-Dog Heritage, 1982; Follow the Wind, 1983; Man of the Shadows, 1983; Daughter of the Eagle, 1984; Moon of Thunder, 1985; The Sacred Hills, 1985; Pale Star, 1986; River of Swans, 1986; Return to the River, 1987; The Medicine Knife, 1988; Flower in the Mountains, 1988; Trail from Taos, 1989; Rivers West: The Smoky Hill, 1989; Song of the Rock, 1989. Add: Rt. 5, Emporia, Kans, 66801, U.S.A.

COLE, Babette. British. Children's fiction. Has worked as an animator for television and illustrator of greeting cards. *Publs:* Basil Brush of the Yard, 1977; Promise Solves the Problem, 1977; Nungu and the Crocodile, 1978; Nungu and the Hippopotmus, 1978; Nungu and the Elephant, 1980; Promise and the Monster, 1981; Beware of the Vet, 1982; Don't Go Out Tonight, 1982; The Trouble with Mum, 1983, in U.S. as The Trouble with Mom, 1984; The Hairy Book, 1984; The Slimy Book, 1985; The Trouble with Dad, 1985; Princess Smartypants, 1986; Prince Cinders, 1987; The Smelly Book, 1987; The Trouble with Gran, 1987; The Trouble with Grandad, 1988; King Change-a-Lot, 1988; Three Cheers for Errol, 1988. Add: c/o Hamish Mailton, 27 Wrights Lane, London W8 5TZ, England.

COLE, Barry. British, b. 1936. Novels/Short stories, Poetry. Worked in the Central Office of Information, London, 1965–70; Fellow in Literature, Univs. of Durham and Newcastle upon Tyne, 1970–72. *Publs:* Blood Ties (poetry), 1967; Ulysses in the Town of Coloured Glass (poetry), 1968; Moonsearch (poetry), 1968; A Run Across the Island (novel), 1968; Joseph Winter's Patronage (novel), 1969; The Search for Rita (novel), 1970; The Visitors (poetry), 1970; The Giver (novel), 1971; Vanessa in the City (poetry), 1971; Doctor Fielder's Common Sense (novel), 1972; Pathetic Fallacies (poetry), 1973; The Rehousing of Scaffardi (poetry), 1976; Dedications (poetry), 1977; The Edge of the Common, 1989. Add: 68 Myddleton Sq., London EC1R 1XP, England.

COLE, Bruce. American, b. 1938. Art. Prof. of Art History, Indiana Univ., Bloomington, since 1977 (Assoc. Prof., 1973–77). Asst. Prof., Univ. of Rochester, N.Y., 1969–73. *Publs:* Giotto and Florentine Painting 1280-1375, 1976; Agnolo Gaddi, 1977; Sienese Painting from Its Origins to the Fifteenth Century, 1980; Masaccio and the Art of Early Renaissance Florence, 1980; The Renaissance Artist at Work, 1983; Sienese Painting in the Age of the Renaissance, 1985. Add: Dept. of Fine Art, Indiana Univ., Bloomington, Ind. 47401, U.S.A.

COLE, Edmund Keith. Australian, b. 1919. History, Anthropology, Biography. Historian, Church Missionary Soc., since 1968; Principal, St. Paul's United Theological Coll., Limuru, Kenya, 1954–60; Archdeacon of Central Kenya, 1961–63; Vice-Principal, Ridley Coll., Univ. of Melbourne, 1964–73; Principal Nungalinya Coll., Darwin, 1973–78; Dir. of Theological Education, Bendigo, Vic., 1978–84; Rector, Broome, W.A., 1985. *Publs:* Mau Mau Mission, 1954; After Mau Mau, 1956; Kenya, Hanging in the Middle Way, 1959; Roper River Mission, 1968; Commissioned to Care, 1969; Cross Over Mount Kenya, 1970; Sincerity My Guide, 1970; Groote Eylandt Pioneer, 1971; Groote Eylandt Mission, 1971; History of CMS Australia, 1971; (ed.) Groote Eylandt Stories, 1972; Oenpelli Stories, 1972; Perriman in Arnhem Land, 1973; Totems and Tamarinds, 1973; Groote Eylandt, 1975; History of Oenpelli,

1975; Oenpelli Jubilee, 1975; Outlines of Christian Doctrine, 1976; Life of Christ, 1976; Winds of Fury, 1977; Worship, 1978; Introducing the Old Testament, 1978; The Aborigines of Arnhem Land, 1979; Cole Family History, 1980; Arnhem Land: Places and People, 1980; Dick Harris: Missionary to the Aborigines, 1980; Seafarers of the Groote Archipelago, 1980; Aborigines: Towards Dignity and Identity, 1981; Aborigines and Mining on Groote Eylandt, 1981; A History of Numbulwar, 1982; The Aborigines of Victoria, 1982; Through Hardship to the Stars, 1984; The Lake Condah Mission, 1984; Fred Gray of Umbakumba, 1985; The Aborigines of Western Australia, 1985; From Mission to Church: The CMS Mission to the Aborigines of Arnhem Land, 1908-1985, 1985; Pethy, Lee, and Mary: Three CMS Missionaries in East Africa, 1986; Crusade Hymns: Their Stories and Their Meanings, 1987; Beneath the Southern Cross: Sacred Hymns, Poetry and Readings, 1988; Letters from China, 1893-1895: The Story of the Sister Martyrs of Ku Cheng, 1988. Add: 28 Woodbury St., Bendigo, Vic. 3550, Australia.

COLE, E(ugene) R(oger). Also writes as Peter E. Locré. American, b. 1930. Plays/Screenplays, Poetry, Theology/Religion. Poet-in-Service, Poets and Writers Inc., since 1974; Freelance writer, editor, researcher, since 1969. Newman Moderator, Central Washington State Coll., Ellensburg, 1958–59; Chmn. of English Dept., Yakima Central High Sch., 1959–66, and Marquette High Sch., 1966–69. Assoc. Ed., The Harvester, 1955; Business Mgr., Experiment Press, 1959–60; Poetry Critic, National Writers Club, 1969–72; Judge, The Poetry Soc. of America, 1970. *Publs:* The Great "O" Antiphons, 1956; What Did St. Luke Mean by Kecharitomene?, 1958; Which End, the Empyrean? (play), 1959; Experiment in Poetry, 1959; (ed.) Experiment: An International Review, 1961; Spring as Ballet: A Dalhousie in-plano, 1961; Three Cycle Poems of Yeats, 1965; Mrs. H. & What Have You, 1966; Woman, you: Illustrapoem, 1967; April Is the Cruelest Month (play), 1970; (ed. with J. Edwards) Grand Slam: 13 Great Short Stories About Bridge, 1975; (ed. with others) In the Beginning, 1978; Falling Up (poetry), 1979; Act and Potency (poetry), 1980; Ding an Sich (anapoems), 1985; Uneasy Camber: Early Poems and Diversions 1943-50, 1986; A Key to Ding an Sich, 1986; Godspeople: Not a Church but a People, 1987; (as Peter E. Locré) Songpoems/poemsongs: new lyrics, 1988; (ed.) Litany: Cynewulf to Vachel Lindsay, 1989; (with Marjorie Zeyen) Earthly Existence, 1990; (ed.) Grand Slam Doubled: A Second Collection of 13 Great Bridge Stories, 1990. Add: P.O. Box 91277, Cleveland, Ohio 44101, U.S.A.

COLE, John Alfred. British, b. 1905. Novels/Short stories, Communications media, Biography, Translations. Civilian Asst. to Gen. Staff, British War Office, 1942–46; Intelligence Officer, Control Commn. for Germany, 1946–50; with British Foreign Office, 1950–56, and German Service, BBC, 1958–73. *Publs:* Come Dungeon Dark, 1935; This Happy Breed, 1937; A Stranger Myself, 1938; Just Back from Germany, 1938; To Make Us Glad, 1941; My Host Michel (in U.S. as Germany My Host), 1955; Nobody Got Into Trouble, 1962; Lord Haw-Haw and William Joyce, 1964, 1987; (trans. and ed.) Hans Dieter Müller: Press Power: A Study of Axel Springer, 1969; The View from the Peak, 1979; Prince of Spies: Henri Le Caron, 1984. Add: 4 Crane Ct., Fleet St, London EC4A 2EJ, England.

COLE, Jonathan. American, b. 1942. Sciences. Prof. of Sociology since 1976, and Provost since 1989, Columbia Univ., NYC (Teaching Asst., 1966–68; Instr., 1968–69; Asst. Prof., 1969–73; Assoc. Prof., 1973–76; Dir. of the Center for Social Sciences, 1979–87; Vice-Pres. for Arts and Sciences, 1987–89). *Publs:* (with Stephen Cole) Social Stratification in Science, 1973; (with Stephen Cole and Leonard Rubin) Peer Review in the National Science Foundation, 1978; Fair Science: Women in the Scientific Community, 1979; (with Paul W. Kingston) The Wages of Writing: Per Word, Per Piece, or Perhaps, 1986. Add: Dept. of Sociology, Columbia Univ., New York, N.Y. 10027, U.S.A.

COLE, Sheila R. American, b. 1939. Novels/Short stories, Psychology, Sociology. Reviewer of children's books, New York Times Sunday Book Review. Reporter, Sunnyvale Daily Standard, 1963–64, and Newport Beach Pilot, 1966–67. *Publs:* Meaning Well, 1974; (ed. with Michael Cole) The Making of Mind: A Personal Account of Soviet Psychology by A.R. Luria, 1979; Working Kids on Working, 1980; When the Tide Is Low, 1985. Add: 522 Glencrest Dr., Solana Beach, Calif. 92075, U.S.A.

COLE, Wayne S. American, b. 1922. History, International relations/Current affairs. Prof. of History, Univ. of Maryland, since 1965. Instr. and Asst. Prof., Univ. of Arkansas, Fayetteville, 1950–54; Asst. Prof., Assoc. Prof., and Prof. of History, Iowa State Univ., Ames, 1954–65. *Publs:* America First, 1953; Senator Gerald P. Nye and American

Foreign Relations, 1962; An Interpretive History of American Foreign Relations, 1968, 1974; Charles A. Lindbergh and the Battle Against American Intervention in World War II, 1974; Roosevelt and the Isolationists 1932-1945, 1983; Norway and the United States, 1989. Add: Dept. of History, Univ. of Maryland, College Park, Md. 20742, U.S.A.

COLE, William. American, b. 1919. Children's non-fiction, Humor/Satire. Book Reviewer, Saturday Review. *Publs:* (ed. with M. Rosenberg) The Best Cartoons from Punch, 1952; (ed.) The Best Humour from Punch, 1953; (ed. with F. Robinson) Women Are Wonderful: A Cartoon History, 1954; (ed.) Humorous Poetry for Children, 1955; (co-ed.) The Poetry-Drawing Book, 1956; (ed.) Story Poems Old and New, 1957; (ed.) I Went to the Animal Fair, 1958; (ed.) The Fireside Book of Humorous Poetry, 1959; (ed.) Poems of Magic and Spells, 1960; (ed.) Poems for Seasons and Celebrations, 1961; (ed.) Folk Songs of England, Ireland, Scotland and Wales, 1961; (ed. with J. Colmore) New York in Photographs, 1961; (ed. with J. Colmore) The Second Poetry-Drawing Book, 1962; (ed.) The Most of A.J. Liebling, 1963; (ed.) Erotic Poetry, 1963; (ed.) The Birds and the Beasts Were There, 1963; A Cat-Hater's Handbook, 1963; Frances Face-Maker, 1963; (ed.) Beastly Boys and Ghastly Girls, 1964; (ed.) A Big Bowl of Punch, 1964; (ed.) A Book of Love Poems, 1965; What's Good for a Six-Year-Old?, 1965; (ed.) Oh, What Nonsense!, 1966; Uncoupled Couplets: A Game of Rhymes, 1966; (ed. with M. Thaler) The Classic Cartoons, 1966; (ed.) The Sea, Ships, and Sailors, 1967; (ed.) D.H. Lawrence Poems Selected for Young People, 1967; (ed.) Poems of W.S. Gilbert, 1967; (ed.) Eight Lines and Under, 1967; (ed.) A Case of the Giggles, 1967; (ed.) Man's Funniest Friend, 1967; What's Good for a Four-Year-Old?, 1967; What's Good for a Five-Year-Old?, 1968; (ed.) Poems of Thomas Hood, 1968; (ed.) A Book of Nature Poems, 1969; (ed.) Pith and Vinegar, 1969; That Pest, Jonathan, 1970; Aunt Bella's Umbrella, 1970; (ed.) Oh, How Silly!, 1970; (ed.) The Poet's Tales, 1971; (ed.) Poetry Brief, 1971; (ed.) Pick Me Up, 1972; (ed.) Oh, That's Ridiculous!, 1972; (ed.) Poems from Ireland, 1972; (ed.) . . . And Be Merry!, 1972; What's Good for a Three-Year-Old?, 1972; (ed.) Poems One Line and Longer, 1973; A Boy Named Mary Jane: Nonsense Verses, 1975; Knock Knock: The Most Ever, 1976; Knock Knocks You've Never Heard Before, 1977; (ed.) An Arkful of Animals: Poems for the Very Young, 1978; Oh, Such Foolishness!, 1978; I'm Mad at You, 1978; Dinosaurs and Beasts of Yore, 1979; The Poetry of Horses, 1979; Good Dog Poems, 1980; (ed.) Poem Stew, 1981; Give Up?, 1981; (with M. Thaler) Monster Knock Knocks, 1982. Add: 201 West 54th St., New York, N.Y. 10019, U.S.A.

COLEBURT, James Russell. British, b. 1920. Philosophy, Theology/Religion. Sr. Classics Master, Stonyhurst Coll., 1947–62; Dir. of Studies, Worth Sch., Crawley, Sussex, 1962–85. *Publs:* An Introduction to Western Philosophy, 1957; The Search for Values, 1960; Christian Evolution, 1967. Add: Archway Lodge, Worth Abbey, Turners Hill, Crawley, Sussex RH10 4SE, England.

COLEGATE, Isabel. British, b. 1931. Novels/Short stories. Occasional book reviewer for Spectator, Times Literary Supplement and the Washington Post. *Publs:* The Blackmailer, 1958; A Man of Power, 1960; The Great Occasion, 1962; Statues in a Garden, 1964; Orlando King, 1968; Orlando at the Brazen Threshold, 1971; Agatha, 1973; News from the City of the Sun, 1979; The Shooting Party, 1980; A Glimpse of Sion's Glory, 1985; Deceits of Time, 1988. Add: c/o A.D. Peters Ltd., 10 Buckingham Street, London WC2, England.

COLEMAN, A(llan) D(ouglass). American, b. 1943. Photography. Vice-Pres., Photography Media Inst., NYC, since 1977; Asst. Prof., Dept. of Photography, Tisch Sch. of the Arts, New York Univ., since 1979; Ed. Emeritus, VIEWS: A New England Journal of Photography, Boston, since 1982 (Founding Ed., 1979–81); Photography Critic, New York Observer, since 1988. Member, Bd. of Dirs., Center for Photography in Woodstock, since 1982, and Los Angeles Center for Photographic Studies, since 1982; Exec. Vice-Pres., and Chmn. of the Membership Cttee., Intnl. Assn. of Art Critics. Photography Critic, The Village Voice, NYC, 1968–73, and the New York Times, 1970–74; Contributing Ed., Camera 35, 1975–82; Member, Bd. of Dirs., Photographic Resource Center, Boston, 1978–82; Member, Bd. of Dirs., and Chairman of the Cttee. on Censorship and Freedom of Vision, Soc. for Photographic Education, 1982–84. *Publs:* The Grotesque in Photography, 1977; Light Readings: A Photography Critic's Writings 1968-1978, 1979; Lee/Model/Parks/Samaras/Turner: Five Interviews Before the Fact, 1979; (with Patricia Grantz and Douglas Sheer) The Photography A-V Program Directory, 1980. Add: 465 Van Duzer St., Staten Island, N.Y. 10304, U.S.A.

COLEMAN, James A. American, b. 1921. Physics. Prof. of Physics and Chmn. of Dept. of Physics, American Intnl. Coll., Springfield, Mass., since 1957. Instr. in Physics and Astronomy, Connecticut Coll. for Women, New London, 1950–57. *Publs:* Relativity for the Layman, 1954; Modern Theories of the Universe, 1963; Early Theories of the Universe, 1967; The Circle (novel), 1970. Add: American Intnl. Coll., Springfield, Mass. 01109, U.S.A.

COLEMAN, James (Samuel). American, b. 1926. Mathematics/Statistics, Sociology. Prof. of Sociology, Univ. of Chicago, since 1973 (Asst. Prof., 1956–59). Assoc. Prof., 1959–62, and Prof. of Social Relations, 1962–73, Johns Hopkins Univ., Baltimore. *Publs:* (with S. Lipset and M. Trow) Union Democracy, 1956; Community Conflict, 1957; The Adolescent Society, 1961; Adolescents and the Schools, 1961; Introduction to Mathematical Sociology, 1964; Models of Change and Response Uncertainty, 1964; (with E. Katz and H. Menzel) Medical Innovation, 1967; (with others) Equality of Educational Opportunity, 1966; Resources for Social Change, 1972; Mathematics of Collective Action, 1973; Power and the Structure of Society, 1973; Youth: Transition to Adulthood, 1974; Longitudinal Data Analysis, 1981; The Asymmetric Society, 1982; (with T. Hoffer and S. Kilgore) High School Achievement, 1982; Individual Interests and Collective Action, 1986; (with T. Hoffer) Public and Private High Schools: The Impact of Communities, 1987. Add: Dept. of Sociology, Univ. of Chicago, Chicago, Ill. 60637, U.S.A.

COLEMAN, Shalom. Australian, b. 1918. Archaeology/Antiquities, Theology/Religion. Chief Rabbi Emeritus, Perth Hebrew Congregation, W.A. Lectr. in Biblical Studies, Dept. of Extension Studies, Univ. of Western Australia, Perth, since 1967. Pres., Assn. of Rabbis and Ministers of Australia and New Zealand, since 1984. Chief Minister, Bloemfontein Hebrew Congregation, S. Africa, 1947–60, and South Head and District Synagogue, Sydney 1961–66; Dayan of Sydney Beth Din, Jewish ecclesiastical court, 1963–66. *Publs:* (ed.) Golden Jubilee Issue Hashomer, 1903-1953, 1953; Hosea Concepts in Midrash and Talmud, 1960; The Dialogue of Habakkuk in Rabbinic Doctrine, 1966; Malachi, a Midrashic Analysis; Trends in Jewish Life and Thought; Spiritual Origins of Man; What Every Jew Should Know, 1974; What Is a Jewish Home, 1978; A Short History of the Karrakatta Cemetery, 1979; What Is A Synagogue, 1982. Add: 38 Bradford St., Mount Lawley, W.A. 6050, Australia.

COLEMAN, Terry. British, b. 1931. Novels, History, Politics, Transportation. Assoc. Ed., The Independent newspaper, London, since 1989. Chief Feature Writer, The Guardian newspaper, London, 1961–74; Special Writer, Daily Mail newspaper, London, 1974–76; Chief Feature Writer, 1976–79, New York Corresp., 1981, and Special Corresp., 1982–89, The Guardian. *Publs:* The Railway Navies, 1965; A Girl for the Afternoons (novel), 1965; (co-author) Providence and Mr. Hardy, 1966; The Only True History, 1969; Passage to America (in U.S. as Going to America), 1972; The Pantheretti (poems), 1973; (ed.) The Poor Man and the Lady, by Thomas Hardy, 1974; The Liners, 1976; The Scented Brawl, 1978; Southern Cross (novel), 1979; Thanksgiving (novel), 1981; Movers and Shakers: Collected Interviews, 1987; Thatcher's Britain, 1987. Add: Lloyd's Bank, Blackheath, London SE3, England.

COLES, John Morton. Canadian, b. 1930. Archaeology/Antiquities. Prof. of European Prehistory, Univ. of Cambridge, 1980–86; Fellow of Fitzwilliam Coll., Cambridge. *Publs:* (with E.S. Higgs) Archaeology of Early Man, 1968; Field Archaeology in Britain, 1972; Archaeology by Experiment, 1973; (with A.F. Harding) The Bronze Age in Europe, 1978; Experimental Archaeology, 1979; (with B. Orme) Prehistory of the Somerset Levels, 1980; The Archaeology of Wetlands, 1984; (with B. Coles) Sweet Track to Glastonbury, 1986; (ed. with A.J. Lawson) European Wetlands in Prehistory, 1987; Meare Village East: The Excavation of A. Bulleid and H.S.G. Gray 1932-1956, 1987; (with B. Coles) People of the Wetlands, 1989. Add: Fursdon Mill Cottage, Thorverton, Devon, England.

COLES, Robert. American, b. 1929. Poetry, Psychiatry, Psychology, Social commentary/phenomena, Sociology, Biography. Research Psychiatrist, Harvard Univ., Cambridge, Mass., since 1964. Chief, Neuropsychiatry Service, Biloxi, Miss. Air Force Base, 1958–60. *Publs:* Children of Crisis: vol. I: A Study in Courage and Fear, 1967, vol. II: Migrants, Sharecroppers, Mountaineers, 1972, vol. III: The South Goes North, 1972, vol. IV: Eskimos, Chicanos, Indians, 1978, vol. V: Privileged Ones: The Well Off and Rich in America, 1978; Dead End School, 1968; Still Hungry in America, 1968; The Grass Pipe, 1969; The Image Is You, 1969; Uprooted Children: The Early Lives of Migrant Farmers, 1970; Drugs and Youth, 1970; Erik H. Erikson: The Growth of His Work, 1970; The Middle Americans, 1971; The Geography of Faith, 1971; A Spectacle unto the World, 1973; The Darkness and the Light, 1974; The Buses Roll, 1974; Irony in the Mind's Life, 1974; Headsparks, 1975; William Carlos Williams, 1975; The Mind's Fate, 1975; A Festering Sweetness (poetry), 1978; Women of Crisis: vol. I: Lives of Struggle and Hope, 1978, vol. II: Lives of Work and Dreams, 1980; The Last and First Eskimos, 1978; Walker Percy: An American Search, 1978; Flannery O'Connor's South, 1980; Dorothea Lange: Photographs of a Lifetime, 1982; The Old Ones of New Mexico, 1984; (with R. Spears) Agee, 1985; (with G. Stokes) Sex and the American Teenager, 1985; The Moral [and Political] Life of Children, 2 vols., 1986; (with H. Levitt) In the Streets, 1987; Simone Weil: A Modern Pilgrimage, 1987; Dorothy Day: A Radical Devotion, 1987. Add: 81 Carr Rd., Concord, Mass. 01942, U.S.A.

COLISH, Marcia Lillian. American, b. 1937. History, Philosophy. Prof. of History since 1975, and Frederick B. Artz Prof. since 1985, Oberlin Coll., Ohio (Instr., 1963–65; Asst. Prof., 1965–69; Assoc. Prof., 1969–75; Chmn. of Dept., 1973–74, 1978–81.) *Publs:* The Mirror of Language: A Study in the Medieval Theory of Knowledge, 1968, 1983; The Stoic Tradition from Antiquity to the Early Middle Ages, 2 vols., 1985. Add: Dept. of History, Oberlin Coll., Oberlin, Ohio 44074, U.S.A.

COLLEDGE, Malcolm (Andrew Richard). British, b. 1939. Art, Classics, History. Prof. of Classics, Westfield Coll., Univ. of London, since 1984 (Lectr., 1967–75; Reader, 1975–84). Asst. Lectr., Univ. Coll. of Swansea, Univ. of Wales, 1964–66. *Publs:* The Parthians, 1967; (co-author) Classics: An Outline for the Intending Student, 1970; The Art of Palmyra, 1976; Parthian Art, 1977; How to Recognize Roman Art, 1979; (co-ed.) Acta of the XI Intnl. Congress of Classical Archaeology, 1979; (co-author) Ancient Rome, 1980; (co-author) The Atlas of Archaeology, 1982; (co-author) The Macmillan Dictionary of Archaeology, 1983; The Parthian Period (Iconography of Religions, XIV, 3), 1986; Pagan Gods and Shrines of the Roman Empire, 1986; (co-author) Hellenism in the East, 1987. Add: Westfield Coll., Univ. of London, Kidderpore Ave., London NW3 7ST, England.

COLLIER, Graham. British, b. 1937. Music. Self-employed composer, musician, bandleader, and writer, since 1963; Dir. of Jazz Studies, Royal Academy of Music, London. *Publs:* Inside Jazz, 1973; Jazz: A Guide for Teachers and Students, 1975; Compositional Devices, 1975; Cleo and John, 1976; Jazz Workshop: The Blues, 1988. Add: 38 Shell Rd., London SE13, England.

COLLIER, James Lincoln. American, b. 1928. Novels/Short stories, Children's fiction, Children's non-fiction, History, Social commentary, Biography. *Publs:* children's fiction—The Teddy Bear Habit, 1967; Rock Star, 1970; Why Does Everybody Think I'm Nutty?, 1971; It's Murder at St. Basket's, 1972; (with Christopher Collier) My Brother Sam Is Dead, 1974; Rich and Famous, 1975; (with Collier) The Bloody Country, 1976; Give Dad My Best, 1976; (with Collier) The Winter Hero, 1978; (with Collier) Jump Ship to Freedom, 1981; Planet Out of the Past, 1983; (with Collier) War Comes to Willie Freeman, 1983; (with Collier) Who Is Carrie?, 1984; When the Stars Begin to Fall, 1986, The Winchesters, 1988; children's non-fiction—Battleground: The United States Army in World War II, 1965; A Visit to the Firehouse, 1967; Which Musical Instrument Shall I Play?, 1969; Danny Goes to the Hospital, 1970; Practical Musical Theory: How Music Is Put Together from Bach to Rock, 1970; The Hard Life of the Teenager, 1972; Inside Jazz, 1973; Jug Bands and Handmade Music 1973; The Making of Man, 1974; Making Music for Money, 1976; CB, 1977; The Great Jazz Artists, 1977; adult novels—Cheers, 1960; Somebody Up There Hates Me, 1962; Fires of Youth, 1968; other, for adults—(with others) The Fine Art of Swindling, ed. by W.B. Gibson, 1966; The Hypocritical American: An Essay on Sex Attitudes in America, 1964; (with others) Sex Education U.S.A.: A Community Approach, 1968; The Making of Jazz: A Comprehensive History, 1978; Louis Armstrong, An American Genius, 1983, in U.K. as Louis Armstrong: A Biography, 1984; Louis Armstrong: An American Success Story, 1985; (with Collier) Decision in Philadelphia: The Constitutional Convention of 1787, 1986; Duke Ellington, 1987. Add: c/o Macmillan Publishing Co., 866 Third Ave., New York, N.Y. 10022, U.S.A.

COLLIER, Jane. *See* **COLLIER,** Zena.

COLLIER, Kenneth (Gerald). British, b. 1910. Education issues. Technical Translator, Stockholm, 1931–32; Schoolmaster, 1933–41; with Royal Ordnance Factories, 1941–44; Physics Master, Lancing Coll., Sussex, 1944–49; Lectr., St. Luke's Coll., Exeter, 1949–59; Principal, Coll. of the Venerable Bede, Durham, 1959–75. Ed., Education for Teaching, 1953–58; Chmn., Assn. of Teachers in Colls. and Depts. of Education,

1964–65; Hon. Fellow, Univ. of East Anglia, Norfolk, 1978–81. *Publs:* The Science of Humanity, 1949; The Social Purposes of Education, 1959; New Dimensions in Higher Education, 1968, 1969; (co-author) Colleges of Education Learning Programmes: A Proposal, 1971; (co-author) The Education of Teachers in Britain, 1973; (ed. and co-author) Innovation in Higher Education, 1974; (co-author and ed., with J. Wilson and P. Tomlinson) Values and Moral Development in Higher Education, 1974; (ed. and co-author) Evaluating the New B. Ed., 1978; (ed. and co-author) The Management of Peer-Group Learning in Higher Education, 1983; Teaching Less, Learnign More: A Guide to Theological Education, 1989. Add: 4 Robson Terrace, Shincliffe, Durham DH1 2NL, England.

COLLIER, Peter (Anthony). American, b. 1939. Novels/Short stories, Social commentary/Phenomena, Biography. Consulting Ed., California Mag., since 1981. Prof., Dept. of English, Univ. of California at Berkeley, 1963–67; Exec. Ed., Ramparts mag., San Francisco, 1967–72. *Publs:* (ed.) Justice Denied, 1971; When Shall They Rest, 1973; The Rockefellers: An American Dynasty, 1976; Downriver (novel), 1978; (with David Horowitz) The Kennedys: An American Drama, 1984; (with W.M. Chace) An Introduction to Literature, 1985; (with Horowitz) The Fords: An American Epic, 1987; (ed. with Horowitz) Second Thoughts: Former Radicals Look Back at the Sixties, 1988; (trans.) Horns Academicus, by P. Bourdieau, 1988; (ed. with E. Timms) Visions and Blueprints: Avant-Garde Culture and Radical Politics in Early Twentieth-Century Europe, 1988; (with Horowitz) Destructive Generation: Second Thoughts about the '60s, 1989. Add: 12294 Willow Valley Rd., Nevada City, Calif. 95959, U.S.A.

COLLIER, Richard. British, b. 1924. Novels, History, Theatre, Autobiography, Biography. Freelance writer. Assoc. Ed., Phoenix Mag. for Forces in S.E. Asia, 1945–46; Ed., Town and Country Mag., London, 1946–48; Member of Features Staff, Daily Mail, 1948–49. *Publs:* Beautiful Friend (novel), 1947; Pay Off in Calcutta (in U.S. as the Solitary Witness), 1948; The Lovely and the Damned (novel), 1949; (with H. Grattidge) Captain of the Queens (autobiography), 1956; Ten Thousand Eyes (history), 1958; The City That Wouldn't Die (history), 1959; A House Called Memory (autobiography), 1960; The Sands of Dunkirk (history), 1961; The Great Indian Mutiny (history), 1963; The General Next to God (biography), 1965; Eagle Day (history), 1966; The River That God Forgot (history), 1968; Duce! (biography), 1971; The Plague of the Spanish Lady (history), 1974; The War in the Desert (history), 1977; Bridge Across the Sky (history) 1978; 1940: The Avalanche (history), 1979; 1941: Armageddon (history), 1981; Four from Buenos Aires (criminology), 1982; The War That Stalin Won, 1983; The Rainbow People (history), 1984; Make Believe: The Magic of International Theatre, 1986; The Warcos (history), 1989; (with Philip Kaplan) The Few (history), 1989. Add: c/o Curtis Brown Ltd., 162-168 Regent St., London W1R 5TB, England.

COLLIER, Zena. (Zena Hampson). Has also written as Jane Collier and Zena Shumsky. American, b. 1926. Novels/Short stories, Children's fiction, Children's non-fiction. *Publs:* (as Zena Shumsky with Lou Shumsky) First Flight, 1962; The Year of the Dream, 1962; (as Zena Shumsky with Lou Shumsky) Shutterbug, 1963; (as Jane Collier) A Tangled Web, 1967; Seven for the People (juvenile non-fiction), 1979; Next Time I'll Know (juvenile fiction), 1981. Add: 83 Berkeley St., Rochester, N.Y. 14607, U.S.A.

COLLIN, Marion (Cripps). British, b. 1928. Historical/Romance/Gothic, Literature. Student nurse, Isle of Wight, 1945–48; medical secty., London, 1948–52; Fiction Ed., Woman's Own mag., London, 1952–56. *Publs:* (with Anne Britton) Romantic Fiction, 1960; Nurse Maria, 1963; Nurse at the Top, 1964; Doctors Three, 1964; Nurse in the Dark, 1965; The Doctor's Delusion, 1967; The Shadow of the Court, 1967; The Man on the Island, 1968; Sun on the Mountain, 1969; Nurse on an Island, 1970; Calling Dr. Savage, 1970; House of Dreams, 1971; Sawdust and Spangles, 1972; Nurses in the House, 1989. Add: 41 Clifton Rd., Heaton Moor, Stockport, Cheshire, England.

COLLINGS, I.J. Australian. Novels/Short stories, Supernatural/Occult topics. *Publs:* The Malevolent Despot, 1968; Astrology and Your Child, 1980. Add: 6 Woodstock House, 11 Marylebone High St., London W1, England.

COLLINGS, Michael (Robert). American, b. 1947. Poetry, Literature. Assoc. Prof. of English, Pepperdine Univ., Malibu, Calif., since 1979. Instr. in English, San Bernadino Valley Coll., Calif., 1976–79, and the Univ. of California at Los Angeles, 1978–79. *Publs:* A Season of Calm Weather (poetry), 1974; (with Judith Collings) Whole Wheat Harvest, 1981; Brian W. Aldiss: A Reader's Guide, 1985; Piers Anthony: A

Reader's Guide, 1985; Stephen King as Richard Bachman, 1985; The Shorter Works of Stephen King, 1985; Naked to the Sun: Dark Visions of Apocalypse (poetry), 1985; The Many Facets of Stephen King, 1986; The Films of Stephen King, 1986; The Annotated Guide to Stephen King, 1986; The Stephen King Phenomenon, 1987. Add: 1089 Sheffield Pl., Thousand Oaks, Calif. 91360 U.S.A.

COLLINGSWOOD, Frederick, M.D. *See* **LAKRITZ,** Esther.

COLLINS, Barry. British, b. 1941. Plays/Screenplays. Teacher, Halifax Education Cttee., 1962–63; Journalist, Halifax Evening Courier, 1963–71. *Publs:* Judgement, 1974, 1980; The Strongest Man in the World, 1977. Add: 7 Golf Cres., Highroad Well, Halifax, Yorks., England.

COLLINS, Carvel. American, b. 1912. Literature. Prof. of English, Univ. of Notre Dame, since 1967. Instr., Colorado State Coll., Fort Collins, 1938–39, and Stephens Coll., Columbia, Mo., 1939–40; Instr., 1942–45, Asst. Dean, 1945, and Asst. Prof., 1946–50, Harvard Univ., Cambridge, Mass.; Assoc. Prof., 1950–56, and Prof., 1956–67, Massachusetts Inst. of Technology, Cambridge. *Publs:* The American Sporting Gallery, 1949; (with others) Literature in the Modern World, 1945; ed.—Sam Ward in the Gold Rush, 1949; William Faulkner's New Orleans Sketches, 1958; William Faulkner, the Unvanquished, 1959; Faulkner's University Pieces, 1961; Erskine Caldwell's Men and Women, 1961; William Faulkner: Early Prose and Poetry, 1962; Faulkner's Mayday, 1977; Introduction to William Faulkner: A Life on Paper, 1980; Faulkner's Helen: A Courtship, 1981. Add: Box 368, Dept. of English, Univ. of Notre Dame, Notre Dame, Ind. 46556, U.S.A.

COLLINS, David R. American, b. 1940. Children's fiction, Children's non-fiction. Instr. in English, Moline Sr. High School, Moline, Illinois, since 1983; Instr. in English, Woodrow Wilson Jr. High School, 1962–83. Pres., Quad Cities Writers Club, since 1973; Vice-Pres., Writers' Studio, since 1973 (Pres., 1967–72); Dir., Mississippi Valley Writers Conference, 1974. *Publs:* Kim Soo and His Tortoise, 1970; Great American Nurses, 1971; Walt Disney's Surprise Christmas Present, 1972; Linda Richards: First American Trained Nurse, 1973; Harry S Truman, People's President, 1974; Abraham Lincoln, 1976; Football Running Backs, 1976; Charles Lindbergh, 1978; If I Could, I Would, 1979; The Wonderful Story of Jesus, 1980; Joshua Poole and Sunrise, 1980; The One Bad Thing About Birthdays, 1981; Joshua Poole and the Special Flowers, 1981; George Meany, Mr. Labor, 1981; Dorothy Day, Catholic Worker, 1981; Thomas Merton, Monk with a Mission, 1981; Super Champ, 1982; George Washington Carver, 1982; Francis Scott Key, 1982; Notable Illinois Women, 1983; The Game of Think, 1984; The Golden Circle, 1984; Johnny Appleseed, 1985; Florence Nightingale, 1985; Not Only Dreams, 1986; Ride a Red Dinosaur, 1987; The Long Legged School Teacher: Lyndon Baines Johnson, From the Texas Hill Country to the White House, 1987; The Country Artist: A Story About Beatrix Potter, 1988; Grover Cleveland: 22nd and 24th President of the United States, 1988; Harry S. Truman: 33rd President of the United States, 1988; To the Point: A Story About E.B. White, 1988. Add: 3403 45th St., Moline, Ill. 61265, U.S.A.

COLLINS, Harold R(eeves). American, b. 1915. Literature. Retired Prof. of English, Kent State Univ., Ohio, since 1955. Asst. Prof. of English, Wilkes Coll., Wilkes-Barre, Pa., 1945–47; Instr. in English, Univ. of Connecticut at Waterbury, 1947–55. *Publs:* Amos Tutuola, 1969. Add: 3121 E. Alpine St., Springfield, Mo. 65804, U.S.A.

COLLINS, Hunt. *See* **HUNTER,** Evan.

COLLINS, Jackie. British. Novels/Short stories. *Publs:* The World Is Full of Married Men, 1968; The Stud, 1969; Sunday Simmons and Charlie Brick, 1971, as Sinners, 1981; Lovehead, 1974, as The Love Killers, 1977; The World Is Full of Divorced Women, 1975; The Hollywood Zoo, 1975; Lovers and Gamblers, 1977; The Bitch, 1979; Chances, 1981; Hollywood Wives, 1983; Lucky, 1985; Hollywood Husbands, 1986; Rock Star, 1987. Add: c/o Simon and Schuster, 1230 Ave. of the Americas, New York, N.Y. 10020, U.S.A.

COLLINS, Joan. British, b. 1933. Novels/Short stories, Fashion/Costume, Biography. Actress: has appeared in films, on the London stage, and on television; has starred as Alexis in the TV series "Dynasty," since 1981. London stage debut, in A Doll's House, 1945; has since appeared in Jassy; The Praying Mantis; The Skin of Our Teeth; The Last of Mrs. Cheyney; etc., principal film appearances include: The Girl in the Red Velvet Swing, 1955; Island in the Sun, 1957; The Man Who Came to

Dinner, 1972; Alfie Darling, 1974; The Big Sleep, 1978; The Stud, 1978; etc., has also appeared in the made-for-TV movies, Paper Dolls, 1982; The Making of a Male Model, 1983; The Cartier Affair, 1984; Sins, 1985. *Publs:* Past Imperfect: An Autobiography, 1978; The Joan Collins Beauty Book, 1980; Katy: A Fight for Life (biography), 1982; Prime Time (novel), 1988. Add: c/o William Morris Agency, 151 El Camino Dr., Beverley Hills, Calif. 90212, U.S.A.

COLLINS, Larry. American, b. 1929. Novels/Short stories, Politics/Government, Social commentary/phenomena. Corresp., U.P.I., Paris, Rome, and Beirut, 1957–59; Middle East Corresp., Newsweek mag., Beirut, 1959–61; Bureau Chief, Newsweek mag., Paris, 1961–65. *Publs:* (with D. Lapierre) Is Paris Burning?, 1965; (with D. Lapierre) Or I'll Dress You in Mourning, 1968; (with D. Lapierre) O Jerusalem, 1972; (with D. Lapierre) Freedom at Midnight, 1975; (with D. Lapierre) The Fifth Horseman (novel), 1980; Fall from Grace, 1985; Maze (novel), 1989. Add: c/o Simon and Schuster, 1230 Ave. of the Americas, New York, N.Y. 10020, U.S.A.

COLLINS, Marva (Delores). American, b. 1936. Education. Principal, private sch., Chicago. Teacher, business subjects, Monroe County Training Sch., Alabama, 1957–59; Medical Secty., Mt. Sinai Hosp., Chicago, 1959–61; Teacher, Chicago Public Schs., 1961–75; founded Daniel Hale Williams Westside Preparatory Sch., Chicago, 1975 (now known as Westside Preparatory Sch.). *Publs:* (with Civia Tamarkin) Marva Collins' Way, 1982. Add: c/o Westside Preparatory Sch., 4146 West Chicago Ave., Chicago, Ill. 60641, U.S.A.

COLLINS, Max Allan. American, b. 1948. Mystery/Crime/Suspense. Has written the comic strips Dick Tracy since 1977, Mike Mist since 1979, and Ms. Tree since 1981, for newspapers and magazines. Musician, with Daybreakers group, 1966–71, and Crusin' group, 1976–79, and since 1986; songwriter, Tree Intnl., Nashville, 1967–71; Reporter, Muscatine Journal, 1968–70; Instr. in English, Muscatine Community Coll., 1971–77. *Publs:* mystery novels—Bait Money, 1973; Blood Money, 1973; The Broker, 1976; The Broker's Wife, 1976; The Dealer, 1976; The Slasher, 1977; Fly Paper, 1981; Hush Money, 1981; Hard Cash, 1981; Scratch Fever, 1982; The Baby Blue Rip-Off, 1983; No Cure for Death, 1983; True Detective, 1983; Kill Your Darlings, 1984; True Crime, 1984; A Shroud for Aquarius, 1985; The Million-Dollar Wound, 1986; Nice Weekend for a Murder, 1986; Midnight Haul, 1986; The Dark City, 1987; Spree, 1987; Primary Target, 1987; Neon Mirage, 1988; other— Dick Tracy Meets Angeltop, 1980; Dick Tracy Meets the Punks, 1980; (ed.) Mike Hammer: The Comic Strip, by Mickey Spillane, 2 vols., 1982– 84; (with Ed Gorman) Jim Thompson: The Killers Inside Him, 1983; (ed.) Tomorrow I Die, by Mickey Spillane, 1984; (with James L. Traylor) One Lonely Knight: Mickey Spillane's Mike Hammer, 1984; The Files of Ms. Tree, 3 vols., 1984–86. Add: 117 Lord Ave., Muscatine, Iowa 52761, U.S.A.

COLLINS, Michael. *See* **LYNDS,** Dennis.

COLLINS, Philip Arthur William. British, b. 1923. Literature. Warden of Vaughan Coll., 1954–62, Sr. Lectr., 1962–64, and Prof. of English, 1964–82, Univ. of Leicester. Member, Bd. of Dirs., The National Theatre, 1976–82. *Publs:* James Boswell, 1956; (ed.) English Christmas, 1956; Dickens and Crime, 1962; Dickens and Education, 1963; The Impress of the Moving Age, 1965; Thomas Cooper the Chartist: Byron and the Poets of the Poor, 1969; A Dickens Bibliography, 1970; (ed.) Dickens: A Christmas Carol: The Public Reading Version, 1971; Bleak House: A Commentary, 1971; (ed.) Dickens: The Critical Heritage, 1971; Reading Aloud: A Victorian Métier, 1972; (ed.) Charles Dickens: The Public Readings, 1975; Charles Dickens: David Copperfield, 1977; (ed.) Charles Dickens: Hard Times, 1978; (ed.) Dickens: Interviews and Recollections, 1981; (ed.) Thackeray: Interviews and Recollections, 1982; Tennyson, Poet of Lincolnshire, 1985; (ed. with Edward Giuliano) The Annotated Dickens, 1986. Add: 26 Knighton Dr., Leicester LE2 3HB, England.

COLLINS, Robert O(akley). American, b. 1933. History. Prof. of History, Univ. of California at Santa Barbara, since 1969 (Assoc. Prof., 1965–69). Member, Editorial Bd., Journal of African Historical Studies, Intnl. Journal of African Historical Studies, and Journal of African Studies. Lectr. in History, 1961, and Asst. Prof. of History, 1963–65, Williams Coll., Williamstown, Mass.; Visiting Asst. Prof. of History, Columbia Univ., NYC, 1962–63. Member, Bd. of Dirs., Intnl. Academy, Santa Barbara, 1968–81. *Publs:* The Southern Sudan 1883-1898, 1962; (with Robert L. Tignor) Egypt and the Sudan, 1967; (ed.) The Nile Basin, by Sir Richard Burton, 1967; (ed.) Problems in African History, 1968; King Leopold, England and the Upper Nile, 1968; (ed.) The Partition of of Africa, 1969; (ed.) An Arabian Diary, by Sir Gilbert Clayton, 1969; (ed.) Problems in the History of Colonial Africa, 1970; Land Beyond the Rivers: The Southern Sudan 1898-1918, 1971; African History: Text and Readings, 1971; Europeans in Africa, 1971; The Southern Sudan in Historical Perspective, 1975; (with Roderick Nash) The Big Drops: Legendary Rapids of the West, 1978; Shadows in the Grass: Britain in the Southern Sudan 1918-1956, 1983; (ed. with Francis Deng) Britain in the Sudan 1898-1956, 1984; The Waters of the Nile: Hydropolitics of the Nile and the Jonglei Canal, 1989. Add: Dept. of History, Univ. of California, Santa Barbara, Calif. 93106, U.S.A.

COLLINSON, Laurence (Henry). British, b. 1925. Novels/Short stories, Plays/Screenplays, Poetry. Columnist, Quorum journal, since 1973. Teacher of English and Maths, Vic. (Australia) Education Dept., 1956–61; Ed., The Educational Mag., Vic. Education Dept., 1961–64; Sub-Ed., Intnl. Publishing Corp., London, 1965–73. *Publs:* Friday Night at the Schrammers', 1949; No Sugar for George, 1949; Poet's Dozen, 1952; The Moods of Love, 1957; A Slice of Birthday Cake, 1963; Who Is Wheeling Grandma?, 1967; The Wangaratta Bunyip, 1970; Cupid's Crescent, 1973; Thinking Straight, 1975; Hovering Narcissus, 1977; One Penny for Israel, 1978. Add: c/o Grandma Press, 4/119 Broadhurst Gardens, London, NW6 3BJ, England.

COLLINSON, Roger (Alfred). British, b. 1936. Children's fiction. Sch. teacher, Essex Co. Council, Leigh-on-Sea, since 1975. *Publs:* A Boat and Bax, 1967; Butch and Bax, 1970; Four Eyes, 1976; Get Lavinia Goodbody!, 1983; Paper Flags and Penny Ices, 1984; Hanky-Panky, 1986. Add: c/o Anderson Press Ltd., Brookmount House, 62-65 Chandos Pl., Covent Garden, London, WC2N 4NW, England.

COLLIS, Louise (Edith). British, b. 1925. Novels/Short stories, Art, History, Biography. Freelance writer and art critic. *Publs:* Without a Voice, 1951; A Year Passed, 1952; After the Holiday, 1954; The Angel's Name, 1955; Seven in the Tower, 1958; The Apprentice Saint, 1964; Soldier in Paradise, 1965; The Great Flood, 1966; A Private View of Stanley Spencer, 1972; Maurice Collis Diaries, 1978; Impetuous Heart: The Story of Ethel Smyth, 1984. Add: 65 Cornwall Gardens, London SW7, England.

COLLOMS, Brenda. Also writes as Brenda Cross and Brenda Hughes. British, b. 1919. Children's non-fiction, Film, Biography. History Lectr., Working Men's Coll., London. Ed. (as Brenda Cross), The Film Star Diary, Cramp publrs., London, 1948–63. *Publs:* (as Brenda Cross) Happy Ever After, 1947; (as Brenda Cross) The Film Hamlet, 1948; (as Brenda Hughes) New Guinea Folk Tales, 1959; (as Brenda Hughes) Folk Tales from Chile, 1962; Certificate History, Books 1-4; Britain and Europe, 1966-70; Israel, 1971; The Mayflower Pilgrims, 1973; Charles Kingsley, 1975; Victorian Country Parsons, 1977; Victorian Visionaries, 1982. Add: 123a Gloucester Ave., London NW1 8LB, England.

COLMAN, E. Adrian M. Australian, b. 1930. Literature. Prof. of English, Univ. of Tasmania, since 1978. Lectr. in English, Univ. of New South Wales, 1962–70; Research Assoc., The Shakespeare Inst., Univ. of Birmingham, 1968–69; Sr. Lectr., 1970–74, and Assoc. Prof., 1974–78, Univ. of Sydney. Chmn. of Bd., Australian Theatre for Young People, 1975–78. *Publs:* Shakespeare's Julius Caesar, 1965; The Structure of Shakespeare's Antony and Cleopatra, 1971; The Dramatic Use of Bawdy in Shakespeare, 1974; (ed.) Poems of Sir Walter Raleigh, 1977; (ed.) King Lear, 1982; (ed.) Henry IV Part I, 1987. Add: Dept. of English, Univ. of Tasmania, Box 252C, G.P.O., Hobart, Australia 7001.

COLMAN, Hila (née Crayder). Also writes as Teresa Crayder. American. Children's fiction, Novels, Documentation/Reportage. Writer since 1949. Publicity/promotion officer, National War Relief Agency, NYC, 1940–45; Exec. Dir., Labor Book Club, NYC, 1945–47. *Publs:* children's fiction—The Big Step, 1957; A Crown for Gina, 1958; Julie Builds Her Castle, 1959; The Best Wedding Dress, 1960; The Girl from Puerto Rico, 1961; Mrs. Darling's Daughter, 1962; Watch That Watch, 1963; Peter's Brownstone House, 1963; Phoebe's First Campaign, 1963; Classmates by Request, 1964; The Boy Who Couldn't Make Up His Mind, 1965; Christmas Cruise, 1965; Bride at Eighteen, 1966; Dangerous Summer, 1966; Car-Crazy Girl, 1967; Thoroughly Modern Millie (novelization of screenplay), 1967; Mixed-Marriage Daughter, 1968; Something Out of Nothing, 1968; Andy's Landmark House, 1969; Claudia, Where Are You?, 1969; The Happenings at North End School, 1970; Daughter of Discontent, 1971; End of the Game, 1971; The Family and the Fugitive, 1972; Benny the Misfit, 1973; Chicano Girl, 1973; Diary of a Frantic Kid Sister, 1973; Friends and Strangers on Location, 1974; After the Wedding, 1975; Ethan's Favorite Teacher, 1975; That's the Way

It Is, Amigo, 1975; The Amazing Miss Laura, 1976; Nobody Has to Be a Kid Forever, 1976; The Case of the Stolen Bagels, 1977; Sometimes I Don't Love My Mother, 1977; Rachel's Legacy, 1978; The Secret Life of Harold, the Bird Watcher, 1978; Tell Me No Lies, 1978; Ellie's Inheritance, 1979; Accident, 1980; What's the Matter with the Dobsons?, 1980; Confessions of a Storyteller, 1981; The Family Trap, 1982; Not for Love, 1983; Just the Two of Us, 1984; Nobody Told Me What I Need to Know, 1984; Weekend Sisters, 1985; Suddenly, 1987; The Double Life of Angela Jones, 1988; Rich and Famous Like My Mom, 1988; works for adults—The Country Weekend Cookbook, 1961; Hanging On, 1977; fiction and other works as Teresa Crayder—Sudden Fame, 1966; Cathy and Lisette, 1964; Cleopatra, 1969; Beauty, Brains and Glamour: A Career in Magazine Publishing, 1988; A Career in Medical Research, 1968; Making Movies: Student Films to Features, 1969; City Planning: What It's All About—In the Planners' Own Words, 1971. Add: c/o Morrow Junior Books, 105 Madison Ave., New York, N.Y. 10016, U.S.A.

COLMAN, John Edward. American, b. 1923. Education. Dir., Govt. and Research Grants, St. John's Univ., Jamaica, N.Y., since 1966 (Assoc. Prof., 1961; Asst. Dean, 1963, Sch. of Education). Instr. of Calculus, Immaculata Coll., Pa., 1946–47; Instr. of Education, Notre Dame, Md., 1956–58; Dean, Niagara Univ., N.Y., 1959–61. *Publs:* (ed.) Teachers and Teaching Today, 1964; The Master Teachers and the Art of Teaching, 1967; (ed.) Talks to Pharmacy, vol. I, 1969, vol. II, 1970. Add: St. John's Univ., Jamaica, N.Y. 11439, U.S.A.

COLMER, John Anthony. British, b. 1921. Literature. Lectr. and Sr. Lectr., Univ. of Khartoum, Sudan, 1949–59; Sr. Lectr., 1961–64, Reader, 1964, and Prof. of English, 1964–86, Univ. of Adelaide, Visiting Prof., National Univ. of Singapore, 1989–90. *Publs:* Coleridge: Critic of Society, 1959; (ed.) Coleridge: Selected Poems, 1965; (co-ed.) Shakespeare: Henry IV, Part I, 1965; (ed.) Approaches to the Novel, 1966; E.M. Forster: A Passage to India, 1967; (co-ed.) New Choice, 1967; (co-ed.) Mainly Modern, 1969; E.M. Forster: The Personal Voice, 1975; (ed.) Coleridge: On the Constitution of the Church and State, 1976; Riders in the Chariot: Patrick White, 1978; Coleridge to Catch-22: Images of Society, 1978; (co-ed.) Pattern and Voice, 1981; Through Australian Eyes, 1984; Patrick White, 1984; (co-ed.) The Penguin Book of Australian Autobiography, 1987; (ed) The Changing Stage, 1988; Australian Autobiography: The Personal Quest, 1989. Add: Dept. of English, Univ. of Adelaide, S.A., 5001, Australia.

COLOMBO, John Robert. Canadian, b. 1936. Poetry, Humor, Social commentary, Translations. Ed. Asst., Univ. of Toronto Press, 1959–60; Asst. Ed., Ryerson Press, 1960–63; Sr. Advisory Ed., McClelland and Stewart, Toronto, 1964–70. Former Ed., The Montrealer, and Exchange; Managing Ed., Tamarack Review, Toronto, 1959–82; Member, Canada Council Arts Advisory Panel, 1968–70. Host, "Columbo Quotes," CBC-TV, 1979. Regular Guest, "Don Harron's Morningside," CBC-Radio, 1980–81. *Publs:* Fragments, 1957; Rubato: New Poems by Young Canadian Poets, 1958; Variations, 1958; This Citadel in Time, 1958; This Studied Self, 1958; In the Streets, 1959; (ed.) The Varsity Chapbook, 1959; Poems and Other Poems, 1959; Two Poems, 1959; This Is the Work Entitled Canada, 1959; Fire Escape, Fire Esc, Fire, 1959; The Impression of Beauty, 1959; Poems to Be Sold for Bread, 1959; Lines for the Last Day, 1960; (ed. with Jacques Godbout) Poesie 64/Poetry 64, 1963; The Mackenzie Poems, 1965; The Great Wall of China: An Entertainment, 1966; Abracadabra, 1967; Miraculous Montages, 1967; (ed. with Raymond Souster) Shapes and Sounds: Poems of W.W.E. Ross, 1968; John Toronto: New Poems by Dr. Strachan, Found by John Robert Colombo, 1969; (ed.) How Do I Love Thee: Sixty Poems of Canada (and Quebec) . . . , 1970; (ed.) New Directions in Canadian Poetry, 1970; Neo Poems, 1970; (ed.) Rhymes and Reasons: Nine Canadian Poets Discuss Their Work, 1971; The Great San Francisco Earthquake and Fire, 1971; Praise Poems and Leonardo's Lists, 1972; (ed.) An Alphabet of Annotations, 1972; (trans.) From Zero to One, by Robert Zend, 1973; Translations from the English, 1974; The Sad Truths, 1974; (ed.) Colombo's Canadian Quotations, 1974, as Concise Canadian Quotations, 1976; (ed.) Colombo's Little Book of Canadian Proverbs, Graffiti, Limericks, and Other Vital Matters, 1975; (trans. with Nikola Roussanoff) Under the Eaves of a Forgotten Village: Sixty Poems from Contemporary Bulgaria, 1975; (ed.) Colombo's Canadian References, 1976; (ed. and trans. with Nikola Roussanoff) The Balkan Range: A Bulgarian Reader, 1976; Mostly Monsters, 1977; Variable Cloudiness, 1977; (trans. with Nikola Roussanoff) The Left-Handed One: Poems by Lyubomir Levchev, 1977; (trans. with Nikola Roussanoff) Remember Me Well: Poems by Andrei Germanov, 1978; (trans. with Nikola Roussanoff) Depths: Poems by Dora Gabe, 1978; (ed.) East and West: Selected Poems by George Faludy, 1978; Private Parts, 1978; (ed.) Colombo's Names and Nicknames, 1978; Colombo's Book of Canada, 1978; The Poets of Canada, 1978; (ed.) The Great Cities of Antiquity, 1979; (ed.) Other Canadas: An Anthology of Science Fiction and Fantasy, 1979; (trans.) Dark Times: Poems of Waclaw Iwaniuk, 1979; (with others) CDN SF&F: A Bibliography of Canadian Science Fiction and Fantasy, 1979; (ed.) Colombo's Hollywood, 1979; (ed.) Colombo's Book of Marvels, 1979; (ed.) The Canada Colouring Book, 1980; (trans.) Such Times: Poems of Ewa Lipska, 1981; (ed.) 222 Canadian Jokes, 1981; (trans.) Far from You: Poems of Pavel Javor, 1981; Blackwood's Books: A Bibliography Devoted to Algernon Blackwood, 1981; (with Michael Richardson) Not to Be Taken at Night, 1981; Poems of the Inuit, 1981; Friendly Aliens, 1981; Years of Light, 1982; Selected Translations, 1982; Selected Poems, 1982; Beyond Labels: Poems of Robert Zend (trans.), 1982; (ed.) Colombo's Last Words, 1982; (ed.) Colombo's Laws, 1982; (ed.) Windigo, 1982; Symmetries: Poems of Marin Sorescu (trans.), 1982; Learn This Poem of Mine by Heart: Poems of George Faludy (trans.), 1983; Colombo's Canadiana Quiz Book, 1983; René Lévesque Buys Canada Savings Bonds and Other Great Canadian Graffiti, 1983; Colombo's 101 Canadian Places, 1983; (ed.) Songs of the Indians, 1983; The Toronto Puzzle Book, 1984; Canadian Literary Landmarks, 1984; Great Moments in Canadian History, 1984; (with Michael Richardson) We Stand on Guard, 1985; 1001 Questions about Canada, 1986; Colombo's New Canadian Quotations, 1987; Off Earth (poetry), 1987; Mysterious Canada, 1988; 999 Questions About Canada, 1989; Extraordinary Experiences, 1989. Add: 42 Dell Park Ave., Toronto, Ont. M6B 2T6, Canada.

COLQUHOUN, Keith. British, b. 1937. Novels/Short stories. *Publs:* The Money Tree, 1959; Point of Stress, 1961; The Sugar Coating, 1973; St. Petersburg Rainbow, 1975; Goebbels and Gladys, 1981; Filthy Rich, 1982; Kiss of Life, 1983; Foreign Wars, 1985. Add: c/o John Murray, 50 Albemarle St., London W1X 4BD, England.

COLSON, Charles W(endell). American, b. 1931. Theology/Religion, Autobiography/Memoirs. Assoc., Fellowship House, Washington, D.C., since 1975; Pres., Prison Fellowship, Washington, since 1976. Admitted to the Bar of Virginia, 1959, Washington, D.C., 1961, and Massachusetts, 1964; Asst. to the Asst. Secty. of the U.S. Navy, 1955–56; Admin. Asst. to U.S. Senator Leverett Saltonstall, 1956–61; Partner, Gadsby and Hannah, Boston, 1961–69; Special Counsel to the President of the United States, Richard Nixon, 1969–73; Partner, Colson and Shapiro, Washington, D.C., 1973–74. *Publs:* Born Again, 1976; Life Sentence, 1979; Loving God, 1983; Who Speaks for God: Confronting the World with Real Christianity, 1985; Dare to Be Different, Dare to Be Christian, 1986; Presenting Belief in an Age of Unbelief, 1986; The Role of Church in Society, 1986; The Struggle for Men's Hearts and Minds, 1986; (with others) Christianity in Conflict: The Struggle for Christian Integrity and Freedom in Secular Culture, 1986; Kingdoms in Conflict, 1987. Add: c/o Prison Fellowship, P.O. Box 17500, Washington, D.C. 20041, U.S.A.

COLSON, Elizabeth. American, b. 1917. Anthropology/Ethnology. Prof. Emeritus of Anthropology, Univ. of California at Berkeley since 1984 (Prof., 1964–84). Dir., Rhodes-Livingstone Inst., 1948–51; Sr. Lectr., Univ. of Manchester, England, 1951–53; Assoc. Prof., Goucher Coll., Towson, Md., 1953–55; Research Assoc. and Assoc. Prof., African Studies Prog., Boston Univ., Mass., 1955–59; Prof., Brandeis Univ., Waltham, Mass., 1959–63; Visiting Prof., Northwestern Univ., Ill., 1963–64; and Univ. of Zambia, 1987. *Publs:* (with M. Gluckman) Seven Tribes of Central Africa, 1951; The Makah, 1953; Marriage and the Family Among the Plateau Tonga, 1958; Social Organization of Gwembe Tonga, 1960; The Plateau Tonga, 1962; Social Consequences of Resettlement, 1971; Tradition and Contract, 1974; (with Thayer Scudder) Secondary Education and the Formation of an Elite, 1980; Voluntary Efforts in Decentralized Management, 1983; (ed.) People in Upheaval, 1987; For Prayer and Profit, 1988. Add: Dept. of Anthropology, Univ. of California, Berkeley, Calif. 94720, U.S.A.

COLT, Clem. See **NYE**, Nelson.

COLT, Zandra. See **STEVENSON**, Florence.

COLTER, Cyrus. American, b. 1910. Novels/Short stories. Commissioner, Illinois Commerce Commn., 1951–73; Prof. of Creative Writing, 1973–76, and Chester D. Tripp Prof. of Humanities, 1976–78, Northwestern Univ., Evanston, Ill. *Publs:* The Beach Umbrella (short stories), 1970; The Rivers of Eros, 1972; The Hippodrome, 1973; Night Studies, 1979; A Chocolate Soldier, 1988. Add: 1115 S. Plymouth Ct., Chicago, Ill. 60605, U.S.A.

COLTHARP, Lurline H(ughes). American, b. 1913. Language/Linguistics. Prof. Emerita of English, Univ. of Texas at El Paso, since 1981 (Instr., 1954–61; Asst. Prof., 1961–65; Assoc. Prof., 1965–70; Prof., 1970–81). Member, Bd. of Mgrs., since 1974, and Vice-Pres., South Central Region, American Name Soc. (National Pres., 1978); Member, Intnl. Cttee. for Onomastic Sciences, since 1978; Member, Bd. of Dirs., American Dialect Soc., 1981–85. Vice-Pres., Mexico-U.S. Educational Assn., 1966–67; Delegate, National Delegate Assembly, Modern Language Assn., 1971–74; Member, Editorial Bd., American Speech mag., 1977–80. *Publs:* The Tongue of the Tirilones, 1965. Add: Dept. of English, Univ. of Texas at El Paso, El Paso, Tex. 79968, U.S.A.

COLTMAN, Will. See **BINGLEY**, David Ernest.

COLTON, Clarence Eugene. American, b. 1914. Theology/Religion. Pastor, Royal Haven Baptist Church, Dallas, Tex., 1939–87, now Pastor Emeritus. Former Head of Bible Dept., Wayland Baptist Coll., Plainview, Tex. *Publs:* The Minister's Mission, 1951; Expository Studies of the Life of Christ, 1957; The Sermon on the Mount, 1960; Questions Christians Ask, 1969; As the Pendulum Swings, 1970; Meditations on the 23rd Psalm, 1978; Revelation: Book of Mystery and Hope, 1979; The Faithfulness of Christ, 1985; How to Be a Good Christian, 1986. Add: 8302 Midway Rd., Dallas, Tex. 75209, U.S.A.

COLTON, James. See **HANSEN**, Joseph.

COLTON, Joel. American, b. 1918. History. Prof. Emeritus, Dept. of History, Duke Univ., Durham, N.C., since 1989 (Chmn. of Dept., 1967–74, Prof., 1947–89). Member, Intnl. Commn. on the History of Social Movement and Social Structures, since 1975 (co-pres., since 1985). Member, Bd. of Eds., Third Republic/Troisième République, since 1975; Member, Advisory Bd., Historical Abstracts, since 1982. Director for Humanities, The Rockefeller Foundation, 1974–81. Member, Bd. of Eds., Journal of Modern History, 1968–71. Member, Bd. of Eds., French Historical Studies, 1985–88. *Publs:* Compulsory Labor Arbitration in France 1936–1939, 1951; (with R.R. Palmer) A History of the Modern World, 1958, 6th ed., 1984; A Study Guide for a History of the Modern World, 1958, 6th ed., 1984; Léon Blum: Humanist in Politics, 1966, 1987; Twentieth Century, 1968, 1980; (ed.) The Contemporary Humanities in International Context, 1976; The Search for a Value Consensus, 1978; The Restoration of the Liberal Arts Curriculum, 1979; (ed. with Stuart Bruchey) Technology, the Economy, and Society: The American Experience, 1986; (with others) The Academic's Handbook, 1988; The French and Spanish Popular Fronts: Comparative Fronts, 1989. Add: 6 Stoneridge Circle, Durham, N.C. 27705, U.S.A.

COLVIN, H(oward) M(ontagu). British, b. 1919. Architecture. Fellow, St. John's Coll., Oxford, since 1948 (Reader in Architectural History, Oxford Univ., 1965–87). Member, Royal Commn. on Ancient and Historical Monuments of Scotland, since 1977. Asst. Lectr., University Coll., London, 1946–48. Member, Royal Fine Art Commn., 1962–72, Royal Commn. on Historical Monuments, England, 1963–76, Historic Bldgs. Council for England, 1970–84, Royal Commn. on Historical Manuscripts, and Historic Bldgs. and Monuments Commn., 1984–86; Pres., Soc. of Architectural Historians of Great Britain, 1979–81. *Publs:* The White Canons in England, 1951; A Biographical Dictionary of English Architects 1660-1840, 1954; (ed.) The History of the King's Works, 6 vols., 1963-82; A History of Deddington, 1963; Catalogue of Architectural Drawings in Worcester College Library, 1964; (with M. Craig) Architectural Drawings in the Library of Elton Hall, 1964; (co-ed.) The Country Seat, 1970; Building Accounts of King Henry III, 1971; A Biographical Dictionary of British Architects 1600-1840, 1978; (co-ed.) Of Architecture, by Roger North, 1981; Unbuilt Oxford, 1983; Calke Abbey, Derbyshire, 1985; The Canterbury Quadrangle, St. John's College, Oxford, 1988; (with J.S.G. Simmons) All Souls: An Oxford College and Its Buildings, 1989. Add: 50 Plantation Rd., Oxford, England.

COMAY, Joan. Israeli. Theology/Religion. *Publs:* Everyone's Guide to Israel, 1963; United Nations in Action, 1965; Ben Gurion and the Birth of Israel, 1967; Who's Who in the Old Testament, 1971; Who's Who in Jewish History, 1974; The Temple of Jerusalem, 1975; The Hebrew Kings, 1977; The Jerusalem I Love, 1977; The World's Greatest Story, 1978; The Diaspora Story, 1981. Add: Nateev-Printing and Publishing Enterprises Ltd., 66 Bnei Dan St. POB 6048, Tel-Aviv, Israel.

COMBE, Gordon Desmond. Australian, b. 1917. Military/Defence, Politics/Government. Writer, Parliament of South Australia Annual, Govt. Printer, since 1962. Officer of Parliament of S.A., 1940–72 (Clerk, House of Assembly, 1953–72). Ombudsman for South Australia, 1972–80. *Publs:* Responsible Government in South Australia, 1957; (with

F.A.Ligertwood and T.J. Gilchrist) The 2/43rd Battalion, 1972.   Add: 98 Penang Ave., Edwardstown, S.A., Australia 5039.

COMFORT, Alex(ander).   British, b. 1920.   Novels/Short stories, Plays/Screenplays, Poetry, Humanities (general), Literature, Medicine/Health, Psychiatry, Sex, Sociology, Essays, Translations. Adjunct Prof., Neuropsychiatric Inst., Univ. of California at Los Angeles, since 1979.   House Physician, London Hosp., 1944; Resident Medical Officer, Royal Waterloo Hosp., 1944–45; Lectr. in Physiology, 1945–51, Hon. Research Assoc., Dept. of Zoology, 1951–73, Dir., Medical Research Council Group on the Biology of Ageing, 1966–70, and Dir. of Research in Gerontology, 1970–73, University Coll., London; Lectr. in Psychiatry, Stanford Univ., California, 1974–83; Prof. of Pathology, Univ. of California Sch. of Medicine, Irvine, 1976–78. *Publs:* The Silver River: Being the Diary of a Schoolboy in the South Atlantic (novel), 1936; No Such Liberty (novel), 1941; France and Other Poems, 1941; The Almond Tree: A Legend (novel), 1942; Into Egypt: A Miracle Play, 1942; (with R. McFadden and I. Serraillier) Three New Poets, 1942; A Wreath for the Living (poetry), 1942; (ed. with Robert Greacen) Lyra: An Anthology of New Lyric, 1942; Cities of the Plain: A Democratic Melodrama, 1943; (ed. with John Bayliss) New Road 1943 (and 1944): New Directions in European Art and Letters, 1943, 1944; The Power House (novel), 1944; Elegies, 1944; The Song of Lazarius (poetry), 1945; The Signal to Engage (poetry), 1946; (trans. with Allan R. Macdougall) The Triumph of Death, by C.F. Ramuz, 1946; Peace and Disobedience, 1946; Letters from an Outpost (short stories), 1947; Art and Social Responsibility: Lectures on the Ideology of Romanticism, 1947; The Novel and Our Time, 1948; Barbarism and Sexual Freedom: Six Lectures on the Sociology of Sex from the Standpoint of Anarchism, 1948; First Year Physiological Techniques, 1948; The Pattern of the Future, 1949; On This Side of Nothing (novel), 1949; The Right Thing to Do, Together with the Wrong Thing to Do, 1949; Authority and Delinquency in the Modern State: Criminological Approach to the Problem of Power, 1950; Sexual Behaviour in Society, 1950, as Sex in Society, 1963; And All But He Departed (poetry), 1951; Delinquency (lecture), 1951; Social Responsibility in Science and Art, 1952; A Giant's Strength (novel), 1952; The Biology of Senescence, 1953, as Ageing: The Biology of Senescence, 1964, 1979; Darwin and the Naked Lady: Discursive Essays on Biology and Art, 1961; Come Out to Play (novel), 1964; (trans.) The Koko Shastra, 1964; The Nature of Human Nature, 1965, in U.K. as Nature and Human Nature, 1966; The Anxiety Makers: Some Curious Preoccupations of the Medical Profession, 1967; (ed.) History of Erotic Art, vol. I, 1969; What Rough Beast? and What Is a Doctor? (lectures), 1971; Poems for Jane, 1975; The Joy of Sex: A Gourmet's Guide to Love Making, 1973; More Joy: A Sequel to "The Joy of Sex", 1974; A Good Age, 1976; (ed.) Sexual Consequences of Disability, 1978; Tetrarch (novel trilogy: Fearful Symmetry, A Grain of Sand, and Beyond the Night of Beulah), 1978; Poems for Jane, 1978; I and That, 1979; A Practise of Geriatric Psychiatry, 1979; (with Jane Comfort) The Facts of Love: Living, Loving, and Growing Up (juvenile), 1979; Reality and Empathy, 1984; Imperial Patient (novel), 1987; The Philosophers (novel), 1989.   Add: The Windmill House, The Hill, Cranbrook, Kent TN17 3AH, England.

COMFORT, Iris Tracy.   American, b. 1917.   Novels/Short stories, Children's fiction, Children's non-fiction, Earth sciences. *Publs:* Earth Treasure: Rocks and Minerals, 1964; Let's Read About Rocks, 1969; Let's Grow Things, 1968; Joey Tigertail, 1973; Echoes of Evil, 1977; Shadow Masque, 1980.   Add: 2902 Oxford St., Orlando, Fla. 32803, U.S.A.

COMINI, Alessandra.   American, b. 1934.   Art, History, Biography. Distinguished Prof. of Art History, Southern Methodist Univ., Dallas, Tex., since 1974.   Asst. Prof., Columbia Univ., NYC, 1969–74. *Publs:* Schiele in Prison, 1962; Egon Schiele's Portraits, 1965; Gustav Klimt, 1975; Egon Schiele, 1974; The Fantastic Art of Vienna, 1978; The Changing Image of Beethoven, 1987.   Add: Dept. of Art History, Southern Methodist Univ., Dallas, Tex. 75275, U.S.A.

COMMAGER, Henry Steele.   American, b. 1902.   History. Simpson Lectr., Amherst Coll., Massachusetts, from 1972 (former Prof. of History from 1956).   Vice-Pres., Cttee. on Effective Congress; Trustee, Friends of Cambridge Univ.   Prof. of History, Columbia Univ., NYC, 1938–56.   Ed., Churchill's History of the English Speaking Peoples, and The Rise of the American Nation, 50 vols. *Publs:* (with Samuel Eliot Morison) The Growth of the American Republic, 2 vols., 1940; Theodore Parker: Yankee Crusader, 1936; (with A. Nevins) The Heritage of America, 1939; (with A. Nevins) America: The Story of a Free People, 1943, 1966; Majority Rule and Minority Rights, 1944; The Story of the Second World War, 1945; The Blue and the Gray, 1950; The American Mind, 1950; Living Ideas in America, 1951; Robert E. Lee, 1951; Freedom, Loyalty,

Dissent, 1954; Joseph Story, 1956; (with G. Brunn) America since 1942, 1954; (with R.B. Morris) The Spirit of Seventy Six, 1958, rev. ed. 1975; Great Declaration, 1958; Great Proclamation, 1960; Crusaders for Freedom, 1962; History: Nature and Purpose, 1965; Freedom and Order, 1966; Search for a Usable Past, 1967; Was America a Mistake?, 1968; The Commonwealth of Learning, 1968; The American Character, 1970; The Discipline of History, 1972; Jefferson, Nationalism and Enlightenment, 1975; American Liberty, 1976; The Defeat of America, 1976; The Empire of Reason, 1977; ed.—The Documents of American History, 1934, 10th ed. 1988; Tocqueville: Democracy in America, 1946; The St. Nicholas Anthology, 1947; America in Perspective, 1947; The Second St. Nicholas Anthology, 1948; Living Ideas in America, 1951, 1964; Atlas of American Civil War, 1959; Immigration in American History, 1961; Why the Confederacy Lost the Civil War; Britain Through American Eyes, 1974.   Add: 405 South Pleasant St., Amherst, Mass. 01002, U.S.A.

COMMONER, Barry.   American, b. 1917.   Environmental science/Ecology, Sciences, Social commentary/phenomena.   Prof. of Earth and Environmental Sciences, and Dir., Center for the Biology of Natural Systems, Queens Coll., Flushing, N.Y., since 1981.   Asst. in Biology, Harvard Univ., Cambridge, Mass., 1938–40; Instr., Queens Coll., NYC, 1940–42; Lt., U.S. Naval Reserve, 1942–46; Assoc. Ed., Science Illustrated, 1946–47.   With Washington Univ., St. Louis: Assoc. Prof. of Plant Physiology, 1947–53; Prof., 1953–81; Dir., Center for the Biology of Natural Systems, 1965–81; Chmn., Dept. of Botany, 1965–69. Visiting Prof. of Community Health, Albert Einstein Coll. of Medicine, NYC, 1981–87. *Publs:* Science and Survival, 1966; The Closing Circle, 1971; Ecology and Social Action, 1973; (ed. with Howard Boksenbaum) Energy and Human Welfare: A Critical Analysis, 3 vols., 1975; The Poverty of Power, 1976; The Politics of Energy, 1979.   Add: CBNS, Queens Coll., Flushing, N.Y. 11367, U.S.A.

COMPTIN, Piers.   British, b. 1903.   Poetry, History, Military/Defence, Theology/Religion, Biography. *Publs:* Twenty Poems, 1927; The Great Religious Orders, 1931; The Genius of Louis Pasteur, 1932, abridged ed. 1939; Sands of Thought, 1932; Father Damien, 1933; Bad Queen Bess, 1933; Camille Desmoulins: A Revolutionary Study, 1933; Marat, 1935; Marshall Ney, 1937; The Turbulent Priest: A Life of St. Thomas of Canterbury, 1957; Harold the King, 1961; (ed.) The University Book 1965, 1964; Colonel's Lady and Camp-Follower: The Story of Women in the Crimean War, 1970; Cardigan of Balaclava, 1972; The Story of Bisham Abbey, 1973; The Last Days of General Gordon, 1974; Victorian Vortex: Pleasure and Peccadilloes of an Age, 1977; The Broken Cross, 1983.   Add: Merlindale, Beamont Rise, Marlow, Bucks., England.

COMPTON, D(avid) G(uy).   Also writes mystery novels as Guy Compton, and romance novels as Frances Lynch.   British, b. 1930. Mystery/Crime/Suspense, Historical/Romance/Gothic, Science fiction/Fantasy. Worked as stage electrician, furniture maker, salesman, docker, and postman; Ed., Reader's Digest Condensed Books, London, 1969–81. *Publs:* (as Guy Compton) Too Many Murders, 1962; (as Guy Compton) Medium for Murder, 1963; (as Guy Compton) Dead on Cue, 1964; (as Guy Compton) Disguise for a Dead Gentleman, 1964; (as Guy Compton) High Tide for a Hanging, 1965; The Quality of Mercy, 1965, 1970; Farewell, Earth's Bliss, 1966; The Silent Multitude, 1966; (as Guy Compton) And Murder Came Too, 1966; Synthajoy, 1968; The Palace, 1969; The Electric Crocodile (in U.S. as The Steel Crocodile), 1970; Chronocules, 1970, in U.K. as Hot Wireless Sets, Aspirin Tablets, The Sandpaper Sides of Used Matchboxes, and Something That Might Have Been Castor Oil, 1971; The Missionaries, 1972; The Unsleeping Eye, 1973, in U.K. as The Continuous Katherine Mortenhoe, 1974; (as Frances Lynch) Twice Ten Thousand Miles, 1974, as Candle at Midnight, 1977; (as Frances Lynch) The Fine and Handsome Captain, 1975; (as Frances Lynch) Stranger at the Wedding, 1977; (as Frances Lynch) A Dangerous Magic, 1978; A Usual Lunacy, 1978; Windows, 1979; (as Frances Lynch) In the House of Dark Music, 1979; Ascendancies, 1980; Scudder's Game, 1985.   Add: c/o Virginia Kidd, Box 278, Milford, Pa. 18337, U.S.A.

COMPTON, Denis (Charles Scott).   British, b. 1918.   Cricket.   Cricket Correspondent, Sunday Express, London, since 1951; Commentator, BBC TV, since 1958.   Advertising Co. Exec., since 1958.   Joined Middlesex Cricket Club (MCC), 1936; member of English Test team (68 matches), 1937–47.   Played Association Football with Arsenal (London), and for England, 1943. *Publs:* Testing Time for England, 1948; Playing for England, 1948; End of an Innings, 1958; Denis Compton's Test Diary, 1964; (co-author) Cricket and All That, 1978.   Add: c/o Sunday Express, Fleet St., London EC4P 4TJ, England.

COMPTON, Guy.   *See* **COMPTON,** D.G.

COMPTON, James V(incent). American, b. 1928. History, International relations/Current affairs. Prof. of History, San Francisco State Univ., since 1969. Konrad Adenauer Fellow in History, Univ. of Munich, 1954–55; Lectr. in History and Government, Univ. of Maryland, College Park, 1956–64; Lectr. in History, and Chmn., Prog. of North American Studies, Univ. of Edinburgh, 1964–68. *Publs:* The Swastika and the Eagle: Hitler, the United States, and the Origins of World War II, 1967; (ed.) America and the Origins of the Cold War, 1972; (consulting ed. with Orville Bullitt) For the President: Personal and Secret Correspondence between Ambassador William C. Bullitt and President Franklin D. Roosevelt, 1973; Anticommunism in American Life since World War II, 1973; (ed.) The New Deal, 1974. Add: 170 Diamond St., San Francisco, Calif. 94114, U.S.A.

CONANT, Ralph W. American, b. 1926. Librarianship, Urban studies. Pres., Public Research Inc., since 1981. Dir. and Prof. of Political Science, Inst. for Urban Studies, Univ. of Houston, since 1969. Prof. of Urban Studies, Rice Univ., Houston, since 1969; Adj. Prof., The Baylor Coll. of Med., Houston; Prof., The Univ. of Texas School of Public Health. Asst. to Dir., Joint Center for Urban Studies, Massachusetts Inst. of Technology and Harvard Univ., Cambridge, 1962–66; Assoc. Dir., Lemberg Center for the Study of Violence, Brandeis Univ., Waltham, Mass., 1967–69; Fnding. Pres., The Southwest Center for Urban Research, Houston, 1969–75; Pres., Shimer Coll., Mt. Carroll, Ill., 1975–78; Pres., Unity Coll., Unity, Maine, 1978–80. *Publs:* (ed.) The Public Library and the City, 1965; (ed. with Molly Apple Levin) Problems of Research in Community Violence, 1968; The Prospects for Revolution, 1971; (ed. with Kathleen Molz) The Metropolitan Library, 1972; The Politics of Community Health, 1968; Urban Perspectives: Politics and Policy, 1975; The Conant Report: A Study of the Education of Librarians, 1980; Using Consultants, 1985; Cutting Loose from Employee to Entrepreneur, 1985; Private Means, Public Ends, 1986. Add: R.D.1, Box 2200, North Vassalboro, Me. 04962, U.S.A.

CONDIT, Carl W(ilbur). American, b. 1914. Architecture, Engineering/Technology. Prof. of History, Art History and Urban Affairs, Northwestern Univ., Evanston, Ill, (Instr. to Prof, 1945–46, 1947–82). Instr. in Mathematics and Mechanics, War Production Sch., Cincinnati, Ohio, 1941–42, and Army Specialized Training Prog., Univ. of Cincinnati, 1942–44; Asst. Designing Engineer, Dept. of Bldg., New York Central Railroad, Cincinnati, Ohio, 1944–45; Asst. Prof., Humanities, Carnegie Institute of Technology, 1946–47. *Publs:* The Rise of the Skyscraper, 1952; American Building Art: The 19th Century, 1960; American Building Art: The 20th Century, 1961; The Chicago School of Architecture, 1964; American Building: Materials and Techniques, 1968; Chicago 1910-1929: Building, Planning and Urban Technology, 1973; Chicago 1930-1970: Building, Planning and Urban Technology, 1974; The Railroad and the City: A Technological and Urbanistic History of Cincinnati, 1977; The Pioneers Stage of Railroad Electrification, 1977; The Port of New York: A History of the Rail and Terminal System from the Beginning to Pennsylvania Station, 1980; The Port of New York: A History of the Rail and Terminal System from the Grand Central Electrification to the Present, 1981. Add: 9300 Linder Ave., Morton Grove, Ill. 60053, U.S.A.

CONDON, Richard (Thomas). American, b. 1915. Novels/Short stories, Plays/Screenplays, Travel/Exploration/Adventure. Publicist in the American film industry for 21 years; theatrical producer, NYC, 1951–52. *Publs:* Men of Distinction (play), 1953; The Oldest Confession, 1958; The Manchurian Candidate, 1959; Some Angry Angel: A Mid-Century Faerie Tale, 1960; A Talent for Living: or, the Great Cowboy Race, 1961; An Infinity of Mirrors, 1964; Any God Will Do, 1966; The Ecstasy Business, 1967; The Summer Music (screenplay), 1960; Mile High, 1969; The Long Loud Silence (screenplay), 1970; The Vertical Smile, 1971; Arigato, 1972; And Then We Moved to Rossenarra: or, The Art of Emigrating, 1973; Winter Kills, 1974; The Star Spangled Crunch, 1974; Money Is Love, 1975; The Whisper of the Axe, 1976; The Abandoned Woman, 1977; Bandicoot, 1978; Death of a Politician, 1979; The Entwining, 1981; Prizzi's Honor, 1982; A Trembling Upon Rome, 1983; Prizzi's Family, 1986; Prizzi's Glory, 1988. Add: 3436 Asbury Ave., Dallas, Tex. 75205, U.S.A.

CONDRY, William (Moreton). British, b. 1918. Natural history, Travel/Exploration, Biography. *Publs:* Thoreau, 1954; Snowdonia National Park, 1966; Birds and Wild Africa, 1967; Exploring Wales, 1970; Woodlands, 1974; Pathway to the Wild, 1975; World of a Mountain, 1977; Natural History of Wales, 1981; Snowdonia, 1987. Add: Ynys Edwin, Eglwysfach, Machynlleth, Powys, Wales.

CONE, Carl B. American, b. 1916. History, Politics/Government. Emeritus Prof. of History, Univ. of Kentucky, Lexington, since 1981 (Prof., 1957–81, Asst. Prof., 1947–49; Assoc. Prof., 1949–57). Asst. Prof. of History, Louisiana State Univ., 1943–47. *Publs:* Torchbearer of Freedom, 1952; Burke and the Nature of Politics, vol. I, 1957, vol. II, 1964; The English Jacobins, 1968; Hounds in the Morning, 1981; A Pictorial History of the University of Kentucky, 1989. Add: 203 Sycamore Rd., Lexington, Ky. 40502, U.S.A.

CONE, Molly. Has also written as Caroline More. American, b. 1918. Children's fiction, Children's non-fiction. *Publs:* Only Jane, 1960; Too Many Girls, 1960; The Trouble with Toby, 1961; Mishmash, 1962; Stories of Jewish Symbols, 1963; (as Caroline More with M. Strachan) Batch of Trouble, 1963; Reeney, 1963; Mishmash and the Substitute Teacher, 1963; The Real Dream, 1964; A Promise Is a Promise, 1964; Who Knows Ten, 1965; Mishmash and the Sauerkraut Mystery, 1965; The Jewish Sabbath, 1966; The Jewish New Year, 1966; Crazy Mary, 1966; Hurry Henrietta, 1966; Purim, 1967; The Other Side of the Fence, 1967; The House in the Tree, 1968; The Green Green Sea, 1968; Mishmash and Uncle Looey, 1968; Annie Annie, 1969; Leonard Bernstein, 1970; Simon, 1970; The Ringling Brothers, 1971; You Can't Make Me If I Don't Want To, 1971; Hear O Israel, 4 vols., 1971–72; Number Four, 1972; Dance Around the Fire, 1974; Mishmash and the Venus Flytrap, 1976; Call Me Moose, 1978; The Amazing Memory of Harvey Bean, 1980; Mishmash and the Robot, 1981; Mishmash and the Big Fat Problem, 1982; Paul Silverman Is a Father, 1983; The Big Squeeze, 1984. Add: P.O. Box 1005, Suguamish, Wash. 98392, U.S.A.

CONEY, Michael G(reatrex). British, b. 1932. Science fiction/Fantasy. Mgmt. Specialist, B.C. Forest Service, since 1973. Auditor, Russell and Co., Birmingham, 1949–56; Sr. Clerk, Pearce Clayton Maunder, Dorchester, Dorset, 1958–61; Accountant, Pontins, Bournemouth, 1962; Tenant, Plymouth Breweries, Totnes, Devon, 1963–66; Accountant, Peplow Warren Fuller, Newton Abbot, Devon, 1966–69; Mgr., Jabberwock Hotel, Antigua, W. Indies, 1969–72; *Publs:* Mirror Image, 1972; Syzygy, 1973; Friends Come in Boxes, 1973; The Hero of Downways, 1973; Winter's Children, 1974; Monitor Found in Orbit (short stories), 1974; The Jaws That Bite, The Claws That Catch (in U.K. as The Girl with a Symphony in Her Fingers), 1975; Hello Summer, Goodbye (in U.S. as Rax), 1975; Charisma, 1975; Brontomek!, 1976; The Ultimate Jungle, 1979; Neptune's Cauldron, 1981; Cat Karina, 1982; Forest Ranger, Ahoy!, 1983; The Celestial Steam Locomotive, 1983; Gods of the Greataway, 1984; Fang, the Gnome, 1988. Add: 2082 Neptune Rd., R.R.3, Sidney, B.C. V8L 3X9, Canada.

CONFORD, Ellen. American, b. 1942. Children's fiction. *Publs:* Impossible Possum, 1971; Why Can't I Be William?, 1972; Dreams of Victory, 1973; Felicia the Critic, 1973; The Luck of Pokey Bloom, 1974; Me and the Terrible Two, 1974; Just the Thing for Geraldine, 1975; Dear Lovey Hart, I Am Desperate, 1975; The Alfred G. Graebner Memorial High School Handbook of Rules and Regulations, 1976; And This Is Laura, 1977; Eugene the Brave, 1978; Hail, Hail Camp Timberwood, 1978; Anything for a Friend, 1979; We Interrupt This Semester for an Important Bulletin, 1979; The Revenge of the Incredible Dr. Rancid and His Youthful Assistant Jeffrey, 1980; Seven Days to a Brand-New Me, 1981; To All My Fans with Love from Sylvie, 1982; Lenny Kandell, Smart Aleck, 1983; If This Is Love, I'll Take Spaghetti, 1983; You Never Can Tell, 1984; Strictly for Laughs, 1985; Why Me?, 1985; A Royal Pain, 1986; A Job for Jenny Archer, 1988; A Case for Jenny Archer, 1988; Jenny Archer, Author, 1989; Genie with the Light Blue Hair, 1989. Add: 26 Strathmore Rd., Great Neck, N.Y. 11023, U.S.A.

CONGER, John (Janeway). American, b. 1921. Psychology. Prof. Emeritus of Clinical Psychology, Univ. of Colorado Health Sciences Center, Denver, since 1953 and Acting Chancellor 1984–85 (Assoc. Dean, 1961–63, Vice Pres. for Medical Affairs, and Dean, 1963–70). Pres., American Psychological Assn., 1981. Vice Chmn., National Motor Vehicle Safety Advisory Council, U.S. Dept. of Transport, 1967–70. *Publs:* Child Development and Personality, 1956, 7th ed. 1990; Readings in Child Development, 1964; Personality, Social Class and Delinquency, 1967; Adolescence and Youth: Psychological Development in a Changing World, 1977, 3rd ed. 1984; Basic and Contemporary Issues in Developmental Psychology, 1975; Adolescence: Generation under Pressure, 1979; Essentials of Child Development and Personality, 1980; Readings in Child and Adolescent Development, 1980. Add: Box C-257, Univ. of Colorado Health Sciences Center, 4200 E. 9th Ave., Denver, Colo. 80262, U.S.A.

CONISTON, Ed. *See* **BINGLEY,** David Ernest.

CONKLIN, John E. American, b. 1943. Criminology. Prof. of

Sociology, Tufts Univ., Medford, Mass., since 1970. Research Assoc., Center for Criminal Justice, Harvard Law Sch., Cambridge, Mass., 1969–70. *Publs:* Robbery and the Criminal Justice System, 1972; (ed.) The Crime Establishment: Organized Crime and American Society, 1973; The Impact of Crime, 1975; Illegal But Not Criminal: Business Crime in America, 1977; Criminology, 1981, 3rd ed. 1989; Sociology: An Introduction, 1984, 1987. Add: Dept. of Sociology, Tufts Univ., Medford, Mass. 02155, U.S.A.

CONN, Stewart. British, b. 1936. Plays/Screenplays, Poetry. Sr. Radio Drama Producer, BBC Scotland, since 1962. Literary Adviser, Edinburgh Royal Lyceum Theatre, 1972. *Publs:* Thunder in the Air: Poems, 1967; The Chinese Tower (poetry), 1967; Stoats in the Sunlight: Poems (in U.S. as Ambush and Other Poems), 1968; The Burning (play), 1971; An Ear to the Ground (poetry), 1972; Thistledown (play), 1975; play Donkey (play), 1977; Under the Ice (poetry), 1978; Herman (play), 1981; The Kibble Palace (poetry), 1987; Hugh Miller 1802-1856 (play), 1988; By the Pool (play), 1988. Add: c/o Harvey Unna and Stephen Durbridge Ltd., 24-32 Pottery Lane, London W11 4LZ, England.

CONNELL, Brian Reginald. British, b. 1916. History, Biography, Translations. Reuters Corresp., Indochina, 1939–42; Bureau Head, Daily Mail, Germany, 1946–50; Roving Corresp., News Chronicle, 1950–55; Profile Writer, The Times, London, 1975–81; Principal Commentator, Independent Television News, 1955–86; Prog. Adviser, Anglia Television, Norwich, 1963–86; former Chmn., Radiopolis, and writer, Sunday Telegraph, London. *Publs:* Manifest Destiny: A Study in Five Profiles of the Rise and Influence of the Mountbatten Family: Knight Errant; A Biography of Douglas Fairbanks, Jr.; Watcher on the Rhine: A Present Day Appraisal of Germany; Portrait of a Whig Peer (in U.S. as Portrait of a Golden Age); The Plains of Abraham: The Victory That Lost America (in U.S. as The Savage Years); Return of the Tiger: The Story of Wartime SOE Raids on Singapore; Regina v Palmerston: The Correspondence Between Queen Victoria and Her Minister 1837-1865; (with Putzi Hanfstaengl) Hitler: The Missing Years 1922-34 (in U.S. as Unheard Witness); (with John, Duke of Bedford) A Silver-Plated Spoon; (with Franz Josef Strauss) The Grand Design; (ed. and trans.) Von Papen: Memoirs; (ed. and trans.) Alain Bombard: The Bombard Story; (ed.) Sir William Napier: History of the War in the Peninsula; (ed.) Captain John Knox: Journal of the Campaigns in North America; (with Geoffrey Knight) The Concorde Story; (with Sir Richard Marsh) Off the Rails, 1978; (with G.I. Smith) Ghosts of Kampala; (with D. Fairbanks, Jr.) Autobiography; (with Lord Forte) Autobiography; (with Kurt Waldheim) Memoirs; (with Lord Wilson) Memoirs. Add: B2 Marine Gate, Marine Drive, Brighton, Sussex BN2 5TQ, England.

CONNELL, Evan S(helby), Jr. American, b. 1924. Novels/Short stories. Ed., Contact mag., Sausalito, Calif., 1960–65. *Publs:* The Anatomy Lesson and Other Stories, 1957; Mrs. Bridge, 1959; The Patriot, 1960; (ed.) I Am a Lover, by Jerry Stoll, 1961; Notes from a Bottle Found on the Beach at Carmel, 1963; At the Crossroads: Stories, 1965; The Diary of a Rapist, 1966; Mr. Bridge, 1969; (ed.) Woman by Three, 1969; Points for a Compass Rose, 1973; The Connoisseur, 1974; Double Honeymoon, 1976; A Long Desire, 1979; The White Lantern, 1980; St. Augustine's Pigeon, 1980; Son of the Morning Star: Custer and the Little Bighorn, 1984. Add: 487 Sherwood Dr., Apt. 310, Sausalito, Calif. 94965, U.S.A.

CONNELL, William (Fraser). Australian, b. 1916. Education. Emeritus Prof. of Education, Univ. of Sydney, since 1977 (Sr. Lectr., 1951–54, Reader, 1954–55; Prof., 1955–77); Fellow, Faculty of Education, Monash Univ., since 1978. Member, Australian Unesco Education Cttee. (Chmn., 1963–73). Lectr. in Education, Univ. of Melbourne, 1945–46, 1950. Ed., Australian Journal of Education, 1957–73; Chmn., Australian National Cttee. on Social Science Teaching, 1970–76; Pres., Australian Assn. for Educational Research, 1973. *Publs:* The Educational Thought and Influence of Matthew Arnold, 1950; Growing Up in an Australian City, 1957; The Foundations of Secondary Education, 1961; (ed.) The Foundations of Education, 1963; (co-author) Social Science for Secondary Schools, 1969; (co-author) China at School, 1974; (co-author) Twelve to Twenty: A Study of Teenagers in Sydney, 1975; The Australian Council for Educational Research 1930-1980; A History of Education in the Twentieth Century World, 1980. Add: 34 Tanti Ave., Mornington, Vic., Australia.

CONNER, Patrick (Roy Mountifort). British, b. 1947. Art, Social sciences. Assoc., Martyn Gregory Gall., since 1986. Keeper of Fine Art, The Royal Pavilion, Art Gallery and Museums, Brighton, 1975–86. *Publs:* Savage Ruskin, 1979; Oriental Architecture in the West, 1979;

People at Home, 1982; People at Work, 1982; (ed.) The Inspiration of Egypt, 1983; Michael Angelo Rooker 1746-1801, 1984; The China Trade, 1986; Hilda May Gordon: A Colourist Abroad, 1987. Add: Martyn Gregory Gallery, 34 Bury St., London SW1, England.

CONNER, Rearden. Also writes as Peter Malin. British, b. 1907. Novels/Short stories, Children's fiction. Fiction Critic, Fortnightly Review, 1936–39; Literary Adviser, Cassell & Co. Ltd., London, 1948–56; Higher Scientific Officer, U.K. Ministry of Defence, until 1972. *Publs:* Shake Hands with the Devil, 1933; Rude Earth, 1934; Salute to Aphrodite, 1935; I Am Death, 1936; Time to Kill, 1936; Men Must Live, 1937; The Sword of Love, 1938; Wife of Colum, 1939; (as Peter Malin) to Kill Is My Vocation, 1939; (as Peter Malin) River Sing Me a Song, 1939; The Devil Among the Tailors, 1947; My Love to the Gallows, 1949; Hunger of the Heart, 1950; (as Peter Malin) Kobo The Brave, 1950; The Singing Stone, 1951; The House of Cain, 1952. Add: 79 Balsdean Rd., Woodingdean, Brighton, Sussex, England.

CONNERS, Kenneth Wray. American, b. 1909. Poetry, Theology/Religion. Advertising Copywriter, 1934–42, Head, File Publ. Section, 1942–47, Mgr., Advertising Div., 1947–69, and Dir. of Public Relations, 1969–74, Leeds and Northrup Co., Pennsylvania. Special Lectr., Dept. of Journalism, Univ. of Pennsylvania, Philadelphia, 1954–60. *Publs:* Pro. Con and Coffee (verse), 1942; (with others) The Church Creative, 1967; Stranger in the Pew, 1970; Who's In Charge Here?, 1973; Lord, Have You Got a Minute?, 1979. Add: 1601 Meadowbrook Rd., Meadowbrook, Pa. 19046, U.S.A.

CONNICK, C(harles) Milo. American. Theology/Religion. Prof. of Religion, Whittier Coll., California, 1946–82; Emeritus Prof. of Religion, 1982. Member, Bd. of Trustees, Whittier College, since 1982. Assoc. Minister, St. Paul's Methodist Church, Lowell, Mass., 1940–41, and Copley Methodist Church, Boston, 1941–42; Head, Bible Dept., Northfield Sch., E. Northfield, Mass., 1944–46. *Publs:* Build on the Rock: You and the Sermon on the Mount, 1960; Jesus: The Man, the Mission and the Message, 1963, 1974; The Message and Meaning of the Bible, 1965; The New Testament: An Introduction to Its History, Literature and Thought, 1972, 1978. Add: 6249 Roundhill Dr., Whittier, Calif. 90601, U.S.A.

CONNOLLY, Paul. *See* **WICKER,** Tom.

CONNOLLY, Peter. British, b. 1935. History. Hon. Research Fellow, Inst. of Archaeology, London, since 1986. Member, Soc. for Promotion of Roman Studies, since 1963, and Soc. for Promotion of Hellenic Studies, since 1974; Fellow, Soc. of Antiquaries, London, since 1985. *Publs:* The Roman Army, 1976; The Greek Armies, 1977; Hannibal and the Enemies of Rome, 1978; Pompeii, 1979; Greece and Rome at War, 1980; Living in the Time of Jesus of Nazareth, 1983; The Legend of Odysseus, 1986; Tiberius Claudius Maximus, 2 vols., 1988. Add: 22 Spring St., Spalding, Lincs. PE11 2XW, England.

CONNOLLY, Ray. British. Novels/Short stories, Plays/Screenplays, Biography. Journalist. *Publs:* A Girl Who Came to Stay: That'll Be the Day (screenplay), 1973; Stardust (screenplay), 1974; Trick or Treat?, 1975; James Dean: The First American Teenager (documentary film), 1975; Newsdeath, 1978; A Sunday Kind of Woman, 1980; Honky Tonk Heroes (TV trilogy), 1980; John Lennon 1940-1980, 1981; The Sun Place, 1981; (ed.) Stardust Memories, 1983; Forever Young (screenplay), 1984; Lytton's Diary (TV series), 1985–86; Defrosting the Fridge (screenplay), 1989. Add: 31 Drayton Gardens, London SW10 9RY, England.

CONNOR, Kevin. *See* **O'ROURKE,** Frank.

CONNOR, Tony. (John Anthony Augustus Connor). British, b. 1930. Plays/Screenplays, Poetry, Translations. Prof. of English, Wesleyan Univ., Middletown, Conn., since 1971 (Visiting Poet and Lectr., 1968–69). Textile designer, Manchester, 1944–60; Asst. in Liberal Studies, Bolton Technical Coll., Lancs., 1961–64; Visiting Poet, Amherst Coll., Mass., 1965–68. *Publs:* With Love Somehow: Poems, 1962; Lodgers: Poems, 1965; (with A. Clarke and Charles Tomlinson) Poems: A Selection, 1964; 12 Secret Poems, 1965; Kon in Springtime: Poems, 1968; Billy's Wonderful Kettle (play), 1971; I Am Real and So Are You, A Visit from the Family, and Crewe Station at 2 A.M. (plays), 1971; In the Happy Valley: Poems, 1971; The Last of the Feinsteins (play), 1973; (trans. with G. Gomori) Love of the Scorching Wind, by Laszlo Nagy, 1973; The Memoirs of Uncle Harry (poetry), 1974; Seven Last Poems from the Memoirs of Uncle Harry, 1974; Dr. Crankenheim's Mixed-up Monster (play), 1974; To Friend Who Asked for a Poem, 1975; David's

Violin (play), 1976; Twelve Villanelles, 1977; Explorations (play), 1982; New and Selected Poems, 1982; Spirits of the Place, 1986. Add: 44 Brainerd Ave., Middletown, Conn. 06457, U.S.A.

CONNORS, Bruton. Pseud. for Edward Rohen. British, b. 1931. Novels/Short stories, Poetry. Served in Korea, 1952–54; Ministry of Supply machine gun inspector, 1954–56; Art Teacher, Ladysmith Jr.-Sr. High Sch., Canada, 1956–57; Head of the Art Dept., St. Bonaventure's Sch., 1958–73; Art Teacher, Ilford County High Sch., 1973–82. *Publs:* Nightpriest, 1965; Bruised Concourse, 1973; Old Drunk Eyes Haiku, 1974; Poems/Poemas, 1976. Add: 57 Kinfauns Rd., Goodmayes, Ilford, Essex, IG3 9QH, England.

CONOT, Robert E. American, b. 1929. Novels/Short stories, Civil liberties/Human rights, History, Biography. Senior Lectr., Univ. of So. California School of Journalism, since 1983. Journalist, 1952–58; Television Writer, 1958–60; Special Consultant, National Advisory Commn. on Civil Disorders, 1967–68. *Publs:* Ministers of Vengeance (novel), 1964; Rivers of Blood, Years of Darkness, 1967; Commission on Civil Disorders, 1968; American Odyssey, 1974; Urban Poverty in Historical Perspective: The Case of the United States, 1975; A Streak of Luck: The Life and Legend of Thomas Alva Edison, 1979; Justice at Nuremberg, 1983; The Nuremberg Gift (novel), 1986. Add: c/o Wayne State Univ. Press, Leonard N. Simons Bldg., 5959 Woodward Ave., Detroit, Mich. 48202, U.S.A.

CONQUEST, Ned (Edwin Parker Conquest, Jr.). American, b. 1931. Novels/Short stories, Plays/Screenplays. Assoc., Milbank, Tweed, Hadley & McCloy, law firm, NYC, 1960–64; Asst. Prof. of English Literature, Georgetown Univ., Washington, D.C., 1967–74. *Publs:* The Gun and Glory of Granite Hendley, 1969; Achilles and Company, 1988. Add: 1547 33rd St. N.W., Washington, D.C. 20007, U.S.A.

CONQUEST, (George) Robert (Acworth). British, b. 1917. Science fiction, Poetry, History, International relations/Current affairs, Literature. With U.K. Army, 1939–46; Diplomatic Service, 1946–56; Fellow, London Sch. of Economics, 1956–58; Literary Ed., The Spectator, London, 1962–63; Fellow, Columbia Univ., 1964–65; and Woodrow Wilson Intnl. Center, 1976–77; Sr. Research Fellow, Hoover Instn., Stanford, Calif., 1977–79, and since 1981. *Publs:* A World of Difference (novel), 1955; Poems, 1955; (ed.) New Lines I, 1956; (ed.) Back to Life, 1958; Common Sense About Russia, 1960; (ed. with Kingsley Amis) Spectrum: A Science Fiction Anthology, 5 vols., 1961–65; Courage of Genius: The Pasternak Affair, 1961; Between Mars and Venus (poetry), 1962; Power and Policy in the U.S.S.R., 1962; (ed.) New Lines II, 1963; (with K. Amis) The Egyptologists (novel), 1965; (ed.) Russia after Khrushchev, 1965; The Great Terror, 1968; (ed.) Soviet Studies Series, 7 vols., 1968; Arias from a Love Opera (poetry), 1969; The Nation Killers, 1970; Lenin, 1972; Kolyma, 1978; Forays (poetry), 1979; Present Danger: Towards a Foreign Policy, 1979; The Abomination of Moab, 1979; We and They, 1980; (with Jon Manchip White) What to Do When the Russians Come: A Survivor's Guide, 1984; Inside Stalin's Secret Police: NKVD Politics 1936-39, 1985; (ed.) The Last Empire: Nationality and the Soviet Future, 1986; The Harvest of Sorrow: Soviet Collectivization and the Terror Famine, 1986; New and Collected Poems, 1988; Stalin and the Kirov Murder, 1989. Add: c/o Brown Shipley and Co., Founders Ct., Lothbury, London EC2, England.

CONRAD, Pam. American, b. 1947. Children's fiction, Civil liberties/Human rights, Women. Full-time writer since 1979. *Publs:* I Don't Live Here!, 1983; Holding Me Here, 1986; Balancing Home and Career, 1986; What I Did for Roman, 1987; Seven Silly Circles, 1987; Tub People, 1988; Machan and the Strawberry Day, 1988; Taking the Ferry Home, 1988; Staying Nine, 1988; (with Robert B. Maddux) Guide to Affirmative Action, 1988. Add: c/o Maria Carvainis Agency, 235 West End Avenue, New York, N.Y. 10023, U.S.A.

CONRAN, Anthony. British, b. 1931. Poetry, Literature, Translations. Research Fellow and Tutor, Univ. Coll. of North Wales, since 1957. *Publs:* Formal Poems, 1960; Metamorphoses, 1961; Icons (opus 6), 1963; Asymptotes (opus 7), 1963; A String o Blethers (opus 8), 1963; Sequence of the Blue Flower, 1963; The Mountain, 1963; For the Marriage of Gerard and Linda, 1963; Stelae and Other Poems, 1965; Guernica, 1966; Collected Poems: vol. I (1951-58), 1966, vol. II (1959-61), 1966, vol. III (1962-66), 1967, vol. IV (1967), 1968; (ed. and trans.) The Penguin Book of Welsh Verse, 1967; Claim, Claim, Claim: A Book of Poems, 1969; Spirit Level, 1974; Poems 1951-67, 1974; Life Fund, 1979; On to the Fields of Praise: Essays on the English Poets of Wales, 1979; The Cost of Strangeness: Essays on the English Poets of Wales, 1982; (trans.)

Welsh Verse, 1987; Blodenwedd and Other poems, 1988. Add: 1 Frondirion, Glanrafon, Bangor, Caenarvonshire, Wales.

CONRAN, Shirley (Ida). British, b. 1932. Novels, Design, Women. Founder and Co-Owner, Conran Fabrics Ltd., since 1957; Editorial Adviser, Sidgwick and Jackson Ltd., London. Home Ed., Daily Mail, London, 1962; Women's Ed., 1964, and Columnist and Feature Writer, 1969–70, Observer, London; Women's Ed., Daily Mail, 1968; Design and Promotion Consultant, Westinghouse Kitchens, London, 1969; Columnist, Vanity Fair mag., 1970–71; Life and Styles Ed., Over 21 mag., 1972; Wrote "Survival" series, Daily Mirror, 1974. Handled publicity for Women in Media campaigns, 1972–74. *Publs:* Printed Textile Design for Studio Publication, 1956; Superwoman, 1975; Superwoman Yearbook, 1976; Superwoman 2 (in U.S. as Superwoman in Action), 1977; (with E. Sidney) Futures: How to Survive Life after Thirty, 1979; Lace (novel), 1982; The Magic Garden, 1983; Lace 2, 1985; Savages, 1987. Add: 39 Ave. Princesse Grace, Monte Carlo, Monaco.

CONROW, Robert W. American, b. 1942. Biography, Medicine/Health. Faculty Member, William James Coll., Grand Valley State Colls., Allendale, Mich. *Publs:* Field Days: The Life, Times and Reputation of Eugene Field, 1974; The Great Diamond Hoax and Other True Tales, 1983; (with A. Hecksel) Herbal Pathfinders: A Sourcebook for the Herbal Renaissance, 1983. Add: Dept. of English, William James Coll., Grand Valley State Colls., Allendale, Mich. 49401, U.S.A.

CONROY, (Donald) Pat(rick). American, b. 1945. Novels/Short stories. *Publs:* The Citadel, 1967; The Boo, 1970; The Water Is Wide, 1972; The Great Santini, 1976; The Lords of Discipline, 1980; The Prince of Tides, 1986. Add: c/o Old New York Book Shop, 1069 Juniper St., Atlanta, GA 30309, U.S.A.

CONSTANT, Stephen. Pseud. for Stephen Constantine Daneff. British, b. 1931. Biography. Special Corresp. for the Daily Express, London, 1956–61, and for the Daily Telegraph, London, 1961–73. *Publs:* Foxy Ferdinand, Tsar of Bulgaria, 1979. Add: 5 Ryecroft St., London SW6, England.

CONSTANTELOS, Demetrios J. American, b. 1927. Human relations, Theology/Religion, Humanities. Charles Cooper Townsend Distinguished Prof. of History and Religious Studies, Stockton State Coll., Pomona, N.J., since 1971. Asst. Prof., and Assoc. Prof. of History, Hellenic Coll., Brookline, Mass., 1965–71; Ed., Greek Orthodox Theological Review, Brookline, 1966–71. *Publs:* The Greek Orthodox Church, 1967; Byzantine Philanthropy and Social Welfare, 1968, 2nd ed. 1989; Marriage, Sexuality and Celibacy, 1975; (ed.) Encyclicals and Documents of the Greek Orthodox Archdiocese 1922-1972, 1976; (ed.) Orthodox Theology and Diakonia, 1981; Understanding the Greek Orthodox Church, 1982; Poverty, Society, and Philanthropy in the Late Medieval Greek World, 1989. Add: 304 Forest Dr., Linwood, N.J. 08221, U.S.A.

CONSTANTINE, K.C. (pseudonym). American. Mystery/Crime/Suspense. *Publs:* The Rocksburg Railroad Murders, 1972; The Man Who Liked to Look at Himself, 1973; The Blank Page, 1974; A Fix Like This, 1975; The Man Who Liked Slow Tomatoes, 1982; Always a Body to Trade, 1983; Upon Some Midnights Clear, 1985; Joey's Case, 1988. Add: c/o Bertha Klausner, 71 Park Ave., New York, N.Y. 10016, U.S.A.

CONSTINER, Merle. American Mystery/Crime/Suspense, Westerns/Adventure, Children's fiction. *Publs:* Hearse of a Different Color (mystery), 1952; Last Stand at Anvil Creek, 1957; The Fourth Gunman, 1958; Short-Trigger Man, 1964; Wolf on Horseback, 1965; Guns at Q Cross, 1965; Outrage at Bearskin Forks, 1966; Rain of Fire, 1966; Top Gun from the Dakotas, 1966; Meeting at the Merry Fifer (juvenile), 1966; The Action at Redstone Creek, 1967; Two Pistols South of Deadwood, 1967; Killer's Corral, 1968; The Rebel Courier and the Redcoats (juvenile), 1968; Sumatra Alley (juvenile), 1971; Steel-Jacket, 1972; The Four from Gila Bend, 1974; Killers Corral, 1978. Add: c/o Ace, Berkley Publishing Group, 200 Madison Ave., New York, N.Y. 10016, U.S.A.

CONVERSE, Philip E. American, b. 1928. Politics. With Univ. of Michigan, Ann Arbor: Prof. of Sociology and Political Science, since 1965; Prog. Dir., Survey Research Center, since 1975; Robert C. Angell Distinguished Prof. of Political Science and Sociology, since 1975; Dir., Center for Political Studies, since 1982 (Asst. Prof. of Sociology, 1960–63; Assoc. Prof., 1963–65). Pres., Intnl. Soc. of Political Psychology, 1980–81; Pres., American Political Science Assn., 1983–84. *Publs:* The American Voter, 1960; The Nature of Belief Systems in Mass Publics,

1964; Elections and the Political Order, 1966; The Human Meaning of Social Change, 1972; The Quality of American Life, 1976; Political Representation in France, 1986. Add: Inst. for Social Research, Univ. of Michigan, Ann Arbor, Mich. 48104, U.S.A.

CONWAY, Alan. British, b. 1920. History. Prof. of American History, Univ. of Canterbury, Christchurch, since 1967, now Emeritus. Publs: The Welsh in America, 1961; (co-author) Hanes yr Unol Daleithiau, 1965; The Reconstruction of Georgia, 1966; History of the Negro in the United States, 1968; (co-author) Soldier-Surgeon: The Crimean War Letters of Douglas A. Reid 1855-56, 1968. Add: 11 Clissold St., Christchurch, New Zealand.

CONWAY, Celine. See BLAIR, Kathryn.

CONWAY, David. British, b. 1939. Philosophy, Supernatural/Occult topics. First Secty., H.M. Diplomatic Service, London, 1972–75; Civil Servant, 1975–77; Principal Dir. (Personnel), European Patent Office, Munich. Publs: Diderot and Stoicism, 1963; Magic: An Occult Primer, 1972; The Magic of Herbs, 1973; Ritual Magic, 1978; Secret Wisdom: The Occult Universe Explored, 1985. Add: c/o Aquarian Press Ltd., Denington Estate, Wellingborough, Northants. NN8 2RQ, England.

CONWAY, E. Carolyn. Pseud. for Evelyn Carolyn Conway Kermond. American, b. 1927. Children's fiction. Publs: Little Ways, 1958; More Little Ways, 1960; Little Ways to Heaven, 1983. Add: 7 Sheffield West, Winchester, Mass. 01890, U.S.A.

CONWAY, Freda. British, b. 1911. Mathematics/Statistics. Lectr., Univ. of Leicester, 1948–64; Lectr., 1965–67, and Sr. Lectr. in Social and Economic Statistics, 1967–75, Univ. of Salford. Publs: Descriptive Statistics, 1963; Sampling: An Introduction for Social Scientists, 1967. Add: 27 Cedars Court, Leicester LE2 1ZD, England.

CONWAY, Laura. See ELSNA, Hebe.

CONWAY, Troy. See AVALLONE, Michael.

COOK, (Sir) Alan (Hugh). British, b. 1922. Physics. Jacksonian Prof. of Natural Philosophy, Univ. of Cambridge, since 1972; Master, Selwyn Coll., Cambridge, since 1983. Supt., Div. of Quantum Metrology, National Physical Lab., Teddington, Middx., 1966–69; Prof. of Geophysics, Univ. of Edinburgh, 1969–72. Publs: Gravity and the Earth, 1969; (with R.H. Tucker, H.M. Iyer, and F.D. Stacey) Global Geophysics, 1970; Interference of Electromagnetic Waves, 1971; Physics of the Earth and Planets, 1973; Celestial Masers, 1977; Interiors of the Planets, 1980; The Motion of the Moon, 1988. Add: The Master's Lodge, Selwyn Coll., Cambridge, England.

COOK, Albert. American, b. 1925. Plays, Poetry, Literature. Prof. of Classics, English and Comparative Literature, Brown Univ., Providence, R.I., since 1978. Asst. Prof. of English, Univ. of California at Berkeley, 1953–56; Assoc. Prof. of English and Comparative Literature, Western Reserve Univ., Cleveland, 1957–63, and State Univ. of New York at Buffalo, since 1963–78. Publs: The Dark Voyage and the Golden Mean, 1949; The Meaning of Fiction, 1960; Progressions (poems), 1963; Oedipus Rex: A Mirror for Greek Drama (textbook), 1963; The Classic Line, 1966; Prisms, 1967; The Odyssey, 1967; The Root of the Thing, 1968; The Charges (poems), 1970; The Death of Trotsky (play), 1971; Enactment: Greek Tragedy, 1971; (co-ed.) Plays for the Greek Theater, 1972; The Odyssey: A Critical Edition, 1973; Shakespeare's Enactment, 1975; Myth and Language, 1980; French Tragedy: The Power of Enactment, 1981; Adapt the Living (poems), 1981; Changing the Signs: The Fifteenth Century Breakthrough, 1985; Thresholds: Studies in the Romantic Experience, 1985; Figural Choice in Poetry and Art, 1985; Dimensions of the Sign in Art, 1988; History/Writing, 1988. Add: 92 Elmgrove Rd., Providence, R.I., 02906, U.S.A.

COOK, Chris(topher). British, b. 1945. History, Politics/Government. Head of Dept., Faculty of Humanities, Polytechnic of N. London, since 1980. Lectr. in Politics, Magdalen Coll., Oxford, 1969–70; Sr. Research Officer, London Sch. of Economics, 1970–80. Publs: (ed. with David McKie) The Decade of Disillusion, 1972; (ed. with John Ramsden) By-Elections in British Politics, 1973; (ed.) Pears Cyclopaedia, 1974–; (with John Paxton) European Political Facts 1918-1973, 1975, and 1918-84, 1985; (ed. with Gillian Peele) The Politics of Reappraisal 1918-1973, 1975; (with Brendan Keith) British Historical Facts 1830-1900, 1975; (with Philip Jones) Sources in British Political History, 6 vols., 1975-85; The Age of Alignment: Electoral Politics in Britain 1922-1929, 1975; A

Short History of the Liberal Party 1900-76, 1976, 2nd ed., 1900-88, 1989; (with John Paxton) European Political Facts 1848-1918, 1977; (with Alan Sked) Post-War Britain: A Political History, 1979; (with John Stevenson) The Slump: Society and Politics During the Depression, 1980 (with John Stevenson) Longman Handbook of Modern British History, 1714-1980, 1983, 2nd ed., 1714-1987, 1988; (with Geoff Pugh) Sources in European Political History, vol. I, The European Left, 1987; Dictionary of Historical Terms, 1989; Facts on File World Political Almanac, 1989. Add: Sch. of History, Polytechnic of North London, London NW5, England.

COOK, David. British, b. 1940. Novels/Short stories. Professional actor since 1961. Writer-in-Residence, St. Martin's Coll., Lancaster, 1982–83. Publs: Albert's Memorial, 1972; Happy Endings, 1974; Walter, 1978; Winter Doves, 1979; Sunrising, 1983; Missing Persons, 1986; Crying Out Loud, 1988. Add: 7 Sydney Pl., London SW7 3NL, England.

COOK, Don. American, b. 1920. Politics/Government, Biography. European Diplomatic Corresp., Los Angeles Times, since 1965. With New York Herald Tribune, Washington, London, Bonn, and Paris, 1943–65. Publs: Floodtide in Europe, 1965; The War Lords: Eisenhower, 1976; Ten Men and History, 1981; Charles De Gaulle: A Biography, 1984. Add: 73 Ave. des Champs-Elysees, Paris 75008, France.

COOK, Dorothy Mary. Writes as D.Y. Cameron, D.M. Carlisle, and Elizabeth Clare. British. Historical/Romance/Gothic. Publs: as D.Y. Cameron—Chasing Shadows, 1962; Out of the Storm, 1963; Strange Byways, 1963; The Unreasonable Heart, 1964; The Searching Heart, 1964; The Loving Cup, 1965; Love Unfolding, 1966; A Puzzled Heart, 1967; Conflicting Tides, 1969; Enchanting Adventure, 1969; Moonlight and March Roses, 1970; Night Scented Air, 1974; Scent of Jasmin, 1975; Music in the Wind, 1978; Jenny's Searching Heart, 1979; A Touch of Spring, 1981; as D.M. Carlisle—Althea's Falcon, 1974; The Secret of the Chateau, 1981; Twisting Paths, 1987; Straws in the Wind, 1983; The Harvest Is Sure, 1985; Harvest Issue, 1986; as Elizabeth Clare—A Land of Stars, 1966; Sunlight Through the Mist, 1967; The Enchanted Way, 1968; In Spring Time, 1968; A Song to the Sun, 1969; Royal Occasion, 1970; Magic of Springtime, 1971; Sunlit Waterways, 1972; Glade in the Woods, 1974; Down by the Willows, 1977; The Delightful Valley, 1980; By the Golden Waters, 1981. Add: c/o Hale, 45-47 Clerkenwell Green, London EC1R 0HT, England.

COOK, Glen (Charles). Has also written as Greg Stevens. American, b. 1944. Novels, Science fiction. Has worked at General Motors, St. Louis, since 1965. Publs: novel—(as Greg Stevens) The Swap Academy, 1970; science-fiction novels—The Heirs of Babylon, 1972; A Shadow of All Night Failing, 1979; October's Baby, 1980; All Darkness Met, 1980; The Swordbearer, 1982; Shadowline, 1982; Starfishers, 1982, Stars' End, 1982; The Fire in His Hands, 1984; The Black Company, 1984; Shadows Linger, 1984; Passage of Arms, 1985; A Matter of Time, 1985; With Mercy Toward None, 1985; The White Rose, 1985; Doomstalker, 1986; Warlock, 1986; Ceremony, 1986; Reap the East Wind, 1987; Sweet Silver Blues, 1987; An Ill Fate Marshalling, 1988; Bitter Gold Hearts, 1988; Cold Copper Tears, 1988; The Dragon Never Sleeps, 1988; Shadow Games, 1989; Old Tin Sorrows, 1989; The Silver Spike, 1989; The Tower of Fear, 1989; Dread Brass Shadows, 1990; Dreams of Steel, 1990. Add: 4106 Flora Pl., St. Louis, Mo. 63110, U.S.A.

COOK, Jeffrey. Canadian, b. 1934. Architecture. Regents Prof., School of Architecture, Coll. of Architecture and Environmental Design, Arizona State Univ., Tempe, since 1988 (Instr., 1961–62; Asst. Prof., 1962–66; Assoc. Prof., 1966–72; Prof., 1972–88). Ed.-in-Chief, Passive Solar Journal of American Solar Energy Soc., 1982–85. Founding Pres., Arizona Assn. of Housing Co-ops, 1965–67; Secty.-Treas., Arizona Solar Energy Soc., 1975–80; Regional Rep., American Inst. of Architects Cttee. on Design, 1976–80. Publs: (with Laurence C. Gerckens) Primer in Architectural Drawing and Design, 1963; Architecture Anthology, 1966, 1969 (Selections, 1973); The Architecture of Bruce Goff, 1978; Cool Houses for Desert Suburbs, 1979; Prize Winning Passive Solar House Designs, 1984; Award Winning Passive Solar Designs, 1984; Passive Cooling, 1989. Add: 3627 Camino Sin Nombre, Paradise Valley, Ariz, 85253, U.S.A.

COOK, (John) Lennox. British, b. 1923. Novels/Short stories, Language/Linguistics, Travel/Exploration/Adventure. Sr. Tutor, Bell Sch. of Languages, 1957–62; Dir., Lennox Cook Sch. of English, Cambridge, 1962–85. Publs: Dark to the Sun, 1951; The World Before Us (travel), 1955; The Lucky Man, 1956; No Language but a Cry, 1958; (as John Lennox Cook with A. Gethin and K. Mitchell) A New Way to Proficiency in English, 1967; A Feeling of Disquiet, 1972; The Bridge, 1974; The

Manipulator, 1978; (as John Lennox Cook, with Gethin and B. Unsworth) The Student's Book of English, 1981; Under Etna, 1982. Add: 35A Grange Rd., Cambridge CB3 9AU, England.

COOK, Lyn. *See* **WADDEL,** Evelyn Margaret.

COOK, Mark. British, b. 1942. Human relations, Psychology, Sex. Lectr. in Psychology, University Coll. of Swansea, since 1973. Asst. Lectr. in Psychology, Univ. of Aberdeen, 1968–69; Research Office, Oxford Univ., 1969–73. *Publs:* Interpersonal Perception, 1971; (with M. Argyle) Gaze and Mutual Gaze, 1976; (with R. McHenry) Sexual Attraction, 1978; (ed. with Glenn Wilson) Love and Attraction, 1979; Perceiving Others: The Psychology of Interpersonal Perception, 1979; (ed. with K. Howells) Adult Sexual Interest in Children, 1980; (ed.) The Bases of Human Sexual Attraction, 1981; (ed.) Issues in Person Perception, 1984; Levels of Personality, 1984; Personal Selection and Productivity, 1988. Add: Dept. of Psychology, University Coll. of Swansea, Singleton Park, Swansea SA2 8PP, Wales.

COOK, Melvin A(lonzo). American, b. 1911. Sciences. Chmn. of the Bd. of Dirs., Cook Assocs., Inc., Salt Lake City, since 1973. Research Chemist, Explosives Dept., Eastern Lab., E.I. duPont de Nemours & Co., Gibbstown, N.J., 1937–47; Prof. of Metallurgy, 1947–70, and Dir., Explosives Research Group, 1951–58, and Inst. of Metals and Explosives Research, 1958–65, Univ. of Utah, Salt Lake City; Pres. and Chmn. of the Bd. of Dirs., Intermountain Research and Engineering Co. Inc., 1958–70; Founder, Pres. 1958–72, and Chmn. of the Bd., 1958–74, IRECO Chemicals, Salt Lake City; Pres. and Chmn. of the Bd., Mesabi Blasting Agents, Inc., Biwabik, Minn., 1960–70. *Publs:* The Science of High Explosives, 1958, 1970; Prehistory and Earth Models, 1966; (with M. Garfield Cook) Science and Mormonism, 1967, 3rd ed. 1973; The Science of Industrial Explosives, 1974. Add: Cook Associates Inc., 2026 Beneficial Life Tower, 36 S. State St., Salt Lake City, Utah 84111, U.S.A.

COOK, Michael. Canadian, b. 1933. Plays/Screenplays. Assoc. Prof. of English, Memorial Univ., St. John's, Nfld., since 1978 (Specialist in Drama, 1967–70, and Lectr., 1970–74; Asst. Prof., 1974–78). Film and Drama Critic, Evening Telegram, St. John's, 1967–82; Member, Editorial Bd., Canadian Theatre Review, Downsview, Ont., since 1973. Artistic Dir., Newfoundland Summer Festival of the Arts, 1970–74; Dir., Newfoundland Arts and Culture Centre productions, 1971–74; One-time host of weekly television review "Our Man Friday," CBC, St. John's; originator and writer for TV series "Up at Ours" 1980–82; Gov., Canadian Conference on the Arts, Ottawa, 1975–79; Vice Chmn., Guild of Canadian Playwrights, 1979; Chmn., Playwrights Canada, 1982–83; Founding member, Nfld. Arts Council, 1980–82. *Publs:* The Head Guts and Soundbone Dance, 1974; Jacob's Wake, 1975; Not as a Dream, 1976; Tiln and Other Plays, 1976; Three Plays, 1977; Terese's Creed, 1977; The Gayden Chronicles, 1979; The Island of Fire, 1980; The Terrible Journey of Frederick Dunglass, 1982; The Fisherman's Revenge, 1985. Add: Dept. of English, Memorial Univ., P.O. Box 4200, St. John's, Newfoundland A/C 557, Canada.

COOK, Robin. (Robert William Arthur Cook). Also writes as Derek Raymond. British, b. 1931. Novels/Short stories, Mystery/Crime/Suspense. *Publs:* The Crust on Its Uppers, 1962; Bombe Surprise, 1963; The Legacy of the Stiff Upper Lip, 1966; Private Parts and Public Places, 1967; State of Denmark, 1970; Tenants of Dirt Street, 1971; Le soleil qui s'eteint, 1983; (as Derek Raymond) He Died with His Eyes Open, 1984; (as Derek Raymond) The Devil's Home on Leave, 1985; How the Dead Live, 1986; Nightmare in the Street, 1987. Add: Toby Eady Assocs., 7 Gledhow Gardens, London SW5 0BL, England.

COOK, Stanley. British, b. 1922. Poetry. Asst. Master, Barrow-in-Furness Grammar Sch., 1944–48; Sixth Form English Master, Bury Grammar Sch., 1948–55; Sr. English Master, Firth Park Sch., Sheffield, 1955–68; Lectr. in English, The Polytechnic, Huddersfield, 1969–81. Ed., Poetry Nottingham, 1981–85. *Publs:* Form Photograph, 1971; Signs of Life, 1972; Staff Photograph, 1976; Alphabet, 1976; Seeing Your Meaning: Concrete Poetry in Language and Education, 1976; Come Along: Poems for Younger Children, 1978; Woods Beyond a Cornfield, 1979; Word Houses: Poems for Juniors, 1979; Woods Beyond a Cornfield and Other Poems, 1981; Come Along Again: More Poems for Younger Children, 1982; Selected Poems 1972-86, 1986; Banresdale, 1987; The Squirrel in Town, 1988; The Northern Seasons, 1988. Add: 600 Barnsley Rd., Sheffield S5 6UA, England.

COOK, Warren Lawrence. American, b. 1925. Anthropology/Ethnology, History. Prof. Emeritus of History and Anthropology, Castleton

State Coll., Vt., since 1960. *Publs:* Flood Tide of Empire: Spain and the Pacific Northwest, 1543-1819, 1973; (ed.) Ancient Vermont: Proceedings of the Castleton Conference, 1978. Add: 9 South St., Castleton, Vt. 05735, U.S.A.

COOKE, (Alfred) Alistair. American (born British), b. 1908. Film, International relations/Current affairs, Social commentary/phenomena, Biography, Essays. Special corresp. in America, BBC, London, since 1938 (BBC Film Critic, 1934–37; Writer-Narrator, BBC-TV series "America: A Personal History of the United States," 1972–73); Television Master of Ceremonies, Masterpiece Theatre, Public Broadcasting Service, U.S., since 1971 (with Omnibus Prog., 1952–61, and U.N. TV Prog., Intnl. Zone, 1961–67). Chief U.S. Correspondent, Guardian newspaper, London, 1948–72. *Publs:* (ed.) Garbo and the Night Watchmen, 1937; Douglas Fairbanks: The Making of a Screen Character, 1940; A Generation on Trial: U.S.A. versus Alger Hiss, 1950; One Man's America (in U.K. as Letters from America), 1951; Christmas Eve, 1952; A Commencement Address, 1954; (ed.) The Vintage Mencken, 1955; Around the World in Fifty Years, 1966; Talk About America, 1968; Alistair Cooke's America, 1973; Six Men, 1977; The Americans, 1979; (with Robert Cameron) Above London, 1980; Masterpieces, 1981; The Patient Has the Floor, 1986; The Fulbright Lecture, 1987. Add: Nassau Point, Cutchogue, L.I., N.Y., U.S.A.

COOKE, Bernard. American, b. 1922. Theology/Religion. Prof. of Religious Studies, Univ. of Calgary, since 1976. Prof. of Theology, and Chmn., Dept. of Theology, Marquette Univ., Milwaukee, Wisc., 1957–69; Prof. of Religious Studies, Univ. of Windsor, Ont., 1970–76. *Publs:* Christian Sacraments and Christian Personality, 1965; Formation of Faith, 1965; New Dimensions in Catholic Life, 1967; Beyond Trinity, 1969; God of Space and Time, 1969; Christian Community: Response to Reality, 1970; Theology in an Age of Revolution, 1971; Rethinking the Faith, 1972; Ministry to Word and Sacraments, 1976; Sacraments and Sacramentality, 1983; Reconciled Sinners: Healing Human Brokenness, 1986. Add: Dept. of Religious Studies, Univ. of Calgary, Calgary, Alta. T2K 1N4, Canada.

COOKE, Jacob Ernest. American, b. 1924. History, Biography. John H. MacCracken Prof. of History, Lafayette Coll., Easton, Pa., since 1963. Ed., A History of the American Colonies, 13 vols., Charles Scribner's Sons Inc., publrs., since 1974. Asst. Prof., Columbia Univ., NYC, 1956–62; Prof. and Head of History Dept., Carnegie-Mellon Univ., Pittsburgh, 1962–63. *Publs:* Frederick Bancroft: Historian, 1956; (ed.) The Federalist, 1962; (assoc. ed.) The Papers of Alexander Hamilton, vols. I-XV, 1963–71; (ed.) Reports of Alexander Hamilton, 1965; (ed.) Alexander Hamilton, 1965; (ed.) The Challenge of History, 1965; A History of the U.S. 1946-1960, 1965; Tench Coxe and the Early American Republic, 1977; Alexander Hamilton, 1982. Add: Dept. of History, Lafayette Coll., Easton, Pa. 18042, U.S.A.

COOKE, William. British, b. 1942. Poetry, Literature, Biography. Lectr., Cauldon Coll. of Further Education, since 1979. Member of faculty, Thistley Hough Sch., 1968–70, and City of Stoke-on-Trent Sixth Form Coll., 1970–79. *Publs:* Edward Thomas: A Critical Biography, 1970; Edward Thomas: A Portrait, 1978; (ed.) Anvil, 1979; Builder (poetry), 1980; Small Ads (poetry), 1980; (ed.) Howlers, 1988. Add: 17 Stuart Ave., Trentham, Stoke-on-Trent ST4 8BG, England.

COOKSON, Catherine (Ann McMullen). Also writes as Catherine Marchant. British, b. 1906. Historical/Romance/Gothic, Children's fiction, Autobiography/Memoirs/Personal. *Publs:* Kate Hannigan, 1950; The Fifteen Streets, 1952; Colour Blind, 1953; A Grand Man, 1954; Maggie Rowan, 1954; The Lord and Mary Ann, 1956; Rooney, 1957; The Devil and Mary Ann, 1958; The Menagerie, 1958; Slinky Jane, 1959; Fanny McBride, 1959; Fenwick Houses, 1960; Love and Mary Ann, 1961; The Garment, 1962; Life and Mary Ann, 1962; (as Catherine Marchant) Heritage of Folly, 1962; The Blind Miller, 1963; (as Catherine Marchant) The Fen Tiger, 1963, in U.S. as the House on the Fens, 1965; (as Catherine Marchant) House of Men, 1963; Marriage and Mary Ann, 1964; Hannah Massey, 1964; Mary Ann's Angels, 1965; The Long Corridor, 1965; (as Catherine Marchant) The Mists of Memory, 1965; Matty Doolin (juvenile), 1965; The Unbaited Trap, 1966; (as Catherine Marchant) Evil at Roger's Cross, 1966; in U.K. as The Iron Façade, 1976; Mary Ann and Bill, 1967; Katie Mulholland, 1967; The Round Tower, 1968; Joe and the Gladiator (juvenile), 1968; The Glass Virgin, 1969; The Nice Bloke, 1969, in U.S. as The Husband, 1976; Our Kate: An Autobiography, 1969, 1982; The Invitation, 1970; The Nipper (juvenile), 1970; The Dwelling Place, 1971; Feathers in the Fire, 1971; Pure as the Lily, 1972; Blue Baccy (juvenile), 1972; The Mallen Girl, 1973; The Mallen Streak,

1973; The Mallen Lot (in U.K. as The Mallen Litter), 1974 (trilogy), in vol. as The Mallen Novels, 1979; Our John Willy (juvenile), 1974; The Invisible Cord, 1975; The Gambling Man, 1975; (as Catherine Marchant) Miss Martha Mary Crawford, 1975; The Tide of Life, 1976; (as Catherine Marchant) The Slow Awakening, 1976; Mrs. Flannagan's Trumpet (juvenile), 1976; Go Tell It to Mrs. Golightly (juvenile), 1977; The Girl, 1977; The Cinder Path, 1978; The Man Who Cried, 1979; Tilly Trotter, (in U.S. as Tilly), 1980; Tilly Trotter Wed (in U.S. as Tilly Wed), 1981; Lanky Jones (juvenile), 1981; Tilly Trotter Widowed (in U.S. as Tilly Alone), 1982; The Whip, 1982; Nancy Nutall and the Mongrel (juvenile), 1982; Hamilton, 1983; The Black Velvet Crown, 1984; Goodbye Hamilton, 1984; A Dinner of Herbs, 1985; Harold, 1985; The Moth, 1985; Bill Bailey, 1985; Catherine Cookson Country, 1986; The Parson's Daughter, 1987; Bill Bailey's Lot, 1987; Bill Bailey's Daughter, 1988; The Cultured Handmaiden, 1988; Let Me Make Myself Plain, 1988. Add: Bristol Lodge, Langley on Tyne, Hexham, Northumberland NE47 5LA, England.

COOLE, W.W. *See* **KULSKI,** Wladyslaw Wszebor.

COOLEY, John Kent. American, b. 1927. History, International relations/Current affairs. Middle East Corresp., The Christian Science Monitor, since 1965 (freelance contrib., 1955–64); Radio News Corresp., Beirut, for ABC News, since 1967. With U.S. Embassy and Defence Dept., Vienna, 1950–53; Editorial Writer, New York Herald Tribune, NYC, 1954; Public Information Officer, U.S. Army Corps of Engineers, Morocco, 1955–58; Contrib., Observer Foreign News Service, London, 1958–64; with United Press Intnl., 1958–60. *Publs:* Baal, Christ and Mohammed: Religion and Revolution in North Africa, 1965; East Wind Over Africa: Red China's African Offensive, 1966; (with others) The Middle East: Its Governments and Politics, 1972; Green March, Black September: The Story of the Palestinian Arabs, 1973; Libyan Sandstorm: The Complete Account of Quddafi's Revolution, 1982. Add: c/o Christian Science Monitor, 1 Norway St., Boston, Mass. 02115, U.S.A.

COOLIDGE, Clark. American, b. 1939. Plays/Screenplays, Poetry. Ed., Joglars Mag., Providence, R.I., 1964–66. *Publs:* Flag Flutter and U.S. Electric, 1966; (Poems), 1967; Ing, 1969; Space, 1970; (with T. Veitch) To Obtain the Value of the Cake Measure from Zero (play), 1970; The So, 1971; Moroccan Variations, 1971; Clark Coolidge Issue of Big Sky 3, 1972; Suite V, 1973; The Maintains, 1974; Polaroid, 1975; Quartz Hearts, 1978; Own Face, 1978; (with others) Smithsonian Depositions and Subject to a Film, 1980; American Ones, 1981; Research, 1982. Add: c/o Tombouctou Books, P.O. Box 265, Bolinas, Calif. 94924, U.S.A.

COOLIDGE, Olivia. American, b. 1908. Children's fiction, History, Biography. English Teacher, Potsdam-Hermannswerder, Germany, 1931–32; Classics Teacher, Wimbledon High Sch., London, 1932–37; Secty., Education Service, Bureau of Camps, NYC, 1938; English Teacher, Low- Heywood Sch., Stamford, Conn., 1939, and Winsor Sch., Boston, 1940–46. Member, Bd. of Trustees, Mills Coll. of Education, 1956–61. *Publs:* Greek Myths, 1949; Legends of the North, 1951; The Trojan War, 1952; Egyptian Adentures, 1954; Cromwell's Head, 1955; Roman People, 1959; Winston Churchill and the Story of Two World Wars, 1960; Caesar's Gallic War, 1961; Men of Athens, 1962; Makers of the Red Revolution, 1963; Edith Wharton, 1964; Lives of the Famous Romans, 1965; People in Palestine, 1965; The King of Men, 1966; Women's Rights, 1966; Eugene O'Neill, 1966; Marathon Looks on the Sea, 1967; George Bernard Shaw, 1968; The Golden Days of Greece, 1968; Tom Paine, Revolutionary, 1969; The Maid of Artemis, 1969; Tales of the Crusades, 1970; Come by Here, 1970; Gandhi, 1971; The Three Lives of Joseph Conrad, 1972; The Apprenticeship of Abraham Lincoln, 1974; The Statesmanship of Abraham Lincoln, 1977. Add: Essex Meadows, Apt. 351, Essex, Conn. 66426, U.S.A.

COOMBS, Patricia. American. Children's fiction. *Publs:* Dorrie series, 20 vols., 1962–83; Waddy and his Brother, 1963; The Lost Playground, 1963; Lisa and the Grompet, 1970; Mouse Café, 1972; Molly Mullett, 1975; The Magic Pot, 1977; Tilabel, 1978; The Magician and McTree, 1983; Dorrie and the Museum Case, 1986. Add: 178 Oswegatchie Rd., Waterford, Conn. 06385, U.S.A.

COOMBS, Philip (Hall). American, b. 1915. Education. Vice Chmn., Intnl. Council for Educational Development, since 1970. Instr., Williams Coll., Williamstown, Mass., 1939, 1940–41; Economist, U.S. Office of Price Admin., 1941–43; Economic Adviser, Office of Economic Stabilization, Washington, 1945–46; Prof. of Economics, Amherst Coll., Mass., 1947–49; Economic Adviser to Gov. Bowles of Connecticut, 1949–50; Exec. Dir., President's Materials Policy Commn., 1950–52; Dir. of Research, Fund for the Advancement of Education, and Program Dir. for

Education, the Ford Foundn., 1952–60; Asst. Secty. of State for Intnl. Educational and Cultural Affairs, Dept. of State, Washington, 1961–62; Fellow of the Council on Foreign Relations, and the Brookings Instn., Washington, 1963; Dir., Intnl. Inst. for Educational Planning, Paris, 1963–68; Dir. of Research for IIEP, based in the U.S., 1969; Co-Founder, Center for Educational Enquiry, Consultant to the World Bank, IIEP, and Unesco, and Visiting Lectr. at Harvard Univ., Cambridge, Mass., Princeton Univ., N.J., and the Intnl. Development Inst. of the World Bank, Washington, 1969–70; Visiting Prof., Inst. of Social Science, Yale Univ., New Haven, Conn., 1970–72. *Publs:* The Fourth Dimension of Foreign Policy, 1964; Education and Foreign Aid, 1965; The New Media: Memo to Educational Planners, 1967; The World Educational Crisis: A Systems Analysis, 1968; (with C. Beeby) The Qualitative Aspects of Educational Planning, 1969; (with others) International Development Targets, 1970; What is Educational Planning, 1970; Educational Cost Analysis, 1971; Managing Educational Costs, 1972; New Paths to Learning for Rural Children and Youth, 1973; Attacking Rural Poverty: How Nonformal Education Can Help, 1974; Education for Rural Development: Case Studies for Planners, 1975; (ed.) Meeting the Basic Needs of the Rural Poor, 1980; The World Crisis in Education: The View from the Eighties, 1985; Cost Analysis in Education: A Tool For Policy and Planning, 1987. Add: 127 River Rd., Essex, Conn. 06426, U.S.A.

COOMER, Joe. American, b. 1958. Novels/Short stories. Full-time Writer. *Publs:* The Decatur Road, 1983; Kentucky Love, 1985; A Flatland Fable, 1986. Add: 101 Ash Creek Dr. W., Azle, Tex. 76020, U.S.A.

COONEY, Ray(mond George Alfred). British, b. 1932. Plays. Actor, since 1946; theatre dir. and producer, since 1965; dir., Ray Cooney Productions Ltd., since 1966; founding artistic dir., Theatre of Comedy, since 1983. *Publs:* (often in collaboration): One for the Pot, 1963; Chase Me, Comrade, 1966; My Giddy Aunt, 1970; Bang Bang Beirut, or Stand by Your Bedouin, 1971; Not Now, Darling, 1971; Charlie Girl, 1972; Move Over, Mrs. Markham, 1972; Why Not Stay for Breakfast?, 1974; There Goes the Bride, 1975; Run for Your Wife, 1984; Two into One, 1985; Wife Begins at Forty, 1986; It Runs in the Family, 1987. Add: 1/3 Spring Gdns., London SW1A 2BD, England.

COOPER, Brian (Newman). British, b. 1919. Mystery/Crime/Suspense, History. Sr. History Master, Moorfield Sch., Bolsover, Derbyshire, 1955–79. *Publs:* fiction—Where the Fresh Grass Grows (in U.S. as Maria), 1955; A Path to the Bridge (in U.S. as Giselle), 1958; The Van Langeren Girl, 1960; A Touch of Thunder, 1961; A Time to Retreat, 1963; Genesis 38 (in U.S. as The Murder of Mary Steers), 1965; A Mission for Betty Smith (in U.S. as Monsoon Murder), 1967; non-fiction—Transformation of a Valley, 1983. Add: 43 Parkland Close, Southlands, Mansfield, Notts., England.

COOPER, Bryan. Canadian, b. 1932. Novels/Short stories, Economics, History, Military/Defence. Ed. and Publr., Petroleum Economist, London, since 1975. Journalist, 1949–54; Public Relations Exec., British Petroleum Co., London. *Publs:* (with T.F. Gaskell) North Sea Oil—The Great Gamble, 1966; The Ironclads of Cambrai, 1967; Battle of the Torpedo Boats, 1970; The Buccaneers, 1970; PT Boats, 1970; Alaska—The Last Frontier, 1972; Tank Battles of World War I, 1973; Fighter, 1973; Bomber, 1974; Stones of Evil (novel), 1974; The Story of the Bomber 1914–45, 1975; E-Boat Threat, 1976; Wildcatters (novel), 1976; The Adventure of North Sea Oil, 1977. Add: 4 Oldlands Hall, Herons Ghyll, Oakfield, East Sussex, TN22 3DA, England.

COOPER, Christopher (Donald Huntington). Australian, b. 1942. Information science/Computers, Mathematics/Statistics. Sr. Lectr., Macquarie Univ., N.S.W., since 1971 (Lectr., 1969–70). *Publs:* Computer Programming, 1968; Infinite Numbers, 1974; Numbers, Their Personalities and Properties, 1974; Permutations, 1974. Add: 31 Epping Ave., Eastwood, N.S.W. 2122, Australia.

COOPER, Colin Symons. Also writes as Daniel Benson. British, b. 1926. Science fiction/Fantasy, Plays/Screenplays. Ed., Classical Guitar mag. *Publs:* Riches and Rags (play), 1957; The Diamond Tooth (play), 1960; The Thunder and Lightning Man, 1968; Outcrop, 1969; Dargason, 1977; The Epping Pyramid, 1978; (as Daniel Benson) The Argyll Killings, 1980. Add: 25 Warner Rd., London N8 7HB, England.

COOPER, Derek (Macdonald). British, b. 1925. Cookery/Gastronomy/Wine, Transportation. Free-lance writer and presenter for radio and television since 1961. Founder member and first Chmn., Guild of Food Writers. Producer, Radio Malaya and Radio Singapore, 1950–60, and Independent Television News, London, 1960–61. *Publs:* The

Bad Food Guide, 1967; The Beverage Report, 1971; Skye, 1971; The Gullibility Gap, 1974; Hebridean Connection, 1977; A Guide to the Whiskies of Scotland, 1978; Road to the Isles, 1979; (with Dione Pattullo) Enjoying Scotch, 1980; Food with Wine, 1980; (with Fay Godwin) The Whisky Roads of Scotland, 1982; Skye Remembered, 1983; The Century Companion to Whiskies, 1983; The World of Cooking, 1983; The Road to Mingulay, 1985; The Gunge File, 1986; A Taste of Scotch, 1987. Add: 4 St. Helena Terrace, Richmond, Surrey TW9 1NR, England.

COOPER, Dominic (Xavier). British, b. 1944. Novels/Short stories. With Decca Record Co. Ltd., 1967–69, and Fabbri & Partners Ltd., 1969–70; Language Teacher, Reykjavik, Iceland, 1970–72; clockmaker, Edinburgh, 1974–78; photographer, 1979–84. Publs: The Dead of Winter, 1975; Sunrise, 1977; Men at Axlir, 1978; The Horn Fellow, 1987. Add: c/o John Johnson Ltd., 45-47 Clerkenwell Green, London EC1R 0HT, England.

COOPER, Henry. See KAYE, Barrington.

COOPER, Jane (Marvel). American, b. 1924. Poetry. Member, Dept. of Literature and Writing, and Poet-in-Residence, Sarah Lawrence Coll., Bronxville, N.Y., 1950–87. Publs: The Weather of Six Mornings, 1969; Maps & Windows, 1974; Calling Me from Sleep: New and Selected Poems 1961–1973, 1974; Threads: Rosa Luxemburg from Prison, 1979; Scaffolding: New and Selected Poems, 1984. Add: 545 W. 111th St., Apt. 8K, New York, N.Y. 10025, U.S.A.

COOPER, Jeremy. British, b. 1946. Antiques/Furnishings. Art Expert and Auctioneer since 1969; Principal, Jeremy Cooper Ltd., London. Lectr. on Antiques and the London Art Market, Associated Speakers, and Speakers Intnl. Head of Furniture and Works of Art Dept., Sotheby's Belgravia, 1971–75. Publs: (co-author) Antiques: A Popular Guide to Antiques for Everyone, 1973; The Complete Guide to London's Antique Street Markets, 1974; Nineteenth Century Romantic Bronzes, 1975; Under the Hammer, 1975; Dealing with Dealers: Ins and Outs of the London Antiques Trade, 1985; Ruth, 1986; Victorian and Edwardian Furniture and Interiors, 1987. Add: c/o Thames and Hudson Ltd., 30 Bloomsbury St., London WC1B 3QP, England.

COOPER, Jilly (Sallitt). British, b. 1937. Historical/Romance/Gothic, Children's fiction, Human relations, Humour/Satire. Columnist, The Mail on Sunday, since 1985 (The Sunday Times, 1969–85). Reporter, Middlesex Independent newspaper, Brentford, 1957–59; also worked as an account exec., copywriter, publrs. reader, receptionist, and typist. Publs: How to Stay Married, 1969; How to Survive from Nine to Five, 1970; Jolly Super, 1971; Men and Super Men, 1972; Jolly Super Too, 1973; Women and Super Women, 1974; Jolly Superlative, 1975; Emily (romance novel), 1975; Super Men and Super Women (omnibus), 1976; Bella (romance novel), 1976; Harriet (romance novel), 1976; Octavia (romance novel), 1977; Work and Wedlock (omnibus), 1977; Superjilly, 1977; Imogen (romance novel), 1978; Prudence (romance novel), 1978; Class: A View from Middle England, 1979; Supercooper, 1980; Little Mabel series (juvenile), 4 vols., 1980–85; (ed. with Tom Hartman) Violets and Vinegar: An Anthology of Women's Writings and Sayings, 1980; (ed.) The British in Love, 1980; Love and Other Heartaches, 1981; Intelligent and Loyal, 1981; Jolly Marsupial, 1982; Animals in War, 1983; The Common Years, 1984; Leo and Jilly Cooper on Rugby, 1984; Riders, 1985; Hotfoot to Zabriskie Point, 1985; Leo and Jilly Cooper o n Cricket, 1985; Horse Mania, 1986; How to Survive Christmas, 1986; Turn Right at the Spotted Dog, 1987; Rivals, 1988. Add: The Mail on Sunday, Carmelite St., London EC4, England.

COOPER, Lee Pelham. American, b. 1926. Children's fiction, Children's non-fiction. Real estate broker, Cooper-Leedy Realtors,. Teacher of Spanish and English, Falmouth High Sch., Va., 1948–50; Librarian, Maury Elementary Sch., Va., 1952–62. Publs: Fun with Spanish, 1960; (with C.B. McIntosh) Fun with French, 1963; (with Green and Beretta) Fun with Italian, 1964; Fun with German, 1965; More Fun with Spanish, 1967; Five Fables from France, 1970; The Chinese Language for Beginners, 1971; The Pirate of Puerto Rico, 1972. Add: 409 William St., Fredericksburg, Va. 22401, U.S.A.

COOPER, Lettice. British, b. 1897. Novels/Short stories, Children's fiction, Children's non-fiction, Biography. Assoc. Ed., Time and Tide, London, 1939–40; served in Public Relations Div., Ministry of Food, London, 1940–45. Pres., English Centre of Intnl. P.E.N., 1977–79. Publs: The Lighted Room, 1925; The Old Fox, 1927; Good Venture, 1928; Likewise the Lion, 1929; The Ship of Truth, 1930; Private Enterprise, 1931; Hark to Rover, 1933; We Have Come to a Country, 1935; The New

House, 1936; National Provincial, 1938; Black Bethlehem. 1947; Robert Louis Stevenson, 1947; Yorkshire: West Riding, 1950; George Eliot, 1951, rev. ed. 1960, 1964; Fenny, 1953; Great Men of Yorkshire, 1955; Three Lives, 1957; The Young Florence Nightingale, 1960; A Certain Compass, 1960; Blackberry's Kitten, 1961; The Young Victoria, 1961; The Double Heart, 1962; The Bear Who Was Too Big, 1963; Bob-a-Job, 1963; James Watt, 1963; Garibaldi, 1964; The Young Edgar Allan Poe, 1964; Contadino, 1964; The Fugitive King, 1965; The Twig of Cypress, 1965; We Shall Have Snow, 1966; A Hand upon Time: A Life of Charles Dickens, 1968; Gunpowder: Treason and Plot, 1970; Robert Louis Stevenson, 1970: Late in the Afternoon, 1972; Tea on Sunday, 1973; Snow and Roses, 1976; Desirable Residence, 1980; Unusual Behaviour, 1986. Add: 95 Canfield Gardens, London NW6 3DY, England.

COOPER, Richard Newell. American, b. 1934. Economics, International relations/Current affairs. Boas Prof. of Intnl. Economics, Harvard Univ., Cambridge, Mass., since 1981. Asst. Prof., 1963–65, Frank Alstchul Prof. of Economics, 1966–77, and Provost, 1972–74, Yale Univ., New Haven, Conn; U.S. Deputy Asst. Secty. of State, 1965–66, and Under Secty. of State for Economic Affairs, 1977–81. Publs: The Economics of Interdependence, 1968; (with others) Britain's Economic Prospects, 1968; Currency Devaluation in Developing Countries, 1971; (ed. and contrib.) A Reordered World: Emerging International Economic Problems, 1973; (with M. Kaji and C. Segre) Toward a Renovated International Monetary System, 1973; Economic Mobility and National Economic Policy, 1974; (with K. Kaiser and M. Kosaka) Towards a Renovated International System, 1977; (ed. and contrib.) The International Monetary System under Flexible Exchange Rates, 1982; Economic Policy in an Independent World, 1986; The International Monetary System, 1987. Add: Harvard University, Cambridge, Mass. 02138, U.S.A.

COOPER, Susan (Mary). British, b. 1935. Novels/Short stories, Children's fiction, Plays/Screenplays. Staff Writer, Sunday Times, London, 1956–63. Publs: Mandrake, 1964; Behind the Golden Curtain: A View of the U.S.A., 1965; Over Sea, Under Stone, 1966; (ed.) Essays of Five Decades, by J.B. Priestley, 1968; J.B. Priestley: Portrait of an Author, 1970; Dawn of Fear, 1970; The Dark is Rising, 1973; Greenwitch, 1974; The Grey King, 1975; Silver on the Tree, 1977; Jethro and the Jumbie, 1979; The Silver Cow, 1983; Seaward, 1983; (with Hume Cronyn) Foxfire: A Play with Songs, 1983; The Selkie Girl, 1986. Add: c/o Margaret J. McElderry, Atheneum, 866 Third Ave., New York, N.Y. 10022, U.S.A.

COOPER, Wendy. British, b. 1919. Children's fiction, Medicine/Health, Social commentary/phenomena, Women. Freelance writer, broadcaster, and lecturer. Publs: The Laughing Lady, 1958; Alibi Children, 1958; The Cat Strikes, 1959; Hair—in Sex, Society, Symbolism, 1971; No Change: A Biological Revolution for Women (in U.S. as Don't Change), 1975, 5th ed. U.K. 1988; The Fertile Years: New Medical Lifelines for Women, 1978; Human Potential: The Limits and Beyond (in U.S. as Beyond Our Limits), 1981; Everything You Need to Know about the Pill, 1984. Add: 9 Applegrove, Reynoldston, W. Glam. SA3 1BZ, Wales.

COOPER, William. Pseud. for Harry Summerfield Hoff. British, b. 1910. Novels/Short stories, Plays/Screenplays, Criminology/Law enforcement/Prisons, Biography. Adjunct Prof., Syracuse Univ., London Center, since 1978. Asst. Commnr., Civil Service Commn., 1945–58; Personnel Consultant, U.K. Atomic Energy Authority, 1958–72, and Central Electricity Generating Bd., London, 1958–72; Asst. Dir., Civil Service Selection Bd., 1973–75; Member, Bd. of Crown Agents, 1975–77; Personnel Adviser, Millbank Technical Services. 1976–78. Publs: (as H.S. Hoff) Trina (in U.S. as It Happened in PRK), 1934; (as H.S. Hoff) Rhea, 1937; (as H.S. Hoff) Lisa, 1937; (as H.S. Hoff) Three Marriages, 1946; Scenes from Provincial Life, 1950; Strawberry Leaves (play), 1951; The Struggles of Albert Woods, 1952; The Ever-Interesting Topic, 1953; Disquiet and Peace, 1956; Young People, 1958; Prince Genji (play), 1958; C.P. Snow, 1959, 1971; Scenes from Married Life (in U.S. as Scenes from Life), 1961; Memoirs of a New Man, 1966; You Want the Right Frame of Reference, 1971; Shall We Ever Know? The Trial of the Hosein Brothers for the Murder of Mrs McKay, 1971; Love On the Coast, 1973; You're Not Alone, 1976; Scenes from Metropolitan Life, 1982; Scenes from Later Life, 1983. Add: 22 Kenilworth Court, Lower Richmond Rd., London SW15, England.

COOPERMAN, Hasye. American. Poetry, Literature. Teacher, American and Comparative Literature, New Sch. for Social Research, NYC, since 1950 (Head, Dept. of Literature, 1960–67). Editorial Researcher, World Publishing Co., NYC, 1937–43; Member, City Coll.,

NYC, 1939–41. *Publs:* The Chase (poetry), 1932; The Aesthetic of Stéphan Mallarmé 1933, 1971; Men Walk the Earth (poetry), 1953; The Making of a Woman (poetry), 1985. Add: 334 West 85th St., New York, N.Y. 10024, U.S.A.

COOVER, Robert. American, b. 1932. Novels/Short stories, Plays/Screenplays. Writer-in-Residence, Brown Univ., Providence, R.I., since 1979. *Publs:* The Origin of the Brunists, 1966; The Universal Baseball Association, Inc., J. Henry Waugh, Prop., 1968; Pricksongs and Descants (short stories), 1969; The Water Pourer: An Unpublished Chapter from The Origin of the Brunists, 1972; A Theological Position (plays), 1972; The Public Burning, 1977; Hair o' the Chine, 1979; After Lazarus, 1980; Charlie in the House of Rue, 1980; A Political Fable, 1980; Spanking the Maid, 1982; The Convention, 1982; In Bed One Night and Other Brief Encounters, 1982; Gerald's Party, 1986; A Night at the Movies, 1987; Whatever Happened to Gloomy Gus of the Chicago Bears?, 1987. Add: c/o Georges Borchardt, 136 E. 57th St., New York, N.Y. 10022, U.S.A.

COOX, Alvin D. American, b. 1924. History, International relations/Current affairs, Military/Defence, Biography. Prof. of History since 1964, Dir., Japan Studies Institute, since 1985, Dir., Center for Asian Studies since 1966, San Diego State Univ. Member, Exec. Cttee., Asian Studies on the Pacific Coast, since 1973. Lectr. in History, Far East Div., Univ. of California, Berkeley, 1954–56, and Far East Div., Univ. of Maryland, College Park, 1956–64. *Publs:* (trans. and co-author with S. Hayashi) Kogun: The Japanese Army in the Pacific War, 1959; Year of the Tiger, 1964; (ed. with M. Schneps) The Japanese Image (anthology), vol. I, 1965, vol. II, 1966; Japan: The Final Agony, 1970; Tojo (biography), 1974; (with others) Diplomats in Crisis, 1974; (with others) Decisive Battles of the Twentieth Century, 1975; (with others) Southeast Asia and the New Balance of Power, 1975; The Anatomy of a Small War: The Soviet-Japanese Struggle for Changkufeng/Khasan, 1977; (ed. with H. Conroy) China and Japan: Search for Balance since World War I, 1978; Nomonhan: Japan Against Russia 1939, 1985. Add: Dept. of History, San Diego State Univ., San Diego, Calif. 92182, U.S.A.

COPE, Jack. South African, b. 1913. Novels/Short stories, Plays/Screenplays, Poetry, Biography, Literature, Translations. Reporter, Natal Mercury, Durban, 1931–35; Corresp. in London, South African Morning Newspapers, 1936–40; Dir., South African Assn. of the Arts, Cape Town, 1946–48. Founder, 1960, and Ed., 1960–80, Contrast, literary quarterly, Cape Town. *Publs:* Comrade Bill, 1943; Lyrics and Diatribes, 1948; Marie: A Satire (verse), 1949; The Fair House, 1955; The Golden Oriole, 1958; The Road to Ysterberg, 1959; Albino, 1963; The Tame Ox, 1966; The Man Who Doubted, 1967; (ed. with U. Krige) The Penguin Book of South African Verse, 1968; The Dawn Comes Twice, 1969; (ed.) Seismograph: New South African Writing in English and Afrikaans, 1970; The Rain-Maker, 1971; The Student of Zend, 1972; My Son Max, 1977; Nona (play) 1978; Recorded in Sun (verse), 1979; The Adversary Within (criticism), 1982; Selected Stories, 1986; Ingrid Jonker: Selected Poems, 1988. Add: 21 Bearton Rd., Hitchin, Herts. SG5 1UB, England.

COPE, Jackson I. American, b. 1925. Literature. Leo S. Bing Prof. of English, Univ. of Southern California at Los Angeles, 1972–87, now Emeritus. Instr., Ohio State Univ. Columbus, 1952–54; Asst. Prof., Washington Univ., 1954–58; Assoc. Prof. and Prof., Rice Univ., Houston, 1958–61, and Johns Hopkins Univ., Baltimore, 1961–72. *Publs:* Joseph Glanvill: Anglican Apologist, 1956; (ed.) Joseph Glanvill: Plus Ultra, 1958; (ed. with Harold Jones) Thomas Sprat's History of the Royal Society, 1958; The Metaphoric Structure of "Paradise Lost", 1962; The Theater and the Dream: From Metaphor to Form in Renaissance Drama, 1973; Joyce's Cities: Archaeologies of the Soul, 1981; (ed. with Geoffrey Green) Novel vs. Fiction: The Contemporary Reformation, 1981; Dramaturgy of the Daemonic: Studies in Anti-Generic Theater from Ruzante to Grimaldi, 1984; Robert Coover's Fictions, 1986. Add: 8200 Manchester Ave., No. 32, Plaza del Rey, Calif. 90291, U.S.A.

COPELAND, Edwin (Luther). American, b. 1916. Theology/Religion. Visiting Prof. of Religion, Baylor Univ., Waco, Texas, since 1987. Prof. of History of Christianity, 1949–56, Pres., 1952–55, and Chancellor, 1976–80, Seinan Gakuin Univ., Fukuoka, Japan; Prof. of Missions and World Religions, Southeastern Baptist Theological Seminary, Wake Forest, N.C., 1956–76; Sr. Prof. of Missions and World Religions, Southern Baptist Theological Seminary, Louisville, 1981–86. *Publs:* Christianity and World Religions, 1963; (with C. Allen West, Jr. and others) Christ for the World, 1963; Frontiers of Advance, 1964; The Crisis of Protestant Missions to Japan 1889-1900, 1965; (with F.R. Bennett and

others) The Mission of the Suburban Church, 1971; (with C.J. Allen and others) Broadman Bible Commentary, vol. 12, 1972; (Roger S. Greenway and others) Discipling the City, 1979; World Mission and World Survival, 1985. Add: 241-101 New Bern Ave., Raleigh, N.C. 27601, U.S.A.

COPELAND, Miles. American, b. 1916. International relations/Current affairs, Politics/Government. Formerly with Central Intelligence Agency. *Publs:* Staffs and Staff Work, 1950; The Game of Nations: The Amorality of Power Politics, 1969; Real Spy World, 1974; Beyond Cloak and Dagger: Inside the CIA, 1975. Add: c/o Simon & Schuster Inc., 1230 Sixth Ave., New York, N.Y. 10022, U.S.A.

COPEMAN, George Henry. British, b. 1922. Administration/Management, Economics. Managing Dir., 1964–69, and Chmn., 1969–74, Business Intelligence Services Ltd., London; Chmn;, Copeman Paterson Ltd., 1977–87. *Publs:* Leaders of British Industry, 1955; Promotion and Pay for Executives, 1957; The Challenge of Employee Shareholding, 1958; The Role of the Managing Director, 1959; Laws of Business Management, 1963; (with F. Hanika) How the Executive Spends his Time, 1964; The Chief Executive and Business Growth, 1971; (with Tony Rumble) Capital as an Incentive, 1972; Employee Share Ownership and Industrial Stability, 1975; The Managing Director, 1978; (co-author) Shared Ownership, 1984. Add: Moonraker, Batts Lane, Mare Hill, W. Sussex RH20 2ED, England.

COPI, Irving M. American, b. 1917. Philosophy. Prof. of Philosophy, Univ. of Hawaii, Honolulu, since 1969. Instr., Univ. of Illinois, 1947–48; Asst. Prof., Assoc. Prof., and Prof., Univ. of Michigan, Ann Arbor, 1948–69; Visiting Prof., U.S. Air Force Univ., Ala., 1958–65. *Publs:* (ed.) Plato's Theaetetus, 1949; (co-author) Language, Thought and Culture, 1958; Introduction to Logic, 1953, 7th ed. 1986; Symbolic Logic, 1954, 5th ed. 1979; (co-author) American Philosophy, 1955; (ed. with J. Gould) Readings on Logic, 1964, 1972; (ed. with R. Beard) Essays on Wittgenstein's Tractacus, 1966; (ed. with J. Gould) Contemporary Readings in Logical Theory, 1967; The Theory of Logical Types, 1971; (ed. with J. Gould) Contemporary Philosophical Logic, 1978. Add: 1618 Kamole St., Honolulu, Hawaii 96821, U.S.A.

COPLESTON, Frederick Charles. British, b. 1907. Philosophy. Emeritus Prof., Univ. of London, since 1974 (Prof., 1939–74, and Principal, 1970–74, Heythrop Coll.; Dean, Univ. Faculty of Theology, 1972–74). Prof. of Metaphysics, Gregorian Univ., Rome, 1962–68; Visiting Prof. of Philosophy, Univ. of Santa Clara, Calif., 1974–82. *Publs:* Friedrich Nietzsche, 1942, 1974; A History of Philosophy: Greece and Rome, 1946, Augustine to Scotus, 1950, Ockham to Suarez, 1953, Descartes to Leibniz, 1958, Hobbes to Hume, 1959, Wolff to Kant, 1960, Fichte to Nietzsche, 1963, Bentham to Russell, 1966, Maine de Biran to Sartre, 1974; Arthur Schopenhauer, 1946; Medieval Philosophy, 1952; Aquinas, 1955; Contemporary Philosophy, 1956, 1972; A History of Medieval Philosophy, 1972; Religion and Philosophy, 1974; Philosophies and Philosophers, 1976; On the History of Philosophy, 1979; Philosophies and Cultures, 1980; Religion and the One, 1982; Philosophy in Russia, 1986; Russian Religious Philosophy, 1988. Add: 114 Mount St., London W1Y 6AH, England.

COPP, Jim (Andrew James Copp III). American. Children's fiction, Children's non-fiction. Owner, Playhouse Records, Los Angeles, since 1958. Columnist and Cartoonist, Los Angeles Times, 1950–58. *Publs:* Martha Matilda O'Toole, 1969; People and Places, 1979. Add: 60 Fremont Pl., Los Angeles, Calif. 90005, U.S.A.

COPPA, Frank John. American, b. 1937. History, Media, Theology/Religion, Urban studies, Biography. Prof. of History, St. John's Univ., NYC, since 1979 (Asst. Prof., 1965–70, Assoc. Prof., 1971–79); also writer for television. *Publs:* (ed. with W. Griffin & B. Bast) From Vienna to Vietnam: War and Peace in the Modern World, 1969; Planning Protectionism and Politics in Liberal Italy: Economics and Politics in the Giolittian Age, 1971; Camillo di Cavour, 1973; (ed. with P. Dolce) Cities in Transition: From the Ancient World to Urban America, 1974; (ed.) Religion in the Making of Western Man, 1974; (ed.) The Immigrant Experience in America, 1976; (ed.) Screen and Society: The Impact of Television upon Aspects of Contemporary Civilization, 1979; Pope Pius IX: Crusader in a Secular Age, 1979; (ed. with R. Hammond) Technology in the Twentieth Century, 1983; Dictionary of Modern Italian History, 1985; (ed.) Studies in Modern Italian History, 1986. Add: Dept. of History, St. John's Univ., Jamaica, Queens, N.Y. 11439, U.S.A.

COPPEL, Alfred. Also writes as Robert Cham Gilman and as Alfred Marin. American, b. 1921. Novels/Short stories, Mystery/-Crime/Suspense, Science fiction/Fantasy. *Publs:* Hero Driver, 1952;

Night of Fire and Snow, 1957; Dark December, 1960; A Certainty of Love, 1966; The Gate of Hell, 1968; (as Alfred Marin) The Clash of Distant Thunder, 1968; (as Robert Cham Gilman) The Rebel of Rhada (science fiction), 1968; Order of Battle, 1969; (as Alfred Marin) Rise with the Wind, 1969; (as Robert Cham Gilman) The Navigator of Rhada (science fiction), 1969; A Little Time for Laughter, 1970; (as Alfred Marin) A Storm of Spears, 1970; Between the Thunder and the Sun, 1971; (as Robert Cham Gilman) The Starkhan of Rhada (science fiction), 1971; The Landlocked Man, 1972; Thirty Four East, 1973; The Dragon, 1977; The Hastings Conspiracy, 1980; The Apocalypse Brigade, 1981; The Burning Mountain, 1983; The Marburg Chronicles, 1985; (as Robert Cham Gilman) The Warlock of Rhada, 1985; The Fates Command Us, 1986; Show Me a Hero, 1987; A Land of Mirrors, 1988. Add: Lescher and Lescher Ltd., 61 Irving Pl., New York, N.Y. 10003, U.S.A.

COPPER, Basil. British, b. 1924. Novels/Short stories, Mystery/Crime/Suspense, Historical/Romance/Gothic, Fantasy. Former journalist and editor. Chmn., Crime Writers Assn. of Great Britain, 1981–82. *Publs:* The Dark Mirror, 1966; Night Frost, 1966; No Flowers for the General, 1967; Scratch on the Dark, 1967; Die Now, Live Later, 1968; Don't Bleed on Me, 1968; Not After Nightfall, 1968; The Marble Orchard, 1969; Dead File, 1970; No Letters from the Grave, 1971; The Vampire in Legend, Fact and Art, 1971; From Evil's Pillow, 1971; Strong Arm, 1972; Big Chill, 1972; Breaking Point, 1973; A Great Year for Dying, 1973; Shock Wave, 1973; A Voice from the Dead, 1974; Feedback, 1974; Ricochet, 1974; The High Wall, 1975; Necropolis (gothic), 1975; The Great White Space (fantasy), 1975; When Footsteps Echo (short stories), 1975; Impact, 1975; A Good Place to Die, 1975; The Lonely Place, 1976; Crack in the Sidewalk, 1976; The Curse of the Fleers (gothic), 1976; Tight Corner, 1976; The Year of the Dragon, 1977; Death Squad, 1977; The Werewolf: In Legend, Fact and Art, 1977; And Afterward, The Dark (short stories), 1977; Murder One, 1978; A Quiet Room in Hell,1978; Here Be Daemons (short stories), 1978; The Dossier of Solar Pons (short stories), 1978; The Big Rip–Off, 1979; The Caligari Complex, 1979; The Further Adventures of Solar Pons, 1979; The Secret Files of Solar Pons, 1979; The Exploits of Solar Pons, 1979; Voices of Doom (short stories), 1980; Flip–Side, 1980; The Long Rest, 1981; The Empty Silence, 1981; Dark Entry, 1981; Hang Loose, 1982; Shoot–Out, 1982; The Far Horizon, 1982; The House of the Wolf (gothic), 1982; Trigger–Man, 1982; Pressure–Point, 1983; The Narrow Corner, 1983; Hard Contract, 1983; Into the Silence (fantasy), 1983; The Hook, 1984; You Only Die Once, 1984; Tuxedo Park, 1984; The Far Side of Fear, 1985; Jet Lag, 1986; Blood on the Moon, 1986; Snow–Job, 1986; Heavy Iron, 1987; Turn Down an Empty Glass, 1987; Bad Scene, 1987; House-Dick, 1988; Print-Out, 1988. Add: Stockdoves, South Park, Sevenoaks, Kent, England.

COPPERUD, Roy H. American, b. 1915. Language/Linguistics, Writing/Journalism. Prof. Emeritus of Journalism, Univ. of Southern California, Los Angeles, since 1980 (joined faculty, 1964). Member, Usage Panel, American Heritage Dictionary, since 1964; Consultant, English Language Inst., since 1967. Journalist, editorial writer, and music critic for various papers, including Baltimore Evening Sun, Milwaukee Journal, Los Angeles Times, and National Observer, 1935–64. *Publs:* Words on Paper, 1958; Dictionary of Usage and Style, 1964; American Usage: The Consensus, 1970; American Usage and Stye, 1980; (with Roy Paul Nelson) Editing the News, 1982. Add: 2782 McNally, Altadena, Calif. 91001, U.S.A.

CORBETT, Edmund V(ictor). British. Librarianship. Borough Librarian, Wandsworth, London, 1952–76. Chmn., Publs. Cttee., 1967–72, Exec. Cttee., 1973–74, and Pres., 1975, Library Assn., London. *Publs:* The Illustrations Collection, 1941; Introduction to Public Librarianship, 1950, 1952; Photocharging, 1957; (ed.) Great True Mountain Stories, 1957; (ed.) Great True Stories of the Sea, 1958; (ed.) Waves of Battle, 1959, 1969; Public Library Finance and Accountancy, 1960; Librarianship, 1961; (ed.) Great True Stories of Tragedy and Disaster, 1961; Public Library and its Control, 1962; 1966; By Car to the Continent, 1962, 1969; Introduction to Librarianship, 1964, 3rd ed. 1971; (ed.) Libraries, Museums and Art Galleries Year Book, 1964, 3rd ed. 1971; Fundamentals of Library Organisation and Administration, 1978. Add: c/o Library Assn., 7 Ridgmount St., London WC1E 7AE, England.

CORBETT, Edward P.J. American, b. 1919. Speech/Rhetoric. Prof. of English, Ohio State Univ., Columbus, since 1966. Pres., Rhetoric Soc. of America, since 1972; Member, Editorial Bd., Philosophy and Rhetoric, since 1972; Ed., College Composition and Communication, since 1974. Prof. of English, Creighton Univ., Omaha, Nebr., 1948–59, 1963–66; Pres., English Assn. of Ohio, 1971–72; Assoc. Ed., Quarterly Journal of Speech, 1972–74, 1986–89; Ed., College Composition and Communication, 1974–79.. *Publs:* Classical Rhetoric for the Modern Student, 1965, 1971; (ed. with G. Tate) Teaching Freshman Composition, 1967; (ed. with J.L. Golden) The Rhetoric of Blair, Campbell, and Whately, 1968, 1980; (ed.) Rhetorical Analysis of Literary Works, 1969; (ed. with G. Tate) Teaching High School Composition, 1970; (ed. with V.M. Burke) The New Century Composition–Rhetoric, 1971; The Little English Handbook: Choices and Conventions, 1973, 4th ed. 1984, 5th ed., 1987; (ed.) The Essay: Subjects and Stances, 1974; The Little Rhetoric Handbook, 1977, 1982; (ed. with Gary Tate) The Writing Teacher's Sourcebook, 1981; The Little Rhetoric and Handbook with Readings, 1983; Selected Essays of Edward P.J. Corbett, ed. by Robert J. Connors, 1989. Add: Dept. of English, Ohio State Univ., Columbus, Ohio 43210, U.S.A.

CORBETT, John Ambrose. British, b. 1908. Language/Linguistics. Dir. of Education, Luton, Beds., 1952–70; Deputy Dir., Centre for Information on Language Teaching, London, 1970–73. *Publs:* Essentials of Modern German Grammar, 1935, rev. ed. 1947; (with Bertil Ekholm Erb) Presse–Querschnitt, 1974; (with Anne Johnson) Basic French Grammar, 1975. Add: 3 Lodge Close, Wateringbury, Maidstone, Kent, England.

CORBETT, Scott. American, b. 1913. Novels/Short stories, Children's fiction, Children's non-fiction, recreation/Leisure/Hobbies. Served as a correspondent, U.S. Army, 42nd (Rainbow) Infantry Div., 1943–46. *Publs:* The Reluctant Landlord, 1950; Sauce for the Gander, 1951; We Chose Cape Cod, 1953; Cape Cod's Way: An Informal History, 1955; The Sea Fox: The Adventures of Cape Cod's Most Colorful Rum-runner, 1956; Susie Sneakers, 1956; Midshipman Cruise, 1956; Tree House Island, 1959; Dead Man's Light, 1960; The Lemonade Trick, 1960; The Mailbox Trick, 1961; Cutlass Island, 1962; Danger Point: The Wreck of the "Birkenhead", 1962; What Makes a Car Go?, 1963; The Disappearing Dog Trick, 1963; The Limerick Trick, 1964; The Baseball Trick, 1965; One by the Sea, 1965; The Cave above Delphi, 1965; What Makes TV Work?, 1965; Pippa Passes, 1966; The Case of the Gone Goose, 1966; What Makes a Light Go On?, 1966; Diamonds Are Trouble,1967; What Makes a Plane Fly?, 1967; The Turnabout Trick, 1968; Cop's Kid, 1968; Ever Ride a Dinosaur?, 1969; The Hairy Horror Trick, 1969; Rhode Island, 1969; The Case of the Fugitive Firebug, 1969; Diamonds Are More Trouble, 1969; What Makes a Boat Float?, 1970; Steady, Freddie, 1970; The Baseball Bargain, 1970; The Mystery Man, 1970; The Case of the Ticklish Tooth, 1971; The Hateful Plateful Trick, 1971; The Big Joke Game, 1972; The Red Room Riddle, 1972; Dead Before Docking, 1972; Run for the Money, 1973; The Home Run Trick, 1973; Dr. Merlin's Magic Shop, 1973; What about the Wankel Engine?, 1974; Take a Number, 1974; The Hockey Trick, 1974; Here Lies the Body, 1974; The Case of the Silver Skull, 1974; The Great Custard Pie Panic, 1974; The Boy with Will Power, 1975; The Case of the Burgled Blessing Box, 1975; The Boy Who Walked on Air, 1975; The Great McGoniggle's Gray Ghost, 1975; The Great McGoniggle's Key Play, 1976; The Black Mask Trick, 1976; The Hockey Girls, 1976; Captain Bucher's Body, 1976; The Great McGoniggle Rides Shotgun, 1977; The Hangman's Ghost Trick, 1977; The Foolish Dinosaur Fiasco, 1978; The Discontented Ghost, 1978; Bridges, 1978; The Donkey Planet, 1979; The Mysterious Zetabet, 1979; Jokes to Read in the Dark, 1980; Home Computers: A Simple and Informative Guide, 1980; The Great McGoniggle Switches Pitches, 1980; The Deadly Hoax, 1981; Grave Doubts, 1982; Jokes to Tell Your Worst Enemy, 1984; Down with Wimps, 1984; The Trouble With Diamonds, 1985; Witch Hunt, 1985. Add: 149 Benefit St., Providence, R.I. 02903, U.S.A.

CORBETT, W(illiam) J(esse). British, b. 1938. Children's fiction. has worked as a merchant seaman, baker's assistant, furniture removal man, slaughterman, and builder. *Publs:* The Song of Pentecost, 1982; Pentecost and the Chosen One, 1984; The End of the Tale and Other Stories, 1985; Pentecost of Lickey Top, 1987; The Bear Who Stood on His Head, 1988; Dear Grumble, 1989. Add: 6 Selborne Grove, Billesley, Birmingham, England.

CORBIN, Claire.American, b. 1913. Marketing. Co-Owner and Partner, Corbin Assocs., Delray Beach, Fla., since 1948; Prof. of Marketing, Coll. of Business Admin., Fordham Univ., Bronx, N.Y., 1957–78, now Emeritus. Freelance Writer, Country Gentleman, Curtis Publishing Co., Philadelphia, 1935–43; Merchandising Exec., R.H. Macy, NYC 1939–40; Asst. Prof., Long Island Univ., Brooklyn, N.Y., 1940–44; own gift packaging business, NYC, 1944–45; Dir. of Sales Training, Loft Candy Corp., Long Island City, N.Y., 1945–46; own food manufacturing and sales business, NYC, 1946; Fashion Ed., Two to Six, children's mag., and Merchandise Ed., Today's Woman, NYC, 1947–48; Publicity and Promotion

Dir., Decorative Fabrics Inst., NYC, 1948–58; Dir., Women's Group Activities, WOR and WOR-TV, NYC, 1948–59; Assoc. Prof., Hofstra Univ., Hempstead, N.Y., 1949–57. Vice-Pres., National Home Fashions League, 1953–54; Ed., Ad Libber, Advertising Women of New York, 1957–58; Chmn., Mass Media Section, American Assn. of Univ. Women, 1959–60; Secty.-Treas., American Assn. of Univ. Professors, 1961–70; Chmn., National Finance Cttee., American Academy of Advertising, 1966–67; Secty.-Treas., American Marketing Assn., 1970–73. *Publs:* (co-author) Principles of Retailing, 1958; Principles of Advertising, 1963; Decision Exercises in Marketing, 1964; New Trends in American Marketing, 1965; Implementing the Marketing Concept, 1973. Add: 6350 Timberlakes Way, Delany Beach, Fla. 33484, U.S.A.

CORCORAN, Barbara. Also writes as Paige Dixon and Gail Hamilton. American, b. 1911. Children's fiction, Novels. Researcher, Celebrity Service, Hollywood, 1945–53; Instr. in English, Univ. of Kentucky, Covington, 1956–57; Researcher, CBS TV, story dept., Hollywood, 1957–59; Instr. in English, Univ. of Colorado, Boulder, 1960–65, and Palomar Coll., Calif., 1965–69. *Publs:* Children's fiction—Sam, 1967; A Row of Tigers, 1969; Sasha, My Friend, 1969; (with Bradford Angier) The Long Journey, 1970; (with Angier) A Star to the North, 1970; The Lifestyle of Robie Tuckerman, 1971; This is a Recording, 1971; Dont' Slam the Door When You Go, 1972; A Trick of Light, 1972; All the Summer Voices, 1973; A Dance to Still Music, 1974; The Winds of Time, 1974; The Clown, 1975, as A Time to Love, A Time to Mourn, 1975, as I Wish You Love, 1977; Meet Me at Tamerlane's Tomb, 1975; Axe-Time, Sword-Time, 1976; Cabin in the Sky, 1976; Faraway Island, 1977; Make No Sound , 1977; (with Angier) Ask for Love, and They Give You Rice Pudding, 1977; Hey, That's My Soul You're Stomping On, 1978; Me and You and a Dog Named Blue, 1979; The Person in the Potting Shed, 1980; Rising Damp, 1980; Making It, 1981; You're Allegro Dead, 1981; Child of the Morning, 1982; A Watery Grave, 1982; Strike!, 1983; Which Witch is Which?, 1983; August, Die She Must, 1984; The Woman in Your Life, 1984; Face the Music, 1985; Mystery on Ice, 1985; The Shadowed Path, 1985; When Darkness Falls, 1985; A Horse Named Sky, 1986; I Am the Universe, 1986; The Hideaway, 1987; The Sky Is falling, 1988; The Private Wars of Lillian Adams, 1989; children's fiction as Paige Dixon—Lion on the Mountain, 1972; Silver Wolf, 1973; Promises to Keep, 1974; The Young Grizzly, 1974; May I Cross Your Golden River?, 1975; Pimm's Cup for Everybody, 1976; The Search for Charlie, 1976; Summer of the White Goat, 1977; The Loner: A Story of the Wolverine, 1978; The Mustang and Other Stories, 1978; Skipper, 1979; Walk My Way, 1980; children's fiction as Gail hamilton—A Candle to the Devil, 1975; Titania's Lodestone, 1975; Love Comes to Eunice K. O'Herlihy, 1977; fiction for adults—Abigail, Abbie in Love, A Husband for Gail (trilogy), 1981; Beloved Enemy, 1981; By the Silvery Moon, 1981; Call of the Heart, 1981; Love Is Not Enough, 1981; Song for Two Voices, 1981. Add: P.O. Box 4394, Missoula, Mont. 59806, U.S.A.

CORCORAN, Gertrude B. American, b. 1923. Education. Prof., San Jose State Univ., Calif., since 1965 (Asst. Prof., 1955–60; Assoc. Prof., 1960–65). Research Assoc., San Jose Unified Sch. District, since 1973. Researcher, U.S. Office of Education, Washington, D.C., 1961–63. *Publs:* Language Arts in the Elementary School: A Modern Linguistic Approach, 1970; Language Experiences for Nursery and Kindergarten Children, 1975. Add: San Jose State Univ., 125 South 7th St., San Jose, Calif. 95192, U.S.A.

CORD, Barry. Pseud. for Peter B. Germano; also writes as Jack Bertin and Jim Kane. American, b. 1913. Westerns/Adventure, Science fiction/Fantasy. Freelance writer since 1946: has written under various house names including Jack Slade and Jackson Cole. *Publs:* Trail Boss from Texas, 1948; The Gunsmoke Trail, 1951; Shadow Valley, 1951; Mesquite Johnny, 1952; Trail to Sundown, 1953; Cain Basin, 1954; The Sagebrush Kid, 1954; Boss of Barbed Wire, 1955; Dry Range, 1955; in U.K. as The Rustlers of Dry Range, 1956; The Guns of Hammer, 1956; The Gunshy Kid, 1957; Sheriff of Big Hat, 1957; Savage Valley, 1957; The Prodigal Gun, 1957; Concho Valley, 1958; Gun-Proddy Hombre, 1958; The Iron Trail Killers, 1959; Starlight Range, 1959; The Third Rider, 1959; Six Bullets Left, 1959; War in Peaceful Valley, 1959; Maverick Gun, 1959; Last Chance at Devil's Canyon, 1959; (as Jim Kane) Gunman's Choice, 1960; (as Jim Kane) Renegade Rancher, 1961; Two Guns to Avalon, 1962; The Masked Gun, 1963; (as Jim Kane) Spanish Gold, 1963; (as Jim Kane) Tangled Trails, 1963; (as Jim Kane) Lost Canyon 1964; (as Jim Kane) Red River Sheriff, 1965; Last Stage to Gomorrah, 1966; A Ranger Called Solitary, 1966; Canyon Showdown, 1967; Gallows Ghost, 1967; The Long Wire, 1968; Trouble in Peaceful Valley, 1968; (as Jim Kane) Rendezvous at Bitter Wells, 1966; (as Jack Bertin) The Interplanetary Adventurers (science fiction), 1970; (as Jim

Kane) Texas Warrior, 1971; The Coffin Fillers, 1972; Brassado Hill, 1972; Desert Knights, 1973; The Running Iron Samaritans, 1973; Hell in Paradise Valley, 1978; Gun Junction, 1979; Deadly Amigos: Two Graves for a Gunman, 1979. Add: 113 Erten St., Thousand Oaks, Calif. 91360, U.S.A.

CORDELL, Alexander. British, b. 1914. Novels/Short stories, Children's fiction. *Publs:* A Thought of Honour, 1954; Rape of the Fair Country, 1959 The Hosts of Rebecca (in U.S. as Robe of Honor), 1959; Race of the Tiger, 1961; The Sinews of Love, 1964; The Bright Cantonese (in U.S as The Deadly Eurasian), 1966; Song of the Earth, 1968; The White Cockade, 1971; Witch's Sabbath, 1972; The Healing Blade, 1972; The Fire People, 1972; If You Believe the Soldiers, 1973; The Traitor Within, 1973; The Dream and the Destiny, 1975; This Sweet and Bitter Earth, 1977; Sea Urchin, 1978; Rogue's March, 1980; To Slay the Dreamer, 1981; Land of My Fathers, 1982; Peerless Jim, 1984; Tunnel Tigers, 1986; This Proud and Savage Land, 1987; Tales from Tiger Bay, 1987; Requiem for a Patriot, 1988; Moll Walbee, 1989. Add: The Conifers, Railway Rd., Rhosddu, Wrexham, Clwyd, Wales.

CORDEN, Warner Max. Australian, b. 1927. Economics. Nuffield Reader in Intnl. Economics, Oxford Univ., 1967–76; Prof., Australian National Univ., Canberra, 1976–88. *Publs:* The Theory of Protection, 1971; Trade Policy and Economic Welfare, 1974; Inflation, Exchange Rates, and the World Economy, 1977, 3rd ed. 1985; Protection, Trade and Growth, 1985. Add: Sch. of Advanced Intnl. Studies, 1740 Massachusetts Ave. N.W., Washington, D.C. 20036, U.S.A.

CORDINGLY, David. British, b. 1938. Art. Head of Exhibitions, National Maritime Museum, London, since 1988 (Asst. Keeper, then Keeper of Pictures, 1980–88). Graphic Designer, Peter Hatch Partnership, 1963–65; Exhibition Designer, British Museum, 1967–71; Keeper of Art Gallery and Museum, Brighton, 1971–78. *Publs:* Marine Painting in England 1700-1900, 1974; Painters of the Sea, 1979; The Art of the Van de Veldes, 1982; Nicholas Pocock, 1986; Captain James Cook, Navigator, 1988. Add: National Maritime Museum, Greenwich, London SE10 9NF, England.

COREN, Alan. British, b. 1938. Children's fiction, Plays/Screenplays, Humour/Satire. TV Critic, The Mail on Sunday, London, since 1983; Ed., The Listener mag., London, since 1988; Columnist, The Times, London, since 1988. Literary Ed., 1967–69, Deputy Ed., 1969–73, and Ed., 1978–87, Punch mag., London., TV Critic, The Times, 1972–78; Columnist, Daily Mail, 1974–77. *Publs:* (co-author) Introduction (short stories), 1961; The Dog It Was That Died, 1965; All Except the Bastard, 1969; The Collected Bulletins of Idi Amin, 1974; The Sanity Inspector, 1974; (ed.) The Punch Book of Kids, 1974; The Further Bulletins of Idi Amin, 1975; Golfing for Cats, 1975; (ed.) Punch in the Country, 1976; The Peanut Papers, 1977; The Lady from Stalingrad Mansions, 1977; The Arthur Books (for children), 1973–81; The Rhinestone as Big as the Ritz, 1979; Tissues for Men, 1980; The Best of Alan Coren, 1980; The Cricklewood Diet, 1982; (ed.) Present Laughter, 1982; (ed.) The Penguin Book of Modern Humour, 1983; Bum, 1984; Something for the Weekend, 1986; Bin Ends, 1987. Add: 199 Old Marylebone Rd., London NW1, England.

COREY, Paul. American, b. 1903. Novels/Short stories, Homes/Gardens. Instr., Napa Coll., Calif., since 1974. *Publs:* Three Miles Square, 1939: The Road Returns, 1940; County Seat, 1941; The Red Tractor, 1944; Buy an Acre, 1944; Five Acre Hill, 1945; Acres of Antaeus, 1946; Build a Home, 1946; The Little Jeep, 1946; Shad Haul, 1947; Corn Gold Farm, 1948; Homemade Homes, 1950; Milk Flood, 1956; (with D. Huff) Home Workshop Furniture Projects, 1957; Holiday Homes, 1967; Planet of the Blind, 1969; Bachelor Bess, My Sister,1975; How to Build Country Homes on a Budget, 1975; Do Cats Think? 1977; Are Cats People?, 1979; Notes of a Cat Watcher, 1979. Add: 267 Cavedale Rd., Sonoma, Calif. 95476, U.S.A.

CORIOLANUS. *See* **McMILLAN,** James.

CORK, Richard (Graham). British, b. 1947. Art. Art Critic, The Listener, London, since 1984. Member, Art Advisory Group, South Bank Bd., London, since 1987; Trustee, Public Art Development Trust, since 1988. Art Critic, Evening Standard, London, 1969–77 and 1980–83; Ed., Studio International, London, 1975–79.Member of Art Panel, Arts Council of Great Britain, 1971–74. *Publs:* Vorticism and Abstract Art in the First Machine Age, 2 vols., 1976; The Social Role of Art, 1979; Art Beyond the Gallery in Early 20th Century England, 1985; David Bomberg, 1987. Add: 24 Milman Rd., London NW6, England.

CORLETT, William. British, b. 1938. Children's fiction, Plays/Screenplays, Children's non-fiction. Repertory and television actor in London and the provinces. *Publs:* The Gentle Avalanche, 1962; Another Round, 1962; Return Ticket, 1962; The Scallop Shell, 1963; Flight of a Lone Sparrow, 1965; Dead Set at Dream Boy, 1965; The Scourging of Matthew Barrow, 1965; Tinker's Curse, 1968; We Never Went to Cheddar Gorge, 1968; The Story Teller, 1969; The Illusionist, 1969; National Trust, 1970; The Deliverance of Fanny Blaydon, 1971; A Memory of Two Loves, 1972; Conversations in the Dark, 1972; The Gate of Eden, 1974; The Land Beyond, 1975; The Ideal Tale, 1975; (with John Moore) The Once and Forever Christmas, 1975; Return to the Gate, 1975; Mr. Oddy, 1975; The Orsini Emeralds, 1975; Emmerdale Farm series, 1975–77; Orlando the Marmalade Cat Buys a Cottage, adaptation of the story by Kathleen Hale, 1975; The Dark Side of the Moon, 1976; Orlando's Camping Holiday, adaptation of the story by Kathleen Hale, 1976; Paper Lads, 1978–79; Questions series (The Question of Religion, The Christ Story, The Hindu Sound, The Judaic Law, The Buddha Way, The Islamic Space), 1978–79; Kids series, 1979; Going Back, 1979; The Gate of Eden, 1980; Barriers series, 1980; Agatha Christie Hour (adaptation of four short stories), 1982; The Machine Gunners (adaptation of Robert Westall book), 1982; Dearly Beloved, 1983; Bloxworth Blue, 1984; Return to the Gate, 1986; The Secret Line, 1988. Add: Cottesbrook, Great Bardfield, nr. Braintree, Essex, England.

CORLEY, Ernest. *See* **BULMER,** Henry Kenneth.

CORLEY, Thomas Anthony Buchanan. British, b. 1923. Business/Trade/Industry, Economics, Biography. Sr. Lectr. in Economics, Univ. of Reading, since 1968 (Lectr., 1962–68). With Bank of England, 1950–56 (sent to Central Bank of Iraq, Baghdad, as Dir., of Issue Dept., 1953–55); with Dept. of Applied Economics, Univ. of Cambridge, 1956–58; Asst. Lectr. and Lectr., Queen's Univ., Belfast, 1958–62. *Publs:* True Book About Napoleon, 1958; Democratic Despot: A Life of Napoleon III, 1961; (ed.) Otto Wolff: Ouvrard, Speculator of Genius, 1962; Domestic Electrical Appliances, 1966; Quaker Enterprise in Biscuits: Huntley & Palmers of Reading 1822-1972, 1972; History of the Burmah Oil Company, 2 vols., 1983, 1988. Add: 30 Allcroft Rd., Reading RG1 5HH, England.

CORMACK, Patrick (Thomas). British, b. 1939. Architecture, History, Politics/Government, Social commentary/phenomena. Member of Parliament (Conservative) for Staffordshire S.W. since 1974 (Member for Cannock, 1970–74). Dir., Watercolour Facsimilies, and of the Watercolour Foundn. Chmn., Parliamentary Heritage Group; Member, Royal Commn. on Historic Manuscripts. Schoolmaster, St. James School, Grimsby, Wrekin College, Shropshire, and Brewood Grammar School, 1961–70. *Publs:* Heritage in Danger, 1976; (ed.) Right Turn, 1978; Westminster: Palace and Parliament, 1981; Castles of Britain, 1982; Wilberforce: The Nation's Conscience, 1983; English Cathedrals, 1984. Add: House of Commons, London SW1, England.

CORMAN, Cid. (Sidney Corman). American, b. 1924. Poetry, Translations. Ed., Origin mag. and Origin Press, Kyoto, Japan, since 1951. Poetry Broadcaster, WMEX, Boston Mass., 1949–51. *Publs:* Subluna, 1945; Thanksgiving Eclogue, 1954; The Precisions, 1955; The Responses, 1956; Stances and Distances, 1957; The Marches, 1957; A Table in Provence, 1958; The Decent from Daimonji, 1959; Clocked Stone, 1959; For Sure, 1959; (trans.) Cool Melon, by Basjo, 1959; (trans.) Cool Gong, 1959; For Instance, 1969; For Good, 1961; Sun Rock Man, 1962; (trans. with Kamike Susumu) Selected Frogs, by Shimpeo Kusano, 1963; In Good Time, 1964; In No Time, 1964; All in All, 1965; Nonce, 1965; For You, 1966; For Granted, 1966; At: Bottom, 1966; Stead, 1966; Words for Each Other, 1967; (trans.) Back Roads to Far Towns, by Basho, 1967; (trans. with Kamile Susumu) Frogs and Others: Poems, by Shimpei Kusano, 1968; Without End, 1968; No Less, 1968; Hearth, 1968; No More, 1969; Plight, 1969; Nigh, 1979; Livingdying, 1970; Of the Breath of, 1970; For Keeps, 1970; For Now, 1971; (trans.) Things, by Francis Ponge, 1971; Out and Out, 1972; Be Quest, 1972; A Language Without Words, 1973; So Far, 1973; (ed.) The Gist of "Origin": An Anthology, 1973; (trans.) Leaves of Hypnos, by Rene Char, 1973; Poems: Thanks to Zukerkandi, 1973; Breathing, 1973; (trans.) Breathings, by Phillippe Jaccottet, 1974; 0/1, 1974 (Lenore Marshall Poetry Prize); Once and For All, 1976; Auspices, 1978; At Their Word: Essays on the Arts of Language, 2 vols., 1977–78; Aegis: Selected Poems 1970–1980, 1983; And the Word, 1987. Add: c/o Black Sparrow Press, Box 3993, Santa Barbara, Calif. 93130, U.S.A.

CORMIER, Robert. American, b. 1925. Novels/Short stories. Children's fiction. Writer, Radio WTAG, Worcester, Mass., 1946–48; Reporter and Columnist, Worcester Telegram and Gazette, 1948–55, and Fitchburg Sentinel and Enterprise, Mass., 1955–78. *Publs:* for adults—Now and at the Hour, 1960; A Little Raw on Monday Morning, 1963; Take Me Where the Good Times Are, 1965; Fade, 1988; for young adults The Chocolate War, 1974; I Am the Cheese, 1977; After the First Death, 1979; Eight Plus One, 1980; The Bumblebee Flies Anyway, 1983; Beyond the Chocolate War, 1985. Add: 1177 Main St., Leominster, Mass., 01453, U.S.A.

CORN, Alfred. American, b. 1943. Poetry. Preceptor, Columbia Coll., NYC, 1968–70; Assoc. Ed., University Review, NYC, 1970; Staff Writer, DaCapo Press, NYC, 1971–72; Asst. Prof., Connecticut Coll., New London, 1978; Visiting Lectr., Yale Univ., New Haven, Conn., 1977, 1978, 1979. *Publs:* All Roads at Once, 1976; A Call in the Midst of the Crowd, 1978; The Various Light, 1980; Notes from a Child of Paradise, 1984; The Metamorphoses of Metaphor: Essays in Poetry and Fiction, 1987; The West Door, 1988. Add: 54 W. 16th St., New York, N.Y. 10011, U.S.A.

CORNETT, R(ichard) Orin. American, b. 1913. Physics, Education. Vice-Pres., 1965–75, Research Prof. since 1965, and Dir., Cued Speech Prog. since 1975, Gallaudet Univ., Washington, D.C., now Emeritus. Specialist, 1958, Exec. Asst. to Dir., 1959–60, and Dir., 1961–65, Div. of Higher Education, and Asst. U.S. Commnr. of Education, 1961–65, U.S. Office Education, Dept. of Health, Education and Welfare, Washington, D.C. *Publs:* (with White, Manning and Weber) Practical Physics, 1943; Algebra: A Second Course, 1945; (with others) Electronic Circuits and Tubes, 1947; (with M.E. Henegar) Cued Speech: Manual for Parents, 1971; (with J. Latt) Cued Speech Manual for Teachers, 1982, (Rev.) 1985. Add: 8702 Royal Ridge Lane, Laurel, Md, 20708, U.S.A.

CORNGOLD, Stanley. American, b. 1934. Literature. Prof. of German and Comparative Literature, Princeton Univ., N.J. since 1981 (Lectr., 1966–67; Asst. Prof., 1967–72; Assoc. Prof., 1972–81). *Publs:* (ed.) Ausgewahlte ProsaMax Frisch, 1968; (ed. and trans.) The Metamorphosis, by Franz Kafka, 1972; The Commentators' Despair: The Interpretation of Kafka's 'Metamorphosis', 1973; (ed. with Richard Ludwig) Thomas Mann, 1875-1975, 1975; (ed. with Michael Curschmann and Theodore Ziolkowski) Aspekte der Goethezeit, 1977; The Fate of the Self: German Writers and French Theory, 1986; Franz Kafka: The Necessity of Form, 1988. Add: 20 Erdman Ave., Princeton, N.J. 08540, U.S.A.

CORNISH, Sam(uel James). American, b. 1935. Children's fiction, Poetry. Ed. Mimeo mag. Consultant in elementary sch. teaching, Central Atlantic Regional Educational Labs. Humanities Prog. Former Ed., Chicory, Enoch Pratt Library publ., Baltimore, Md. *Publs:* In This Corner: Sam Cornish and Verses, 1961; People Under the Window, 1962; Generations, 1964; Angles, 1965; Winters, 1968; (ed. with L.W. Dixon) Chicory: Young Voices from the Black Ghetto, 1969; (ed. with H. Fox) The Living Underground: An Anthology of Contemporary American Poetry, 1969; Your Hand in Mine, 1970; Generations: Poem, 1971; Streets, 1973; Sometimes: Ten Poems, 1973; Grandmother's Pictures (children's fiction), 1974; Sam's World, 1978. Add: c/o Bookstore Press, Box 191, R.F.D.I, Freeport, Maine 04032, U.S.A.

CORNWELL, Bernard. British, b. 1944. Romance/Historical fiction. Producer, London, 1969–76, and Head of Current Affairs, Belfast, 1976–79, BBC Television; News Ed., Thames TV. London, 1979–80. *Publs:* Sharpe's Eagle, 1981; Sharpe's Gold, 1982; Sharpe's Company, 1982; Sharpe's Sword, 1983; Sharpe's Enemy, 1984; Sharpe's Honour, 1985; Sharpe's Regiment, 1986; Sharpe's Siege, 1987; Sharpe's Rifles, 1988; Redcoat, 1988; Wildtrack, 1988; Sharpe's Revenge, 1989; Sea Lord, 1989. Add: c/o Collins, 8 Grafton St., London W1X 3LA, England.

CORREN, Grace. *See* **HOSKINS,** Robert.

CORREY, Lee. *See* **STINE,** G. Harry.

CORRIGAN, Robert W(illoughby).American, b. 1927. Theatre, Translations. Dean, Sch. of Arts and Humanities, Univ. of Texas at Dallas, Richardson, since 1984. Arts, Univ. of Wisconsin, Milwaukee, since 1974. Chmn. of the Bd., SPACE for Innovative Development, NYC. Andrew Mellon Prof. and Head, Dept. of Drama, Carnegie Inst. of Technology, Pittsburgh, 1961–64; Prof. of Dramatic Literature, 1964–68, and Dean, Sch. of the Arts, 1965–68, New York Univ., NYC; Dir., Critics' Prog. for National Endowment for the Humanities, 1967–68; Pres., California Inst. of the Arts, Valencia, 1968–74. *Publs:* (ed.) The New Theatre of Europe, vol. I, 1962; (trans. with M.D. Dirks) Appia's Music and the Art of the Theatre, 1962; (trans.) Chekhov: Six Plays, 1962; The Theatre in the Twentieth Century, 1963; (ed.) The New Theatre of Europe, vol. II, 1964; (ed. with J.L. Rosenberg) The Art of the Theatre, 1964; (ed. with J.L. Rosenberg) The Context and Craft of Drama, 1964; The Modern Theatre, 1964; (ed.) New American Plays, vol. I, 1965; (ed.) Comedy: Meaning and Form, 1965, 1981; (ed.) Tragedy: Vision and Form, 1965, 1981; (ed.) Laurel British Drama: 20th Century, 1965; (ed.) Laurel British Drama: 19th Century, 1967; (ed.) Masterpieces of the Modern Theatre, 9 vols., 1967; (ed.) The New Theatre of Europe, vol. III, 1968; Arthur Miller, 1969; (ed. with G. Loney) Comedy: A Critical Anthology, 1971, 1980; (ed. with G. Loney) Tragedy: A Critical Anthology, 1971, 1980; (ed. with G. Loney) The Forms of Drama, 1972; The Theatre in Search of a Fix, 1973; The World of the Theatre, 1979; The Making of Theatre: From Drama to Performance, 1980; (ed.) Classical Comedy, 1987. Add: Univ. of Texas at Dallas, Sch. of Arts and Humanities, P.O. Box 830688 JO 45, Richardson, Tex. 75083, U.S.A.

CORRINGTON, John William. American, b. 1932. Novels/Short stories, Plays/Screenplays, Poetry. Former member of faculty, Louisiana State Univ., Baton Rouge, and Univ. of California, Berkeley. *Publs:* Where We Are (poetry), 1962; The Anatomy of Love and Other Poems, 1964; Mr. Clean and Other Poems, 1964; And Wait for the Night (novel), 1964; Lines to the South and Other Poems, 1965; (ed. with M. Williams) Southern Writing in the Sixties, 2 vols., 1966–67; The Upper Hand (novel), 1967; The Lonesome Traveler and Other Stories, 1968; The Bombardier (novel), 1970; (with J.F. Corrington) Richthofen or Brown (screenplay), 1970; (with J.F. Corrington) The Omega Man (screenplay), 1972; (with J.F. Corrington) Box Car Bertha (screenplay), 1972; (with J.F. Corrington) The Arena (screenplay), 1973; (with P. Dehn) Battle for the Planet of the Apes (screenplay), 1973; The Deadly Bees (television play), 1974; The Actes and Monuments (stories), 1978; The Southern Reporter Stories, 1981; Shad Sentell, 1984; (with J.F. Corrington) So Small a Carnival, 1986; All My Trials, 1987; (with J.H. Corrington) A Civil Death, 1987; (with J.H. Corrington) A Project Named Desire, 1987. Add: 1724 Valence St., New Orleans, La. 70115, U.S.A.

CORSO, Gregory. American, b. 1930. Novels/Short stories, Plays/Screenplays, Poetry. Manual labourer, 1950–51; Reporter, Los Angeles Examiner, Calif., 1951–52; Merchant Seaman, 1952–53; Member of English Dept., State Univ. of New York, Buffalo, 1965–70. *Publs:* The Vestal Lady on Brattle and Other Poems, 1955; This Hung-Up Age (play), 1955; Gasoline, 1958; Bomb, 1958; (with H. Marsman) A Pulp Magazine for the Dead Generation: Poems, 1959; The Happy Birthday of Death, 1960; The American Express (novel), 1961; (with Anselm Hollo and Tom Raworth) The Minicab War (parodies), 1961; (ed. with R. Hollerer) Junge Amerikanische Lyrik, 1961; Long Live Man, 1962; Selected Poems, 1962; (with Lawrence Ferlinghetti and Allen Ginserg) Penguin Modern Poets 5, 1963; The Mutation of the Spirit, 1964; There is Yet Time to Run Back Through Life and Expiate All That's Been Sadly Done, 1965; 10 Times a Poem, 1967; That Little Black Door on the Left (play), 1968; Elegiac Feelings American, 1970; Egyptian Cross, 1971; Ankh, 1971; The Last Night Was at Its Nightest, 1972; Earth Egg, 1974; The Japanese Notebook, 1974; Herald of the Autochthonic Spirit, 1981; Writings from Ox, 1981. Add: c/o New Directions, 80 Eighth Ave., New York, N.Y. 10011, U.S.A.

CORSON, Richard. American. Fashion/Costume, Theatre. Adjunct Prof. of Theatre, Southern Methodist Univ., Dallas, Tex., 1971–87. Artist Prof. in Residence, California State Univ., Long Beach, 1968–69. *Publs:* Fashions in Hair, 1965, 3rd ed. 1980; Fashions in Eyeglasses, 1967, 1980; Fashions in Makeup, 1972; Stage Makeup, 8th ed. 1989. Add: c/o Prentice-Hall Inc., Englewood Cliffs, N.J. 07632, U.S.A.

CORWIN, Norman. American, b. 1910. Plays/Screenplays, Poetry, Songs, lyrics and libretti. Creator, writer, and dir., Norman Corwin Presents, TV series; Visiting Prof., Univ. of Southern California Sch. of Journalism, Los Angeles, since 1980; Gov., Academy of Motion Picture Arts and Sciences, 1981–89. *Publs:* They Fly Through the Air, 1939; Thirteen by Corwin, 1940; More by Corwin, 1942; On a Note of Triumph, 1945; The Warrior (libretto), 1946; Untitled and Other Radio Dramas, 1947; The Plot to Overthrow Christmas, 1952; Dog in the Sky, 1952; The Rivalry, 1958; The World of Carl Sandburg, 1961, 1965; Overkill and Megalove, 1963; Prayer for the 70s, 1969; Cervantes, 1973; Holes in a Stained Glass Window, 1978; Trivializing America, 1984; screenplays—The Blue Veil; The Grand Design; Scandal in Scourie; Lust for Life, 1956; The Story of Ruth, 1960. Add: 1840 Fairburn, Los Angeles, Calif. 90025, U.S.A.

CORY, Desmond. *See* **McCARTHY,** Shaun.

COSBY, Bill. American, b. 1937. Children's non-fiction, Human relations, Humor. Began career as stand-up comic, 1962; television and film actor. *Publs:* You Are Somebody Special, ed. by Charlie W. Shedd (for children), 1978; Fatherhood, 1986; Time Flies, 1988. Add: c/o NBC-TV, Press Dept., 30 Rockefeller Plaza, Room 1420, New York, N.Y. 10112, U.S.A.

COSER, Lewis A. American, b. 1913. Sociology. Distinguished Prof. Emeritus of Sociology, State Univ. of New York at Stony Brook, since 1987 (Distinguished Prof. since 1969). Adj. Prof. of Sociology, Boston Coll., since 1987. Advisory Ed. for Social Sciences, New American Library Inc., NYC; Member, Editorial Bd., Dissent mag. Instr., Univ. of Chicago, 1948–50; Member of faculty, 1951–68, and Prof. of Sociology, 1960–68, Brandeis Univ., Waltham, Mass. Pres., American Sociological Assn., 1974–75. *Publs:* The Functions of Social Conflict, 1956; (with B. Rosenberg) Sociological Theory, 1957, 5th ed. 1975; (with I. Howe) The American Communist Party: A Critical History, 1957, 1963; (ed.) Max Scheler: Ressentiment, 1961; (ed.) Sociology Through Literature, 1963, 1972; Men of Ideas, 1965; (ed.) Georg Simmel, 1965; (ed.) Political Sociology, 1967; Continuities in the Study of Social Conflict, 1967; Masters of Sociological Thought, 1970, 1977; Greedy Organizations, 1974; (with Charles Kadushin and Walter W. Powell) The Culture and Commerce of Publishing, 1982; Refuge Scholars in America: Their Impact and Their Experiences, 1984; A Handful of Thistles, 1988. Add: 27 Shepard St., Cambridge, Mass. 02138, U.S.A.

COSGRAVE, Patrick. Irish, b. 1941. Mystery/Crime/Suspense, Literature, Politics/Government, Biography. Managing Ed., Quartet Crime Books Ltd., London, since 1979. Special Adviser to Margaret Thatcher, 1975–79. *Publs:* The Public Poetry of Robert Lowell, 1970; Churchill at War, 1974; Margaret Thatcher: A Tory and Her Party, 1978; Cheyney's Law (novel), 1977; The Three Colonels (novel), 1979; Origins, Evolution, and Future of Israeli Foreign Policy, 1979; R.A. Butler: An English Life, 1981; Adventure of State (novel), 1984; Thatcher: The First Term, 1985; Carrington: A Life and a Policy, 1985; The Lives of Enoch Powell, 1989. Add: c/o Curtis Brown, 162-168 Regent St., London W1R 5TA, England.

COSH, (Ethel Eleanor) Mary. British. Novels/Short stories, History, Travel/Exploration/Adventure. Lectr. on architecture and local history. *Publs:* The Real World (novel), 1961; (with Ian G. Lindsay) Inveraray and the Dukes of Argyll, 1973; (with Anna Butkovsky- Hewitt) With Gurdjiev in St. Petersburg and Paris, 1978; Historical Walks: Clerkenwell, 1980, Barnsbury, 1981, The New River, 1982; (ed.) Angus McBean in Islington, 1983. Add: 63 Theberton St., London N1, England.

COSTELLO, David F. American, b. 1904. Natural history. Instr. in Biology, Marquette Univ., Milwaukee, Wisc., 1926–32; Range and Wildlife Researcher, U.S. Forest Service, 1934–64. *Publs:* The World of the Porcupine, 1966; The World of the Ant, 1968; The Prairie World, 1969, 1980; The World of the Prairie Dog, 1970; The World of the Gull, 1971; The Desert World, 1972; The Mountain World, 1975; The Seashore World, 1980. Add: 4965 Hogan Dr., Fort Collins, Colo. 80525, U.S.A.

COSTIGAN, Daniel M. American, b. 1929. Engineering/Technology, History, Information science. Information Systems Designer since 1962; Ed./Columnist, Rahway, N.J. News-Record/Clark Patriot, since 1987. Chmn., Publs. Cttee., National Micrographics Assn., 1978–80. *Publs:* FAX: The Principles and Practice of Facsimile Communication, 1971; Micrographic Systems, 1975, 1980; (ed.) Guide to Micrographic Equipment, 1977–79; Electronic Delivery of Documents and Graphics 1978; Encore for a Worthy Performer, 1984. Add: 8 Wyndmoor Way, Edison, N.J. 08820, U.S.A.

COSTLEY, Bill. (William Kirkwood Costley, Jr.) American, b. 1942. Plays/Screenplays, Poetry. Communications Consultant, since 1976. Formerly, medical technician, library asst., English instr., and technical editor/writer. *Publs:* Knosh I Cir (verse), 1975; Rag(a)s (verse), 1978; Hard Currency (play), 1985; The 4th (play), 1986; A(Y)S(H)A (verse), 1988. Add: c/o Arts End Books, P.O. Box 162, Waban, Mass. 02168, U.S.A.

COTES, Peter. British. Theatre, Autobiography/Memoirs/Personal, Biography. Sr. Drama Dir., Associated Rediffusion Television, 1955–57; Sr. Drama Dir., ARTV; Contract Producer/Dir., Assoc. British Picture Corp.; Supervising Producer, Channel 7, Melbourne, 1961–62. *Publs:* No Star Nonsense (autobiography), 1949; (co-author) The Little Fellow: Charlie Chaplin, 1951; (ed.) A Handbook of the Amateur Theatre, 1957; George Robey, 1972; (ed.) Trial of Elvira Barney, 1976; (co-author) Circus, 1977; J.P.: The Man Called Mitch, 1978; The Diminutive One, 1980;

(with H. Atkins) The Barbirollis, 1983; Old Stagers (radio series), 1982–87; Sincerely Dickie, 1989. Add: 7 Hill Lawn Ct., Chipping Norton, Oxon. OX7 5NF, England.

COTTER, James Finn. American, b. 1929. Literature. Prof. of English, Mount Saint Mary Coll., Newburgh, N.Y., since 1963. Contr. writer for The Hudson Review. Fulbright-Hays Lectr., Algeria, 1970–71. *Publs:* Inscape: The Christology and Poetry of Gerard Manley Hopkins, 1972; (trans.) Divine Comedy, 1988. Add: 372 Grand St., Newburgh, N.Y. 12550, U.S.A.

COTTERELL, Geoffrey. British, b. 1919. Novels/Short stories. *Publs:*Then a Soldier, 1944; This is the Way, 1947; Randle in Springtime, 1949; Strait and Narrow, 1950; Westward the Sun, 1952; The Strange Enchantment, 1956; Tea at Shadow Creek, 1958; Tiara Tahiti, 1960; Go, Said the Bird, 1966; Bowers of Innocence, 1970; Amsterdam, 1972. Add: 2 Fulbourne House, Blackwater Rd., Eastbourne, Sussex, England.

COTTLE, Thomas J. American, b. 1937. Education, Psychology, Sociology. Research sociologist and practicing psychotherapist. Children's Defense Fund of Washington Research Project, Cambridge, Mass. Consultant, ABC-TV, since 1972. Asst. Prof. of Social Relations, Harvard Univ., Cambridge, Mass., 1965–69; Fellow, Center for Advanced Study, Univ. of Illinois, Urbana, 1969–70; Research Sociologist, Massachusetts Inst. of Technology, Cambridge, 1970–73. *Publs:* Time's Children: Impressions of Youth, 1971; The Prospect of Youth: Contexts for Sociological Inquiry, 1972; (with C.R. Eisendrath) Out of Discontent: Visions of the Contemporary University, 1972; The Abandoners: Portraits of Loss, Separation and Neglect, 1973; The Voices of School: Educational Issues Through Personal Accounts, 1973; (with S.L. Klineberg) The Present of Things Future: Explorations of Time in Human Experience, 1974; Black Children, White Dreams, 1974; A Family Album: Portraits of Intimacy and Kinship, 1974; Lovers From Denver, 1974; The Horizons of Time: Inquiries and Speculations, 1974; Busing, 1976; Barred from School, 1976; Perceiving Time, 1976; Children in Jail, 1977; College: Reward and Betrayal, 1977; (ed.) Readings in Adolescent Psychology, 1977; Private Lives and Public Accounts, 1977; (co-ed.) Psychotherapy, 1979; Black Testimony, 1980; Children's Secrets, 1980; Divorce and the Jewish Child, 1981; Like Fathers, Like Sons, 1981. Add: c/o WCVB, 5 TV Place, Needham, Mass. O2192, U.S.A.

COTTON, Billy. *See* **ANDREWS**, Allen.

COTTON, John. British, b. 1925. Poetry, Literature. Tutor for the Arvon Foundn. Treasurer, Poetry Soc., London since 1986 (Chmn., 1972–74, 1977). Advisory Ed., Contemporary Poets of the English Language, St. James Press, London, since 1970. Ed., Priapus mag., 1962–72; Chmn., Poetry Soc., 1972–74 and 1977. *Publs:* Fourteen Poems, 1967; Outside the Gates of Eden, 1969; Poetry Introduction I, 1969; Old Movies and Other Poems, 1971; British Poetry since 1965, 1973; Kilroy Was Here, 1975; (with Fred Sedgwick and Freda Downie) A Berkhamsted Three, 1978; Catullus at Sirmio, 1982; Day Book, 1983; The Storyville Portraits, 1984; The Crystal Zoo, 1984; Dust, 1986; Oh Those Happy Feet, 1986; The Poetry File, 1989. Add: 37 Lombardy Dr., Berkhamstead, Herts. HP4 2LQ, England.

COTTRELL, (Sir) Alan (Howard). British, b. 1919. Earth sciences, Environmental science/Ecology, Physics. Prof. of Physical Metallurgy, Univ. of Birmingham, 1949–55; Deputy Head of Metallurgy Div., Atomic Research Establishment, Harwell, 1955–58; Goldsmiths' Prof. of Metallurgy, Univ. of Cambridge, 1958–65; Chief Adviser, Studies, Ministry of Defence, 1965–67; Deputy Chief Scientific Adviser, 1968–71, and Chief Scientific Adviser to H.M. Govt., 1971–74; Master of Jesus Coll., Cambridge, 1974–86. *Publs:* Theoretical Structural Metallurgy, 1948; Dislocations and Plastic Flow in Crystals, 1953; The Mechanical Properties of Matter, 1964; Theory of Crystal Dislocations, 1964; An Introduction to Metallurgy, 1967; Portrait of Nature, 1975; Environmental Economics, 1978; How Safe Is Nuclear Energy?, 1981; Introduction to the Modern Theory of Metals, 1988. Add: Jesus Coll., Cambridge, England.

COUGHLAN, (John) Robert. American, b. 1914. Art, History, Literature, Social commentary/phenomena. Assoc. Ed., Fortune Mag., 1938–43; Articles Ed. 1943–49, and Sr. Staff Writer 1949–69, Life Mag., NYC. *Publs:* Wine of Genius, 1951; The Private World of William Faulkner, 1954; Tropical Africa, 1962; The World of Michelangelo, 1966; Empresses of Russia, Elizabeth and Catherine, 1974; (with Rose Kennedy) Times to Remember, 1974; Kennedy Roots, 1989. Add: Madison St., P.O. Box 847, Sag Harbor, N.Y. 11963, U.S.A.

COULSON, John H(ubert) A(rthur). Writes as John Bonett. British, b. 1906. Mystery/Crime/Suspense. Admiralty contracts Officer, 1940–45; Sales Promotion Exec., 1945–62. *Publs:* all with Felicity Carter as John and Emery Bonett—Dead Lion, 1949; A Banner for Pegasus (in U.S. as Not in the Script), 1951; No Grave for a Lady, 1959; Better Dead (in U.S. as Better Off Dead), 1964; The Private Face of Murder, 1966; This Side Murder? (in U.S. as Murder on the Costa Brava), 1967; The Sound of Murder, 1970; No Time to Kill, 1972; Perish The Thought, 1984. Add: Las Adelfas 28A, Calpe (Alicante), Spain.

COULSON, Juanita. American, b. 1933. Historical/Romance/Gothic, Science fiction/Fantasy. Publr., Forum mag., Science Fiction Writers of America, 1971–72. *Publs:* Crisis on Cheiron (science fiction), 1967: The Singing Stones (science fiction), 1968; The Secret of Seven Oaks, 1972; Door into Terror, 1972; (contrib.) The Comic-Book Book, 1973; Stone of Blood, 1975; Unto the Last Generation (science fiction), 1975; Space Trap (science fiction), 1976; Fear Stalks the Bayou, 1976; Intersection Point, 1976; Dark Priestess, 1977; The Web of Wizardry (Fantasy), 1978; Fire of the Andes, 1979; The Death God's Citadel (Fantasy), 1980; Tomorrow's Heritage (science fiction), 1981; Outward Bound (science fiction), 1982; Legacy of Earth (science fiction), 1989; The Past of Forever (science fiction), 1989. Add: 2677W-500N, Hartford City, Ind. 47348, U.S.A.

COULSON, Robert (Stratton). Also writes as Thomas Stratton. American, b. 1928. Mystery/Crime/Suspense, Science fiction/Fantasy. Publisher, Comic Buyer's Guide, since 1984. Office Worker, Overhead Door Co. of Indiana, 1965–86. Ed., SWFA Forum, 1971–72, and Secty., 1972–74, Science Fiction Writers of America. *Publs:* (as Thomas Stratton) The Invisibility Affair: Man from U.N.C.L.E. No. 11, 1967; (as Thomas Stratton) The Mindtwisters Affair: Man from U.N.C.L.E. No. 12, 1967; (with Gene De Weese) Now You See It/Him/Them, 1975; The Gates of the Universe, 1976; To Renew the Ages, 1977; (with Piers Anthony) But What of Earth?, 1977; (with Gene Weese) Charles Fort Never Mentioned Wombats, 1977; Amazing Stories (book reviews), 1983–86; (with Gene DeWeese) Nightmare Universe, 1985; High Spy, 1987. Add: 2677W—500N, Hartford City, Ind., 47348, U.S.A.

COULTER, Stephen. Also writes as James Mayo. British, b. 1914. Novels/Short stories, Mystery/Crime/Suspense. Reporter in the British home counties; joined Reuters as a Parliamentary Staff Correspondent, 1937; Staff Correspondent for Kemsley Newspapers, in Paris, 1945–65. *Publs:* mystery novels, as Stephen Coulter—The Loved Enemy, 1962; Threshold, 1964; Offshore!, 1965; A Stranger Called the Blues (in U.S. as Players in a Dark Game), 1968 (as U.K. paperback Death in the Sun, 1970); Embassy, 1969; An Account to Render, 1970; The Soyuz Affair, 1977; Blood Tie, 1988; mystery novels as James Mayo—The Quickness of the Hand, 1952; Rebound, 1961; A Season of Nerves, 1962; Hammerhead, 1964; Let Sleeping Girls Lie, 1965; Shamelady, 1966; Once in a Lifetime (in U.S. as Sergeant Death), 1968; The Man above Suspicion, 1969; Asking for It, 1971; other novels, as Stephen Coulter—Damned Shall Be Desire: The Loves of Guy de Maupassant, 1958; The Devil Inside: A Novel of Dostoevsky's Life, 1960; other—The Chateau, 1974. Add: c/o Grafton Books, 8 Grafton St., London W1X 3LA, England.

COUNT, Earl W(endel). American, b. 1899. Anthropology/Ethnology. Prof. Emeritus of Anthropology, Hamilton Coll., Clinton, N.Y., since 1968 (Prof. and Chmn. of Dept., 1947–68); also Episcopal Clergyman, since 1933; Member, Book Cttee., The Key Reporter, Phi Beta Kappa, since 1959. Instr. to Asst. Prof. of Biology and Zoology, San Jose State Coll., Calif., 1928–37; Asst. Prof. to Assoc. Prof. of Human Anatomy, New York Medical Coll., NYC, 1937–45. *Publs:* 4000 Years of Christmas, 1948; This Is Race, 1950; (ed. with G.T. Bowles) Fact and Theory in Social Science: Essays Honoring Douglas Haring, 1964; Das Biogramm, 1970; Being and Becoming Human, 1973. Add: 2616 Saklan Indian Dr., Walnut Creek, Calif. 94595, U.S.A.

COUNTRYMAN, Vern. American, b. 1917. Law, Politics/Government. Prof. of Law, Harvard Law Sch., Cambridge, Mass., since 1963. Prof. of Law, Yale Univ., New Haven, Conn., 1947–55; Dean of Law Sch., Univ. of New Mexico, Albuquerque, 1959–63. *Publs:* Un-American Activities in the State of Washington, 1951; (with W. Gellhorn) The States and Subversion, 1952; Douglas of the Supreme Court, 1959; Debtor and Creditor, 1964, 1974; (with T. Finman) The Lawyer in Modern Society, 1966; Discrimination and the Law, 1965; (with P. Weinstein) Featherbedding and Technological Change, 1965; (with A. Kaufman and Z. Wiseman) Commercial Law, 1971, 1982; The Judicial Record of Judge William O. Douglas, 1974; The Douglas Opinions, 1977. Add: Harvard

Sch., Cambridge, Mass. 02138, U.S.A.

COUPER, J(ohn) M(ill). Australian, b. 1914. Novels/Short stories, Poetry. Assoc. Prof. of English, Macquarie Univ., North Ryde, N.S.W., since 1969. Lectr. in Education, Univ. of Queensland, Brisbane, 1951–53; Headmaster, Knox Grammar Sch., Sydney, 1954–55; Lectr. in English, Sydney Teachers' Coll., 1955–57, and Univ. of New South Wales, Sydney, 1958–68. *Publs:* East of Living, 1967; The Book of Bligh, 1969; The Thundering Good Today (in U.S. as Lottery in Lives), 1970; Looking for a Wave, 1973; In from the Sea, 1974; The Lee Shore, 1979; Canterbury Folk, 1984. Add: 9 Dudley St., Asquith, N.S.W., Australia 2078.

COURTER, Gay (Eleanor). American, b. 1944. Novels, Cookery/Gastronomy/Wine, Homes/Gardens. Secty-Treas., Courter Films and Assocs., Crystal River, Fla., since 1972, and Pres., Courter Media Corp., Crystal River, since 1978. Documentary scriptwriter, PBS. *Publs:* The Beansprout Book, 1973; The Midwife (novel), 1981; River of Dreams (novel), 1984; Code Ezra (novel), 1986. Add: 121 N.W. Crystal St., Crystal River, Fla. 32629, U.S.A.

COURTNEY, Caroline. British, b. 1920. Historical/Romance/Gothic. *Publs:* Duchess in Disguise, 1979; A Wager for Love, 1979; Love Unmasked, 1979; Guardian of the Heart, 1979; Dangerous Engagement, 1979; The Fortunes of Love, 1980; Forbidden Love, 1980; Love Triumphant, 1980; The Romantic Rivals, 1980; Love's Masquerade, 1981; Heart of Honour, 1982; Libertine in Love, 1982; Destiny's Duchess, 1982; Love in Waiting, 1982; A Lover's Victory, 1982; The Daring Heart, 1983; Love of My Life, 1985; The Tempestuous Affair, 1985; The Courier of Love, 1986; Conspiracy of Kisses, 1986. Add: c/o Warner Books, 75 Rockefeller Plaza, New York, N.Y. 10019, U.S.A.

COURTNEY, Gwendoline. British. Children's fiction. *Publs:* Torley Grange, 1935; The Grenville Garrison, 1940; The Denehurst Secret Service, 1940; Well Done, Denehurst!, 1941; Sally's Family, 1946; Stepmother (U.S. as Those Verney Girls), 1948; Long Barrow, 1950; A Coronet for Cathie, 1950; At School with the Stanhopes, 1951; The Girls of Friar's Rise, 1952; The Chiltons, 1953; The Wild Lorings at School, 1954; The Wild Lorings, Detectives, 1956; Passage of Arms (TV). Add: Silverstones, Green Lane, Stour Row, Shaftesbury, Dorset, England.

COUSINS, Margaret. Has also written as Avery Johns. American, b. 1905. Children's fiction, Children's non-fiction, Biography. Ed., Pictorial Review, McCall's and Good Housekeeping mags., 1937–58; Sr. Ed., Doubleday & Co., NYC, 1961–70; Fiction/Book Ed., Ladies Home Journal, 1971–73. *Publs:* Uncle Edgar and the Reluctant Saint, 1948; Ben Franklin of Old Philadelphia, 1952; Christmas Gift, 1952; We Were There at the Battle of the Alamo, 1958; (with M. Truman) Souvenir (biography), 1955; (as Avery Johns) Traffic with Evil, 1962; (ed.) Stories of Love and Marriage, 1961; The Story of Thomas Edison, 1965; The Boy in the Alamo, 1983. Add: Box 1468, San Antonio, Tex. 78295, U.S.A.

COUSINS, Norman. American, b. 1915. Literature, Social commentary/phenomena, Biography. Adjunct Prof., School of Medicine, Univ. of California, Los Angeles, since 1978. Pres., World Federalist Assn., since 1980. Ed., Saturday Review, 1940–71, World Mag., 1972–73, Saturday Review/World, 1973–74, and Saturday Review, 1975–78. Vice-Pres., P.E.N. American Center, 1952–55; Co-Chmn, National Cttee. for Sane Nuclear Policy, 1957–63; Chmn., Bd. of Dirs., National Educational Television, 1969–70. *Publs:* The Good Inheritance, 1942; (ed.) A Treasure of Democracy, 1942; (ed. with W.R. Benet) The Poetry of Freedom, 1948; Modern Man Is Obsolete, 1945; Talks with Nehru, 1951; Who Speaks for Man, 1953; In God We Trust, 1958; Dr. Schweitzer of Lambarene, 1960; In Place of Folly, 1961; Present Tense, 1967; The Improbable Triumvirate, 1972; The Celebration of Life, 1974; Anatomy of an Illness, 1979; Human Options, 1981; The Physician in Literature, 1982; The Healing Heart, 1983; (ed.) The Words of Albert Schweitzer, 1984; Albert Schweitzer's Mission: Healing and Peace, 1985; The Pathology of Power, 1987. Add: Dean's Office, School of Medicine, 12-138 CHS, UCLA, Los Angeles, Calif. 90024, U.S.A.

COUSINS, Peter Edward. British, b. 1928. Theology/Religion. Editorial Dir., Paternoster Press, since 1975. Head of Religious Education Dept., Mayfield Sch., Putney, London, 1961–66; Ed., Spectrum mag., 1968–74; Sr. Lectr., 1966–71, and Principal Lectr., 1971–75, Dept. of Religious Studies, Gipsy Hill Coll., Kingston upon Thames. *Publs:* A Christian's Guide to the Death of Christ, 1967; Education and Christian Parents, 1969; Christianity and Sexual Liberation, 1972; (with Pamela Cousins) The Power of the Air, 1978; The Brethren, 1982. Add: The Paternoster Press Ltd., Paternose House, 3 Mount Radford Cres., Exeter,

Devon EX2 4JW, England.

COUZYN, Jeni. Canadian (born South African), b. 1942. Poetry. Tutor, Arvon Foundn., since 1973. *Publs:* (ed.) Twelve to Twelve: Poems Commissioned for Poetry D-Day, Camden Arts Festival, 1970, 1970; Flying, 1970; Monkey's Wedding, 1972, 1978; Christmas in Africa, 1975; House of Changes, 1978; The Happiness Birds, 1978; A Time to Be Born, 1981; Life by Drowning: Selected Poems, 1983, 1985; (ed.) The Bloodaxe Book of Contemporary Women Poets, 1985; Tom-Cat-Lion (children's book), 1987; Bad Day (juvenile), 1988. Add: c/o Bloodaxe Books, P.O. Box 1SN, Newcastle upon Tyne NE99 1SN, England.

COVER, Arthur Byron. American, b. 1950. Science fiction. Member of the extension faculty, Univ. of California at Los Angeles. Interviewer, Vertex, Los Angeles, 1974–75. *Publs:* Autumn Angels, 1975; The Sound of Winter, 1976; The Platypus of Doom and Other Nihilists (short stories), 1976; An East Wind Coming, 1979; Flash Gordon, 1980; The Kings of Saturn (juvenile), 1985; (ed. with Martin Greenberg) The Best of the New Wave, 1986. Add: c/o Jayne Rotrosen Agency, 226 E. 32nd St., New York, N.Y. 10016, U.S.A.

COVINGTON, James W. American, b. 1917. History. Dana Prof. of History, Univ. of Tampa, since 1976 (Assoc. Prof., 1950–53; Dean, Evening Div., 1961–64; Prof., 1954–76). Historian, Apollo History, National Aeronautics and Space Admin., Kennedy Space Center, 1968–70. *Publs:* (co-author) Story of the University of Tampa, 1955; Story of Southwestern Florida, 1957; The British Meet the Seminoles, 1961; (ed.) Pirates, Indians and Spaniards, 1963; Under the Minarets, 1982; The Billy Bowlegs War, 1983. Add: 2901 S. Beach Dr., Tampa, Fla. 33629, U.S.A.

COWAN, Edward (James). British, b. 1944. History, Biography. Prof. of History, Univ. of Guelph, since 1983 (Assoc. Prof., 1979–83). Lectr. in Scottish History, Univ. of Edinburgh, 1967–79. *Publs:* Montrose: For Covenant and King, 1977; The People's Past: Scottish Folk in Scottish History, 1980. Add: Dept. of History, Univ. of Guelph, Guelph, Ont. N1G 2W1, Canada.

COWAN, Gordon. British, b. 1933. Education. Head of Student Services, Manchester Polytechnic, since 1983. Teacher in Liverpool Secondary Schs., 1955–65; Lectr. in Education, 1965–68, and Head of Education Dept., 1968–72, C.F. Mott Coll. of Education; Deputy Principal, Manchester Coll. of Education, 1972–77; Asst. Principal, Manchester Coll. of Higher Education, 1977–83. *Publs:* Project Work in the Secondary School, 1967; A Centennial History of Sale Moor Cricket Club, 1987. Add: 39 Barwell Rd., Sale, Cheshire M33 5EE, England.

COWAN, Henry (Jacob). Australian, b. 1919. Engineering, Technology. Ed., Architectural Science Review, since 1958. Prof. and Head, Dept. of Architectural Science, Univ. of Sydney, 1953–84. *Publs:* The Theory of Prestressed Concrete Design, 1956; (with P.R. Smith) Design of Reinforced Concrete, 1963, 3rd ed. 1976; Reinforced and Prestressed Concrete in Torsion, 1965, 2nd ed. 1972; An Historical Outline of Architectural Science, 1966, 3rd ed. 1976; (with P.R. Smith) The Design of Prestressed Concrete, 1966; (with J.S. Gero, G.D. Ding and R.W. Muncey) Models in Architecture, 1968; Architectural Structures, 1971; 3rd ed. 1980; Dictionary of Architectural Science, 1973; (with J.S. Gero) Design of Building Frames, 1976; The Master Builders, 1977, 1985; Science and Building, 1978; (with J.F. Dixon) A Building Science Laboratory Manual, 1978; Solar Energy Applications in the Design of Buildings, 1980; (with F. Wilson) Structural Systems, 1981; Design of Reinforced Concrete Structures, 1982, 1989; (with P.R. Smith) Environmental Systems, 1983; Predictive Methods for the Energy Conserving Design of Buildings, 1983; Energy Conservation in the Design of Multi-Story Buildings, 1984; (with P.R. Smith) Dictionary of Architectural and Building Technology, 1986; Encyclopedia of Building Technology, 1987; (with P.R. Smith) The Science and Technology of Building Materials, 1988. Add: Dept. of Architectural Science, Univ. of Sydney, N.S.W. 2006, Australia.

COWAN, Ian B(orthwick). Scottish, b. 1932. History. Prof. of Scottish History, Univ. of Glasgow, since 1983 (Lectr., 1962–70 Sr. Lectr., 1970–77; Reader, 1977–83). Treas., Scottish Historical Conference Trust, since 1952, and Scottish History Soc., since 1965; Member of Advisory Cttee. on Papal Registers, Irish Manuscript Commn., Dublin, since 1971; Vice-Pres., Historical Assn., London, since 1982. Asst. Lectr. in Scottish History, Univ. of Edinburgh, 1956–57; Lectr. in History, Newbattle Abbey Coll., Dalkeith, Scotland, 1959–62. Pres., Historical Assn., Glasgow Branch, 1968–70, and Scottish Church History Soc., 1971–74. *Publs:* (ed.) Blast and Counterblast, 1960; (ed.) The Parishes of Medieval

Scotland, 1967; (ed. with A.I. Dunlop) Calendar of Scottish Supplications to Rome, 1970; The Enigma of Mary Stuart, 1971; (ed. with D.E. Easson) Medieval Religious Houses—Scotland, 1976; The Scottish Covenanters 1660-1688, 1976; Regional Aspects of the Scottish Reformation, 1978; The Scottish Reformation, 1982; (ed. with D. Shaw) Renaissance and Reformation Scotland, 1982; (co-ed.) The Knights of St. John of Jerusalem in Scotland, 1983; Ayrshire Abbeys: Crossraguel and Kilwinning 1986; Mary Queen of Scots, 1987. Add: Dept. of Scottish History, Univ. of Glasgow, 9 University Gardens, Glasgow G12 8QH, Scotland.

COWAN, James C. American, b. 1927. Literary Criticism/History. Adj. Prof. of English, Univ. of North Carolina, Chapel Hill, since 1983. Instr., 1963–64, and Asst. Prof., 1964–66, Tulane Univ., New Orleans; Asst. Prof., 1966–67, Assoc. Prof., 1967–72, and Prof., 1972–83, Univ. of Arkansas, Fayetteville. Ed., D.H. Lawrence Review, 1968–83. *Publs:* D.H. Lawrence's American Journey: A Study in Literature and Myth, 1970; D.H. Lawrence: An Annotated Bibliography of Writings About Him, 2 vols., 1982, 1985; D.H. Lawrence and the Trembling Balance, 1990. Add: Dept. of English, Univ. of North Carolina, Chapel Hill, N.C. 27514, U.S.A.

COWAN, Peter. Australian, b. 1914. Novels/Short stories, Biography. Research Fellow, Dept. of English, Univ. of Western Australia, since 1979 (Member of Faculty, 1962–79). Sr. English Master, Scotch Coll., Swanbourne, W.A., 1950–62. *Publs:* Drift Stories, 1944; The Unploughed Land: Stories, 1959; Summer, 1964; (ed.) Short Story Landscape: The Modern Short Story, 1964; The Empty Street: Stories, 1965; Seed, 1966; (co-ed.) Spectrum One to Three, 1970–79; (ed.) Today: Contemporary Short Stories, 1971; The Tins and Other Stories, 1973; (ed.) A Faithful Picture: Letters of Eliza and Thomas Brown, Swan River Colony 1841-1851, 1977; Unique Position: A Biography of Edith Dircksey Cowan, 1978; (ed.) Westerly 21, 1978; Mobiles (stories), 1979; (ed.) Perspectives One (short fiction), 1985; A Window in Mrs. X's Place (short stories), 1986; The Color of The Sky (novel), 1986; Maitland Brown: A View of 19th Century Western Australia (biography), 1988; Voices (stories), 1988. Add: English Dept., Univ. of Western Australia, Nedlands, W.A. 6009, Australia.

COWAN, Tom Keith. New Zealander, b. 1916. Accountancy/Money/Finance. Prof. of Accountancy, Univ. of Otago, Dunedin, since 1961, now Emeritus. Writer of series of textbooks on Accounting Exercises and Discussion Topics, for Cowan & Valentine. Public Accountant and part-time lectr., 1945–60. *Publs:* (with B. Popoff) Management Accounting: Objectives, Systems, Analysis of Relevant Costs, 1971; Financial Analysis: Data for Decisions, 1972; (with W.G. Kenley) Case Studies in Financial Accounting, 1976; (with Popoff) Analysis and Interpretation of Financial Statements, 1981, 1985; Commerce at Otago 1912–1987: A Personal Perspective, 1988. Add: 48 Elliot St., Dunedin, New Zealand.

COWASJEE, Saros. Canadian, b. 1931. Novels/Short stories, Plays/Screenplays, Literature. Prof. of English, Univ. of Regina, Regina, Sask., Canada, since 1971 (joined faculty, 1963). Asst. Ed., Times of India Press., Bombay, India, 1961–63; Managing Ed., Wascana Review, 1966–70; Research Assoc., Univ. of California, Berkeley, 1970–71; Gen. Ed., Arnold-Heinemann's (New Delhi) 'Literature of The Raj' series, since 1984. *Publs:* Sean O'Casey: The Man Behind the Plays, 1963; O'Casey, 1966; Stories and Sketches, 1970; (ed.) Author to Critic: The Letters of Mulk Raj Anand, 1973; Goodbye to Elsa (novel), 1974; Coolie: An Assessment, 1976; So Many Freedoms: A Study of the Major Fiction of Mulk Raj Anand, 1977; Nude Therapy (short stories), 1978; The Last of the Maharajas (screenplay), 1980; (ed. with Vasant Shahane) Modern Indian Fiction, 1981; Suffer Little Children (novel), 1982; (ed.) Stories from the Raj, 1982; (ed. with Shiv. K. Kumar) Modern Indian Short Stories, 1982; (ed.) The Raj and After (anthol.), 1986; (ed.) More Stories from the Raj and After (anthol.), 1986; (ed. with K.S. Duggal) When the British Left, 1987; (ed.) Women Writers of the Raj: Short Fiction (anthol.), 1989. Add: Dept. of English, Regina Univ., Regina, Sask. S4S 0A2, Canada.

COWDREY, (Michael) Colin. British, b. 1932. Sports/Physical education/Keeping fit. Executive, Barclays Bank. Captain, Tonbridge Cricket Team, 1946–50, Kent Cricket Team, 1950–70, Oxford Cricket Team, 1952–54 and England Cricket Team, 1954–70. Pres., MCC (Marylebone Cricket Club), 1986–87. *Publs:* Cricket Today, 1961; Time for Reflection; Tackle Cricket This Way; Incomparable Game; Autobiography of a Cricketer, 1976. Add: 54 Lombard St., London EC3, England.

COWEN, Frances. Also writes historical romance as Eleanor Hyde.

British, b. 1915. Mystery/Crime/Suspense, Historical/Romance/Gothic, Children's fiction. Asst. Secty., Royal Literary Fund, London, 1955–66. *Publs:* juvenile—In the Clutch of the Green Hand, 1929; The Wings That Failed, 1931, abridged ed. as The Plot That Failed, 1933; The Milhurst Mystery, 1933; The Conspiracy of Silence, 1935; The Perilous Adventure, 1936; Children's Book of Pantomimes, 1936; Laddie's Way: The Adventures of a Fox Terrier, 1939; The Girl Who Knew Too Much, 1940; Mystery Tower, 1945; Honor Bound, 1946; Castle in Wales, 1947; The Secret of Arrivol, 1947; Mystery at the Walled House, 1951; The Little Countess, 1954; The Riddle of the Rocks, 1956; Clover Cottage, 1958; The Secret of Grange Farm, 1961; The Secret of the Loch, 1963; mystery and romance novels for adults—The Little Heiress, 1961; The Balcony, 1962; A Step in the Dark, 1962; The Desperate Holiday, 1962; The Elusive Quest, 1965; The Bitter Reason, 1966; Scented Danger, 1966; The One Between, 1967; The Gentle Obsession, 1968; The Fractured Silence, 1969; The Daylight Fear, 1969; The Shadow of Polperro, 1969; Edge of Terror, 1970; The Hounds of Carvello, 1970; The Nightmare Ends, 1970; The Lake of Darkness, 1971; The Unforgiving Moment, 1971; (as Eleanor Hyde) Tudor Maid, 1972; (as Eleanor Hyde) Tudor Masquerade, 1972; (as Eleanor Hyde) Tudor Mayhem, 1973; The Curse of the Clodaghs, 1973; Shadow of Theale, 1974; The Village of Fear, 1974; (as Eleanor Hyde) Tudor Mystery, 1974; The Secret of Weir House, 1975; The Dangerous Child, 1975; The Haunting of Helen Farley, 1976; The Medusa Connection, 1976; Sinister Melody, 1976; (as Eleanor Hyde) Tudor Myth, 1976; The Silent Pool, 1977; The Lost One, 1977; (as Eleanor Hyde) Tudor Mausoleum, 1977; (as Eleanor Hyde) Tudor Murder, 1977; Gateway to Nowhere, 1978; The House Without a Heart, 1978; (as Eleanor Hyde) Tudor Mansion, 1978; (as Eleanor Hyde) Tudor Malice, 1979; (as Eleanor Hyde) The Princess Passes, 1979; House of Larne, 1980; Wait for Night, 1980; The Elusive Lover, 1981; Sunrise at Even, 1982. Add: Flat 1, 13 Thornton Hill, Wimbledon, London SW19, England.

COWEN, Ron(ald). American, b. 1944. Plays/Screenplays. *Publs:* Summertree, 1968; Saturday Adoption, 1969; The Book of Murder, 1974; (with Daniel Lipman) An Early Frost, 1985. Add: Dramatists Play Service Inc., 440 Park Ave. South, New York, N.Y. 10016, U.S.A.

COWEN, Zelman. Australian, b. 1919. Law. Provost, Oriel Coll., Oxford, since 1982. Chmn., British Press Council, since 1983. Prof. of Public Law, and Dean of Faculty of Law, Univ. of Melbourne, 1951–66; Vice-Chancellor, Univ. of New England, 1967–70; Vice Chancellor, Univ. of Queensland, 1970–77; Gov.-Gen. of Australia, 1977–82. *Publs:* (specialist ed.) Dicey: Conflict of Laws, 6th ed. 1949; Australia and the United States: Some Legal Comparisons, 1954; (with P.B. Carter) Essays on the Law of Evidence, 1956; American-Australian Private International Law, 1957; Federal Jurisdiction in Australia, 1959, (with Leslie Zines) 1978; (with D. Mendes da Costa) Matrimonial Causes Jurisdiction, 1961; The British Commonwealth of Nations in a Changing World, 1964; Sir John Latham and Other Papers, 1965; Sir Isaac Isaacs, 1967; The Private Man (ABC Boyer Lectures), 1969; Individual Liberty and the Law (Tagore Law Lectrs.), 1975; The Virginia Lectures, 1984; Reflections on Medicine, Biotechnology and the Law, 1986; A Touch of Healing, 3 vols., 1986. Add: Oriel Coll., Oxford, England.

COWIE, Evelyn Elizabeth. British. Children's non-fiction, Cookery/Gastronomy/Wine. Lectr. in Education, King's Coll., Univ. of London, 1965–84 (Sr. Lectr., Goldsmiths' Coll., 1957–65). Writer of Living Through History, 12 vols., Cassell, London, 1964–75. *Publs:* Breakfasts, 1958; Leftovers, 1959; Man and Roads, 1963; Man and Shops, 1964; Man and Crusades, 1969; Examining the Evidence: Education, 1974; (with Leonard W. Cowie) The Environment through Photographs: Architecture, 1974; History and the Slow-Learning Child, 1979. Add: 38 Stratton Rd., London SW19 3JG, England.

COWIE, Hamilton Russell. Australian, b. 1931. History. Sr. Lectr. in Education, Univ. of Queensland, St. Lucia, since 1972. Asst. to Headmaster, Church of England Grammar Sch., Brisbane, 1970–72. *Publs:* Frankfurt to Fra Mauro: A Thematic History of the Modern World, 1975; Revolutions in the Modern World, 1979; Crossroads: Nationalism and Internationalism in the Modern World, Economic Trends in the Modern World, Asia and Australia in World Affairs, The Historical Background to Problems of Contemporary Society, Imperialism and Race Relations, 5 vols., 1979–82; (with K. Cowie) Discovering Brisbane, 1981; Obedience or Choice: The Major Issues of the Modern World, 1987. Add: c/o Dept. of Education, Univ. of Queensland, Brisbane, Qld. 4067, Australia.

COWIE, Leonard Wallace. British, b. 1919. History, Theology/Religion, Biography. Sr. Lectr. in History, Whiteland's Coll., London, 1969–82. *Publs:* Henry Newman: An American in London

1708-1743; About the Bible; Seventeenth-Century Europe; Eighteenth-Century Europe; Hanoverian England: The March of the Cross; The Reformation; Martin Luther; (with J.S. Gummer) The Christian Calendar, 1974 (with Evelyn E. Cowie) The Environment Through Photographs: Architecture, 1974; Decisive Battles, 1976; Sixteenth-Century Europe, 1977; The Railway Age, 1978; History in Close-Up, 1981; (with Robert Wolfson) Years of Nationalism, 1985; The Age of Exploration and Discovery, 1986; The Age of Scientific Discovery, 1987; The French Revolution, 1988. Add: 38 Stratton Rd., London SW19 3JG, England.

COWIE, Mervyn. British, b. 1909. Natural history, Autobiography/Memoirs/Personal. Trustee, East African Wild Life Soc.; Vice-Pres., Fauna Preservation Soc.; Consultant, World Wildlife Fund. Founder and former Dir., National Parks of Kenya, 1946–66; Member, Kenya Legislative Council, 1951–60; Financial Dir., Flying Doctor Service, Nairobi, 1972–79. *Publs:* Fly Vulture, 1961; I Walk with Lions, 1964; African Lion, 1966. Add: Flint Cottage, Benhall, Saxmundham, Suffolk, IP17 1JB, England.

COWLES, Fleur. American. Art, Autobiography/Memoirs/Personal, Biography. Freelance painter and writer. Ed., Flairbook, U.S.A., 1952; Founder and Ed., Flair Mag., 1950–51; Asst. Ed., Look mag., U.S.A., 1949–55. *Publs:* Bloody Precedent, 1951; The Case of Salvador Dali, 1959; The Hidden World of Hadhramoutt, 1964; I Can Tell It Now, 1965; Treasures of the British Museum, 1966; Tiger Flower, 1969; Lion and Blue, 1974; Friends and Memories, 1975; Romany Free, 1977; The Love of Tiger Flower, 1980; All Too True, 1980; The Flower Game, 1983; Flowers, 1985; People as Animals, 1985; To Be a Unicorn, 1986; An Artist's Journey, 1988. Add: A5 Albany, Piccadilly, London W1, England.

COWLIN, Dorothy. British, b. 1911. Novels/Short stories, Children's fiction, Children's non-fiction. *Publs:* Penny to Spend; Winter Solstice; The Holly and the Ivy; Rowanberry Wine; The Slow Train Home; An End and a Beginning; Draw the Well Dry; The Pair of Them; Greenland Seas; A Woman in the Desert; Elizabeth Barrett Browning; Cleopatra, 1970. Add: 14 Littledale, Pickering, N. Yorks., England.

COWPER, Richard. *See* MURRY, Colin Middleton.

COX, Alfred Bertram. Australian, b. 1902. History, Politics/Government, Travel/Exploration/Adventure, Autobiography/Memoirs/Personal. *Publs:* Farming is Fun, 1952, 1975; The Other Half, 1956; The Better Half, 1958; Siestas and Fiestas, 1961; Local Government in South Australia, 1964, 1965; Figures Aren't Funny, 1966; Out of the Rough, 1975; Fairways on the Mount, 1977; The First Hundred Years, 1981; Links with a Past, 1987. Add: Cooinda, 2 Nioka Ct., Beaumont, S.A. 5066, Australia.

COX, Archibald. American, b. 1912. Law. Emeritus Prof., Harvard Univ., Cambridge, Mass., since 1984 (Lectr., 1945–46, Prof. of Law, 1946–58, Royal Prof. of Law, 1958–65, Williston Prof. of Law, 1965–67, Carl M. Loeb Univ. Prof., 1976–84); Visiting Prof. of Law, Boston Univ. since 1984. Member, Bd. of Dirs., Harvard Univ. Press; Chmn. Bd. of Govs., Common Cause, since 1980. Admitted to the Massachusetts Bar, 1937; with Law firm of Ropes, Gray, Best, Coolidge and Rugg, Boston, 1938–41; Attorney, Office of the Solicitor-Gen., U.S. Dept. of Justice, 1941–53; Assoc. Solicitor, U.S. Dept. of Labor, 1943–45; Solicitor- Gen. of the U.S., 1961–65; Special Prosecutor, Watergate Special Prosecution Force, U.S. Dept. of Justice, Washington, D.C., 1973; Visiting Pitt Prof. of American History, Cambridge Univ., England, 1974–75. Chmn., Wage Stabilization Bd., 1952, and Advisory Panel to Senate Cttee. on Education and Labor, 1958–59; Member, Bd. of Overseers, Harvard Univ.,1962–65. *Publs:* (with Derek Bok) Cases in Labor Law, 1948, (with Derek Bok and Robert German) 9th ed. 1981; Law and the National Labor Policy, 1960; (with Mark DeWolfe Howe and J.R. Wiggins) Civil Rights, the Constitution, and the Courts, 1967; The Warren Court: Constitutional Decision as an Instrument of Reform, 1968; The Role of the Supreme Court in American Government, 1976; Freedom of Expression, 1981; The Court and the Constitution, 1987. Add: Harvard Law Sch., Cambridge, Mass. 02138, U.S.A.

COX, Charles Brian. British, b. 1928. Poetry, Education (not textbooks on other subjects), Literature. Prof. of English Literature, Univ. of Manchester since 1966. Co-Ed., Critical Quarterly, since 1959; Dir., Manchester Poetry Centre; since 1971. Lectr., and Sr. Lectr., Univ. of Hull, 1954–66. *Publs:* The Free Spirit, 1963; (with A.E. Dyson) Modern Poetry, 1963; Conrad's "Nostromo", 1964; (with A.E. Dyson) The Practical Criticism of Poetry, 1965; (ed with A.E. Dyson) Poems of This Cen-

tury, 1968; (ed. with A.E. Dyson) Word in the Desert, 1968; (ed. with A.P. Hinchliffe) "The Waste Land": A Casebook, 1968; (ed. with A.E. Dyson) The Black Papers on Education, 1971; (ed. with A.E. Dyson) The Twentieth Century Mind, 3 vols., 1972; (ed.) Conrad: "Youth", "Heart of Darkness", and "The End of the Tether", 1974; Joseph Conrad: The Modern Imagination, 1974; (ed. with R. Boyson) Black Paper 1975, 1975; (ed. with R. Boyson) Black Paper 1977, 1977; Conrad, 1977; Every Common Sight (verse), 1981; Two Headed Monster (verse), 1985. Add: 20 Park Gates Dr., Cheadle Hulme, Cheshire, England.

COX, Christopher Barry. British, b. 1931. Biogeography/Palaeontology, Zoology. Prof. since 1976, and Head of Dept. of Biology, 1984–88, King's Coll., London (Lectr., 1956–66; Sr. Lectr., 1966–69; Reader, 1969–76). *Publs:* Prehistoric Animals, 1969; (with I.N. Healey and P.D. Moore) Biogeography—An Ecological and Evolutionary Approach, 1973, 4th ed. (with P.D. Moore) 1985; Prehistoric World, 1985; Macmillan Illustrated Encyclopedia of Dinosaurs and Prehistoric Animals, 1988; Atlas of the Living World, 1989. Add: Div. of Biosphere Sciences, King's Coll., Campden Hill Rd., London W8 7AH, England.

COX, Constance. British, b. 1915. Plays/Screenplays. *Publs:* Miss Letitia; The Caliph's Minstrel; The Desert Air; What Brutes Men Are; Parson Brontë's Daughters; adaptations—Vanity Fair, 1946; Spring at Marino, 1951; The Picture of Dorian Gray, 1953; Jane Eyre, 1959; Lord Arthur Savile's Crime; Pride and Prejudice; Northanger Abbey; Mansfield Park; Wuthering Heights; Because of the Lockwoods; Trilby; The Woman in White; The Three-Cornered Hat; A Christmas Carol; A Miniature Beggar's Opera; Maria Marten; Everyman; Three Knaves of Normandy; The Murder Game; Lady Audley's Secret; A Time for Loving. Add: 2 Princes Ave., Hove, Sussex BN3 4GD, England.

COX, (Sir) Geoffrey (Sandford). New Zealander, b. 1910. History. Reporter, Foreign and War Corresp., News Chronicle, 1935–37, and Daily Express, 1937–40; Political Corresp., News Chronicle, 1945; Asst. Ed., News Chronicle, 1954; Regular Contrib., B.B.C. radio and T.V., 1945–56; Ed. and Chief Exec., Independent Televison News, 1956–68; Deputy Chmn., Yorkshire Television, 1968–71; Chmn., Tyne & Tees Television, 1971–74 and London Broadcasting Co., 1977–81. *Publs:* Defence of Madrid, 1937; Red Army Moves, 1941; Road to Trieste, 1946; Race for Trieste, 1977; See It Happen, 1983; A Tale of Two Battles, 1987; Countdown to War, 1988. Add: Amadines, Coln St. Dennis, Glos., England.

COX, Harvey. American, b. 1929. Theology/Religion. Victor Thomas Prof. of Divinity, Harvard Univ., Cambridge, Mass., since 1970 (Assoc. Prof., 1965–70). Dir., Religious Activities, Oberlin Coll., Ohio, 1955–58; Prog. Assoc., American Baptist Home Mission Soc., 1958–62; Fraternal Worker, Gossner Mission, East Berlin, 1962–63; Asst. Prof., Andover Newton Theological Sch., Mass., 1963–65. *Publs:* The Secular City, 1965; God's Revolution and Man's Responsibility, 1965; The Feast of Fools, 1969; The Seduction of the Spirit: The Use and Misuse of People's Religion, 1973; Turning East: The Promise and Peril of the New Orientalism, 1977; Just As I Am, 1983; Religion in the Secular City, 1984; Many Mansions: A Christian's Encounter with Other Faiths, 1988; The Silencing of Leonardo Boff: The Vatican and the Future of World Christianity, 1988. Add: Harvard Univ. Divinity Sch., Cambridge, Mass. 02140, U.S.A.

COX, Kevin Robert. British, b. 1939. Geography. Prof. of Geography, Ohio State Univ., Columbus, since 1971 (Asst. Prof. 1965–68; Assoc. Prof. 1968–71). *Publs:* (co-ed. with R.G. Golledge) Behavioral Problems in Geography: A Symposium, 1969; Man, Location and Behavior: An Introduction to Human Geography, 1972; Conflict, Power and Politics in the City: A Geographic View, 1973; (co-ed. with D. Reynolds and J. Rokkan) Locational Approaches to Power and Conflict, 1974; (ed.) Urbanization and Conflict in Market Societies, 1978; Location and Public Problems: A Political Geography of the Contemporary World, 1979; (ed. with R.G. Golledge) Behavioral Problems in Geography Revisited, 1981; (ed. with R.J. Johnston) Conflict, Politics and the Urban Scene, 1982. Add: 111 Forest Ridge, Worthington, Ohio 43085, U.S.A.

COX, Richard (Hubert Francis). British, b. 1931. Novels/Short stories, International relations/Current affairs, Travel/Exploration/Adventure. Managing Dir., Thornton Cox Ltd., Publishers, London, since 1972. Defence Corresp., Daily Telegraph, London, 1966–72. *Publs:* Pan Africanism in Practice, 1964; Kenyatta's Country, 1965; Traveller's Guide to East Africa, 1966, 7th ed., as Traveller's Guide to Kenya and N. Tanzania, 1987; Sealion: The German Invasion of Britain, 1940, 1974; Sam 7, 1977; Auction, 1979; The Time It Takes, 1980; The KGB Directive,

1981; The Ice Raid, 1983; Ground Zero, 1984; The Columbus Option, 1986; An Agent of Influence, 1988. Add: P.O. Box 88, Alderney, Channel Islands, United Kingdom.

COX, Roger (Kenneth). British, b. 1936. Business/Trade/Industry. Marketing Consultant, since 1975. Retail Development Mgr., John Menzies, 1968–71; Group Marketing Officer, Development, ADA Halifax, 1973–75. *Publs:* Retail Site Assessment, 1968; Retail Development, 1971; Retailing, 1978; Running Your Own Shop, 1985; (with J.P.R. Brittain) Retail Management, 1988. Add: 30 London Rd., Westerham, Kent TN16 1BD, England.

COX, William R(obert), Also writes as Mike Frederic, Joel Reeve, Roger G. Spellman and Jonas Ward. American, b. 1901. Mystery/Crime/Suspense, Westerns/Adventure, Children's fiction, Sports/Physical education/Keeping fit, Biography. Freelance writer. Former Pres., Western Writers of America. *Publs:* western novels—The Lusty Men, 1957; Comanche Moon: A Novel of the West, 1959; The Duke, 1962; The Outlawed, 1963, as Navajo Blood, 1973; Bigger Than Texas, 1963; (as Roger G. Spellman) Tall for a Texan, 1965; The Gunsharp, 1965; Black Silver, 1967; Day of the Gun, 1967; Firecreek (novelization of screenplay), 1968; Moon of the Corbre, 1969; Law Comes to Razor Edge, 1970; (as Jonas Ward) Buchanan's War, 1970; (as Jonas Ward) Trap for Buchanan, 1971; The Sixth Horseman, 1972; Buchanan's Gamble, 1972; Jack o' Diamonds, 1972; Buchanan's Siege, 1972; Buchanan on the Run, 1973; Get Buchanan, 1973; The Gunshop, 1973; Buchanan Takes Over, 1974; Buchanan Calls the Shots, 1975; Buchanan's Big Showdown, 1975; Buchanan's Texas Treasure, 1976; Buchanan's Stolen Railway, 1977; Buchanan's Manhunt, 1978; Buchanan's Range War, 1979; Buchanan's Big Fight, 1980; mystery novels—Make My Coffin Strong, 1954; The Tycoon and the Tigress, 1958; Hell to Pay, 1958; Murder in Vegas, 1960; Death Comes Early, 1961; Death on Location, 1962; Way to Go, Doll Baby!, 1966; Hot Times (novel of era, 1932), 1973; juvenile novels—Five Were Chosen: Basketball Story, 1956; Gridiron Duel, 1959; The Wild Pitch, 1963; Tall on the Court, 1964; Third and Eight to Go, 1964; Big League Rookie, 1965 (as Mike Frederic) Frank Merriwell, Freshman Quarterback, 1965; (as Mike Frederic) Frank Merriwell, Freshman Pitcher, 1965; (as Mike Frederic) Frank Merriwell, Sports Car Racer, 1965; Trouble at Second Base, 1966; The Valley Eleven, 1966; (as Joel Reeves) Goal Ahead, 1967; Jump Shot Joe, 1968; Rookie in the Backcourt, 1970; Big League Sandlotters, 1971; Third and Goal, 1971; Playoff, 1972; Gunner on the Court, 1972; The Running Back, 1972; Chicano Cruz, 1972; The Backyard Five, 1973; Game, Set, and Match, 1973; The Unbeatable Five, 1974; Battery Mates, 1978; Home Court Is Where You Find It, 1980; otherLuke Short and His Era, 1961, in U.K. as Luke Short: Famous Gambler of the Old West, 1962; The Mets Will Win the Pennant, 1964; (ed.) Rivers to Cross, 1966; Cemetery Jones, 1985; Buchanan's Black Sheep, 1985; Buchanan's Stage Line, 1986. Add: 3974 Beverly Glen, Sherman Oaks, Calif. 91423, U.S.A.

COX, William Trevor. *See* **TREVOR,** William.

COXE, Louis (Osborne). American, b. 1918. Plays/Screenplays, Poetry, usLiterature, Biography. Pierce Prof. of English, Bowdoin Coll., Brunswick, Me., since 1956 (Prof., 1955–56). Briggs-Copeland Fellow, Harvard Univ., Cambridge, Mass., 1948–49; Asst. Prof., and Assoc. Prof., Univ. of Minnesota, Minneapolis, 1949–55; Fulbright Lectr., Trinity Coll., Dublin, 1959–60. *Publs:* The Sea Faring and Other Poems, 1947; (with R. Chapman) Billy Budd (play) (in U.K. as The Good Sailor), 1951; The General (play), 1954; The Witchfinders (play), 1955; The Second Man and Other Poems, 1955; The Wilderness and Other Poems, 1958; The Middle Passage, 1960; Edwin Arlington Robinson, 1962; (ed.) Chaucer, 1963; The Last Hero and Other Poems, 1965; Nikal Seyn, Decoration Day: A Poem and a Play, 1966; Edwin Arlington Robinson: The Life of Poetry, 1969; Enabling Acts: Selected Essays, 1976; Passage: Selected Poems 1943–1978, 1979. Add: Dept. of English, Bowdoin Coll., Brunswick, Me. 04011. U.S.A.

COXETER, Harold Scott Macdonald. British, b. 1907. Mathematics. Emeritus Prof. of Mathematics, Univ. of Toronto, Ont., since 1980 (Asst. Prof., 1936–43; Assoc. Prof., 1943–48; Prof., 1948–80). Fellow of Trinity Coll., Cambridge, 1931–36; Ed., Canadian Journal of Mathematics, 1948–57. *Publs:* (co-author) The Fifty-Nine Icosahedra, 1938, 1982; (with Rouse Ball) Mathematical Recreations and Essays, 1939, 13th ed. 1987; Non-Euclidean Geometry, 1942, 1965; Regular Polytopes, 1948, 1973; The Real Projective Plane, 1949, 1955; (with W. Moser) Generators and Relations for Discrete Groups, 1957, 4th ed., 1980; Introduction to Geometry, 1961, 1969; Projective Geometry, 1968, 1974; (with S.L. Greitzer) Geometry Revisited, 1967, 1975; Twelve Geometric Essays, 1968;

Regular Complex Polytopes, 1974, 1989; (with R. Frucht and D. Powers) Zero-symmetric Graphs, 1981; (co-ed.) M.C. Escher: Art and Science, 1986. Add: 67 Roxborough Dr., Toronto M4W 1X2, Canada.

CRABB, Edmund William. British, b. 1912. Children's fiction, Theology/Religion, Travel/Exploration/Adventure. Headmaster, The Hyde Sch., London, 1948–53, and Stanburn Sch., Stanmore, Middx., 1953–73. *Publs:* Good News from God, 1949; Workers for God, 1949; Telling the Good News, 1950; Founder of the Faith, 1951; Jesus and the Chosen Nation, 1951; The Way of Life, 1952; Heralds of the Way, 1952; The Christian Faith, 1953; Train Up a Child, 1954; The Challenge of the Summit, 1957; The Secret of the Plateau, 1961; Living in Old Testament Times, 1962; Living in New Testament Times, 1962; Religious Education for the C.S.E. Year, 1966; Shadow in the Sunshine, 1968; Lion Encyclopedia of the Bible, 1978. Add: 36 Ridgeway, Kenton, Harrow, Middx. HA3 OLL, England.

CRABB, Henry Stuart Malcolm. British, b. 1922. Medicine/Health. Lectr. in Clinical Dentistry, Univ. of Bristol, 1950–60; Consultant Dental Surgeon, United Bristol Hosps., 1957–60; Prof. of Conservative Dentistry, Univ. of Leeds, 1961–86. *Publs:* (with A.I. Darling) The Pattern of Progressive Mineralisation of Human Dental Enamel; Emergency Dental Treatment. Add: Sch. of Dentistry, Dept. of Restorative Dentistry, Clarendon Way, Leeds LS2 9LU, England.

CRACKNELL, Basil Edward. British, b. 1925. Agriculture/Forestry, Natural history, Third World problems. Economist, Ministry of Agriculture, 1952–65; Sr. Research Fellow, Univ. of Nottingham, 1966–69; Sr. Economic Adviser, Overseas Development Admin., London, 1969–85. *Publs:* Canvey Island: The Story of a Marshland Community, 1958; Portrait of London River: The Tidal Thames from Teddington to the Sea, 1968; (with D.K. Britton) Cereals in the United Kingdom: Production, Marketing, and Utilisation, 1969; Portrait of Surrey, 1970, 3rd ed. 1980; Dominica, 1973; The West Indies: How They Live and Work, 1974. Add: c/o Hale, 45-47 Clerkenwell Green, London EC1R 0HT, England.

CRAFT, Robert. American, b. 1923. Music. Orchestral conductor, Europe, Japan, and U.S.A., since 1952. *Publs:* (with A. Piovesan and R. Vlad) Le Musiche religiose di Igor Stravinsky con il catalogo analitico completo di tutte le sue opere di Craft, Piovesan, Vlad, 1957; Conversations with Igor Stravinsky, 4 vols., 1959; Memories and Commentaries, 1960; Expositions and Developments, 1962; Dialogues and a Diary, 1963; Table Talk, 1965; Themes and Episodes, 1966; (with A. Newman) Bravo Stravinsky, 1967; Retrospectives and Conclusions, 1969; Stravinsky: The Chronicle of a Friendship 1948–71, 1972; Prejudices in Disguise, 1974; Current Convictions: Views and Reviews, 1977; (ed.) Stravinsky: Selected Correspondence, 3 vols., 1981–85; A Stravinsky Scrapbook, 1984; Present Perspectives: Critical Writings, 1985; (ed.) Dearest Bubushkin: The Correspondence of Vera and Igor Stravinsky 1921-1954, with Excerpts from Vera Stravinsky's Diaries 1922–1971 (trans. by L. Davidova), 1985. Add: c/o Alfred A. Knopf Inc., 201 East 50th St., New York, N.Y. 10022, U.S.A.

CRAGG, (Albert) Kenneth. British, b. 1913. Theology/Religion, Translations. Warden, St. Augustine's Coll., Canterbury, 1960–67; Bye-Fellow, Gonville and Caius Coll., Cambridge, 1969–73; Reader in Religious Studies, Univ. of Sussex, Brighton, 1973–78. *Publs:* The Call of the Minaret, 1956; Sandals at the Mosque, 1958; (trans.) Kamil Husain: City of Wrong, 1959; The Dome and the Rock, 1964; (trans.) Muhammad Abduh: The Theology of Unity, 1964; Counsels in Contemporary Islam, 1965; Christianity in World Perspective, 1968; The Privilege of Man, 1968; The House of Islam, 1969; Alive to God; The Event of the Quran, 1970; The Mind of the Quran, 1973; The Christian and Other Religion, 1977; (trans.) Passage to France, 1977; (trans.) The Hallowed Valley, 1977; Islam from Within, 1980; This Year in Jerusalem, 1982; Muhammad and the Christian, 1984; The Pen and the Faith, 1985; Jesus and the Muslim, 1985; The Christ and the Faiths, 1986; Readings in the Qur'an, 1988; What Decided Christianity, 1989. Add: Appletree Cottage, Ascott under Wychwood, Oxon OX7 6AG, England.

CRAGO, Thomas Howard. Australian, b. 1907. Theology/Religion, Biography. Baptist Minister, since 1934. Leader Writer, The Age, Melbourne, since 1976. Publ. Dir. and Ed., Baptist Bd. of Christian Education, 1957–1974; Ed., Victorian Baptist Witness, 1958–66. *Publs:* Real Discipleship, 1940; (with W. Bligh) Champions of Liberty, 1946; Wind in the Tree Tops, 1954; The Road Winds Uphill, 1956; The Story of F.W. Boreham, 1961; Spare a Minute, 1986. Add: 14 Gareth Dr., East Burwood, Vic. 3151, Australia.

CRAIB, Ian. British, b. 1945. Sociology. Lectr. in Sociology, Univ. of Essex, since 1973. *Publs:* Sociology and Existentialism: A Study of Jean-Paul Sartre, 1976; Modern Social Theory, 1984. Add: Dept. of Sociology, Univ. of Essex, Colchester CO4 3SQ, England.

CRAIG, Alisa. *See* **MacLEOD,** Charlotte.

CRAIG, David. *See* **TUCKER,** James.

CRAIG, Edward Anthony. Also writes as Edward Carrick. British, b. 1905. Film, Theatre, Biography. Former dir. to major film producing companies. *Publs:* as Edward Carrick—Designing for Moving Pictures, 1941, 2nd ed. as Designing for Films, 1950; (compiler with G. Bradley) Meet the Common People, 1942; Art and Design in the British Film, 1948; as Edward Craig—Gordon Craig: The Story of His Life, 1968; (ed.) Fabrizio Carini Motta, Trattato Sopra La Struttura De'Teatri, 1972; William Nicholson's Alphabet, 1978; William Nicholson's An Almanac of Twelve Sports, 1980; Baroque Theatre Construction, 1982; (ed.) Edward Gordon Craig: The Last Eight Years, 1983. Add: Southcourt Cottage, Aylesbury, Bucks. HP18 9AQ, England.

CRAIG, Mary (Francis Young). Also writes as M.S. Craig, Alexis Hill, and Mary Francis Shura. American, b. 1923. Mystery/Crime/Suspense, Historical/Romance/Gothic, Children's fiction. *Publs:* all as Mary Francis Shura unless otherwise noted—Simple Spigott, 1960; The Garret of Greta McGraw, 1961; Mary's Marvelous Mouse, 1962; The Nearsighted Knight, 1964; Run Away Home, 1965; Shoe Full of Shamrock, 1965; A Tale of Middle Length, 1966; Backwards for Luck, 1967; Pornada, 1968; The Valley of the Frost Giants, 1971; The Seven Stone, 1972; Topcat of Tam, 1972; The Shop on Threnody Street (suspense), 1972; (as Mary Craig) A Candle for the Dragon (romance), 1973; (as Mary Craig) Ten Thousand Several Doors (suspense), 1973, as Mistress of Lost River, 1976; (as Mary Craig) The Cranes of Ibycus (suspense), 1974, as Shadows of the Past, 1976; The Riddle of Raven's Gulch, 1974, as The Riddle of Raven's Hollow, 1976; The Season of Silence, 1976; The Gray Ghosts of Taylor Ridge, 1978; (as Mary Craig) Were He a Stranger (suspense), 1978; Mister Wolf and Me, 1979; The Barkley Street Six-Pack, 1979; (as Alexis Hill) Passion's Slave (romance), 1979; (as Alexis Hill) The Untamed Heart (romance), 1980; Chester, 1980; Happles and Cinnamunger, 1981; (as M.S. Craig) The Chicagoans: Dust to Diamonds (historical saga), 1981; (as Mary S. Craig) Lyon's Pride, 1983; (as Mary S. Craig) Pirate's Landing, 1983; (as M.S. Craig) To Play the Fox (suspense), 1982; (as M.S. Craig) Gillian's Chain (suspense), 1983; (as M.S. Craig) The Third Blonde (suspense), 1985; (as Meredith Hill) The Silent Witness (Juvenile Fiction), 1983; Eleanor, 1983; Jefferson, 1984; Jessica, 1984; Marilee, 1985; The Search for Grissi, 1985; The Josie Gambit, 1986; (as Mary Craig) Flash Point, 1987; Don't Call Me Toad, 1987; Gabrielle, 1987; The Sunday Doll, 1988; Diana, 1988. Add: 301 Hinsdale Dr., No. 112, Clarendon Hills, Ill. 60514, U.S.A.

CRAIG, Patricia. British, b. 1943. Literature. Freelance writer. Formerly, Children's Books Ed., The Literary Review, London. *Publs:* Elizabeth Bowen, 1986; (with Mary Cadogan) You're a Brick, Angela! A New Look at Girls' Fiction 1839-1975, 1976; Women and Children First: The Fiction of Two World Wars, 1978; The Lady Investigates: Women Detectives and Spies in Fiction, 1981. Add: c/o Oxford Univ. Press, Walton St., Oxford, OX2 6DP, England.

CRAIG, Robert Charles. American, b. 1921. Education, Psychology. Prof., Counseling, Personnel Services and Educational Psychology, Michigan State Univ., East Lansing, since 1967 (Asst. Dir., Sch. for Advanced Studies, Coll. of Education, 1966–67; Dept. Chmn., 1969–81). Asst. Prof., State Univ. of Washington, 1952–55; Research Scientist, and Prog. Dir. for Education, American Inst. for Research, Pittsburgh, Pa., 1955–58; Assoc. Prof., and Prof., Marquette Univ., Milwaukee, Wisc., 1958–66. *Publs:* Transfer Value of Guided Learning, 1953; (with A. Dupuis) American Education, Origins and Issues, 1963; Psychology of Learning in the Classroom, 1966; (with H. Clarizio and W. Mehrens) Contemporary Issues in Educational Psychology, 1970, 5th ed. 1987; (with H. Clarizio and W. Mehrens) Contemporary Educational Psychology, 1975; (with V. Noll and D. Scannell) Introduction to Educational Measurement, 4th ed., 1979. Add: 185 Maplewood Dr., East Lansing, Mich. 48823, U.S.A.

CRAIK, T(homas) W(allace). British, b. 1927. Literature. Prof. of English, Univ. of Durham, since 1977. Asst. Lectr., 1953–55, and Lectr., 1955–65, Univ. of Leicester; Lectr., 1965–67, and Sr. Lectr., 1967–73, Univ. of Aberdeen; Prof. of English, Univ. of Dundee, 1973–77; *Publs:* The Tudor Interlude: Stage, Costume and Acting, 1958, 3rd ed. 1967;

The Comic Tales of Chaucer, 1964; (ed.) A New Way to Pay Old Debts, by Massinger, 1964, 1981; (ed.) The City Madam, by Massinger, 1964; (ed.) Selected Poetry and Prose of Sir Philip Sidney, 1965; (ed.) The Jew of Malta, by Marlowe, 1966, 1979; (ed.) Minor Elizabethan Tragedies, 1974; (ed., with J.M. Lothian) Twelfth Night, by Shakespeare, 1975; (ed., with C. Leech and Lois Potter) The 'Revels' History of Drama in English, 6 vols., 1975–83; (ed. with R.J. Craik) John Donne: Selected Poetry and Prose, 1986; (ed.) The Maid's Tragedy, by Beaumont and Fletcher, 1988; (ed.) The Merry Wives of Windsor, by Shakespeare, 1989. Add: Dept. of English, Univ. of Durham, Elvet Riverside, New Elvet, Durham DH1 3JT, England.

CRAIK, Wendy Ann. British, b. 1934. Literature. Sr. Lectr. in English, Univ. of Aberdeen, since 1972 (Asst. Lectr., 1965–66; Lectr., 1966–72). Asst. Teacher of English, Kibworth Beauchamp Grammar Sch., Leics., 1962–63; Head of English Dept., Oadby Beauchamp Grammar Sch., Leicester, 1963–65. *Publs:* Jane Austen: The Six Novels, 1965; The Brontë Novels, 1968; Jane Austen in her Time, 1969; (ed.) Jane Austen: Persuasion, 1969; (ed.) Jane Austen: Sense and Sensibility, 1972; (ed.) Jane Austen: Mansfield Park, 1972; Elizabeth Gaskell and the 19th Century Provincial Novel, 1974. Add: Dept. of English, King's Coll., Univ. of Aberdeen, Old Aberdeen, Scotland.

CRAMER, Stanley H. American, b. 1933. Education. Prof., State Univ. of New York at Buffalo, since 1965. *Publs:* (with E.L. Herr) Guidance of the College Bound: Problems, Practices, and Perspectives, 1968; (with E.L. Herr, C.N. Morris and T.T. Frantz) Research and the School Counselor, 1970; (co-ed, with J.D. Hansen) Group Guidance and Counseling in the Schools, 1971; (with E.L. Herr) Vocational Guidance and Career Development in the Schools: Toward a Systems Approach, 1972; (with E.L. Herr) Career Guidance Through the Lifespan: Systematic Approaches, 1979, 3rd ed. 1987; (with E.L. Herr) Controversies in the Mental Health Professions, 1987. Add: 21 Foxboro Lane, East Amherst, N.Y. 14051, U.S.A.

CRAMPTON, Helen. *See* **CHESNEY,** Marion.

CRANDALL, Norma (Rand). American. Biography. Freelance writer; Editorial Consultant for English and French manuscripts, Harcourt, Brace, publ. and to individual writers, since 1939. Member, The Poetry Society of America and The Brontë Society of England. *Publs:* Emily Brontë, 1970, 3rd ed. 1978. Add: 44 East 63rd St., New York, N.Y. 10021, U.S.A.

CRANE, Caroline. American, b. 1930. Novels/Short stories, Children's fiction. *Publs:* Lights down the River, 1963; Pink Sky at Night, 1964; A Girl Like Tracy, 1966; Wedding Song, 1967; Don't Look at Me that Way, 1970; Stranger on the Road, 1971; Summer Girl, 1979; The Girls Are Missing, 1980; Coast of Fear, 1981; Wife Found Slain, 1981; The Foretelling, 1982; The Third Passenger, 1983; Trick or Treat, 1983; Woman Vanishes, 1984; Something Evil, 1984; Someone at the Door, 1985; Circus Day, 1986; Man in the Shadows, 1987; The People Next Door, 1988. Add: 317 W. 93rd St., New York, N.Y. 10025, U.S.A.

CRANE, Richard (Arthur). British, b. 1944. Plays/Screenplays, Songs/Lyrics/Libretti. Dir. of plays in Bradford, Edinburgh, and London, and actor, in London, and in repertory, on TV, and in films, since 1966; Founder Member, Brighton Combination and Pool, Edinburgh; Assoc. Dir., Brighton Theatre, since 1980; Bd. of Dirs., Edinburgh Festival Fringe Soc., since 1973. Fellow in Theatre, Univ. of Bradford, Yorkshire, 1972–74; Playwright-in-Residence, National Theatre, London, 1974–75; Fellow in Creative Writing, Univ. of Leicester, 1976; Literary Mgr., Royal Court Theatre, London, 1978–79; Dramaturge, Tron Theatre, Glasgow, 1983–84. *Publs:* Thunder: A Play of the Brontës, 1976; Gunslinger: A Wild West Show, 1978; Mutiny (recording), 1983. Add: c/o Margaret Ramsay Ltd., 14a Goodwin's Ct., London WC2N 4LL, England.

CRANFIELD, Charles Ernest Burland. British, b. 1915. Theology/Religion. Emeritus Prof., Univ. of Durham, since 1980 (Lectr. in Theology, 1950–62; Sr. Lectr., 1962–66; Reader, 1966–78; Prof. of Theology, 1978–80). Jt. Gen. Ed., Intnl. Critical Commentary, new series, since 1966. Ordained, Methodist Church, 1941; Minister in Shoeburyness, 1940–42; Forces Chaplain, 1942–46; Minister in Cleethorpes, 1946–50; admitted to Presbyterian Church of England (now part of United Reformed Church), 1954. *Publs:* The First Epistle of Peter, 1950; The Gospel According to St. Mark, 1959; I and II Peter and Jude, 1960; A Critical and Exegetical Commentary on the Epistle to the Romans, 2 vols., 1975–79; Romans: A Shorter Commentary, 1985; The Bible and Christian

Life (essays), 1985; If God Be For Us (sermons), 1985. Add: 30 Western Hill, Durham DH1 4RL, England.

CRANSTON, Maurice (William). British, b. 1920. Philosophy, Politics/Government. Editorial Adviser, Encounter, since 1970. Lectr., Univ. of London, 1950–69; Prof. of Political Science, London Sch. of Economics, 1969–86; Prof. of Political Science, European Univ. Inst., Florence, 1978–81. Literary Adviser, Methuen & Co. Ltd., publrs., London, 1959–69. Vice Chmn., English PEN Centre, 1968–77; Registrar, Royal Literary Fund, 1974–78. *Publs:* Freedom, 1953; John Locke, 1957; Sartre, 1962; (ed.) Western Political Philosophers, 1964; (co-ed with Sanford Lakoff) A Glossary of Political Ideas, 1965; (trans.) Rousseau's Social Contract, 1968; Political Dialogues, 1968; Philosophy and Language, 1969; The Quintessence of Sartrism, 1969; (ed.) The New Left, 1970; (co-ed. with R.S. Peters) Hobbs and Rousseau, 1972; The Mask of Politics, 1973; Jean-Jacques Rousseau, 1984; Philosophers and Pamphleteers, 1987. Add: 1A Kent Terr., Regent's Park, London NW1, England.

CRATTY, Bryant J. American. b. 1929. Education, Psychology, Sports/Physical education/Keeping fit. Prof. of Kinesiology, and Dir., Perceptual-Motor Learning Lab., Univ., of California, Los Angeles, since 1967 (Inst., 1958–61; Asst. Prof., 1961–65; Assoc. Prof., 1965–67). Ed., Research Quarterly: The Journal of Motor Behavior. *Publs:* Movement Behavior and Motor Learning, 1967, 3rd ed. 1973; Motor Activity and the Education of Retardates, 1969, 1974; Psychology and the Superior Athlete, 1969; Perceptual and Motor Development of Infants and Children, 1970, 1979; Children and Youth in Competitive Sport; Movement and Spatial Awareness in Blind Children and Youth, 1971; Active Learning, 1971, 1985; Physical Expressions of Intelligence, 1972; (with J.S. Breen) Educational Activities for the Physically Handicapped, 1972; Psychology in Contemporary Sport, 1973, 3rd ed. 1989; Teaching Motor Skills, 1973; Intelligence in Action, 1973; Psychomotor Behavior in Education and Sport: Selected Papers, 1974; Teaching Human Behavior via Active Games, 1975; Remedial Motor Activity for Children: Theory, Evaluation and Remediation, 1975; The Athlete in the Sports Team, 1980; Social Psychology in Athletics, 1980; Adapted Physical Education for Handicapped Children and Youth, 1980, 1989; Psychological Preparation and Athletic Excellence, 1984; (with Rob Piggot) Student Projects in Sports Psychology, 1984. Add: Perceptual-Motor Learning Lab., Dept. of Kinesiology, 405 Hilgard Ave., Univ. of California, Los Angeles, Calif. 90024, U.S.A.

CRAWFORD, Alan. British, b. 1943. Architecture, Design, Crafts. Research Fellow, Victorian Studies Centre, Univ. of Leicester, 1970–72; Lectr. in History of Design, Birmingham Polytechnic, 1972–78. Chmn. Victorian Soc., 1982–86. *Publs:* (with Robert Thorne) Birmingham Pubs 1890-1939, 1975; (ed.) By Hammer and Hand: The Arts and Crafts Movement in Birmingham, 1984; C.R. Ashbee: Architect, Designer and Romantic Socialist, 1985; (with Robert Thorne and Michael Dunn) Birmingham Pubs 1880-1939, 1986. Add: 20 Ravenshaw St., London NW6 1NN, England.

CRAWFORD, Christina. American, b. 1939. Novels, Autobiography. Pres., The Hermitage Co. Inc., Los Angeles, since 1978. Actress, 1958–72; in corporate communications, 1975–78. Member, Alumni Bd. of Govs., Univ. of Southern California, Los Angeles, 1975–78; Pres., ICAN Assocs. Charity, Los Angeles, 1979–85; Los Angeles County Commissioner for Children's Services, 1984–87; *Publs:* Mommie Dearest (autobiography), 1978; Black Widow (novel), 1982; Survivor (autobiography), 1988. Add: c/o The Hermitage Co. Inc., 4630 Mirador Pl., Tarzana, Calif. 91356, U.S.A.

CRAWFORD, John Richard. Also writes as J. Walker. American, b. 1932. Money/Finance, Theology/Religion, Autobiography/Memoirs/Personal. Chmn., Div. of Social Sciences, and Prof. of History, Montreat-Anderson Coll., Montreat, N.C., since 1970. Former Asst. Dean of Chapel and Asst. Prof. of Religion, Austin Coll., Sherman, Tex.; Prof. of Ecclesiastical History and Vice Dean, Faculté de Theologie, Univ. Libre du Congo (now Univ. Nationale du Zïre), 1960–69. *Publs:* (as J. Walker) Only by Thumb (autobiography), 1964; A Christian and His Money, 1967; Protestant Missions in Congo, 1878-1969, 1970; Dieu et Votre Argent, 1973. Add: 100 Sunrise Terrace, Black Mountain, N.C. 28711, U.S.A.

CRAWFORD, Robert. *See* **RAE,** Hugh C.

CRAWFORD, William P. American, b. 1922. Law, Marine science/Oceanography, Meteorology/Atmospheric sciences, Recrea-

tion/Leisure/Hobbies. Dir., Crawford Nautical Center, San Francisco, since 1958. Member, National Transportation Bd., since 1979. Shipmaster and deck officer, 1941–46; Proctor in Admiralty, California, 1949–58. *Publs:* Mariner's Rules of the Road, 1960, 1983; Mariner's Notebook, 1960, 5th ed. 1971; Mariner's Celestial Navigation, 1972; Sea Marine Atlas, 1972, 1979; Boat-owner's Legal guide, 1975; Mariner's Weather, 1979. Add: 1557 White Oak Way, San Carlos, Calif. 94070, U.S.A.

CRAWLEY, Aidan (Merivale). British, b. 1908. Novels/Short stories, Plays/Screenplays, History, Biography. Dir., Independent Television News (Founder Ed., 1955–56). Labour M.P. (U.K.) for Buckingham, 1945–51; Under Secty. for Air, 1950–51; Delegate to the Council of Europe, 1948–49; engaged in making documentaries for BBC TV, 1957–60; Conservative M.P. (U.K.) for West Derbyshire, 1962–67; Chmn., 1967–71, and Pres., 1971–75, London Weekend Television. *Publs:* Escape from Germany, 1955; India's Challenge (TV series), 1953; The Inheritors (TV series), 1953–54; Viewfinder (TV series); De Gaulle (biography), 1968; The Philippines (film script), 1972–75; The Rise of Western Germany 1945–72, 1973; The Three Himalayan Kingdoms (film script); Dial 200-200 (novel), 1980; Leap Before You Look, 1987. Add: Oak Cottage, Queens St, Farthinghoe, Brackley, NN13 5NY, England.

CRAY, Edward. American, b. 1933. Civil liberties/Human rights, Law, Mythology/Folklore, Social commentary/phenomena. Assoc. Prof., Sch. of Journalism, Univ. of Southern California. Los Angeles, since 1982 (Sr. Lectr., 1976–82). Dir. of Publications, American Civil Liberties Union of Southern California, 1965–70; Dir. of Publicity, Southern California Symphony, Hollywood Bowl Assn., 1970–71. *Publs:* The Big Blue Line, 1967; (ed.) The Erotic Muse, 1968; In Failing Health, 1971; The Enemy in the Streets, 1972; Burden of Proof, 1973; Levi's, 1978; Chrome Colossus, 1980. Add: 10436 Kinnard Ave., Los Angeles, Calif. 90024, U.S.A.

CRAYDER, Teresa. *See* **COLMAN,** Hila.

CREAGER, Clara. American, b. 1930. Crafts. Asst. Prof., Dept. of Art, Ohio State Univ., Columbus, since 1972. *Publs:* Weaving: A Creative Approach for Beginners, 1974; All About Weaving, 1984. Add: 75 W. College Ave., Westerville, Ohio 43081, U.S.A.

CREAMER, Robert W. American, b. 1922. Sports, Biography. Spec. Contrib., Sports Illustrated mag., NYC, since 1985 (Sr. Ed., 1954–84). *Publs:* (ghost writer) Mickey Mantle: The Quality of Courage, 1964; (with J. Conlan) Jocko, 1967; (with R. Barber) Rhubarb in the Catbird Seat, 1968; Babe: The Legend Comes to Life, 1974; (co-author) The Yankees, 1979; Stengel: His Life and Times, 1984; (with R. Houk) Season of Glory: The Amazing Saga of the 1961 New York Yankees, 1988. Add: c/o Sports Illustrated, Time & Life Bldg., Rockefeller Center, New York, N.Y. 10020, U.S.A.

CRECY, Jeanne. *See* **WILLIAMS,** Jeanne.

CREELEY, Robert (White). American, b. 1926. Novels/Short stories, Plays/Screenplays, Poetry, Literature. Gray Prof. of Poetry and Letters, State Univ. of New York, Buffalo, since 1978 (Visiting Prof., 1966–67; Prof. of English, 1967–78). Operated Divers Press, Palma de Mallorca, 1953–55; Ed., Black Mountain Review, N.C., 1954–57; Visiting Lectr., 1961–62, and Lectr., 1963–66 and 1968–69, Univ. of New Mexico, Albuquerque; Lectr., Univ. of British Columbia, Vancouver, 1962–63. *Publs:* Le Fou, 1952; The Kind of Act of, 1953; The Immoral Proposition, 1953; (ed.) Mayan Letters, by Charles Olson, 1953; The Gold Diggers (short stories), 1954; A Snarling Garland of Xmas Verses, 1954; All That Is Lovely in Men, 1955; If You, 1956; The Whip, 1957; A Form of Women, 1959; For Love: Poems 1950-60, 1962; The Island (novel), 1963; Distance, 1964; Two Poems, 1964; Mister Blue (short stories), 1964; The Gold Diggers and Other Stories, 1965; (ed. with D. Allen) New American Story, 1965; Hi There!, 1965; Words, 1965; (ed.) Selected Writings, by Charles Olson, 1966; About Women, 1966; Poems, 1950–65, 1966; For Joel, 1966; A Sight, 1967; Words, 1967; Robert Creeley Reads, 1967; (ed. with D. Allen) The New Writing in the U.S.A., 1967; The Finger, 1968; 5 Numbers, 1968; The Charm: Early and Uncollected Poems, 1968; The Boy, 1968; Numbers, 1968; Divisions and Other Early Poems, 1968; Pieces, 1968; Contexts of Poetry, 1968; Hero, 1969; A Wall, 1969; Mary's Fancy, 1970; In London, 1970; The Finger: Poems 1966–69, 1970; For Betsy and Tom, 1970; For Benny and Sabina, 1970; As Now It Would Be Snow, 1970; America, 1970; Christmas: May 10, 1970, 1970; A Quick Graph: Collected Notes and Essays, 1970; A Day Book, 1970; St. Martin's, 1971; Sea, 1971; 1,2,3,4,5,6,7,8,9,0, 1971; For the Graduation, 1971; Listen (play), 1972; Change, 1972; One Day After Another, 1972; A Day Book, 1972; For My Mother, 1973; Kitchen, 1973; The Creative,

1973; A Sense of Measure (essays), 1973; Contexts of Poetry: Interviews 1961–71, 1973; (ed.) Whitman, 1973; Sitting Here, 1974; Thirty Things, 1974; Inside Out: Notes on the Autobiographical Mode, 1974; Presences: A Text for Marisol, 1976; Mabel: A Story, 1976; Selected Poems, 1976; Myself, 1977; Hello, 1978; Later, 1978; Was That a Real Poem and Other Essays, 1978; Desultory Days, 1978; Later, 1979; Charles Olson and Robert Creeley: The Complete Correspondence, 7 vols., 1980–86; Mother's Voice, 1981; Echoes, 1982; The Collected Poems of Robert Creeley 1945–1975, 1982; Mirrors, 1983; The Complete Prose, 1984; Memory Gardens, 1986. Add: Dept. of English, State Univ. of New York, Buffalo, N.Y. 14260, U.S.A.

CREGAN, David (Appleton Quartus). British, b. 1931. Novels/Short stories, Plays/Screenplays. Head of English Dept., Palm Beach Private Sch., Florida, 1955–57; Asst. English Master, Burnage Boys' Grammar Sch., Manchester, 1957; Asst. English Master and Head of Drama Dept., 1958–62, and Part-time Drama Teacher, 1962–67, Hatfield Sch., Herts.; Salesman and Clerk at the Automobile Assn., 1958; has worked with Cambridge Footlights, 1953, 1954, The Royal Court Theatre Studio, London, 1964 and 1968, and the Midlands Arts Centre, Birmingham, 1971; conducted three-week studio at the Royal Shakespeare Company Memorial Theatre, Stratford upon Avon, 1971. Member, Drama Panel, West Midlands Arts Assn., 1972–75, Eastern Arts, 1981–86. *Publs:* Ronald Rossiter (novel), 1959; Miniatures, 1965; Transcending, and The Dancers, 1966; Three Men for Colverton, 1966; The Houses by the Green, 1968; How We Held the Square: A Play for Children, 1973; The Land of Palms and Other Plays, 1973; Poor Tom and Tina, 1976; Play Nine, 1980; Sleeping Beauty, 1984; Red Riding Hood, 1985; Jack and the Beanstalk, 1987; Beauty and the Beast, 1987. Add: 76 Wood Close, Hatfield, Herts., England.

CREIGHTON, Don. *See* **DRURY,** Maxine Cole.

CREMIN, Lawrence. American, b. 1925. Education. Prof., since 1957, and Frederick A.P. Bernard Prof. of Education, since 1961, Teachers Coll., Columbia Univ., New York (Instr., 1949–51; Asst. Prof. of Education, 1951–54; Assoc. Prof., 1954–57; Pres., 1974–84). Pres., Spencer Foundn., Chicago, since 1985. *Publs:* The Transformation of the School: Progressivism in American Education 1876-1957, 1961; American Education: The Colonial Experience 1607-1783, 1970; American Education: The National Experience 1783-1876, 1980; The Metropolitan Experience 1876-1980, 1988. Add: Teachers Coll., Columbia Univ., 525 W. 120th St., New York, N.Y. 10027, U.S.A.

CRENSHAW, James L. American, b. 1934. Theology/Religion. Prof. of Old Testament, Duke Divinity Sch., Durham, N.C., since 1987. Asst. Prof. of Religion, Atlantic Christian Coll., Wilson, N.C., 1964–65; Asst. Prof. to Assoc. Prof., Mercer Univ., Macon, Ga., 1965–69; Asst. Prof. to Prof., Vanderbilt Divinity Sch., Nashville, Tenn., 1970–87. Assoc. Ed., 1976–78, and Ed. 1978–84, Soc. of Biblical Literature Monograph Series. *Publs:* Prophetic Conflict: Its Effect Upon Israelite Religion, 1971; (co-author) Old Testament Form Criticism, 1974; (co-ed) Essays in Old Testament Ethics, 1974; Hymnic Affirmation of Divine Justice, 1975; Studies in Ancient Israelite Wisdom, 1976; Gerhard von Rad, 1978; Samson: A Secret Betrayed, A Vow Ignored, 1978; (co-ed) The Divine Helmsman, 1980; Old Testament Wisdom, 1981; (with others) Theodicy in the Old Testament, 1983; A Whirlpool of Torment, 1984; Story and Faith, 1986; Ecclesiastes, 1987; (ed.) Perspectives on the Hebrew Bible, 1988. Add: 8 Beckford Pl., Durham, N.C. 27705, U.S.A.

CRESSWELL, Helen. British, b. 1936. Children's fiction. Cttee. Member, Children's Group, Soc. of Authors, since 1973. *Publs:* Sonya-by-the-Shore, 1960; Jumbo Spencer, 1963; The White Sea Horse, 1964; Jumbo Back to Nature, 1965; Pietro and the Mule, 1965; Where the Wind Blows, 1966; Jumbo Afloat, 1966; The Pie Makers, 1967; A Day on Big O, 1967; A Tide for the Captain, 1967; The Signposters, 1968; The Sea Piper, 1968; Jumbo and the Big Dig, 1968; Rug is a Bear, 1968; Rug Plays Tricks, 1968; The Night Watchmen, 1969; A Game of Catch, 1969; A Gift from Winklesea, 1969; A House for Jones. 1969; Rug Plays Ball, 1969; Rug and a Picnic, 1969; The Outlanders, 1970; The Wilkses, 1970; Rainbow Pavement, 1970; John's First Fish, 1970; Up the Pier, 1971; The Weather Cat, 1971; The Bird Fancier, 1971; At the Stroke of Midnight, 1971; The Beachcombers, 1972; Jane's Policeman, 1972; The Long Day, 1972; Short Back and Sides, 1972; Blue Birds Over Pit Row, 1972; Roof Fall, 1972; Lizzie Dripping series, 5 vols., 1972–74; The White Sea Horse and Other Tales of the Sea, 1972; The Bongleweed, 1973; The Bower Bird, 1973; The Key, 1973; The Trap, 1973; The Beetle Hunt, 1973; The Two Hoots series, 6 vols., 1974–77; Cheap Day Return, 1974; Shady Deal, 1974; Butterfly Chase, 1975; The Winter of the Birds, 1975;

Jumbo Spencer (television play), 1976; Two Hoots and the King, 1977; Bagthorpe series, 4 vols., 1977–79; Donkey Days, 1977; Absolute Zero, 1978; The Flyaway Kite, 1979; My Aunt Polly by the Sea, 1980; Dear Shrink, 1982; The Secret World of Polly Flint, 1982; Ellie and the Hagwitch, 1984; Bagthorpes Abroad, 1984; Bagthorpes Haunted, 1985; Whodunnit?, 1986; Moondial, 1987; Time Out, 1987; Bagthorpes Liberated, 1988. Add: Old Church Farm, Eakring, Newark, Notts., NG22 0DA, England.

CREW, Louie. American, b. 1936. Poetry, Essays. Dir. of the Writing Program, Chinese Univ. of Hong Kong, since 1984. Founder, Integrity: Intnl. Ministry of Lesbian and Gay Anglicans, since 1974; Member of Bd., Journal of Homosexuality, since 1978. Master of English and Bible, Darlington Sch., Rome, Ga., 1959–62; Master of English and Sacred Studies, St. Andrew's Sch., Middletown, Del., 1962–65; Instr. of English, Penge Secondary Modern Sch., London; 1965–66; Instr. of English, Univ. of Alabama, Tuscaloosa, 1966–70; Dir., Independent Study in England for Experiment in Intnl. Living, 1970–71; Prof. of English, Claflin Coll., Orangeburg, S.C., 1971–73; Assoc. Prof. of English, Fort Valley State Col., Ga., 1973–79; Assoc. Prof. of English, Univ. of Wisconsin at Stevens Point, 1979–84. Member of Bd., National Gay Task Force, 1976–78; and National Council of Teachers of English, 1976–80. *Publs:* Sunspots (poetry), 1976; The Gay Academic (essays), 1978. Add: P.O. Box 754, Stevens Point-on-the-Wisconsin, Wisc. 54481, U.S.A.

CREWS, Frederick C(ampbell). American, b. 1933. Literature. Prof. of English, Univ. of California, Berkeley, since 1966 (Instr., 1958–60, Asst. Prof., 1960–63, and Assoc. Prof., 1963–66). Fellow, Center for Advanced Studies in the Behavioral Sciences, 1965–66. *Publs:* The Tragedy of Manners: Moral Drama in the Later Novels of Henry James, 1957; E.M. Forster: The Perils of Humanism, 1962; The Pooh Perplex: A Freshman Casebook (parodies), 1963; The Sins of the Fathers: Hawthorne's Psychological Themes, 1966; (ed.) Great Short Works of Nathaniel Hawthorne, 1967; The Patch Commission (satire), 1968; (ed. with Orville Schell) Starting Over: A College Reader, 1970; (ed.) Psychoanalysis and Literary Process, 1970; The Random House Handbook, 1974, 5th ed. 1988; Out of My System: Psychoanalysis, Ideology, and Critical Method, 1975; (ed.) The Random House Reader, 1981; (with Sandra Schor) The Borzoi Handbook for Writers, 1985, 1989; Skeptical Engagements, 1986. Add: 636 Vincente Ave., Berkeley, Calif. 94707, U.S.A.

CREWS, Harry (Eugene). American, b. 1935. Novels/Short stories, History. Prof. of English, Univ. of Florida, Gainesville, since 1974 (Assoc. Prof., 1968–74). English Teacher, Broward Junior Coll., Fort Lauderdale, Fla., 1962–68. *Publs:* The Gospel Singer, 1968; Naked in Garden Hills, 1969; This Thing Don't Lead to Heaven, 1970; Karate Is a Thing of the Spirit, 1971; Car, 1972; The Hawk Is Dying, 1973; The Gypsy's Curse, 1974; A Feast of Snakes, 1976; A Childhood: The Biography of a Placeon Macon County, Ga., 1978; Blood and Grits (nonfiction), 1979; Florida Frenzy, 1982; Two, 1984; All We Need of Hell, 1987; The Knockout Artist, 1988. Add: 1800 N.W. 8th Ave., Gainesville, Fla. 36201, U.S.A.

CREWS, Judson. American, b. 1917. Poetry. Lectr. in Social Development Studies, Univ. of Zambia, Lusaka. Publr., Motive Press, and Este Es Press, Texas and New Mexico, 1946–66; Printer, Taos Star, El Crepusculo, and Taos News, all N.M. 1948–66. *Publs:* Psalms for a Late Season, 1942; The Southern Temper, 1946; No is the Night, 1949; Come Curse to the Moon, 1952; The Anatomy of Proserpine, 1955; (with M. Tolbert and W.B. Anderson) Patrocinio Barela: Taos Wood Carver, 1955, rev. ed. 1962; The Wrath Wrenched Splendor or Love, 1956; The Heart in Naked Hunger, 1958; To Wed Beneath the Sun, 1958; A Sheaf of Christmas Verse; The Ogres Who Were His Henchmen, 1958; Inwade to Briney Garth, 1960; The Feel of Sun and Air upon Her Body, 1960; A Unicorn When Needs Be, 1963; Hermes Past the Hour, 1963; Selected Poems, 1964; You, Mark Anthony, Navigator upon the Nile, 1964; Angels Fall, They Are Towers, 1965; (with W.B. Anderson and C. Farallon) Three on a Match, 1966; The Stones of Konarak, 1966; Nations and Peoples, 1976; Nolo Contendere, 1978; The Noose, 1980; If I, 1981; The Clock of Moss, 1983. Add: P.O. Box 4435, Albuquerque, N.M. 87196, U.S.A.

CRICHTON, James (Dunlop). British, b. 1907. Theology/Religion. Roman Catholic Priest, since 1932. Hon. Fellow, Inst. of Liturgy and Worship, Birmingham Univ. Ed., Liturgy-Life and Worship, 1951–72; Parish Priest, Holy Redeemer Parish, Pershore, 1955–77. *Publs:* The Church's Worship, 1964; Changes in the Liturgy, 1965; (ed.) The Mass and the People of God, 1966; Companion to the New Order of Baptism, 1970; The Liturgy of Holy Week, 1971; Christian Celebration: The Mass,

1971; Christian Celebration: The Sacraments, 1973; The Ministry of Reconciliation, 1974; Christian Celebration: The Prayer of the Church, 1976; The Once and the Future Liturgy, 1977; Praying and Singing, 1980; The Dedication of a Church, 1980; A Short History of the Mass, 1983; The Living Christ, 1987; Worship in a Hidden Church, 1988. Add: 40 Bridge St., Pershore, Worcs. WR10 1RT, England.

CRICHTON, (John) Michael. Also writes as Jeffrey Hudson and John Lange, and with Douglas Crichton as Michael Douglas. American, b. 1942. Novels/Short stories, Science fiction/Fantasy, Plays/Screenplays, Medicine/Health. Physician. Post-Doctoral Fellow, Salk Inst., La Jolla, 1969–70. Visiting Writer, Massachusetts Inst. of Technology, Cambridge, 1988. *Publs:* (as John Lange) Odds On, 1966; (as John Lange) Scratch One, 1967; (as John Lange) Easy Go, 1968; (as Jeffrey Hudson) A Case of Need, 1968; The Andromeda Strain, 1969; (as John Lange) Zero Cool, 1969; (as John Lange) The Venom Business, 1969; (as John Lange) Drug of Choice, 1970; (as John Lange) Grave Descend, 1970; Five Patients: The Hospital Explained, 1970; (as Michael Douglas) Dealing: or, The Berkeley-to-Boston Forty-Brick Lost-Bag Blues, 1972; (as John Lange) Binary, 1972; The Terminal Man, 1972; Westworld (screenplay), 1973; The Great Train Robbery, 1975; Eaters of the Dead, 1976; Jasper Johns, 1977; Congo, 1980; Looker (screenplay), 1980; Electronic Life: How to Think about Computers, 1983; Runaway (screenplay), 1954; Sphere, 1987; Travels, 1988. Add: 2049 Century Park E., No. 4000, Los Angeles, Calif. 90067, U.S.A.

CRICHTON, Robert. American, b. 1925. Novels/Short stories, Autobiography/Memoirs/Personal, Biography. *Publs:* The Great Impostor (biography), 1958; The Rascal and the Road (autobiography), 1960; The Secret of Santa Vittoria, 1966; The Camerons, 1972; Memoirs of a Bad Soldier (autobiography), 1979. Add: 320 West 71st Street, New York, N.Y., U.S.A.

CRICK, Bernard. British, b. 1929. Politics/Government, Social commentary/phenomena, Biography. Prof. of Politics, Birkbeck Coll., Univ. of London, 1971–84. Joint Ed., Political Quarterly, London, 1967–80. *Publs:* The American Science of Politics, 1958; In Defence of Politics, 1962, 1964; The Reform of Parliament, 1964, 1968; (ed.) Essays on Reform, 1967; (ed.) Protest and Discontent, 1970; (ed.) Machiavelli: The Discourses, 1971; Theory and Practice: Essays in Politics, 1972; (ed.) Taxation Theory, 1973; Basic Forms of Government, 1973; (ed. with William Robson) China in Transition, 1975; Crime, Rape, and Gin: Reflections on Contemporary Attitudes to Violence, Pornography, and Addiction, 1977; (ed. with Alex Porter) Political Education and Political Literacy, 1978; George Orwell, 1980, 1982; (ed.) Unemployment, 1981; (ed. with Audrey Coppard) Orwell Remembered, 1984; Socialism, 1987; (with Tom Crick) What Is Politics? 1987; Politics and Literature, 1989; Political Thoughts and Polemics, 1989. Add: 8A Bellevue Terrace, Edinburgh EH7 4DT, Scotland.

CRICK, Donald Herbert. Australian, b. 1916. Novels/Short stories, Plays/Screenplays. Member, Bd. of Management, Australian Soc. of Authors; Dir., Australian Film Council. *Publs:* Bikini Girl, 1963; Martin Place, 1964; Period of Adjustment, 1966; A Different Drummer, 1972; The Moon to Play With, 1981; The Veronica (screenplay), 1983. Add: 1/1 Elamang Ave., Kirribilli, N.S.W., 2061, Australia.

CRICK, F(rancis) H(arry) C(ompton). British, b. 1916. Biology. W. Kieckhefer Distinguished Prof., Salk Inst. for Biological Studies, Univ. of California at San Diego, since 1977 (Non-Resident Fellow, 1962–73; Fernkauf Foundn. Visiting Prof., 1976–77). Scientist, British Admiralty, 1940–47, and Strangeways Research Lab., Cambridge Univ., 1947–49; Member, Research Council Lab. of Biology, Cambridge, 1949–77. Recipient, with Watson and Wilkins, Nobel Prize for Medicine, 1962. *Publs:* Of Molecules and Men, 1966; Life Itself, 1981. Add: Salk Inst., P.O. Box 85800, San Diego, Calif. 92138, U.S.A.

CRIGHTON, John Clark. American, b. 1903. Education, History, Politics/Government. Instr. in History, Lynchburg Coll., Virginia, 1930–32; Prof. of Social Studies, Stephens Coll., Columbia, Mo., 1935–42, 1946–70; Historical Feature Writer, Columbia Daily Tribune, Mo., 1972–77. *Publs:* (with Joseph J. Senturia) Business and Government, 1935; Missouri and the World War 1914-1917, 1947; Stephens: A Story of Educational Innovation, 1970; A History of Columbia and Boone County, 1988. Add: 601 Manor Dr., Columbia, Mo. 65203, U.S.A.

CRINKLEY, Richmond Dillard. American, b. 1940. Biography. Chairman, Cerberus Productions, since 1984 (Pres., 1978–84); Member, Ed. Bd., Shakespeare Quarterly, and Advisory Commn., U.S. Bicentennial

Commn. of Kennedy Center. Asst. Prof. of English, Univ. of North Carolina, Chapel Hill, 1967–69; Dir. of Progs., Folger Shakespeare Library, Washington, D.C., 1969–73; Producer, Kennedy Center for the Performing Arts, Washington, D.C., 1970–73; Exec. Dir., American National Theatre and Academy, 1976–78; Dir., Lincoln Center Theater Co., Lincoln Center, New York, 1978–84. *Publs:* Walter Pater, Humanist, 1971. Add: 59 W. 71st St., New York, N.Y. 10023, U.S.A.

CRISCUOLO, Anthony Thomas. Writes as Tony Crisp and Mark Western. British, b. 1937. Recreation/Leisure/Hobbies, Supernatural/Occult topics. Group Psychotherapy Leader, since 1971. Founder-Dir., Ashram Yoga and Human Growth Centre, 1972–82. *Publs:* (as Mark Western) Mystic Man, 1966; (as Tony Crisp) Relax with Yoga, 1970; (as Tony Crisp) Do You Dream, 1971; (as Tony Crisp) Yield, 1974; (as Tony Crisp) Yoga and Childbirth, 1975; (as Tony Crisp) The Instant Dream Book, 1984; (as Tony Crisp) Mind and Movement: The Practice of Coex, 1987; (as Tony Crisp) The Dictionary of Dreams, 1989. Add: Ashram, King St., Combe Martin, Devon EX34 OAG, England.

CRISP, Tony. *See* CRISCUOLO, Anthony Thomas.

CRISPO, John. Canadian, b. 1933. Economics, Humanities, industrial relations, and business-government relations. Prof. of Political Economy, Faculty of Mgmt. Studies and Dept. of Economics, Univ. of Toronto, since 1965 (Asst. Prof., 1961–64; Assoc. Prof., 1964–65; Founding Dir., Centre for Industrial Relations, 1965–72; First Dean, Faculty of Management Studies, 1970–75). *Publs:* (ed.) Industrial Relations: Challenges and Responses, 1966; (ed.) Collective Bargaining and the Professional Employee, 1966; International Unionism: A Study in Canadian-American Relations, 1967; The Role of International Unionism, 1967; (co-author) Construction Labour Relations, 1969; (co-author) Canadian Industrial Relations: The Report of the Prime Minister's Task Force on Labour Relations, 1969; Fee-setting by Independent Practitioners, 1972; The Public Right to Know: Accountability in the Secretive Society, 1975; The Canadian Industrial Relations System, 1978; Industrial Democracy in Western Europe, 1978; Mandate for Canada, 1978; National Consultation: Problems and Prospects, 1985. Add: 1127 Mt. Pleasant Rd., Toronto, Ont. M4P 2M8, Canada.

CRIST, Judith. American, b. 1922. Film. Critical Columnist, Coming Attractions, since 1985. Adjunct Prof., Grad. Sch. of Journalism, Columbia Univ., NYC, since 1964. Reporter, 1943–60, Ed., 1960–63, and Film Critic, 1963–66, New York Herald Tribune; Film and Theatre Critic NBC-TV Today Show, 1963–73; Film Critic, New York Mag., 1968–75; Saturday Review, 1975–78, 1980–84; 50 Plus, 1978–83. Contrib. Ed. and Film Critic, TV Guide, 1966–88; Arts Critic, WWOR-TV, 1981–87. *Publs:* The Private Eye, the Cowboy, and the Very Naked Girl: Movies from Cleo to Clyde, 1968; Judith Crist's TV Guide to the Movies, 1974; Take 22: Moviemakers on Moviemaking, 1984. Add: 180 Riverside Dr., New York, N.Y. 10024, U.S.A.

CRISTOFER, Michael. Pseud. for Michael Procaccino. American, b. 1946. Plays/Screenplays. *Publs:* The Shadow Box, 1977; Black Angel, 1984; The Lady and the Clarinet, 1985. Add: c/o Dramatists Play Service, 440 Park Ave. S., New York, N.Y. 10016, U.S.A.

CRITCHFIELD, Richard. American, b. 1931. Social commentary/phenomena. Freelance writer and Contrib., The Christian Science Monitor, The New York Times, Los Angeles Times, Wall Street Journal, Reader's Digest and The Economist, London. Reporter, Cedar Valley Daily Times, 1955–56; Washington Corresp., Salt Lake City Desert News, 1957–58; Acting Asst. Prof., Univ. of Nagpur, India, 1960–62; Asia and Natnl. Corresp., The Washington Star, 1963–72 (White House Corresp., 1968–69). *Publs:* The Indian Reporters Guide, 1962; (ed. and illustrator) Lore and Legend of Nepal, 1962; The Long Charade: Political Subversion in the Vietnam War, 1968; The Golden Bowl Be Broken: Peasant Life in Four Cultures, 1974; Shahhat: An Egyptian, 1978; Villages, 1981; Those Days: An American Album, 1986. Add: c/o Peggy Ann Trimble, 4532 Airlie Way, Annandal, Va. 22003, U.S.A.

CRITCHLEY, Thomas Alan. British, b. 1919. Criminology/Law enforcement/Prisons, Public/Social administration. Justice of the Peace for Middx., since 1977. Principal Private Secty. to the Home Secty., 1958–60; Secty., Royal Commn. of Police, 1960–62, and Lord Denning's Enquiry into the Profumo Affair, 1963; Dir., Uganda Resettlement Bd., 1972–74; Asst. Under-Secty. of State, 1974–76. *Publs:* The Civil Service Today, 1951; A History of Police in England and Wales, 1967, 1978; The Conquest of Violence, 1970; (with P.D. James) The Maul and the Pear Tree, 1971, 1986; (co-author) The Police We Deserve, 1973. Add: 26

Temple Fortune Lane, London NW11, England.

CROCKER, Lester G(ilbert). American, b. 1912. Intellectual history, Language/Linguistics, Literature, Biography. Kenan Prof. of French Emeritus, Univ. of Virginia, Charlottesville; Visiting Prof. of History, Graduate Center, City Univ. of New York, 1985. Prof. and Chmn., Dept. of Modern Languages, Goucher Coll., Towson, Md., 1950–60; Fulbright Research Scholar and Guggenheim Fellow, 1954–55; Member, Inst. for Advanced Study, Princeton, N.J., 1958–59; Winifred G. Leutner Distinguished Prof. of Romance Languages, 1960–71, Chmn., Dept. of French, 1960–63, Dean of the Grad. Sch., 1963–67, and Dean of Humanities, 1967–71, Case Western Reserve Univ., Cleveland, Ohio. Benjamin Franklin Fellow, Royal Society of Arts, London, 1968; Pres. American Soc. for Eighteenth-Century Studies, 1969–71; Pres., International Soc. for the Study of the Eighteenth Century, 1971–75; Visiting Prof. of French Literature, Univ. de Paris-Sorbonne, 1975–76. *Publs:* La Correspondence de Diderot: son intérêt documentaire, psychologique et littéraire, 1939; Two Diderot Studies: Ethics and Esthetics, 1953; (consulting ed.) Larousse: Pocket Books French Dictionary, 1955; (ed.) Cervantes: Don Quixote, 1957; (ed.) The Confessions of Rousseau, 1957; (with L. Seibert) Skills and Techniques for Reading French, 1958; (ed.) Candide, 1958; (ed.) Montaigne: Selected Essays, 1959; An Age of Crisis: Man and World in Eighteenth Century French Thought, 1959; (ed.) The Traveler's Phrase Books: Spanish/English and French/English, 1961; (ed.) Voltaire: Candide and Zadig, 1962; (ed.) Balzac: Père Goriot, 1962; (ed.) Machiavelli: The Prince, 1963; (ed. with L. Seibert) Histoire d'une revanche, 1963; (ed. with L. Seibert) Le Fils du fauconnier, 1963; (ed.) Stendhal: The Red and the Black, 1963; Nature and Culture: Ethical Thought in the French Enlightenment, 1963; (ed.) Diderot's Selected Writings, 1966; Jean-Jacques Rousseau: The Quest 1712-1758, 1968; Rousseau's "Social Contract": An Interpretive Essay, 1968; (ed.) The Age of Enlightenment, 1969; (ed.) Anthologie de la littérature française du XVIII siècle, 1972; Jean-Jacques Rousseau: The Prophetic Voice 1758-1778, 1973; Diderot's Chaotic Order: Approach to Synthesis, 1974. Add: 930 Fifth Ave., New York, N.Y. 10021, U.S.A.

CROCKER, (Sir) Walter (Russell). Australian, b. 1902. International relations/Current affairs, Politics/Government, Autobiography/Memoirs/Personal, Biography. Formerly in Australian Diplomatic Service: High Commnr. in India, 1952–55; Ambassador to Indonesia, 1955–57; High Commnr. in Canada, 1957–58; High Commnr. in India and Ambassador to Nepal, 1958–62; Ambassador to the Netherlands and Belgium, 1962–65; Ambassador to Ethiopia and High Commnr. in Kenya and Uganda, 1965–67; Ambassador to Italy, 1967–70. Lt. Gov. of South Australia, 1973–82. *Publs:* The Japanese Population Problem, 1931; Nigeria, 1936; On Governing Colonies, 1946; Self Government for the Colonies, 1949; Race as Factor in International Relations, 1956; Nehru, 1966; Australian Ambassador, 1971; Memoirs, 1980; Sir Thomas Playford, 1983. Add: 256 East Terrace, Adelaide, S.A. 5000, Australia.

CROCOMBE, Ronald Gordon. New Zealand, b. 1929. Anthropology/Ethnology, Politics/Government. Research Fellow, Austalian National Univ., Canberra, 1961–64; Prof., Univ. of California, 1964–65; Field Dir., New Guinea Research Unit, 1965–69; Prof. of Pacific Studies, 1969–88, now Emeritus and Dir., Inst. of Pacific Studies, 1975–86, Univ. of the South Pacific, Suva. *Publs:* Land Tenure in the Cook Islands, 1963; Improving Land Tenure, 1968, 1973; (with M. Crocombe) The Works of Ta'unga, 1968; Land Tenure in the Pacific, 1971, 1986; The South Pacific, 1973, 1987; (with others) Holy Torture in Fiji, 1975; (ed.) Cook Islands Politics, 1978; (ed.) Pacific Indians, 1980; (ed.) Politics of the Pacific Islands Series, 1982–87. Add: Univ. of the South Pacific, Box 130, Rarotonga, Cook Islands.

CROMBIE, Alistair Cameron. British, b. 1915. Sciences. Research Officer, Zoological Laboratory, Univ. of Cambridge, 1941–46; Lectr. in History and Philosophy of Science, Univ. Coll., Univ. of London, 1946–53; Fellow, Trinity Coll., and Univ. Lectr. in the History of Science, Oxford Univ., 1953–83; Prof. of History of Science and Medicine, Smith Coll., Northampton, Mass., 1982–85. Ed., British Journal for the Philosophy of Science, 1949–54; Ed., History of Science, 1961–72. Pres., British Soc. for the History of Science, 1964–66; Pres., Intnl. Academy for the History of Science, 1968–71. *Publs:* Augustine to Galileo, 1952, 4th ed. 1979; Robert Grosseteste and the Origins of Experimental Science, 1953, 3rd ed. 1971; Scientific Change, 1963; The Mechanistic Hypothesis and the Scientific Study of Vision, 1967; The Rational Arts of Living, 1987; Science, Optics, and Music in Medieval and Early Modern Thought, 1989; Styles of Scientific Thinking in the European Tradition, 1989. Add: Orchardlea, Boars Hill, Oxford, England.

CROMPTON, Louis. American, b. 1925. Literature. Prof. of English, Univ. of Nebraska at Lincoln, since 1964 (Asst. Prof. 1955–60; Assoc. Prof. 1960–64). *Publs:* (ed.) Great Expectations, by Charles Dickens, 1964; Shaw the Dramatist, 1969; (ed.) The Road to Equality: Ten Unpublished Lectures and Essays, 1884-1918, by Bernard Shaw, 1971; (ed.) The Great Composers, by Bernard Shaw, 1978; Byron and Greek Love: Homophobia in 19th Century England, 1985. Add: 5840 Locust St., Lincoln, Nebr. 68516, U.S.A.

CROMWELL, Elsie. *See* **LEE,** Elsie.

CRONIN, Anthony. Irish, b. 1926. Novels/Short stories, Plays/Screenplays, Poetry, Literature. Cultural and Artistic Adviser, Irish Prime Minister, since 1980. Formerly, Assoc. Ed., The Bell, Dublin, and Literary Ed., Time and Tide, London; Columnist, Irish Times, Dublin, 1974–80. *Publs:* Poems, 1957; (ed.) The Courtship of Phelim O'Toole and Other Stories, by William Carleton, 1962; The Life of Riley (novel), 1964; A Question of Modernity (literary criticism), 1966; The Shame of It (play), 1971; Collected Poems 1950-1973, 1973; Dead as Doornails: A Chronicle of Life, 1976; Identity Papers (novel), 1979; Reductionist Poem, 1980; 41 Sonnet-Poems 82, 1982; R.M.S. Titanic (poem), 1982; Heritage Now: Irish Literature in the English Language, 1982; New and Selected Poems, 1982; The Irish Eye: Viewpoints, 1985. Add: 18 Curzon St., Dublin 8, Ireland.

CRONKITE, Walter (Leland, Jr.) American, b. 1916. Communications media, International relations/Current affairs, Autobiography/Memoirs/Personal. CBS News Corresp., 1950–81, and Special Corresp., since 1981, NYC. Chief Corresp., Nuremberg War Crimes Trials, 1945–46. *Publs:* Challenges of Change, 1970; I Can Hear It Now: The Sixties, 1970; Eye on the World, 1971; South by Southeast, North by Northeast, 1986. Add: CBS, 51 W. 52nd St., New York, N.Y. 10019, U.S.A.

CRONON, William. American, b. 1954. History. Assoc. Prof. of History, Yale Univ., New Haven, since 1986. *Publs:* Changes in the Land: Indians, Colonists, and the Ecology of New England, 1983. Add: Dept. of History, Box 1504A Yale Station, Yale Univ., New Haven, Conn. 06520, U.S.A.

CROOK, Joseph Mordaunt. British, b. 1937. Architecture. Prof. of Architectural History, Royal Holloway and Bedford New Coll., Univ. of London, since 1981 (Research Fellow, 1962–63; Lectr., 1965–75; Reader, 1975–81). Research Fellow, Inst. of Historical Research, London, 1961–62; Asst. Lectr., Leicester Univ., 1963–65. Member, Historic Buildings Council for England, 1974–80. *Publs:* (ed.) History of the Gothic Revival, by C.L. Eastlake, 1970, 1978; The British Museum, 1971; Victorian Architecture: A Visual Anthology, 1972; The Greek Revival: Neo-Classical Attitudes in British Architecture 1760-1870, 1972; (ed.) Six Essays by J.T. Emmett, 1972; (ed.) The Gentleman's House, by R. Kerr, 1972; (with M.H. Port) The History of the King's Works, vol. VI, 1782-1851, 1973; (with H.M. Colvin, J. Newman and K. Downes) The History of the King's Works, vol. V, 1660-1782, 1976; William Burges and the High Victorian Dream, 1981; (with C.A. Lennox-Boyd) Axel Haig and the Victorian Vision of the Middle Ages, 1983; The Dilemma of Style, 1987. Add: 55 Gloucester Ave., London NW1, England.

CROSBY, Alfred W., Jr. American, b. 1931. History. Prof. of American Studies, Univ. of Texas at Austin, since 1977. Assoc. Prof. of History, Washington State Univ., Pullman, 1969–77. *Publs:* America, Russia, Hemp and Napoleon, 1965; The Columbian Exchange: Biological and Cultural Consequences of 1492, 1972; Epidemic and Peace 1918, 1976; Ecological Imperialism: The Biological Expansion of Europe 900-1900, 1987. Add: American Studies, Univ. of Texas, Austin, Tex. 78712, U.S.A.

CROSBY, Harry C. *See* **ANVIL,** Christopher.

CROSBY, John (Campbell). American, b. 1912. Novels/Short stories. Columnist and TV Critic, New York Herald Tribune, 1936–65. *Publs:* Out of the Blue, 1952; With Love and Loathing, 1963; Sappho in Absence, 1970; The Literary Obsession, 1973; Contract on the President, 1973; An Affair of Strangers, 1975; Nightfall, 1976; Company of Friends, 1977; Dear Judgment, 1978; Party of the Year, 1979; Penelope Now, 1981; Men in Arms, 1983; Take No Prisoners, 1985; Family Worth, 1987; Wingwalker, 1988. Add: Esmont, Va., U.S.A.

CROSLAND, Margaret. British. Literature, Biography, Translations. *Publs:* Madame Colette, 1953; Jean Cocteau, 1955; (trans.) First Poems by Minou Drouet, 1956; (co-trans. with Sinclair Road) Opium by Jean Cocteau, 1957; (trans) Then There Was Fire by Minou Drouet, 1957; (trans.) The Story of Renard by Maurice Genevoix, 1959; Louise of Stolberg, 1962; (ed.) Marquis de Sade, Selected Letters, 1965; (ed.) A Traveller's Guide to Literary Europe (in U.S. as A Guide to Literary Europe), 1965; (ed. and trans.) My Contemporaries by Jean Cocteau, 1967; (trans.) Donatella by Minou Drouet, 1969; (trans.) Hebdomeros, by G. de Chirico; (trans. and ed.) A Mania for Solitude by Cesare Pavese, 1969; (trans. and ed.) Memoirs of Giorgio de Chirico, 1971; (trans.) The Other Woman by Colette, 1971; (trans. and ed.) Cocteau's World 1972; (co-trans. with David Le Vay) The Thousand and One Mornings by Colette, 1973; Colette: The Difficulty of Loving, 1973; (trans. and ed.) Retreat from Love, by Colette, 1974; (trans. and ed.) Duo, by Colette, 1974; Women of Iron and Velvet, 1976; Raymond Radiguet, 1976; (ed.) The Leather Jacket, by Cesare Pavese, 1980; Beyond the Lighthouse, 1981; Piaf, 1985. Add: The Long Croft, Upper Hartfield, Sussex, England.

CROSLAND, Maurice P. British, b. 1931. History, Sciences. Prof. of the History of Science, and Dir. of the Unit for History, Philosophy and Social Relations of Science, Univ. of Kent at Canterbury, since 1974. Lectr., 1963–69, and Reader in the History of Science, 1969–74, Univ. of Leeds. Pres., British Soc. for the History of Science, 1974–76. *Publs:* Historical Studies in the Language of Chemistry, 1962, 1978; The Society of Arcueil: A View of French Science at the Time of Napoleon I, 1967; (ed.) Science in France in the Revolutionary Era, Described by Thomas Bugge, 1969; (ed.) The Science of Matter: A Historical Survey, 1971; (ed.) The Emergence of Science in Western Europe, 1975; Gay-Lussac, Scientist and Bourgeois, 1978. Add: Unit for History of Science, Physics Bldg., Univ. of Kent at Canterbury, Canterbury, Kent CT2 7NR, England.

CROSS, Amanda. See **HEILBRUN,** Carolyn G.

CROSS, Anthony Glenn. British, b. 1936. History, Literature. Prof. of Slavonic Studies, Cambridge Univ, since 1985. Co-ed., Journal of European Studies, since 1971; Ed., Newsletter of the Study Group on Eighteenth Century Russia, since 1973. Lectr., 1964–69, Sr. Lectr., 1969–72, and Reader in Russian, 1972–81, Univ. of East Anglia Norwich; Prof. of Russian, Univ. of Leeds, 1981–85. *Publs:* (gen. ed.) Russia Through European Eyes, 1553-1917 (series), 1968–72; N.M. Karamzin: A Study of His Literary Career, 1783-1803, 1971; (ed.) Russia under Western Eyes, 1517-1825, 1971; (ed.) Russian Literature in the Age of Catherine the Great: Collection of Essays, 1976; Anglo-Russian Relations in the Eighteenth Century, 1977; (ed.) Great Britain and Russia in the Eighteenth Century: Contacts and Comparisons, 1978; "By the Banks of the Thames": Russians in Eighteenth-Century Britain, 1980; The 1780's: Russia under Western Eyes, 1981; The Tale of the Russian Daughter and Her Suffocated Lover, 1982; (ed.) Russian and the West in the Eighteenth Century, 1983; The Russian Theme in English Literature, 1985; (co-ed.) Russia and the World of the Eighteenth Century, 1988. Add: Dept. of Slavonic Studies, Sedgwick Ave., Cambridge CB3 9DA, England.

CROSS, (Alan) Beverley. British, b. 1931. Plays/Screenplays, Songs, lyrics and libretti. *Publs:* Mars in Capricorn: An Adventure and an Experience (novel), 1955; The Nightwalkers (novel), 1956; One More River, 1958; Strip the Willow, 1960; The Singing Dolphin, and The Three Cavaliers, 1960; (adaptor) Boeing-Boeing, 1961; Half a Sixpence, 1963; The Mines of Sulphur, 1965; Jorrocks, 1966; All the King's Men, 1969; Victory, 1970; The Rising of the Moon, 1970; Catherine Howard (TV play), 1970; The Great Society, 1974; Haworth, 1978; (adaptor) Happy Birthday, 1978; The Scarlet Pimpernel, 1985; Miranda, 1987. Add: c/o Curtis Brown Ltd., 162-168 Regent St., London W1R 5TB, England.

CROSS, Brenda. See **COLLOMS,** Brenda.

CROSS, (Margaret) Claire. British, b. 1932. History. Lectr., then, Prof. in History, Univ. of York, since 1965. County Archivist, Cambs., 1958–61; Intnl. Fellow, American Assn. of Univ. Women, 1961–62; Research Fellow, Reading Univ., 1962–65. *Publs:* The Free Grammar School of Leicester, 1953; The Puritan Earl: The Life of Henry Hastings, Third Earl of Huntingdon 1536-1595, 1966; (ed.) The Letters of Sir Francis Hastings, 1574-1604, 1969; (ed. and contrib.) The Royal Supremacy in the Elizabethan Church, 1969; Church and People 1450-1660, 1976. Add: Dept. of History, Univ. of York, Heslington, York, England.

CROSS, Gillian (Clare). British, b. 1945. Children's fiction. *Publs:* The Runaway, 1979; The Iron Way, 1979; Revolt at Ratcliffe's Rags, 1980; Save Our School, 1981; A Whisper of Lace, 1981; The Dark Behind the Curtain, 1982; The Demon Headmaster, 1982; The Mintyglo Kid, 1983; Born of the Sun, 1983; On the Edge, 1984; The Prime Minister's Brain, 1985; Swimathon, 1986; Chartbreak, 1986; Roscoe's Leap, 1987; A Map of Nowhere, 1988. Add: 41 Essex Rd., Gravesend, Kent DA11 OSL, England.

CROSS, Ian. New Zealander, b. 1925. Novels/Short stories. Chmn., Broadcasting Corporation of New Zealand, since 1977. Public Relations Officer, New Zealand Police and Justice Depts., 1956–58. *Publs:* The God Boy, 1957; The Backward Sex, 1960; After Anzac Day, 1961; The City of No (TV play), 1970. Add: P.O. Box 98, Wellington, New Zealand.

CROSS, James. See **PARRY,** Hugh Jones.

CROSS, K. Patricia. American, b. 1926. Education. Prof. of Education and Dept. Chair., Harvard Univ., Cambridge, Mass., since 1981; Asst. Dean of Women, Univ. of Illinois, Urbana, 1953–59; Dean of Students, Cornell Univ., Ithaca, N.Y., 1959–63; Dir., Coll. and Univ. Progs., 1963–66, and Sr. Research Psychologist, 1963–81, Educational Testing Service, Berkeley, Calif.; Research Educator, Center for Research and Development in Higher Education, 1967–77, and Lectr. on Higher Education, 1978–81, Univ. of California, Berkeley. *Publs:* The Junior College Student: A Research Description, 1968; Beyond the Open Door: New Students to Higher Education, 1971; Explorations in Nontraditional Study, 1972; (with S. Gould) New Students and New Needs in Higher Education, 1972; Integration of Earning and Learning: Cooperative Education and Nontraditional Study, 1973; Planning for Nontraditional Programs: An Analysis of the Issues, 1974; (with John Valley) Accent on Learning: Improving Instruction and Reshaping the Curriculum, 1976; The Missing Link, 1978; Adults as Learners, 1981; (with A.M. McCartan) Adult Learning: State Policies and Institutional Practices, 1984. Add: 409 Gutman Library, Harvard Grad. Sch. of Education, Cambridge, Mass. 02138, U.S.A.

CROSS, Richard K. American, b. 1940. Literature. Prof. of English, Univ. of Maryland, College Park, since 1983 (Chmn. of the Dept., 1983–88). Instr. in English, Dartmouth Coll., Hanover, N.H., 1966–68; Asst. Prof., 1968–74, Assoc. Prof. 1974–80 and Prof. of English, 1980–83, Univ. of California at Los Angeles. *Publs:* Flaubert and Joyce: The Rite of Fiction, 1971; Malcolm Lowry: A Preface to His Fiction, 1980. Add: Dept. of English, Univ. of Maryland, College Park, Md. 20742, U.S.A.

CROSS, Thomas B. American, b. 1949. Communications media, Information science/Computers, Technology. Managing Dir., Cross Information Co., Boulder, Colo., since 1980; also, Vice-Pres., Intelligent Buildings Corp., Faculty member, Univ. of Colorado and Univ. of Denver. Dir. of Telecommunications for City and County Govt., Boulder, 1974–77; Telecommunications Mgr., Storage Technology Corp., Louisville, Colo., 1977–78; Program Mgr., Telecommunications Systems, STC Communications Corp., Louisville, 1978–80. *Publs:* Intelligent Buildings and Information Systems I, 1984; Strategies for Telecommunications Management, 1984; Telecommunications Outlook, 1985; (with Marjorie Raizman) Networking: An Electronic Mail Handbook, 1985; (with Kathleen Kelleher) Tele/Conferencing: Linking People Together Electronically, 1985; (ed.) Tele/Conferencing Report, 1985; (with Marjorie Raizman) Telecommuting: Work Strategies for the Information Organization, 1986; Centrex II: Strategic Directions, 1986; (ed.) Centrex I: Strategic Outlook, 1986; (with Michelle D. Gouin) Intelligent Buildings: Strategies for Technology and Architecture, 1986; The Softside of Software, 1986; (with James R. Weidlein) Networking Personal Computers in Organizations: An Executive Perspective, 1986; Telecommuting: The Future Technology of Work, 1986; CTO: Chief Telecommunications Officer, 1987; Knowledge Engineering, 1987. Add: c/o Simon and Schuster Inc., 1230 Ave. of the Americas, New York, N.Y. 10020, U.S.A.

CROSS, Victor. See **COFFMAN,** Virginia.

CROSS, Wilbur (Lucius) (III). American, b. 1918. Antiques/Furnishings, Children's non-fiction, Education, History, Medicine/Health, Travel/Exploration/Adventure. Sr. Ed., Conoco, Stamford, Conn., since 1969. Asst. Ed., Life mag., NYC, 1953–62; Founder and Editorial Dir., Books for Business Inc., NYC, 1962–69. *Publs:* Challengers of the Deep, 1959; Ghost Ship of the Pole, 1960; Naval Battles and Heroes, 1960; John Diebold: Breaking the Confines of the Possible, 1965; White House Weddings, 1968; Lost Men of Anatahan, 1969; (co-author) The New Age of Medical Discovery, 1972; (co-author) The Complete Book of Paper Antiques, 1973; A Guide to Unusual Vacations, 1973; The Weekend Education Source Book, 1976; You Are Never Too Old to Learn,

1978; Kids and Booze, 1979; (co-author) Presidential Courage, 1980; Egypt, 1982; Coal, 1983; Petroleum, 1983; Brazil (children's), 1984; Solar Energy, (children's), 1984; Space Shuttle (children's), 1985; Commitment to Excellence: The Remarkable Amway Story, 1986; (with M. Kosser) The Conway Twitty Story, 1987. Add: c/o Benjamin Co., Inc., 1 Westchester Plaza, Elmsford, N.Y. 10523, U.S.A.

CROSSAN, G(regory) D(ixon). New Zealander, b. 1950. Literature. Lectr. in English, Massey Univ., Palmerston North, since 1977. Asst. Lectr. in English, Univ. of Canterbury, Christchurch, 1973–76. *Publs:* A Relish for Eternity (on the poetry of John Clare), 1976. Add: Dept. of English, Massey Univ., Palmerston North, New Zealand.

CROSSLEY-HOLLAND, Kevin (John William). British, b. 1941. Children's fiction, Poetry, Travel/Exploration/Adventure, Translations. Ed., Macmillan & Co., Publishers, London, 1962–69; Gregory Fellow in Poetry, 1969–71; Talks Producer, BBC, London, 1972; Editorial Dir., Victor Gollancz, Publishers, Ltd., London, 1972–77. *Publs:* Havelok the Dane, 1964; King Horn, 1965; (trans.) The Battle of Maldon and Other Old English Poems, 1965; The Green Children, 1966; The Callow Pit Coffer, 1968; (ed.) Running to Paradise: An Introductory Selection of the Poems of W.B. Yeats, 1968; Beowulf, 1968; (with Jill Paton Walsh) Wordhoard, 1969; (ed.) Winter's Tales for Children 3, 1969; (trans.) Storm and Other Old English Riddles, 1970; Norfolk Poems, 1970; The Pedlar of Swaffham, 1972; Pieces of Land: Journeys to Eight Islands, 1972; The Rain-Giver and Other Poems, 1972; The Sea-Stranger, 1973; The Fire-Brother, 1974; Green Blades Rising: The Anglo-Saxons, 1975; The Wildman, 1976; The Dream-House, 1976; (ed.) The Faber Book of Northern Legends, 1977; (trans.) The Exeter Riddle Book, 1978; (ed.) The Faber Book of Northern Folk-Tales, 1980; The Norse Myths, 1981; Between My Father and My Son, 1982; The Dead Moon, 1982; Beowulf, 1982; (ed.) The Riddle Book, 1982; The Anglo-Saxon World, 1982; Time's Oriel (poetry), 1983; (with Gwyn Thomas) Tales from the Mabinogion, 1984; Axe-Man, Wolf-Age: A Selection for Children from the Norse Myths, 1985; Storm, 1985; (ed.) Folk-Tales of the British Isles, 1985; (ed.) Oxford Book of Travel Verse, 1986; Waterslain and Other Poems, 1986; The Painting Room (poetry), 1988. Add: c/o Deborah Rogers Literary Agency, 43 Blenheim Cres., London W11 2EF, England.

CROUCH, Marcus S. British, b. 1913. Children's non-fiction, History, Literature, Travel/Exploration/Adventure. Branch Librarian, Tonbridge, Kent, 1939–48; Deputy County Librarian, Kent County Council, 1948–77. *Publs:* Treasure Seekers and Borrowers, 1962; Britain in Trust, 1963; Rivers of England and Wales, 1965; (ed.) Chosen for Children, 1967; Kent, 1967; Fingerprints of History, 1968; Beatrix Potter, 1969; Heritage of Sussex, 1969; Canterbury, 1970; Detective in the Landscape: South East England, 1972; The Nesbit Tradition, 1972; Cream of Kent, 1973; (with Wyn F. Bergess) Victorian and Edwardian England, 1974; The Home Counties, 1975; (with William Stobbs) Brer Rabbit, 1977; (with Stobbs) Six Against the World, 1978; (with Stobbs) The Ivory City, 1980; (with Stobbs) Rainbow Warrior's Bride, 1981; The Whole World Storybook, 1983; Rich Man, Poor Man, 1985; Ivan: Stories of Old Russia, 1989; Kentish Books, Kentish Writers, 1989. Add: Ty'n Llidiart, Pentre Celyn, Ruthin, Clwyd, Wales.

CROUSE, William H. American, b. 1911. Plays/Screenplays, Engineering/Technology. Consulting Ed., Automotive Books, McGraw-Hill Book Co., NYC; First Ed.-in-Chief, McGraw-Hill Encyclopedia of Science and Technology, since 1956 (ed. of Technical Books, 1946–53). Dir. of Field Education, Delco-Remy Div. of General Motors, 1937–46. *Publs:* Automotive Electrical Equipment, 1941, 10th ed., 1985; Automotive Mechanics, 1946, 9th ed. 1985; Everyday Automobile Repairs, 1946; Home Guide to Repair, Upkeep and Remodeling, 1947; Understanding Science, 1948, 4th ed. 1973; Electrical Appliance Servicing, 1950; Workbook for Automotive Electricity, 1950, 6th ed. 1980; Workbook for Automotive Tools, 1951, 6th ed. 1980; Workbook for Automotive Engines, 1951, 7th ed. 1985; Workbook for Automotive Chassis, 1951, 3rd ed. 1966; Workbook for Automotive Service and Trouble Diagnosis, 1951, 6th ed. 1980; Everyday Household Appliance Repairs, 1952; Automotive Chassis and Body, 1955, 7th ed. 1985; Automotive Engines, 1955, 7th ed. 1985; Automotive Fuel, Lubricating and Cooling Systems, 1955, 7th ed. 1986; Automotive Transmissions and Power Trains, 1955; 7th ed. 1986; Science Marvels of Tomorrow, 1963; (with D. Anglin) Testbook for Automotive Mechanics, 1965, 3rd ed. 1980; Automotive Emission Control; Automotive Engine Design; Automotive Service Business: Operation and Management; (with D. Anglin) Workbook for Automotive Mechanics; Workbook for Automotive Transmissions and Power Trains; Workbook for Small Engines: Operation and Maintenance; (with R. Worthington and M. Margules) General Power Mechanics; Small Engines:

Operation and Maintenance; Study Guide for Automotive Mechanics; The Auto Book; (with D. Anglin) Auto Shop Workbook; Auto Study Guide; (with D. Anglin) Auto Test Book; Automotive Brakes; Automotive Electrical Systems; Automotive Engine Systems; Automotive Transmissions and Power Trains; Automotive Steering Systems; Automotive Suspension Systems; Engines and Fuel Systems; Up the Sex Ladder (play); You Live only Once, or Twice, or Maybe (play); Automotive Tune Up, 1977, 1986; Automotive Emission Control, 1977, 1986; Automotive Air Conditioning, 1978, 1986; Motor Vehicle Inspection, 1978; Auto Body Repair and Refinishing, 1979, 1985; Motorcycle Mechanics, 1979. Add: 1285 Gulf Shore Blvd., Naples, Fla. 33940, U.S.A.

CROWDER, Richard H(enry). American, b. 1909. Literature, Biography. Emeritus Prof. of English, Purdue Univ., West Lafayette, Ind., since 1976 (Instr., 1937–45; Asst. Prof., 1945–50; Assoc. Prof., 1950–58; Prof., 1958–76). Fulbright Lectr. in American Poetry, Univ. of Bordeaux, France, 1963–65. *Publs:* Those Innocent Years . . . James Whitcomb Riley, 1957; No Featherbed to Heaven: Michael Wigglesworth, 1631–1705, 1962; Carl Sandburg, 1964; (ed. with R.B. Browne, V.L. Lokke and W.T. Stafford) Frontiers of American Culture, 1968. Add: 1525 Sheridan Rd., West Lafayette, Ind. 47906, U.S.A.

CROWE, Cecily Bentley (Teague). American. Romance/Gothic. *Publs:* Miss Spring, 1953; The Tower of Kilraven, 1965; Northwater, 1968; The Twice-Born, 1972; Abbeygate, 1977; The Talisman, 1979; Bloodrose House, 1985. Add: Brick House, Mirror Lake, N.H. 03853, U.S.A.

CROWE, John. *See* **LYNDS**, Dennis.

CROWLEY, John. American, b. 1942. Science fiction/Fantasy. Freelance writer since 1966. Photographer and commercial artist, 1964–66. *Publs:* The Deep, 1975; Beasts, 1976; Engine Summer, 1979; Little, Big, 1981; A Egypt, 1987; Egypt, 1987. Add: Box 395, Conway, Mass. 01341, U.S.A.

CROWLEY, Mart. American, b. 1935. Plays/Screenplays. *Publs:* The Boys in the Band, 1968; A Breeze from the Gulf, 1974. Add: 1355 N. Laurel Ave., Los Angeles, CA, U.S.A.

CROWN, David Allan. American, b. 1928. Criminology/Law enforcement. Adjunct Prof., American Univ., Washington, D.C., 1971–75; Adjunct Prof., Antioch Sch. of Law, Washington, 1977–81; Pres., Crown Forensic Labs. Inc., Fairfax, Va. Assoc. Ed., Journal of Forensic Science, since 1973. Asst. Dir., Identification Lab., U.S. Postal Inspection Service, San Francisco, Calif., 1957–67; Dir., Questioned Documents Lab., U.S. Dept. of the Army, Washington, D.C., 1967–72; Dir., Questioned Documents Staff, INR/DDC, Dept. of State, Washington, 1972–77; Chief, Questioned Documents Lab., Office of Technical Services, Washington, 1977–82. *Publs:* The Forensic Examination of Paints and Pigments, 1968; (co-author) Forensic Sciences, 1982; (co-author) Legal Medicine Annual, 1985. Add: 3103 Jessie Ct., Fairfax, Va. 22030, U.S.A.

CROWSON, P(aul) S(piller). British, b. 1913. History, International relations/Current affairs. Schoolmaster, Chillon Coll., Montreux, Switzerland, 1937–39, Watford Grammar Sch., England, 1939–45, and Radley Coll., Abingdon, England, 1945–74. *Publs:* A History of the Russian People, 1948; Tudor Foreign Policy, 1973; Animals in Focus, 1980. Add: Tarvers, Crofts Lane, Adderbury, Banbury, Oxon OX17 3ND, England.

CROWTHER, Harold Francis. American, b. 1920. Novels/Short stories. Retired Lawyer, Salina, Kans., since 1983. With U.S. Navy, 1939–45; Probation Officer, Salina County Juvenile Court, 1956–59. *Publs:* The Oblique Equalizer or Some for Me, 1965. Add: Box 216, Pierce City, Missouri 65723, U.S.A.

CROXTON, C(live) A(nthony). British, b. 1945. Language, Physics. Assoc. Prof., Dept. of Mathematics, Univ. of Newcastle, N.S.W., since 1974. Fellow, Jesus Coll., Cambridge, 1969–74. *Publs:* Liquid State Physics: A Statistical Mechanical Introduction, 1974; Introductory Eigenphysics, 1974; Introduction to Liquid State Physics, 1975; (ed.) Progress in Liquid Physics, 1978; Statistical Mechanics of the Liquid Surface, 1980; Russian for the Scientist and Mathematician, 1985; Fluid Interfacial Phenomena, 1986. Add: Dept. of Mathematics, Univ. of Newcastle, Newcastle, N.S.W. 2308, Australia.

CROZIER, Andrew. British, b. 1943. Poetry. Lectr. in English, Univ. of Sussex, Brighton. *Publs:* Loved Litter of Time Spent, 1967; Train

Rides, 1968; Walking on Grass, 1969; (with John James and Tom Phillips) In One Side and Out the Other, 1970; Neglected Information, 1973; The Veil Poem, 1974; Printed Circuit, 1974; (with Ian Potts) Seven Contemporary Sun Dials, 1975; Pleats, 1975; Duets, 1976; High Zero, 1978; Were There, 1978; Residing, 1976; Utamaro Variations, 1982; Majority, 1985; (ed. with Tim Longville) A Various Art (anthology), 1987. Add: Arts B, Univ. of Sussex, Brighton, Sussex BN1 9RH, England.

CROZIER, Brian. Also writes as John Rossiter. British, b. 1918. International relations/Current affairs, Third World problems, Biography, Novels. Columnist, National Review, New York since 1978. Staff member: Reuters, 1943–44; News Chronicle, 1944–48; Sydney Morning Herald, 1948–51, Reuters-AAP, 1951–52, Straits Times, 1952–53, The Economist, 1954–64, BBC, 1954–65; Dir., Inst. for the Study of Conflict, London, 1970–79. *Publs:* The Rebels: A Study of Post-War Insurrections, 1960; The Morning After: A Study of Independence, 1963; Neo-Colonialism, 1964; South-East Asia in Turmoil, 1965; The Struggle for the Third World, 1966; Franco, 1967; The Masters of Power, 1969; (ed.) We Will Bury You: A Study of Left-wing Subversion Today, 1970; The Future of Communist Power (in U.S. as After Stalin), 1970; De Gaulle, 2 vols., 1973–74, in U.S., 1 vol., 1973; A Theory of Conflict, 1974; The Man Who Lost China: A Biography of Chiang Kai-shek, 1978; Strategy of Survival, 1978; The Minimum State, 1979; Franco: Crepusculo de un Hombre, 1980; The Price of Peace, 1980; (co-author) Socialism Explained, 1984; (co-author) This War Called Peace, 1984; (as John Rossiter) The Andropov Deception (novel), 1984, U.S. ed. as Brian Crozier, 1986; Socialism: Dream and Reality, 1987; (ed.) The Grenada Documents, 1987. Add: Kulm House, Dollis Avenue, London N3 1DA, England.

CRUICKSHANK, Charles Greig. Pseud.: Charles Greig. British, b. 1914. Novels/Short stories, Mystery/Crime/Suspense, Military/Defence, Sports. With U.K. Bd. of Trade, 1946–51; Trade Commnr., Ceylon, 1951–55, and Canada, 1955–58; Sr. Trade Commnr., New Zealand, 1958–63; Exec. Secty., Commonwealth Economic Cttee., 1964–66; Dir., Commodities Div., Commonwealth Secretariat, 1967–68; Regional Export Dir., London and South-East, Bd. of Trade, 1969–71; Inspector, Foreign and Commonwealth Office, 1971–72. *Publs:* Elizabeth's Army, 1966; Army Royal: Henry VIII's Expedition to France, 1969; The English Occupation of Tournai, 1971; (co-author) A Guide to the Sources of British Military History, 1971; The German Occupation of the Channel Islands 1940–45, 1975; Greece 1940–41, 1976; The V-Mann Papers, 1976; The Tang Murders, 1976; The Fourth Arm: Psychological Warfare, 1938–1945, 1977; The Ebony Version, 1978; The Deceivers, 1978; Deception in World War II, 1979; SOE in the Far East, 1983; Kew for Murder, 1984; Scotch Murder, 1985; SOE in Scandinavia, 1986; History of Royal Wimbledon Golf Club, 1986. Add: 15 McKay Rd., Wimbledon Common, London SW20 0HT, England.

CRUICKSHANK, John. British, b. 1924. History, Literature. Prof. of French, Univ. of Sussex, Brighton, since 1962. *Publs:* Albert Camus and the Literature of Revolt, 1959; (ed.) Critical Readings in the Modern French Novel, 1961; (contrib. ed.) The Novelist as Philosopher: Essays in French Fiction, 1935–1960, 1962; Montherlant, 1964; (ed.) Vigny: Servitude et Grandeur Militaires, 1966; (contrib. ed.) French Literature and its Background, 6 vols., 1968–70; (ed.) Aspects of the Modern European Mind, 1969; (coed. with E.M. Beaumont and J.M. Cocking) Order and Adventure in Post-Romantic French Poetry, 1973; Benjamin Constant, 1974; (with W.D. Howarth and H.M. Peyre) French Literature from 1600 to the Present, 1974; Variations on Catastrophe: Some French Responses to the Great War, 1982; Pascal: Pensées, 1983. Add: Woodpeckers, East Hoathly, Sussex BN8 6QL, England.

CRUMLEY, James. American, b. 1939. Mystery/Crime/Suspense. Asst. Prof. of English, Univ. of Texas at El Paso, since 1981. Instr. in English, Univ. of Montana, Missoula, 1966–69; Asst. Prof. of English, Univ. of Arkansas, Fayetteville, 1969–70, and Colorado State Univ., Ft. Collins, 1971–74; freelance writer, 1974–76; Visiting Writer, Reed Coll., Portland, Ore., 1976–77, and Carnegie-Mellon Univ., Pittsburgh, 1979–80. *Publs:* One to Count Cadence (non-mystery novel), 1969; The Wrong Case, 1975; The Last Good Kiss, 1978; Dancing Bear, 1983. Add: P.O. Box 9278, Missoula, Mont. 59807, U.S.A.

CRUMP, Barry (John). New Zealander, b. 1935. Novels/Short stories. Hunter, goldminer, and radio announcer. *Publs:* A Good Keen Man, 1961; Hang on a Minute Mate, 1962; One of Us, 1963; Two in One, 1964; There and Back, 1965; Gulf, 1966; Scrapwagon, 1966: The Odd Spot of Bother, 1967; No Reference Intended, 1968; Warm Beer (short stories), 1969; A Good Keen Girl, 1970; Bastards I Have Met, 1971; Fred, 1972; The Best of Barry Crump, 1974; Shorty, 1980; Puha Road, 1981;

Adventures of Sam Cash, 1985; Wild Pork and Watercress, 1986. Add: c/o Beckett Sterling Publishers, 28 Poland Rd., Glenfield, Auckland, New Zealand.

CRUZ, Victor Hernandez. Puerto Rican, b. 1949. Poetry. Instr., San Francisco State Univ., Calif., since 1973. Former Ed., Umbra mag., NYC. *Publs:* Papo Got His Gun, 1966; Snaps: Poems, 1969; (ed. with H. Kohl) Stuff: A Collection of Poems, Visions and Imaginative Happenings from Young Writers in Schools—Opened and Closed, 1970; Mainland, 1973; Tropicalization, 1976; By Lingual Wholes, 1982. Add: P.O. Box 40148, San Francisco, Calif. 94140, U.S.A.

CRYSTAL, David. British, b. 1941. Children's non-fiction, Language/Linguistics, Medicine/Health, Speech/Rhetoric. Professorial Fellow, University Coll. of North Wales, Bangor, since 1985. Ed., Child Language Teaching and Therapy, since 1985, and Linguistics Abstracts, since 1985; Consultant Ed., English Today, since 1986. Asst. Lectr., Coll. of North Wales, 1963–65; Lectr. and Reader, 1965–75, and Prof. of Linguistic Science, 1976–85, Univ. of Reading. *Publs:* (with R. Quirk) Systems of Prosodic and Paralinguistic Features in English, 1964; Linguistics, Language and Religion, 1965; What Is Linguistics?, 1968, 6th ed. 1985; (with D. Davy) Investigating English Style, 1969; Prosodic Systems and Intonation in English, 1969; (ed. with W. Bolton) The English Language, vol. 2, 1969; Linguistics, 1971, 1985; The English Tone of Voice, 1975; (with D. Davy) Advanced Conversational English, 1975; (with P. Fletcher and M. Garman) The Grammatical Analysis of Language Disability, 1976, 1981; Child Language, Learning, and Linguistics, 1976; Working with LARSP, 1979; Eric Partridge: In His Own Words, 1980; A First Dictionary of Linguistics and Phonetics, 1980; Introduction to Language Pathology, 1980; Clinical Linguistics, 1981; Directions in Applied Linguistics, 1981; Linguistic Controversies, 1981; Profiling Linguistic Disability, 1982; Linguistic Encounters with Language Handicap, 1984; Language Handicap in Children, 1984; Who Cares about English Usage?, 1984; Listen to Your Child, 1986; (ed., with W. Bolton) The English Language, 1987; Cambridge Encyclopedia of Language, 1987; Rediscover Grammar, 1988; The English Language, 1988; Pilgrimage, 1988; children's non-fiction—(with J. Bevington) Skylarks, 1975; (with John Foster) Heat, Light, Sound, Roads, Railways, Canals, Monasteries, Manors, Castles, Money, Parliament, Newspapers, The Romans, The Greeks, The Ancient Egyptians, Air, Food, Volcanoes, Deserts, Electricity, Motorcycles, Computers, Horses and Ponies, The Normans, The Vikings, The Celts, The Anglo-Saxons, The Stone Age, Fishing, 29 vols., 1979–85. Add: P.O. Box 5, Holyhead, Gwynedd LL65 1RG, Wales.

CUA, Antonio S. American, b. 1932. Philosophy. Prof. of Philosophy, Catholic Univ. of America, Washington, D.C., since 1969. Co-Ed., Journal of Chinese Philosophy; Ed. Consultant, American Philosophical Quarterly, and Philosophy East and West. Instr. to Asst. Prof., Ohio Univ., 1958–62; Prof. and Chmn., Dept. of Philosophy, Oswego Coll., State Univ. of New York, 1962–68; Pres., Soc. for Asian and Comparative Philosophy, 1978–80; Pres., Intl. Soc. for Chinese Philosophy, 1983–85. *Publs:* Reason and Virtue, 1966; Dimensions of Moral Creativity, 1978; The Unity of Knowledge and Action, 1982; Ethical Argumentation, 1985. Add: Sch. of Philosophy, Catholic Univ. of America, Washington, D.C. 20017, U.S.A.

CUBETA, Paul (Marsden). American, b. 1925. Literature. Prof. of English since 1964, Dir., Bread Loaf Sch. of English since 1964, and College Prof. of Humanities since 1979, Middlebury Coll. (joined faculty, 1952, Asst. Dir., Bread Loaf Writers' Conference, 1955–64; Dean of Faculty, 1967–70; Academic Vice-Pres., 1970–76; Vice Pres., 1976–79). *Publs:* Modern Drama for Analysis, 1950; 3rd ed., 1962; Twentieth Century Interpretations of Richard II, 1971. Add: 39 Seminary St., Middlebury, Vt. 05753, U.S.A.

CUDDON, J(ohn) A(nthony). British, b. 1928. Novels/Short stories, Plays/Screenplays, Literature, Sports/Physical education/Keeping fit, Travel/Exploration/Adventure. *Publs:* The Owl's Watchsong (travel), 1960, 1986; A Multitude of Sins, 1961; Testament of Iscariot, 1962; Acts of Darkness, 1963; The Six Wounds, 1964; The Bride of Battersea, 1967; Jugoslavia, 1968, 1986; Dictionary of Literary Terms, 1977, 1979; Dictionary of Sport and Games, 1980; (ed.) Penguin Book of Ghost and Horror Stories, 2 vols., 1984. Add: 43 Alderbrook Rd., London SW12, England.

CULLER, Jonathan Dwight. American, b. 1944. Literary Criticism/History. Prof. of English and Comparative Literature, Cornell Univ., Ithaca, since 1977. Fellow, and Dir. of Studies in Modern Languages Selwyn, Coll., Cambridge, 1969–74; Visiting Prof., Yale Univ., New Haven, Conn., 1975; Fellow, Brasenose Coll. and University Lectr. in French, Oxford, 1974–77. Dir., Soc. for the Humanities, 1984–90. *Publs:* Flaubert: The Uses of Uncertainty, 1974; Structuralist Poetics: Structuralism, Linguistics and the Study of Literature, 1975; Saussure, 1976; The Pursuit of Signs: Semiotics, Literature, Deconstruction, 1981; On Deconstruction: Theory and Criticism after Structuralism, 1982; Roland Barthes, 1983. Add: 643 Jacksonville Rd., Jacksonville, N.Y. 14854, U.S.A.

CULLINGFORD, Guy. Pseud. for Constance Lindsay Taylor. British, b. 1907. Novels/Short stories, Mystery/Crime/Suspense. *Publs:* mystery novels—(as C. Lindsay Taylor) Murder with Relish, 1948; If Wishes Were Hearses, 1952; Post Mortem, 1953; Conjurer's Coffin, 1954; Framed for Hanging, 1956; The Whipping Boys, 1958; A Touch of Drama, 1960; Third Party Risk, 1962; Brink of Disaster, 1964; The Stylist, 1968; other novel—The Bread and Butter Miss, 1979. Add: c/o A. M. Heath, 79 St. Martin's Lane, London WC2N 4AA, England.

CULLINGWORTH, J(ohn) Barry. British, b. 1929. Regional/Urban planning. Unidel Prof. of Urban Affairs and Public Policy, Univ. of Delaware, since 1983. Research Asst., Asst. Lectr. and Lectr. in Social Admin., Univ. of Manchester, 1955–60; Lectr. in Social Studies, Univ. of Durham, 1960–63; Sr. Lectr. to Reader in Urban Studies, Univ. of Glasgow, 1963–66; Dir. of the Centre for Urban and Regional Studies 1966–72, and Prof. of Urban and Regional Studies 1968–72, Univ. of Birmingham; Dir. of the Scottish Planning Exchange, 1972–75; Official Historian, Cabinet Office, London, 1974–77; Chmn., Urban and Regional Planning, Univ. of Toronto, 1977–80; Prof. of Geography, Univ. of Toronto, 1980–83. *Publs:* Housing Needs and Planning Policy, 1960; Housing in Transition, 1963; Town and Country Planning in England and Wales, 1964, 10th ed., 1988; English Housing Trends, 1965; Housing and Local Government, 1966; Scottish Housing in 1965, 1967; A Profile of Glasgow Housing, 1968; (with Valerie A. Karn) The Ownership and Management of Housing in the New Towns, 1968; Housing and Labour Mobility, 1969; (ed. with Sarah C. Orr) Regional and Urban Studies, 1969; (with C.J. Watson) Housing in Clydeside, 1971; Problems of an Urban Society, 3 vols., 1973; Official History of Environmental Planning 1939-1969: vol. 1: Reconstruction and Land Use Planning, 1976, vol. II: British New Towns Policy, 1980, vol. IV: Land Values, Compensation and Betterment, 1980; Essays on Housing Policy, 1979; (with J.R. Miron) Rent Control, 1983; Canadian Planning and Public Participation, 1984; Urban and Regional Planning in Canada, 1987. Add: College of Urban Affairs and Public Policy, Univ. of Delaware, Newark, Del. 19716, U.S.A.

CULP, John H(ewett, Jr.). American, b. 1907. Westerns/Adventure. Sch. teacher, Norman, Okla., 1934–41; owner of a music store, Ardmore, Okla., 1941–42, and Shawnee, Okla., 1946–68; then full-time writer. *Publs:* Born of the Sun, 1959; The Men of Gonzales, 1960; The Restless Land, 1962; The Bright Feathers, 1965; A Whistle in the Wind, 1968; Timothy Baines, 1969; The Treasurer of the Chisos, 1971; Oh, Valley Green!, 1972. Add: 1805 N. Louisa, Shawnee, Okla. 74801, U.S.A.

CULVER, Timothy, J. *See* **WESTLAKE,** Donald E.

CULYER, A(nthony) J(ohn). British, b. 1942. Economics, Medicine/Health. Prof. of Economics, Univ. of York, since 1979 (Lectr. and Reader, 1969–79; Deputy Dir., Inst. of Social and Economic Research, 1971–82). Tutor and Asst. Lectr., Exeter Univ., 1965–69; Visiting Prof. at Queen's Univ., Kingston, Ont., 1976, Otago Univ., New Zealand, 1979, Australian National Univ., Canberra, 1979, and Trent Univ., Peterborough, Ont., 1985–86. *Publs:* The Economics of Social Policy, 1973; (with M.H. Cooper) Health Economics, 1973; Economic Policies and Social Goals, 1974; Need and the National Health Service, 1976; (with J. Wiseman and A. Walker) Annotated Bibliography of Health Economics, 1977; (with V. Halberstadt) Human Resources and Public Finance, 1977; Measuring Health: Lessons for Ontario, 1978; (ed., with K. Wright) Economic Aspects of Health Services, 1978; The Political Economy of Social Policy, 1980; (ed.) Health Indicators, 1983; (with B. Horisberger) Economic and Medical Evolution of Health Care Technologies, 1983; (ed., with G. Terny) Public Finance and Social Policy, 1985; Economics, 1985; (ed., with B. Jonsson) Public and Private Health Services, 1986; (with others) The International Bibliography of Health Economics, 1986; Health Care Expenditure in Canada: Myth and Reality, Past and Future, 1988. Add: The Laurels, Barmby Moor, York YO4 5EJ, England.

CUMBERLAND, Kenneth B(railey). New Zealander, b. 1913. Agriculture/Forestry, Geography. Prof. Emeritus of Geography, Univ. of Auckland (Sr. Lectr. in Charge, 1946–49; Prof., 1949–78). Asst. Lectr. in Geography, Univ. Coll., London, 1937–38; Lectr., Univ. of Canterbury, 1938–45. *Publs:* Soil Erosion in New Zealand, 1944; A Regional Geography of New Zealand, 1948; New Zealand in Outline, 1949, in later eds. as This Is New Zealand; Southwest Pacific, 1954, 5th ed. 1968; (with J.W. Fox) New Zealand: A Regional View, 1959, 5th ed. 1970; (co-ed with J.W. Fox) Land, Life and Agriculture in Western Samoa, 1961; (with J.S. Whitelaw) World Landscapes: New Zealand, 1970; Planning a Future for the Land and Agriculture, 1971; (ed.) New Zealand: Pacific Land Down Under, 1973; Landmarks, 1981. Add: Kettlewelldale, Brookby, Manurewa, New Zealand.

CUMBERLEGE, Marcus (Crossley). British, b. 1938. Poetry. English Teacher, British Council, Lima, Peru, 1957–58 and 1962–63; Advertising Exec., Ogilvy & Mather, London, 1964–67; English Teacher, Lycée Intnl., St. Germain, 1968–70; Lectr., Univ. of Lugano, 1978–82. *Publs:* Oases, 1968; Poems for Quena and Tabla, 1970; Running Towards a New Life, 1973; The Poetry Millionaire, 1977; Firelines, 1977; La Nuit Noire, 1977; Twintig Vriendelijke Vragen, 1977; (with Owen Davis) Bruges, Brugge, 1978; Northern Lights, 1981; Flemish Fables, 1982; Sweet Poor Hobo, 1984. Add: Westmeers 84, 8000 Bruges, Belgium.

CUMMING, Primrose (Amy). British, b. 1915. Children's fiction. *Publs:* Doney, 1934; Spider Dog, 1936; Silver Snaffles, 1937; Silver Eagle Riding School, 1938; Rachel of Romney, 1939; The Wednesday Pony, 1939; Ben, 1939; Silver Eagle Carries On, 1940; The Chestnut Filly, 1942; Owls Castle Farm, 1943; The Great Horses, 1946; Trouble at Trimbles, 1949; Four Rode Home, 1951; No Place for Ponies, 1954; Rivals to Silver Eagle, 1954; The Deep Sea Horse, 1956; The Mystery Pony, 1957; Flying Horseman, 1959; The Mystery Trek, 1964; Foal of the Fjords, 1966; Penny and Pegasus, 1979. Add: Wynberg, Sandhurst, Hawkhurst, Kent, England.

CUMMING, William P(atterson). American, b. 1900. Geography, History. Irvin Prof. of English Emeritus, Davidson Coll., N.C., since 1968 (Asst. Prof., 1927–29; Assoc. Prof., 1929–37; Prof., 1937–68). *Publs:* (ed.) The Revelations of St. Birgitta, 1929; The Southeast in Early Maps, 1958, 1962; (ed.) The Discoveries of John Lederer (travel literature), 1958; North Carolina in Maps, 1966, 1985; Captain James Wimble and the Colonial Cartography of the North Carolina Coast, 1969; (with R.A. Skelton and D.B. Quinn) The Discovery of North America, 1971, 1972; (ed. with H. Wallis) A Map of the British Empire in America, by H. Popple, 1972; British Maps of Colonial America, 1974; (with Quinn, S. Hiller and G. Williams) The Exploration of North America, 1630-1776, 1974; (with H.F. Rankin) The Fate of a Nation: The American Revolution Through Contemporary Eyes, 1975; (ed. with D. Marshall) North America at the Time of the American Revolution: A Collection of Eighteenth Century Maps, 1975; Mapping the North Carolina Coast: Sixteenth Century Cartography and the Roanoke Voyages, 1988; Add: 400 Avinger Lane, Apt. 108, Davidson, N.C. 28036, U.S.A.

CUMMINGS, Milton C(urtis) Jr. American, b. 1933. Politics/Government. Prof. of Political Science, Johns Hopkins Univ., Baltimore, since 1968 (Assoc. Prof., 1965–68; Chmn. of the Dept., 1970–72); Consultant, NBC-News, 1962–74. Staff Member, Brookings Instn., Washington, D.C., 1959–65. *Publs:* (co-author) The Image of the Federal Service, 1964; (co-author) Source Book of a Study of Occupational Values and the Image of the Federal Service, 1964; Congressman and the Electorate, 1966; (ed.) The National Election of 1964, 1966; (with D. Wise) Democracy Under Pressure: An Introduction to the American Political System, 1971, 4th ed. 1981; (ed. with R.S. Katz) The Patron State: Government and the Arts in Europe, North America, and Japan, 1987. Add: 2811 35th St. N.W., Washington, D.C. 20007, U.S.A.

CUNLIFFE, Barry. British, b. 1939. Archaeology/Antiquities. Prof. of European Archaeology, Univ. of Oxford, since 1972. Lectr. in Archaeology, Bristol Univ., 1963–66; Prof. of Archaeology, Southampton Univ., 1966–72. *Publs:* Roman Bath Discovered, 1971, 1985; Fishbourne: Roman Palace and its Gardens, 1971; The Cradle of England, 1973; The Making of the English, 1973; The Regni, 1973; Iron Age Communities in Britain, 1974; Rome and the Barbarians, 1975; Iron Age Sites in Central South Britain, 1976; (with Trevor Rowley) The Origins of Urbanization in Barbarian Europe, 1976; Hengistbury Head, 1978; Rome and Her Empire, 1978; The Celtic World, 1979; Danebury: Anatomy of an Iron Age Hillfort, 1983; Heywood Sumner's Wessex, 1985; The City of Bath, 1986; Greeks, Romans and Barbarians, 1988. Add: Inst. of Archaeology, 36 Beaumont St., Oxford, England.

CUNLIFFE, John (Arthur). British, b. 1933. Children's fiction.

Full-time writer since 1988. Branch Librarian, Earby, Yorkshire, 1951–54; Mobile Librarian, Wooler, Northumberland, 1955–56; Deputy Information Officer, Decca Radar Research Laboratories, Tolworth, Surrey, 1957–58; Sr. Asst. Librarian, Hendon, London, 1958; Mgr., Rare Books Dept., Foyle's booksellers, London, 1958–59; Regional Children's Librarian, Bletchley, Bucks., 1959–62; Librarian in charge of work with young people, Reading, Berks., 1962–64, and Brighton, Sussex, 1967–73; Librarian, British Council, Belgrade, 1964–66; Education Librarian, Newcastle upon Tyne, 1966–67; Teacher, Castle Park Sch., Kendal, Cumbria, 1975–79; Teacher-Organizer, Manchester Education Cttee., 1979–80; Deputy Head Teacher, Crowcroft Park Primary Sch., Manchester, 1981–85; Advisory Teacher, Manchester Education Service, 1985–88. *Publs:* Farmer Barnes Buys a Pig, 1964; Farmer Barnes and Bluebell, 1966; Farmer Barnes at the County Show (in U.S. as Farmer Barnes at the County Fair), 1969; The Adventures of Lord Pip, 1970; The Giant Who Stole the World, 1971; Farmer Barnes and the Goats, 1971; Riddles and Rhymes and Rigamaroles, 1971; The Giant Who Swallowed the Wind, 1972; Farmer Barnes Goes Fishing, 1972; Giant Kippernose and Other Stories, 1972; The King's Brithday Cake, 1973; The Great Dragon Competition and Other Stories, 1973; The Farmer, The Rooks, and the Cherry Tree, 1974; Small Monkey Tales, 1974; Farmer Barnes and the Snow Picnic, 1974; Giant Brog and the Motorway, 1976; Farmer Barnes Fells a Tree, 1977; Farmer Barnes and the Harvest Doll, 1977; Mr. Gosling and the Runaway Chair, 1978; Farmer Barnes' Guy Fawkes Day, 1978; Mr. Gosling and the Great Art Robbery, 1979; Sara's Giant and the Upside-Down House, 1980; Our Sam: The Daftest Dog in the World, 1980; Postman Pat and the Mystery Thief, 1981; Postman Pat's Treasure Hunt (Secret, Rainy Day, Difficult Day, and Foggy Day), 5 vols., 1981–82; Play Logo, 1984; Standing on a Strawberry, 1987; Fog Lane School and the Great Racing-Car Disaster, 1988. Add: 64 Goulden Rd., Withington, Manchester M20 9YF, England.

CUNLIFFE, Marcus (Falkner). British, b. 1922. History, Literature, Military/Defence. Univ. Prof., George Washington Univ., Washington, D.C., since 1980. NTE Lectr. and Prof., Univ. of Manchester, 1949–64; Prof. of American Studies, Univ. of Sussex, Brighton, 1965–80. *Publs:* The Royal Irish Fusiliers, 1953; The Literature of the United States, 1954, 4th ed. 1986; George Washington: Man and Monument, 1958, 1982; The Nation Takes Shape, 1789-1837, 1960; (ed.) Weems' Life of Washington, 1962; Soldiers and Civilians: The Martial Spirit in America, 1775-1865, 1968, 1973; American Presidents and the Presidency, 1968, 1976, rev. ed. as The Presidency, 1987; (co-ed. with Robin Winks) Past-Masters: Some Essays on American Historians, 1969; (ed.) The Times History of Our Times, 1971; The Age of Expansion, 1848-1917, 1974; (ed.) Sphere History of English Literature, vols. 8 and 9, 1974; American Literature to 1900, 1974, 1986; American Literature from 1900, 1975, 1987; Chattel Slavery and Wage Slavery: The Anglo-American Context 1830-1860, 1979. Add: 1823 Lamont St. N.W., Washington, D.C. 20010, U.S.A.

CUNNINGHAM, Cathy. *See* **CUNNINGHAM,** Chet.

CUNNINGHAM, Chet. Also writes as Cathy Cunningham American, b. 1928. Mystery/Crime/Suspense, Westerns/Adventure, Recreation/-Leisure/Hobbies, Sciences. Freelance writer since 1960; Columnist "Truck Talk" since 1956, and "Your Car", since 1959. Chmn., San Diego Writers Workshop, since 1962. City Ed., Foret Grove News-Times, 1954–55; Writer, Jam Handy, Detroit, 1955,19659; motion picture writers, Convair, San Diego, 1959–. *Publs:* Bushwackers at Circle K, 1969; Killer's Range, 1970; The Gold wagon, 1972; Blood on the Strip, (suspense), 1973; Fatal Friday (suspense), 1973; Die of Gold (suspense) 1973; (as Cathy Cunningham) The Demons of Highpoint House (suspense), 1973; Dead Start Scramble (non-fiction), 1973; Your Wheels: How to Keep Your Car Running, 1973; Hijacking Manhattan (suspense), 1974; Y'Terror in Tokyo (suspense), 1974; Baja Bika (non-fiction), 1974; Your Bike: How to Keep Your Motorcycle Running, 1975; Bloody Gold, 1975; The Patriots, 1976; The Gold and the Glory, 1977; The Power and the Price, 1977; Seeds of Rebellion, 1977; The Poker Club, 1978; Beloved Rebel, 1978; Rainbow Saga, 1979; This Splendid Land, 1979; Devil's Gold, 1980; Die of Gole, 1980; Cheyenne Payoffn, 1981; Gold Train, 1981; The Silver Mistress, 1981; Tucson Temptress, 1981; 222 Ways to Save Gas and Get the Best Possible Mileage, 1981. Add:c/o Don Sheperd, 18645 Sherman Way, Suite 210, Reseda, calif. 91335, U.S.A.

CUNNINGHAM, E.V. *See* **FAST,** Howard.

CUNNINGHAM, Julia W(oolfolk). American, b. 1916. Children's fiction. Bookseller and children's book buyer, Tecolote Book Shop, Santa Barbara, Calif., from 1957, now retired. Clerk, Guaranty Trust Co., NYC, 1937–40; Co-ordinating Ed., G. Schirmer, music publishers, NYC, 1940–44; Assoc. Ed., Dell Publishing Co., NYC, 1944–47; Secty., Air Reduction Co., NYC, 1947–49; Asst. to the Advertising Mgr., Sherman Clay and Co., San Francisco, 1950–51; freelance writer in France, 1952; Salesperson, Metropolitan Museum of Art, NYC, 1953–56. *Publs:* The Vision of Francois the Fox, 1960; Dear Rat, 1961; Macaroon, 1962; Candle Tales, 1964; Dorp Dead, 1965; Viollet, 1966; Onion Journey, 1967; Burnish Me Bright, 1970; Wings of the Morning, 1971; Far in the Day, 1972; The Treasure Is the Rose, 1973; Maybe, A Mole, 1974; Come to the Edge, 1977; Tuppenny, 1978; A Mouse Called Junction, 1980; Flight of the Sparrow, 1980; The Silent Voice, 1981; Wolf Roland, 1983; Oaf, 1986. Add: 122a W. Valerio St., Santa Barbara, Calif. 93101, U.S.A.

CUNNINGHAM, Marion (Elizabeth). American, b. 1922. Cookery/Gastronomy. Cookbook author and restaurant consultant. *Publs:* (ed.) The Fannie Farmer Cookbook, 12th ed. 1979; The Fannie Farmer Baking Book, 1984; The Breakfast Book, 1987. Add: 1147 Northgate Rd., Walnut Creek, Calif. 94598, U.S.A.

CUNNINGHAM, Merce. American, b. 1919. Dance/Ballet. Choreographer, and dancer. Founder, Merce Cunningham Dance Co., 1953, and Cunningham Sch. 1959, NYC. *Publs:* Changes: Notes on Choreography, 1969; La Danseur et la Danse, 1980, English ed. 1984. Add: Cunningham Dance Foundn. Inc., 463 West St., New York, N.Y. 10014, U.S.A.

CUOMO, George (Michael). American, b. 1929. Novels/Short stories, Poetry. Prof. of English, Univ. of Massachusetts at Amherst, since 1973. Prof. of English, California State Univ. at Hayward, 1965–73. *Publs:* Becoming a Better Reader, 1960; Jack Be Nimble (novel), 1963; Bright Day, Dark Runner (novel), 1964; Among Thieves (novel), 1968; Sing, Choirs of Angels (short stories), 1970; The Hero's Great Great Great Great Grandson (novel), 1971; Geronimo and the Girl Next Door (poetry), 1974; Pieces from a Small Bomb (novel), 1976; Becoming a Better Reader and Writer, 1978; Family Honor (novel), 1983. Add: Dept. of English, Univ. of Massachusetts, Amherst, Mass. 01003, U.S.A.

CUOMO, Mario (Matthew). American, b. 1932. Politics/Government, Urban studies. Governor of New York State since 1983. Lawyer: Partner, Corner, Finn, Cuomo & Charles, NYC, 1963–75; Secty. of State, New York, 1975–78; Lt. Gov. of New York, 1979–82. Prof. of Law, St. John's Univ. Sch. of Law, Jamaica, N.Y., 1963–73. *Publs:* The Forest Hills Controversy, 1972; Forest Hills Diary: The Crisis of Low-Income Housing, 1974; Diaries of Mario M. Cuomo: The Campaign for Governor, 1984. Add: State Capitol, Albany, N.Y. 12224, U.S.A.

CURL, James Stevens. British, b. 1937. Architecture, Urban studies. Prof. of Architectural History, and Dir. of the Historical Architecture Research Unit., Leicester Sch. of Architecture, since 1987 (Sr. Lectr., 1978–87). Architectural Ed., Survey of London, 1970–73; Architectural Adviser, European Architectural Heritage Year, Scottish Civic Trust, 1973–75; Sr. Planning Officer, Herts. County Council, 1975–78. *Publs:* European Cities and Society: The Influence of Political Climate on Town Design, 1970; The Victorian Celebration of Death, 1972; (with T.M. Richards) City of London Pubs, 1973; Victorian Architecture: Its Practical Aspects, 1973; The Erosion of Oxford, 1977; English Architecture: An Illustrated Glossary, 1977; Mausolea in Ulster, 1978; Moneymore and Draperstown, 1979; Celebration of Death, 1980; Classical Churches in Ulster, 1980; The History, Architecture, and Planning of the Estates of the Fishmongers Company in Ulster, 1981; The Egyptian Revival, 1982; The Life and Works of Henry Roberts, (1803-76), Architect, 1983; The Londonderry Plantation, 1609-1914: The History, Architecture and Planning of the Estates of the City of London and Its Livery Companies in Ulster, 1986; English Architecture, 1987. Add: 2 The Coach House, Burley-on-the-Hill, Oakham, Rutland, Leics. LE15 7SJ, England.

CURLING, Bill. (Bryan William Richard Curling). British, b. 1911. Sports/Physical education/Keeping fit, Biography. Racing Corresp. as Julius, Yorkshire Post, Leeds, 1936–39; served with Royal Navy, 1939–45; Racing Corresp. as Hotspur, Daily Telegraph, London, 1946–65; Public Relations Officer, Jockey Club, London, 1965–69, and Hampshire County Scout Council, 1973–81. *Publs:* British Racecourses, 1951; The Captain: A Biography of Sir Cecil Boyd-Rochfort, Royal Trainer, 1970; (with Clive Graham) The Grand National: An Illustrated History of the Greatest Steeplechase in the World, 1972; Derby Double: The Story of Racehorse Trainer Arthur Budgett, 1977; All the Queen's Horses, 1978; Royal Champion: The Story of Steeplechasing's First Lady, 1980; The Sea Pigeon Story, 1982. Add: Fullerton Manor, nr. Andover, Hants., England.

CURNOW, Allen. New Zealander, b. 1911. Plays, Poetry. Reporter and Sub-Ed., 1935–48, and Drama Critic, 1945–47, The Press, Christchurch; Reporter and Sub-Ed., News Chronicle, London, 1949; Lectr., 1951, Sr. Lectr., 1954–66, and Assoc. Prof. of English, 1967–76, Auckland Univ. *Publs:* Valley of Decision, 1933; Three Poems, 1934-1936, 1937; Not in Narrow Seas, 1939; Island and Time, 1941; (with A.R.D. Fairburn, R.A.K. Mason and Denis Glover) Recent Poems, 1941; Sailing or Drowning, 1943; (ed.) A Book of New Zealand Verse 1923-1945, 1945, 1951; Jack Without Magic, 1946; The Axe: A Verse Tragedy, 1949; At Dead Low Water, and Sonnets, 1949; Poems 1947-57, 1957; (ed.) The Penguin Book of New Zealand Verse, 1960; A Small Room with Large Windows : Selected Poems, 1962; Four Plays: The Axe, The Overseas Expert, The Duke's Miracle, Resident of Nowhere, 1972; Trees, Effigies, Moving Objects: A Sequence of Eighteen Poems, 1972; An Abominable Temper and Other Poems, 1973; Collected Poems 1933-1973, 1974; An Incorrigible Music: A Sequence of Poems, 1979; You Will Know When You Get There: Poems 1979-81, 1982; Selected Poems, 1982; The Loop in Lone Kauri Road, Poems 1983-1986, 1986; Look Back Harder: Critical Writings 1935-84, 1987; Continuous New and Later Poems 1972-1988, 1988. Add: 62 Tohunga Cres., Parnell, Auckland 1, New Zealand.

CURNOW, Frank. *See* **ATKINSON**, Frank.

CURRAN, Charles E. American, b. 1934. Philosophy, Theology/Religion. Prof. of Moral Theology, Catholic Univ. of America, Washington, D.C., since 1972 (Asst. Prof., 1966–68; Assoc. Prof., 1968–72). Pres., Catholic Theological Soc. of America, 1969–70, and American Soc. of Christian Ethics, 1971–72; Sr. Research Scholar, Kennedy Center for Bioethics, Georgetown Univ., Washington, D.C., 1972. *Publs:* Christian Morality Today, 1966; (ed.) Absolutes in Moral Theology?, 1968; A New Look at Christian Morality, 1968; (co-author) Dissent in and for the Church, 1969; (with J.W. Hunt and T.R. Connelly) The Responsibility of Dissent: The Church and Academic Freedom, 1969; (ed.) Contraception: Authority and Dissent, 1969; Contemporary Problems in Moral Theology, 1970; (ed. with G.J. Dyer) Shared Responsibility in the Local Church, 1970; Catholic Moral Theology in Dialogue, 1972; Crisis in Priestly Ministry, 1972; Politics, Medicine and Christian Ethics: A Dialogue with Paul Ramsey, 1973; New Perspectives in Moral Theology, 1974; Ongoing Revision in Moral Theology, 1975; Themes in Fundamental Moral Theology, 1977; Issues in Sexual and Medical Ethics, 1978; Transition and Tradition in Moral Theology, 1979; (ed. with R.A. McCormick) Readings in Moral Theology, 5 vols., 1979–86; American Catholic Social Ethics, 1982; Critical Concerns in Moral Theology, 1983; Moral Theology: A Continuing Journey, 1983; Directions in Catholic Social Ethics, 1985; Directions in Fundamental Moral Theology, 1985; Faithful Dissent, 1986; Toward an American Catholic Theology, 1987; Tensions in Moral Theology, 1988. Add: Caldwell Hall, Catholic Univ., Washington, D.C. 20064, U.S.A.

CURRAN, Francis X. American, b. 1914. Theology/Religion. Prof. of History, Fordham Univ., NYC, since 1966 (Asst. Prof., 1955–62; Assoc. Prof., 1962–66). Historian of the New York Province, Soc. of Jesus, since 1951. *Publs:* Major Trends in American Church History, 1946; The Churches and the Schools, 1954; (ed.) Catholics in Colonial Law, 1963; The Return of the Jesuits, 1966. Add: Dept. of History, Fordham Univ., New York, N.Y. 10458, U.S.A.

CURRAN, Peter Malcolm. British, b. 1922. Language/Linguistics. Sr. Tutor, Davies's Sch. of English, Hove, Sussex. *Publs:* English Notes and Exercises, 1964; Do You Speak English?, 1967; Beware of Idioms, 1970; Proverbs in Action, 1972; English Structure Stories, 1975; English Idiom Stories, 1977. Add: 29 The Drive, Hove, Sussex, England.

CURREY, R(alph) N(ixon). British, b. 1907. Poetry, Literature, Biography. Schoolmaster, retired 1972; frequent broadcaster. *Publs:* Tiresias and Other Poems, 1940; This Other Planet, 1945; (co-ed. with R.V. Gibson) Poems from India by Members of the Forces, 1945; Indian Landscape, 1947; (trans.) Formal Spring: French Renaissance Poems, 1950; Poets of the 1939-45 War, 1960, rev. ed. 1967; (ed.) Letters of a Natal Sheriff: Thomas Phipson 1815-76, 1968; The Africa We Knew, 1973; Vinnicombe's Trek, 1988. Add: Beverley Rd., Colchester, Essex CO3 3NG, England.

CURRY, Avon. *See* **BOWDEN**, Jean.

CURRY, Jane (Louise). American, b. 1932. Children's fiction. Lectr., Stanford Univ., California, since 1987 (Teaching Asst., 1959–61, 1964–65 and 1967–68; Acting Inst., 1967–68; Instr., 1983–84). Art Instr., Los Angeles City Schs., Calif., 1955–59. Fulbright Fellow, Royal Holloway Coll., 1965–66, and Leverhulme Fellow, University Coll.,

1965–66, Univ. of London. *Publs:* Down from the Lonely Mountain: California Indian Tales, 1965; Beneath the Hill, 1967; The Sleepers, 1968; The Change-Child, 1969; The Daybreakers, 1970; Mindy's Mysterious Miniature, (in U.K. as the Housenapper), 1970; Over the Sea's Edge, 1971; The Ice Ghosts Mystery, 1972; The Lost Farm, 1974; Parsley Sage, Rosemary and Time, 1975; The Watchers, 1975; The Magical Cupboard, 1976; Poor Tom's Ghost, 1977; The Birdstones, 1977; The Bassumtyte Treasure, 1978; Ghost Lane, 1979; The Wolves of Aam, 1981; The Shadow Dancers, 1983; The Great Flood Mystery, 1985; The Lotus Cup, 1986; Back in the Beforetime: Tales of the California Indians, 1987; Me, Myself and I, 1987. Add: c/o Macmillan, 866 Third Avenue., New York, N.Y. 10022, U.S.A.

CURRY, Lerond. American, b. 1938. Theology/Religion, Autobiography/Memoirs/Personal. Campus Minister and Assoc. Prof. of Religion, Averett Coll., Danville, Va., since 1970. Asst. Prof. of History, Western Kentucky Univ., Bowling Green, 1967–70. *Publs:* Protestant-Catholic Relations in America: World War I Through Vatican II, 1972; From Pipes to Podiums: Confessions of a Gamesman, 1974; Will the Real Evangelical Please Stand Up?, 1976; Humanities and Religion, 1976. Add: 1025 Blake, Bowling Green, Ky. 42101, U.S.A.

CURRY, Richard O(rr). American, b. 1931. History. Prof. of American History, Univ. of Connecticut, Storrs, since 1971 (Asst. Prof., 1963–66; Assoc. Prof., 1966–71). Instr., Pennsylvania State Univ., University Park, 1960–62; Asst. Prof., Univ. of Pittsburgh, 1962–63. *Publs:* A House Divided: A Study of Statehood Politics and the Copperhead Movement in West Virginia, 1964; (ed.) The Abolitionists: Reformers or Fanatics?, 1965, as The Abolitionists, 1973; (contrib. and ed.) Racism and Party Realignment: The Border States During Reconstruction, 1969, 1973; (with J. Sproat and K. Cramer) The Shaping of America, 1972; (with J. Sproat and K. Cramer) The Shaping of American Civilization, 2 vols., 1972; (contrib. and co-ed.) Conspiracy: The Fear of Subversion in American History, 1972; (co-ed.) Slavery in America: Theodore Weld's American Slavery As It Is, 1972, 1979; (ed. and co-author) Freedom at Risk: Secrecy, Censorship and Repression in the 1980's, 1988. Add: Dept. of History, Univ. of Connecticut, Storrs, Conn. 06268, U.S.A.

CURTEIS, Ian (Bayley). British, b. 1935. Novels, Plays/Screenplays. Acted and directed in theatres around Britain, 1956–64; Dir., B.B.C. and I.T.V. television, 1963–66. *Publs:* Beethoven (television play); Sir Alexander Fleming (television play), 1972; Mr. Rolls and Mr. Royce (television play); Long Voyage Out of War (trilogy); The Folly (television play); Second Time Around (television play); Inferno, 1973; The State Visit (novel), 1974; Philby, Burgess, and Maclean (television play); Hess (television play); Churchill and the Generals (television play); Suez, 1956 (television play); The Spaghetti House Siege (screenplay), 1978; Miss Morrison's Ghosts (television play), 1982; A Personal Affair (stage play), 1982; Man's Estate (screenplay), 1982; Berenson and Duveen (television trilogy), 1982; The Man Within (screenplay), 1983; The Falklands Play (television play), 1984; Lost Empires (screenplay), 1984; The Nightmare Years (screenplay), 1989; also various television series. Add: c/o Mrs Casarotto, Douglas Rae Management Ltd., 28 Charing Cross Rd., London WC2, England.

CURTIS, Anthony. British, b. 1926. Literature. Literary Ed., The Financial Times, London, since 1970. Literary Ed., The Sunday Telegraph, London, 1961–69. *Publs:* New Developments in the French Theatre: Sartre, Camus, de Beauvoir and Anouilh, 1948; The Pattern of Maugham, 1974; (ed. and contrib.) The Rise and Fall of the Matinee Idol, 1974; Somerset Maugham, 1977; Spillington and the Whitewash Clowns, 1981; Somerset Maugham (Writers and Their Work), 1982; (ed., with John Whitehead) Somerset Maugham: The Critical Heritage, 1987. Add: 9 Essex Villas, London W8 7BP, England.

CURTIS, Tony. British, b. 1946. Novels/Short stories, Poetry, Literature. Sr. Lectr. in English, The Polytechnic of Wales, Pontypridd, since 1974. Exec. Member, since 1977, and Pres., since 1984, Yr Academi Gymreig (National Assn. of Writers in Wales). Teacher, Wilmslow Grammar Sch., Cheshire, 1969–71; Teacher, Maltby Grammar Sch., Yorkshire, 1971–74. *Publs:* Walk Down a Welsh Wind, 1972; Album, 1974; (with Duncan Bush and Nigel Jenkins) Three Young Anglo-Welsh Poets, 1974; (ed.) Pembrokeshire Poems, 1975; Out of the Dark Wood (fiction), 1977; The Deer Slayers, 1978; Carnival, 1978; Preparations, 1980; (ed.) The Art of Seamus Heaney, 1982; Letting Go, 1983; Dannie Abse, 1985; Wales—The Imagined Nation: Essays in Cultural and National Identity, 1986; Selected Poems 1970-1985, 1986; Poems: Selected and New, 1986; The Last Candles (poems), 1989; (ed.) The Poetry of

Pembrokeshire, 1989; (ed.) The Poetry of Snowdonia, 1989; How to Study Modern Poetry, 1989. Add: The Polytechnic, Pontypridd, CF37 1DL, Wales.

CURTIS, Wade. *See* **POURNELLE,** Jerry.

CURTIS, Will. *See* **NUNN,** William Curtis.

CURTIS, William J.R. British, b. 1948. Architecture, Art. Asst. Prof. of Art History, Boston Univ., 1975–76, and Harvard Univ., Cambridge, 1976–82; Visiting Assoc. Prof., Washington Univ., St. Louis, School of Architecture, 1982–83. *Publs:* Le Corbusier: English Architecture of the 1930's, 1975; (with Denys Lasdun) A Language and a Theme: The Architecture of Denys Lasdun and Partners, 1976; (with E.F. Sekler) Le Corbusier at Work: The Genesis of the Carpenter Center for the Visual Arts at Harvard University, 1978; Boston: Fifty Years of Modern Architecture, 1980; Modern Architecture since 1900, 1982; Le Corbusier: Ideas and Forms, 1986. Add: Carpenter Center for the Visual Arts, Harvard Univ., Cambridge, Mass. 02138, U.S.A.

CURTISS, Vienna Ione. American, b. 1909. Art, History, Travel/Exploration/Adventure. Interior Designer, Hollywood, Calif., 1930–37; Prof. of Design in Art, Arizona State Univ., Tempe, 1937–40; Prof. and Head, Dept. of Design in Art, Univ. of Maryland, College Park, 1940–75. *Publs:* Life's Great Show!; Zip, Zing, Ping, Pop!, 1966; Pageant of Art: Visual History of Western Culture, 1976; I Should Be Glad to Help You, Madame: Europe Minus One's Wardrobe, 1979; Cappy: Rollicking Rancher Atop Arizona's Mighty Rim, 1980. Add: 1727 Massachusetts NW, Washington, D.C. 20036, U.S.A.

CURTO, Josephine. American, b. 1929. Children's fiction, Plays/Screenplays, Writing/Journalism. Prof., Tallahassee Community Coll., Fla., since 1967. Columnist, Tallahassee Democrat, since 1970; Book Review Ed., United Teacher mag., since 1975. Teacher, Miami Beach High Sch., 1955–62; Assoc. Prof., and Dept. Chmn., Miami Dade Jr. Coll., 1962–66. *Publs:* (co-author) Reading Forward, 1965; Writing with Understanding, 1966; (co-author) Ladder of Language, 1967; (co-author) Handbook for Reader and Writing, 1968; The Coming, 1971; Count Ten, 1972; Biography of an Alligator, 1975; Hard Times Notes, 1981; How to Become a Single Parent: A Guide for Single People Considering Adoption or Natural Parenthood Alone, 1983. Add: 2109 Croydon Dr., Tallahassee, Fla. 32303, U.S.A.

CURZON, Lucia. *See* **STEVENSON,** Florence.

CUSHMAN, Dan. American, b. 1909. Historical/Romance/Gothic, Westerns/Adventure, Country life/Rural societies, History. Worked in mining as prospector, assayer, and geologist; then journalist and freelance writer. *Publs:* Montana, Here I Be!, 1950; Badlands Justice, 1951; Naked Ebony, 1951; Jewel of the Java Sea, 1951; The Ripper from Rawhide, 1952; Savage Interlude, 1952; Stay Away, Joe, 1953; Timberjack, 1953; Jungle She, 1953; The Fabulous Finn, 1954; Tongking!, 1954; Port Orient, 1955; The Fastest Gun, 1955; The Old Copper Collar, 1957; The Silver Mountain, 1957; Tall Wyoming, 1957; The Forbidden Land, 1958; Goodbye, Old Dry, 1959, in paperback as the Con Man, 1960; The Half-Caste, 1960; Brothers in Kickapoo, 1962, in U.K. as Boomtown, in U.S. paperback as On the Make, 1963; 4 for Texas (novelization of screenplay), 1963; The Grand and the Glorious, 1963; Opium Flower, 1963; North Fork to Hell, 1964; The Great North Trail: America's Route of the Ages (non-fiction), 1966; The Long Riders, 1967; Cow Country Cook Book (non-fiction), 1967; Montana: The Gold Frontier (non-fiction), 1973; Plenty of Room and Air (non-fiction), 1975; The Muskrat Farm, 1977; Rusty Irons, 1984. Add: Box 2054, Great Falls, Mont. 69403, U.S.A.

CUSSLER, Clive (Eric). American, b. 1931. Novels. Owner, Bestgen & Cussler Advertising, Newport Beach, Calif., 1961–65; Copy Dir., Darcy Advertising, Hollywood, Calif., and Instr. in Advertising Communications, Orange Coast Coll., 1965–67; Advertising Dir., Aquatic Marine Corp., Newport Beach, Calif., 1967–69; Vice-Pres. and Creative Dir. of Broadcast, Meffon, Wolff and Weir Advertising, Denver, 1970–73. *Publs:* The Mediterranean Caper, 1973; Iceberg, 1975; Raise the Titanic, 1976; Vixen O-Three, 1978; Night Probe, 1981; Pacific Vortex, 1983; Deep Six, 1984; Cyclops, 1986; Treasure, 1988. Add: P.O. Box 635, Golden, Colo. 80402, U.S.A.

CUTLER, Ivor. Scottish, b. 1923. Short stories, Children's fiction. Numerous plays on BBC Radio, since 1980. *Publs:* Gruts (stories), 1962, 1986; Cockadoodledon't!!! (stories), 1966; Meal One (children's fiction), 1971; Many Flies Have Feathers (verse), 1973; Balooky Klujypop (children's fiction), 1974; The Animal House (children's fiction), 1986; A Flat Man (verse), 1977; Private Habits (poetry), 1981; Life in a Scotch Sitting Room vol. II, 1984; Large et Puffy (verse) (children's stories), 1984; Herbert the Chicken (children's stories), 1984; Herbert the Elephant, 1984; Fresh Carpet (stories), 1986; Fremsley (stories), 1987; One and a Quarter (children's stories), 1987; Herbert (children's stories), 1988; Nice Wee Present from Scotland (poetry), 1988; Glasgow Dreamer (short stories), 1989. Add: c/o BBC, London W1A 1AA, England.

CUTT, Margaret Nancy. Canadian, b. 1913. Literature, Mythology/Folklore. Faculty Member, Univ. of Alberta, Edmonton, 1946–48, and 1958–63, and Univ. of Victoria, B.C., 1963 until her retirement in 1973; with Govt. of Alberta, 1951–59. *Publs:* Mrs. Sherwood and Her Books for Children, 1974; (with W.T. Cutt) The Hogboon of Hell and Other Strange Orkney Tales, 1978; Ministering Angels: Study of 19th Century Evangelical Writing for Children, 1980. Add: 624 Cornwall St., Victoria, B.C. V8V 4LI, Canada.

CUTTER, Tom. *See* **RANDISI,** Robert J.

D

DABNEY, Joseph Earl. American, b. 1929. History. Information Writer, and Ed., Lockheed Aeronautical Systems Co., Marietta, Ga., since 1965. Newspaperman in Georgia and South Carolina, 1949–65. *Publs:* Mountain Spirits: A Chronicle of Corm Whiskey from King James' Ulster Plantation to America's Appalachians, 1974, vol. 2, 1980, reissued as More Mountain Spirits, 1986; HERK, Hero of the Skies, 1979, 1987. Add: 3966 St., Clair Ct., Atlanta, Ga., 30319, U.S.A.

DABNEY, Virginius. American, b. 1901. History, Autobiography/Memoirs/Personal, Biography. Chmn., Advisory Bd., U.S. Historical Soc.; Member, Bd. of Virginia Commonwealth Univ., Richmond (Rector, 1968–69), and Virginia Historical Soc. Pres., American Soc. of Newspaper Eds., 1957–58, and Virginia Historical Soc., 1969–72. Recipient, Pulitzer Prize, 1947. *Publs:* Liberalism in the South, 1932; Below the Potomac, 1942; Dry Messiah: The Life of Bishop Cannon, 1949; Virginia: The New Dominion, 1971; (ed.) The Patriots: The American Revolution, Generation of Genius, 1975; Richmond: The Story of a City, 1976; Across the Years: Memories of a Virginian, 1978; The Jefferson Scandals: Rebuttal, 1981; Mr. Jefferson's University: A History, 1981; The Last Review: The Confederate Reunion, Richmond, 1932, 1984; Virginia Commonwealth University: A Sesquicentennial History, 1987; Pistols and Pointed Pens: The Oldtime Dueling Virginia Editors, 1987. Add: 5621 Cary Street Rd., No. 213, Richmond, Va. 23226, U.S.A.

DABYDEEN, Cyril. Canadian (born British Guyana), b. 1945. Novels/Short stories, Poetry. Former elementary school teacher in Guyana; has also worked as a consultant for the Canadian govt.; Reviewer, Ottawa Journal, 1975–78. *Publs:* Poems in Recession, 1972; Distances, 1977; Still Close to the Island, 1980; Elephants Make Good Stepladders, 1982; To Monkey Jungle, 1985; The Wizard Swarmi, 1985; Islands Lovelier Than a Vision, 1987. Add: 23-2 Montcalm, Ottawa, Ont. K1S 5K9, Canada.

DACE, Tish. American, b. 1941. Literature, Theatre. Prof. of English and Drama, Southeastern Massachusetts Univ., N. Darmouth, since 1986 (Dean, Coll. of Arts and Sciences, 1980–86). Theatre Critic: The Advocate, Los Angeles, Cal., since 1982; The New York Native, NYC, since 1983; Plays and Players, London, since 1984; Plays International, London, since 1986. Instr. in Speech and Assoc. Dir. of Theatre, Kansas State Univ., 1967–71; Asst. Prof., 1971–74, Assoc. Prof. of Speech, Drama and English, 1975–80, and Chmn., Dept. of Speech and Theatre, 1979–80, John Jay Coll. of Criminal Justice, City Univ. of New York. Theatre Ed., Greenwich Village News, NYC, 1976–77; Theatre Critic, Soho Weekly News, NYC, 1977–82, Other Stages, NYC, 1978–82, The Villager, 1982–83, and Plays and Players, London, 1984–86. *Publs:* LeRoi Jones (Imamu Amiri Baraka): A Checklist of Works by and about Him, 1971; (co-author) The Theatre Student: Modern Theatre and Drama, 1973; The Osborne Generation: A Bibliography of Works by and about Twenty Contemporary British and Irish Playwrights, with a List of Production Data, 1986. Add: Coll. of Arts and Sciences, Southeastern Massachusetts Univ., N. Dartmouth, Mass. 02747, U.S.A.

DACEY, Philip. American, b. 1939. Poetry. Member of the English Dept., now Prof. of English, Southwest State Univ., Marshall, Minn., since 1970. *Publs:* The Beast with Two Backs, 1969; Fist, Sweet Giraffe, The Lion, Snake, and Owl, 1970; Four Nudes, 1971; How I Escaped from the Labyrinth and Other Poems, 1977; The Condom Poems, 1979; Men at Table, 1979; The Boy under the Bed, 1981; Gerard Manley Hopkins Meets Walt Whitman in Heaven and Other Poems, 1982; Fives, 1984;

(ed. with David Jauss) Strong Measures: Contemporary American Poetry in Traditional Forms, 1985; The Man with Red Suspenders, 1986; The Condom Poems II, 1989. Add: English Dept., Southwest State Univ., Marshall, Minn. 56258, U.S.A.

DACRE OF GLANTON, Baron. *See* **TREVOR-ROPER,** Hugh.

DAEMER, Will. *See* **WADE,** Robert.

DAENZER, Bernard J(ohn). American, b. 1916. Marketing, Money/Finance. Pres., Daenzer Associates, Key Largo, Fla., since 1980. Dir., RLI Corp., Peoria, Ill., since 1975; underwriting member of Lloyd's, since 1968; Ed. and Columnist, Weekly Underwriter, since 1961. Former Exec. Vice-Pres. and Dir., Security-Connecticut Companies, Hartford; Pres. and Dir., Alexander Howden Group Ltd., 1957–80. *Publs:* Ethics and Insurance, 1953; Insurance Marketing in the U.S., 1963; Cover Notes, 1964; Fact Finding Techniques in Risk Analysis, 1971; Excess and Surplus Lines Manual, 1970; Strategies in Insurance Coverages, 1985. Add: 29 Angelfish Cay Dr., Key Largo, Fla. 33037, U.S.A.

DAHL, Curtis. American, b. 1920. Literature. S.V. Cole Prof. of English Literature, Wheaton Coll., Norton, Mass., since 1966 (Asst. Prof., 1948–53; Assoc. Prof., 1953–58; Prof., 1958–66). Pres., New England Coll. English Assn., 1951–52, and New England American Studies Assn., 1962–64. *Publs:* Robert Montgomery Bird, 1963; (ed.) "There She Blows": A Narrative of a Whaling Voyage, 1971. Add: Dept. of English, Wheaton Coll., Norton, Mass. 02766, U.S.A.

DAHL, Roald. British, b. 1916. Novels/Short stories, Children's fiction, Plays/Screenplays. Member of the Eastern Staff, Shell Co., London, 1933–37, and Shell Co. of East Africa, Dar es Salaam, 1937–39. *Publs:* The Gremlins, 1943; Over to You: 10 Stories of Flyers and Flying, 1946; Sometime Never: A Fable for Supermen, 1948; Someone Like You, 1953, 1961; The Honeys (play), 1955; Kiss, Kiss, 1960; James and the Giant Peach, 1961; Charlie and the Chocolate Factory, 1964; The Magic Finger, 1966; You Only Live Twice (screenplay), 1967; Twenty-Nine Kisses, 1969; Selected Stories, 1970; The Night-Digger (screenplay), 1970; Fantastic Mr. Fox, 1970; The Lightning Bug (screenplay), 1971; Willy Wonka and the Chocolate Factory (screenplay), 1971; Charlie and the Great Glass Elevator: The Further Adventures of Charlie Bucket and Willy Wonka, Chocolate-Maker Extraordinary, 1972; Switch Bitch, 1974; Danny the Champion of the World, 1975; The Wonderful Story of Henry Sugar, 1977; The Enormous Crocodile, 1978; The Best of Roald Dahl, 1978; Tales of the Unexpected, 1979; My Uncle Oswald (novel), 1979; The Twits, 1980; George's Marvellous Medicine, 1981; Revolting Rhymes, 1982; The BFG, 1982; The Witches, 1983; Boy, 1984; The Giraffe and the Pelly and Me, 1985; Going Solo, 1986; Matilda, 1988. Add: Gipsy House, Great Missenden, Bucks. HP16 0PB, England.

DAHL, Robert (Alan). American, b. 1915. Economics, Politics/Government. Sterling Prof. of Political Science, Yale Univ., New Haven, since 1964 (joined faculty, 1946; Eugene Meyer Prof. of Political Science, 1955–64). Mgmt. Analyst, U.S. Dept. of Agriculture, Washington, D.C., 1940; Economist, Office of Production Management, War Production Bd., 1940–42; with U.S. Army, 1943–45. *Publs:* Congress and Foreign Policy, 1950; (with Ralph Brown) Domestic Control of Atomic Energy, 1951; (with D.E. Lidblom) Politics, Economics Welfare, 1953; A Preface to Democratic Theory, 1956; (with Haire and Lazarsfeld) Social Science Research on Business, 1959; Who Governs?

Democracy and Power in an American City, 1961; Modern Political Analysis, 1963, 4th ed. 1984; Political Oppositions in Western Democracies, 1966; Pluralist Democracy in the United States, 1967, 4th ed. 1981; After the Revolution, 1970; Polyarchy: Participation and Opposition, 1971; Size and Democracy, 1973; Dilemmas of Pluralistic Democracy, 1983; A Preface to Economic Democracy, 1985; Controlling Nuclear Weapons, 1985; Democracy, Liberty and Equality, 1986. Add: 17 Cooper Rd., North Haven, Conn. 06473, U.S.A.

DAHLIE, Hallvard. Canadian, b. 1925. Literature. Prof. of English, Univ. of Calgary, since 1967 (Head of Dept., 1974–79). *Publs:* Brian Moore, 1969; (ed. with R. Chadbourne) The New Land as Literary Theme, 1978; Brian Moore, 1981; Alice Munro and her Works, 1985; Varieties of Exile: The Canadian Experience, 1986. Add: Dept. of English, Univ. of Calgary, Calgary, Alta. T2N 1N4, Canada.

DAHRENDORF, (Sir) Ralf. British (born German), b. 1929. Sociology. Warden, St. Antony's Coll., Oxford. Univ. Lectr., Saarbrucken, 1957; Fellow, Center for Advanced Study in the Behavioral Sciences, Stanford Univ., Calif., 1957–58; Prof. of Sociology, Hamburg, 1958–60; Visiting Prof., Columbia Univ., NYC, 1960; Prof. of Sociology, Tubingen, 1960–64; Vice-Chmn., Founding Cttee. of the Univ. of Constance, 1964–66; Parliamentary Secty. of State, Foreign Office, W. Germany, 1969–70; Member, Commn. of the European Communities, Brussels, 1970–74; Dir., London Sch. of Economics, 1974–84. *Publs:* Marx in Perspective, 1953; Industrie und Betriebssoziologie, 1956; Soziale Klassen und Klassenkonflikt, 1957; Homo Sociologicus, 1959; Sozialstruktur des Betriebes, 1959; Gesellschaft und Freiheit, 1961; Uber den Ursprung der Ungleichheit, 1961; Die Angewandte Aufklarung, 1963; Das Mitbestimmungsproblem in der Deutschen Sozialforschung, 1963; Arbeiterkinder an Deutschen Universitäten, 1965; Bildung ist Burgerrecht, 1965; Gesellschaft und Demokratie in Deutschland, 1965; Markt und Plan, 1966; Confict after Class, 1967; Essays in the Theory of Society, 1967; Pfade aus Utopia, 1967; Die Soziologie und der Soziologe, 1967; Fur eine Erneuerung der Demokratie in der Bundesrepublik, 1968; Konflikt und Freiheit, 1972; Plädoyer für die Europäische Union, 1973; The New Liberty, 1975; Life Changes, 1979; On Britain, 1982; Die Chancender Krise, 1983; Reisen nach innen und aussen, 1984; Law and Order, 1985; The Modern Social Conflict, 1988. Add: St. Antony's Coll., Oxford OX2 6JF, England.

DAICHES, David. British, b. 1912. Literature, History, Biography. Asst. in English, Edinburgh Univ., 1935–36; Andrew Bradley Fellow, Balliol Coll., Oxford, 1936–37; Asst. Prof., Univ. of Chicago, 1939–43; Second Secty., British Embassy, Washington, 1944–46; Prof., Cornell Univ., Ithaca, N.Y., 1945–51; Lectr., Cambridge Univ., 1951–61; Fellow, Jesus Coll., Cambridge, 1957–62; Dean, Sch. of English and American Studies, 1961–67, and Prof. of English, 1961–77, Univ. of Sussex; Dir. Inst. for Advanced Studies, Edinburgh Univ., 1980–86. *Publs:* The Place of Meaning in Poetry, 1935; New Literary Values, 1936; Literature and Society, 1938; The Novel and the Modern World, 1939, 1960; Poetry and the Modern World, 1940; The King James Version of the Bible: A Study of Its Sources and Development, 1941; Virginia Woolf, 1942; Robert Louis Stevenson, 1947; A Study of Literature, 1948; (ed.) Poems in English, 1950; Robert Burns, 1951; (ed.) A Century of the Essay, 1951; Willa Cather, 1951; Two Worlds, 1956; Critical Approaches to Literature, 1956; Literary Essays, 1956; Milton, 1957; The Present Age, 1958; A Critical History of English Literature, 1960; George Eliot's Middlemarch, 1963; English Literature, 1964; (ed.) The Idea of a New University, 1964; The Paradox of Scottish Culture, 1964; More Literary Essays, 1968; Scotch Whisky, 1969; Some Late Victorian Attitudes, 1969; A Third World, 1971; (ed.) Penguin Companion to Literature: Great Britain and the Commonwealth, 1971; Sir Walter Scott and His World, 1971; Robert Burns and His World, 1971; Charles Edward Stuart, 1973; Robert Louis Stevenson and His World, 1973; Was, 1975; Moses: Man in the Wilderness (in U.S. as Moses: The Man and His Vision), 1975; James Boswell and His World, 1976; Scotland and the Union, 1977; Glasgow, 1977; Edinburgh, 1978; Literary Landscapes of the British Isles, 1979; (ed.) Fletcher of Saltoun: Selected Writings, 1979; Literature and Gentility in Scotland, 1982; Robert Fergusson, 1982; God and the Poets, 1984; Edinburgh: A Travellers' Companion, 1986. Add: 12 Rothsay Place, Edinburgh EH3 7SQ, Scotland.

DAILEY, Janet. American, b. 1944. Historical/Romance/Gothic, Western. *Publs:* No Quarter Asked, 1974; Savage Land, 1974; Something Extra, 1975; Fire and Ice, 1975; Boss Man from Ogallala, 1975; After the Storm, 1975; Land of Enchantment, 1975; Sweet Promise, 1976; The Homeplace, 1976; Dangerous Masquerade, 1976; Show Me, 1976; Valley of the Vapours, 1976; The Night of the Cotillion, 1976; Fiesta

San Antonio, 1977; Bluegrass King, 1977; A Lyon's Share, 1977; The Widow and the Wastrel, 1977; The Ivory Cane, 1977; Six White Horses, 1977; To Tell the Truth, 1977; The Master Fiddler, 1977; Giant of Medabi, 1978; Beware of the Stranger, 1978; Darling Jenny, 1978; The Indy Man, 1978; Reilly's Woman, 1978; For Bitter or Worse, 1978; Tidewater Lover, 1978; The Bride of the Delta Queen, 1978; Green Mountain Man, 1978; Sonora Sundown, 1978; Summer Mahogany, 1978; The Matchmakers, 1978; Big Sky Country, 1978; Low Country Liar, 1979; Strange Bedfellow, 1979; For Mike's Sake, 1979; Sentimental Journey, 1979; Sweet Promise, 1979; Bed of Grass, 1979; That Boston Man, 1979; Kona Winds, 1979; A Land Called Deseret, 1979; Touch the Wind, 1979; Difficult Decision, 1980; Enemy in Camp, 1980; Heart of Stone, 1980; Lord of the High Lonesome, 1980; The Mating Season, 1980; Southern Nights, 1980; The Thawing of Mara, 1980; One of the Boys, 1980; The Rogue, 1980; Wild and Wonderful, 1980; Ride the Thunder, 1981; A Tradition of Pride, 1981; The Travelling Kind, 1981; Dakota Dreamin', 1981; The Hostage Bride, 1981; Night Way, 1981; Lancaster Men, 1981; For the Love of God, 1981; Calder saga: This Calder Sky, 1981, This Calder Range, 1982, Stands a Calder Man, 1982; Northern Magic, 1982; With a Little Luck, 1982; That Carolina Summer, 1982; Terms of Surrender, 1982; Wildcatter's Woman, 1982; Calder Born, Calder Bred, 1983; Foxfire Light, 1982; The Second Time, 1982; Mistle Toe and Holly, 1982; Separate Cabins, 1983; Western Man, 1983; Best Way to Lose, 1983; Leftover Love, 1984; Silver Wings, Santiago Blue, 1984; The Pride of Hannah Wade, 1985; The Glory Game, 1985; The Great Alone, 1986; Heiress, 1987; Rivals, 1989. Add: c/o William Dailey, Star Rt. 4, Box 2197, Branson, Mo. 65616, U.S.A.

DAINTON, (Lord) Frederick. British, b. 1914. Chemistry, Education. Chancellor, Univ. of Sheffield, since 1978. H.O. Jones Lectr. in Physical Chemistry, and Fellow of St. Catharine's Coll., Cambridge, 1944–50; Prof. of Physical Chemistry, Univ. of Leeds, 1950–65; Vice-Chancellor, Univ. of Nottingham, 1965–70; Chmn., Council for Scientific Policy, 1969–73; Dr. Lee's Prof. of Chemistry in the Univ. of Oxford, 1970–73; Chmn., Univ. Grants Cttee., London, 1973–78. Chmn., National Radiological Protection Bd., and British Library Bd., 1978–85. *Publs:* Chain Reactions, 1956, 1966; (author and ed.) Chain Kinetics and Photochemistry, 1967; Choosing a British University, 1980; Universities and the National Health Service, 1983. Add: Fieldside, Water Eaton Lane, Oxford OX5 2PR, England.

DALCOURT, Gerard Joseph. American, b. 1927. Philosophy. Prof., Seton Hall Univ., South Orange, N.J., since 1975 and Dept. Chmn., since 1988 (Asst. Prof., 1962–66; Assoc. Prof., 1966–75). Librarian, Univ. of Kansas, Lawrence, 1954–56; Instr., Villanova Univ., Pa., 1957–62. *Publs:* The Philosophy of St. Thomas Aquinas, 1965; (ed. and trans.) The Great Dialogue of Nature and Space, 1970; The Methods of Ethics, 1983. Add: 579 Prospect, Maplewood, N.J. 07040, U.S.A.

DALE, Antony. British, b. 1912. Architecture, History. Hon. Secty., Regency Soc. of Brighton and Hove, since 1946. Investigator, 1946–61, and Chief Investigator of Historic Buildings, 1961–76, U.K. Dept. of Environment. *Publs:* Fashionable Brighton: 1820-60, 1947; The History and Architecture of Brighton, 1950; About Brighton, 1951; James Wyatt, 1953; Brighton Old and New, 1976; Brighton Town and Brighton People, 1977; The Theatre Royal, Brighton, 1980; The Wagners of Brighton, 1983; Brighton Churches, 1988. Add: 38 Prince Regent's Close, Brighton, Sussex BN2 5JP, England.

DALE, Peter. British, b. 1938. Poetry, Translations. Head of English Dept., Hinchley Wood Sch., Esher, Surrey, since 1972. Ed., Agenda, London, since 1971. *Publs:* Walk from the House, 1962; The Storms, 1968; Mortal Fire, 1970; (trans.) The Legacy and Other Poems of Fran#ois Villon, 1971; (co-trans. with Kokilam Subbiah) The Seasons of Cankam, 1974; Mortal Fire: New and Selected Poems and Translations, 1976; Cross Channel, 1977; One Another (sonnets), 1978; (trans.) Selected Poems of Villon, 1978; Two Much of Water: Poems 1976–82, 1984; (trans.) The Poems of Laforgue, 1986; (trans.) Narrow Straits, 1986. Add: 10 Selwood Rd., Sutton, Surrey SM3 9JU, England.

DALE, Richard. American, b. 1932. International relations/Current affairs, Politics/Government. Assoc. Prof., Dept. of Political Science, Southern Illinois Univ., Carbondale, since 1971 (Adjunct Prof., 1966–67; Asst. Prof., 1967–71). Member, Editorial Advisory Bd., Journal of Contemporary African Studies, since 1980. Instr., Dept. of Govt., Univ. of New Hampshire, Durham, 1962–63; Asst. Prof. of Political Science, Northern Illinois Univ., DeKalb, 1963–66. Member of the Council, South African Inst. of Race Relations, 1974–81; Member, Advisory Bd., Univ. Press of America, Washington, D.C., 1976–81. *Publs:* Botswana and Its Southern Neighbor: The Patterns of Linkage and the Options in Statecraft (monograph), 1970; The Racial Component of Botswana's Foreign Policy, 1971; (ed. with C.P. Potham) Southern Africa in Perspective: Essays in Regional Politics, 1972. Add: Dept. of Political Science, Southern Illinois Univ., Carbondale, Ill. 62901, U.S.A.

DALE, William. *See* **DANIELS,** Norman A.

DALESKI, H.M. Israeli, b. 1926. Literature. Prof. of English, Hebrew Univ., Jerusalem, since 1976 (Asst. Lectr. to Assoc. Prof., 1958-76; Chmn., Dept. of English, 1968-70, 1984-85; Provost, Sch. for Overseas Students, 1973-76). *Publs:* The Forked Flame: A Study of D.H. Lawrence, 1965; Dickens and the Art of Analogy, 1970; Joseph Conrad: The Way of Dispossession, 1977; The Divided Heroine: A Recurrent Pattern in Six English Novels, 1984; Unities: Studies in the English Novel, 1985. Add: Dept. of English, The Hebrew Univ., Jerusalem, Israel.

DALEY, Brian C. American, b. 1947. Science fiction. Has worked as awaiter, housepainter, laborer, and case worker. *Publs:* The Doomfarers of Coramonde, 1977; The Starfollowers of Coramonde, 1979; Han Solo at Stars' End, 1979; Han Solo's Revenge, 1979; Han Solo and the Lost Legacy, 1980; Tron (novelization of screenplay), 1982; A Tapestry of Magics, 1983; Requiem for a Ruler of Worlds, 1985; Jinx on a Terran Inheritance, 1985; Fall of the White Ship Avatar, 1987. Add: c/o Ballantine/del Rey Books, 201 E. 50th St., New York, N.Y. 10022, U.S.A.

DALEY, Robert (Blake). American, b. 1930. Novels/Short stories. Publicity Dir., New York Giants, 1953-58; Foreign and War Corresp. in Europe and N. Africa, New York Times, 1959-64; Deputy Commnr., New York Police Dept., 1971-72. Photographs exhibited at Baltimore Museum, Art Inst. of Chicago, and N.Y. Gallery of Modern Art, 1968-69. *Publs:* The World Beneath the City, 1959; Cars at Speed, 1961; The Bizarre World of European Sports, 1963; The Cruel Sport, 1963; The Swords of Spain, 1965; The Whole Truth, 1967; Only a Game, 1967; A Priest and a Girl, 1969; A Star in the Family, 1971; Target Blue, 1973; Strong Wine Red as Blood, 1974; To Kill a Cop, 1976; Treasure, 1977; The Fast One, 1978; Prince of the City, 1979; An American Saga, 1980; Year of the Dragon, 1981; The Dangerous Edge, 1983; Hands of a Stranger, 1985; Man with a Gun, 1988. Add: c/o Esther Newburg, ICM, 40 W. 57th St., New York, N.Y. 10019, U.S.A.

DALGLISH, Edward Russell. American, b. 1913. Theology/Religion. Macon Prof. of Religion, Baylor Univ., Waco, Tex., since 1984 (Prof. of Old Testament and Hebrew, 1966-84; Chmn., Univ. Libraries Cttee., 1970; Coordinator, Major Library Acquisition, 1975-80). Prof., Gordon Divinity Sch., Boston, Mass., 1946-52; Prof. of Old Testament Interpretation, Eastern Baptist Theological Seminary, Philadelphia, Pa., 1952-66 (Visiting Prof., 1986-87). Visiting Prof., Goldengate Baptist Seminary, Mill Valley, Calif., 1985. *Publs:* Psalm Fifty-One in the Light of Ancient Near Eastern Patternism, 1962; The Book of Judges, 1972; The Book of Nahum, 1972; The Great Deliverance: A Concise Study of the Book of Exodus, 1978; Jeremiah: Lamentations, 1983. Add: 316 Guittard Ave., Waco, Tex. 76706, U.S.A.

DALITZ, Richard Henry. British, b. 1925. Physics. Research Prof., The Royal Soc., London, since 1963. Reader in Mathematical Physics, Univ. of Birmingham, 1955-56; Prof. of Physics, Enrico Fermi Inst. for Nuclear Studies, Univ. of Chicago, 1955-66. *Publs:* Strange Particles and Strong Interactions, 1962; Nuclear Interactions of the Hyperons, 1965; (co-author) Nuclear Energy Today and Tomorrow, 1971. Add: 1 Keble Rd., Oxford, England.

DALLAS, Ruth. Pseud. for Ruth Mumford. New Zealander, b. 1919. Children's fiction, Poetry. *Publs:* Country Road and Other Poems, 1953; The Turning Wheel, 1961; Day Book: Poems of a Year, 1966; Shadow Show, 1968; The Children in the Bush, 1969; Ragamuffin Scarecrows, 1969; A Dog Called Wig, 1970; The Wild Boy in the Bush, 1971; The Big Flood in the Bush, 1972; The House on the Cliffs, 1975; Walking on the Snow, 1976; Songs for a Guitar, 1976; Shining Rivers, 1979; Steps of the Sun, 1979; Holiday Time in the Bush, 1983; Collected Poems, 1987. Add: 448 Leith St., Dunedin, New Zealand.

DALLEK, Robert. American, b. 1934. International relations/Current affairs, Biography. Prof. of History, Univ. of California at Los Angeles (joined faculty as Asst. Prof., 1964). Member, Bd. of Editors, Reviews in American History; Member of the Council, Soc. for Historians of American Foreign Relations, and Cttee. on the History of the Second World War. Instr. in History, Columbia Univ., NYC, 1960-64. *Publs:*

Democrat and Diplomat: The Life of William E. Dodd, 1968; (ed.) The Roosevelt Diplomacy and World War II (reader), 1970; (ed.) Western Europe, vol. I of Dynamics of World Power: A Documentary History of American Foreign Policy 1945-1973, 1973; Franklin D. Roosevelt and American Foreign Policy 1932-45, 1979; The American Style of Foreign Policy: Cultural Politics and Foreign Affairs, 1983; Ronald Reagan: The Politics of Symbolism, 1984; (co-author) The Great Republic: A History of the American People, 3rd ed. 1985. Add: Dept. of History, Univ. of California, Los Angeles, Calif. 90024, U.S.A.

DALLY, Ann. British, b. 1926. Medicine/Health, Psychiatry, Psychology, Women, Biography. Psychiatrist in private practice, London. *Publs:* A-Z of Babies, 1961; (with R. Sweering) A Child is Born, 1965, (in U.S., as The Birth of a Baby, 1969); Intelligent Person's Guide to Modern Medicine, 1967; Ciceley: The Story of a Doctor, 1968; Mothers: Their Power and Influence, 1976; The Morbid Streak (in U.S. as Understanding), 1978; Why Women Fail, 1979; Inventing Motherhood, 1982; Doctor into Rebel, 1989. Add: 13 Devonshire Pl., London W1, England.

DALRYMPLE, Jean. American, b. 1902. Cookery/Gastronomy/Wine, Theatre, Autobiography/Memoirs/Personal. Dir. and Publicity Dir., New York City Center of Music and Drama, 1943-68; Publicity Dir., Berlin Arts Festival, 1951; Dir., American Theatre, Brussels World's Fair, 1958. *Publs:* September Child (autobiography), 1963; Careers and Opportunities in the Theatre, 1970; The Jean Dalrymple Pinafore Farm Cookbook, 1971; (with F. Lavan) The Folklore and Facts of Natural Nutrition; From the Last Row, 1975; The Complete Community Theatre Handbook, 1977. Add: 150 West 55th St., New York, N.Y. 10019, U.S.A.

DALRYMPLE, Willard. American, b. 1921. Medicine/Health. Dir., Univ. Health Services, Coordinator, Premed. Advising, and Courtesy Staff Member, Princeton Medical Center, Princeton Univ., N.J., all since 1961; Asst. Prof., Rutgers Univ. Medical Sch., New Brunswick, N.J., since 1961; Ed., Journal of the American Coll. Health Assn., since 1973. Pres., American Coll. Health Assn., 1972-73. *Publs:* The Foundations of Health, 1959; Sex Is For Real, 1969; (with Harold S. Diehl) Healthful Living, 9th ed. 1973; (ed. with Elizabeth F. Purcell) Campus Health Programs, 1976. Add: Princeton Medical Center, Princeton, N.J. 08540, U.S.A.

DALTON, G(raham) E(yre). British, b. 1942. Agriculture. Head, Agricultural Economics Div., North of Scotland Coll. of Agriculture, Aberdeen, since 1981 (Deputy Head, 1976-80), and Hon. Sr. Lectr., Univ. of Aberdeen, since 1976. Lectr. in Farm Management, Univ. of Reading, 1966-76; Lectr., Univ. of Ghana, 1970-71. Council Member, 1974-76, and Chmn., 1975-76, Farm Management Assn.; Member, Exec. Cttee., Agricultural Economics Soc., 1974-76; Consultant (on Ghana), World Bank, 1980; Consultant (on Pakistan), Agricultural Prices Commn., 1982. *Publs:* (ed.) Study of Agricultural Systems, 1975; Managing Agricultural Systems, 1982. Add: Agricultural Economics Div., Sch. of Agriculture, Aberdeen AB9 1UD, Scotland.

DALTON, Priscilla. *See* **AVALLONE,** Michael.

DALY, Cahal Brendan. Irish, b. 1917. Theology/Religion. Roman Catholic Bishop of Down and Connor, since 1982. Chmn., Christus Rex. Soc., 1941-66; Lectr., then Reader in Scholastic Philosophy, Queen's Univ., Belfast, 1946-67; Canon of Diocesan Chapter of Down and Connor, 1966; R.C. Bishop of Ardagh and Clanmacnois, 1967-82; former Peritus, Second Vatican Council. *Publs:* Morals, Law and Life, 1962; Natural Law Morality Today, 1965; Intellect and Hope, 1968; New Essays in Religious Language, 1969; Understanding the Eucharist, 1969; Violence in Ireland and Christian Conscience, 1973; Peace: The Work of Justice, 1979. Add: Lisbreen, 73 Somerton Rd., Belfast, Northern Ireland.

DALY, Leo (Arthur). Irish, b. 1920. Novels, Literature, Travel/Exploration/Adventure. Broadcaster, Radio-Telefis-Eireann. *Publs:* The Aran Islands, 1975; James Joyce and the Mullingar Connection, 1975; (ed.) The Midlands, 1979; Titles, 1981; (ed.) The Westmeath Examiner Centenary Edition, 1982; The Rock Garden (novel), 1984; The Sign Writer (novel), 1989. Add: 10 Mary St., Mullingar, Co. Westmeath, Ireland.

DALY, Lowrie J. American, b. 1914. History, Politics/Government, Theology/Religion. Prof. of History, St. Louis Univ., since 1963, now Emeritus. Asst. Ed., Manuscripta, since 1957. *Publs:* The Medieval University, 1961; The Political Theory of John Wycliff, 1962; (with V. Daly) Meditations for Educators, 1965; Benedictine Monasticism, 1965;

(with V. Daly) Meditations; Advent to Lent, 1966.   Add: St. Louis Univ., 221 N. Grand Ave., St. Louis, Mo. 63103, U.S.A.

DALY, Mary. American, b. 1928. Theology/Religion, Women. Assoc. Prof. of Theology, Boston Coll., Chestnut Hill, Mass., since 1969 (Asst. Prof., 1966–69). Visiting Lectr., St. Mary's Coll., Notre Dame, Ind., 1952–54; Member of faculty, Cardinal Cushing Coll., Brookline, Mass., 1954–59; Teacher of theology and philosophy, U.S. jr. year abroad progs., Fribourg, Switzerland, 1959–66. *Publs:* Natural Knowledge of God in the Philosophy of Jacques Maritain, 1966; The Church and the Second Sex, 1968, reissued as The Church and the Second Sex: With a New Feminist Postchristian Introduction by the Author, 1975; Beyond God the Father: Toward a Philosophy of Women's Liberation, 1973, 1985; Gyn/Ecology; The Metaethics of Radical Feminism, 1978; Pure Lust: Elemental Feminist Philosophy, 1984; Webster's First New Intergalactic Wickedary of the English Language, 1987.   Add: 34 Brookside Ave., Newton, Mass. 02160, U.S.A.

DALY, Maureen. American. Novels/Short stories, Children's fiction. Freelance journalist and script writer. Police Reporter and Columnist, Chicago Tribune, 1946–48; Assoc. Ed., Ladies' Home Journal, Philadelphia, 1948–54; Editorial Consultant, Saturday Evening Post, Philadelphia, 1960–69. *Publs:* Seventeenth Summer, 1942; Smarter and Smoother: A Handbook on How to Be That Way, 1944; The Perfect Hostess: Complete Etiquette and Entertainment for the Home, 1948; (ed.) My Favorite Stories, 1948; (ed.) Profile of Youth, 1951; What's Your P.Q. (Personality Quotient)?, 1952; Twelve Around the World, 1957; (as Maureen Daly McGivern, with William P. McGivern) Mention My Name in Mombasa: The Unscheduled Adventures of an American Family Abroad, 1958; Patrick series, 4 vols., 1959–63; Spanish Roundabout, 1960; Moroccan Roundabout, 1961; Sixteen and Other Stories, 1961; The Ginger Horse, 1964; (ed.) My Favorite Mystery Stories, 1966; The Small War of Sergeant Donkey, 1966; Rosie, The Dancing Elephant, 1967; (ed.) My Favorite Suspense Stories, 1968; (with William McGivern) The Seeing, 1981; Acts of Love, 1986; Promises to Keep, 1987; How to Understand the Law, 1989.   Add: 73-305 Ironwood, St., Palm Desert, Calif. 92260, U.S.A.

D'AMATO, Anthony A. American, b. 1937. Plays/Screenplays, Law, Philosophy, Politics/Government. Prof. of Law, Northwestern Univ. School of Law, Chicago, since 1968 (formerly Asst. Prof., and subsequently Assoc. Prof.). *Publs:* (ed. with W. Christopher Beal) The Realities of Vietnam, 1968; The Concept of Custom in International Law, 1971; (with Robert M. O'Neil) The Judiciary and Vietnam, 1972; (co-author) The Politics of Ecosuicide, 1972; (co-author) The Political Calculus (philosophy), 1972; (co-author) International Law and Vietnam, vol. 3, 1973; The Magic Man (play), 1974; (with others) Desegregation from Brown to Alexander: An Exploration of Supreme Court Strategies, 1978; (with Burns Weston and Richard Falk) International Law and World Order, 1980; R.S.V.P. Broadway (musical play), 1981; Assyrian Case for Autonomy, 1982; Jurisprudence: A Descriptive and Normative Analysis of Law, 1984; International Law: Process and Prospect, 1987; How to Understand the Law, 1989.   Add: Sch. of Law, Northwestern University, Chicago, Ill. 60611, U.S.A.

DAMAZ, Paul F. American, b. 1917. Architecture, Art. Principal, Paul Damaz Assoc. Architects and Planners. Vice-Pres., Fine Arts Fedn. of New York. Former Vice-Pres., Architectural League of New York; former Pres., Adasco Tech Intnl., from 1976. *Publs:* Art in European Architecture, 1956; Art in Latin American Architecture, 1962. Add: 302 East 88th St., New York, N.Y. 10028, U.S.A.

DAMERST, William A. American, b. 1923. Writing/Journalism. Prof. Emeritus of English, Pennsylvania State Univ., University Park, since 1985 (Instr., 1955–60; Asst. Prof., 1960–65; Assoc. Prof., 1965–72; Prof., 1972–85). Fellow, since 1972, and Pres., 1972, American Business Communication Assn. *Publs:* Good Gulf Letters and Reports, 1959; Resourceful Business Communication, 1966; Clear Technical Reports, 1972, 1986.   Add: 248 Waring Ave., State College, Pa. 16801, U.S.A.

DAMES, Michael. British, b. 1938. Anthropology/Ethnology, Art. Lectr. in Prehistoric Design, Sheffield Polytechnic, 1964–68; Sr. Lectr. in Art History, Birmingham Polytechnic, 1971–76. *Publs:* The Silbury Treasure: The Great Goddess Rediscovered, 1976; The Avebury Cycle, 1977.   Add: 60 Poplar Rd., Kings Heath, Birmingham B14 7AG, England.

DANA, Robert (Patrick). American, b. 1929. Poetry. Prof. of English and Poet-in-Residence, Cornell Coll., Mt. Vernon, Iowa since 1968

(joined faculty, 1953). Contrib. Ed., American Poetry Review, since 1971. Ed., Hillside Press, 1957–67, and North American Review, 1964–68, Mt. Vernon, Iowa. *Publs:* My Glass Brother and Other Poems, 1957; The Dark Flags of Waking, 1964; Journeys from the Skin: A Poem in Two Parts, 1966; Some Versions of Silence: Poems, 1967; The Power of the Visible, 1971; In a Fugitive Season, 1980; What the the Stones Know, 1984; Blood Harvest, 1986; Against the Grain: Interviews with Maverick American Publishers, 1986; Starting Out for the Difficult World, 1987.   Add: Dept. of English, Cornell Coll., Mt. Vernon, Iowa 52314, U.S.A.

DANAHER, Kevin. (Caoimhín O'Danachair). Irish, b. 1913. Anthropology/Ethnology. Lectr. in Regional and Comparative Ethnology, University Coll., National Univ. of Ireland, Dublin, since 1972, now retired. Ed., "Life and Culture" series, Irish Govt., since 1965. Ed., Irish Sword, 1960–71. *Publs:* In Ireland Long Ago, 1962; (ed. with J.G. Simms) The Danish Force in Ireland 1691-1692, 1963; Gentle Places and Simple Things, 1964; Irish Country People, 1966; Folktales of the Irish Countryside, 1967; The Pleasant Land of Ireland, 1970; The Year in Ireland, 1972; Irish Vernacular Architecture, 1976; (ed.) Folk and Farm, 1976; A Bibliography of Irish Ethnology and Folk Tradition, 1978; That's How It Was, 1984; The Hearth and Stool and All!, 1985.   Add: 22 Calderwood Ave., Dublin 9, Ireland.

DANBURY, Iris. British. Historical/Romance/Gothic. Full-time writer. Former typist, secty., and owner of a typing business. *Publs:* The Gentle Invader, 1957; My Heart a Traitor, 1958; One Enchanted Summer, 1958; Feather in the Wind, 1959; The Rose-Walled Castle, 1959; The Rainbow Shell, 1960; The Silent Nightingale, 1961; Hotel Belvedere, 1961; Bride of Kylsaig, 1963; Story de Luxe, 1963; Home from the Sky, 1964; The Marble Mountain, 1964; Bonfire in the Dusk, 1965; Illyrian Summer, 1965; Doctor at Drumlochan, 1966; The Eagle of Segarra, 1966; Doctor at Villa Ronda, 1967; Rendezvous in Lisbon, 1967; Feast of the Candles, 1968; Hotel by the Loch, 1968; Chateau of Pines, 1969; Isle of Pomegranates, 1969; Island of Mermaids, 1970; Serenade at Santa Rosa, 1970; The Legend of Roscano, 1971; Summer Comes to Albarosa, 1971; Jacaranda Island, 1972; Mandolins of Mantori, 1973; The Silver Stallion, 1973; The Fires of Torretta, 1974; The Amethyst Meadows, 1974; A Pavement of Pearl, 1975; The Scented Island, 1976; The Windmill of Kalakos, 1976; The Painted Palace, 1977.   Add: c/o Mills and Boon Ltd., Eton House, 18-24 Paradise Rd., Richmond, Surrey TW9 1SR, England.

DANBY, Mary. Also writes as Mary Calvert, Simon Reed, and Andy Stevens. British, b. 1941. Novels/Short stories, Children's fiction, Children's non-fiction. Consultant Ed., Armada Books, London, since 1973. Television Production Asst., 1962–69; Fiction Ed., Fontana Books, London, 1969–72. *Publs:* as Mary Danby—(ed.) Fontana Books of Great Horror Stories, 5-15, 1970–82; (with D. Dickens) The Armada Quiz and Puzzle Book, 1-8, 1970–80; (ed.) The Armada Ghost Book, 3-14, 1970–82; (ed.) The Armada Book of Fun, 1-3, 1971–75; A Single Girl, 1972; (ed.) The Armada Book of Cartoons, 1-3, 1972–77; Fun on Wheels, 1973; (ed.) Frighteners, 1-2, 1974–76; The Best of Friends, 1975; (ed.) The Armada Book of Christmas Fun, 1975; (ed.) The Armada Book of Limericks, 1-2, 1977–78; (ed.) 65 Great Tales of the Supernatural, 1979; (ed.) The Awful [Even More Awful, Most Awful] Joke Book, 3 vols, 1979–84; (with Jane Allen) Hello to Ponies, 1979; (with Jane Allen) Hello to Riding, 1980; (ed.) The Armada Funny Story Book, 1980; (with C. Bostock-Smith) Metal Mickey's Boogie Book, 1981; (ed.) 65 Great Tales of Horror (and Terror), 2 vols., 1981–82; (ed.) The Funniest Fun Book, 1984; (ed.) The Batty Book [and Cartoon Book], 2 vols., 1985–86; How Trivial Can You Get?, 1986; (ed.) Nightmares 1-3, 1983–85; The Batty Cartoon Book, 1986; as Mary Calvert—Turnip Tom and Big Fat Rosie, 1972; The Big Fat Rosie Storybook, 1977; as Andy Stevens—(with E. Sticklee) World of Stars, 1980; as Simon Reed—(with D. Dickens) Quick Quiz, 1981.   Add: Noakes Hill Cottage, Ashampstead, Berks. RH8 8RY, England.

DANCE, Stanley. British, b. 1910. Music. Reviewer, Jazz Times, Washington, D.C., since 1980. Reviewer, Jazz Journal, London, 1948–77, The Saturday Review, NYC, 1962–72, and Music Journal, NYC, 1962–79. *Publs:* (ed.) Jazz Era, 1961; (with D. Wells) The Night People, 1971; The World of Duke Ellington, 1970; The World of Swing, 1974; The World of Earl Hines, 1977; (with M. Ellington) Duke Ellington in Person, 1978; The World of Count Basie, 1980; (with Charlie Barnet) Those Swinging Years, 1984.   Add: 1745 Bittersweet Hill, Vista, Calif. 92084, U.S.A.

DANCER, J.B. *See* **HARVEY,** John B.

DANE, Eva. *See* **DARRELL,** Elizabeth.

DANE, Mark. *See* **AVALLONE**, Michael.

DANFORTH, Paul M. *See* **ALLEN**, John E.

DANIEL, Pete. American, b. 1938. History. Curator, National Museum of American History, Washington, D.C., since 1982. Asst. Prof. 1971–73, Assoc. Prof., 1973–78, and Prof., 1978–79, Univ. of Tennessee, Knoxville. Asst. Ed., Booker T. Washington Papers, 1969–70. *Publs:* The Shadow of Slavery: Peonage in the South 1901-69, 1972; (with Raymond Smock) A Talent for Detail, 1974; Deep'n as It Come: The 1927 Mississippi River Flood, 1977; Breaking the Land: The Transformation of Cotton, Tobacco and Rice Cultures since 1880, 1985; Standing at the Crossroads: Southern Life in the Twentieth Century, 1986; (with others) Official Images: New Deal Photography, 1987. Add: 1367 Emerald St. N.E., Washington, D.C. 20002, U.S.A.

DANIELS, Dorothy (Smith). Also writes as Danielle Dorsett, Angela Gray, Cynthia Kavanaugh, Helaine Ross, Suzanne Somers, Geraldine Thayer, and Helen Gray Weston. American, b. 1915. Mystery/Crime/Suspense, Historical/Romance/Gothic. Formerly, actress and sch. teacher. *Publs:* (as Geraldine Thayer) The Dark Rider, 1961; (as Suzanne Somers) The Caduceus Tree, 1961 (as Dorothy Daniels) A Nurse for Doctor Keith, 1962; (as Suzanne Somers) House of Eve, 1962; Jennifer James, R.N., 1962; (as Helaine Ross) No Tears Tomorrow, 1962; Eve Originals, 1962; Cruise Ship Nurse, 1963; Country Nurse, 1963; (as Suzanne Somers) Image of Truth, 1963; World's Fair Nurse, 1964; Island Nurse, 1964; The Tower Room, 1965; The Leland Legacy, 1965; Shadow Glen, 1965; Marriott Hall, 1965; Darkhaven, 1965; The Unguarded, 1965; The Mistress of Falcon Hill, 1965; Dance in Darkness, 1965; Cliffside Castle, 1965; The Lily Pond, 1965; Marble Leaf, 1966, as The Marble Angel, 1970; Midday Moon, 1966; Knight in Red Armor, 1966; Nurse at Danger Mansion, 1966; Dark Villa, 1966; (as Cynthia Kavanaugh) Bride of Lenore, 1966; (as Cynthia Kavanaugh) The Deception, 1966; (as Helen Gray Weston) Mystic Manor, 1966; The Templeton Memoirs, 1966; This Ancient Evil, 1966; The Last of the Mansions, 1966; as Survivors of Darkness, 1969; (as Suzanne Somers) The Mists of Mourning, 1966; (as Helen Gray Weston) House of False Faces, 1967; House of Stolen Memories, 1967, as Mansion of Lost Memories, 1969; The Sevier Secrets, 1967; Screen Test for Laurel, 1967; Traitor's Road, 1967; House of Seven Courts, 1967; The Eagle's Nest, 1967; Mostly by Moonlight, 1968; Blue Devil Suite, 1968; Affair at Marrakesh, 1968; Candle in the Sun, 1968; Lady of the Shadows, 1968; Duet, 1968; Strange Paradise, 1969; Affair in Hong Kong, 1969; Voice in the Wind, 1969; The Carson Inheritance, 1969; The Tormented, 1969; The Curse of Mallory Hall, 1970; The Man from Yesterday, 1970; The Dark Stage, 1970; Emerald Hill, 1970; Willow Weep, 1970; Island of Evil (novelization of TV series), 1970; Raxl, Voodoo Princess (novelization of TV series), 1970; The Raging Waters, 1970; The Attic Rope, 1970; The Unearthly, 1970; Journey into Terror, 1971; Key Diablo, 1971; The House of Many Doors, 1971; The Bell, 1971; Diablo Manor, 1971; Witch's Castle, 1971; The Beaumont Tradition, 1971; The Lattimer Legend, 1971; Shadows of Tomorrow, 1971; (as Suzanne Somers) The Romany Curse, 1971; (as Angela Gray) The Ghost Dancers, 1971; (as Angela Gray) The Golden Packet, 1971; (as Angela Gray) The Lattimore Arch, 1971; (as Danielle Dorsett) Dueling Oaks, 1972; The Spanish Chapel, 1972; Conover's Folly, 1972; The House of Broken Dolls, 1972; The Lanier Riddle, 1972; Castle Morvant, 1972; Maya Temple, 1972; The Larrabee Heiress, 1972; Shadows from the Past, 1972; The House on Circus Hill, 1972; Dark Island, 1972; Witch's Island, 1972; (as Angela Gray) Blackwell's Ghost, 1972; The Stone House, 1973; The Duncan Dynasty, 1973; The Silent Halls of Ashenden, 1973; The Possession of Tracy Corbin, 1973; Hills of Fire, 1973; The Prisoner of Malville Hall, 1973; Jade Green, 1973; The Caldwell Shadow, 1973; Image of a Ghost, 1973; (as Suzanne Somers) The House on Thunder Hill, 1973; (as Suzanne Somers) Touch Me, 1973; (as Suzanne Somers) Until Death, 1973; (as Angela Gray) Ashes of Falconwyck, 1973; (as Angela Gray) The Watcher in the Dark, 1973; (as Angela Gray) Nightmare at Riverview, 1973; (as Angela Gray) Ravenswood Hall, 1973; (as Angela Gray) The Warlock's Daughter, 1973; The Apollo Fountain, 1974; Island of Bitter Memories, 1974; Child of Darkness, 1974; Ghost Song, 1974; The Two Worlds of Peggy Scott, 1974; The Exorcism of Jenny Slade, 1974; A Web of Peril, 1974; Illusion at Haven's Edge, 1975; The Possessed, 1975; The Guardian of Willow House, 1975; The Unlamented, 1975; The Tide Mill, 1975; Shadow of a Man, 1975; Marble Hills, 1975; Blackthorn, 1975; Whistle in the Wind, 1976; Night Shade, 1976; The Vineyard Chapel, 1976; Circle of Guilt, 1976; Juniper Hill, 1976; Portrait of a Witch, 1976; The Summer House, 1976; Terror of the Twin, 1976; Dark Heritage, 1976; Twilight at the Elms, 1976; Poison Flower, 1977; Nightfall, 1977; Wines of Cyprien, 1977; A Woman in Silk and Shadows, 1977; In the Shadows, 1978; The Lonely Place, 1978; Hermitage Hill,

1978; Perrine, 1978; The Magic Ring, 1978; Meg, 1979; The Cormac Legend, 1979; Yesterday's Evil, 1979; Veil of Treachery, 1979; The Purple and the Gold, 1980; Legend of Death, 1980; Valley of the Shadows, 1980; Bridal Black, 1980; House of Silence, 1980; Nicola, 1980; (as Angela Gray) The Love of the Lion, 1980; Sisters of Valcour, 1981; Saratoga, 1981: Monte Carlo, 1981; For Love and Valcour, 1983; Crisis at Valcour, 1985. Add: 6107 Village 6, Camarillo, Calif. 93010, U.S.A.

DANIELS, Elizabeth Adams. American, b. 1920. Biography. Prof. Emeritus of English, Vassar Coll., Poughkeepsie, N.Y. (Instr., 1948–54; Asst. Prof., 1954–60; Assoc. Prof., 1960–65; Prof. from 1965); Vassar Historian, since 1986. *Publs:* Jessie White Mario: Risorgimento Revolutionary, 1973; Posseduta dall'angelo, 1977; (ed.) Vassar: The Remarkable Growth of a Man and his College, 1984; Main to Mudd, 1987. Add: Vassar Coll., Poughkeepsie, N.Y. 12601, U.S.A.

DANIELS, John S. *See* **OVERHOLSER**, Wayne D.

DANIELS, Mary. American, b. 1937. Animals/Pets. Feature Writer and Columnist, Chicago Tribune, since 1969. *Publs:* Morris: An Intimate Biography: The Nine Lives of Morris the Cat, 1974; Cat Astrology, 1976. Add: Chicago Tribune, 435 N. Michigan Ave., Chicago, Ill. 60611, U.S.A.

DANIELS, Max. *See* **GELLIS**, Roberta.

DANIELS, Norman. *See* **LEE**, Elsie.

DANIELS, Norman A. Also writes as William Dale, Peter Grady, Harrison Judd, and Robert Wallace. American. Novels/Short stories, Mystery/Crime/Suspense. *Publs:* mystery novels—The Mausoleum Key, 1942; (as William Dale) John Doe—Murderer, 1942; Mistress on a Deathbed, 1952; The Captive, 1959; The Deadly Game, 1959; Lady for Sale, 1960; Lover, Let Me Live, 1960; Some Die Running, 1960; Spy Hunt, 1960; Suddenly by Shotgun, 1961; (as Harrison Judd) Shadow of a Doubt, 1961; The Detectives (novelization of TV series), 1962; Something Burning, 1963; Arrest and Trial (novelization of TV series), 1963; The Hunt Club, 1964; The Missing Witness (novelization of TV play), 1964; Overkill, 1964; The Secret War, 1964; Spy Ghost, 1965; (as Robert Wallace) Murder under the Big Top, 1965; Operation K, 1965; Operation N, 1965; The Baron of Hong Kong, 1967; A Killing in the Market, 1967; Operation T, 1967; Operation VC, 1967; Baron's Mission to Peking, 1968; The Magnetic Man (novelization of TV play), 1968; The Kono Diamond, 1969; Moon Express (novelization of TV play), 1969; The Tape of a Town, 1970; One Angry Man, 1971; Operation S-L, 1971; Meet the Smiths (novelization of TV play), 1971; License to Kill, 1972; Chase (novelization of TV series), 1974; other novels—Colt Law, 1956; (as Peter Grady) Two Trails to Bannack, 1956; (as Peter Grady) The Marshal of Winter Gap, 1962; County Hospital, 1963; Showdown, 1963; Dr. Kildare's Finest Hour (novelization of TV play), 1963; Dr. Kildare's Secret Romance (novelization of TV play), 1963; Jennifer James, R.N., 1963; Gun Empire, 1963; The Hunt Club, 1964; Battalion, 1965; Moments of Glory, 1965; Strike Force, 1965; Dark Desire, 1967; The Tarnished Scalpel, 1968; The Deadly Ride, 1968; Law of the Lash, 1968; Master of Wyndward, 1969; Jubal, 1970; Slave Rebellion, 1970; Voodoo Slave, 1970; Wyndward Passion (includes Law of the Lash and Master of Wyndward), 1978; Wyndward Fury, 1979; Wyndward Glory, 1981. Add: 6107 Village 6, Camarillo, Calif. 93010, U.S.A.

DANIELS, Olga. *See* **SINCLAIR**, Olga Ellen.

DANIELS, Robert (Vincent). American, b. 1926. History. Prof. Emeritus of History, Univ. of Vermont, Burlington, since 1988 (joined faculty, 1956). State Senator, Vermont, 1973–82. *Publs:* The Conscience of the Revolution, 1960; (ed.) A Documentary History of Communism, 1960, 1984; The Nature of Communism, 1962; Understanding Communism, 1964; Russia, 1964; (ed.) The Stalin Revolution, 1965; (ed.) Marxism and Communism, 1966; Studying History, 1966; Red October, 1967, 1984; (ed.) The Russian Revolution, 1972; Europe Talking, 1975; (co-ed.) The Dynamics of Soviet Politics, 1976; Russia: The Roots of Confrontation, 1985; Is Russia Reformable?, 1988; Year of the Heroic Guerilla, 1989. Add: 195 S. Prospect St., Burlington, Vt., U.S.A.

DANIELS, Sarah. British, b. 1957. Plays. Writer-in-Residence, Royal Court Theatre, London, 1983–84. *Publs:* Masterpieces, 1984, 1986; Ripen Our Darkness and The Devil's Gateway, 1986; Neaptide, 1986; Byrthrite, 1987; The Gut Girls, 1989. Add: c/o Judy Daish Assocs., 83 Eastbourne Mews, London W2 6LQ, England.

DANN, Colin (Michael). British, b. 1943. Children's fiction, Natural history. *Publs:* (with C. Guthrie) Looking at Insects, 1978; The Animals of Farthing Wood, 1979; In the Grip of Winter, 1981; Fox's Feud, 1982; Fox Cub Bold, 1983; The Siege of White Deer Park, 1985; Ram of Sweetriver, 1986. Add: 76 Bardsley Close, Croydon, Surrey, England.

DANN, Jack. American, b. 1945. Science fiction/Fantasy, Poetry. Freelance writer and lectr. Instr. of writing and science fiction, Broome Community Coll., Binghamton, N.Y., 1972; Asst. prof., Cornell Univ., Ithaca, N.Y., 1973. Managing Ed., SFWA Bulletin, 1970–75. *Publs:* (ed.) Wandering Stars: An Anthology of Jewish Fantasy and Science Fiction, 1974; (ed. with Gardner Dozois) Future Power, 1976; (ed. with George Zebrowski) Faster Than Light: An Anthology of Stories about Interstellar Travel, 1976; (ed.) Immortal, 1977; Starhiker (novel), 1977; Christs and Other Poems, 1978; Timetipping (short stories), 1980; (ed. with G. Dozois) Aliens!, 1980; Junction, 1981; The Man Who Melted, 1984; (ed. with G. Dozois) Unicorns! 1984; (ed. with G. Dozois) Magicats! 1984; (ed. with G. Dozois) Bestiary!, 1985; (ed. with G. Dozois) Mermaids!, 1986; (ed. with G. Dozois) Sorcerers!, 1986; (ed. with Jeanne Dann) In the Field of Fire, 1987; (ed. with Dozois) Demons!, 1987; Hellhounds, 1988. Add: 825 Front St., Binghamton, N.Y. 13905, U.S.A.

DANTO, Arthur C(oleman). American, b. 1924. Philosophy. Johnsonian Prof. of Philosophy, Columbia Univ., NYC (joined faculty, 1951). Art Critic, The Nation Mag., NYC. *Publs:* Analytical Philosophy of History, 1965; Nietzsche as Philosopher, 1965; Analytical Philosophy of Knowledge, 1968; What Philosophy Is, 1968; Mysticism and Morality, 1972; Analytical Philosophy of Action, 1974; Jean-Paul Sartre, 1975; The Transfiguration of the Commonplace, 1981; Narration and Knowledge, 1985; The Philosophical Disenfranchisement of Art, 1986; The State of the Art, 1987; Connections to the World, 1989. Add: 420 Riverside Dr., New York, N.Y. 10025, U.S.A.

DANZIGER, Paula. American, b. 1944. Children's fiction. Formerly a teacher in a junior high sch. *Publs:* The Cat Ate My Gymsuit, 1974; The Pistachio Prescription, 1978; Can You Sue Your Parents for Malpractice?, 1979; There's a Bat in Bunk Five, 1980; The Divorce Express, 1982; It's an Aardvaak-Eat-Turtle World, 1985; This Place Has No Atmosphere, 1986; Remember Me to Harold Square, 1987. Add: c/o Delacorte Press, 1 Dag Hammarskjold Plaza, 245 E. 47th St., New York, N.Y. 10017, U.S.A.

DARBY, Catherine. *See* PETERS, Maureen.

DARBY, (Sir Henry) Clifford. British, b. 1909. Geography. Emeritus Prof. of Geography, Univ. of Cambridge, since 1976 (Lectr., 1931–45; Prof., 1966–76). Prof. of Geography, Liverpool Univ., 1945–49, and Univ. Coll., Univ. of London, 1949–66. *Publs:* (ed. and contrib.) An Historical Geography of England before AD 1800, 1936; The Medieval Fenland, 1940; The Draining of the Fens, 1940; (gen. ed. and contrib.) The Domesday Geography of England, 7 vols., 1952–77; (ed. with H. Fullard) The Library Atlas, 15th ed. 1981; (with H. Fullard) The New Cambridge Modern History Atlas, 1970; (ed. with H. Fullard) The University Atlas, 22nd ed. 1983; (ed. and contrib.) A New Historical Geography of England, 1973; The Changing Fenland, 1983. Add: 60 Storey's Way, Cambridge CB3 ODX, England.

DARBY, John. British, b. 1940. History, Social sciences (general). Dir. of the Centre for the Study of Conflict since 1984, and Prof. of Social Administration and Policy, since 1984, Univ. of Ulster, Coleraine (Lectr. in Social Admin., 1974–84). Research-Publications Officer, Northern Ireland Community Relations Commn., 1971–74. *Publs:* Conflict in Northern Ireland, 1976; Violence and the Social Services in Northern Ireland, 1978; Northern Ireland: Background to the Conflict, 1983; Dressed to Kill: Cartoonists and the Northern Irish Conflict, 1983; Intimidation and the Control of Conflict in Northern Ireland, 1986. Add: Social Admin. Dept., Univ. of Ulster, Coleraine, Northern Ireland.

DARCY, Clare. American. Historical/Romance/Gothic. *Publs:* Georgina, 1971; Cecily, or A Young Lady of Quality, 1972; Lydia, or Love in Town, 1973; Victoire, 1974; Allegra, 1975; Lady Pamela, 1975; Regina, 1976; Elyza, 1976; Cressida, 1977; Eugenia, 1977; Gwendolen, 1978; Rolande, 1978; Letty, 1980; Caroline and Julia, 1982. Add: c/o Walker & Co., 720 Fifth Ave., New York, N.Y. 10019, U.S.A.

D'ARCY, Margaretta. Plays/Screenplays, Autobiography. Founder-member, Galway Women's Entertainment, 1982, and Women's Scéal

Radio, 1986. *Publs:* Tell Them Everything (prison memoirs), 1981; with John Arden—The Happy Haven, 1961; Business of Good Government, 1962; Ars Longa Vita Brevis, 1964; The Royal Pardon, 1966; Friday's Hiding, 1967; The Hero Rises Up, 1969; The Island of the Mighty, 1974; The Non-Stop Connolly Show, 1975; Vandaleur's Folly, 1978; The Little Grey Home in the West, 1979; Whose Is the Kingdom?, 1988; Awkward Corners, 1988. Add: c/o Margaret Ramsay 14a Goodwins Court, London WC2N 4LL, England.

D'ARCY, Pamela. *See* ROBY, Mary Linn.

DARDIS, Thomas (Anthony). American, b. 1926. Film, Literature. Prof., John Jay Coll., NYC, since 1980. Assoc. Ed., Avon Books, NYC, 1952–55; Exec. Ed., 1955–60, and Ed.-in-Chief, 1960–72, Berkley Books, NYC. *Publs:* Some Time in the Sun, 1976; Keaton: The Man Who Wouldn't Lie Down, 1979; Harold Lloyd: The Man on the Clock, 1983; The Thirsty Muse, 1989. Add: 2500 Johnson Ave., New York, N.Y. 10463, U.S.A.

DARKE, Marjorie (Sheila). British, b. 1929. Children's fiction. Textile designer, John Lewis Partnership, London, 1951–54. *Publs:* Ride the Iron Horse, 1973; The Star Trap, 1974; Mike's Bike, 1974; A Question of Courage, 1975; What Can I Do?, 1975; The Big Brass Band, 1976; Kipper's Turn, 1976; My Uncle Charlie, 1977; The First of Midnight, 1977; A Long Way to Go, 1978; Kipper Skips, 1979; Carnival Day, 1979; Comeback, 1981; Tom Post's Private Eye, 1983; Messages: A Collection of Shivery Tales, 1984; Imp, 1985; The Rainbow Sandwich, 1989. Add: c/o Rogers Coleridge and White Ltd., 20 Powis Mews, London W11 1JN, England.

DARKE, Nick. British, b. 1948. Plays. Actor, Belfast, 1970; actor and dir., Victoria Theatre, Stoke-on-Trent, 1971–78. *Publs:* The Body, 1983; High Water (in Plays Introduction), 1984; Ting Tang Mine and Other Plays, 1987. Add: St. Julians, Sevenoaks, Kent TN15 0RX, England.

DARLING, Lois. American, b. 1917. Environmental science/Ecology, Natural history. Freelance writer and illustrator; work in permanent collection: Beinecke Library, Yale Univ. and Kerlan Collection, Univ. of Minnesota. Formerly, Staff Artist, Dept. of Paleontology, American Museum of Natural History, NYC., 1952–54. *Publs:* with Louis Darling—Before and After Dinosaurs, 1959; Sixty Million Years of Horses, 1960; The Science of Life, 1961; Bird, 1962; Turtles, 1962; Coral Reefs, 1963; The Sea Serpents Around Us, 1965; A Place in the Sun, 1968; Worms, 1972. Author/Illustrator—The Beagle: A Search for a Lost Ship, 1960; H.M.S. Beagle: Further Research or Twenty Years a-Beagling, 1977; H.M.S. Beagle 1820-1870: Voyages Summarized, Research and Reconstruction, 1984. Add: 4 Smith Neck Rd., Old Lyme, Conn. 06371, U.S.A.

DARNAY, Arsen. American. Science fiction/Fantasy, Environmental science/Ecology, Information Science/Computers, Mathematics/Statistics. *Publs:* (with William E. Franklin) The Role of Non-packaging Paper in Solid Waste Management 1966 to 1970, 1971; (with William E. Franklin) Salvage Markets for Materials in Solid Wastes, 1972; Recycling Assessment and Prospects for Success, 1972; A Hostage for Hinterland, 1976; The Karma Affair, 1978; The Siege of Faltara, 1978; The Purgatory Zone, 1981. Add: 259 McKinley, Grosse Pointe Farms, Mich. 48236, U.S.A.

DARNTON, Robert. American, b. 1939. History, Literature. Shelby Collum Davis Prof. of European History, Princeton Univ., New Jersey. *Publs:* Mesmerism and the End of the Enlightenment in France, 1968; The Business of Enlightenment: A Publishing History of the Encyclopédie, 1979; The Literary Underground of the Old Regime, 1982; The Great Cat Massacre and Other Episodes in French Cultural History, 1984. Add: Dept. of History, Princeton Univ., Princeton, N.J. 08540, U.S.A.

DARRELL, Elizabeth. Also writes as Emma Drummond, Eva Dane, and Edna Dawes. British. Romance/Historical fiction. *Publs:* (as Eva Dane) A Lion by the Mane, 1975; (as Eva Dane) Shadows in the Fire, 1975; (as Edna Dawes) Dearest Tiger, 1975; (as Edna Dawes) Pink Snow, 1975; (as Edna Dawes) A Hidden Heart of Fire, 1976; (as Emma Drummond) Scarlet Shadows, 1978; (as Edna Dawes) Fly with My Love, 1978; (as Eva Dane) The Vaaldorp Diamond, 1978; (as Emma Drummond) The Burning Land, 1979; The Jade Alliance, 1979; The Gathering Wolves, 1980; (as Emma Drummond) The Rice Dragon, 1980; (as Emma Drummond) Beyond All Frontiers, 1983; At the Going Down of the Sun, 1984; (as Emma Drummond) Forget the Glory, 1985; And in the Morning, 1986;

(as Emma Drummond) The Bridge of a Hundred Dragons, 1986; (as Emma Drummond) A Captive Freedom, 1987; (as Emma Drummond) Some Far Elusive Dawn, 1988; The Flight of the Flamingo, 1989. Add: c/o Gollancz Ltd., 14 Henrietta St., London WC2E 8QJ, England.

DARY, David Archie. American, b. 1934. History, Media, Social commentary/Phenomena. Prof. of Journalism, Univ. of Oklahoma, Norman, and Dir., Sch. of Journalism and Mass Communication, since 1989. Reporter and Ed., CBS News 1960–63, and Mgr. of Local News, NBC News 1963–67, Washington, D.C. Prof. of Journalism, Univ. of Kansas, Lawrence, 1969–89. Pres., Western Writers of America, 1989–90. *Publs:* Radio News Handbook, 1967, 1970; TV News Handbook, 1971; How to Write News for Broadcast and Print Media, 1973; The Buffalo Book, 1974; Tales of the Old-Time Plains, 1979; Cowboy Culture, 1981; True Tales of Old-Time Kansas, 1984; Entrepreneurs of the Old West, 1986; More True Tales of Old Time Kansas, 1987. Add: 1101 West 27th St., Lawrence, Kans. 66046, U.S.A.

DAS, D(eb) K(umar). Indian, b. 1935. Poetry, Philosophy. Dir., U.S. National Utilization Project for post-secondary education, Seattle, Wash., since 1972. Member, Mgmt. Staff, I.C.I., Calcutta, 1959–61; Teaching Asst., Univ. of Washington, Seattle, 1961–63; Instr., and Supt., S.O.I.C., Seattle, 1967–70; Deputy Dir., and Dir. of Research and Planning, State Bd. for Community Coll. Education, Seattle, 1970–72. *Publs:* The Night Before Us: Poems, 1960; Through a Glass Darkly: Poems, 1965; The Eyes of Autumn: An Experiment in Poetry, 1968; Navbharat Papers: A Political Programme for a New India, 1968; Freedom and Reality, parts I to VI, 1968; (trans.) Sankaracharya: A Discourse on the Real Nature of Self, 1970; The Fire Canto, 1970; The First Philosopher: Yajnravalka, 1971; The Labyrinths, 1971; (trans.) The Isa and Kena Upanisads, 1971; The Agony of Arjun and Other Essays, 1971; Svatvavada: Towards a Theory of Property, 2000 B.C.-1800 A.D.: An Essay in Three Parts, 1972; An Essay on the Forms of Individualism, 1973; What Final Frontier? or, The Future of Man in Space, 1973; Beginnings of Human Thought: The Rig Vedas, 1973; (trans.) On Exploring Reality: The Jabala and Paingala Upanisads, 1976; Always Once Was: Experiments in Metapoetics, 1977. Add: c/o Writers Workshop, 162–92 Lake Gardens, Calcutta 700045, India.

DAS, Kamala. Indian, b. 1934. Novels, Poetry. Poetry Ed., Illustrated Weekly of India, Bombay, 1971–72, 1978–79. *Publs:* Fifty Poems, 1965; The Descendents, 1967; The Old Playhouse, 1973; Driksakshi Panna (for children), 1973; My Story, 1976; A Doll for the Child Prostitute (stories), 1977; Alphabet of Lust (novel), 1977; Tonight This Savage Rite: The Love Poetry of Kamala Das and Pritish Nandy, 1979. Add: c/o K. Madhava Das, The Reserve Bank of India, Bombay 1, India.

DATHORNE, O(scar) R(onald). British, b. 1934. Novels/Short stories, Poetry, Literature. Prof. of English, Univ. of Miami, Coral Gables, Fla., since 1977. Assoc. Prof., Ahmadu Bello Univ., Zaria, 1959–63, and Univ. of Ibadan, 1963–66, Nigeria; Unesco Consultant to the Govt. of Sierra Leone, 1967–68; Prof. of English, Njala Univ. Coll., Univ. of Sierra Leone, 1968–69; Prof. of African Literature, Howard Univ., 1970; Prof. of Afro-American Literature, Univ. of Wisconsin, Madison, 1970–71; Prof. of English and Black Literature, Ohio State Univ., Columbus, 1971–74; Prof. of English, Florida Intnl. Univ. 1974–75; Prof. of English and Black Literature, Ohio State Univ., 1975–77. *Publs:* Dumplings in the Soup (novel), 1963; The Scholar Man (novel), 1964; (ed.) Caribbean Narrative, 1965; (ed.) Caribbean Verse, 1967; (ed. with W. Feuser) Africa in Prose, 1969; The Black Mind, 1975; African Literature in the Twentieth Century, 1976; Dark Ancestor, 1981; Dele's Child, 1985. Add: Dept. of English, Univ. of Miami, Coral Gables, Fla. 33124, U.S.A.

DAUBE, David. British, b. 1909. Law, Theology/Religion. Prof. of Law and Dir. of the Robbins Hebrew and Roman Collection, Univ. of California at Berkeley, 1970–81, now Emeritus. Hon. Prof. of History, Univ. of Konstanz, Germany, since 1966. Fellow, Caius Coll., Cambridge, 1938–46; Lectr. in Law, Univ. of Cambridge, 1946–51; Prof. of Jurisprudence, Univ. of Aberdeen, 1951–55; Regius Prof. of Civil Law, Univ. of Oxford and Fellow, All Souls Coll., Oxford, 1955–70. *Publs:* Shakespeare on Aliens Learning English, 1942; Studies in Biblical Law, 1947, 1969; (ed.) Background and Eschatology of the New Testament, 1955, 1964; The New Testament and Rabbinic Judaism, 1956, 1973; Forms of Roman Legislation, 1956; Defence of Superior Orders in Roman Law, 1956; (ed.) Studies in the Roman Law of Sale, 1958, 1977; Sin, Ignorance and Forgiveness in the Bible, 1960; The Exodus Pattern in the Bible, 1963; Suddenness and Awe in Scripture, 1964; The Sudden in the Scriptures, 1964; Collaboration with Tyranny in Rabbinic Law,

1965; He That Cometh, 1966; Roman Law, 1969; Legal Problems in Medical Advance, 1971; Gewaltloser Frauenwiderstand in Altertum, 1971; Civil Disobedience in Antiquity, 1972; Ancient Hebrew Fables, 1973; Wine in the Bible, 1975; Medical and Genetic Ethics, 1976; The Duty of Procreation, 1977; Typologie im Work des Flavius Josephus, 1977; (with B.S. Jackson) Ancient Jewish Law, 1981; Sons and Strangers, 1984; (with C. Carmichael) Witnesses in Bible and Talmud, 1986; Appeasement or Resistance and Other Essays on New Testament Judaism, 1987. Add: Sch. of Law, 225 Boalt Hall, Univ. of California, Berkeley, Calif. 94720, U.S.A.

DAUGHTREY, Anne Scott. American, b. 1920. Admin./Management, Business/Trade/Industry, Economics. Emeritus Prof. of Management, Old Dominion Univ., Norfolk, Va., since 1988 (Asst. Prof., 1959–63; Assoc. Prof., 1963–66; Prof., 1966–88). *Publs:* Basic Business and Economic Education, 1965, 3rd ed. (with Ristau) 1989; (with S.J. DeBrum, P. Haines and D. Malsbary) General Business for Economic Understanding, 11th ed. 1976, 12th ed. (with Ristau and DeBrum), 1981; (with Ristau and Eggland) Introduction to Business, 1985; (with B. Ricks) Contemporary Supervision: Managing People and Technology, 1989. Add: 1304 Harmott, Norfolk Va. 23509, U.S.A.

DAVENPORT, Guy (Mattison, Jr.) American, b. 1927. Short stories, Poetry, Literature, Translations. Prof. of English, Univ. of Kentucky, Lexington, since 1963. Contrib. Ed., National Review, since 1962. *Publs:* (trans.) Carmina Archolochi: The Fragments of Archilochos, 1964; (trans.) Sappho: Songs and Fragments, 1965; Flowers and Leaves (verse), 1966; Cydonia Florentia, 1966; Pennant Key-Indexed Guide to Homer's Iliad [and Odyssey], 2 vols., 1967; Do You Have a Poem Book on E.E. Cummings?, 1969; Jonathan Williams, Poet, 1969; Tatlin! (stories), 1974; Da Vinci's Bicycle (stories), 1979; (trans.) Archilochos, Sappho, Alkman, 1980; (trans.) Herakleitos and Diogenes, 1980; (trans.) The Mimes of Herondas, 1981; The Geography of the Imagination (essays), 1981; Eclogues (stories), 1981; Trois Caprices (stories), 1981; Cities on Hills (literary criticism), 1983; Apples and Pears (stories), 1984; Thasos and Ohio: Poems and Translations, 1985; Every Force Evolves a Form (essays), 1986; The Jules Verne Steam Balloon (stories), 1987. Add: Dept. of English, Univ. of Ky., Lexington, Ky. 40506, U.S.A.

DAVENPORT, John (Chester). British, b. 1938. Medicine/Health. Sr. Lectr. in Dental Prosthetics, Univ. of Birmingham, and Consultant, Birmingham Area Health Authority, since 1979 (Lectr. in Dental Prosthetics, Univ. of Birmingham, and Sr. Registrar, Birmingham Area Health Authority, 1966–79). In general dental practice, Cambridge, 1963–64; Sr. House Officer, 1964, and Registrar, 1965–66, Bristol Dental Sch. *Publs:* (with R.M. Basker and H.R. Tomlin) Prosthetic Treatment of the Edentulous Patient, 1976, 1983; A Colour Atlas of Removable Partial Dentures, 1988. Add: Dental Sch., St. Chad's Queensway, Birmingham B4 6NN, England.

DAVENPORT, Marcia (Gluck). American, b. 1903. Novels, Children's non-fiction, Autobiography/Memoirs/Personal, Biography. Copywriter in Philadelphia, 1924–27; Staff Member, The New Yorker mag., 1927–30; Music Critic, Theatre Guild Newsletter (later called Stage), 1930–38; Commentator for Salzburg and Metropolitan Opera broadcasts, 1936–37. *Publs:* Mozart (biography), 1932, 1956; Of Lena Geyer, 1936; 2nd U.K. ed. as Lena Geyer, 1949; The Valley of Decision, 1942; East Side, West Side, 1947; My Brother's Keeper, 1954; Garibaldi, Father of Modern Italy (juvenile), 1957; The Constant Image, 1960; Too Strong for Fantasy (autobiography), 1967. Add: c/o Brandt and Brandt, 1501 Broadway, New York, N.Y. 10036, U.S.A.

DAVENPORT, William H(enry). American, b. 1908. Social commentary/Phenomena. Instr., Carnegie Inst., Pittsburgh, Pa., 1931–35, and Smith Coll., Northampton, Mass., 1938; Asst. Prof. of English, 1938–42, Assoc. Prof., 1942–49, Prof., 1959–57, and Chmn. of Dept., 1955–57, Univ. of Southern Calif., Los Angeles; Prof. of English and Chmn., Dept. of Humanities and Social Sciences, 1957–68, and Prof. of Literature and Willard W. Keith Jr. Fellow in the Humanities, 1968 until retirement, Harvey Mudd Coll., Claremont, Calif. *Publs:* (ed.) Modern Omnibus, 1946; (ed.) Modern Exposition, 1946; (ed.) Dominant Types in British and American Literature, 1949; (ed.) Nine Modern American Plays, 1951; (ed.) Voices in Court, 1958; (ed.) The Good Physician, 1962; (ed.) Biography: Past and Present, 1965; (ed.) Engineering: Its Role and Function in Human Society, 1967; The One Culture, 1970; (ed.) Technology and Culture, 1972. Add: 616 Purdue Dr., Claremont, Calif. 91711, U.S.A.

DAVEY, Frank(land Wilmot). Canadian, b. 1940. Poetry, Literature. Assoc. Prof., then Prof., York Univ., Toronto, since 1970, and Chmn. of the Dept. of English, since 1985 (Coordinator of the Creative Writing Program, 1976–79). Gen. Ed., Quebec Translations series, since 1973; Member of the Editorial Bd., Coach House Press, Toronto, since 1975; Gen. Ed., New Canadian Criticism series, Talonbooks, Vancouver, since 1977. Lectr., 1963–66, and Asst. Prof., 1967–69, Royal Roads Military Coll., Victoria; Writer-in-Residence, Sir George Williams Univ., Montreal, 1969–70. Ed., Tish mag., Vancouver, 1961–63, and Open Letter mag., Toronto, 1965–82. *Publs:* D-Day and After, 1962; City of the Gulls and Sea, 1964; Bridge Force, 1965; The Scarred Hull, 1966; Four Myths for Sam Perry, 1970; Weeds, 1970; Five Readings of Olson's "Maximus" (criticism), 1970; Earle Birney (criticism), 1971; Griffon, 1972; King of Swords, 1972; L'An Trentiesme: Selected Poems 1961-1970, 1972; Arcana, 1973; The Clallam; or, Old Glory in Juan de Fuca, 1973; From There to Here: A Guide to English-Canadian Literature since 1960, 1974; (ed.) Tish 1-19, 1975; (ed.) Mrs. Dukes' Million, by Wyndham Lewis, 1977; War Poems, 1979; The Arches: Selected Poems, 1980; Louis Dudek and Raymond Souster (criticism), 1981; The Contemporary Canadian Long Poem, 1981; Capitalistic Affection!, 1982; Surviving the Paraphrase, 1983; Edward and Patricia, 1984; Margaret Atwood: A Feminist Poetics, 1984; The Louis Riel Organ and Piano Company, 1985; The Abbotsford Guide to India, 1986; Reading Canadian Reading, 1988. Add: 334 Stong Coll., York Univ., Downsview, Ont. M35 1P3, Canada.

DAVEY, Jocelyn. *See* **RAPHAEL,** Chaim.

DAVID, Elizabeth. British. Cookery/Gastronomy/Wine. *Publs:* A Book of Mediterranean Food, 1950; French Country Cooking, 1951; Italian Food, 1954; Summer Cooking, 1955; French Provincial Cooking, 1960; English Cooking, Ancient and Modern, vol. I: Spices, Salt and Aromatics in the English Kitchen, 1970; English Bread and Yeast Cookery, 1977; An Omelette and a Glass of Wine, 1984. Add: Penguin Books, Harmondsworth, Middx., England.

DAVID, Heather M. American, b. 1937. Military/Defence, Biography. Exec. Vice-Pres., Wagner & Baroody Public Affairs, Washington, D.C., since 1974. Assoc. Ed., Missiles and Rockets mag., 1959–67; Pentagon Corresp., Capital City Broadcasting Co., and Fairchild Publs., both 1967–70; Washington Bureau Chief, Electronics Design mag., 1972–74; Washington Corresp., Computer Decisions mag., and Laboratory Medicine mag., both 1973–74. *Publs:* Werner von Braun, 1963; Admiral Richover and the Nuclear Navy, 1969; Operation Rescue, 1971. Add: Route 2, Box 69, Leesburg, Va. 22075, U.S.A.

DAVIDSON, Alan Eaton. British, b. 1924. Cookery/Gastronomy/-Wine, International relations/Current affairs, Natural history. Managing Dir., Prospect Books Ltd., since 1980. Joined British Diplomatic Service, 1948; Counsellor and Head of Chancery, U.K. Delegation to NATO, 1968–71; Head of Defence Dept., FCO, 1972–73; Visiting Fellow, Centre for Contemporary European Studies, Univ. of Sussex, 1971–72; British Ambassador, Vientiane, Laos, 1973–75. *Publs:* Seafish of Tunisia and the Central Mediterranean, 1963; Snakes and Scorpions Found in the Land of Tunisia, 1964; Mediterranean Seafood, 1972; The Role of the Uncommitted European Countries in East/West Relations, 1972; Fish and Fish Dishes of Laos, 1974; Seafood of South East Asia, 1977; (with Jane Davidson) Dumas on Food, 1978; North Atlantic Seafood, 1979; (co-ed.) Traditional Recipes of Laos, 1981; On Fasting and Feasting, 1988; A Kipper with My Tea, 1988. Add: 45 Lamont Rd., London SW10, England.

DAVIDSON, Avram. American, b. 1923. Science fiction/Fantasy. Ed., Fantasy and Science Fiction mag., NYC, 1962–64. *Publs:* (with Ward Moore) Joyleg, 1962; Or All the Seas with Oysters (short stories), 1962; (ed.) Best from Fantasy and Science Fiction 12-14, 2 vols., 1963–65; Mutiny in Space, 1964; What Strange Stars and Skies (short stories), 1965; Rogue Dragon, 1965; Rork!, 1965; Masters of the Maze, 1965; The Enemy of My Enemy, 1966; Clash of Star-Kings, 1966; The Kar-Chee Reign, 1966; The Island under the Earth, 1969; The Phoenix and the Mirror; or, The Enigmatic Speculum, 1969; Peregrine: Primus, 1971; Strange Seas and Shores (short stories), 1971; Ursus of Prima Thule, 1973; The Enquiries of Dr. Eszterhazy (short stories), 1975; The Redward Edward Papers (short stories), 1978; The Best of Avram Davidson (short stories), 1979; Collected Fantasies of Avram Davidson, 1982; (ed.) Magic for Sale, 1983; Vergil in Averno, 1987. Add: c/o E.J. Carnell Literary Agency, Danescroft, Goose Lane, Little Hallingbury, Bishops Stortford, Herts. CM22 7RG, England.

DAVIDSON, Basil. British, b. 1914. Novels/Short stories, History, International relations/Current affairs, Travel/Exploration/Adventure, Biography. Hon. Fellow, Univ. of Birmingham. Paris Corresp., 1945–47,

and Chief Foreign Leader Writer, 1947–49, The Times, London; Special Corresp., New Statesman, London, 1949–53; Leader Writer, Daily Mirror, London, 1959–61. *Publs:* Partisan Picture, 1946; Highway Forty (novel), 1949; Germany: From Potsdam to Partition, 1950; Golden Horn (novel), 1952; Report on Southern Africa, 1952; Daybreak in China, 1953; (ed. with A. Ademola) The New West Africa, 1953; The African Awakening, 1954; The Rapids (novel), 1955; Turkestan Alive, 1957; Lindy (in U.S. as Ode to a Young Love), 1958; Old Africa Rediscovered, 1959; Black Mother: The African Slave Trade, 1961; (with Paul Strand) Tir a Mhurain: The Outer Hebrides, 1962; A Guide to African History, 1963; Which Way Africa?, 1964, 1971; The African Past, 1964; A History of West Africa to 1800, 1965; Africa: History of a Continent, 1966, rev. ed. as Africa in History: Themes and Outlines, 1968; The Andrassy Affair (novel), 1966; A History of Eastern and Central Africa to the Late 19th Century, 1967; The Africans: An Entry to Cultural History (in U.S. as The African Genius), 1969; The Liberation of Guiné, 1969; Discovering Our African Heritage, 1971; In the Eye of the Storm: Angola's People, 1972; Black Star: View of the Life and Times of Nkrumah, 1973; Can Africa Survive? Arguments Against Growth Without Development, 1974; (with Paul Strand) Ghana: An African Portrait, 1976; Discovering Africa's Past, 1978; Africa in Modern History, 1978 (in U.S., as Let Freedom Come); Special Operations Europe, 1980; The People's Cause, 1981; Modern Africa, 1982; The Story of Africa, 1984; The Fortunate Isles, 1989. Add: Old Cider Mill, N. Wootton, Somerset BA4 4HA, England.

DAVIDSON, Donald (Herbert). American, b. 1917. Philosophy. Slusser Prof., Univ. of California, Berkeley, since 1981. Asst. Prof. to Prof. of Philosophy, Stanford Univ., California, 1951–67; Prof. of Philosophy, 1967–70, Chmn. of Dept. of Philosophy, 1968–70, and Lectr. with rank of Prof., 1970–76, Princeton Univ., New Jersey; Prof. of Philosophy, Rockefeller Univ., New York, 1970–76; University Prof., Univ. of Chicago, 1976–81. *Publs:* (with Patrick Suppes) Decision Making: An Experimental Approach, 1957; (ed. with Jaakko Hintikka) Words and Objections: Essays on the Work of W.V. Quine, 1969, 1975; (with others) Essays in Honor of Carl G. Hempel, 1970; (ed. with Gilbert Harman) Semantics of Natural Language, 1972; (ed. with Gilbert Harman) The Logic of Grammar, 1975; Essays on Actions and Events, 1980; Inquiries into Truth and Interpretation, 1984. Add: Philosophy Dept., Univ. of California, Berkeley, Calif. 94720, U.S.A.

DAVIDSON, Eugene. American, b. 1902. History. Chmn., Conference on European Problems, Park Coll., Mo., since 1970, Honorary Pres. since 1987. Ed., Yale Univ. Press, New Haven, Conn., 1931–59; Ed., Modern Age, 1960–70; Former Pres., Foundn. for Foreign Affairs. *Publs:* The Death and Life of Germany, 1959; The Trial of the Germans, 1966; The Nuremberg Fallacy, 1973; The Making of Adolf Hitler, 1977. Add: 780 Riven Rock Rd., Santa Barbara, Calif. 93108, U.S.A.

DAVIDSON, Frank Geoffrey. Australian, b. 1920. Business/Trade/Industry, Economics. Emeritus Prof., La Trobe Univ., Bundoora, Vic., since 1985 (Prof. of Economics, 1966–85; Dean of Social Sciences, 1970–71; Dean of Economics, 1977–81). Asst. Secty., and subsequently First Asst. Secty., Commonwealth Dept of Labour, 1960–66. *Publs:* The Industrialization of Australia, 1957, 4th ed. 1969; (with B.R. Stewardson) Economics and Australian Industry, 1974, 1979. Add: Dept. of Economics, La Trobe Univ., Bundoora, Vic., Australia, 3083.

DAVIDSON, Jeffrey P. American, b. 1951. Business/Trade/Industry, Marketing. Full-time author. Dir., National Capital Speakers, and Washington Independent Writers; Vice-Pres., Inst. of Management Consultants, Washington, D.C.; Project Mgr., Profiles Inc., Vernon, Conn., 1975–77; Sr. project Mgr., Emay Corp., Washington, D.C., 1977–80; Vice-Pres., Marketing, IMR Systems, Falls Church, Va., 1980–84. *Publs:* (ed.) A Writer's Guide to Washington, 1983; (co-author) Reducing Energy Costs in Small Business, 1983; (with Richard A. Connor) Marketing Your Consulting and Professional Services, 1985; Marketing Your Business to the Fortune 500, 1986; Checklist Manager: The 8-Hour Manager, 1986; (with Richard A. Connor) Getting New Clients, 1987; (with Don Beveridge) The Achievement Challenge, 1987; Blow Your Own Horn, 1987; Avoiding the Pitfalls of Starting Your Own Business, 1988; Marketing on a Shoestring, 1988. Add: 3709 S. George Mason Dr., Suite 315E, Falls Church, Va. 22041, U.S.A.

DAVIDSON, Lionel. Also writes as David Line. British, b. 1922. Novels/Short stories, Mystery/Crime/Suspense, Children's fiction. *Publs:* The Night of Wenceslas, 1960; The Rose of Tibet, 1962; A Long Way to Shiloh (in U.S. as The Menorah Men), 1966; Making Good Again, 1968; Smith's Gazelle, 1971; The Sun Chemist, 1976; The Chelsea Murders (in U.S. as Murder Games), 1978; children's fiction, as David Line—

Soldier and Me, 1965; Run for Your Life, 1966; Mike and Me, 1974; (as Lionel Davidson) Under Plum Lake, 1980; Screaming High, 1985. Add: c/o Curtis Brown Ltd., 162-168 Regent St., London W1R 5TA, England.

DAVIDSON, Michael. American. b. 1944. Poetry, Literature. Research Historian since 1975, and Assoc. Prof. since 1981, Univ. of California at San Diego (Asst. Prof., 1976–81). Lectr., San Diego State Univ., 1973–76. *Publs:* Exchanges, 1972; Two Views of Pears, 1973; The Mutabilities and the Foul Papers, 1976; Summer Letters, 1976; Grillwork, 1980; Discovering Motion, 1980; The Prose of Fact, 1981; The Landing of Rochambeau, 1985; The World, the Flesh, and Myself, 1985; Analogy of the Ion, 1988. Add: 1220 Hygeia, Leucadia, Calif. 92024, U.S.A.

DAVIDSON, Mildred. British, b. 1935. Children's fiction, Literature. Sr. Lectr., in English, Middlesex Polytechnic, since 1973. Lectr., Baghdad Univ., 1964–65; Lectr. and Sr. Lectr. in English, Hendon Coll. of Technology, 1966–73. *Publs:* The Poetry Is in the Pity, 1972; The Last Griffin, 1974; Dragons and More, 1976; Link of Three, 1980. Add: c/o Chatto and Windus, 30 Bedford Sq., London WC1B 3RP, England.

DAVIDSON, Roger H(arry). American, b. 1936. Politics/Government, Public/Social administration. Prof. of Govt. and Politics, Univ. of Maryland, College Park, since 1987. Asst. Prof. of Govt., Dartmouth Coll., Hanover, N.H., 1962–68; Research Assoc., W.E. Upjohn Inst. for Employment Research, 1965–66; Scholar in Residence, National Manpower Policy Task Force, Washington, D.C., 1970–71; Staff member, Select Cttee. on Cttees., U.S. House of Reps., Washington, D.C., 1973–74; Prof. of Political Science, Univ of Calif., Santa Barbara, 1971–83 (Assoc. Prof., 1968–71; Chmn., 1976–78; Assoc. Dean, 1978–80); Sr. Specialist, American Govt. and Public Admin., Congressional Research Service, Library of Congress, Washington, D.C., 1980–88. *Publs:* (with D.M. Kovenock and M.K. O'Leary) Congress in Crisis: Politics and Congressional Reform, 1966; (with J.F. Bibby) On Capitol Hill: Studies in the Legislative Process, 1967, 1972; The Role of the Congressman, 1969; The Politics of Comprehensive Manpower Legislation, 1972; (with W.J. Oleszek) Congress Against Itself, 1977; (with S.P. Patterson and R.B. Ripley) A More Perfect Union, 1979, 4th ed. 1989; (with W.J. Oleszek) Congress and Its Members, 1981, 3rd ed. 1989; (with W.J. Oleszek) Governing, 1987. Add: 2141 LeFrak Hall, College Park, Md. 20742, U.S.A.

DAVIDSON, Sol M. American, b. 1924. Human relations, Social commentary/phenomena, Humor/Satire, Children's fiction. Pres., Davidson Assocs., mgmt. consultants, Des Moines, since 1976. Vice-Pres., and Dir. of Operations, Dial Finance Co., Des Moines, 1959–74 Exec. Asst., Northwestern Bell Telephone Co., Des Moines, 1974–76. *Publs:* Culture and the Comic Strips, 1959; The Cultivation of Imperfection, 1965; The Value of Friction, 1968; Philbert the Flea, 1989; Wild Jake Hiccup: America's First Frontiersman, 1989; Grandpa Sol's Not-for-Children Stories, 1989; Soloman and Eucalyptus, 1989. Add: Box 5115, Des Moines, Iowa 50306, U.S.A.

DAVIE, Donald (Alfred). British, b. 1922. Poetry, Language/Linguistics, Literature. Lectr. in English, 1950–57, and Fellow, Trinity Coll., 1954–57, Dublin Univ.; Lectr. in English, 1958–64, and Fellow of Gonville and Caius Coll., 1959–64, Cambridge Univ.; Prof. of English, 1964–68, and Pro-Vice-Chancellor, 1964–68, Univ. of Essex, Colchester; Prof. of English, Stanford Univ., California, 1968–78; Mellon Prof. of the Humanities, Vanderbilt Univ., Nashville, 1978–88. *Publs:* Purity of Diction in English Verse, 1952; (Poems), 1954; Brides of Reason (poetry), 1955; Articulate Energy: An Enquiry into the Syntax of English Poetry, 1955; A Winter Talent and Other Poems, 1957; (ed.) The Late Augustans: Longer Poems of the Later Eighteenth Century, 1958; The Forests of Lithuania (poetry adaptation), 1959; (ed.) Poems: Poetry Supplement, 1960; A Sequence for Francis Parkman, 1961; New and Selected Poems, 1961; The Heyday of Sir Walter Scott, 1961; (ed.) Poetics Poetyka, 1961; (ed.) Selected Poems of Wordsworth, 1962; The Language of Science and the Language of Literature, 1700-1740, 1963; Ezra Pound: Poet as Sculptor, 1964, 1976; Events and Wisdoms: Poems 1957-1963, 1965; (ed.) Russian Literature and Modern English Fiction: A Collection of Critical Essays, 1965; (trans.) The Poems of Dr. Zhivago, by Boris Pasternak, 1965; (ed. with A. Livingstone) Pasternak, 1969; Poems, 1969; Essex Poems 1963-1967, 1970, 1972; Thomas Hardy and British Poetry, 1972; Orpheus (poetry), 1974; The Shires: Poems, 1974; (ed.) The Augustan Lyric, 1974; The Poet in the Imaginary Museum: Essays of Two Decades, 1976; In the Stopping Train (poetry), 1976; A Gathered Church: The Literature of the English Dissenting Interest 1700-1930, 1978; (ed.) Collected Poems, by Yvor Winters, 1978; Trying to Explain, 1979; Three

for Water-Music (poems), 1981; (ed.) The New Oxford Book of Christian Verse, 1981; Dissentient Voice: Enlightenment and Christian Dissent, 1982; These the Companions: Recollections, 1982; Collected Poems: 1970-1983, 1984; Selected Poems, 1985; Czeslaw Milosz and the Insufficiency of Lyric, 1986; To Scorch or Freeze, 1988. Add: 4 High St., Silverton, Exeter EX5 4JB, England.

DAVIE, Ian. British, b. 1924. Plays, Poetry, Philosophy. Schoolmaster, Ampleforth Coll., York, since 1968. Head of English Dept. Marlborough Coll., 1965–68. *Publs:* Piers Prodigal (poetry), 1961; A Play for Prospero: Shakespearean Parable, 1965; Roman Pentecost (poetry), 1970; Theology of Speech, 1973; Jesus Purusha (Vedanta doctrine), 1986; Angkor Apparent (poetry), 1988. Add: Alba, Acklam, Malton, N. Yorks, England.

DAVIE-MARTIN, Hugh. *See* **McCUTCHEON,** Hugh.

DAVIES, Andrew (Wynford). British, b. 1936. Children's fiction, Plays/Screenplays. Teacher, St. Clement Danes Grammar Sch., 1958–61, and Woodberry Down Sch., 1961–63, both in London; Lectr., Coventry Coll. of Education and Univ. of Warwick, Coventry, 1963–87. *Publs:* children's fiction—The Fantastic Feats of Doctor Boox, 1972; Conrad's War, 1978; Marmalade and Rufus, 1979, as Marmalade Atkins' Dreadful Deeds, 1982; Marmalade Atkins in Space, 1982; Educating Marmalade, 1983; Danger! Marmalade at Work, 1984; Alfonso Bonzo, 1986; plays— Marmalade Atkins in Space, 1982; for adults—A Very Peculiar Practice, 1987; A Very Peculiar Practice: The New Frontier, 1988; Getting Hurt, 1989. Add: 21 Station Rd., Kenilworth, Warwicks. CV8 1JJ, England.

DAVIES, Christie. (John Christopher Hughes Davies). British, b. 1941. Criminology/Law enforcement/Prisons, Sociology, Humour/Satire. Prof. of Sociology, Univ. of Reading, since 1985 (Lectr. and Sr. Lectr., 1972– 81; Reader, 1981–85). Radio Producer, BBC Third Prog., 1967–69; Lectr. in Sociology, Univ. of Leeds, Yorks., 1969–72. *Publs:* (with Ruth Brandon) Wrongful Imprisonment, Mistaken Convictions and Their Consequences, 1973; (with Russell Lewis) The Reactionary Joke Book, 1973; Permissive Britain: Social Change in the 60s and 70s, 1975; Welsh Jokes, 1978; (with Rajeev Dhavan) Censorship and Obscenity, 1978; Jokes Are about Peoples, 1989. Add: Dept. of Sociology, Univ. of Reading, Whiteknights, Reading, Berks. RG6 2AA, England.

DAVIES, Daniel R. American, b. 1911. Education. Pres., Davies-Brickell Assocs. Ltd., Tucson, since 1972. Teacher and Head, English Dept., Forty Four High Sch., Pennsylvania, 1934–44; Asst. Supt. of Schs., Briarcliff, N.Y., 1944–45; Prof. of Education, Teachers Coll., Columbia Univ., NYC, 1946–62; Visiting Lectr., Univ. of Arizona, Tucson, 1961–64; Vice-Pres. and Dir. of Research, Croft Educational Services, Inc., 1965– 71. *Publs:* (with W.S. Elsbree) Instructional Personnel Record, 1945; (with W.F. Hosler) The Challenge of School Board Membership, 1949; The School Board Member in Action, 1949; (with E. Prestwood) Practical School Board Procedures, 1951; (with K. Herrold) The Dynamics of Group Action (8 vols.), 1954–56; (with V. Anderson) Patterns of Educational Leadership, 1956; (with H.M. Brickell) Davies-Brickell System for School Board Policy Making and Administrative Regulations, 1957; 6th ed. 1987; (with R.T. Livingston) You and Management, 1958; The Administrative Internship, 1962; (with M. Handlong) Teaching of Art, 1962; (with J.T. Greer and F. Hall) Recruiting Teachers, 1967; (with J.B. Deneen) New Patterns for Catholic Education, 1968; (with H.M. Brickell) Davies-Brickell System for School Board Policy Making, 1968; (with C.D. Armistead) In-Service Education, 1975. Add: San Jose Sq. #11, Bisbee, Ariz. 85603, U.S.A.

DAVIES, David Margerison. British, b. 1923. Medicine/Health. Ed., Adverse Drug Reactions and Acute Poisoning Review, since 1982; Hon. Lectr., Univ. of Newcastle upon Tyne; Ed., Adverse Drug Reaction Bulletin, since 1966. Consultant Physician, Shotley Bridge Gen. Hosp., Consett, Co. Durham, 1962–86; Dir., Northern Regional Clinical Pharmacology Unit, 1977–86. Prof. of Clinical Pharmacology, Chinese Univ. of Hong Kong, 1986–88. *Publs:* (co-author) Antibiotic and Sulphonamide Therapy, 1959; Medicine Today, 1961; Medicine as a Career, 1962; (ed.) Textbook of Adverse Drug Reactions, 1977, 3rd ch. 1985. Add: 79 Queens Rd., Consett, Co. Durham DH8 0BW, England.

DAVIES, E(benezer) T(homas). British, b. 1903. Education, Theology/Religion. Retired clergyman; Examining Chaplain to the Bishop of Monmouth since 1952; Consultant Archivist to the Church of Wales, and Canon of Monmouth, since 1953. Hon., Ed., Historical Soc. of the Church of Wales, 1953–73. *Publs:* The Political Ideas of Richard Hooker, 1945; Episcopacy and the Royal Supremacy in the Church of

England in the Sixteenth Century, 1950; Education and Schools in Monmouthshire to 1870, 1953; (ed.) The Story of the Church in Glamorgan, 1962; An Ecclesiastical History of Monmouthshire: Part I, 1953; Religion and the Industrial Revolution in South Wales, 1963; Religion and Society in Wales in the Nineteenth Century. Add: 11 Ty Brith Gardens, Usk, Gwent, Wales.

DAVIES, Horton (Marlais). American, b. 1916. Literature, Theology/Religion. Prof. Emeritus, Princeton Univ., N.J., since 1984 (Prof. of Religion, 1956–59; Putnam Prof., 1959–84). Prof. and Dean, Faculty of Divinity, Rhodes Univ., Grahamstown, S. Africa, 1946–53. Sr. Lectr., and Head of Dept., Mansfield and Regent's Park Colls., Oxford Univ., 1953–56. Publs: The English Free Churches, 1952, 1964; Christian Deviations, 1954, 4th rev. ed. 1974; A Mirror of the Ministry in Modern Novels, 1959; Worship and Theology in England, 5 vols., 1961–75; (with H. Davies) Sacred Art in a Secular Century, 1978; (with M.-H. Davies) Holy Days and Holidays, 1982; Catching the Conscience, 1985; Like Angels on a Cloud, 1985. Add: 120 McCosh Circle, Princeton, N.J. 08544, U.S.A.

DAVIES, Hunter. British. Novels, Children's fiction, Travel, Biography. Journalist, Sunday Times, London, 1960–84; Columnist, Punch, 1979–89; Presenter, Bookshelf, BBC, 1983–86. Publs: Here We Go Round the Mulberry Bush, 1966, screenplay, 1967; The Other Half, 1966; The New London Spy, 1966; The Beatles, 1968; The Rise and Fall of Jake Sullivan, 1969; I Knew Daisy Smuten, 1970; A Very Loving Couple, 1971; The Glory Game, 1972; Body Charge, 1972; A Walk Along the Wall, 1974; George Stephenson, 1975; The Creighton Report, 1976; The Sunday Times Book of Jubilee Year, 1977; A Walk Around the Lakes, 1979; The Book of British Lists, 1980; William Wordsworth, 1980; The Grades, 1981; Father's Day, 1981; A Walk Along the Tracks, 1982; Green Britain: A Celebration, 1982; Flossie Treacle's Fur Coat, 1982; A Walk Round London's Parks, 1983; The Joy of Stamps, 1983; The Good Guide to the Lakes, 1984; Flossie Teacake Strikes Back, 1984; Come On Ossie, 1985; The Grand Tour, 1986; Ossie Goes Supersonic, 1986; The Good Quiz Book to the Lakes, 1987; Back in the USSR, 1987; Beatrix Potter's Lakeland, 1988; Saturday Night, 1989. Add: 11 Boscastle Rd., London NW5, England.

DAVIES, John Gordon. British, b. 1919. Theology/Religion. Emeritus Prof., Univ. of Birmingham, since 1986 (joined faculty, 1948; Lectr. to Reader, 1950–60; Edward Cadbury Prof. and Head of Dept. of Theology, 1960–86). Dir., Inst. for the Study of Worship and Religious Architecture, 1962–86. Publs: The Theology of William Blake, 1948; The Origin and Development of Early Christian Church Architecture, 1952; Daily Life in the Early Church, 1952; Daily Life of Early Christians, 1953; Social Life of Early Christians, 1954; The Spirit, the Church and the Sacraments, 1954; He Ascended into Heaven: A Study in the History of Doctrine, 1958; Members One of Another: Aspects of Koinonia, 1958; (with G. Cope and T. Tytler) An Experimental Liturgy, 1959; The Making of the Church, 1960; Intercommunion, 1961; The Architectural Setting of Baptism, 1962; God's Will and Gift, 1962; Holy Week: A Short History, 1963; The Early Christian Church, 1965; A Select Liturgical Lexicon, 1965; Worship and Mission, 1966; Dialogue with the World, 1967; The Early Christian Church, 1967; The Secular Use of Church Buildings, 1968; (ed.) A Dictionary of Liturgy and Worship, 1972; Every Day God: Encountering the Holy in World and Worship, 1973; Christians, Politics and Violent Revolution, 1976; New Perspectives on Worship Today, 1978; Temples, Churches, and Mosques, 1982; Liturgical Dance, 1984; (ed.) New Westminster Dictionary of Liturgy and Worship, 1986; Pilgrimage Yesterday and Today, 1988. Add: 28 George Rd., Birmingham B15 1PJ, England.

DAVIES, John Tasman. British, b. 1924. Engineering, Sciences. Prof., since 1960, and Research Prof. of Chemical Engineering, since 1983, Univ. of Birmingham (Head of Dept., 1960–83). Lectr. in Chemical Engineering, Univ. of Cambridge, 1955–60. Publs: (co-author) Interfacial Phenomena, 1963; The Scientific Approach, 1965, 1973; Turbulence Phenomena, 1972. Add: Dept. of Chemical Engineering, Univ. of Birmingham, Birmingham B15 2TT, England.

DAVIES, L(eslie) P(urnell). Also writes as Leslie Vardre. British, b. 1914. Novels/Short stories, Mystery/Crime/Suspense. Former sub-postmaster, optician and tobacconist. Publs: The Paper Dolls, 1964; Man Out of Nowhere (in U.S. as Who Is Lewis Pinder?), 1965; The Artificial Man, 1965; Psychogeist, 1966; The Lampton Dreamers, 1966; (in U.K. as Leslie Vardre) Tell It to the Dead (in U.S. as The Reluctant Medium), 1966; Twilight Journey, 1967; (in U.K. as Leslie Vardre) The Nameless Ones (in U.S. as A Grave Matter), 1967; The Alien, 1968; Dimension

A, 1969; Stranger to Town, 1969; Genesis Two, 1969; The White Room, 1969, Adventure Holidays Ltd., 1970; The Shadow Before, 1970; Give Me Back Myself, 1971; The Silver Man, 1972; What Did I Do Tomorrow?, 1972; Assignment Abacus, 1975; Possession, 1976; The Land of Leys, 1979; Morning Walk, 1983. Add: Apt. K-1, Edificio Alondra, El Botanico, Puerto de la Cruz, Tenerife, Canary Islands.

DAVIES, Mansel Morris. British, b. 1913. Chemistry, Physics, Sciences. Emeritus Prof. of Chemistry, Univ. of Wales at Aberystwyth, since 1978 (Sr. Lectr., 1955–65; Reader, 1965–69; Prof., 1969–78). Publs: Outline of the Development of Science, 1948; (with Rhiannon Davies) Hanes Datblygiad Gwyddoniaeth, 1948; The Physical Principles of Gas Liquefaction and Low Temperature Rectification, 1959; Electrical and Optical Aspects of Molecular Behaviour, 1965; (ed. and contrib.) Infra-Red Spectroscopy, 1963; (ed. and contrib.) Dielectric Properties and Molecular Behaviour, 1969; (ed. and contrib.) Relaxation Processes, 1970; (ed.) Specialist Progress Reports: Dielectrics and Related Studies, vol. I 1972, vol. II 1974, vol. III 1978. Add: 14 Marine Terr., Criccieth LL52 0EF, North Wales.

DAVIES, Margaret (Constance). British, b. 1923. Novels/Short stories, Literature. Prof. of French, Univ. of Reading, since 1974 (Lectr., 1964–70; Reader in French Studies, 1970–74). Publs: Two Gold Rings, 1958; Colette, 1961; Apollinaire, 1964; Une Saison en Enfer, 1974. Add: Dept. of French Studies, Univ. of Reading, Whiteknights, Reading, Berks. RG6 2AA, England.

DAVIES, Martin (Brett). British, b. 1936. Social work, Sociology. Prof. of Social Work, Univ. of East Anglia, Norwich, since 1979 (Dir. of Social Work Prog., 1975–79). Ed., Social Work Monographs, since 1982. Research Officer, Home Office, London 1964–71; Sr. Lectr., Univ. of Manchester, 1971–75. Publs: Probationers in Their Social Environment, 1969; Financial Penalties and Probation, 1970; Social Enquiry Reports and the Probation Service, 1973; An Index of Social Environment, 1973; Social Work in the Environment, 1974; Prisoners of Society, 1974; Support Systems in Social Work, 1977; The Essential Social Worker, 1980, 1985; Towards a Classification of Unemployment, 1986; Skills, Knowledge and Qualities in Probation Practice, 1988. Add: Sch. of Economic and Social Studies, Univ. of East Anglia, Norwich, England.

DAVIES, Nigel. British, b. 1920. Anthropology/Ethnology, Archaeology/Antiquities, History. Conservative M.P. (U.K.) for Epping, 1950–51. Publs: The Aztecs, 1973; The Toltecs, 1977; Voyagers to the New World, 1979; The Toltec Heritage, 1980; Human Sacrifice, 1981; The Ancient Kingdoms of Mexico, 1983; The Rampant God, 1984; The Aztec Empire, 1987. Add: Sonora 75, Colonia Chapultepec, Tijuana, Mexico.

DAVIES, Norman. British, b. 1939. History, International Relations. Prof., School of Slavonic and East European Studies, Univ. of London, since 1971. Research Fellow, St. Antony's Coll., Oxford, 1969–71. Publs: White Eagle, Red Star, 1972, 1983; Poland Past and Present: Select Bibliography of Works in English, 1976; God's Playground: A History of Poland, 2 vols., 1981; Heart of Europe: A Short History of Poland, 1984. Add: Sch. of Slavonic and East European Studies, Senate House, Malet St., London WC1E 7HU, England.

DAVIES, P(aul) C(harles) W(illiam). British, b. 1946. Astronomy, Physics. Prof. of Theoretical Physics, Univ. of Newcastle upon Tyne, since 1980. Visiting Fellow, Inst. of Theoretical Astronomy, Cambridge Univ., 1970–72; Lectr. in Mathematics, King's Coll., Univ. of London, 1972–80. Publs: The Physics of Time Asymmetry, 1974, 1977; Space and Time in the Modern Universe, 1977; The Runaway Universe, 1978; in paperback as Stardoom, 1979; the Forces of Nature, 1979, 1986; Other Worlds, 1980; The Search for Gravity Waves, 1980; The Edge of Infinity, 1981; (with N.D. Birrell) Quantum Fields in Curved Space, 1982; The Accidental Universe, 1982; God and the New Physics, 1983; Superforce, 1984; Quantum Mechanics, 1984; (ed. with J.R. Brown) The Ghost in the Atom, 1987; The Cosmic Blueprint, 1987; Fireball, 1987 (ed. with J.R. Brown) Superstrings: A Theory of Everything?, 1988; (ed.) The New Physics, 1989. Add: Dept. of Physics, The University, Newcastle upon Tyne, England.

DAVIES, Piers Anthony David. New Zealander, b. 1941. Plays, Screenplays, Poetry. Barrister and Solicitor, Jordan, Smith & Davies, Auckland (qualified 1965). Chmn., Short Film Fund, New Zealand Film Commn., since 1987. Publs: East and Other Gong Songs, 1967; (with Peter Weir) Life and Flight of Rev. Buck Shotte (screenplay), 1969; Day Trip from Mount Meru, 1969; (with Peter Weir) Homesdale (screenplay), 1971; (with Peter Weir) The Cars That Ate Paris (screenplay), 1973;

Diaspora, 1974; Bourgeois Homage to Dada, 1974; (ed.) Central Almanac, 1974; Skin Deep (screenplay), 1978; R.V. Huckleberry Finn (video documentary), 1979; Olaf's Coast (documentary), 1982; Jetsam, 1984; The Lamb of God (screenplay), 1985. Add: 16 Crocus Pl., Remuera, Auckland 5, New Zealand.

DAVIES, Robert William. British, b. 1925. Economics. Dir. 1963–79, and Prof. of Soviet Economic Studies since 1965, Centre for Russian and East European Studies, Univ. of Birmingham (Research Fellow 1956–59; Lectr. 1959–62; Sr. Lectr. 1962–63). *Publs:* The Development of the Soviet Budgetary System, 1958; (with E.H. Carr) Foundations of a Planned Economy 1926-1929, vol. I, 1969; (with E. Zaleski and others) Science Policy in the U.S.S.R., 1969; (co-ed.) The Technological Level of Soviet Industry, 1977; (ed.) The Soviet Union, 1978, 1989; The Socialist Offensive: The Collectivization of Soviet Agriculture, 1929-1930, 1980; The Soviet Collective Farm 1929-1930, 1980; (ed.) Soviet Investment for Planned Industrialisation 1929-37, 1984; (co-ed.) Materials for a Balance of the Soviet National Economy 1928-30, 1985; (ed.) E.H. Carr's What Is History?, 2nd ed., 1986; The Soviet Economy in Turmoil 1929-1930, 1989; Soviet History in the Gorbachev Revolution, 1989. Add: Centre for Russian and East European Studies, Univ. of Birmingham, Birmingham 15, England.

DAVIES, Robertson. Canadian, b. 1913. Novels/Short stories, Plays Screenplays, Literature, Theatre. Prof. of English and Master of Massey Coll, Univ. of Toronto, Ont., 1963–81, now Emeritus Prof. Actor and Teacher, Old Vic Theatre Co., London, 1938–40, Literary Ed., Saturday Night, 1940–42; Ed., 1942–58, and Publr., 1958–68, Peterborough Examiner. *Publs:* Shakespeare's Boy Actors, 1939; Shakespeare for Young Players, 1942; The Diary of Samuel Marchbanks, 1947; The Table Talk of Samuel Marchbanks, 1949; Eros at Breakfast and Other Plays, 1949; Fortune My Foe (play), 1949; At My Heart's Core (play), 1950; Tempest Tost (novel), 1951; A Masque of Aesop (play), 1952; (with Tyrone Guthrie) Renown at Stratford, 1953; (with Tyrone Guthrie) Twice Have the Trumpets Sounded, 1954; A Jig for the Gypsy (play), 1954; Leaven of Malice (novel), 1954; (with Tyrone Guthrie) Thrice the Brinded Cat Hath Mew'd, 1955; A Mixture of Frailties (novel), 1958; A Voice from the Attic, 1960; The Personal Art, 1961; A Masque of Mr. Punch (play), 1963; Samuel Marchbanks' Almanack, 1967; Stephen Leacock, 1970; Feast of Stephen (anthology), 1970; Fifth Business (novel), 1970; Hunting Stuart and Other Plays, 1972; The Manticore (novel), 1972; World of Wonders (novel), 1975; Question Time (play), 1975; One Half of Robertson Davies, 1977; The Enthusiasms of Robertson Davies, 1979; Robertson Davies: The Well-Tempered Critic, 1981; The Rebel Angels (novel), 1981; High Spirits: A Collection of Ghost Stories, 1982; The Mirror of Nature (lecture), 1983; What's Bred in the Bone (novel), 1985; The Papers of Samuel Marchbanks, 1985; The Lyre of Orpheus (novel), 1988. Add: Massey Coll., 4 Devonshire Pl., Toronto, Ont. M5S 2E1, Canada.

DAVIES, Rupert E(ric). British, b. 1909. Theology/Religion. Methodist Minister of Religion, since 1935; Co-Ed., The History of the Methodist Church in Great Britain, since 1954; Joint Ed., Wesley's Works, Abingdon Press, since 1972. Chaplain of Kingswood Sch., Bath, 1935–47; Principal, Wesley Coll., Bristol, 1967–73; Pres. Methodist Conference, 1970–71. *Publs:* The Problem of Authority in the Continental Reformers, 1946; Reading Your Bible, 1948; (ed. with R.N. Flew) The Catholicity of Protestantism, 1950; Praying Together, 1952; (ed.) An Approach to Christian Education, 1956; (ed.) John Scott Lidgett, 1957; The Sunday School Today; A Colony of Heaven; Studies in I Corinthians; Methodism, 1963, 3rd. ed. 1985; (co-ed.) The History of the Methodist Church in Great Britain, 4 vols., 1965–88; (ed.) I Believe in God, 1968; Religious Authority in an Age of Doubt, 1968; A Christian Theology of Education, 1975, 1986; What Methodists Believe, 1977; The Church in Our Times, 1979; (ed.) The Testing of the Churches 1932-1982, 1983; The Church of England Observed, 1985; (with M. Morgan) Will You Walk a Little Faster?, 1985; Making Sense of the Creeds, 1987. Add: 6 Elmtree Dr., Bishopsworth, Bristol BS13 8LY, England.

DAVIES, Walter Merlin. British, b. 1910. Theology/Religion. Warden, St. Hilda's Retreat House, Northcote, Auckland, since 1977. Canon of Auckland Cathedral; Hon. Adviser, Friends of F.D. Maurice. Bristol Diocesan Dir. of Religious Education, 1946–49; Vicar of Berkswich, Staffs., 1949–59; Vicar of Avonside, 1959–74, Archdeacon of Akaroa and Ashburton, 1959–69, and of Sumner, 1969–74, Diocese of Christchurch; Dir. of Post Ordination Training, Diocese of Christchurch, 1959–69; Warden, St. John's Coll., Auckland, 1973–77. *Publs:* An Introduction to F.D. Maurice's Theology, 1964; Priorities in Praying, 1984. Add: 20 Queen St., Northcote, Auckland 9, New Zealand.

DAVIN, Dan(iel Marcus). British, b. 1913. Novels/Short stories, History, Literature. Deputy Secty. to Delegates of Oxford Univ. Press, 1970–78 (Jr. Asst. Secty., 1946–48; Asst. Secty., Clarendon Press, 1948–69). Emeritus Fellow of Balliol Coll., Oxford. *Publs:* Cliffs of Fall, 1945, For the Rest of Our Lives, 1947; The Gorse Blooms Pale, 1947; Introduction to English Literature, 1947; Roads from Home, 1949; Crete, 1953; (ed.) New Zealand Short Stories, 1953; (ed.) Katherine Mansfield's Short Stories, 1953; The Sullen Bell, 1956; (with W.K. Davin) Writing in New Zealand: The New Zealand Novel, 1956; (ed.) English Short Stories of Today: Second Series, 1958; Katherine Mansfield in Her Letters, 1959; No Remittance, 1959; Not Here, Not Now, 1970; Brides of Price, 1972; Breathing Spaces, 1975; Selected Stories, 1981; (ed.) Short Stories from the Second World War, 1982; Closing Times, 1986; The Salamander and the Fire, 1987. Add: 103 Southmoor Rd., Oxford, England.

DAVINSON, Donald (Edward). British, b. 1932. Librarianship. Asst. Dir., Leeds Polytechnic, since 1985 (Lectr., 1962–68; Head of Sch. of Librarianship, 1968–85). Chmn., Council for National Academic Awards, Librarianship Bd., 1971–80, and Assn. of British Library and Information Science Schs., 1974–76. *Publs:* Periodicals: A Manual of Practice for Librarians, 1959; Commercial Information, 1964, 1964; Academic and Legal Deposit Libraries, 1969; The Periodicals Collection, 1969, 1978; (with A. Thompson) Technical College Libraries, 1971; Bibliographic Control, 1975, 1981; Theses and Dissertations, 1977; Reference Service, 1980; (with N. Roberts) Education for Information, 1985. Add: Meadowfields, Main St., S. Duffield, Yorks. Y08 7ST, England.

DAVIS, Allen F. American, b. 1931. History, Biography. Prof. of History, Temple Univ., Philadelphia, Pa., since 1968. Inst., Wayne State Univ., Detroit, Mich., 1959–60; Assoc. Prof. of History, Univ. of Missouri, Columbia, 1960–68. Exec. Secty., American Studies Assn., 1972–77; Visiting Prof., Univ. of Texas at Austin, 1983. Pres., American Studies Assn., 1989–90. John Adams Chair, Univ. of Amsterdam. *Publs:* (with J. Cooke and R. Daly) March of American Democracy, vol. 5, 1965; (ed. with H. Woodman) Conflict and Consensus in American History, 1966, 7th ed., 1988; Spearheads for Reform, 1967, 1982; (ed. with M. McCree) Eighty Years at Hill House, 1969; American Heroine: The Life and Legend of Jane Addams, 1973; (ed. with M. Haller) The Peoples of Philadelphia, 1973; (with J. Watts) Generations, 1974, 1983; (ed.) Jane Addams on Peace, War and International Understanding, 1976; (ed.) For Better or Worse, 1981, (co-author) Still Philadelphia, 1983; (co-author) The American People, 1986, 1990; (co-author) Philadelphia Stories, 1988; (co-author) One-Hundred Years at Hull House, 1989. Add: 1730 Delancy Place, Philadelphia, Penn. 19103, U.S.A.

DAVIS, Burke. American, b. 1913. Novels/Short stories, Children's non-fiction, History, Biography. Ed., Feature Writer and Sports Ed., Charlotte News, N.C., 1937–47; Reporter, Baltimore Evening Sun, Md., 1947–52; Reporter, Greensboro News, N.C., 1951–60; Writer and Historian, Colonial Williamsburg, Va., 1960–78. *Publs:* Whisper My Name, 1949; The Ragged Ones, 1951; Yorktown, 1952; They Called Him Stonewall, 1954; Gray Fox, 1956; Roberta E. Lee, 1956; Jeb Stuart, The Last Cavalier, 1957; To Appomattox, 1959; Our Incredible Civil War, 1960; Marine!, 1961; The Guilford Courthouse-Cowpens Campaign, 1962; America's First Army, 1962; Appomattox: Closing Struggle of the Civil War, 1963; The Summer Land, 1965; (co-author) Rebel Raider, 1966; The Billy Mitchell Affair, 1967; A Williamsburg Galaxy, 1967; (co-author) The World of Currier & Ives, 1968; Get Yamamoto, 1969; Yorktown: The Winning of American Independence, 1969; Billy Mitchell Story, 1969; The Campaign That Won America: Yorktown, 1970; Heroes of the American Revolution, 1971; Jamestown, 1971; Thomas Jefferson's Virginia, 1971; Amelia Earhart, 1972; Biography of a Leaf, 1972; Three for Revolution, 1975; Biography of a Kingsnake, 1975; George Washington and the American Revolution, 1975; Newer and Better Organic Gardening, 1976; Biography of a Fish Hawk, 1976; Black Heroes of the American Revolution, 1976; Old Hickory: A Life of Andrew Jackson, 1977; Mr. Lincoln's Whiskers, 1978; Sherman's March, 1980; The Long Surrender, 1985; The Southern Railway, 1985; War Bird: The Life and Times of Elliott White Springs, 1986. Add: c/o Harold Matson Co., 276 Fifth Ave., New York, N.Y. 10001, U.S.A.

DAVIS, Christopher. American, b. 1928. Novels, Plays. Teacher of writing, Bryn Mawr Coll., Pennsylvania, since 1977. *Publs:* Lost Summer, 1958; First Family, 1959; A Kind of Darkness, 1962; Belmarch, 1964; Sad Adam-Glad Adam (children's fiction), 1966; The Shamir of Dachau, 1966; Ishmael, 1967; A Peep into the 20th Century, 1971; The Producer (theatre), 1972; The Sun in Mid-Career, 1975; Suicide Note, 1977; Waiting for It (on the death penalty), 1980; Private Territory (play),

1984; A Peep into the 20th Century (play), 1988; Dog, Horse, Rat, 1990. Add: c/o Curtis Brown, 10 Astor Pl., New York, N.Y. 10003, U.S.A.

DAVIS, David Brion. American, b. 1927. History, Literature. Sterling Prof. of History, Yale Univ., New Haven, Conn., since 1978 (Prof. and Farnum Prof., 1969–78). Ernest I. White Prof. of History, Cornell Univ., Ithaca, N.Y. 1963–69; Harold Vyvyan Harmsworth Prof., Oxford Univ., 1969–70; Chair in American Civilization, Ecole de Hautes Etudes en Sciences Sociales, Paris, 1980–81. *Publs:* Homicide in American Fiction, 1957; (ed.) Ante-Bellum Reform, 1967; The Problem of Slavery in Western Culture, 1967; The Slave Power Conspiracy and the Paranoid Style, 1969; (ed.) The Fear of Conspiracy, 1971; The Problem of Slavery in the Age of Revolution, 1975; (co-author) The Great Republic, 1977, 1980; (ed.) Antebellum American Culture, 1979; Slavery and Human Progress, 1984; From Homicide to Slavery: Studies in American Culture, 1986; Slavery in the Colonial Chesapeake, 1986. Add: Dept. of History, Yale Univ., New Haven, Conn. 06520, U.S.A.

DAVIS, David (Howard). American, b. 1941. Politics/Government. Assoc. Prof. of Political Science, Univ. of Wyoming, Laramie. Ed., Social Science Journal, since 1986. Member of Staff, Environmental Protection Agency, 1973–74; Asst. Prof. of Political Science, Rutgers Univ., New Jersey, 1971–77; Assoc. Prof. of Government, Cornell Univ., Ithaca, N.Y., 1977–78; Member of Staff, Congressional Research Service, Library of Congress, 1979–80; Deputy Asst. Secty. of Interior, Energy and Minerals, Washington, D.C., 1980–81. *Publs:* How the Bureaucracy Makes Foreign Policy, 1972, 1978; Energy Politics, 1974; 3rd ed. 1982. Add: 1422 Sublette St., Laramie, Wyo. 82070, U.S.A.

DAVIS, Dick. British, b. 1945. Poetry, Translations. Teacher in Italy, Greece and Iran, 1970–78. *Publs:* (with Clive Wilmer and Robert Wells) Shade Mariners, 1970; In the Distance, 1975; Seeing the World, 1980; (ed.) The Selected Writings of Thomas Traherne, 1980; Wisdom and Wilderness: The Achievement of Yvor Winters, 1983; Hold'em Poker Bible, 1983; What the Mind Wants, 1984; The Covenant, 1984; (trans.) The Little Virtues, by Natalia Ginzburg, 1985; (ed. with David Williams) New Writing from the North, 1988. Add: c/o Anvil Press Poetry, 69 King George St., London SE10 8PX, England.

DAVIS, Dorothy Salisbury. American, b. 1916. Mystery/Crime/-Suspense, Historical/Romance/Gothic. Pres., 1956–57, and Exec. Vice Pres., 1976–79, Mystery Writers of America. *Publs:* The Judas Cat, 1949; The Clay Hand, 1950; A Gentle Murderer, 1951; A Town of Masks, 1952; Men of No Property, 1956; Death of an Old Sinner, 1957; (ed.) A Choice of Murders, 1958; A Gentleman Called, 1959; Old Sinners Never Die, 1959; The Evening of the Good Samaritan, 1961; Black Sheep White Lamb, 1963; The Pale Betrayer, 1965; Enemy and Brother, 1966; (with J. Ross) God Speed the Night, 1968; Where the Dark Streets Go, 1969; (ed.) Crime Without Murder, 1970; Shock Wave, 1972; The Little Brothers, 1973; A Death in the Life, 1976; Scarlet Night, 1980; Lullaby of Murder, 1984; Tales for a Stormy Night, 1985; The Habit of Fear, 1987. Add: Snedens Landing, Palisades, N.Y. 10964, U.S.A.

DAVIS, Douglas (Matthew). American, b. 1933. Architecture, Art. Artist and critic, NYC. Sr. Writer, Newsweek mag., NYC, since 1980 (Art Critic, 1966–77; Gen. Ed., 1977–80). Artistic Dir., Intnl. Network for the Arts, since 1976. *Publs:* Art and the Future, 1973; Artculture: Essays on the Post-Modern, 1977; Modern Redux, 1986. Add: 80 Wooster St., New York, N.Y. 10012, U.S.A.

DAVIS, Gerry. British. Science fiction/Fantasy. *Publs:* (with Kit Pedler) Mutant 59, The Plastic Eaters, 1971; Doctor Who and the Cybermen, 1974; (with Kit Pedler) Brainrack, 1974; (with Kit Pedler) The Dynostar Menace, 1975; Doctor Who and the Tenth Planet, 1976; Doctor Who and the Tomb of the Cybermen, 1978. Add: c/o W.H. Allen, 44 Hill St., London W1X 8LB, England.

DAVIS, Gita. See **ROSE,** Evelyn Gita.

DAVIS, Gordon. See **HUNT,** E. Howard.

DAVIS, Hope Hale. American. Short stories. Instr. in Writing, Radcliffe Seminars, since 1985. Ed., Consumers' Guide, Dept. of Agriculture, 1933–37. *Publs:* The Dark Way to the Plaza (short stories), 1968. Add: 1600 Massachusetts Ave., Cambridge, Mass. 02138, U.S.A.

DAVIS, Horace Bancroft. American, b. 1898. Economics, Industrial relations. Dean, Faculty of Social Sciences, Univ. of Guyana, Georgetown, 1963–65; Special Prof. of Economics, Hofstra Univ., Hempstead,

N.Y., 1966–71. *Publs:* Labor and Steel, 1934; NRA: Fascismo E Comunismo, 1934; Shoes: The Workers and the Industry, 1941; Nationalism and Socialism, 1967; Toward a Marxist Theory of Nationalism, 1978. Add: Box 226, Sandwich, Mass. 02563, U.S.A.

DAVIS, Jack (Leonard). Australian, b. 1917. Plays, Poetry. Stockman; dir., Aboriginal Centre, Perth, 1967–71; ed., Aboriginal Publs. Foundn., 1972–77; co-ed., Identity mag., 1973–79. Pres., Aboriginal Writers and Dramatists Assoc., 1980–84. *Publs:* The First-Born and Other Poems, 1970; Jagardoo: Poems from Aboriginal Australia, 1977; The Dreamers, and Kullark (Home) (plays), 1982; (co-ed.) Aboriginal Writing Today, 1985; No Sugar (play), 1986; Bununquis (play), 1988; John Pat and Other Poems, 1988; Moonli and the Leprechaun, 1989. Add: 22 Knutsford Ave., Rivervale, W.A. 6103, Australia.

DAVIS, John David. British, b. 1937. Psychology, Translations. Sr. Lectr., Dept. of Psychology, Univ. of Warwick, Coventry, since 1977; Practising Clinical Psychologist and Psychotherapist, Coventry Area Health Authority. Fellow in Medical Psychology, Langley Porter Neuropsychiatric Inst., Univ. of California Medical Sch. at San Francisco, 1966–67; Sr., Lectr. in Psychology, Oxford Polytechnic, England, 1968–69; Lectr., Dept. of Psychology, Univ. of Sheffield, 1969–77. *Publs:* (trans.) Mathematical Analysis: A Special Course by G. Ye. Shilov, 1965: The Interview as Arena: Strategies in Standardized Interviews and Psychotherapy, 1971. Add: Dept. of Psychology, Univ. of Warwick, Coventry CV4 7AL, England.

DAVIS, John Gilbert. British. Bacteriology, Chemistry. Consultant Bacteriologist and Chemist, Reading, since 1953. Former Head of Metabolism Section, National Inst. for Research in Dairying, Reading. *Publs:* A Dictionary of Dairying, 1950, 1955, supplementary vol. 1965; (with F.J. Macdonald) Richmond's Dairy Chemistry, 5th ed. 1953; Milk Testing, 1953, 1959; Laboratory Control of Dairy Plant, 1956; Cheese, 4 vols., 1965–76; Quality Control in the Food Industry, 1986; Dairy Microbiology, 1989. Add: 52 London Rd., Reading, Berks. RG1 5AS, England.

DAVIS, Julia. Also writes as F. Draco. American, b. 1900. Novels/Short stories, Plays/Screenplays, Children's non-fiction. *Publs:* Swords of the Vikings (children's non-fiction), 1928; Vaino (children's non-fiction), 1929; Mountains Are Free (children's non-fiction), 1930; Stonewall Jackson, 1932; Remember and Forget (children's non-fiction), 1937; Peter Hale, 1939; The Sun Climbs Slow, 1942; The Winds and the Grass, 1943; The Shenandoah, 1945; Cloud on the Land, 1951; (as F. Draco) The Devil's Church, 1951; (as F. Draco) Cruise with Death, 1952; Bridle the Wind, 1953; Eagle on the Sun, 1956; Legacy of Love, 1961; Ride with the Eagle, 1963; The Anvil (play), 1963; A Valley and a Song, 1963; Mount Up, 1967; Never Say Die, 1980. Add: 624 S. Mildred St., Charles Town, W. Va. 25414, U.S.A.

DAVIS, Keith. American, b. 1918. Administration/Management, Business/Trade/Industry. Emeritus Prof. of Mgmt., Arizona State Univ., Tempe, since 1980 (Prof., 1958–80). Personnel Specialist, Howard Hughes Industries, 1940–42; Assoc. Prof. of Mgmt., Univ. of Texas, 1946–51; Prof. of Mgmt., Indiana Univ., Bloomington, 1951–58. Consulting Ed., Series in Mgmt., McGraw-Hill Book Co., Inc., NYC, 1957–87. *Publs:* (with H.M. Cruickshank) Cases in Management, 1954, 3rd ed. 1962; (with John W. Newstrom) Human Behavior at Work, 1957; 8th ed., 1989; (with William C. Frederick and James E. Post) Business and Society, 1966, 6th ed. 1988; (ed.) The Challenge of Business, 1975; (with William B. Werther, Jr.) Personnel Management and Human Resources, 1981, 3rd ed., 1989. Add: 331 Aepli Dr., Tempe, Ariz. 85282, U.S.A.

DAVIS, Margaret (Thomson). British. Novels/Short stories. *Publs:* The Breadmakers, 1972; A Baby Might Be Crying, 1973; A Sort of Peace, 1973; The Prisoner, 1974; The Prince and the Tobacco Lords, 1976; Roots of Bondage, 1977; Scorpion in the Fire, 1977; The Dark Side of Pleasure, 1981; The Making of a Novelist, 1982; A Very Civilized Man, 1982; Light and Dark, 1984; Rag Woman, Rich Woman, 1987; Mothers and Daughters, 1988; Wounds of War, 1989. Add: c/o London Management, 235-241 Regent St., London W1A 2JT, England.

DAVIS, Martyn P(aul). British, b. 1929. Advertising/Public relations, Media. Head of Marketing Services, Coll., for the Distributive Trades, London, since 1984 (Head of Marketing and Advertising Studies, 1960–84); Trustee, Inter-Varsity Club. Publicity Controller, Buland Publishing Co., 1953–56; Assoc. Dir., Robert Brandon & Partners, 1956–58, and Sr. Exec., T. Booth Waddicor and Partners, 1958–60. *Publs:* (ed.) Impact Yellow Book, 1957; A Career in Advertising, 1963; Handbook for Media Representatives, 1967; The Effective Use of Advertising Media, 1980,

1985. Add: 10 Kildare Ct., Kildare Terr., London W2 5JU, England.

DAVIS, Michael Justin. British, b. 1925. Literature. Teacher, 1949–85, Head of English Dept., 1958–62, and Housemaster, 1962–75, Marlborough Coll., Wilts. *Publs:* (ed.) Tennyson: In Memoriam, 1956; (ed.) The Harrap Book of Humorous Prose, 1962; (ed.) Milton: Areopagitica and Of Education, 1963; (supervisory ed.) The Kennet Shakespeare, 1964; (ed.) Shakespeare: Macbeth, 1964; (ed.) Shakespeare: Twelfth Night, 1966; (ed.) Milton: Samson Agonistes, 1968; (ed. with Christopher Campling) Words for Worship (anthology), 1969; (ed.) Shakespeare: Hamlet, 1974; William Blake: A New Kind of Man, 1977; (ed.) More Words for Worship, 1980; (ed.) Alfred Williams: In a Wiltshire Village, 1981; (ed.) Alfred Williams: Round About Middle Thames, 1982; The Way to the Tree of Life, 1983; To the Cross, 1984; (ed.) Alfred Williams: Life in a Railway Factory, 1984; The Landscape of William Shakespeare, 1987. Add: Hyde Lodge, Hyde Lane, Marlborough, Wilts, SN8 1JN, England.

DAVIS, Mildred (B.). American, b. 1930. Mystery/Crime/Suspense. *Publs:* The Room Upstairs, 1948; They Buried a Man, 1953; The Dark Place, 1955; The Voice on the Telephone, 1964; The Sound of Insects, 1966; Strange Corner, 1967; Walk into Yesterday, 1967, as Nightmare of Murder, 1969; The Third Half, 1969; Three Minutes to Midnight, 1972; The Invisible Border, 1974; Tell Them What's-Her-Name Called, 1975; Scorpion, 1977; (with Katherine Davis) Lucifer Land (non-mystery novel), 1977. Add: Millertown Rd., Bedford, N.Y. 10506, U.S.A.

DAVIS, Ossie. American, b. 1917. Plays/Screenplays. Film dir., and stage, television and film actor. Writer and co-host, With Ossie and Ruby PBS-TV series, 1982. *Publs:* Purlie Victorious, 1961, with P. Rose and P. Udell as Purlie, 1970; Escape to Freedom, 1978; Langston: A Play, 1982. Add: The Artists Agency, 10000 Santa Monica Blvd., Suite 305, Los Angeles, Calif. 90067, U.S.A.

DAVIS, Patrick. British, b. 1925. Travel/Exploration/Adventure, Autobiography/Memoirs/Personal. Publs. Officer, London Sch. of Economics and Political Science, since 1964. *Publs:* A Child at Arms, 1970, 1986; An Experience of Norway, 1974. Add: 6 Mt. Harry Rd., Sevenoaks, Kent, England.

DAVIS, Patti. American, b. 1952. Novels. Actress. Daughter of former U.S. President, Ronald Reagan, and Nancy Davis Reagan. *Publs:* (with Maureen Strange Foster) Home Front, 1986. Add: c/o Crown Publishers, Inc., 225 Park Ave. S., New York, N.Y. 10003, U.S.A.

DAVIS, Ralph Henry Carless. British, b. 1918. History. Fellow and Tutor, Merton Coll., Oxford, 1956–70; Prof. of Medieval History, Univ. of Birmingham, 1970–84. Ed., History, 1968–78; Pres., The Historical Assn., 1979–82. *Publs:* The Kalendar of Abbot Samson of Bury St. Edmunds, 1954; A History of Medieval Europe, 1957; King Stephen, 1967; (ed. with H.A. Crome) Regesta Regum Anglo-Normannorum, vols. 3 and 4, 1968–69; The Normans and Their Myth, 1976; (jt. ed.) The Writing of History in the Middle Ages, 1981; The Medieval Warhorse, 1989. Add: 349 Banbury Rd., Oxford OX2 7PL, England.

DAVIS, Richard. British. Novels/Short stories, Literature. Critic and Columnist, Films and Filming, 1964–71; Story Ed., BBC Television, London, 1966–68. *Publs:* (ed.) Tandem Horror, 2-3, 1968–69; Viola, 1968; (ed.) Year's Best Horror Stories, 1-3, 1971–73; (ed.) Space 1-7, 1973–81; (ed.) Spectre, 1-4, 1973–77; (ed.) Science Fiction, 1-4, 1975–77; (ed.) Orbit Book of Horror Stories, 1, 1976; (ed. with Vincent Price) Price of Fear, 1976; (ed.) The John Pertwee Book of Monsters, 1978; Encyclopedia of Horror, 1981; Animal Ghosts, 1982. Add: 77 St. Quintin Ave., London W10, England.

DAVIS, Richard Whitlock. American, b. 1935. History. Prof. of History, Washington Univ., St. Louis, Mo., since 1973 (Assoc. Prof., 1969–73; Dept. Chmn., 1974–77). Supvr. in History, Christ's Coll., Cambridge, 1960–62; Instr., Univ. of Rhode Island, Kingston, 1962–64; Asst. Prof., Univ. of California at Riverside, 1964–69. Distinguished Visiting Prof., Christ's College, Cambridge, England, 1981–82. *Publs:* Dissent in Politics 1760-1830, 1971; Political Change and Continuity 1760-1885, 1972; Disraeli, 1976; The English Rothschilds, 1983. Add: Dept. of History, Washington Univ., St. Louis, Mo. 63130, U.S.A.

DAVIS, Robert Prunier. Also writes as Joe Brandon. American, b. 1929. Novels/Short stories, Plays/Screenplays. *Publs:* Day of the Painter (screenplay), 1961; Apes on a Tissue-Paper Bridge, 1963; Goodbye, Bates McGee, 1967; The Dingle War, 1968; (as Joe Brandon) Cock-

A-doodle-Dew, 1972; (as Joe Brandon) Paradise in Flames; The Pilot, 1976; Cat Five, 1977; The Divorce, 1980; Control Tower, 1981. Add: 2488 Pine Way Dr., Palm Beach, Fla., U.S.A.

DAVIS, Vincent. American, b. 1930. International relations/Current affairs, Politics/Government. Dir., and Patterson Chair Prof. of Intnl. Studies, Patterson Grad. Sch. of Diplomacy and Intnl. Commerce, Univ. of Kentucky, Lexington, since 1971. Faculty member, Princeton Univ., N.J., 1959–61, Dartmouth Coll., Hanover, N.H., 1961–62, and Grad. Sch. of Intnl. Studies, Denver Univ., Colo., 1962–69; Visiting Prof., Princeton Univ., N.J., 1969–70; Visiting Nimitz Chair Prof., U.S. Naval War Coll., 1970–71. Pres.-Elect and Pres., Intnl. Studies Assn., 1975–77. *Publs:* Postwar Defense Policy and the U.S. Navy 1943-46, 1966; The Admirals Lobby, 1967; (ed. with A.N. Gilbert) Basic Courses in International Relations, 1968; (ed. with J.N. Rosenau and M.A. East, and contrib.) The Analysis of International Politics, 1971; (ed. and contrib.) The Post-Imperial Presidency, 1980; (co-ed.) Reorganizing America's Defense: Leadership in War and Peace, 1985. Add: 3533 Gloucester Dr., Lexington, Ky. 40510, U.S.A.

DAVIS, Wayne Harry. American, b. 1930. Environmental science/Ecology, Zoology. Prof. of Zoology, Univ. of Kentucky, Lexington, since 1961. Research Assoc., Univ. of Minnesota, Minneapolis, 1957–59; Instr. in Biology, Middlebury Coll., Vermont, 1959–61. *Publs:* (with R.W. Barbour) Bats of America, 1969; (ed.) Reading in Human Population Ecology, 1971; (with R.W. Barbour) Mammals of Kentucky, 1974. Add: 130 Jesselin Dr., Lexington, Ky. 40503, U.S.A.

DAVIS, William. British, b. 1933. Business/Trade/Industry, Money/Finance, Travel. Ed. and Publisher of High Life, since 1973, and Chmn., Headway Publications, London, since 1977; also, Ed., and Publisher, Business Life, since 1986. On staff of the Financial Times, London, 1954–59; Ed., Investor's Guide, 1959–60; City Ed., Evening Standard newspaper, London, 1960–65; Financial Ed., The Guardian, London, 1965–68; Ed., Punch, London, 1968–77; Ed.-in-Chief, Financial Weekly, 1977–80. Presenter, Money Programme, BBC-TV, 1967–69. *Publs:* Three Years Hard Labour: The Road to Devaluation, 1968; Merger Mania, 1970; Money Talks, 1972; Have Expenses, Will Travel, 1975; It's No Sin to Be Rich, 1976; (ed.) The Best of Everything, 1980; Money in the 1980's, 1981; The Rich: A Study of the Species, 1982; Fantasy: A Practical Guide to Escapism, 1984; The Corporate Infighter's Handbook, 1984; Best Business Hotels: A World Guide, 1985; The Super Salesman's Handbook, 1986; The Business Innovators, 1987. Add: c/o Headway Publications, Athene House, 66-73 Shoe Lane, London EC4P 4AB, England.

DAVIS, W(illiam) Jackson. American, b. 1942. Environmental science/Ecology. Prof. of Biology and Brain and Cognitive Sciences, Univ. of California at Santa Cruz, since 1969. *Publs:* The Seventh Year: Industrial Civilization in Transition, 1979. Add: Dept. of Biology, Univ. of California at Santa Cruz, Santa Cruz, Calif. 95064, U.S.A.

DAVISON, Dennis. British, b. 1923. Plays, Literature, Translation. Sr. Lectr. in English, Monash Univ., Clayton, since 1964. Theatre Critic, and Book Reviewer, The Australian. Lectr. in English, Rhodes Univ., Grahamstown, South Africa, 1953–56; Sr. Lectr. in English, New England Univ., Armidale, N.S.W., 1957–64. *Publs:* (ed.) Andrew Marvell: Selected Poetry and Prose, 1952; The Poetry of Andrew Marvell, 1963; Dryden, 1968; W.H. Auden, 1970; (ed.) Restoration Comedies, 1970; (ed.) The Penguin Book of Eighteenth-Century English Verse, 1973; (trans.) Parisian Lady, by Becque, 1977; Come into the Garden, Maud (play), 1979; (trans.) A Month in the Country, by Turgenev, 1980; (trans.) Independence, by Scribe, 1980; Weekend Affair (play), 1981; (ed.) Reverses, by Marcus Clarke, 1985; Strawberry Punch (play), 1981; Happy Easter, Antigone! (play), 1982; Overnight Loan Only (play), 1984; Lord for a Week (play), 1984; The Third Lady Rutland (play), 1985; (ed.) A Daughter of Eve, by Marcus Clarke, 1985; One Russian Summer (play), 1985; (trans.) French Spoken Here (play, by Bernard), 1986; (ed.) Hedda Gabler (play, by Ibsen), 1987; (ed.) Miss Julie (play, by Strindberg), 1987; (ed.) Hazard (play, by Cooper), 1987; Miss Dresden's Revenge (play), 1987; Come Live with Me (play), 1987; Maid in Australia (play), 1988. Add: English Dept., Monash Univ., Clayton, Vic. 3168, Australia.

DAVISON, Geoffrey. Also writes as George Duncan. British, b. 1927. Mystery/Crime/Suspense, Adventure. *Publs:* The Spy Who Swopped Shoes; Nest of Spies; The Chessboard Spies; The Fallen Eagles; The Honourable Assassins; Spy Puppets; The Berlin Spy Trap, 1974; No Names on Their Grave, 1978; (as George Duncan) The Bloody Legionnaires, 1981. Add: 95 Cheviot View, Ponteland, Newcastle upon Tyne NE20 9BH, England.

DAVISON, Peter (Hubert). American, b. 1928. Poetry, Autobiography/Memoirs/Personal. Consulting Ed., Houghton Mifflin Co., Boston, since 1985; Poetry Ed., Atlantic Monthly mag., Boston, Mass., since 1972. Ed., Harcourt Brace, publrs., NYC, 1950–51 and 1952–55; Asst. to Dir., Harvard Univ. Press, Cambridge, Mass., 1955–56; Ed., Atlantic Monthly Press, Boston, 1956–85. *Publs:* The Breaking of the Day and Other Poems, 1964; The City and the Island: Poems, 1966; Pretending to Be Asleep: Poems, 1970; Dark Houses, 1971; Half Remembered: A Personal History, 1973; Walking the Boundaries: Poems 1957-1974, 1974; A Voice in the Mountain, 1977; (ed.) The Collected Poems of L.E. Sissman, 1978; (ed.) The World of Farley Mowat, 1980; Barn Fever and Other Poems, 1981; Praying Wrong: New and Selected Poems 1959-1984, 1984; The Great Ledge, 1989. Add: 70 River St., Boston, Mass. 02108. U.S.A.

DAWE, (Donald) Bruce. Australian, b. 1930. Short stories, Poetry. Sr. Lectr. in Literature, Inst. of Advanced Education, Darling Heights, Toowoomba. Formerly worked as labourer, gardener, and postman. *Publs:* No Fixed Address, 1962; A Need of Similar Name, 1965; An Eye for Tooth: Poems, 1968; Beyond the Subdivision: Poems, 1969; Heat Wave, 1970; Condolences of the Season, 1971; (ed.) Dimensions, 1974; Just a Dugong at Twilight, 1975; Sometimes Gladness: Collected Poems 1954-1978, 1978, 3rd ed. 1987; Over Here, Harv! and Other Stories, 1983; Towards Sunrise: Poems 1979-1986, 1986; (ed.) Speaking in Parables: A Reader, 1987. Add: 30 Cumming St., Toowoomba, Qld., Australia.

DAWES, Edna. *See* **DARRELL**, Elizabeth.

DAWES, Edward Naasson. Australian, b. 1914. Administration/Management, Law, Accounting. Practising Barrister at Law, 1939–58; Master, Equity Div., and Protective Div., Supreme Court of New South Wales, 1958–76. *Publs:* Dawes' Australian Proprietary and Private Companies Law and Management, 1955, consulting ed. 1964; (consulting ed.) Purvis on Proprietary Companies, 1973. Add: 108 Prince Alfred Parade, Newport, N.S.W., Australia 2106.

DAWIDOWICZ, Lucy S. American, b. 1915. History, International relations/Current affairs. Asst. to the Research Dir., Yivo Inst. for Jewish Research, NYC, 1940–46; Educational Officer, American Jewish Joint Distribution Cttee., Germany, 1946–47; Research Analyst, then Research Dir., American Jewish Cttee., NYC, 1949–69; Assoc. Prof. of History, 1969–74, Holder of the Paul and Leah Lewis Chair in Holocaust Studies, 1970–75, Prof. of Social History, 1974–78, and Holder of the Eli and Diana Z. Borowski Chair in Interdisciplinary Holocaust Studies, 1976–78, Yeshiva Univ., NYC. *Publs:* (with Leon J. Goldstein) Politics in a Pluralist Democracy, 1963; (ed., with Joshua A. Fishman) For Max Weinreich: Studies in Jewish Languages, Literature and Society, 1964; (ed.) The Golden Tradition: Jewish Life and Thought in Eastern Europe, 1967; The War Against the Jews, 1933-1945, 1975; (ed.) A Holocaust Reader, 1976; The Jewish Presence: Essays on Identity and History, 1977; The Holocaust and the Historians, 1981; On Equal Terms; Jews in America 1881-1981, 1982; From That Time and Place, 1989. Add: 200 W. 86th St., New York, N.Y. 10024, U.S.A.

DAWISHA, Adhid (Isam). Iraqi, b. 1944. International relations/Current affairs. Asst. Dir. of Studies, Royal Inst. of Intnl. Affairs, London, since 1979. Lectr. in Intnl. Relations, Lancaster Univ., 1974–76. *Publs:* Egypt in the Arab World: The Elements of Foreign Policy, 1976; Saudi Arabia's Search for Security, 1979; Syria and the Lebanese Crisis, 1980; Islam in Foreign Policy, 1983. Add: c/o Cambridge Univ. Press, Shaftesbury Rd., Cambridge CB2 2RU, England.

DAWSON, Elizabeth. *See* **GEACH**, Christine.

DAWSON, George Glenn. American, b. 1925. Economics. Emeritus Prof. of Economics and Dean, Empire State Coll., State Univ. of New York, Old Westbury, since 1975. Asst. Prof. 1959–64, Assoc. Prof. 1964–65, and Prof. and Head, Div. of Social Studies, and Dir., Center for Economic Education 1965–70; New York Univ., NYC; Ed., Economic Education Experiences of Enterprising Teachers, vols. 4-15, 1966–78. *Publs:* (ed.) Communism (readings), 1962; (ed.) Freedom (readings), 1962; (with R. McClain) Guide to Economics, 1963; Economics: Book One, 1965, Book Two, 1965; (with McClain) Economics for Businessmen and Investors, 1966; College Level Economics, 1968; Our Nation's Wealth, 1968; Foundations of the American Economy, 1969; (with S. Gordon and J. Witchel) The American Economy, 1969; (with Gordon) Introductory Economics, 1972, 6th ed. 1987; (with E. Prehn) Teaching Economics in American History, 1973, 1984; (with L. Leamer) Suggestions for a Basic Economics Library, 1973; (ed.) Economics and Our Community, 1973; (ed.) Government and the Economy, 1974. Add: 2292 Arby Ct., Bellmore, N.Y. 11710, U.S.A.

DAWSON, Jennifer. British. Novels/Short stories. Former social worker, teacher, and publisher's editor. *Publs:* The Ha-Ha, 1961; Fowler's Snare, 1963; The Cold Country, 1966; Strawberry Boy, 1976; Hospital Wedding (short stories), 1978; A Field of Scarlet Poppies, 1979; The Upstairs People, 1988; Judasland, 1989. Add: c/o Virago Press, 41 William IV St., London WC2N 4DB, England.

DAWSON, Linda. British, b. 1949. Children's fiction. Teacher, Guy's Hospital School, London, since 1979. Primary sch. teacher in Inner London, 1970–72, 1975–79; Teacher, American Intnl. Sch., Amsterdam, 1972–75. *Publs:* (with Terry Furchgott) Phoebe and the Hot Water Bottles, 1977. Add: c/o André Deutsch, 105 Great Russell St., London, WC1, England.

DAY, James F. American, b. 1917. Psychology, Sociology. Prof. Emeritus of Educational Psychology, Univ. of Texas, at El Paso, since 1982 (Prof., 1955–82). Dir. of Guidance, Visalia Coll., Calif., 1947–48; Instr., of Psychology, Stanford Univ., Calif., 1948; Dir. of Psychological Clinic, Eastern Washington State Coll., Cheney, 1949–50; Asst. Prof. of Psychology, Arizona State Univ., Tempe, 1950–51; Asst. Prof., San Francisco State Coll., Calif., 1952–54. *Publs:* Teacher Retirement in the United States, 1971; Migrant Education, 1975; Problems of the Mexican Border, 1976. Add: Box 91, Univ. of Texas at El Paso, El Paso, Tex. 79968, U.S.A.

DAY, John Robert. British, b. 1917. Transportation. Mgr., London Transport Collection of Historical Vehicles, since 1974 (Head, Technical Press Section, 1957–64; Sr. Asst. to Press Officer, 1964–74). Asst. Ed., The Railway Gazette, 1954–57. *Publs:* (with B.G. Wilson) Unusual Railways, 1957; (with B.K. Cooper) Railway Signaling Systems, 1958; (with B.K. Cooper) Railway Locomotives, 1960; More Unusual Railways, 1960; Railways of Southern Africa, 1962; Railways Under the Ground, 1963; The Story of London's Underground, 1963; Railways of Northern Africa, 1964; (with P. Duff and M. Hill) Transport Today and Tomorrow, 1967; Trains, 1969; The Story of the Victoria Line, 1969; The Last Drop, 1971; The Story of the London Bus, 1973; London's Trams and Trollybuses, 1977; Engines, 1980; Source Book of Underground Railways (London Transport) 2 vols., 1980–82. Add: c/o Ward Lock, 8 Clifford St., London W1X 1RB, England.

DAY, Michael Herbert. British, b. 1927. Archaeology/Antiquities. Prof. of Anatomy, United Medical and Dental Schs., St. Thomas's Campus, London, since 1972. Sr. Lectr. in Anatomy, 1964–69, and Reader in Physical Anthropology, 1969–72, Middlesex Hosp. Medical Sch., London. *Publs:* Guide to Fossil Man, 1965, 1967, 1977, 1986; (ed.) Human Evolution, 1973. Add: Div. of Anatomy, United Medical and Dental Schs., St. Thomas's Campus, London SE1 7EH, England.

DAY, Robert P. American, b. 1941. Westerns/Adventure. *Publs:* The Last Cattle Drive, 1977; The Four Wheel Drive Quartet, 1986. Add: c/o Washington Coll., Chestertown, Md. 21620, U.S.A.

DAY, (Sir) Robin. British, b. 1923. Communications Media, Autobiography/Memoirs/Personal. With B.B.C. television since 1959, specialising in political interviews and reports (Introducer of current affairs prog., Panorama, 1967–73). Pres., Oxford Union Soc., 1950; called to the Bar, 1952; Information Asst., British Embassy Press Office, Washington, 1953–54; Freelance Broadcaster and Journalist, 1954–55, B.B.C. Radio Talk Producer, 1955; Newscaster and Parliamentary Corresp., ITV News, 1955–59. *Publs:* Television: A Personal Report, 1961; The Case for Televising Parliament, 1964; Day by Day: A Dose of My Own Hemlock, 1975. Add: c/o B.B.C. TV Studios, Lime Grove, W12, England.

DAY, Stacey B. American (born British), b. 1927. Novels/Short stories, Plays/Screenplays, Poetry, Medicine/Health, Sociology. Pres., Intnl. Foundn. for Biosocial Development and Human Health. Former Conservator, and Head, Bell Museum of Pathobiology; former Assoc. Prof. of Pathology and Laboratory Medicine, Univ. of Minnesota Medical Sch., Minneapolis; former Prof., Cornell Univ. Medical Coll., NYC, Univ. of Calabar (Nigeria), Univ. of Arizona, and Meharry Medical Coll., Nashville; and former Member and Head, Biosciences Communications and Medical Education, Sloan Kettering Inst., NYC. Ed.-in-Chief, Biosciences Communication, Karger, Basel, Switzerland, 1975–80. *Publs:* Collected Lines, 1966; By the Waters of Babylon, 1966; American Lines, 1967; The Music Box, 1967; Rosalita, 1968; Poems and Etudes, 1968; The Idle Thoughts of a Surgical Fellow, 1968; Edward Stevens: Gastric Physiologist, Physician and American Statesman, 1969; Bellechasse, 1970; (with B.G. MacMillan and W.A. Altmeier) Curling's Ulcer: An Experiment of Nature, 1971; Ten Poems and a Letter from America, 1971; (with R.A. Good) Membranes and Viruses in Immunopathology, 1972; (ed.) Death and Attitudes Towards Death, 1972; (ed.) Ethics in Medicine in a Changing Society, 1973; Tuluak and Amaulik: Dialogues on Death and Mourning with the Innuit Eskimo of Point Barrow, Alaska, 1974; (ed.) Trauma: Clinical and Biological Aspects, 1975; (with R.A. Good and J. Yunis) Molecular Pathology, 1975; (ed.) Communication of Scientific Information, 1975; (series ed. with R.A Good) Comprehensive Immunology, 1975; East of the Navel and Afterbirth: Reflections and Song Poetry from Rapa Nui (Easter Island), 1976; Cancer Invasion and Metastasis: Biologic Mechanisms and Therapy, 1977; The American Biomedical Network: Health Care Systems in America, Present and Future, 1978; A Companion to the Life Sciences, vol. I, 1978; Health Communications, 1979; (with J. Taché and Hans Selye) Cancer, Stress, and Death, 1979, 1986; (ed.) Readings in Oncology, 1980; Integrated Medicine, 1980; Biopsychosocial Health, 1981; The Biopsychosocial Imperative: Understanding the Biologos and General Systems Approach to Biocommunications as the Psychospiritual Anatomy of Good Health, 1981; (ed.) Computers for Medical Office and Patient Management, 1982; (ed.) Life Stress, 1982; The Way of a Physician: The Biologos, Biopsychosocial Way, Survival, and the Parasympathetic Towards an Ethic and a Way of Life, 1982; Creative Health and Health Enhancement, 1982; Man in Search of Health, 1983; Primary Health Care Guide Lines, 1984, 1986; (ed. with T.A. Lambo) Contemporary Issues in International Health, 1989. Add: 6 Lomond Ave., Spring Valley, N.Y. 10977, U.S.A.

DEACON, Richard. *See* **McCORMICK,** Donald.

DEAK, Istvan. American (born Hungarian), b. 1926. History. Prof. of History, Columbia Univ., NYC, since 1971 (Instr., 1963–64; Asst. Prof., 1964–67; Assoc. Prof., 1967–71; Dir., Inst. on East Central Europe, 1967–78). *Publs:* Weimar Germany's Left-wing Intellectuals: A Political History of the Weltbühne and Its Circle, 1968; (co-ed.) Eastern Europe in the 1970's, 1972; (ed. with A. Mitchell) Everyman in Europe: Essays in Social History, 2 vols., 1974, 1981; The Lawful Revolution: Louis Kossuth and the Hungarians 1848-49, 1979 (trans. into Hungarian, 1983). Add: 410 Riverside Dr., New York, N.Y. 10025, U.S.A.

DEAKIN, (Sir) (Frederick) William. British, b. 1913. History. Fellow, Wadham Coll., Oxford, 1935–49; Warden, St. Antony's Coll., Oxford, 1950 until retirement, 1968. *Publs:* The Brutal Friendship: Mussolini, Hitler and the Fall of Italian Fascism, 1962; (with Storry) The Case of Richard Sorge, 1966; The Embattled Mountain, 1971. *Publs:* 83330 Le Beausset, Le Castellet, Var, France.

DEAN, Anabel. American, b. 1915. Children's fiction, Children's nonfiction. Kindergarten teacher, Enterprise Elementary Sch. District, Redding, Calif., since 1959. *Publs:* About Paper, 1968; Exploring and Understanding Oceanography, 1970; Exploring and Understanding Heat, 1970; Willie Cannot Squirm, 1971; Willie Can Ride, 1971; Willie Can Fly, 1971; Men Under the Sea, 1972; Hot Rod, 1972; Drag Race, 1972; Destruction Derby, 1972; Stock Car Race, 1972; Road Race, 1972; Indy 500, 1972; The Pink Paint, 1973; Saddle Up, 1974; Junior Rodeo, 1974; Horse Show, 1974; Harness Race, 1974; Steeplechase, 1974; The Horse Race, 1974; Bats: The Night Flyers, 1974; Strange Partners, 1974; Animals That Fly, 1975; Motorcycle Scramble, 1976; Motorcycle Racer, 1976; Baja 500, 1976; Safari Rally, 1976; Grand Prix, 1976; Le Mans Race, 1976; Strange Partners: The Story of Symbiosis, 1976; Submerge! The Story of Divers and Their Crafts, 1976; How Animals Communicate, 1977; Fire! How Do They Fight It?, 1978; Animals' Defenses, 1978; Emergency Squad, 1980; Emergency Ambulance 10, 1980; Emergency Life Support Unit, 1980; Emergency Air Ambulance, 1980; Emergency Firefighters, 1980; Emergency Rescue Team, 1980; Up, Up and Away: The Story of Ballooning, 1980; Going Underground: Caves and Caving, 1984. Add: 2993 Sacramento Dr., Redding, Calif. 96001, U.S.A.

DEAN, Beryl. British, b. 1911. Crafts. Part-time embroidery teacher and lectr., I.L.E.A., since 1934; Freelance ecclesiastical embroiderer and designer since 1952. *Publs:* Ecclesiastical Embroidery, 1958; Church Needlework, 1962; Ideas for Church Embroidery, 1968; Creative Appliqué 1970; Embroidery in Religion and Ceremonial, 1981; Church Embroidery, 1982. Add: 59 Thornhill Sq., London N1, England.

DEAN, Dwight G(antz). American, b. 1918. Sociology. Prof. of Sociology, Iowa State Univ., Ames, since 1968. Member of faculty, Chicago City Jr. Coll. (Wright Branch), 1949–51; Grad. Asst., Ohio State Univ., Columbus, 1951–53; Instr., to Asst. Prof., Capital Univ., Columbus, Ohio, 1953–59; Asst. Prof., to Assoc. Prof., 1959–68; and Chmn. of Dept. 1965–68, Denison Univ., Granville, Ohio. *Publs:* (with D.M. Valdes) Experiments in Sociology, 1963, 3rd ed. 1976; (co-author) Sociology in Use, 1965; Dynamic Social Psychology, 1969. Add: Dept. of Sociology, Iowa State Univ., Ames, Iowa 50011, U.S.A.

DEAN, Phillip Hayes. American. Plays. Taught acting, Univ. of Michigan, Ann Arbor. *Publs:* This Bird of Dawning Singeth All Night Long, 1971; The Sty of the Blind Pig, 1972; American Night Cry: Thunder in the Index, The Minstrel Boy, 1972; Freeman, 1973; The Owl Killer, 1973; The Sty of the Blind Pig and Other Plays, 1973; Every Night When the Sun Goes Down, 1976; Paul Robeson, 1978. Add: c/o Dramatists Play Service, 440 Park Ave. S., New York, N.Y. 10016, U.S.A.

DEAN, Shelley. *See* **WALKER,** Lucy.

DEAN, William Denard. American, b. 1937. Theology/Religion. Prof. of Religion, Gustavus Adolphus Coll., St. Peter, Minn., since 1980 (Asst. Prof., 1968–73; Assoc. Prof., 1973–80). Asst. Prof. of Philosophy and Religion, Northland Coll., Ashland, Wisc., 1966–68; Research Scholar, The Inst. for Advanced Study of Religion, Univ. of Chicago, 1984–85. *Publs:* Coming To: A Theology of Beauty, 1972; Love Before the Fall, 1976; American Religious Empiricism, 1986; (co-ed.) The Size of God: The Theology of Bernard Loomer in Context, 1987; History Making History: The New Historicism in American Religious Thought, 1988. Add: Gustavus Adolphus Coll., St. Peter, Minn. 56082, U.S.A.

DeANDREA, William L(ouis). Also writes as Lee Davis Willoughby. American, b. 1952. Novels/Short stories, Mystery/Crime/Suspense. Freelance writer since 1976. Reporter, Westchester-Rockland Newspapers, New York, 1969–70; factory worker, Electrolux Corp., Old Greenwich, Conn., 1975–76. *Publs:* mystery novels—Killed in the Ratings, 1978; The HOG Murders, 1979; The Lunatic Fringe, 1980; Killed in the Act, 1981; Five o'Clock Lightning, 1981; Killed with a Passion, 1983; Killed on the Ice, 1984; Cronus, 1984; The Lunatic Fringe, 1985; Snark, 1985; Azrael, 1987; Killed in Paradise, 1988; novel—(as Lee Davis Willoughby) The Voyageurs, 1983. Add: c/o Meredith Bernstein, 33 Riverside Dr., New York, N.Y. 10024, U.S.A.

DEANE-DRUMMOND, Anthony (John). British, b. 1917. International relations/Current affairs, Autobiography/Memoirs/Personal. With the British Army until 1971 (Major General); Dir., Paper and Paper Products Ltd., Potters Bar, Herts., 1971–79; Dir., Cotswold Conversions, 1983–88. *Publs:* Return Ticket, 1955; Riots, 1974. Add: Royal Bank of Scotland, 67 Lombard St., London EC3, England.

DEARDEN, James Shackley. British, 1931. Literature. Curator, Ruskin Galleries, Bembridge Sch., Isle of Wight, since 1957; Printer, Yellowsands Press, Bembridge Sch., since 1958; Curator, Brantwood, Coniston, Cumbria, since 1959; Ed., Ruskin Newsletter, Bembridge Sch., since 1969; Ed., Ruskin Research Series, since 1979. Dir., Guild of St. George, since 1979. *Publs:* (ed.) The Professor: Arthur Severn's Memoir of John Ruskin, 1967; A Short History of Brantwood, 1967; (ed.) Iteriad, or Three Weeks Among the Lakes, by John Ruskin, 1969; Facets of Ruskin, 1970; (with K.G. Thorne) Ruskin and Coniston, 1971; John Ruskin, 1973, 1981; Turner's Isle of Wight Sketchbook, 1979; John Ruskin und die Schweiz, 1988. Add: Hillway House, Bembridge, Isle of Wight, England.

DEATS, Richard. American, b. 1932. Human relations, International relations/Current affairs, Theology/Religion, Third World problems. (US-USSR reconciliation). Dir. of Inter-Faith Activities, Fellowship of the Reconciliation, since 1984 (and 1972–79; Exec. Secty., 1979–84). Prof. of Social Ethics, Union Theological Seminary, Manila, Philippines 1959–72, and Southeast Asia Grad. Sch. of Theology, 1968–72. *Publs:* The Story of Methodism in the Philippines, 1964; Nationalism and Christianity in the Philippines, 1967; (co-ed. and contrib.) The Filipino in the Seventies: An Ecumenical Perspective, 1973; (contrib.) What About the Russians?, 1982. Add: 523 N. Broadway, Nyack, N.Y. 10960, U.S.A.

DeBAKEY, Michael Ellis. American, b. 1908. Medicine/Health. Chmn. of the Dept. of Surgery since 1948, and Chancellor since 1979. Baylor Coll. of Medicine, Houston (Pres., 1969–79). Chmn., Editorial Cttee., Cardiovascular Research Center Bulletin; Ed., Section on Cardiovascular Surgery, Contemporary Surgery, and Surgical Section on Cardiovascular Disease, Contemporary Therapy. Ed., Year Book of Gen. Surgery, Year Book Publrs., Chicago, 1957–71. *Publs:* The Blood Bank and the Technique and Therapeutics of Transformations, 1942; (co-author) Battle Casualties: Incidence Morality and Logistic Considerations, 1952; (co-author) Cold Injury: Cold Type, 1958; (co-ed.) Christopher's Minor Surgery, 8th ed. 1959; (co-author) Buerger's Disease, 1962; A Surgeon's Diary of a Visit to China, 1974; The Living Heart, 1977; (ed.) Advances in Cardiac Valves, 1983; (with Anthony M. Gotto, Jr.) Factors Influencing the Course of Myocardial Ischemia, 1983; The Living Heart Diet, 1984. Add: One Baylor Plaza, Houston, Tex. 77030, U.S.A.

DeBLASIS, Celeste (Ninette). American, b. 1946. Novels/Short stories. *Publs:* The Night Child, 1975; Suffer a Sea-Change, 1976; The Proud Breed, 1978; The Tiger's Woman, 1981; Wild Swan, 1984; Swan's Chance, 1985; A Season of Swans, 1989. Add: c/o Jane Rotrosen Agency, 318 E. 51st St., New York, N.Y. 10022, U.S.A.

de BLIJ, Harm J(an). American, (born Dutch), b. 1935. Geography. Prof. of Geography, Univ. of Miami, since 1969. Ed., National Geographic Research, since 1984. Prof. and Assoc. Dir., African Studies Center, Michigan State Univ., 1961–69. Councillor, 1970–72, and Secty., 1972–75, Assn. of American Geographers. *Publs:* Africa, South, 1962; Dar es Salaam: A Study in Urban Geography, 1963; A Geography of Subsaharan Africa, 1964; Systematic Political Geography, 1967, 4th ed. 1988; Mombasa: An African City, 1968; Geography: Regions and Concepts, 1971, 5th ed. 1988; Essentials of Geography, 1973; Man Shapes the Earth, 1974; (with D. Greenland) The Earth in Profile: A Physical Geography, 1977; (with A.C.G. Best) African Survey, 1977; Human Geography: Culture, Society, and Space, 1977, 3rd ed. (with P.O. Muller) 1986; The Earth: A Topical Geography, 1980; (with E.B. Martin) African Perspectives, 1981; Wine: A Geographical Appreciation, 1983; Wine Regions of the Southern Hemisphere, 1985; World Geography, 1989. Add: P.O. Box 249057, Univ. of Miami, Coral Gables, Fla., U.S.A.

DeBOER, John C. American, b. 1923. Administration/Management, Environmental science/Ecology, Theology/Religion. Exec. Dir., Joint Strategy and Action Cttee. Inc., NYC, since 1977. Pres., Cornucopia Network of N.J. Inc. *Publs:* Discovering Our Missions, 1967; Let's Plan, 1970; How to Succeed in the Organization Jungle Without Losing Your Religion, 1972; (ed. with Alexander Greendale) Are New Towns for Lower Income Americans, Too?, 1974; Energy Conservation Manual for Congregations, 1980; Primer on Food Stewardship, 1981. Add: 475 Riverside Dr., New York, N.Y. 10115, U.S.A.

de BOISSIÈRE, Ralph (Anthony Charles). Australian (born Trinidadian), b. 1907. Novels. Accounts clerk, 1927–28, and salesman, 1929–39, Standard Brands, Trinidad; clerk, Trinidad Clay Products, 1940–47; auto assembler, General Motors-Holden, 1948, cost clerk in car repair shops, 1949–55, freelance writer, 1955–60, and statistical clerk, Gas and Fuel Corp., 1960–80, all in Melbourne. *Publs:* Crown Jewel, 1952; Rum and Coca-Cola, 1956; No Saddles for Kangaroos, 1964. Add: 10 Vega St., North Balwyn, Vic. 3104, Australia.

deBONO, Edward (Francis Charles). British, b. 1933. Administration/Management, Technology, Philosophy. Asst. Dir. of Research, Dept. of Investigative Medicine, Univ. of Cambridge, since 1964. Dir., Cognitive Research Trust. *Publs:* The Five Day Course in Thinking, 1967; The Use of Lateral Thinking (in U.S. as New Think), 1967; The Mechanism of Mind, 1969; Lateral Thinking: A Textbook of Creativity (in U.S. as Lateral Thinking: Step by Step Creativity), 1972; (ed.) Technology Today, 1972; Lateral Thinking for Management, 1972; The Dog Exercising Machine, 1972; Po: Beyond Yes and No, 1972; Children Solve Problems, 1973; Practical Thinking, 1973; The Case of the Disappearing Elephant, 1974; (ed.) Eureka!: History of Inventions, 1974; The Greatest Thinkers, 1976; The Happiness Purpose, 1977; Opportunities: A Handbook of Business Opportunity Search, 1978; Future Positive, 1979; Atlas of Management Thinking, 1981; DeBono's Course in Thinking, 1982; Tactics: The Art and Science of Success, 1984; Conflicts: A Better Way to Resolve Them, 1985; Six Thinking Hats, 1985; Masterthinker's Handbook, 1985; Letters to Thinkers, 1987. Add: L2 Albany, London W1V 9RR, England.

DEBRECZENY, Paul. American, b. 1932. Historical Novels, Literature. Alumni Distinguished Prof. of Russian, Univ. of North Carolina, Chapel Hill, since 1983 (Assoc. Prof., 1967–74; Prof., 1974–83). Asst. to Assoc. Prof. of Russian, Tulane Univ., New Orleans, La., 1960–67. *Publs:* Nikolay Gogol and his Contemporary Critics, 1966; (trans. and ed. with Jesse Zeldin) Literature and National Identity: Nineteenth-Century Russian Critical Essays, 1970; (co-ed.) Chekhov's Art of Writing:

A Collection of Critical Essays, 1977; (trans. and ed.) Alexander Pushkin: Complete Prose Fiction, 1983; The Other Pushkin: A Study of Alexander Pushkin's Prose Fiction, 1983; Temptations of the Past (historical novel), 1982; (ed.) American Contributions to the Ninth International Congress of Slavists Kiev, vol. II: Literature, Poetics, History, 1983. Add: 304 Hoot Owl Lane, Chapel Hill, N.C. 27514, U.S.A.

DEBREU, Gerard. American (b. French), b. 1921. Economics. Prof. of Economics since 1962, and of Mathematics since 1975, Univ. of California, Berkeley (Miller Inst. Prof., 1973–74). Research Assoc., Cowles Commn. for Research in Economics, Univ. of Chicago, 1950–55; Assoc. Prof. of Economics, Cowles Foundn. for Research in Economics, Yale Univ., New Haven, 1955–60; Fellow, Center for Advanced Study in the Behavioral Sciences, Stanford, Calif., 1960–61. Vice Pres. and Pres., Econometric Soc., 1969–71; Pres., American Economic Assn., 1989. Recipient, Nobel Prize in Economics, 1983. *Publs:* Theory of Value, 1959, 1971; Mathematical Economics, 1983. Add: Dept. of Economics, Univ. of California, 250 Barrows Hall, Berkeley, Calif. 94720, U.S.A.

DEBUS, Allen George. American, b. 1926. Intellectual history, Medicine/Health, Music, Philosophy. Morris Fishbein Prof. of the History of Science and Medicine, Univ. of Chicago, since 1978 (Asst. Prof., 1961–65; Assoc. Prof., 1965–68; Prof., 1968–78; Dir., Morris Fishbein Center, 1971-77). *Publs:* The English Paracelsians, 1965, 1966; (with Robert P. Multhauf) Alchemy and Chemistry in the 17th Century, 1966; The Chemical Dream of the Renaissance, 1968, 1972; (ed.) Science and Education in the Seventeenth Century: The Webster-Ward Debate, 1970; (ed. and contrib.) Science, Medicine and Society in the Renaissance, 2 vols., 1972; (with Brian A.L. Rust) The Complete Entertainment Discography: from the mid-1890s to 1942, 1973; (ed. and contrib.) Medicine in 17th Century England, 1974; Chemical Philosophy: Paracelsian Science and Medicine in the Sixteenth and Seventeenth Centuries, 2 vols., 1977; Man and Nature in the Renaissance, 1978, 1986; Robert Fludd and His Philosophical Key, 1979; Music of Victor Herbert, 1979; Science and History: A Chemist's Appraisal, 1984; Chemistry, Alchemy and the New Philosophy, 1550-1700, 1987; (ed. with Ingrid Merkel, and contrib.) Hermeticism and the Renaissance: Intellectual History and the Occult in Early Modern Europe, 1988. Add: Social Sciences 209, Univ. of Chicago, 1126 E. 59th St., Chicago, Ill. 60637, U.S.A.

de CAMP, Catherine Crook. American, b. 1907. Children's fiction, Children's non-fiction. *Publs:* (with L.S. de Camp) Ancient Ruins and Archaeology (in U.K. as Citadels of Mystery), 1964; (with L.S. de Camp) Spirits, Stars and Spells, 1966; (with L.S. de Camp) Story of Science in America, 1967; (with L.S. de Camp) The Day of the Dinosaur, 1968; (ed. with L.S. de Camp) 3,000 Years of Fantasy, 1972; The Money Tree, 1972; (with L.S. de Camp) Darwin and His Great Discovery, 1972; (ed. with L.S. de Camp) Tales Beyond Time, 1973; Teach Your Child to Manage Money, 1974; (ed.) Creatures of the Cosmos, 1977; (with L.S. de Camp) Footprints on Sand, 1981; (with L.S. de Camp) The Bones of Zora, 1983; (with L.S. de Camp) Dark Valley Destiny, 1983; (with L.S. de Camp) The Incorporated Knight, 1987; (with L.S. de Camp) The Stones of Nomuru, 1988. Add: 3453 Hearst Castle Way, Plano, Texas 75025, U.S.A.

de CAMP, L(yon) Sprague. American, b. 1907. Novels/Short stories, Historical, Science fiction/Fantasy, Poetry, History, Sciences, Biography. Instr., Inventors Foundn. Inc., 1933–36. *Publs:* (with A.K. Berle) Inventions and their Management, 1937–51; Lest Darkness Fall, 1941; (with F. Pratt) The Incomplete Enchanter, 1941; (with F. Pratt) The Land of Unreason, 1942; The Evolution of Naval Weapons, 1947; (with F. Pratt) The Carnelian Cube, 1948; Divide and Rule, 1948; The Wheels of If, 1948; (with F. Pratt) The Castle of Iron, 1950; (with P.S. Miller) Genus Homo, 1950; The Undesired Princess, 1951; Rogue Queen, 1951; (with W. Ley) Lands Beyond, 1952; Science-Fiction Handbook, 1953; The Continent Makers,1953; (with F. Pratt) Tales from Gavagan's Bar, 1953; The Tritonian Ring, 1953; Lost Continents: The Atlantis Theme in History, Science and Literature, 1954; Cosmic Manhunt, 1954; Sprague de Camp's New Anthology, 1954; (with R.E. Howard) Tales of Conan, 1955; (with B. Nyberg) The Return of Conan, 1957; Solomon's Stone, 1957; The Tower of Zanid, 1958; An Elephant for Aristotle, 1958; (with A.K. Berle) Inventions, Patents and their Management, 1959; Engines, 1959; The Bronze God of Rhodes, 1960; The Glory that Was, 1960; (with F. Pratt) Wall of Serpents, 1960; The Heroic Age of American Invention, 1961; The Dragon of the Ishtar Gate, 1961; Energy and Power, 1962; The Search for Zei, 1962; A Gun for Dinosaur and Other Imaginative Tales, 1963; Swords and Sorcery, 1963; (with Catherine C. de Camp) Ancient Ruins and Archaeology (in U.K. as Citadels of Mystery), 1964; Elephant, 1964;

The Arrows of Hercules, 1965; The Spell of Seven, 1965; (with C.C. de Camp) Spirits, Stars and Spells, 1966; Conan the Adventurer, 1966; (with C.C. de Camp) The Story of Science in America, 1967; Conan, 1967; Conan the Warrior, 1967; (with R.E. Howard) Conan the Conqueror, 1967; Conan the Ursurper, 1967; The Goblin Tower, 1968; (with L. Carter) Conan of the Isles, 1968; (with B. Nyberg) Conan the Avenger, 1968; The Conan Reader, 1968; Conan the Freebooter, 1968; Conan the Wanderer, 1968 (with C.C. de Camp) The Day of the Dinosaur, 1968; Conan of Cimmeria, 1969; The Golden Wind, 1969; Demons and Dinosaurs, 1970; Warlocks and Warriors, 1970; (with G.H. Scithers) The Canon Swordbook, 1970; The Clocks of Iraz, 1971; (with L. Carter) Conan the Buccaneer, 1971; (with G.H. Scithers) The Conan Grimoire, 1972; (with C.C. de Camp) Darwin and His Great Discovery, 1972; Phantoms and Fancies, 1972; Scriblings, 1972; Great Cities of the Ancient World, 1972; (ed. with C.C. de Camp) Tales Beyond Time, 1973; The Fallible Fiend, 1973; (ed. with C.C. de Camp) 3,000 Years of Fantasy and Science Fiction, 1973; Lovecraft: A Biography, 1975; Science Fiction Handbook, 1975; Literary Swordsmen and Sorcerers, 1976; The Queen of Zamba, 1977; The Hostage of Zir, 1977; The Best of L. Sprague de Camp, 1978; The Great Fetish, 1978; The Purple Pterodactyls, 1979; Conan and the Spider God, 1980; The Ragged Edge of Science, 1980; The Hand of Zei, 1981; Heroes and Hobgoblins, 1981; (with L. Carter and C.C. de Camp) Conan the Barbarian, 1982; The Prisoner of Zhamanak, 1982; The Unbeheaded King, 1982; The Fringe of the Unknown, 1983; (with C.C. de Camp) The Bones of Zora, 1983; (with C.C. de Camp) Dark Valley Destiny, 1983; (with C.C. de Camp) The Incorporated Knight, 1987; (with C.C. de Camp) The Stones of Nomuru, 1988. Add: 3453 Hearst Castle Way, Plano, Texas 75025, U.S.A.

De CAUX, Len (Howard). American, b. 1899. Industrial relations. National Publicity Dir. and Ed., CIO News, Congress of Industrial Orgs., Washington, D.C., 1935–47. *Publs:* Labor Radical—From the Wobblies to CIO, 1970; The Living Spirit of the Wobblies, 1978. Add: 800-B East Windsor Rd., Glendale, Calif. 91205, U.S.A.

de CHAIR, Somerset (Struben). British, b. 1911. Novels/Short stories, Poetry, Military/Defence, Biography, Translations. Member of Parliament (U.K.), 1935–45, 1950–51; Parliamentary Private Secty. to Minister of Production, 1942–44. *Publs:* The Impending Storm, 1930; Divided Europe, 1931; Peter Public, 1933; Enter Napoleon, 1935; Red Tie in the Morning, 1937; The Golden Carpet: Iraq Campaign, 1943; The Silver Crescent: Syrian Campaign, 1943; A Mind on the March, 1945; (ed.) Napoleon's Memoirs, 2 vols., 1945; (ed. and trans.) The First Crusade, 1946; The Teetotalitarian State, 1947; The Dome of the Rock, 1948; The Millennium, 1949; (ed.) Julius Caesar's Commentaries, 1952; The Story of a Lifetime, 1954; The Waterloo Campaign, 1957; (ed.) The Sea Is Strong: Admiral de Chair's Memoirs, 1961; Bring Back the Gods, 1962; Collected Verse, 1970; Friends, Romans, Concubines, 1973; The Star of the Wind (novel), 1974; Legend of the Yellow River, 1979; Buried Pleasure (autobiography), 1985; Morning Glory (autobiography), 1988; Getty on Getty: A Man in a Billion, 1989. Add: St. Osyth Priory, Essex, England.

DECKER, William. American, b. 1926. Westerns/Adventure. *Publs:* To Be a Man, 1967; The Holdouts, 1979. Add: c/o Little Brown, 34 Beacon St., Boston, Mass. 02106, U.S.A.

de CRESPIGNY, (Richard) Rafe (Champion). Australian, b. 1936. History. Reader in Chinese since 1973, Australian National Univ., Canberra (Lectr., 1964–70, and Sr. Lectr., 1970–73). *Publs:* The Biography of Sun Chien, 1966; (with H.H. Dubs) Official Titles of the Former Han Dynasty, 1967; The Last of the Han, 1969; The Records of the Three Kingdoms, 1970; China: The Land and Its People, 1971; China This Century: A History of Modern China, 1975; Portents of Protest, 1976; Northern Frontier, 1984. Add: 5 Rous Crescent, Forrest, A.C.T., Australia 2603.

DeCRISTOFORO, Romeo John. American, b. 1917. Engineering/Technology, Recreation/Leisure/Hobbies. Consulting Ed., Popular Science Mag. since 1971, and Popular Science Encyclopedia since 1974. *Publs:* Power Tool Woodworking for Everyone, 1953; The New Handy Man's Carpentry Guide, 1959; Handy Man's Concrete and Masonry Handbook, 1960; Home Carpentry Handbook, 1960; How to Choose and Use Power Tools, 1960; Fun with a Saw, 1961; Concrete and Masonry Ideas for the Homeowner, 1962; How to Build Your Own Furniture, 1965; Carpentry Handbook, 1967; DeCristoforo's Complete Book of Power Tools, 1972; Concrete and Masonry Techniques and Design, 1973; The Hand Tool Book, 1975; Power Tools, 1975; DeCristoforo's Housebuilding Illustrated, 1977; Woodworking Techniques: Joints and Their Applications, 1979; The Magic of Your Radial Arm Saw, 1980; Power Tool Woodwork-

ing for Everyone, 1984; The Complete Book of Stationary and Portable Power Tool Techniques, 2 vols., 1985–86; The Portable Router Book, 1987; The Table Saw Book, 1988; The Bank Saw Book, 1989. Add: 27861 Natoma Rd., Los Altos Hills, Calif. 94022, U.S.A.

DeCROW, Karen. American, b. 1937. Education, Women. Lawyer: Member, Panel of Arbitrators, American Arbitration Assn.; Chancellor's Affirmative Action Cttee., Syracuse Univ. Fashion and Resorts Ed., Golf Digest mag., Norwalk, Conn., 1959–60; Ed., Zoning Digest, American Soc. of Planning Officials, Chicago, 1960–61; Writer and Ed., Center for the Study of Liberal Education for Adults, Chicago, 1961–64; Ed. of Social Studies and Adult Education, Holt, Reinhart and Winston Inc., NYC, 1965–66; Textbook Ed., L.W. Singer Co. Inc., NYC, 1965–66; Writer, Eastern Regional Instn. for Education, Syracuse, N.Y., 1967–69. Past Pres., National Organization for Women. *Publs:* (with Roger De-Crow) University Adult Education: A Selected Biography, 1967; (ed.) The Pregnant Teenager, by Howard Osofsky, 1968; The Young Women's Guide to Liberation, 1971; (ed.) Corporate Wives, Corporate Casualties, by Robert Seidenberg, 1973; Sexist Justice, 1974; (with Robert Seidenberg) Women Who Marry Houses: Panic and Protest in Agoraphobia, 1983. Add: 7 Fir Tree Lane, Jamesville, N.Y. 13078, U.S.A.

DECTER, Midge (Rosenthal). American, b. 1927. Sociology, Women. Sr. Ed., Basic Books, NYC, since 1974. Exec. Dir., Cttee. for the Free World, since 1980. Asst. Ed., Midstream mag., 1956–58; Managing Ed., Commentary mag., 1961–62; Ed., Hudson Inst., 1965–66; Ed., CBS Legacy Books, 1966–68; Exec. Ed., Harper's mag., 1968–71; Literary Ed., Saturday Review, NYC, 1972–74. *Publs:* The Liberated Woman and Other Americans, 1971; The New Chastity and Other Arguments Against Women's Liberation, 1973, as The New Chastity, 1974; Liberal Parents, Radical Children, 1975. Add: 120 E. 81st St., New York, N.Y. 10028, U.S.A.

DEER, M.J. *See* **SMITH,** George H.

DEFORD, Frank. American, b. 1938. Novels/Short stories, Social Commentary/Phenomena, Sports. Sr. Writer, Sports Illustrated mag., NYC, since 1969. *Publs:* (with Don Budge) A Tennis Memoir, 1968; Five Strides on the Banked Track, 1971; There She Is: The Life and Times of Miss America, 1971; Cut 'n' Run, 1973; (with Arthur Ashe) Portrait in Motion, 1975; Big Bill Tilden, 1976; The Owner, 1976; (with Jack Kramer) The Game, 1980; Everybody's All-American, 1981; (with Billie Jean King) The Autobiography, 1982; Alex: The Life of a Child, 1983; The Spy in the Deuce Court, 1986; The World's Tallest Midget, 1987; Casey on the Loose, 1989. Add: 73 Clapboard Hill Rd., Westport, Conn., U.S.A.

DeFREES, Madeline. Also writes as Sister Mary Gilbert. American, b. 1919. Poetry, Autobiography/Memoirs/Personal. Full-Time Writer. Retired from the Univ. of Massachusetts, Amherst (Prof. of English, 1979–85; Dir. of M.F.A. Writing Program, 1980–83). With Holy Names Coll., Spokane, Wash., 1950–67; Assoc. Prof., 1967–71, and Prof. of English, Univ. of Montana, Missoula, 1971–79. *Publs:* as Sister Mary Gilbert—Springs of Silence (autobiography), 1953; Later Thoughts from the Springs of Silence, 1962; From the Darkroom (poetry), 1964; as Madeline DeFrees—When Sky Lets Go, 1978; Imaginary Ancestors, 1978; Magpie on the Gallows, 1982. Add: c/o Copper Canyon Press, Box 271, Port Townsend, Wash. 98368, U.S.A.

DEGENHARDT, Henry W. British, b. 1910. Politics/Government. Managing Dir., College of Careers, Cape Town, 1950–62; Writer, Keesing's Contemporary Archives, 1962–80. *Publs:* (compiler) South African Fishing Industry Handbook and Buyers' Guide, 1951; (ed.) Treaties and Alliances of the World, 1968, 4th ed. 1986; (ed. with Alan J. Day) Political Parties of the World, 1980, 3rd Ed. 1988; (with others) Border and Territorial Disputes, 1982, 1987; (compiler) Political Dissent: An International Guide to Dissident, Extra-Parliamentary, Guerrilla and Illegal Political Movements, 1983; Maritime Affairs: A World Handbook, 1986; Revolutionary and Dissident Movements, 1988. Add: 3 Horsecombe Brow, Bath BA2 5QY, England.

DeGEORGE, Richard T(homas). American, b. 1933. Philosophy. Univ. Prof. of Philosophy, Univ. of Kansas, Lawrence, since 1972 (Asst. Prof., 1959–62; Assoc. Prof., 1962–64; Prof., 1964–72). *Publs:* (ed.) Classical and Contemporary Metaphysics, 1962; (co-ed.) Reflections on Man, Part II: Dialectical Thought, 1966; Patterns of Soviet Thought, 1966; (co-author) Science and Ideology in Soviet Society, 1967; (ed.) Ethics and Society, 1966; The New Marxism, 1968; Soviet Ethics and Morality, 1969; Guide to Philosophical Bibliography and Research, 1971; (ed. with

F.M. DeGeorge) The Structuralists from Marx to Lévi-Strauss, 1972; (ed. with J.P. Scanlan) Marxism and Religion in Eastern Europe, 1976; (ed. with J. Pichler), Ethics, Free Enterprise and Public Policy, 1978; The Philosopher's Guide, 1980; (ed.) Semiotic Themes, 1981; Business Ethics, 1982, 1986; The Nature and Limits of Authority, 1985. Add: Dept. of Philosophy, Univ. of Kansas, Lawrence, Kans. 66045, U.S.A.

De GRAEFF, Allen. *See* **BLAUSTEIN,** Albert P(aul).

de GRAFT-HANSON, J(ohn) O(rleans). Ghanaian, b. 1932. Children's Fiction. *Publs:* The Secret of Opokuwa, 1967; The Little Sasabonsam, 1972; Papa Ewusi and the Magic Marble, 1973; Papa and the Animals, 1973; The Fetish Hide-Out, 1975; The People from the Sea, 1988. Add: c/o Ghana Publishing Corp., Barnes Rd., P.O. Box 4348, Accra, Ghana.

de HAMEL, Joan (Littledale). British, b. 1924. Children's fiction. Lectr. in French, Dunedin Teachers Coll., 1967–80. *Publs:* 'X' Marks the Spot, 1973; Take the Long Path, 1978; Hemi's Pet, 1985; The Third Eye, 1987. Add: 25 Howard St., Macandrew Bay, Dunedin, New Zealand.

DEHN, Olive. British, b. 1914. Children's fiction. *Publs:* Tales of Sir Benjamin Bulbous, Bart, 1935; The Basement Bogle, 1935; The Nixie from Rotterdam, 1937; Tales of the Taunus Mountains, 1937; The Well-Behaved Witch, 1937; Come In, 1946; Higgly-Piggly Farm, 1957; The Pike Dream, 1958; The Caretakers (and the Poacher, and the Gipsy, to the Rescue, and of Wilmhurst), 5 vols., 1960–67; Spectacles for the Mole, 1968; Good-bye Day, 1980. Add: Lear Cottage, Colemans Hatch, Hartfield, Sussex, England.

DEIGHTON, Len. British, b. 1929. Novels/Short stories, Mystery/Crime/Suspense, Cookery/Gastronomy/Wine, History. *Publs:* The Ipcress File, 1962; Horse Under Water, 1963; Funeral in Berlin, 1964; Action Cook Book: Len Deighton's Guide to Eating (in U.S. as Cookstrip Cook Book), 1965; Ou est le Garlic: or, Len Deighton's French Cook Book, 1965; rev. ed. as Basic French Cooking, 1978; The Billion Dollar Brain, 1966; An Expensive Place to Die, 1967; (ed.) London Dossier, 1967; Only When I Larf, 1968; (compiled by Victor and Margaret Pettit) Len Deighton's Continental Dossier: A Collection of Cultural, Culinary, Historical, Spooky, Grim and Preposterous Facts, 1968; Bomber, 1970; Declarations of War (stories), 1971; Close-Up, 1972; Spy Story, 1974; Yesterday's Spy, 1975; Twinkle, Twinkle, Little Spy, 1976; Fighter: The True Story of the Battle of Britain, 1977; SS-GB, 1978; (with Arnold Schwartzman) Airshipwreck, 1978; Blitzkrieg: From the Rise of Hitler to the Fall of Dunkirk, 1979; Battle of Britain, 1980; XPD, 1981; Goodbye Mickey Mouse, 1982; Berlin Game, 1983; Mexico Set, 1984; London Match, 1985; Winter, 1987; ABC of French Food, 1989. Add: c/o Century-Hutchinson, 62-65 Chandos Pl., London WC2N 4NW, England.

DEISS, Joseph Jay. American, b. 1915. Novels/Short stories, Archaeology/Antiquities, Biography. Ed., U.S. Govt., 1938–45; Vice-Dir., American Academy in Rome, 1965–69; Writer-in-Residence, Currier House, Harvard Univ., Cambridge, Mass., 1975. *Publs:* (ed. with H.H. Miller) Report of the President's Commission on Farm Tenancy, 1937; A Washington Story, 1950; The Blue Chips, 1957; The Great Infidel: Frederick II of Hohenstaufen (novel), 1963; Captains of Fortune: Profiles of Six Italian Condotieri, 1965; Herculaneum: Italy's Buried Treasure, 1966, 1985; The Roman Years of Margaret Fuller, 1969; The Town of Hercules (juvenile), 1974. Add: Thoreau House, Wellfleet, Mass. 02667, U.S.A.

DE JONG, Meindert. American, b. 1906. Children's fiction. Served in the U.S. Army Air Corps during World War II; Historian of the Chinese-American Wing, 14th Air Force. *Publs:* The Big Goose and the Little White Duck, 1938; Dirk's Dog Bello, 1939; Wheels Over the Bridge, 1941; Bells of the Harbor, 1941; The Cat That Walked a Week, 1943; The Little Stray Dog, 1943; Billy and the Unhappy Bull, 1946; Bible Days, 1949; Good Luck Duck, 1950; Tower by the Sea, 1950; Smoke Above the Lane, 1951; Shadrach, 1953; Hurry Home, Candy, 1953; The Wheel on the School, 1954; The Little Cow and the Turtle, 1955; The House of Sixty Fathers, 1956; Along Came a Dog, 1958; The Mighty Ones: Great Men and Women of Early Bible Days, 1959; The Last Little Cat, 1961; The Singing Hill, 1962; Nobody Plays with a Cabbage, 1962; Far Out the Long Canal, 1964; Puppy Summer, 1966; Journey from Peppermint Street, 1968; A Horse Came Running, 1970; The Easter Cat, 1971; The Almost All-White Rabbity Cat, 1972. Add: 351 Grand St., Allegan, Mich. 49010, U.S.A.

de JONGE, Alex. British, b. 1938. Literature, Biography. Fellow and Tutor, New Coll., Oxford, since 1965. *Publs:* (with others) Nineteenth Century Russian Literature, 1973; Nightmare Culture, Lautréamont and Les Chants de Maldoror, 1973; Dostoevsky and the Age of Intensity, 1975; Prince of Clouds: A Biography of Baudelaire, 1976; The Weimar Chronicle: Prelude to History, 1977; Napoleon's Last Will and Testament, 1977; Fire and Water: A Life of Peter the Great, 1979; The Life and Times of Grigorii Rasputin, 1982; Stalin and the Shaping of the Soviet Union, 1986. Add: New Coll., Oxford, England.

DEKKER, Carl. *See* **LYNDS,** Dennis.

DEKKER, George. American, b. 1934. Literature. Prof. of English since 1974, and Atha Prof. in Humanities since 1988, Stanford Univ., California. (Assoc. Prof., 1972–74). Lectr., University Coll., Swansea, Wales, 1962–64; Lectr., 1964–66, Sr. Lectr., 1966–70, and Reader in Literature, 1970–72, Univ. of Essex, Colchester. *Publs:* Sailing After Knowledge: The Cantos of Ezra Pound, 1963; James Fenimore Cooper: The Novelist, 1967; (ed. with Larry Johnston) The American Democrat, by James Fenimore Cooper, 1969; (ed. with John McWilliams) James Fenimore Cooper: The Critical Heritage, 1973; Coleridge and the Literature of Sensibility, 1978; (ed.) Donald Davie and the Responsibilities of Literature, 1984; The American Historical Romance, 1987. Add: Dept. of English, Stanford Univ., Stanford, Calif. 94305, U.S.A.

DELAHAYE, Michael (John). British, b. 1946. Mystery/Crime/-Suspense. Full-time writer and broadcaster. Teacher of English, British Inst., Florence, 1968–69; Television Reporter and Correspondent, BBC, News and Current Affairs Dept., London, 1969–79. *Publs:* The Sale of Lot 236, 1981; On the Third Day (in U.K. as The Third Day), 1984; Stalking-Horse, 1987. Add: c/o David Higham Assocs., 5-8 Lower John St., London W1R 4HA, England.

DELANEY, Denis. *See* **GREEN,** Peter.

DELANEY, Joseph H. American, b. 1932. Science fiction. Full-time writer since 1983. Practising lawyer for 31 years: member of the bar of Maryland, Illinois, and Texas. *Publs:* (with Marc Stiegler) Valentina, 1984; In the Face of My Enemy, 1985; Lords Temporal, 1987. Add: Box 957, Alpine, Texas 79831, U.S.A.

DELANEY, Mary Murray. Also writes short stories and articles as Mary D. Lane. American, b. 1913. Social commentary/phenomena. Vice-Pres., Delaney, Joyce and O'Dell Inc., Travel Agents, St. Paul, Minn., since 1961. *Publs:* Of Irish Ways, 1973; Family Album, 1989. Add: 1606 Highland Parkway, St. Paul, Minn. 55116, U.S.A.

DELANEY, Norman Conrad. American, b. 1932. Biography. Prof., Del Mar Coll., Corpus Christi, Tex., since 1967; Adjunct Prof., Naval War Coll., since 1984. *Publs:* John McIntosh Kell of the Raider Alabama, 1973. Add: 3747 Aransas St., Corpus Christi, Tex. 78411, U.S.A.

DELANEY, Shelagh. British, b. 1930. Plays/Screenplays. *Publs:* A Taste of Honey, 1959; The Lion in Love, 1961; Sweetly Sings the Donkey, 1963; The House That Jack Built, 1977. Add: c/o Tessa Sayle, 11 Jubilee Place, London SW3 3TE, England.

DELANO, Anthony. British, b. 1930. Novels/Short stories, Documentaries/Reportage. Managing Ed., Daily Mirror, London, 1978–84. Dir., Mirror Group, 1984–87. (Rome Corresp., 1956–60; Paris Corresp., 1960–63; American Corresp., 1963–70; London Diary Ed., 1970–74; Roving Corresp., 1970–74; Chief American Corresp., 1974–78). *Publs:* Breathless Diversions (novel), 1975; Slip-Up (documentary), 1977; Manacled Mormon, 1978; Maxwell, 1988. Add: c/o Dasha Shenkman Assocs., 56 Queen's Gate Terrace, London SW7 5PJ, England.

DELANY, Samuel R(ay). American, b. 1942. Science fiction/Fantasy. *Publs:* The Jewels of Aptor, 1962, unabridged ed., 1968; The Fall of the Towers, vol. I, Captives of the Flames, 1963, as Out of the Dead City, 1968, vol. II, The Towers of Toron, 1964, vol. III, City of a Thousand Suns, 1965; The Ballad of Beta-2, 1965; Empire Star, 1966; Babel-17, 1966; The Einstein Intersection, 1967; Nova, 1968; Driftglass: Ten Tales of Speculative Fiction, 1971; Dhalgren, 1975; Triton, 1976; The Jewel-Hinged Jaw: Notes on the Language of Science Fiction, 1977; The American Shore, 1978; Empire, 1978; (ed.) Nebula Award Winners 13, 1979; Distant Stars, 1981; Stars in My Pocket Like Grains of Sand, 1984; Starboard Wine: More Notes on the Language of Science Fiction, 1984; The Splendor and Misery of Bodies, 1985; Flight from Nevèrÿon, 1985;

The Bridge of Lost Desire, 1987; The Motion of Light in Water, 1988; The Straits of Messina, 1988; Wagner-Artaud: A Play of 19th and 20th Century Critical Fictions, 1988. Add: c/o Bantam Books, 666 Fifth Ave., New York, N.Y. 10019, U.S.A.

de la TORRE, Lillian. Pseud. for Lillian Bueno McCue. American, b. 1902. Mystery/Crime/Suspense, Plays/Screenplays, Cookery/-Gastronomy/Wine, Biography. Teacher, NYC, 1923–34; Instr., Colorado Coll., Colorado Springs, 1937, and the Univ. of Colorado Extension, 1937–41; Technical Adviser, Twentieth Century Fox, Hollywood, Calif., 1945. *Publs:* mysteries—Elizabeth Is Missing, 1945; Dr. Sam: Johnson, Detector (stories), 1946; The Heir of Douglas, 1952; The Truth About Belle Gunness, 1955; The Detections of Dr Sam: Johnson (stories), 1960; The Return of Dr. Sam: Johnson, Detector (stories), 1985; The Exploits of Dr. Sm: Johnson, Detector (stories), 1987; plays—Goodbye, Miss Lizzie Borden, 1948; Cheat the Wuddy, 1948; Remember Constance Kent, 1949; The Sally Cathleen Claim, 1952; The Coffee Cup, 1955; The Queen's Choristers, 1961; The Jester's Apprentice, 1962; The Bar-Room Floor, 1964; The Stroller's Girl, 1966; other—(with Carol Truax) The 60 Minute Chef, 1947; Villainy Detected, 1947; The White Rose of Stuart (juvenile), 1954; The Actress (juvenile), 1957; (with Carol Truax) The New 60 Minute Chef, 1975. Add: 16 Valley Pl., Apt. 302, Colorado Springs, Colo. 80903, U.S.A.

DELBANCO, Nicholas F(ranklin). American, b. 1942. Novels/Short stories, Plays/Screenplays. Prof. of English, Univ. of Michigan, Ann Arbor, since 1985; Member of faculty, Dept. of Language and Literature, Bennington Coll., Vt., since 1966. Visiting Prof., Columbia and Iowa Univs., Skidmore, Trinity and Williams Colleges. *Publs:* The Martlet's Tale, 1966, screenplay, 1970; Grasse, 3/23/66, 1968; Consider Sappho Burning, 1969; News, 1970; In the Middle Distance, 1971; Fathering, 1973; Small Rain, 1975; Possession, 1977; Sherbrookes, 1978; Stillness, 1980; Group Portrait: Conrad, Crane, Ford, James, and Wells, 1982; About My Table and Other Stories, 1983; The Beaux Arts Trio: A Portrait, 1985; Running in Place: Scenes from the South of France, 1989. Add: 428 Concord St., Ann Arbor, Mich. 48104, U.S.A.

DELDERFIELD, Eric R. British, b. 1909. Animals/Pets, History, Travel/Exploration/Adventure. Managing Dir., ERD Publs. Ltd., Exmouth, Devon, since 1965. Dir., David & Charles Ltd., Newton Abbot, 1965–72. *Publs:* Cavalcade by Candlelight, 1950; North Devon Story, 1952; Lynmouth Flood Disaster, 1953; Exmoor Wanderings, 1956; The Cotswolds—Its Villages and Churches, 1961; British Inn Signs and Their Stories, 1965; Kings and Queens of England, 1966; Church Treasure, 1966; Cotswold Countryside and Its Characters, 1967; Fascinating Facts and Figures of the Bible, 1967; West Country Historic Houses and Their Families, 3 vols., 1968, 1970, 1973; Introduction to Inn Signs, 1969; Eric Delderfield's True Animal Stories, 2 vols., 1970, 1972; Stories of Inns and Their Signs, 1974; Inns and Their Signs: Facts and Fiction, 1975; Animal Stories, 1979; Devon and Cornwall, 1980; Brief Guide to British Inn Signs, 1986. Add: 3 Oldfields, Exmouth, Devon, EX8 2EG, England.

DELEAR, Frank J. American, b. 1914. Air/Space topics. Publicity Rep., Chance Vought Aircraft, 1942–47; Asst. to Public Relations Dir., United Aircraft, 1947–48; Asst. Public Relations Dir., Hamilton Standard Div., 1953–57. Aviation Ed., Post Telegram, Bridgeport, Conn., 1937–42; Writer, Socony-Vacuum Oil Co., N.Y., 1948–52; Public Relations Dir., Sikorsky Aircraft Div. of United Technologies, Stratford, Conn., 1957–77. *Publs:* The New World of Helicopters, 1967; Igor Sikorsky: His Three Careers in Aviation, 1969; Imaka (screenplay), 1970; Holland Heartbeat (screenplay), 1973; Helicopters and Airplanes of the U.S. Army, 1977; Famous First Flights Across the Atlantic, 1979; Airplanes and Helicopters of the U.S. Navy, 1982. Add: 308 Patriot Way, Centerville, Mass. 02632, U.S.A.

DeLILLO, Don. American, b. 1936. Novels/Short stories. *Publs:* Americana, 1971; End Zone, 1972; Great Jones Street, 1973; Ratner's Star, 1976; Players, 1977; Running Dog, 1978; The Names, 1982; White Noise, 1985; Libra, 1988. Add: c/o Wallace Agency, 177 E. 70th St., New York, N.Y. 10021, U.S.A.

DELINSKY, Barbara (Ruth, née Greenberg). Also writes as Bonnie Drake and Billie Douglass. American, b. 1945. Romance/Historical fiction. Sociological researcher, Children's Protective Services, Boston, 1968–69; Instr. in Photography, Dover-Sherborn Sch. System, Massachusetts, 1978–82. *Publs:* (as Bonnie Drake) Sensuous Burgundy, 1981; (as Bonnie Drake) Surrender by Moonlight, 1981; (as Bonnie Drake) Sweet Ember, 1981; (as Bonnie Drake) The Passionate Touch, 1981; (as Bonnie Drake) Amber Enchantment, 1982; (as Bonnie Drake)

Lilac Awakening, 1982; (as Bonnie Drake) The Ardent Protector, 1982; (as Bonnie Drake) Whispered Promise, 1983; (as Billie Douglass) A Time to Love, 1982; (as Billie Douglass) Knightly Love, 1982; (as Billie Douglass) Search for a New Dawn, 1982; (as Billie Douglass) An Irresistible Impulse, 1983; (as Billie Douglass) Beyond Fantasy, 1983; (as Billie Douglass) Fasting Courting, 1983; (as Billie Douglass) Flip Side of Yesterday, 1983; (as Billie Douglas) Sweet Serenity, 1983; (as Billie Douglass) The Carpenter's Lady, 1983; (as Bonnie Drake) Gemstone, 1983; (as Bonnie Drake) Lover from the Sea, 1983; (as Bonnie Drake) Passion and Illusion, 1983; (as Bonnie Drake) Moment to Moment, 1984; (as Billie Douglass) Variation on a Theme, 1984; Bronze Mystique, 1984; A Special Something, 1984; Fingerprints, 1984; Secret of the Stone, 1986; First, Best and Only, 1987; Twelve Across, 1987; Twilight Whispers, 1987; T.L.C., 1988. Add: c/o Harlequin, 225 Duncan Mill Rd., Don Mills, Ont. M3B 3K9, Canada.

DELIUS, Anthony (Ronald St. Martin). South African, b. 1916. Novels/short stories, Plays/Screenplays, Poetry, Travel/Exploration/Adventure. Freelance broadcaster and journalist. Member of Editorial Bd., Contrast mag., Cape Town, since 1962. Staff Member, Port Elizabeth Evening Post, 1947–50; Parliamentary Corresp., Cape Times, Cape Town, 1951–54 and 1958–68; banned from South Africa House of Assembly for Cape Times political commentary. Lectr. on African govt., Univ. of Cape Town, 1964–66; Talks Writer, B.B.C. Africa Service, London, 1968–77. *Publs:* The Young Traveller in South Africa, 1947, 1959; An Unknown Border: Poems, 1954; The Long Way Round (travel), 1956; The Fall: A Play About Rhodes, 1957; The Last Division (poetry), 1959; Upsurge in Africa, 1960; A Corner of the World: Thirty-Four Poems, 1962; The Day Natal Took Off: A Satire (novel), 1963; Black South-Easter (poetry), 1966; Border (historical novel), 1977. Add: 30 Graemesdyke Ave., London SW14 7BJ, England.

DELL, Belinda. *See* **BOWDEN,** Jean.

DELL, Edmund. British, b. 1921. Business/Trade/Industry, Institutions/Organizations, Politics/Government. Labour M.P. (U.K.) for Birkenhead, 1964–79: Parliamentary Secty., Ministry of Technology, 1966–67; Joint Parliamentary Under-Secty. of State, Dept. of Economic Affairs, 1967–68; Minister of State, Bd. of Trade, 1968–69, and Dept. of Employment and Productivity, 1969–70; Chmn., Cttee. of Public Accounts, House of Commons, 1972–74; Paymaster Gen., 1974–76; Secty. of State for Trade, 1976–78; Chmn., Guinness Peat Group, London, 1979–82; and Channel Four Television, 1980–82. *Publs:* (ed. with J.E.C. Hill) The Good Old Cause, 1949, 1971; Political Responsibility and Industry, 1973; (co-author) Report on European Institutions, 1979; The Politics of Economic Interdependence, 1987. Add: 4 Reynolds Close, London NW11 7EA, England.

DELL, Sidney. British, b. 1918. Economics, Money/Finance. Sr. Fellow, U.N. Inst. for Training and Research, NYC, since 1985 (Asst. Dir., Bureau of Gen. Economic Research and Policies, 1961–64; Dir. of Research, Centre for Industrial Development, 1964–65; Dir., New York Office, Conference on Trade and Development, 1965–73; Asst. Admin., Development Prog., 1973–76; Special Adviser, 1977–82, and Exec. Dir., 1982–84, U.N. Center of Transnational Corps). *Publs:* Problemas de un Mercado Común en América Latina, 1959; Trade Blocs and Common Markets, 1963; A Latin American Common Market?, 1966; The Inter-American Development Bank: A Study in Development Financing, 1972; (with Roger Lawrence) The Balance of Payments Adjustments Process in Developing Countries, 1980; On Being Grandmotherly: The Evolution of IMF Conditionality, 1981; (ed.) The International Monetary System and Its Reform, parts I-III, 1987; (ed.) Policies for Development, 1988; The United Nations and International Business, 1989. Add: U.N. Inst. for Training and Research, New York, N.Y. 10017, U.S.A.

DEL MAR, Norman (Rene). British, b. 1919. Music. Prof., Royal Coll of Music, London. Orchestral conductor: Asst. to Sir Thomas Beecham, 1947; English Opera Group, 1949–54, Guildhall School of Music, 1953–60, Yorkshire Symphony Orchestra, 1954, BBC Scottish Orchestra, 1960–65, Royal Academy of Music, 1974–77, Academy of BBC, 1974–77; Artistic Dir., Norfolk and Norwich Triennial Festival, 1979, 1982; Artistic Dir. and Chief Conductor, Aarhus Symphony Orch., 1985–88; many guest appearances. *Publs:* Richard Strauss: A Critical Commentary on His Life and Works, 3 vols., 1962–72; Mahler's Sixth Symphony: A Study, 1980; Orchestral Variations: Confusion and Error in the Orchestral Repertoire, 1981; Anatomy of the Orchestra, 1981; A Companion to the Orchestra, 1987. Add: c/o Faber and Faber Ltd., 3 Queen Sq., London WC1N 3AU, England.

DELMAR, Viña (Croter). American, b. 1905. Historical/Romance/-Gothic, Plays/Screenplays, Autobiography/Memoirs/Personal. Freelance writer. Former typist, switchboard operator, usher, actress, and theatre mgr. *Publs:* Bad Girl, 1928; Kept Woman, 1929, in U.K. as The Other Woman, 1930; Loose Ladies (romantic short stories) (in U.K. as Women Who Pass By), 1929; Women Live Too Long, 1932, 2nd U.S. ed. as The Restless Passion, 1947; The Marriage Racket, 1933; Mystery at Little Heaven, 1933; The End of the World, 1934; The Rich, Full Life (play), 1945; The Love Trap, 1949; New Orleans Lady, 1949; About Mrs. Leslie, 1950; Stangers in Love, 1951; The Marcaboth Women, 1951; The Laughing Stranger, 1953; Ruby, 1953; Mid-Summer (play), 1954; Beloved, 1956; The Breeze from Camelot, 1959; Warm Wednesday (play), 1959; The Big Family, 1961; The Enchanted, 1965; Grandmère, 1967; The Becker Scandal: A Time Remembered (autobiography), 1968; The Freeways, 1971; Time for Titans, 1974; McKeever, 1976. Add: c/o Harcourt Brace Jovanovich, 1250 Sixth Ave., San Diego, CA 92101, U.S.A.

DELOUGHERY, Grace L. American, b. 1933. Medicine/Health. Assoc. Prof., Indiana Univ., since 1985. Public Health Nurse, Minneapolis, 1955–59; Research Fellow, Univ. of Minnesota, Minneapolis, 1960–63; Consultant, Riverside County Sch., 1966–67; Assoc. Prof., Univ. of North Dakota, Grand Forks, 1967–68; Asst. Prof. in Residence, Univ. of California, Los Angeles, 1968–72. *Publs:* Study of Development and Implementation of Health Insurance for Braceros, 1967; (with K. Gebbie and B. Neuman) Consultation and Community Organization in Community Mental Health Nursing, 1971; (with Gebbie) Political Dynamics: The Nurse in Organizations, 1975; History and Trends of Professional Nursing, 1977. Add: Rt. 2, Circle Dr., Georgetown, Ind. 47122, U.S.A.

del REY, Lester (Ramon Felipe San Juan Mario Silvio Enrico Alvarez-del Rey). Also writes as Edson McCann, Philip St. John, Erik Van Lhin, and Kenneth Wright. American, b. 1915. Science fiction/Fantasy, Children's fiction, Children's non-fiction, Sciences. Ed., Del Rey Books (Ballantine Books), since 1977 (Fantasy Ed., 1975–77). Book Reviewer, Analog, since 1974. Sheet metal worker, McDonnell Aircraft Corp., St. Louis, Mo., 1942–44; author's agent, Scott Meredith Literary Agency, NYC, 1947–50; Ed., Space Science Fiction, London, 1952–53; Publr., as R. Alvarez, 1952, and Ed., as Philip St. John, 1952–53, Science Fiction Adventures; Assoc. Ed., as John Vincent, 1953, and as Cameron Hull, with Harry Harrison, 1953, Fantasy Fiction; Ed., as Wade Kaempfert, Rocket Stories, 1953; Managing Ed., International Science Fiction, 1968; Managing Ed., 1968–69, and Features Ed., 1969–74, Galaxy and If; Ed., Worlds of Fantasy, 1968; Instr. of Fantasy Fiction, New York Univ., 1972–73; Ed., Garland Press science fiction series, 1975. *Publs:* . . . and Some Were Human (short stories), 1948; It's Your Atomic Age, 1951; A Pirate Flag for Monterey (juvenile), 1952; Marooned on Mars (juvenile), 1952; (as Philip St. John) Rocket Jockey (juvenile), 1952, in U.K. as Rocket Pilot, 1955; (as Kenneth Wright) The Mysterious Planet (juvenile), 1953; Attack from Atlantis (juvenile), 1953; (as Erik Van Lhin) Battle on Mercury (juvenile), 1953; Step to the Stars (juvenile), 1954; (as Philip St. John) Rockets to Nowhere (juvenile), 1954; (ed. with Cecile Matschat and Carl Carmer) The Year After Tomorrow, 1954; (as Edson McCann, with Frederik Pohl) Preferred Risk, 1955; Mission to the Moon (juvenile), 1956; (as Erik Van Lhin) Police Your Planet, 1956, (as Lester del Rey) 1975; Nerves, 1956, 1976; Rockets Through Space (juvenile), 1957, 1960; The Cave of Spears (juvenile), 1957; Robots and Changelings (short stories), 1958; Day of the Giants, 1959; Space Flight (juvenile), 1959; The Mysterious Earth (Sea, Sky), 3 vols., 1960–64; Rocks and What They Tell Us (juvenile), 1961; Moon of Mutiny (juvenile), 1961; The Eleventh Commandment, 1962, 1970; The Sky Is Falling, Badge of Infamy, 1963; Outpost of Jupiter (juvenile), 1963; (with Paul W. Fairman) The Runaway Robot (juvenile), 1964; Mortals and Monsters (short stories), 1965; Rocket from Infinity (juvenile), 1966; (with Paul W. Fairman) The Scheme of Things, 1966; The Infinite Worlds of Maybe, 1966; (with Paul W. Fairman) Siege Perilous, 1966, as The Man Without a Planet, 1969; (with Paul W. Fairman) Tunnel Through Time (juvenile), 1966; (with Paul W. Fairman) Prisoners of Space (juvenile), 1968; Pstalemate, 1971; (ed.) Best Science Fiction Stories of the Year, 5 vols., 1972-76; Gods and Golems (short stories), 1973; Early del Rey (short stories), 1975; The Best of Later del Rey (short stories), 1978; (with Raymond F. Jones) Weeping May Tarry, 1978; The World of Science Fiction 1926-1976: The History of a Subculture, 1979. Add: c/o Ballantine Books, 201 E. 50th St., New York, N.Y. 10022, U.S.A.

DELZELL, Charles F. American, b. 1920. History. Prof. of History, Vanderbilt Univ., Nashville, Tenn., since 1952 (Chmn., Dept. of History, 1970–73, 1983, 1986; Acting Dir., Center for European Studies, 1985–86). Asst. Prof. of History, Univ. of Hawaii, Honolulu, 1949–50; Instr. in History, Univ. of Oregon, Eugene, 1950–51. *Publs:* The Meaning of Yalta:

Big Three Diplomacy and the New Balance of Power, 1956, 3rd ed. 1965; Mussolini's Enemies: The Italian Anti-Fascist Resistance, 1961, 1974; Italy in Modern Times, 1964; (ed.) The Unification of Italy, 1959-1961, 1965; Mediterranean Fascism, 1919-1945, 1970; (with H.A. Schmitt) Historians of Modern Europe, 1971; (with W.S. Sworakowski) World Communism: A Handbook 1918-1965, 1973; (ed.) The Papacy and Totalitarianism Between The Two World Wars, 1974; (ed.) The Future of History, 1977; Italy in the Twentieth Century, 1980. Add: Dept. of History, Vanderbilt Univ., Nashville, Tenn. 37235, U.S.A.

DEMARAY, Donald E(ugene). American, b. 1926. Theology/Religion, Biography. Fisher Prof. of Preaching, Asbury Theological Seminary, Wilmore, Ky., since 1967 (Assoc. Prof. of Preaching, 1966–67; Dean of Students, 1967–75). Minister of Youth, Seattle First Free Methodist Church, 1952–53; Dean, Sch. of Religion, Seattle Pacific Coll., Wash., 1959–66. *Publs:* (ed.) Prayers and Devotions of John Wesley, 1957; Basic Beliefs, 1958; Loyalty to Christ, 1958; Amazing Grace, 1958; The Acts, 1959; (ed.) A Pulpit Manual, 1959; (ed.) Prayers and Devotions of C.H. Spurgeon, 1960; Questions Youth Ask, 1961; Acts (in Aldersgate series), 2 vols., 1961; Layman's Guide to the Bible, 1964, reissued as Sourcebook of the Bible, 1971; Alive to God Through Prayer, 1965, Rev. ed. as How Are You Praying?, 1986; Preacher Aflame!, 1972; Pulpit Giants, 1973; An Introduction to Homiletics, 1974; A Guide to Happiness: Paraphrase of the Book of James, 1974; The Minister's Ministries, 1974; The Practice of the Presence of God (paraphrase of the work by Brother Lawrence), 1975; (ed.) Blow, Wind of God (anthology of Billy Graham's writings), 1975; Near Hurting People: The Pastoral Ministry of Robert Moffat Fine, 1978; Proclaiming the Truth: Guides to Scriptural Preaching, 1980; Watch Out for Burnout, 1983; Snapshots: The People Called Free Methodist, 1985; Laughter, Joy, and Healing, 1986; The Innovation of John Newton 1725-1807, 1988. Add: Asbury Theological Seminary, Wilmore, Ky. 40390, U.S.A.

DEMARIS, Ovid. American, b. 1919. Mystery/Crime/Suspense, Social commentary/phenomena, Biography. *Publs:* mystery novels—Ride the Gold Mare, 1956; The Hoods Take Over, 1957; The Lusting Drive, 1958; The Long Night, 1957; The Slasher, 1959; The Enforcer, 1960; The Extortioners, 1960; The Gold-Plated Sewer, 1960; Candyleg, 1961 (as Machine Gun McCanin, 1970); The Parasite, 1963; The Organization, 1965 (as The Contract, 1970); The Overlord, 1972; other—Lucky Luciano, 1960; The Lindbergh Kidnapping Case, 1961; The Dillinger Story, 1961; (with Edward Reid) The Green Felt Jungle, 1963; (with Garry Wills) Jack Ruby, 1968; Captive City: Chicago in Chains, 1969; America the Violent, 1970; Poso del Mundo: Inside the Mexican-American Border, 1970; Dirty Business: The Corporate-Political Money-Power Game, 1974; The Director: An Oral Biography of J. Edgar Hoover, 1975; Brothers in Blood: The International Terrorist Network, 1977; My Story (by Judith Exner as told to Demaris), 1977; The Last Mafioso: The Treacherous World of Jimmy Fratianno, 1981; The Vegas Legacy, 1983; The Boardwalk Jungle, 1986; Ricochet, 1988. Add: c/o Bantam Books, Inc., 666 Fifth Ave., New York, N.Y. 10103, U.S.A.

DEMETILLO, Ricardo. Filipino, b. 1920. Novels/Short stories, Plays/Screenplays, Poetry, Literature. Prof. of Humanities, Univ. of the Philippines, Diliman, Quezon City, since 1975 (Asst. Prof., 1959–70; Chmn., Dept. of Humanities, 1961–62; Assoc. Prof., 1970–75). *Publs:* No Certain Weather: A Collection of Poetry, 1956; La Via: A Spiritual Journey, 1958; Daedalus and Other Poems, 1961; Barter in Panay (poetry), 1961; The Authentic Voice of Poetry, 1962; Masks and Signature (poetry), 1968; The Sacre-Crow Christ (poetry), 1973; The Heart of Emptiness Is Black (play), 1973; The City and the Thread of Light (poetry), 1974; Lazarus, Troubadour (poetry), 1974; The Genesis of a Troubled Vision (novel), 1976. Add: 38 Balacan St., West Ave., Quezon City, Philippines.

DEMIJOHN, Thom. *See* **DISCH,** Thomas M. and **SLADEK,** John.

de MILLE, Richard. American, b. 1922. Short stories, Sciences (general), Biography. Writer, since 1953. Television Dir., KTLA, 1946–50; Psychometrician, Univ. of Southern California, Los Angeles, 1961–62; Lectr. in Psychology, Univ. of California, Santa Barbara, 1962–65; Scientist, Gen. Research Corp., 1967–70; Consulting Ed., 1973–84. *Publs:* Put Your Mother on the Ceiling: Children's Imagination Games, 1967; Two Qualms and a Quirk, 1973; Castaneda's Journey, 1976; The Don Juan Papers, 1980. Add: 960 Lilac Dr., Montecito, Calif. 93108, U.S.A.

DEMING, Robert H. American, b. 1937. Literature. Prof. of English, State Univ. Coll. at Fredonia, N.Y. since 1970. Asst. Prof. of English, Miami Univ., Oxford, Ohio, 1965–70. *Publs:* Bibliography of James

Joyce Studies, 1964, 1977; (ed.) James Joyce, 1970; Ceremony and Art: Robert Herrick's Poetry, 1974. Add: 1801 N. Stadium Blvd., Columbia, Mont. 65201, U.S.A.

DeMORDAUNT, Walter J(ulius). American, b. 1925. Literature, Writing/Journalism. Prof. Emeritus of English, Southern Oregon State Coll., Ashland, since 1967 (Dir. of Composition, 1968–70). *Publs:* Assignments in Rhetoric, 1963; A Writer's Guide to Literature, 1965. Add: 18026 Alyssum Dr., Sun City West, Ariz. 85375, U.S.A.

DEMOTT, Benjamin (Hailer). American, b. 1924. Novels, Literary criticism, Social commentary. Member of the faculty, Amherst Coll., Massachusetts. Contributing Ed., Atlantic Monthly, Boston, since 1977 (Columnist, 1973–80); Columnist, Harper's mag., NYC, since 1982 (also, 1962–64). *Publs:* The Body's Cage (novel), 1959; Hells and Benefits (essays), 1962; You Don't Say (essays), 1966; A Married Man (novel), 1968; Supergrow (essays), 1969; Surviving the Seventies (essays), 1972; Scholarship for Society, 1974; America in Literature, 1977; Close Imaging: An Introduction to Literature, 1987. Add: Dept. of English, Amherst Coll., Amherst, Mass. 01002, U.S.A.

DEMPSEY, David (Knapp). American, b. 1914. Novels/Short stories, History, Psychology, Biography. Staff member, Reader's Digest, 1942–43, Time mag., 1947–48, and New York Times Book Review, 1950–53; Book Ed., The Unicorn Year Book, 1952–57; Columnist, Saturday Review, 1961–69. *Publs:* (contrib.) The U.S. Marines on Iwo Jima, 1945; (contrib.) Uncommon Valor, 1946; History of the Fourth Marine Division, 1946; Flood, 1956; All That Was Mortal (novel), 1958; (with R.P. Baldwin) Triumphs and Trials of Lotta Crabtree, 1968; (co-author) An Introduction to Environmental Psychology, 1974; The Way We Die, 1975; (with P.G. Zimbardo)—Psychology and You, 1978. Add: 12 Hayward Pl., Rye, N.Y. 10580, U.S.A.

de NATALE, Francine. *See* **MALZBERG,** Barry.

DENBIGH, Kenneth George. British, b. 1911. Sciences. Lectr. Univ. of Cambridge, 1948–55; Prof., Univ. of Edinburgh, 1955–60; Prof., Imperial Coll., 1960–66, and Principal, Queen Elizabeth Coll., 1966–77, Univ. of London. *Publs:* The Thermodynamics of the Steady State, 1951; The Principles of Chemical Equilibrium, 1955; Science, Industry and Social Policy, 1963; Chemical Reactor Theory, 1966; An Inventive Universe, 1975; Three Concepts of Time, 1981; Entropy in Relation to Incomplete Knowledge, 1985. Add: 19 Sheridan Rd., London SW19 3HW, England.

DEN BOER, James D. American, b. 1937. Poetry. Research Information Officer, Univ. of California, Santa Barbara, since 1973. Instr. of Adult Education, Santa Barbara Community Coll. District. Information Officer, U.S. Public Health Service, 1963–67; Estate Gardener, Montecito, Calif., 1967–68; Asst. Dir., Unicorn Press, Santa Barbara, 1968–69; Member, White House Conference on Children and Youth, Washington, D.C., 1970–71; Freelance writer, 1971–73. *Publs:* Learning The Way, 1968; Trying to Come Apart, 1971; Nine Poems, 1972; (ed.) A Letter from Charles Olson, 1975; Firewood, 1976; Lost in Blue Canyon, 1979. Add: 228 Ortega Ridge Rd., Santa Barbara, Calif. 93108, U.S.A.

DENENBERG, Herbert. American, b. 1929. Advertising/Public relations, Marketing, Money/Finance. Consumer Ed., WCAU-TV, since 1975; Columnist, Delaware County Daily Times, since 1987. Attorney, Denenberg & Denenberg, Omaha, Neb., 1954–55; Asst. Prof. of Insurance, Univ. of Iowa, Iowa City, 1961–62; Prof. Wharton Sch. of Finance and Commerce, Univ. of Pennsylvania, 1962–71; Insurance Commnr., Commonwealth of Pennsylvania, 1971–74; Public Utility Commissioner, Commonwealth of Pennsylvania, 1975; Columnist, Philadelphia Bulletin, 1975–79; Consumer Expert, WCAU-Radio, 1976–82. *Publs:* Risk and Insurance, 1964, 1974; (ed. with S.L. Kimball) Insurance, Government and Social Policy: Studies in Insurance Regulation, 1969; The Insurance Trap, 1972; Cover Yourself: The Moneysworth Guide to Buying Insurance, 1974; Shopper's Guidebook to Life Insurance, Health Insurance, Auto Insurance, Homeowner's Insurance, Doctors, Lawyers, Dentists, Pension Plans, Etc., 1974; Herb Denenberg's Smart Shopper's Guide, 1980. Add: P.O. Box 146, Wynnewood, Pa. 19096, U.S.A.

de NEUFVILLE, Richard. American, b. 1939. Engineering/Technology, Transportation. Prof. and Chmn., Technology and Policy Prog., Massachusetts Inst. of Technology, Cambridge, since 1975 (Asst. to Assoc. Prof., 1966–75). White House Fellow, Washington, D.C., 1965–66; Visiting Prof., London Graduate Sch. of Business, 1973–74, and Univ. of California, Berkeley, 1974–75, 1978; Ecole Centrale de Paris, 1981–82. *Publs:* (with J. Stafford) Systems Analysis for Engineers

and Managers, 1971; (with D.H. Marks) Systems Planning and Design, 1974; Airport Systems Planning, 1976; Applied Systems Analysis, 1989. Add: Room E40-251, MIT, Cambridge, Mass. 02139, U.S.A.

DENHOLM, David. Also writes as David Forrest. Australian, b. 1924. Novels/Short stories, History. Sr. Lectr. in History, Riverina-Murray Inst. of Advanced Education, Wagga Wagga, N.S.W. *Publs:* (as David Forrest) The Last Blue Sea, 1959; (as David Forrest) The Hollow Woodheap, 1962; The Colonial Australians, 1979. Add: Riverina-Murray Inst., P.O. Box 588, Wagga Wagga, N.S.W., Australia 2650.

DENISOFF, R. Serge. American, b. 1939. Media, Sociology. Assoc. Prof., then Prof. of Sociology, Bowling Green State Univ., Ohio, since 1970. Ed., Popular Music & Society. Asst. Prof., California State Univ., Los Angeles, 1969–70. *Publs:* (compiler) Protest Songs of War and Peace: Bibliography and Discography, 1970; Great Day Coming: Folk Music and the American Left, 1971; (with Gary B. Rush) Social and Political Movements, 1971; (contrib. ed. with Richard A. Peterson) The Sounds of Social Change: The Uses of Music in Contemporary Society, 1972; (contrib. ed.) Sociology: Theories in Conflict, 1972; (ed. with Charles H. McCaghy) Deviance, Criminality and Conflict: The Sociology of Criminality and Non-Conformity, 1973; (contrib. ed. with M. Levine and O. Callahan) Theories and Paradigms of Contemporary Sociology, 1974; (ed.) The Sociology of Dissent, 1974; Solid Gold: The Popular Record Industry, 1975; (with R. Wahrman) An Introduction to Sociology, 1975, 3rd ed., 1982; Sing a Song of Social Significance, 1983; Waylon: A Biography, 1983; Tarnished Gold: The Record Industry Revisited, 1986; Inside MTV, 1988. Add: 7 Valley View Dr., Bowling Green, Ohio 43402, U.S.A.

DENISON, Edward F(ulton). American, b. 1915. Economics. Sr. Fellow Emeritus, Brookings Instn., Washington, D.C., since 1979 (Sr. Fellow, 1962–78). Economist, 1941–47, and Acting Chief, 1948, National Income Div., U.S. Dept. of Commerce; Asst. Dir., Office of Business Economics, 1949–56; Economist, Cttee. for Economic Development, 1956–62; Assoc. Dir., Bureau of Economic Analysis, 1979–82—all Washington, D.C. *Publs:* (co-author) The Effects of Strategic Bombing on the German War Economy, 1945; The Sources of Economic Growth in the United States and the Alternatives Before Us, 1962; Why Growth Rates Differ: Postwar Experience in Nine Western Countries, 1967; Guideposts for Wages and Prices: Criteria and Consistency, 1968; Accounting for United States Economic Growth 1929-1969, 1974; (co-author) How Japan's Economy Grew So Fast, 1976; Accounting for Slower Economic Growth, 1979; Trends in American Economic Growth, 1929-82, 1985; Estimates of Productivity Change by Industry: An Evaluation and an Alternative, 1988. Add: 560 N St., S.W., Apt. N-902, Washington, D.C. 20024, U.S.A.

DENISON, (John) Michael (Terence Wellesley). British, b. 1915. Theatre, Autobiography. Actor; Dir., New Shakespeare Co., since 1971. Member of the Council, 1949–77, and Vice Pres., 1952, 1961–63, 1973, British Actors Equity Assn.; Member, Drama Panel, Arts Council, 1975–79. *Publs:* (with Dulcie Gray) The Actor and His World, 1964; Overture and Beginners (memoirs), 1973; Double Act (memoirs), 1985. Add: Shardeloes, Amersham, Bucks, England.

DENKER, Henry. American, b. 1912. Novels/Short stories, Plays/Screenplays. Member of the Council, Dramatists' Guild, 1970–73, Author's League, 1984–89. *Publs:* I'll Be Right Home, Ma, 1947; My Son, The Lawyer, 1949; Salome: Princess of Galilee, 1951; The First Easter, 1951; Time Limit! (play), 1957; Far Country (play), 1961; A Case of Libel (play), 1963; What Did We Do Wrong? (play), 1967; The Director, 1970; The Kingmaker, 1972; A Place for the Mighty, 1974; The Physicians, 1975; The Experiment, 1976; The Headhunters (play), 1976; The Starmaker, 1977; The Scofield Diagnosis, 1977; The Second Time Around (play), 1977; The Actress, 1978; Error of Judgement, 1979; Horowitz and Mrs. Washington, 1979, as play, 1980; The Warfield Syndrome, 1981; Outrage, 1982, as play, 1983, as film, 1985; The Healers, 1983; Kincaid, 1984; Robert, My Son, 1985; Judge Spencer Dissents, 1986; The Choice, 1987; The Retreat, 1988; Gift of Life, 1989. Add: 241 Central Park W., New York, N.Y. 10024, U.S.A.

DENMAN, Donald Robert. British, b. 1911. Economics. Prof. Emeritus of Land Economy, Univ. of Cambridge (joined faculty, 1947). *Publs:* Tenant Right Valuation in History and Modern Practice, 1942; Tenant Right Valuation and Current Legislation, 1948; Estate Capital: The Contribution of Landownership to Agricultural Finance, 1957; Origins of Ownership: A Brief History of Landownership and Tenure, 1958; (co-author) Bibliography of Rural Land Economy and Landownership, 1900-

1957, 1958; (co-author) Farm Rents: A Comparison of Current and Past Farm Rents in England and Wales, 1959; (ed. and contrib.) Landownership and Resources, 1960; (ed. and contrib.) Contemporary Problems of Land-ownership, 1963; Land in the Market, 1964; (Co-author) Commons and Village Greens: A Study in Conservation and Management, 1967; (ed. and contrib.) Land and People, 1967; Rural Land Systems: A General Classification of Rural Land Systems in Relation to the Surveyor's Profession and Rural Land Reform, 1968; Land Use and the Constitution of Property, 1969; Land Use: An Introduction to Proprietary Land Use Analysis, 1971; Human Environment: The Surveyor's Response, 1972; The King's Vista (Persian Land Reform), 1973; Prospects of Cooperative Planning, 1973; Land Economy: An Edcucation and a Career, 1975; The Place of Property, 1978; Land in a Free Society, 1980; The Fountain Principle (rural planning), 1982; Markets under the Sea?, 1984; Survival and Responsibility, 1986; After Government Failure?, 1988; Planning Fails the Inner Cities, 1988. Add: Pembroke Coll., Cambridge, England.

DENNING, Lord; Alfred Thompson Denning. British, b. 1899. Law. Called to Bar, 1923; King's Counsel, 1938; Judge of the High Court of Justice, 1944; a Lord Justice of Appeal, 1948–57; a Lord of Appeal in Ordinary, 1957–62; Master of the Rolls, 1962–82. *Publs:* (joint ed.) Smith's Leading Cases, 1929; (joint ed.) Bullen and Leake's Precedents, 1935; Freedom under the Law (Hamlyn Lectures), 1949; The Changing Law, 1953; The Road to Justice, 1955; The Discipline of Law, 1979; The Due Process of Law, 1980; The Family Story, 1981; What Next in the Law, 1982; The Closing Chapter, 1983; Landmarks in the Law, 1984; Leaves from My library, 1986. Add: The Lawn, Whitchurch, Hants. RG28 7AS, England.

DENNIS, Nigel (Forbes). British, b. 1912. Novels/Short stories, Plays/Screenplays, Poetry, Literature. Drama Critic, Encounter, London, since 1960 (Joint Ed., 1967–70); Staff Book Reviewer, The Sunday Telegraph, London, since 1961. Staff Book Reviewer, Time, NYC, 1940–59. *Publs:* Boys and Girls Come Out to Play (in U.S. as Sea Change), 1949; Cards of Identity, 1955; Two Plays and a Preface, 1958; Dramatic Essays, 1962; August for the People (play), 1962; Jonathan Swift's A Short Character, 1964; A House in Order, 1966; Exotics: Poems, 1971; An Essay on Malta, 1972. Add: c/o A.M. Heath & Co., 40-42 William IV St., London WC2N 4DD, England.

DENNIS-JONES, Harold. Also writes as Paul Hamilton. British, b. 1915. Language/Linguistics, Travel/Exploration/Adventure, Translations. Member, News Staff, Kewsley Newspapers, London, 1945–57; Travel Corresp., Geographical Mag., London, 1951–62, and Cambridge Evening News, 1968–70; Ed., mainly as Paul Hamilton, Fodor's Modern Guides, Yogoslavia, 1968–77, and Morocco, 1968–71; Asst. Ed., Travel Asia Pacific, 1977–78; Managing Dir., Tourplan Ltd., London 1974–82. *Publs:* (trans.) New Roads; (Trans.) School for Parents, 1963; Your Guide to the Dalmatian Coast, 1963; Your Guide to Denmark, 1964; Your Guide to Brittany, 1964; Your Guide to Morocco, 1965; Romania, 1968; Bulgaria, 1968; Israel, 1970, 4th ed. 1977; Portugal, 1974, 6th ed., 1983; Morocco and Tunisia, 1974; 3rd ed. 1979; Costa del Sol, 1974, 6th ed., 1983; Costa Brava, 1974; 6th ed., 1983; Majorca and the Balearic Islands, 6th ed. 1983; Holland, 1974, 6th ed. 1983; France, 1975, 6th ed. 1983; Denmark, 1975, 6th ed. 1983; Northern Spain, 1977, 1979; Amsterdam, 1977, 4th ed. 1986; Letts Speak French (Italian, Spanish), 3 vols., 1977; Spain, 1987; Yugoslavia, 1988. Add: 38 Broadwater Down, No. 14, Tunbridge Wells, kent, TN2 5NX, England.

DENSEN-GERBER, Judianne. American, b. 1934. Sociology, Autobiography/Memoirs/Personal. Founder and Exec. Dir., Odyssey House, NYC, since 1967; Founder and Pres., Odyssey Inst. Inc., since 1974. Visiting Assoc. Prof. of Law, Univ. of Utah Law Sch., Salt Lake City, Adjunct Assoc. Prof. of Law, New York Law Sch., NYC, and Founder and Pres., Inst. of Women's Wrongs, all since 1973. Columnist, New York Law Journal, 1971–72, and Manchester Union Leader, N.H., 1971–73. *Publs:* (with T.A. Baden) Drugs, Sex, Parents and You, 1972; (co-author) We Mainline Dreams: The Odyssey House Story, 1973; Walk in My Shoes: An Odyssey into Woman-life, 1976; Child Abuse and Neglect as Related to Parental Drug Abuse and Other Antisocial Behavior, 1978; (with David Sandberg) The Role of Child Abuse in Delinquency and Juvenile Court Decision-Making, 1984. Add: Odyssey Inst., 817 Fairfield Ave., Bridgeport, Conn. 06604, U.S.A.

DENT, Harold, Collett. British, b. 1894. Education. Ed. Times Educational Supplement, 1940–51; Prof. of Education, and Dir., Inst. of Education, Sheffield Univ., 1956–60. *Publs:* A New Order in English Education, 1942; Education in Transition, 1943; The Education Act, 1944, 1944; Secondary Education for All, 1949; Secondary Modern Schools:

An Interim Report, 1958; Universities in Transition, 1961; The Educational System of England and Wales, 1961; 1870-1970: Century of Growth in English Education, 1970; The Training of Teachers in England and Wales 1800-1975; Education in England and Wales, 1977. Add: Barns Croft, Goblin Lane, Cullompton, Devon EX15 1BB, England.

DENVER, Drake, C. *See* **NYE,** Nelson.

DENVER, Lee. *See* **GRIBBLE,** Leonard.

dePAOLA, Tomie. (Thomas Anthony dePaola). American, b. 1934. Children's Fiction, Children's Non-fiction. Freelance artist and designer, since 1956. Instr., 1962–63, and Asst. Prof. of Art, 1963–66, Coll. of the Sacred Heart, Newton, Mass.; Asst. Prof. of Art, San Francisco Coll. for Women, 1967–70; Instr. in Art, Chamberlayne Jr. Coll., Boston, 1972–73; Assoc. Prof. in Speech and Theatre, Colby-Sawyer Coll., New London, N.H., 1973–76; Assoc. Prof. of Art, 1976–78, and Artist-in-Residence, 1978–79, New England Coll., Henniker, New Hampshire. *Publs:* fiction for children—The Wonderful Dragon of Timlin, 1966; Fight the Night, 1968; Joe and the Snow, 1968; Parker Pig, Esquire, 1969; The Journey of the Kiss, 1970; The Monsters' Ball, 1970; Nana Upstairs and Nana Downstairs, 1973; Andy (That's My Name), 1973; The Unicorn and the Moon, 1973; Charlie Needs a Cloak, 1974; Watch Out for the Chicken Feet in Your Soup, 1974; Michael Bird-Boy, 1975; When Everyone Was Fast Asleep, 1976; Four Stories for Four Seasons, 1977; Helga's Dowry: A Troll Love Story, 1977; Bill and Pete, 1982; Pancakes for Breakfast, 1978; Oliver Button Is a Sissy, 1979; Big Anthony and the Magic Ring, 1979; Flicks, 1979; Songs of the Fog maiden, 1979; The Knight and the Dragon, 1980; The Friendly Beast, 1981; The Hunter and the Animals, 1981; Sing, Pierrot, Sing, 1983; The Vanishing Pumpkin, 1984; Merry Christmas, Strega Nona, 1986; non-fiction for children—The Wind and the Sun, 1972; The Cloud (Quid, Popcorn, Kids' Cat, Family Christmas Tree) Book, 5 vols., 1975–80; Strega Nona: An Old Tale, 1975, in U.K. as The Magic Pasta Pot, 1979; Things to Make and Do for Valentine's Day, 1976; The Christmas Pageant, 1978; The Clown of God: An Old Story, 1978; Criss-Cross, Applesauce, 1979; The Lady of Guadalupe, 1980; The Prince of the Dolomites: An Old Italian Tale, 1980; The Legend of Old Befana: An Italian Christmas Story, 1980; Fin M'Coul: The Giant of Knockmany Hill, 1981; The Comic Adventures of Old Mother Hubbard and Her Dog, 1981; Giorgio's Village, 1982; Francis, The Poor Man of Assisi, 1982; Strega Nona's Magic Lessons, 1982; The Legend of the Bluebonnet, 1983; Noah and the Ark, 1983; The Story of the Three Wise Kings, 1983; Country Farm, 1984; Mother Goose Story Streamers, 1984; The Mysterious Giant of Barletta, 1984; David and Goliath, 1984; The First Christmas, 1984; Mother Goose, 1985; Favorite Nursery Tales, 1986; Queen Esther, 1986; Bill and Pete Go Down the Nile, 1987; Kitten Kids, 4 vols., 1987; Book of Christmas Carols, 1987; An Early American Christmas, 1987; The Parables [and miracles] of Jesus, 2 vols., 1987. Add: c/o Putnam, 200 Madison Ave., New York, N.Y. 10016, U.S.A.

DE PRÉ, Jean-Anne. *See* **AVALLONE,** Michael.

de REGNIERS, Beatrice Schenk. Also writes as Tamara Kitt. American, b. 1914. Children's fiction, Poetry, Children's non-fiction. Dir. of Educational Materials, American Heart Assn., NYC, 1949–61; Ed., Lucky Book Club, Scholastic Book Services, NYC, 1961–81. *Publs:* The Giant Story, 1953; A Little House of Your Own, 1954; What Can You Do with a Shoe?, 1955; Was It a Good Trade?, 1956; A Child's Book of Dreams, 1957; Something Special, 1958; Cats Cats Cats Cats Cats, 1958; The Snow Party, 1959; What Happens Next?, 1959; The Shadow Book, 1960; Who Likes the Sun?, 1961; (as Tamara Kitt) The Secret Cat, 1961; The Little Book, 1961, reissued as Going for a Walk 1982; (as Tamara Kitt) The Adventures of Silly Billy, 1961; (as Tamara Kitt) The Surprising Pets of Billy Brown, 1962; (as Tamara Kitt) Billy Brown: The Baby Sitter, 1962; The Little Girl and Her Mother, 1963; (as Tamara Kitt) The Boy Who Fooled the Giant, 1963; (as Tamara Kitt) The Boy, the Cat, and the Magic Fiddle, 1964; May I Bring a Friend?, 1964; The Abraham Lincoln Joke Book, 1965; David and Goliath, 1965; How Joe the Bear and Sam the Mouse Got Together, 1965; Penny, 1966, 1987; Circus, 1966; The Giant Book, 1966; (as Tamara Kitt) A Special Birthday Party for Someone Very Special, 1966; (as Tamara Kitt) Sam and the Impossible Thing, 1967; The Day Everybody Cried, 1967; Willy O'Dwyer Jumped in the Fire, 1968; (as Tamara Kitt) Jake, 1968; Catch a Little Fox, 1969; Poems Children Will Sit Still For, 1969; The Boy, the Rat, and the Butterfly, 1971; Red Riding Hood Retold in Verse for Boys and Girls to Read Themselves, 1972; It Does Not Say Me-ow and Other Animal Riddle Rhymes, 1972; The Enchanted Forest, 1974; Little Sister and the Month Brothers, 1976; A Bunch of Poems and Verses, 1977; Laura's Story, 1979;

Everyone Is Good for Something, 1979; Picture Book Theater, 1982; Waiting for Mama, 1984; So Many Cats, 1985; This Big Cat and Other Cats I've Known, 1985; Jack and the Beanstalk Retold in Verse, 1985; A Week in the Life of Best Friends and Other Poems of Friendship, 1986; Jack the Giant Killer Retold in Verse and Other Useful Information about Giants, 1987; The Way I Feel. . . Sometimes, 1988. Add: 180 West 58th St., New York, N.Y. 10019, U.S.A.

DERFLER, (Arnold) Leslie. American, b. 1933. History. Prof. of History, Florida Atalntic Univ., Boca Raton, since 1969. Member of faculty, Carnegie Mellon Univ., Pittsburgh, 1962–68, and Univ. of Massachusetts, Amherst, 1968–69. *Publs:* (ed.) The Dreyfus Affair: Tragedy of Errors, 1963; The Third French Republic 1870-1940, 1966; Socialism Since Marx, 1973; Alexandre Millerand: The Socialist Years, 1977; (ed.) Hindi, 1977; President and Parliament: A Short History of the French Presidency, 1984. Add: Dept. of History, Florida Atlantic Univ., Boca Raton, Fla. 33431, U.S.A.

DERHAM, Arthur Morgan. British, b. 1915. Children's fiction. Theology/Religion. Editorial Secty., The Scripture Union, 1947–66; Information Officer, United Bible Socs., 1968–73; Editorial Secty., Leprosy Mission, 1973–80. *Publs:* On The Trail of the Windward, 1948; The Cruise of the Clipper, 1950; Bluewater Mere, 1952; No Darker Rooms, 1954; The Mature Christian, 1957; A Christian's Guide to Bible Study, 1960; A Christian's Guide to Love, Sex, and Marriage, 1962. Add: 50 Firs Rd., West Mersea, Essex, England.

de ROO, Anne (Louise). New Zealander, b. 1931. Children's fiction. Full-time writer. Library Asst., Dunedin Public Library, 1956; Asst. Librarian, Dunedin Teachers' Coll., 1957–59; Governess and part-time gardener, Shropshire, England, 1962–68; Part-time secty., Hertfordshire, England, 1969–73. *Publs:* The Gold Dog, 1969; Moa Valley, 1969; Boy and the Sea Beast, 1971; Cinnamon and Nutmeg, 1972; Mick's Country Cousins, 1974; Scrub Fire, 1977; Traveller, 1979; Because of Rosie, 1980; Jacky Nobody, 1983; Friend Troll, Friend Taniwha, 1986; The Bat's Nest, 1986. Add: 38 Joseph St., Palmerston North, New Zealand.

DERRETT, (John) Duncan (Martin). British, b. 1922. Law, Theology/Religion. Prof. of Oriental Laws, Univ. of London, 1965–82 (Lectr. in Hindu Law, Sch. of Oriental and African Studies, 1949–56; Reader in Oriental Laws, 1956–65); Lectr. in Hindu Law, Inns of Court Sch. of Law, London, 1965–79; Wilde Lectr. in Natural and Comparative Religion, Univ. of Oxford, 1978–81. *Publs:* The Hoysalas, 1957; Hindu Law Past and Present, 1957; Introduction to Modern Hindu Law, 1963; (ed. and co-author) Studies in the Law of Succession in Nigeria, 1965; Religion, Law and the State in India, 1968; (ed. and co-author) Introduction to Legal Systems, 1968; Law in the New Testament, 1970; Critique of Modern Hindu Law, 1970; Jesus's Audience, 1973; (trans. and ed.) Law of India, by R. Lingat, 1973; Henry Swinburne 1551-1624, Civil Lawyer of York, 1973; Dharmasastra and Juridical Literature, 1973; Bharuci's Commentary on the Manusmrti, 1975; Essays in Classical and Modern Hindu Law, 4 vols., 1976–78; Studies in the New Testament, 5 vols., 1977–89; Death of a Marriage Law, 1978; (ed. and co-author) The Concept of Duty in South Asia, 1978; Beitrage zu Indischem Rechtsdenken, 1979; The Anastasis, 1982; A Textbook for (Buddhist) Novices, 1983; The Making of Mark, 1985; New Resolutions of Old Conundrums (on Luke), 1986; The Ascetic Discourse, 1989. Add: Half Way House, High St., Blockley, Moreton-in-Marsh, Glos. GL56 9EX, England.

DERRIMAN, James Parkyns. British, b. 1922. Advertising/Public relations, Law. Barrister since 1947; Secty. and Group Personnel Dir., Charles Barker Group, London, 1975–82, now retired (Joint Manag. Dir., 1968–73, and Joint Vice-Chmn., 1973–74, Charles Barker City Ltd.). Pres., Inst. of Public Relations, 1973–74; Hon. Vice-Pres., European Confedn. of Public Relations since 1981. *Publs:* Pageantry of the Law, 1955; Discovering the Law, 1962; Public Relations in Business Management, 1964; Company-Investor Relations, 1969; (ed. with George Pulay) The Bridge Builders: Public Relations Today, 1980. Add: 34 Mossville Gardens, Morden, Surrey SM4 4DG, England.

DERRY, John (Wesley). British, b. 1933. History, Biography. Reader in History, Univ. of Newcastle upon Tyne, since 1977 (Lectr., 1970–73; Sr. Lectr., 1973–77). Research Fellow, Emmanuel Coll., Cambridge, 1959–61; Asst. Lectr., 1961–63, and Lectr., 1963–65, London Sch. of Economics; Dir. of Studies in History, and Fellow, Downing Coll., Cambridge, 1965–70. *Publs:* William Pitt, 1962; Reaction and Reform, 1963, 3rd ed. 1970; The Regency Crisis and the Whigs, 1963; Parliamentary Reform, 1966; The Radical Tradition, 1967; Political Parties, 1968; (ed.) Cobbett's England. 1968; Charles James Fox, 1972; Castlereagh,

1976; English Politics and the American Revolution, 1976. Add: Dept. of History, Univ. of Newcastle upon Tyne, Newcastle NE1 7RU, England.

DERRY, Thomas Kingston. British, b. 1905. History, International relations/Current affairs. Headmaster, Mill Hill Sch., 1938–40; with Political Intelligence Dept., Foreign Office, London, 1941–45; Asst. Master, St. Marylebone Grammar Sch., London, 1945–65. *Publs:* (with T. Jarman) The European World, 1950; The Campaign in Norway, 1952; A Short History of Norway, 1957; (with T. Williams) A Short History of Technology, 1960; The United Kingdom Today, 1961; A Short Economic History of Britain, 1965; (with E. Knapton) Europe 1815-1914, 1965; Europe 1914 to the Present, 1966; (co-author) The Making of Britain, 3 vols., 1959–69; A History of Modern Norway 1814-1972, 1973; A History of Scandinavia, 1979; (with T. Jarman) Modern Britain, 1979. Add: Nils Lauritssons vei 27, 0854 Oslo 8, Norway.

DERSHOWITZ, Alan M. American, b. 1938. Civil liberties/Human rights, Criminology, Law, Psychiatry. Civil liberties lawyer since 1963; Prof. of Law, Harvard Univ., Cambridge, Mass., since 1967 (Assoc. Prof., 1964–67). Consultant, National Inst. of Mental Health; syndicated columnist, United Features Syndicate; Columnist ("Justice"), Penthouse mag. *Publs:* (with Jay Katz and others) Psychoanalysis, Psychiatry and the Law, 1967; (with Joseph Goldstein and Richard Schwartz) Criminal Law: Theory and Process, 1974; (with others) Fair and Certain Punishment: Report of the Twentieth-Century Fund Task Force on Criminal Sentencing, 1976; (with Telford Taylor) Courts of Terror, 1976; The Best Defense, 1982; Reversal of Fortune: Inside the Von Bulow Case, 1986; Taking Liberties: A Compendium of Hard Cases, Legal Dilemmas and Bum Raps, 1988. Add: Law Sch., Harvard Univ., Griswold 302, Cambridge, Mass. 02138, U.S.A.

DESAI, Anita. Indian, b. 1937. Novels/Short stories, Children's fiction. *Publs:* Cry, The Peacock, 1963; Voices in the City, 1965; Bye-Bye, Blackbird, 1971; The Peacock Garden, 1974; Where Shall We Go This Summer?, 1975; Cat on a Houseboat, 1976; Fire on the Mountain, 1977; Games at Twilight, 1978; Clear Light of Day, 1980; A Village by the Sea, 1982; In Custody, 1984; Baumgantner's Bombay, 1988. Add: c/o Deborah Rogers Ltd., 49 Blenheim Cres., London W11 2EF, England.

de ST. JORRE, John. British, b. 1936. Novels/Short stories, History. Freelance journalist and writer. Formerly Foreign Corresp. with the Observer newspaper. *Publs:* The Nigerian Civil War (in U.S. as The Brothers' War), 1972; (with B. Shakespeare) The Patriot Game, 1973; A House Divided: South Africa's Uncertain Future, 1977; The Guards, 1981. Add: c/o Deborah Rogers Ltd., 49 Blenheim Cres., London W11 2EF, England.

DESANI, G(ovindas) V(ishnoodas). American, b. 1909. Novels/ Short stories, Plays/Screenplays. Prof. of Philosophy, Univ. of Texas at Austin, 1969–79, now Emeritus (Fulbright-Hays Lectr., 1968). Columnist, and Special Contrib., Illustrated Weekly of India, Bombay, 1960–68. *Publs:* All About H. Hatterr (in U.S. as All About H. Hatterr: A Gesture), 1948, 6th ed. 1970; Hali (play), 1950. Add: Dept. of Philosophy, Univ. of Texas, Austin, Tex. 78712, U.S.A.

DeSANTIS, Vincent P. American, b. 1916. History. Prof. of American History, Univ. of Notre Dame, since 1949 (Chmn., Dept. of History, 1963–71). *Publs:* Republicans Face the Southern Question: The New Departure Years 1877-1897, 1959; (co-author) Our Country , 1960; (co-author) Roman Catholicism and the American Way of Life, 1960; (co-author) America's Ten Greatest Presidents, 1961; (co-author) The Gilded Age: A Reappraisal, 1963; The Democratic Experience, 1963, 5th ed. 1981; (co-author) America Past and Present, 2 vols., 1968; (co-author) American Foreign Policy in Europe, 1969; (co-author) America's Eleven Greatest Presidents, 1971; (compiler) The Gilded Age, 1973; The Shaping of Modern America 1877-1914, 1973, 3rd ed. 1989; (co-author) Six Presidents from the Empire State, 1974; (co-author) The Heritage of 1776, 1976; (co-author) A History of United States Foreign Policy, 4th ed. 1979. Add: Dept. of History, Univ. of Notre Dame, Notre Dame, Ind. 46556, U.S.A.

DeSANTO, Robert S. American, b. 1940. Environmental science/Ecology, Zoology. Chief Scientist, De Leuw, Cather Co., East Hartford, Conn., since 1977. Ed. of the Springer Series on Environmental Management, since 1979. Asst. Prof., Connecticut Coll., New London, 1968–72; Chief Ecologist, Maguire Inc., Weathersfield, Conn., 1972–74, and Comsis Corp., Glastonbury, Conn., 1974–77. *Publs:* (ed. with P. Knauth and D. McAdo) Lesser Invertebrates, and Protochordates and the Echnioderms, vols. 18 and 19 of the Illustrated Encyclopedia of the Animal

Kingdom, 1971; (with R.V. Tait) Elements of Marine Ecology, 1974; Concepts of Applied Ecology, 1978. Add: 8 Sylvan Glen, East Lyme, Conn. 06333, U.S.A.

DeSEYN, Donna E. American, b. 1933. Earth sciences, Natural history. Science teacher since 1960, and Dept. Chmn. since 1974, Fairport Central Sch., N.Y. (Elementary Science Consultant, 1962–69; Dir., Earth-Space Science Center, 1969–71). Staff member, Phelps Central Sch., 1955–59. *Publs:* Termite Works for His Colony, 1968; Teaching Earth Science with Investigations and Behavioral Objectives, 1973; Trees of Sonnenberg Gardens, 1977. Add: 5 Tamarack Dr., Canandaigua, N.Y. 14424, U.S.A.

DESSAUER, John Paul. American, b. 1904. Business/Trade/Industry. Pres., John P. Dessauer Inc., since 1972. Contrib. Ed., Publishers Weekly, NYC, since 1970. Assoc. Dir., Indiana Univ. Press, Bloomington, 1960–67; Dir., Univ. Press of Kansas, Lawrence, 1967–69. *Publs:* Book Publishing—What It Is, What It Does, 1974, 1981; Book Industry Trends, 1983; International Strategies for American Investors, 1986. Add: P.O. Box 2174, Vineyard Haven, Mass. 02568, U.S.A.

DETHIER, Vincent G(aston). American, b. 1915. Novels/Short stories, Children's fiction, Natural history, Zoology. Prof. of Zoology, Univ. of Massachusetts, Amherst, since 1975. Assoc. Prof., 1947–51, and Prof. of Biology, 1951–58, Johns Hopkins Univ., Baltimore, Md.; Prof. of Biology and Psychology, Univ. of Pennsylvania, Philadelphia, 1957–68; Prof. of Biology, Princeton Univ., New Jersey, 1968–75. *Publs:* Chemical Insect Attractants and Repellents, 1947; (co-author) Animal Behavior, 1961; To Know a Fly, 1962; The Physiology of Insect Senses, 1963; Fairweather Duck, 1970; Biological Principles and Processes, 1971; Buy Me a Volcano (novel), 1972; Man's Plague, 1975; The Hungry Fly: A Physiological Analysis, 1975; The Ant Heap (novel), 1979; The World of the Tent Makers: The Natural History of Tent Caterpillars, 1980; Newberry: The Life and Times of a Maine Clam (juvenile), 1981; The Ecology of a Summer House, 1984; A University in Search of Civility, 1984; Ten Masses: Impressions, 1988. Add: Dept. of Zoology, Univ. of Massachusetts, Amherst, Mass. 01003, U.S.A.

de TREVINO, Elizabeth (Borton). American, b. 1904. Novels/Short stories, Children's fiction, Children's non-fiction, Autobiography/Memoirs/Personal. Reporter, Jamaica Plain Journal, Boston; apprentice in production and advertising, Ginn and Co., publishers; Boston; Interviewer, Boston Herald American, for several years. *Publs:* Pollyanna series, vols., 1931–51; Our Little Aztec Cousin of Long Ago, 1934; Our Little Ethiopian Cousin: Children of the Queen of Sheba, 1935; About Bellamy, 1940; My Heart Lies South: The Story of My Mexican Marriage, 1953; A Carpet of Flowers, 1955; Even As You Love, 1957; The Greek of Toledo: A Romantic Narrative about El Greco, 1959; Where The Heart Is (memoirs), 1962; Nacar, The White Deer, 1963; I, Juan de Pareja, 1965; The Fourth Gift, 1966; Casilda of the Rising Moon: A Tale of Magic and of Faith of Knights and a Saint in Medieval Spain, 1967; Turi's Poppa, 1968; The House on Bitterness Street, 1970; Here Is Mexico, 1970; Beyond the Gates of Hercules: A Tale of the Lost Atlantis, 1971; The Music Within, 1973; Juarez, Man of Law, 1974; The Hearthstone of My Heart (memoirs), 1977; The Heart Possessed: A Love Story, 1978; Among the Innocent, 1981; El Güero, 1989. Add: c/o Farrar, Straus and Giroux, 19 Union Square West, New York, N.Y. 10003, U.S.A.

DETWEILER, Robert. American, b. 1932. Literature. Prof. of Comparative Literature, Emory Univ., Atlanta, since 1973. Asst. Prof. of English, Univ. of Florida, Gainesville, 1963–65; Asst. Prof. of English, Hunter Coll. of City Univ. of New York, 1965–66; Assoc. Prof. of Literature, Florida Presbyterian Coll., St. Petersburg, 1966–70; Fulbright Prof. of American Studies, Univ. of Salzburg, Austria, 1971–72. *Publs:* Four Spiritual Crises in Mid-Century American Fiction, 1964; Saul Bellow, 1967; Iris Murdoch's The Unicorn, 1969; John Updike, 1973, 1984; Story, Sign and Self: Phenomenology and Structuralism as Literary Critical Methods, 1978; (ed. with G. Meeter) Faith and Fiction: The Modern Story, 1979; (ed.) Derrida and Biblical Studies, 1982; (ed.) Art/Literature/Religion: Life on the Borders, 1983; (ed.) Reader Response Approaches to Biblical and Secular Texts, 1985; Breaking the Fall: Religious Readings of Contemporary Fiction, 1989. Add: Emory Univ., Atlanta, Ga. 30322, U.S.A.

DETZ, Joan (Marie). American. Speech/Rhetoric, Writing/Journalism. Dir., Joan Detz Communications Consulting, since 1985. Teacher, James Blair Sch., Williamsburg, Va., 1974–76; Writer and Researcher, Wells,

Rich and Greene Advertising, NYC, 1976–80; Speechwriter, Brooklyn Union Gas, N.Y., 1980–85. *Publs:* How to Write and Give a Speech, 1984; You Mean I Have to Stand Up and Say Something?, 1986. Add: 573 Second St., No. 2, Brooklyn, N.Y. 11215, U.S.A.

DEUTSCH, Karl (Wolfgang). American, b. 1912. Politics/Government. Stanford Prof. of Intnl. Peace, Harvard Univ., Cambridge, since 1971; and Dir., Intnl. Inst. for Comparative Social Research, West Berlin. Prof. of Political Science, Yale Univ., New Haven, 1958–67. Vice-Pres., 1970–76, and Pres., 1976–79, Intnl. Political Science Assn. Pres., American Political Science Assn., 1969–70. *Publs:* Political Community and the North Atlantic Area, 1957; Germany Rejoins the Powers, 1959; The Nerves of Government, 2nd ed., 1966; The Analysis of International Relations, 1968, 3rd ed. 1988; Politics and Government, 1974, 3rd ed. 1980; (co-author and ed.) Mathematical Approaches to Politics, 1973; (ed.) Eco-Social Systems and Eco-Politics, 1977; Tides Among Nations, 1978; (with M. Kochen) Decentralization, 1980; (co-author and ed.) Fear of Science—Trust in Science, 1980; (with others) Comparative Government, 1981; (ed. with others) Advances in the Social Sciences since 1900, 1984. Add: 25 Lakeview Ave., Cambridge, Mass. 02138, U.S.A.

DEUTSCHER, Irwin. American, b. 1923. Sociology. Prof. of Sociology, Univ. of Akron, 1975–83, now Emeritus. Dir. of Research in Health and Welfare, Community Studies Inc., Kansas City, Mo., 1954–59; Dir., Youth Development Center, and Prof. of Sociology, Syracuse Univ., N.Y., 1959–68; Prof. of Sociology, Case Western Reserve Univ., Cleveland, 1968–75. *Publs:* (with E.C. and H.M. Hughes) Twenty Thousand Nurses Tell Their Story, 1958; (ed. with E.J. Thompson) Among the People: Encounters with the Poor, 1968; What We Say/What We Do: Sentiments and Acts, 1973. Add: Dept. of Sociology, Univ. of Akron, Akron, Ohio 44325, U.S.A.

DEVERAUX, Jude. Pseudonym for Jude Gilliam White. American, b. 1947. Novels. *Publs:* The Enchanted Land, 1978; The Black Lyon, 1980; The Velvet Promise, 1981; Casa Grande, 1982; Highland Velvet, 1982; Velvet Song, 1983; Velvet Angel, 1983; Sweetbriar, 1983; Counterfeit Lady, 1984; Lost Lady, 1985; River Lady, 1985; Twin of Ice, 1985; Twin of Fire, 1985; The Temptress, 1986; The Raider, 1987; The Princess, 1987; The Maiden, 1988; The Awakening, 1988. Add: 1937 Tijeras Rd., Santa Fe, N.M. 87501, U.S.A.

de VINCK, José M.G.A. (Baron de Vinck). Belgian, b. 1912. Poetry, Human relations, Theology/Religion, Translations. Owner, Alleluia Press, Allendale, N.J. Prof. of Philosophy, Seton Hall Univ., 1950–54; Ed., Trans. and Designer, St. Anthony Guild Press, Paterson, N.J. 1955–70; Prof. of Philosophy and Theology, Tombrock Coll., Paterson, N.J., 1967–74; Assoc. Ed., Sunday Publs., Fairfield, N.J., 1974. *Publs:* Images, 1940; (with Etienne du Bus de Warnaffe) Le Cantique de la Vie, 1943; (co-ed and trans. with J. Raya) Byzantine Missal for Sundays and Feast Days, 1958; (trans.) The Works of Bonaventure, 5 vols., 1960–70; The Virtue of Sex, 1966; (with J.T. Catoir) The Challenge of Love, 1969; (co-ed. and trans. with J. Raya) Byzantine Daily Worship, 1969; The Yes Book: An Answer to Life, 1972; The Words of Jesus, 1977; (ed.) Byzantine Altar Gospel, 1979; (ed.) Byzantine Altar Epistles, 1980; Revelations of Women Mystics, 1985. Add: 672 Franklin Turnpike, Allendale, N.J. 07401, U.S.A.

DeVITO, Joseph. American, b. 1938. Language/Linguistics, Speech/Rhetoric. Prof., Hunter Coll. of City Univ. of New York, since 1985. Prof., Queens Coll. of City Univ. of New York, 1972–85. *Publs:* The Psychology of Speech and Language, 1970, 1981; General Semantics, 1971, 1974; Psycholinguistics, 1971; (ed.) Communication, 1971, 3rd ed. 1981; (ed.) Language, 1973; The Interpersonal Communication Book, 1976, 5th ed. 1985; Human Communication: The Basic Course, 1978, 4th ed. 1988; Elements of Public Speaking, 1981, 3rd ed. 1987; Communication Handbook: A Dictionary, 1986; The Nonverbal Communication Workbook, 1989. Add: 140 Nassau St., New York, N.Y. 10038, U.S.A.

DEVLIN, Anne. British/Irish, b. 1951. Short Stories, Plays. Writer Assoc., Royal Court Theatre, London, since 1985; Visiting Lectr. in Playwriting, Univ. of Birmingham, since 1987. *Publs:* Ourselves Alone and Other Plays, 1986; The Way Paver (short stories), 1986. Add: 70 Woodstock Rd., Moseley, Birmingham B13 9BN, England.

DEVLIN, Lord; Patrick Arthur Devlin. British, b. 1905. History, Law. High Steward, Cambridge Univ., since 1966. Called to the Bar, Gray's Inn, London, 1929; Prosecuting Counsel to the Mint, 1931–39; served in the Legal Dept., Ministry of Supply, 1940–42; Jr. Counsel, Ministries of War Transport, Food and Supply 1942–45; King's Counsel, 1945; Master of the Bench, Gray's Inn, 1947; Attorney Gen., Duchy of Cornwall, 1947–48; Justice of the High Court, Queen's Bench Div., London, 1948–60; Chmn., Wiltshire Quarter Sessions, 1955–71; Pres., Restrictive Practices Court, 1956–60; a Lord Justice of Appeal, 1960–61; a Lord of Appeal in Ordinary, 1961–64; Chmn. of the Press Council, 1964–69. Chmn. of the Council, Bedford Coll., Univ. of London, 1953–59; Chmn., Cttee. of Inquiry into Dock Labour Scheme, 1955–56, Nyasaland Inquiry Commn., 1959, and Cttee. of Inquiry into Port Transport Industry, 1964–65; Chmn., Assn. of Average Adjusters, 1966–67; Chmn., Joint Bd. for the National Newspaper Industry, 1965–69; Chmn., Intnl. Labour Office Comm. to Examine Complaints Concerning Observance by Greece of Freedom of Association Conventions, 1969–71; Chmn., Commn. of Inquiry into Industrial Representation, 1971–72. *Publs:* Trial by Jury (Hamlyn Lectures), 1956; Criminal Prosecution in England (Sherrill Lectures), 1957; Samples of Lawmaking (Lloyd Roberts and other Lectures), 1962; The Enforcement of Morals (Maccabean and other Lectures), 1965; The House of Lords and the Naval Prize Bill, 1911 (Rede Lecture), 1968; Too Proud to Fight: Woodrow Wilson's Neutrality, 1974; The Judge (lectures), 1979; Easing the Passing: The Trial of Dr. John Bodkin Adams, 1985. Add: West Wick House, Pewsey, Wilts., England.

DE VORSEY, Louis, Jr. American, b. 1929. Geography. Prof. of Geography, Univ. of Georgia, Athens, since 1967, now Emeritus. *Publs:* The Indian Boundary in the Southern Colonies, 1763-1775, 1966; De Brahm's Report of the General Survey in the Southern District of North America, 1971; (ed.) The Atlantic Pilot, 1974; The Georgia-South Carolina Boundary, 1982; (ed. with John Parker) In the Wake of Columbus, 1985; (ed. with Dorinda Dallmeyer) Rights to Oceanic Resources, 1989. Add: 355 King's Rd., Athens, Ga. 30606, U.S.A.

DE VRIES, Peter. American, b. 1910. Novels/Short stories, Plays/Screenplays. Candy vending machine operator, and radio actor, Chicago, 1931–38; Assoc. Ed., 1938–42. and Co-ed., 1942–44, Poetry mag., Chicago; Member, Editorial Staff, The New Yorker mag., N.Y.C., 1944–87. *Publs:* But Who Wakes the Bugler?, 1940; The Handsome Heart, 1943; Angels Can't Do Better, 1944; No But I Saw the Movie (short stories), 1952; The Tunnel of Love, 1954; Comfort Me with Apples, 1956; (with J. Fields) The Tunnel of Love (play), 1957; The Mackerel Plaza, 1958; The Tents of Wickedness, 1959; Through the Fields of Clover, 1961; The Blood of the Lamb, 1962; Reuben, Reuben, 1964; Let Me Count the Ways, 1965; The Vale of Laughter, 1967; The Cat's Pajamas and Witch's Milk, 1968; Mrs. Wallop, 1970; Into Your Tent I'll Creep, 1971; Forever Panting, 1973; The Glory of the Hummingbird, 1974; I Hear America Swinging, 1976; Madder Music, 1977; Consenting Adults, 1980; Sauce for the Goose, 1981; Slouching Towards Kalamazoo, 1982; The Prick of Noon, 1985; Peckham's Marbles, 1986. Add: 170 Cross Hwy., Westport, Conn. 06880, U.S.A.

de VRIES, Rachel (Guido). American, b. 1947. Novels/Short stories, Poetry, Essays. Part-time English Instr., Syracuse Univ., New York, since 1978. Co-Founder and Co-Dir., Community Writers' Project, Syracuse, since 1984; Poet-in-Residence, Alternate Literary Programs in the Schools, since 1984. Nurse, in the U.S. and in Kenya, 1968–78; Resident Faculty Member and Co-Dir. of the Women's Writers' Center, Cazenovia, N.Y., 1978–82; Instr., Morrisville Coll., State Univ. of New York, 1985. *Publs:* An Arc of Light, 1978; (with others) Learning Our Way: Essays in Feminist Education, 1983; Tender Warriors, 1986. Add: c/o Firebrand Books, 141 The Commons, Ithaca, N.Y. 14850, U.S.A.

De WAAL, Ronald Burt. American, b. 1932. Literature. Special Collections Librarian, Univ. of New Mexico, Albuquerque, 1958–59; Head Librarian, New Mexico Military Inst., Roswell, 1959–60, Sperry Utah Co., Salt Lake City, 1961–64, and Westminster Coll., Salt Lake City, 1964–66; Humanities Librarian, and Exhibits Coordinator, Colorado State Univ., Fort Collins, 1966–88. *Publs:* The World Bibliography of Sherlock Holmes and Dr. Watson: A Classified and Annotated List of Materials Relating to Their Lives and Adventures, 1887-1972, 1974; The International Sherlock Holmes, 1980. Add: 638 Twelfth Ave., Salt Lake City, Utah 84103, U.S.A.

DEWALD, Paul A. American, b. 1920. Psychiatry. Private practitioner of psychoanalysis, St. Louis, Mo., since 1961; Clinical Prof. of Psychiatry, Sch. of Medicine, St. Louis Univ., since 1969; Medical Dir., St. Louis Psychoanalytic Inst., 1972–83. *Publs:* Psychotherapy: A Dynamic Approach, 1964, 1969; The Psychoanalytic Process, 1972; Learning Process in Psychoanalytic Supervision, 1987. Add: 4524 Forest Park, St. Louis, Mo. 63108, U.S.A.

DEWAR, Michael J(ames Steuart). American, b. 1918. Chemistry. Robert A. Welch Prof. of Chemistry, Univ. of Texas at Austin, since 1963. Prof. of Chemistry, and Head of Dept., Queen Mary Coll., Univ. of London 1951–59; Prof. of Chemistry, Univ. of Chicago, 1959–63. *Publs:* The Electronic Theory of Organic Chemistry, 1949; Hyperconjugation, 1962; An Introduction to Modern Chemistry, 1965; The Molecular Orbital Theory of Organic Chemistry, 1969; (with R. Jones) Computer Compilation of Molecular Weights and Percentage Compositions for Organic Compounds, 1969, (with R.C. Dougherty) The PMO Theory of Organic Chemistry, 1975. Add: Dept. of Chemistry, Univ. of Texas at Austin, Austin, Tex., 78712, U.S.A.

DEWART, Leslie. Canadian, b. 1922. Philosophy, Theology/Religion. Prof. of Philsopy and Religious Studies, Univ. of Toronto, since 1956, Emeritus since 1988. Assoc. Ed., Intnl. Zialog Zeitschrift, since 1967; Contrib. Ed., The Ecumenist, since 1968; Assoc. Ed., Continuum, 1964–70. *Publs:* Christianity and Revolution, 1963; The Future of Belief, 1966; The Foundations of Belief, 1969; Religion, Language and Truth, 1970; Evolution and Consciousness, 1989. Add: 14 Prospect St., Toronto, Ont. M4X 1C6, Canada.

DEWDNEY, John Christopher. British, b. 1928. Geography. Prof. of Geography, Univ. of Durham, since 1986 (Lectr., 1953–68; Sr. Lectr., 1968–71; Reader, 1971–86). Prof. of Geography, Fourah Bay Coll., Univ. of Sierra Leone, 1965–67. *Publs:* (with H. Bowen-Jones and W.B. Fisher) Maltas-Background for Development, 1961; A Geography of the Soviet Union, 1965, 1971, 1979; (ed.) Durham County and City with Teesside, 1970; Turkey, 1971; The U.S.S.R., 1976, 1979; (ed. with D. Rhind) People in Durham: A Census Atlas, 1976; (with others) People in Britain: A Census Atlas, 1980; U.S.S.R. in Maps, 1982. Add: Dept. of Geography, Science Labs., South Rd., Durham City, England.

DeWEESE, Gene. (Thomas Eugene DeWeese). Also writes with Robert Coulson under joint pseud. Thomas Stratton, and writes gothic novels as Jean DeWeese and, with Connie Kugi, as Victoria Thomas. American, b. 1934. Romance/Gothic, Science fiction/Fantasy, Children's fiction, Crafts. Electronics Technician, Delco Radio, Kokomo, Ind., 1954–59; Technical Writer, Delco Electronics, Milwaukee, 1959–74. *Publs:* (as Thomas Stratton) The Invisibility Affair: Man from U.N.C.L.E. No. 11, 1967; (as Thomas Stratton) The Mind-Twisters Affair: Man from U.N.C.L.E. No. 12, 1967; (with Robert Coulson) Now You See It/Him/Them . . ., 1975; (with Gini Rogowski) Making American Folk Art Dolls, 1975; (as Jean DeWeese) The Reimann Curse, 1975, expanded version as A Different Darkness, 1982; (as Jean DeWeese) The Carnelian Cat, 1975; (as Jean DeWeese) The Moonstone Spirit, 1975; (as Jean DeWeese) The Doll with Opal Eyes, 1976; (as Jean DeWeese) Cave of the Moaning Wind, 1976; (as Jean DeWeese) Web of Guilt, 1976; Jeremy Case, 1976; (with Robert Coulson) Charles Fort Never Mentioned Wombats, 1977; (as Jean DeWeese) Nightmare in Pewter, 1978; Major Corby and the Unidentified Flapping Object (juvenile), 1979; The Wanting Factor, 1980; The Adventures of a Two-Minute Werewolf (juvenile), 1980; (as Jean DeWeese) Hour of the Cat, 1980; Nightmares From Space (juvenile), 1981; (as Jean DeWeese) The Blackhoe Gothic, 1981; Adventures of a Two-Minute Werewolf, 1983; Something Answered, 1983; Computers in Entertainment and the Arts (juvenile non-fiction), 1984; Black Suits from Outer Space (juvenile science fiction), 1985; (with Robert Coulson) Nightmare Universe, 1985; The Dandelion Caper (juvenile science fiction), 1986; (as Victoria Thomas) Ginger's Wish, 1987; The Calvin Nullifier (juvenile science fiction), 1987; Chain of Attack (Star Treks, No. 32), 1987; The Peacekeepers (Star Trek: The Next Generation No. 2), 1988; The Final Nexus (Star Trek No. 43), 1988. Add: 2718 N. Prospect, Milwaukee, Wisc. 53211, U.S.A.

DeWEESE, Jean. *See* **DeWEESE,** Gene.

DEWEY, Donald O(dell). American, b. 1930. History. Prof. of History since 1969, and Dean of Natural and Social Sciences since 1983, California State Univ., Los Angeles (Asst. Prof. 1962–65; Assoc. Prof. 1966–69). Asst. Ed. 1960, and Assoc. Ed. 1960–62, The Papers of James Madison. *Publs:* (co-ed.) The Papers of James Madison, 3 vols., 1962–64; (co-ed.) The Continuing Dialogue, 2 vols., 1964–65; (ed.) Union and Liberty: Documents in American Constitutionalism, 1969; Marshall Versus Jefferson: The Political Background of Marbury v. Madison, 1970; (co-author) Becoming Informed Citizens: Lessons on the Constitution for Junior High School Students, 1988. Add: Dept. of History, California State Univ., Los Angeles, Calif. 90032, U.S.A.

DEWEY, Thomas B(lanchard). Also writes as Tom Brandt and Cord Wainer. American, b. 1915. Mystery/Crime/Suspense. Self-employed writer, 1952–71, and since 1977. Prof., Arizona State Univ., Tempe, 1971–77. *Publs:* Hue and Cry, 1944 (in U.K. as the Murder of Marion Mason, 1951; in U.S. paperback, Room for Murder, 1950); As Good as Dead, 1946; Draw the Curtain Close, 1947 (in U.S. paperback, Dame in Danger, 1958); Mourning After, 1950; Handle with Fear, 1951; Every Bet's a Sure Thing, 1953; (as Cord Wainer) Mountain Girl, 1953; (as Tom Brandt) Kiss Me Hard, 1954; (as Tom Brandt) Run, Brother, Run!, 1954; Prey for Me (in U.S. paperback, The Case of the Murdered Model, 1955); The Mean Streets, 1955; The Brave, Bad Girls, 1956; My Love Is Violent, 1956; And Where She Stops, 1957 (in U.K. as I.O.U. Murder, 1958); You've Got Him Cold, 1958; (with Harold M. Imerman) What Women Want to Know (non-fiction), 1958; The Case of the Chased and the Unchaste, 1959; Go to Sleep Jeannie, 1959; The Girl Who Wasn't There, 1960 (in U.S. paperback, The Girl Who Never Was, 1962); Too Hot for Hawaii, 1960; The Golden Hooligan (in U.K. as Mexican Slayride), 1961; Hunter at Large, 1961; Go, Honeylou, 1962; How Hard to Kill, 1962; The Girl with the Sweet Plump Knees, 1963; A Sad Song Singing, 1963; Don't Cry for Long, 1964; The Girl in the Punchbowl, 1964; Only on Tuesdays, 1964; Nude in Nevada, 1965; Can a Mermaid Kill?, 1965; Portrait of a Dead Heiress, 1965; Deadline, 1966; A Season for Violence, 1966; (ed.) Sleuths and Consequences, 1966; Death and Taxes, 1967; The King-Killers, 1968 (in U.K. as Death Turns Right, 1969); The Love-Death Thing, 1969; The Taurus Trip, 1970; A Sad Song Singing, 1982; Deadline, 1984. Add: c/o Simon and Schuster, 1230 Sixth Ave., New York, N.Y. 10020, U.S.A.

DEWHIRST, Ian. British, b. 1936. Poetry, History. Reference Librarian, Keighley Public Library, since 1967 (Library Asst., 1960–65; Lending Librarian, 1965–67). Member Cttee. of Yorkshire Dialect Soc., since 1964. Member, Editorial Bd., Orbis, 1970–75. *Publs:* The Handloom Weaver and Other Poems, 1965; The Haworth Water-Wolf, and Other Yorkshire Stories, 1967; (ed.) A Poet Passed . . . Poems by Alfred Holdsworth, 1968; Scar Top, and Other Poems, 1968; (compiler) Old Keighley in Photographs, 1972; Gleanings from Victorian Yorkshire, 1972; (compiler) More Old Keighley in Photographs, 1973; A History of Keighley, 1974; Yorkshire Through the Years, 1975; The Story of a Nobody, 1980; You Don't Remember Bananas, 1985. Add: 14 Raglan Ave., Fell Lane, Keighley, W. Yorks. BD22 6BJ, England.

DEWHURST, Keith. British, b. 1931. Novels/Short stories, Plays/Screenplays. Sports writer, Evening Chronicle, Manchester, 1955–59; Granada Television presenter, 1968–69; Arts Columnist, The Guardian, London, 1969–72; BBC2 Television presenter, London, 1972; Writer-in-Residence, Western Australia A.P.A., Perth, 1984. *Publs:* Lark Rise to Candleford (2 plays), 1980; Captain of the Sands (novel), 1981; Don Quixote (play), 1982; McSullivan's Beach (novel), 1986. Add: c/o London Management, 235-241 Regent St., London W1A 1JT, England.

DEWLEN, Al. American, b. 1921. Western/Adventure. Freelance writer and lectr. Reporter, Daily News, Amarillo, Tex., 1946–47; City Ed., Amarillo Times, 1947–51; Night Ed., United Press, Dallas, 1951–52. *Publs:* The Night of the Tiger, 1956, in paperback as Ride Beyond Vengeance, 1966; The Bone Pickers, 1958; in paperback as The Golden Touch, 1959; Twilight of Honor, 1961; Servants of Corruption, 1971; Next of Kin, 1977; The Session, 1981. Add: 7720 Croftwood Dr., Austin, Tex. 78749, U.S.A.

DEXTER, (Norman) Colin. British, b. 1930. Mystery/Crime/-Suspense. Sr. Asst. Secty. to the Oxford Delegacy of Local Examinations, Summertown, since 1966. Asst. Classics Master, Wyggeston Sch., Leicester, 1954–57; Sixth Form Classics Master, Loughborough Grammar Sch., 1957–59; Sr. Classics Master, Corby Grammar Sch., Northants, 1959–66. *Publs:* Last Bus to Woodstock, 1975; Last Seen Wearing, 1976; The Silent World of Nicholas Quinn, 1977; Service of All the Dead, 1979; The Dead of Jericho, 1981; The Riddle of the Third Mile, 1983; The Secret of Annexe 3, 1986. Add: 456 Banbury Rd., Oxford OX2 7RG, England.

DEXTER, John. *See* **BRADLEY,** Marion Zimmer.

DEXTER, Lewis Anthony. American, b. 1915. Education, Politics/Government, Sociology. Itinerant visiting prof.; Research Consultant on social science research projects, mental retardation, and in political campaign field, since 1950. *Publs:* Tyranny of Schooling, 1964; (co-ed.) People, Society, and Mass Communications, 1964; How Organizations Are Represented in Washington, 1969, 1987; Sociology and Politics of Congress, 1970; Elite and Specialized Interviewing, 1970 (with R. Bauer and I. Pool) American Business and Public Policy, 2nd ed., 1972; Representation Versus Direct Democracy in Fighting About Taxes, 1982.

Add: c/o J. Cullen, Tucker Anthony, One Beacon St., Boston, Mass. 02108, U.S.A.

DHAVAMONY, Mariasusai. Indian, b. 1925. Philosophy, Theology/Religion. Prof. of History of Religions and Hinduism, Gregorian Univ., since 1968. Chief Ed., Studia Missionalia periodical, and Chief Dir.-Ed., Documenta Missionalia series, since 1968. *Publs:* Subjectivity and Knowledge According to St. Thomas Aquinas (philosophy), 1965; Love of God According to Saiva Sidhanta, 1971; (with C. Papali and P. Fallon) For Dialogue with Hinduism, 1972; (ed.) Evangelization, Dialogue and Development, 1972; Phenomenology of Religion, 1973; Classical Hinduism, 1982; (ed.) Prospettive di Missiologia oggi, 1982; La luce di Dio nell'Indivismo, 1987. Add: Gregorian Univ., Piazza della Pilotta 4, Rome 00187, Italy.

D'HONDT, John Patrick. American, b. 1953. Novels. Production Mgr., Hycomb Productions, San Francisco, since 1988. VISTA Volunteer in Iowa and New Mexico, 1976–78; Child Care Worker, May Inst., Chatham, Mass., 1978–79; Clerk, Pacific Stock Exchange, San Francisco, 1979–83; Volunteer Journalist, Haight-Ashbury Collective Perspective, San Francisco, 1980–82; Corporate Writer, Pacific Stock Exchange, San Francisco, 1983–87. *Publs:* Amber Screen, 1986. Add: 940 Jones St., No. 6, San Francisco, Calif. 94109, U.S.A.

DHONDY, Farrukh. Indian, b. 1944. Children's fiction. Teacher, later Head of English, Archibishop Temple Sch., Lambeth, London, 1974–80; regular contributor to Debonair and Economic and Political Weekly, both Bombay, and Race Today, London. *Publs:* East End at Your Feet, 1976; The Siege of Babylon, 1978; Come to Mecca and Other Stories, 1978; Poona Company, 1980; Trip Trap, 1982; also, stage and television plays for adults. Add: c/o Gollancz, 14 Henrietta St., London WC2E 8QJ, England.

DIAMANT, Lincoln. American, b. 1923. Advertising/Public relations, Media. Pres., Spots Alive Consultants, Inc., NYC, since 1969. Adjunct Prof. in Television, Hofstra Univ., Hempstead, N.Y. and Pace Univ., NYC. *Publs:* Introduction to Aristotle, 1960; (co-author) Effective Advertising, 1965; The Anatomy of a Television Commercial, 1970; Television's Classic Commercials: The Golden Age, 1971; (ed.) The Broadcast Communications Dictionary, 1974, 1978; (co-author) Messages and Meaning, 1975; Bernard Romans: Forgotten Patriot of the American Revolution, 1985. Add: 342 Madison Ave., New York, N.Y. 10173, U.S.A.

DIAMANT, R(udolph) M(aximilian) E(ugen). British, b. 1925. Engineering, Technology. Formerly Lectr. in Applied Chemistry, Univ. of Salford. *Publs:* Applied Chemistry for Engineers, 1962, 3rd ed., 1972; Insulation of Buildings, 1964; Industrialised Building, vol. 1, 1965, vol. 2, 1967, vol. 3, 1969; (with J. McGarry) Space and District Heating, 1969; Home Insulation, 1969, 1975; Understanding SI Metrication, 1970; Total Energy, 1970; Chemistry of Building Materials, 1970; Prevention of Corrosion, 1971; Internal Environment of Dwellings, 1971; Rust and Rot, 1972; Prevention of Pollution, 1974; Insulation Deskbook, 1977; (with D. Kut) District Heating and Cooling for Energy Conservation, 1981; Atomic Energy, 1982; Energy Conservation Equipment, 1984; Thermal and Acoustic Insulation, 1986. Add: 7 Goodwood Ave., Manchester, M23 9JQ, England.

DIBBLE, J(ames) Birney. American, b. 1925. Novels/Short stories, Travel/Exploration/Adventure. Surgeon, Eau Claire, Wisc., since 1957. *Publs:* In This Land of Eve, 1964; The Plains Brood Alone, 1973; Pan (fiction), 1980; Brain Child (fiction), 1987. Add: Rt. 4, Box 222, Eau Claire, Wisc. 54701, U.S.A.

DI CERTO, J(oseph) J(ohn). American, b. 1933. Novels/Short stories, Children's fiction, Air/Space topics, Media, Social commentary/phenomena. Dir. of Communications, CBS Broadcast Intnl., since 1981 (Dir of Sales Promotions, CBS TV stations, 1978–80; Dir. of Communications, CBS Cable, 1980–81). Sr. Technical Writer, Curtiss Wright Corp., 1956–59; Technical Writer and Ed., American Machine and Foundry, 1959–62; Publs. Engineer, Sperry Gyroscope, 1962–66; Advertising Supvr., Sylvania Electric Products, NYC, 1966–74; Mgr. of Special Projects, Sperry Rand Corp, Advertising Agencies, NYC 1974–78. *Publs:* Planning and Preparing Data Flow Diagrams, 1963; Missile Base Beneath the Sea, 1967; The Electric Wishing Well: The Energy Crisis, 1976; From Earth to Infinity, 1980; Star Voyage, 1981; Looking into TV, 1983; The Wall People (for children), 1985; Hoofbeats in the Wilderness, 1988; (with Gene Barnes) The Emmy Award Book, 1990. Add: 1646 1st Ave., New York, N.Y. 10028, U.S.A.

DI CESARE, Mario A. American, b. 1928. Literature. Prof. of English and Comparative Literature, Harpur Coll., State Univ. of New York, Binghamton, since 1968 (Inst., 1959–61; Asst. Prof., 1961–64; Assoc. Prof., 1964–68; Master of Newing Coll., Harpur Coll., 1967–68; Chmn., English Dept., 1968–73). Dir. and Gen. Ed., Medieval and Renaissance Texts and Studies. *Publs:* Vida's Christiad and Vergilian Epic, 1964; (trans. with R. Mignani) Juan Ruiz, The Book of Good Love, 1970; Biblioteca Vidiana: A Critical Bibliography of Marco Girolamo Vida, 1974; The Altar and the City: A Reading of Vergil's Aeneid, 1974; (with R. Mignani) A Concordance to the Complete Writings of George Herbert, 1977; (with E. Fogel) A Concordance to the Poems of Ben Jonson, 1978; George Herbert and the Seventeenth-Century Religious Poets; A Norton Critical Edition, 1978; (with R. Fehrenbach and L.A. Boone) A Concordance to the Plays, Poems and Translations of Christopher Marlowe, 1982; (with Amy Charles) The Bodleian Manuscript of George Herbert's The Temple, 1984. Add: 69 Bennett Ave., Binghamton, N.Y. 13905, U.S.A.

DICHTER, Ernest. American, b. 1907. Psychology. Pres., Ernest Dichter Motivations, Inc., Peekskill, N.Y. Formerly, Pres., Inst. for Motivation Research, NYC. *Publs:* Successful Living; Strategy of Desire, 1960; Handbook of Consumer Motivations, 1964; Motivating Human Behavior, 1971; The Naked Manager, 1974; The New World of Packaging, 1975; Getting Motivated, 1979; Dichter on Consumer Motivations, 1985; Are You a Hot Manager?, 1985. Add: 24 Furnace Brook Dr., Peekskill, N.Y. 10566, U.S.A.

DICK, Bernard. American, b. 1935. Film, Literature. Prof. of English and Comparative Literature, Fairleigh Dickinson Univ. Teaneck, N.J., since 1973 (Assoc. Prof., 1970–73). Instr. to Assoc. Prof. and Chmn., Classics Dept., Iona Coll., New Rochelle, N.Y., 1961–70. *Publs:* William Golding, 1967, 1987; The Hellenism of Mary Renault, 1972; The Apostate Angel: A Critical Study of Gore Vidal, 1974; Anatomy of Film, 1978; Billy Wilder, 1980; (ed.) Dark Victory (screenplay), 1981; Hellman in Hollywood, 1982; Joseph L. Mankiewicz, 1983; The Star-Spangled Screen, 1985; Radical Innocence: A Critical Study of the Hollywood Ten, 1988. Add: 580 Wyndham Rd., Jeaneck, N.J. 07666, U.S.A.

DICK, Kay. British, b. 1915. Novels/Short stories, Literature, Biography. Ed., The Windmill series, and other anthologies. *Publs:* By the Lake, 1949; Young Man, 1951; An Affair of Love, 1953; Solitaire, 1958; Pierrot, 1960; Sunday, 1962; (ed.) Bizarre and Arabesque: Selections from Edgar Allen Poe, 1967; Ivy and Stevie, 1971; (ed.) Writers at Work, 1972; Friends and Friendship, 1974; They, 1977; The Shelf, 1984. Add: Flat 5, 9 Arundel Terr., Brighton, Sussex BN2 1GA, England.

DICK, Robert C(hristopher). American, b. 1938. Recreation/Leisure/Hobbies, Speech/Rhetoric. Prof. and Chmn., Dept. of Communication and Theatre, Indiana-Purdue Univ., Indianapolis, since 1975. Consulting Ed., Western Speech: Journal of the Western Speech Communication Assn., since 1973. Instr. in Speech and Dir. of Forensics, Texas Technological Coll., Lubbock, 1961–62; Instr. in Speech, Stanford Univ., California, 1962–65; Lectr. in Speech, San Francisco State Coll., 1966–67; Asst. Prof. of Speech, 1965–71, Dir. of Forensics, 1967–71, and Assoc. Prof. of Speech Communication, 1971–75, Univ. of New Mexico, Albuquerque. *Publs:* Argumentation and Rational Debating, 1972; (contrib.) Language, Communication and Rhetoric in Black America, 1972; Black Protest: Issues and Tactics, 1974; (contrib.) Responsible Public Speaking, 1983. Add: Dept. of Communication and Theatre, Indiana-Purdue Univ., Indianapolis, Ind., U.S.A.

DICKE, Robert H. American, b. 1916. Physics. Cyrus Fogg Brackett Prof. of Physics, then Albert Einstein Univ. Prof. of Science, Princeton Univ. (Chmn. of Dept. of Physics, 1967–70). Engaged in Microwave radar development, Massachusetts Inst. of Technology, Cambridge, 1941–46; Member, Advisory Panel for Physics, National Science Foundn., 1959–61; Chmn., NASA Cttee. on Physics, 1963–66. *Publs:* (with Purcell and Montgomery) Principles of Micro-Wave Circuits (radar series), 1948; (with Wittke) An Introduction of Quantum Mechanics, 1960; The Theoretical Significance on Experimental Relativity, 1965; Gravitation and the Universe (lecture series), 1970. Add: Joseph Henry Labs., Physics Dept., Jadwin Hall, Princeton Univ., Princeton, N.J. 08544, U.S.A.

DICKENS, Arthur Geoffrey. British, b. 1910. History. Fellow, British Academy, since 1966. Fellow, Keble Coll., Oxford, 1932–49; Prof. of History, Univ. of Hull, 1949–62; Prof. of History, King's Coll., 1962–67; Dir., Inst. of Historical Research, Univ. of London, 1967–77. *Publs:* Lubeck Diary, 1947; (ed.) The Register of Butley Priory, 1951;

The East Riding of Yorkshire, 1954; Lollards and Protestants, 1959; Thomas Cromwell, 1959; (ed.) Tudor Treatises, 1960; (ed.) Clifford Letters, 1962; The English Reformation, 1964, 1989; Reformation and Society in Sixteenth Century Europe, 1966; Martin Luther and the Reformation, 1967; The Counter-Reformation, 1968; The Age of Humanism and Reformation, 1972; The German Nation and Martin Luther, 1974; (ed.) The Courts of Europe, 1977; Reformation Studies, 1982; (with J.M. Tonkin) The Reformation in Historical Thought, 1985. Add: Inst. of Historical Research, Senate House, London WC1E 7HU, England.

DICKENS, Monica (Enid). British, b. 1915. Novels/Short stories, Children's fiction, Autobiography/Memoirs/Personal. Columnist, Woman's Own mag., London, 1946–65. *Publs:* One Pair of Hands (autobiography), 1939; Marianna (in U.S. as the Moon Was Low), 1940; One Pair of Feet (autobiography), 1942; The Fancy (in U.S. as Edward's Fancy), 1943; Thursday Afternoons, 1945; The Happy Prisoner, 1946; Joy and Josephine, 1948; Flowers on the Grass, 1949; My Turn to Make the Tea (autobiography), 1951; No More Meadows (in U.S. as The Nightingales Are Singing), 1953; The Winds of Heaven, 1955; The Angel in the Cobbler's Dream, 1964; Kate and Emma, 1964; The Room Upstairs, 1966; My Fair Lady, 1967; The Landlord's Daughter, 1968; The Listeners (in U.S. as The End of the Line), 1970; The Great Fire, 1970; The House at World's End, 1970; The Great Escape, 1971; Summer at World's End, 1971; Follyfoot, 1971; World's End in Winter, 1972; Dora at Follyfoot, 1972; Cape Cod, 1972; Last Year When I Was Young, 1974; Talking of Horses, 1974; The Horse of Follyfoot, 1975; (with W. Berchen) Cape Cod, 1975; Stranger at Follyfoot, 1976; (ed. with R. Sutcliff) Is Anyone There?, 1978; An Open Book, 1978; Miracles of Courage, 1985; The Messenger, 1985; Ballad of Favour, 1985; Dear Doctor Lily, 1988; Enchantment, 1989; Closed at Dusk, 1990. Add: Lavender Cottage, Pudding Lane, Brightwalton, Berks. RG6 0BY, England.

DICKERSON, John. British, b. 1939. Crafts. Chmn., Dept of Fine Arts, Richmond American Coll., London, since 1977. Instr. in Ceramics and Painting, Pratt Inst., NYC, 1966–68; Lectr. in Fine Arts, Borough Rd. Coll., Isleworth, Middx., 1969–77. *Publs:* Raku Handbook: A Practical Approach to the Ceramic Art, 1972; Pottery Making: A Complete Guide, 1974; Some Aspects of Rukuware, 1974; Pottery in Easy Steps, 1976. Add: 23 Greystoke Ct., Hanger Lane, London W5, England.

DICKEY, James (Lafayette). American, b. 1923. Novels/Short stories, Plays/Screenplays, Poetry, Children's non-fiction, Literature. Prof. of English and Poet-in-Residence, Univ. of South Carolina, Columbia, since 1969. Member of faculty, Rice Univ., Houston, Tex., 1950 and 1952–54, and Univ. of Florida, Gainesville, 1955–56; Poet-in-Residence, Reed Coll., Portland, Ore., 1962–64, and San Fernando Valley State Coll., Northridge, Calif., 1964–66; Consultant in Poetry, Library of Congress, Washington, D.C. 1966–68. *Publs:* Into the Stone and Other Poems, 1960; Drowning with Others: Poems, 1962; Helmets: Poems, 1964; Two Poems of the Air, 1964; The Suspect in Poetry, 1964; Buckdancer's Choice (poetry), 1965; A Private Brinkmanship, 1965; Poems 1957-67, 1967; Spinning the Crystal Ball: Some Guesses at the Future of American Poetry, 1967; The Achievement of James Dickey: A Comprehensive Selection of His Poems, with a Critical Introduction, 1968; Metaphor as Pure Adventure: A Lecture . . . , 1968; Babel to Byzantium: Poets and Poetry Now, 1968; The Eye-Beaters, Blood, Victory, Madness, Buckhead and Mercy, 1970; Self-Interviews, 1970; Deliverance (novel), 1970; Sorties (essays), 1971; Exchanges . . . : Being in the Form of a Dialogue with Joseph Trumbull Stickney, 1971; (trans.) Stolen Apples, by Evgenii Evtushenko, 1971; Jericho: The South Beheld, 1974; The Zodiac, 1976; God's Images, 1977; The Strength of Fields, 1977, 1979; Tucky the Hunter (juvenile), 1978; Deliverance: A Screenplay, 1981; Puella, 1982; Night Hurdling, 1983; The Imagination as Glory: The Poetry of James Dickey, 1984; Bronwen, The Traw, and the Shape-Shifter (poetry for children), 1986; Alnilam (novel), 1987; Wayfarer (prose), 1988. Add: 4620 Lelia's Ct., Lake Katherine, Columbia, S.C. 29206, U.S.A.

DICKEY, William. American, b. 1928. Poetry. Prof. of English and Creative Writing, San Francisco State Univ. (joined faculty, 1962; Chmn., Creative Writing Dept., 1974–77). Instr. Cornell Univ., Ithaca, N.Y. 1956–59; Asst. Prof., Denison Univ., Granville, Ohio, 1960–62. *Publs:* Of the Festivity, 1959; Interpreter's House, 1964; Rivers of the Pacific Northwest, 1969; More Under Saturn, 1971; The Rainbow Grocery, 1978; Sacrifice Consenting, 1981; Six Philosophical Songs, 1983; Joy, 1983; Brief Lives, 1985; The King of the Golden River, 1986 Add: Dept of Creative Writing, San Francisco State Univ., 1600 Holloway, San Francisco, Calif. 94132, U.S.A.

DICKINSON, Harry Thomas. British, b. 1939. History, Biography.

Prof. of History, Edinburgh Univ., since 1980 (Lectr. and Reader, 1966–80); concurrently, Prof. of History, Nanjing Univ., China, since 1987. History Master, Washington Grammar Sch., Co. Durham, 1961–64; Earl Grey Research Fellow, Univ. of Newcastle upon Tyne, 1964–66. *Publs:* (ed.) Correspondence of Sir James Clavering, 1967; Bolingbroke, 1970; Walpole and the Whig Supremacy, 1973; (ed.) Politics and Literature in the 18th Century, 1974; Liberty and Property, 1977; (ed.) The Political Works of Thomas Spence, 1982; British Radicalism and the French Revolution, 1985; Caricatures and the Constitution 1760-1832, 1986; (ed.) Britain and the French Revolution 1789-1815, 1989. Add: 44 Viewforth Terr., Edinburgh 10, Scotland.

DICKINSON, Margaret. *See* **MUGGESON,** Margaret Elizabeth.

DICKINSON, Patric (Thomas). British, b. 1914. Plays/Libretti, Poetry, Autobiography/Personal, Translations. Schoolmaster, 1936–39; Producer, 1942–45, and Poetry Ed., 1945–48, BBC, London; Gresham Prof. of Rhetoric, City Univ. of London, 1964–67. *Publs:* The Seven Days of Jericho (poetry), 1944; Theseus and the Minotaur (radio play), 1945; (ed.) Soldiers' Verse, 1945; Theseus and the Minotaur and Other Poems, 1946; Stone in the Midst and Poems, 1948; (ed.) Byron: Poems, 1949; A Round of Golf Courses, 1951; The Sailing Race and Other Poems, 1952; Robinson (play), 1953; The Scale of Things: Poems, 1955; (ed. with E. Marx and J.C. Hall) New Poems 1955, 1955; (trans.) Aristophanes Against War: Three Plays, 1956; (ed.) Poetry Supplement, 1958; (ed. with S. Shannon) Poems to Remember, 1958; The Golden Touch (play), 1959; The World I See (poetry), 1960; (trans.) The Aeneid of Virgil, 1961; A Durable Fire (play), 1962; This Cold Universe: Poems, 1964; The Good Minute: An Autobiographical Study, 1965; Pseudolus (play), 1966; (ed. with S. Shannon) Poets' Choice: An Anthology of English Poetry from Spenser to the Present Day, 1967; (ed.) C. Day Lewis: Selections from His Poetry, 1967; Selected Poems, 1968; More Than Time (poetry), 1970; (trans.) The Complete Plays of Aristophanes, 2 vols., 1971; A Wintering Tree (poetry), 1973; Ode to St. Catharine (libretto), 1973; Creation (libretto), 1973; The Miller's Secret (libretto), 1973; The Bearing Beast (poetry), 1976; The Return of Odysseus (libretto), 1976; Our Living John (poetry), 1979; (ed.) The Selected Poems of Henry Newbolt, 1981; A Rift in Time (poetry), 1982; To Go Hidden (poetry), 1984; A Sun Dog (poetry), 1988. Add: 38 Church Sq., Rye, Sussex, England.

DICKINSON, Peter. British, b. 1927. Novels/Short stories, Mystery/Crime/Suspense, Science fiction/Fantasy, Children's fiction, Poetry. Asst. Ed., Punch mag., London, 1952–69. Chmn., Soc. of Authors, 1979–80. *Publs:* Skin Deep, 1968; The Weathermonger, 1968; A Pride of Heroes, 1969; Heartsease, 1969; The Seals, 1970; The Devil's Children, 1970; Sleep and His Brother, 1971; Emma Tupper's Diary, 1971; The Lizard in the Cup, 1972; The Dancing Bear, 1972; The Green Gene, 1973; The Gift, 1973; The Iron Lion, 1973; The Poison Oracle, 1974; Chance, Luck and Destiny, 1975; The Lively Dead, 1975; The Blue Hawk, 1976; King and Joker, 1976; Annerton Pit, 1977; Walking Dead, 1977; Hepzibah, 1978; One Foot in the Grave, 1979; Tulku, 1979; The Flight of the Dragons, 1979; City of Gold, 1980; A Summer in the Twenties, 1981; The Last House-Party, 1982; Healer, 1983; Hindsight, 1983; Death of a Unicorn, 1984; A Box of Nothing, 1985; Tefuga, 1986; Perfect Gallows, 1988; Merlin Dreams, 1988; Eva, 1988. Add: 61a Ormiston Grove, London W12 0JP, England.

DICKSON, Gordon (Rupert). American, b. 1923. Science fiction/Fantasy, Children's fiction. *Publs:* Alien from Archturus, 1956; Mankind on the Run, 1956; (with Poul Anderson) Earthman's Burden, 1957; Secret Under the Sea, 1960; Time to Teleport, 1960; The Genetic General, 1960; Delusion World, 1960; Spacial Delivery, 1961; Naked to the Stars, 1961; Necromancer, 1962; Secret Under Antarctica, 1963; Secret Under the Caribbean, 1964; Space Winners, 1965; The Alien Way, 1965; Mission to Universe, 1965; (with Keith Laumer) Planet Run, 1967; Soldier, Ask Not, 1967; The Space Swimmers, 1967; None But Man, 1969; Spacepaw, 1969; Wolfling, 1969; Hour of the Horde, 1970; Danger—Human (also known as The Book of Gordon R. Dickson), 1970; Mutants, 1970; Sleepwalker's World, 1971; The Tactics of Mistake, 1971; The Outposter, 1972; The Pritcher Mass, 1972; The Star Road, 1973; Alien Art, 1973; The R-Master, 1973; (with Ben Bova) Gremlins, Go Home!, 1974; Ancient, My Enemy, 1974; Three to Dorsai, 1975; (ed.) Combat SF, 1975; (with Poul Anderson) Star Prince Charlie, 1975; (with Harry Harrison) The Lifeship, 1976; The Dragon and the George, 1976; Time Storm, 1977; (ed.) Nebula Award Stories Twelve, 1978; The Far Call, 1978; Home from the Shore, 1978; Spirit of Dorsai, 1979; Masters of Everon, 1979; Lost Dorsai, 1980; In Iron Years, 1981; Love Not Human, 1981; The Space Swimmers, 1982; The Outposter, 1982; The Pritcher Mass, 1983; Beyond the Dar Al-Harb, 1985; Steel Brother, 1985; The Forever Man, 1986; The Dorsai Companion, 1986; Way of the Pilgrim, 1987. Add: P.O. Box 1569, Twin Cities Airport, Minn. 55111, U.S.A.

DICKSON, Mora Agnes. British, b. 1918. Sociology, Travel/Exploration/Adventure, Biography. Self-employed author and artist. *Publs:* New Nigerians, 1960; Baghdad and Beyond, 1961; A Season in Sarawak, 1962; A World Elsewhere, 1964; Israeli Interlude, 1966; Count Us In, 1968; Longhouse in Sarawak, 1971; Beloved Partner, 1974; (ed.) A Chance to Serve, 1977; The Inseparable Grief, 1977; Assignment in Asia, 1979; The Powerful Bond, 1980; The Aunts, 1981; Teacher Extraordinary, 1986. Add: 19 Blenheim Rd., London W4, England.

DICKSON, Naida. American, b. 1916. Children's fiction, Children's non-fiction. Founder and Dir., Dickson Feature Service newspaper syndicate, since 1977 and writer of word puzzles, since 1970. Former teacher and social worker. Author of 32 quarterly puzzle mags. published by Circle-A-Word, Old Lyme, Conn., since 1973; Co-Dir., Dickson Bennett Intnl. newspaper syndicate, 1980–83. *Publs:* The Littlest Helper, 1971; I'd Like, 1971; In the Meadow, 1971; The Story of Harmony Lane, 1972; Just the Mat for Father Cat, 1972; Doctors of Long Ago (biography), 1972; The Happy Moon (poetic-scientific prose), 1973; Big Sister and Tagalong Teddy, 1973; Biography of a Honeybee, 1974; How to Cope with Smokers, 1979; Daisie Stout Richardson 1884-1984, a Centennial Memorial, 1984; My Pet Hippotamus, 1987; Penelope, the Stout Princess, 1988. Add: 17700 S. Western 69, Gardena, Calif. 90248, U.S.A.

DICKSON, Paul. American, b. 1939. Recreation/Leisure/Hobbies, Social commentary/phenomena, Speech/Rhetoric. Ed., McGraw-Hill Publs., NYC, 1964–69. *Publs:* Think Tanks, 1971; The Great American Ice Cream Book; The Future of the Workplace; The Electronic Battlefield; The Mature Person's Guide to Kites, Yo-Yo's, Frisbees and Other Childlike Diversions; The Future of This World; Chow; The Official Rules; The Official Explanations; Toasts; Words; (with Joseph C. Gouldon) There Are Alligators in Our Sewers; Jokes; On Our Own; Names; The Library in America. Add: Box 80, Garrett Park, Md. 20896, U.S.A.

DI CYAN, Erwin. American, b. 1918. Medicine/Health, Psychology. Author and consultant in drug research and psychotherapy. East Coast Ed., Brain/Mind Bulletin; Assoc. Ed., Psychosomatic Medicine and Dentistry. *Publs:* (with Robert Moser) Adventures in Medical Writing, 1970; Staying Young with Vitamin E; Vitamin E and Aging, 1972; Vitamins in Your Life, 1972; (with Lawrence Hessman) Without Prescription, 1972; Creativity: Road to Self-Discovery, 1978; A Beginner's Introduction to Trace Minerals, 1984. Add: 1486 E. 33rd St., Brooklyn, N.Y. 11234, U.S.A.

DIDION, Joan. American, b. 1934. Novels/Short stories, Social commentary/phenomena. Assoc. Feature Ed., Vogue mag., NYC, 1956–63. *Publs:* Run River, 1963; Slouching Towards Bethlehem (essays), 1968; Play It as It Lays, 1970; A Book of Common Prayer (novel), 1977; Telling Stories, 1978; The White Album, 1979; Salvador, 1983; Democracy (novel), 1984; Essays and Interviews, 1984; Miami, 1987. Add: c/o Wallace Literary Agency, 177 E. 70th St., New York, N.Y. 10021, U.S.A.

DIEBOLD, John. American, b. 1926. Administration/Management, Information science/Computers, Technology. Founder, and Chmn. of Bd., Diebold Group Inc., mgmt. consultants, NYC, since 1954; Founder, and Chmn., John Diebold Inc., mgmt. and investment, since 1967; Chmn., DCL Inc., holding co. of Diebold Computer Leasing Inc., since 1967; Dir., Genesco. With Griffenhagen and Assocs., mgmt. consultants, NYC and Chicago, 1951–60: Owner, 1957–60. *Publs:* Automation: The Advent of the Automatic Factory, 1952; Beyond Automation, 1964; Man and the Computer: Technology as an Agent of Social Change, 1969; Business Decisions and Technological Change, 1970; (ed.) World of the Computer, 1973; Management, 1973; Automation, 1983; Making the Future Work, 1984; Managing Information, 1985; Business in the Age of Information, 1985. Add: Diebold Group, 475 Park Ave. S., New York, N.Y. 10016, U.S.A.

DIERENFIELD, Richard Bruce. American, b. 1922. Education, Theology/Religion. Prof. of Education, Macalester Coll., St. Paul, Minn., since 1951. *Publs:* Religion in American Public Schools, 1962; (co-author) The High School Curriculum, 3rd ed. 1964; (co-author) The Sociology of Religion, 1967; Learning to Teach, 1981. Add: 1566 Red Cedar Rd., St. Paul, Minn. 55101, U.S.A.

DIETRICH, Robert. *See* **HUNT,** E. Howard.

DI LELLA, Alexander Anthony. American, b. 1929. Language/Linguistics, Theology/Religion. Prof. of Old Testament, Catholic Univ. of America, Washington, D.C., since 1976. Assoc. Prof. of Semitic Languages, Catholic Univ. of America, Washington, D.C. 1966–76. Fellow, American Sch. of Oriental Research, 1962–63; Guggenheim Fellow, 1972–73; Pres., Catholic Biblical Assn. of America, 1975–76. *Publs:* The Hebrew Text of Sirach: A Text-Critical and Historical Study, 1966; (with L.F. Hartman) The Book of Daniel, 1978; Proverbs, in The Old Testament in Syriac, 1979; (with P.W. Skehan) The Wisdom of Ben Sira, 1987. Add: Curley Hall, Catholic Univ. of America, Washington, D.C. 20064, U.S.A.

DI LEO, Joseph H. American, b. 1902. Pediatrics. Dir., Developmental Clinic, New York Foundling Hosp., NYC, 1945–78; Asst. Clinical Prof. of Pediatrics, New York Univ., 1947–80; Instr., Cornell Univ. Coll. of Medicine, NYC, 1954–71; Lectr., Teachers Coll., Columbia Univ. NYC, 1963–80. Member Community Services Bd., New York City Dept. of Mental Health, 1973–81; Member, Bd. of Dirs., St. Joseph's Sch. for the Deaf, 1980. *Publs:* Young Children and Their Drawings, 1970; Physical Factors in Growth and Development, 1970; Children's Drawings as Diagnostic Aids, 1973; Child Development: Analysis and Synthesis, 1977; Interpreting Children's Drawings, 1983. Add: 49 E. 86th St., New York, N.Y. 10028, U.S.A.

DILKE, Caroline (Sophia). British, b. 1940. Novels/Short stories. *Publs:* The Sly Servant, 1975. Add: Houseboat Viva, 106 Cheyne Walk, London SW10 0DG, England.

DILKE, Oswald Ashton Wentworth. British, b. 1915. Classics, Literature, History of Cartography. Prof. of Latin, Univ. of Leeds, 1967–80, now Emeritus. Lectr. in Classics, Univ. Coll., Hull, 1946–50; Lectr. and Sr. Lectr. in Humanity, 1950–67, Univ. of Glasgow. *Publs:* (with E. Mercanti) La Scuola nel Mondo: 5. Inghilterra, 1949; (ed.) Statius, Achilleid, 1954; (ed.) Horace Epistles I, 1954, 3rd ed. 1966; (ed.) Lucan, De Bello Civili VII, 1960,1978; The Roman Land Surveyors, 1971; The Ancient Romans: How They Lived and Worked, 1975; Roman Books and Their Impact, 1977; Greek and Roman Maps, 1985; Reading the Past: Mathematics and Measurement, 1987; (co-author) The History of Cartography, vol. 1, 1987. Add: Moorfield, Huby, Leeds LS17 OBP, England.

DILLARD, Annie. American, b. 1945. Novels/Short stories, Poetry, Literature, Autobiography/Memoirs/Personal. Prof., Wesleyan Univ., since 1979. Contributing Ed., Harper's Mag., 1973–82. *Publs:* Tickets for a Prayer Wheel, 1974; Pilgrim at Tinker Creek, 1974; Holy the Firm, 1977; Living by Fiction, 1978; Teaching a Stone to Talk, 1978; Encounters with Chinese Writers, 1984; An American Childhood, 1987. Recipient of Pulitzer Prize, 1974. Add: c/o Blanche Gregory, 2 Tudor City Place, New York, N.Y. 10017, U.S.A.

DILLARD, R(ichard) H(enry) W(ilde). American, b. 1937. Novels/Short stories, Plays/Screenplays, Poetry. Chmn. of Grad. Prog. in Contemporary Literature and Creative Writing since 1971, and Prof. of English since 1974, Hollins Coll., Va. (Asst. Prof., 1964–68; Assoc. Prof., 1968–74). Vice Pres., The Film Journal, NYC, since 1973. Instr. in English, Univ. of Virginia, Charlottesville, 1961–64. Contrib. Ed., The Hollins Critic, 1966–77. *Publs:* The Day I Stopped Dreaming About Barbara Steele and Other Poems, 1966; (with G. Garrett and J. Rodenbeck) Frankenstein Meets the Space Monster (screenplay), 1966; (ed. with L.D. Rubin) The Experience of America: A Book of Readings, 1969; News of the Nile (poetry), 1971; (ed. with G. Garrett and J.R. Moore) The Sounder Few: Essays from "The Hollins Critic", 1971; After Borges (poetry), 1972; The Book of Changes (novel), 1974; Horror Films, 1976; The Greeting: New and Selected Poems, 1981; The First Man on the Sun (novel), 1983; Understanding George Garrett (criticism), 1988. Add: Box 9671, Hollins College, Va. 24020, U.S.A.

DILLENBERGER, John. American, b. 1918. Art, Theology/Religion. Prof. Emeritus, Graduate Theological Seminary, since 1983. Asst. Prof of Religion, 1949–52, Dept. Rep., Columbia Coll., 1949–54, Assoc. Prof., 1952–54, and Asst. Secty., Ph.D. Prog., 1951–54, Columbia Univ. and Union Theological Seminary; Assoc. Prof. of Theology, 1954–57, and Parkman Prof. of Theology, 1957–58, Divinity Sch., and Chmn., Prof. in History and Philosophy of Religion, Faculty of Arts and Sciences, 1955–58, Harvard Univ., Cambridge, Mass.; Ellen S. James Prof. of Systematic and Historical Theology, Drew Univ., Madison, N.J., 1958–62; Dean of Grad. Studies, Dean of Faculty, and Prof. of Historical Theology, San Francisco Theological Seminary, Calif., 1962–64; Dean, 1963–69, Prof. of Historical Theology, 1963–78, and Pres., 1967–72, Grad. Theological Union, Berkeley Calif; Pres., Hartford Seminary, 1978–83.

Publs: God Hidden and Revealed, 1953; (with C. Welch) Protestant Christianity, 1954, 1988. Protestant Thought and Natural Science, 1960; (ed.) Martin Luther: Selections from His Writings, 1961; Contours of Faith, 1969; (ed.) John Calvin: Selections from His Writings, 1971; (with Jane Dillenberger) Perceptions of the Spirit in 20th Century American Art, 1977; Benjamin West: The Context of His Life's Work, 1977; The Visual Arts and Christianity in America, 1984, 1989; A Theology of Artistic Sensibilities, 1986. Add: 1536 Le Roy, Berkeley, Calif. 94708, U.S.A.

DILLINGHAM, William B. American, b. 1930. Literature. Charles Howard Candler Prof. of American Literature, Emory Univ., Atlanta, since 1956. *Publs:* Frank Norris: Instinct and Art, 1969; An Artist in the Rigging: The Early Work of Herman Melville, 1972; Practical English Handbook, 7th ed. 1986; Humor of the Old Southwest, 2nd ed. 1975; Melville's Short Fiction, 1853-1856, 1978; Melville's Later Novels, 1986. Add: 1416 Vistaleaf Dr., Decatur, Ga. 30033, U.S.A.

DILLON, Eilis. Irish, b. 1920. Novels/Short stories, Children's fiction, Plays/Screenplays. Lectr. in creative writing, Trinity Coll., Dublin, 1971–72. Member, Arts Council of Ireland, 1973–79. *Publs:* An Choill Bheo (The Live Forest), 1948; Midsummer Magic, 1950; Oscar agus an Coiste Se nEasog (Oscar and the Six-Weasel Coach), 1952; The Lost Island, 1952; Death at Crane's Court, 1953; The San Sebastian, 1953; Sent to His Account, 1954; Ceol na Coille (The Song of the Forest), 1955; The House on the Shore, 1955; The Wild Little House, 1955; Death in the Quadrangle, 1956; The Island of Horses, 1956; Plover Hill, 1957; The Bitter Glass, 1958; Aunt Bedelia's Cats, 1958; The Singing Cave, 1959; Manna (radio play), 1960; The Head of the Family, 1960; King Big-Ears, 1961; A Pony and a Trap, 1962; The Cat's Opera, 1963; The Coriander, 1963; A Family of Foxes, 1964; Bold John Henebry, 1965; The Sea Wall, 1965; The Lion Cub, 1966; The Road to Dunmore, 1966; A Page of History (play), 1966; The Cruise of the Santa Maria, 1967; The Key, 1967; Two Stories: The Road to Dunmore and The Key, 1968; The Seals, 1968; Under the Orange Grove, 1968; A Herd of Deer, 1969; The Wise Man on the Mountain, 1969; The Voyage of Mael Duin, 1969; The King's Room, 1970; The Five Hundred, 1972; Across the Bitter Sea, 1973; Living in Imperial Rome (in U.S. as Rome under the Emperors), 1975; (ed.) The Hamish Hamilton Book of Wise Animals, 1975; The Shadow of Vesuvius, 1977; Blood Relations, 1977; Wild Geese, 1981; Inside Ireland, 1982; Down in the World, 1983; Citizen Burke, 1984; The Horse Fancier, 1985; The Seekers, 1986; The Interloper, 1987. Add: 7 Templemore Ave., Dublin 6, Ireland.

DILLON, Wilton Sterling. American, b. 1923. Anthropology/Ethnology. Dir. of Interdisciplinary Studies, Smithsonian Instn., Washington, D.C., since 1969; Vice-Pres., Literary Soc. of Washington, since 1984. Adjunct Prof. of Anthropology, Univ. of Alabama, Tuscaloosa, since 1971; Trustee Emeritus, Phelps-Stokes Fund of New York (Exec. Secty., 1957–63), Member of Editorial Bd., Teachers College Record, Columbia Univ., NYC, since 1974. Pres Emeritus, Inst. for Intercultural Studies, American Museum of Natural History, NYC. *Publs:* Gifts and Nations, 1968; (ed. with John F. Eisenberg) Man and Beast: Comparative Social Behavior, 1972; (ed.) The Cultural Drama: Modern Identities and Social Ferment, 1974. Add: Smithsonian Instn., Washington, D.C. 20560, U.S.A.

DIMBLEBY, Jonathan. British, b. 1944. International relations/Current affairs, Biography. Freelance journalist, broadcaster and writer. Pres., U.N. Assn. of Great Britain, 1977–78; Member, National Commn. for Unesco, 1978–79. *Publs:* Richard Dimbleby, 1975; The Palestinians, 1979. Add: c/o David Higham Assocs. Ltd., 5-8 Lower John St., Golden Sq., London W1R 4HA, England.

DIMENT, Adam. British. Mystery/Crime/Suspense. *Publs:* The Dolly Dolly Spy, 1967; The Bang Bang Birds, 1968; The Great Spy Race, 1968; Think Inc., 1971. Add: c/o Michael Joseph, 45 Bedford Sq., London WC1B 3DU, England.

DIMOCK, Marshall Edward. American, b. 1903. Business/Trade/Industry, Politics/Government, Public/Social administration, Autobiography/Memoirs/Personal. Faculty member, Univ. of California, Los Angeles, 1928–32, and Univ. of Chicago, 1932–41; Lectr., Sch. of Public Law and Admin., 1941–44, and Prof. and Head, Dept. of Govt., 1955–62, New York Univ., NYC; Prof. of Political science, Northwestern Univ., Evanston, Ill., 1944–48; Member, Vermont Legislature, 1949–50, and U.N., 1953–54. *Publs:* Congressional Investigating Committees, 1929; British Public Utilities and National Development, 1933; (with J.M. Gaus and L.D. White) Frontiers of Public Administration, 1936; Modern Politics and Administration, 1937; The Executive in Action, 1945; (with

G.O. Dimock) American Government in Action, 1946, 1951; Business and Government, 1949, 4th ed. 1961; Free Enterprise and the Administrative State, 1951; (with G.O. Dimock) Public Administration, 1953, 5th ed. 1982; A Philosophy of Administration, 1959; Administrative Vitality, 1959; The New American Political Economy, 1961; The Japanese Technocracy, 1969; Games Cats Play and Other Scrivelsby Tales, 1980; Law and Dynamic Administration, 1980; The Center of My World: An Autobiography, 1981; (with E.N. Jackson) Doubting Is Not Enough, 1982. Add: Scrivelsby, Bethel, Vt. 05032, U.S.A.

DIMONT, Penelope. *See* **MORTIMER,** Penelope.

DINERMAN, Beatrice. American, b. 1933. Medicine/Health, Politics/Government, Urban studies. Dir., Strategic Planning Analysis, Cedars-Sinai Medical Center, Los Angeles, since 1981. Public Admin. Analyst, Bureau of Governmental Research, 1956–62, and Research Assoc., Sch. of Public Health, 1966–67, Univ. of California, Los Angeles; Dir., Ford Foundn. Project on Priority Planning, Welfare Planning Council of Los Angeles, 1962–65; Social Science Research Analyst, Economic and Youth Opportunities Agency, Los Angeles, 1965–66; Consultant, Health Planning Assn. of Southern California, Los Angeles, 1967–68; Research Assoc., Sch. of Public Admin., 1968–69, and Research Consultant, Regional Research Inst. in Social Welfare, 1970–72, Univ. of Southern California, Los Angeles; Chief, Research and Information, Comprehensive Health Planning Council of Los Angeles County, 1972–75; Dir., Dept. of Health Planning, Pacific Health Resources, 1975–80; Independent Mgmt. Consultant, 1980–81. *Publs:* Chambers of Commerce in the Modern Metropolis, 1958; Hospital Development and Communities, 1961; Administrative Decentralization in City and County Government, 1961; Structure and Organization of Local Government in the United States, 1961; (co-author) Southern California Metropolis, 1963; Citizen Participation in the Model Cities Program, 1971. Add: 15434 Vista Haven Pl., Sherman Oaks, Calif. 91403, U.S.A.

DINGLE, Graeme. New Zealander, b. 1945. Recreation, Sports/-Fitness. Mountaineer, mountain guide and photojournalist, since 1968; Founder and Dir., Outdoor Pursuits Centre of New Zealand, since 1972. Co-Founder, Trustee, and Dir., Foundn. for Youth Development, since 1986. *Publs:* Two Against the Alps, 1972; The Wall of Shadows, 1976; The Seven Year Adventure, 1981; (with Peter Hillary) First Across the Roof of the World, 1982; The Outdoor World of Graeme Dingle, 1983; Chomolungma, 1986. Add: Hodder and Stoughton, 47 Bedford Sq., London WC1B 3DP, England.

DINGWELL, Joyce. Australian, b. 1912. Also writes as Kate Starr. Historical/Romance/Gothic. *Publs:* Australian Hospital, 1955; Greenfingers Farm, 1955; Second Chance, 1956; Wednesday's Children, 1957, in Can. as Nurse Trent's Children, 1961; Will You Surrender?, 1957; The Coral Tree, 1958; If Love You Hold, 1958, in Can. as Doctor Benedict, 1962, 2nd Can. ed. as Love and Doctor Benedict, 1978; The Girl at Snowy River, 1959; The House in the Timberwoods, 1959; Nurse Jess, 1959; Tender Conquest, 1960; The Third in the House, 1961; The Wind and the Spray, 1961; The Boomerang Girl, 1962; River Nurse, 1962; The New Zealander, 1963; The Timber Man, 1964; The English Boss, 1964; The Kindly Giant, 1964; The Man from the Valley, 1966; The Feel of Silk, 1967; I and My Heart, 1967; Clove Orange, 1967; A Taste for Love, 1967; Hotel Southerly, 1968; Venice Affair, 1968; Nurse Smith, Cook, 1968, in Can. as No Females Wanted, 1970; The Drummer and the Song, 1969; One String for Nurse Bow, 1969, in Can. as One String for Her Bow, 1970; Spanish Lace, 1969; Crown of Flowers, 1969; Demi-Semi Nurse, 1969; September Street, 1969; West of the River (in Can. as Guardian Nurse), 1970; Pool of Pink Lilies, 1970; Nickel Wife, 1970; Mr. Victoria, 1970; Sister Pussycat, 1971; A Thousand Candles, 1971; Red Ginger Blossom, 1972; Wife to Sim, 1972; Friday's Laughter, 1972; There Were Three Princes, 1972; The Mutual Look, 1973; The Cattleman, 1974; The New Broom, 1974; Flamingo Flying South, 1974; The Habit of Love, 1974; The Kissing Gate, 1975; Cane Music, 1975; Love and Lucy Brown, 1975; Corporation Boss, 1975; Inland Paradise, 1976; Deep in the Forest, 1976; The Road Boss, 1976; A Drift of Jasmine, 1977; The Truth Game, 1978; All the Days of Summer, 1978; Remember September, 1978; The Tender Winds of Spring, 1978; The Boss's Daughter, 1978; Year of the Dragon, 1978; The Angry Man, 1979; The All-the-Way Man, 1980; Come Back to Love, 1980; A Man Like Brady, 1981; The Yes Look, 1983; Brother Wolf, 1983; The Arousing Touch, 1983; A Thousand Ways of Loving, 1986; Indian Silk, 1986; as Kate Starr—Dolan of Sugar Hills, 1961; The Nurse Most Likely, 1962; Satin for the Bride, 1963; The Enchanted Trap, 1963; Sister for the Cruise, 1964; Dalton's Daughter, 1964; Patricia and the Rosefields, 1964; Bells in the Wind, 1966; Wrong Doctor John, 1966. Add: c/o Mills and Boon Ltd., Eton House, 18-24 Paradise Rd., Richmond,

Surrey TW9 1SR, England.

DINHOFER, Alfred D. American, b. 1930. Children's non-fiction, Travel/Exploration/Adventure, Humor/Satire. Pres., Caribbean World Communication Inc., since 1970; Ed./Publisher, Walking Tours of San Juan, since 1980. Columnist, San Juan Star, 1959–64; Ed. and Publr., Caribbean Beachcomber Mag., 1964–70. *Publs:* Our Man in San Juan, 1963; (with J.R. Ullman) Caribbean Here and Now, 1972, 3rd ed. 1974; (with E. Dinhofer) Kids in the Kitchen, 1972; Explore the Caribbean and Bahamas, 1973. Add: Caribbean World Communications Inc., First Federal Bldg., Suite 301, 1519 Ponce de Leon Ave., Santurce, Puerto Rico 00909.

DINNERSTEIN, Leonard. American, b. 1934. History. Prof. of American History, Univ. of Arizona, Tucson, since 1972 (Assoc. Prof., 1970–72). Inst., New York Inst. of Technology, NYC, 1960–65; Asst. Prof., Fairleigh Dickinson Univ., Teaneck, N.J., 1967–70. *Publs:* The Leo Frank Case, 1968; (ed. with F.C. Jaher) The Aliens, 1970, as Uncertain Americans, 1977; (ed. with K.T. Jackson) American Vistas, 1971, 5th ed. 1987; (ed.) Antisemitism in the United States, 1971; (ed. with M.D. Palsson) Jews in the South, 1973; (ed. with J. Christie) Decisions and Revisions, 1975; (with D.M. Reimers) Ethnic Americans: A History of Immigration and Assimilation, 1975, 3rd ed. 1988; (with R.L. Nichols and D.M. Reimers) Natives and Strangers, 1979, 1990; America and the Survivors of the Holocaust, 1982; Uneasy at Home, 1987. Add: 5821 East 7th St., Tucson, Ariz. 85711, U.S.A.

DINTENFASS, Mark. American, b. 1941. Novels/Short stories. Asst. Prof. of English, Lawrence Univ., Appleton, Wisc., since 1968. *Publs:* Make Yourself an Earthquake, 1969; The Case Against Org., 1970; Figure 8, 1974; Montgomery Street, 1978; Old World, New World, 1982; The Loving Place, 1986. Add: Dept. of English, Lawrence Univ., Appleton, Wisc. 54911, U.S.A.

DI PIETRO, Robert Joseph. American, b. 1932. Language/Linguistics. Prof., Linguistics Dept., Univ. of Delaware, Newark, since 1985 (joined faculty, 1978). Project Linguist, Center for Applied Linguistics, Arlington, Va., 1960–61; Prof. of Linguistics and Italian, Georgetown Univ., Washington, D.C., 1961–78. *Publs:* (with F.B. Agard) The Sounds of English and Italian, 1965, 1969; (with F.B. Agard) The Grammatical Structures of English and Italian, 1965, 1969; Language Structures in Contrast, 1971; Language as Human Creation, 1976; Linguistics and the Professions, 1982; (with E. Ifkovic) Ethnic Perspectives in American Literature, 1983; Strategic Interaction, 1987. Add: Linguistics Dept., Univ. of Delaware, Newark, Del. 19716, U.S.A.

di PRIMA, Diane. American, b. 1934. Short stories, Plays/-Screenplays, Poetry, Translations. Instr., New Coll. of California, San Francisco, since 1980. Contrib. Ed., Kulchur mag., NYC, 1960–61; Co.Ed., Floating Bear mag., NYC, 1961–69; Ed. and Publr., Poets Press, NYC, 1964–69; Publr., Eidolon Editions, San Francisco, 1972–76. Dir., New York Poets Theatre, 1961–65. *Publs:* This Kind of Bird Flies Backward, 1958; (ed.) Various Fables from Various Places, 1960; Murder Cake (play), 1960; Paideuma (play), 1960; The Discontent of a Russian Prince (play), 1961; Dinners and Nightmares (short stories), 1961, 1974; The Monster, 1961; The New Handbook of Heaven, 1963; Poets Vaudeville, 1964; Like (play), 1964; (trans.) Seven Love Poems from the Middle Latin, 1965; Combination Theatre Poem and Birthday Poem for Ten People, 1965; Haiku, 1967; Earthsong: Poems 1957-59, 1968; Hotel Albert: Poems, 1968; New Mexico Poem, June-July 1967, 1968; The Star, The Child, The Light, 1968; (ed.) War Poems, 1968; Memoirs of a Beatnik (novel), 1969; Revolutionary Letters, 1969; L.A. Odyssey, 1969; New As . . . , 1969; Notes on a Summer Solstice, 1969; Kerhonkson Journal 1966, 1971; Prayer to the Mothers, 1971; So Fine, 1971; The Calculus of Variation (novel), 1972; Poems for Freddie, 3 vols., 1972–78; Loba, part 1, 1973; (ed.) The Floating Bear: A Newsletter, Numbers 1-37, 1974; Selected Poems, 1956-75, 1975; Loba as Eve, 1975; Loba, Part 2, 1976; Loba, Parts 1-8, 1978. Add: Box 15068, Suite 103, San Francisco, Calif. 95115, U.S.A.

DISCH, Thomas M(ichael). Also writes as Leonie Hargrave, and with John Sladek under joint pseuds. Thom Demijohn and Cassandra Knye. American, b. 1940. Novels/Short stories, Science fiction/Fantasy, Poetry, Songs, lyrics and libretti, Literature. Freelance writer and lectr., since 1964. Theatre Critic, The Nation mag., NYC. Formerly, draftsman and copywriter. *Publs:* The Genocides, 1965; Mankind Under the Leach, 1966, later as Puppies of Terra; One Hundred and Two H-Bombs (short stories), 1966 as White Fang Goes Dingo, 1971; (as Cassandra Knye) The House That Fear Built (novel), 1966; Echo Round His Bones, 1967;

Camp Concentration, 1968; Under Compulsion (short stories), 1968, in U.S. as Fun with Your New Head, 1971; (as Thom Demijohn) Black Alice (suspense novel), 1968; The Prisoner, 1969; (with Marilyn Hacker and Charles Platt) Highway Sandwiches (poetry), 1970; The Right Way to Figure Plumbing (poetry). 1971; (ed.) The Ruins of Earth: An Anthology of the Immediate Future, 1971; 334, 1972; (ed.) Bad Moon Rising, 1973; Getting into Death (short stories), 1973; (ed.) The New Improved Sun; An Anthology of Utopian Science Fiction, 1975; (as Leonie Hargrave) Clara Reeve, 1975; (ed. with Charles Naylor) New Constellations, 1976; (ed. with Charles Naylor) Strangeness, 1977; On Wings of Song, 1979; Triplicity (omnibus), 1980; Fundamental Disch (short stories), 1980; (with Charles Naylor) Neighboring Lives (historical novel), 1981; ABCDEFGHIJKLMNOPQRSTUVWXYZ (poetry), 1981; Orders of the Retina (poetry), 1982; Burn This (poetry), 1982; The Man Who Had No Idea (short stories), 1982; Frankenstein (libretto for opera by Gregory Sandow), 1982; Ringtime, 1983; The Businessman: A Tale of Terror, 1984; Torturing Mr Amberwell, 1985; The Brave Little Toaster (children's book), 1986; Amnesia (computer-interactive novel), 1986; The Tale of Dan De Lion (children's book), 1986; The Silver Pillow, 1984; The Brave Little Toaster Goes to Mars, 1988; Yes, Let's: New and Selected Poems, 1989. Add: 31 Union Sq. W., No. 11E, New York, N.Y. 10003, U.S.A.

DISNEY, Dorothy Cameron. American, b. 1903. Mystery/Crime/-Suspense. *Publs:* (with Milton MacKaye) Guggenheim (non-fiction), 1927; Death in the Back Seat, 1936; The Golden Swan Murder, 1939; Strawstick, 1939; The Balcony, 1940; (with George Sessions Perry) Thirty Days Hath September, 1942; Crimson Friday, 1943; The Seventeenth Letter, 1945; Explosion, 1948; (with Milton MacKaye) Mary Roberts Rinehart (non-fiction), 1948; The Hangman's Tree, 1949; (with Paul Popenoe) Can This Marriage Be Saved? (non-fiction), 1960. Add: c/o Macmillan, 866 Third Ave., New York, N.Y. 10022, U.S.A.

DITTERICH, (Eric) Keith. Australian, b. 1913. Theology/Religion. Chmn., Bd. of Treasurers, Uniting Church Beneficiary Fund, and Dir., Aldersgate Press, Melbourne. Uniting Church clergyman. Pres., Victoria and Tasmania Conference, 1969–70. *Publs:* The Church on Active Service, 1945; Some Distortions of the Christian Faith, 1954; Methodist Members' Manual, 1956; Three Curious Creeds, 1961; When We Go to Communion, 1961; The Methodist Background, 1963; Mixed Marriage: A Positive Approach, 1964; Our Faith and Its Fruits, 1965; John Cope, 1969; The Radio Church of God and the Teachings of Herbert W. Armstrong, 1970; Inflation, The Church, and the Ministry, 1973; Daniel Draper: Master Builder, 1974; The Supernumerary Fund: What More Can Be Done?, 1975; Conferences in Contrast, 1875 and 1975, 1976. Add: 1574 High St., Glen Iris, Vic., Australia 3146.

DITTON, James. *See* **CLARK,** Douglas.

DIVALE, William T(ulio). American, b. 1942. Anthropology/Ethnology, Autobiography/Memoirs/Personal. Assoc. Prof. of Anthropology, York Coll. of City Univ. of New York (joined faculty, 1973). *Publs:* I Lived Inside the Campus Revolution, 1970; Warfare in Primitive Societies, 1973; Matrilocal Residence in Pre-literate Society, 1984. Add: Dept. of Anthropology, York Coll., City Univ. of New York, 94-20 Guy Brewer Blvd., Jamaica, N.Y. 11451, U.S.A.

DIVINE, Robert A(lexander). American, b. 1929. History. George W. Littlefield Prof. in American History, Univ. of Texas at Austin, since 1981 (Instr., 1954–57; Asst. Prof., 1957–61; Assoc. Prof., 1961–63; Prof. of History, 1963–80). Fellow, Inst. for Advanced Study in the Behavioral Sciences, Stanford, Calif., 1962–63. *Publs:* American Immigration Policy 1924-52, 1957; (ed.) American Foreign Policy, 1960; The Illusion of Neutrality, 1962; The Reluctant Belligerent, 1965, 1979; Second Chance, 1967; (ed.) The Age of Insecurity, 1968; (ed. with J.A. Garraty) Twentieth Century America, 1968; Roosevelt and World War II, 1969; (ed.) Causes and Consequences of World War II, 1969; (ed.) American Foreign Policy since 1945, 1969; (ed.) The Cuban Missile Crisis, 1971; Foreign Policy and U.S. Presidential Elections 1940-1960, 2 vols., 1974; Since 1945, 1975, 1979; Blowing on the Wind, 1978; Eisenhower and the Cold War, 1981; (ed.) Exploring the Johnson Years, 1981; (with T.H. Breen, G.M. Frederickson and R.H. Williams) America: Past and Present, 1984; (ed.) The Johnson Years, vol. 2, 1987. Dept. of History, Univ. of Texas, Austin, Tex. 78712, U.S.A.

DIXON, Bernard. British, b. 1938. Medicine/Health, Sciences. European Ed., The Scientist, Washington, D.C., since 1986. Research Fellow, Univ. of Newcastle upon Tyne, 1965; Asst. Ed., and Deputy Ed., World Medicine, London, 1965–68; Deputy Ed., 1968–69, and Ed., 1969–79, New Scientist, London; European Ed., Biotechnology, New York,

1980–86. Chmn., Assn. of British Science Writers, 1971–72. *Publs:* (ed.) Journeys in Belief, 1968; What Is Science For?, 1973; Magnificent Microbes, 1976; Invisible Allies, 1976; Beyond the Magic Bullet, 1979; Ideas of Science, 1984; Health and the Human Body, 1986; Engineered Organisms in the Environment, 1988; How Science Works, 1989; Science and Society, 1989; (ed.) Words About Science, 1989. Add: 130 Cornwall Rd., Ruislip Manor, Middlesex HA4 6AW, England.

DIXON, Dougal. British, b. 1947. Science fiction/Fantasy, Earth sciences, Natural history. Freelance writer since 1980. Researcher and Editor, Mitchell Beazley Ltd., 1973–78, and Blandford Press, 1978–80; part-time tutor in earth sciences, Open University, 1976–78. Chmn., Bournemouth Science Fiction and Fantasy Group, 1981–82. *Publs:* Doomsday Planet (comic strip), 1980; After Man: A Zoology for the Future, 1981; Discovering Earth Sciences, 1982; Science World: Geology, 1982; Science World: Geography, 1983; Picture Atlas: Mountains, 1984; Picture Atlas: Forests, 1984; Picture Atlas: Deserts, 1984; Find Out About Prehistoric Reptiles, 1984; Find Out About Jungles, 1984; (with Jane Burton) The Age of Dinosaurs (in U.S. as Time Exposure), 1984; Nature Detective Series: Minerals, Rocks, and Fossils, 1984; Time Machine 7: Ice Age Explorer, 1985; Secrets of the Earth, 1986; Find Out About Dinosaurs, 1986; The First Dinosaurs, 1987; Hunting the Dinosaurs, 1987; The Jurassic Dinosaurs, 1987; The Last Dinosaurs, 1987; Be a Dinosaur Detective, 1987; The Dinosaurs: An Alternative Evolution, 1988; Dino Dots, 1988; (ed.) The Macmillan Illustrated Encyclopedia of Dinosaurs and Prehistoric Animals, 1988. Add: c/o Hamlyn, 69 London Rd., Twickenham, Middx TW1 3SB, England.

DIXON, Eustace A(ugustus). American, b. 1934. Environmental science/Ecology. Medical/Health. Safety and Health Manager, Philadelphia Naval Ship Engineering Center. *Publs:* New Jersey: Environment and Cancer, 1982; (ed.) The Association of Human Mortality with Air Pollution, 1984; Syndromes for the Layperson: Now I Know What's Wrong with Me, 1989; The First Book of Belches (humor), 1989. Add: P.O. Box 372, Mantua, N.J. 08051, U.S.A.

DIXON, Norman (Frank). British, b. 1922. Psychology. Emeritus Prof. of Psychology, University Coll., London (joined faculty, 1954). Commissioned, Royal Engineers, 1945–54. *Publs:* Subliminal Perception: The Nature of a Controversy, 1971; On the Psychology of Military Incompetence, 1976; Preconscious Processing, 1981. Add: Dept. of Psychology, University Coll., London WC1E 6BT, England.

DIXON, Paige. *See* **CORCORAN,** Barbara.

DIXON, Roger. Also writes as John Christian, and as Charles Lewis. British, b. 1930. Novels/Short stories, Plays/Screenplays. *Publs:* The Marble Clock (radio play), 1959; The Old Boy Net (radio play), 1960; All for a Penny (radio play), 1961; Duet for Mixed Voices (radio play), 1961; The Devil Finds Work (radio play), 1962; The God Machine (television play), 1966; Billingsgate (television play), 1966; The Mobius Twist (radio play), 1970; and other TV and radio plays and series including The Trigger, The Mars Project, and The Commander; novels— Noah II, 1970; Christ on Trial, 1973; The Messiah, 1974; (as John Christian) Five Gates to Armageddon, 1975; (as Charles Lewis) The Cain Factor, 1975; Going to Jerusalem, 1977. Add: Badgers, Warren Lane, Cross-in-Hand, Heathfield, Sussex, England.

DIXON, Stephen. American, b. 1936. Novels/Short stories. Assoc. Prof. of English, Johns Hopkins Univ., Baltimore, since 1984 (Asst. Prof., 1980–83). Worked at various jobs, including bartender, waiter, jr. high school teacher, technical writer, news ed., etc., 1953–79; Lectr., New York Univ. Sch. of Continuing Education, 1979–80. *Publs:* No Relief (short stories), 1976; Work (novel), 1977; Too Late (novel), 1978; Quite Contrary: The Mary and Newt Story (short stories), 1979; 14 Stories, 1980; Movies (short stories), 1983; Time to Go (short stories), 1984; Fall and Rise (novel), 1985; Garbage (novel), 1988; The Play and Other Stories, 1988; Love and Will (short stories), 1989. Add: Writing Seminars, Gilman 135, Johns Hopkins Univ., Baltimore, Md. 21218, U.S.A.

DIZENZO, Charles (John) American, b. 1938 Children's fiction, Plays/Screenplays. Instr. in Playwriting, New York Univ., NYC, 1970–71. *Publs:* The Drapes Come, 1965; An Evening for Merlin Finch, 1968; A Great Career, 1968; The Last Straw, and Sociability, 1970; Big Mother and Other Plays, 1970; (with Patricia Dizenzo) Phoebe (children's fiction), 1970. Add: c/o Helen Harvey, 410 W. 24th St., New York, N.Y. 10014, U.S.A.

DOAK, Wade (Thomas) New Zealander, b. 1940 Marine

science/Oceanography. Publr., Dive South Pacific Underwater Mag. *Publs:* Elingamite and Its Treasure, 1969; Beneath New Zealand Seas, 1971; Fishes of the New Zealand Region, 1972, rev. ed. 1978; Sharks and Other Ancestors, 1975; Islands of Survival, 1976; The Cliffdwellers, 1979; Dolphin, Dolphin, 1981; The Burning of the Boyd, 1984; Ocean Planet, 1984; Encounters with Whales and Dolphins, 1988. Add: P.O. Box 20, Whangarei, New Zealand.

DOAN, Eleanor Lloyd. American. Children's non-fiction, Crafts, Theology/Religion. Promotional Publicist, Gospel Light Publs., Glendale, Calif., 1975–85 (Merchandising Mgr., 1945–75; Editorial Dir., 1951–66; Marketing Research Mgr., 1966–71; Mgr. of Special Projects, 1971–75). *Publs:* Fascinating Finger Fun, 1951; Teaching Twos and Threes, 1951; Series I: Twos and Threes, 1951; 261 Crafts and Fun, 1953; How to Plan a Junior Church, 1954; Series II: Twos and Threes, 1956; Fun to Do Handcrafts, 1957; Hobby Fun, 1958; Sourcebook for Speakers, 1960; Handcraft Encyclopedia, 1961; (co-author) How to Plan a Primary Church, 1961; Equipment Encyclopedia, 1962; Pattern Encyclopedia, 1962; (co-author) Missy Stories for Preschoolers, 1962; (co-author) Missy Stories for Primaries, 1962; (co-author) Missy Stories for Juniors, 1962; (co-author) Missy Stories for Youth, 1962; Teaching Juniors, 1962; Teaching Junior Highs, 1962; Teaching Adults, 1962; Fun and Food Crafts, 1963; Teaching Fours and Fives, 1963; Teaching Primaries, 1964; More Handicrafts, 1966; Visual Aid Encyclopedia, 1966, Sourcebook for Mothers, 1969; New Sourcebook for Speakers, 1969; Kid Stuff, 1970; Treasury of Inspiration, 1970; Bible Story Picture Book, 1971; 145 Fun to Do Crafts, 1972; Creative Crafts for Young Children, 1973; Creative Crafts for Children, 1973; Creative Crafts for Juniors, 1973; Creative Crafts for Youth, 1973; 157 More Fun to Do Crafts, 1973; Mothers Treasury Inspiration, 1973; Treasury of Verse for Children, 1978, 1987; Find the Words Puzzle Book, 1980. Add: 10749 Galvin St., Ventura, Calif., U.S.A.

DOBBS, Betty Jo (Teeter). American, b. 1930. History. Prof. of History, Northwestern Univ., Evanston, Ill., since 1986 (Asst. Prof., 1975–76; Assoc. Prof., 1976–86). NATO Postdoctoral Fellow in the History of Science, Univ. of Cambridge, 1974–75; Fellow, National Humanities Center, 1978–79, and the Huntington Library, 1987–88. *Publs:* The Foundations of Newton's Alchemy; or "The Hunting of the Greene Lyon", 1975; The Janus Faces of Genius and the Role of Alchemy in Newton's Thought, 1989. Add: Dept. of History, Harris Hall, Northwestern Univ., Evanston, Ill. 60201, U.S.A.

DOBSON, James C., Jr. American, b. 1936. Medicine/Health, Psychology. Assoc. Clinical Prof. of Pediatrics (Child Development), Univ. of Southern California Sch. of Medicine, Los Angeles; Member, Attending Staff, Div. of Medical Genetics, Children's Hosp. of Los Angeles. Teacher, 1960–63, and Psychometrist, 1962–63, Hudson Sch. District, Hacienda Heights, Calif.; Psychometrist-Counselor, 1963–64, and Sch. Psychologist and Coordinator of Pupil Personnel Services, 1964–66, Charter Oak Unified Sch. District, Covina, Calif. *Publs:* Dare to Discipline, 1970; (ed. with R. Koch) The Mentally Retarded Child and His Family: A Multidisciplinary Handbook, 1971; Discipline with Love, 1972; Hide or Seek, 1974; What Wives Wish Their Husbands Knew About Women, 1975; The Strong-Willed Child, 1978; Preparing for Adolescence, 1978; Prescription for a Tired Housewife, 1978; Straight Talk to Men and Their Wives, 1980; Emotions: Can You Trust Them?, 1980; Dr. Dobson Answers Your Questions, 1982; Raising Teenagers Right, 1988. Add: 41 E. Foothill, Arcadia, Calif., U.S.A.

DOBSON, Julia. *See* **TUGENDHAT,** Julia.

DOBSON, R(ichard) Barrie. British, b. 1931. History. Prof. of Medieval History, Cambridge Univ., since 1988; Lectr. in Mediaeval History, Univ. of St. Andrews, Scotland, 1958–64; Lectr., 1964–68; Sr. Lectr., 1968–71; Reader, 1971–76, and Prof. of History, 1976–88, Univ. of York. *Publs:* Selby Abbey and Town, 1969; (ed.) The Peasants' Revolt of 1381, 1970; (with M.J. Angold) The World of the Middle Ages, 1970; Durham Priory 1400-1450, 1973; The Jews of Medieval York and the Massacre of March 1190, 1974; (with J. Taylor) Rymes of Robyn Hood: An Introduction to the English Outlaw, 1976; York City Chamberlains' Account Rolls 1396-1500, 1981; (ed.) The Church, Politics, and Patronage in the Fifteenth Century, 1984; (with S. Donaghey) The Nunnery of Clementhorpe, 1984. Add: Christ's Coll., Cambridge CB2 3BU, England.

DOBSON, Rosemary. Australian, b. 1920. Poetry, Translations. *Publs:* In a Convex Mirror, 1944; The Ship of Ice and Other Poems, 1948; Child with a Cockatoo and Other Poems, 1955; Rosemary Dobson: Australian Poets Series, 1963; Cock Crow: Poems, 1965; Rosemary Dobson Reads

Her Own Work, 1970; Focus on Ray Crooke, 1971; Selected Poems, 1973; (trans. with David Campbell) Moscow Trefoil, 1975; Greek Coins: A Sequence of Poems, 1977; Over the Frontier: Poems, 1978; (trans. with David Campbell) Seven Russian Poets, 1979; (ed.) Sisters Poets 1, 1979; The Three Fates and Other Poems, 1984; Summer Press (for children), 1987. Add: 61 Stonehaven Cres., Deakin, Canberra, A.C.T., Australia, 2600.

DOBYNS, Henry F. American, b. 1925. Anthropology/Ethnology, History. Dir., Native American Historical Demography Project, Newberry Library, since 1981. Research Assoc. to Lectr., Dept. of Anthropology, Cornell Univ., Ithaca, N.Y., 1959–66; Prof. and Chmn., Dept. of Anthropology, Univ. of Kentucky, Lexington, 1966–70; Prof., Prescott Coll., Ariz., 1970–73; Visiting Prof., Univ. of Wisconsin-Parkside, Kenosha, 1974–75; Visiting Prof., Univ. of Florida, Gainesville, 1977–79; Sr. Fellow, Center for the History of the American Indian, Newberry Library, Chicago, 1979–80; Adjunct Prof., Univ. of Oklahoma, Norman, 1988. *Publs:* Papagos in the Cotton Fields, 1950; 1951; (ed.) Hepah, Calfornia! The Journal of Cave Johnson Couts from Monterey, Nuevo Leon, Mexico, to Los Angeles, California, during the Years 1848-1849, 1961; (with M.C. Vazquez) Migración e Integración en el Perú, 1963; The Social Matrix of Peruvian Indigenous Communities, 1964; (with M.E. Opler and Lauriston Sharp) Recommendations for Future Research on the Processes of Cultural Change, 1966; (with Holmberg, Opler and Sharp) Some Principles of Cultural Change, 1967; (with Holmberg, Opler and Sharp) Strategic Intervention in the Cultural Change Process, 1967; (with Holmberg, Opler and Sharp) Methods for Analyzing Cultural Change, 1967; (with R.C. Euler) The Ghost Dance of 1889 Among the Pai Indians of Northwestern Arizona, 1967; (with S.C. Bourque, L.A. Brownrigg and E.A. Maynard) Factions and Faenas: The Developmental Potential of Checras District, Peru, 1967; (with E.W. Morris, L.A. Brownrigg and S.C. Bourque) Coming Down the Mountain: The Social Worlds of Mayobamba, 1968; Comunidades Campesinas del Peru, 1970; (with R.C. Euler) Wauba Yuma's People: The Comparative Socio-Political Structure of the Pai Indians of Arizona, 1970; The Havasupai People, 1971; The Apache People, 1971; (with R.C. Euler) The Hopi People, 1971; (with P.L. Doughty and H.D. Lasswell) Peasants, Power, and Applied Social Change: Vicos as a Model, 1971; The Navajo People, 1972; The Papago People, 1972; The Mescalero Apache People, 1973; Prehistoric Indian Occupation within the Eastern Area of the Yuman Complex: A Study of Applied Archaeology, 1974; (with P.L. Doughty) Peru: A Cultural History, 1976; (with R.C. Euler) The Walapai People, 1976; Spanish Colonial Tucson: A Demographic History, 1976; Native American Historical Demography: A Critical Bibliography, 1976; (with Juan B. Climent and others) The Case of the Burned Out Water Pump, 1979; (with R.C Euler) Indians of the Southwest: A Critical Biography, 1980; (ed.) Spanish Colonial Frontier Research, 1981; From Fire to Flood, 1981; Their Number Become Thinned, 1983. Add: c/o Newberry Library, 60 W. Walton St., Chicago, Ill. 60610, U.S.A.

DOBYNS, Stephen. American, b. 1941. Novels/Short stories, Poetry. Member of the faculty, Warren Wilson Coll., Swannanoa, N.C., since 1982; Prof. of English, Syracuse Univ., N.Y., since 1987. Visiting Writer, Univ. of New Hampshire, 1973–75, Univ. of Iowa, 1977–78, Boston Univ., 1978–79, 1980–81, and Syracuse Univ., 1986. *Publs:* Concurring Beasts (poetry), 1972; A Man of Little Evils (novel), 1973; Griffon (poetry), 1976; Saratoga Swimmer (novel), 1981; The Balthus Poems, 1982; Dancer with One Leg (novel), 1983; Black Dog, Red Dog (poetry), 1984; Saratoga Headhunter (novel), 1985; Cold Dog Soup (novel), 1985; Saratoga Snapper (novel), 1986; Cemetery Nights (poetry), 1986; A Boat off the Coast, 1987; Saratoga Longshot, 1987; Saratoga Bestiary, 1988; The Two Deaths of Senora Puccini, 1988. Add: 20 Brattle Rd., Syracuse, N.Y. 13203, U.S.A.

DOCTOROW, E(dgar) L(aurence). American, b. 1931. Novels/Short stories, Westerns/Adventure, Plays/Screenplays. Prof. of English, NYU, N.Y.C., since 1982. Dir., Authors Guild of America, and American P.E.N. Sr. Ed., New American Library, NYC, 1959–64; Ed.-in-Chief, 1964–69, and Publr., 1969, Dial Press, NYC; Writer-in-Residence, Univ. of California at Irvine, 1969–70; Member of Faculty, Sarah Lawrence Coll., Bronxville, N.Y., 1971–78. *Publs:* Welcome to Hard Times, 1960; Big as Life, 1966; The Book of Daniel, 1971; Ragtime, 1975; Drinks Before Dinner (play), 1979; Loon Lake, 1980; Lives of the Poets: Six Stories and a Novella, 1984; World's Fair, 1985; Billy Bathgate, 1989. Add: 170 Broadview Ave., New Rochelle, N.Y. 10804, U.S.A.

DODD, Arthur Edward. British, b. 1913. Poetry, Crafts, Travel. Chief Information Officer, British Ceramic Research Assn., Stoke-on-Trent, 1938–70, now retired. *Publs:* Poems from Belmont, 1955; Three Journeys,

1958; Flower-Spun Web (play), 1960; Words and Music, 1963; Dictionary of Ceramics, 1964; To Build a Bridge (play), 1965; Weaver Hills, 1967; Fifth Season, 1971; Gold in Gun Street (play), 1973; (with E.M. Dodd) Peakland Roads and Trackways, 1974; Beacon Stoop, 1985. Add: Hall Lodge, Upper Ellastone, Ashbourne, Derbyshire, England.

DODD, Lynley (Stuart, née Weeks). New Zealander, b. 1941. Children's fiction. Art teacher and freelance illustrator. *Publs:* The Nickle Nackle Tree, 1978; Titimus Trim, 1979; The Smallest Turtle, 1982; Hairy Maclary from Donaldson's Dairy, 1983; Hairy Maclary's Bone, 1984; Hairy Maclary, Scattercat, 1985; The Apple Tree, 1985; Wake Up, Bear, 1986; Hairy Maclary's Caterwaul Caper, 1987; A Dragon in a Wagon, 1988; Hairy Maclary's Rumpus at the Vet, 1989. Add: 60 Pomare Rd., Belmont, Lower Hutt, New Zealand.

DODD, Susan M. American, b. 1946. Novels/Short stories. Instr., Vermont Coll., since 1984. Instr. in Creative Writing, Univ. of Iowa, Iowa City, 1985. *Publs:* Old Wives' Tales, 1984; No Earthly Notion, 1986; Mamaw, 1988. Add: c/o Philip G. Spitzer, 1465 Third Ave., New York, N.Y. 10028, U.S.A.

DODD, Wayne D. Has also written as Donald Wayne. American, b. 1930. Novels/Short stories, Children's fiction, Poetry. Prof. of English, Ohio Univ., Athens. Ed., The Ohio Review. *Publs:* (as Donald Wayne) The Adventures of Little White Possum, 1970; We Will Wear White Roses, 1974; Made in America, 1975; A Time of Hunting, 1975; The Names You Gave It, 1980; The General Mule Poems, 1980; Sometimes Music Rises, 1986. Add: 11292 Peach Ridge Rd., Athens, Ohio, U.S.A.

DODGE, Bertha S(anford). American, b. 1902. Cultural/Ethnic topics, Medicine/Health, Sciences. *Publs:* Introduction to Chemistry, 1948; Story of Nursing, 1954, 1965; Plants That Changed the World, 1959; Engineering Is Like This, 1963; Hands That Help; Careers for Medical Workers, 1967; Potatoes and People, 1970; Big Is So Big, 1972; Tales of Vermont Ways and People, 1977; Marooned . . ., 1979, 1986; It Started in Eden, 1979; The Road West: Saga of the 35th Parallel, 1980; Cotton: The Plant That Would Be King, 1984; Vermont by Choice, 1987; Quests for Spices and New Worlds, 1988. Add: 42 The Terrace, Shelburne, Vt. 05482, U.S.A.

DODGE, David (Francis). American, b. 1910. Mystery/Crime/-Suspense, Travel/Exploration/Adventure, Humor/Satire. Full-time writer. *Publs:* mystery novels—Death and Taxes, 1941; Shear the Black Sheep, 1942; Bullets for the Bridegroom, 1944; It Ain't Hay, 1946 (in U.K. as A Drug on the Market, 1949); The Long Escape, 1948; Plunder of the Sun, 1949; The Red Tassel, 1950; To Catch a Thief, 1952; The Lights of Skaro, 1954; Angel's Ransom, 1956; Loo Loo's Legacy, 1960; Carambola (in U.K. as High Corniche), 1961; Hooligan, 1969 (in U.K. as Hatchetman, 1970); Troubleshooter, 1971; other—How Green Was My Father: A Sort of Travel Diary, 1947; How Lost Was My Weekend: A Greenhorn in Guatemala, 1948; The Crazy Glasspecker; or, High Life in the Andes, 1949 (in U.K. as High Life in the Andes, 1951); 20,000 Leagues Behind the 8 Ball, 1951; With a Knife and Fork down the Amazon, 1952; The Poor Man's Guide to Europe, 1953 and later editions; Time Out for Turkey (in U.K. as Talking Turkey), 1955; The Rich Man's Guide to the Riviera, 1962; The Poor Man's Guide to the Orient, 1965; Fly Down, Drive Mexico, 1968; rev. ed. as The Best of Mexico by Car, 1969. Add: 706 Kingston Rd., Princeton, N.J. 08540, U.S.A.

DODGE, Peter. American, b. 1926. History, Sociology. Assoc. Prof. of Sociology, Univ. of New Hampshire, Durham, since 1964. Instr., 1958–61 and Asst. Prof., 1961–64, Harpur Coll., State Univ. of New York, Binghamton; Social Science Research Council Grantee to Brazil, 1968–69. *Publs:* Beyond Marxism: The Faith and Works of Hendrik de Man, 1966; (ed. and trans.) Hendrik de Man, Socialist Critic of Marxism: A Documentary Study, 1979. Add: Falls House, Lee, R.F.D. Newmarket, N.H. 03857, U.S.A.

DODGSHON, Robert A(ndrew). British, b. 1941. Geography, History. Prof. of Geography, Univ. Coll. of Wales, Aberystwyth (joined faculty, 1970). Asst. Keeper, Museum of English Rural Life, Univ. of Reading, 1966–70. Ed., HGRG Research Monograph Series, 1978–82. *Publs:* (ed. with R.A. Butlin) An Historical Geography of England and Wales, 1978; The Origins of British Field Systems, 1980; Land and Society in Early Scotland, 1981; The European Past: Social Evolution and Spatial Order, 1987. Add: Dept. of Geography, University College of Wales, Aberystwyth SY23 3DB, Wales.

DODSON, Daniel B. American, b. 1918. Novels/Short stories. Prof.

of English, Columbia Univ., NYC. *Publs:* The Man Who Ran Away, 1961; Malcolm Lowry (criticism), 1965; The Dance of Love, 1974; Scala Dei, 1975; On a Darkling Plain, 1976; Looking for Zoe, 1980; Dancers in the Dark, 1983; The Drunken Boats, 1987. Add: Place Jean Alcard, Solliès-Ville 83210, France.

DODSON, Kenneth (MacKenzie). American, b. 1907. Historical/Romance/Gothic, Children's non-fiction, Biography. Master mariner in command of ocean tramps, 1938–42; former Capt., U.S. Navy. *Publs:* Away All Boats, 1954; Stranger to the Shore, 1956; Hector the Stowaway Dog, 1958; The China Pirates, 1960; Hawaii's Wreath of Love; From Make-Believe to Reality (The Bill Roberts Story), 1973; Carl Sandburg: A Friendship, 1987. Add: 1342 Rosario Rd., Anacortes, Wash. 98221, U.S.A.

DOHAN, Mary Helen. American, b. 1914. History, Language/Linguistics. Freelance writer. *Publs:* Our Own Words, 1974; Mr. Roosevelt's Steamboat, 1981. Add: 321 Audubon Blvd., New Orleans, La. 70125, U.S.A.

DOHERTY, Bertie. British, b. 1943. Children's fiction. Social worker and English teacher. *Publs:* How Green You Are!, 1982; The Making of Fingers Finnigan, 1983; Tilly Mint Tales, 1984; White Peak Farm, 1984; Children of Winter, 1985; Tough Luck, 1987; Tilly Mint and the Dodo, 1988; Granny Was a Buffer Girl, 1988; Paddiwak and Cosy, 1988; Spellhorn, 1989. Add: 38 Banner Cross Rd., Sheffield, York., S11 9HR, England.

DOLL, (Sir) (William) Richard (Shaboe). British, b. 1912. Medicine. Hon. Assoc. Physician, Central Middlesex Hosp., London, 1949–69; Dir., Medical Research Council's Statistical Unit, 1961–69; Regius Prof. of Medicine, Oxford Univ., 1969–79; Warden, Green Coll., Oxford, 1979–83. *Publs:* (with F. Avery Jones and M.M. Buckatzsch) Occupational Factors in the Aetiology of Gastric and Duodenal Ulcers, 1951; (with W.M. Court Brown) Leukaemia and Aplastic Anaemia in Patients Irradiated for Ankylosing Spondylitis, 1957; (with F.G.J. Hayhoe and D. Quaglino) The Cytology and Cytochemistry of Acute Leukaemias, 1964; (co-ed.) Cancer Incidence in Five Continents, vol. 1, 1966, vol. 2, 1970; Prevention of Cancer: Pointers from Epidemiology, 1967; The Epidemiology of Leukaemia, 1972; (ed. with I. Vodopija) Host Environment Interactions in the Aetiology of Cancer in Man, 1974; (ed. D.J. Jussawalla) International Seminar on Epidemiology of Oesophageal Cancer; (with R. Peto) The Causes of Cancer, 1981 Add: 12 Rawlinson Rd., Oxford, England.

DOLL, Ronald C. American, b. 1913. Writer on education curriculum. Prof. of Education Emeritus, Richmond Coll., City Univ. of New York, since 1976 (Prof., Hunter Coll., City Univ. of New York, 1961–67; Prof., Richmond Coll., 1967–76). Admin., West Orange Public Schs., N.J., 1944–52; Curriculum Specialist, Citizenship Education Project, Columbia Univ., NYC, 1952–53; Asst. Supt., Montclair Public Schs., N.J., 1953–57; Prof. of Education, New York Univ., NYC, 1957–61; Prof. of Curriculum, Georgian Court Coll., Lakewood, N.J., 1976–79. *Publs:* (with A.H. Passow and S.M. Corey) Organizing for Curriculum Improvement, 1953; (with T. Pollock, M. Sheridan and F. Hunter) The Art of Communicating, 1955, 1961; (with J. Macdonald) Cues to Effective Teaching and Teacher Education, 1961; (ed.) Individualizing Instruction, 1964; Curriculum Improvement: Decision-Making and Process, 1964, 7th ed. 1989; (ed. with R.S. Fleming) Children Under Pressure, 1966; Leadership to Improve Schools, 1972; (with R.C. Cook) The Elementary School Curriculum, 1973; (with others) Issues in Secondary Education, 1976; Supervision for Staff Development: Ideas and Application, 1983. Add: 1081A Argyll Circle, Lakewood, N.J. 08701, U.S.A.

DOMAN, Glenn. American, b. 1919. Education, Psychology. Founder, 1955, and since 1980 Chmn. of the Bd., Institutes for the Achievement of Human Potential, Philadelphia; Assoc. Dir., Centro de Reabilitacao Nossa Senhora da Gloria, Rio de Janeiro, since 1959. Staff Member, Temple Univ. Hosp., Philadelphia, 1941, and Pennsylvania Hosp., 1945–48; Dir., Norwood Rehabilitation Center, Philadelphia, 1948–55; Prof. of Human Development, Univ. of Plano, 1965–72. Pres., Intnl. Rehabilitation Forum, 1959, and World Org. for Human Potential, 1968–72. *Publs:* How to Teach Your Baby to Read, 1964, 1979; Nose Is Not Toes (children's book), 1964; What to Do About Your Brain-Injured Child, 1974; Teach Your Baby Math, 1979, (with J. Michael Armentrout) The Universal Multiplication of Intelligence, 1980; How to Multiply Your Baby's Intelligence, 1984; In a Word: Answers to 1001 Questions Parents Ask About their Brain-injured Children, 1987; How to Teach Your Baby to be Physically Superb, 1988. Add: Inst. for the Achievement of Human

Potential, 8801 Stenton Ave., Philadelphia, Pa. 19118, U.S.A.

DOMAR, Evsey D(avid). American, b. 1914. Economics. Ford Prof. Emeritus of Economics, Massachusetts Inst. of Technology, Cambridge, Mass., since 1984 (Prof., 1958–72; Ford Prof., 1972–84). Research Assoc., Russian Research Center, Harvard Univ., Cambridge, Mass., since 1958. Asst. Prof. of Economics, Carnegie Inst. of Technology, Pittsburgh, Pa., 1946–47, and Univ. of Chicago, 1947–48; Assoc. Prof. of Political Economy, 1948–55, and Prof., 1955–58, Johns Hopkins Univ., Baltimore, Md. *Publs:* Essays in the Theory of Economic Growth, 1957. Add: 264 Heath's Bridge Rd., Concord, Mass. 01742, U.S.A.

DOMINIAN, Jack. British, b. 1929. Human relations, Psychology. Consultant Physician, Central Middlesex Hosp., London, since 1965. *Publs:* Psychiatry and the Christian, 1962; Christian Marriage, 1967; Marital Breakdown, 1968; (co-author) The Future of Christian Marriage, 1969; The Church and the Sexual Revolution, 1971; Cycle of Affirmation, 1975; The Marriage Relationship Today, 1974; Depression, 1976; Authority: A Christian Interpretation, 1976; Marital Pathology, 1980; Marriage, Faith, and Love, 1981; The Growth of Love and Sex, 1982; Make or Break, 1984; The Capacity to Love, 1985; Sexual Integrity: The Answer to AIDS, 1987. Add: Pefka, The Green, Croxley Green, Rickmansworth, Herts., England.

DOMINIC, R.B. *See* **LATHEM,** Emma.

DOMINY, Eric Norman. British, b. 1918. Recreation/Leisure/Hobbies, Sports/Physical education/Keeping fit. Vice Chmn., British Judo Assn. (Holder of 6th Dan; Coach, London area; Team Mgr., 1954; Team Business Mgr., 1955). Exec. Officer, U.K. Civil Service, London, now retired. Gen. Secty., London Judo Soc. and London Karate Kai. *Publs:* The Art of Judo, 1952; Judo, 1954; Self-Defence, 1957; Judo Basic Principles, 1958; Judo: Beginner to Black Belt, 1958; Judo Throws and Counters, 1960; Camping: Home and Abroad, 1965; Judo: Contest Techniques and Tactics, 1966; Karate, 1967; Camping, 1972; Judo for Beginners, 1983. Add: 18 Hamilton Way, London N3 1AN, England.

DOMMERMUTH, William P. American, b. 1925. Marketing. Prof. of Marketing, Univ. of Missouri, St. Louis, since 1986. Assoc. Prof., Univ. of Texas at Austin, 1961–67; Assoc. Prof., Univ. of Iowa, Iowa City, 1967–68; Prof., Southern Illinois Univ., Carbondale, 1968–86. *Publs:* The Road to the Top, 1965; (with J.B. Kernan and M.S. Sommers) Promotion: An Introductory Analysis, 1970; (ed. with R.C. Andersen) Distribution Systems: Firms, Functions and Efficiencies, 1972; (with B. Marcus) Modern Marketing, 1975; The Use of Sampling in Marketing Research, 1975; (with others) Modern Marketing Management, 1980; Promotion: Analysis, Creativity and Strategy, 1984, 1989. Add: SSB 1304, Univ. of Missouri, St. Louis, Mo. 63121, U.S.A.

DONAHUE, Francis James. American, b. 1917. Literature. Prof. of Spanish, California State Univ., Long Beach, since 1960. Asst. Prof., U.S. Merchant Marine Academy, Kings Point, N.Y., 1948–54; Cultural Attaché U.S. Embassies, Caracas and Havana, 1954–60. *Publs:* Washington Irving: Su Mundo de Romance y Leyenda, 1958; The Dramatic World of Tennessee Williams, 1964; (ed.) Leandro F. de Moratín: El Si de las Niñas y La Comedia Nueva, 1967; Diez Figuras Ilustres de la Literatura Norteamericana, 1965; Alfonso Sastre: Dramaturgo y Preceptista, 1973. Add: Dept. of Spanish, California State Univ., Long Beach, Calif. 90801, U.S.A.

DONALD, William (Spooner). British, b. 1910. Plays/Screenplays, Autobiography/Memoirs/Personal. Freelance journalist since 1949. Officer, Royal Navy, 1924–49; Mgr., Castle Fisheries, Cumberland, 1951–57; Secty., Anglers Co-operative Assn., Scottish Branch, 1957–64. *Publs:* Hong Kong Cocktail (play), 1951; Pickled Salts (play), 1951; The Slings and Arrows (play), 1954; Stand By for Action (naval memoirs), 1956; Hanky Panky in the Highlands (play), 1968. Add: Troutlets, Church St., Keswick, Cumbria CA12 4DT, England.

DONALDS, Gordon. *See* **SHIRREFFS,** Gordon Donald.

DONALDSON, Frances. British, b. 1907. Agriculture/Forestry, History, Theatre, Autobiography/Memoirs/Personal, Biography. *Publs:* Approach to Farming, 1941; Four Years' Harvest, 1945; Milk without Tears, 1955; Freddy Lonsdale, 1957; Child of the Twenties, 1959; The Marconi Scandal, 1962; Evelyn Waugh: Portrait of a Country Neighbour, 1967; (with J.G.S. Donaldson) Farming in Britain Today, 1969; Actor-Managers, 1970; Edward VIII, 1974; P.G. Wodehouse, 1982; The British Council: The First Fifty Years, 1984; The Royal Opera House in the Twentieth

Century, 1988. Add: 17 Edna St., London SW11, England.

DONALDSON, Gordon. British, b. 1913. History, Biography. H.M. Historiographer in Scotland, since 1979. Emeritus Prof. of Scottish History and Palaeography, Univ. of Edinburgh, since 1979 (Lectr., 1947–55; Reader, 1955–63; Prof., 1963–79). Asst. Keeper, Scottish Record Office, 1938–47. *Publs:* The Making of the Scottish Prayer Book 1637, 1954; (ed.) The Register of the Privy Seal of Scotland, Vols. V-VIII, 1957–82; Shetland Life Under Earl Patrick, 1958; Scotland: Church and Nation Through Sixteen Centuries, 1960, 1972; The Scottish Reformation, 1960, 1972; Scotland: James V to James VII, 1965, 1978; The Scots Overseas, 1966; Northwards by Sea, 1966, 1978; Scottish Kings, 1967, 1977; Memoirs of Sir James Melville, 1969; The First Trial of Mary, Queen of Scots, 1969; Scottish Historical Documents, 1970; Who's Who in Scottish History, 1974; Mary, Queen of Scots, 1974; Scotland: The Shaping of a Nation, 1974, 1980; Dictionary of Scottish History, 1977; All the Queen's Men, 1983; Isles of Home, 1983; Scottish Church History, 1985; Sir William Fraser, 1985; Reformed by Bishops, 1987. Add: 6 Pan Ha', Dysart, Fife, Scotland.

DONALDSON, Norman. American, b. 1922. Chemistry, Biography. Sr. Ed., Chemical Abstracts Service, American Chemical Soc., Columbus, Ohio, since 1957. Chemist, ICI Ltd (Dyestuffs Div.), Manchester, England, 1950–57. *Publs:* Chemistry and Technology of Naphthalene Compounds, 1958; In Search of Dr. Thorndyke (biography), 1971; Goodbye, Dr. Thorndyke (pastiche), 1972; The Queen's Treasure, 1975; (with B. Donaldson) How Did They Die?, 1979. Add: 1358 Inglis Ave., Columbus, Ohio 43212, U.S.A.

DONALDSON, Scott. American, b. 1928. Literature, Social commentary/phenomena, Biography. Louise G.T. Cooley Prof. of English, Coll. of William and Mary, Williamsburg, Va., since 1984 (Prof., 1974–84; Asst. Prof., 1966–69; Assoc. Prof., 1969–74). Exec. Ed., Sun newspapers, Minn., 1961–64. *Publs:* The Suburban Myth, 1969; Poet in America: Winfield Townley Scott, 1972; By Force or Will: The Life and Art of Ernest Hemingway, 1977; (with A. Massa) American Literature: Nineteenth and Early Twentieth Centuries, 1978; (ed.) On the Road, by Jack Kerouac, 1979; Fool for Love, F. Scott Fitzgerald, 1983; (ed.) Critical Essays on F. Scott Fitzgerald's *The Great Gatsby*, 1984; (ed.) Conversations with John Cheever, 1987; John Cheever: A Biography, 1988. Add: Dept. of English, Coll. of William and Mary, Williamsburg, Va. 23185, U.S.A.

DONALDSON, Stephen R. Also writes novels as Reed Stephens. American, b. 1947. Mystery/Crime/Suspense, Science fiction/Fantasy. Assistant Dispatcher, Transportation Dept., Akron City Hosp., Ohio, 1968–70; Teaching Fellow, Dept. of English, Kent State Univ., Ohio, 1971; Assoc. Instr., Ghost Ranch Writers' Workshops, Abiquiu, N. Mex., 1973–75; Acquisitions Ed., Tapp-Gentz Assoc., West Chester, Penn., 1973. *Publs:* The Chronicles of Thomas Covenant the Unbeliever: Lord Foul's Bane, 1977, The Illearth War, 1977, and The Power That Preserves, 1977; The Second Chronicles of Thomas Covenant: The Wounded Land, 1980; (as Reed Stephens) The Man Who Killed His Brother, 1980; The One Tree, 1982; White Gold Wielder, 1983; Daughter of Regals and Other Tales, 1984; (as Reed Stephens) The Man Who Risked His Partner, 1984; Mordant's Need: The Mirror of Her Dreams, 1986; A Man Rides Through, 1987. Add: c/o Del Rey Books, Ballantine Books, 201 E. 50th St., New York, N.Y. 10022, U.S.A.

DONKIN, Nance (Clare) Australian, b. 1915. Children's fiction. Journalist, Daily Mercury, Maitland, and Morning Herald, Newcastle. Pres., Children's Book Council, Victoria, 1968–76. *Publs:* Araluen Adventures, 1946; No Medals for Meg, 1947; Julie Stands By, 1948; Blue Ribbon Beth, 1951; (ed.) The Australian Children's Annual, 1963; Sheep, 1967; Sugar, 1967; An Emancipist, 1968; A Currency Lass, 1969; House by the Water, 1969; An Orphan, 1970; Johnny Neptune, 1971; The Cool Man, 1973; A Friend for Petros, 1974; Margaret Catchpole, 1974; Patchwork Grandmother, 1975; Green Christmas, 1976; Yellowgum Girl, 1976; A Handful of Ghost, 1976; The Best of the Bunch, 1978; The Maidens of Pefka, 1979; Nini, 1979; Stranger and Friend (for adults), 1983; We of the Never Never Retold for Children, 1983; Two at Sullivan Bay, 1985; Blackout, 1987; A Family Affair: The Women Were There (for adults), 1988. Add: 8/8 Mooltan Ave., Balaclava, Vic. 3183, Australia.

DONLEAVY, J(ames) P(atrick). Irish, b. 1926. Novels/Short stories, Plays/Screenplays, Social commentary/phenomena. *Publs:* The Ginger Man, 1955, complete ed. 1963; The Ginger Man (play), 1961, in U.K. as What They Did in Dublin, with the Ginger Man, 1962: Fairy Tales of New York (play), 1961; A Singular Man, 1963; A Singular Man (play), 1965; Meet My Maker the Mad Molecule (short stories), 1964; The Saddest Summer of Samuel S., 1966; The Beastly Beatitudes of Balthazar B., 1968; The Onion Eaters, 1971; The Collected Plays of J.P. Donleavy, 1972; A Fairy Tale of New York, 1973; The Unexpurgated Code: A Complete Manual of Survival and Manners, 1975; The Destinies of Darcy Dancer, Gentleman, 1977; Schultz, 1979; Leila, 1983; De Alfonce Tennis, 1984; J.P. Donleavy's Ireland, 1986; Are You Listening Rabbi Low, 1987. Add: Levington Pk., Mullinger, Co. Westmeath, Ireland.

DONNACHIE, Ian. British, b. 1944. Economics, History. Sr. Lectr., The Open Univ. in Scotland, since 1985 (Staff Tutor in History, 1970–85). Research Asst., Dept. of History, Strathclyde Univ., 1967–68; Lectr. in History, Napier Coll., Edinburgh, 1968–70; Lectr. in Social Sciences, Deakin Univ., Vic., 1982; Visiting Fellow, Deakin Univ., and Univ. of Sydney, N.S.W., 1985. Asst. Ed., Industrial Archaeology, 1968–73, and Industrial Archaeology Review, 1975–78. *Publs:* (with J. Butt and J. Hume) Industrial History: Scotland, 1968; (with J. Butt) The Industries of Scotland, 1969; (ed. with J. Butt) Industrial Archaeology, 5 vols., 1969–73; Industrial Archaeology of Galloway, 1971; War and Economic Growth in Britain 1793-1815, 1973; (with I. Macleod) Old Galloway, 1974; Roads and Canals, 1976; (with Alasdair Hogg) The War of Independence and the Scottish Nation, 1976; (with John Hume and Michael Moss) Historic Industrial Scenes: Scotland, 1977; A History of the Brewing Industry in Scotland, 1979; (with John Butt) Industrial Archaeology in the British Isles, 1979; (with Innes Macleod) Victorian and Edwardian Scottish Lowlands in Old Photographs, 1979; (with G. Hewitt) Scottish History 1560-1980, 1982; (with C. Harvie and I.S. Wood) Forward! Labour Politics in Scotland 1888-1988, 1989; (with G. Hewitt) Companion to Scottish History, 1989. Add: The Open Univ. in Scotland, 60 Melville St., Edinburgh EH3 7HF, Scotland.

DONNELLY, Austin S(tanislaus). Has also written as Bullen Bear. Business/Trade/Industry, Money/Finance. Managing Dir., Donnelly Money Management Pty, Ltd., since 1983. Queensland Mgr., A.F.T. Ltd., and Development Finance Corp. Group, 1958–69; Managing Dir., Capital Services Ltd., 1969–83. *Publs:* The Practice of Public Accounting, 1953, 1961; Profitable Business Writing, 1955; Guide to Business Management, 1956; Direct Costing, 1957; Secretarial Practice, 1958; Trends in Public Accounting Practice, 1958; Financial Management, 1959, 3rd ed. 1968; Communication in Financial Management, 1960; Australian Secretarial Practice, 2nd ed. 1962; (with Sheila Donnelly) The Executive's Private Secretary, 1963; Profit Through Cost Analysis and Direct Costing, 1965; How to Make Your Association Profitable, 1966; You and Your Money, 1966; (as Bullen Bear) How to Make Money in Investments, 1967; Investing for Profit, 1969; Successful Investment in Industrial and Mining Shares, 1970; Investing—How to Make Profit with Your Spare Money, 1971; Strategic Investing, 1973; Investing for Profit in the Seventies, 1975; Seven Steps to Investment Success, 1975; Successful Investment in Industrial and Mining Shares, 1977; Practical Financial Management, 1978; Managing Cash Flow, 1979; Personal Money Management, 1979; Planning and Financing a Secure Retirement, 1980; Treasury Management, 1981; How to Generate and Control Cash Flow, 1982; Where to Park Your Cash, 1982; The Three R's of Investing: Return, Risk and Relativity, U.S. ed., 1984, and Australian rev. ed., 1985; Australian Investment Planning Guide, 1985. Add: 31 King Arthur Terr., Tennyson, Qld., 4105, Australia.

DONNELLY, James S., Jr. American, b. 1943. Economics, History. Prof. of History, Univ. of Wisconsin-Madison, since 1980 (Asst. Prof., 1972–75; Assoc. Prof., 1975–80). Asst. Prof. of History, Univ. of Tennessee, Chattanooga, 1969–72. *Publs:* Landlord and Tenant in Nineteenth-Century Ireland, 1973; The Land and the People of Nineteenth-Century Cork: The Rural Economy and the Land Question, 1975; (ed.) Irish Peasants: Violence and Political Unrest, 1780-1914, 1983. Add: Dept. of History, Univ. of Wisconsin-Madison, 3211 Humanities Bldg., 455 North Park St., Madison, Wisc. 53706, U.S.A.

DONNELLY Jane. British. Romance/Historical fiction. Former journalist; television critic. *Publs:* A Man Apart, 1968; Don't Walk Alone, 1969; Shadows from the Sea, 1970; Take the Far Dream, 1970; Halfway to the Stars, 1971; Never Turn Back, 1971; The Man in the Next Room, 1971; The Mill in the Meadow, 1972; A Stranger Came, 1972; The Long Shadow, 1973; Rocks Under Shining Water, 1973; A Man Called Mallory, 1974; Collision Course, 1975; The Man Outside, 1975; Ride Out the Storm, 1975; Dark Pursuer, 1976; The Silver Cage, 1976; Dear Caliban, 1977; Four Weeks in Winter, 1977; The Intruder, 1977; Forest of the Night, 1978; Love for a Stranger, 1978; Spell of the Seven Stones, 1978; The Black Hunter, 1978; Touched by Fire, 1978; A Man to Watch, 1979;

A Savage Sanctuary, 1979; Behind a Closed Door, 1979; No Way Out, 1980; When Lightning Strikes, 1980; Flash Point, 1981; So Long a Winter, 1981; The Frozen Jungle, 1981; Diamond Cut Diamond, 1982; A Fierce Encounter, 1983; Call Up the Storm, 1983; Face the Tiger, 1983; Moon Lady, 1984; Ring of Crystal, 1985; To Cage a Whirlwind, 1985; Force Field, 1987; The Frozen Heart, 1987; Ride a Wild Horse, 1987; No Place to Run, 1988; Fetters of Gold, 1988; When We're Along, 1989. Add: c/o Mills and Boon Ltd., Eton House, 18-24 Paradise Rd., Richmond, Surrey TW9 1SR, Emgland.

DONNISON, David Vernon. British, b. 1926. Social sciences. Prof. of Town and Regional Planning, Univ. of Glasgow, since 1980. Prof. of Social Admin., London Sch. of Economics, 1961–69; Chmn., Public Schs. Commn., 1968–70; Chmn., Supplementary Benefits Commn., 1975–80. *Publs:* The Neglected Child and the Social Services, 1954; Welfare Services in a Canadian Community, 1958; The Government of Housing, 1965; (ed. with D. Eversley) London: Urban Patterns, Problems and Policies, 1973; Social Policy and Administration Revisited, 1975; (with P. Soto) The Good City: A Study of Urban Development and Policy in Britain, 1979; The Politics of Poverty, 1982; (with C. Ungerson) Housing Policy, 1982; (ed. with Alan Middleton) Regenerating the Inner City: Glasgow's Experience, 1987. Add: The Old Manse, Ardentinny, Argyll PA23 8TR, Scotland.

DONNISON, Frank Siegfried Vernon. British, b. 1898. History. With the Indian Civil Service, Burma, 1922–46; Historian, Cabinet Office, London, 1949–66, now retired. *Publs:* Public Administration in Burma, 1953; British Military Administration in the Far East 1943-46, 1956; Civil Affairs and Military Government North-West Europe 1944-46, 1961; Civil Affairs and Military Government Central Organization and Planning, 1966; Burma, 1970. Add: Lower Cross Farmhouse, East Hagbourne, Didcot, Oxon OX11 9LD, England.

DONNITHORNE, Audrey Gladys. British/Australian, b. 1922. Economics. Exec. Dir., Assn. for Intnl. Technological, Economic and Cultural Exchange, Hong Kong, since 1988. Research Asst., 1948–51, Lectr. in Political Economy, 1951–66, and Reader in Chinese Economic Studies, 1966–68, Univ. Coll., Univ. of London; Professorial Fellow, 1969–85, and Foundn. Head, Contemporary China Centre, 1970–77; Australian National Univ., Canberra. *Publs:* (with G.C. Allen) Western Enterprise in Far Eastern Economic Development: China and Japan, 1954; (with G.C. Allen) Western Enterprise in Indonesia and Malaya, 1957; British Rubber Manufacturing, 1958; China's Economic System, 1967; China's Grain: Output, Procurement, Transfers and Trade, 1970; The Budget and the Plan in China: Central-Local Economic Relations, 1972; Centre-Provincial Economic Relations in China, 1981. Add: Flat A3, 18th Floor, 73 Bonham Rd., Hong Kong.

DONOGHUE, Denis. Irish, b. 1928. Literature. Henry James Prof. of English and American Letters, New York Univ., since 1979. Administrative Officer, Irish Dept. of Finance, Dublin, 1951–54; Music Critic, Irish Times, Dublin, 1957; University Lectr. and Fellow of King's Coll., Cambridge, 1964–65; Lectr., 1954–64, and Prof., 1965–79, University Coll., Dublin. Dir. of Yeats Intnl. Summer Sch., Dublin, 1960; Visiting Scholar, Univ. of Pennsylvania, Philadelphia, 1962–63; Member of the Bd., Abbey Theatre, Dublin. *Publs:* The Third Voice: Modern British and American Verse Drama, 1959; Connoisseurs of Chaos: Ideas of Order in Modern American Literature, 1965; (ed., with J.R. Mulryne) An Honoured Guest: New Essays on W.B. Yeats, 1965; (ed.) Swift Revisited, 1968; The Ordinary Universe: Soundings in Modern Literature, 1968; Jonathan Swift: A Critical Introduction, 1969; Emily Dickinson, 1969; William Butler Yeats, 1971; (ed.) Jonathan Swift: A Critical Anthology, 1971; (ed.) Memoirs, by W.B. Yeats, 1973; Thieves of Fire, 1973; The Sovereign Ghost: Studies in Imagination, 1976; Ferocious Alphabets, 1981; The Arts Without Mystery, 1983; Reading America: Essays on American Literature, 1987; England, Their England: Commentaries on English Language and Literature, 1988; We Irish: On Irish Literature and Society, 1988; (ed.) Selected Essays of R.P. Blackmur, 1988; (ed. with others) American in Theory, 1988. Add: Dept. of English, New York Univ., New York, N.Y. 10003, U.S.A.

DONOGHUE, Mildred R(ansdorf). American, b. 1929. Education, Language. Prof. of Education, California State Univ., Fullerton, since 1971 (Asst. Prof., 1962–66; Assoc. Prof. 1966–71). Assoc. Ed., MLABSTRACTS, 1962–69. *Publs:* Foreign Languages and the Schools, 1967; Foreign Languages and the Elementary School Child, 1968; The Child and the English Language Arts, 1971, 1975, 1979, 1985, 1990; Second Languages in Primary Education, 1979. Add: California State Univ., Fullerton, Calif. 92634, U.S.A.

DONOUGHUE, (Lord) Bernard. British, b. 1934. Politics/Government, Biography. Exec. Vice-Chmn., London and Bishopsgate Intnl., since 1988. Member, Editorial Staff, The Economist, London, 1959–60; Sr. Research Officer, Political and Economic Planning (PEP), London, 1960–63; Sr. Lectr. in Politics, London Sch. of Economics, 1963–74; Sr. Policy Adviser to the Prime Minister, 1974–79; Dir., Economist Intelligence Unit, London, 1979–81; Asst. Ed., The Times, London, 1981–82; Head of Research, Kleinwort Grieveson & Co., 1982–88. *Publs:* (ed.) Oxford Poetry 1956, 1956; British Politics and the American Revolution, 1963; (co-author) The People into Parliament, 1964; (co-author) Herbert Morrison: Portrait of a Politician, 1973; Prime Minister, 1987. Add: 7 Brookfield Park, London NW5, England.

DONOVAN, John. Pseud: Hugh Hennessey. American, b. 1919. Novels/Short stories, History, Travel/Exploration/Adventure, Biography. Freelance public relations consultant. *Publs:* Eichmann, Man of Slaughter, 1960; Red Machete, 1963; Not for Eternity (novel), 1971; International Businessman's Travel Guide, 1972; (ed.) U.S. and Soviet Policy in the Middle East, vol. I, 1972; vol. II, 1974; There's Money in Your House, 1976; Bitter Sweet Temptation, 1980. Add: 4925 38th Way S., St. Petersburg, Fla. 33711, U.S.A.

DONOVAN, John. American, b. 1928. Children's fiction. Pres., Children's Book Council. *Publs:* The Little Orange Book, 1961; I'll Get There, It Better Be Worth the Trip, 1969; Wild in the World, 1971; Remove Protective Coating a Little at a Time, 1973; Good Old James, 1975; Family, 1976. Add: Children's Book Council, 67 Irving Place, New York, N.Y. 10003, U.S.A.

DOOB, Leonard W. American, b. 1909. Psychology. Prof. of Psychology, Yale Univ., New Haven, since 1934. Ed., Journal of Social Psychology, since 1966. *Publs:* Propaganda, 1935; (co-author) Competition and Cooperation, 1937; (co-author) Frustration and Aggression, 1939; Plans of Men, 1940; Public Opinion and Propaganda, 1948; Social Psychology, 1952; Becoming More Civilized, 1960; Communication in Africa, 1961; Patriotism and Nationalism, 1964; (ed.) Ants Will Not Eat Your Fingers, 1966; (ed.) A Crocodile Has Me by the Leg, 1967; (ed.) Resolving Conflict in Africa, 1970; Patterning of Time, 1971; Pathways to People, 1975; Panorama of Evil, 1978; (ed.) Ezra Pound Speaking, 1978; The Pursuit of Peace, 1980; Personality, Power and Authority, 1983; Slightly Beyond Skepticism, 1987; Inevitability, 1988. Add: Dept. of Psychology, Box 11A, Yale Station, New Haven, Conn. 06520, U.S.A.

DORLAND, Henry. *See* **ASH,** Brian.

DORMAN, Luke. *See* **BINGLEY,** David Ernest.

DORMAN, Michael L. American, b. 1932. Politics/Government. Newspaper reporter and ed., 1950–64. *Publs:* We Shall Overcome, 1964; The Secret Service Story, 1967; The Second Man, 1968; King of the Courtroom, 1969; Under 21, 1970; Payoff: The Role of Organized Crime in American Politics, 1972; The Making of a Slum, 1972; Confrontation, 1974; Vesco: The Infernal Money-Making Machine, 1975; Witch Hunt, 1976; The George Wallace Myth, 1976; Detectives of the Sky, 1976; Dirty Politics: From 1776 to Watergate, 1979. Add: 7 Lauren Ave. South, Dix Hills, N.Y. 11746, U.S.A.

DORMAN, Sonya (Hess). American, b. 1924. Science fiction, Children's fiction, Poetry. Formerly stable maid, kennel owner, receptionist, cook, dancer, greenhouse asst., and housekeeper. *Publs:* Poems, 1970; Stretching Fence, 1975; A Paper Raincoat, 1976; Planet Patrol (juvenile science fiction), 1978; The Far Traveler, 1980; Palace of Earth, 1984. Add: c/o John Schaffner, 114 E. 28th St., New York, N.Y. 10016, U.S.A.

DORN, Ed(ward Merton). American, b. 1929. Poetry, Anthropology/Ethnology, Literature, Translations. Member of the English Dept., Univ. of Colorado, Boulder, since 1977. Visiting Prof. of American Literature, 1965–68, and member of English Dept., 1974–75, Univ. of Essex, Wivenhoe, U.K.; Visiting Poet, Univ. of Kansas, Lawrence, 1968–69. *Publs:* What I See in the Maximus Poems, 1960; The Newly Fallen: Poems, 1961; Hands Up!, 1964; From Gloucester Out, 1964; (with M. Rumaker and W. Tallman) Prose I, 1964; The Rites of Passage: A Brief History, 1965, rev. ed. as By the Sound, 1971; Idaho Out, 1965; Geography, 1965; The Shoshoneans: The People of the Basin-Plateau, 1966; The North Atlantic Turbine, 1967; (trans. with G. Brotherston) Our Word: Guerrilla Poems from Latin America, 1968; Gunslinger, Book I, 1968; Gunslinger, Book II, 1969; Gunslinger, Books I and II, 1969; Twenty-Four Love Songs, 1969; (trans. with G. Brotherston) Tree Between the Two Walls, by José Emilio Pacheco, 1969; The Midwest Is That Space Between the Buffalo Statler and the Lawrence Eldridge, 1969; The Cosmology of Finding Your Spot, 1969; Songs: Set Two, A Short Count, 1970; Spectrum Breakdown: A Microbook, 1971; A Poem Called Alexander Hamilton, 1971; The Cycle, 1971; Some Business Recently Transacted in the White World (short stories), 1971; The Hamadryas Baboon at the Lincoln Park Zoo, 1972; Gunslinger, Book III: The Winterbook Prologue to the Great Book IV Kornerstone, 1972; Recollections of Gran Apacheria, 1973; Gunslinger, Books I, II, III, IV, 1975; Collected Poems of Edward Dorn, 1975; (with Jennifer Dunbar) Manchester Square (poetry), 1975; (trans., with Gordon Brotherston) Selected Poems, by Vallejo, 1976; Hello, La Jolla (poetry), 1978; Views, Interviews, 2 vols., 1978; Selected Poems, 1978; (trans.) Images of the New World, 1979; Yellow Lola, 1981. Add: c/o Four Seasons Foundation, P.O. Box 31190, San Francisco, Calif. 94131, U.S.A.

DORNBERG, John. American, b. 1931. History, International relations/Current affairs, Politics/Government, Biography. Freelance Foreign Corresp, Toronto Star. Managing Ed., The Overseas Weekly, Frankfurt, Germany, 1956–63; Corresp. in Bonn and Bureau Chief in Vienna, Moscow, and Munich, Newsweek mag., 1965–72. *Publs:* Schizophrenic Germany, 1961; The Other Germany, 1968; The New Tsars: Russia Under Stalin's Heirs, 1972; Brezhnev: The Masks of Power, 1974; The Two Germanys, 1974; The New Germany, 1975; The Soviet Union Today, 1976; Eastern Europe: A Communist Kaleidoscope, 1980; The Putsch That Failed: Munich 1923, 1982. Add: Kafka Str. 8, 8 Munich, Germany.

DOROSHKIN, Milton. American, b. 1914. Sociology. Prof. Emeritus of Sociology and Psychology, Bronx Community Coll., City Univ. of New York, since 1960. *Publs:* Yiddish in America: Social and Cultural Foundations, 1970. Add: 2560 S. Ocean Blvd., Apt. 301, Palm Beach, Fla. 33480, U.S.A.

DORSEN, Norman. American, b. 1930. Civil liberties/Human rights, Law. Stokes Prof. of Law, New York Univ. Sch. of Law, NYC, since 1961. Pres., American Civil Liberties Union, NYC, since 1976. Law Assoc., Dewey, Ballantine, Bushby, Palmer & Wood, NYC, 1958–60. Chmn., Cttee. for Public Justice, 1972–73; Pres., Soc. of American Law Teachers, 1973–75; Chmn., Review Panel on New Drug Regulation, Dept. of Health, Education, and Welfare, 1975–77. *Publs:* (with others) Political and Civil Rights in the U.S., 3rd ed. 1967, 4th ed. 1979, supplement 1982; Frontiers of Civil Liberties, 1968; Discrimination and Civil Rights, 1969; (ed.) The Rights of Americans, 1971; (with Leon Friedman) Disorder in the Court, 1973; (co-ed. with Stephen Gillers) None of Your Business—Governments, Secrecy in America, 1974; (ed.) Our Endangered Rights: The ACLU Report on Civil Liberties Today, 1984; (with Stephen Gillers) Regulation of Lawyers, 1985; (ed.) The Evolving Constitution, 1987. Add: 40 Washington Sq. South, New York, N.Y. 10012, U.S.A.

DORSET, Phyllis (Flanders). American, b. 1924. History. Technical Writer and Ed., SRI Intnl., California, 1956–65 and since 1966. Technical Writer and Ed., Sandia Corp., 1952–56, Technical Operations, 1963–66, Arthur D. Little Inc., 1964–66, and Physics Intnl. Inc., 1968–74. *Publs:* Historic Ships Afloat, 1967; The New Eldorado: The Story of Colorado's Gold and Silver Rushes, 1970; (ed.) My Life at Fort Ross, 1987. Add: 460 Sherwood Way, Menlo Park, Calif. 94025, U.S.A.

DORSETT, Danielle. *See* **DANIELS,** Dorothy.

DOSS, Margot P(atterson). American, b. 1920. Travel/Exploration/Adventure. Columnist, San Francisco Chronicle, since 1961; Lectr. in Natural History, Calif. Acad. of Science; Commissioner, Golden Gate National Recreation Area, since 1976. Lectr., Univ. of Calif., 1970–83; Performer and Outdoor Ed., KPIX-TV Evening mag., 1977–83. *Publs:* San Francisco at Your Feet, 1964, 4th ed. 1990; Walks for Children in San Francisco, 1970; Bay Area at Your Feet, 1970, 3rd ed. 1986; Golden Gate Park at Your Feet, 1970, 1978; Paths of Gold, 1974; There, There, 1978; A Walker's Yearbook, 1984; Beijing at Your Feet, 1989. Add: 120 Horseshoe Hill Rd., Bolinas, Calif. 94924, U.S.A.

DOTTS, Maryann J. American, b. 1933 Children's non-fiction, Education, Theology/Religion. Dir. of Christian Education, First Methodist Church, Erie, Pa., 1956–58, and Arlington Heights, Ill., 1958–61; Teacher and Supvr., Children's Section of Education Staff, Riverside Church, NYC, 1965–67; Dir. of Christian Ed., Belle Meade United Methodist Church, Nashville, 1975–79; Dir. of Christian Ed., Andrew Price United Methodist Church, Nashville, 1980–84; Dir. of Christian Education, First

United Methodist Church, Cape Coral, Fla., 1985–89. Pres., Church and Synagogue Library Assn., 1978–79. *Publs:* I Am Happy, 1971; (with M. Franklin) Clues to Creativity: Providing Learning Experiences for Children, 3 vols., 1974; Church Resource Library, 1975, 1988; When Jesus Was Born, 1979; You Can Have a Church Library, 1988. Add: Settlers Colony 2658, Gulf Breeze, Fla. 32561, U.S.A.

DOUBTFIRE, Dianne (Joan). British, b. 1918. Novels/Short stories, Children's fiction, Writing. Lectr. in Creative Writing, Univ. of Surrey, since 1986. Lectr. on Creative Writing, Isle of Wight County Council Adult Education 1965–85. *Publs:* Lust for Innocence, 1960; Reason for Violence, 1961; Kick a Tin Can, 1964; The Flesh Is Strong, 1966; Behind the Screen, 1969; Escape on Monday, 1970; This Jim, 1974; Girl in Cotton Wool, 1975; A Girl Called Rosemary, 1977; Sky Girl, 1978; The Craft of Novel-Writing, 1978; Girl in a Gondola, 1980; Sky Lovers, 1981; Teach Yourself Creative Writing, 1983; The Wrong Face, 1985; Overcoming Shyness: A Woman's Guide, 1988. Add: April Cottage, Beech Hill, Headley Down, Hampshire GU35 8EQ, England.

DOUGHTY, Robin W. British, b. 1941. Geography, Zoology, Environmental science/Ecology. Assoc. Prof. of Geology, Univ. of Texas at Austin, since 1974 (Asst. Prof., 1971–74). Visiting Lectr., Oxford Univ., 1976–77. *Publs:* Feather Fashions and Bird Preservation: A Study in Nature Protection, 1975; Wildlife and Man in Texas: Environmental Change and Conservation, 1983; (with Larry L. Smith) The Amazing Armadillo: Geography of a Folk Critter, 1984; At Home in Early Texas: Early Views of the Land, 1987; State Birds: The Mockingbird, 1987. Add: Dept. of Geography, Univ. of Texas, Austin, Tex. 78712, U.S.A.

DOUGLAS, Barbara. *See* **LAKER,** Rosalind.

DOUGLAS, James Dixon. British, b. 1922. Theology/Religion. Lectr. in Ecclesiastical History, Univ. of St. Andrews, Scotland, 1955–56; Librarian Tyndale House, Cambridge, 1958–61; British Editorial Dir., 1961–69, and Ed.-at-Large, 1969–83, Christianity Today. *Publs:* (ed.) New Bible Dictionary, 1962; (ed.) Evangelicals and Unity, 1964; Light in the North, 1964; (ed.) New International Dictionary of the Christian Church, 1974; Completing the Course, 1976; (ed.) The Work of an Evangelist, 1984; (ed.) The Calling of an Evangelist, 1987; (ed.) New International Dictionary of the Bible, 1988; (co-author) Compact Dictionary of Church History and Theology, 1989. Add: 2 Doocot Rd., St. Andrews KY16 8QP, Scotland.

DOUGLAS, John (Frederick James). British, b. 1929. Geography, Photography, Third World problems, Travel/Exploration/Adventure. Photographer and travel consultant, since 1955; Library Dir., Geoslides Photo Agency, London, since 1969. *Publs:* South Downs, 1969; The Arctic Highway, 1972; Town and Village in Northern Ghana, 1973; Water Problems in the Third World, 1973; Kampong Tengah, a Malay Village, 1974; Kuala Lumpur, A Third World City, 1974; A Dyak Longhouse in Borneo, 1975; Environmental Viewpoint: Water, 1976; Shelter and Subsistence, 1976; Ice and Snow, 1976; Expedition Photography, 1979; Creative Techniques in Travel Photography, 1982. Add: GeoGroup, 4 Christian Fields, London SW16 3JZ, England.

DOUGLAS, Michael. *See* **CRICHTON,** Michael.

DOUGLAS-HAMILTON, (Lord) James Alexander. British, b. 1942. History. Advocate, Faculty of Advocates, Edinburgh. Councillor, City of Edinburgh; M.P. for Edinburgh West since 1974, and Minister for Home Affairs and the Environment, Scottish Office, since 1987 (Lord Commnr. of the Treasury, 1979–81; Personal Private Secty. to Secty. of State for Scotland, 1986–87). With 6/7 Battalion, Cameronians Scottish Rifles, 1961–67; Capt., Cameronian Company 2nd Battalion, Lowland Volunteers, 1971–74. *Publs:* Motive for a Mission: The Story Behind Hess's Flight to Britain, 1971; (ed.) The Air Battle for Malta, 1981; Roof of the World, 1983. Add: 12 Quality St. Lane, Edinburgh, Scotland.

DOUGLAS-HOME, Alec. *See* **HOME,** Lord.

DOUGLASS, Billie. *See* **DELINSKY,** Barbara.

DOVER, (Sir) K(enneth) J(ames). British, b. 1920. Classics. Prof. of Classics (winter quarter) Stanford Univ., California, since 1987. Fellow and Tutor, Balliol Coll., Oxford, 1948–55; Prof. of Greek, Univ. of St. Andrews, Scotland, 1955–76; Pres., Corpus Christi Coll., Oxford, 1976–86. Co-Ed., Classical Quarterly, 1962–68; Pres., Hellenic Soc., 1971–74, Classical Assn., 1976, and British Academy, 1978–81. *Publs:* Greek Word Order, 1960; (ed.) Thucydides Book VI, 1965; (ed.) Thucydides

Book VII, 1965; (ed.) Aristophanes' Clouds, 1968; Lysias and the Corpus Lysiacum, 1968; (with A.W. Gomme and A. Andrewes) Historical Commentary on Thucydides, vol. IV, 1970; (ed.) Theocritus: Select Poems, 1971; Aristophanic Comedy, 1972; Greek Popular Morality, 1975; Greek Homosexuality, 1978; The Greeks, 1980; (co-author) Ancient Greek Literature, 1980; Greek and the Greeks (Collected Papers, vol. I), 1987. Add: 49 Hepburn Gardens, St. Andrews, Fife KY16 9LS, Scotland.

DOW, Marguerite (Ruth). Canadian, b. 1926. Literature, Social commentary/phenomena, Theatre. Prof. of English and Drama, Faculty of Education, Univ. of Western Ontario, London, since 1972 (Assoc. Prof., 1965–72). *Publs:* Light from Other Windows, 1964; The Magic Mask, 1966; Courses of Study in the Theatre Arts, 1969; We Are Canada/Nous Sommes Canadiens, 1981. Add: 1231 Richmond St., Apt. 909, London, Ont. N6A 3L9, Canada.

DOWDEN, Anne Ophelia Todd. American, b. 1907. Botany. Freelance botanical artist and author, since 1952. Head of Art Dept., Manhattanville Coll., N.Y., 1932–53. *Publs:* The Little Hill, 1961; Look at a Flower, 1963; The Secret Life of the Flowers, 1964; Roses, 1965; Wild Green Things in the City: A Book of Weeds, 1972; The Blossom on the Bough: A Book of Trees, 1975; State Flowers, 1978; This Noble Harvest: A Chronicle of Herbs, 1979; From Flower to Fruit, 1984; The Clover and the Bee: A Book of Pollination, 1990. Add: 205 West 15th St., New York, N.Y. 10011, U.S.A.

DOWDESWELL, Wilfrid Hogarth. British, b. 1914. Biology, Environmental science/Ecology. Emeritus Prof. of Education, Bath Univ., since 1979 (Sr. Lectr., 1969–72; Prof., 1972–79). Ed., Heinemann Scholarship Series of Monographs. Sr. Biology Master, 1950–57, and Head of the Science Dept., 1957–69, Winchester Coll., Hants. *Publs:* Introduction to Animal Ecology, 1952, 1959; Practical Animal Ecology, 1959, 1963; The Mechanism of Evolution, 1955, 4th ed. 1972; Projects in Biological Science, 1970; Teaching and Learning Biology, 1981; The Life of the Meadow Brown, 1981; Ecology: Principles and Practice, 1984; Evolution: A Modern Synthesis, 1984; Hedgerows and Verges, 1987. Add: The Old Forge, Atworth, Melksham, Wilts. SN12 8HY, England.

DOWLER, James R. American, b. 1925. Westerns/Adventure. Advertising Mgr., Shell Chemical Co., div. of Shell Oil Co., U.S.A., since 1954. *Publs:* Partner's Choice, 1958; Fiddlefoot Fugitive, 1970; Laredo Lawman, 1970; The Copperhead Colonel, 1972. Add: 5061 Heather Rd., S.E., Smyrna, Ga. 30080, U.S.A.

DOWLING, Basil (Cairns). New Zealander, b. 1910. Poetry. Head of English Dept., Raine's Foundn. Grammar Sch., London, since 1965 (Asst. Master, 1954–65). Librarian, Otago Univ., Dunedin, 1947–52; Asst. Master, Downside Sch., Surrey, England, 1952–54. *Publs:* A Day's Journey, 1941; Signs and Wonders: Poems, 1955; Canterbury and Other Poems, 1949; Hatherley: Recollective Lyrics, 1968; A Little Gallery of Characters, 1971; Bedlam: A Mid-Century Satire, 1972; The Unreturning Native, 1973; The Stream, 1979; Windfalls, 1983. Add: 12 Mill Rd., Rye, Sussex, England.

DOWNES, Bryan. American, b. 1939. Public/Social administration, Urban studies. Prof. of Public Affairs, Dept. of Planning, Public Policy and Management, Univ. of Oregon, since 1981 (Assoc. Prof., 1976–78; Assoc. Dean and Prof. of Community Service and Public Affairs, 1978–80). Asst. Prof., San Francisco State Coll., Calif., 1966–67; Asst. Prof. 1967–70, and Assoc. Prof. 1970–71, Michigan State Univ., East Lansing; Assoc. Prof. of Political Science, Univ. of Missouri, St. Louis, 1971–76. *Publs:* (ed.) Cities and Suburbs: Selected Readings in Local Politics and Public Policy, 1971; Politics, Change, and Urban Crisis, 1975. Add: Dept. of Planning, Public Policy and Management, Univ. of Oregon, Eugene, Ore. 97403, U.S.A.

DOWNES, David A(nthony). American, b. 1927. Literature. Dean of Humanities since 1968, Prof. of English since 1972, Dir. of Grad. Studies since 1977, and Chmn., Dept. of English since 1978, California State Univ., Chico. Chmn., Dept. of English, Seattle Univ., Wash., 1964–68. Ed. University Journal, 1975–77. *Publs:* Gerard Manley Hopkins: A Study of His Ignatian Spirit, 1960; Victorian Portraits: Hopkins and Pater, 1965; The Temper of Victorian Belief: Studies in the Religious Novels of Pater, Kingsley and Newman, 1972; Ruskin's Beatific Landscapes, 1980, 1984; The Great Sacrifice, 1983; Hopkins' Sanctifying Imagination, 1985; The Ignatian Personality of G.M. Hopkins, 1989. Add: Dept. of English, California State Univ., Chico, Calif. 95926, U.S.A.

DOWNES, (John) Kerry. British, b. 1930. Architecture, Art. Prof. of

History of Art, Univ. of Reading, since 1978 (Lectr., 1966–71; Reader, 1971–78). Member, Royal Commn. on Historical Monuments (England), since 1981. Member of library staff, Courtauld Inst. of Art, London, 1954–58; Librarian, Barber Inst. of Fine Arts, Univ. of Birmingham, 1958–66. *Publs:* Hawksmoor, 1959, 1979; English Baroque Architecture, 1966; Christopher Wren, 1971; Vanbrugh, 1977; The Georgian Cities of Britain, 1979; Rubens, 1980; The Architecture of Wren, 1982; Sir John Vanbrugh, A Biography, 1987. Add: Dept. of History of Art, Reading University, Reading RG1 5AQ, England.

DOWNES, Quentin. *See* **HARRISON**, Michael.

DOWNEY, Fairfax Davis. American, b. 1893. Children's fiction, Animals/Pets, Military/Defence, Biography, Humor/Satire. Staff member, Kansas City Star, Mo., 1918–21, and New York Tribune, and Herald Tribune, NYC, 1921–27. *Publs:* A Comic History of Yale, 1923; Father's First Two Years, 1925; When We Were Rather Older, 1926; Young Enough to Know Better, 1927; The Grande Turke: Suleyman the Magnificent, 1919; Burton, Arabian Nights Adventurer, 1931; Richard Harding Davis: His Day, 1933; Portrait of an Era, 1936; Disaster Fighters, 1938; Indian-Fighting Army, 1941; (with W.A. James) Reunion in Print, 1942; War Horse, 1942; Dog of War, 1943; Jezebel the Jeep, 1944; Army Mule, 1945; Cavalry Mount, 1946; (ed.) Laughing Verse, 1946; Our Lusty Forefathers, 1947; The Seventh's Staghound, 1948; Horses of Destiny, 1949; Clash of Cavalry: The Battle of Brandy Station, 1949; Cats of Destiny, 1950; Free and Easy, 1951; Trail of the Iron Horse, 1952; A Horse for General Lee, 1953; Mascots, 1954; The Shining Filly, 1954; (ed.) Julia Marlowe's Story, by E.H. Southern, 1954; Dogs for Defense, 1955; Sound of the Guns, 1955; General Crook: Indian Fighter, 1957; The Guns at Gettysburg, 1958; Famous Horses of the Civil War, 1959; Storming of the Gateway: Chattanooga, 1960; (ed.) My Kingdom for a Horse, 1960; Guns for General Washington, 1961; Texas and the War with Mexico, 1961; (ed.) Great Dog Stories of all Time, 1962; Indian Wars of the U.S. Army, 1776-1865, 1964; Louisbourg, Key to a Continent, 1966; It Happened in New Hampshire, 1981; The Color-bearers, 1982. Add: West Springfield, N.H. 03284, U.S.A.

DOWNIE, Freda (Christina). British, b. 1929. Poetry. *Publs:* Night Music, 1974; A Sensation, 1975; Night Sucks Me In, 1976; A Stranger Here, 1977; (with Fred Sedgwick and John Cotton) A Berkhamsted Three, 1978; Man Dancing with the Moon, 1979; Plainsong, 1981. Add: 32 Kings Rd., Berkhamsted, Herts. HP4 3BD, England.

DOWNIE, Leonard, Jr. American, b. 1942. Law, Urban studies, Writing/Journalism. Managing Ed., Washington Post, since 1984 (on staff since 1964). *Publs:* Justice Denied: The Case for Reform of the Courts, 1971; Mortgage on America, 1974; The New Muckrakers, 1976. Add: The Washington Post, 1150 15th St., Washington, D.C. 20005, U.S.A.

DOWNIE, Mary Alice. Canadian, b. 1934. Children's fiction, Children's non-fiction, Homes/Gardens. *Publs:* (with B. Robertson) The Wind Has Wings: Poems from Canada, 1968; Scared Sarah, 1974; (trans.) The Magical Adventures of Pierre, 1974; Dragon on Parade, 1974; The Witch of the North: Folktales from French Canada, 1975; The King's Loon, 1980; The Last Ship, 1980; (with Mary Hamilton) And Some Brought Flowers: Plants in a New World, 1980; (with John Downie) Honor Bound, 1971; (with George Rawlyk) A Proper Acadian, 1981; (with Jillian Hulme Gilliland) Seeds and Weeds: A Book of Country Crafts, 1981; The Wicked Fairy Wife, 1983; (with John Downie) Alison's Ghosts, 1984; Jenny Greenteeth, 1984; (with Jillian Hulme Gilliland) Stones and Cones: Country Crafts for Kids, 1984; (with B. Robertson) The New Wind Has Wings, 1984; (with Elizabeth Greene and M.-A. Thompson) The Window of Dreams, 1986; (with B. Robertson) The Well-Filled Cupboard: Everyday Pleasures of Home and Garden, 1987; How the Devil Got His Cat, 1988. Add: 190 Union St., Kingston, Ont. K7L 2P6, Canada.

DOWNING, John (Allen). British, b. 1922. Education, Psychology. Prof. of Education, Univ. of Victoria, B.C., since 1970. Dir., Reading Research Unit, Univ. of London, 1960–67; Visiting Prof., Univ. of California, Berkeley, 1967–68; Sr. Lectr. in Psychology, Univ. of London, 1968–69. *Publs:* The Initial Teaching Alphabet Explained and Illustrated, 1964; The Initial Teaching Alphabet Reading Experiment, 1964; First International Reading Symposium, 1966; (ed. with A.L. Brown) The Second International Reading Symposium, 1967; Evaluating the Initial Teaching Alphabet: A Study of the Effects of English Orthography on Learning to Read and Write, 1967; (ed. with A.L Brown) The Third International Reading Symposium, 1968; (with A.L. Brown and J. Sceats) Words Children Want to Use, 1971; Comparative Reading, 1973; (with D.V. Thackray) Reading Readiness, 1974; Learning to Read with Under-

standing, 1976; Reading and Reasoning, 1979; (with C.K. Leong) Psychology of Reading, 1982; (with I. Gross and A. d'Heurle) Sex Role Attitudes and Cultural Change, 1983; (with J. Fijalkov) Lire et Raisonner, 1984; (with R. Valtin) Language Awareness and Learning to Read, 1984. Add: Faculty of Education, Univ. of Victoria, P.O. Box 1700, Victoria, B.C., Canada.

DOWNS, Robert (C.S.) American, b. 1937 Novels/Short stories. Prof. of English, Pennsylvania State Univ., since 1980. Instr. in English, Phillips Exeter Academy, Exeter, N.H., 1962–63; Lectr. in English, Hunter Coll., City Univ., NYC, 1965–66; Sales Promotion Writer, Life mag., NYC, 1966–68; Asst. Prof. of English, Colby Jr. Coll., New London, N.H., 1968–73; Assoc. Prof. of English, Univ. of Arizona, 1973–79. *Publs:* Going Gently, 1973; Peoples, 1974; Country Dying, 1976; White Mama, 1980; Living Together, 1983. Add: 764 W. Hamilton Ave., State College, Penn. 16801, U.S.A.

DOWNS, Robert B(ingham) American, b. 1903 Education, Librarianship, Travel/Exploration/Adventure, Biography. Dean of Library Admin. Emeritus, Univ. of Illinois, Urbana, since 1971 (Dir. of the Library and Library Sch., 1943–58; Dean of Library Admin., 1958–71). Librarian, Colby Coll., Waterville, Maine, 1929–31, and Univ. of North Carolina, Chapel Hill, 1932–38; Dir., New York Univ. Libraries, NYC, 1938–43. Pres., Assn. of College and Research Libraries, 1940–41, American Library Assn., 1952–53, and Illinois Library Assn., 1955–56. *Publs:* Resources of Southern Libraries, 1938; Resources of New York City Libraries, 1942; (ed.) Union Catalogs in the United States, 1942; American Library Resources, 1951–81; Books That Changed the World, 1956, 1978; (ed.) The First Freedom: Liberty and Justice in the World of Books and Reading, 1960; Molders of the Modern Mind, 1961; Famous Books, Ancient and Medieval, 1964; (ed.) The Bear Went Over the Mountain (folklore), 1964; How to Do Library Research, 1966; Resources of Canadian Academic and Research Libraries, 1967; (ed. with France B. Jenkins) Bibliography: Current State and Future Trends, 1967; Books That Changed America, 1970; Famous American Books, 1971; British Library Resources, 1973; Horace Mann, Champion of Public Schools, 1974; Heinrich Pestalozzi, Father of Modern Pedagogy, 1975; Books That Changed the South, 1976; Henry Barnard, 1977; Friedrich Froebel, 1978; In Search of New Horizons: Epic Tales of Travel and Exploration, 1978; Australian and New Zealand Library Resources, 1979; British and Irish Library Resources, 1981, 1982; Landmarks in Science, 1982; (co-author) Memorable Americans, 1983; (ed. with Ralph E. McCoy) The First Freedom Today, 1984; (co-author) More Memorable Americans, 1985; Images of America: Travelers from Abroad in the New World, 1987; Scientific Enigmas, 1988. Add: 708 W. Pennsylvania Ave., Urbana, Ill. 61801, U.S.A.

DOWSE, Robert Edward. British. Politics/Government, Sociology. Prof., Univ. of Western Australia, Perth, since 1986. Lectr., Univ. of Exeter, 1965–86; also, Lectr., Univ., of Edinburgh, 1959–60, Univ., of Hull, 1960–64, State Univ. of New York, 1966, and Univ. of Connecticut, 1974. *Publs:* Left in the Centre, 1966; (ed. with R. Benewick) Readings on British Politics, 1968; Modernization in Ghana and the U.S.S.R., 1969; (co-author) Political Sociology, 1972, 1986; (ed.) The Labour Ideal, 1974. Add: Dept. of Politics, Univ. of Western Australia, Perth, W.A., Australia.

DOWTY, Alan K. American, b. 1940. International relations/Current affairs, Politics/Government. Prof. of Government and Intl. Studies, Univ. of Notre Dame, Indiana, since 1978 (Assoc. Prof., 1975–78). Lectr. 1972–75, and Chmn. of the Intl. Relations Dept., 1974–75, Hebrew Univ. of Jerusalem. *Publs:* (ed. and Trans.) Nuclear War and Nuclear Peace, 1966; The Limits of American Isolation, 1971; The Role of Great Power Guarantees in International Peace Agreements, 1974; Middle-East Crisis: U.S. Decision-Making in 1958, 1970, and 1973, 1984; Closed Borders: The Contemporary Assault on Free Movement, 1987; Democracy in Israel Today, 1987. Add: Dorwood Dr., South Bend, Ind. 46617, U.S.A.

DOYLE, Brian. Canadian, b. 1935. Children's fiction. Teacher and Head of English Dept., Glebe Collegiate Inst., since 1969. *Publs:* Hey Dad!, 1978; You Can Pick Me up at Peggy's Cove, 1979; Up to Low, 1982; Angel Square, 1984; Easy Avenue, 1988. Add: c/o Groundwood Books, 3rd Floor, 26 Lennox Str., Toronto, Ont. M6G 1J4, Canada.

DOYLE, Charles (Desmond). Also writes as Mike Doyle. Canadian, b. 1928. Poetry, Literature, Politics/Government, Biography. Prof. of English, Univ. of Victoria, B.C. Ed., Tuatara mag., 1969–74. *Publs:* A Splinter of Glass: Poems 1951-55, 1956; Distances: Poems 1956-61, 1963; (ed.) Recent Poetry in New Zealand, 1965; Messages for Herod,

1965; A Sense of Place: Poems, 1965; (as Mike Doyle) Noah, 1970; R.A.K. Mason, 1970; Earth Meditations, 1971; Abandoned Sofa, 1971; Earthshot, 1972; Preparing for the Ark, 1973; Planes, 1975; Stonedancer, 1976; James K. Baxter, 1976; (ed.) William Carlos Williams: The Critical Heritage, 1980; William Carlos Williams and the American Poem, 1982; A Steady Hand, 1983; (co-ed.) The New Reality: The Politics of Restraint in British Columbia, 1984; (ed.) Wallace Stevens: The Critical Heritage, 1985; (co-ed.) After Bennett: A New Politics for British Columbia, 1986; Richard Aldington: A Biography, 1989. Add: 759 Helvetia Cres., Victoria, B.C. V8Y 1MI, Canada.

DOYLE, Mike. *See* **DOYLE,** Charles.

DOYLE, Paul A. American, b. 1925. Literature. Prof. of English, Nassau Coll., State Univ. of New York, since 1962. Contrib. Ed., Best Sellers, since 1962; Consultant, Choice, since 1966; Ed.-in-Chief, Evelyn Waugh Newsletter, since 1967, and Nassau Review, since 1970. Asst. Prof. of English, Fordham Univ., Bronx, N.Y., 1948–60, and Assoc. Prof., St. John's Univ., Jamaica, N.Y., 1960–62. *Publs:* (co-author) Basic College Skills, 2 vols., 1958; (co-ed.) Alexander Pope's Iliad: An Examination, 1960; (ed.) Readings in Pharmacy, 1962; Pearl S. Buck, 1965, 1980; (ed.) A Concordance to the Collected Poems of James Joyce, 1966; Evelyn Waugh: An Introduction, 1968; Sean O'Faolain, 1968; Liam O'Flaherty, 1971; Paul Vincent Carroll: A Critical Introduction, 1972; (co-ed.) Henry David Thoreau: Studies and Commentaries, 1972; (ed.) Liam O'Flaherty: An Annotated Bibliography, 1972; (co-ed.) Evelyn Waugh: A Checklist of Primary and Secondary Criticism, 1972; Guide to Basic Bibliography in English Literature, 1976; (co-ed.) A Bibliography of Evelyn Waugh, 1986; A Reader's Companion to Evelyn Waugh's Novels and Short Stories, 1989. Add: 161 Park Ave., Williston Park, N.Y. 11596, U.S.A.

DOYLE, Richard. British, b. 1948. Novels. *Publs:* Deluge, 1976; Imperial 109, 1978; Havana Special, 1982; Pacific Clipper, 1987. Add: c/o Arlington Books, 15 King St., London SW1, England.

DOZIER, Zoe. *See* **BROWNING,** Dixie Burns.

DOZOIS, Gardner. American, b. 1947. Science fiction/Fantasy. Reader, Dell and Award publrs., and for Galaxy, If, Worlds of Fantasy, and Worlds of Tomorrow, 1970–73; Co-Founder and Assoc. Ed., Isaac Asimov's Science Fiction Mag., 1976–77. *Publs:* (ed.) A Day in the Life, 1972; (ed.) Beyond the Golden Age; (with Geo. Alec Effinger) Nightmare Blue, 1975; (ed. with Jack Dann) Future Power, 1976; (ed.) Another World (juvenile), 1977; The Visible Man (short stories), 1977; The Fiction of James Tiptree, Jr., 1977; (ed.) Best Science Fiction Stories of the Year 6-9, 4 vols., 1977–80; Strangers, 1978; (ed. with Jack Dann) Aliens!, 1980; (ed. with Jim Frenkel) The Year's Best Science Fiction, 1984, 1988; (ed.) The Mammoth Book of Best New Science Fiction, 1987; Ripper!, 1988. Add: 401 Quince St., Philadelphia, Pa. 19147, U.S.A.

DRABBLE, Margaret. British, b. 1939. Novels/Short stories, Plays/Screenplays, Literature, Biography. *Publs:* A Summer Bird-Cage, 1963; The Garrick Year, 1964; The Millstone, 1965; Wordsworth, 1966; Jerusalem the Golden, 1967; The Waterfall, 1969; Bird of Paradise (play), 1969; Touch of Love (screenplay), 1969; The Needle's Eye, 1972; Arnold Bennett, 1974; The Realms of Gold, 1975; The Ice Age, 1977; For Queen and Country (juvenile), 1978; A Writer's Britain, 1979; The Middle Ground, 1980; (ed.) The Oxford Companion to English Literature, 1985; The Radiant Way, 1987; A Natural Curiosity, 1989. Add: c/o A.D. Peters, The Chambers, Chelsea Harbour, Lots Rd., London SW10 0XF, England.

DRACKETT, Phil(ip Arthur). Also writes as Paul King. British, b. 1922. Children's non-fiction, Sports, Travel, Biography. *Publs:* Fighting Days, 1942; (with Matt Wells) Come Out Fighting, 1944; Speedway, 1951; Motor Racing, 1952; Motoring, 1955; (with Leslie Webb) You and Your Car, 1958; Great Moments in Motoring, 1958; (with A. Thompson) You and Your Motorcycle 1959; Automobiles Work Like This, 1960; Veteran Cars, 1961; Motor Rallying, 1963; Passing the Test, 1964; Young Car Drivers' Companion, 1964; (as Paul King) Taking Your Car Abroad, 1965; Let's Look at Cars, 1966; Slot Car Racing, 1968; (ed.) International Motor Racing, 4 vols., 1969–72; Like Father, Like Son, 1969; Rally of the Forests, 1970; Car Care Tips, 1973; (ed.) Motor Racing Champions, 2 vols., 1973–74; Book of the Veteran Car, 1973; Purnell Book of Great Disasters, 1978; Purnell Book of Dangermen, 1979; (ed.) Encyclopaedia of the Motor Car, 1979; Wonderful World of Cars, 1979; Inns and Harbours of North Norfolk, 1980; The Car Makers, 1980; The Story of the RAC International Rally, 1980; Vintage Cars, 1981; The Classic Mercedes-Benz, 1983; Brabham: Story of a Racing Team, 1985; Flashing Blades: The Story of British Ice Hockey, 1987. Add: Seafret Cottage,

Victoria Rd., Mundesley-on-Sea, Norfolk, England.

DRACO, F. *See* **DAVIS,** Julia.

DRAKE, Albert (Dee). American, b. 1935. Novels/Short stories, Poetry. Prof. of English, Michigan State Univ., East Lansing (joined faculty, 1966). Research Asst., Oregon Research Inst., Eugene, 1963–64; Teaching Asst., Univ. of Oregon, 1965–66. *Publs:* (ed.) Michigan Signatures, 1969; Three Northwest Poets, 1970; Riding Bike, 1973; The Postcard Mysteries, 1976; Tillamook Burn, 1977; In the Time of Surveys, 1978; One Summer, 1979; Beyond the Pavement, 1981; The Big Little GTO Book, 1982; Street Was Fun in Fifty-One, 1982; I Remember the Day James Dean Died and Other Stories, 1983. Add: 1790 Grand River Ave., Okemos, Mich. 48864, U.S.A.

DRAKE, Bonnie. *See* **DELINSKY,** Barbara.

DRAKE, Charles D. British, b. 1924. Law. Prof. of English Law, Univ., of Leeds, since 1972 (Dean, Faculty of Law, 1974–78; Head of Dept., 1979–82). Visiting Prof., Univ. of South Carolina, Columbia, 1978–79, and Vanderbilt Univ., Nashville, Tenn., 1981. 1985–86; ILO Expert, Mission to Fiji Islands, 1981. *Publs:* Law of Partnership, 1972, 1976; Labour Law, 2nd ed., 1973, 3rd ed. 1981; (with B. Bercusson) The Employment Acts 1974-1980, 1981; (with F. Wright) Law of Health and Safety at Work, 1982; Trade Union Acts, 1985. Add: 16 Elmete Ave., Roundhay, Leeds 8, Yorks, England.

DRAKE, David A. American, b. 1945. Novels/Short stories, Science fiction/Fantasy. Freelance writer, since 1981. Asst. Town Attorney, Chapel Hill, 1972–80. *Publs:* The Dragon Lord, 1979; Hammer's Slammers (short stories), 1979; Time Safari, 1982; Skyripper, 1983; From the Heart of Darkness (short stories), 1983; The Forlorn Hope, 1984; Cross the Stars, 1984; Birds of Prey, 1984; (with Karl Edward Wagner) Killer, 1984; (with Janet Morris) Active Measures, 1985; Bridgehead, 1985; At Any Price, 1985; Ranks of Bronze, 1986; Lacey and His Friends (short stories), 1986; Counting the Cost, 1987; (with Janet Morris) Kill Ratio, 1987; Fortress, 1987; Dagger, 1988; The Sea Hag, 1988; (ed.) Men Hunting Things, 1988; (ed.) Things Hunting Men, 1988; (ed. with Bill Fawcett) The Fleet, 1988; (ed. with Bill Fawcett) Counterattack, 1988; Vettius and His Friends (short stories), 1989; Rolling Hot, 1989; (with Janet Morris) Target, 1989; (ed. with Bill Fawcett) Breakthrough, 1989; (ed. with Sandra Miesel) A Separate Star, 1989; (ed. with M.H. Greenberg and Charles Waugh) Space Gladiators, 1989. Add: Box 904, Chapel Hill, N.C. 27514, U.S.A.

DRAKE, Joan. Pseud. for Joan H. Davies. British. Children's fiction. *Publs:* The Story of Wimpy a Wump, 1940; More About Wimpy, 1941; Wimpy Goes on Holiday, 1946; Wimpy Goes Abroad, 1954; Jiggle Woggle Bus, 1957; Mr. Grimpwinkle, 1958; Mr. Grimpwinkle's Marrow, 1959; Mr. Grimpwinkle: Pirate Cook, 1960; Mr Grimpwinkle Buys a Bus, 1961; Mr. Grimpwinkle's Holiday, 1963; Mr. Grimpwinkle's Visitor, 1964; Jiggle Woggle Saves the Day, 1966; Sally Seal's Summer, 1968; James and Sally Again, 1970; Mr. Bubbus and the Apple-Green Engine, 1971; Miss Hendy's House, 1974; Mr. Bubbus and the Railway Smugglers, 1976; Mr. Bubbus and the Railway Rescue, 1978; Fire!, 1978. Add: Castle Rock, 46 Marine Dr., Barry, Glamorgan, Wales.

DRAKE, W(alter) Raymond. British, b. 1913. Supernatural/Occult topics. Surveyor, H.M. Customs and Excise, Sunderland, 1954–75. *Publs:* Gods or Spaceman?, 1964; Gods and Spacemen in the Ancient East, 1968; Gods and Spacemen in the Ancient West, 1974; Gods and Spacemen in the Ancient Past, 1975; Gods and Spacemen Throughout History, 1975; Ancient Israel, 1976; Gods and Spacemen in Greece and Rome, 1976; Gods and Spacemen of the Ancient Past, 1975; Messengers from the Stars, 1977; Cosmic Continents, 1986. Add: 2 Peareth Grove, Roker, Sunderland, England.

DRAKE, William Earle. American, b. 1903. Education. Prof., Univ. of Texas at Austin, from 1957, now retired. (Chmn., Dept. of History and Philosophy of Education, 1959–69). Prof., Univ. of Missouri, 1939–57. *Publs:* The American School in Transition, 1955; Higher Education in North Carolina Before 1860, 1964; Intellectual Foundations of Modern Education, 1967; (ed.) Sources for Intellectual Foundations of Modern Education, 1967; When Darkness Came, 1980; Betrayal on Mt. Parnassus, 1983; The Challenge of Marriage, 1987. Add: 5806 Trailridge Circle, Austin, Tex. 78731, U.S.A.

DRAPER, Alfred Ernest. British, b. 1924. Novels/Short stories, Biography. Formerly journalist, Daily Herald, Daily Mail, B.B.C., and Daily

Express, London. *Publs:* Swansong for a Rare Bird, 1969; The Death Penalty, 1972; Smoke Without Fire (biography), 1974; The Prince of Wales, 1975; The Story of the Goons, 1976; Operation Fish, 1978; Amritsar, 1981; Grey Seal, 5 vols., 1981–85; The Con Man, 1987; Dawns Like Thunder, 1987; Scoops and Swindles, 1988. Add: 31 Oakridge Ave., Radlett, Herts., England.

DRAPER, Cena C(hristopher). American, b. 1907. Children's fiction, Children's non-fiction. *Publs:* Plays of Fancy, 1948; Deep in the Dingle Dell, 1951; Ridge Willoughby, 1952; Papa Says, 1956; Children's Plays, 1960; Mother the Overseer, 1962; Rim of the Ridge, 1965; The Golden Hoop; Rugby and the Snook; Bells of Melodoon; Wizards of Taboo; From the Singing Hills, 1973; Dandy and the Mystery of the Locked Room, 1974; The Worst Hound Around, 1979; A Holiday Year, 1988. Add: Conquistador, Bldg. 6-203, Stuart, Fla. 33494, U.S.A.

DRAPER, Hal. American, b. 1914. History, Social commentary/phenomena. Ed., New International, NYC, 1948–49, and Labor Action, NYC, 1949–57; Librarian, Univ. of California Library, 1960–71. *Publs:* Berkeley: The New Student Revolt, 1965, 1969; (with A. Draper) The Dirt on California: Agribusiness and the University, 1966; (ed. and trans.) Writings on the Paris Commune, by Karl Marx and Friedrich Engels, 1971; Karl Marx's Theory of Revolution, vol. I, 1977, vol. II, 1978, vol. III, 1986; The Marx-Engels Encyclopedia, 1981; (ed. and trans.) The Complete Poems of Henrich Heine: A Modern English Version, 1982; (ed. with Center for Socialist History) The Marx-Engels Chronicle [Register, Glossary], 3 vols., 1985–86; The "Dictatorship of the Proletariat" from Marx to Lenin, 1987. Add: 2450 Warring St., Berkeley, Calif. 94704, U.S.A.

DRAPER, Hastings. *See* **JEFFRIES**, Roderic.

DRAPER, R(onald) P(hilip). British, b. 1928. Literature. Prof. of English, Univ. of Aberdeen, since 1973. Lectr. in English, Univ. of Adelaide, S. Australia, 1955–57; Lectr., then Sr. Lectr., Univ. of Leicester, 1957–73. *Publs:* D.H. Lawrence, 1964; D.H. Lawrence (Profile series), 1969; (ed.) D.H. Lawrence: The Critical Heritage, 1970; (ed.) Hardy: The Tragic Novels, 1975; (ed.) The Mill on the Floss and Silas Marner, by George Eliot, 1977; (ed.) Tragedy, 1980; Lyric Tragedy, 1985; The Winter's Tale: Text and Performance, 1985; Sons and Lovers, 1986; Twelfth Night, 1988; (ed.) The Literature of Region and Nation, 1988. Add: King's Coll., Univ. of Aberdeen, Old Aberdeen AB9 2UB, Scotland.

DRESNER, Samuel (Hayim). American, b. 1925. History, Theology/Religion. Rabbi, Moriah Congregation, Deerfield, Ill., since 1977. Ed., Conservative Judaism mag., 1954–64. *Publs:* Prayer, Humility and Compassion, 1957, 1969; Jewish Dietary Laws, 1959; Three Paths of God and Man, 1960; The Zaddik, 1960, 1974; The Jew in American Life, 1963; God, Man and Atomic War, 1966, 1970; The Sabbath, 1970; Between the Generations, 1971; Levi Yitzhak of Berditchev: Portrait of a Hasidic Master, 1974; Judaism: The Way of Sanctification, 1978. Add: c/o Shapolsky Publishing, 56 E. 11th St., New York, N.Y. 10003, U.S.A.

DREW, Fraser (Bragg Robert). American, b. 1913. Literature. Distinguished Teaching Prof. of English, State Univ. of New York, Coll. at Buffalo, 1973–83, now Emeritus (Instr., 1945–47; Asst. Prof., 1947–52; Prof., 1952–73; Chmn., English Dept., 1957–63). *Publs:* John Masefield: Interpreter of England and Englishmen, 1952; John Masefield's England: A Study of the National Themes in his Work, 1973. Add: Tralee House, 16 Gothic Ledge, Lockport, N.Y. 14094, U.S.A.

DREW, Nicholas. *See* **HARLING**, Robert.

DREW, Philip. Australian, b. 1943. Architecture. Australian Correspondent, Architecture and Urbanism, Tokyo, since 1978. Technical Ed., The Architectural Press., London, 1970–71; Sr. Lectr. in Architecture, Univ. of Newcastle, N.S.W., 1974–82; Asst. Prof., Washington Univ., St. Louis, 1982–83. *Publs:* Third Generation: The Changing Meaning of Architecture, 1973; Frei Otto: Form and Structure, 1976; Tensile Architecture, 1979; Two Towers: Harry Seidler, 1980; The Architecture of Arata Isozaki, 1982; Leaves of Iron: Glenn Murcutt, Pioneer of an Australian Architectural Form, 1985. Add: 12 View St., Annandale, N.S.W. 2038, Australia.

DREWE, Robert. Australian, b. 1943. Novels/Short stories. Journalist: cadet reporter, Perth West Australian, 1961–64; Reporter, 1964–65, and Head of the Sydney Bureau, 1965–70, The Age, Melbourne; daily columnist, 1970–73, Features Ed., 1971–72, and Literary Ed., 1972–74, The Australian, Sydney; Special Writer, 1975–76, and Contributing Ed.,

1980–82, The Bulletin, Sydney; Writer-in-Residence, Univ. of Western Australia, Perth, 1979; Columnist, Mode, Sydney, 1981–82, and Sydney City Monthly, 1981–83. *Publs:* The Savage Crows (novel), 1976; A Cry in the Jungle Bar (novel), 1979; The Bodysurfers (short stories), 1984; Fortune (novel), 1986; The Bay of Contented Men (short stories), 1989. Add: c/o Hickson Assocs. Pty. Ltd., P.O. Box 271, Woollahra, N.S.W. 2025, Australia.

DREXLER, Rosalyn. Also writes as Julia Sorel. American, b. 1926. Novels/Short stories, Plays/Screenplays. Painter, sculptor, and singer. *Publs:* (with others) I Am the Beautiful Stranger (novel), 1965; The Line of Least Existence and Other Plays, 1967; The Investigation, and Hot Buttered Roll, 1969; One or Another (novel), 1970; The Bed Was Full, 1972; Skywriting, 1968; To Smithereens (novel), 1972; She Who Was He, 1973; The Cosmopolitan Girl (novel), 1975; (as Julia Sorel) Unwed Widow (novelization), 1975; Dawn (novelization), 1976; Rocky (novelization), 1976; Alex (novelization), 1977; See How She Runs (novelization), 1978; Forever Is Sometimes Temporary When Tomorrow Rolls Around, 1979; Starburn (novel), 1979; Bad Guy, 1982; Transients Welcome (plays), 1984; (with Thomas W. Sokolowski) Rosalyn Drexler: Intimate Emotions, 1986. Add: c/o Georges Borchardt Inc., 136 E. 57th St., New York, N.Y. 10022, U.S.A.

DREYFUS, Edward A. American, b. 1937. Psychology. Clinical Psychologist, since 1964; Consultant, California Sch. of Professional Psychology, since 1970; Asst. Clinical Prof., Dept. of Psychology (Legal), Neuropsychiatric Inst., Univ. of California at Los Angeles, since 1976. Psychologist, Palo Alto Veterans Admin. Hosp., 1964–65; Assoc. Dir., Student Counseling Center, Univ. of California, Los Angeles, 1965–73. *Publs:* Youth: Search for Meaning, 1972; Adolescence: Theory and Experience, 1976. Add: 10817 Santa Monica Blvd., Los Angeles, Calif. 90025, U.S.A.

DRINKROW, John. *See* **HARDWICK**, Michael.

DRINKWATER, Penny. British (born S. African) b. 1929. Cookery/Gastronomy/Wine. *Publs:* To Set Before a King; Time for a Party; Making and Mixing Drinks; Basic Cookery; (with Elaine Self) A Passion for Garlic, 1980. Add: 59 Maresfield Gardens, London NW3 5TE, England.

DRISCOLL, Peter. British, b. 1942. Mystery/Crime/Suspense. Reporter, Rand Daily Mail, Johannesburg, S. Africa, 1959–67; Sub-Ed. and Scriptwriter, ITV News, London, 1969–73. *Publs:* The White Lie Assignment, 1971; The Wilby Conspiracy, 1972; In Connection with Kilshaw, 1974; The Barboza Credentials, 1976; Pangolin, 1979; Heritage, 1982; Spearhead, 1988. Add: c/o David Higham Assocs., 5-8 Lower John St., London W1R 4HA, England.

DRIVER, C(harles) J(onathan). British (born South African), b. 1939. Novels/Short stories, Poetry, Biography. Master, Wellington Coll., since 1989. Pres., National Union of South African Students, 1963–64; Housemaster, Intnl. Sixth Form Centre, Sevenoaks Sch., Kent, 1968–73; Dir. of Sixth-Form Studies, Matthew Humberstone Comprehensive Sch., 1973–77; Principal, Island Sch., Hong Kong, 1978–83. Headmaster, Berkhamsted Sch., Hertfordshire, 1983–89. Member, Literature Panel, Arts Council, 1975–77; Chmn., Literature Panel, Lincs. and Humberside Arts Council, 1977. *Publs:* Elegy for a Revolutionary, 1969; Send War in Our Time, O Lord, 1970; Death of Fathers, 1972; A Messiah of the Last Days, 1974; (with J. Cope) Occasional Light (poems), 1979; I Live Here Now (poems), 1979; Patrick Duncan (biography), 1980; Hong Kong Portraits (poems), 1986. Add: Wellington Coll., Crowthorne, Berks. RG11 7PU, England.

DRIVER, Christopher (Prout). British, b. 1932. Food, Social commentary/phenomena. Personal Page Ed., The Guardian, London, since 1988 (Features Ed., 1964–68; Food and Drink Ed., 1984–88). Ed., The Good Food Guide, London, 1969–82. *Publs:* A Future for the Free Churches?, 1962; The Disarmers, 1964; The Exploding University, 1971; The British at Table 1940–1980, 1983; (with M. Berriedale-Johnson) Pepys at Table, 1984; Twelve Poems, 1985. Add: 6 Church Rd., London N6 4QT, England.

DROPPERS, Carl H. American, b. 1918. Architecture, Theology/Religion. Practicing architect with Droppers and Assocs. Asst. Prof., 1946–66, and Assoc. Prof., 1946–72, Dept. of Architecture, Case Western Reserve Univ., Cleveland. *Publs:* (with Bruggink) Christ and Architecture, 1965; (with Bruggink) When Faith Takes Form, 1971. Add: 345 Prospect St., Berea, Ohio 44017, U.S.A.

DROWER, Margaret Stefana. (Margaret Hackforth-Jones). British, b. 1911. Archaeology, History, Biography. Hon. Research Fellow, Univ. Coll., Univ. of London, since 1979 (Asst. Lectr., 1937–40; Lectr. 1940–58; Sr. Lectr., 1958–66; Reader in Ancient History, 1966–79). Vice-Pres., Egypt Exploration Soc., since 1971 (Hon. Secty., 1958–71; Chmn., 1978–82). *Publs:* (trans. and ed.) P. Montet: Everyday Life in Egypt, 1958; Egypt in Colour, 1964; (Reviser) M. Rostovtzeff's Storia del Mondo Antica, 1965; Nubia, A Drowning Land, 1967; Flinders Petrie: A Life in Archaeology, 1985. Add: Dept. of History, Univ. Coll. London, Gower St., London WC1, England.

DRUCKER, Daniel Charles. American, b. 1918. Education, Engineering. Graduate Research Prof., Univ. of Florida, Gainesville, since 1984. Asst., Columbia Univ., NYC, 1938–39; Instr. in Mechanics of Engineering, Cornell Univ., Ithaca, N.Y., 1940–43; Supvr. of Mechanics of Solids, 1943–45, and Asst. Prof. of Mechanics, 1946–47, Armour Research Foundn., Illinois Inst. of Technology; Assoc. Prof. of Engineering, 1947–50, Prof., 1950–68, Chmn., Div. of Engineering, 1953–59, and Physical Sciences Council, 1961–63, and L. Herbert Ballou Univ. Prof., 1963–68, Brown Univ., Providence, R.I.; Dean, Coll. of Engineering, Univ. of Illinois, Urbana, 1968–84. *Publs:* Introduction to Mechanics of Deformable Solids, 1967. Add: 231 Aerospace, Univ. of Florida, Gainesville, Flor. 32611, U.S.A.

DRUCKER, H. M. American, b. 1942. Politics/Government. Dir., Development Office, Oxford Univ. Formerly, Sr. Lectr., Dept. of Politics, Univ. of Edinburgh. *Publs:* The Political Uses of Ideology, 1974; The Scottish Government Yearbook, 6 vols., 1976–82; Breakaway: The Scottish Labour Party, 1978; Doctrine and Ethos in the Labour Party, 1979; Multi-Party Britain, 1979; (with Brown) The Politics of Nationalism and Devolution, 1980; (ed.) Developments in British Politics, 1983, vol. II, 1986. Add: Oxford Univ. Development Office, University Offices, Wellington Square, Oxford OX1 2JD, England.

DRUCKER, Peter (Ferdinand) American, b. 1909 Novels, Administration/Management. Mgmt. Consultant (own firm), since 1940; Clarke Prof. of Social Science, Claremont Grad. Sch., Calif., since 1971. Prof. of Politics and Philosophy, Bennington Coll., Vt., 1942–49; Prof. of Mgmt., 1950–72, and Chmn. of the Dept., 1956–62, New York Univ. Pres., Soc. of History of Technology, 1965–66. *Publs:* The End of Economic Man, 1939; The Future of Industrial Man, 1942; Concept of the Corporation, 1946; The New Society, 1950; The Practice of Management, 1954; America's Next Twenty Years, 1959; The Landmarks of Tomorrow, 1960; Managing for Results, 1964; The Effective Executive, 1966; The Age of Discontinuity, 1969; Technology, Management and Society, 1970; The New Markets, 1971; Management: Tasks, Responsibilities, Practices, 1974; The Unseen Revolution, 1976; People and Performance, 1977; Adventures of a Bystander, 1979; Managing in Turbulent Times, 1980; Toward the Next Economics, 1981; The Changing World of the Executive, 1982; The Last of All Possible Worlds (novel), 1982; The Temptation to Do Good (novel), 1984; Innovation and Entrepreneurship, 1986; Frontiers of Management, 1986; The New Realities, 1989. Add: 636 Wellesley Dr., Claremont, Calif. 91711, U.S.A.

DRUKS, Herbert. American, b. 1937. History, international relations, and the city in history. Assoc. Prof. of Judaic Studies, Brooklyn Coll., N.Y., Formerly Faculty Member and Adviser to the Pres., Sch. of Visual Arts, N.Y.C. *Publs:* Harry S Truman and the Russians, 1967, 1981; From Truman Through Johnson, 2 vols., 1971; The City in Western Civilization, 1971; The Failure to Rescue, 1977; The U.S. and Israel: A Diplomatic History, 1979, 1987; Jewish Resistance During the Holocaust, 1983; Not in Vain: A Holocaust Documentary, 1984. Add: c/o R. Speller, 30 E. 23rd St., New York, N.Y. 10010, U.S.A.

DRUMMOND, Emma. See **DARRELL**, Elizabeth.

DRUMMOND, Ian M. Canadian, b. 1933. Economics. Prof. of Economics, Univ. of Toronto, since 1971 (Lectr. in Economics, 1960–62; Asst. Prof., 1962–65; Assoc. Prof., 1965–71). Instr. in Economics, Yale Univ., New Haven, Conn., 1958–60. Managing Ed., 1966–69 and Member, Bd. of Eds., 1969–73, Canadian Journal of Economics. *Publs:* The Canadian Economy, 1966, 1972; Canada's Trade with the Communist Countries of Eastern Europe, 1966; British Economic Policy and the Empire 1919-1939, 1972; Imperial Economic Policy 1917-1939: Studies in Expansion and Protection, 1974; Economics: Principles and Policies in an Open Economy, 1976; The Floating Pound and the Sterling Area 1931-39, 1981; (with R.S. Bothwell and J. English) Canada since 1945, 1981, and Canada 1900-1945, 1987; Political Economy at Toronto, 1982; The Gold Standard and the International Monetary System 1900-1939, 1986;

Progress Without Planning, 1987; (with Norman Hillmer) Negotiating Freer Trade, 1989. Add: Dept. of Economics, Univ. of Toronto, Toronto, Ont. M5S 1A1, Canada.

DRUMMOND, Ivor. See **LONGRIGG**, Roger.

DRUMMOND, June. South African, b. 1923. Mystery/Crime/Suspense. Journalist, Woman's Weekly and Natal Mercury, both in Durban, 1946–48; secretary in London, 1948–50, and with the Durban Civil Orchestra, 1950–53; Asst. Secty., Church Adoption Soc., London, 1954–60; Chmn., Durban Adoption Cttee., Indian Child Welfare Soc., 1963–74. *Publs:* The Black Unicorn, 1959; Thursday's Child, 1961; A Time to Speak, 1962; A Cage of Humming-Birds, 1964; Welcome, Proud Lady, 1964; Cable-Car, 1965; The Saboteurs, 1967; The Gantry Episode (in U.S. as Murder on a Bad Trip), 1968; The People in Glass House, 1969; Farewell Party, 1971; Bang! Bang! You're Dead, 1973; The Boon Companions, 1974 (in U.S. as Drop Dead, 1976); Slowly the Poison, 1975; Funeral Urn, 1976; The Patriots, 1979; I Saw Him Die, 1979; Such a Nice Family, 1980; The Trojan Mule, 1982; The Bluestocking, 1985; Junta, 1989. Add: 24 Miller Grove, Durban, Natal, South Africa.

DRUMMOND, V(iolet) H(ilda). (Mrs. Anthony Swetenham). British, b. 1911. Children's fiction. Chmn., V.H. Drummond Productions Ltd., London, since 1965. *Publs:* Phewtus the Squirrel, 1939, 1987; Mrs. Easter's Parasol, 1944; Miss Anna Truly, 1945; Lady Talavera, 1946; Tidgie's Innings, 1947; The Charming Taxicab, 1947; The Mountain That Laughed, 1947; The Flying Postman, 1948; Mr. Finch's Pet Shop, 1953; Mrs. Easter and the Storks, 1957; Little Laura's Cat, 1960; Little Laura on the River, 1960; Little Laura and the Thief, 1963; Little Laura and Her Best Friend, 1963; Little Laura and the Lonely Ostrich, 1963; Miss Anna Truly and the Christmas Lights, 1968; Mrs. Easter and the "Golden Bounder", 1970; Mrs. Easter's Christmas Flight, 1972; Mrs. Easter's Parasol, 1977; I'll Never Be Asked Again, 1979. Add: 24 Norfolk Rd., London NW8 6HG, England.

DRURY, Allen (Stuart). American, b. 1918. Novels, Politics/Government. Ed., The Tulare Bee (Calif.), 1939–41; County Ed., The Bakersfield Californian (Calif.), 1941–42; served in the U.S. Army, 1942–43; Member, United Press Senate Staff, Washington, D.C., 1943–45; Freelance Writer, 1946; National Ed., Pathfinder mag., Washington, D.C. 1947–53; Member, National Staff, Washington Evening Star, 1953–54, Senate Staff, New York Times, 1954–59; Political Corresp., The Reader's Digest, 1959–64. Member, National Council on the Arts, 1982–88. *Publs:* Advise and Consent, 1959 (Pulitzer Prize); A Shade of Difference, 1962; A Senate Journal, 1943-45, 1963; Three Kids in a Cart: A Visit to Ike and Other Diversions, 1965; That Summer, 1965; Capable of Honor, 1966; "A Very Strange Society": A Journey to the Heart of South Africa, 1967; Preserve and Protect, 1968; Courage and Hesitation: Notes and Photographs of the Nixon Administration, 1971; The Throne of Saturn, 1971; Come Nineveh, Come Tyre: The Presidency of Edward M. Jason, 1973; The Promise of Joy, 1975; A God Against the Gods, 1976; Anna Hastings, 1977; Return to Thebes, 1977; Mark Coffin, U.S.S., 1979; Egypt, 1980; The Hill of Summer, 1981; Decision, 1983; The Roads of Earth, 1984; Pentagon (in U.K. as The Destiny Makers), 1986. Add: c/o Lantz Office, 888 Seventh Ave., New York, N.Y. 10106, U.S.A.

DRURY, Maxine Cole. Also writes as Don Creighton. American, b. 1914. Children's fiction, Children's non-fiction. *Publs:* (with J. Drury) Danger Afloat, 1951; (with J. Drury) The Rosemont Riddle, 1953; Marty and the Major, 1955; George and the Long Rifle, 1957; (with J. Drury) A Career for Carol, 1958; Half a Team, 1960; Glory for Gil, 1964; To Dance, to Dream, 1965; (as Don Creighton) Little League Giant, 1965; (as Don Creighton) The Secret Little Leaguer, 1966; Liberty Boy, 1967; (as Don Creighton) Little League Old-Timers, 1967; (as Don Creighton) Little League Ball Hawk, 1968. Add: P.O. Box 89, Thomaston, Me. 04861, U.S.A.

DUANE, Diane. American. Science fiction. *Publs:* The Door into Fire, 1979; The Wounded Sky, 1983; So You Want to Be a Wizard, 1983; The Door into Shadow, 1984; My Enemy, My Ally, 1984; Deep Wizardry, 1985; Star Trek: The Romulan Way, 1987. Add: c/o Bluejay Books, 130 W. 42nd St., New York, N.Y. 10036, U.S.A.

DRYDEN, Pamela. See **ST. JOHN**, Nicole.

DUBERMAN, Martin. American, b. 1930. Plays/Screenplays, History, Literature. Distinguished Prof., Lehman Coll., City Univ. of New York, since 1971. Tutor, Harvard Univ., Cambridge, Mass., 1955–57; Instr. and Asst. Prof., Yale Univ., New Haven, Conn., 1957–62; Asst. Prof., 1962–

65, Assoc. Prof., 1965–67, and Prof. of History, 1967–71, Princeton Univ., N.J. *Publs:* Charles Francis Adams, 1807-1886, 1961; In White America, 1964; (ed.) The Antislavery Vanguard: New Essays on the Abolitionists, 1965; James Russell Lowell, 1966; Metaphors, 1968; The Colonial Dudes, 1969; The Uncompleted Past (essays), 1969; The Memory Bank, 1970; Guttman Ordinary Scale, 1972; Black Mountain: An Exploration in Community (non-fiction), 1972; Male Armor: Selected Plays 1968-1974, 1975; Visions of Kerouac, 1977; About Time: Exploring the Gay Past, 1986; Paul Robeson, 1989. Add: History Dept., Lehman Coll., New York, N.Y. 10468, U.S.A.

DUBERSTEIN, Helen (Laura). American, b. 1926. Plays/Screenplays, Poetry. Artistic Dir., Theatre for the New City, 1974–75; Pres., Playwrights Group, Inc., 1974–76; Playwright-in-Residence, Hartford Univ., Conn., 1977–78. *Publs:* Street Scene (play), 1971; Succubus/Incubus (poetry), 1972; The Human Dimension (poetry), 1972; The Affair (play), 1973; The Guillotine (play), 1978; The Voyage Out (poetry), 1978; Changes (poetry), 1978. Add: 463 West St., New York, N.Y. 10014, U.S.A.

DUBIE, Norman (Evans, Jr.). American, b. 1945. Poetry. Prof. of English, Arizona State Univ., Tempe, since 1980 (Writer-in-Residence, 1975–76; Dir. of the Grad. Writing Program, 1976–77). Teaching Asst., 1969–71, and Lectr. in Creative Writing, 1971–74, Univ. of Iowa, Iowa City; Asst. Prof., Ohio Univ., Athens, 1974–75. *Publs:* The Horsehair Sofa, 1969; Alehouse Sonnets, 1971; The Prayers of the North American Martyrs, 1975; Popham of the New Song and Other Poems, 1975; In the Dead of the Night, 1975; The Illustrations, 1977; A Thousand Little Things and Other Poems, 1978; Odalisque in White, 1978; The City of the Olesha Fruit, 1979; The Everlastings, 1980; The Selected and New Poems, 1983; The Springhouse: Poems, 1986. Add: Dept. of English, Arizona State Univ., Tempe, Ariz. 85281, U.S.A.

DUBOIS, M. See **KENT,** Arthur.

du BOIS, William Pène. American, b. 1916. Children's fiction. Served in the U.S. Army, 1941–45; Corresp., Yank mag.; Art Ed., and Designer, Paris Review. *Publs:* Elizabeth, The Cow Ghost, 1936; Otto series, 5 vols., 1936–70; The Three Policemen; or, Young Bottsford of Farbe Island, 1938; The Great Geppy, 1940; The Flying Locomotive, 1941; The Twenty-One Balloons, 1947; Peter Graves, 1950; Bear Party, 1951; Squirrel Hotel, 1952; The Giant, 1954; Lion, 1956; The Alligator Case, 1965; Lazy Tommy Pumpkinhead, 1966; The Horse in the Camel Suit, 1967; Pretty Pretty Peggy Moffitt, 1968; Porko von Popbutton, 1969; Call Me Bandicoot, 1970; Bear Circus, 1971; (with Lee Po) The Hare and the Tortoise, and the Tortoise and the Hare, 1972; The Forbidden Forest, 1978; Gentleman Bear, 1986. Add: c/o Penguin Books, 40 W. 23rd St., New York, N.Y. 10010, U.S.A.

DUBUS, Andre. American, b. 1936. Novels/Short stories. Full-time writer. Visiting teacher at the Univ. of Alabama, Boston Univ., etc., since 1984. Commissioned Lt., U.S. Marine Corps, 1958: served until 1964 (rank of Capt.); teacher of modern fiction and creative writing, Bradford Coll., Massachusetts, 1966–84. *Publs:* novels/novells—The Lieutenant, 1967; (with David R. Godine) Voices from the Moon, 1984; short stories—Separate Flights, 1975; Adultery and Other Choices, 1977; Finding a Girl in America, 1980; The Times Are Never So Bad, 1983; We Don't Live Here Anymore, 1984; Land Where My Fathers Died, 1984; The Last Worthless Evening: Four Novella and Two Short Stories, 1986; Selected Stories of Andre Debus, 1988; New Traditions, 1988. Add: 753 E. Broadway, Haverhill, Mass. 01830, U.S.A.

DUCHENE, Louis-François. British/Swiss, b. 1927. Economics, Literature, Politics/Government. Leader Writer, The Economist, London, 1963–67; Dir. Intnl. Inst. for Strategic Studies, 1969–74; Dir., Sussex European Research Centre, Sussex Univ., Brighton, 1974–82. *Publs:* (ed.) The Endless Crisis: America in the Seventies, 1970; The Case of the Helmeted Airman: A Study of W.H. Auden's Poetry, 1972; (co-ed.) Europe's Industries, 1983; New Limits on European Agriculture, 1985; (co-ed.) Managing Industrial Change in Western Europe, 1987. Add: 3 Powis Villas, Brighton, Sussex BN1 3HD, England.

DUCKHAM, Baron Frederick. British, b. 1933. History, Transportation. Prof. of History, St. David's University Coll., Lampeter, since 1978. Lectr. in Further Education, 1958–62; Lectr., Doncaster Coll. of Education, 1962–66; Part-time Lectr., Univ. of Sheffield, 1964–66; Lectr., 1966–71, and Sr. Lectr., 1971–78, Dept. of Economic History, Univ. of Strathclyde, Glasgow. Ed., Transport History, 1968–73. *Publs:* Navigable Rivers of Yorkshire: Their History and Traditions, 1964; The

Yorkshire Ouse: The History of a River Navigation, 1967; The Transport Revolution 1750-1830, 1967, rev. ed. 1973; Yorkshire Ports and Harbours: A Short Historical Guide, 1967; A History of the Scottish Coal Industry 1700-1815, 1970; The Inland Waterways of East Yorkshire 1700-1900, 1973; (with H. Duckham) Great Pit Disasters: Great Britain 1700 to the Present Day, 1973; (with H. Duckham) Learning about the History of Land Transport, 1974; (with R. Hume) Steam Entertainment, 1974. Add: Dept. of History, St. David's University Coll., Lampeter, Dyfed, Wales.

DUDEK, Louis. Canadian, b. 1918. Communications Media, Poetry, Literature. Greenshields Prof. of English, McGill Univ., Montreal (joined faculty, 1951). Publr., DC Books, Montreal. With First Statement mag., 1941–43; Instr. in English, City Coll. of New York, 1946–51; Ed., Delta mag., 1957–66; former Publr., Contact Press, Toronto, and Delta Canada Press, Montreal. *Publs:* East of the City, 1946; (ed. with I. Layton) Canadian Poems, 1850-1952, 1952; The Searching Image, 1952; (with I. Layton and R. Souster) Cerberus, 1952; Twenty-Four Poems, 1952; Europe, 1954; (ed.) Selected Poems, by Raymond Souster, 1956; The Transparent Sea, 1956; En México, 1958; Laughing Stalks, 1958; Literature and the Press: A History of Printing, Printed Media, and Their Relation to Literature, 1960; (trans.) Montreal, Paris d'Amérique, by Michel Regnier, 1961; (ed.) Poetry of Our Time: An Introduction to Twentieth Century Poetry, Including Modern Canadian Poetry, 1966; Atlantis, 1967; The First Person in Literature, 1967; (ed. with M. Gnarowski) The Making of Modern Poetry in Canada: Essential Articles on Contemporary Canadian Poetry in English, 1967; Collected Poetry, 1971; (ed.) All Kinds of Everything, 1973; Epigrams, 1975; Selected Poems, 1975; Selected Essays and Criticism, 1978; Technology and Culture, 1979; Cross-Section: Poems 1940-1980, 1980; Poems from Atlantis, 1980; Continuation I, 1981, Ideas for Poetry, 1983; Zembla's Rocks, 1987; Infinite Worlds, 1988; In Defence of Art, 1988. Add: 5 Ingleside Ave., Montreal, Que., H3Z 1N4, Canada.

DUDER, Tessa (née Stavely). New Zealander, b. 1940. Children's fiction. Ed., Spirit of Adventure Trust, Auckland, since 1986. Book Reviewer, Dominion Sunday Times, Wellington, since 1986. *Publs:* Kawau, 1980; Night Race to Kawau, 1985; The Book of Auckland, 1985; Spirit of Adventure, 1985; Jellybean, 1985; Play It Again, Sam, 1987; Dragons, 1987; Alex, 1988; Simply Messing About in Boats, 1988; Waimata: Harbour of Sail, 1989. Add: 94-A Shakespeare Rd., Milford, Auckland, New Zealand.

DUDLEY, Geoffrey A(rthur). British, b. 1917. Language/Linguistics, Psychology, Sports/ Physical education/Keeping fit. Dir. of Studies, R. and W. Heap (Publishing) Co. Ltd., Marple, Stockport, Cheshire, since 1951 (Tutor, 1942–51). *Publs:* Dreams: Their Meaning and Significance (in U.S. as How to Understand Your Dreams), 1956; The Right Way to Interpret Your Dreams, 1961; Self-Help for Self-Mastery, 1962; Your Personality and How to Use It, 1962; Rapid Reading, 1964; Use Your Imagination, 1965; Increase Your Learning Power, 1966; Dreams: Their Mysteries Revealed, 1969; (with E. Pugh) How To Be a Good Talker, 1971; (with G. Fischhof) Psychogenes Training, 1974; (with Thelma A. Farison) New Course in Practical English, 1975; (with Donald R. Low) Effective Speaking and Writing, 1978; Dudleys: A Family History, 1984; Double Your Learning Power, 1986. Add: 1 Thornton Dr., Handforth, Wilmslow, Cheshire SK9 3DA, England.

DUDLEY-SMITH, Timothy. British, b. 1926. Theology/Religion. Bishop of Thetford, since 1981. Archdeacon of Norwich, 1973–81. Ed., Crusade mag., 1954–59. *Publs:* Christian Literature and the Church Bookstall, 1963; What Makes a Man a Christian?, 1965; A Man Named Jesus, 1971; Someone Who Beckons, 1978; Lift Every Heart, 1984; A Flame of Love, 1987; Songs of Deliverance, 1988. Add: Rectory Meadow, Bramerton, Norwich, England.

DUFAULT, Peter Kane. American, b. 1923. Poetry. Critic-in-Residence, Williams Coll., Williamstown, Mass., 1968–69; Poet-in-Residence, Cheltenham Festival of Literature, England, 1978. *Publs:* Angel of Accidence, 1953; For Some Stringed Instrument, 1957; On Balance, 1978; Memorandum to the Age of Reason, 1988; Selected Poems, 1989. Add: R.D. 2, Hillsdale, N.Y. 12529, U.S.A.

DUFFIELD, Gervase E. British, b. 1935. History, Theology/Religion. Ed., News Today, since 1980; Ed., News Extra, 1964–79 and since 1985. Member, Gen. Synod of Church of England for Oxford Diocese, 1960–80. Ed., News Extra, 1964–79; Ed., The Churchman, 1967–72. *Publs:* The Work of William Tyndale, 1963; The Work of Thomas Cranmer, 1965; Admission to Holy Communion, 1964; (ed.) The Paul Report Considered, 1964; Martin Bucer's Psalter of David 1530, 1973; (ed.) Why Not? Priesthood and the Ministry of Women, 1978; (ed.) Across the Divide, 1978; Bunyan of Bedford, 1978; (ed.) The Prayer Book Noted 1550, by John Marbeck, 1982; (ed.) William Barlowe's Dialogue of Lutheran Factions 1531, 1983; Tyndale's 1525 New Testament Fragment, 1989; The Work of Peter Martyr, 1989. Add: Appleford, Abingdon, Oxford OX14 4PB, England.

DUFFY, Maureen (Patricia). British, b. 1933. Novels/Short stories, Plays/Screenplays, Poetry, Translations. Teacher, 1951–53 and 1956–60. *Publs:* That's How It Was, 1962; (trans.) A Blush of Shame, by Domenico Rea, 1963; The Single Eye, 1964; The Microcosm, 1966; The Paradox Players, 1967; Lyrics for the Dog Hour: Poems, 1968; Wounds, 1969; Lovechild, 1971; The Venus Touch (poetry), 1971; I Want to Go to Moscow, 1973; Capital, 1975; Evesong (poetry), 1976; The Passionate Shepherdess, 1977; House-spy, 1978; Memorials of the Quick and the Dead (poetry), 1979; The Erotic World of Faery, 1980; Inherit the Earth, 1980; Gorsaga, 1981; Men and Beasts, 1984; Collected Poems 1949-84, 1985; Change (novel), 1987. Add: 18 Fabian Rd., London SW6 7TZ, England.

DUGAN, Alan. American, b. 1923. Poetry. Staff Member for Poetry, Fine Arts Work Center, Provincetown, Mass., since 1971. Member of faculty, Sarah Lawrence Coll., Bronxville, N.Y., 1967–71. *Publs:* General Prothalamion in Populous Times, 1961; Poems, 1961; Poems, 2, 1963; Poems 3, 1967; Collected Poems, 1969; Poems 4, 1974; Sequence, 1976; Collected Poems 1961-1983, 1983; Poems 6, 1989. Add: Box 97, Truro, Mass. 02666, U.S.A.

DUGDALE, Norman. British, b. 1921. Poetry. Chmn., Bryson House, since 1985; Member, British Council, since 1986. Permanent Secty., Dept. of Health and Social Services, Northern Ireland, 1970–84 (Asst. Secty., 1955–64; Sr. Asst. Secty., 1964–68; Second Secty., 1968–70). *Publs:* Disposition of the Weather, 1967; A Prospect of the West, 1970; Night Ferry, 1974; Corncrake in October, 1978; Running Repairs, 1983. Add: 16 Massey Park, Belfast BT4 2JX, Northern Ireland.

DUHL, Leonard J. American, b. 1926. Medicine/Health, Psychology, Urban studies. Physician: Prof. of Urban Social Policy and Public Health, Univ. of California, Berkeley, since 1968. Chief, Office of Planning, National Inst. of Mental Health, Bethesda, Md., 1964–66; Special Asst. to the Secty., Dept. of Housing and Urban Development, Washington, D.C., 1966–68. *Publs:* Approaches to Research in Mental Retardation, 1959; The Urban Condition: People and Policy in the Metropolis, 1963; Urban America and the Planning of Mental Health Services, Symposium No. 10, 1964; Mental Health and Urban Social Policy, 1968; (ed.) A Symposium on the Urban Crisis, 1969; (with M. Myerson, C. Rapkin and J. Collins) The City and the University, 1969; Making Whole: Health for a New Epoch, 1980; The Mental Health Complex: It's a New Ball Game, 1985; Healthy Social Change, 1985; Health Planning and Social Change, 1986; (co-ed.) The Future of Mental Health Care, 1987; (with Erma Olafson) In the Time of a Parenthesis: The Entrepreneurship of Change, 1989; The Urban Condition—20 Years Later, 1989. Add: c/o Sch. of Public Health, Warren Hall, Univ. of California, Berkeley, Calif. 94720, U.S.A.

DUKE, Donald. American, b. 1929. Transportation. Pubr., Golden West Books and Athletic Press, San Marino, Calif., since 1964; Ed., Westerners Branding Iron Quarterly, 1972–78 and since 1987. *Publs:* Southern Pacific Steam Locomotives, 1955; The Pacific Electric Railway, 1955; Night Train, 1961; Santa Fe: Steel Rails to California, 1963; George Westinghouse and Electric Traction, 1967; Trails of the Iron Horse, 1975; American Narrow Gauge, 1978; Water Trails West, 1980. Add: c/o Golden West Books, P.O. 80250, San Marino, Calif. 91108, U.S.A.

DUKE, Madelaine (Elizabeth). Also writes as Alex Duncan. British, b. 1925. Novels/Short stories, Mystery/Crime/Suspense. Chmn., Crime Writers Assn., 1983–84. *Publs:* novels—Azael and the Children, 1958; No Margin for Error, 1959; A City Built to Music, 1960; Ride the Brooding Wind, 1961; Thirty Pieces of Nickel, 1962; The Sovereign Lords, 1963; Sobaka, 1965; The Lethal Innocents, 1968; Because of Fear in the Night, 1973; novels, as Alex Duncan—It's a Vet's Life, 1961; The Vet Has Nine Lives, 1962; Vets in the Belfry, 1964; Vet Among the Pigeons, 1977; Vets in Congress, 1978; Vet in the Manger, 1978; Vet in a State, 1979; Vet on Vacation, 1979; To Be a Country Doctor, 1980; God and the Doctor, 1981; The Diary of a Country Doctor, 1982; The Doctor's Affairs All Told, 1983; mystery novels—Claret, Sandwiches and Sin, 1964; This Business of Bomfog, 1967; Death of a Holy Murderer, 1975; Death at the Wedding, 1976; The Bormann Receipt, 1977; Death of a Dandie Dinmont, 1978; Flashpoint, 1982; other—The Secret Mission,

1954; Slipstream: The Story of Anthony Duke, 1955; No Passport: The Story of Jan Felix, 1957; Beyond the Pillars of Hercules: A Spanish Journey, 1957; The Secret People (juvenile), 1967; The Sugar Cube Trap (juvenile), 1969. Add: c/o Mondial Books Ltd., Norman Alexander and Co., 19 Bolton St., London W1Y 8HD, England.

DUKE, Will. *See* GAULT, William Campbell.

DUKERT, Joseph M(ichael). American, b. 1929. Engineering/Technology, Sciences. *Publs:* Atompower, 1962; This Is Antarctica, 1965, rev. ed., 1971; Nuclear Ships of the World, 1973; A Short Energy History of the United States and Some Thoughts About the Future, 1980; High Energy Costs: Uneven, Unfair, Unavoidable?, 1981. Add: 4709 Crescent St., Bethesda, Md. 20816, U.S.A.

DUKES, Paul. British, b. 1934. History. Prof. of History, Univ. of Aberdeen. *Publs:* Catherine the Great and the Russian Nobility, 1967; The Emergence of the Super-Powers, 1970; A History of Russia, 1974; (ed.) Russia Under Catherine the Great, 2 vols., 1977–78; October and the World, 1979; The Making of Russian Absolutism, 1982; A History of Europe, 1985; The Last Great Game: USA Versus USSR, 1989. Add: History Dept., Univ. of Aberdeen, Aberdeen AB9 2UB, Scotland.

DUKORE, Bernard F. American, b. 1931. Literature, Theatre. Univ. Distinguished Prof. of Theatre, Virginia Tech., Blacksburg, since 1986. Instr. of Speech and Drama, Hunter Coll., Bronx, N.Y., 1957–60; Asst. Prof. of Drama, Univ. of Southern California, Los Angeles, 1960–62; Assoc. Prof of Drama, California State Univ. at Los Angeles, 1962–66; Visiting Assoc. Prof. of Drama, Stanford Univ., Calif., 1965–66; Prof. of Drama, City Univ. of New York, 1966–72, and Univ., of Hawaii, Honolulu, 1972–86. *Publs:* (ed.) The Man of Mode (play), 1962; (ed.) A Bibliography of Theatre Arts Publications in English, 1963; (ed. with Ruby Cohn) Twentieth Century Drama: England, Ireland, the U.S. (anthology), 1966; (ed. with M. Rohrberger and S.H. Woods, Jr.) Introduction to Literature, 1968; (ed.) Saint Joan: A Screenplay by Bernard Shaw, 1968; (ed. with Robert O'Brien) Tragedy (anthology), 1969; ed. with D.C. Gerould) Avant-Garde Drama (anthology), 1969, 1976; (ed. with John Gassner) A Treasury of the Theatre: vol. II, 1970; (ed.) Drama and Revolution (anthology with commentary), 1971; (ed.) Documents for Drama and Revolution (anthology with commentary), 1971; Bernard Shaw, Director, 1971; Bernard Shaw, Playwright, 1973; (ed.) Dramatic Theory and Criticism, 1974; (ed.) Seventeen Plays, 1976; Where Laughter Stops: Pinter's Tragicomedy, 1976; Money and Politics in Ibsen, Shaw and Brecht, 1980; (ed.) The Collected Screenplays of Bernard Shaw, 1980; The Theatre of Peter Barnes, 1981; (compiler) Bernard Shaw's Arms and the Man: A Composite Production Book, 1982; Harold Pinter, 1982; American Dramatists 1918-1945, 1984; Death of a Salesman and The Crucible: Text and Performance, 1989. Add: Dept. of Theatre Arts, Virginia Tech, Blacksburg, Va. 24061, U.S.A.

DULLES, Avery. American, b. 1918. Theology/Religion. McGinley Prof. of Religion and Society, Fordham Univ., NYC, since 1988. Asst. Prof., 1960–62, Assoc. Prof., 1962–69, and Prof., 1969–74, Systematic Theology, Woodstock Coll., Maryland; Prof. of Systematic Theology, Catholic Univ. of America, Washington, D.C., 1974–88, now Emeritus. *Publs:* Princeps Concordiae, 1941; A Testimonial to Grace, 1946; (with J.M. Demske and R.J. O'Connell) Introductory Metaphysics, 1955; Apologetics and the Biblical Christ, 1963; The Dimensions of the Church, 1967; Revelation and the Quest for Unity, 1968; Revelation Theology: A History, 1969; (with W. Pannenberg and C.E. Braaten) Spirit, Faith, and Church, 1970; The Survival of Dogma, 1971; A History of Apologetics, 1971; Models of the Church, 1974; Church Membership as a Catholic and Ecumenical Problem, 1974; The Resilient Church, 1977; A Church to Believe In, 1982; Models of Revelation, 1983; (with Patrick Granfield) The Church: A Bibliography, 1985; The Catholicity of the Church, 1985; The Reshaping of Catholicism, 1988. Add: Jesuit Community, Fordham Univ., Bronx, New York, N.Y. 10458, U.S.A.

DUMAS, Claudine. *See* MALZBERG, Barry.

DUMMETT, M(ichael) A(nthony) E(ardley). British, b. 1925. Philosophy, Recreation. Fellow, New College, Oxford, and Wykeham Prof. of Logic, Oxford Univ., since 1979 (Fellow, 1950–79, Sub-Warden, 1974–76, All Souls Coll.; Reader in the Philosophy of Mathematics, Oxford Univ., 1962–74). Asst. Lectr., Birmingham Univ., 1950–51. *Publs:* Frege: Philosophy of Language, 1973; The Justification of Deduction, 1973; Elements of Intuitionism, 1977; Truth and Other Enigmas, 1978; Immigration: Where the Debate Goes Wrong, 1978; Catholicism and the World Order, 1979; The Game of Tarot, 1980; Twelve Tarot

Games, 1980; The Interpretation of Frege's Philosophy, 1981; Voting Procedures, 1984; The Visconti-Sforza Tarot Cards, 1986.. Add: 54 Park Town, Oxford, England.

DUNBAR, Andrea. British, b. 1961. Plays. *Publs:* The Arbor, 1980; Rita, Sue, and Bob Too, 1982, screenplay, 1988. Add: 7 Edge End Gdns., Buttershaw, Bradford BD6 2BB, England.

DUNBAR, Charles Stuart. British, b. 1900. Transportation. Transport consultant and freelance writer. Founder and Managing Dir., Red Arrow Deliveries, Ltd., and Central Carriers Ltd., 1933–43; Area Road Haulage Officer, Ministry of Transport, 1944–45; Road Transport Expert, European Central Inland Transport Org., 1945–47; Ed., Buses Illustrated, 1949–50; Transport Officer, Colonial Development Corp., 1950–52; Ed., Passenger Transport, 1961–63. *Publs:* Tramways in Wandsworth and Battersea, 1945, 3rd ed. 1971; London's Tramway Subway, 1948, 3rd ed. 1976; Goods Vehicle Operation, 1949; Buses, Coaches and Lorries, 1960; Road Haulage, 1960; Transport Oddities, 1962; Idealism and Competition: The Fares Policy of the London County Council Tramways, 1967; Buses, Trolleys and Trams, 1967; The Rise of Road Transport 1919-39, 1981. Add: 9 Christchurch Rd., Malvern, Worcs, WR14 3BH, England.

DUNBAR, Maxwell (John). Canadian, b. 1914. Environmental science/Ecology, Marine Science/Oceanography. Prof. of Oceanography, Inst. of Oceanography, McGill Univ., Montreal. Arctic Explorer, 1935–58; Canadian Consul, Greenland, 1941–46. *Publs:* Marine Distributions, 1963; Ecological Development in Polar Regions, 1968; Environment and Good Sense, 1971; (ed.) Polar Oceans, 1977; (ed.) Marine Production Mechanisms, 1979. Add: 488 Strathcona Ave., Montreal, Que. H3Y 2X1, Canada.

DUNBOYNE, Lord. Wrote as Patrick Butler before 1945. British, b. 1917. Genealogy/Heraldry, Law. Genealogical Asst., Butler Soc.; Pres., Irish Genealogical Research Soc., since 1971. Recorder of Hastings, 1961–71; Deputy Chmn., Middlesex Sessions, 1963–65, Kent Sessions, 1963–70, and Inner London Sessions, 1971; Diocesan Commissary-Gen. of Canterbury, 1959–71; Circuit Judge, 1972–86. Fellow, Irish Genealogical Research Soc., 1982. *Publs:* The Trial of John George Haigh: The Acid Bath Murder, 1953; Butler Family History, 1966, 5th ed. 1982; Happy Families, 1983. Add: 36 Ormonde Gate, London SW3 4HA, England.

DUNCAN, A(lastair) R(obert) C(ampbell). Canadian, b. 1915. Philosophy, Translations. Emeritus Prof. of Philosophy, Queen's Univ., Kingston, since 1980 (Prof., 1949–80; Dean, Faculty of Arts and Science, 1959–64). Pres., Canadian Philosophical Assn., 1961 and 1967. *Publs:* Practical Reason and Morality, 1957; (trans.) The Development of Kantian Thought, by J.J. de Vleeschauwer, 1962; Moral Philosophy, 1965. Add: 68 Kensington Ave., Kingston, Ont., Canada.

DUNCAN, Alex. *See* **DUKE,** Madelaine.

DUNCAN, Anthony Douglas. British, b. 1930. Poetry, Theology/Religion. Vicar of Whitley St. Helen, since 1987. Hon. Chaplain to Bishop of Oxford since 1972. Regular Army Officer, British Army, 1953–60; Curate, Tewkesbury Abbey, 1962–65; Vicar, Parkend, Glos., 1965–69; Rector, Higham, Glos., 1969–73; Vicar, St. John the Baptist Church, Newcastle upon Tyne, 1973–79; Vicar, Warkworth, 1979–87. *Publs:* Over the Hill (poetry), 1964; Pray and Live, 1966; The Whole Christ, 1968; The Christ, Psychotherapy and Magic, 1969; (ed.) New Dimensions (Report of Willesdon Commn.), 1972; The Lord of the Dance, 1972; The Priesthood of Man, 1973; The Fourth Dimension, 1975; The Lover Within (poetry), 1981; Jesus: Essential Readings, 1986. Add: Whitley Vicarage, Hexham, Northumberland NE46 2LA, England.

DUNCAN, A(rchibald) A(lexander) M(cBeth). British, b. 1926. History. Prof. of Scottish History and Literature, Univ. of Glasgow, since 1962 (Dean, Faculty of Arts, 1973–76; Clerk of Senate, 1978–83). Gov., Morrison's Academy, Criff, Scotland, since 1963; Commnr., Royal Commn. on Ancient and Historical Monuments, Scotland, since 1969. Lectr., Balliol Coll., Oxford, 1950–51; Queen's Univ., Belfast, 1951–53, and Univ. of Edinburgh, 1953–62; Pres., Scottish History Soc., 1976–81. *Publs:* (ed. with J.M. Webster) Regality of Dumfermline Court Book 1531-1538, 1953; (ed.) Scottish Independence 1100-1328, 1971; Scotland: The Making of the Kingdom, 1975; (ed.) Formulary E: Scottish Letters and Brieves, 1286-1424, 1976; (ed.) Scotland from the Earliest Times to 1603, by W.C. Dickinson, 3rd. rev. ed., 1977; (ed.) Regestor Repum Scottrum, V, The Acts of Robert I, 1306-29, 1988. Add: Dept. of Scottish

History, Univ. of Glasgow, Glasgow G12 8QQ, Scotland.

DUNCAN, David. American, b. 1913. Novels/Short stories, Screenplays, Science fiction/Fantasy. Freelance writer since 1946; screen and television writer (screenplays include The Time Machine and Fantastic Voyage). *Publs:* Remember the Shadows, 1944; The Shade of Time (science fiction), 1946; The Bramble Bush, 1948, as Sweet, Low, and Deadly, 1949; The Madrone Tree (science fiction), 1949, as Worse Than Murder, 1954; The Serpent's Egg, 1950; None But My Foe, 1950; Wives and Husbands, 1952; Dark Dominion (science fiction), 1954; Beyond Eden (science fiction), 1955, in U.K. as Another Tree in Eden, 1956; The Trumpet of God, 1956; Occam's Razor (science fiction), 1957; Yes, My Darling Daughters, 1959; The Long Walk Home from Town, 1964. Add: 2214 7th St., Everett, Wash. 98201, U.S.A.

DUNCAN, Lois. Also writes as Lois Kerry. American, b. 1934. Novels/Short stories, Mystery/Crime/Suspense, Children's fiction. Freelance writer; Contributing Ed., Woman's Day. Instr., Journalism Dept., Univ. of New Mexico, 1970–82. *Publs:* (as Lois Kerry) Love Song for Joyce, 1958; Debutante Hill, 1958; (as Lois Kerry) A Promise for Joyce, 1959; The Littlest One in the Family, 1960; The Middle Sister, 1961; Game of Danger, 1962; Silly Mother, 1962; Giving Away Suzanne, 1963; Season of the Two-Heart, 1964; Ransom, 1966; Point of Violence, 1966; They Never Came Home, 1969; Major André, Brave Enemy, 1969; Peggy, 1970; A Gift of Magic, 1971; Hotel for Dogs, 1971; I Know What You Did Last Summer, 1973; When the Bough Breaks, 1973; Down a Dark Hall, 1974; Summer of Fear (screenplay), 1976; Killing Mr. Griffin, 1978; Daughters of Eve, 1979; How to Write and Sell Your Personal Experiences, 1979; Stranger with My Face, 1981; Chapters: My Growth as a Writer, 1982; From Spring to Spring, 1982; The Terrible Tales of Happy Days School, 1983; The Third Eye, 1984; Locked In Time, 1985; Horses of Dreamland, 1985; The Twisted Window, 1987; Wonder Kid Meets the Evil Lunch Snatcher, 1988; Songs from Dreamland, 1989; Don't Look Behind You, 1989; The Birthday Moon, 1989. Add: c/o Dell Publishing, 666 Fifth Ave., New York, N.Y. 10103, U.S.A.

DUNCAN, Robert L(ipscomb). Also writes as James Hall Roberts. American, b. 1927. Novels/Short stories, Mystery/Crime/Suspense, Biography. *Publs:* novels—The Voice of Strangers, 1961; If It Moves Salute It, 1961; The General and the Coed, 1962; (as W.R. Duncan, with Wanda Duncan) The Queen's Messenger, 1982; suspense novels—(as James Hall Roberts) The Q Document, 1964; (as James Hall Roberts) The Burning Sky, 1966; (as James Hall Roberts) The February Plan, 1967; The Day the Sun Fell, 1970; The Dragons at the Gate, 1975; Temple Dogs, 1977; Fire Storm, 1978; Brimstone, 1980; In the Enemy Camp, 1985; In the Blood, 1986; China Dawn, 1988; short stories—The Dicky Bird Was Singing, 1952; Buffalo Country, 1959; other—(with Wanda Duncan) Castles in the Air: The Memoirs of Irene Castle, 1958; The Life and Times of Albert Pike, 1961. Add: P.O. Box 5569, Norman, Okla. 73070, U.S.A.

DUNCAN, Terrence. *See* **NOLAN** William F.

DUNCAN, William (Robert). British, b. 1944. Business/Trade/Industry, Marketing, Travel. Founder and Principal, Duncan Publishing, since 1980; Editor-in-Chief for Japan, Export Times, since 1980. Information officer and travel writer and tour manager, mainly concerning the Far East 1966–70; Ed., Egon Ronay Organisation, 1971–75; Ed., Kluwer Publishing, 1975–79, and Oyez Publishing, 1979–80. *Publs:* A Guide to Japan, 1970; Japanese Markets Review, 1974; Doing Business with Japan, 1976; Thailand: A Complete Guide, 1976. Add: 40 Bonham Court, Kettering, Northants NN16 8NJ, England.

DUNDY, Elaine. American, b. 1927. Novels/Short stories, Plays/Screenplays, Biography. *Publs:* The Dud Avocado, 1958; My Place (play), 1962; The Old Man and Me, 1964; The Injured Party, 1974; Finch, Bloody Finch (biography), 1980; Elvis and Gladys (biography), 1985. Add: c/o Andrew Hewson, John Johnson Agency, 45 Clerkenwell Green, London EC1, England.

DUNHAM, (Sir) Kingsley (Charles). British, b. 1910. Earth sciences. Prof. Emeritus of Geology, Univ. of Durham, since 1968 (Prof. of Geology, 1950–66). Chief Petrographer, Geological Survey, 1948–50, and Dir., 1967–75, Inst. of Geological Sciences, London; Miller Prof., Univ. of Illinois, Urbana, 1956. Foreign Secty, Royal Soc., 1971–76; Pres., British Assn. for the Advancement of Science, 1972–73; Chmn., Council for Environmental Science and Engineering, 1973–75. *Publs:* Geology of the Organ Mountains, 1936; (ed.) Geology, Paragenesis and Reserves of the Ores of Lead and Zinc, 1948; Geology of the Northern Pennine

Orefield, Vol. 1, 1949, Vol. 2, 1985; Fluorspar, 1952; (with G.A.L. Johnson) Geology of Moor House, 1963; (with F.W. Anderson) Geology of Northern Skye, 1966; (with W.C.C. Rose) Geology and Hematite Deposits of South Cumbria, 1977; Geological Aspects of World Energy, 1978; Geology in the Real World, 1986. Add: Charleycroft, Quarryheads Lane, Durham DH1 3DY, England.

DUNLAP, Leslie W. American, b. 1911. Librarianship. Dean of Library Admin., Univ. of Iowa, Iowa City, 1970–82, now Emeritus. Assoc. Dir., Univ. of Illinois Libraries, 1951–58. Member, National Commn. on Libraries and Information Sciences, 1970–74. *Publs:* Letters of Willis Gaylord Clark and Lewis Gaylord Clark, 1940; American Historical Societies, 1944; Readings in Library History, 1972; The Wallace Papers: An Index, 1975; The Publication of American Historical Manuscripts, 1976; Your Affectionate Husband, J.F. Culver, 1978; Our Vice-Presidents and Second Ladies, 1988. Add: 640 Stuart Court, Apt. 2, Iowa City, Iowa, 52245, U.S.A.

DUNLEAVY, Patrick. British, b. 1952. Education, Humanities, Politics/Government, Social sciences, Urban topics. Reader in Government, London Sch. of Economics, since 1986 (Lectr., 1979–86). Lectr. in Urban Studies, Open Univ., Milton Keynes, 1978–79. *Publs:* Urban Political Analysis, 1980; The Politics of Mass Housing in Britain 1945-1975: A Study of Corporate Power and Professional Influence in the Welfare State, 1981; (with others) Developments in British Politics, 2 vols., 1983, 1986; (with C.T. Husbands) British Democracy at the Crossroads: Voting and Party Competition in the 1980's, 1985; Studying for a Degree in the Humanities and Social Sciences, 1986; (with Brendan O'Leary) Theories of the State: The Politics of Liberal Democracy, 1987; Democracy, the State, and Public Choice, 1988. Add: 70 Ulyett Pl., Oldbrook, Milton Keynes, Bucks., England.

DUNLOP, Eileen (Rhona). British, b. 1938. Children's fiction, History, Travel. Teacher, Preparatory School of Dollar Academy, Clackmannan, since 1980. *Publs:* Children's fiction—Robinsheugh, 1975; A Flute in Mayferry Street, 1976; Fox Farm, 1978; The Maze Stone, 1982; Clementina, 1985; The House on the Hill, 1987; other—(with Antony Kamm) Edinburgh, 1982; (ed. with Antony Kamm) A Book of Old Edinburgh, 1983; (with Antony Kamm) Kings and Queens of Scotland, 1984; (with Antony Kamm) Scottish Heros and Heroines of Long Ago, 1984; (with Antony Kamm) The Story of Glasgow, 1984; (with Antony Kamm) Scottish Homes Through the Ages, 1985; (ed. with Antony Kamm) The Scottish Collection of Verse to 1800, 1985; (ed.) Scottish Traditional Rhymes, 1985. Add: 46 Tarmangie Dr., Dollar, Clackmannan FK14 7BP, Scotland.

DUNLOP, Ian (Geoffrey David). British, b. 1925. Architecture. Canon and Chancellor of Salisbury Cathedral, since 1972. Chaplain, Westminster Sch., 1959–62; Vicar of Bures, Suffolk, 1962–72. *Publs:* Versailles, 1956, 1970; Palaces and Progresses of Elizabeth I, 1962; Chateaux of the Loire, 1969; Collins Companion Guide to the Ile de France, 1979; The Cathedrals' Crusade, 1982; Royal Palaces of France, 1985; Thinking It Out: Christianity in Thin Slices, 1986. Add: 24 The Close, Salisbury, Wilts, England.

DUNLOP, John T(homas). American, b. 1914. Economics, Industrial relations. Prof. of Economics since 1950, Chmn. of the Wertheim Cttee. on Industrial Relations since 1945, and Lamont University Prof. since 1971, Harvard Univ., Cambridge (Instr., 1938–45, Assoc. Prof., 1945–50, Chmn., Dept. of Economics, 1961–66, Chmn., Cttee. on Governance, 1969–72, Dean, Faculty of Arts and Sciences, 1970–73). U.S. Secty. of Labor, 1975–76. Pres., Industrial Relations Research Assn., 1960; Chmn., Construction Industry Joint Conference, Washington, D.C., 1959–68; Member, Bd. of Medicine, National Academy of Sciences, 1967–69; Chmn., President's National Commn. on Productivity, Washington, 1973–74; Dir., Cost of Living Council, Washington, 1973–74; Pres., Intnl. Industrial Relations Assn., 1973–76. *Publs:* Wage Determination Under Trade Unions, 1944; Cost Behavior and Price Policy, 1955; (co-author) Collective Bargaining: Principles and Cases, 1949; The Wage Adjustment Board, 1950; (ed.) The Theory of Wage Determination, 1957; Industrial Relations Systems, 1958, 1971; (ed.) Potentials of the American Economy, 1960; (co-author) Industrialism and Industrial Man, 1960; (ed.) Economic Growth in the United States, 1961; (ed.) Automation and Technological Change, 1962; (co-ed.) Frontiers of Collective Bargaining, 1967; (co-author) Labor and the American Community, 1970; (ed.) Lessons of Wage and Price Controls, 1977; (ed.) Labor in the Twentieth Century, 1978; (ed.) Business and Public Policy, 1980; Dispute Resolution, Negotiation and Consensus Building, 1984. Add: 208 Littauer Center, Harvard Univ.,

Cambridge, Mass. 02138, U.S.A.

DUNMORE, John. New Zealander, b. 1923. Education (not textbooks on other subjects), History, Biography. Exec. Member, New Zealand Playwrights' Assn. Prof. of French, Massey Univ., Palmerston North, 1966–84 (Sr. Lectr. 1961–66). Pres., Australasian Language and Literature Assn., 1980–82. *Publs:* (ed.) The Map Drawn by the Chief Tukitahua; Le Mystère d'Omboula; French Explorers in the Pacific, 2 vols.; Aventures dans le Pacifique; Success at University, Success at School; The Fateful Voyage of the St. Jean Baptiste, 1969; Norman Kirk: A Portrait; (ed.) An Anthology of French Scientific Prose; (trans.) In Search of the Maori; Meurtre à Tahiti; The Expedition of the St. Jean-Baptiste to the Pacifique, 1769-70; How to Succeed as an Extra-Mural Student; Pacific Explorer: the Life of Jean-François de la Pérouse; New Zealand: The North Island; New Zealand: The South Island. Add: 35 Oriwa St., Waikanae, New Zealand.

DUNMORE, Spencer S. Canadian, b. 1928. Novels/Short stories. *Publs:* Bomb Run, 1971; Tower of Strength (in U.S. as The Last Hill), 1973; Collision, 1974; Final Approach (in U.S. as Ashley Landing), 1976; Means of Escape, 1978; Ace, 1981; The Sound of Wings, 1984; No Holds Barred, 1987. Add: 44 Ravenscliffe Ave., Hamilton, Ont. L8P 3M4, Canada.

DUNN, Charles W(illiam). American, b. 1915. Language/Linguistics, Literature. Emeritus Prof., Harvard Univ., Cambridge, Mass., since 1984 (Chmn., Dept. of Celtic Languages and Literatures, 1963–84). Instr. of English, Cornell Univ., Ithaca, N.Y., 1943–46; Prof. of English, Univ. of Toronto, Ont., 1946–56, and New York Univ., NYC, 1956–63. *Publs:* A Chaucer Reader: Selections from the Canterbury Tales, 1952; Highland Settler: A Portrait of the Scottish Gael in Nova Scotia, 1953; The Founding and the Werewolf: A Literary-Historical Study of Guillaume de Palerne, 1960; (ed.) The Actor's Analects, 1970; (with E. Byrnes) Middle English Literature, 1973; American Political Theology: Historical Perspective and Theoretical Analysis, 1984. Add: 25 Longfellow Rd., Cambridge, Mass. 01238, U.S.A.

DUNN, Douglas (Eaglesham). British, b. 1942. Poetry. Reviewer, Glasgow Herald, since 1985; Hon. Prof., Univ. of Dundee, since 1987. Library Asst., Renfrew County Library, Paisley, 1959–62, and Andersonian Library, Glasgow, 1962–64; Asst. Librarian, Akron Public Library, Ohio 1964–66, and Brynmor Jones Library, Univ. of Hull, 1969–71; Poetry Reviewer, Encounter mag., London, 1971–78. *Publs:* Terry Street, 1969; Backwaters, 1971; Night, 1971; The Happier Life, 1972; (ed.) New Poems 1972-73, 1973; Love or Nothing, 1974; (ed.) A Choice of Byron's Verse, 1974; (ed.) Two Decades of Irish Writing, 1975; (ed.) What Is to Be Given: Selected Poems of Delmore Schwartz, 1976; (ed.) The Poetry of Scotland, 1979; Barbarians, 1979; St. Kilda's Parliament, 1981; Europa's Lover, 1982; Elegies, 1985; Secret Villages, 1985; Selected Poems, 1986; Northlight, 1988. Add: c/o Faber & Faber Ltd., 3 Queen Sq., London WC1N 3AU, England.

DUNN, Hugh Patrick. New Zealander, b. 1916. Children's fiction, Sex. Obstetrician and Gynaecologist, National Women's Hosp, Auckland, since 1955. *Publs:* The Capture of Black Pete, 1968; The School Detective, 1980; Sex and Sensibility, 1982; So You're Pregnant . . ., 1985; A Woman and Her Doctor, 1988; Ethics for Doctors and Nurses, 1989. Add: 168 Upland Rd., Auckland 5, New Zealand.

DUNN, Nell (Mrs. Nell Sandford). British, b. 1936. Novels/Short stories, Children's fiction, Plays/Screenplays, Women. *Publs:* Up the Junction (short stories), 1963; Talking to Women, 1965; Poor Cow, 1967; Freddy Gets Married, 1969; The Incurable, 1971; (with Adrien Henri) I Want, 1972; Tear His Head Off His Shoulders, 1974; Different Drummers, 1978; The Only Child, 1978; Steaming (play), 1981. Add: c/o Jonathan Cape, 32 Bedford Sq., London WC1B 3EL, England.

DUNN, Peter Norman. American (born British), b. 1926. Literature. Prof. of Romance Languages, Wesleyan Univ., Middletown, Conn., since 1977. Asst. Lectr., and Lectr. in Spanish, Univ. of Aberdeen, 1949–65; Prof. of Spanish Literature, Univ. of Rochester, N.Y., 1966–77. *Publs:* Castillo Solorzano and the Decline of the Spanish Novel, 1952; (ed.) Calderon, El alcalde de Zalamea, 1966; Fernando de Rojas, and La Celestina, 1975; The Spanish Picaresque Novel, 1979. Add: Dept. of Romance Languages, Wesleyan Univ., Middletown, Conn. 06457, U.S.A.

DUNN, S(amuel) Watson. American, b. 1918. Advertising/Public relations. Instr., Univ. of Western Ontario, London, 1946–47; Prof., Univ. of Pittsburgh, 1947–49; Prof., Univ. of Illinois, Urbana, 1949–51; Prof.,

Univ. of Wisconsin, Madison, 1951–66; Prof. and Head, Dept. of Advertising, Univ. of Illinois, Urbana, 1966–77; Prof. and former Dean, Coll. of Business and Public Admin., Univ. of Missouri, Columbia, 1977–88. *Publs:* Advertising Copy and Communication, 1956; (ed.) International Handbook of Advertising, 1964; Advertising: Its Role in Modern Marketing, 1961, 6th ed. (with A.M. Barban), 1986; How Fifteen Transnational Corporations Manage Public Affairs, 1979; (ed.) International Advertising and Marketing, 1979; Public Relations, 1986. Add: George Washington Univ., 403 Monroe, Wash., D.C. 20052, U.S.A.

DUNN, Stephen. American, b. 1939. Poetry. Assoc. Prof., then Prof., and Poet-in-Residence, Stockton State Coll., Pomona, N.J., since 1974. Visiting Lectr. Syracuse Univ., N.Y., 1973–74: Asst. Prof., Southwest Minnesota State Coll., Marshall, 1970–73; Visiting Prof., Univ. of Washington, 1981; Adjunct Prof. of Poetry, Columbia Univ., NYC, 1984–87. *Publs:* Five Impersonations, 1971; Looking for Holes in the Ceiling, 1974; Full of Lust and Good Usage, 1976; (ed.) A Cat of Wind, an Alibi of Gifts (poetry), 1977; (ed.) Silence Has a Rough, Crazy Weather (poetry), 1978; A Circus of Needs, 1978; Work and Love, 1981; Not Dancing, 1984; Local Time, 1986; Between Angels, 1989. Add: 445 Chestnut Neck Rd., Port Republic, N.J. 08241, U.S.A.

DUNNE, John Gregory. American, b. 1932. Novels, Essays. Freelance writer, journalist and screen writer. *Publs:* Delano: The Story of the California Grape Strike, 1967; The Studio, 1969; Vegas: A Memoir of a Dark Season (novel), 1974; True Confessions (novel), 1977; Quintana and Friends (essays), 1979; Dutch Shea, Jr. (novel), 1982; The Red White and Blue (novel), 1987; Harp, 1989. Add: c/o Lynn Nesbit, Janklow-Nesbit, 598 Madison Ave., New York, N.Y. 10022, U.S.A.

DUNNE, John S(cribner). American, b. 1929. Theology/Religion. Prof. of Theology, Univ. of Notre Dame, Ind., since 1969 (Instr., 1957–60; Asst. Prof., 1960–65; Assoc. Prof., 1965–69). Visiting Lectr., and holder of Riggs Chair, Yale Univ., New Haven, Conn., 1972–73; Sarum Lectr., Oxford Univ., U.K., 1976–77. *Publs:* The City of the Gods, 1965; A Search for God in Time and Memory, 1969; The Way of All the Earth, 1972; Time and Myth, 1973; The Reasons of the Heart, 1978; The Church of the Poor Devil, 1982; The House of Wisdom, 1985; The Homing Spirit, 1987. Add: Theology Dept., Univ. of Notre Dame, Notre Dame, Ind. 46556, U.S.A.

DUNNETT, Alastair M(acTavish). British, b. 1908. Novels/Short stories, Plays, Travel, Autobiography. Dir., Thomson Scottish Petroleum Ltd., Edinburgh (Chmn., 1972–79). Journalist in Scotland from 1935; Chief Press Officer, Secty. of State for Scotland, 1940–46; Ed.; Daily Record, 1946–55; Ed., The Scotsman, 1956–72; Managing Dir., 1962–70, and Chmn., 1970–74; Scotsman Publications Ltd.; Member, Exec. Bd., Thomson Org. Ltd., 1973–78; Dir., Scottish Television, 1975–79. *Publs:* Treasure at Sonnach, 1935; Heard Tell, 1946; Quest by Canoe, 1950; Highlands and Islands of Scotland, 1951; The Original John Mackay (play), 1956; Fit to Print (play), 1962; The Duke's Day, 1970; No Thanks to the Duke, 1978; Among Friends (autobiography), 1984; (with Dorothy Dunnett) The Scottish Highlands, 1988; End of Term, 1989. Add: 87 Colinton Rd., Edinburgh EH10 5DF, Scotland.

DUNNETT, Dorothy (Halliday). British, b. 1923. Mystery/Crime/Suspense, Historical/Romance/Gothic. Professional portrait painter since 1950; Dir., Scottish Television; Trustee, National Library of Scotland. Worked for Public Relations Dept., Secty. of State in Scotland, Edinburgh, 1940–46, and Research Dept. Bd. of Trade, Glasgow, 1946–55. *Publs:* The Game of Kings, 1961; Queens' Play, 1964; The Disorderly Knights, 1966; Dolly and the Singing Bird, 1968; Pawn in Frankincense, 1960; Dolly and the Cookie Bird, 1970; The Ringed Castle, 1971; Dolly and the Doctor Bird, 1971; Dolly and the Starry Bird, 1973; Checkmate, 1975; Dolly and the Nanny Bird, 1976; King Hereafter, 1982; Dolly and the Bird of Paradise, 1983; Niccolo Rising, 1986; The Spring of the Ram, 1987; (with Alastair M. Dunnett) The Scottish Highlands, 1988; Race of Scorpions, 1989. Add: 87 Colinton Rd., Edinburgh EH10 5DF, Scotland.

DUNNING, John H. British, b. 1927. Economics. ICI Research Prof. in Intnl. Investment and Business Studies, Univ. of Reading, since 1987 (Foundn. Prof. of Economics, 1964–74; Esmee Fairbairn Prof. of Intnl. Investment and Business Studies, 1975–87). Chmn. and Dir., Economists Advisory Group. Former Lectr., Univ. of Southampton. Adviser, National Economic Development Office, England, 1973, U.N., 1973–74, and OECD, 1974–85; Dir. of research project, United Nations Conference on Trade and Development (UNCTAD), 1974–75, and Sr. Consultant to U.N. Centre for Transnational Corporations, 1977–87. *Publs:* American In-

vestment in British Manufacturing Industry, 1958; Studies in International Investment, 1970; (ed.) Readings in International Investment, 1972; (ed.) Economic Analysis and the Multinational Enterprise, 1974; United Kingdom Multinationals and Trade Flows of Less Developed Countries, 1976; (with T. Houston) United Kingdom Industry Abroad, 1976; United States Industry in Britain, 1976; International Production and the Multinational Enterprise, 1981; (co-ed.) International Capital Movements, 1982; (with R.D. Pearce) The World's Largest Industrial Companies, 1985; Multinational Enterprises, Economic Structure, and International Competitiveness, 1985; Japanese Participation in British Industry, 1986; (co-ed.) The IRM Directory of Statistics on International Investment and Production, 1987; Explaining International Production, 1988; Multinationals: Technology and Competitiveness, 1988. Add: Dept. of Economics, Univ. of Reading, Reading RG6 2AH, England.

DUPRE, Catherine. British. Novels/Short stories, Biography. *Publs:* The Chicken Coop, 1967; Jelly Baby, 1968; A Face Full of Flowers, 1969; Matt Jones Is Nobody, 1970; The Child of Julian Flynn, 1972; John Galsworthy, 1976; Gentleman's Child, 1980. Add: 16 South St., Osney, Oxford OX2 0BE, England.

DUPRÉ, Louis. American. Philosophy, Theology/Religion. Prof. in the Philosophy of Religion, Yale Univ., New Haven, Conn., since 1973. Instr., 1958–59, Asst. Prof., 1959–64, Assoc. Prof., 1964–67, and Prof. in Philosophy, Georgetown Univ., Washington, D.C. *Publs:* Het Vertrekpunt der Marxistische Wijsbegeerte, 1954; Kierkegaard as Theologian, 1963; Contraception and Catholics, 1964; The Philosophical Foundations of Marxism, 1966; (ed.) Faith and Reflection, 1969; The Other Dimension, 1972; Transcendent Selfhood, 1976; A Dubious Heritage, 1977; The Deeper Life, 1981; Terugkeer naar Innerlijkheid, 1981; Marx's Social Critique of Culture, 1983; The Common Life, 1984; (co-ed.) Light from Light, 1987. Add: 67 N. Racebrook Rd., Woodbridge, Conn. 06525, U.S.A.

DUPUIS, Adrian M(aurice). American, b. 1919. Education. Prof. of Education, Marquette Univ., Milwaukee, since 1957. Prof., Coll. of St. Teresa, Winona, Minn., 1948–57. *Publs:* (with R.C. Craig) American Education: Origins and Issues, 1963; (with R.B. Nordberg) Philosophy and Education, 1964, 3rd ed. 1973; Philosophy of Education in Historical Perspective, 1966, 1985; (ed.) Nature, Aims and Policies, 1970. Add: Sch. of Education, Marquette Univ. Milwaukee, Wisc. 53233, U.S.A.

DUPUY, T(revor) N(evitt). American, b. 1916. History, Military/Defence. Pres., and Exec. Dir., and Member of the Bd., Historical Evaluation and Research Org., Washington, D.C., since 1962; Pres., Data Memory Systems, Inc., since 1983. Col., U.S. Army, 1938–58; Prof. of Military Science and Tactics, Harvard Univ., Mass., 1952–56; Dir., Ohio State Univ. Military History Course, 1956–57: with Intnl. Studies Div., Inst. for Defense Analyses, 1960–62. *Publs:* (co-author) To the Colors, 1942; Faithful and True, 1949; (co-author) Military Heritage of America, 1956; Campaigns of the French Revolution and of Napoleon, 1956; (co-author) Brave Men and Great Captains, 1960; (co-author) Compact History of the Civil War, 1960; Civil War Land Battles, 1960; Civil War Naval Actions, 1961; Military History of World War II, 19 vols., 1962–65; Compact History of the Revolutionary War, 1963; (ed. co-author) Holidays, 1965; Military History of World War I, 12 vols., 1967; The Battle of Austerlitz, 1968; Modern Libraries for Modern Colleges: Research Strategies for Design and Development, 1968; Ferment in College Libraries: The Impact of Information Technology, 1968; Military History of the Chinese Civil War, 1969; Military Lives Series, 12 vols., 1969–70; (co-author) Encyclopedia of Military History, 1970, 1977; (co-author) Revolutionary War Land Battles, 1970; (co-author) Revolutionary War Naval Battles, 1970; (ed. and co-author) Almanac of World Military Power, 1970, 1972, 1974, 1978; (co-ed.) Documentary History of Arms Control and Disarmament, 1973; (co-author) People and Events of the American Revolution, 1974; (co-author) Outline History of the American Revolution, 1975; A Genius for War: The German Army and General Staff, 1977; Numbers, Predictions, and War, 1978; Elusive Victory: The Arab-Israeli Wars 1947-1974, 1978, 1984; The Evolution of Weapons and Warfare, 1980; (co-author) Great Battles on the Eastern Front, 1982; Options of Command, 1984; (with Paul Martell) Flawed Victory: The 1982 War in Lebanon, 1986; (with others) Dictionary of Military Terms, 1986; Understanding War: History and Theory of Combat, 1987. Add: 1324 Kurtz Rd., Mclean, Va. 22101, U.S.A.

DURAC, Jack. *See* **RACHMAN,** Stanley Jack.

DURACK, (Dame) Mary. (Mary Miller). Australian, b. 1913. Children's fiction, Songs, lyrics and libretti, History. Hon. Life Member,

Fellowship of Australian Writers (Pres., W.A. Branch, 1958–63). *Publs:* All About, 1935; Chunuma, 1936; Son of Djaro, 1938; The Way of the Whirlwind, 1941; Piccaninnies, 1943; The Magic Trumpet, 1944; (with F. Rutter) Child Artists of the Australian Bush, 1952; Keep Him My Country, 1955; Kings in Grass Castles, 1959; To Ride a Fine Horse, 1963; Kookanoo and Kangaroo, 1963; The Courteous Savage, 1964, as Yagan of the Bibbulmun, 1976; An Australian Settler, also as A Pastoral Emigrant, 1964; Dalgerie (libretto), 1966; The Ship of Dreams (libretto), 1968; The Rock and the Sand, 1969; Swan River Saga, 1972; (with Ingrid Drysdale) The End of Dreaming, 1974; To Be Heirs Forever, 1976; The Way of the Whirlwind, 1979; Sons in the Saddle, 1983; (with others) The Land Beyond Time, 1984; (with others) The Stockman, 1984. Add: 12 Bellevue Ave., Nedlands, W.A. 6009, Australia.

DURANG, Christopher. American, b. 1949. Plays/Screenplays. *Publs:* (with Albert Innaurato) The Idiots Karamazov (musical play), 1974, 1981; A History of the American Film, 1978; The Vietnamization of New Jersey, 1978; The Nature and Purpose of the Universe/Death Comes to Us All, Mary Agnes/'dentity Crisis: Three Short Plays, 1979; Sister Mary Ignatius Explains It All for You, 1980; Christopher Durang Explains It All for You, 1983; Baby with the Bathwater, 1984; The Marriage of Bette and Boo, 1985; Laughing Wild, 1988. Add: c/o Helen Merrill, 435 W. 23rd St., No. 1a, New York, N.Y. 10011, U.S.A.

DURANT, David (Norton). British, b. 1925. Architecture, Biography. *Publs:* Bess of Hardwick, 1977; Arbella Stuart, 1978; (co-ed.) The Building of Hardwick Hall, 2 vols., 1980–84; Ralegh's Lost Colony, 1981; Living in the Past, 1988. Add: The Old Hall, Bleasby, Nottingham NG14 7FU, England.

DURBAND, Alan. British, b. 1927. Literature, Theatre. Head of English Dept., Liverpool Inst., 1953–63; Sr. Lectr., 1963–66, and Principal Lectr., 1966–80, City of Liverpool Coll. of Higher Education. Chmn., Everyman Theatre, Liverpool, 1974–84. *Publs:* English Workshop Books 1-3, 1959; (ed.) New Directions: Five One-Act Plays in the Modern Idiom, 1961; Contemporary English Books 1-2, 1962; Shorter Contemporary English, 1964; New English Books 1-4, 1966; (ed.) Playbill 1-3, 1969; (ed.) Second Playbill 1-3, 1973; (ed.) Prompt 1-3, 1975; (ed.) Wordplays 1-2, 1982; (ed.) Shakespeare Made Easy (12 plays), 1984–88. Add: Ty-Nant, Llansilin, Oswestry, Salop SY10 7QQ, England.

DURBRIDGE, Francis (Henry). British, b. 1912. Mystery/Crime/-Suspense, Plays/Screenplays. Full-time writer. *Publs:* mystery novels—Paul Temple series, 7 vols., 1938–70; The Back Room Girl, 1950; Beware of Johnny Washington, 1951; Design for Murder, 1951; (with Douglas Rutherford; as Paul Temple) The Tyler Mystery, 1957; The Other Man, 1958; (with Douglas Rutherford; as Paul Temple) East of Algiers, 1959; A Time of Day, 1959; The Scarf, 1960 (as The Case of the Twisted Scarf, 1961); Portrait of Alison, 1962; The World of Tim Frazer, 1962; My Friend Charles, 1963; Tim Frazer Again, 1964; Another Woman's Shoes, 1965; The Desperate People, 1966; Dead to the World, 1967; My Wife Melissa, 1967; The Pig-Tail Murder, 1969; A Man Called Harry Brent (novelization of tv series), 1970; The Geneva Mystery, 1971; Bat Out of Hell, 1972; The Curzon Case, 1972; A Game of Murder, 1975; The Passenger, 1977; Tim Frazer Gets the Message, 1978; The Breakaway, 1981; The Doll, 1982; plays—Suddenly at Home, 1971; The Gentle Hook, 1974; Murder with Love, 1976; House Guest, 1982; Deadly Nightcap, 1986; A Touch of Danger, 1988; numerous screenplays, radio plays and television serials. Add: c/o Harvey Unna and Stephen Durbridge Ltd., 24 Pottery Lane, London W11 4LZ, England.

DURDEN, Robert F(ranklin). American, b. 1925. History, Biography. Prof. of History, Duke Univ., Durham, N.C., since 1952 (Chmn. of the Dept., 1974–80). *Publs:* James Shepherd Pike: Republicanism and the American Negro, 1850-1882, 1957; Reconstruction Bonds and Twentieth-Century Politics: South Dakota and North Carolina (1904), 1962; The Climax of Populism: The Election of 1896, 1965; (ed.) The Prostrate State: South Carolina Under Negro Government, 1968; The Gray and the Black: The Confederate Debate on Emancipation, 1972; The Dukes of Durham, 1865-1929, 1975; (co-author) Maverick Republican in the Old North State: Political Biography of Daniel L. Russell, 1977; The Self-Inflicted Wound: Nineteenth Century Southern Politics, 1985. Add: History Dept., Duke Univ., Durham, N.C. 27706, U.S.A.

DURFEE, David A(rthur). American, b. 1929. Sociology. Instr., Marymount Coll., Tarrytown, N.Y., since 1976. Communications Officer, U.S. Navy, 1951–54; Teacher, Public Schs. of Great Neck, N.Y., 1955–63; Social Studies Chmn., Sleepy Hollow High Sch., N.Y., 1963–

68; Social Studies Co-ordinator, Public Schs. of the Tarrytowns, N.Y., 1968–85; Instr., United States Intnl. Univ., San Diego, Calif., 1971–74. *Publs:* Poverty in the Affluent Society, 1970, 1976; (ed.) William Henry Harrison and John Tyler (documents), 1970; Power in American Society, 1976. Add: Rd. 2, Box 149, Rte. 346, Peterburg, N.Y. 12138, U.S.A.

DURGNAT, Raymond (Eric). British/Swiss, b. 1932. Film. Lectr., 1964–71, and Head of Dept. of Gen. Studies, 1971–73, St. Martin's Sch. of Art, London. *Publs:* Nouvelle Vague—The First Decade, 1963; (with John Kobal) Greta Garbo, 1965; The Marx Brothers, 1966; Eros in the Cinema, 1966; Luis Bunuel, 1966; Franju, 1967; Films and Feelings, 1967; The Crazy Mirror, 1970; A Mirror for England, 1971; Sexual Alienation in the Cinema, 1974; The Strange Case of Alfred Hitchcock, 1974; Jean Renoir, 1974; Durgnat on Film, 1975; (with Scott Simmon) King Vidor, American, 1988. Add: 84 St. Thomas's Rd., London N4, England.

DURHAM, Marilyn (Wall). American, b. 1930. Novels/Short stories, Westerns/Adventure. *Publs:* The Man Who Loved Cat Dancing, 1972; Dutch Uncle, 1973; Flambard's Confession, 1982; A Season in Eden, 1988. Add: 1508 Howard St., Evansville, Ind. 47713, U.S.A.

DURNBAUGH, Donald F. American, b. 1927. Theology/Religion. Ziegler Prof. of Religion and History, Elizabethtown Coll., Pennsylvania, since 1988. Dir. of Prog. Brethren Service Commn., Austria, 1953–56; Asst. Prof. of History, Juniata Coll., Pa., 1958–62; Assoc. Prof., 1962–69, and Prof. of Church History, 1970–88, Bethany Theological Seminary, Oak Brook, Ill. Dir. in Europe, Brethren Colls. Abroad, Marburg and Strasburg, Germany, 1964–65; Adjunct Prof., Northern Baptist Theological Seminary, 1968–71; Assoc., Center for Reformation and Free Church Studies, Chicago Theological Seminary, 1966–78; Moderator, Church of the Brethren, 1985–86. *Publs:* (ed. and trans.) European Origins of the Brethren, 1958; (ed. and trans.) The Brethren in Colonial America, 1967; The Believers' Church, 1968, 1985; (ed. and co-author) Die Kirche der Brüder, 1971; (ed. and co-author) The Church of the Brethren Past and Present, 1971; (ed. and trans.) Every Need Supplied, 1974; (ed.) To Serve the Present Age, 1975; (ed.) On Earth Peace, 1978; (ed.) The Brethren Encyclopedia, 3 vols., 1983–84; Meet the Brethren, 1984. (ed.) Church of the Brethren: Yesterday and Today, 1986; Pragmatic Prophet: The Life of Michael Robert Zigler, 1989. Add: Elizabethtown Coll., Elizabethtown, Pa. 17022, U.S.A.

DURR, William K. American, b. 1924. Writer on education. Prof. Emeritus of Education, Michigan State Univ., East Lansing (Prof., from 1955). Sr. Author, Houghton Mifflin Readers, since 1971. Member, Bd. of Dirs., 1968–71, Pres., 1972–73, Intnl. Reading Assn. *Publs:* The Gifted Student, 1964; Reading Instructions: Dimensions and Issues, 1967; Reading Difficulties: Diagnosis, Correction, and Remediation, 1970. Add: 3377 Gulf Shore Blvd. N., Naples, Fla. 33940, U.S.A.

DURRELL, Gerald (Malcolm). British, b. 1925. Novels/Short stories, Children's fiction, Animals/Pets, Natural history, Autobiography/Memoirs/Personal. Founder and Dir., Jersey Wildlife Preservation Trust (formerly Jersey Zoo Park), since 1959. *Publs:* The Overloaded Ark, 1951; Three Singles to Adventure, 1953; The Bafut Beagles, 1953; The Drunken Forest, 1955; My Family and Other Animals, 1956; The New Noah, 1956; Encounters with Animals, 1959; A Zoo in My Luggage, 1960; Island Zoo, 1961; The Whispering Land, 1962; My Favourite Animal Stories, 1963; Menagerie Manor, 1964; Two in the Bush, 1966; Rosy is My Relative, 1968; The Donkey Rustlers, 1968; Birds, Beasts and Relatives, 1969; Fillets of Plaice, 1971; Catch Me a Colobus, 1972; Beasts in My Belfry, 1973; The Talking Parcel, 1974; The Stationary Ark, 1975; Golden Bats and Pink Pigeons, 1977; Garden of the Gods, 1978; The Picnic and Suchlike Pandemonium, 1979; The Mockery Bird, 1981; The Amateur Naturalist, 1982; How to Shoot an Amateur Naturalist, 1984; Durrell in Russia, 1986; The Fantastic Flying Journey, 1987. Add: Jersey Wildlife Preservation Trust, Les Augres Manor, Trinity, Jersey, Channel Islands.

DURRELL, Jacqueline (Sonia). British, b. 1929. Animals/Pets, Travel/Exploration/Adventure. Personal Asst. Business Mgr. for Gerald Durrell, 1954–79. *Publs:* Beasts in My Bed, 1965; Intimate Relations, 1976. Add: c/o Richard Simon, Scott Simon Agency, 32 College Cross, London N1, England.

DURRELL, Lawrence (George). Wrote one novel as Charles Norden. British, b. 1912. Novels/Short stories, Plays/Screenplays, Poetry, Travel/Exploration/Adventure, Translations. Formerly with the U.K. Foreign Service in Greece, Egypt, Argentina, and Yugoslavia; Dir. of

Public Relations, and Ed. of Cyprus Review, Govt. of Cyprus, 1954–56. *Publs:* Quaint Fragment: Poems Written Between the Ages of Sixteen and Nineteen, 1931; Ten Poems, 1932; Bromo Bombastes, 1933; Transition: Poems, 1934; Pied Piper of Lovers, 1935; (as Charles Norden) Panic Spring, 1937; The Black Book: An Agon, 1938; A Private Country, 1943; Prospero's Cell: A Guide to the Landscape and Manners of the Island of Corcyra, 1945; Cities, Plains and People, 1946; Cefalu (in U.S. as The Dark Labyrinth), 1947; On Seeming to Presume, 1948; Deus Loci, 1950; Sappho: Play in Verse, 1950; Key to Modern Poetry (in U.S. as A Key to Modern British Poetry), 1952; Reflections on a Marine Venus: A Companion to the Landscape of Rhodes, 1953; Private Drafts, 1955; The Tree of Idleness and Other Poems, 1955; Selected Poems, 1956; White Eagles Over Serbia, 1957; The Alexandria Quartet: Justine, 1957, Balthazar, 1958, Mountolive, 1958, and Clea, 1960; Esprit de Corps: Sketches from Diplomatic Life, 1957; Bitter Lemons, 1957; Stiff Upper Lip: Life Among the Diplomats, 1958; Art and Outrage: A Correspondence About Henry Miller Between Alfred Perles and Lawrence Durrell, with an Intermission by Henry Miller, 1959; (ed.) A Henry Miller Reader (in U.S. as The Best of Henry Miller), 1959; Collected Poems, 1960, 1968; (with E. Jennings and R.S. Thomas) Penguin Modern Poets 1, 1962; An Irish Faustus: A Morality in Nine Scenes, 1963; Beccafico Le Becfigue, 1963; Lawrence Durrell and Henry Miller: A Private Correspondence, 1963; (ed.) New Poems 1963; A P.E.N. Anthology of Contemporary Poetry, 1963; La Descente du Styx, 1964; Selected Poems 1935-63, 1964; Acte (play), 1965; Sauve Qui Peut, 1966; The Ikons: New Poems, 1966; Aut Tunc Aut Nunquam: Tunc, 1968, and Nunquam, 1970; Spirit of Place: Letters and Essays on Travel, 1969; The Red Limbo Lingo: Poetry Notebook for 1968-1970, 1971; On the Suchness of the Old Boy, 1972; Vega and Other Poems, 1973; Monsieur, 1974; Selected Poems, 1977; Livia, 1978; The Greek Islands, 1978; A Smile in the Mind's Eye, 1980; Collected Poems 1931-1974, 1980; Literacy Lifelines: The Richard Aldington/Lawrence Durrell Correspondence, 1981; Constance; or, Solitary Practices, 1982; Sebastian; or, Ruling Passions, 1983; Quinx; or, The Ripper's Tale, 1985; Antrobus Complete (short stories), 1985. Add: c/o Grindlay's Bank, 13 St. James's Sq., London SW1, England.

DURST, Paul. Also writes as Peter Bannon, John Chelton, Jeff Cochran and John Shane. American, b. 1921. Mystery/Crime/Suspense, Westerns/Adventure, History, Autobiography/Memoirs/Personal. Chief Editorial Writer and Newscaster, St. Joseph News-Press, 1946–48; Advertising Supvr., Southwestern Bell Telephone Co., Kansas City and St. Louis, 1948–50; Advertising Mgr., Crofts Engineering, Bradford, 1958–60, and J.G. Graves, mail order firm, Sheffield, 1960–62. *Publs:* Die, Damn You!, 1952; Bloody River, 1953; Trail Herd North, 1953; (as Jeff Cochran) Guns of Circle 8, 1954; (as John Shane) Along the Yermo Rim, 1954; (as John Chelton) My Deadly Angel (crime), 1955; Showdown, 1955; Justice, 1956; Kid from Canadian, 1956; Prairie Reckoning, 1956; (as John Shane) Sundown in Sundance, 1956; (as John Shane) Six-Gun Thursday, 1956; (as John Shane) Gunsmoke Dawn, 1957; John Law, Keep Out, 1957; Ambush at North Platte, 1957; The River Flows West, 1957; (as Peter Bannon) They Want Me Dead (crime), 1958; (as Peter Bannon) If I Should Die (crime), 1958; Kansas Guns, 1958; Dead Man's Range, 1958; The Gun Doctor, 1959; Johnny Nation, 1960; (as Peter Bannon) Whisper Murder Softly (crime), 1963; Backlash (crime), 1967; Badge of Infamy (crime), 1968; Intended Treason: What Really Happened in the Gunpowder Plot, 1970; A Roomful of Shadows (autobiography), 1975; The Florentine Table (crime), 1980; Paradiso County (crime), 1985. Add: The Keep, West Wall, Presteigne, Powys LD8 2BY, Wales.

DUTTON, Geoffrey (Piers Henry). Australian, b. 1922. Novels/Short stories, Children's fiction, Poetry, Art, Literature, Travel/Exploration/Adventure, Biography. Editorial Dir., Sun Books, Melbourne (Co-Founder, 1965); Ed., Sydney Morning Herald Literary Supplement, since 1980. Sr. Lectr. in English, Univ. of Adelaide, 1954–62; Ed., Penguin Australia, Melbourne, 1961–65. Co-Founder, Australian Letters, Adelaide, 1957, and Australian Book Review, Kensington Park, 1962; Member, Australian Council for the Arts, 1968–70; Ed., Bulletin Literary Supplement, Sydney, 1980–85, and The Australian Literary Quarterly, 1985–88. *Publs:* Nightfight and Sunrise, 1945; The Mortal and the Marble, 1950; A Long Way South, 1953; Antipodes in Shoes, 1955; Africa in Black and White, 1956; State of the Union, 1958; Founder of a City: The Life of William Light, 1960; Patrick White, 1961; Walt Whitman, 1961; Paintings of S.T. Gill, 1962; Russell Drysdale, 1962; Flowers and Fury, 1963; (ed.) The Literature of Australia, 1964; Tisi and the Yabby, 1965; Seal Bay, 1966; (ed.) Modern Australian Writing, 1966; The Hero as Murderer: The Life of Edward John Eyre, Australian Explorer and Governor of Jamaica 1815-1901, 1967; On My Island: Poems for Children, 1967; Andy, 1968; Poems Soft and Loud, 1968; Tisi and the Pageant, 1968; (ed. with M. Harris) The Vital Decade: 10 Years of Australian Art and Letters, 1968; Tamara,

1970; Findings and Keepings, 1970; Queen Emma of the South Seas, 1976; A Body of Words, 1977; A Taste of History: Geoffrey Dutton's South Australia, 1978; (with Harri Peccinotti) Patterns of Australia, 1979; Impressions of Singapore, 1981; The Australian Heroes, 1981; S.T. Gill's Australia, 1981; The Eye-Opener, 1982; The Prowler, 1982; Country Life in Old Australia, 1982; In Search of Edward John Eyre, 1982; Snow on the Saltbush, 1984; Selective Affinities (poetry), 1985; The Innovators, 1986. Add: c/o Curtis Brown Ltd., P.O. Box 19, Paddington, N.S.W. 2021, Australia.

DUVAL, Jeanne. *See* **COFFMAN,** Virginia.

DUVALL, Evelyn Millis. American, b. 1906. Human relations, Sex. Founder and Consultant, Sarasota Inst. of Lifetime Learning, since 1972; Incorporator and Vice-Pres., Sarasota Council on Aging, since 1973. Founding Dir., Assn. for Family Living, 1940–45; Exec., National Council on Family Relations, 1945–51; Distinguished Prof. of Family Life, Southern Illinois Univ., 1962. *Publs:* (with R. Hill) When You Marry, 1945; Family Living, 1950, 1961; Facts of Life and Love, 1950; In-Laws: Pro and Con, 1954; Family Development, 1957, 6th ed. as Marriage and Family Development, 1983; The Art of Dating, 1958, 1967; (with R. Hill) Being Married, 1960; (S. Duvall) Sex Ways in Fact and Faith, 1961; (with S. Duvall) Sense and Nonsense About Sex, 1962; Love and the Facts of Life, 1963; Why Wait Till Marriage?, 1965; Today's Teenagers, 1966; Faith in Families, 1970; Coping with Kids, 1974; Handbook for Parents, 1974; Parent and Teenager, 1976. Add: Plymouth Harbor Apts. 804-805, 700 John Ringling Blvd., Sarasota, Fla. 34236, U.S.A.

DuVAUL, Virginia C. *See* **COFFMAN,** Virginia.

DVORETZKY, Edward. American, b. 1930. Literature, Translations. Prof. Dept. of German, Univ. of Iowa, since 1967. Teaching Fellow in German, Harvard Univ., Cambridge, Mass., 1954–56; Instr. 1956–59, Asst. Prof. 1959–64, and Assoc. Prof. 1964–67, Rice Univ., Houston, Tex. *Publs:* (trans.) Emilia Galotti, by Gotthold Ephraim Lessing, 1962; The Enigma of Emilia Galotti, 1963; The Eighteenth-Century English Translations of Emilia Galotti, 1966; (ed.) Lessing: Dokumente zur Wirkungsgeschichte 1755-1968, 2 vols., 1971, 1972; (trans.) Philotas, by Lessing, 1979; (ed.) Lessing Heute: Beitrage zur Wirkungsgeschichte, 1981; Der Teufel und sein Advokat: Gedichte und Prosa, 1981; Tief im Herbstwald (poetry), 1983. Add: 102 Schaeffer Hall, Univ. of Iowa, Iowa City, Iowa 52242, U.S.A.

DWORKIN, Ronald (Myles). American, b. 1931. Law. Prof. of Jurisprudence, Oxford Univ., and Fellow of University Coll., Oxford, since 1969; Prof. of Law, New York Univ., since 1976. Assoc., Sullivan and Cromwell, NYC, 1958–62; Assoc. Prof., 1962–65, Prof. of Law, 1965–68, and Wesley N. Hohfield Prof. of Law, 1968–69, Yale Univ., New Haven; Prof.-at-Large, Cornell Univ., Ithaca, N.Y., 1976–82. *Publs:* Taking Rights Seriously, 1977; (ed.) The Philosophy of Law, 1977; A Matter of Principle, 1985; Law's Empire, 1986. Add: New York Univ. Law Sch., Washington Square, New York, N.Y. 10012, U.S.A.

DWYER, Deanna. *See* **KOONTZ,** Dean R.

DWYER, K.R. *See* **KOONTZ,** Dean R.

DYEN, Isidore. American, b. 1913. Language/Linguistics. Prof. Emeritus of Comparative Linguistics and Austronesian Languages, 1984; Yale Univ., New Haven, Conn (Research Fellow 1939–42; Instr. in Malay, 1942–43; Asst. Prof. of Malayan Languages, 1943–57; Prof., 1957–58; Prof. of Malayopolynesian and Comparative Linguistics, 1958–73). Vice-Pres., American Oriental Soc., 1965–66. Adjunct Research Prof., Univ. of Hawaii-Manoa, 1985–89. *Publs:* Spoken Malay, 1945; The Proto-Malayo-Polynesian Laryngeals, 1953; (with E. Schafer, H. Fernald and H. Glidden) Index to Journal of the American Oriental Society, vols. 21-60, 1955; A Lexicostatistical Classification of the Austronesian Languages, 1965; A Sketch of Trukese Grammar, 1965; Beginning Indonesian, 4 vols., 1967; A Descriptive Indonesian Grammar, 1967; (ed.) Lexicostatistics in Genetic Linguistics: Proceedings of the Yale Conference, 1973; (with D. Aberle) Lexical Reconstruction: The Case of the Athapaskan Kinship System, 1974; Linguistic Subgrouping and Lexicostatistics, 1975. Add: Dept. of Linguistics, Univ. of Hawaii, Honolulu, Hawaii 96822, U.S.A.

DYER, Charles (Raymond). British, b. 1928. Novels/Short stories, Plays/Screenplays. Freelance actor and dir. *Publs:* Time, Murderer, Please, 1956; Wanted, One Body, 1956; Rattle of a Simple Man, 1962, novel, 1964; Staircase (play), 1966, novel as Charlie Always Told Harry

Almost Everything (in U.S. as Staircase: or, Charlie Always Told Harry Almost Everything), 1969; Mother Adam, 1971; Lovers Dancing, 1984; Loving Leopold (play), 1987. Add: Old Wob, Gerrards Cross, Bucks., England.

DYER, Frederick C(harles). American, b. 1918. Administration/Management, Writing/Journalism. Full-time Writer. Contrib. Ed., The Pope Speaks mag., 1954–64; Professorial Lectr. in Communications, George Washington Univ., Washington, D.C. 1956–60; Adjunct Prof. in Communications, Drexel Univ., Philadelphia, Pa., 1962–67; Dir., Prog. Analysis, Navy Publs. and Printing Service, 1968–74; Professorial Lectr., American Univ., Washington, D.C., 1969–72; Contrib. Ed., The Wall Street Review of Books, 1975–84. *Publs:* (with H.F. Cope) The Petty Officer's Guide, 1953, 6th ed. 1966; (with R. Evans and D. Lovell) Putting Yourself Over in Business, 1957; Executive's Guide to Handling People, 1958; Executive's Guide to Effective Speaking and Writing, 1962; (with J.M. Dyer) Export Financing, 1964; Blueprint for Executive Success, 1964; (with J.M. Dyer) Bureaucracy vs. Creativity: The Dilemma of Modern Leadership, 1965, 1969; (with C.A. Dailey) How to Make Decisions About People, 1966; (with J.M. Dyer) The Enjoyment of Management, 1971, 1982. Add: 4509 Cumberland Ave., Town of Somerset, Md. 20815-5459, U.S.A.

DYER, James (Frederick). British, b. 1934. Archaeology/Antiquities, Children's non-fiction, History. Freelance writer and broadcaster. Archaeological Ed., Shire Publs., Princes Risborough, Bucks, since 1968. Ed., The Bedfordshire Mag., 1965–74; Principal Lectr. in Archaeology, Putteridge Bury Coll. of Education, Luton, 1966–76. *Publs:* (with J. Dony) The Story of Luton, 1964, 3rd ed. 1975; Discovering Archaeology in England and Wales, 1969, 5th ed. 1985; Discovering Regional Archaeology; Eastern England, 1969, 1973; Discovering Regional Archaeology: The Cotswolds and Upper Thames, 1970; (with L.V. Grinsell) Discovering Regional Archaeology: Wessex, 1971; Discovering Archaeology in Denmark, 1972; Southern England: An Archaeological Guide, 1973; Your Book of Prehistoric Britain, 1974; (ed.) From Antiquary to Archaeologist: William Cunnington 1754-1810, 1974; Worthington Smith 1835-1917, 1978; The Penguin Guide to Prehistoric England and Wales, 1981; Hillforts of England and Wales, 1981; Teaching Archaeology in Schools, 1983; Shire Guide to Bedfordshire, 1987. Add: 6 Rogate Rd., Cassel Park, Luton, Beds., LU2 8HR, England.

DYER, John M(artin). American, b. 1920. Business/Trade/Industry, Marketing. Prof. of Marketing, Univ. of Miami, Coral Gables, since 1969; Attorney. *Publs:* United States-Latin America Trade and Financial Relations, 1961; (with F.C. Dyer) Export Financing, 1963; (with F.C. Dyer) Bureaucracy vs. Creativity: The Dilemma of Modern Leadership, 1965; Guidelines to Operating in Latin America, 1970; (with F.C. Dyer) The Enjoyment of Management, 1971; Materials for International Finance and Marketing, 2nd ed. 1978; Materials on International Finance, Law, and Marketing, 4th ed. 1980. Add: Marketing Dept., P.O. Box 248147, Univ. of Miami, Coral Gables, Fla. 33124, U.S.A.

DYER, Wayne W(alter). American, b. 1940. Novels/Short stories, Psychology. Resource Teacher and Counselor, Pershing High Sch., Detroit, 1965–67; Instr. in Counselor Education and Practicum Supvr., Wayne State Univ., Detroit, 1969–71; Dir. of Guidance and Counseling, Mercy High Sch., Farmington, Mich., 1967–71; Education Counselor and Asst. Prof., 1971–74, and Assoc. Prof., 1974–77, St. John's Univ., Jamaica, N.Y.; Staff Consultant, Drug Information and Service Center, Bd. of Cooperative Educational Services, Dix Hills, N.Y., 1972–75; Staff Consultant, Mental Health Assn. of Nassau Co. and Nassau Co. Dept. of Drug and Alcohol Addiction, 1973–75; Trainer and Staff Consultant of Guidance and Sch. Psychological Personnel, Half Hollow Sch. District, Huntington, N.Y., 1973–75; Staff Consultant, Detroit Hosp. Drug Treatment Prog., Herman Kiefer Hosp., Detroit, 1974–75; Member of the Teaching Staff and Adjunct Consultant, Drug Treatment and Education Center, North Shore Univ. Hosp., Manhasset, N.Y., 1974–75. *Publs:* (with Jon Vriend) Counseling Effectively in Groups, 1973; (with John Vriend) Counseling Techniques That Work: Application to Individual and Group Counseling, 1974; Your Erroneous Zones: Bold But Simple Techniques for Eliminating Unhealthy Behavior Patterns, 1976; Pulling Your Own Strings, 1977; The Sky's the Limit, 1980; Gifts from Eykis (novel), 1982; Group Counseling for Personal Mastery, 1980; What Do You Really Want for Your Children, 1985; Happy Holidays, 1986. Add: The Shore Club, Tower House C, 1905 N. Atlantic Blvd., Ft. Lauderdale, Fla. 33305, U.S.A.

DYKEMAN, Wilma. American. Novels/Short stories, Sociology,

Travel/Exploration/Adventure, Biography. Editorial Columnist, News-Sentinel, Knoxville, Tenn., since 1962; Tennessee State Historian, since 1981; also, Prof. of Special Programs in English, Univ. of Tennessee, Knoxville, since 1986. *Publs:* The French Broad, 1955; (with J. Stokely) Neither Black nor White, 1957; The Tall Woman (novel), 1962; Seeds of Southern Change, 1962; The Far Family (novel), 1966; Prophet of Plenty, 1966; Look to This Day (essays), 1968; The Border States, 1968; Return the Innocent Earth (novel), 1973; Too Many People, Too Little Love, 1974; Tennessee: A Bicentennial History, 1976; (with Jim Stokely) Highland Homeland: The People of the Great Smokies, 1977; (with Dykeman Stokely) The Appalachian Mountains, 1980; Explorations, 1984. Add: 405 Clifton Heights, Newport, Tenn. 37821, U.S.A.

DYLAN, Bob. (Robert Zimmerman). American, b. 1941. Poetry, Songs, lyrics and libretti. Freelance singer and composer; devised and popularized folk-rock. Records for Columbia Records. *Publs:* numerous songs; published verse—Tarantula, 1966; Writing and Drawings by Bob Dylan, 1973; The Songs of Bob Dylan 1966-1975, 1976; Bob Dylan in His Own Words, 1978; XI Outlined Epitaphs, and Off the Top of My Head, 1981; Lyrics 1962-1985, 1985. Add: P.O. Box 870, Cooper Station, New York, N.Y. 10276, U.S.A.

DYMOKE, Juliet. Pseud. for Juliet Dymoke de Schanschieff. British, b. 1919. Historical/Romance, Children's fiction, History. *Publs:* Sons of the Tribune (juvenile), 1956; London in the 18th Century (juvenile), 1958; The Orange Sash, 1958; Born for Victory, 1960, 1974; Treason in November, 1961; Bend Sinister, 1962; The Cloisterman, 1969; Of the Ring of Earls, 1970; Henry of the High Rock, 1971; Serpent in Eden, 1973; The Lion's Legacy, 1974; Prisoner of Rome (juvenile), 1974; Shadows on a Throne, 1976; A Pride of Kings, 1978; The Royal Griffin, 1978; The White Cockade, 1979; Lady of the Garter, 1979; The Lion of Mortimer, 1979; The Lord of Greenwich, 1980; The Sun in Splendour, 1980; A Kind of Warfare, 1981; The Queen's Diamond, 1985; March to Corunna, 1985; Two Flags for France, 1986; A Border Knight, 1987; The Spanish Boy (juvenile), 1987. Add: Heronswood, Chapel Lane, Forest Row, East Sussex, England.

DYRNESS, William A. American, b. 1943. Art, Theology/Religion. Minister to Students, Hinson Memorial Baptist Church, Portland, Ore., 1971–73; Guest Instr., Regent Coll., Vancouver, 1972–74; Prof. of Theology, Asian Theological Seminary, Manila, 1972–82; Prof. of Theology, New College, Berkeley, Calif., 1986–9 (Pres., 1982–86). *Publs:* Rouault: A Vision of Suffering and Salvation, 1971; Christian Critique of American Culture, 1974; Themes of Old Testament Theology, 1979; Christian Art in Asia, 1979; Let the Earth Rejoice! 1983; A Christian Apologetics in a World Community, 1983; How Does America Hear the Gospel?, 1989; Learning About Theology from the Third World, 1990. Add: 1335 M.L. King, Berkeley, Calif. 94709, U.S.A.

DYSON, A(nthony) E(dward). British, b. 1928. Literature. Hon. Fellow, formerly Reader in English, Univ. of East Anglia, Norwich. Co-ed., Critical Quarterly, since 1959. Lectr. in English, University Coll. of North Wales, Bangor, 1955–63. *Publs:* (with C.B. Cox) Modern Poetry, 1963; The Crazy Fabric: Essays in Irony, 1965; The Practical Criticism of Poetry, 1965; (ed.) Modern Judgements on Dickens, 1968; (ed. with C.B. Cox) Word in the Desert, 1968; Casebook on Bleak House, 1969; (ed. with C.B. Cox) Black Papers on Education, 3 vols., 1969–70; The Inimitable Dickens, 1970; Between Two Worlds: Aspects of Literary Form, 1972; (ed. with C.B. Cox) Twentieth Century Mind, 3 vols., 1972; (ed.) English Poetry: Select Bibliographical Guides, 1973; (ed.) English Novel: Select Bibliographical Guides, 1974; (ed. with Julian Lovelock) Casebook of Paradise Lost, 1974; Freedom in Love, 1975; (with Julian Lovelock) Masterful Images: Metaphysicals to Romantics, 1975; (ed. with Julian Lovelock) Education and Democracy, 1975; Yeats, Eliot, and R.S. Thomas: Riding the Echo, 1981; Casebook on "Poetry Criticism and Practice: Developments Since the Symbolists", 1986. Add: c/o Macmillan, 4 Little Essex St., London WC2R 3LF, England.

DYSON, Freeman (John). American, b. 1923. Physics, Autobiography/Memoirs/Personal. Prof. of Physics, Inst. for Advanced Study, Princeton, since 1953. Civilian Scientist, RAF Bomber Command, High Wycombe, Bucks., England, 1943–45; Prof. of Physics, Cornell Univ., Ithaca, N.Y., 1951–53. *Publs:* Disturbing the Universe (autobiography), 1979; Weapons and Hope, 1984; Origins of Life, 1986; Infinite in All Directions, 1988; Recipient of National Book Critics Circle Award for Non-fiction, 1984. Add: 105 Battle Rd. Circle, Princeton, N.J. 08540, U.S.A.

E

EABORN, Colin. British, b. 1923. Chemistry. Prof. of Chemistry, Univ. of Sussex, since 1962 (Dean of Molecular Sciences, 1964–68 and 1978–79; Pro-Vice Chancellor (Science), 1968–73). Regional Ed., Journal of Organometallic Chemistry since 1963, Elsevier, Netherlands. Asst. Lectr. 1947–50, Lectr. 1950–54, and Reader in Chemistry 1954–62, Univ. of Leicester. *Publs:* Organosilicon Compounds, 1960. Add: Sch. of Chemistry and Molecular Sciences, Univ. of Sussex, Brighton BN1 9QJ, England.

EAGLESFIELD, Francis. *See* **GUIRDHAM,** Arthur.

EAGLETON, Terence (Francis). British, b. 1943. Novels, Literature, Politics/Government. Tutor in English, Wadham Coll., Oxford, since 1969, and Lectr. in Critical Theory, Oxford Univ., since 1988. Poetry Reviewer, Stand mag. Tutor in English, Jesus Coll., Cambridge, 1964–69. *Publs:* Shakespeare and Society, 1966; The New Left Church, 1966; Exiles and Emigrés, 1970; The Body as Language, 1970; Myths of Power: A Marxist Study of the Brontës, 1974; Marxism and Literary Criticism, 1976; Criticism and Ideology, 1976; Brecht and Company (play), 1979; Walter Benjamin: or, Towards a Revolutionary Criticism, 1981; The Rape of Clarissa, 1982; Literary Theory, 1983; The Function of Criticism, 1984: William Shakespeare, 1985; Against the Grain, 1986; Saints and Scholars (novel), 1987. Add: Linacre Coll., Oxford, England.

EARHART, H. Byron. American, b. 1935. Theology/Religion. Prof. of Religion, Western Michigan Univ., since 1975 (Asst. Prof., 1966–69; Assoc. Prof. 1969–75). Adviser on Far Eastern Religion, Encyclopaedia Britannica. Asst. Prof. of Religion, Vanderbilt Univ., Nashville, Tenn., 1965–66. *Publs:* Japanese Religion: Unity and Diversity, 1969, 3rd ed. 1982; A Religious Study of the Mount Haguro Sect of Shugendo: An Example of Japanese Mountain Religion, 1970; The New Religions of Japan: A Bibliography of Western Language Materials, 1970, 2nd ed. 1983; Religion in the Japanese Experience: Sources and Interpretations, 1974; (trans.) Japanese Religion in the Modern Century, by Shigeyoshi Murakami, 1980; (ed. with Hitoshi Miyake) Dentoteki shukyo no saisei, 1983; Religions of Japan: Many Traditions within One Sacred Way, 1984; (ed.) Religious Traditions of the World, 8 vols., 1984–87; Gedatsu-Ki and Religion in Contemporary Japan: Returning to the Center, 1989. Add: Dept. of Religion, Western Michigan Univ., Kalamazoo, Mich. 49008, U.S.A.

EARLE, William Alexander. American, b. 1919. Philosophy. Prof. of Philosophy, Northwestern Univ., Evanston, Ill, since 1960 (Assoc. Prof. 1948–80). Rockefeller Foundation Fellow, 1947–48; Carnegie Foundation Fellow, 1965–66. *Publs:* Objectivity, 1956, 1968; Christianity and Existentialism, 1963; Autobiographical Consciousness, 1972; Public Sorrows and Private Pleasures, 1976; Mystical Reason, 1980; A Surrealism of the Movies, 1986. Add: Dept. of Philosophy, Northwestern Univ., Evanston, Ill. 60201, U.S.A.

EARLEY, Tom. (Thomas Powell Earley). Welsh, b. 1911. Poetry. Member, Welsh Academy, since 1972. Teacher, St. Dunstan's Coll., London, 1945–71. *Publs:* Welshman in Bloomsbury, 1966; The Sad Mountain, 1970; Rebel's Progress, 1979. Add: 21 Bloomsbury Sq., London, WC1, England.

EARNSHAW, Anthony. British, b. 1924. Novels/Short stories, Autobiography/Memoirs/Personal. Part-time Lectr. in Fine Art, Leeds Polytechnic, since 1970. *Publs:* (with E. Thacker) Musrum, 1968; (with

E. Thacker) Wintersol, 1971; Seven Secret Alphabets (drawings), 1972; Twenty five Poses (drawings), 1973; Flick Knives and Forks, 1981. Add: 8 King George Gardens, Leeds LS7 4NS, England.

EASMON, R(aymond) Sarif. Sierra Leonean. Novels/Short stories, Plays/Screenplays. Practising Physician. *Publs:* Dear Parent and Ogre, 1961; The New Patriots, 1965; The Burnt-Out Marriage (novel), 1967; The Feud, 1981. Add: 31 Bathurst St., Freetown, Sierra Leone.

EAST, John (Marlborough). British, b. 1937. Theatre, Biography. Radio and television broadcaster, since 1955; controls publicity company handling many publishers, show business personalities and companies. Former actor. *Publs:* Neath the Mask, 1967; Cheeky Chappie, Max Miller, 1977. Add: 22 Gibson's Hill, Norbury, London SW16 3JP, England.

EAST, Michael. *See* **WEST,** Morris.

EAST, William Gordon. British, b. 1902. Geography, History, International relations/Current affairs. Prof. Emeritus of Geography, Birkbeck Coll., Univ. of London, since 1970 (joined faculty, 1947). Admin. Officer, Ministry of Economic Welfare, and Foreign Office, 1941–45; Reader in Geography, London Sch. of Economics, 1945–47. *Publs:* The Union of Moldavia and Wallachia 1859, 1929; An Historical Geography of Europe, 1935, 4th ed. 1966; The Geography Behind History, 1938, rev. ed. 1965; Mediterranean Problems, 1938; (ed. with O.H.K. Spate and C.A. Fisher) The Changing Map of Asia, 1950, 5th ed. 1971; (with S.W. Wooldridge) The Spirit and Purpose of Geography, 1951, 3rd ed. 1966; (ed. with A.E. Moodie) The Changing World, 1956; (ed.) The Caxton Atlas, 1960; The Soviet Union, 1963; The Destruction of Cities in the Mediterranean World, 1971; (with J.R.V. Prescott) Our Fragmented World, 1975. Add: Wildwood, Danes Way, Oxshott, Surrey, England.

EASTAUGH, Kenneth. British, b. 1929. Plays/Screenplays, Film, Biography. Film Critic, Prima mag., and Music Critic, Classical Music Weekly, both since 1976. Television Critic, 1965–67, and Show Business Writer, 1967–70, Daily Mirror, London; Chief Show Business Writer, The Sun, London, 1970–73; TV Columnist, The Times, London, 1977; Chief Show Business Exec., Daily Star, London, 1978–83. Member of Exec. Council, Writers' Guild of Great Britain, 1975. *Publs:* The Event (television play), 1968; Better than a Man (television play), 1970; Dapple Downs (radio serial), 1973–74; Awkward Cuss (play), 1976; Havergal Brian: The Making of a Composer (biography), 1976; The Carry On Book (cinema), 1978; Havergal Who? (TV documentary), 1980; Mr. Love (novel, also screenplay), 1986. Add: c/o Curtis Brown, 162-168 Regent St., London W1R 5TB, England.

EASTLAKE, William (Derry). American, b. 1917. Novels/Short stories, Poetry, Essays. Writer-in-Residence, Knox Coll., Galesburg, Ill., 1967–68; Lectr., Univ. of New Mexico, Albuquerque, 1968–69; Writer-in-Residence, Univ. of Arizona, Tucson, 1969–71. *Publs:* Go in Beauty, 1956; The Bronc People, 1958; Portrait of an Artist with Twenty-Six Horses, 1963; Castle Keep, 1964; The Bamboo Bed, 1970; A Child's Garden of Verses for the Revolution (poetry and essays), 1971; Dancers in the Scalp House, 1975; The Long Naked Descent into Boston, 1977; Jack Armstrong in Tangier, 1984; Pretty Fields (novella), 1987. Add: 15 Coy Rd., Bisbee, Ariz. 85603, U.S.A.

EASTON, David. Canadian, b. 1917. Politics/Government. Andrew

MacLeish Distinguished Service Prof., Dept. of Political Science, Univ. of Chicago, 1955–84, now Emeritus (Asst.-Prof., 1947–53; Assoc. Prof., 1953–55); Distinguished Prof. of Political Science, Univ. of California at Irvine, since 1982. Vice-Pres., American Academy of Arts and Sciences, since 1985. Member Bd. of Eds., Behavioral Science, since 1956; Youth and Society, since 1970, Journal of Political Methodology, since 1972, and International Political Science Abstracts, since 1972. Jointly, Sir Edward Peacock Prof. of Political Science, Queen's Univ., Canada, 1971–80. Pres., American Political Science Assn., 1968–69; Pres., Intl. Cttee. on Social Science Documentation, 1969–71. *Publs:* The Political System: An Inquiry into the State of Political Science, 1953, 1971; A Framework for Political Analysis, 1965; A Systems Analysis of Political Life, 1965; (ed.) Varieties of Political Theory, 1966; (with J. Dennis) Children in the Political System; Origins of Political Legitimacy, 1969. Add: Sch. of Social Sciences, Univ. of California, Irvince, Calif. 92715, U.S.A.

EASTON, Loyd D. American, b. 1915. Philosophy. Duvall Prof. of Philosophy, Ohio Wesleyan Univ., Delaware, 1978–80, now Emeritus Prof. (joined faculty, 1946). Pres., Ohio Philosophical Assn., 1964–67. *Publs:* Ethics, Policy, and Social Ends, 1955; Hegel's First American Followers: The Ohio Hegelians, 1966; (ed. and trans. with K. Guddat) Writings of the Young Marx on Philosophy and Society, 1967; (ed.) Philosophical Analysis and Human Welfare: Selected Essays and Chapters from Six Decades, by D.S. Miller, 1975. Add: 998 Braumiller Rd., Delaware, Ohio 43015, U.S.A.

EASTON, Robert. American, b. 1915. Novels/Short stories (historical fiction), Western/Adventure, History, Natural history, Biography. *Publs:* The Happy Man (novel), 1943, 1977; (with M. Brown) Lord of Beasts, 1961; (with others) The Book of the American West, 1963; The Hearing (novel), 1964; (with D. Smith) California Condor, 1964; (ed.) Max Brand's Best Stories, 1967; (ed. with M. Brown) Bullying the Moqui: Charles F. Lummis' Defense of the Hopi, 1968; Max Brand, 1970; Black Tide: The Santa Barbara Oil Spill and Its Consequences, 1972; Guns, Gold and Caravans, 1978; China Caravans: An American Adventurer in Old China, 1982; This Promised Land (novel), 1982; Life and Work (autobiography), 1988; Power and Glory (novel) 1989. Add: 2222 Las Canoas Rd., Santa Barbara, Calif. 93105, U.S.A.

EATON, Charles Edward. American, b. 1916. Novels/Short stories, Poetry, Art, Biography. Instr. of Creative Writing, Univ. of Missouri, Columbia, 1940–42; Vice Consul, American Embassy, Rio de Janeiro 1942–46; Prof. of Creative Writing, Univ. of North Carolina, Chapel Hill, 1946–51. *Publs:* The Bright Plain, 1942; Write Me from Rio, 1959; The Shadow of the Swimmer, 1951; The Greenhouse in the Garden, 1956; Countermoves, 1963; The Edge of the Knife, 1970; Karl Knaths, 1971; The Girl from Ipanema, 1972; Karl Knaths: Five Decades of Painting, 1973; The Man in the Green Chair, 1977; The Case of the Missing Photographs, 1978; Colophon of the Rover, 1980; The Thing King, 1983; The Work of the Wrench, 1985; New and Selected Poems, 1942-1987, 1987; New and Selected Stories 1959-1989, 1989. Add: 808 Greenwood Rd., Chapel Hill, N.C. 27514, U.S.A.

EATON, George L. *See* **VERRAL,** Charles Spain.

EATON, John Herbert. British, b. 1927. Theology/Religion. Reader, Dept., of Theology, Univ. of Birmingham, since 1977 (Asst. Lectr., 1956–59; Lectr., 1959–69; Sr. Lectr., 1969–77). Teacher, St. George's Upper Sch., Jerusalem 1953–56. *Publs:* Obadiah, Nahum, Habakkuk and Zephaniah: Introduction and Commentary, 1961; Psalms: Introduction and Commentary, 1967; Kingship and the Psalms, 1976, 1986; Festal Drama in Deutero-Isaiah, 1979; First Studies in Biblical Hebrew, 1980; Vision in Worship, 1981; Readings in Biblical Hebrew, 1982; The Psalms Come Alive, 1984; Job, 1985. Add: Dept. of Theology, Univ. of Birmingham, Birmingham B15 2TT, England.

EATON, Richard Behrens. American, b. 1914. History, Law, Biography. Lectr., Shasta Coll., since 1953, and Dir., Shasta Historical Soc., since 1952, and Dir., Redding Museum and Art Center since 1963—all Redding, Calif. Superior Court Judge, State of California, 1951–76. *Publs:* Court of Sessions 1851-54, 1947; The Four Court Houses of Shasta County, 1958; The Six School Houses of Shasta, 1959; Law in Action: The Juvenile Court, 1959; Discovery of Gold at Readings Bar 1848, 1964; Mae Helene Bacon Boggs: Pioneer-Philanthropist-Centenarian, 1964; A Town Is Born (play), 1965; Colonel William Magee, 1965; People on Foot, 1974; Charles H. Behrens, 1979; Shasta County in 1930, 1980; Redding Museum and Art Center, 1986; Naming of Redding—Incorporation of Redding, 1987. Add: 1520 West St., Redding, Calif. 96001, U.S.A.

EATON, Trevor (Michael William). British, b. 1934. Language/Linguistics, Literature. Ed., Journal of Literary Semantics, since 1970; Convenor, Intnl. Assn. of Literary Semantics, since 1987. Lectr. in English, Univ. of Erlangen, Germany, 1958–60; Lectr. in English Language, Univ. of New South Wales, Newcastle, 1961–65; Teacher, 1965–87, and Head of the Philosophy Dept., 1974–87, Norton Knatchbull Sch. Section Convenor, Linguistics and Literature Section, Linguistics Assn., of Great Britain, 1972–76. *Publs:* The Semantics of Literature, 1966; The Foundations of Literary Semantics, 1970; Theoretical Semics, 1972; (ed.) Poetries: Their Media and Ends, by I.A. Richards, 1974; (ed.) Essays in Literary Semantics, 1978. Add: Honeywood Cottage, 35 Seaton Ave., Hythe, Kent CT21 5HH, England.

EBBETT, Eve. Also wrote as Eva Burfield. New Zealander, b. 1925. Novels/Short stories, History. *Publs:* as Eva Burfield—Yellow Kowhai, 1957; A Chair to Sit On, 1958; The Long Winter, 1964; Out of Yesterday, 1965; After Midnight, 1965; The White Prison, 1966; The New Mrs. Rainier, 1967; The Last Day of Summer, 1968; as Eve Ebbett—Give Them Swing Bands, 1969; To the Garden Alone, 1970; In True Colonial Fashion, 1977; Victoria's Daughters: New Zealand Women of the Thirties, 1981; When the Boys Were Away, 1984. Add: 908 Sylvan Rd., Hastings, New Zealand.

EBEL, Suzanne. Also writes as Suzanne Goodwin and Cecily Shelbourne. British. Historical/Romance, Travel. *Publs:* Love, the Magician, 1956; Journey from Yesterday, 1963; The Half-Enchanted, 1964; The Love Campaign, 1965; The Dangerous Winter, 1965; A Perfect Stranger, 1966; A Name in Lights, 1968; A Most Auspicious Star, 1968; Somersault, 1971; Portrait of Jill, 1972; Dear Kate, 1972; To Seek a Star, 1973; The Family Feeling, 1973; (with Doreen Impey) Explore the Cotswolds by Bicycle (non-fiction), 1973; Girl by the Sea, 1974; Music in Winter, 1975; (with Doreen Impey) London's Riverside, from Hampton Court in the West to Greenwich Palace in the East (non-fiction), 1975, as A Guide to London's Riverside, 1985; A Grove of Olives, 1976; River Voices, 1976; The Double Rainbow, 1977; A Rose in Heather, 1978; (as Suzanne Goodwin) The Winter Spring, 1978, in U.S. (as Cecily Shelbourne) Stage of Love, 1978; (as Suzanne Goodwin) The Winter Sisters, 1980; (as Suzanne Goodwin) Emerald, 1980; Julia's Sister, 1982; The Provençal Summer, 1982; (as Suzanne Goodwin) Floodtide, 1983; (as Suzanne Goodwin) Sisters, 1985; House of Nightingales, 1986; (as Suzanne Goodwin) Cousins, 1986; The Clover Field, 1987; (as Suzanne Goodwin) Daughters, 1987; (as Suzanne Goodwin) Reflections in a Lake, 1989. Add: 52A Digby Mansions, Hammersmith Bridge Rd., London W6 9DF, England.

EBERHART, Mignon G. American, b. 1899. Mystery/Crime/-Suspense, Historical/Romance/Gothic. Self-employed writer since 1930. Past Pres., Mystery Writers of American. *Publs:* The Patient in Room 18, 1929; The Mystery of Hunting's End, 1930; While the Patient Slept, 1930; From This Dark Stairway, 1931; Murder by an Aristocrat, 1932, in U.K. as Murder of My Patient, 1934; The Dark Garden, 1933, in U.K. as Death in the Fog, 1934; The White Cockatoo, 1933; The Cases of Susan Dare (short stories), 1934; The House on the Roof, 1935; Fair Warning, 1936; Danger in the Dark (in U.K. as Hand in Glove), 1937; The Pattern, 1937; in U.S. paperback as Pattern of Murder, 1948; The Glass Slipper, 1938; Hasty Wedding, 1938; (with Fred Ballard) 320 College Avenue (play), 1938; Brief Return, 1939; The Chiffon Scarf, 1939; The Hangman's Whip, 1940; Strangers in Flight, 1941; Speak No Evil, 1941; With This Ring, 1941; (with Robert Wallsten) Eight O'Clock Tuesday (play), 1941; Wolf in Man's Clothing, 1942; Deadly Is the Diamond (short stories), 1942; The Man Next Door, 1943; Unidentified Woman, 1943; Escape the Night, 1944; Wings of Fear, 1945; Five Passengers from Lisbon, 1946; The White Dress, 1946; Another Woman's House, 1947; House of Storm, 1949; Five of My Best (omnibus), 1949; Hunt with the Hounds, 1950; Never Look Back, 1951; Dead Men's Plans, 1952; The Unknown Quantity, 1953; Man Missing, 1954; Postmark Murder, 1956; Another Man's Murder, 1957; Deadly Is the Diamond and Three Other Novelettes of Murder, 1958; The Crimson Paw (short stories), 1959; Melora, 1959, in U.S. paperback, The Promise of Murder, 1961; Jury of One, 1960; The Cup, The Blade, or The Gun, 1961, in U.S. as The Crime at Honotassa, 1962; Enemy in the House, 1962; Run Scared, 1963; Call after Midnight, 1964; R.S.V.P. Murder, 1965; Witness at Large, 1966; Woman on the Roof, 1968; Message from Hong Kong, 1969; El Rancho Rio, 1970; Two Little Rich Girls, 1972; The House by the Sea, 1972; Murder in Waiting, 1973; Danger Money, 1975; Family Fortune, 1976; Nine O'-Clock Tide, 1978; The Bayou Road, 1979; Casa Madrone, 1980; Family Affair, 1981; Next of Kin, 1982; The Patient in Cabin C, 1983; Alpine Condo Cross-Fire, 1984; A Fighting Chance, 1986; Three Days for Emerald, 1988. Add: c/o Random House, 201 E. 50th St., New York,

N.Y. 10022, U.S.A.

EBERHART, Richard (Ghormley). American, b. 1904. Poetry, Plays/Screenplays. Prof. of English Emeritus, Dartmouth Coll., Hanover, N.H., since 1970 (Prof. and Poet-in-Residence, 1956–68; Class of 1925 Prof., 1968–70). Dir., Yaddo Corp., since 1964; Hon. Pres., Poetry Soc. of America, since 1972; Tutor to son of King Prajadhipik of Siam, 1930–31; English Teacher, St. Mark's Sch., Southboro, Mass., 1933–41, and Cambridge Sch., Kendal Green, Mass., 1941–42; Asst. Mgr. to Vice-Pres., Butcher Polish Co., Boston, 1946-52; Visiting Prof., Univ. of Washington, Seattle, 1952–53, 1967, 1972; Prof. of English, Univ. of Connecticut, Storrs, 1953–54; Visiting Prof., Wheaton Coll., Norton, Mass., 1954–55; Resident Fellow and Gauss Lectr., Princeton Univ., N.J., 1955–56; Consultant in Poetry, 1959–61, and Hon. Consultant in American Letters, 1963–69, Library of Congress, Washington, D.C. *Publs:* A Bravery of Earth, 1931; Reading the Spirit, 1936; Song and Idea, 1940; Poems, New and Selected, 1944; (ed. with S. Rodman) War and the Poet: An Anthology of Poetry Expressing Man's Attitude to War from Ancient Times to the Present, 1945; Burr Oaks,1947; Brotherhood of Men, 1949; An Herb Basket, 1950; The Apparition (play), 1951; Selected Poems, 1951; The Visionary Farms (play), 1952; Undercliff: Poems 1946–1953, 1953; Triptych (play), 1955; Great Praises, 1957; The Oak: A Poem, 1957; (ed.) . . . Dartmouth Poems, 12 vols., 1958–59, 1962–71; Collected Poems, 1930-1960, Including 51 New Poems, 1960; The Mad Musician, and Devils and Angels (plays), 1962; Collected Verse Plays, 1962; The Quarry: New Poems, 1964; The Bride from Mantua (play), 1964; The Vastness and Indifference of the World, 1965; Fishing for Snakes, 1965; Selected Poems 1930-1965, 1965; Thirty One Sonnets, 1967; Shifts of Being: Poems, 1968; The Achievement of Richard Eberhart: A Comprehensive Selection of His Poems, 1968; Three Poems, 1968; Fields of Grace, 1972; Collected Poems 1930-1976, 1976, 1986; Poems to Poets, 1976; Of Poetry and Poets, 1979; Ways of Light, 1980; Richard Eberhart: A Celebration (festschrift), 1980; Four Poems, 1980; Survivors, 1980; New Hampshire: Nine Poems, 1980; Chocorua, 1981; Florida Poems, 1981; The Long Reach: New Poems, 1984; Richard Eberhart Symposium, Negative Capability, 1986; Collected Poems 1930-1986, 1988; Maine Poems, 1989. Add: 5 Webster Terr., Hanover, N.H. 03755, U.S.A.

EBERSOHN, Wessel (Schalk). South African, b. 1940. Novels/Short stories, Mystery/Crime/Suspense. Freelance writer since 1979. Technician, Dept. of Posts and Telecommunications, Pretoria, 1956–62, for Gowlett Alpha, Johannesburg, 1962–69, and for the Dept. of Posts of Telecommunications, Durban, 1970–79. *Publs:* A Lonely Place to Die (mystery novel), 1979; The Centurion (mystery novel), 1979; Store Up the Anger (novel), 1981; Divide the Night (mystery novel), 1981; Klara's Visitors (novel), 1987. Add: Private Bag X001, Wittedrif 6603, South Africa.

EBERT, Alan. American, b. 1935. Novels/Short stories, Human relations. *Publs:* The Homosexuals, 1977; (with Ron Fletcher) Every Body Is Beautiful, 1978; Intimacies, 1979; Traditions (novel), 1981; The Long Way Home (novel), 1984; Marriages (novel), 1987. Add: 353 W. 56th St., New York, N.Y. 10019, U.S.A.

EBERT, James D(avid). American, b. 1921. Chemistry, Medicine/Health. Hon. Prof. of Biology, since 1956, and Dir. of Chesapeake Bay Inst., since 1987, Johns Hopkins Univ., Baltimore. Vice-Pres., National Academy of Sciences, since 1981. Assoc. Prof. of Zoology, Indiana Univ., Bloomington, 1951–55; Pres. and Dir., Marine Biological Lab., Woods Hole, Mass., 1970–78; Pres., Carnegie Instn. of Washington, 1978–87. Chmn., Assembly of Life Sciences, National Academy of Sciences, 1973–77. *Publs:* (ed. with B.L. Strehler, H.B. Glass and N.W. Shock) The Biology of Aging, 1960; (with I.M. Sussex) Interacting Systems in Development, 1965, 1970; (with A. Loewy, R.S. Miller and H.A. Schneiderman) Biology, 1973; (ed. with M. Marois) Tests of Teratogenicity in Vitro, 1976; (ed. with T.S. Okada) Mechanisms of Cell Change, 1979. Add: Chesapeake Bay Inst., Johns Hopkins Univ., 4800 Atwell Rd., Shady Side, Md. 20764, U.S.A.

EBERT, Roger (Joseph). American, b. 1942. Plays/Screenplays, Film, History. Film Critic, Chicago Sun Times, since 1967, and New York Daily News, since 1988; Lectr. on Film, Univ. of Chicago Fine Arts Prog., since 1969; Co-Host, Siskel and Ebert, syndicated TV prog., since 1986. Juror, Chicago Film Festival, since 1968; Member, Bd., of Advisors, Film Center, Art Inst. of Chicago, since 1973. Staff Writer, News-Gazette, Champaign-Urbana, Ill., 1958–66; Ed., Daily Illinois, Chicago, 1963–64; Instr. in English, Chicago City Coll., 1967–68; Pres., U.S. Student Press Assn., 1963–64; Co-Host, Sneak Previews, PBS-TV, 1977–82, and At the Movies, 1982–86. Member, Bd. of Dirs., Univ. of Illinois Alumni Assoc.,

1975–77. *Publs:* An Illinois Century, 1967; Beyond the Valley of the Dolls (screenplay), 1970; A Kiss Is Still a Kiss: Roger Ebert at the Movies, 1984; Roger Ebert's Movie Home Companion, 1989; The Perfect London Walk, 1986; Two Weeks in the Midday Sun, 1987. Add: Chicago Sun-Times, 401 North Wabash, Chicago, Ill. 60611, U.S.A.

EBON, Martin. American, b. 1917. Supernatural/Occult topics, Biography. Lectr., Div. of Social Sciences, New Sch. for Social Research, NYC, 1949–50, 1955–56, and 1967; Information Officer, U.S. Information Agency, 1950–52; Account Exec., Hill and Knowlton Inc., NYC, 1952–53; Administrative Secty., 1953–59, and Exec. Ed., Intnl. Journal of Parapsychology, 1959–65, Parapsychology Foundn. Inc., NYC; Member of Editorial Bd., Intnl. Report, 1960–67; Pres., Lombard Assocs. Inc., NYC, 1962–82; Consulting Ed., New American Library, NYC, 1966–85; Exec. Ed., Playboy Press, Chicago, 1971–72. *Publs:* World Communism Today, 1948; Malenkov: Stalin's Successor, 1953; Svetlana: The Story of Stalin's Daughter, 1967; (ed.) True Experiences in Prophecy, 1967; (ed.) True Experiences in Telepathy, 1967; Prophecy in Our Time, 1968; (ed.) Beyond Space and Time, 1968; (ed.) The Psychic Reader, 1969; (ed.) Reincarnation in the Twentieth Century, 1969; Ché: The Making of a Legend, 1969; Lin Piao: China's New Ruler, 1970; The Last Days of Luther, 1970; (ed.) Test Your ESP, 1970; They Knew the Unknown, 1971; (ed.) Witchcraft Today, 1971; (ed.) Psychic Discoveries by the Russians, 1971; The Truth about Vitamin E, 1972; Which Vitamins Do You Need?, 1974; The Essential Vitamin Counter, 1974; The Devil's Bride: Exorcism, Past and Present, 1974; (ed.) Exorcism: Fact, Not Fiction, 1974; The Psychic Scene, 1974; Five Chinese Communist Plays, 1975; Saint Nicholas: Life and Legend, 1975; (ed.) The Amazing Uri Geller, 1975; (ed.) The Riddle of the Bermuda Triangle, 1975; The Relaxation Controversy, 1976; (ed.) The Satan Trap: Dangers of the Occult, 1976; (ed.) TM: How to Find Peace of Mind Through Meditation, 1976; (ed.) Mysterious Pyramid Power, 1976; The Evidence for Life after Death, 1977; (ed.) Doomsday, 1977; (ed.) Atlantis: The New Evidence, 1977; (ed.) Demon Children, 1978; The Cloning of Man, 1978; (ed.) The Signet Book of Parapsychology, 1978; (ed.) The World's Weirdest Cults, 1979; (ed.) Miracles, 1981; The Man from the Other Shore, 1981; The Andropov File, 1983; Psychic Warfare: Threat or Illusion, 1983; The Soviet Propaganda Machine, 1987. Add: 5615 Netherland Ave., New York, N.Y. 10471, U.S.A.

ECCLES, (Sir) John (Carew). Australian, b. 1903. Medicine/Health. Distinguished Prof. of Biophysics and Physiology Emeritus, State Univ. of New York, Buffalo, since 1975 (Prof., 1968–75). Prof. of Physiology, Univ. of Otago Medical Sch., Dunedin, N.Z., 1944–51, and Australian National Univ., Canberra, 1951–66; Member, American Medical Assn./Education and Research Foundn. Inst. for Biomedical Research, Chicago, 1966–68. Pres., Australian Academy of Sciences, 1957–61. Recipient, Nobel Prize, 1963. *Publs:* (with others) Reflex Activity of the Spinal Cord, 1932; The Neurophysiological Basis of Mind: The Principles of Neurophysiology, 1953; Physiology of Nerve Cells, 1957; The Physiology of Synapses, 1964; (ed.) Brain and Conscious Experience, 1966; (with others) The Cerebellum as a Neuronal Machine, 1967; The Inhibitory Pathways of the Central Nervous System, 1969; Facing Reality: Philosophical Adventures by a Brain Scientist, 1970; The Understanding of the Brain, 1973; (co-author) The Self and the Brain, 1977; The Human Mystery, 1978; (co-author) The Molecular Neurobiology of the Mammalian Brain, 1978; The Human Psyche, 1979; (co-author) Sherrington: His Life and Work, 1979; (co-author) The Wonder of Being Human: Our Brain, Our Mind, 1984; (co-ed.) Upper Motor Neuron Functions and Dysfunctions, 1985; Evolution of the Brain: Creation of the Self, 1989. Add: Ca'a la Gra', CH-6646 Contra, Ticino, Switzerland.

ECHERUO, Michael (Joseph Chukwudalu). Nigerian, b. 1937. Poetry, Literature. Vice-Chancellor, Imo State Univ., Okigwe, since 1981. Founding Pres., Nigerian Assn. for African and Comparative Literature. Lectr., Nigerian Coll. of Arts and Technology, Enugu, 1960–61; Lectr., 1961–70, Sr. Lectr., 1970–73, and Prof., 1973–74, Univ. of Nigeria, Nsukka; Prof. of English, 1974–80, and Dean of the Postgrad. Sch., 1978–80, Univ. of Ibadan. *Publs:* Mortality: Poems, 1968; (ed.) Igbo Traditional Life, Literature, and Culture, 1972; Joyce Cary and the Novel of Africa, 1973; Distances: New Poems, 1975; Victorian Lagos, 1977; The Conditioned Imagination from Shakespeare to Conrad, 1978; Joyce Cary and the Dimensions of Order, 1979; (ed.) Shakespeare's The Tempest, 1980. Add: Office of the Vice-Chancellor, Imo State Univ., Okigwe, Nigeria.

ECHEVERRIA, Durand. American, b. 1913. Literature. Prof. of French and Comparative Literature Emeritus, Brown Univ., Providence, R.I., since 1978 (Secty. of Faculty, 1962–64; Chmn., Dept. of French, 1964–67; Prof., 1962–78). *Publs:* Mirage in the West: A History of the

French Image of American Society to 1815; (ed. and co-trans.) New Travels in the United States of America 1788, by J.P. Brissot de Warville; The Maupeou Revolution: A Study in the History of Libertarianism, France 1770-1774, 1985. Add: RR No. 1, E. Main St., Wellfleet, Mass. 02667, U.S.A.

ECKARDT, A(rthur) Roy. American, b. 1918. Philosophy, Theology/Religion. Prof. of Religion Studies Emeritus, Lehigh Univ.; Visiting Scholar, Centre for Hebrew Studies, Univ. of Oxford, 1982–88. Ed., Journal of the American Academy of Religion, 1961–69. *Publs:* Christianity and the Children of Israel, 1948; The Surge of Piety in America, 1958; Elder and Younger Brothers, 1967, 1973; (ed.) The Theologian at Work, 1968; (with Alice Eckardt) Encounter with Israel, 1970; Your People, My People, 1974; (with Alice Eckardt) Long Night's Journey into Day, 1982, 1988; Jews and Christians, 1986; For Righteousness' Sake, 1987; Black-Woman-Jew, 1989. Add: Beverly Hill Rd., Box 619A, Coopersburg, Pa. 18036, U.S.A.

ECKBLAD, Edith G. American, b. 1923. Children's fiction, Children's non-fiction. Teacher of creative writing, Gateway Technological Inst., Racine, Wisc., 1972–74, 1976–78. *Publs:* Living with Jesus, 1955; Something for Jesus, 1959; Danny's Straw Hat, 1962; Kindness Is a Lot of Things, 1965; A Smile Is to Give, 1969; Danny's Orange Christmas Camel, 1970; Soft as the Wind, 1974; Qu'Est-ce Qui Est Doux?, 1976; God Listens and Knows, 1981. Add: 5224 Spring St., Racine, Wisc. 53406, U.S.A.

ECKBO, Garrett. American, b. 1910. Architecture (Environmental Design). Landscape Architect and Environmental Planner, since 1935. Prof. VI, Coll. of Environmental Design, Dept. of Land Architecture, Univ. of California, Berkeley, since 1965, now Emeritus. Sr. Founding Principal, Eckbo Dean Austin & Williams (landscape architects), San Francisco, Honolulu, Minn., and Los Angeles, Calif., 1942–73; Member of faculty, Sch. of Architecture, Univ. of Southern California, Los Angeles, 1948–56; Partner, Eckbo-Kay Assocs., San Francisco, Calif., 1979–82. *Publs:* Landscape for Living, 1950; The Art of Home Landscaping, 1956; Urban Landscape Design, 1964; The Landscape We See, 1964; Home Landscape, 1964; Environment and Design (in Japanese), 1969; Public Landscape, 1977. Add: 1006 Cragmont Ave., Berkeley, Calif. 94708, U.S.A.

ECKELS, Jon. American. Poetry. Writer and teacher, Mills Coll., Merritt Coll., Stanford Univ., all California, 1968–1974. United Methodist Minister, 1964–1968. *Publs:* This Time Tomorrow, 1966; Home Is Where the Soul Is, 1969; Black Right On, 1969; Our Business in the Streets, 1970; Firesign—For the Free I Will Be, 1973; Pursuing the Pursuit, 1977. Add: c/o Alford, 1925 Miller, Indianapolis, Ind. 46221, U.S.A.

ECONOMOU, George. American, b. 1934. Poetry, Literature. Prof. of English, Long Island Univ., Brooklyn, N.Y. (joined faculty, 1961). Lectr., Wagner Coll., NYC, 1958–60; Ed., Chelsea Review, NYC, 1958–60, and Trobar, NYC, 1960–64. *Publs:* The Georgics, 1968; Landed Natures, 1969; Poems for Self-Therapy, 1972; The Goddess Natura in Medieval Literature, 1972; (ed.) Geoffrey Chaucer: A Collection of Criticism, 1975; Ameriki: Book One and Selected Earlier Poems, 1977; (ed.) An Anthology of Troubadour Poetry, 1986. Add: S.U.N. 347 W. 39th St., New York, N.Y. 10018, U.S.A.

EDDINS, Dwight. American, b. 1939. Poetry, Literature. Prof. of English, Univ. of Alabama, since 1976 (Instr., 1966–67; Asst. Prof. 1967–70; Assoc. Prof., 1972–76). *Publs:* Yeats: The Nineteenth Century Matrix, 1971; Of Desire, and the Circles of Hell, 1980. Add: 262 Cedar Crest, Tuscaloosa, Ala, 35401, U.S.A.

EDEL, Abraham. American, b. 1908. Philosophy. Research Prof. of Philosophy, Univ. of Pennsylvania, Philadelphia, since 1974. Prof. of Philosophy Emeritus, City Coll. since 1973 (joined faculty, 1931), and Distinguished Prof. of Philosophy Emeritus, Grad. Sch. since 1973 (Distinguished Prof., 1970–73), City Univ. of New York. *Publs:* Theory and Practice of Philosophy, 1946; Ethical Judgement: The Use of Science in Ethics, 1955; (with M. Edel) Anthropology and Ethics, 1959, as Anthropology and Ethics: The Quest for Moral Understanding, 1970; (ed. with Y.H. Krikorian) Contemporary Philosophic Problems: Selected Readings, 1959; Science and the Structure of Ethics, 1961; Method in Ethical Theory, 1963; (ed. and contrib.) Aristotle, 1967; Analyzing Concepts in Social Science, 1979; Exploring Fact and Value, 1980; Aristotle and His Philosophy, 1982; Interpreting Education, 1985; (with E. Flowen and F.W. O'Connor) Morality, Philosophy, and Practice: Historical and Contem-

porary Readings and Studies, 1989. Add: Dept. of Philosophy, 305 Logan Hall, Univ. of Pennsylvania, Philadelphia, Pa. 19104, U.S.A.

EDEL, (Joseph) Leon. American, b. 1907. Literature, Biography. Henry James Prof. of English and American Letters Emeritus, New York Univ., NYC, since 1971; Citizens Prof. of English Emeritus, Univ. of Hawaii, Honolulu, since 1978. *Publs:* James Joyce: The Last Journey, 1947; The Life of Henry James: The Untried Years, 1953, The Conquest of London, 1962, The Middle Years, 1963, The Treacherous Years, 1969, The Master, 1972; (with Brown) Willa Cather, 1953; The Psychological Novel, 1955; Literary Biography, 1957; Henry D. Thoreau, 1970; Bloomsbury: A House of Lions, 1979; Stuff of Sleep and Dreams, 1982; Henry James in Westminster Abbey, 1976; Writing Lives: Principia Biographica, 1984; Henry James, A Life, 1985; ed.—The Complete Plays of Henry James, 1949; Selected Letters of Henry James, 1956; The Complete Tales of Henry James, 1962–65; The Diary of Alice James, 1964; Literary History and Literary Criticism, 1965; The American Scene, 1968; Henry James: Stories of the Supernatural, 1970; Henry James Letters, 4 vols., 1974–84; The Bodley Head Henry James, 11 vols., 1980. Add: c/o William Morris Agency, 1350 Sixth Ave., New York, N.Y. 10019, U.S.A.

EDELMAN, Murray J. American, b. 1919. Politics/Government. Prof. of Political Science, Univ. of Wisconsin, Madison, since 1966. Instr., 1948–49, Asst. Prof., 1949–53, Assoc. Prof. 1953–58, and Prof. 1958–66, Dept. of Political Science, Univ. of Illinois, Urbana. *Publs:* The Licensing of Radio Services in the United States, 1927-1947, 1950; Channels of Employment, 1952; National Economic Planning by Collective Bargaining, 1954; The Symbolic Uses of Politics, 1964; (with R.W. Fleming) The Politics of Wage-Price Decisions, 1965; Politics as Symbolic Action, 1971; (with Kenneth Dolbeare) American Politics: Public Policy, Conflict, and Change, 1971, 5th ed. 1985; Political Language, 1977; Constructing the Political Spectacle, 1987. Add: 1824 Vilas Ave., Madison, Wisc. 53711, U.S.A.

EDEY, Maitland A(rmstrong). American, b. 1910. Biology, Natural history, Zoology, Photography. Freelance writer, Time-Life Books, NYC, since 1970. Dir. of Conservation Foundation, Washington, D.C., since 1969. Mayor, Inc. Village of Upper Brookville, N.Y., 1958–62. *Publs:* American Songbirds, 1940; American Waterbirds, 1941; (with F. Clark Howell) Early Man, 1965; The Cats of Africa, 1968; The Northeast Coast, 1972; The Missing Link, 1973; The Sea Traders, 1974; The Lost World of the Aegean, 1975; Great Photographic Essays, 1978; (with Donald C. Johanson) Lucy: The Beginnings of Humankind, 1981. Add: Seven Gates Farm, Vineyard Haven, Mass. 02568, U.S.A.

EDGAR, David. British, b. 1948. Plays/Screenplays. Sr. Research Fellow, Univ. of Birmingham, since 1988. Lectr. Reporter, Telegraph and Argus, Bradford, Yorkshire, 1969–72; Creative Writing Fellow, Leeds Univ., 1972–74; Resident Playwright, Birmingham Repertory Theatre, 1974–75; Playwriting Tutor, Univ. of Birmingham, 1975–78. *Publs:* Dick Deterred, 1974; Destiny, 1976; The Jail Diary of Albie Sachs, 1978; Ball Boys, 1978; Mary Barnes, 1979; (with Susan Todd) Teendreams, 1979; Nicholas Nickleby, 1982; Maydays, 1983; Entertaining Strangers, 1985; That Summer, 1987; The Second Time as Farce, 1988. Add: c/o Michael Imison, 28 Almeida St., London N1 1TD, England.

EDGAR, Josephine. *See* **HOWARD,** Mary.

EDGERTON, Harold E(ugene). American, b. 1903. Photography. Inst. Prof. Emeritus, Massachusetts Inst. of Technology, Cambridge, Mass. (joined faculty, 1927). *Publs:* (with J.R. Killian) Flash, 1939, 1954; Electronic Flash Strobe, 1970, 3rd ed. 1987; (with J.R. Killian) Moments of Vision, 1979; Sonar Images, 1986; Stopping Time, 1987. Add: 100 Memorial Dr., Apt. 11-7a, Cambridge, Mass. 02142, U.S.A.

EDGINGTON, Eugene Sinclair. American, b. 1924. Statistics, Psychology. Prof. of Psychology, Univ. of Calgary, Alta., since 1968 (Assoc. Prof., 1963–68). Asst. Prof. of Psychology, Oregon State Univ., Corvallis, 1957–59; Asst. and Assoc. Prof. of Psychology, Kansas State Teachers Coll., Emporia, 1959–63. *Publs:* Statistical Inference: The Distribution-Free Approach, 1969; Randomization Tests, 1980, 1987. Add: Dept. of Psychology, Univ. of Calgary, Calgary, Alta. T2N 1N4, Canada.

EDMOND, Lauris (Dorothy). New Zealander, b. 1924. Poetry. Off-Campus Tutor and Lectr., Massey Univ., Palmerston North, since 1980. Teacher, Huntly Coll., 1968–69, and Heretaunga Coll., Wellington, 1971–72; Ed., New Zealand Post-Primary Teachers Journal, 1973–80. Writer-in-Residence, Deakin Univ., Melbourne, 1985, and at Victoria Univ. of

Wellington, New Zealand, 1987. *Publs:* (ed.) Dancing to My Tune: Verse and Prose, by Denis Glover, 1974; In Middle Air (verse), 1975; The Pear Tree and Other Poems, 1977; (ed.) Young Writing, 1979; (ed.) A Remedial Persiflage, by Chris Ward, 1980; Salt from the North (verse), 1980; Seven (verse), 1980; (ed.) The Letters of A.R.D. Fairburn, 1981; Wellington Letter (verse), 1983; Selected Poems, 1984; High Country Weather (novel), 1984; (ed.) Women in Wartime, 1986; Seasons and Creatures (verse), 1986; Summer Near the Arctic Circle (poetry), 1988; Hot October (autobiography), 1989. Add: 22 Grass St., Oriental Bay, Wellington, New Zealand.

EDMONDS, Charles. *See* **CARRINGTON,** Charles Edmund.

EDMONDS, Walter D(umaux). American, b. 1903. Novels/Short stories, Children's fiction, History. *Publs:* Rome Haul, 1929; The Big Barn, 1930; Erie Water, 1933; Mostly Canallers (short stories), 1934; Drums Along the Mohawk, 1936; Chad Hanna, 1940; The Matchlock Gun, 1941; Tom Whipple, 1942; Young Ames, 1942; Two Logs Crossing, 1943; Wilderness Clearing, 1945; In the Hands of the Senecas, 1947; The Wedding Journey, 1947; The First Hundred Years, 1948; Cadmus Henry, 1949; Mr. Benedict's Lion, 1950; The Boyds of Black River, 1953; Hound Dog Moses and the Promised Land, 1954; Uncle Ben's Whale, 1955; They Had a Horse, 1962; The Musket and the Cross, 1968; Time to Go House, 1969; Seven American Stories, 1970; Wolf Hunt, 1970; Beaver Valley, 1971; The Story of Richard Storm, 1974; Bert Breen's Barn, 1975; The Night Raider and Other Stories, 1980; The South African Quirt, 1985. Add: 27 River St., Concord, Mass. 01742, U.S.A.

EDMONDSON, G.C. (José Mario Garry Ordonez Edmondson y Cotton). Also writes western, crime, and gothic novels as Kelly P. Gast; also writes as J.B. Masterson and Jake Logan. Mystery/Crime/Suspense, Historical/Romance/Gothic, Westerns/Adventure, Science fiction/Fantasy. American, b. 1922. *Publs:* Stranger Than You Think (short stories), 1965; The Ship That Sailed the Time Stream, 1965; Chapayeca, 1971, as Blue Face, 1972; T.H.E.M., 1974; The Aluminum Man, 1975; (as Kelly P. Gast) Dil Dies Hard, 1975; (as Kelly P. Gast) The Long Trail North, 1976; (as Kelly P. Gast) Murphy's Trail, 1976; (as Kelly P. Gast) Last Stage from Opal, 1978; (as Kelly P. Gast) Murder at Magpie Flats, 1978; (as Kelly P. Gast) Paddy, 1979; (as J.B. Masteron) Rudge, 1979; (as Jake Logan) Slocum's Slaughter, 1980; (with C.M. Kotlan) The Takeover, 1984; (with C.M. Kotlan) The Black Magician, 1986. Add: 12328 Rockcrest, Lakeside, Calif. 92040, U.S.A.

EDMONSON, Munro S. American, b. 1924. Anthropology/Ethnology. Prof. of Anthropology, Tulane Univ., New Orleans, since 1951. Assoc., Middle America Research Inst., since 1952. *Publs:* Los Manitos, 1957; Status Terminology, 1958; (ed. with John H. Rohrer) The Eighth Generation, 1959; Quiche-English Dictionary, 1965; Lore (folklore), 1971; (trans.) The Book of Counsel (Mayan mythology), 1971; (ed.) Meaning in Mayan Languages, 1973; (ed.) Sixteenth-Century Mexico, 1974; (trans.) The Ancient Future of the Itza, 1982; Heaven Born Merida and Its Destiny, 1986; The Book of the Year, 1988. Add: 901 Cherokee St., New Orleans, La. 70118, U.S.A.

EDSON, J(ohn) T(homas). British, b. 1928. Westerns/Adventure. *Publs:* Floating Outfit series—Trail Boss, 1961; The Ysabel Kid, 1962; Quiet Town, 1962; Rio Guns, 1962; The Texan, 1962; Waco's Debt, 1962; The Hard Riders, 1962; The Half Breed, 1963; Gun Wizard, 1963; The Rio Hondo Kid, 1963; Gunsmoke Thunder, 1963; Wagons to Backsight, 1964; Trigger Fast, 1964; The Rushers, 1964; The Rio Hondo War, 1964; Troubled Range, 1965; The Wildcats, 1965; The Trouble Busters, 1965; The Peacemakers, 1965; The Fortune Hunters, 1965; The Man from Texas, 1965; A Town Called Yellowdog,1966; The Law of the Gun, 1966; Return to Backsight, 1966; Guns in the Night, 1966; Sidewinder, 1967; The Fast Gun, 1967; The Floating Outfit, 1967; Terror Valley, 1967; The Hooded Raiders, 1968; Rangeland Hercules, 1968; McGraw's Inheritance, 1968; The Bad Bunch, 1968; The Making of a Lawman, 1968; Goodnight's Dream, 1969; From Hide and Horn, 1969; Cuchilo, 1969; The Small Texan, 1969; The Town Tamers, 1969; A Horse Called Mogollon, 1971; Hell in the Palo Duro, 1971; Go Back to Hell, 1972; The South Will Rise Again, 1972; .44 Calibre Man, 1973; Set Texas Back on Her Feet (in U.S. as Viridian's Trail), 1973; The Hide and Tallow Men, 1974; The Quest for Bowie's Blade, 1974; Beguinage, 1978; Beguinage Is Dead!, 1978; Viridian's Trail, 1978; The Gentle Giant, 1979; Master of Triggernometry, 1981; White Indian, 1981; Old Moccasins on the Trail, 1981; Diamonds, Emeralds, Cards and Colts, 1986; No Finger on the Trigger, 1987; Waco series—Sagebrush Sleuth, 1962; Arizona Ranger, 1962; The Drifter, 1963; Waco Rides In, 1964; Hound Dog Man, 1967; Doc Leroy, M.D., 1977; Waco's Badge, 1981; Civil War series—The Fastest Gun in

Texas, 1963; The Devil Gun, 1966; The Colt and the Sabre, 1966; Comanche, 1967; The Rebel Spy, 1968; The Bloody Border, 1969; Back to the Bloody Border, (in U.S. as Renegade), 1970; Kill Dusty Fog!, 1970; Under the Stars and Bars, 1970; You're in Command Now, Mr. Fog, 1973; The Big Gun, 1973; A Matter of Honour, 1981; Decision for Dusty Fog, 1986; Calamity Jane series—The Bull Whip Breed, 1965; Trouble Trail, 1965; The Cow Thieves, 1965; The Big Hunt, 1967; Calamity Spells Trouble, 1968; Cold Deck, Hot Lead, 1969; White Stallion, Red Mare, 1970; The Remittance Kid, 1978; The Whip and the War Lance, 1979; Rockaby County series—The Professional Killers, 1968; The 1/4 Second Draw, 1969; The Deputies, 1969; Point of Contact, 1970; The Owlhoot, 1970; Run for the Border, 1971; Bad Hombre, 1971; The Sixteen Dollar Shooter, 1974; The Sheriff of Rockabye County, 1981; The Lawmen of Rockabye County, 1982; Old Devil Hardin series—Young Ole Devil, 1975; Get Urrea, 1975; Old Devil and the Caplocks, 1976; Old Devil and the Mule Train, 1976; Old Devil at San Jacinto, 1977; Old Devil's Hands and Feet, 1982; Cap Fog series—Cap Fog, Meet Mr. J.G. Reeder, 1977; You're a Texas Ranger, Alvin Fog, 1979; Rapido Clint, 1980; The Justice of Company "Z", 1981; The Return of Rapido Clint and Mr J.G. Reeder, 1984; Decision for Dusty Fog, 1987; Bunduki series—Bunduki and Dawn, 1975; Sacrifice for the Quagga God, 1975; Bunduki, 1975; Fearless Master of the Jungle, 1978; miscellaneous titles—Slaughter's Way, 1965; Slip Gun, 1971; Two Miles to the Border, 1972; Blonde Genius, 1973; J.T.'s Hundredth, 1979; J.T.'s Ladies, 1980; The Hide and Horn Saloon, 1983; Cut One, They All Bleed, 1983; Wanted! Belle Starr, 1983; Buffalo Are Coming, 1984; Is-A-Man, 1985; More J.T.'s Ladies, 1987. Add: P.O. Box 13, Melton Mowbray, Leics. LE13 0HY, England.

EDSON, Russell. American, b. 1935. Novels, Plays, Poetry. *Publs:* Appearances: Fable and Drawings, 1961; A Stone Is Nobody's: Fables and Drawings, 1961; The Boundry, 1964; The Very Thing That Happens: Fables and Drawings, 1964; The Brain Kitchen: Writings and Woodcuts, 1965; What a Man Can See, 1969 The Childhood of an Equestrian, 1973; The Clam Theater, 1973; The Falling Sickness (plays), 1975; The Intuitive Journey, 1976; The Reason Why the Closet-Man Is Never Sad, 1977; With Sincerest Regrets, 1980; Wuck Wuck Wuck!, 1984; Gulping's Recital, 1984; The Wounded Breakfast, 1985. Add: 149 Weed Ave., Stamford, Conn. 06902, U.S.A.

EDWARDS, Allen Jack. American, b. 1926. Psychology. Prof. of Psychology, Southwest Missouri State Univ., Springfield, since 1973. Asst. Prof., 1958–62, and Assoc. Prof. of Education, 1962–63, Univ. of Kansas, Lawrence; Assoc. Prof., Southern Illinois Univ., Carbondale, 1963–65; Assoc. Prof. and subsequently Prof. of Education, Univ. of Missouri-Columbia, 1965–72. *Publs:* (co-author) Educational Psychology: The Teaching-Learning Process, 1968; Individual Mental Testing: part I: History and Theories, 1971, part II: Measurement, 1972; (ed. and contrib.) Selected Writings of David Wechser, 1974. Add: 3325 S. Delaware, Springfield, Mo. 65804, U.S.A.

EDWARDS, Anne. American, b. 1927. Novels/Short stories, Historical/Gothic, Children's non-fiction, Autobiography/Memoirs/Personal, Biography. Member of Council, 1978–81, and Pres., 1981–85, The Authors Guild. *Publs:* (adaptor) A Child's Bible, 1967; The Survivors, 1968; Miklos Alexandrovitch Is Missing (in U.K. as Alexandrovitch Is Missing), 1969; Shadow of a Lion, 1971; Haunted Summer, 1972; The Hesitant Heart, 1974; Judy Garland: A Biography, 1974; (with Stephen Citron) The Inn and Us (reminiscences), 1975; Child of Night (in U.K. as Ravenwings), 1975; P.T. Barnum (juvenile), 1976; The Great Houdini (juvenile), 1977; Vivien Leigh: A Biography, 1977; Sonya: The Life of the Countess Tolstoy, 1981; The Road to Tara: The Life of Margaret Mitchell, 1983; Matriarch: Queen Mary and the House of Windsor, 1984; Road to Tara: The Life of Margaret Mitchell, 1985; A Remarkable Woman: Katherine Hepburn, 1986; Early Reagan, 1987; Shirley Temple: American Princess, 1988; The DeMilles: An American Family, 1989. Add: c/o International Creative Mgmt. Inc., 40 W. 57th St., New York, N.Y. 10019, U.S.A.

EDWARDS, Betty. American, b. 1926. Art. Prof. in Art, California State Univ., Long Beach. *Publs:* Drawing on the Right Side of the Brain, 1979; (with E. Coleman) Brief Encounters, 1980; Drawing on the Artist Within, 1986. Add: Art Dept., Calif. State Univ., Long Beach, Calif. 90840, U.S.A.

EDWARDS, Donald. British, b. 1904. Autobiography/Memoirs/Personal. Ed., News and Current Affairs, BBC, 1958–67; Managing Dir., Independent Television News, London, 1968–71. *Publs:* Two Worlds of Donald Edwards, 1970. Add: Spindles, Miles Lane, Cobham, Surrey, England.

EDWARDS, Harvey. American, b. 1929. Children's non-fiction, Sports/Physical education/Keeping fit, Travel/Exploration/Adventure, Translations. Owner, Edwards Films, Eagle Bridge, N.Y.; freelance writer, journalist and filmmaker, former European Ed., Skiing mag., NYC, and Corresp. for Ski mag., NYC, and Mountain Gazette, Denver, Colo.; Asst. to Dir., Jewish Braille Inst., NYC, 1956–58. *Publs:* Scandinavia: The Challenge of Welfare, 1968; Lars Olav: A Norwegian Boy, 1969; Leise: A Danish Girl from Dragoer, 1970; France and the French, 1972; Skiing to Win, 1973; 100 Hikes in the Alps, 1979; documentary films: Ten Days Around Mont Blanc, 1974; The Great Traverse, 1975; High Route Adventure, 1975; Personnalite Rossignol, 1976; If You Can Walk, 1976; Free and Easy, 1977; Race Day, 1978; Skiing Across the French Alps, 1978; Powder Hound, 1979; The Return of Powder Hound, 1980; Marathon Fever, 1981; Marathon Symphony, 1982; Winners/Losers, 1982; Bicycle Racing U.S.A., 1983; Life Among the BMXers, 1984; Bicycle Dancin', 1985; Skating and Striding: Cross Country Skiing in America, 1986; Why We Love Cross Country Skiing, 1986; Last Ride, 1987; Living Poetry, 1988. Add: R.D.1, Eagle Bridge, N.Y. 12057, U.S.A.

EDWARDS, Iorwerth (Eiddon Stephen). British, b. 1909. Archaeology/Antiquities, History. Co-Ed., Cambridge Ancient History, since 1970. Keeper of Egyptian Antiquities, British Museum, London 1955–74, now retired. *Publs:* Hieroglyphic Texts in the British Museum, Part VIII, 1939; The Pyramids of Egypt, 1947, 3rd ed. 1985; Hieratic Papyri in the British Museum (4th series), 1960; The Treasures of Tutankhamun, 1972; Tutankhamun's Jewelry, 1976; Tutankhamun: His Tomb and its Treasures, 1976. Add: Dragon House, The Bull Ring, Deddington, Oxon, OX5 4TT, England.

EDWARDS, Joseph Castro. American, b. 1909. Medicine/Health. Retired from private practice of internal medicine, cardiologist. Asst. prof. of Clinical Medicine, Washington Univ., St. Louis, Mo., 1968–70. *Publs:* Management of Hypertensive Disease, 1960. Add: 610 W. Polo Dr., St. Louis, Mo. 63105, U.S.A.

EDWARDS, June. *See* **BHATIA,** Jamunadevi.

EDWARDS, Michael. British, b. 1938. Poetry, Literature. Prof. of English, Univ. of Warwick. Formerly, Reader, Dept. of Literature, Univ. of Essex, Colchester. Co-Ed., Prospice Review, 1973–82. *Publs:* La Thébaide de Racine, 1965; Common-place (verse), 1971; La Tragédie racinienne (criticism), 1972; To Kindle the Starling (verse), 1972; Where (verse), 1975; (ed.) French Poetry Now, 1975; Eliot/Language, 1975; (co-ed.) Directions in Italian Poetry, 1975; The Ballad of Mobb Conroy (verse), 1977; (ed.) Raymond Queneau, 1978; (ed.) Words/Music, 1979; (ed.) Languages, 1981; Towards a Christian Poetics, 1984; The Magic, Unquiet Body (verse), 1985; Poetry and Possibility, 1988. Add: 4 Northumberland Rd., Leamington Spa CV32 6HA, England.

EDWARDS, Monica. British, b. 1912. Children's fiction. *Publs:* No Mistaking Corker, 1947; Wish for a Pony, 1947; The White Riders, 1950; Black Hunting Whip, 1950; Cargo of Horses, 1951; Hidden in a Dream, 1952; Spirit of Punchbowl Farm, 1952; Storm Ahead, 1953; The Wanderer, 1953; Joan Goes Farming, 1954; No Entry, 1954; Punchbowl Harvest, 1954; The Unsought Farm, 1954; Rennie Goes Riding, 1956; Punchbowl Midnight, 1956; The Nightbird, 1956; Frenchman's Secret, 1956; Strangers to the Marsh, 1957; Operation Seabird, 1957; The Cownappers, 1958; Killer Dog, 1959; No Going Back, 1960; The Outsider, 1961; The Hoodwinkers, 1962; Dolphin Summer, 1963; The Badgers of Punchbowl Farm, 1966; Fire in the Punchbowl, 1965; Under the Rose, 1968; A Wind Is Blowing, 1969; The Valley and the Farm, 1971; Badger Valley, 1976. Add: Cowdray Cross, Thursley, Godalming, Surrey, England.

EDWARDS, Norman. *See* **WHITE,** Ted.

EDWARDS, Page, Jr. American, b. 1941. Novels/Short stories. Dir., St. Augustine Historical Soc., Florida, since 1984. Formerly, Reference Librarian, Haverhill Public Library, Massachusetts. *Publs:* The Mules that Angels Ride, 1972; Touring, 1974; Staking Claims, 1980; Peggy Salte, 1983; Scarface Joe, 1985; The Lake, 1986. Add: c/o Marion Boyars, 26 East 33rd St., New York, N.Y. 10016, U.S.A.

EDWARDS, Philip (Walter). British, b. 1923. Literature. King Alfred Prof. of English Literature, Univ. of Liverpool, since 1974. Prof. of English Literature, Trinity Coll., Dublin, 1960–66; Prof. of Literature, Univ. of Essex, 1966–74. *Publs:* Sir Walter Raleigh, 1953; (ed.) Thomas Kyd: The Spanish Tragedy, 1959; Thomas Kyd and Early Elizabethan Tragedy, 1966; Shakespeare and the Confines of Art, 1968; Person and

Office in Shakespeare's Plays, 1970; (with C.A Gibson) Plays and Poems of Philip Massinger, 1976; (ed.) Shakespeare, Pericles Prince of Tyre, 1976; Threshold of a Nation, 1979; (ed.) Shakespeare, Hamlet, 1985; Shakespeare: A Writer's Progress, 1986; Last Voyages, 1988. Add: Dept. of English Literature, Univ. of Liverpool, P.O. Box 147, Liverpool, England.

EDWARDS, Ronald George. Australian, b. 1930. Cultural/Ethnic topics, Music. *Publs:* Overlander Songbook, 1956; Index to Australian Folksong, 1970; Australian Folk Songs, 1972; Australian Bawdy Ballads, 1974; Australian Traditional Bush Crafts, 1975; The Big Book of Australian Folk Songs, 1976; Australian Yarns, 1977; Skills of the Australian Bushman, 1979; The Stock Saddle, 1980; Yarns and Ballads of the Australian Bush, 1981; (with Lin Wei-Nao) Mud Brick and Earth Building the Chinese Way, 1984; Bush Leatherwork, 1984; The Convict Maid, 1987; Wild Master and the Bongo Multiwagon, 1987; Index of Australian Folksong 1788-1988, 1988; Bushcraft 3, 1988; A Handful of Oranges, 1988. Add: Box 274, Kuranda, Qld. 4872, Australia.

EDWARDS, Thomas R(obert). American, b. 1928. Literature. Prof. of English, Rutgers Univ., New Brunswick, N.J., since 1966 (Assoc. prof., 1964–66); Exec. Ed., Raritan: A Quarterly Review, since 1981. *Publs:* This Dark Estate: A Reading of Pope, 1963; Imagination and Power, 1971. Add: c/o Raritan Review, 165 College Ave., New Brunswick, N.J. 08903, U.S.A.

EFFINGER, George Alec. American, b. 1947. Novels/Short stories, Science fiction/Fantasy. Teacher of Science Fiction Course, Tulane Univ., New Orleans, 1973–74, and Univ. of New Orleans, since 1987. *Publs:* What Entropy Means to Me, 1972; Relatives, 1973; Mixed Feelings (short stories), 1974; (with G. Dozois) Nightmare Blue, 1975; Irrational Numbers (short stories), 1976; Those Gentle Voices, 1976; Felicia, 1976; Death in Florence, 1978, as Utopia Three, 1980; Dirty Tricks (short stories), 1978; Heroics, 1979; The Wolves of Memory, 1981; Idle Pleasures (short stories), 1983; The Nick of Time, 1985; The Bird of Time, 1986; When Gravity Fails, 1987; Shadow Money, 1988; A Fire in the Sun, 1989. Add: Box 15183, New Orleans, La. 70175, U.S.A.

EGAN, Ferol. American, b. 1923. Novels/Short stories, History, Biography. *Publs:* (ed.) Incidents of Travel in New Mexico, 1969; The El Dorado Trail, 1970; (ed.) A Sailor's Sketch of the Sacramento Valley in 1842, 1971; (ed.) California, Land of Gold, or, Stay At Home and Work Hard, 1971; (ed.) A Dangerous Journey, 1972; Sand in a Whirlwind: The Paiute War of 1860, 1972; (ed.) Overland Journey to Carson Valley and California, 1973; (ed.) Across the Rockies with Fremont, 1975; Fremont: Explorer for a Restless Nation, 1977; The Taste of Time, 1977. Add: 1199 Grizzly Peak Blvd., Berkeley, Calif. 94708, U.S.A.

EGBUNA, Obi (Benedict). Nigerian, b. 1938. Novels/Short stories, Plays/Screenplays, Race relations. *Publs:* Wind Versus Polygamy: Where "Wind" Is the "Wind of Change" and "Polygamy" Is the "Change of Eves" (novel), 1964, as Elina, 1978; The Anthill, 1965; The Murder of Nigeria: An Indictment, 1968; Daughters of the Sun and Other Stories, 1970; Destroy This Temple: The Voice of Black Power in Britain, 1971; Emperor of the Sea and Other Stories, 1973; Menace of the Hedgehog, 1973; The ABC of Black Power Thought, 1973; Emperor of the Sea and Other Stories, 1974; The Minister's Daughter (short story), 1975; Diary of a Homeless Prodigal (short story), 1976; Black Candle for Christmas (short story), 1980; The Rape of Lysistrata (novel), 1980; The Madness of Didi (novel), 1980. Add: c/o Fontana, William Collins, 8 Grafton St., London W1X 3LA, England.

EGLER, Frank E(dwin). American, b. 1911. Environmental science/Ecology. Dir. in Charge, Aton Forest, Norfolk, Conn., since 1943. Consulting Vegetationist, since 1949 (Technical Adviser, R/W Maintenance Corp., Buffalo, N.Y., 1949–54; Research Assoc., Dept. of Conservation, American Museum of Natural History, New York, 1951–55). Chmn., Rightofway Resources of America, 1963–66; Consultant, Electric Power Research Inst., 1982–86. *Publs:* The Way of Science, 1971; The Plight of the Right-of-Way Domain, 2 vols., 1975; The Nature of Vegetation: Its Management and Mismanagement, 1977. Add: Aton Forest, Norfolk, Conn. 06058, U.S.A.

EGLETON, Clive. Also writes as Patrick Blake and John Tarrant. British, b. 1927. Mystery/Crime/Suspense. Served in the British Army, rising to the rank of Lt. Col., 1945–75. *Publs:* A Piece of Resistance, 1970; Last Post for a Partisan, 1971; The Judas Mandate, 1972; Seven Days to a Killing, 1973 (in U.S. paperback, The Black Windmill, 1974); The October Plot (in U.S. as The Bormann Brief), 1974; Skirmish, 1975;

State Visit, 1976; (as John Tarrant) The Rommel Plot, 1977; The Mills Bomb, 1978; (as John Tarrant) The Clauber Trigger, 1978; Backfire, 1979; (as Patrick Blake) Escape to Athena, 1979; The Winter Touch (in U.S. as The Eisenhower Deception),1981; A Falcon for the Hawk, 1982; (as John Tarrant) China Gold, 1982; (as Patrick Blake) Double Griffin, 1982; The Russian Enigma, 1982; A Conflict of Interests, 1983; Troika, 1984; A Different Drummer, 1985; Picture of the Year, 1987; Gone Missing, 1988. Add: Dolphin House, Beach House Rd., Bembridge, Isle of Wight PO35 5TA, England.

EHLE, John. American, b. 1925. Novels, Biography. Member of the faculty, Univ. of North Carolina, Chapel Hill, 1951–64. Member, Exec. Cttee., National Book Cttee., 1972–75. *Publs:* Move Over Mountain, 1957; The Survivor, 1958; Kingstree Island, 1959; Shepherd of the Streets, 1960; Lion on the Hearth, 1961; The Land Breakers, 1964; The Free Men, 1965; The Road, 1967; Time of Drums, 1970; The Journey of August King, 1971; The Cheeses and Wines of England and France with Notes on Irish Whiskey, 1972; The Changing of the Guard, 1975; The Winter People, 1982; Last One Home, 1984; Trail of Tears: The Rise and Fall of the Cherokee Nation, 1988; The Widow's Trial, 1989. Add: 125 Westview Drive NW, Winston-Salem, N.C. 27104, U.S.A.

EHLERS, Henry James. American, b. 1907. Education, Philosophy. Prof. of Philosophy Emeritus, Univ. of Minnesota, Duluth, since 1975 (joined faculty, 1947; Prof. of Philosophy, 1955–75). Music Teacher, Conroy Jr. High Sch., Pittsburgh, Pa., 1936–41; Prof., and Head of Dept. of Music, State Teacher Coll., Plattsburg, 1941–44; Head of Music Dept., Eastern Oregon Coll., La Grande, 1944–47. *Publs:* (ed.) Crucial Issues in Education, 1955, 7th ed., 1981; Logic by Way of Set Theory, 1968; Logic: Modern and Traditional, 1976. Add: 1809 Woodland Ave., Duluth, Minn. 55803, U.S.A.

EHRET, Christopher. American, b. 1941. History, Language/Linguistics. Assoc. Prof., then Prof., Univ. of California, Los Angeles, since 1968. *Publs:* Southern Nilotic History: Linguistic Approaches to the Study of the Past, 1971; Ethiopians and East Africans: The Problem of Contacts, 1974; The Historical Reconstruction of Southern Cushitic Phonology and Vocabulary, 1980; (with Merrick Posnarisky) The Archaeological and Linguistic Reconstruction of African History, 1982. Add: Dept. of History, Univ. of California, 405 Hilgard Ave., Los Angeles, Calif. 90024, U.S.A.

EHRLICH, Bettina. *See* **BETTINA.**

EHRLICH, Eugene. American, b. 1922. Language/Linguistics, Writing/Journalism. Assoc., Dept. of English, Columbia Univ., NYC, since 1948. *Publs:* How to Study Better, 1960, 1976; (with D. Murphy) The Art of Technical Writing, 1962; (with D. Murphy) Researching and Writing Term Papers and Reports, 1964; (with D. Murphy and D. Pace) College Developmental Reading, 1966; (with D. Murphy) Basic Grammar for Writing, 1970; (with D. Murphy) Concise Index to English, 1974; Basic Vocabulary Builder, 1975; English Grammar, 976; Punctuation, Capitalization, and Spelling, 1977; (with others) Oxford American Dictionary, 1980; (with Gorton Carruth) The Oxford Illustrated Literary Guide to the United States, 1982; Speak for Success, 1984; Amo, Amas, Amat, & More, 1985; The Bantam Concise Handbook of English, 1986. Add: 15 Park Rd., Scarsdale, N.Y., U.S.A.

EHRLICH, Jack. (John Gunther Ehrlich). American, b. 1930. Mystery/Crime/Suspense, Westerns/Adventure. Lawyer: now Sr. Asst. District Attorney, Suffolk County, N.Y. Reporter, Newsday, NYC, 1955–60. *Publs:* Revenge, 1958; Court-Material, 1959; Parole, 1960; Slow Burn, 1961; Cry, Baby, 1962; The Girl Cage, 1967; The Drowning, 1970; The Fastest Gun in the Pulpit, 1972; Bloody Vengeance, 1973; The Laramie River Crossing, 1973; The Chatham Killing, 1976; Rebellion at Cripple Creek, 1979. Add: 15 Deer Park Ave., Babylon, N.Y. 11702, U.S.A.

EHRLICH, Paul. American, b. 1932. Biology, Environmental science/Ecology. Bing Prof. of Population Studies, Stanford Univ., Calif., since 1976 (Asst. Prof. and Assoc. Prof., 1959–66; Prof., 1966–76). Consulting Ed. in Population in Biology, McGraw-Hill Book Co., NYC, since 1966 (Advisor in the Biological Sciences, 1966–75). Hon. Pres., Zero Population Growth, since 1970 (Pres., 1969–70); Member, National Acad. of Sciences; Fellow, American Acad. of Arts and Sciences. *Publs:* How to Know the Butterflies, 1961; Process of Evolution, 1963, 1974; Principles of Modern Biology, 1968; Population Bomb, 1968; Population, Resources, Environment: Issues in Human Ecology, 1970; How to Be a Survivor, 1971; The Bomb, 1977; Ecoscience: Population, Resources, En-

vironment, 1977; Golden Door: International Migration, Mexico and the United States, 1980; Extinction, 1981; (with others) The Cold and the Dark: The World After Nuclear War, 1984; The Machinery of Nature, 1986; Earth, 1987; The Science of Ecology, 1987; The Birder's Handbook, 1988; New World, New Mind, 1989. Add: Dept. of Biological Sciences, Stanford Univ., Stanford, Calif. 94305, U.S.A.

EHRLICHMAN, John. American, b. 1925. Novels, Politics, Memoirs. Attorney, 1952–74; Counsel to the President of the U.S., 1969; Asst. to the President for Domestic Affairs, 1969–73. *Publs:* The Company (novel) 1976, as Washington Behind Closed Doors, 1978; (contributor) The American Electoral Process, 1977; The Whole Truth (novel), 1979; Witness to Power: The Nixon Years (memoir), 1983; The China Card (novel), 1986; Sketches and Notes: Washington 1969-1973 (ink drawings and text), 1987. Add: P.O. Box 5559, Santa Fe, N.M. 87502, U.S.A.

EHRMAN, John (Patrick William). British, b. 1920. History, Biography. Chmn., Royal Commn. on Historical Manuscripts, since 1973; Member, Panizzi Foundn. Selection Council, since 1983. Fellow, Trinity Coll., Cambridge, 1947–52; Historian, Cabinet Office, 1948–56; Lees Knowles Lectr., Cambridge Univ., 1957–58; Vice Pres., Navy Records Soc., 1968–70 and 1974–76; Member, Reviewing Cttee. on Export of Works of Art, 1970–76; Trustee, National Portrait Gallery, London, 1971–85; Chmn., Advisory Cttee., British Library Reference Div., 1975–84; James Ford Special Lectr., Oxford Univ., 1976–77. *Publs:* The Navy in the War of William III, 1689-1697, 1953; Grand Strategy, 1943-1944, 1956; Grand Strategy, 1944-45, 1956; Cabinet Government and War, 1890-1940, 1958; The British Government and Commercial Negotiations with Europe, 1783-1793, 1962; The Younger Pitt, The Years of Acclaim, 1969; The Reluctant Transition, 1983. Add: The Mead Barns, Taynton, Burford, Oxon, England.

EICHNER, Hans. Canadian, b. 1921. Literature. Prof. since 1967, and Chmn. since 1973, Dept. of German, Univ. of Toronto, Ont. Gen. Ed., Canadian Studies in German Language and Literature, since 1970. Asst. Lectr., Bedford Coll., Univ. of London, 1948–50; Asst. Prof., 1950–56, Assoc. Prof., 1956–62, and Prof, and Head of Dept. of German, 1962–67, Queen's Univ., Kingston, Ont. *Publs:* Thomas Mann: Eine Einfuhrung in sein Werk, 1953, 1961; Friedrich Schlegal: Literary Notebooks 1797-1801, 1957; (with H. Hein) Reading German for Scientists, 1959; ed. Kritische Friedrich Schlegel-Ausgabe, vols. II-VI, 1959–74, vol. XVI, 1981; Four Modern German Authors: Mann, Rilke, Kafka, Brecht, 1964; Friedrich Schlegel, 1970; (ed. with Lisa Kahn) Studies in German in Memory of Robert L. Kahn, 1971; (ed.) Romantic and Its Cognates: The European History of a Word, 1972. Add: 97 St. George St., Univ. of Toronto, Toronto, Ont. M5S 1A1, Canada.

EIGNER, Larry (Laurence Joel Eigner). American, b. 1927. Short stories, Poetry. *Publs:* (some are broadsides): From the Sustaining Air, 1953, augmented ed. 1967; Look at the Park, 1958; On My Eyes: Poems, 1960; Murder Talk: The Reception: Suggestions for a Play; Five Poems, Bed Never Self Made, 1964; The Music, The Rooms, 1965; The Memory of Yeats, Blake, DHL, 1965; Six Poems, 1967; Another Time in Fragments, 1967; The—/ Towards Autumn, 1967; Air the Trees, 1968; The Breath of Once Live Things, in the Field With Poe, 1968; A Line That May Be Cut, 1968; Clouding, 1968; Farther North, 1969; Valleys, Branches, 1969; Flat and Round, 1969, 1980; Over and Over, Ends, As the Wind May Sound, 1970; Poem Nov. 1968, 1970; Circuits: A Microbook, a Microbook, 1971; Looks Like Nothing, The Shadow Through Air, 1972; What You Hear, 1972; Selected Poems, 1972; Words Touching Ground Under, 1972; Shape Shadow Elements Move, 1973; Things Stirring Together or Far Away, 1974; Anything on Its Side, 1974; No Radio, 1974; My God the Proverbial, 1975; Suddenly It Gets Light and Dark in the Street: Poems 1961-74, 1975; The Music Variety, 1976; The World and Its Streets, Places, 1977; Watching How or Why, 1977; Cloud, Invisible Air, 1978; Flagpole Riding, 1978; Running Around, 1978; Heat Simmers Cold, 1978; Time, Details of a Tree, 1979; Country-Harbour-Around (prose), 1978; Earth Birds, 1981; now there's-a-morning-hulk of the the sky, 1981; Waters-Places-A Time, 1983; Larry Eigner Letters, 1987. Add: 2338 McGee Ave., Berkeley, Calif, 94703, U.S.A.

EILERS, Hazel Kraft. American, b. 1910. Genealogy/Heraldry. Certified genealogist. Columnist on heraldry, Hobbies: The Mag. for Collectors, Chicago, 1953–83. Budget Chmn., National Bd., National League of American Pen Women Inc., 1970–72, and Pres., Chicago Chapter, 1968–70. *Publs:* The Kraft/Krafft Family Genealogy, 1962; Place Notes, 1968; The Descendants of Isaac Place and Henry Love, 1968; All Name Index to Stephenson County, Illinois History 1880, 1973; House of Sanger, vol. II, 1976; NSDAC Bicentennial Ancestor Index, 1976; Ancestry and Descendants of Johann Dirk Eilers (1815-1885) including Allied Families of Geistfeld, Boatsman, Menken, and Janssen, 1982. Add: 2522 Thayer St., Evanston, Ill. 60201, U.S.A.

EILON, Samuel. British, b. 1923. Administration/Management. Chief Ed., OMEGA, Intnl. Journal of Mgmt. Science. Sr. Research Fellow, Imperial Coll., London (Head, Dept. of Mgmt. Science, 1963–87). *Publs:* Industrial Engineering Tables, 1962; Elements of Production Planning and Control, 1962; (with J.R. King and R.I. Hall) Exercise in Industrial Management: A Series of Case Studies, 1966; (with J.R. King) Industrial Scheduling Abstracts, 1967; (with W. Lampkin) Inventory Control Abstracts, 1968; (with C.D.T. Watson-Gandy and N. Christofides) Distribution Management—Mathematical Modelling and Practical Analysis, 1971; Management Control, 1971, 1979; (with T.R. Fowkes) Applications of Management Science and Banking and Finance, 1972; (with B. Gold and J. Soesan) Applied Productivity Analysis for Industry, 1976; Aspects of Management, 1977, 1979; The Act of Reckoning, 1984; Management Assentions and Aversions, 1985. Add: Dept. of Mechanical Engineering, Imperial Coll., Exhibition Rd., London SW7 2BX, England.

EINBOND, Bernard Lionel. American, b. 1937. Poetry, Literature. Assoc. Prof. of English, Lehman Coll. of the City Univ. of New York, Bronx, since 1973 (Asst. Prof., 1968–72; Chmn., 1976–79). Preceptor, Columbia Univ., NYC, 1961–63; Instr., Hunter Coll. of the City Univ. of New York, 1964–68. *Publs:* Samuel Johnson's Allegory, 1971; The Coming Indoors and Other Poems, 1979. Recipient of British Keats Poetry Prize, 1975. Add: P.O. Box 307, Ft. George Station, New York, N.Y. 10040, U.S.A.

EISENBERG, Larry. American, b. 1919. Novels/Short stories, Poetry, Humor/Satire. Co-Chmn., Dept of Electronics and Computer Sciences, Rockefeller Univ., NYC, since 1970 (Research Assoc., 1960–66; Asst. Prof., 1966–70). *Publs:* (with George Gordon) Limericks for the Loo, 1965; (with Gordon) Games People Shouldn't Play (fiction humor), 1966; Best Laid Schemes (short stories), 1970. Add: 315 East 88th St., New York, N.Y. 10128, U.S.A.

EISENHOWER, John S(heldon) D(oud). American, b. 1922. History, Autobiography/Memoirs. Brigadier general, U.S. Army Reserves, since 1974 (Reserve officer, since 1963; Regular officer, 1944–63). Asst. staff secretary at the White House, Washington D.C., 1958–61; U.S. Ambassador to Belgium, 1969–81. *Publs:* The Bitter Woods: A Comprehensive Study of the War in Europe, 1969; Strictly Personal (memoir), 1974; Allies: Pearl Harbor to D-Day, 1982; So Far from God: The U.S. War with Mexico, 1846-1848, 1987. Add: P.O. Box 278, Kimberton, Pa. 19442, U.S.A.

EISENMAN, Peter D. American, b. 1932. Architecture. Dir. of the Inst. for Architecture and Urban Studies, NYC, since 1967; Ed., Oppositions mag., NYC, since 1973; Adjunct Prof., The Coopers Union, NYC, since 1975 (Lectr., 1967–75); Principal, Eisenman Robertson, Architects, 1980–1985, and Eisenman Architects, since 1988. Worked for Percival Goodman, NYC, 1957–58, and The Architects Collaborative, Cambridge, Mass., 1959; Asst. Lectr., 1960–63, Cambridge Univ., Asst. Prof., 1963–67, Princeton Univ., New Jersey. *Publs:* Giuseppe Terragni, 1979; House of Cards, 1980; John Hejduk: Seven Houses, 1980; House X, 1982. Add: Eisenman Architects, 40 West 25th St., New York, N.Y. 10010, U.S.A.

EISENSON, Jon. American, b. 1907. Communications media/Broadcasting, Psychology. Emeritus Prof. of Hearing and Speech Sciences, Stanford Univ., since 1973 (Prof., 1962–73). Consultant, Veterans Admin., Clinical Psychology and Speech Pathology; Licensed Psychologist, State of Calif. Member of faculty, Brooklyn Coll., N.Y., 1935–42; Prof. of Speech and Dir., Queens Speech and Hearing Center, Queens Coll., City Univ. of New York, 1946–62; Lectr., Coll. of Physicians and Surgeons, 1947–60; Distinguished Prof. of Special Education, San Francisco State Univ., Calif., 1973–84. *Publs:* Confirmation and Information in Rewards and Punishments, 1935; The Psychology of Speech, 1938; (with Pinter and Stanton) The Psychology of the Physically Handicapped, 1940; (with Berry) The Defective in Speech, 1942; Examining for Aphasia, 1945, 1954; Basic Speech, 1950, 2nd ed. with P. Boase, 1964, 3rd ed. 1975; (with Berry) Speech Disorders, 1956; Improvement of Voice Diction, 1957, 5th ed. 1985; (with M. Oglivie) Speech Correction for the Schools, 1957, and as Communicative Disorders in Children, 1983; (ed. and contrib.) Stuttering: A Symposium, 1958; (with J.J. Auer and J. Irwin) Psychology of Communication, 1963; Aphasia in Children, 1972, 1984; Adult Aphasia: Assessment and Treatment in Adults, 1973, 1984; Voice and Diction: A Program for Improvement, 1974, 5th ed. 1985; Stuttering: A Second Symposium, 1975; Is Your

Child's Speech Normal, 1976; Reading for Meaning, 1984; A Special Zoo (children's poetry), 1985; Language and Speech Disorders in Children, 1986; Gerontic Reflections (verses and poems), 1988; Really Now, Why Can't Our Johnnies Read, 1989. Add: 82 Pearce Mitchell Pl., Stanford Calif. 94305, U.S.A.

EISENSTADT, Shmuel Noah. Israeli. Sociology. Prof. of Sociology, Hebrew Univ., Jerusalem, since 1959 (Lectr., 1951–57; Assoc. Prof., 1957–59). *Publs:* The Absorption of Immigrants, 1954; From Generation to Generation, 1956; Essays on Sociological Aspects of Political and Economic Development, 1961; The Political Systems of Empires, 1963; Essays on Compative Institutions, 1965; Modernization, Protest and Change, 1966; Israeli Society, 1968; The Protestant Ethic and Modernization, 1968; Political Sociology of Modernization, 1968; (ed.) Comparative Perspectives on Social Change, 1968, (ed.) Charisma and Institution Building; Selections from Max Weber, 1968; (ed.) Political Sociology, 1971; Social Differentiation and Stratification, 1972; Tradition, Change and Modernity, 1973; (ed. with S. Rokkan) Building States and Nations; Models and Data Resources, 1973; (ed. with S. Graubard) Intellectuals and Traditions, 1973; Post-Traditional Societies, 1974; (ed. with Y. Atzmon) Socialism and Tradition, 1975; (with M. Curelaru) The Form of Sociology, 1976; Revolution and the Transformation of Societies, 1978; (co-author) Patrons, Clients, and Friends, 1984; Transformation of Israeli Society, 1985; (co-author) Society, Culture, and Urbanisation, 1986; (with M. Abitbol and N. Chazan) The Origins of the State Reconsidered, 1986; (with others) Social Change in Latin American Societies: Comparative Perspective, 1986; (with A. Shachar) Society, Culture and Urbanization, 1987; European Civilization in a Comparative Perspective, 1987; (ed. with L. Roniger and A. Seligman) Centre Formation, Protest Movements and Class Structure in Europe and the United States, 1987; (ed.) Patterns of Modernity, 2 vols., 1987; (ed. with M. Abitbol and N. Chazan) The Early State in African Perspective: Culture, Power and Division of Labor, 1988; (ed. with I. Silber) Knowledge and Society: Studies in the Sociological Culture, Past and Present, 1988. Add: Rechov, Radak 30, Jerusalem, Israel.

EISENSTEIN, Phyllis (Kleinstein). American, b. 1946. Science fiction. Teacher of Science fiction, Columbia Coll., Chicago, 1979–80; Teacher, Clarion Workshop in Science Fiction and Fantasy Writing, Michigan State Univ., East Lansing, 1983. Anthology Trustee, Science Fiction Writers of America, 1976–81; Co-Founder and Dir., Windy City SF Writers Conference, Chicago, 1972–77. *Publs:* Born to Exile, 1978; Sorcerer's Son, 1979; Shadow of Earth, 1979; In the Hands of Glory, 1981; The Crystal Palace, 1988; In the Red Lord's Reach, 1989. Add: 6208 N. Campbell, Chicago, Ill. 60659, U.S.A.

EISNER, Gisela. British, b. 1925. Economics. Member of staff, Manchester Univ., 1951–56. *Publs:* Jamaica 1830-1930: A Study in Economic Growth, 1961. Add: 69 Macclesfield Rd., Buxton, Derbyshire, England.

EISNER, Robert. American, b. 1922. Economics. William R. Kenan Prof. of Economics, Northwestern Univ., Evanston, Ill., since 1974 (Asst. Prof., 1952–54; Assoc. Prof., 1954–60; Prof., 1960–74). *Publs:* Determinants of Capital Expenditures, 1963; Some Factors in Growth Reconsidered, 1966; Factors in Business Investment, 1977; How Real Is the Federal Deficit?, 1986; The Total Incomes System of Accounts, 1989. Add: Dept. of Economics, Northwestern Univ., Evanston, Ill. 60208, U.S.A.

EITNER, Lorenz E.A. American, b. 1919. Art. Chmn., Art Dept., Stanford Univ., Calif., and Dir., Stanford Univ. Museum, since 1963. Prof., Art Dept., Univ. of Minnesota, Minneapolis, 1949–63. *Publs:* Neoclassicism and Romanticism, 2 vols., 1970; Gericault's Raft of the Medusa, 1972; (ed.) Gericault, étude Biographique et critique, 1973; Gericault: His Life & Work, 1982; An Outline of Nineteenth Century Painting, 1987. Add: 684 Mirada, Stanford, Calif. 94305, U.S.A.

EKIRCH, Arthur A., Jr. American, b. 1915. History, Intellectual history, Politics/Government. Emeritus Prof. of History, State Univ. of New York, Albany, since 1986 (Prof., 1965–86). Prof. of History, American Univ., Washington, D.C., 1947–65. *Publs:* Idea of Progress in America 1815-1860, 1944; Decline of American Liberalism, 1955; The Civilian and the Military, 1956; Man and Nature in America, 1963; The American Democratic Tradition, 1963; Ideas, Ideals, and American Diplomacy, 1966; Ideologies and Utopias: The Impact of the New Deal on American Thought, 1969; Challenge of American Democracy, 1973; Progressivism in America, 1974. Add: 24 Tierney Dr., Delmar, N.Y. 12054, U.S.A.

EKLUND, Gordon. American, b. 1945. Science fiction/Fantasy. *Publs:* The Eclipse of Dawn, 1971; A Trace of Dreams, 1972; Beyond the Resurrection, 1973; (with Paul Anderson) Inheritors of Earth, 1974; All Times Possible, 1974; Serving in Time, 1975; Falling Toward Forever, 1975; The Grayspace Beast, 1976; (with G. Benford) If the Stars Are God, 1977; Starless World, 1978; Devil World, 1979; (with F.P. Wilson) Twilight River, 1979; Garden of Winter, 1980; Find the Changeling, 1980. Add: c/o Kirby McCauley Ltd., 432 Park Ave. S., New York, N.Y., 10016, U.S.A.

EKWENSI, Cyprian. Nigerian, b. 1921. Novels/Short stories, Children's fiction. Dir. of Information Services, Federal Ministry of Information, Enugu, since 1966 (Dir. of Information, Lagos, 1961–66). Lectr. in Pharmacognosy and Pharmaceutics, Sch. of Pharmacy, Lagos, 1949–56; Pharmacist, Nigerian Medical Service, and Head of Features, Nigerian Broadcasting Corp., 1956–61; Managing Dir., Star Printing and Publishing Co. Ltd., 1974–79; Managing Dir., Ivory Trumpet Publishing Co. Ltd., 1981–83. Chmn., East Central State Library Bd., 1972; Chmn., Hosps. Mgmt. Bd., 1986. *Publs:* When Love Whispers, 1947; Ikolo the Wrestler, 1947; The Leopard's Claw, 1950; People of the City, 1954; The Drummer Boy, 1960; The Passport of Mallam Ilia, 1960; Jagua Nana, 1961; Burning Grass: A Story of the Fulani of Northern Nigeria, 1962; An African Night's Entertainment: A Tale of Vengeance, 1962; Yaba Round-about Murder, 1962; Beautiful Feathers, 1963; Great Elephant Bird, 1965; The Rainmaker and Other Stories, 1965; Iska, 1966; Lokotown and Other Stories, 1966; Trouble in Form Six, 1966; The Boa Suitor, 1966; Juju Rock, 1966; Restless City and Christmas Gold, 1975; The Rainbow-Tinted Scarf and Other Stories, 1975; Samankwe and the Highway Robbers, 1975; Survive the Peace, 1976; (ed.) Festac Anthology of Nigerian New Writing, 1977; Motherless Baby, 1980; Divided We Stand, 1980; Jagua Nana's Daughter, 1986; For a Roll of Parchment, 1987; Behind the Convent Wall, 1987. Add: 12 Hillview, Independence Layout, P.O. Box 317, Enugu, Nigeria.

ELATH, Eliahu. Israeli, b. 1903. History, Autobiography/Memoirs/Personal. Prof. Emeritus, Hebrew Univ. of Jerusalem, since 1966 (Pres., 1960–66). Israeli Ambassador to the U.S., 1948–50, and to the U.K., 1950–59. *Publs:* The Bedouin: Their Customs and Manners, 1933; Trans-Jordan, 1934; Israel and Her Neighbours, 1957; (ed. with N. Bentwich and D. May) Memories of Sir Wyndham Deedes, 1958; The Political Struggle for Inclusion of Elath in the Jewish State, 1967; San Francisco Diary, 1971; British Routes to India, 1971; Zionism and the Arabs, 1974; Zionism and the U.N., 1977; The Struggle for Statehood, 1982. Add: 17 Bialik St., Jerusalem, Israel.

ELBERT, Joyce. American. Novels/Short stories. *Publs:* The Crazy Ladies, 1960; A Martini on the Other Table, 1963; Drunk in Madrid, 1972; Getting Rid of Richard, 1972; The Goddess Hang-Up, 1973; The Three of Us, 1973; The Crazy Lovers, 1979; A Very Cagey Lady, 1980; Red Eye Blues, 1982; Return of the Crazy Ladies, 1984. Add: c/o New American Library, 1633 Broadway, New York, N.Y. 10019, U.S.A.

ELCOCK, Howard (James). British, b. 1942. History, Politics/Government. Head of Government Section, Dept. of Economics and Govt., Newcastle upon Tyne Polytechnic, since 1981. Lectr. and Sr. Lectr. in Politics, Univ. of Hull, 1966–81. Member, Humberside County council, 1973–77. *Publs:* Administrative Justice, 1969; Portrait of a Decision: The Council of Four and the Treaty of Versailles, 1972; Political Behaviour, 1976; (with S. Haywood) The Buck Stops Where? Accountability and Control in the NHS, 1980; (with M. Wheaton) Local Government, 1982, 1986; (ed. with E. Jordan) Learning from Local Authority Budgeting, 1987. Add: Dept. of Economics and Government, Newcastle upon Tyne Polytechnic, Newcastle-upon-Tyne, England.

ELDER, John (William). New Zealander, b. 1933. Earth sciences. Prof. of Geophysics, Geology Dept., Univ. of Manchester, since 1970. Worked for the New Zealand Defence Scientific Corp., 1955–61; Prof. of Physics, Medical Coll., Mosul, Iraq, 1961–62; Postgrad. Fellow, Inst. of Geophysics and Planetary Physics, Univ. of California at San Diego, 1963–65; Research Asst., Dept. of Applied Mathematics and Theoretical Physics, Cambridge Univ., 1966–70, and Atlas Laboratory Fellow and Sr. Research Fellow, Churchill Coll., Cambridge, 1969–70. *Publs:* Hydrothermal Systems, 1966; The Bowels of the Earth, 1976; Geothermal Systems, 1980; The Structure of the Planets, 1987. Add: Geology Dept., Univ. of Manchester, Manchester M13 9PL, England.

ELDER, Lonne III. American, b. 1931. Plays/Screenplays. Coordinator, Playwrights-Dirs. Unit, Negro Ensemble Co., NYC, 1967–69; Writer, 1968, and Writer and Producer, 1971, Talent Assocs.; Writer and Producer, Cinema Center Films, Hollywood, Calif., 1969–70; Writer, Universal Pictures, 1970–71; Radnitz-Mattel Productions, 1971, and MGM Pictures, and Columbia Pictures, 1972, all Hollywood, Calif. *Publs:* Ceremonies in Dark Old Men, 1969. Add: c/o Farrar Straus and Giroux, 19 Union Sq. W., New York, N.Y. 10003, U.S.A.

ELDER, Michael Aiken. British, b. 1931. Science fiction/Fantasy, Children's fiction, Biography. Freelance writer, actor and broadcaster. Dir., Edinburgh Film Festival, 1962–64; Ed., The Scottish Life-Boat, 1967–84. *Publs:* The Affair at Invergarroch, 1951; Tony Behind the Scenes, 1955; The Cabin at Barton Bridge, 1956; The Phantom in the Wings, 1957; For Those in Peril, 1963; The Young Martin Luther, 1966; The Young James Barrie, 1967; Paradise Is Not Enough, 1970; The Alien Earth, 1971; The Everlasting Man, 1972; Nowhere on Earth, 1972; The Perfumed Planet, 1973; Down to Earth, 1973; A Different World, 1974; The Seeds of Frenzy, 1974; Centaurian Quest, 1975; The Island of the Dead, 1975; Double Time, 1976; Mindslip, 1976; Oil-Seeker, 1977; Mindquest, 1978; Oil-Planet, 1978; Danger in the Glen, 1984; Mist on the Moorland, 1985; The Man from France, 1986; The Last of the Lairds, 1987. Add: 20 Zetland Place, Edinburgh EH5 3LY, Scotland.

ELDRIDGE, Colin Clifford. British, b. 1942. History. Sr. Lectr. in History, Saint David's Univ. Coll., Univ. of Wales, Lampeter, since 1975 (Lectr., 1968–75). Post-Doctoral Fellow, Univ. of Edinburgh, 1966–68. *Publs:* England's Mission: The Imperial Idea in the Age of Gladstone and Disraeli, 1868-80, 1973; Victorian Imperialism, 1978; (ed.) British Imperialism in the Nineteenth Century, 1984. Add: Tanerdy, Ciliau Aeron, Lampeter, Dyfed, Wales.

ELDRIDGE, John E.T. British, b. 1936. Sociology. Prof. of Sociology, Univ. of Glasgow, since 1972. Lectr. and Sr. Lectr., Univ of York, 1964–69; Prof., Univ. of Bradford, 1969–72. *Publs:* Industrial Dispute: Essays in the Sociology of Industrial Relations, 1968; (ed.) Max Weber: The Interpretation of Social Reality, 1971; Sociology and Industrial Life, 1971; (with A.D. Crombie) Sociology of Organizations, 1974; (with Glasgow Univ. Media Group) Bad News, 1976; (with Glasgow Univ. Media Group) More Bad News, 1980; Recent British Sociology, 1980; C. Wright Mills, 1983; (with Glasgow Univ. Media Group) War and Peace News, 1985; (co-author) Just Managing, 1985. Add: Dept. of Sociology, Adam Smith Bldg., Univ. of Glasgow G12 8QQ. Scotland.

ELEGANT, Robert (Sampson). British/American, b. 1928. Novels, History, Biography, Reportage. Journalist: War Corresp., Korea, Overseas News Agency, Intnl. News Service, 1951–53; South Asian Corresp. and Chief of New Delhi Bureau, 1956–57, Southeast Asian Corresp., and Chief of Hong Kong Bureau, 1958–61, and Chief, Central European Bureau, Bonn, 1962–64, Newsweek mag.; Chief, Hong Kong Bureau, 1965–69; Foreign Affairs Commentator, 1965–76, Los Angeles Times. *Publs:* China's Red Masters (in U.K. as China's Red Leaders), 1951; The Dragon's Seed, 1959; The Centre of the World, 1963, 1968; A Kind of Treason, 1966; The Seeking, 1969; Mao's Great Revolution, 1971; Mao vs. Chiang: The Battle for China, 1972; Dynasty, 1977; Hong Kong, 1977; Manchu, 1980; Mandarin, 1983; White Sun, Red Star, 1986. Add: The Manor House, Middle Green, near Langley, Bucks. SL3 6BS, England.

ELGIN, (Patricia Anne) Suzette Haden (Wilkins). American, b. 1936. Science fiction/Fantasy, Language/Linguistics. Assoc. Prof Emeritus, San Diego State Univ. Publisher, producer and writer, The Lonesome Node newsletter, since 1981. Asst. Prof., then Assoc. Prof., San Diego State Univ., since 1972. Formerly TV folk music performer, instr. of music and guitar, and instr. of linguistics. *Publs:* The Communipaths, 1970; Furthest, 1971; At the Seventh Level, 1972; (with John T. Grinder) Guide to Transformational Grammer: History, Theory, Practice, 1973; What Is Linguistics?, 1973, 1979; A Primer of Transformational Grammer for Rank Beginners, 1975; (ed.) Pouring Down Words, 1975; Star-Anchored, Star-Angered, 1979; The Gentle Art of Verbal Self-Defense, 1980; Ozark Fantasy Trilogy, 3 vols., 1981; More on the Gentle Art of Self-Defense, 1983; Native Tongue, 1984; Yonder Comes the Other End of Time, 1986; The Last Word on the Gentle Art of Self-Defense, 1987; Native Tongue II: The Judas Rose, 1987. Add: P.O. Box 1137, Huntsville, Ark. 72740, U.S.A.

ELKIN, Benjamin. American, b. 1911. Children's fiction, Children's non-fiction. Personnel Office, U.S. Social Security Bd., Washington, D.C., 1936–39; English teacher in high schs., Chicago, Ill., 1939–48; Inst. in Military Admin., U.S. Army, Savanna, Ill., 1942–45; Principal, Philip Rogers Sch., Chicago, 1948–72; Lectr., Roosevelt Univ., Chicago, 1950–53. *Publs:* Loudest Noise in the World, 1954; Gillespie and the Guards, 1956; Six Foolish Fishermen, 1957; Big Jump and Other Stories, 1958;

True Book of Schools, 1960; True Book of Money, 1960; King's Wish and Other Stories, 1960; Man Who Walked Around the World, 1961; Lucky and the Giant, 1962; Al and the Magic Lamp, 1963; Why the Sun Was Late, 1966; Such Is the Way of the World, 1967; Wisest Man in the World, 1968; Magic Ring, 1969; How the Tsar Drinks Tea, 1971; King Who Could Not Sleep, 1975; Add: 1522 First St., Apt. M-209, Coronado, Calif., 92118, U.S.A.

ELKIN, Stanley (Lawrence). American, b. 1930. Novels/Short stories, Plays/Screenplays. Prof. of English, Washington Univ., St. Louis, since 1968 (joined faculty, 1960). Visiting Lectr., Smith Coll., Northampton, Mass., 1964–65. *Publs:* Boswell, 1964; Criers and Kibitzers Kibitzers and Criers (short stories), 1966; A Bad Man, 1967; The Six-Year-Old Man (filmscript), 1969; (ed.) Stories from the Sixties, 1971; The Dick Gibson Show, 1971; The Making of Ashenden, 1972; Searchers and Seizures, 1973, 1974; Eligible Men (short stories), 1974; The Franchiser, 1976; The Living End, 1979; Stanley Elkin's Greatest Hits, 1980; George Mills, 1982; The Magic Kingdom, 1985; Early Elkin, 1985; The Rabbi of Lud, 1987. Add: Dept. of English, Washington Univ., St. Louis, Mo. 63130, U.S.A.

ELKINS, Dov Peretz. American, b. 1937. Psychology, Theology/Religion. Founder and Dir., Growth Assocs., Rochester, since 1976; Sr. Rabbi, The Park Synagogue, Cleveland, since 1987. Rabbi, Temple Bethel, Rochester, N.Y., 1972–76. *Publs:* (with A. Eisenberg) Worlds Lost and Found (Biblical archaeology), 1964; So Young to Be a Rabbi, 1969; (with A. Eisenberg) Treasures from the Dust (Biblical archaeology), 1972; (ed.) Rejoice with Jerusalem (reading and prayers), 1972; A Tradition Reborn (sermons and essays). 1972; God's Warriors, Stories of Military Chaplains (children), 1974; Glad to Be Me: Building Self-Esteem in Yourself and Others, 1976, 1989; Teaching People to Love Themselves, 1977; Clarifying Jewish Values, 1977; Jewish Consciousness Raising, 1979; Self Concept Sourcebook, 1979; Loving My Jewishness, 1978; Experiential Programs for Jewish Groups, 1979; Twelve Pathways to Feeling Better About Yourself, 1980; My Seventy-Two Friends, 1989. Add: Box 18429, Rochester, N.Y. 14618-0429, U.S.A.

ELLER, Vernard. American, b. 1927. Theology/Religion. Prof. of Religion, Univ. of La Verne, since 1958. *Publs:* Kierkegaard and Radical Discipleship, 1968; His End Up: Getting God into the New Theology, 1969; The Promise: Ethics in the Kingdom of God, 1970; The Mad Morality: The 10 Commandments Revisited, 1971; The Sex Manual for Puritans, 1971; In Place of Sacraments: A Study of Baptism and the Lord's Supper, 1972; King Jesus' Manual of Arms for the Armless: War and Peace from Genesis to Revelation, 1973; The Simple Life: The Christian Stance Towards Possessions, 1973; The Most Revealing Book of the Bible: Making Sense Out of Revelation, 1974; Cleaning Up the Christian Vocabulary, 1976; The Outward Bound: Caravaning as the Style of the Church, 1980; The Kingdom Come: A Blumhardt Reader, 1980; War and Peace from Genesis to Revelation, 1981; The Language of Canaan and the Grammar of Feminism, 1982; A Pearl of Christian Counsel for the Brokenhearted, 1982; Towering Babble: God's People Without God's Word, 1983; Proclaim Good Tidings: Evangelism for the Faith Community, 1987; Christian Anarchy: Jesus' Primacy Over the Powers, 1987; The Beloved Disciple: His Name, His Story, His Thought, 1987; Eller's Ethical Elucidations: A Reader in Christian Ethics, 1989. Add: Univ. of La Verne, La Verne, Calif. 91750, U.S.A.

ELLERBECK, Rosemary (Anne L'Estrange). Also writes as Nicola Thorne, Anna L'Estrange, and Katherine Yorke. British. Historical/Romance/Gothic. Fulltime writer since 1975. Formerly, publrs. reader and ed. *Publs:* Inclination to Murder, 1965; (as Nicola Thorne) The Girls, 1967; (as Nicola Thorne) Bridie Climbing, 1969; (as Nicola Thorne) In Love, 1973; Hammersleigh, 1976; Rose, Rose Where Are You?, 1977; (as Anna L'Estrange) Return to Wuthering Heights, 1978; (as Katherine Yorke) The Enchantress, 1979; (as Nicola Thorne) A Woman Like Us, 1979; (as Katherine Yorke) Falcon Gold, 1980; (as Nicola Thorne) The Perfect Wife and Mother, 1980; (as Nicola Thorne) The Daughters of the House, 1981; (as Katherine Yorke) Lady of the Lakes, 1981; (as Nicola Thorne) Where the Rivers Meet, 1982; (as Nicola Thorne) Affairs of Love, 1983; (as Katherine Yorke) A Woman's Place, 1983; (as Katherine Yorke) The Pair Bond, 1984; (as Nicola Thorne) The Askham Chronicles: Never Such Innocence, 1985; Yesterday's Promises, 1986, Bright Morning, 1986, and A Place in the Sun, 1987; (as Katherine Yorke) Swift Flows the River, 1988; (as Nicola Thorne) Pride of Place, 1988; (as Nicola Thorne) Champagne, 1989. Add: c/o Richard Scott Simon Ltd., 43 Doughty St., London WC1N 2LF, England.

ELLINGER, John Henry. British, b. 1919. Design (general). Con-

sultant Project Engineer, since 1973. Engineer, Ministry of Works, London, 1950–59, and Atomic Energy Establishment, Dorchester, 1959–66; Staff Design Engineer, Aero Engine Div., Rolls Royce Ltd., Derby, 1966–70; Project Engineer, Queen Mary Coll., London, 1970–73. *Publs:* Design Synthesis, 1968. Add: c/o The Secty., Soc. of Authors, 84 Drayton Gardens, London SW10, England.

ELLIOT, Alistair. British, b. 1932. Poetry. Freelance writer since 1983. Actor and Stage Mgr., English Children's Theatre, London, 1957–59; Asst. Librarian, Kensington, London, 1959–61; Cataloguer, Keele Univ. Library, 1961–65; Accessions Librarian, Pahlavi Univ. Library, Shiraz, Iran, 1965–67; Special Collections Librarian, Univ. of Newcastle upon Tyne, 1967–82. *Publs:* (trans.) Alcestis by Euripides, 1965; (trans.) Peace, by Aristophanes, in Greek Comedy, 1965; Air in the Wrong Place (verse), 1968, (ed.) Poems by James I and Others, 1970. (ed.) Lines on the Jordan, 1971; Contentions (verse), 1978; Kisses (verse), 1978; (trans.) Femmes/Hombres, Women/Men, by Verlaine, 1979; (trans.) The Lazarus Poems, by Heinrich Heine, 1979; (ed.) The Georgics with John Dryden's Translation, by Virgil, 1981; Talking to Bede (verse), 1982; Talking Back (verse), 1982; On the Appian Way (verse), 1984; My Country: Collected Poems, 1989. Add: 27 Hawthorn Rd., Newcastle upon Tyne NE3 4DE, England.

ELLIOT, Jeffrey M. American, b. 1947. Politics, International relations/Current affairs. Prof. of Political Science, North Carolina Central Univ., Durham, since 1981. Ed., Journal of Black Political Studies, since 1985; Adviser on Foreign Affairs, U.S. House of Representatives, Washington, D.C., since 1985. Asst. Prof. of History and Political Science, Univ. of Alaska, Anchorage, 1972–74; Asst. Dean of Academic Affairs, Miami-Dade Community Coll., 1974–76; Asst. Prof. of Political Science, Wesleyan Coll., Norfolk, Va., 1978–79; Sr. Curriculum Specialist, Educational Development Center, Newton, Mass., 1979–81. *Publs:* Keys to Economic Understanding, 1977; Literary Voices, 1980; Political Ideals, Policy Dilemmas, 1981; Fantasy Voices, 1981; Deathman Pass Me By, 1983; Tempest in a Teapot: The Falkland Islands War, 1983; Kindred Spirits, 1984; The Presidential-Congressional Political Dictionary, 1984; Black Voices in American Politics, 1985; Urban Society, 1985; Fidel Castro: Nothing Can Stop the Course of History, 1985; The Work of R. Reginald: An Annotated Bibliography and Guide, 1985; The Analytical Congressional Directory, 1986; Discrimination in America: An Annotated Resource Guide, 1986; Fidel Castro: Resources on Contemporary Persons, 1986. Add: 1419 Barliff Pl., Durham, N.C. 27712, U.S.A.

ELLIOTT, Brian Robinson. Australian, b. 1910. Novels/Short stories. Literature, Biography. Formerly, Reader in Australian Literary Studies, Univ. of Adelaide, S.A. *Publs:* Leviathan's Inch (novel), 1946; Singing to the Cattle, and Other Australian Essays, 1947; (ed.) Coast to Coast: Australian Stories 1948, 1949; Marcus Clarke, 1958; The Landscape of Australian Poetry, 1967; (ed. with Adrian Mitchell) Bards in the Wilderness: Australian Poetry to 1920, 1970; Colonial Poets: Adam Lindsay Gordon, 1973; (ed.) Clarke: For the Term of His Natural Office, 1973; Portable Australian Authors: The Jindyworobaks, 1979; (trans.) Primitive Mythology, by Lucien Lévy-Bruhl, 1981. Add: 25 Glenuga Ave., Glenuga, S.A., Australia.

ELLIOTT, C. Orville. American, b. 1913. Information science/Computers. Prof. of Accounting and Information Science, Western Illinois Univ. Coll. of Business, Macomb, since 1967 (Chmn., Dept. of Accounting and Information Sciences, 1967–69). *Publs:* Card Punching and Verifications, 1965, 1974; (with R.S. Wasley) Business Information Systems Professional, 1970; Introduction to Data Processing, 1970, 3rd ed. 1979. Add: Dept. of Accountancy and Information Sciences, Western Illinois Univ., Macomb, Ill. 61455, U.S.A.

ELLIOTT, Jan Walter. American, b. 1939. Economics. Sheldon B. Lubar Prof., Univ. of Wisconsin-Milwaukee, since 1976 (Asst. Prof., 1968–72; Assoc. Prof., 1973–75). Asst. Prof., California State Coll., Los Angeles, 1966–67. *Publs:* Economic Analysis for Management Decision, 1973; Macroeconomic Analysis, 1975, 1979; Money, Banking and Financial Markets, 1984. Add: Dept. of Economics, Univ. of Wisconsin-Milwaukee, Milwaukee, Wisc. 53201, U.S.A.

ELLIOTT, Janice. British, b. 1931. Novels/Short stories, Children's fiction. Staff Journalist, House and Garden, House Beautiful, Harper's Bazaar, and the Sunday Times, London, 1954–62; Book Reviewer, New Statesman, London, 1967–68; Columnist, Twentieth Century mag., London, 1968–72. Book Reviewer, Sunday Telegraph, London, 1969–86. *Publs:* Cave with Echoes, 1962; The Somnambulists, 1964; The Godmother, 1966; The Buttercup Chain, 1967; The Singing Head, 1968; Angels Falling, 1969; The Kindling, 1970; The Birthday Unicorn, 1970; A State of Peace, 1971; Private Life, 1972; Alexander in the Land of Mog, 1973; Heaven on Earth, 1975; A Loving Eye, 1977; The Honey Tree, 1978; Summer People, 1980; Secret Places, 1981; The Country of Her Dreams, 1982; The Incompetent Dragon, 1982; Magic, 1983; The Italian Lesson, 1985; Dr. Gruber's Daughter, 1986; The King Awakes, 1987; The Sadness of Witches, 1987; The Empty Throne, 1988. Add: c/o Hodder & Stoughton, 47 Bedford Sq., London WC1B 3DP, England.

ELLIOTT, John Huxtable. British, b. 1930. History. Prof., Sch. of Historical Studies, Inst. for Advanced Study, Princeton, N.J., since 1973. Lectr. in History, Cambridge Univ., 1957–67; Prof. of History, King's Coll., Univ. of London, 1968–72. *Publs:* Imperial Spain, 1963; The Revolt of the Catalans, 1963; Europe Divided, 1559-1598, 1968; The Old World and the New, 1492-1650, 1970; (with H.G. Koenigsberger) The Diversity of History, 1970; Memoriales y Cartas del Conde Duque de Olivares, 1978–80; (with Jonathan Brown) A Palace for a King, 1980; Richelieu and Olivares, 1984; The Count-Duke of Olivares, 1986. Add: Sch. of Historical Studies, Inst. for Advanced Study, Princeton, N.J. 08540, U.S.A.

ELLIOTT, Sumner Locke. American (b. Australian), b. 1917. Novels/Short stories, Science fiction/Fantasy, Plays/Screenplays. Professional actor until 1948. *Publs:* Interval (play), 1942; Buy Me Blue Ribbons (play), 1952; Careful, He Might Hear You, 1963; Some Doves and Pythons, 1966; Edens Lost, 1969; The Man Who Got Away, 1972; Going (SF novel), 1975; Water under the Bridge, 1977; Signs of Life, 1981; About Tilly Beamis, 1984; Waiting for Childhood (novel), 1988. Add: c/o Harper and Row, 10 E. 53rd St., New York, N.Y. 10022, U.S.A.

ELLIOTT, William Rowcliffe. British, b. 1910. History. H.M. Inspector of Schs., 1936–48, Staff Inspector, 1948–57, Chief Inspector, 1957–68, and Sr. Chief Inspector, 1968–72, Dept. of Education and Science, London. *Publs:* (trans. with K.T. Elliott) Pupil Guidance: Facts and Problems, by M. Reuchlin, 1964; Monemvasia: The Gibraltar of Greece, 1971; Chest Tombs and "Tea Caddies" by Cotswold and Severn, 1977. Add: Astwick House, Farthinghoe, Brackley, Northants NN13 5NY, England.

ELLIOTT-BINNS, Michael Ferrers. British, b. 1923. Theology/Religion. Charity Consultant, since 1983. Asst. Secty. to the Church Assembly 1949–63, Legal Secty., 1963–70, and Asst. Secty. to the Gen. Synod, 1970–76; Coordinator, Chiswick Family Rescue, 1978–80; Liaison Worker, Brixton Circle Projects, 1981–83. *Publs:* The Layman in Church Government, 1956; Guide to the Pastoral Measure, 1968; The Layman and His Church, 1970; North Downs Church, 1983. Add: 22 Wilton Rd., Edinburgh EH16 5NX, Scotland.

ELLIS, Albert. American, b. 1913. Human relations, Psychology, Sex. Psychotherapist and Exec. Dir., Inst. for Rational-Emotive Therapy, NYC, since 1959. Adjunct Prof. of Psychology, Rutgers Univ., New Brunswick, N.J. In private practice of pyschotherapy, and marriage and family counseling, NYC, 1943–68; Chief Psychologist, New Jersey State Diagnostic Center, 1949–50, and New Jersey State Dept. of Instns. and Agencies, 1950–52. *Publs:* Introduction to the Scientific Principles of Psychoanalysis, 1950; Folklore of Sex, 1951; (ed. with A.P. Pillay) Sex, Society and the Individual, 1953; American Sexual Tragedy, 1954; (ed. and contrib.) Sex Life of the American Woman and the Kinsey Report, 1955; (with R. Brancale) Psychology of Sex Offenders, 1956; How to Live with a "Neurotic", 1957, 1975; Sex Without Guilt, 1958; The Art and Science of Love, 1960; (with R.A. Harper) Creative Marriage, 1961; as A Guide to Successful Marriage, 1966; (with R.A Harper) A Guide to Rational Living, 1961; (with A. Abarbanel) The Encyclopedia of Sexual Behavior, 1961; Reason and Emotion in Psychotherapy, 1962; The Intelligent Woman's Guide to Man-Hunting, 1963; Sex and the Single Man, 1963; The Origins and Development of the Incest Taboo, 1963; If This Be Sexual Heresy . . . , 1963; (with E. Sagarin) Nymphomania: A Study of the Oversexed Woman, 1964; Homosexuality, 1965; Suppressed: Seven Key Essays Publishers Dared Not Print, 1965; The Case for Sexual Liberty, 1965; The Search for Sexual Enjoyment, 1966; (with J.L. Wolfe and S. Moseley) How to Prevent Your Child from Becoming a Neurotic Adult, 1966; (with R.O. Conway) The Art of Erotic Seduction, 1967; Is Objectivism a Religion?, 1968; (with J.M. Gullo) Murder and Assassination, 1971; Growth Through Reason, 1971; Executive Leadership: A Rational Approach, 1972; The Civilized Couple's Guide to Extramarital Adventure, 1972; How to Master Your Fear of Flying, 1972; (with F. Seruya and S. Losher) Sex and Sex Education: Bibliography, 1972; Humanistic Psychotherapy: The Rational-Emotive Approach, 1973; (with R.A. Harper) A New Guide to Rational Living, 1975; Sex and the Liberated Man, 1976; (with W. Knaus) Overcoming Procrastination, 1977; (with R. Grieger) Handbook of Rational Emotive Therapy, 1977, vol. 2, 1986; (with E. Abrams) Brief Psychotherapy in Medical and Health Practice, 1978; The Intelligent Woman's Guide to Dating and Mating, 1979; Theoretical and Empirical Foundations of Rational-Emotive Therapy, 1979; (with I. Becker) A Guide to Personal Happiness, 1982; (with M.E. Bernard) Rational-Emotive Approaches to the Problems of Childhood, 1983; (with M.E. Bernard) Clinical Applications of Rational-Emotive Therapy, 1985; Overcoming Resistance, 1985; (with Windy Dryden) The Practice of Rational-Emotive Therapy, 1987; (with J. McInerny, R. Di Giuseppe, and R. Yeager) Rational-Emotive Treatment of Alcoholism and Substance Abuse, 1988; (with R. Yeager) Why Some Therapies Don't Work: The Dangers of Transpersonal Psychology, 1989; (with others) Rational-Emotive Couples Therapy, 1989. Add: 45 East 65th St., New York, N.Y. 10021, U.S.A.

ELLIS, Alec (Charles Owen). British, b. 1932. Librarianship, Education, History. Deputy Dir., Academic Affairs, Sch. of Information Science and Technology, Liverpool Polytechnic, since 1988 (Lectr. 1965–68; Sr. Lectr. 1968–72; Principal Lectr., 1972–78; Head of Dept., Sch. of Librarianship and Information Studies, 1978–88). Asst. Librarian, Liverpool City Libraries, 1949–61; Librarian, St. Katharine's Coll. of Education, Liverpool, 1961–64. *Publs:* How to Find Out About Children's Literature, 1966, 3rd ed. 1973; A History of Children's Reading and Literature, 1968; Library Services for Young People in England and Wales 1830-1970, 1971; Books in Victorian Elementary Schools, 1971; Public Libraries and the First World War, 1975; The Parish of All Hallows Allerton, 1976; (co-author) Chosen for Children, 1977; Public Libraries at the Time of the Adams Report, 1978; Educating Our Masters, 1985. Add: 53 Beechfield Rd., Calderstones, Liverpool L18 3EQ, England.

ELLIS, Alice Thomas. Pseud. for Anna Margaret Haycraft; also writes as Anna Haycraft. British. Novels, Cookery, Humour. Columnist ("Home Life"), The Spectator, London. *Publs:* Natural Baby Food: A Cookery Book, 1977; The Sin Eater (novel), 1977; (as Anna Haycraft; with Caroline Blackwood) Darling, You Shouldn't Have Gone to So Much Trouble (cookery), 1980; The Birds of the Air (novel), 1980; The 27th Kingdom (novel), 1982; (ed.) Mrs. Donald, by Mary Keene, 1983; The Other Side of the Fire (novel), 1983; Unexplained Laughter (novel), 1985; (with Tom Pitt-Aikens) Secrets of Strangers (psychology), 1986; Home Life (humour), 1986; More Home Life, 1987; The Clothes in the Wardrobe (novel), 1987; The Skeleton in the Cupboard (novel), 1988; Home Life Three, 1988. Add: c/o Duckworth, 43 Gloucester Cres., London NW1 7DY, England.

ELLIS, Audrey. British. Cookery/Gastronomy/Wine. Regular contrib. to Parents. Former Managing Ed., Hamlyn Publishing Group Cookery Books. *Publs:* Modern Cake Decorating, 1965; (ed.) Woman's Own Book of Cake Making and Cake Decorating, 1966; Casserole Cookery, 1967, (ed.) Woman's Own Book of Casserole Cookery, 1967; 101 Easy to Use Cookery Hints, 1968; Home Guide to Food Freezing, 1968; All About Home Freezing, 1969; Meals to Enjoy from Your Freezer, 1969; Cooking for Your Freezer, 1970; (with M. Berry and A. Body) Hamlyn All Colour Cook Book, 1970; Step by Step Guide to Home Freezing, 1971; Farmhouse Kitchen, 1971; Entertaining from Your Freezer, 1972; Kitchen Garden Cook Book, 1972; Step by Step Guide to Meat Cooking, 1973; Easy Freeze Cooking, 1973; Complete Book of Home Freezing, 1973; French Family Cooking, 1974; Wine Lovers Cook Book, 1975; Home Freezing Through the Year, 1975; Colourful Entertaining, 1975; Four Seasons Series: Autumn, 1975, Winter, 1975, Spring, 1976, Summer, 1976; Cooking to Make Kids Slim, 1976; Freezing Calendar, 1976; Starting with Home Freezing, 1976; The Kid Slimming Book, 1976; The Magpie History of Food, 1977; Encyclopedia of Freezing, 1977; Hamlyn All Colour Freezer Cook Book, 1977; Oven-to-Table Cooking, 1977; Budget Cookery, 1977; Cooking for Your Outline, 1977; Cookery for All Seasons, 1977; 500 Recipes and Hints for Freezing, 1978; Table Layout and Decoration, 1978; The Best of Dial-a-Recipe, 1978; Sweet Success Slimming for All the Family, 1979; Menu Planners Series, 1979; The Great Country Cookbook, 1979; Hints for Modern Cooks, 1979; Record Pasta Cookbook, 1980; Cooking Made Easy for Disabled, 1981; The Great Little Cookbook, 1982; Cooking Through the Year, 1982; The Pasta Book, 1985; Traditional British Cookery, 1986; Pearls Are for Tears, 1987; Table Decorations, 1988. Add: The Hermitage, Petersham Rd., Richmond, Surrey TW10 7AW, England.

ELLIS, Bret Easton. American, b. 1964. Novels/Short stories. Writer. *Publs:* Less Than Zero, 1985; The Rules of Attraction, 1987. Add: c/o Amanda Urban, International Creative Management, 40 W. 57th St., New York, N.Y. 10019, U.S.A.

ELLIS, Edward Robb. American, b. 1911. History, Sociology. Reporter and feature writer for various wire services and newspapers in U.S., 1927–47; with New York World-Telegram and Sun, 1947–62. *Publs:* (with George N. Allen) Traitor Within: Our Suicide Problem (sociology), 1961; The Epic of New York City, 1966; A Nation in Torment: The Great American Depression, 1929-1939, 1970; Echoes of Distant Thunder: Life in the United States, 1914-18, 1974. Add: 441 West 21st Street, New York, N.Y. 10011, U.S.A.

ELLIS, Ella T(horp). American. Novels/Short stories, Children's fiction, Autobiography/Memoirs/Personal. Instr. in Creative Writing, San Francisco State Univ., and Univ. of California Extension, Berkeley. *Publs:* Roam the Wild Country, 1967; Riptide, 1969; Celebrate the Morning, 1972; Where the Road Ends, 1974; Hallelujah, 1976; Sleepwalter's Moon, 1980; Hugo and the Princess Nena, 1983. Add: 1438 Grizzly Peak Blvd., Berkeley, Calif. 94708, U.S.A.

ELLIS, Gwynn Pennant. British. Chemistry. Reader, Univ. of Wales, Cardiff, since 1962. Co-ed., Progress in Medicinal Chemistry, since 1961. Research Chemist, I.C.I., 1953–57; Head of Chemistry Research, Fisons Pharmaceuticals, 1957–62. *Publs:* Modern Textbook of Organic Chemistry, 1966; (co-author) Qualitative Organic Chemical Analysis, 1967; Medicinal Chemistry Reviews, 1972; Spectral and Chemical Characterisation of Organic Compounds, 1976, 1980; Chromenes, Chromanones, and Chromones, 1977; Chromans and Tocopherols, 1981; Synthesis of Fused Heterocycles, 1987. Add: Dept. of Applied Chemistry, Univ. of Wales, P.O. Box 13, Cardiff CF1 3XF, Wales.

ELLIS, Harold. British, b. 1926. Medicine/Health. Prof. of Surgery, Westminster Medical Sch., Univ. of London, since 1962. Surgical Tutor, Univ. of Oxford, 1959–61. *Publs:* Clinical Anatomy, 1961; Anatomy for Anaesthetists, 1963; History of the Bladder Stone, 1968; (with S. Feldman) Principles of Resuscitation, 1969; (with Roy Calne) Lecture Notes on General Surgery, 1974; Intestinal Obstruction, 1982; Maingot's Abdominal Operations, 1985; Famous Operations, 1985. Add: Surgical Unit, Westminster Medical Sch., London SW1 2AP, England.

ELLIS, Harry Bearse. American, b. 1921. Children's non-fiction, Economics, History. Television Commentator on national and Intnl. affairs, Public Broadcasting System, since 1972; Radio Commentator for the BBC from Washington, since 1972. Corresp., Christian Science Monitor, 1952–84; Radio Commentator, for NBC from Beirut and Paris, 1958–64, and for CBS and Westinghouse Broadcasting Co., from Bonn, 1965–71. *Publs:* Heritage of the Desert: Arabs and the Middle East, 1956; Israel and the Middle East, 1957; The Arabs, 1958; Challenge in the Middle East, 1960; The Common Market, 1965; Ideals and Ideologies: Communism, Socialism, and Capitalism, 1968; The Dilemma of Israel, 1970; Israel: One Land, Two Peoples, 1973. Add: Box 370, Chatham, Ma. 02633, U.S.A.

ELLIS, Humphry Francis. British, b. 1907. Humour/Satire. Contrib., New Yorker mag., since 1954. Member of Editorial Staff, Punch mag., London, 1933–53 (Contrib., 1931–68; Literary and Deputy Ed., 1949–53). *Publs:* So This Is Science, 1932; (co-ed.) The Royal Artillery Commemoration Book, 1950; (ed.) The Manual of Rugby Union Football, 1952; Twenty Five Years Hard, 1960; Mediatrics, 1961; The World of A.J. Wentworth, 1964; A.J. Wentworth, B.A., 1980; Swan Song of A.J. Wentworth, 1982; A Bee in the Kitchen, 1983. Add: Hill Croft, Kingston St. Mary, Taunton, Somerset, England.

ELLIS, Julie. Also writes as Alison Lord; Jeffrey Lord; Susan Marino; Julie Marvin; Susan Marvin; Susan Richard. American, b. 1933. Historical/Romance. *Publs:* The Women Around R.F.K., 1967; (as Alison Lord) DeeDee, 1969, as The Strip in London, 1970; (as Julie Marvin) Revolt of the Second Sex, 1970; (as Jeffrey Lord) Jeb, 1970; Evil at Hillcrest, 1971; (as Susan Marino) Vendetta Castle, 1971; The Jeweled Dagger, 1973; Walk into Darkness, 1973; Kara, 1974; Eden, 1975; Walk a Tightrope, 1975; Elulaie, 1976; The Magnolias, 1976; The Girl in White, 1976; Rendezvous in Vienna, 1976; Wexford, 1976; Savage Oaks, 1977; Long Dark Night of the Soul, 1978; The Hampton Heritage, 1978; The Hampton Women, 1980; Glorious Morning, 1982; East Wind, 1983; Maison Jennie, 1984; Rich Is Best, 1985; The Only Sin, 1986; The Velvet Jungle, 1987; A Daughter's Promise, 1988; novels, as Susan Marvin—The Secret of the Villa Como, 1966; Chateau in the Shadows, 1969; Summer of Fear, 1971; The Secret of Chateau Laval, 1973; Where Is Holly Carleton?, 1974; Chateau Bougy-Villars, 1975; novels, as Susan Richard—Ashley Hall, 1967; Intruder at Maison Benedict, 1967; The Secret of Chateau Kendall, 1967; Chateau Saxony, 1970; Terror at Nelson Woods, 1973; Secret of the Chateau Laval, 1975. Add: c/o William Morrow,

105 Madison Ave., New York, N.Y. 10016, U.S.A.

ELLIS, Keith. British, b. 1927. History, Money/Finance, Psychology. Staff Writer, John Bull mag., London, 1950–60. *Publs:* How to Make Money in Your Spare Time, 1967; The American Civil War, 1971; Warriors and Fighting Men, 1971; The Making of America, 1973; Man and Measurement, 1973; Man and Money, 1973; Prediction and Prophecy, 1973; Thomas Telford, 1974; Thomas Edison, 1974; Science and the Supernatural, 1974; Number Power, 1977; How to Cope with Insomnia, 1983. Add: 3 Belmont Hill, St. Albans, Herts., England.

ELLIS, Mark (Karl). British, b. 1945. Novels/Short stories, Language/Linguistics. Sr. Partner, Language Training Services, Bath, since 1980. Asst. Lectr. in English, Univ. of Libya, 1970–73, and Asian Inst. of Technology, Bangkok, 1973–78. *Publs:* Bannerman, 1973; A Fatal Charade, 1974; The Adoration of the Hanged Man, 1975; Survivors Beyond Babel, 1979; (co-author) Language Guide to the Economist, 1982; Nelson Reading Skills Series, 1982–84; Professional English, 1984; (co-author) English, 1984; (co-author) Counterpoint, 4 vols., 1985; Longman Business Skills Series, 1987. Add: 39 St. Martin's, Marlborough, Wilts., England.

ELLIS, Richard N. American, b. 1939. History. Dir., Center of Southwest Studies, Fort Lewis Coll., Durango, Colo. Assoc. Ed., Red River Valley Historical Review, since 1973; Book Review Ed., New Mexico Historical Review, since 1975; former Prof. of History, and Dir. of the New Mexico Oral History Project, Univ. of New Mexico, Albuquerque. Asst. Prof. of American History, Murray State Univ., Ky., 1967–68. *Publs:* General Pope and U.S. Indian Policy, 1970; (ed.) New Mexico: Past and Present, 1971; (ed. and contrib.) The Western American Indian, 1972; (ed.) New Mexico Historic Documents, 1975. Add: Center of Southwest Studies, Fort Lewis Coll., Durango, Colo. 81301, U.S.A.

ELLIS, Royston. British, b. 1941. Novels, Poetry, Air/Space Topics. Freelance travel writer since 1986. Freelance Poet, Lectr., and television and radio interviewer, 1956–61; Asst. Ed., Jersey News and Features Agency, 1961–63; Assoc. Ed., Canary Island Sun, 1963–66; Project Dir., Emerald Hillside Estates, 1966–74, and Agent and Attorney for Marquis of Bristol, Dominica, W. Indies, 1974–75; Producer and Broadcaster, Radio Dominica, 1973–76; Assoc. Ed., The Educator, Dominica, 1974–76; Dir. Dominica Broadcasting Services, 1976–78; Ed., Wordsman Ltd., Guernsey, 1977–86. *Publs:* Jiving to Gyp, 1959; Drifting with Cliff Richard, 1959; Rave, 1960; Rainbow Walking Stick, 1961; The Big Beat Scene, 1961; The Shadows by Themselves, 1961; Rebel, 1962; The Seaman's Suitcase, 1963; Myself for Fame, 1964; The Flesh Merchants, 1966; The Rush at the End, 1967; The Cherry Boy, 1967; The Small Business Institute Guide to Import/Export, 1976; The Bondmaster, 1977; Blood of the Bondmaster, 1977; Bondmaster Breed, 1979; Fleur, 1979; Bondmaster Fury, 1982; The Bondmaster's Revenge, 1983; Bondmaster Buck, 1984; Master of Black River, 1984; Black River Affair, 1985; Black River Breed, 1985; Bloodheart, 1985; Bloodheart Royal, 1986; Bloodheart Feud, 1987; Giselle, 1988; Guide to Mauritius, 1988; India by Rail, 1989. Add: BM Box 235, London WC1N 3XX, England.

ELLISON, Harlan (Jay). American, b. 1934. Novels/Short stories, Science fiction/ Fantasy. Freeelance writer and lectr., Book Critic, Los Angeles Times, since 1969; Pres., Kilmanjaro Corp., since 1979. Ed., Rogue mag., Chicago, 1959–60; Founding Ed., Regency Books, publrs., Chicago, 1960–61; television series and movie scriptwriter, 1962–77; Weekly Columnist. "The Glass Teat" TV column, 1968–71, and "Harlan Ellison Hornbook," 1972–73, Los Angeles Free Press newspaper; Instr., Clarion Writers Workshops, Michigan State Univ., East Lansing, 1969–77; Editorial Commentator, CBC-TV, 1972–78; Creator and Ed., Harlan Ellison Discovery Series of First Novels, Pyramid Books, 1973–77; Creative Consultant and screenwriter, The Twilight Zone, CBS-TV, 1984–85. *Publs:* science fiction—The Man with Nine Lives, 1960; A Touch of Infinity (short stories), 1960; Ellison Wonderland (short stories), 1962, as Earthman, Go Home, 1964; Paingod and Other Delusions (short stories), 1965; Doomsman, 1967; I Have No Mouth, and I Must Scream (short stories), 1967; From the Land of Fear (short stories), 1967; Love Ain't Nothing but Sex Misspelled (short stories), 1968; The Beast That Shouted Love at the Heart of the World (short stories), 1969; Over the Edge: Stories from Somewhere Else, 1970; Alone Against Tomorrow (short stories). 1971, in U.K. as All the Sound of Fear, and The Time of the Eye, 2 vols., 1973–74; Partners in Wonder: Harlan Ellison in Collaboration with . . . (short stories), 1971; (with Edward Bryant) Approaching Oblivion: Road Signs on the Treadmill Toward Tomorrow (short stories), 1974; Deathbird Stories: A Pantheon of Modern Gods, 1975; No Doors, No Windows (short stories), 1975; (with Edward Bryant) Phoenix Without

Ashes, 1975; The City on the Edge of Forever (novelization of TV play), 1977; Strange Wine (short stories), 1978; The Illustrated Harlan Ellison (short stories), 1978; Blood's a Rover, 1980; Night and the Enemy, 1987; Angry Candy (short stories), 1988; other—Rumble, 1958; The Deadly Streets (short stories), 1958; Rockabilly, 1961, as Spider Kiss, 1975; The Juvies (short stories), 1961; Gentlemen Junkie and Other Stories of the Hung-up Generation, 1961, 1975; Memos from Pergatory: Two Journeys of Our Time (non-fiction), 1961; Demon with a Glass Hand (novelization of TV play), 1967; Kill Machine, 1967; Perhaps Impossible (short stories), 1967; (ed.) Dangerous Visions, 1967; The Glass Teat: Essays of Opinion on the Subject of Television, 1970; (ed.) Again, Dangerous Visions, 1972; The Other Glass Teat: Further Essays of Opinion on Television, 1975; Shatterday, 1980; Stalking of the Nightmare, 1982; Web of the City, 1983; An Edge in My Voice, 1984; Sleepness Nights in the Procrustean Bed: Essays, 1984; The Essential Ellison, 1987.   Add: 3484 Coy Dr., Sherman Oaks, Calif. 91423, U.S.A.

ELLISON, Joan Audrey. Also writes as Elspeth Robertson. British, b. 1928.   Cookery/Gastronomy/Wine. Microbiologist, 1948–50; Lectr., Queen Elizabeth Coll., Univ of London. 1950–54; Information Officer, Norway Food Centre, London, 1966–72; Ed. with M. Costa, Time-Life Foods of the World series, 1970–72; Food Consultant, food industries in U.K. and Scandinavia; Head, Dept. of Nutrition and Home Economics, Flour Advisory Bureau Ltd., London, 1972–78; Secty., Royal Soc. of Health, London, 1980–82. *Publs:* (trans. and ed.) The Great Scandinavian Cook Book, 1966; (as Elspeth Robertson) The Findus Book of Fish Cookery, 1968, 1973; (trans.) The Best of Scandinavian Cookery; (trans. and ed.) Norway's Delights, 1969, 1980; (co-author) Growing for the Kitchen, 1978; The Colman Book of British Traditional Cooking, 1980; The Bread Book, 1987; Patisserie of Scandinavia, 1989.   Add: 135 Stevenage Rd., London SW6 6PB, England.

ELLISON, Ralph (Waldo). American, b. 1914. Novels/Short stories, Essays. Prof. Emeritus, New York Univ., since 1979 (Albert Schweitzer Prof. in the Humanities, 1970–79). Inst. of Russian and American Literature, Bard Coll., Annandale-on-Hudson, N.Y., 1958–61; Visiting Prof. of Writing, Rutgers Univ., New Brunswick, N.J., 1962–64; Chmn., Literary Grants Ctte., National Inst. of Arts and Letters, 1964–67; Member, National Council of the Arts. 1965–67, Editorial Bd., American Scholar, Washington, D.C.., 1966–69, and Carnegie Commn. on Educational Television, 1966–67; Hon. Consultant in American Letters, Library of Congress, Washington, D.C. 1966–72. *Publs:* Invisible Man, 1952; Shadow and Act (essays), 1964; Going to the Territories (essays), 1986. Add: 730 Riverside Dr., New York, N.Y. 10031, U.S.A.

ELLISON, Virginia Howell (Mrs. M.J. Reis). Also writes as Virginian Tier Howell, Leong Gor Yun, Mary A. Mapes, Virginia T.H. Mussey, and V.H. Soskin. American, b. 1910. Children's fiction, Children's non-fiction. Part owner and Ed., Howell, Soskin Publs. Inc., NYC, 1940–48; Ed., Crown Publs. Inc. and Lothrop Lee & Shephard Co., 1948–55; Dir. of Publs. and Promotion, CWU, National Council of Churches, NYC, 1961–64. *Publs:* (as Virginia T.H. Mussey) The Exploits of George Washington, 1933; (with Y.K. Chu as Leong Gor Yun) Chinatown Inside Out, 1936; (as Virginia Howell) Falla, a President's Dog, 1941; (as Mary A. Mapes) Fun with Your Child, 1943; (as Mary A. Mapes) Surprise!, 1944; (as Virginia Howell) Who Likes the Dark, 1945; (as Virginia Howell) Training Pants, 1946; The Pooh Cook Book, 1969; The Pooh Party Book, 1971; The Pooh Get-Well Book, 1973. Add: 92 Mather Rd., Stamford, Conn. 06903, U.S.A.

ELLSWORTH, Ralph E. American, b. 1907. Librarianship. Dir. of Libraries, Univ of Iowa, Iowa City, 1943–58; Dir. of Libraries and Prof. of Library Science, Univ. of Colorado, Boulder, 1958 until retirement. *Publs:* (with D.E. Bean) Modular Planning for College and Small University Libraries, 1948; The State of the Library Art: Buildings, 1960; Planning the College and University Library Building, 1960; (with S. Harris) The American Right Wing, 1961; (with H.D. Wagener) The School Library: Faculties for Independent Study in the Secondary School, 1963; The School Library, 1965; The Economics of Book Storage, 1972; Academic Library Buildings: A Guide to Architectural Issues and Solutions, 1973; Planning Manual for Academic Library Buildings, 1973. Add: 860 Willowbrook, Boulder, Colo, 80301, U.S.A.

ELMSLIE, Kenward. American, b. 1929. Novels/Short stories, Plays, Screenplays, Poetry, Songs, lyrics and libretti. *Publs:* The Power Plant Poems, 196; Lizzie Borden (libretto), 1967; Miss Julie (libretto), 1967; Album, 1969; Circus Nerves, 1971; Motor Disturbance, 1971; City Junket, 1972; The Grass Harp, 1972; The Orchid Stories, 1973; The Sweet Bye and Bye (libretto), 1973; Penguin Modern Poets 24, 1974; The Seagull

(libretto), 1974; Tropicalism, 1975; Washington Square (libretto), 1976; The Alphabet Work, 1977; Communications Equipment, 1979; Moving Right Along, 1980; Bimbo Dirt, 1982; Lola (libretto), 1982; Three Sisters (libretto), 1986; 26 Bars, 1987; Sung Sex, 1989. Add: Poet's Corner, Calais, Vt. 05648, U.S.A.

ELSEN, Albert Edward. American, b. 1927. Art. Walter A. Haas Prof. of Art History, Stanford Univ., California, since 1968. Asst. Prof. of Art History, Carleton Coll., Northfield, Minn., 1952–58; Prof. of Art History, Indiana Univ., Bloomington, 1958–68. Pres., College Art Assn., 1974–74. *Publs:* Rodin's Gates of Hell, 1960; Purposes of Art, 1962, 4th ed. 1981; Rodin, 1963; (ed.) Auguste Rodin: Readings on His Life and Work, 1965; The Partial Figure in Modern Sculpture: From Rodin to 1969, 1969; Seymour Lipton, 1970; (with K. Varnedoe) Rodin Drawings, 1972; The Sculpture of Henri Matisse, 1972; Paul Jenkins, 1973; (with S. McGough and S. Wander) Rodin and Balzac, 1973; Pioneers of Modern Sculpture, 1973; rev. ed. as Origins of Modern Sculpture; Pioneers and Premises, 1974; Modern European Sculpture, 1918-1945, 1979; In Rodin's Studio, 1980; (with J.H. Merryman) Law, Ethics and the Visual Arts, 2 vols., 1979, 2nd ed., 1987; Rodin Rediscovered, 1981; The Gates of Hell by Auguste Rodin, 1986; Rodin's Thinker and the Dilemmas of Modern Public Sculpture, 1985. Add: 10 Peter Coutts Circle, Stanford, Cal. 94305, U.S.A.

ELSNA, Hebe. Pseud. for Dorothy Phoebe Ansle; also writes as Laura Conway, Vicky Lancaster, and Lyndon Snow. Historical/Romance/Gothic, Plays/Screenplays, Biography. *Publs:* Child of Passion, 1928; The Third Wife, 1928; Sweeter Unpossessed, 1929; Strait-Jacket, 1930; Study of Sara, 1930; We Are the Pilgrims, 1931; (as Laura Conway) as I Know Not Whither, 1979; Other People's Fires, 1931; All Swans, 1933; Upturned Palms, 1933; You Never Knew, 1933; Women Always Forgive, 1934; Half Sisters, 1934; Receipt for Hardness, 1935; Uncertain Lover, 1935; Crista Moon, 1936; (as Vicky Lancaster) Gypsy Virtue, 1936; The Silver Boy and Other Stories, 1936; Brief Heroine, 1937; People Are So Respectable, 1937; The Price of Pleasure, 1937; (as Vicky Lancaster) Dawn Through the Shutters, 1937; Men Are So Strange, 1937; All Visitors Ashore, 1938; Like Summer Brave, 1938; This Clay Suburb, 1938, as Bid Time Return, 1979; (as Vicky Lancaster) Heartbreaker, 1938; (as Vicky Lancaster) Masquerade for Love, 1938; (as Vicky Lancaster) This Wild Enchantment, 1938; The Wedding Took Place, 1939; (as Vicky Lancaster) Daughter at Home, 1939; (as Vicky Lancaster) Three Roads to Heaven, 1939; The First Week in September, 1940; (as Vicky Lancaster) Farewell to Veronica, 1940; (as Lyndon Snow) Young Love Wakes, 1940; (as Vicky Lancaster) Sometimes Spring Returns, 1940; Lady Misjudged, 1941; Everyone Loves Lorraine, 1941; (as Laura Conway) as Portrait of Lorraine, 1971; (as Vicky Lancaster) Must the Dream End, 1941; (as Lyndon Snow) Follow Your Star, 1941; (as Lyndon Snow) Second Thoughts, 1941; Our Little Life, 1942; (as Lyndon Snow) as Yesterday and Tomorrow, 1971; None Can Return, 1942; See My Shining Palace, 1942; (as Vicky Lancaster) Sweet Shipwreck, 1942; (as Lyndon Snow) But Joy Kissed Me, 1942; Young and Broke, 1943; No Fields of Amaranth, 1943, (as Lyndon Snow), 1971; (as Vicky Lancaster) Beggar Girl's Gift, 1943; (as Vicky Lancaster) The Happy Cinderella, 1943; (as Lyndon Snow) Three Latch Keys, 1978; The Happiest Year, 1944; I Have Lived Today, 1944, (as Lyndon Snow) as The Songless Wood, 1979; (as Vicky Lancaster) Lady-Look Ahead, 1944; (as Vicky Lancaster) They Loved in Donegal, 1944; (as Lyndon Snow) Dream Daughter, 1944; Echo from Afar, 1945; The Gilded Ladder, 1945; (as Lyndon Snow) Christening Party, 1945; Cafeteria, 1946; (as Vicky Lancaster) The Sunset Hour, 1946; (as Vicky Lancaster) Fixed as the Stars, 1946; (as Lyndon Snow) Dear Yesterday, 1946; (as Lyndon Snow) Early Blossom, 1946; Clemency Page, 1947; The Dream and the World, 1947; as A Link in the Chain, 1975; (as Vicky Lancaster) So Many Worlds, 1948, (as Laura Conway) as The Sisters, 1971; (as Lyndon Snow) Two Walk Apart, 1948; (as Lyndon Snow) The Gift of My Heart, 1948; Midnight Matinée, 1949; The Soul of Mary Olivane, 1949, as Mary Olivane, 1973; (as Vicky Lancaster) All Past Years, 1949; (as Vicky Lancaster) Perfect Marriage, 1949; (as Lyndon Snow) Come to My Wedding, 1949; The Door Between, 1950, 1971; No Shallow Stream, 1950, (as Lyndon Snow) as The World of Christy Pembroke, 1978; (as Vicky Lancaster) Draw Back the Curtain, 1950; (as Vicky Lancaster) Short Lease, 1950; (as Lyndon Snow) Golden Future, 1950; (as Lyndon Snow) All in the Day's Work, 1950; Happy Birthday to You, 1951, (as Lyndon Snow) as The Conjuror's Daughter, 1979; (as Vicky Lancaster) Homecoming, 1951, (as Laura Conway) as Journey Home, 1978; (as Lyndon Snow) A Year of Her Life, 1951; (as Lyndon Snow) Poor Butterfly, 1951; The Convert, 1952; A Day of Grace, 1952; (as Vicky Lancaster) They Were Not Divided, 1952; (as Laura Conway), 1972;

(as Lyndon Snow) Honoured Guest, 1952; (as Lyndon Snow) Made in Heaven, 1952; (as Laura Conway) Love Calls Me Home, 1952; A Girl Disappears, 1953; Gail Talbot, 1953, (as Laura Conway) as If This Be Sin, 1975; (as Vicky Lancaster) The Career of Stella Merlin, 1953; (as Vicky Lancaster) Passing Sweet, 1953; (as Lyndon Snow) Dearest Enemy, 1953, (as Laura Conway) as The Case Is Closed, 1980; (as Lyndon Snow) Wayward Love, 1953; (as Laura Conway) Loving You Always, 1953; (as Laura Conway) Innocent Enchantress, 1953; Consider These Women, 1954; A Shade of Darkness, 1954; The Season's Greetings, 1954, as play, 1954; (as Vicky Lancaster) Lover's Staff, 1954; (as Vicky Lancaster) Many a Human Heart, 1954; (as Lyndon Snow) Always Remember, 1954; (as Lyndon Snow) Do Not Forget Me, 1954; (as Laura Conway) Love's Prisoner, 1954; The Sweet Lost Years, 1955; I Bequeath, 1955; (as Vicky Lancaster) Lovers in Darkness, 1955; (as Vicky Lancaster) In Search of Love, 1955; (as Vicky Lancaster) Suspicion, 1955; (as Lyndon Snow) Love Me for Ever, 1955; (as Lyndon Snow) Alone with You, 1955; (as Laura Conway) So New to Love, 1955; Strange Visitor, 1956, (as Laura Conway), 1973; The Love Match, 1956; (as Vicky Lancaster) The Way of a Man, 1956; (as Lyndon Snow) So Fair My Love, 1956; (as Lyndon Snow) Tomorrow's Promise, 1956; (as Laura Conway) Enchantment, 1956; (as Laura Conway) Hard to Win, 1956; My Dear Lady, 1957; The Marrying Kind, 1957; (as Vicky Lancaster) Women in Love, 1957; (as Vicky Lancaster) Princess in Love, 1957; (as Vicky Lancaster) Royal Deputy, 1957; (as Lyndon Snow) For Love Alone, 1957; (as Lyndon Snow) Romance Is Always Young, 1957, 1975; (as Laura Conway) Be True to Me, 1957; (as Laura Conway) When Next We Meet, 1957; Mrs. Melbourne, 1958, 1972; The Gay Unfortunate, 1958; (as Vicky Lancaster) All Our Tomorrows, 1958; (as Vicky Lancaster) The Amazing Marriage, 1958; (as Lyndon Snow) Silence Is Golden, 1958; (as Lyndon Snow) A Heart to Be Won, 1958; (as Laura Conway) Wish upon a Dream, 1958, in U.S. as Dark Dream, 1976; (as Laura Conway) No Regrets, 1958; The Younger Miss Nightingale, 1959; (as Vicky Lancaster) The Unbroken Link, 1959; (as Vicky Lancaster) The Past Must Die, 1959; (as Lyndon Snow) Moonlight Witchery, 1959; (as Lyndon Snow) Stealer of Hearts, 1959; (as Laura Conway) The Sun Still Shines, 1959; (as Laura Conway) By Love Transformed, 1959; Marks upon Snow, 1960; Time Is-Time Was, 1960; (as Vicky Lancaster) Secret Lives, 1960; (as Vicky Lancaster) Sweet Wine of Youth, 1960; (as Lyndon Snow) Happy Event, 1960; (as Lyndon Snow) Some Day You'll Love Me, 1960; (as Laura Conway) Bargain in Love, 1960; (as Laura Conway) The Turn of the Road, 1960; The Little Goddess, 1961; The Lonely Dreamer, 1961, (as Laura Conway), 1972; Vicky, 1961, as The Eldest Daughter, 1974; (as Vicky Lancaster) The Cobweb Mist, 1961; (as Vicky Lancaster) Snake in the Grass, 1961; (as Lyndon Snow) The Fabulous Marriage, 1961; (as Lyndon Snow) After All, 1961; (as Laura Conway) Teach Me to Forget, 1961; (as Laura Conway) Shadow Marriage, 1961; Beyond Reasonable Doubt, 1962; Take Pity upon Youth, 1962; (as Vicky Lancaster) Doctor in Suspense, 1962; (as Vicky Lancaster) Love's Second Chance, 1962; (as Vicky Lancaster) No Good as a Nurse, 1962; (as Lyndon Snow) Anything Can Happen, 1962; (as Lyndon Snow) My Dream Fulfilled, 1962; (as Laura Conway) It's Lonely Without You, 1962; (as Laura Conway) Lovers in Waiting, 1962; Minstrel's Court, 1963, (as Lyndon Snow), 1974; (with Margaret Barnes) Lady on the Coin, 1963; A House Called Pleasance, 1963, in U.S. (as Laura Conway), 1979; (as Lyndon Snow) Prima Donna, 1963; (as Lyndon Snow) Difficult to Love, 1963; (as Laura Conway) A Way Through the Maze, 1963; (as Laura Conway) Safety for My Love, 1963; Unwanted Wife: A Defence of Mrs. Charles Dickens (biography), 1963; The Undying Past, 1964, in U.S. (as Laura Conway), 1980; Too Well Beloved, 1964, in U.S. (as Laura Conway), 1979; (as Lyndon Snow) My Brother's Wife, 1964; (as Laura Conway) Loving Is Different, 1964; (as Laura Conway) A Butterfly's Hour, 1964; The Brimming Cup, 1965; The China Princess, 1965; (as Lyndon Snow) The One Who Looked On, 1965; (as Lyndon Snow) Bright Face of Honour, 1965; (as Lyndon Snow) His Shadow on the Wall, 1965; (as Laura Conway) Two Fair Daughters, 1965; (as Laura Conway) Gifted Friends, 1965; Saxon's Folly, 1966; (as Lyndon Snow) My Cousin Lola, 1966; (as Lyndon Snow) Spinster of This Parish, 1966; (as Laura Conway) Heiress Apparent, 1966; (as Laura Conway) Five Mrs. Lorrimers, 1966; The Queen's Ward, 1967; (as Lyndon Snow) The Head of the House, 1967; (as Laura Conway) For a Dream's Sake, 1967; (as Laura Conway) The Unforgotten, 1967; Catherine of Braganza, Charles II's Queen (biography), 1967; The Heir of Garlands, 1968; (as Lyndon Snow) Poor Relations, 1968; (as Lyndon Snow) Moment of Truth, 1968, in U.S. (as Laura Conway), 1975; The Pursuit of Pleasure, 1969; The Abbot's House, 1969, in U.S. (as Laura Conway), 1974; (as Laura Conway) Dearest Mamma, 1969; (as Laura Conway) The Night of the Party, 1969; Take Heed of Loving Me, 1970, in U.S. (as Laura Conway),

1976; Sing for Your Supper, 1970; The Mask of Comedy, 1970; (as Lyndon Snow) Francesca, 1970, in U.S. (as Laura Conway), 1973; The King's Bastard, 1971; Prelude for Two Queens, 1972; (as Lyndon Snow) An Arrow in My Heart, 1972; (as Laura Conway) Living with Paula, 1972; The Elusive Crown, 1973; (as Lyndon Snow) Trial and Error, 1973; (as Laura Conway) Dark Symmetry, 1973; (as Laura Conway) Acquittal, 1973; The Cherished One, 1974; (as Lyndon Snow) Don't Shut Me Out, 1974; Distant Landscape, 1975; (as Laura Conway) A Link in the Chain, 1975; Cast a Long Shadow, 1976, in U.S. (as Laura Conway), 1978; (as Lyndon Snow) Best Loved Person, 1976; Heiress Presumptive, 1981; Red-Headed Bastard, 1981. Add: c/o Curtis Brown Ltd., 162-168 Regent St., London W1R 5TB, England.

ELSOM, John (Edward). British. Plays, Literature, Theatre. Sr. Lectr., City Univ., London. Chmn., British Liberal Party's Arts & Broadcasting Cttee.; Pres., Intnl. Assn. of Theatre Critics, since 1985. Theatre Critic for London Mag., 1964–70, The Observer, London, 1972, The Listener, 1972–82, and The Mail on Sunday, 1983. *Publs:* Theatre Outside London, 1971; One More Bull (plays, trilogy), 1972; Erotic Theatre, 1973; Post-War British Theatre, 1976: (with N. Tomalin) The History of the National Theatre, 1978; (ed.) Post-War Theatre Criticism, 1980; The Man of the Future Is Dead, 1985. Add: c/o Campbell, Thomson & Mc-Laughlin Ltd., 31 Newington Green, London N16 9PU, England.

ELSON, Edward L.R. American, b. 1906. Theology/Religion. Chaplain, U.S. Senate, Washington, D.C., 1969–81. *Publs:* One Moment with God, 1951; America's Spiritual Recovery, 1954; And Still He Speaks, 1960; The Inevitable Encounter, 1962; Prayers in the U.S. Senate During the 91st Congress, 1971; Prayers in the U.S. Senate During the 92nd Congress, 1973; Prayers in the U.S. Senate During the 93rd Congress, 1975; Prayers in the U.S. Senate During the 94th Congress, 1976; Prayers in the U.S. Senate During the 95th Congress, 1979; Prayers in the U.S. Senate During the 96th Congress, 1981; Wide Was His Parish (autobiography), 1987. Add: The Westchester, 4000 Cathedral Ave. N.W., Washington D.C. 20016, U.S.A.

ELSON, R.N. *See* **NELSON**, Ray.

ELSTOB, Peter. British, b. 1915. Novels, History. Vice-Pres. Intnl. P.E.N., since 1982 (Press Officer, 1970–74; Secty.-Gen., 1974–82). Dir., Archive Press Ltd., since 1965. Dir., Arts Theatre Club, London, 1946–54; Dir., Trade Winds Films, 1958–62. *Publs:* Spanish Prisoner, 1939; (co-author) The Flight of the Small World, 1959; Warriors for the Working Day, 1960; The Armed Rehearsal, 1964; Bastogne, the Road Block, 1968; The Battle of the Reichswald, 1970; Hitler's Last Offensive, 1971; (ed.) A Register of the Regiments and Corps of the British Army, 1972; Condor Legion, 1973; (ed.) The Survival of Literature, 1979; Scoundrel, 1986. Add: Burley Lawn House, Burley Lawn, Ringwood, Hants BH24 4AR, England.

ELSY, (Winifred) Mary. British. Travel/Exploration/Adventure. Producer's Asst., Realist Film Unit, 1957–58, and Assoc.-Rediffusion, Television, London, 1958–59; Writer and Sub-Ed., Fleetway Publs., 1960–62, B.P.C., 1963–64, and Evans Bros., 1965–66; Children's Book Ed., Abelard-Schuman Ltd., London, 1967–68. *Publs:* Travels in Belgium and Luxembourg, 1966; Brittany and Normandy, 1974; Travels in Normandy, 1988; Travels in Brittany, 1988; Travels in Alsace Lorraine, 1989; Travels in Burgundy, 1989. Add: 519C Finchley Rd., Hampstead, London NW3 7BB, England.

ELTON, (Sir) Geoffrey Rudolph. British, b. 1921. History. Regius Prof. of Modern History, Cambridge Univ., 1983–88 (Lectr., Reader and Prof. in History, 1949–83). Pres., Royal Historical Soc., 1972–76, and Selden Soc., 1982–85. *Publs:* The Tudor Revolution in Government, 1953; England under the Tutors, 1955; Star Chamber Stories, 1958; (ed.) New Cambridge Modern History, vol. II, 1958; The Tudor Constitution, 1960, 1982; Reformation Europe, 1963; (ed.) Ideas and Institutions: Renaissance and Reformation, vol. III, 1963; The Practice of History, 1967; Sources of History: England 1200-1640, 1969; Political History: Principles and Practice, 1970; Modern Historians on British History 1485-1945, 1970; Policy and Police: The Enforcement of the Reformation in the Age of Thomas Cromwell, 1972; Reform and Renewal: Thomas Cromwell and the Common Weal, 1973; Studies in Tudor and Stuart Politics and Government, vol. 2, 1974, vol. 3, 1983; Reform and Reformation: England 1509-1558, 1977; F.W. Maitland, 1985; The Parliament of England 1559-1581, 1986. Add: Clare Coll., Cambridge CB2 1TL, England.

ELTRINGHAM, S(tewart) K(eith). British, b. 1929. Environmental science/Ecology, Marine science/Oceanography, Natural history, Zoology. Univ. Lectr. in Zoology, Cambridge Univ., since 1989 (Univ. Lectr. in Applied Biology, 1973–89). Pilot-biologist, The Wildfowl Trust, Slimbridge, Glos., 1957–61; Lectr. in Zoology, King's Coll., Univ. of London, 1962–67; Dir., Nuffield Unit of Tropical Animal Ecology, Queen Elizabeth National Park, Uganda, 1966–71; Dir., Uganda Inst. of Ecology Queen Elizabeth National Park, Uganda, and Chief Research Officer, Uganda National Parks, 1971–73. *Publs:* (ed. with E.B. Gareth Jones) Marine Borers, Fungi and Fouling Organisms of Wood, 1971; Life in Mud and Sand, 1971; The Ecology and Conservation of Large African Mammals, 1979; Elephants, 1982; Wildlife Resources and Economic Development, 1984. Add: Dept. of Zoology, Cambridge Univ., Downing St., Cambridge CB2 3EJ, England.

ELWOOD, Ann. American, b. 1931. Children's fiction, Children's non-fiction. Advertising Mgr., Glencoe Press, Calif., 1967–72. *Publs:* (with John Raht) Walking Out, 1980; (with Carol Orsag and Sidney Solomon) The Macmillan Illustrated Almanac for Kids, 1981; (with Linda C. Wood) Windows in Space, 1982; (with Carol Orsag) Brainstorms and Thunderbolts: How Creative Genius Works, 1983. Add: 2442 Montomery Ave., Cardiff, Calif. 92007, U.S.A.

ELY, David. American, b. 1927. Novels/Short stories. Reporter, St. Louis Post-Dispatch, Mo., 1949–50, 1952–54 and 1955–56; Administrative Asst., Development and Resources Corp., NYC, 1956–59. *Publs:* Trot, 1963; Seconds, 1963; The Tour, 1967; Time Out (short stories), 1968; Poor Devils, 1970; Walking Davis, 1972; Mr. Nicholas, 1974. Add: P.O. Box 1387, East Dennis, Mass. 02641, U.S.A.

EMANUEL, James A(ndrew, Sr.). American, b. 1921. Poetry, Literature. Prof. of English, City Coll. of New York, since 1972 (Instr., 1957–62; Asst. Prof., 1962–70; Assoc. Prof., 1970–72). Civilian Chief, Pre-Induction Section, Army and Air Force Induction Station, Chicago, 1951–53; Instr., Harlem YWCA Business Sch., NYC, 1954–56; Fulbright Prof. of American Literature, Univ., of Grenoble, France, 1968–69; Visiting Prof. of English, Univ. of Toulouse, France, 1971–73, 1979–81. *Publs:* Langston Hughes, 1967; (ed. with T.L. Gross) Dark Symphony: Negro Literature in America, 1968; The Treehouse and Other Poems, 1968; At Bay, 1969; Panther Man, 1970; (with MacKinlay Kantor and L. Osgood) How I Write 2, 1972; Black Man Abroad: The Toulouse Poems, 1979; A Chisel in the Dark, 1980; The Broken Bowl: New and Uncollected Poems, 1983; A Poet's Mind, 1983. Add: Dept. of English, City Coll. of New York, Convent Ave., New York, N.Y. 10031, U.S.A.

EMBEY, Philip. *See* PHILIPP, Elliott Elias.

EMECHETA, (Florence Onye) Buchi. British, b. 1944. Novels/Short stories, Sociology, Autobiography/Memoirs/Personal. Youth Worker and Sociologist, Inner London Education Authority since 1969. Library Officer, British Museum, London, 1965–69. *Publs:* In the Ditch, 1972; Second Class Citizen, 1974; The Bride Price, 1976; The Slave Girl, 1977; Titch the Cat, 1979; Joys of Motherhood, 1979; Nowhere to Play, 1980; The Moonlight Bride, 1981; Destination Biafra, 1982; Naira Power, 1982; Double Yoke, 1982; The Rape of Shavi, 1983; Head Above Water (autobiography), 1986. Add: 7 Briston Grove, London N8 9EX, England.

EMENEAU, Murray Barnson. American, b. 1904. Anthropology, Ethnology, Language/Linguistics, Mythology/Folklore. Prof. Emeritus, Univ. of California, Berkeley, since 1971 (Asst. Prof. of Sanskrit and Gen. Linguistics, 1940–43; Assoc. Prof., 1943–46; Prof., 1946–71). *Publs:* Jambhaladatta's Version of Vetalapancavinsati, 1934; A Union List of Printed Indic Texts and Translations in American Libraries, 1935; Kota Texts, 1944–46; Studies in Vietnamese Grammar, 1951; Sanskrit Sandhi and Exercises, 1952; 4th ed. 1968; Kolami, a Dravidian Language, 1955; (with T. Burrow) A Dravidian Etymological Dictionary, 1961, 1966, supplement 1968, 2nd ed. 1984; (with T. Burrow) Dravidian Borrowing from Indo-Aryan, 1962; Brahui and Dravidian Comparative Grammar, 1962; India and Historical Grammar, 1965; Dravidian Linguistics, Ethnology, and Folktales: Collected Papers, 1967; Dravidian Comparative Phonology: A Sketch, 1970; Toda Songs, 1971; Ritual Structure and Language Structure of the Todas, 1974; Language and Linguistic Area: Selected Essays, 1980; Toda Grammer and Texts, 1984; Sanskrit Studies: Selected Papers, 1988. Add: 909 San Benito Rd., Berkeley, Calif. 94707, U.S.A.

EMERSON, David. British, b. 1900. Novels/Short stories. *Publs:* Regency Windows, 1930; The Distant Storm, 1931; Fitzwarren, 1932; Dark Bright Rose, 1951; The Pride of Parson Carnaby, 1953; The Curate of Wakefield, 1954; The Surgeon of Sedbridge, 1955; Miss Marlow from Court, 1956; The Warden of Grey's, 1957; The Esplanade House, 1958;

The Trouble at Sheplinch, 1959; The Wisteria Woman, 1961; Julie and the General, 1963; Scrope and the Spinster, 1964; Sweet Orchard, 1965; The Obliging Housemaid, 1966; Young Sweetly, 1967; Old Man's Darling, 1968; Cartwright's Wicked Aunt, 1969; A Murder in the Family, 1970; Little Brother Claude, 1971; Nancy in London, 1972; Aunt Campbell's Young Man, 1973; A Nice Little Widow, 1974; The Fate of Esther Fox, 1976; The Schoolhouse Sofa, 1978; The Gate of Honour, 1980. Add: 15 St. Andrew's Rd., Burnham-on-Sea, Somerset, England.

EMERSON, Earl W. American, b. 1948. Mystery/Crime/Suspense. Lieutenant, Seattle Fire Dept., Wash., since 1978. *Publs:* The Rainy City, 1985; Poverty Bag, 1985; Nervous Laughter, 1986; Fat Tuesday, 1987; Black Hearts and Slow Dancing, 1988; Deviant Behaviour, 1988. Add: c/o Dominick Abel, 498 West End Ave., Suite 12C, New York, N.Y. 10024, U.S.A.

EMERSON, Thomas I. American, b. 1907. Civil liberties/Human rights, Politics/Government. Lines Prof. of Law, Yale Law Sch., Yale Univ., New Haven, Conn., since 1946. *Publs:* Political and Civil Rights in the United States, 2 vols., 4th ed. 1976–79, supplement 1980; Toward a General Theory of the First Amendment, 1967; The System of Freedom of Expression, 1970. Add: Yale Law Sch., New Haven, Conn. 06520, U.S.A.

EMERY, Kenneth (Orris). American, b. 1914. Marine science/Oceanography. Sr. Scientist, Woods Hole Oceanographic Instn., 1963–79, now Emeritus (Geologist, 1962–63, Acting Dean of Grad. Studies, 1968). Asst. Geologist, Illinois State Geological Survey, 1941–43; Asst. Marine Geologist, to Assoc. Geologist, Univ. of California Div. of War Research, San Diego, 1943–45; Asst. Prof., to Prof., Univ. of Southern California, Los Angeles, 1945–62; Geologist, U.S. Geological Survey, 1946–60; Oceanographer, Navy Ordnance Test Center, Pasadena, Calif. 1960–62. Member, Navy Research and Development Bd., 1948–52; Councillor, Geological Soc. of America, 1967–69; Member, Advisory Bd., The Cousteau Soc., 1975. *Publs:* (with F. Shepard) Submarine Topography Off the California Coast, 1941; The Sea Off Southern California: A Modern Habitat of Petroleum, 1960; Marine Geology of Guam, 1962; A Coastal Pond, Studied by Oceanographic Methods, 1969; (with E. Uchupi) Western North Atlantic Ocean: Topography, Rocks, Structure, Water, Life and Sediments, 1972; (with B.J. Skinner) Mineral Deposits of the Deep-Ocean Floor, 1978; (with E. Uchupi) The Geology of the Atlantic Ocean, 1984; (with D. Neev and N. Babler) Mediterranean Coasts of Israel and Sinai, 1987; (with T.M. Hamilton) Eighteenth-Century Gunflints from Fort Michilimackinac and Other Colonial Sites, 1988. Add: Woods Hole Oceanographic Instn., Woods Hole, Mass. 02543, U.S.A.

EMERY, Robert Firestone. American, b. 1927. Economics. Economist, Federal Reserve System, Washington, D.C., 1955–88. Adjunct Prof. of Economics, Southeastern Univ., Washington, D.C., since 1960 (Chmn., Dept. of Financial Admin., 1963–65; Dean, Sr. Div., 1965–68). *Publs:* The Financial Institutions of Southeast Asia: A Country-by-Country Study, 1970; The Japanese Money Market, 1984. Add: 3421 Shepherd St., Chevy Chase, Md. 20815, U.S.A.

EMMERICH, André. American, b. 1924. Art. Pres., André Emmerich Gallery, NYC, since 1954. Pres., Art Dealers of America, 1972–74. *Publs:* Art Before Columbus, 1963; Sweat of the Sun and Tears of the Moon: Gold and Silver in Pre-Columbian Art, 1965. Add: 41 E. 57th St., New York, N.Y. 10022, U.S.A.

EMMET, Dorothy Mary. British. Philosophy. Fellow, Lucy Cavendish Coll., Cambridge, since 1966. Lectr. in Philosophy, King's Coll., Newcastle upon Tyne, 1932–38; Lectr., 1938–46, and Univ. Prof. of Philosophy, 1946–66, Univ. of Manchester. Ed., Theoria to Theory journal, London, 1966–81. *Publs:* Whitehead's Philosophy of Organism, 1932; Philosophy and Faith, 1936; The Nature of Metaphysical Thinking, 1946; Function, Purpose and Powers, 1957; Rules, Roles and Relations, 1966; (ed. with A. MacIntyre) Sociological Theory, 1970; The Moral Prism, 1979; The Effectiveness of Causes, 1984. Add: 11 Millington Rd., Cambridge, England.

EMSHWILLER, Carol (Fries). American, b. 1921. Science fiction/Fantasy. Teacher of short story writing at New York Univ. and visiting teacher of writing at Sarah Lawrence Coll., Bronxville, N.Y. National Endowment for Arts Grant, 1980. *Publs:* Joy in Our Cause, 1974; Carmen Dog, 1988; Verging on Pertinent, 1989. Add: 260 E. 10th St., No. 10, New York, N.Y. 10009, U.S.A.

ENGDAHL, Sylvia L(ouise). American, b. 1933. Children's fiction, Science fiction, Sciences (general). *Publs:* Enchantress from the Stars, 1970 (Newbery Honor Book); Journey Between Worlds, 1970; The Far Side of Evil, 1971; This Star Shall Abide (in U.K. as Heritage of the Star), 1972; Beyond the Tomorrow Mountains, 1973; The Planet-Girded Suns: Man's View of Other Solar Systems, 1974; (ed. with R. Roberson) Universe Ahead: Stories of the Future, 1975; (ed.) Anywhere, Anywhen: Stories of Tomorrow, 1976; (with R. Roberson) The Subnuclear Zoo: New Discoveries in High Energy Physics, 1977; (with R. Roberson) Tool for Tomorrow: New Knowledge About Genes, 1979; Our World Is Earth, 1979; The Doors of the Universe, 1981. Add: 3088 Delta Pines Dr., Eugene, Or. 97401, U.S.A.

ENGEL, Bernard F. American, b. 1921. Literature. Prof., Dept. of American Thought and Language, Michigan State Univ., East Lansing, since 1957 (Chmn., 1967–77). *Publs:* (ed.) History of the 413th Infantry, 1946; Marianne Moore, 1964, 1989; The Achievement of Richard Eberhart, 1970; Richard Eberhart, 1972; (ed.) A New Voice for a New People: Midwestern Poetry 1800-1910, 1985. Add: Dept. of American Thought and Language, Bessey Hall, Michigan State Univ., East Lansing, Mich. 48823, U.S.A.

ENGEL, Monroe. American, b. 1921. Novels/Short stories, Literature. Sr. Lectr. on English, Harvard Univ., Cambridge, Mass., since 1955. Assoc. Ed., Reynal & Hitchcock, 1946–47, and Viking Press, NYC, 1947–51; Lectr., Princeton Univ., N.J., 1954–55. *Publs:* A Length of Rope (novel), 1952; Visions of Nicholas Solon (novel), 1959; The Maturity of Dickens, 1959; Voyager Belsky (novel), 1962; (ed.) The Uses of Literature, 1974; Fish (novel), 1981; Statutes of Limitations (novel), 1988. Add: 17 Hilliard St., Cambridge, Mass. 02138, U.S.A.

ENGELHARDT, (Sister) M. Veronice. American, b. 1912. Children's non-fiction. Chmn., Communications Bd., Third Franciscan Order, Syracuse, N.Y. (Dir., Reading Clinic, 1962–84; Asst. Mother Gen., 1965–71; Personnel Dir., 1972–75). Dean of Women, and Head, Dept. of Education and Psychology, Chaminade Coll., Honolulu, Hawaii, 1957–60; Chmn., Dept. of Education and Psychology, Maria Regina Coll., Syracuse, 1962–68. *Publs:* Looking at God's World; Creatures in God's World; Learning More About God's World; (co-author) Songs about God's World. Add: 1024 Court St., Syracuse, N.Y. 13208, U.S.A.

ENGELS, John (David). American, b. 1931. Poetry. Prof. of English, St. Michael's Coll., Winooski Park, Vt., since 1970 (Asst. Prof., 1962–70). Secty., 1971–72, and Trustee, 1971–75, Vermont Council on the Arts. *Publs:* (with Norbert Engels) Writing Techniques, 1962; (with Norbert Engels) Experience and Imagination, 1965; The Homer Mitchell Place (verse), 1968; (ed.) The Merrill Guide to William Carlos Williams, 1969; (ed.) The Merrill Checklist of William Carlos Williams, 1969; (ed.) The Merrill Studies in Paterson, 1971; Signals from the Safety Coffin (verse), 1975; Vivaldi in Early Fall (verse), 1977; Blood Mountain (verse), 1977; Vivaldi in Early Fall (collection), 1981; The Seasons in Vermont (verse), 1982; Weather-Fear: New and Selected Poems 1958-1982, 1983; Cardinals in the Ice Age (verse), 1987. Add: Dept. of English, St. Michael's Coll., Winooski Park, Vt. 05404, U.S.A.

ENGLAND, Barry. British, b. 1934. Novels/Short stories, Plays, Screenplays. *Publs:* End of Conflict, 1964; Figures in a Landscape (novel), 1968; Conduct Unbecoming, 1971. Add: c/o Patricia Macnaughton, M.L.R., 194 Old Brompton Rd., London SW5 0AS, England.

ENGLE, Eloise. (Mrs. Lauri Paananen). American, b. 1923. Novels/Short stories, Military/Defence. *Publs:* Dawn Mission, 1962; Princess of Paradise, 1962; Sea Challenge, 1962; Countdown for Cindy, 1962; Escape, 1963; (with M. Ransom) Sea of the Bear, 1964; Pararescue, 1964; (with K. Drummond) Sky Rangers, 1965; Earthquake, 1966; Medic, 1967; The House that Half-Jack Built, 1971; (ghostwriter) The Do's and Don'ts of Delightful Dieting, 1972; Parachutes: How They Work, 1972; (with L.A. Paananen) The Winter War: The Russo-Finnish conflict of 1939-40, 1973; (with A. Lott) America's Maritime Heritage, 1976; Man in Flight: Biomedical Achievements in Aerospace, 1979; Earthquake Technology, 1982; Of Cabbages and the King, 1984; The Baltimore One-Day Trip Book, 1985. Add: 6348 Crosswoods Dr., Falls Church, Va. 22044, U.S.A.

ENGLE, Paul (Hamilton). American, b. 1908. Novels/Short stories, Children's fiction, Plays/Screenplays, Poetry, Literature. Prof. of English, 1946–77, and Dir. of Intnl. Writing Prog. 1966–77, Univ. of Iowa, Iowa City. *Publs:* Worn Earth, 1932; American Song: A Book of Poems, 1934; Break the Heart's Anger, 1936; Corn, 1939; New Englanders, 1940; Always the Land (novel), 1941; West of Midnight, 1941; American Child, 1944; American Child: A Sonnet Sequence, 1945, rev. ed. as American Child: Sonnets for My Daughter, with Thirty Six New Poems, 1956; The Word of Love, 1951; (ed.) Prize Stories: The O. Henry Award, 6 vols., 1954–59; (ed. with W. Carrier) Reading Modern Poetry, 1955, 1968; For the Iowa Dead (play), 1956; Book and Child: Three Sonnets, 1956; (ed.) Homage to Baudelaire, on the Centennial of "Les Fleurs du Mal", from the Poets at the State University of Iowa, 1957; Poems in Praise, 1959; Robert Frost, 1959; Golden Child (play), 1960, novel, 1962; A Prairie Christmas, 1960; (ed. with Henri Coulette) Midland: Twenty-Five Years of Fiction and Poetry from the Writing Workshops of the State University of Iowa, 1961; Christmas Poems, 1962; (ed. with J. Langland) Poet's Choice, 1962; Who's Afraid?, 1963; An Old-Fashioned Christmas, 1964; (ed.) On Creative Writing, 1964; Woman Unashamed and Other Poems, 1965; Embrace: Selected Love Poems, 1969; (trans. with Hualing Nieh) Poems of Mao Tse-Tung, 1972; (with John Zielinski) Portrait of Iowa, 1976; Women in the American Revolution, 1976; (ed. with others) Writing from the World, 1976; Images of China: Poems Written in China, April–June 1980, 1981. Add: 1104 North Dubuque, Iowa City, Iowa 52240, U.S.A.

ENGLE, Thelburn L. American, b. 1901. Psychology. Prof. Emeritus of Psychology, Indiana Univ., Fort Wayne, since 1972 (Prof., 1938–72). *Publs:* (with Harold J. Mahoney) Points for Decision, 1957, 1961; Psychology: Its Principles and Applications, 1945, 8th ed. 1984; Teacher's Manual and Objective Tests, 1945, 9th ed. 1989; Workbook in Psychology, 1951; Record of Activities and Experiments, 1958; (with L. West and O. Milton) Record of Activities and Experiments with Programmed Units, 1964; (with L. Snellgrove) Psychological Experiments and Experiences, 1969, 7th ed. 1979; (with L. Snellgrove) Student Handbook: Activities and Review, 8th ed. 1984; (with L. Snellgrove) Teacher's Guide and Resource Guide, 9th ed., 1989. Add: 1025 Northlawn Dr., Fort Wayne, Ind. 46805, U.S.A.

ENGLISH, Barbara (Anne). British, b. 1933. History, Military/Defence. Lect. and Sr. Lectr., Univ. of Hull, since 1982 (Research Fellow, 1980–82). Archivist, National Register of Archives, West Riding (Northern Section), Yorks., 1958–62; Asst. ed., Thomas Nelson & Sons Ltd., publrs., Edinburgh, 1962–64. *Publs:* John Company's Last War (in U.S. a The War for a Persian Lady), 1971; The Lords of Holderness, 1980; (co-author) Beverley: An Archaeological and Architectural Study, 1982; (co-author) Strict Settlement: A Guide for Historians, 1983; Yorkshire Enclosure Awards, 1985. Add: Westwood Close, Beverley, Yorks., England.

ENGLISH, Brenda H. British. Novels/Short stories. Former medical practitioner, now retired. *Publs:* Into the North, 1966; The Gabriel Hounds, 1966; The Goodly Heritage, 1967; The Proper Standard, 1968; These Yellow Sands, 1969; Crying in the Wilderness, 1970; Hob of High Farndale, 1971; Sins of the Fathers, 1972; This Freedom, 1973; Except Ye Repent, 1974; Five Generations of a Whitby Medical Family, 1977; Rhymes of a Rural Railway, 1987. Add: Groves Banks, Sleights, Whitby, N. Yorks, Y021 1RY, England.

ENGLISH, Isobel. British, b. 1925. Novels/Short stories, Plays. *Publs:* The Key that Rusts, 1954; Every Eye, 1956; Four Voices, 1961; (with B. Jones) Gift Book, 1964; Life After All and Other Stories, 1973; Meeting Point (play), 1976. Add: 10 Gardnor Rd., London NW3, England.

ENRIGHT, D(ennis) J(oseph). British, b. 1920. Novels, Poetry, Literature, Travel, Autobiography/Memoirs/Personal, Translations. Prof. of English, Univ. of Singapore, 1960–70; Co-Ed., Encounter mag., London, 1970–72; Dir., Chatto and Windus, 1973–82; Hon. Prof. of English, Warwick Univ., 1975–80. *Publs:* A Commentary on Goethe's "Faust", 1949; The Laughing Hyena and Other Poems, 1953; Academic Year, 1955; The World of Dew: Aspects of Living Japan, 1955; Literature for Man's Sake: Critical Essays, 1955; (ed.) Poetry of the 1950s; An Anthology of New English Verse, 1955; Bread Rather than Blossoms, 1956; Heaven Knows Where, 1957; The Apothecary's Shop, 1957; (ed. with T. Ninomiya) The Poetry of Living Japan, 1957; Insufficient Poppy, 1960; Some Men Are Brothers, 1960; Addictions, 1962; (ed. with E. de Chickera) English Critical Texts: 16th Century to 20th Century, 1962; Figures of Speech, 1965; The Old Adam, 1965; Conspirators and Poets, 1966; Unlawful Assembly, 1968; Selected Poems, 1969; Memoirs of a Mendicant Professor, 1969; Shakespeare and the Students, 1970; The Typewriter Revolution and Other Poems, 1971; Daughters of Earth, 1972; The Terrible Shears, 1973; Sad Ires and Others, 1975; The Joke Shop (juvenile), 1976; Wild Ghost Chase (juvenile), 1978; Paradise Illustrated and Other Poems, 1978;

Beyond Land's End (juvenile), 1979; A Faust Book (verse), 1979; (ed.) The Oxford Book of Contemporary Verse 1945-1980, 1980; Collected Poems, 1981; (ed.) The Oxford Book of Death, 1983; A Mania for Sentences, 1983; Instant Chronicles (verse), 1985; (ed.) Fair of Speech: The Uses of Euphemism, 1985; The Alluring Problem: An Essay on Irony, 1986; Collected Poems 1987, 1987; Fields of Vision: Essays on Literature, Language and Television, 1988. Add: 35-A Viewfield Rd., London SW18 5JD, England.

ENSLIN, Theodore (Vernon). American, b. 1925. Poetry. *Publs:* The Work Proposed, 1958; New Sharon's Prospect, 1962; The Place Where I Am Standing, 1964; This Do (and The Talents), 1966; New Sharon's Prospect and Journals, 1966; To Come to Have Become, 1966; The Four Temperaments, 1966; Characters in Certain Places, 1967; The Diabelli Variations and Other Poems, 1967; 2/30-6/31; Poems 1967, 1967; Agreement and Back: Sequences, 1969; The Poems, 1970; Forms, 4 vols., 1970–73; Views 1-7, 1970; The Country of Our Consciousness, 1977; Etudes, 1972; Views, 1973; Sitio, 1973; In the Keepers House, 1973; With Light Reflected, 1973; The Swamp Fox, 1974; The Mornings, 1974; Fever Poems, 1974; The Last Days of October, 1974; The Median Flow: Poems 1943-1973, 1974; Synthesis 1-24, 1975; Mahler, 1975; Landler, 1975; Papers, 1976; The July Book, 1976; Ranger, 2 vols., 1979–81; Markings, 1983; Music for Several Occasions, 1985; The Waking of the Eye, 1986; The Weather Within, 1986; Case Book, 1987. Add: R.F.D. Box 289, Kansas Rd., Milbridge, Me. 04658, U.S.A.

ENTWISLE, Eric Arthur. British, b. 1900. Crafts. Dir., The Wall Paper Manufactures Ltd., 1935–61 (joined firm 1918). Fellow, Soc. of Antiquaries of London. *Publs:* The Crace Papers, 1939; The Book of Wallpaper, 1954; A Literary History of Wallpaper, 1961; Wallpapers of the Victorian Era, 1964; French Scenic Wallpapers, 1972. Add: 23 Downsview Ave., Storrington, Sussex, England.

ENYEART, James L. American, b. 1943. Photography. Dir., Intl. Museum of Photography, George Eastman House, Rochester, NY., Charter Dir., Albrecht Gallery of Art, St. Joseph, Mo., 1967–68; Curator of Photography, Univ. of Kansas Museum of Art, 1969–76; Exec. Dir., Friends of Photography, Carmel, Calif., 1976–77. Dir., Centre for Creative Photography, and Adjunct Prof. of Art, Univ. of Arizona, Tucson, from 1977. National Conference Chmn. 1976, and Member of the Bd. of Dirs., 1978–82, National Soc. for Photographic Education. *Publs:* Karsh (catalogue), 1970; Kansas Landscape (catalogue), 1971; Invisible in America (catalogue), 1973; Language of Light (catalogue), 1974; No Mountains in the Way (catalogue), 1975; (ed.) Kansas Album, 1977; Francis Bruguiere, 1977; (ed.) Kansas Album, 1977; George Fiske, Yosemite Photographer, 1980; Photography of the Fifties: An American Perspective, 1980; (ed.) Heinecken, 1980; W. Eugene Smith: Master of the Photographic Essay, 1981; Jerry Uelsmann: Twenty-Five years, A Retrospective, 1982; Aaron Siskind: Terrors and Pleasures 1931-1980, 1982; (with R.D. Monroe and Philip Stoker) Three Classic American Photographs: Texts and Contexts, 1982; (with others) Edward Weston Omnibus, 1984; Edward Weston's California Landscapes, 1984; Judy Dater: Twenty Years, 1986; Andreas Feininger: A Retrospective, 1986; (co-ed.) Henry Holmes Smith: Collected Writings 1935-1985, 1986; Decade by Decade, 1989. Add: Intl. Museum of Photography, George Eastman House, Rochester, NY 14607, U.S.A.

EPHRON, Delia. Also writes as Delia Brock. American, b. 1944. Children's fiction and children's non-fiction. *Publs:* (as Delia Brock, with Lorraine Bodger) The Adventurous Crocheter, 1972; (with Bodger) Glad Rags, 1975; How to Eat Like a Child, and Other Lessons in Not Being a Grown-up, 1978; (with Bodger) Crafts for All Seasons, 1980; Teenage Romance: Or How to Die of Embarrassment, 1981; Santa and Alex, 1983; Funny Sauce: Us, The Ex, the Ex's New Mate, the New Mate's Ex & the Kids, 1986, 1988. Add: c/o Penguin, 40 W. 23rd St., New York, N.Y. 10010, U.S.A.

EPP, Eldon Jay. American, b. 1930. Theology/Religion. Harkness Prof. of Biblical Literature, Case Western Reserve Univ., Cleveland, Ohio, since 1971 (Assoc. Prof., 1968–71; Dean of Humanities and Social Sciences, 1979–84). Assoc. Ed., Journal of Biblical Literature, since 1971. Asst. Prof., and Assoc. Prof. of Religion, 1962–67, and Assoc. Prof. of Classics, 1966–68, Univ. of Southern California, Los Angeles. *Publs:* The Theological Tendency of Codex Bezae Cantabrigiensis in Acts, 1966; (ed. with G.D. Fee) New Testament Textual Criticism: Its Significance for Exegesis: Essays in Honour of Bruce M. Metzger, 1981; (ed. with G.M. MacRae) The New Testament and Its Modern Interpreters, 1989. Add: Dept. of Religion, Case Western Reserve Univ., Cleveland, Ohio 44106, U.S.A.

EPP, Margaret Agnes. Canadian, b. 1913. Novels/Short stories, Children's fiction, Travel/Exploration/Adventure, Autobiography/Memoirs/Personal, Biography. *Publs:* Peppermint Sue, 1955; Jack Tandy of Baskatong, 1955; North to Sakitawa, 1955; Come Back, Jonah, 1956; Light on Twin Rocks, 1956; The Long Chase, 1956; The Sign of the Tumbling T, 1956; Thirty Days Hath September (short stories), 1956; Vicki Arthur, 1956; Sap's Running, 1956; Anita and the Driftwood House, 1967; No-Hand Sam, 1959; All in the April Evening (short stories), 1959; Mystery at Pony Ranch, 1963; But God Hath Chosen (biography), 1963; Come to My Party (adult non-fiction), 1964; The Brannans of Bar Lazy B, 1965; A Fountain Sealed (novel), 1965; The North Wind and the Caribou, 1966; Jungle Call, 1966; Trouble on the Flying M, 1966; Search Down the Yukon, 1967; Walk in My Woods (autobiography), 1967; Prairie Princess, 1967, as Sarah and the Magic Twenty-Fifth, 1977; The Princess and the Pelican, 1968, as Sarah and the Pelican, 1977; This Mountain Is Mine (biography), 1969; The Princess Rides a Panther, 1970, as Sarah and the Lost Friendship, 1979; No Help Wanted, 1968; Call of the Wahoe (children's short stories), 1971; The Great Frederick (children's short stories), 1971; Runaway on the Running K, 1972; Into All the World (travel), 1973; The Earth Is Round (historical novel), 1974; Proclaim Jubilee! (history), 1976; 8 Tulpengasse (adult non-fiction), 1978; Sarah and the Mystery of the Hidden Boy, 1979; Sarah and the Darnley Boys, 1981; Sarah and the Persian Shepherd, 1982. Add: P.O. Box 178, Waldheim, Sask., Canada.

EPPLE, Anne Orth. American, b. 1927. Children's non-fiction, Crafts. *Publs:* Nature Quiz Book, 1955; Modern Science Quiz Book, 1958; The Beginning Knowledge Book of Ants, 1969; The Beginning Knowledge Book of Fossils, 1969; The Lookalikes, 1971; Nature Crafts, 1974; Something from Nothing Crafts, 1976; The Amphibians of New England, 1983. Add: 1927 Leisure World, Mesa, Ariz. 85206, U.S.A.

EPSTEIN, Charlotte. American, b. 1921. Mystery, Education, Human Relations, Health. Prof. Emeritus, Temple Univ., Philadelphia, since 1985 (Asst. Prof. of Human Relations and Staff Assoc. of the Greenfield Center for Human Relations, 1957–61; Assoc. Prof. of Curriculum and Instruction, 1966–69, Prof. of Curriculum and Instruction and Adjunct Prop. of Nursing, 1969–74; Prof. of Elementary Education, 1974–85). *Publs:* Intergroup Relations for Police Officers, 1961; Intergroup Relations for the Classroom Teacher, 1968; Affective Subjects in the Classroom: Exploring Race, Sex, and Drugs, 1972; Effective Interaction in Contemporary Nursing, 1974; Nursing the Dying Patient, 1975; Learning to Care for the Aged, 1977; Classroom Management and Teaching: Persistent Problems and Rational Solutions, 1979; Introduction to the Human Services, 1981; The Nurse Leader: Philosophy and Practice, 1982; Special Children in Regular Classrooms: Mainstreaming Skills for Teachers, 1984; Murder in China (mystery novel), 1986. Add: Prof. of Elementary Education Emeritus, Temple Univ., Philadelphia, Penn. 19122, U.S.A.

EPSTEIN, Cynthia Fuchs. American, b. 1933. Sociology, Women. Prof., Dept. of Sociology, Graduate Center, City Univ. of NY, since 1975. Ed., Signs, Dissent and Work and Occupations; Ed., Sex Roles quarterly journal, Plenum Press, NYC, since 1975. Instr. in Anthropology, Finch Coll., NYC, 1961–62; Assoc. in Sociology, Columbia Univ. Sch. of Gen. Studies, NYC, 1964–65; Consultant, The White House Conference on Children, 1970; White House Appointee, Advisory Cttee. on the Economic Role of Women, 1972–73; Prof., Dept. of Sociology, Queens Coll., City Univ. of NY, 1975–84 (Instr., 1966–67, Asst. Prof., 1968–70; Assoc. Prof., 1970–75); Fellowship, Center for Adv. Study in the Behavioral Sciences, 1977–78; Sr. Research Assoc., Center for Social Sciences, Columbia Univ, NYC, 1977–82; Resident Scholar, Russell Sage Foundn., 1982–88. *Publs:* Woman's Place: Options and Limits in Professional Careers, 1970; (ed. with William J. Goode) The Other Half: Roads to Women's Equality, 1971; (ed. with Rose L. Coser) Access to Power: Cross National Studies on Women and Elites, 1981; Women in Law, 1981: Deceptive Distinctions: Sex Gender and the Social Order, 1988. Add: 425 Riverside Dr., New York, N.Y. 10025, U.S.A.

EPSTEIN, Helen. American, b. 1947. History. Assoc. Prof. of Journalism, New York Univ., since 1980 (joined faculty, 1974; Asst. Prof., 1976–79). Freelance contrib. to New York Times, Washington Post, Esquire mag., Ms. mag., and the Soho News, since 1970. Reporter, The Jerusalem Post, 1968–70. *Publs:* Children of the Holocaust, 1979; The Companies She Keeps: Tina Packer Builds a Theater, 1985; Music Talks: Conversations with Musicians, 1987. Add: c/o McGraw-Hill, 1221 Ave. of the Americas, New York, N.Y. 10020, U.S.A.

EPSTEIN, Joseph. American, b. 1937. Essays, Social commentary. Visiting Lectr. in literature and writing, Northwestern Univ., Evanston,

Ill., since 1974. Ed., American Scholar, Wash., D.C., since 1975. *Publs:* Divorced in America: Marriage in an Age of Possibility, 1974; Familiar Territory: Observations on American Life, 1979; Ambition: The Secret Passion, 1980; (ed.) Masters: Portraits of Great Teachers, 1981; The Middle of My Tether: Familiar Essays, 1983; Plausible Prejudices: Essays on American Writing, 1985; Once More Around the Block: Familiar Essays, 1987; Partial Payments: Essays Arising from the Pleasures of Reading, 1989. Add: Dept. of English, Northwestern Univ., 633 Clark St., Evanston, Ill. 60201, U.S.A.

EPSTEIN, Seymour. American, b. 1917. Novels/Short stories. Prof. Emeritus, Univ. of Denver, Colo. *Publs:* Pillar of Salt, 1960; The Successor, 1961; Leah, 1964; A Penny for Charity, 1964; Caught in That Music, 1967; The Dream Museum, 1971; Looking for Fred Schmidt, 1973; Love Affair, 1979; A Special Destiny, 1986; September Faces, 1987. Add: 3205 S. St. Paul, Denver, Colo. 80210, U.S.A.

ERDMAN, Paul E. American, b. 1932. Mystery/Crime/Suspense, Money/Finance. Intnl. Economist, Stanford Research Inst., 1959–61; Exec. Vice Pres., Electronics Intnl. Capital, 1962–65; Vice-Chmn., Salik Bank, 1965–69; Vice Chmn., United California Bank in Basel, 1969–70. *Publs:* Swiss-American Economic Relations, 1959; The Billion Dollar Sure Thing (in U.K. as the Billion Dollar Killing), 1973; The Silver Bears, 1974; The Crash of '79, 1976; The Last Days of America, 1981; Paul Erdman's Money Book, 1984; Panic of Eighty Three, 1987; The Palace, 1987. Add: 1817 Lytton Springs Rd., Healdsburg, Calif. 95448, U.S.A.

ERDRICH, Louise. American, b. 1954. Novels, Poetry. Writer. *Publs:* Jacklight (poems), 1984; Love Medicine, 1984 (National Book Critics Award); The Beet Queen, 1986; Tracks, 1988. Add: c/o Michael Dorris, 307 Barlett, Dartmouth College, Hanover, N.H. 03755, U.S.A.

ERENS, Patricia. American, b. 1938. Art, Cinema, Women's Studies. Assoc. Prof., Communication Arts and Sciences, Rosary Coll., River Forest, Ill, since 1985 (Part-time Teacher, 1977; Asst. Prof., 1984–85). Advisory Bd. Member, Film Center, Art Institute of Chicago, since 1972, and National Center for Jewish Film, since 1981; Exec. Cttee. Member, American Jewish Cttee., since 1981; Artistic Dir., Chicago Jewish Film Festival, since 1983. Member, Bd. of Dirs., Midwest Women's Center, 1981–85. *Publs:* The Films of Shirley MacLaine, 1978; Akira Kurosawa: A Guide to References and Resources, 1979; (ed.) Sexual Stratagems: The World of Women in Film, 1979; Masterpieces: Famous Chicagoans and Their Paintings, 1979; The Jew in American Cinema, 1984. Add: Rosary Coll., 7900 W. Division, River Forest, Ill. 60305, U.S.A.

ERHARD, Tom. American, b. 1923. Novels/Short stories, Plays/-Screenplays, Literature. Prof. of Drama, New Mexico State Univ., Las Cruces, since 1960. Information Dir., Albuquerque Public Schs., N.M., 1953–57; Assistant Dir., for Press and Radio, National Education Assn., Washington, D.C., 1957–58. *Publs:* For the Love of Pete, 1954; The High White Star, 1957; Rocket in His Pocket, 1960, 1964; The Electronovac Gasser, 1963; A Wild Fight for Spring, 1966; In Search of Leaders, 1967; Stress and Campus Response, 1968; The Agony and Promise, 1969; the Cataclysmic Loves of Cooper and Looper and Their Friend Who Was Squashed by a Moving Van, 1969; The Troubled Campus, 1970; Lynn Riggs: Southwestern Playwright, 1970; The New Decade, 1971; 900 Plays: A Synopsis—History of American Theatre, 1978; Pomp and Circumstances, 1982; I Saved a Winter Just for You, 1984; A Merry Medieval Christmas, 1985; Laughing Once More, 1986 Add: 2110 Rosedale Dr., Las Cruces, N.M. 88005, U.S.A.

ERI, Vincent (Serei). Papua New Guinean, b. 1936. Novels. Personnel Dir., Harrisons and Crosfield Ltd., since 1982. Teacher, 1956–66; Chief of Operations, Education Dept., 1972–73, and Dir., Information Dept., 1973–74, both Port Moresby; with Papua New Guinea Foreign Service: Consul-Gen. in Sydney, 1974–76, and High Comissioner in Canberra, 1976–79; Head of the Dept. of Transport and Civil Aviation, 1980, and Dept. of Defence, 1981–82, both Port Moresby. *Publs:* The Crocodile, 1970. Add: P.O. Box 586, Lae, Papua New Guinea.

ERICKSON, Charlotte J(oanne). American, b. 1923. History. Paul Mellon Prof. of American History, Cambridge Univ., since 1983. Instr., Vassar Coll., Poughkeepsie, N.Y., 1950–52; Research Fellow, Natl. Inst. of Economic and Social Research, 1952–55; Asst. Lectr., 1955–58, Lectr., 1958–66, Sr. Lectr., 1966–75, Reader, 1975–79, and Prof. of Economic History, 1979–82, London School of Economics. *Publs:* American Industry and the European Immigrant, 1860-1885, 1957, 1969; British Industrialists, Steel and Hosiery 1850-1950, 1958, 1986; Invisible Immigrants, 1972; Emigration from Europe 1815-1914, 1976. Add: Cor-

pus Christi College, Cambridge CB2 1RH, England.

ERICKSON, Steve. American, b. 1950. Novels. *Publs:* Days Between Stations, 1985; Rubicon Beach, 1986; Tours of the Black Clock, 1989; Leap Year, 1989. Add: c/o Melanie Jackson Agency, 250 W. 57th St., Suite 1119, New York, N.Y. 10107, U.S.A.

ERICKSON, Walter. *See* **FAST,** Howard.

ERICSON, Julia. *See* **LEISY,** James Franklin.

ERIKSON, Erik H(omburger). American, b. 1902. Psychiatry, Psychology. Prof. Emeritus of Human Development and Lectr. on Psychiatry, Harvard Univ., Cambridge, Mass., since 1970 (Prof., 1960–70). Research Assoc. in Child Development, and Lectr. in Psychiatry to Prof. of Psychology, Univ. of California, Berkeley, 1939–51; Visiting Prof. of Psychiatry, Univ. of Pittsburgh Medical Sch., 1951–60. *Publs:* Childhood and Society, 1950, 1963; Young Man Luther: A Study in Psychoanalysis and History, 1958; Identity and the Lifecycle, 1959, 1980; (ed.) Youth: Change and Challenge, 1963; Insight and Responsibility, 1964; Identity: Youth and Crisis, 1968; Gandhi's Truth, 1969; (with Huey P. Newton) In Search of Common Ground, 1973; Life History and the Historical Moment, 1975; Toys and Reasons: Stages in the Ritualization of Experience, 1977; (ed.) Adulthood, 1978; Dimensions of a New Identity, 1979; The Lifecycle Completed, 1982; (with Joan M Erikson and Helen Kivnick) Vital Involvement in Old Age, 1987. Add: c/o Norton, 500 Fifth Ave., 6th Floor, New York, N.Y. 10110, U.S.A.

ERITH, John. British, b. 1904. Photography. Theatrical and illustrative photographer. Past member, Council and Qualifications Bd., British Inst. of Professional Photographers; Past Chmn., Portrait and Theatrical Panel of Qualifications Bd., Royal Photographic Soc. *Publs:* Erith on Portraiture, 1948; Erith on Pictorial Photography, 1951; (ed. and contrib.) Modern Control in Photography, 1951. Add: Smugglers House, Smugglers Walk, Worthing, Sussex, England.

ERNENWEIN, Leslie. Westerns/Adventure. *Publs:* Gunsmoke Galoot, 1941; Kinkaid of Red Butte, 1942; as Kinkaid, 1975; Boss of Panamint, 1942; The Faro Kid, 1944; Bullet Breed, 1946; Rio Renegade, 1946; Revels Ride Proudly, 1947, as Trigger Justice, 1949; Rebel Yell, 1948; Horseshoe Combine, 1949; Ambush at Jubilo Junction, 1950; Renegade Ramrod, 1950, as Big T Ramrod, 1955; Gunfighter's Return, 1950; Gunsmoke, 1950; Gunhawk Harvest, as Gun Hawk, 1952; The Texas Gun, 1951; Hell for Leather, 1951; Savage Justice, 1952; Give a Man a Gun, 1952; Mystery Rider, 1953; Rampage, 1954; Bullet Barricade, 1955; Hell-Town in Texas, 1955; Texas Guns, 1956; High Gun, 1956; The Gun-Hung men, 1957; Ramrod from Hell, 1958; Warrior Basin, 1959; Rampage West, 1963; The Way They Died, 1978; Gun Hawk, 1979; Rebel Yell, 1979. Add: c/o Chivers, Windsor Bridge Rd., Bath BA2 3AX, England.

ERNO, Richard B(ruce). American, b. 1923. Novels/Short stories, Children's fiction. Prof. Emeritus of English, Arizona State Univ., Tempe (member of staff, 1957–62). Held teaching positions at McCook Jr. Coll., Nebraska, 1953–55, George Washington Univ., Washington D.C., 1955–57, and Northern Montana Coll., Havre, 1962–63. *Publs:* My Old Man, 1955; The Hunt, 1960; The Catwalk, 1965; Johnny Come Jingl-O, 1967; Billy Lightfoot (children's fiction), 1969; An Ultimate Retreat (reminiscences), 1971. Add: 4467 Diablo Dr., Cottonwood, Ariz. 86327, U.S.A.

ERNST, Robert. American, b. 1915. History, Biography. Instr., 1946–47, Asst. Prof., 1947–54, Assoc. Prof., 1954–58 and Prof. of History, 1958–83, Adelphi Univ., Garden City, N.Y. Member, Editorial Bd., New York History, since 1976. *Publs:* Immigrant Life in New York City 1825-1863, 1949; Rufus King: American Federalist, 1968. Add: 26 Butler St., Westbury, N.Y. 11590, U.S.A.

ERSKINE, Margaret. Pseudonym for Margaret Wetherby Williams. British. Mystery/Crime/Suspense. *Publs:* And Being Dead, 1938 (in U.S. as The Limping Man, 1939; in U.S. paperback, The Painted Mask, 1972); The Whispering House (in U.S. as The Voice of the House), 1947; I Knew MacBean, 1948 (in U.S. paperback, Caravan of Night, 1972); Give Up the Ghost, 1949; The Disappearing Bridegroom, 1950 (in U.S. as The Silver Ladies, 1951); Death of Our Dead One (in U.S. as Look Behind You, Lady), 1952 (in U.S. paperback, Don't Look Behind You, 1972); Dead by Now, 1953; Fatal Relations (in U.S. as Old Mrs. Ommanney Is Dead and [book club edition] The Dead Don't Speak), 1955; The Voice of Murder, 1956; Sleep No More, 1958; The House of the

Enchantress (in U.S. as A Graveyard Plot), 1959; The Woman at Belguardo, 1961; The House in Belmont Square (in U.S. as No. 9 Belmont Square), 1963; Take a Dark Journey, 1965 (in U.S. as The Family at Tammerton, 1966); Case with Three Husbands, 1967; The Ewe Lamb, 1968; The Case of Mary Fielding, 1970; The Brood of Folly, 1971; Besides the Wench Is Dead, 1973; Harriet Farewell, 1975; The House in Hook Street, 1977. Add: c/o A.M. Heath and Co. Ltd., 79 St. Martins Lane, London WC2N 4AA, England.

ERSKINE, Rosalind. *See* **LONGRIGG,** Roger.

ESHBACH, Lloyd Arthur. American, b. 1910. Science fiction/Fantasy. Worked for dept. stores, 1925–41; Advertising Copywriter, Glidden Paint Co., Reading, Pa., 1941–50; Publisher, Fantasy Press, Reading, 1950–58, and Church Center Press, Myerstown, Pa., 1958–63; Advertising Mgr., 1963–68, and Sales Rep., 1968–75, Moody Press, Chicago; Clergyman, for 3 small churches in eastern Pa., 1975–78. *Publs:* (ed.) Of Worlds Beyond: The Science of Science-Fiction Writing, 1947; The Tyrant of Time, 1955; Over My Shoulder, Reflections on a Science Fiction Era, 1983; The Land Beyond the Gate, 1984; The Armlet of the Gods, 1986; The Sorceress of Scath, 1988; The Scroll of Lucifer, 1989. Add: 220 S. Railroad St., Myerstown, Pa. 17067, U.S.A.

ESHLEMAN, Clayton. American, b. 1935. Poetry, Translations. Prof. of Creative Writing, Eastern Michigan Univ., Ypsilanti, since 1986. Ed., Sulfur Mag., since 1981. Instr., in English, Matsushita Electric Corp., Osaka, 1962–64; Instr., New York Univ. American Language Inst., NYC, 1966–68; Ed. and Publr., Caterpillar mag., NYC, 1967–70, and Sherman Oaks, Calif., 1970–73; Member, Sch. of Critical Studies, California Inst. of the Arts, Valencia, 1970–72; taught at the Univ. of California at Los Angeles, 1974–77; Dreyfus Poet in Residence and Lectr. in Creative Writing, California Inst. of Technology, 1979–84, Ed., Caterpillar Mag., 1967–73. *Publs:* Mexico and North, 1962; (trans.) Residence on Earth, by Pablo Neruda, 1962; The Chavin Illumination, 1965; Lachrymae Mateo: 3 Poems for Christmas 1966, 1966; (trans. with D. Kelly) State of the Union, by Aimé Césaire, 1966; Walks, 1967; The Crocus Bud, 1967; Brother Stones, 1968; Cantaloups and Splendour, 1968; (trans.) Poemas Humanos/Human Poems, by César Vallejo, 1968; T'ai, 1969; The House of Okumura, 1969; Indiana: Poems, 1969; The House of Ibuki: A Poem, New York City, 14 March-30 Sept. 1967, 1969; The Yellow River Record, 1969; A Pitchblende, 1969; (ed.) A Caterpillar Anthology: A Selection of Poetry and Prose from Caterpillar Magazine, 1971; The Wand, 1971; Bearings, 1971; Altars, 1971; The Sanjo Bridge, 1972; Coils, 1973; Human Wedding, 1973; (trans. with J.R. Barcia) Spain, Take This Cup from Me, by César Vallejo, 1974; Aux Morts, 1974; Realignment, 1974; Portrait of Francis Bacon, 1975; The Gull Wall: Poems and Essays, 1975; Cogollo, 1976; The Woman Who Saw Through Paradise, 1976; Grotesca, 1977; Core Meander, 1977; What She Means, 1978; Our Lady of the Three-Pronged Devil, 1981; Hades in Manganese, 1981; Foetus Graffiti, 1981; (trans. with Norman Glass) Four Texts, by Artaud, 1982; Fracture, 1983; (trans. with Annette Smith) The Collected Poetry, by Aimé Césaire, 1983; Visions of the Fathers of Lascaux, 1983; (trans.) Sea-Urchin Harakiri, by Bernard Bador, 1984; (trans.) Given Giving: Selected Poems of Michel Deguy, 1984; The Name Encanyoned River: Selected Poems 1960-1985, 1986; (trans., with Annette Smith) Lost Body, by Aimé Césaire, 1986; Conductors of the Pit: Major Works by Rimbaud, Vallejo, Césaire, Artaud and Itolan, 1988; Antiphonal Swing: Selected Prose 1962-1987, 1989; Novices: A Study of Poetic Apprenticeship, 1989; Hotel Cro-Magnon, 1989. Add: 210 Washtenaw Ave., Ypsilanti, Mich. 48197, U.S.A.

ESKIN, Frada. British, b. 1936. Medicine/Health. Dir., Centre for Professional Development, Dept. of Community Medicine, Univ. of Manchester. Sr. Medical Officer, Derbyshire County Council, 1966–68, and Sheffield County Borough, 1968–70; Asst. Sr. Medical Officer, Sheffield Regional Hosp. Bd., 1970–74; former Specialist in Community Medicine, Barnsley Area Health Authority. *Publs:* Medical Notes for Social Workers, 1971; Doctors and Management Skills, 1981. Add: 62 The Glen, Endcliffe Vale Rd., Sheffield 10, England.

ESLER, Anthony James. American, b. 1934. Novels, History. Prof. of History, Coll. of William & Mary, Williamsburg, Va., since 1972 (Asst. prof., 1962–67; Assoc. prof., 1967–72). Fulbright Post-doctoral Research Fellow, Univ. of London, 1961–62; American Council of Learned Societies Research Fellow, Chicago, 1969–70; William and Mary Research Fellow, 1975–76; Fulbright Travel Grant, Ivory Coast and Tanzania, 1983. *Publs:* The Aspiring Mind of the Elizabethan Younger Generation, 1966; Bombs, Beards and Barricades: 150 Years of Youth in Revolt, 1971; (ed.) The Youth Revolution: The Conflict of Generations

in Modern History, 1974; The Blade of Castlemayne, 1974; Hellbane, 1975; Lord Libertine, 1976; Forbidden City, 1977; The Freebooters, 1979; Generational Studies: A Basic Bibliography, 1979; Babylon, 1980; Bastion, 1980; Generations in History: An Introduction to the Concept, 1982; The Generation Gap in Society and History: A Select Bibliography, 2 vols., 1984; The Human Venture: A World History, 2 vols., 1986; (co-author) A Survey of Western Civilization, 1987. Add: Dept. of History, Coll. of William and Mary, Williamsburg, Va. 23185, U.S.A.

ESMOND, Harriet. *See* **BURKE,** John.

ESPELAND, Pamela (Lee). American, b. 1951. Children's fiction, Poetry, Children's non-fiction, Education, Medicine/Health, Mythology/Folklore. Freelance Writer and Ed., Minneapolis, since 1976. *Publs:* The Story of Cadmus, 1980; The Story of Arachne, 1988; The Story of King Midas, 1980; The Story of Pygmalion, 1981; The Story of Baucis and Philemon, 1981; Theseus and the Road to Athens, 1981; Why Do We Eat?, 1981; (with Marilyn Waniek) Hundreds of Hens and Other Poems for Children, 1982; (with Marilyn Vaniek) The Cat Walked Through the Casserole and Other Poems for Children, 1984; (with Jacquelyn Saunders) Bringing Out the Best: A Resource Guide for Parents of Young Gifted Children, 1986; (with Evelyn Leife) Different Like Me: A Book for Teens Who Worry About Their Parents' Use of Alcohol-Drugs, 1987. Add: 3351 Colfax Ave., S., Minneapolis, Minn. 55408, U.S.A.

ESPEY, John (Jenkins). American, b. 1913. Novels/Short stories, Business/Trade/Industry, Literature. Prof. Emeritus of English, Univ. of California, Los Angeles, since 1973 (joined faculty, 1948). *Publs:* Minor Heresies, 1945; Tales Out of School, 1947; The Other City, 1950; Ezra Pound's Mauberley: A Study in Composition, 1955; The Anniversaries, 1963; An Observer, 1965; (with C. Gullans) A Checklist of Trade Bindings Designed by Margaret Armstrong, 1968; The Decorative Designers 1895-1932, 1970; The Empty Box Haiku, 1980; (with R. Ellmann) Oscar Wilde: Two Approaches, 1977; (with C. See and L.S. Kendall) Lotus Land, 1983; (with C. See and L.S. Kendall) 110 Shanghai Road, 1986; (with C. See and L.S. Kendall) Greetings from Southern California, 1988; The Nine Lives of Algernon, 1988; (with C. See) Two Schools of Thought: Some Tales of Learing and Romance, 1989. Add: Dept. of English, Univ. of California, 405 Hilgard Ave., Los Angeles, Calif. 90024, U.S.A.

ESPINO, Federico (Liesi, Jr.). Filipino, b. 1939. Short stories, Poetry. Asst. Ed., Mirror Mag., Manila, 1969–72. *Publs:* In Three Tongues: A Folio of Poems in Tagalog, English, and Spanish, 1963; Apocalypse in Ward 19 and Other Poems, 1965; The Shuddering Clavier, 1965; Sa Paanan ng parnaso, 1965; Toreng Bato, Kastilyong Pawid, 1966; Balalayka ni Pasternak at iba pang tula, 1967; A Rapture of Distress, 1968; Alak na buhay, hinog no abo, phoenix na papel, 1968; Dark Sutra, 1969; Burnt Alphabets: Poems in English, Tagalog, and Spanish, 1969; Dawn and Downsitting: Poems, 1969; Counterclockwise: Poems 1965-1969, 1969; The Country of Sleep (short stories), 1969; A Manner of Seeing: A Folio of Poems, 1970; Caras y Caretas de Amor, 1970; The Winnowing Rhyme, 1970; Makinilya at lira, tuluyan at tula, 1970; Percussive Blood (short stories), 1972; Letter and Nocturnes: Poems, 1972-73, 1973; Puente del Diablo, 1973; In the Very Torrent, 1975; Opus 27, 1976; Tambor de Sangre, 1977; Ritmo ng lingkaw, 1978; Dalitan at tuksuhan, 1979; Lightning-Rods, Pararrayos, 1980; Siddhartha in Saigon, Christ in Manila: New Poems, 1983; Rhapsody on Themes of Brecht, Recto, and Others, 1983; The Woman Who Had Many Birthdays and Other Works, 1983. Add: 178 Marcelo H. del Pilar, Pasig, Rizal, Philippines.

ESSEX, Harry J. American, b. 1915. Novels/Short stories, Plays, Screenplays. Writer, MGM, Bill Cosby Co., Frank Sinatra Artanis Productions, etc. *Publs:* Something for Nothing, 1937; Dragnet, 1947; He Walked by Night, 1948; (with F. Niblo, Jr., G.W. George and R.B. Altman) Bodyguard, 1948; (with Leonard Lee and R.H. Andrews) Wyoming Mail, 1950; (with F. Rosenwald) Undercover Girl, 1950; The Killer That Stalked New York, 1951; The Fat Man, 1951; (with R. Bradbury) It Came from Outer Space, 1953; Devil's Canyon, 1953; I Put My Right Foot In (novel) 1954; The Creature from the Black Lagoon, 1954; (with R. Hill) Raw Edge, 1956; (with R. Smith) The Lonely Man, 1957; Neighborhood Affair, 1960; One for the Dame, 1965; (with W.H. Right, A. Weiss and T. Jennings) The Sons of Katie Elder, 1965; Man and Boy, 1971; Fatty, 1974; Marina, 1981; Terror in the Skies (for television), 1986. Add: 9303 Readcrest Dr., Beverly Hills, Calif. 90210, U.S.A.

ESSEX-CATER, Antony John. British, b. 1923. Medicine/Health. Chmn., National Assn. for Maternal and Child Welfare, London; Vice-Pres., National Assn. for Maternal and Child Welfare. Deputy Medical Officer of Health, City of Manchester, 1961–68; County Medical Officer,

Monmouthshire County Council, 1968–74; Medical Officer of Health and Consultant Venereologist, Jersey, Channel Islands, 1974–88. *Publs:* Synopsis of Public Health and Social Medicine, 1961, 1967, 3rd ed. as Manual of Public and Community Medicine, 1979. Add: c/o Honfleur, Mont Cambrai, St. Lawrence, Jersey, Channel Islands.

ESSLIN, Martin (Julius). British (b. Hungarian), b. 1918. Literature, Theatre. Prof. of Drama, Stanford Univ., California, since 1977. Producer and Scriptwriter, European Div., 1941–55, Asst. Head of the European Productions Dept., 1955, Asst. Head of Drama (Sound), 1961, and Head of Drama (Radio), 1963–77, BBC, London. *Publs:* Brecht: A Choice of Evils: A Critical Study of the Man, His Work, and His Options, 1959 (in US as Brecht: The Man and His Work, 1960); The Theatre of the Absurd, 1961, 1968; (ed. with others) Sinn oder Unsinn? Das Groteske im Modernen Drama, 1961; (ed.) Samuel Beckett: A Collection of Critical Essays, 1965; (ed.) Absurd Drama, 1965; Harold Pinter, 1967; (ed.) The Genius of the German Theatre, 1968; Bertolt Brecht, 1969; Reflections: Essays of Modern Theatre, 1969, in U.K. as Brief Chronicles: Essays on Modern Theatre, 1970; The Peopled Wound: The Work of Harold Pinter, 1970 (in U.S. as Pinter: A Study of His Plays, 1973); (ed.) The New Theatre of Europe, vol. 4, 1970; An Anatomy of Drama, 1976; Artaud, 1976; Mediations, 1980; The Age of Television, 1982; The Field of Drama, 1987. Add: 64 Loudoun Rd., London NW8, England.

ESSOP, Ahmed. Indian, b. 1931. Novels/Short stories, Poetry. Teacher at a secondary sch. in Eldorado Park, Johannesburg, South Africa, 1980–85. *Publs:* (as Ahmed Yousuf) The Dark Goddess (poetry), 1959; The Hajji and Other Stories, 1978; The Visitation (novel), 1980; The Emperor (novel), 1984. Add: P.O. Box 1747, Lenasia, Johannesburg 1820, South Africa.

ESTES, William (Kaye). American, b. 1919. Psychology. Prof. of Psychology, Harvard Univ., Cambridge, since 1979. Member of Faculty, 1946–62, Prof. of Psychology, 1955–60, and Research Prof., 1960–62, Univ. of Indiana, Bloomington; Prof. of Psychology, and Member of Inst. of Mathematical Studies in Social Sciences, Stanford Univ., Calif., 1962–68; Prof. of Psychology, Rockefeller Univ., NYC, 1968–79. Pres., Midwestern Psychological Assn., 1956–57; Pres., Div. of Experimental Psychology, American Psychological Assn., 1958–59; Assoc. Ed., Journal of Experimental Psychology, 1958–62; Ed., Journal of Comparative and Physiological Psychology, 1962–68; Ed., Psychological Review, 1977–82. *Publs:* An Experimental Study of Punishment, 1944; (co-author) Modern Learning Theory, 1954; (co-ed.) Studies in Mathematical Learning Theory, 1959; Stimulus Sampling Theory, 1967; Learning Theory and Mental Development, 1970; Handbook of Learning and Cognitive Processes, 6 vols., 1975–78; Models of Learning, Memory, and Choice, 1982. Add: 95 Irving St., Cambridge, Mass. 02138, U.S.A.

ESTLEMAN, Loren D. American, b. 1952. Mystery/Crime/Suspense, Westerns/Adventure. Reporter, The Press, Ypsilanti, 1973; Ed., Community Foto-News, Pinckney, Mich., 1975–76; Special Writer, Ann Arbor News, 1976–77; staff writer, Dexter Leader, 1977–80. *Publs:* The Oklahoma Punk, 1976; Sherlock Holmes Versus Dracula, or The Adventure of the Sanguinary Count, 1978; The Hider, 1978; The High Rocks, 1979; Dr. Jekyll and Mr. Holmes, 1979; Stamping Ground, 1980; Motor City Blue, 1980; Angel Eyes, 1981; Aces and Eights, 1981; The Wolfer, 1981; Murdock's Law, 1982; The Midnight Man, 1982; Mister St. John, 1983; The Glass Highway, 1983; This Old Bill, 1984; The Stranglers, 1984; Sugartown, 1984; Kill Zone, 1984; Roses Are Dead, 1985; Gun Man, 1985; Every Brilliant Eye, 1985; Any Man's Death, 1986; Lady Yesterday, 1987; The Wister Trace (non-fiction), 1987; Downriver, 1988; Bloody Season, 1988; General Murders: Ten Amos Walker Mysteries, 1988; Silent Thunder, 1989; Best Western Stories, 1989. Add: c/o Ray Peekner Literary Agency, 3210 S. Seventh St., Milwaukee, Wisc, 53215, U.S.A.

ESTORIL, Jean. *See* **ALLAN,** Mabel Esther.

ESTRIDGE, Robin. Writes mystery novels as Philip Loraine, also writes as Robert York. British. Novels/Short stories, Mystery/Crime/Suspense. *Publs:* novels, as Robin Estridge—The Future Is Tomorrow, 1947; The Publican's Wife, 1948; Meeting on the Shore, 1949; Return of a Hero (in U.S. as Sword Without Scabbard), 1950; The Olive Tree, 1953; A Cuckoo's Child, 1969; novels, as Robert York—The Swords of December, 1978; My Lord the Fox, 1985; mystery novels, as Philip Loraine—White Lie the Dead (in U.S. And to My Beloved Husband), 1950; Exit with Intent: The Story of a Missing Comedian, 1950; The Break in the Circle, 1951 (in U.S. paperback, Outside the Law, 1953); The Dublin Nightmare (in U.S. as Nightmare in Dublin), 1952; The Angel of Death, 1961; Day of the Arrow, 1964 (in U.K. paperback, The Eye

of the Devil, 1966); W.I.L. One to Curtis, 1967; The Dead Men of Sestos, 1968; A Mafia Kiss, 1969; Photographs Have Been Sent to Your Wife, 1971; Voices in an Empty Room, 1973; Ask the Rattlesnake (in U.S. as Wrong Man in the Mirror), 1975; Lions' Ransom, 1980; Sea Change, 1982; Death Wishes, 1983; Loaded Questions, 1985; Last Shot, 1986. Add: c/o Serafina Clarke, 98 Tunis Rd., London W12 7EY, England.

ETS, Marie Hall. American, b. 1893. Children's fiction, Children's non-fiction. *Publs:* Mister Penny, 1935; Story of a Baby, 1939; In the Forest, 1944; (with E. Terry) My Dog Rinty, 1946; Oley the Sea Monster, 1947; Little Old Automobile, 1948; Mr. T.W. Anthony Woo, 1951; Beasts and Nonsense, 1952; Another Day, 1953; Play with Me, 1955; Mister Penny's Race Horse, 1956; Cow's Party, 1958; (with A. Labastida) Nine Days to Christmas, 1959; Mr. Penny's Circus, 1961; Gilberto and the Wind, 1963; Automobiles for Mice, 1964; Just Me, 1965; Bad Boy, Good Boy, 1967; Talking Without Words, 1968; Rosa: The Life of an Italian Immigrant, 1970; Elephant in a Well, 1971; Jay Bird, 1974. Add: c/o Viking/Penguin, 40 W. 23rd St., New York, N.Y. 10010, U.S.A.

ETTER, Dave. (David Pearson Etter). American, b. 1928. Poetry. Former writer for the Encyclopedia Britannica, Chicago. *Publs:* Go Read the River, 1966; The Last Train to Prophetstown, 1968; Strawberries, 1970; (with J. Knoepfle and L. Mueller) Voyages to the Inland Sea, 1971; Crabtree's Woman, 1972; Well You Needn't, 1975; Bright Mississippi, 1975; Central Standard Time: New and Selected Poems, 1978; Alliance, Illinois, 1978; Open to the Wind, 1978; Riding the Rock Island Through Kansas, 1979; Cornfields, 1980; West of Chicago, 1981; Boondocks, 1982; Alliance, Illinois, 1983; Home State, 1985; Live at the Silver Dollar, 1986; Selected Poems, 1987; Midlanders, 1988; Electric Avenue, 1988. Add: 414 Gates St., Elburn, Ill. 60119, U.S.A.

ETTINGER, Elzbieta. Polish. Novels/Short stories, Translations. Assoc. Prof., Massachusetts Inst. of Technology, Cambridge, Mass., since 1973. With Radcliffe Seminars, Harvard Extension, Cambridge, Mass., since 1970 (Sr. Fellow, Radcliffe Inst., 1972–74). *Publs:* Kindergarten, 1970; (trans.) Nullum Crimen Sine Lege, 1975; (ed. and trans.) Comrade and Lover: Rosa Luxemburg's Letters to Leo Jogiches, 1979; Rosa Luxemburg: A Life, 1986. Add: MIT, 14N-328, Cambridge, Mass., U.S.A.

ETZIONI, Amitai. American (born German), b. 1929. Sociology. Univ. Prof., George Washington Univ., Washington, D.C., since 1980; Dir., Center for Policy Research, since 1968. Sponsor, The Atlantic Council of the United States, since 1964; Member of the Bd., Canadian Peace Research Inst., since 1964; Member, Editorial Bd., Administration and Mental Health, since 1972; Member, Governing Council of the American Jewish Congress, and the National Advisory Bd. of the National Alliance for Safer Cities, since 1973; Member, Advisory Panel of the Population Soc., and the Intnl. Soc. for Research in Aggression, since 1973. Instr. to Prof., Columbia Univ., NYC, 1958–80. Core-member, American Academy of Arts and Sciences, Summer Inst., 1962; Member, National Bd., Americans for Democratic Action, 1963–68; Member, Editorial Bd., Journal of Peace Research, 1965–72, and the Administrative Science Quarterly, 1964–68; Assoc. Ed., American Sociological Review, 1964–68; Member, Editorial Bd., Sociological Inquiry, 1967–74; Assoc. Ed. Sociological Abstracts, 1968–71; Member, Commn. on Urban Affairs, American Jewish Congress, 1969–71; Member, Science Information Council, National Science Foundn., 1969–74; Member, Social Problems Research Review Cttee., National Inst., of Mental Health, 1970–72; Member, Editorial Bd., Science, 1970–72; Member, Editorial Bd., Sage Professional Papers on Administrative and Policy Studies, 1973. *Publs:* A Diary of a Commando Soldier, 1951; A Comparative Analysis of Complex Organizations, 1961, 1975; (ed.) Complex Organizations: A Sociological Reader, 1961, 3rd ed. 1980; The Hard Way to Peace: A New Strategy, 1962; Winning Without War, 1964; Modern Organizations, 1964; The Moon-Doggie: Domestic and International Implications of the Space Race, 1964; Political Unification: A Comparative Study of Leaders and Forces, 1965; Studies in Social Change, 1966; (ed.) International Political Communities, 1966; The Active Society: A Theory of Societal and Political Processes, 1968; (ed.) Readings on Modern Organizations, 1969; (ed.) The Semi-Professions and Their Organization: Teachers, Nurses, Social Workers, 1969; Demonstration Democracy, 1971; Genetic Fix, 1973; Social Problems, 1976; The Organizational Structure of the Kibbutz, 1980; Capital Corruption: An Assault on American Democracy, 1984; The Moral Dimension, 1988. Add: Dept. of Sociology, George Washington Univ., Washington, D.C. 20052, U.S.A.

EUSTIS, Helen (White). American, b. 1916. Mystery/Crime/Suspense. *Publs:* The Horizontal Man (novel), 1946; The Captains and the Kings Depart and Other Stories, 1949; The Fool Killer (novel), 1954; (trans.) When I Was Old, by Georges Simenon, 1971; Mr. Death and the Redheaded Woman (juvenile), 1983. Add: c/o Green Tiger Press, 1061 India St., San Diego, Calif. 92101, U.S.A.

EVANOFF, Vlad. American, b. 1916. Sports. *Publs:* Surf Fishing, 1948, 1974; Natural Baits for Fishermen, 1952, 3rd ed. 1959; How to Make Fishing Lures, 1959, 2nd ed. as Make Your Own Fishing Lures, 1975; A Complete Guide to Fishing, 1961, 1981; Modern Fishing Tackle, 1961; How to Fish in Salt-Water, 1962; Fishing Secrets of the Experts, 1962; Spinfishing, 1963; Hunting Secrets of the Experts, 1964; 1001 Fishing Tips and Tricks, 1966; Another 1001 Fishing Tips and Tricks, 1970; Best Ways to Catch More Fish, 1975; Fishing with Natural Baits, 1975; 500 Fishing Experts and How They Catch Fish, 1978; Fresh-Water Fishing Rigs, 1984; Salt-Water Fishing Rigs, 1985. Add: Box 9032, Coral Springs, Fla. 33065, U.S.A.

EVANS, Alan. Pseud. for Alan Stoker. British, b. 1930. Novels/Short stories, Children's fiction. Civil Servant, H.M. Govt. *Publs:* The End of the Running, 1966; Mantrap, 1967; Bannon, 1968; Vicious Circle, 1970; The Big Deal, 1971; Running Scared (juvenile), 1975; Kidnap! (juvenile), 1977; Escape at the Devil's Gate (juvenile), 1978; Thunder at Dawn, 1978; Ship of Force, 1979; Dauntless, 1980; Seek Out and Destroy, 1982; Deed of Glory, 1984; Audacity, 1985; Eagle at Taranto, 1987; Night Action, 1989. Add: 9 Dale Rd., Walton-on-Thames, Surrey, England.

EVANS, Anthony Meredith. British, b. 1929. Earth sciences. Sr. Lectr. in Geology, Univ. of Leicester, since 1957. *Publs:* An Introduction to Ore Geology, 1980, 1987; (ed.) Metallization Associated with Acid Magmatism vol. 6, 1982. Add: Dept. of Geology, Univ. of Leicester, Leicester, England.

EVANS, David Ellis. British, b. 1930. Language/Linguistics. Prof. of Celtic, Univ. of Oxford, and Fellow, Jesus Coll., since 1978. Ed., Language and Literature Section, The Bulletin of the Board of Celtic Studies, since 1972. Asst. Lectr., 1957–59, Lectr., 1960–68, Reader, 1968–74, and Prof. of Welsh, 1974–78, University Coll. of Swansea, Wales. *Publs:* Gaulish Personal Names: A Study of Some Continental Celtic Formations, 1967; (ed.) Cofiant Agricola, Lywodraethwr Prydain, 1974; The Labyrinth of Continental Celtic, 1981; (ed.) Proceedings of the Seventh International Congress of Celtic Studies, Oxford 1983, 1986. Add: Jesus Coll., Oxford, England.

EVANS, David Stanley. British, b. 1916. Astronomy. Jack S. Josey Centennial Prof. of Astronomy, Univ. of Texas at Austin, since 1984 (Assoc. Dir. for Research, McDonald Observatory, 1968–81). Second Asst., Radcliffe Observatory, Pretoria, South Africa, 1946–51; Chief Asst., Royal Observatory, Cape of Good Hope, South Africa, 1951–68. *Publs:* Frontiers of Astronomy, 1946; Teach Yourself Astronomy, 1952, 4th ed. 1975; (ed. with T.J. Deeming, B.H. Evans and S. Goldfarb) Herschel at the Cape, 1969; (ed.) The Shadow of the Telescope, 1970; (ed. with D. and B. Wills) International Astronomical Union Symposium No. 44: External Galaxies and Quasistellar Objects, 1972; (ed.) Photometry, Kinematics and Dynamics of Galaxies, 1979; (ed.) Proceeding of XI Texas Symposium on Relativistic Astrophysics, 1984 (with J.D. Mulholland) Big and Bright: A History of McDonald Observatory, 1986; Under Capricorn: A History of the Southern Hemisphere, 1988. Add: 6001 Mountainclimb Dr., Austin, Tex. 78731, U.S.A.

EVANS, E(myr) Estyn. British, b. 1905. Anthropology/Ethnology, Archaeology/Antiquities, Geography, History, Travel/Exploration/Adventure. Prof. Emeritus of Irish Studies, and Hon. Fellow, Queen's Univ., Belfast (Prof. of Geography, 1945–65; Prof. of Irish Studies, 1965–70). Trustee, Ulster Museum, and Ulster Folk and Transport Museum, 1965–70. Recipient: Victoria Medal, Royal Geographical Soc. *Publs:* France: A Geographical Introduction, 1937; (ed. with H.J. Fleure) South Carpathian Studies, 1939; (ed. with D.A. Chart) A Preliminary Survey of the Ancient Monuments of Northern Ireland, 1940; Irish Heritage, 1941; Northern Ireland: Festival of Britain Guide, 1951; Mourne Country, 1951; Lyles Hill: A Late Neolithic Site in County Antrim, 1953; Irish Folkways, 1957; Florin Guide to Northern Ireland, 1965; Prehistoric and Early Christian Ireland, 1966; (ed.) Lord George Hill's Facts from Gweedore, 1971; The Personality of Ireland, 1973; (ed.) Harvest Home: The Last Sheaf, 1974; (ed.) Ireland's Eye: The Photographs of Robert John Welch, 1977. Add: 98A Malone Rd., Belfast BT9 5HP, Northern Ireland.

EVANS, Eric J(ohn). British, b. 1945. History. Prof. of Social History, Univ. of Lancaster, since 1985 (Lectr., 1970–80; Sr. Lectr., 1980–84; Reader in Modern British History, 1984–85). Asst. Ed., Studies in Social History series, Routledge and Kegan Paul Ltd., London, since 1972; Jt. Ed., Lancaster Pamphlets, Methuen Co., since 1983. Lectr. in History, Univ. of Stirling, 1969–70. *Publs:* Tillicoultry: A Centenary History 1871-1971, 1971; The Contentious Tithe: The Tithe Problem and British Agriculture, 1976; Social Policy 1830-1914, 1978; A Social History of Britain in Postcards 1870-1930, 1980; The Forging of the Modern State: Early Industrial Britain, 1783-1870, 1983; The Great Reform Act of 1832, 1983; Political Parties in Britain 1783-1867, 1985; Britain Before the Reform Act: Politics and Society 1815-32, 1989. Add: Dept. of History, Univ. of Lancaster, Bailrigg, Lancaster LA1 4YG, England.

EVANS, Frances. *See* **CARTER,** Frances Monet.

EVANS, Grose. American, b. 1916. Art. Adjunct Prof., George Washington Univ., Washington, D.C., 1973–90 (Professorial Lectr. in Art History, 1953–61). Curator, National Gallery of Art, Washington, D.C., 1946–73. *Publs:* Benjamin West and the Taste of His Time, 1959; Vincent Van Gogh, 1968. Add: 2308 Glasgow Rd., Alexandria, Va. 22307, U.S.A.

EVANS, Harold (Matthew). British, b. 1928. Media, Writing/Journalism. Ed.-in-Chief, Condé-Nast's Traveler, since 1986. Asst. Ed., Manchester Evening News, 1958–61; Ed., The Northern Echo, 1961–66; Ed.-in-Chief, North of England Newspaper Co., 1963–66; Ed., The Sunday Times, London, 1967–81 (Chief Asst. to the Ed., and Managing Ed., 1966; Ed., The Times 1981–82). *Publs:* The Active Newsroom, 1961; The Suez Crisis: A Study in Press Performance, 1967; Newspaper Editing and Design, 5 vols., 1972–78; (ed.) Eye Witness; We Learned to Ski, 1974; Good Times, Bad Times, 1983; Front Page News, 1984; (ed.) Eyewitness Two: Three Decades Through World Press Photos, 1986. Add: c/o Condé-Nast's Traveler, 360 Madison Ave., New York, N.Y. 10017, U.S.A.

EVANS, James Allan S. Canadian, b. 1931. Classics, History. Prof. of Classics, since 1972, and Head of Dept., since 1986, Univ. of British Columbia, Vancouver. Ed., Studies in Medieval and Renaissance History, since 1978. Ed., Assn. of Ancient Historians Newsletters, 1979–82. *Publs:* Social and Economic History of an Egyptian Temple in Greco-Roman Egypt, 1961; Procopius, 1972; (ed.) Polis and Imperium: Studies in Honour of Edward Togo Salmon, 1974; Herodotus, 1982. Add: Dept. of Classics, Univ. of British Columbia, Vancouver, B.C. V6T 1W5, Canada.

EVANS, Julia. Also writes as Polly Hobson. British, b. 1913. Mystery/Crime/Suspense, Children's fiction. *Publs:* (all as Polly Hobson): Brought Up in Bloomsbury, 1959; The Mystery House, 1963; Murder Won't Out, 1964; Titty's Dead (in U.S. as A Terreble Thing Happened to Miss Dupont), 1968; The Three Graces, 1970; (with J. Rendel) Henry Bada-Bada, 1971; Venus and Her Prey, 1975; Sarah's Story, 1983. Add: 21 The Close, Chequens Park, Wye, nr. Asford, Kent, England.

EVANS, Kathleen Marianne. British, b. 1911. Education. Reader in Education, Univ. Coll., Cardiff, 1950–72. *Publs:* Sociometry and Education, 1962; Attitudes and Interests in Education, 1965; Planning Small Scale Research, 1968, 3rd ed. 1984. Add: 33 Axminster Rd., Cardiff CF2 5AR, Wales.

EVANS, Mari. American. Children's fiction, Poetry, Plays. Producer, Writer, and Dir., The Black Experience television prog., Indianapolis, Ind, 1968–73; Asst. Prof. and Writer-in-Residence, Indiana Univ., Bloomington, 1970–78; Asst. Prof., Purdue Univ., Lafayette, Ind., 1978–80; Cornell Univ., Ithaca, NY, 1981–85; Assoc. Prof., State Univ. of New York at Albany, 1985–86. *Publs:* Where Is All the Music? (poetry), 1968; I Am a Black Woman (poetry), 1970; JD (juvenile), 1973; I Look at Me, 1973; Rap Stories, 1973; Singing Black, 1976; Jim Flying High (juvenile), 1979; Whisper (poetry), 1979; Nightstar (poetry), 1981; (ed.) Black Women Writers 1950-1980: A Critical Evaluation, 1984; Boochie (play), 1985; Portrait of a Man (play), 1985. Add: P.O. Box 483, Indianapolis, Ind. 46206, U.S.A.

EVANS, Max. American, b. 1925. Westerns/Adventure, Biography. Independent painter. Vice-Pres., Taos Minerals Inc., 1955–58, and Pres., Solar Metals Inc., 1957–59, both in Taos, N.M. *Publs:* Southwest Wind (short stories), 1958; Long John Dunn of Taos, 1959; The Rounders, 1960; The Hi Lo Country, 1961; Three Short Novels: The Great Wedding, The One-Eyed Sky, My Pardner, 1963; The Mountain of Gold, 1965; Shadow of Thunder, 1969; Bobby Jack Smith, You Dirty Coward!, 1974; The

White Shadow, 1977; Three West: Conversations with Vardis Fisher, Max Evans, Michael Straight, 1970; Sam Peckinpah, Master of Violence, 1972; Xavier's Folly and Other Stories, 1984; Super Bull and Other True Escapades, 1985. Add: 1111 Ridgecrest Dr. S.E. Albuquerque, N.M. 87108, U.S.A.

EVANS, Robert Owen. American, b. 1919. Novels/Short stories, Literature, Translations. Retired Prof. of English, Univ. of New Mexico, Albuquerque, since 1985 (Prof., 1978–84). Prof. of English, Univ. of Kentucky, Lexington, 1954–78. *Publs:* (with D. Crabb) Norfolk Billy, 1952; (ed.) Graham Greene: Some Critical Considerations, 1964; (ed. with J.M. Patrick) Style, Rhetoric and Rhythm, 1966; Milton's Elisions, 1966; The Osier Cage, 1966; Romeo and Juliet: A Commentary, 1967; King Lear: Commentary, 1967; (ed.) The English Secretary, by Angel Day, 1967; (ed. with J.M. Patrick) Attic and Baroque Prose Style, 1970; (ed. and trans. with L.C. Keating) Introduction to American Literature, by Borges, 1973; (ed. with Jack I. Biles) William Golding: Some Critical Considerations, 1978. Add: P.O. Box 4, Macatawa, Mich. 49434, U.S.A.

EVANS, Rowland, Jr. American, b. 1921. Politics/Government, Biography. Syndicated columnist, since 1963. *Publs:* (with R. Novak) Lyndon B. Johnson: The Exercise of Power, 1955; Nixon in the White House: The Frustration of Power, 1971; The Reagan Revolution, 1981. Add: 3125 O St. N.W., Washington, D.C. 20007, U.S.A.

EVANS, Tabor. *See* **KNOTT**, William C.

EVANS, William McKee. American, b. 1923. History. Prof. of History, California State Polytechnic Univ., Pomona, since 1968. *Publs:* Ballots and Fence Rails: Reconstruction on the Lower Cape Fear, 1967; To Die Game: The Story of the Lowry Band, Indian Guerrillas of Reconstruction, 1971. Add: Dept. of History, California State Polytechnic Univ., Pomona, Calif. 91768, U.S.A.

EVANSEN, Virginia B(esaw). American. Novels/Short stories, Children's fiction. *Publs:* Laura Reynolds, M.D., 1963; Nancy Kelsey, 1965; Sierra Summit, 1967; The Flea Market Mystery, 1978; (with Elsie E. Wolfers) The Organization Organizer, 1981. Add: 513 Pierce, West Plains, Mo. 65775, U.S.A.

EVARTS, Hal G(eorge, Jr.). American, b. 1915. Westerns/Adventure, Children's fiction, History. Screenwriter and reporter, staff member, Paris ed. of the New York Herald-Tribune, 1939–40; then full-time writer. Vice-Pres., Western Writers of America, 1959–60. *Publs:* Rolling Ahead (combat history), 1945; Highgrader, 1954; Apache Agent, 1955; Fugitive's Canyon (short stories), 1955; Ambush Rider, 1956; The Night Raiders, 1956; The Man Without a Gun, 1957; The Long Rope, 1959; The Man from Yuma, 1959; Jedediah Smith, Trail Blazer of the West (juvenile), 1959; Jim Clyman (juvenile), 1959; The Blazing Land, 1960; Turncoat, 1962; The Silver Concubine, 1962; Massacre Creek, 1962; The Secret of the Himalayas (juvenile), 1962; Colorado Crossing, 1963; Treasure River (juvenile), 1963; The Branded Man, 1965; The Talking Mountain (juvenile), 1966; Smuggler's Road, 1968; The Sundown Kid, 1969; Mission to Tibet (juvenile), 1970; The Pegleg Mystery (juvenile), 1972; Big Foot (juvenile), 1973; The Purple Eagle Mystery (juvenile), 1976; Jay-Jay and the Peking Monster (juvenile), 1978. Add: 6625 Muirlands Dr., La Jolla, Calif. 92037, U.S.A.

EVELING, (Harry) Stanley. British, b. 1925. Plays/Screenplays, Theatre. Fellow, Edinburgh Univ. Asst. Lectr., Dept. of Logic and Metaphysics, King's Coll. Aberdeen Univ., 1955–57; Lectr., Dept. of Philosophy, University Coll. of Wales, Aberystwyth, 1957–60. *Publs:* Poems, 1956; The Lunatic, the Secret Sportsman and the Woman Next Door, and Vibrations, 1970; The Balachites, and The Strange Case of Martin Richter, 1970; Come and Be Killed, and Dear Janet Rosenberg, Dear Mr. Kooning, 1971; The Total Theatre (non-fiction), 1972; Mister, in A Decade's Drama, 1980; The Buglar Boy and His Swish Friend, 1983. Add: 30 Comely Bank, Edinburgh EH4 1AS, Scotland.

EVERDELL, M(aurice) H(enry). British, b. 1917. Chemistry. Sr. Lectr. in Physical Chemistry, Univ. of Aston, Birmingham, since 1960 (Warden, Gracie Hall, 1960–68). *Publs:* Fundamental Thermodynamics for Engineers, 1958; Introduction to Chemical Thermodynamics, 1965; Statistical Mechanics and Its Chemical Applications, 1975. Add: 44 High Point, Richmond Hill Rd., Edgbaston, Birmingham 15, England.

EVEREST, Allan S. American, b. 1913. Architecture, History, Biography. Prof. of History, State Univ. Coll. of Arts and Science, Plattsburgh, N.Y., 1947–83. Instr., Green Mountain Jr. Coll., Poultney, Vt.,

1938–41. *Publs:* Morgenthau, The New Deal and Silver, 1950, 1973; (ed.) Recollections of Clinton County and the Battle of Plattsburgh, 1964; Pioneer Homes of Clinton County, New York, 1966, 1971; (ed.) A Doctor at All Hours, 1970; Our North Country Heritage, 972; (ed.) The Journal of Charles Carroll of Carrollton, 1976; Moses Hazen and the Canadian Refugees in the American Revolution, 1976; Rum Across the Border, 1978; Henry Delord and His Family, 1979; The War of 1812 in the Champlain Valley, 1981; Briefly Told: Plattsburgh, New York 1784-1984, 1984. Add: 20 S. Catherine St., Plattsburgh, N.Y., U.S.A.

EVERETT, Douglas Hugh. British, b. 1916. Chemistry. Emeritus Prof. of Physical Chemistry, Univ. of Bristol, since 1982 (Leverhulme Prof. of Physical Chemistry 1954–82). Prof. of Physical Chemistry, Dundee Univ., 1948–54. *Publs:* (trans. and co-author) Chemical Thermodynamics, 1954; (ed. with F.S. Stone) Colston Papers Vol. X: Structure and Properties of Porous Materials, 1958; Introduction to the Study of Chemical Thermodynamics, 1959, 1971; (trans. and co-author) Surface Tension and Adsorption, 1966; (ed. with R.H. Ottewill) Surface Area Determination, 1970; Basic Principles of Colloid Science, 1988. Add: Sch. of Chemistry, Univ. of Bristol, Cantock's Close, Bristol BS8 1TS, England.

EVERETT, Peter. British, b. 1931. Novels/Short stories, Plays/-Screenplays. *Publs:* A Day of Dwarfs, 1962; The Instrument, 1962; Negatives, 1964; The Fetch, 1966; The Last of the Long-Haired Boys (screenplay), 1971; Visions of Heydrich, 1979; A Death in Ireland, 1981. Add: c/o Little Brown, 34 Beacon St., Boston, Mass. 02106, U.S.A.

EVERETT, Wade. *See* **LUTZ**, Giles A.

EVERITT, Alan Milner. British, b. 1926. History. Prof. and Head of Dept. of English Local History, Univ. of Leicester, 1968–84 (Research Fellow in Urban History, 1960–65; Lectr. in Local History, 1965–68). *Publs:* Suffolk and the Great Rebellion 1640-60, 1961; The Community of Kent and the Great Rebellion, 1640-60, 1966; The Local Community and the Great Rebellion, 1969; Perspectives in English Urban History, 1973; The Pattern of Rural Dissent: The Nineteenth Century, 1972; Landscape and Community in England, 1985; Continuity and Colonization: The Evolution of Kentish Settlement, 1986. Add: Kimcote, Leics., England.

EVERNDEN, Margery (Gulbransen). American, b. 1916. Children's fiction. Prof. Emeritus of English, Univ. of Pittsburgh, Pa.; freelance writer. *Publs:* novels—Secret of the Porcelain Fish; Sword with the Golden Hilt; The Runaway Apprentice; Knight of Florence; Lyncoya; The Kite Song, 1984; The Dream Keeper, 1985; plays—King Arthur and the Magic Sword; Secret of Han Ho; Davy Crockett and His Coonskin Cap; The Frog Princess and the Witch, 1985. Add: 63 Hathaway Ct., Pittsburgh, Pa. 15235, U.S.A.

EVERSON, Ronald (Gilmour). Canadian, b. 1903. Poetry. Managing Dir., 1936–47, and Pres., 1947–63, Johnston, Everson & Charlesworth Ltd., Toronto; Dir., Ryerson Press, Toronto, 1960–65; Chmn., Communications-6 Inc., Montreal, 1964–72. *Publs:* Three Dozen Poems, 1957; A Lattice for Momos, 1958; Blind Man's Holiday, 1963; Four Poems, 1963; Wrestle with an Angel, 1965; Incident on Cote des Neiges, 1966; Raby Head and Other Poems, 1967; The Dark Is Not So Dark, 1969; Selected Poems, 1970; Indian Summer, 1976; Carnival, 1978; Everson at Eighty, 1984. Add: 459 Wicklow Rd., Burlington, Ont. L7L 2H9, Canada.

EVERSON, William (Oliver). Also writes as Brother Antoninus. American, b. 1912. Poetry, Literature. Co-Founder, Untide Press, Waldport, Ore.; Dominican lay brother, 1951–69; Poet-in-Residence, Kresge Coll., Univ. of California, Santa Cruz, 1971–81. *Publs:* as Brother Antoninus—At the Edge, 1958; A Fragment for the Birth of God, 1958; An Age Insurgent, 1959; The Crooked Lines of God: Poems 1949-1954, 1959; The Hazards of Holiness: Poems 1959-1960, 1962; The Poet Is Dead: A Memorial for Robinson Jeffers, 1964; The Rose of Solitude, 1964; The Rose of Solitude (collection), 1967; The Achievement of Brother Antoninus: A Comprehensive Selection of His Poems with a Critical Introduction, 1967; Canticle to the Waterbirds, 1968; The City Does Not Die, 1969; The Last Crusade, 1969; Who Is She that Looketh Forth as the Morning, 1972; as William Everson—These Are the Ravens, 1935; San Joaquin, 1939; The Masculine Dead: Poems 1938-40, 1942; Waldport Poems, 1944; War Elegies, 1944; Residual Years, Poems 1934-1946, 1948; A Privacy of Speech: Ten Poems in Sequence, 1949; Triptych for the Living, 1951; There Will Be Harvest, 1960; The Year's Declension, 1961; The Blowing of the Seed, 1966; Single Source: The Early Poems of William Everson, 1934-1940, 1966; The Vision of Felicity, 1966; In the Fictive Wish, 1967; The Springing of the Blade, 1968; The Residual Years: Poems, 1934-1948, 1968; Robinson Jeffers: Fragments of an Older Fury, 1968; (with J. Burns) If I Speak Truth: An Inter View-ing, 1968; (ed.) Cawdor and Medea, By Robinson Jeffers, 1970; Earth Poetry, 1971; (ed.) Californians, by Robinson Jeffers, 1971; Tendril in the Mesh, 1973; Black Hills, 1973; (ed.) The Alpine Christ, by Robinson Jeffers, 1973; (ed.) Tragedy Has Obligations, by Robinson Jeffers 1973; (ed.) Brides of the South Wind, by Robinson Jeffers, 1975; Man-Fate: The Swan Song of Brother Antoninus, 1974; (ed.) Granite and Cypress, by Robinson Jeffers, 1975; Archetype West: The Pacific Coast as a Literary Region, 1976; River-Root: A Syzygy for the Bicentennial of These States, 1976; (ed.) The Double Axe, by Robinson Jeffers, 1977; The Mate-Flight of Eagles, 1977; The Veritable Years: Poems 1949-1966, 1978; Cutting the Firebreak, 1978; Blame It on the Jet Stream, 1978; The Masks of Drought, 1980; Earth Poetry: Selected Essays and Interviews 1950-77, 1980; Eastward the Armies: Selected War Poems 1935-42, 1980; Sixty-Five, 1980; (ed.) American Bard, by Walt Whitman: The Original Preface to Leaves of Grass Arranged as Verse, 1981; Cougar, 1982; Birth of a Poet, 1982; On Writing the Waterbirds 1935-81, 1983; Renegade Christmas, 1984; In Medias Res: Canto One: Dust Shall Be the Serpent's Food, 1984; The High Embrace, 1986. Add: 312 Swanton Rd., Davenport, Calif. 95017, U.S.A.

EVERWINE, Peter (Paul). American, b. 1930. Poetry. Prof. of English, California State Univ., Fresno, since 1962. Instr. in English, Univ. of Iowa, Iowa City, 1959–62. *Publs:* The Broken Frieze, 1958; In the House of Light: Thirty Aztec Poems, 1970; Collecting the Animals, 1973; Keeping the Night, 1977; (ed. and trans.) The State Element: Selected Poems of Natan Zach, 1982. Add: Dept. of English, California State Univ., Fresno, Calif. 93710, U.S.A.

EVERY, George. British, b. 1909. Poetry, Literature, Theology/Religion. Part-time Lectr., Oscott Coll., Birmingham, since 1973. Librarian, 1953–73, and Tutor, 1929–72, Kelham Coll., Newark, Notts.; Assoc. Ed., Theoria to Theory, 1966–68; Ed., Eastern Churches Review, 1968–78. *Publs:* Christian Discrimination, 1940; (with S.L. Bethell and J.D.C. Pellow) Selected Poems, 1943; Byzantine Patriarchate, 1947, 1962; Poetry and Personal Responsibility, 1949; Lamb to the Slaughter, 1957; Baptismal Sacrifice, 1959; (ed.) Basic Liturgy, 1961; Misunderstandings Between East and West, 1965; Christian Mythology, 1970, 1987; The Mass, 1978; Understanding Eastern Christianity, 1978, 1980. Add: 7 Lenton Ave., The Park, Nottingham, England.

EWART, Gavin (Buchanan). British, b. 1916. Poetry. With British Council, 1946–62; Advertising copywriter, 1952–71. *Publs:* Poems and Songs, 1939; (ed.) Forty Years On: An Anthology of School Songs, 1964; Londoners, 1964; Throwaway Lines, 1964; Two Children, 1966; Pleasures of the Flesh, 1966; The Deceptive Grin of the Gravel Porters, 1968; Twelve Apostles, 1970; The Gavin Ewart Show, 1971; (co-author) Folio, 1971; Venus, 1972; The Select Party, 1972; Alphabet Soup, 1972; (with B.S. Johnson and Zulfikar Ghose) Penguin Modern Poets 25, 1974; Be My Guest!, 1975; Question Partly Answered, 1976; (ed.) The Batsford Book of Children's Verse, 1976; No Fool Like An Old Fool, 1976; (ed.) New Poems, 1977-1978: A P.E.N. Anthology, 1977; Or Where a Young Penguin Lies Screaming, 1977; The First Eleven, 1977; (ed.) The Batsford Book of Light Verse for Children, 1978; All My Little Ones: The Shortest Poems of Gavin Ewart, 1979; (ed.) The Penguin Book of Light Verse, 1980; The Collected Ewart 1933-1980, 1980; The New Ewart: Poems 1980-82, 1982; More Little Ones: Short Poems, 1982; Capital Letters, 1983; The Ewart Quarto, 1984; The Young Pobbles Guide to His Toes, 1985; The Complete Little Ones of Gavin Ewart, 1986; The Gavin Ewart Show: Selected Poems, 1986; The Learned Hippopotamus: Poems for Children, 1987; Late Pickings, 1987; Selected Poems, 1933-1988, 1988; Penultimate Poems, 1989. Add: 57 Kenilworth Ct., Lower Richmond Rd., London SW15, England.

EWING, David Walkley. American, b. 1923. Administration/Management, Personnel management. Managing Ed., Harvard Business Review, Boston, Mass. (Asst. Ed., 1949–64; Assoc. Ed., 1964–68; Sr. Assoc. Ed., 1968–72). *Publs:* (ed.) Long-Range Planning for Management, 1964; (ed.) Effective Marketing Action, 1958; (co-ed.) Incentives for Executives, 1962; The Managerial Mind, 1964; (ed. and contrib.) Long-Range Planning for Management, 1964, 1972; The Practice of Planning, 1968; The Human Side of Planning, 1969; (ed.) Technological Change and Management, 1970; (ed.) Science Policy and Business, 1973; Writing for Results: In Business, Government, and the Professions, 1974; Freedom Inside the Organization, 1977; Do It My Way or You're Fired! Add: 195 Cambridge St., Winchester, Mass. 01890, U.S.A.

EWING, Elizabeth Cameron. British, b. 1906. Fashion/Costume. Reporter, Feature Writer, and Columnist, Allied newspapers (now Thomson), 1929–35; Freelance journalist and public relations consultant, 1936–70. *Publs:* Fashion in Underwear, 1972; A History of Twentieth Century Fashion, 1974; Women in Uniform Through the Centuries, 1975, 1987; History of Children's Costume, 1977; Dress and Undress: A History of Women's Underwear, 1978; Fur in Dress, 1981; Everyday Dress 1650-1900, 1984. Add: 25 Westfield Way, Ruislip, Middex. HA4 6HW, England.

EXTON, Clive (Jack Montague). British, b. 1930. Plays/Screenplays. Worked in advertising, 1946–48; Actor, 1951–59. *Screenplays:* No Fixed Abode (play), 1959; Night Must Fall, 1963; (with Melvyn Bragg) Isadora, 1968; Entertaining Mr. Sloane, 1969; Have You Any Dirty Washing, Mother Dear (play), 1969; Ten Rillington Place, 1970; Doomwatch, 1971; (with D. Hemmings) Running Scared, 1971; (with T. Nation) Nightmare Park, 1973; Legacies, 1973; Breakthrough, 1975; When Greek Meets Greek, 1975; The Root of All Evil, 1975; A Chance for Mr. Lever, 1976; The Overnight Bag, 1976; The Killers series, 1976; The Crezz series, 1976; Stigma, 1977; Henry Intervening, 1978; The Awakening, 1979; Red Sonja, 1984; Bucks, 1985; One Fine Day, 1985. Add: c/o A.D. Peters, 10 Buckingham St., London WC2N 6BU, England.

EXTON, William (Philip), Jr. American, b. 1907. Administration/Management. Principal Sr. Consultant, William Exton, Jr. and Assocs., NYC, since 1948. *Publs:* He's with the Destroyers Now, 1943; Audio-Visual Aids to Instruction, 1947; The Age of Systems: The Human Dilemma, 1972; Motivational Leverage: A New Approach to Managing People, 1975; Cost-Effective Error Reduction, 1979; Selling Leverage: How to Motivate People to Buy, 1984; The Future of Management, 1982; The Future of Language, 1983; Coping with the Future: Toward Greater Mastery of Problem-Situations, 1984; The Future of Conflict Resolution, 1986; A General Semantics Approach to "Critical Thinking", 1986; Situation Management, 1986; The Ultimate Task of Management: The Takeover of the Evolutionary Future of the Human Species, 1986. Add: 40 Central Park South, New York, N.Y. 10019 or Box 175, RFD 1, Dover Plains, N.Y. 12522, U.S.A.

EYCK, Frank. Canadian, b. 1921. History. Prof. of History, Univ. of Calgary, Alta, since 1968, Emeritus since 1987. Lectr. in Modern European History, Exeter Univ., U.K., 1959–68. Vice-Chmn. of the Council, Inter-Univ. Centre of Post-Grad. Studies, Dubrovnik, 1974–79. *Publs:* The Prince Consort: A Political Biography, 1959; The Frankfurt Parliament 1848-49, 1968; (ed.) The Revolutions of 1848-49, 1972; (ed.) Frederick Hertz: The German Public Mind in the Nineteenth Century, 1975; G.P. Gooch, 1982. Add: Dept. of History, Univ. of Calgary, Calgary, Alta. T2N 1N4, Canada.

EYEN, Tom. American, b. 1941. Plays/Screenplays. Playwright and Director. Teacher of drama, Metropolitan Television Arts, NYC, 1962; Former publicity agent; Founder, Theatre of the Eye (affiliated with the La Mama group), NYC, 1965; Writer, Mary Hartman, Mary Hartman, television series, 1970–77. *Publs:* Sarah B. Divine! and Other Plays, 1971; Women Behind Bars, 1974; The Dirtiest Musical, 1975; 2008 (A Spaced Odyssey), 1976; The Neon Woman, 1978; Milliken Breakfast Show, 1977; Dreamgirls, 1981. Add: c/o Bridget Aschenberg, Intnl. Creative Management, 40 W. 57th St., New York, N.Y. 10019, U.S.A.

EYRE, Annette. *See* **WORBOYS**, Anne.

EYRE, S. Robert. British, b. 1922. Geography. Lectr., 1952–66, and Sr. Lectr., 1966 until retirement 1982, Univ. of Leeds. Pres., Geography Section, British Assn. for the Advancement of Science, 1970–71. *Publs:* (author and ed. with G.R.J. Jones) Geography as Human Ecology, 1966; Vegetation and Soils: A World Picture, 2nd ed. 1968; (ed.) World Vegetation Types, 1971; (with J. Palmer) The Face of North East Yorkshire, 1973; The Real Wealth of Nations, 1978. Add: Rokeby Cott, Husthwaite, York, England.

EYSENCK, H(ans) J(urgen). British, b. 1916. Psychiatry, Psychology. Prof. of Psychology, Inst. of Psychiatry, Univ. of London, since 1955. *Publs:* Dimensions of Personality, 1947; The Scientific Study of Personality, 1952; The Structure of Human Personality, 1952; Uses and Abuses of Personality, 1953; The Psychology of Politics, 1954; Sense and Nonsense in Psychology, 1956; The Dynamics of Anxiety and Hysteria, 1957; (with G. Granger and J.C. Brengelmann) Perceptual Processes and Mental Illness, 1957; (ed.) Handbook of Abnormal Psychology, 1960, 1972; (ed.) Experiments in Personality, 2 vols., 1960; (ed.) Behaviour Therapy and the Neuroses, 1960; Know Your Own I.Q., 1962;

(ed.) Experiments with Drugs, 1963; (ed.) Experiments in Motivation, 1964; (ed.) Experiments in Behaviour Therapy, 1964; Crime and Personality, 1964, 1970; (with S. Rachman) Causes and Cures of Neuroses, 1965; Fact and Fiction in Psychology, 1965; Smoking, Health and Personality, 1965; Check Your Own I.Q., 1966; The Effects of Psychotherapy, 1966; The Biological Basis of Personality, 1967; (with S.B.G. Pesenck) Personality Structure and Measurement, 1969; Readings in Extraversion/Introversion, 3 vols., 1971; Race, Intelligence and Education, 1971; Psychology Is About People, 1972; (ed.) Lexicon der Psychologie, 1972; The Inequality of Man, 1973; (with G. Wilson) The Experimental Study of Freudian Theories, 1973; (with G. Wilson) Know Yourself, 1975; (ed.) Case Studies in Behaviour Therapy, 1976; (with S.B.G. Eysenck) Psychoticism as a Dimension of Personality, 1976; Personality and Sex, 1977; You and Neurosis, 1977; The Measurement of Personality, 1977; (with D.K. Nias) Sex, Violence and the Media, 1978; (with G. Wilson) Psychological Basis of Ideology, 1978; The Structure and Measurement of Intelligence, 1979; (with G. Wilson) The Psychology of Sex, 1979; (with L. Evans) The Causes and Effects of Smoking, 1980; (ed.) A Model for Personality, 1981; (with M.W. Eysenck) Mindwatching, 1981; (with L. Kamin) The Battle for the Mind, 1981; Personality, Genetics, and Behaviour: Selected Papers, 1982; (with C. Sargent) Explaining the Unexplained, 1982; (with C. Sargent) Know Your Own PSI-Q, 1983; (with M.W. Eysenck) Personality and Individual Differences, 1985; The Decline and Fall of the Freudian Empire, 1985. Add: 10 Dorchester Dr., London SE24, England.

EZEKIEL, Nissim. Indian, b. 1924. Plays/Screenplays, Poetry, Literature. Lectr., Khalsa Coll., Bombay, 1947–48; Ed., Quest mag., 1955–57; Assoc. Ed., Imprint mag., 1961–67; Prof. of English and Vice-Principal, Mithibai Coll., Bombay, 1916–61; Art Critic, The Times of India, Bombay, 1964–67; Reader, then Prof. of American Literature, Bombay Univ., 1972–85; Writer in Residence, National Univ. of Singapore, 1988–89. *Publs:* A Time to Change and Other Poems, 1952; Sixty Poems, 1953; The Third, 1958; The Unfinished Man: Poems Written in 1959, 1960; (ed.) A New Look at Communism, 1963; (ed.) Indian Writers in Conference, 1964; (ed.) Writing in India, 1965; The Exact Name: Poems 1960-64, 1965; (ed.) An Emerson Reader, 1965; (ed.) A Martin Luther King Reader, 1969; Three Plays, 1969; (ed.) All My Sons, by Arthur Miller, 1972; The Actor: A Sad and Funny Story for Children of Most Ages, 1974; Hymns in Darkness, 1976; Latter-Day Psalms, 1982; Collected Poems, 1952-88, 1989. Add: 18 Kala Niketan, 6th Floor, 47-c Bhulabhai Desai Rd., Bombay 400026, India.

F

FABER, John. American, b. 1918. Photography. Historian, National Press Photographers Assn., since 1956; Press Photography Adviser, Smithsonian Inst., Washington, D.C. since 1960. Chief Photographer, Alabama Ordnance Works, 1941–43; Chief Photographer, Birmingham Aircraft Modification Center, Ala., 1943–46; Photographic Dir., Birmingham News and T.V. Station, WAFM-TV, 1946–50; Photo-Press Rep., Eastman Kodak Co., Rochester, N.Y., 1950–83; Faculty Assoc., Sch. of Modern Photography, 1970–75. *Publs:* Industrial Photography, 1948; Great Moments in News Photography, 1960; Humor in News Photography, 1961; Travel Photography, 1971; Great News Pictures and Their Stories, 1978. Add: Isle of Pines, Smith Mountain, Lake Route 1, Box 255, Moneta, Va. 24121, U.S.A.

FABRIZIUS, Peter. *See* **FABRY,** Joseph B.

FABRY, Joseph B. Also writes as Peter Fabrizius. American, b. 1909. Psychology, Translations. Ed. Independent Logotherapist since 1968. Ed., Logotherapy Journal; Dir., Logotherapy Inst. Script writer, Voice of America, 1944–48; Ed., Univ. of California, 1948–72. *Publs:* with M. Knight as Peter Fabrizius: Der schwarze Teufel, 1942, Der Komet, 1942, Die siebzehn Kamele, 1949, Wer zuletzt lacht, 1952, and Lacht am besten, 1957; (trans. with M. Knight) Johann Nestroy: Three Comedies, 1967; (trans.) In Psychotherapy and Existentialism, 1967; The Pursuit of Meaning, 1968, 1980; (trans. with M. Knight) Bertolt Brecht, 1970; (trans. with M. Knight) In These Great Times, 1976; (ed. with R. Bulka and W. Sahakian) Logotherapy in Action, 1979; Swingshift, 1982; Wege zur Selbstfindung, 1985; (as Peter Fabrizius) One and One Make Three, 1988; Guideposts to Meaning, 1988. Add: 315 Carmel Ave., El Cerrito, Calif. 94530, U.S.A.

FACKENHEIM, Emil L(udwig). Canadian, b. 1916. Philosophy, Theology/Religion. Fellow, Inst. of Contemporary Jewry, Hebrew Univ. of Jerusalem; Prof. of Philosophy Emeritus, Univ. of Totonto, since 1983 (Lectr., 1948–53; Asst Prof., 1953–57; Assoc. Prof., 1957–60; Prof. 1960–83). *Publs:* Paths to Jewish Belief, 1960; Metaphysics and Historicity, 1961; The Religious Dimension in Hegel's Thought, 1967; Quest for Past and Future: Essays in Jewish Theology, 1967; God's Presence in History: Jewish Affirmations and Philosophical Reflections, 1970; Encounters Between Judaism and Modern Philosophy: A Preface to Future Jewish Thought, 1973; The Jewish Return into History, 1978; To Mend the World: Foundations of Future Jewish Thought, 1983; What Is Judaism? An Interpretation for the Present Age, 1987. Add: 3 Alroi St., Jerusalem 92108, Israel.

FADIMAN, Clifton. American, b. 1904. Wine, Intellectual history, Essays. Member, Bd. of Editors, Encyclopaedia Britannica, Chicago, since 1959. Ed., Simon and Schuster, NYC, 1929–35; Book Ed., The New Yorker, 1933–43; Regents Lectr., UCal. at Los Angeles, 1967; Book Reviewer, Signature, 1981–84 (columnist, 1981); Commentator, First Edition (TV show), 1983–84, 1986. *Publs:* (ed.) Reading I've Liked, 1941; (ed.) The American Treasury, 1955; Party of One, 1955; Any Number Can Play, 1957; (ed.) Fantasia Mathematica, 1958; The Lifetime Reading Plan, 1959, 3rd ed. 1988; Enter Conversing, 1962; (ed.) The Mathematical Magpie, 1962; (ed.) Dionysus, 1962; Willy the Wordworm, 1964; (ed.) Fifty Years, 1965; (co-author) The Joys of Wine, 1975; Wine-Buyer's Guide, 1977; Empty Pages, 1979; (ed.) World Treasury of Children's Literature, 2 vols., 1984; (ed.) The Little Brown Book of Anecdotes, 1985; (ed.) The World of the Short Story, 1986. Add: 3222 Campanil Dr., Santa Barbara, Calif. 93109, U.S.A.

FAGAN, Brian Murray. American (b. British), b. 1936. Anthropology/Ethnology, Archaeology/Antiquities, History. Prof. of Anthropology, Univ. of California, Santa Barbara, since 1969 (Assoc. Prof., 1967–69). Keeper of Prehistory, Livingstone Museum, Zambia, 1959–65; former Dir., Bantu Studies Project, British Inst. in Eastern Africa; Visiting Assoc. Prof., Univ. of Illinois, 1965–66. *Publs:* (ed.) Victoria Falls Handbook, 1964; Southern Africa During the Iron Age, 1966; (ed.) A Short History of Zambia, 1966, 1968; (with S.G.H. Daniels and D.W. Phillipson) Iron Age Cultures in Zambia, vol. I, 1967, vol. II, 1969; (with F. Van Noten) The Hunter-Gatherers of Gwisho, 1971; In the Beginning, 1972, 3rd ed. 1978; People of the Earth, 1974, 1976; The Rape of the Nile, 1975; Elusive Treasure, 1977; Quest for the Past, 1978; Archaeology: A Brief Introduction, 1978; Return to Babylon, 1979; The Aztecs, 1984; Clash of Cultures, 1984; The Adventure in Archaeology, 1985; Bareboating, 1985; Anchoring, 1985; The Great Journey, 1987. Add: Dept. of Anthropology, Univ. of California, Santa Barbara, Calif. 93106, U.S.A.

FAGE, John Donnelly. British, b. 1921. History. Prof. of History, Univ. Coll. of Ghana, 1955–59; Lectr. in African History, Sch. of Oriental and African Studies, Univ. of London, 1959–63; Prof. of African History Emeritus, Univ of Birmingham, since 1984 (Prof., 1963–84; Dir., Centre of West African Studies, 1963–82; Pro-Vice-Chancellor, 1979–84). Gen Ed., with Roland Oliver, Cambridge History of Africa, 1966–86. *Publs:* An Introduction to the History of West Africa, 1955, 3rd ed. 1962; An Atlas of African History, 1958, 1978; Ghana: An Historical Interpretation, 1959; (with Roland Oliver) A Short History of Africa, 1962, 6th ed. 1988; On the Nature of African History, 1965; a History of West Africa, 1969; (ed.) Africa Discovers Her Past, 1970; (ed. with Roland Oliver) Papers on African Prehistory, 1970; States and Subjects in Sub-Saharan African History, 1974; A History of Africa, 1978, 1988. Add: Centre of West African Studies, Univ. of Birmingham, Birmingham B15 2TT, England.

FAHN, Abraham. Israeli, b. 1916. Botany. Prof. of Botany since 1965, and Otto Warburg Prof. of Botany since 1976, Hebrew Univ. of Jerusalem (joined faculty, 1945; Instr., 1949–52; Lectr., 1952–55; Sr. Lectr., 1955–60; Assoc. Prof., 1960–65; Dean of the Faculty of Science, 1963–65; Head, Dept. of Botany, 1965–72; Pro-Rector, 1969–70). Pres., Botanical Soc. of Israel, 1981–84. *Publs:* (with M. Zohary) Cultivated Plants of Israel (in Hebrew), 1957, 1980; Plant Anatomy, 1967, 3rd ed. 1982; Secretory Tissues in Plants, 1979; (with E. Werker and P. Baas) Wood Anatomy and Identification of Trees and Shrubs from Israel and Adjacent Regions, 1986. Add: Dept. of Botany, Hebrew Univ. of Jerusalem, Jerusalem, Israel.

FAINLIGHT, Ruth. American, b. 1931. Short stories, Poetry, Translations. Poet-in-Residence, Vanderbilt Univ., Nashville, Tenn., 1985 *Publs:* A Forecast, A Fable, 1958; Cages, 1966; 18 Poems from 1966, 1967; (trans. with Alan Sillitoe) All Citizens Are Soldiers (play), 1967; To See the Matter Clearly, 1968; (with A. Sillitoe and Ted Hughes) Poems, 1971; Daylife and Nightlife (short stories), 1971; The Region's Violence, 1973; 21 Poems, 1973; Another Full Moon, 1976; Two Fire Poems, 1977; The Function of Tears, 1979; Sibyls and Others, 1980; Climates, 1983; Fifteen to Infinity, 1983; (trans.) Navigacions, by Sophia de Mello Breyner Andresen, 1983; (trans.) Marine Rose, by Sophia de Mello Breyner Andresen, 1987; Selected Poems, 1988. Add: 14 Ladbroke Terr., London W11 3PG, England.

FAIRBAIRN, Douglas. American, b. 1926. Novels/Short stories,

Animals/Pets. *Publs:* A Man's World, 1956; The Joy Train, 1957; Money Mables and Chalk, 1958; The Voice of Charlie Pont, 1961; A Gazelle on the Lawn, 1964; A Squirrel of One's Own, 1971; Shoot, 1973; A Squirrel Forever, 1973; Street 8, 1977. Add: c/o Roberta Pryor, Intnl. Creative Mgmt., 40 W. 57th St., New York, N.Y. 10019, U.S.A.

FAIRBAIRNS, Zoë (Ann). British, b. 1948. Novels/Short stories, Science fiction, Social commentary/phenomena. Ed., CND newspaper Sanity, London, 1973–75; Poetry Ed., Spare Rib, London, 1978–82. Writer-in-Residence, Rutherford Sch., London, 1977–78, Bromley schools, Kent, 1981–82, Deakin Univ., Melbourne, Vic., 1983, and Sunderland Polytechnic, 1983–85. *Publs:* Live as Family (novel), 1968; Down: An Explanation (novel), 1969; Study War No More, 1974; (with Jim Wintour) No Place to Grow Up, 1977; (with others) Tales I Tell My Mother, 1978; Benefits (science fiction), 1979; Stand We at Last (novel), 1983; Here Today (novel), 1984; (with Ed Barber and James Cameron) Peace Moves: Nuclear Protest in the 1980's, 1984; Closing (novel), 1987. Add: c/o A.M. Heath, 79 St. Martins Lane, London WC2N 4AA, England.

FAIRBURN, Eleanor. Also writes as Catherine Carfax, Emma Gayle, and Elena Lyons. Tutor in Practical Writing, Univ. of Leeds Adult Education Centre, Middlesborough, since 1985. British, b. 1928. Novels/Short stories, Mystery/Crime/Suspense, Historical/Romance/-Gothic. *Publs:* The Green Popinjays, 1962; The White Seahorse, 1964; The Golden Hive, 1966; Crowned Ermine, 1968; (as Catherine Carfax) A Silence with Voices, 1969; The Rose in Spring, 1971; White Rose, Dark Summer, 1972; (as Catherine Carfax) The Semper Inheritance, 1972; (as Catherine Carfax) To Die a Little, 1972; (as Catherine Carfax) The Sleeping Salamander, 1973; (as Catherine Carfax) The Locked Tower, 1974; The Rose at Harvest End, 1975; Winter's Rose, 1976; (as Emma Gayle) Cousin Caroline, 1980; (as Elena Lyons) The Haunting of Abbotsgarth, 1980; (as Emma Gayle) Frenchman's Harvest, 1980; (as Elena Lyons) A Scent of Lilacs, 1982. Add: 199 Oxford Rd., Linthorpe, Middlesborough, Cleveland TS5 5EG, England.

FAIRE, Zabrina. *See* STEVENSON, Florence.

FAIRFAX, John. British, b. 1930. Poetry, Literature. Dir., Phoenix Press, Newbury, Berks., since 1967; Dir., Writers Studio, Newbury, Berks. Co-Founding Dir., Arvon Foundn., Devon, since 1968. Sch. teacher, 1955–62. *Publs:* (ed.) Listen to This: A Contemporary Anthology, 1967; This I Say: Twelve Poems, 1967; The 5th Horseman of the Apocalypse, 1969; (ed.) Stop and Listen: An Anthology of Thirteen Living Poets, 1969; (ed.) Frontier of Going: An Anthology of Space Poetry, 1969; (ed.) Horizons, 1971; (with Michael Baldwin and Brian Patten) Double Image, 1972; Adrift on the Star Brow of Taliesin (poems), 1975; Bone Harvest Done, 1980; (with J. Moat) The Way to Write, 1981; Wild Children (poems), 1986; Writer in Residence for West Berk, 1988; Creative Writing, 1989; Grotesque Tournament and Other Poems, 1989. Add: The Thatched Cottage, Hermitage, Newbury, Berks., England.

FAIRFIELD, Darrell. *See* LARKIN, Rochelle.

FAIRLEY, James S(tewart). British, b. 1940. Animals, Natural history, Zoology. Lectr. in Zoology, University Coll., Galway, Ireland, since 1968. Research Fellow, Queen's Univ., Belfast, 1966–68. *Publs:* Irish Wild Mammals: A Guide to the Literature, 1972; An Irish Beast Book, 1975, 1984; (ed.) The Experienced Huntsman, 1977; Irish Whales and Whaling, 1981. Add: Dept. of Zoology, University Coll., Galway, Ireland.

FAIRMAN, Joan Alexandra (Mrs. George T. Mitchell, Jr.). American, b. 1935. Children's fiction. Consultant, Towers, Perrin, Forster & Crosby, Inc. (mgmt. consultants), Philadelphia, since 1970. Exec. Secty., Curtis Publishing Co., Philadelphia, 1953–70. *Publs:* (contrib.) Widening Circles, 1970, 1974; A Penny Saved, 1971. Add: 430 Wayland Rd., Cherry Hill, N.J. 08034, U.S.A.

FALCK, Colin. British, b. 1934. Poetry, Literature. Adjunct Prof. in English Literature, Syracuse Univ. London Centre, since 1985. Lectr. in Sociology, London Sch. of Economics, 1961–62; Lectr. in Humanities, Chelsea Coll., London, 1964–84. Assoc. Ed., The Review, Oxford and London, 1962–72. *Publs:* The Garden in the Evening (poetry adaptations), 1964; Promises, 1969; Backwards into the Smoke, 1973; (ed. with Ian Hamilton) Poems since 1900: An Anthology, 1975; In This Dark Light, 1978; (ed.) Robinson Jeffers: Selected Poems, 1987; Myth, Truth and Literature: Towards a True Post-Modernism, 1989. Add: 20 Thurlow Rd., London NW3 5PP, England.

FALK, Candace. American, b. 1947. History, Women, Biography. Ed. and Dir., The Emma Goldman Papers, National Historical Publications and Records Commn., National Archives and Univ. of California at Berkeley, since 1980. Ed., Socialist Review, San Francisco, then Oakland, Calif., 1972–79; Ed., Southeast Asia Chronicle, Berkeley, Calif., 1976–79. *Publs:* Love, Anarchy, and Emma Goldman, 1984; Selected Papers of Emma Goldman, 1992. Add: c/o Emma Goldman Papers, Univ. of California, 2224 Piedmont, Berkeley, Calif. 94720, U.S.A.

FALK, Signi Lenea. American, b. 1906. Literature, Theatre, Biography. Prof. Emerita of English, Coe Coll., Cedar Rapids, Iowa, since 1971 (joined faculty, 1947). *Publs:* Tennessee Williams, 1961, 1978; Archibald Macleish, 1965, 1989. Add: 1846 C Ave. N.E., Cedar Rapids, Iowa 52402, U.S.A.

FALK, Stanley Lawrence. American, b. 1927. History, International relations/Current affairs, Military/Defence. Historical Consultant, since 1982, Historian, Office of Chief of Military History, Dept. of the Army, 1949–54, Bureau of Social Science Research, American Univ., 1954–56, and Historical Div., Joint Chiefs of Staff, 1956–59; Sr. Historian, Office of Chief of Military History, Dept. of the Army, 1959–62—all in Washington, D.C.; Educational Specialist, 1962–65, Assoc. Prof. of National Security Affairs, 1965–70, and Prof. of Intnl. Relations, Resident Sch., 1970–74, all with Industrial Coll. of the Armed Forces, Washington, D.C.; Chief Historian, U.S. Air Force, Washington, D.C. 1974–80; Deputy Chief Historian for Southeast Asia, U.S. Army Center of Military History, Washington, D.C., 1980–82. *Publs:* Bataan: The March of Death, 1962; (co-author) Organization for National Security, 1963; The International Arena, 1964; Human Resources for National Strength, 1966; Decision at Leyte, 1966; The National Security Structure, 1967, rev. ed. 1972; The Environment of National Security, 1968, rev. ed. 1973; (ed.) The World in Ferment: Problem Areas for the United States, 1970, 1974; Defense Military Manpower, 1970; The Liberation of the Philippines, 1971; Bloodiest Victory: Palaus, 1974; Seventy Days to Singapore: The Malayan Campaign, 1975. Add: 2310 Kimbro St., Alexandria, Va. 22307, U.S.A.

FALK, Ze'ev W(ilhelm). Israeli, b. 1923. Law. Berman Prof. of Family and Succession Law, Hebrew Univ. of Jerusalem, since 1970. Hon. Pres., Intnl. Soc. of Family Law, since 1975; Co-Ed., Diné Israel: Annual of Jewish Law and Israeli Family Law; Member of Editorial Bd., Petahim: Journal of Jewish Thought, and Immanuel: Journal of Jewish-Christian Relations. Legal Adviser, Ministries of Social Welfare and Interior, Israel, 1955–68. *Publs:* Hebrew Law in Biblical Times, 1964; Jewish Matrimonial Law in the Middle Ages, 1966; Introduction to Jewish Law of the Second Commonwealth, vol. 1, 1972, vol. 2, 1978; Law and Religion: The Jewish Experience, 1981. Add: 10 Harav Berlin St., Jerusalem, Israel.

FALKIRK, Richard. *See* LAMBERT, Derek.

FALLON, George. *See* BINGLEY, David Ernest.

FALLON, Martin. *See* PATTERSON, Henry.

FAMILY DOCTOR. *See* HUTCHIN, Kenneth Charles.

FANCUTT, Walter. British, b. 1911. History, Theology/Religion. Editorial Consultant, Leprosy Mission, London, since 1970 (Editorial Secty., 1957–70). Gen. Secty., Southern Baptist Assn. Baptist Minister, London and Hampshire, 1934–57. *Publs:* (ed.) Kingsgate Pocket Poets, 9 vols., 1943; Then Came Jesus, 1943; From Vision to Advance, 1951; Whitchurch Baptist Church 1652-1952, 1952; In This Will I Be Confident, 1957; Beyond the Bitter Sea, 1959; Present to Heal, 1962; (ed.) Escaped as a Bird, 1963; Daily Remembrance, 1966; The Imprisoned Splendour, 1973; The Southern Baptist Association, 1974; With Strange Surprise, 1974; The Luminous Cloud, 1980; His Excellent Greatness, 1982; East Dene, 1982. Add: 10 Homewright House, Crocker St., Newport, Isle of Wight PO30 5GA, England.

FANE, Bron. *See* FANTHORPE, R. Lionel.

FANE, Julian. British, b. 1927. Novels/Short stories. *Publs:* Morning; Letter; Memoir in the Middle of the Journey; Gabriel Young; Tug-of-War; Hounds of Spring, 1976; Happy Endings, 1979; Revolution Island, 1979; Gentleman's Gentleman, 1981; Memories of My Mother, 1987; Rules of Life, 1987; Cautionary Tales for Women, 1988. Add: Rotten Row House, Lewes, Sussex BN7 1TN, England.

FANNING, Odom. American, b. 1920. Environmental science/Ecology. Ed. and Publr., Fanning Features; Syndicated columnist on consumer affairs, Science Writer and Gen. Reporter, Atlanta Journal, Ga., 1939–49; Public Information Officer, Centers for Disease Control, Atlanta, 1949–53, Georgia Inst. of Technology, Atlanta, 1953–55, and Midwest Research Inst., Kansas City, Mo., 1955–60; involved in public relations and advertising, CBS Labs., Stamford, Conn., 1960–62, and Baird-Atomic Inc., Cambridge, Mass., 1962–65; writer for U.S. Govt. Dept. of Energy, 1965–82; now retired. *Publs:* (ed.) Marine Science Affairs: A Year of Plans and Progress, 1968; Opportunities in Oceanographic Careers, 1969; Opportunities in Environmental Careers, 1971, 1985; (ed.) Environmental Quality: The First Annual Report, 1970; Man and His Environment: Citizen Action, 1975. Add: 9206 Bulls Run Parkway, Bethesda, Md. 20817, U.S.A.

FANTHORPE, R(obert) Lionel. Also writes as Erle Barton; Lee Barton; Thornton Bell; Leo Brett; Bron Fane; Mel Jay; Marston Johns; Victor LaSalle; Robert Lionel; John E. Muller; Phil Nobel; Lionel Robert; Neil Thanet; Trebor Thorpe; Pel Torro; Olaf Trent; and Karl Zeigfried. British, b. 1935. Science fiction. English teacher, Hellesdon High School, Norfolk, since 1972. Worked as a machine operator, farm worker, warehouseman, journalist, salesman, and storekeeper during the 1950's; school teacher in Dereham, 1963–67; Industrial Training Officer, Phoenix Timber Co., Rainham, 1969–72. *Publs:* science-fiction novels—(as Victor LaSalle) Menace from Mercury, 1954; The Waiting World, 1958; Alien from the Stars, 1959; Hyperspace, 1959; Space-Borne, 1959; Fiends, 1959; (as Lionel Roberts) Dawn of the Mutants, 1959; (as Lionel Roberts) Time-Echo, 1959, in U.S. as Robert Lionel, 1964; Doomed World, 1960; Satellite, 1960; Asteroid Man, 1960; Out of the Darkness, 1960; Hand of Doom, 1960; (as Trebor Thorpe) Five Faces of Fear, 1960; (as Trebor Thorpe) Lightning World, 1960; (as Lionel Roberts) Cyclops in the Sky, 1960; (as Lionel Roberts) The In-World, 1960; (as Lionel Roberts) The Face of X, 1960, in U.S. as Robert Lionel, 1965; (as Leo Brett) Exit Humanity, 1960; (as Leo Brett) The Microscopic Ones, 1960; (as Leo Brett) Faceless Planet, 1960; (as Bron Fane) Juggernaut, 1960, in U.S. as Blue Juggernaut, 1965; (as Bron Fane) Last Man on Earth, 1960; (as Pel Torro) Frozen Planet, 1960; (as Pel Torro), World of the Gods, 1960; Flame Mass, 1961; The Golden Chalice, 1961; (as Lionel Roberts) The Last Valkyrie, 1961; (as Lionel Roberts) The Synthetic Ones, 1961; (as Lionel Roberts) Flame Goddess, 1961; (as Leo Brett) March of the Robots, 1961; (as Leo Brett) Wind Force, 1961; (as Leo Brett) Black Infinity, 1961; (as Bron Fane) Rodent Mutation, 1961; (as Pel Torro) The Phantom Ones, 1961; (as John E. Muller) The Ultimate Man, 1961; (as John E. Muller) The Uninvited, 1961; (as John E. Muller) Crimson Planet, 1961, (as Jon E. Muller) The Venus Venture, 1961, in U.S. as Marston Johns, 1965; (as John E. Muller) Forbidden Planet, 1961; Space Fury, 1962; (as Leo Brett) Nightmare, 1962; (as Leo Brett) Face in the Night, 1962; (as Leo Brett) The Immortals, 1962; (as Leo Brett) They Never Came Back, 1962; (as Pel Torrro) Legion of the Lost, 1962; (as John E. Muler) The Return of Zeus, 1962; (as John E. Muller) Perilous Galaxy, 1962; (as John E. Muller) Uranium 235, 1962; (as John E. Muller) The Man Who Conquered Time, 1962; (as John E. Muller) Orbit One, 1962, in U.S. as Mel Jay, 1966; (as John E. Muller) The Eye of Karnak, 1962; (as John E. Muller) Micro Infinity, 1962; (as John E. Muller) Beyond Time, 1962, in U.S. as Marston Johns, 1966; (as John E. Muller) Infinity Machine, 1962; (as John E. Muller) The Day the World Died, 1962; (as John E. Muller) Vengeance of Siva, 1962; (as John E. Muller) The X-Machine, 1962; (as Karl Zeigfried) Walk Through Tomorrow, 1962; (as Karl Zeigfried) Android, 1962; (as Karl Zeigfried) Gods of Darkness, 1962; (as Karl Zeigfried) Atomic Nemesis, 1962; (as Karl Zeigfried) Zero Minus X, 1962; Negative Minus, 1963; (as Leo Brett) The Forbidden, 1963; (as Leo Brett) From Realms Beyond, 1963; (as Leo Brett) The Alien Ones, 1963; (as Leo Brett) Power Sphere, 1963; (as Bron Fane) The Intruders, 1963; (as Bron Fane) Somewhere Out There, 1963; (as Bron Fane) Softly by Moonlight, 1963; (as Pel Torro) The Strange Ones, 1963; (as Pel Torro) Galaxy 666, 1963; (as Pel Torro) Formula 29X, 1963, in U.S. as Beyond the Barrier of Space, 1969; (as Pel Torro) Through the Barrier, 1963; (as Pel Torro) The Timeless Ones, 1963; (as Pel Torro) The Last Astronaut, 1962; (as Pel Torro) The Face of Fear, 1963; (as John E. Muller) Reactor Xk9, 1963; (as John E. Muller) Special Mission, 1963; (as Karl Zeigfried) Escape to Infinity, 1963; (as Karl Zeigfried) Radar Alert, 1963; (as Karl Zeigfried) World of Tomorrow, 1963, in U.S. as World of the Future, 1964; (as Karl Zeigfried) The World That Never Was, 1963; (as Erle Barton) The Planet Seekers, 1964; (as Lee Barton) The Unseen, 1964; (as Thornton Bell) Space Trap, 1964; (as Thornton Bell) Chaos, 1964; (as Neil Thanet) Beyond the Veil, 1964; (as Neil Thanet) The Man Who Came Back, 1964; (as Bron Fane) Unknown Destiny, 1964; (as Bron Fane) Nemesis, 1964; (as Bron Fane) Suspension, 1964; (as Bron Fane) The Macabre Ones!, 1964; (as Pel Torro) The Return, 1964, in U.S. as Exiled in Space, 1968; (as Bron Fane)

Space No Barrier, 1964, in U.S. as Man of Metal, 1970; (as John E. Muller) Dark Continuum, 1964; (as John E. Muller) Mark of the Beast, 1964; (as Karl Zeigfried) Projection Barrier, 1964; (as Karl Zeigfried) No Way Back, 1964; Neuron World, 1965; The Triple World, 1965; The Unconfined, 1965;(as Pel Torro) Force 97X, 1965; (as John E. Muller) The Exorcists, 1965; (as John E. Muller) The Man from Beyond, 1965; (as John E. Muller) Beyond the Void, 1965; (as John E. Muller) Spectre of Darkness, 1965 (as John E. Muller) Out of the Night, 1965; (as Karl Zeigfried) Barrier 346, 1965; The Watching World, 1966; (as Lee Barton) The Shadow Man, 1966; (as Bron Fane) U.F.O. 517, 1966; (as John E. Muller) Phenomena X, 1966; (as John E. Muller) Survival Project, 1966; (as Karl Zeigfried) The Girl from Tomorrow, 1966; (with Patricia Fanthorpe) The Black Lion, 1979; science-fiction short stories—(as Lionel Roberts) The Incredulist, 1954; Resurgam, 1957; Secret of the Snows, 1957; The Flight of the Valkyries, 1958; Watchers of the Forest, 1958; Call of the Werewolf, 1958; The Death Note, 1958; (as Lionel Roberts) Guardians of the Tomb, 1958; (as Trebor Thorpe) The Haunted Pool, 1958; (as Lionel Roberts) The Golden Warrior, 1958; Mermaid Reef, 1959; The Ghost Rider, 1959; (as Leo Brett) The Druid, 1959; (as Leo Brett) The Return, 1959; The Man Who Couldn't Die, 1960; Werewolf at Large, 1960; Whirlwind of Death, 1960; (as Bron Fane) The Crawling Fiend, 1960; (as Trebor Thorpe) Voodoo Hell Drums, 1961; Fingers of Darkness, 1961; Face in the Dark, 1961; Devil from the Depths, 1961; Centurion's Vengeance, 1961; The Grip of Fear, 1961; Chariot of Apollo, 1962; Hell Has Wings, 1962; Graveyard of the Damned, 1962; The Darker Drink, 1962; Curse of the Totem, 1962; (as Leo Brett) The Frozen Tomb, 1962; (as Bron Fane) Storm God's Fury, 1962, Goddess of the Night, 1963; Twilight Ancestor, 1963; Sands of Eternity, 1963; (as Leo Brett) Phantom Crusader, 1963; (as Bron Fane) The Thing from Sheol, 1963; Moon Wolf, 1964; (as Olaf Trent) Roman Twilight, 1964; (as Phil Nobel) The Hand from Gehenna, 1964; Avenging Goddess, 1964; Death Has Two Faces, 1964; The Shrouded Abbott, 1964; Bitter Reflection, 1964; (as Bron Fane) The Walking Shadow, 1964; Call of the Wild, 1965; Vision of the Damned, 1965; The Sealed Sarcophagus, 1965; Stranger in the Shadow, 1966; Curse of the Khan, 1966; other publications, all with P.A. Fanthorpe—Spencer's Metric and Decimal Guide, 1970; Metric Conversion Tables, 1970; Spencer's Office Guide, 1971 Spencer's Metric Decimal Companion, 1971; Decimal Payroll Tables, 1971; The Holy Grail Revealed: The Real Secret of Rennes-le-Chateau, 1982. Add: 48 Fairways, Hellesdon, Norwich NR6 5PN, England.

FANTHORPE, U(rsula) A(skham). British, b. 1929. Poetry. Asst. English Teacher, 1954–62, and Head of English, 1962–70, Cheltenham Ladies Coll.; clerk in various businesses in Bristol, 1972–74; hospital clerk and receptionist, Bristol, 1974–83; Arts Council Creative Writing Fellow, St. Martin's Coll., Lancaster, 1983–85. *Publs:* Side Effects, 1978; Four Dogs, 1980; Standing To, 1982; Voices Off, 1984; Selected Poems, 1986; A Watching Brief, 1987. Add: Culverhay House, Wotton under Edge, Glos., England.

FANTONI, Barry (Ernest). Also writes as Sylvie Krin and E.J. Thribb. British, b. 1940. Mystery/Crime/Suspense, Humor/Satire. Asst. Ed., Private Eye mag., London. Cartoonist, The Times Diary, since 1983. Chmn., Chelsea Arts Club, London, 1978–80. *Publs:* (with Richard Ingrams) Bible for Motorists, 1967; (with Richard Ingrams; as Sylvie Krin) Love in the Saddle, 1974; Private Eye Cartoons, 1975; (with John Wells) Lional (musical), 1977; (as E.J. Thribb) So Farewell Then, and Other Poems, 1977; Mike Dime (crime novel), 1980; (as Sylvie Krin) Born to Be Queen, 1981; (with G. Melly) The Media Mob, 1981; Stickman (crime novel), 1982; (ed.) Colemanballs, 3 vols., 1982–86; The Times Cartoons, 1984; Chinese Horoscopes, 1985, 1986, 1987; Barry Fantoni Cartoons, 1987; The Royal Chinese Horoscopes, 1988; Colemanballs 4, 1988; (as Sylvie Krin) Heir of Sorrows, 1988. Add: 3 Franconia Rd., London SW4 6NB, England.

FARAH, Nuruddin. Somalian, b. 1945. Novels. Clerk-typist, Ministry of Education, 1964–65, and secondary sch. teacher, 1969–71, both Mogadiscio, Somalia; Lectr. in Comparative Literature, Afgoi Coll. of Education, 1971–74; thereafter, Assoc. Prof., Univ. of Ibadan, Jos, Nigeria. *Publs:* From a Crooked Rib, 1970; A Naked Needle, 1976; Sweet and Sour Milk, 1979; Sardines, 1981; Close Sesame, 1983; Maps, 1986. Add: Pantheon Bks., Random House, Inc., 201 E. 50th St., New York, N.Y. 10022, U.S.A.

FARELY, Alison. *See* **POLAND,** Dorothy.

FARICY, Robert L. American, b. 1926. Theology/Religion. Prof.,

Gregorian Univ., since 1971. *Publs:* Teilhard de Chardin's Theology of the Christian in the World, 1967; Building God's World, 1976; Spirituality for Religious Life, 1976; Praying, 1979; Praying for Inner Healing, 1979; (with M. Flick and G. O'Collins) The Cross Today, 1978; All Things in Christ: The Spirituality of Teilhard de Chardin, 1981; Christian Faith in My Everyday Life, 1981; The End of the Religious Life, 1983; Wind and Sea Obey Him, 1983; Seeking Jesus in Contemplation and Discernment, 1983; (with L. Rooney) Mary, Queen of Peace: Is Our Lady Appearing at Medjugorje?, 1984; (with L. Rooney) Medjugorje Unfolds, 1985, in U.S. as Medjugorje Up Close, 1986; (with S. Blackborow) The Healing of the Religious Life, 1985; (with L. Rooney) The Contemplative Way of Prayer, in U.K. as Personal Prayer, 1986; (with R. Wicks) Contemplating Jesus, 1986; (with L. Rooney) Medjugorje Journal, 1988; The Lord's Dealing: The Primacy of the Feminine in Christian Spirituality, 1988; (with L. Rooney) Lord Jesus, Teach Me to Pray, 1989; (with L. Rooney) Medjugorje Retreat, 1989; A Spring of Love, 1989. Add: Gregorian Univ., Piazza della Pilotta 4, 00187 Rome, Italy.

ARIDI, Shah Nasir(uddin Mohammad). Indian, b. 1929. Economics, History, Language/Linguistics. Lectr., Shuaib Mohammadia Coll., Agra, since 1950. *Publs:* Spotlight on Forms of English Prose, 1954; Popular Set of General English, 4 parts, 1954; Economic Welfare of Indian Moslems, 1965; Hindu History of Urdu Literature, 1965; College Translation and Composition; Islam and Non-Moslem Intellectuals, 1972; From Bahadur Shah to Lal Bahadur. Add: Dept. of Economics, Shuaib Mohammadia Coll., Agra (U.P.), India.

FARISH, Donald J(ames). Canadian, b. 1942. Biology. Prof. of Biology and Dean of the Sch. of Natural Sciences, Sonoma State Univ., since 1983. Instr. to Assoc. Prof., Div. of Biological Sciences, Univ. of Missouri, Columbia, 1968–79; Assoc. Dean of Coll. of Arts and Sciences, Univ. of Rhode Island, Kingston, 1979–83. *Publs:* Biology: The Human Perspective, 1978; Introduction to Biology: A Human Perspective, 1984. Add: School of Natural Sciences, Sonoma State Univ., Rohnert Park, Calif. 94928, U.S.A.

FARLEY, Carol. American, b. 1936. Children's fiction. *Publs:* Mystery of the Fog Man, 1966; Mystery in the Ravine, 1967; Sergeant Finney's Family, 1969; The Bunch on McKellahan Street, 1971; The Most Important Thing in the World, 1974; The Garden Is Doing Fine, 1975; Loosen Your Ears, 1977; Settle Your Fidgets, 1977; Ms. Isabelle Cornell, Herself, 1980; Twilight Waves, 1981; Mystery of the Fiery Message, 1983; Korea: A Land Divided, 1983; Mystery of the Melted Diamonds, 1985; The Case of the Vanishing Villain, 1986; The Case of the Lost Lookalike, 1987. Add: c/o Avon Books, 105 Madison Ave., New York, N.Y. 10016, U.S.A.

FARLEY, Walter (Lorimer). American, b. 1920. Children's fiction, Animals/pets. Served in the Fourth Armoured Div., and as staff member of Yank mag., U.S. Army, 1942–46. *Publs:* The Black Stallion series, from 1941; Larry and the Undersea Raider, 1942; Son of the Black Stallion, 1947; The Island Stallion, 1948; The Black Stallion and Satan, 1949; The Blood Bay Colt, 1950; The Island Stallion's Fury, 1951; The Black Stallion's Filly, 1952; The Black Stallion Revolts, 1953; The Black Stallion's Sulky Colt, 1954; The Black Stallion's Courage, 1955; The Island Stallion Races, 1955; The Black Stallion Challenged, 1956; The Black Stallion Mystery, 1957; The Horse-Tamer, 1958; The Black Stallion and Flame, 1960; Little Black, A Pony, 1961; Man o'War, 1962; Little Black Goes to the Circus, 1963; The Horse That Swam Away, 1965; The Great Dane, Thor, 1966; The Little Black Pony Races, 1968; The Black Stallion's Ghost, 1969; The Black Stallion and the Stranger, in U.S. as The Black Stallion and the Stranger Girl, 1971; How to Stay Out of Trouble with Your Horse, 1980; The Black Stallion Picture Book, 1980; The Black Stallion Returns: Movie Storybooks, 1982; The Black Stallion Legend, 1983; The Black Stallion: Comic Book Album, 1983; The Black Stallion Returns: A Comic Book Album, 1984; The Black Stallion: Beginning Reader Book, 1986. Add: c/o Random House Inc., 201 E. 50th St., New York, N.Y. 10022, U.S.A.

FARMER, Bertram Hughes. British, b. 1916. Geography. Fellow, St. John's Coll., Cambridge, since 1948 (Tutor, 1958–61; President, 1967–71). Ed., Geographical Journal, since 1980. Lectr. in Geography, Univ. Coll., Swansea, 1946–48; Univ. Demonstrator in Geography, 1948–52, Lectr., 1952–67, Reader, 1967–83, and Dir of the Centre of South Asian Studies, 1964–83, Cambridge Univ. Member, Ceylon Land Commn., 1955–58; Chmn., Gal Oya Project Evaluation Cttee., Ceylon, 1968–69; Ed., 1961–66, Vice-Pres., 1970–71, and Pres., 1972, Inst. of British Geographers. *Publs:* Pioneer Peasant Colonization in Ceylon, 1957; Ceylon: A Divided Nation, 1963; Agricultural Colonization in India since Independence, 1974; (ed.) Green Revolution? Technology and Change in Rice-growing Areas of Tamil Nadu and Sri Lanka, 1977; An Introduction to South Asia, 1983. Add: St. John's Coll., Cambridge CB2 1TP, England.

FARMER, Penelope. British, b. 1939. Novels/Short stories, Children's fiction. Teacher, London, 1961–63. *Publs:* for children—The China People, 1960; The Summer Birds, 1962; The Magic Stone, 1964; Saturday Shillings, 1965; The Seagull, 1965; Emma in Winter, 1966; Charlotte Sometimes, 1969; The Dragonfly Summer, 1971; Daedalus and Icarus, 1971; Serpent's Teeth: The Story of Cadmus, 1971; A Castle of Bone, 1972; William and Mary, 1974; Heracles, 1974; August the Fourth, 1974; Year King, 1977; The Coal Train, 1977; (ed.) Beginnings: Creation Myths of the World, 1978; The Runaway Train, 1980; adult novels—Standing in the Shadow, 1984; Eve: Her Story, 1985; Away from Home, 1987; Glasshouses, 1988. Add: 39 Mount Ararat Rd., Richmond, Surrey, England.

FARMER, Philip José. Also writes as Kilgore Trout. American, b. 1918. Novels/Short stories, Science fiction/Fantasy, Autobiography/Memoirs/Personal. Freelance writer since 1969. Electro-mechanical technical writer for defense-space industry: Gen. Electric Co., Syracuse, N.Y., 1956–58; Motorola, Scottsdale, Ariz., 1959–62; Bendix, Ann Arbor, Mich., 1962; Motorola, Phoenix, Ariz., 1962–65; and McDonnell-Douglas, Santa Monica, Calif., 1965–69. *Publs:* The Green Odyssey, 1957; Flesh, 1960; A Woman a Day, 1960, as The Day of Timestop, 1968, in U.K. as Timestop!, 1974; Strange Relations (short stories), 1960; The Lovers, 1961; Cache from Outer Space, 1962; The Alley God (short stories), 1960; The Celestial Blueprint and Other Stories, 1962; Fire and the Night (novel), 1962; Inside Outside, 1964; Tongues of the Moon, 1964; Dare, 1965; The Maker of Universes, 1962, 1980; The Gate of Time, 1966, as Two Hawks from Earth, 1979; The Gates of Creation, 1966; Night of Light, 1966; The Image of the Beast, 1968; A Private Cosmos, 1968; Blown, 1968; A Feast Unknown, 1969; Behind the Walls of Terra, 1970; Lord Tyger, 1970; Lord of the Trees, the Mad Goblin, 1970; The Stone God Awakens, 1970; Love Song (novel), 1970; Down in the Black Gang, and Others (short stories), 1971; To Your Scattered Bodies Go, 1971; The Fabulous Riverboat, 1971; The Wind Whales of Ishmael, 1971; Tarzan Alive: A Definitive Biography of Lord Greystoke, 1972; Time's Last Gift, 1972; The Other Log of Phineas Fogg, 1973; Traitor to the Living, 1973; Doc Savage: His Apocalyptic Life, 1973; The Book of Philip José Farmer (short stories), 1973; The Adventure of the Peerless Peer by John H. Watson, M.D., 1974; Hadon of Ancient Opar, 1974; (as Kilgore Trout) Venus on the Half-Shell, 1974; (ed.) Mother Was a Lovely Beast, 1974; Flight to Opar, 1976; The Dark Design, 1977; The Lavalite World, 1977; Dark Is the Sun, 1979; Jesus on Mars, 1979; The Magic Labyrinth, 1979; Riverworld and Other Stories, 1979; Riverworld War (short stories), 1980; A Barnstormer in Oz, 1982; Greatheart Silver, 1982; Stations of the Nightmare, 1982; The Purple Book, 1982; Father to the Stars, 1982; The Unreasoning Mask, 1983; River of Eternity, 1983; Gods of Riverworld, 1983; Dayworld, 1983; Fantastic Voyage II, 1985; Two Hawks from Earth, 1985; Traitor to the Living, 1985; Dayworld Rebel, 1987. Add: c/o Berkley Publishing Group, 200 Madison Ave., New York, N.Y. 10010, U.S.A.

FARMER, William R(euben). American, b. 1921. Theology/Religion. Prof. of New Testament, Southern Methodist Univ., Dallas, Tex., since 1964 (Assoc. Prof., 1959–64). Chmn., Gospels Research Group, and Resident Fellow, Center for the Study of Religion in the Greco-Roman World, since 1984. Pastor, Methodist Church, Coatesville, Ind., 1952–55; Visiting Instr. in Theology, De Pauw Univ., Greencastle, Ind., 1952–55; Visiting Instr. in Theology, Drew Univ., Madison, N.J., 1955–59. Co-Chmn., Intnl. Inst. for the Renewal of Gospel Studies, 1980–87. *Publs:* Maccabees, Zealots, and Josephus: An Inquiry into Jewish Nationalism in the Greco-Roman Period, 1956; The Synoptic Problem: A Critical Analysis, 1964; (ed. with C.F.D. Moule and R.R. Niebuhr, and contrib.) Christian History and Interpretation: Studies Presented to John Knox, 1967; (ed.) Synopticon: The Verbal Agreement Between the Greek Texts of Matthew, Mark and Luke Contextually Exhibited, 1969; (ed.) The Great Roman-Jewish War: A.D. 66-70, by Flavius Josephus, 1970; The Last Twelve Verses of Mark, 1974; Jesus and the Gospel: Tradition, Scripture, and the Canon, 1982; (ed. and contrib.) New Synoptic Studies: The Cambridge Gospel Conference and Beyond, 1983; (with Denis Farkasfalvy) The Formation of the New Testament Canon: An Ecumenical Approach, 1983; (ed. with F. Neirynck and M.E. Boismard) Papers from the Jerusalem Bible Conference, 1987; (ed.) Mark as Composer, by D.B. Peabody, 1987; The Two Gospel Hypothesis, 1988. Add: 4103 Emerson, Dallas, Tex. 75205, U.S.A.

FARMILOE, Dorothy. Canadian, b. 1920. Poetry, Writing/Journalism.

Teacher, St. Clair Coll., Windsor, Ont., 1969–78. *Publs:* The Lost Island, 1966; (co-author) 21 x 3, 1967; Poems for Apartment Dwellers, 1970; (ed.) Contraverse, 1971; Winter Orange Mood, 1972; Blue Is the Colour of Death, 1973; And Some in Fire, 1974; Creative Communication, 1974; Elk Lake Diary Poems, 1976; Adrenalin of Weather, 1978; How to Write a Better Anything, 1979; Words for My Weeping Daughter, 1980; Communication for Business Students, 1981; Elk Lake Lore and Legend, 1984; Isabella Valancy Crawford: The Life and the Legends, 1984; Dragons and Dinosaurs and Other Poems, 1988. Add: P.O. Box 94, Elk Lake, Ont. P0J 1G0, Canada.

FARNDALE, James. *See* **FARNDALE,** W.A.J.

FARNDALE, W(illiam) A(rthur) J(ames). Also writes as James Farndale. British, b. 1916. Law, Medicine/Health. Part-time Lectr., London Sch. of Insurance and Arbitration, Polytechnic of Central London, and Bromley and Croydon Colleges, since 1983. Chmn., Ravenwood Publs., Ravenswood Circle, and Ravenswood Charitable Trust, since 1971; Principal Lectr. in Health Service Admin. and Law, Polytechnic of the South Bank, London, 1962–81. Deputy House Gov. and Secty., Bd. of Govs., Bethlem Royal Hosp. and Maudsley Hosp., London, 1948–60. *Publs:* Day Hospital Movement in Great Britain, 1961; (co-ed.) Trends in the Mental Health Services, 1962; (ed.) Trends in the National Health Service, 1963; (co-ed.) Trends in the Services for Youth, 1966; (co-ed.) New Aspects of the Mental Health Services, 1967; Series on Hospital Laundry Services, 1967–71; Medical Negligence, 1969; Law on Human Transplants, 1970; Law on Redundancy Payments, 1971; Health Services Travelogue, 1972; (co-ed.) International Medical Care, 1972; French Hospitals, 1975; Law on Accidents to Health Service Staff and Volunteers, 1977; Law on Hospital Consent Forms, 1978; Aspects of Health Service Law, 1981; West German Hospitals and European Medical Care Services, 1983; Appreciation of the Personal Insurance Arbitration Service, 1986. Add: 58 Ravenswood Ave., West Wickham, Kent BR4 0PW, England.

FARNES, Eleanor. Historical/Romance/Gothic. *Publs:* Merry Goes the Time, 1935; Tangled Harmonies, 1936; Three Happy Pilgrims, 1937; Romantic Melody, 1938; Hesitation Waltz, 1939; The Crystal Spring, 1940; Walk the Mountain Tops, 1940; Bloom on the Gorse, 1941; Reckless Adventure, 1942; Fruits of the Year, 1942; The Doctor's Wife, 1943; Summer Motley, 1943; Brief Excursion, 1944; The Quiet Valley, 1944; Stormcloud and Sunrise, 1945; Journey for Two Travellers, 1946; Mistress of the House, 1946; The Deep, Wide River, 1947; The Opening Flower, 1948; The Wayward Stream, 1949; The Faithless Friend, 1949; Captive Daughter, 1950; The Dream and the Dancer, 1951; The Golden Peaks, 1951; The House by the Lake, 1952; Magic Symphony, 1952; The Wings of Memory, 1953; The Young Intruder, 1953; A Home for Jocely, 1953; Song of Summer, 1954, in Can. as Doctor's Orders, 1963; Sister of the Housemaster, 1954; The Fortunes of Springfield, 1955; The Mist of Morning, 1955; Secret Heiress, 1956; The Constant Heart, 1956; A Season of Enchantment, 1956; The Way Through the Forest, 1957; The Persistent Lover, 1957; The Blessing in Disguise, 1958; The Happy Enterprise, 1958; The Flight of the Swan, 1959; A Stronger Spell, 1959; The Painted Ceiling, 1960; The Red Cliffs, 1961; Lovers' Meeting, 1962; A Change of Heart (in Can. as Doctor Max), 1963; The Tangled Web, 1963; The Daring Deception, 1965; The Pursuit and the Capture, 1966; Loving and Giving, 1968; The Rose and the Thorn, 1968; Rubies for My Love, 1969; The Doctor's Circle, 1970; The Enchanted Island, 1970; A Castle in Spain, 1971; Serpent in Eden, 1971; The Valley of the Eagles, 1972; The Shadow of Suspicion, 1972; The Splendid Legacy, 1973; The Runaway Visitors, 1973; Homeward Bound, 1975; This Golden Estate, 1975; The Amaranth Flower, 1979. Add: c/o Mills and Boon Ltd., 15-16 Brooks Mews, London W1A 1DR, England.

FARR, Alfred Derek. British, b. 1930. Medicine/Health, Theology/Religion, Transportation. Sr. Chief Scientific Officer, North East Scotland Blood Transfusion Service, Aberdeen, since 1961. Formerly, Lectr. in Blood Transfusion Techniques, Robert Gordon's Inst. of Technology, and Aberdeen Technical Coll. Ed., Medical Laboratory Sciences. *Publs:* Laboratory Handbook of Blood Transfusion Techniques, 1961; Synopsis of Blood Group Theory and Serological Techniques, 1963; The Royal Deeside Line, 1968; Campbeltown and Machrihanish Light Railway, 1969; Stories of Royal Deeside's Railway, 1971; God, Blood and Society, 1972; Let Not the Deep, 1973; (ed.) Founders of Medical Laboratory Science, 1978; "Learn That You May Improve": The History of the Institute of Medical Laboratory Sciences, 1982; (ed.) Quality Assurance and Control in Clinical Laboratories, 1984; Science Writing for Beginners, 1985; (ed.) Quality Control and Assurance in Clinical Laboratories: Three Years On, 1988; Dictionary of Medical Laboratory

Sciences, 1988. Add: Tullochvenus House, Lumphanan, Aberdeenshire, Scotland.

FARR, Diana. *See* **PULLEIN-THOMPSON,** Diana.

FARRAN, Roy Alexander. Canadian, b. 1921. Novels/Short stories, Military/Defence. Chmn., Alberta Racing Commn. since 1979; Columnist, Edmonton Journal and Calgary Herald. Minister of Telephones and Utilities, Govt. of Alberta, 1973–75; Solicitor-Gen., Govt. of Alberta, 1975–79. *Publs:* History of the Calgary Highlanders; Jungle Chase, 1951; Winged Dagger, 1954; The Day After Tomorrow, 1956; The Search, 1958; Operation Tombola, 1960; Never Had a Chance, 1968. Add: P.O. Box 9, Site 7, R.R. 8, Calgary, Alta T2H 0G3, Canada.

FARRAR, Ronald T(ruman). American, b. 1935. Communications Media, Biography. Reynolds-Faunt Prof. of Journalism, Univ. of South Carolina, Columbia since 1986. Asst. Prof. then Assoc. Prof., Indiana Univ., Bloomington, 1964–70; Prof. and Chmn., Dept. of Journalism, Southern Methodist Univ., Dallas, Tex., 1970–73; Prof. and Dir., Sch. of Journalism, Univ. of Kentucky, 1977–86. *Publs:* Reluctant Servant: The Story of Charles G. Ross, 1968; (co-author) Mass Media and the National Experience, 1971; College 101, 1984; Mass Communication: An Introduction to the Field, 1988. Add: 105 Holly Ridge Lane, W., Columbia, S.C. 29169, U.S.A.

FARRELL, Ben. *See* **CEBULASH,** Mel.

FARRELL, David. *See* **SMITH,** Frederick E.,

FARREN, Mick. British, b. 1943. Novels/Short stories, Science fiction/Fantasy, Cultural/Ethnic topics. Short order cook, London Zoo, 1965; painter, 1965–67; Lead Singer, Deviants rock band, 1967–73; Consulting Ed., New Musical Express, London, 1975–77. *Publs:* (with Edward Barker) Watch Out Kids (non-fiction), 1972; The Texts of Festival, 1973; The Tale of Willy's Rats (novel), 1975; (ed.) Get on Down, 1976; The Quest of the DNA Cowboys, 1976; The Synaptic Manhunt, 1976; The Neutral Atrocity, 1977; (ed. with Pearce Marchbank) Elvis in His Own Words, 1977, in U.S. as Elvis Presley, 1978; The Feelies, 1978; (with George Snow) Rock 'n' Roll Circus (non-fiction), 1978; The Song of Phaid the Gambler, 1981; (with Roy Carr) Elvis Presley: The Complete Illustrated Record, 1982; Protectorate, 1984; The Black Jacket Goes On Forever (non-fiction), 1985; Citizen Phaid, 1987; (with Dirk Vellenga) Elvis and the Colonel, 1988; The Armageddon Crazy, 1989; The Last Stand of the DNA Cowboys, 1989. Add: c/o Abner Stein, 10 Roland Gardens, London SW7 3PH, England.

FARRIMOND, John. British, b. 1913. Novels/Short stories. *Publs:* Dust in My Throat, 1963; The Hollow Shell, 1964; Kill Me a Priest, 1965; Pick and Run, 1966; No Friday in the Week, 1967; Dust Is Forever, 1969; The Unending Track, 1970; The Hills of Heaven, 1978; The Weathermakers, 1980. Add: 102 Algernon St., Hindley, nr. Wigan, Lancs., England.

FARRINGTON, Ian S(tewart). British, b. 1947. Agriculture, Archaeology/Antiquities. Lectr., St. David's University Coll., Univ. of Wales, Lampeter, since 1974. Research Fellow, Centre for Latin American Studies, Univ. of Liverpool. *Publs:* (with W.M. Bray and E.H. Swanson) The New World, 1975; (ed.) Prehistoric Intensive Agriculture in the Tropics, 1985. Add: Dept. of Geography, St. David's University Coll., Univ. of Wales, Lampeter, Dyfed, Wales.

FARROW, James S. *See* **TUBB,** E.C.

FARSON, Daniel (Negley). British, b. 1927. Novels/Short stories, Children's non-fiction, Biography, Autobiography. Parliamentary and Lobby Correspondent for Central Press, 1945–46; Feature Writer, Stars and Stripes, Germany, 1947; started Panorama mag., Cambridge Univ., 1949–51; Photographer, Picture Post; Freelance journalist; TV interviewer with such series as Farson's Guide to the British, Farson in Australia, Time Gentlemen Please, etc., 1956–64; TV Critic, The Mail on Sunday, London, 1983–84; Columnist, Sunday Today, 1986–87. *Publs:* Jack the Ripper, 1972; Marie Lloyd and Music Hall, 1972; (ed.) Wanderlust, by Negley Farson, 1972; Out of Step (autobiography), 1974; The Man Who Wrote Dracula (biography), 1975; Vampires, Zombies, and Monster Men, 1976; The Dan Farson Black and White Picture Show, 1976; In Praise of Dogs (anthology), 1976; A Window on the Sea, 1977; Horror, 1977; Ghosts, 1978; The Clifton House Mystery, 1978; (as Matilda Excellent) The Dog Who Knew Too Much (satire), 1979; Curse (novel), 1980; Transplant (novel), 1981; Henry (biography of Henry Williamson), 1982;

Monsters, 1984; A Traveller in Turkey, 1985; Swansdowne (fiction), 1985; Soho in the Fifties, 1987; The Collins Guide to Turkey, 1988; Sacred Monsters, 1988. Add: Appledore, N. Devon, England.

FAST, Howard. Also writes as E.V. Cunningham and Walter Erickson. American, b. 1914. Novels/Short stories, Mystery/Crime/Suspense, Science fiction/Fantasy, Plays/Screenplays, History. Member, Fellowship for Reconciliation. Film writer, Universal, Paramount, Pennybaker, and for Alfred Hitchcock, 1958–67; Founder, World Peace Movement, and member, World Peace Council, 1950–55. *Publs:* Two Valleys, 1933; Strange Yesterday, 1934; Place in the City, 1937; Conceived in Liberty: A Novel of Valley Forge, 1939; The Last Frontier, 1941; The Romance of a People, 1941; Lord Baden-Powell of the Boy Scouts, 1941; Haym Solomon, Son of Liberty, 1941; (with B. Fast) The Picture-Book History of the Jews, 1942; Goethals and the Panama Canal, 1942; The Unvanquished, 1942; The Tall Hunter, 1942; Citizen Tom Paine, 1943; Freedom Road, 1944; The Incredible Tito, 1945; Patrick Henry and the Frigate's Keel and Other Stories of a Young Nation, 1945; The American: A Middle Western Legend, 1946; (with W. Gropper) Never to Forget: The Story of the Warsaw Ghetto, 1946; (ed.) The Selected Works of Tom Paine, 1946; The Children, 1947; Clarkton, 1947; (ed.) Best Stories of Theodore Dreiser, 1947; My Glorious Brothers, 1948; Tito and His People, 1948; Departures and Other Stories, 1949; The Proud and the Free, 1950; The Hammer (play), 1950; Literature and Reality, 1950; Spartacus, 1951, screenplay with Dalton Trumbo, 1960; Thirty Pieces of Silver (play), 1951; Peekskill, U.S.A.: A Personal Experience, 1951; (as Walter Erickson) Fallen Angel, 1952; The Passion of Sacco and Vanzetti: A New England Legend, 1953; Silas Timberman, 1954; The Last Supper and Other Stories, 1955; The Story of Lola Gregg, 1956; George Washington and the Water Witch (play), 1956; The Naked God: The Writer and the Communist Party, 1957; Moses, Prince of Egypt, 1958; The Winston Affair, 1959; The Golden River, 1960; (as E.V. Cunningham) Sylvia, 1960; The Howard Fast Reader, 1960; April Morning, 1961; The Edge of Tomorrow, 1961; Power, 1962; (as E.V. Cunningham) Phyllis, 1962; The Crossing (play), 1962; (as E.V. Cunningham) Alice, 1963; Agrippa's Daughter, 1964; (as E.V. Cunningham) Shirley: An Entertainment, 1964; (as E.V. Cunningham) Lydia: An Entertainment, 1964; The Hill (screenplay), 1964; (as E.V. Cunningham) Penelope: An Entertainment, 1965; Torquemada, 1966; (as E.V. Cunningham) Helen, 1966; (as E.V. Cunningham) Margie, 1966; The Hunter and the Trap, 1967; (as E.V. Cunningham) Sally, 1967; (as E.V. Cunningham) Samantha, 1967; (as E.V. Cunningham) Cynthia, 1968; The Jews: Story of a People, 1969; (as E.V. Cunningham) The Assassin Who Gave Up His Gun, 1969; The General Zapped an Angel, 1970; The Crossing, 1971; The Hessian (screenplay), 1971, novel, 1972; A Touch of Infinity: Thirteen New Stories of Fantasy and Science Fiction, 1973; (as E.V. Cunningham) Millie, 1973; Time and the Riddle: Thirty-Two Zen Stories, 1975; The Immigrants (novel), 1978; The Second Generation (novel), 1978; (as E.V. Cunningham) The Case of the Poisoned Eclairs, 1979; The Establishment (novel), 1979; (as E.V. Cunningham) The Case of the Three Penny Orange, 1979; (as E.V. Cunningham) The Case of the Russian Diplomat, 1980; (as E.V. Cunningham) The Case of the Sliding Pool. 1981; The Legacy (novel), 1981; Max (novel), 1982; (as E.V. Cunningham) The Case of the Kidnapped Angel, 1982; (as E.V. Cunningham) The Case of the Murdered MacKenzie, 1984; The Outsider (novel), 1984; The Immigrant's Daughter (novel), 1985; (as E.V. Cunningham) The Wabash Factor, 1986; The Dinner Party, 1987. Add: c/o Sterling Lord Agency, 1 Madison Ave., 22nd Fl., New York, N.Y. 10010, U.S.A.

FAST, Jonathan (David). American, b. 1948. Novels, Science fiction, Screenplays. Independent composer and writer. *Publs:* The Secrets of Synchronicity, 1977; Mortal Gods, 1978; The Inner Circle, 1979; The Beast, 1980; The Golden Fire: A Novel of Ancient India, 1986; The Jade Stalk: A Novel of Tang China, 1988. Add: Sterling Lord Agency, 1 Madison Ave., 22nd Fl., New York, N.Y. 10010, U.S.A.

FATCHEN, Max. Australian, b. 1920. Children's fiction, Poetry. Journalist, Adelaide News and Sunday Mail, Adelaide, 1946–55; Literary Ed., The Advertiser, Adelaide, 1971–81. *Publs:* Driver and Trains (verse), 1963; Keepers and Lighthouses (verse), 1963; The Plumber (verse), 1963; The Electrician (verse), 1963; The Transport Driver (verse), 1965; The Carpenter (verse), 1965; Peculia Australia: Verses, 1965; The River Kings (fiction), 1966; Just Fancy, Mr. Fatchen! A Collection of Verse, Prose and Fate's Cruel Blows, 1967; Conquest of the River (fiction), 1970; The Spirit Wind (fiction), 1973; Chase Through the Night (fiction), 1977; The Time Wave (fiction), 1979; Songs for My Dog and Other People (nonsense verse), 1980; Closer to the Stars (fiction), 1981; Wry Rhymes for Troublesome Times (verse), 1983; Forever Fatchen, 1983; A Paddock of Poems, 1987; Had Yer Jabs (short stories), 1987; A Pocketful of Rhymes,

1989. Add: 15 Jane St., Smithfield, S.A. 5114, Australia.

FATIO, Louise. American, b. 1904. Children's fiction. *Publs:* The Christmas Forest, 1950; Anna the Horse, 1951; The Happy Lion series, 8 vols., 1954–71; A Doll for Marie, 1957; Red Bantam, 1963; Hector Penguin, 1973; Hector and Christina, 1976; The Happy Lioness, 1980. Add: P.O. Box 116, Gladstone, N.J. 07934, U.S.A.

FATOUROS, Arghyrios A. Greek, b. 1932. International relations/Current affairs, Law. Prof. of Intnl. Economic Law and European Organizations, Aristotelian Univ. of Thessaloniki, since 1980; Permanent Representative of Greece to the OECD, since 1982. Lectr., 1960–62, and Asst. Prof. of Law, 1962–63, Univ. of Western Ontario, London; Asst. Prof., 1964–68, and Prof. of Law, 1968–80, Indiana Univ., Bloomington. *Publs:* Government Guarantees to Foreign Investors, 1962; (with R.N. Kelson) Canada's Overseas Aid, 1964; Diethnes Dikaio Anaptyxeos (International Law of Development), 1977; (co-author) Dimosioo Diethnes Dikaio (Public International Law), vol. I, 1973; (with P.N. Stangos) Diethnes Oikonomiko Dikaio (International Economic Law), vol. I, 1984, vol. II, 1985. Add: Faculty of Law and Economics, Aristotelian univ. of Thessaloniki, Thessaloniki, Greece.

FAULK, Odie B. American, b. 1933. History, Translations. Prof. of History, Northeastern State Univ., Tahlequah, Okla. since 1979. Instr., Texas A & M Univ., College Station, 1962–63; Research Historian, Arizona Historical Soc., 1963–67; Head of Dept., Arizona Western Coll., Yuma, 1967–68; Prof., and Head, Dept. of History, Oklahoma State Univ., Stillwater, 1968–78. Dir., Memphis State Univ. Press, 1978–79. *Publs:* Tom Green: A Fightin' Texan, 1963; The Last Years of Spanish Texas 1778-1921, 1964; (co-author) Government by the People (rev. ed.); A Successful Failure, 1965; Texas After Spindletop, 1965; Lancers for the King: A Study of the Frontier Military System of Northern New Spain, 1965; Too Far North—Too Far South: The Controversial Boundary Survey and the Gadsden Purchase, 1967; (trans. and ed.) The Constitution of Occidente: The First Constitution of Arizona, Sonora, and Sinaloa 1825-1831, 1967; Land of Many Frontiers: A History of the American Southwest, 1968; The Geronimo Campaign, 1969; Derby's Report on the Opening of the Colorado 1850-51, 1969; Arizona: A Short History, 1970, 1977; The Leather Jacket Soldier: Spanish Military Equipment and Institutions of the Late 18th Century; North America Divided: The Mexican War 1846-1848; Tombstone: Myth and Reality; The Mexican War: Changing Interpretations; This Beats Working for a Living; Destiny Road: The Gila Trail and the Opening of the Southwest; Crimson Desert: Indian Wars of the American Southwest; Never at a Loss for an Opinion; (co-author) A Short History of the American West, 1974; (co-author) The Australian Alternative, 1975; The Camel Corps: An Army Experiment, 1976; (co-author) Home of the Brave: A Patriot's Guide to American History, 1976; The Modoc People, 1976; (co-author) Miracle of the Wilderness: The Continuing American Revolution, 1977; Dodge City: The Most Western Town of All, 1977; (co-author) The McMan: The Lives of Robert M. McFarlin and James A. Chapman, 1977; (with J.A. Carroll) A Home of the Brave, 1977; (co-author) The Life a Successful Bank, 1978; (ed.) Early Military Forts and Ports in Oklahoma, 1978; (co-author) The Gentleman: The Life of Joseph A. LaFortune, 1979; (ed.) One Man in His Time: The Autobiography of Jack T. Conn, 1979; A Man of Vision: The Life and Career of O.W. Coburn, 1980; The Making of a Merchant: R.A. Young and T.G. and Y. Stores, 1980; A Specialist in Everything: The Life of Fred S. Watson, M.D., 1981; A Full-Service Banker: The Life of Louis W. Duncan, 1981; (co-author) Coletta: A Sister of Mercy, 1981; Dear Everybody: The Life of Henry B. Bass, 1982; Muskogee: City and County, 1983; Jennys to Jets: The Life of Clarence E. Page, 1983; (co-author) Fort Smith: An Illustrated History, 1983; (co-author) Tahlequah, NSU, and the Cherokees, 1984; (co-author) The Cherokees: An Illustrated History, 1984; Oklahoma: Land of the Fair God, 1986. Add: Dept. of History, Northeastern State Univ., Tahlequah, Okla. 74464, U.S.A.

FAULKNER, Charles Herman. American, b. 1937. Anthropology/Ethnology, Archaeology/Antiquities. Prof. of Anthropology, Univ. of Tennessee, Knoxville, since 1976 (Asst. Prof., 1964–70; Assoc. Prof., 1971–76). Instr. of Sociology and Anthropology, St. Lawrence Univ., Canton, N.Y., 1963–64. *Publs:* An Archaeological Survey of Marshall County, Indiana, 1961; (with J.B. Graham) Excavations, in the Nickajack Reservoir, 1965; The Old Stone Fort: Exploring an Archaeological Mystery, 1968; The Late Prehistoric Occupation of Northwestern Indiana, 1972; (with C.R. McCollough) Excavations of the Higgs and Doughty Sites: I-75 Salvage Archaeology, 1973; Introductory Report of the Normandy Reservoir Salvage Project, 1972, 3rd to 6th reports, 1976–78; (with Carol K. Buckles) Glimpses of Southern Appalachian Folk Culture:

Papers in Memory of Norbert F. Riedl, 1978; (with Gerald W. Kline and Gary D. Crites) The McFarland Project: Early Middle Woodland Settlement and Subsistence in the Upper Duck River Valley in Tennnessee, 1982 (ed.) The Prehistoric Native American Art of Mud Glyph Cave, 1986. Add: Dept. of Anthropology, Univ. of Tennessee, Knoxville, Tenn. 37916, U.S.A.

FAULKNOR, (Chauncey) Cliff(ord Vernon). Canadian, b. 1913. Children's fiction, Country life/Rural societies. Member, Alberta Land Compensation Bd., since 1978. Assoc. Ed., Country Guide mag., Winnipeg, Man., 1954–75. *Publs:* The White Calf, 1965; The White Peril, 1966; The Romance of Beef, 1966; The In-Betweener, 1976; The Smoke Horse, 1968; West to Cattle Country, 1975; Pen and Plow, 1976; Turn Him Loose, 1977; Alberta Hereford Heritage, 1981; Johnny Eagleclaw, 1982. Add: 2919-14th Ave. N.W., Calgary, T2N 1N3, Canada.

FAUST, Irvin. American, b. 1924. Novels/Short stories. Dir., Guidance and Counseling, Garden City High Sch., N.Y., since 1960. Guidance Counselor, Lynbrook High Sch., N.Y. 1956–60. *Publs:* Roar Lion Roar, 1965; The Steagle, 1966; The File on Stanley Patton Buchta, 1970; Willy Remembers, 1971; Foreign Devils, 1973; A Star in the Family, 1975; Newsreel, 1980; The Year of the Hot Jock, 1985. Add: 417 Riverside Dr., New York, N.Y. 10025, U.S.A.

FAY, Allen. American, b. 1934. Psychiatry, Psychology. Clinical Psychiatrist, in private practice, NYC. Asst. Attending Clinical Psychiatrist, since 1975, and Asst. Clinical Prof. of Psychiatry, Mount Sinai Hosp., NYC, since 1977 (Instr., Sch. of Medicine, 1966–75; Staff Psychiatrist, 1968; Sr. Clinical Asst., 1970–75). *Publs:* (with Arnold A. Lazarus) I Can If I Want To, 1975; Making Things Better by Making Them Worse, 1978; PQR: Prescription for a Quality Relationship, 1990. Add: 250 E. 87th St., New York, N.Y. 10028, U.S.A.

FAZAL, Muhammad Abul. Bangladeshi, b. 1939. Law, Politics/Government, Public/Social administration. Principal Lectr. in Law, Trent Polytechnic, Nottingham, since 1970 (Lectr. in Law, 1967–70). Fellow in Politics, Dacca Univ., Bangladesh, 1960–63. *Publs:* Judicial Control of Administrative Action in India and Pakistan, 1969. Add: 48 Wookbank Dr., Wollaton, Nottingham, England.

FEARON, Peter (Shaun). British, b. 1942. Economics. Sr. Lectr. in Economic History, Univ. of Leicester, since 1980 (Lectr., 1966–80). *Publs:* (ed. with Derek H. Aldcroft) Economic Growth in Twentieth Century Britain, 1969; (ed. with Derek H. Aldcroft) Growth and Fluctuations in the British Economy 1790-1939, 1971; The Origins and Nature of the Great Slump 1929-1932, 1979; War, Prosperity and Depression: The U.S. Economy 1917-1945, 1987. Add: 148 Knighton Church Rd., Leicester, England.

FEATHER, Leonard (Geoffrey). American (born British), b. 1914. Music. Writer for Melody Maker, London, since 1933, Down Beat, since 1951, Intnl. Musician, since 1961, and Contemporary Keyboard, since 1976 (has also written for Esquire, 1943–56, Playboy, 1956–62, Show Mag., 1962–66, and Rolling Stone, 1975–77). Script writer, Jazz Scene U.S.A. TV series, 1962–63. Member, Bd. of Govs., Academy of Recording Arts and Sciences, 1968–69. *Publs:* Inside Jazz, 1949; Encyclopedia of Jazz, 1955; New Yearbook of Jazz, 1958; Book of Jazz, 1960; New Encyclopedia of Jazz, 1960; Laughter from the Hip, 1964; The Encyclopedia of Jazz in the '60's, 1966: From Satchmo to Miles, 1972; The Pleasures of Jazz, 1976; The Encyclopedia of Jazz in the '70's, 1977; The Passion for Jazz, 1981; The Jazz Years, 1986. Add: 13833 Riverside Dr., Sherman Oaks, Calif. 91423, U.S.A.

FEAVER, William (Andrew). British, b. 1942. Art. Art Critic, The Observer, London, since 1975. James Knott Research Fellow, Univ. of Newcastle upon Tyne, 1971–73; Art Critic, The Listener, and the Financial Times. Art Adviser, Sunday Times mag., London. *Publs:* The Art of John Martin, 1975; When We Were Very Young, 1977; Masters of Caricature, 1981. Add: c/o The Observer, 8 St. Andrew's Hill, London EC4V 5JA, England.

FECHER, Constance. *See* **HEAVEN,** Constance.

FEDDER, Norman Joseph. American, b. 1934. Plays/Screenplays, Literature, Theatre. Prof. of Theatre, Kansas State Univ., Manhattan, since 1980 (Assoc. Prof., 1970–80). Chairperson, Religion and Theatre Program, American Theatre Assn.; Pres., Ecumenical Council for Drama and Other Arts. *Publs:* The Eternal Kick, 1963; The Influence of D.H. Lawrence on Tennessee Williams, 1966; My Old Room, 1967; A Thousand

at the Branches, 1969; We Can Make Our Lives Sublime, 1969; Some Events Connected with the Early History of Arizona, 1969; The Planter May Weep, 1970; Earp!, 1971 (with M. McCarthy) Monks, 1972; PUBA, 1973; The Betrayal, 1974; The Decision, 1974; The Matter with Kansas, 1975; The Kansas Character, 1976; Tennessee Williams' Dramatic Technique, 1977; A Jew in Kansas, 1978; American Jewish Theatre, 1979; Next Thing to Kinfolks, 1980; Beyond Absurdity and Sociopolitics: The Religious Theatre Movement in the Seventies, 1980; (with R. Lippman) The Buck Stops Here, 1982; (with R. Lippman) Abraham! Abraham! 1985; No Other Gods: A Midrash on Moses, 1987. Add: Speech Dept., Kansas State Univ., Manhattan, Kans. 66506, U.S.A.

FEDER, Bernard. American, b. 1924. Medicine/Health, Sciences, Social sciences. Teacher of Social Studies, secondary schs. in NYC, 1949–66; Asst. Prof. 1966–69, and Assoc. Prof. of Education 1969–70, Hofstra Univ., Hempstead, N.Y. *Publs:* (author and ed.) Viewpoints: U.S.A., 1967, 1972; (author and ed.) Viewpoints in World History, 1967, 1974; The Process of American Government, 1972; Bucking the System: Politics of Dissent, 1973; Price of Maintaining Poverty: Politics of Welfare, 1973; A Matter of Life and Breath, 1973; Walking the Straight Line: Politics of Drug Control, 1973; Policeman and Citizen: Politics of Law and Order, 1973; Then and Now: Cases in the American Experience, 1974; The Complete Guide to Taking Tests, 1979; (with Elaine Feder) The Expressive Arts Therapies, 1981, 1984; (ed.) Medguide, 1984; (with Dr. David Stutz) Between You and Your Doctor: A Guide to Effective Decision Making in Your Medical Care, 1989. Add: 615 Waterside Way, Siesta Key, Sarasota, Fla. 34242, U.S.A.

FEDERMAN, Raymond. American, b. 1928. Novels/Short stories, Poetry, Literature, Translations. Prof. of English and Comparative Literature, State Univ. of New York, Buffalo, since 1973 (Assoc. Prof. of French, 1964–68); Prof. of French and Comparative Literature, 1968–73). Jazz saxophonist, 1947–50; Lectr. to Asst. Prof., Univ. of California at Santa Barbara, 1959–64. Ed., Mica mag., Santa Barbara, Calif., 1959–64; Dir., Fiction Collective, 1977–80. *Publs:* Journey to Chaos: Samuel Beckett's Early Fiction, 1965; (trans.) Temporary Landscapes, by Y. Caroutch, 1965; Among the Beasts (poetry), 1967; Samuel Beckett: His Work and His Critics, 1970; (ed.) Cinq Nouvelles Nouvelles, 1971; Double or Nothing, 1971; Amer Eldorado (in French), 1974; (ed.) Surfiction: Fiction Now and Tomorrow, 1975, 1981; Take It or Leave It, 1976; Me Too (poetry), 1976; (ed. with Tom Bishop) Samuel Beckett, 1976; (ed. with Lawrence Graver) Samuel Beckett: The Critical Heritage, 1979; The Voice in the Closet, 1979; The Twofold Vibration, 1982; Smiles on Washington Square (novel), 1985. Add: 46 Four Seasons West, Eggertsville, N.Y. 14226, U.S.A.

FEHL, Philipp P. American, b. 1920. Art. Prof. of Art History, Univ. of Illinois at Urbana-Champaign, since 1969; Dir., Leopoldo Cicognana Program, since 1987. Pres., Intnl. Survey of Jewish Monuments, since 1977. Assoc. Prof., Univ. of Nebraska, Lincoln, 1963–66; Prof., Univ. of North Carolina, Chapel Hill, 1966–69. *Publs:* (ed. and trans.) A Course in Drawing, by Nicolas Cochin and Denis Diderot, 1954; The Bird (drawings), 1970; Capricci (drawings), 1971; The Classical Monument: Reflections on the Connection between Mortality and Art in Greek and Roman Sculpture, 1972; Franciscus Junius: The Literature of Ancient Art, 1989; Decorum and Wit: The Poetry of Venetian Painting, 1989. Add: Dept. of Art, Univ. of Illinois, Champaign, Ill. 61820, U.S.A.

FEHRENBACH, T(heodore) R(eed). Also writes as Thomas Freeman. American, b. 1925. History, Military/Defence, Money/Finance. Pres., Royal Poinciana Corp., San Antonio, Tex., since 1971; Chmn., Texas Historical Commn., since 1987. *Publs:* Battle of Anzio, 1962; U.S. Marines in Action, 1962; (as Thomas Freeman) Crisis in Cuba, 1963; This Kind of War, 1963; Swiss Banks, 1966; Crossroads in Korea, 1966; This Kind of Peace, 1967; F.D.R.'s Undeclared War, 1967; Lone Star, 1968; Greatness to Spare, 1968; UN in War and Peace, 1968; Fight for Korea, 1969; Fire and Blood, 1973; Comanches, 1974; The San Antonio Story, 1978; Seven Keys to Texas, 1983; Texas: A Salute from Above, 1985. Add: 131 Mary D. Ave., P.O. Box 6698, San Antonio, Tex. 78209, U.S.A.

FEHRENBACHER, Don Edward. American, b. 1920. History, Biography. Coe Prof. Emeritus of History and American Studies, Stanford Univ., Calif., since 1984 (Asst. prof., 1953–57: Assoc. Prof., 1957–62; Prof., 1962–66; Coe Prof., 1966–84). Asst. Prof. of History, Coe Coll., Cedar Rapids, Iowa, 1949–53. Harmsworth Prof. of History, Oxford, 1967–68; Harrison Prof. of History, Coll. of William and Mary, Virginia, 1973–74. *Publs:* Chicago Giant: A Biography of Long John Wentworth, 1957; Prelude to Greatness: Lincoln in the 1850s, 1962; A Basic History of California, 1964; (ed.) Abraham Lincoln: A Documentary Portrait,

1964; (with N. Tutorow) California: An Illustrated History, 1968; The Era of Expansion, 1800-1848, 1969; (compiler) Manifest Destiny and the Coming of the Civil War, 1970; (ed.) The Leadership of Abraham Lincoln, 1970; (ed. with C.N. Degler) The South and the Concurrent Majority, by David M. Potter, 1972; (ed.) History and American Society: Essays of David M. Potter, 1973; (completed and edited) The Impending Crisis, by David M. Potter, 1976 (ed.) Freedom and Its Limitations in America, by David M. Potter, 1976; (ed. with R.M. Brown) Tradition, Conflict, and Modernization, 1977; The Dred Scott Case: Its Significance in American Law and Politics, 1978, Pulitzer Prize for History, 1979; The South and Three Sectional Crises, 1980; Slavery, Law, and Politics: The Dred Scott Case in Historical Perspective, 1981; Lincoln in Text and Context: Collected Essays, 1987. Add: Dept. of History, Stanford, Univ., Stanford, Calif. 94305, U.S.A.

FEIFFER, Jules. American, b. 1929. Novels/Short stories, Plays/Screenplays, Humor/Satire. Cartoonist, Village Voice, NYC, since 1956; Syndicated cartoonist since 1959. Freelance cartoonist, 1951–56; Faculty member, Yale Univ. Drama Sch., New Haven, Conn., 1973–74. *Publs:* Sick, Sick, Sick, 1958; Passionella and Other Stories, 1959; The Explainers, 1960, Boy, Girl, Boy, Girl, 1961; Munro (animated cartoon strip), 1961; Hold Me!, 1963; Feiffer's Album, 1963; Harry, the Rat with Women (novel), 1963; The Unexpurgated Memoirs of Bernard Mergendeiler, 1965; The Great Comic Book Heroes, 1965; The Penguin Feiffer, 1966; Feiffer on Civil Rights, 1966; Little Murders, 1968; Feiffer's Marriage Manual, 1967; The White House Murder Case (play), 1970; Carnal Knowledge: A Screenplay, 1971; Pictures at a Prosecution: Drawings and Text from the Chicago Conspiracy trial, 1971; Feiffer on Nixon, 1974; Knock, Knock (play), 1977; Hold Me (play), 1977; Ackroyd (novel), 1977; Tantrum (cartoon novel), 1979; Popeye (screenplay), 1980; Jules Feiffer's America from Eisenhower to Reagan, 1982; Marriage is an Invasion of Privacy and Other Dangerous Views, 1984; Feiffer's Children, 1986; Elliot Loves, 1989. Add: c/o Universal Press Syndicate, 4400 Johnson Dr., Fairway, Kans. 66205, U.S.A.

FEIGL, Herbert. American, b. 1902. Philosophy, Sciences. Prof. Emeritus, Univ. of Minnesota, Minneapolis, since 1971 (Asst. Prof., 1932–38; Assoc. Prof., 1938–40; Prof. of Philosophy, 1940–67; Regent's Prof., 1967–71). Dir., Minnesota Center for the Philosophy of Science, since 1973. Lectr., People's Inst., Vienna, 1927–30, Harvard Univ., Cambridge, Mass., 1930, and Univ. of Iowa, Iowa City, 1931–32. Vice Pres., American Assn. for the Advancement of Science, 1959; Pres., American Philosophical Assn., 1962–63. *Publs:* Theorie and Erfahrung in der Physik, 1929; (ed. with Wilfrid Sellars) Readings in Philosophical Analysis, 1949; (ed. with Max Brodbek) Readings in the Philosophy of Science, 1953; (ed.) Minnesota Studies in the Philosophy of Science, 3 vols., 1956–58; (ed. with Grover Maxwell) Scientific Explanation, Space, and Time, 1962; The "Mental" and the "Physical": The Essay and a Postscript, 1967; (ed. with Wilfrid Sellars and Keith Lehrer) New Readings in Philosophical Analysis, 1972; Inquiries and Provocations: Selected Writings, 1929-1974, 1981. Add: 5601 Dupont Ave. S., Minneapolis, Minn. 55419, U.S.A.

FEIKEMA, Feike. *See* **MANFRED,** Frederick Feikema.

FEIN, Richard J. American, b. 1929. Literature. Prof. of English, State University Coll. of New York at New Platz, since 1963. *Publs:* Robert Lowell, 1971, 1979; The Dance of Leah, 1986; (trans.) Selected Poems of Yankev Glatshteyn, 1987. Add: Dept. of English, State University of New York, New Platz, N.Y. 12561, U.S.A.

FEINBERG, Barry. South African, b. 1938. Poetry, Biography. Dir. of Research, Intnl. Defence and Aid Fund for Southern Africa, since 1977. Ed., Bertrand Russell's Literary Executors and Estate, 1966–75. *Publs:* (ed.) The Archives of Bertrand Russell (bibliography), 1967; (ed. with Ronald Kasrils) Dear Bertrand Russell (letters), 1969; (ed.) The Collected Stories of Bertrand Russell, 1972; (with Ronald Kasrils) Bertrand Russell's America, vol. I, 1973, vol. II (his Transatlantic Travels and Writings, 1945–70), 1985; (ed.) Poets to the People: South African Freedom Poems, 1974, 1980. Add: 6 Carlton Mansions, 73 Chichele Rd., London NW2, England.

FEINBERG, Gerald. American, b. 1933. Physics. Prof. of Physics, Columbia Univ., NYC, since 1959. *Publs:* The Prometheus Project, 1969; What Is the World Made Of?, 1977; Consequences of Growth, 1977; (with R. Shapiro) Life Beyond Earth, 1980; Solid Clues, 1985; (with Jeremy Bernstein) Cosmological Constants, 1986. Add: Physics Dept., Columbia Univ., New York, N.Y. 10027, U.S.A.

FEINBERG, Leonard. American, b. 1914. Literature. Retired Emeritus Dist. Prof. in Humanities, Iowa State Univ., (Prof. of English, 1957–82). Fulbright Lectr., Univ., of Ceylon, 1957–58. *Publs:* The Satirist, 1963; Introduction to Satire, 1967; (ed.) Asian Laughter, 1971; The Secret of Humor, 1978. Add: 111 Lynn St., Ames, Iowa 50010, U.S.A.

FEINGOLD, Eugene. American, b. 1931. Medicine, Health. Prof. of Medical Care Org. since 1971. Univ. of Michigan, Ann Arbor (Instr. in Political Science, 1960–63; Asst. Prof. of Political Science, 1963–66; Assoc. Prof. of Medical Care Org., 1966–71; Assoc. Dean of the Grad. Sch., 1977–84; Acting Dean, 1979–80). *Publs:* Medicare: Policy and Politics, 1966. Add: Dept. of Health Services Management and Policy, Sch. of Public Health, Univ. of Michigan, Ann Arbor, Mich. 48109, U.S.A.

FEINGOLD, S. Norman. American. Psychology, Women. Pres., National Career-Counseling Services, since 1980. National Dir., B'nai B'rith Career-Counseling Services, Washington, D.C., 1958–80. Member, President's Cttee. on Employment of the Handicapped, 1985–88. *Publs:* A Career Conference for Your Community, 1964; (ed.) The Vocational Expert in the Social Security Disability Program, 1969; (with Sol Swerdloff) Occupations and Careers, 1969; (with Dora R. Evers) Your Future in Exotic Occupations, 1972; A Counselor's Handbook: Readings in Counseling Student Aid and Rehabilitation, 1972; (consulting ed.) Rehabilitation in Israel, 1974; (ed. with William B. Silverman) A Legend in His Own Time, 1976; (with Alice Fins) Your Future in More Exotic Occupations, 1978; Counseling for Careers in the 1980's, 1979; (with Shirley Levin) What to Do Until the Counselor Comes, 1980; (with Lenard G. Perlman) Making It on Your Own, 1981; Wither Guidance: Future Directions, 1981; (with Norma R. Miller) Your Future: A Guide for the Handicapped Teenager, 1981; (with Glenda Ann Hansard-Winkler) 900,000 Plus Jobs, 1982; (with Marie Feingold) Scholarships, Fellowships and Loans, vol. 7, 1982, vol. 8, 1987, vol. 9, 1989; (with Avis J. Nicholson) The Professional and Trade Association Job Finder, 1983; (with Avis J. Nicholson) Getting Ahead: A Woman's Guide to Career Success, 1983; New Emerging Careers: Today, Tomorrow and in the 21st Century, 1988; Futuristic Exercises: A Work Book for Emerging Lifestyles and Careers in the 21st Century and Beyond, 1989. Add: 9707 Singleton Dr., Bethesda, Md. 20817, U.S.A.

FEINSTEIN, Elaine. British, b. 1930. Novels/Short stories, Poetry, Biography. Editorial Staff member, Cambridge Univ. Press, 1960–62; Lectr. in English, Bishop's Stortford Training Coll., Herts., 1963–66; Asst. Lectr. in Literature, Univ. of Essex, Wivenhoe, 1967–70. *Publs:* In a Green Eye, 1966; (ed.) Selected Poems of John Clare, 1968; The Circle (novel), 1970; (trans.) The Selected Poems of Marina Tsvetayeva, 1971; The Magic Apple Tree, 1971; At the Edge, 1972; The Amberstone Exit (novel), 1972; Matters of Chance (short stories), 1972; The Celebrants and Other Poems, 1973; The Glass Alembic (in U.S. as The Crystal Garden) (novel), 1973; The Children of the Rose (novel), 1974; The Ecstasy of Miriam Garner (novel), 1976; Some Unease and Angels (poems), 1977; The Shadow Master (novel), 1978; (trans.) Three Russian Poets, 1978; (ed. with Fay Weldon) New Stories 4, 1979; The Silent Areas (short stories), 1980; The Feast of Euridice (poems), 1980; The Survivors (novel), 1982; The Border (novel), 1984; Bessie Smith, 1985; A Captive Lion: The Life of Marina Tsvetayeva, 1987; (co-trans.) First Draft: Poems, by Nika Turbina, 1987; Mother's Girl (novel), 1988; (ed.) PEN New Poetry 2, 1988. Add: c/o Century Hutchinson Publishing Group Ltd., 62-65 Chandos Pl., London WC2N 4NW, England.

FELD, Werner J. American, b. 1910. International relations/Current Affairs, Politics/Government. Prof. and Chmn., Dept. of Political Science, Univ. of New Orleans. Pres., Dixie Speciality Co. Inc., 1948–61; Adjunct Prof., Univ. of Colorado, Colorado Springs, 1965– 86. *Publs:* Reunification and West German-Soviet Relations, 1963; The Court of the European Communities: New Dimension in International Adjudication, 1964; The European Common Market and the World, 1967; Transnational Business Collaboration Among Common Market Countries, 1970; Nongovernmental Forces and World Politics: A Study of Business, Labor, and Political Groups, 1972; The European Community in World Affairs: Economic Power and Political Influence, 1976; Domestic Political Realities and European Unification: A Study of Mass Publics and Elites in the European Community Countries, 1977; The Foreign Policies of West European Socialist Parties, 1978; International Relations: A Transnational Approach, 1979; Multinational Corporations and U.N. Politics, 1980; (ed. and contrib.) Comparative Regional Systems, 1980; (ed.) Western Europe's Global Reach, 1980; West Germany and the European Community, 1981; NATO and the Atlantic Defense: Perceptions and Illusions, 1981; International Organizations: A Comparative Approach,

1983; American Foreign Policy: Aspirations and Reality, 1983; Congress and National Defense, 1985; (co-author) Europe in the Balance, 1986; Arms Control and the Atlantic Community, 1987. Add: 3743 Blue Merion Ct., Colorado Springs, Co. 80906, U.S.A.

FELDMAN, Edwin Barry. American, b. 1925. Pres., Service Engineering Assoc. Inc., Atlanta, Ga., since 1960. *Publs:* Industrial Housekeeping, 1963; How to Use Your Time to Get Things Done, 1968; Housekeeping Handbook for Institutions, Business and Industry, 1969; Building Design for Maintainability, 1975; Energy Saving Handbook for Homes, Businesses and Industry, 1979; Supervisor's Guide to Custodial and Building Maintenance Operations, vol. I 1982, vol. II 1987; The Supervisor's Handbook, 1982; (ed.) Programmed Cleaning Guide, 1984. Add: 1023 Burton Dr. N.E., Atlanta, Ga. 30329, U.S.A.

FELDMAN, Gerald D(onald). American, b. 1937. History. Prof. of History, Univ. of California, Berkeley, since 1963. *Publs:* Army, Industry and Labor in Germany, 1914-1918, 1966; (ed.) German Imperialism, 1914-1918: The Development of an Historical Debate, 1972; (ed. with T.G. Barnes) A Documentary History of Modern Europe, 4 vols., 1972; Iron and Steel in the German Inflation 1916-1923, 1977; (with H. Homburg) Industrie und Inflation: Studien und Dokumente zur Politik der Deutschen Unternehmer 1916-1923, 1977; (ed. with Otto Busch) historische Prozesse der Deutschen Inflation, 1978; Vom Weltkrieg zur Weltwirtschaftskrise: Studien zur deutschen Wirtschafts-und Sozialgeschichte 1914-1932, 1984; (with Irmgard Steinisch) Industrie und Gewerkschaften 1918-1924; Die überforderte Zentralartbeitsgemeinschaft, 1985; Armee, Industrie und Arbeiterschaft in Deutschland 1914 bis 1918, 1985. Add: Dept. of History, Univ. of California, Berkeley, Calif. 94720, U.S.A.

FELDMAN, Irving (Mordecai). American, b. 1928. Poetry. Prof. of English, State Univ. of New York, Buffalo, since 1964. Member of faculty, Univ. of Puerto Rico, Rio Piedras, 1954–56, Univ. of Lyons, France, 1957–58, and Kenyon Coll., Gambier, Ohio, 1958–64. *Publs:* Work and Days and Other Poems, 1961; The Pripet Marshes and Other Poems, 1965; Magic Paper and Other Poems, 1970; Lost Originals, 1972; Leaping Clear and Other Poems, 1976; New and Selected Poems, 1979; Teach Me, Dear Sister, 1983; All of Us Here, 1986. Add: Dept. of English, State Univ. of New York, Buffalo, N.Y. 14260, U.S.A.

FELICE, Cynthia. American, b. 1942. Science fiction. Technical Communications Mgr., United Technologies Microelectronics Center, Colorado Springs, since 1981. Sales Engineer, Lindgren and Assocs., Chicago, 1962–71; Owner and Mgr., Glen Russ Motel, Colorado Springs, 1972–78; Technical Writer, Kaman Sciences Corp., Colorado Springs, 1978–79; Technical Communications Mgr., Inmos Corp., Colorado Springs, 1979–81. *Publs:* Godsfire, 1978; The Sunbound, 1981; (with Connie Willis) Water Witch, 1982; Eclipses, 1982; Downtime, 1985; Double Nocturne, 1986; (with Connie Willis) Light Raid, 1989. Add: 5025 Park Vista Blvd., Colorado Springs, Colo. 80928, U.S.A.

FELL, Barry. New Zealander, b. 1917. Also writes as H. Barraclough Fell. Anthropology/Ethnology. Environmental science/Ecology, Marine science/Oceanography. Prof. Emeritus, Harvard Univ., Cambridge, Mass., since 1977 (Prof. of Invertebrate Zoology, 1965–77). Pres., Epigraphic Soc., since 1974. Assoc. Prof. of Zoology, Univ. of Wellington, New Zealand, 1947–64. Pres., New Zealand Assn. of Scientists, 1949. *Publs:* America B.C., 1976; (with Douglas Faulkner) Dwellers in the Sea, 1976; Saga America, 1979; Bronze Age America, 1982. Add: c/o Epigraphic Soc., 6625 Bamburgh Dr., San Diego, Calif. 92117, U.S.A.

FELLOWS, Catherine. Historical/Romance/Gothic. *Publs:* Leonora, 1972; The Marriage Masque, 1974; The Heywood Inheritance, 1975, in U.S. as The Love Match, 1977; Vanessa, 1978; Entanglement, 1979. Add: c/o Hodder and Stoughton, Mill Rd., Dunton Green, Sevenoaks, Kent TN13 2YA, England.

FELLOWS, Malcolm Stuart. British, b. 1924. Plays/Screenplays, Film, Literature. Justice of the Peace, since 1973. Ed., Laurel and Hardy mag. Former Chmn., Education Cttee., and Member, Exec. Council, Writers' Guild of Great Britain. *Publs:* The Truth About Helen (TV play), 1961; Shame in Summer, 1964; Projects for School, 1965; (ed.) Eight Plays, 1965; Behind the Wheel, 1968; Come Fly with Me, 1968; (ed.) Red Lion Plays, 1968; Home Movies, 1973; Success, 1976. Add: Denham, 42 Queens Walk, Kingsbury, London NW9 8ER, England.

FELSTEIN, Ivor. British, b. 1933. Medicine/Health, Psychology, Sex.

Private psychotherapist; Sr. Physician, Bolton Health Authority, since 1963. Consulting Ed., British Journal of Sexual Medicine, 1973– 77. Medical Registrar, Kingston Group Hosps., Surrey, 1960–63. *Publs:* Later Life: Geriatrics Today and Tomorrow, 1969; Snakes and Ladders: Medical and Social Aspects of Modern Management, 1971; A Change of Face and Figure, 1971; Living to Be a Hundred, 1973; Sex in Later Life, 1973; (with J. Mitson and M. Barnard) The Medical Shorthand Typist, 1974; Sexual Pollution: The Fall and Rise of Venereal Diseases; Looking at Retirement, 1977; (contrib.) Visual Dictionary of Sex, 1978; (with others) B.M.A. Book of Executive Health, 1979; Sex in Later Life, 1980; (co-author) Well Being, 1982; (co-author) Foot Health, 1989. Add: Consulting Rooms, 11 Chorley New Rd., Bolton, Lancs BL1 4QR, England.

FELVER, Charles Stanley. American, b. 1916. Literature, Biography. Prof. of English, California State Univ., Chico, since 1961 (English Dept. Head, 1961–68; Language Arts Div., Chmn., 1961–67. Lectr. in English, Univ. of Michigan, 1952–55; Asst. to Assoc. Prof. of English, Kent State Univ., Ohio, 1955–61. *Publs:* Robert Armin, Shakespeare's Fool: A Biographical Essay, 1961; (with M.K. Nurmi) Poetry: An Introduction and Anthology, 1967; Joseph Crawhall: The Newcastle Wood Engraver, 1821-1896, 1973. Add: 1069 Woodland Ave., Chico, California 95928, U.S.A.

FENBY, Eric (William). British, b. 1906. Music, Autobiography/Memoirs/Personal. Amanuensis of Frederick Delius, 1928–34; Musical Adviser, Boosey & Hawkes Ltd., 1936–39; Dir. of Music, North Riding Training Coll., 1948–62; Artistic Dir., Delius Centenary Festival, 1962; Prof. of Composition, Royal Academy of Music, London, 1964–77. *Publs:* Delius as I Knew Him, 1936, 3rd. ed. 1981; A Song of Summer (screenplay based on Delius as I Knew Him), 1968; Menuhin's House of Music, 1969; Delius, 1971. Add: 1 Raincliffe Ct., Stepney Rd., Scarborough YO12 5BY, England.

FENIGER, Siegmund. *See* **NYANAPONIKA**.

FENN, Charles. American, b. 1907. Novels/Short stories, Plays/Screenplays, Biography. *Publs:* The Sea Breeze, 1949; Fire-Eaters, 1950; The Final Ace, 1951; School for Scoundrels, 1954; The Pleasure Dome, 1955; The Sorcerer's Apprentice, 1956; A for Angel, 1957; The Golden Rule of General Wong, 1960; Crimson Joy, 1961; Skyrocket, 1962; Tropic Zero, 1963; Floating Pagoda-Boat, 1965; Pyramid of Night, 1967; Journal of a Voyage to Nowhere, 1971; Ho Chi Minh, 1973; Add: The Standing Stone, Schull, Co. Cork, Ireland.

FENNARIO, David. Canadian. Plays/Screenplays, Autobiography/Memoirs/Personal. *Publs:* Without a Parachute (memoirs), 1974; On the Job, 1976; Nothing to Lose, 1977; Balconville, 1981; (with Daniel Adams) Blue Mondays, 1984. Add: c/o Black Rock Creations, P.O. Box 244, Verdun, Quebec H4G 3E9, Canada.

FENNELL, John Lister Illingworth. British, b. 1918. History, Language, Literature. Prof. of Russian, Oxford Univ., since 1968 (Lectr. in Russian, 1956–58; Fellow of Univ. Coll., 1964–68). Asst. Lectr., Dept. of Slavonic Studies, Cambridge Univ., 1947–52; Reader in Russian, and Head of Dept. of Slavonic Languages, Univ. of Nottingham, 1952–56. *Publs:* Correspondence Between Prince A.M. Kurbsky and Ivan IV, 1564-1579, 1955; Ivan the Great of Moscow, 1961; The Penguin Russian Course, 1961; Pushkin, 1964; (ed.) Kurbsky's History of Ivan IV, 1965: The Emergence of Moscow, 1969; (co-author) Historical Russian Reader, 1969; (ed. and author) 19th Century Russian Literature, 1973; (ed. and author) Early Russian Literature, 1974; The Crisis of Medieval Russia, 1983. Add: 8 Canterbury Rd., Oxford, England.

FENNER, Carol. Pseud. for Carol Williams. American, b. 1929. Children's fiction. Freelance publicist and writing instructor. *Publs:* Tigers in the Cellar, 1963; Christmas Tree on the Mountain, 1966; Lagalag the Wanderer, 1968; Gorilla Gorilla, 1973; The Skates of Uncle Richard, 1978; Saving Amelia Earhart, 1982; Cat's Party, 1985; Deer Flight, 1986; A Summer of Horses, 1989. Add: 190 Rebecca Rd., Battle Creek, Mich. 49015, U.S.A.

FENNER, Frank John. Australian, b. 1914. Medicine/Health. Visiting Fellow, Australian National Univ., Canberra, since 1980 (Prof. of Microbiology, 1949–73, and Dir., 1967–73, John Curtin Sch. of Medical Research; Dir., Centre for Resource and Environmental Studies, 1973–79). *Publs:* (with F.M. Burnet) The Production of Antibodies, 1949; (with F.N. Ratcliffe) Myxomatosis, 1965; The Biology of Animal Viruses, 1968; (with B.R. McAuslan, C.A. Mims, J.F. Sambrook and D.O. White)

1974; (with D.O. White) Medical Virology, 1970, 3rd ed. 1986; Classification and Nomenclature of Viruses, 1976; (ed. with A.L.G. Rees) The Australian Academy of Sciences: The First Twenty-Five Years, 1980; (with P.A. Bachman, E.P.G. Gibbs, F.A. Murphy, M.J. Studdert and D.O. White) Veterinary Virology, 1987; (with others) Smallpox and Its Eradication, 1988; (with R. Wittek and K.R. Dumbell) The Orthopox Viruses, 1988; (with Z. Jezek) Human Monkeypox, 1988; (ed. with A. Gibbs) Portraits in Virology, 1988. Add: Box 334, G.P.O., Canberra, A.C.T., Australia.

FENNER, James R. *See* **TUBB,** E.C.

FENNER, Roger T(heedham). British, b. 1943. Engineering, Technology. Reader in Mechanical Engineering, Imperial Coll., Univ. of London, since 1979 (Lectr., 1968–79). Technical Officer, Imperial Chemical Industries Ltd., Plastics Div., Welwyn Garden City, 1965–68. *Publs:* Extruder Screw Design, 1970; Computing for Engineers, 1974; Finite Element Methods for Engineers, 1975; Principles of Polymer Processing, 1979; Engineering Elasticity, 1986; Mechanics of Solids, 1989. Add: Mechanical Engineering Dept., Imperial Coll., Exhibition Rd., London SW7 2BX, England.

FENTEN, D.X. American, b. 1932. Children's non-fiction, Homes/Gardens, Horticulture. Author, Weekend Gardener, and Columnist, Newsday Newspaper, since 1974, and Garden Ed., since 1978; syndicated newspaper columnist, "Computer Bits." *Publs:* Better Photography for Amateurs, 1960; Electric Eye Still Camera Photography, 1961; Flower and Garden Photography, 1966; Aviation Careers, 1969; Greenhorn's Guide to Gardening, 1969; Harvesting the Sea, 1970; Sea Careers, 1970; The Clear and Simple Gardening Guide, 1971; Making of a Police Officer, 1972; (with Barbara Fenten) The Organic Grow It, Cook It, Preserve It Guidebook, 1972; Gardening . . . Naturally, 1973; Ms—M.D., 1973; (with Barbara Fenten) The Concise Guide to Natural Foods, 1974; First Book of Indoor Gardening, 1974; Ins and Outs of Gardening, 1974; Ms—ATT'Y, 1974; The Concise Guide to TV and Radio Careers, 1975; The Concise Guide to Volunteer Work, 1975; Strange Differences, 1975; The Weekend Gardener, 1976; Greenhousing for Purple Thumbs, 1976; (with B. Fenten) Careers in the Sports Industry, 1977; The Children's Complete How Does Your Garden Grow Guide to Plants and Planting, 1977; Ms—Architect, 1977; (with B. Fenten) Tourism and Hospitality Careers Unlimited, 1978; Behind the Scenes, 10 vols., 1980; Easy to Make House Plants, 1981; (with B. Fenten) The Team Behind the Great Parades, 1981. Add: 27 Bowden Road, Greenlawn, N.Y. 11740, U.S.A.

FENTON, Edward. American, b. 1917. Novels/Short stories, Children's fiction, Poetry, Translations. Staff member in the print dept., Metropolitan Museum of Art, NYC, 1950–55. *Publs:* Soldiers and Strangers: Poems, 1945; The Double Darkness, 1945; Us and the Duchess, 1947; Aleko's Island, 1948; Hidden Trapezes, 1950; Nine Lives, or, The Celebrated Cat of Beacon Hill, 1951; The Golden Doors (in U.K. as Mystery in Florence), 1957; Once Upon a Saturday, 1958; Fierce John, 1959; The Nine Questions, 1959; The Phantom of Walkaway Hill, 1961; An Island for a Pelican, 1963; The Riddle of the Red Whale, 1966; The Big Yellow Baloon, 1967; A Matter of Miracles, 1967; (trans.) Petro's War, by Alki Zei, 1968; Penny Candy, 1970; Anne of a Thousand Days (novel), 1970; Duffy's Rocks, 1974; (trans.) The Sound of the Dragon's Feet, 1979; The Refugee Summer, 1982; The Morning of the Gods, 1987. Add: 24 Evrou St., Athens 610, Greece.

FENTON, James (Martin). British, b. 1949. Poetry, History, Literature, Theatre, Translations. Chief Literary Critic, The Times, London, since 1984. Freelance journalist, Indo-China, 1973–75; Political Columnist, New Statesman, London, 1976–78; German Correspondent, Guardian, London, 1978–79; Theatre Critic, Sunday Times, London, 1979–84. *Publs:* Our Western Furniture, 1968; Put Thou Thy Tears into My Bottle, 1969; Terminal Moraine, 1972; A Vacant Possession, 1978; Dead Soldiers, 1981; A German Requiem, 1981; (trans.) Rigoletto, 1982; The Memory of War, 1982; Children in Exile, 1983; The Memory of War and Children in Exile: Poems 1968-83, 1983, in U.S. as Children in Exile, 1984; You Were Marvellous (theatre reviews), 1983; The Fall of Saigon, 1985; The Snap Revolution (on the Philippines), 1986; (with John Fuller) Partingtime Hall, 1987; All the Wrong Places: Adrift in the Politics of Asia, 1987. Add: 1 Bartlemas Rd., Oxford OX4 1XU, England.

FENTON, John Charles. British, b. 1921. Theology/Religion. Canon, Christ Church, Oxford, since 1978. Principal, Lichfield Theological Coll., 1958–65; Principal, St. Chad's Coll., Durham, 1965–78. *Publs:* Preaching the Cross, 1958; The Passion According to John, 1961; The Gospel of St. Matthew, 1963; The Gospel According to John, 1970; (with M.H. Duke) Good News, 1976; Finding the Way Through John, 1988. Add: Christ Church, Oxford OX1 1DP, England.

FENWICK, Elizabeth. Also writes as E.P. Fenwick. American, b. 1920. Mystery/Crime/Suspense. *Publs:* (as E.P. Fenwick) The Inconvenient Corpse, 1943; (as E.P. Fenwick) Murder in Haste, 1944; (as E.P. Fenwick) Two Names for Death, 1945; The Long Wing, 1947; Afterwords, 1950; Days of Plenty, 1956; Poor Harriet, 1957; A Long Way Down, 1959; Friend of Mary Rose, 1961; A Night Run, 1961; The Silent Cousin, 1962; The Make-Believe Man, 1963; Cockleberry Castle (juvenile novel), 1963; The Passenger, 1967; Disturbance on Berry Hill, 1968; Goodbye, Aunt Elva, 1968; Impeccable People, 1971; The Last of Lysandra, 1973. Add: c/o Gollancz, 14 Henrietta St., London WC2E 8QJ, England.

FENWICK, Ian (Graham Keith). British, b. 1941. Education. Dean of Students, Christchurch Coll., Canterbury. Lectr., 1971–80, and Sr. Lectr. in Education, 1980–85, Univ. of Leeds. *Publs:* The Comprehensive School 1944-1970, 1976; The Government of Education, 1981. Add: Christchurch Coll., Canterbury, Kent, England.

FERGUSON, Everett. American, b. 1933. Theology/Religion. Prof., Abilene Christian Univ., Tex. since 1962. Ed., The Second Century, since 1981. *Publs:* Early Christians Speak, 1971; (with A.J. Malherbe) Gregory of Nyssa: The Life of Moses, 1978; Demonology of the Early Christian World, 1984; Backgrounds of Early Christianity, 1987; (ed.) Encyclopaedia of Early Christianity, 1989. Add: 609 East North 16th St., Abilene, Tex. 79601, U.S.A.

FERGUSON, Peter. British, b. 1933. Novels/Short stories. Formerly, Sr. Lectr. in English, Hertfordshire Coll. of Higher Education. *Publs:* Autumn for Heroes, 1959; Monster Clough, 1962; A Week Before Winter (In the Year of the Great Reaping), 1971. Add: 74 West Riding, Bricket Wood, St. Albans, Herts. AL2 3QQ, England.

FERLINGHETTI, Lawrence. American, b. 1919. Novels/Short stories, Plays/Screenplays, Poetry. Owner and Ed.-in-Chief, City Lights books, San Francisco, Calif.; also painter. *Publs:* Pictures of the Gone World, 1955; A Coney Island of the Mind, 1958; (trans.) Selections from Paroles by Jacques Prevert, 1958; Tentative Description of a Dinner Given to Promote the Impeachment of President Eisenhower, 1958; (ed.) Beatitude Anthology, 1960; Her (novel), 1960; Howl of the Censor, 1961; One Thousand Fearful Words of Fidel Castro, 1961; Berlin, 1961; Starting from San from San Francisco: Poems, 1961, 1967; Unfair Arguments with Existence: Seven Plays for a New Theatre, 1963; (with others) Penguin Modern Poets 5, 1963; Routines (play and short pieces), 1964; Where Is Vietnam?, 1965; To Fuck Is to Love Again: Kyrie Eleison Kerista: or, The Situation in the West: Followed by a Holy Proposal, 1965; An Eye on the World: Selected Poems, 1967; After the Cries of the Birds, 1967; Moscow in the Wilderness, Segovia in the Snow, 1967; The Secret Meaning of Things, 1969; Tyrannus Nix?, 1969; The Mexican Night: Travel Journal, 1970; Back Roads to Far Places, 1971; Love Is No Stone on the Moon, 1971; Open Eyes, Open Heart, 1973; Who Are We Now?, 1976; Northwest Ecolog, 1978; Landscape of Living and Dying, 1979; Endless Life: Selected Poems, 1981; A Trip to Italy and France, 1981; Mule Mountain Dreams, 1981; The Populist Manifestos, 1981; (with Nancy J. Peters) Literary San Francisco, 1981; Leaves of Life: Drawings from the Model, 1983; Seven Days in Nicaragua Libre, 1984; Over All the Obscene Boundaries: European Poems and Transitions, 1984; Love in the Days of Rage (novel), 1988. Add: City Lights Books, 261 Columbus Ave., San Francisco, Calif. 94133, U.S.A.

FERLITA, Ernest. American, b. 1927. Plays/Screenplays, Songs, lyrics and libretti, Film, Translations. Jesuit Priest since 1962. Prof. of Drama and Speech since 1969, and Chmn. of the Dept. since 1970, Loyola Univ., New Orleans. *Publs:* Songs of Hiroshima, 1970; The Theatre of Pilgrimage, 1971; The Krewe of Dionysus (play), 1974; (with J.R. May) Film Odyssey, 1976; The Way of the River, 1977; (with J.R. May) The Parables of Lina Wertmuller, 1977; (verse trans.) The Spiritual Marriage of the Shepherd Peter and the Mexican Church, 1977; Quetzal, 1979; (with others) Religion in Film, 1982; Gospel Journey, 1982; Introduction to Poems of Gerard Manley Hopkins, 1986. Add: Loyola Univ., 6363 St. Charles Ave., New Orleans, La. 70118, U.S.A.

FERRAR, Harold. American, b. 1935. Literature. Member of Faculty, New Sch. for Social Research, NYC. Asst. Prof., Columbia Univ., NYC, 1968–74. *Publs:* Denis Johnston's Irish Theatre, 1973; John Osborne, 1973; (with B. Clarke) The Dublin Drama League, 1978. Add: 210 Riverside Dr., Apt. 5G, New York, N.Y. 10025, U.S.A.

FERRARS, Elizabeth. British, b. 1907. Mystery/Crime/Suspense. *Publs:* Give a Corpse a Bad Name, 1940; Remove the Bodies, 1940; Death in Botanist's Bay, 1941; Don't Monkey with Murder, 1942; Your Neck in a Noose, 1942; I, Said the Fly, 1945; Murder Among Friends, 1946; With Murder in Mind, 1948; The March Hare Murders, 1949; Milk of Human Kindness, 1950; Alibi for a Witch, 1952; The Clock that Wouldn't Stop, 1952; Murder in Time, 1953; The Lying Voices, 1954; Enough to Kill a Horse, 1955; Always Say Die, 1956; Murder Moves In, 1956; Count the Cost, 1957; Furnished for Murder, 1957; Hunt the Tortoise, 1958; A Tale of Two Murders, 1959; The Sleeping Dogs, 1960; Fear the Light, 1960; The Wandering Widows, 1962; The Busy Body, 1962; The Doubly Dead, 1963; Legal Fiction, 1964; Ninth Life, 1965; No Peace for the Wicked, 1966; Zero at the Bone, 1967; The Swaying Pillars, 1968; The Seven Sleepers, 1970; Breath of Suspicion, 1972; Foot in the Grave, 1973; Alive and Dead, 1974; Hanged Man's House, 1974; The Cup and the Lip, 1975; Blood Flies Upward, 1976; Murders Anonymous, 1977; Pretty Pink Shroud, 1977; Last Will and Testament, 1978; In at the Kill, 1978; Witness Before the Fact, 1979; Frog in the Throat, 1980; Experiment with Death, 1981; Thinner Than Water, 1981; Skeleton in Search of a Cupboard (in U.S. as Skeleton in Search of a Closet), 1982; Death of a Minor Character, 1983; Something Wicked, 1983; Root of All Evil, 1984; The Crime and the Crystal, 1985; I Met Murder, 1985; Other Devil's Name, 1987; Come and Be Killed, 1987; A Murder Too Many, 1988; Trial by Fury, 1989. Add: 5 Treble House Terrace, London Rd., Blewbury, Didcot, Oxon. OX11 9NZ, England.

FERRÉ, Frederick. American, b. 1933. Philosophy. Research Prof. of Philosophy, Univ. of Georgia, since 1988 (Head of Dept. of Philosophy and Religion, 1980–88). Dana Prof. of Philosophy, Dickinson Coll., Carlisle, Pa., 1962–80. Pres., American Theological Soc., 1975–76. *Publs:* Language, Logic and God, 1961, 3rd ed. 1981; (with K. Bendall) Exploring the Logic of Faith: A Dialogue on the Relation of Modern Philosophy to Christian Faith, 1962; (ed.) William Paley's Natural Theology, 1963; Basic Modern Philosophy of Religion, 1967; (ed.) Comte: Introduction to Positive Philosophy, 1970; Shaping the Future, 1976; The Challenge of Religion, 1982; (ed. with Rita H. Mataragnon) God and Global Justice: Religion and Poverty in an Unequal World, 1985; The Philosophy of Technology, 1988. Add: 275 Davis Estates Rd., Athens, Ga. 30606, U.S.A.

FERRIS, Paul. British, b. 1929. Novels/Short stories, Plays/-Screenplays, Medicine/Health, Biography. Freelance writer. *Publs:* A Changed Man, 1958; The City, 1960; Then We Fall, 1960; The Church of England, 1962; A Family Affair, 1963; The Doctors, 1965; The Destroyer, 1965; The Nameless: Abortion in Britain Today, 1966; The Dam, 1967; Men and Money: Financial Europe Today (in U.S. as The Money Men of Europe), 1968; The House of Northcliffe, 1971; The New Militants: Crisis in the Trade Unions, 1972; Very Personal Problems, 1973; The Cure, 1974; The Detective (in U.S. as High Places), 1976; Dylan Thomas, 1977; Talk to Me About England, 1979; Richard Burton, 1981; A Distant Country, 1983; Gentlemen of Fortune (in U.S. as The Master Bankers), 1984; (ed.) Collected Letters of Dylan Thomas, 1985; TV plays—The Revivalist, 1975; Dylan, 1978; Nye, 1982; The Extremist, 1983; The Fasting Girl, 1984; Children of Dust, 1988. Add: c/o Curtis Brown Ltd., 162-168 Regent St., London W1R 5TB, England.

FERRIS, Timothy. American, b. 1944. Astronomy, Sciences, Writing/Journalism. Assoc. Prof. of Journalism, Univ. of Southern California, Los Angeles, since 1982. Reporter, United Press Intnl., NYC, 1967–69, and New York Post, 1969–71. Assoc. Ed., Rolling Stone mag., NYC, 1971–73 (Contrib. Ed., 1973–80); Prof., Brooklyn Coll. of the City Univ. of New York, 1974–82. *Publs:* The Red Limit: The Search for the Edge of the Universe, 1977, 1983; Galaxies, 1980; Spaceshots: The Beauty of Nature Beyond Earth, 1984; (with Bruce Porter) The Practice of Journalism: A Guide to Reporting and Writing the News, 1988; Coming of Age in the Milky Way, 1988. Add: Sch. of Journalism, Univ. of Southern California, Los Angeles, Calif. 90089, U.S.A.

FERRISS, Abbott Lamoyne. American, b. 1915. Sociology. Prof. Emeritus, Dept. of Sociology, Emory Univ., since 1982 (Prof., 1970–82); Ed., SINET, Social Indicators Network News quarterly, since 1984. Assoc. Study Dir., National Science Foundn., 1962–67; Research Sociologist, social indicator project, Russell Sage Foundn., 1967–70; Ed., The Sociologist, 1965–68; Ed., Southern Sociologist quarterly, 1980–84. *Publs:* (co-ed.) Reducing Traffic Accidents by Use of Group Discussion-Decision: An A Priori Evaluation, 1957; (with Charles Proctor et al) National Recreation Survey, 1962; Indicators of Trends in American Education, 1969; Indicators of Change in the American Family, 1970; Indicators of Trends in the Status of American Women, 1971; (ed.) Re-

search and the 1970 Consus, 1971. Add: Dept. of Sociology, Emory Univ., Atlanta, Ga. 30322, U.S.A.

FERRY, John Douglass. American, b. 1912. Chemistry. Emeritus Prof. of Chemistry, Univ. of Wisconsin, Madison, since 1982 (Asst. Prof., 1946; Assoc. Prof., 1946–47; Prof., 1947–82; Chmn., Dept. of Chemistry, 1959–67; Farrington Daniels Research Prof., 1973–82). Instr., 1936–38, member, Soc. of Fellows, 1938–41, and Research Assoc., 1942–45, Harvard Univ., Cambridge, Mass.; Assoc. Chemist, Woods Hole Oceanographic Instn., 1941–45. *Publs:* Viscoelastic Properties of Polymers, 1961, 3rd ed. 1980. Add: 1101 University Ave., Madison, Wisc. 53706, U.S.A.

FESPERMAN, John T(homas). American, b. 1925. Music. Curator of Musical Instruments, Smithsonian Instn., Washington, D.C., since 1965 (Concert Dir., 1965–66). Member, Organ and History Faculty, New England Conservatory, Boston, Mass., 1959–65; Dir. of Music, Old North Church, Boston, Mass., 1960–65. *Publs:* The Organ as Musical Medium, 1961; Two Essays on Organ Design, 1965; A Snetzler Chamber Organ of 1761, 1970; Organs in Mexico, 1980; Flentrop in America, 1982; Organ Planning (Hymnal Studies IV), 1984. Add: Div. of Musical Instruments, Smithsonian Instn., Washington, D.C. 20560, U.S.A.

FETHERLING, Doug. Canadian (b. Virgin Islands), b. 1947. Poetry, Literature. With House of Anansi Press, Toronto, 1967–69; Writer, Canadian Broadcasting Corp., Toronto, 1969–70; Book Page Ed., Toronto Star, 1973, 1974. *Publs:* Cafe Terminus, 1973; The Five Lives of Ben Hecht, 1977; (ed.) A George Woodcock Reader, 1980, Variorum: New Poems and Old 1965–85; The Blue Notebook: Reports on Canadian Culture, 1985; (ed. with Dale Fetherling) Carl Sandburg at the Movies: A Poet in the Silent Era 1920-27, 1985; Moving Towards the Vertical Horizon, 1986; (ed.) Documents in Canadian Art, 1987. Add: Box 367, Station F, Toronto, Ont. M4Y 2L8, Canada.

FEUERSTEIN, Georg W. German, b. 1947. Cultural/Ethnic topics, Philosophy, Social commentary, Theology/Religion, Translations. Dir., Integral Publishing, Lower Lake, Calif., since 1986. Co-Dir., California Center for Jean Gebser Studies, since 1986. Dir., Yoga Research Centre, Univ. of Durham, England, 1975–80; Editorial Dir., Dawn Horse Press, Clearlake, Calif., 1981–86. *Publs:* Yoga: Sein Wesen und Werden, 1969; (with J. Miller) A Reappraisal of Yoga: Essays in Indian Philosophy, 1969, reissued as Yoga and Beyond: Essays in Indian Philosophy, 1972; The Essence of Yoga: A Contribution to the Psychohistory of Indian Civilization, 1974; The Bhagavad-Gita: Its Philosophy and Cultural Setting, 1974, reissued as the Bhagavad-Gita: An Introduction, 1983; Textbook on Yoga, 1975; Yoga-Sutra: An Exercise in the Methodology of Textual Analysis, 1979; The Bhagavad-Gita: A Critical Rendering, 1980; (ed. and trans.) The Yoga-Sutra of Patanjali: A New Translation and Commentary, 1980; The Philosophy of Classical Yoga, 1980; (with Patricia Feuerstein) Remembrance of the Divine Names of Da, 1982; Structures of Consciousness: The Genius of Jean Gebser: An Introduction and Critique, 1987; Guru, God and Sex, 1987. Add: c/o Nancy Stodart, Fourth Lloyd Prods., 350 School Rd., Novato, Calif. 94947, U.S.A.

FEUERWERKER, Albert. American, b. 1927. History. A.M. and H.P. Bentley Prof. of History, Univ. of Michigan, Ann Arbor, since 1984 (Assoc. Prof., 1960–63; Dir., Center for Chinese Studies, 1961–67, 1972–84; Prof. of History, 1963–86). *Publs:* China's Early Industrialization, 1958; (with S. Cheng) Chinese Communist Studies of Modern Chinese History, 1961; (ed. and contrib.) Modern China, 1964; (ed. with R. Murphey and M.C. Wright, and contrib.) Approaches to Modern Chinese History, 1967; (ed. and contrib.) History in Communist China, 1968; The Chinese Economy, circa 1870-1911, 1969; Rebellion in Nineteenth Century China, 1975; State and Society in Eighteenth-Century China: The Ching Empire in Its Glory, 1976; The Foreign Establishment in China in the Early Twentieth Century, 1976; Economic Trends in the Republic of China 1912-1949, 1977; (ed. and contrib.) Chinese Social and Economic History from the Song to 1900, 1982; (ed., with J.K. Fairbanks, and contrib.) Cambridge History of China, Vol. 13, 1986. Add: Center for Chinese Studies, Univ. of Michigan, 104 Lane Hall, Ann Arbor, Mich. 48109, U.S.A.

FEYERABEND, Paul K(arl). Austrian, b. 1924. Philosophy, Sciences. Prof. of Philosophy, Univ. of California, Berkeley, since 1962; Prof. of Philosophy of Science, Federal Inst. of Technology, Zurich, since 1980. Lectr. in Philosophy, Bristol Univ., England, 1955–58; Prof. and Chmn. of Dept., University Coll., London, 1966–69; Prof. of History and Philosophy, and Chmn. of the Dept., Free Univ. of Berlin, 1969–70; Prof. of Philosophy, Yale Univ., New Haven, Conn., 1969–70. *Publs:* Against

Method: Outline of an Anarchistic Theory of Knowledge, 1975; Science in a Free Society, 1978; Realism, Rationalism and Scientific Method: Philosophical Papers, Vol. 1, 1981; Problems of Empiricism: Philosophical Papers, Vol. 2, 1981; (ed. with Grover Maxwell) Mind, Matter, and Method: Essays in Philosophy and Science in Honor of Herbert Feigl, 1981; Farewell to Reason, 1987. Add: Dept. of Philosophy, University of California, Berkeley, Calif. 94720, U.S.A.

FIACC, Padraic. Pseud. for Patrick Joseph O'Connor. Irish, b. 1924. Poetry, Literature. *Publs:* By the Black Stream, 1969; Odour of Blood, 1973; (ed.) The Wearing of the Black, 1974; Nights in the Bad Place, 1977; Selected Poems, 1979; Missa Terriblis, 1986. Add: 43 Farmley Park, Glengormley, Newtownabbey, Co. Antrim, Northern Ireland.

FICHTER, George S. Pseud: George Kensinger, Matt Warner, and Marc Ziliox. American, b. 1922. Environmental science/Ecology, Natural history, Sports/Physical education/Keeping fit. Instr. of Zoology and Conservation, Miami Univ., Ohio, 1948–50; Vice Pres. and Ed.-in-Chief, Fisherman Press Inc., 1950–55; Asst. Exec. Vice Pres., Sport Fishing Inst., Washington, D.C., 1955–57; Freelance writer, and Ed., Florida Outdoors mag., 1957–63; Ed., 1963–67, and Dir., 1967–68, Golden Guides, Western Publishing Co. *Publs:* Fishing, 1954; (co-author) Good Fishing, 1959; Reptiles and How They Live, 1960; Fishes and How They Live, 1960; Flying Animals, 1961; (managing ed.) Golden Encyclopedia of Natural History, 16 vols., 1962; Snakes, 1963; Fishes, 1963; (managing ed.) Golden Bookshelf of Natural History, 16 vols., 1963; Insects, 1964; Reptiles, Questions and Answers, 1965; (co-author) Fishing, 1965; Insect Pests, 1966; Rocks, 1966; Animal Kingdom, 1968; Snakes and Other Reptiles, 1968; Airborne Animals, 1969; Exploring Biology, 1970; Exploring with a Microscope, 1970; Your World—Your Survival, 1970; Birds of Florida, 1971; Earth and Ecology, 1972; The World of Animals, 1972; (co-author) Bicycling, 1972; Cats, 1973; (co-author) Ecology, 1973; The Florida Cookbook, 1973; Reptiles and Amphibians, 1974; Insects, 1975; Flowers, Trees, and Garden Plants, 1975; (co-author) Fresh and Salt Water Fishes of the World, 1976; Cats of the World, 1976; (co-ed.) How to Build an Indian Canoe, 1976; (co-author) Inside Bicycling, 1977; Changing World for Wildlife, 1977; Strangest Creatures in the World, 1977; Dangerous Animals of the Sea, 1977; The Human Body, 1977; Bicycles and Bicycling, 1978; (co-author) Bicycle Racing, 1978; Fishing the Four Seasons, 1978; The Future Sea, 1978; Iraq, 1978; Music the Indians Gave Us, 1978; Snakes, 1979; Keeping Amphibians and Reptiles as Pets, 1979; Working Dogs, 1979; Florida: A Visual Geography, 1979; Racquetball, 1979; Life Science, 1979; The Plains Indians and How They Lived, 1980; The Bulge of Africa, 1981; Disastrous Fires, 1981; Space Shuttle, 1981; Poisonous Snakes of the World, 1982; Karts and Karting, 1982; Comets and Meteors, 1982; Birds, 1982; Rocks and Minerals, 1982; Reptiles and Amphibians, 1982; Wildflowers of North America, 1982; Comets and Meteors, 1982; The Florida Living Cookbook, 1985; Underwater Farming, 1988; First Steamboat Down the Mississippi, 1989; Whales, Dolphins and Other Marine Mammals, 1990. Add: P.O. Box 3280, DeLand, Fla. 32720, U.S.A.

FICKERT, Kurt J. American, b. 1920. Literature. Prof., Wittenberg Univ., Springfield, Ohio, since 1956 (Chmn. of the Dept. of Foreign Languages, 1969–75). Instr. in German, Hofstra Univ., Hempstead, N.Y., 1947–53; Asst. Prof. of German, Florida State Univ., Tallahassee, 1953–54, and Kansas State Univ., Fort Hays, 1954–56. *Publs:* To Heaven and Back: The New Morality in the Plays of Friedrich Durrenmatt, 1972; Herman Hesse's Quest: The Evolution of the Dichter Figure in His Work, 1978; Kafka's Doubles, 1979; Signs and Portents: Myth in the Work of Wolfgang Borchert, with a Translation of His Poems, 1980; Franz Kafka: Life, Work and Criticism, 1984; Neither Left Nor Right: The Politics of Individualism in Uwe Johnson's Work, 1987. Add: 33 South Kensington Pl., Springfield, Ohio 45504, U.S.A.

FIEDLER, Fred E. American, b. 1922. Administration/Management, Psychology. Prof. of Psychology, and of Mgmt. and Org., Univ. of Washington, Seattle, since 1969. Prof. of Psychology, Univ. of Illinois, Urbana, 1951–69. *Publs:* Leader Attitudes and Group Effectiveness, 1958; (with E.P. Godfrey and D.M. Hall) Boards, Management and Company Success, 1959; A Theory of Leadership Effectiveness, 1967; (with M.M. Chemers) Leadership and Effective Management, 1974; (ed. with others) Managerial Control and Organizational Democracy, 1976; (with others) Improving Leadership Effectiveness: The Leader Match Concept, 1977, 1984; (with J.E. Garcia) New Approaches to Effective Leadership: Cognitive Resources and Organizational Performance, 1987. Add: Dept. of Psychology, Univ. of Washington, Seattle, Wash. 98195, U.S.A.

FIEDLER, Leslie A(aron). American, b. 1917. Novels/Short stories,

Literature, Social commentary/phenomena. Prof. of English, State Univ. of New York at Buffalo, since 1965. Asst. Prof., 1947–48, Assoc. Prof., 1948–52, Prof. of English, 1953–64, and Chmn. of Dept., 1954–56, Montana State Univ., Missoula; Fulbright Lectr., Univ. of Rome, 1951–52, Univ. of Bologna and Ca Foscari Univ., 1952–53, and Univ. of Athens, 1961–62; Gauss lectr., Princeton Univ., N.J., 1956–57; Advisory Ed., Ramparts mag., NYC, 1958–61; Literary Advisor, St. Martin's Press, NYC, 1958–61; Visiting Prof., Univ. of Vincennes, Paris, 1970–71. *Publs:* An End to Innocence: Essays on Culture and Politics, 1955; (ed.) The Art of the Essay, 1958; rev. ed. 1969; (ed.) Selections from the Leaves of Grass, by Walt Whitman, 1959; The Jew in the American Novel, 1959; Love and Death in the American Novel, 1960; rev. ed. 1966; No! In Thunder: Essays on Myth and Literature,1960; The Riddle of Shakespeare's Sonnets, 1962; Pull Down Vanity and Other Stories, 1962; The Second Stone: A Love Story, 1963; Waiting for the End (in U.K. as Waiting for the End: The American Literary Scene from Hemingway to Baldwin), 1964; Back to China (novel), 1965; (ed. with J. Vinocur) The Continuing Debate: Essays on Education, 1965; The Last Jew in America (short stories), 1966; (ed. with A. Zeiger) O Brave New World, 1967; The Return of the Vanishing American, 1968; Nude Croquet and Other Stories, 1969; Being Busted, 1970; Collected Essays, 1971; The Stranger in Shakespeare, 1971; To the Gentiles, 1972; Cross the Border, Close the Gap, 1972; The Messenger Will Come No More (novel), 1974; A Fiedler Reader, 1977; Freaks, Myths, and Images of the Secret Self, 1977; An Inadvertent Epic, 1980; Olaf Stapledon, 1982; What Was Literature?, 1982. Add: 154 Morris Ave., Buffalo, N.Y. 14214, U.S.A.

FIELD, D.M. *See* **GRANT,** Neil.

FIELD, Edward. American, b. 1924. Novels, Poetry. Former Lectr., YM-YWHA Poetry Center, NYC. *Publs:* Stand Up, Friend, with Me, 1963; Variety Photoplays, 1967; (ed. and trans.) Eskimo Songs and Stories, 1973; Sweet Gwendolyn and the Countess, 1977; A Full Heart, 1977; Stars in My Eyes, 1978; (ed.) A Geography of Poets, 1979; (co-author) Village (novel), 1982; (co-author) The Office (novel), 1987; New and Selected Poems, 1987. Add: 463 West St., D518, New York, N.Y. 10014, U.S.A.

FIELD, Joanna. *See* **MILNER,** Marion.

FIELD, John. American, b. 1910. Archaeology/Antiquities, Natural history. *Publs:* Two Seas: Nature and Man Around the Mediterranean and the Caribbean, 1970; Cap and Bells, 1974. Add: Apt. 315, 4540 Bee Ridge Rd., Sarasota, Fla. 33583, U.S.A.

FIELD, John. British/New Zealander, b. 1928. Administration/Management, Money/Finance. Lectr., 1958–60, Sr. Lectr., 1960–72, and Assoc. Prof. of Accounting, 1972–86, Univ. of Auckland. *Publs:* Management Accounting: An Information Service, 1962, 3rd ed. 1974; (co-ed.) Corporate Accounting and Financial Institutions: A Bibliography and Review, 1979. Add: 17 Grenada Ave., Auckland 10, New Zealand.

FIELD, Mark G(eorge). American, b. 1923. Medicine/Health, Sociology. Prof. of Sociology, Boston Univ., Mass since 1962, now Emeritus; Asst. Sociologist, Massachusetts Gen. Hosp., Boston, since 1964; Fellow, or Assoc., Russian Research Center, since 1962, Adjunct Prof., Sch. of Public Health, since 1988, Harvard Univ., Cambridge, Mass. (Research Assoc., Russian Research Center, 1959–61; Lectr. on Sociology, Medical Sch., 1971–72). *Publs:* Doctor and Patient in Soviet Russia, 1957; The Social Environment and Its Effect on the Soviet Scientist, 1959; Soviet Socialized Medicine: An Introduction, 1967; Technology, Medicine and Society: Effectiveness, Differentiation and Depersonalization, 1968; (with R.E. Berry, Jr., D. Koch-Weser, J. Karefa-Smart and M. Thompson) Evaluating Health Program Impact: The U.S.-Yugoslav Cooperative Research Effort, 1974; (ed.) The Social Consequences of Modernization in Community Societies, 1976; Soviet Infant Mortality: A Mystery Story, 1986; (with A. d'Houtaud) La Sauté: Approche Psychosociologique, 1989; (ed.) Success and Crisis in National Health Systems, 1989. Add: 40 Peacock Farm Rd., Lexington, Mass. 02173, U.S.A.

FIELD, Peter. *See* **MINES,** Samuel.

FIELDER, Mildred. American, b. 1913. Poetry, History, Biography. Columnist, In Focus, Pen Woman Mag., 1978–81. *Publs:* Wandering Foot in the West (poetry), 1955; Railroads of the Black Hills, 1960, 7th ed., 1985; The Edzards Family and Related Lines, 1965; Wild Bill and Deadwood, 1965, 1969; The Treasure of Homestake Gold, 1970, 1975;

A Guide to the Black Hills Ghost Mines, 1972, 1983; The Chinese in the Black Hills, 1972, 1982; Potato Creek Johnny, 1973, 1980; Hiking Trails in the Black Hills, 1973, 1981; Wild Bill Hickok, Gun Man, 1974, 1979; Theodore Roosevelt in Dakota Territory, 1974; Deadwood Dick and the Dime Novels, 1974, 1984; Sioux Indian Leaders, 1975, 1983; Plant Medicine and Folklore, 1975, 1982; Poker Alice, 1978; Silver Is the Fortune, 1978; Lost Gold, 1978; Preacher Smith of Deadwood, 1981; Fielder's Herbal Helper for Hunters, Trappers, and Fisherman, 1982; The Legend of Lame Johnny Creek, 1982; Wild Fruits: An Illustrated Guide and Cookbook, 1983; Captain Jack Crawford, Poet and Military Scout, 1983; Invitation to Fans, 1988. Add: 264 San Jacinto Dr., Los Osos, Calif. 93402, U.S.A.

FIELDHOUSE, David K(enneth). British, b. 1925. History, Third World Problems. Fellow, Jesus Coll., Cambridge, and Vere Harmsworth Prof. of Imperial and Naval History, Cambridge Univ., since 1981. History teacher, Haileybury Coll., 1950–52; Lectr., Univ. of Canterbury, Christchurch, New Zealand, 1953–57; Beit Lectr. in Commonwealth History, 1958–81, and Fellow, Nuffield Coll., 1966–81, Oxford Univ. Publs: The Colonial Empires, 1966, 1982; The Theory of Capitalist Imperialism, 1967, 1969; Economics and Empire, 1973; Unilever Overseas, 1978; Colonialism 1870-1945, 1981; Black Africa 1945-1980, 1986. Add: Jesus College, Cambridge, England.

FIELDING, A(lexander) W(allace). Also writes as Xan Fielding. British, b. 1918. Travel/Exploration/Adventure, Translations. Publs: as Xan Fielding—The Stronghold: An Account of the Four Seasons in the White Mountains of Crete, 1953; Hide and Seek: The Story of a Wartime Agent, 1954; Corsair Country: The Diary of a Journey Along the Barbary Coast, 1958; The Money Spinner: Monte Carlo Casino, 1977; (ed.) Best of Friends: The Brenan-Partridge Letters, 1986; translations from French as A.W. Fielding—The Walnut Trees of Altenburg, by Andrew Malraux, 1952; In Spite of Blasphemy, by Michel Mourre, 1953; translations from French as Xan Fielding—The Bridge on the River Kwai, by Pierre Boulle, 1954; William Conrad, by Pierre Boulle, 1955; Saving Face, by Pierre Boulle, 1956; White Man's Test, by Pierre Boulle, 1957; Reap the Whirlwind, by Jean Hougron, 1958; Sacrilege in Malaya, by Pierre Boulle, 1959; For a Noble Cause, by Pierre Boulle, 1961; The Centurions, by Jean Larteguy, 1961; The Chinese Executioner, by Pierre Boulle, 1962; Mariners' Prison, by Michael Mohrt, 1963; The Praetorians, by Jean Larteguy, 1963; Monkey Planet, by Pierre Boulle, 1964; Clochemerle les Bains, by Gabriel Chevallier, 1964; Yellow Fever, by Jean Larteguy, 1965; The Garden on the Moon, by Pierre Boulle, 1965; The Hounds of Hell, by Jean Larteguy, 1966; Time Out of Mind and Other Stories, by Pierre Boulle, 1966; The Bronze Drums, by Jean Larteguy, 1967; The Source of the River Kwai, by Pierre Boulle, 1967; An Impartial Eye, by Pierre Boulle, 1968; Sauveterre, by Jean Larteguy, 1968; Farewell to the King, by Pierre Schoendorffer, 1970; Victory at Le Mans, by Bernard Clavel, 1971; No Peace on Earth, by Jean Larteguy, 1971; The Freedom Fighters, by Jean Larteguy, 1972; Furioso, by Valdemar Lestienne, 1972; Don Fernando, by Fernando Fournier-Aubry, 1973; Presumed Dead, by Jean Larteguy, 1974. Add: Apartado 73, Ronda (Malaga), Spain.

FIELDING, Raymond. American, b. 1931. Plays/Screenplays, Film/Media. Prof. and Dir. of the Sch. of Communications, Univ. of Houston, since 1978. Trustee, Univ. Film Foundn., since 1981; Fellow, Soc. of Motion Picture and Television Engineers, since 1976; Member, Academy of Motion Picture Arts and Sciences, since 1981. Lectr., 1957–61, Asst. Prof., 1961–65, and Assoc. Prof., 1965–66, Univ. of California at Los Angeles; Assoc. Prof., Univ. of Iowa, Iowa City, 1966–69; Prof. of Communications, Temple Univ., Philadelphia, 1969–78. Pres., Univ. Film Assn., 1967–68, and Soc. for Cinema Studies, 1972–74. Publs: The Honorable Mountain (screenplay), 1956; The Technique of Special Effects Cinematography, 1965, 4th ed., 1985; (ed.) A Technological History of Motion Pictures and Television, 1967 (Venice Intnl. Film Festival); The American Newsreel, 1911-67, 1972, screenplays, 1975, 1978; The March of Time 1935-1951, 1978. Add: Sch. of Communication, Univ. of Houston, Houston, Tex. 77004, U.S.A.

FIELDS, Victor Alexander. American, b. 1901. Music. Prof. Emeritus of Voice and Diction, City Coll. of New York (joined faculty, 1926). Publs: (with Brommall) Taking the Stage, 1939; Training the Singing Voice, 1947; (with Bender) Voice and Diction, 1949; The Singer's Glossary, 1957; Foundations of the Singer's Art, 1977. Add: Kennedy Plaza, Apt. 1514, Utica, N.Y. 13502, U.S.A.

FIENNES, (Sir) Ranulph (Twisleton-Wykeham-). British, b. 1944. Travel/Exploration/Adventure, Autobiography/Memoirs/Personal. Explorer: led British expeditions to the White Nile, 1969; Jostedalsbre Glacier, 1970; Headless Valley, 1971; towards North Pole, 1977; Transglobe Expedition, 1979–82; first polar circumnavigation of earth. Exec. Consultant to Chmn. of Occidental Petroleum, Inc., 1984–87. Publs: A Talent for Trouble, 1970; Icefall in Norway, 1972; The Headless Valley, 1973; Where Soldiers Fear to Tread, 1975; Hell on Ice, 1979; To the Ends of the Earth, 1983; Bothie, the Polar Dog, 1984; Living Dangerously, 1987. Add: Greenlands, Exford, Minehead, Somerset TA2X 7NU, England.

FIENNES, Richard (Nathaniel Twisleton-Wykeham-). British, b. 1909. Environmental science/Ecology, Medicine/Health, Zoology. Former Head, Dept. of Pathology, Nuffield Inst. of Comparative Medicine, Zoological Soc., Regent's Park, London. Publs: Man, Nature and Disease, 1964; (ed.) Some Recent Developments in Comparative Medicine, 1966; Zoonoses of Primates, 1967; (with A.I. Fiennes) Natural History of the Dog, 1968; (ed.) Biology of Nutrition, 1972; (ed.) Pathology of Simian Primates, 1972; Ecology and Earth Nistory, 1975; Order of Wolves, 1977; Environment of Man, 1977; Zoonoses, and the Origins and Ecology of Human Disease, 1979; Infectious Cancers of Animals and Man, 1982. Add: Tixall Farm House, Tixall, Stafford ST18 0X4, England.

FIERSTEIN, Harvey (Forbes). American, b. 1954. Plays. Gay activist and actor, since 1970. Publs: Torch Song Trilogy, 1981, as film, 1988; La Cage aux Folles, 1983; Forget Him, 1984; Safe Sex, 1987; Spookhouse, 1987. Add: c/o George Lane, William Morris Agency, 1350 Ave. of the Americas, New York, N.Y. 10019, U.S.A.

FIGES, Eva. British, b. 1932. Novels/Short stories, Children's fiction, Women. Publs: Equinox, 1966; Winter Journey, 1967; The Banger, 1968; Konek Landing, 1969; Patriarchial Attitudes: Women in society, 1970; Scribble Sam, 1971; B, 1972; Days, 1974; Tragedy and Social Evolution, 1975; Nelly's Version, 1977; Little Eden: A Child at War, 1978; Waking, 1981; Sex and Subterfuge, 1982; Light, 1983; The Seven Ages, 1986; Ghosts, 1988. Add: 24 Fitzjohn's Ave., London NW3, England.

FIGUEROA, John (Joseph Maria). Jamaican and British, b. 1920. Poetry, Education, Literature, Philosophy. Adviser to the Manchester Education Authority since 1984. Former teacher and lectr. in U.S., and Lectr. in English and Philosophy, Univ. of London; Sports Reporter, since 1945, and Broadcaster, BBC, London; Prof. of Education, Univ. of the West Indies, Kingston, Jamaica, 1957–73; Prof. of Humanities, El Centro Caribeno de Estudios Postgraduados, Puerto Rico, 1973–76; Prof. of Education and Acting Dean, Univ. of Jos, Nigeria, 1976–79; Visiting Prof., Bradford Coll., Yorkshire, 1979–80; Member, Third World Studies Course Team, Open Univ., Milton Keynes, Bucks., 1980–83. Advisor to Manchester Education Council on Education of Caribbean Heritage People, and Hon. Lectr., Manchester Univ., 1983–85; Hon. Fellow, Univ. of Warwich, 1988. Publs: Love Leaps Here, 1962; Staffing and Examination in Secondary Schools in the British Caribbean, 1964; (ed.) Caribbean Voices: An Anthology of West Indian Poetry, 2 vols., 1966-70, 1982; Society, Schools and Progress in the West Indies, 1971; Ignoring Hurts, 1976; (ed. with others) Caribbean Writers, 1979; (ed.) An Anthology of African and Caribbean Writing in English, 1982; (ed.) Caribbean Sampler, 1983. Add: 77 Station Rd., Woburn Sands, Bucks, MK17 8SH, England.

FILBY, P. William. American, b. 1911. Genealogy/Heraldry, History, Transportation. Consultant, Gale Research Co., Detroit, and to Scholarly Resources, Wilmington, Del. Librarian, 1965–72, and Dir., 1972–78, Maryland Historical Soc.; Fellow of the Society of Genealogists, London, 1984. Fellow of National Genealogical Soc., 1985; Fellow of the Manuscript Soc., 1986. Publs: Calligraphy and Handwriting in America, 1710-1962, 1963; (with D. Miner and V. Carlson) 2,000 Years of Calligraphy, 1965; American and British Genealogy and Heraldry, 1970, 3rd ed., 1982, supplement, 1986; (with E.G. Howard) Star-Spangled Books: The History of the Star-Spangled Banner, 1972; Passenger and Immigration Lists Index, 6 vols., suppls., 1982–87; Passenger and Immigration Lists Bibliography 1538-1900, 1981, suppl., 1984–88; (with M.K. Meyer) Who's Who in Genealogy and Heraldry, 1981; Philadelphia Naturalization Records, 1982; Bibliography of American County Histories, 1985; Directory of Libraries with Genealogical Collections, 1988; (with Ira Glazier) Germans to America 1850-1855, 10 vols., 1988–89. Add: 8944 Madison St., Savage, Md. 20763, U.S.A.

FILOSA, Gary (Fairmont Randolph de Marco, II). American, b. 1931. Novels/short stories, Plays/Screenplays, Education, Sports/Physical education/Keeping fit. Author and Editor, The Filosa Newsletter, since 1986. Account Exec. and Ed. of house publication, Robertson, Buckley and Gotsch Inc., Chicago, 1953–54; Account Exec. and Copywriter, Fuller, Smith and Ross Inc., NYC, 1954–55; Ed., Apparel Arts mag., Esquire Inc., NYC, 1955–56; Pres. and Chmn. of the Bd., Filosa Publications, NYC, 1956–61; Publisher, Teenage, Teenlife, Talent, Campus Personalities, Stardust, Mystery Digest, Rock and Roll Roundup, and Rustic Rhythm mags., NYC, 1956–60; Pres., Monclaire Sch., 1958–60; Exec. Asst. to Benjamin A. Javits, 1961–62; Dean of Administration, Postgraduate Center for Mental Health, NYC, 1962–64; Dir., Filosa Films Intnl., 1964–67; Vic Pres. of Academic Affairs, World Academy, San Francisco, 1967–68; Asst. Headmaster and Instr. in Latin, San Miguel Sch., 1968–69; Assoc. Prof. of Philosophy, Art Coll., San Francisco, 1969–70; Vice Pres. of Academic Affairs and Dean of Faculty, Intnl. Inst., Phoenix 1968–73; Pres., Université Universelle, 1970–73; Vice Pres. of Academic Affairs and Dean of Summer Sch., Intnl. Community Coll., Los Angeles, 1970–72; Vice-Pres. for Academic Affairs, Intnl. Inst., 1970–83. Chmn., United Shareowners of America, 1961–67, the Social Directory of the United States, 1967–75, and the Social Directory of California, 1969–75. Pres., American Assn. of Social Directories, 1970–81; Pres., American Surfing Assn., and U.S. Surfing Foundn., 1974–86. *Publs:* Let Me Call Ethel (drama), 1955; (lyricist) Feather Light (musical), 1966; (with Eric Javits) SOS: New York, 1961; No Public Funds for Nonpublic Schools, 1968; Creative Function of the College President, 1969; Corby Price (novel), 1971; Duke Kahanamoku (screenplay), 1973; The Surfers Almanac, 1976; Payne of Florida (TV series), 1985. Add: Viana House, P.O. Box 2042, Miami Beach, Fla. 33140, U.S.A.

FINCH, Christopher. British, b. 1939. Art, Film, Biography. Curator, Walker Art Center, Minneapolis, 1968–69. *Publs:* Pop Art: Object and Image, 1968; Image as Language, 1968; Patrick Caulfield (art), 1971; The Art of Walt Disney, 1973; Rainbow: The Stormy Life of Judy Garland, 1975; Norman Rockwell's America, 1976; Walt Disney's America, 1978; (with Linda Rosenkrantz) Gone Hollywood, 1979; Norman Rockwell's 332 Magazine Covers, 1979; Of Muppets and Men, 1981; The Making of The Dark Crystal, 1983; Special Effects, 1984; American Watercolors, 1986; Twentieth-Century Watercolours, 1988. Add: c/o Abbeville Pr., 505 Park Ave., New York, N.Y. 10022, U.S.A.

FINCH, Matthew. *See* **FINK,** Merton.

FINCH, Merton. *See* **FINK,** Merton.

FINCH, Peter. British, b. 1947. Poetry, Language/Linguistics, Literature. Mgr., Oriel Bookshop, Welsh Arts Council, since 1973. Ed., Second Aeon Publs., since 1966; Treas., Assn. of Little Presses, since 1970. Treas., Yr Academi Gymreig, 1978–81. *Publs:* (with Steve Morris) Wanted, 1968; Pieces of the Universe, 1969; Cycle of the Suns, 1970; Beyond the Silence, 1970; An Alteration in the Way I Breathe, 1970; (with J.W. Rushton) The Edge of Tomorrow, 1971; The End of the Vision, 1971; Whitesung, 1972; Blats, 1973; Anatarktika, 1973; (ed.) Typewriter Poems, 1973; Trowch Eich Radio Ymlaen, 1977; How to Learn Welsh, 1978; (ed., with Meic Stephens). The Green Horse, 1978; Connecting Tubes, 1980; Blues and Heartbreakers, 1981; Big Band Dance Music, 1981; Collected Visual Poetry 1930-50, 1981; Between 35 and 42, 1982; Dances Interdites, 1983; Some Music and a Little War, 1984; On Criticism, 1985; How to Publish Your Poetry, 1985; Reds in the Bed, 1986; Selected Poems, 1987; How to Publish Yourself, 1988. Add: 19 Southminister Rd., Penylan, Cardiff CF2 5AT, Wales.

FINCH, Robert (Duer Claydon). Canadian, b. 1900. Poetry, Literature. Prof. Emeritus of French, Univ. of Toronto, since 1968 (Lectr., 1928–30; Asst. Prof., 1931–42; Assoc. Prof., 1943–51; Prof., 1952–67). *Publs:* (with others) New Provinces, 1936; Poems, 1946; The Strength of the Hills, 1948; A Century Has Roots, 1953; (ed. with C.R. Parsons) René, 1957; Acis in Oxford, 1959, 1961; Dover Beach Revisited, 1961; Silverthorn Bush, 1966; The Sixth Sense, Individualism in French Poetry 1686-1760, 1966, 1968; (ed. with E. Joliat) French Individualist Poetry, 1971; Sir Politick Would-be, 1978; Les Opéra, 1979; Variations and Theme, 1980; Has and Is, 1981; Twelve for Christmas, 1982; The Grand Duke of Moscow's Favorite Solo, 1983; Double Tuning, 1984; For the Back of a Likeness, 1986; Sail-boat and Lake, 1988. Add: Massey Coll., 4 Devonshire Pl., Univ., of Toronto, Toronto, Ont. M5S 2E1, Canada.

FINDLEY, Timothy. Canadian, b. 1930. Novels/Short stories, Plays. Stage, television, and radio actor, 1951–62; Playwright-in-Residence, National Arts Centre, Ottawa, 1974–75; Writer-in-Residence, Univ. of Toronto, 1979–80, Trent Univ., Peterborough, Ont., 1984, and Univ. of Winnipeg, 1985. *Publs:* The Last of the Crazy People (novel), 1967;

The Butterfly Plague (novel), 1969; The Wars (novel), 1977; Can You See Me Yet? (play), 1977; Famous Last Words (novel), 1981; Not Wanted on the Voyage (novel), 1984; Dinner Along the Amazon (short stories), 1984; The Telling of Lies (novel), 1986; Stones (short stories), 1988; also numerous plays, screenplays, and radio and TV plays and documentaries. Add: Box 419, Cannington, Ont. LOE 1EO, Canada.

FINE, Anne. British, b. 1947. Novels, Children's Fiction. Teacher, Cardinal Wiseman Secondary Sch., Coventry, 1968–69, and Saughton Prison, Edinburgh, 1971–72; Information Officer, Oxfam, Oxford, 1969–71. *Publs:* children's fiction—The Summer-House Loon, 1978; The Other, Darker Ned, 1979; The Stone Menagerie, 1980; Round Behind the Ice-House, 1981; The Granny Project, 1983; Scaredy-Cat, 1985; Anneli the Art Hater, 1986; Madame Doubtfire, 1987; Crummy Mummy & Me, 1987; A Pack of Liars, 1988; Goggle-Eyes, 1989; Bill's New Frock, 1989; adult fiction—The Killjoy, 1986. Add: c/o Murray Pollinger, 4 Garrick St., London WC2E 9BH, England.

FINE, Sidney. American, b. 1920. History, Industrial relations. Andrew Dickson White Distinguished Prof. of History, Univ. of Michigan, Ann Arbor, since 1974 (Instr., 1948–51; Asst. Prof., 1951–55; Assoc. Prof., 1955–59; Prof., 1959–74). *Publs:* Laissez Faire and the General Welfare State: A Study of Conflict in American Thought, 1865-1901, 1956; (co-ed.) The American Past: Conflicting Interpretations of the Great Issue, 1961, 4th ed. 1976; (ed.) Recent America, 1962, 1967; The Automobile Under the Blue Eagle: Labor, Management and the Automobile Manufacturing Code, 1963; Sit-Down: The General Motors Strike of 1936-1937, 1969; Frank Murphy: The Detroit Years, 1975; Frank Murphy: The New Deal Years, 1979; Frank Murphy: The Washington Years, 1984. Add: Dept. of History, Univ. of Michigan, Ann Arbor, Mich. 48109, U.S.A.

FINEGAN, Jack. American, b. 1908. Archaeology/Antiquities, Theology/Religion. Minister, First Christian Church, Ames, Iowa, 1934–39; Prof. and Head of Dept. of Religious Education, Iowa State Coll., Ames, 1939–46; Frederick Billings Prof. of New Testament History and Archeology, Pacific Sch. of Religion, Berkeley, Calif., 1946–75; Pastor, University Christian Church, Berkeley, 1949–74. *Publs:* Die Ueberlieferung der Leidens und Auferstehungsgeschichte Jesu, 1934; Light from the Ancient Past, The Archeological Background of the Hebrew-Christian Religion, 1946, rev. ed. 1959; Book of Student Prayers, 1946; A Highway Shall Be There, 1946; Youth Asks About Religion, 1949; Like the Great Mountains, 1949; The Archeology of World Religions, 1952; Rediscovering Jesus, 1952; Clear of the Brooding Cloud, 1953; The Orbits of Life, 1954; India Today, 1955; Wanderer Upon Earth (novel), 1956; Beginnings in Theology, 1956; Christian Theology, 1957; 40 Questions and Answers on Religion, 1958; Space, Atoms, and God, 1959; First Steps in Theology, 1960; Step by Step in Theology, 1962; In the Beginning, 1962; Let My People Go, 1963; At Wit's End, 1963; The Three R's in Christianity, 1964; Jesus, History and You, 1964; Handbook of Biblical Chronology, 1964; Hidden Records of the Life of Jesus, 1969; The Archeology of the New Testament: The Life of Jesus, and the Beginning of the Early Church, 1969; Mark of the Taw (novel), 1972; The Christian Church, 1973; Encountering New Testament Manuscripts, 1974; Archeological History of the Ancient Middle East, 1978; The Archeology of the New Testament: The Mediterranean World of the Early Christian Apostles, 1981; Discovering Israel: An Archeological Guide to the Holy Land, 1981; Tibet: A Dreamt-of Image, 1986; Myth and Mystery: An Introduction to the Pagan Religions of the Biblical World, 1989; An Archaeological History of Religions of Indian Asia, 1989. Add: 1798 Scenic Ave., Berkeley, Calif. 94709, U.S.A.

FINER, Samuel (Edward). British, b. 1915. Politics/Government. Gladstone Prof. of Politics, Oxford Univ., 1974–82, now Emeritus. Lectr. in Politcs, 1946–49, and Jr. Research Fellow, 1949–50, Balliol Coll., Oxford; Prof. of Political Institutions, 1950–66, and Deputy Vice Chancellor, 1962–64, Univ. of Keele, Staffs; Prof. of Government, Univ. of Manchester, 1966–74. Chmn., Political Studies Assn. of the U.K., 1965–69. *Publs:* A Primer of Public Administration, 1950; The Life and Times of Sir Edwin Chadwick, 1952; (with Sir J. Maud) Local Government in England and Wales, 1953; Anonymous Empire: A Study of the Lobby in Britain, 1958, 1966; Private Industry and Political Power, 1958; (with D. Bartholomew and H. Berrington) Backbench Opinion in the House of Commons 1955-59, 1961; The Man on Horseback: The Role of the Military in Politics, 1962, 1988; (ed.) Sieves: What Is the Third Estate, 1963; Great Britain in Modern Political Systems: Europe (ed. by Macridis and Ward), 1963, 1980; (ed.) Pareto: Sociological Writings, 1966; Comparative Government, 1970; Adversary Politics and Electoral Reform, 1975; Five Constitutions, 1979; The Changing British Party Systems, 1980; The British Party System, 1986.   Add: All Souls Coll., Oxford; 48 Lonsdale Road, Oxford, England.

FINGER, Seymour (Maxwell). American, b. 1915. International relations/Current affairs, Politics/Government, Essays. Prof. of Political Science, the Grad. Sch. and the Coll. of Staten Island, City Univ. of New York, and Dir. of the Ralph Bunche Inst. on the United Nations. Pres., Inst. for Mediterranean Affairs, since 1971. Formerly, career office in the U.S. Foreign Service: Vice-Consul, Stuttgart, 1946–49; Second Secty., American Embassy, Paris, 1949–51, American Legation, Budapest, 1951–53, and American Embassy, Rome, 1954–55; First Secty., American Embassy, Laos, 1955–56; Sr. Adviser on Economics and Social Affairs, U.S. Mission to the U.N., 1956–65; Counselor of Mission, 1965–67; Ambassador and Sr. Adviser to the U.S. Permanent Rep. to the U.N., 1967–71. *Publs:* (ed. and contrib.) The New World Balance and Peace in the Middle East, 1975; (ed. with Yonah Alexander) Terrorism: Interdisciplinary Perspectives, 1977; (ed. with Joseph R. Harbert and contributor) U.S. Policies in International Institutions, 1978; Your Man at the U.N.: People, Politics and Bureaucracy in the Making of American Foreign Policy, 1980, rev. ed. as American Ambassadors at the U.N., 1986; American Jewry During the Holocaust, 1984. Add: c/o Holmes and Meier, 30 Irving Pl., New York, N.Y. 10003, U.S.A.

FINK, Augusta. American, b. 1916. Children's fiction, History, Biography. With Los Angeles County Civil Service Dept., 1945–60; Owner and Mgr., Shorebird Bookstore, Palos Verdes Peninsula, Calif., 1960–67. *Publs:* The Pales Verdes Peninsula: Time and the Terraced Land, 1966, 1987; To Touch the Sky (children), 1971; Monterey—The Presence of the Past, 1972; Adobes in the Sun (history), 1972; Room and Time Enough: The Land of Mary Austin, 1979; I, Mary: A Biography of Mary Austin, 1983. Add: Del Mesa Carmel 60, Carmel, Calif. 93921, U.S.A.

FINK, Merton. Writes as Matthew Finch and Merton Finch. British, b. 1921. Novels/Short stories, Historical/Romance/Gothic, Education (not textbooks on other subjects), Humor/Satire. Dental Surgeon, National Health Service, since 1952. *Publs:* all as Matthew Finch except as noted—Dentist in the Chair, 1955; Teething Troubles, 1956; The Third Set, 1957; Hang Your Hat on a Pension, 1958; Empire Builder, 1959; Snakes and Ladders, 1960; Solo Fiddle, 1961; Beauty Bazaar, 1962; The Match Breakers, 1963; Five as the Symbols, 1964; Chew This Over, 1965; The Succubus, 1966; Eye with Mascara, 1967; (as Merton Finch) Simon Bar Cochba, 1971; A Fox Called Flavius, 1974; (with Bill Tidy) Open Wide, 1975; Matilda the Ironside, 1975; Molly on the Seashore, 1983. Add: Quill Cottage, 27 Harbutts, Bathampton, Bath BA2 6TA, England.

FINKEL, Donald. American, b. 1929. Poetry. Poet-in-Residence, Washington Univ., St. Louis, Mo., since 1960. Instr., Univ. of Iowa, Iowa City, 1957–58, and Bard Coll., Annandale-on-Hudson, N.Y., 1958–60; Visiting Lectr., Bennington Coll., Vt., 1966–67, and Princeton Univ., N.J., 1985. *Publs:* The Clothing's New Emperor and Other Poems, 1959; The Jar (play), 1961; Simeon: Poems, 1964; A Joyful Noise: Poems, 1966; Answer Back, 1968; The Garbage Wars: Poems, 1970; Adequate Earth, 1972; A Mote in Heaven's Eye, 1975; Going Under and Endurance, 1978; What Manner of Beast, 1981; The Detachable Man, 1984; The Wake of the Electron, 1987; Selected Shorter Poems, 1987. Add: 6943 Columbia Pl., St. Louis, Mo. 63130, U.S.A.

FINLAY, Ian. British, b. 1906. Architecture, Arts, Crafts, History. Prof. of Antiquities to the Royal Scottish Academy. Secty., Royal Fine Art Commn. for Scotland, 1953–61; Keeper, Dept. of Art and Ethnology, 1955–61, and Dir., 1961–71, Royal Scottish Museum, Edinburgh. Member, Scottish Arts Council, 1947–60. *Publs:* Scotland, 1945, rev. ed. 1957; Scottish Art, 1945; Art in Scotland, 1948; Scottish Crafts, 1948; Scottish Tradition in Silver, 1948; Scottish Architecture, 1951; Treasures in Edinburgh, 1951; Scotland, 1953, 1956; A History of Scottish Gold and Silver Work, 1956; The Lothians, 1960; The Highlands, 1963; The Young Robert Louis Stevenson, 1965; The Lowlands, 1967; Celtic Art: An Introduction, 1973; Priceless Heritage: The Future of Museums, 1977; Columba, 1979. Add: Currie Riggs, Balerno, Midlothian EH14 5AG, Scotland.

FINLAY, Ian Hamilton. British, b. 1925. Short stories, Poetry. Publr., Wild Hawthorn Press, Dunsyre, Lanarkshire (formerly in Edinburgh and Easter Ross), since 1961. *Publs:* The Sea-Bed and Other Stories, 1958; The Dancers Inherit the Party, 1960; Glasgow Beasts, an a Burd, 1961; Concertina, 1962; Rapel, 1963; Canal Stripe Series 3 and 4, 1964; Telegrams from My Windmill, 1964; Ocean Stripe Series 2 and 3, 1965; Cythera, 1965; Autumn Poem, 1966; 6 Small Pears for Eugene Gomringer, 1966; 6 Small Songs in 3's, 1955; Tea-Leaves and Fishes, 1966;

Ocean Stripe Series 4, 1966; 4 Sails, 1966; Headlines, Eavelines, 1967; Stonechats, 1967; Ocean Stripe Series 5, 1967; Canal Game, 1967; The Collected Coaltown of Challange Tri-kai, 1968; Air Letters, 1968; The Blue and the Brown Poems, 1968; 3/3's, 1969; A Boatyard, 1969; Lanes, 1969; Wave, 1969; Rhymes for Lemons, 1970; "Fishing News" News, 1970; 30 Signatures to Silver Catches, 1971; Poems to Hear and See, 1971; A Sailor's Calendar, 1971; The Olsen Exerpts, 1971; A Memory of Summer, 1971; From "An Island Garden", 1971; Evening/Sail 2, 1971; The Weed Boat Masters Ticket, Preliminary Text (Part Two), 1971; Sail/Sundial, 1972; Jibs, 1972; Honey by the Water, 1973; Butterflies, 1973; A Family, 1973; Exercise X, 1974; So You Want to Be a Panzer Leader, 1975; Airs Waters-Graces, 1975; The Wild Hawthorn Wonder Book of Boats, 1975; A Master of Hankies, 1975; The Axis, 1975; Trombone Carrier, 1975; Homage to Watteau, 1975; Three Sundials, 1975; Imitations, Variations, Reflections, Copies, 1976; The Wild Hawthorn Art Test, 1977; Heroic Emblems, 1977; The Boy's Alphabet Book, 1977; The Wartime Garden, 1977; Trailblazers, 1978; Homage to Poussin, 1978; Peterhead Fragments, 1979; "SS", 1979; Dzaezl, 1979; Woods and Seas, 1979; Two Billows, 1979; Romances, Emblems, Enigmas, 1981; Developments, 1982. Add: Stoneypath, Dunsyre, Lanarkshire, Scotland.

FINLAY, William. *See* MACKAY, James Alexander.

FINLAY, Winifred (Lindsay Crawford). British, b. 1910. Children's fiction. Schoolmistress, Newcastle upon Tyne, 1933–35, Stratford-upon-Avon, 1941–44, and Leeds, 1944–48. *Publs:* The Castle and the Cave, 1961; Alison in Provence, 1963; Mystery in the Middle Marches, 1964; Castle for Four, 1966; Folk Tales from the North, 1968; Danger at Black Dyke, 1968; Summer of the Golden Stag, 1969; Cry of the Peacock, 1969; Folk Tales from Moor and Mountain, 1969; Singing Stones, 1970; Beadbonny Ash, 1973; Cap o' Rushes, 1974; Tattercoats, 1976; (with Gillian Hancock) Ghosts, Ghouls, and Spectres, 1976; (with Hancock) Spies and Secret Agents, 1977; (with Hancock) Treasure Hunters, 1977; (with Hancock) Clever and Courageous Dogs, 1978; Tales from the Hebrides and Highlands, 1978; (with Hancock) Famous Flights of Airships and Balloons, 1979; Tales from the Borders, 1979; Tales of Sorcery and Witchcraft, 1980; Tales of Fantasy and Fear, 1981; Fight for Life, 1981; Secret Rooms and Hiding Places, 1982; Werewolves, Vampires and Phantoms of the Night, 1983. Add: The Old House, Walgrave, Northampton, England.

FINLAYSON, Roderick (David). New Zealander, b. 1904. Novels/Short stories, History, Literature. *Publs:* Brown Man's Burden, 1938; Our Life in This Land, 1940; Sweet Beulah Land, 1942; Tidal Creek, 1948; The Schooner Came to Atia, 1952; (with Joan Smith) The Maori of New Zealand, 1959; The Springing Fern, 1965; D'Arcy Cresswell, 1972; Brown Man's Burden and Later Stories, 1973; Other Lovers (stories), 1976. Add: 46 McLeod Rd., Weymouth, Manurewa, New Zealand.

FINLEY, Glenna. American, b. 1925. Historical/Romance/Gothic. Freelance writer since 1957. Announcer, KEVR-Radio, Seattle, 1941–42; Producer, NBC Intnl. Div., NYC, 1945–47; Film Librarian, March of Time newsreel series, NYC, 1947–48; News Bureau Staff Member, Time Inc., NYC, 1948–49. *Publs:* Death Strikes Out, 1957; Career Wife, 1964, in paperback title as A Tycoon for Ann; Nurse Pro Tem, 1967; Journey to Love, 1970; Love's Hidden Fire, 1971; Treasure of the Heart, 1971; Love Lies North, 1972; Bridal Affair, 1972; Kiss a Stranger, 1972; Love in Danger, 1973; When Love Speaks, 1973; The Romantic Spirit, 1973; Surrender My Love, 1974; A Promising Affair, 1974; Love's Magic Spell, 1974; The Reluctant Maiden, 1975; The Captured Heart, 1975; Holiday for Love, 1976; Love for a Rogue, 1976; Storm of Desire, 1977; Dare to Love, 1977; To Catch a Bride, 1977; Master of Love, 1978; Beware My Heart, 1978; The Marriage Merger, 1978; Wildfire of Love, 1979; Timed for Love, 1979; Love's Temptation, 1979; Stateroom for Two, 1980; Affairs of Love, 1980; Midnight Encounter, 1981; Return Engagement, 1981; One Way to Love, 1982; Taken by Storm, 1982; A Business Affair, 1983; Wanted for Love, 1983; A Weekend for Love, 1984; Love's Waiting Game, 1985; A Touch of Love, 1985; Diamonds for My Love, 1986; Secret of Love, 1987. Add: P.O. Box 866182, Plano, Tex. 75086, U.S.A.

FINN, R(alph) L(eslie). British, b. 1922. Novels/Short stories, Sports, Autobiography/Memoirs/Personal. Freelance advertising and publicity consultant; Tutor in English. Feature writer, Reynolds News, 1937–40, People, 1941–47, Birmingham Daily Mail, and Daily Mail, London, 1953–55; Creative Dir., various advertising agencies, 1955–70. *Publs:* Out of the Depths; Down Oxford Street; He Said, What's Blue?; Time Marches Sideways; Twenty Seven Stairs; The Peephole; After the Sickness; And the Ants Came; Freaks v. Supermen; Captive on a Flying Saucer: The Lunatic Lover and Poet; Waiting Room; And All Is Mist; Return to Earth; I Sent You Red Roses; Death of a Dream; Bleu; My Greatest Game; World Cup 1954; Spurs Supreme; Spurs Go Marching On; Spurs Again; Arsenal: Chapman to Mee; Champions Again: Manchester United 1965; England World Champions 1966; London's Cup Final 1967; World Cup 1970; Official History of Tottenham Hotspur 1972; History of Chelsea; No Tears in Aldgate; Spring in Aldgate; Saturday Afternoon (screenplay); Punch Drunk (screenplay); Time Remembered, Grief Forgotten, 1985. Add: 7 Red Lodge, Red Road, Elstree, Herts., WD6 4SN, England.

FINNEGAN, Frances (Elizabeth). British, b. 1941. Sociology, Urban studies. Research Fellow, Univ. of New York, 1975–76. *Publs:* (with E.M. Sigsworth) Poverty and Social Policy, 1978; Poverty and Prostitution: Study of Victorian Prostitutes in New York, 1979; Poverty and Prejudice: Irish Immigrants in York 1840-1875, 1981. Add: Mount Alto, Woodstown, Co. Waterford, Ireland.

FINNERAN, Richard J(ohn). American, b. 1943. Literature. Hodges Chair of Excellence Prof. of English, Univ. of Tennessee, Knoxville, since 1988. Instr., Univ. of Florida, 1967–68; Instr., New York Univ., 1968–70; Asst. Prof., 1970–74, Assoc. Prof., 1974–77, and Prof. of English, 1977–88, Newcomb Coll., Tulane Univ., New Orleans. *Publs:* (ed.) John Sherman and Dhoya by W.B. Yeats, 1969; (ed.) William Butler Yeats: The Byzantium Poems, 1970; The Prose Fiction of W.B. Yeats: The Search for "Those Simple Forms", 1973; (ed.) Letters of James Stephens, 1974; (ed.) Anglo-Irish Literature: A Review of Research, 1976; (ed.) The Correspondence of Robert Bridges and W.B. Yeats, 1977; (ed. with George Mills Harper and William M. Murphy) Letters to W.B. Yeats, 1977; (ed.) Recent Research in Anglo-Irish Writers, 1982; (ed.) Yeats Annual, since 1982; Editing Yeats's Poems 1983; (ed.) The Poems of W.B. Yeats, 1983, 1989; (ed.) Critical Essays on W.B. Yeats, 1986; (ed.) W.B. Yeats, Collected Poems, 1989; Editing Yeats's Poems: A Reconsideration, 1989. Add: 243 Evangeline Dr., Mandeville, La. 70448, U.S.A.

FINNEY, Jack. (Walter Braden Finney). American, b. 1911. Novels/Short stories, Mystery/Crime/Suspense, Science fiction. *Publs:* Five Against the House (mystery novel), 1954; The Body Snatchers (novel), 1955; Telephone Roulette (play), 1956; The House of Numbers (mystery novel), 1957; The Third Level (short stories), 1957 (in U.K. as The Clock of Time, 1958); Assault on a Queen (mystery novel), 1959; Good Neighbor Sam (novel), 1963; I Love Galesburg in the Springtime (short stories), 1963; The Woodrow Wilson Dime (novel), 1968; Time and Again (novel), 1970; Marion's Wall (novel), 1973; The Night People (mystery novel), 1977; Forgotten News: The Crime of the Century and Other Lost Stories, 1983. Add: c/o Harold Matson Co., 276 Fifth Ave., New York, N.Y. 10001, U.S.A.

FINNEY, Patricia (Deirdre Emoke). British, b. 1958. Novels/Short stories. Freelance journalist. *Publs:* A Shadow of Gulls, 1977; The Crow Goddess, 1978. Add: c/o Collins, 8 Grafton St., London W1X 3LA, England.

FINNIGAN, Joan. Canadian, b. 1925. Children's fiction, Poetry, Area studies (oral history and Canadian culture), Children's non-fiction. Poet, oral historian. Former schoolteacher and journalist. *Publs:* poetry—A Dream of Lilies, 1965; Through the Glass, Darkly, 1965; Entrance to the Greenhouse, 1968; In the Brown Cottage on Loughborough Lake, 1970; It Was Warm and Sunny When We Set Out, 1970; Living Together, 1976; A Reminder of Familiar Faces, 1978; This Series Has Been Discontinued, 1980; The Watershed Collection, 1988; other—(as Michelle Bedard) Canada in Bed, 1967; Kingston: Celebrate This City, 1976; I Come from the Valley, 1976; Canadian Colonial Cooking, 1976; Some of the Stories I Told You Were True, 1981; Giants of Canada's Ottawa Valley, 1981; Look! The Land is Growing Giants, 1983; Laughing All the Way Home, 1984; Legacies, Legends and Lies, 1985; Tell Me Another Story (oral history), 1988; Finnigan's Guide to the Ottawa Valley, 1988; The Dog That Wouldn't Be Left Behind (children's), 1989. Add: Hartington, Ont. K0H 1W0, Canada.

FIORE, Peter A(madeus). American, b. 1927. Literature. Prof. of English, Siena Coll., Loudonville, N.Y., since 1971 (Instr., 1957–58; Asst. Prof., 1961–66; Chmn. of Dept., 1962–67; Assoc. Prof., and Dean of Arts, 1966–71). Roman Catholic Priest, Order of Friars Minor. *Publs:* Th'Up-right Heart and Pure, 1967; (ed.) Just So Much Honor: Essays Commemorating the 400th Anniversary of the Birth of John Donne, 1972; Milton and Augustine: Patterns of Augustinian Thought in Milton's Paradise Lost, 1981. Add: Siena Coll., Loudonville, N.Y. 12211, U.S.A.

FIRCHOW, Peter. American, b. 1937. Literature, Translations. Prof. of English and Comparative Literature, Univ. of Minnesota, Minneapolis (joined faculty, 1967). Asst. Prof. of English, Univ. of Michigan, Ann Arbor, 1965–67. Pres., Midwest Modern Language Assn., 1977–78; Visiting Prof., National Cheng Kung Univ., Taiwan, 1982–83. *Publs:* (trans. and author of introduction) Lucinde and the Fragments, 1971; Aldous Huxley, Satirist and Novelist, 1972; (ed. and interviewer) The Writer's Place, 1974; (ed. and trans. with E.S. Firchow) East German Short Stories: An Introductory Anthology, 1979; The End of Utopia: A Study of Huxley's Brave New World, 1984; The Death of the German Cousin: Variations on a Literary Stereotype, 1890-1920, 1986. Add: 135 Birnamwood Dr., Burnsville, Minn. 55337, U.S.A.

FIRESIDE, Harvey F. American, b. 1929. Politics/Government. Charles A. Dana Prof. of Politics, Ithaca Coll., N.Y., since 1977 (Asst. Prof., 1968–70; Assoc. Prof., 1970–74; Prof., 1974–77). Asst. Prof. of Social Science, New York Inst. of Technology, NYC, 1964–68. *Publs:* Icon and Swastika: The Russian Orthodox Church Under Nazi and Soviet Control, 1971; Soviet Psychoprisons, 1979. Add: Dept. of Politics, Ithaca Coll., Ithaca, N.Y. 14850, U.S.A.

FIRESTONE, O. J(ohn). Canadian, b. 1913. Advertising/Public relations, Economics. Prof. of Economics, Univ. of Ottawa, Ont., since 1960 (Vice Dean, Faculty of Social Sciences, 1964–70). Economist, Dir. of Economic Research, and Economic Adviser, Govt. of Canada, 1942–60; Member, Royal Commn. on Health Services, 1961–64. *Publs:* Private and Public Investment in Canada 1926-1951, 1951; Residential Real Estate in Canada, 1951; Canada's Economic Growth, 1965; Broadcast Advertising in Canada: Past and Future Growth, 1966; The Economic Implications of Advertising, 1967; Industry and Education: A Century of Canadian Development, 1969; The Public Persuader, 1970; Economic Implications of Patents, 1971; (ed. and contrib.) Economic Growth Reassessed, 1972; (ed. and contrib.) Regional Economic Development, 1974; Canada's Anti-Inflation Program and Kenneth Galbraith, 1977; The Other A.Y. Jackson, 1979. Add: Dept. of Economics, Faculty of Social Sciences, Univ. of Ottawa, 550 Cumberland St., Ottawa, Canada.

FIREY, Walter Irving. American, b. 1916. Sociology. Retired Prof. of Sociology, Univ. of Texas, Austin, since 1985 (Asst. Prof., 1946–47; Assoc. Prof., 1947–59). Asst. Prof., Michigan State Univ., East Lansing, 1945–46; Fellow, Center for Advanced Study in the Behavioral Science, 1959–60; Advisory Ed., Social Science quarterly, 1967–85. *Publs:* Land Use in Central Boston, 1946; (co-ed.) Selected Readings in an Introduction to Sociology, 1954; Man, Mind and Land: A Theory of Resource Use, 1960; Law and Economy in Planning, 1965; The Study of Possible Societies, 1977. Add: Dept. of Sociology, Univ. of Texas, Austin, Tex. 78712, U.S.A.

FIRKINS, Peter Charles. Australian, b. 1926. History, Military/-defence. Business exec. Dir., Perth Chamber of Commerce, 1963–82. Gen. Secty., Liberal Party of Australia, Hobart, 1957–62. *Publs:* Strike and Return, 1964; The Australians in Nine Wars, 1971; Of Nautilus and Eagles, 1975; From Hell to Eternity, 1979; (ed.) A History of Commerce and Industry in Western Australia, 1979; The Golden Eagles, 1980; Service Above Self, 1987. Add: 22 Sudbury Way, City Beach, W.A. 6009, Australia.

FIRTH, (Sir) Raymond (William). British, b. 1901. Anthropology/Ethnology, Sociology. Prof. Emeritus, London School of Economics, since 1968 (Lecturer in Anthropology, 1933–35; Reader, 1935–44; Prof., 1944–68). Honorary Secretary, 1936–39, and President, 1953–55, Royal Anthropological Institute; Life President, Assn. of Social Anthropologists of the Commonwealth. *Publs:* The Kauri-Gum Industry: Some Economic Aspects, 1924; Primitive Economics of the New Zealand Maori, 1929, as Economics of the New Zealand Maori, 1959; (ed., with E.E. Evans-Pritchard and others) Essays Presented to C.G. Seligman, 1934; Art and Life in New Guinea, 1936; We the Tikopia: A Sociological Study of Kinship in Primitive Polynesia, 1936, 1961; Human Types: An Introduction to Social Anthropology, 1938, 1975; Primitive Polynesian Economy, 1939; The Work of the Gods in Tikopia, 1940, 1967; Malay Fishermen: Their Peasant Economy, 1946, 1966; Elements of Social Organization, 1951, 3rd ed. 1971; The Fate of the Soul: An Interpretation of Some Primitive Concepts, 1955; (ed. and contributor) Two Studies of Kinship in London, 1956; (ed. and contributor) Man and Culture: An Evaluation of the Work of Bronislaw Malinowski, 1957; Social Anthropology as Science and as Art, 1958; Social Change in Tikopia: A Re-Study of a Polynesian Community After a Generation, 1959; History and Traditions of Tikopia, 1961; (with James Spillius) A Study in Ritual Modification: The Work of the Gods in Tikopia in 1929 and 1952, 1963; Essays on Social Organization and Values, 1964, 1969; (ed., with B.S. Yamey, and contributor) Capital, Saving, and Credit in Peasant Societies from Asia, Oceania, the Caribbean, and Middle America, 1964; Tikopia Ritual and Belief, 1967; (ed. and contributor) Themes in Economic Anthropology, 1967; (ed. and commentator) Kinship and Social Organization by William Halse Rivers, 1968; (ed., with Jane Hubert and Anthony Forge) Families and Their Relatives: Kinship in a Middle-Class Sector of London—An Anthropological Study, 1969; Rank and Religion in Tikopia, 1970; The Skeptical Anthropologist? Social Anthropology and Marxist Views on Society, 1972; Symbols: Public and Private, 1973; Tikopia—English Dictionary, 1985. Add: 33 Southwood Ave., London N6 5SA, England.

FISCH, Harold. British/Israeli, b. 1923. Literature. Prof. of English, Bar-Ilan Univ., Israel, since 1964 (Assoc. Prof., 1957–64; Rector of Univ., 1968–71). Lectr. in English Language and Literature, Univ. of Leeds, 1947–57. *Publs:* The Dual Image, 1959, 1971; Jerusalem and Albion (literary history), 1964; (trans.) Haggada, 1965, 1973; (ed.) The Five Books of the Tora and the Haftarot, 1967; (ed.) Mans Mortalitie, by Richard Overton, 1968; (ed.) The Koren Jerusalem Bible, 1969; Hamlet and the Word, 1971; S.Y. Agnon, 1975; The Zionist Revolution, 1978; A Remembered Future, 1984; Poetry with a Purpose, 1988. Add: 4 Shmaryahu Levin St., Jerusalem, Israel.

FISCHER, Bruno. Has also written as Russell Gray. American, b. 1908. Mystery/Crime/Suspense. *Publs:* So Much Blood, 1939 (in U.S. paperback, Stairway to Death, 1951); The Hornet's Nest, 1944; Quoth the Raven, 1944 (in U.K. as Croaked the Raven, 1947; in U.S. paperback, The Fingered Man, 1953); The Dead Men Grin, 1945; Kill to Fit, 1946; The Pigskin Bag, 1946; The Spider Lily, 1946; More Deaths Than One, 1947; The Bleeding Scissors, 1948 (in U.K. as The Scarlet Scissors, 1950); The Restless Hands, 1949; (as Russell Gray) The Lustful Ape, 1950, as Bruno Fischer 1959; The Angels Fell, 1950 (in U.S. paperback, The Flesh Was Cold, 1951); House of Flesh, 1950; The Silent Dust, 1950; Fools Walk In, 1951; The Lady Kills, 1951; The Paper Circle, 1951 (in U.S. paperback, Stripped for Murder, 1953); The Fast Buck, 1952; (ed.) Crooks' Tour, 1953; Run for Your Life, 1953; So Wicked My Love, 1954; Knee-Deep in Death, 1956; Murder in the Raw, 1957; Second-Hand Nude, 1959; The Girl Between, 1960; The Evil Days, 1974. Add: 19 Twin Pines Rd., Putnam Valley, N.Y. 10579, U.S.A.

FISCHER, Edward A. American, b. 1914. Plays/Screenplays, Film, History, Travel/Exploration/Adventure. Prof., Dept. of Communication Arts, Univ. of Notre Dame, Ind., since 1947. *Publs:* Shake Down the Thunder (screenplay), 1954; Life Without Germs (screenplay), 1956; The Poetry of Polymers (screenplay), 1957; The Screen Arts, 1960; War on Gobbledygook (screenplay), 1964; Elements of Film (screenplay), 1965; Visual Language of Film (screenplay), 1965; The Nature of the Film Medium (screenplay), 1965; Film as an Art (screenplay), 1965; Film as Insight, 1972; Why Americans Retire Abroad, 1974; Light in the Far East, 1976; Everybody Steals from God, 1977; Mindanano Mission, 1978; Mission in Burma, 1980; Fiji Revisited, 1981; Maybe a Second Spring, 1983; Japan Journey, 1984; Journeys not Regretted, 1986; Notre Dame Remembered (autobiography), 1987; Life in the Afternoon, 1987. Add: Dept. of American Studies, Univ. of Notre Dame, Notre Dame, Ind. 46556, U.S.A.

FISCHER, Robert H. American, b. 1918. Theology/Religion, Biography, Memoirs/Personal, Translations. Minister, Hartland Community Parish, Vt., 1944–45; Asst. Pastor, Zion Lutheran Church, Sunbury, Pa., 1947–49; Prof. of Church History, Lutheran Sch. of Theology, Chicago, 1949–86. *Publs:* (trans. and ed.) Luther's Large Catechism, in the Lutheran Book of Concord, 1959; (trans. and ed.) Luther's Works, vol. 37, 1961; (trans.) Luther by Franz Lau, 1963; (trans.) Melanchthon by Robert Stupperich, 1965; (ed.) Luther, 1966; (ed.) Franklin Clark Fry, 1972; (ed.) A Tribute to Arthur Voobus, 1977. Add: 5324 Central Ave., Western Springs, IL. 60558, U.S.A.

FISH, Stanley E(ugene). American, b. 1938. Law, Literature. Arts and Sciences Distinguished Prof. of English, and Prof. of Law, and Chmn. of the Dept. of English, Duke Univ., Durham, since 1988. Member of the editorial board, Milton Quarterly, Milton Studies, Medievalia et Humanistica, Journal on Law and Literature, and Poetics Today. Asst. Prof., 1963–67, and Assoc. Prof., 1967–74, Univ. of California, Berkeley; Leonard S. Bing Visiting Prof., Univ. of Southern California, Los Angeles, 1973–74; Prof. of English, 1974–78, and Kenan Prof. of English and Humanities, 1978–85; Johns Hopkins Univ., Baltimore; Adjunct Prof., Univ. of Maryland Law Sch., 1976–85; Visiting Prof., Columbia Univ., NYC, 1983,19688. *Publs:* John Skelton's Poetry, 1965; Surprised by

Sin: The Reader in Paradise Lost, 1967; Self-Consuming Artifacts: The Experience of Seventeenth-Century Literature, 1972; The Living Temple: George Herbert and Catechizing, 1978; Is There a Text in This Class? The Authority of Interpretive Communities, 1980; Doing What Comes Naturally: Change, Rhetoric, and the Practice of Theory in Legal and Literary Studies, 1989. Add:

FISHBURN, Angela Mary. British, b. 1933. Crafts, Homes/Gardens. Part-time tutor in Adult Education, Herts. and Bucks. County Councils, since 1964. *Publs:* Lampshades: Technique and Design, 1975; The Batsford Book of Soft Furnishings (Home Furnishings), 2 vols, 1978–82; Curtains and Window Treatments, 1982; Batsford Book of Lampshades, 1984; Creating Your Own Soft Furnishings, 1984; Soft Furnishings for the Bedroom, 1988. Add: Oak Farm, Ashley Green, nr. Chesham, Bucks., England.

FISHER, A. Stanley T. Also writes as Michael Scarrott. British, b. 1906. Novels/Short stories, Poetry, History, Theology/Religion. Asst. Master, St. Paul's Sch., Darjeeling, 1929–31, Bryanston Sch., Dorset, 1931–34, and Little Messenden Abbey Sch., Buckinghamshire, 1935–36; Principal, Brickwall Sch., Sussex, 1936–37; Asst. Master and Chaplain, Leeds Grammar Sch., Yorkshire, 1937–43, De Aston Sch., Market Rasen, Lincs., 1943–46, and Magdalen Coll. Sch., Oxford, 1946–60; Rector of Westwell, and Vicar of Holwell, West Oxfordshire, 1961–74. *Publs:* An Anthology of Prayers, 1934. 5th ed. 1950; The Reach of Words (verse), 1935; Voice and Verse: An Anthology in Three Parts for Community-Speaking in Schools, 1946; The Comet and Earlier Poems, 1948; Happy Families: The Story of Sex for Boys and Girls, 1950; (as Michael Scarrott) Ambassador of Loss (novel), 1955; Notes on Three Gospels and The Acts, 1956; The Story of Life, 1957; Fifty Days to Easter, 1964; History of Broadwell, Oxfordshire, with Filkins, Kelmscott and Holwell, 1968; The History of Kencot, 1970; The History of Westwell, 1972; (with D.G.O. Ayerst) Records of Christianity, vol. I, In the Roman Empire, 1970, vol. II, Christendom, 1977; Selected Poems, 1978. Add: 72 Rosamund Rd., Oxford OX2 8NX, England.

FISHER, Aileen (Lucia). American, b. 1906. Children's fiction, Plays/Screenplays, Poetry. Dir., Women's National Journalistic Register, Chicago, 1929–32; Research Asst., Labor Bureau of the Middle West, Chicago, 1931–32. *Publs:* children's fiction—Over the Hills to Nugget, 1949; Trapped by the Mountain Storm, 1950; Homestead of the Free: The Kansas Story, 1953; Timber! Logging in Michigan, 1955; Off to the Gold Fields, 1955, retitled as Secret in the Barrel, 1965; Cherokee Strip: The Race for Land, 1956; A Lantern in the Window, 1957; Skip, 1958; Fisherman of Galilee, 1959; Summer of Little Rain, 1961; My Cousin Abe, 1962; Arbor Day, 1965; (with Olive Rabe) Human Rights Day, 1966; plays—The Squanderbug's Christmas Carol, 1943; The Squanderbug's Mother Goose, 1944; A Tree to Trim: A Christmas Play, 1945; What Happened to Toyland, 1945; Nine Cheers for Christmas: A Christmas Pageant, 1945; Before and After: A Play About the Community School Lunch Program, 1945; All Set for Christmas, 1946; Here Comes Christmas! A Varied Collection of Christmas-Program Materials for Elementary Schools, 1947; Witches, Beware: A Hallowe'en Play, 1948; Set the Stage for Christmas: A Collection of Pantomimes, Skits, Recitations, Readings, Plays and Pageants, 1948; Christmas in Ninety-Nine Words (lyrics only), 1949; The Big Book of Christmas: A Collection of Plays, Songs, Readings, Recitations, Pantomimes, Skits, and Suggestions for Things to Make and Do for Christmas, 1951; Health and Safety Plays and Programs, 1953; Holiday Programs for Boys and Girls, 1953; (with Olive Rabe) United Nations Plays and Programs, 1954; (with Olive Rabe) Patriotic Plays and Programs, 1956; Christmas Plays and Programs, 1960; Plays About Our Nation's Songs, 1962; The King's Toothache, and One-Ring Circus, in Thirty Plays for Classroom Reading, 1956; Time for Mom, and Young Abe Lincoln, in Fifty Plays for Holidays, 1969; Bicentennial Plays and Programs, 1975; verse—The Coffee-Pot Face, 1933; Inside a Little House, 1938; That's Why, 1946; Up the Windy Hill: A Book of Merry Verse and Silhouettes, 1953; Runny Days, Sunny Days, Merry Verses, 1958; Going Barefoot, 1960; Where Does Everyone Go?, 1961; I Wonder How, I Wonder Why, 1962; Like Nothing at All, 1962; I Like Weather, 1963; Cricket in a Thicket, 1963; Listen Rabbit, 1964; In the Middle of the Night, 1965; In the Woods, In the Meadow, In the Sky: Poems, 1965; Best Little House, 1966; Skip Around the Year, 1967; My Mother and I, 1967; Up, Up the Mountain, 1968; We Went Looking, 1968; Clean as a Whistle, 1969; In One Door and Out the Other: A Book of Poems, 1969; Sing, Little Mouse, 1969; But Ostriches . . ., 1970; Feathered Ones and Furry, 1971; Do Bears Have Mothers Too?, 1973; My Cat Has Eyes of Sapphire Blue, 1973; Once We Went on a Picnic, 1975; I Stood upon a Mountain; Out in the Dark and Daylight, 1980; Anybody Home?, 1980; other—Guess Again! (riddles), 1941; All on a Mountain Day, 1956; We

Dickinsons: The Life of Emily Dickinson as Seen Through the Eyes of Her Brother Austin, 1965; Valley of the Smallest: The Life Story of a Shrew, 1966; We Alcotts: The Life of Louisa May Alcott as Seen Through the Eyes of "Marmee" . . . , 1968; Easter, 1968; Jeanne d'Arc, 1970; The Ways of Animals, 10 vols., 1973–74; The Ways of Plants, 10 vols., 1977; I Stood upon a Mountain, 1979; Out in the Dark and Daylight, 1980; Anybody Home?, 1980; Rabbits, Rabbits, 1983; (ed.) Year-Round Programs for Young Players, 1985; My First Hanukkah Book, 1985; When It Comes to Bugs, 1986; (ed.) Holiday Programs for Boys and Girls, 1986; The House of a Mouse, 1988. Add: 505 College Ave., Boulder, Colo. 80302, U.S.A.

FISHER, Alan W. American, b. 1939. History. Prof. of History, Michigan State Univ., East Lansing, since 1978; (joined faculty, 1967). Publs: The Russian Annexation of the Crimea: 1772-1783, 1970; The Crimean Tatars, 1978, 1987; Ottoman Studies Directory, 3 vols., 1979–83. Add: Dept. of History, Michigan State Univ., East Lansing, Mich. 48824, U.S.A.

FISHER, Allen. British, b. 1944. Poetry. Co-Publisher, Aloes Books, London, since 1972, and Spanner, London, since 1974. Co-Publisher, New London Price, 1975–81. Publs: Thomas Net's Tree-Birst, 1971; Before Ideas, Ideas, 1971; Spaces for Winter Solstice (Blueprint), 1972; Sicily, 1973; Place, 1974; Long Shout to Kernewek, 1975; 5 Plages 'shun, 1975; Paxton's Beacon, 1976; Gripping the Rail, 1976; "Der Verolene" Operation, 1976; Stane, 1977; Fire-Place (with Hearth-Work by Pierre Joris), 1977; Self-Portraits, Pink 149, 1977; Doing, 1977; Samuel Matthews, 1977; Docking, 1978; London Blight, 1978; Convergences, in Place, of the Play, 1978; Becoming, 1978; The Apocalyptic Sonnets, 1978; Intermediate Spirit Receiver, 1980; Hooks (Taken Out of Place 32), 1980; Eros, Father, Pattern, 1980; Imbrications, 1981; Unpolished Mirrors, 1981; The Art of Flight VI-IX, 1982; Poetry for Schools, Including Black Light, Shorting-Out, and Other Poems, 1982; Bending Windows, 1982; Defamiliarising, 1983; African Boog, 1983; Banda, 1983; Brixton Fractals, 1985; Buzzards and Bees, 1987. Add: 64 Lancercost Rd., London SW2 3DN, England.

FISHER, Clay. See ALLAN, Henry Wilson.

FISHER, David. American, b. 1946. Novels, Criminology/Law enforcement/Prisons, Politics, Sports. On staff of Life mag., 1970–72. Publs: (with Jhan Robbins) Without Pills, 1972; (with Jhan Robbins) How to Make and Break Habits, 1973; (with "Joey") Killer, 1973; (with "Joey") Hit No. 29, 1974; (with Jack Clouser) The Most Wanted Man in America, 1974; (with Cecile Milete) Louie's Widow, 1975; The Pack (novel), 1976; Joey Collects, 1980; (with Reg Bragonier) What's What (reference), 1982; The War Magician (novel), 1983; (with Ron Luciano) The Umpire Strikes Back, 1984; (with Tommy Lasordo) The Artful Dodger, 1985; (with Ron Luciano) Strike Two, 1986; (with Ron Luciano) The Fall of the Roman Empire, 1987; (with George Burns) Gracie: A Love Story, 1988; (with Ron Luciano) Remembrance of Swings Past, 1988. Add: 357 W. 19th St., New York, N.Y. 10011, U.S.A.

FISHER, David E. American, b. 1932. Novels/Short stories, Plays/Screenplays, Sciences. Prof., Univ. of Miami, Fla., since 1966. Publs: The Courtesy Not to Bleed, 1970; Crisis, 1971; Compartments, 1972; A Fearful Symmetry, 1974; The Last Flying Tiger, 1976; The Creation of the Universe, 1977; The Creation of Atoms and Stars, 1979; The Ideas of Einstein, 1980; The Man You Sleep With, 1980; Variation on a Theme, 1981; Katie's Terror, 1982; Grace for the Dead, 1984; The Third Experiment: Is There Life on Mars?, 1985; The Birth of the Earth, 1987; A Place on the Edge of Time, 1987; The Origin and Evolution of Our Own Particular Universe, 1988. Add: 9650 Kendale Blvd., Miami, Fla., U.S.A.

FISHER, Franklin M. American, b. 1934. Economics. Prof. of Economics, Massachusetts Inst. of Technology, Cambridge, since 1965 (Asst. Prof., 1960–62; Assoc. Prof., 1962–65). Asst. Prof. of economics, Univ. of Chicago, 1959–60. Assoc. Ed., Journal of the American Statistical Assn., and American Ed., Review of Economic Studies, 1965–68; Ed., Econometrica, 1968–77; Vice-Pres., Econometics Soc., 1977–78, and Pres., 1979. Publs: A Priori Information and Time Series Analysis: Essays in Economic Theory and Measurement, 1962; A Study in Econometrics: The Demand for Electricity in the United States, 1962; (with A. Ando and H.A. Simon) Essays on the Structure of Social Science Models, 1963; Supply and Costs in the United States Petroleum Industry: Two Econometric Studies, 1964; The Identification Problem in Econometrics, 1966; (with K. Shell) The Economic Theory of Price Indices, 1972; (with J.M. Gowan and J. Greenwood) Folded, Spindled, and

Mutilated: Economic Analysis and U.S. v. IBM, 1983; (with R. Mancke and J. McKie) IBM and the U.S. Data Processing Industry: An Economic History, 1983; Disequilibrium Foundations of Equilibrium Economics, 1983; (ed.) Antitrust and Regulation: Essays in Memory of John T. McGown, 1985. Add: Dept. of Economics, E52-359, Massachusetts Inst. of Technology, Cambridge, Mass. 02139, U.S.A.

FISHER, Leonard Everett. American, b. 1924. Children's fiction and Children's non-fiction. Dean Emeritus, Paier Coll. of Art, Connecticut, since 1982 (joined faculty, 1966; Prof. of Fine Arts and Dean of Academic Affairs, 1978–82); Delegate-at-Large, White House Conference on Library and Information Sciences, 1979. Publs: Pumpers, Boilers, Hooks and Ladders, 1961; Pushers, Spads, Jennies and Jets, 1961; Head Full of Hats, 1962; The Glassmakers, 1964; The Silversmiths, 1964; The Papermakers, 1965; The Printers, 1965; The Wigmakers, 1965; The Hatters, 1965; The Tanners, 1966; The Weavers, 1966; The Cabinetmakers, 1966; The Shoemakers, 1967; The Schoolmasters, 1967; The Peddlers, 1968; The Doctors, 1968; The Potters, 1969; The Limners, 1969; The Architects, 1970; Two if by Sea, 1970; Revolutionary War Heroes, 1970; The Shipbuilders, 1971; The Death of Evening Star, 1972; The Homemakers, 1973; The Art Experience: Oil Painting, 1973; The Warlock of Westfall, 1974; Sweeney's Ghost, 1975; Across the Sea from Galway, 1975; The Blacksmiths, 1976; The Liberty Book, 1976; Letters from Italy, 1977; Noonan, 1978; Alphabet Art, 1978; The Railroads, 1979; The Factories, 1979; The Hospitals, 1980; The Sports, 1980; A Russian Farewell, 1980; Storm at the Jetty, 1980; The Newspapers, 1981; The Seven Days of Creation, 1981; The Unions, 1982; Number Art, 1982; The Schools, 1983; Star Signs, 1983; Boxes! Boxes!, 1984; The Olympians, 1984; Symbol Art, 1985; The Statue of Liberty, 1985; Masterpieces of American Painting, 1985; The Great Wall of China, 1986; Ellis Island, 1986; Look Around, 1986; Remington and Russell, 1986; Calendar Art, 1987; The Tower of London, 1987; The Alamo, 1987; The White House, 1989; The Wailing Wall, 1989. Add: 7 Twin Bridge Acres Rd., Westport, Conn. 06880, U.S.A.

FISHER, Louis. American, b. 1934. Politics/Government. Sr. Specialist (Separation of Powers), Congressional Research Service, Library of Congress, Washington, D.C., since 1988 (Analyst, 1970–74; Specialist, 1974–88). Asst. Prof. of Political Science, Queens Coll., Flushing, N.Y., 1967–70; Prof. of Political Science, the American Univ., Washington, D.C., 1975–77, Georgetown Univ., Washington, 1976–77, Catholic Univ., Washington, 1980–87, and Indiana Univ., Bloomington, 1987. Publs: President and Congress: Power and Policy, 1972; Presidential Spending Power, 1975; The Constitution Between Friends, 1978; The Politics of Shared Power: Congress and the Executive, 1981, 2nd ed., 1987; Constitutional Conflicts Between Congress and the President, 1985; Constitutional Dialogues: Interpretation as Political Process, 1988. Add: 4108 Southend Rd., Rockville, Md. 20853, U.S.A.

FISHER, Marvin. American, b. 1927. History, Literature. Prof. of English since 1958, Arizona State Univ., Tempe (Chmn. of Dept., 1977–83). Publs: Workshops in the Wilderness: The European Response to American Industrialization 1830-1860, 1967; Going Under: Melville's Short Fiction and the American 1850's, 1977; Continuities: Essays and Ideas in American Literature, 1986; Herman Melville: Life, Work and Criticism, 1988. Add: Dept. of English, Arizona State Univ., Tempe, Ariz. 85287, U.S.A.

FISHER, (Sir) Nigel. British, b. 1913. Politics, Biography. Conservative M.P. (U.K.) for Surbiton, 1955–74, for Hitchin, 1950–55, and for Kingston-upon-Thames, 1974–83: Parliamentary Private Secty. to Minister of Food, 1951–54, and to Home Secty. 1954–57; Parliamentary Under-Secty. of State for the Colonies 1962–63, and for Commonwealth Affairs 1963–64; Front Bench Opposition Spokesman for Commonwealth and Colonial Affairs 1964–66. Publs: Iain Macleod, 1973; The Tory Leaders, 1977; Harold Macmillan, 1982. Add: 45 Exeter House, Putney Heath, London SW15, England.

FISHER, Ralph Talcott, Jr. American, b. 1920. History, Politics/Government. Prof. of History and Dir., Russian and East European Center, Univ. of Illinois, Urbana, since 1960, Emeritus since 1987 (Assoc. Prof., 1958–60). Member, Editorial Bd., Russian Review, since 1959, and Slavic Review, 1969–79. Asst., Instr., then Asst. Prof. of History, Yale Univ., New Haven, Conn., 1950–58. Secty., 1960–69, Vice-Pres., 1978–80, and Pres., 1979–80, American Assn. for the Advancement of Slavic Studies. Publs: Pattern for Soviet Youth: A Study of the Congresses of the Komsomol 1918-1954, 1959; (ed. with G. Vernadsky) Dictionary of Russian Historical Terms, by Pushkarev, 1970; (co-ed.) Source Book for Russian History from the Early Times to 1917, 3

3 vols., 1972. Add: 2115 Burlison Dr., Urbana, Ill. 61801, U.S.A.

FISHER, Roger (Dummer). American, b. 1922. International relations/Current affairs. Samuel Williston Prof. of Law, Harvard Univ., Cambridge, since 1976 (Lectr., 1958–60; Prof., 1960–76); Dir., Harvard Negotiation Project, since 1980. Sr. Consultant, and Dir., Conflict Management, Inc., since 1984. Member, Bd. of Trustees, Hudson Inst., since 1963; Member, Bd. of Dirs., Council for a Livable World, Washington, D.C., since 1969. Asst. to the Gen. Counsel, Economic Cooperation Admin., Paris, 1948–49; Assoc., law firm of Covington and Burling, Washington, D.C., 1950–56; Asst. to the Solicitor-Gen. of the U.S., Dept. of Justice, Washington, 1956–58. Member, Exec. Council, American Soc. of Intnl. Law, 1961–64, 1966–69; Originator and exec. Ed., The Advocates, TV series, 1969–70; Vice-Pres., World Affairs Council, Boston, 1972–74; Member, Gov.'s Commn. on Citizen Participation, Mass., 1973. *Publs:* (ed.) International Conflict and Behavioral Science, 1964; International Conflict for Beginners, 1969 (in U.K., as Basic Negotiating Strategy, 1971); Dear Israelis, Dear Arabs, 1972; Points of Choice, 1978; Improving Compliance with International Law, 1981; Getting to Yes, 1981; Getting Together, 1988. Add: 16 Fayerweather St., Cambridge, Mass. 02138, U.S.A.

FISHER, Roy. British, b. 1930. Poetry. Pianist with jazz groups since 1946. Sch. and coll. teacher, 1953–56; Principal Lectr. and Head of Dept. of English and Drama, Bordesley Coll. of Education, Birmingham, 1963–71; Member, Dept. of American Studies, Univ. of Keele, Staffs, 1971–82. *Publs:* City, 1961; Then Hallucinations: City 2, 1962; The Ship's Orchestra, 1966; Ten Interiors with Various Figures, 1967; The Memorial Fountain, 1967; Collected Poems, 1968; The Ghost of a Paper Bag, 1969; Titles, 1969; Correspondence, 1970; Matrix, 1971; Metamorphoses, 1971; The Cut Pages, 1971; Also There, 1972; Bluebeard's Castle, 1972; Cultures, 1975; Neighbours!, 1976; 19 Poems and an Interview, 1976; Barnardine's Reply, 1977; The Thing About Joe Sullivan: Poems, 1971-1977, 1978; Comedies, 1979; Poems 1955-1980, 1980; Talks for Words, 1980; Consolidated Comedies, 1981; (with Ronald King) The Half-Year Letters: An Alphabet Book, 1983; Turning the Prism, 1985; A Furnace, 1986; (with Ronald King) The Left-Handed Punch, 1986; (with Paul Lester) A Birmingham Dialogue, 1986; Poems 1955-1987, 1988. Add: Four Ways, Earl Sterndale, Buxton, Derbyshire, England

FISHLOCK, David Jocelyn. British, b. 1932. Air/Space topics, Technology, Medicine/Health, sciences (general). Science Ed., The Financial Times, London, since 1967. Technology Ed., New Scientist, London, 1962–67. *Publs:* Metal Colouring, 1962; (with K.W. Hards) New Ways of Working Metals, 1965; The New Materials, 1967; (ed.) A Guide to the Laser, 1967; Taking the Temperature, 1967; (ed.) A Guide to Superconductivity, 1969; Man Modified, 1969; (ed.) A Guide to Earth Satellites, 1971; (ed.) The New Scientists, 1971; The Business of Science, 1974; The Business of Biotechnology, 1982; (co-author) Biotechnology: Strategies for Life, 1986. Add: Traveller's Joy, Copse Lane, Jordans, Bucks., England.

FISK, Nicholas. British, b. 1923. Children's fiction. Children's nonfiction. Has worked as an actor, journalist, musician, ed., and publr.; also, illustrator of his own books and others. *Publs:* Look at Cars, 1959, 1969; Look at Newspapers, 1962: Cars, 1963; The Young Man's Guide to Advertising, 1963; The Bouncers (novel), 1964; The Fast Green Car (novel), 1965; There's Something on the Roof! (novel), 1966; Making Music, 1966; Space Hostages, 1967; Lindbergh the Lone Flier, 1968; Richtofen the Red Baron, 1968; Trillions, 1971; Grinny, 1973; High Way Home, 1973; Emma Borrows a Cup of Sugar (novel), 1973; Little Green Spaceman, 1974; Time Trap, 1976; Wheelie in the Stars, 1976; The Witches of Wimmering (novel), 1976; Antigrav, 1978; Escape from Splatterbang, 1978, as Flamers, 1979; Monster Maker, 1979; A Rag, a Bone, and a Hank of Hair, 1980; Leadfoot (novel), 1980; Robot Revolt, 1981; Starstormers series, 5 vols., 1981; Catfang, 1981; Sweets from a Stranger, 1982; Snatched, 1983; On the Flip Side, 1983; You Remember Me, 1984; Bonkers Clocks, 1985; Dark Sun, Bright Sun, 1986; Mindbenders, 1987; Backlash, 1987; Living Fire, 1987; The Talking Car, 1988; The Telly Is Watching You, 1989; The Worm Charmers, 1989; The Model Village, 1989. Add: 59 Elstree Rd., Bushey Heath, Herts. WD2 3QX, England.

FISKE, Sharon. *See* **HILL,** Pamela.

FISON, David Charles. Australian, b. 1908. Medicine/Health. Chairman. Medical Committee, Royal Queensland Bush Children's Health Scheme, since 1974. Resident Medical Officer, 1937–38, Medical Registrar, 1939–45, and Medical Supt., 1946–74, Royal Children's Hosp., Brisbane. *Publs:* History of the Royal Children's Hospital Brisbane, 1970. Add: 16 Hope St., Ormiston, Qld., Australia 4160.

FISS, Owen M(itchell). American, b. 1938. Law. Alexander M. Bickel Prof. of Public Law, Yale Univ. New Haven, Conn., since 1984 (Prof. of Law, 1974–84). Member, Editorial Bd., Foundation Press, and Philosophy and Public Affairs, Law, Economics, and Organization, etc.; Member, Exec. Bd., Lawyers Cttee. for Civil Rights under Law. Law Clerk to Thurgood Marshall, then Judge of the U.S. Court of Appeals, Second Circuit, 1964–65; Law Clerk to Justice Brennan, U.S. Supreme Court, 1965–66; Special Asst. to John Doar, Asst. Attorney-Gen., U.S. Dept. of Justice, 1966–68; Prof. of Law, Univ. of Chicago, 1968–74. *Publs:* Injunctions, 1972, (with Douglas Rendleman) 1984; The Civil Rights Injunction, 1978; (with R.M. Cover) The Structure of Procedure, 1979; (with R.M. Cover and J. Resnik) Procedure, 1988. Add: Yale Law Sch., New Haven, Conn. 06520, U.S.A.

FITTER, Richard (Sidney Richmond). British, b. 1913. Natural history. Biography. Member since 1963, and Chmn. of the Steering Cttee. 1975–88, Species Survival Commn., Intnl. Union for Conservation of Nature. Open Air Corresp., The Observer, London, 1958–66; Dir., Intelligence Unit, Council for Nature, 1959–63; Trustee, World Wildlife Fund (U.K.), 1977–83; Chmn., Fauna and Flora Preservation Soc., 1983–88. *Publs:* London's Natural History, 1945; London's Birds, 1949; Pocket Guide to British Birds, 1952; Pocket Guide to Nests and Eggs, 1954; (with D. McClintock) Pocket Guide to Wild Flowers, 1956; The Ark in Our Midst, 1959; Six Great Naturalists, 1959; Guide to Bird Watching, 1963; Wildlife in Britain, 1963; Britain's Wildlife: Rarities and Introductions, 1966; (with M. Fitter) The Penguin Dictionary of British Natural History 1967; Vanishing Wild Animals of the World, 1968; Finding Wild Flowers, 1971; (with H. Heinzel and J. Parslow) The Birds of Britain and Europe, with North Africa and the Middle East, 1972; (with A. Fitter and M. Blamey) The Wild Flowers of Britain and Northern Europe, 1974; The Penitent Butchers, 1978; Handguide to the Wild Flowers of Britain and Northern Europe, 1979; (with M. Blamey) Gem Guide to Wild Flowers, 1980; (with N. Arlott and A. Fitter) The Complete Guide to British Wildlife, 1981; (with J. Wilkinson and A. Fitter) Collins Guide to the Countryside, 1984; (with A. Fitter and A. Farrer) Guide to the Grasses, Sedges, Rushes, and Ferns of Britain and Northern Europe, 1984; Wildlife for Man, 1986; (with R. Manuel) Field Guide to the Freshwater Life of Britain and North-west Europe, 1986; (with A. Fitter) A Field Guide to the Countryside in Winter, 1988. Add: Drifts, Chinnor Hill, Oxford OX9 4BS, England.

FITZGEORGE-PARKER, Tim. British, b. 1920. Sports/Physical education/Keeping fit, Biography. Corresp.-in-Chief, Pacemaker, since 1973. Writer of own syndicated racing column, since 1974. Chief Racing Corresp., Daily Mail, London, 1960–71; Racing Columnist, The Sun, London, 1972–73. *Publs:* The Spoilsports, 1968; Steeplechase Jockeys: The Great Ones, 1971; Flat Race Jockeys: The Great Ones, 1973; Training the Racehorse, 1973; Vincent O'Brien: A Long Way from Tipperary, 1975; Great Racehorse Trainers, 1975; Grundy, 1976; The Guv'nor: Biography of Sir Noel Murless, 1980; Jockeys of the Seventies, 1980; No Secret So Close: The Biography of Bruce Hobbs M.C., 1984; Ever Loyal: The Biography of Neville Crump, 1987. Add: c/o Pelham Books, 27 Wright's Lane, London W8 5DZ, England.

FITZGERALD, Charles Patrick. British, b. 1902. Anthropology/Ethnology, History, International relations/Current affairs. Emeritus Prof. of Far Eastern History, Austrian National Univ., Canberra, since 1969 (Reader in Oriental Studies, 1951–54; Prof., 1954–69). With UK Foreign Office, 1939–46, and British Council, North China, 1946–51. *Publs:* Son of Heaven: Biography of T'ang T'ai Tsung, 1932; China: Short Cultural History, 1935, 3rd ed. 1961; Tower of Five Glories: The Minchia of Yunna, 1940; Revolution in China, 1952, reissued as Birth of Communist China, 1960; The Empress Wu, 1956, 1968; Floodtide in China, 1959; The Third China, 1960; The Chinese View of Their Place in the World, 1964, 4th ed. 1969; East Asia, 1966; Barbarian Beds: The Origin of the Chair in China, 1967; History of China, 1969, Southward Expansion of the Chinese People, 1972; (with Myra Roper) China: A World So Changed, 1973; A Concise History of East Asia, 1974; Mao Tse-Tung and China, 1977; Ancient China, 1978; Why China?: Recollections of China 1923-51, 1985. Add: 4 St. Paul's St., Randwick, N.S.W. 2031, Australia.

FITZGERALD, Ernest Abner. American, b. 1925. Theology/Religion. Bishop, The United Methodist Church Altanta Area, Georgia. *Publs:*

There's No Other Way, 1970; The Structures of Inner Peace, 1973; Living Under Pressure, 1975; You Can Believe, 1975; A Time to Cross the River, 1977; How to Be a Successful Failure, 1978; God Writes Straight with Crooked Lines, 1980; Diamonds Everywhere, 1983; Keeping Pace: Inspirations in the Air, 1988. Add: 159 Ralph McGill Blvd., Atlanta, Ga. 30308, U.S.A.

FITZGERALD, Frances. American, b. 1940. Military/Defence, Politics/Government, Social commentary. Freelance journalist. Member, Congress for Cultural Freedom, Paris, 1962–64; Reporter, Herald Tribune Sunday Mag., NYC, 1964–66; Instr. in Journalism, Univ. of California, Berkeley, 1978. Regular contrib. to The New Yorker. *Publs:* Fire in the Lake: The Vietnamese and the Americans in Vietnam (1972 National Book Award; Pulitzer Prize); America Revised, 1980; Cities on a Hill, 1986. Add: c/o Simon and Schuster Inc., 1230 Ave. of the Americas, New York, N.Y. 10020, U.S.A.

FITZGERALD, Garret. Irish, b. 1926. Politics/Government. Fine Gael Member of the Dail Eireann (Irish Parliament) for Dublin S.E., since 1969 (Member, Seanad Eireann, Irish Senate, 1965–69, and former Member, Senate Electoral Law Commn.; Member, Dail Cttee. on Public Acounts, 1969–73; Minister for Foreign Affairs, 1973–77; Pres., Fine Gael Party, 1977–87; Prime Minister of Ireland, 1981–82, 1982–87). Dir., Guinness Peat Aviation; Assoc., Arthur Young O'Hare Barry. Dir., Trade Development Inst., Dublin, and Intnl. Inst. for Economic Development, London. With Aer Lingus, Irish Airlines, 1947–58; Lectr., Dept. of Political Economy, University Coll. Dublin, 1959–73. Pres., Council of Ministers of EEC, 1975, and of the European Council, 1984. *Publs:* State-Sponsored Bodies, 1959; Planning in Ireland, 1968; Towards a New Ireland, 1972; Unequal Partners, 1978; Estimates for Baronies of Minimum Level of Irish-Speaking Amongst Successive Decennial Cohorts 1771-1781 to 1861-1871, 1984. Add: 30 Palmerston Rd., Dublin 6, Ireland.

FITZGERALD, Julia. Pseudonym for Julia Watson; also writes as Jane de Vere and Julia Hamilton. Historical/Romance, Health. Co-ordinator and editor, Amy Intnl. Productions (film series). Has worked as artist, jewelry designer, model, and adviser to Sphere Books. *Publs:* as Julia Watson—The Lovechild, 1967; Medici Mistress, 1968; A Mistress for the Valois, 1969; The King's Mistress, 1970; The Wolf and the Unicorn, 1971; Winter of the Witch, 1971; The Tudor Rose, 1972; Saffron, 1972; Love Song, 1981; as Jane de Vere—The Scarlet Women, 1969; as Julia Hamilton—The Last of the Tudors, 1971; Katherine of Aragon, 1972, as Katherine the Tragic Tudor, 1974; Anne of Cleves, 1972; Son of York, 1973; The Changeling Queen, 1977; The Emperor's Daughter, 1978; The Pearl of the Habsburgs, 1978; The Snow Queen, 1978; The Habsburg Inheritance, 1980; as Julia Fitzgerald—Royal Slave, 1978; Scarlet Woman, 1979; Slave Lady, 1980; Salamander, 1981; Fallen Woman, 1981; Venus Rising, 1982; The Princess and the Pagan, 1982; Firebird, 1983; The Jewelled Serpent, 1984; Taboo, 1985; Desert Queen, 1986; Daughter of the Gods, 1986; Flame of the East, 1986; Pasadoble, 1986; A Kiss from Aphrodite, 1986; Castle of the Enchantress, 1986; Beauty of the Devil, 1986; Healthy Signs (non-fiction), 1987; Earth Queen, Sky King, 1989. Add: 22 Lyndhurst Close, Downley, High Wycombe, Bucks., HP13 5JD, England.

FITZGERALD, Nigel. Irish, b. 1906. Mystery/Suspense. *Publs:* Midsummer Malice, 1953; The Rosey Pastor, 1954; The House Is falling, 1955; Imagine a Man, 1956; The Student Body, 1958; Suffer a Witch, 1958; This Won't Hurt You, 1959; The Candles Are All Out, 1960; Ghost in the Making, 1960; Black Welcome, 1961; The Day of the Adder, 1963 (in U.S. as Echo Answers Murder, 1965); Affairs of Death, 1967. Add: c/o Collins, 8 Grafton St., London W1X 3LA, England.

FITZGERALD, Penelope (Mary Knox). British, b. 1916. Novels/Short stories. Biography. Teacher with Westminster Tutors, London. *Publs:* Edward Burne-Jones: A Biography, 1975; The Knox Brothers: Edmund ("Evoe") 1881-1971, Dillwyn 1883-1943, Wilfred 1886-1950, Ronald 1888-1957 (biography), 1977; The Golden Child, 1977; The Bookshop, 1978; Offshore, 1979; Human Voices, 1980; At Freddie's 1982; Charlotte Mew and Her Friends (biography), 1984; Innocence, 1986; The Beginning of Spring, 1988. Add: c/o William Collins and Co. Ltd., 8 Grafton St., London W1X 3LA, England.

FITZGERALD, Robert D(avid). Australian, b. 1902. Poetry, Literature. Surveyor, FitzGerald & Blair, 1926–30; Native Lands Comm. Surveyor, Fiji, 1931–36; Municipal Surveyor, 1936–39 Surveyor, Australian Dept. of the Interior, 1939–65, now retired. *Publs:* The Greater Apollo, 1927; To Meet the Sun, 1929; Moonlight Acre, 1938 (Australian Litera-

ture Soc. Gold Medal); (ed.) Australian Poetry, 1942, 1942; (ed.) Selected Verse, by Mary Gilmore, 1948, rev. ed. 1969; Heemskerck Shoals, 1949; Between Two Tides, 1952 (Grace Leven Prize); This Night's Orbit: Verses, 1953; The Wind at Your Door: A Poem, 1959; Southmost Twelve, 1962; The Elements of Poetry, 1963; Of Some Country: 27 Poems, 1963; Selected Poems, 1963; Forty Years' Poems, 1965; (ed.) The Letters of Hugh McCrae, 1970; Of Places and Poetry, 1976; Product (verse), 1979; Portable Selection, by Julian Craft, 1987. Add: 4 Prince Edward Parade, Hunters Hill, N.S.W. 2110, Australia.

FITZGERALD, Valerie. Historical/Romance/Gothic. *Publs:* Zemindar, 1981. Lives in Canada. Add: c/o Bodley Head Ltd., 32 Bedford Sq., London WC1B 3EL, England.

FitzGIBBON, (Joanne Eileen) Theodora (Winifred). Irish, b. 1916. Novels/Short stories, Cookery/Gastronomy/Wine, Autobiography. Feature writer, Irish Times, since 1968, and Image magazine, since 1975. *Publs:* Cosmopolitan Cookery, 1952; Weekend Cooking, 1956; (with M. Hemans) The High Protein Diet and Cookery Book, 1957; Country House Cooking, 1958; The Young Cook's Book, 1958; Game Cooking, 1963; The Art of British Cooking, 1965; The Flight of the Kingfisher (novel), 1967; A Taste of Ireland (Scotland, Wales, England: The West Country, London, Paris, Rome, the Sea, Yorkshire, the Lake District), 11 vols., 1968–80; Eat Well and Live Longer, 1969; Theodora FitzGibbon's Cookery Book, 1972; Making the Most of It, 1978; Crockery Pot Cooking, 1978; The Irish Kitchen, 1978; (compiler) The Food of the Western World, 1978; Traditional Scottish Cookery, 1981; The Pleasures of the Table, 1981; Traditional West Country Cookery, 1982; With Love (autobiography), 1982; Savouries, 1982; Traditional Irish Food, 1983; Love Lies a Loss (autobiog.), 1985; (with Elizabeth Ayrton) Traditional British Cookery, 1985; Your Favourite Recipes, 1985; A Taste of England, 1986. Add: The Mill House, Mill Lane, Shanganagh Bridge, Shankill, Co. Dublin, Ireland.

FITZSIMONS, Raymund. British. Plays, Biography. *Publs:* The Baron of Piccadilly, 1967; Barnum in London, 1970; Charles Dickens Show, 1970; Edmund Kean: Fire from Heaven, 1976; Death and the Magician: The Mystery of Houdini, 1980; Edmund Kean (play), 1983. Add: 62 Scotby Rd., Scotby, Carlisle, Cumbria CA4 8BD, England.

FJELDE, Rolf (Gerhard). American, b. 1926. Plays/Screenplays, Poetry, Literature, Translations. Prof. of English and Drama, Pratt Inst., Brooklyn, N.Y., since 1969 (Instr., 1954–58; Asst. Prof., 1958–64; Assoc. Prof., 1964–69). Teacher of drama history, Academic Faculty, Juilliard Sch., NYC, since 1973. Pres., Ibsen Soc. of America, since 1979; Ed., Ibsen News and Comment, since 1979. Founding Ed., Yale Poetry Review, 1945–49, and Poetry New York, 1949–51. *Publs:* Washington (poetry), 1955; The Imaged Word (poetry), 1962; (trans.) Peer Gynt, by Ibsen, 1964, 1980; (trans.) Four Major Plays, by Ibsen, vol. I, 1965, vol. II, 1970; (ed.) Ibsen: A Collection of Critical Essays, 1965; Washington (play), 1966; The Rope Walk (play), 1967; Rafferty One by One (play), 1975; (trans.) Complete Major Prose Plays, by Ibsen, 1978; The Bellini Look (play), 1982. Add: 261 Chatterton Parkway, White Plains, N.Y. 10606, U.S.A.

FLADELAND, Betty. American, b. 1919. History, Biography. Distinguished Prof. of History, Southern Illinois Univ., Carbondale, since 1985 (Lectr., 1962–64; Assoc. Prof., 1964–68; Prof., 1968–85). Member of faculty, Wells Coll., Aurora, N.Y., 1952–55, and Central Michigan Univ., Mount Pleasant, 1955–59, and Central Missouri State Coll., Warrensburg, 1959–62. *Publs:* James Gillespie Birney: Slaveholder to Abolitionist, 1955, 1969; Men and Brothers: Anglo-American Antislavery Co-operation, 1972; Abolitionists and Working-Class Problems in the Age of Industrialization, 1984. Add: Dept. of History, Southern Illinois Univ., Carbondale, Ill. 62901, U.S.A.

FLANAGAN, Patrick Joseph. Irish, b. 1940. Environmental science/Ecology, Transportation. Research officer, An Foras Forbartha, National Planning Inst., since 1970. Asst. Lectr., Dept. of Civil Engineering, Univ. Coll., Dublin, 1965–70. *Publs:* The Cavan and Leitrim Railway, 1966; (co-author) Dublin's Buses, 1968; Transport in Ireland, 1880-1910, 1969; The Ballinamore and Ballyconnell Canal, 1972; (with P.F. Toner) The National Survey of Irish Rivers: A Report (and Second Report) on Water Quality, 2 vols., 1972–74. Add: 33 Fortfield Park, Dublin 6, Ireland.

FLANAGAN, Thomas (James Bonner). American, b. 1923. Novels/Short stories, Literature. Prof. of English, State Univ. of New York at Stony Brook, since 1978. Instr. to Asst. Prof., Columbia Univ.,

1952–60; Asst. Prof. to Assoc. Prof., 1960–73, Prof., 1973–78, and Chmn., 1973–76, Univ. of California at Berkeley. *Publs:* The Irish Novelists 1800-1850, 1959; The Year of the French (novel), 1979; The Tenants of Time (novel), 1988. Add: Robin Straus, 229 E. 79th St., New York, N.Y. 10021, U.S.A.

FLEISCHMAN, Harry. American, b. 1914. Civil liberties/Human rights, Economics, Sociology. National Secty., Socialist Party, USA, 1942–50; Ed., Socialist Call, 1947–50; Labor Ed., Voice of America, 1950–53; Race Relations and Labor Dir., American Jewish Cttee., 1953–79; Exec. Dir., National Alliance for Safer Cities, 1970–79. *Publs:* (with J.L. Kornbluh and B.D. Segal) Security, Civil Liberties and Unions, 1956; (with J. Rorty) We Open the Gates: Labor's Fight for Equality, 1958; Unions and Discrimination, 1959; Is Labor Color-Blind?, 1960; Let's Be Human, 1960; Labor and Civil Liberties, 1963; Norman Thomas: A Biography, 1964, 1969; Civil Rights Story—1964, 1965; Civil Rights Story—1966, 1966; Negroes and Jews: Brotherhood or Bias, 1967; Anti-Semitism in the United States, 1967; Negro Anti-Semitism and the White Backlash, 1968; (with M. Gross) 22 Steps to Safer Neighbourhoods, 1973; How to Combat Racism and Bigotry, 1975; Norman Thomas: The Legacy of a Prophet, 1977; The Challenge of Crime, 1977; Out of Work: The Impact of Unemployment and What's Being Done About It, 1978; Steps to Safer Neighbourhoods and Schools, 1979; Brown and Intergroup Relations, 1979; American Labor and the U.S. Political Scene, 1980; Labor in the 80's—Victor or Victim, 1981; Reagan versus Labor, 1984; A Socialist Witness, 1984; Norman Thomas at 100, 1984; Norman Thomas and the Jews, 1984; Remembering Norman Thomas, 1984. Add: 11 Wedgewood Lane, Wantagh, N.Y. 11793, U.S.A.

FLEISCHMAN, Paul. American, b. 1952. Children's fiction. Has worked as janitor, bagel baker, bookstore clerk, and proofreader. *Publs:* The Birthday Tree, 1979; The Half-a-Moon Inn, 1980; Graven Images: Three Stories, 1982; Animal Hedge, 1983; Finzel the Farsighted, 1983; Path of the Pale Horse, 1983; Phoebe Danger, Detective, in the Case of the Two-Minute Cough, 1983; Coming-and-Going Men: Four Tales of Itinerates, 1985; Rear-View Mirrors, 1986; Rondo in C, 1988; verse for children—I Am Phoenix: Poems for Two Voices, 1985; Joyful Noise: Poems for Two Voices, 1988. Add: 855 Marino Pines Rd., Pacific Grove, Calif. 93950, U.S.A.

FLEISCHMAN, (Albert) Sid(ney). American, b. 1920. Novels/Short stories, Children's fiction, Plays/Screenplays. Magician in vaudeville and night clubs, 1938–41; reporter, San Diego Daily Journal, 1949–50; Assoc. Ed., Point mag., San Diego, 1950–51. *Publs:* The Straw Donkey Case, 1948; Murder's No Accident, 1949; Shanghai Flame, 1951; Look Behind You, Lady (in U.K. as Chinese Crimson), 1952; Danger in Paradise, 1953; Counterspy Express, 1954; Malay Woman (in U.K. as Malayan Manhunt), 1954; Blood Alley (novel and screenplay), 1955; Good-bye My Lady (screenplay), 1956; Lafayette Escadrille (screenplay), 1958; Yellowleg, 1960; The Deadly Companions (screenplay), 1961; children's fiction—Mr. Mysterious and Company, 1962; By the Great Horn Spoon!, 1963, retitled as Bullwhip Griffin, 1967; The Ghost in the Noonday Sun, 1965; McBroom series, 9 vols. 1966–80; Chancy and the Grand Rascal, 1966; Longbeard the Wizard, 1970; Jingo Django, 1971; The Wooden Cat Man, 1972; The Ghost on a Saturday Night, 1974; Mr. Mysterious's Secret of Magic (in U.K. as Secrets of Magic), 1975; Me and the Man on the Moon-Eyed Horse, 1977; Humbug Mountain, 1978; The Hey Hey Man, 1979; The Case of the Cackling Ghost (Princess Tomorrow, Flying Clock, Secret Message), 4 vols., 1981; The Case of the 264-Pound Burglar, 1982; McBroom's Almanac, 1984; The Whipping Boy, 1986; The Scarebird, 1988. Add: 305 Tenth St., Santa Monica, Calif. 90402, U.S.A.

FLEISHMAN, Avrom. American, b. 1933. Literature. Prof. of English, Johns Hopkins Univ., Baltimore, Md., since 1970 (Assoc. Prof., 1968–70). Instr., Columbia Univ., NYC, 1958–59, and Hofstra Univ., Hempstead, N.Y., 1960–63; Asst. Prof., Univ. of Minnesota, Minneapolis, 1963–66, and Michigan State Univ., East Lansing, 1966–67. *Publs:* A Reading of Mansfield Park: An Essay in Critical Synthesis, 1967; Conrad's Politics: Community and Anarchy in the Fiction of Joseph Conrad, 1967; The English Historical Novel: Walter Scott to Virginia Woolf, 1971; Virginia Woolf: A Critical Reading, 1975; Fiction and the Ways of Knowing: Essays on British Novels, 1978; Figures of Autobiography: The Language of Self-Writing in Victorian and Modern England, 1983. Add: English Dept., Johns Hopkins Univ., Baltimore, Md. 21218, U.S.A.

FLEMING, Alice (Carew Mulcahey). American, b. 1928. Children's fiction, Children's non-fiction, Social commentary/phenomena. *Publs:* The Key to New York, 1960; Wheels, 1960; A Son of Liberty, 1961;

Doctors in Petticoats, 1964; Great Women Teachers, 1965; The Senator from Maine, 1969; Alice Freeman Palmer: Pioneer College President, 1970; Reporters at War, 1970; General's Lady, 1971; Highways into History, 1971; Pioneers in Print, 1971; Ida Tarbell: First of the Muckrakers, 1971; Psychiatry: What's It All About?, 1972; (ed.) Hosannah the Home Run!, 1972; Nine Months, An Intelligent Woman's Guide to Pregnancy, 1972; The Moviemakers, 1973; Trials That Made Headlines, 1974; Contraception, Abortion, Pregnancy, 1974; New on the Beat, 1975; Alcohol: The Delightful Poison, 1975; (ed.) America Is Not All Traffic Lights, 1976; Something for Nothing, 1978; The Mysteries of ESP, 1980; What to Say When You Don't Know What to Say, 1982; Welcome to Grossville, 1985; The King of Prussia and a Peanut Butter Sandwich, 1988. Add: c/o Raines & Raines, 71 Park Ave., New York, N.Y. 10016, U.S.A.

FLEMING, Caroline. *See* **MATHER,** Anne.

FLEMING, Laurence William Howie. British, b. 1920. Novels/Short stories; Gardens. Freelance artist and designer, gardens, landscapes, wood carving and embroidery. With British Council, 1961–64, with Roberto Burle Marx, Rio de Janeiro, 1965–66, and Ian Mylles & Assoc., Landscape Designers, London, 1967–71. *Publs:* A Diet of Crumbs, 1959; (with Alan Gore) The English Garden (book and TV script), 1979; The One Hour Garden, 1985; (with Clay Perry and Ann Gore) Old English Villages, 1986. Add: c/o Lloyds Bank Ltd., 112 Kensington High St., London W8, England.

FLEMING, Thomas. American, b. 1927. Novels/short stories, History, Biography. Full-time writer since 1961. Assoc. Ed., 1954, and Exec. Ed., 1958–61, Cosmopolitan Mag. Pres., Soc. of Magazine Writers, 1967–68; Chmn., American Revolution Round Table, 1970–81; Pres., American Center, P.E.N., 1971–73. *Publs:* Now We Are Enemies (history), 1960; All Good Men (novel), 1961; The God of Love (novel), 1963; Beat the Last Drum (history), 1963; One Small Candle (history), 1964; King of the Hill (novel), 1966; A Cry of Whiteness (novel), 1967; (ed.) Affectionately Yours, George Washington, 1967; West Point: The Man and Times of the U.S. Military Academy, 1969; The Man from Monticello (biography), 1969; Romans, Countrymen, Lovers (novel), 1969; The Sandbox Tree (novel), 1970; The Man Who Dared the Lightning (biography, 1971; (ed.) Benjamin Franklin: A Biography in His Own Words, 1972; The Forgotten Victory (history), 1973; The Good Shepherd (novel), 1974; 1776: Year of Illusions (history), 1975; Liberty Tavern (novel), 1976; Rulers of the City (novel), 1977; New Jersey (history), 1977; Promises to Keep (novel), 1978; A Passionate Girl (novel), 1979; The Officers' Wives (novel), 1981; Dreams of Glory (novel), 1983; The Spoils of War (novel), 1984; Time and Tide (novel), 1987. Add: 315 E. 72nd St., New York, N.Y. 10021, U.S.A.

FLEMING, William (Coleman). American, b. 1909. Art, Music. Centennial Prof. of Fine Arts, Syracuse Univ., New York, 1969–76, now Emeritus (Chmn., Dept. of Fine Arts, 1947–69); Music Critic, Syracuse Post-Standard, 1948–76; William Kenan, Jr., Distinguished Prof. of Humanities, William and Mary Coll., Williamsburg. Va., 1983. *Publs:* Arts and Ideas, 7th ed., 1986; (co-author) Understanding Music, 1958; Art, Music and Ideas, 1970; Concerts of the Arts: Modes of Interrelationship, 1990; (co-author) Musical Arts and Styles, 1990. Add: 112 Hillcrest Rd., Syracuse, N.Y. 13224, U.S.A.

FLESCH, Y. Pseud. for Yolande (Catarina) Flesch. Also writes as Yvonne Greene. American, b. 1950. Children's fiction, Children's non-fiction, Homes/Gardens, Biography. Affiliated with Flesch Inc., NYC, since 1986. Fashion model, NYC, 1968–87. *Publs:* (as Yvonne Greene) Little Sister, 1981; Free Things for Homeowners, 1981; (as Yvonne Greene) Cover Girl, 1982; (as Yvonne Greene) Love Hunt, 1985; Julian Lennon, 1985; (as Yvonne Greene) The Sweet Dreams Model's Handbook, 1985; (as Yvonne Greene) Kelly Blake, Teen Model, 1986. Add: Flesch Inc., 853 Seventh Ave., Apt. 3B, New York, N.Y. 10019, U.S.A.

FLESCH, Yolande (Caterina). *See* **FLESCH,** Y.

FLESCHER, Irwin. American, b. 1926. Human relations, Psychology. Clinical Psychologist, private practice, N.Y., since 1959. Counseling Psychologist, New York State Dept. of Labor, 1952–55; Psychologist, Bureau of Child Guidance, NYC, 1955–58; Sch. and Research Psychologist, East Williston Public Schs., N.Y., 1960–86; Adjunct Assoc. Prof., Long Island Univ., N.Y., 1971–74. *Publs:* Children in the Learning Factory: The Search for a Humanizing Teacher, 1972. Add: 33 Canterbury Lane, Roslyn Heights, N.Y. 11577, U.S.A.

FLETCHER, Colin. American (b. British), b. 1922. Natural history,

Walking, Biography. Served (as Captain) in the Royal Marines, 1940–47; Farmed in Kenya, 1948–52; Prospector, Canada, 1954–56; Santa Claus, San Francisco dept. store, 1956; Janitor, San Francisco hosp., 1957–58. *Publs:* The Thousand Mile Summer, 1964; The Man Who Walked Through Time, 1968; The Complete Walker, 1968; The Winds of Mara, 1973; The New Complete Walker, 1974; The Man from the Cave, 1981; The Complete Walker III, 1984; The Secret Worlds of Colin Fletcher, 1989. Add: c/o Brandt and Brandt, 1501 Broadway, New York, N.Y. 10036, U.S.A.

FLETCHER, John Walter James. British, b. 1937. Literature, Translations. Prof. of Comparative Literature, Univ. of East Anglia, Norwich, since 1969 (Lectr. in French, 1966–68; Reader in French, 1968–69; Pro-Vice-Chancellor, 1974–79). Lectr. in English, Univ. of Toulouse, 1961–64; Lectr. in French, Univ. of Durham, 1964–66. Ed., Critical Appraisals series, Calder & Boyars, London, 1974–79. *Publs:* The Novels of Samuel Beckett, 1964, 1970; Samuel Beckett's Art, 1967; A Critical Commentary on Flaubert's Trois Contes, 1968; New Directions in Literature, 1968; (with R. Federman) Samuel Beckett: His Works and His Critics, 1970; (ed. with B.S. Fletcher) Samuel Beckett: Fin de partie, 1970; (ed.) Samuel Beckett: Waiting for Godot, 1971; (ed.) Forces in Modern French Drama, 1972; (with J. Spurling) Beckett: A Study of His Plays, 1972, 3rd ed. 1985; Claude Simon and Fiction Now, 1975; (with others) A Student's Guide to the Plays of Samuel Beckett, 1978, 1985; Novel and Reader, 1980; Alain Robbe-Grillet, 1983. Add: Sch. of Modern Languages and European History, Univ. of East Anglia, Norwich NR4 7TJ, England.

FLETCHER, Lucille. American, b. 1912. Mystery/Crime/Suspense, Plays/Screenplays. *Publs:* (with Norman Corwin) My Client Curley (radio play), 1940; The Hitch-Hiker (radio play), 1941; Sorry, Wrong Number (radio play), 1944, screenplay, 1948; The Daughters of Jasper Clay (novel), 1958; Blindfold (mystery novel), 1960; . . . and Presumed Dead (mystery novel), 1963; The Strange Blue Yawl (mystery novel), 1964; The Girl in Cabin B54 (mystery novel), 1968; Night Watch (play), 1972; Eighty Dollars to Stamford (mystery novel), 1975; Mirror Image (supense novel), 1988. Add: Avon Light, Oxford, Md. 21654, U.S.A.

FLETCHER, Ronald. British, b. 1921. Plays/Screenplays, Poetry, Sociology. Freelance writer, ed., and broadcaster, since 1969; Prof. Emeritus, Univ. of Reading; Consultant to the Intnl. Commn. (Unesco) for Scientific and Cultural History of Mankind, since 1980. Gen. Ed., Making of Sociology series, Michael Joseph Ltd., publrs., London. Lectr. in Sociology, Bedford and Birkbeck Colls., Univ. of London, 1953–63; Prof. and Head of Dept. of Sociology, Univ. of York, 1964–68; Visiting Prof., Univ. of Essex, Colchester, 1968–69. *Publs:* Issues in Education, 1960; The Family and Marriage in Britain, 1962; Human Needs and Social Order, 1965; The Parkers of Saltram: Everyday Life in an Eighteenth Century House, 1970; The Making of Sociology, 2 vols., 1971; (ed.) John Stuart Mill: Logical Critique of Sociology, 1971; (ed.) The Science of Society and the Unity of Mankind, 1974; (ed.) The Crisis of Industrial Civilization, 1974; The Akenham Burial Case; What's Wrong with Higher Education?, 1975; The Framework of Society, 1976; The Biography of a Victorian Village, 1977; In a Country Churchyard, 1978; Old Pathways (verse), 1979; The East Anglians, 1980; Margaret Catchpole: Two Worlds Apart (opera libretto), 1980; Sociology, 2 vols., 1980; Education in Society, 1984; Sheridan's First Edition: A Plan of Education, 1987; The Shaking of the Foundations: Family and Society, 1988; The Abolitionists: The Family and Marriage under Attack, 1988. Add: Cranmere, Halesworth Rd., Reydon, Southwold, Suffolk IP18 6NH, England.

FLETCHER-COOKE, (Sir) John. British, b. 1911. Politics/Government, Autobiography/Memoirs/Personal. With U.K. Colonial Office 1934–36, and Overseas Civil Service, 1937–61; served in Malaya, Malta, Palestine, Cyprus, and Tanganyika. Conservative M.P. (U.K.) for Southampton Test, 1964–66; Dir., Progs, in Diplomacy, Carnegie Endowment for Intnl. Peace, NYC, 1967–68. *Publs:* (co-author) Parliament as an Export, 1966; The Emperor's Guest 1942-45 (autobiography), 1971, 3rd. ed. 1982 (also issued as Talking Book for the Blind, 1982). Add: c/o Lloyds Bank, 111 Old Broad St., London EC2N 1AU, England.

FLEW, Antony (Garrard Newton). British, b. 1923. Education, Philosophy, Psychology. Emeritus Prof., Univ. of Reading, since 1983 (Prof. of Philosophy, 1973–82). Prof., Univ. of Keele, Staffs, 1954–72; Prof., Univ. of Calgary, Alta., 1972–73; Distinguished Research Fellow, Social Philosophy and Policy Center, Bowling Green State Univ., Ohio, 1986–88. *Publs:* A New Approach to Psychical Research, 1953; Hume's Philosophy of Belief, 1961; God and Philosophy, 1966; Evolutionary Ethics, 1967; An Introduction to Western Philosophy, 1971; (ed.) Malthus on Population, 1971; Crime or Disease?, 1973; Thinking About Thinking, 1975; Sociology, Equality, and Education, 1976; The Presumption of Atheism, 1976; A Rational Animal, 1978; (ed.) Dictionary of Philosophy, 1979; The Politics of Procrustes, 1981; Darwinian Evolution, 1984; Thinking About Social Thinking, 1985; David Hume: Philosopher of Moral Science, 1986; The Logic of Mortality, 1987. Add: 26 Alexandra Rd., Reading RG1 5PD, England.

FLEXNER, James Thomas. American, b. 1908. Art, History, Biography. *Publs:* Doctors on Horseback: Pioneers of American Medicine, 1937; America's Old Masters, 1939, 1982; (with Simon Flexner) William Henry Welch and the Heroic Age of American Medicine, 1942; Steamboats Come True: American Inventors in Action, 1944, 1978; First Flowers of Our Wilderness, 1947; John Singleton Copley, 1948; The Pocket History of American Painting, 1950; The Traitor and the Spy, 1953, 1975; American Painting: The Light of Distant Skies, 1954; Treason 1780 (television drama), 1954; Gilbert Stuart, 1955; Mohawk Baronet: Sir William Johnson of New York, 1959; The Wilder Image: The Painting of America's Native School from Thomas Cole to Winslow Homer, 1962; George Washington: The Forge of Experience, 1732-1775, 1965; (co-author) The World of Winslow Homer, 1836-1910, 1966; George Washington in the American Revolution, 1775-1783, 1968; George Washington and the New Nation, 1783-1793, 1970; Nineteenth Century American Painting, 1970; George Washington: Anguish and Farewell, 1793-1799 (Natnl. Book Award; Pulitzer Prize), 1972; Washington: The Indispensable Man, 1974; (with L. Samter) The Face of Liberty, 1975; (with others) Institute to University: A Seventy-Fifth Anniversary Colloquium, 1977; The Young Hamilton, 1978; States Dyckman, American Loyalist, 1980; Asher B. Durand: An Engraver's and a Farmer's Art, 1983; An American Saga: The Story of Helen Thomas and Simon Flexner, 1984. Add: c/o New American Library, 1633 Broadway, New York, N.Y. 10019, U.S.A.

FLEXNER, Stuart B. American, b. 1928. Language/Linguistics. Ed.-in-Chief, Reference Book Div., Random House Inc., NYC, since 1980. Prof., Cornell Univ., Ithaca, N.Y., 1951–55; Sr. Ed., Macmillan Publishers, NYC, 1955–59; Pres., Libros y Jugetas S.A., Mexico City, 1959–65; Vice-Pres., Random House Inc., NYC, 1965–73; Vice-Pres. and Member of the Bd., The Hudson Group, Pleasantville, N.Y., 1973–80. *Publs:* (with H. Wentworth) The Dictionary of American Slang, 1960, 3rd. ed. 1975; (sr. ed.) The Random House Unabridged Dictionary, 1966, ed.-in-chief, 1987 ed.; (sr. ed.) The Random House College Dictionary, 1968; (sr. ed.) The Random House School Dictionary, 1971; How to Increase Your Word Power, 1971; The Family Word Finder, 1975; I Hear America Talking (history of American language), 1976; (ed.) The Oxford American Dictionary, 1980; Listening to America, 1982. Add: Random House, Inc., 201 E. 50th St., New York, N.Y. 10022, U.S.A.

FLIER, Michael Stephen. American, b. 1941. Cultural/ethnic topics, Language/Linguistics. Prof. of Slavic Languages and Literatures, Univ. of California, Los Angeles, since 1979 (Asst. Prof. of Slavic Languages, 1968–73; Assoc. Prof., 1973–79; Chmn. of Dept., 1978–84 and since 1987). Co-Investigator, NSF Russian Morphology Project, 1977. *Publs:* Aspects of Nominal Determination in Old Church Slavic, 1974; Slavic Forum: Essays in Linguistics and Literature, 1974; Say It in Russian, 1982; (ed.) American Contributions to the Ninth Intnl. Congress of Slavists 1983, vol. I: Linguistics, 1983; (ed. with Henrik Birnbaum) Medieval Russian Culture, 1984; (ed. with Richard D. Brecht) Issues in Russian Morphosyntax, 1985; (ed., with Alan Timberlake) The Scope of Slavid Aspect, 1985; (ed., with Dean S. Worth) Slavic Linguistics, Poetics, Cultural History, 1985; (ed. with Simon Karlinsky) Language, Literature, Linguistics: In Honor of Francis J. Whitfield, 1987. Add: Dept. of Slavic Languages and Literatures, Univ. of California, Los Angeles, Calif. 90024, U.S.A.

FLIESS, Peter Joachim. American, b. 1915. Civil liberties/Human rights, History, International relations/Current affairs. Prof. Emeritus of Political Science, Univ. of Massachusetts, Amherst, since 1982 (Prof., 1967–82). Prof., Louisiana State Univ., Baton Rouge, 1948–67; Ed., POLITY, Journal of the Northeastern Political Science Assn., 1975–80. *Publs:* Freedom of the Press in the German Republic, 1918-1933, 1955; Thucydides and the Politics of Bipolarity, 1966; International Relations in the Bipolar World, 1968. Add: 6 Winston Ct., Amherst, Mass. 01002, U.S.A.

FLINDERS, Neil J. American, b. 1934. Education, Human relations, Speech/Rhetoric, Theology/Religion. Dir. of Long Range Planning and Analysis, Church Educational System, Salt Lake City; Asst. Prof.,

Brigham Young Univ., Provo, Utah. Seminary Principal, 1960–62, Inst. Instr., and Teacher Trainer, 1963–67, and member of Grad. Faculty, 1968–70, Church of Jesus Christ of the Latter Day Saints, Provo, Utah; Prof. of Education, Brigham Young Univ., Provo, Utah, 1979–85. *Publs:* Personal Communications: How to Understand and Be Understood, 1966; Leadership and Human Relations: A Handbook for Parents, Teachers and Executives, 1969; Continue in Prayer, 1975; Moral Perspective and Educational Practice, 1979; A Piece of Cowardice, 1982; My Decision: An Act of Faith or A Piece of Cowardice, 1984; Teach the Children: An Agency Approach to Education, 1989. Add: 9784 N. 4000 W., Pleasant Grove, Utah 84062, U.S.A.

FLINT, Betty Margaret. Canadian, b. 1920. Psychology. Prof. Emeritus, Inst. of Child Study, Faculty of Education, Univ. of Toronto (joined faculty, 1948). *Publs:* The Child and the Institution: A Study of Deprivation and Recovery; The Flint Infant Security Scale; The Security of Infants; New Hope for Deprived Children, 1978. Add: 18 Apsley Rd., Toronto, Ont., M5M 2X8, Canada.

FLINT, John Edgar. Canadian, b. 1930. History, Third World problems, Biography. Prof. of History, Dalhousie Univ., Halifax, N.S. since 1967. Asst. Lectr., and Reader in Colonial History, King's Coll., Univ. of London, 1954–67; Prof. and Head, History Dept., Univ. of Nigeria, 1963–64. *Publs:* Sir George Goldie and the Making of Nigeria, 1960; Mary Kingsley: A Reassessment, 1963; Nigeria and Ghana, 1966; Books on the British Empire and Commonwealth, 1968; (ed. with G. Williams) Perspectives of Empire: Essays Presented to Gerald S. Graham, 1973; Cecil Rhodes, 1974; (ed.) Cambridge History of Africa, vol. V, 1977. Add: Dept. of History, Dalhousie Univ., Halifax, N.S., Canada.

FLOOD, Charles Bracelen. American, b. 1929. Novels/Short stories, History, Biography. Instr. in Creative Writing and World Literature, Sophia Univ., Tokyo, 1963–65. *Publs:* Love Is a Bridge, 1953; A Distant Drum, 1957; Tell Me, Stranger, 1959; Monmouth, 1961; More Lives Than One, 1967; The War of the Innocents, 1970; Trouble at the Top, 1972; Rise, and Fight Again, 1976; Lee: The Last Years, 1981. Add: Box 8, Richmond, Ky. 40475, U.S.A.

FLORA, James (Royer). American, b. 1914. Children's fiction. Art Dir., Computer Design Publishing Co., since 1962. Co-Founder, Little Man Press, 1939–42; Art Dir., Columbia Recording Corp., 1942–50; Consultant Art Dir., Benwill Publishing Corp., 1957–62. *Publs:* The Fabulous Firework Family, 1955, film, 1959; The Day the Cow Sneezed, 1957; Charlie Yup and His Snip-Snap Boys, 1959; Leopold, The See-Through Crumbpicker, 1961, film, 1972; Kangaroo for Christmas, 1962; My Friend Charlie, 1964; Gandpa's Farm: Four Tall Tales, 1965; Sherwood Walks Home, 1966; Fishing with Dad, 1967; The Joking Man, 1968; Little Hatchy Hen, 1969; Pishtosh, Bullwash, and Wimple, 1972; Stewed Goose, 1973; The Great Green Turkey Creek Monster, 1976; Grandpa's Ghost Stories, 1978; Wanda and the Bumbly Wizard, 1980; Grandpa's Witched-Up Christmas, 1982. Add: St. James Pl., Bell Island, Rowayton, Conn., U.S.A.

FLORA, Joseph M(artin). American, b. 1934. Literature. Prof. of English, since 1977, and Chmn. of Dept., since 1980, Univ. of North Carolina, Chapel Hill (Instr., 1962–64; Asst. Prof., 1964–67; Assoc. Prof., 1967–77; Asst. Dean of Grad Sch., 1967–72; Assoc. Dean, 1977–78). *Publs:* Vardis Fisher, 1965; William Ernest Henley, 1970; Frederick Manfred, 1974; (co-ed.) Southern Writers: A Biographical Dictionary, 1979; Hemingway's Nick Adams, 1982; (ed.) The English Short Story 1880-1945, 1985. Add: 505 Caswell Rd., Chapel Hill, N.C. 27514, U.S.A.

FLOREN, Lee. Also writes as Brett Austin, Claudia Hall, Wade Hamilton, Matthew Whitman Harding, Felix Lee Horton, Stuart Jason, Grace Lang, Marguerite Nelson, Lew Smith, Maria Sandra Sterling, Lee Thomas, Len Turner, Will Watson, and Dave Wilson. American, b. 1910. Novels/Short stories, Mystery/Crime/Suspense, Historical/Romance/Gothic, Biography. *Publs:* has written over 300 novels, of which the following are the most recent—Gambler with a Gun, 1971; Wyoming Showdown, 1972; The Bloodskinners, 1972; (as Maria Sandra Sterling) War Drum, 1973; Trail to High Pine, 1974; (as Felix Lee Horton) Long Knife and Musket, 1974; (as Matthew Whitman Harding) Muskets on the Mississippi, 1974; (as Stuart Jason) Valley of Death, 1974; (as Stuart Jason) Deadly Doctor, 1974; Boothill Riders, 1979; Renegade Gambler, 1979; Gun Chore, 1979; High Border Riders, 1979; Powdersmoke Attorney, 1979; (as Matt Harding) Edge of Gunsmoke, 1979; (as Grace Lang) Nedra, 1979; (as Marguerite Nelson) Mercy Nurse, 1979; Rope the Wild Wind, 1980; The Bushwhackers, 1980; High Trail to

Gunsmoke, 1980; (as Marguerite Nelson) Hard Rock Nurse, 1980; Smoky River, 1980; (as Wade Hamilton) Ride Against the Rifles, 1980; The High Gun, 1980; North to Powder River, 1981; Broomtail Basin, 1981; Cowthief Clanton, 1982; Renegade Rifles, 1983; Buckskin Challenge, 1983; Boothill Brand, 1984; Gun Quick, 1985; West of Barbwire, 1985; Wyoming Gun Law, 1985; (as Lee Thomas) The Gringo, 1985; The Saddle Wolves, 1985; Fighting Ramrod, 1986; Bring Bullets, Texan, 1986; The Tall Texan, 1986. Add: c/o Hale, 45-47 Clerkenwell Green, London EC1R 0HT, England.

FLORENCE, Ronald. American, b. 1942. History. Assoc. Prof. of History, State Univ. of New York, Coll. at Purchase, since 1971. Research Fellow, Joint Center for Urban Studies, MIT and Harvard Univ., Cambridge, Mass., 1965–66; Prof. of History, Sarah Lawrence Coll., Bronxville, N.Y., 1968–71. *Publs:* Fritz: the Story of a Political Assassin, 1971; Marx's Daughters, 1975; Zeppelin, 1982; The Gypsy Man, 1985; The Optimum Sailboat, 1987. Add: c/o Ballantine Books, 201 E. 50th St., New York, N.Y. 10022, U.S.A.

FLORES, Ivan. American, b. 1923. Information science/Computers. Pres., Flores Assocs., since 1960; Prof. of Statistics and Computer Information Science, Baruch Coll., City Univ. of New York, since 1968. Ed., Modern Data, since 1968, and Journal of Computer Languages, since 1973. Adjunct Prof. of Electrical Engineering, 1958–62, and Assoc. Prof., 1961–63, Polytechnic Inst. of Brooklyn, N.Y.; Ed., Journal of Assn. for Computing Machinery, 1963–67; Adjunct Prof. of Electrical Engineering, New York Univ., NYC, 1963–64; Assoc. Prof. of Electrical Engineering, Stevens Inst. of Technology, Hoboken, N.J., 1965–67. *Publs:* Computer Logic, 1960; Logic of Computer Arithmetic, 1963; Computer Software, 1965; Computer Programming, 1966; Computer Design, 1967; Computer Sorting, 1969; Computer Organization, 1969; Data Structure and Management, 1970, 1977; BAL and Assemblers, 1971; JCL and File Definition, 1971; Computer Programming, 1971; The BAL Machine, 1972; OS/MVT, 1973; Peripheral Devices, 1973; Data Base Architecture, 1981; (with Chris Terry) Microcomputer Systems, 1982; Word Processing Handbook, 1982; (with Arthur Seedman) The Handbook of Computers and Computing, 1984; The Professional Microcomputer Handbook, 1986. Add: 441 Redmond Rd., South Orange, N.J. 07079, U.S.A.

FLOWER, Jake. *See* **BOLD,** Alan.

FLOWER, John Matthew. Australian, b. 1929. Business/Trade/Industry. Secty., Australian Inst. of Petroleum, since 1976. Dir., Petroleum Information Bureau, Melbourne, 1968–76 (Deputy Dir., S.A., 1960–61, and N.S.W., 1961–68). *Publs:* (ed.) This Age of Oil, 1960; Petroleum and Natural Gas in Australia, 1967. Add: 39 Stawell St., Kew, Vic., 3101, Australia.

FLOWERDEW, Phyllis. British. Children's fiction, Children's nonfiction. Freelance writer. Formerly teacher in Surrey, and adviser in primary schs. in Oxfordshire. *Publs:* (with F.J. Schonell) Wide Range Readers, 12 books, 1958–53, 1965; (with R. Ridout) Reading to Some Purpose, 6 books, 1952–57; (with F.J. Schonell) Happy Venture Playbooks, books; (with S. Stewart) Reading On, 4 books, 1958–63; Stories for Sounds, 1958; Flamingo Books, 20 books, 1965–66; Stories for Telling, 1966; (with F.J. Schonell and A.E. Cannon) Wide Range Interest, 4 books, 1966–67; Poetry Is All Around, 1967; More Stories for Telling, 1968; New Interest Books, 4 books, 1972; New Interest Activity Books, 4 books, 1974; Trug Books, 12 books, 1974; Pedro Books, 8 books, 1974; Goodbye Candlelight, 1974; More Interest Books, 4 books, 1977–78; Wide Range Red Books, 8 books, 1978–82; Wide Range Quiz, 6 books, 1980; Wide Range Starter, 6 books, 1985. Add: Fallows, Chartway, Sevenoaks, Kent, England.

FLYNN, Frank. (Francis Stanislaus Flynn). Australian, b. 1906. Anthropology/Ethnology, Medicine/Health, Travel/Exploration/Adventure, Autobiography/Memoirs/Personal. Medical Missionary, Northern Territory, Aust., 1946–67, and since 1977 (in Papua New Guinea, 1968–77). House Surgeon, Sydney Hosp., 1930–31; Ophthalmic Specialist, Moorfields Ophthalmic Hosp., London, 1932–34; Admin., Darwin Cathedral, 1946–67, and Port Moresby Cathedral, 1968–70; Deputy Chmn., Museum and Art Gallery, Bd. of N.T., 1966–77; Pres., Papua New Guinea Medical Soc., 1969–70; Deputy Chmn., Medical Bd. of Papua New Guinea, 1970–71. *Publs:* Distant Horizons, 1957; (with K. Wiley) Northern Gateway, 1963; (with K. Wiley) The Living Heart, 1964; The Darwin Cathedral, 1964; (with K. Wiley) Northern Frontiers, 1968; Guide to Port Moresby Cathedral, 1973. Add: P.O. Box 547, Darwin, 0801, N.T., Australia.

FLYNN, Jackson. *See* **SHIRREFFS,** Gordon Donald.

FLYNN, James Robert. American/New Zealander, b. 1934. Philosophy, Politics/Government, Psychology. Prof. and Chmn., Political Studies Dept., Univ. of Otago, Dunedin, since 1967. Asst. Prof. of Political Science, Eastern Kentucky State Univ., 1957–61, Wisconsin State Coll., Whitewater, 1961–62, and Lake Forest Coll., Ill., 1962–63; Lectr. to Sr. Lectr., Univ. of Canterbury, Christchurch, 1963–67. *Publs:* American Politics: A Radical View, 1967; Humanism and Ideology, 1973; Race, IQ, and Jensen, 1980. Add: Dept. of Political Studies, Univ. of Otago, P.O. Box 56, Dunedin, New Zealand.

FLYNN, Leslie Bruce. American (b. Canadian), b. 1918. Theology/Religion. Pastor, Grace Conservative Baptist Church, Nanuet, N.Y., since 1949. Regional Ed., Christian Life Mag., since 1944. *Publs:* Did I Say That?, 1959, 1986; Serve Him with Mirth, 1960; Your God and Your Gold, 1961; The Power of Christ-like Living, 1962; Did I Say Thanks?, 1963; Christmas Messages, 1964; Day of Resurrection, 1965; How to Save Time in the Ministry, 1966; Your Influence is Showing, 1967; You Can Live Above Envy, 1970; A Source Book of Humorous Stories, 1973; 19 Gifts of the Spirit, 1974; It's About Time, 1974; Now a Word from Our Creator, 1976; Great Church Fights, 1976; Man: Ruined and Restored, 1978; God's Will: You Can Know It, 1979; Joseph: God's Man in Egypt, 1979; The Gift of Joy, 1980; From Clay to Rock, 1981; You Don't Have to Go It Alone, 1981; Dare to Care Like Jesus, 1982; The Twelve, 1982; Worship, Together We Celebrate, 1983; Your Inner You, 1984; The Sustaining Power of Hope, 1985; Holy Contradictions, 1987; When the Saints Come Storming In, 1988; The Other Twelve, 1988; Come Alive with Illustrations, 1987. Add: 32 Highview Ave., Nanuet, N.Y. 10954, U.S.A.

FLYNN, Robert (Lopez). American, b. 1932. Westerns/Adventure. Prof. and Novelist-in-Residence, Trinity Univ., San Antonio, Tex., since 1963. Instr., Gardner-Webb Coll. Boiling Springs, N.C., 1957–59; Asst. Prof., Baylor Univ., Waco, Tex., 1959–63. *Publs:* North to Yesterday, 1967; In the House of the Lord, 1969; The Sounds of Rescue, The Signs of Hope, 1970; Seasonal Rain and Other Stories, 1986. Add: c/o Knopf, 201 E. 50th St., New York, N.Y. 10022, U.S.A.

FM-20 30, Pseud. for F. M. Esfandiary. American. Future studies, Social commentary. Lectr., New Sch. for Social Research, NYC, and Univ. of California at Los Angeles. *Publs:* Day of Sacrifice, 1959; The Beggar, 1965; Identity Card, 1966; Optimism One, 1970; Up Wingers, 1973; (co-author) Woman: Year 2,000, 1974; Telespheres, 1977; Are You a Transhuman?, 1989. Add: P.O. Box 24421, Los Angeles, Calif. 90024, U.S.A.

FOGARTY, Michael Patrick. British/Irish, b. 1916. Economics, Industrial relations. Research Officer, Social Reconstruction Survey, 1941–44, and Official Fellow, 1944–51, Nuffield Coll., Oxford; Prof. of Industrial Relations, Univ. of Wales, Cardiff, 1951–66; Consultant, Political and Economic Planning, London, 1966–68; Dir. and Prof., Economic and Social Research Inst., Dublin, 1968–72; Sr. Fellow, Centre for Studies in Social Policy, 1973–78; Deputy Dir., Policy Studies Inst., 1978–82; Dir., Inst. for Family and Environmental Research, 1981–84. *Publs:* Prospects of the Industrial Areas of Great Britain, 1945; Plan Your Own Industries, 1957; Town and Country Planning, 1948; (ed.) Further Studies in Industrial Organization, 1948; Economic Control, 1955; Personality and Group Relations in Industry, 1956; Christian Democracy in Western Europe, 1820-1953, 1957; Under-Governed and Over-Governed, 1962; The Just Wage, 1962; The Rules of Work, 1963; Company and Corporation—One Law?, 1965; Companies Beyond Jenkins, 1965; Wider Business Objectives, 1966; A Companies Act 1970?, 1967; (with R. and R. Rapaport) Sex, Career and Family, 1971; (ed.) Women in Top Jobs, 1971; Women and Top Jobs: The Next Move, 1972; Irish Entrepreneurs Speak for Themselves, 1974; Forty to Sixty, 1975; Company Responsibility and Participation—A New Agenda, 1975; How We Waste the Middle-Aged, 1975; Pensions—Where Next?, 1976; (with E. Reid) Differentials for Managers and Skilled Manual Workers in the U.K., 1980; Retirement Age and Retirement Costs, 1980; (ed.) Women in Top Jobs 1968-79, 1981; (ed.) Retirement Policy—The Next Fifty Years, 1982; (with L. Ryan and J. Lee) Irish Values and Attitudes, 1984; (with S. Harding and D. Phillips) Contrasting Values in Western Europe, 1986; (with D. Brooks) Trade Unions and British Industrial Development, 1986. Add: Red Copse, Boars Hill, Oxford, England.

FOGG, Gordon Elliott. British, b. 1919. Biology, Botany, Marine science/Oceanography. Reader in Botany, Univ. Coll., 1953–60, and Prof. of Botany, Westfield Coll., 1960–71, Univ. of London; Prof. of Marine Biology, University Coll., of North Wales, 1971–85. *Publs:* The

Metabolism of Algae, 1953; The Growth of Plants, 1963, 1970; (ed.) Cell Differentiation, 1963; Algal Cultures and Phytoplankton Ecology, 1965, 1975, 3rd ed., with B.A. Thake, 1987; (ed.) The State and Movement of Water in Living Organisms, 1965; Photosynthesis, 1968, 1972; (with W.D.P. Stewart, P. Fay and A.E. Walsby) The Blue-Green Algae, 1973. Add: Marine Science Labs., Menai Bridge, Anglesey, Wales.

FOLEY, (Mary) Louise Munro. American (b. Canadian), b. 1933. Novels/Short stories, Children's fiction. Ed. of Publs., Inst. for Human Service Mgmt., California State Univ., Sacramento, 1975–80. *Publs:* The Caper Club, 1969; No Talking, 1970; Sammy's Sister, 1970; A Job for Joey, 1970; Somebody Stole Second, 1972; (ed.) Stand Close to the Door, 1976; Tackle 22, 1978; (ed.) Women in Skilled Labor, 1980; The Train of Terror, 1982; The Sinister Studies of KESP-TV, 1983; The Lost Tribe, 1983; The Mystery of the Highland Crest, 1984; The Mystery of Echo Lodge, 1985; Danger at Anchor Mine, 1985; Forest of Fear, 1986; The Mardi Gras Mystery, 1987; Mystery of the Sacred Stones, 1988; Australia, 1988. Add: 5010 Jennings Way, Sacramento, Calif. 95819, U.S.A.

FOLLETT, Ken(neth Martin). Has also written as Symon Myles and Zachary Stone. British, b. 1949. Mystery/Crime/Suspense. Full-time writer since 1977. Reporter and rock music columnist, South Wales Echo, Cardiff, 1970–73; Reporter, London Evening News, 1973–74; Editorial Dir., 1974–76, and Deputy Managing Ed., 1976–77, Everest Books, London. *Publs:* (as Symon Myles) The Big Black, 1974; (as Symon Myles) The Big Needle, 1974; (as Symon Myles) The Big Hit, 1975; The Shakeout, 1975; The Bear Raid, 1976; The Secret of Kellerman's Studio (juvenile), 1976; (as Zachary Stone) The Modigliani Scandal, 1976, published in U.S. as by Ken Follett, 1985; (as Zachary Stone) Paper Money, 1977; Storm Island (in U.S. as Eye of the Needle), 1978; Triple, 1979; The Key to Rebecca, 1980; The Man from St. Petersburg, 1982; On Wings of Eagles, 1983; Lie Down with Lions, 1985. Add: P.O. Box 708, London SW10 0DH, England.

FOLSOM, Franklin Brewster. Also writes as Benjamin Brewster, Michael Gorham, Lyman Hopkins, and Troy Nesbit. American, b. 1907. Children's fiction, Archaeology/Antiquities, Children's non-fiction, History. Freelance writer since 1948. English Instr., Swarthmore Coll., Pa., 1928–30; Exec. Secty., League of American Writers, 1937–42; Staff Writer, Tass News Agency, 1946–48. Chmn., Council on Inter-racial Books for Children, 1965–69; Member, Bd. of Dirs., Great Peace March for Global Nuclear Disarmament, 1986; Visiting Lectr., English Dept., Univ. of Colorado, Boulder, 1987. *Publs:* (co-author) Life of the Party (in later eds. as 72 Sure Fire Ways of Having Fun), 1934; (as Benjamin Brewster) The First Book of Baseball, 1950; (as Benjamin Brewster) The First Book of Cowboys, 1950; (as Benjamin Brewster) The First Book of Indians, 1950; (ghost writer) The Cowboy and His Horse, 1951; (as Lyman Hopkins) Real Book About Baseball, 1951; (as Michael Gorham) Real Book About Abraham Lincoln, 1951; (as Benjamin Brewster) The Big Book of Real Boats and Ships, 1951; (as Benjamin Brewster) The First Book of Firemen, 1951; (as Troy Nesbit) Sand Dune Pony, 1952, as Sand Dune Pony Mystery, 1960; (as Troy Nesbit) Forest Fire Mystery, 1952; (as Michael Gorham) Real Book About Cowboys, 1952; (as Michael Gorham) Real Book of American Tall Tales, 1952; (co-author as Benjamin Brewster) The Big Book of the Real Circus, 1953; (as Benjamin Brewster) The First Book of Eskimos, 1953; (as Michael Gorham) Real Book About Indians, 1953; (as Michael Gorham) Real Book of Great American Journeys, 1953; (as Troy Nesbit) The Jinx of Payrock Canyon, 1954, as the Mystery of Payrock Canyon, 1962; (as Troy Nesbit) Indian Mummy Mystery, 1954; (ghost writer) The American Indian, 1954; Search in the Desert, 1955; (as Troy Nesbit) Diamond Cave Mystery, 1956; (as Troy Nesbit) The Hidden Ruin, 1957; (as Troy Nesbit) Mystery at Rustler's Fort, 1957; The Explorations of America, 1958; (as Troy Nesbit) Wagon Train, 1959; (as Troy Nesbit) Fury and the Mystery at Trapper's Hole, 1959; (co-author) The Story of Archaeology in the Americas, 1960; Exploring American Caves, 1962; Famous Pioneers, 1963; The Language Book, 196; Men Who Won the West, 1963; (co-author) The Answer Book of Geography, 1964; The Soviet Union: A View from Within, 1965; (co-author) The Answer Book of History, 1966; Science and the Secret of Man's Past, 1966; (co-author) Flags of All Nations and the People Who Live Under Them, 1967; Beyond the Frontier, rev. ed. 1968; (co-author) If You Lived in the Days of the Wild Mammoth Hunters, 1968; America's Accent Treasures: Guide to Archaeological Sites and Museums, 1983; Power on the Rio Grande: The Native American Revolution of 1680, 1973; The Life and Legend of George McJunkin: Black Cowboy, 1973; Give Me Liberty: Our Colonial Heritage, 1974; Some Basic Rights of Soviet Citizens, 1983; (co-author) The Great Peace March: An American Odyssey, 1988. Add: 1186a Monroe Dr., No. 212, Boulder,

Colo. 80303, U.S.A.

FONDA, Jane. American, b. 1937. Sports/Physical Education/Keeping fit. Motion picture actress; films include: Tall Story, 1960; A Walk on the Wild Side, 1962; Period of Adjustment, 1962; Sunday in New York, 1963; The Love Cage, 1963; La Ronde, 1964; Histoires extraordinaries, 1967; Barbarella, 1968; They Shoot Horses Don't They, 1969; Klute, 1970; Steelyard Blues, 1972; Tout va bien, 1972; A Doll's House, 1973; The Blue Bird, 1975; Dick and Jane, 1976; Julia, 1977; Coming Home, 1978; California Suite, 1978; The Electric Horseman, 1979; The China Syndrome, 1979; Nine to Five, 1980; On Golden Pond, 1981; Roll-Over, 1981. *Publs:* Jane Fonda's Work Out Book, 1982; (with Mignon McCarthy) Women Coming of Age, 1984; Jane Fonda's Year of Fitness, Health and Nutrition, 1985; Jane Fonda's New Workout and Weight-Loss Program, 1986; Jane Fonda's New Low Impact Workout and Weight Loss Program, 1988. Add: Fonda Films, P.O. Box 491355, Los Angeles, Calif. 90049, U.S.A.

FONER, Eric. American, b. 1943. History, Race relations. Dewitt Clinton Prof. of History, Columbia Univ., NYC, since 1982 (Instr., and subsequently Asst. Prof. and Assoc. Prof., 1969–73). Prof. of History, City Coll., City Univ. of New York, 1973–82. *Publs:* Free Soil, Free Labor, Free Men: The Ideology of the Republican Party Before the Civil War, 1970; (ed.) America's Black Past: A Reader in Afro-American History, 1970; (ed.) Nat Turner, 1971; Tom Paine and Revolutionary America, 1976; Politics and Ideology in the Age of the Civil War, 1980; Nothing but Freedom, 1983; Reconstruction: America's Unfinished Revolution, 1988. Add: 606 West 116th St., New York, N.Y., U.S.A.

FONER, Philip S. American, b. 1910. History, Industrial relations, Race relations. Instr. in History, City Coll. of New York, 1933–41; Educational Dir., Fur and Leather Workers Union, 1941–45; Publisher, The Citadel Press, NYC, 1945–67; Prof. of Pennsylvania History, Lincoln Univ., Pennsylvania, 1967–79. *Publs:* Business and Slavery, 1941; The Basic Writings of Thomas Jefferson, 1943; The Selected Writings of Thomas Jefferson, 1943; The Selected Writings of Abraham Lincoln, 1944; The Complete Writings of Thomas Paine, 2 vols., 1945; History of the Labor Movement in the United States, 7 vols., 1947–87; The Fur and Leather Workers Union, 1950; The Life and Writings of Frederick Douglass, 4 vols., 1950–52; Jack London: American Rebel, 1953; Jews in American History, 1954; Mark Twain: Social Critic, 1958; The Case of Joe Hill, 1965; The Letters of Joe Hill, 1965; History of Cuba and Its Relations with the United States, 2 vols., 1962–64; The Bolshevik Revolution, 1967; The Haymarket Autobiographies, 1969; The Black Panthers Speak, 1970; W.E.B. Du Bois Speaks, 2 vols., 1970; American Labor and the War in Indochina, 1971; The Voice of Black America: Major Speeches of Negroes in the United States 1969-1971, 1972; When Karl Marx Died: Comments in 1883, 1973; Organized Labor and the Black Worker 1619-1973, 1974; History of Black Americans, vol. I, 1975; Jose Marti, Inside the Monster, 1975; American Labor Songs of the Nineteenth Century, 1975; We the Other People: Alternative Declarations of Independence, 1976; Formation of the Workingmen's Party of the United States, 1976; Blacks and the American Revolution, 1976; The Great Labor Uprising of 1877, 1977; Frederick Douglass and Women's Rights, 1977; The Factory Girls, 1977; Our America, 1977; Antonio Maceo, 1977; Labor and the American Revolution, 1977; American Socialism and Black Americans, 1977; The Black Worker: A Documentary History from Colonial Times to the Present, 4 vols., 1978–85; (with Ronald L. Lewis) Women and the American Labor Movement, 2 vols., 1979–80; (with George E. Walker) Proceedings of the Black State Conventions 1840-1865, 2 vols., 1979–80; On Art and Literature, 1982; Major Poems, 1982; British Labor and the American Civil War, 1982; Wilhelm Liebknecht: Letters to the Chicago Workingmen's Advocate, 1983; From the Emergence of the Cotton Kingdom to the Eve of the Compromise in 1850, 1983; From the Compromise of 1850 to the End of the Civil War, 1983; Mother Jones Speaks, 1983; Black Socialist Preacher, 1983; The Anti-Imperialist Reader, 1984; First Facts of American Labor, 1984; Clara Zetkin, Selected Writings, 1984; May Day: A Short History of the International Workers Holiday 1886-1986, 1986; The Literary Anti-Imperialists, 1986; Proceedings of Black National and State Conventions 1865-1900, vol. 1, 1986; American Communism and Black Americans 1919-1929, 1987. Add: Park Plaza 3900, Ford Rd., Philadelphia, Pa. 19131, U.S.A.

FONSECA, Aloysius (Joseph). Indian, b. 1915. Economics, Politics/Government. Jesuit: Member, Editorial Bd., La Civilta Cattolica, Roma; Prof. of Economics, Pontifical Gregorian Univ., Rome. *Publs:* Citizen and State; Indian Administration and Civics, Wage Determination and Organized Labor in India; (ed.) Report of the Food and

Health Seminar; The Challenge of Poverty in India; Wage Issues in a Developing Economy; The Marxian Dilemma; Food Aid for Relief and Development; (ed.) Multinationals in Third-World Countries. Add: La Civilta Cattolica, Via di Porta Pinciana 1, 00187 Rome, Italy.

FONSECA, John dos Reis. American, b. 1925. Law, Money/Finance. Prof. of Law and Banking Emeritus, State Univ. of New York, Albany, since 1968. With Dun & Bradstreet, U.S. and South America, 1952–53; Financial Analyst, Chase Manhattan Bank, NYC, 1953–56; Ed. and Admin. of Trusts and Estates, Univ. of Pennsylvania, Philadelphia, 1959–60; Legal Ed., The Banking Law Journal, 1967–72; Ed., Banking Law Journal Digest, 1967–72; Ed.-in-Chief, Uniform Commercial Code Law Journal, 1968–72; Assoc. Ed., Criminal Law Bulletin, 1969–71. *Publs:* (ed. and contrib.) Banking Manual, 1956; Law of Contracts, 1965; (ed.-in-chief) Pert-Cost, 1965; (ed.-in-chief) Artillery Course, 1965; Fire Insurance, 1966; Negotiable Instruments, 1967; (ed.) Encyclopedia of Banking Laws, 1968–71; (ed.) Encyclopedia of Commercial Laws, 1968–71; (ed.) Brady on Bank Checks, 1968–69; Law of Business Organizations, 1971; Law and Society, 1972; (co-author) Handling Consumer Credit Cases, 1972, 2 vols., 3rd ed. 1986; Proof of Cases: Massachusetts, 1972–81; Environment Law, 1972; New York Evidence, 1972–86; (co-author) Automobile Insurance and No-Fault Law, 1974; Legal Environment of Business, 1974; Consumer Credit Compliance Manual, 1975, 1984; Law of Modern Commercial Practices, 1975-86, 2 vols., 1981. Add: El Rancho, Greenfield Center, N.Y. 12833, U.S.A.

FONTENAY, Charles L(ouis). American, b. 1917. Science fiction/Fantasy, Philosophy, Biography. Rewriter, The Tennessean, since 1968 (Political Reporter, 1946–64; City Ed., 1964–68). *Publs:* Twice Upon a Time, 1958; Rebels of the Red Planet, 1961; The Day the Oceans Overflowed, 1964; Epistle to the Babylonians, 1969; The Kayen of Fu Tze, 1977; Estes Kefauver: A Biography, 1980. Add: 1708 20th Ave. N., St. Petersburg, Fl. 33713, U.S.A.

FONTENOT, Mary Alice. American, b. 1910. Children's fiction, Cultural/Ethnic topics, History, Biography. *Publs:* Clovis Crawfish series, 9 vols., 1962–82; The Ghost of Bayou Tigre, 1965; The Cat and St. Landry, 1972; Acadia Parish: A History to 1900, 1976; Acadia Parish: A History to 1920, vol. II, 1979; Cajun Accent (cookbook), 1979; The Louisiana Experience: An Introduction to the Culture of the Bayou State, 1983; The Star Seed: A Story of the First Christmas, 1985; The Tensas Story, 1987. Add: 431 Holden Ave., Lafayette, La. 70506, U.S.A.

FOON, Dennis. American, b. 1951. Children's fiction, Children's nonfiction. Co-Founder and Artistic Dir., Green Thumb Theatre for Young People, Vancouver, since 1975. Instr. in Playwriting, Univ. of British Columbia Centre for Continuing Education, 1974–79; Playwright-in-Residence, Young People's Theatre, Toronto, 1983–84; Canadian Vice-Pres., Intnl. Assn. of Theatres for Children and Youth, 1979–82. *Publs:* plays for children—The Last Days of Paul Bunyan, 1978; The Windigo, 1978; Heracles, 1978; New Canadian Kid, 1982; The Hunchback of Notre Dame (adaptation of the novel by Victor Hugo), 1983; Trummi Kaput (adaptation of the play by Volker Ludwig), 1983; Skin, 1988; Liars, 1988; others for children—(with B. Knight) Am I the Only One?: A Young People's Book About Sex Abuse (non-fiction), 1985; The Short Tree and the Bird That Could Not Sing, 1986. Add: 647 E. 12th Ave., Vancouver, B.C. V5T 2H7, Canada.

FOOT, Michael. British, b. 1913. History, Politics/Government, Biography. Labour Member of Parliament (U.K.), 1945–55, and since 1960 (Secty. of State for Employment, 1974–76, and leader of the House of Commons, 1976–79; Leader of the Labour Party, 1980–83). Managing Dir., Tribune newspaper, London, 1952–74; Literary Critic, Evening Standard newspaper, London, 1964–74. *Publs:* Armistice 1918-39, 1940; (with Frank Owen and Peter Howard) Guilty Men, 1940; Trial of Mussolini, 1943; Brendan and Beverley, 1944; Still at Large, 1950; Full Speed Ahead, 1950; (with M. Jones) Guilty Men, 1957; The Pen and the Sword, 1957; Parliament in Danger, 1959; Aneurin Bevan, 2 vols., 1962–74; Debts of Honours, 1979; Another Heart and Other Pulses, 1984; Loyalists and Loners, 1986; The Politics of Paradise: A Vindication of Byron, 1988. Add: House of Commons, London SW1, England.

FOOT, Michael Richard Daniell. British, b. 1919. History, International relations/Current affairs, Biography. Prof. of Modern History, Manchester Univ., 1967–73. *Publs:* (with J.L. Hammond) Gladstone and Liberalism, 1952; British Foreign Policy since 1898, 1956; Men in Uniform, 1961; SOE in France, 1966, 1968; (ed.) Gladstone Diaries, vols. I & II: 1825-1839, 1968 (with H.C.G. Matthew) vols. III & IV: 1840-1855, 1975; (ed.) War and Society, 1973; Resistance, 1976, 1978; Six Faces of Courage, 1978; (with J.M. Langley) MI9, 1979; SOE: An Outline History, 1984. Add: 45 Countess Rd., London NW5 2XH, England.

FOOTE, Geoffrey. British, b. 1950. Politics/Government. Adult Education Tutor, City Univ., London, since 1983, and Open Univ., since 1985. Private teacher of politics and economics, 1979–83. *Publs:* The Labour Party's Political Thought: A History, 1985; A Chronology of British Politics 1945-1986, 1987. Add: 52 Beauchamp Pl., Oxford OX4 3NE, England.

FOOTE, Horton. American, b. 1916. Novels, Plays/Screenplays, Actor, 1939–42; workshop dir., King Smith Sch. of Creative Arts, 1944, and mgr., Productions Inc., 1945–48, both in Washington D.C. *Publs:* plays—The Chase, 1952; The Trip to Bountiful, 1954; The Traveling Lady, 1955; A Young Lady of Property: Six Short Plays, 1955; Harrison, Texas: Eight Television Plays, 1956; Flight (in Television Plays for Writers), 1957; The Midnight Caller, 1959; Three Plays, 1962; The Screenplay of To Kill a Mockingbird, 1964; The Roads to Home, 1982; Courtship, Valentine's Day 1918, 1987; Selected One-Act Plays, 1988; Roots in Parched Ground, Convicts, Lily Dale, and The Widow Claire, 1988; Cousins, and The Death of Papa, 1989; To Kill a Mockingbird, Tender Mercies, and The Trip to Bountiful: Three Screenplays, 1989; novel—The Chase, 1956. Add: c/o Lucy Kroll, 390 West End Ave., New York, N.Y. 10024, U.S.A.

FOOTE, Shelby. American, b. 1916. Novels/Short stories, Plays/Screenplays, History. Playwright-in-Residence, Arena Stage, Washington, D.C., 1963–64; Writer-in-Residence, Hollins Coll., Virginia, 1968. *Publs:* Tournament, 1949; Follow Me Down, 1950; Love in a Dry Season, 1951; Shiloh, 1952; Jordan County, 1954; The Civil War: A Narrative, vol. I, Fort Sumter to Perryville, 1958; vol. II, Fredericksburg to Meridian, 1963, vol. III, Red River to Appomattox, 1974; Jordan County: A Landscape in the Round (play), 1964; September September, 1978; The Novelist's View of History, 1981. Add: 542 East Parkway South, Memphis, Tenn. 38104, U.S.A.

FORBES, Bryan. British, b. 1926. Novels/Short stories, Chldren's fiction, Plays/Screenplays, Autobiography/Memoirs/Personal, Biography. Film Dir., since 1959. Pres., National Youth Theatre of Great Britain. Stage and screen actor, 1942–60; Managing Dir., and Head of Production, EMI Films, 1969–71. *Publs:* Truth Lies Sleeping, 1951; The Distant Laughter (novel), 1972; Notes for a Life (autobiography), 1974; The Slipper and the Rose (fiction for children), 1976; Ned's Girl (on Dame Edith Evans), 1977; International Velvet (novel), 1978; Familiar Strangers (novel), 1979; That Despicable Race (on the British Acting Tradition), 1980; The Rewrite Man, 1984; The Endless Game, 1986. Screenplays—The Angry Silence, 1960; The League of Gentlemen, 1961; Only Two Can Play, 1961; The L-Shaped Room, 1962; Seance on a Wet Afternoon, 1963; King Rat, 1964; The Whisperers, 1966; Deadfall, 1967; The Raging Moon (in U.S. as Long Ago Tomorrow), 1970; The Stepford Wives, 1974; The Slipper and the Rose, 1976; International Velvet, 1978; Ménage à Trois, 1981; The Naked Face, 1984; The Endless Game, 1988. Add: c/o Pinewood Studios, Iver Heath, Bucks., England.

FORBES, Colin. British. Novels/Short stories. *Publs:* Tramp in Armour, 1969; The Heights of Zervos, 1970; The Palermo Ambush, 1972; Target Five, 1973; Year of the Golden Ape, 1974; The Stone Leopard, 1975; Avalanche Express, 1977; The Stockholm Syndicate, 1981; Double Jeopardy, 1982; The Leader and the Damned, 1983; Terminal, 1984; Cover Story, 1985; The Janus Man, 1987; Deadlock, 1988; The Greek Key, 1989. Add: c/o Elaine Greene Ltd., 31 Newington Green, London N16 9PU, England.

FORBES, Daniel. *See* **KENYON,** Michael.

FORBES, John. Australian, b. 1950. Poetry. Ed., Surfer's Paradise, 1974–83. *Publs:* Tropical Skiing, 1976; On the Beach, 1977; Drugs, 1980; Stalin's Holidays, 1981. Add: c/o 74 Corruna Rd., Stanmore, N.S.W. 2048, Australia.

FORBES, (Deloris) Stanton. Also writes as Forbes Rydell and Tobias Wells. American, b. 1923. Mystery/Crime/Suspense. Co-Proprietor, Pierre Lapin fashion shop, St. Martin, since 1973. Asst. Ed., Wellesley Townsman (weekly newspaper), Mass., 1958–73. *Publs:* with Helen Rydell under joint pseudonym Forbes Rydell—Annalisa, 1960; If She Should Die, 1962; No Questions Asked, 1963; as Stanton Forbes—They're Not Home Yet, 1963; Grieve for the Past, 1964; Terrors of the Earth, 1964; Relative to Death, 14; Terror Touches Me, 1964; A Business of Bodies, 1964; Encounter Darkness, 1967; If Two of Them are Dead,

1968; Go to Thy Deathbed, 1968, filmscript as Reflection of Fear; The Name's Death, Remember Me, 1969; She Was Only the Sheriff's Daughter, 1969; If Laurel Shot Hardy the World Would End, 1969; The Sad Sudden Death of My Fair Lady, 1971; All for One and One for Death, 1971; A Deadly Kind of Lonely, 1971; But I Wouldn't Want to Die There, 1972; Welcome My Dear to Belfrey House, 1972; Some Poisoned by Their Wines, 1974; Bury Me in Gold Lamé, 1975; Buried in So Sweet a Place, 1977; The Will and Last Testament of Constance Cobble, 1980; as Tobias Wells—A Matter of Love and Death, 1966; What Should You Know of Dying, 1967; Dead by the Light of the Moon, 1967; Murder Most Fouled Up, 1968; Die Quickly Dear Mother, 1969; The Young Can Die Protesting, 1969; Dinky Died, 1969; What to Do Till the Undertaker Comes, 1971; The Foo Dog, 1971; A Die in the Country, 1972; How to Kill a Man, 1972; Brenda's Murder, 1973; Have Murcy Upon Us, 1974; Hark, Hark, Watchdogs Bark, 1975; A Creature Was Stirring, 1977. Add: Goetz House, Grand Case, St. Martin, French West Indies.

FORBUS, Ina B. American. Children's fiction. *Publs:* The Magic Pin, 1956; The Secret Circle, 1958; Melissa, 1962; Tawny's Trick, 1965. Add: 109 Forestwood Dr., Durham, N.C. 27707, U.S.A.

FORCHÉ, Carolyn (Louise). American, b. 1950. Poetry. Visiting Lectr., Michigan State Univ., E. Lansing, 1974; Visiting Lectr., 1975, and Asst. Prof., 1976–78, San Diego State Univ.; Visiting Lectr., Univ. of Virginia, Charlottesville, 1979, 1982–83; Asst. Prof., 1980, and Asst. Prof., 1981, Univ. of Arkansas, Fayetteville; Visiting Lectr., New York Univ., 1983, Vassar Coll., Poughkeepsie, N.Y., 1984, and Columbia Univ., NYC, 1984–85. *Publs:* Gathering the Tribes, 1976; Undisclosed No. 24, 1977; The Country Between Us, 1983. Add: c/o Yale Univ. Press, 302 Temple St., New Haven, Conn. 06520, U.S.A.

FORCIONE, Alban Keith. American, b. 1938. Literature. Walker S. Carpenter Jr. Prof. of the Language, Literature, and Civilization of Spain, Princeton Univ., New Jersey, since 1985 (Emory L. Ford Prof. of Spanish and Comparative Literature, 1965–82). Prof. of Spanish and Comparative Literature, Stanford Univ., Calif., 1983–85. *Publs:* Cervantes, Aristotle, and the Persiles, 1970; Cervantes' Christian Romance, 1972; Cervantes and the Humanist Vision, 1982; Cervantes and the Mystery of Lawlessness, 1984. Add: Princeton Univ., Princeton, N.J. 08544, U.S.A.

FORD, Alec George. British, b. 1926. Economics. Prof. of Economics, Univ. of Warwick, since 1970 (Reader, 1965–70; Pro-Vice-Chancellor, 1977–89). Lectr. in Economics, Univ. of Leicester, 1953–65. *Publs:* The Gold Standard, 1880-1914: Britain and Argentina, 1962; (ed. and author with W. Birmingham) Planning and Growth in Rich and Poor Countries, 1966; Income, Spending and the Price Level, 1971. Add: Dept. of Economics, Univ. of Warwick, Coventry CV4 7AL, England.

FORD, Boris. British, b. 1917. Education. Prof. of Education, Univ. of Bristol, 1974–82, now retired. Chief Ed., and Dir., Bureau of Current Affairs, 1946–51; Information Officer, Technical Assistance Bd., U.N., 1951–53; Head of Schs. Progs., ITV, 1957–58; Dir., Inst. of Education, Sheffield Univ., 1960–63; Prof. of Education, Univ. of Sussex, 1963–74. Ed., Pelican Guide to English Literature, 7 vols., Penguin Publrs., 1954–61, rev. ed., in 11 vols., 1982–88; Ed., Cambridge Guide to the Arts in Britain, 9 vols., 1988–90. Ed., Universities Quarterly, 1955–86. *Publs:* Discussion Methods, 1949; Teachers Handbook to Human Rights, 1950; Liberal Education in a Technical Age, 1955; (ed.) Young Readers/Young Writers, 1960. Add: 35 Alma Vale Rd., Clifton, Bristol, England.

FORD, Brian John. British, b. 1939. Biology, Physics, Sciences, Humor/Satire. Research scientist and consultant in microscopy; intnl. science consultant, since 1961. Fellow, and Member of Court of Govs., Cardiff Univ.; former Pres., European Union of Science Journalists' Assns., Brussels. *Publs:* German Secret Weapons: Blueprint for Mars, 1969; Microbiology and Food, 1970; Allied Secret Weapons, The War of Science, 1970; (co-author) The Recovery, Removal and Reconstruction of Human Skeletal Remains—Some New Techniques, 1970; (co-author) History of English-Speaking Peoples, 1971; Nonscience . . ., or How to Rule the World (satire), 1971; V1, V2, 1972; The Optical Microscope Manual—Past and Present Uses and Techniques, 1973; The Earth Watchers, 1973; (co-author) The Revealing Lens, Mankind and the Microscope, 1973; (co-author) The Cardiff Book, 1973; Microbe Power: Tomorrow's Revolution, 1976; Patterns of Sex: The Mating Urge and Our Sexual Future, 1980; The Cult of the Expert, 1982; (co-author) Viral Pollution of the Environment, 1983; 101 Questions About Science, 1983; 101 More Questions About Science, 1984; Single Lens: The Story of the Simple Microscope, 1985; Compute: How, Why, Do I Need to?, 1985;

The Food Book, 1986; Leeuwenhoek Legacy, 1989. Add: Rothay House, Mayfield Rd., Eastrea, Cambridge PE7 2AY, England.

FORD, Charles Henri. American, b. 1913. Poetry. Ed., Blues, Columbus, Miss., 1929–30, and View, New York City, 1940–47. *Publs:* The Garden of Disorder, 1938; The Overturned Lake, 1941; (ed.) A Night with Jupiter and Other Fantastic Stories, 1945; Sleep in a Nest of Flames, 1949; Spare Parts, 1966; Silver Flower Coo, 1968; Flag of Ecstasy, 1971; Om Krishna, II and III, 1979–82; Haiku and Imprints, 1984; Handshakes from Heaven, 1985; Emblems of Arachne, 1985. Add: 1 West 72nd St., New York, N.Y. 10023, U.S.A.

FORD, Daniel (Francis). American, b. 1931. Novels/Short stories, History. *Publs:* Now Comes Theodora, 1965; Incident at Muc Wa, 1967, screenplay as Go Tell the Spartans, 1978; (ed.) Carter's Coast of New England, by R. Carter, 1969; The High Country Illuminator, 1971; The Country Northward, 1976; Tiger in the Jungle, 1989. Add: 433 Bay Rd., Durham, N.H. 03824, U.S.A.

FORD, David. *See* **GILMAN,** George G.

FORD, Douglas (William Cleverley). Writes as D.W. Cleverley Ford. British, b. 1914. Theology/Religion. Minister of Religion, since 1937. Lectr. in Old Testament and Hebrew, London Coll. of Divinity, 1937–39, 1942–43 and 1952–58; Vicar, Holy Trinity Church, Hampstead, London, 1942–55; Vicar, Holy Trinity Church, South Kensington, London, 1955–74; Dir., Coll. of Preachers, London, 1960–73; Chaplain to the Queen, 1973–84, Sr. Chaplain to the Archbishop of Canterbury, 1975–80. *Publs:* Why Men Believe in Jesus Christ, 1950; A Key to Genesis, 1951; An Expository Preacher's Notebook, 1960; A Theological Preacher's Notebook, 1962; (with Cant, Perry and Sargent) The Churchman's Companion, 1964; A Pastoral Preacher's Notebook, 1965; A Reading of St. Luke's Gospel, 1967; Preaching at the Parish Communion, 3 vols., 1967–69; Preaching Today, 1969; Preaching Through the Christian Year, 1971; Praying Through the Christian Year, 1973; Have You Anything to Declare, 1973; Preaching on Special Occasions, 2 vols., 1975–82; New Preaching from the Old Testament, 2 vols., 1976, 1983; New Preaching from the New Testament, 2 vols., 1977–82; The Ministry of the Word, 1979; Preaching Through the Acts of the Apostles [Psalms, Life of Christ], 3 vols., 1980–85; Preaching on Devotional Occasions, 1986; From Strength to Strength, 1987; Preaching the Risen Christ, 1988; Preaching the Great Themes, 1989. Add: Rostrevor, Lingfield, Surrey RH7 6BZ, England.

FORD, Elbur. *See* **HOLT,** Victoria.

FORD, George H(arry). American, b. 1914. Literature. Prof. of English, Univ. of Rochester, N.Y., since 1958. Member, American Academy of Arts and Sciences, since 1980. Pres., Intnl. Soc. for the Study of Time, 1981–84. *Publs:* Keats and the Victorians, 1944; Dickens and His Readers, 1955; (ed.) Thackeray, Vanity Fair, 1958; (ed.) Dickens' David Copperfield, 1958; Double Measure: The Novels of D.H. Lawrence, 1965; (ed. with L. Lane) The Dickens Critics, 1966; (co-ed.) Dickens' Hard Times, 1970; (co-ed.) The Norton Anthology of English Literature, 1974, 4th ed., 1979, 5th ed., 1985; (ed.) Selected Poems of John Keats; (ed.) Dickens' Bleak House, 1978; (ed.) Victorian Fiction: A Second Guide to Research, 1978; The Making of a Secret Agent, 1978. Add: 2230 Clover St., Rochester, N.Y. 14618, U.S.A.

FORD, Gordon Buell, Jr. American, b. 1937. Language/Linguistics, Translations. Reimbursement Financial Management Specialist, Humana Inc., The Hosp. Co., Louisville, since 1978; Dir., Southeastern Investment Trust Inc., Louisville, since 1979. Asst. Prof. of Indo-European and Baltic Linguistics, 1965–72, and Asst. Prof. of Anthropology, Evening Divs., 1971–72, Northwestern Univ., Evanston, Ill.; Visiting Asst. Prof. of Medieval Latin, 1966–67, and Extension Lectr. in Linguistics, 1966–67 and 1970–72, Univ. of Chicago; Prof. of English, Univ. of Northern Iowa, Cedar Falls, 1972–76. *Publs:* The Ruodlieb: The First Medieval Epic of Chivalry from Eleventh-Century Germany, 1965; The Ruodlieb: Facsimile Edition, 1965, 1967; The Wolfenbuttel Lithuanian Postile Manuscript of the Year 1573, vols. I-III, 1965–66; The Ruodlieb: Linguistic Introduction, Latin Text, and Glossary, 1966; Isidore of Seville's History of the Goths, Vandals, and Suevi, 1966, 1970; Baltramiejus Vilentas Lithuanian Translation of the Gospels and Epistles (1579), vols. I-II, 1966; (trans.) Jan Gonda: A Concise Elementary Grammar of the Sanskrit Language with Exercises, Reading Selections and a Glossary, 1966; (trans.) Antoine Meillet: The Comparative Method in Historical Linguistics, 1967; Old Lithuanian Texts of the Sixteenth and Seventeenth Centuries with a Glossary, 1969; The Old Lithuanian Catechism of Baltramiejus Vilentas (1579): A Phonological, Morphologi-

cal, and Syntactical Investigation, 1969; The Letters of St. Isidore of Seville, 1966, 1970; The Old Lithuanian Catechism of Martynas Mazvydas (1547), 1971; (trans.) Manfred Mayrhofer: A Sanskrit Grammar, 1972; Isidore of Seville: On Grammar, 1972. Add: 3619 Brownsboro Rd., Louisville, Ky. 40207, U.S.A.

FORD, Herbert (Paul). American, b. 1927. History, Biography. Prof. of Journalism, and Vice-Pres., Development and Alumni Relations, Pacific Union Coll., Angwin, Calif., since 1984 (Assoc. Prof. of Journalism, 1974–84). Public Relations Dir., Seventh-day Adventists' Conferences, 1954–69, and The Voice of Prophecy, 1969–74; Dir., Corporate Communications, Adventist Health System-West, 1983. *Publs:* Wind High, Sand Deep, 1965; Flee the Captor, 1966; No Guns on Their Shoulders, 1968; Crimson Coats and Kimonos, 1968; Affair of the Heart, 1969; Rudo the Reckless Russian, 1970; Man Alive, 1971; For the Love of China, 1971; Pitcairn, 1972; The "Miscellany" of Pitcairn's Island, 1980. Add: Development Dept., Pacific Union Coll., Angwin, Calif. 94508, U.S.A.

FORD, Hilary. *See* **CHRISTOPHER,** John.

FORD, James Allan. British, b. 1920. Novels/Short stories, Essays. Entered U.K. Civil Service, 1938; Asst. Secty., Dept. of Agriculture for Scotland, Edinburgh, 1958–66; Registrar Gen. for Scotland, 1966–69; Dir. of Establishments, Scottish Office, Edinburgh, 1969–79. Pres., Scottish Centre, Intnl. P.E.N., 1970–73, and 1983–86. *Publs:* The Brave White Flag, 1961; Season of Escape, 1963; A Statue for a Public Place, 1965; A Judge of Men, 1968; The Mouth of Truth, 1971. Add: 29 Lady Rd., Edinburgh EH16 5PA, Scotland.

FORD, Jesse Hill (Jr.). American, b. 1928. Novels/Short stories, Plays/Screenplays. Reporter, Nashville Tennesseean, 1950–51; Editorial News Writer, Univ. of Florida, Gainesville, 1953–55; Medical News Writer, Tennessee Medical Assn., Nashville, 1955–56; Public Relations Exec., American Medical Assn., Chicago, 1956–57. Writer-in-Residence, Vanderbilt Univ., Nashville, Tenn., 1987. *Publs:* Mountains of Gilead, 1961; The Conversion of Buster Drumwight: The Television and Stage Scripts, 1964; The Liberation of Lord Byron Jones, 1965, screenplay as The Liberation of L.B. Jones, 1969; Fishes, Birds and Sons of Men: Stories, 1967; The Feast of Saint Barnabas, 1969; The Raider, 1975; Mr. Potter and His Bank, 1977; Drumwight (musical), 1982. Add: Box 43, Bellevue, Tenn. 37021, U.S.A.

FORD, Kirk. *See* **SPENCE,** William John Duncan.

FORD, Lee Ellen. American, b. 1917. Animals/Pets, Law. Attorney-at-Law, since 1972. Assoc. Prof. of Biology, Gustavus Adolphus Coll., 1950–61; Anderson Coll.,1952–55; Univ. of Alberta, Calgary, 1955–56, and Pacific Lutheran Univ., Parkland, Wash., 1956–62; Ed., Breeder's Journal, 1958–63; Prof. of Biology and Cytogenetics, Mississippi State Coll. for Women, 1962–64; Chief Cytogeneticist, Pacific Northwest Research Foundn., Seattle, Wash., 1964–65; Dir., Canine Genetics Conservation Service, Parkland, Wash., 1963–69; Manpower Economist, Nevada Dept. of Labor, and Head, Research Unit, Nevada Employment Security Div., Carson City, 1966–68; Dir., Chromosome Lab., Inst. for Basic Research in Mental Retardation, 1968–69; Ed., New Dimensions in Legislation, 1969–70; Pres., Ford Assocs., Butler, Ind., 1972–78; Exec. Asst. to the Gov. of Indiana, 1973–75; Ed., Record Herald weekly paper, Butler, Ind., 1973–76; Ed., Women in the Eighties series, 1975–86; Ed., Animal Rights in the Eighties, 1975–86. *Publs:* (compiler and ed.) Animal Welfare Encyclopedia, 21 series, 1956–83; Anthology of Collie Genetics and Breeding, 1955; The Dog in Research, 1955; Color Inheritance in Collies, 1955; Master Pedigree Method of Analysis, 1955; Showing and Judging Collies, 1955; Whelping, 1955; Shamrock Smooth Collie Leader Dog Handbook, 1956; Leader Dog Puppy Pretests, 1956; Leader Dog Schools in U.S.A., 1956; Advanced Leader Dog Training, or Leader Dogs Abroad, 1956; Handbook of Shamrock Collie College, 1956; Shamarock Collie Research Laboratory, 1956; Shamrock Collie Research Laboratory Dogs, 1957; Shamrock Collie Research Laboratory Litter Data, 1957; Novice Obedience, 1957; The White Collie, 1957; The Female Canine, 1957; Cryptorchidism, Heredity and Variation, 1957; Eyes, Heredity and Variation, 1957; The Smooth Collie, 1957; The Blue Merle Collie, 1957; Bonus: The Shamrock Collie Research Laboratory's Ten Smooth Leader Dog Pups Grow Up, 1957; Illustrated History of Collies; Elementary Genetic Lessons, 2 vols.; Geriatrics; Advanced Obedience Training; Coat Color and Pigment Studies; Companion Collie: Second Year; The Gray Collie; (ed.) Directory of Women Law Graduates and Attorneys in the U.S.A., 24 Series, 1971–83; Indiana Dog Laws, 1981; (ed.) Directory of Indiana Humane Societies, 1981. Add: 824 E. 7th St. Auburn, Ind.

46706, U.S.A.

FORD, Richard. American, b. 1944. Novels/Short stories, Essays. Jr. Fellow, Soc. of Fellows, 1971–74, and Lectr., 1974–76, Univ. of Michigan, Ann Arbor; Lectr., Princeton Univ., New Jersey, 1979–80. *Publs:* A Piece of My Heart, 1976; The Ultimate Good Luck, 1981; The Sportswriter, 1986; Rock Springs (stories), 1987. Add: c/o Intnl. Creative Mgmt., 40 W. 57th St., New York, N.Y. 10019, U.S.A.

FORD, R(obert) A(rthur) D(ouglass). Canadian, b. 1915. Poetry, Translations. Member, Palme Commn. on Disarmament and Security Issues; Member, Bd. of Dirs., Intnl. Inst. of Geopolitics. Joined Canadian Dept. of External Affairs, 1940; Served in Rio de Janeiro, Moscow and London, 1940–51; Head of European Div., Ottawa, 1954–57; Ambassador to Colombia, 1957–58, Yugoslavia, 1959–61, and United Arab Republic, 1961–63, and Soviet Union, 1964–80; Special Adviser on East-West Relations, 1980–84. *Publs:* A Window on the North, 1956; The Solitary City, 1969; Holes in Space, 1979; Needle in the Eye, 1983; (ed. and trans.) Russian Poetry, 1984; Doors, Words and Silence, 1985; Dostoevsky and Other Poems, 1988; Our Man in Moscow: A Diplomat's Reflections on the Soviet Union, 1989. Add: La Poivriere, Randan 63310, France.

FORD, Robert N(icholas). American, b. 1909. Administration/Management. Dir., Work Org. Research, American Telephone & Telegraph Co., NYC, 1947–74. *Publs:* Motivation Through the Work Itself, 1969; (with John R. Maher) New Horizons in Job Enrichment, 1971; Why Jobs Die and What to Do About It: Job Redesign and Future Productivity, 1979. Add: 2194 Bayou Rd., Punta Gorda, Fla., U.S.A.

FORDE-JOHNSTON, James. British, b. 1927. Anthropology/Ethnology, Archaeology/Antiquities. Keeper of Ethnology, Univ. of Manchester, 1958 until retirement. Asst. Keeper of Archaeology, Liverpool Museum, 1954–56; Investigator, Royal Commn. on Historical Monuments, 1956–58. *Publs:* Neolithic Cultures of North Africa, 1959; History from the Earth: An Introduction to Archaeology, 1974; Hillforts of the Iron Age in England and Wales, 1974; Prehistoric Britain and Ireland, 1976; Hadrian's Wall, 1977; Castles and Fortifications of Britain and Ireland, 1977; (ed.) A Bibliography of Archery; Brazilian Indian Archery, 1977; (ed.) The Manchester Museum Mummy Project, 1979; Great Medieval Castles of Britain, 1979; Guide to the Castles of England and Wales, 1981. Add: 6 Greystoke Ave., Sale, Cheshire, England.

FORDER, Anthony. British, b. 1925. Public/Social administration, Social work. Probation Officer, London Probation Service, 1953–59; Lectr. London Sch. of Economics, 1959–63; Sr. Lectr., Oppenheimer Coll. of Social Service, Zambia, and Univ. of Zambia, 1963–66; Lectr. in Social Administration, Liverpool Univ., 1966–70; Head, Dept. of Applied Social Studies, Millbank Coll. of Commerce, 1971–72; Principal Lectr., 1972–76; and Head of the Dept. of Social Work, 1976–84; Liverpool Polytechnic. *Publs:* Social Casework and Administration, 1966, 1970; (ed. and co-author) Penelope Hall's Social Social Services of England and Wales, 7th ed. 1969, 10th ed. 1983; Concepts in Social Administration: A Framework for Analysis, 1974; (co-author) Theories of Welfare, 1984 (ed.) Working with Parents of Handicapped Children, 1985. Add: 29 Lyndhurst Rd., Wallasey L45 6XB, England.

FORDER, Charles Robert. British, b. 1907. History, Theology/Religion. Archdeacon Emeritus, Church of England, since 1972 (Archdeacon of York, 1957–72). *Publs:* History of Paston School, North Walsham, 1934; The Parish Priest at Work, 1947; Synods in Action, 1970; Churchwardens: In Church and Parish, 1976. Add: Dulverton Hall, St. Martin's Sq., Scarborough YO11 2DQ, England.

FORDIN, Hugh. American, b. 1935. Film, Music. *Publs:* (ed. with Gloria Kravitz) Film TV Daily Yearbook of Motion Pictures and Television, vol. 52, 1970; The New Jerome Kern Song Book, 1974; M.G.M.'s That's Entertainment Song Book, 1974; Hollywood's Royal Family: The Freed Unit, 1974; Oscar Hammerstein II: Getting to Know Him, 1976; The World of Entertainment: Hollywood's Greatest Musicals, 1976. Add: c/o Ungar, 370 Lexington Ave., New York, N.Y. 10017, U.S.A.

FOREMAN, Michael. British, b. 1938. Children's fiction. Art Dir., Ambit, London, since 1960. Lectr., St. Martin's Sch. of Art, London, 1963–65, London Sch. of Painting, 1967, Royal Coll. of Art, 1968–70, and Central Sch. of Art, London, 1971–72; Art Dir., Playboy, Chicago, 1965, and King, London, 1966. *Publs:* The Perfect Present, 1967; The Two Giants, 1967; The Great Sleigh Robbery, 1968; Horatio (in U.S. as The Travels of Horatio), 1970; Moose, 1971; Dinosaurs and All That Rub-

bish, 1972; War and Peas, 1974; All the King's Horses, 1976; Panda's Puzzle, 1977; Trick a Tracker, 1979; Winter's Tales, 1979; Panda and the Odd Lion, 1981; Land of Dreams, 1982; Panda and the Bunyips, 1984; Cat and Canary, 1984; Private Zoo, 1985; Panda and the Bushfire, 1986; Ben's Box, 1986; Ben's Baby, 1987; The Angel and the Wild Animal, 1988. Add: 5 Church Gate, London SW6, England.

FOREMAN, Richard. American, b. 1937. Plays/Screenplays. Founding Dir., Ontological-Hysteric Theatre, NYC, since 1968. *Publs:* Richard Foreman: Plays and Manifestos, 1976; Richard Foreman: Reverberation Machines, More Plays and Manifestos, 1985. Add: 152 Wooster St., New York, N.Y. 10012, U.S.A.

FOREST, Antonia. British. Children's fiction. *Publs:* Autumn Term, 1948; The Marlows and the Traitor, 1953; Falconer's Lure, 1957; End of Term, 1959; Peter's Room, 1961; The Thursday Kidnapping, 1963; The Thuggery Affair, 1965; The Ready-Made Family, 1967; The Player's Boy, 1970; The Players and the Rebels, 1971; The Cricket Term, 1974; The Attic Term, 1976; Run Away Home, 1982. Add: c/o Faber & Faber Ltd., 3 Queen Sq., London WC1N 3AU, England.

FORMAN, Charles William. American, b. 1916. Theology/Religion. Prof. of Missions, now Emeritus, Yale Univ. Divinity Sch., New Haven, Conn., since 1953 (Acting Dean, 1960–62). *Publs:* A Faith for the Nations, 1958; The Nation and the Kingdom, 1964; Christianity and the Non-Western World, 1967; The Island Churches of the South Pacific, 1982; The Voice of Many Waters, 1986. Add: 329 Downs Rd., Bethany, CT 06525, U.S.A.

FORMAN, Joan. British. Children's fiction, Plays/Screenplays, Paranormal/Occult topics. Educational Admin. of Bursar of teachers' training coll., Lancs., until 1953; Poetry Page Ed., John o'Londons, 1958–62, and Time and Tide, 1962–63. *Publs:* (ed.) Galaxy Anthology, 4 vols.; See for Yourself, 2 vols.; The Wise Ones; The Old Girls; Night of the Fox; The Accusers; Midwinter Journey; Maid in Arms; Mr. Browning's Lady; The Pilgrim Women; Guests of Honour; Portrait of the Late; Ding Dong Belle; The End of a Dream; The Walled Garden; A Search for Comets; The Turning Tide; The Freedom of the House; (ed.) Look Through a Diamond; The Princess in the Tower, 1973; Haunted East Anglia, 1974; The Mask of Time, 1978; The Haunted South, 1978; Haunted Royal Homes, 1987; Royal Hauntings, 1987; The Golden Shore, 1988. Add: c/o Jarrold, Barrack St., Norwich NR3 1TR, England.

FORNÉS, Maria Irene. American (b. Cuban), b. 1930. Plays/Screenplays. Playwright-Dir., Theater for the New City, Padua Hills Festival, INTAR, and American Place Theatre, 1965–87. *Publs:* Promenade and Other Plays, 1971; Fefu and Her Friends, 1978; Plays, 1986. Add: 1 Sheridan Sq., New York, N.Y. 10014, U.S.A.

FORREST, David. *See* **DENHOLM,** David.

FORREST, Leon. American, b. 1937. Novels. Prof. since 1984, and Chmn. of the Dept. of African-American Studies since 1985, Northwestern Univ., Evanston (Assoc. Prof., 1973–84). Ed. of community newspaper, Chicago, 1965–69; Assoc. Ed., 1969–72, and Managing Ed., 1972–73, Muhammad Speaks (Black Muslim newspaper), Chicago. *Publs:* There Is a Tree More Ancient Than Eden, 1973; The Bloodworth Orphans, 1977; Two Wings to Veil My Face, 1984. Add: Dept. of African-American Studies, Northwestern Univ., Arthur Andersen Hall, 2003 Sheridan Rd., Evanston, Ill. 60201, U.S.A.

FORREST, Richard (Stockton). Also writes as Stockton Woods. American, b. 1932. Mystery/Crime/Suspense. Full-time writer since 1972. Branch Mgr., Lawyers Title Insurance Co., Hartford, Conn., 1958–68; Vice-Pres., Chicago Title Insurance Co., Hartford, 1968–72. *Publs:* Who Killed Mr. Garland's Mistress?, 1974; A Child's Garden of Death, 1975; The Wizard of Death, 1977; Death Through the Looking Glass, 1978; The Death in the Willows, 1979; The Killing Edge, 1980; (as Stockton Woods) The Laughing Man, 1980; Death at Yew Corner, 1981; (as Stockton Woods) Game Bet, 1981; (as Stockton Woods) The Man Who Heard Too Much, 1983; Death Under the Lilacs, 1985; Lark, 1986. Add: Box 724, Old Saybrook, Conn. 06475, U.S.A.

FORREST, William George Grieve. British, b. 1925. History. Wykeham Prof. of Ancient History, Oxford Univ., since 1977. Fellow and Tutor, Wadham Coll., Oxford, 1951–77 (Dean, 1962–68; Sr. Tutor, 1970–72). *Publs:* (ed.) Herodotus: History of the Greek and Persian War, 1963; The Emergence of Greek Democracy, 1966; A History of Sparta, 1968. Add: New Coll., Oxford, England.

FORRESTER, Helen. *See* **BHATIA**, Jamunadevi.

FORRESTER, Rex (Desmond). New Zealander, b. 1928. Sports/Physical education/Keeping fit, Autobiography/Memoirs/Personal, Hunting and Fishing Officer, NZ Govt. Tourist and Publicity Dept., since 1965. Trapper, bounty hunter, and ranger, 1945–56; Owner, NZ Safaris, 1956–65. *Publs:* Hunter for Hire; Hunting in New Zealand; Trout Fishing in New Zealand, 1979; True Adventure Hunting with Rex Forrester, 1979; The Chopper Boys, 1983. Add: 81 Grand Vue Rd., Kawaha Point, Rotorua, New Zealand.

FORRESTER, William Ray. American, b. 1911. Law. Robert S. Stevens Prof. of Law Emeritus, Cornell Univ., Ithaca, N.Y., since 1978 (Dean of Law Sch., 1963–73; Robert S. Stevens Prof. of Law, 1963–78); Prof. of Law, Univ. of California, Hastings, since 1978. Dean of Law Sch., Vanderbilt Univ., Nashville, Tenn., 1949–52; Dean and W.R. Irby Prof., Tulane Univ. Law Sch., New Orleans, La., 1952–63. *Publs:* (with Dobie and Ladd) Forrester's Edition of Dobie and Ladd's Cases and Materials on Federal Jurisdiction and Procedure, 1950; Cases and Materials on Constitutional Law, 1959; (with Currier) Cases and Materials on Federal Jurisdiction and Procedure, 1962, with Currier and Moye, 1970, supplement, 1973, with Moye, rev. ed., 1977, supplements 1981, 1985. Add: 198 McAllister St., San Francisco, Calif. 94102, U.S.A.

FORSBERG, (Charles) Gerald. British, b. 1912. Recreation/Leisure/Hobbies. With Merchant Navy, 1928–38, and Royal Navy, 1938–62; Deputy Dir., 1958–72, and Asst. Dir., Marine Services (Naval), 1972–75, U.K. Ministry of Defence. *Publs:* Long Distance Swimming, 1957; First Strokes in Swimming, 1961; (co-author) Swimming, 1961; Modern Long Distance Swimming, 1963; Salvage from the Sea, 1977; Pocket Book for Seamen, 1981; Thirty Years of Long Distance Swimming, 1986. Add: c/o Barclays, 19 Euston Rd., Morecambe, Lancs. LA4 5DE, England.

FORSTCHEN, William R. American. Science fiction. *Publs:* Ice Prophet, 1983; The Flame Upon the Ice, 1984; The Darkness Upon the Ice, 1985; The Gamester Wars Series (The Alexandrian Rig, The Assassin Gambit), 2 vols., 1987–88. Add: c/o Ballantine Books, 201 E. 50th St., New York, N.Y. 10022, U.S.A.

FORSTER, Margaret. British, b. 1938. Novels, Biography. Fiction Reviewer, Evening Standard, London, 1977–80. *Publs:* Dames Delight, 1964; The Bogey Man; Fenella Fizackerly; Georgy Girl; Miss Owen-Owen is at Home; Mr. Bone's Retreat; The Park; The Travels of Maudie Tipstaff; The Rash Adventurer; The Rise and Fall of Charles Edward Stuart, 1973; The Seduction of Mrs. Pendlebury, 1974; Thackeray: Memoirs of a Vistorian Gentleman, 1978; Mother, Can You Hear Me?, 1979; The Bride of Lowther Fell, 1980; Marital Rites, 1981; Significant Sisters: Active Feminism 1839–1939, 1984; Private Papers, 1986; Elizabeth Barrett Browning: A Biography, 1988; Have the Men Had Enough? (novel), 1989. Add: c/o Chatto and Windus, 30 Bedford Sq., London WC1B 3RP, England.

FORSYTH, Frederick. British, b. 1938. Novels/Short stories, Mystery/Crime/Suspense. Former staff member, BBC, London. *Publs:* The Biafra Story (non-fiction), 1969; Day of the Jackal, 1971; The Odessa File, 1972; The Dogs of War, 1974; The Shepherd, 1975; The Devil's Alternative, 1979; No Comebacks: Collected Short Stories, 1982; The Fourth Protocol, 1984; The Negotiator, 1989. Add: c/o Century Hutchinson Publishing Group, 62-65 Chandos Pl., London WC2N 4NW, England.

FORSYTH, James (Law). British, b. 1913. Plays/Screenplays, Biography. Dramatist-in-residence, Old Vic Co., London, 1946–48, and Howard Univ., Washington, D.C., 1961–62, and Florida State Univ., 1964; Dir., Tufts Univ. Prog. in London, 1967–71; Artistic Dir., Forsyths' Barn Theatre, Ansty, Sussex, 1972–83. *Publs:* Emmanuel: A Nativity Play, 1952; Three Plays: The Other Heart, Heloise, Adelaise, 1957; The Road to Emmaus: A Play for Eastertide, 1958; Joshua, 1959; (adaptor) Brand, by Ibsen, 1960; Dear Wormwood, 1961, as Screwtape, 1973; (adaptor) Cyrano de Bergerac, by E. Rostand, 1968; The Last Journey, 1972; Defiant Island, 1975; Tyrone Guthrie: A Biography, 1976; Back to the Barn: The Story of a Country Theatre; also radio and TV plays. Add: Grainloft, Ansty, nr. Haywards Heath, Sussex RH17 5AG, England.

FORWARD, Robert L. American, b. 1932. Science fiction. Science Consultant, Forward Unlimited, Malibu, since 1987. Sr. Scientist, Hughes Research Labs., Malibu, 1974–87. (Technical Staff Member, 1956–66; Assoc. Mgr., Theoretical Studies Dept., 1966–67; Mgr., Exploratory Studies Dept., 1967–74). *Publs:* Dragon's Egg, 1980; The

Flight of the Dragonfly, 1984; Starquake, 1985; Future Magic, 1988; (with Joel Davis) Mirror Matter: Pioneering Antimatter Physics, 1988. Add: Forward Unlimited, P.O. Box 2783, Malibu, Calif. 90265, U.S.A.

FOSKETT, Daphne. British, b. 1911. Art, Biography. *Publs:* British Portrait Miniatures, 1963, 1968; John Smart, the Man and His Miniatures, 1964; Dictionary of British Miniature Painters, 2 vols., 1972; Samuel Cooper, 1974; John Harden of Brathay Hall, 1974; Samuel Cooper and His Contemporaries, 1974; Collecting Miniatures, 1979; Miniatures: Dictionary and Guide, 1987. Add: Field Broughton Pl., Field Broughton, Grange-over-Sands, Cumbria, England.

FOSKETT, Douglas John. British, b. 1918. Information science, Librarianship. Dir. of Central Library Services and Goldsmiths' Librarian, Univ. of London, 1978–83, now retired. Asst. Librarian, Illford Municipal Libraries, 1940–48; Information Officer, Metal Box Co. Ltd., 1948–57; Librarian, Inst. of Education, Univ. of London, 1957–78. *Publs:* Assistance to Readers, 1952; Information Science in Libraries, 1952, 1967; Science, Humanism and Libraries, 1964; How to Find Out: Educational Research, 1965; Classification and Indexing in the Social Sciences, 1975; Pathways for Communication, 1984. Add: 1 Daleside, Gerrards Cross, Bucks., England.

FOSSUM, Robert H. American, b. 1923. Poetry, Literature. Prof. of English and American Literature, Claremont McKenna Coll., and Claremont Graduate Sch., Calif., since 1963, Emeritus since 1987. Assoc. Prof., Dept. of English, Beloit, Wisc., 1950–62; Assoc. Prof. of English, California State Univ., Los Angeles, 1962–63. *Publs:* William Styron: A Critical Essay, 1968; Hawthorne's Inviolable Circle, 1972; (with Sy Kahn) Facing Mirrors, 1980; (with John Roth) The American Dream, 1981; (with John Roth) American Ground, 1988. Add: Bauer Center, Claremont McKenna Coll., Claremont, Calif. 91711, U.S.A.

FOSTER, Alan Dean. American, b. 1946. Science fiction/Fantasy. Instr. of English and Film, Univ. of California at Los Angeles, intermittently, since 1971. Head Copywriter, Headlines Ink Agency, Studio City, Calif., 1970–71; Instr. of English and Film, Los Angeles City Coll., 1972–76. *Publs:* The Tar-Aiym Krang, 1972; Bloodhype, 1973; Icerigger, 1974; Luana, 1974; Dark Star, 1974; Star Trek Log One to Ten, 10 vols., 1974–78; Midworld, 1975; (as George Lucas) Star Wars, 1976; Orphan Star, 1977; The End of the Matter, 1977; With Friends Like These (collection), 1977; Splinter of the Mind's Eye, 1978; Mission to Moulokin, 1979; Alien, 1979; The Black Hole, 1979; Cachalot, 1980; Clash of the Titans, 1981; Outland, 1981; The Thing, 1982; Nor Crystal Tears, 1982; For Love of Mother-Not, 1983; Spellsinger at the Gate (Spellsinger and The Hour at the Gate), 1983; Krull, 1983; The Man Who Used the Universe, 1983; The I Inside, 1984; Voyage to the City of the Dead, 1984; Slipt, 1984; The Last Starfighter, 1984; The Day of the Dissonance, 1984; Who Needs Enemies (collection), 1984; The Moment of the Magician, 1984; Starman, 1984; Shadowkeep, 1984; Pale Rider, 1985; Sentenced to Prism, 1985; The Paths of the Perambulator, 1985; Aliens, 1986; Into the Out of, 1986; The Time of the Transference, 1986; The Deluge Drivers, 1987; Glory Lane, 1987; Quozal, 1987; Maori, 1988; Flinx in Flux, 1988; Alien Nation, 1988; To the Vanishing Point, 1988; Quozl, 1989; Counting the Damned, 1990. Add: c/o Thranx, Inc., 4001 Pleasant Valley Dr., Prescott, Ariz. 86301, U.S.A.

FOSTER, David Manning. Australian, b. 1944. Novels. Intnl. Postdoctoral Research Fellow, U.S. Public Health Service, Philadelphia, Pa., 1970–71; Sr. Research Officer, Medical Sch., Univ. of Sydney, N.S.W., 1971–72. *Publs:* North South West, 1973; The Pure Land, 1974; The Fleeing Atlanta (poetry), 1975; Escape to Reality, 1977; (with D. Lyall) The Empathy Experiment, 1977; Moonlite, 1981; Plumbum, 1983; Dog Rock, 1985; Christian Rosy Cross, 1986; Testostero, 1987. Add: Ardara, Victoria St., Bundanoon, N.S.W., Australia.

FOSTER, David William. American, b. 1940. Literature. Prof. of Spanish, since 1966, and Chmn., Editorial Bd., Center for Latin American Studies, since 1972, Arizona State Univ., Tempe. Ed., Rocky Mountain Review of Language and Literature, since 1980. Asst. Prof. of Spanish, Univ. of Missouri, 1964–66. *Publs:* (co-author) Research on Language Teaching, 1962, 1965; Forms of the Novel in the Work of Camilo Jose Cela, 1967; Myth of Paraguay in the Fiction of Augusto Roa Bastos, 1969; (with V.R. Foster) Manual of Hispanic Bibliography, 1970, 1977; (with V.R. Foster) Research Guide to Argentine Literature, 1970, 1982; A Bibliography of the Works of Jorge Luis Borges, 1971; Christian Allegory in Early Hispanic Poetry, 1971; The Marqués de Santillana, 1971; (with G.L Bower) Haiku in Western Languages, 1972; Early Spanish Ballad, 1972; Unamuno and the Novel as Expressionist Conceit, 1973; (with V.R.

Foster) Modern Latin American Literature, 1975; Currents in the Contemporary Argentine Novel, 1975; Twentieth Century Spanish-American Novel: A Bibliography, 1975; (ed.) A Dictionary of Contemporary Latin American Authors, 1975; (with H.J. Becco) La nueva narrativa hisposmericana: Bibliograffa, 1976; Chilean Literature: A Working Bibliography, 1978; Augusto Roa Bastos, 1978; Studies in the Contemporary Spanish American Short Story, 1979; Mexican Literature: A Bibliography of Secondary Sources, 1981; Peruvian Literature: A Bibliography of Secondary Sources, 1981; (with Roberto Reis) A Dictionary of Contemporary Brazilian Authors, 1982; (ed.) Sourcebook of Hispanic Culture in the United States, 1982; (ed.) Marqués de Santillana: Poesia (selection), 1982; Para una lectura semiótica del ensayo latinoamericano, 1983; (ed. with Francisco Arturo Rosales) Hispanics and the Humanities in the Southwest: A Directory of Resources, 1983; Jorge Luis Borges: An Annotated Primary and Secondary Bibliography, 1984; Estudios sobre teatro mexicano contemporàneo: semiologia de la competencia teatral, 1984; Cuban Literature: A Research Guide, 1984; Alternate Voices in the Contemporary Latin American Narrative, 1985; The Argentine Teatro Independiente, 1930-1955, 1986; Social Realism in the Argentine Narrative, 1986; Handbook of Latin American Literature, 1987. Add: Dept. of Foreign Languages, Arizona State Univ., Tempe, Ariz. 85287, U.S.A.

FOSTER, Don. American, b. 1948. Poetry. *Publs:* Laugh, 1971; The Train, the Locust Tree, and the Dark Country Beyond, 1982. Add: 2405 Fowler St., Denton, Tex. 26201, U.S.A.

FOSTER, Edward Halsey. American, b. 1942. Literature. Prof. of English and American Literature, since 1985, and Dir. of the program in English and American Literature since 1988, Stevens Institute of Technology, Hoboken (Assoc. Prof., 1975–84). Ed., Talisman: A Journal of Contemporary Poetry and Poetics, since 1988. Visiting Fulbright Prof., Univ. of Istanbul, Turkey, 1985–86. *Publs:* Catharine Maria Sedgwick, 1974; The Civilized Wilderness, 1975; (ed., with Geoffrey W. Clark) Hoboken, 1976; Josiah Gregg and Lewis H. Garrard, 1977; Susan and Anna Warner, 1978; Richard Brautigan, 1983; Cummington Poems, 1982; William Saroyan, 1984. Add: Dept. of Humanities, Stevens Inst. of Technology, Hoboken, N.J. 07030, U.S.A.

FOSTER, Elizabeth Read. American, b. 1912. History. Prof. of History, 1966–81, and Dean of Grad. Sch. of Arts and Sciences, 1966–72, Bryn Mawr College., Pa. *Publs:* (ed.) Proceedings in Parliament 1610, 2 vols., 1966; The Painful Labour of Mr. Elsying, 1972; The House of Lords 1603-1649, 1983. Add: 205 Strafford Ave., Wayne, Pa. 19087, U.S.A.

FOSTER, George. See **HASWELL,** Chetwynd John Duke.

FOSTER, Iris. See **POSNER,** Richard.

FOSTER, M(ichael) A(nthony). American, b. 1939. Science fiction, Poetry. Full-time writer since 1984. Served in the U.S. Air Force, 1957–62, 1965–76: Captain; Dept. Mgr., Allied Stores, Greensboro, N.C., 1976–78; Salesman, Sunox Inc., 1978–84. *Publs:* poetry—Shards from Byzantium, 1969; The Vaseline Dreams of Hundifer Soames, 1970; science fiction—The Warriors of Dawn, 1975; The Gameplayers of Zan, 1977; The Day of the Klesh, 1979; Waves, 1980; The Morphodite, 1981; Transformer, 1983; Preserver, 1985; Owl Time (short stories), 1985. Add: 5409 Amberhill Dr., Greensboro, N.C. 27405, U.S.A.

FOSTER, Malcolm Burton. Canadian, 1931. Children's fiction, Literature, Biography. Prof. of English, Concordia Univ., Montreal, since 1976. Pres., Canadian Authors Assn., 1974–76. *Publs:* The Prince with a Hundred Dragons, 1963; Alan Paton: A Critical Study, 1965; Joyce Cary: A Biography, 1968; The Italian White Horse, 1979; The Anderson Affair: A Personal Study, 1979; The Bird Whose Feathers Were Stolen, 1979. Add: Dept. of English, Concordia Univ., Loyola Campus, 7141 Sherbrooke St., Montreal, Que. H4B 1R6, Canada.

FOSTER, Paul. American, b. 1931. Novels/Short stories, Plays/Screenplays. Pres., La Mama Experimental Theater Club, NYC, since 1962. *Publs:* Minnie the Whore, The Birthday, and Other Stories, 1963; The Madonna in the Orchard, 1965; Balls and Other Plays: The Recluse, Hurrah for the Bridge, The Hessian Corporal, 1967; Tom Paine, 1967; Helmskringa; or, The Stoned Angels, 1970; Satyricon, 1972; Elizabeth I, 1972; Silver Queen Saloon, 1975; Marcus Brutus, 1976; The House on Lake Geneva, 1978; Cop and the Anthem (film script), 1982; Cinderella Story (film script), 1983; Smile (film script), 1984; The Dark and Mr. Stone, 3 vols., 1985–86; (trans.) Faith, Hope and Charity, by Odon von Horvath, 1987. Add: 242 E. 5th St., New York, N.Y. 10003, U.S.A.

U.S.A.

FOSTER, Ruel E. American, b. 1916. Literature. Benedum Prof., Dept. of English, West Virginia Univ., Morgantown, since 1974 (Prof. and Chmn., 1967–74). *Publs:* (co-author) Work in Progress, 1948; (co-author) William Faulkner: A Critical Appraisal, 1951; Elizabeth Madox Roberts, American Novelist, 1956; Author: Jesse Stuart, 1969. Add: 1110 Windsor Ave., Morgantown, W. VA., U.S.A.

FOSTER, Simon. See **GLEN,** Duncan.

FOTHERGILL, Brian. British, b. 1921. History, Biography. Member of the Council, since 1977, and Chmn., since 1986, Royal Soc. of Literature. *Publs:* The Cardinal King, 1958; Nicholas Wiseman, 1963; Mrs. Jordan: Portrait of an Actress, 1965; Sir William Hamilton: Envoy Extraordinary, 1969; The Mitred Earl, 1974; Beckford of Fonthill, 1979; (ed.) Essays by Divers Hands XLI, 1980; The Strawberry Hill Set, 1983. Add: 7 Union Square, London N1 7DH, England.

FOULDS, Elfrida Vipont. Also writes as Charles Vipont and Elfrida Vipont. British, b. 1902. Children's fiction, Children's non-fiction, Theology/Religion. *Publs:* (all as Elfrida Vipont unless otherwise noted)—Good Adventure, 1931; Colin Writes to Friends House, 1934, 3rd rev. ed. 1957; (as Charles Vipont) Blow the Man Down, 1939; The Lark in the Morn, 1948, 1970; Sparks Among the Stubble, 1950; The Lark on the Wing, 1950, 1970; (as Elfrida Vipont Foulds) The Birthplace of Quakerism, 1952, 3rd ed., 1987; The Story of Quakerism, 1652-1952, 1954; rev. ed. as The Story of Quakerism Through Three Centuries, 1960; The Family at Dowbiggins, 1955; (as Charles Vipont) The Heir of Craigs, 1955; Arnold Rowntree: A Life, 1955; The Spring of the Year, 1957; The High Way, 1957; The Secret of Orra, 1957; More About Dowbiggins, 1958, retitled A Win for Henry Conyers, 1969; Bless This Day, 1958; Henry Purcell and His Times, 1959; Ackworth School, 1959; Changes at Dowbiggins, 1958; retitled Boggarts and Dreams, 1969; Flowering Spring, 1960; The Story of Christianity in Britain, 1960; What About Religion?, 1961; The Bridge, 1962; Search for a Song, 1962; A Faith to Live By (in U.K. as Quakerism: A Faith to Live By), 1962; Some Christian Festivals, 1963; Stevie, 1965; Larry Lopkins, 1965; Rescue for Mittens, 1965; The Offcomers, 1965; Weaver of Dreams, 1966; Terror by Night (in U.S. as Ghosts High Noon), 1966; The Secret Passage, 1967; A Child of the Chapel Royal, 1967; Children of the Mayflower, 1969; Michael and the Dogs, 1969; The Pavilion, 1969; The Elephant and the Bad Baby, 1969; Towards a High Attic, 1970; Lancashire Hotpot, 1973; Bed in Hell, 1974; George Fox and the Valiant Sixty; 1975; A Little Bit of Ivory, 1977. Add: Green Garth, Yealand Conyers, nr. Carnforth, Lancs. LA5 9SG, England.

FOULKES, (Albert) Peter. British, b. 1936. Literature. Prof. of German, Univ. of Wales, Cardiff, since 1977. Asst. Prof. of German, Univ. of Mississippi, University, 1961–63, and Univ. of Illinois, Urbana, 1963–65; Asst. Prof., 1965–67, Assoc. Prof., 1967–72, and Prof. of German Studies, 1972–77, Stanford Univ., California; Alexander von Humboldt Sr. Research Fellow, Univ. of Constance, 1972–74. *Publs:* The Reluctant Pessimist: A Study of Franz Kafka, 1967; (ed. with Edgar Lohner) Deutsche Novellen von Tieck bis Hauptmann. 1969; (ed. with Lohner) Das deutsche Drama von Kleist bis Hauptmann, 1973; the Search for Literary Meaning, 1976; (ed.) The Uses of Criticism, 1977; Literature and Propaganda, 1983. Add: University Coll., Cardiff CF1 1XL, Wales.

FOWKE, Edith Margaret. Canadian, b. 1913. Mythology/Folklore. Prof. Emeritus of English, York Univ., Downsview, Ont., since 1983 (Assoc. Prof., 1971–74; Prof., 1977–83). Ed., Canadian Folk Music Journal. *Publs:* (ed. with R. Johnson) Folk Songs of Canada, 1954; (ed. with R. Johnston) Folk Songs of Quebec, 1957; (ed.) Logging with Paul Bunyan, 1957; (with A. Mills) Canada's Story in Song, 1960; (ed. with J. Glazer) Songs of Work and Freedom, 1960; Traditional Singers and Songs from Ontario, 1965; (ed. with R. Johnston) More Folk Songs from Canada, 1967; (ed.) Sally Go Round the Sun, 1969; Lumbering Songs from the Northern Woods, 1970; (ed.) Penguin Book of Canadian Folk Songs, 1974; Folklore of Canada, 1976; Ring Around the Moon, 1977; Folktales of French Canada, 1979; (ed. with C. Carpenter) A Bibliography of Canadian Folklore in English, 1982; (ed.) Songs and Ballads from Nineteenth-Century Nova Scotia, 1982; (with C. Carpenter) Explorations in Canadian Folklore, 1985; Tales Told in Canada, 1987; Red Rover, Red Rover: Children's Games in Canada, 1988; Canadian Folklore, 1988. Add: Toronto, Ont. M4B 2M7, Canada.

FOWLER, Alastair (David Shaw). British, b. 1930. Poetry, Literature. Regius Prof. of Rhetoric and English Literature, Univ. of Edinburgh, from

1971, now Emeritus; Visiting Prof., Univ. of Virginia, Charlottesville, since 1985. Jr. Research Fellow, Queen's Coll., Oxford, 1955–59; Fellow and Tutor in English, Brasenose Coll., Oxford, 1962–71. *Publs:* (trans. and ed.) Richard Will's De Re Poetica, 1958; Spenser and the Numbers of Time, 1964; (ed.) C.S. Lewis's Spenser's Images of Life, 1967; (ed. with John Carey) The Poems of John Milton, 1968'; Triumphal Forms, 1970; (ed.) Silent Poetry, 1970; (ed. with I.C. Butler) Topics in Criticism, 1971; Seventeen (poetry), 1971; Conceitful Thought, 1975; Catacomb Suburb, 1976; Spenser, 1978; From the Domain of Arnheim, 1982; Kinds of Literature, 1982; A History of English Literature, 1987. Add: Dept. of English, Univ. of Edinburgh, David Hume Tower, George Sq., Edinburgh EH8 9JX, Scotland.

FOWLER, Don D. American, b. 1936. Anthropology/Ethnology, History, Photography. Mamie Kleberg Prof. of Historic Preservation, Univ. of Nevada, Reno, since 1978 (Research Prof. of Anthropology, 1972–78); Research Assoc., Smithsonian Instn., Washington, D.C., since 1970. Asst. Prof., 1964–67, and Assoc. Research Prof., 1968–72, Univ. of Nevada, Reno; Pres., Society for American Archaeology, 1985–87. *Publs:* (ed.) Down the Colorado: John Wesley Powell's Diary of the First Trip Through the Grand Canyon, 1969; (ed.) Photographed All the Best Scenery: Jack Hiller's Diary of the Powell Expedition, 1972; In a Sacred Manner We Live—Edward S. Curtis's Photographs of North American Indians, 1972; Myself in the Water: J.K. Hillers' Photographs 1871-1900, 1989. Add: Historic Preservation Prog., Univ. of Nevada, Reno, Nev. 89557, U.S.A.

FOWLER, Gene. American, b. 1931. Poetry. Served five years in San Quentin Prison. *Publs:* Field Studies, 1965; Quarter Tones, 1966; Shaman Songs, 1967; Her Majesty's Ship, 1969; Fires, 1971; Vivisection, 1974; Felon's Journal, 1975; Fires: Selected Poems 1963-1976, 1975; Return of the Shaman, 1981; Waking the Poet, 1981; The Quiet Poems, 1982. Add: 1432 Spruce St., Berkeley, Calif. 94709, U.S.A.

FOWLES, John. British, b. 1926. Novels/Short stories, Poetry, Translations. *Publs:* The Collector, 1958; The Aristos: A Self-Portrait in Ideas, 1964; The Magus, 1966; The French Lieutenant's Woman, 1969; The Ebony Tower: Collected Novellas, 1974; Poems, 1974; (trans.) Perault: Cinderella 1974; Shipwreck, 1974; Daniel Martin, 1977; Islands, 1978; The Tree, 1979; The Enigma of Stonehenge, 1980; A Brief History of Lyme, 1981; (co-ed.) Monumenta Britannica, by John Aubrey, 2 vols., 1981–82; A Short History of Lyme Regis, 1982; Mantissa, 1982; Land, 1985; A Maggot, 1985. Add: c/o Jonathan Cape Ltd., 30 Bedford Sq., London WC1B 3EL, England.

FOX, Aileen. British, b. 1907. Archaeology/Antiquities, Children's non-fiction. Hon. Archaeologist, Auckland Museum, NZ, since 1974. Lectr., University Coll., Cardiff, 1940–45; Sr. Lectr., Exeter Univ., 1947–72; Visiting Lectr., Auckland Univ., 1973–74. *Publs:* Roman Exeter, 1952; (with Alan Sorrell) Roman Britain, 1961; South West England: 3500 BC-AD 600, 1964, 1973; Exeter in Roman Times, 1973; Prehistoric Maori Fortifications, 1976; Carved Maori Burial Chests, 1983. Add: 2 The Retreat, Topsham, Exeter, Devon, England.

FOX, Alan. British, b. 1920. Administration/Management, Economics, Industrial relations. Lectr. in Sociology, Univ. of Oxford, since 1963. Lectr., Ruskin Coll., 1951–57; Research Fellow, Nuffield Coll., 1957–63; Fellow in Industrial Sociology, Oxford Centre for Mgmt. Studies, 1965–73, all Oxford. *Publs:* History of the National Union of Boot and Shoe Operatives 1874-1957, 1958; (with H.A. Clegg and A.F. Thompson) History of British Trade Unions 1889-1910, 1964; A Sociology of Work in Industry, 1971; Beyond Contract: Work, Power, and Trust Relations, 1974; Man Mismanagement, 1974, 1985; Socialism and Shop Floor Power, 1978; History and Heritage: The Social Origins of the British Industrial Relations System, 1985. Add: Dept. of Social and Admin. Studies, Barnett House, Wellington Sq., Oxford OX1 2ER, England.

FOX, Anthony. *See* **FULLERTON, Alexander.**

FOX, C(harles) P(hilip). American, b. 1913. Children's fiction, History. Member, Bd. of Dirs., State Historical Soc. of Wisconsin, and Circus World Museum, Barabo, Wisc., since 1983. Dir., Circus World Museum, 1960–72; Dir. of Circus Research, Ringling Bros. and Barnum and Bailey, Washington, D.C., 1973–83; now retired. Vice-Pres., Circus Historical Soc., 1954–59; Pres., Milwaukee County Zoological Soc., 1959–61. *Publs:* Children's books—Frisky Try Again, 1959; Come to the Circus, 1959; A Fox in the House, 1960; Mr. Stripes the Gopher, 1961; When Winter Comes, 1962; Birds Will Come to You, 1962; Mr. Duck's Big Day, 1963; Snowball the Trick Pony, 1963; When Spring Comes, 1964; When Summer Comes, 1966; When Autumn Comes, 1966;

Opie Possums Trick, 1968; pictorial histories—Circus Trains, 1948; Circus Parades, 1960; Performing Horses, 1961; The Circus Comes to Town, 1963; (with Tom Parkinson) The Circus in America, 1969; (with F. Beverly Kelley) The Great Circus Street Parade, 1978; Circus Posters, 1978; (with Tom Parkinson) The Circus Moves by Rail, 1978; Old Time Circus Cuts, 1979; Circus Baggage Stock, 1983; (with Tom Parkinson) Circus Advertising, 1985; Horses in Harness, 1988. Add: 2122 Jefferson St., Baraboo, Wisc., 53913, U.S.A.

FOX, Connie. *See* **FOX, Hugh.**

FOX, Hugh (Bernard). Also writes as Connie Fox. American, b. 1932. Novels/Short stories, Plays/Screenplays, Poetry, Literature, Autobiography/Memoirs/Personal. Prof. of American Thought and Language, Michigan State Univ., East Lansing, since 1968. Member of faculty, Loyola Univ., of Los Angeles, Calif., 1958–68; Smith-Mundt Prof. of American Studies, Inst. Pedagogico and Univ. Catolica, Caracas, Venezuela, 1964–66. *Publs:* 40 Poems, 1966; A Night with Hugh Fox, 1966; Eye into Now, 1967; Soul Catcher Songs, 1967; Apotheosis of Olde Towne, 1968; Henry James, 1968; Permeable Man, 1969; Open Letter to a Closed System, 1969; (ed.) Anthology 2, 1969; Countdown of an Empty Streetcar, 1969; Charles Bukowski, 1969; Mind Shaft, 1969; Son of Camelot Meets the Wolfman, 1969; (with S. Schott) Ghost Dance; Portfolio I, 1969; (with A. Cortina) Ghost Dance: Portfolio II, 1970; Ecological Suicide Bus, 1970; (with E.A. Vigo) Handbook Against Gorgons, 1971; (with G. Deisler) The Industrial Ablution, 1971; Paralytic Grandpa Dream Secretions, 1971; The Omega Scriptures, 1971; Icehouse, 1971; Kansas City Westport Mantras, 1971; Survival Handbook, 1972; Just, 1972; Caliban and Ariel, 1972; Peeple, 1973–74; (ed.) The Living Underground, 1973; Gods of the Cataclysm, 1975; (ed.) The Diamond Eye, 1975; Huaca, 1977; First Fire, 1978; Mom-Honeymoon, 1978; Leviathan: An Indian Ocean Whale Journal, 1981; The Dream of the Black Topaz Chamber (poetry), 1982; The Guernica Cycle: The Year Franco Died, 1982; Lyn Lifshin: A Critical Study, 1985; (as Connie Fox) Babishka: A Poem-cycle, 1985; Papa Funk (chapbook), 1986; The Voyage to the House of the Sun, 1988. Add: ATL/EBH, Michigan State Univ., East Lansing, Mich. 48823, U.S.A.

FOX, Karl A(ugust). American, b. 1917. Economics. Distinguished Prof. of Economics, Iowa State Univ., Ames, since 1968, Emeritus since 1987 (Head, Dept. of Economics, 1955–72). Assoc. Head, 1947–51, and Head, 1951–54, Div. of Statistical and Historical Research, U.S. Bureau of Agricultural Economics. Chmn., Social Science Research Council Cttee. on Areas for Social and Economic Statistics, 1964–67. *Publs:* Econometric Analysis for Public Policy, 1958; (with M. Ezekiel) Methods of Correlation and Regression Analysis, 3rd ed., 1959; (with E. Thorbecke and J. Sengupta) The Theory of Quantitative Economic Policy, 1966, 1973; Intermediate Economic Statistics, 1968, 2nd ed. (with T. Karl), 2 vols., 1980; (with J. Sengupta) Economic Analysis and Operations Research: Optimization Techniques in Quantitative Economic Models, 1969; (ed. with D. Johnson) Readings in the Economics of Agriculture, 1969; (ed. with J. Sengupta and G. Narasimham) Economic Models, Estimation and Risk Programming: Essays in Honor of Gerhard Tintner, 1969; (with W. Merrill) Introduction to Economic Statistics, 1970; (ed. and contrib.) Economic Analysis for Educational Planning: Resource Allocation in Nonmarket Systems, 1972; Social Indicators and Social Theory: Elements of an Operational System, 1974; Social System Accounts, 1985; (ed., with Don G. Miles) Systems Economics: Concepts, Models, and Multidisciplinary Perspectives, 1987; Demand Analysis, Econometrics, and Policy Models: Selected Writings of Karl A. Fox, vol. 1, 1989. Add: Dept. of Economics, Iowa State Univ., Ames, Iowa 50010, U.S.A.

FOX, Len. (Leonard Phillips Fox). Australian, b. 1905. Poetry, Art, Economics, Politics/Government. Former Ed., Common Cause, Miners' Fedn. *Publs:* Monopoly, 1940; (with Nettie Palmer) Australians in Spain, 1948; Chung of Vietnam, 1957; Friendly Vietnam, 1958; Gumleaves and Bamboo, 1959; Strange Story of the Eureka Flag, 1963; Vietnam Neighbors, 1966; Gumleaves and People, 1967; E. Phillips Fox, 1969; Eureka and Its Flag, 1973; Australia Taken Over?, 1974; (with others) Depression Down Under, 1977; Gumleaves and Dreaming, 1978; Old Sydney Windmills, 1978; Multinationals Take Over Australia, 1981; Broad Left, Narrow Left, 1982; E. Phillips Fox and His Family, 1985. Add: 10 Little Surrey St., Potts Point, N.S.W. 2011, Australia.

FOX, Levi. British, b. 1914. History, Literature. Dir. and Secty., Shakespeare Birthplace Trust, since 1945. Gen. Ed., Dugdale Soc., since 1945. *Publs:* Leicester Abbey, 1938; Administration of the Honour of Leicester in the Fourteenth Century, 1940; Leicester Castle, 1943; (with P. Russell) Leicester Forest, 1945; Coventry's Heritage, 1946; Stratford-upon-Avon, 1949; Shakespeare's Town, 1949; Oxford, 1951; Shakespeare's Stratford-upon-Avon, 1951; Shakespeare's Country, 1953; The Borough Town of Stratford-upon-Avon, 1953; (ed.) English Historical Scholarship in the 16th and 17th Centuries, 1956; Shakespeare's Town and Country, 1959, 1976; Stratford-upon-Avon: An Appreciation, 1963, 1976; The 1964 Shakespeare Anniversary Book, 1964; Celebrating Shakespeare, 1965; Correspondence of the Reverend Joseph Greene, 1965; A Country Grammar School, 1967; The Shakespeare Book, 1969; (ed.) Shakespeare's Sonnets, 1970; Shakespeare's England, 1972; In Honour of Shakespeare, 1972, 1982; (compiler) The Shakespeare Treasury, 1972; (compiler) The Stratford-upon-Avon Shakespeare Anthology, 1975; Stratford: Past and Present, 1975; Shakespeare's Flowers, 1978; Shakespeare's Birds, 1978; The Shakespeare Centre, 1982; Shakespeare in Medallic Art, 1982; Shakespeare's Magic, 1982; The Early History of King Edward VI School, Stratford-upon-Avon, 1984; Coventry Constables' Presentments, 1986; Historic Stratford-upon-Avon, 1986; Stratford-upon-Avon: Shakespeare's Town, 1986; Oxford in Colour, 1987. Add: The Shakespeare Center, Stratford-upon-Avon, England.

FOX, M(ichael) W. British, b. 1937. Children's fiction, Animals/Pets. Dir., Inst. for the Study of Animal Problems, Humane Soc. of the U.S., Washington, D.C., since 1976. Assoc. Prof. of Psychology, Washington Univ., St. Louis, 1969–76. *Publs:* Canine Behavior, 1965; Canine Pediatrics, 1966; (ed.) Abnormal Behavior in Animals, 1968; Integrative Development of Brain and Behavior in the Dog, 1971; Behavior of Wolves, Dogs and Related Canids, 1971; Understanding Your Dog, 1972; The Wolf (children's fiction), 1973; Vixie, The Story of a Little Fox (children's fiction), 1973; Understanding Your Cat, 1974; (ed.) The Wild Canids, 1974; Concepts in Ethology: Animal and Human Behavior, 1974; Ramu and Chennai, 1975; Sundance Coyote (children's fiction); What Is Your Cat Saying, 1977; Wild Dogs Three, 1977; Between Animal and Man, 1976; What Is Your Dog Saying, 1977; Understanding Your Pet, 1978; (ed.) On the Fifth Day: Animal Rights and Human Obligations, 1978; Whitepaws: A Coyote-Dog (children's fiction), 1979; One Earth One Mind, 1980; Returning to Eden: Animal Rights and Human Responsibilities, 1980; The Soul of the Wolf, 1980; Dr. Fox's Fables: Lessons from Nature (children's fiction), 1980; The Touchlings, 1981; The Way of the Dolphin (children's fiction), 1981; How To Be Your Pet's Best Friend, 1981; Dr. Michael Fox's Massage Program for Cats and Dogs, 1981; Love Is a Happy Cat, 1982; The Healing Touch, 1983; Farm Animals: Husbandry, Behavior and Veterinary Practice, 1983; The Whistling Hunters, 1984; The Animal Doctor's Answer Book, 1984; Agricide: The Hidden Crisis that Affects Us All, 1986; Laboratory Animal Husbandry, 1986; (ed. with L.D. Mickley) Advances in Animal Welfare Science 1985, 1986; (ed. with Mickley) Advances in Animal Welfare Science 1986-87, 1987. Add: 2100 L St. N.W., Washington, D.C., U.S.A.

FOX, Mona Alexis. *See* **BRAND**, Mona.

FOX, Paula. American, b. 1923. Novels/Short stories, Children's fiction. *Publs:* Maurice's Room, 1966; Poor George, 1966; A Likely Place, 1967; Dear Prosper, 1967; How Many Miles to Babylon, 1967; The Stone-Faced Boy, 1968; Portrait of Ivan, 1969; The King's Falcon, 1969; Desperate Characters, 1969; The Western Coast, 1972; Blowfish Live in the Sea, 1972; The Slave Dancer, 1973; The Widow's Children, 1976; The Little Swineherd and Other Tales, 1978; A Place Apart, 1980; A Servant's Tale, 1984; One-Eyed Cat, 1984; The Moonlight Man, 1986. Add: 306 Clinton St., Brooklyn, N.Y. 11201, U.S.A.

FOX, Robert. British, b. 1938. History, Sciences. Prof. of History of Science, Oxford Univ., since 1988. Lectr., 1966–72; Sr. Lectr., 1972–75; Reader, 1975–85, and Prof. of History of Science and Technology, 1986–88, Univ. of Lancaster. Ed., The British Journal for the History of Science, 1971–77; Pres., British Soc. for the History of Science, 1980–82. *Publs:* The Caloric Theory of Gases from Lavoisier to Regnault, 1971; (ed.) Réflexions sur la puissance motrice du feu, by Sadi Carnot, 1978; (ed. with George Weisz) The Organization of Science and Technology in France 1808-1914, 1980; (trans. and ed.) Reflexions on the Motive Power of Fire, by Sadi Carnot, 1986. Add: Modern History Faculty, Broad St., Oxford OX1 3BD, England.

FOX, Samuel. American, b. 1908. Law, Money/Finance, Politics/Government. Attorney-at-Law, and CPA, since 1963. Univ. Prof., Roosevelt Univ., Chicago, since 1972. Member of faculty, Univ. of Illinois, Chicago, 1946–72. *Publs:* Law of Decedents' Estates, 1937; Proportional Representation and the Principles of American Representative Government, 1950; Fundamental Cost Accounting Stipes, 1958; Advanced Cost Accounting, 1959; C.P.A. Law Review Manual, 1959; Management and the Law, 1966; Workbook on Managerial Law, 1971;

(with N.G. Rueschhoff) Principles of International Accounting, 1986. Add: Suite 7311, John Hancock Center, 175 East Delaware Pl., Chicago, Ill. 60611, U.S.A.

FOX, Stephen R. American, b. 1945. Advertising/Public relations, Criminology, Environmental science/Ecology, History. Asst. Prof. of American Studies, Univ. of Kansas, 1971–73. Member of the Board, Alliance of Independent Scholars, Cambridge, Mass., 1984–88. *Publs:* The Guardian of Boston: William Monroe Trotter, 1970; John Muir and His Legacy: The American Conservation Movement, 1981; The Mirror Makers: A History of American Advertising and Its Creators, 1984; Blood and Power: Organized Crime in Twentieth-Century America, 1989. Add: c/o William Morrow and Co., 105 Madison Ave., New York, N.Y. 10016, U.S.A.

FOX, Ted. (Theodore J. Fox). American, b. 1954. Music. Freelance writer. Music feature Sr. Editor, Audio. *Publs:* Showtime at the Apollo, 1983; In the Groove: The Men Behind the Music, 1986. Add: c/o Perry Knowlton, Curtis Brown Ltd., 10 Astor Pl., New York, N.Y. 10003, U.S.A.

FOX, Theodore J. *See* **FOX**, Ted.

FOXALL, Raymond. British, b. 1916. Novels/Short stories, Biography. Journalist, 1936–52; Reporter and Feature Writer, Sunday Express, Manchester, 1958–73. *Publs:* Here Lies the Shadow, 1957; Song for a Prince, 1959; The Devil's Smile, 1960; John McCormack, 1962; The Wicked Lord, 1962; The Devil's Spawn, 1965; Squire Errant, 1968; The Little Ferret, 1968; Brandy for the Parson, 1970; The Dark Forest, 1972; The Silver Goblet, 1974; Society of the Dispossessed, 1976; The Amorous Rogue, 1977; The Noble Pirate, 1978; The Last Jacobite, 1979; The Amateur Commandos, 1980; The Guinea Pigs: Britain's First Paratroop Raid, 1982. Add: The Old Crossings House, Balgowan, nr. Perth PH1 1QW, Scotland.

FOXELL, Nigel. British, b. 1931. Novels/Short stories, Literature. Asst. Keeper, Ashmolean Museum, 1956–58; Lektor in English, Tübingen Univ., 1958–66; Asst. Prof., Univ. of Saskatchewan, 1966–67; Asst. Prof., Long Island Univ., 1967–69. *Publs:* Ten Poems Analysed, 1966; Carnival, 1968; (trans.) Art and Confrontation, 1970; Schoolboy Rising, 1973; Sermon in Stone: John Donne's Monument in St. Paul's Cathedral, 1978; The Marriage Seat, 1978; Loving Emma, 1986; Emma Expects, 1987. Add: 1 Child's Pl., London SW5 9RX, England.

FOX-GENOVESE, Elizabeth. American, b. 1941. History, Area Studies (French political science and biography), Women's Studies, Translations. Prof. of History, State Univ. of New York at Binghamton, since 1980. Teaching fellow, Harvard Univ., Cambridge, 1965–69; Asst. Ed. in History, Houghton Mifflin Co., NYC, 1966–67; Asst. Prof. of History and Liberal Arts, 1973–76, and Assoc. Prof., 1976–80, Univ. of Rochester, N.Y. Dir., Project on Integrating Materials on Women into Traditional Survey Courses; developer and Chairperson, Cluster on Interdisciplinary Study on Women in Culture and Society, 1978–80. *Publs:* The Origins of Physiocracy: Economic Revolution and Social Order in Eighteenth-Century France, 1976; (with others) Girondins et Montagnards, 1982; (with Eugene D. Genovese) Fruits of Merchant Capital: Slavery and Bourgeois Property in the Rise and Expansion of Capitalism, 1983; (trans. and co-ed.) The Autobiography of Pierre Samuel Du Pont De Nemours, 1983; Within the Plantation Household: Black and White Women of the Old South, 1988. Add: 115 E. Upland Rd., Ithaca, N.Y. 14850, U.S.A.

FOXX, Jack. *See* **PRONZINI**, Bill.

FRAENKEL, Jack R. American, b. 1932. Criminology/Law enforcement/Prisons, Education. Prof. of Interdisciplinary Studies in Education, since 1971, and Dir. of the Research and Development Center since 1987, San Francisco State Univ. (Assoc. Prof., 1966–71). Series Ed., Inquiry into Crucial American Problems, Prentice-Hall, Englewood Cliffs, N.J., since 1970, and Crucial Issues in American Govt., Allyn & Bacon Inc., Boston, Mass. *Publs:* (ed.) The U.S. War with Spain 1898: Was Expansionism Justified?, 1969; (ed. with Richard E. Gross and Walter McPhie) Teaching the Social Studies: What, Why and How, 1969; Crime and Criminals, 1970, 1976; (with Betty Reardon and Margaret Carter) Peacekeeping, 1970; (with Hilda Taba, Anthony McNaughton and Mary Durkin) Teacher's Handbook to Elementary Social Studies, 1971; Helping Students Think and Value, 1973; (with Betty Reardon and Margaret Carter) Human Rights: A Study of Values, 1974; How to Teach About Values: An Analytic Approach, 1977; Decision-Making in American Government, 1983, 1985; Civics, 1983, 1986; Toward Improving Research in Social Studies Education, 1988; How to Design and Evaluate

Research in Education, 1990. Add: DAIS Sch. of Education, San Francisco State Univ., San Francisco, Calif. 94132, U.S.A.

FRAKES, George Edward. American, b. 1932. Environmental science/Ecology, History, Race relations. Prof. of History and Geography, Santa Barbara City Coll., since 1973 (Instr. in History, 1962–65; Asst. Prof., 1967–69; Assoc. Prof. of History and Geography, 1969–71; Chmn., Dept. of History, 1971–73, and 1986–87; Chmn., Social Science Div., 1973–76). Supvr. of Student Teachers, Univ. of California Santa Barbara Campus, 1965–66. *Publs:* (with Alexander DeConde) Instructor's Manual for Patterns in American History, 1968; Laboratory for Liberty . . . , 1970; (ed. with Curtis B. Solberg) Pollution Papers, 1971; (ed. with Solberg) Minorities in California History, 1971; (with W. Royce Adams) Colombus to Aquarius: An Interpretive History, 2 vols., 1976. Add: 735 Willow Glen Rd., Santa Barbara, Calif. 93105, U.S.A.

FRAME, Donald Murdoch. American, b. 1911. Literature, Translations. Prof. Emeritus of French, Columbia Univ., NYC, since 1980 (joined faculty, 1938; Prof., 1958–75; Moore Collegiate Prof., 1975–80); Fellowship (resident), NHC, Research Triangle Park, N.C., 1982–83; Trans. Fellowship, NEA, 1984–86. *Publs:* Montaigne in France 1812-1852, 1940; (trans. and ed.) Montaigne: Selected Essays, 1943; (trans. and ed.) Montaigne: Selections from the Essays, 1948; (ed.) Montaigne: Selected Works, 1953; Montaigne's Discovery of Man, 1955; (trans.) Montaigne: The Complete Works, 1957, 1983; (trans.) Voltaire: Candide, Zadig, and Selected Stories, 1961; (trans.) Prévost: Manon Lescaut, 1961; (trans. and ed.) Montaigne: Essays and Selected Writings, 1963; Montaigne: A Biography, 1965, 1984; (trans.) Molière: Tartuffe and Other Plays, 1967; (trans.) Molière: The Misanthrope and Other Plays, 1968; Montaigne's Essais: A Study, 1969; François Rabelais: A Study, 1977; (co-ed.) Columbia Montaigne Conference Papers, 1981; (trans.) Rabelais: Complete Works, 1990. Add: 2218 Windsor Rd., Alexandria, Va. 22307, U.S.A.

FRAME, Janet. New Zealander, b. 1924. Novels/Short stories, Children's fiction, Poetry. *Publs:* The Lagoon: Stories, 1951, rev. ed. as The Lagoon and Other Stories, 1961; Owls Do Cry, 1957; Faces in the Water, 1961; The Edge of the Alphabet, 1961; Scented Gardens for the Blind, 1963; The Reservoir: Stories and Sketches, and Snowman, Snowman: Fables and Fantasies, 1963; The Adaptable Man, 1965; A State of Siege, 1966; The Reservoir and Other Stories, 1966; The Pocket Mirror: Poems, 1967; The Rainbirds (in U.S. as Yellow Flowers in the Antipodean Room), 1968; Mona Minim and the Small of the Sun, 1969; Intensive Care, 1970; Daughter Buffalo, 1972; Living in the Maniototo, 1979; To the Is-land (Autobiography), 1982; An Angel at My Table (Autobiography), 1984; You Are Now Entering the Human Heart (short stories), 1984; The Envoy from the Mirror City (Autobiography), 1985; The Carpathians, 1988. Add: 276 Glenfield Rd., Auckland 10, New Zealand.

FRANCIS, C.D.E. *See* **HOWARTH,** Patrick.

FRANCIS, Clare. British, b. 1946. Novels, Travel/Exploration/Adventure, Autobiography/Memoirs/Personal. *Publs:* Come Hell or High Water, 1977; Come Wind or Weather, 1978; The Commanding Sea, 1981; Night Sky, 1983; Red Crystal, 1985; Wolf Winter, 1987. Add: c/o William Heineman, 81 Fulham Rd., London SW3 6RB, England.

FRANCIS, Dick. British, b. 1920. Mystery/Crime/Suspense, Autobiography/Memoirs/Personal. Amateur steeplechase jockey, 1946–48; Professional steeplechase jockey, 1948–57; Racing Columnist, Sunday Express, London, 1957–73. *Publs:* The Sport of Queens (autobiography), 1957; Dead Cert, 1962; Nerve, 1964; For Kicks, 1965; Odds Against, 1965; Flying Finish, 1966; (ed. with J. Welcome) Best Racing and Chasing Stories, 1966; Blood Sport, 1967; Forfeit, 1968; Enquiry, 1969; (with J. Welcome) Best Racing and Chasing Stories 2, 1969; (ed. with J. Welcome) The Racing Man's Bedside Book, 1969; Rat Race, 1970; Bonecrack, 1971; Smoke-screen, 1972; Slay-Ride, 1973; Knock Down, 1974; High Stakes, 1975; In the Frame, 1976; Risk, 1977; Trial Run, 1978; Whip Hand, 1979; Reflex, 1980; Twice Shy, 1981; Banker, 1982; The Danger, 1983; Proof, 1984; Break In, 1985; Bolt, 1986; A Jockey's Life (biog. of Lester Piggott), 1986; Hot Money, 1987; The Edge, 1988. Add: 5100 N. Ocean Blvd., No. 609, Fort Lauderdale, Fla. 33308, U.S.A.

FRANCIS, Dorothy Brenner. Also writes as Sue Alden, Ellen Goforth and Pat Louis. American, b. 1926. Mystery/Crime/Suspense, Historical/Romance/Gothic, Children's fiction. *Publs:* Adventure at Riverton Zoo, 1966; Mystery of the Forgotten Map, 1968; Laugh at the Evil Eye, 1970; Another Kind of Beauty, 1970; Hawaiian Interlude, 1970; Studio Affair, 1972; Blue Ribbon for Marni, 1973; Nurse on Assignment, 1973; Nurse Under Fire, 1973; Murder in Hawaii, 1973; Nurse in the Caribbean, 1974; Golden Girl, 1974; Nurse of the Keys, 1974; Nurse at Spirit Lake, 1975; Keys to Love, 1975; Legacy of Merton Manor, 1976; Nurse at Playland Park, 1976; (as Sue Alden) The Magnificent Challenge, 1976; Two Against the Arctic, 1976; The Flint Hills Foal, 1976; (as Sue Alden) Nurse of St. John, 1977; Piggy Bank Minds, 1977; Run of the Sea Witch, 1978; The Boy with the Blue Ears, 1979; Shoplifting: The Crime Everybody Pays For, 1980; (as Ellen Goforth) Path of Desire, 1980; New Boy in Town, 1981; Special Girl, 1981; (as Ellen Goforth) A New Dawn, 1982; Say Please, 1982; Captain Morgana Mason, 1982; (as Pat Louis) Treasure of the Heart, 1982; Ghost of Graydon Place, 1982; A Secret Place, 1982; A Blink of the Mind, 1982; Just Friends, 1983; Promises and Turtle Shells, 1984; The Warning, 1984; The Magic Circle, 1984; Kiss Me Kit, 1984; Bid For Romance, 1985; Write On, 1986; Stop Thief!, 1986; The Tomorrow Star, 1986; Fellow Your Heart, 1986; Computer Crime, 1987; The Right Kind of Girl, 1987; Vonnie and Monique, 1987; Suicide: The Preventable Tragedy, 1988. Add: 1505 Brentwood Terr., Marshalltown, Iowa 50158, U.S.A.

FRANCIS, H(erbert) E(dward), Jr. American, b. 1924. Novels/Short stories, Literature, Translations. Prof. of English, Univ. of Alabama, Huntsville, since 1966. Contrib. Ed., Poem Mag. Instr. of English, Pennsylvania State Univ., 1950–52, Univ. of Tennessee, 1952–56, and Northern Illinois Univ., 1956–58; Asst. Prof. of English, Emory Univ., Atlanta, Ga., 1958–65; Fulbright Visiting Prof. to Univ. Nacional de Cuyo, Mendoza, Argentina, 1964, 1965–66 and 1969, and to Cordoba, Argentina, 1969–70. *Publs:* The Itinerary of Beggars, 1973 (Iowa Sch. of Letters Award for Short Fiction); Naming Things, 1980; A Disturbance of Gulls, 1983. Add: 508 E. Clinton Ave., Huntsville, Ala. 35801, U.S.A.

FRANCIS, Marilyn. American, b. 1920. Poetry. Poetry Ed., The Arizonian, Scottsdale, 1958–60; Sedona Ed., The Verde Independent newspaper, 1968–69; Dir., Winged Arts Gallery of Contemporary Art, 1969–73. *Publs:* Thunder in the Superstitions, 1959; Tangents at Noon, 1961; Space for Sound, 1962; Mirror Without Glass, 1964; Symbols for Instants, 1965; Radius: Red Rocks, 1972; Rivers of Remembrance, 1980; Water and Windfalls, 1982. Add: c/o Mosaic Pr., 358 Oliver Rd., Cincinnati, Ohio 45215, U.S.A.

FRANCK, Frederick. Has also written as Dr. Frank Fredericks. American, b. 1909. Art, Theology/Religion, Biography. Freelance writer and artist. *Publs:* (as Dr. Frank Fredericks) Open Wide, Please, 1957; (with L. Begue) Au Pays de Soleil, 1958; Days with Albert Schweitzer, 1959; My Friend in Africa, 1960; African Sketchbook, 1961; My Eye Is in Love, 1963; Outsider in the Vatican, 1965; Au Fil de l'Eau, 1965; I Love Life, 1967; Exploding Church, 1967; (with L. Begue) Croquis Parisiens, 1969; (with G. Simenon) Simenon's Paris, 1970; Tussen Broek en Brooklyn, 1971; Tutte le Strade portano a Roma, 1970; The Zen of Seeing, 1973; Pilgrimage to Now/Here, Christ-Buddha and the True Self of Man: Confrontations and Meditations on an Inward Journey to India, Ceylon, the Himalayas, and Japan, 1973; The Book of Angelus Silesius, 1976; Zen and Zen Classics, 1978; Everyone: The Timeless Myth of Everyman Reborn, 1978; The Awakened Eye, 1979; Art as a Way: A Return to the Spiritual Roots, 1981; The Buddha Eye: An Anthology of the Kyoto School, 1982; The Supreme Koan: Confessions of a Journey Inward, 1982; Messenger of the Heart: The Book of Angelus Silesius, 1982; De Zen Van het Zien (in Dutch), 1982; Echoes from the Bottomless Well, 1985; De Droomzolder, Oog met Venetie (in Dutch), 1985. Add: Pacem in Terris, 96 Covered Bridge Rd., Warwick, N.Y. 10990, U.S.A.

FRANCK, Thomas Martin. American, b. 1931. International relations/Current affairs, Law, Politics/Government. Prof. of Law, Sch. of Law, and Dir., Center for Intnl. Studies, 1965–73 and since 1974, New York Univ., NYC; on leave from NYU: Dir. of Research, U.N. Inst. for Training and Research, 1980–82. Dir., Intnl. Law Prog., Carnegie Endowment for Intnl. Peace, 1975–79 (Acting Dir., 1973–75); Visiting Prof. Osgoode Hall Law Sch., York Univ., Toronto, 1972–76. *Publs:* Race and Nationalism, 1960; (co-author) The Role of the United Nations in the Congo, 1963; (co-author) African Law, 1963; East African Unity Through Law, 1964; Comparative Constitutional Process, 1968; The Structure of Impartiality, 1968; (co-author) A Free Trade Association, 1968; (co-author) Why Federations Fail, 1968; (co-author) Word Politics: Verbal Strategy Among the Superpowers, 1971; (co-ed.) Secrecy and Foreign Policy, 1974; (co-author) Resignation in Protest, 1975; (co-author) Foreign Policy by Congress, 1979; (co-author) U.S. Foreign Relations Law, vols. I-III, 1980– 81, vols. IV-V, 1984; The Tethered Presidency, 1982; Human Rights in Third World Perspective, 3 vols., 1982; (co-author) Foreign Relations Law, vols. IV-V, 1984; Nation Against Nation, 1985; Judging the World Court, 1986; Foreign Relations and National

Security Laws, 1987. Add: 15 Charlton St., New York, N.Y. 10014, U.S.A.

FRANCOEUR, Robert Thomas. American, b. 1931. Human relations, Medicine/Health, Sex. Prof. of Human Sexuality, Embryology and Allied Health Science, Fairleigh Dickinson Univ., Madison, N.J., since 1974 (joined faculty, 1965). *Publs:* (ed.) The World of Teilhard de Chardin, 1961; Perspectives in Evolution, 1965; Evolving World, Converging Man, 1970; Utopian Motherhood: New Trends in Human Reproduction, 1972; Eve's Rib: 20 Faces of Sex, Marriage and Family, 1972; (with Anna K Francoeur) Hot and Cool Sex: Cultures in Conflict, 1974; (ed. with A.K. Francoeur) The Future of Sexual Relations, 1974; Becoming a Sexual Person, 1982, 1989; Biomedical Ethics: A Guide to Decision Making, 1983; Becoming a Sexual Person: A Brief Edition, 1984; (ed.) Taking Sides: Clashing Views on Controversial Issues in Human Sexuality, 1987, 1989; A Descriptive Dictionary of Sexology, 1989. Add: Two Circle Dr., Rockaway, N.J. 07866, U.S.A.

FRANEY, Ros(alind). British, b. 1946. Novels, Social commentary, Researcher for documentaries, Yorkshire Television, London, since 1985. Journalist, IPC Magazines, London, 1972–74; Information Officer, UNICEF, Ethiopia, 1974–75; Journalist, Shelter, London, 1977–82; freelance writer and journalist in London, 1982–85. *Publs:* Poor Law: The Mass Arrest of Homeless Claimants in Oxford, 1983; Cry Baby (novel), 1987; (with Grant McKea) Time Bomb: Irish Bombers, English Justice and the Guildford Four, 1988. Add: 78 Marquis Rd., London NW1, England.

FRANK, André Gunder. West German, b. 1929. Economics, History, Politics/Government, Social sciences, Third World problems. Prof. of Development Studies, Univ. of East Anglia, Norwich, since 1978; Prof. of Development Economics, Univ. of Amsterdam, since 1982. Instructor, Iowa State Univ., Ames, 1956–57; Lectr. and Asst. Prof. of Economics, Michigan State Univ., East Lanssing, 1957–61; Assoc. Prof. of Sociology, Univ. of Brasilia, 1963; Prof. of Sociology and Economics, Univ. of Chile, Santiago, 1968–73; Research Assoc., Max Planck Institut, Starnberg, 1974–78. *Publs:* Capitalism and Underdevelopment in Latin America, 1967, 1969; Latin America: Underdevelopment or Revolution, 1969; Sociology of Development and Underdevelopment of Sociology, 1969; Lumpenbourgeoisie: Lumpendevelopment: Dependence, Class, and Politics in Latin America (trans. from Spanish by M.D. Berdicio), 1972; (with D. Johnson and J. Cockcroft) Dependence and Underdevelopment, 1972; On Capitalist Underdevelopment, 1975; Economic Genocide in Chile, 1976; World Accumulation 1492-1789, 1978; Dependent Accumulation and Underdevelopment, 1978; Mexican Agriculture 1521-1630, 1979; Crisis: In the World Economy, 1980; Crisis: In the Third World, 1981; Reflections on the World Economic Crisis, 1981; (with others) Dynamics of Global Crisis, 1982; The European Challenge: From Atlantic Alliance to Pan-European Entente for Peace and Jobs, 1984. Add: 23 Camberley Rd., Norwich NR4 65J, England.

FRANK, Charles R(aphael, Jr.). American, b. 1937. Economics, International relations/Current affairs. Vice-Pres., Salomon Bros. Inc., NYC, since 1978. Prof. of Economics, Yale Univ., New Haven, Conn., 1965–67; Prof. of Economics and Intnl. Affairs, Princeton Univ., N.J., 1967–74; Sr. Fellow, Brookings Inst., Washington, D.C. 1972–74; Deputy Asst.-Secty. of State, Washington, D.C., 1974–78. *Publs:* The Sugar Industry in East Africa, 1965; (with B. Van Arkadie) Economic Accounting and Development Planning, 1966, 1969; Production Theory and Indivisible Commodities, 1969; Statistics and Econometrics, 1971; Foreign Trade Regimes and Economic Development: The Case of Korea, 1975; Foreign Trade and Domestic Aid, 1977. Add: Salomon Bros. Inc., 1 New York Plaza, New York, N.Y. 10004, U.S.A.

FRANK, Helmut J. American. Economics. Prof. Emeritus of Economics, Univ. of Arizona, Tucson, since 1984 (Asst. Prof., 1961–63; Assoc. Prof., 1963–67; Prof., 1967–83; Dir. of Economic and Business Research, 1978–80). Ed., The Energy Journal, since 1980. Economist, W.J. Levy Consultants, New York, 1950–56, and Paris, 1960–61, and Univ. of Denver Research Inst., 1967–68. *Publs:* Crude Oil Prices in the Middle East, 1966; (with J.J. Schanz) U.S.-Canadian Energy Trade, 1978; (with J.H. Lichtblau) Outlook for World Oil in the 21st Century, 1978. Add: Dept. of Economics, Univ. of Arizona, Tucson, Ariz. 85721, U.S.A.

FRANK, Joseph (Nathaniel). American, b. 1918. Literature. Prof. of Slavic Languages and Literature and Comparative Literature, Stanford Univ., Calif., since 1986. Ed., Bureau of National Affairs, Washington, D.C., 1942–50; Special Researcher, American Embassy, Paris, 1951–52;

Lectr., Dept. of English, Princeton Univ., 1955–56; Asst. Prof. of English, Univ. of Minnesota, 1958–61; Assoc. Prof. and Prof., Dept. of Comparative Literature, Rutgers—The State Univ., New Jersey, 1961–66; Prof. of Comparative Literature, 1966–86, and Dir. of Christian Gauss Seminars in Criticism, 1966–83, Princeton Univ., New Jersey. *Publs:* The Widening Gyre: Crisis and Mastery in Modern Literature, 1963; (ed.) A Primer of Ignorance by R.P. Blackmur, 1967; F.M. Dostoevsky: The Seeds of Revolt 1821-1849, 1976, The Years of Ordeal 1850-1859, 1983, and The Stir of Liberation, 1860-1865, 1986. Add: Dept. of Slavic Literature and Languages, Stanford Univ., Stanford, Calif. 94305, U.S.A.

FRANKE, Carl Wilfred. American, b. 1928. Psychology, Theology/Religion. Clergyman, Pecatonia United Methodist Church, Illinois, 1979–85. *Publs:* How to Stay Alive All Your Life, 1967; Defrost Your Frozen Assets, 1969; Christian, Be a Real Person, 1974; Surviving My Heart Attack, 1987. Add: 905 Roncevalles Ave., Rockford, Ill. 61107, U.S.A.

FRANKEL, Joseph. British, b. 1913. International relations. Emeritus Prof., Univ. of Southampton (Prof. of Politics, 1962–78). Sr. Assoc. Member, St. Antony's, Oxford Univ., since 1985. Research Assoc., Royal Inst. of Intnl. Affairs, 1950 and 1972–73; Lectr., Univ. of Aberdeen, 1951–61, 1962–78. *Publs:* The Making of Foreign Policy, 1962, 1967; International Relations, 1964, 1972; International Politics: Conflict and Harmony, 1969, 1971; National Interest, 1970; Contemporary International Theory and the Behaviour of States, 1973; British Foreign Policy 1945-1973, 1975; International Relations in a Changing World, 1980. Add: Well Cottage, Lockinge, Wantage, Oxon. OX12 8QD, England.

FRANKEL, Sandor. American, b. 1943. Law, Money/Finance. Attorney, in private practice, New York, since 1971. Temporary Counsel to National Commn. for Reform of Federal Criminal Laws, 1968. Staff member, White House Task Force on Crime, 1967; Asst. U.S. Attorney for District of Columbia, 1968–71. *Publs:* Beyond a Reasonable Doubt, 1972; The Aleph Solution, 1978; How To Defend Yourself Against the I.R.S., 1985. Add: 225 Broadway, New York, N.Y. 10007, U.S.A.

FRANKEL, William. British, b. 1917. Area studies. London Corresp., The Statesman, India; Ed., Survey of Jewish Affairs annual. Ed., Jewish Chronicle, London, 1958–77; Special Adviser, The Times, London, 1977–81. *Publs:* (ed.) Friday Nights (a Jewish Chronicle anthology), 1973; Israel Observed: An Anatomy of the State, 1980; Israel: The First Forty Years, 1987. Add: 131-135 Temple Chambers, Temple Ave., London EC4Y 0DT, England.

FRANKEN, Rose (Dorothy Lewin). Also wrote with W(illiam) B(rown) Meloney (died, 1970) as Margaret Grant, and under joint pseud. Franken Meloney. American, b. 1895. Historical/Romance/Gothic, Plays/Screenplays, Medicine/Health, Autobiography/Memoirs/Personal. *Publs:* Pattern, 1925; Another Language (play), 1932; (with Jane Lewin) Mr. Dooley, Jr. (juvenile play), 1932; Twice Born, 1935; (as Margaret Grant) Call Back Love, 1937; Of Great Riches, 1937, in U.K. as Gold Pennies, 1938; Claudia: The Story of a Marriage, 1939, as Claudia (play), 1941; (as Franken Meloney) Strange Victory, 1939; Claudia and David, 1940; (as Franken Meloney) When Doctors Disagree, 1940; (as Franken Meloney) American Bred, 1941; Another Claudia, 1943; Outrageous Fortune (play), 1944; Soldier's Wife (play), 1945; Young Claudia, 1946; The Marriage of Claudia, 1948; The Hallams (play), 1948; From Claudia to David, 1949; The Fragile Years (in U.K. as Those Fragile Years), 1952, 2nd U.K. ed. as The Return of Claudia, 1957; Rendezvous (in U.K. as The Quiet Heart), 1954; Intimate Story, 1955; The Antic Years, 1958; When All Is Said and Done (autobiography), 1962; You're Well Out of Hospital (non-fiction), 1966. Add: 5026 Arlington Ave., Riverdale, N.Y., U.S.A.

FRANKHOUSER, Floyd Richard. American, b. 1944. Poetry. Production Scheduler, Geo. W. Bollman & Co. Inc., Adamstown, Pa., since 1967 (Shipping Clerk, 1963–64; Office Clerk, 1964–65; Asst. Production Scheduler, 1965–67). *Publs:* Folk Singer, 1973; Beyond Shadows, 1974; Crumbs, and Pieces of Cake, 1976; Love's Hand, 1978; Brothers, 1982. Add: R.F.D. 1, Box 416, Denver, Pa. 17517, U.S.A.

FRANKLAND, (Anthony) Noble. British, b. 1922. Military/Defence, Biography. Official Military Historian, 1951–60; Deputy Dir. of Studies, Royal Inst. of Intnl. Affairs, London, 1956–60; Dir., Imperial War Museum, London, 1960–82; Consultant, World at War television series, London, 1971–74. *Publs:* (ed.) Documents on International Affairs, 1955, 1956, 1957, 1958–60; Crown of Tragedy: Nicholas II (in U.S. as Imperial Tragedy: Nicholas II, Last of the Tsars), 1961; (with Charles

Webster) The Strategic Air Offensive Against Germany 1939-45, 4 vols., 1961; The Bombing Offensive Against Germany: Outlines and Perspectives, 1965; Bomber Offensive: The Devastation of Europe, 1970; (ed. with Christopher Dowling) The Politics and Strategy of the Second World War, 8 vols., 1974–78; Decisive Battles of the 20th Century, 1976; Prince Henry, Duke of Gloucester, 1980. Add: Thames House, Eynsham, Oxford, England.

FRANKLIN, Alexander John. British, b. 1921. Plays/Screenplays. Songs, lyrics and libretti, Theatre. Lectr., South-West Essex Technical Coll., London, 1949–57; Sr. Lectr. 1957–70, and Head of Drama 1975–78, Furzedown Coll. of Education, London; Scriptwriter and Ed., ILEA Television Service, London, 1970–75. *Publs:* (ed.) Far East Survey, 1945; (adaptor) Noah's Flood, 1952; (compiler and ed.) Choral Verse, 1962; (adaptor and ed.) Seven Miracle Plays, 1963; (ed. with F. Palmer) Looking Around, 1969; (compiler with P. Franklin) Ways, 2 vols., 1973; Ways: Teacher's Book, 1973; Three Letters and a Postcard (film), 1974; Barbara's Diary (film), 1974; Home at a Price (film), 1975; The Shepherds (opera libretto), 1976. Add: 23 Abinger Pl., Lewes, Sussex BN7 2QA, England.

FRANKLIN, John H(ope). American, b. 1915. History, Race relations. Instr., Fisk Univ., Nashville, Tenn., 1936–37; Prof. of History, St. Augustine's Coll., Raleigh, N.C., 1939–43; Prof. of History, North Carolina Coll., 1943–47; Prof. of History, Howard Univ., Washington, D.C., 1947–56; Prof. and Chmn., Dept. of History, Brooklyn Coll., NYC, 1956–64; Prof. of American History, 1964–82, and Chmn. of Dept. of History, 1967–70, Univ. of Chicago; James B. Duke Prof. of History, Duke Univ., Durham, N.C., 1982–85. *Publs:* The Free Negro in North Carolina, 1790-1860, 1943, 1969; (ed.) The Civil War Diary of James T. Ayers, 1947; From Slavery to Freedom: A History of Negro Americans, 1947, 6th ed. 1987; The Militant South 1800-1860, 1956; Reconstruction After the Civil War, 1961; (ed.) A Fool's Errand, by Albion Tourgee, 1961; (ed.) Army Life in a Black Regiment, by T.W. Higginson, 1962; The Emancipation Proclamation, 1963; (with J.W. Caughey and E.R. May) Land of the Free, 1965; (ed.) Three Negro Classics, 1965; (ed., with I. Star) The Negro in the Twentieth Century, 1967; 8ed.) Color and Race, 1968; (ed.) The Suppression of the African Slave Trade, by W.E.B. Du Bois, 1969, (ed.) Reminiscences of an Active Life: The Autobiography of John R. Lynch, 1970; Illustrated History of Black Americans, 1970; Racial Equality in America, 1976; Southern Odyssey: Travelers in the Antebellum North, 1976; George Washington Williams: A Biography, 1985. Add: Dept. of History, Duke Univ., Durham, N.C. 27708, U.S.A.

FRANKLIN, Linda Campbell. American, b. 1941. Antiques, Design. Ed., The Ephemera News quarterly, 1981–83; Ed., Show Forth bimonthly, 1983–84; Ed. and Publisher, Kitchen Collectibles News bimonthly, 1984–86. *Publs:* From Hearth to Cookstove, 1976, 1979; Antiques and Collectibles: A Bibliography of Works in English, 1978; Our Old Fashioned Country Diary, 1980, 10th ed. 1988; Library Display Ideas, 1980; A Baby Book, 1980; A Wedding Notebook, 1980; A Birthday Book, 1981; Our Christmas Book, 1981; Address Book, 1981; Our Old Fashioned Country Diary for 1986, 1982; 300 Years of Kitchen Collectibles, 1981, 1984, 1987; A Travel Diary, 1983; Wedding Memory Keepbook, 1985; Display and Publicity Ideas for Libraries, 1985. Add: P.O. Box 383, Murray Hill Station, New York, N.Y. 10156, U.S.A.

FRANKLIN, Richard Langdon. Australian, b. 1925. Philosophy. Emeritus Prof. of Philosophy, Univ. of New England, Armidale, since 1986. (Prof. 1968–86). Lectr., Univ. of Western Australia, Perth, 1956–67. *Publs:* Freewill and Determinism, 1968. Add: Philosophy Dept., Univ. of New England, Armidale, N.S.W., Australia 2351.

FRANKLIN, Samuel Harvey. New Zealander, b. 1928. Geography, Sociology. Prof., Dept. of Geography, Victoria Univ. of Wellington, since 1967. *Publs:* Rural Societies, 1971; The European Peasantry, 1975; Trade, Growth, and Anxiety: New Zealand Beyond the Welfare State, 1978; Cul de Sac: The Question of New Zealand's Future, 1985. Add: Victoria Univ. of Wellington, Dept. of Geography, Box 600, Wellington, New Zealand.

FRANTZ, Joe B. American, b. 1917. History, Biography. Prof. of History, Univ. of Texas, Austin (joined faculty, 1949; Asst. Prof. to Assoc. Prof., 1949–59; Chmn., Dept. of History, 1959–65). Dir., Texas State Historical Assn; Member, Advisory Bd., National Park Service, Pres., Phi Alpha Theta, 1962–64, Southwestern Social Science Assn., 1963–64, and Texas Inst. of Letters, 1967–69; Consultant in History, The White House, 1968–69. *Publs:* Gail Borden: Dairyman to a Nation, 1951; (with J.E. Choate, Jr.) The American Cowboy: The Myth and the Reality, 1955;

(ed.) An Honest Preface and Other Essays, 1959; (ed. with Duke) 6000 Miles of Fence, 1961; (co-ed.) Readings in American History, 1964; (co-author) The Heroes of Texas, 1964; (co-author) Turner, Bolton and Webb: Three Historians of the American Frontier, 1965; LBJ: 37 Years of Public Service, 1973; Texas, 1976; Aspects of the American West, 1976; The Forty-Acre Follies, 1983; (with M. Cox) Lure of the Land: Texas County Maps and the History of Settlement, 1988. Add: 4301 Edgemond, Austin, Tex. 78731, U.S.A.

FRANTZEN, Allen J. American, b. 1947. Literary criticism/History. Assoc. Prof. of English, Loyola Univ. of Chicago, since 1983 (Asst. Prof., 1978–82; Dir., Graduate Progs. in English, 1984–89). Asst. Prof. of English, Oberlin Coll., Ohio, 1976–78. Pres., Edgewater Community Council, Chicago, 1984–85. *Publs:* The Literature of Penance in Anglo-Saxon England, 1983; King Alfred, 1986; The Desire for Origins and the History of Anglo-Saxon Studies, 1990. Add: Dept. of English, Loyola Univ. of Chicago, 6525 N. Sheridan Rd., Chicago, Ill. 60626, U.S.A.

FRASER OF TULLYBELTON, Lord. *See* **FRASER**, Walter Ian Reid.

FRASER, Anthea. Also writes as Lorna Cameron; Vanessa Graham. British. Novels/Short stories. Secty., Crime Writers Assn. *Publs:* Designs of Annabelle, 1971; In the Balance, 1973; Laura Possessed, 1974; Home Through the Dark, 1974; Whistler's Lane, 1975; Presence of Mind, 1979; Breath of Brimstone, 1979; Island in Waiting, 1979; (as Vanessa Graham) Time of Trial, 1979; The Stone, 1980; (as Lorna Cameron) Summer in France, 1981; (as Vanessa Graham) Second Time Round, 1982; (as Vanessa Graham) The Stand-In, 1984; A Shroud for Delilah, 1984; A Necessary End, 1985; Pretty Maids All in a Row, 1986; Death Speaks Softly, 1987; The Nine Bright Shiners, 1987; Six Proud Walkers, 1988. Add: c/o Laurence Pollinger Ltd., 18 Maddox St., London W1R 0EU, England.

FRASER, (Lady) Antonia. British, b. 1932. Mystery/Crime/Suspense, Children's fiction, History, Biography. Pres., English P.E.N. since 1988. Member, Arts Council, 1970–72; Chmn., Cttee. of Mgmt., Soc. of Authors, London, 1974–75; Gen. Ed., Kings and Queens of England series, Weidenfeld and Nicolson, publishers, London, 1974–75; Chmn., Crime Writers Assn., 1985–86. *Publs:* King Arthur, 1954; Robin Hood, 1955; Dolls, 1963; History of Toys, 1966; Mary, Queen of Scots, 1969; Cromwell Our Chief of Men (in U.S. as Cromwell the Lord Protector), 1973; Mary, Queen of Scots, and the Historians, 1974; King James VI and I, 1974; (ed.) Scottish Love Poems, 1975; (ed.) Love Letters, 1976; Quiet as a Nun (mystery), 1977; The Wild Island (mystery), 1978; King Charles II (in U.S. as Royal Charles), 1979; A Splash of Red (mystery), 1981; (ed.) Mary, Queen of Scots in Poetry, 1981; Cool Repentance (mystery), 1982; (ed.) Oxford and Oxfordshire in Verse, 1982; The Weaker Vessel: Woman's Lot in Seventeenth Century England, 1984; Oxford Blood (mystery), 1985; Jemima Shore's First Case (mystery), 1986; Your Royal Hostage (mystery), 1987; Boadicea's Chariot: The Warrior Queens, 1988. Add: c/o Curtis Brown, 162-168 Regent St., London W1R 5TB, England.

FRASER, Conon. British, b. 1930. Children's fiction, Travel/Exploration/Adventure. Freelance writer. Television Producer, New Zealand Broadcasting Corp., 1964–69; Film Producer and Director, New Zealand National Film Unit, 1969–86. *Publs:* Dead Man's Cave, 1954; The Green Dragon, 1955; Shadow of Danger, 1956; The Underground Explorers, 1957; The Underground River, 1959; The Scoter Island Adventure, 1959; Lim of Hong Kong, 1960; Oyster-Catcher Bay, 1962; With Captain Cook in New Zealand, 1963; Brave Rescue, 1964; Looking at New Zealand, 1969; (co-author) Gardens of New Zealand, 1975; Beyond the Roaring Forties, 1986. Add: Matapuna Rd., Horopito, R.D.6 Raetihi, New Zealand.

FRASER, Douglas. British, b. 1910. Poetry. *Publs:* Landscape of Delight, 1967; Rhymes o'Auld Reekie, 1973; Where the Dark Branches Part, 1977; Treasure for Eyes to Hold, 1981. Add: 2 Keith Terr., Edinburgh EH4 3NJ, Scotland.

FRASER, George MacDonald. British, b. 1925. Novels/Short stories, Screenplays. Deputy Ed., Glasgow Herald newspaper, 1964–69. *Publs:* Flashman, 1969; Royal Flash, 1970, screenplay, 1975; The General Danced at Dawn, 1970; Flash for Freedom, 1971; Steel Bonnets, 1971; Flashman at the Charge, 1973; The Three Musketeers (screenplay), 1973; The Four Musketeers (screenplay), 1974; McAuslan in the Rough, 1974; Flashman in the Great Game, 1975; The Prince and the Pauper (screenplay), 1976; Flashman's Lady, 1977; Mr. American, 1980; Flashman and the Redskins, 1982; Octopussy (screenplay), 1983; The Pyrates, 1983; Flashman and the Dragon, 1985; Casanova (TV screenplay), 1987; The Hollywood History of the World, 1988; The Sheikh and the Dustbin, 1988; The Return of the Musketeers (screenplay), 1989. Add: Baldrine, Isle of Man, British Isles.

FRASER, Harry. British, b. 1937. Crafts. Joint Managing Dir., Potclays Ltd., Stoke-on-Trent, since 1983 (Dir. since 1976). Production Mgr., Twyfords Ltd., Etruria, Stoke-on-Trent, 1959–62; Mgr. Armitage-Shanks Ltd., Armitage, Rugeley, Staffs., 1962–65; Divisional Mgr., Wengers Ltd., Etruria, 1965–66, and Podmore & Sons Ltd., Shelton, 1966–73, Stoke-on-Trent; Managing Dir., Harry Fraser Ltd., 1973–77. *Publs:* Kilns and Kiln Firing for the Craft Potter, 1969; Glazes for the Craft Potter, 1973; Electric Kilns, 1974; Electric Kilns and Firing, 1978; Ceramic Faults and Their Remedies, 1986. Add: Redferns, 12 Leyfield Rd., Trentham, Stoke-on-Trent, Staffs. ST4 8HQ, England.

FRASER, Ian Watson. New Zealander, b. 1907. Theology/Religion. Minister, St. Andrew's Church, Levin, 1933–39; Minister, Presbyterian Church, Wyndham, 1939–41; Chaplain, St. Andrew's Coll., Christchurch, 1941–48; Minister, St. John's Church, Paptoetoe, 1948–61, and St. Stephen's Church, Lower Hutt, 1961–73; Moderator, Presbyterian Church of New Zeand, 1968–69. *Publs:* Understandest Thou?, The Bible in Our Time; Understanding the Old Testament; Journey into the Shadows, The Story of Nansen Home, 1984. Add: 19A Bloomfield Terr., Lower Hutt, New Zealand.

FRASER, James. *See* **WHITE,** Alan.

FRASER, Jane. *See* **PILCHER,** Rosamunde.

FRASER, Kathleen. American, b. 1937. Poetry. Prof. of Creative Writing, San Francisco State Univ., since 1987 (Dir. of the Poetry Center, 1972–75, and Founder, American Poetry Archive, 1974; Assoc. Prof., 1975–87). Visiting Prof., Writers Workshop, Univ. of Iowa, Iowa City, 1969–71; Writer-in-Residence, Reed Coll., Portland, Ore., 1971–72. *Publs:* Change of Address and Other Poems, 1966; Silts, Somersaults, and Headstands: Game Poems Based on a Painting by Peter Breughel (juvenile), 1968; In Defiance of the Rains, 1969; Little Notes to You from Lucas Street, 1972; What I Want, 1974; Magritte Series, 1978; New Shoes, 1978; Each Next (narratives), 1980; Something (even human voices) in the foreground, a lake, 1984; Boundary, 1987; Notes Preceding Trust, 1987. Add: Dept. of English, San Francisco State Univ., 1600 Holloway Ave., San Francisco, Calif. 94132, U.S.A.

FRASER, Morris. British, b. 1941. Psychiatry. Sr. Registrar in Psychiatry, the London Hosp., since 1976. Psychiatrist, Springfield Hosp., London, since 1973; Consultant Psychiatrist, University Coll Hosp., London, since 1979. Sr. Registrar in Child Psychiatry, Royal Belfast Hosp. for Sick Children, Northern Ire., 1971–73; Psychiatrist, Springfield Hosp., London, 1973–76. *Publs:* Children in Conflict, 1973; The Death of Narcissus, 1977; ECT: A Clinical Guide, 1983; Dementia: Its Nature and Management, 1987. Add: 14 Northchurch Terrace, London N1, England.

FRASER, Russell A(lfred). American, b. 1927. Literature. Austin Warren Prof. of English, Univ. of Michigan, Ann Arbor, since 1968 (Chmn., Dept. of English Language and Literature, 1968–73). Instr., Univ. of California at Los Angeles, 1950; Asst. Prof., Duke Univ., Durham, N.C., 1951–56; Asst. Prof. and Assoc. Prof., Princeton Univ., N.J., 1956–65 (Assoc. Dean, Graduate Sch., 1962–65); Prof. and Chmn. of English Dept., Vanderbilt Univ., Nashville, Tenn, 1965–68. *Publs:* The Court of Venus, 1955; The Court of Virtue, 1962; Shakespeare's Poetics, 1962; King Lear (criticism), 1963; (ed.) Selected Writings of Oscar Wilde, 1969; The War Against Poetry, 1970; An Essential Shakespeare, Nine Plays and the Sonnets, 1972; The Dark Ages and the Age of Gold, 1973; (with N. Rabkin) Drama of the English Renaissance, 2 vols., 1976; The Language of Adam, 1976; A Mingled Yarn: The Life of R.P. Blackmur, 1981; The Three Romes, 1985; (ed.) All's Well That Ends Well, 1985; Young Shakespeare, 1988. Add: Dept. of English, Univ. of Michigan, Ann Arbor, Mich. 48109, U.S.A.

FRASER, W. Hamish. British, b. 1941. History, Industrial relations. Sr. Lectr., Univ. of Strathclyde, since 1977 (Lectr., 1966–77). *Publs:* Trade Union and Society: The Struggle for Acceptance 1850-1880, 1974; Workers and Employers: Documents on Trade Unions and Industrial Relations in Britain since the 18th Century, 1980; The Coming of the Mass Market 1850-1914, 1982; Conflict and Class: Scottish Workers 1700-1838, 1988. Add: Dept. of History, Univ. of Strathclyde, Glasgow G1

1XQ, Scotland.

FRASER, Walter Ian Reid (Lord Fraser of Tullybelton). British, b. 1911. Law. Privy Counsellor, since 1975. Dean of Faculty of Advocates, Queen's Counsel, until 1964; Senator of Coll. of Justice in Scotland, 1964–74; Lord of Appeal in Ordinary, 1975–85. *Publs:* Outline of Constitutional Law, 1938, 1948. Add: Tullybelton House, Bankfoot, Perthshire, Scotland.

FRATCHER, William Franklin. American, b. 1913. Law. Prof. Emeritus, Univ. of Missouri, Columbia, since 1983 (Assoc. Prof., 1947–49; Prof., 1949–71; R.B. Price Distinguished Prof. of Law, 1971–83). Gen. Reporter for the Intnl. Encyclopedia of Comparative Law, since 1966. Visiting Prof. of Law, Univ. of Puget Sound, Tacoma, Wash., 1983–85, and at Western New England College School of Law, Springfield, Mass., 1986–87. *Publs:* The National Defense Act, 1945; Perpetuities and Other Restraints, 1954; (with Simes) Cases and Other Materials on the Law of Fiduciary Administration, 1956; (ed.) The Law of Future Interests, by Simes and Smith, biennial supplements, since 1961; Trusts and Estates in England, 1968; (co-author) Uniform Probate Code, 1970; Trust, 1974; (co-author) Uniform Probate Code Practice Manual, 1977; The Law Barn, 1978, 1988; The Luncheon Guest, 1979; (co-author) Trusts and Trust-Like Devices, 1981; (ed.) The Law of Trusts, by Scott, annual supplements, since 1982; (ed.) Scott on Trusts, 8 vols., 1986–88 (vols. 9-12 forthcoming); (co-author) International Symposium on Trusts, Equity and Fiduciary Relationships, 1989. Add: Sch. of Law, Univ. of Missouri, Columbia, Mo. 65211, U.S.A.

FRATTI, Mario. American (b. Italian), b. 1927. Plays/Screenplays, Poetry. Prof., Hunter Coll., NYC, since 1967. Trans., Rubelli publrs., Venice, 1953–63; Drama critic, Sipario, Milan, 1963–66; Drama Critic, Ridotto, Venice, Paese Sera, Rome, and L'Ora, Palermo, 1963–73; Prof., Adelphi Coll., NYC, 1967–68. *Publs:* Il Ritorno (in U.S and U.K. as The Return), 1961; Il Suicidio (in U.S. and U.K. as The Suicide), 1962; La Gabbia (in U.S. as The Cage), 1963; The Academy, 1963; Le Vedova Bianca (in U.S. as Mafia), 1963; Le Telefonata (in U.S. as The Gift), 1965; I Frigoriferi (in U.S. as The Refrigerators), 1965; Eleonora Duse, 1967; Il Ponte (in U.S. as The Bridge), 1967; The Victim, 1968; Four Plays, 1972; Races: Six New Plays, 1972; Birthday, 1978; American Scenes, 2 vols., 1980; Nine (Tony Award), 1982; Mario Fratti (biography), 1983; Young Wife, Mothers and Daughters, Three Beds, 1984; Paganini, 1985; Lovers, 1985; A.I.D.S., 1986; 500: A Musical about Columbus, 1988; Friends, 1989. Add: 145 W. 55th St., Apt. 15D, New York, N.Y. 10019, U.S.A.

FRAYN, Michael. British, b. 1933. Novels, Plays/Screenplays, Humor/Satire, Translations. Reporter, 1957–59, and Columnist, 1959–62, The Guardian, Manchester and London; Columnist, The Observer, London, 1962–68. *Publs:* The Day of the Dog, 1962; (ed.) The Best of Beachcomber, by J.B. Morton, 1963; The Book of Fub (in U.S. as Never Put Off to Gomorrah), 1963; On the Outskirts, 1964; The Tin Men, 1965; The Russian Interpreter, 1966; Towards the End of the Morning (in U.S. as Against Entropy), 1967; At Bay in Gear Street, 1967; A Very Private Life, 1968; The Two of Us (plays), 1970; Sweet Dreams, 1974; Constructions (essays), 1974; Alphabetical Order (play), 1975; Clouds (play), 1976; (trans.) The Cherry Orchard, 1978; (trans.) The Fruits of Enlightenment, 1979; Make and Break (play), 1980; Noises Off, 1982; (trans.) Three Sisters, 1983; The Original Michael Frayn, 1983; (trans.) Wild Honey, 1984; Benefactors (play), 1984; One (collection), 1985; Clockwise (film), 1986; (trans.) The Seagull, 1986; Balmoral (play), 1987; (trans.) Uncle Vanya, 1987; (trans.) Chekhov: Plays, 1988; (trans.) The Sneeze, 1989. Add: c/o Fraser and Dunlop Scripts Ltd., 91 Regent St., London W1R 8RU, England.

FRAZEE, (Charles) Steve. Also writes as Dean Jennings. American, b. 1909. Westerns/Adventure, Science fiction/Fantasy, Children's fiction, Children's non-fiction. Dir., Salida Bldg. and Loan Assn.; freelance writer since 1946. Heavy construction and mining worker, 1926–36, 1941–43; Journalism Teacher, La Junta High Sch., Colo., 1937–41; Bldg. Inspector, City of Salida, 1950–63. Pres., 1954, and Vice-Pres., 1962, Western Writers of America. *Publs:* (as Dean Jennings) Range Trouble, 1951; Shining Mountains, 1951; Pistolman, 1952; Lawman's Feud, 1953; Sharp the Bugle Calls, 1953, as Gold at Kansas Gulch, 1958; The Sky Block (science fiction novel), 1953; The Gun-Throwers (western short stories), 1954; Cry Coyote, 1955; Many Rivers to Cross, 1955; Spur to the Smoke, 1955; Tumbling Range Woman, 1956; He Rode Alone, 1956; Running Target, 1957; High Cage, 1957; Desert Guns, 1957, in U.K. as Gold of the Seven Saints, 1961; Rendezvous, 1958; Walt Disney's Zorro (novelization of TV play; juvenile), 1958; Smoke in the Valley, 1959;

The Alamo, 1960; More Damn Tourists, 1960; First Through the Grand Canyon (juvenile), 1960; Year of the Big Snow (juvenile), 1962; Killer Lion (juvenile), 1966; Bragg's Fancy Woman, 1966, in U.K. as A Gun for Bragg's Woman, 1967; Outcasts, 1967; Lassie: The Mystery of the Bristlecone Pine (juvenile), 1967; Where Are You? All about Maps (juvenile), 1968; Utah Hell Guns, 1968; Flight 409, 1969; Fire in the Valley, 1972; Many Rivers to Cross, 1978; Lassie: Lost in the Snow, The Secret of the Smuggler's Cave, Trouble at Panter's Lake, 3 vols., 1979; Best Western Stories, 1984.   Add: c/o Scott Meredith Literary Agency, 1845 Third Ave., New York, N.Y. 10022, U.S.A.

FRAZIER, Arthur. *See* **BULMER,** Henry Kenneth.

FREDERIC, Mike. *See* **COX,** William R.

FREDERICKS, Dr. Frank. *See* **FRANCK,** Frederick.

FREDERICKS, P.C. *See* **PRIMMER,** Phyllis.

FREEBORN, Richard (Harry). British, b. 1926. Novels/Short stories, History, Literature. Prof. of Russian Literature, Univ. of London, 1967–88. Vice-Pres., British Universities Assn. of Slavists (Pres., 1969–72); Hon. Vice-Pres., Assn. of Teachers of Russian. University Lectr. in Russian, and Hulme Lectr. in Russian, Brasenose Coll., Oxford, 1954–64; Visiting Prof., Univ. of California at Los Angeles, 1964–65; Sir William Mather Chair of Russian Studies, Univ. of Manchester, 1965–67. *Publs:* Turgenev: A Study, 1960; Two Ways of Life (novel), 1962; The Emigration of Sergey Ivanovich (novel), 1963; A Short History of Modern Russia, 1966; (trans.) Ivan Turgenev: Sketches from a Hunter's Album, 1967; (trans.) Ivan Turgenev: Home of the Gentry, 1970; The Rise of the Russian Novel, 1974; (contrib.) The Age of Realism, 1974; (trans.) Ivan Turgenev: Rudin, 1974; (ed. and contrib.) Russian Literary Attitudes from Pushkin to Solzhenitsyn, 1976; (ed. with Charles Ward) Russian and Slavic Literature to 1917, vol. I, 1976; Russian Roulette (novel), 1979; (trans.) The Russian Revolutionary Novel: Turgenev to Pasternak, 1982, 1985; (trans.) Love and Death: Six Stories by Ivan Turgenev, 1983; The Russian Crucifix (novel), 1987.   Add: Sch. of Slavonic and East European Studies, Univ. of London, Malet St., London WC1E 7HU, England.

FREED, Lynn Ruth. American, b. 1945. Novels. *Publs:* Heart Change, 1982; Home Ground, 1986.   Add: 57 Ashbury Terrace, San Francisco, Calif. 94117, U.S.A.

FREEDBERG, Sydney Joseph. American, b. 1914. Art. Emeritus Prof., Harvard Univ., Cambridge, Mass., since 1984 (member of the faculty, 1938–40, 1953–83; Prof. of Fine Arts, 1960–83; Arthur Kingsley Porter Prof., 1979–83); Chief Curator, National Gallery of Art, Washington, D.C., 1983–88, Emeritus since 1988. Asst. Prof., 1946–49, and Assoc. Prof. of Art, 1950–54, Wellesley Coll., Mass. *Publs:* Parmigianino: His Works in Painting, 1950; Painting of the High Renaissance in Rome and Florence, 2 vols., 1961; Andrea del Sarto, 2 vols., 1963; Painting in Italy 1500-1600, 1971; Circa 1600, 1983.   Add: 3328 Reservoir Rd. N.W., Washington, D.C. 20007, U.S.A.

FREEDGOOD, Morton. Writes suspense as John Godey; has also written as Stanley Morton. American, b. 1912. Novels/Short stories, Mystery/Crime/Suspense, Autobiography/Memoirs/Personal. *Publs:* suspense novels—The Gun and Mr. Smith, 1947; The Blue Hour, 1948 (in U.S. paperback, Killer at His Back, 1955; in U.K. paperback, The Next to Die, 1975); The Man in Question, 1951 (in U.S. paperback, The Blonde Betrayer, 1955); This Year's Death, 1953; The Clay Assassin, 1959; The Fifth House, 1960; The Reluctant Assassin, 1966; A Thrill a Minute with Jack Albany, 1967; Never Put Off till Tomorrow What You Can Kill Today, 1970; The Three Worlds of Johnny Handsome, 1972; The Taking of Pelham One Two Three, 1973; The Talisman, 1976; The Snake, 1978; Nella, 1981; Fatal Beauty, 1984; other—(as Stanley Morton; with Stanley Freedgood) Yankee Trader (novel), 1947; (as Morton Freedgood) The Wall-to-Wall Trap (novel), 1957; The Crime of the Century and Other Misdemeanors (autobiography), 1973.   Add: c/o Curtis Brown Ltd., 10 Astor Pl., New York, N.Y. 10003, U.S.A.

FREEDLAND, Michael. British, b. 1934. Biography. Producer and Ed., You Don't Have to be Jewish, BBC Radio, London. *Publs:* Al Jolson, 1972; Irving Berlin, 1974; James Cagney, 1975; Fred Astaire, 1976; Sophie: The Story of Sophie Tucker, 1978; Jerome Kern, 1978; Errol Flynn, 1979; Gregory Peck, 1980; (with Morecambe and Wise) There's No Answer to That, 1981; Maurice Chevalier, 1982; Peter O'Toole, 1982; The Warner Brothers, 1983; So Let's Hear the Applause: The Story of the Jewish Entertainer, 1983; Jack Lemmon, 1984; Dino: The Dean Martin

Story, 1984; Katharine Hepburn, 1985; The Secret Life of Danny Kaye, 1985; Shirley Maclaine, 1986; Linda Evans, 1986; The Goldwyn Touch, 1986; Jane Fonda, 1987.   Add: 35 Hartfield Ave., Elstree, Herts., England.

FREEDMAN, Mervin Burton. American, b. 1920. Education, Psychology. Prof. of Psychology, San Francisco State Univ., since 1965. Lectr., Univ. of California, Berkeley, 1950–53; Research Assoc., 1953–58, and Dir., 1958–60, Mary Conover Mellon Foundn. for the Advancement of Education; Fellow, Center for Advanced Study in the Behavioral Sciences, Stanford, Calif., 1960–61; Sr. Fulbright Research Fellow, Univ. of Oslo, Norway, 1961–62, Asst. Dean of Undergrad. Education, Stanford Univ., Calif., 1962–65; Dean, Grad. Sch., Wright Inst., Berkeley, Calif., 1969–79. *Publs:* The College Experience, 1967; (co-author) Search for Revelance, 1969; (ed.) Facilitating Faculty Development, 1973; Academic Culture and Faculty Development, 1978; Human Development in Social Settings, 1982; Social Change and Personality Development, 1985.   Add: Dept. of Psychology, San Francisco State Univ., Calif. 94132, U.S.A.

FREEDMAN, Nancy. American, b. 1920. Novels/Short stories, Science fiction/Fantasy. *Publs:* (with Benedict Freedman) Back to the Sea, 1941; (with B. Freedman) Mrs. Mike, 1947; (with B. Freedman) This and No More, 1950; (with B. Freedman) The Spark and the Exodus, 1954; (with B. Freedman) Lootville, 1957; (with B. Freedman) Tresa, 1958; (with B. Freedman) The Apprentice Bastard, 1966; (with B. Freedman) Cyclone of Silence, 1969; Joshua Son of None, 1973; The Immortals, 1976; Prima Donna, 1981.   Add: 5837 Latigo Canyon Rd., Malibu, Calif. 90267, U.S.A.

FREEDMAN, Ronald. American, b. 1917. Sociology. Roderick D. McKenzie Distinguished Prof. of Sociology Emeritus, since 1978, Univ. of Michigan, Ann Arbor (Instr., to Assoc. Prof., 1946–53; Prof., 1954–78; Dir., Population Studies Center, 1962–73). Dir., Detroit Area Study, 1951–53. *Publs:* Recent Migration to Chicago, 1950; (with A. Hawley, W. Landecker, G. Lenski and H. Miner) Principles of Sociology, rev. ed. 1956; (with P.K. Whelpton and A.A. Campbell) Family Planning, Sterility, and Population Growth, 1959; (with others) Family Planning in Taiwan: An Experiment in Social Change, 1969.   Add: Population Studies Center, Univ. of Michigan, 1225 S. University, Ann Arbor, Mich. 48109, U.S.A.

FREELING, Nicolas. British, b. 1927. Mystery/Crime/Suspense, Cookery/Gastronomy/Wine. Hotel and Restaurant cook, throughout Europe, 1945–60. *Publs:* Love in Amsterdam, 1962; Because of the Cats, 1963; Gun Before Butter (in U.S. as Question of Loyalty), 1963; (as F.R.E. Nicholas in U.K.) Valparaiso, 1964; Double Barrel, 1964; Criminal Conversation, 1965; The King of the Rainy Country, 1966; The Dresden Green, 1966; Strike Out Where Not Applicable, 1967; This Is the Castle, 1968; Tsing-Boum (in U.S. as Tsing-Boom!), 1970; Kitchen Book, 1970; Over the High Side (in U.S. as The Lovely Ladies), 1971; Cook Book, 1972; A Long Silence (in U.S. as Auprès de ma Blonde), 1972; A Dressing of Diamond, 1974; What Are the Bugles Blowing For (in U.S. as The Bugles Blowing), 1975; Lake Isle (in U.S. as Sabine), 1976; Gadget, 1977; The Night Lords, 1978; The Widow, 1979; Castang's City, 1980; One Damn Thing After Another (in U.S. as Arlette), 1981; Wolfnight, 1982; The Back of the North Wind, 1983; No Part in Your Death, 1984; A City Solitary, 1985; Cold Iron, 1986; Lady Macbeth, 1987; Not as Far as Velma, 1989; Sandcastles, 1989.   Add: Grandfontaine, 67130 Schirmeck, France.

FREEMAN, Barbara C(onstance). British, b. 1906. Children's fiction. *Publs:* Two-Thumb Thomas, 1961; Timi, 1961; A Book by Georgina, 1962; Broom-Adelaide, 1963; The Name on the Glass, 1964; Lucinda, 1965; The Forgotten Theatre, 1967; Tobias, 1967; The Other Face, 1975; A Haunting Air, 1976; A Pocket of Silence, 1977; The Summer Travellers, 1978; Snow in the Maze, 1979; Clemency in the Moonlight, 1981.   Add: Shirley, 62 Hook Rd., Surbiton, Surrey KT6 6BH, England.

FREEMAN, Bill (William Bradford Freeman). Canadian, b. 1938. Children's fiction, Politics/Government. Financial consultant, 3rd St. Funding, Toronto, since 1984. Probation officer, Hamilton, Ontario, 1964–69; community organizer, Hamilton Welfare Rights, 1970; Lectr., McMaster Univ., 1971–73; teacher, Vanier College, Montreal, 1977–86. *Publs:* children's fiction—Shantymen of Cache Lake, 1975; The Last Voyage of the Scotian, 1976; Cedric and the North End Kids, 1978; First Spring on the Grand Banks, 1978; Trouble at Lachine Mill, 1983; Danger on the Tracks, 1987; for adults—(ed. with Marsha Hewitt) Their Town: The Mafia, the Media, and the Party Machine, 1978; 1005: Political Life of a Local Union, 1982.   Add: 16 Third St., Ward's

Island, Toronto, Ont. M5J 2B2, Canada.

FREEMAN, David. Canadian, b. 1945. Plays/Screenplays. *Publs:* Creeps, 1972; Battering Ram, 1972; You're Gonna Be Alright, Jamie Boy, 1974; Flytrap, 1980. Add: c/o John Goodwin and Assoc., 4235 Ave. de l'Esplanade, Montreal, Que. H2W IT1, Canada.

FREEMAN, Gillian. Also wrote as Eliot George and Elaine Jackson. British, b. 1929. Novels/Short stories, Plays/Screenplays, Children's non-fiction, Literature, Sociology. *Publs:* The Liberty Man, 1955; Fall of Innocence, 1956; Jack Would Be a Gentleman, 1959; The Story of Albert Einstein, 1960; (as Eliot George) The Leather Boys, 1961; The Campaign, 1963; The Leader, 1965; The Undergrowth of Literature, 1967; The Leather Boys (screenplay), 1967; Cold Day in the Park (screenplay), 1968; Pursuit (play), 1969; I Want What I Want (screenplay), 1970; The Alabaster Egg, 1970; Marriage Machine, 1975; The Schoolgirl Ethic, 1976; Nazi Lady (in U.S. as Confessions of Elisabeth von S.), 1978; An Easter Egg Hunt, 1981; (as Elaine Jackson) Lovechild, 1984; Day after the Fair (screenplay), 1986; ballet scenarios—Mayerling, 1978; Isadora, 1981; (with Edward Thorpe) Ballet Genius, 1988; Termination Rock, 1989. Add: c/o Richard Scott Simon, 32 College Cross, London N1, England.

FREEMAN, Jo. American, b. 1945. Politics/Government, Women. Lawyer; political scientist; also lecturer, photographer and consultant. *Publs:* The Politics of Women's Liberation, 1975; (ed.) Women: A Feminist Perspective, 1975, 4th ed., 1989; (ed.) Social Movements of the Sixties and Seventies, 1983; Quest for Equality, 1991; (ed.) How Institutions Work, 1991. Add: 410 East 8th St., Brooklyn, N.Y. 11218, U.S.A.

FREEMAN, Lucy. American, b. 1916. Mystery/Crime/Suspense, Psychiatry, Autobiography/Memoirs/Personal, Biography. Reporter, New York Times, NYC, 1941–54. *Publs:* Fight Against Fears, 1951; Before I Kill More, 1955; (co-author) Emotional Maturity in Love and Marriage, 1961; (co-author) Remember Me to Tom, 1963; Why People Act That Way, 1965; The Cry for Love, 1969; Farewell to Fear, 1969; (ed.) Celebrities on the Couch, 1970; The Dream, 1971; The Story of Anna O., 1972; (co-author) Sparks, 1973; The Psychiatrist Says Murder, 1973; (ed.) Killers of the Mind, 1975; The Case on Cloud Nine, 1975 Betrayal, 1976 The Sorrow and the Fury, 1978; What Do Women Want?, 1978; Who Is Sylvia?, 1979; Freud Rediscovered, 1980; Too Deep for Tears, 1980; Freud and Women, 1981; Belle: The Biography of Belle Case La Follette, 1986; Guilt, 1986; Letting Go, 1986; The Power of Fantasy, 1988; The Beloved Prison, 1989. Add: 210 Central Park South, New York, N.Y. 10019, U.S.A.

FREEMAN, Roger A. American, b. 1904. Economics, Public/Social administration. Sr. Fellow Emeritus, Hoover Inst. of War, Revolution and Peace, Stanford Univ., California, since 1975 (Sr. Fellow, 1962–75). Special Asst. to the Gov., State of Washington, 1950–55; Asst. in the White House Office, 1955–56; Vice-Pres., Inst. for Social Science Research, Washington, D.C., 1957–61; Special Asst. to the U.S. Pres., 1969–70. *Publs:* Your Dollar's Worth of State Government, 1952; School Needs in the Decade Ahead, 1958; Taxes for the Schools, 1960; Crisis in College Finance, 1965; Socialism and Private Enterprise in Equatorial Asia, 1968; Tax Loopholes: The Legend and the Reality, 1973; The Growth of American Government, 1975; The Wayward Welfare State, 1981; Does America Neglect Its Poor?, 1987. Add: Hoover Inst., Stanford Univ., Stanford, Calif. 94305, U.S.A.

FREEMAN, Thomas. *See* FEHRENBACH, T.R.

FREEMAN ALLEN, Geoffrey. British, b. 1922. Transportation. Ed., Jane's World Railways, since 1982, and Railway Technology Intnl., since 1988. Ed., Modern Railways, London, 1950–69; Publishing Dir., Ian Allan Ltd., Shepperton, Middx., 1969–77 . *Publs:* Modern Railways the World Over, 1956, 1968; British Railways Today and Tomorrow, 1959, 3rd ed. 1962; British Rail after Beeching, 1966; Salute to the LNER, 1978; The Fastest Trains in the World, 1978; The Illustrated History of Railways in Britain, 1978; The Western (Eastern and Southern) since 1948, 3 vols., 1979–87; Modern Railways, 1980; The Riddles Standard Types in Traffic, 1982; Railways Past, Present and Future, 1982; Railways of the Twentieth Century, 1983 British Railfreight Today and Tomorrow, 1984. Add: Barton Cottage, Station Rd., Blockley, Glos. GL56 9DT, England.

FREEMAN-GRENVILLE, Greville Stewart Parker. British, b. 1918. History. Hon. Fellow, Univ. of York, since 1969 (Sr. Research Fellow,

1966–69). With H.M. Overseas Civil Service, 1951–64 (Educational Advisor, Aden Protectorate, 1961–64); Sr. Research Fellow, Univ. of Ghana, 1964–66; Prof. of African History, State Univ. of New York, New Paltz, 1969–74. *Publs:* The Medieval History of the Coast of Tanganyika, 1962; (ed. and trans.) The East African Coast: Select Documents, 1962, 1975; The Muslim and Christian Calendars, 1963, 1977; The French at Kilwa Island, 1965; Chronology of African History, 1973; Chronology of World History, 1975, 1978, 1989; A Modern Atlas of African History, 1976; The Queen's Lineage, 1977; Atlas of British History, 1979; The Mombasa Rising Against the Portuguese 1631, 1980; The Beauty of Cairo, 1981; (ed. and trans.) Buzurg ibn Shahriyar: The Book of Wonders of India (c. 953), 1982; (ed.) Emily Said-Ruete: Memoirs of an Arabian Princess (1888), 1982; The Beauty of Jerusalem and the Holy Places of the Gospels, 1982, 1988; The Stations of the Cross, 1982; The Beauty of Rome, 1988; The Swahili Coast, 1988. Add: North View House, Sheriff Hutton, York, England.

FREEMANTLE, Brian (Harry). Pseudonyms: Jonathan Evans, Richard Gant, John Maxwell, and Jack Winchester. British, b. 1936. Mystery/Crime/Suspense, Plays/Screenplays. Reporter, the New Milton Advertiser, 1953–58, the Bristol Evening World, 1958; the London Evening News, 1958–61, and the Daily Express, London, 1961–63; Asst. Foreign Ed., Daily Express, 1963–69; Foreign Ed., the Daily Sketch, London, 1969–71, and the Daily Mail, London, 1971–75. *Publs:* (as Richard Gant) Sean Connery: Gilt-Edged Bond, 1967; The Touchables, 1968; Goodbye to an Old Friend, 1973; Face Me When You Walk Away, 1974; The Man Who Wanted Tomorrow, 1975; The November Man, 1976; Charlie Muffin, 1977; (as John Maxwell) H.M.S. Bounty, 1977; Clap Hands, Here Comes Charlie (in U.S. as Here Comes Charlie M), 1978; The Inscrutable Charlie Muffin, 1979; (as John Maxwell) The Mary Celeste, 1979; (as Jack Winchester) The Solitary Man, 1980; Charlie Muffin's Uncle Sam, 1980; (as Jonathan Evans) Misfire, 1980; Madrigal for Charlie Muffin, 1981; (as Jonathan Evans) The Midas Men, 1981; (as Jonathan Evans) Chairman of the Board, 1982; Deakin's War, 1982; KGB (non-fiction), 1982; CIA (non-fiction), 1983; Vietnam Legacy, 1984; The Lost American, 1984; The Fix, 1985;The Blind Run, 1986; Dirty White, 1986; See Charlie Run, 1987; The Bearpit, 1988. Add: c/o Jonathan Clowes, 22 Prince Albert Rd., London NW1 7ST, England.

FREMANTLE, Anne. American, b. 1910. Theology/Religion, Biography, Translations. Ed., Catholic Book Club, NYC, since 1947. With London Mercury, England, 1931; Reviewer, Times Literary Supplement, London, 1930–40; Writer for Manchester Guardian, and London Times, 1932–35; Research Asst., Indian Section of British Embassy, Washington, D.C., 1942–45; Lectr. in Dept. of Communication Arts, Fordham Univ., N.Y., 1948–61; Assoc. Ed., Commonweal, 1950–57; Ed. for the U.N., 1950–61; own prog. on NBC, 1961–62; Sr. History Fellow, Center for Advanced Studies, Wesleyan Univ., Middletown, Conn., 1966; Visiting Prof., New York Univ., 1970–72; Visiting Assoc. Prof., NYU, 1979–80. *Publs:* Poems, 1931; George Eliot, 1933; (ed.) Sicily, by Frederick H. Jackson, 4th ed., 1935; Loyal Enemy: The Life of Marmaduke Pickthall, 1938; Come to Dust, 1941; (trans.) Face of the Saints, by Wilhelm Schamoni, 1947; James and Joan, 1948; Desert Calling, 1949 (in U.K. as Desert Calling: The Life of Charles de Foucauld); (ed.) The Commonwealth Reader, 1949; (ed.) The Greatest Bible Stories: A Catholic Anthology From World Literature, 1951; (trans. with Christopher Fremantle) Lives of the Saints, by Omer Englebert, 1951; (ed.) Mothers: A Catholic Treasury of Great Stories, 1951; (ed.) The Wynne Diaries 1789-1820, 1952; (ed.) Christian Conversation: Catholic Thoughts for Every Day of the Year, 1953; (ed.) A Treasury of Early Christianity, 1953; (ed.) Visionary Novels: Lilith and Phantastes, by George Macdonald, 1954; Europe: A Journey with Pictures, 1954; The Age of Belief: The Medieval Philosophers, 1955; (ed.) Christmas Is Here: A Catholic Selection of Stories and Poems, 1955; (ed.) The Papal Encyclicals in Their Historical Context, 1956; By Grace of Love, 1957; This Little Band of Prophets: The British Fabians, 1960; (trans. with Christopher Fremantle) Fountain of Arethusa, by Maurice Zermatten, The Social Teachings of the Church, 1963; Holiday in Europe, 1963; The Protestant Mystics, 1964; The Island of Cats (children's fiction), 1964; (with others) The Age of Faith, 1965; (trans. with Christopher Fremantle) A Time of Glory: The Renaissance in France 1488-1559, 1967; (trans.) The Pope Speaks, by Jean Guitton, 1968; Pilgrimage to People, 1968; Three Cornered Heart (biography), 1970; (ed.) Communism: Basic Writing, 1970; (ed.) Glenarvon, by Caroline Lamb, 1973; A Primer of Linguistics, 1974; Woman's Way to God, 1976; Saints Alive!, 1978; (with C. Fremantle) In Love With Love: One Hundred of the World's Greatest Spiritual Poems, 1978. Add: 252 E. 78th St., New York, N.Y. 10021, U.S.A.

FREMGEN, James Morgan. American, b. 1933. Administration/Management, Money/Finance. Prof. of Accounting, Naval Postgrad. Sch., Monterey, Calif., since 1969 (Assoc. Prof., 1965–69). Faculty Lectr. in Accounting, Indiana Univ., Bloomington, 1959–61; Asst. Prof. of Accounting, 1961–64, and Assoc. Prof., 1964–65, Univ. of Notre Dame, Ind. *Publs:* Accounting for Managerial Analysis, 1972, 3rd ed. 1976; (with S.S. Liao) The Allocation of Corporate Indirect Costs, 1981. Add: Code 54, Naval Postgrad. Sch., Monterey, Calif. 93943, U.S.A.

FREMLIN, Celia. British, b. 1914. Mystery/Crime/Suspense. *Publs:* The Seven Chars of Chelsea, 1940; The Hours Before Dawn, 1958; Seven Lean Years, 1961; Uncle Paul; The Trouble-Makers, 1963; The Jealous One, 1965; Prisoner's Base, 1967; Possession, 1969; Don't Go to Sleep in the Dark, 1970; Appointment with Yesterday, 1972; By Horror Haunted, 1974; The Long Shadow, 1975; The Spider Orchid, 1977; With No Crying, 1980; The Parasite Person, 1982; A Lovely Day to Die and Other Stories, 1984. Add: 11 Parkhill Rd., London NW3 2YH, England.

FRENCH, Alfred. British, b. 1916. History, Literature. Fellow, Univ. Coll., Cambridge, 1968–69; Reader in Classics, Univ. of Adelaide, S.A., 1964–81. *Publs:* (ed.) A Book of Czech Verse, 1958; (trans.) V. Nezval: Sunset Over Atlantis 1960; The Growth of the Athenian Economy, 1964; The Poets of Prague, 1969; The Athenian Half-Century, 1971; (ed.) Czech Poetry, vol. I, 1973; Czech Writers and Politics, 1982; The Poet's Lamp, 1986; Sixth Century Athens, 1987. Add: Univ. of Adelaide, S.A., Australia.

FRENCH, David. Canadian, b. 1939. Plays/Screenplays. *Publs:* Leaving Home, 1972; Of the Fields, Lately, 1973; One Crack Out, 1976; (trans.) The Seagull, by Anton Chekhov, 1978; Jitters, 1980; Salt-Water Moon, 1985. Add: c/o Tarragon Theatre, 30 Bridgman Ave., Toronto, Ont. M5R 1X3, Canada.

FRENCH, Fiona. British, b. 1944. Children's fiction. Children's art therapy teacher, Long Grove Psychiatric Hosp., Epsom, Surrey, 1967–69; Design teacher, Wimbledon Sch. of Art, London, 1970–71, and Leicester and Brighton Polytechnics, 1973–74. *Publs:* Jack of Hearts, 1970; Huni, 1971; The Blue Bird, 1972; King Tree, 1973; City of Gold, 1975; Aio the Rainmaker, 1975; Matteo, 1976; Hunt the Thimble, 1978; Oscar Wilde's "Star Child", 1979; The Princess and the Musician, 1981; John Barley Corn, 1982; Future Story, 1983; Fat Cat, 1984; Going to Squintums, 1985; Maid of the Wood, 1985; Snow White in New York, 1986; Song of the Nightingale, 1986; Cinderella, 1987; Rise, Shine, 1989. Add: 33 Hungate St., Aylsham, Norfolk NR11 6AA, England.

FRENCH, Marilyn. American, b. 1929. Novels/Short stories, Literature. Instr. in English, Hofstra Univ., Hempstead, N.Y., 1964–68; Teaching Asst., Harvard Univ., Cambridge, Mass., 1970–72; Asst. Prof. of English, College of the Holy Cross, Worcester, Mass., 1972–76; Mellon Fellow in English, Harvard Univ., Cambridge, Mass., 1976–77. *Publs:* The Book as World: James Joyce's Ulysses, 1976; The Women's Room (novel), 1977; The Bleeding Heart (novel), 1980; Shakespeare's Division of Experience, 1981; Beyond Power: On Women, Men and Morals, 1985; Her Mother's Daughter, 1987. Add: c/o Sheedy Literary Agency, 41 King St., New York, N.Y. 10041, U.S.A.

FRENCH, Philip (Neville). British, b. 1933. Film, Literature. Sr. Talks and Documentary Producer, BBC Radio, since 1959; Film Critic, The Observer, London, since 1978. *Publs:* (co-ed.) The Age of Austerity 1945–51, 1963; (ed.) The Novelist as Innovator, 1966; The Movie Moguls, 1969; Westerns: Aspects of a Movie Genre, 1974, 1977; Three Honest Men: Portraits of Edmund Wilson, F.R. Leavis, and Lionel Trilling, 1980; (ed.) The Third Dimension: Voices from Radio 3, 1983. Add: 62 Dartmouth Park Rd., London NW5 1SN, England.

FRENCH, Simon. Australian, b. 1957. Children's fiction. Teacher, New South Wales, since 1988. *Publs:* Hey, Phantom Singlet, 1975; Cannily, Cannily, 1981; All We Know, 1986. Add: 24 Burdekin Rd., Wilberforce, N.S.W. 2756, Australia.

FRENCH, Warren G. American, b. 1922. Film, Literature. Hon. Research Prof., Univ. of Wales.; Emeritus Prof., Indiana Univ., Indianapolis, since 1986 (joined faculty, 1970). Ed., Twayne Film Series, and Twayne United States Authors Series, since 1975. Member of faculty, Univ. of Mississippi, University, 1948–50, Univ. of Kentucky, Lexington, 1954–56; Stetson Univ., Deland, Fla., 1956–58, Univ. of Florida, Gainesville, 1958–62, Kansas State Univ., Manhattan, 1962–65, and Univ. of Missouri, Kansas City, 1965–70. *Publs:* John Steinbeck, 1961, 1975; Frank Norris, 1962; J.D. Salinger, 1963, 1988; (ed.) A Companion to "The Grapes of

Wrath", 1963; The Social Novel at the End of an Era, 1966; (ed.) The Thirties: Fiction, Poetry, Drama, 1969; (ed. with W. Kidd) American Winners of the Nobel Literary Prize, 1968; Season of Promise, 1968; (ed.) The Forties: Fiction, Poetry, Drama, 1969; Filmguide to "The Grapes of Wrath", 1973; (ed.) The Twenties: Fiction, Poetry, Drama, 1975; (ed.) The South and Film, 1981; Jack Kerouac, 1986. Add: 23 Beechwood Rd., Uplands, Swansea SA2 0HL, Wales.

FREND, William (Hugh Clifford). British, b. 1916. Theology/Religion. Vicar of Barnwell, since 1984. Univ. Lectr. in Divinity, Univ. of Cambridge, 1956–69; Fellow, 1956–69, and Dir. of Studies in Archaeology and Anthropology, 1961–69, Gonville and Caius Coll., Cambridge; Prof. of Ecclesiastical History, 1969–84, and Dean of Divinity, Univ. of Glasgow. Ed., The Modern Churchman, 1963–82. Fellow of the British Academy, 1983 *Publs:* The Donatist Church, 1952, 1971, 1985; Martyrdom and Persecution in the Early Church, 1964, 1981; The Early Church, 1965, 1981; The Rise of the Monophysite Movement, 1972, 1979; Religion Popular and Unpopular in the Early Christian Centuries, 1976; Town and Countryside in the Early Christian Centuries, 1980; The Rise of Christianity, 1984; Saints and Sinners in the Early Church, 1985; History and Archaeology in the Study of Early Christianity, 1988. Add: Barnwell Rectory, Peterborough, England.

FRERE, S(heppard) S(underland). British, b. 1916. Archaeology, History. Taught at Epsom Coll., 1938–40, and Lancing Coll., 1945–54; Lectr., Manchester Univ., 1954–55; Reader, Inst. of Archaeology, 1955–62, and Professor, 1963–66, Univ. of London; Prof. of the Archaeology of the Roman Empire, Oxford Univ., 1966–83. Dir., excavations at Canterbury, 1946–60, and at Verulamium, 1955–61; Member, Royal Commn. on Historical Monuments (England), 1966–83, and Ancient Monuments Bd. (England), 1966–82; Pres., Royal Archaeological Inst., 1978–81; Pres., Soc. for the Promotion of Roman Studies, 1983–86. *Publs:* (ed.) Problems of the Iron Age in Southern Britain, 1961; Britannia: A History of Roman Britain, 1967, 1974; Verulamium Excavations, 3 vols., 1972–84; Excavations on the Roman and Medieval Defences of Canterbury, 1982; Excavations at Canterbury, 7 vols., most recent, 1987; (with J.K. St. Joseph) Roman Britain from the Air, 1983; (with F.A. Leppel) Trajan's Column, 1988. Add: Netherfield House, Marcham, Abingdon, Oxford, England.

FREUD, (Sir) Clement (Raphael). British, b. 1924. Children's fiction, Food, Humour. Columnist, Financial Times, since 1964, Daily Telegraph, since 1968, and The Times, since 1988; broadcaster, "Just a Minute", since 1968. Liberal Member of Parliament (U.K.) for the Isle of Ely, 1973–83, and for Cambridgeshire N.E., 1983–87; Liberal spokesman on education, the arts and broadcasting. Rector, Univ. of Dundee, 1974–80. *Publs:* Grimble, 1968; Grimble at Christmas, 1973; Freud on Food, 1978; Clicking Vicky, 1980; The Book of Hangovers, 1981; Below the Belt, 1983. Add: 22 Wimpole St., London W1, England.

FREUDENBERGER, Herman. American, b. 1922. Economics. Prof. of Economics, Tulane Univ., New Orleans, La., since 1966 (Assoc. Prof., 1962–66; Chmn., Dept. of Economics, 1966–70). Pres., Business History Conference, 1978–79. *Publs:* The Waldstein Woolen Mill, 1963; (co-author) Von der Provinzstadt zur Industrieregion, 1975; The Industrialization of a Central European City, 1977. Add: Tulane Univ., New Orleans, La. 70118, U.S.A.

FREUND, Philip. American, b. 1909. Novels/Short stories, Plays/Screenplays, Poetry, Literature. Prof. Emeritus of Communications, Fordham Univ., NYC. *Publs:* The Merry Communist, 1934; The Snow and Other Stories, 1935; The Evening Heron, 1936; The Zoltans (trilogy), 1937–45; Dreams of Youth, 1938; The Young Greek and Creole, 1943; Three Exotic Tales, 1944; Easter Island, 1947; A Man of Taste, 1949; Prince Hamlet, 1955; Private Speech, 1955; The Volcano God (trilogy), 1956–60; The Beholder, 1962; The Devious Ways, 1963; Myths of Creation, 1964; The Spymaster and Other Stories, 1965; The Art of Reading the Novel, 1965; Myths of Creation, 1965; The Young Artists and Other Stories, 1967; Three Off-Broadway Plays, 1969; Three Poetic Plays, 1970; Searching, 1972; More Off-Broadway Plays, 1974. Add: 1025 Fifth Ave., New York, N.Y. 10028, U.S.A.

FREWER, Glyn (Mervyn Louis). Also writes as Mervyn Lewis. British, b. 1931. Mystery/Suspense, Children's fiction, Plays/-Screenplays. Proprietor, antiquarian and secondhand bookshop since 1985. Student officer, British Council, Oxford, 1955; Copywriter, various advertising agencies, 1955–74; Advertising agency Assoc. Dir., 1974–85. *Publs:* The Hitch-Hikers (radio play), 1957; Adventure in Forgotten Valley, 1962; Adventure in the Barren Lands, 1964; The Last of the Wispies,

1965; The Token of Elkin, 1970; Crossroad, 1970; (as Mervyn Lewis) Death of Gold, 1970; The Square Peg, 1972; The Raid, 1976; The Trackers, 1976; Simon in the Land of Chalk Drawings (tv series), 1976; Tyto: The Odyssey of an Owl, 1978; Bryn of Brockle Hanger, 1980; Fox, 1984; The Call of the Raven, 1987. Add: Fairfield Cottage, Brook End, Chadlington, Oxon, England.

FRICK, C.H. *See* **IRWIN,** Constance.

FRIDAY, Nancy. American. Human relations, Sex, Women. *Publs:* My Secret Garden (women's sexual fantasies), 1973; Forbidden Flowers (women's sexual fantasies), 1975; My Mother/My Self (study of the mother-daughter relationship), 1977, 1987; Men in Love: Men's Sexual Fantasies: The Triumph of Love over Rage, 1980; Jealousy, 1985. Add: c/o Bantam Books, Inc., 666 Fifth Ave., New York, N.Y. 10103, U.S.A.

FRIEDAN, Betty. American, b. 1921. Women, Autobiography/Memoirs/Personal. Contrib. Ed., McCalls Mag., since 1971. Founding Pres., Natl. Org. For Women, 1966-70. *Publs:* The Feminine Mystique, 1963, 1983; It Changed My Life: Writings on the Women's Movement, 1976, 1985; The Second Stage, 1982, 1986. Add: 1 Lincoln Pl., No. 40K, New York, N.Y. 10023, U.S.A.

FRIEDBERG, Gertrude (Tonkonogy). American. Science fiction/Fantasy. Plays/Screenplays. Former high sch. mathematics teacher, NYC Bd. of Education. *Publs:* Three-Cornered Moon (play), 1933; Town House (play), 1948; The Revolving Boy, 1966. Add: 1185 Park Ave., New York, N.Y. 10128, U.S.A.

FRIEDBERG, Maurice. American, b. 1929. International relations/Current affairs, Literature, Translations. Prof. of Slavic Languages and Literatures, and Dept. Head, Univ. of Illinois, Urbana, since 1975. Assoc. Prof. of Russian, and Chmn. of Russian Div., Hunter Coll., City Univ. of New York, 1955-65; Fulbright Visiting Prof. of Russian Literature, Hebrew Univ., Jerusalem, 1965-66; Prof. of Slavic Languages and Literatures, 1966-75, and Dir. of the Russian and East European Inst. 1967-71, Indiana Univ., Bloomington; Dir. d'Etudes Associé, Ecole des Hautes Etudes en Sciences Sociales, Paris, 1984-85. *Publs:* Russian Classics in Soviet Jackets, 1962; (ed.) A Bilingual Edition of Russian Short Stories, 1965, vol. II, ed. and trans. with R.A. Maguire, 1965, 1966; The Jew in Post Stalin Soviet Literature, 1970; (ed. and co-author) Encyclopedia Judaica, 16 vols., 1971-72; (ed.) The Young Lenin, by Leon Trotsky, 1972; A Decade of Euphoria: Western Literature in Post-Stalin Russia, 1977; Russian Culture in the 1980's, 1985; (co-ed.) Soviet Society Under Gorbachev, 1987; (co-ed.) The Red Pencil: Artists, Scholars and Censors in the U.S.S.R., 1989. Add: 3001 Meadowbrook Ct., Champaign, Ill. 61821, U.S.A.

FRIEDEN, Bernard J. American, b. 1930. Regional/Urban planning. Prof. Dept. of Urban Planning, Massachusetts Inst. of Technology, Cambridge, since 1969 (Asst. Prof., 1961-65; Assoc. Prof., 1965-69; Research Dir., MIT Centre for Real Estate Development, 1985-87). Dir., Massachusetts Inst. of Technology-Harvard Univ. Joint Center for Urban Studies, 1971-75. Ed., Journal of the American Inst. of Planners, 1962-65. *Publs:* The Future of Old Neighborhoods, 1964; (ed. with R. Morris) Urban Planning and Social Policy, 1968; (ed. with W. Nash) Shaping an Urban Future, 1969; (with M. Kaplan) The Politics of Neglect, 1975, 1977; (ed. with W. Anderson and M. Murphy) Managing Human Services, 1977; The Environmental Protection Hustle, 1979. Add: 245 Highland Ave., West Newton, Mass. 02165, U.S.A.

FRIEDLAND, William H(erbert). American, b. 1923. Industrial relations, Sociology. Prof. of Community Studies and Sociology, Univ. of California, Santa Cruz, since 1969. Asst. Prof., and Assoc. Prof., Cornell Univ., Ithaca, N.Y., 1961-69. *Publs:* Unions and Industrial Relations in Underdeveloped Countries, 1963; (ed. with C.G. Rosberg) African Socialism, 1964; Vuta Kamba: The Development of Trade Unions in Tanganyika, 1969; (with I.L. Horowitz) The Knowledge Factory, 1970; (with D. Nelkin) Migrant: Agriculture America's Northeast, 1971; (with A. Barton and R. Thomas) Manufacturing Green Gold: Capital, Labor, and Technology in the Lettuce Industry, 1981; Revolutionary Theory, 1982. Add: Social Science Div., Univ. of California, Santa Cruz, Calif. 95064, U.S.A.

FRIEDLANDER, Albert H(oschander). American, b. 1927. Songs, lyrics and libretti, Theology/Religion, Biography. Rabbi, Westminster Synagogue, London; Dean and Sr. Lectr. in History and Theology, Leo Baeck Coll., London. Ed., European Judaism journal, since 1966. *Publs:* Leo Baeck: Teacher of Theresienstadt, 1968; (ed.) Never Trust a God Over 30: Religion on the Campus, 1968; (ed.) Leo Baeck's This People

Israel, 1968; (ed. and trans.) Out of the Whirlwind: Literature of the Holocaust, 1969; The Five Seasons of God (libretti), 1972-76; (ed.) Meir Gertner: An Anthology, 1978; Existenz nach Auschwitz, 1980; (ed.) Georg Salzberger: Leben und Werke, 1982; (ed. with H. Bronstein) The Five Scrolls, 1983; (with R. von Weizsaecker and H. Kohl) Versoehnung mit der Geschichte, 1985; Kaddish for the Children of Terezin (libretti), 1986; The Death Camps and Theology, 1985. Add: Kent House, Rutland Gardens, London SW7, England.

FRIEDMAN, Alan Warren. American, b. 1939. Literature. Prof. of English, since 1976, and Chmn. of the Faculty Senate since 1987, Univ. of Texas, Austin (Instr., 1964-66; Asst. Prof., 1966-69; Assoc. Prof., 1969-76). *Publs:* Lawrence Durrell and The Alexandria Quartet: Art for Love's Sake, 1970; (ed.) Forms of Modern British Fiction: A Symposium, 1975; (ed. with C. Rossman) Mario Vargas Llosa: A Collection of Critical Essays, 1978; Multivalance: The Moral Quality of Form in the Modern Novel, 1978; William Faulkner, 1984; (ed. with Charles Rossman and Dina Sherzer) Beckett Translating/Translating Beckett, 1987. Add: Dept. of English, Univ. of Texas, Austin, Tex. 78712, U.S.A.

FRIEDMAN, B(ernard) H(arper). American, b. 1926. Novels/Short stories, Art, Literature, Biography. Lectr., Cornell Univ., Ithaca, N.Y., 1966-67. *Publs:* (ed.) School of New York, 1969; Circles, reprinted as I Need to Love (novel), 1962; Yarborough (novel), 1964; Whispers (novel), 1972; Jackson Pollock: Energy Made Visible, 1972; Alfonso Ossorio, 1973; Museum (novel), 1974; Almost a Life (novel), 1975; Gertrude Vanderbilt Whitney, 1978; The Polygamist (novel), 1981; Coming Close (short stories), 1982. Add: 439 E. 51st St., New York, N.Y. 10022, U.S.A.

FRIEDMAN, Bruce Jay. American, b. 1930. Novels/Short stories, Plays/Screenplays. Editorial Dir., Mag. Mgmt. Co., publrs., NYC, 1953-64. *Publs:* Stern, 1962; Far from the City of Class and Other Stories, 1963; Mother's Kisses, 1964; (ed.) Black Humor, 1965; 23 Pat O'Brian Movies, 1966; Black Angels, 1966; Scuba Duba: A Tense Comedy, 1967; Steambath (play), 1970; The Dick, 1970; About Harry Towns, 1975; The Lonely Guy's Book of Life, 1979; Let's Hear It for a Beautiful Guy, 1984; Tokyo Woes, 1985; The Current Climate, 1989. Add: P.O. Box 746, Water Mill, N.Y. 11976, U.S.A.

FRIEDMAN, Elias. *See* **FRIEDMAN,** Jacob Horace.

FRIEDMAN, Jacob Horace. Writes as Elias Friedman, John Friedman, and Elias Pater. South African, b. 1916. Poetry, Theology/Religion, Translations. Ordained Roman Catholic priest, 1953. Conventual, Stella Maris Monastery, Discalced Carmelite Order, Haifa, since 1954. Medical officer, Camp Hosp., Robben Island, and Cape Town Castle, Cape Town, 1944-46. *Publs:* (as John Friedman) The Redemption of Israel, 1947; (trans. as Elias Friedman) The Diocese of the Latin Patriarchate of Jerusalem, by P. Medebielle, 1963; (as Elias Pater) In Praise of Night, 1969; (trans. as Elias Pater) Variations of Bialik Themes, 1970; (trans. as Elias Pater) Selected Poems of Rachel, 1974; (as Elias Friedman) Jewish Identity, 1974; as (Elias Friedman) The Latin Hermits of Mount Carmel, 1979; (as Elias Pater) Mount Carmel: Poems from a Garden, 1988. Add: Stella Maris Monastery, P.O. Box 9047, Haifa 31090, Israel.

FRIEDMAN, John. *See* **FRIEDMAN,** Jacob Horace.

FRIEDMAN, Lawrence M. American, b. 1930. Law, Politics/Government. Prof. of Law since 1968, and Kirkwood Prof. since 1976, Stanford Univ., California. *Publs:* Contract Law in America, 1965; Government and Slum Housing: A Century of Frustration, 1968; (ed. with S. Macaulay) Law and the Behavioral Sciences, 1969, 1977; A History of American Law, 1973, 1985; The Legal System: A Social Science Perspective, 1975; Law and Society: An Introduction, 1977; (ed. with H.N. Scheiber) American Law and Constitutional Order, 1978, 1988; (ed. with J. Merryman and D. Clark) Law and Social Change in Mediterranean Europe and Latin America, 1980; (with Robert V. Percival) The Roots of Justice: Crime and Punishment in Alameda County, California, 1870-1910, 1981; American Law, 1984; Total Justice, 1985; Your Time Will Come, 1985. Add: Stanford Law Sch., Stanford, Calif. 94305, U.S.A.

FRIEDMAN, Melvin J. American, b. 1928. Literature. Prof. of Comparative Literature and English, Univ. of Wisconsin, Milwaukee, since 1966 (Asst. Prof. of English, Madison, 1960-62). Member of Editorial Bd., Journal of Popular Culture, since 1970, Renascence, since 1972, and Studies in the Novel, since 1973. Ed., Wisconsin Studies in Contemporary Literature, 1960-62; Assoc. Prof. of English and Comparative Literature, Univ. of Maryland, College Park, 1962-66; Ed., Comparative

Literature Studies, 1963–66. *Publs:* Stream of Consciousness: A Study in Literary Method, 1955; (ed.) Configuration critique de Samuel Beckett, 1964; (ed. with L.A. Lawson) The Added Dimension: The Art and Mind of Flannery O'Connor, 1966; (ed. with A.J. Nigro) Configuration critique de William Styron, 1967; (ed. with J.B. Vickery) The Shaken Realist: Essays in Modern Literature in Honor of Frederick J. Hoffman, 1970; (ed.) Samuel Beckett Now: Critical Approaches to His Novels, Poetry, and Plays, 1970, 1975; (ed. with I. Malin) William Styron's The Confession of Nat Turner: A Critical Handbook, 1970; (ed.) The Vision Obscured: Perceptions of Some Twentieth-Century Catholic Novelists, 1970; (with J.R. Bryer, P. Hoy and R.J. Davis) Calepins de Bibliographie Samuel Beckett, 1972; William Styron, 1974 (ed. with R.C. Lamont) The Two Faces of Ionesco, 1978; (ed. with Beverly L. Clark) Critical Essays on Flannery O'Connor, 1985. Add: 1211 East Courtland Pl., Milwaukee, Wisc. 53211, U.S.A.

FRIEDMAN, Milton. American, b. 1912. Economics. Paul Snowden Russell Distinguished Service Prof. Emeritus of Economics, Univ. of Chicago, since 1983 (Assoc. Prof., 1946–48; Prof., 1948–63; Paul Snowden Russell Distinguished Service Prof., 1963–83). Sr. Research Fellow, Hoover Instn., Stanford, Calif., since 1976. Assoc. Economist, National Resources Cttee., 1935–37; Member of Research Staff, National Bureau of Economic Research Inc., 1937–45 and 1948–81; Visiting Prof. of Economics, Univ. of Wisconsin, Madison, 1940–41; Principal Economist, Div. of Tax Research, U.S. Treasury Dept., 1941–43; Assoc. Dir., Statistical Research Group, Div. of War Research, Columbia Univ., NYC, 1943–45; Assoc. Prof., Univ. of Minnesota, Minneapolis, 1945–46; Columnist and Contrib. Ed., Newsweek, NYC, 1966–84. *Publs:* (with S. Kuznets) Income from Independent Professional Practice, 1946; (with H.A. Freeman, F. Mosteller and W.A. Wallis) Sampling Inspection, 1948; Essays in Positive Economics, 1953; (ed.) Studies in the Quantity Theory of Money, 1956; A Theory of the Consumption Function, 1957; A Program for Monetary Stability, 1960; Capitalism and Freedom, 1962; Price Theory: A Provisional Text, 1962, 1976; (with A.J. Schwartz) A Monetary History of the United States, 1867-1960, 1963; (with R.V. Roosa) The Balance of Payments: Free versus Fixed Exchange Rates, 1967; Dollars and Deficits: Inflation, Monetary Policy and the Balance of Payments, 1968; The Optimum Quantity of Money and Other Essays, 1969; (with W.W. Heller) Monetary versus Fiscal Policy, 1969; (with A.J. Schwartz) Monetary Statistics of the United States, 1970; A Theoretical Framework for Monetary Analysis, 1971; (with W.J. Cohen) Social Security: Universal or Selective?, 1972; An Economist's Protest: Columns on Political Economy, 1972, 1975, 1983; Money and Economic Development, 1973; Tax Limitation, Inflation and the Role of Government, 1978; (with Rose Friedman) Free to Choose, 1980; (with A.J. Schwartz) Monetary Trends in the United States and the United Kingdom, 1982; (with Rose D. Friedman) Tyranny of the Status Quo, 1984. Add: Hoover Instn., Stanford, Calif. 94305, U.S.A.

FRIEDMAN, Norman. American, b. 1925. Poetry, Literature, Psychology. Prof. of English, Queens Coll., City Univ. of New York, Flushing, since 1963, Emeritus since 1988; Exec.-Dir., Gestalt Therapy Center of Queens, N.Y., since 1984; also psychotherapist. Member of Faculty, Dept. of English, Univ. of Connecticut, Storrs, 1952–63; New Sch. for Social Research, NYC, 1964–66; Fulbright Lectureship, Nantes and Nice, France, 1966–67. *Publs:* E.E. Cummings: The Art of His Poetry, 1960; (with C.A. McLaughlin) Poetry: An Introduction to Its Form and Art, 1961; (with C.A. McLaughlin) Logic, Rhetoric, and Style, 1963; E.E. Cummings: Growth of a Writer, 1964; (ed.) E.E. Cummings: A Collection of Critical Essays, 1972; Form and Meaning in Fiction, 1975; The Magic Badge: Poems 1953-1984, 1984. Add: 33-54 164th St., Flushing, N.Y. 11358, U.S.A.

FRIEDMAN, Paul. American, b. 1937. Short Stories. Prof., Univ. of Illinois, Urbana (member of the faculty, since 1968); Asst. Prof., Univ. of Wisconsin, Stevens Point, 1964–68. *Publs:* And I Defeated Alleged Fraud (short stories), 1971; Serious Trouble (short stories), 1986. Add: 310 W. Illinois St., Urbana, Ill. 61801, U.S.A.

FRIEDMAN, Rosemary. Also writes as Robert Tibber and Rosemary Tibber. British, b. 1929. Novels/Short stories. *Publs:* as Robert Tibber—No White Coat, 1957; Love on My List, 1959; We All Fall Down, 1960; Patients of a Saint, 1961; The Fraternity, 1963; The Commonplace Day, 1964; Aristide, 1966; The General Practice, 1967; as Rosemary Tibber—Practice Makes Perfect, 1969; As Rosemary Friedman—The Life Situation, 1977; The Long Hot Summer, 1980; Proofs of Affection, 1982; A Loving Mistress, 1983; Rose of Jericho, 1984; A Second Wife, 1985; To Live in Peace, 1987; Aristide, 1987; Aristide in Paris, 1987; An

Eligible Man, 1989. Add: 2 St. Katharine's Precinct, London NW1 4HH, England.

FRIEDMANN, Yohanan. Israeli, b. 1936. Islamic Studies. Assoc. Prof., then Prof., Inst. of Asian and African Studies, Hebrew Univ., Jerusalem, since 1966; (Dean, Faculty of Humanities, 1985–88). *Publs:* Shaykh Ahmad Sirhindi: An Outline of His Thought and a Study of His Image in the Eyes of Posterity, 1971; Prophecy Continuous: Aspects of Ahmadi Religious Thought and Its Medieval Background, 1987. Add: Inst. of Asian and African Studies, Hebrew Univ., Jerusalem, Israel.

FRIEDRICH, Paul. American, b. 1927. Poetry, Anthropology/Ethnology, Language/Linguistics. Faculty member, Univ. of Chicago, since 1962. Faculty member, Harvard Univ. Cambridge, Mass., 1957–58, and Univ. of Pennsylvania, Philadelphia, 1959–62. *Publs:* Proto-Indo-European Trees, 1970; Agrarian Revolt in a Mexican Village, 1970, 1978; The Tarascan Suffixes of Locative Space: Meaning and Morphotactics, 1971; Neighboring Leaves Ride This Wind, 1976; The Meaning of Aphrodite, 1978; Language, Context, and the Imagination, 1979; Bastard Moons, 1979; Redwing, 1982; The Language Parallax, 1986; The Princes of Naranja, 1987. Add: 1126 East 59th St., Chicago, Ill. 60637, U.S.A.

FRIEL, Brian. Irish, b. 1929. Short stories, Plays/Screenplays. Full-time writer since 1960; Founder with Stephen Rea, Field Day Theatre Co., Northern Ireland, 1980. School teacher in primary and intermediate schs. in Derry, N. Ireland, 1950–60. *Publs:* A Saucer of Larks (short stories), 1962; The Enemy Within, 1962; Philadelphia, Here I Come!, 1964; The Gold in the Sea (short stories), 1966; The Loves of Cass McGuire, 1966; Lovers: Part I: Winners: Part II: Losers, 1967; Crystal and Fox, 1968; The Mundy Scheme, 1969; The Gentle Island, 1971; The Freedom of the City, 1973; Volunteers, 1975; Faith Healer, 1976; Living Quarters, 1977; Selected Stories, 1979; Aristocrats, 1979; Translations, 1981; (trans.) Three Sisters, 1981; The Diviner (short stories), 1982; The Communication Cord, 1983; Selected Plays of Brian Friel, 1986; Fathers and Sons (after Turgenev), 1987; (ed.) The Last of the Name, 1987; Making History, 1988. Add: Drumaweir House, Greencastle, Co. Donegal, Ireland.

FRIEND, Robert. American, b. 1913. Poetry, Translations. Assoc. Prof., Hebrew Univ., Jerusalem, 1951–82. *Publs:* Shadow on the Sun, 1941; Salt Gifts, 1964; The Practice of Absence, 1971; Selected Poems, 1975; (trans.) Leah Goldberg: Selected Poems, 1976; (trans.) Natan Alterman: Selected Poems, 1978; Somewhere Lower Down, 1980; (trans.) Sunset Possibilities, by Gabriel Preil, 1985. Add: 2 Itzhak Elhanan St., 92225 Jerusalem, Israel.

FRIENDLY, Fred W. American, b. 1915. Civil liberties/Human rights, Writing/Journalism, Documentation/Reportage. Edward R. Murrow Prof. of Journalism, Columbia Univ., NYC, since 1966. Announcer and Newscaster, WEAN-Radio, Providence, R.I., 1937–41; collaborated with Edward R. Murrow in album "I Can Hear It Now" (Columbia Records), and NBC Radio prog. "Who Said That?", 1948–49; Joint Producer with Edward R. Murrow, "Hear It Now" radio series, then "See It Now" and "Small World" television series, 1951–58; Exec. Producer, CBS Reports 1959–64; Pres. of CBS News, 1964–66; Chmn. of the Broadcast Prog., Ford Foundn., NYC, 1966–80. *Publs:* (with Edward R. Murrow) See It Now, 1955; Due to Circumstances Beyond Our Control, 1967; The Good Guys, the Bad Guys and the First Amendment: Free Speech vs. Fairness in Broadcasting, 1976; Minnesota Rag: The Dramatic Story of the Landmark Supreme Court Case That Gave New Meaning to Freedom of the Press, 1981; (with Martha J. Elliott) The Constitution: That Delicate Balance, 1984. Add: c/o Graduate Sch. of Journalism, Columbia Univ., 116th St. and Broadway, New York, N.Y. 10027, U.S.A.

FRIERMOOD, Elisabeth H(amilton). American, b. 1903. Children's fiction, Autobiography/Memoirs/Personal. Children's librarian, 1925–42. *Publs:* The Wabash Knows the Secret, 1951; Geneva Summer, 1952; Hoosier Heritage, 1954; Candle in the Sun, 1955; That Jones Girl, 1956; Head High, Ellen Brody, 1958; Jo Allen's Predicament, 1959; Promises in the Attic, 1960; The Luck of Daphne Tolliver, 1961; Ballad of Calamity Creek, 1962; The Wild Donahues, 1963; Whispering Willows, 1964; Doc Dudley's Daughter, 1965; Molly's Double Rainbow, 1966; Focus the Bright Land, 1967; Circus Sequins, 1968; Peppers' Paradise, 1969; One of Fred's Girls, 1970; Promises in the Attic, 1975; Frier and Elisabeth: Sportsman and Storyteller (autobiography), 1979. Add: 3030 Park Ave., 2W16, Bridgeport, Conn. 06604, U.S.A.

FRIIS, Erik J(ohan). American, b. 1913. History, Translations. Ed. and Publr., The Scandinavian-American Bulletin; Contrib. Ed., Explorers

Journal, since 1980; General Ed., "The Library of Nordic Literature" series, since 1983; Ed., Norwegian Trade Bulletin, since 1983. Business Mgr., 1946–48, Assoc. Ed., 1948–51, and Ed. and Dir. of Publs., 1951–78, The American-Scandinavian Review, NYC. *Publs:* The American-Scandinavian Foundation 1910-1960: A Brief History, 1960; (author and ed. with Carl F. Bayerschmidt) Scandinavian Studies, 1965; (trans.) The Secret Transmitter, by Olaf Rynning-Tonnesen (juvenile), 1965; (trans.) China's Red Guard, by Hans Granqvist, 1967; (co-trans.) Body and Clothes, by R. Broby Johansen, 1968; (trans.) Westward to Vinland, by Helge Ingstad, 1969; (trans.) The Lost Musicians, by William Heinesen (fiction), 1971; (trans.) Cleng Peerson I-II, by Alfred Hauge, 1975; (ed.) The Scandinavian Presence in North America, 1976; (trans.) The Moment of Truth, by K. Arne Blom, 1977; (co-trans.) Changing, by Liv Ullmann, 1977; (trans.) Red Harvest, by Olav Nordra, 1978; (trans.) Wooden Boat Designs, by Chr. Nielsen, 1980; (ed. and trans.) Nordic Democracy, 1981; (trans.) Dreams of Roses and Fire, by Eyvind Johnson, 1984; (trans.) How to Deep-Freeze a Mammoth, by Björn Kurtén, 1986. Add: 19 Shadow Lane, Montvale, N.J. 07645, U.S.A.

FRINTA, Mojmir S. American, b. 1922. Art. Prof. of Art History, State Univ. of New York at Albany, since 1969 (Asst. Prof., 1963–65; Assoc. Prof., 1965–69). *Publs:* The Genius of Robert Campin, 1966. Add: 150 Maple Ave., Altamont, N.Y. 12009, U.S.A.

FRISBY, Terence. British, b. 1932. Plays/Screenplays. Professional actor, director, and producer since 1957. *Publs:* The Subtopians, 1964; There's a Girl in My Soup, 1968; The Bandwagon, 1973; It's All Right If I Do It, 1977; Seaside Postcard, 1978; Just Remember Two Things: It's Not Fair and Don't Be Late, 1989. Add: c/o Harvey Unna and Stephen Dunbridge Ltd., 24 Pottery Lane, London W11, England.

FRITH, Harold James. Australian. Natural history. Chief, Div. of Wildlife Research, Commonwealth Scientific Industrial Research Org., Canberra, 1961–81, now retired (joined staff 1946). *Publs:* The Mallee Fowl, 1959; Waterfowl in Australia, 1967; (co-author) Kangaroos, 1969; (ed.) Birds in the Australian High County, 1969; (co-ed.) Conservation, 1971; Wildlife Conservation, 1973; (co-ed.) The Murray Waters, 1974; (ed. with B.S. Hetzel) The Nutrition of Aborigines in Relation to the Ecosystem of Central Australia, 1979; Pigeons and Doves in Australia, 1982. Add: c/o Rigby, 176 S. Creek Rd., P.O. Box 60, Dee Why, N.S.W. 2099, Australia.

FRITSCH, Albert J(oseph). American, b. 1933. Environmental science/Ecology. Dir., Appalachia-Science in the Public Interest, since 1977. Research Assoc., Chemistry Dept., Univ. of Texas, Austin, 1969–70, and Center for Study of Responsive Law, 1970–71; Dir., Center for Science in the Public Interest, 1971–77. *Publs:* Theology of the Earth, 1972; The Contrasumers: A Citizen's Guide to Resource Conservation, 1974; 99 Ways to a Simple Lifestyle, 1976; Household Pollutants Guide, 1978; Environmental Ethics, 1980; Green Space, 1982; Appalachia: A Meditation, 1986; Renew the Face of the Earth, 1987; Ethnic Atlas of the United States, 1989; Earthen Vessels, 1989. Add: P.O. Box 298, Livingston, Ky. 40445, U.S.A.

FRITZ, Jean. American, b. 1915. Children's fiction, Children's nonfiction. Research Asst., Silver Burdett Co., NYC, 1938–41; Children's Librarian, Dobbs Ferry Library, NYC, 1955–57; Teacher, The Jean Fritz Writer's Workshop, Katonah, N.Y., 1962–70, and Bd. of Cooperative Educational Services, Westchester Co., N.Y., 1971–73; Book Reviewer, New York Times. *Publs:* Bunny Hopwell's First Spring (fiction), 1954; Help Mr. Willy Nilly (fiction), 1955; Growth Up, 1956; The Late Spring (fiction), 1957; The Cabin Faced West (fiction), 1958; (with Tom Clute) Champion Dog, Prince Tom (fiction), 1958; The Animals of Dr. Schweitzer, 1958; How to Read a Rabbit (fiction), 1959; Brady (fiction), 1960; Tap, Tap, Lion—One, Two, Three (fiction), 1962; San Francisco, 1962; I, Adam (fiction), 1963; Magic to Burn (fiction), 1964; Surprise (reader), 1965; The Train (reader), 1965; Early Thunder (fiction), 1967; George Washington's Breakfast (fiction), 1969; Cast for a Revolution: Some American Friends and Enemies 1728-1814, 1972; And Then What Happened, Paul Revere?, 1973; Why Don't You Get a Horse, Sam Adams?, 1974; Where Was Patrick Henry on the 29th of May?, 1975; Who's That Stepping on Plymouth Rock?, 1975; Will You Sign Here, John Hancock?, 1976; What's the Big Idea, Ben Franklin?, 1976; Can't You Make Them Behave, King George?, 1977; Brendan the Navigator, 1979; Stonewall, 1979; Where Do You Think You're Going, Christopher Columbus?, 1980; The Man Who Loved Books (fiction), 1981; Stonewall, 1981; Traitor: The Case of Benedict Arnold, 1981; The Good Giants and the Bad Pukwudgies (fiction), 1982; Homesick: My Own Story (fiction), 1982; The Double Life of Pocahontas, 1983; China Homecoming, 1985; Make Way

for Sam Houston, 1986; Shh! We're Writing the Constitution, 1987; China's Long March, 1988. Add: 50 Bellewood Ave., Dobbs Ferry, N.Y. 10522, U.S.A.

FROME, Michael. American, b. 1920. Environmental science/Ecology, Travel/Exploration/Adventure. Columnist, Defenders of Wildlife mag., since 1975. News Reporter, Washington Post, 1945–46; Conservation Ed., and Columnist, Field and Stream, 1968–74. *Publs:* Whose Woods These Are, 1962, 1984; Strangers in High Places, 1966, 1980; Virginia, 1966, 3rd ed. 1971; National Park Guide, annually since 1968; The Varmints, 1970; The Forest Service, 1972, 1984; Battle for the Wilderness, 1974, 1984; (with D. Muench) The National Parks, 1977, 1979; Promised Land: Adventures and Encounters in Wild America, 1985; Conscience of a Conservationist, 1989. Add: c/o Huxley Coll. of Environmental Studies, Western Washington Univ., Bellingham, WA 98225, U.S.A.

FROST, Alan. Australian, b. 1943. History. Sr. Lectr., La Trobe Univ., Bundoora, Vic., since 1975. *Publs:* Convicts and Empire, 1980; Dreams of a Pacific Empire, 1981; (co-ed.) The Journal of Daniel Paine 1794-1797, 1983. Add: c/o History Dept., La Trobe Univ., Bundoora, Vic. 3083, Australia.

FROST, David (Paradine). British, b. 1939. Social commentary/phenomena, Humor/Satire. Television performer, producer and actor. Joint Founder, London Weekend Television; Chmn. and Chief Exec., David Paradine Ltd., London, since 1966; Joint Deputy Chmn., Equity Enterprises, since 1973. *Publs:* That Was the Week That Was, 1963; How to Live Under Labour, 1964; Talking with Frost, 1967; To England with Love, 1967; The Presidential Debate, 1968; The Americans, 1970; Whitlam and Frost, 1974; I Gave Them a Sword, 1978; I Could Have Kicked Myself, 1982; Who Wants to Be a Millionaire?, 1983; (with others) The Mid-Atlantic Companion, 1986; (with others) The Rich Tide, 1986; The World's Shortest Books, 1987. Add: David Paradine Ltd., 115-123 Bayham Street, London NW1, England.

FROST, Stanley Brice. Canadian, b. 1913. History, Theology/Religion. Prof. of Old Testament, McGill Univ., Montreal, since 1956 (Dean of Grad. Studies and Research, 1963–69; Vice Principal Admin. and Professional Faculties, 1969–74). Dir., History of McGill Project, since 1974. *Publs:* Old Testament Apocalyptic, Its Origin and Growth, 1952; The Beginning of the Promise, Eight Lectures on Genesis, 1960; Patriarchs and Prophets, 1963; Standing and Understanding: A Reappraisal of the Christian Faith, 1969; For the Advancement of Learning: McGill University, 2 vols., 1980–84. Add: McGill Univ., 3459 McTavish St., Montreal, Que. H3A 1Y1, Canada.

FRUCHTER, Benjamin. American, b. 1914. Mathematics/Statistics, Psychology. Prof. of Educational Psychology, Univ of Texas at Austin, since 1949. Lectr., Univ. of Southern California, Los Angeles, 1946–48; Assoc. Dir. of Research, U.S. Air Force, Human Resources Center, 1948–49. *Publs:* Introduction to Factor Analysis, 1967; (co-author) Fundamental Statistics in Psychology and Education, 6th ed., 1978. Add: 2704 Valley Springs Rd., Austin, Tex. 78746, U.S.A.

FRUMKIN, Gene. American, b. 1928. Poetry. Prof. of English, Univ. of New Mexico, Albuquerque, since 1987 (Lectr., 1966–67; Asst. Prof., 1967–71; Assoc. Prof., 1971–87). *Publs:* The Hawk and the Lizard, 1963; The Orange-Tree, 1965; The Rainbow-Walker, 1969; Dostoevsky and Other Nature Poems, 1972; Locust Cry: Poems 1958-65, 1973; The Mystic Writing Pad, 1977; Loops, 1979; Clouds and Red Earth, 1981; A Lover's Quarrel with America, 1985; A Sweetness in the Air, 1987. Add: 3721 Mesa Verde N.E., Albuquerque, N.M. 87110, U.S.A.

FRUTON, Joseph S(tewart). American, b. 1912. Biology, Chemistry. Eugene Higgins Prof. Emeritus of Biochemistry, Yale Univ., New Haven, Conn., since 1982 (Assoc. Prof. of Physiological Chemistry, 1945–50; Prof. of Biochemistry, 1950–57; Eugene Higgins Prof., 1957–82). Assoc., Rockefeller Inst. for Medical Research, 1934–45. *Publs:* (with S. Simmonds) General Biochemistry, 1953, 1958; Molecules and Life: Historical Essays on the Interplay of Chemistry and Biology, 1972; Selected Bibliography of Biographical Data for the History of Biochemistry since 1800, 1974, 1982, supplement 1985; Contrasts in Scientific Style: Research Groups in the Chemical and Biochemical Sciences, 1988. Add: 123 York St., New Haven, Conn. 06511, U.S.A.

FRY, Christopher. British, b. 1907. Plays/Screenplays, Poetry, Songs, lyrics and libretti, Autobiography/Memoirs/Personal, Translations. Teacher, Bedford Froebel Kindergarten, 1926–27; Schoolmaster, Hazelwood Sch., Limpsfield, Surrey, 1928–31; Secty. to H. Rodney Bennett, 1931–32; Founding Dir., Tunbridge Wells Repertory Players, 1932–35; Lectr., and ed. of schs. mag., Dr. Barnardo's Homes, 1934–39; Dir., 1946, and Visiting Dir., 1945–46. Oxford Playhouse. *Publs:* Open Door, 1936; The Boy with a Cart: Cuthman, Saint of Sussex, 1938; Thursday's Child: A Pageant, 1939; Phoenix Too Frequent, 1946; The Firstborn, 1946; The Lady's Not for Burning, 1948; Thor, with Angels, 1948; Venus Observed, 1950; (adaptor and trans.) Ring Round the Moon: A Charade with Music, 1950; A Sleep of Prisoners, 1951; The Beggar's Opera (screenplay), 1953; The Queen Is Crowned (screenplay), 1953; The Dark Is Light Enough: A Winter Comedy, 1954; (trans.) The Lark, 1955; (trans.) Tiger at the Gates, 1955; (trans.) Duel of Angels, 1958; Ben Hur (screenplay), 1959; Curtmantle, 1961; Barabbas (screenplay), 1962; (trans.) Judith, 1962; (trans.) Colette, the Boy and the Magic, 1964; The Boat That Mooed, 1966; The Bible: Original Screenplay, 1966 (filmed as The Bible: In the Beginning); (trans.) Peer Gynt, 1970; A Yard of Sun: A Summer Comedy, 1970; The Brontës of Haworth (TV plays), 1975; (trans.) Edmond Rostand: Cyrano de Bergerac, 1975; Sister Dora (TV play), 1977; The Best of Enemies (TV play), 1977; Can You Find Me: A Family History, 1978; Paradise Lost (opera), 1978; One Thing More, or Caedmon Construed, 1986. Add: The Toft, East Dean, Nr. Chichester, Sussex PO18 0JA, England.

FRY, Edward B. American, b. 1925. Education. Visiting Prof., Univ. of California at Riverside, since 1988. Assoc. Prof. of Education, Loyola Univ., Los Angeles, Calif., 1955–63; Dir. of the Reading Center, Rutgers Univ., New Brunswick, N.J. 1963–87. *Publs:* Teaching Machine and Programmed Instruction, 1963; Teaching Faster Reading, 1963; Reading Faster: A Drill Book, 1963; The Emergency Reading Treachers Manual, 1969, 1980; Typing Course for Children, 1969; Reading for Classroom and Clinic, 1972; Elementary Reading Instruction, 1977; Skimming and Scanning, 1978; Dictionary Drills, 1980; Graphical Comprehension, 1981; The Reading Teachers Book of Lists, 1984; Everyday Words, 1985; Vocabulary Drills, 1985; The New Reading Teachers Book of Lists, 1985; Fry's Instant Word Puzzles and Activities, 1987. Add: 245 Grandview Ave., Laguna Beach, CA 92651, U.S.A.

FRY, Rosalie K(ingsmill). British, b. 1911. Children's fiction. Freelance writer and illustrator. *Publs:* Bumblebuzz, 1938; Ladybug! Ladybug!, 1940; Bandy Boys Treasure Island, 1941; In a Rock Pool; Adventures Downstream; The Little Gipsy; Cherrywinkle; Two Little Pigs, Pipkin Sees the World, 1951; Cindrella's Mouse and Other Tales, 1953; The Wind Call, 1955; Deep in the Forest, 1955; Lucinda and the Painted Bell, 1956; Child of the Western Isles, 1957; Lucinda and the Sailor Kitten, 1958; Secret of the Forest, 1958; The Mountain Door, 1960; Fly Home, Columbina, 1960; Princess in the Forest, 1961; The Echo Song, 1962; The Riddle of the Figurehead, 1963; Promise of the Rainbow, 1965; September Island, 1965; The Castle Family, 1965; Gypsy Princess, 1969; Snowed Up, 1970; Mungo, 1972; Secrets, 1973. Add: Lark Rise, 15 East Cliff, Southgate, Swansea SA3 2AS, Wales.

FRY, William Finley, Jr. American, b. 1924. Literature. Assoc. Clinical Prof., Stanford Univ., California, since 1959, now Emeritus. Dir., Intnl. Gelotology Inst., Nevada City, Calif. Comedy Consultant, Summer Inst., American Conservatory Theatre, San Francisco, 1969; Member, Bd. of Dirs., Mental Research Inst., Palo Alto, Calif., 1975–83 (Dir. of Education, 1962–67), and Workshop Library of Humor, Washington, D.C. *Publs:* Sweet Madness: A Study of Humor, 1963; (with Melanie Allen) Make 'Em Laugh: Life Studies of Comedy Writers, 1976; (with Waleed Salameh) Handbook of Humor and Therapy, 1983. Add: 156 Grove St., Nevada City, CA 95959, U.S.A.

FRYE, (Charles) Alton. American, b. 1936. History, International relations/Current affairs, Politics/Government. Vice-Pres., Sr. Fellow and Washington Dir., Council of Foreign Relations, Washington, D.C., since 1973 (Intnl. Affairs Fellow, 1971–73). Consultant, U.S. Senate, since 1983; Bd. member, Patterson School of Diplomacy, Univ. of Ky., since 1980, and Mershon Center for National Security Studies, Ohio State Univ., since 1982. Radio Reporter and Announcer, WNAH and WMAK, Nashville, Tenn., KXLW and WTMV, St. Louis, Mo., and WELI, New Haven, Conn., 1953–61; Personnel Supvr., City of St. Louis, Mo., 1956–58; Staff member, Rand Corp., 1962–68; Research Fellow, Center for Intnl. Affairs, and Lectr., Dept. of Govt., Harvard Univ., Cambridge, Mass., 1965–66; Legislative and Administrative Asst. to Sen. Edward W. Brooke, 1968–71; Fellow, Woodrow Wilson Intnl. Center for Scholars, 1971–73; Dir., Policy Planning, National Unity Campaign (Anderson for Pres.), 1980. *Publs:* The Hazards of Atomic Wastes: Perspectives and Proposals on Oceanic Disposal, 1962; Nazi Germany and the American Hemisphere, 1933-1941, 1967; A Responsible Congress: The Politics of

National Security, 1975. Add: 11 Dupont Circle N.W., Suite 900, Washington, D.C. 20036, U.S.A.

FRYE, (Herman) Northrop. Canadian, b. 1912. Literature. Univ. Prof., Univ. of Toronto, since 1967 (Lectr., Prof., and Principal of Victoria Coll., Univ. of Toronto, 1939–67); Chancellor, Victoria Univ., since 1978. Ed., Canadian Forum, 1948–52. *Publs:* Fearful Symmetry: Study on William Blake, 1947; Anatomy of Criticism: Four Essays, 1957; The Well-Tempered Critic, 1963; The Educated Imagination, 1963; T.S. Eliot, 1963; Fables of Identity, 1963; A Natural Pespective: Essays on the Development of Shakespearean Comedy and Romance, 1965; The Return of Eden: Five Essays on Milton's Epics, 1965; Fools of Time: Studies in Shakespearean Tragedy, 1967; The Modern Century, 1967; A Study of English Romanticism, 1968; The Stubborn Structure: Essays on Criticism and Society, 1970; The Bush Garden: Essays on the Canaian Imagination, 1971; The Critical Path: An Essay on the Social Context of Literary Criticism, 1976; The Seecular Scripture: A Study of the Structure of Romance, 1976; Spiritus Mundi: Essays on Literature, Myth and Society, 1976; Northrop Frye on Culture and Literature: A Collection of Review Essays, 1978; Creation and Recreation, 1980; The Great Code: The Bible and Literature, 1982; Divisions on a Ground, 1982; The Myth of Deliverance: Reflections on Shakespeare's Problem Comedies, 1983; Northrop Frye on Shakespeare, 1986; No Uncertain Sounds, 1988; Northrop Frye on Education, 1988. Add: Massey Coll., 4 Devonshire Pl., Toronto, Ont. M5S 2E1, Canada.

FRYE, Richard Nelson. American, b. 1920. Archeology/Antiquities, History. Aga Khan Prof. of Iranian, Harvard Univ., Cambridge, Mass., since 1957. Pres., Asia Inst., Pahlavi Univ., Shiraz, Iran, 1969–74. *Publs:* Notes on the Early Coinage of Transoxiana, 1949; The Near East and the Great Powers, 1951; (with L.V. Thomas) The United States and Turkey and Iran, 1952; Iran, 1953; (with R.P. Blake) History of the Nation of Archers, 1954; The History of Bukhara, 1954; The Heritage of Persia,1962; Bukhara, the Medieval Achievement, 1965; (ed.) Islam and the West, 1966 (author and ed.) The Histories of Nishapur, 1966; (ed.) Corpus Inscriptionum: Inscriptions of Dura Europos, 1969; (ed.) Corpus Inscriptionum Iranicarum: Seals in the Collection of Mohsen Foroughi, 1971; Sasanian Remains from Qasr-i Abu Nasr, 1973; Neue Methodologie in der Iranistik, 1974; (ed.) Cambridge History of Iran, vol. 4, 1975; Islamic Iran and Central Asia (7th-12th Centuries), 1979; Ancient Iran: Handbuch der Altertumswissenschaft, 1983. Add: Dept. of Near Eastern Languages and Civilizations, Harvard Univ., 6 Divinity Ave., Cambridge, Mass. 02138, U.S.A.

FRYE, Roland (Mushat). American, b. 1921. Literature. Prof. Emeritus of English Literature, Univ. of Pennsylvania, Philadelphia. Instr. in English, Howard Coll., Birmingham, Ala., 1947–48; Asst. Prof. to Prof. of English, Emory Univ., Altanta, Ga., 1952–61; Research Consultant: 1961–62, and Research Prof., 1962–65, Folger Shakespeare Library, Washington. *Publs:* God, Man, and Satan: Patterns of Christian Thought and Life in Paradise Lost, Pilgrim's Progress, and the Great Theologians, 1960; Perspective on Man: Literature and the Christian Tradition, 1961; Shakespeare and Christian Doctrine, 1963; The Bible: Selections from the King James Version for Study as Literature, 1965; Shakespeare's Life and Times: A Pictorial Record, 1967; Shakespeare: The Art of the Dramatist, 1970; Milton's Imagery and the Visual Arts, 1970; (ed.) The Reader's Bible, 1979; Is God a Creationist? The Religious Case Against Creation Science, 1983; The Renaissance Hamlet: Issues and Responses in 1600, 1985. Add: 226 W. Valley Rd., Wayne, Pa. 19087, U.S.A.

FRYER, Jonathan. British, b. 1950. History, Third world problems, Biography. Freelance journalist, working mainly for BBC Radio (World Service and Radio 4). Member, Bromley Council, since 1986; Member of the Exec., English P.E.N., since 1989. Reuters Correspondent, London and Brussels, 1973–74; Visiting Lectr., Univ. of Nairobi, Kenya, 1976; Consultant, World Council of Churches, Geneva, 1979–82; Ed., Earthscan Features, London, 1986–87. *Publs:* The Great Wall of China, 1975; Isherwood, 1977; (with Rona Dobson) Brussels as Seen by Naif Artists, 1979; Food for Thought, 1981. Add: 9 Felstead Rd., Orpington, Kent BR6 9AA, England.

FRYKENBERG, Robert E(ric). American, b. 1930. History. Prof., Dept. of History and South Asian Studies, Univ. of Wisconsin, Madison, since 1971 (Asst. Prof., 1962–67; Assoc. Prof. 1967–71; Chmn., Dept. of South Asian Studies, 1970–73; Dir., Center for South Asian Studies, 1970–73). Trustee, American Inst. of Indian Studies, 1970–81. *Publs:* Guntur District 1788-1848: A History of Local Influence and Central Authority in South India, 1965; Today's World in Focus: India, 1968;

Land Control and Social Structure in Indian History, 1969: Land Tenure and Peasants in South Asia, 1979 (ed.) Delhi Through the Ages: Essays on Urban Culture and Society, 1986. Add: Univ. of Wisconsin, 3211 Humanities Bldg., 435 N. Park, Madison, Wisc. 53706, U.S.A.

FUCHS, Lucy. American, b. 1935. Historical/Romance, Children's fiction, Education. Instr. in Sociology and French, Hillsborough Community Coll., Hillsborough, Fla., since 1972; Prof., St. Leo Coll., St. Leo Fla., since 1980. High Sch. French teacher, Cincinnati, Ohio, 1966–69; Counsellor, Florida State Univ., Tallahassee, 1969–71. *Publs:* Wild Winds of Mayaland, 1978; Dangerous Splendour, 1978; Shadow of the Walls, 1980; Pictures of Fear, 1981; Teaching Reading in Secondary School, 1987. Add: 505 S. Oakwood Ave., Brandon, Fla. 33511, U.S.A.

FUCHS, Daniel. American, b. 1909. Novels/Short stories, Plays/Screenplays. Scripwriter, Hollywood, Calif., since 1937. *Publs:* Summer in Williamsburg, 1934; Homage to Blenholt, 1936; Low Company (in U.K. as Neptune Beach), 1937; (with P. Viertel) The Hard Way (screenplay), 1943; Hollow Triumph (screenplay), 1948; Panic in the Streets (screenplay), 1950; Love Me or Leave Me (screenplay), 1955; (with S. Levien and J. Fante) Jeanne Engels (screenplay), 1957; West of the Rockies, 1971; The Apathetic Bookie Joint (stories), 1979. Add: 430 S. Fuller Ave., Apt. 9-C, Los Angeles, Calif. 90036, U.S.A.

FUCHS, (Sir) Vivian. British, b. 1908. Travel/Exploration/Adventure. Dir., British Antarctic Survey, London, 1947–73. *Publs:* (with Sir Edmund Hillary) The Crossing of Antarctica, 1958; Antarctic Adventure, 1959; (ed.) Forces of Nature, 1977; Of Ice and Men, 1982. Add: 106 Barton Rd., Cambridge CB3 9LH, England.

FUEGI, John. American/Swiss/British, b. 1936. Literature. Dir., Univ. of Maryland Research Ctr. for the Arts and Humanities, College Park, since 1986 (Prof., and Dir. of Comparative Literature Prog., 1976–86). Prof. of Comparative Literature, Univ. of Wisconsin, Milwaukee, 1974–76 (joined faculty as Asst. Prof., 1967). Visiting Prof., Harvard Univ., Cambridge, Mass. since 1974. Lectr. in American Literature, Freie Universität, Berlin, 1965–67. *Publs:* The Wall (documentary film), 1961; The Essential Brecht, 1972; (ed.) Brecht Today, 3 vols., 1972–74; Brecht the Director, 1986; Bert's People (tv series), 1988. Add: Univ. of Maryland Research Ctr. for Arts and Humanities, College Park, Md. 20742, U.S.A.

FUGARD, Athol. South African, b. 1932. Novels/Short stories, Plays/Screenplays. Actor, dir., and playwright, since 1959; Dir., Serpent Players, Port Elizabeth, since 1965. Co-founder, The Space experimental theatre, Cape Town, 1972. *Publs:* The Blood Knot, 1963; Hello and Goodbye, 1966; People Are Living There, 1969; Boesman and Lena, 1969; Three Plays, 1972, reissued as Three Port Elizabeth Plays, 1974; Statements (3 plays), 1974; (with J. Kani and W. Ntshona) Two Plays: Sizwe Bansi Is Dead and The Island, 1976; Dimetos and Two Early Plays, 1977; The Guest (screenplay), 1977; Tsots (novel), 1980; A Lesson from Aloes, 1981; Master Harold and the Boys, 1982; Marigolds in August (screenplay), 1982; Notebooks 1960-1977, 1983; The Road to Mecca, 1985; Selected Plays, 1987. Add: P.O. Box 5090, Walmer, Port Elizabeth, South Africa.

FUKUDA, Haruko. Japanese, b. 1946. Economics, Third World. With Nikko Securities (Europe) since 1988; Dir., Foreign and Colonial Investment Trust plc, since 1988. Research Officer, Trade Policy Research Centre, 1968–70; Research Officer, Overseas Development Inst., 1970–71; Economics Dept., IBRD (World Bank), Washington, D.C., 1971–72; Economist, Vickers da Costa & Co., Ltd., 1972–74; Member of Staff, 1974–88, and Partner, 1980–88, James Capel and Co., London. *Publs:* Britain in Europe: Impact on the Third World, 1973; Japan & World Trade: The Years Ahead, 1974. Add: Creems, Wissington, Nayland, Suffolk, England.

FUKUTAKE, Tadashi. Japanese, b. 1917. Economics, Sociology. Prof. of Sociology, Univ. of Tokyo, 1970–77, Emeritus, since 1977 (Asst. Prof., 1948–56; Assoc. Prof., 1956–60). *Publs:* Man and Society in Japan, 1962; (with T. Ouchi and C. Nakane) The Socio-Economics Structure of the Indian Village: Surveys of Villages in Gujarat and West Bengal, 1964; Asian Rural Society: China, India, Japan, 1967; Japanese Rural Society, 1967; Japanese Society Taday, 1974, 1981; (ed. with K. Morioka) Sociology and Social Development in Asia: Proceedings of the Symposium, 1974; Rural Society in Japan, 1980; Japanese Social Structure 1870-1980, 1982. Add: 6-31-20 Daita, Setagaya-Ku, Tokyo, Japan.

FULBRIGHT, J(ames) William. American, b. 1905. Politics/Government. Special Attorney, Anti-Trust Div., U.S. Dept. of Justice, Washington, 1934–35; Instr. in Law, George Washington Univ., Washington, 1935–36; Lectr. in Law, and Pres., Univ. of Arkansas, Fayetteville, 1936–41; Member. 3rd District of Arkansas, U.S. House of Reps., Washington, 1942–45; Jr. Senator from Arkansas (Democrat), U.S. Senate, Washington, 1945–1975: Chmn., Foreign Relations Cttee., and Member, Senate Finance Cttee. and Joint Congressional Economic Cttee. (Chmn., Banking and Currency Cttee.), 1955–59). *Publs:* Old Myths and New Realities, 1964; Prospects for the West, 1965; The Arrogance of Power, 1967; The Pentagon Machine, 1970. Add: 555-13th St., N.W., Washington, D.C. 20004, U.S.A.

FULLER, Charles. American, b. 1939. Plays. Loan collector, counselor at Temple Univ., and city housing inspector, all in Philadelphia; co-founder dir., Afro-American Arts Theatre, Philadelphia, 1967–71; writer and dir., Black Experience program, WIP Radio, 1970–71. *Publs:* The Rise (in New Plays from the Black Theatre), 1969; Zooman and the Sign, 1982; A Soldier's Play, 1982. Add: c/o Esther Sherman, William Morris Agency, 1350 Ave. of the Americas, New York, N.Y. 10019, U.S.A.

FULLER, Edmund. American, b. 1914. Novels/Short stories, History, Literature, Biography. *Publs:* A Pageant of the Theatre, 1941, rev. ed. 1965; John Milton, 1944; A Star Pointed North (novel), 1946; George Bernard Shaw: Critic of Western Morale, 1950; Brothers Divided (novel), 1951; Vermont: A History of the Green Mountain State, 1952; Tinkers and Genius: The Story of the Yankee Inventors, 1955; (ed.) The Christian Idea of Education; Man in Modern Fiction: Some Minority Opinions on Comtemporary American Writing, 1958; (ed.) Bulfinch's Mythology, 1959; Books with the Men Behind Them, 1962; The Corridor (novel), 1963; Successful Calamity: A Writer's Follies on a Vermont Farm, 1966; Commentary on Charles Williams' All Hallows Eve, 1967; (with D.E. Green) God in the White House: The Faiths of the American Presidents, 1968; Flight (novel), 1970; Prudence Crandall: An Incidence of Racism in Nineteenth Century Connecticut, 1972; Time of Turbulence: Research Cases for Freshman English, 1972; Myth, Allegory and Gospel: An Interpretation of J.R.R. Tolkien, C.S. Lewis, G.K. Chesterton and Charles Williams, 1974. Add: c/o Random House Inc., 201 East 50th St., New York, N.Y. 10022, U.S.A.

FULLER, Jean (Violet) Overton. British, b. 1915. Poetry, History, Biography. Founding Dir., Fuller d' Arch Smith Ltd., London, rare book sellers and publrs., since 1969. Examiner, Postal Censorship, 1941–45; Lectr. in Phonetics, 1951–52. *Publs:* Madeleine, 1952, rev. ed. as Noor-un-Nisa Inayat Khan, 1971; The Starr Affair (in U.S. as No. 13 Bob), 1954; Double Webs, 1958; Horoscope for a Double Agent, 1960; Venus Protected, 1964; The Magical Dilemma of Victor Neuburg, 1965; Carthage and the Midnight Sun, 1966; Shelley: A Biography, 1968; Swineburne: A Biography, 1968; African Violets, 1968; Darun and Pitar, 1970; Tintagel, 1970; Conversations with a Captor, 1973; The German Penetration of SOE, 1975; Shiva's Dance, 1979; Sir Francis Bacon, 1981; That the Gods May Remember, 1982; The Comte de Saint-Germain, 1985; Blavastsky and Her Teachers, 1988; Dericourt, The Chequered Spy, 1989. Add: 6 Church Lane, Wymington, Rushden, Northants NN10 9LW, England.os

FULLER, John (Harold). British, b. 1916. Catering, Hotelkeeping, Cuisine. Hon. Catering Adviser, R.A.F., since 1971. Catering Books Adviser, Hutchinson Publrs. Ltd., London, since 1964; Editorial Bd., Hospitality Management, since 1974. Ed., Journal of the Hotel and Catering Inst., 1949–54, and Food and Cookery Review, 1957–58; Prof. of Hotel Mgmt., and Dir., Scottish Hotel Sch., Univ. of Strathclyde, 1959–70. *Publs:* The Chef's Manual of Kitchen Management, 1962; (with E. Renold) The Chef's Compendium of Professional Recipes, 1963; The Caterer's Potato Manual, 1963; Guéridon and Lamp Cookery, 1965; (with A. Currie) The Waiter, 1965; Hotelkeeping and Catering as a Career, 1965; (ed.) Catering Management in the Technological Age, 1967; (ed.) Pellaprat's Great Book of the Kitchen, 1968; (ed. with J. Steel) Productivity and Profit in Catering, 1968; (ed.) Catering and Hotelkeeping, 2 vols., 1975; (with D. Gee) A Hotel and Catering Career, 1976; Professional Kitchen Management, 1981; Modern Restaurant Service, 1982; (ed.) Meat Dishes in International Cuisine, 1984; Pub Catering, 1985; Essential Table Service, 1986. Add: 61 Lime Walk, Oxford OX3 7AB, England.

FULLER, John (Leopold). British, b. 1937. Novels/Short stories, Plays/Screenplays, Poetry, Literature. Fellow of Magdalen Coll., Oxford, since 1966; Publr., Sycamore Press, Oxford. Visiting Lectr., State Univ. of New York, Buffalo, 1962–63; Asst. Lectr., Manchester Univ., 1963–66. *Publs:* (ed.) Light Blue Dark Blue, 1960; (ed.) Oxford Poetry,

1960, 1960; Fairground Music, 1961; (ed.) Poetry Supplement, 1962; The Tree That Walked, 1967; Herod Do Your Worst (play), 1967; The Art of Love, 1968; (ed. with Harold Pinter and Peter Redgrove) New Poems 1967, 1968; The Labours of Hercules: A Sonnet Sequence, 1969; Three London Songs, 1969; Annotations of Giant's Town, 1970; The Wreck, 1970; Half a Fortnight, 1970; A Reader's Guide to W.H. Auden, 1970; (ed.) Poetry Supplement, 1970; The Spider Monkey Uncle King (play), 1971; (ed.) Nemo's Almanac, 17 vols., 1971–87; Cannibals and Missionaries, 1972; Boys in a Pie, 1972; Fox-Trot (play), 1972; The Sonnet, 1972; Hut Groups, 1973; (with Adrian Mitchell and Peter Levi) Penguin Modern Poets 22, 1973; Epistles to Several Persons, 1973; Poems and Epistles, 1974; Squeaking Crust, 1974; The Queen in the Golden Tree (play), 1974; The Mountain in the Sea, 1975; The Last Bid, 1975; Carving Trifles, 1976; Bel and the Dragon, 1977; The Wilderness, 1977; Lies and Secrets, 1979; The Illusionists, 1980; The Extraordinary Wood Mill and Other Stories, 1980; The January Divan, 1980; The Ship of Sounds, 1981; Waiting for the Music, 1982; The Beautiful Inventions, 1983; Flying to Nowhere (novel), 1983; Come Aboard and Sail Away (for children), 1983; Poets in Hand (for children), 1985; The Adventures of Speedfall (stories), 1985; Selected Poems 1954–82, 1985; Partingtime Hall, with James Fenton, 1987; Tell It Again (novel), 1988; The Grey Among the Green (poems), 1988; The Burning Boys (novel), 1989. Add: 4 Benson Pl., Oxford, England.

FULLER, Reginald Horace. British, b. 1915. Theology/Religion. Retired Prof. of New Testament, Virginia Theological Seminary, Alexandria, 1972–85. Prof. of Theology, St. David's Coll., Lampeter, Wales, 1950–55; Prof. of New Testament, Seabury-Western Theological Seminary, Evanston, Ill., 1955–66; Baldwin Prof. of Sacred Literature, Union Theological Seminary, New York, 1966–72. *Publs:* (with R.P.C. Hanson) The Church of Rome: A Dissuasive, 1948; (trans.) The Cost of Discipleship, by D. Bonhoffer, 1948; (trans.) Kerygma and Myth I, 1963; The Mission and Achievement of Jesus, 1954; (trans.) Bonhoffer's Letters and Papers from Prison, 1954; (trans.) Primitive Christianity, 1956; (trans.) Unknown Sayings of Jesus, 1957; What Is Liturgical Preaching?, 1957; (with G.E. Wright) The Book of the Acts of God, 1957; Luke's Witness to Jesus Christ, 1958; (trans.) Modern Catholicism, 1959; The New Testament in Current Study, 1962; (trans.) Kerygma and Myth II, 1962; Interpreting the Miracles, 1963; The Foundations of New Testament Christology, 1965; A Critical Introduction to the New Testament, 1966; (with B. Rice) Christianity and the Affluent Society, 1966; (trans. with I. Fuller) Two Studies in the Theology of Bonhoeffer, 1967; The Formation of the Resurrection Narratives, 1971; (trans.) Reverence for Life, by A. Schweitzer, 1971; (trans. with I. Fuller) Church and Theology; (trans. with I. Fuller) The New Testament: A Guide to Its Writings, by G. Bornkamm, 1973; Preaching the New Lectionary, 1974; Proclamation 2: Advent and Christmas, 1979; (trans. with I. Fuller) The Holy Spirit, by E. Schweizer, 1980; The Use of the Bible in Preaching, 1980; (with P. Perkins) Who Is This Christ?, 1983; Preaching the Lectionary, 1984. Add: 5001 East Seminary Ave., Richmond, Va. 23227, U.S.A.

FULLER, Roy (Broadbent). British, b. 1912. Mystery/Crime/Suspense, Children's fiction, Poetry, Literature, Autobiography. Asst. Solicitor, 1938–58, Solicitor, 1958–69, and Dir., 1969–87, Woolwich Equitable Building Soc. Chmn., Legal Advisory Panel, 1958–69, and Vice Pres., 1969–88, Building Socs. Assn. Prof. of Poetry, Oxford Univ., 1968–73. Chmn., Literature Panel, Arts Council of Great Britain, 1976–77; Member, Bd. of Govs., BBC, 1972–79. *Publs:* Poems, 1939; The Middle of War, 1942; A Lost Season, 1944; Savage Gold, 1946; With My Little Eye, 1948; Epitaphs and Occasions, 1949; The Second Curtain, 1953; Counterparts, 1954; Fantasy and Fugue (in U.S. as Murder in Mind), 1954; Image of a Society, 1956; Brutus's Orchard, 1957; The Ruined Boys (in U.S. as That Distant Afternoon), 1959; The Father's Comedy, 1961; Collected Poems, 1936-1961, 1962; The Perfect Fool, 1963; My Child, My Sister, 1965; Buff, 1965; Catspaw, 1966; New Poems, 1968; Off Course, 1969; The Carnal Island, 1970; Owls and Artificers: Oxford Lectures on Poetry, 1971; Seen Grandpa Lately?, 1972; Professors and Gods: Last Oxford Lectures on Poetry, 1973; From the Joke Shop, 1975; The Joke Shop Annexe, 1975; An Ill-Governed Coast: Poems, 1976; Poor Roy, 1977; The Other Planet, 1979; Retreads, 1979; Souvenirs (memoirs), 1980; The Reign of Sparrows, 1980; More About Tompkins and Other Light Verse, 1981; Vamp Till Ready: Further Memoirs, 1982; The Individual and His Times: A Selection of the Poetry of Roy Fuller, 1982; House and Shop, 1982; As from the Thirties, 1983; (with Barbara Giles and Adrian Rumble) Upright, Downfall, 1983; Mianserin Sonnets, 1984; Home and Dry: Memoirs III, 1984; New and Collected Poems 1934-84, 1985; Subsequent to Summer, 1985; Consolations, 1987; Available for Dreams, 1989; Collected Poems for Children, 1989. Add: 37 Langton Way, London SE3, England.

FULLER, Samuel (Michael). American, b. 1911. Novels/Short stories, Mystery/Crime/Suspense, Plays/Screenplays. Film writer, producer and director, since 1936. *Publs:* novels—Burn, Baby, Burn!, 1935; Test Tube Baby, 1936; Make Up and Kiss, 1938; The Rifle, 1969; mystery novels—The Dark Page, 1944 (in U.S. paperback, Murder Makes a Deadline, 1952); The Naked Kiss (novelization of screenplay), 1964; Crown of India, 1966; 144 Piccadilly, 1971; Dead Pigeon on Beethoven Street (novelization of screenplay), 1974; The Big Red One, 1980; The Rifles, 1981; Pecos Bill and the Soho Kid, 1986. Also numerous screenplays, 1937–72. Add: c/o Charles Silverberg, One Century Plaza, No. 1900, 2029 Century Park, E. Los Angeles, Calif. 90067, U.S.A.

FULLERTON, Alexander (Fergus). Has also written as Anthony Fox. British, b. 1924. Novels/Short stories. *Publs:* Surface!, 1953; Bury the Past, 1954; Old Moke, 1954; No Man's Mistress, 1955; A Wren Called Smith, 1957; The White Men Sang, 1958; The Yellow Ford, 1959; The Waiting Game, 1961; Soldier from the Sea, 1962; The Thunder and the Flame, 1964; Lionheart, 1965; Chief Executive, 1969; The Publisher, 1970; Store, 1971; The Escapists, 1972; Other Men's Wives, 1973; Piper's Leave, 1974; The Blooding of the Guns, 1976; Sixty Minutes for Saint George, 1977; Patrol to the Golden Horn, 1978; Storm Force to Narvik, 1979; (as Anthony Fox) Threat Warning Red, 1979; Last Lift from Crete, 1980; (as Anthony Fox) Kingfisher Scream, 1980; All the Drowning Seas, 1981; A Share of Honour, 1982; Regenesis, 1983; The Torch Bearers, 1983; The Gatecrashers, 1984; The Aphrodite Cargo, 1985; Special Deliverance, 1986; Special Dynamic, 1987; Special Deception, 1988; Johnson's Bird, 1989. Add: c/o John Johnson Ltd., 45-47 Clerkenwell Green, London EC1R 0HT, England.

FULLERTON, Gail. Also writes as Gail J. Putney. American, b. 1927. Human relations, Psychology. Prof. of Sociology since 1972, and Pres. since 1978, San Jose State Univ., Calif. (Asst. Prof., 1963–68; Assoc. prof., 1968–72; Dean of Grad. Studies and Research, 1972–76; Exec. Vice-Pres., 1977–78). Asst. Prof. of Sociology, Florida State Univ., Tallahassee, 1957–60. *Publs:* (as Gail J. Putney with Snell Putney) Normal Neurosis, 1964; The Adjusted American, 1966; Survival in Marriage, 1972, 1977. Add: Office of the President, San Jose State Univ., San Jose, Calif. 95192, U.S.A.

FULLMER, J(une) Z(immerman). American, b. 1920. Sciences. Prof. of the History of Science, Ohio State Univ., Columbus, since 1966. Assoc. Prof. of Chemistry, and Head, Dept. of Chemistry, Newcomb Coll., Tulane Univ., New Orleans, La., 1955–64. *Publs:* Sir Humphry Davy's Published Works, 1969. Add: Dept. of History, 106 Dulles Hall, Ohio State Univ., Columbus, Ohio 43210, U.S.A.

FULTON, Robin. British, b. 1937. Poetry, Literature, Translations. Ed., Lines Review, Edinburgh, 1967–76, and Lines Review Editions, 1970–78. *Publs:* A Matter of Definition, 1963; (trans.) An Italian Quartet: Versions After Saba, Ungaretti, Montale, Quasimodo, 1966; Instances, 1967; (trans.) Blok's Twelve, 1968; Inventories, 1969; The Spaces between the Stones, 1971; Quarters, 1971; The Man with the Surbahar, 1971; (ed.) Trio: New Poets from Edinburgh, 1971; (trans.) Selected Poems, by Lars Gustafsson, 1972; (trans.) Selected Poems, by Gunnar Harding, 1973; (trans.) Selected Poems, by Tomas Transtömer, 1974; Tree Lines, 1974; Contemporary Scottish Poetry: Individuals and Contexts, 1974; (trans.) Selected Poems by Östen Sjöstrand, 1975; (trans.) Selected Poems by Werner Aspenström, 1976; Between Flights, 1976; Places to Stay In, 1978; Following a Mirror, 1979; Selected Poems 1963-1978, 1980; (trans.) Baltics, by Transtömer, 1980; (trans.) Family Tree, by Johannes Edfelt, 1981; (trans.) Selected Poems, by Transtömer, 1981; (trans.) The Blue Whale, by W. Aspenström, 1981; Fields of Focus, 1982; (ed.) Selected Poems, by I.C. Smith, 1982; (ed.) The Complete Poems, by R. Garioch, 1982; (trans.) Starnberger See, by Gunnar Harding, 1983 (trans.) The Truth Barrier, by Transtömer, 1984; (trans.) Don't Give Me the Whole Truth, by Olav Hauge, 1985; (trans.) Béla Bartók Against the Third Reich, by Kjell Espmark, 1985; (ed.) A Garioch Miscellany, 1986; (trans.) The Complete Poems, by Transtömer, 1987; (trans. with others) Toward the Solitary Star: Selected Poetry and Prose of Östen Sjöstrand, 1988; (trans.) German Autumn, by Stig Dagerman, 1988; (trans.) Guest of Reality, by Pär Lagerkvist, 1989; The Way the Words Are Taken: Selected Essays, 1989. Add: P.O. Box 467, N 4001 Stavanger, Norway.

FUMENTO, Rocco. American, b. 1923. Novels/Short stories, Film. Assoc. Prof. of English, Univ. of Illinois, Urbana, since 1964 (joined faculty, 1952). *Publs:* Devil by the Tail, 1954; Tree of Dark Reflection, 1962; (ed.) Introduction to the Short Story, 1962; (ed.) 42nd Street, 1980. Add: 307 South Garfield Ave., Champaign, Ill. 61821 U.S.A.

FURNISH, Victor Paul. American, b. 1931. Theology/Religion. University Distinguished Prof. of New Testament, Perkins Sch. of Theology, Southern Methodist Univ., Dallas, since 1983 (Instr., 1959–60; Asst. Prof., 1960–65; Assoc. Prof., 1965–71; Prof., 1971–83). *Publs:* Theology and Ethics in Paul, 1968; The Love Command in the New Testament, 1972; (with J.H. Snow) Easter, 1975; (ed. with K. Crim and L. Bailey) The Interpreter's Dictionary of the Bible, Supplementary vol., 1976; The Moral Teaching of Paul, 1979, 1985; (with R.L. Thulin) Pentecost, 1981; (with Leander E. Keck) The Pauline Letters, 1984; II Corinthians, 1984; Lent, 1986. Add: Kirby Hall, Southern Methodist Univ., Dallas, Tex. 75275, U.S.A.

FURST, Lilian R(enee). American, b. 1931. Literature. Marcel Bataillon Prof. of Comparative Literature, Univ. of North Carolina, Chapel Hill, since 1986. Taught at the Queen's Univ. of Belfast, 1955–66, Univ. of Manchester, 1966–71, Dartmouth Coll., Hanover, N.H., 1971–72, and the Univ. of Oregon, Eugene, 1972–75; Prof. of Comparative Literature, Univ. of Texas at Dallas, 1975–86. Chmn., 19th Century Comparative Literature Section, Modern Language Assn. of America, 1979; Flora Stone Mather Visiting Prof., Case Western Reserve Univ., 1978–79; Visiting Prof. at Stanford Univ., 1981–82, and Harvard Univ., 1983–84; Kenan Distinguished Prof. in the Humanities, Coll. of William and Mary, 1985–86. *Publs:* Romanticism in Perspective, 1969, 1979; Romanticism, 1969, 1976; (with Peter N. Skrine) Naturalism, 1971; Counterparts: The Dynamics of Franco-German Literary Relations 1770-1895, 1977; The Contours of European Romanticism, 1979; European Romanticism: Self-Definition, 1980; Fictions of Romantic Irony, 1984. Add: 106 Arbutus Place, Chapel Hill, N.C. 27514, U.S.A.

FURTH, George. American, b. 1932. Plays. Actor from 1956; taught in drama dept., Univ. of Southern California, Los Angeles. *Publs:* Company, 1972; Twigs, 1972; The Supporting Cast, 1982. Add: 3030 Durand Dr., Hollywood, Calif. 90068, U.S.A.

FUSON, Ben(jamin) W(illis). American, b. 1911. Literature. Assoc. Prof. of English, Mary Baldwin Coll., Staunton, Va., 1942–44; Bridgewater Coll., Va., 1944–46; Lynchburg Coll., Va., 1946–48; Park Coll., Parkville, Mo., 1948–58; Visiting Prof. of American Studies, Meshed Univ., Iran, 1958–60; Prof. of English, Kansas Wesleyan Univ., Salina, 1960–76; Visiting Prof. of English, Kobe Coll., Nishinomiya, Japan, 1966–67 and 1973–74; Lectr. in Asian Literature, Univ. of Kentucky, 1977–79. *Publs:* Browning and His English Predecessors in the Dramatic Monolog, 1948; Centennial Bibliography of Kansas Literature, 1961; Oriental Literature Study Guide, 1969, 1970; Anti-War Asian Poetry, 1974; Islamic Literature Study Guide, 1978; Contacts with Ghandi and Nehru, 1983. Add: Rt. 1, Box 5860, Louisa, Ky. 41230, U.S.A.

FUSSELL, George Edwin. British, b. 1889. Agriculture/Forestry, Country life/Rural societies, History. Civil Servant, Ministry of Agriculture, London, 1909–49, now retired. Co-founder, British Agricultural History Soc., 1952. *Publs:* The Exploration of England 1570-1815, 1936; (ed.) Robert Loder's Farm Accounts 1610-20, 1936; The Old English Farming Books, 1523-1730, 4 vols., 1947–85; Life in an 18th Century Village, 1947; Tolpuddle to T.U.C., 1948; (ed.) Sir Hugh Plat, Delightes for Ladies, 1609, 1948; English Rural Labourer, 1949; More Old English Farming Books 1730-1793, 1950; The Farmer's Tools 1500-1900, 1952; The English Countrywomen, 1953; The English Countryman 1500-1900, 1955; The Story of Farming, 1969; Crop Nutrition, Science and Practice Before Liebig; The Classical Tradition in West European Farming, 1972; Jethro Tull: His Influence on Mechanised Agriculture, 1973; James Ward, R.A.: Animal Painter 1767-1859 and His England, 1974; Farms, Farmers, and Society, 1976; Agricultural History in Great Britain and Western Europe Before 1914, 1983; Landscape Art and the Agricultural Revolution, 1985. Add: 3 Nightingale Rd., Horsham, Sussex RH12 2NW, England.

FUSSELL, Paul. American, b. 1924. Literary criticism/History, Social commentary. Donald T. Regan Prof. of English Literature, Univ. of Pennsylvania, Philadelphia, since 1983. Instr. in English, Connecticut Coll., New London, 1951–54; Asst. Prof., 1955–59, Assoc. Prof., 1959–64, Prof. of English, 1964–76, and John DeWitt Prof. of English Literature, 1976–83, Rutgers Univ., New Brunswick, N.J.; Fulbright Lectr., Univ. of Heidelberg, 1957–58; Regional Chmn., Woodrow Wilson National Fellowship Foundn., 1962–64; Consulting Ed., Random House, Inc., 1964–65. *Publs:* Theory of Prosody in Eighteenth-Century England, 1954; (co-author) The Presence of Walt Whitman, 1962; The Rhetorical World of Augustan Humanism: Ethics and Imagery from Swift to Burke, 1965; Poetic Meter and Poetic Form, 1965, 1979; Samuel Johnson and the Life of Writing, 1971, 1986; The Great War and Modern Memory, 1975 (National Book Award); (ed.) The Ordeal of Alfred M. Hale, 1975; Abroad: British Literary Traveling Between the Wars, 1980; The Boy Scout Handbook and Other Observations, 1982; (ed.) Siegfried Sassoon's Long Journey: Selections from the Sherston Memoirs, 1983; Class: A Guide Through the American Status System, 1983, in the U.K. as Caste Marks: Style and Status in the USA, 1984; (ed.) The Norton Book of Travel, 1987; Thank God for the Atom Bomb and Other Essays, 1988. Add: 2020 Walnut St., Philadelphia, Pa. 19103, U.S.A.

FUSSNER, Frank Smith. American, b. 1920. History. Prof. Emeritus of History, Reed Coll., Portland, Ore. (joined faculty, 1950). Rancher, Circle-S Ranch, Spray, Ore. Ed., Wheeler County Historical Commn. *Publs:* The Historical Revolution, 1962; Tudor History and the Historians, 1970; (ed. and contrib.) Glimpses of Wheeler County's Past, 1975. Add: Circle-S Ranch, Spray, Ore. 97874, U.S.A.

FYSON, J(enny) G(race). British, b. 1904. Children's fiction. *Publs:* Saul and David (2 radio interludes for schools), 1952; The Three Brothers of Ur, 1964; The Journey of the Eldest Son, 1965; Friend, Fire and the Dark Wings, 1983. Add: c/o Oxford Univ. Press, Walton St., Oxford OX2 6DP, England.

G

GAAN, Margaret. Spanish, b. 1914. Novels/Short stories, Autobiography. Exec. Secty., China Mercantile Co., Shanghai, 1940–49; Programme Officer, 1950–65, Chief of the Asia Desk, 1966–68, and Deputy Regional Director for East Asia and Pakistan, 1969–74, United Nations Children's Fund; now retired. *Publs:* Last Moments of a World (autobiography), 1978; Little Sister (novel), 1983; Red Barbarian (novel), 1984; White Poppy (novel), 1985; Blue Mountain (novel), 1987. Add: 3325 Northrop Ave., Sacramento, Calif. 95864, U.S.A.

GABLIK, Suzi. American, b. 1934. Art. *Publs:* (with John Russell) Pop Art Redefined, 1970; Magritte, 1970; Progress in Art, 1976; Has Modernism Failed?, 1984. Add: 5 Westmoreland St., London W1, England.

GABRIEL, Jüri (Evald). British, b. 1940. Antiques/Furnishings, Communications/Media, Travel/Exploration/Adventure. Freelance writer, photographer, trans. and ed., literary agent and lectr; Cameraman, Associated Rediffusion Television (programme contractors), London, 1963–65; Ed., Thames & Hudson Ltd., publrs., London, 1965–67. *Publs:* Victoriana, 1969; (with L. Hemmant) Europa: Gastronomic Guide to Europe, 3 vols., 1971; Thinking About Television, 1973; (ed.) RAC Guide to British and Continental Camping and Caravanning Sites, 6 vols., 1974–81; Unqualified Success: Comprehensive Guide to Jobs for School Leavers, 1984. Add: 16 Roseneath Rd., Battersea, London SW11, England.

GADDIS, Vincent Hayes. American, b. 1913. Animals/Pets, Supernatural/Occult topics. *Publs:* Invisible Horizons, 1965; Mysterious Fires and Lights, 1967; Wide World of Magic, 1967; (with M. Gaddis) Strange World of Animals and Pets, 1970; (with M. Gaddis) Curious World of Twins, 1972; Courage in Crisis, 1973; American Indian Myths and Mysteries, 1977. Add: P.O. Box 429, Garberville, Calif. 95440, U.S.A.

GADDIS, William. American, b. 1922. Novels. *Publs:* The Recognitions, 1955; J.R. 1975; Carpenter's Gothic, 1985. Add: c/o Candida Donadio Literary Agency, 231 W. 22nd St., New York, N.Y. 10011, U.S.A.

GADNEY, Reg. British, b. 1941. Mystery/Crime/Suspense, Screenplays, Art, History. Research Fellow and Instr., Sch of Architecture and Planning, Massachusetts. Inst. of Technology, Cambridge, 1966–67; Deputy Controller, National Film Theatre, London, 1967–68; Sr. Tutor and Fellow, 1968–78, and Pro-Rector, 1978–83, Royal Coll. of Art, London Regular Contributor, London Magazine, 1964–87. *Publs:* mystery novels—Drawn Blanc, 1970; Somewhere in England, 1972; Seduction of a Tall Man, 1972; Something Worth Fighting For, 1974; The Last Hours Before Dawn (in U.S. as Victoria), 1975; The Champagne Marxist (in U.S. as The Cage), 1976; Nightshade, 1987; on art—Constable and His World, 1976; A Catalogue of Drawings and Watercolours by John Constable, R.A., with a Selection of Mezzotints by David Lucas after Constable for "English Landscape Scenery" in the Fitzwilliam Museum, Cambridge, 1976; screenplays—Forgive Our Foolish Ways, 1981; The Bell, 1982; Last Love, 1983; Kennedy, 1983; Drummonds, 1985. 2nd series, 1987; history—Kennedy, 1983; Cry Hungary!, 1986; Goldeneye, 1989; High Desire, 1989. Add: c/o Peters Fraser and Dunlop, The Chambers, Chelsea Harbour, Lots Rd., London SW10 0XF, England.

GAGE, Wilson. *See* **STEELE,** Mary Quintard.

GAGLIANO, Frank. American, b. 1931. Novels, Plays/Screenplays.

Benedum Prof. of Playwriting, West Virginia Univ., Morgantown, since 1976. Playwright-in-Residence, Royal Shakespeare Co., London, 1967–69; Asst. Prof. of Drama, Playwright-in-Residence, and Dir. of Contemporary Playwright's Center, Florida State Univ., Tallahassee, 1969–73; Lectr. in Playwriting and Dir. of the Conkle Workshop for Playwrights, Univ. of Texas, Austin, 1973–75; Distinguished Visiting Prof., Univ. of Rhode Island, 1975. *Publs:* The City Scene (3 plays), 1966; Night of the Dunce, 1967; Father Uxbridge Wants to Marry, 1968; The Hide-and-Seek Odyssey of Madeleine Gimple, 1970; Big Sur, 1970; The Prince of Peasantmania, 1970; The Private Eye of Hiram Bodini (TV play), 1971; Quasimodo (musical), 1971; Anywhere the Wind Blows (musical), 1972; In the Voodoo Parlour of Marie Laveau, 1974; The Commedia World of Lafcadio B., 1974; The Resurrection of Jackie Cramer (musical), 1974; Congo Square (musical), 1975; The Total Immersion of Madelaine Favorini, 1981; San Ysidro (dramatic cantata), 1985; From the Bodoni County Songbook Anthology, 1986, musical version 1987; Anton's Leap (novel), 1988; My Chekhov Light (play; monologue), 1988. Add: c/o Howard Buck Agency, 80 Eighth Ave., Suite 1170, New York, N.Y. 10011, U.S.A.

GAGLIARDO, John G. American, b. 1933. History. Prof. of History, Boston Univ., since 1970 (Assoc. Prof. 1968–70). Instr. and Asst. Prof. of History, Amherst Coll., Mass., 1960–65; Asst. Prof. and Assoc. Prof. of History, Univ. of Illinois at Chicago Circle, 1965–68. *Publs:* Enlightened Despotism, 1967; From Pariah to Patriot: The Changing Image of the German Peasant, 1770-1840, 1969; Reich and Nation: The Holy Roman Empire as Idea and Reality 1763-1806, 1980. Add: 10 Emerson Pl., Apt 7C, Boston, Mass. 02114, U.S.A.

GAIL, Barbara. *See* **KATZ,** Bobbi.

GAINES, Ernest J. American, b. 1933. Novels/Short stories. *Publs:* Catherine Carmier, 1964; Of Love and Dust, 1967; Bloodline (short stories), 1968; The Autobiography of Miss Jane Pitman, 1971; A Long Day in November, 1971; In My Father's House, 1978; A Gathering of Old Men, 1983. Add: 932 Divisadero St., San Francisco, Calif. 94115, U.S.A.

GAINHAM, Sarah. Pseud. for Rachel Ames. British, b. 1922. Novels/Short stories, Mystery/Crime/Suspense. Central European Corresp. for the Spectator, London, 1956–65. *Publs:* Time Right Deadly (mystery novel), 1956; The Cold Dark Night (mystery novel), 1957; The Mythmaker (mystery novel), 1957, in U.S. as Appointment in Vienna, 1958; The Stone Roses (mystery novel), 1959; The Silent Hostage (mystery novel), 1960; Night Falls on the City, 1969; A Place in the Country (novel), 1969; Takeover Bid (novel), 1972; Private Worlds (novel), 1971; Maculan's Daughter (novel), 1973; To the Opera Ball (novel), 1975; The Habsburg Twilight: Tales from Vienna, 1979; The Liger, Life, 1983. Add: Altes Forsthaus, Schlosspark, A2404 Petronell, Austria.

GAJDUSEK, D(aniel) Carleton. American, b. 1923. Medicine/Health, Autobiography/Memoirs/Personal. Chief, Study of Child Growth, Development and Behavior, and Disease Patterns in Primitive Cultures, and Dir., Lab. of Slow, Latent and Temperate Virus Infections, National Inst. of Health, Bethesda, Md., since 1958. *Publs:* Acute Infectious Hemorrhagic Fevers and Mycotoxicoses in the U.S.S.R., 1953; Journals, 1954-85, 39 vols., 1960–87; (ed. with C.J. Gibbs and M. Alpers) Slow, Latent and Temperate Virus Infections, 1965; Correspondence on the Discovery and Original Investigations of Kuru, 1975; (with J. Farquhar) Kuru, 1980. Add: National Inst. of Health, Bethesda, Md. 20205, U.S.A.

GALANTE, Pierre. French, b. 1909. International relations/Current affairs, Biography. Secty. Gen., Paris Match mag. *Publs:* The Blue Men, 1956; The Berlin Wall, 1965; The General; Malraux, 1973; Mademoiselle Chanel; Marseilles Mafia, 1975; Is Hitler Dead?: The German Generals Against Their Fuhrer, 1980; Operation Walkyrie, 1983; The American Years on the Riviera, 1985; Voices from the Bunker, 1989. Add: Paris-Match, 65 Champs Elysées, Paris 8, France.

GALBRAITH, Jean. Australian, b. 1906. Children's fiction. Poetry, Botany, Children's non-fiction. *Publs:* Garden in a Valley, 1939; Wildflowers of Victoria, 1950, 3rd rev. ed. 1967; Grandma Honeypot, 1962; From Flower to Fruit, 1962; Fruits, 1966; The Wonderful Butterfly, 1968; (co-author) Music of Faith, 2nd ed. 1960. (ed.) Bushland Notes, by Winifred Waddell, 1975; Field Guide to the Wildflowers of South East Australia, 1977; A Gardener's Year, 1985, 1987; Letters to My Friends (Known and Unknown), 1989. Add: Tyers, Vic. 3844, Australia.

GALBRAITH, J(ohn) Kenneth. American, b. 1908. Novels/Short stories, Art, Economics, International relations/Current affairs. Pres., American Academy and Inst. of Arts and Letters, since 1984. Prof. of Economics, 1949–59, and Paul M. Warburg Prof. of Economics, 1959–60, and 1963–75, now Emeritus Prof., Harvard Univ., Cambridge, Mass. (Instr. and Tutor, 1934–39). Asst. Prof. of Economics, Princeton Univ., N.J., 1939–42; Economic Adviser, National Defense Advisory Commn., 1940–41; Member, Bd. of Eds., Fortune mag., 1943–48; U.S. Ambassador to India, 1961–63. *Publs:* American Capitalism: The Concept of Countervailing Power, 1951; A Theory of Price Control, 1952; The Great Crash 1929, 1955; The Affluent Society, 1958, 3rd ed. 1978; Journey to Poland and Yugoslavia, 1959; The Liberal Hour, 1960; (under pseudonym) The McLandress Dimension (satire); Made to Last, 1964; The Economic Discipline, 1967; The New Industrial State, 1967, 3rd ed. 1979; The Triumph (novel), 1968; Ambassador's Journal, 1969; (with M.S. Randawa) Indian Painting, 1969; Economics and the Public Purpose, 1973; A China Passage, 1973; Money: Whence It Came, Where It Went, 1975; The Age of Uncertainty, 1977; (with N. Salinger) Almost Everyone's Guide to Economics, 1978; The Nature of Mass Poverty, 1979; Annals of an Abiding Liberal, 1979; The Galbraith Reader, 1979; The Nature of Mass Poverty, 1979; A Life in Our Times, 1981. The Anatomy of Power, 1983; The Voice of the Poor: Essays in Economic and Political Persuasion, 1983; A View from the Stands: Of People, Politics, Military Power, and the Arts, 1986; A History of Economics, 1987. Add: 30 Francis Ave., Cambridge, Mass. 02138, U.S.A.

GALENSON, Walter. American, b. 1914. Economics, Industrial relations. Asst. Prof. of Economics, Harvard Univ., Cambridge, Mass., 1946–51; Prof. of Economics, Univ. of California, Berkeley, 1951–66; Prof. of Economics, Cornell Univ., Ithaca, N.Y., 1966–85. *Publs:* Rival Unionism in the United States, 1940; Labor in Norway, 1949; The Danish System of Labor Relations, 1952; (ed.) Comparative Labor Movements, 1952; Labor Productivity in Soviet and American Industry, 1955; (ed.) Labor and Economic Development, 1959; The CIO Challenge to the AFL, 1960; Trade Union Democracy in Western Europe, 1961; (ed.) Labor in Developing Economics, 1962; (with F.G. Pyatt) The Quality of Labor, 1964; Primer on Employment and Wages, 1966; (ed. with A Eckstein and T.C. Liu) Economic Trends in Communist China, 1968; (with N.R. Chen) The Chinese Economy Under Communism, 1969; (ed.) Essays on Employment, 1971; (ed.) Incomes Policy: What Can We Learn from Europe?, 1973; (ed.) Labor in the Twentieth Century, 1979; (ed.) Economic Growth and Structural Change in Taiwan, 1979; The International Labor Organization: An American View, 1981; The International Labor Organization: Mirroring the U.N.'s Problems, 1982; The United Brotherhood of Carpenters and Joiners, 1983; (ed.) Foreign Trade and Investment: Economic Growth in the Newly Industrializing Asian Countries, 1985; A Welfare State Strikes Oil: The Norwegian Experience, 1986. Add: 1150 Park Ave., New York, N.Y. 10128, U.S.A.

GALINSKY, G. Karl. American, b. 1942. Classics. Prof. of Classics since 1972, and Chmn. since 1974, Univ. of Texas at Austin (Asst. Prof., 1966–68; Assoc. Prof., 1968–72). Member, Advisory Council to the Classical Sch. of the American Academy in Rome, since 1968; Member of Editorial Bd., Vergilius, since 1973. Instr., Princeton Univ., N.J., 1965–66. *Publs:* Aeneas, Sicily and Rome, 1969, 1971; (ed. with F.W. Lenz) Albii Tibulli Aliorumque carminum libri tres, 1971; The Herakles Theme, 1972; (ed.) Perspectives of Roman Poetry, 1974; (ed.) Ovid's Metamorphoses, 1975. Add: 4850 Edgemont, Austin, Tex. 78731, U.S.A.

GALLACHER, Tom. British, b. 1934. Novels/Short stories, Plays/Screenplays. Writer-in-Residence, Pitlochry Festival Theatre, 1975–78, and Royal Lyceum Theatre, Edinburgh, 1978–81. *Publs:* plays—Mr. Joyce Is Leaving Paris, 1972; Revival! and Schellenbrack, 1978; Jenny, 1980; fiction—Hunting Shadows, 1981; Apprentice, 1983; Journeyman, 1984; Survivor, 1985; The Jewel Maker, 1986; The Wind on the Heath, 1987. Add: c/o Michael Imison Playwrights Ltd., 28 Almeida St., London N1 1TD, England.

GALLAGHER, James Roswell. American, b. 1903. Medicine/Health, Psychology. Chief Emeritus, Adolescents' Unit, Children's Hosp. Medical Centre, Boston, Mass., since 1969 (Chief, 1951–67); Clinical Prof. Emeritus of Pediatrics, Yale Univ. Sch. of Medicine, New Haven, Conn., since 1971 (Prof., 1967–71). Sch. Physician, Phillips Academy, Andover, Mass., 1934–50; Clinical Prof. of Pediatrics, Harvard Medical Sch., Boston, Mass., 1951–67. *Publs:* Understanding Your Son's Adolescence, 1951; (with H.I. Harris) Emotional Problems of Adolescence, 1958, 3rd ed. 1975; Medical Care of the Adolescent, 1960, 3rd ed. (with F. Heald and D. Garrell) 1975; (with I. Goldberger and G. Hallock) Health for Life, 1961; (ed. with T.E. Cone and R.P. Masland) The Medical Clinics of North America: The Medical Care of the Adolescent, 1965. Add: 67 Mill Rock Rd., New Hamden, Conn. 06517, U.S.A.

GALLAGHER, Patricia. American. Historical/Romance/Gothic. *Publs:* The Sons and the Daughters, 1961; Answer to Heaven, 1964; The Fires of Brimstone, 1966; Shannon., 1967; Shadows of Passion, 1971; Summer of Sighs, 1971; The Thicket, 1974; Castles in the Air, 1976; Mystic Rose, 1977; No Greater Love, 1979; All for Love, 1981; Echoes and Embers, 1983; On Wings of Dreams, 1985; Love Springs Eternal, 1985; A Perfect Love, 1987. Add: c/o Richard Curtis Assocs., 164 E. 64th St., New York, N.Y. 10021, U.S.A.

GALLAGHER, Tess. American. Novels/Short stories, Plays/-Screenplays, Poetry, Essays. Lectr., Syracuse Univ., N.Y., since 1980. Taught at St. Lawrence Univ., Canton, N.Y., 1974–75, Kirkland Coll., Clinton, N.Y., 1975–77, Univ. of Montana, Missoula 1977–78, and Univ. of Arizona, Tucson, 1979–80. *Publs:* Stepping Outside, 1974; Instructions to the Double, 1976; Under Stars, 1978; Portable Kisses, 1978; Willingly, 1984; A Concert of Tenses: Essays on Poetry, 1986; The Lover of Horses, 1986; Amplitude: New and Selected Poems, 1987. Add: English Dept., Syracuse Univ., Syracuse, N.Y. 13210, U.S.A.

GALLAHER, Art, Jr. American, b. 1925. Anthropology/Ethnology. Prof. of Anthropology since 1963, and Chancellor, since 1981, Univ. of Kentucky, Lexington (Deputy Dir., Center for Developmental Change, 1966–70; Chmn., Dept. of Anthropology, 1970–72; Dean of Coll. of Arts and Sciences, 1972–80). Asst. to Assoc. Prof., Dept. of Sociology and Anthropology, Univ. of Houston; Assoc. Prof., Univ. of Nebraska, 1962–63. *Publs:* Plainville Fifteen Years Later, 1961; (ed.) Perspectives in Developmental Change, 1968; (ed. with Harland Padfield) The Dying Community, 1980. Add: Office of the Chancellor, Univ. of Kentucky, Lexington, Ky. 40506, U.S.A.

GALLANT, Mavis. Canadian, b. 1922. Novels/Short stories. Regular Contrib., The New Yorker mag., NYC, since 1951. *Publs:* The Other Paris (short stories), 1956; Green Water, Green Sky, 1959; My Heart Is Broken: Eight Stories and a Short Novel (in U.K. as An Unmarried Man's Summer), 1964; A Fairly Good Time, 1970; The Pegnitz Junction: A Novella and Five Short Stories, 1973; The End of the World and Other Stories, 1975; From the Fifteenth District: A Novella and Eight Short Stories, 1979; Home Truths, 1981; Overhead in a Balloon (stories), 1985; Paris Notebooks: Essays and Reviews, 1987; In Transit (stories), 1988. Add: 14 rue Jean Ferrandi, Paris VI, France.

GALLANT, Noelle. *See* **BERMAN,** Clare.

GALLANT, Roy Arthur. American, b. 1924. Astronomy, Biology, Chemistry, Children's non-fiction, Earth sciences, Environmental science/Ecology, Zoology, Biography. Dir., Southworth Planetarium, and Adjunct Prof. of English, Univ. of Southern Maine, since 1980. Member of faculty, American Museum-Hayden Planetarium, 1972–80. Managing Ed., Scholastic Teacher mag., 1954–57; Exec. Ed., Aldus Books Ltd., London, 1959–62; Ed.-in-Chief, The Natural History Press, 1962–64. *Publs:* Exploring the Moon, 1955; Exploring Mars, 1956; Exploring the Universe, 1956; Exploring the Weather, 1957; Exploring the Sun, 1958; Exploring the Planets, 1958; Exploring Chemistry, 1958; Man's Reach into Space, 1959; Exploring Under the Earth, 1960; (ed. with Fisher & Sir J. Huxley) Nature, 1960; (ed. with F. Debenham) Discovery and Exploration, 1960; (ed. with F. Manley) Geography, 1961; Antarctic,

1962; The ABC's of Astronomy, 1963; (ed. with G.E.R. Deacon) Seas, Maps and Men, 1963; The ABC's of Chemistry, 1963; (ed. with H. Garnott) Treasures of Yesterday, 1964; (ed. with T.F. Gaskell) World Beneath the Oceans, 1964; (ed. with C.A. Ronan) Man Probes the Universe, 1964; (ed. with R. Clark) Explorers of the World, 1964; (with C.J. Schuberth) Discovering Rocks and Minerals, 1967; (ed. with McElroy) Foundations of Biology, 1968; Man Must Speak, 1969; (ed. with C.E. Swartz) Measure and Find Out 1-3, 1969; (ed.) Charting the Universe, 1969; (ed.) The Universe in Motion, 1969; (ed.) Gravitation, 1969; (ed.) The Message of Starlight, 1969; (ed.) The Life Story of a Star, 1969; (ed.) Galaxies and the Universe, 1969; Man's Reach for the Stars, 1971; Me and My Bones, 1971; Man the Measurer, 1972; Charles Darwin, 1972; Explorers of the Atom, 1973; (with R.A. Suthers) Biology: The Behavioral View, 1973; Astrology: Sense or Nonsense?, 1974; How Life Began, 1975; Beyond Earth, 1977; Fires in the Sky, 1978; Earth's Changing Climate, 1979; The Constellations, 1979; You and Your Memory, 1980; The National Geographic Atlas of Our Universe, 1980; (with Isaac Asimov) Ginn Science Program (grades 4-8), 1981; The Planets, 1982; Once Around the Galaxy, 1982; (contrib.) Science and Evolution, 1984; 101 Questions About the Universe, 1984; Lost Cities, 1985; Fossils, 1985; Ice Ages, 1985; Macmillan Book of Astronomy, 1986; Our Restless Earth, 1986; From Living Cells to Dinosaurs, 1986; The Rise of Mammals, 1986; Private Lives of the Stars, 1986; Rainbows, Mirages and Sundogs, 1987; When the Sun Dies: The Story of Evolution, 1989; Ancients Indians, 1989; The Peopling of Planet Earth, 1989. Add: P.O. Box 228, Rangeley, Me. 04970, U.S.A.

GALLEYMORE, Frances. British, b. 1946. Novels. Freelance novelist and television playwright. *Publs:* The Orange Tree, 1970; Ground Wave Sailing, 1975. Add: Peter Fraser and Dunlop, The Chambers, Chelsea Harbour, Lots Rd., London SW10 0XF, England.

GALLOWAY, Allan Douglas. British, b. 1920. Theology/Religion. Prof. of Divinity, Univ. of Glasgow, 1968–82, now Emeritus (Sr. Lectr., 1960–66; Reader in Divinity, 1966–68; Gifford Lectr., 1984); Principal of Trinity Coll., Glasgow, 1972–82. Prof. of Religious Studies, Univ. of Ibadan, Nigeria, 1954–60. *Publs:* The Cosmic Christ, 1951; Basic Readings in Theology, 1964; Faith in a Changing Culture, 1966; Wolfhart Pannenberg, 1973; History of Christian Theology, Vol. 1, Pt. III, 1986. Add: 5 Straid Bheag, Clynder, Helensburgh, Dunbartonshire GQ4 0QX, Scotland.

GALLUN, Raymond Z(inke). American, b. 1911. Science fiction/Fantasy. Science Fiction magazine writer, since 1929. Construction worker for Army Corps of Engineers, 1942–43; marine blacksmith, Pearl Harbor Navy Yard, 1944; Technical Writer, EDO Corp., College Point, N.Y., 1964–75. *Publs:* (as William Callahan) The Machine That Thought (short stories), 1940; People Minus X, 1957; The Planet Strappers, 1961; The Eden Cycle, 1974; The Best of Raymond Z. Gallun (short stories), 1978; Skyclimber, 1981; Bioblast, 1985; Science Fiction and Me (autobiography), 1985. Add: 110-20 71st St., Forest Hills, N.Y. 11375, U.S.A.

GALLWEY, W. Timothy. American, b. 1938. Sports/Physical education/Keeping fit. Founding Pres., Inner Game Resources, Westwood, Calif., since 1974. English Teacher, Phillips Exeter Academy, Exeter, N.H., 1960–61; Dir. of Admissions, Mackinac Coll., Michigan, 1965–69; tennis professional, Meadowbrook Swim and Tennis Club, Seaside, Calif., 1970–71. *Publs:* The Inner Game of Tennis, 1974; Inner Tennis: Playing the Game, 1976; (with R. Kriegel) Inner Skiing, 1977; The Inner Game of Golf, 1981; (with B. Green) The Inner Games of Music, 1986. Add: c/o Doubleday and Co., Inc., 666 Fifth Ave., New York, N.Y. 10103, U.S.A.

GALVIN, Brendan. American, b. 1938. Poetry. Prof. of English, Central Connecticut State Univ., New Britain (member of the faculty since 1969). Instr. in English, Northeastern Univ., Boston, 1964–65; Asst. Prof. of English, Slippery Rock State Coll., Pennsylvania, 1968–69. *Publs:* The Narrow Land, 1971; The Salt Farm, 1972; No Time for Good Reasons, 1974; The Minutes No One Owns, 1977; Atlantic Flyway, 1980; Winter Oysters, 1983; A Birder's Dozen, 1984; Seals in the Inner Harbor, 1986; Raising Irish Walls, 1989; Wampanoag Traveler, 1989. Add: P.O. Box 54, Durham, Conn. 06422, U.S.A.

GALWEY, Geoffrey (Valentine). British, b. 1912. Novels/Short stories, Plays/Screenplays, Songs, lyrics and libretti. Copy Writer and Account Exec., 1933, and Dir., 1936–76, Lovell and Rupert Curtis Ltd., advertising agency, London. Ed., The Bulldozer mag., 1941–42; Co-ed. with H.S. Coleman, Modelcraft Mag., 1947–49. *Publs:* Murder on

Leave, 1947; The Lift and the Drop, 1948; Full Fathom Five, 1949; (with H.S. Coleman) Ship Modelmaking; Babel (play), 1970; Heart of Oak, 1982. Add: Tower Cottage, Palmers Lane, Walberswick, Southwold, Suffolk IP18 6TQ, England.

GAMBLE, Andrew Michael. British, b. 1947. Economics, History, Politics/Government, Social commentary/phenomena. Prof., Univ. of Sheffield, since 1986 (Reader, 1982–86). *Publs:* (with P. Walton) From Alienation to Surplus Value, 1972; The Conservative Nation, 1974; (with P. Walton) Capitalism in Crisis: Inflation and the State, 1976; An Introduction to Modern Social and Political Thought, 1981; Britain in Decline, 1981; (with S.A. Walkland) The British Party System and Economic Policy 1945-83, 1984; The Free Economy and the Strong State, 1988. Add: Dept. of Politics, Univ. of Sheffield, Sheffield S10 2TN, England.

GAMSON, William A(nthony). American, b. 1934. Politics/Government, Social sciences. Prof. of Sociology, Boston College, Chestnut Hill, Mass., since 1982. Research Assoc. in Social Psychology, Harvard Univ., Cambridge, Mass., 1959–62; Research Sociologist, Center for Research on Conflict Resolution, 1962–71; Prof. of Sociology, Univ. of Michigan, Ann Arbor, 1966–82 (Asst. Prof., 1962–64; Assoc. Prof., 1964–66; Chmn., 1974–78). *Publs:* Power and Discontent, 1968; SIMSOC: Simulated Society, 1969, 3rd ed. 1978; (with Andre Modigliani) Untangling the Cold War, 1971; (with Modigliani) Conceptions of Social Life: A Text-Reader for Social Psychology, 1974; The Strategy of Social Protest, 1975; (with B. Fireman and S. Rytina) Encounters with Unjust Authority, 1982; What's News: A Game Simulation of TV News, 1984. Add: R.F.D. 1, Box 11A, Chilmark, Mass. 02535, U.S.A.

GAMST, Frederick Charles. American, b. 1936. Anthropology/Ethnology. Prof. of Anthropology, Univ. of Massachusetts, Boston, since 1975 (Assoc. Provost for Graduate Studies, 1978–83). Instr., 1966–67, Asst. Prof., 1967–71, and Assoc. Prof., 1971–75, Rice Univ., Houston. Acting Dir., Houston Inter-Univ. African Studies Prog. 1968–71. *Publs:* Travel and Research in Northwestern Ethiopia, Notes for Anthropologists and Other Field Workers in Ethiopia No. 2, 1965; The Qemant: A Pagan-Hebraic Peasantry of Ethiopia, 1969; Peasants in Complex Society, 1974; Studies in Cultural Anthropology, 1975; (with E. Norbeck) Ideas of Culture, 1976; The Hoghead: An Indstrial Ethnology of the Locomotive Engineer, 1980. Add: Dept. of Anthropology, Univ. of Massachusetts, Harbor Campus, Boston, Mass. 02125, U.S.A.

GANDEVIA, Bryan Harle. Australian, b. 1925. Medicine/Health. Sr. Fellow, Occupational Health, Univ. of Melbourne, 1958–62; Assoc. Prof. of Respiratory Medicine, Univ. of New South Wales, 1963–85. *Publs:* The Melbourne Medical Students, 1862-1942, 1948; Tears Often Shed: Child Health and Welfare in Australia since 1788, 1978; (with A. Holster and S. Simpson) Annotated Bibliography of the History of Medicine and Health in Australia, 1984; Life in the First Settlement at Sydney Cove, 1985. Add: Cregganduff, Mt. York Rd., Mount Victoria, N.S.W. 2786, Australia.

GANDLEY, Kenneth Royce. *See* **ROYCE,** Kenneth.

GANN, Ernest K(ellogg). American, b. 1910. Novels, Historical/Romance, Plays/Screenplays, Air/Space topics, Autobiography/Memoirs. Freelance writer, since 1939. Captain, U.S. Air Force Air Transport Command, 1942–46. *Publs:* Island in the Sky, 1945, as screenplay, 1953; Blaze at Noon, 1947; Benjamin Lawless, 1948; Fiddler's Green, 1950; Twilight for the Gods, 1950, as screenplay, 1958; The Raging Tide (screenplay), 1951; The High and the Mighty, 1953, as screenplay, 1954; Soldier of Fortune, 1954, as screenplay, 1955; Trouble with Lazy Ethel, 1958; Of Good and Evil, 1963; In the Company of Eagles, 1967; The Song of the Siren, 1968; The Antagonists, 1970; Band of Brothers, 1973; Brain 2000, 1980; The Aviator, 1981; The Magistrate, 1982; Gentlemen of Adventure, 1983; The Triumph, 1986; The Bad Angel, 1987; other—Sky Roads, 1940; All American Aircraft, 1941; Getting Them into the Blue, 1942; Fate Is the Hunter (memoirs), 1961; Flying Circus, 1974; A Hostage to Fortune (memoirs), 1978; The Black Watch: America's Spy Pilots and Their Planes, 1989. Add: Box 727, Friday Harbour, Wash. 98250, U.S.A.

GANN, Lewis Henry. American, b. 1924. History. Sr. Fellow, Hoover Inst., Stanford Univ., Calif., since 1964. Member, Editorial Bd., Intercollegiate Review. *Publs:* The Birth of a Plural Society: The Development of Northern Rhodesia Under the British South Africa Company 1894-1914, 1958; (with P. Duignan) White Settlers in Tropical Africa, 1962; A History of Northern Rhodesia: Early Days to 1953, 1964; (with M. Gelfand) Huggins of Rhodesia: The Man and His Country, 1964; A

History of Southern Rhodesia: Early Days to 1934, 1965; (with P. Duignan) Burden of Empire: An Appraisal of Western Colonialism in Africa South of the Sahara, 1967; Central Africa: The Former British States, 1971; Guerrillas in History, 1971; (with P. Duignan) Africa and the World at Large: An Introduction to the History of the Sub-Saharan Africa from Antiquity to 1840, 1972; (with P. Duignan) Colonialism in Africa 1870-1960, 5 vols., 1969–73; (with P. Duignan) The Rulers of German Africa 1884-1914, 1977; (with P. Duignan) The Rulers of British Africa 1870-1914, 1978; (with P. Duignan) South Africa: War, Revolution or Peace, 1978; (with P. Duignan) The Rulers of Belgian Africa 1884-1914, 1979; (with P. Duignan) Why South Africa Will Survive, 1981; (with T. Henriksen) The Struggle for Zimbabwe, 1981; (with P. Duignan) The U.S. and Africa: A History, 1984; (with P. Duignan) The Hispanics in the U.S., 1986; (with Arthur J. Knoll) Germans in the Tropics: Essays in German Colonial History, 1987. Add: Hoover Inst., Stanford Univ., Stanford, Calif. 94305, U.S.A.

GANNETT, Ruth Stiles. American, b. 1923. Children's fiction. Medical Technician, Boston City Hosp.; Radar Research Technician, Massachusetts Inst. of Technology, Cambridge; Staff member, Children's Book Council, NYC. *Publs:* My Father's Dragon, 1948; The Wonderful House-Boat-Train, 1949; Elmer and the Dragon, 1950; The Dragons of Blueland, 1951; Katie and the Sad Noise, 1961. Add: BD-2, Box 334, Trumansburg, N.Y. 14886, U.S.A.

GANS, Eric L. American, b. 1941. Literature. Prof. of French, since 1976, and Chmn. of Dept., 1974–77, and 1981–86, Univ. of California at Los Angeles (Asst. Prof., 1969–73; Assoc. Prof., 1973–76). Instr. in French, State Univ. of New York at Fredonia, 1965–67; Asst. Prof., Dept. of French and Italian, Indiana Univ., Blooming, 1967–69. *Publs:* The Discovery of Illusion: Flaubert's Early Works 1835-1837, 1971; Un Pari Contre l'Histoire: Les Premières Nouvelles de Mérimée, 1972; Musset et le Drame Tragique, 1974; Le Paradoxe de Phèdre, 1975; Essais d'esthétique paradoxale, 1977; The Origin of Language: A Formal Theory of Representation, 1981; The End of Culture: Toward a Generative Anthropology, 1985; Madame Bovary: The End of Romance, 1989. Add: Dept. of French, Univ. of Calfornia at Los Angeles, Los Angeles, Calif. 90024, U.S.A.

GANS, Herbert J(ulius). American, b. 1927. Sociology. Robert S. Lynd Prof. of Sociology, Columbia Univ., NYC, since 1985 (Prof. of Sociology-Ford Foundn. Urban Chair, 1971–85). Advisory Ed., Ethnic and Racial Studies, Journal of Contemporary Ethnography, Journal of Communications, and Social Policy (Film Critic, 1971–78). Research Asst., American Soc. of Planning Officials, Chicago, 1950; Asst. Planner, Chicago Housing Authority, 1950–51; Chief Research Planner, P.A.C.E. Assocs., Chicago, 1951–52; Field Rep., Div. of Slum Clearance, U.S. Housing and Home Finance Agency, Washington, 1952–53; Research Assoc., Inst. for Urban Studies, 1953–57, Lectr., Dept. of City Planning, 1956–57, Asst. Prof. of City Planning, Inst. for Urban Studies and Dept. of City Planning, 1958–61, Lectr., Dept. of Sociology, 1958–59, and Research Assoc. Prof. of City Planning and Urban Studies, 1961–64, Univ. of Pennsylvania, Philadelphia; Assoc. Prof. of Sociology and Education, 1964–66, Research Assoc., Inst. of Urban Studies, 1964–65, and Adjunct Prof. of Sociology and Education, 1966–69, Teachers' Coll., Columbia Univ., NYC; Prof. of Sociology and Planning, Dept. of Urban Studies and Planning, Massachusetts Inst. of Technology, and Faculty Assoc., M.I.T.-Harvard Joint Center for Urban Studies, Cambridge, Mass., 1969–71. Member of the Council, American Sociological Assn., 1968–71; Member of Exec. Cttee., Soc. for the Study of Social Problems, 1968–71; Pres., Eastern Sociological Soc 1972–73; Pres., American Sociological Assn., 1987–88. *Publs:* The Urban Villagers, 1962, 1982; The Levittowners, 1967, 1982; People and Plans, 1968; More Equality, 1973; Popular Culture and High Culture, 1974; Deciding What's News, 1979; (co-ed.) On the Making of Americans, 1979; Middle American Individualism, 1988. Add: Dept. of Sociology, Columbia Univ., New York, N.Y. 10027, U.S.A.

GANT, Jonathan. *See* **ADAMS,** Clifton.

GANT, Richard. *See* **FREEMANTLE,** Brian.

GANTNER, Neilma. *See* **SIDNEY,** Neilma.

GARB, Solomon. American, b. 1920. Medicine/Health. Assoc. Clinical Prof. of Medicine, Univ. of Colorado Medical Center, since 1974. Research Fellow in Pharmacology, 1949–50, Instr. in Pharmacology, 1950–53, Asst. Prof. of Clinical Pharmacology, 1953–56, and Asst. Prof. of Pharmacology, 1956–57, Cornell Univ. Medical Coll.; Assoc. Prof. of

Pharmacology, Albany Medical Coll., 1957–61; Assoc. Prof. of Pharmacology, 1961–66, Prof. of Pharmacology and Assoc. Prof. of Community Health, 1966–70, Univ. of Missouri Medical Sch.; Scientific Dir., American Medical Center, Denver, 1970–80. *Publs:* Laboratory Tests in Common Use, 1956, 6th ed. 1976; Essentials of Therapeutic Nutrition, 1958; (with B. Chrim) Pharmacology and Patient Care, 1962, 3rd ed. 1970; (with E. Eng) Disaster Handbook, 1964, 1969; A Cure for Cancer—A National Goal, 1968; Clinical Guide to Undesirable Drug Interactions, 1971, 1974; Abbreviations and Acronyms in Medicine and Nursing, 1976; (with S. Gross) Cancer Treatment and Research in Humanistic Perspective, 1985. Add: 6401 West Colfax Ave., Lakewood, Colo, 80214, U.S.A.

GARD, Janice. *See* **LATHAM,** Jean Lee.

GARD, Joyce. Pseud. for Joyce Reeves. British, b. 1911. Children's fiction, Translations. Asst., Foreign Rights Dept., Curtis Brown Ltd., London, 1934–35; Teacher, Varndean Sch. for Girls, Brighton, 1935–37; lived in Paris, 1937–39; Trans. and contrib., XX Siècle art review, Paris, 1939–70; Temporary Administrative Asst., Ministry of Economic Warfare, London, 1939–45; Civil Servant, Frankfurt and Hamburg, 1945–47; Apprentice, Winchcombe Pottery, Glos., 1947–48; Studio Potter, London and Newhaven, Sussex, 1948–56; Part-time Private Secty. and research Asst. to Roland Penrose, London, 1956–72. *Publs:* Woorroo, 1961; (trans.) Journey to the Centre of the Earth, by Jules Verne, 1961; The Dragon of the Hill, 1963; Talargain, The Seal's Whelp, 1964; Smudge of the Fells, 1965; The Snow Firing, 1967; The Mermaid's Daughter, 1969; (trans. as Joyce Reeves) Marc Chagall: Drawings and Water Colours for the Ballet, by Jacques Lassaigne, 1969; Handysides Shall Not Fall, 1975; The Hagwaste Donkeys, 1976. Add: 1 Eliza Cottages, Charing, Ashford, Kent TN27 0JG, England.

GARDAM, Jane. British, b. 1928. Novels/Short stories, Children's fiction. Sub-Ed., Weldons Ladies Journal, London, 1952–53; Asst. Literary Ed., Time and Tide, London, 1953–55. *Publs:* A Few Fair Days, 1971; A Long Way from Verona, 1971; The Summer After the Funeral, 1973; Black Faces, White Faces, 1975; Bilgewater, 1977; God on the Rocks, 1978; The Sidmouth Letters (short stories), 1980; Bridget and William, 1981; The Hollow Land, 1981; Horse, 1982; The Pangs of Love and Other Stories, 1983; Kit, 1983; Crusoe's Daughter, 1985; Kit in Boots, 1986; Swan, 1987; Through the Doll's House Door, 1987; Showing the Flag, 1989. Add: Haven House, Sandwich, Kent, England.

GARDEN, Bruce. *See* **MACKAY,** James Alexander.

GARDEN, Edward (James Clarke). British, b. 1930. Music. Prof. of Music since 1975, and Dean of the Faculty of Arts since 1988, Univ. of Sheffield. Member of Music Staff, Clifton Coll., Bristol, 1954–57; Dir. of Music, Loretto, nr. Edinburgh, 1957–66; Sr. Lectr. in Music, Univ. of Glasgow, 1966–75. *Publs:* Balakirev: A Critical Study of His Life and Music, 1967; Tchaikovsky, 1973; Tschaikowsky: Leben und Werk, 1986. Add: 91 Millhouses Lane, Sheffield, England.

GARDEN, Nancy. American, b. 1938. Children's fiction, Children's non-fiction. Contrib. Ed., Junior Scholastic mag., NYC, 1969–70; contrib. Ed., American Observer mag., 1970–72; Ed., Houghton Mifflin Co., Boston, 1971–76. *Publs:* Berlin: City Split in Two, 1971; What Happened in Marston, 1971; The Loners, 1972; Vampires, 1973; Werewolves, 1973; Witches, 1975; Devils and Demons, 1976; Fours Crossing, 1980; The Kid's Code and Cipher Book, 1981; Annie on My Mind, 1982; Watersmeet, 1983; Prisoner of Vampires, 1984; Peace, O River, 1985; The Door Between, 1987; Mystery of the Night Raiders, 1987; Mystery of the Midnight Menace, 1988; Mystery of the Secret Masks, 1989. Add: c/o McIntosh & Otis, Inc., 310 Madison Ave., New York, N.Y. 10017, U.S.A.

GARDINER, Patrick. British, b. 1922. Philosophy. Fellow and Tutor in Philosophy, Magdalen Coll., Oxford, since 1958 (Lectr., Wadham Coll., 1949–52; Research Fellow, St. Antony's Coll., 1952–58). *Publs:* The Nature of Historical Explanation 1952; (ed.) Theories of History, 1959; Schopenhauer, 1963; (ed.) Nineteenth-Century Philosophy, 1969; (ed.) The Philosophy of History, 1974; Kierkegaard, 1988. Add: Magdalen Coll., Oxford, England.

GARDNER, (Robert) Brian. British, b. 1931. History, Biography. Feature Writer, Western Mail, 1956–57; Reporter, Sunday Times, 1957; Feature Writer, Sunday Express, 1957–61; Television Critic, Daily Sketch, 1963–64. *Publs:* The Big Push, 1961; German East, 1963; The Wasted Hour, 1963; (anthologist) Up the Line to Death, 1964; Allenby, 1965;

(anthologist) The Terrible Rain, 1966; Mafeking, 1966; The Quest for Timbuctoo, 1968; (anthologist) Churchill in His Time, 1968; The Lion's Cage, 1969; The African Dream, 1970; The East India Company, 1971; The Public Schools, 1973. Add: c/o Methuen, 11 New Fetter Lane, London EC4P 4EE, England.

GARDNER, Edward Clinton. American, b. 1920. Theology/Religion. Prof. of Christian Ethics, Candler Sch. of Theology, Emory Univ., Atlanta, Ga., since 1954. Pastor, South Meriden Methodist Church, Conn., 1948–49; Asst. Prof., of Philosophy and Religion, North Carolina State Coll., Raleigh, 1949–54. *Publs:* Biblical Faith and Social Ethics, 1960; The Church as a Prophetic Community, 1967; Christocentrism in Christian Social Ethics, 1983. Add: 2504 Tanglewood Rd., Decatur, Ga. 30033, U.S.A.

GARDNER, Herb(ert). American, b. 1934. Novels, Plays/Screenplays. *Publs:* plays—The Elevator, 1952; A Thousand Clowns, 1962; Who Is Harry Kellerman and Why Is He Saying Those Terrible Things About Me? (screenplay), 1971; The Goodbye People, 1974; Thieves, 1979; I'm Not Rappaport, 1985; novel—A Piece of the Action, 1958. Add: c/o Samuel French Inc., 45 W. 25th St., New York, N.Y. 10010, U.S.A.

GARDNER, John (Edmund). British, b. 1926. Mystery/Crime/-Suspense, Autobiography/Memoirs/Personal. Theatre Critic and Arts Ed., Stratford-upon-Avon Herald, 1959–65. *Publs:* Spin The Bottle (autobiography), 1964; The Liquidator, 1964; The Understrike, 1965; Amber Nine, 1966; Madrigal, 1967; Hideaway (stories) 1968; A Complete State of Death, 1969; Founder Member, 1969; The Censor, 1969; Traitor's Exit, 1970; The Airline Pirates (in U.S. as Air Apparent), 1970; Every Night's a Bullfight (in U.S. as Every Night's a Festival), 1971; The Assassination File (stories) 1974; The Corner Men, 1974; The Return of Moriarty, 1974; A Killer for a Song, 1975; the Revenge of Moriarty, 1975; To Run a Little Faster, 1976; The Werewolf Trace, 1977; The Dancing Dodo, 1978; The Nostradamus Traitor, 1979; The Garden of Weapons, 1980; License Renewed, 1981; For Special Services, 1982; The Quiet Dogs, 1982; Icebreaker, 1983; Flamingo, 1983; Role of Honour, 1984; The Secret Generations, 1985; Nobody Lives Forever, 1986; Scorpius, 1988; The Secret Houses, 1988; Licence to Kill (book of film), 1989; The Secret Families, 1989; Win Lose or Die, 1989. Add: c/o Desmond Elliott, Kingsbury House, 15-17 King St., St. James's, London SW1Y 6QU, England.

GARDNER, Miriam. *See* **BRADLEY,** Marion Zimmer.

GARDNER, Nancy Bruff. *See* **BRUFF,** Nancy.

GARDNER, Paul. British, b. 1930. Recreation/Leisure/Hobbies, Social commentry/phenomena, Sports/Physical education/Keeping fit. Executive Ed., KICK Mag., NYC, since 1983. Fellow, Pharmaceutical Soc. of Great Britain, since 1952. Asst. Ed., Pharmacy Digest, London, 1953–59; Asst. Managing Ed., MD of Canada, N.Y. and Montreal, 1960–64. *Publs:* (with P. Woosnam) Soccer, 1972; Pele: The Master and His Method, 1973; Nice Guys Finish Last, 1975; The World of Soccer, 1975; The Simplest Game, 1976; (co-ed.) The International Book of Soccer, 1977. Add: 73 W. 82nd St., Apt. 5W, New York, N.Y. 10024, U.S.A.

GARDNER, Ralph D. American, b. 1923. Literature, Biography. Pres., Ralph Gardner Advertising, NYC, since 1955. Host, Ralph Gardner's Bookshelf, WVNJ-Radio, NYC. Staff member, New York Times, 1942–55. *Publs:* Horatio Alger, or the American Hero Era, 1964, 1978; Road to Success: The Bibliography of the Works of Horatio Alger, 1971; Introduction to Silas Snobden's Office Boy, 1973; Introduction to Cast Upon the Breakers, 1974; A Fancy of Hers, 1981; History of Street and Smith, 1981; Struggling Upward, 1984; Writers Talk to Ralph D. Gardner, 1989. Add: 135 Central Park West, New York, N.Y., 10023, U.S.A.

GARDNER, Richard A. American, b. 1931. Children's fiction, Children's non-fiction, Medicine/Health, Psychiatry. Private practice, adult and child psychiatry and psychoanalysis, Cresskill, N.J., since 1963. Attending Psychiatrist, Presbyterian Hosp., NYC; Prof. of Psychiatry, Div. of Child Psychiatry, Columbia Univ. Coll. of Physicians and Surgeons, NYC; Assoc. Attending Psychiatrist, New York State Psychiatric Inst. Formerly, Member of faculty, William W. White Psychoanalytic Inst., NYC. *Publs:* The Child's Book About Brain Injury, 1966; The Boys' and Girls' Book About Divorce, 1970; Therapeutic Communication with Children: The Mutual Storytelling Technique, 1971; Dr. Gardner's Stories About the Real World, 1972; MBD: The Family Book About Minimal Brain Dysfunction, 1973; Understanding Children: A Parents' Guide

to Child Rearing, 1973; Dr. Gardner's Fairy Tales for Today's Children, 1974; Psychotherapeutic Approaches to the Resistant Child, 1975; Psychotherapy with Children of Divorce, 1976; Dr. Gardner's Modern Fairy Tales, 1977; The Parents' Book About Divorce, 1977; The Boys' and Girls' Book about One-Parent Families, 1977; The Objective Diagnosis of Minimal Brain Dysfunction, 1979; Dorothy and the Lizard of Oz, 1980; The Boys' and Girls' Book about Stepfamilies, 1981; Dr. Gardner's Fables for Our Times, 1981; Family Evaluation in Child Custody Litigation, 1982; Separation Anxiety Disorder, 1985; Psychotherapeutic Techniques, 1986; Child Custody Litigation: A Guide to Parents and Mental Health Professionals, 1986; Hyperactivity, The So-Called Attention Deficit Disorder, and The Group of MBD Syndromes, 1987; The Parental Alienation Syndrome, 1987; Psychotherapy with Adolescents, 1988; Family Evaluation in Child Custody Mediation, Arbitration, and Litigation, 1989. Add: P.O. Box R, Cresskill, N.J. 07626, U.S.A.

GARDONS, S.S. *See* **SNODGRASS,** W.D.

GARFIELD, Brian (F.W.). Also writes as Bennett Garland, Alex Hawk, John Ives, Drew Mallory, Frank O'Brian, Jonas Ward, Brian Wynne, and Frank Wynne. American, b. 1939. Mystery/Crime/Suspense, Historical/Romance/Gothic, Westerns/Adventure, Plays/Screenplays, Film, History. Pres., Shan Productions Co. Inc. (motion picture productions), and Dir., Mystery Writers of America, Inc., both since 1974. Vice-Pres., 1965–66, Pres., 1966–67, and Dir., 1967–68, Western Writers of America Inc; Pres., Mystery Writers of America, Inc., 1983. *Publs:* Range Justice, 1960; The Arizonans, 1961; (as Frank Wynne) Massacre Basin, 1961; (as Frank Wynne) The Big Snow, 1962; (as Frank O'Brian) The Rimfire Murders, 1962; The Lawbringers, 1962; (as Frank Wynne) Arizona Rider, 1962; Trail Drive, 1962; (as Bennett Garland) Seven Brave Men, 1962, under own name, 1969; Vultures in the Sun, 1963; Apache Canyon, 1963; (as Frank Wynne) Dragoon Pass, 1963; (as Bennett Garland, with T.V. Olsen) High Storm, 1963, under own name, 1969; (as Frank Wynne) Rio Concho, 1964; (as Frank Wynne) Rails West, 1964; (as Bennett Garland) The Last Outlaw, 1964, under own name, 1969; (as Brian Wynne) Mr. Sixgun, 1964; The Vanquished, 1964; (as Frank Wynne) Lynch Law Canyon, 1965; (as Brian Wynne) The Night It Rained Bullets, 1965; (as Frank O'Brian) Bugle and Spur, 1966; (as Frank Wynne) The Wolf Pack, 1966; The Last Bridge, 1966; (as Frank Wynne) Call Me Hazard, 1966; (as Frank Wynne) The Lusty Breed, 1966; (as Brian Wynne) The Bravos, 1966; (as Brian Wynne) The Proud Riders, 1967; (as Brian Wynne) A Badge for a Badman, 1967; (as Jonas Ward) Buchanan's Gun, 1968; (ed.) War Whoop and Battle Cry, 1968; (as Alex Hawk) Savage Guns, 1968; (as Brian Wynne) Brand of the Gun, 1968; (as Bennett Garland) Rio Chama, 1969; (as Frank O'Brian) Arizona, 1969; (as Brian Wynne) Gundown, 1969; (as Brian Wynne) Big Country, Big Men, 1969; The Thousand-Mile War, 1969; Valley of the Shadow, 1970; The Villiers Touch, 1970; Sliphammer, 1970; The Hit, 1971; What of Terry Conniston?, 1971; Sweeny's Honour, 1971; Gun Down, 1971, as the Last Hard Men, 1976; Deep Cover, 1971; Relentless, 1972, screenplay, 1977; Line of Succession, 1972; Death Wish, 1972, screenplay, 1974; Tripwire, 1973, screenplay, 1976; (with Donald W. Westlake) Gangway, 1973; Kolchak's Gold, 1974; The Threepersons Hunt, 1974; The Romanov Succession, 1974; Hopscotch (novel; and screenplay with Bryan Forbes), 1975; (as Drew Mallory) Target Manhattan, 1975; (as Frank O'Brian) Act of Piracy, 1975; Death Sentence, 1976; Recoil, 1977; (as John Ives) Fear in a Handful of Dust, 1977; (ed.) I Witness, 1978; Wild Times, 1979; (as John Ives) The Marchand Woman, 1979; The Paladin, 1980; Checkpoint Charlie, 1981; Western Films: A Complete Guide, 1982; (ed.) The Crime of My Life, 1983; Necessity, 1984; Manifest Destiny, 1989. Add: c/o Jane Cushman, JCA Agency Inc., 242 W. 27th St., New York, N.Y. 10001, U.S.A.

GARFIELD, Leon. British, b. 1921. Children's fiction. *Publs:* Jack Holborn, 1964; Devil-in-the-Fog, 1966; Smith, 1967; Black Jack, 1968; Mister Corbett's Ghost, 1969; The Boy and the Monkey, 1969; Drummer Boy, 1970; The Strange Affair of Adelaide Harris, 1971; (with E. Blishen) The God Beneath the Sea, 1971; The Ghost Downstairs, 1972; (with D. Proctor) Child O'War, 1972; (ed.) Kaleidoscope, 1973; The Captain's Watch, 1973; Lucifer Wilkins, 1973; (with E. Blishen) Golden Shadow, 1973; The Sound of Coaches, 1974; The Prisoners of September, 1975; The Lamplighter's Funeral, 1976; Mirror, Mirror, 1976; The Pleasure Garden, 1976; The Cloak, 1976; Moss and Blister, 1976; The House of Hanover, 1976; The Dumb Cake, 1977; Tom Titmarsh's Devil, 1977; The Fool, 1977; Rosy Starling, 1977; The Valentine, 1977; Labour in vain, 1977; An Adelaide Ghost, 1977; The Apprentices, 1978; The Enemy, 1978; Filthy Beast, 1978; The Confidence Man, 1978; Bostock and Harris, 1979; John Diamond (in U.S. as Footsteps), 1980; Fair's Fair, 1981; King

Nimrod's Tower, 1982; The House of Cards, 1982; The Writing on the Wall, 1983; The King in the Garden, 1984; Guilt and Gingerbread, 1984; The Wedding Ghost, 1985; Shakespeare Stories, 1985; The December Rose, 1986; The Empty Sleeve, 1988; Blewcoat Boy, 1988. Add: c/o John Johnson Ltd., 45-47 Clerkenwell Green, London EC1R OHT, England.

GARFITT, Roger. British, b. 1944. Poetry. Ed., Poetry Review, London, 1978–81. Writer-in-Residence, Sunderland Polytechnic, 1978–80. *Publs:* Caught on Blue, 1970; West of Elm, 1975; Unwritten Histories, 1980; The Broken Road, 1982. Add: 2 Mount Pleasant, St. Leonards, Hereford HR2 8PH, England.

GARFORTH, Francis William. British, b. 1917. Education, Philosophy. Sr. Lectr., Dept. of Education, Univ. of Hull, 1949–84, now retired. Teacher, St. George's Sch., Harpenden, Herts., 1939–45, and Bristol Grammar Sch., 1945–49. *Publs:* Education and Social Purpose, 1962; (ed.) Locke's Thoughts Concerning Education, 1964; (ed.) John Locke's Of the Conduct of the Understanding, 1966; (ed.) John Dewey: Selected Educational Writings, 1966; (ed.) Bede's Historia Ecclesiastica: A Selection, 1967; (ed.) Education for the Seventies, 1969; (ed.) John Stuart Mill on Education, 1971; The Scope of Philosophy, 1971; John Stuart Mill's Theory of Education, 1979; Educative Democracy: John Stuart Mill on Education in Society, 1980; Aims, Values, and Education, 1985. Add: Arkangel, Westerdale, Castleton, N. Yorks. YO21 2DT, England.

GARLAND, Bennett. *See* **GARFIELD,** Brian.

GARLAND, George. *See* **ROARK,** Garland.

GARLICK, Raymond. British, b. 1926. Poetry, Literature. Founding Ed., Dock Leaves, later the Anglo-Welsh Review, 1949–60; Head, English Dept., Intnl. Sch., Kasteel Eerde, Ommen, The Netherlands, 1961–67; Sr. Lectr. in English, 1967–72, and Dir. of Welsh Studies and Principal Lectr., 1972–86, Trinity Coll., Carmarthen. *Publs:* Poems from the Mountain-House, 1950; The Welsh-Speaking Sea, 1954; Blaenau Observed, 1957; Landscapes and Figures, 1964; A Sense of Europe: Collected Poems, 1954-1968, 1968; An Introduction to Anglo-Welsh Literature, 1970, rev. ed. 1972; Sense of Time: Poems and Antipoems 1969-72, 1972; Incense: Poems 1972-1975, 1976, (ed. with Roland Mathias) Anglo-Welsh Poetry 1480-1980, 1984; The Hymn to the Virgin, 1985; Collected Poems, 1987. Add: 30 Glannant House, College Road, Carmarthen SA31 3EF, Wales.

GARLINSKI, Jozef. Polish, b. 1913. Novels/Short stories, History. Chmn., Union of Polish Writers Abroad, since 1975. Chmn., Exec. Cttee., Polish Home Army Circle, London, 1954–65; Cultural Vice-Chmn., Polish Cultural and Social Centre, London, 1970–79. *Publs:* Dramat i Opatrznosc, 1961; Matki i zony, 1962; Ziemia (novel), 1964; Miedzy Londynem i Warszawa, 1966; Poland, SOE and the Allies, 1969; Fighting Auschwitz, 1975; Hitler's Last Weapons, 1978; Intercept: Secrets of the Enigma War, 1979; The Swiss Corridor: Espionage Networks in Switzerland During World War II, 1981; Polska w Drugiej Wojnie Swaiatowej, 1982; Poland in the Second World War, 1985. Add: 94 Ramillies Rd., London W4 1JA, England.

GARNER, Alan. British, b. 1934. Children's fiction, Songs, lyrics and libretti, Mythology/Folklore. *Publs:* The Weirdstone of Brisingamen, 1960; The Moon of Gomrath, 1963; Elidor, 1965; Holly from the Bongs, 1966; The Owl Service, 1967; (with R. Hill) The Old Man of Mow, 1967; (ed.) The Hamish Hamilton Book of Goblins: An Anthology of Folklore, 1969; Red Shift, 1973; (ed.) The Guizer, 1975; (with A. Trowski) The Breadhorse, 1975; The Stone Book, 1976; Tom Fobble's Day, 1977; Granny Reardun, 1977; The Aimer Gate, 1978; Fairytales of Gold, 1979; The Lad of the Gad, 1980; A Book of British Fairy Tales, 1984; A Bag of Moonshine, 1986; It's O.K. to Say No to Drugs, 1987. Add: c/o William Collins, 8 Grafton St., London W1X 3LA, England.

GARDNER, Helen. Australian, b. 1942. Novels/Short Stories. Feature Writer, The Age, Melbourne, since 1981. Member, Australia Council Literature Bd., since 1985. Taught at Werribee High Sch., 1966–67, Upfield High Sch., 1968–69, and Fitzroy High Sch., 1971–72, all Victoria; Writer-in-Residence, Griffith Univ., Nathan, Qld., 1983. and Univ. of Western Australia, Nedlands, 1984; Melbourne Theatre Critic, National Times, Sydney, 1982–83. *Publs:* Monkey Grip (novel), 1977; Honour, and Other People's Children: Two Stories, 1980; Moving Out (novelization of screenplay), 1983; The Children's Bach (novel), 1984; Postcards from Surfers (short stories), 1985. Add: 849 Drummond St., North Carlton, Vic. 3054, Australia.

GARNER, Wendell (Richard). American, b. 1921. Psychology. James Rowland Angell Prof. of Psychology, Yale Univ., New Haven. *Publs:* (co-author) Applied Experimental Psychology, 1949; Uncertainty and Structure as Psychological Concepts, 1962; The Processing of Information and Structure, 1974; (ed.) Ability Testing, 1982. Add: Dept. of Psychology, Yale Univ., New Haven, Conn. 06520, U.S.A.

GARNER, William. British, b. 1920. Mystery/Crime/Suspense. Formerly in intnl. business. *Publs:* Overkill, 1966; The Deep Deep Freeze, 1968; The Us or Them War, 1969; The Puppet-Masters (in U.S. as The Manipulators), 1970; The Andra Fiasco (in U.S. as Strip Jack Naked), 1971; Ditto, Brother Rat, 1972; A Big Enough Wreath, 1974; The Mobius Trip, 1978; Think Big, Think Dirty, 1982; Rats' Alley, 1984; Zones of Silence, 1986 (last 3 vols. reissued as The Morpurgo Trilogy, 1987); Paper Chase, 1988. Add: c/o Elaine Greene Ltd., 31 Newington Green, London N16 9PU, England.

GARNETT, Eve C.R. British. Children's fiction, Children's non-fiction. Autobiography/Memoirs/Personal. Freelance writer and illustrator. *Publs:* The Family from One End Street, 1937; Is It Well with the Child?, 1938; In and Out and Roundabout: Stories of a Little Town, 1948; (ed.) Further Adventures of the Family from One End Street, 1956; A Book of the Seasons: An Anthology, 1956; Holiday at the Dew Drop Inn: A One End Street Story, 1962; To Greenland's Icy Mountains: The Story of Hans Egede, Explorer, Colonizer, Missionary, 1968; Lost and Found: Four Stories, 1974; First Affections (memoirs), 1982. Add: c/o Lloyd's Bank Ltd., Lewes, Sussex, England.

GARNETT, Richard (Duncan Carey). British, b. 1923. Children's fiction, Translations. Dir., Macmillan Publrs., 1982 until retirement, 1988 (Ed. 1966–82, and Dir., 1972–82, Macmillan London). Production Mgr. 1951–59, and Dir. 1954–66, Rupert Hart-Davis Ltd.; Dir., Adlard Coles Ltd., 1963–66. *Publs:* (ed.) Goldsmith: Selected Works, 1950; (trans.) Robert Gruss: The Art of the Aqualung, 1955; The Silver Kingdom (in U.S. as The Undersea Treasure), (trans.) Bernard Heuvelmans: On the Track of the Unknown Animals, 1958; The White Dragon, 1963; Jack of Dover, 1966; (trans.) Bernard Heuvelmans: In the Wake of the Sea-Serpents, 1968; (ed. with Reggie Grenfell) Joyce, 1980. Add: Hilton Hall, Hilton, Huntingdon, Cambridgeshire PE18 9NE, England.

GARNHAM, Percy Cyril Claude. British, b. 1901. Zoology. Prof. Emeritus, Imperial Coll. of Science and Technology, London, since 1968 (Prof. of Medical Protozoology, 1951–68). Dir., Insect-Borne Diseases, Medical Research Lab., Nairobi, 1925–47; Dir., Dept. of Parasitology, London Sch. of Tropical Medicine and Hygiene, 1951–68. *Publs:* Immunity to Protozoa, 1963; Malaria Parasites, 1966; Progress in Parasitology, 1971; Catalogue Raisonné Malaria Parasites and Haemosporidea, 1986; In the Wake of Poe, 1990. Add: Southernwood, Farnham Common, Bucks., England.

GARRARD, Lancelot Austin. British, b. 1904. Theology/Religion, Translations. Principal, Manchester Coll., Oxford, 1956–65; Prof. of Philosophy and Religion, Emerson Coll., Boston, 1965–71. Ed., The Hibbert Journal, 1951–62. *Publs:* Duty and the Will of God, 1935; The Interpreted Bible, 1946; The Gospels Today, 1953; The Historical Jesus, 1956; (trans.) H. von Camperhausen: The Fathers of the Greek Church, 1963; Athens or Jerusalem?. 1965; (trans.) Albert Schweitzer: The Kingdom of God and Primitive Christianity, 1968; An Index to the Hibbert Journal, 1987. Add: 7 Bancroft Ct., Reigate, Surrey RH2 7RW, England.

GARRETT, Florence Rome. American, b. 1912. Poetry. Secty., Walt Whitman Soc. of America, 1943–44; Pres., Long Island Branch, 1954–56, and Poetry Chmn., Connecticut Pioneer Branch, 1960–62, National League of American Pen Women. *Publs:* Edge of Day, 1954; More than the Quiet Pond, 1969; On the Hill, 1977; The Mill and Us, 1978; Japanese Sketches, 1981; Bridgewater Morning, 1986. Add: 40 Hut Hill Rd., Bridgewater, Conn. 06752, U.S.A.

GARRETT, George (Palmer, Jr.). American, b. 1929. Novels/Short stories, Plays/Screenplays, Poetry, Literature. Henry Hoyns Prof. of Creative Writing, Univ. of Virginia, since 1984. Contrib. Ed., Contempora, Atlanta, Ga., since 1970, and The Film Journal, NYC, since 1971; Co-ed., Worksheet, Columbia, S.C., since 1972. Asst. Prof., Wesleyan Univ., Middletown, Conn., 1956–60; U.S. Poetry Ed., Transatlantic Review, Rome, London and NYC, 1958–71; Visiting Lectr., Rice Univ., Houston, Tex., 1961–62; Assoc. Prof., Univ. of Virginia, Charlottesville, 1962–67; Contemporary Poetry Series Ed. Univ. of North Carolina Press,

Chapel Hill, 1963–68; Writer-in-Residence, Princeton Univ., N.J., 1964–65; Prof. of English, and Dir. of Writing Prog., Hollins Coll., Va., 1967–71; Prof. of English and Writer-in-Residence, Univ. of South Carolina, Columbia, 1971–73; Sr. Fellow, Council of the Humanities, Princeton Univ., New Jersey, 1974–76; Adjunct Prof., Sch. of the Arts, Columbia Univ., NYC, 1976–77; Writer-in-Residence, Univ. of Michigan, Ann Arbor, 1978–79; Prof. of English, Bennington College, Vt., 1979–80; Eminent Scholar, Virginia Military Inst., 1983–84. *Publs:* The Reverend Ghost: Poems, 1957; The Sleeping Gypsy and Other Poems, 1958; King of the Mountain (short stories), 1958; The Finished Man, 1959; Which Ones Are the Enemy?, 1961; In the Briar Patch (short stories), 1961; Abraham's Knife and Other Poems, 1961; Sir Slob and the Princess: A Play for Children, 1962; Garden Spot, U.S.A. (play), 1962; (ed.) New Writing from Virginia, 1963; The Young Lovers (screenplay), 1964; Do, Lord, Remember Me, 1965; The Playground (screenplay), 1965; Frankenstein Meets the Space Monster (screenplay), 1966; (ed.) The Girl in the Black Raincoat, 1966; For a Bitter Season: New and Selected Poems, 1967; (ed. with W.R. Robinson) Man and the Movies, 1967; A Wreath for Garibaldi (short stories), 1969; Death of the Fox, 1971; (ed. with R.H.W. Dillard and J. Moore) The Sounder Few: Selected Essays from the Hollins Critic, 1971; (ed. with O.B. Hardison and J. Gelfman) Film Scripts One, Two, Three and Four, 1971–72; (ed. with W. Peden) New Writing in South Carolina, 1971; (ed. with J. Graham) Craft So Hard to Learn, 1972; (ed. with J. Graham) The Writer's Voice, 1973; Magic Striptease, 1973; (ed. with V. Walton) Intro 5, 1974; (ed. with K.G. Biddle) The Botteghe Oscure Reader, 1974; (ed.) Intro 6: Life as We Know It, 1974; (ed.) Intro 7: All of Us and None of You, 1975; (ed. with S. Kendrick) Intro 8: The Liar's Craft, 1977; (ed. with M. Mewshaw) Intro 8: Close to Home, 1978; Welcome to the Medicine Show: Postcards, Flashcards, Snapshots (verse), 1978; To Recollect a Cloud of Ghosts: Christmas in England 1602/03, 1979; Luck's Shining Child: A Miscellany of Poems and Verses, 1981; Enchanted Ground (play), 1982; The Succession (novel), 1983; The Collected Poems of George Garrett, 1984; James Jones (biography), 1984; An Evening Performance: New and Selected Short Stories, 1985; Poison Pen, 1986; Understanding Mary Lee Settle, 1988. Add: Dept. of English, Univ. of Virginia, Charlottesville, Va. 22903, U.S.A.

GARRETT, Leslie. American, b. 1932. Novels/short stories. *Publs:* The Beasts, 1966. Add: 1409 Clinch Ave., Knoxville, Tenn. 37916, U.S.A.

GARRETT, Richard. British, b. 1920. History, Biography. *Publs:* Fast and Furious, 1968; The Motor Racing Story, 1969; The Rally-Go-Round, 1970; Anatomy of a Grand Prix Driver, 1970; Motoring and the Mighty, 1971; Atlantic Jet, 1971; Great Sea Mysteries, 1971; Cross Channel, 1972; Hoaxes and Swindles, 1972; True Tales of Detection, 1972; The Search for Prosperity, 1973; Narrow Squeaks, 1973; Stories of Famous Ships, 1974; Heroines, 1974; General Gordon, 1974; Queen Victoria, 1974; Famous Characters of the Wild West, 1975; General Wolfe, 1975; The British Sailor, 1975; Stories of Famous Natural Disasters, 1976; Robert Clive, 1976; Clash of Arms, 1976; Famous Rescues at Sea, 1977; Submarines, 1977; Scharnhorst and Gneisenau: The Elusive Sisters, 1978; Mrs Simpson, 1979; The Raiders, 1980; P.O.W., 1981; File on Spies, 1981; File on Forgery, 1982; Royal Travel, 1982; Jailbrakers, 1983; The Story of Britain, 1983; Atlantic Disaster, 1986; Flight Into Mystery, 1986; Voyage Into Mystery, 1987; Great Escapes of World War II, 1989; The Final Betrayal, 1989. Add: The White Cottage, 27A Broadwater Down, Tunbridge Wells, Kent TN2 5NL, England.

GARRISON, Omar V. American, b. 1913. Civil liberties/Human Rights, Philosophy, Supernatural/Occult topics, Biography. *Publs:* Tantra, 1964, 3rd ed. 1971; Spy Government, 1967; The Dictocrats, 1970; Howard Hughes in Las Vegas, 1970; Medical Astrology, 1971; Balboa: Conquistador, 1971; Hidden Story of Scientology, 1973; (ed.) Lost Gems of Secret Knowledge, 1973; (as Marten Steinbach) Medical Palmistry, 1975; The Secret World of Interpol, 1976; The Encyclopedia of Prophecy, 1978, Playing Dirty: The Secret War Against Beliefs, 1980. Add: 1099 W. Cedar Knolls, Cedar City, Utah 84720, U.S.A.

GARROW, David J. American, b. 1953. Human rights, Politics, Race relations. Prof. of Political Science, City Coll. of New York and City Univ. Graduate Center, since 1987 (Asoc. Prof., 1984–87). Visiting Member, Inst. for Advanced Study, Princeton, N.J., 1979–80; Asst. Prof. of Political Science, Univ. of North Carolina, Chapel Hill, 1980–84; Visiting Fellow, Joint Center for Political Studies, Washington, D.C., 1984. *Publs:* Protest at Selma: Martin Luther King, Jr., and the Voting Rights Act of 1965, 1978; The FBI and Martin Luther King, Jr.: From "Solo" to Memphis, 1981; Bearing the Cross: Martin Luther King, Jr., and the

Southern Christian Leadership Conference, 1986; (ed.) The Montgomery Bus Boycott and the Women Who Started It: The Memoir of JoAnn Gibson Robinson, 1987; (co-ed.) Eyes on the Prize: American's Civil Rights Years, 1987. Add: Political Science Dept., City Coll. of New York, New York, N.Y. 10031, U.S.A.

GARTHOFF, Raymond L(eonard). American, b. 1929. International relations/Current affairs, Politics/Government. Sr. Fellow, Brookings Inst., since 1980. U.S. Dept. of State, Washington, D.C. 1961–77 (Special Asst. for Soviet Political-Military Affairs, 1961–1967; Counselor, U.S. Mission to NATO, 1968–70; Sr. State Dept. Advisor, U.S. SALT Delegation, 1969–72; Deputy Dir., Bureau of Political-Military Affairs, 1970–73; Sr. Foreign Service Inspector, 1974–77; U.S. Ambassador to Bulgaria, 1977–79). Professorial Lectr., Inst. for Sino-Soviet Studies, George Washington Univ., 1963–64, and Sch. for Advanced Intnl. Studies, Johns Hopkins Univ., 1964–67, both Washington, D.C. *Publs:* Soviet Military Doctrine, 1953; How Russia Makes War, 1954; Soviet Strategy in the Nuclear Age, 1958; The Soviet Image of Future War, 1959; (ed. and trans.) Science and Technology in Contemporary War, by Maj. Gen. G. Pokrovsky, 1959; (ed. and trans.) Military Strategy, by Marshal V.D. Sokolovsky, 1963; Soviet Military Policy: A Historical Analysis, 1966; (ed. and co-author) Sino-Soviet Military Relations, 1966; Perspectives on the Strategic Balance, 1983; Detente and Confrontation: American-Soviet Relations from Nixon to Reagan, 1985; Reflections on the Cuban Missile Crisis, 1987. Add: 2128 Bancroft Pl. N.W., Washington, D.C. 20008, U.S.A.

GARTNER, Chloe Maria. American, b. 1916. Novels/Short stories, Plays/Screenplays. *Publs:* Perchance to Dream (play), 1983; The Infidels, 1960; Drums of Khartoum, 1967; Die Lange Sommer, 1970; Woman from the Glen, 1973; Mistress of the Highlands, 1976; Anne Bonny, 1977; The Image and the Dream, 1980; Still Falls the Rain, 1982; Greenleaf, 1987; Lower Than the Angels, 1989. Add: c/o John Hawkins and Assocs., 71 W. 23rd St., Suite 1600, New York, N.Y. 10010, U.S.A.

GARVE, Andrew. Pseud. for Paul Winterton; also writes as Roger Bax and Paul Somers. British, b. 1908. Mystery/Crime/Suspense, International relations/Current affairs. Staff Member, Economist, London, 1929–33; Reporter, Leader Writer, and Foreign Corresp., News Chronicle, London, 1933–46. *Publs:* No Tears for Hilda, 1950; No Mask for Murder (in U.S. as Fontego's Folly), 1950; Murder in Moscow (in U.S. as Murder Through the Looking Glass), 1951; A Press of Suspects (in U.S. as By-line for Murder), 1951; A Hole in the Ground, 1952; The Cuckoo Line Affair, 1953; Death and the Sky Above, 1953; The Riddle of Samson, 1954; The End of the Track, 1956; The Megstone Plot, 1956; The Narrow Search, 1957; The Galloway Case, 1958; A Hero for Leanda, 1959; The Far Sands, 1960; The Golden Deed, 1960; The House of Soldiers, 1961; Prisoner's Friend, 1962; The Sea Monks, 1963; Frame-Up, 1964; The Ashes of Loda, 1965; Murderer's Fen (in U.S. as Hide and Go Seek), 1966; A Very Quiet Place, 1967; The Long Short Cut, 1968; The Ascent of D-13, 1969; Boomerang, 1969; The Late Bill Smith, 1971; The Case of Robert Quarry, 1972; The File on Lester, 1974; Home to Roost, 1976; Counterstroke, 1978; as Roger Bax—Death Beneath Jerusalem, 1938; Red Escapade, 1940; Disposing of Henry, 1946; Blueprint for Murder (in U.S. as The Trouble with Murder), 1948; Came the Dawn (in U.S. as Two If by Sea), 1949; A Grave Case of Murder, 1951; as Paul Somers—Beginner's Luck, 1958; Operation Piracy, 1958; The Shivering Mountain, 1959; The Broken Jigsaw, 1961; as Paul Winterton—A Student in Russia, 1931; Russia—with Open Eyes, 1937; Mending Minds: The Truth About Our Mental Hospitals, 1938; Eye-Witness on the Soviet War-Front, 1943; Report on Russia, 1945; Inquest on an Ally, 1948. Add: Collins, 8 Grafton Street., London W1X 3LA, England.

GASCOIGNE, Bamber. British, b. 1935. Novels/Short stories, History, Literature, Theatre. Presenter, Conniosseur, BBC2-TV, since 1988. Drama Critic, Spectator, 1961–63, and Observer, 1963–64, both London; Chmn., University Challenge, Granada TV, Manchester, 1962–87. *Publs:* Twentieth Century Drama, 1962; World Theatre, 1968; The Great Moghuls, 1971; Murgatreud's Empire, 1972; Treasures and Dynasties of China, 1973; The Heyday, 1973; Ticker Khan, 1974; The Christians, 1977; Images of Richmond, 1978; Images of Twickenham, 1981; Why the Rope Went Tight, 1981; Fearless Freddie's Magic Wish (and Sunken Treasure), 1982; Quest for the Golden Hare, 1983; Cod Streuth, 1986; How to Identify Prints, 1986. Add: St. Helena Terr., Richmond TW19 1NR, England.

GASCOYNE, David (Emery). British, b. 1916. Novels/Short stories, Plays/Screenplays, Poetry, literature, Autobiography/Memoirs/Personal. *Publs:* Roman Balcony and Other Poems, 1932; Opening Day (novel), 1933; Short Survey of Surrealism, 1935; (trans. with H. Jennings) A

Bunch of Carrots: Twenty Poems, by Benjamin Peret, rev. ed. as Remove Your Hat, 1936; (trans.) What Is Surrealism?, by André Breton, 1936; Man's Life Is This Meat, 1936; Holderlin's Madness (poetry), 1938; Poems 1937-42, 1943; (ed.) Outlaw of the Lowest Planet, by Kenneth Patchen, 1946; The Hole in the Fourth Wall: or Talk, Talk, Talk (play), 1950; A Vagrant and Other Poems, 1950; Thomas Carlyle, 1952; Night Thoughts, 1956; Collected Poems, 1965; (with Kathleen Raine and W.S. Graham) Penguin Modern Poets 17, 1970; The Sun at Midnight, 1970; Collected Verse Translations, 1970; 3 Poems, 1976; Paris Journal 1937-39, 1978; Journal 1936-37, 1980; Early Poems, 1980; Collected Poems, 1982; Three Translations, 1988. Add: 48 Oxford St., Northwood, Cowes, Isle of Wight, England.

GASH, Jonathan. Pseudonym for John Grant; also writes as Graham Gaunt. British, b. 1933. Mystery/Crime/Suspense. Physician; General practitioner, London, 1958–59; pathologist, London and Essex, 1959–62; Clinical Pathologist, Hannover and Berlin, 1962–65; Lectr. and Head of the Div. of Clinical Pathology, Univ. of Hong Kong, 1965–68; microbiologist, Hong Kong and London, 1968–71; Microbiologist, Faculty of Medicine, Univ. of London, 1971–88. Publs: The Judas Pair, 1977; Gold from Gemini, 1978, in U.S. as Gold by Gemini, 1979; The Grail Tree, 1979; Spend Game, 1980; The Vatican Rip, 1981; (as Graham Gaunt) The Incomer, 1981; Firefly Gadroon, 1982; The Sleepers of Erin, 1983; The Gondola Scam, 1983; Pearlhanger, 1985; Moonspender, 1986; Jade Woman, 1988. Add: c/o William Collins, 8 Grafton St., London W1X 3LA, England.

GASH, Norman. British, b. 1912. History, Biography. Lectr. in Modern History, Univ. Coll., London, 1936–40; Lectr. in Modern History, Univ. of St. Andrews, 1946–53; Prof. of Modern History, Univ. of Leeds, 1953–55; Prof. of History, Univ. of St. Andrews, 1955–80. Publs: Politics in the Age of Peel, 1953; Mr. Secretary Peel, 1961; Reaction and Reconstruction in English Politics 1832-1852, 1965; Age of Peel, 1968; Sir Robert Peel, 1973; (with others) The Conservative Leadership, 1974; Peel, 1976; (with others) The Conservatives, 1977; Aristocracy and People: Britain 1815-1865, 1979; Lord Liverpool, 1984; Pillars of Government, 1986. Add: Old Gatehouse, Langport, Somerset, England.

GASKELL, Jane. British, b. 1941. Novels/Short stories. Roving corresp., Daily Mail, London. Former feature writer, Daily Express, London. Publs: Strange Evil, 1957; King's Daughter, 1958; Attic Summer, 1958; The Serpent, 1963; The Shiny Narrow Grin, 1964; The Fabulous Heroine, 1965; Atlan, 1965; The City, 1966; All Neat in Black Stockings, 1966; A Sweet Sweet Summer, 1969; Summer Coming, 1974; Some Summer Lands, 1977. Add: c/o Futura Publications, Div. of MacDonald and Co., Greater London House, Hampstead Rd., London NW1 7QX, England.

GASKELL, (John) Philip (Wellesley). British, b. 1926. History, Librarianship. Fellow since 1967, Librarian, 1967–86, and Tutor, 1973–83, Trinity Coll., Cambridge (Fellow, King's Coll., 1953–61). Part-time Prof. of Literature, California Inst. of Technology, 1983–88. Publs: William Mason, 1951; John Baskerville, 1959; The Foulis Press, 1964; Morvern Transformed, 1968; A New Introduction to Bibliography, 1972; From Writer to Reader, 1978; Trinity College Library: The First 150 Years, 1980. Add: Trinity Coll., Cambridge CB2 1TQ, England.

GASKIN, Catherine. Irish, b. 1929. Historical/Romance/Gothic, Mystery/Crime/Suspense. Publs: This Other Eden, 1947; With Every Year, 1949; Dust in Sunlight, 1950; All Else Is Folly, 1951; Daughter of the House, 1952; Sara Dane, 1955; Blake's Reach, 1958; Corporation Wife, 1960; I Know My Love, 1962; The Tilsit Inheritance, 1963; The File on Devlin, 1965; Edge of Glass, 1967; Fiona, 1970; A Falcon for a Queen, 1972; The Property of a Gentleman, 1974; The Lynmara Legacy, 1975; The Summer of the Spanish Woman, 1977; Family Affairs, 1980; Promises, 1982; The Ambassador's Women, 1985; The Charmed Circle, 1988. Add: White Rigg, E. Ballaterson, Maughold, Isle of Man, U.K.

GASPERINI, Jim. American, b. 1952. Children's fiction. Software Developer, Trans Fiction Systems, NYC, since 1986. Technician, Stichting Video Heads, Paris, 1974–75; Video Ed., Video in Paris, 1976–77; Asst., Sterling Lord Agency, Inc., NYC, 1978–80; Ed., Byron Preiss Visual Publications, NYC, 1981–82; Regional Mgr., Ballen Booksellers Intnl., Commack, N.Y., 1983–86. Publs: Secret of the Knights, 1984; Sail with Pirates, 1984; The Mystery of Atlantis, 1985. Add: c/o Victoria Pryor, Arcadia Ltd., 221 W. 82nd St., Suite 7D, New York, N.Y. 10024, U.S.A.

GASS, Ian (Graham). British, b. 1926. Earth Sciences. Prof. of Earth Sciences, The Open Univ., Milton Keynes, since 1969. Geologist, Sudan Geological Survey, 1952–55, and Cyprus Geological Survey, 1955–60; Lectr./Sr. Lectr. in Earth Sciences, Univ. of Leeds, 1961–69; Pres., Intnl. Assn. of Volcanology and Chemistry of the Earth's Interior, 1983–87. Publs: (ed. with others) African Magmatism and Tectonics, 1970; (ed. with others) Understanding the Earth, 1970; (ed. with others) Ophiolites and Oceanic Lithosphere, 1984. Add: Dept. of Earth Sciences, The Open Univ., Walton Hall, Milton Keynes, Bucks. MK7 6AA, England.

GASS, William (Howard). American, b. 1924. Novels/Short stories, Literature. David May Distinguished Prof. in Humanities, Washington Univ., St. Louis, Mo., since 1979 (Prof. of Philosophy, 1969–79). Instr. in Philosophy, Coll. of Wooster, Ohio, 1950–54; Asst. Prof., 1955–58, Assoc. Prof., 1960–65, and Prof. of Philosophy, 1966–69; Purdue Univ., Lafayette, Ind.; Visiting Lectr. in English and Philosophy, Univ. of Illinois, Urbana, 1958–59. Publs: Omen-setter's Luck, 1966; In the Heart of the Heart of the Country and Other Stories, 1968; Willie Masters' Lonesome Wife, 1968; Fiction and Figures of Life, 1971; On Being Blue, 1976; The World Within the Word, 1978; (with P. Eisenman) The House VI Book, 1979; the First Winter of My Married Life (stories), 1979; Habitations of the Word: Essays, 1985. Add: 6304 Westminster, University City, Mo. 63130, U.S.A.

GASTON, Bill. See GASTON, William James.

GASTON, Edwin Willmer, Jr. American, b. 1925. Literature, Biography. Prof. of English Emeritus, Stephen F. Austin State Univ., Nacogdoches, Tex., since 1986 (Prof. of English, 1950–86, and Vice Pres. for Academic Affairs, 1981–86). Fulbright Lectr. in American Literature, Univ. of Helsinki, 1964–65. Pres., Alpha Chi national Scholarship Soc., 1967–79. Chmn., Editorial Bd., Southwestern American Literature Journal, 1972–3. Publs: The Early Novel of the Southwest, 1961; A Manual of Style, 1961; Conrad Richter, 1965, 1989; Eugene Manlove Rhodes, 1967; Southwestern American Literature: A Bibliography, 1980. Add: 709 Bostwick, Nacogdoches, Tex. 75961, U.S.A.

GASTON, William James. Also writes as Bill Gaston and Jack Bannatyne. British, b. 1927. Mystery/Crime/Suspense, Westerns/-Adventure. Planning engineer, Rolls-Royce Ltd., East Kilbride, 1954–83. Publs: Deep Green Death, 1963; Drifting Death, 1964; Death Crag, 1965; The Death Dealers, 1967; Dark Roots of Fear, 1969; Shabby Eagles, 1973; (as Jack Bannatyne) Torpedo Squadron, 1975; Winter of the Wildcat, 1977; (as Jack Bannatyne) Intruder Squadron, 1978; Winter and the White Witch, 1979; (as Jack Bannatyne) Strike Force Squadron, 1981; Winter and the Wild Rover, 1982; (as Jack Bannatyne) The Mountain Eagles, 1983; Winter and the Widowmakers, 1984; (as Jack Bannatyne) Find, Strike, and Sink, 1984; Winter and the Wanderer, 1986. Add: 9 Falstaff, East Kilbride, Glasgow, Scotland.

GATCH, Milton McCormick, Jr. American, b. 1932. Literature, theology/Religion. Prof. of Church History and Academic Dean, Union Theological Seminary, NYC, since 1978. Chaplain and Chmn. of Humanities, Shimer Coll., Mount Carroll, Ill., 1964–67; Assoc. Prof. of English, Northern Illinois Univ., DeKalb, 1967–68; Assoc. Prof. 1968–72, Prof. of English, 1972–78, and Chmn. of the Dept., 1971–74, Univ. of Missouri, Columbia. Publs: Death: Meaning and Mortality in Christian Thought and Contemporary Culture; Loyalties and Traditions: Man and His World in Old English Literature; Preaching and Theology in Anglo-Saxon England: Aelfric and Wulfstan, 1977; (ed. with C.T. Berkhout) Anglo-Saxon Scholarship: The First Three Centuries, 1982. Add: Union Theological Seminary, 3041 Broadway, New York, N.Y. 10027, U.S.A.

GATENBY, Greg. Canadian, b. 1950. Poetry. Artistic dir. Harbourfront Reading Series, since 1975, and Artistic dir., Harbourfront Intnl. Festival of Authors, Toronto, since 1980. Publs: Rondeaus for Erica, 1976; Adrienne's Blessing, 1976; (ed.) 52 Pickup, 1976; (ed.) Whale Sound: An Anthology of Poems About Whales and Dolphins, 1977; The Brown Stealer, 1977; The Salmon Country, 1978; Growing Still, 1981; (ed.) Whales: A Celebration, 1983. Add: c/o Harbourfront Reading Series, 410 Queen's Quay W., Toronto, Ont. M5V 2Z3, Canada.

GATES, Henry Louis. American, b. 1950. Literature. DuBois Prof. of Literature, N.Y., since 1988 (Prof. of English, Comparative Literature and Africana Studies, Cornell Univ., Ithaca, N.Y., 1985–88). Assoc. Prof. of English and Afro-American Studies, Yale Univ., New Haven, Conn., 1979–85. Publs: (ed.) Black Is the Color of the Cosmos: Charles T. Davis's Essays on Black Literature and Culture 1942-1981, 1982; (ed.) Our Nig; or, Sketches from the Life of a Free Black, 1983; (ed.) Black Literature and Literary Theory, 1984; (ed. with Charles T. Davis) The Slave's Narrative: Texts and Contexts, 1985; (ed.) "Race," Writing, and

Difference, 1986; (co-author) Wole Soyinka: A Bibliography, 1986; Figures in Black: Words, Signs, and the Racial Self, 1987; (ed.) The Classic Slave Narratives, 1987; The Signifying Monkey: Towards a Theory of Afro-American Literary Criticism, 1988; (ed.) In the House of Osugbo: Critical Essays on Wole Soyinka, 1988. Add: Dept. of English, Rockefeller Hall, Cornell Univ., Ithaca, N.Y. 14853, U.S.A.

GATES, Norman T(immins). American, b. 1914. Literature. Prof. of English, Rider Coll., Lawrenceville, N.J., 1977–85, now Emeritus (Asst. Prof., 1969; Assoc. Prof., 1974). *Publs:* The Poetry of Richard Aldington: Critical Evaluation and an Anthology of Uncollected Poems, 1974; A Checklist of the Letters of Richard Aldington, 1977. Add: 520 Woodland Ave., Haddonfield, N.J. 08033, U.S.A.

GATES, Paul W(allace). American, b. 1901. Agriculture/Forestry, History. Prof. of American History Emeritus, Cornell Univ., Ithaca, N.Y. since 1971 (John Stambaugh Prof. of American History, 1944–71; Chmn., Dept. of History, 1946–56). Consultant and Expert Historian, Public Land Law Review Commn., 1966–68; Visiting Prof., Univ. of Wisconsin, Madison, 1969–70, and Univ. of Kansas, Lawrence, 1971–72. *Publs:* The Illinois Central Railroad and its Settlement Work, 1934; Fifty Million Acres: Conflicts Over Kansas Land Policy, 1854-1890, 1954; The Farmers' Age: Agriculture, 1815-1860, 1960; Agriculture and the Civil War, 1965; The Wisconsin Pine Lands of Cornell University, 1968; History of Public Land Law Development, 1968; California Ranchos and Farms, 1968; Landlords and Tenants on the Prairie Frontier, 1974; Pressure Groups and American Land Policies 1945-1978, 1980; The Intermountain West Against Itself, 1985; The Intermountain West Against Itself, 1985. Add: McGraw Hall, Cornell Univ., Ithaca, N.Y. 14850, U.S.A.

GATHORNE-HARDY, Jonathan. British, b. 1933. Novels/Short stories, Children's fiction, History, Social commentary/phenomena. *Publs:* One Foot in the Clouds, 1961; Jane series, 3 vols., 1966–74; Chameleon, 1967; The Office, 1970; The Rise and Fall of the British Nanny (in U.S. as The Unnatural History of the Nanny), 1972; The Public School Phenomenon (in U.S. as The Old School Tie), 1977; Cyril Bonhamy series, 5 vols., 1978–87; Marriage, Love, Sex, and Divorce, 1981; The Centre of the Universe is 18 Baedekerstrasse, 1981; Doctors, 1984; The City Beneath the Skin, 1986. Add: 31 Blacksmith's Yard, Binham, Fakenham, Norfolk NR21 0AL, England.

GATLAND, Kenneth William. British, b. 1924. Air/Space topics. Ed., Technical Publications, British Aerospace PLC, Military Aircraft Div., Kingston upon Thames, since 1981. Ed., Astronautics Section, The Aeroplane, 1959–62; Ed., Spaceflight, 1959–81; Space Corresp., Sunday Telegraph, 1959–85, and Aviation and Space Corresp., Telegraph Sunday mag., 1963–86; Contrib. Ed., Astronautics, 1962–64. *Publs:* Development of the Guided Missile, 1952; (with A.M. Kunesch) Space Travel, 1953; (with D.D. Dempster) The Inhabited Universe, 1957; Astronautics in the Sixties, 1962; Spacecraft and Boosters, 2 vols., 1963–64; Manned Spacecraft, 1968; (with P. Bono) Frontiers of Space, 1969; Robot Explorers, 1969; (with D.D. Dempster) Frontiers of Knowledge (in U.S. as Worlds in Creation), 1974; Missiles and Rockets, 1975; Space Shuttle Handbook, 1979; Illustrated Encyclopedia of Space Technology, 1981; Illustrated Diary of Space Exploration, 1989. Add: 10 Brook Mead, Ewell, Epsom, Surrey, England.

GATOS, Stephanie. *See* **KATZ**, Steve.

GATTEY, Charles Neilson. British, b. 1921. Historical/Novels, Plays/Screenplays, Social commentary/phenomena, Biography. Pres., Soc. of Civil Service Authors, London, since 1981. *Publs:* (with J. Lawrence) The White Falcon, 1952; (with Z. Bramley-Moore) The Eleventh Hour, 1952; (with Z. Bramley-Moore) In the Maze, 1953; (with J. Lawrence) Queen's Night, 1953; (with Z. Bramley-Moore) Tidings of Canute, 1954; (with J. Lawrence) The Birth of Elizabeth, 1954; (with J. Lawrence) Queen of a Thousand Dresses, 1955; (with Z. Bramley-Moore) A Spell of Virtue, 1955; (with Z. Bramley-Moore) The Birth of the Bloomer, 1955; (with Z. Bramley-Moore) Mightier than the Sword, 1955; (with Z. Bramley-Moore) Mrs. Adams and Eve, 1955; (with Z. Bramley-Moore) Treasure from France, 1956; (with Z. Bramley-Moore) Man in a Million, 1956; (with Z. Bramley-Moore) Farewell, Pots and Pans, 1956; (with Z. Bramley-Moore) True Love or The Bloomer, 1958; (with Z. Bramley-Moore) By a Hand Unknown, 1958; (with Z. Bramley-Moore) Life with Alfredo, 1958; (with Z. Bramley-Moore) The Cloak of Courage, 1959; (with Z. Bramley-Moore) The Landlady's Brother, 1959; (with Z. Bramley-Moore) The Colour of Anger, 1963; (with Z. Bramley-Moore) Fair Cops, 1965; The Bloomer Girls, 1967; Gauguin's Astonishing

Grandmother, 1970; (with Z. Bramley-Moore) The King Who Could Not Stay the Tide, 1971; A Bird of Curious Plumage, 1971; The Incredible Mrs. Van Der Elst, 1973; They Saw Tomorrow, 1977; Queens of Song, 1979; The Elephant That Swallowed a Nightingale, 1981; Peacocks on the Podium, 1982; Great Dining Disasters, 1984; Foie Gras and Trumpets, 1984; 'Farmer' George's Black Sheep, 1986; Excess in Food, Drink and Excess, 1986. Add: Garrick Club, London WC2E 9AY, England.

GAULDIE, Enid Elizabeth. British, b. 1928. Architecture, Business/Trade/Industry, Country life/Rural societies. *Publs:* (ed.) The Dundee Textile Industry from the Papers of Peter Carmichael of Arthurstone, 1969; (co-author) Dundee and Its Textile Industry, 1850-1914, 1969; Cruel Habitations: A History of Working Class Housing, 1780-1918, 1974; The Scottish Country Miller: History of Water-powered Meal Milling in Scotland, 1980; The Quarries and the Fens, 1981. Add: Waterside, Invergowrie, Dundee, Scotland.

GAULT, William Campbell. Also writes as Will Duke and has written as Dial Forest and Roney Scott. American, b. 1910. Mystery/Crime/Suspense, Children's fiction. Full-time writer since 1939. *Publs:* mystery novels—Don't Cry for Me, 1952; The Bloody Bokhara, 1952, in U.K. as the Bloodstained Bokhara, 1953; The Canvas Coffin, 1953; Blood on the Boards, 1953; Run, Killer, Run, 1954; Ring Around Rosa, 1955 (in U.S. paperback, Murder in the Raw, 1956); Square in the Middle, 1956; Day of the Ram, 1956; (as Will Duke) Fair Prey, 1956; The Convertible Hearse, 1957; The Atom and Eve, 1958; End of a Call Girl, 1958, in U.K. as Don't Call Tonight, 1960; Night Lady, 1958; Death Out of Focus, 1959; Sweet Wild Wench, 1959; The Wayward Widow, 1959; Come Die with Me, 1959; Million Dollar Tramp, 1960; The Hundred-Dollar Girl, 1961; Vein of Violence, 1961; County Kill, 1962; Dead Hero, 1963; The Bad Samaritan, 1982; The Cana Diversion, 1982; The Chicano War, 1984; children's fiction—Thunder Road, 1952; Mr. Fullback, 1953; Gallant Colt, 1954; Mr. Quarterback, 1955; Speedway Challenge, 1956; Bruce Benedict, Halfback, 1957; Dim Thunder, 1958; Rough Road to Glory, 1958; Drag Strip, 1959; Dirt Track Summer, 1961; Through the Line, 1961; Road-Race Rookie, 1962; Two-Wheeled Thunder, 1962; Little Big Foot, 1963; Wheels of Fortune: Four Racing Stories, 1963; The Checkered Flag, 1964; The Karters, 1965; The Long Green, 1965; Sunday's Dust, 1966; Backfield Challenge, 1967; The Lonely Mound, 1967; The Oval Playground, 1968; Stubborn Sam, 1969; Quarterback Gamble, 1970; The Last Lap, 1972; Trouble at Second, 1973; Gasoline Cowboy, 1974; Wild Willie, Wide Receiver, 1974; The Black Stick, 1975; Underground Skipper, 1975; Showboat in the Backcourt, 1976; Cut-Rate Quarterback, 1977; Thin Ice, 1978; Sunday Cycles, 1979; Superbowl Bound, 1980; Death in Donegal Bay, 1984; The Dead Seed, 1985; The Chicano War, 1986; Cat and Mouse, 1988. Add: 482 Vaquero Lane, Santa Barbara, Calif. 93111, U.S.A.

GAUNT, Graham. *See* **GASH**, Jonathan.

GAVIN, Catherine. British, b. 1907. Historical/Romance/Gothic, History, Biography. Former lectr. in history, and war corresp. *Publs:* Louis Philippe, King of the French (biography), 1933; Clyde Valley, 1938; The Hostile Shore, 1940; Edward the Seventh: A Biography, 1941; Britain and France: A Study of Twentieth Century Relations, The Entente Cordiale, 1941; The Black Milestone, 1941; The Mountain of Light, 1944; Liberated France, 1955; The Second Empire Quartet: Madeleine, 1957, The Cactus and the Crown, 1962, The Fortress, 1964, The Moon into Blood, 1966; The Devil in Harbour, 1968; The House of War, 1970; Give Me the Daggers, 1972; The Snow Mountain, 1973; Traitor's Gate, 1976, None Dare Call It Treason, 1978, and How Sleep the Brave, 1980 (trilogy); The Sunset Dream, 1983; A Light Woman, 1986; The Glory Road, 1987; A Dawn of Splendour, 1989. Add: 1201 California St., San Francisco, Calif., U.S.A.

GAVRONSKY, Serge. American, b. 1932. Poetry, History, Translations. Prof. of French, Barnard Coll., Columbia Univ., NYC, since 1975 (Assoc. Prof., 1960–75). *Publs:* The French Liberal Opposition and the American Civil War, 1968; (ed. and trans.) Poems and Texts, 1969; Lectures et compte rendu, 1973; (ed. with J-M. Blanchard) Le Moyen Age, 1974; (ed. and trans. with P. Terry) Modern French Poetry, 1975; (ed. and trans.) Francis Ponge: The Sun Placed in the Abyss and Other Texts, 1977; (ed. and trans.) Francis Ponge: The Power of Language, 1979; (ed. and trans.) Ten Poems, Dix Poèmes de Francis Ponge, 1983; Culture/Ecriture, essais critiques, 1983; The German Friend (novel), 1984; Ecrire l'homme, essais critiques, 1986. Add: 525 West End Ave., New York, N.Y. 10024, U.S.A.

GAWRON, Jean Mark. American, b. 1953. Science fiction/Fantasy.

Publs: An Apology for Rain, 1974; Algorithm, 1978. Add: c/o Berkley Publishing Co., 200 Madison Ave., New York, N.Y. 10016, U.S.A.

GAY, Amelia. *See* **HOGARTH,** Grace.

GAY, Kathlyn R. American, b. 1930. Children's fiction, Plays/Screenplays, Social commentary/phenomena, Sociology. *Publs:* Girl Pilot, 1967; Money Isn't Everything, 1967; Meet Your Mayor, 1967; Meet Your Governor, 1968; Beth Donnis: Speech Therapist, 1968; Careers in Social Service, 1969; Where the People Are: Cities and Their Future, 1969; The Germans Helped Build America, 1971; (with E. Wolk) Core English: English for Speakers of Other Languages, 1972; (co-author) Young American Basic Reading series: Grades 1-3, 1972; A Family Is for Living, 1972; A Proud Heritage on Parade, 1972; (co-author) Young American Basic Reading Series: Grades 1-3, 1972; (with L. Senesh) Our Working World, 1973; Body Talk, 1974; Be a Smart Shopper, 1974; (with B. Barnes) The River Flows Backward, 1975; Look Mom! No Words, 1977; Care and Share: Teenagers and Volunteerism, 1977; (with Martin and Marla Gay) Get Hooked on Vegetables, 1978; English for a Changing World, 1979, 1980; (with Ben Barnes) Your Fight Has Just Begun, 1980; (with Ben Barnes) Beginner's Guide to Better Boxing, 1980; (with Martin Gay) Eating What Grows Naturally, 1980; (co-author) I Like English, 1981; Boxes and More Boxes, 1981; (co-author) Family Living, 1982; Junkyards, 1982; Acid Rain, 1983; Cities Under Stress, 1985; Will the U.S Be Ready for the Year 2000?: The School Crisis, 1986; Ergonomics, 1986; The Greenhouse Effect, 1986; The Rainbow Effect: Interracial Families, 1987; Changing Families: Meeting Today's Challenges, 1988; Science in Ancient Greece, 1988; Silent Killers: Radon and Other Hazards, 1988; Bigotry, 1989. Add: 1711 E. Beardsley Ave., Elkhart, Ind. 46514, U.S.A.

GAY, Peter. American, b. 1923. Art, History, Intellectual history. Prof. of Comparative European Intellectual History since 1969, Durfee Prof. of History since 1970 and Sterling Prof. since 1984, Yale Univ., New Haven, Conn. Fellow, American Council of Learned Socs., 1959-60; and Center for Advanced Study in the Behavioral Sciences, 1963-64; Overseas Fellow, Churchill Coll., Cambridge, England, 1970-71. *Publs:* The Dilemma of Democratic Socialism: Edward Bernstein's Challenge to Marx, 1952; Voltaire's Politics: The Poet as Realist, 1959; The Party of Humanity: Essays in the French Enlightenment, 1964; A Loss of Mastery: Puritan Historians in Colonial America, 1966; The Enlightenment, vol. I: The Rise of Modern Paganism, 1966, vol. II: The Science of Freedom, 1969; Deism: An Anthology, 1968; Weimar Culture: The Outsider as Insider, 1968; The Bridge of Criticism: Dialogues on the Enlightenment, 1970; (with R.K. Webb) Modern Europe, 1973; Art and Act: On Causes in History—Manet, Gropius, Mondrian, 1976; Style in History, 1976; Freud, Jews, and Other Germans, 1978; The Bourgeois Experience: Victoria to Freud, vol. I, Education of the Senses, 1984, vol. II, The Tender Passion, 1986; Freud for Historians, 1985; A Godless Jew: Freud, Atheism, and the Making of Psychoanalysis, 1987; Freud: A Life in Our Time, 1988. Add: 105 Blue Trail, Hamden, Conn. 06518, U.S.A.

GAYDON, Alfred Gordon. British, b. 1911. Chemistry, Physics. Emeritus Prof., Imperial Coll., London, since 1973 (Prof. of Molecular Spectroscopy, 1961–73). Warren Research Fellow, Royal Soc., 1945–74. *Publs:* (with R.W.B. Pearse) The Identification of Molecular Spectra, 1941, 4th ed. 1976; Spectroscopy and Combustion Theory, 1942; Dissociation Energies and Spectra of Diatomic Molecules, 1947; (with H.G. Wolfhard) Flames, Their Structure, Radiation and Temperature, 1953, 1979; The Spectroscopy of Flames, 1957; (with I.R. Hurle) The Shock Tube in High-Temperature Chemical Physics, 1963; (co-ed.) Shock Tube Research—Proceedings of The Eight International Shock Tube Symposium, 1971. Add: Dale Cottage, Shellbridge Rd., Slindon Common, Nr. Arundel, Sussex, England.

GAYLE, Emma. *See* **FAIRBURN,** Eleanor.

GAYLIN, Willard. American, b. 1925. Civil liberties/Human rights, Law, Psychology. Clinical Prof. of Psychiatry, Columbia Psychoanalytic Sch., NYC, since 1972 (joined faculty, 1956). Co-Founder and Pres., The Hastings Center (Inst. of Soc., Ethics and the Life Sciences), since 1970. Formerly Adjunct Prof. of Psychiatry, Union Theological Seminary, NYC; Adjunct Prof. of Psychiatry and Law, Columbia Univ. Sch of Law, NYC, 1970. *Publs:* (with H. Hendrin and A. Carr) Psychoanalysis and Social Research, 1965; The Meaning of Despair, 1968, 2nd ed. as Psychodynamic Understanding of Depression: The Meaning of Despair, 1984; In the Service of Their Country: War Resisters in Prison, 1970; (with R. Veatch and C. Morgan) The Teaching of Medical Ethics, 1973; Partial Justice: A Study of Bias in Sentencing, 1975; (with

J. Meister and R. Neville) Operating on the Mind: The Psychosurgery Conflict, 1975; Caring, 1976; (with I. Glasser, S. Marcus and D.J. Rothman) Doing Good: The Limits of Benevolence, 1978; Feelings: Our Vital Signs, 1979; (ed. with others) Violence and the Politics of Research, 1981; (ed. with R. Macklin) Who Speaks for the Child?: The Problems of Proxy Consent, 1982; The Killing of Bonnie Garland: A Question of Justice, 1982; The Rage Within: Anger in Modern Life, 1984; Rediscovering Love, 1986; (ed. with E. Person) Passionate Attachments: Thinking About Love, 1988. Add: Hastings Center, Hastings-on-Hudson, N.Y. 10706, U.S.A.

GAYRE OF GAYRE AND NIGG, Robert. British, b. 1907. Anthropolbogy/Ethnology, Genealogy/Heraldry, Military/Defence, Autobiography. Ed., The Armorial, since 1959, and The Mankind Quarterly, since 1977 (Ed., 1959–77). Life Pres., Heraldic Soc. of Malta, since 1970. Prof. of Anthropology, and Head of Dept. of Anthropo-Geography, Univ. of Saugor, India, 1954–56. *Publs:* Teuton and Slav on the Polish Frontier, 1944; Italy in Transition, 1946; Gayre's Booke, 4 vols., 1948–59; Wassail! In Mazers of Mead, 1948; The Heraldry of the Knights of St. John, 1956; Heraldic Standards and Other Ensigns, 1959; The Nature of Arms, 1961; Heraldic Cadency, 1961; The Armorial Who Is Who, 1961, 4th ed. 1980; Who Is Who in Clan Gayre, 1962; A Case of Monarchy, 1962; Roll of Scottish Arms, Part I, vol. I, 1964; Part II, vol. I, 1969; Ethnological Elements in Africa, 1966; Zimbabwe, 1972; Miscellaneous Ethnological Papers, 2 vols., 1972–73; More Ethnological Elements in Africa, 1973; The Knightly Twilight, 1973; The Lost Clan, 1974; Minard Castle, 1978; Mackays of the Rhinns of Islay, 1979; An Autobiography, 1987; The Power Beyond, 1989. Add: Minard Castle, Minard Argyll, Scotland.

GAZE, R(aymond) Michael. British, b. 1927. Biology. Head, Medical Research Council Neural Development and Regeneration Group, Univ. of Edinburgh, since 1984. Lectr., 1955–62, and Reader, 1966–70, Dept. of Physiology, Edinburgh Univ., Head of the Div. of Developmental Biology, 1970–83, and Deputy Dir., 1977–83, National Inst. for Medical Research, London. *Publs:* The Formation of Nerve Connections, 1970. Add: 37 Sciennes Rd., Edinburgh EH9 INS, Scotland.

GEACH, Christine. Also writes as Elizabeth Dawson, Anne Lowing, and Christine Wilson. British, b. 1930. Historical/Romance/Gothic. Freelance writer. *Publs:* (as Christine Wilson) Broken Vows; (as Anne Lowing) Masked Ball, 1966; (as Christine Wilson) Trial of Love; (as Christine Wilson) A Husband for Charlotte; (as Anne Lowing) The Denbigh Affair, 1967; (as Christine Wilson) A Deeper Love; (as Christine Wilson) Love's True Face; (as Christine Wilson) The Doubting Heart; (as Anne Lowing) Yasmin, 1969; (as Christine Wilson) Nurse Emma in Love; (as Christine Wilson) Dr. Mary's Dilemma; (as Christine Wilson) Watch for Me by Moonlight; (as Christine Wilson) The Driven Clouds; (as Christine Wilson) Where Is Tomorrow; (as Christine Wilson) The Gift of Happy Rain; (as Anne Lowing) Shadow on the Wind, 1970; (as Christine Wilson) Is This My Island?; (as Christine Wilson) The Lonely Tower; (as Anne Lowing) The Gossamer Thread; (as Christine Wilson) This Nearly Was Mine; (as Christine Wilson) Some Other Spring; (as Anne Lowing) Melyonen; (as Christine Wilson) The Man Beyond Price; (as Elizabeth Dawson) Isle of Dreams; (as Elizabeth Dawson) Wine in a Crystal Goblet; (as Anne Lowing) The Captain's Pawn; (as Anne Lowing) The Napoleon Ring; (as Anne Lowing) The Branch and the Briar, 1976; (as Christine Wilson) The Man in the Blue Car, 1978; (as Anne Lowing) Copper Moon, 1979; (as Christine Wilson) Proud Swells the Tide, 1979; (as Elizabeth Dawson) The Bending Reed, 1979; (as Christine Wilson) The Light in the Window, 1980; (as Anne Lowing) Girl in the Shadows, 1984. Add: 6 Seaview Dr., Wembury, Plymouth PL9 0JR, England.

GEARHEART, Bill R. American, b. 1928. Education. Prof. of Special Education, Univ. of Northern Colorado, Greeley. *Publs:* (with E. Willenberg) Application of Pupil Assessment Information, 1970, 3rd ed. 1980; (ed. and contrib.) Education of the Exceptional Child: History, Present Practices and Trends, 1972; Learning Disabilities: Educational Strategies, 1973, 5th ed., 1989; Organization and Administration of Programs for the Exceptional Child, 1974, 1979; (with F. Litton) Trainable Mentally Retarded: A Foundation Approach, 1975, 1979; The Exceptional Student in the Regular Classroom, 1976, 4th ed. 1988; Teaching the Learning Disabled: A Combined Task-Process Approach, 1976; (with G. Marsh and C. Gearhart) The Learning Disabled Adolescent, 1978; Special Education for the '80's, 1980; (with James De Ruiter) Teaching Mildly and Moderately Handicapped Students, 1986; (with C. Gearheart) Assessment Principles and Practices, 1990. Add: 2209 20th St., Rd., Greeley, Colo. 80631, U.S.A.

GÉBLER, Ernest. Irish, b. 1915. Novels/,-Short stories, Plays/-

Screenplays. *Publs:* He Had My Heart Scalded, 1946; The Plymouth Adventure: The Voyage of the Mayflower, 1949; A Week in the Country: The Love Investigator; The Old Man and the Girl; Girl with Green Eyes (screenplay), 1962; Day of Freedom (screenplay), 1968; Call Me Daddy (TV play), 1968 (U.S. "Emmy"); Hoffman (play), 1976; Cry for Help (play), 1976; A Civilized Life (novel), 1979; Not the End of the World (novel), 1985.   Add: 92 Coliemore Rd., Dalkey, Dublin, Ireland.

GEDDES, Gary. Canadian, b. 1940. Stories, Poetry. Prof. of English, Concordia Univ., Montreal, since 1979 (Visiting Assoc. Prof., 1978–79). Gen. Ed., Studies in Canadian Literature series, for Douglas and McIntyre, Vancouver.   Visiting Asst. Prof., Trent Univ., Peterborough, Ont., 1968–69; Lectr., Carleton Univ., Ottawa, 1971–72, and Univ. of Victoria, B.C. 1972–74; Writer-in-Residence, 1976–77, and Visiting Assoc. Prof., 1977–78, Univ. of Alberta, Edmonton. *Publs:* (ed.) 20th Century Poetry and Poets, 1969, 3rd ed. 1985; (ed., with Phyllis Bruce) 15 Canadian Poets, 1970, 3rd ed. 1988; Poems, 1970; Rivers Inlet (verse), 1972; Snakeroot (verse), 1973; Letter of the Master of Horse (verse), 1973; (ed.) Skookum Wawa: Writings of the Canadian Northwest, 1975; War and Other Measures (verse), 1976; (ed.) Divided We Stand, 1977; Conrad's Later Novels, 1980; The Acid Test (verse), 1981; (ed.) The Inner Ear: An Anthology of New Canadian Poets, 1983; The Terracotta Army (verse), 1984; (co-trans.) I Didn't Notice the Mountain Growing Dark, 1985; Changes of State (verse), 1986; (ed.) Vancouver: Soul of a City, 1986; The Unsettling of the West (stories), 1986; Hong Kong (verse), 1987.   Add: Dept. of English, Concordia Univ., 1455 de Maisonneuve Blvd. W., Montreal, Que. H3G 1M8, Canada.

GEE, Maggie (Mary). British, b. 1948. Novels. Writing Fellow, Univ. of East Anglia, Norwich, 1982. *Publs:* Dying in Other Words, 1981; (ed.) For Life on Earth, 1982; The Burning Book, 1983; Light Years, 1985; Grace, 1987.   Add: c/o William Heinemann Ltd., 81 Fulham Rd., London SW3 6RB, England.

GEE, Maurice (Gough). New Zealander, b. 1931. Novels/Short stories, Children's fiction. Full-time writer since 1975, Librarian and teacher, 1955–75. *Publs:* The Big Season, 1962; A Special Flower, 1965; In My Father's Den, 1972; A Glorious Morning, Comrade: Stories, 1975; Games of Choice, 1976; Plumb, 1978; Under the Mountain, 1979; The World Around the Corner, 1980; Meg, 1981; The Halfmen of O, 1982; Sole Survivor, 1983; The Priests of Ferris, 1984; Motherstone, 1985; Collected Stories, 1986; The Fireraiser, 1986; Prowlers, 1987; The Champion, 1989.   Add: 125 Cleveland Terrace, Nelson, New Zealand.

GEE, Shirley. British, b. 1932. Plays/Screenplays. Actress, 1952–66. *Publs:* Typhoid Mary (in Best Radio Plays of 1979), 1980; Never in My Lifetime (in Best Radio Plays of 1983), 1984, as stage play, 1987; Ask for the Moon, 1987.   Add: 28 Fernshaw Rd., London SW10 0TF, England.

GEERING, R(onald) G(eorge). Australian, b. 1918. Literature. Vice-Pres., English Assn., Sydney, since 1974 (Member, Exec. Cttee., 1957–67; Pres., 1968–74). Lectr., 1952–57, Sr. Lectr., 1957–68, and Assoc. Prof. of English, 1969–78, Univ. of New South Wales, Sydney. *Publs:* Christina Stead, 1969, 1979; (ed.) The Miner's Right by Rolf Boldrewood, 1973; Recent Fiction, 1974; (ed.) Southern Lights and Shadows, by Frank Fowler, 1975; (ed.) Ocean of Story, by Christina Stead, 1985; (ed.) I'm Dying Laughing, by Christina Stead, 1986.   Add: 11 Burgoyne St., Gordon, N.S.W. 2072, Australia.

GEERTZ, Clifford (James). American, b. 1926. Anthropology. Prof. of Social Science, Inst. for Advanced Study, Princeton, N.J., since 1970. Research Associate, Center for International Studies, Massachusetts Institute of Technology, in Indonesia, 1957–58; Fellow, Center for Advanced Study in the Behavioral Sciences, Stanford, Calif., 1958–59; Asst. Prof. of Anthropology, Univ. of California, Berkeley, 1959–60; Asst. Prof. of Anthropology, 1960–61, Assoc. Prof., 1961–64, and Prof., 1964–70, Univ. of Chicago. Eastman Prof., Oxford Univ., 1978–79. Chairman, Committee for the Comparative Study of New Nations, 1968–69. *Publs:* The Rotating Credit Association: An Instrument for Development, 1956; The Development of the Javanese Economy: A Socio-Cultural Approach, 1956; The Social Context of Economic Change: An Indonesian Case Study, 1956; Modjokuto: Religion in Java, 1960; Agricultural Involution: The Process of Ecological Change in Indonesia, 1963; (ed.) Old Societies and New States, 1963; Peddlers and Princes: Social Change and Economic Modernization in Two Indonesian Towns, 1963; The Social History of an Indonesian Town, 1965; Person, Time and Conduct in Bali: An Essay in Cultural Analysis, 1966; Islam Observed: Religious Development in Morocco and Indonesia, 1968; The Interpretation of Cultures, 1973; (ed.)

Myth, Symbol and Culture, 1974; (with Hildred Geertz) Kinship in Bali, 1975; (with L. Rosen and Hildred Geertz) Meaning and Order in Moroccan Society, 1979; Negara: The Theatre State in Nineteenth-Century Bali, 1980; Local Knowledge, 1983; Works and Lives: The Anthropologist as Author, 1988.   Add: Sch. of Social Science, Inst. for Advanced Study, Princeton, N.J. 08540, U.S.A.

GEHMAN, Christian. American, b. 1948. Novels/Short Stories, Children's fiction. Contributing Ed., Style Weekly, Richmond, since 1984. Pres., The Woodstock Youth Center, 1965–66; Sports Writer, Kingston Daily Freeman, Kingston, N.Y., 1966–67; Syndicated Food Columnist, 1969–74. *Publs:* Beloved Gravely (novel), 1984; Isengard and Northern Gondor, 1984; Riders of Rohan (children's), 1985; A Southern Celebration: Charleston and Savannah Proclaimed (photographic essay), 1985.   Add: 300 N. Lombardy, Richmond, Va. 23220, U.S.A.

GEIGER, Don Jesse. American, b. 1923. Poetry, Literature. Prof. of Rhetoric, Univ. of California, Berkeley, since 1950. Consulting Ed. in Speech, Random House Publrs. Ed., Western Speech, 1955–57; Assoc. Ed., Quarterly Journal of Speech, 1960–62 and 1969–71. *Publs:* The Age of the Splendid Machine, 1960; The Sound, Sense and Performance of Literature, 1963; The Dramatic Impulse in Modern Poetics, 1967; Hero's Way, 1971.   Add: c/o Louisiana State Univ. Press, Highland Rd., Baton Rouge, La. 70893, U.S.A.

GEISERT, Arthur (Frederick). American, b. 1941. Children's fiction. Artist and writer. Former Art Teacher, Concordia Coll., River Forest, Ill., Concordia Coll., Seward, Nebr., and Clark Coll., Dubuque, Iowa. *Publs:* (self-illustrated) Pa's Balloon and Other Pig Tales, 1984; Alphabet Book, 1985; (self-illustrated) Pigs from A to Z, 1986; (self-illustrated) The Building of Noah's Ark, 1988; The Ark, 1988.   Add: P.O. Box 3, Galena, Ill. 61036, U.S.A.

GEISLER, Norman (Leo). American, b. 1932. Philosophy, Theology/Religion. Dean of Liberty Center for Christian Scholarship, Lynchbury VA. Formerly: Prof. of Systematic Theology, Dallas Theological Seminary; Asst. Prof., 1966–70, and Professor and Chmn., from 1970, Philosophy of Religion Dept., Trinity Evangelical Divinity Sch., Deerfield, Ill. *Publs:* (co-author) General Introduction to the Bible, 1968; Ethics: Alternatives and Issues, 1971; The Christian Ethic of Love, 1973; Philosophy of Religion, 1974; (co-author) From God to Us, 1974; Christ, The Key to Interpreting the Bible, 1975; Christian Apologetics, 1976; Roots of Evil, 1977; A Popular Survey of the Old Testament, 1977; (with P. Feinberg) Introduction to Philosophy, 1979; (ed.) Inerrancy, 1979; (ed.) Biblical Errancy, 1981; Options in Contemporary Christian Ethics, 1981; The Roots of Evil, 1981; Decide for Yourself: How History Views the Bible, 1982; Miracles and Modern Thought, 1982; (ed.) What Augustine Says, 1982; The Creator in the Courtroom, 1982; Cosmos: Carl Sagan's Religion for the Scientific Mind, 1983; (with J. Amano) The Religion of the Force, 1983; Is Man the Measure? An Evaluation of Contemporary Humanism, 1983; (with W. Watkins) Perspectives, 1984; False Gods of Our Time, 1985; (with J. Amano) The Reincarnation Sensation, 1986; (with K. Anderson) Origin Science, 1987; To Drink or Not to Drink, 1987; Signs and Wonders, 1988; World's Apart, 1988.   Add: 7 Fairwinds Ct., Forest, VA 24551, U.S.A.

GEISMAR, Ludwig Leo. American, b. 1921. Sociology. Prof. of Social Work and Sociology, and Dir., Social Work Research Center, Graduate Sch. of Social Work and Dept. of Sociology, Rutgers Univ., New Brunswick, N.J., since 1963 (Assoc. Prof., 1959–62). Coordinator of Social Research, Ministry of Social Welfare, Israel, 1954–56; Research Dir., Family Centered Project, St. Paul, Minn., 1956–59. *Publs:* (with M.A. LaSorte) Understanding the Multi-Problem Family: A Conceptual Analysis and Exploration in Identification, 1964; (with J. Krisberg) The Forgotten Neighborhood: Site of an Early Skirmish in the War on Poverty, 1967; Preventive Intervention in Social Work, 1969; Family and Community Functioning, 1971, 1980; (with Lagay, Wolock, Gerhart and Fink) Early Supports for Family Life, 1972; 555 Families: A Social Psychological Study of Young Families in Transition, 1973; (with S. Geismar) Families in an Urban Mold, 1979; (ed. with M. Dinerman) A Quarter Century of Social Work Education, 1984; (with K. Wood) Family and Delinquency: Resocializing the Young Offender, 1986; (with K. Wood) Families at Risk: Treating the Multiproblem Family, 1989.   Add: 347 Valentine St., Highland Park, N.J. 08904, U.S.A.

GEIST, Harold. American, b. 1916. Medicine/Health, Psychiatry, Psychology. Private practice in clinical psychology, Berkeley, Calif., since 1954. Staff Research Psychologist, Gladman Memorial Hosp. and

Foundn., Oakland, Calif., since 1970; Prof., California Univ. of Advanced Studies, since 1986. Clinical Psychologist, Lawson Gen. Hosp., Atlanta, Ga., 1943–44, and 305 Gen. Hosps., Tacoma, Washington, France, Philippines and Japan, 1944–46; Assoc. Advisement and Guidance Officer, Central Office, Veterans Admin., Washington, D.C., 1946–47; Psychologist Jr. Coll., Vallejo, Calif., 1947–48; Chief Clinical Psychologist, Mare Island Naval Hosp., Calif., 1951–53; Consultant, Unified Sch. District, Pittsburg, Calif., 1956–59; Principal Investigator, Picture Interest Research Project for the Deaf, Berkeley Sch. for the Deaf, Calif., 1959–61; San Francisco State Univ., 1966–82, and Lectr., Univ. of San Francisco, 1982–83. *Publs:* The Etiology of Idiopathic Epilepsy, 1962; The Psychological Aspects of Diabetes, 1964; A Child Goes to the Hospital, 1965; The Psychological Aspects of Rheumatoid Arthritis, 1966; The Psychological Aspects of Retirement, 1968; The Psychological Aspects of the Aging Process, 1968; From Eminently Disadvantaged to Eminence, 1973; Tennis Psychology, 1974; The Emotional Aspects of Heart Disease, 1975; Emotional Aspects of Migraine, 1980; Bahian Adventure (novel), 1982; Manual for Retirement Counselors, 1988. Add: 2255 Hearst Ave., Berkeley, Calif. 94709, U.S.A.

GELBART, Larry. American, b. 1928. Plays/Screenplays. *Publs:* My L.A., 1950; The Conquering Hero, 1960; The Notorious Landlady (screenplay), 1960; A Funny Thing Happened on the Way to the Forum (musical comedy), 1961; The Wrong Box (screenplay), 1966; Not with My Wife You Don't (screenplay), 1966; MASH (TV series), 1972–76; Sly Fox (play), 1977; Oh, God! (screenplay), 1978; Movie, Movie (screenplay), 1979; United States (TV series), 1980; Tootsie (screenplay), 1982; Blame It on Rio (screenplay), 1984; Mastergate (play), 1989. Add: 807 N. Alpine Dr., Beverly Hills, Calif. 90210, U.S.A.

GELBER, Jack. American, b. 1932. Novels/Short stories, Plays/Screenplays. Prof. of Drama, Brooklyn Coll., NYC, since 1972. Assoc. Prof. of Drama, Columbia Univ., NYC, 1966–72. *Publs:* The Connection, 1960; The Apple, 1961; On Ice (novel), 1964; Square in the Eye, 1965; The Cuban Thing, 1968; Sleep, 1972; Rehearsal, 1976; Starters, 1982; Big Shot, 1988. Add: 215 Marlborough Rd., Brooklyn, N.Y. 11226, U.S.A.

GELLHORN, Martha. American, b. 1908. Novels/Short stories, Autobiography/Memoirs/Personal. War Corresp., Collier's Weekly, NYC, in Spain, 1937–38, Finland, 1939. China, 1940–41, England, Italy, France and Germany, 1943–45, and Java, 1946; and for the Guardian newspaper, London, in Vietnam, 1966, and Israel, 1967. *Publs:* What Mad Pursuit, 1934; The Trouble I've Seen, 1936; A Stricken Field, 1940; The Heart of Another, 1941; Liana, 1944; The Wine of Astonishment, 1948; The Honeyed Peace, 1953; Two by Two, 1958; The Face of War, 1959; His Own Man, 1961; Pretty Tales for Tired People, 1965; The Lowest Trees Have Tops, 1969; The Weather in Africa, 1978; Travels with Myself and Another, 1978; The View from the Ground, 1988. Add: 72 Cadogan Sq., London SW1, England.

GELLIS, Roberta (Leah Jacobs). Also writes as Max Daniels, Priscilla Hamilton, and Leah Jacobs. American, b. 1927. Historical/Romance/Gothic, Science fiction/Fantasy. Freelance ed., Macmillan Co., NYC, 1956–58, and since 1971. Chemist, Foster D. Snell Inc., NYC, 1947–53; Ed., McGraw-Hill Book Co., NYC, 1953–56; freelance ed., Academic Press, NYC, 1956–70. *Publs:* Knight's Honor, 1964; Bond of Blood, 1965; (as Leah Jacobs) The Psychiatrist's Wife, Sing Witch, Sing Death, 1975; The Sword and the Swan, 1977; The Roselynde Chronicles: Roselynde, 1978, Alinor, 1978, Joanna, 1978, Gilliane, 1979, Rhiannon, 1982; Sybelle, 1983; (as Max Daniels) Space Guardian (science fiction), 1978; (as Max Daniels) Offworld! (science fiction), 1979; (as Priscilla Hamilton) Love Token, 1979; Heiress Series: The English Heiress, 1980, The Cornish Heiress, 1981, The Kent Heiress, 1982, Fortune's Bride, 1983, A Woman's Estate, 1984; Siren's Song, 1981; Winter Song, 1982; Fire Song, 1984; A Tapestry of Dreams, 1985; The Rope Dancer, 1986; Fires of Winter, 1987; Masques of Gold, 1988; A Silver Mirror, 1989. Add: Box 483, Roslyn Heights, N.Y. 11577, U.S.A.

GELL-MANN, Murray. American, b. 1929. Physics. Prof. since 1956 and Robert A. Millikan Prof. of Physics since 1967, California Institute of Technology, Pasadena (Assoc. Prof., 1955–56). Dir., MacArthur Foundn., Chicago, since 1979. Instructor, 1952–53, Asst. Prof., 1953–54, and Assoc. Prof., 1954–55, Univ. of Chicago. Member, President's Science Advisory Committee, 1969–72. Regent, Smithsonian Inst., Washington, D.C., 1974–88. Recipient, Nobel Prize in Physics, 1969. *Publs:* Lectures on Weak Interactions of Strongly Interacting Particles, 1961; (with Yuval Ne'eman) The Eightfold Way: A Review with a Collection of Reprints, 1964. Add: Dept. of Physics,

California Inst. of Technology, Pasadena, Calif. 91125, U.S.A.

GELLNER, Ernest (André). British, b. 1925. Philosophy, Sociology. William Wyse Prof. of Social Anthropology, and Fellow of King's Coll., Cambridge, since 1984. Asst. Lectr., 1949–51, Lectr., 1951–57, Reader, 1957–62, and Prof., 1962–84, London Sch. of Economics. *Publs:* Words and Things, 1959; Thought and Change, 1965; Saints of the Atlas, 1969; Cause and Meaning in the Social Sciences, 1973; Contemporary Thought and Politics, 1974; The Devil in Modern Philosophy, 1974; Legitimation of Belief, 1975; Spectacles and Predicaments, 1979; Muslim Society, 1981; Nations and Nationalism, 1982; The Psychoanalytic Movement, 1985; Concept of Kinship and Other Essays, 1987; Culture, Identity, and Politics, 1987; Plough, Sword and Book, 1988; State and Society in Soviet Thought, 1988. Add: King's Coll., Cambridge, England.

GELPI, Albert. American, b. 1931. Literature. Coe Prof. of American Literature, Stanford Univ., Calif., since 1978 (Assoc. Prof., 1968–74; Prof., 1974–78). Ed., Cambridge Studies in American Literature and Culture. Asst. Prof., Harvard Univ., Cambridge, Mass., 1962–68. *Publs:* Emily Dickinson: The Mild of the Poet, 1965; The Poet in America: 1950 to Present, 1973; (ed. with Barbara Charlesworth Gelpi) The Poetry of Adrienne Rich, 1975; The Tenth Muse: The Psyche of the American Poet, 1975; (ed.) Wallace Stevens: The Poetics of Modernism, 1986; A Coherent Splendor: The American Poetic Renaissance 1910-1950, 1988. Add: Dept. of English, Stanford Univ., Stanford, Calif. 94305, U.S.A.

GEMS, Pam. British, b. 1925. Novels/Short stories, Plays/Screenplays. *Publs:* Dusa, Fish, Stas, and Vi, 1977; Piaf, 1979; (adaptor) Uncle Vanya, by Chekhov, 1979; Queen Christina, 1980; Camille, Piaf, Loving Woman, 1984; Mrs. Frampton (novel), 1989. Add: c/o ACTAC, 16 Cadogan Lane, London SW1, England.

GENAUER, Emily. American. Art, Dance/Ballet. Arts Critic and Columnist for the Newsday Syndicate, NYC, since 1967. Member of Exec. Bd., Connecticut Coll. Sch. of Dance; Member of Bd., Martha Graham Sch. of Contemporary Dance; Member of Advisory Bd., Columbia Univ. Sch. of Journalism. Staff Writer and Art Feature Writer, New York World, 1929–31; Art Critic and Ed., New York World-Telegram, 1932–49; Art Critic, New York Herald Tribune, 1949–66; Art Critic and Ed., New York World-Journal-Tribune, 1966–67. *Publs:* The Best of Art, 1947; Chagall, 1957; Hommage à l'Ecole de Paris, 1962; Chagall at the Met, 1971; Tamayo, 1973; American Ballet Theatre, 1976. Add: 243 E. 49th St., New York, N.Y. 10017, U.S.A.

GENTLE, Mary. British, b. 1956. Science fiction, Children's fiction. Has worked as a movie projectionist, clerk, and civil servant. *Publs:* A Hawk in Silver (for children), 1977; Golden Witchbreed, 1983; Ancient Light, 1987. Add: 56 Coombe Rd., Flat 3, Croydon, Surrey, England.

GENTLEMAN, David. British, b. 1930. Children's fiction, Architecture, Travel/Exploration/Adventure. Freelance graphic designer and painter. *Publs:* Fenella in France, 1964; Fenella in Spain, 1964; Fenella in Greece, 1964; Fenella in Ireland, 1964; Design in Miniature, 1972; Everyday Architecture in Towns, 1975; Everyday Architecture in the Country, 1975; Everyday Architecture at the Seaside, 1975; Everyday Industrial Architecture, 1975; David Gentleman's Britain, 1982; David Gentleman's London, 1985; A Special Relationship, 1987; David Gentleman's Coastline, 1988. Add: 25 Gloucester Cres., London NW1 7DL, England.

GENTRY, Curt. American. Science fiction/Fantasy, History, Biography. Freelance writer since 1961. Head of Mail Order Dept., Paul Elder Books, San Francisco, 1954–57; Mgr., Harper Books, San Francisco, 1957–61. *Publs:* The Dolphin Guide to San Francisco and the Bay Area: Present and Past, 1962, 1969; The Madams of San Francisco: An Irrevent History of the City by the Golden Gate, 1964; (with John M. Browning) John M. Browning, American Gunmaker, 1964; The Vulnerable Americans, 1966; Frame-Up: The Incredible Case of Tom Mooney and Warren Billings, 1967; The Killer Mountains: A Search for the Legendary Lost Dutchman Mine, 1968; The Last Days of the Late, Great State of California (science fiction novel), 1968; (with Francis Gary Powers) Operation Overflight, 1970; (ed.) King of Loving, by Toni L. Scott, 1970; (with Edward R. Murphy, Jr.) Second in Command, 1971; (with Vincent Bugliosi) Helter Skelter, 1974, in U.K. as The Manson Murders, 1975. Add: 1955 Stockton St., San Francisco, Calif. 94133, U.S.A.

GEORGE, Claude S(wanson), Jr. American, b. 1920. Administration/Management. Prof., Sch. of Business Admin., Univ. of North

Carolina, Chapel Hill, 1954–80 (Assoc. Dean, 1958–77). Member, mgmt. staff, Western Electric Co., 1946–50; Prof., Univ. of Texas, Austin, 1953–54. *Publs:* Management in Industry, 1959, 1964; History of Management Thought, 1968; 1972; Management for Business and Industry, 1970; Supervision in Action, 1977, 4th ed. 1985; Action Guide for Supervisors, 1981. Add: Sch. of Business Admin., Univ. of North Carolina, Chapel Hill, N.C. 27514, U.S.A.

GEORGE, Eliot. *See* **FREEMAN**, Gillian.

GEORGE, Emily. *See* **KATZ**, Bobbi.

GEORGE, Graham Elias. Canadian (b. British), b. 1912. Music. Prof. of Music Emeritus, Queen's Univ., Kingston, Ont. (Prof. 1946–77). Pres., Canadian Folk Music Soc., 1965–68; Secty-Gen., Intnl. Folk Music Council, 1969–80; Pres., Royal Canadian Coll. of Organists, 1972–74. *Publs:* Tonality and Musical Structure, 1970; Twelve-Note Tonal Species Counterpoint, 1975. Add: 151 Earl St., Kingston, Ont. Canada.

GEORGE, Jean Craighead. American, b. 1919. Children's fiction, Children's non-fiction, Natural history. Reporter, Intnl. News Service, 1942–44, and Washington Post, 1943–46, both Washington, D.C.; Artist Pageant Magazine, NYC, 1946–47; Staff Writer, 1969–74, and Roving Ed., 1974–81, Reader's Digest, Pleasantville, N.Y. *Publs:* (with John L. George) Vulpes the Red Fox, 1948; (with John L. George) Vison the Mink, 1949; (with John L. George) Masked Prowler: The Story of a Raccoon, 1950; (with John L. George) Meph, The Pet Skunk, 1952; (with John L. George) Bubo the Great Horned Owl. 1954; (with John L. George) Dipper the Copper Creek, 1956; Snow Tracks, 1958; My Side of the Mountain, 1959; The Summer of the Falcon, 1962; Red Robin Fly Up!, 1963; Gull Number 737, 1964; Hold Zero, 1966; Spring Comes to the Ocean, 1966; The Thirteen Moons (The Moon of the Owls, Bears, Salamander, Chicadee, Monarch, Butterfly, Fox Pups, Wild Pigs, Mountain Lion, Deer, Alligator, Wolves, Winter Bird, and Mole), 13 vols., 1967–69; The Hole in the Tree, 1967; Coyote in Manhattan, 1968; Beastly Inventions: A Surprising Investigation into How Smart Animals Really Are (in U.K. as Animals Can Do Anything), 1970; All upon a Stone, 1971; Who Really Killed Cock Robin?, 1971; Julie of the Wolves, 1972; Everglades Wildguide, 1972; All upon a Sidewalk, 1974; Hook a Fish, Catch a Mountain, 1975; Going to the Sun, 1976; The Wentletrap Trap, 1977; The American Walk Book, 1977; The Wounded Wolf, 1978; River Rats, 1979; Journey Inward (autobiography), 1982; The Wild Wild Book Cookbook, 1982; The Grizzly Bear with the Golden Ears, 1982; The Talking Earth, 1983; One Day in the Desert Alpine Tundra, Prairie, 3 vols., 1983–87; How to Talk to Your Animals, 1986; Water Sky, 1987; Shark Beneath the Reef, 1988. Add: 20 William St., Chappaqua, N.Y. 10514, U.S.A.

GEORGE, Jonathan. *See* **BURKE**, John.

GEORGE, Wilma (Beryl). British, b. 1918. Sciences, Zoology, Biography. Fellow and Tutor in Zoology, Lady Margaret Hall, and Univ. Lectr., Univ. of Oxford, since 1958. *Publs:* Elementary Genetics, 1951, 1965; Animal Geography, 1962; Biologist Philosopher: The Life and Writings of A.R. Wallace, 1964; Eating in Eight Languages, 1968; Animals and Maps: A Study of Early Cartographers and Their Contributions to Zoogeography, 1969; Gregor Mendel and Heredity, 1975; Darwin, 1982. Add: Lady Margaret Hall, Oxford, England.

GERAS, Adele (Daphne, née Weston). British, b. 1944. Children's fiction, Poetry. French teacher, Fairfield High Sch., Droylsden, Lancashire, 1968–71. *Publs:* Tea at Mrs. Manderby's, 1976; Apricots at Midnight and Other Stories from a Patchwork Quilt, 1982; Beyond the Cross Stitch Mountains, 1977; The Girls in the Velvet Frame, 1979; The Painted Garden, 1979; A Thousand Yards of Sea, 1981; The Rug That Grew, 1981; The Green Behind the Glass, 1982, in U.S. as Snapshots of Paradise: Love Stories, 1984; Other Echoes, 1982; The Christmas Cat, 1983; Voyage, 1983; Letters of Fire and Other Unsettling Stories, 1984; Happy Endings, 1986; Little Elephant's Moon, 1986; Ritchie's Rabbit, 1986; Finding Annabel, 1987; Fishpie for Flamingoes, 1987; The Fantora Family Files, 1988; The Strange Bird, 1988; The Coronation Picnic, 1989; other for adults—(with Pauline Stainer) Up on the Roof (poetry), 1987. Add: 10 Danesmoor Rd., Manchester M20 9JS, England.

GERAS, Norman (Myron). British, b. 1943. Politics/Government. Sr. Lectr. in Govt., Univ. of Manchester, since 1984 (Lectr., 1967–84). Member, Editorial Cttee., New Left Review, since 1976. *Publs:* The Legacy of Rosa Luxemburg, 1976; Marx and Human Nature, 1983; Literature of Revolution, 1986. Add: Dept. of Govt., Univ. of Manchester,

Manchester M13 9PL, England.

GERBER, Douglas E. Canadian, b. 1933. Classics, Literature. Prof. in Classics, since 1969, Univ. of Western Ontario, London (Lectr., 1959–60, Asst. Prof., 1960–64; Assoc. Prof., 1964–69). Member, American Philological Assn. (Ed., Transactions of the American Philological Assn., 1974–82), Classical Assn. of Canada, and Classical Assn. (Great Britain). Lectr. in Greek, Univ. Coll., Univ. of Toronto, Ont., 1958–59. *Publs:* A Bibliography of Pindar, 1513-1966, 1969; (ed.) Euterpe: An Anthology of Early Greek Lyric, Elegiac and Iambic Poetry, 1970; Emendations in Pindar, 1513-1972, 1974; Pindar's Olympian One: A Commentary, 1982; Lexicon in Bacchylidem, 1984. Add: Dept. of Classics, Univ. of Western Ontario, London, Ont. N6A 3K7, Canada.

GERBER, John C(hristian). American, b. 1908. Literature, Writing/Journalism. Instr., Univ. of Pittsburgh, 1931–36; Instr., Univ. of Chicago, 1938–42; Asst. Prof., 1944–47, Assoc. Prof., 1947–49, Prof., 1949–76, now Emeritus, Chmn. of the Dept., 1961–76, and Dir. of Sch. of Letters, 1967–76, Univ. of Iowa, Iowa City; Prof. of English, 1976–84, and Chmn. of the Dept., 1976–81, State Univ. of New York at Albany. Member of the Editorial Bd., College English, 1947–48, 1965–71, and American Quarterly, 1963–68; Editorial Adviser, Philological Quarterly, 1951–57. Pres., National Council of Teachers of English, 1955; Member of the Exec. Council, Modern Language Assn., 1972–75. *Publs:* (with Walter Blair) Factual Prose, 1945; Literature, 1948; Writers Resource Book, 1953; (co-author) Toward Better Writing,1958; (co-author) Speakers Resource Book, 1960; (ed.) Twentieth Century Interpretations of The Scarlet Letter, 1968; Studies in Huckleberry Finn, 1971; (ed.) Iowa-California Ed. of the Works of Mark Twain: Mark Twain, 1988; (with others) Pictorial History of the University of Iowa, 1988. Add: 359 Magowan Ave., Iowa City, Iowa 52240, U.S.A.

GERBER, William. American, b. 1908. Philosophy, Politics/Government. Staff, Office of Historical Adviser, Div. of Research and Publ., 1930–41, Asst. to Chief of Div., 1942–44, Asst. Chief of Current Research, Div. of Historical Policy Research, 1946–48, Chief, Special Studies Section, Historical Div., 1948–57, and Foreign Service Officer, 1957–60, U.S. Dept. of State; Chief, British Commonwealth Section, Div. of Foreign Labor Conditions, 1958–60, Chief of Research Branch, 1960–62, Acting Deputy Chief of Div., 1962–65, and Deputy Chief, 1965–68, U.S. Dept. of Labor; Writer and Indexer, Editorial Research Reports, 1968–71, and Congressional Quarterly, 1971–73, Washington, D.C. *Publs:* The Department of State of the United States, 1942; The Domain of Reality (philosophy), 1946; (with Letitia A. Lewis) Freedom of Information in American Policy and Practice, 1948; (with Edwin S. Costrell) The Department of State: 1930-1955, 1955; (compiler) The Mind of India, 1967, 1977; American Liberalism, 1975, 1987; Serenity, 1986. Add: 3077 Chestnut St. N.W., Washington, D.C. 20015, U.S.A.

GERLACH, Don. R. American, b. 1932. History. Prof. of History, Univ. of Akron, Ohio, since 1972 (Asst. Prof., 1962–65; Assoc. Prof., 1965–72). *Publs:* Philip Schuyler and the Amerian Revolution in New York 1733-1777, 1964; Twenty Years of the "Promotion of Literature": The Regents of the University of the State of New York 1784-1804, 1974; Proud Patriot: Philip Schuyler and the War of Independence 1775-1783, 1987. Add: Univ. of Akron, Ohio 44325, U.S.A.

GERNSHEIM, Helmut (Erich Robert). British, b. 1913. Photography, Biography. Founder, Gernsheim Collection, 1945, since 1964 at the Univ. of Texas at Austin. Adviser to the Ed., Encyclopaedia Britannica, since 1968; Trustee of the Swiss Foundation of Photography, since 1975, and Alimari Museum, Florence, since 1985. Co-ed., Photography Year Book, London 1952–54; Lectr. of the History of Photography and African Art, Franklin Coll., Lugano, 1971–72; Prof., History of Art, Univ. of Texas, Austin, 1979, at Arizona State Univ., 1982, at Univ. of California, Riverside, 1984, at Univ. of California, Santa Barbara, 1985, 1989. *Publs:* New Photo Vision, 1942; (with C. Bell) Twelfth Century Wall paintings, 1947; The Main Behind the Camera, 1948; 1979; Julia Margaret Cameron, 1948, 3rd ed. 1987; Focus on Architecture and Sculpture, 1949; Lewis Carroll—Photographer, 1949, 1969; Beautiful London, 1950; Masterpieces of Victorian Photography, 1951; (with Q. Bell) Those Impossible English, 1952; (with A. Gernsheim) Roger Fenton, 1954, 1973; (with R. Churchill) Churchill, His Life in Photographs, 1955; (with A. Gernsheim) The History of Photography, 1955, 3rd ed. 1983; (with A. Gernsheim) L.J.M. Daguerre, 1956; rev. ed. 1968; (with A. Gernsheim) Queen Victoria, 1959; (with A. Gernsheim) Historic Events (in U.S. as The Recording Eye), 1960; (with A. Gernsheim) Edward VII and Queen Alexandra, 1962; Creative Photography, 1962, 3rd ed. 1987; Concise History of Photography, 1965, 3rd ed. 1986; (with A. Gernsheim) Alvin

Langdon Coburn, Photographer, 1966, 1978; (ed.) Photo-Graphic Editions, 1970–73; The Origins of Photography, 1981; Incunabula of British Photographic Literature 1839-75, 1984; The Rise of Photography, 1988. Add: Via Tamporiva 28, CH 6976 Castagnola-Lugano, Switzerland.

GERRISH, Brian Albert. American (born British), b. 1931. Theology/Religion. John Nuveen Prof. of Historical Theology, Univ. of Chicago, since 1985 (Assoc. Prof. 1965–68; Prof., 1968–85). Instr., 1958–59, Asst. Prof., 1959–63, and Assoc. Prof. of Church History, 1963–65, McCormick Theological Seminary, Chicago. Co-ed., Journal of Religion, 1972–85. Pres., American Soc. of Church History, 1979. *Publs:* Grace and Reason: a Study in the Theology of Luther, 1962; (ed.) The Faith of Christendom: A Source Book of Creeds and Confessions, 1963; (ed.) Reformers in Profile, 1967; Tradition and the Modern World: Reformed Theology in the Nineteenth Century, 1978; (ed.) Reformatio Perennis: Essays on Calvin and the Reformation in Honor of Ford Lewis Battles, 1981; The Old Protestantism and the New: Essays on the Reformation Heritage, 1982; A Prince of the Church: Schleiermacher and the Beginnings of Modern Theology, 1984. Add: Swift Hall, Univ. of Chicago, Chicago, Ill. 60637, U.S.A.

GERROLD, David. American, b. 1944. Science fiction/Fantasy, Literature. Computer Columnist, CIT Profiles, since 1984. Columnist, Starlos and Galileo mags.; Story Ed., Land of the Lost TV series, 1974; also freelance writer of SF short stories, screenplays and TV plays. *Publs:* (with Larry Niven) The Flying Sorcerers, 1971; (ed. with Stephen Goldin) Protostars, 1971; (ed.) Generation, 1972; Space Skimmer, 1972; Yesterday's Children 1972; When Harlie Was One, 1972; With a Finger in My I (short stories), 1972; Battle for the Planet of the Apes (novelization of screenplay), 1973; The Man Who Folded Himself, 1973; The Trouble with Tribbles, 1973; The World of Star Trek, 1973; (ed. with Stephen Goldin) Science Fiction Emphasis 1, 1974; (ed. with Stephen Goldin) Alternities, 1974; (ed. with Stephen Goldin) Ascents of Wonder, 1977; Deathbeast, 1978; The Galactic Whirlpool, 1980; The War Against the Chtorr: A Matter for Man, 1983; A Day for Damnation, 1984; When Harlie Was Two, 1987; Chess with a Dragon, 1988. Add: Box 1190, Hollywood, Calif. 90028, U.S.A.

GERSHON, Karen. British, b. 1923. Novels/Short stories, Poetry, Social commentary/phenomena. *Publs:* (with C. Levenson and I. Crichton Smith) New Poets 1959, 1960; Selected Poems, 1966; (ed.) We Came as Children: A Collective Autobiography, 1966; (ed.) Postscript: A Collective Account of the Lives of Jews in West Germany Since the Second World War, 1969; Legacies and Encounters: Poems 1966-1971, 1972; My Daughters, My Sisters, 1975; Coming Back from Babylon, 1979; Burn Helen (novel) 1980; The Bread of Exile (novel), 1985; The Fifth Generation (novel), 1987. Add: c/o Victor Gollancz Ltd., 14 Henrietta St., London WC2E 8QJ, England.

GERSTENBERGER, Donna. American, b. 1929. Literature. Prof. of English, Univ. of Washington, Seattle, since 1960 (Chmn., Undergrad. Studies, 1971–74; Assoc. Dean, Coll. of Arts and Sciences, and Dir., Coll. Honors and Office of Undergrad. Studies, 1974– 76; Chmn., Dept. of English, 1976–83; Vice-Chmn. Faculty Senate, 1984–85, and Chmn. 1985–86). Editor, Swallow Series in Bibliography, since 1974. Assoc. Ed., Abstracts of English Studies, 1958–68. *Publs:* (co-author) Directory of Periodicals, 1959, 4th ed. 1975; (co-author) The American Novel: A Checklist of Twentieth-Century Criticism, 2 vols., 1961; John Millington Synge, 1964, 1988; (co-author) Microcosm: An Anthology of the Short Story, 1969; The Complete Configuration: Modern Verse Drama, 1974; Iris Murdoch, 1975; Richard Hugo, 1982. Add: Dept. of English, GN-30, Univ. of Washington, Seattle, Wash. 98195, U.S.A.

GESCH, Roy (George). American, b. 1920. Theology/Religion, Travel/Exploration/Adventure. Lutheran clergyman, since 1944. Assoc. Dir., Messengers of Christ, Lutheran Bible Translators, Inc., Aurora, Ill., since 1986 (Exec. Dir., 1976–86). *Publs:* On Active Duty, 1967; A Husband Prays, 1968; A Wife Prays, 1968; Parent Pray, 1968; God's World Through Young Eyes, 1969; Help! I'm in College, 1970; Man at Prayer, 1970; Lord of the Young Crowd, 1971; (with J. Nelesen) And Yet the Church Goes On, 1972; (with D. Gesch) Discover Europe, 1973; Service Prayer Book, 1981; Confirmed in Christ, 1984; To Love and To Cherish, 1985; Made for Each Other, 1987; Silver Reflections, 1989. Add: 1572 Skyline Dr., Laguna Beach, Calif. 92651, U.S.A.

GESNER, Carol. American, b. 1922. Poetry, Literature. Prof. of English, Berea Coll., since 1967 (Instr., 1954–56; Asst. Prof., 1956–61; Assoc. Prof., 1961–67). *Publs:* The Crystal Spectrum (poetry), 1964–64; Shakespeare and the Greek Romance: A Study of Origins, 1970;

Plymouth, 1977. Add: c/o 2800 N. Flagler Dr., West Palm Beach, FL 33407, U.S.A.

GESSNER, Lynne. Also writes as Merle Clark. American, b. 1919. Children's fiction. *Publs:* Trading Post Girl, 1968; Lightning Slinger, 1968; (as Merle Clark) Ramrod, 1969; Bonnie's Guatemala, 1970; Navajo Slave, 1976; Yamadan, 1976; Malcolm Yucca Seed, 1977; To See a Witch, 1978; Danny, 1978; Edge of Darkness, 1979; Brother to the Navajo, 1979. Add: 6507 East Holly St., Scottsdale, Ariz. 85257, U.S.A.

GESTON, Mark S(ymington). American, b. 1946. Science fiction/Fantasy. Attorney, Eberle Berlin Kading, Turnbow and Gillespie, Boise, Idaho. *Publs:* Lords of the Starship, 1967; Out of the Mouth of the Dragon, 1969; The Day Star, 1972; The Siege of Wonder, 1976. Add: Box 1368, Boise, Idaho 83701, U.S.A.

GEYER, Georgie Anne. American, b. 1935. International relations/Current affairs, Politics/Government, Writing/Journalism, Autobiography/Memoirs, Documentation/Reportage. Syndicated Columnist, Universal Press Syndicate, since 1980; also, radio and television news commentator. Trustee, American Univ., Washington, D.C., since 1981. Society Desk Reporter, 1959–60, City Desk Gen. Assignment Reporter, 1960–64, and Foreign Corresp., 1964–75, Chicago Daily News; Syndicated Columnist, Los Angeles Times Syndicate, 1975–80; Lyle M. Spencer Prof. of Journalism, Syracuse Univ., New York, 1976. *Publs:* The New Latins: Fateful Change in South and Central America, 1970; The New 100 Years War, 1972; The Young Russians, 1976; Buying the Night Flight: The Autobiography of a Woman Foreign Correspondent, 1983; The First War We Can Drive To, 1988; Fidel!, 1988. Add: The Plaza, 800 25th St., N.W. Washington, D.C. 20037, U.S.A.

GEYMAN, John P. American, b. 1931. Medicine/Health. Prof. and Chmn., Dept. of Family Medicine, Sch. of Medicine, Univ. of Washington, Seattle, since 1976. Ed., Journal of Family Practice, since 1974. Assoc. Prof. and Chmn., Div. of Family Practice, Univ. of Utah Coll. of Medicine, Salt Lake City, 1971–72; Prof. and Vice-Chmn., Dept. of Family Practice, Sch. of Medicine, Univ. of California at Davis, 1972–76. *Publs:* The Modern Family Doctor and Changing Medical Practice, 1971; Content of Family Practice, 1976; Family Practice in the Medical School, 1977; Research in Family Practice, 1978; Preventive Medicine in Family Practice, 1979; Profile of the Residency-Trained Family Physician, 1980; Family Practice: Foundation of Changing Health Care, 1980; Behavioral Science in Family Practice, 1980; Funding Patient Care, Education and Research in Family Practice, 1981; Family Practice: An International Perspective in Developed Countries, 1982. Add: 2325 92nd Ave., Bellevue, Wash. 98004, U.S.A.

GHISELIN, Brewster. American, b. 1903. Poetry, Literature. Prof. Emeritus, Univ. of Utah, Salt Lake City, since 1971 (Instr., 1934–38; Lectr., 1938–39; Asst. Prof., 1939–46; Assoc. Prof., 1946–50; Dir. of Writers' Conference, 1947–66; Prof. of English, 1950–71; Distinguished Research Prof., 1967–68); Ed. Adv. Bd., Concerning Poetry, since 1968. Poetry Ed., 1937–46, and Assoc. Ed., 1946–49, Rocky Mountain Review (later Western Review), Salt Lake City, and Lawrence, Kans. *Publs:* Against the Circle, 1946; (ed.) The Creative Process: A Symposium, 1952, 1985; The Nets, 1955; Writing, 1959; (with E. Leuders and C. Short) Images and Impressions, 1969; Country of the Minotaur, 1970; Light, 1978; Windrose: Poems 1929-1979, 1980. Add: Dept. of English, Univ. of Utah, Salt Lake City, Utah 84112, U.S.A.

GHOSE, Zulfikar. Pakistani, b. 1935. Novels/Short stories, Poetry, Literature, Autobiography/Memoirs/Personal. Prof. in English, Univ. of Texas at Austin, since 1969. Cricket Corresp., The Observer, London, 1960–65; Teacher in London, 1963–69. *Publs:* (with B.S. Johnson) Statement Against Corpses, 1964; The Loss of India (verse) 1964; Confessions of a Native-Alien, 1965; The Contradictions (novel), 1966; The Murder of Aziz Khan (novel), 1967; Jets from Orange (verse), 1967; The Incredible Brazilian, Book I (novel) 1972; The Violent West (verse), 1972; (with Gavin Ewart and B.S. Johnson) Penguin Modern Poets 25, 1974; Crump's Terms (novel), 1975; The Beautiful Empire (novel), 1975; Hamlet, Prufrock, and Language, 1978; A Different World (novel), 1978; Hulme's Investigations into the Bogart Scipt (novel), 1981; A New History of Torments (novel), 1982; The Fiction of Reality (criticism), 1983; Don Bueno (novel), 1983; A Memory of Asia (poetry), 1984; Figures of Enchantment (novel), 1986. Add: Dept. of English, Univ. of Texas, Austin, Tex. 78712, U.S.A.

GHOSH, Amitav. Indian, b. 1956. Novels. Lectr., Dept. of Sociology, Delhi Sch. of Economics, Delhi Univ., since 1986. *Publs:* The

Circle of Reason, 1986. Add: c/o Dept. of Sociology, Delhi Sch. of Economics, Delhi Univ., Delhi 110007, India.

GHOSH, Arun Kumar. Indian, b. 1930. Economics, Money/Finance. Asst. Dir. of Research, Inst. of Cost and Works Accountants of India, since 1970, and Ed. of the Inst.'s Bulletin, since 1982 (Tutor and Lectr. in Economics, 1965–70 and 1971–72). Asst. Teacher, Burdwan Town Sch., 1951; Lect. in Economics and Commerce, Jaipuria Coll., 1955–56 and Research Asst. in Industrial Finance, Dept. of Economics, 1956–66, Calcutta Univ. *Publs:* Fiscal Problem of Growth with Stability, 1959; Fiscal Policy and Economic Growth: A Cross-Section Study, part I 1962, part II 1963; Monetary Policy of the Research Bank of India, 1964; Inflation and Price Control, 1975; Cost Accounting in Commercial Banking Industry, 1979. Add: "Punascha", 72/1 B.C. Road, Burdwan, West Bengal, India.

GIANAKARIS, Constantine John. American, b. 1934. Literature. Prof. of English and Theatre, Western Michigan Univ., Kalamazoo, since 1972 (Assoc. Prof., 1966–72; Assoc. Dean Coll. of Arts and Sciences, 1979–82). Co-Ed., Comparative Drama quarterly, since 1966. Assoc. Prof. of English, Illinois State Univ., Normal, 1961–66. *Publs:* (ed.) Antony and Cleopatra, 1969; Plutarch, 1970; (author and ed.) Foundations of Drama, 1974; (co-ed.) Drama in the Middle Ages, 1984; (co-ed.) Drama in the Twentieth Century, 1985; (co-ed.) Drama in the Renaissance, 1985. Add: Dept. of English, Western Michigan Univ., Kalamazoo, Mich. 49008, U.S.A.

GIANNARIS, George. American, b. 1936. Poetry, Literature, Music, Translations. Lectr. in Comparative Literature, Fordham Univ., and Lectr. in Greek Literature, Queens Coll. of the City Univ. of New York, since 1972; Asst. Prof. of Comparative Literature, Deree Coll., Athens, since 1975. *Publs:* (trans.) The Ballad of the Dead Brother, by Mikis Theodorakis (musical drama), 1970; (trans.) The Greek Easter of Spiro Agnew, by Vassilis Vassilikos (play), 1970; Mikis Theodorakis: Music and Social Change, 1972; Frontiers (poems), 1973; Americadomina (poetry), 1974; Tropoi (poetry), 1976; Diavimata (poetry), 1976; Heterotropa (poetry), 1976; Anthropographia (poetry), 1979; Hydrovio Soma (poetry), 1980; Ho Epaphos (poetry), 1982; Jean Moreas, 1984; The House of Chan (poetry), 1985; Melopoiimeni Poiisi (essays), 1985; Kimon Friar, 1985. Add: 21-72 Steinway St., Long Island City, N.Y. 11105, U.S.A.

GIBBERD, Kathleen. British, b. 1897. Novels/Short stories, Education, Social commentary/phenomena. Education Corresp., Sunday Times, 1956–61; and New Statesman, 1961–70, both London; freelance writer and broadcaster on the needs of old people, 1970–80. *Publs:* Vain Adventure (novel), 1928; The People's Government; Young Citizens; Citizenship Through the Newspaper, The League in Our Time; The I.L.O.; Soviet Russia: An Introduction; English on the Job; The People's English; Politics on the Blackboard, 1954; (ed.) About Your Schools; (ed.) Your Teenage Children; No Place Like School; Teaching Religion in Schools. Add: Southease, nr. Lewes, Sussex, England.

GIBBONS, Stella (Dorothea). British, b. 1902. Novels/Short stories, Poetry, Humour/Satire. Feature Writer, Evening Standard, London, 1926–28; Drama and Literary Critic, The Lady, London, 1928–31. *Publs:* The Mountain Beast and Other Poems, 1930; Cold Comfort Farm, 1932; Bassett, 1934; The Priestess and Other Poems, 1934; The Untidy Gnome, 1935; Enbury Heath, 1935; Miss Linsey and Pa, 1936; Roaring Tower and Other Short Stories, 1937; Nightingale Wood, 1938; The Lowland Venus and Other Poems, 1938; My American: A Romance, 1939; Christmas at Cold Comfort Farm and Other Stories, 1940; The Rich House, 1941; Ticky, 1943; The Bachelor, 1944; Westwood: or, The Gentle Powers (in U.S. as The Gentle Powers), 1946; The Matchmaker, 1949; Conference at Cold Comfort Farm, 1949; The Swiss Summer, 1951; Collected Poems, 1951; Fort of the Bear, 1953; Beside the Pearly Water, 1954; The Shadow of a Sorcerer, 1955; Here Be Dragons, 1956; White Sand and Grey Sand, 1958; Pink Front Door, 1959; The Weather at Tregulla, 1962; The Wolves Were in the Sledge, 1964; The Charmers, 1965; Starlight, 1967; The Snow Woman, 1969; The Woods in Winter, 1970. Add: 19 Oakeshott Ave., London N6 6NT, England.

GIBBS, Alonzo (Lawrence). American, b. 1915. Novels/Short stories, Poetry, Songs, lyrics and libretti. Contrib. Ed., Long Island Forum, since 1964. Poetry Reviewer, Voices Mag. 1953–64; Ed. and Publr., The Kinsman literary quarterly, 1961–63. *Publs:* Weather-House, 1959; The Fields Breathe Sweet, 1963; Monhegan, 1963; The Least Likely One, 1964; Dolphin off Hippo (libretto), 1965; A Man's Calling, 1966; By a Sea-Coal Fire, 1969; Drift South, 1969; Son of a Mile-Long Mother, 1970;

One More Day, 1971; Sir Urian's Letters Home, 1974; The Rumble of Time Through Town, 1980; (with Iris Gibbs) Harking Back, 1983. Add: HC60, Box 20, Waldoboro, Me. 04572, U.S.A.

GIBBS, Anthony Matthews. Australian, b. 1933. Literature. Prof. of English, Macquarie Univ., N.S.W., since 1975. Fellow, Australian Acad of the Humanities, since 1982 (Vice-Pres., 1988–89). Lectr. in English, 1960–66, and Ed. with K.B. Magarey, Southern Review, 1963–64, Univ. of Adelaide; Lectr., Univ. of Leeds, 1966–69; Prof. of English and Head of Dept., Univ. of Newcastle, N.S.W., 1969–75. *Publs:* Shaw, 1969; (ed.) Sir William Davenant: The Shorter Poems, and Songs from the Plays and Masques, 1972; The Art and Mind of Shaw, 1983. Add: Sch. of English and Linguistics, Macquarie Univ., North Ryde, N.S.W. 2109, Australia.

GIBBS, R(onald) Darnley. British, b. 1904. Biology, Botany, Chemistry. Prof. of Botany Emeritus, McGill Univ., Montreal, since 1971 (joined staff as demonstrator, 1925). *Publs:* (with E.J. Holmes) A Modern Biology, 1937; Botany: An Evolutionary Approach, 1950; Chemotaxonomy of Flowering Plants, 1974. Add: 32 Orchards Way, Southampton SO2 1RD, England.

GIBSON, Charles E(dmund). British, b. 1916. Children's fiction, History. Head of Dept., Scott Lidgett Sch., London, since 1969 (with I.L.E.A. since 1948). With Royal Navy, 1940–46. *Publs:* The Story of the Ship, 1948; The Secret Tunnel, 1948; Wandering Beauties, 1960; The Clash of Fleets, 1961; Knots and Splices, 1962; Plain Sailing, 1963; Daring Prows, 1963; Be Your Own Weatherman, 1963; The Two Olafs of Norway: With a Cross on Their Shields, 1964; The Ship with Five Names, 1965; Knots and Splices, 1979; Death of a Phantom Raider, 1987. Add: 59 Victoria Rd., Shoreham-by-Sea, Sussex, England.

GIBSON, Josephine. *See* **JOSLIN,** Sesyle.

GIBSON, Miles. British, b. 1947. Novels, Poetry. *Publs:* The Guilty Bystander, 1970; Permanent Damage, 1973; The Sandman, 1984; Dancing with Mermaids, 1985; Vinegar Soup, 1987. Add: c/o Jonathan Clowes, 22 Prince Albert Rd., London NW1 7ST, England.

GIBSON, Quentin. Australian, b. 1913. Philosophy. Lectr., Univ. of Western Australia, 1937–44, and Canberra Univ. Coll., 1945–48; Sr. Lectr., 1951–60, and Assoc. Prof. of Philosophy, 1960–78, Australian National Univ., Canberra. *Publs:* Facing Philosophical Problems, 1948, rev. ed. 1961; The Logic of Social Enquiry, 1960. Add: Dept. of Philosophy, Arts Faculty, Australian National Univ., Box 4, G.P.O., Canberra, A.C.T. 2601, Australia.

GIBSON, Robert. British, b. 1927. Literature, Biography. Prof. of French, Univ. of Kent at Canterbury, since 1965. Asst. Lectr., Univ. of St. Andrews, 1954–55; Lectr., Queen's Coll., Dundee, 1955–58, and Aberdeen Univ., 1958–61; Prof. of French, Queen's Univ., Belfast, 1961–65. *Publs:* The Quest of Alain-Fournier, 1953; Roger Martin du Gard; (ed.) C. Aveline: Le Bestiaire Inattendu, 1961; (compiler) Modern French Poets on Poetry, 1961; (ed.) C. Aveline: Brouart et Le Desordre, 1962; (ed.) J. Giraudoux: Provinciales, 1965; (ed.) Alain-Fournier: Le Grand Meaulnes, 1968; The Land Without a Name, 1975; (ed.) Studies in French Fiction, 1988; Annals of Ashdon, 1988. Add: 7 Sunnymead, Tyler Hill, Canterbury, Kent, England.

GIBSON, Walter Samuel. American, b. 1932. Art. Mellon Prof. of the Humanities, Case Western Reserve Univ., Cleveland, since 1978 (Asst. Prof., 1966–71; Acting Chmn., 1970–71; Assoc. Prof., 1971–78; Chmn., 1971–79); Clark Visiting Prof. of Art History, Williams Coll., Williamstown, MA, 1989. *Publs:* Hieronymus Bosch, 1973; The Paintings of Cornelis Engebrechtsz, 1977; Bruegel, 1977; Hieronymus Bosch: An Annotated Bibliography, 1983; "Mirror of the Earth", The World Landscape in 16th Century Flemish Painting, 1988; Pieter Bruegel the Elder: Two Studies, 1989. Add: Dept. of Art, Mather House, Case Western Reserve Univ., Cleveland, Ohio 44106, U.S.A.

GIBSON, William. American, b. 1914. Novels/Short stories, Plays/Screenplays, Poetry. *Publs:* I Lay in Zion, 1943; Dinny and the Witches: A Frolic on Grave Matters, 1945, 1959; Winter Crook (poetry), 1948; A Cry of Players, 1948; The Cobweb (novel and screenplay), 1954; The Miracle Worker (television play), 1957, stage play, 1959, screenplay, 1962; The Seesaw Log: A Chronicle of the Stage Production with the Text of Two for the Seesaw, 1959; (with Clifford Odets) Golden Boy, 1964; A Mass for the Dead, 1968; American Primitive, 1969; A Season in Heaven (chronicle), 1974; The Body and the Wheel, 1975; The Butterfingers Angel, Mary and Joseph, Herod the Nut, and the Slaughter of

12 Hit Carols in a Pear Tree (play), 1975; Golda (play), 1978; Shakespeare's Game (criticism), 1978; Monday After the Miracle, 1983. *Publs:* Stockbridge, Mass. 01262, U.S.A.

GIBSON, William (Ford). American, b. 1948. Science fiction. *Publs:* Neuromancer, 1984; Count Zero, 1985; Burnig Chrome, 1986; Mona Lisa Overdrive, 1987. Add: 2630 W. 7th Ave., Vancouver, B.C. V6K 1Z1, Canada.

GIDDINGS, John Calvin. American, b. 1930. Chemistry, Environmental science/Ecology. Prof. of Chemistry, Univ. of Utah, Salt Lake City, since 1966 (Asst. Prof., 1957–59; Assoc. Prof., 1959–62; Research Prof., 1962–66). Ed., Advances in Chromatography, since 1965, and Separation Science and Technology since 1966. *Publs:* Dynamics of Chromatography, 1965; (ed. with M.B. Monroe) Our Chemical Environment, 1972; Chemistry, Man, and Environmental Change, 1973. Add: Dept. of Chemistry, Univ. of Utah, Salt Lake City, Utah 84112, U.S.A.

GIELGUD, (Sir Arthur) John. British, b. 1904. Theatre, Autobiography/Memoirs/Personal. Actor and Dir. *Publs:* Early Stages, 1938; (ed.) The Cherry Orchard, by Chekhov, 1954; Stage Directions, 1963; (ed.) Ivanov, by Chekhov, 1966; Distinguished Company, 1973; An Actor and His Time (autobiography), 1979. Add: S. Pavilion, Wotton Underwood, Aylesbury, Bucks, England.

GIFFORD, Denis. British, b. 1927. Communications Media, Film, Literature. Creator and compiler, Looks Familiar, and Quick on the Draw series for Thames TV, and Sounds Familiar for BBC Radio; Scriptwriter for Yorkshire Television series: The Witch's Brew, Junior Showtime, and the Laughing Policeman; Writer, The Crazy Gang, BBC TV. Founder, Assn. of Comics Enthusiasts. *Publs:* Space Patrol Handbook, 1952; (author and artist) Adventures of Baron Munchausen, 1958; Cinema Britanico, 1963; British Cinema, 1968; Movie Monsters, 1969; Science Fiction Film, 1971; Discovering Comics, 1971; Stap Me! The British Newspaper Strip, 1971; Test Your N.Q., 1972; 50 Years of Radio Comedy, 1972; (ed.) Six Comics of World War One, 1972; A Pictorial History of Horror Movies, 1973; The British Film Catalogue 1895-1970, 1973, 1986; Karloff: The Man, The Monster, The Movies, 1973; (ed.) Film Pictorial 1933 Souvenir Edition, 1973; The Movie-Makers: Chaplin, 1974; The Armchair Odeon, 1974; (ed.) Penny Comics of the Thirties, 1974; Victorian Comics, 1975; The Great Cartoon Stars: A Who's Who!, 1975; Happy Days! One Hundred Years of Comics, 1975; The British Comic Catalogue 1874-1974, 1975; (ed.) Run Adolf Run: World War Two Fun Book, 1975; (ed.) Ally Sloper Magazine, 1976; (ed.) Best of Eagle, 1977; Stewpot's Fun Book, 1977; Monsters of the Movies, 1977; Morecambe and Wise Comic Book, 1977; Quick on the Draw, 1978; Two Ronnies Comic Book, 1978; Eric and Ernie's TV Fun Book, 1978; The Illustrated Who's Who in British Films, 1979; (ed.) Money Fun Comic, 1981; British Comics and Story Paper Price Guide, 1982; The International Book of Comics, 1984; The Golden Age of Radio, 1985; British Animated Films, 1985; The Complete Catalogue of British Comics, 1986; Encyclopedia of Comic Characters, 1987; (ed.) Eagle Book of Cutaways, 1988; Comics at War, 1988. Add: 80 Silverdale, Sydenham, London SE26 4SJ, England.

GIFFORD, Edward Stewart, Jr. American, b. 1907. History, Mythology/Folklore, Autobiography/Memoirs/Personal. Assoc. Prof. of Ophthalmology, Univ. of Penn., Philadelphia, since 1983. Medical practitioner, Philadelphia, since 1934; Consulting Ophthalmologist, Pennsylvania Hosp., since 1973 (Chief Ophthalmologist, 1954–73). *Publs:* The Evil Eye: Studies in the Folklore of Vision, 1958; The Charms of Love, 1962; Father Against the Devil, 1966; The American Revolution in the Delaware Valley, 1976. Add: 1913 Spruce St., Philadelphia, Pa. 19103, U.S.A.

GIFFORD, Thomas (Eugene). American, b. 1937. Mystery/Crime/Suspense. Full-time writer since 1975. Textbook salesman, Minneapolis, 1960–68; Ed.-in-Chief, Twin Citian, Minneapolis, 1968–69; Dir. of Public Relations, Tyrone Guthrie Theatre, Minneapolis, 1970; Ed. and Columnist, Sun Newspapers, Minneapolis, 1971–75. *Publs:* Benchwarmer Bob (sports biography), 1974; The Wind Chill Factor, 1975; The Cavanaugh Quest, 1976; The Man from Lisbon, 1977; The Glendower Legacy, 1978; Hollywood Gothic, 1979. Add: c/o Julian Bach Literary Agency, 747 Third Ave., New York, N.Y. 10017, U.S.A.

GIL, David Georg. American, b. 1924. Social Sciences. Prof. of Social Policy, Brandeis Univ., since 1969 (Asst. Prof., 1964–66; Assoc. Prof., 1966–69; Dir., Social Policy Study Prog., 1969–73); Dir., Center for Social Change, Practice and Theory, since 1983. Dir., Nationwide Epidemologic Study of Child Abuse, Brandeis Univ. and U.S. Children's Bureau, 1965–69; Pres., Assn. for Humanist Sociology, 1981. *Publs:* Violence Against Children, Physical Child Abuse in the United States, 1970; Unravelling Social Policy, Theory, Analysis, and Political Action Toward Social Equality, 1973; The Challenge of Social Equality, 1976; (ed.) Child Abuse and Violence, 1978; Beyond the Jungle, 1979; (ed. with Eva A. Gil) Toward Social and Economic Justice, 1985; (ed. with Eva A. Gil) The Future of Work, 1987. Add: Brandeis Univ., Waltham, Mass. 02254, U.S.A.

GIL, Federico Guillermo. American, b. 1915. International relations/Current affairs, Politics/Government. Research Prof., Inst. for Research in Social Science, since 1956, Dir., Inst. of Latin American Studies, since 1959, and Kenan Prof. of Political Science since 1966, Univ. of North Carolina, Chapel Hill (Instr., Political Science, 1943–45; Asst. Prof., 1945–49; Assoc. Prof., 1949–55; Prof., 1955–66). Gen. Ed., Latin American Politics Series, Allyn & Bacon Inc., Boston, Mass., since 1968. *Publs:* (with W.W. Pierson) The Governments of Latin America, 1957; Genesis and Modernization of Political Parties in Chile, 1962; (with C. Parrish) The Chilean Presidential Elections of September 4, 1964, 1965; The Political System of Chile, 1966; Instituciones y desarrollo politico de America Latina, 1966; Latin American-United States Relations, 1971; Chile at the Turning Point, 1979. Add: P.O. Box 1001, Chapel Hill, N.C. 27514, U.S.A.

GILBERT, Alan (Graham). British, b. 1944. Geography, Regional/Urban planning. Reader in Geography at University Coll. and the Inst. of Latin American Studies, since 1969. *Publs:* Latin American Development: A Geographical Perspective, 1974; (ed.) Development Planning and Spatial Structure, 1976; (with J. Gugler) Cities, Poverty, and Development, 1982; (with P. Ward) Housing, the State, and the Poor, 1985; (with P. Healey) The Political Economy of Land, 1985. Add: Dept. of Geography, University Coll., 26 Bedford Way, London WC1H 0AP, England.

GILBERT, Anna. Pseud. for Marguerite Lazarus. British, b. 1916. Historical/Romance/Gothic. Grammar sch. English teacher 1938–73. *Publs:* Images of Rose, 1974; The Look of Innocence, 1975; A Family Likeness, 1977; Remembering Louise, 1978; The Leavetaking, 1979; Flowers for Lilian, 1980; Miss Bede Is Staying, 1982; The Long Shadow, 1984; A Walk in the Wood, 1989. Add: Oakley Cottage, Swainsea Lane, Pickering, N. Yorks., England.

GILBERT, Benjamin Franklin. American, b. 1918. History. Prof. of History, San Jose State Univ., Calif., 1950–88, now Emeritus. Assoc. and Regional Ed., Journal of the West, 1962–84. Historical Consultant, Office of the Attorney-Gen., State of Calif., 1972–79. *Publs:* Pioneers for One Hundred Years: San Jose State College 1857-1957, 1957; The Mining Frontier, 1958; Alaska History 1741-1910, 1961; Scientific Discoveries and Inventions in the United States, 1600-1913, 1964; (with H.B. Melendy) The Governors of California: Peter H. Burnett to Edmund G. Brown, 1965; Teacher's Manual: Problems in American History, 1966; (with the National Park Service) Prospector, Cowhand, and Sodbuster: Historic Places Associated with the Mining, Ranching, and Farming Frontiers in the Trans-Mississippi West, 1967; The State of California, 1974; Santa Teresa Laboratory: A Place in History, 1977; (with C.B. Burdick) Washington Square, 1857-1979: The History of San Jose State University, 1980; The Craft of History at San Jose State, 1981; (with K.J. Bauer) Ports in the West, 1982; (with A.T. Turhollow and K.J. Bauer) History of Navigation and Navigation Improvements on the Pacific Coast, 1983. Add: 736 Cambrian Dr., Campbell, Calif. 95008, U.S.A.

GILBERT, Bentley Brinkerhoff. American, b. 1924. History. Prof. of History since 1967, and Chmn. of the Dept. since 1988, Univ. of Illinois at Chicago (Assoc. Dean of Grad. Coll., 1971–72). Exec. Secty., National Conference on British Studies; Ed., Journal of British Studies. Assoc. Prof., Dept. of History, Colorado Coll., Colorado Springs, 1955–67. *Publs:* The Evolution of National Insurance in Great Britain, 1966; Britain Since 1918, 1967; British Social Policy, 1914-1939, 1971; The Heart of the Empire, 1973, 1981; David Lloyd George: A Political Life, vol. I, The Architect of Change, 1987. Add: 830-D Forest Ave., Evanston, Ill. 60202, U.S.A.

GILBERT, Creighton Eddy. American, b. 1924. Art, Translations. Prof. of History of Art, Yale Univ., New Haven, Conn., since 1981. Assoc. Prof., 1961–65, and Sidney and Ellen Wien Prof. of the History of Art, 1965–69, Brandeis Univ., Waltham, Mass.; Prof. of the History of Art, Queens Coll. of the City Univ. of New York, 1969–77; Jacob Gould Schurman Prof. of History of Art, Cornell Univ., Ithaca, N.Y., 1977–81. Ed.,

The Art Bulletin, 1980–85. *Publs:* (trans.) Complete Poems and Selected Letters of Michelangelo, 1963; Michelangelo, 1967; Change in Piero della Francesca, 1968; (ed.) Renaissance Art, 1970; History of Renaissance Art, 1972; (ed.) Italian Art 1400-1500: Sources and Documents, 1980; The Works of Girolamo Savoldo, 1986. Add: Dept. of History of Art, 56 High St., Yale Univ., New Haven, Conn. 06520, U.S.A.

GILBERT, Douglas L. American, b. 1925. Agriculture/Forestry, Environmental science/Ecology, Zoology. Prof. and Chmn., Fishery and Wildlife Biology, Coll. of Forestry and Natural Resources, Colorado State Univ., Fort Collins, since 1975 (Asst. Prof. of Wildlife Mgmt., 1956–62; Assoc. Prof. of Wildlife Biology, 1962–66; Prof. and Chmn., Wildlife Biology 1966–69). Prof. of Wildlife Science and Extension Dir., 1969–71, and Prof. of Wildlife Biology and Asst. Dean, 1971–78, Coll. of Forestry and Natural Resources, Cornell Univ., Ithaca, N.Y. *Publs:* Economics, Ecology and Biology of the Black Bear in Colorado, 1953; (ed.) Forester's Handbook, 1957; (with R. Tigner) A Contribution Toward the Bibliography of the Black Bear, 1960; (with W.E. Martin) Field Wildlife Studies in Colorado, 1961; Public Relations and Communications in Wildlife Management, 1962; Public Relations and Communications in Natural Resource Management, 1964; (with D.R. Smith) Field Wildlife Studies in Colorado, 1967; (ed.) Proceedings of Third Annual Short Course in Game and Fish Management, 1967; Natural Resources and Public Relations, 1971; (ed.) Forestry and Natural Resources Professions, 1973; (ed.) Big Game Management and Ecology, 1978; (with J.R. Fazio) Public Relations for Natural Resources Personnel, 1981. Add: 1205 Ellis St., Fort Collins, Colo. 80521, U.S.A.

GILBERT, Glenn G(ordon). American, b. 1936. Language/Linguistics. Prof. of Linguistics, since 1970, and Chmn. of the Dept. since 1987, Southern Illinois Univ., Carbondale. Founder and Ed., Journal of Pidgin and Creole Languages, since 1986. Instr. to Asst. Prof. in Germanic Languages, Univ. of Texas, Austin, 1963–70. *Publs:* (ed.) Texas Studies in Bilingualism: Thirteen Studies of Romance, Germanic, and Slavic Immigrant Languages Spoken in Texas, Louisiana, and Oklahoma, 1970; (ed.) The German Language in America, 1971; Linguistic Atlas of Texas German, 1972; (co-ed.) Problems in Applied Educational Sociolinguistics: Readings on Language and Culture Problems of United States Ethnic Groups, 1974; (ed. and trans.) Pidgin and Creole Languages: Selected Essays of Hugo Schuchardt, 1980; (ed.) Pidgin and Creole Languages: Essays in Memory of John E. Reinecke, 1987. Add: R.R.4, Box 371, Carbondale, Ill. 62901, U.S.A.

GILBERT, Harriett. British, b. 1948. Novels. Literary Ed., New Statesman, London, 1986–88. *Publs:* I Know Where I've Been, 1972; Hotels with Empty Rooms, 1973; An Offence Against the Persons, 1974; Tide Race, 1977; Running Away, 1979; The Riding Mistress, 1983; A Women's History of Sex, 1987. Add: c/o Richard Scott Simon Ltd., 43 Doughty St., London WC1N 2LF, England.

GILBERT, John Raphael. British, b. 1926. Natural history, Travel, Translations. *Publs:* Modern World Book of Animals, 1947; Cats, Cats, Cats, 1961; Famous Jewish Lives, 1970; Myths of Ancient Rome, 1970; Pirates and Buccaneers, 1971, 1975; Highwaymen and Outlaws, 1971; Charting the Vast Pacific, 1971; National Costumes of the World, 1972; (trans.) World of Wildlife, 1972–74; Miracles of Nature, 1975; Knights of the Crusades, 1978; Vikings, 1978; Prehistoric Man, 1978; (trans.) Leonardo da Vinci, 1978; (trans.) La Scala, 1979; Dinosaurs Discovered, 1980; (trans.) Macdonald Encyclopedia of Trees, 1983; Macdonald Encyclopedia of House Plants, 1986; Theory and Use of Colour, 1986; Macdonald Encyclopedia of Roses, 1987; Gardens of Britain, 1987; (trans.) Macdonald Encyclopedia of Butterflies and Moths, 1988. Add: 28 Lyndale Ave., London NW2, England.

GILBERT, Martin. British, b. 1936. History, Biography. Fellow, Merton Coll., Oxford, since 1962. *Publs:* (with R. Gott) The Appeasers, 1963; Britain and Germany Between the Wars, 1964; The European Powers 1900-1945; Plough My Own Furrow: The Life of Lord Allen of Hurtwood, 1965; Servant of India: A Study of Imperial Rule 1905-1910, 1966; The Roots of Appeasement, 1966; (ed.) A Century of Conflict: Essays Presented to A.J.P. Taylor, 1966; Recent History Atlas 1860-1960, 1966; Winston Churchill (for young people), 1966; Churchill, 1967; Lloyd George, 1968; British History Atlas, 1968; American History Atlas, 1968; Jewish History Atlas, 1969; First World War Atlas, 1970; Winston S. Churchill (biography), vols. 3-8, 1971–88; Russian History Atlas, 1972; Sir Horace Rumbold: Portrait of a Diplomat, 1973; The Coming of War in 1939, 1973; Churchill: Photographic Portrait, 1974; The Arab-Israel Conflict: Its History in Maps, 1974; Churchill and Zionism, 1974; The Jews in Arab Lands: Their History in Maps, 1975; Jerusalem Illustrated History Atlas, 1977; Exile and Return: The Struggle for a Jewish Homeland, 1978; Final Jouney: The Fate of the Jews in Nazi Europe, 1979; Children's Illustrated Bible Atlas, 1979; Auschwitz and the Allies, 1981; Churchill's Political Philosophy, 1981; Churchill: The Wilderness Years, 1981; Atlas of the Holocaust, 1982; The Jews of Hope: The Plight of Soviet Jewry Today, 1984; Jerusalem: Rebirth of a City 1838-1898, 1985; Scharansky: Hero of Our Time, 1986; The Holocaust: The Jewish Tragedy, 1987. Add: Merton Coll., Oxford, England.

GILBERT, Sister Mary. *See* **De FREES,** Madeline.

GILBERT, Michael. British, b. 1912. Mystery/Crime/Suspense. Solicitor, Trower Still & Keeling, since 1947 (Partner since 1952). Founder Member, Crime Writers Assn., 1953. *Publs:* Close Quarters, 1947; They Never Looked Inside, 1948; The Doors Open, 1949; Smallbone Deceased, 1950; Death Has Deep Roots, 1951; Death in Captivity, 1952; Fear to Tread, 1953; Sky High, 1955; Be Shot for Sixpence, 1956; The Tichborne Claimant, 1957; Blood and Judgement, 1958; After the Fine Weather, 1963; The Crack in the Teacup, 1965; The Dust and the Heat, 1967; Game Without Rules (stories), 1967; The Etruscan Net, 1969; The Body of a Girl, 1972; The Ninety Second Tiger, 1973; Amateur in Violence (stories), 1973; Flash Point, 1975; The Night of the Twelfth, 1976; Petrella at Q (stories), 1977; The Empty House, 1978; Death of a Favourite Girl (in U.S. as The Killing of Katie Steelstock), 1980; Mr. Calder and Mr. Behrens (stories), 1982; The Final Throw (in U.S. as End-Game), 1982; The Black Seraphim, 1983; The Long Journey Home, 1985; (ed.) The Oxford Book of Legal Anecdotes, 1986; Trouble, 1987. Add: Luddesdown Old Rectory, Cobham, Kent, England.

GILBERT, Ruth. New Zealander, b. 1917. Poetry. Formerly physiotherapist in New Zealand, 1938–46. Past Pres., New Zealand P.E.N. *Publs:* Lazarus and Other Poems, 1949; The Sunlit Hour, 1955; The Luthier, 1966; Collected Poems, 1984. Add: 23 Teece Dr., Motueka, New Zealand.

GILCHRIST, Ellen. American, b. 1935. Novels/Short stories, Poetry. Broadcaster on National Public Radio; also journalist. *Publs:* The Land Surveyor's Daughter (poetry), 1979; In the Land of Dreamy Dreams: Short Fiction, 1981; The Annunciation (novel), 1983; Victory Over Japan (short stories), 1984; Drunk with Love (short stories), 1986; Falling Through Space (journal), 1987; The Anna Papers (novel), 1988; Light Can Be Both Wave and Particle (short stories), 1989. Add: c/o Little Brown, 34 Beacon St., Boston, Mass. 02108, U.S.A.

GILDERSLEEVE, Thomas. American, b. 1927. Information science/Computers. Dir., Financial Systems Applications. Controller's Office. Columbia Univ., NYC, since 1979. *Publs:* (co-author) System Design for Computer Applications, 1963; Design of Sequential File Systems, 1971; Decision Tables and Their Practical Application in Data Processing, 1971; Data Processing Project Management, 1974, 1985; Successful Data Processing System Analysis, 1978; The CICS Companion: A Reference Guide to COBOL Command Level Programming, 1987. Add: 56 Witch Lane, Rowayton, Conn. 06853, U.S.A.

GILDNER, Gary. American, b. 1938. Novels/Short stories, Poetry. Prof. of English, Drake Univ., Des Moines (member of the faculty since 1966). Visiting Prof. and Writer-in-Residence, Reed Coll., Portland, Ore., 1983–85, and Michigan State Univ., E. Lansing, 1987. *Publs:* First Practice (poetry), 1969; Digging for Indians (poetry), 1971; Eight Poems, 1973; Nails (poetry), 1975; (ed. with Judith Gildner) Out of This World: Poems from the Hawkeye State, 1975; Letters from Vicksburg (poetry), 1976; The Runner (poetry), 1978; Toads in the Greenhouse, 1978; Jabon (poetry), 1981; The Crush (short stories), 1983; Blue Like the Heavens: New and Selected Poems, 1984; The Second Bridge (novel), 1987; A Week in South Dakota (short stories), 1987. Add: 2915 School St., Des Moines, Iowa 50311, U.S.A.

GILES, John. British, b. 1921. History. Local Govt. Councillor, Bromley, 1963–66; Sr. Contracts Negotiator, Air Products Ltd., New Malden, Surrey, 1966–72. *Publs:* The Ypres Salient, 1970, as The Ypres Salient: Flanders Then and Now, 1979, 3rd ed., 1987; The Somme, Then and Now, 1975, 3rd ed. 1988. Add: Guilton Mill, Poulton Lane, Ash, Nr. Canterbury, Kent CT3 2HN, England.

GILL, B.M. *See* **TRIMBLE,** Barbara Margaret.

GILL, Bartholomew. *See* **McGARRITY,** Mark.

GILL, Brendan. American, b. 1914. Novels/Short stories, Poetry, Architecture, Biography. Regular contrib. since 1936, and Theatre Critic since 1968, New Yorker mag. (Film Critic, 1961–67). *Publs:* Death in April and Other Poems, 1935; The Trouble of One House, 1950; The Day the Money Stopped, 1957; La Belle (play), 1962; (with R. Kimball) Cole: A Book of Cole Porter Lyrics and Memorabilia (in U.K. as Cole: A Biographical Essay), 1971; Tallulah, 1972; The Malcontents, 1973; (ed.) Happy Times, 1973; Ways of Loving: Two Novellas and Eighteen Stories, 1974; Here at The New Yorker, 1975; (ed.) States of Grace: Eight Plays by Philip Barry, 1975; Lindbergh Alone, 1977; Summer Places, 1978; The Dream Came True, 1980; John F. Kennedy Center for the Performing Arts, 1982; A Fair Land to Build In: The Architecture of the Empire State, 1984; Many Masks: A Life of Frank Lloyd Wright, 1987. Add: c/o The New Yorker, 25 West 43rd St., New York, N.Y. 10036, U.S.A.

GILL, David (Lawrence William). British, b. 1934. Poetry. Lectr., Buckinghamshire Coll. of Higher Education, High Wycombe, since 1971. Teacher, Bedales Sch., Hants, 1960–62, Nyakasura Sch., Fort Portal, Uganda, 1962–64, and Magdalen Coll. Sch., Oxford, 1965–71. *Publs:* Men Without Evenings, 1966; The Pagoda and Other Poems, 1969; Peaches and Aperçus, 1974; (ed. and trans.) In the Eye of the Storm, 1976; The Upkeep of the Castle, 1978; (with Dorothy Clancy) One Potato, Two Potato, 1985. Add: 32 Boyn Hill Rd., Maidenhead, Berks., England.

GILL, Jerry H. American, b. 1933. Film, Philosophy, Theology/Religion. Prof. of Christianity and Culture, Eastern Coll., St. davids, Pa., since 1977. Prof. of Philosophy, Coll. of St. Rose, Albany, N.Y. Clergyman, ordained 1956. Asst. Prof., Seattle Pacific Coll., Wash., 1960–64, and Southwestern at Memphis, Tenn., 1966–69; Prof. of Philosophy, Eckerd Coll., 1969–77. *Publs:* Ingmar Bergman and the Search for Meaning, 1967; (ed.) Philosophy and Religion: Some Contemporary Perspectives, 1968; (ed.) Philosophy Today, 3 vols., 1968–70; (ed.) Essays on Kierkegaard, 1969; The Possibility of Religious Knowledge, 1971; (ed.) Christian Empiricism (anthology of essays by Ian T. Ramsey), 1974; Ramsey: The Religious Use of Language, 1975; Wittgenstein and Metaphor, 1981; On Knowing God, 1981; Toward Theology, 1982; Metaphilosophy, 1982; Faith in Dialogue: A Christian Apologetic, 1985. Add: Dept. of Philosophy, Eastern Coll., St. David's, Pa. 19087, U.S.A.

GILL, Joseph. British, b. 1901. History, Theology/Religion. Prof. in Greek Language and Byzantine History, Pontifical Oriental Inst., Rome, 1938–39, 1946–68; Lectr. in Anglican Theology, Gregorian Univ., Rome, 1946–66. *Publs:* Acta graeca concilii Florentini, 1953; The Council of Florence, 1959; Eugenius IV, Pope of Christian Union, 1961; Personalities of the Council of Florence, 1964; Constance et Bâle-Florence, 1965; Orationes Georgii Scholarii in Concilio Florentino habitae, 1965; (co-author) Handbuch der Ostkirchenkunde, 1971; (co-author) Byzantium: An Introduction, 1971, 1981; (co-author) Relations Between East and West in the Middle Ages, 1973; (co-author) Das Konstánzer Konzil, 1977; Church Union: Rome and Byzantium 1204-1453, 1979; Byzantium and the Papacy 1198-1400, 1979. Add: 10 Albert Rd., Birmingham B17, England.

GILL, Myrna Lakshmi. Canadian, b. 1943. Poetry. Member, League of Canadian Poets, since 1966. Instr. in English, Notre Dame Univ., Nelson, B.C., 1965–67; Departmental Asst., English Dept., Mt. Allison Univ., Sackville, N.B., 1971–75; Teacher, St. Francis Xavier Chinese Sch., Vancouver, B.C., 1980–82. *Publs:* Rape of the Spirit, 1962; During Rain, I Plant Chrysanthemums, 1966; Mind Walls, 1970; First Clearing, An Immigrant's Tour of Life, 1972; Novena to St. Jude Thaddeus, 1979; (ed.) Land of the Morning, 1980. Add: 587 Colby St., New Westminster, B.C., Canada.

GILL, Peter. British, b. 1939. Plays/Screenplays. Co-Dir., Olivier and Cottesloe Theatres, National Theatre, London, since 1980. Actor, 1957–65; Riverside Studios, London, 1976–80. *Publs:* The Sleeper's Den, 1965; Over Gardens Out, 1970; Drop in the Ocean: The Work of Oxfam 1960-1970, 1970; Small Change, 1979; Small Change, and Kick for Touch, 1985; Mean Tears, 1987. Add: c/o Margaret Ramsey Ltd., 14a Goodwin's Ct., London WC2N 4LL, England.

GILL, Ronald Crispin. British, b. 1916. Country Life/Rural Societies, History. Asst. Ed., The Western Morning News, 1950–70. Ed., The Countryman, 1971–81. *Publs:* The West Country, 1962; Plymouth: A New History, 1966; (with F. Booker and T. Soper) The Wreck of the Torrey Canyon, 1967; Plymouth in Pictures, 1968; Mayflower Remembered, 1970; Sutton Harbour, 1970; (ed.) Dartmoor: A New Study, 1970; The Isles of Scilly, 1975; (ed.) The Countryman's Britain, 1976; Dartmoor, 1976; The Countryman's Britain in Pictures, 1977; Plymouth:

A New History, vol. II, 1979; (ed.) The Duchy of Cornwall, 1987. Add: 14 Harbourside Ct., Hawkes Ave., Plymouth PL4 0QT, England.

GILLEN, Lucy. *See* **STRATTON**, Rebecca.

GILLESPIE, Gerald (Ernest Paul). American, b. 1933. Literature, Translations. Prof. of German Studies and Comparative Literature, Stanford Univ., Calif., since 1974. Assoc. Prof. and Prof. of German and Comparative Literature, State Univ. of New York at Binghamton, 1965–74. Secty., and Vice Pres., Intnl. Comparative Literature Assn., 1979–88. *Publs:* Daniel Casper von Lohenstein's Historical Tragedies, 1965; College Level German Grammar, 1966; German Baroque Poetry, 1971; (ed. and trans.) Die Nachtwachen des Bonaventura, 1972; (trans. and ed.) Der gestiefelte Kater, by L. Tieck, 1974; (ed. and trans. with A. Zahareas) Luces de Bohemia, by R.M. del Valle-Inclan, 1976; (ed. with E. Lohner) Herkommen und Erneuerung: Essays Für Oskar Seidlin, 1976; (ed. with G. Spellerberg) Studien zum Werk D.C. von Lohenstein, 1983; Garden and Labyrinth of Time: Studies in Renaissance and Baroque Literature, 1987; Ouzhou Changpian de Yanhua (Evolution of the European Novel), 1988. Add: Bldg. 242G, Stanford Univ., Stanford, Calif. 94305, U.S.A.

GILLESPIE, Robert B. American. Mystery/Crime. *Publs:* The Crossword Mystery, 1979; Little Sally Does It Again, 1982; Print-Out, 1983; Cryptopic Crosswords (puzzles), 1983; Heads You Lose, 1985; Empress of Coney Island, 1986; The Hell's Kitchen Connection, 1987; The Last of the Honeywells, 1988. Add: 226 Bay St., Douglaston, N.Y. 11363, U.S.A.

GILLETT, Charlie. British, b. 1942. Music. Co-Dir., Oval Records. Radio Presenter, since 1972 (Presenter, The Late Shift, Channel 4, 1988). Lectr. in Social Studies, film making, and athletics, Kingsway Coll. of Further Education, London, 1966–71; BBC-TV Production Asst., 1971–72. *Publs:* (ed.) All in the Game (sport), 1970; The Sound of the City: The Rise of Rock and Roll, 1970, 1983; (ed.) Rock File, 5 vols., 1972–78; Making Tracks: The Story of Atlantic Records, 1974, 1986. Add: 11 Liston Rd., London SW4 0DG, England.

GILLETT, Margaret. Canadian, b. 1930. Novels/Short stories, Education. Macdonald Prof. of Education, McGill Univ., Montreal, since 1982 (Prof., 1964–82). Education Officer, Commonwealth Office of Education, Australia, 1954–57; Asst. Prof., Dalhousie Univ., Halifax, N.S., Canada, 1961–62; Registrar, Haile Selassie I Univ., Ethiopia, 1962–64; Ed., McGill Journal of Education, 1966–77. *Publs:* A History of Education: Thought and Practice, 1966; (co-author) The Laurel and the Poppy (novel), 1968; (ed.) Readings in the History of Education, 1969; (co-ed.) Foundation Studies in Education: Justifications and New Directions, 1973; Educational Technology: Toward Demystification, 1973; We Walked Very Warily: A History of Women at McGill, 1981; A Fair Shake: Autobiographical Essays by McGill Women, 1984; Dear Grace: A Romance of History, 1986. Add: Faculty of Education, McGill Univ., Montreal PQ H3A 1Y2, Canada.

GILLETTE, Bob. *See* **SHAW**, Bynum G(illette).

GILLIATT, Penelope. British. Novels/Short stories, Plays/Screenplays, Film. Film Critic, The New Yorker mag., NYC, since 1967. Film Critic, 1961–65 and 1966–67, and Theatre Critic, 1965–66, The Observer newspaper, London. *Publs:* One by One, 1965; A State of Change, 1967; What's It Like Out? and Other Stories (in U.S. as Come Back If It Doesn't Get Better), 1968; Sunday Bloody Sunday (screenplay), 1971; Nobody's Business: Stories, 1972; Jean Renoir, 1975; Jacques Tati, 1975; Splendid Lives, 1978; The Cutting Edge, 1978; Three-Quarter Face, 1980; Quotations from Other Lives, 1982; They Sleep Without Dreaming, 1985; 22 Stories, 1986; Making Sunday Bloody Sunday, 1986; A Woman of Singular Occupation, 1988. Add: c/o The New Yorker, 25 West 43rd St., New York, N.Y. 10036, U.S.A.

GILLIE, Christopher. British, b. 1914. Literature. Coll. Lectr., Trinity Hall, Cambridge. *Publs:* Character in English Literature, 1965; Longman's Companion to English Literature, 1972; Jane Austen: A Preface Book, 1974, 1985; English Literature 1900-1939, 1975; E.M. Forster: A Preface Book, 1983. Add: Trinity Hall, Cambridge, England.

GILLIES, Valerie. Scottish, b. 1948. Poetry. Writer-in-Residence, Boroughmuir Sch., Edinburgh. *Publs:* (with Roderick Watson and Paul Mills) Trio: New Poets from Edinburgh, 1971; Each Bright Eye: Selected Poems, 1977; (ed.) Scottish Short Stories 1979 and 1980, 2 vols., 1979–80; Kim: Notes, 1981; Bed of Stone, 1984. Add: c/o Canongate Publishing Ltd., 17 Jeffrey St., Edinburgh EH1 1DR, Scotland.

GILLILAND, Alexis A(rnaldus). American, b. 1931. Science fiction. Freelance writer since 1982; also a cartoonist. Thermochemist, National Bureau of Standards, 1956–67, and Chemist and Specification Writer, Federal Supply Service, 1967–82, both in Washington, D.C. *Publs:* novels—The Revolution from Rosinante, 1981; Long Shot for Rosinante, 1981; The Pirates of Rosinante, 1982; The End of the Empire, 1983; Wizenbeak, 1986; cartoons—The Iron Law of Bureaucracy, 1979; Who Says Paranoia Isn't "In" Anymore, 1985. Add: 4030 Eighth St. S., Arlington, Va. 22204, U.S.A.

GILLON, Adam. American, b. 1921. Novels/Short stories, Poetry, Literature, Translations. Emeritus Prof. of English and Comparative Literature, State Univ. of New York at New Paltz (joined faculty, 1962). Pres., Joseph Conrad Soc. of America, and Ed., Joseph Conrad Today, since 1975. Member of Editorial Bd., Inst. for Textual Studies, Texas Technical Univ., Lubbock. Prof. of English and Head of Dept., Acadia Univ., Nova Scotia, 1957–62. Ed., Polish Series, Twayne Publrs. Inc., 1963–72; Regional Ed., Conradiana, 1968–72. *Publs:* Joseph Conrad (radio play), 1959; The Bet (radio play), 1969; The Eternal Solitary: A Study of Joseph Conrad, 1960, 1966; A Cup of Fury (novel), 1962; Selected Poems and Translations, 1962; (ed., trans. and contrib.) Introduction to Modern Polish Literature, 1964, 1982; In the Manner of Haiku: Seven Aspects of Man, 1967, 1970; (author and trans.) The Dancing Socrates and Other Poems, by Julian Tuwim, 1968; (ed., trans. and contrib.) Poems of the Ghetto: A Testament of Lost Men, 1969; The Solitary (radio play), 1969; Daily New and Old: Poems in the Manner of Haiku, 1971; Strange Mutations: In the Manner of Haiku, 1973; (ed.) Joseph Conrad: Commemorative Essays, 1975; Summer Morn . . . Winter Weather: Poems 'Twixt Haiku and Senryu, 1975; Conrad and Shakespeare and Other Essays, 1976; Joseph Conrad, 1982; The Withered Leaf: A Medley of Haiku and Senryu, 1982; (co-author) The Conspirators (screenplay), 1985; Jared (novel), 1989; Dark Country (screenplay), 1989. Add: Lake Illyria, Sparkling Ridge Rd., New Paltz, N.Y. 12561, U.S.A.

GILMAN, Dorothy. Writes children's fiction as Dorothy Gilman Butters. Mystery/Crime/Suspense, Children's fiction. American, b. 1923. Mystery novelist, and writer of fiction for children. *Publs:* novels—The Unexpected Mrs. Pollifax, 1966 (in U.K. as Mrs. Pollifax, Spy, 1971); Uncertain Voyage, 1967; The Amazing Mrs. Pollifax, 1970; The Elusive Mrs. Pollifax, 1971; A Palm for Mrs. Pollifax, 1973; A Nun in the Closet, 1975 (in U.K. as A Nun in the Cupboard, 1976); The Clairvoyant Countess, 1975; Mrs. Pollifax on Safari, 1977; A New Kind of Country (non-mystery novel), 1978; The Tightrope Walker, 1979; Mrs. Pollifax on the China Station, 1983; Mrs. Pollifax and the Hong Kong Buddha, 1985; for children—Enchanted Caravan, 1949; Carnival Gypsy, 1950; Ragamuffin Alley, 1951; The Calico Year, 1953; Four-Party Line, 1954; Papa Dolphin's Table, 1955; Girl in Buckskin, 1956; Heartbreak Street, 1958; Witch's Silver, 1959; Masquerade, 1961; Ten Leagues to Boston Town, 1962; The Bells of Freedom, 1963; The Maze in the Heart of the Castle, 1983. Add: c/o Howard Morhaim Agency, 175 Fifth Ave., New York, N.Y. 10010, U.S.A.

GILMAN, George G. Pseud. for Terry (William) Harknett; also writes western fiction as Frank Chandler, William M. James, Charles R. Pike, and William Terry, crime fiction as Jane Harman, Joseph Hedges, William Pine, and Thomas H. Stone, and non-fiction as David Ford and James Russell. British, b. 1936. Mystery/Crime/Suspense, Westerns/-Adventure, Travel/Exploration/Adventure. Freelance writer since 1972. Copyboy, Reuters, 1952; clerk, Newspaper Features Ltd., 1952–54; typist, Reuters Comtelburo, 1956–57; publicity ast. 20th-Century Fox, 1957–58; ed., Newspaper Features Ltd., 1958–61; reporter and features ed., National Newsagent, 1961–72: all London. *Publs:* westerns—Edge series—The Loner, 1972; Ten Thousand Dollars, American (in U.S. as Ten Grand), 1972; Apache Death, 1972; Killer's Breed, 1972; Blood on Silver, 1972; The Blue, The Grey, and the Red (in U.S. as Red River), 1973; California Killing, 1973, in U.S. as California Kill, 1974; Seven Out of Hell (in U.S. as Hell's Seven), 1973; Bloody Summer, 1973; Vengeance Is Black, 1973, in U.S. as Black Vengeance, 1974; Sioux Uprising, 1974; The Biggest Bounty (in U.S. as Death's Bounty), 1974; A Town Called Hate, 1974, in U.S. as The Hated, 1975; The Big Gold, 1974, in U.S. as Tiger's Gold, 1975; Blood Run (in U.S. as Paradise Loses), 1975; The Final Shot, 1975; Vengeance Valley, 1975; Ten Tombstones to Texas, 1975, in U.S. as Ten Tombstones, 1976; Ashes and Dust, 1976; Sullivan's Law, 1976; Rhapsody in Red, 1976; Slaughter Road, 1977; Echoes of War, 1977; The Day Democracy Died, 1977, in U.S. as Slaughterday, 1978; Violence Trail, 1978; Savage Dawn, 1978; Eve of Evil, 1978; The Living, The Dying, and the Dead, 1978; Waiting for a Train (in U.S. as Towering Nightmare), 1979; The Guilty Ones, 1979; The Frightened Gun, 1979; The Hated, 1979, in U.S. as Red Fury, 1980; A Ride in the Sun, 1980;

Death Deal, 1980; Two of a Kind: Edge Meets Steele, 1980; Town on Trial, 1981; Vengeance at Ventura, 1981; Massacre Mission, 1981; The Prisoners, 1981; Montana Melodrama, 1982; Matching Pair: Edge Meets Adam Steele, 1982; The Killing Claim, 1982; Bloody Sunrise, 1982; Arapaho Revenge, 1983; The Blind Side, 1983; House on the Range, 1983; The Godforsaken, 1982; Edge Meets Steele No. 3 Double Action, 1984; The Moving Cage, 1984; School for Slaughter, 1985; Revenge Ride, 1985; Shadow of the Gallows, 1985; A Time for Killing, 1986; Brutal Border, 1986; Hitting Paydirt, 1986; Backshot, 1987; Uneasy Riders, 1987; Doom Town, 1987; Dying Is Forever, 1987; The Desperadoes, 1988; Terror Town, 1988; The Breed Woman, 1989; The Rifle, 1989; Adam Steele series—The Violent Peace, 1974, in U.S. as Rebels and Assassins Die Hard, 1975; The Bounty Hunter, 1974; Hell's Junction, 1974; Valley of Blood, 1975; Gun Run, 1975; The Killing Art, 1975; Cross-Fire, 1975; Comanche Carnage, 1976; Badge in the Dust, 1976; The Losers, 1976; Lynch Town, 1976; Death Trail, 1977; Bloody Border, 1977; Delta Duel, 1977; River of Death, 1977; Nightmare at Noon, 1978; Satan's Daughters, 1978; The Hard Way, 1978; The Tarnished Star, 1979; Wanted for Murder, 1979; Wagons East, 1979; The Big Game, 1979; Fort Despair, 1979; Manhunt, 1980; Steele's War: The Woman, The Preacher, The Storekeeper, The Stranger, 4 vols., 1980–81; The Big Prize, 1981; The Killer Mountains, 1982; The Cheaters, 1982; The Wrong Man, 1982; The Valley of the Shadow, 1983; The Runaway, 1983; Stranger in a Strange Town, 1983; The Hellraisers, 1984; Canyon of Death, 1985; High Stakes, 1985; Rough Justice, 1985; The Sunset Ride, 1986; The Killing Strain, 1986; The Big Gunfight, 1987; The Hunted, 1987; Code of the West, 1987; The Outcasts, 1987; The Return, 1988; Trouble in Paradise, 1988; Going Back, 1989; The Long Shadow, 1989; The Undertaker series—Black as Death, 1981; Destined to Die, 1981; Funeral by the Sea, 1982; Three Graves to a Showdown, 1982; Back from the Dead, 1982; Death in the Desert, 1982; as William Terry—A Town Called Bastard (novelization of screenplay), 1971; Hannie Caulder (novelization of screenplay), 1971; Red Sun (novelization of screenplay), 1972; (as Frank Chandler) A Fistful of Dollars (novelization of screenplay), 1972; as Charles R. Pike, Jubal Cade series—The Killing Trail, 1974; Double Cross, 1974; The Hungry Gun, 1975; as William M. James, Apache series—The First Death, 1974; Duel to the Death, 1974; Fort Treaachery, 1975; Sonora Slaughter, 1976; Blood on the Tracks, 1977; All Blood Is Red, 1977; The Best Man, 1979; crime novels: as Terry Harknett—The Benevolent Blackmailer, 1962; The Scratch on the Surface, 1962; Invitation to a Funeral, 1963; Dead Little Rich Girl, 1963; The Evil Money, 1964; The Man Who Did Not Die, 1964; (as William Terry) Once a Copper, 1965; Death of an Aunt, 1967; The Two-Way Frame, 1967; (as William Pine) The Protectors, 1967; The Softcover Kill, 1971; (as Jane Harman) W.I.T.C.H., 1971; Promotion Tour, 1972; (as William Terry) The Weekend Game, 1972; Crown series: The Sweet and Sour Kill, Macao Mayhem, Bamboo Shoot-Out, 3 vols, 1974–75; as Thomas H. Stone—Dead Set, 1972; One Horse Race, 1973; Stopover Murder, 1973; Black Death, 1973; Squeeze Play, 1973; as Joseph Hedges—Funeral Rites, 1973; Arms for Oblivion, 1973; The Chinese Coffin, 1974; The Gold-Plated Hearse, 1974; Rainbow-Coloured Shroud, 1974; Corpse on Ice, 1975; The Mile-Deep Grave, 1975; Mexican Mourning, 1975; The Stainless Steel Wreath, 1975; The Chauffeur-Driven Pyre, 1976; non-fiction—(as Terry Harknett) The Caribbean, 1972; (as James Russell) The Balearic Islands, 1972; (as David Ford) Cyprus, 1973; ghostwriter—The Hero, by Peter Haining, 1973; The Savage, and Doomsday Island, both by Alex Peters, 1979. Add: Mill Gate House, Annings Lane, Burton Bradstock, Bridport, Dorset DT6 4QN, England.

GILMAN, Richard. American, b. 1925. Literature, Theatre, Autobiography. Prof. of Drama, Yale Univ., New Haven, Conn., since 1967. Pres., 1981–83, and Vice Pres., 1983–85, P.E.N., New York. *Publs:* The Confusion of Realms, 1969; Common and Uncommon Masks, 1970; The Making of Modern Drama, 1974; Decadence: The Strange Life of an Epithet, 1979; Faith, Sex, Mystery: A Memoir. Add: Yale Sch. of Drama, New Haven, Conn. 06520, U.S.A.

GILMAN, Robert Cham. *See* **COPPEL,** Alfred.

GILPIN, Alan. Australian, b. 1924. Economics, Environmental science/ Ecology, Technology. Consultant and Adviser on Environmental Planning since 1989. Gen. Ed., Australian Environment Series, Univ. of Queensland Press, since 1972. Dir., Air Pollution Control, Queensland, 1965–72; Chmn., Environment Protection Authority, Victoria, 1972–74; Asst. Secty., Natural Resources Branch, Commonwealth Dept. of Environment, Housing and Community Development, Canberra, 1975–76; Asst. Dir (Environmental Control), N.S.W. State Pollution Control Commn., 1977–81; Commnr. of Inquiry, N.S.W., 1980–89. *Publs:* Control of Air Pollution, 1963; Dictionary of Economic Terms, 1966; 4th ed. 1977; Dictionary of Fuel Technology, 1969, as Dictionary of Energy, 1979; Air

Pollution, 1971, 1978; Dictionary of Environmental Terms, 1975; Environmental Policy in Australia, 1978; The Australian Environment: Twelve Controversial Issues, 1979; Dictionary of Economics and Financial Markets, 1985; Environmental Planning: A Condensed Encyclopedia, 1986; Australian Dictionary of Environment and Planning, 1989. Add: P.O. Box 17, South Bexley, N.S.W. 2207, Australia.

GILROY, Frank D(aniel). American, b. 1925. Novels/Short stories, Plays/Screenplays. Member of Council, Dramatists Guild, NYC, since 1964 (Pres., 1969–71). *Publs:* Who'll Save the Plowboy?, 1962; The Subject Was Roses, 1962; About Those Roses: or, How Not to Do a Play and Succeed, and the Text of The Subject Was Roses, 1965; That Summer—That Fall, 1967; The Only Game in Town, 1968: A Matter of Pride, 1970; Private (novel), 1970; (with Ruth C. Gilroy) Little Ego (book for children), 1970; Present Tense, 1972; From Noon Till Three (novel), 1973, in U.K. as For Want of a Horse, 1975; The Next Contestant, 1979; Dreams of Glory, 1980. Add: c/o Dramatists Guild, 234 W. 44th St., New York, N.Y. 10036, U.S.A.

GIMBEL, John. American, b. 1922. International relations/Current affairs. Prof. of History, Humboldt State Univ., Arcata, Calif., since 1959. Prof. of History, Luther Coll., Decorah, Iowa, 1954–59. *Publs:* A German Community Under American Occupation: Marburg, 1945-52, 1961; The American Occupation of Germany: Politics and the Military, 1945-49, 1968; (ed. with J.C. Hennessey) From Coalition to Confrontation: Readings in Cold War Origins, 1973; Origins of Marshall Plan, 1976. Add: 1145 Chester Ave., Arcata, Calif. 95521, U.S.A.

GINDIN, James. American, b. 1926. Literature. Prof. of English, Univ. of Michigan, Ann Arbor, since 1968 (Instr., 1956–59; Asst. Prof., 1959–63; Assoc. Prof., 1963–68). *Publs:* Postwar British Fiction: New Accents and Attitudes, 1962; (ed.) The Return of the Native, by T. Hardy, 1969; Harvest of a Quiet Eye: The Novel of Compassion, 1971; The English Climate: An Excursion into a Biography of John Galsworthy, 1979; John Galsworthy's Life and Art: An Alien's Fortress, 1987. Add: 1615 Shadford Rd., Ann Arbor, Mich. 48104, U.S.A.

GINGER, Ann F(agan). American, b. 1925. Law, Biography. Dir., Meiklejohn Civil Liberties Inst., Berkeley, Calif., since 1965. Chairperson, Berkeley Commn. on Peace and Justice, since 1987. Supervising Ed., California Continuing Education of the Bar, Berkeley, 1961–70; Adjunct Law Prof., University of California-Hastings Coll. of Law, 1972–76, and Univ. of San Francisco School of Law, 1974, 1989; Assoc. Dean, New Coll. of California Sch. of Law, San Francisco, 1975–78; Visiting Prof., Univ. of California, Berkeley, 1988. *Publs:* (ed.) Civil Rights and Liberties Handbook: Pleadings and Practice, 3 vols., 1963; (with others) Legal Aspects of the Civil Rights Movement, 1964; (ed.) California Criminal Law Practice I, 1964, II, 1969, 1977; (ed.) Bill of Rights Citator, 1967; (ed.) The New Draft Law: A Manual for Lawyers and Counselors, 1967, 6th ed. 1971; (with others) Police Misconduct Litigation: Plaintiff's Remedies, 1968; (ed). Civil Liberties Docket 1969, 1970; (ed.) Human Rights Casefinder: The Warren Court Era, 1972; (ed.) The Relevent Lawyers, 1972; The Law, the Supreme Court and the People's Rights, 1974, 1977; (ed.) DeFunis v. Odegaard: The Complete Record, 3 vols., 1974; (ed.) Angela Davis Case Collection, 1974; (ed.) Pentagon Papers Case Collection, 1975; (ed.) Human Rights Docket U.S. 1979, 1979; Issues for the Eighties: Six Speeches, 1981; Jury Selection in Civil and Criminal Trials, 2 vols., 1984–85; (with others) The Cold War Against Labor, 2 vols., 1987; (with others) The National Lawyers Guild: From Roosevelt through Reagan, 1987; Peace Law Docket 1945-1988, 1988. Add: 1715 Francisco St., Berkeley, Calif. 94703, U.S.A.

GINSBERG, Allen. American, b. 1926. Poetry, Literature, Autobiography/Memoirs/Personal. Associated with Beat movements and San Francisco Renaissance in 1950s; Co-Founder and Co-Dir., Jack Kerouac Sch. of Disembodied Poetics, Naropa Inst., Boulder, Colo., 1974. *Publs:* Howl and Other Poems, 1956; Siesta in Xbalba and Return to the States, 1956; Empty Mirror: Early Poems, 1961; Kaddish and Other Poems, 1958-1960, 1961; Reality Sandwiches, 1953-60, 1963; (with Lawrence Ferlinghetti and Gregory Corso) Penguin Modern Poets 5, 1963; (with William S. Burroughs) The Yage Letters, 1963; Kral Majales, 1965; Prose Contribution to Cuban Revolution, 1966; T.V. Baby Poems, 1967; Wales—A Visitation, July 29, 1967, 1968; Scrap Leaves, Tasty Scribbles, 1968; Planet News, 1961-67, 1968; Airplane Dreams: Compositions from Journal, 1968; Ankor-Wat, 1969; Indian Journals: March 1962-May 1963: Notebooks, Diary, Blank Pages, Writings, 1970; The Moments Return: A Poem, 1970; Notes After an Evening with William Carlos Williams, 1970; Improvised Poetics, 1971; Iron Horse, 1972; Kaddish (play), 1972; The Gates of Wrath (Early Rhymed Poems, 1948-1951), 1972; The Fall

of America: Poems of These States, 1973; Gay Sunshine Interview with Allen Young, 1974; Allen Verbatim: Lectures on Poetry, Politics, Consciousness, 1974; The Visions of the Great Rememberer, 1974; Chicago Trial Testimony, 1975; First Blues, 1975; To Eberhart form Ginsberg 1976; Journals: Early Fifties, Early Sixties, 1977; (with N. Cassady) As Ever, 1977; Mind Breaths: Poems 1971-76, 1978; Poems All Over the Place: Mostly Seventies, 1978; (with Peter Orlovsky) Straight Hearts Delight, 1980; Composed on the Tongue, 1980; Collected Poems 1947-1980, 1985; White Shroud, 1986; (with Robert Creeley) The Centos 125 to 143, 1986. Add: P.O. Box 582, Stuyvesant Station, New York, N.Y. 10009, U.S.A.

GINSBURGS, George. American, b. 1932. History, International relations/Current affairs, Law. Distinguished Prof. of Law, Rutgers Univ., Camden, N.J. Prof. of Political Science, New Sch. for Social Research, NYC, 1966–73. *Publs:* (with M. Mathos) Communist China and Tibet, The First Dozen Years, 1964; Soviet Citizenship Law, 1968; Soviet Works on Korea, 1945-1970, 1973; (ed. with D. Barry and W. Butler) Contemporary Soviet Law, Essays in Honor of John N. Hazard, 1974; The Legal Framework of Trade Between the USSR and the People's Republic of China, 1976; (with R. Kim) Calendar of Diplomatic Affairs, Democratic People's Republic of Korea, 1945-1975, 1977; (C.F. Pinkele) The Sino-Soviet Territorial Dispute 1949-1964, 1978; (with R.M. Slusser) A Calendar of Soviet Treaties 1958-1973, 1981; The Citizenship Law of the USSR, 1984. Add: c/o Kluwer Academic Publs., 101 Philip Dr., Assinippi Pk., Norwell, Mass. 02061, U.S.A.

GINZBERG, Eli. American, b. 1911. Economics, Sociology. Emeritus A. Barton Hepburn Prof. of Economics and Special Lect., since 1979 (A. Barton Hepburn Prof., 1967–79), and Dir. of the Conservation of Human Resources Project, since 1950, Columbia Univ., NYC. Consultant to U.S. Depts. of State, Defense, Labor, Health, Education, and Welfare. Gov., Hebrew Univ. of Jerusalem, 1953–59; Chmn., National Manpower Advisory Cttee., 1962–74; Chmn., National Commn. for Manpower Policy (since 1978, National Commn. for Employment Policy), 1974–81. *Publs:* Studies in the Economics of the Bible, 1932; The House of Adam Smith, 1934; The Illusion of Economics Stability, 1939; Grass on the Slag Heaps: The Story of the Welsh Miners, 1942; Report to American Jews: On Overseas Relief, Palestine, and Refugees in the U.S., 1942; Unemployed, 1943; The Labor Leader, 1948; A Pattern for Hospital Care, 1949; Agenda for American Jews, 1950; Occupational Choice, 1951; The Uneducated, 1953; Psychiatry and Military Manpower Policy, 1953; What Makes an Executive, 1955; The Negro Potential, 1956; Effecting Change in Large Organizations, 1957; Human Resources: The Wealth of a Nation, 1958; The Ineffective Soldier: Lessons for Management and the Nation, 1959; (ed.) The Nation's Children, 3 vols., 1960; (ed.) Values and Ideals of American Youth, 1961; Planning for Better Hospital Care, 1961; The Optimistic Tradition and American Youth, 1962; The American Worker in the Twentieth Century, 1963; Democratic Values and the Rights of Management, 1963; (ed.) Technology and Social Change, 1964; The Troublesome Presence: American Democracy and the Negro, 1964; Talent and Performance, 1964; (ed.) The Negro Challenge to the Business Community, 1964; The Pluralistic Economy, 1965; Keeper of the Law: Louis Ginzberg, 1966; Life-Styles of Educated Women, 1966; Educated American Women: Self Portraits, 1966; The Development of Human Resources, 1966; Manpower Strategy for Developing of Nations, 1967; The Middle-Class Negro in the White Man's World, 1967; Manpower Agenda for America, 1968; Men, Money and Medicine, 1969; Urban Health Services: The Case of New York, 1970; Career Guidance, 1971; Manpower for Development: Perspectives on Five Continents, 1971; Manpower Advice for Government, 1972; New York Is Very Much Alive, 1973; (ed.) Corporate Lib: Women's Challenge to Management, 1973; The Manpower Connection: Education and Work, 1975; The Human Economy, 1976; The Limits of Health Reform: The Search for Realism, 1977; Regionalization and Health Policy, 1977; Health Manpower and Health Policy, 1978; Good Jobs, Bad Jobs, No Jobs, 1979; Employing the Unemployed, 1980; The School-Work Nexus, 1980; Tell Me About Your School, 1980; American Jews: The Building of a Voluntary Community (in Hebrew), 1980; Home Health Care: Its Role in the Changing Service Market, 1984; The Coming Physician Surplus: In Search of a Policy, 1984; Beyond Human Scale: The Large Corporation at Risk, 1985; Local Health Policy in Action, 1985; Technology and Employment, 1986; Young People at Risk: Is Prevention Possible?, 1987; (ed.) Medicine and Society: Clinical Decisions and Societal Values, 1987; The Skeptical Economist, 1987; Executive Talent: Developing and Keeping the Best People, 1988; The Financing of Biomedical Research, 1989; My Brother's Keeper: A Personal Memoir of a Public Life, 1989; Does Job Training Work: The Clients Speak Out, 1989. Add: 525 Uris, Columbia Univ., New York, N.Y. 10027, U.S.A.

GIOVANNI, Nikki (Yolande C., Jr.). American, b. 1943. Children's fiction, Poetry, Race relations, Biography. Assoc. Prof. of English, Livingston Coll., Rutgers Univ., New Brunswick, N.J., 1968–70; former Editorial Consultant, Encore mag., Albuquerque, N.M. *Publs:* Black Judgement, 1968; Black Feeling, Black Talk, 1968; (ed.) Night Comes Softly, 1970; Re: Creation, 1970, Black Feeling Black Talk/Black Judgement, 1970; Poem of Angela Yvonne Davis, 1970; Spin a Soft Black Song, 1971; Gemini: An Extended Autobiographical Statement on My First Twenty-Five Years of Being a Black Poet, 1971; My House, 1972; Ego Tripping and Other Poems for Young Readers, 1973; A Dialogue: James Baldwin and Nikki Giovanni, 1973; A Poetic Equation: Conversations Between Nikki Giovanni and Margaret Walker, 1974; The Women and the Men, 1975; Cotton Candy on a Rainy Day, 1978; Vatican Time, 1980; Those Who Ride the Night Winds, 1982; Sacred Cows (essays), 1988. Add: c/o William Morrow Inc., 105 Madison Ave., New York, N.Y. 10016, U.S.A.

GIRLING, John (Lawrence Scott). British-Australian, b. 1926. International relations. Third World problems. Sr. Fellow, Dept. of Intnl. Relations, Research Sch. of Pacific Studies, Australian National Univ., Canberra, since 1966. Member, Research Staff, Foreign Office, London, 1952–66. *Publs:* People's War: Conditions and Consequences in China and Southeast Asia, 1969; America and the Third World: Revolution and Intervention, 1980; The Bureaucratic Polity in Modernising Societies: Similarities, Differences and Prospects in the Asean Region, 1981; Thailand: Society and Politics, 1981; Capital and Power: Political Economy and Social Transformation, 1987. Add: Dept. of Intnl. Relations, Australian National Univ., G.P.O. Box 4, Canberra, A.C.T. 2601, Australia.

GISH, Lillian (Diana). American, b. 1906. Autobiography/Memoirs/-Personal. Stage and film actress. *Publs:* The Movies, Mr. Griffith and Me, 1969; Dorothy and Lillian Gish, 1973; (with S. Lanes) An Actor's Life For Me! (childrens), 1987. Add: 430 E. 57th St., New York, N.Y. 10022, U.S.A.

GITTELSOHN, Roland B. American, b. 1910. Human relations, Theology/Religion. Rabbi Emeritus Temple Israel, Boston, Mas., since 1977 (Rabbi, 1953–77); Rabbi, Central Synagogue of Nassau County, 1936–53. *Publs:* Modern Jewish Problems, 1943; Little Lower Than the Angels, 1954; Man's Best Hope, 1961; Consecrated Unto Me, 1965; My Beloved Is Mine, 1969; Wings of the Morning, 1969; Fire in My Bones, 1969; The Meaning of Judaism, 1970; The Modern Meaning of Judaism, 1978; Love, Sex and Marriage, 1980; The Extra Dimension, 1982; Here I Am—Harnessed to Hope, 1988. Add: Temple Israel, Boston, Mass. 02215, U.S.A.

GITTINGS, Robert (William Victor). British, b. 1911. Plays/Screenplays, Poetry, History, Literature, Biography. Research Student and Research Fellow, 1933–38, and Supvr. in History, 1938–40, Jesus Coll., Cambridge; Producer and Scriptwriter, BBC, London, 1940–63. *Publs:* The Roman Road and Other Poems, 1932; The Story of Psyche, 1936; Wentworth Place: Poems, 1950; The Seven Sleepers (play), 1950; The Makers of Violence (play), 1951; (with Jo Manton) The Peach Blossom Forest and Other Chinese Legends, 19151; Through a Glass, Lightly (play), 1952; Famous Meeting: Poems, Narrative and Lyric, 1953; Man's Estate: A Play of Saint Richard of Chichester, 1954; John Keats: The Living Year, 21 September 1818 to 21 September 1819, 1954; Out of This Wood: A Country Sequence of Five Plays, 1955; The Mask of Keats: A Study of Problems, 1956; (with J. Manton) Windows on History, 4 vols., 1959–61; Shakespeare's Rival: A Study in Three Parts, 1960; (ed.) The Living Shakespeare, 1960; This Tower My Prison and Other Poems, 1961; Love's a Gamble: A Ballad Opera, 1961; (ed. with Evelyn Hardy) Some Recollections, by Emma Hardy, 1961; (with J. Manton) The Story of John Keats, 1962; The Keats Inheritance, 1964; (with J. Manton) Makers of the Twentieth Century, 1966; (ed.) Selected Poems and Letters of John Keats, 1966; John Keats, 1968; Matters of Love and Death, 1968; (ed.) Omniana: or, Horae otiosiores, by Robert Southey and Samuel Taylor Coleridge, 1969; (ed.) Letters of John Keats: A New Selection, 1970; The Odes of Keats and Their Earliest Known Manuscripts in Facsimile, 1970; Conflict at Canterbury: An Entertainment in Sound and Light, 1970; American Journey: Twenty-Five Sonnets, 1972; Young Thomas Hardy, 1975; Collected Poems, 1976; (with Jo Manton) The Flying Horses, 1977; The Older Hardy, 1978; The Nature of Biography, 1978; (with Jo Manton) The Second Mrs. Hardy, 1979; (ed. with James Reeves) Selected Poems of Thomas Hardy, 1981; (with Jo Manton) Dorothy Wordsworth, 1985; People, Places, Personal, 1985. Add: The Stables, East Dean, Chichester, Sussex, England.

GITTLER, Joseph B. American, b. 1912. Philosophy, Social commentary/phenomena, Sociology. Distinguished Prof. of Sociology since 1978, and Dir. of the Center for the Study of Race and Ethnic Relations since 1987, George Mason Univ., Fairfax. Co-Ed., Intnl. Journal of Group Tensions, since 1985. Instr., Asst. Prof., and Assoc. Prof. of Sociology, 1936–43, Univ. of Georgia, Athens; Prof. of Sociology and Head of Dept., Drake Univ., Des Moines, Iowa, 1943–45; Ed., Midwest Sociologist, 1945–48; Assoc. Prof. and Prof. of Sociology, 1945–54, and Dir. of Research Project, Intergroup Relations in Rural Areas, 1952–55, Iowa State Univ., Ames; Prof. and Chmn., Dept. of Sociology and Anthropology, 1954–61, Chmn., Univ. Reorganization Cttee., 1956–58, and Dir., Center for the Study of Group Relations, 1954–60, Univ. of Rochester, N.Y.: Dean of Faculty, Queensborough Community Coll., City Univ. of New York, 1961–66; Dean, Ferkauf Grad. Sch. of Humanities and Social Sciences, and Univ. Prof. of Sociology, Yeshiva Univ., NYC, 1966–78. *Publs:* Social Thought Among the Early Greeks, 1940; Social Dynamics, 1952; (with L. Gittler) Your Neighbor Near and Far, 1955; (ed.) Understanding Minority Groups, 1956, 1964; (ed.) Review of Sociology: Analysis of a Decade, 1957; Ethnic Minorities in the U.S., 1977; Perspectives from the Social Sciences; Jewish Life in the U.S.: Perspectives from the Social Sciences, 1981; Problems of Racial and Ethnic Relations Among High School Youth, 1983; Educational Curricula for Multi-Ethnic Societies, 1984; Integration in the Social Sciences, 1987; A Schematic Framework for Studying Human Social Conflict Resolution, 1988. Add: Dept of Sociology, George Mason Univ., Fairfax, Va. 22030, U.S.A.

GLADSTONE, Arthur M. Writes as Margaret Sebastian; Maggie Gladstone; Cilla Whitmore; and Lisabet Norcross. American, b. 1921. Historical/romance/gothic. Full-time writer since 1973. Major, U.S. Air Force, retired (enlisted, 1943): Research Chemist, American Cyanamid, Bridgeville, Pa., 1947–48; Research Supervisor, Pittsburgh Coke and Chemical, 1948–53; Product Mgr., Nopco Chemical, Newark, N.J., 1953–59; Vice-Pres., Anchor Serum, St. Joseph, Mo., 1959–61; Advanced Rocket Propulsion Marketer, Hercules, Rocket City, W. Va., 1962–68; Product Development Consultant, 1969–73. *Publs:* as Margaret Sebastian—The Honorable Miss Clarendon, 1975; Meg Miller, 1976; Bow Street Gentleman, 1977; Bow Street Brangle, 1977; Miss Letty, 1977; My Lord Rakehell, 1977; Lord Orlando's Protegée, 1977; The Young Lady from Alton-St. Pancras, 1977; That Savage Yankee Squire!, 1978; The Poor Relation, 1978; Lord Dedringham's Divorce, 1978; The Courtship of Colonel Crowne, 1978; Her Knight on a Barge, 1978; The Awakening of Lord Dalby, 1979; Dilemma in Duet, 1979; Byway to Love, 1980; The Plight of Pamela Pollworth, 1980; Miss Keating's Temptation, 1981; A Keeper for Lord Linford, 1982; as Maggie Gladstone—The Scandalous Lady, 1978; The Fortunate Belle, 1978; The Love Duel, 1978; The Reluctant Debutante, 1979; The Impudent Widow, 1979; The Love Tangle, 1980; The Lady's Masquerade, 1980; The Reluctant Protegée, 1980; A Lesson in Love, 1981; as Lisabet Norcross—Masquerade of Love, 1978; Heiress to Love, 1978; My Lady Scapegrace, 1979; as Cilla Whitmore—The Lady and the Rogue, 1978; Manner of a Lady, 1979; His Lordship's Landlady, 1979; Mansion for a Lady, 1980. Add: 1701 Owensville Rd., Charlottesville, Va. 22901, U.S.A.

GLADSTONE, Maggie. *See* **GLADSTONE**, Arthur M.

GLADWYN, Lord. (Hubert Miles Gladwyn Jebb). British, b. 1900. International relations/Current affairs, Autobiography/Memoirs/Personal. Deputy Leader, Liberal Party, House of Lords, 1965–87. Hon. Gov., Atlantic Inst., Chmn., Campaign for Europe; Vice Pres., Atlantic Treaty Assn.; Vice Chmn., British Council for the European Movement. Entered U.K. Diplomatic Service, 1924, and served in Tehran, Rome, and at the Foreign Office, London; Private Secty. to the Permanent Under Secty. of State, 1937–40; Head, Reconstruction Dept., Foreign Office, 1942–45; Exec. Secty., Preparatory Commn. of the U.N., 1945; Acting Secty.-Gen., U.N., 1946; Deputy to the Secty. of State for Peace Treaties, 1946; Asst. Under Secty. of State and U.N. Adviser, 1946–47; U.K. Rep., Brussels Treaty Permanent Commn., 1948; Deputy Under Secty. of State, 1949–50; U.K. Rep. to the U.N., 1950–54; British Ambassador to France, 1954–60; Member of the European Parliament, 1973–76. *Publs:* Is Tension Necessary, 1960; Peaceful Co-existence, 1962; The European Idea, 1967; Halfway to 1984, 1968; Europe after de Gaulle, 1969; The Memoirs of Lord Gladwyn, 1972. Add: 62 Whitehall Ct., London SW1, England.

GLAHE, Fred R. American, b. 1934. Economics. Prof. of Economics, Univ. of Colorado, Boulder, since 1965. *Publs:* (with Malcom Dowling) Reading in Econometric Theory, 1970; (ed.) Collected Paper of Kenneth E. Boulding: Economics, 2 vols., 1971; Macroeconomics: Theory and Policy, 1973, 1985; (ed.) Adam Smith and the

Wealth of Nations, 1978; (with Dwight Lee) Microeconomics: Theory and Applications, 1981, 1989; (ed. with Joseph Peden) The American Family and the State, 1986. Add: Dept. of Economics, Univ. of Colorado, Boulder, Colo. 80309, U.S.A.

GLANVILLE, Brian (Lester). British, b. 1931. Novels/Short stories, Sports/Physical education/Keeping fit. Sports Columnist and Chief Football Writer, Sunday Times newspaper, London, since 1958. Literary Adviser, Bodley Head Ltd., publrs., London, 1958-62. *Publs:* (with Cliff Bastin) Cliff Bastin Remembers, 1950; The Reluctant Dictator, 1952; Henry Sows the Wind, 1954; Soccer Nemesis, 1955; Along the Arno, 1956; The Bankrupts, 1958; (with Jerry Weinstein) World Cup, 1958; After Rome, Africa, 1959; Soccer Round the Globe, 1959; A Bad Streak and Other Stories, 1961; Diamond, 1962; The Rise of Gerry Logan, 1963; The Director's Wife and Other stories, 1963; Goalkeepers Are Crazy: A Collection of Football Stories, 1964; The King of Hackney Marshes and Other Stories, 1965; Know About Football, 1965; A Second Home, 1965; A Roman Marriage, 1966; The Artist Type, 1967; People in Sport, 1967; Soccer: A Panorama, 1968; The Olympian, 1969; A Betting Man, 1969; A Cry of Crickets, 1970; Puffin Book of Football, 1970; Goalkeepers Are Different, 1971; The Financiers, 1972; Brian Glanville's Book of World Football, 1972; World Football Handbook, 1972; The Sunday Times History of the World Cup (in U.S. as History of the Soccer World Cup), 1973; The Thing He Loves and Other Stories, 1973; The Comic, 1974; The Dying of the Light, 1976; Target Man (children's novel), 1978; A History of Soccer (in U.S. as A Book of Soccer), 1979; Never Look Back, 1980; A Visit to the Villa (play), 1981; Underneath the Arches (musical play), 1981; (with Kevin Whitney) The British Challenge, 1984; Love Is Not Love and Other Stories, 1985; Kissing America, 1985; (ed.) The Joy of Football, 1986; The Catacomb, 1988. Add: 160 Holland Park Ave., London W11, England.

GLASER, Comstock. See **GLASER**, Kurt.

GLASER, Kurt. Wrote as Comstock Glaser until 1946. American, b. 1914. International relations/Current affairs, Politics/Government, Public/Social administration. Prof. of Govt., Southern Illinois Univ. Edwardsville, since 1965 (Lectr., 1959-60; Assoc. Prof., 1960-65). Assoc. Ed., Modern Age, Chicago; Bd. Member, Foundn. for the Study of Plural Socs. Chief, Methods Section, Personnel Div., Social Security Bd., Washington, D.C., 1941-46; Govt. Affairs Officer, U.S. Military Govt. for Germany, 1946-50; Research Project Leader, Govt. Affairs, Inst., Washington, D.C., 1953-54; Asst. Prof. of Govt., Univ. of Maryland, College Park, 1956-59. *Publs:* (with Arnold Brecht, as Comstock Glaser) The Art and Technique of Administration in German Ministries, 1940; Administrative Procedure, 1941, Adaptation as Administrative Technique, 1951; Land and Local Government in the United States Zone of Germany, 1947; (ed. and author) Government and Administration in the Soviet Zone of Germany, 1947, 1948; Comparative Federal Constitutions, 1948; The Iron Curtain and American Policy, 1953; Czecho-Slovakia: A Critical History, 1961; (ed. with D.S. Collier) Berlin and the Future of Western Europe, 1963; (trans. and ed.) Europe's Road to Potsdam, by Wenzel Jaksch, 1963; (ed. with D.S. Collier) Western Integration and the Future of Eastern Europe, 1964; World War II and the War-Guilt Question, 1965; (ed. with D.S. Collier) Western Policy and Eastern Europe, 1966; (with D.S. Collier) Elements of Change in Eastern Europe, 1968; (with D.S. Collier) the Conditions for Peace in Europe: Problems of Detente and Security, 1969; (ed. with J. Barratt); (with S.T. Possony) Victims of Politics: The State of Human Rights, 1979. Add: 660 Chase Rd., N. Dartmouth, Mass. 02747, U.S.A.

GLASER, William Arnold. American, b. 1925. Social Sciences. Sr. Research Assoc., Bureau of Applied Social Research, Columbia Univ., NYC, since 1956 (Exec. Dir., Council of Social Sciences Data Archives, 1965-68). Asst. Prof., Michigan State Univ., 1952-56. *Publs:* (co-ed.) Readings in Social Science, 1956; (co-author) Public Opinion and Congressional Elections, 1962; (co-ed.) The Government of Associations, 1966; Sheltered Employment of the Disabled, 1966; Pre-Trial Discovery and the Adversary System, 1968; Social Settings and Medical Organization 1970; The Brain Drain and Study Abroad, 1975; Health Insurance Bargaining: Foreign Lessons for Americans, 1978; Paying the Hospital: The Organization, Dynamics, and Effects of Differing Financial Arrangements, 1987. Add: c/o Jossey-Bass, Inc., 350 Sansome St., San Francisco, Calif. 94104, U.S.A.

GLASKIN, G(erald) M(arcus). Also writes as Neville Jackson. Australian, b. 1923. Novels/Short stories, Plays/Screenplays, Supernatural/Parapsychology, Travel/Exploration/Adventure. Partner, Lyall & Evatt, Stockbrokers, Singapore, 1951-59. Pres., Fellowship of Australian Writers in Western Australia, 1968-69. *Publs:* A World of Our Own, 1955; A Minor Portrait, 1957; A Change of Mind, 1959; A Lion in the Sun, 1960; A Waltz Through the Hills, 1961; The Land That Sleeps, 1961; The Beach of Passionate Love, 1962; A Small Selection, 1962; Flight to Landfall, 1963; O Love, O Loneliness, 1964; (as Neville Jackson) No End to the Way, 1965; The Man Who Didn't Count, 1965; Turn on the Heat (play), 1967; The Road to Nowhere, 1967; A Bird in My Hands, 1967; Windows of the Mind, 1974; Two Women: Turn on the Heat and The Eaves of Night, 1975; Worlds Within, 1976; A Door to Eternity, 1979; One Way to Wonderland, 1984. Add: 1 Warnham Heights, 14 Warnham Rd., Cottesloe, W.A. 6011, Australia.

GLASRUD, Clarence A. American, b. 1911. Literature. Prof. of English Emeritus, Moorhead State Univ., Minnesota (Prof. of English, 1947-77; Chmn., Dept. of English, 1949-71); Dir. of Research, Red River Valley Historical Soc., Moorhead, since 1978. Advisory Ed., Studies in American Fiction, Boston, since 1972; Member, Bd. of Publications, Norwegian-American Historical Assn., Northfield, Minn., since 1973. *Publs:* (ed.) The Age of Anxiety, 1960; Hjalmar Hjorth Boyesen: A Biographical and Critical Study, 1963; (ed.) A Heritage Deferred: The German-American in Minnesota, 1981; (ed.) Roy Johnson's Red River Valley, 1982; (ed.) A Special Relationship, 1983; (ed.) A Heritage Fulfilled, 1984; (ed.) L'Heritage Tranquille, 1987; The Moorhead Normal School: A History, 1987; Moorhead State Teachers College 1921-1957: A History, 1989. Add: 422 6th St. S., Moorhead, Minn. 56560, U.S.A.

GLASSCOCK, Anne. See **BONNER**, Michael.

GLASSON, T(homas) Francis. British, b. 1906. Theology/Religion, Biography. Methodist Minister, since 1937. Lectr. in New Testament Studies, New Coll., Univ. of London, 1960-72. *Publs:* Thomas Glasson: Lay Preacher, 1943; The Second Advent: The Origin of the New Testament Doctrine, 1945, 3rd ed. 1963; His Appearing and His Kingdom: The Christian Hope in the Light of Its History, 1953; Greek Influence in Jewish Eschatology, 1961; Moses in the Fourth Gospel, 1963; The Revelation of John, 1965; Jesus and the End of the World, 1980. Add: 29 Bear Cross Ave., Bournemouth BH11 9NU, England.

GLAZE, Andrew Louis. American, b. 1920. Novels, Plays, Poetry. Press Officer, British Tourist Authority, NYC, 1958-82. *Publs:* Lines, 1964; Damned Ugly Children, 1966; Miss Pete (play), 1966; Kleinhoff Demonstrates Tonight (play), 1971; Masque of Surgery, 1974; The Trash Dragon of Shensi, 1978; I Am the Jefferson County Courthouse, 1980; A City, 1982; Uneasy Lies (play), 1983; Earth That Sings: The Poetry of Andrew Glaze, 1985. Add: 825 N.W. 14th St., Miami, Fla. 33125, U.S.A.

GLAZEBROOK, Philip. British, b. 1937. Novels/Short stories. *Publs:* Try Pleasure, 1968; The Eye of the Beholder, 1974; The Burr Wood, 1977; Byzantine Honeymoon, 1979; Journey to Kars, 1984; Captain Vinegar's Commission, 1987; The Gate at the End of the World, 1989. Add: Strode Manor, Bridport, Dorset, England.

GLAZER, Nathan. American, b. 1923. Race relations, Sociology, Urban studies. Prof. of Education and Social Structure, Harvard Univ., Cambridge Mass., since 1969. Co-Ed., The Public Interest, since 1973; Staff Member, Commentary Mag., 1944-53; Ed. and Editorial Advisor, Doubleday Anchor Books, 1954-57; Editorial Adviser, Random House, publrs., 1958-62; Urban Sociologist, Housing and Home Finance Agency, Washington, D.C., 1962-63; Prof. of Sociology, Univ. of California at Berkeley, 1963-69. *Publs:* (with David Riesman and Reuel Denney) The Lonely Crowd, 1950; (with D. Riesman) Faces in the Crowd, 1952; American Judaism, 1957, 1972; (ed. with D. McEntire) Studies in Housing and Minority Groups, 1960; The Social Basis of American Communism, 1961; (with Daniel P. Moynihan) Beyond the Melting Pot, 1963, 1970; Remembering the Answers, 1970; (ed. with D.P. Moynihan) Ethnicity: Theory and Experience, 1975; Affirmative Discrimination: Ethnic Inequality and Public Policy, 1976; (ed. with William Gorham) The Urban Predicament, 1976; Ethnic Dilemmas 1964-1982, 1983; Clamor at the Gates: The New American Immigration, 1985; (ed. with Mark Lilla) The Public Face of Architecture, 1987. Add: Grad. Sch. of Education, Harvard Univ., Cambridge, Mass. 02138, U.S.A.

GLEAVE, John T. British, b. 1917. Geography. Gen. Ed., Evans Bros., and Macmillan Ltd. Lectr. in Education, Coll. of St. Mark and St. John, London, 1946-47; Asst. Education Officer, Ipswich, 1947-48; H.M. Overseas Civil Service, Uganda, 1949-62; Deputy Dir. of Education, 1958-62; Dir. of Extramural Classes and Courses, 1962-69, and Dir. of Special Courses, 1969-82, Univ. of Leeds. *Publs:* Geography for

Uganda Schools, Books I & II; Introducing Geography, Uganda, Books I & II: (adaptor) Civics for East African Schools; Visual Geography of East Africa: (co-author) Uganda Our Homeland. Add: Fulwith Close, Harrogate, N. Yorks., England.

GLECKNER, Robert F(rancis). American, b. 1925. Literature. Prof. of English, Duke Univ., Durham, N.C., since 1978 (Acting Chmn. of Dept., 1983). Advisory Ed., Criticism, since 1962, Blake Studies, since 1970, Studies in Romanticism, since 1977, and of Milton and the Romantics (now Nineteenth-Century Contexts), since 1980. Instr. in English, Johns Hopkins Univ., Baltimore, Md., 1949–51, Univ. of Cincinnati, Ohio, 1952–54, and Univ. of Wisconsin, Madison, 1954–57; Ed., Research Studies Inst., Maxwell Air Force Base, Ala., 1951–52; Asst. Prof., and Assoc. Prof. of English, Wayne State Univ., Detroit, Mich., 1957–62; Prof. of English, 1962–78, Chmn. of the Dept. of English, 1962–66, Assoc. Dean of the Coll. of Letters and Science, 1966–68, and Dean of the Coll. of Humanities, 1968–75, Univ. of California at Riverside. *Publs:* The Piper and the Bard: A Study of William Blake, 1957; (ed. with G.E. Enscoe) Romanticism: Points of View, 1962, rev. ed. as sole ed. 1970, 3rd ed. 1975; (ed.) Selected Writings of William Blake, 1967, 1970; Byron and the Ruins of Paradise, 1967, 1982; (ed.) Complete Poetical Works of Lord Byron, 1975; Blake's Prelude: "Poetical Sketches", 1982; Blake and Spenser, 1985; Approaches to the Teaching of Blake's "Songs", 1989. Add: English Dept., Duke Univ., Durham, N.C. 27706, U.S.A.

GLEN, Duncan (Munro). Also writes as Simon Foster and Ronald Eadie Munro. British, b. 1933. Poetry, Literature. Typographer, H.M.S.O., 1958–60; Asst. Lectr. in Typographic Design, Watford Coll. of Technology, 1960–63; Ed., Robert Gibson & Sons Ltd., Educational Publrs., 1963–65; Lectr., 1965–69, Sr. Lectr., 1969–74, and Principal Lectr. in Graphic Design, 1974–78, Preston Polytechnic, Lancashire; Head, Dept. of Visual Communication, Trent Polytechnic, Nottingham, 1978–86, now Emeritus Prof. Ed. Akros poetry mag., 1965–83. *Publs:* Hugh MacDiarmid: Rebel Poet and Prophet, 1962; Hugh MacDiarmid and the Scottish Renaissance, 1964; The Literary Masks of Hugh MacDiarmid, 1964; (as Ronald Eadie Munro) Stanes, 1966; (as Simon Foster) Scottish Poetry Now, 1966; (ed.) Poems Addressed to Hugh MacDiarmid, 1967; (as Ronald Eadie Munro) Idols, 1967; Sunny Summer Sunday Afternoon in the Park?, 1969; (ed.) Selected Essays of Hugh MacDiarmid, 1969; Unnerneath the Bed, 1970; A Small Press and Hugh MacDiarmid, 1970; (with H. MacDiarmid) The MacDiarmids: A Conversation, 1970; (ed.) The Akros Anthology of Scottish Poetry, 1965-70, 1970; In Appearances, 1971; Clydesdale, 1971; Feres, 1971; The Individual and the Twentieth-Century Scottish Literary Tradition, 1971; (ed.) Whither Scotland?, 1971; (ed.) Hugh MacDiarmid: A Critical Survey, 1972; A Journey Past, 1972: A Cled Score, 1974; (compiler) A Bibliography of Scottish Poets from Stevenson to 1974, 1974; Mr. and Mrs. J.L. Stoddart at Home: A Poem, 1975; (with John Brook) Preston's New Buildings, 1975; Buits and Wellies: A Sequence of Poems, 1976; Follow! Follow! Follow! and Other Poems, 1976; Spoiled for Choice: Poems, 1976; (ed. with Nat Scammacca) La Nuova Poesia Scozzese, 1976; Five Literati, 1976; Weddercock: A Poem, 1976; Gaitherings: Poems in Scots, 1977; (ed.) Preston Polytechnic Poets, 1977; Forward from Hugh MacDiarmid, 1977; Hugh MacDiarmid: An Essay for 11 August 1977, 1977; Traivellin Man: A Sequence of Poems, 1977; In Place of Wark: A Sequence of Thirty Pairts, 1977; Of Philosophers and Tinks: A Sequence of Poems, 1977; (ed.) Graphic Designers as Poets, 1977; (ed.) Typoems, 1977; The Inextinguishable, part 14 of Realities Poems, 1977; Ten Sangs, 1978; Ither Sangs, 1978; Ten Bird Sangs, 1978; Ten Sangs of Luve, 1978; Realities Poems, 1980; On Midsummer Evenin Merriest of Nichts?, 1981; (ed.) Akros Verse 1965-1982, 1982; Facts Are Chiels, 1983; The State of Scotland, 1983; Portraits, 1983; The Stones of Time, 1984; Nottingham, 1984; Situations, 1984; In the Small Hours, 1984; Eden, 1985; Frae a Suburban Gairden, 1985; The Turn of the Earth, 1985; Geeze!, 1985; The Autobiography of a Poet, 1986; Tales to Be Told, 1987; (ed. with Peter France) European Poetry in Scotland, 1989; A Journey into Scotland, 1989. Add: 18 Warrender Park Terrace, Edinburgh EH9 1EF, Scotland.

GLEN, Frank Grenfell. New Zealander, b. 1933. Theology/Religion, Autobiography/Memoirs/Personal, Biography. Ordained Minister of Methodist Conference of New Zealand, since 1960; Police Chaplain, since 1983; Minister, Thames Union Parish, New Zealand. Chaplain to NZ Territorial Army, 1962–66; Supt., Methodist Far West Mission and Flying Padre, N.S.W., 1966–70; Chaplain, Royal Australian Air Force, 1970–76; with the New Zealand Dept. of Justice, 1976–84; Chaplain, Presbyterian Support Services, 1985–86. *Publs:* Methodism in Southland, 1956; Methodist in Auckland during Maori Wars, 1860-64, 1958; Methodism in the Coal Field of Southland, 1960; Journal of Rev. F. Glen 1960–62 in the Fiords of Southland; Rev. J.T. Luxford, Chaplain to the Forces,

1966; (ed.) Journal of Rev. J. Harris Under Sail to New Zealand in 1874, 1966; Holy Joe's People, 1968, 3rd ed. 1975; Fly High Reach Far, 1971; Study of the Chaplain's Role and Religion in the R.A.A.F., 1973; Bush in Our Yard, 1981; For Glory and a Farm, 1984. Add: P.O. Box 544, Thames, New Zealand.

GLIAUDA, Jurgis. American, b. 1906. Novels/Short stories, Plays/Screenplays, Poetry, Social commentary/phenomena. *Publs:* Ave America! (poetry), 1950; Ora pro nobis, 1952; The Expiring Sun (short stories), 1954; Seed-Corns of Character, 1955; The Throne of Bats, 1960; House Upon the Sand, 1963; Agony (history), 1965; Under the Sign of the Dolphin, 1966; Sonata of Icarus, 1968; Amphorae of Despair, 1969; Goblins and the Forest, 1969; The Masked Ball (play), 1969; The Searchers of Happiness (play), 1970; Simas (social comment), 1971; The Burden of Twilight, 1972; The Morning of Peace (short stories), 1972; The Most Difficult Way, 1973; The Night (play), 1974; Under the Wind, 1975; The Trial in June (social comment), 1977; The Daring to Live, 1978; The Republic of Perloja, 1979; The Punishment (short stories), 1980; The White Flags (novel) 1984; The March Fourth (novel), 1984; The Pastor and the Wolves (novel), 1986. Add: 946 E. Herring Ave., West Covina, Calif. 91790, U.S.A.

GLICK, Edward Bernard. American, b. 1929. Middle East studies, International relations/Current affairs, Military/Defence, Politics/Government. Prof. of Political Science, Temple Univ., Philadelphia, since 1968. Human Factors Scientist, System Development Corp., Washington, D.C., 1959–64; Sr. Political Scientist, Office of National Security Studies of the Bendix Corp., Washington, D.C., 1964–65. *Publs:* Latin America and the Palestine Problem, 1958; Straddling the Isthmus of Tehuantepec, 1959; (with R.H. Davis and R. Boguslaw) Plans: Planning and Negotiation Studies, 1966; Peaceful Conflict: The Non-Military Use of the Military, 1967; Soldiers, Scholars, and Society: The Social Impact of the American Military, 1971; Between Israel and Death, 1974; Israel and Her Army, 1977; The Triangular Connection: America, Israel, and American Jews, 1982. Add: Dept. of Political Science, Temple Univ., Ambler Campus, Ambler Pa. 19002, U.S.A.

GLICKSBERG, Charles Irving. American, b. 1900. Literature, Writing/Journalism. Adjunct Prof. in Comparative Literature, Grad. Div., and Prof. Emeritus, Dept. of English, Brooklyn Coll., City Univ. of New York, since 1971 (Asst. Prof. of English, 1946–50; Assoc. Prof. of English, 1950–58; Prof. of English, 1958–71; Member of the doctoral faculty in English, 1963–71). Member of faculty, New Sch. for Social Research, 1947–64; Dir., Vermont Writers Conference, 1954–56; Fulbright Lectr. in American Literature, Bar-Ilan Univ., 1958–59. *Publs:* (ed.) Walt Whitman and the Civil War, 1933; (ed.) American Literary Criticism 1900-1950, 1951; Writing the Short Story, 1953; (ed. with B. Weber) American Vanguard, 1953; (ed.) New Voices 3, 1958; (ed.) New Voices 4, 1960; Creative Writing, 1961; Literature and Religion, 1961; The Tragic Vision in Twentieth-Century Literature, 1963; The Self in Modern Literature, 1963; Modern Literature and the Death of God, 1966; The Ironic Vision in Modern Literature, 1969; The Sexual Revolution in Modern American Literature, 1971; Modern Literary Perspectivism, 1971; Literature and Society, 1972; The Sexual Revolution in Modern English Literature, 1973; The Literature of Nihilism, 1974; The Literature of Commitment, 1976. Add: 210 West 101st St., New York, N.Y. 10025, U.S.A.

GLIEWE, Unada G. Writes as Unada. American, b. 1927. Children's fiction. Staff Artist, O'Brien Advertising Agency, Rochester, N.Y. 1950–55, and Lutheran Bd. of Paris Education, 1955–67. Illustrator of more than 30 books. *Publs:* Ricky's Boots; Andrew's Amazing Boxes; The Marvelous Monster of Mulligan Heights, 1981. Add: 2300 Pine St., Philadelphia, Pa. 19103, U.S.A.

GLOAG, Julian. British, b. 1930. Novels, Plays. *Publs:* Our Mother's House, 1963; A Sentence of Life, 1966; Maundy, 1969; A Woman of Character, 1973; Sleeping Dogs Lie, 1980; Lost and Found, 1981; Blood for Blood, 1985; Only Yesterday, 1986. Add: c/o Michelle Lapautre, 6 rue Jean Carriès, 75007 Paris, France.

GLOCK, Marvin David. American, b. 1912. Education. Prof. Emeritus of Educational Psychology, Cornell Univ., Ithaca, N.Y., since 1949. Prof., Michigan State Univ., East Lansing, 1946–49. *Publs:* Guiding Learning, 1971; Evaluating Pupil Growth, 6th ed. 1981; PROBE: Developmental Reading Program, rev. ed., 1983. Add: 308 Roberts Hall, Cornell Univ., Ithaca, N.Y. 14853, U.S.A.

GLOVACH, Linda. American, b. 1947. Children's fiction, Children's non-fiction. Freelance painter, 1965–69. *Publs:* Hey! Wait for Me, I'm

Amelia (non-fiction), 1970; The Cat and the Collector, 1972; The Little Witch series, 15 vols., 1972–88; Let's Make a Deal, 1976; Potions, Lotions, Tonics and Teas, 1979. Add: 233 8th Ave., Sea Cliff, N.Y. 11579, U.S.A.

GLOVER, Janet Reaveley. British, b. 1912. History. Head Mistress, Laurel Bank Sch., Glasgow, 1946–59; Head Mistress, Sutton High Sch. for Girls, Surrey, 1959–73. Pres., Assn. of Head Mistresses, 1970–72. *Publs:* (ed. with J.A. Wilson) A Constribution to the History of Lanarkshire, 1937; (ed. with others) Laurel Bank School 1903-1953, 1953; The Story of Scotland, 1960, 1976. Add: 73 Christchurch Mt., Epsom, Surrey KT19 8LP, England.

GLOVER, Judith. British, b. 1943. Historical novels, History, Language/Linguistics, Travel. *Publs:* The Place Names of Sussex, 1974; The Place Names of Kent, 1975; Colour Book of Sussex, 1975; Colour Book of Kent, 1976; (with Anthony Kersting) Sussex in Photographs, 1976; Drink Your Own Garden, 1979; The Stallion Man, 1982; Sisters and Brothers, 1984; To Everything a Season, 1986; Birds in a Gilded Cage, 1987; The Imagination of the Heart, 1989. Add: 9 Barclay Close, Albighton, West Midlands, WV7 3PX, England.

GLOVER, Michael. British, b. 1922. History, Military/Defence, Biography. With British Army, 1941–46, and British Council, 1947–70. *Publs:* Wellington's Peninsular Victories, 1963; Wellington as Military Commander, 1968; Britannia Sickens, 1971; Legacy of Glory, 1971; (with U. Pericoli) 1815—The Armies at Waterloo, 1973; An Assemblage of Indian Army Soldiers and Uniforms, 1973; The Peninsular War, A Concise History, 1974; Wellington's Army, 1977; A Very Slippery Fellow: Sir Robert Wilson, 1978; A Gentleman Volunteer: The Letters of George Hennel, 1979; The Napoleonic Wars: An Illustrated History 1792-1815, 1979; Warfare from Waterloo to Mons, 1980; Warfare in the Age of Bonaparte, 1981; The Velvet Glove: The Decline and Fall of Moderation in War, 1982; The Fight for the Channel Ports: Calais to Brest 1940, 1985; An Improvised War: Ethiopia 1940-41, 1987; Guide to the Battlefields of France and the Low Countries, 1987; That Astonishing Infantry: The Royal Welch Fusiliers 1689-1989, 1989. Add: Bidcombe, France Lynch, Glos. GL6 8LY, England.

GLÜCK, Louise. American, b. 1943. Poetry. Member of the Faculty, Williams Coll., Williamstown, MA, since 1983. *Publs:* Firstborn, 1968; The House of Marshland, 1974; The Garden, 1976; Descending Figure, 1980; The Triumph of Achilles, 1985. Add: Creamery Rd., Plainfield, Vt. 05667, U.S.A.

GLUT, Don(ald) F. American, b. 1944. Novels/Short stories, Art, Film, Literature, Creator of many comic strip characters including Tragg, Simbar, Dagar, Durak, Dr. Spektor, and Baron Tibor. Assoc. Ed., Monsters of the Movies mag., Marvel comic Group, since 1974. Musician/singer, actor, book store clerk, asst. copyrwriter, 1965–71; Contrib. Ed., Castle of Frankenstein, 1969–71. *Publs:* Frankenstein Lives Again (novels), 1971; Terror of Frankenstein, and sequels, 1971; (with Jim Harmon) The Great Movie Serials: Their Sound and Fury, 1972; True Vampires of History, 1972; The Dinosaur Dictionary, 1972, rev. ed. as The New Dinosaur Dictionary, 1982; The Frankenstein Legend: A Tribute to Mary Shelley and Boris Karloff, 1973; (contrib.) The Comic-Book Book, 1973; Bugged! (science fiction), 1974; The Dracula Book, 1974; Spawn (novel), 1976; Classic Movie Monsters, 1978; The Empire Strikes Back (novel), 1980; The Dinosaur Scrapbook, 1980; with Sylvia Massey Dinosaurs, Mammoths, and Cavemen: The Art of Charles R. Knight, 1982; The Frankenstein Catalog, 1984. Add: 2805 N. Keystone St., Burbank, Calif. 91504, U.S.A.

GLUYAS, Constance. American (b. British), b. 1920. Historical/Romance/Gothic. *Publs:* The King's Brat, 1972; Born to Be King, 1974; My Lady Benbrook, 1975; Brief Is the Glory, 1975; The House on Twyford Street, 1976; My Lord Foxe, 1976; Savage Eden, 1976; Rogue's Mistress, 1977; Woman of Fury, 1978; Flame of the South, 1979; Madame Tudor, 1979; Lord Sin, 1980; The Passionate Savage, 1980; The Bridge to Yesterday, 1981; Brandy Kane, 1985. Add: c/o Teresa Kralik, New American Library, 1633 Broadway, New York, N.Y. 10019, U.S.A.

GLYN, (Sir) Anthony (Geoffrey Leo Simon). British, b. 1922. Novels/Short stories, Plays/Screenplays, Travel/Exploration/Adventure, Biography. *Publs:* Romanza, 1953; The Jungle of Eden, 1954; Elinor Glyn, 1955; The Ram in the Thicket, 1957; I Can Take It All, 1959; Kick Turn, 1963; The Terminal, 1965; The Seine, 1966; The Dragon Variation, 1969; The British, 1970; The Companion Guide to Paris, 1985. Add: Marina Brie des Anges, Ducal Apt. U-03, 06270 Villeneuve Loubet,

France.

GMELCH, George. American, b. 1944. Anthropology/Ethnology. Assoc. Prof. of Anthropology, Union Coll., Schenectady, N.Y., since 1981. Research Fellow, Inst. of Social and Economic Research, Memorial Univ. of Newfoundland, St. John's, Canada, 1971–73; Asst. Prof., McGill Univ., Montreal, 1973–75; Asst. Prof., State Univ. of New York, Albany, 1975–80; Research Assoc., Leicester Polytechnic, England, 1980–81. *Publs:* Irish Tinkers: The Urbanization of an Itinerant People, 1977, 1985; To Shorten the Road: Traveller Folk Tales from Ireland, 1978; (ed.) J.M. Synge: In Wicklow, West Kerry and Connemara, 1980; (with W.P. Zenner) Urban Life: Readings in Urban Anthropology, 1980, 1988. Add: Dept. of Sociology and Anthropology, Union Coll., Schenectady, N.Y. 12308, U.S.A.

GMELCH, Sharon (Bohn). American, b. 1947. Anthropology/Ethnology. Assoc. Prof., Union Coll., Schenectady, N.Y., since 1981. *Publs:* Tinkers and Travellers, 1975; Irish Life: The People and Places of Ireland, 1979; (ed.) Irish Life and Traditions, 1986; Nan: The Life of an Irish Travelling Woman, 1986. Add: Dept. of Sociology, Union Coll., Schenectady, N.Y. 12308, U.S.A.

GNAROWSKI, Michael. Canadian, b. 1934. Poetry, Literature. Prof. of English, Carleton Univ., and Vice-Pres. and Gen. Ed., Carleton Univ. Press, Ottawa. Ed., Critical Views on Canadian Writers series, McGraw-Hill Ryerson Press, Toronto. Former Assoc. Prof. and Coordinator of Canadian Studies, Sir George Williams Univ., Montreal. Founding Co-Ed., Yes: A Magazine of Poetry and Prose, 1956–64, and Canadian Poetry: Studies, Documents and Reviews, 1977–83. *Publs:* Postscript for St. James Street (poetry), 1965; Contact 1952-1954: Being an Index to the contents of "Contact", a Little Magazine edited by Raymond Souster, 1966; (ed. with L. Dudek) The Making of Modern Poetry in Canada: Essential Articles on Contemporary Canadian Poetry in English, 1967; (ed.) The Rising Village of Oliver Goldsmith: A New Edition, 1968; The Gentlemen Are Also Lexicographers (poetry), 1969; (ed.) Archibald Lampman, 1970; (ed.) Selected Stories of Raymond Knister, 1972; (comp.) Concise Bibliography of English-Canadian Literature, 1973, 1978; (ed.) New Provinces: Poems of Several Authors, 1976; (ed.) Leonard Cohen: The Artist and His Critics, 1976. Add: 409 Oxford St. E., Kemptville, Ont., Canada.

GOACHER, Denis. British, b. 1925. Poetry, Translations. *Publs:* (with Peter Whigham) The Marriage Rite, 1960; (trans.) Inferno (Cantos 29-31), by Dante, 1965; Logbook, 1972; Transversion, 1973; Night of the 12th, 13th, 1973; (ed.) Soldier On, 1973; Three Songs from the Romany King of Wembworthy, 1976; To Romany, 12976; If Hell, Hellas, 1980. Add: Dioné House, Wembworthy, Chulmleigh, North Devon, England.

GOAMAN, Muriel. Pseud. for Edith Muriel Cox. British. Children's non-fiction, History, Recreation/Leisure/Hobbies. Mayor, Councillor, Alderman, and Justice of the Peace, Devon, 1948–64. *Publs:* 15 educational books for children, 1947–68; Thomas Guy, 1959; English Clocks, 1967; Through the Ages—Food, 1968; Fun with Chess, 1968; Old Bideford and District, 1968; Through the Ages—Transport, 1970; Fun with Time, 1970; Fun with Travel, 1971; Picture Signs and Symbols, 1971; Touch Wood—A Book of Everyday Superstitions, 1973; Chess Made Easy, 1973; Never So Good; or, How Children Were Treated, 1974. Add: Stone Cottage, Durrant Lane, Northam, Bideford, Devon EX39 2RL, England.

GODBER, John (Harry). British, b. 1956. Plays/Screenplays. Artistic Dir., Hull Truck Theatre co., since 1984. Teacher, Minsthorpe High Sch., 1981–83. *Publs:* Up 'n' Under, 1985; Bouncers, and Shakers, 1987. Add: Hull Truck, Spring St. Theatre, Spring St., Hull, Yorks. HU2 8RW, England.

GODBOLD, E(dward) Stanly, Jr. American, b. 1942. History, Biography. Prof. of History, Mississippi State Univ., since 1977. Asst. Prof., Univ. of Tennessee at Chattanooga, 1969–70; Assoc. Prof., Valdosta State Coll., Ga., 1970–77. *Publs:* Ellen Glasgow and the Woman Within, 1972; (co-ed.) Essays in Southern History in Honor of Robert H. Woody, 1974; (with Robert H. Woody) Christopher Gadsden and the American Revolution, 1982. Add: Dept. of History, Mississippi State Univ., Miss. 39762, U.S.A.

GODDEN, Geoffrey Arthur. British, b. 1929. Antiques/Furnishings. *Publs:* Victorian Porcelain, 1961; Victorian Pottery, 1962; Encyclopaedia of British Poetry and Porcelain Marks, 1964; Antique China and Glass

Under Pounds, 1966; An Illustrated Encyclopaedia of British Pottery and Porcelain, 1966; The Handbook of British Pottery and Porcelain Marks, 1968; Minton Pottery and Porcelain of the First Period, 1793-1850, 1968; Caughley and Worcester Porcelains 1775-1800, 1969; Coalport and Coalbrookdale Porcelains, 1970; Stevengraphs and Other Victorian Silk Pictures, 1971; Jewitt's Ceramic Art of Great Britain 1800-1900, 1972; British Porcelain—An Illustrated Guide, 1973; British Pottery—An Illustrated Guide, 1974; Godden's Guide to English Porcelain, 1978; Oriental Export Market Porcelain, 1979; Mason's China and the Ironstone Wares, 1980; Chamberlain-Worcester Porcelain, 1982; Staffordshire Porcelain, 1983; English China, 1985; Encyclopaedia of British Porcelain Manufacturers, 1988. Add: 19A Crescent Rd., Worthing, Sussex, England.

GODDEN, (Margaret) Rumer. British, b. 1907. Novels/Short stories, Children's fiction, Poetry, Autobiography/Memoirs/Personal, Documentaries/Reportage, Translations. *Publs:* Chinese Puzzle (novel), 1936; The Lady and the Unicorn (novel), 1937; Black Narcissus (novel), 1939; Gypsy, Gypsy (novel), 1940; Breakfast with the Nikolides (novel), 1942; Rungli-Rungliot (Thus Far and No Further), 1943, in U.S. as Rungli-Rungliot Means in Paharia, Thus Far and No Further, 1946, 2nd U.K. ed. as Thus Far and No Further, 1961; A Fugue in Time (novel) (in U.S. as Take Three Tenses: A Fugue in Time), 1945; Bengal Journey: A Story of the Part Played by Women in the Province 1939-1945, 1945; The River (novel), 1946; The Doll's House (juvenile), 1947; A Candle for St. Jude (novel), 1948; In Noah's Ark (poetry), 1949; The Mousewife (juvenile), 1951; A Breath of Air (novel), 1950; Kingfishers Catch Fire (novel), 1953; Impunity Jane: The Story of a Pocket Doll (juvenile), 1954; An Episode of Sparrows (novel), 1955; Hans Christian Andersen: A Great Life in Brief, 1955; The Fairy Doll (juvenile), 1956; Mouse House (juvenile), 1957; Mooltiki and Other Stories and Poems of India, 1957; The Story of the Holly and Ivy (juvenile), 1958; The Greengage Summer (novel), 1958; Candy Floss (juvenile), 1960; Miss Happiness and Miss Flower (juvenile), 1961; China Court: The Hours of a Country House (novel), 1961; St. Jerome and the Lion (juvenile poetry), 1961; (trans.) Prayers from the Ark (poetry), by Carmen de Gasztold, 1962; Little Plum (juvenile), 1963; The Battle of the Villa Fiorita (novel), 1963; Home Is the Sailor (juvenile), 1964; (trans.) The Creatures' Choir (poetry), by Carmen de Gasztold, 1965, in U.S. as The Beasts' Choir, 1967; (with Jon Godden) Two Under the Indian Sun (autobiography), 1966; (ed.) Round the Day, Round the Year, The World Around: Poetry Programmes for Classroom or Library, 6 vols., 1966–67; Swans and Turtles: Stories (in U.S. as Gone: A Thread of Stories), 1968; (ed.) A Letter to the World: Poems for Young Readers, by Emily Dickinson, 1968; (ed.) Mrs Manders' Cookbook, by Olga Manders, 1968; The Kitchen Madonna (juvenile), 1969; Operation Sippacik (juvenile), 1969; In This House of Brede (novel), 1969; (ed.) The Raphael Bible, 1970; The Tale of the Tales: The Beatrix Potter Ballet, 1971; (with Jon Godden) Shiva's Pigeons: An Experience of India (autobiography), 1972; The Old Woman Who Lived in a Vinegar Bottle (juvenile), 1972; The Diddakoi (juvenile), 1972; Mr McFadden's Hallowe'en (juvenile), 1975; The Peacock Spring (novel), 1975; The Rocking Horse Secret (juvenile), 1977; The Butterfly Lions: The Story of the Pekingese in History, Legend and Art, 1977; A Kindle of Kittens (juvenile), 1978; Five for Sorrow, Ten for Joy (novel), 1979; Gulbadan: Portrait of a Rose Princess at the Mughal Court, 1981; The Dragon of Og (juvenile), 1981; The Dark Horse (novel), 1981; Thursday's Children, 1984; Memoirs: vol. I, A Time to Dance: No Time to Weep, 1987, and vol. II, A House with Four Rooms, 1989. Add: Ardnacloich, Moniaive, Thornhill, Dumfriesshire D63 4HZ, Scotland.

GODEY, John. *See* **FREEDGOOD,** Morton.

GODFREY, Dave. Canadian, b. 1938. Novels/Short stories. Co-Founder and Dir., Press Porcepic, Toronto, since 1971. Prof. of Creative Writing, Univ. of Victoria, B.C., since 1968. Acting Head of English Dept., Adisadel Coll., Cape Coast, Ghana, 1963–65; Asst. Prof. of English, Trinity Coll., Univ. of Toronto, 1966–75. *Publs:* Death Goes Better with Coca-Cola (short stories), 1967; (with B. McWhinney) Man Deserves Man, 1967; The New Ancestors, 1970; (ed.) Gordon to Watkins to You, 1970; I Ching Kanada, 1976; Dark Must Yield, 1977; Gutenberg Two, 1981, 1982, 1983, 1985; The Telidon Book, 1982; The Elements of CAL, 1982; Computer-Aided Learning Using the NATAL Language, 1984. Add: 4355 Gordon Head Rd., Victoria, B.C. V8V 3Y4, Canada.

GODLEY, W(ynne) A(lexander) H(ugh). British, b. 1926. Economics. Fellow, King's College, Cambridge, since 1970, and Prof. of Applied Economics, Cambridge Univ., since 1980. (Dir., 1970–75, and Acting Dir., 1985–87, Dept. of Applied Economics). Professional oboist, 1950; Member, 1956–70, and Deputy Dir., 1967–70, Economic Section,

Treasury Dept; Dir., Investing in Success Equities Ltd., 1970–83. Dir., Royal Opera House, Covent Garden, 1976–87. *Publs:* (with T.F. Cripps) Local Government Finance and Its Reform, 1976; The Planning of Telecommunications in the United Kingdom, 1978; (with K.J. Coutts and W.D. Nordhaus) Pricing in the Trade Cycle, 1978; (with T.F. Cripps) Macroeconomics, 1983. Add: 16 Eltisley Ave., Cambridge, England.

GOLDMAN, Albert. American, b. 1927. Cultural/Ethnic topics, Literary criticism/history, Music, Social commentary, Biography. Assoc. Prof. of English, Columbia Univ., NYC, 1963–72; moderator and writer of "Wednesday Review", weekly television cultural prog., WNDT, NYC; pop music critic, Life mag., 1970–73. *Publs:* (ed. with E. Sprinchorn) Wagner on Music and Drama (trans. by H.A. Ellis), 1964; The Mine and the Mint: Sources for the Writings of Thomas De Quincey, 1965; Freakshow: The Rocksoulbluesjazzsickjewblackhumorsexpoppsych Gig and Other Scenes from the Counterculture, 1971; Ladies and Gentlemen—Lenny Bruce!!, 1974; Carnival in Rio, 1978; Grass Roots: Marijuana in America Today, 1979; Disco, 1979; Elvis, 1981; The Lives of John Lennon, 1988. Add: c/o Paul R. Reynolds Inc., 12 E. 41st St., New York, N.Y. 10017, U.S.A.

GODMAN, Arthur. British, b. 1916. Information science/Computers, Mathematics/Statistics, Medicine/health, Sciences (general). Chief Examiner, Univ. of Cambridge Local Examinations Syndicate, 1970–83 (Examiner, 1952–70). With H.M. Overseas Civil Service, Malaya, 1946–58, and Hong Kong, 1958–63. *Publs:* (with Hobson) Everyday Science for the Tropics, 1956; Health Science for the Tropics, 1962; (with Copeland) Upper Primary Arithmetic, 1964; (with Hobson) Everyday Science for Malaysia, 1965; (with Talbert) Malaysian General Mathematics, 1965; (with H. Lau) Remove Mathematics, 1967; (with Johnson & Chua) General Science Certificate Course, 1968; (with Muraguri) Practical Certificate Chemistry, 1969; (with Bajah) Chemistry: A New Certificate Approach, 1969; (with Johnson) Junior Tropical Biology, 1970; Longman Certificate Notes; Health Science, 1970; (with Talbert) Additional Mathematics, 1971; Physical Science, 1972; Certificate Human and Social Biology, 1973; (with Folivi) New Certificate Physics, 1974; (with Gutteridge) A New Health Science for Africa, 1979; (with Payne) Longman Dictionary of Scientific Usage, 1979; Longman Illustrated Science Dictionary, 1981; Longman Illustrated Dictionary of Chemistry, 1981; The Colour Coded Guide to Microcomputers, 1984; Cambridge Illustrated Thesaurus of Computer Science, 1984; (with Denny) Cambridge Illustrated Thesaurus of Science and Technology, 1985; (with Denny) Cambridge Illustrated Thesaurus of Chemistry, 1985; (with Treyean) Cambridge Illustrated Dictionary for Young Computer Users, 1986. Add: Sondes House, Patrixbourne, Canterbury, Kent CT4 5DD, England.

GODSEY, John Drew. American, b. 1922. Theology/Religion. Prof. of Systematic Theology, Wesley Theological Seminary, Washington, D.C., since 1971, Emeritus since 1988 (Assoc. Dean and Prof. of Systematic Theology, 1968–71). Instr., 1956–59, Asst. Prof., 1959–64, Assoc. Prof., 1964–66, and Prof., 1966–68, of Systematic Theology, Drew Univ., Madison, N.J. *Publs:* The Theology of Dietrich Bonhoeffer, 1960; (ed.) Karl Barth's Table Talk, 1963; Preface to Bonhoeffer: The Man and Two of His Shorter Writings, 1965; (ed.) How I Changed My Mind, by Karl Barth, 1966; The Promise of H. Richard Niebuhr, 1970; (co-ed.) Ethical Responsibility: Bonhoeffer's Legacy to the Churches, 1981. Add: 8306 Bryant Dr., Bethesda, Md. 20817, U.S.A.

GODWIN, Gail. American, b. 1937. Novels/Short stories. Reporter, Miami Herald, 1959–60; Consultant, U.S. Travel Service, London, 1962–65; Research, Saturday Evening Post, NYC, 1966; Instr., Univ. of Iowa, Iowa City, 1967–70; Instr. and Fellow, Center for Advanced Studies, Univ. of Illinois, Urbana, 1971–72; Lectr., Writers' Workshop, Univ. of Iowa, 1972–73; Vassar Coll., Poughkeepsie, N.Y., 1975, and Columbia Univ., NYC, 1978. *Publs:* The Perfectionists, 1970; Glass People, 1972; The Odd Woman, 1974; Dream Children (short stories), 1976; Violet Clay, 1978; A Mother and Two Daughters, 1982; Mr. Bedford and the Muses, 1983; The Finishing School, 1985; A Southern Family, 1987. Add: c/o William Morrow, 105 Madison Ave., New York, N.Y. 10016, U.S.A.

GODWIN, John. British, b. 1922. Air/Space topics, Education, Biography, Local History. Commenced teaching career 1948, now retired. Headmaster, Mawnan Village Sch., nr. Falmouth, 1955–58; Deputy Headmaster, Corley Residential Sch. for Delicate Children, 1958–61; Headmaster, St. George's Primary Sch., Stamford, 1961–69; Headmaster, St. Michael's Primary Sch., Lichfield, Staffs., 1970–81. *Publs:* Battling Parer, 1968; Wings to the Cape, 1971; Give Your Child a Better Start, 1973; Lives to Inspire, 1978; More Lives to Inspire, 1980; The Murder of Christina Collins, 1981; Lessons from Life and Legend, 1982;

Beaudesert and the Pagets, 1982; Some Staffordshire Characters, 1982; More Staffordshire Characters, 1983; Some Notable 18th Century Staffordshire M.P.'s, 1984; Early Aeronautics in Staffordshire, 1986; Still More Lives to Inspire, 1987. Add: Lark Rise, 10 Church Lane, Etching Hill, Rugeley, Staffs. WS15 2TH, England.

GODWIN, Tom. American, b. 1915. Science fiction/Fantasy. Freelance writer, mainly of SF short stories. Formerly, prospector. *Publs:* The Survivors, 1958, as Space Prison, 1960; The Space Barbarians, 1964; Beyond Another Sun, 1971. Add: Lives in Nevada.

GOEDICKE, Patricia (McKenna). (Mrs. Leonard Robinson). American, b. 1931. Poetry. Assoc. Prof. in Creative Writing, Univ. of Montana, Missoula, since 1983 (Poet-in-Residence, 1981–83). Editorial Asst., Harcourt Brace & World publrs., NYC, 1953–54, and T.Y. Crowell publrs., NYC, 1955–56; Co-Ed., Page mag., Athens, Ohio, 1961–66; Faculty Member, Ohio Univ., Athens, 1962–68, Hunter Coll., NYC, 1969–71, Institute Allende, 1972–79, Sarah Lawrence Coll., Bronxville, N.Y., 1980–81. *Publs:* Between Oceans, 1968; For the Four Corners, 1976; The Trail That Turns on Itself, 1978; The Dog That Was Barking Yesterday, 1980; Crossing the Same River, 1980; The King of Childhood, 1984; The Wind of Our Going, 1985; Listen Love, 1986; The Tongues We Speak, 1989. Add: 310 McLeod Ave., Missoula, Mont. 59801, U.S.A.

GOEN, Clarence C. American, b. 1924. History, Theology/Religion. Prof., Wesley Theological Seminary, Washington, D.C., since 1966 (Asst. Prof., 1960–62; Assoc. Prof., 1962–66). Adjunct Prof. of U.S. Intellectual History, American Univ., Washington, D.C., 1971–74. *Publs:* Revivalism and Separatism in New England 1740-1800, 1962, 1987; (ed.) The Great Awakening, vol. 4, The Works of Jonathan Edwards, 1972; (ed.) Pilgrimage of Faith, 1984; Broken Churches, Broken Nation, 1985. Add: 4500 Massachusetts Ave. N.W., Washington, D.C. 20016, U.S.A.

GOFF, Martyn. British, b. 1923. Novels/Short stories, History, Music, Sociology. Chmn., Henry Satheran, booksellers, London. Dir., National Book League, 1970–86; former Chief Exec., Book Trust. Member, Literature Panel of the Arts Council, 1970–78; Chmn., The New Fiction Soc., 1975–82. *Publs:* The Plaster Fabric, 1956; A Short Guide to Long Play, 1956; A Season with Mammon, 1957; A Further Guide to Long Play, 1957; A Sort of Peace, 1959; Long Playing Collecting, 1959; The Youngest Director, 1961; Red on the Door, 1963; Flint Inheritance, 1965; Indecent Assault, 1967; Why Conform?, 1969; Victorian Surrey, 1972; Record Choice, 1974; The Liberation of Rupert Bannister, 1977; Tar and Cement (novel), 1988. Add: 75 Sisters Ave., London SW11 5SW, England.

GOFORTH, Ellen. *See* **FRANCIS**, Dorothy Brenner.

GOHEEN, Robert (Francis). American, b. 1919. Classics, Education. Prof. of Classics, Emeritus, since 1972, and Sr. Fellow, Woodrow Wilson Sch., Princeton Univ., since 1982 (Instr. in Classics, 1948–50; Asst. Prof., 1950–57; Prof. and Pres. of the Univ., 1957–72). Chmn., Council on Foundations, NYC, 1972–77; U.S. Ambassador to India, 1977–80. *Publs:* The Imagery of Sophocles' Antigone, 1951; The Human Nature of a University, 1969. Add: 1 Orchard Circle, Princeton, N.J. 08540, U.S.A.

GOKAK, Vinayak Krishna. Indian. Poetry, Language/Linguistics, Literature. Vice-Chancellor, Bangalore Univ., 1966–69. *Publs:* The Poetic Approach to Language, 1952; In Life's Temple, 1965; English in India, 1965; (ed.) The Golden Treasury of Indo-Anglian Poetry, 1971; India and World Culture, 1972; Narahari Prophet of New India, 1972; (ed.) A Value Orientation to Our System of Education, 1973; Sri Aurobindo: Seer and Poet, 1973; Coleridge's Aesthetics, 1974; An Integral View of Poetry, 1974; The Concept of Indian Literature, 1979. Add: Meera Cottage, 525 RMV Extension, Bangalore, India.

GOLANT, William. American, b. 1937. History. Lectr. in History, Univ. of Exeter, 1964–87. *Publs:* The Long Afternoon, 1975; Image of Empire: The Early History of the Imperial Institute, 1984. Add: 317 S. Maple Dr., Beverley Hills, CA 90212, U.S.A.

GOLD, Herbert. American, b. 1924. Novels/Short stories, Autobiography/Memoirs/Personal, Essays. Lectr. in Philosophy and Literature, Western Reserve Univ., Cleveland, Ohio, 1951–56. *Publs:* Birth of a Hero, 1951; The Prospect Before Us, 1954; The Man Who Was Not with It (in paperback as The Wildlife), 1956; (with R.V. Cassill and J.B. Hall) 15-3 (short stories), 1957; The Optimist, 1959; (ed.) Fiction of the Fifties: A Decade of American Writing, 1959; Therefore Be Bold, 1960; Love

and Like (short stories), 1960; (ed. with D.L. Stevenson) Stories of Modern America, 1961, rev. ed. 1963; The Age of Happy Problems (essays), 1962; (ed.) First Person Singular: Essays for the Sixties, 1963; Salt, 1963; The Fathers: A Novel in the Form of a Memoir, 1967; The Great American Jackpot, 1970; The Magic Will: Stories and Essays of a Decade, 1971; My Last Two Thousand Years (autobiography), 1972; The Young Prince and the Magic Cone, 1973; Swiftie the Magician, 1974; Waiting for Cordelia, 1977; Slave Trade, 1979; He/She, 1980; A Walk on the West Side (essays), 1981; Family (novel), 1981; True Love, 1982; Mister White Eyes, 1984; Stories of Misbegotten Love, 1985; Lovers and Cohorts, 1986; A Girl of Forty, 1986; Dreaming, 1988. Add: 1051-A Broadway, San Francisco, Calif. 94133, U.S.A.

GOLD, H(orace) L(eonard). American (b. Canadian), b. 1914. Science fiction/Fantasy. Asst. Ed., Thrilling Wonder Stories, Startling Stories, and Captain Future, and Assoc. Ed., Standard Mags., NYC, 1939–41; Managing and Contrib. Ed., Scoop Publs., NYC, 1941–43; Ed., A and S Comics, NYC, 1942–44; Contract Writer, Molle Mystery Theatre, 1943–44; Pres., Rossard Co., NYC, 1946–50; Ed., Galaxy, and Galaxy Science Fiction Novels, NYC, 1950–61; and If, Beyond Fiction, 1953–55, and If, 1959–61. *Publs:* (ed.) Galaxy Reader 1-6, 2 vols., 1952–54, 4 vols., 1958–62; The Old Die Rich and Other Science Fiction Stories, 1955; (ed.) Five Galaxy Short Novels, 1958; (ed.) The World That Couldn't Be and Eight Other Novelets from Galaxy, 1959; (ed.) Bodyguard and Four Other Short Novels from Galaxy, 1960; (ed.) Mind Partner and Eight Other Novelists from Galaxy Science Fiction, 1961; What Will They Think of Last? (editorials from Galaxy), 1977. Add: P.O. Box 461536, Los Angeles, Calif. 90046, U.S.A.

GOLDBARTH, Albert. American, b. 1948. Poetry. Visiting Prof. of Creative Writing, Univ. of Texas at Austin, since 1977. Member of Advisory Panel to Literature Cttee., National Endowment for the Arts, Instr. in English, Elgin Community Coll., Illinois, 1971–72; Instr., Central YMCA Community Coll., 1971–73; Instr. in Creative Writing, Univ. of Utah, Salt Lake City, 1973–74; Asst. Prof. of Creative Writing, Cornell Univ., Ithaca, N.Y., 1974–76. Co-Dir., Illinois Arts Council Traveling Writers Workshop, 1971–72. *Publs:* Under Cover, 1973; Coprolites, 1974 Optics, 1974; Jan. 31, 1974; Keeping, 1975; Coming Back, 1976; Curve: Overlapping Narratives, 1977; Different Fleshes, 1980; Eurekas, 1980; Who Gathered and Whispered Behind Me, 1981; Original Light: New and Selected Poems 1973-83, 1983; Arts and Sciences, 1986. Add: Dept. of English, Univ. of Texas, Austin, Tex. 78712, U.S.A.

GOLDBERG, Arthur J(oseph). American, b. 1908. International relations/Current affairs, Law. Lawyer in private practice, Washington. Chmn., Bd. of Trustees, Inst. of Intnl. Education, NYC. Admitted to Illinois Bar, 1929; Engaged in private law practice, Chicago, 1929–48; Member, firm of Goldberg, Devoe, Shadur and Mikva, Chicago, 1945–61; Gen. Counsel, Congress of Industrial Workers, 1948–55, United Steel Workers, 1948–61; Member of firm of Goldberg, Feller and Bredhoff, Washington, 1952–61; Special Counsel, AFL-CIO, 1955–61; Secty. of Labor, 1961–62; Assoc. Justice of the U.S. Supreme Court, 1962–65; U.S. Representative to the U.N., 1965–68; Partner, Paul, Weiss, Goldberg, Rifkind, Wharton and Garrison, NYC, 1968–71. *Publs:* AFL Labor United, 1956; Defenses of Freedom: The Public Papers of Arthur J. Goldberg, 1964; Equal Justice: The Warren Era of the Supreme Court, 1972. Add: 2801 New Mexico Ave. N.W., Washington, D.C. 20007, U.S.A.

GOLDBERG, Louis. Australian, b. 1908. Accounting. Prof. of Accounting Emeritus, Univ. of Melbourne, since 1973 (Part-time Tutor, 1931–45; Lectr., 1946–48; Sir Lectr., 1949–57; Assoc. Prof., 1957–58; Prof., 1958–73). *Publs:* A Philosophy of Accounting, 1939; Accounting Principles, 1946; Classification of Accounts and the Planning of Accounting Systems, 1946; (with V.R. Hill) Elements of Accounting, 1947; An Outline of Accounting, 1957; Concepts of Depreciation, 1960; An Inquiry into the Nature of Accounting, 1965; (ed. with R.J. Chambers and R.L. Mathews) The Accounting Frontier, 1965; (ed.) Fitzgerald's Accounting, 1967; S. Vaidyanath Aiyar Memorial Lectures, 1971; The Fluorescent Decade, 1981; (with S.A. Leech) An Introduction to Accounting Method, 1984; (with S.A. Leech and P.J. Colvin) The TAC System, 1985; Dynamics of an Entity: History of AAANZ, 1987. Add: 5 Kemsley Ct., Hawthorn, Vic. 3123, Australia.

GOLDBERG, Samuel Louis. British, b. 1926. Literature. Sr. Fellow, Research Sch. of Social Sciences, Australian National Univ., Canberra, since 1976. Ed., The Critical Review, since 1958, and Australian Cultural History, since 1981. Challis Prof. of English Literature, Univ. of Sydney, 1963–66; Wallace Prof. of English, Univ. of Melbourne, 1966–76.

Publs: The Classical Temper: A Study of James Joyce's Ulysses, 1961; Joyce, 1962; An Essay on King Lear, 1974. Add: Dept. of Philosophy, Australian National Univ., P.O. Box 4, Canberra, A.C.T. 2601, Australia.

GOLDENSON, Robert M. American, b. 1908. Psychiatry, Psychology. Psychotherapist in private practice. Consultant, United Cerebral Palsy, since 1969; Prof., Intnl. Grad. Sch. of Behavioral Science, since 1975. Prof of Psychology, Hunter Coll., City Univ. of New York, 1940–60; Dir. of Educational Activities, Book-of-the-Month Club, NYC, 1960–68. *Publs:* (with L.K. Frank and R.E. Hartley) Understanding Children's Play, 1952; Helping Your Child to Read Better, 1957; (with R.E. Hartley) The Complete Book of Children's Play, 1957, 1963; All About the Human Mind, 1963; The Encyclopaedia of Human Behavior: Psychology, Psychiatry and Mental Health, 2 vols., 1970; Mysteries of the Mind, 1973; (ed.-in-chief) The Disability and Rehabilitation Handbook, 1978; The Longman Dictionary of Psychology, Psychiatry, and Psychoanalysis, 1983; (with K.N. Anderson) The Language of Sex from A to Z, 1986. Add: 551-A, Sheldon Way, Jamesburg, N.J. 08831, U.S.A.

GOLDFARB, Ronald (Lawrence). American, b. 1933. Law, Media, Politics/Government. Partner, Goldfarb Kaufmann and O'Toole, Washington, D.C., since 1966. Judge Advocate, Gen. Corps. U.S. Air Force, 1957–60; Special Prosecutor, U.S. Dept. of Justice, 1961–64; admitted to D.C. bar, 1965. *Publs:* The Contempt Power, 1963; Ransom: A Critique of the American Bail System, 1965; (with A. Friendly) Crime and Publicity: The Impact of News on the Administration of Justice, 1967; (with L. Singer) After Conviction: A Review of the American Correction System, 1973; Jails: The Ultimate Ghetto, 1975; Migrant Farm Workers, A Caste of Despair, 1981; (with J. Raymond) Clear Understandings: Guide to Legal Writing, 1982; The Writer's Lawyer, 1989. Add: Goldfarb Kaufman and O'Toole, 918 16th St. N.W., Washington, D.C. 20006, U.S.A.

GOLDFARB, Russell M. American, b. 1934. Literature. Prof. of English Literature, Western Michigan Univ., since 1971 (Instr., 1960–61; Asst. Prof., 1961–64; Assoc. Prof., 1964–71). *Publs:* Sexual Repression and Victorian Literature, 1970; Spiritualism and Nineteenth-Century Letters, 1978. Add: Western Michigan Univ., Kalamazoo, Mich. 49001, U.S.A.

GOLDIN, Augusta. American, b. 1906. Children's non-fiction, Education. Educational columnist for Staten Island Advance, since 1968, Principal, Public Sch. 39R, NYC, 1944–71; Asst. Prof. of Education, St. John's Univ., NYC, 1971–74. *Publs:* My Toys, 1955; Spider Silk, 1964; Ducks Don't Get Wet, 1965; Salt, 1965; Straight Hair, Curly Hair, 1965; The Bottom of the Sea, 1966, 1988; Where Does Your Garden Grow?, 1967; The Sunlit Sea, 1968; How to Release the Learning Power in Children, 1970; Let's Go to Build a Skyscraper, 1974; Grass, The Everything Everywhere Plant, 1977; The Shape of Water, 1979; Oceans of Energy, 1980; Geotherman Energy: A Hot Prospect, 1981; Water: Too Much, Too Little, Too Polluted?, 1983; Small Energy Sources: Choices That Work, 1988. Add: 590 Bard Ave., Staten Island, N.Y. 10310, U.S.A.

GOLDIN, Stephen. American, b. 1947. Science fiction/Fantasy. Dir., Merrimont House creative consultations; freelance writer, mainly of SF short stories. Physicist, Navy Space Systems Actvity, El Segundo, Calif., 1968–71; Mgr., Circle K. Grocery Store, Rosemead, Calif., 1972; Ed., Jaundice Press, Van Nuys, Calif., 1973–74; Ed., San Francisco Ball, 1973–74, and SFWA Bulletin, 1975–77. *Publs:* (ed. with David Gerrold) Protostars, 1971; (ed.) The Alien Condition, 1973; (ed. with David Gerrold) Science Fiction Emphasis 1, 1974; (ed. with David Gerrold) Alternities, 1974; Herds, 1975; Caravan, 1975; Scavenger Hunt, 1975; Finish Line, 1976; Imperial Stars, 1976; Strangler's Moon, 1976; The Clockwork Traitor, 1976; Assault on the Gods, 1977; Getaway World, 1977; (ed. with David Gerrold) Ascents of Wonder, 1977; Mindfight, 1978; Appointment at Bloodstar (in U.K. as The Bloodstar Conspiracy), 1978; The Purity Plot, 1978; Trek to Madworld, 1979; The Eternity Brigade, 1980; A World Called Solitude, 1981; And Not Make Dreams Your Master, 1981; Planet of Treachery, 1982; (with Kathleen Sky) The Business of Being a Writer (non-fiction), 1982; Eclipsing Binaries, 1984; The Omicron Invasion, 1984; Revolt of the Galaxy, 1985. Add: 389 Florin Rd., No. 22, Sacramento, Calif. 95831-1406, U.S.A.

GOLDING, Peter. British, b. 1947. Communications media, Sociology. Sr. Research Fellow, Centre for Mass Communication Research, Leicester Univ., since 1970. *Publs:* The Mass Media, 1974; Making the News, 1979; Images of Welfare: Press and Public Attitudes to Poverty, 1982; Excluding the Poor, 1986; Communicating Politics: Mass Communication and the Political Process, 1986; The Politics of the Urban

Crisis, 1988. Add: Centre for Mass Communication Research, 104 Regent Rd., Leicester, England.

GOLDING, Raymund Marshall. Australian, b. 1935. Chemistry, Physics. Vice-Chancellor, James Cook Univ., since 1986. Prof. of Theoretical and Physical Chemistry, 1968–86, and Pro-Vice-Chancellor, 1978–86, Univ. of New South Wales. Staff member, Dept. of Scientific and Industrial Research, Wellington, 1957–68. *Publs:* Applied Wave Mechanics, 1969; (co-author) Multistrand Science of the Senior High School Students, 1975. Add: James Cook Univ., Townsville, Queensland 4811, Australia.

GOLDING, (Sir) William (Gerald). British, b. 1911. Novels/Short stories, Plays/Screenplays, Poetry, Travel/Exploration/Adventure. Schoolmaster, Bishop Wordsworth's Sch., Salisbury, Wilts., 1939–40 and 1945–61. *Publs:* Poems, 1934; Lord of the Flies, 1954; The Inheritors, 1955; Pincher Martin (in U.S. as The Two Deaths of Christopher Martin), 1956; The Brass Butterfly (plays), 1958; Free Fall, 1960; The Spire, 1965; The Hot Gates and Other Occasional Pieces, 1965; The Pyramid, 1967; The Scorpion God (short stories), 1971; Darkness Visible, 1979; Rites of Passage, 1980; The Paper Men, 1984; An Egyptian Journal, 1985; Close Quarters, 1987; Fire Down Below, 1989. Recipient, Nobel Prize for Literature, 1983. Add: c/o Faber and Faber, 3 Queen Sq., London WC1N 3AU, England.

GOLDMAN, Arnold (Melvyn). American, b. 1936. Literature. Hon. Prof. of American Studies, Univ. of Kent at Canterbury, since 1985. Faculty member, Univ. of Manchester, 1961–65, and Univ. of Sussex, 1966–74; Prof. of American Studies, Univ. of Keele, 1975–82; Deputy Chief Exec., Council for National Academic Awards, 1983–88. *Publs:* The Joyce Paradox, 1966; James Joyce, 1968; (ed.) Twentieth Century Interpretations of Absalom Absalom!, 1971; (co-ed.) Charles Dickens' American Notes, 1972; (ed.) Tender Is the Night, by F. Scott Fitzgerald, 1982; (ed.) American Literature in Context, 4 vols., 1982–83. Add: 8 St. Stephen's Hill, Canterbury, Kent CT2 7AX, England.

GOLDMAN, Charles R(emington). American, b. 1930. Environmental science/Ecology, Marine science/Oceanography. Prof. of Limnology, Univ. of California, Davis, since 1966, now Chmn., Div. of Environmental Studies (Member of the Faculty, since 1958; Dir., Inst. of Ecology, 1966–69). Dir., Tahoe Research Group, since 1973. Teaching Fellow, Fisheries, Univ. of Michigan, 1955–58; Fishery Research Biologist, U.S. Fish and Wildlife Service, Alaska, 1957–58. Pres., American Soc. of Limnology and Oceanography, 1967–68. *Publs:* Primary Productivity in Aquatic Environments, 1966; Environmental Impact and Water Development, 1973; (with A. Horne) Limnology, 1982; (ed.) Freshwater Crayfish V, 1983. Add: 2094 Alta Loma, Davis, Calif. 95616, U.S.A.

GOLDMAN, Eric F(rederick). American, b. 1915. History, Social commentary/phenomena, Biography. Rollins Prof. of History, Princeton Univ., N.J., since 1962 (Asst. prof., 1943–47; Assoc. Prof., 1947–55; Prof., 1955–62). Pres., Soc. of American Historians, 1962–69; Special Consultant to the Pres., Washington, D.C., 1963–66. *Publs:* Historiography and Urbanization, 1941; Charles J. Bonaparte: Patrician Reformer, 1943; John Bach McMaster: American Historian, 1943; (with F.C. Lane) The World's History, 1947; Rendezvous with Destiny: A History of Modern American Reform, 1952; The Crucial Decade: America 1945-55, 1956; The Crucial Decade—and After: America 1945-60, 1961; The Tragedy of Lyndon Johnson, 1969. Add: 213 Palmer Hall, Princeton Univ., Princeton, N.J. 08540, U.S.A.

GOLDMAN, James. American, b. 1927. Novels/Short stories, Plays/Screenplays. Member of Council, Dramatists Guild, since 1966, and Authors League of America, since 1966. *Publs:* Waldorf (novel), 1965; The Lion in Winter, 1967, screenplay, 1968; They Might Be Giants (screenplay), 1970; (with S. Sondheim) Follies, 1972; The Man from Green and Roman (novel), 1974; Robin and Marian (screenplay), 1976; Myself as Witness (novel), 1980; Fulton County (novel), 1989. Add: c/o Sam Cohn, Intnl. Creative Mgmt., 40 W. 57th St., New York, N.Y. 10019, U.S.A.

GOLDMAN, Marshall I(rwin). American, b. 1930. Economics, Environmental science/Ecology. Prof. of Economics, Wellesley Coll., Mass., since 1968 (Instr., 1958–60; Asst. Prof., 1961–65; Assoc. Prof., 1966–68). Assoc. Dir., Russian Research Center, Harvard Univ., Cambridge, Mass., since 1975 (Assoc., 1957–75). *Publs:* Soviet Marketing: Distribution in a Controlled Economy, 1963; (ed.) Comparative Economic Systems: Reader, 1964, 1971; Soviet Foreign Aid, 1967; (ed.) Controlling Pollution: The Economics of a Cleaner America, 1967; The

Soviet Economy: Myth and Reality, 1968; (ed.) Ecology and Economics: Controlling Pollution in the 70s, 1972; The Spoils of Progress: Environmental Pollution in the Soviet Union, 1972; Detente and Dollars: Doing Business with the Soviets, 1975; The Enigma of Soviet Petroleum: Half Full or Half Empty, 1980; The Soviet Union in Crisis: The Failure of an Economic System, 1983; Gorbachev's Challenge: Economic Reform in the Age of High Technology, 1987. Add: 17 Midland Rd., Wellesley, Mass. 02181, U.S.A.

GOLDMAN, William. Also writes as Harry Longbaugh. American, b. 1931. Novels/Short stories, Children's fiction, Plays/Screenplays, Theatre. *Publs:* The Temple of Gold, 1957; Your Turn to Curtsy, My Turn to Bow, 1958; Soldier in the Rain, 1960; (with James Goldman) Blood, Sweat and Stanley Poole (play), 1961; (with J. Goldman and J. Kander) A Family Affair (play), 1962; Boys and Girls Together, 1964; (as Harry Longbaugh) No Way to Treat a Lady, 1964, as William Goldman, 1968; The Thing of It Is . . ., 1967; The Season: A Candid Look at Broadway, 1969; Father's Day, 1971; The Prince's Bride: S. Morgenstern's Classic Tale of True Love and High Adventure, The "Good Parts" Version, Abridged, 1974; Marathon Man, 1974; Wigger (children's fiction), 1974; The Great Waldo Pepper, 1975; Magic, 1976; Tinsel, 1979; Control, 1982; Adventures in the Screen Trade (non-fiction), 1983; (as S. Morgenstern) The Silent Goldoliers, 1983; The Color of Light, 1984; Heat (in England as Edged Weapons), 1985; Brothers (novel), 1986. Add: 50 E. 77th St., New York, N.Y. 10021, U.S.A.

GOLDRING, Patrick (Thomas Zachary). British, b. 1921. Sociology, Travel/Exploration/Adventure. *Publs:* Yugoslavia, 1967; The Broiler-house Society, 1969; Friend of the Family: The Work of Family Service Units, 1973; Multipurpose Man, 1974; Britain by Train, 1982. Add: c/o Arrow Books Ltd., Brookmount House, 62-65 Chandos Pl., London WC2N 4NW, England.

GOLDSCHMIDT, Yaaqov. Israeli, b. 1927. Administration/Management, Economics. With Inter-Kibbutz Unit for Management Services, and Faculty of Management, Tel-Aviv Univ. *Publs:* Introduction to Production Economics on the Farm, 1963; Information for Management Decisions: A Systems for Economic Analysis and Accounting Procedures, 1970; Costing Theory: Accounting, Economics and Behavioral Aspects, 1974, 1980; Profit Measurement During Inflation, 1977; Tools for Financial Management, 1983; The Impact of Inflation on Financial Activity in Business with Application to the U.S. Farm Sector, 1986. Add: 11 Dan St., Ramat Hasharon 47204, Israel.

GOLDSMITH, Arthur. American, b. 1926. Photography. Editorial Dir., Popular Photography and Photography Annual, NYC, since 1972, and Ed.-at-Large for Popular Photography, since 1986. Chmn., Intnl. Relations Cttee., American Soc. of Magazine Photographers, since 1984. Exec. Ed., Popular Photograph, 1951–60; Picture Ed., This Week, NYC, 1960–61; Pres. and Dir., Famous Photographers Sch., Westport, Conn., 1961–72. *Publs:* (co-author) How to Take Better Pictures, 1956; (with Alfred Eisenstaedt) The Eye of Eisenstaedt, 1969; The Photography Game, 1971; The Nude in Photography, 1975; The Camera and Its Images, 1979; (ed.) Photojournalism: The World Gallery of Photography, 1983. Add: c/o Popular Photography, 1515 Broadway, New York, N.Y. 10036, U.S.A.

GOLDSMITH, Barbara. American, b. 1931. Novels, History, Biography. Member, President's Council, Museum of the City of New York, since 1970; Dir., National Dance Inst., NYC, since 1980; Trustee, New York Public Library; Member, Bd. of Overseers, Wellesley Coll., Massachusetts; Member, Exec. Bd., American P.E.N. Entertainment Ed., Woman's Home Companion, NYC, 1954–57; Founding Ed., New York Mag., 1968–73; Sr. Ed., Harpers Bazaar, NYC, 1970–74. *Publs:* The Straw Man (novel), 1975; Little Gloria, Happy at Last, 1980; Johnson v. Johnson, 1987. Add: c/o Morton L. Janklow Assoc., 598 Madison Ave., New York, N.Y. 10022, U.S.A.

GOLDSMITH, Immanuel. Canadian, b. 1921. Law. Barrister and Solicitor; Queen's Counsel, since 1970. *Publs:* (trans.) The Earliest Illustrated Haggadah, 1940; (trans.) Hebrew Incunables, 1948; Damages for Personal Injuries and Death in Canada, 1959, 4th ed. 1981; Canadian Building Contracts, 1968, 1983; Patents of Invention, 1981; Trademarks and Industrial Designs, 1982. Add: 400 Walmer Rd., Toronto M5P 2X7, Canada.

GOLDSTEIN, Abraham S. American, b. 1925. Law. Sterling Prof. of Law, Yale Univ., New Haven (Dean of Yale Law Sch., 1970–75). *Publs:* The Insanity Defense, 1967; (with J. Goldstein) Crime, Law and

Society: Readings, 1971; (with Orland) Criminal Procedure, 1974; The Passive Judiciary: Prosecutorial Discretion and the Guilty Plea, 1981. Add: Yale Law Sch., New Haven, Conn. 06520, U.S.A.

GOLDSTEIN, Harvey. British, b. 1939. Education, Mathematics/Statistics. Prof. of Statistics, Univ. of London Inst. of Education, since 1977. Jt. Ed., Statistics in Society, since 1987. Lectr. in Statistics, Inst. of Child Health, Univ. of London, 1964–71; Head of the Statistics Section, National Children's Bureau, 1971–77. Member of the Council, 1973–77, and Chmn. of the Social Statistics Section, 1978–80, Royal Statistical Soc. *Publs:* (with R. Davie and N.R. Butler) From Birth to Seven; (with others) Assessment of Skeletal Maturity and Prediction of Adult Height; (ed. with L. Moss) The Recall Method in Social Surveys; The Design and Analysis of Longitudinal Studies; (with C. Gipps) Monitoring Children; (ed. with P. Levy) Tests in Education; Multilevel Models in Educational and Social Research, 1987. Add: Dept. of Mathematics, Statistics and Computing, Inst. of Education, 20 Bedford Way, London WC1H 0AL, England.

GOLDSTEIN, Jerome. American, b. 1931. Environmental science/Ecology. Ed./Publisher, The JG Press Inc., Emmaus, since 1978. Trustee, Inst. on Man and Science, since 1980. Exec. Ed. and Vice-Pres., Rodale Press Inc., Emmaus, 1952–78. *Publs:* Garbage as You Like It, 1970; How to Manage Your Company Ecologically, 1971; New Food Chain, 1972; Sensible Sludge, 1977; (with Rill Goldstein) The Least Is Best Pesticide Stragety, 1978; Recycling Book, 1979; New American Business Dream, 1981; In Business for Yourself, 1982; How to Start a Family Business and Make It Work, 1983. Add: The JG Press Inc., Box 351, Emmaus, Pa. 18049, U.S.A.

GOLDSTEIN, Jonathan Amos. American, b. 1929. History, Translations. Prof. of History and Classics, Univ. of Iowa, Iowa City, since 1962. Instr. in History, Columbia Univ., NYC, 1960–62. *Publs:* The Letters of Demosthenes, 1968; (ed. and trans.) The First Book of Maccabees, 1976; (ed. and trans.) The Second Book of Maccabees, 1982. Add: Dept. of History, Schaffer Hall, Univ. of Iowa City, Iowa 52242, U.S.A.

GOLDSTEIN, Joseph. American, b. 1923. Law. Sterling Prof. of Law, Yale Univ. Law Sch., New Haven, since 1978 (Assoc. Prof., 1956–59; Prof., 1959; Justus H. Hotchkiss Prof. of Law, 1968–69; Walton Hale Hamilton Prof. of Law, Science, and Social Policy, 1969–78). Admitted to Virginia Bar, 1953; Acting Asst. Prof., Stanford Law Sch., Calif., 1954–56; Exec. Secty. and Research Dir., Govt. of Conn. Prison Study Cttee., 1956–67. *Publs:* The Government of a British Trade Union, 1952; (with R. Donnelly and R. Schwartz) Criminal Law, 1962; (with J. Katz) The Family and the Law, 1965; (with J. Katz and A. Dershwitz) Psychoanalysis, Psychiatry and Law, 1966; (with A.S. Goldstein) Crime, Law and Society, 1971; (with Anna Freud and A.J. Solnit) Beyond the Best Interests of the Child, 1973, 1978; (with Anna Freud and A.J. Solnit) Before the Best Interests of the Child, 1980; (co-author) In the Best Interests of the Child, 1986. Add: Yale Univ. Law Sch., 127 Wall St., New Haven, Conn. 06520, U.S.A.

GOLDSTEIN, Sidney. American, b. 1927. Demography, Sociology. Prof. of Sociology since 1960, Dir., Population Studies and Training Center, since 1966, and George Hazard Crooker Univ. Prof. since 1977, Brown Univ. (Asst. Prof., 1955–57; Assoc. Prof., 1957–60; Chmn. of Dept., 1963–70). Member, Cttee. on Population, National Research Council of National Accademy of Sciences, since 1983. Pres., Population Assn. of America, 1975–76; Consultant, UN Economic and Social Commn. for Asia and the Pacific, 1977–82; Distinguished Scholar, Cttee. on Scholarly Communication with China, National Academy of Sciences, 1981. *Publs:* Patterns of Mobility, 1910-1950: A Method for Measuring Migration and Occupational Mobility in the Community, 1958; The Norristown Study, An Experiment in Interdisciplinary Research Training, 1961; (with Kurt B. Mayer) The First Two Years: Problems of Small Business Growth and Survival, 1961; (with Calvin Goldscheider) Jewish-Americans: Three Generations in a Jewish Community, 1968; A Population Survey of the Greater Springfield Jewish Community, 1968; Urbanization in Thailand, 1970; The Demography of Bangkok, 1972; (with A. Speare and W. Frey) Residential Mobility, Migration and Metropolitan Change, 1975; (ed. with D. Sly) Basic Data Needed for the Study of Urbanization, 1975; (ed. with D. Sly) Measurement of Urbanization and the Projection of Urban Population, 1975; (ed. with D. Sly) Patterns of Urbanization: Comparative Country Studies, 1976; Circulation in the Context of Total Mobility in Southeast Asia, 1978; (with A. Goldstein) A Test of the Potential Use of Multiplicity in Research on Population Movement, 1979; (with A. Goldstein) Surveys of Migration in Developing Countries: A Methodological Review, 1981; (with A. Goldstein) Migration and Fertility in Peninsular Malaysia; (with A. Goldstein) Urbanization in China: New Insights From the 1982 Census; (with A. Goldstein) Migration in Thailand: A 25-Year Review, 1986. Add: Population Studies and Training Center, Brown Univ., Providence, R.I. 02912, U.S.A.

GOLDSTEIN-JACKSON, Kevin. British, b. 1946.Recreation/Leisure/-Hobbies, Humor. Worked on seven series of networked children's prog., How, for southern television in the U.K.; also on documentaries, religious series, political discussions, worked on television prog., HK-TVB, Hong Kong, 1973; Head of Film, Dhofar Region Television Service, Sultanate of Oman, 1975–76; Asst. to Head of Drama, Anglia Television, U.K. 1977–81; Dir. of Progs. and Chief Exec., Television South West Holdings PLC, Plymouth, 1981–85. *Publs:* The Right Joke for the Right Occasion, 1973; Ridiculous Facts, 1974; Encyclopaedia of Ridiculous Facts, 1975; Experiments with Everyday Objects, 1976; Joke After Joke After Joke, 1977; Things to Make with Everyday Objects, 1978; Magic with Everyday Objects, 1979; Activities with Everyday Objects, 1980; The Dictionary of Essential Quotations, 1983; Jokes for Telling, 1986. Add: c/o Barclays Bank, 49 St. Leonard's Rd., Windsor, Berks., England.

GOLDWATER, Barry M(orris). American, b. 1909. Politics/-Government, Travel/Exploration/Adventure. Senator from Arizona (Republican), U.S. Senate, Washington, D.C., 1952–64, and 1969–87. Chmn. of the Bd., Goldwater Inc., Phoenix, Ariz., since 1953. *Publs:* Arizona Portraits, 2 vols., 1940; Journey Down the River of Canyons, 1940; Speeches of Henry Ashurst: The Conscience of a Conservative, 1960; Why Not Victory, 1962; Where I Stand, 1964; The Face of Arizona, 1964; People and Places, 1967; The Conscience of a Majority, 1970; Delightful Journey, 1971; Barry Goldwater and the Southwest, 1976; The Coming Breakpoint, 1976; With No Apologies, 1979; (with Jack Casserly) Goldwater, 1988. Add: P.O. Box 1601, Scottsdale, Ariz. 85252, U.S.A.

GOLDWIN, Robert (Allen). American, b. 1922. International relations/Current affairs, Politics/Government. Resident Scholar and Dir., Constitutional Studies, American Enterprise Inst., Washington, D.C., since 1976. Dir., Public Affairs Conference Center, Univ. of Chicago, 1960–66; Assoc., Prof., Kenyon Coll., Gambier, Ohio, 1966–69; Dean, St. John's Coll., Annapolis, Md., 1969–73; Special Adviser to the Ambassador, U.S.A. Mission to NATO, Brussels, 1973–74; Special Consultant to the President of the U.S., 1974–76. *Publs:* (ed.) Readings in World Politics, 1959, 1970; (ed.) Readings in American Foreign Policy, 1959, 1971; (ed.) Readings in Russian Foreign Policy, 1959; A Nation of States, 1963; America Armed, 1963; Why Foreign Aid?, 1963; Political Parties USA, 1964; Beyond the Cold War, 1964; 100 Years of Emancipation, 1965; Left, Right and Center, 1967; Higher Education and Modern Democracy, 1967; Representation and Misrepresentation, 1968; A Nation of Cities, 1968; On Civil Disobedience, 1969; How Democratic Is America?, 1971; Bureaucrats, Policy Analysts, Statesmen: Who Leads?, 1980; Political Parties in the Eighties, 1980; How Democratic Is the Constitution?, 1980; How Capitalistic Is the Constitution?, 1982; How Does the Constitution Secure Rights?, 1985; Separation of Powers—Does It Still Work?, 1986; How Does the Constitution Protect Religious Liberty?, 1987; How Federal Is the Constitution?, 1987; Slavery and Its Consequences: The Constitution, Equality, and Race, 1988. Add: c/o American Enterprise Inst., 1150 17th St., Washington, D.C. 20036, U.S.A.

GOLE, Victor Leslie. Australian, b. 1903. Administration/Management, Money/Finance. Dir., V.L. Gole Pty. Ltd. since 1935. *Publs:* (ed.) Fitzgerald's Analysis and Interpretation of Financial Statements; Fundamentals of Financial Management in Australia; Accounting for Businessmen: Australian Proprietary Companies Management Finance and Taxation; Valuation of Businesses, Shares and Property, 1980; Questions on Financial Management, 1983; Solutions to Questions on Financial Management, 1983. Add: 72 Canberra Grove, Brighton, Vic. 3187, Australia.

GOMBRICH, (Sir) Ernst (Hans Josef). British, b. 1909. Art, Biography. Sr. Research Fellow, 1946–48, Lectr., 1948–54, Reader, 1954–56, Special Lectr. and Durning Lawrence Prof. of History of Art, 1956–59, and Dir. of the Warburg Inst., and Prof. of the History of the Classical Tradition, 1959–76, Univ. of London. Slade Prof. of Fine Art, Univ. of Oxford, 1950–53, and Univ. of Cambridge, 1961–63. *Publs:* Weltgeschichte: Wissenschaft für Kinder, 1936; (with E. Kris) Caricature, 1940; The Story of Art, 1950, 13th rev. ed. 1978; Art and Illusion, 1960; Meditations on a Hobby Horse, 1963; Norm and Form, 1966; In Search of Cultural History, 1969; Aby Warburg: An Intellectual Biography, 1970; Symbolic Images, 1972; (with Richard Gregory) Illusion in Nature and

Art, 1973; The Sense of Order, 1979; Ideals and Idols, 1979; The Image and the Eye, 1982; Tributes, 1984; New Light on Old Masters, 1986; Reflections on the History of Art, 1987. Add: 19 Briardale Gardens, London NW3, England.

GONZÁLEZ, Justo L(uis). American, b. 1937. Theology/Religion, Visiting Prof. of Theology, Interdenominational Theological Center, since 1977. Ed., Apuntes. Prof. of Historical Theology, 1966–69, and Dean, 1967–69, Evangelical Seminary of Puerto Rico; Asst. Prof., 1969–71, and Assoc. Prof., 1971–77). Emory Univ., Atlanta. *Publs:* (in English): The Development of Christianity in the Latin Caribbean, 1969; A History of Christian Thought, 3 vols., 1970–79, 1987; (with C.G. González) Their Souls Did Magnify the Lord, 1977; (with C.G. González) Vision at Patmos, 1978; (with C.G. González) Rejoice in Your Savior, 1979; (with C.G. González) Liberation Preaching, 1980; (with C.G. González) In Accord, 1981; (ed.) Proclaiming the Acceptable Years, 1982; The Story of Christianity, 2 vols., 1984–85; The Crusades: Piety Misguided, 1988; Monasticism: Patterns of Piety, 1988. Add: 475 Riverside Dr., Suite 832, New York, N.Y. 10115, U.S.A.

GOOCH, Brison D(owling). American, b. 1925. History. Prof. since 1973, Texas A and M Univ. (Head of the Dept. of History, 1973–75; Assoc. Dean of Liberal Arts, 1975–81). Instr., and Asst. Prof., Massachusetts Inst. of Technology, Cambridge, 1954–60; Assoc. Prof., and Prof., Univ. of Oklahoma, Norman, 1960–69; Prof. and Head of Dept., Univ. of Connecticut, Storrs, 1969–73. *Publs:* The New Bonapartist Generals in the Crimean War, 1959; (ed.) Napoleon III: The Man of Destiny, 1963; Belgium and the February Revolution, 1963; (ed.) Napoleonic Ideas, 1967; (gen. ed. and contrib.) Interpreting European History, 2 vols., 1967; (gen. ed. and contrib.) Interpeting Western Civlization, 2 vols., 1967; The Reign of Napoleon III, 1969; (ed.) The Origins of the Crimean War, 1969; Europe in the Nineteenth Century: A History, 1970; (gen. ed. and contrib.) The World of Europe, 1973; (ed.) Proceedings of the Western Society for French History, 1975, 1976. Add: Dept. of History, Texas A & M Univ., College Station, Tex. 77843, U.S.A.

GOOCH, Stanley (Alfred). British, b. 1932. Biology, Psychology, Supernatural/Occult topics. Publisher's reader. Head of Modern Languages, Highbury County Boys Sch., London, 1958–61; Teacher, Colebrooke Row Sch. for Maladjusted Children, London, 1961–63; Sr. Research Psychologist, National Children's Bureau, London, 1964–68. *Publs:* Four Years On, 1966; Total Man, 1972; The Neanderthal Question, 1977; The Paranormal, 1978; Guardians of the Ancient Wisdom, 1979; The Double Helix of the Mind, 1980; The Secret Life of Humans, 1981; Creatures from Inner Space, 1984; The Child with Asthma, 1986; Cities of Dreams, 1989. Add: 11 Crossfield Rd., Hampstead, London NW3 4NS, England.

GOOCH, Steve. British, b. 1945. Plays/Screenplays. Asst. Ed., Plays and Players mag., London, 1972–73; Resident Dramatist, Half Moon Theatre, 1973–74, and Greenwich Theatre, 1974–75, both in London, Solent Peoples Theatre, Southampton, 1982, Theatre Venture, London, 1983–84, and Warehouse Theatre, Croyden, 1986–87. *Publs:* (trans.) Big Wolf, 1972; (trans.) The Mother, 1973; Female Transport, 1974; (with Paul Thompson) The Motor Show, 1974; Will Wat, If Not, What Will?, 1975; (trans.) Wolf Biermann's Poems and Ballads, 1977; The Women Pirates, 1978; (trans.) Wallraff: The Undesirable Journalist, 1978; Fast One, 1982; Landmark, 1982; (trans.) Gambit 39, 1982; Writing a Play, 1988; All Together Now, 1984. Add: c/o Margaret Ramsay Ltd., 14a Goodwins Ct., St. Martin's Lane, London WC2N 4LL, England.

GOOD, Carter V(ictor). American, b. 1897. Education. Dean and Prof. of Education Emeritus, Univ. of Cincinnati, Ohio (faculty member, since 1930). Prof. of Education, Miami Univ., 1925–30. *Publs:* The Supplementary Reading Assignment, 1927; How to Do Research in Education, 1928; Teaching in College and University, 1929; (with Barr and Scates) The Methodology of Educational Research, 1936; (ed.) A Guide to Colleges, Universities, and Professional Schools in the U.S., 1945; (ed.) Dictionary of Education, 1945, 3rd ed. 1973; (with Scates) Methods of Research, 1954; Introduction to Educational Research, 1959, 1963; Essentials of Educational Research, 1966, 1972. Add: 1012 Brayton Ave., Wyoming, Ohio 45215, U.S.A.

GOOD, Irving John. British, b. 1916. Mathematics/Statistics. Research Prof. since 1967, and Univ. Distinguished Prof. since 1969, Virginia Polytechnic Inst. and State Univ., Blacksburg. Served in the U.K. Foreign Office, 1941–45; Lectr. in Mathematics and Electronic Computing, Manchester Univ., 1945–48; with Govt. Communications Headquarters, 1948–59, and Admiralty Research Lab., 1959–62, all in U.K.;

Consultant, Communications Research Div., Inst. of Defense Analyses, Princeton, N.J. 1962–64; Sr. Research Fellow, Trinity Coll., Oxford, and Atlas Computer Lab., Science Research Council, 1964–67. *Publs:* Probability and the Weighing of Evidence, 1950; (gen. ed.) The Scientist Speculates: An Anthology of Partly Baked Ideas, 1962; The Estimation of Probabilities: An Essay in Modern Bayesian Methods, 1965; (with D.B. Osteyee) Information, Weight of Evidence, The Singularity Between Probability Measures, and Signal Detection, 1974; Good Thinking, 1983. Add: Dept. of Statistics, Virginia Polytechnic Inst. and State Univ., Blacksburg, Va. 24061, U.S.A.

GOODACRE, Elizabeth Jane. Australian, b. 1929. Children's fiction, Children's non-fiction, Education. Prof. of Education, Middlesex Polytechnic. Consultant, Centre for the Teaching of Reading, Sch. of Education, Univ. of Reading, since 1968. Research Psychologist, National Foundn. for Educational Research, 1958–65. *Publs:* Reading in Infant Classes, 1967; Teachers and Their Pupils' Home Background, 1968; School and Home, 1970; Provision for Reading, 1971; Children and Learning to Read, 1971; Pictures and Words, 1971; (with F. Schonell) The Psychology and Teaching of Reading, 1974; (ed. with A. Blackwood) Beanstalk Books, 1974. Add: 24 Brookside Cres., Cuffley, Potters Bar, Herts. EN6 4QN, England.

GOODE, Kenneth G(regory). American, b. 1932. Administration/Management, Education, History. Asst. Vice-Chancellor, Administrative Services, Univ. of California, Berkeley, since 1973 (Instr. in Afro-American History, Extension Div., 1967–68; Asst. to Exec. Vice Chancellor, 1968–69; Asst. Chancellor, Special Services, 1970–73). Contract Admin., U.S. Atomic Energy Commn., Berkeley, 1963–67; Instr. in Political Science and Afro-American History, Laney Coll., Oakland, Calif., 1964–67. *Publs:* From Africa to the United States and Then, 1967, 1969; (contrib.) The Rumble of California Politics, 1970; (contrib.) The Disadvantaged Workers, 1971; (contrib.) The Teacher's Handbook, 1971; (contrib.) An Assessment of Educational Opportunity Programs in California Public Higher Education, 1973; (contrib.) Handbook on Contemporary Education, 1974; California's Black Pioneers, 1974. Add: 200 California Hall, Office of the Chancellor, Univ. of California, Berkeley, Calif. 94720, U.S.A.

GOODE, Richard. American, b. 1916. Economics. Guest Scholar, Brookings Instn., Washington, D.C., since 1981 (Sr. Staff member, 1959–65). Fiscal Analyst, U.S. Bureau of the Budget, 1941–45; Economist, U.S. Treasury Dept., 1945–47; Asst. Prof. of Economics, Univ. of Chicago, 1947–51; Asst. Chief, then Chief, Finance Div. Research Dept., 1951–58, Asst. Dir., Asian Dept., 1958–59, and Dir., Fiscal Affairs Dept., 1965–81, Intnl. Monetary Fund, Washington, D.C. *Publs:* The Corporation Income Tax, 1951; The Individual Income Tax, 1964, 1976; Government Finance in Developing Countries, 1984; Economic Assistance to Developing Countries Through the IMF, 1985. Add: 4301 Massachusetts Ave. N.W., Washington, D.C. 20016, U.S.A.

GOODENOUGH, Ward Hunt. American, b. 1919. Anthropology/Ethnology. Univ. Prof. of Anthropology, Univ. of Pennsylvania, Philadelphia, since 1980 (Asst. Prof., 1949–54; Assoc. Prof., 1954–62; Prof., 1962–80). Curator of Oceanian Ethnology, Univ. Museum, Univ. of Pennsylvania, since 1962 (Asst. Curator, 1950–54; Assoc. Curator, 1954–62). *Publs:* Property, Kin, and Community on Truk, 1951; Cooperation in Change, 1963; (ed.) Explorations in Cultural Anthropology, 1964; Description and Comparison in Cultural Anthropology, 1970; Culture, Language, and Society, 1971; Trukese-English Dictionary, 1980. Add: Dept. of Anthropology, Univ. of Pennsylvania, Philadelphia, Pa. 19104, U.S.A.

GOODERS, John. British, b. 1937. Natural history, Photography. Ed., Birds of the World Encyclopedia, 1969–71; Consultant Ed., Encyclopedia of Birds, 1977–78; Writer, "Survival", television series. *Publs:* Where to Watch Birds, 1967; Where to Watch Birds in Europe, 1969; How and Why of Birds, 1971; How and Why of the Spoilt Earth, 1972; (with E. Hosking) Wildlife Photography, 1973; The Bird-Watcher's Book, 1974; Wildlife Paradises of the World, 1975; How to Watch Birds, 1976; Birds of Mountain and Moorlands Ocean and Estuary, Marsh and Shore, Hedgerow and Garden, 4 vols., 1978–79; (with P. Alden) Finding Birds Around the World, 1979; A Day in the Country, 1979; (with S. Keith) Collins Bird Guide, 1980; Bird Seeker's Guide, 1980; Collins British Birds, 1982; The New Where to Watch Birds in Britain, 1986; (with T. Boyer) Ducks of North America and the Northern Hemisphere, 1986; Field Guide to the Birds of Britain and Ireland, 1986. Add: Lattenden Farm, Ashburnham, Battle, E. Sussex, England.

GOODFIELD, (Gwyneth) June. British, b. 1927. Novels/Short stories, Sciences. Adjunct Prof., Cornell Univ. Medical Coll., since 1977; Adjunct Member, Memorial Sloan Kettering Cancer Center, since 1981. Pres., Intnl. Health and Biomedicine Ltd. Asst. Dir., Unit for the History of Ideas, Nuffield Foundn., England, 1961–64; Rebecca Bachrach Treves Prof., Wellesley Coll., Mass., 1965–68; Prof. of Philosophy and Medicine, Coll. of Human Medicine, Michigan State Univ., East Lancing, 1968–77; Sr. Research Assoc., Rockefeller Univ., N.Y.C., 1976–83. *Publs:* The Growth of Scientific Physiology, 1960; (co-author) The Fabric of the Heavens, 1961; (co-author) The Architect of Matter, 1962; (co-author) The Discovery of Time, 1965; Courier to Peking, 1973; The Siege of Cancer, 1974; Playing God, 1977; Reflections on Science and the Media, 1980; An Imagined World: A Story of Scientific Creativity, 1980; From the Face of the Earth, 1984; Quest for the Killers, 1985; The Planned Miracle, 1989. Add: The Manor House, Alfriston, Polegate, E. Sussex, England.

GOODHEART, Barbara. American, b. 1934. Medicine/Health, Writing. *Publs:* A Year on the Desert, 1969; The Complete Guide to Writing Non-Fiction, 1983. Add: 15 Sheffield Ct., Lincolnshire, Deerfield, Ill. 60015, U.S.A.

GOODHEART, Eugene. American, b. 1931. Literature. Edytha Macy Gross Prof. of Humanities, Brandeis Univ., Waltham, Mass., since 1983. Instr., then Asst. Prof., Bard Coll., Annandale-on-Hudson, N.Y., 1958–62; Asst. Prof., Univ. of Chicago, 1962–66; Assoc. Prof., Mount Holyoke Coll., South Hadley, Mass., 1966–67; Assoc. Prof., 1967–70, Prof., 1970–74, and Co-Dir., Cambridge Humanities Seminar, 1973–82, Massachusetts Inst. of Technology, Cambridge; Prof. of English, and Chmn. of Dept., Boston Univ., 1974–80. *Publs:* The Utopian Vision of D.H. Lawrence, 1963; The Cult of the Ego: The Self in Modern Literature, 1968; Culture and the Radical Conscience, 1973; The Failure of Criticism, 1978; The Skeptic Disposition in Contemporary Criticism, 1985; Pieces of Resistance, 1987. Add: National Humanities Ctr., 7 Alexander Dr., Research Triangle Park, N.C. 27709, U.S.A.

GOODING, Judson. American, b. 1926. Sociology. Head, Trend Analysis Assocs., Bedford, N.Y., since 1975. Reporter, Minneapolis Tribune, 1954–57; Reporter, Life mag., North and South America, Africa and Europe, 1957–62; Corresp., Time mag., Paris Bureau, 1962–66; Bureau Chief, Time-Life News Service, San Francisco, 1966–68; Contrib. Ed., Time mag., 1968–69; Assoc. Ed., Fortune mag., NYC, 1969–73; Ed., The Trend Report, Chicago, 1973–75; Exec. Ed., Next mag., NYC, 1979–81; Member, U.S. Delegation to Unesco, Paris, 1982–84. *Publs:* The Job Revolution, 1972. Add: N. Main St., P.O. Box 745, Walpole, N.H. 03608, U.S.A.

GOODLAD, John I. American, b. 1920. Education. Prof. of Education, Univ. of Washington, Seattle, since 1985. Prof. of Education and Dir. of the University Elementary Sch., 1960–85, and Dean of the Grad. Sch. of Education, 1967–83, Univ. of California at Los Angeles. Member, Bd. of Editors, Child's World, 1952–75; Chmn., Editorial Advisory Bd., New Standard Encyclopedia, 1953–75; Contrib. Ed., Progressive Education, 1955–58; Member, Bd. of Eds., Sch. Review, 1956–58, and Journal of Teacher Education, 1958–60; Member of the Exec. Cttee., 1958–64, and Pres., 1962–63, National Soc. of Coll. Teachers of Education; Member, Editorial Bd., American Educational Research Journal, 1964–66; Pres., American Educational Research Assn., 1967–68; Member, Editorial Advisory Bd., The Education Digest, 1968–70, and Editorial Bd., The Educational Forum, 1969–71; Contrib. Ed., Educational Technology, 1970–72; Member, Governing Bd., Unesco Inst. of Education, Hamburg, 1972–79. *Publs:* (co-author) The Elementary School, 1956; (co-author) Educational Leadership and the Elementary School Principal, 1956; (co-author) The Non-graded Elementary School, 1959, rev. ed. 1963; Planning and Organizing for Teaching, 1963; School Curriculum Reform in the United States, 1964; (ed.) The Changing American School, 1966; (co-author) Computers and Information Systems in Education, 1966; School, Curriculum, and the Individual, 1966; The Changing School Curriculum, 1966; The Development of a Conceptual System for Dealing with Problems of Curriculum and Instruction, 1966; (co-author) Behind the Classroom Door, 1970, rev. ed. as Looking Behind the Classroom Door, 1974; (co-ed.) The Elementary School in the United States, 1973; (co-author) Early Schooling in England and Israel, 1973; (co-author) Early Schooling in the United States, 1973; (co-author) Toward a Mankind School: An Adventure in Humanistic Education, 1974; (co-author) The Conventional and the Alternative in Education, 1975; The Dynamics of Educational Change: Toward Responsive Schools, 1975; Facing the Future: Issues in Education and Schooling, 1976; (co-author) Curriculum Inquiry: The Study of Curriculum Practice, 1979; What Schools Are For,

1979; (ed.) Individual Differences and the Common Curriculum, 1983; A Place Called School, 1984; (ed.) The Ecology of School Renewal, 1987; (co-ed.) School-University Partnerships in Action, 1988; (co-ed.) Access to Knowledge, 1989. Add: Coll. of Education, Univ. of Washington, Seattle, WA 98102, U.S.A.

GOODMAN, Elliot R. American, b. 1923. Politics/Government. Prof. of Political Science, Brown Univ., Providence, R.I., since 1970 (joined faculty, 1955). *Publs:* The Soviet Design for a World State, 1960; The Fate of the Atlantic Community, 1975. Add: 45 Amherst Rd., Cranston, R.I. 02920, U.S.A.

GOODMAN, Jonathan. British, b. 1933. Novels/Short stories, Plays/Screenplays, Poetry, Criminology. Gen. Ed., Celebrated Trials Series, David & Charles (Publrs.) Ltd., Newton Abbott, Devon, from 1972. Theatre dir. and television producer, various companies in the U.K., 1951–64. *Publs:* Matinee Idylls (poetry), 1954; Instead of Murder (novel), 1961; Criminal Tendencies (novel), 1964; Hello Cruel World Goodbye (novel), 1964; The Killing of Julia Wallace, 1969; Bloody Versicles, 1971; Posts-Mortem, 1971; (ed.) Trial of Ian Brady and Myra Hindley, 1973; (ed.) Trial of Ruth Ellis, 1975; The Burning of Evelyn Foster, 1977; The Last Sentence (novel), 1978; The Stabbing of George Harry Storrs, 1982; The Pleasures of Murder, 1983; Railway Murders, 1984; Who-He?, 1984; Seaside Murders, 1985; (ed.) The Crippen File, 1985; (with I. Will) Underworld, 1985; (ed.) Christmas Murders, 1986; The Moors Murders, 1986; Acts of Murder, 1986; Murder in High Places, 1986; The Slaying of Joseph Bowne Elwell, 1987; The Country House Murders, 1987; The Vintage Car Murders, 1988; Murder in Low Places, 1988; The Oscar Wilde File, 1988. Add: 43 Ealing Village, London W5 2LZ, England.

GOODMAN, Louis Wolf. American, b. 1942. Sociology. Visiting Asst. Prof. of Sociology, Yale Univ., New Haven, since 1979. Asst. Prof. of Sociology, Yale Univ., New Haven, Conn., 1969–74; Staff Assoc., Social Science Research Council, NYC, 1974–78. *Publs:* (ed.) Selected Studies in Marriage and the Family, 1968; (ed.) Workers and Managers in Latin America, 1973; The Structure of Human Society, 1975; (co-ed.) Multi-National Corporations and Development, 1976; The Alien Doctors, 1978; Small Nations and Giant Firms, 1987. Add: Dept. of Sociology, Yale Univ., New Haven, Conn. 06520, U.S.A.

GOODMAN, (Henry) Nelson. American, b. 1906. Philosophy. Prof. Emeritus, Harvard Univ., Cambridge, Mass., since 1977 (Director, Project Zero, Graduate School of Education, 1967–71). Assoc. Prof., 1946–51 and Prof., 1951–64, Univ. of Pennsylvania, Philadelphia; Henry Austryn Wolfson Prof., Brandeis Univ., Waltham, Mass, 1964–67. Vice-President, Assn. for Symbolic Logic, 1951–52; President, Eastern Division, American Philosophical Assn., 1967. *Publs:* The Structure of Appearance, 1951; Fact, Fiction and Forecast, 1955; Languages of Art: An Approach to a Theory of Symbols, 1968; Problems and Projects, 1972; Ways of Worldmaking, 1978; Of Mind and Other Matters, 1983; (with Catherine Z. Elgin) Reconceptions: In Philosophy and Other Arts and Sciences, 1988. Add: Emerson Hall, Harvard Univ., Cambridge, Mass., 02138, U.S.A.

GOODMAN, Roger B. American, b. 1919. Poetry, Language/Linguistics, Writing/Journalism. Assoc. Exec. Ed., Hungarian Heritage Review. Chmn., Dept. of English, Stuyvesant High Sch., NYC, 1960–75; now retired. *Publs:* (ed.) Just for Laughs, 1952; (with D. Lewin) New Ways to Greater Word Power, 1955; (ed.) 75 Short Masterpieces from the World's Literature, 1961; A Concise Handbook of Better English, 1962; (ed.) World-Wide Short Stories, 1966; (ed.) The World's Best Short-Short Stories, 1967; (ed.) American's Today, 1969; Cast of Characters (poetry), 1978; (with C. Spiegler) A Matter for Judgment, 1979; An O'Henry Reader (adaptation), 1980; A Bed for the Wind (for children), 1988. Add: 2005 Pearson St., Brooklyn, N.Y. 11234, U.S.A.

GOODWIN, Geoffrey (Lawrence). British, b. 1916. International relations/Current affairs. Emeritus Prof. of Intnl. Relations, London Sch. of Economics, Univ. of London, since 1978 (Member of Faculty, L.S.E., since 1948; Montague Burton Prof., 1962–78). Served in Foreign Office, London, 1945–48; Principal, St. Catherine's Cumberland Lodge, Windsor Great Park, 1971–72. *Publs:* (ed.) The University Teaching of International Relations, 1951; Britain and the United Nations, 1958; (ed.) New Dimensions of World Politics, 1975; (ed.) A New International Commodity Regime, 1979; (ed.) Ethics and Nuclear Deterrance, 1982. Add: 8 Latham Rd., Selsey, Chichester, W. Sussex, England.

GOODWIN, Suzanne. *See* **EBEL,** Suzanne.

GOODWIN, Trevor W(alworth). British, b. 1916. Biology, Chemistry. Johnston Prof. of Biochemistry, Univ. of Liverpool, 1966–83, now Emeritus. Ed., Phytochemistry, Protoplasma, and Photosynthetica. Former Prof. of Biochemistry, Univ. Coll. of Wales, Aberystwyth. *Publs:* Biochemistry of Carotenoids, 1954, 1980, 1983; Recent Advances in Biochemistry, 1959; Biosynthesis of Vitamins, 1963; (co-author) Introduction to Plant Biochemistry, 1972, 1982; (ed.) Chemistry and Biochemistry of Plant Pigments, 1965, 3rd ed. 1987; (ed.) Biochemistry of Chloroplasts, 2 vols.; (ed.) Aspects of Insect Biochemistry; (ed.) Instrumentation in Biochemistry; (ed.) Metabolic Rates of Citrate; (ed.) British Biochemistry Past and Present; (co-ed.) Biological Structure and Function: History of the Biochemical Society 1911-1986, 1987. Add: Monzar, Woodlands Close, Parkgate, South Wirral, Cheshire, England.

GOODY, John R(ankine). British, b. 1919. Anthropology. Fellow, St. John's Coll., Cambridge, since 1960 (Asst. Lectr., 1954–59, Lectr., 1959–71, Dir. of the African Studies Centre, 1966–73, Smuts Reader in Commonwealth Studies, 1972, and William Wyse Prof. of Social Anthropology, 1973–84, Cambridge Univ.). *Publs:* The Social Organisation of the LoWiili, 1956; (ed.) The Developmental Cycle in Domestic Groups, 1958; Death, Property, and the Ancestors, 1962; (ed.) Succession to High Office, 1966; (with J.A. Braimah) Salaga: The Struggle for Power, 1967; (ed.) Literacy in Traditional Societies, 1968; Comparative Studies in Kinship, 1969; Technology, Tradition, and the State in Africa, 1971; The Myth of the Bagre, 1972; (with S.J. Tambiah) Bridewealth and Dowry, 1973; (ed.) The Character of Kinship, 1973; (ed.) Changing Social Structure in Ghana, 1975; Production and Reproduction, 1977; The Domestication of the Savage Mind, 1977; (with J.W.D.K. Gandah) Une Recitation du Bagré 1981; Cooking, Cuisine, and Class, 1982; The Development of the Family and Marriage in Europe, 1983; The Logic of Writing and the Organization of Society, 1986; The Interface Between the Oral and the Written, 1987; The Oriental, the Ancient and the Primitive, 1989. Add: St. John's College, Cambridge, England.

GOOSSENS, Eugene (Coons). American, b. 1920. Art. Prof. of Art and Chmn., Art Dept., Hunter Coll., NYC, since 1961. Member, Advisory Cttees., Archives of American Art, since 1965, and NYC Cultural Council, since 1969. Critic Corresp., Monterey Peninsula Herald, Calif., 1948–58; Dir. of Exhibitions and Lectr., Benington Coll., Vt. 1958–61. Guest Exhibitions Dir., Museum of Modern Art, 1967–68, 1971–73, and Whitney Museum of American Art, 1968–69, NYC, and Detroit Inst. of the Arts, 1973. *Publs:* Ellsworth Kelly, 1958; Stuart Davis, 1959; Three American Sculptors, 1959; Art of the Real, 1968; Helen Frankenthaler, 1969; Ellsworth Kelly, 1973. Add: R.D. 1, Buskirk, N.Y. 12028, U.S.A.

GOPAL, Sarvepalli. Indian, b. 1923. History, Biography. Prof. of History, Jawaharlal Nehru Univ., New Delhi, 1972–83, now Emeritus. Fellow of St. Antony's Coll., Oxford, since 1986. Former Chmn., National Book Trust of India. Reader in S. Asian History, Oxford Univ., England, 1966–71. *Publs:* The Permanent Settlement in Bengal, 1949; The Vice Royalty of Lord Ripon, 1953;The Vice Royalty of Lord Irwin, 1957; British Policy in India 1858-1905, 1965; Modern India, 1967; Jawaharlal Nehru, 3 vols., 1975–84; (ed.) Nehru: An Anthology, 1981; (ed.) Selected Works by Nehru, 4 vols., 1985–87. Add: 97 Radhakrishnan Salal, Mylapore, Madras 4, India.

GORAN, Morris. American, b. 1916. Sciences, Biography. Prof. and Chmn., Dept. of Physical Science, Roosevelt Univ., Chicago, since 1945. Chemist, Dearborn Chemical Co., 1941–42; Asst. Prof. of Physics, Univ. of Indiana, 1942–43; Scientist, Manhattan District Corps of Engineers, Oak Ridge, Tenn., 1943–45; Lectr., George Williams Coll., and Elmhurst Coll., Illinois. Pres., Lincolnwood, Ill. Bd. of Education, 1959–68. *Publs:* The Story of Fritz Haber, 1967; The Future of Science, 1971; Science and Anti-Science, 1974; A Preface to Astronomy, 1975; The Modern Myth: Ancient Astronauts and UFOs, 1978; Fact, Fraud, and Fantasy, 1978; The Occult and Pseudo-Sciences, 1979; Ten Lessons of the Energy Crisis, 1980; The Conquest of Pollution, 1981; Can Science Be Saved, 1981; A Treasury of Science Jokes, 1987. Add: 7330 N. Bilbourne St., Lincolnwood, Ill. 60646, U.S.A.

GORDIMER, Nadine. South African, b. 1923. Novels/Short stories. *Publs:* Face to Face: Short Stories, 1949; The Soft Voice of the Serpent and Other Stories, 1952; The Lying Days, 1953; Six Feet of the Country, 1956; A World of Strangers, 1958; Friday's Footprint and Other Stories, 1960; Occasion for Loving, 1963; Not for Publication and Other Stories, 1965; The Late Bourgeois World, 1966; (ed. with L. Abrahams) South African Writing Today, 1967; A Guest of Honour, 1970; Livingston's Companions: Stories, 1971; The Conservationist, 1974; Selected Stories, 1975; Some Monday for Sure (stories), 1976; Burger's Daughter, 1979;

A Soldier's Embrace (stories), 1980; July's People, 1981; Something Out There (stories), 1984; A Sport of Nature (novel), 1987; The Essential Gestures (essays), 1988. Add: 7 Frere Rd., Parktown West, Johannesburg, South Africa.

GORDIS, Robert. American, b. 1908. Theology/Religion. Founder, 1950, and Ed., since 1970, Judaism, American Jewish Congress, NYC (Chmn., Bd. of Eds., 1950–59). Prof. of Bible and of Philosophies of Religion, Jewish Theological Seminary, NYC, 1974–81, now Emeritus. Rabbi, Temple Bath-El, Rockaway Park, N.Y., 1931–68; Adjunct Prof. of Religion, Columbia Univ., NYC, 1950–59; Prof. of Religion, Temple Univ., Philadelphia, 1968–74. *Publs:* The Biblical Text in the Making, 1937, 1971; The Jew Faces a New World, 1941; The Wisdom of Ecclesiates, 1945; Conservative Judaism—An American Philosophy, 1945; Koheleth—The Man and His World, 1951; Song of Songs, 1954; Judaism and the Modern Age, 1955; A Faith for Moderns, 1960; The Root and the Branch: Judaism and the Free Society, 1962; The Book of God and Man: A Study of Job, 1965; Judaism in the Christian World, 1966; Sex and the Family in Jewish Tradition, 1967; Leave a Little to God, 1967; Poets, Prophets and Sages— Essays in Biblical Interpretation, 1971; (ed. with Ruth B. Waxman) Faith and Reason, Essays in Judaism, 1973; The Song of Songs and Lamentations: A Commentary and Translation, 1974; Love and Sex: A Modern Jewish Perspective, 1978; The Book of Job: Commentary and Translation, 1978; Understanding Conservative Judaism, 1978; Judaic Ethics for a Lawless World, 1986. Add: 150 West End Ave., New York, N.Y. 10023, U.S.A.

GORDON, Barry (Lewis John). Australian, b. 1934. Economics, Industrial Relations. Assoc. Prof. of Economics, Univ. of Newcastle, N.S.W., since 1968 (Lectr., then Sr. Lectr., 1956–68). Dir., Datex Research Co-op, Newcastle, since 1976. *Publs:* Non-Ricardian Political Economy, 1967; (ed. with K. Lindgren and E. Mason) The Corporation in Australian Society, 1974; Economic Analysis Before Adam Smith: Hesiod to Lessius, 1975; Political Economy in Parliament 1819-1823, 1976; Economic Doctrine and Tory Liberalism 1824-1830, 1979; (ed. with M.T. Gordon) The Shortage of Skilled People, 1980; (ed. with M.T. Gordon) Policy Priorities for Australian Steel Regions, 1983; (ed. with W.C. Dunlop) Small Business Research, 1984. Add: Dept. of Economics, Univ. of Newcastle, N.S.W. 2308, Australia.

GORDON, Cyrus Herzl. American, b. 1908. History, Language/Linguistics, Literature. Prof. of Hebraic Studies, since 1973, and Dir., Center for Ebla Research, since 1982, New York Univ., NYC (Visiting Prof., 1970–73). Field Archeologist, American Schs. of Oriental Research, Jerusalem and Baghdad, 1931–35; Prof of Assyriology and Egyptology, Dropsie Univ., Philadelphia, Pa., 1946–56; Prof. of Mediterranean Studies, and Dept. Chmn., Brandeis Univ., Waltham, Mass., 1956–73. *Publs:* Nouns in the Nuzi Tablets, 1936; Ugaritic Grammar, 1940; The Living Past, 1941; Loves and Wars of Baal and Anat, 1943; Ugaritic Handbook, 1947; Lands of the Cross and Crescent, 1948; Ugaritic Literature, 1949; Smith College Tablets, 1952; Introduction to Old Testament Times, 1953; Ugaritic Manual, 1955; Hammurapi's Code, 1957; World of the Old Testament, 1958; New Horizons in Old Testament Literature, 1960; Before the Bible, 1962; Common Background of Greek and Hebrew Civilizations, 1965; The Ancient Near East, 1965; Ugarit and Minoan Crete, 1966; Evidence for the Minoan Language, 1966; Homer and the Bible, 1967; Ugaritic Textbook, 1967; Forgotten Scripts, 1968. 3rd ed. 1982; Poetic Legends and Myths from Ugarit, 1977; The Pennsylvania Tradition of Semitics, 1986; (ed. and contrib.) Publications of the Center for Ebla Research, vol. 1, 1987, vol. 2, 1989. Add: 130 Dean Rd., Brookline, Mass. 02146, U.S.A.

GORDON, Diana. *See* **ANDREWS,** Lucilla.

GORDON, Donald. *See* **PAYNE,** Donald Gordon.

GORDON, Donald C(raigie). American, b. 1911. History. Prof. of History, Univ. of Maryland, College Park, since 1961 (Asst. Prof., 1946–55; Assoc. Prof., 1955–61). Member of faculty, Coll. of William and Mary, Norfolk Div., 1938–46. *Publs:* The Australian Frontier in New Guinea, 1951; (author and ed. with W. Gewehr, D. Sparks and R. Stromberg) The United States: A History of a Democracy, 1957, 1960; The Dominion Partnership in Imperial Defense, 1965; Moment of Power: Britain's Imperial Defense, 1965; Moment of Power; Britain's Imperial Epoch, 1970. Add: History Dept., Univ. of Maryland, College Park, Md. 20742, U.S.A.

GORDON, Donald (Ramsay). Canadian, b. 1929. Media. Freelance writer and consultant, since 1975. Writer and Filing Ed., Canadian Press,

Toronto, 1949–55; Asst. Ed., Financial Post, Toronto, 1955–56; European Corresp. based in London, CBC, 1957–63; Asst. Prof., 1963–65, and Assoc. Prof. of Political Science, 1965–66, Univ. of Calgary; Asst. Prof., 1966–67, Assoc. Prof. of Political Science, 1967–71, and Assoc., Prof. of Communications Studies, 1971–75, Univ. of Waterloo, Ont. *Publs:* Language, Logic and the Mass Media, 1966; The New Literacy, 1971; Fine Swine, 1984; The Rock Candy Bandits, 1984; S.P.E.E.D., 1985. Add: 134 Iroquois Pl., Waterloo, Ont. N2L 2S5, Canada.

GORDON, Ernest. American, b. 1916. Novels/Short stories, Theology/Religion, Travel/Exploration/Adventure, Autobiography/Memoirs/-Personal. Dean, Princeton Univ. Chapel, N.J., since 1955. Pres., CREED (Christian Relief Efforts for the Emancipation of Dissidents in the USSR). *Publs:* A Living Faith for Today, 1956; Through the Valley of the Kwai (in U.K. as Miracle on the River Kwai), 1962; Guidebook for the New Christian, 1972; Solan (novel), 1973; Islands Apart, 1977; Me, Myself and Who?, 1980; (co-author) Education for Decision, 1963; (co-author) The Church in the Modern World; Beyond Hatred (autobiography). Add: 787 Princeton Kingston Rd., Princeton Township, N.J. 08540, U.S.A.

GORDON, Ethel E(dison). American, b. 1915. Historical/Romance Gothic, Children's fiction. Freelance writer, mainly of romantic short stories for women's mags., since 1947. *Publs:* Where Does the Summer Go (juvenile), 1967; So Far from Home (juvenile), 1968; Freer's Cove, 1972; The Chaperone, 1973; The Birdwatcher, 1974; The Freebody Heiress, 1974; The French Husband, 1977; The Venetian Lover, 1982. Add: 105 Lake Dr., Hewlett Harbor, N.Y. 11557, U.S.A.

GORDON, Fritz. *See* **JARVIS,** Frederick J.H.

GORDON, George N. American, b. 1926. Media, Social commentary/phenomena. Prof., Dept. of Communications, Fordham Univ., Bronx, N.Y. (Former Chmn. of Dept.). Former Prof., Communications Arts Dept., Hofstra Univ., Hempstead, N.Y. *Publs:* (with L. Costello) Teach with Television, 1961, 1965; (with I. Falk and W. Hodapp) The Idea Invaders, 1963; A Logical and Psychological Examination, 1969; (with I. Falk) Your Career as a Film Maker, 1969; Classroom Television, 1970; Persuasion: The Theory and Practice of Manipulative Communications, 1971; (with I. Falk) Videocasette Technology in American Education, 1972; (with I. Falk) The War of Ideas: America's International Identity Crisis, 1973; Communications and Media, 1975; The Communication Revolution, 1977; Erotic Communications Studies in Sex, Sin and Censorship, 1980; (with Goran Tamm and Hans Ingvar Hanson) Man in Focus: New Approaches to Commercial Communications, 1980. Add: P.O. Box 203 Newtown, Conn. 06470, U.S.A.

GORDON, Giles (Alexander Esme). British. b. 1940. Novels/Short stories, Children's fiction, Poetry, Literature. Literary Agent and Dir., Anthony Sheil Assocs., London, since 1972. Advertising Exec. Secker and Warburg, Publrs., London, 1962–63; Ed., Hutchinson Publishing Group, London, 1963–64; Ed., Penguin Books, 1964–66; Editorial Dir., Victor Gollancz Ltd., London, 1967–72; Ed., Drama mag., 1982–84; Theatre Critic, The Spectator, 1983–84, and Punch, 1985–87; Lectr., Hollins Univ-in-London, 1983–86. *Publs:* Landscape Any Date (poetry), 1963; Two and Two Make One (poetry), 1966; Two Elegies, 1968; Book 2000: Some Likely Trends in Publishing, 1969; Eight Poems for Gareth, 1970; Pictures from an Exhibition (short stories), 1970; The Umbrella Man, 1971; About a Marriage, 1972; Twelve Poems for Callum, 1972; One Man, Two Women (poetry), 1974; Girl with Red Hair, 1974; (with M. Gordon) Walter and the Balloon, 1974; (ed. with A. Hamilton) Factions, 1974; Farewell, Fond Dreams (short stories), 1975; (ed.) Beyond the Words, 1975; (ed. with D. Barber) Members of the Jury, 1975; (ed. with B.S. Johnson and M. Bakewell) You Always Remember the First Time, 1975; 100 Scenes from Married Life, 1976; (ed.) Prevailing Spirits, 1976; (ed.) A Book of Contemporary Nightmares, 1977; Enemies, 1977; The Oban Poems, 1977; Couple (short stories), 1978; The Illusionist and Other Fictions, 1978; (ed. with Fred Urquhart) Modern Scottish Short Stories, 1978; Ambrose's Vision, 1980; (ed.) Modern Short Stories 2, 1940-1980, 1982; (ed.) Shakespeare Stories, 1982; (ed. with David Hughes) Best Short Stories 1986, 4 vols., 1986–89; (ed.) English Short Stories: 1900 to the Present, 1988. Add: 9 St. Ann's Gardens, London NW5 4ER, England.

GORDON, Gordon. Wrote with Mildred Gordon (now deceased) as The Gordons. American, b. 1906. Mystery/Crime/Suspense, Criminology/Law enforcement/Prisons. Full-time writer since 1945. Reporter, 1930–31, and Managing Ed., 1931–35, Daily Citizen, Tucson, Ariz.; Publicist, Twentieth Century Fox, Hollywood, 1935–42; Counter-

Espionage Agent, F.B.I., Washington D.C. and Chicago, 1942–45. *Publs:* (all with Mildred Gordon, as The Gordons): mystery novels—The Little Man Who Wasn't There, 1946; Make Haste to Live, 1950; FBI Story, 1950; Campaign Train, 1952 (in U.S. paperback, Murder Rides the Campaign Train, 1976); Case File: FBI, 1953; The Case of the Talking Bug (in U.K. as Playback), 1955; The Big Frame, 1957; Captive, 1957; Tiger on My Back, 1960; Operation Terror, 1961 (in U.S. paperback, Experiment in Terror, 1962); Menace, 1962 (in U.K. as Journey with a Stranger, 1963); Undercover Cat, 1963 (in U.S. and U.K. paperback, That Darn Cat, 1966); Power Play, 1965; Undercover Cat Prowls Again, 1966; Night Before the Wedding, 1969; The Tumult and the Joy, 1971; The Informant, 1973; Catnapped: The Further Adventures of Undercover Cat, 1974; Ordeal, 1976; Night After the Wedding, 1979; (with Mary Dorr Gordon) Race for the Golden Tide, 1983: Freedoms Foundation of Valley Forge Award for Best Novel; other—(with Judge Louis H. Burke) With This Ring, 1958; (ed.) A Pride of Felons, 1963. Add: 6145 Jochums Dr., Tucson, Ariz. 85718, U.S.A.

GORDON, Ian Alistair. New Zealander/British, b. 1908. Language/Linguistics, Literature, Biography. Weekly Columnist, The New Zealand Listener. Prof. of English, Univ. of Wellington, 1936–74. Ed., New Zealand New Writing, Wellington, 1943–45; Vice-Chancellor, Univ. of New Zealand, 1947–52; Chmn., New Zealand Literary Fund, 1950–74. *Publs:* John Skelton, 1943; The Teaching of English, 1947; (ed.) English Prose Technique, 1948; (ed.) Shenstone's Miscellany, 1952; Katherine Mansfield, 1954; The Movement of English Prose, 1966; (ed.) John Galt: The Entail, 1970; John Galt, 1972; (ed.) John Galt: The Provost, 1973; (ed.) Undiscovered Country: The New Zealand Stories of Katherine Mansfield, 1974; (ed.) John Galt: The Member, 1975; (ed.) John Galt: The Last of the Lairds, 1976; (ed.) John Galt: Selected Short Stories, 1978; (ed.) Katherine Mansfield: The Urewera Notebook, 1979; (ed.) Word Finder, 1979; A Word in Your Ear, 1980; (ed.) Collins Compact New Zealand Dictionary of the English Language, 1985. Add: 91 Messines Rd., Wellington 5, New Zealand.

GORDON, Jane. *See* **LEE**, Elsie.

GORDON, John Fraser. British, b. 1916. Animals/Pets. Managing Dir., Dongora Mill Co. Ltd., London, and J.F. Gordon (London) Ltd., since 1963. *Publs:* Staffordshire Bull Terrier Handbook, Bull Terrier Handbook, Bulldog Handbook, Dandie Dinmont Terrier Handbook, 1952–59; Staffordshire Bull Terriers, 1964; Miniature Schnauzers, 1966; Spaniel Owner's Encyclopedia, 1967; Staffordshire Bull Terrier Owner's Encyclopedia, 1967; The Beagle Guide, 1968; The Miniature Schnauzer Guide, 1968; All About the Boxer, 1970; The Staffordshire Bull Terrier, 1970; All About the Cocker Spaniel, 1971; The Pug, 1973; The Irish Wolfhound; The Borzoi; Some Rare and Unusual Breeds; The Bull Terrier; The Bulldog; The Dandie Dinmont Terrier; The German Shepherd, 1978; The Pyrenean Mountain Dog, 1978; The Alaskan Malamute, 1979; Schnauzers, 1982; All About the Staffordshire Bull Terrier, 1984; All About the Cairn Terrier, 1987. Add: 72 Clyde Way, Romford, Essex RM1 4UT, England.

GORDON, John (William). British, b. 1925. Children's fiction. *Publs:* The Giant Under the Snow, 1968; The House on the Brink, 1970; The Ghost on the Hill, 1976; The Waterfall Box, 1978; The Spitfire Grave, 1979; The Edge of the World, 1983; Catch Your Death, 1984; The Quelling Eye, 1986; The Grasshopper, 1987; Ride the Wind, 1989; Blood Brothers, 1989. Add: 99 George Borrow Rd., Norwich, Norfolk NR4 7HU, England.

GORDON, Katharine. British, b. 1916. Historical/Romance/Gothic. Secty. to E.A. Army Wardens, Nairobi, 1950–51; Immigration Officer, Immigration Dept., Nairobi, 1954–57; Consular Clerk, British Embassy, Khartoum, 1964–69. *Publs:* The Emerald Peacock, 1978; Peacock in Flight, 1979; In the Shadow of the Peacock, 1980; The Peacock Ring, 1981; Peacock in Jeopardy, 1983; Cheetah, 1986. Add: Box 132, Girne, Turkey.

GORDON, Lew. *See* **BALDWIN**, Gordon C.

GORDON, Lois G. American, b. 1938. Literature. Prof. of English and Comparative Literature, since 1968, and Chmn. of Dept. since 1982, Fairleigh Dickinson Univ., Teaneck, N.J. Consultant, Doubleday, Prentice-Hall, Kennikat, and Fairleigh Dickinson Univ., Press publrs. Lectr., City Coll. of New York, NYC, 1964–66; Asst. Prof., Univ. of Missouri, Kansas City, 1966–68; Asst. Ed., Literature and Psychology, 1968–70. *Publs:* Stratagems to Undercover Nakedness: The Dramas of Harold Pinter, 1969; Donald Barthelme, 1981: Robert Coover: The Universal Fic-

tion-making Process, 1982; American Chronicle: Six Decades in American Life 1920-1980, 1987. Add: 300 Central Park West, New York, N.Y. 10024, U.S.A.

GORDON, Mary (Catherine). American, b. 1949. Novels/Short Stories. English Teacher, Dutchess Community Coll., Poughkeepsie, N.Y., 1974–78. *Publs:* Final Payments, 1978; The Company of Women, 1981; Men and Angels, 1985; Temporary Shelter (stories), 1987. Add: c/o Random House, 205 E. 50th St., New York, N.Y. 10022, U.S.A.

GORDON, Ray. *See* **WAINWRIGHT**, Gordon Ray.

GORDON, Rex. *See* **HOUGH**, S.B.

GORDON, Richard. Pseudonym for Gordon Ostlere. British, b. 1921. Novels/Short stories, Medicine/Health. Sr. Resident Anaesthetist, St. Bartholomew's Hosp., London, 1945–48; Asst. Ed., British Medical Journal, 1949–50; Ship's surgeon, 1950–51; Research Asst. and Deputy First Asst., Nuffield Dept. of Anasthetics, Oxford Univ., 1951–52. *Publs:* Doctor in the House series, 14 vols., 1952–82; The Captain's Table, 1954; Nuts in May, 1964; The Summer of Sir Lancelot, 1965; Love and Sir Lancelot, 1966; (with Mary Ostlere) A Baby in the House: A Guide to Practical Parenthood, 1966; The Facemaker, 1967; Surgeon at Arms, 1968; The Facts of Life, 1969; The Medical Witness, 1971; The Sleep of Life, 1975; Good Neighbours, 1976; Invisible Victory, 1977; Bedside Manners, 1982; Good Dr. Bodkin Adams (television screenplay). Add: c/o Curtis Brown Ltd., 162-168 Regent St., London W1R 5TA, England.

GORDON, Stewart. *See* **SHIRREFFS**, Gordon Donald.

GORDON, Stuart. Pseud. for Richard Gordon; also writes as Alex R. Stuart. British, b. 1947. Novels/Short stories, Science fiction/Fantasy. *Publs:* Time Story, 1972; (as Alex R. Stuart) The Bike from Hell (novel), 1973; (as Alex R. Stuart) The Devil's Rider, 1973; One-Eye, 1973; Two-Eyes, 1974; Three-Eyes, 1975; Suaine and the Crow-God, 1975; Smile on the Void, 1981; Fire in the Abyss, 1983; The Book of the Watchers (series); vol. 1, Archon, 1987; vol. II, The Hidden World, 1988; vol. III, The Mask, 1989; vol. IV, Eye in the Stone, 1990. Add: c/o Maggie Noach, 21 Redan St., London W14, England.

GORDON, Sydney. British, b. 1914. Children's non-fiction. Educational Adviser, Barnsley Co. Borough, since 1967. Deputy Headmaster until 1966. *Publs:* Leonardo da Vinci, 1966; Thomas Edison, 1966; Galileo Galilei, 1968; Isaac Newton, 1968; Michael Faraday, 1969; Orville and Wilbur Wright, 1969; Jean Henri Fabre, 1971; Archimedes, 1971. Add: Flat 6, 10 York Rd., Birkdale, Southport, England.

GORDON, Thomas. American, b. 1918. Human relations. Pres., Effectiveness Training Inc., Solana Beach. Asst. Prof., 1949–54, and Assoc. Prof., 1954, Univ. of Chicago. *Publs:* Group-Centred Leadership, 1955; Parent Effectiveness Training, 1970; Teacher Effectiveness Training, 1974; P.E.T. in Action, 1976; Leader Effectiveness Training, 1977; Teaching Children Self-Discipline, 1989. Add: 531 Stevens Ave., Solana Beach, Calif. 92075, U.S.A.

GORDONE, Charles. American, b. 1925. Plays/Screenplays. Dir. and actor. Instr., Cell Block Theatre, Yardville and Bordontown Prisons, N.J., 1977–78, and New School for Social Research, NYC, 1978–9. Co-Founder, Cttee. for the Employment of Negro Performers, 1962. *Publs:* No Place to Be Somebody: A Black-Black Comedy, 1969; Gordone Is a Muthah (in The Best Short Plays 1973), 1973. Add: 17 W. 100th St., New York, N.Y. 10025, U.S.A.

GORDONS, The. *See* **GORDON**, Gordon.

GOREN, Charles H(enry). American, b. 1901. Recreation/Leisure/-Hobbies. Contrib. Ed. of Bridge World; Member, Editorial Advisory Bd. of the Bridge Encyclopedia. Admitted to the Pennsylvania Bar, 1923, and practised law in Philadelphia until 1936; entered tournament bridge competitions, 1931, and won first national events, U.S. Bridge Assn. and American Bridge League Open Teams, 1933; subsequently played in all major U.S. bridge competitions and lead master point winners list, 1944–62; also known for his syndicated newspaper column, for columns in Sports Illustrated and McCall's mag., and for the series of television shows Championship Bridge with Charles Goren. *Publs:* Winning Bridge Made Easy, 1936; Better Bridge for Better Players, 1942; Standard Book of Bidding, 1944; Contract Bridge Made Easy: A Self-Teacher, 1948; Point Count Bidding in Contract Bridge, 1949; Goren Presents the Italian Bridge System, 1958; New Contract Bridge in a Nutshell, 1959,

1972; Sports Illustrated Book of Bridge, 1961; Goren's Winning Partnership Bridge, 1961; Charles Goren's Bridge Complete, 1963; Bridge Is My Game, 1965; Go with the Odds, 1969; Charles Goren Presents the Precision System, 1971; Goren's Modern Backgammon Complete, 1974; Goren on Play and Defense, 1974; Play as You Learn Bridge, 1979; Fundamentals of Contract Bridge, 1981; Goren's Bridge Complete, 1981; (with Ronald P. Porter) Introduction to Competitive Bidding, 1984. Add: 18361 Lake Encino Dr., Encino, CA 91316, U.S.A.

GORES, Joe. (Joseph N. Gores). American, b. 1931. Mystery/Crime/Suspense. Full-time writer. Private investigator, L.A. Walker Co., San Francisco, 1955–57, and David Kikkert and Assocs., San Francisco, 1959–62, 1965–67; English Teacher, Kakamega Boys Secondary Sch., Kenya, 1963–64; Mgr., Automobile Auction Co., San Francisco, 1968–76. Pres., Mystery Writers of America, 1986. Extensive film and TV writing, including scripts for Kojak, Mike Hammer, Magnum, p.i., Remington Steele, and T.J. Hooker. *Publs:* mystery novels—A Time of Predators, 1969; Dead Skip, 1972; Final Notice, 1973; Interface, 1974; Hammett: A Novel, 1975; Gone, No Forwarding, 1978; Come Morning, 1986; other—Marine Salvage, 1971; (ed.) Honolulu: Port of Call, 1974; (ed. with Bill Pronzini) Tricks or Treats, 1976, in U.K. as Mystery Writers' Choice, 1977; Wolf Time, 1989. Add: 401 Oak Crest Rd., San Anselmo, Calif. 94960, U.S.A.

GOREY, Edward (St. John). Pseuds.: Edward Bluting, Mrs. Regera Dowdy and Ogdred Weary. American, b. 1925. Humor/Satire. Designer and illustrator. *Publs:* The Unstrung Harp, 1953; The Listing Attic, 1954; The Doubtful Guest, 1957; The Object-Lesson, 1958; The Bug Book, 1960; The Fatal Lozenge, 1960; The Hapless Child, 1961; (as Ogdred Weary) The Curious Sofa, 1961; (as Ogdred Weary) The Beastly Baby, 1962; The Willowdale Handcar, 1962; The Vinegar Works, 1963; The Wuggly Ump, 1963; The Sinking Spell, 1965; The Remembered Visit, 1965; The Inanimate Tragedy, 1966; (as Edward Bluting) The Evil Garden, 1966; (as Mrs. Regera Dowdy) The Pious Infant, 1966; The Utter Zoo, 1967; (with Victoria Chess) Fletcher and Zenobia, 1967; Other Statue, 1968; Blue Aspic, 1968; The Epileptic Bicycle, 1969; Amphiogorey, 1972; The Black Doll, 1973; Category, 1973; The Glorious Nosebleed, 1975; The Broken Spoke, 1976; The Loathsome Couple, 1977; Gorey Endings, 1978; Dracula, 1979; The Gilded Bat, 1979; (with L. Evans) Gorey Endings, 1979; Dancing Cats and Neglected Murderesses, 1980; Amphigorey Too, 1980; The Awdrey-Gore Legacy, 1982; The Dwindling Party, 1982; Amphigorey Also, 1983; The Tunnel Calamity, 1984; The Eclectic Abecedarium, 1985; The Insect God, 1986; The Gashlycrumb Tinies, 1986; The Raging Tide, 1987. Add: Box 146, Yartmouthport, Mass. 02675, U.S.A.

GORHAM, Michael. *See* FOLSOM, Franklin Brewster.

GORMAN, Clem. (Brian Gorman). Australian, b. 1942. Plays/Screenplays, Human Relations, Music. Arts administrator in the U.K. and Australia; playwriting tutor. *Publs:* The Book of Ceremonies, 1969, rev. ed. as Making Ceremonies, 1972, and the Book of Ceremony, 1972; Making Communes: Survey/Manual, 1971; People Together, 1975; Backstage Rock: Behind the Scenes with the Bands, 1978; plays—A Manual of Trench Warfare, 1979; A Night in the Arms of Raeleen, and The Harding Woman, 1983; The Motivators, 1983; The Last Night-Club, 1985. Add: 505/3 Greenknowe Ave., Potts Point, N.S.W. 2011, Australia.

GORMAN, Ginny. *See* ZACHARY, Hugh.

GORNICK, Vivian. American, b. 1935. Social commentary/phenomena, Women. *Publs:* (ed. with Barbara K. Moran) Woman in Sexist Society, 1971; In Search of Ali Mahomud: An American Woman in Egypt, 1973; The Romance of American Communism, 1977; Essays in Feminism, 1978; Women in Science, 1983; Fierce Attachments, 1987. Add: 175 W. 12th St., New York, N.Y. 10011, U.S.A.

GORRELL, Robert (Mark). American, b. 1914. Language/Linguistics, Literature. Emeritus Prof. of English and former Vice-Pres. for Academic Affairs, Univ. of Nevada, Reno (joined faculty, 1945). Instr., Deep Springs Coll., Calif., 1939–42; Instr., Indiana Univ., Bloomington, 1942–45; Fulbright Prof., Univ. of Sydney, Aust., 1954–55; Consultant, Portlant Sch. District, Ore., 1959–61; Fulbright Prof., Univ. of Helsinki, Finland, 1961–62. *Publs:* (with C. Emery and K.N. Cameron) Practice in English Communication, 2 vols., 1944, rev. ed. in 1 vol., 1947; (with C. Laird) Modern English Handbook, 1953, 7th ed. 1988; (with C. Laird) Modern English Workbook, 1957, 1962; (with C. Laird) A Course in Modern English, 1960; (with C. Laird) English as Language, 1961; (with A. Kitzhaber and P. Roberts) Education for College, 1961; (with C. Laird

and P. Pflug) A Basic Course in Modern English, 1963; (with C. Laird and W. Lutz) Modern English Reader, 1970, 1977; (with C. Laird) Reading About Language, 1971; (with M.M. Brown) Writing and Language: Books I and II, 1971; (with C. Laird) Writing Modern English, 1973. Add: 3855 Skyline Blvd., Reno, Nev. 89509, U.S.A.

GOSLING, J.C.B. British, b. 1930. Philosophy. Principal, St. Edmund Hall, Oxford Univ., since 1982 (Fellow and Tutor, 1960–82). *Publs:* Pleasure and Desire, 1969; Plato, 1973; Plato: Philebus, 1975; The Greeks on Pleasure, 1982. Add: St. Edmund Hall, Oxford, England.

GOSLING, Paula. Also writes as Ainslie Skinner. American, b. 1939. Mystery/Crime/Suspense. Full-time writer. Copywriter, Mitchell's Advertising, 1964–67, Pritchard-Wood Advertising, 1967–68, and David Williams Advertising, 1968–69, all London; Copy Consultant, Mitchell's Advertising, 1969–70, and ATA Advertising, Bristol, 1977–79; Chmn., Crime Writers Assn., 1988–89. *Publs:* A Running Duck (in U.S. as Fair Game), 1978; The Zero Trap, 1979; Loser's Blues, 1980, in U.S. as Solo Blues, 1981; (as Ainslie Skinner) Mind's Eye, 1980, in U.S. as The Harrowing, 1981; The Woman in Red, 1983; Monkey Puzzle, 1985; The Wychford Murders, 1986; Hoodwink, 1988; Backlash, 1989. Add: c/o Elaine Greene Ltd., 31 Newington Green, London N16 9PU, England.

GOTLIEB, Phyllis (Fay). Canadian, b. 1926. Novels/Short stories, Science fiction/Fantasy, Poetry. *Publs:* Within the Zodiac, 1964; Sunburst (novel), 1964; Why Should I Have All the Grief (novel), 1969; Ordinary, Moving, 1969; Garden Varieties, 1972; Doctor Umlaut's Earthly Kingdom, 1974; O Master Caliban (novel), 1976; The Works (poetry), 1978; Judgement of Dragons (novel), 1980; Emperor, Swords, Pentacles (novel), 1982; Son of the Morning and Other Stories (short stories), 1983; The Kingdom of the Cats (novel), 1985. Add: 19 Lower Village Gate, PH06, Toronto, Ont. M5P 3L9, Canada.

GOTSCHALK, Felix C. American, b. 1929. Science fiction/Fantasy. Freelance writer of SF short stories. Retired Psychologist, private practice in Winston-Salem, N.C., 1970–84. Draftsman, Vepco, Richmond, Va., 1946–47, 1949–51; pianist, Chelf's, 1951–56, and On the Road, 1956–58, both in Richmond; Asst. Prof. of Psychology, Nicholls State Univ., Thibodaux, La., 1958–62, and at Bowman-Gray Medical Sch., Winston-Salem, 1962–70. *Publs:* Growing Up in Tier 3000, 1975; The Last Americans, 1980. Add: 3103 Hungary Spring Rd., Richmond, Va. 23228, U.S.A.

GOTT, Richard (Willoughby). British, b. 1938. International relations/Current affairs, Third World problems. Features Ed., The Guardian, since 1978. Research Asst., Royal Inst. of Intnl. Affairs, London, 1962–65; Leader Writer, Guardian newspaper, London, 1964–66; Research Fellow, Inst. of Intnl. Studies, Univ. of Chile, Santiago, 1966–69; Foreign Ed., The Standard, Dar Es Salaam, Tanzania, 1970–72; Dir., Latin American Newsletters Ltd., 1976–80. *Publs:* (co-ed.) Documents on International Affairs, 1960; (with M. Gilbert) The Appeasers, 1963; (with J. Gittings) NATO's Final Decade, 1964; (with J. Gittings) The End of the Alliance, 1965; Mobuto's Congo, 1968; Guerilla Movements in Latin America, 1970; Close Your Frontiers: Development as the Ideology of Imperialism, 1983. Add: c/o The Guardian, 119 Farringdon Rd., London EC1, England.

GOTTSCHALK, Laura Riding. *See* RIDING, Laura.

GOTTSHALL, Franklin H. American, b. 1902. Crafts. Retired teacher of Industrial Arts. *Publs:* Simple Colonial Furniture, 1931; How to Design Period Furniture, 1937; Design for the Craftsman, 1940; (with A.W. Hellum) You Can Whittle and Carve, 1942; Making Useful Things of Wood, 1950; Woodwork for the Beginner, 1952; Craftwork in Metal, Wood, Leather, Plastics, 1954; Heirloom Furniture, 1957; Wood Carving and Whittling Made Easy, 1963; Furniture of Pine, Poplar, and Maple, 1966; How to Make Colonial Furniture, 1971; Reproducing Antique Furniture, 1971; Wood Carving and Whittling for Everyone, 1977; Masterpiece Furniture Making, 1979; Provincial Furniture: Design and Construction, 1983. Add: 604 E. 4th St., Boyertown, Pa. 19512, U.S.A.

GÖTZ, Ignacio L. Venezuelan, b. 1933. Education. Prof. of Philosophy of Education since 1977, and Dir. Special Studies Prog., Hofstra Univ., Hempstead, N.Y. (Adjunct Asst. Prof., 1966–68; Asst. Prof., 1968–72; Assoc. Prof., 1972–77). Ordained Roman Catholic Priest, 1962. *Publs:* (trans.) Pavitra Gulabmâlâ, 1962; Joseph Fletcher's Situation Ethics and Education, 1968; (ed.) No Schools, 1971; The Psychedelic Teacher, 1972; Creativity, 1978. Add: 386 California Ave., Uniondale, N.Y. 11553, U.S.A.

GOULART, Ron(ald Joseph). Also writes as Josephine Kains, Howard Lee, Kenneth Robeson, Frank S. Shawn, and Con Steffanson. American, b. 1933. Novels/Short stories, Mystery/Crime/Suspense, Science fiction/Fantasy, Literature. Full-time writer since 1968. Formerly, advertising copywriter. *Publs:* fiction—The Sword Swallowers, 1968; After Things Fell Apart, 1970; The Fire Eater, 1970; What's Become of Screwloose and Other Stories, 1971; Ghost Breaker (short stories), 1971; If Dying Was All, 1971; Gadget Man, 1971; Death Cell, 1971; Clockwork's Pirates, 1971; Broke Down Engine (stories), 1971; Hawkshaw, 1972; Too Sweet to Die, 1972; Plunder, 1972; The Chameleon Corps (stories), 1972; Wildsmith, 1972; The Same Lie Twice, 1973; Cleopatra Jones (novelization of screenplay), 1973; Shaggy Planet, 1973; A Talent for the Invisible, 1973; (as Howard Lee) Superstition (novelization of tv play), 1973; The Tin Angel, 1973; (as Frank S. Shawn) The Veiled Lady, 1973; (as Frank S. Shawn) The Golden Circle, 1973; (as Frank S. Shawn) The Mystery of the Sea Horse, 1973; One Grave Too Many, 1974; (as Kenneth Robeson) The Man from Atlantis, 1974; (as Kenneth Robeson) Red Moon, 1974; (as Kenneth Robeson) The Purple Zombie, 1974; (as Kenneth Robeson) Dr. Time, 1974; (as Kenneth Robeson) The Nightwitch Devil, 1974; (as Kenneth Robeson) Black Chariots, 1974; (as Kenneth Robeson) The Cartoon Crimes, 1974; (as Kenneth Robeson) The Iron Skull, 1974; Flux, 1974; (as Frank S. Shawn) The Hydra Monster, 1974; (as Frank S. Shawn) The Goggle-Eyed Pirates, 1974; (as Frank S. Shawn) The Swamp Rats, 1974; (as Con Steffanson) The Lion Men of Mongo, 1974 (as Con Steffanson) The Plague of Sound, 1974; (as Con Steffanson) The Space Circus, 1974; Cleopatra Jones and the Casino of Gold (novelization of screenplay), 1975; Spacehawk, Inc., 1975; (as Kenneth Robeson) The Death Machine, 1975; (as Kenneth Robeson) The Blood Countess, 1975; (as Kenneth Robeson) The Glass Man, 1975; (as Kenneth Robeson) Demon Island, 1975; Odd Job: 101 and Other Future Crimes and Intriques (stories), 1975; When the Waker Sleeps, 1975; The Tremendous Adventures of Bernie Wine, 1975; Bloodtalk (novelization of comic strip), 1975; On Alien Wings (novelization of comic strip), 1975; The Hellhound Project, 1975; A Whiff of Madness, 1975; Nutzenbolts (stories), 1975; The Enormous Hourglass, 1976; Quest of the Gypsy, 1976; Deadwalk (novelization of comic strip), 1976; (as Con Steffanson) Laverne and Shirley: Teamwork (Easy Money, Gold Rush), 3 vols. (novelization of a tv play), 1976; Crackpot, 1977; The Emperor of the Last Days, 1977; The Panchronicon Plot, 1977; Nemo, 1977; Eye of the Vulture, 1977; Calling Dr. Patchwork, 1978; The Wicked Cyborg, 1978; (as Josephine Kains) The Devil Mask Mystery, 1978; (as Josephine Kains) Curse of the Golden Skull, 1978; (as Josephine Kains) Green Lama Mystery, 1979; Cowboy Heaven, 1979; Hello, Lemuria, Hello, 1979; Empire 99, 1980; Hail Hibbler, 1980; Skyrocket Steele, 1980; The Cyborg King, 1981; Brinkman, 1981; Upside Down, 1982; Big Bang, 1982; Greetings from Earth, 1983; Experiment in Terra, 1984; The Long Patrol, 1984; Hellquad, 1984; The Prisoner of Blackwood Castle, 1984; Gravey and of My Own, 1985; Galaxy Jane, 1986; The Wiseman Originals, 1989; other—(ed.) The Hardboiled Dicks: An Anthology and Study of Pulp Detective Fiction, 1965; (ed.) Lineup Tough Guys, 1966; The Assault on Childhood, 1969; Cheap Thrills: An Informal History of the Pulp Magazines, 1972; An American Family, 1973; The Adventurous Decade: Comic Strips in the Thirties, 1975; (ed.) The Great British Detective, 1982; Great History of Comic Books, 1986; The Great Comic Book Artists, 1986; The Dime Detectives, 1988. Add: 30 Farrell Rd., Weston, Conn. 06883, U.S.A.

GOULD, Cecil (Hilton Monk). British, b. 1918. Art. Asst. Keeper, 1946–52, Deputy Keeper, 1962–73, and Keeper and Deputy Dir., 1973–78, The National Gallery, London. *Publs:* An Introduction to Italian Renaissance Painting, 1957; Trophy of Conquest, 1965; Leonardo da Vinci, 1975; The Paintings of Correggio, 1976; Bernini in France, 1981. Add: Jubilee House, Thornecombe, Somerset TA20 4PP, England.

GOULD, James A. American, b. 1922. Philosophy, Politics/Government. Prof. and Chmn., Dept. of Philosophy, Univ of South Florida, since 1967 (Assoc. Prof., 1964–67). Instr., Univ. of Miami, Coral Gables, 1952–57; Asst. Prof., Emory Univ., Atlanta, Ga., 1957–62; Assoc. Prof., Florida State Univ., Tallahassee, 1962–64. *Publs:* (with I. Copi) Readings on Logic, 1964, 1972; (with Copi) Contemporary Readings in Logical Theory, 1967; Eleven Philosophical Problems, 1968; (with V. Thursby) Contemporary Political Thought, 1969; (with A.K. Bierman) Philosophy for a New Generation, 1970, 4th ed. 1981; (with R. Dewey) Freedom: The Philosophical Problems, 1970; (with C. Kiefer) The Western Humanities, vols. I & II, 1971; Classical Philosophical Questions, 1971, 6th ed. 1989; (with I. Deer) Person to Person Reader, 1972; (with J.J. Iorio) Love, Sex, and Identity, 1972; (with Iorio) Violence and Literature in the 20th Century, 1972; (with Bierman and J. Needleman) Religion for a New Generation, 1973, 1977; (with W. Truitt) Political

Philosophies, 1973; (with Truitt) Existentialism, 1973; (with I. Copi) Contemporary Philosophical Logic, 1978. Add: Dept. of Philosophy, Univ. of South Florida, Tampa, Fla. 33620, U.S.A.

GOULD, Jean R. American, b. 1919. Children's fiction, Art, Children's non-fiction, Literature, Biography. Involved in editorial and re-write work, National Education Office, 1952–62, and Ed., Legislative Newsletter, 1957–58, Amalgamated Clothing Workers union. *Publs:* Fairy Tales, 1944; Miss Emily, 1946; Jane, 1947; Young Thack, 1949; Sidney Hillman: Great American, 1952; Fisherman's Luck, 1954; (co-author and ed.) Homegrown Liberal, 1954; Young Mariner Melville, 1956; That Dunbar Boy, 1958; A Good Fight: FDR's Conquest of Polio, 1960; Winslow Homer: A Portrait, 1962; Robert Frost: The Aim Was Song, 1964; Modern American Playwrights, 1966; The Poet and Her Book: A Biography of Edna St. Vincent Millay, 1969; (with L. Hickok) Walter Reuther: Labor's Rugged Individualist, 1972; Amy: The World of Amy Lowell and the Imagist Movement, 1975; American Women Poets: Pioneers of Modern Poetry, 1980; Modern American Women Poets, 1985. Add: c/o Dodd Mead & Co., 71 Fifth Ave., 6th Fl., New York, N.Y. 10003, U.S.A.

GOULD, Lois. American. Novels/Short stories, Social commentary/phenomena, Essays, Humor/Satire. *Publs:* (with Waldo L. Fielding) Sensible Childbirth (non-fiction), 1962; So You Want to Be a Working Mother! (humour), 1966; Such Good Friends, 1970; Necessary Objects, 1972; Final Analysis, 1974; A Sea-Change, 1976; Not Responsible for Personal Articles (essays), 1978; X: A Fabulous Child's Story, 1979; La Presidenta, 1981. Add: c/o Carol E. Rinzler, Remban and Curtis, 19 W. 44th St., New York, N.Y. 10036, U.S.A.

GOULD, Peter (Robin). British, b. 1932. Environmental science/Ecology, Human Relations, Philosophy, Regional/Urban planning, Social sciences, Transportation. Evan Pugh Prof. of Geography, Pennsylvania State Univ., University Park, since 1963. Consulting Ed., Environment and Planning, Geographical Analysis, L'Espace Geographique, Geografia, Mappemond, Journal of Geography in Higher Education, and Journal of Geography; Dir., Social Science Research Council, 1977–80 (Member of Corp., 1980). *Publs:* Transportation in Ghana, 1960; Africa: Continent of Change, 1961; Spatial Diffusion, 1969; (with J. Adams and R. Abler) Spatial Organisation: The Geographer's View of the World, 1971; (with G. Tonqvist, R. Nordbeck and B. Rystedt) Multiple Location Analysis, 1972; (with R. White) Mental Maps, 1974; People in Information Space, 1974; (with G. Olsson) A Search for Common Ground, 1982; (with J. Johnson and G. Chapman) The Structure of Television, 1984; The Geographer at Work, 1985. Add: 306 Walker Bldg., University Park, Pa. 16802, U.S.A.

GOULD, Stephen Jay. American, b. 1941. Biology, Earth Sciences, Zoology. Prof. of Geology, Alexander Agassiz Prof. of Zoology, and Curator of Invertebrate Paleontology, Museum of Comparative Zoology, Harvard Univ., Cambridge, since 1973 (Asst. Prof. of Geology and Asst. Curator, 1967–71; Assoc. Prof. of Geology and Assoc. Curator, 1971–73). Pres., Paleontological Soc; Columnist ("This View of Life"), Natural History Magazine, since 1974. *Publs:* Ontogeny and Phylogeny, 1977; Ever Since Darwin, 1977; The Panda's Thumb, 1980 (American Book Award); The Mismeasure of Man, 1981 (National Book Critics Circle Award); Hen's Teeth and Horse's Toes, 1983; The Flamingo's Smile, 1985; Time's Arrow, Time's Cycle, 1987. Add: Museum of Comparative Zoology, Harvard Univ., Cambridge, Mass. 02138, U.S.A.

GOULDEN, Joseph C. American, b. 1934. History, Institutions/Organizations, Military/Defence. *Publs:* The Curtis Caper, 1965; Monopoly: A Muckraking Study of AT & T, 1968; Truth Is the First Casualty: The Tonkin Gulf Incidents, 1969; The Money Givers: The Great American Foundations, 1971; The SuperLawyers: The Small and Powerful World of the Great Washington Law Firms, 1972; Meany: The Unchallenged Strong Man of American Labor, 1972; The Benchwarmers: The Private World of the Federal Judiciary, 1974; The Best Years, 1976; (ed.) Mencken's Last Campaign, 1976; The Million Dollar Lawyers, 1978; Korea: The Untold Story, 1982; (with Paul A. Dickson) There Are Alligators in Our Sewers, 1983; The Death Merchant, 1984; (as Henry S.A. Becket) A Dictionary of Espionage, 1986; Fit to Print: A. M. Rosenthal and His Times, 1988. Add: 1534 29th St., N.W., Washington, D.C. 20007, U.S.A.

GOULDING, Peter Geoffrey. British, b. 1920. Country Life, Sports. Freelance writer and photographer. Former Asst. ed., Shooting Times, and Country Magazine. *Publs:* The British Heavy Horse, 1976; Sporting

Hotels and Inns, 1980. Add: Glebe Cottage, Romansleigh, S. Molton, N. Devon, England.

GOURDIE, Tom. British, b. 1913. Design. Freelance writer, lectr., and artist. Visiting Prof. of Calligraphy, Southeastern Massachusetts Univ. Art Master, The High Sch., Kirkcaldy, 1946–74. *Publs:* Italic Handwriting, 1955; Puffin Book of Lettering, 1961; Das Schift Schreiben, 1963; The Simple Modern Hand, 1965; The Ladybird Book of Handwriting, 1968; Guide to Better Handwriting, 1969; Handwriting for Today, 1971; I Can Write, 1974; Improve Your Handwriting, 1974; (with Ronald Ridout) Introductory Books to Write in English, 1977; Modern Primary English for Hong Kong, 1977; Twenty Favourite Songs and Poems of Robert Burns, 1978; Calligraphic Styles, 1978; Calligraphy for Beginners, 1979; The Alpha Lettering Books, 1979; Practice in Handwriting, 1980; Puffin Book of Handwriting, 1980; Teaching Children to Write, 1981; Remedial Handwriting, 1982; Complete Guide to Calligraphy, 1984. Add: 3 Douglas St., Kirkcaldy, Fife, Scotland.

GOURLAY, David. British, b. 1922. Novels/Short stories, Plays. Head of Dept. of History and English, Rudolph Steiner Sch. of Edinburgh, since 1979. Asst. Lectr., Dept. of Biblical Studies, 1952–55, and Chaplain, 1955–63, Glasgow Univ.; Member, Editorial Staff, 1964–68, and Education Corresp., 1966–68, The Guardian newspaper, London; Warden, Melbourne Univ. Union, 1968–71; Member, English Dept., Queen Elizabeth Coll., Palmerston North, New Zealand, 1971–74; Warden, Carrington Hall, Univ. of Otago, New Zealand, 1974–76. *Publs:* The Beatitudes, 1952; Circle of Grace (radio play), 1954; Busload of Saints (radio play), 1956; Once Upon a Subway, 1960; The Chancellor Regrets, 1970; Once a Wolf Always a Wolf, 1973; The Fan, 1974; Ballista, 1982; The Forth Estate, 1984; The Paradise Trust, 1986. Add: 16 Bell Place, Stockbridge, Edinburgh, Scotland.

GOVER, (John) Robert. American, b. 1929. Novels/Short stories. Reporter on newspapers in Pa. and Md., until 1961. *Publs:* One Hundred Dollar Misunderstanding, 1962; The Maniac Responsible, 1963; Here Goes Kitten, 1964; Poorboy at the Party, 1966; J.C. Saves, 1968; (ed.) The Portable Walter: From the Poetry and Prose of Walter Lowenfels, 1968; Luke Small Tells All, 1973; Going for Mr. Big, 1973; (as O. Govi) Tomorrow Now Occurs Again, 1975; (as O. Govi) Getting Pretty on the Table, 1975; Bring Me the Head of Rona Barrett (stories), 1981. Add: Gen. Delivery, Carpinteria, Calif. 93013.

GOW, Ronald. British, b. 1897. Plays/Screenplays. *Publs:* Breakfast at Eight, 1920; The Sausage, 1924; Under the Skull and Bones: A Piratical Play with Songs, 1929; Higgins: The Highwayman of Cranford, 1930; Henry: or, The House on the Moor, 1931; Five Robin Hood Plays, 1932; The Golden West, 1932; The Vengeance of the Gang, 1933; Plays for the Classroom, 1933; O.H.M.S., 1933; Gallows Glorious (in U.S. as John Brown), 1933; My Lady Wears a White Cockade, 1934; (adaptor) Love on the Dole, 1934; Compromise, 1935; The Marrying Sort, 1935; The Miracle on Watling Street: A Play for the Open Air, 1935; Ma's Bit o' Brass, 1938; Scuttleboom's Treasure, 1938; Grannie's a Hundred, 1939; The Lawyer of Springfield, 1940; (adaptor) Ann Veronica, 1951; (adaptor) The Edwardians, 1959; (adaptor) A Boston Story, 1964. Add: 9 Stratton Rd., Beaconsfield, Bucks., England.

GOWANS, Alan. American, b. 1923. Architecture, Art. Instr., Rutgers Univ., New Jersey, 1948–53; Asst. Prof., Middlebury Coll., Vermont, 1953–54; Asst. Prof. and Dir. of the Univ. Museum, Univ. of Vermont, 1954–56; Assoc. Prof. and Chmn., 1956–60, and Prof. and Chmn. Assoc., 1960–66, Univ. of Delaware; Prof. of History in Art, Univ. of Victoria, 1966–88. Secty., 1957–64, First Vice-Pres., 1968–70, and Pres., 1970–74, Soc. of Architectural Historians. *Publs:* Church Architecture in France, 1955; Looking at Architecture in Canada, 1958; The Face of Toronto (photographs by Ralph Greenhill), 1960; Images of American Living: Four Centuries of Architecture and Furniture, 1964; Architecture in New Jersey, 1964; The Restless Art: A Study of Painting and Painters in Society 1750-1950, 1966; Building Canada: An Architectural History of Canadian Life, 1967; King Carter's Church, 1969; The Unchanging Arts: A Study of the Living Arts of Society, 1971; On Parallels in Universal History Discoverable in Arts and Artifacts, 1974; Learning to See, 1981; Prophetic Allegory: E.C. Segar's Popeye and the American Dream, 1982; The Comfortable House: Suburban Architecture 1890-1930, 1986. Add: 524-2020 St. N.W., Washington, D.C. 20006, U.S.A.

GOWER, Iris. Pseud. for Iris Davies. British, b. 1939. Historical/Romance. *Publs:* The Copper Cloud, 1976; Return to Tip Row, 1977; Beloved Captive, 1981; Beloved Traitor, 1981; Sweyn's Eye series—Copper Kingdom, 1983; Proud Mary, 1984; Spinner's Wharf, 1985; Morgan's

Woman, 1986; Fiddler's Ferry, 1987; Black Gold, 1988. Add: 16 Major St., Manselton, Swansea, W. Glamorgan SA5 9NN, Wales.

GOWING, (Sir) Lawrence (Burnett). British, b. 1918. Art. Trustee, National Portrait Gallery, since 1960. Prof. of Fine Art, Univ. of Durham, and Principal of King Edward VII Sch. of Art, Newcastle upon Tyne, 1948–58; Principal, Chelsea Sch. of Art, London, 1958–65; Trustee, 1953–60 and 1961–64, Keeper of the British Collection, and Deputy Dir., 1965–67, Tate Gallery, London; Prof. of Fine Arts, Univ. of London, 1967–75; Slade Prof. of Fine Art, University Coll., London, 1975–85. Member, Art Panel, 1953–58, 1959–65 and 1969–72, Member, Deputy Chmn., and Chmn. of the Art Films Cttee., 1970–72, Arts Council of Great Britain; Chmn., Advisory Cttee. on Painting, Gulbenkian Foundn., 1958–64; Member, National Council for Diplomas in Art and Design, 1961–65. *Publs:* Renoir, 1947; Vermeer, 1952, 1961; Constable, 1960; Goya, 1965; Turner: Imagination and Reality, 1966; Matisse, 1966; Hogarth, 1971; Watercolours by Cezanne, 1973; Matisse, 1979; Lucian Freud, 1982; (ed.) The Encyclopedia of Visual Arts, 2 vols., 1983; The Originality of Thomas Jones, 1986; Paintings in the Louvre, 1987; Paul Cezanne: The Basic Sketchbooks, 1988; Cezanne: The Early Years, 1988. Add: 49 Walham Grove, London SW6, England.

GOWING, Margaret Mary. British, b. 1921. Business/Trade/Industry, Economics, Sciences, Technology. Trustee, National Portrait Gallery, London, since 1978. Civil servant, 1941–45; Historian, U.K. Cabinet Office, 1945–59; Historian and Archivist, U.K. Atomic Energy Authority, 1959–66; Reader in Contemporary History, Univ. of Kent, 1966–73; Prof. of History of Science, Oxford Univ., 1973–86. *Publs:* (with Sir Keith Hancock) British War Economy, 1949; (with E.L. Hargreaves) Civil Industry and Trade, 1952; Britain and Atomic Energy 1939–1945; 1964; Independence and Deterence: vol. I—Policy Making, vol. II—Policy Execution, 1974. Add: Linacre Coll., Oxford, England.

GOYDER, George Armin. British, b. 1908. Economics, Sociology, Theology/Religion. Chmn. and Managing Dir., British Intnl. Paper Ltd., 1935–71; Gen. Mgr., Newsprint Supply Co., 1940–47. *Publs:* The Future of Private Enterprise, 1951, 1954; The Responsible Company, 1961; The People's Church, 1966; The Responsible Worker, 1975; The Just Enterprise, 1987. Add: Mansel Hall, Long Melford, Sudbury, Suffolk, England.

GRACE, Patricia (Frances). New Zealand, b. 1937. Novels/Short Stories, Children's fiction. Teacher in primary and secondary schools in King Country, Northland, and Porirua. *Publs:* Waiariki (short stories), 1975; Mutuwhenua: The Moon Sleeps (novel), 1978; The Dream Sleepers and Other Stories, 1980; The Kuia and the Spider (for children), 1981; Wahine Toa: Women of Maori Myth (for children), 1984; Watercress Tuna and the Children of Champion Street (for children), 1984; He aha te mea nui? Ma wai? Ko au tenei, and Ahakoa he iti (Maori readers for children), 4 vols., 1985; Potiki (novel), 1986; Electric City (short stories), 1987. Add: c/o Penguin New Zealand Ltd., Private Bag, Takapuna, Auckland 9, New Zealand.

GRACY, David B(ergen) II. American, b. 1941. History. Assoc. Ed., Military History of Texas and the Southwest, since 1962; Dir., Texas State Archives, since 1977; Lectr. to Sr. Lectr., Grad. Sch. of Library and Information Science, Univ. of Texas at Austin, since 1980; Coordinator, Texas Historical Records Advisory Bd., since 1979; U.S. Resp., Archives Cttee., Pan American Inst. of Geography and History, since 1962. Member, Bd. of Dirs., Historical Soc. of the Episcopal Church, since 1978; Editorial Asst., Southwestern Historical Quarterly, Austin, Tex., 1963–66; Archivist, Southwest Collection, Texas Tech Univ., Lubbock, 1966–71; Archivist, Asst. Prof., and Assoc. Prof. of Urban Life, Georgia State Univ., Atlanta, 1971–77. Pres., Soc. of Georgia Archivists, 1972–74; Ed., Georgia Archive: Journal of the Soc. of Georgia Archivists, 1972;76; Adjunct Prof. of History, DeKalb Community Coll., 1973–74; Member, Georgia Historical Records Advisory Bd., 1976; Member, Editorial Bd., American Archivist, 1976–79; Member of Council, 1976–80; and Vice-Pres. to Pres., 1982–84, Soc. of American Archivists; Member, National Cttee. for the Preservation of Architectural Records, 1978–80; Member, National Historial Publs. and Records Cmmn., 1980–85. *Publs:* (ed.) Maxey's Texas, 1965; Littlefield Lands, 1968; (ed.) Establishing Austin's Colony, 1970; Archives and Manuscripts: Arrangement and Description, 1977; (with J. Carefoot) Ships of the Texas Navy, 1979; An Introduction to Archives and Manuscripts, 1981. Add: Texas State Archives, Box 12927, Austin, Tex. 78711, U.S.A.

GRADY, Peter. *See* **DANIELS,** Norman A.

GRAEBNER, Norman Arthur. American, b. 1915. International relations/Current affairs, Politics/Government. Contrib. Ed., Current History. Asst. Prof. to Prof., Iowa State Univ., Ames, 1948–56; Prof. of History, 1956–67, and Chmn., Dept. of History, 1961–63; Univ. of Illinois, Urbana; Prof. of History, Univ. of Virginia, Charlottesville, 1967–86. Harmsworth Prof. of American History, Oxford Univ., 1978–79. *Publs:* Empire on the Pacific, 1955; The New Isolationism, 1956; (ed.) The Enduring Lincoln, 1959; (ed.) An Uncertain Tradition: American Secretaries of State in the Twentieth Century, 1961; (ed.) Politics and the Crisis of 1860, 1961; Cold War Diplomacy, 1962, 1977; (ed.) The Cold War: Conflict of Ideology and Power, 1963, 1976; Ideas and Diplomacy, 1964; (ed.) Manifest Destiny, 1968; (with G.C. Fite and P.L. White) A History of the United States, 2 vols., 1970; (with G.C. Fite and P.L. White) A History of the American People, 1970, 1975; (with G.C. Fite) Recent United States History, 1972; (ed.) Nationalism and Communism in Asia: The American Response, 1977; (ed.) Freedom in America: A 200-Year Perspective, 1977; (ed.) American Diplomatic History Before 1900, 1978; The Age of Global Power, 1979; America as a World Power, 1984; (ed.) Traditions and Values: American Diplomacy 1790-1945, 2 vols., 1985; Foundations of American Foreign Policy, 1985; (ed.) The National Security: Its Theory and Practice in the United States 1945-1960, 1986. Add: 542 Worthington Dr., Charlottesville, VA 22901, U.S.A.

GRAEME, Roderic. *See* **JEFFRIES,** Roderic.

GRAFF, Henry Franklin. American, b. 1921. History. Prof. of History, Columbia Univ., NYC, since 1961 (joined faculty, 1946; Chmn., Dept. of History, 1961–63). *Publs:* Bluejackets with Perry in Japan, 1952; (with J. Barzun) The Modern Researcher, 1962, 4th ed. 1985; (with C. Lord) American Themes, 1963; Thomas Jefferson, 1968; The Free and the Brave, 1967, 4th ed., 1980; (ed.) American Imperialism and the Philippine Insurrection, 1969; The Tuesday Cabinet: Deliberation and Decision on Peace and War under Lyndon B. Johnson, 1970; (with J.A. Krout) The Adventure of the American People, 3rd ed., 1973; (with P.J. Bohannan) The Grand Experiment, vol. I, The Call of Freedom, and vol. II, The Promise of Democracy, 1978; This Great Nation, 1983; The Presidents: A Reference History, 1984; America: The Glorious Republic, 1985, 3rd ed. 1990. Add: Dept. of History, Columbia Univ., 617 Fayerweather Hall, New York, N.Y. 10027, U.S.A.

GRAHAM, Ada. American, b. 1931. Children's non-fiction. Developer and Writer, Audubon Adventures (National Audubon Society), since 1984. Vice-Chmn., Maine State Commn. on the Arts, 1975–80; Bd. Member, New England Foundn. for the Arts, 1977–80; Member, Bd. of Dirs., Maine Family Planning Assn., 1973–80. *Publs:* (with Frank Graham) The Great American Shopping Cart, 1969; (with F. Graham) Wildlife Rescue, 1970; (with F. Graham) Puffing Island, 1971; The Mystery of the Everglades, 1972; Dooryard Garden, 1974; Let's Discover the Winter Woods, 1974; Let's Discover the Floor of the Forest, 1974; Let's Discover Changes Everywhere, 1974; Let's Discover Birds in Our World, 1974; The Careless Animal, 1974; (with F. Graham) The Milkweed and Its World of Animals, 1976; Foxtails, Ferns and Fishscales: A Handbook of Art and Nature Projects, 1976; Whale Watch, 1978; Bug Hunters, 1978; Coyote Song, 1978; Falcon Flight, 1978; (with F. Graham) Audubon Readers, 6 vols., 1978–81; (with F. Graham) Alligators, 1979; (with F. Graham) Careers in Conservation, 1980; (with F. Graham) Birds of the Northern Seas, 1981; Bears, 1981; (with F. Graham) The Changing Desert, 1981; (with F. Graham) Jacob and the Owl, 1981; (with F. Graham) Three Million Mice, 1981; Six Little Chickadees, 1982; (with F. Graham) Busy Bugs, 1983; (with F. Graham) The Big Stretch, 1985; (with F. Graham) We Watch Squirrels, 1985. Add: Milbridge, Me. 04658, U.S.A.

GRAHAM, Alexander John. British, b. 1930. History. Prof. of Classical Studies, Univ. of Pennsylvania, Philadelphia, since 1977. Asst. Lectr. in Classics, Bedford Coll., Univ. of London, 1955–57; Lectr., in History, Univ. of Manchester, 1957–77. *Publs:* Colony and Mother City in Ancient Greece, 1964; (ed.) Polis und Imperium Beiträge zur alten Geschichte, by Victor Ehrenberg, 1965; An Attic Country House, Below the Cane of Pan at Vari, 1974. Add: Dept. of Classical Studies, 720 Williams Hall, Univ. of Pennsylvania, Philadelphia, Pa. 19104, U.S.A.

GRAHAM, Billy. (William F. Graham). American, b. 1918. Theology/Religion. Evangelist; Founder, Billy Graham Evangelistic Assn., since 1950; Leader of the weekly radio program, Hour of Decision, since 1950; Author of the syndicated newspaper column, My Answer, since 1952; known for world evangelistic campaigns. Ordained Southern Baptist Minister, 1940; Pastor, First Baptist Church, Western Springs, Ill., 1943–45; First Vice-Pres., Youth for Christ Intn., Chicago, 1945–50; Pres., Northwestern Coll., Minneapolis, 1947–52. *Publs:* Peace with God, 1953; The Secret of Happiness, 1955; My Answer, 1960; World Aflame, 1965; The Challenge, 1969; The Jesus Generation, 1971; Angels: God's Secret Agents, 1976; Billy Graham Talks to Teenagers, 1976; How to Be Born Again, 1977; The Holy Spirit, 1979; Till Armageddon, 1981; Approaching Hoofbeats: The Four Horseman of the Apocalypse, 1983; A Biblical Standard for Evangelists, 1984; Unto the Hills, 1986; Facing Death and the Life After, 1987; Answers to Life's Problems, 1988. Add: 1300 Harmon Pl., Minneapolis, Minn. 55403, U.S.A.

GRAHAM, Bob. (Robert Graham). Australian, b. 1942. Children's fiction, Children's non-fiction, Literary criticism/history. Artist, New South Wales. Govt. Printers, Sydney, 1973–75; Resource Designer, Dept. of Technical Education, Sydney, 1975–82; Illustrator, Five Mile Press, Melbourne, 1982–85. *Publs:* Children's fiction (all self-illustrated)—A Boggle of Bunyips, 1981; Pete and Roland, 1981; Here Comes John, 1983; Here Comes Theo, 1983; Pearl's Place, 1983; Libby, Oscar and Me, 1984; Bath Time for John, 1985; First There Was Frances, 1985; Where Is Sarah?, 1985; The Wild, 1986; The Adventures of Charlotte and Henry, 19876; Crusher Is Coming!, 1987; The Red Woollen Blanket, 1987; Has Anyone Seen William?, 1988; children's non-fiction (readers)—I Can series: Actions 1, Actions 2, Babies, Bikes, Colour, Families, Helping, In the Water, My Senses, Pets, School, Shopping, 12 vols., 1984, in U.K. as Reading Is Fun series, 12 vols., 1986; Science Early Learners series: Heat, Moving, Push, Senses, Sound, Water, Wheels, 7 vols., 1985–86; Busy Day Board Books: Playing, Sleeping, Waking, 3 vols., 1988; other—(ed.) A First Australian Poetry Book, 1983. Add: Lot 8, Mt. Dandenong Rd., Mt. Dandenong, Vic. 3767, Australia.

GRAHAM, Brother. *See* **JEFFERY,** Graham.

GRAHAM, Charles S. *See* **TUBB,** E.C.

GRAHAM, Desmond. British, b. 1940. Literature, Biography. Sr. Lectr. in English Literature, Univ. of Newcastle upon Tyne, since 1971. Visiting Lectr., Munich Univ., Germany, 1968–70; Mannheim Univ., 1970–71, and Gdansk Univ., Poland, 1984. Corresp., Opera News, NYC, 1969–71. *Publs:* Introduction to Poetry, 1968; Keith Douglas 1920-1944: A Biography, 1974; (ed.) The Complete Poems of Keith Douglas, 1978; (ed.) Alamein to Zem Zem, by Keith Douglas, 1979; The Truth of War: Owen, Blunden, and Rosenberg, 1984; (ed.) A Prose Miscellany, by Keith Douglas, 1985. Add: 7 Swinburne Pl., Newcastle upon Tyne NE4 6AE, England.

GRAHAM, Frank, Jr. American, b. 1925. Children's non-fiction, Environmental science/Ecology. Field Ed., Audubon mag., since 1968. *Publs:* (with M. Allen) It Takes Heart, 1959; Disaster by Default, 1966; (with Ada Graham) The Great American Shopping Cart, 1969; Since Silent Spring, 1970; (with A. Graham) Wildlife Rescue, 1970; (with A. Graham) Puffin Island, 1971; Man's Dominion, 1971; (with A. Graham) The Mystery of the Everglades, 1972; Where the Place Called Morning Lies, 1973; (with A. Graham) Aububon Primers, 4 vols., 1974; (with A. Graham) The Careless Animal, 1975; Gulls: A Social History, 1975; Potomac: The Nation's River, 1976; (with A. Graham) The Milkweed and Its World of Animals, 1976; The Adirondack Park: A Political History, 1978; (with A. Graham) Audubon Readers, 6 vols., 1978–81; (with A. Graham) Careers in Conservation, 1980; (with A. Graham) Birds of the Northern Seas, 1981; A Farewell to Heroes, 1981; (with A. Graham) The Changing Desert, 1981; (with A. Graham) Jacob and the Owl, 1981; (with A. Graham) Three Million Mice, 1981; (with A. Graham) Busy Bugs, 1983; The Dragon Hunters, 1984; (with A. Graham) The Big Stretch, 1985; (with A. Graham) We Watch Squirrels, 1985. Add: Milbridge, Me. 04658, U.S.A.

GRAHAM, Henry. British, b. 1930. Poetry. Lectr. in Art History, Liverpool Polytechnic, since 1969. Poetry Ed., Ambit mag., London. Former artist. *Publs:* (with J. Mangnall) Soup City Zoo: Poems, 1968; Good Luck to You Kafta/You'll Need It Boss, 1969; Passport to Earth, 1971; Europe after Rain, 1982; The Very Fragrant Death of Paul Gauguin, 1986. Add: 37 Lindale Rd., Liverpool 7, England.

GRAHAM, Hugh (Davis). American, b. 1936. Politics/Government, History. Prof. of History, Univ. of Maryland, Baltimore County, since 1972 (Dean of Social Sciences, 1971–77, Dean of Grad. Studies and Research, 1982–85), Assoc. Prof., 1967–71, and former Acting Dir., Inst. of Southern History, Johns Hopkins Univ., Baltimore, Md. *Publs:* Crisis in Print, 1967; (co-ed.) Violence in America, 1969, 1979; (ed.) Huey Long, 1970; (ed.) Violence, 1971; Since 1954: School Desegregation, 1972; (co-author) Southern Politics and the Second Reconstruction, 1975; (ed.) Government and Politics, 1975; (co-ed.) Southern Elections, 1978;

The Uncertain Triumph, 1984. Add: 205 Tunbridge, Baltimore, Md. 21212, U.S.A.

GRAHAM, James. *See* **PATTERSON**, Henry.

GRAHAM, John. American, b. 1926. Children's fiction, Literature. Assoc. Prof., Dept. of Rhetoric, Univ. of Virginia, since 1967 (Instr. in English, 1958–61; Asst. Prof., 1961–67). *Publs:* A Crowd of Cows (for children), 1968; (ed.) Great American Speeches, 1970; (ed. and contrib.) Studies in A Farewell to Arms, 1971; (ed. and contrib.) Studies in Second Skin, 1971; Craft So Hard to Learn (interviews), 1972; The Writer's Voice (interviews), 1973; I Love You Mouse (for children), 1976; Lavater's Essays on Physiognomy, 1979. Add: 1 Dawson's Row, Univ. of Virginia, Charlottesville, Va. 22903, U.S.A.

GRAHAM, Jorie. American, b. 1951. Poetry. Member of staff, University of Iowa, since 1983. Formerly taught at California State Univ., Humboldt, 1979–81, and Columbia Univ., NYC, 1981–83. *Publs:* Hybrids of Plants and of Ghosts, 1980; Erosion, 1983; The End of Beauty, 1987. Add: 436 EPB, Univ. of Iowa, Iowa City, Iowa 52242, U.S.A.

GRAHAM, Lorenz. American, b. 1902. Children's fiction, Children's non-fiction. Teacher, Monrovia Coll., Liberia, Africa, 1924–29; Teacher, Advisor, and Admin. in U.S. Govt. education progs., Virginia and Pennsylvania, 1933–43; Social Worker, New York, 1944–56; Probation officer, Los Angeles, 1957–67; Lectr., English Dept., California State Univ., Pomona, 1970–78. Pres. Los Angeles Center, P.E.N. Intnl., 1970–72. *Publs:* How God Fix Jonah, 1946; Tales of Momolu, Life of an African Boy, 1947; The Story of Jesus, 1955; The Ten Commandments, 1956; South Town, 1958; North Town, 1965; I, Momolu, 1966; Whose Town?, 1969; Every Man Heart Lay Down, 1970; Road Down in the Sea, 1971; God Wash the World, 1971; David He No Fear, 1971; Hongry Catch the Foolish Boy, 1973; John Brown's Raid, 1972; Song of the Boat, 1975; Return to South Town, 1976; John Brown: A Cry for Freedom, 1980. Add: 1400 Niagara Ave., Claremont, Calif. 91711, U.S.A.

GRAHAM, Robert. *See* **HALDEMAN**, Joe.

GRAHAM, Victor Ernest. Canadian, b. 1920. Literature. Prof. of French, Univ. of Toronto, since 1958, now Emeritus (Chmn. Grad. Dept. of French, 1965–67; Assoc. Dean, Sch. of Grad. Studies, 1967–69; Vice Principal, Univ. Coll., 1969–70). Prof. of French, Univ. of Alberta, Calgary, 1948–58. *Publs:* (ed.) Phillippe Desportes: Cartels et Masquarades, 1958; (ed.) Desportes: Les Amours de Diane, vols. 1 & 2, 1959 (ed.) Desportes: Les Amours d'Hippolyte, 1960; (ed.) Desportes: Les Elégies, 1961; (ed.) Desportes: Cléonice, Dernières Amours, 1962; (ed.) Representative French Poetry, 1962; (ed.) Desportes: Diverses Amours, 1963; (ed.) Sixteenth Century French Poetry, 1964; (ed.) André Chamson: Le Chiffre de nos jours, 1965; The Imagery of Proust, 1966; (ed.) Pernette du Guillet: Rimes, 1968; (with W. McAllister Johnson) Estienne Jodelle: Le Recueil des inscriptions 1558, 1972; (with W. McAllister Johnson) The Paris Entries of Charles IX and Elisabeth of Austria 1571, 1974; (with W. McAllister Johnson) The Royal Tour of France by Charles IX and Catherine de'Medici: Festivals and Entries 1564-66, 1979. Add: French Dept., Univ. Coll., Univ. of Toronto, Toronto, Ont., M5S 1AI, Canada.

GRAHAM, W(illiam) Fred. American, b. 1930. History, Theology/Religion. Prof., Michigan State Univ., East Lansing, since 1973 (Instr., 1963–64; Asst. Prof., 1964–69; Assoc. Prof., 1969–73). Ordained Presbyterian Minister, 1955; Pastor, Bethel United Presbyterian Church, Waterloo, Iowa, 1955–61. Pres., Sixteenth-Century Studies Soc., 1988–89. *Publs:* The Constructive Revolutionary: John Calvin and His Socio-Economic Impact, 1971; Picking Up the Pieces: A Christian Stance in a 'Godless' Age, 1975. Add: 332 Chesterfield Parkway, East Lansing, Mich. 48823, U.S.A.

GRAHAM, Winston (Mawdsley). British. Novels/Short stories, Mystery/Crime/Suspense, Historical. Chmn., Soc. of Authors, London, 1967–69. *Publs:* The House with the Stained-Glass Windows, 1934; Into the Fog, 1935; The Riddle of John Rowe, 1935; Without Motive, 1936; Dangerous Pawn, 1937; Giant's Chair, 1938; Strangers Meeting, 1939; Keys of Chance, 1939; No Exit: An Adventure, 1940; Night Journey, 1941; My Turn Next, 1942; The Merciless Ladies, 1944; The Forgotten Story (in U.S. as The Wreck of the Grey Cat), 1945; Ross Poldark; A Novel of Cornwall 1783-1787 (in U.S. as Renegade), 1945; Demelza: A Novel of Cornwall 1788-1790, 1946; Take My Life, 1947; Cordelia, 1949; Night Without Stars, 1950; Jeremy Poldark: A Novel of Cornwall 1790-1791 (in U.S. As Venture Once More: A Novel of Cornwall 1790-1791),

1950; Warleggan: A Novel of Cornwall 1792-1793 (in U.S. as The Last Gamble), 1953; Fortune Is a Woman, 1953; The Little Walls, 1955; The Sleeping Partner, 1956; Greek Fire, 1957; The Tumbled House, 1959; Marnie, 1961; The Grove of Eagles, 1963; After the Act, 1965; The Walking Stick, 1967; Angell, Pearl and Little God, 1970; The Japanese Girl and Other Stories, 1971; The Spanish Armadas, 1972; The Black Moon: A Novel of Cornwall 1794-1799, 1974; Woman in the Mirror, 1975; The Four Swans, 1976; The Angry Tide, 1977; The Stranger from the Sea, 1981; The Miller's Dance, 1982; Poldark's Cornwall, 1983; The Loving Cup, 1984; The Green Flash, 1986; Cameo, 1988. Add: Abbotswood House, Buxted, Sussex, England.

GRAMPP, William D. American, b. 1914. Economics. Prof. Emeritus of Economics, Univ. of Illinois, Chicago (Prof., 1947–84); Visiting Prof. of Economics, Univ. of Chicago, since 1980. Member, Editorial Advisory Bd., History of Political Economy. Member of Editorial Staff, Akron Time-Press, Ohio, 1937–38; Instr. in Economics, Adelphi Univ., Garden City, N.Y., 1942; Asst. Prof. of Economics, Elmhurst Coll., Ill., 1942–44; Vice-consul in Economics Section, American Embassy, Rome, Italy, 1944–45; Assoc. Prof., De Paul Univ., Chicago, 1945–47. *Publs:* (ed. with E.T. Weiler) Economic Policy, 1953, 1961; The Manchester School of Economics, 1960; Economic Liberalism, 1965; Pricing the Priceless: Art, Artists, and Economics, 1989. Add: 5426 Ridgewood Ct., Chicago, Ill. 60615, U.S.A.

GRANADOS, Paul. *See* **KENT**, Arthur.

GRANDOWER, Elissa. *See* **WAUGH**, Hillary.

GRANGE, Peter. *See* **NICOLE**, Christopher.

GRANGER, Bill. Also writes as Bill Griffith. American, b. 1941. Mystery/Crime/Suspense. Columnist for the Chicago Tribune. *Publs:* The November Man, 1979; Sweeps, 1980; Public Murders, 1980; Schism, 1981; Queen's Crossing, 1982; The Shattered Eye, 1982; (as Bill Griffith) Time for Frankie Coolin, 1982; The British Cross, 1983; The Zurich Numbers, 1984; Dead of Winter, 1986; There Are No Spies, 1986; The Magic Feather, 1986; Hemingway's Notebook, 1986; The El Murders, 1987; The Enfant of Prague, 1987; Henry McGee Is Not Dead, 1988. Add: Box 1214, Oak Park, Ill. 60304, U.S.A.

GRANGER, Bruce Ingham. American, b. 1920. Literature. Prof. Emeritus of English. Univ. of Oklahoma, Norman, since 1982 (Assoc. Prof., 1953–61; Prof., 1961–82). Instr. in English, Univ. of Wisconsin, Madison, 1946–50; Asst. Prof., Univ. of Denver, 1950–53. *Publs:* Political Satire in the American Revolution, 1763-1783, 1960; Benjamin Franklin: An American Man of Letters, 1964; (ed. with M. Hartzog) Oldstyle/Salmagundi (vol. VI of the Complete Works of Washington Irving), 1977; American Essay Serials from Franklin to Iriving, 1978. Add: 944 Chautauqua Ave., Norman, Okla. 73069, U.S.A.

GRANICK, David. American, b. 1926. Administration/Management, Economics. Prof. of Economics, Univ. of Wisconsin, Madison, since 1962 (Assoc. Prof., 1959–62). Assoc. Prof. of Economics, Fisk Univ., Nashville, Tenn., 1951–57; Asst. Prof., Carnegie Inst. of Technology (now Carnegie-Mellon Univ.), Pittsburgh, Pa., 1957–59; with Ecole des Hautes Etudes Commerciales, Univ. of Montreal, 1975–76. *Publs:* Management of the Industrial Firm in the U.S.S.R., 1954; The Red Executive, 1960; The European Executive, 1962; Soviet Metal-Fabricating and Economic Development, 1967; Managerial Comparison of Four Developed Countries, 1972; (ed.) East European Managers, 1973; Enterprise Guidance in Eastern Europe, 1976; Job Rights in the Soviet Union: Their Consequences, 1987; Chinese Regional Property Rights and Industrial Enterprises, 1989. Add: Dept. of Economics, Social Science Bldg., Univ. of Wisconsin, Madison, Wisc. 53706, U.S.A.

GRANITE, Tony. *See* **POLITELLA**, Dario.

GRANOVETTER, Mark S. American, b. 1943. Sociology. Prof. of Sociology, State Univ. of New York at Stony Brook, since 1984 (Assoc. Prof., 1977–84). Asst. Prof. of Sociology, Harvard Univ., 1973–77. *Publs:* Getting a Job: A Study of Contacts and Careers, 1974. Add: Dept. of Sociology, State Univ. of New York, Stony Brook, N.Y. 11794, U.S.A.

GRANT, Anthony. *See* **CAMPBELL**, Judith.

GRANT, Bruce (Alexander). Australian, b. 1925. International relations/Current affairs, Politics/Government. Consultant to the Australian

Minister for Foreign Affairs and Trade, since 1988. Formerly with The Age newspaper, Melbourne: Film Theatre Critic, 1949–53; Foreign Correspondent in Europe and Middle East (based in London), 1954–57; Foreign Correspondent in Asia for The Age and Sydney Morning Herald (based in Singapore), 1959–63; Washington Correspondent, 1964–72; and Columnist on Public Affairs (Melbourne based), 1968–72; High Commnr. for Australia in India, and Ambassador to Nepal, 1973–76; Assoc., Intnl. Inst. for Strategic Studies, London, 1976–77; Writer-in-Residence, Monash Univ., Australia, 1980; Arts Adviser, Govt. of Victoria, 1982–86; Pres., Spoleto Melbourne Festival of Three Worlds, 1985–87. *Publs:* Indonesia, 1964; A Crisis of Loyalty, 1972; Arthur and Eric, 1977; The Security of South-East Asia, 1978; The Boat People, 1979; Cherry Bloom, 1980; Gods and Politicians, 1982; The Australian Dilemma, 1983; What Kind of Country?, 1988. Add: 11/63 Domain St., South Yarra, Vic. 3141, Australia.

GRANT, Charles L. American, b. 1942. Novels/Short stories, Science fiction/Fantasy. Freelance writer, mainly of SF short stories since 1975. English Teacher, Toms River High Sch., N.J., 1964–70, Chester High Sch., N.J., 1970–72, and Mt. Olive High Sch., N.J., 1972–73; English and History Teacher, Roxbury High Sch., N.J. 1974–75. *Publs:* The Shadow of Alpha (SF novel), 1976; The Curse, 1976; The Hour of the Oxrun Dead, 1977; (ed.) Writing and Selling Science Fiction, 1977; Ascension (SF novel), 1977; The Ravens of the Moon (SF novel), 1978; The Sound of Midnight, 1978; (ed.) Shadows 1-9, 9 vols., 1978–86; (ed.) Nightmares, 1979; The Last Call of Mourning, 1979; Legion (SF novel), 1979; Tales from the Nightside, 1981; Glow of Candles and Other Stories, 1981; Nightmare Seasons (SF novel), 1982; Night Songs (SF novel), 1984; The Tea Party, 1985; The Pet, 1986; The Orchard, 1986; For Fear of the Night, 1988; In a Dark Dream, 1989. Add: 51-J, The Village Green, Budd Lake, N.J. 07828, U.S.A.

GRANT, David. *See* **THOMAS,** Craig.

GRANT, James Russell. British, b. 1924. Poetry, Translations. Medical practitioner, London, since 1958. Registrar, The Maudsley Hosp., Inst. of Psychiatry, London, 1954–55; Psychiatrist, Provincial Guidance Clinic, Red Deer, Alta., Canada, 1955–57. *Publs:* Hyphens, 1958; Poems, 1959; (trans.) Zone, by Apollinaire, 1962; The Excitement of Being Sam, 1977; Myths of My Age, 1985; Hattonrig Road, 1986. Add: 255 Creighton Ave., London N2, England.

GRANT, John Webster. Canadian, b. 1919. Theology/Religion. Prof. of Church History, Emeritus, Emmanuel Coll. of Victoria Univ., Toronto, since 1984 (Prof., 1963–84). Prof. of Church History, Union Coll. of British Columbia, Vancouver, 1949–59; Ed.-in-Chief, Ryerson Press, Toronto, 1959–63. Managing Ed., Studies in Religion/Science Religieuses, 1971–76; Ed., Die Unierten Kirchen, 1973. *Publs:* Free Churchmanship in England, 1955; God's People in India, 1959; The Ship Under the Cross, 1960; George Pidgeon, 1962; (ed.) The Churches and the Canadian Experience, 1965; (compiler) God Speaks . . . We Answer, 1965; The Canadian Experience of Church Union, 1967; (ed.) Salvation! O the Joyful Sound: Selected Writings of John Carroll, 1967; The Church in the Canadian Era, 1972; Moon of Wintertime, 1984; A Profusion of Spires, 1988. Add: 86 Gloucester St., Apt. 1002, Toronto, Ont. M4Y 2S2, Canada.

GRANT, Julius. British, b. 1901. Business/Trade/Industry, Chemistry. Managing Dir., Hehner & Cox Ltd. Consulting Scientist, London, since 1950. Asst. to A. Chaston Chapman, Analytical and Consulting Chemist, 1922–30; in paper industry, 1931–49; with Censorship Dept., 1939–43. Pres., Forensic Science Soc., 1972–73; Pres., Medico-Legal Soc., 1973–74. *Publs:* Measurement of Hydrogen Ion Concentration, 1930; Qualitative Chemical Analysis, 1935; Books and Documents, 1941; Science for the Prosecution, 1941; Clowes and Coleman's Quantitative Analysis, 15th ed. 1947; Sutton's Volumetric Chemical Analysis, 13th ed. 1955; Pregl's Organic Microanalysis, 5th ed. 1955; Cellulose Pulp and Allied Products, 3rd ed. 1958; Fluorescence Analysis in Ultra-violet Light, 4th ed. 1961; Chemical Dictionary, 4th ed. 1970; (ed.) Paper and Board Manufacture, 1978. Add: 500 Chesham House, 150 Regent St., London W1R 5FA, England.

GRANT, Landon. *See* **GRIBBLE,** Leonard.

GRANT, Margaret. *See* **FRANKEN,** Rose.

GRANT, Michael. British, b. 1914. Classics, History. Fellow, Trinity Coll., Cambridge, 1938–49; Prof. of Humanity, Univ. of Edinburgh, 1948–59; Vice-Chancellor, Univ. of Khartoum, Sudan, 1956–58; Vice-Chancel-

lor, Queen's Univ. of Belfast, 1959–66. Pres., Virgil Soc., 1963–66, and Classical Assn., 1977–78. *Publs:* From Imperium to Auctoritas, 1946, 1969; Aspects of the Principate of Tiberius, 1950; Roman Anniversary Issues, 1950; Ancient History, 1952; The Six Main Aes Coinages of Augustus, 1953; Roman Imperial Money, 1954; Roman Literature, 1954; (trans.) Tacitus: Annals, 1956; Roman History from Coins, 1958; (with D. Pottinger) Greeks, 1958; (with D. Pottinger) Romans, 1960; (trans.) Cicero: Selected Works, 1960; The World of Rome, 1960; Myths of the Greeks and Romans, 1962; (ed. and contrib.) The Birth of Western Civilisation, 1964, reprinted as Greece and Rome, 1986; The Civilizations of Europe, 1965; Cambridge, 1966; The Gladiators, 1967; The Climax of Rome, 1969; The Ancient Mediterranean, 1969; Julius Caesar, 1969; (trans.) Cicero: Selected Political Speeches, 1969; The Ancient Historians, 1970; The Roman Forum, 1970; Nero, 1970; Cities of Vesuvius, 1971; Herod the Great, 1971; Roman Myths, 1971; (trans.) Cicero on the Good Life, 1971; Cleopatra, 1972; The Jews in the Roman World, 1973; (with J. Hazel) Who's Who in Classical Mythology (in U.S. as Gods and Mortals in Classical Mythology), 1973; (ed.) Greek Literature (in Translation), 1973; Caesar, 1974; The Army of the Caesars, 1974; The Twelve Caesars, 1975; (trans.) Cicero: Murder Trials, 1975; The Fall of the Roman Empire, 1976; Saint Paul, 1976; Jesus, 1977; History of Rome, 1978; (ed.) Latin Literature (in Translation), 1979; Greek and Latin Authors, 1980; The Etruscans, 1980; The Dawn of the Middle Ages, 1981; From Alexander to Cleopatra, 1982; The History of Ancient Israel, 1984; The Roman Emperors, 1985; A Guide to the Ancient World, 1986; The Rise of the Greeks, 1988. Add: Le Pitturacce, Gattaiola, 55050 Lucca, Italy.

GRANT, Neil. Also writes as D.M. Field, David Mountfield, and Gail Trenton. British, b. 1938. Antiques/Furnishings, Art, Children's nonfiction, History, Travel/Exploration/Adventure. *Publs:* Disraeli, 1969; Emperor Charles V, 1970; English Explorers of North America, 1970; Victoria, 1970; The Renaissance, 1971; Munich 1938, 1971; Kings and Queens of England, 1971; Cathedrals, 1972; Guilds, 1972; Easter Rising, 1972; World Leaders, 1972; Howards of Norfolk, 1972; Barbarossa, 1972; History Alive: Lives, 3 vols., 1972; The Industrial Revolution, 1973; Partition of Palestine, 1973; Basic Atlas (author of text), 1973; The New World Held Promise, 1974; David Livingstone, 1974; (as David Mountfield) A History of Polar Exploration, 1974; (as David Mountfield) Antique Collectors Dictionary, 1974; The Campbells of Argyll, 1975; Neil Grant's Book of Spies and Spying, 1975; The German-Soviet Pact, 1975; (as David Mountfield) A History of African Exploration, 1976; (as David Mountfield) The Coaching Age, 1976; Buccaneers, 1976; Stagecoaches, 1977; Children's History of Britain, 1977; (as David Mountfield) Brief Histories of Great Nations: England, 1978; Smugglers, 1978; (with Nigel Viney) An Illustrated History of Ball Games, 1978; (as David Mountfield) Everyday Life in Elizabethan England, 1978; (as D.M. Field) Great Masterpieces of World Art, 1979; (as David Mountfield) The Partisans, 1979; (as David Mountfield) London, 1979; (as David Mountfield) Britain, 1979; (as David Mountfield) The Railway Barons, 1979; The Discoverers, 1979; Explorers, 1979; The Savage Trade, 1980; (with Peter Womersley) Collecting Stamps, 1980; Conquerers, 1981; (as D.M. Field) The Nude in Art, 1981; Great Palaces, 1982; (as Gail Trenton) Whispers at Twilight, 1982; Everyday Life in the 18th Century, 1983; (as Gail Trenton) The White Bear, 1983; (as Gail Trenton) Reflections in the Stream, 1983; Scottish Clans and Tartans, 1987; 500 Questions and Answers About the Bible, 1988; (as David Mountfield; with Rixi Markus) A Vulnerable Game, 1988; People and Places: The United Kingdom, 1988. Add: 2 Avenue Rd., Teddington, Middx., England.

GRANT, Nigel (Duncan Cameron). British, b. 1932. Education. Prof. of Education, Univ. of Glasgow, since 1978. Teacher of English, Glasgow schs., 1957–60; Lectr., Jordanhill Coll. of Education, 1960–65; Lectr., 1965–72, and Reader in Educational Studies, 1972–78, Univ. of Edinburgh. *Publs:* Soviet Education, 1964, 4th ed. 1979; Society, Schools and Progress in Eastern Europe, 1969; (ed. and author with J. Lowe and T.D. Williams) Education and Nation-Building in the Third World, 1971; Other People's Curricula, 1973; (with R.E. Bell) A Mythology of British Education, 1974; (with R.E. Bell) Patterns of Education in the British Isles, 1977; The Crisis of Scottish Education, 1982. Add: Dept. of Education, The University, Glasgow W12 8QQ, Scotland.

GRANT, Richard. *See* **FREEMANTLE,** Brian.

GRANT, Roderick. British, b. 1941. Novels/Short stories, Travel/Exploration/Adventure, Biography. Sub-Ed., Weekly Scotsman, 1965–67. *Publs:* Adventure in My Veins, 1968; Seek Out the Guilty, 1969; Where No Angels Dwell, 1969; Gorbals Doctor, 1970; (with Alexander Highlands) The Dark Horizon, 1971; The Lone Voyage of Betty Mouat,

1973; The Stalking of Adrian Lawford, 1974; The Clutch of Caution, 1975, 1985; The 51st Highland Division at War, 1976; Strathalder: A Highland Estate, 1978; A Savage Freedom, 1978; The Great Canal, 1978; A Private Vendetta, 1978; (with C. Cole) But Not in Anger, 1979; Clap Hands for the Singing Molecatcher, 1989. Add: 3 Back Lane Cottages, Bucks Horn Oak, Farnham, Surrey, England.

GRANT, Verne. American, b. 1917. Biology, Botany, Zoology. Prof. of Botany, Univ. of Texas, Austin, since 1970, Emeritus since 1987. Geneticist and Experimental Taxonomist, Rancho Santa Ana Botanic Garden, Claremont, Calif., 1959–67; Asst. Prof., and subsequently Prof. of Botany, Claremont Grad. Sch., 1952–67; Prof. of Biology, Inst. of Life Science, Texas A. & M. Univ., Coll. Station, 1967–68; Dir., Boyce Thompson Southwestern Aboretum, and Prof. of Biological Sciences, Univ. of Arizona, Superior, 1968–70. *Publs:* Natural History of the Phlox Family, 1959; The Origin of Adaptations, 1963; The Architecture of the Germplasm, 1964; (with Karen Grant) Flower Pollination in the Phlox Family, 1965; (with Karen Grant) Hummingbirds and Their Flowers, 1968; Plant Speciation, 1971, 1981; Genetics of Flowering Plants, 1975; Organismic Evolution, 1977; The Evolutionary Process, 1985. Add: Dept. of Botany, Univ. of Texas, Austin, Tex. 78712, U.S.A.

GRATUS, Jack. British, b. 1935. Novels, Plays. Tutor in charge of Non-Fiction Writing, City Literary Inst., London, since 1974. Exec. Councillor, Writers' Guild of Great Britain, since 1978. Organizing Tutor of Creative Writing Course, Glamorgan Summer Sch., South Wales, 1968–77. *Publs:* A Man in His Position, 1968; The Victims, 1969; Mister Landlord Appel, 1971; (with T. Preston) Night Hair Child, 1971; The Great White Lie: History of the Anti-Slave Trade Campaign, 1973; The False Messiahs, 1976; The Joburgers, 1979; The Redneck Rebel, 1980. Add: 32 The Grove, Ealing, London W5 5LH, England.

GRAU, Shirley Ann. American, b. 1929. Novels/Short stories. *Publs:* The Black Prince and Other Stories, 1955; The Hard Blue Sky, 1958; The House on Coliseum Street, 1961; The Keepers of the House, 1964; The Condor Passes, 1971; The Wind Shifting West (short stories), 1973; Evidence of Love, 1977; Nine Women, 1986. Add: c/o Brandt & Brandt, 1501 Broadway, New York, N.Y. 10036, U.S.A.

GRAUBARD, Mark. American, b. 1904. Medicine/Health, Sciences. Dir., Food and Nutrition Labor Education Prog., 1942–46; Former National Lectr., Extension Service, U.S. Dept. of Agriculture, Washington, D.C.; Prof. of Natural Science, 1947–57, and Chmn., Dept. of Natural Science, 1957–68. Univ. of Minnesota, Minneapolis. *Publs:* Man's Food: Its Rhyme or Reason, 1943; Astrology and Alchemy: Two Fossil Sciences, 1953; The Foundations of Life Science, 1958; Circulation and Respiration: The Evolution of an Idea, 1964; Motivations, Tools and Theories of Ancient Science, 1967; Campustown, USA, at Midcentury, 1971; Campustown in the Throes of the Counter-Culture, 1974; Witchcraft and the Nature of Man, 1984. Add: 2928 Dean Parkway, Minneapolis, Minn. 55416, U.S.A.

GRAVER, Lawrence Stanley. American, b. 1931. Film, Literature, Biography. Prof. of English, Williams Coll., Williamstown, Mass., since 1964. *Publs:* Conrad's Short Fiction, 1969; Carson McCullers, 1969; Mastering the Film, 1977; (with R. Federman) Samuel Beckett: the Critical Heritage, 1978; Beckett: Waiting for Godot, 1989. Add: Dept. of English, Williams Coll., Williamstown, Mass. 01267, U.S.A.

GRAVES, Valerie. *See* **BRADLEY,** Marion Zimmer.

GRAY, Alasdair (James). British, b. 1934. Novels/Short stories, Plays. Freelance writer and painter since 1979. Art teacher, Lanarkshire and Glasgow, 1958–62; scene painter, Pavilion and Citizens' theatres, Glasgow, 1962–63; freelance painter and writer, Glasgow, 1963–76; artist recorder, People's Palace Local History Museum, Glasgow, 1976–77; Writer-in-Residence, Univ. of Glasgow, 1977–79. *Publs:* The Comedy of the White Dog (short stories), 1979; Lanark: A Life in Four Books (novel), 1981; Unlikely Stories, Mostly, 1983; 1982, Janine (novel), 1984; The Fall of Kelvin Walker (novel), 1985; (with Agnes Owens and James Kelman) Lean Tales, 1985; Five Scottish Artists (catalogue), 1986; Saltire Self-Portrait 4 (autobiographical sketch), 1988; Old Negatives (four verse sequences), 1989; The Anthology of Prefaces: A History of English Literature, 1989; Something Leather (novel), 1989. Add: 39 Kersland St., Glasgow G12 8BP, Scotland.

GRAY, Alfred Orren. American, b. 1914. History, Writing/Journalism. Emeritus Prof. of Journalism. Whitworth Coll., Spokane, Wash., since 1980 (Prof., and Chmn. of Dept., 1946–80); Communications and Re-

search Consultant, since 1980. Member, Bd. of Dirs., The Presbyterian Historical Society, since 1984, and Chmn. of its National Historical Sites Cttee., since 1986. Member, Editorial Advisory Bd., Today, since 1988. Dir. of Whitworth Coll. News Bureau, 1952–58; Ed., The Synod Story, 1953–55; Dir., Inland Empire Publications Clinic, 1959–74. *Publs:* Historyof U.S. Ordnance Service in the European Theater of Operations During World War II, 1946; Techniques of Communications for the Church, 1957; Not by Might: The Story of Whitworth College, 1965; The Whitworthian: A Crash Course in Leadership, 1980; Eight Generations from Gondelsheim: A Genealogical Study, 1980; (co-author) Many Lamps, One Light: A Centennial History, 1984. Add: W. 304 Hoerner Ave., Spokane, Wash. 99218, U.S.A.

GRAY, Angela. *See* **DANIELS,** Dorothy.

GRAY, Clayton. Canadian, b. 1918. History, Travel/Exploration/Adventure. Historian, David M. Stewart Museum and Macdonald-Stewart Foundn., Que., since 1955. Ed., Canadian Press News Bureau, 1944–45; Lectr., History of Canadian Literature, Concordia Univ., 1954–61; Vice-Pres., Lake St. Louis Historical Society, 1954–75; Member, National Liberal Club, London, 1982–83. Hon. Secty., P.E.N. Canadian Centre, 1979–80. *Publs:* The Montreal Story, 1949; Montréal qui disparait, 1952; Conspiracy in Canada, 1959; Le Vieux Montréal, 1964; Montreal During the American Civil War, 1965; The Louisiana Affair, 1984; The Canadian Guide to Britain, vol. I, England, 1985; Le Castor Fait Tout, 1987. Add: 1495 Ste. Croix, Montreal, Que. H41 3Z5, Canada.

GRAY, Douglas. British, b. 1930. Language, Literature. J.R.R. Tolkien Prof. of English Literature and Language, Oxford Univ., and Professorial Fellow, Lady Margaret Hall, Oxford, since 1980 (Lectr., Pembroke and Lincoln Colls., 1956–61; Fellow, Pembroke Coll., 1961–80; Univ. Lectr. in English Language, 1976–80). Member of the Council, Early English Texts Society, since 1981. Pres., Soc. for Study of Mediaeval Languages and Literature, 1982–86. *Publs:* (ed.) The Faerie Queene, Book 1, by Spenser, 1969; Themes and Images in the Medieval English Religious Lyric, 1972; (ed.) A Selection of Religious Lyrics, 1975; (co-author) A Chaucer Glossary, 1979; Robert Henryson, 1979; (ed.) The Oxford Book of Late Medieval Verse and Prose, 1985. Add: Lady Margaret Hall, Oxford, England.

GRAY, Dulcie. British, b. 1920. Mystery/Crime/Suspense, Plays/Screenplays. Actress, since 1939. *Publs:* Murder on the Stairs, 1957; Love Affair (play). 1957; Murder in Melbourne, 1958; Baby Face, 1959; Epitaph for a Dead Actor, 1960; Murder on a Saturday, 1961; Murder in Mind, 1963; The Devil Wore Scarlet, 1964; (with Michael Denison) The Actor and the World, 1964; No Quarter for a Star, 1964; The Murder of Love, 1967; Died in the Red, 1968; Murder on Honeymoon, 1969; For Richer for Richer, 1970; Deadly Lampshade, 1971; Understudy to Murder, 1972; Dead Give Away, 1974; Ride on a Tiger, 1957; Stage-Door Fright (stories), 1977; Death in Denims, 1977; Butterflies on My Mind (non-fiction), 1978; Dark Calypso, 1979; The Glanville Women, 1982; Anna Starr, 1984; Mirror Image, 1987. Add: Shardeloes, Amersham, Bucks., England.

GRAY, Elizabeth Janet. *See* **VINING,** Elizabeth Gray.

GRAY, Francine du Plessix. American, b. 1930. Novels/Short stories, History. Reporter, United Press Intnl., NYC, 1952–54; Asst. Ed., Réalités mag., Paris, 1954–55; Book Ed., Art in America, NYC, 1962–64; Visiting Prof., City Univ. of New York, 1975, Yale Univ., New Haven, Conn., 1981, and Columbia Univ., New York, 1983; Ferris Prof., Princeton Univ., N.J., 1986. *Publs:* Divine Disobedience: Profiles in Catholic Radicalism, 1970; Hawaii: The Sugar-Coated Fortress, 1972; Lovers and Tyrants, 1976; World Without End, 1981; October Blood, 1985; Adam and Eve and the City, 1987. Add: c/o Georges Borchardt Inc., 136 E. 57nd St., New York, N.Y. 10022, U.S.A.

GRAY, Harold James. British, b. 1907. Business/Trade/Industry, Economics, Physics. Under-Secty., U.K. Bd. of Trade, 1954–60; Sr. Trade Commnr. and Economic Advisor to the U.K. High Commnr. in Australia, 1954–58, and in South Africa, 1958–60; Dir., National Assn. of British Manufacturers, 1961–65; Dir. of Legal Affairs, Confedn. of British Industry, London, 1965–72. *Publs:* (with S.G. Starling) Electricity in the Service of Man, 1949; (ed. and contrib.) Economic Survey of Australia, 1955; (ed. and contrib.) Dictionary of Physics, 1958; Britain's Small Firms, 1968; Problems of Small Firms, 1970; Earnings-Related Security, 1970; Small Firms and the Common Market, 1972; (ed. with A. Isaacs) New Dictionary of Physics, 1974. Add: Copper Beeches, Rudor Ave., Maidstone, Kent ME14 5HJ, England.

GRAY, Jack. Canadian, b. 1927. Plays/Screenplays. Pres., John Gray Productions Ltd., Toronto; Ed., Canadian Play Series, Univ. of Toronto Press; Pres., League of Canadian Communications, since 1984. Asst Ed., Maclean's Mag., Toronto, 1953–57; Prof. of Integrated Studies, Univ. of Waterloo, Ont., 1969–71; Secty. Gen., Canadian Theatre Centre, Toronto, 1971–73; Pres., Alliance of Canadian Cinema, Television and Radio Artist (ACTRA), 1978–82. *Publs:* Chevalier Johnstone (produced as Louis-bourg), 1972; Susannah, Agnes and Ruth, 1972; Striker Schneiderman, 1973; (with A. Fortier) The Third Strategy, 1984. Add: 65 Pine St., Brockville, Ont. K6V 166, Canada.

GRAY, John. Canadian, b. 1946. Novels, Plays/Screenplays.Founding Dir., Tamahnous Theatre, Vancouver, 1972–74; theatre dir. *Publs:* Billy Bishop Goes to War (play), 1981; Dazzled (novel), 1984. Add: 3392 W. 37th Ave., Vancouver, B.C. V6N 2V6, Canada.

GRAY, Nicolete. British, b. 1911. Art, Children's non-fiction, Design. Lectr. on Lettering, Central Sch. of Art and Design, London, 1966–80. *Publs:* XIXth Century Ornamented Types and Title Pages, 1938; rev. ed. 1974; Rossetti, Dante and Ourselves, 1947; The Paleography of Latin Inscriptions in VIII, IX, X Centuries in Italy, 1948; Jacob's Ladder: A Bible Picture Book from Anglo-Saxon and XII Century English Manuscripts, 1949; Lettering on Buildings, 1960; (adaptor) The Desecra-tion of Christ, by R. Egenter, 1967; Lettering as Drawing, 1970; Helen Sutherland Collection: Catalogue, 1970; The Painted Inscriptions of David Jones, 1981; A History of Lettering, 1986. Add: Dawbers House, Long Wittenham, Abingdon, Oxon OX14 4QQ, England.

GRAY, (John) Richard. British, b. 1929. History, Race relations. Prof. of African History, Sch. of Oriental and African Studies, Univ. of London, since 1972 (Fellow, 1961–63; Reader, 1963–72; Chmn., Centre for African Studies, 1974–77; Chmn., Centre of Religion and Philosophy, Univ. of London, since 1986. Lectr., Univ. of Kartoum, 1959–61; Chmn., African Centre, Covent Garden, London, 1967–72; Ed., Journal of African His-tory, 1968–71; Chmn., Britain-Zimbabwe Soc., 1981–85. *Publs:* The Two Nations: Aspects of the Development of Race Relations in the Rhodesias and Nyasaland, 1960; A History of the Southern Sudan, 1839-1889, 1961; (with D. Chambers) Materials for West African History in Italian Archives, 1965; (ed. with D. Birmingham) Pre-Colonial African Trade, 1970; (ed.) Cambridge History of Africa, vol. IV, 1975; (ed., with E. Fashole-Luke and others) Christianity in Independent Africa, 1978. Add: 39 Rotherwick Rd., London NW11 7DD, England.

GRAY, Richard Butler. American, b. 1922. International relations/Cur-rent affairs, Politics/Government. Prof. of Political Science, Florida State Univ., Tallahassee, since 1958, now Emeritus (Dir. of Intnl. Affairs, 1958–85). Staff Member, U.S. State Dept., Dominican Republic, 1949–51; Asst. Prof., C.W. Post Coll., Long Island Univ., N.Y., 1957–58. *Publs:* Jose Marti, Cuban Patriot, 1962; (ed.) International Security Sys-tems, Concepts and Models of World Order, 1969; (co-ed.) Security in a World of Change: Notes and Readings in International Relations, 1969; (ed.) Latin American and the United States in the 1970s, 1971. Add: Dept. of Political Science, 545 Bellamy Bldg., Florida State Univ., Tal-lahassee, Fla. 32306-2049, U.S.A.

GRAY, Robert. Australian, b. 1945. Poetry. *Publs:* Introspect, Retrospect, 1970; Creekwater Journal, 1974; Grass Script, 1978; The Skylight, 1984: Selected Poems 1963-83, 1985; (ed. with Geoffrey Leh-mann) The Younger Australian Poets, 1983; Piano, 1988. Add: c/o Angus and Robertson, P.O. Box 290, North Ryde, N.S.W. 2113, Australia.

GRAY, Russell. *See* **FISCHER,** Bruno.

GRAY, Simon (James Holliday). Also writes as Hamish Reade. British, b. 1936. Novels/Short stories, Plays/Screenplays. Lectr. in English, Queen Mary Coll., Univ. of London, since 1966. Ed., Delta mag., Cambridge, since 1964. Lectr., Univ. of British Columbia, Van-couver, 1963–64; Supvr. in English, Trinity Coll., Cambridge, 1964–66. *Publs:* Colmain, 1963; Simple People, 1965; (ed. with Keith Walker) Selected English Prose, 1967; Little Portia, 1968; Wise Child (play), 1968; Sleeping Dog (play), 1968; (as Hamish Reade) A Comeback for Stark, 1969; Dutch Uncle (play), 1969; The Idiot (play), 1970; Spoiled (play), 1971; Butley (play), 1971; Otherwise Engaged and Other Plays, 1975; Dog Days, 1976; Molly (play), 1977; The Rear Column and Other Plays, 1978, in U.S. as The Rear Column, Dog Days, and Other Plays, 1979; Stage Struck (play), 1979; Close of Play, and Pig in a Poke (plays), 1979; Quartermaine's Terms (play), 1981; The Common Pursuit (play), 1984; An Unnatural Pursuit (journal of a production), 1985; Plays One, 1986; After Pilkington, 1987; Melon (play), 1987; How's That for Telling

'Em, Fat Lady? (non-fiction), 1988. Add: c/o Judy Daish Assoc., 83 Eastbourne Mews, London W2 6LQ, England.

GRAY, Spalding. American, b. 1941. Plays/Screenplays. Actor from 1965; co-founder, Wooster Group, NYC, 1975. *Publs:* In Search of the Monkey Girl, 1982; Swimming to Cambodia, 1985; Rivkala's Ring, 1986; Sex and Death to the Age 14 (collection), 1986. Add: c/o Suzanne Gluck, ICM, 40 W. 57th St., New York, N.Y., 10019, U.S.A.

GRAY, Tony (George Hugh). Irish, b. 1922. Novels/Short stories, His-tory, Sociology, Biography. Former Features Ed., Daily Mirror, London. *Publs:* Starting from Tomorrow, 1965; The Real Professionals, 1966; Gone the Time, 1967; The Irish Answer, 1967; (adaptor) Interlude, 1968; (with L. Villa) The Record Breakers, 1970; The Last Laugh, 1972; The Orange Order, 1972; Psalms and Slaughter, 1972; (with H. Ward) Buller, 1974; No Surrender, 1975; Champions of Peace, 1976; (with C. McBride) The White Lions of Timbavati, 1977; (with T. Murphy) Some of My Best Friends Are Animals, 1979; (with C. McBride) Operation White Lion, 1981; The Road to Success: Alfred McAlpine, 1935-85, 1987; Fleet Street, 1989. Add: 3 Broomfield Rd., Kew Gardens, Richmond, Surrey, England.

GRAYLAND, Valerie (Merle). Also writes as Lee Belvedere, Valerie Spanner, and Valerie Subond. New Zealander. Mystery/Crime/-Suspense, Children's fiction, History, Travel/Exploration/Adventure. *Publs:* (as Valerie Spanner) The First Strawberry, 1954; John and Hoani, 1962; Dead Men of Eden, 1962; Early One Morning, 1963; Night of the Reaper, 1963; Baby Sister, 1964; The Grave-Digger's Apprentice, 1964; Jest of Darkness, 1965; (with E. Grayland) Coromandel Coast, 1965; (with E. Grayland) Historic Coromandel, 1969; (with E. Grayland) Tarawera, 1971; (as Lee Belvedere) Farewell to a Valley, 1971; (as Lee Belvedere) Meet a Dark Stranger, 1971; (as Lee Belvedere) Thunder Beach, 1972; (as Lee Belvedere) Fringe of Heaven, 1972; (as Valerie Subond) Heights of Havenrest, 1972; (as Lee Belvedere) The Smiling House, 1973; (as Lee Belvedere) Return to Moon Bay, 1973; (as Valerie Subond) House Over Hell Valley, 1974; (as Valerie Subond) House at Haunted Inlet, 1978. Add: 4031 Great North Rd., Kelston, Auckland, New Zealand.

GREAVES, Margaret. British, b. 1914. Children's fiction, Literature. Principal Lectr. in English, 1946–70, and Head of Dept., 1960–70, St. Mary's Coll. of Education, Cheltenham; now retired. *Publs:* The Blazon of Honour, 1964; Regency Patron, 1966; Gallery, 1968; Gallimaufry, 1971; The Dagger and the Bird, 1971; The Grandmother Stone (in U.S. as Stone of Terror), 1972; Little Jacko, 1973; The Gryphon Quest, 1974; Curfew, 1975; Nothing Ever Happens on Sundays, 1976; The Night of the Goat, 1976; A Net to Catch the Wind, 1979; The Abbottsbury Ring, 1979; Charlie and Emma series, 5 vols., 1980–87; Cat's Magic, 1980; The Snake Whistle, 1980; Once There Were No Pandas, 1985; Nicky's Knitting Grannary, 1986; The Mice of Nibbling Village, 1986; Hetty Pegler, 1987. Add: 8 Greenways, Winchcombe GL54 5LG, England.

GREBSTEIN, Sheldon Norman. American, b. 1928. Literature. Pres., and Prof. of Literature, State Univ. of New York Coll. at Purchase, since 1981. Instr., and Asst. Prof., Univ. of Kentucky, Lexington, 1953–62; Asst. Prof., Univ. of South Florida, Tampa, 1962–63; Assoc. Prof., 1963–68, Dir. of English Grad. Studies, 1966–72, Prof., 1968–81, and Dean of Arts and Science, 1975–81, State Univ. of New York, Binghamton. *Publs:* (ed.) Monkey Trial, 1960; Sinclair Lewis, 1962; John O'Hara, 1966; (ed.) Perspectives in Contemporary Criticism, 1968; (ed.) Studies in For Whom the Bell Tolls, 1971; Hemingway's Craft, 1973. Add: Of-fice of the Pres., State Univ. of New York at Purchase, N.Y. 10577, U.S.A.

GREELEY, Andrew (Moran). American, b. 1928. Novels, Education, Sociology, Theology/Religion. Dir., Center for the Study of American Pluralism, National Opinion Research Center, Univ. of Chicago, since 1971 (Sr. Study Dir., 1962–68, and Prog. Dir. in Higher Education, 1968–70, National Opinion Research Center; Lectr. in Sociology, Univ. of Chicago, 1963–72); Prof. of Sociology, Univ. of Arizona, Tucson, since 1978. Ed., Ethnicity; Syndicated columnist, "People and Values", Chicago Sun Times, since 1985; Past Pres., Catholic Sociological Soc. *Publs:* Religion and Career: A Study of College Graduates, 1963; (with P. Rossi) The Education of Catholic Americans, 1966; The Catholic Ex-perience: A Sociologist's Interpretation of the History of American Catholicism, 1967; The Changing Catholic College, 1967; The Student in Higher Education, 1968; (with M. Marty and S. Rosenberg) What Do We Believe?, 1968; From Backwater to Mainstream: A Profile of Catholic Higher Education, 1969; Religion in the Year 2000, 1969; (with J. Spaeth) Recent Alumni and Higher Education: Survey of College Graduates, 1970; Why Can't They Be Like Us?, 1971; The Denominational Society, 1972;

Unsecular Man, 1972; Priests in the United States: Reflections on a Survey, 1972; That Most Distressing Nation: The Taming of the American Irish, 1972; American Priests, 1972; The New Agenda, 1973; Sexual Intimacy, 1973; Building Coalitions, 1974; Ecstasy: A Way of Knowing, 1974; Ethnicity in the United States, 1975; The Devil, You Say, 1976; The Communal Catholic, 1976; Love and Play, 1977; The Mary Myth, 1977; Great Mysteries: Essential Catechism, 1977; The Making of the Popes, 1978; The Magic Cup, 1979; Women I've Met, 1979; The Cardinal Sins, 1981; Thy Brother's Wife, 1982; Ascent into Hell, 1983; A Piece of My Mind, 1983; Virgin and Martyr, 1985; Angels of September, 1986; Patience of a Saint, 1986; The Final Planet, 1987; Rite of Spring, 1988; Angel Fire, 1988; Love Song, 1988. Add: c/o Warner Books, Inc., 666 Fifth Ave., New York, N.Y. 10103, U.S.A.

GREEN, Andrew M(alcolm). British, b. 1927. Supernatural/Occult topics. Development Chemist, Thermionic Products, London, 1948–52; Sale Exec., Thorn Electrical Industries, London, 1952–57; Sales Office Mgr., Crypto, London, 1957–59; Publicity Mgr., Stanley-Bridges, London, 1959–63; Press Relations Officer, Industrial and Trade Fairs, London, 1963–65; Ed., Trade and Technical Press, Morden, Surrey, 1965–68; Editorial Dir., Perry Press Productions, London, 1968–72; Founder, Ealing Psychical Research Soc., and Co-founder, National Fedn. of Psychical Research Societies, 1951. *Publs:* Mysteries of Surrey, 1972, 1973; Ghost Hunting, 1973, 1976; Our Haunted Kingdom, 1973, 3rd ed. 1975; Mysteries of Sussex, 1973; Mysteries of London, 1973; Haunted Houses, 1975, 4th ed. 1989; Ghosts of the South East, 1976, 1981; Phantom Ladies, 1977; Ghosts of Tunbridge Wells, 1978; The Ghostly Army, 1979; Ghosts of Today, 1980. Add: 3 Church Cottages, Mountfield, Robertsbridge, Sussex TN32 5JS, England.

GREEN, Benny. British, b. 1927. Novels/Short stories, Music, Biography. Musician (saxophonist); Scriptwriter and broadcaster for BBC, and BBC-TV, London; TV Critic. Punch mag.; Literary Critic, Spectator mag. Jazz Critic, Observer newspaper, 1958–77. *Publs:* The Reluctant Art, 1962; Blame It on My Youth, 1967; 58 Minutes to London, 1969; Drums in My Ears, 1973; I've Lost My Little Willie, 1976; Swingtime in Tottenham, 1976; (ed.) Cricket Addicts Archive, 1977; Shaw's Companions, 1978; Fred Astaire, 1979; (ed.) Wisden Anthology, 4 vols., 1979–83; P.G. Wodehouse: A Literary Biography, 1981; Wisden Book of Obituaries, 1986; (ed.) The Last Empires, 1986; (ed.) The Lord's Companion, 1987; (ed.) A Hymn to Him, 1987. Add: c/o BBC, Broadcasting House, Portland Place, London W1, England.

GREEN, Brian *See* **CARD,** Orson Scott.

GREEN, Celia (Elizabeth). British, b. 1935. Psychology, Sciences. Dir., Inst. of Psychophysical Research, Oxford, since 1961. *Publs:* Lucid Dreams, 1968; Out-of-the-Body Experiences, 1968; The Human Evasion, 1969; (with Charles McCreery) Apparitions, 1975; The Decline and Fall of Science, 1976; Advice to Clever Children, 1981. Add: Inst. of Psychophysical Research, 118 Banbury Rd., Oxford OX2 6JU, England.

GREEN, David E. American, b. 1942. International relations/Current affairs. Prof. of History, Univ. of Saskatchewan, Saskatoon, since 1977 (Special Lectr. in history, 1969–70; Asst. Prof. of History, 1970–72; Assoc. Prof., 1972–77). Asst. Prof. of History, Ohio State Univ., Columbus, 1967–68; Fellow, Centre for Advanced Study in the Behavioural Sciences, Stanford, Calif., 1971–72. *Publs:* The Containment of Latin America: A History of the Myths and Realities of the Good Neighbor Policy, 1971. Add: Dept. of History, Univ. of Saskatchewan, Saskatoon S7N 0W0, Canada.

GREEN, D(ennis) H(oward). British, b. 1922. Literature, Fellow, Trinity Coll., Cambridge, since 1949, and Schröder Prof. of German, since 1979, Cambridge Univ. (Asst. Lectr., 1950–54; teaching fellow, 1952–66; Head of Dept. of Other Languages, 1956–79; Prof. of Modern Languages, 1966–79). Lectr. in German, St. Andrews Univ., 1949–50. *Publs:* The Carolingian Lord, 1965; The Millstätter Exodus: A Crusading Epic, 1966; (with L.P. Johnson) Approaches to Wolfram von Eschenbach, 1978; Irony in the Medieval Romance, 1979; The Art of Recognition in Wolfram's Parzival, 1982. Add: Trinity College, Cambridge, England.

GREEN, Donald Ross. American, b. 1924. Education, Psychology. Sr. Research Psychologist since 1967, and Dir. of Research since 1968, CTB/McGraw-Hill, Monterey, Calif. Assoc. in Education, Univ. of California, Berkeley, 1956–57; Instr. to Assoc. Prof. of Education, 1957–67, and Assoc. Prof. of Psychology, 1963–67, Emory Univ., Atlanta. *Publs:* Educational Psychology, 1964; (with R.L. Henderson) Reading for Meaning in the Elementary School, 1969; (ed. with M.P. Ford and G.B.

Flamer) Measurement and Piaget, 1971; (ed.) The Aptitude-Achievement Distinction, 1974; (ed. with M.J. Wargo) Achievement Testing of Disadvantaged and Minority Students for Educational Program Evaluation, 1978. Add: CTB/McGraw-Hill, Del Monte Research Park, Monterey, Calif. 93940, U.S.A.

GREEN, Dorothy (Auchterlonie). Writes verse as Dorothy Auchterlonie. British, b. 1915. Poetry, Literature. Hon. Visiting Fellow, Royal Military Coll., Duntroon, Canberra, since 1980 (Lectr. in English, 1987–80). Teacher, 1933–38; Journalist, Sydney Daily Telegraph, 1941; News Ed., Australian Broadcasting Commn., Brisbane, 1942–44; Teacher, then Co-Principal, Presbyterian Girls' Coll., Warwick, Qld., 1955–60; Lectr. in English, Monash Univ., Melbourne, 1960–63; Sr. Lectr. in English and Australian Literature, Australian National Univ., Canberra, 1964–72. *Publs:* Kaleidoscope (verse), 1940; (with H.M. Green) Fourteen Minutes, 1950; The Dolphin (verse), 1967; (ed.) Australian poetry, 1968; Ulysses Bound: A Study of Henry Handel Richardson and Her Fiction, 1973, 1986; The Music of Love (essays), 1985; Something to Someone (verse), 1984; A History of Australian Literature 1789-1950, 2 vols., 1985. Add: 18 Waller Crescent, Campbell, A.C.T. 2601, Australia.

GREEN, Elizabeth A(dine) H(erkimer). American, b. 1906. Music. Teacher of Stringed Instruments and Orchestra Conductor, East High Sch., Waterloo, Iowa, 1928–42; Instr., Asst. Prof., and Assoc. Prof., 1943–57, and Prof. of Music, 1957–75, Univ. of Michigan, Ann Arbor (now Emeritus). *Publs:* The Modern Conductor, 1961, 4th ed., 1987; Teaching Stringed Instruments in Classes, 1966, 1987; (with N. Malko) The Conductor and His Score, 1975, 2nd ed. retitled The Conductor's Score, 1985; The Dynamic Orchestra, 1987. Add: 1225 Ferdon Rd., Ann Arbor, Mich. 48104, U.S.A.

GREEN, Frederick Pratt. British, b. 1903. Poetry. Methodist Minister, now retired. *Publs:* This Unlikely Earth, 1952; The Skating Parson, 1963; 26 Hymns, 1971; The Old Couple, 1976; Hymns and Ballads, 1982. Add: 96 Hillcrest Rd., Thorpe St. Andrew, Norwich NR7 0JR, England.

GREEN, Gerald. American, b. 1922. Novels/Short stories. With Intnl. News Service to 1950; Producer and Writer, NBC-TV, 1950–64. *Publs:* Sword and the Sun, 1954; The Last Angry Man, 1957; The Lotus Eaters, 1959; The Heartless Light, 1961; The Portofino PTA, 1962; The Legion of Nobel Christians, 1965; (with Lawrence Klingman) His Majesty O'Keefe, 1968; To Brooklyn with Love, 1968; Faking It, 1971; The Stones of Zion, 1971; Blockbuster, 1972; Tourist, 1973; The Hostage Heart; 1976; Girl, 1977; Holocaust, 1978; Cactus Pie, 1979; The Artists of Terezin, 1979; The Healers, 1980; Murfy's Men, 1981; Karpov's Brain, 1982; Not in Vain, 1984; East and West, 1986. Add: c/o Scott Meredith Literary Agency, 845 Third Ave., New York, N.Y. 10022, U.S.A.

GREEN, J.C.R. British, b. 1949. Poetry, Medicine/Health, Sports/Physical education/Keeping fit, Biography, Translations. Managing Ed., Prospice mag.; Dir. and Ed., Aquila Publishing Co. Ltd., Ed., The Phaethon Press and Helius Designs; Publr., Skye Island Publs; and Johnston Green and Co. Ltd. Dir., 1970–71, and Chmn., 1971–72, Birmingham Poetry Centre; Vice-Chmn., Poetry Cttee., Birmingham and Midland Inst. of Mgmt., 1971–72; Producer, BBC Poetry Progs., 1971–73. *Publs:* (with A. Jackson and C. Lewis) Go Dig Your Own Grave, 1968; A Notebook for Glider Pilots, 1968; The Vegetarian Diet, 1968; (ed. with J. Dalton) Come Together: Poetry for International Youth Year, 1970; Into the Darkness, 1971; Death of Bishop Bowie, 1971; (ed. with S. Morris) Ecology, 1972; (ed. with M. Booth and M. Edwards) Prospice One, 1973; (ed. with M. Booth and M. Edwards) Prospice Two, 1974; By Weight of Reason, 1974; The Keeper of Flocks, 1975; (trans.) Lisbon Revisited, by Fernando Pessoa, 1975; (trans.) The Maritime Ode, by Alvaro de Campos, 1975; Fernando Pessoa, 1975; Prospice 5, 1976; (trans.) The Ancient Rhythm, by Fernando Pessoa, 1977; Prospice 7, 1977; (trans.) The Tobacconist, by Fernando Pessoa, 1977; A Beaten Image: Poems for Several Places 1968–1976, 1977; Garlic Miscellany, 1982; Sixty Haiku, 1982; (ed.) New Mexican [Portuguese, Spanish] Poetry, 3 vols., 1982–84. Add: Sachnahanaid, by Portree, Isle of Skye, Scotland.

GREEN, James L(eroy). American, b. 1919. Economics. Prof. of Economics, Coll. of Business Admin., Univ. of Georgia, Athens, since 1960. Academic Dir., Chamber of Commerce of U.S. Inst. for Org. Mgmt., since 1963. Prof. of Economics, Michigan Technological Univ., 1953–56; Economic and Financial Adviser to Minister of Finance, Colombia, South America, 1956–57; Prof. and Head, Dept. of Economics, Grad. Sch. of Business, Air Force Inst. of Technology, Ohio, 1957–60. *Publs:* Metropolitan Economic Republics, 1965; Economic Ecology, 1969. Add: Dept. of Economics and Statistics, Coll. of Business Admin., Univ.

of Georgia, Athens, Ga. 30601, U.S.A.

GREEN, Joseph (Lee). American, b. 1931. Science fiction/Fantasy. Public Affairs Science Writer, Kennedy Space Center, Fla., since 1965. Lab. Technician, Intnl. Paper Co., Panama City, Fla., 1949–51; welder and shop worker, Panama City, 1952–54; millwright in Fla., Tex., and Ala., 1955–58; Sr. Supvr., Boeing Co., Seattle, 1959–63. *Publs:* The Loafers of Refuge, 1965; An Affair with Genius (short stories), 1969; Gold the Man (in U.S. as The Mind Behind the Eye), 1971; Conscience Interplanetary, 1972; Star Probe, 1976; The Horde, 1976. Add: 1390 Holly Ave., Merritt Island, Fla. 32952, U.S.A.

GREEN, Judith. *See* **RODRIGUEZ,** Judith.

GREEN, Martin (Burgess). British, b. 1927. Novels/Short stories, Literature, Biography. Prof. of English, Tufts Univ., Medford, Mass., since 1968. Instr., Wellesley Coll., Mass., 1957–61; Lectr., Birmingham Univ., U.K., 1965–68. *Publs:* Mirror for Anglo-Saxons, 1960; Reappraisals, 1965; Science and the Shabby Curate of Poetry, 1965; The Problem of Boston, 16; Yeat's Blessings on von Hügel, 1968; Cities of Light and Sons of the Morning, 1972; The von Richthofen Sisters, 1974; Children of the Sun, 1975; The Earth Again Redeemed (novel), 1976; Transatlantic Patterns, 1977; The Challenge of the Mahatmas, 1978; Dreams of Adventure, Deeds of Empire, 1979; (ed.) The Old English Elegies, 1983; Tolstoy and Gandhi, 1983; The Great American Adventure, 1984; Mountains of Truth, 1986; (wish J. Swan) The Triumph of Pierrot, 1986; The Origins of Non-Violence: Tolstoy and Gandhi in Their Historical Setting, 1986; The English Novel in the 20th Century: The Doom of Empire, 1987; New York, 1913: The Armory Show and the Paterson Strike Pageant, 1988. Add: 8 Boylston Terrace, Medford, Mass. 02144, U.S.A.

GREEN, Michael (Frederick). British, b. 1927. Novels/Short stories, Humour/Satire. *Publs:* Art of Coarse Rugby, 1960; Art of Coarse Sailing, 1962; Even Coarser Rugby, 1963; Art of Coarse Acting, 1965; Don't Print My Name Upside Down (novel), 1965; Art of Coarse Sport, 1966; Art of Coarse Golf, 1967; Art of Coarse Moving, 1969; Rugby Alphabet, 1972; Art of Coarse Drinking, 1973; Squire Haggard's Journal (satire), 1975; Art of Coarse Cruising, 1976; Even Coarser Sport, 1978; Four Plays for Coarse Actors, 1978; The Coarse Acting Show 2, 1980; Art of Coarse Sex, 1981; Tonight Josephine, 1982; Don't Swing from the Balcony, Romeo, 1983; The Art of Coarse Office Life, 1985; The Third Great Coarse Acting Show, 1986; The Boy Who Shot Down an Airship, 1988. Add: 78 Sandall Rd., London W5 1JB, England.

GREEN, Peter (Morris). Also writes as Denis Delaney. British, b. 1924. Novels/Short stories, Children's non-fiction, Classics, Biography, Translations. James R. Dougherty Centennial Professor of Classics, Univ. of Texas at Austin, since 1982 (Prof., 1972–82). Ed., Cambridge Review, 1950–51; Dir. of Studies in Classics, Selwyn Coll., Cambridge, 1952–53; Fiction Critic, Daily Telegraph, London, 1953–63; Literary Adviser, Bodley Head Ltd., publrs., London, 1957–58; Consultant Ed., Hodder & Stoughton Ltd., publrs., London, 1960–63; Television Critic, The Listener, London, and Film Critic, John o'London's, 1961–63; Prof. of Greek History and Literature, Coll. Year in Athens, 1966–71. *Publs:* (ed.) Poetry from Cambridge, 1947–50, 1951; The Expanding Eye: A First Journey to the Mediterranean, 1953; Achilles His Armour, 1955; (as Denis Delaney) Cat in Gloves, 1956; The Sword of Pleasure, 1957; Sir Thomas Browne, 1959; Kenneth Grahame 1859-1932: A Study of His Life, Work and Times (in U.S. as Kenneth Grahame: A Biography), 1959; Essays in Antiquity, 1960; (ed.) Appreciations: Essays by Clifton Fadiman, 1962; Habeas Corpus (short stories), 1962; Look at the Romans, 1963; The Laughter of Aphrodite, 1965; (trans.) Juvenal: The Sixteen Satires, 1967, 1974; Alexander the Great, 1970; Armada from Athens, 1970; The Year of Salamis, 480-479 B.C., 1970; The Shadow of the Parthenon: Studies in Ancient History and Literature, 1972; The Parthenon, 1973; A Concise History of Ancient Greece (in U.S. as Ancient Greece: An Illustrated History), 1973; Alexander of Macedon 356-323 BC, 1974; (trans.) Ovid: The Erotic Poems, 1982. Add: c/o Dept. of Classics, Univ. of Texas, Waggener Hall, Austin, Tex. 78712, U.S.A.

GREEN, Richard. American, b. 1936. Psychiatry, Sex. Prof. of Psychiatry and Psychology, State Univ. of New York at Stony Brook; Founder, Intnl. Academy of Sex Research. Formerly Prof. of Psychiatry in Residence, and Dir., Gender Identity Research and Treatment Prog., Univ. of California Sch. of Medicine, Los Angeles. Ed., Archives of Sexual Behavior. *Publs:* (ed., with J. Money) Transsexualism and Sex Reassignment, 1969; Sexual Identity Conflict in Children and Adults, 1973; Human Sexuality, 1979; (with G. Wagner) Impotence, 1981; The "Sissy Boy Syndrome" and the Development of Homosexuality, 1986. Add: Dept. of Psychiatry, State Univ. of New York, Stony Brook, N.Y. 11794, U.S.A.

GREEN, Roger James. British, b. 1944. Children's fiction, Paranormal. Deputy Head Teacher, Wisewood Primary Sch., Sheffield, since 1977. Teacher and Head of Language Studies, middle sch., Sheffield, 1973–77. *Publs:* The Fear of Samuel Walton, 1984; The Lengthening Shadow, 1986; The Devil Finds Work, 1987; They Watched Him Die, 1988. Add: 268 Abbeydale Rd. S., Sheffield S17 31N, England.

GREEN, Timothy (S.) British, b. 1936. Money/Finance, Natural history, Travel/Exploration/Adventure. London Corresp., Horizon, and American Heritage, 1959–62, and Life, 1962–64; Ed., Illustrated London News, 1964–66. *Publs:* The World of God, 1968; The Smugglers 1969; Restless Spirit (in U.K. as The Adventurers) 1970; The Universal Eye, 1972; World of Gold Today, 1973; How to Buy Gold, 1975; The Smuggling Business 1977; The World of Diamonds, 1981; The New World of Gold, 1982, 1985; (with Maureen Green) The Good Water Guide, 1985; The Prospect for Gold, 1987. Add: c/o Rosendale Press, Premier House, Greycoat Pl., London SW1, England.

GREEN, Vivian (Hubert Howard). British, b. 1915. History, Theology/Religion. Fellow and Tutor in History, Lincoln Coll., Oxford, since 1951 (Chaplain, 1951–69; Sr. Tutor, 1953–62, 1974–77; Sub-Rector, 1970–83; Rector, 1983–87). *Publs:* Bishop Reginald Pecock, 1945; The Hanoverians, 1948; From St. Augustine to William Temple, 1948; Renaissance and Reformation, 1952; The Later Plantagenets, 1955; Oxford Common Room, 1957; The Young Mr. Wesley, 1961; The Swiss Alps, 1961; Martin Luther and the Reformation, 1964; John Wesley, 1964; Religion at Oxford and Cambridge, 1964; The Universities, 1969; Medieval Civilization in Western Europe, 1971; History of Oxford University, 1974; The Commonwealth of Lincoln College, Oxford 1427-1977, 1979; Love in a Cool Climate: The Letters of Mark Pattison and Meta Bradley, 1985; (ed.) Memoirs of an Oxford Don: Mark Pattison, 1988; (with William Scoular) A Question of Guilt: The Murder of Nancy Eaton, 1989. Add: Calendars, Burford, Oxon, England.

GREENBAUM, Sidney. British, b. 1929. Language/Linguistics. Quain Prof. of English Language and Literature, and Dir. of the Survey of English Usage, since 1983, and Dean, Faculty of Arts, since 1988, University Coll., London. Assoc. Prof., 1969–72, and Prof., 1972–83, English Dept., Univ. of Wisconsin, Milwaukee. *Publs:* Studies in English Adverbial Usage, 1969; Verb-Intensifier Collocations in English: An Experimental Approach, 1970; (with Randolph Quirk) Elicitation Experiments in English: Linguistic Studies in Use and Attitude, 1970; (with Randolph Quirk, Geoffrey Leech and Jan Svartvik) A Grammar of Contemporary English, 1972; (with Quirk) A Concise Grammar of Contemporary English (in U.K. as A University Grammar of English), 1973; (ed.) Acceptability in Language, 1977; (ed. with Leech and Svartvik) Studies in English Linguistics, 1980; The English Language Today, 1984; (with Quirk, Leech, and Svartik) A Comprehensive Grammar of the English Language, 1985; (with Charles Cooper), Studying Writing: Linguistic Approaches, 1986; (with Janet Whitcut), rev. ed. of Gower's Complete Plain Words, 1986; (with Janet Whitcut) Guide to English Usage, 1988; Good English and the Grammarian, 1988; A College Grammar of English, 1989. Add: Dept. of English, University Coll., Gower St., London WC1E 6BT, England.

GREENBERG, Alvin. American, b. 1932. Novels/Short stories, Poetry, Libretti. Prof. of English, Macalester Coll., St. Paul, Minn. (joined faculty, 1965). Instr., Univ. of Kentucky, Lexington, 1963–65; Ed., 1967–71, and Fiction Ed., 1971–73, The Minnesota Review. *Publs:* The Small Waves (novel), 1965; The Metaphysical Giraffe (poetry), 1968; Going Nowhere (novel), 1971; The House of the Would-Be Gardener (poetry), 1972; Dark Lands (poetry), 1973; Metaform (poetry), 1975; The Invention of the West (novel), 1976; In Direction (poetry), 1978; The Discovery of America (stories), 1980; And Yet (poetry), 1981; Detta Q (stories), 1983; The Man in the Cardboard Mask (stories), 1985; Heavy Wings (poetry), 1988. Add: Dept. of English, Macalester College, St. Paul, Minn. 55105, U.S.A.

GREENBERG, Clement. American, b. 1909. Art. Assoc. Ed., Commentary, 1945–57. *Publs:* Joan Miro, 1948; Matisse, 1953; Hans Hofmann, 1961; Art and Culture, 1961; Collected Essays and Criticism, 2 vols., 1986. Add: c/o Beacon Press, 25 Beacon St., Boston, Mass. 02108, U.S.A.

GREENBERG, Ira (Arthur). American, b. 1934. Psychology.

Founder and Exec. Dir., Thyrsus Publishing Co., Beverley Hills, Calif., since 1968; Mgmt. Consultant, Behavioral Studies Inst., Los Angeles, since 1970; Founder and Exec. Dir., Psychodrama Center for Los Angeles Inc., since 1971; Founder and Exec. Dir., Group Hypnosis Center for Los Angeles, since 1976; part-time clinical Psychologist, Camarillo State Hosp., Calif.; Lectr., California Sch. of Professional Psychology; Producer-Host, tv show Crime and Public Safety, since 1983. Member, Bd. of Dirs., Southern Calif. Soc. of Clinical Hypnosis (Pres., 1977–78); Calif. State Humane Officer (Peace Officer) with Animal Protection Inst. of America, since 1979. Reporter, Columbus, Ga. Enquirer, 1951–55, Louisville, Ky. Courier-Journal, 1952–56, and Los Angeles Times, 1956–62; Counselor, Psychological Clinic and Counseling Center, The Claremont Colleges, Calif., 1964–65; Assoc., Staff, and Supervising Psychologist, Camarillo State Hosp., Calif., 1967–72; Part-time Asst. Prof., San Fernando Valley State Coll., Northridge, Calif., 1967–69; Psychologist, The Free Clinic, Los Angeles, 1968–70; Lectr., Univ. of California at Santa Barbara, 1968–70; Member, Directing Staff, California Inst. of Psychodrama, Los Angeles, 1969–71; Consultant, Bd. of Dirs., Topanga Center for Human Development, Los Angeles, 1971–74. *Publs:* Psychodrama and Audience Attitude Change, 1968; Psychodrama: Theory and Therapy, 1974; Group Hypnotherapy and Hypnodrama, 1977. Add: Box A-369, Camarillo State Hosp., Camarillo, Calif. 93010, U.S.A.

GREENBERG, Joanne. American, b. 1932. Novels/Short stories. Teacher of experimental class in etymology, Jefferson County Sch. System, Colorado, since 1963. *Publs:* The King's Persons, 1963; I Never Promised You a Rose Garden, 1964; The Monday Voices, 1965; Summering, 1966; In This Sign, 1970; Rites of Passage, 1971; Founder's Praise, 1976; High Crimes and Misdemeanours, 1979; A Season of Delight, 1981; The Far Side of Victory, 1983; Simple Gifts, 1986; Age of Consent, 1987; Of Such Small Differences, 1988. Add: 29221 Rainbow Hills Rd., Golden, Colo. 80401, U.S.A.

GREENBERG, Joseph (Harold). American, b. 1915. Anthropology/Ethnology, Language/Linguistics. Ray Lyman Wilbur Prof. of the Social Sciences in Anthropology, Stanford Univ., California, since 1971 (Prof. of Anthropology, since 1962; Chmn., Cttee on Africa Studies, 1964–70; Chmn. of the Dept. of Anthropology, 1971–73). Instr., then Asst. Prof., Univ. of Minnesota, 1946–48; Asst. Prof. to Prof., Columbia Univ., NYC, 1948–62. Member of Exec. Cittee., Linguistic Soc. of America, 1953–55; Dir., West African Languages Survey, 1959–60; Pres., West African Linguistic Soc., 1955–70, and African Studies Assn., 1964–65. *Publs:* The Influence of Islam on a Sudanese Religion, 1946; Studies in African Linguistic Classfication, 1955; Essays in Linguistics, 1957; Universals of Language, 1963; The Languages of Africa, 1963; Anthropological Linguistics: An Introduction, 1968; Language, Culture, and Communication, 1971; Language Typology, 1974; A New Introduction to Linguistics, 1977; Universals of Human Language, 4 vols., 1978; Language in the Americas, 1987. Add: Dept. of Anthropology, Stanford Univ., Stanford, Calif., U.S.A.

GREENBERGER, Howard. American. Novels, Plays/Screenplays, Biography. Writer and Dir., La Mama Experimental Theatre Club and Caffé Cino. Employed in public relations, Motivational Programmers Inc., NYC, 1948–51; Copy Chief, Robert Whitehill Advertising Inc. NYC, 1951–55 and 1958–61; Television and Radio Producer, Arkwright Advertising Co. Inc., NYC, 1955–58, and American Cancer Soc., 1961–65. *Publs:* Birthday of Eternity (novel), 1944; Shadow on the Moon (play), 1944; Gay Masquerade (musical), 1944; The End of the Circle (play), 1946; Turning Points (radio series); Once Upon a Tune (TV series), 1950; Inside Times Square, 1955 (TV Series); A Celebration for Emily (television play), 1968; (with Robert Rheinhold) Our Play on the Future Has No Name (musical), 1970; Everything's the Same—Only Different (musical), 1971; The Off-Broadway Experience, (history), 1971; Bogey's Baby (biography), 1976; (with Robert Rheingold) Grow with Me (play), 1980; Getting Your Foot in the Door, 4 vols. Add: 404 E. 55th St., New York, N.Y. 10022, U.S.A.

GREENE, A.C. American, b. 1923. History, Autobiography/Memoirs/Personal. Radio and Television Commentator since 1970; Essayist, MacNeil-Lehrer News Hour, since 1983; Historical Columnist, Dallas News, since 1983; Co-Dir., Center for Texas Studies, Univ. of North Texas, since 1986. Member of staff, 1948–52, and Amusements Ed., 1952–59, Abilene Reporter-News, Tex.; Book Ed. and Editorial Columnist, 1960–68, and Ed. of Editorial Page, 1963–65, Dallas Times Herald, Tex.; Television Producer, KERA-Television, Dallas, 1970–71; Host, A.C. Greene's Historic Moments, WFAA-Radio, Dallas, 1982–83. *Publs:* A Personal Country (reminiscences), 1969, rev. ed. 1979; (ed. and contrib.) Living Texas: A Gathering of Experiences, 1970; The Last Cap-

tive (history) 1972; The Santa Claus Bank Robbery (history) 1972; A Christmas Tree (reminiscences), 1973, 1978; Dallas: The Deciding Years, 1973; Views in Texas, 1974; A Place Called Dallas, 1975; (with Roger Horchow) Elephants in Your Mailbox, 1980; The Fifty Best Books on Texas, 1981; The Highland Park Woman (fiction), 1983; Dallas U.S.A., 1984; Texas Sketches, 1985. Add: 4359 Shirley Dr., Dallas, Tex. 75229, U.S.A.

GREENE, Bette. American, b. 1934. Children's fiction. *Publs:* Summer of My German Soldier, 1973; Philip Hall Likes Me, I Reckon Maybe, 1974; Morning Is a Long Time Coming, 1978; Bette Green's Survival Kit: 303 Tips from One Writer to Another, 1980; Get on Out of Here, Philip Hall, 1981; Them That Glitter and Them That Don't, 1983; I've Already Forgotten Your Name, Philip Hall, 1983. Add: 338 Clinton Rd., Brookline, Mass. 02146, U.S.A.

GREENE, Constance C(larke). American, b. 1924. Novels, Children's fiction. *Publs:* A Girl Called Al, 1969; Leo the Lioness, 1970; Good Luck Bogie Hat, 1971; Unmaking of Rabbit, 1972; Isabelle the Itch, 1973; The Ears of Louis, 1974; I Know You, Al, 1975; Beat the Turtle Drum, 1976; Getting Nowhere, 1977; I and Sproggy, 1978; Your Old Pal, Al, 1979; Dotty's Suitcase, 1980; Double-Dare O'Toole, 1981; Al(exandra) the Great, 1982; Ask Anybody, 1983; Isabelle Shows Her Stuff, 1984; Star Shine, 1985.; Other Plans (for adults), 1985; Just Plain Al, 1986; The Love Letters of J. Timothy Owen, 1986; Monday I Love You, 1988; Isabelle and Little Orphan Frannie, 1988. Add: c/o Viking Press Inc., 40 W. 23rd St., New York, N.Y. 10010, U.S.A.

GREENE, Graham. British, b. 1904. Novels/Short stories, Mystery/Crime/Suspense, Children's fiction, Plays/Screenplays, Poetry, Film, Autobiography/Memoirs/ Personal, Biography. Staff Member, The Times, London, 1926–30; Film Critic, 1937–40, and Literary Ed., 1940–41, Spectator, London; Dir., Eyre & Spottiswoode, publrs., 1944–48, and The Bodley Head, publrs., 1958–68, both London. *Publs:* Babbling April: Poems, 1925; The Man Within, 1929; The Name of Action, 1930; Rumour at Nightfall, 1931; Stamboul Train: An Entertainment (in U.S. as Orient Express: An Entertainment), 1932; It's a Battlefield, 1934; England Made Me, 1935; The Basement Room and Other Stories, 1935; The Bear Fell Free, 1935; Journey Without Maps: A Travel Book, 1936; A Gun for Sale: An Entertainment (in U.S. as This Gun for Hire: An Entertainment), 1936; Brighton Rock (in U.S. as Brighton Rock: An Entertainment), 1938; The Confidential Agent, 1939; (with J. Laver and S. Townsend) Twenty-Four Stories, 1939; The Lawless Roads: A Mexican Journey (in U.S. as Another Mexico), 1939; The Power and the Glory (in U.S. as The Labyrinthine Ways), 1940 British Dramatists, 1942; The Ministry of Fear: An Entertainment, 1943; The Little Train, 1946; Nineteen Stories, 1947, augmented ed. as Twenty-One Stories, 1954; The Heart of the Matter, 1948; Why Do I Write: An Exchange of Views Between Elizabeth Bowen, Graham Greene and V.S. Pritchett, 1948; After Two Years, 1949; For Christmas, 1950; The Little Fire Engine (in U.S. as The Little Red Fire Engine), 1950; The Third Man: An Entertainment, 1950; The Third Man and The Fallen Idol, 1950; The End of the Affair, 1951; The Lost Childhood and Other Essays, 1951; The Little Horse Bus, 1952; The Little Steam Roller: A Story of Mystery and Detection, 1953; Essais Catholiques, 1953; The Living Room, 1953; Loser Takes All: An Entertainment, 1955; The Quiet American, 1955; The Potting Shed, 1957; Our Man in Havana: An Entertainment, 1959; A Visit to Morin, 1959; The Complaisant Lover, 1959; In Search of a Character: Two African Journals, 1961; A Burnt-Out Case, 1961; The Revenge: An Autobiographical Fragment, 1963; A Sense of Reality, 1963; Carving a Statue, 1964; Victorian Detective Fiction: A Catalogue of the Collection made by Dorothy Glover and Graham Greene, 1966; The Comedians 1966; May We Borrow Your Husband? and Other Comedies of the Sexual Life, 1967; (with Carol Reed) The Third Man: A Film, 1969; Travels with My Aunt, 1969; Collected Essays, 1969; A Sort of Life, 1971; The Pleaure Dome: Collected Film Criticism 1935-40, 1972; Collected Stories, 1972; The Honorary Consul, 1973; Lord Rochester's Monkey: A Biography of John Wilmot, Second Earl of Rochester, 1974; The Return of A.J. Raffles: An Edwardian Comedy in Three Acts (play), 1975; Shades of Greene (short stories), 1975; (ed.) An Impossible Woman: The Memories of Dottoressa Moor, 1975; The Human Factor, 1978; Doctor Fischer of Geneva, 1980; Ways of Escape, 1980; The Great Jowett (play), 1981; J'Accuse, 1982; Monsignor Quixote, 1982; Getting to Know the General: A Friendship in Panama, 1984; The Tenth Man, 1985; The Captain and the Enemy, 1988. Add: c/o Reinhardt Books Ltd., 27 Wright's Lane, London W8 5TZ, England.

GREENE, James H. American, b. 1915. Engineering/Technology. Prof. of Industrial Engineering, Purdue Univ., West Lafayette, Ind., since

1948. Former Fulbright Lectr., Finland Inst. of Technology. *Publs:* (ed.) Production and Inventory Control Handbook; Production Control Systems and Decisions, 1965, 1974; Operations Planning and Control, 1967; Operations Management for Productivity and Profit, 1984; Production and Inventory Control Handbook, 1987. Add: 555 N 400 W, West Lafayette, Ind. 47906, U.S.A.

GREENE, Jonathan (Edward). American, b. 1943. Poetry. Founding Ed. and Dir., Gnomon Press, Frankfort, Ky., since 1965. Ed., Kentucky Renaissance, 1976. *Publs:* The Reckoning, 1966; Instance, 1968; The Lapidary, 1969; A 17th Century Garner, 1969; An Unspoken Complaint, 1970; (trans.) The Poor in Church, by Arthur Rimbaud, 1973; Scaling the Walls, 1974; Glossary of the Everyday, 1974; Peripatetics, 1978; (ed.) Jonathan Williams: A 50th Birthday Celebration, 1979; Once a Kingdom Again, 1979; Quiet Goods, 1980; Idylls, 1983; Small Change for the Long Haul, 1984; Trickster Tales, 1985. Add: P.O. Box 475, Frankfort, Ky. 40602, U.S.A.

GREENE, Judith. British, b. 1936. Language/Linguistics, Psychology, Travel/Exploration/Adventure Prof. of Psychology, Open Univ., since 1976. Lect. in Psychology, Birkbeck Coll., Univ. of London, 1966–75. Publicity Mgr., Andre Deutsch, publrs., London, 1959–60; Admin., Intnl. Sugar Council, 1960–62. *Publs:* Psycholinguistics: Chomsky and Psychology, 1972; Thinking and Language, 1975; (with M. D'Oliveira) Learning to Use Statistics, 1982; (with C. Hicks) Basic Cognitive Processes, 1984; Language Understanding, 1986; Memory, Thinking, and Language, 1987; Gen. Ed. of Cape's 'Travellers Guide to': Sicily, 1965; Finland, 1965; Malta and Gozo, 1967; Sardinia, 1967; Cyprus, 1967; The Channel Islands, 1968; Yugoslavia, 1969; Crete, 1969; Rhodes and the Dodecanese, 1970; Corfu and the Ionian Islands, 1971; Morocco, 1972; Tunisia, 1973; Turkey 1975; Balearics, 1975; Cyclades, 1986; Egypt, 1987. Add: c/o Open Univ., Milton Keynes, England.

GREENE, Nathanael. American, b.1935. History. Prof. of History since 1974, and Vice-Pres. for Academic Affairs since 1977, Wesleyan Univ., Middletown, Conn. (Instr., 1963–64; Asst. Prof., 1964–68; Assoc. Prof., 1968–74). *Publs:* (ed.) Fascism: An Anthology, 1968; Crisis and Decline: The French Socialist Party in the Popular Front Era, 1969; From Versailles to Vichy: The Third French Republic, 1919-1940, 1970; (ed.) European Socialism Since World War I, 1971. Add: Dept. of History, Wesleyan Univ., Middletown, Conn. 06457, U.S.A.

GREENE, Victor. American, b 1933. History. Prof., History Dept., Univ. of Wisconsin, Milwaukee, since 1977 (Assoc. Prof., 1971–77). Asst. Prof., 1963–68, and Assoc. Prof., 1968–71, Kansas State Univ. *Publs:* Slavic Community on Strike, 1968; (ed. with others) American Immigration Collection: Series 2, 33 vols., 1970; For God and Country: Polish and Lithuanian Ethnic Consciousness in America, 1975; American Immigrant Leaders, 1987. Add: Dept. of History, Univ. of Wisconsin, Milwaukee, Wisc. 53201, U.S.A.

GREENE, Yvonne. *See* FLESCH, Y.

GREENER, Michael John. British, b. 1931. Business/Trade/Industry, Law. Managing Dr., Greener & Sons Ltd., retail jewellers and booksellers, since 1971. Sr. Audit Clerk, Deloitte Plender Griffiths, Cardiff, 1953–57; Asst. to Secty., Western Mail Echo Ltd., Cardiff, 1957–60; Lectr. in Accounting, Coll. of Commerce, Wednesbury, 1960–63. *Publs:* Between the Lines of the Balance Sheet, 1968, 1980; Problems for Discussion in Mercantile Law, 1968; Penguin Dictionary of Commerce, 1970, 1980; Penguin Business Dictionary, 1987. Add: 33 Glan Hafren, The Knap, Barry, S. Glam. CF6 8TA, Wales.

GREENFIELD, Eloise. American, b. 1929. Children's fiction. *Publs:* The Last Dance, 1971; Love, Oh, Love, 1972; Bubbles, 1972, reissued as Good News, 1977; Rosa Parks (biography), 1973; Sister, 1974; She Come Bringing Me That Little Baby Girl, 1974; Me and Nessie, 1975; Paul Robeson, 1975; First Pink Light, 1976; Mary McLeod Bethune, 1977; African Dream, 1977; (with L.J. Little) I Can Do It By Myself, 1978; Honey, Love, and Other Love Poems, 1978; Talk About a Family, 1978; Childtimes, 1979; Grandmama's Joy, 1980; Darlene, 1980; Daydreamers, 1981; Nathaniel Talking, 1988; Under the Sunday Tree (verse), 1988; Grandpa's Face, 1988. Add: c/o Maria Brown Assocs., 412 W. 154th St., New York, N.Y. 10034, U.S.A.

GREENFIELD, Jerome. American, b. 1923. Novels/Short stories, History. Assoc. Prof. of English, State Univ. of New York Coll. at New Paltz. *Publs:* The Chalk Line (novel), 1963; Wilhelm Reich vs. the U.S.A., 1974. Add: 31 Beechwood Park, Poughkeepsie, N.Y. 12601, U.S.A.

GREENHILL, Basil Jack. British, b. 1920. History, Recreation/Leisure/Hobbies. Joined Commonwealth Service, subsequently Diplomatic Service, 1946; Served in Dacca, 1950–52; Peshawar, 1952–53, Karachi, 1953–54, U.K. Delegation to the U.N., 1954, Tokyo, 1955–58, and U.K. Delegation to the Conference on Law of the Sea, Geneva, 1958; Deputy High Commnr. in E. Pakistan, 1958–59, and in Ottawa, 1961–64; with Commonwealth Office, London, 1965–66; Dir., National Maritime Museum, Greenwich, London, 1967–83. *Publs:* The Merchant Schooners, vols., 1951–57, 4th ed., 1987; (ed.) W.J. Slade's Out of Appledore, 1959; Sailing for a Living, 1962; (with Ann Giffard) Westcountrymen in Prince Edward's Isle, 1967; (with Ann Giffard) Women Under Sail, 1970; Captain Cook, 1970; Boats and Boatmen of Pakistan, 1971; (with Ann Giffard) Travelling by Sea in the Nineteenth Century, 1972; (with P.W. Brock) Sail and Steam, 1973; (with W.J. Slade) West Country Coasting Ketches, 1974; Victorian Maritime Album, 1974; A Quayside Camera, 1975; (with Lionel Willis) The Coastal Trade: Sailing Craft of British Waters 900-1900, 1975; Archaeology of the Boat, 1976; (with Ann Giffard) Victorian and Edwardian Sailing Ships, 1976; (with Ann Giffard) Victorian and Edwardian Ships and Harbours, 1978; (ed.) The Last Tall Ships, by Georg Kahre, 1978; (with Ann Giffard) Victorian and Edwardian Merchant Steamships, 1979; Schooners, 1980; The Life and Death of the Sailing Ship, 1980; (with D. Stonham) Seafaring Under Sail, 1981; Karlsson, 1982; The Grain Races, 1986; The Woodshipbuilders, 1988; The British Assault on Finland: A Forgotten Naval War, 1988. Add: West Boetheric Farm, St. Dominic, Cornwall PL12 6SZ, England.

GREENLEAF, Stephen (Howell). American, b. 1942. Mystery/-Crime/Suspense. Admitted to the Bar of California, 1968, and Iowa, 1977; Research, Multnomah County Legal Aid, Portland, Ore., 1969–70; Assoc. Attorney, Thompson and Hubbard, Monterey, Calif., 1970–71, and Sullivan Jones and Archer, San Francisco, 1972–76; Adjunct Prof. of Trial Advocacy, Univ. of Iowa, 1979–81. *Publs:* Grave Error, 1979; Death Bed, 1980; State's Evidence, 1982; Fatal Obsession, 1983; The Ditto List, 1985; Beyond Blame, 1986; Toll Call, 1987; Impact, 1989. Add: c/o Esther Newberg, ICM, 40 W. 57th St., New York, N.Y. 10019, U.S.A.

GREENLEAF, William. American. Science fiction. *Publs:* Time Jumper, 1981; The Tartarus Incident, 1983; The Pandora Stone, 1984; Starjacked!, 1987. Add: 525 E. Stonebridge Dr., Gilbert, Ariz. 85234, U.S.A.

GREENLEE, J(acob) Harold. American, b. 1918. Language/Linguistics, Theology/Religion. Christian Missionary, OMS Intnl., since 1969; Adjunct Prof. of Linguistics, Univ. of Texas at Arlington, since 1978. Trans. Consultant, Wycliffe Bible Translators. Prof. of New Testament Greek, Asbury Theological Seminary, Wilmore, Ky., 1947–65, and Oral Roberts Univ., 1965–69. *Publs:* The Gospel Text of Cyril of Jerusalem, 1955; Concise Exegetical Grammar of New Testament Greek, 1963; An Introduction to New Testament Textual Criticism, 1964; Nine Uncial Palimpsests of the Greek New Testament, 1969; A New Testament Greek Morpheme Lexicon, 1983; Scribes, Scrolls, and Scripture, 1985. Add: 715 Kennedy Ave., Duncanville, Tex. 75116, U.S.A.

GREENWALT, Tibor J. American, b. 1914. Medicine/Health. Prof. Emeritus of Internal Medicine and Pathology, Univ. of Cincinnati Coll. of Medicine; Dir., Hoxworth Blood Center of Univ. of Cincinnati, 1979–87, and Deputy Dir. of Research since 1987. Clinical Prof. of Medicine, George Washington Univ. Sch. of Medicine, Washington, D.C., and American Red Cross Blood Services, Sr. Scientific Advisor and Dir., 1967–79; Sr. Member, Inst. of Medicine, NAS, 1984. *Publs:* (with W. Dameshek and C. Dreyfus) Hemolytic Syndromes, 1942; (with Shirley A. Johnson) Coagulation and Transfusion in Clinical Medicine, 1965; (ed. and contrib.) Immunogenetics, 1968; (with G.A. Jamieson) Red Cell Membrane: Structure and Function, 1969; (with G.A. Jamieson) Formation and Descrution of Blood Cells, 1970; (ed. with G.A. Jamieson) Glycoproteins of Blood Cells and Plasma, 1971; (ed. with G.A. Jamieson) The Human Red Cell in Vitro, 1973, 1974; Transmissible Disease and Blood Transfusions, 1975; (ed. with E.A. Steane) Handbook in Clinical Laboratory Science: Blood Banking, 3 vols., 1977–81; Trace Components of Plasma, 1976; The Granulocyte: Function and Clinical Utilization, 1977; Blood Substitutes and Plasma Expanders, 1978; The Blood Platelet in Transfusion Therapy, 1978; Blood Transfusions, 1988. Add: 3231 Burnet Ave., Cincinnati, Ohio 45267, U.S.A.

GREENWOOD, Duncan. British, b. 1919. Plays/Screenplays. Asst. Chief Engineer, Dept. of Transport, London 1968–79 (Sr. Engineer 1963–66; Superintending Engineer 1966–68). *Publs:* Cat Among Pigeons, 1957; Strike Happy, 1960; Murder Delayed, 1962; (with Robert King)

No Time for Fig Leaves, 1966; (with Derek Parkes) Surprise Package, 1976; (with Robert King) Murder by the Book, 1983; Waiting for Yesterday, 1985. Add: 58 High View, Pinner, Middx. HA5 3PB, England.

GREENWOOD, Norman Neill. British, b. 1925. Chemistry. Prof. and Head of Dept. of Inorganic and Structural Chemistry, Univ. of Leeds, since 1971. Resident Tutor and Lectr. in Chemistry, Trinity Coll., Melbourne, 1946–48; Sr. Harwell Research Fellow, 1951–53; Lectr. and Sr. Lectr. in Inorganic Chemistry, Univ. of Nottingham, 1953–61; Prof. and Head of Dept., Univ. of Newcastle upon Tyne, 1961–71. *Publs:* Principles of Atomic Orbitals, 1964, 4th ed. 1980; (ed. and co-author) Spectroscopic Properties of Inorganic and Organometallic Compounds, 9 vols., 1967–75; Ionic Crystals, Lattic Defects and Non-Stoichiometry, 1968; (with T.C. Gibb) Mossbauer Spectroscpy, 1971; (with W.A. Campbell) Contemporary British Chemists, 1971; Periodicity and Atomic Structure, 1971; (with E.J.F. Ross) Index of Vibrational Spectra of Inorganic and Organometallic Compounds, 3 vols., 1972, 1974, 1977; Boron, 1973; (with A. Earnshaw) Chemistry of the Elements, 1984. Add: Sch. of Chemistry, Univ. of Leeds, Leeds LS2 9JT, England.

GREENWOOD, Ted. (Edward Alister Greenwood). Australian, b. 1930. Children's fiction. Primary sch. teacher, Melbourne, 1948–56; Lectr. in art education, Melbourne Teachers' Coll., 1956–60, and Toorak Teachers' Coll., Melbourne, 1960–68. *Publs:* Obstreperous, 1969; Alfred, 1970; V.I.P.: Very Important Plant, 1971; Joseph and Lulu and the Prindiville House Pigeons, 1972; Terry's Brrrmmm GT, 1974; The Pochetto Coat, 1978; Ginnie, 1979; Curious Eddie, 1979; The Boy Who Saw God, 1980; Everlasting Circle, 1981; Flora's Treasures, 1982; Marley and Friends, 1983; (with S. Fennessy) Warts and All, 1984; Ship Rock, 1985; (with Fennessy) I Don't Want to Know, 1986; Windows, 1989. Add: 50 Hilton Rd., Ferny Creek, Vic. 3786, Australia.

GREER, Germaine. Australian, b. 1939. Women. Sr. Tutor, Sydney Univ., 1963–64; Lectr. in English, Univ. of Warwick, Coventry, 1967–73; Columnist, Sunday Times newspaper, London 1971–73; Dir., Tulsa Centre for the Study of Women's Literature, 1980–82. *Publs:* The Female Eunuch, 1970; The Obstacle Race, 1979; Sex and Destiny, 1984; Shakespeare, 1985; The Madwoman's Underclothes, 1986; Daddy We Hardly Knew You, 1988. Add: c/o Aitken and Stone, 29 Fernshaw Rd., London SW10 0TG, England.

GREET, Kenneth Gerald. British, b. 1918. Theology/Religion. With the Conference of the British Methodist Church, London: Secty. of Social Responsibility Dept., 1954–71; Secty. of the Conference, 1971–84; Pres. of the Conference, 1981–81. Religious Adviser, Thames Television, London, 1967–84. *Publs:* The Mutual Society, 1962; Man and Wife Together, 1962; Large Petitions, 1964; Guide to Loving, 1965; The Debate About Drink, 1969; The Sunday Question, 1970; The Art of Moral Judgment, 1970; When the Spirit Moves, 1975; A Lion from a Thicket, 1978; The Big Sin, 1982; Under the Rainbow Arch, 1984; What Shall I Cry?, 1986. Add: 89 Broadmark Lane, Rustington, Sussex BN16 2JA, England.

GREGG, Davis Weinert. American, b. 1918. Money/Finance. Distinguished Prof. of Economics, The American Coll., Bryn Mawr, Pa. (Asst. Dean, 1949–51; Dean, 1951–54; Pres., 1954–82). Consulting Ed., Irwin Series in Insurance and Economic Security, 1949–82. *Publs:* Group Life Insurance, 1950, 1962; Insurance Courses in Colleges and Universities Outside the United States, 1960; (co-ed.) Life and Health Insurance Handbook, 3rd ed. 1973. Add: 270 Bryn Mawr Ave., Bryn Mawr, Pa. 19010, U.S.A.

GREGG, Hubert. British, b. 1914. Novels/Short stories, Plays/-Screenplays, Songs, lyrics and libretti, Autobiography. Actor, director and broadcaster. *Publs:* April Gentleman (novel), 1951; A Day's Loving (novel), 1974; Agatha Christie and All That Mousetrap, 1981; Thanks for the Memory, 1983; Geliebtes Traumbild (play), 1984; Maybe It's Because (autobiography), 1989; also author of stage plays and musicals, and songs. Add: c/o Garrick Club, London WC2, England.

GREGG, Pauline. British. History, Biography. *Publs:* Social and Economic History of Britain from 1760 to the Present Day, 1950, 8th rev. ed. 1981; The Chain of History, 1958; Freeborn John: A Biography of John Lilburne, 1961; The Welfare State, 1963; Modern Britain, 1967; A Social and Economic History of England from the Black Death to the Industrial Revolution, 1975; King Charles the First, 1981; Oliver Cromwell, 1988. Add: c/o Weidenfeld and Nicolson, 91 Clapham High St., London SW4 7TA, England.

GREGG, Richard (Alexander). American, b. 1927. Literature. Prof. of Russian, and Chmn. of Russian Dept., Vassar Coll., Poughkeepsie, N.Y., since 1969. Instr., 1960–62, Asst. Prof., 1962–66, and Assoc. Prof. of Russian Language and Literature, 1967–69, Columbia Univ., NYC. *Publs:* Fedor Tiutchev: The Evolution of a Poet, 1965. Add: 64 Boardman Rd., Poughkeepsie, N.Y. 12603, U.S.A.

GREGG, Sidney John. British, b. 1902. Chemistry. Lectr., 1940–47, and Reader, 1948–67, Dept. of Chemistry, Univ. of Exeter. *Publs:* (trans.) Physical Chemistry, 1932; The Adsorption of Gases by Solids, 1934; The Surface Chemistry of Solids, 1951, 1961; (co-author) Adsorption, Surface Area and Porosity, 1967, 1982; (co-author) Concise Etymological Dictionary of Chemistry, 1976. Add: 45 Pennsylvania Rd., Exeter EX4 6DB, England.

GREGOR, Arthur. American, b. 1923. Poetry, Plays, Children's fiction. Assoc. Prof., Hofstra Univ., Hempstead, N.Y., since 1973. Sr. Ed., Macmillan Co., publrs., NYC, 1962–70. *Publs:* Fire (play), 1952; Octavian Shooting Targets, 1954; 1 2 3 4 5, 1956; The Little Elephant, 1956; Declensions of a Refrain, 1957; Animal Babies, 1959; Basic Movements, 1966; Figure in the Door, 1968; Continued Departure (play), 1968; The Door Is Open (play), 1970; A Bed by the Sea, 1970; Selected Poems, 1971; The Past Now, 1975; Embodiment, 1982; A Longing in the Land, 1983; Secret Citizen, 1989. Add: 250 W. 94th St., New York, N.Y. 10025, U.S.A.

GREGORY, Cedric E. American, b. 1908. Earth sciences, Engineering/Technology. Prof. Emeritus of Mining Engineering, Univ. of Idaho, Moscow, since 1974 (prof., 1968–74); Prof., King Abdulaziz Univ., Jeddah, Saudi Arabia, since 1977. Assoc. Prof., Univ. of Queensland, Brisbane, 1956–66; Prof., Colorado Sch. of Mines, 1967–68; Prof., Virginia Polytechnic Inst. and State Univ., 1974–77. *Publs:* Explosives for Australasian Engineers, 1966, 3rd ed. 1977; Explosives for North American Engineers, 1973, 3rd ed. 1984; A Concise History of Mining, 1980; Bucolic Bull, 1982; Rudiments of Mining Practice, 1983. Add: Edificio Phoenix del Mar 411, Los Arenales del Sol, Alicante, Spain.

GREGORY, Dick. American, b. 1932. Civil liberties/Human rights, Race relations, Social commentary/phenomena. Comedian and civil rights activist. Pres., Dick Gregory Enterprises, Chicago. *Publs:* From the Back of the Bus, 1964; Nigger, 1964; What's Happening, 1965; The Shadow That Scares Me, 1971; Write Me In, 1971; No More Lies, 1971; Dick Gregory's Political Primer, 1971; Natural Diet, 1973; Up from Nigger, 1976; (with M. Lane) Code Name Zorro: The Murder of Martin Luther King, 1971; Dick Gregory's Bible Tales, 1978. Add: P.O. Box 266, Tower Hill Farm, Plymouth, Mass. 02360, U.S.A.

GREGORY, James Stothert. British, b. 1912. Children's non-fiction, Geography, Translations. Sr. Lectr. in Geography, Furzedown Coll. of Education, London, since 1965. Teacher of Geography, Manchester and London schs., 1937–42; Research Asst., National Farm Survey of U.K., 1943–44; Sr. Admin. Officer, U.N. Relief and Rehabilitation Admin., London and Yugoslavia, 1945–48; Sr. Admin, Officer, UNICEF Mission to Yugoslavia, 1949–50; freelance journalist and broadcaster, 1950–52; Sr. Lectr., Teachers' Training Coll., Bangkok, 1952–55; Teacher of Geography, Kitimat, B.C., Canada, 1955–57; Headmaster of sch. in Samoa, S. Pacific, 1957–60; Sr. Lectr., Univ. of Singapore, 1960–63; Ed., Teaching and Learning monthly journal, Univ. of Singapore, 1961–63; Sr. Lectr., Univ. of Ghana, 1963–65. *Publs:* (with D.W. Shave) The U.S.S.R.: A Geographical Survey, 1948; Land of the Soviets, 1949; (with K.A. Wilkins) Aspects of Modern Soviet Geography, 4 vols., 1974–75; (trans. and ed.) Geography of the U.S.S.R.: An Outline, 1974. Add: 189 Manggate Lane, Shepperton, Mddx., England.

GREGORY, John. *See* **HOSKINS,** Robert.

GREGORY, Richard Langton. British, b. 1923. Biology, Psychology, Sciences. Prof. of Neuropsychology, Univ. of Bristol, and Dir., Brain and Perception Lab., Medical Research Council, since 1970, now Emeritus. Fellow, Corpus Christi Coll., Cambridge. Lectr. in Psychology, Univ. of Cambridge, 1959–67; Prof. of Bionics, Dept. of Machine Intelligence and Perception, Univ. of Edinburgh, 1967–70. *Publs:* (with J. Wallace) Recovery from Early Blindness, 1963; Eye and Brain, 1966, 3rd ed. 1977; The Intelligent Eye, 1970; (ed. with E.H. Gombrich) Illusions in Nature and Art, 1973; Concepts and Mechanisms of Perception, 1974; Mind in Science, 1981; Odd Perceptions, 1986; Oxford Companion to the Mind, 1987. Add: 23 Royal York Crescent, Clifton, Bristol BS8 4JX, England.

GREGORY, Roy. British, b. 1935. Politics/Government. Prof. of Politics, Univ. of Reading, since 1973 (Lectr., 1964–73; Reader, 1973–76). Lectr., Queen's Coll., Dundee, 1962–64. *Publs:* The Miners and British Politics, 1906-1914, 1968; The Price of Amenity: Five Studies in Conservation and Government, 1971; The Parliamentary Ombudsman, 1975. Add: Dept. of Politics, Univ. of Reading, Whiteknights Park, Reading, Berks., England.

GREGORY, Stephan. *See* PENDLETON, Don.

GREIG, Charles. *See* CRUICKSHANK, Charles Greig.

GREIG, Doreen (Edith). South African, b. 1917. Architecture. Member of the Exec., South African Council for Architects, since 1971 (Pres., 1975–77); Pres. of the Convocation, Univ. of the Witwatersrand, Johannesburg, since 1978. Pres., Transvaal Inst. of Architects, 1959–60, 1965–66; Pres.-in-Chief, Inst. of South African Architects, 1972–74. *Publs:* Herbert Baker in South Africa, 1970; A Guide to Architecture in South Africa, 1971; The Reluctant Colonists, 1986. Add: 45 Talbragar Ave., Craighall 2196, Johannesburg, South Africa.

GRENVILLE, John A.S. British, b. 1928. Screenplays, History, International relations/Current affairs. Prof. of Modern History, Univ. of Birmingham, since 1969. Lectr., Univ. of Nottingham, 1953–66; Fellow, Yale Univ., New Haven, Conn., 1960–64; Prof. of Intnl. History, Univ. of Leeds, 1966–69. *Publs:* (with Joan Fuller) The Coming of the Europeans, 1962; Lord Salisbury and Foreign Policy, 1964; (with G.B. Young) Politics Strategy and American Diplomacy 1873-1917, 1966; (with Nicholas Pronay) The Munich Crisis 1938 (film), 1968; (with N. Pronay) The End of Illusions, from Munich to Dunkirk (film), 1970; The Major International Treaties, 1914-1973; A History and Guide with Texts, 1974, rev. ed. in 2 vols., 1987; Europe Reshaped 1848-1878, 1976, and subsequent eds.; Film as Evidence: "Tomorrow the World" (film, 1977); World History of the Twentieth Century, vol. I 1900-1945, 1980. Add: Sch. of History, Univ. of Birmingham, P.O. Box 363, Birmingham B15 2TT, England.

GRESSER, Seymour. American, b. 1926. Poetry. Freelance sculptor, since 1948. Resident Sculptor, Mt. Rushmore, S. Dakota, 1980. *Publs:* Stone Elegies, 1955; Coming of the Atom, 1957; Poems from Mexico, 1964; Voyages, 1969; A Garland for Stephen, 1970; Departure for Sons, 1973; Fragments and Other Poems, 1982. Add: 1015 Ruatan St., Silver Spring, Md. 20903, U.S.A.

GREX, Leo. *See* GRIBBLE, Leonard.

GREULACH, Victor A(ugust). American, b. 1906. Botany. Prof. Emeritus of Botany, Univ. of North Carolina, Chapel Hill, since 1974 (Assoc. Prof., 1949–51; Prof., 1951–74; Chmn., Dept. of Botany, 1960–72). Instr. in Botany, Muskingum Coll. New Concord, Ohio, 1933–35; Asst. Prof., 1935–40, Assoc. Prof. of Biology, 1940–46, and Chmn. of the Div. of Biological Sciences, 1944–46, Univ. of Houston; also, Dir., Houston Museum of Natural History, 1942–46; Assoc. Prof. of Plant Physiology, Texas A and M Univ., 1946–49. Exec. Dir., Commn. on Undergrad. Education in the Biological Sciences, Washington, D.C., 1964–65. *Publs:* Laboratory Manual for Elementary Plant Physiology, 1952; (with J. Edison Adams) Plants: An Introduction to Modern Botany, 1962, 3rd ed. 1976; Botany Made Simple, 1968; Plant Function and Structure, 1973, (with T.K. Scott), 1983; (with V.J. Chiapetta) Biology, 1977. Add: Dept. of Botany, Univ. of North Carolina, Chapel Hill, N.C. 27514, U.S.A.

GREY, Anthony. British, b. 1938. Novels/Short stories, Autobiography/Memoirs/Personal. Journalist, Eastern Daily Press, 1960–64; Foreign Corresp., East Berlin and Prague, 1965–67, and Peking, 1967–69, for Reuters, London; radio and television reporter and presenter. *Publs:* Hostage in Peking (autobiography), 1970; A Man Alone (short stories), 1972; Some Put Their Trust in Chariots, 1973; The Bulgarian Exclusive, 1976; The Chinese Assassin, 1978; Saigon, 1982; The Prime Minister Was a Spy (non-fiction), 1983; Peking, 1988. Add: The Chambers, Lots Rd., London SW10 0XF, England.

GREY, (Dame) Beryl (Elizabeth). British, b. 1927. Dance/Ballet, Travel/Exploration/Adventure. Chmn., Imperial Soc. of Teachers of Dancing; Vice-Pres., Royal Academy of Dancing; Pres., Dance Council of Wales. Prima Ballerina, Royal Ballet (formerly Sadlers Wells Ballet), London, 1941–59; Dir., Gen. Arts Education Trust, 1966–68; Artistic Dir., London Festival Ballet, 1968–79 (formerly prima ballerina and guest producer). *Publs:* Red Curtain Up, 1958; Through the Bamboo Curtain, 1965; My Favourite Ballet Stories, 1981. Add: "Fernhill", Priory Rd.,

Forest Row, Sussex, England.

GREY, Brenda. *See* MACKINLAY, Leila.

GREY, Charles. *See* TUBB, E.C..

GREY, Georgina. *See* ROBY, Mary Linn.

GREY, Ian. British. History, Biography. Staff member, Foreign and Commonwealth Office, London, 1946–51; Secty. to the Council, Royal Inst. of Intnl. Affairs, London, 1951–55; Publications Ed., and Deputy Secty.-Gen., Commonwealth Parliamentary Assn., 1955–83. *Publs:* Peter the Great, 1960; Catherine the Great, 1961; Ivan the Terrible, 1963; Ivan III and the Unification of Russia, 1964; The First Fifty Years: Soviet Russia 1917-1967, 1967; The Romanovs: The Rise and Fall of the Dynasty, 1970; A History of Russia, 1970; Boris Godunov: The Tragic Tsar, 1973; Stalin: Man of History, 1979; The Parliamentarians: The History of the Commonwealth Parliamentary Association, 1986. Add: 10 Alwyn Ave., London W4, England.

GREY, Jerry. American, b. 1926. Air/Space topics, Engineering/Technology, Sciences. Dir., Science and Technology Policy, American Inst. of Aeronautics and Astronautics, since 1978; Dir., Applied Solar Energy Corp., since 1979. Vice-Pres., Intnl. Academy of Astronautics, since 1983. Instr., Cornell Univ., Ithaca, N.Y., 1947–49; Engineer, Fairchild Engine Div., 1949–50; Hypersonic Aerodynamicist, Galcit, 1950–51; Sr. Engineer, Marquardt Aircraft, 1951–52; Prof., Princeton Univ., New Jersey, 1952–67; Pres., Greyrad Corp., 1959–71; Administrator, Public Policy, American Inst. of Aeronautics and Astronautics, 1971–82; Pres., Calprobe Corp., 1972–83; Adjunct Prof., Long Island Univ., 1976–82. Vice Pres., 1978–84, and Pres., 1984–86, Intnl. Astronautical Fedn.; Deputy Secty. Gen., U.N. Conference on the Exploration and Peaceful Uses of Outer Space, 1982. *Publs:* (ed. with V. Grey) Space Flight Report to the Nation, 1962; Nuclear Propulsion, 1970; (ed.) Offshore Airport Center Planning, 1971; The Race for Electric Power, 1972; (ed. with J.P. Layton) New Space Transportation Systems, 1973; The Facts of Flight, 1973; (ed. with A. Henderson) Solar System Exploration, 1974; (ed.) Aircraft Fuel Conservation, 1974; Noise, Noise, Noise!, 1975; (co-ed.) Solar Energy for Earth, 1975; (ed.) The Role of Technology in Civil Aviation Policy, 1976; (ed.) Advanced Energy Conservation Technology, 1976; (ed. with R. Downey and B. Davis) Space: A Resource for Earth, 1976; (ed.) Space Manufacturer Facilities, 4 vols., 1977–81; (ed. with M. Newman) Aerospace Technology Transfer to the Public Sector, 1978; (ed. with R. Salkeld and D. Patterson) Space Transportation 1980-2000, 1978; Enterprise, 1979; (co-ed.) Alternative Fuels for Transportation, 1979; (ed. with C. Krop) Aerospace Technology and Marine Transport, 1979; Aeronautics in China, 1981; Space Tracking and Data Systems, 1981; (co-ed.) International Aerospace Review, 1982; (co.-ed.) Working in Space, 1982; (co-ed.) Global Applications of Space Activities, 1982; Beachheads in Space, 1983; (co-ed) Aerospace Technology and Commercial Nuclear Power, 1983. Add: 1 Lincoln Plaza, New York, N.Y. 10023, U.S.A.

GREY, Louis. *See* GRIBBLE, Leonard.

GREY-WILSON, Christopher. British, b. 1944. Botany. Principal Scientific Officer (Taxonomic Botanist), Royal Botanic Gardens, Kew, since 1968. *Publs:* Dionysia, 1970; Alpine Flowers of Britain and Europe, 1979; Impatiens of Africa, 1980; (with B. Mathew) Bulbs, 1981; (with V. Matthews) Gardening on Walls, 1983; Garden Flowers, 1986; The Genus Cyclamen, 1988; (ed.) A Manual of Alpine and Rock Garden Plants, 1988; (with M. Blaney) The Illustrated Flora of Britain and Northern Europe, 1988. Add: Herbarium, Royal Botanic Gardens, Kew, Richmond, Surrey TW9 3AE, England.

GRIBBLE, Leonard (Reginald). Also writes as Sterry Browning, Lee Denver, Landon Grant, Leo Grex, Louis Grey, and Dexter Muir. British, b. 1908. Mystery/Crime/Suspense, Western/Adventure. Full-time writer. Founding Member, Crime Writers Assn., 1953. *Publs:* mystery novels—The Case of the Marsden Rubies, 1929; The Gillespie Suicide Mystery (in U.S as The Terrace Suicide Mystery), 1929; The Grand Modena Murder, 1930; Is This Revenge?. 1931 (in U.S. as The Serpentine Murder, 1931); (as Leo Grex) The Tragedy at Draythorpe, 1931; (as Leo Grex) The Nightborn, 1931; The Stolen Home Secretary (in U.S. as The Stolen Statesman), 1932; The Secret of Tangles, 1933; The Yellow Bungalow, 1933; (as Leo Grex) The Londly Inn Mystery, 1933; (as Leo Grex) The Madison Murder, 1933; The Death Chime, 1934; The Riddle of the Ravens, 1934; (as Louis Grey) The Signet of Death, 1934; (as Leo Grex) The Man from Manhattan, 1934; (as Leo Grex) Murder in the Sanctuary,

1934; Mystery at Tudor Arches, 1935; (as Leo Grex) Crooner's Swan Song, 1935; (as Leo Grex) Stolen Death, 1936; The Case of the Malverne Diamonds, 1936; Riley of the Special Branch, 1936; Who Killed Oliver Cromwell?, 1937; (as Leo Grex) Transatlantic Trouble, 1937; The Case-Book of Anthony Slade (short stories), 1937; Tragedy in E Flat, 1938; The Arsenal Stadium Mystery, 1939, 1950; (as Leo Grex) The Carlent Manor Crime, 1939; (as Leo Grex) The Black-Out Murders, 1940; Atomic Murder, 1947; (as Leo Grex) The Stalag Mites, 1947; (as Leo Grex) King Spiv, 1948; (as Dexter Muir) The Pilgrims Meet Murder, 1948; (as Leo Grex) Crooked Sixpence, 1949; (as Dexter Muir) The Speckled Swan, 1949; Hangman's Moon, 1950; They Kidnapped Stanley Matthews, 1950; The Frightened Chameleon, 1951; Mystery Manor, 1951; (as Sterry Browning) Crime at Cape Folly, 1951; The Glass Alibi, 1952; Murder Out of Season, 1952; The Velvet Mask and Other Stories, 1952; (as Leo Grex) Ace of Danger, 1952; She Died Laughing, 1953; (with Janet Green) Murder Mistaken, 1953; (as Dexter Muir) Rosemary for Death, 1953; (as Sterry Browning) Sex Marks the Spot, 1954; The Inverted Crime, 1954; (with Geraldine Laws) Sally of Scotland Yard, 1954 Superintendent Slade Investigates (short stories), 1956; Death Pays the Piper, 1956; Stand-In for Murder, 1957; (as Leo Grex) Thanks for the Felony, 1958; Don't Argue with Death, 1959; (as Leo Grex) Larceny in Her Heart, 1959; Wantons Die Hard, 1961; (as Leo Grex) Terror Wears a Smile, 1962; (as Leo Grex) The Brass Knuckle, 1964; Heads You Die, 1964; The Violent Dark, 1965; Strip-Tease Macabre, 1967; (as Leo Grex) Violent Keepsake, 1967; A Diplomat Dies, 1969; (as Leo Grex) The Hard Kill, 1969; Alias the Victim, 1971; (as Leo Grex) Kill Now—Pay Later, 1971; Programmed for Death, 1973; (as Leo Grex) Die—as in Murder, 1974; You Can't Die Tomorrow, 1975; The Cardinal's Diamonds, 1976; (as Leo Grex) Death Throws No Shadow, 1976; Midsummer Slay Ride, 1976; The Deadly Professionals, 1976; Compelled to Kill, 1977; Crime on Her Hands, 1977; The Dead End Killers, 1978; (as Leo Grex) Mix Me a Murder, 1978; Death Needs No Alibi, 1979; Dead End in Mayfair, 1981; The Dead Don't Scream, 1983; (as Leo Grex) Hot Ice, 1983; western novels, as Landon Grant—Rustler's Gulch, 1935; Wyoming Deadline, 1939; Texas Buckeroo, 1948; Ramrod of the Bar X, 1949; Scar Valley Bandit, 1951; The Rawhide Kid, 1951; Gunsmoke Canyon, 1952; Outlaws of Silver Spur, 1953; Marshall of Mustang, 1954; Thunder Valley Deadline, 1956; western novels as Lee Denver—Cheyenne Jones, Maverick Marshal, 1977; Cheyenne's Sixgun Justice, 1980; Cheyenne's Trail to Perdition, 1982; Cheyenne's Two-Gun Shoot-Out, 1983; Cheyenne at Dull-Knife Pass, 1982; Other—Queens of Crime, 1932; Famous Feats of Detection and Deduction, 1933; (with Nancy Gribble) All the Year Round Stories, 1935; Heroes of the Fighting R.A.F., 1941; Epics of the Fighting R.A.F., 1943; Heroes of the Merchant Navy, 1944; Battle Stories of the R.A.F., 1945; Toy Folk and Nursey People (verse), 1945; Great Detective Feats, 1946; Murder First Class, 1946; On Secret Service, 1946; (as Sterry Browning) Coastal Commandoes (novel), 1946; The Secret of the Red Mill (juvenile), 1948; The Missing Speed Ace (juvenile), 1950; The Riddle of the Blue Moon (juvenile), 1950; Speed Dermot, Junior Reporter (juvenile), 1951; (as Sterry Browning) Santa Fe Gunslick (novel), 1951; Famous Manhunts: A Century of Crime, 1953; Adventures in Murder Undertaken by Some Notorious Killers in Love, 1954; Triumphs of Scotland Yard: A Century of Detection, 1955; Famous Judges and Their Trials: A Century of Justice, 1957; The True Book About Scotland Yard (juvenile), 1957; Dangerous Mission (novel), 1957; Great Detective Exploits, 1958; Murders Most Strange, 1959; The True Book About the Old Bailey,1959; Hands of Terror: Notable Assassinations of the Twentieth Century, 1960; The True Book About the Mounties, 1960; Clues That Spelled Guilty, 1951; (ed.) Stories for Boys, 1961; (ed.) Stories for Girls, 1961; (ed.) Famous Stories of High Adventure (juvenile), 1962; (ed.) Famous Stories of the Sea and Ships, 1962; The True Book About Great Escapes, 1962; When Killers Err, 1962; Stories of Famous Detectives, 1963; They Challenged the Yard, 1963; The True Book About Smugglers and Smuggling, 1963; The True Book about The Spanish Main, 1963; Stories of Famous Spies, 1964; Such Women Are Deadly, 1965; Great Manhunters of the Yard, 1966; Stories of Famous Explorers, 1966; (ed.) Great War Adventures, 1966; Famous Stories of the Wild West (juvenile), 1967; They Had a Way with Women, 1967; Stories of Famous Conspirators, 1968; Famous Stories of Police and Crime, 1968; Famous Historical Mysteries, 1969; Famous Stories of Scientific Detection, 1969; Stories of Famous Modern Trials, 1970 (in U.S. as Justice?, 1971); Strange Crimes of Passion, 1970; Famous Detective Feats, 1971; They Got Away with Murder, 1971; More Famous Historical Mysteries, 1972; Sisters of Cain, 1971; Famous Feats of Espionage, 1972; The Hallmark of Horror, 1973; Stories of Famous Master Criminals, 1973; Such Was Their Guilt, 1974; Famous Stories of the Murder Squad, 1974; They Conspired to Kill, 1975; (as Leo Grex) Murder Stranger Than Fiction, 1975; Famous Mysteries of Detection, 1976; Famous Mysteries of Modern Times, 1976; (as Leo Grex) Detection Stranger Than Fiction, 1977;

Crimes Stranger Than Fiction, 1981; Notorious Killers in the Night, 1983; Mysteries Behind Notorious Crimes, 1984; Notorious Crimes, 1985; Such Lethal Ladies, 1985; They Shot to Slay, 1986. Add: Chandons, Firsdown Close, High Salvington, Worthing, Sussex, England.

GRIDBAN, Volsted. *See* **TUBB**, E.C.

GRIEB, Kenneth J. American, b. 1939. History, International relations/Current affairs, Literature, Politics/Government. Prof. of History and Intnl. Studies since 1974, Coordinator of Intnl. Studies since 1977. Dir. of the Interdisciplinary Center since 1978, and John McNaughton Rosebush Univ. Prof. since 1983, Univ. of Wisconsin-Oshkosh (Asst. Prof., 1966–70; Assoc. Prof. 1970–74; Coordinator of Latin American Studies, 1968–77). Member, Bd. of Eds., The Americas, since 1976, and The Historian, since 1981; Consulting Ed., the World of Latin America series, since 1982. Resident Lectr. in History, Indiana Uiv., South Bend, 1965–66. *Publs:* The United States and Huerta, 1969; (co-ed.) Latin American Government Leaders, 1970, 1974; (co-author) Essays on Miguel Angel Asturias (literary criticism), 1972; The Latin American Policy of Warren G. Harding, 1976, 1977; Guatemalan Caudillo: The Regime of Jorge Ubico, 1979; (ed.) Research Guide to Central America and the Caribbean, 1985. Add: Intnl. Studies Program, Univ. of Wisconsin, Oshkosh, Wisc. 54901, U.S.A.

GRIER, Eldon (Brockwill). Canadian, b. 1917. Poetry. A painter: has taught at the Montreal Museum of Art. *Publs:* A Morning from Scraps, 1955; Poems, 1956; The Ring of Ice, 1957; Manzanillo and Other Poems, 1958; A Friction of Lights, 1963; Pictures on the Skin, 1967; Selected Poems 1955-1970, 1971; The Assassination of Colour, 1978. Add: 6221 St. George's Pl., W. Vancouver, B.C. V7W 1Y6, Canada.

GRIERSON, Edward. Also writes as John P. Stevenson. British, b. 1914. Novels/Short stories, History, Travel/Exploration/Adventure. Deputy Chmn., Northumberland Quarter Sessions, 1963–72. *Publs:* Reputation for a Song, 1951; The Lilies and the Bees (in U.S. as The Hastening Wind; in paperback as The Royalist), 1953; Far Morning, 1955; The Second Man, 1956; The Captain General, 1958; Dark Torrent of Glencoe, 1961; The Massingham Affair, 1962; A Crime of One's Own, 1967; The Fatal Inheritance, 1969; The Imperial Dream (in U.S. as Death of the Imperial Dream), 1972; Confessions of a Country Magistrate, 1972; King of Two Worlds: Philip II of Spain, 1974; Companion Guide to Northumbria, 1976. Add: Greystead, Tarset, Hexham, Northumberland, England.

GRIERSON, Philip. British, b. 1910. History, Money. Fellow, Gonville and Caius Coll., Cambridge, since 1935; Honorary Keeper of the Coins, Fitzwilliam Museum, Cambridge, since 1949 (Librarian, 1944–69, and Pres., 1966–76, Gonville and Caius Coll.; Lectr. in History, 1945–59, Reader in Medieval Numismatics, 1959–71, and Prof. of Numismatics, 1971–78, now Emeritus, Cambridge Univ.); Adviser in Byzantine Numismatics to the Dumbarton Oaks Library and Collections, Harvard Univ., Washington, D.C., since 1955. Prof. of Numismatics and the History of Coinage, Univ. of Brussels, 1948–81. Literary Dir., Royal Historical Soc., 1945–55; Pres., Royal Numismatic Soc., 1961–66. *Publs:* Les Annales de Saint-Pierre de Gand, 1937; Books on Soviet Russia 1917-42, 1943; Sylloge of Coins of the British Isles, vol. I, 1958; Bibliographie numismatique, 1966, 1979; English Linear Measures: A Study in Origins, 1973; (with A.R. Bellinger) Catalogue of the Byzantine Coins in the Dumbarton Oaks Collection and in the Whittemore Collections, 3 vols., 1966–73; Numismatics, 1975; Monnaies du Moyen Age, 1976; The Origins of Money, 1977; Dark Age Numismatics, 1979; Later Medieval Numismatics, 1979; Byzantine Coins, 1982; (with M. Blackburn) Medieval European Coinage, vol. I, 1986. Add: Gonville and Caius Coll., Cambridge CB2 1TA, England.

GRIFFIN, Donald R. American, b. 1915. Biology, Zoology. Asst. Prof., 1946–47, Assoc. Prof., 1947–52, and Prof., 1952–53, Cornell Univ., Ithaca, N.Y.; Prof. of Zoology, Harvard Univ., Cambridge, Mass., 1953–65; Prof., Rockefeller Univ., NYC, 1965–86. *Publs:* Listening in the Dark, 1958, 3rd ed. 1986; Echoes of Bats and Men, 1959; Animal Structure and Function, 2nd ed. 1962; Bird Migration, 1964, 1974; The Question of Animal Awareness, 1976; Animal Thinking, 1984. Add: Rockefeller Univ., New York, N.Y. 10021-6399, U.S.A.

GRIFFIN, (Arthur) Harry. British, b. 1911. Natural history, Sports/Physical education/Keeping fit, Travel/Exploration/Adventure. Chief Northern Corresp., United Newspapers Publs., 1946–76. *Publs:* Inside the Real Lakeland, 1961; In Mountain Lakeland, 1963; Pageant of Lakeland, 1966; The Roof of England, 1968; Still the Real Lakeland,

1970; Long Days in the Hills, 1974; Discovering Lakeland, 1974; A Lakeland Notebook, 1975; A Year in the Fells, 1976; Freeman of the Hills, 1978; Adventuring in Lakeland, 1980. Add: 19 High Fellside Ct., Kendal, Cumbria, England.

GRIFFIN, Jonathan. Pseud. for Robert John Thurlow Griffin. British, b. 1906. Poetry, Translations. Dir. of European Intelligence, BBC, London, 1940-44; Second Secty., British Embassy, Paris, 1945-51. *Publs:* Britain's Air Policy: Present and Future, 1935; Alternative to Rearmament, 1936; Glass Houses and Modern War, 1938; The Czechoslovak-German Frontier: Its Strategic Importance, 1938; (with Joan Griffin) Lost Liberty? The Ordeal of the Czechs and the Future of Freedom, 1939; (trans.) The Hussar on the Roof, by Jean Giono, 1953; (trans.) Christ Recrucified, by Nikos Kazantzakes (in U.S. as The Greek Passion), 1954; The Hidden King: A Poem for the Stage in the Form of a Trilogy, 1955; (trans.) Freedom and Death, by Nikos Kazantzakes (in U.S. as Freedom or Death), 1956; The Rebirth of Pride (verse), 1957; (trans.) The Roots of Heaven, by Romain Gary, 1958; (trans.) For the Time Being, by Vercors, 1960; The Oath and Other Poems, 1963; (trans.) Fernando Pessoa I-IV, 1971; (trans.) Selected Poems, by Fernando Pessoa, 1974; In Time of Crowding: Selected Poems 1963-1974, 1975; (trans.) Camoes: Some Poems, 1976; In This Transparent Forest (verse), 1977; Outsing the Howling: An Interlude (verse), 1979; The Fact of Music (verse), 1980; Commonsense of the Senses (verse), 1982. Add: c/o Menard Press, 8 The Oaks, Woodwide Ave., London N12 8AR, England.

GRIFFIN, Keith B(roadwell). British, b. 1938. Economics, Third World problems. Prof. and Head, Economics Dept., Univ. of California at Riverside, since 1988. Pres., Magdalen Coll., Oxford, 1979-88. *Publs:* Underdevelopment in Spanish America, 1969; (with John Enos) Planning Development, 1970; (ed.) Financing Development in Latin America, 1971; (ed. with A.R. Khan) Growth and Inequality in Pakistan, 1972; The Political Economy of Agrarian Change, 1974; Land Concentration and Rural Poverty, 1976; International Inequality and National Poverty, 1978; (with J. James) The Transition to Egalitarian Development, 1981; (with A. Saith) Growth and Equality in Rural China, 1981; (ed.) Institutional Reform and Economic Development in the Chinese Countryside, 1984; World Hunger and the World Economy, 1987; Alternative Strategies for Economic Development, 1989. Add: Dept. of Economics, Univ. of California, Riverside, CA, U.S.A.

GRIFFITH, Arthur Leonard. Canadian, b. 1920. Theology/Religion. Retired Minister. Minister, Trinity United Church, Grimsby, 1947-50, Chalmers United Church, Ottawa, 1950-60, City Temple, London, U.K., 1960-66, and Deer Park United Church, Toronto, 1966-75; Minister, St. Paul's Anglican Church, Bloor St., Toronto, 1975-85. *Publs:* The Roman Letter Today, 1959; God and His People, 1960; Beneath the Cross of Jesus, 1961; What Is a Christian?, 1962; Barriers to Christian Belief, 1962; A Pilgrimage to the Holy Land, 1962; The Eternal Legacy, 1963; Pathways to Happiness, 1964; God's Time and Ours, 1964; The Crucial Encounter, 1965; This Is Living, 1966; God Is Man's Experience, 1968; Illusions of Our Culture, 1969; The Need to Preach, 1971; Hang on to the Lord's Prayer, 1973; We Have This Ministry, 1973; Ephesians: A Positive Affirmation, 1975; Gospel Characters, 1976; Reactions to God, 1979; Take Hold of the Treasure, 1981; From Sunday to Sunday, 1987. Add: 71 Old Mill Rd., Etobicoke, Ont. M8X 1G9, Canada.

GRIFFITH, Bill. See **GRANGER,** Bill.

GRIFFITH, Ernest S. American, b. 1896. Politics/Government. Consulting Ed., Westview Press, formerly Praeger Library of Govt. Depts. and Agencies, since 1967; Writer, National Academy of Public Admin., Washington, D.C., since 1974. Dean of the Grad. Sch., and Prof. of Political Science, American Univ., Washington, D.C., 1935-40. Dir., Legislative Reference Service, Library of Congress, 1940-58; Visiting Prof., Oxford Univ., 1950-57; Dean, Sch. of Intnl. Service, American Univ., Washington, D.C., 1958-65. *Publs:* Modern Development of City Government, 2 vols., 1927; Current Municipal Problems, 1933; History of American Colonial City Government, 1938; Impasse of Democracy, 1939; Modern Government in Action, 1942; Research in Political Science, 1948; Congress: Its Contemporary Role, 1951, 5th ed. 1975; (with K. Kilmer) Congressional Anthology, 1955, 1958; American System of Government, 1955, 6th ed. 1983; History of American City Government 1870-1920, 1974; (with C. Adrian) History of American City Government 1775-1870, 1975; The American Presidency, 1977; High School Crossroads, 1981. Add: 211 Russell Ave., Gaithersburg, Md. 20877, U.S.A.

GRIFFITH, Helen V(irginia). American, b. 1934. Children's fiction.

Secty. and Treasurer, S.G. Williams and Bros., Wilmington, since 1976. *Publs:* Mine Will, Said John, 1980; Alex and the Cat, 1982; Alex Remembers, 1983; More Alex and the Cat, 1983; Foxy, 1985; Nata, 1985; Georgia Music, 1986; Grandaddy's Place, 1987; Journal of a Teenage Genius, 1987; Emily and the Enchanted Frog, 1989. Add: 410 Country Club Dr., Wilmington, Del. 19803, U.S.A.

GRIFFITH, Thomas Gwynfor. British, b. 1926. Language/Linguistics, Literature, Translations. Prof. of Italian Language and Literature, Univ. of Manchester, since 1971, Emeritus since 1988. Univ. Lectr. in Italian, Oxford Univ., 1958-65; Fellow, St. Cross Coll., 1965; Prof. of Italian, Hull Univ., 1966-71. *Publs:* (ed. and trans.) Boccaccio: Detholion o'r Decameron, 1951: Bandello's Fiction: An Examination of the Novelle, 1955; Avventure Linguistiche del Cinquecento, 1961; Italian Writers and the Italian Language, 1967; (ed. with P.R.J. Hainsworth) Petrarch: Selected Poems, 1971, 1979; (with B. Migliorini) The Italian Language, 1984. Add: Dept. of Italian Studies, Univ. of Manchester, Manchester M13 9PL, England.

GRIFFITH, William E(dgar). American, b. 1920. International relations/Current affairs, Politics/Government. Ford Prof. of Political Science, Mass. Inst. of Technology, Cambridge, since 1972 (Research Assoc., Center of Intnl. Studies, 1958-65; Prof. of Political Science, 1965-72); also Gen. Ed., M.I.T. Studies in Communism, Revisionism, and Revolution; Adjunct Prof. of Diplomatic History, Fletcher Sch. of Law and Diplomacy, Tufts Univ., Medford, Mass., since 1962. Roving Ed., Reader's Digest. Teaching Fellow, Harvard Univ., Cambridge, 1948-50; Asst. to the Pres., Free Europe Cttee., 1950-51; Political Adviser, Radio Free Europe, Munich, 1951-58; Sr. Adviser to the Ambassador, U.S. Embassy, Bonn, 1985-86. *Publs:* Albania and the Sino-Soviet Rift, 1963; The Sino-Soviet Rift, 1964; (ed.) Communism in Europe, vol. I, 1964; vol. II, 1966; Sino-Soviet Relations 1964-1965, 1967; Cold War and Coexistence: Russia, China and the United States, 1971; The World and the Great Power Triangle, 1975; The Soviet Empire, 1976; The European Left, 1979; Die Ostpolitik, 1981; The Superpowers and Regional Tensions: The U.S.S.R., the United States, and Europe, 1981; Central and Eastern Europe: The Opening Curtain?, 1989. Add: 19 Peacock Farm Rd., Lexington, Mass. 02173, U.S.A.

GRIFFITHS, Bryn(lyn David). British, b. 1933. Poetry. *Publs:* The Mask of Pity, 1966; The Stones Remember, 1967; (ed.) Welsh Voices, 1967; Scars, 1969; The Survivors, 1971; Beasthoods, 1972; Starboard Green, 1973; The Dark Convoys: Sea Poems, 1974; Love Poems, 1980. Add: 13 Pleasant St., Morriston, Swansea, South Wales.

GRIFFITHS, Helen. British, b. 1939. Children's fiction. Secty., Blackstock Engineering, Cockfosters, London, 1958-59; Office Worker, Selfridges, London, 1959, and Oliver and Boyd, publishers, London, 1959-60; Teacher of English as a foreign language, Madrid, 1973-76. *Publs:* Horse in the Clouds, 1957; Wild and Free, 1958; Moonlight, 1959; Africano, 1961; The Wild Heart, 1963; The Greyhound, 1964; The Wild Horse of Santander, 1966; The Dark Swallows (novel), 1966; Leon, 1967; Stallion of the Sands, 1968; Moshie Cat: The True Adventures of a Majorcan Kitten, 1969; Patch, 1970; Federico, 1971; Russian Blue, 1973; Just a Dog, 1974; Witch Fear (in U.S. as Mysterious Appearance of Agnes), 1074; Pablo (in U.S. as Running Wild), 1977; The Kershaw Dogs (in U.S. as Grip: A Dog Story), 1978; The Last Summer, 1979; Blackface Stallion, 1980; Dancing Horses, 1981; Hari's Pigeon, 1982; Rafa's Dog, 1983; Jesus, as Told by Mark, 1983; Dog at the Window, 1984; Caleb's Lamb, 1984; If Only, 1987. Add: 42 Newbridge Rd., Bath, Avon, England.

GRIFFITHS, John Gwyn. Welsh, b. 1911. Poetry, Classics. Co-ed., Yflam, Welsh literary journal, 1941-47; lectr., Sr. Lectr. and Reader, 1946-72, and Prof. of Classics and Egyptology, 1973-79, University Coll., Univ. of Wales. Lady Wallis Budge Research Lectr., Univ. Coll., Oxford, 1957-58; Ed., The Welsh Nation, 1964-65; Guest Prof. in Classics and Egyptology, Univ. of Cairo, 1965-66; Ed., Journal of Egyptian Archaeology, 1970-78; Visiting Fellow, All Souls Coll., Oxford, 1976-77. *Publs:* The Conflict of Horus and Seth, 1960; Dragon's Nostrils, 1961; Songs of Cairo, 1970; (ed.) Plutarch's de Iside et Osiride, 1970; (ed.) The Isis-Book of Apuleius, 1975; Aristotle's Poetics, 1978; The Origins of Osiris and His Cult, 1980. Add: 3 Long Oaks Ave., Abertawe, Swansea, Wales.

GRIFFITHS, Richard (Mathias). British, b. 1935. History, Literature, Translations. Prof. of French, Univ. Coll., Cardiff, since 1974. Fellow, 1960-66, and Dean, 1962-65, Selwyn Coll., Cambridge; Fellow,

Brasenose Coll., Oxford, 1966–74. *Publs:* (trans.) Parisian Sketches, by Huysmans, 1961; The Reactionary Revolution, 1966; (ed.) Claudel: A Reappraisal, 1968; Marshal Petain, 1970; The Dramatic Technique of Montchrestien, 1970; (ed.) Montherlant: Port-Royal, 1976; Fellow Travellers of the Right, 1980; (ed.) Le Diable au Corps, by Radiguet, 1983; (ed.) Les Juifres, by Garnier, 1986. Add: Dept. of French, Univ. Coll., Cardiff, Wales.

GRIFFITHS, Sally. British, b. 1934. Novels/Short stories. Reporter, Western Telegraph, Pembs., 1954–56; Sub-Ed., Amalgamated Press, London, 1956–57. *Publs:* The Tree and the Flood, 1966; Winter Day in a Glasshouse, 1968. Add: Rosewood, Maes y Forwen, Upper Solva, St. David's, Haverfordwest, Dyfed, Wales.

GRIFFITHS, Trevor. British, b. 1935. Plays/Screenplays. Education Officer, BBC, London, 1965–72. *Publs:* Occupations, and The Big House, 1972; (with others) Lay By, 1972; Tip's Lot (children's fiction), 1972; The Party, 1974; Comedians, 1976, 1979; All Good Men, and Absolute Beginners, 1977; Through the Night, and Such Impossibilities, 1977; The Cherry Orchard (new English version), 1978; Apricots, and Thermidor, 1978; (with Howard Brenton and others) Deeds, 1978; Country, 1981; Oi for England, 1982; Sons and Lovers (TV version), 1982; Judgement Over the Dead, 1985; Real Dreams, 1987; Fatherland, 1987; Collected Plays for Television, 1988. Add: c/o A.D. Peters, The Chambers, Chelsea Harbour, Lots Rd., London SW10 0XF, England.

GRIGG, John (Edward Poynder). British, b. 1924. History, Politics. Journalist and author. *Publs:* Two Anglican Essays, 1958; The Young Lloyd George, 1973; Lloyd George: The People's Champion, 1978; 1943: The Victory That Never Was, 1980; Nancy Astor: Portrait of a Pioneer, 1980; Lloyd George: From Peace to War, 1985. Add: 32 Dartmouth Row, London SE10 8AW, England.

GRIGSON, Jane. British, b. 1928. Cookery/Gastronomy, Translations. Cookery Corresp., The Observer newspaper Colour Mag., London, since 1968. Asst., Heffers Art Gallery, Cambridge, 1950–51, Walker's Art Gallery, London, 1952–53, George Rainbird Ltd., London, 1953–54, and Thames & Hudson Ltd., London, 1954–55. *Publs:* (trans.) Scano Boa, by Giovanni A. Cibotto, 1963; (trans.) On Crimes and Punishments, by Cesare Beccaria, 1964; (with Geoffrey Grigson) Shapes and Stories, 1965; (with Geoffrey Grigson) More Shapes and Stories, 1967; Charcuterie and French Pork Cookery (in U.S. as Art of Charcuterie), 1967; Good Things, 1971; Fish Cookery, 1973; English Food, 1974, 1979; The Mushroom Feast, 1975; Jane Grigson's Vegetable Book, 1978; Food with the Famous, 1979; Jane Grigson's Fruit Book, 1982; The Observer Guide to European Cookery, 1983; Jane Grigson's British Cookery, 1984; (with Charlotte Knox) Exotic Fruits and Vegetables, 1986. Add: c/o David Higham Assoc., 5-8 Lower John St., London W1R 3PE, England.

GRIMBLE, Ian. British, b. 1921. History, Travel/Exploration/Adventure, Biography Intelligence Corps, 1942–46; Librarian, House of Commons Library, 1947–55; Producer, BBC, 1955–59. *Publs:* The Harington Family, 1957; The Trial of Patrick Sellar, 1962; Chief of Mackay, 1965; Denmark, 1966; (co-ed. and co-author) The Future of the Highlands, 1968; Regency People, 1972; Scottish Clans and Tartans, 1973; The Sea Wolf, 1978; The World of Rob Donn, 1979; Clans and Chiefs, 1980; Highland Man, 1980; Scottish Islands, 1985; Castles of Scotland, 1987. Add: 14 Seaforth Lodge, High St., London SW13, England.

GRIMES, Alan P. American, b. 1919. History, Politics/Government. Prof. of Political Science, Michigan State Univ., East Lansing, since 1949, now Emeritus. *Publs:* The Political Liberalism of the New York Nation 1865-1932, 1953; American Political Thought, 1955; (ed. with R. Horwitz) Modern Political Ideologies, 1959; Equality in America, 1964; (ed.) Liberalism, by L.T. Hobhouse, 1964; The Puritan Ethic and Woman Suffrage, 1967; Democracy and the Amendments to the Constitution, 1978. Add: Political Science Dept., Michigan State Univ., East Lansing, Mich. 48824, U.S.A.

GRIMOND, Jo(seph); (Lord Grimond). British, b. 1913. Politics/Government, Autobiography/Memoirs/Personal. Liberal M.P. (U.K.) for Orkney and Shetland, since 1950 (Leader, Parliamentary Liberal Party, 1956–67). Chancellor, Univ. of Kent, since 1970. European Dir. of Personnel, U.N. Relief and Rehabilitation Admin., 1945–47; Secty., National Trust for Scotland, 1947–50; Liberal M.P. (U.K.) For Orkney and Shetland, 1950–83: Leader of the Parliamentary Liberal Party, 1956–67, 1976. Rector, Univ. of Edinburgh, 1960–63, and of Aberdeen, 1970–73. *Publs:* The Liberal Future, 1959; The Liberal Challenge, 1967; (with Brian Neve) The Referendum, 1975; (with others) The

Prime Ministers, 1976; (with others) My Oxford, 1977; The Common Welfare, 1978; Memoirs, 1979; A Personal Manifesto, 1983; Britain: A View from Westminster, 1986. Add: Old Manse of Firth, Kirkwall, Orkney, Scotland.

GRIMSTEAD, Hettie. Also writes as Marsha Manning. British. Historical/Romance/Gothic. *Publs:* Painted Virgin, 1931; The Journey Home, 1950; Navy Blue Lady, 1951; The Twisted Road, 1951; The Captured Heart, 1952; Strangers May Kiss, 1952; The Passionate Summer, 1953; Song of Surrender, 1953; Candles for Love, 1954; Winds of Desire, 1954; Enchanted August, 1955; The Tender Pilgrim, 1955; The Burning Flame, 1956; Escape to Paradise, 1956; The Reluctant Bride, 1957; Scales of Love, 1957; The Unknown Heart, 1958; Tinsel Kisses, 1958; (as Marsha Manning) Kisses for Three, 1958; (as Marsha Manning) Passport to Love, 1958; Dream Street, 1959; A Kiss in the Sun, 1959; (as Marsha Manning) The Heart Alone, 1959; (as Marsha Manning) Skyscraper Hotel; The Path to Love, 1960; (as Marsha Manning) Because You're Mine, 1960; Sweet Prisoner, 1961; (as Marsha Manning) Magic of the Moon, 1961; (as Marsha Manning) Star of Desire, 1961; The Golden Moment, 1962; Love Has Two Faces, 1962; (as Marsha Manning) Circle of Dreams, 1962; (as Marsha Manning) Roses for the Bride, 1962; Wedding for Three, 1963; Whisper to the Stars, 1963; (as Marsha Manning) Flower of the Heart, 1963; When April Sings, 1964; (as Marsha Manning) Lucy in London, 1964; (as Marsha Manning) Our Miss Penny, 1964; The Door of the Heart, 1965; Once upon a Kiss, 1965; (as Marsha Manning) Sister Marion's Summer, 1965; (as Marsha Manning) Lover Come Lonely, 1965; Shake Down the Moon, 1966; The Sweetheart Tree, 1966; (as Marsha Manning) Full Summer's Kiss, 1966; (as Marsha Manning) The Proud Lover, 1966; Orchids for the Bride, 1967; The Tender Chord, 1967; (as Marsha Manning) Four of Hearts, 1967; (as Marsha Manning) Dreams in the Sun, 1967; Chase a Rainbow, 1968; Portrait of Paula, 1968; (as Marsha Manning) Friends of the Bride, 1968; (as Marsha Manning) Some Day My Love, 1968; September's Girl, 1969; (as Marsha Manning) Yesterday's Lover, 1969; (as Marsha Manning) Holiday Affair, 1969; The Lovely Day, 1970; Roses for Breakfast, 1970; (as Marsha Manning) To Catch a Dream, 1970; Island Affair, 1971; (as Marsha Manning) Summer Song, 1971; The Winter Rose, 1972; (as Marsha Manning) The Smiling Moon, 1972; (as Marsha Manning) Sweet Friday, 1972; Fires of Spring, 1973; Tuesday's Child, 1973; (as Marsha Manning) The Magic City, 1973; The Tender Vine, 1974; (as Marsha Manning) Dance of Summer, 1974; (as Marsha Manning) Wedding of the Year, 1974; Sister Rose's Holiday, 1975; (as Marsha Manning) Chance Encounter, 1975; (as Marsha Manning) Day of Roses, 1976; (as Marsha Manning) The Passionate Rivals, 1978; The Heart Alone, 1981. Add: c/o Curtis Brown Ltd., 162-168 Regent St., London W1R 5TB, England.

GRIMWADE, Arthur Girling. British, b. 1913. Crafts. Hon. Expert Adviser, Soc. of Silver Collectors, since 1958; Member, Council of Jewish Museum, since 1974; Asst., Worshipful Co. of Goldsmiths, since 1975 (Prime Warden, 1984–85). Dir., Christie, Manson and Woods Ltd., London, 1954–78. *Publs:* (co-author) Treasures of a London Temple, 1951; The Queen's Silver, 1953; Rococo Silver, 1973; London Goldsmiths 1697-1837, 1976. Add: Christie, Manson & Woods Ltd., 8 King St., London SW1, England.

GRINDROD, Muriel (Kathleen). British, b. 1902. History, Translations, Italian Specialist, and Ed. of Periodicals, Royal Inst. of Intnl. Affairs, London, 1931–39, 1945–62; with Italian Section, Research Dept., Foreign Office, London, 1939–45; Asst. Ed., Annual Register of World Events, 1962–73. *Publs:* The Rebuilding of Italy 1940-54, 1954; (trans.) A History of Italian Fascism, by F. Chabod, 1963; Italy: Modern World Series, 1964, 1966; (trans.) Pope John and His Council, by C. Falconi, 1964; (trans.) The Popes in the Twentieth Century, by C. Falconi, 1967; Italy: Nations of the Modern World Series, 1968; (trans.) Napoleon Is Dead in Russia, by G. Artom, 1970; (trans.) The Fontana Economic History of Europe, by C.M. Cipolla, 1970; (trans.) Rome, by G. Carandente, 1971; (trans.) Journey Among the Economists, by A. Levi, 1973. Add: 45 Lancaster Grove, London NW3, England.

GRITSCH, Eric W(alter). American, b. 1931. Theology/Religion. Prof. of Church History, Lutheran Theological Seminary, Gettysburg, Pa., since 1961. Dir., Inst. for Luther Studies, since 1970. *Publs:* (ed. with R. Gritsch) Luther's Works, vol. 39, 1966, vol. 41, 1970; Reformer Without a Church, 1967; (ed. with Roland H. Bainton) Bibliography of the Continental Reformation; (trans. with R. Gritsch) Heinrich Bornkamm: Luther and the Old Testament, 1969; The Continuing Reformation, 1971; (with R. Jenson) Lutheranism, 1976; (ed.) Encounters with Luther, vols. 1-3, 1980–86; Born Againism, 1982; Martin Luther in Retrospect: God's Court Jester, 1983; Thomas Muentzer: A Tragedy of

Errors, 1989. Add: Lutheran Theological Seminary, Gettysburg, Pa. 17325, U.S.A.

GROB, Gerald N. American, b. 1931. History. Prof. of History, Rutgers Univ., New Brunswick, N.J., since 1969. Instr. to Prof. of History, Clark Univ., Worcester, Mass., 1957–69. *Publs:* Workers and Utopia: A Study of Ideological Conflict in the American Labor Movement 1865-1900, 1961; (ed. with R.N. Beck) American Ideas, 2 vols., 1963, 1970; The State and the Mentally Ill, 1966; (ed. and author with G.A. Billias) Interpretations of American History; Patterns and Perspectives, 2 vols., 1967, 5th ed. 1987; (ed.) Statesmen and Statecraft of the Modern West, 1967; (compiler) American Social History Before 1860, 1970; (ed. with G.A. Billias) American History: Retrospect and Prospect, 1971; (ed.) Insanity and Idiocy in Massachusetts: Report of the Commission on Lunacy, 1855, by E. Jarvis, 1971; Mental Institutions in America: Social Policy to 1875, 1973; Edward Jarvis and the Medical World of Nineteenth-Century America, 1978; Mental Illness and American Society 1875-1940, 1983; The Inner World of American Psychiatry 1890-1940, 1985. Add: Inst. for Health, Health Care Policy, and Aging Research, Rutgers Univ., New Brunswick, N.J. 08903, U.S.A.

GROHSKOPF, Bernice. American. Children's fiction, Archaeology. Ed. Staff, William James Edition, Harvard Univ. Press, since 1984. Banister Writer-in-Residence, Sweet Briar Coll., Virginia, 1980–82. *Publs:* Seeds of Time, 1963; From Age to Age, 1968; The Treasure of Sutton Hoo (non-fiction), 1970; Shadow in the Sun, 1975; Notes on the Hauter Experiment, 1975; Children in the Wind, 1977; Blood and Roses, 1979; Tell Me Your Dream, 1981; End of Summer, 1982. Add: 116 Turtle Creek Rd., No. 11, Charlottesville, Va. 22901, U.S.A.

GROSE, Peter (Bolton). American, b. 1934. History, Politics/Government. Managing Ed., Foreign Affairs, NYC, since 1984. Sr. Fellow, Council on Foreign Relations, NYC, since 1982. Correspondent, Paris Bureau, 1963, Chief Correspondent in Vietnam, 1964–65, Chief of the Moscow Bureau, 1965–67, Diplomatic Correspondent, Washington Bureau, 1967–70, Chief of the Israel Bureau, 1970–72, Member of the Editorial Bd., 1972–77, and Chief of the United Nations Bureau, 1977—all with the New York Times; Deputy Dir., Policy Planning Staff, U.S. Dept. of State, 1977–78; Research Assoc., Middle East Inst., Columbia Univ., NYC, 1978–81; Dir. of Studies, Seven Springs Center, Mt. Kisco, N.Y., 1981–82; Dir. of Middle East Studies, Council on Foreign Relations, NYC, 1982–84. *Publs:* Israel in the Mind of America, 1983; (co-author) The End of the Palestine Mandate, 1985; A Changing Israel, 1985. Add: 58 E. 68th St., New York, N.Y. 10021, U.S.A.

GROSS, Joel. American, b. 1951. Novels/Short stories, Plays/Screenplays. *Publs:* Bubble's Shadow, 1970; The Young Man Who Wrote Soap Operas, 1975; 1407 Broadway, 1978; The Books of Rachel, 1979; Maura's Dream, 1981; Home of the Brave, 1982; This Year in Jerusalem, 1983; The Lives of Rachel, 1984; Spirit in the Flesh, 1986; Sarah, 1987. Add: 165 East 66th St., New York, N.Y. 10021, U.S.A.

GROSS, John (Jacob). British, b. 1935. Literature, Biography. Member, Editorial Staff, New York Times Book Review, since 1983. Ed., Victor Gollancz Ltd., London, 1956–58; Asst. Lectr., Queen Mary Coll., Univ. of London, 1959–62; Fellow, King's Coll., Cambridge, 1962–65; Literary Ed., New Statesman, London, 1973, Ed., Times Literary Supplement, London, 1974–81; Editorial Consultant, Weidenfeld and Nicolson, publishers, London, 1982. *Publs:* The Rise and Fall of the Man of Letters, 1969; James Joyce, 1971; (ed.) The Oxford Book of Aphorisms, 1983. Add: 24A St. Petersburgh Place, London W2, England.

GROSS, Ludwik. American, b. 1904. Medicine/Health. Head, Cancer Research Unit, since 1948, Veterans Admin. Hosp., Bronx, N.Y. (Sr. Medical Investigator, 1960–77, and V.A. Distinguished Physician, 1977–81); Research Prof. Emeritus of Medicine, Mount Sinai Sch. of Medicine, City Univ. of New York, since 1973 (research Prof., 1971–73). Research Assoc., Inst. for Medical Research, Christ Hosp., Cincinnati, Ohio, 1941–43; Consultant, 1953–56 and Assoc. Scientist, 1957–60, Sloan-Kettering Inst., NYC. *Publs:* Humanity Fighting for Life (in Polish), 1932, 1934; Sowers of Death and Disease (in Polish), 1934; Oncogenic Viruses, 1961, 3rd ed. 1983. Add: Cancer Research Unit, Veterans Admin. Medical Center, 130 W. Kingsbridge Rd., Bronx, N.Y. 10468, U.S.A.

GROSS, Richard (Edmund). American, b. 1920. Education, History, Social sciences. Prof., Sch. of Education, Stanford Univ., Calif. (joined faculty, 1955). *Publs:* (with M. Rodehaver and W. Axtell) The Sociology of the School, 1957; (with L.B. Zeleny) Educating Citizens for Democracy, 1958; (ed.) Report of the State Central Committee on Social Studies, 1959; (ed. and contrib.) The Heritage of American Education, 1962; United States History, 1964; (ed. and contrib.) British Secondary Education, 1965; (with V. Devereaux) Civics in Action, 1965, rev. ed. 1971; (with F. MacGraw) Man's World: A Physical Geography, 1966; (with W. McPhie and J. Fraenkel) Teaching the Social Studies: What, Why, and How, 1969; (with J. Chapin and R. McHugh) Quest for Liberty, 1971, 3rd rev. ed. 1973; (ed. with R. Muessig) Problem-Centered Social Studies Instruction: Approaches to Reflective Teaching, 1971; (ed. with L. de la Cruz) Social Studies Dissertations, 1963-69, 1971; (with J. Chapin) Teaching Social Studies Skills, 1973; (with D. Weitzman) Man's World, 1973; The Human Experience, 1973; American Citizenship: The Way We Govern, 1978; Social Studies for Our Times, 1978; (with D. Duffy) Learning to Live in Society, 1980; (with T. Dynneson) What Should We Be Teaching in the Social Studies?, 1983. Add: 26304 Esperanza Dr., Los Altos, Calif. 94022, U.S.A.

GROSSINGER, Tania. American, b. 1937. Psychology, Travel, Autobiography/Memoirs/Personal. Public relations consultant. Dir. of Broadcast Promotion, Playboy Mag., NYC, 1963–69; Dir. of Publicity, Stein & Day Inc., publrs., NYC, 1970–72. *Publs:* The Book of Gadgets, 1974; Growing Up at Grossinger's, 1975; The Great Gadget Catalogue, 1978; (co-author) Weekend, 1980. Add: 1 Christopher St., New York, N.Y. 10014, U.S.A.

GROSSKURTH, Phyllis. Canadian, b. 1924. Literary criticism/history, Biography. Asst. Prof. of English, Univ. of Toronto, since 1965. Lectr., Carleton Univ., Ottawa, Ont., 1964–65. *Publs:* John Addington Symonds: A Biography, 1964, as The Woeful Victorian, 1965; Notes on Browning's Works, 1967; Leslie Stephen, 1968; Gabrielle Roy, 1969; Havelock Ellis: A Biography, 1980; (ed.) The Memoirs of John Addington Symonds: The Secret Homosexual Life of a Leading 19th Century Man of Letters, 1984; Melanie Klein: Her Work and Her World, 1986. Add: 147 Spruce St., Toronto, Ont. M5A 26J, Canada.

GROSSMAN, Alfred. American, b. 1927. Novels/Short stories. Ed., New York Times Almanac, since 1968. Ed., East Europe Mag., NYC, 1954–61. *Publs:* Acrobat Admits, 1959; Many Slippery Errors, 1963; Marie Beginning, 1964; The Do-Gooders, 1968. Add: c/o Times Books, 201 E. 50th St., New York, N.Y. 10022, U.S.A.

GROSSMAN, Sebastian P. American, b. 1934. Phychology. Prof. of Biopsychology, Univ. of Chicago, since 1967 (Assoc. Prof., 1964–67). Asst. Prof., Univ. of Iowa, 1961–64. *Publs:* A Textbook of Physiological Psychology, 1967; Essentials of Physiological Psychology, 1973. Add: Cttee. on Biopsychology, Univ. of Chicago, Chicago, Ill. 60637, U.S.A.

GROSSMANN, Reinhardt. American, b. 1931. Philosophy. Prof. of Philosophy, Indiana Univ., Bloomington, since 1970 (joined faculty as Asst. Prof., 1962). Instr. 1958–61, and Asst. Prof. 1961–62, Univ. of Illinois, Urbana. *Publs:* (co-author) Essays in Ontology, 1963; The Structure of Mind, 1965; Reflections on Frege's Philosophy, 1969; Ontological Reduction, 1973; Meinong, 1974; The Categorial Structure of the World, 1983; Phenomenology and Existentialism: An Introduction, 1984. Add: Dept. of Philosophy, Indiana Univ., Bloomington, Ind. 47405, U.S.A.

GROUNDS, Roger. British, b. 1938. Horticulture. Garden designer. *Publs:* Gardening for Beginners, 1972; Simple Greenhouse Gardening, 1972; (ed.) Complete Handbook of Pruning, 1973; (ed.) Making and Planning a Small Garden, 1973; (ed.) Gardening in Colour, 1973; The Perfect Lawn, 1974; Shrubs and Decorative Evergreens, 1974; Trees for Smaller Gardens, 1974; Ferns, 1974; Bottle Gardens, 1974; Grow Your Own Vegetables, 1975; The Natural Garden, 1976; Growing Vegetables and Herbs, 1977; Everyday Gardening, 1977; Ornamental Grasses, 1979, 1989; The Private Life of Plants, 1980; The Multi-Coloured Garden, 1982; The White Garden, 1990. Add: Laurence Pollinger Ltd., 18 Maddox St., London W1R 0EU, England.

GROVE, Fred(erick Herridge). American, b. 1913. Westerns/Adventure. Reporter and Sports Ed., Daily Citizen, Cushing, Okla., 1937–40; reporter, Morning News, Shawnee, Okla., 1940–42; Sports Ed., Star, Harlingen, Tex., 1942; reporter, 1943–44, and Managing Ed., 1944–45, Morning News and Star, Shawnee; on copy desk, Times and Daily Oklahoman, Oklahoma City, 1946–47; Sr. Asst., Univ. of Oklahoma Public Relations Office, 1947–53; part-time Instr. of Journalism, Univ. of Oklahoma, 1964–68; Dir. of Public Information, Oklahoma Educational Television Authority, Norman, 1969–74. *Publs:* Flame of the Osage, 1958; Sun Dance, 1958; No Bugles, No Glory, 1959; Comanche Captives, 1961; The Land Seekers, 1963; Buffalo Spring, 1967; The Buffalo Runners,

1968; War Journey, 1971; The Child Stealers, 1973; Warrior Road, 1974; Drums Without Warriors, 1976; The Great Horse Race, 1977; Bush Track, 1978; The Running Horses, 1980; Phantom Warrior, 1981; Match Race, 1982; A Far Trumpet, 1985; Search for the Breed, 1986; Deception Trail, 1988. Add: P.O. Box 1248, Silver City, N.M. 88062, U.S.A.

GROVER, Philip. British, b. 1929. Literature. Sr. Lectr. in English Literature, Sheffield Univ., since 1975 (Lectr., 1969–75). *Publs:* Henry James and the French Novel, 1973; (with Omar Pound) Wyndham Lewis: A Descriptive Bibliography, 1978; (ed.) Ezra Pound: The London Years, 1978 Add: Dept. of English, Sheffield Univ., Sheffield S10 2TN, England.

GROVES, Georgina. *See* **SYMONS,** Geraldine.

GRUBB, Norman Percy. British, b. 1895. Theology/Religion, Biography. Intnl. Secty. Emeritus, Worldwide Evangelization Crusade, Gerrards Cross, Bucks. (with Crusade since 1919). *Publs:* C.T. Studd, Cricketer and Pioneer; Rees Howells, Intercessor, 1982; Alfred Buxton; Jack Harrison; Edith Moules; Rees Howells, Intercessor; J.D. Drysdale; Abram Vereide; With Christ in Congo Forests; After C.T. Studd; Touching the Invisible; The Law of Faith; The Liberating Secret; The Deep Things of God; God Unlimited; The Spontaneous You; Who Am I?, 1974; Yes I Am, 1982. Add: 709 Pennsylvania Ave., Fort Washington, Pa. 19034, U.S.A.

GRUBERG, Martin. American, b. 1935. Politics/Government. Prof., Political Science, Univ. of Wisconsin, Oshkosh (Asst. Prof. 1963–66; Assoc. Prof. 1966–69). Instr., Political Science, Hunter Coll. NYC, 1961–62. *Publs:* Women in American Politics, 1968; (ed.) Encyclopedia of American Government, 3rd ed. 1985. Add: 1545 Maricopa Drive, Oshkosh, Wisc. 54904, U.S.A.

GRUMBACH, Doris. American, b. 1918. Novels, Literature, Biography. Title-writer, MGM, 1940; Assoc. Ed., Architectural Forum, 1941; Prof. of English, College of St. Rose, Albany, N.Y., 1952–70; Literary Ed., New Republic, 1973–75; Columnist, Saturday Review, 1975–76, and New York Times Book Review, 1977–80; Prof. of English, American Univ., Washington, D.C., 1976–85. *Publs:* The Spoil of the Flowers, 1962; The Short Throat, the Tender Mouth, 1964; The Company She Kept (biography of Mary McCarthy), 1967; Chamber Music, 1979; The Missing Person, 1981; The Ladies, 1984; The Magician's Girl, 1987. Add: 909 North Carolina Ave. S.E., Washington, D.C. 20003, U.S.A.

GRUMLEY, Michael. American, b. 1941. Novels, Mythology/Folklore, Social Commentary/phenomena. *Publs:* (with R. Ferro) Atlantis: The Auto-biography of a Search, 1970; There Are Giants in the Earth, 1974; Hard Corps, 1977; After Midnight, 1978; Life Drawing (novel), 1988. Add: 55 W. 95th St., No. 24, New York, N.Y. 10025, U.S.A.

GRÜNBAUM, Adolf. American, b. 1923. Philosophy. Andrew Mellon. Prof. of Philosophy since 1960, Chmn. of Center for Philosophy of Science since 1978, and Research Prof. of Psychiatry since 1979, Univ. of Pittsburgh (Dir., Center for Philosophy of Science, 1960–78). Fellow, American Academy of Arts and Sciences, since 1976. Member, Governing Bd., Philosophy of Science Assn. (Pres., 1965–70), Exec. Cttee., Intnl. Union for History and Philosophy of Science. Selfridge Prof. of Philosophy, Lehigh Univ., Bethlehem, Pa., 1956–60. Vice-Pres., American Assn. for the Advancement of Science, 1963; Pres., American Philosophical Assn., 1982–83; Gifford Lectr., St. Andrews Coll., Scotland, 1985. *Publs:* Philosophical Problems of Space and time, 1963, rev. ed. 1974; Modern Science and Zeno's Paradoxes, 1967, rev. British ed. 1968; Geometry and Chronometry in Philosophical Perspective, 1968; The Foundations of Psychoanalysis: A Philosophical Critique, 1984; Psychoanalyse in wissenschaftstheoretischer Sicht, 1987. Add: 2510 Cathedral of Learning, Univ. of Pittsburgh, Pittsburgh, Pa. 15260, U.S.A.

GRUNDSTEIN, Nathan (David). American, b. 1913. Administration/Management, Law. Prof. of Mgmt. Policy, Sch. of Mgmt., Case Western Reserve Univ., since 1979, now Emeritus (Prof. of Management, 1964–79; Chmn., Policy Cttee., 1969–70). Prof., Dept. of Public Law and Admin., Wayne State Univ., Detroit, 1947–58; Visiting Prof., 1958–60, and Prof. of Admin. 1960–64, Grad. Sch. of Public and Intnl. Affairs, Univ. of Pittsburgh. *Publs:* (with J. Forrester Davison) Administrative Law: Cases and Readings, 1952, 1970; (ed. and contrib.) The Executive and Administrative Practice, 1955; Presidential Delegation of Authority in Wartime, 1961; (ed. with J. Forrester Davison) Administrative Law and the Regulatory System 1966, 1968; Ethical Decisions of City Managers, 1968; The Managerial Kant: The Kant Critiques and the

Managerial Order, 1982; Futures of Prudence, 1984. Add: Sch. of Mgmt., Case Western Reserve Univ., Cleveland, Ohio 44106, U.S.A.

GRUNDY, Joan. British, b. 1920. Literature. Prof. of English Literature, Royal Holloway, Coll., Univ. of London, 1979–80, now Emeritus (Reader, 1965–79). Asst. Lectr. in English, Univ. of Edinburgh, 1947–50; Lectr. in English, Univ. of Liverpool, 1950–65. *Publs:* The Poems of Henry Constable, 1960; The Spenserian Poets, 1969; Hardy and the Sister Arts, 1979. Add: Rose Cottage, Lamb Park, Rosside, Ulverston, Cumbria LA12 7NR, England.

GRUNFELD, Frederic V. American, b. 1929. Art, Music, Travel/Exploration/Adventure. Radio Commentator, WQXR, NYC, 1950–55; Cultural Corresp., Reporter Mag., 1958–67; Consulting Ed., 1964–70, and Ed., 1970, Queen Mag.; Roving Ed., Horizon Mag., 1967–77, and Connoisseur mag., 1982. *Publs:* Music and Recordings, 1955; The Art and Times of the Guitar, 1970; The Hitler File, 1974; Music, 1974; Berlin (The Great Cities), 1976; Prophets Without Honour, 1979; Vienna, 1981; Wayfarers of the Thai Forest: The Akha, 1982; The Kings of France, The Princes of Germany, The Spanish Kings, 3 vols., 1983–84; Rodin: A Biography, 1987; Wild Spain, 1989. Add: Son Rullan, Deya, Mallorca, Spain.

GUARE, John. American, b. 1938. Plays/Screenplays. *Publs:* The Loveliest Afternoon of the Year, and Something I'll Tell You Tuesday, 1968; Muzeeka, and Other Plays, 1969; Kissing Sweet, and A Day for Surprises, 1970; The House of Blue Leaves, 1979; (with Mel Shapiro) Two Gentlemen of Verona (adaptation), 1973; (with Milos Forman) Taking Off (screenplay), 1971; Marco Polo Sings and Solo, 1977; The Landscape of the Body, 1978; Bosoms and Neglect, 1980; Three Exposures, 1982; Lydie Breeze, 1982; Gardenia, 1982; The Talking Dog, 1986. Add: c/o Dramatists Play Service, 440 Park Ave. S., New York, N.Y. 10016, U.S.A.

GUBRIUM, Jaber F(andy). Canadian, b. 1943. Sociology. Assoc. Prof. of Sociology, Marquette Univ., Milwaukee, since 1974 (Asst. Prof., 1970–74). *Publs:* The Myth of the Golden Years: A Socio-Environmental Theory of Aging, 1973; (ed.) Late Life: Communities and Environmental Policy, 1974; Living and Dying at Murray Manor, 1976; Toward Maturity, 1977; Describing Care, 1982; Old Timers and Alzheimers: The Descriptive Organization of Senility, 1986. Add: c/o Sage Publications, 2111 W. Hillcrest Dr., Newbury Park, Calif. 91320, U.S.A.

GUENTHER, Charles (John). American, b. 1920. Poetry, Literature, Translations. Midwest Regional Vice-Pres., Poetry Soc. of America, since 1977. Head, Archives Unit, 1943–45, Head, Research Unit, 1945–47, Asst. Chief and Chief of Library, 1945–57, and Chief of the Technical Library, 1957–75, Defense Mapping Agency Aerospace Center, St. Louis; Asst. Prof., St. Louis Univ., 1977–78. Pres., St. Louis Writers' Guild, 1959, 1976–77; Vice-Pres., 1971–73, and Pres., 1973–74, Missouri Writers' Guild; Pres., St. Louis Poetry Center, 1974–76. *Publs:* (trans. and ed.) Modern Italian Poets, 1961; (trans. with Samuel Beckett et al) Alain Bosquet: Selected Poems, 1963; (trans.) Paul Valéry in English, 1970; Phrase/Paraphrase, 1970; The Pluralism of Poetry, 1974; (trans.) High Sundowns: Twelve Poems of Death and Resurrection from Juan Ramon Jiminez, 1974; (trans. and ed.) Voices in the Dark (poetry and essay), 1974; Jules Laforgue: Selected Poems, 1984; The Hippopotamus: Selected Translations, 1986. Add: 2935 Russell Blvd., St. Louis, Mo. 63104, U.S.A.

GUERARD, Albert (Joseph). American, b. 1914. Novels/Short stories, Literature, Biography. Prof. of Literature, Stanford Univ., Calif., since 1961, now Emeritus. Faculty member, English Dept., Harvard Univ., Cambridge, Mass., 1938–61. *Publs:* The Past Must Alter (novel), 1937; Robert Bridges, 1942; The Hunted (novel), 1944; Maquisard (novel), 1945; Joseph Conrad, 1947; Thomas Hardy, 1949; Night Journey (novel), 1950; André Gide, 1951; The Bystander (novel), 1958; Conrad the Novelist, 1958; The Exiles (novel), 1963; (co-ed.) The Personal Voice, 1964; The Triumph of the Novel, 1976; The Touch of Time: Myth, Memory, and the Self, 1980; Christine/Annette (novel), 1985. Add: 635 Gerona Rd., Stanford, Calif. 94305, U.S.A.

GUEST, Anthony Gordon. British, b. 1930. Law. Prof. of English Law, King's Coll., Univ. of London, since 1966. Barrister-at-law, since 1955. Fellow and Praelector, Univ. Coll. Oxford, 1955–65; Reader in Common Law, Council of Legal Education, Inns of Court, London, 1967–80. U.K. Delegate to UN Commn. on Intnl. Trade Law, 1968–84. *Publs:* (ed.) Anson's Law of Contract, 21st to 26th eds., 1959–84; (gen. ed.) Oxford Essays in Jurisprudence, 1961; The Law of Hire-Purchase,

1966; (gen. ed.) Chitty on Contracts, 23rd-26th eds., 1968–89; (gen. ed.) Benjamin's Sale of Goods, 1974, 3rd ed. 1987; (with others) Introduction to the Law of Credit and Security, 1978; Encyclopedia of Consumer redit, 1979. Add: 16 Trevor Pl., London SW7, England.

GUEST, Barbara. American, b. 1920. Novels/Short stories, Poetry, Plays, Biography. Editorial Assoc., Art News, NYC, 1951–54. *Publs:* The Ladies Choice (play), 1953; The Location of Things, 1960; Poems, 1962; (with B.H. Friedman) Robert Goodnough, Painter, 1962; The Office (play), 1963; Port (play), 1965; The Blue Stairs, 1968; (with S. Isham) I Ching: Poems and Lithographs, 1969; Moscow Mansions (poetry), 1973; The Countess from Minneapolis (poetry), 1977; Seeking Air (novel), 1978; The Turler Losses (poetry), 1979; Biography (poetry), 1981; Quilts (poetry), 1981; Herself Defined: The Poet H.D. and Her World, 1984. Add: 37 Pleasant Lane, Southampton, N.Y. 11968, U.S.A.

GUEST, Harry. (Henry Bayly Guest). British, b. 1932. Novels/Short stories, Poetry. Head of Modern Languages, Exeter Sch., since 1972. Asst. Master, Felsted Sch., Essex, 1955–61; Head of Modern Languages Dept., Lancing Coll., Sussex, 1961–66; Asst. Lectr., Yokohama National Univ. Japan, 1966–72. *Publs:* Private View, 1962; A Different Darkness, 1964; Arrangements, 1968; Another Island Country, 1970; The Cutting-Room, 1970; (with Matthew Mead and Jack Beeching) Penguin Modern Poets 16, 1970; The Place, 1971; (trans. with Lynn Guest and Kajima Shozo) Post-War Japanese Poetry, 1972; The Inheritance (radio play), 1972; The Achievements of Memory, 1974; The Enchanted Acres, 1975; The Emperor of Outer Space (radio play), 1976; A House Against the Night, 1976; English Poems, 1976; Two Poems, 1977; Days (novel), 1978; The Hidden Change, 1978; Zeami in Exile, 1978; Elegies, 1980; Lost and Found: Poems 1975-1982, 1983; The Emperor of Outer Space, 1983; The Distance, The Shadows, 1981; Dealings with the Real World, 1987; Mastering Japanese, 1989. Add: 1 Alexandra Terr., Exeter, Devon EX4 6SY, England.

GUEST, Ivor (Forbes). British, b. 1920. Dance/Ballet. Solicitor. Chmn., Royal Academy of Dancing, since 1969. Vice-Chmn., British Theatre Museum, 1966–77, *Publs:* Napoleon III in England, 1962; The Ballet of the Second Empire, 1858-70, 1953, 1974; The Romantic Ballet in England, 1954; 1972, The Ballet of the Second Empire, 1847-58, 1955, 1974; Fanny Cerrito, 1956, 1974; Victorian Ballet Girl, 1957; Adeline Genée, 1958; The Alhambra Ballet, 1959; The Dancer's Heritage, 1960; (ed. and co-author) La Fille mal Gardée, 1960; The Empire Ballet, 1962; A Gallery of Romantic Ballet, 1965; The Romantic Ballet in Paris, 1966, 1980; Dandies and Dancers, 1969; Carlotta Zambelli, 1969; Two Coppélias, 1970; Fanny Elssler, 1970; Pas de quatre, 1970; Le Ballet de l'Opéra de Paris, 1976; The Divine Virginia, 1977; Adeline Genée: A Pictorial Record, 1978; Lettres d'un Maître de Ballet, 1978; Adventures of a Ballet Historian, 1982; Jules Perrot, 1984; Gautier on Dance, 1986; Gautier on Spanish Dancing, 1987. Add: 17 Holland Park, London W11 3TD, England.

GUEST, Judith. American, b. 1936. Novels/Short stories, Essays. *Publs:* Ordinary People, 1976; Second Heaven, 1982; (with Rebecca Hill) Killing-Time in St. Cloud, 1988; Mythic Family (essay), 1988. Add: c/o Viking-Penguin Inc., 40 W. 23rd St., New York, N.Y. 10017, U.S.A.

GUFFIN, Gilbert Lee. American, b. 1906. Theology/Religion. Emeritus Dean of Religion, Samford Univ., Birmingham, Ala., since 1971 (Founder and Dir., Extension Div., 1947–50; Dean of Religion, 1961–71). Pres., Eastern Baptist Theological Seminary, Philadelphia, 1950–61, and Eastern Coll., St. Davids, Pa., 1952–61. *Publs:* How to Run a Church, 1948; Called of God, 1951, 1965; Pastor and Church, 1955; (ed.) What God Hath Wrought, 1960; The Gospel in Isaiah, 1968; The Bible: God's Missionary Message to Man, vol. I, 1973, vol. II, 1974. Add: 3605 Ratliff Rd., Birmingham, Ala. 35210, U.S.A.

GUIDO, Cecily Margaret. British, b. 1912. Archaeology/Antiquities *Publs:* Syracuse: A Handbook to Its History and Principal Monuments, 1958; Sardinia, 1964; Sicily: An Archaeological Guide, 1967; Southern Italy: An Archaeological Guide, 1972; The Glass Beads of the Prehistoric and Roman Periods in Britain and Ireland, 1978. Add: 44 Long St., Devizes, Wilts. SN10 1NP, England.

GUILES, Fred Lawrence. American, b. 1922. Film, Biography. *Publs:* Norma Jean: The Life of Marilyn Monroe, 1969; Marion Davies, 1973; Hanging On in Paradise, 1975; Tyrone Power: The Last Idol, 1979; Stan: The Life of Stan Laurel, 1981; Jane Fonda: The Actress in Her Time, 1982; Legend: The Life and Death of Marilyn Monroe, 1984. Add: c/o Berkeley Publishing Group, 200 Madison Ave., New York, N.Y. 10016,

U.S.A.

GUIN, Wyman (Woods). American, b. 1915. Science fiction/Fantasy. Planning Admin., L.W. Erolich-Intercon Intnl., since 1964. Technician in Pharmacology, Advertising Writer, Advertising Mgr., and Marketing Vice-Pres., Lakeside Labs, Inc., Milwaukee, 1938–62; Vice-Pres., Medical Television Communications Inc., Chicago, 1962–64. *Publs:* Living Way Out (short stories), 1967, in U.K. as Beyond Bedlam, 1973; The Standing Joy, 1969. Lives in Tarrytown, N.Y. Add: c/o Avon Books, 959 Eighth Ave., New York, N.Y. 10019, U.S.A.

GUINNESS, Bryan (Walter). (Baron Moyne of Bury St. Edmunds). British, b. 1905 Novels/Short stories, Children's fiction, Plays/-Screenplays, Poetry. Member, House of Lords, London. Joined Bd. of Arthur Guinness Son & Co. Ltd., Dublin, 1934: Vice-Chmn., 1949–67; Joint Vice-Chmn., 1967–79. *Publs:* 23 Poems, 1931; Singing out of Tune, 1933; Landscape with Figures, 1934; Under the Eyelid, 1935; Johnny and Jemima, 1936; A Week by the Sea, 1936; Lady Crushwell's Companion, 1938; The Fragrant Concubine (play), 1939; The Children in the Desert, 1947; Reflexions, 1947; The Animals' Breakfast, 1940; (with D. MacCarthy) Story of a Nutcracker, 1953; A Riverside Charade (play), 1954; Collected Poems, 1956; A Fugue of Cinderellas, 1956; (with R. Pym) Catriona and the Grasshopper, 1957; (with R. Pym) Priscilla and the Prawn, 1960; Leo and Rosabelle, 1961; The Giant's Eye, 1964; The Rose in the Tree, 1964; The Girl with the Flower, 1966; The Engagement, 1969; The Clock, 1973; (sic) Dairy Not Kept, 1975; Hellenic Flirtation, 1978; Potpourri from the Thirties, 1982; Personal Patchwork, 1987. Add: Knockmaroon House, Castleknock, Co. Dublin, Ireland.

GUIRDHAM, Arthur. Also writes as Francis Eaglesfield. British, b. 1905. Novels, Medicine. Former Sr. Consultant Psychiatrist, Bath Clinical Area, National Health Service. *Publs:* Disease and the Social System, 1942; The Lights Were Going Out (novel) 1944; These Paid (novel), 1946; I, A. Stranger (novel), 1949; A Theory of Disease, 1957; Christ and Freud, 1959; Man: Divine or Social, 1960; Cosmic Factors in Disease, 1963; The Nature of Healing, 1964; (as Francis Eaglesfield) Silent Union, 1966; The Cathars and Reincarnation, 1970; The Gibbet and the Cross (novel), 1971; Obsession, 1972; A Foot in Both Worlds, 1973; We Are One Another, 1974; The Lake and the Castle, 1976; The Great Heresy, 1977; The Psyche in Medicine, 1978; Paradise Found, 1980; The Psychic Dimensions in Mental Illness, 1982. Add: 742 Corton Denham, Sherborne, Dorset, England.

GULLANS, Charles (Bennett). American, b. 1929. Poetry, Design, Translations. Prof. of English, Univ of California at Los Angeles, since 1961; Publisher, Symposium Press. Faculty member, Univ. of Washington, Seattle, 1955–61. *Publs:* Moral Poems, 1957; (co-trans.) Last Letters from Stalingrad, 1962; Arrivals and Departures (poetry), 1962; (ed.) The English and Latin Poems of Sir Robert Ayton, 1963; (co-author) A Checklist of Trade Bindings Designed by Margaret Armstrong, 1968; (co-author) The Decorative Designers, 1895-1932: An Essay, 1970; A Bibliography of the Published Writings of J.V. Cunningham, 1973, 1988; Imperfect Correspondences (verse), 1978; Many Houses (poetry), 1981; A Diatribe to Dr. Steele (poetry), 1982; The Bright Universe (poetry), 1983; Under Red Skies (poetry), 1983; Local Winds (poetry), 1985; The Wrong Side of the Rug (translations), 1986; (co-author) A Bibliography of the Published Works of Turner Cassity 1952-1988, 1988. Add: Dir. of Creative Writing, Dept. of English, Univ. of California, 405 Hilgard Ave., Los Angeles, Calif. 90024, U.S.A.

GUNDRY, Dudley William. British, b. 1916. Theology/Religion. Canon of Leicester Cathedral, since 1963. Warden of Reichel Hall, Univ. Coll of North Wales, Bangor, 1947–60; Dean, Bangor Sch. Theology, 1956–60; Prof. of Religious Studies, Univ. of Ibadan, Nigeria, 1960–63; Religious Affairs Corresp., Daily Telegraph, 1978–86. Co-Founder and Hon. Secty., British Assn. for the History of Religions, 1954–60 *Publs:* Religions: An Historical and Theological Study, 1958, 1966; The Teacher and the World Religions, 1968. Add: 28 Stoneygate Court, Leicester LE2 2AH, England.

GUNN, James E(dwin). American, b. 1923 Science fiction/Fantasy, Literature. Prof. of English, Univ. of Kansas, since 1970 (Managing Ed., Alumni Publs., 1955–58; Administrative Asst. to Chancellor for Univ. Relations, 1958–70). Chmn., Campbell Award Jury, 1978–80 and since 1984. Ed., Western Printing and Lithographing Co., Racine, Wisc., 1951–52. Pres., Science Fiction Writers of America, 1971–72; Pres., Science Fiction Research Assn., 1980–82. *Publs:* This Fortress World, 1955; (with J. Williamson) Star Bridge, 1955; Station in Space, 1958; The Joy Makers, 1961; The Immortals, 1962; Future Imperfect (short stories), 1964; (ed.) Man and the Future, 1968; The Immortal (novelization of TV series), 1970 The Witching Hour (short stories), 1970; The Burning, 1972; Breaking Point (short stories), 1972; The Listeners, 1972; Some Dreams Are Nightmares (short stories), 1974; Alternate Worlds: The Illustrated History of Science Fiction, 1975; (ed.) Nebula Award Stories 10, 1975; The End of the Dreams (3 short novels), 1975; The Magicians, 1976; Kampus, 1977; (ed.) The Road to Science Fiction 4 vols., 1977–82; The Dreamers, 1981; Isaac Asimov: The Foundations of Science Fiction, 1982; Crisis!, 1986; (ed.) The New Encyclopedia of Science Fiction, 1988. Add: 2215 Orchard Lane, Lawrence, Kans. 66044, U.S.A.

GUNN, Thom(son William). British, b. 1929. Poetry, Literature. Member of English Dept., Univ. of California, Berkeley, 1958–66, and since 1975. Poetry Reviewer, Yale Review, New Haven, Conn., 1958–64. *Publs:* (ed.) Poetry from Cambridge 1951-52: A Selection of Verse by Members of the University, 1952; (Poems), 1953; Fighting Terms, 1954, 1958; The Sense of Movement, 1957; My Sad Captains and Other Poems, 1961; (with Ted Hughes) Selected Poems, 1962; (ed. with T. Hughes) Five American Poets, 1963; A Geography, 1966; (with A. Gunn) Positives, 1966; Touch, 1967; The Garden of the Gods, 1968; (ed.) Selected Poems of Fulke Greville, 1968; The Explorers: Poems, 1969; The Fair in the Woods, 1969; Poems 1950-66: A Selection, 1969; Sunlight, 1969; Last Days at Teddington, 1971; Moly, 1971; Moly and My Sad Captains, 1973; (ed.) Ben Jonson, 1974; Mandrakes, 1974; Song Book, 1974; To the Air, 1974; Jack Straw's Castle and Other Poems, 1976; Games of Chance, 1979; Selected Poems 1950-1975, 1979; The Passages of Joy, 1982; The Occasions of Poetry (prose), 1982; The Hurtless Trees, 1986; Undesirables, 1988. Add: 1216 Cole St., San Francisco, Calif. 94117, U.S.A.

GUNSTON, Bill. (William Tudor Gunston). British, b. 1927. Air/Space topics, Military/Defence, Technology, Transportation, Biography. Asst. Compiler, Jane's All the World's Aircraft, since 1969; European Ed., Aircraft (Australia), since 1973. Technical Ed., Flight Intnl., London, 1951–63; Technology Ed., Science Journal, London, 1964–70. *Publs:* Your Book of Light, 1968; Hydrofoils and Hovercraft, 1969; The Jet Age, 1971; Transport Technology, 1972; Transport Problems and Prospects, 1972; (ed.) Atlas of the Earth, 1972; (with F. Howard) Conquest of the Air, 1973; Bombers of the West, 1973; Shaping Metals, 1974; Attack Aircraft of the West, 1974; Philatelist's Companion, 1975; Supersonic Fighters, 1975; Submarines in Colour, 1975; F-4 Phantom, 1976; Night Fighters, 1976; Encyclopedia of Combat Aircraft, 1976; Modern Military Aircraft, 1977; Aircraft of World War II, 1978; (with Bill Sweetman) Soviet Air Power, 1978; Spotting Planes, 1978; F-111, 1978; Bombers, 1978; By Jupiter (biography of Sir Roy Fedden), 1978; Tornado, 1979; Encyclopedia of Missiles and Rockets, 1979; (ed.) St. Michael Encyclopedia of Aviation, 1979; (ed.) The Flyer's Handbook, 1979; Find Out About Trains and Railways, 1979; Find Out about Aircraft, 1979; Water, 1980; Aircraft of World War 2, 1980; (ed.) Encyclopedia of World Air Power, 1980; (ed.) The Colour Encyclopedia of Aviation, 1980; The Plane Makers, 1980; Jane's Aerospace Dictionary, 1980, 3rdd ed. 1988; Harrier, 1980; Coal, 1981; Motor Cycles, 1981; Modern Warplanes, 1981; Airliners, 1981; (ed.) The Illustrated History of Propeller Airliners Jet Airliners, Fighters, 3 vols., 1981; Fighters of the Fifties, 1981; Bombers of World War II, 1981; Military Helicopters, 1981; Fighters 1914-1945, 1982; Record Breakers (Land), 1982; (with Anthony Wood) Hitler's Luftwaffe, 1982; St. Michael Airliners, 1982; Aeroplanes, Balloons and Rockets, 1982; The Israeli Air Force, 1982; Family Library of Aviation, 1982; St. Michael Modern Air Combat, 1982; F-16 Fighting Falcon, 1982; Air-Launched Missiles, 1982; Warships, 1982; (main contributor) The Arms Yearbook, 1982; Fighter Aircraft in Colour, 1983; Aircraft of the Soviet Union, 1983; Spyplanes and RPVs, 1983; Fact File F-111, 1983; Missiles and Rockets of World War III, 1983; Encyclopedia of Modern Air Combat, 1983; Helicopters of the World, 1983; Naval and Maritime Aircraft, 1983; Falklands: The Aftermath, 1984; Fact File Harrier, 1984; Not Much of an Engineer (biography of Sir Stanley Hooker), 1984; Big Book of Fighter Planes, 1984; First Questions: Transport, 1984; Future Fighters and Combat Aircraft, 1984; Encyclopedia of Modern Fighting Aircraft, 1984; (with David Taylor) The Guinness Book of Speed Facts and Feats, 1984; Aircraft of the RAF: Phantom, 1984; Air Superiority, 1985; F/A-18 Hornet, 1985; (with others) Advanced Technology Warfare, 1985; Commercial Aircraft, 1985; Military Aircraft, 1985; A Century of Flight, 1985; Warplanes of the Future, 1985; (co-author) Encyclopedia of Modern Weapons, 1985; Technology Series; Aircraft, 1985; Grumman X-29, 1985; World Encyclopedia of Aero Engines, 1986, 1989;

Water Travel, 1986; EAP, 1986; Encyclopedia of Modern Fighting Helicopters, 1986; Encyclopedia of American Warplanes, 1986; MiG-21, 1986; British German, Japanese, US Aircraft of World War 2, 4 vols., 1986; Modern European Aircraft, 1986; Modern Soviet Aircraft, 1986; Modern US Aircraft, 1986; (with John Golley) Whittle: The True Story, 1987; MiG-23 Flogger, 1987; AH-64A Apache, 1987; Aircraft of the Vietnam War, 1987; Encyclopedia of Aircraft Armament, 1987; British Midland (airways), 1987; Topics: Railways, 1987; Stealth Warplanes, 1987; One of a Kind (history of Grumman aircraft), 1987; Airbus, 1988; Modern Combat Arms: Carriers and Fighters, 2 vols., 1988; American Military Aircraft, 1988; Guide to Modern Bombers, 1988; Flight Without Formulae (update), 1988; Anatomy of Aircraft, 1988; (with Lindsay Peacock) Encyclopedia of Fighter Missions, 1988; History of Rolls-Royce Aero Engines, 1989. Add: High Beech, Kingsley Green, Haslemere, Surrey GU27 3LL, England.

GUNSTONE, Frank Denby. British, b. 1923. Chemistry. Prof. of Chemistry, St. Andrews Univ., Fife, since 1971 until retirement, 1989 (Lectr. 1954–59; Sr. Lectr. 1959–65; Reader 1965–70). Lectr., Univ. of Glasgow, 1946–54. *Publs:* An Introduction to the Chemistry of Fats and Fatty Acids, 1958; (with John Read) A Text-Book of Organic Chemistry, 1958; Programmes in Organic Chemistry, 6 vols., 1966–74; An Introduction to the Chemistry and Biochemistry of Fatty Acids and Their Glycerides, 1967; (ed.) Topics in Lipid Chemistry, 3 vols., 1970–72; (with J.T. Sharp and D.M. Smith) An Introductory Course in Practical Organic Chemistry, 1970; Guidebook to Stereochemistry, 1975; (with F.A. Norris) Lipids in Foods, 1983; (co-ed.) The Lipid Handbook. Add: Dept. of Chemistry, St. Andrews Univ., St. Andrews, Fife, Scotland.

GUNTER, Pete (Addison Yancey). American, b. 1936. Novels, Environmental science/Ecology, Philosophy. Prof. of Philosophy, Univ. of North Texas, Denton, since 1969 (Chmn., 1969–76). Exec. Dir., Foundn. for Philosophy of Creativity, since 1982. Book Reviewer, Dallas Morning News, Fort Worth Star-Telegram; Environmental Adviser, National Forum. Fellow, Yale Univ., New Haven, Conn. 1960–62; Asst. Prof., Auburn Univ., Ala. 1962–65; Assoc. Prof., Univ. of Tennessee, Knoxville 1965–69. Pres., Southwestern Philosophical Soc., 1978–79. *Publs:* (ed. and translator) Bergson and the Evolution of Physics, 1969; The Big Thicket: A Challenge for Conservation, 1972; Henri Bergson: Bibliography, 1974, 1986; (with J.R. Sibley) Process Philosophy: Basic Writings, 1978; (ed. with Robert Calvert) The Memoirs of W.R. Strong; River in Dry Grass (novel), 1985; (with A. Papanicolaou) Bergson and Modern Thought: Towards a Unification of the Sciences, 1987. Add: 225 Jagoe, Denton, Tex. 76201, U.S.A.

GUNTHER, A(lbert) E(verard). British, b. 1903. Sciences (general), Biography. Geologist and Admin., Shell Intnl. Group of Petroleum Cos., 1925–61. *Publs:* The German War for Crude Oil in Europe, 1947; Rolfe Family Records, 1962; Early Science in Oxford, vol. 15, 1967; A Century of Zoology in the British Museum, 1975; The Life of William C. M'Intosh 1838-1931, 1975; The Founders of Science at the British Museum 1753-1900, 1980; An Introduction to the Life of the Rev. Thomas Birch 1705-1766, 1984. Add: Park House, Heacham, King's Lynn, Norfolk, England.

GUNTHER, Gerald. American (b. German), b. 1927. Law. William Nelson Cromwell Prof. of Law, Stanford Law Sch., Stanford, Calif., since 1972 (faculty member, since 1962). Member, Editorial Bd., University Casebook Series, The Foundation Press Inc., since 1972. Instr. of Political Science and Constitutional Law, Brooklyn Coll., and City Coll. of New York, 1949–59, 1951; Ed., Harvard Law Review, 1951–53; Law Clerk, Judge Learned Hand, U.S. Court of Appeals for the Second Circuit, 1953–54; Law Clerk, Chief Justice Earl Warren, U.S. Supreme Court, 1954–55; Assoc., Cleary, Gottlieb, Friendly and Hamilton, law firm, NYC, 1953, 1954, 1955–56; Assoc. Prof. of Law, 1956–59, and Prof. of Law, 1959–62, Columbia Univ. Sch. of Law, N.Y. Member, Harvard Law Review Bd. of Overseers, 1967–74, and Harvard Overseers' Cttee. to Visit Harvard Law Sch., 1974–80. *Publs:* (co-ed.) Selected Essays on Constitutional Law, 1938-62, 1963; John Marshall's Defense of McCulloch v. Maryland, 1969; Constitutional Law, 7th-11th eds., 1965–85; Individual Rights in Constitutional Law, 1975, 4th ed. 1986. Add: Stanford Law Sch., Stanford, Calif. 94305, U.S.A.

GUPPY, Nicholas (Gareth Lechmere). British, b. 1925. Travel/Exploration/Adventure. Research Assoc., New York Botanical Garden, 1953–55; Leader or Member, 8 expeditions in northern South Africa; Advisory Ed., Animal mag. (now Wildlife), 1963–81. Chmn., Sovereign-American Arts Corp., New York, 1969–70; Founder/Chmn., Survival Intnl., 1970. *Publs:* Wai-Wai: Through the Forests North of the Amazon, 1958; Calder Gouaches, 1962; (co-author) The Amazon, 1970; A Young Man's Journey, 1974; (with Yseult Bridges) Child of the Tropics, 1980; (co-author) Growth Without Ecodisaster, 1980. Add: 21a Shawfield St., London SW3, England.

GURNEY, A(lbert) R(amsdell), Jr. American, b. 1930. Novels/Short stories, Plays/Screenplays. Prof. of Literature, Massachusetts Inst. of Technology, Cambridge, since 1970 (Member of the faculty since 1960). *Publs:* The Comeback, 1965; The Rape of Bunny Stuntz, 1966; The David Show, 1966; The Golden Fleece, 1968; The Problem, 1969; The Open Meeting, 1969; The Love Course, 1970; Scenes from American Life, 1970; The House of Mirth (screenplay), 1972; The Old One-Two, 1973; Children, 1974; The Gospel According to Joe (novel), 1974; Richard Cory, 1976; Entertaining Strangers (novel), 1976; The Wayside Motor Inn, 1977; The Middle Ages, 1977; The Dining Room, 1982; What I Did Last Summer, 1983; The Golden Age, 1984; Four Plays, 1984; The Snow Ball (novel), 1985; Sweet Sue, 1986; The Perfect Lady, 1986; Another Antigone, 1987; The Cocktail Hour, 1988; Love Letters, 1989. Add: Wellers Bridge Rd., Roxbury, Conn. 06783, U.S.A.

GURR, A(ndrew) J(ohn). New Zealander, b. 1936. Literature. Prof. and Head, Dept. of English Language and Literature, Univ. of Reading, since 1976. Ed., Journal of Commonwealth Literature, since 1979. Lectr. in English, Univ. of Leeds, 1962–76; Prof. and Head, Dept. of Literature, Univ. of Nairobi, 1969–73. *Publs:* (ed.) The Knight of the Burning Pestle, by Beaumont and Fletcher, 1968; (ed.) The Maid's Tragedy, by Beaumont and Fletcher, 1969; (ed.) Philaster, by Beaumont and Fletcher, 1969; The Shakespearean Stage 1574-1642, 1970, 1980; (ed. with Pio Zirimu) Black Aesthetics, 1973; (ed., with Angus Calder) Writers in East Africa, 1974; "Hamlet" and the Distracted Globe, 1978; Writers in Exile, 1981; (with Clare Hanson) Katherine Mansfield, 1981; (ed.) Richard II, by Shakespeare, 1984; Playgoing in Shakespeare's London, 1987. Add: Dept. of English, Univ. of Reading, Whiteknights Park, Reading RG6 2AA, England.

GUSTAFSON, Ralph. Canadian, b. 1909. Novels/Short stories, Poetry. Music critic, C.B.C., since 1960. Prof. of English, Bishop's Univ., Lennoxville, Que., 1963–79. Poetry Delegate, to U.K., 1972, 1985, to U.S.S.R., 1976, to Washington, D.C., 1977, to Italy, 1981, 1982. *Publs:* Flight into Darkness, 1944; (ed.) Anthology of Canadian poetry, 1942; (ed.) Little Anthology of Canadian Poetry, 1943; (ed.) Canadian Accent (poetry and prose), 1944; (ed.) Penguin Book of Canadian Verse, 1958, 4th ed., 1984; Rivers Among Rocks, 1960; Rocky Mountain Poems, 1960; Sift in an Hourglass, 1966; Ixion's Wheel, 1969; Theme and Variations for Sounding Brass, 1972; Selected Poems, 1972; Fire on Stone, 1974; The Brazen Tower (short stories), 1974; Corners in the Glass, 1977; Soviet Poems, 1978; Sequences, 1979; Landscape with Rain, 1980; The Vivid Air (short stories), 1980; Conflicts of Spring, 1981; Gradations of Grandeur, 1982; The Moment Is All: Selected Poems 1944-1983, 1983; Directives of Autumn, 1984; At the Ocean's Verge, 1984; Impromptus, 1984; A Literary Friendship: The Correspondence of Ralph Gustafson and W.W.E. Ross, 1984; Plummets and Other Partialities (essays), 1987; Collected Poems, 1987; Winter Prophecies, 1987; The Celestial Corkscrew, 1989. Add: P.O. Box 172, North Hatley, Que., Canada.

GUTHRIE, A(lfred) B(ertram), Jr. American, b. 1901. Novels/Short stories, Westerns/Adventure. Reporter, 1926–29, City Ed. and Editorial Writer, 1929–45, and Exec. Ed., 1945–47, Leader newspaper, Lexington, Ky.; Fellow and Lectr., Bread Loaf Writers' Conference. Vt., 1945–47; Prof. of Creative Writing, Univ. of Kentucky, Lexington, 1947–52. *Publs:* Murders at Moon Dance, 1943; The Big Sky, 1947; The Way West, 1949; Shane (screenplay), 1951; The Kentuckian (screenplay), 1953; These Thousand Hills, 1956; The Big It and Other Stories, 1960; The Blue Hen's Chick, 1965; Arfive, 1971; Once Upon a Pond (children's fiction), 1973; Wild Pitch, 1973; The Last Valley, 1975; The Genuine Article, 1977; No Second Wind, 1980; Fairland, Fairland, 1982; Playing Catch-up, 1985; Four Miles to Far Mountain (poetry), 1987; Murder in the Cotswold, 1989. Add: Star Route 1, Box 30, Choteau, Mont. 59422, U.S.A.

GUTHRIE, John. British, b. 1908. Engineering. Seagoing Engineer with various shipping lines, 1930–38; Marine Surveyor, Lloyd's Register of Shipping, 1939–72. *Publs:* Bizarre Ships of the Nineteenth Century, 1970; History of Marine Engineering, 1971. Add: 8 De Walden Ct., 51 Meads Rd., Eastbourne, Sussex BN20 7QB, England.

GUTMAN, Judith Mara. American, b. 1928. History, Photography. Freelance writer, lectr., and reviewer; regular contributor to the Intnl. Herald Tribune, since 1983. Former Lectr., Hunter Coll., NYC, Dir., Montefiore Nursery Sch., NYC, and Instr., Univ. of Wisconsin, Madison. *Publs:* The Colonial Venture, 1966; Lewis W. Hine and the American Social Conscience, 1967; (with E. Rozwenc) The Making of American Society, 1972; Is America Used Up?, 1973; Lewis W. Hine: Two Perspectives, 1974; Buying, 1975; Ethnic Heritage: Immigration, Migration and the Growth of Cities (film strip), 1975; Through Indian Eyes (Photographic exhibition catalogue), 1982. Add: 97 Sixth Ave., Nyack, N.Y. 10960, U.S.A.

GUTMAN, Robert W. American, b. 1925. Biography. Dean of Grad. Studies, Fashion Inst. of Technology, State Univ. of New York, NYC, 1980–88 (joined faculty, 1957; Dean of Art and Design Div., 1974–80). Founder and former Lectr., Master Classes of Bayreuth Festival. *Publs:* (ed.) Volsunga Saga, 1962; Richard Wagner: The Man, His Mind, and His Music, 1968, 1972. Add: 37 West 12th St., New York, N.Y. 10011, U.S.A.

GUTTERIDGE, Don(ald George). Canadian, b. 1937. Novels/Short stories, Poetry, Language/Linguistics. Prof. of English, Univ. of Western Ontario, London. *Publs:* Riel: A Poem for Voices, 1968; The Village Within, 1970; Language and Expression, 1970; Death at Quebec, 1971; Saying Grace, an Elegy, 1972; Coppermine: The Quest for North, 1973; Bus-Ride, 1974; Borderlands, 1975; Tecumseh, 1976; A True History of Lambton County, 1977; Mountain and Plain, 1978; The Country of the Young, 1978; Rites of Passage, 1979; All in Good Time, 1980; God's Geography, 1982; Brave Season, 1983; The Exiled Heart, 1986; Incredible Journeys, 1986; St. Vitus Dance, 1987; Shaman's Ground, 1988; The Dimension of Delight, 1988. Add: 114 Victoria St., London, Ont. N6A 2B5, Canada.

GUTTERIDGE, Richard (Joseph Cooke). British, b. 1911. Theology/Religion. Tutor, Queen's Coll., Birmingham, 1935–37; Principal, Blue Coat Sch., Birmingham, 1941–45; Rector, Brampton, Huntingdon, 1945–52; Chaplain, R.A.F., 1952–68, Bampton Fellow, Univ. of Oxford, 1969–71. *Publs:* Open Thy Mouth for the Dumb: The German Evangelical Church and the Jews 1879-1950. Add: 1 Croftgate, Fulbrooke Rd., Cambridge CB3 9EG, England.

GUTTERIDGE, William Frank. British, b. 1919. International relations/Current affairs. Dir. of Complementary Studies 1971–80, and Prof. of Intnl. Studiies, 1976–82, now Emeritus, Univ. of Aston in Birmingham; Editorial Consultant, Inst. for the Study of Conflict, since 1982. Lectr. and Sr. Lectr. of Commonwealth History and Govt., Royal Military Academy Sandhurst, Camberley, Surrey, 1949–63; Head of Dept. of Languages and Modern Studies, Lanchester Polytechnic, Coventry, 1963–71. *Publs:* Armed Forces in New States, 1962; Military Institutions and Power in the United States, 1965; The Military in African Politics, 1969; Military Regimes in Africa, 1975; (ed.) European Security, Nuclear Weapons and Public Confidence, 1982; Mineral Resources and National Security, 1984; South Africa: Evolution or Revolution?, 1985; The South African Crisis: Time for International Action, 1985; The New Terrorism, 1986. Add: 26 St. Mark's Rd., Leamington Spa CV32 6DL, England.

GUTTMANN, Allen. American, b. 1932. History, Literature, Sports. Prof. of English and American Studies, Amherst Coll., Massachusetts, since 1959. *Publs:* The Wound in the Heart: America and the Spanish Civil War, 1962; The Conservative Tradition in America, 1967; The Jewish Writer in America, 1971; From Ritual to Record: The Nature of Modern Sports, 1978; (co-ed.) Life of George Washington, by Washington Irving, 5 vols., 1981; The Games Must Go On: Avery Brundage and the Olympic Movement, 1984; Sports Spectators, 1986; A Whole New Ball Game: An Interpretation of American Sports, 1988. Add: 6 Lead Mine Hill Rd., Rt. 3, Amherst, Mass. 01002, U.S.A.

GUY, Rosa (Cuthbert). American, b. 1928. Children's fiction, Plays/Screenplays. Founding Pres., Harlem Writer's Guild. *Publs:* Venetian Blinds (play), 1954; Bird at My Window, 1966; (ed.) Children of Longing, 1971; The Friends, 1973; Ruby, 1976; Edith Jackson, 1978; The Disappearance, 1979; Mirror of Her Own, 1981; (trans.) Mother Crocodile, by B. Diop, 1981; New Guys Around the Block, 1983; A

Measure of Time, 1983; Paris, Pee Wee and Big Dog, 1984; My Love, My Love, 1985. Add: c/o Ellen Levine, 432 Park Ave. S., Suite 1205, New York, N.Y. 10016, U.S.A.

GWALTNEY, John Langston. American, b. 1928. Anthropology, Race relations. Assoc. to Prof. of Anthropology, Syracuse Univ., N.Y., since 1971. Member, Resource Group, Project on the Handicapped, American Assn. for the Advancement of Science, Washington D.C., since 1975. Asst. and Assoc. Prof., Dept. of Sociology and Anthropology, State Univ. of New York, Cortland, 1967–71; Past Chmn., Presidential Advisory Cttee., on the Caste Disadvantaged, Cortland Coll., N.Y. *Publs:* The Thrice Shy: Cultural Accommodation to Blindness and other Disasters in a Mexican Community, 1970; Drylongso: A Self Portrait of Black America, 1980; The Dissenters: Voices from Contemporary America, 1986. Add: Dept. of Anthropology, Syracuse Univ., Syracuse, N.Y. 13210, U.S.A.

GWYN, William Brent. American. Politics/Government. Prof. of Political Science since 1969, Tulane Univ., New Orleans, (Assoc. Prof., 1963–69; Chmn. of Dept., 1975–79). Asst. Prof., Bucknell Univ., Lewisburg, Pa., 1957–63. *Publs:* Democracy and the Cost of Politics in Britain, 1962; The Meaning of the Separation of Powers, 1965; Barriers to Establishing Urban Ombudsmen, 1974; (co-ed.) Perspectives on Public Policy, 1975; (co-ed.) Britain: Progress and Decline, 1980. Add: 8011 Jeannette St., New Orleans, La. 70118, U.S.A.

GWYNNE, Peter. British, b. 1941. Engineering, Physics. Pres., Peter Gwynne Ltd., Boston, since 1981; Dir., Editorial Operations, The Scientist, Washington, D.C., since 1986. Science Ed., Boston Herald-Traveler, 1968–69; Assoc. Ed., 1969–72, and Science Ed., 1972–81, Newsweek mag., NYC; freelance writer, 1981–83; Managing Ed., Technology Review, MIT, Cambridge, Mass., 1983–86. *Publs:* (co-ed.) Advances in Materials Science, 1967; (co-author) Physics and the Physical Perspectives, 1980. Add: 2013 37th St., Washington, D.C. 20007, U.S.A.

GYLDENVAND, Lily M. American, b. 1917. Theology/Religion. Ed., SCOPE mag., 1960–79. *Publs:* Beyond All Doubt, 1949; What Am I Saying?, 1952; Of All Things, 1956; So You're Only Human, 1957; What Am I Praying?, 1964; If God So Loved Me, 1965; (with A. Storaasli) Established in the Faith, 1966; (with A. Storaasli) Called to Be Agents of Reconciliation, 1966; (with A. Storaasli) Growing in Prayer, 1967; Call Her Blessed, 1967; Invitation to Joy, 1969; Prayer Scrapbook, 1974; Stewardship Scrapbook, 1978; Free Gift, 1980; Martin Luther: Giant of Faith, 1981; Joy in His Presence, 1981. Add: 2545 Fry St., Roseville, Minn. 55113, U.S.A.

H

HAAC, Oscar A. American, b. 1918. History, Literature, Biography. Asst. Prof. of Romance Languages, Pennsylvania State Univ., University Park, 1948–54; Prof. of Romance Languages, Emory Univ., Atlanta, 1954–62; Prof. of French, State Univ. of New York, Stony Brook, 1965–88 (Chmn., Romance Languages, 1965–68); Visiting Prof., New York Univ., 1989. *Publs:* Les Principes Inspirateurs de Michelet, 1951; Jules Michelet: Cours Professé au College de France 1839, 1954; (translator and author) Max Scheler: Philosophical Perspectives, 1958; P.-S. Ballanche: La Theodicée, 1959; (co-author) Points de Vue, 1959; (co-author) Perspectives de France, 1968, 3rd ed. 1982; Marivaux, 1973; (with A. Bieler) Actualité et Avenir: A Guide to France, 1975; Michelet, 1982; (contrib. ed.) Oeuvres Complètes, by Michelet (Cours, Histoire de la Revolution), 1989. Add: 138 E. 36th St., New York, N.Y. 10016, U.S.A.

HAAR, Charles M(onroe). American, b. 1920. Regional/Urban planning. Louis D. Brandeis Prof. of Law, Harvard Univ., Cambridge, since 1972 (Assoc. Prof., 1952–54; Prof., 1954–56 and 1966–72); Chmn., Joint Center for Urban Studies, Massachusetts Inst. of Technology/Harvard Univ., Cambridge, since 1969. Admitted to New York Bar, 1949; in law practice, NYC, 1949–52; Asst. Secty., Metropolitan Development, U.S. Dept. of Housing and Urban Development, Washington, 1966–69. Former Chmn., President's Task Force on Natural Beauty, and President's Commn. on Suburban Problems. *Publs:* Land Planning Law in a Free Society, 1959; Land-Use Planning, 1959, 3rd ed. as Land Use Planning: A Casebook on the Use, Misuse and Reuse of Urban Land, 1977; Federal Credit and Private Housing, 1960; Law and Land, 1964, 2nd ed. as Property and Law, 1985; Golden Age of American Law, 1966; The End of Innocence, 1972; Housing the Poor in Suburbia, 1974; Between the Idea and the Reality, 1975; (with others) Transfer of Development Rights: A Primer, 1981; (ed.) Housing in the Eighties: Financial and Institutional Perspective, 1984; (ed.) Cities, Law, and Social Policy: Learning from the British, 1984; (ed.) Judges, Politics and Flounders: Perspectives on the Cleaning up of Boston Harbor, 1986; (with D.W. Fessler) Wrong Side of the Tracks, 1986; (with D.W. Fessler) Fairness and Justice: Law in the Service of Equality, 1987; (with J.S. Kayden) Landmark Justice: The Influence of William J. Brennan Jr. on America's Communities, 1988; (ed. with Kayden) Zoning at Sixty: Mediating Public and Private Rights, 1990. Add: 1 Kennedy Rd., Cambridge, Mass. 02138, U.S.A.

HAAR, James. American, b. 1929. Music. Prof. of Music, Univ. of North Carolina, Chapel Hill, since 1978. Member, Exec. Bd., Grove's Dictionary of Music and Musicians, 6th ed. Instr., 1960–63, and Asst. Prof., 1963–67, Harvard Univ., Cambridge, Mass.; Assoc. Prof., Univ. of Pennsylvania, Philadelphia, 1967–69; Prof. of Music, New York Univ., NYC, 1969–78. *Publs:* (ed.) Chanson and Madrigal 1480-1530, 1964; The Tugendsterne of Harsdörffer and Staden, 1965; (co-ed.) The Duos of Gero, 1980; (ed. with L.F. Bernstein) Il Primo Libro de Madrigali Italiani e Canzone Francese a Due Voci: Masters and Monuments of the Renaissance, by Ihan Gero, 1980; Essays on Italian Poetry and Music in the Renaissance: 1350-1600, 1986. Add: Dept. of Music, Univ. of North Carolina, Chapel Hill, N.C. 27514, U.S.A.

HABAKKUK, John Hrothgar. British, b. 1915. Economics, Technology. Principal, Jesus Coll., Oxford, 1968–84 (Chicele Prof. of Economic History and Fellow of All Souls Coll., 1950–67; Vice-Chancellor, Oxford Univ., 1973–77). Pres., Royal Historical Soc., 1976–80. *Publs:* American and British Technology in the Nineteenth Century, 1962; (ed. with M.M. Postan) Cambridge Economic History of Europe, vol. VI, 1966; Population Growth and Economic Development since 1750, 1971.

Add: 28 Cunliffe Close, Oxford OX2 7BL, England.

HABERLER, Gottfried. Austrian, b. 1900. Economics. Prof. Emeritus of Economics, Harvard Univ., Cambridge, Mass., since 1971 (Prof. 1936–57, Galen L. Stone Prof. of Intnl. Trade, 1957–71); Resident Scholar, American Enterprise Inst., Washington, since 1971. Hon. Pres., Intnl. Economic Assn., since 1953 (Pres., 1950–51); Consultant to the Dept. of Treasury, Washington, since 1965. Lectr., later Prof. of Economics and Statistics, Univ. of Vienna, 1928–36; Visiting Lectr., Harvard Univ., Cambridge, 1931–32; Expert attached to Financial Section, League of Nations, Geneva, 1934–36; worked as Expert in Bd. of Govs, Federal Reserve System, Washington, 1943–44. Pres., National Bureau of Economics, New York, 1955; Pres., American Economic Assn., 1963. *Publs:* Der Sinn Der Indexzahlen, 1927; Der Internationale Handel: Theorie der Weltwirtschaftlichen Zusammenhänge Sowie Darstellung und Analyse über Aussenhandelspolitik, 1933; Prosperity and Depression, 1937, 4th ed. 1958; Consumer Instalment Credit and Economic Fluctuations, 1942; Problemas de Conjuntura e De Política Econômica, 1948; (with S. Verosta) Liberale und Planwirtschaftliche Handelspolitik, 1934; Inflation: Its Causes and Cures, rev. ed. as With A New Look at Inflation in 1966, 1966; (with T. Willett) U.S. Balance of Payments Policies and International Monetary Reform: A Critical Analysis, 1971; (with T. Willett) A Strategy for U.S. Balance of Payments Policy, 1971; Incomes Policy and Inflation: An Analysis of Basic Principles, 1972; (with M. Parkin and H. Smith) Inflation and the Unions, 1972; Economic Growth and Stability, 1974; The World Economy, Money, and the Great Depression: 1919–1939, 1976; The Problem of Stagflation, 1985; Selected Essays, 1985. Add: 4108 48th St. N.W., Washington, D.C. 20036, U.S.A.

HABERMAN, Richard. American, b. 1945. Mathematics. Prof. of Mathematics, Southern Methodist Univ., Dallas, since 1985 (Assoc. Prof., 1978–85). Asst. Prof. of Mathematics, Rutgers Univ., New Brunswick, N.J. 1972–77, and Ohio State Univ., Columbus, 1977–78. *Publs:* Mathematical Models: Mechanical Vibrations, Population Dynamics, and Traffic Flow: An Introduction to Applied Mathematics, 1977; Elementary Applied Partial Differential Equations (with Fourier Series and Boundary Value Problems), 1983, 1987. Add: Dept. of Mathematics, Southern Methodist Univ., Dallas, Tex. 75275, U.S.A.

HABGOOD, John Stapylton. British, b. 1927. Sciences, Theology/Religion. Anglican clergyman: Archbishop of York since 1983. Vice-Principal, Westcott House, Cambridge, 1956–62; Rector of St. John's Church, Jedburgh, 1962–67; Principal of The Queen's Coll., Birmingham, 1967–73; Bishop of Durham, 1973–83. *Publs:* (co-author) Soundings, 1962; Religion and Science, 1964, 1972; (co-author) The Bible Tells Me So, 1967; (co-author) Christianity and Change, 1971; (co-author) Queen's Sermons, 1973; The Proliferation of Nuclear Technology, 1977; A Working Faith, 1980; (co-author) Explorations in Ethics and International Relations, 1981; Church and Nation in a Secular Age, 1983; (co-author) In Search of Christianity, 1986; (co-author) Changing Britain, 1987; Confessions of a Conservative Liberal, 1988. Add: Bishopthorpe, York YO2 1QE, England.

HACKER, Andrew. American, b. 1929. Economics, Politics/Government. Prof. of Political Science, Queens Coll., City Univ. of New York, since 1971. Consultant, National Industrial Conference Bd., Brookings Instn., Rockefeller Bros. Fund, etc. Instr. in Government, 1955–56, Asst. Prof., 1956–60, Assoc. Prof., 1960–66, and Prof., 1966–71, Cornell Univ., Ithaca, N.Y. *Publs:* Political Theory: Philosophy, Ideology, Science,

1960; Congressional Districting, 1963; The Corporation Take-Over, 1964; The End of the American Era, 1970; (ed.) Democracy in America, by A. De Tocqueville, 1971; The Study of Politics, 1973; The New Yorkers, 1975; Free Enterprise in America, 1977; (with others) Nuclear Power in American Thought, 1980; (co-ed.) U.S: A Statistical Portrait of the American People, 1983. Add: Dept. of Political Science, Queens Coll., City Univ. of N.Y., Flushing, N.Y. 11367, U.S.A.

HACKER, Marilyn. American, b. 1942. Poetry. Has worked as a teacher, editor, and antiquarian bookseller. *Publs:* The Terrible Children, 1967; (with Thomas M. Disch and Charles Platt) Highway Sandwiches, 1970; Presentation Piece, 1974; Separations, 1976; Taking Notice, 1980; Assumptions, 1985; Love, Death, and the Changing of the Seasons, 1986. Add: c/o Frances Collin Agency, 110 W. 40 St., New York, N.Y. 10016, U.S.A.

HACKER, Rose. British, b. 1906. Human relations, Medicine/Health. Formerly social worker and marriage guidance counsellor. Councillor, Greater London Council, 1973–77. *Publs:* Telling the Teenagers, 1957, 1966; The Opposite Sex, 1960, 4th ed. 1967; You and Your Daughter, 1965; Health and Happiness, 1967. Add: 19 West Hill Ct., London N6 6JJ, England.

HACKETT, Cecil Arthur. British, b. 1908. Literature. Emeritus Prof. of French, Univ. of Southampton, since 1970 (Prof. 1952–70). *Publs:* Le lyrisme de Rimbaud, 1938; Rimbaud l'Enfant, 1948; (ed.) An Anthology of Modern French Poetry: From Baudelaire to the Present Day, 1952, 4th ed. 1976; Rimbaud, 1957; Autour de Rimbaud, 1967; (ed.) New French Poetry, 1973; Rimbaud: A Critical Introduction, 1981; (ed.) Rimbaud: Oeuvres Poétiques, 1986. Add: Shawford Close, Shawford, Winchester, Hants, England.

HACKETT, (Gen. Sir) John (Winthrop). British, b. 1910. History, Military/Defence. Visiting Prof. in Classics, King's Coll., Univ. of London (Principal, King's Coll., 1968–75). Career in the British Army: commissioned as a regular officer, 8th Hussars, 1931; served in Palestine, 1936; with the Transjordan Frontier Force, 1937–39, in Syria, 1941, and the Western Desert, 1942; Comdr., 4th Parachute Brigade, 1943–45; Gen. Officer Comdg., 7th Armoured Div., 1956–58; Commandant, Royal Military Coll. of Science, 1958–61; Gen. Officer Comdg.-in-Chief, Northern Ireland Command, 1961–63; Deputy Chief of the Gen. Staff, 1964–66; Comdr.-in-Chief, British Army of the Rhine, 1966–68. Pres., U.K. Classical Assn., 1971, and English Assn., 1973–74. *Publs:* The Profession of Arms, 1963, 1984; Some Thoughts on Change, 1968; (with others) The Armed Forces, 1969; Reflections on Epic Warfare, 1971; The Military in the Service of the State, 1971; Sweet Uses of Adversity, 1974; I Was a Stranger, 1977; (with others) The Third World War 1985 ("fictional cautionary tale"), 1978; The Third World War: The Untold Story, 1982; (ed.) Warfare in the Ancient World, 1989. Add: Coberley Mill, nr. Cheltenham, Glos. GL53 9NH, England.

HADINGHAM, Evan. British, b. 1951. Air/Space topics, Archaeology/Antiquities. Archeologist and freelance writer. *Publs:* The Fighting Triplanes, 1968; Ancient Carvings in Britain, 1974; Circles and Standing Stones: An Illustrated Exploration of Megalith Mysteries of Early Britain, 1975; Secrets of the Ice Age, 1980; Early Man and the Cosmos: Explorations in Astroarchaeology, 1984; Lines to the Mountain Gods: Nazca and the Mysteries of Peru, 1986. Add: 153 Walden St., Cambridge, Mass. 02140, U.S.A.

HADLEY, Leila (E.B.). American, b. 1929. Travel/Exploration/Adventure. Assoc. Ed., Diplomat Mag., 1965–67, and Saturday Evening Post, 1967–68. *Publs:* Give Me the World, 1958; How to Travel with Children in Europe, 1964, 1984; (co-author) Manners for Young People, 1964; Fielding's Guide to Traveling with Children in Europe, 1972, 1974; Traveling with Children in the U.S.A.: A Guide to Pleasure, Adventure, Discovery, 1977; Tibet: 20 Years after the Chinese Takeover, 1979; Fielding's Europe with Children, 1984. Add: c/o William Morrow, 105 Madison Ave., New York, N.Y. 10016, U.S.A.

HAEBERLE, Erwin J. German, b. 1936. Literature, Sex. Dir. of Historical Research, The Institute for Advanced Study of Human Sexuality, San Francisco, since 1977; Research Assoc., Alfred C. Kinsey Inst. for Sex Research, Indiana Univ., Bloomington, since 1981. Research Fellow in American Studies, Yale Univ., New Haven, Conn., 1966–68, 1970–71; Research Fellow in Japanese and Korean Studies, Univ. of California, Berkeley, 1968–69, 1971–72. *Publs:* Das szenische Werk Thornton Wilders, 1967; (with M. Goldstein) The Sex Book: A Modern Pictorial Encyclopedia, 1972; The Sex Atlas, 1978, 1983. Add: Inst. for Advanced

Study of Human Sexuality, 1523 Franklin St., San Francisco, Calif. 94109, U.S.A.

HAGA, Enoch John. American, b. 1931. Information science/Computers. Teacher, and Chmn., Business Education and Mathematics Depts., Amador Valley High Sch. District, Pleasanton, Calif., since 1964; Instr., Chabot Coll., Hayward, Calif., since 1970. Asst. Prof. of Business, Stanislaus State Coll., Turlock, Calif., 1960–61; Engineering Writer, Sr. Publs. Engineer, Sr. Admin. Analyst, and Procedures Analyst, Hughes Aircraft Co., Lockheed Missiles & Space Co., Gen. Precision Inc., and Holmes & Narver Inc., 1961–64. Vice-Pres., California Inst. of Asian Studies, 1972–75; Co-Ed., Automedica, 1972–76. *Publs:* (ed.) Total Systems, 1962; Understanding Automation: A Data Processing Curriculum Guide and Reference Text, 1965; (ed.) Automated Educational Systems, 1967; Simplified Computer Arithmetic; Simplifed Computer Logic; Simplified Computer Input; Simplified Computer Flowcharting; (ed.) Computer Techniques in Biomedicine and Medicine, 1973. Add: 983 Venus Way, Livermore, Calif. 94550, U.S.A.

HAGAR, Judith. *See* **POLLEY,** Judith Anne.

HAGEN, Uta. German, b. 1919. Cookery/Gastronomy/Wine, Theatre. Actress. Teacher of Acting, Herbert Berghof Studio, NYC, since 1947. *Publs:* (with Haskel Frankel) Respect for Acting, 1973; Love for Cooking, 1976; Sources: A Memoir, 1983. Add: Herbert Berghof Studio, 120 Bank St., New York, N.Y. 10014, U.S.A.

HAGGARD, Paul. *See* **LONGSTREET,** Stephen.

HAGGARD, William. Pseud. for Richard Henry Michael Clayton. British, b. 1907. Mystery/Crime/Suspense. Served in the Indian Civil Service, 1931–39, and Indian Army, 1939–45; worked for the Board of Trade, London, 1947–69: Controller of Enemy Property, 1965–69. *Publs:* Slow Burner, 1958; The Telemann Touch, 1958; Venetian Blind, 1959; Closed Circuit, 1960; The Arena, 1961; The Unquiet Sleep, 1962; The High Wire, 1963; The Antagonists, 1964; The Powder Barrel, 1965; The Hard Sell, 1965; The Power House, 1966; The Conspirators, 1967; A Cool Day for Killing, 1968; The Double Disciple, 1969; The Hardliners, 1970; The Bitter Harvest, 1971 (in U.S. as Too Many Enemies, 1972); The Protectors, 1973; The Old Masters (in U.S. as The Notch on the Knife), 1973; The Kinsmen, 1974; The Scorpion's Tail, 1975; Yesterday's Enemy, 1976; The Poison People, 1978; Visa to Limbo, 1978; The Median Line, 1979; The Money Men, 1981; The Mischief Makers, 1982; The Heirloom, 1983; The Need to Know, 1984; The Meritocrats, 1985; The Martello Tower, 1986; The Diplomatist, 1987; The Expatriates, 1989. Add: 3 Linkside, Holland Rd., Frinton-on-Sea, Essex CO13 9EN, England.

HAGON, Priscilla. *See* **ALLAN,** Mabel Esther.

HAGUE, (Sir) Douglas (Chalmers). British, b. 1926. Economics, Administration/Management. Chairman, Oxford Strategy Network, since 1984. Asst. Lectr., 1947–50, Lectr., 1950–57, and Reader in Political Economy, 1957, University Coll., London; Newton Chambers Prof. of Economics, 1957–63, Head of Dept. of Business Studies, 1962–63, Univ. of Sheffield; Prof. of Managerial Economics 1965–81, and Deputy Dir. 1978–81, Manchester Business Sch., Univ. of Manchester; Professorial Fellow, Oxford Centre for Management Studies, 1981–83 (Assoc. Fellow, since 1983). British Chmn., Carnegie Corp's Anglo-American Project on Accountability, 1969–72. *Publs:* (with A. Stonier) A Textbook of Economic Theory, 1953; The Essentials of Economics, 1955; The Economics of Man-Man Fibres, 1957; Managerial Economics, 1969; (with B. Smith) The Dilemma of Accountability in Modern Government, 1971; Pricing in Business, 1971; (with W.J.M. Mackenzie and A. Barker) Public Policy and Private Interests: The Institutions of Compromise, 1975; (with G. Wilkinson) The IRC: An Experiment in Industrial Rationalization, 1983. Add: Templeton Coll., Oxford OX1 5NY, England.

HAHN, Emily. American, b. 1905. Social sciences, Autobiography/Memoirs/Personal, Biography. Member of staff, New Yorker mag., NYC. Lectr., Yale Univ., New Haven, Conn., 1969–74, Univ. of Virginia, Charlottesville, 1974, and the Univ. of Missouri, St. Louis, 1975. *Publs:* The Soong Sisters, 1943; China to Me (autobiography), 1944; Raffles of Singapore, 1945; On the Side of the Apes (social sciences), 1971; Times and Places (autobiography), 1974; Lorenzo, 1975; Mabel, 1976; Love of Gold, 1980; The Islands, 1981. Add: 16 West 16th St., Apt. 12 N South, New York, N.Y. 10011, U.S.A.

HAHN, Frank H(orace). British, b. 1925. Economics. Fellow, Churchill Coll., Cambridge, since 1960, and Prof. of Economics, Cambridge Univ., since 1972. Reader, Univ. of Birmingham, 1948–60; Lectr., Cambridge Univ., 1960–67; Prof. of Economics, London School of Economics, 1967–72. Member, Council for Scientific Policy, later Advisory Bd., of Research Councils, 1972–75; Pres., Econometric Soc., 1968–69; Managing Ed., Review of Economic Studies, 1965–86; President, Royal Economic Society, since 1986. *Publs:* (with K.J. Arrow) General Competitive Analysis, 1971; The Share of Wages in the National Income, 1972; Money and Inflation, 1982; Equilibrium and Macro-economics, 1984; Money, Growth and Stability, 1985. Add: 16 Adams Rd., Cambridge CB3 9AD, England.

HAHN, Mary Downing. American, b. 1937. Children's fiction. Children's Librarian Asst., Prince George's County Memorial Library System, Laurel, Md., since 1975. *Publs:* The Sara Summer, 1979; The Time of the Witch, 1982; Daphne's Book, 1983; The Jellyfish Season, 1985; Wait Till Helen Comes: A Ghost Story, 1986; Tallahassee Higgins, 1987; Following the Mystery Man, 1988; December Stillness, 1988. Add: 9746 Basket Ring Rd., Columbia, Md. 21045, U.S.A.

HAIBLUM, Isidore. American, b. 1935. Mystery/Crime, Science fiction/Fantasy. Freelance writer of SF novels, essays and book reviews. Formerly interviewer, script writer, and folk-singers' agent. *Publs:* The Tsaddik of the Seven Wonders, 1971; The Return, 1973; Transfer to Yesterday, 1973; The Wilk Are Among Us, 1975; Interworld, 1977; Nightmare Express, 1979; Outerworld, 1979; (with Stuart Silver) Faster Than a Speeding Bullet: An Informal History of Radio's Golden Age, 1980; The Mutants Are Coming, 1984; The Identity Plunderers, 1984; The Hand of Ganz, 1985; Murder in Yiddish, 1988. Add: 160 W. 77th St., New York, N.Y. 10024, U.S.A.

HAILEY, Arthur. Canadian and British, b. 1920. Novels/Short stories, Plays/Screenplays. Freelance writer since 1956. Ed., MacLean Hunter, publrs., Toronto, 1947–53; Sales Promotion Mgr., Trailmobile Canada, Toronto, 1953–56. *Publs:* (with John Castle) Flight into Danger, 1958, in U.S. as Runway Zero Eight, 1959; The Final Diagnosis, 1959, in U.K. paperback as The Young Doctors, 1962; Close-up on Writing for Television: Collected Plays, 1960; In High Places, 1962; Hotel, 1965; Airport, 1968; Wheels, 1971; The Moneychangers, 1975; Overload, 1979; Strong Medicine, 1984; The Evening News, 1989. Add: Lyford Cay, P.O. Box N7776, Nassau, Bahamas.

HAILEY, Elizabeth Forsythe. American, b. 1938. Novels/short stories. *Publs:* A Woman of Independent Means, 1978 (also screenplay, 1983); Life Sentences, 1982; Joanna's Husband and David's Wife, 1986. Add: 11747 Canton Pl., Studio City, Calif. 91604, U.S.A.

HAILEY, Oliver. American, b. 1932. Plays/Screenplays. *Publs:* Hey You, Light Man!, 1963; First One Asleep, Whistle, 1966; Who's Happy Now?, 1967; Picture, Animal, Crisscross, 3 Plays, 1970; Continental Divide, 1970; Father's Day, 1970, rev. rd., 1981; For the Use of the Hall, 1974; Red Rover, Red Rover, 1978; I Won't Dance, 1981; About Time, 1983; Twenty-Four Hours—AM and PM, 1983. The Father (freely adapted from Strindberg), 1984; The Bar Off Melrose, 1987; Kith and Kin, 1988. Add: 11747 Canton Pl., Studio City, Calif. 91604, U.S.A.

HAILSHAM, Lord, of St. Marylebone. *See* **HOGG,** Quintin.

HAINES, Gail Kay. American, b. 1943. Children's non-fiction. *Publs:* The Elements, 1972; Fire, 1975; Explosives, 1976; Supercold/Superhot, 1976; What Makes a Lemon Sour?, 1977; Natural and Synthetic Poisons, 1978; Brain Power, 1979; Cancer, 1980; Baking in a Box, Cooking on a Can, 1981; Test Tube Mysteries, 1982; The Great Nuclear Power Debate, 1985; Which Way Is Up, 1987; Micro Mysteries, 1988. Add: 4145 Lorna Ct. SE, Olympia, Wash. 98503, U.S.A.

HAINES, John (Meade). American, b. 1924. Poetry, Literature, Translations. Homesteader in Alaska, 1947–69; Poet-in-Residence, Univ. of Alaska, Anchorage, 1972–73; Visiting Prof. of English, Univ. of Washington, Seattle, 1974; Visiting Lectr., Univ. of Montana, Missoula, 1974–75; Guggenheim Fellowship, 1984–85; Distinguished Visiting Lectr., Univ. of California, Santa Cruz, 1986; Writer-in-Residence, Montalvo Center for the Arts, 1987–88; Writer-in-Residence, Djerassi Foundn., 1988; Visiting Prof., Ohio Univ., 1989. *Publs:* Winter News: Poems, 1966; (trans.) El Amor Ascendia, by Miguel Hernandez, 1967; Suite for the Pied Piper, 1967; The Legend of Paper Plates, 1970; The Mirror, 1971; The Stone Harp, 1971; Twenty Poems, 1971; Leaves and Ashes: Poems, 1974; In Five Years Time, 1976; The Sun on Your Shoulder, 1976; Cicada, 1977; In a Dusty Light, 1977; Living Off the Country: Essays on Poetry and Place, 1981; Of Traps and Snares (essays), 1981; Other Days (essays), 1982; News from the Glacier: Selected Poems 1960–1980, 1982; Forest Without Leaves, 1984; Stories We Listened To, 1986; The Stars, The Snow, The Fire, 1989; Meditation On a Skull Carved In Crystal, 1989. Add: Mile 68, Richardson Hwy., Fairbanks, Alaska 99701, U.S.A.

HAINES, Pamela Mary. British, b. 1929. Historical/Romance/Gothic. *Publs:* Tea at Gunter's, 1974; A Kind of War, 1976; Men on White Horses, 1978; The Kissing Gate, 1981; The Diamond Waterfall, 1984; The Golden Lion, 1986; Daughter of the Northern Fields, 1987. Add: 57 Middle Lane, London N8, England.

HAINES, Walter Wells. American, b. 1918. Economics. Prof. of Economics, New York Univ., NYC, since 1960 (Asst. Prof., 1947–49; Assoc. Prof., 1949–60; Chmn., Dept. of Economics, 1956–68). Fulbright Prof., Univ. of Peshawar, Pakistan, 1962–63; Administrator, Friends Hosp., Kaimosi, Kenya, 1969–70; Fulbright Prof., Middle East Technical Univ., Ankara, Turkey, 1973–74. *Publs:* Money, Prices and Policy, 1961, 1966; The Economic Effect of Trade Liberalization in Benzenoid Chemicals, 1968. Add: RR2, Box 407A, Averhill Park, N.Y. 12018, U.S.A.

HAINING, Peter Alexander. British, b. 1940. Novels/Short stories, Supernatural topics. Editorial Dir., New English Library, publrs., London, 1970–73. *Publs:* (ed.) The Hell of Mirrors, 1966; (ed.) Where Nightmares Are, 1966; (ed.) Summoned from the Tomb, 1966; (ed.) Beyond the Curtain of Dark, 1966; (ed.) The Future Makers, 1968; (ed.) The Gentlewomen of Evil, 1967; (ed.) The Evil People, 1968; (ed.) The Midnight People, 1968; (ed.) The Unspeakable People, 1969; (ed.) The Witchcraft Reader, 1969; (ed.) A Circle of Witches, 1970; (ed.) The Hollywood Nightmare, 1970; (ed.) The Freak Show, 1970; (ed.) The Wild Night Company, 1970; (ed.) A Thousand Afternoons, 1970; (ed.) The Necromancers, 1970; (ed.) Witchcraft and Black Magic, 1970; The Clans of Darkness, 1971; (ed.) The Ghouls, 1971; The Warlock's Book, 1971; (ed.) Tales of Terror, 2 vols., 1972; (ed.) The Magicians, 1972; (ed.) Anatomy of Witchcraft, 1972; The Lucifer Society, 1972; (ed.) Nightfrights, 1972; (ed.) The Nightmare Reader, 1973; Eurotunnel: An Illustrated History of the Channel Tunnel Project, 1973; (ed.) The Dream Machines: An Illustrated History of Ballooning, 1973; (ed.) The Magic Valley Travellers, 1974; (ed.) The Monster Makers, 1974; (ed.) The Hashish Club, 1974; (ed.) The Sherlock Holmes Scrapbook, 1974; The Hero (novel), 1974; The Witchcraft Papers, 1974; Ghosts: An Illustrated History, 1974 (ed.) The Fantastic Pulps, 1975; (ed.) The Ghost's Companion, 1975; (ed.) An Illustrated History of Witchcraft, 1975; The Ancient Mysteries Reader, 1975; (ed.) Black Magic Omnibus, 1976; The Great English Earthquake, 1976; The Compleat Birdman, 1976; (ed.) Weird Tales, 1976; (ed.) First Book (and Second) of Unknown Tales of Horror, 1977–78; The Monster Trap, 1977; (ed.) Deadly Nightshade, 1977; Spring Heeled Jack, 1977; The Restless Bones, 1978; (ed.) The Shilling Shockers, 1978; Movable Books, 1979; Superstitions, 1979; (ed.) M.R. James Book of the Supernatural, 1979; The Leprechaun's Kingdom, 1979; The Man Who Was Frankenstein, 1980; Sweeney Todd, 1980; (ed.) The Edgar Allan Poe (and Gaston Leroux) Bedside Companion, 2 vols., 1980; Buried Passions, 1980; (ed.) The Final Adventures of Sherlock Holmes, 1981; (ed.) The Best Short Stories of Rider Haggard, 1981; (ed.) Dead of Night, 1981; Dictionary of Ghosts, 1982; (ed.) Greasepaint and Ghosts, 1982; (ed.) Lost Stories of W. S. Wilbert, 1982; (ed.) The Legend of Charlie Chaplin, 1982; (ed.) Shades of Dracula, 1982; (ed.) The Complete Ghost Stories of Charles Dickens, 1982; (ed.) Nightcaps and Nightmares, 1983; (ed.) Paths to the River Bank, 1983; The Traction Engine Companion, 1983; The Legend of Brigitte Bardot, 1983; (ed.) Christmas Spirits, 1983; Doctor Who: A Celebration, 1983; (ed.) Ghost Tour, 1984; The Last Gentleman, 1984; Raquel Welch, 1984; (ed.) Halloween Hauntings, 1984; Doctor Who: The Key to Time, 1984; (ed.) Tune In for Fear, 1985; Goldie Hawn, 1985; (ed.) Zombie!, 1984; (ed.) Vampire!, 1984; Eyewitness to the Galaxy, 1985; The Spitfire Log, 1985; (ed.) The Ghost Ship, 1985; For Mother, With Love, 1986; The Race for Mars, 1986; (ed.) Supernatural Sleuths, 1986; (ed.) Tales of Dungeons and Dragons, 1986; The Television Sherlock Holmes, 1986; The Doctor Who File, 1986; (ed.) Laughter Before Wicket, 1986; The Savage (novel), 1986; (ed.) Book of Learned Nonsense, 1987; (ed.) Supernatural Tales of Rudyard Kipling, 1987; James Bond: A Celebration, 1987; (ed.) Werewolf!, 1987; Elvis in Private, 1987; Doctor Who: The Time Traveller's Guide, 1987; The Dracula Centenary Book, 1987; (ed.) Supernatural Tales of Sir Arthur Conan Doyle, 1987; (ed.) Poltergeist!, 1987; (ed.) Movie Monsters, 1988; Doctor Who: 25 Glorious Years, 1988; (ed.) Hole in Fune, 1988; (ed.) The Mummy!, 1988; The Scarecrow, 1988; (ed.) The Supernatural Tales of Thomas Hardy, 1988. Add: Peyton House, Boxford, Suffolk, England.

HAIRE, Wilson John. British, b. 1932. Plays/Screenplays. *Publs:* Within Two Shadows, 1974; Bloom of the Diamond Stone, 1973; Lost Worlds, 1978. Add: 61 Lulot Gardens, London N19 5TS, England.

HALAM, Ann. Pseud. for Gwyneth A. Jones. British, b. 1952. Children's fiction, Novels. *Publs:* children's fiction—Ally Ally, Aster, 1981; The Alder Tree, 1982; King Death's Garden, 1986; The Daymaker, 1987; Transformations, 1988; as Gwyneth A. Jones—Water in the Air, 1977; The Influence of Ironwood, 1978; The Exchange, 1979; Dear Hill, 1980; The Hidden Ones, 1988; novels as Gwyneth A. Jones—Escape Plans, 1986; Divine Endurance, 1987; Kairos, 1988. Add: c/o Herta Ryder, Toby Eady Assocs., 7 Gledhow Gardens, London SW5 0BL, England.

HALBERSTAM, David. American, b. 1934. International relations/Current affairs, Politics/Government, Biography. Member of staff, Daily Times Leader, West Point, Miss., 1955–56, and Nashville Tennessean, 1956–60; Foreign Corresp. in Congo, Vietnam and Eastern Europe, New York Times, NYC, 1960–67; Contrib. Ed., Harper's Mag., NYC, 1967–71. *Publs:* The Noblest Roman, 1961; The Making of a Quagmire, 1965, 2nd ed. as The Making of a Quagmire: America and Vietnam During the Kennedy Era, 1987; One Very Hot Day, 1968; The Unfinished Odyssey of Robert Kennedy, 1969; Ho, 1971; The Best and Brightest, 1972; The Powers That Be, 1979; The Breaks of the Game, 1981; The Amateurs, 1985; The Reckoning, 1986. Add: c/o William Morrow, 105 Madison Ave., New York, N.Y. 10016, U.S.A.

HALDEMAN, Jack C(arroll, II). American, b. 1941. Science fiction/Fantasy, Poetry. Freelance writer, mostly of sports, SF short stories. Research Asst., Johns Hopkins Univ. School of Hygiene and Public Health, 1963–68; Medical Technician, Univ. of Maryland Hospital, 1968–73; has also worked as a statistician, photographer, and printer's devil. Former Pres., Washington Science Fiction Assn. *Publs:* Between Pearl Harbor and Christmas (poetry); Vector Analysis, 1978; Perry's Planet, 1980; (with Joe Haldeman) There Is No Darkness, 1983. Add: c/o Kirby McCauley Ltd., 432 Park Ave. South, New York, N.Y. 10016, U.S.A.

HALDEMAN, Joe (William). Has also written as Robert Graham. American, b. 1943. Science fiction/Fantasy. Freelance writer, since 1970. Adjunct Prof., Mass. Inst. of Technology, since 1983. Teaching Asst., Univ. of Iowa, Iowa City, 1975; Ed., Astronomy mag., Milwaukee, 1976. Former Treas., Science Fiction Writers of America. *Publs:* War Year, 1972, 1977; (ed) Cosmic Laughter, 1974; The Forever War, 1975; (as Robert Graham) Attar 1: Attar's Revenge, 1975; (as Robert Graham) Attar 2: War of Nerves, 1975; Mindbridge, 1976; Planet of Judgment, 1977; (ed.) Study War No Nore, 1977; All My Sins Remembered, 1977; Infinite Dreams (short stories), 1978; World Without End, 1979; Worlds, 1981; (with Jack C. Haldeman) There Is No Darkness, 1983; Worlds Apart, 1983; The Forever War (stage play), 1984; (ed.) Nebula Awards 17, 1984; Dealing in Futures (short stories), 1985; Tool of the Trade, 1987; Buying Time, 1989; The Hemingway Hoax, 1990. Add: 5412 NW 14th Ave., Gainesville, Fla. 32605, U.S.A.

HALE, Allean Lemmon. American, b. 1914. Plays, Women. Ed., Alumni Magazine, Columbia Coll., Mo., 1951–56; Instr. in Writing, Univ. of Iowa, 1960–62; Instr. in Creative Writing, Parkland Coll., Champaign, Ill., 1979–80; Editorial Bd., The Tennessee Williams Literary Journal, 1989. *Publs:* The Hero (play), 1934; Last Flight Over (play), 1935, 1949; Petticoat Pioneer, 1956, rev. ed., 1968; Remind Me To Live (play), 1960; Two In A Trap (play), 1966; A Whole New Life (play), 1969; (ed.) A Death in the Sanchez Family, by Oscar Lewis, 1969; The Second Coming of Mrs. C. (play), 1971; The Battle at Liberty Courthouse (play), 1975. Add: 22 G.H. Baker Dr., Urbana, Ill. 61801, U.S.A.

HALE, John. British, b. 1926. Novels/Short stories, Plays. Freelance writer and dir. since 1964. Founder and Artistic Dir., Lincoln Theatre, 1955–58; Artistic Dir., Arts Theatre, Ipswich, 1958–59, and Bristol Old Vic, 1959–61; Member, Bd. of Govs., and Assoc. Artistic Dir., Greenwich Theatre, London, 1963–71. *Publs:* Kissed the Girls and Made Them Cry, 1963; The Grudge Fight, 1964; A Fool at the Feast, 1966; The Paradise Man, 1969; The Fort, 1973; The Love School, 1974; Lovers and Heretics, 1976; The Whistle Blower, 1984. Add: c/o Stephen Durbridge, Harvey Unna and Stephen Durbridge Ltd., 24 Pottery Lane, London W11 4LZ, England.

HALE, Michael. *See* **BULLOCK,** Michael.

HALEY, Alex (Palmer). American, b. 1921. History, Autobiography/Memoirs/Personal. Founder and Pres., Kinte Corp., Beverly Hills,

Calif., since 1972. Enlisted United States Coast Guard, 1939, and advanced to Chief Journalist, 1949; retired, 1959. *Publs:* The Autobiography of Malcolm X, 1965; Roots, 1976; Roots: The Saga of an American Family, 1979; A Different Kind of Christmas, 1988. Add: Kinte Corp., P.O. Box 3338, Beverly Hills, Calif. 90212, U.S.A.

HALEY, Gail E(inhart). American, b. 1939. Children's fiction. Vice Pres., Manuscript Press, NYC, since 1965; currently, Writer-in-Residence and Curator of the Gail Haley Collection of the Culture of Childhood, Appalachian State Univ., Boone. N.C. *Publs:* My Kingdom for a Dragon, 1962; The Wonderful Magical World of Marguerite, 1964; Round Stories about Things That Live on Land and in Water, 1966; Round Stories about Things that Grow, 1966; Round Stories about Our World, 1966; A Story, A Story: An African Tale, Retold, 1970; Noah's Ark, 1971; Jack Jouett's Ride, 1973; The Abominable Swamp Man, 1975; The Post Office Cat, 1976; Go Away, Stay Away, 1977; Costumes for Plays and Playing, 1977; The Green Man, 1980; Birdsong, 1984; Margeurite, 1988; (retold by and illus.) Jack and the Fire Dragon, 1988. Add: c/o A.P. Watt, 26-28 Bedford Row, London WC1R 4HL, England.

HALEY, Kenneth (Harold Dobson). British, b. 1920. History, Biography. Prof. of Modern History, Sheffield Univ., 1962–82 (Asst. Lectr. 1947–50; Lectr. 1950–60; Sr. Lectr 1960–62). *Publs:* William III and the English Opposition, 1672-1674, 1953; Charles II, 1966; The First Earl of Shaftesbury, 1968; The Dutch in the Seventeenth Century, 1972; (ed.) The Historical Association Book of the Stuarts, 1973; Politics in the Reign of Charles II, 1985; An English Diplomat in the Low Countries: Sir William Temple and John de Witt, 1665-1672, 1986; The British and the Dutch, 1988. Add: 15 Haugh Lane, Sheffield S11 9SA, England.

HALL, Adam, *See* **TREVOR,** Elleston.

HALL, Angus. British, b. 1932. Novels/Short stories, Mythology/Folklore. Ed., I.P.C., publrs., since 1971, and B.P.C., publrs., since 1972, both London. Film and Theatre Critic, London Daily Sketch, 1958–61. *Publs:* Love in Smoky Regions, 1962; High-Bouncing Lover, 1966; Live Like a Hero, 1967; Come-uppance of Arthur Hearne, 1967; Qualtrough, 1968; Late Boy Wonder, 1969; Devilday, 1970; To Play the Devil, 1971; Scars of Dracula, 1971; Long Way to Fall, 1971; On the Run, 1974; Signs of Things to Come: A History of Divination, 1975; Monsters and Mythic Beasts, 1976; Strange Cults, 1977; The Rigoletto Murder, 1978; Crime Busters, 1984; Self-Destruct, 1985. Add: c/o Treasure Press, Michelin House, 81 Fulham Rd., London SW3 6RB, England.

HALL, Anthony Stewart (also writes as Tony Hall). British, b. 1945. Social sciences, Sociology. Dir., Central Council for Education and Training in Social Work, London. Lectr. in Social Admin., Univ. of Bristol, 1973–78. Lectr. in Mgmt. and Org. Studies, National Inst. for Social Work. Dir., British Agencies for Adoption and Fostering, London, since 1978; Series Ed., Child Care Policy and Practice, 1980–86. *Publs:* A Management Game for the Social Services, 1974; The Point of Entry, 1975; (as Tony Hall) Part-Time Social Work, 1980. Add: 115 Babington Rd., London SW16, London.

HALL, Aylmer. Pseud. for Norah E.L. Hall. British, b. 1914. Children's fiction, History. Personal Asst. to the Secty., New Commonwealth Inst., London, 1936; Asst. Press Librarian, Royal Inst. of Intnl. Affairs, London, 1937–39; Chief Press Librarian in Reference Div., Ministry of Information, London, 1939–40. *Publs:* (ed. as Norah Hall) The Chronology of the Second World War, 1947; The Mystery of Torland Manor, 1952; The Admiral's Secret, 1953; The K.F. Conspiracy, 1955; The Sword of Glendower (in U.S. as The Search for Lancelot's Sword), 1960; The Devilish Plot, 1965; The Tyrant King: A London Adventure, 1967; The Marked Man, 1967; Colonel Bull's Inheritance, 1968; Beware of Moonlight, 1969; The Minstrel Boy, 1970. Add: 28 Burghley Rd., London SW19, England.

HALL, Claudia. *See* **FLOREN,** Lee.

HALL, Donald (Andrew, Jr.). American, b. 1928. Children's fiction, Poetry, Art, Literature. Poetry Ed., Paris Review, Paris and NYC, 1953–62; Jr. Fellow, Soc. of Fellows, Harvard Univ., Cambridge, Mass., 1954–57; Asst. Prof., 1957–61, Assoc. Prof., 1961–66, and Prof. of English, 1966–76, Univ. of Michigan, Ann Arbor. Member of Editorial bd. for Poetry, Wesleyan Univ. Press, Middletown, Conn., 1958–64. *Publs:* (ed.) The Harvard Advocate Anthology, 1950; (Poems), 1952; Exile, 1952; To the Loud Wind and Other Poems, 1955; Exiles and Marriages, 1955; The Dark Houses, 1958; (ed. with R. Pack and L. Simpson) New Poets of

England and America, 1957; Andrew the Lion Farmer, 1959; String Too Short to Be Saved: Childhood Reminiscences, 1961; (ed.) Whittier, 1961; (ed. with R. Pack) New Poets of England and America: Second Selection, 1962; (ed.) Contemporary American Poetry, 1962, 1971; (ed. with Stephen Spender) The Concise Encyclopedia of English and American Poets and Poetry, 1963, 1970; (ed. with W. Taylor) Poetry in English, 1963, 1970; A Roof of Tiger Lilies: Poems, 1964; An Evening's Frost (play), 1965; (ed.) The Faber Book of Modern Verse, rev. ed. 1965; Henry Moore: The Life and Work of Great Sculptor, 1966; The Alligator Bride, 1968; (ed.) A Choice of Whitman's Verse, 1968; (ed.) The Modern Stylists: Writers on the Art of Writing, 1968; (ed.) Man and Boy: An Anthology, 1968; The Alligator Bride: Poems New and Selected, 1969; (ed.) American Poetry, An Introductory Anthology, 1969; Marianne Moore: The Cage and the Animal, 1970; As the Eye Moves: A Sculpture by Henry Moore, 1970; The Yellow Room Love Poems, 1971; (ed.) The Pleasures of Poetry, 1971; The Gentleman's Alphabet Book, 1972; Writing Well, 1973; Playing Around, 1974; A Blue Wing Tilts at the Edge of the Sea, 1975; Dock Ellis in the Country of Baseball, 1976; Remembering Poets, 1978; Goatfoot Milktongue Twinbird: Interviews, Essays, and Notes on Poetry 1970–76, 1978; Kicking the Leaves, 1978; Ox Cart Man, 1979; To Keep Moving, 1980; (ed.) To Read Literature, 1981; (ed.) The Oxford Book of American Literary Anecdotes, 1981; (ed.) To Read Poetry, 1982; (ed.) Writing Well, 5th ed. 1985; (ed.) A Writer's Reader, 4th ed., 1985; The Weather for Poetry, 1982; The Contemporary Essay, 1984; The Man Who Lived Alone, 1984; Fathers Playing Catch with Sons, 1985; The Oxford Book of Children's Verse in America, 1985; The Happy Man, 1986; To Read Fiction, 1987; The Ideal Bakery, 1987; The Bone Ring, 1987; Seasons at Eagle Pond, 1987; Poetry and Ambition, 1988; The One Day, 1988. Add: Eagle Pond Farm, Danbury, N.H. 03230, U.S.A.

HALL, Evan. *See* **HALLERAN,** E.E.

HALL, Gimone. American, b. 1940. Novels/Short stories. *Publs:* The Blue Taper, 1970; Witch's Suckling, 1970, 3rd ed. 1973; Devil's Walk, 1971; The Silver Strand, 1974; The Juliet Room, 1975; Hide My Savage Heart, 1976; Rapture's Mistress, 1978; Fury's Son, Passion's Moon, 1979; Ecstasy's Empire, 1980; The Jasmine Veil, 1982; Rules of the Heart, 1984; The Kiss Flower, 1985. Add: Million Wishes Farm, Box 212, Route 1, Mountain View Dr., Ottsville, Pa. 18942, U.S.A.

HALL, James. British, b. 1918. Art, History. *Publs:* Dictionary of Subjects and Symbols in Art, 1974; (ed.) Ehresmann's Pocket Dictionary of Art Terms, 1980; A History of Ideas and Images in Italian Art, 1983. Add: 19 Milton Rd., Harpenden, Herts. AL5 5LA, England.

HALL, James B(yron). American, b. 1918. Novels/Short stories, Poetry. Writer-in-Residence, Miami Univ., 1948–49; Instr., Cornell Univ., Ithaca, N.Y. 1952–53; Writer-in-Residence, Univ. of North Carolina, Greensville, 1954; Asst. Prof., 1954–57, Assoc. Prof., 1958–60, and Prof. of English, 1960–65, Univ. of Oregon, Eugene; Co-Founding Ed., Northwest Review, Eugene, Ore., 1957–60; Founder and Dir., Univ. of Oregon Summer Academy of Contemporary Arts, Eugene, 1959–64; Dir., The Writing Center, and Prof. of English, Univ. of California, Irvine, 1965–68; Prof. of Literature and Writer-in-Residence, Univ. of California at Santa Cruz, 1968–84, Emeritus since 1985; Provost, Porter Coll., 1970–77; Writer-in-Residence, Kansas State Univ., since 1978. West Coast Grievance Officer, National Writer's Union, since 1986. *Publs:* Not by the Door, 1954; TNT for Two, 1956; (ed. with J. Langland) The Short Story, 1956; (with Herbert Gold and R.V. Cassill) 15 x 3 (short stories), 1957; Racers to the Sun, 1960; Us He Devours (short stories), 1964; (ed.) Realm of Fiction: 61 Short Stories, 1965, as Realm of Fiction: 65 Short Stories, 1970, 3rd ed. as 71 Short Stories, 1976; (ed. with B. Ulanov) Modern Culture and the Arts, 1967, 1975; Mayo Sergeant, 1967; The Hunt Within: Poems, 1973; The Short Hall: Stories, 1981. Add: 1670 E. 27th Ave., Eugene, Ore. 97403, U.S.A.

HALL, Jerome. American, b. 1901. Law. Prof., Hastings Coll. of the Law, San Francisco, since 1970. Prof. of Law, 1939–57, and Distinguished Service Prof. of Law, Indiana Univ., 1957–70. Visiting Prof., King's Coll., London, 1954–55, and Univ. of Freiburg, W. Germany, 1961. *Publs:* Theft, Law and Society, 1935, 1952; (ed.) Readings in Jurisprudence, 1938; General Principles of Criminal Law, 1947, 1960; Living Law of Democratic Society, 1949; Studies in Jurisprudence and Criminal Theory, 1958; Comparative Law and Social Theory, 1963; Foundations of Jurisprudence, 1973; Law, Social Science and Criminal Theory, 1982; (with others) Cases and Readings on Criminal Law and Procedure, 4th ed., 1983; (ed.) 20th Century Legal Philosophy Series, 8 vols. Add: 1390 Market St., San Francisco, Calif. 94102, U.S.A.

HALL, J(ohn) C(live). British, b. 1920. Poetry, Literature, Biography. Member of staff, Encounter mag., London, since 1955. Former book publr. *Publs:* (with K. Douglas and N. Nicholson) Selected Poems, 1943; The Summer Dance and Other Poems, 1951; (ed. with P. Dickinson and E. Marx) New Poems 1955, 1955; Edwin Muir, 1956; (ed. with W. Muir) Collected Poems of Edwin Muir, 1921–1958, 1960; The Burning Hare, 1966; (ed. with G.S. Fraser and J. Waller) The Collected Poems of Keith Douglas, rev. ed. 1966; A House of Voices, 1973; Selected and New Poems 1939–1984, 1985. Add: 9 Warwick Rd., Mount Sion, Tunbridge Wells, Kent TN1 1YL, England.

HALL, John Ryder. *See* **ROTSLER,** William.

HALL, Kathleen (Mary). British, b. 1924. Literature. Asst. Lectr., Queen's Univ., Belfast, 1953–55; Lectr., 1955–69, Sr. Lectr. in French 1969–85, Univ. of Southampton. *Publs:* Pontus de Tyard and His Discours Philosophiques, 1963; (ed. with K. Cameron and F. Higman) Théodore de Bèze: Abraham sacrifiant, 1967; (ed. with C.N. Smith) Jean de la Taille: Dramatic Works, 1972; (ed.) Estienne Jodelle: Cleopatre Captive, 1980; (with M.B. Wells) Du Bellay: Poems, 1985; Rabelais: Pantagruel and Gargantua, 1989. Add: 37 Granville Ct., Oxford OX3 OHS, England.

HALL, Lynn. American, b. 1937. Children's fiction. Copywriter, Ambro Ad Agency, Des Moines, Iowa, 1963–67. *Publs:* The Shy Ones, 1967; The Secret of Stonehouse, 1968; Ride a Wild Dream, 1969; Too Near the Sun, 1970; Gently Touch the Milkweed, 1970; A Horse Called Dragon, 1971; Sticks and Stones, 1972; The Famous Battle of Bravery Creek, 1972; Dog Stories, 1972; The Siege of Silent Henry, 1972; Flash— Dog of Old Egypt, 1973; Barry—The Bravest St. Bernard, 1973; Riff Remember, 1973; To Catch a Tartar, 1973; Troublemaker, 1974; Bob— Watchdog of the River, 1974; Stray, 1974; Kids and Dog Shows, 1975; New Day for Dragon, 1975; Captain, Canada's Flying Pony, 1976; Flowers of Anger, 1976; Owney, The Traveling Dog, 1977; Dragon Defiant, 1977; Shadows, 1977; Careers for Dog Lovers, 1978; The Mystery of Pony Hollow (the Lost and Found Hound, the Schoolhouse Dog, the Stubborn Old Man, the Plum Park Pony, the Caramel Cat), 1978–80; Dog of the Bondi Castle, 1979; The Leaving, 1980; Dragon's Delight, 1980; The Horse Trader, 1980; The Haunting of the Green Bird, 1980; The Disappearing Grandad, 1980; The Mysterious Moortown Bridge, 1980; The Ghost of the Great River Inn, 1980; Danza!, 1981; Half the Battle, 1982; Tin Can Tucker, 1982; Denison's Daughter, 1983; Uphill All the Way, 1983; Megan's Mare, 1983; The Boy in the Off-White Hat, 1984; The Something-Special Horse, 1985; The Giver, 1985; Tazo and Me, 1985; Just One Friend, 1985; If Winter Comes, 1986; The Solitary, 1986; Letting Go, 1987; Flyaway, 1987; Ride a Dark Horse, 1987; In Trouble AGAIN, Zelda Hammersmith, 1987; Zelda Strikes Again, 1988; The Secret Life of Dagmar Schultz, 1988; Murder at the Spaniel Show, 1988; Where Have All the Tigers Gone, 1989; Dagmar Schultz and the Powers of Darkness, 1989; Here Comes Zelda Claus, 1989; Murder in a Pig's Eye, 1989. Add: Touchwood, Rt. 2, Elkader, Iowa 52043, U.S.A.

HALL, Marie Boas. British (b. American), b. 1919. History. Asst. Prof. of History, Brandeis Univ., Waltham, Mass., 1952–57; Assoc. Prof. of History of Science, Univ. of California, Los Angeles, 1957–61; Prof. of History and Logic of Science, Indiana Univ., Bloomington, 1961–63; Reader in History of Science and Technology, Imperial Coll., Univ. of London, 1963–80. *Publs:* Robert Boyle and 17th Century Chemistry, 1958; The Scientific Renaissance, 1540-1630, 1962; (ed. with A.R. Hall) Unpublished Scientific Papers of Isaac Newton, 1962; (ed.) Robert Boyle's Experiments and Considerations Touching Colours, 1964; (with A.R. Hall) A Brief History of Science, 1964; Robert Boyle on Natural Philosophy, 1965; (ed. with A.R. Hall). The Correspondence of Henry Oldenburg, 13 vols., 1965–86; (ed.) Henry Power's Experimental Philosophy, 1966; Nature and Nature's Laws: Documents of the Scientific Revolution, 1970; (ed.) The Pneumatics of Hero of Alexandria, 1971; All Scientists Now: The Royal Society in the 19th Century, 1984. Add: 14 Ball Lane, Tackley, Oxford OX5 3AG, England.

HALL, Marjory. Also writes as Carol Morse. American, b. 1908. Historical/Romance/Gothic, Children's fiction. With Curtis Publishing Co., Philadelphia, Pa., 1931–42, and Humphrey, Alley & Richards, advertising agency, Boston, Mass., 1942–56; Travel Ed., Yankee Mag., 1945–72. *Publs:* Success in Reserve, 1941; Bread and Butter, 1942; After a Fashion, 1944; Model Child, 1945; Copy Kate, 1947; Your Young Life, 1949; Linda Clayton, 1951; Saralee's Silver Spoon, 1952; A Year From Now, 1952; Greetings from Glenna, 1953; Star Island, 1953; Orchids for Anita, 1954; Paper Moon, 1954; Picnic for Judy, 1955; Star Island Again, 1955; Morning Glory, 1956; Mirror, Mirror, 1956; Cathy and Her Castle, 1957; Straw Hat Summer, 1957; Three Stars for Star Island, 1958; (as Carol Morse) Glass House, 1958; (as Carol Morse) Carnival Cruise, 1958; (as Carol Morse) Roundabout Robin, 1959; Romance at Courtesy Bend, 1959; White Collar Girl, 1959; Magic Word, 1959; Hatbox for Mimi, 1960; Tomorrow is Another Day, 1960; Bright Red Ribbon, 1961; Whirl of Fashion, 1961; (as Carol Morse) Green Light for Sandy, 1961; Rita Rings a Bell, 1962; To Paris and Love, 1962; Fanfare for Two, 1963; See the Red Sky, 1963; One Perfect Rose, 1964; A Hatful of Gold, 1964; (as Carol Morse) Judy North: Drum Majorette, 1964; (as Carol Morse) Double Trouble, 1964; A Valentine for Vinnie, 1965; Drumbeat on the Shore, 1965; Clotheshorse, 1966; Treasure Tree, 1966; (as Carol Morse) Three Cheers for Polly, 1966; Look at Me! 1967; Mystery at Lions Gate, 1967; Another Kind of Courage, 1967; The Gold-Lined Box, 1968; The Whistle Stop Mystery, 1969; The Seventh Star, 1969; Quite Contrary, 1970; Beneath Another Sun, 1970; The Carved Wooden Ring, 1972; The Other Girl, 1974; Rosamunda, 1974; The April Ghost, 1975; Mystery at October House, 1977. Add: 572 Commonwealth Lane, Sarasota, Fla. 34242, U.S.A.

HALL, Oakley (Maxwell). Also writes as Jason Manor and O.M. Hall. American, b. 1920. Mystery/Crime/Suspense, Westerns/Adventure, Plays/Screenplays/Songs/Librettos. Prof. of English since 1977, and Dir. of Programs in Writing, 1970–77, and since 1982, Univ. of California at Irvine Founding Dir., Squaw Valley Community of Writers, 1970. Publs: (as O.M. Hall) Murder City, 1949; So Many Doors, 1950; Corpus of Joe Bailey, 1953; (as Jason Manor) Too Dead to Run, 1953; (as Jason Manor) The Red Jaguar, 1954, in paperback as The Girl in the Red Jaguar, 1955; Mardios Beach, 1955; (as Jason Manor) The Pawns of Fear, 1955, in paperback as No Halo for Me, 1956; (as Jason Manor) The Tramplers, 1956; Warlock (western), 1958; The Downhill Racers, 1963; The Pleasure Garden, 1966; A Game for Eagles, 1970; Report from Beau Harbor, 1971; The Adelita (western), 1975; Angle of Repose (musical play; adaptation of novel by W. Stegner), 1976; The Bad Lands (western), 1978; Lullaby, 1982; The Children of the Sun, 1983; The Coming of the Kid (western), 1985; Apaches (western), 1986. Add: P.O. Box 2101, Olympic Valley, Calif. 95730, U.S.A.

HALL, Peter (Geoffrey). British, b. 1932. Geography, Regional/Urban planning. Prof. of City and Reg. Planning, Univ. of Cal., Berkeley, since 1980. Reader in Geography, London Sch. of Economics, 1965–67. Prof. of Geography, Univ. of Reading, 1968–89. Publs: The Industries of London, 1962; London 2000, 1963, rev. ed. 1969; (ed.) Labour's New Frontiers, 1964; (ed.) Land Values, 1965; The World Cities, 1966, 3rd ed. 1984; (ed.) Von Thunen's Isolated State, 1966; (co-author) An Advanced Geography of North-West Europe, 1967; Theory and Practice of Regional Planning, 1970; (co-author) Containment of Urban England: Urban and Metropolitan Growth Processes or Megalopolis Denied, 1973; (co-author) Containment of Urban England: The Planning System: Objectives, Operations, Impacts, 1973; (with M. Clawson) Planning and Urban Growth: An Anglo-American Comparison, 1973; Urban and Regional Planning: An Introduction, 1974, 1982; Europe 2000, 1977; Great Planning Disasters, 1980; Growth Centres in the European Urban System, 1980; (ed. with D. Banister) Transport and Public Policy Planning, 1980; (ed.) The Inner City in Context, 1981; (ed.) Silicon Landscapes, 1985; (co-author) Can Rail Save the City, 1985; (co-author) High-Tech America, 1986; (co-author) London 2001, 1986; (co-author) Western Sunrise, 1987; (co-author) Cities of Tomorrow, 1988. Add: Inst. of Urban and Regional Development, Univ. of California, Berkeley, Calif. 94720, U.S.A.

HALL, Richard. British, b. 1925. Politics/Government, Biography. Ed., Africa Analysis, since 1986. Ed., Africa Mail, Lusaka, and Times of Zambia, 1960–68; Corresp., Gemini News Service, 1968–70; Ed., Observer Colour Mag., 1970–73; Columnist, Financial Times, London, 1976–79; Commonwealth Corresp., The Observer, London, 1982–1986. Publs: Kaunda, Founder of Zambia, 1964; Zambia, 1965; The High Price of Principles, 1969; Discovery Africa, 1970; (ed.) South-West Africa, Namibia: Proposals for Action, 1972; Stanley: An Adventurer Explored, 1974; (with Hugh Peyman) The Great Uhuru Railway, 1976; Lovers on the Nile, 1980; My Life with Tiny, 1987. Add: 21 Earls Terr., London W8, England.

HALL, Rodney. Australian, b. 1935. Novels/Short stories, Poetry, Literature, Race relations, Biography. Freelance Scriptwriter and Actor, 1957–67, and Film Critic, 1966–67, A.B.C., Brisbane; Advisory Ed., Overland mag., Melbourne, 1962–75; Poetry Ed., The Australian, Sydney, 1967–78. Tutor, New England Univ. Sch. of Music, Armidale, N.S.W., 1967–71; Youth Officer, Australian Council for the Arts, 1971–73. Publs: Penniless till Doomsday, 1962; Forty Beads on a Hangman's Rope:

Fragments of Memory, 1963; (with S. Andrews) Social Services and the Aborigines, 1963; Eyewitness: Poems, 1967; The Autobiography of a Gorgon, 1968; Focus on Andrew Sibley, 1968; (ed. with T. Shapcott) New Impulses in Australian Poetry, 1968; The Law of Karma: A Progression of Poems, 1968; Heaven, In a Way, 1970; (ed.) Australian Poetry 1970, 1970; The Ship on the Coin (novel), 1971; (ed.) Poems from Prison, 1973; The Soapbox Omnibus, 1973; Selected Poems, 1975; A Place among People (novel), 1976; Black Bagatelles, 1978; J.S. Manifold (biography), 1978; The Most Beautiful World (verse), 1981; (ed.) The Collins Book of Australian Poetry, 1981; Just Relations (novel), 1982; (with David Moore) Australia: Image of a Nation, 1983; Captivity Captive (novel), 1988; Kisses of the Enemy (novel), 1988; Journey Through Australia, 1988. Add: c/o Faber and Faber Ltd., 3 Queens Sq., London WC1N 3AU, England.

HALL, Roger (Leighton). New Zealander, b. 1939. Plays/Screenplays. Freelance writer and editor. Formerly worked in insurance, as a wine waiter, in factories, and as a teacher; Teaching Fellow, Univ. of Otago, Dunedin, 1979–89. Publs: Glide Time, 1978; Middle-Age Spread, 1978; State of the Play, 1979; Prisoners of Mother England, 1981; Fifty-Fifty, 1981; Hot Water, 1982; Footrot Flats (musical), 1983; Multiple Choice, 1984; Dream of Sussex Downs, 1986; Love off the Shelf (musical), 1986; The Share Club, 1987; After the Crash, 1988. Add: c/o Douglas Rae Mgmt., 28 Charing Cross Rd., London WC2H 0DB, England.

HALL, Thor. American, b. 1927. Theology/Religion. LeRoy A. Martin Distinguished Prof. of Religious Studies, Univ. of Tennessee at Chattanooga, since 1972. Asst. Prof. of Preaching and Theology, 1962–68, and Assoc. Prof., 1968–72, Duke Univ., Durham, N.C. Publs: (ed.) The Unfinished Pyramid, Ten Sermons by Charles P. Bowles, D.D., 1967; A Theology of Christian Devotion, 1969, 1972; A Framework for Faith, 1970; The Future Shape of Preaching, 1971, 1973; Whatever Happened to the Gospel?, 1973; Advent–Christmas, 1975; Directory of Systematic Theologians in North America, 1977; Anders Nygren, 1978, 1985; Systematic Theology Today, 1978; The Evolution of Christology, 1982. Add: 1102 Montvale Circle, Signal Mountain, Tenn. 37377, U.S.A.

HALL, Trevor Henry. British, b. 1910. History, Literature. Sr. Partner, V. Stanley Walker and Son, chartered surveyors, Leeds, 1945–82, now retired. Dir., Huddersfield Bldg. Soc., 1958–82; Dir., Legal and Gen. Assurance Soc., North Regional and Scottish Bd., 1962–82. Justice of the Peace, Leeds; Pres., Leeds Library, since 1969. Cecil Oldman Memorial Lectr. in Bibliography and Textual Criticism, Univ. of Leeds, 1972–73. Regional Chmn., National Trust, Leeds District, 1966–68. Publs: A Bibliography of Books on Conjuring in English from 1580 to 1850, 1957; The Spiritualists: The Story of Florence Cook and William Crookes, 1962; The Strange Case of Edmund Gurney, 1964, 1980; (with J.L. Campbell) Strange Things, 1968; Sherlock Holmes: Ten Literary Studies, 1969; Mathematical Recreations, 1633: An Exercise in 17th Century Bibliography, 1969; The Late Mr. Sherlock Holmes, 1971; Old Conjuring Books, 1973; The Early Years of the Huddersfield Building Society, 1974; The Winder Sale of Old Conjuring Books, 1975; (with Percy H. Muir) Some Printers and Publishers of Conjuring Books and Other Ephemera 1800-1850, 1976; Search for Harry Price, 1978; Sherlock Holmes and His Creator, 1978; Dorothy L. Sayers: Nine Literary Studies, 1980; The Strange Story of Ada Goodrich Freer, 1980; Twelve Friends, 1981; The Leeds Library: A Checklist of Publications Relating to its History from 1768 to 1777, 1983; Daniel Home: A Victorian Enigma, 1984; The Medium and the Scientist, 1984; The Last Case of Sherlock Holmes, 1986. Add: The Lodge, Selby, N. Yorks. YO8 0PW, England.

HALL, Willis. British, b. 1929. Children's fiction, Plays/Screenplays, Sports. Publs: Final at Furnell, 1954; Poet and Pheasant, 1955; The Gentle Knight, 1957; The Play of the Royal Astrologers, 1958; The Long and the Short and the Tall, 1958; (with I.O. Evans) They Found the World, 1959; A Glimpse of the Sea, and Last Days in Dreamland, 1959; Return to the Sea, 1960; The Royal Astrologers: Adventures of Father Mole-Cricket or the Malayan Legends, 1960; The Days Beginning: An Easter Play, 1963; Come Laughing Home, 1964; (with M. Parkinson) The A to Z of Soccer, 1970; (with B. Monkhouse) The A to Z of Television, 1971; The Railwayman's New Clothes, 1974; My Sporting Life, 1975; Walk On, Walk On, 1976; The Summer of the Dinosaur, 1977; The Last Vampire, 1982; The Inflatable Shop, 1984; Dragon Days: The Return of the Antelope, 1985; The Antelope Company Ashore, 1986; Spooky Rhymes 1987; The Antelope Company at Large, 1987; Henry Hollins and the Dinosaur, 1988; Doctor Jekyll and Mr. Hollins, 1988; with Keith Waterhouse—Billy Liar, 1960; England, Our England, 1962; Squat Betty, 1962; The Sponge Room, 1962; All Things Bright and Beautiful, 1962; Say Who You Are (in U.S. as Help Stamp Out Marriage), 1965; (eds.) The

Writers' Theatre, 1967; Whoopsa-Daisy, 1968; Children's Day, 1969; Who's Who, 1971; (adaptors) Saturday, Sunday, Monday, by Eduardo de Filippo, 1973; (adaptors) The Card, by Arnold Bennett, 1973; The Incredible Kidnapping (children), 1975; Kidnapped at Christmas, Christmas Crackers, and A Right Christmas Caper (trilogy of children's plays), 1975–77; (adaptors) Filumena, 1977; The Television Adventures of Worzel Gummidge (juvenile), 2 vols., 1979; The Trials of Worzel Gummidge (juvenile), 1980; Worzel Gummidge at the Fair (juvenile), 1980; (adaptors) Worzel Gummidge (juvenile), 1981. Add: c/o London Mgmt., 235-241 Regent St., London W1, England.

HALLAHAN, William H(enry). American. Mystery/Crime/Suspense. *Publs:* The Dead of Winter, 1972; The Ross Forgery, 1973; The Search for Joseph Tully, 1974; Catch Me, Kill Me, 1977; Keeper of the Children, 1978; The Trade, 1981; The Monk, 1983. Add: c/o William Morrow Inc., 105 Madison Ave., New York, N.Y. 10016, U.S.A.

HALLAM, Elizabeth M. British, b. 1950. History. Asst. Keeper of Public Records Office, London, since 1976. *Publs:* Capetian France 987-1328, 1980; The Itinerary of Edward II and His Household 1307-23, 1984; The Domesday Project Book, 1986; Domesday Book: Through Nine Centuries, 1986; (ed.) The Plantagenet Chronicles, 1986; (ed.) The Four Gothic Kings: The Turbulent History of Medieval England and the Plantagenet Kings 1216-1377, 1987; The War of the Roses: From Richard II to the Fall of Richard III at Bosworth Field, 1988. Add: c/o Public Records Office, Chancery Lane, London WC2L 1LR, England.

HALLER, Bill. *See* **BECHKO,** P.A.

HALLERAN, E(ugene) E(dward). Also writes as Evan Hall. American, b. 1905. Westerns/Adventure. Social Studies Teacher, Ocean City High Sch., N.J., 1928–49. *Publs:* No Range Is Free, 1944; Prairie Guns, 1944; Outposts of Vengeance, 1945; Thirteen Toy Pistols (novel), 1945; Shadow of the Badlands, 1946; Double Cross Trail, 1946; Outlaw Guns, 1947; Rustlers' Canyon, 1948; Outlaw Trail, 1949, in U.K. as The Outlaw, 1952; High Prairie, 1950; Smoky Range, 1951; Gunsmoke Valley, 1952; Straw Boss, 1952; Colorado Creek, 1953 (as Evan Hall) Logan, 1956; Winter Ambush, 1954; Blazing Border, 1955; Devil's Canyon, 1956; Wagon Captain, 1956; The Hostile Hills, 1957; Spanish Ridge, 1957; Shadow of the Big Horn, 1960; The Dark Raiders, 1960; Warbonnet Creek, 1960; Convention Queen (novel), 1960; Blood Brand (in U.S. as Gringo Gun), 1961; Boot Hill Silver, 1962; Crimson Desert, 1962; The Far Land, 1963; Indian Fighter (Spur Award for Best Western), 1964; Summer of the Sioux, 1965; High Iron, 1965; Red River Country, 1966; The Pistoleros, 1967; Outlaws of Empty Poke, 1969; Cimarron Thunder, 1970. Add: 2600 S.E. Ocean, Apt. JJ-12, Stuart, Fla. 4996, U.S.A.

HALLETT, Graham. British, b. 1929. Agriculture/Forestry, Economics. Sr. Lectr. in Economics, Univ. Coll., Cardiff, since 1967. *Publs:* The Economics of Agricultural Land Tenure, 1960; The Economics of Agricultural Policy, 1968, 1981; (with J. Gwyn) Farming for Consumers, 1969; (with P. Randall) Maritime Industry and Port Development in South Wales, 1970; The Social Economy of West Germany, 1973; Housing and Land Policies in West Germany and Britain, 1977; Urban Land Economics, 1979; Second Thoughts on Regional Policy, 1981; (ed.) Land and Housing Policies in Europe and North America: A Comparative Analysis, 1988. Add: Dept. of Economics, University Coll., Cardiff, Wales.

HALLETT, Robin. British, b. 1926. History. Freelance writer since 1979. Tutor-Organiser, Norfolk WEA, 1951–52; Resident Tutor, Northern Nigeria, Dept. of Extra-Mural Studies, Univ. of Ibadan, 1956–59; Asst. Rep., British Council, Tanganyika and Zanzibar, 1959–61; Research Officer, Inst. of Commonwealth Studies, Oxford Univ., 1965–71; Sr. Lectr., Dept. of History, Univ. of Cape Town, 1972–78. *Publs:* Records of the African Association 1788-1831, 1964; The Penetration of Africa, 1965; The Niger Journal of Richard and John Lander, 1965; People and Progress in West Africa, 1966; (with E.W. Bovill) Golden Trade of the Moors, 1968; Africa to 1875, 1971, as Africa since 1875, 1974. Add: Yearlet, Cunnery Rd., Church Stretton, Shropshire SY6 6AH, England.

HALLGARTEN, S(iegfried Salomon) F(ritz). British, b. 1902. Cookery/Gastronomy/Wine, Travel/Exploration/Adventure. Lawyer: Former Chmn. and Managing Dir., House of Hallgarten Group of Companies (founder 1933). *Publs:* Rhineland-Wineland, 1952, 4th ed. 1967; Alsace and Its Winegardens, 1957; 1966; Wines of Germany, Israel, Luxembourg, Alsace; (with André Simon) The Great Wines of Germany, 1963, 1967; (with André Simon) Wines of the World, 1967–72; German

Wine Law, 1969, 1970; A Guide to the Vineyards, Estates and Wines of Germany, 1974; German Wines, 1976, 1981; Alsace: Its Winegardens, Cellars and Cuisine, 1977; (with F.L. Hallgarten) Wines and Winegardens of Austria, 1979; Der Konflikt zwischen geographiscen Herkunftsausgabe und Warenzeichen, 1985; Wine Scandal, 1986. Add: 20 Bracknell Gardens, London NW3, England.

HALLIDAY, William R(oss). American, b. 1926. Natural history, Recreation, Travel/Exploration. Asst. Dir., Intnl. Glaciospeleological Survey, since 1981. Dir., Western Speleological Survey, 1955–81; thoracic surgeon, in private practice, Seattle, Wash., 1957–65; Medical Consultant, 1965–71, and Chief Medical Consultant and Medical Dir., Dept. of Labor and Industries, Olympia and Seattle, Wash., 1971–76; Medical Dir., Washington State Div. of Vocational Rehabilitation, 1976–82. *Publs:* Adventure Is Underground, 1959; Depths of the Earth, 1966; American Caves and Caving, 1974; (with Frank K. Walsh) Oregon Caves: Discovery and Exploration, 1982. Add: 11569 N. Shore Dr., Reston, Va. 22090, U.S.A.

HALLIN, Emily Watson. American, b. 1919. Children's fiction, Children's non-fiction. Ed. of Publs. and Public Relations Rep., Chance Vought Aircraft, and Pratt & Whitney Aircraft, 1944–52. *Publs:* (with Robert Buell) Wild White Wings, 1965; (with Robert Buell) Follow the Honey Bird, 1967; Moya and the Flamingoes, 1969; Love at First Sight, 1980; We Belong Together, 1981; Be My Valentine, 1982; Light of My Life, 1982; The Mystery Kiss, 1982; Short Stop for Romance, 1982; Bunny Hug, 1983; Fireworks, 1983; Turkey Trot, 1983; Christmas Date, 1983; The Ghost of Gamma Rho, 1984; Lover's Lake, 1984; Janine, 1984; The Phantom Skateboard, 1985; Orinoco Adventure, 1985; Homecoming, 1985; Coral Island, 1986; Birds of Paradise, 1987; No Easy Answers, 1987; Wanted: Tony Roston, 1988; A Dark Horse, 1988; Queen Bee, 1989; Partners, 1989; Changes, 1989. Add: 13861 Cicerone, Los Altos Hills, Calif. 94022, U.S.A.

HALLIWELL, David. British, b. 1936. Plays/Screenplays. Dir., Quipu Theatre, London, 1966–76. Visiting Fellow, Reading Univ., 1969–70. *Plays:* Little Malcolm and His Struggle Against the Eunuchs (in U.S. as Hail Scrawdyke), 1965; K.D. Dufford Hears K.D. Dufford Ask K.D. Dufford How K.D. Dufford'll Make K.D. Dufford, 1969; A Who's Who of Flapland and Other Plays, 1971; The House, 1979. Add: 8 Crawborough Villas, Charlbury, Oxford OX7 3TS, England.

HALLO, William W. American, b. 1928. Archaeology/Antiquities, History. Curator, Babylonian Collection, since 1963; Ed., Yale Near Eastern Researches, since 1968, and Laffan Prof. of Assyriology and Babylonian Literature since 1975, Yale Univ., New Haven, Conn. (Prof. of Assyriology, 1965–75). Instr. 1956–58 and Asst. Prof. 1958–62, Hebrew Union Coll.-Jewish Inst. of Religion, Cincinnati. *Publs:* Early Mesopotamian Royal Titles, 1957; (ed.) Essays in Memory of E.A. Speiser, 1968; (with J.J.A. van Dijk) The Exaltation of Inanna, 1968; (trans.) The Star of Redemption, by Franz Rosenzweig, 1971; (with William Kelly Simpson) The Ancient Near East: A History, 1971; Sumerian Archival Texts, 1973; (ed. with Carl D. Evans and John B. White) Scripture in Context: Essays on the Comparative Method, 1980; (with W. Gunther Plant and Bernard T. Bamberger) The Torah: A Modern Commentary, 1981; (with Briggs Buchanan) Early Near Eastern Seals in the Yale Babylonian Collection, 1981; (ed. with James C. Moyer and Leo G. Perdue) Scripture in Context II: More Essays on the Comparative Method, 1983; (with Scott G. Beld and Piotr Michalowski) The Tablets of Ebla: Concordance and Bibliography, 1984; (with David B. Ruderman and Michael Stanislawski) Heritage: Civilization and the Jews (2 vols.), 1984. Add: Babylonian Collection, Yale Univ., New Haven, Conn. 06520, U.S.A.

HALLS, Geraldine. *See* **JAY,** Geraldine Mary.

HALLS, Wilfred Douglas. British, b. 1918. Education, History, Literature. Supernumerary Fellow, St. Antony's Coll., Oxford Univ., since 1985. Research Fellow, Bedford Coll., Univ. of London, 1955–56; Sr. Lectr., Royal Naval Coll., Dartmouth, 1956–59. Ed., Comparative Education, 1964–72, and Oxford Review of Education, 1974–84. Lectr. in Educational Studies, Oxford Univ., 1959–86. *Publs:* Maurice Maeterlink: Study of His Life and Thought, 1960; (trans.) Hubert & Mauss: The Nature and Function of Sacrifice, 1964; Society, Schools and Progress in France, 1965; (trans.) J. Capelle: Tomorrow's Education: The French Experience, 1967; (trans.) C. Führ: Educational Reform in the Federal Republic of Germany, 1970; Foreign Languages and Education in Western Europe, 1971; International Equivalences in Access to Higher Education, 1971; (with A.D.C. Peterson) The Education of Young People in Europe,

1973; A World Guide to Higher Education, 1976; Education, Culture and Politics in Modern France, 1976; The Youth of Vichy France, 1981; (trans.) E. Durkheim: The Rules of Sociological Method, 1982; (trans.) E. Durkheim: The Division of Labor in Society, 1984; (trans.) Durkheim and Politics, 1986; (trans.) M. Mauss: A Category of the Human Mind, 1986; (trans.) R. Aron: Macht, Power, Puissance in S. Lukes, Power, 1986; La Jeunesse sous Vichy, 1987; (ed.) Comparative Education: Contemporary Issues and Trends, 1988. Add: St. Anthony's College, Oxford, England.

HALPERN, Daniel. American, b. 1945. Poetry. Ed., Antaeus mag., NYC, since 1969; Ed.-in-Chief, Ecco Press, NYC, since 1971; Chmn., Graduate Writing Division, Columbia Univ. Sch. of the Arts, NYC (staff member, since 1976). Dir., National Poetry Series, NYC, since 1978. Instr., New Sch. for Social Research, NYC, 1971–76; Visiting Prof., Princeton Univ., New Jersey, 1975–76, 1988. *Publs:* Traveling on Credit, 1972; (ed., with Norman Thomas di Giovanni and Frank MacShane) Borges on Writing, 1973; (as Angela McCabe) The Keeper of Height, 1974; (trans.) Songs of Mririda, Courtesan of the High Atlas, by Mririda n'Ait Attik, 1974; (ed.) The American Poetry Anthology, 1975; The Lady Knife-Thrower, 1975; (with Gerda Mayer and Florence Elon) Treble Poets 2, 1975; Street Fire, 1975; Life among Others, 1978; Seasonal Rights, 1982; (ed.) The Art of the Tale, 1986; (ed.) The Antaeus Poetry Anthology, 1986; Tango, 1987; Writers on Artists, 1989. Add: 26 W. 17th St., New York, N.Y. 10001, U.S.A.

HALSALL, Eric. British, b. 1920. Animals/Pets, Country life/Rural societies. Freelance journalist; Press Officer, Ribblesdale Farmers Club. Staff Journalist, Burnley Express, 1946–51: Estate Surveyor with National Coal Bd., 1951–81. Regular broadcasts, BBC, on sheepdogs and sheep; Weekly column in Farmer's Guardian, Sheepdog Trials. *Publs:* Hill Dog, 1961; Meg of Lonktop, 1967; Sheepdogs, My Faithful Friends, 1980; Sheepdog Trials, 1982; Gael, Sheepdog of the Hills, 1985. Add: 528 Red Lees Rd., Cliviger, nr. Burnley, Lancs., England.

HALSEY, A(lbert) H(enry). British, b. 1923. Sociology. Dir., Dept. of Social and Admin. Studies, Univ. of Oxford, since 1962. Professorial Fellow, Nuffield Coll., Oxford. Lectr. and Sr. Lectr., Univ. of Birmingham, 1954–62; Fellow, Center for Advanced Study of the Behavioral Sciences, Palo Alto, Calif., 1956–57; Visiting Prof., Univ. of Chicago, 1959–60. *Publs:* (with J.E. Floud and F.M. Martin) Social Class and Educational Opportunity, 1956; (with J.E. Floud and C.A. Anderson) Education, Economy and Society, 1961; Ability and Educational Opportunity, 1962; (with G.N. Ostergaard) Power in Co-operatives, 1965; (with M. Trow) The British Academics, 1971; (ed.) Trends in British Society since 1900, 1972; (ed.) Educational Priority, 1972 (with J. Karabel) Power and Ideology in Education, 1977; (ed.) Heredity and Environment, 1977; (with A.F. Heath and J.M. Ridge) Origins and Destinations, 1980; Change in British Society, 1981, 3rd ed., 1986; (with N. Dennis) English Ethical Socialism, 1988; British Social Trends since 1900, 1988. Add: Nuffield Coll., Oxford, England.

HALTRECHT, Montague. British, b. 1932. Novels/Short stories, Biography. Reviewer, Times Literary Supplement, since 1982. Fiction Reviewer, Sunday Times, London, 1965–68. *Publs:* Jonah and His Mother, 1964; A Secondary Character, 1965; The Devil Is a Single Man, 1969; The Edgware Road, 1970; The Quiet Showman: Sir David Webster of the Royal Opera House, 1975. Add: c/o TLS, Prioty Hse., St. John's Lane, London EC1M 4BX, England.

HALVORSON, Marilyn. Canadian, b. 1948. Children's fiction. Teacher, Sundre High Sch., Alberta, since 1973. *Publs:* Cowboys Don't Cry, 1984; Let It Go, 1985; Nobody Said It Would Be Easy, 1987; Hold on, Geronimo, 1988. Add: Box 364, Sundre, Alberta T0M 1X0, Canada.

HAM, Wayne Albert. American, b. 1938. Theology/Religion. *Publs:* Enriching Your New Testament Studies, 1965; Man's Living Religion, 1965; Faith and the Arts, 1968; The Call to Covenant, 1969; Publish Glad Tidings, 1970; The First Century Church. 1971; Where Faith and World Meet, 1972; Listening for God's Voice, 1973; On the Growing Edge, 1973; Yesterday's Horizons, 1975; More Than Burnt Offerings, 1978; My Million Faces, 1985; Studies in Genesis, 2 vols., 1987. Add: P.O. Box 1059, Independence, Mo. 64051, U.S.A.

HAMBURGER, Michael (Peter Leopold). British, b. 1924. Poetry, Literature, Autobiography/Memoirs, Translations. Asst. Lectr. in German, Univ. Coll., London, 1952–55; Lectr., and Reader in German, Univ. of Reading, Berks, 1955–64; and subsequent visiting professorships. *Publs:* (ed. and trans.) Poems of Hölderlin, 1943; Later Hogarth, 1945;

Flowering Cactus: Poems 1942–49, 1950; (ed. and trans.) Beethoven: Letters, Journals, and Conversations, 1951, rev. eds. 1966, 1984; Poems 1950–51, 1952; (ed. and trans.) Hölderlin: Poems, 1952; The Dual Site: Poems, 1957; Reason and Energy: Studies in German Literature, 1957, rev. ed. (in U.S. as Contraries: Studies in German Literature) 1971; (ed. and trans.) Holderlin: Selected Poems, 1961; (ed. and trans. with Christopher Middleton) Modern German Poetry, 1910–1960: An Anthology with Verse Translations, 1962; Weather and Season: New Poems, 1963; Hugo von Hofmannsthal: Zwei Studien, 1964; In Flashlight: Poems, 1965; From Prophecy to Exorcism: The Premisses of Modern German Literature, 1965; (ed.) Das Werks: Sonette, Lieder, Erzählungen, by Jesse Thoor, 1965; Zwischen den Sprachen: Essays und Gedichte, 1966; (ed. and trans.) Hölderlin: Poems and Fragments, 1966, 1980; In Massachusetts, 1967; Feeding the Chickadees, 1968; Travelling: Poems 1963–68, 1969; (with Alan Brownjohn and Charles Tomlinson) Penguin Modern Poets 14, 1969; Home, 1969; The Truth of Poetry: Tensions in Modern Poetry from Baudelaire to the 1960s, 1969; Travelling I-V, 1972; (ed. and trans.) East German Poetry: An Anthology in German and English, 1972; Ownerless Earth: New and Selected Poems 1950–72, 1973; Conversations with Charwomen, 1973; A Mug's Game: Intermittent Memoirs, 1973; (ed.) Selected Poems, by Thomas Good, 1974; Art as Second Nature: Occasional Pieces 1950–1974, 1975; Real Estate: Poems, 1977; Moralities: Poems, 1977; (ed. and trans.) German Poetry 1910–75, 1977; (trans.) Paul Celan: Poems, 1980; An Unofficial Rilke, 1981; Variations: Poems, 1981; In Suffolk: A Poem, 1982; Goethe: Poems and Epigrams, 1983; A Proliferation of Prophets: German Literature from Nietzsche to the Second World War, 1983; Collected Poems 1941–1983, 1984; After the Second Flood: Essays on Post-War German Literature, 1986; Trees (poetry) 1988; Selected Poems, 1988; (trans.) Poems of Paul Celan (enlarged trans.), 1989; Testimonies (essays), 1989. Add: Marsh Acres, Middleton, Saxmundham, Suffolk, England.

HAMBURGER, Philip. American, b. 1914. Cultural/ethnic topics, Biography, Essays, Humor/Satire. Staff member, New Yorker mag., NYC, since 1939. *Publs:* The Oblong Blur and Other Odysseys, 1949; J.P. Marquand, Esquire, 1952; Mayor Watching and Other Pleasures, 1958; Our Man Stanley, 1963; An American Notebook, 1965; Curious World: A New Yorker at Large. Add: c/o The New Yorker, 25 West 43rd St., New York, N.Y. 10036, U.S.A.

HAMBY, Alonzo L(ee). American, b. 1940. History, Biography. Prof. of History, Ohio Univ., Athens, since 1975 (Asst. Prof., 1965–69; Assoc. Prof., 1969–75. Chmn. of Dept., 1980–83). *Publs:* (ed.) The New Deal: Analysis and Interpretation, 1969, 1980; Beyond the New Deal: Harry S. Truman and American Liberalism, 1973; (ed.) Harry S. Truman and the Fair Deal, 1974; The Imperial Years: The United States since 1939, 1976; (ed.) Access to the Papers of Recent Public Figures, 1977; Liberalism and its Challengers: F.D.R. to Reagan, 1985. Add: Dept. of History, Ohio Univ., Athens, Ohio 45701, U.S.A.

HAMBY, Wallace Bernard. American, b. 1903. Medicine/Health, Translations. Prof. of Neurosurgery, Univ. of Buffalo Medical Sch., N.Y., 1940–60; Head, Dept. of Neurosurgery, Cleveland Clinic Foundn., Ohio, 1960–68. *Publs:* The Hospital Care of Neurosurgical Patients, 1940, 1948; Intracranial Aneurysms, 1952; Case Reports and Autopsy of Ambroise Paré 1965; Carotid-Cavernous Fistula, 1966; Ambroise Paré: Surgeon of the Renaissance, 1967; The French Disease, 1980; (trans. with A. Fournier) Jean de Vigo: Le Mal Français, Selections from Ancient Syphilographers, 1980. Add: 3001 N.E. 47th Ct., Ft. Lauderdale, Fla. 33308, U.S.A.

HAMELL, Patrick Joseph. Irish, b. 1910. Theology/Religion. Roman Catholic Parish Priest, Birr, Co. Offaly, since 1967; Vicar Gen., Killaloe Diocese, since 1969. Prof. of Ancient Classics, 1937–43, and of Dogmatic Theology, 1943–67, Maynooth Coll.; Prof. of Theology, National Univ. of Ireland, and Vice-Pres., St. Patrick's Coll. Maynooth, 1959–67. *Publs:* Index to the Irish Ecclesiastical Record 1864-1964, 1200 vols., 1959–62; (ed.) Sermons for Sundays and Feastdays, 1963; (ed.) Sunday and Feastday Homilies, 1965; Index to Maynooth Students and Ordinations 1795-1984, 2 vols., 1967, 1985; Patrology: An Introduction, 1967. Add: St. Brendan's, Birr, Co. Offaly, Ireland.

HAMILL, Ethel. *See* **WEBB,** Jean Francis.

HAMILTON, Bernard. British, b. 1932. History. Reader in History, Univ. of Nottingham. *Publs:* Monastic Reform, Catharism, and the Crusades, 1979; The Latin Church in the Crusader States, 1980; The Medieval Inquisition, 1981; Religion in the Medieval West, 1986. Add: Dept. of History, The University, Nottingham, England.

HAMILTON, Charles. American, b. 1913. History, Recreation/Leisure/Hobbies. Pres., Hamilton Galleries, NYC. *Publs:* (ed.) Cry of the Thunderbird: The American Indian's Own Story, 1950; Men of the Underworld: The Professional Criminal's Own Story, 1952; Braddock's Defeat, 1959; Collecting Autographs and Manuscripts, 1961; (with L. Ostendorf) Lincoln in Photographs, 1963; The Robot That Helped to Make President, 1965; Scribblers and Scoundrels, 1968; (with D. Hamilton) Big Name Hunting, 1973; Collecting Autographs and Manuscripts, 1974; The Book of Autographs, 1978; The Signature of America, 1979; Great Forgers and Famous Fakes, 1980; Auction Madness, 1981; American Autographs: Signers of the Declaration of Independence, Revolutionary War Leaders, Presidents, 2 vols, 1983; Leaders and Personalities of the Third Reich: Their Biographies, Portraits and Autographs, Vol. 1, 1984; In Search of Shakespeare: A Reconnaissance into the Poet's Life and Handwriting, 1985; The Illustrated Letter, 1987. Add: c/o Harcourt Brace Jovanovich, Inc., 1250 6th Ave., San Diego, Calif. 92101, U.S.A.

HAMILTON, David. American, b. 1918. Economics. Prof. of Economics, Univ. of New Mexico, Albuquerque, since 1962 (Asst. Prof. 1949–56; Assoc. Prof. 1956–62). Contrib. Ed., New Mexico Independent newspaper. Instr., Univ. of Pittsburgh, Pa. 1946–47; Instr., Univ. of Texas, Austin, 1947–49. *Publs:* Newtonian Classicism and Darwinian Institutionalism, 1953, 1975; The Consumer in Our Economy, 1962; A Primer on the Economics of Poverty, 1968; Evolutionary Economics, 1970. Add: Dept. of Economics, Univ. of New Mexico, Albuquerque, N.M. 87131, U.S.A.

HAMILTON, Donald (Bengtsson). American, b. 1916. Mystery/Crime/Suspense, Westerns/Adventure, Sports. Full-time writer and photographer since 1946. *Publs:* mystery novels—Date with Darkness, 1947; The Steel Mirror, 1948; Murder Twice Told, 1950; Night Walker (in U.K. as Rough Company), 1954; Line of Fire, 1955; Assignment: Murder, 1956 (as Assassins Have Starry Eyes, 1966); Death of a Citizen, 1960; The Wrecking Crew, 1960; The Removers, 1961; Murderer's Row, 1962; The Silencers, 1962; The Ambushers, 1963; The Ravagers, 1964; The Shadowers, 1964; The Devastators, 1965; The Betrayers, 1966; The Menacers, 1968; The Interlopers, 1969; The Poisoners, 1971; The Intriguers, 1973; The Intimidators, 1974; The Terminators, 1975; The Retaliators, 1976; The Terrorizers, 1977; The Mona Intercept, 1980; The Revengers, 1982; The Annihilators, 1983; The Infiltrators, 1984; The Detonators, 1985; The Vanishers, 1986; The Demolishers, 1987; The Frighteners, 1989; western novels—Smoky Valley, 1954; Mad River, 1956; The Big Country, 1957; The Man from Santa Clara, 1960 (as The Two-Shoot Gun, 1971); Texas Fever, 1960; others— (ed.) Iron Men and Silver Stars, 1967; Donald Hamilton On Guns and Hunting, 1970; Cruises with Kathleen, 1980. Add: 984 Acequia Madre, P.O. Box 1045, Santa Fe, New Mexico, U.S.A.

HAMILTON, Elizabeth. British, b. 1906. Novels/Short stories, Autobiography/Memoirs/Personal, Biography, Translations. Freelance coach in Latin and Greek. *Publs:* The Year Returns, 1952; A River Full of Stars, 1954; Simon, 1956; Put off Thy Shoes, 1960; An Irish Childhood, 1960; The Great Teresa: Biography of St. Teresa of Avila, 1960; Héloïse, 1966; The Desert Thy Dwelling Place: Biography of Charles de Foucauld, 1970; (trans.) The Need for Contemplation, by R. Voillaume, 1973; I Stay in the Church, 1974; Cardinal Suenens: A Portrait (in U.S. as Suenens: A Portrait), 1975; (ed.) Servants of Love: Teresa of Avila and the Spiritual Life, 1975; Voice of the Spirit: The Spirituality of St. John of the Cross, 1976; Ways of the Spirit: The Spirituality of Cardinal Suenens, 1976; (ed. and trans. with E. Jones) Microcosmus: An Essay Concerning Man and His Relation to the World, by Hermann Lotze, 2 vols., 1976; Your God?, Cardinal Suenens Oxford Mission 1977, 1978; In Celebration of Cats, 1978; The Priest of the Moors, 1981; The Life of Saint Teresa of Avila, 1982. Add: 84 Vicarage Court, London W8 4HG, England.

HAMILTON, Franklin W. American, b. 1923. Novels/Short stories, Poetry. English teacher, Mott Community Coll., Flint, Mich., since 1956. Ed., Huron Review, and Walden Press, Flint, Mich. Instr. of English, Coll. of Emporia, Kans., 1953–55; Illinois State Univ., Normal, 1955–56, and Univ. of Kansas, Lawrence, 1960–61. *Publs:* Leaf Scar, 1965; Thoreau on the Art of Writing, 1967; Love Cry–Poems, 1970; End of the River, 1974. Add: 423 South Franklin Ave., Flint, Mich. 48503, U.S.A.

HAMILTON, Gail. *See* CORCORAN Barbara.

HAMILTON, (Robert) Ian. British, b. 1938. Poetry, Literature, Biog-

raphy. Ed., The Review, later The New Review, London, 1962–79; Poetry and Fiction Ed., Times Literary Supplement, London, 1965–73; Lectr. in Poetry, Univ. of Hull, 1972–73; Presenter, Bookmark, BBC TV, 1984–87. *Publs:* A Poetry Chronicle: Essays and Reviews, 1963; Pretending not to Sleep: Poems, 1964; (ed.) The Poetry of War, 1939–45, 1965; (ed.) Selected Poetry and Prose, by Alun Lewis, 1966; (ed.) The Modern Poet: Essays from "The Review", 1968; (ed.) Eight Poems, 1968; The Visit: Poems, 1970; Anniversary and Vigil, 1971; (ed.) Selected Poems, by Robert Frost, 1973; (ed. with Colin Falck) Poems since 1900: An Anthology, 1974; The Little Magazines: A Study of Six Editors, 1976; Robert Lowell: A Biography, 1982; (ed.) Yorkshire in Verse, 1984; In Search of J.D. Salinger, 1988. Add: 54 Queens Rd., London SW19, England.

HAMILTON, James Robertson. British, b. 1921. Classics, History. Lectr. 1951–56, Sr. Lectr. 1956–63, and Reader 1963–70, Univ. of Otago, Dunedin. Assoc. Prof. of Classics, Univ. of Auckland, 1970–87. *Publs:* Plutarch, Alexander: A Commentary, 1969; (ed.) Arrian: The Campaigns of Alexander, 1971; Alexander the Great, 1973. Add: 8 Glenveagh Dr., Mt. Roskill, Auckland 4, New Zealand.

HAMILTON, Julia. *See* FITZGERALD, Julia.

HAMILTON, Kenneth (Morrison). Canadian, b. 1917. Literature, Theology/Religion. Prof. Emeritus of Theology and Literature, Univ. of Winnipeg, since 1982 (Asst. Prof., 1958–62; Assoc. Prof., 1962–68; Prof. of Religious Studies, 1968–82). Minister of Religion, Nottingham, 1943–48, Wallington, Surrey, 1948–51, and Nova Scotia, 1951–58. *Publs:* The Protestant Way, 1956; The System and the Gospel: A Critique of Paul Tillich, 1963; Revolt Against Heaven, 1965; God Is Dead: The Anatomy of a Slogan, 1966; In Search of Contemporary Man, 1967; J.D. Salinger: A Critical Essay, 1967; (with A. Hamilton) John Updike: A Critical Essay, 1967; What's New in Religion, 1968; Life in One's Stride: A Short Study in Dietrich Bonhoffer, 1968; The Promise of Kierkegaard, 1969; (with A. Hamilton) The Elements of John Updike, 1970; Words and the Word, 1971; To Turn from Idols, 1973; (with A. Hamilton) To Be a Man—To Be a Woman, 1975; (with A. Hamilton) Condemned to Life: The World of Samuel Beckett, 1976; Earthly Good, 1989. Add: 4-237 Thomas Berry St., Winnipeg, Man. R2H 0P9, Canada.

HAMILTON, Mary (E.). Canadian, b. 1927. Novels, Children's fiction, Poetry. Freelance ed. since 1952. Ed., Toronto Star, 1946–48; Ed., News of the World, Cambridge, England, 1950–52. *Publs:* The Sky Caribou, 1980; (with M. A. Downie) And Some Brought Flowers, 1980; The Tin-Lined Truck, 1980; The New World Bestiary, 1985. Add: 50 Edgehill St., Kingston, Ont. K7L 2T5, Canada.

HAMILTON, Paul. *See* DENNIS-JONES, Harold.

HAMILTON, Priscilla. *See* GELLIS, Roberta.

HAMILTON, (George) Ronald. British, b. 1909. History, Travel/Exploration/Adventure, Biography. Asst. Master, 1933–39 and 1946–69, and House Master, 1946–64, Winchester Coll., Hants. *Publs:* Frederick the Great, 1936; (with Colin Badcock) Pendlebury and the Plaster Saints, 1959; (ed. and co-author) Budge Firth: A Memoir and Some Sermons, 1960; Now I Remember: A Holiday History of Britain (in U.S. as A Visitor's History of Britain), 1964; A Holiday History of France, 1971; Summer Pilgrimage, 1973; A Holiday History of Scotland, 1975; The Pluscarden Story, 1977. Add: Cherry Orchard Cottage, Broad Campden, Glos. GL55 6UU, England.

HAMILTON, Virginia (Esther). American, b. 1936. Children's fiction, Biography. *Publs:* Zeely, 1967; The House of Dies Drear, 1968; The Time-Ago Tales of Jahdu, 1969; The Planet of Junior Brown, 1971; W.E.B. Du Bois: A Biography, 1972; Time-Ago Lost: More Tales of Jahdu, 1973; M.C. Higgins, The Great, 1974; Paul Robeson: The Life and Times of a Free Black Man, 1974; (ed.) The Writings of W.E.B. Du Bois, 1975; Arilla Sun Down, 1976; Illusion and Reality (lecture), 1976; The Justice Cycle: Justice and Her Brothers, 1978, Dustland, 1980, and the Gathering, 1980; Jahdu, 1980; Sweet Whispers, Brother Rush, 1982; The Magical Adventures of Pretty Pearl, 1983; Willie Bea and the Time the Martians Landed, 1983; A Little Love, 1984; Junius over Far, 1985; The People Could Fly: American Black Folktales, 1985; In the Beginning: Creation Stories from Around the World, 1988; Anthony Burns: The Defeat and Triumph of a Fugitive Slave, 1988. Add: Box 293, Yellow Springs, Ohio 45387, U.S.A.

HAMILTON, Wade. *See* FLOREN, Lee.

HAMILTON-EDWARDS, Gerald (Kenneth Savery). British, b. 1906. Poetry, Genealogy/Heraldry, History, Biography. Asst. Librarian, Queen Mary Coll., Univ. of London, 1945–47; Regional Librarian, Devon County Library, 1947–55; Councillor, Oxford City, 1967–72; Gov., Oxford Polytechnic, and Magdalen Coll. Sch., 1970–72. *Publs:* Twelve Men of Plymouth, 1951; The Leisured Connoisseur: William Cotton of Ivybridge, 1954; (ed.) A Cadet in the Baltic, Frederick Edwards: Letters 1855-1857, 1956; (ed.) My Memory Walks Beside Me, by Nona Louisa Edwards, 1963; In Search of British Ancestry, 1966, 4th ed. 1982; Tracing Your British Ancestors, 1967; In Search of Scottish Ancestry, 1970, 1983; In Search of Army Ancestry, 1977; Perthshire Marriage Contracts 1687-1809, 2nd ed., 1979; Paris in My Youth and Other Poems, 1982; In Search of Welsh Ancestry, 1985. Add: 32 Bowness Ave., Headington, Oxford OX3 0AL, England.

HAMMER, Emanuel F. American, b. 1926. Psychology. In private psychoanalytic practice, NYC, since 1954. Clinical Prof., Post-Doctoral Program in Psychotherapy, Inst. of Advanced Psychological Studies, Adelphi Univ., New York, since 1980. Sr. Research Scientist, New York State Psychiatric Inst., 1952–55; Chief Psychologist, Lincoln Inst. for Psychotherapy, 1955–66; Research Consulant, Art Dept., 1958–61, and Adjunct Assoc. Prof. of Psychology, Grad. Sch. of Arts and Science, 1970–76, New York Univ.; Dir. of Training, New York Center for Psychoanalytic Training, 1966–75; Adjunct Prof., Grad. Art Therapy Dept., Pratt Inst., Brooklyn, N.Y., 1977–81. *Publs:* The House-Tree-Person Clinical Research Manual, 1955; The Clinical Application of Projective Drawings, 1958; Creativity, 1961; (ed.) Personality Dimensions of Creativity, 1962; (ed. with John N. Buck) Advances in the House-Tree-Person Test: Variations and Applications, 1968; (ed.) Use of Interpretation in Treatment: Its Role, Depth, Timing and Art, 1968; (ed.) Anti-achievement: Perspectives on School Drop-outs, 1970; Creativity, Talent, and Personality, 1984; Reaching the Affect: Style and Art in the Psychodynamic Therapies, 1989. Add: 381 West End Ave., New York, N.Y. 10024, U.S.A.

HAMMES, John A. American, b. 1924. Psychology, Theology/Religion. Prof. of Psychology, Univ. of Georgia, Athens, since 1968 (Asst. Prof., 1956–62; Assoc. Prof. of Psychology and Dir., Civil Defense Research, 1962–68). *Publs:* To Help You Say the Rosary Better, 1962; To Help You Follow the Way of the Cross, 1964; Humanistic Psychology: A Christian Interpretation, 1971; Human Destiny: Exploring Today's Value Systems, 1978; The Way of the Cross in Scriptural Meditation, 1979; In Praise of God, 1983; Ascend to Your Father, 1986; In Praise of God (vol. II), 1987. Add: Dept. of Psychology, Univ. of Georgia, Athens, Ga. 30602, U.S.A.

HAMMOND, Jane. *See* POLAND, Dorothy.

HAMMOND, Mac. American, b. 1926. Poetry. Prof. of English, State Univ. of New York at Buffalo, since 1963. *Publs:* The Horse Opera, 1966; Cold Turkey, 1969; Six Dutch Hearts, 1977; Mappamundi, 1989. Add: 314 Highland Ave., Buffalo, N.Y. 14222, U.S.A.

HAMMOND, Nicholas (Geoffrey Lempriere). British, b. 1907. Archaeology/Antiquities, Classics, History. Prof. of Greek Emeritus, Univ. of Bristol, since 1973 (Prof. 1962–73). Fellow and Tutor, Clare Coll., Cambridge, 1930–54 (Hon. Fellow, 1974); Headmaster, Clifton Coll., Bristol, 1954–62. *Publs:* Sir John Edwin Sandys, 1933; A History of Greece, 1959, 3rd ed. 1986; (ed.) Centenary Essays on Clifton College, 1962; Epirus, 1967; (ed. with H.H. Scullard) The Oxford Classical Dictionary, 2nd ed. 1970; (co-ed.) The Cambridge Ancient History, 7 vols., 3rd ed. 1970–88; A History of Macedonia I, 1972. II, 1978, III, 1988; Studies in Greek History, 1973; The Classical Age of Greece, 1975; Migrations and Invasions in Greece, 1976; Alexander the Great, 1980; Atlas of the Greek and Roman World in Antiquity, 1981; Three Historians of Alexander the Great, 1983; Venture into Greece with the Guerrillas 1943–44, 1983. Add: 3 Belvoir Terr., Trumpington Rd., Cambridge, England.

HAMMOND, Ralph. *See* HAMMOND INNES, Ralph.

HAMMOND INNES, Ralph. Writes as Hammond Innes and Ralph Hammond. British, b. 1913. Novels/Short stories, Children's fiction, History, Travel/Exploration/Adventure. Staff Member, Financial News, London, 1935–40. *Publs:* all as Hammond Innes unless specified—Doppelganger, 1937; Air Disaster, 1937; Sabotage Broadcast, 1938; All Roads Leads to Friday, 1939; Wreckers Must Breathe (in U.S. as Trapped), 1940; The Trojan Horse, 1940; Attack Alarm, 1941; Dead and Alive, 1946; The Killer Mine, 1947; The Lonely Skier (in U.S. as Fire in the Snow), 1947;

Maddon's Rock (in U.S. as Gale Warning), 1948; The Blue Ice, 1948; The White South (in U.S. as The Survivors), 1949; The Angry Mountain, 1950; (as Ralph Hammond) Cocos Gold, 1950; (as Ralph Hammond) Isle of Strangers (in U.S. as Island of Peril), 1953; Air Bridge, 1951; Campbell's Kingdom, 1952; (as Ralph Hammond) Saracen's Gold (in U.S. as Cruise of Danger), 1952; (as Ralph Hammond) Black Gold on the Double Diamond, 1953; The Strange Land (in U.S. as The Naked Land), 1954; The Mary Deare (in U.S. as The Wreck of the Mary Deare), 1956; The Land God Gave to Cain, 1958; The Doomed Oasis, 1960; Harvest of Journeys, 1960; Atlantic Fury, 1962; The Strode Venturer, 1965; Sea and Islands, 1967; The Conquistadors, 1969; Hammond Innes Introduces Australia, 1971; Levkas Man, 1971; North Star, 1974; Golden Soak, 1973; North Star, 1974; The Big Footprints, 1977; The Last Voyage, 1978; Solomons Seal, 1980; The Black Tide, 1982; High Stand, 1985; Hammond Innes' East Anglia, 1986; Medusa, 1988. Add: Ayres End, Kersey, Suffolk 1P7 6EB, England.

HAMMONTREE, Marie. American, b. 1913. Children's non-fiction. Secty., Mayor's Office, City of Indianapolis, since 1978. Worked for Bobbs-Merrill Co., Indianapolis, Ind., 1934–42, Indiana Univ. Medical Center, Indianapolis, 1942–48, and Travel Enterprises Inc., NYC, 1949–50; Secty., U.S. Dept. of Justice, 1950–75. *Publs:* Will and Charlie Mayo, Boy Doctors, 1954; A.P. Giannini, Boy of San Francisco, 1956; Albert Einstein, Young Thinker, 1961; Mohandas Gandhi, Boy of Principle, 1966; Walt Disney, Young Movie Maker, 1969. Add: 8140 Township Line Rd., Indianapolis, Ind. 46260, U.S.A.

HAMPSCH, George (Harold). American, b. 1927. Philosophy, Politics/Government (Peace and Conflict). Prof. of Philosophy, Coll. of the Holy Cross, Worcester, Mass. since 1970 (Chmn. of the Dept., 1979–83, 1987–88). Asst. Prof., 1961–65, and Assoc. Prof., 1965–70, John Carroll Univ., Cleveland, Ohio. *Publs:* Theory of Communism, 1965; Preventing Nuclear Genocide, 1988. Add: Dept. of Philosophy, Coll. of the Holy Cross, Worcester, Mass. 01610, U.S.A.

HAMPSHIRE, (Sir) Stuart (Newton). British, b. 1914. Philosophy. Warden, Wadham Coll., Oxford, 1970–84 (Fellow of All Souls Coll., and Lectr. in Philosophy, 1936–40, Fellow, New Coll., 1950–55, and Domestic Bursar and Research Fellow, All Souls Coll., 1955–60). Personal Asst. to Minister of State, Foreign Office, London, 1945; Lectr. in Philosophy, University Coll., London, 1947–50; Grote Prof. of Philosophy of Mind and Logic, Univ. of London, 1960–63; Prof. of Philosophy, Princeton Univ., New Jersey, 1963–70. *Publs:* Spinoza, 1951; Thought and Action, 1959; Freedom of the Individual, 1965; Modern Writers and Other Essays, 1969; Freedom of Mind and Other Essays, 1971; (co-ed.) The Socialist Idea, 1975; Two Theories of Morality, 1977; (ed.) Public and Private Morality, 1978; Morality and Conflict, 1983. Add: 79 Old High St., Headington, Oxford, England.

HAMPSON, Anne. British. Historical/Romance/Gothic. Full-time writer. Formerly café owner, sewing factory worker, and teacher. *Publs:* Eternal Summer, 1969; Precious Waif, 1969; Unwary Heart, 1969; The Autocrat of Melhurst, 1969; Gates of Steel, 1970; By Fountains Wild, 1970; Heaven Is High, 1970; Love Hath an Island, 1970; The Hawk and the Dove, 1970; Beyond the Sweet Waters, 1970; When the Bough Breaks, 1970; An Eagle Swooped, 1970; Isle of the Rainbows, 1970; Dark Hills Rising, 1971; The Rebel Bride, 1971; Stars of Spring, 1971; Wings of the Night, 1971; Follow a Shadow, 1971; Gold Is the Sunrise, 1971; Petals Drifting, 1971; South of Mandraki, 1971; Waves of Fire, 1971; The Fair Island, 1972; Enchanted Dawn, 1972; Beloved Rake, 1972; The Plantation Boss, 1972; There Came a Tyrant, 1972; Dark Avenger, 1972; Wife for a Penny, 1972; Hunter of the East, 1973; Boss of Bali Creek, 1973; Blue Hills of Sintra, 1973; Dear Stranger, 1973; Stormy the Way, 1973; When Clouds Part, 1973; Master of Moonrock, 1973; Windward Crest, 1973; A Kiss from Satan, 1973; The Black Eagle, 1973; Dear Plutocrat, 1973; After Sundown, 1974; Stars over Sarawak, 1974; Fetters of Hate, 1974; Pride and Power, 1974; The Way of a Tyrant, 1974; Moon Without Stars, 1974; Not Far from Heaven, 1974; Two of a Kind, 1974; Autumn Twilight, 1975; Flame of Fate, 1975; Jonty in Love, 1975; Reap the Whirlwind, 1975; South of Capricorn, 1975; Sunset Cloud, 1976; Song of the Waves, 1976; Dangerous Friendship, 1976; Satan and the Nymph, 1976; A Man to Be Feared, 1976; Isle at the Rainbow's End, 1976; Hills of Kalamata, 1976; Fire Meets Fire, 1976; Dear Benefactor, 1976; Call of the Outback, 1976; Call of the Veld, 1977; Harbour of Love, 1977; The Shadow Between, 1977; Sweet is the Web, 1977; Moon Dragon, 1978; To Tame a Vixen, 1978; Master of Forrestmead, 1978; Under Moonglow, 1978; For Love of a Pagan, 1978; Leaf in the Storm, 1978; Above Rubies, 1978; Fly Beyond the Sunset, 1978; Isle of Desire, 1978; South of the Moon, 1979; Bride for a Night, 1979; Chateau in the Palms, 1979; Coolibah

Creek, 1979; A Rose from Lucifer, 1979; Temple of Dawn, 1979; Call of the Heathen, 1980; The Laird of Locharrun, 1980; Pagan Lover, 1980; The Dawn Steals Softly, 1980; Stormy Masquerade, 1980; Second Tomorrow, 1980; Man of the Outback, 1980; Where Eagles Nest, 1980; Payment in Full, 1980; Beloved Vagabond, 1981; Man Without Heart, 1981; Shadow of Apollo, 1981; Love So Rare, 1983; The Dawn is Golden, 1983; Dreamtime, 1983; Spell of the Island, 1983; Soft Velvet Night, 1983; To Buy a Memory, 1983; When Love Comes, 1983; There Must Be Showers, 1983; Sweet Secome Love, 1984. Add: c/o Hodder and Stoughton Ltd., Mill Rd., Dunton Green, Sevenoaks, Kent TN13 2YA, England.

HAMPSON, Norman. British, b. 1922. History, Biography. Prof. of History, Univ. of York, since 1974. Prof. of Modern History, Univ. of Newcastle upon Tyne, 1967–74. *Publs:* La Marine de l'An II, 1959; A Social History of the French Revolution, 1963; Pelican History of European Thought: Volume IV, The Enlightenment, 1968; The First European Revolution, 1969; The Life and Opinions of Maxmilien Robespierre, 1974; A Concise History of the French Revolution, 1974; Danton, 1978; Will and Circumstance: Montesquieu, Rousseau, and the French Revolution, 1983; Prelude to Terror, 1988. Add: History Dept., Univ. of York, Heslington, York YO1 5DD, England.

HAMPTON, Christopher (James). British, b. 1946. Plays/Screenplays. Resident Dramatist, Royal Court Theatre, London, 1968–70. *Publs:* When Did You Last See My Mother?, 1967; Total Eclipse, 1969; The Philanthropist, 1970; Savages, 1974; Treats, 1976; Able's Will (television play), 1979; The Portage to San Cristobal of A.H., 1983; Tales from Hollywood, 1983; Les Liaisons Dangereuses, 1985; translations—Marya, 1969; Uncle Vanya, 1971; Hedda Gabler, 1971; A Doll's House, 1971; Don Juan, 1972; Tales from the Vienna Woods, 1977; Don Juan Comes Back from the War, 1978; The Wild Duck, 1980; Ghosts, 1983; Tartuffe, 1984; Dangerous Liaisons: The Film, 1989. Add: c/o Margaret Ramsay Ltd., 14a Goodwin's Ct., London WC2N 4LL, England.

HAMPTON, Christopher (Martin). British, b. 1929. Children's fiction, Poetry, History, Literature, Politics/Government. Lectr. in English, Polytechnic of Central London, since 1968. Poetry Adviser, Globe Playhouse Trust, since 1972. Teacher of English and Dir. of Studies, Shenker Inst., Rome, 1962–66; Lectr. in English, Davies Sch. of English, London, 1966–68. Member of the Council, Poetry Soc., London, 1969–75. *Publs:* (trans.) The Fantastic Brother, 1961; Island of the Southern Sun, 1962; (co-author) A Group Anthology, 1963; The Etruscans and the Survival of Etruria (in U.S. as The Etruscan Survival), 1969; (ed.) Poems for Shakespeare, 1972; An Exile's Italy, 1972; (ed.) Poems for Shakespeare, 1978; A Cornered Freedom, 1980; Socialism in a Crippled World, 1981; (ed.) The Penguin Radical Reader: The Struggle for Change in England 1381-1914, 1983. Add: c/o Penguin, 27 Wright's Lane, London W8 5TZ, England.

HAMPTON, William (Albert). British, b. 1929. Politics/Government. Prof., Univ. of Sheffield, since 1983 (Asst. Lectr. 1963–64; Lectr. 1964–70; Sr. Lectr., 1970–77; Reader, 1977–83). *Publs:* Democracy and Community, 1970; (co-author) Public Participation in Local Services, 1982; (ed.) Local Democracies, 1983; Local Government and Urban Politics, 1987. Add: Div. of Continuing Education, Univ. of Sheffield, Sheffield S10 2TN, England.

HAMRE, Leif. Norwegian, b. 1914. Children's fiction. Retired Colonel, Royal Norwegian Air Force, since 1974 (commissioned 1943). *Publs:* all have won Norwegian State Prize for Best Juvenile Book of the Year—Leap into Danger (in U.K., Otter Three Two Calling), 1957; Edge of Disaster (in U.K., Blue Two—Bale Out), 1958; Perilous Wings (in U.K., Ready for Take Off) 1959; Contact Lost, 1965; Operation Arctic, 1971. Add: Syrinvegan 10, 3408 Tranby, Norway.

HANBURY, Harold Grenville. British, b. 1898. Law. Vinerian Prof. Emeritus of English Law, Oxford Univ. (Fellow of Lincoln Coll., 1921–49; Vinerian Prof. and Fellow of All Souls Coll., 1949–64). Dean of the Law Faculty, Univ. of Nigeria, 1964–66. *Publs:* Le Système actuel de l'équité dans le système juridique de l'Angleterre, 1929; Essays in Equity, 1934; Modern Equity, 1935, 12th ed. 1985; (with R. Moureaux) Traité Pratique des Divorces et des Successions Droit Anglais, 1939, 1952; English Courts of Law, 1944, 5th ed. (with Yardley) 1979; Principles of Agency, 1952, 1960; The Vinerian Chair and Legal Education, 1958; Biafra: A Challenge to the Conscience of Britain, 1968; (ed.) Precedent in English Law and Other Essays, 1969; Shakespeare as Historian, 1985. Add: 14 Dan Picenaar Rd., Kloof 3610, Natal, South Africa.

HANBURY-TENISON, Robin. British, b. 1936. Human rights, Travel/Exploration/Adventure. Farmer, since 1960. Member of Council, Royal Geographical Soc., since 1968; Pres. Survival Intnl., since 1969. *Publs:* The Rough and the Smooth (exploration), 1969; A Question of Survival for the Indians of Brazil, 1973; A Pattern of Peoples: A Journey Among the Tribes of the Outer Indonesian Islands, 1975; Mulu: The Rain Forest, 1980; The Aborigines of the Amazon Rain Forest: The Yanomami, 1982; Worlds Apart, 1984; White Horses over France, 1985; A Ride along the Great Wall, 1987; Fragile Eden: A Ride Through New Zealand, 1989. Add: Maidenwell, Cardinham, Bodmin, Cornwall PL30 4DW, England.

HAND, Geoffrey Joseph Philip. Irish, b. 1931. History, Law. Barber Prof. of Jurisprudence, Univ. of Birmingham, since 1980. Asst. Lectr., Univ. of Edinburgh, 1960–61; Lectr., Univ. of Southampton, 1961–65; Lectr. and Prof., University Coll., Dublin, 1965–76; Prof. of Law, University Inst., Florence, 1976–80. Chmn., Arts Council of the Republic of Ireland, 1974–75. *Publs:* English Law in Ireland, 1290-1324, 1967; (ed.) Report of the Irish Boundary Commission 1924, 1970; (ed. with Lord Cross of Chelsea) Radcliffe and Cross's English Legal System 5th ed. 1971; 6th ed. (with D.J. Bentley) 1977; (with J. Georgel and C. Sasse) Handbook to the Electoral Systems of the Nine Member-States of the European Community, 1979; (co-author) The European Parliament: Towards a Uniform Procedure for Direct Elections, 1981. Add: Faculty of Law, Univ. of Birmingham, Birmingham B15 2TT, England.

HANDFORD, Michael Anthony. British, b. 1944. Transportation. Managing Dir., The Waterways Bookshop Ltd. Sr. Lectr. in History, Leicester Polytechnic. Former Lectr. in History, Bristol Polytechnic. *Publs:* Coal, Clothiers and the Navigations to Stroud, 1973; The Stroudwater Navigation, 1976–79; Towpath Guide to the Stroudwater, Thames, and Severn Canals, 1982. Add: Studio Flat, 52 Park St., Bristol BS1 5JN, England.

HANDLEY, Eric Walter. British, b. 1926. Classics. Regius Prof. of Greek, Cambridge Univ., since 1984. Lectr., 1949–61, Reader, 1961–67, and Prof. of Greek and Dir. of the Inst. of Classical Studies, 1967–84, University Coll., London. Foreign Secty., British Academy, 1979–88. *Publs:* (with J. Rea) The Telephus of Euripides, 1957; The Dyskolos of Menander, 1965. Add: Trinity Coll., Cambridge CB2 1TQ, England.

HANDLEY, Graham Roderick. British, b. 1926. Literature. Head of English Dept., Borehamwood Grammar Sch., Herts., 1957–62, and Hatfield Sch., Herts., 1962–67; Sr. Lectr., 1967–76, and Principal Lectr. in English, 1967–80, Coll. of All Saints, Tottenham, London; Research Officer in English, Birbeck Coll., Univ. of London, 1981–83. *Publs:* Golding's Lord of the Flies, 1965; Lawrence's Sons and Lovers, 1967; Notes on This Day and Age, 1968; Mrs. Gaskell's Sylvia's Lovers, 1968; Dickens' Hard Times, 1969; (with E. Newton) A Guide to Teaching Poetry, 1971; Huxley's Brave New World, 1977; Steinbeck's The Grapes of Wrath and Of Mice and Men and The Pearl, 1977; Hemingway's For Whom the Bell Tolls, 1977; Greene's The Power and the Glory, 1977; Heller's Catch 22, 1977; Hines' A Kestrel for a Knave, 1977; Joyce's A Portrait of the Artist as a Young Man, 1977; (with Stanley King) Kesey's One Flew Over the Cuckoo's Nest, 1977; Waterhouse's Billy Liar, 1977; Dickens' Oliver Twist, 1977; George Eliot's The Mill on the Floss, 1978; Fitzgerald's The Great Gatsby, 1978; Selected Poems and Letters of John Keats, 1978; Auden's Selected Poems, 1978; Poems of Thomas Hardy, 1978; Mann's Death in Venice and Tonio Kruger, 1978; (with Stanley King) Dickens' Bleak House, 1978; (with Paul Harris) Selected Tales of D.H. Lawrence, 1978; Blake's Songs of Innocence and Experience, 1978; Wilde's Importance of Being Earnest, 1978; Congreve's The Way of the World, 1978; Shakespeare's Sonnets, 1978; Dickens' Dombey and Son, 1978; Dickens' Our Mutual Friend, 1979; An Informal History of the College of All Saints, 1978; Dickens' Little Dorrit, 1979; (with Stanley King) O'Casey's Shadow of a Gunman and The Plough and the Stars, 1980; (with Stanley King) Graham Greene's The Quiet American, 1980; (with Barbara Handley) Wilkie Collins' The Woman in White, 1980; (ed.) Short Stories on Sport, 1980; The Metaphysical Poets, 1981; (ed.) Wuthering Heights, 1982; (ed.) Daniel Deronda, by George Eliot, 1984; Thackeray's Vanity Fair, 1985; Harper Lee's To Kill a Mockingbird, 1985; (ed.) The Mill on the Floss, by George Eliot, 1985; Shakespeare's Macbeth, 1985; Shakespeare's Twelfth Night, 1985; George Eliot's Silas Marner, 1985; George Eliot's Middlemarch, 1985; Shakespeare's As You Like It, 1985; Hardy's Tess of the D'Urbervilles, 1986; Wycherley's The Country Wife, 1986; Chaucer's The Pardoner's Tale, 1986; Trollope's Barchester Towers, 1987; Hartley's The Go-Between, 1987; Hardy's The Woodlanders, 1987; Fielding's Tom Jones, 1987; Dickens' David Copperfield, 1987; Mrs. Gaskell's North and South, 1988; John Christopher's

The Death of Grass, 1988; Hardy's Far from the Madding Crowd, 1988; (with Derek Jones) The Modern World: Ten Great Writers, 1988; Scott Fitzgerald's Tender Is the Night, 1989; Lawrence's Women in Love, 1989; (ed.) Trollopes' The Three Clerks, 1989. Add: Glasgow Stud Farmhouse, Crews Hill, Enfield, Middx., England.

HANDY, Rollo. American, b. 1927. Philosophy, Psychology. Pres., American Inst. for Economic Research, Great Barrington, Mass. since 1976. Asst. Prof. to Prof. and Head, Philosophy Dept., Univ. of South Dakota, Vermillion, 1954–60; Assoc. Prof., Union Coll., 1960–61; Chmn. and Prof., Philosophy Dept., 1962–67, and Provost, Faculty of Educational Studies, 1967–76, State Univ. of New York at Buffalo. *Publs:* A Current Appraisal of the Behavioral Sciences, (with P. Kurtz) 1964, (with E.C. Harwood) 1973; Methodology of the Behavioral Sciences, 1964; (with E.C. Harwood) Useful Procedures of Inquiry, 1964; (co-ed.) Philosophical Perspectives on Punishment, 1968; (co-ed.) The Behavioral Sciences, 1968; (co-ed.) The Idea of God, 1968; Value Theory and the Behavioral Sciences, 1969; The Measurement of Values, 1970. Add: American Inst. for Economic Research, Great Barrington, Mass. 01230, U.S.A.

HANES, Frank Borden. American, b. 1920. Novels, Poetry. Involved in real estate and farming. Chmn., Arts and Sciences Foundation, Univ. of No. Carolina, Chapel Hill. Past Chmn., North Carolina Writers' Conference; Past Pres., North Carolina Literary and Historical Assn.; Trustee, John M. Morehead Foundn. and North Carolina Zoological Soc.; Dir., Chatham Mfg. Co., and Hanes Dye & Finishing Co. *Publs:* Abel Anders, 1951; The Bat Brothers, 1953; Journey's Journal, 1956; The Fleet Rabble, 1961; Jackknife John, 1965; The Seeds of Ares, 1977; The Garden of Nonentities, 1983. Add: 1057 W. Kent Rd., Winston-Salem, N.C. 27104, U.S.A.

HANEY, William Valentine Patrick. American, b. 1925. Communications/Media, Administration/Management. Pres., William V. Haney Assocs., since 1969. Faculty member, Beloit Coll., Wisc., 1950–51, and DePaul Univ., Chicago, 1953–57; Prof. of Communication and Admin., Grad. Sch. of Mgmt., Northwestern Univ., Evanston, Ill., 1957–69. *Publs:* Communication: Patterns and Management Action, 1966; Communication and Organizational Behavior, 3rd ed. 1973; Communication and Interpersonal Relations, 5th ed. 1986. Add: 2453 Cardinal Lane, Wilmette, Ill. 60091, U.S.A.

HANFF, Helene. American, b. 1916. Social commentary. Freelance writer, NYC, since the 1960's. *Publs:* 84 Charing Cross Road, 1971; Duchess of Bloomsbury, 1973; Apple of My Eye, 1977; Underfoot in Show Business, 1980; Q's Legacy, 1985. Add: 305 E. 72nd St., Apt. 8G, New York, N.Y. 10021, U.S.A.

HANLEY, Clifford. Also writes as Henry Calvin. British, b. 1922. Novels/Short stories, Children's fiction, Plays/Screenplays, Autobiography/Memoirs/Personal. Reporter, Scottish Newspaper Services, Glasgow, 1940–45; Sub-Ed., Scottish Daily Record, Glasgow, 1945–57; Feature Writer, TV Guide, Glasgow, 1957–58; Columnist, Glasgow Evening Citizen, 1958–60; Member, Close Theatre Mgmt. Cttee., Glasgow, 1965–71, and Inland Waterways Council, 1967–71. *Publs:* Dancing in the Streets (autobiography), 1958; The Durable Element, 1958; Love from Everybody, 1959; The Taste of Too Much, 1960; (as Henry Calvin) The System, 1962; (as Henry Calvin) It's Different Abroad, 1963; Nothing But the Best (in U.S. as Second Time Around), 1964; Saturmacnalia, 1965; A Skinful of Scotch, 1965; Oh for an Island, 1966; (as Henry Calvin) The Italian Gadget, 1966; The Hot Month, 1967; (as Henry Calvin) The DNA Business, 1967; (as Henry Calvin) A Nice Friendly Town, 1967; (as Henry Calvin) Miranda Must Die, 1968; (as Henry Calvin) The Chosen Instrument (in U.S. as Boka Lives), 1969; The Redhaired Bitch, 1969; (as Henry Calvin) The Poison Chasers, 1970; Oh Glorious Jubilee, 1970; The Clyde Moralities, 1972; (as Henry Calvin) Take Two Popes, 1973; The Unspeakable Scot, 1977; Poems of Ebenezer McIlwham, 1978; Prissy, 1978; The Biggest Fish in the World (children's fiction), 1979; The Scots, 1980; Another Street Another Dance, 1983; Glasgow: A Celebration, 1984. Add: 36 Munro Rd., Glasgow W3, Scotland.

HANLEY, Gerald (Anthony). Irish, b. 1916. Novels/Short stories, Plays/Screenplays, Travel/Exploration/Adventure. *Publs:* Monsoon Victory, 1946; The Consul at Sunset, 1951; The Year of the Lion, 1954; Drinkers of Darkness, 1955; Without Love, 1957; The Journey Homeward, 1961; Gilligan's Last Elephant, 1962; A Voice from the Top (radio play), 1962; Gandhi (screenplay), 1964; The Blue Max (screenplay), 1966; See You in Yasukuni, 1970; Warriors and Strangers (travel), 1971; Noble Descents, 1982. Add: c/o/ Gillon Aitken, Aitken

and Stone Ltd., 29 Fernshaw Rd., London SW10 0TG, England.

HANLEY, William. American, b. 1931. Novels/Short stories, Plays/Screenplays. *Publs:* Mrs. Dally Has a Lover, and Other Plays, 1963; Slow Dance on the Killing Ground, 1964; Flesh and Blood, 1968; No Answer, 1968; Blue Dreams; or, The End of Romance and the Continued Pursuit of Happiness (novel), 1971; Mixed Feelings (novel), 1972; Leaving Mount Venus (novel), 1977. Add: c/o Leo Bookman, William Morris Agency, 1350 Ave. of the Americas, New York, N.Y. 10019, U.S.A.

HANNAH, Barry. American, b. 1942. Novels/Short stories. Member of the English Dept., Clemson Univ., South Carolina, 1967–73; Writer-in-Residence, Middlebury Coll., Vermont, 1974–75; member of the English Dept., Univ. of Alabama, 1975–80; writer for the director Robert Altman, Hollywood, 1980; Writer-in-Residence, Univ. of Iowa, Iowa City, 1981, Univ. of Mississippi, Oxford, 1982, 1984, 1985, and Univ. of Montana, Missoula, 1982–83. *Publs:* Geronimo Rex (novel), 1972; Nightwatchmen (novel), 1973; Airships (short stories), 1978; Ray (novel), 1981; Black Butterfly (short stories), 1982; The Tennis Handsome (novel), 1983; Power and Light (novel), 1983; Captain Maximus (short stories), 1985; Hey Jack! (novel), 1987; Boomerany (novel), 1989. Add: c/o Houghton Mifflin, 2 Park St., Boston, Mass. 02108, U.S.A.

HANNAM, Charles Lewis. British. Education, Psychology. Sr. Lectr., Univ. of Bristol, since 1973 (Lectr., 1959–73). *Publs:* (with P. Smyth and N. Stephenson) Young Teachers and Reluctant Learners, 1971; Parents and Mental Handicap, 1974, 3rd ed., 1988; (with P. Smyth and N. Stephenson) First Year of Teaching, 1975; A Boy in Your Situation, 1977; Almost an Englishman, 1979; Refugees, Evacuees, 1989. Add: Sch. of Education, Univ. of Bristol, Bristol BS8 1JA, England.

HANNAN, Edward James. Australian, b. 1921. Mathematics/Statistics. Prof., Australian National Univ., Canberra, 1959–86 (Research Fellow, 1953–56; Fellow, 1956–58). *Publs:* Time Series Analysis, 1960; Group Representations and Applied Probability, 1965; Multiple Time Series, 1970; (with M. Deistler) Statistical Theory of Linear Systems. Add: Statistics Dept., Faculty of Economics, Australian National Univ., Canberra, A.C.T. 2601, Australia.

HANNIBAL, Edward L. American, b. 1936. Novels. *Publs:* Chocolate Days, Popsicle Weeks, 1970; Dancing Man, 1973; Liberty Square Station, 1977, paperback as Better Days, 1979; (with R. Boris) Blood Feud, 1979; A Trace of Red, 1982. Add: 118 Pantigo Rd., East Hampton, N.Y. 11937, U.S.A.

HANNON, Ezra. *See* **HUNTER**, Evan.

HANRAHAN, Barbara. Australian, b. 1939. Novels. Writer and artist: 24 one-woman exhibitions in Australia, England, and Italy, since 1964; represented in the collections of the Australian National Gallery, Canberra, and in Australian state galleries. *Publs:* The Scent of Eucalyptus, 1973; Sea-Green, 1974; The Albatross Muff, 1977; Where the Queens All Strayed, 1978; The Peach Groves, 1980 The Frangipani Gardens, 1980; Dove, 1982; Kewpie Doll, 1984; Annie Magdalene, 1985; Dream People (short stories), 1987. Add: c/o Chatto and Windus Ltd., 30 Bedford Sq., London WC1B 3RP, England.

HANSEN, Ann Natalie. American, b. 1927. History. Publr., At the Sign of the Cock, since 1974. Research Asst. and Ed., Martha Kinney Cooper Ohioana Library Assn., 1951–54; on Editorial Staff, Columbus Dispatch, Ohio, 1954–58. *Publs:* (ed.) Ohio, 1954, 1955; Westward the Winds: Being Some of the Main Currents of Life in Ohio, 1788-1873, 1974; So You're Going Abroad: How To Do It, 1984; The English Origins of the "Mary and John" Passengers, 1985; The Dorchester Group: Puritanism and Revolution, 1987. Add: 2341 Brixton Rd., Columbus, Ohio 43221, U.S.A.

HANSEN, Barbara (Joan). American. Cookery/Gastronomy/Wine. Staff writer, Los Angeles Times, since 1968. Teacher in Mexican foods and cultures, Extension Div., Univ. of California at Los Angeles, 1975; consultant, Mexican foods project, General Mills, 1976. *Publs:* Cooking California Style, 1971; Good Bread, 1976; Mexican Cookery, 1980, 1988; Barbara Hansen's Taste of Southeast Asia: Brunei, Indonesia, Malaysia, The Phillipines, Singapore, Thailand and Vietnam, 1987. Add: Food Dept., Los Angeles Times, Times-Mirror Sq., Los Angeles, Calif. 90053, U.S.A.

HANSEN, Chadwick. American, b. 1926. Area Studies, History, Literature. Prof. of English, Univ. of Illinois at Chicago, 1974–75, and since 1976. Instr., to Prof., Pennsylvania State Univ., 1955–71; Prof., Univ. of Minnesota, Minneapolis, 1971–74; Prof. of English, Univ. of Iowa, Iowa City, 1975–76. *Publs:* (with D. Austin and R.W. Condee) Modern Fiction: Form and Idea in the Contemporary Novel and Short Story, 1959; (with others) The American Renaissance: The History and Literature of an Era, 1961; Witchcraft at Salem, 1969; (ed. with A. Hodes) Selections from the Gutter: Portraits from the Jazz Record, 1977. Add: English Dept., Univ. of Illinois, Box 4348, Chicago, Ill. 60680, U.S.A.

HANSEN, Joseph. Also writes as Rose Brock and James Colton. American, b. 1923. Novels/Short stories, Mystery/Crime/Suspense, Historical/Romance/Gothic. Full-time writer. *Publs:* (as James Colton) Lost on Twilight Road, 1964; (as James Colton) Strange Marriage, 1965; (as James Colton) The Corrupter and Other Stories, 1968; (as James Colton) Known Homosexual, 1968 (as Stranger to Himself, 1978 and Pretty Boy Dead, 1984); (as James Colton) Cocksure, 1969; (as James Colton) Hang-Up, 1969; (as James Colton) Gard, 1969; Fadeout (mystery), 1970; (as Rose Brock) Tarn House, 1971; (as James Colton) The Outward Side, 1971; (as James Colton) Todd, 1971; Death Claims (mystery), 1973; (as Rose Brock) Longleaf, 1974; Troublemaker (mystery), 1975; One Foot in the Boat (verse), 1977; The Man Everybody Was Afraid of (mystery), 1978; Skinflick (mystery), 1979; The Dog and Other Stories, 1979; A Smile in His Lifetime (novel), 1981; Gravedigger (mystery), 1982; Backtrack (mystery), 1982; Job's Year (novel), 1983; Brandstetter and Others (short stories), 1984; Steps Going Down (mystery), 1985; The Little Dog Laughed, 1986; Early Graves, 1987; Bohannon's Book (short stories), 1988; Obedience (mystery), 1988. Add: 2638 Cullen St., Los Angeles, Calif. 90034, U.S.A.

HANSEN, Joyce. American, b. 1942. Children's fiction. English teacher, NYC, since 1973; Mentor, Empire State Coll., Brooklyn, N.Y., since 1987. *Publs:* The Gift-Giver, 1980; Home Boy, 1982; Which Way Freedom?, 1986; Yellowbird and Me, 1986; Out from This Place, 1988. Add: c/o Walker and Co., 720 Fifth Ave., New York, N.Y. 10019, U.S.A.

HANSON, Earl D(orchester). American, b. 1927. Biology. Prof. of Biology and Science in Society, since 1981, and Fisk Prof. of Natural Science since 1972, Wesleyan Univ., Middletown (Assoc. Prof., 1960–63; Prof. of Biology, 1963–81). Instr. of Zoology, 1954–57, and Asst. Prof. of Zoology, 1957–60, Yale Univ., New Haven, Conn. Member, Ed. Cttee., American Inst. of Biological Sciences, 1978–82; Council for Intnl. Exchange of Scholars, Life Sciences, 1981–84. *Publs:* Animal Diversity, 1961, 3rd ed. 1972; (ed. with others) The Lower Metazoa: Comparative Biology and Phylogeny, 1963; The Origin and Early Evolution of Animals, 1977; (with J.D. Lockard and P.F. Jensch) Biology: The Science of Life, 1980; Understanding Evolution, 1981; (ed.) Recombinant DNA Research and the Human Prospect, 1983. Add: Science in Society Prog., Wesleyan Univ., Middletown, Conn. 06457, U.S.A.

HANSON, Joan. American, b. 1938. Children's fiction, Children's non-fiction. *Publs:* The Monster's Nose Was Cold, 1971; Alfred Snood, 1972; I Don't Like Timmy, 1972; Synonyms, 1972; Antonyms, 1972; Homographs, 1972; British-American Synonyms, 1972; More Synonyms, 1973; More Antonyms, 1973; More Homonyms, 1973; Homographic Homophones, 1973; I Won't Be Afraid, 1974; I'm Going to Run Away, 1976; Still More Antonyms, 1976; Still More Homonyms, 1976; Sound Words, 1976; Similes, 1976; Plurals, 1979; More Sound Words, 1979; More Similes, 1979; Possessives, 1979; The Cat's Out of the Bag, 1986. Add: 15707 Afton Hills, Afton, Minn., U.S.A.

HANSON, Kenneth O. American, b. 1922. Poetry, Translations. Prof. of Literature and Humanities, Reed Coll. Portland, Ore., since 1956. *Publs:* 8 Poems 1958, 1958; Poems, 1959; The Distance Anywhere, 1967; Saronikos and Other Poems, 1970; (ed.) Clear Days: Poems by Palama and Elytis, in Versions by Nikos Tselepides, 1972; The Uncorrected World, 1973; (trans.) Growing Old Alive: Poems by Han Yu, 1978; (with La Verne Krause) Portraits: Friend: Artists, 1978; Lighting the Night Sky, 1983. Add: Dept. of English, Reed Coll., Portland, Ore. 97202, U.S.A.

HANSON, Pauline. American. Poetry. Asst. to the Dir., Yaddo, Saratoga Springs, N.Y., 1950–76. *Publs:* The Forever Young, 1948; The Forever Young and Other Poems, 1957; Across Countries of Anywhere, 1971. Add: 221 Freeman St., Brookline, Mass. 02146, U.S.A.

HANSON, Philip. British, b. 1936. Economics. Prof. of Soviet Economics, Univ. of Birmingham, since 1987 (Lectr., 1968–73; Sr. Lectr., 1973–81; Reader, 1981–87). Economic Asst., H.M. Treasury, 1960–61; Lectr. in Economics, Univ. of Exeter, 1961–67; Visiting Prof., Univ. of Michigan, 1967–68, 1977; Sr. Research Officer, Foreign and Common-

wealth Office, 1971–72; Sr. Mellon Fellow, Harvard Univ., Cambridge, Mass., 1986–87. Member of the Editorial Bd., Cambridge Univ. Press Soviet and East European Studies Monograph Series, 1973–77; Contributing Ed., Soviet Economy, since 1985. *Publs:* The Wage-Packet: How the Economy Works, 1968; The Consumer in the Soviet Economy, 1968; Advertising and Socialism, 1974; U.S.S.R.: The Foreign Trade Implications of the 1976–80 Plan, 1976; Trade and Technology in Soviet-Western Relations, 1981; (ed. with K. Dawisha) Soviet-East European Dilemmas, 1981; (with K. Pavitt) The Comparative Economics of Research, Development, and Innovation in East and West, 1987; (ed. with M. Kirkwood) Alexander Znoviev as Writer and Thinker, 1987; Western Economic Statecraft in East–West Relations, 1988. Add: Centre for Russian and East European Studies, Univ. of Birmingham, Birmingham 15, England.

HAN SUYIN. Pseudonym for Guanghu/Elizabeth Zhou. British (b. Chinese), b. 1917. Novels/Short stories, International Relations/Current affairs, Travel/Exploration/Adventure, Autobiography. Medical practitioner, in London, Hong Kong, Singapore and Malaya, 1948–63; full-time writer since 1963. *Publs:* Destination Chungking, 1942; A Many-Splendoured Thing, 1952; And the Rain My Drink, 1956; The Mountain Is Young, 1958; Asia Today, 1960; Cast But One Shadow, 1962; Winter Love, 1963; Four Faces, 1964; The Crippled Tree, 1965; A Mortal Flower, 1967; China in 2001, 1967; Birdless Summer, 1969; Asia Today, 1969; The Morning Deluge, 1972; Wind in the Tower, 1975; Lhasa, The Open City, 1976; La Peinture Chinoise, 1977; La Chine au Mille Visages, 1978; Chine: Terre, Eau et Hommes, 1980; My House Has Two Doors, 1981; Phoenix Harvest, 1981; Till Morning Comes, 1982; The Enchantress, 1985; A Share of Loving, 1987; Han Suyin's China, 1988; Fleur de Soleil, 1988. Add: c/o Jonathan Cape, 32 Bedford Sq., London WC1B 3EL, England.

HAPGOOD, David. American, b. 1926. International relations/Current affairs (popular history), Translations. Fellow, Inst. of Current World Affairs, 1961–63; Conference Ed., Center for Intnl. Studies, Massachusetts Inst. of Technology, 1964, 1968. *Publs:* Africa from Independence to Tomorrow, 1965; Africa, 1965; (with M.F. Millikan) No Easy Harvest: The Dilemma of Agriculture in Underdeveloped Countries, 1967; (with M. Bennett) Agents of Change: A Close Look at the Peace Corps, 1968; (ed.) Popular Participation in Development, 1969; Diplomatism, 1971; (ghostwriter) Tender Loving Greed, by Mary Adelaide Mondelson, 1974; The Screwing of the Average Man, 1974; The Average Man Fights Back, 1978; (trans.) The Totalitarian Temptation, by J.-F. Revel, 1978; (with B. Weider) The Murder of Napoleon, 1984; Monte Cassino, 1986. Add: 2 Washington Sq., New York, N.Y. 10012, U.S.A.

HARBERGER, Arnold C. American, b. 1924. Economics. Prof. of Economics, Univ. of Chicago, since 1959 (Assoc. Prof., 1953–59), and Univ. of California, Los Angeles, since 1984. Asst. Prof. of Political Economy, Johns Hopkins Univ., Baltimore, Md., 1949–53. *Publs:* (ed.) Demand for Durable Goods, 1960; (ed. with M.J. Bailey) Taxation of Income from Capital, 1969; Project Evaluation, 1972; Taxation and Welfare, 1974; World Economic Growth, 1985. Add: Dept. of Economics, Univ. of California, 405 Hilgard Ave., Los Angeles, Calif. 90024, U.S.A.

HARBINSON, Robert. *See* **BRYANS,** Robin.

HARBOTTLE, Michael Neale. British, b. 1917. International relations/Current affairs, Military/Defence, Autobiography/Memoirs/Personal. Dir., London Centre for Intnl. Peacebuilding. Consultant for Special Projects, Intnl. Peace Academy, since 1972 (former Dir. of Studies in Peacekeeping; Vice Pres., 1972–74). Officer in British Army, 1937–68; Brig., Chief of Staff, United Nations Force in Cyprus, 1966 until retirement in 1968; Chief Security Officer, Sierra Leone Selection Trust Mines, 1969–70. *Publs:* The Impartial Soldier, 1970; The Blue Berets, 1972; (co-author) The Thin Blue Line, 1974; The Knaves of Diamonds, 1976; (compiler) Peacekeeper's Handbook, 1978; Ten Questions Answered, 1983; (ed.) Arms Race to Armageddon, 1984. Add: 9 West St., Crippins Norton, Oxon OX7 5LH, England.

HARBURY, Colin. British, b. 1922. Economics. Prof. of Economics, The City Univ., London, since 1971; Gen. Ed., Economics and Society, Allen and Unwin; Gen. Ed., Fontana Introduction to Modern Economics. Pres., Economics Assn., 1978–80. *Publs:* Descriptive Economics, 1957, 7th ed. 1986; The Industrial Efficiency of Rural Labour, 1959; Workbook in Introductory Economics, 1969, 4th ed. 1987; (with D. Hitchins) Inheritance and Wealth Inequality in Britain, 1979; Economic Behaviour, 1980; (with R. Lipsey) An Introduction to the UK Economy, 1983, 1986. Add: Dept. of Social Science, The City Univ., St. Johns St., London EC1, England.

HARCOURT, Geoffrey Colin. Australian, b. 1931. Economics. Univ. Lectr. in Economics and Politics, and Fellow, Jesus College, Cambridge, since 1982; Pres. since 1988. Joint Ed., Australian Economic Papers, since 1967; Joint Ed., Cambridge Journal of Economics, since 1983 (Assoc. Ed., 1976–1982); Member, Academic Bd., Journal of Post Keynesian Economics, since 1977; Corresp. Ed., The Manchester School of Economic and Social Studies, since 1982. Editorial Bd., Political Economy, since 1985. Advisory Bd., Journal of Economic Surveys, since 1986. Lectr. to Prof. of Economics, Univ. of Adelaide, 1958–81 (Prof. Emeritus, 1988); Univ. Lectr. in Economics and Politics, and Fellow, Trinity Hall, Cambridge, 1963–66. *Publs:* (with P.H. Karmel and R.H. Wallace) Economic Activity, 1967; (ed. with R.H. Parker) Readings in the Concept and Measurement of Income, 1969, 2nd ed. (ed. with Parker and G. Whittington) 1986; (ed. with N.F. Laing) Capital and Growth: Selected Readings, 1971; Some Cambridge Controversies in the Theory of Capital, 1972; (ed.) The Microeconomic Foundations of Macroeconomics, 1977; The Social Science Imperialists, 1982; (ed.) Keynes and His Contemporaries, 1985; Controversies in Political Economy, 1986; (ed. with Jon S. Cohen) International Monetary Problems and Supply-Side Economics: Essays in Honour of Lorie Tarshis, 1986. Add: Jesus College, Cambridge, England.

HARCOURT, Palma. Also writes in collaboration with her husband as John Penn. British. Mystery/Crime/Suspense. *Publs:* Climate for Conspiracy, 1974; A Fair Exchange, 1975; Dance for Diplomats, 1976; At High Risk, 1977; Agents of Influence, 1978; A Sleep of Spies, 1979; Tomorrow's Treason, 1980; A Turn of Traitors, 1981; (as John Penn) Notice of Death, 1982; The Twisted Tree, 1982; Shadows of Doubt, 1983; (as John Penn) Deceitful Death, 1983; (as John Penn) A Will to Kill, 1983; The Distant Stranger, 1984; (as John Penn) Mortal Term, 1985; (as John Penn) A Deadly Sickness, 1985; A Cloud of Doves, 1985; A Matter of Conscience, 1986; (as John Penn) Unto the Grave, 1986; (as Jon Penn) Barren Revenge, 1986; Limited Options, 1987; (as John Penn) Accident Prone, 1987; Clash of Loyalties, 1988; (as John Penn) Outrageous Exposure, 1988; Cover for a Traitor, 1989; (as John Penn) A Feast of Death, 1989. Add: c/o Murray Pollinger, Literary Agent, 4 Garrick St., London WC2E 9BH, England.

HARDCASTLE, Michael. Also writes as David Clark. British, b. 1933. Children's fiction, Children's non-fiction. Literary Ed., Bristol Evening Post, 1959–65; Chief Feature Writer, Liverpool Daily Post, 1965–67. *Publs:* Soccer Is Also a Game, 1966; Shoot on Sight, 1967; Redcap, 1967; Aim for the Flat, 1967; The Chasing Game, 1968; Goal, 1969; Dive to Danger, 1969; Shilling a Mile, 1969; Stop that Car!, 1970; Reds and Blues, 1970; Strike, 1970; Smashing, 1970; Don't Tell Me What To Do, 1970; The Hidden Enemy, 1970; Come and Get Me, 1971; Live in the Sky, 1971; Shelter, 1971; A Load of Trouble, 1971; Blood Money, 1971; It Wasn't Me, 1971; In the Net, 1971; (as David Clark) Goalie, 1972; (as David Clark) Splash, 1972; Playing Ball, 1972; Goals in the Air, 1972; Island Magic, 1973; (as David Clark) Run, 1973; (as David Clark) Top Spin, 1973; United!, 1973; Away from Home, 1974; Free Kick, 1974; The Demon Bowler, 1974; The Big One, 1974; The Chase, 1974; On the Run, 1974; Heading for Goal, 1974; Last Across, 1974; The Match, 1974; Dead of Night, 1974; Road Race, 1974; A Hard Man, 1974; Catch, 1974; Day in the Country, 1974; The Long Drop, 1974; (as David Clark) Grab, 1974; (as David Clark) Winner, 1974; Flare Up, 1975; Get Lost, 1975; (as David Clark) Volley, 1975; (as David Clark) Roll Up, 1975; Life Underground, 1975; Money for Sale, 1975; Where the Action Is, 1976; The First Goal, 1976; Breakaway, 1976; Go and Find Him, 1977; River of Danger, 1977; The Great Bed Race, 1977; Night Raid, 1977; On the Ball, 1977; Shooting Star, 1977; The Saturday Horse, 1977; Strong Arm, 1977; Fire on the Sea, 1977; Holiday House, 1977; Crash Car, 1977; Goal in Europe, 1978; Soccer Special, 1978; Top of the League, 1979; Top Soccer, 1979; The Switch Horse, 1980; Top Fishing, 1980; Go for Goal, 1980; Racing Bike, 1980; Snake Run, 1980; Hot Wheels, 1980; Half a Team, 1980; Behind the Goal, 1980; Kick Off, 1980; Top Speed, 1980; Gigantic Hit, 1982; Roar to Victory, 1982; Attack!, 1982; Fast from the Gate, 1983; Caught Out, 1983; The Team That Wouldn't Give In, 1984; Hooked!, 1984; Tiger of the Track, 1985; Double Holiday, 1985; Winning Rider, 1985; One Kick, 1986; James and the TV Star, 1986; No Defence, 1986; The Shooters, 1986; Snookered!, 1987; Quake, 1987; Mascot, 1987; The Rival Games, 1988; The Magic Party, 1988; The Green Machine, 1989; Kickback, 1989; Splashdown, 1989; Jump In, 1989; Lucky Break, 1990; Joanna's Goal, 1990; Mark England's Cap, 1990; Walking the Goldfish, 1990. Add: 17 Molescroft Park, Beverley, North Humberside HU17 7EB, England.

HARDEN, Donald B(enjamin). British, b. 1901. Archaeology/Antiquities. Asst. Keeper, 1929–45, and Keeper, 1945–56, Dept. of Antiq-uities, Ashmolean Museum, Oxford; Dir., London Museum, 1956–70. *Publs:* Roman Glass from Karanis, 1936; (with E.T. Leeds) The Anglo-Saxon Cemetery at Abingdon, Berkshire, 1936; Sir Arthur Evans, 1951, 1983; (ed.) Dark-Age Britain: Studies Presented to E.T. Leeds, 1956; The Phoenicians, 1962, 3rd ed. 1980; (co-author) Masterpieces of Glass, 1968; Catalogue of Greek and Roman Glass in the British Museum, 1981; Glass of the Caesars (catalogue), 1987. Add: 12 St. Andrew's Mansions, Dorset St., London W1H 3FD, England.

HARDEN, O(leta) Elizabeth (McWhorter). American, b. 1935. Literature. Prof. of English since 1972, Wright State Univ., Dayton (faculty member, since 1966; Exec. Dir., Gen. Univ. Services, 1974–76). Taught at Univ. of Arkansas, Fayetteville, Southwest Missouri State Coll., Murray Kentucky Univ., Northeastern State Coll., Okla., and Wichita State Univ., Kans. *Publs:* Maria Edgeworth's Art of Prose Fiction, 1971; Maria Edgeworth, 1984. Add: Dept. of English, Wright State Univ., 7751 Colonel Glenn Highway, Dayton, Ohio, 45435, U.S.A.

HARDIE, Frank. British, b. 1911. History, Politics/Government. *Publs:* (co-author) Young Oxford and War, 1934; (co-author) New Trends in Socialism, 1935; The Political Influence of Queen Victoria 1861-1901, 1935; Is Britain a Democracy?, 1942; (co-author) Socialism: The British Way, 1948; The Political Influence of the British Monarchy 1868-1952, 1970; The Abyssinian Crisis, 1974; (ed.) The Prints of Martin Hardie, 1975; (co-author) Britain and Zion: The Fateful Entanglement, 1980. Add: 18 Kensington Gate, London W8 5NA, England.

HARDIN, Clement. *See* **NEWTON,** D.B.

HARDIN, Clifford M. American, b. 1915. Agriculture/Forestry. Chmn., Institutional Policy Cttee., Stifel, Nicolaus and Co., St. Louis, Mo., since 1980. Dir., Michigan State Agricultural Experiment Station, East Lansing 1949–53; Dean of Agriculture, Michigan State Univ., Lansing 1953–54; Chancellor, Univ. of Nebraska, Lincoln 1954–69; Secty., U.S. Dept. of Agriculture 1969–71; Vice-Chmn. of the Bd., Ralston Purina Co., St. Louis, Mo., 1971–80. Scholar-in-Residence, Center for the Study of American Business, Washington Univ., 1983–85. (Dir. of Center, 1981–83). *Publs:* (ed.) Overcoming World Hunger, 1969. Add: 10 Roan Lane, St. Louis, Mo. 63124, U.S.A.

HARDING, D(enys) (Clement) W(yatt). British, b. 1906. Literature, Psychology, Translations. Prof. Emeritus, Univ. of London, since 1968 (Prof. of Psychology, 1945–68). Investigator and Member of the Research Staff, National Inst. of Industrial Psychology, London, 1928–33; Asst., later Lectr. in Social Psychology, London Sch. of Economics, 1933–38; Sr. Lectr. in Psychology, Univ. of Liverpool, 1938–45; part-time Lectr. in Psychology, Univ. of Manchester, 1940–41, and 1944–45; Clark Lectr., Trinity Coll., Cambridge, 1971–72. Member, Editorial Bd., Scrutiny, Cambridge, 1933–47; Hon. General Secty., British Psychological Soc., 1944–48; Ed., British Journal of Psychology (Gen. Section), London, 1948–54. *Publs:* (trans. with Erik Mesterton) The Eternal Smile, by Pär Lagerkvist, 1934; (trans. with Erik Mesterton) Guest of Reality, by Pär Lagerkvist, 1936; (ed. with Gordon Bottomley) The Collected Works of Isaac Rosenberg, 1937; The Impulse to Dominate, 1941; (ed. with Gordon Bottomley) The Collected Poems of Isaac Rosenburg, 1949; Social Psychology and Individual Values, 1953; Experience into Words: Essays on Poetry (criticism), 1963; (ed.) Persuasion, by Jane Austen, 1965; Words into Rhythm: English Speech Rhythm in Verse and Prose, 1976. Add: Ashbocking Old Vicarage, nr. Ipswich, Suffolk IP6 9LG, England.

HARDING, James. British, b. 1929. Literature, Music, Biography. Sr. Lectr. in French, Thames Polytechnic, London, since 1966. *Publs:* Saint-Saens and His Circle, 1965; Sacha Guitry, The Last Boulevardier, 1968; The Duke of Wellington, 1968; (ed.) The Maid of Sker, 1968; Massenet, 1970; The Astonishing Adventure of General Boulanger, 1971; Rossini, 1971; The Ox on the Roof, 1972; (ed.) Lord Chesterfield's Letters to His Son, 1973; Gounod, 1973; Lost Illusions: Paul Léautaud and His World, 1974; Erik Satie, 1975; (trans.) Poulenc: My Friends and Myself, 1978; Folies de Paris: The Rise and Fall of French Operetta, 1979; Offenbach, 1980; Maurice Chevalier, 1982; Jacques Tati: Frame by Frame, 1984; James Agate, 1986; Ivor Novello, 1987; Cochran, 1988; Gerald du Maurier, 1989. Add: 100 Ridgmount Gardens, Torrington Pl., London WC1E 7AZ, England.

HARDING, John. British, b. 1948. Plays/Screenplays. Actor. *Publs:* with John Burrows—The Golden Pathway Annual, 1975. Add: c/o Michael Imison Playwrights Ltd., 28 Almeida St., London N1 1TD, England.

HARDING, Lee (John). Also writes as Harold G. Nye. Australian, b. 1937. Science fiction/Fantasy, Children's fiction, Autobiography. Freelance writer of SF novels, short stories, and radio plays. Freelance photographer, 1953–70. *Publs:* The Fallen Spaceman (juvenile), 1973, 1980; A World of Shadows, 1975; Future Sanctuary, 1976; The Children of Atlantis (juvenile), 1976; The Frozen Sky (juvenile), 1976; Return to Tomorrow (juvenile), 1976; (ed.) Beyond Tomorrow: An Anthology of Modern Science Fiction, 1976; (ed.) The Altered I: An Encounter with Science Fiction, 1976, 1978; The Weeping Sky, 1977; (ed.) Rooms of Paradise, 1978; Displaced Person (in U.S. as Misplaced Persons), 1979; The Web of Time (juvenile), 1979; Waiting for the End of the World (juvenile), 1983; Born a Number: Autobiography, 1986. Add: c/o Virginia-Kidd, 538 E. Hartford St., Milford, Pa. 18337, U.S.A.

HARDING, Matthew Whitman. *See* **FLOREN,** Lee.

HARDING, Michael. Irish, b. 1953. Novels. Teacher and social worker, 1974–77. Ordained Catholic Priest, 1981. *Publs:* Priest (novel), 1986. Add: Farnham Rd., Cavan, Ireland.

HARDING, Walter. American, b. 1917. Literature. Prof. Emeritus of American Literature, State Univ. of New York at Geneseo, since 1982 (Assoc. Prof., 1956–59; Prof. and Chmn., English Dept., 1959–66; Univ. Prof., 1966–72; Distinguished Prof., 1972–82). Secty., Thoreau Soc., since 1941. Instr., Rutgers Univ., New Brunswick, N.J. 1947–51; Asst. Prof., Univ. of Virginia, Charlottesville, 1951–56; Ed.-in-Chief, The Writings of Henry D. Thoreau, 1965–72. *Publs:* A Thoreau Handbook, 1959; (ed.) Alcott's Essays on Education, 1960; (ed.) Thoreau: Man of Concord, 1960; (with M. Meltzer) A Thoreau Profile, 1962; (ed.) Variorum Walden, 1963; (ed.) The Thoreau Centennial, 1965; The Days of Henry Thoreau, 1965; (ed.) Poems of Ellery Channing, 1967; (ed.) Emerson's Library, 1967; (ed.) Variorum Civil Disobedience, 1967; (ed.) Henry David Thoreau: A Profile, 1971; (ed.) The Selected Works of Thoreau, 1975; (with Michael Meyer) The New Thoreau Handbook, 1980; In the Woods and Fields of Concord, 1982; Thoreau's Journal, 1984. Add: State Univ. of New York, Geneseo, N.Y. 14454, U.S.A.

HARDISON, Osborne B. Also writes as H.O. Bennett. American, b. 1928. Mystery/Crime/Suspense, Poetry, Literature. University Prof. of English, Georgetown Univ., Washington, D.C., since 1985. Editorial Bd., Crofts Classics, and Series Ed., Goldentree Bibliographies, AHM Press, Chicago; Member, Editorial Bd., Film Journal, Milton Studies, English Literary Renaissance. Dir., Folger Shakespeare Library, Washington, D.C., 1969–84. *Publs:* Lyrics and Elegies, 1958; The Enduring Monument, 1962; (ed.) Modern Continental Literary Criticism, 1962; (ed.) English Literary Criticism, 1963; (ed. with A. Preminger and F. Warnke) The Princeton Encyclopedia of Poetry and Poetics, 1965, 1975; Christian Rite and Christian Drama in the Middle Ages, 1965; Practical Rhetoric, 1965; (as H.O. Bennett) The Last Drop, 1967; (ed. with J. Mills) The Forms of Imagination, 1972; Toward Freedom and Dignity, 1972; (author and trans. with L. Golden) Classical and Medieval Literary Criticism, 1974; Pro Musica Antiqua, 1979; Entering the Maze: Identity and Change in Modern Culture, 1981; Prosody and Purpose in the English Renaissance, 1989; Disappearing Through the Skylight: Technology and Culture in the Twentieth Century, 1989. Add: Dept. of English, Georgetown Univ., Washington, D.C. 20057, U.S.A.

HARDMAN, David Rennie. British. Poetry, History, Literature. Labour Member of Parliament (U.K.) for Darlington, and Parliamentary Secty., Ministry of Education, 1945–51; Prof. of English Literature, Elmira Coll., N.Y. 1964–66; Barclay Acheson Prof. of Intnl. Studies, Macalester Coll., Minn., 1966–67. Secty., Sir Ernest Cassel Educational Trust, 1956–86. *Publs:* What About Shakespeare?, 1939; Poems of Love and Affairs, 1951; Telscombe, Story of a Sussex Village, 1968. Add: Bankyfield, Hurstpierpoint, Sussex, England.

HARDON, John A(nthony). American, b. 1914. Theology/Religion. Research Prof., Jesuit Sch. of Theology, Chicago, since 1974, and Prof. of Dogmatic Theology, Inst. for Advanced Studies in Catholic Doctrine, St. John's Univ., Jamaica, N.Y since 1974; Prof., Notre Dame (Pontifical Catechetical) Inst., Va., since 1981. Theological Dir., Mark Communications Inc., Toronto, since 1973. Ordained Priest, Roman Catholic Church, Soc. of Jesus, 1947; Assoc. Prof. of Theology, West Baden, Indiana Theologate, 1951–62; Assoc. Prof. in Religion, Western Michigan Univ., 1962–67; Assoc. Prof. in Fundamental Theology, Ballarmine Sch. of Theology, North Aurora, Ill., 1968–73. *Publs:* Christianity in Conflict, 1959; All My Liberty, 1959, 1982; For Jesuits, 1963; The Hungry Generation, 1966; The Spirit and Origins of American Protestantism, 1968; Protestant Churches in America, 1968, 1982; Religions of the World, 2nd ed. 1969, 3rd ed. 1982; Religions of the Orient: A Christian View, 1970; (ed.) Gospel Witness, 1971; American Judaism, 1971; Christianity in the Twentieth Century, 2nd ed. 1972, 3rd ed. 1978; The Catholic Catechism, 1975, 3rd ed. 1978; Holiness in the Church, 1976; Religious Life Today, 1977; Salvation and Sanctification, 1978; Theology of Prayer, 1978; Modern Catholic Dictionary, 1980; The Question and Answer Catholic Catechism, 1981; Spiritual Life in the Modern World, 1982; Pocket Catholic Dictionary, 1985; The Treasury of Catholic Wisdom, 1987; The Lifetime Catholic Reading Plan, 1988. Add: Georgetown Univ., Washington, D.C. 20057, U.S.A.

HARDWICK, Elizabeth (Bruce). American, b. 1916. Novels/Short stories, Literature. Adjunct Assoc. Prof., Barnard Coll., NYC. Founder and Ed., New York Review of Books. *Publs:* The Ghostly Lover, 1945; The Simple Truth, 1955; (ed.) The Selected Letters of William James, 1961; View of My Own (essays), 1962; Seduction and Betrayal: Women and Literature, 1974; Sleepless Nights, 1979; Bartleby in Manhattan and Other Essays, 1983; (ed. with Robert Atwan) The Best American Essays 1986, 1986. Add: 15 W. 67th St., New York, N.Y. 10023, U.S.A.

HARDWICK, Michael. Also writes as John Drinkrow. British, b. 1924. Novels/Short stories, Plays/Screenplays, Literature, Music, Biography. Writer and Dir., New Zealand National Film Unit, 1947–52; Drama Producer, and with Script Dept., BBC, London, 1958–63. *Publs:* (with Mollie Hardwick) The Sherlock Holmes Companion, 1962; (with M. Hardwick) Sherlock Holmes Investigates, 1963; (with M. Hardwick) The Man Who Was Sherlock Holmes, 1964; (with M. Hardwick) Four Sherlock Holmes Plays, 1964; (with M. Hardwick) The Charles Dickens Companion, 1965; (with M. Hardwick) Writers' Houses, 1968; (with M. Hardwick) Alfred Deller: A Singularity of Voice, 1968, 1980; (with M. Hardwick) The Game's Afoot (plays), 1969; (with M. Hardwick) Dickens's England, 1970; (with M. Hardwick) Plays from Dickens, 1970; (with M. Hardwick) The Private Life of Sherlock Holmes, 1970; The Osprey Guide to Gilbert and Sullivan, 1972; (as John Drinkrow) The Vintage Operetta Book, 1972; The Osprey Guide to Jane Austen, 1973; (with M. Hardwick) The Charles Dickens Encyclopedia, 1973; The Osprey Guide to Oscar Wilde, 1973; (with M. Hardwick) Four More Sherlock Holmes Plays, 1973; (as John Drinkrow) The Vintage Musical Comedy Book, 1973; A Literary Atlas and Gazetteer of the British Isles, 1973; Upstairs, Downstairs: Mr. Hudson's Diaries, 1973; The Osprey Guide to Anthony Trollope, 1974; Upstairs, Downstairs: Mr. Bellamy's Story, 1974; The Inheritors, 1974; (abridger) The Pallisers, 1974; (with M. Hardwick) The Charles Dickens Quiz Book, 1974; (with M. Hardwick) The Bernard Shaw Companion, 1974; The Four Musketeers, 1975; The Man Who Would Be King, 1975; Upstairs, Downstairs: On with the Dance, 1975; Upstairs, Downstairs: Endings and Beginnings, 1975; (with M. Hardwick) The Upstairs, Downstairs Omnibus, 1975; (with M. Hardwick) The Gaslight Boy, 1976; Regency Royal, 1978; Prisoner of the Devil, 1979; Regency Rake, 1979; Regency Revenge, 1980; The Chinese Detective, 1981; Bergerac, 1981; Regency Revels, 1982; (with M. Hardwick) The Hound of the Baskervilles and Other Sherlock Holmes Plays, 1982; (abridger) The Barchester Chronicles, 1982; The Private Life of Dr. Watson, 1983; Last Tenko, 1984; Sherlock Holmes: My Life and Crimes, 1984; The Complete Guide to Sherlock Holmes, 1986; The Revenge of the Hound, 1987. Add: 2 Church St., Wye, Kent TN25 5BJ, England.

HARDWICK, Mollie. British. Novels/Short stories, Historical/Romance/Gothic, Plays/Screenplays, Literature, Biography. Announcer, 1943–46, and Producer and Script Ed., Drama Dept., 1946–62, BBC, London. *Publs:* (with Michael Hardwick) The Sherlock Holmes Companion, 1962; (with M. Hardwick) Sherlock Holmes Investigates, 1963; (with M. Hardwick) The Man Who Was Sherlock Holmes, 1964; (with M. Hardwick) Four Sherlock Holmes Plays, 1964; (with M. Hardwick) The Charles Dickens Companion, 1965; (compiler) Stories from Dickens, 1967; (with M. Hardwick) Alfred Deller: A Singularity of Voice, 1968, 1980; (with M. Hardwick) Writers' Houses, 1968; Emma, Lady Hamilton, 1969; (with M. Hardwick) Dickens's England, 1970; (with M. Hardwick) Plays from Dickens, 1970; Mrs. Dizzy, 1972; (with M. Hardwick) The Charles Dickens Encyclopedia, 1973; Upstairs, Downstairs: Sarah's Story, 1973; (with M. Hardwick) Four More Sherlock Holmes Plays, 1973; Upstairs, Downstairs: The Years of Change, 1974; (with M. Hardwick) The Bernard Shaw Companion, 1974; (with M. Hardwick) The Charles Dickens Quiz Book, 1974; Upstairs, Downstairs: Mrs. Bridges' Story, 1975; Upstairs, Downstairs: The War to End Wars, 1975; (with M. Hardwick) The Upstairs, Downstairs Omnibus, 1975; World of Upstairs, Downstairs, 1976; Beauty's Daughter, 1976; The Duchess of Duke Street: The Way Up, 1976; The Duchess of Duke Street: The Golden Years, 1976; (with M. Hardwick) The Gaslight Boy, 1976;

The Duchess of Duke Street: The World Keeps Turning, 1977; Charlie Is My Darling, 1977; The Atkinson Heritage, 1978; The Atkinson Heritage: Sisters in Love, 1979; Thomas and Sarah, 1979; Lovers Meeting, 1979; Willowood, 1980; The Atkinson Heritage: Dove's Nest, 1980; Juliet Bravo 1, 1980; Juliet Bravo 2, 1980; Calling Juliet Bravo, 1981; Monday's Child, 1981; I Remember Love, 1982; The Shakespeare Girl, 1983; By the Sword Divided, 1983; The Merrymaid, 1984; Girl with a Crystal Dove, 1985; Malice Domestic, 1986; Parson's Pleasure, 1987; Blood Royal, 1988; Uneaseful Death, 1988; The Bandersnatch, 1989. Add: 2 Church St., Wye, Kent TN25 5BJ, England.

HARDY, Adam. *See* **BULMER**, Henry Kenneth.

HARDY, Barbara (Gladys). British. Literature. Prof. of English, Birkbeck Coll., Univ. of London, since 1970 (Prof., Royal Holloway Coll., Univ. of London, 1965–70). *Publs:* The Novels of George Eliot: A Study in Form, 1959; Twelfth Night, 1962; Wuthering Heights, 1963; The Appropriate Form: An Essay on the Novel, 1964; Jane Eyre, 1964; (ed.) Middlemarch: Critical Approaches to the Novel, 1967; (ed.) Daniel Deronda, by George Eliot, 1967; Charles Dickens: The Later Novels, 1968; (ed.) Critical Essays on George Eliot, 1970; The Moral Art of Dickens, 1970; The Exposure of Luxury: Radical Themes in Thackeray, 1972; (ed.) The Trumpet Major, by Thomas Hardy, 1974; Tellers and Listeners: The Narrative Imagination, 1975; (ed.) Laodicean, by Hardy, 1975; A Reading of Jane Austen, 1976; The Advantage of Lyric: Essays on Feeling in Poetry, 1976; Particularities: Readings in George Eliot, 1983; Forms of Feeling in Victorian Fiction, 1985; Narrators and Novelists: Collected Essays, Vol. 1, 1987; (ed.) Not So Quiet..., by Helen Zenna Smith, 1988. Add: Birkbeck Coll., Malet St., London WC1E 7HX, England.

HARDY, Bobbie (Marjorie Enid Hardy). Australian, b. 1913. History. *Publs:* Water Carts to Pipelines, 1968; West of the Darling, 1970; Their Work Was Australian: The Story of the Hudson Family, 1970; Lament for the Barkindji, 1976; The World Owes Me Nothing, 1979; Early Hawkesbury Settlers, 1985. Add: Unit 402, 349 New South Head Rd., Double Bay, N.S.W. 2038, Australia.

HARDY, Frank. (Francis Joseph Hardy). Australian, b. 1917. Novels/Short stories. Freelance writer: Pres., Realist Writers Group, Melbourne and Sydney, 1945–74; Co-Founder, Australian Soc. of Authors, Sydney, 1968–74; Pres., Carringbush Writers, Melbourne, 1980–83. *Publs:* Power Without Glory (novel), 1950; The Man from Clinkapella and Other Prize-Winning Stories, 1951; The Four-Legged Lottery (novel), 1958; Legends from Benson's Valley, 1963; The Yarns of Billy Borker, 1965; Billy Borker Yarns Again, 1967; The Outcasts of Foolgarah (novel), 1971; The Great Australian Lover and Other Stories, 1972; It's Moments Like These (short stories), 1972; But the Dead Are Many: A Novel in Fugue Form, 1975; Warrant of Distress (novel), 1983; The Obsession of Oscar Oswald (novel), 1983; The Loser Now Will Be Later to Win (short stories), 1985; other—Journey into the Future (on the Soviet Union), 1952; The Hard Way: The Story Behind Power Without Glory, 1961; The Unlucky Australians (on the Gurindji), 1968, 1972; (with Athol George Mulley) The Needy and the Greedy: Humorous Stories of the Racetrack, 1975; (with Fred Trueman) You Nearly Had Him That Time and Other Cricket Stories, 1978; (ed. by C. Semmler) A Frank Hardy Swag, 1982. Add: 9/76 Elizabeth Bay Rd., Elizabeth Bay, N.S.W. 2011, Australia.

HARDY, John Philips. Australian, b. 1933. Literature. Prof. of English, Australian National Univ., A.C.T., since 1972. Jr. Research Fellow, Magdalen Coll., Oxford, 1962–65; Visiting Asst. Prof., Univ. Coll., Univ. of Toronto, 1965–66; Prof. of English, Univ. of New England, Armidale, N.S.W., 1966–72. *Publs:* (ed. with others) Johnson, Boswell and Their Circle: Essays Presented to Lawrence Fitzroy Powell, 1965; (ed.) The Political Writings of Dr. Johnson: A Selection, 1968; (ed.) The History of Rasselas, Prince of Abissinia, 1968; Reinterpretations: Essays on Poems by Milton, Pope and Johnson, 1971; (ed.) Johnson's Lives of the Poets: A Selection, 1971; Samuel Johnson: A Critical Study, 1979; (co-ed.) The Classical Temper in Western Europe, 1983; Jane Austen's Heroines: Intimacy in Human Relationships, 1984. Add: 30 Elroy Circuit, Hawker, A.C.T. 2614, Australia.

HARDY, Laura. *See* **HOLLAND**, Sheila.

HARDY, Richard Earl. American, b. 1938. Psychology, Sociology. Chmn., Dept. of Rehabilitation Counseling, Virginia Commonwealth Univ., Richmond, since 1969. Ed., Social and Rehabilitation Psychology series, Charles C. Thomas Publishing, Springfield, Ill., since 1972. Rehabilitation Counselor, Richmond, Va. 1961–63; Rehabilitation Advisor, Dept. of Health, Education and Welfare, Washington, D.C. 1963–66; Chief Psychologist, South Carolina Dept. of Rehabilitation, Columbia, 1966–68. Licensed Clinical Psychologist, ABPP Diplomate in Counseling Psychology. *Publs:* all with J.G. Cull—The Big Welfare Mess: Public Assistance & Rehabilitation Approaches; Introduction to Correctional Rehabilitation, 1972; Drug Dependence and Rehabilitation Approaches, 1972; Rehabilitation of the Drug Abuser with Delinquent Behavior; Climbing Ghetto Walls; Vocational Rehabilitation: Profession and Process; Alcohol Dependence and Rehabilitation Approaches; Behavior Modification of the Mentally Ill; Drug Language and Lore; Counseling Strategies with Special Populations: The Neglected Older American; (with Gandy and Martin) Rehab Counseling and Services, 1987; Hemingway: A Psychological Portrait, 1988. Add: 9214 Groundhog Dr., Richmond, Va. 23235, U.S.A.

HARE, David. British. b. 1947. Plays/Screenplays. Dir., Portable Theatre, London, 1968–71; Literary Mgr., 1969–70, and Resident Dramatist, 1970–71, Royal Court Theatre, London; Resident Dramatist, Nottingham Playhouse, 1973; Co-founder, Joint Stock Theatre Group, 1975–80; Co-Founder, Greenpoint Films, 1983; Assoc. Dir., National Theatre, London, 1984–88. *Publs:* Slag, 1970; (with others) Lay By, 1971; The Great Exhibition, 1972; (with Howard Brenton) Brassneck, 1974; Knuckle, 1974, 1978; Teeth 'n' Smiles, 1976; Fanshen, 1976; Licking Hitler, 1978; Plenty, 1978, 1979; Dreams of Leaving, 1980; Saigon, 1981; A Map of the World, 1982; The History Plays, 1984; Wetherby (screenplay), 1985; (with Howard Brenton) Pravda, 1985; The Asian Plays, 1986; The Bay at Nice and Wrecked Eggs, 1987; The Secret Rapture, 1988; Paris by Night, 1989; Strapless, 1989. Add: 33 Ladbroke Rd., London W11, England.

HARE, R(ichard) M(ervyn). British, b. 1919. Philosophy. Prof., Univ. of Florida, Gainesville, since 1983. White's Prof. of Moral Philosophy, Univ. of Oxford, 1966–83. *Publs:* The Language of Morals, 1952; Freedom and Reason, 1963; Practical Inferences, 1971; Essays on Philosophical Method, 1971; Essays on the Moral Concepts, 1972; Applications of Moral Philosophy, 1972; Moral Thinking, 1981; Plato, 1982; Essays in Ethical Theory, 1989; Essays on Political Morality, 1989. Add: Dept. of Philosophy, Univ. of Florida, Gainesville, FL 32611, U.S.A.

HARE DUKE, Michael (Geoffrey). British, b. 1925. Psychology, Theology/Religion. Bishop of United Diocese of St. Andrews, Dunkeld and Dunblane, since 1969. Member, Scottish Inst. of Human Relations, since 1974. Ordained Deacon, 1952; Priest, 1953; Curate, St. Johns Wood Church, 1952–56; Vicar, St. Mark's Bury, 1956–62; Vicar, St. Paul's Daybrook, 1964–69; Officiating Chaplain to the Forces, E. Midlands Headquarters, 1968–69. Pastoral Dir., 1962–64, and Consultant, 1964–69, Clinical Theology Assn.; Chmn., Scottish Pastoral Assn., 1972–76; Chmn., Scottish Assn. for Mental Health, 1978–85. *Publs:* (co-author) The Caring Church, 1963; (co-author) First Aid in Counselling, 1968; Understanding the Adolescent, 1969; The Break of Glory, 1970; Freud, 1972; Good News, 1978; Stories, Signs, and Sacraments in the Emerging Church, 1982. Add: Bishop's House, Fairmount Rd., Perth PH2 7AP, Scotland.

HAREVEN, Tamara K. American, b. 1937. History, Sociology, Biography. Prof. of History, Clark Univ., Worcester, Mass., since 1976 (Assoc. Prof., 1969–76); Research Assoc., Center for Population Studies, Harvard Univ., Cambridge, Mass. (Fellow, Charles Warren Center for Studies in American History, 1967–69); Ed., Journal of Family History; Exec. Bd. Member, National Council on Family Relations; Chmn., Family History and Historical Demography Network, Social Science History Assn. Instr. in History, Ohio State Univ., Columbus, 1962–65; Asst. Prof. and Assoc. Prof. of History, Dalhousie Univ., Halifax, 1965–67. *Publs:* Eleanor Roosevelt: An American Conscience, 1968; (ed.) Anonymous Americans: Explorations in American Social History, 1971; (ed. with Robert H. Bremner) Children and Youth in America, 1974; (ed. with Alice Rossi and Jerome Kagan) The Family, 1978; (ed.) Transitions: The Family and the Life Course in Historical Perspective, 1978; (with Randolph Langenbach) Amoskeag: Life and Work in an American Factory City, 1978; (ed. with M. Vinovskis) Family and Population in 19th-Century America, 1978; (ed.) Themes in the History of the Family, 1978; Family Time and Industrial Time: The Relationship Between the Family and Work in a New England Community, 1982; (co-ed.) Aging and Life Course Transitions, 1982; (ed. with A. Plakans) Family History at the Crossroads, 1987. Add: Clark Univ., Dept. of History, Worcester, Mass. 01610, U.S.A.

HARGRAVE, Leonie. *See* **DISCH**, Thomas M.

HARGREAVES, John D(esmond). British, b. 1924. History. Joint Ed., Oxford Studies in African Affairs. Lectr., Univ. of Manchester, 1948–52; Sr. Lectr., Fourah Bay Coll., Sierra Leone, 1952–54; Visiting Prof., Union Coll., Schenectady, N.Y., 1960–61, and the Univ. of Ibadan, 1970–71; Prof. of History, Univ. of Aberdeen, 1962–85. Pres., African Studies Assn. (U.K.) 1972–73. *Publs:* A Life of Sir Samuel Lewis, 1958; Prelude to the Partition of West Africa, 1963; West Africa: The Former French States, 1967; (ed.) France and West Africa, 1970; West Africa Partitioned, 2 vols., 1974–85; The End of Colonial Rule in West Africa: Essays in Contemporary History, 1979; Aberdeenshire to Africa, 1981; Decolonization in Africa, 1987. Add: 22 Raemoir Rd., Banchory, Aberdeen AB3 3UJ, Scotland.

HARGROVE, Erwin C. American, b. 1930. Politics/Government. Dir., Inst. for Public Policy Studies, and Prof. of Political Science, Vanderbilt Univ., Nashville, Tenn. Formerly, Sr. Fellow, The Urban Inst., Washington, D.C.; Prof. of Political Science, Brown Univ., Providence, R.I. *Publs:* Presidential Leadership: Personality and Political Style, 1966; The Power of the Modern Presidency, 1974; The Missing Link, 1975; The Presidency, 1976; (co-ed.) TVA 50 Years of Grass-Roots Bureaucracy, 1984; (with M. Nelson) Presidents, Politics, and Policy, 1984; (co-ed.) The President and the Council of Economic Advisors, 1984; (co-ed.) Leadership and Innovation, 1987; Jimmy Carter as President, 1988. Add: Dept. of Political Science, Vanderbilt Univ., Nashville, Tenn. 37235, U.S.A.

HÄRING, Bernard. German, b. 1912. Theology/Religion. Prof. of Moral Theology, Academia Alfonsiana, Lateran Univ., Rome, since 1949. Visiting Prof., Yale Univ., New Haven, Conn., 1966–67, Union Theological Seminary, NYC, 1967–68, and Joseph Kennedy Inst. for Bioethics, Washington, D.C., 1974, 1975. *Publs:* Das Heilige und das Gute, 1950; Das Gesetz Christi, 3 vols., 1954; Ehe in dieser Zeit, 1956; Christian Renewal in a Changing World, 1962; Shalom: Peace: Sacrament of Reconciliation, 1966; Acting on the Word, 1968; The Christian Existentialist, 1968; A Theology of Protest, 1970; Morality is for Persons, 1971; Hope is the Remedy, 1971; Faith and Morality in the Secular Age, 1973; Medical Ethics, 1973; Sin in the Secular Age, 1974; Evangelization Today, 1974; Prayer: Integration of Faith and Life, 1975; Ethics of Manipulation, 1976; Free and Faithful in Christ: Moral Theology for Priests and Laity, 3 vols., 1978–81; The Eucharist and Our Everyday Life, 1978; Called to Holiness, 1982; The Sacred Heart of Jesus and the Redemption of the World, 1983; Christian Maturity: Holiness in Today's World, 1983; Healing and Revealing: Wounded Healers Sharing in Christ's Mission, 1984; The Healing Power of Peace and Nonviolence, 1986. Add: Kirchplatz 10, D-8096 Gars am Inn, West Germany.

HARING, Joseph E. American, b. 1931. Economics. Pres., Pasadena Research Inst., Calif., since 1966. Asst. Prof. of Economics, 1959–64, and Chmn., Dept. of Economics, 1962–73, and Richard W. Millar Prof. of Economics and Finance, 1965–78, Occidental Coll., Los Angeles. Visiting Prof., Univ. of Southern California, Los Angeles, 1964–66, Univ. of Munich, and Univ. of Vienna, 1974–75. *Publs:* (ed.) An Approach to an Orderly and Efficient Transportation System for the Southern California Metropolis, 1960; Jobs for the Future, 1962; Migration and the Southern California Economy, 1964; Crisis in School Finance, 1966; The New Economics of Regulated Industries, 1968; Arresting Slums, 1968; New Shape of Southern California, 1971; Crime, Police and the Judiciary, 1972; (co-ed. and co-author) Utility Regulation During Inflation, 1971; (ed. and author) Urban and Regional Economics, 1972. Add: 607 Laguna Rd., Pasadena, Calif. 91105, U.S.A.

HARINGTON, Joy. British, b. 1914. Novels/Short stories. Freelance writer, dir. and actress, since 1970. Actress, Hollywood, London, and NYC, 1933–50; Dialogue Dir., MGM and Paramount, Hollywood, 1942–45; TV Dir. and Scriptwriter, BBC, London, 1950–70. *Publs:* Jesus of Nazareth (novel); Paul of Tarsus (novel). Add: 41 Primrose Mansions, London SW11 4EF, England.

HARKEY, Ira Brown, Jr. American, b. 1918. Autobiography/Memoirs/Personal, Biography. Reporter, Rewriter and Mag. Writer, New Orleans Times-Picayune, 1940–42 and 1946–49; Ed., Pascagoula, Miss. Chronicle, 1949–66; received Pulitzer Prize for distinguished editorial writing, 1963. *Publs:* The Smell of Burning Crosses, 1967; Pioneer Bush Pilot: The Story of Noel Wien, 1974; (co-author) Dr. Alton Ochsner: A Biography, 1989. Add: HCR 5, Box 574-540, Kerrville, Tex. 78028, U.S.A.

HARKNESS, David W. British, 1937. History. Prof. of Irish History, Queen's Univ. of Belfast, since 1975. Joint Ed., Irish Historical Studies,

1978–88. Lectr., 1965–72, and Sr. Lectr. in History, 1972–75, Univ. of Kent, Canterbury. *Publs:* The Restless Dominion: The Irish Free State and the British Commonwealth of Nations 1921–31, 1969; The Post-war World, 1974; (ed. with M. O'Dowd) The Town in Ireland, 1981; Northern Ireland since 1920, 1983. Add: Dept. of Modern History, Queen's Univ., Belfast BT7 1NN, Northern Ireland.

HARLAN, Glen. *See* **CEBULASH**, Mel.

HARLE, Elizabeth. *See* **ROBERTS**, Irene.

HARLING, Robert. Has also written as Nicholas Drew. British, b. 1910. Novels/Short stories, Mystery/Crime/Suspense, Art, Design (general), Homes/Gardens. Ed., House and Garden mag., London, since 1957. Former design consultant to the Times Literary Supplement and The Sunday Times, London. *Publs:* The London Miscellany: A Nineteenth-Century Scrapbook, 1937; Home: A Victorian Vignette, 1938; (as Nicholas Drew) Amateur Sailor, 1944; Notes on the Wood-Engravings of Eric Ravilious, 1946; The Steep Atlantick Stream (wartime autobiography), 1946; Edward Bawden, 1950; The Paper Palace (mystery novel), 1951; The Dark Saviour (mystery novel), 1952; The Enormous Shadow (mystery novel), 1955; The Endless Colonnade (mystery novel), 1958; (ed.) House and Garden's Interiors and Colour, 1959; (ed., with others) Small Houses, 1961; (ed.) House and Garden Book of Interiors, 1962; (ed.) House and Garden Book of Cottages, 1963; (ed.) The Modern Interior, 1964; (ed.) House and Garden Garden Book, 1965; (ed.) House and Garden First Cook Book, 1965; (ed.) House and Garden Book of Modern Houses and Conversions, 1966; (ed.) House and Garden Guide to Interior Decoration, 1967; The Hollow Sunday (mystery novel), 1967; (ed.) House and Garden Book of Holiday and Weekend Houses, 1968; (ed.) Historical Houses: Conversations in Stately Homes (in U.S. as The Great Houses and Finest Rooms in England), 1969; (ed.) House and Garden Modern Furniture and Decoration (in U.S. as Modern Furniture and Decoration), 1971; (ed.) House and Garden Dictionary of Design and Decoration (in U.S. as Studio Dictionary of Design and Decoration), 1973; The Athenian Widow (mystery novel), 1974; The Letter Forms and Type Design of Eric Gill, 1976; The Summer Portrait (novel), 1979; (with Miles Hadfield and Leonie Highton) British Gardeners: A Biographical Dictionary, 1980; (co-author) House and Gardens Book of Romantic Rooms, 1985. Add: c/o House and Garden, Vogue House, Hanover Sq., London W1R 0AD, England.

HARMAN, Jane. *See* **GILMAN**, George G.

HARMON, Maurice. Irish, b. 1930. Literature. Assoc. Prof. of Anglo-Irish Literature and Drama, University Coll., Dublin, since 1976 (Lectr. in English, 1964–76); Ed., Irish University Review, since 1970 (Ed., University Review, 1964–68). Member, Exec. Cttee., American Cttee. for Irish Studies; Member, Royal Irish Acad., since 1976. Teaching Fellow and Research Asst., Harvard Univ., Cambridge, Mass., 1955–58; Instr., Dept. of English, Lewis and Clark Coll., Portland, Ore., 1958–61; Asst. Prof., Dept. of English, Univ. of Notre Dame, Indiana, 1961–64. Chmn., Intnl. Assn. for the Study of Anglo-Irish Literature, 1979–82. *Publs:* Sean O'Faolain: A Critical Introduction, 1967, 1985; Modern Irish Literature, 1967; (ed.) Fenians and Fenianism (essays), 1968; (ed.) The Celtic Master (essays), 1969; (ed.) King Lear, by Shakespeare, 1970; (ed.) Romeo and Juliet, by Shakespeare, 1970; (ed.) J.M. Synge Centenary Papers 1971, 1971; (ed.) King Richard II, by Shakespeare, 1971; (ed.) Coriolanus, by Shakespeare, 1972; The Poetry of Thomas Kinsella, 1974; (ed. with Patrick Rafroidi) The Irish Novel in Our Times, 1976; Select Bibliography for the Study of Anglo-Irish Literature and its Background, 1976; (ed.) Richard Murphy: Poet of Two Traditions, 1978; (ed.) Irish Poetry after Yeats: Seven Poets, 1979; (ed.) Image and Illusion: Anglo-Irish Literature and Its Contexts, 1979; (with Roger McHugh) A Short History of Anglo-Irish Literature from Its Origins to the Present, 1982; (ed.) The Irish Writer and the City, 1985; Austin Clarke: A Critical Introduction, 1989. Add: Dept. of English, University Coll., Dublin 4, Ireland.

HARMSTON, Olivia. *See* **WEBER**, Nancy.

HARNACK, Curtis. American, b. 1927. Novels/Short stories, History, Autobiography/Memoirs/Personal. Fulbright Prof. of American Literature, Univ. of Tabriz, Iran, 1958–59; Lectr., Univ. of Iowa Writers' Workshop, Iowa City, 1959–60; Member of Literature Faculty, Sarah Lawrence Coll., Bronxville, N.Y., 1960–71; Exec. Dir., Corp of Yaddo, Saratoga Springs, N.Y., 1971–87. *Publs:* (ed. with Paul Engle) Prize Stories: The O. Henry Memorial Collection, 1958, and 1959; The Work of an Ancient Hand, 1960; Love and Be Silent, 1962; Persian Lions, Persian Lambs, 1965; We Have All Gone Away, 1973; Under My Wings Everything Prospers, 1977; Limits of the Land, 1979; Gentlemen on the Prairie, 1985. Add: 205 West 57th St., New York, N.Y. 10019, U.S.A.

HARNESS, Charles L(eonard). American, b. 1915. Science fiction/Fantasy, Earth sciences, Marketing. Mineral Economist, U.S. Bureau of Mines, Washington, D.C., 1941–47; Patent Attorney, American Cyanamid Co., Stamford, Conn., 1947–53, and W.R. Grace and Co., Columbia, Md., 1953–81. *Publs:* (with Nan C. Jensen) Marketing Magnesite and Allied Products, 1943; (with F.M. Barsigian) Mining and Marketing of Barite, 1946; Flight into Yesterday, 1953, as The Paradox of Men, 1955, in U.K. with Dome Around America, 1964; The Rose (short stories), 1966; The Ring of Ritornel, 1968; Wolfhead, 1978; The Catalyst, 1980; Firebird, 1981; The Venetian Court, 1984; Redworld, 1986; Krono, 1988. Add: 6705 White Gate Rd., Clarksville, Md. 21029, U.S.A.

HARPER, Daniel. *See* **BROSSARD,** Chandler.

HARPER, George Mills. American, b. 1914. Literature. Distinguished Prof. of English, Florida State Univ., Tallahassee, since 1978 (Prof. since 1970; Chmn. of Dept., 1970–73). Formerly, Dean of Arts and Sciences, Virginia Polytechnic Inst., Blacksburg. *Publs:* The Neoplatonism of William Blake, 1961; Yeats' Quest for Eden, 1966; (co-ed.) Selected Writings of Thomas Taylor the Platonist, 1969; Yeat's Golden Dawn, 1974; The Mingling of Heaven and Earth: Yeat's Theory of Theatre, 1975; Yeats and the Occult, 1976; (co-ed.) Letters to W.B. Yeats, 2 vols., 1977; (co-ed.) A Critical Edition of Yeats's "A Vision," 1978; W.B. Yeats and W.T. Horton, 1980; The Making of Yeats's A Vision, 1987. Add: 407 Plantation Rd., Tallahassee, Fla. 32303, U.S.A.

HARPER, Michael S(teven). American, b. 1938. Poetry. Dir. of Writing Prog., and Prof. of English since 1971, and Kapstein Prof. since 1980, Brown Univ., Providence, R.I. Member of faculty, Contra Costa Coll., San Pablo, Calif., 1964–68, and Reed Coll. and Lewis and Clark Coll., Portland, Ore., 1968–69. *Publs:* Dear John, Dear Coltrane, 1970; History is Your Own Heartbeat, 1971; Photographs: Negatives: History as Apple Tree, 1972; Song: I Want a Witness, 1972; Debridement, 1973; Nightmare Begins Responsibility, 1974; (ed.) Heartblow: Black Veils, 1974; Images of Kin: New and Selected Poems, 1977; (ed. with Robert B. Stepto) Chant of Saints: A Gathering of Afro-American Literature, Art, and Scholarship, 1979; (ed.) The Collected Poems of Sterling A. Brown, 1980; Rhode Island: Eight Poems, 1981; Healing Song for the Inner Ear, 1986. Add: Box 1852, Brown Univ., Providence, R.I. 02912, U.S.A.

HARRE Rom. British, b. 1927. Psychology, Sciences. Univ. Lectr. in Philosophy of Science, and Fellow, Linacre Coll., Oxford, since 1960; Adjunct Prof., State Univ. of N.Y., Binghamton, since 1973. Lectr., Univ. of Leicester, 1957–59. *Publs:* An Introduction to the Logic of the Sciences, 1960; Theories and Things, 1961; Matter and Method, 1964; The Anticipation of Nature, 1965; (ed.) The Principles of Linguistic Philosophy, by F. Waismann, 1965; (ed.) The Sciences, 1967; (ed.) How I See Philosophy, by F. Waismann, 1968; (ed.) Scientific Thought 1900-1960, 1969; The Method of Science, 1970; The Principles of Scientific Thinking, 1970; The Philosophies of Science, 1972; (with P.F. Second) The Explanation of Social Behaviour, 1972; (with E.H. Maddern) Casual Powers, 1972; (ed.) Problems of Scientific Revolution, 1975; Social Being, 1979; Personal Being, 1983; Varieties of Realism, 1986. Add: Linacre Coll., Oxford, OX1 3JA, England.

HARRELL, David Edwin, Jr. American, b. 1930. History, Race relations, Theology/Religion. Univ. Scholar and Chmn. of the Dept. of History, Univ. of Alabama at Birmingham, since 1985. Assoc. Prof. of History, East Tennessee State Univ., 1964–66; Assoc. Prof. of History, Univ. of Oklahoma, 1966–67; Assoc. Prof., Univ. of Georgia, Athens, 1967–70; Prof. of History and Chmn. of Dept., Univ. of Alabama, Birmingham, 1970–76, Univ. Scholar, 1976–81; Distinguished Prof. of History, Univ. of Arkansas, 1981–85. *Publs:* Quest for a Christian America, 1966; White Sects and Black Men in the Recent South, 1971; The Social Sources of Division in the Disciples of Christ, 1973; A Social History of the Disciples of Christ 1866-1900, 1974; All Things Are Possible, 1975; (ed.) The Varieties of Southern Evangelism, 1981; Oral Roberts: An American Life, 1985; Pat Robertson: A Personal Religious and Political Portrait, 1987. Add: 5253 Kirkwall, Birmingham, Ala. 35243, U.S.A.

HARRELL, Irene Burk. American, b. 1927. Poetry, Theology/Religion. Pres., Star Books, Inc., since 1982. Ed., Logos Intnl., 1969–79. *Publs:* Prayerables: Meditations of a Homemaker, 1967; Good Marriages Grow, 1968; Lo, I Am with You (also titled Miracles Through Prayer), 1970; (ed.) God Ventures, 1970; (ed.) Diary of Hope, by Luce Gray, 1970; (ed.) Some Gall and Other Recflections on Life, by James Buckingham, 1970; Ordinary Days with an Ordinary God: Prayerables II, 1971; (with Allen W. Harrell) The Opposite Sex, 1972; (with Floyd Miles) Black Tracks, 1972; (with Herbert Walker) God's Living Room, 1972; Security Blankets—Family Size, 1973; (with Michael Esses) Phenomenon of Obedience, 1973; Muddy Sneakers and Other Family Hassles, 1974; (with Harold Hill) How to Live Like a King's Kid, 1974; (with M. Esses) Jesus in Genesis, 1975; (with Iverna Tompkins) How To Be Happy in No Man's Land, 1975; Windows of Heaven, 1975; (with H. Hill) From Goo to You by Way of the Zoo? (also titled How Did It All Begin), 1976; (with S. Roth) Something for Nothing, 1976; (with M. Esses) Next Visitor to Planet Earth, 1976; Multiplied by Love: Lessons Learned Through the Holy Spirit, 1976; (with H. Hill) How to Be a Winner, 1976; (ed.) Make It Happen, by Ernst Schmidt, 1976; (with I. Tompkins) How to Live with Kids and Enjoy It, 1977; (with M. Esses) Jesus in Exodus, 1977; (with H. Hill) How to Live in High Victory, 1977; Super-Prayerables: To Add a Glow to Your Life, 1977; (with I. Tompkins) God and I: A Book About Faith and Prayer, 1978; (with H. Hill and G. Black) Instant Answers for King's Kids in Training, 1978; (with K. Golbeck), Lord, How Will You Get Me Out of This Mess?, 1978; (with H. Hill and G. Black) How to Flip Your Flab—Forever, 1979; (with Colleen Townsend Evans) The Vine Life, 1980; (with Nora Lam) China Cry, 1980; (with H. Hill) How to Live the Bible Like a King's Kid, 1980; (with K. Golbeck) Hopeless? Never!, 1981; (with Charlene Curry) The General's Lady, 1981; (with H. Hill) God's in Charge Here, 1982; (with Tommy Lewis) Isn't It Amazin'—? A Book about the Love of God, 1983; (with Mickey Jordan) Let Yesterday Go, 1984; (with B.J. Smith) Divorced!, 1983; (with Harold Hill) The Money Book for King's Kids, 1984; (with Harold Hill) ABC's for King's Kids, 1985; (with Gloria Phillips) A Heart Set Free, 1985; (ed. with Alie Harrell Benson) The Manufacturer's Handbook: The 4-in-1 Gospel for King's Kids, 1987, reissued as This Man Jesus, 1988. Add: 408 Pearson St., Wilson, N.C. 27893, U.S.A.

HARRELSON, Walter Joseph. American, b. 1919. Theology/Religion. Prof. of Old Testament since 1960, and Distinguished Prof. since 1975, Vanderbilt Univ. (Chmn., Dept. of Religion, Grad. Sch., 1961–62, 1964–67; Dean of the Divinity Sch., 1967–75). Instr. in Philosophy, Univ. of North Carolina, 1947; ordained Baptist Minister, 1949; Instr. in Old Testament, Union Theological Seminary, 1950; Instr., then Prof. of Old Testament, Andover Newton Theological Sch., 1951–55; Assoc. Prof. of Old Testament and Dean, Divinity Sch., Univ. of Chicago, 1955–60. Ed., Newsletter, American Soc. for the Study of Religion, 1964–67; Dir., Microfilming Project in Ethiopia, 1972–84; Ed., Religious Studies Review, 1974–79. *Publs:* Jeremiah: Prophet to the Nations, 1959; Interpreting the Old Testament, 1964; Teaching the Biblical Languages, 1967; From Fertility Cult to Worship, 1969, 1980; The Ten Commandments and Human Rights, 1980. Add: The Divinity Sch., Vanderbilt Univ., Nashville, Tenn. 37240, U.S.A.

HARRIFORD, Daphne. *See* **HARRIS,** Marion Rose.

HARRIS, Albert J. American, b. 1908. Language/Linguistics, Psychology. Prof. Emeritus, City Univ. of New York, since 1968 (Instr. to Asst. Prof. and Supvr., Remedial Reading Service, City Coll., 1935–49; Dir., Queens Coll. Educational Clinic, 1949–64; Prof. and Dir., Office of Educational Research and Evaluation, City Coll., 1964–68). Pres., Intnl. Reading Assn., 1957–58. *Publs:* (with E.R. Sipay) How to Increase Reading Ability, 1940, 8th ed. 1985; (with E.R. Sipay) Effective Teaching of Reading, 1962; (ed. with E.R. Sipay) Readings on Reading Instruction, 1963, 3rd ed., 1984; (co-author) The Macmillan Reading Program, 1965–74; (co-author) A Continuation of the CRAFT Project, 1968; (ed.) Casebook on Reading Disability, 1970; (with M.D. Jacobson) Basic Elementary Reading Vocabularies, 1972; (with E.R. Sipay) How to Teach Reading: A Competency Based Approach, 1978; (with M.D. Jacobson) Basic Reading Vocabularies, 1982. Add: Wellington G233, Century Village, West Palm Beach, Fla. 33417, U.S.A.

HARRIS, Aurand. American, b. 1915. Plays, Children's non-fiction. Drama teacher, Gary public schs., Indiana, 1939–41; Head of the Drama Dept., William Woods Coll., Fulton, Mo., 1942–45; Drama Teacher, Grace Church Sch., NYC, 1946–77; Teacher of Playwrighting and Dir., Univ. of Texas at Austin, 1977–1987; Univ. of Kansas, 1979; Calif. State Univ., Northridge, 1981; Purdue Univ.—Indiana Univ.—Indianapolis, 1985, New York Univ., 1988. Associated with summer theatre in Cape May, N.J., 1946, Bennington, Vt., 1947, Peaks Island, Me., 1948, Harwich, Mass., 1963–86; Cleveland Play House, Ohio, 1984–87; Akron Children's Theatre, Ohio, 1986–87. *Plays:* (all children's plays unless otherwise noted): Pinocchio and the Fire-Eater, 1949; Once upon a Clothesline, 1944; Ladies of the Mop (adult play), 1945; The Doughnut Hole, 1947; The Moon Makes Three, 1947; Seven League Boots, 1947; Circus Days, 1948, rev. ed. as Circus in the Wind, 1960; Madam Ada (adult play), 1948; Pinocchio and the Indians, 1949; And Never Been Kissed (adult play), 1950; Simple Simon; or Simon Big-Ears, 1952; Buffalo Bill, 1953; We Were Young That Year, 1954; The Plain Princess, 1954; The Flying Prince, 1958, 1985; Junket (No Dogs Allowed), 1959; The Brave Little Tailor, 1960; Pocahontas, 1961; Androcles and the Lion, 1964; Rags to Riches, 1965; A Doctor in Spite of Himself, 1966; The Comical Tragedy or Tragical Comedy of Punch and Judy, 1969; Just So Stories, 1971; Ming Lee and the Magic Tree, 1971; Steal Away Home, 1972; Peck's Bad Boy, 1973; Robin Goodfellow, 1974; Yankee Doodle, 1975; Star Spangled Minstrel, 1975; Six Plays for Children, 1977; A Toby Show, 1978; Romancers (adaptations, adult), 1978; Ralph Roister Doister, 1978; Candada, 1979; (co-ed.) Plays Children Love: An Anthology, 1979; Cyrano De Bergerac, 1980; The Arkansaw(sic) Bear, 1980; The Magician's Nephew, 1984; Ride a Blue Horse, 1986; Huck Finn's Story, 1988; Plays Children Love: An Anthology (vol.2), 1988; Monkey Magic, 1989. Add: c/o Anchorage Press, Box 8067, New Orleans, La. 70182, U.S.A.

HARRIS, Bruce Fairgray. New Zealander, b. 1921. Classics, History. Hon. Visiting Fellow in History, Macquarie Univ., since 1986 (Sr. Lectr., 1970–71; Assoc Prof., 1972–86; Head of the Sch. of History, Philosophy, and Politics, 1979–84). Australian Ed., Prudentia journal, 1969–87. *Publs:* Cicero as an Academic: A Study of De Natura Deorum, 1961; Bithynia under Trajan: Greek and Roman Views of the Principate, 1963; (ed. and contrib.) Auckland Classical Essays: Presented to E.M. Blaiklock, 1970; (ed.) The Idea of a University, 1983. Add: Sch. of History, Philosophy and Politics, Macquarie Univ., Sydney, N.S.W. 2109, Australia.

HARRIS, Chauncy D(ennison). American, b. 1914. Geography. Samuel N. Harper Distinguished Service Prof. of Geography Emeritus, Univ. of Chicago, since 1984 (on faculty, 1943–84; Dean, Social Sciences, 1954–60; Dir., Center for Intnl. Studies, 1966–84; Vice-Pres., Academic Resources, 1975–78). *Publs:* (ed.) Economic Geography of the USSR, edited by S.S. Balzak, V.F. Vasyutin and Ya. G. Feigin, 1949; (compiler with J.D. Fellman) International List of Geographical Serials, 1960, 3rd ed. 1980; (compiler) Annotated World List of Selected Current Geographical Serials, 1960, 4th ed. 1980; (ed.) Soviet Geography: Accomplishments and Tasks, edited by I.P Gerasimov, 1962; Cities of the Soviet Union: Studies of Their Functions, Size, Density and Growth, 1970; (compiler) Guide to Geographical Bibliographies and Reference Works in Russian or on the Soviet Union, 1975; Bibliography of Geography, part I: General Aids, 1976, and Regional, part II: vol. 1, U.S.A., 1984; (ed.) A Geographical Bibliography for American Libraries, 1985; (ed.) Directory of Soviet Geographers 1946–1987, 1988. Add: Dept of Geography, Univ. of Chicago, 5828 University Ave., Chicago, Ill. 60637, U.S.A.

HARRIS, Christie (Lucy Irwin). Canadian (b. American), b. 1907. Children's fiction, Mythology/Folklore. School-teacher, British Columbia, 1925–32; freelance scriptwriter, CBC, 1936–62; Women's Ed. of a newspaper, British Columbia, 1951–57. *Publs:* Cariboo Trail, 1957; Once upon a Totem (Indian legends), 1963; You Have to Draw the Line Somewhere, 1964; West with the White Chiefs, 1965; Raven's Cry, 1966; Confessions of a Toe-Hanger, 1967; Forbidden Frontier, 1968; Let X Be Excitement, 1969; (with Moira Johnston) Figleafing Through History: The Dynamics of Dress, 1971; (with Tom Harris) Mule Lib, 1972; Secret in the Stlalakum Wild, 1972; Once More Upon a Totem (Indian legends), 1973; Sky Man on the Totem Pole?, 1975; Mouse Woman and the Vanished Princesses (Indian legends), 1976; Mouse Woman and the Mischief Makers (Indian legends), 1977; Mystery at the Edge of Two Worlds, 1978; Mouse Woman and the Muddleheads (Indian legends), 1979; The Trouble with Princesses (Indian legends), 1980; The Trouble with Adventurers (Indian legends), 1982. Add: Suite 1604, 2045 Nelson St., Vancouver, B.C. V6G 1N8, Canada.

HARRIS, Dudley Arthur. South African, b. 1925. Chemistry. With South African Council for Scientific and Industrial Research, 1948–51; Dir. and Analytical and Consulting Chemist, J. Muller Labs., Cape Town, 1953–81. *Publs:* Hydroponics: The Gardening Without Soil, 1966, 4th ed. 1974; Hydroponics, 1975, 7th ed., 1987. Add: 55 Geneva Dr., Camps Bay, Cape Town, South Africa.

HARRIS, Fred R. American, b. 1930. Politics/Government. Prof. of Political Science, Univ. of New Mexico, since 1976. Admitted to Oklahoma Bar, 1954; Sr. Partner in law firm of Harris, Newcombe, Redman and Doolin, Lawton, Okla., 1954–64; Member, Oklahoma State Senate,

1956–64; Senator from Oklahoma (Democrat), U.S. Senate, 1964–72; served on the Senate Finance Cttee., Govt. Operations Cttee., and Select Cttee. on Small Business. Chmn., Democratic National Cttee., 1969. *Publs:* Alarms and Hopes, 1968; Now Is the Time, 1971; The New Populism, 1973; Social Science and Public Policy, 1973; Potomac Fever, 1976; America's Democracy: The Ideal and Reality, 1980, 1983, 1986; America's Legislative Processes: Congress and the States, 1983; Readings on the Body Politic, 1987; Understanding American Government, 1988; Race and Poverty in the United States, 1988. Add: P.O. Box 1203, Corrales, N.M. 87048, U.S.A.

HARRIS, Geraldine. British, b. 1951. Children's fiction, Children's non-fiction, Mythology, Geography. Freelance Egyptologist. *Publs:* White Cranes Castle, 1979; Prince of the Godborn, 1982; The Children of the Wind, 1982; The Dead Kingdom, 1983; The Seventh Gate, 1983; Gods and Pharaohs from Egyptian Mythology, 1983; The Junior Atlas of Ancient Egypt, 1989; New Kingdom Votive Offerings to Hathor, 1989. Add: c/o Macmillan Publishers, 4 Little Essex St., London WC2R 3LF, England.

HARRIS, Helen(a) (Barbara Mary). British, b. 1927. Agriculture, Archaeology, Local history/Rural topics. Hon. Ed., The Devon Historian, since 1985. Dairy Adviser, Ministry of Agriculture, 1948–56. *Publs:* The Industrial Archaeology of Dartmoor, 1968, 1986; The Industrial Archaeology of the Peak District, 1971; (with Monica Ellis) The Bude Canal, 1972; The Grand Western Canal, 1973. Add: Hirondelles, 22 Churchill Rd., Whitchurch, Tavistock, Devon, England.

HARRIS, Herbert. British, b. 1911. Mystery/Crime/Suspense. Chmn., Freelance Section, Inst. of Journalists, 1957; Founder, 1956, and former Hon. Ed., Red Herrings journal, and Chmn., 1969–70, Crime Writers Assn. *Publs:* Who Kill to Live, 1962; Painted in Blood, 1972; Serpents in Paradise, 1975; (ed.) John Creasey's Mystery Bedside Book (10 vols.), 1966–75; The Angry Battalion, 1976, (ed.) John Creasey's Crime Collection, 13 vols., 1977–89; (ed.) Great Short Stories of Scotland Yard (in U.S. as Great Cases of Scotland Yard), 1978; (ed.) A Handful of Heroes: Five Short Stories, 1978; 3,000 short stories published in 16 languages in 30 countries. Add: 20 Castle Ct., Ventnor, Isle of Wight, England.

HARRIS, Jana. American, b. 1947. Novels/Short stories, Poetry. Director, Writers in Performance Series, Manhattan Theatre Club, NYC, since 1980. Educational Mathematics Consultant, Project SEED Inc., Lawrence Hall of Science, Univ. of California, Berkeley, 1970–76; Instr., Poetry in the Schools, San Francisco State Univ., 1972–78; Instr. in Creative Writing, Modesto Jr. Coll., California, 1975–78; Poet-in-Residence, Alameda County Neighborhood Arts, California, 1977–78; Instr. in Creative Writing, New York Univ., 1980. *Publs:* This House That Rocks with Every Truck on the Road (poetry), 1976; Letters from the Promised Land: Alaska Poems, 1976; Pin Money (poetry), 1977; The Book of Common People: Poems in a Dime Store Sack, 1978; The Clackamas (poetry), 1980; Alaska (novel), 1980; Who's That Pushy Bitch? (poetry), 1981; Manhattan as a Second Language, and Other Poems, 1982; The Sourlands (poetry), 1989. Add: 32814 120 St. S.E., Sultan, Wash. 98294, U.S.A.

HARRIS, John. Also writes as Mark Hebden and Max Hennessy. Novels/Short stories, Mystery/Crime/Suspense, Children's fiction, History. History teacher, journalist, and cartoonist, then full-time writer. *Publs:* The Lonely Corner, 1951; Hallelujah Corner, 1952; The Sea Shall Not Have Them (in USA as The Undaunted), 1953; The Claws of Mercy, 1955; Getaway (in USA as Close to the Wind), 1956; The Sleeping Mountain, 1958; Road to the Coast (in USA as Adventure's End), 1959; Sunset at Sheba, 1960; Covenant with Death, 1961; The Spring of Malice, 1962; The Unforgiving Wind, 1964; Vardy, 1964; The Cross of Lazzaro, 1965; The Old Trade of Killing, 1966; Light Cavalry Action, 1967; Right of Reply, 1968; The Mercenaries (in USA as The Jade Wind), 1969; The Courtney Entry, 1970; The Mustering of the Hawks, 1972; A Kind of Courage, 1972; The Professionals, 1973; Smiling Willie and the Tiger, 1974; Ride Out the Storm, 1974; The Victors, 1975; Take or Destroy!, 1976; Army of Shadows, 1977; The Fox from His Lair, 1978; The Revolutionaries, 1978; Corporal Cotton's Little War, 1979 (in USA as Cotton's War, 1980); Swordpoint, 1980; North Strike, 1981; Live Free or Die!, 1982; Harkaway's Sixth Column, 1983; Up for Grabs, 1985; A Funny Place to Hold a War, 1986; China Seas, 1987; The Thirty Days War, 1988; Picture of Defeat, 1988; So Far From God, 1989; novels as Max Hennessy—The Lion at Sea (trilogy): The Lion at Sea, 1977, The Dangerous Years, 1978, and Back to Battle, 1979; Soldier of the Queen, 1980; Blunted Lance, 1981; The Iron Stallions, 1982; The Bright Blue Sky, 1982; The Challenging Heights, 1983; Once More the hawks, 1984;

The Crimson Wind, 1985; crime novels as Mark Hebden—What Changed Charley Farthing, 1965; Eyewitness, 1966; The Errant Knights, 1968; Portrait in a Dusty Frame, 1969, in USA as Grave Journey, 1970; Mark of Violence, 1970; A Killer for the Chairman, 1972; The Dark Side of the Island, 1973; A Pride of Dolphins, 1974; The League of 89, 1977; Death Set to Music, 1979; Pel and the Faceless Corpse, 1979; Pel under Pressure, 1980; Pel Is Puzzled, 1981; Pel and the Staghound, 1982; Pel and the Bombers, 1982; Pel and the Predators, 1984; Pel and the Pirates, 1984; Pel and the Prowler, 1985; Pel and the Paris Mob, 1986; Pel among the Pueblos, 1987; Pel and the Touch of Pitch, 1988; Pel and the Picture of Innocence, 1988; for children—The Charge of the Light Brigade, 1965; The Wonderful Ice Cream, 1966; The Sword of General Frapp, 1967; Sir Sam and the Dragon, 1968; Sam and the Kite, 1968; The Fledglings, 1971; A Matter of Luck, 1971; A Tale of a Tail, 1975; The Interceptors, 1977; other—The Somme: Death of a Generation, 1966; The Big Slump, 1967; The Gallant Six Hundred, 1973; The Indian Mutiny, 1973; Much Sounding of Bugles: The Siege of Chitral 1895, 1975; Dunkirk, 1980; Without Trace, 1981; The Court Martial of Lord Lucan, 1987; Scapegoat, 1988. Add: Beaumont, Rookwood Rd., West Wittering, Sussex, England.

HARRIS, John F(rederick). British, b. 1931. Architecture, Art, Crafts, Homes/Gardens. Member of the Council, Victorian Soc., since 1974; Trustee, American Museum in Britain, since 1974; Ed., Studies in Architecture, since 1976; Pres., Intnl. Confederation on Architectural Museums, since 1981; Chmn., Colnaghi & Co., since 1982. Mellon Lectr., Natl. Gallery, Washington, D.C., 1981; Slade Prof. of Fine Art, Oxford Univ., 1982–83. Member of the Council, Drawing Soc. of America, 1962–68; Member, Paul Mellon's Advisory Bd., 1966–78; Member of Natl. Council, Intnl. Council of Monuments and Sites, 1976–83. Curator, British Architectural Library Drawing Collection and Heinz Gallery, London, 1960–86. Publs: English Decorative Ironwork, 1960; Regency Furniture Designs, 1961; (ed.) The Prideaux Collection of Topographical Drawings, 1963; Georgian Country Houses, 1968; Sir William Chambers, Knight of the Polar Star, 1970; (ed.) The Rise and Progress of the Present State of Planting, 1970; (co-ed.) The Country Seat, 1970; Catalogue of British Drawings for Architecture, Decoration, Sculpture, and Landscape Gardening in American Collections, 1971; A Country House Index, 1971, 1979; Catalogue of the Drawings Collection RIBA: Colin Campbell, 1973; Headfort House and Robert Adam, 1973; Gardens of Delight: The Art of Thomas Robins, 1976, and The Rococo English Landscape of Thomas Robins, 1978; (ed. with A.A. Tait) Catalogue of the Drawings by Inigo Jones, 1979; A Garden Alphabet, 1979; (ed.) The Garden Show, 1979; The Artist and the Country House, 1979; The English Garden 1530-1840, 1981; The Palladians, 1981; William Talman: Maverick Architect, 1982; Architectural Drawings in the Cooper Hewitt Museum, New York, 1982; (ed. with G. Stops) Britannia Illustrated, 1984; The British Country House, 1985; Town Reeves of Bungay 1725-1986: Study of a Unique and Ancient Office and Those Who Have Occupied It, 1986. Add: 10 Limerston St., London SW10 0HH, England.

HARRIS, Jonathan. American, b. 1921. Children's non-fiction, History, Politics/Government, Social commentary, Sports. Fulltime writer since 1983. Social Studies Teacher, Paul D. Schreiber High School, Port Washington, N.Y., 1962–83. Publs: Hiroshima: A Study in Science, Politics, and the Ethics of War, 1970; Scientists in the Shaping of America, 1971; Judgement: A Simulated Trial of Harry S. Truman, 1977; The New Terrorism: Poltics of Violence, 1983; Super Mafia: Organized Crime Threatens America, 1984; A Statue for America: The First 100 Years of the Statue of Liberty, 1986; Drugged Athletes: The Crisis in American Sports, 1987; The Land and the People of France, 1988. Add: Hillside Ave., Roslyn Heights, N.Y. 11577, U.S.A.

HARRIS, Larry Mark. See JANIFER, Laurence M.

HARRIS, Lavinia. See ST. JOHN, Nicole.

HARRIS, Leonard. American, b. 1929. Novels, Screenplays. Freelance journalist, and writer, critic, and host for network-and cable-television and radio; also actor. Writer, CBS This Morning, since 1987. Reporter, Writer, and Ed., Hartford Courant, Connecticut, 1958–60; Reporter, and Critic, New York World Telegram & Sun, 1960–66. Critic, WCBS-TV News, NYC, 1966–74; Adjunct Assoc. Prof., Fordham Univ., Bronx, N.Y., 1969–74, and Hunter Coll., NYC, 1974–75; NYC Theatre Critic, Soho News, NYC, 1977–78, and The Hollywood Reporter, 1982; Media Commentator, Entertainment Tonight, 1983–84; Writer, CBS Morning Program, 1986–87. Publs: The Masada Plan, 1976; Don't Be No Hero, 1978; The Hamptons, 1981. Add: 330 E. 71st St., New York, N.Y. 10021, U.S.A.

HARRIS, MacDonald. American, b. 1921. Novels/Short stories. Publs: Private Demons, 1961; Mortal Leap, 1964; Trepleff, 1968; They Sailed Alone (travel), 1972; Bull Fire, 1973; The Balloonist, 1976; Yukiko, 1977; Pandora's Galley, 1979; The Treasure of Sainte Foy, 1980; Herma, 1981; Screenplay, 1982; Tenth, 1984; The Little People, 1986; Glowstone, 1987; The Cathay Stories and Other Fictions, 1988. Add: c/o William Morrow, 105 Madison Ave., New York, N.Y. 10016, U.S.A.

HARRIS, Marilyn. American, b. 1931. Novels/Short stories, Historical/Romance/Gothic, Children's fiction. Publs: King's Ex (short stories), 1967; In the Midst of Earth, 1969; The Peppersalt Land (juvenile), 1970; The Runaway's Diary (juvenile), 1971; Hatter Fox, 1973; The Conjurers, 1974; Bledding Sorrow (romance), 1976; Eden series (romance): This Other Eden, 1977, The Prince of Eden, 1978, The Eden Passion, 1979, The Women of Eden, 1980, Eden Rising, 1982; The Last Great Love, 1982; The Portent, 1982; The Diviner, 1984; Warrick, 1985; Night Games, 1987; American Eden, 1987. Add: 1846 Rolling Hills, Norman, Okla. 73069, U.S.A.

HARRIS, Marion (Rose). Also writes as Rose Young, Henry Charles, Daphne Harriford, and Keith Rogers. British, b. 1925. Novels/Short stories, Children's non-fiction, Cookery/Gastronomy/Wine, Homes/Gardens. Ed. and Proprietor, Regional Feature Service, 1964–72; Editorial Controller, W. Foulsham & Co. Ltd., publishers, Slough, Bucks., 1974–83. Publs: Fresh Fruit Dishes, 1963; Making a House a Home, 1964; The Awful Slimmer, 1967; Flower Arranging, 1968; (as Daphne Harriford) Around the Home, 1974; (as Keith Rogers) Plumbing Repairs and Maintenance, 1974; Love Can Conquer, 1974; (as Henry Charles) Easy Guide to Growing Vegetables, 1975; When the Clouds Clear, 1975; Secret of Abbey Place, 1976; Captain of Her Heart, 1976; Just a Handsome Stranger, 1983; The Queen's Windsor, 1985; Soldiers' Wives, 1986; Officers' Ladies, 1987; Nesta, 1988; Amelda, 1989; Megan, 1990. Add: Walpole Cottage, Long Dr., Burnham, Bucks. SL1 8AJ England.

HARRIS, (Evelyn) Marjorie. (Viscountess St. Davids). British, b. 1919. Business/Trade/Industry, Industrial relations. Publs. Officer, and Information and Publs. Officer, 1948–60, Ed., 1960–67, Mgr., Publishing and Press, 1967–77, and Asst. Dir., Services, 1978–79, Inst. of Personnel Mgmt., London. Publs: Married Women in Industry, 1954; (ed.) Equal Pay, 1955; (ed.) The Realities of Productivity Bargaining, 1968; How to Get a Job: A Practical Guide for Young People, 1971; How to Get a Job, 1976, 1979; (with D. MacKenzie Davey) Judging People, 1982; (with J. Batten) Everyday Law, 1987. Add: 15 St. Mark's Cres., London NW1, England.

HARRIS, Mark. American, b. 1922. Novels/Short stories, Plays/Screenplays, Autobiography/Memoirs/Personal, Biography. Prof. of English, Arizona State Univ., Tempe, since 1980. Teacher, San Francisco State Coll., Calif., 1954–68, Purdue Univ., Lafayette Ind., 1967–70, California Inst. of the Arts, Valencia, 1970–73, Immaculate Heart Coll., Los Angeles, 1973–74, and Univ. of Southern California, Los Angeles, 1973–75; Prof. of English, Univ. of Pittsburgh, 1975–80. Publs: Trumpet to the World, 1946; City of Discontent, 1952; The Southpaw, 1953; Bang the Drum Slowly, 1956; Something About a Soldier, 1957; A Ticket for a Seamstitch, 1957; Wake Up, Stupid, 1959; Friedman & Son (play), 1963; Mark the Glove Boy, or The Last Days of Richard Nixon (autobiography), 1964; Twentyone Twice: A Journal, 1966; The Goy, 1970; Killing Everybody, 1973; Best Father Ever Invented: An Autobiography, 1976; (co-ed.) The Design of Fiction (anthology), 1976; It Looked Like For Ever, 1979; Short Work of It: Selected Writings, 1979; (ed.) The Heart of Boswell, 1980; Saul Bellow: Drumlin Woodchuck (non-fiction), 1980; Lying in Bed, 1984. Add: c/o Fox Chase Agency, Public Ledger Bldg., Independence Sq., Philadelphia, Pa. 19106, U.S.A.

HARRIS, Peter Bernard. British, b. 1929. International relations/Current affairs, Politics/Government. Prof. and Head, Dept. of Political Science, Univ. of Hong Kong, since 1970. Journalist, since 1960. Sr. Lectr., Univ. of Natal Durban, 1964–67; Prof., and Head of Dept., Univ. Coll. of Rhodesia, Salisbury, 1967–70. Publs: Interest Groups in South African Politics, 1968; The Withdrawal of the Major European Powers from Africa, 1969; (co-author) Studies in African Politics, 1970; (co-author) South African Government and Politics, 1971; The Commonwealth: Political Realities, 1975; Foundations of Political Science, 1976; Hong Kong: A Study in Bureaucratic Politics, 1978; Political China Observed, 1980; Public Affairs and Public Administration in Hong Kong, 1982; Hong Kong: Bureaucracy and Politics, 1988. Add: 2 University Dr., Hong Kong.

HARRIS, Philip Robert. American, b. 1926. Administration/Management, Education. Pres., Harris Intnl. Ltd., La Jolla, Calif., since 1972; Sr. Research Assoc., Calif. Space Inst., since 1984. Vice Pres., St. Francis Coll., Brooklyn, N.Y., 1956–64; Co-author, Insight Series, Harcourt Brace Jovanovich, NYC, 1957–65; Co-author, Challenge Series, St. Paul Publs., Allahabad, India, 1963; Visiting Prof., Pennsylvania State Univ., University Park, 1965–66; Senior Assoc., Leadership Resources Inc., 1966–69; Visiting Prof., Temple Univ., Philadelphia, 1967–69; Vice Pres., Copley Intnl. Corp., 1970–71. *Publs:* (ed.) Regents Study Guide to State Scholarships, 1949, 1965; (ed.) Official Guide to Catholic Educational Institutions, 1959; (co-author) It's Your Future, 1964; (ed.) Impact (textbook), 1965; Organizational Dynamics, 1973; Effective Management of Change, 1976; (with D. Harris) Improving Management Communication Skills, 1978; (with R. Moran) Managing Cultural Differences, 1979, 1987; (ed. with G. Malin) Innovations in Global Consultation, 1980; (with R.T. Moran) Managing Cultural Synergy, 1982; New Worlds, New Ways, New Management, 1983; (ed.) Global Strategies for Human Resource Development, 1984; Innovations in Global Consultation, 1984; Management in Transition, 1985; High Performance Leadership, 1989; (ed.) Human Enterprise in Space, 1990. Add: 2702 Costebelle Drive, La Jolla, Calif. 92037, U.S.A.

HARRIS, Ronald Walter. British, b. 1916. History, Intellectual history, Politics/Government. Head of History Dept., and Master of Studies, King's Sch., Canterbury, Kent, since 1946. Gen. Ed., Blandford History Series, Blandford History and Literature, and Gollancz Men and Ideas Series. *Publs:* Science, Mind and Matter, 1960; Political Ideas 1760-92, 1963; England in the 18th Century, 1963; Absolutism and Enlightenment, 1964; Introduction to the Twentieth Century, 1966; Reason and Nature, 1968; Romanticism and the Social Order, 1969; Clarendon and the English Revolution, 1983. Add: 14 Barton Rd., Canterbury, Kent, England.

HARRIS, Rosemary (Jeanne). British, b. 1923. Historical/Romance/Gothic, Children's fiction, Mythology/Folklore. Formerly, picture restorer, Reader for Metro-Goldwyn-Mayer, 1951–52, and Children's Book Reviewer, The Times, London, 1970–73. *Publs:* The Summer-House (romance), 1956; Voyage to Cythera (romance), 1958; Venus with Sparrows (romance), 1961; All My Enemies (romance), 1967; The Nice Girl's Story (romance), 1968, in U.S. as Nor Evil Dreams, 1974; The Moon in the Cloud, 1968; A Wicked Pack of Cards (romance), 1969; The Shadow on the Sun, 1970; The Seal-Singing, 1971; The Child in the Bamboo Grove, 1972; The Bright and Morning Star, 1972; The King's White Elephant, 1973; The Double Snare (romance), 1974; The Lotus and the Grail: Legends from East to West (abridged ed. in U.S. as Sea Magic and Other Stories of Enchantment), 1974; The Flying Ship, 1975; The Little Dog of Fo, 1976; Three Candles for the Dark (romance), 1976; I Want to Be a Fish, 1977; A Quest for Orion, 1978; Beauty and the Beast (folklore), 1979; Green Finger House, 1980; Tower of the Stars, 1980; The Enchanted Horse, 1981; Janni's Stork, 1981; Zed, 1982; Summers of the Wild Rose, 1987; (ed.) Love and the Merry-Go-Round (poetry anthology), 1988. Add: c/o A.P. Watt Ltd., 20 John St., London WC1N 2DR, England.

HARRIS, Roy. British, b. 1931. Language/Linguistics. Fellow, Worcester Coll., Oxford, and Prof. of General Linguistics, Oxford Univ., since 1978 (Medieval and Modern Languages faculty, 1961–76, and Prof. of the Romance Languages, 1976–77, Oxford Univ.; Fellow and Tutor, Keble Coll., Oxford, 1967–76). Ed., Language and Communication, since 1980. Lectr., Ecole Normale Superieure, Paris, 1956–57; Asst. Lectr., 1957–58, and Lectr., 1958–60, Univ. of Leicester. Member of the Council, Philological Soc., 1978–82. *Publs:* Synonymy and Linguistic Analysis, 1973; Communication and Language, 1978; The Language-Makers, 1980; The Language Myth, 1981; (trans.) Course in General Linguistics, by de Saussure, 1983; The Origin of Writing, 1986; Reading Saussure, 1987; Language, Saussure and Wittgenstein, 1988; (ed.) Linguistic Thought in England, 1914–1945, 1988. Add: 2 Paddox Close, Oxford OX2 7LR, England.

HARRIS, Sheldon H. American, b. 1928. History, International relations/Current affairs, Music. Prof. of American History, California State Univ. at Northridge, since 1970 (Asst. Prof., 1963–66; Assoc. Prof., 1967–70). Visiting Prof., Univ. of California at Los Angeles, since 1965. *Publs:* Paul Cuffe: Black America and the African Return, 1972; Intervention: President Johnson's Decision to Intervene in Vietnam, 1972; The Prohibition Era: A Study of Law and Private Morality, 1974; Blues Who's Who, 1979; (with Clyde Bernhardt) I Remember, 1986. Add: 17144 Nanette St., Granada Hills, Calif. 91344, U.S.A.

HARRIS, Walter A. American, b. 1929. Economics, Politics/Government. Principal, Sheepshead Bay High Sch., NYC, since 1974.

Teacher, Social Studies, Midwood High Sch., NYC, 1957–65; Asst. Principal, Port Richmond High Sch., NYC, 1965–74. *Publs:* Workbook: The Modern Economy in Action, 1968; Introductory Economics, 1970; Economics for Everybody, 1973; Current Issues in American Democracy, 1975; Western Civilization, 1982. Add: 194 Melhorn Rd., Staten Island, N.Y. 10314, U.S.A.

HARRIS, (Theodore) Wilson. British, b. 1921. Novels/Short stories, Poetry, Literature. Sr. Surveyor, Govt. of British Guiana, 1955–58. *Publs:* Fetish (poetry), 1951; Eternity to Season (poetry), 1954, 1978; Palace of the Peacock, 1960; The Far Journey of Oudin, 1961; The Whole Armour, 1962; The Secret Ladder, 1963; Heartland, 1964; The Eye of the Scarecrow, 1965; Tradition and the West Indian Novel, 1965; Tradition, The Writer and Society: Critical Essays, 1967; The Waiting Room, 1967; Tumatumari, 1968; Ascent to Omai, 1970; The Sleepers of Roraima, 1970; The Age of the Rainmakers, 1971; Companions of the Day and Night, 1975; Da Silva da Silva's Cultivated Wilderness and Genesis of the Clowns, 1977; The Tree of the Sun, 1978; Explorations: A Selection of Talks and Articles, 1981; The Angel at the Gate, 1982; The Womb of Space: The Cross-Cultural Imagination, 1983; Carnival, 1985; The Infinite Rehearsal, 1987. Add: c/o Faber & Faber Ltd., 3 Queen Sq., London WC1N 3AU, England.

HARRISON, Bernard. British, b. 1933. Literature, Philosophy. Prof. of Philosophy, Univ. of Sussex, since 1985 (Lectr., 1963–71; Reader, 1971–85). Lectr., Univ. of Toronto, 1960–62; Asst. Lectr., Univ. of Birmingham, 1962–63; Assoc. Prof., Univ. of Cincinnati, 1967–68. *Publs:* (co-author) Violence (philosophical essays), 1971; Meaning and Structure: An Essay on the Philosophy of Language, 1972; Form and Content, 1973; Fielding's "Tom Jones": The Novelist as Moral Philosopher, 1975; (co-author) The Modern English Novel, 1976; (co-author) Communication and Understanding, 1978; An Introduction to the Philosophy of Language, 1979; (co-author) Philosophers of the Enlightenment, 1979; (co-author) Codes, Languages, Traductions, 1980. Add: Dept. of Philosophy, Univ. of Sussex, Brighton, Sussex, England.

HARRISON, Brian Fraser. British, b. 1918. Business/Trade/Industry, Law. Military artist, since 1983. Partner, Mace & Jones, Solicitors, Liverpool, 1948–83. *Publs:* Advocacy at Petty Sessions, 1952, 1959; Work of a Magistrate, 1964, 3rd. ed. 1975; A Business of Your Own, 1968; A Business of Your Own Today, 1973; How to Make Money as a Freelance Book-Keeper, 1982; How to Select your Professional Advisers . . . and Then Get the Best Out of Them, 1982; How to Be a Successful Outside Caterer, 1983; How to Make Money as a Neighbourhood Handyman, 1983; How to Sell Your Car Successfully, 1983; How to Choose a Second Hand Car, 1983; How to Get What You *Really* Want Out of Life, 1984; Become Slim—Stay Slim, 1985. Add: Peddars Cottage, The Street, Hessett, Bury St. Edmunds, Suffolk IP30 9AX, England.

HARRISON, Chip. *See* **BLOCK,** Lawrence.

HARRISON, David Lakin. British, b. 1926. Natural history, Travel/Exploration/Adventure. Gen. medical practitioner, since 1956. Dir., Harrison Zoological Museum, Sevenoaks. House Physician, St. Thomas's Hosp., London, 1951–52. *Publs:* Footsteps in the Sand: The Mammals of Arabia, 3 vols.; Mammals of the Arabian Gulf. Add: Bowerwood House, St. Botolph's Road, Sevenoaks, Kent, England.

HARRISON, Elizabeth Fancourt. Romance. *Publs:* Coffee at Dobree's, 1965; The Physicians, 1966; The Ravelston Affair, 1967; Emergency Call, 1970; Accident Call, 1971; Ambulance Call, 1972; Surgeon's Call, 1973; On Call, 1974; Hospital Call, 1975; Dangerous Call, 1976; To Mend a Heart, 1977; Young Doctor Goddard, 1978; A Doctor Called Caroline, 1979; A Surgeon Called Amanda, 1982; A Surgeon's Life, 1983; Marrying a Doctor, 1984; Surgeon's Affair, 1985; A Surgeon at St. Marks, 1986; The Surgeon She Married, 1988. Add: 71 Wingfield Rd., Kingston upon Thames, Surrey KT2 5LR, England.

HARRISON, Everett F(alconer). American, b. 1902. Theology/Religion. Prof. Emeritus of New Testament, Fuller Theological Seminary, Pasadena, Calif., since 1972 (Prof., 1947–67; Sr. Prof., 1967–72). New Testament Ed., revision of Intnl. Standard Bible Encyclopaedia, since 1965. Prof. of New Testament, Dallas Theological Seminary, Tex., 1935–40 and 1944–47. *Publs:* The Son of God among the Sons of Men, 1949, as Jesus and His Contemporaries, 1970; (ed.) Alford's Greek Testament, 1958; (ed.) Dictionary of Theology, 1960; John: A Brief Commentary, 1962; (ed. with Charles F. Pfeiffer) Wycliffe Bible Commentary, 1962; Introduction to the New Testament, 1964, 1971; A Short Life of Christ, 1968; Colossians: Christ All-Sufficient, 1971;

Acts: The Expanding Church, 1975; The Apostolic Church, 1985. Add: 2889 San Pasqual St., Pasadena, Calif. 91107, U.S.A.

HARRISON, Harry. Pseud. for Henry Maxwell Dempsey. American, b. 1925. Science fiction/Fantasy, Children's fiction. Vice Pres., Science Fiction Writers of America, 1968–69. *Publs:* Deathworld, 3 vols. 1960–68; The Stainless Steel Rat series, 7 vols.,1961–87; Planet of the Damned, 1962; War with the Robots (short stories), 1962; Bill, the Gallactic Hero, 1965; Two Tales and 8 Tomorrows (short stories), 1965; Plague From Space, 1966; Make Room! Make Room!, 1966; The Technicolor Time Machine, 1967; (ed.) World of Wonder (juvenile), 1968; Captive Universe, 1969; In Our Hands the Stars, 1970; Prime Number (short stories), 1970; One Step From Earth (short stories), 1970; Spaceship Medic (children), 1970; A Transatlantic Tunnel, Hurrah!, 1972; Stonehenge, 1972; Montezuma's Revenge, 1972; Star Smashers of the Galaxy Rangers, 1973; The Men from P.I.G. and R.O.B.O.T. (children), 1974; The California Iceberg (children), 1974; Queen Victoria's Revenge, 1974; (ed. with Brian Aldiss) Best SF: 1967 to 1975, 1975; (with G. Dickson) The Lifeship, 1976; The Best of Harry Harrison, 1976; Skyfall, 1977; Great Balls of Fire, 1977; Mechanismo, 1978; (with M. Edwards) Spacecraft in Fact and Fiction, 1979; Planet Story, 1979; The QE2 Is Missing, 1980; Wheelworld, 1980; Homeworld, 1980; Starworld, 1981; Planet of No Return, 1981; Invasion, Earth, 1982; Rebel in Time, 1983; West of Eden, 1984; Winter in Eden, 1986; Return to Eden, 1988. Add: Nat Sobel Assocs., 146 E. 19th St., New York, N.Y. 10003, U.S.A.

HARRISON, Jim. (James Thomas Harrison). American, b. 1937. Novels/Short stories, Poetry. Former Asst. Prof. of English, State Univ. of New York, Stony Brook. *Publs:* Plain Song, 1965; Locations, 1968; Walking, 1969; Outlyers and Ghazals, 1971; Wolf (novel), 1971; A Good Day to Die (novel), 1973; Letters to Yesenin, 1973; Farmer (novel), 1976; Legends of the Fall (novel), 1979; Warlock (novel), 1981; New and Selected Poems, 1982; (with Diana Guest) Natural World, 1983; Sundog (novel), 1984; The Theory & Practice of Rivers (poetry), 1986; Dalva (novel), 1988. Add: Box 120a, Lake Leelanau, Mich. 49653, U.S.A.

HARRISON, John F(letcher) C(lews). British, b. 1921. History. Deputy Dir., Extra Mural Dept., Leeds Univ., 1958–61; Prof., Univ. of Wisconsin, Madison, 1961–70; Prof. of History, Univ. of Sussex, Brighton, 1970–85, now Emeritus. *Publs:* History of the Working Men's College 1854-1954, 1954; Learning and Living 1790-1960, 1961; Society and Politics in England 1780-1960, 1965; Robert Owen and the Owenites, 1969; The Early Victorians 1832-1851, 1971; Birth and Growth of Industrial England 1714-1867, 1973; The Second Coming 1780-1850, 1979; The Common People, 1984. Add: 13 Woodlands, Barrowfield Dr., Hove, Sussex BN3 6TJ, England.

HARRISON, Keith (Edward). Australian, b. 1932. Poetry. Prof. of English and Poet-in-Residence, Carleton Coll., Northfield, Minn. (joined faculty as Asst. Prof., 1968; former Dir. of Arts Prog.) Tutor, Univ. of London Extra-Mural Dept., 1963–65; Lectr. in English, York Univ., Toronto, 1966–68. *Publs:* Points in a Journey and Other Poems, 1967; Two Variations on a Ground, 1968; Songs from the Drifting House, 1972; The Basho Poems, 1975; The Sense of Falling, 1980; At the Wedding of Peleus and Thetis, 1981; The Water Man (radio play), 1981. Add: Rt. 1, Northfield, Minn. 55057, U.S.A.

HARRISON, Kenneth (Cecil). British, b. 1915. Librarianship. Consultant Librarian, Commonwealth Library Assoc., since 1983 (Pres., 1972–75). Advisory Ed., Libri, since 1972; Pres., Library Assn., since 1973. Chief Librarian, Hyde, 1939–47, Hove, 1947–50, Eastbourne, 1950–55, and Hendon, 1958–61; City Librarian, Westminster, 1960–81. Ed., Library World, 1961–71. *Publs:* First Steps in Librarianship, 1950, 5th ed. 1980; Libraries in Scandinavia, 1961, 1969; Public Libraries Today, 1963; The Library and the Community, 1963, 3rd ed. 1976; Facts at Your Fingertips: Everyman's Guide to Reference Books, 1964; British Public Library Buildings, 1966; Libraries in Britain, 1969; Public Relations for Librarians, 1973, 1982; (ed.) Prospects for British Librarianship, 1976; Public Library Policy, 1981; Public Library Buildings, 1975–83, 1987; International Librarianship, 1989. Add: 5 Tavistock, Devonshire Pl., Eastbourne, E. Sussex BN21 4A6, England.

HARRISON, Lowell H. American, b. 1922. History, Biography. Instr., New York Univ., NYC, 1948–51; Head of Dept. 1957–67, and Chmn., Social Sciences Div., 1962–67, West Texas State Univ., Canyon (joined faculty, 1952). Prof. of History, Western Kentucky Univ., Bowling Green, 1967–88. *Publs:* John Breckinridge, Jeffersonian Republican, 1969; The Civil War in Kentucky, 1975; George Rogers Clark and the War in the West, 1976; (co-ed.) A Kentucky Sampler, 1977; The

Anti-Slavery Movement in Kentucky, 1978; (ed.) Kentucky's Governors, 1985. Western Kentucky University, 1987. Add: 704 Logan Way, Bowling Green, Ky. 42101, U.S.A.

HARRISON, Michael. Also writes as Quentin Downes; has also written as Michael Egremont. Irish, b. 1907. Novels/Short stories, Mystery/Crime/Suspense, Cookery/Gastronomy/Wine, History, Literature, Recreation/Leisure/Hobbies, Supernatural/Occult topics, Biography. Formerly, editor, market research executive, industrial and technical consultant, and creative dir. of an advertising agency; now retired. *Publs:* novels—Weep for Lycidas, 1934; Spring in Tartarus: An Arabesque, 1935; All the Trees Were Green, 1936; (as Michael Egremont) The Bride of Frankenstein, 1936; What Are We Waiting For?, 1939; Vernal Equinox, 1939; Battered Caravanserai, 1942; Reported Safe Arrival: The Journal of a Voyage to Port X, 1943; So Linked Together, 1944; Higher Things, 1945; The House in Fishergate, 1946; Treadmill, 1947; Sinecure, 1948; There's Glory for You!, 1949; Things Less Noble: A Modern Love Story, 1950; Long Vacation, 1951; The Brain, 1953; The Dividing Stone, 1954; A Hansom to St. James's, 1954; mystery novels—The Darkened Room, 1952; (as Quentin Downes) No Smoke, No Fire, 1952; (as Quentin Downes) Heads I Win, 1953; (as Quentin Downes) They Hadn't a Clue, 1954; other—Transit of Venus (short stories), 1936; Dawn Express: There and Back, 1938; (ed.) Under Thirty (short story anthology), 1939; Gambler's Glory: The Story of John Law of Lauriston, 1940; Count Cagliostro, Nature's Unfortunate Child, 1942; They Would be King, 1947; Post Office, Mauritius 1847: The Tale of Two Stamps, 1947; The Story of Christmas: Its Growth and Development from Earliest Times, 1951; Airborne at Kitty Hawk: The Story of the First Heavier-than-Air Flight Made by the Wright Brothers, 1953; Charles Dickens, 1953; (with Douglas Armstrong) A New Approach to Stamp Collecting, 1953; Beer Cookery, 1954; Peter Cheyney, Prince of Hokum: A Biography, 1954; In the Footsteps of Sherlock Holmes, 1958, 1971; The History of the Hat, 1960; London Beneath the Pavement, 1961, 1971; Rosa (biography of Rosa Lewis), 1962; Painful Details: Twelve Victorian Scandals, 1962; London by Gaslight 1861-1911, 1963, 1987; London Growing: The Development of a Metropolis, 1965; Mulberry: The Return in Triumph, 1965; Lord of London: A Biography of the Second Duke of Westminster, 1966; Technical and Industrial Publicity, 1968; The Exploits of Chevalier Dupin (mystery short stories), 1968 (in U.K., expanded version, as Murder in the Rue Royale, 1972); The London That Was Rome: The Imperial City Recreated by the New Archaeology, 1971; Fanfare of Strumpets, 1971; Clarence: The Life of H.R.H. the Duke of Clarence and Avondale 1864-1892, 1972 (in U.S. as Clarence: Was He Jack the Ripper?, 1974); The London of Sherlock Holmes, 1972; The Roots of Witchcraft, 1973; The World of Sherlock Holmes, 1973; Theatrical Mr. Holmes: The World's Greatest Consulting Detective, Considered Against the Background of the Contemporary Theatre, 1974; Fire from Heaven; or How Safe Are You from Burning, 1976, rev. ed. 1977; (ed.) Beyond Baker Street: Sherlockian Anthology, 1976; I, Sherlock Holmes, 1977; Vanishings: An Adventure in the Paranormal, 1981; A Study in Surmise: The Making of Sherlock Holmes, 1983; Immortal Sleuth: Sherlockian Musings and Memories, 1987. Add: 5A Palmeira Ct., Palmeira Sq., Hove, Sussex BN3 2JP, England.

HARRISON, M(ichael) John. British, b. 1945. Science fiction/Fantasy. Literary Ed., and Reviewer, New Worlds mag. *Publs:* The Committed Men, 1971; The Pastel City, 1971; The Centauri Device, 1974; The Machine in Shaft Ten And Other Stories, 1975; A Storm of Wings, 1980; In Viriconium, 1982; The Floating Gods, 1983; The Ice Monkey and Other Stories, 1983; Viriconium Nights, 1984. Add: c/o Anthony Sheil Assocs., 43 Doughty St., London WC1N 2LF, England.

HARRISON, Rex (Carey). British, b. 1908. Autobiography/Memoirs/Personal. Stage and film actor. *Publs:* Rex, 1974. Add: 5 Impasse de la Fontaine, Monte Carlo 98000, Monaco.

HARRISON, Sir Richard (John). British, b. 1920. Biology. Trustee, British Museum of Natural History, London, since 1978 (Chmn. of the Bd., 1984–88). Prof. of Anatomy, London Hosp. Medical Coll., Univ. of London, 1954–68; Fullerian Prof. of Physiology, Royal Instn., 1961–67; Prof. of Anatomy, Cambridge Univ., 1968–82; Fellow, Downing Coll., Cambridge, 1968–82, and Hon. Fellow since 1982. *Publs:* (with E.J. Field) Anatomical Terms, 1947, 3rd ed. 1968; The Child Unborn, 1951; Man the Peculiar Animal, 1958; (ed. with F. Goldby) Recent Advances in Anatomy, 1961; (with J.E. King) Marine Mammals, 1965, 1980; Reproduction and Man, 1967; (ed. and co-author) The Behavior and Physiology of Pinnipeds, 1968; (with W. Montagna) Man, 1969; (ed.) Functional Anatomy of Marine Mammals, 3 vols., 1972–77; (ed. with S.H. Ridgway) Handbook of Marine Mammals: Sea Lions, Seals, 3 vols.,

1981; Whales, 1985, 1989; (ed. with M.M. Bryden) Research on Dolphins, 1986; (ed. with M.M. Bryden) Whales, Dolphins and Porpoises, 1988. Add: The Beeches, Woodlands Rd., Great Shelford, Cambs., England.

HARRISON, Roger. British, b. 1938. Biology, Chemistry. Reader in Biochemistry, Sch. of Biological Sciences, Univ. of Bath (appointed Lectr., 1967). Research Fellow, State Univ. of New York at Buffalo, 1962–63; Visiting Scientist, National Insts. of Health, Bethesda, Md., 1963–64; Alexander von Humboldt Fellow, 1964–65, and Member of the teaching staff, 1965–66, Univ. of Hamburg, Germany; Research Fellow, Univ. of Loughborough, 1966–67. *Publs:* (with G.G. Lunt) Biological Membranes: Their Structure and Function, 1975. Add: Biochemistry Dept., Sch. of Biological Sciences, Univ. of Bath, Bath BA2 7AY, England.

HARRISON, Rosina. British, b. 1899. Autobiography/Memoirs/Personal. Young Ladies Maid to Maj. John and Lady Tufton of Appleley Castle, 1918–22; Ladies Maid to Viscountess Crawborne (later the Lady Salisbury), 1923–28; Young Ladies Maid to Hon. Phyliss Astor, 1928, and Ladies Maid to Viscountess Astor, M.P., 1929–64. *Publs:* Rose: My Life in Service, 1975; Gentlemen's Gentlemen: My Friends in Service, 1976. Add: 2 Homefield Rd., Worthing, Sussex BN11 2HZ, England.

HARRISON, Royden John. British, b. 1927. History, Politics/Government. Prof. of Social History and Dir., Centre for the Study of Social History, Univ. of Warwick, since 1970. Co-Founder and Co-Ed., Bulletin of the Soc. for the Study of Labour History, since 1960. Reader in Political Theory and Instns., Univ. of Sheffield, 1968–70. *Publs:* Before the Socialists, 1965; The English Defence of the Commune, 1972; (ed.) The Warwick Guide to British Labour Periodicals, 1978; The Independent Collier, 1979; (co-ed.) Divisions of Labour: Skilled Workers and Technological Change in Nineteenth Century Britain, 1985. Add: Centre for the Study of Social History, Univ. of Warwick, Coventry CV4 7AL, England.

HARRISON, Sarah. British, b. 1946. Novels/Short stories, Children's fiction. Journalist, IPC Magazines, London, 1969–72. *Publs:* The Flowers of the Field (novel), 1980; In Granny's Garden (children's book), 1980; A Flower That's Free (novel), 1984; Hot Breath (novel), 1985; Laura from Lark Rise series (children's books), 4 vols., 1986; An Imperfect Lady (novel), 1988. Add: Holmcrest, 17 Station Rd., Steeple Morden, Royston, Herts., England.

HARRISON, Sydney Gerald. British, b. 1924. Botany. Keeper, Dept. of Botany, National Museum of Wales, Cardiff, since 1962. Scientific Officer, then Sr. Scientific Officer, Royal Botanic Gardens, Kew, 1949–62. *Publs:* Garden Shrubs and Trees, 1960; (with W. Dallimore and A.B. Jackson) A Handbook of Coniferae and Ginkgoaceae, 1966; (with H.A. Hyde and A.E. Wade) Welsh Ferns, 1969, 1978; (with G.B. Masefield and M. Wallis) The Oxford Book of Food Plants, 1969; (with H.A. Hyde) Welsh Timber Trees, 1977. Add: 8 Queen Wood Close, Cyncoed, Cardiff, Wales.

HARRISON, Tony. British, b. 1937. Plays, Poetry, Translations. Lectr. in English, Ahmadu Bello Univ., Zaria, North Nigeria, 1962–66, and Charles Univ., Prague, 1966–67; Co-Ed., Stand, Newcastle upon Tyne, 1968–69; Resident Dramatist, National Theatre, London, 1977–79. Pres., Classical Assn., 1988. *Publs:* Earthworks, 1964; (with J. Simmons) Aikin Mata (play), 1965; Newcastle Is Peru, 1969; The Loiners, 1970; Voortrekker, 1972; The Misanthrope, 1973; (ed. and trans.) Poems of Palladas of Alexandria, 1973; Phaedra Britannica (play), 1975; Bow Down (music theatre), 1977; The Passion (play), 1977; The Bartered Bride (libretto), 1978; The School of Eloquence (poems), 1978; Oresteia (adaptation), 1981; Continuous, 1981; A Kumquat for John Keats, 1981; U.S. Martial, 1981; Selected Poems, 1984; The Fire Gap, 1985; Dramatic Verse 1973–1985, 1985; The Mysteries, 1985; Theatre Works, 1973–1985, 1986; The Trackers of Oxyrhynchus, 1988. Add: 9 The Grove, Gosforth, Newcastle upon Tyne NE3 1NE, England.

HARRISS, C(lement) Lowell. American, b. 1912. Economics, Money/Finance. Emeritus Prof. of Economics, Columbia Univ., NYC (joined faculty, 1938). Dir. since 1950, Vice-Pres. since 1972, and Life Hon. Member since 1978, Intnl. Inst. of Public Finance; Sr. Advisor, Academy of Political Science, since 1987 (Exec. Dir., 1981–87); Dir. Manhattan Inst. for Policy Research, Robert Schalkenbach Foundn., Inst. for Research on the Economics of Taxation and N.Y. Council for Economic Education. Fulbright Prof., Netherlands Sch. of Economics, now Erasmus Univ., 1953–54, Univ. of Strasbourg, France, 1960–61. Economic Consultant, Tax Foundn. Inc., 1963–80; Consultant, Lincoln Inst. of Land Policy, Cambridge, Mass., 1971–87. Pres., National Tax

Assn.—Tax Inst. of America, 1972. Numerous governmental advisory groups. *Publs:* Gift Taxation in the U.S., 1941; (ed.) Income Distribution in the U.S., 1943; (with W.J. Shultz) American Public Finance, 5th ed. 1948, 8th ed. 1965; The History and Policies of the Home Owners Loan Corporation, 1951; The American Economy, 1953, 6th ed. 1968; Selected Readings in Economics, 1954, 3rd ed. 1968; Money and Banking, 1961, 1965; Economics, 1962, 3rd ed. 1970; (ed.) Government Spending and Land Values, 1973; (ed.) The Good Earth of America, 1974; (ed.) Inflation, 1975; (ed.) The Property Tax and Local Finance, 1983; (ed.) Control of Federal Spending, 1985. Add: 14 Plateau Circle, Bronxville, N.Y. 10708, U.S.A.

HARROD-EAGLES, Cynthia. Also writes as Elizabeth Bennett and Emma Woodhouse. British, b. 1948. Historical/Romance, Novels. *Publs:* The Waiting Game, 1972; Shadows on the Mountain, 1973; Hollow Night, 1980; Deadfall, 1982; Dynasty series—The Founding, 1980; The Dark Rose, 1981; The Princeling, 1981, in the U.S.A. as The Distant Wood, 1982; The Oak Apple, 1982, in the U.S.A. as The Crystal Crown, 1982; The Black Pearl, 1982; The Long Shadow, 1983; The Chevalier, 1984; The Maiden, 1985; The Flood-Tide, 1986; The Tangled Thread, 1987; The Emperor, 1988; The Victory, 1989; as Emma Woodhouse—A Rainbow Summer, 1976; A Well-Painted Passion, 1976; Romany Magic, 1977; Love's Perilous Passage, 1978; On Wings of Love, 1978; Never Love a Stranger, 1978; as Elizabeth Bennett—Title Role, 1980; The Unfinished, 1983; Even Chance, 1984; Last Run, 1984. Add: c/o Macdonald and Co. Ltd., Headway House, 66-73 Shoe Lane, London EC4P 4AP, England.

HARRON, Don(ald Hugh). Canadian, b. 1924. Plays/Screenplays, Humor/Satire. Actor, since 1936; freelance writer, since 1950. *Publs:* Anne of Green Gables (adaptation), 1955; Turvey (adaptation), 1956; The Broken Jug (adaptation), 1958; Spring Thaw '67 (revue), 1967; Once (screenlay), 1971; Charlie Farquharson's History of Canada, 1972; Atuk (screenplay), 1973; Charlie Farquharson's Jogfree of Canda the Wirld and Other Places, 1974; Charlie Farquharson's KORN Allmynack, 1976; Olde Charlie Farquharson's Testament, 1978; The Wonder of It All (musical), 1979; Yer Last Decadent: Comic History 1972–1982, 1982; De Bunk's Canadian Establishment (parody), 1984. Add: 125 Dupont St., Toronto, Ont. SWR 1V4, Canada.

HARROWER, Elizabeth. Australian, b. 1928. Novels/Short stories. Staff member, A.B.C., Sydney, 1959–60, and Macmillan & Co. Ltd., publrs., Sydney, 1961–67. *Publs:* Down in the City, 1957; The Long Prospect, 1958; The Catherine Wheel, 1960; The Watch Tower, 1966. Add: 5 Stanley Ave., Mosman, N.S.W. 2088, Australia.

HARSENT, David. British, b. 1942. Novels, Poetry. Full-time writer. Fiction Critic, Times Literary Supplement, London, 1965–73, and Poetry Critic, Spectator, London, 1970–73. *Publs:* Tonight's Lover, 1968; A Violent Country, 1969; Ashbridge, 1970; After Dark, 1973; Truce, 1973; Dreams of the Dead, 1977; Mister Punch, 1984; From an Inland Sea (novel), 1985; Selected Poems, 1989. Add: c/o Jonathan Clowes Agency, 22 Prince Albert Rd., London NW1 7ST, England.

HART, H(erbert) L(ionel) A(dolphus). British, b. 1907. Law, Philosophy, Politics/Government. Honorary Fellow, University Coll., Oxford, since 1973, Brasenose Coll., Oxford, since 1978, and New College, Oxford, since 1969 (Fellow and Tutor in Philosophy, New Coll., Oxford, 1945–52; University Lectr. in Philosophy, 1948, and Prof. of Jurisprudence, 1952–68, Oxford Univ.; Fellow, 1952–68, and Resident Fellow, 1969–73, University Coll., Oxford; Principal, Brasenose Coll., Oxford, 1973–78). Practised at the Chancery Bar, 1932–40; served in the War Office, 1940–45; Queen's Counsel (Q.C.), 1982. Pres., Aristotelian Soc., 1959–60; Vice-Pres., British Academy, 1976–77. *Publs:* (with A.M. Honore) Causation in the Law, 1959, 1984; The Concept of Law, 1961; Law, Liberty and Morality, 1963; The Morality of the Criminal Law, 1965; Punishment and Responsibility, 1968; (ed. with J.H. Burns) Jeremy Bentham: An Introduction to the Principles of Morals and Legislation, 1970; (ed.) Jeremy Bentham: Of Laws in General, 1970; A Comment on the Commentaries and A Fragment on Government, 1977; Essays on Bentham: Jurisprudence and Political Theory, 1982; Essays in Jurisprudence and Philosophy, 1983. Add: University Coll., Oxford, England.

HART, John Fraser. American, b. 1924. Geography. Prof. of Geography, Univ. of Minnesota, Minneapolis, since 1967. Faculty member, Univ. of Georgia, Athens, 1949–55 and Indiana Univ., 1955–67; Ed., Annals of the Assn. of American Geographers, 1970–75. *Publs:* The British Moorlands, 1955; The Southeastern United States, 1967; U.S. and Canada,

1967; (ed.) Regions of the United States, 1972; The Look of the Land, 1975; The South, 1977. Add: Dept. of Geography, Univ. of Minnesota, Minneapolis, Minn. 55455, U.S.A.

HART, John. *See* **HARVEY**, John B.

HART, Judith (Baroness Hart of South Lanark). British, b. 1924. International relations/Current affairs. Labour Member of Parliament U.K. for Lanark, 1959–83, and for Clydesdale, 1983–87 (Joint Parliamentary Under Secty. of State of Scotland, 1964–66; Minister of State for Commonwealth Affairs, 1966–67; Minister of Social Security, 1967–68; Paymaster-Gen., 1968–69; Minister of Overseas Development, 1969–70, 1974–75, 1977–79). *Publs:* Aid and Liberation, 1973. Add: 3 Ennerdale Rd., Richmond, Surrey TW9 3PG, England.

HART, Kevin. Australian, b. 1954. Poetry, Literary critcism. Lectr. in Literary Studies, Deakin Univ., since 1987. Co-ordinator, Dept. of Philosophy and Religious Studies, Geelong Coll., Victoria, 1979–83; Part-time Lectr., Dept. of Philosophy, 1984–85 and Lectr., Dept. of English, 1986–87, Univ. of Melbourne. *Publs:* Nebuchadnezzar, 1976; The Departure, 1978; The Lines of the Hand: Poems 1976–79, 1981; Your Shadow, 1984; The Trespass of the Sign, 1989. Add: School of Humanities, Deakin Univ., Vic. 3217, Australia.

HARTCUP, Adeline. British, b. 1918. Biography, Translations. Member, Editorial Staff, Times Educational Supplement, London, 1946–50. *Publs:* Angelica, 1954; (trans.) The Labour and the Wounds, 1957; (with John Hartcup) Morning Faces, 1963; (trans.) European Porcelain, 1969; (trans.) Oriental Carpets, 1969; (trans.) Historic Villas, 1969; Below Stairs in the Great Country Houses, 1980; Children of the Great Country Houses, 1982; Love and Marriage in the Great Country Houses, 1984; (with John Hartcup) Spello: Life Today in Ancient Umbria, 1985. Add: 10 Winchelsea Close, Chantfield Ave., London SW15 6HE, England.

HARTCUP, Guy. British, b. 1919. Military/Defence, Sciences. Historian, Air Ministry, 1948–60; English Ed., Intnl. Atomic Energy Agency, Vienna, 1961–62; Asst. Historian, Cabinet Office Historical Section, 1963–64; Historian, H.M. Treasury, London, 1965–77. *Publs:* Origins and Development of Operational Research in the Royal Air Force, 1963; The Challenge of War, 1970; The Achievement of the Airship, 1974; Code Name Mulberry, 1977; Camouflage, 1979; (with T.E. Allibone) Cockcroft and the Atom, 1984; The War of Invention, 1988. Add: 16 Temple Sheen, East Sheen, London SW14 7RP.

HARTCUP, John. British, b. 1915. Biography. Chief Sub-Ed., Times Educational Supplement, London, 1949–52; with Macmillan & Co., publrs., London, 1953–55, and Bank of England, 1967–72. *Publs:* Love is Revolution: Biography of Camille Desmoulins, 1950; (with Adeline Hartcup) Morning Faces, 1963; (ed.) The Water Babies, by Charles Kingsley, 1965; (ed.) Robinson Crusoe, by Daniel Defoe, 1965; (with Adeline Hartcup) Spello: Life Today in Ancient Umbria, 1985. Add: 10 Winchelsea Close, Chantfield Ave., London SW15 6HE, England.

HART-DAVIS, Duff. British, b. 1936. Novels/Short stories, History, Biography. Feature writer 1972–76, Literary Ed., 1976–77 and Asst. Ed., 1977–78, Sunday Telegraph, London. *Publs:* The Megacull, 1968; The Gold of St. Matthew (in U.S. as The Gold Trackers), 1968; Spider in the Morning, 1972; Ascension: The Story of a South Atlantic Island, 1972; Peter Fleming (biography), 1974; Monarchs of the Glen, 1978; The Heights of Rimring, 1980; (with C. Strong) Fighter Pilot, 1981; Level Five, 1982; Fire Falcon, 1984; The Man-Eater of Jassapur, 1985; Hitler's Games, 1986; (ed.) End of an Era: Letters and Journals of Sir Alan Lascelles 1887-1920, 1987; Armada, 1988; Country Matters, 1988; (ed.) In Royal Service: Letters and Journals of Sir Alan Lascelles, Vol. 2, 1920–36, 1989. Add: Owlpen Farm, Uley, Dursley, Glos., England.

HART-DAVIS, (Sir) Rupert (Charles). British, b. 1907. Literature, Autobiography, Biography. Actor, 1928–29; staff member, William Heinemann, publishers, London, 1929–31; Manager, Book Soc., London, 1932; Dir., Jonathan Cape, London, 1933–40; Founding Dir., Rupert Hart-Davis Ltd., publishers, London, 1946–68. *Publs:* Hugh Walpole: A Biography, 1952; (ed.) George Moore: Letters to Lady Cunard, 1957; (ed.) The Letters of Oscar Wilde, 1962; (ed.) Max Beerbohm: Letters to Reggie Turner, 1964; A Catalogue of the Caricatures of Max Beerbohm, 1972; (ed.) The Autobiography of Arthur Ransome, 1976; The Lyttelton Hart-Davis Letters, 6 vols., 1978–84; The Arms of Time (memoir), 1979; (ed.) Selected Letters of Oscar Wilde, 1979; Two Men of Letters, 1979; (ed.) Siegfried Sassoon Diaries 1920–22, 1981, 1915–18, 1983, 1923–25, 1985; (ed.) The War Poems of Siegfried Sassoon, 1983;

A Beggar in Purple: Commonplace Book, 1983; More Letters of Oscar Wilde, 1985; Siegfried Sassoon Letters to Max Beerbohm, 1986; Letters of Max Beerbohm, 1988. Add: The Old Rectory, Marske-in-Swaledale, Richmond, N. Yorkshire, England.

HARTE, Marjorie. *See* **McEVOY**, Marjorie.

HARTHOORN, Antonie Marinus. British, b. 1923. Medicine/Health, Natural history. Trustee, Mlilwane Wildlife Sanctuary, since 1969. Pres., Uganda Veterinary Soc., 1958–60; Secty. and Corresponding Member for Uganda, Uganda Div., British Veterinary Assn., 1958–61; Head, Dept. of Physiology and Biochemistry, Univ. of East Africa, Nairobi, 1961–71; Chief Professional Officer, Research, Nature Conservation Div., Pretoria, 1971–81; Gov., Baharini Wildlife Sanctuary, Kenya, 1968–72. *Publs:* Application of Pharmacological and Physiological Principals in Restraint of Wild Animals, 1965; The Flying Syringe, 1970; Chemical Capture of Animals, 1976. Add: 239 End St., Hatfield 0083, South Africa.

HARTLAND, Michael. British, b. 1941. Mystery/Crime/Suspense. Full-time writer since 1982. In British Govt. service, 1963–78 (Private Secty. to Jennie Lee, Minister for the Arts, 1966–68; Planning Unit of Margaret Thatcher, Secty. of State for education, 1970–73; then diplomatic duties overseas, intelligence and counter-terrorism); Dir., U.N. Intl. Atomic Energy Agency, Vienna, 1978–82. FRSA 1982. Hon. Fellow, Univ. of Exeter, 1985. Book reviewer fot The Times, Sunday Times, Today and Western Morning News. *Publs:* Down Among the Dead Men (dramatised for TV), 1983; Seven Steps to Treason (dramatised for BBC Radio-4 Saturday Night Theatre; South West Arts Literary Award); The Third Betrayal (dramatised for TV), 1986; Frontier of Fear, 1989. Add: Cotte Barton, Branscombe, Devon EX12 3BH, England.

HARTLEY, Marie. British, b. 1905. Country life/Rural societies, History. *Publs:* with Ella Pontefract—Swaledale, 1934, Wensleydale, 1936, Wharfedale, 1938, Yorkshire Tour, 1939, Yorkshire Cottage, 1942; Yorkshire Heritage, 1950; with Joan Ingilby—Old Hand-Knitters of the Dales, 1951, Yorkshire Village, 1953, The Yorkshire Dales, 1956, The Wonders of Yorkshire, 1959, Yorkshire Portraits, 1961, Getting to Know Yorkshire, 1964, Life and Tradition in the Yorkshire Dales, 1968, Life in the Moorlands of North-East Yorkshire, 1972; Life and Tradition in West Yorkshire, 1976; A Dale's Heritage, 1982; Dales Memories, 1986; Yorkshire Album, 1988. Add: Coleshouse, Askrigg, Leyburn, North Yorks., England.

HARTMAN, Geoffrey H. American (b. German), b. 1929. Literary criticism/History, Poetry. Prof. of English and Comparative Literature, Yale Univ., New Haven, since 1967 and Karl Young Prof. since 1974 (Sterling Fellow, 1952–53; Instr., 1955–60; Morse Faculty Fellow, 1958; Asst. Prof., 1961–62). Fulbright Fellow, Univ. of Dijon, France, 1951–52; Visiting Asst. Prof., Univ. of Chicago, 1960–61; Assoc. Prof., 1962–64, and Prof., 1964–65, Univ. of Iowa, Iowa City; Prof., Cornell Univ., Ithaca, N.Y., 1965–67. *Publs:* The Unmediated Vision: An Interpretation of Wordsworth, Hopkins, Rilke, and Valery, 1954; André Malraux, 1960; Wordsworth's Poetry 1787-1814, 1964; (ed.) Hopkins: A Collection of Critical Essays, 1966; Beyond Formalism: Literary Essays 1958–1970, 1970; (ed.) Selected Poetry and Prose of William Wordsworth, 1970; (ed.) New Perspectives on Coleridge and Wordsworth, 1972; (ed.) Romanticism: Vistas, Instances, Continuities, 1973; The Fate of Reading and Other Essays, 1975; Akiba's Children (poetry), 1978; Criticism in the Wilderness, 1980; Saving the Text, 1981; Easy Pieces, 1985; Psychoanalysis and the Question of the Text, 1985; (ed.) Midrash and Literature, 1986; (ed.) Bitburg in Moral and Political Perspective, 1986; The Unremarkable Wordsworth, 1987. Add: 260 Everit St., New Haven, Conn. 06511, U.S.A.

HARTMANN, Ernest L. American, b. 1934. Psychiatry, Psychology. Dir., Schizophrenia Lab., Sleep and Dream Lab., Boston State Hosp., Mass., since 1967. Prof of Psychiatry, Tufts Univ. Sch. of Medicine, Medford, Mass., since 1975 (Assoc. Prof., 1969–75). Residency in Psychiatry, Massachusetts Mental Health Center, Boston, 1960–62; Clinical Assoc., 1962–64, and Career Investigator, 1964–69, National Inst. of Mental Health, Bethesda, Md. *Publs:* The Biology of Dreaming, 1967; (with B. Glasser, M. Greenblatt, M. Solomon and D. Levinson) Adolescents in a Mental Hospital, 1968; (ed.) Sleep and Dreaming, 1970; The Functions of Sleep, 1973; The Sleeping Pill, 1978; Tryptophan in Neurology and Psychiatry, 1981; The Nightmare, 1985; The Sleep Book, 1987. Add: 20 Claremont St., Newton, Mass. 02158, U.S.A.

HARTMANN, Michael (John). British, b. 1944. Novels/Short stories, Plays/Screenplays. Crown Counsel, Attorney-General's Chambers,

Hong Kong. Formerly, Attorney and Notary Public, Kantor & Immerman, Harare, Zimbabwe, and Lectr. in Company Law, Univ. of Zimbabwe, from 1971. *Publs:* Pepper in a Milkshake (play), 1966; Feather in a Battered Cap (play), 1972; Game for Vultures, 1975; Leap for the Sun, 1976; Shadow of the Leopard, 1978; Days of Thunder, 1980; Web of Dragons, 1987; The Phoenix Pact, 1988. Add: 13B Glendale, 8 Deep Water Bay Drive, Hong Kong.

HARTNACK, Justus. Danish, b. 1912. Philosophy. Univ. Prof., State Univ. of New York Coll., Brockport, since 1970 (Prof. of Philosophy, 1968–70). Visiting Lectr., 1946–50, and Asst. Prof., 1950–54, Colgate Univ., Hamilton, N.Y.; Prof. of Philosophy, 1954–72, and Head of Dept., 1954–68, Aarhus Univ., Denmark; Visiting Prof., Vassar Coll., Poughkeepsie, N.Y., 1958–59, and New York Univ., 1966–67. *Publs:* The Problems of Perception in British Empiricism, 1950; Philosophical Problems, 1962; Wittgenstein and Modern Philosophy, 1965, 1985; Kant's Theory of Knowledge 1967; Language and Philosophy, 1973; History of Philosophy, 1973, 1976; Immanuel Kant, 1974; From Radical Empiricism to Kant's Critical Idealism, 1986. Add: Dept. of Philosophy, State Univ. of New York Coll., Brockport, N.Y. 14420, U.S.A.

HARTNETT, Michael. Irish, b. 1941. Poetry. Teacher, National Coll. of Physical Education, Limerick. Worked as civil servant, security guard, dishwasher, postman, teaboy, and housepainter, 1961–68; Co-Ed., Arena mag., Dublin, 1963–65. *Publs:* Anatomy of a Cliché, 1968; Tao: A Version of the Chinese Classic of the Sixth Century B.C., 1969; The Hag of Beare: A Rendition of the Old Irish, 1969; (ed. with D. Egan) Choice, 1973; Selected Poems, 1976; Poems in English, 1977; Prisoners, 1978; Adharca Broic, 1978; Farewell to English, 1978; Daoine, 1979; (ed.) This Was Arena, 1982; O Bruadair, 1985; Collected Poems, 1985. Add: c/o Gallery Press, 19 Oakdown Rd., Dublin 14, Ireland.

HARTSHORNE, Charles. American, b. 1897. Philosophy, Theology/Religion. Prof. Emeritus, Univ. of Texas at Austin, since 1976 (Ashbel Smith Prof. of Philosophy, 1962–76). Instructor to Prof. of Philosophy, Univ. of Chicago, 1928–55; Prof. of Philosophy, Emory Univ., Atlanta, 1955–62. President, Western Division, American Philosophical Assn., 1949; Charles Peirce Society, 1950–51; and Metaphysical Society of America, 1954–55. *Publs:* (ed. with Paul Weiss) Collected Papers of Charles Sanders Peirce, 6 vols., 1931–35; The Philosophy and Psychology of Sensation, 1934; Beyond Humanism: Essays in the New Philosophy of Nature, 1937; Man's Vision of God and the Logic of Theism, 1941; The Divine Relativity: A Social Conception of God, 1948; (with others) Whitehead and the Modern World: Science, Metaphysics, and Civilization: Three Essays on the Thought of Alfred North Whitehead, 1953; (ed. with William L. Reese) Philosophers Speak of God, 1953; Reality as Social Process: Studies in Metaphysics and Religion, 1953; The Logic of Perfection, 1962; Anselm's Discovery: A Re-Examination of the Ontological Proof for God's Existence, 1965; Aquinas to Whitehead: Seven Centuries of Metaphysics of Religion, 1970; Creative Synthesis and Philosophical Method, 1970; Whitehead's Philosophy: Selected Essays 1935–1970, 1972; Born to Sing: An Interpretation and World Survey of Bird Song, 1973; Whitehead's View of Reality, 1981; Creativity in American Philosophy, 1984. Add: 313 Wagener Hall, Univ. of Texas, Austin, Texas 78712, U.S.A.

HARTSHORNE, Richard. American, b. 1899. Geography. Emeritus Prof. of Geography, Univ. of Wisconsin, Madison, since 1970 (Assoc. Prof., 1940–41; Prof., 1941–70). Instr., 1924–27, Asst. Prof., 1927–37, and Assoc. Prof., 1937–40, Dept. of Geography, Univ. of Minnesota, Minneapolis. *Publs:* (with S.N. Dicken) Syllabus in Economic Geography, 1933, 1936; The Nature of Geography, 1939, 3rd ed. 1961; Perspective on the Nature of Geography, 1959; The Academic Citizen, 1970. Add: 3218 Topping Rd., Madison, Wisc. 53705, U.S.A.

HARTSHORNE, Thomas L. American, b. 1935. Intellectual history. Assoc. Prof. of History, Cleveland State Univ., Ohio, since 1969 (Asst. Prof. of History, 1966–69). Instr. in History, 1962–65, and Asst. Prof. of History, 1965–66, Kent State Univ., Ohio. *Publs:* The Distorted Image: Changing Conceptions of the American Character since Turner, 1968; (co-ed.) the Social Fabric, 5th ed., 1987. Add: Dept. of History, Cleveland State Univ., Cleveland, Ohio 44115, U.S.A.

HART-SMITH, William. Australian, b. 1911. Poetry. Radio Copywriter and Announcer, Station 2CH, Sydney, 1937–41; Freelance writer, Sydney, 1943–46; Tutor Organiser, Adult Education Dept., Canterbury Univ., New Zealand, 1948–55; Advertising Copywriter, Jack Penny Ltd., Christchurch, 1956–60; Mgr., Christchurch Office, 1960–62, and Advertising Mgr., Sydney, 1962–66, Charles Kidd & Co.; Radio Technician,

Amalgamated Wireless of Australia, Sydney, 1966–70; Part-time Lectr. in Creative Writing, Western Australian Inst. of Technology, Perth, 1973–76; Writer-in-Residence, Univ. of Western Australia, Perth, 1976. Pres., Poetry Soc. of Australia, 1963–64. *Publs:* Columbus Goes West, 1943; Harvest, 1945; The Unceasing Ground: Poems, 1946; Christopher Columbus: A Sequence of Poems, 1948; On the Level: Mostly Canterbury Poems, 1950; Poems in Doggerel, 1955; Poems of Discovery, 1959; The Talking Clothes: Poems, 1966; (with Judith Wright and Randolph Stow) Poetry from Australia: Pergamon Poets 6, 1969; Mini-poems, 1974; (with Mary Morris) Let Me Learn the Steps: Poems from a Psychiatric Ward, 1977. Add: c/o Angus and Robertson, P.O. Box 290, North Ryde, N.S.W. 2113, Australia.

HARTSTON, William Roland. British, b. 1947. Recreation/Leisure/Hobbies. Industrial psychologist; Chess Columnist, The Mail on Sunday. Research Officer, Industrial Training Research Unit, Cambridge, 1974–81. *Publs:* (with L. Barden and R. Keene) The King's Indian Defence, 1969, 1973; The Benoni, 1969, 1973; The Grunfeld Defence, 1971, 1973; (with R. Keene) Karpov-Korchnoi, 1974; (with H. Golombek) The Best Games of C.H. O'D. Alexander, 1975; How to Cheat at Chess, 1976; The Battle of Baguio City, 1978; Soft Pawn, 1979; The Penguin Book of Chess Openings, 1980; Play Chess 1 and 2, 2 vols., 1980–81; (with S. Reuben) London 1980: Phillips and Drew Kings Chess Tournament, 1980; (with J. James) The Master Game Book Two, 1981; Karpov v. Korchnoi, 1981; (with P.C. Wason) The Psychology of Chess, 1983; (with J. Dawson) The Ultimate Irrelevant Encyclopaedia, 1984; Teach Yourself Chess, 1985; Kings of Chess, 1985; Chess: The Making of a Musical, 1986. Add: 14 Willow Walk, Cambridge CB1 1LA, England.

HARVEY, Caroline. *See* **TROLLOPE,** Joanna.

HARVEY, John (Hooper). British, b. 1911. Architecture, Art, Horticulture, Biography. Self-employed architect and writer, since 1970; Consultant Architect to Winchester Coll., Hants., 1947–86; Lectr. on Mediaeval Bldgs., Univ. Coll., London, 1950–59; Member and Secty., Archbishop of York's Commn. on Redundant Churches in the City of York, 1964–69. *Publs:* Henry Yevele, 1944, 1946; Gothic England, 1947, 1948; The Plantagenets, 1948, 3rd rev. ed. 1972; Dublin, 1949, 1972; Tudor Architecture, 1949; (with H. Felton) English Cathedrals, 1950; The Gothic World, 1950; English Mediaeval Architects, 1954, 1984 (supplement, 1987); English Cathedrals, 1956, rev. ed. 1963; (with H. Felton) A Portrait of English Cathedrals, 1957; The Cathedrals of Spain, 1957; (ed. and trans.) William Worcestre: Itineraries, 1969; Catherine Swynford's Chantry, 1971; The Master Builders, 1971; The Mediaeval Architect, 1972; Conservation of Buildings, 1972; Early Gardening Catalogues, 1972; Man the Builder, 1973; Sources for the History of Houses, 1974; Cathedrals of England and Wales, 1974, 1988; Medieval Craftsmen, 1975; York, 1975; Early Nurserymen, 1975; The Black Prince and His Age, 1976; The Perpendicular Style, 1978; Medieval Gardens, 1981; The Georgian Garden, 1983; Restoring Period Gardens, 1988. Add: 32 Christchurch St. E., Frome, Somerset BA11 1QH, England.

HARVEY, John B. Also writes as Jon Barton, William S. Brady, L.J. Coburn, J.B. Dancer, John Hart, William M. James, James Mann, John J. McLaglen, Thom Ryder, J.D. Sandon, and Jonathan White. British, b. 1938. Novels/Short stories, Mystery/Crime/Suspense, Westerns/Adventure, Children's fiction, Poetry. English and drama teacher in London, Heanor, Derbyshire, Andover, Hants., and Stevenage, Herts., 1963–74; part-time film and literature teacher, Nottingham Univ., 1979–86; film reviewer, Nottingham News and Trader, 1981–86. *Publs:* western novels, as John J. McLaglen, Herne the Hunter series—River of Blood, 1976; Shadow of the Vulture, 1977; Death in Gold, 1977; Criss-Draw, 1978; Vigilante!, 1979; Sun Dance, 1980; Billy the Kid, 1980; Till Death . . . , 1980; as J.B. Dancer, Lawmen series—Evil Breed, 1977; Judgement Day, 1978; The Hanged Man, 1979; as L.J. Coburn, Caleb Thorn series—The Raiders, 1977; Bloody Shiloh, 1978; as William S. Brady, Hawk series—Blood Money, 1979; Killing Time, 1980; Blood Kin, 1980; Desperadoes, 1981; Dead Man's Gold, 1981; Sierra Gold, 1981; Peacemaker series—Whiplash, 1981; as William M. James, Apache series—Blood Rising, 1979; Blood Brother, 1980; Death Dragon, 1981; as J.D. Sandon, Gringos series—Cannons in the Rain, 1979; Border Affair, 1979; Mazatlan, 1980; Wheels of Thunder, 1981; as John B. Harvey, Hart the Regulator series—Cherokee Outlet, 1980; Blood Trail, 1980; Tago, 1980; The Silver Lie, 1980; Blood on the Border, 1980; Ride the Wide Country, 1981; Arkansas Breakout, 1982; John Wesley Hardin, 1982; California Bloodlines, 1982, The Skinning Place, 1982; other—(as Thom Ryder) Avenging Angel, 1975; (as Thom Ryder) Angel Alone, 1975; Amphetamines and Pearls, 1976; The Geranium Kiss, 1976; One of Our

Dinosaurs Is Missing (novelization of screenplay), 1976; (as Jon Barton) Kill Hitler, 1976; (as Jonathan White) Double Trouble, 1976; (as Jonathan White) Double Dutch, 1976; (as Jonathan White) Double Exposure, 1976; Junkyard Angel, 1977; Neon Madman, 1977; Herbie Rides Again (novelization of screenplay), 1977, as Herbie Goes to Monte Carlo, 1978; (as Jon Barton) Forest of Death, 1977; (as Jon Barton) Lightning Strikes, 1977; (as Jonathan White) Double Up, 1977; (as Jonathan White) Double Act, 1977; (as Jon Hart) Black Blood, 1977; (as Jon Hart) High Slaughter, 1977; (as Jon Hart) Triangle of Death, 1977; (as Jon Hart) Guerilla Attack!, 1977; (as Jon Hart) Death Raid, 1978; (as Jonathan White) Double Bed, 1978; Provence (poetry), 1978; What about It, Sharon (juvenile), 1979; Frame, 1979; (as James Mann, with Laurence James) Endgame, 1982; Reel Love (juvenile), 1982; Sundae Date (juvenile), 1983; What Game Are You Playing? (juvenile), 1983; Footwork (juvenile), 1984; The Old Postcard Trick (poems), 1984; (as Terry Lennox) Dancer Draws a Wild Card, 1985; Duty Free (novelisation), 1985; More Duty Free (novelisation), 1986; Wild Love (juvenile), 1986; Last Summer, First Love (juvenile), 1986; Kidnap! (juvenile), 1987; Daylight Robbery! (juvenile), 1987; Hot Property! (juvenile), 1987; Neil Sedaka Lied (poetry), 1987; Terror Trap! (juvenile), 1988; Downeast to Danger (juvenile), 1988; Runner! (juvenile), 1988; Taking the Long Road Home (poetry), 1988; Lonely Hearts (novel), 1989; (with Sue Dymoke) Sometime Other Than Now (poetry), 1989; The Downeast Poets (poetry), 1989. Add: Flat 4, 1 Park Valley, Nottingham NG7 1BS, England.

HARVEY, John F(rederick). American, b. 1921. Librarianship. Intnl. Library Consultant, since 1967. Prof. and administrator in library science, Drexel Univ., Philadelphia, 1958–67, Univ. of Tehran, 1967–71, Univ. of New Mexico, Albuquerque, 1972–74, Hofstra Univ., Hempstead, N.Y., 1974–76. *Publs:* (with others) The Library Periodical Directory, 1955, 1967; (with L. Shores and R. Jordan) The Library College, 1964; Data Processing in College and Public Libraries, 1966; Comparative and International Library Science, 1977; Church and Synagogue Libraries, 1980; (with E.M. Dickinson) Affirmative Action in Libraries, 1982; (with P. Spyers-Duran) Austerity Management in Academic Libraries, 1984; (with F.L. Carroll) Internationalizing Library and Information Science Education, 1987. Add: P.O. Box 122, Lyndonville, Vt. 05851, U.S.A.

HARVEY, Nigel. Also writes as Hugh Willoughby. British, b. 1916. Agriculture/Forestry, Country life/Rural societies. On staff of Agricultural Research council, 1958 until retirement, 1976. On staff of Ministry of Agriculture, Fisheries and Food, 1944–58. *Publs:* The Story of Farm Buildings, 1953; Ditches, Dykes and Deep-Drainage, 1955; The Farming Kingdom, 1955; Farm Work Study, 1958; (as Hugh Willoughby) Amid the Alien Corn, 1958; A History of Farm Buildings in England and Wales, 1970, 1984; Old Farm Buildings, 1975, 1987; Fields, Hedges and Ditches, 1976, 1987; Farms and Farming, 1977; Discovering Farm Livestock, 1979; The Industrial Archaeology of Farming in England and Wales, 1980; Trees, Woods, and Forests, 1981; (ed.) Agricultural Research Centres, 1983; Historic Farm Buildings Study: Sources of Information, 1986. Add: 41 Corringham Rd., Golders Green, London, NW11, England.

HARVEY, P(aul) D(ean) A(dshead). British, b. 1930. Geography, History. Prof. Emeritus of Medieval History, Univ. of Durham, since 1985 (Prof. 1978–85). Gen. Ed., Portsmouth Record Series, since 1969. Asst. Archivist, Warwick County Record Office, 1954–56; Asst. Keeper, Dept. of Manuscripts, British Museum, London, 1957–66; Lectr., 1966–70, and Sr. Lectr., 1970–78, in Medieval Economic and Social History, Univ. of Southampton. *Publs:* (with H. Thorpe) Printed Maps of Warwickshire 1576-1900, 1959; A Medieval Oxfordshire Village: Cuxham 1240-1400, 1965; (with William Albert) Portsmouth and Sheet Turnpike Commissioners' Minute Book 1711-1754, 1973; Manorial Records of Cuxham, Oxfordshire, circa 1200-1359, 1976; The History of Topographical Maps: Symbols, Pictures and Surveys, 1980; Manorial Records, 1984; (ed.) The Peasant Land Market in Medieval England, 1984; (ed. with R.A. Skelton) Local Maps and Plans from Medieval England, 1986. Add: Lyndhurst, Farnley Hey Rd., Durham DH1 4EA, England.

HARWOOD, (Henry) David. British, b. 1938. Children's fiction, Children's non-fiction. Lectr., and Marketing Coordinator, Filton Technical Coll., Bristol, Avon, since 1974. Administrative Officer, Medical Research Council, London, 1960–66; freelance writer and photographer, 1966–70; Youth and Community Service Officer, Wiltshire County Council, 1970–74. *Publs:* Scouts in Action, 1963; Scouts on Safari, 1965; The Scout Handbook, 1967; Scouts Indeed!, 1967; Alert to Danger!, 1969; Cub Scouts, 1970; How to Read Maps, 1970; Discover Your Neighbourhood, 1970; Scouts, 1971; The Extension Activities Handbook, 1972; (ed. with V. Peters) The Bronze Arrow, 1973; (ed. with V. Peters) The Silver Arrow, 1973; (ed. with V. Peters) The Gold Arrow, 1973; Camping, 1977;

(ed.) The Cub Scout Annual, 1977–89; Car Games, 1978; (ed.) The International Cub Scout Book, 1980. Add: 4 Prospect Close, School Rd., Frampton Cotterell, Bristol BS17 2DQ, England.

HARWOOD, Gwen(doline Nessie). Australian, b. 1920. Poetry, Songs, lyrics and libretti. Former medical secty. *Publs:* Poems, 1964; The Fall of the House of Usher (libretto), 1965; Poems vol. II, 1968; Commentaries on Living (song text), 1971; Choral Symphony (song text), 1972; Lenz (libretto), 1974; Sea Changes (libretto), 1974; Selected Poems, 1975; Fiery Tales (libretto), 1976; Voices in Limbo (libretto), 1980; The Golem (libretto), 1981; The Lion's Bride, 1981; Stations, 1981. Add: Halcyon, Kettering, Tas. 7155, Australia.

HARWOOD, Lee. British, b. 1939. Poetry, Translations. *Publs:* verse —Title Illegible, 1965; The Man with Blue Eyes, 1966; The White Room, 1968; The Beautiful Atlas, 1969; Landscapes, 1969; The Sinking Colony, 1970; (with John Ashbery and Tom Raworth) Penguin Modern Poets 19, 1971; The First Poem, 1971; New Year, 1971; Captain Harwood's Log of Stern Statements and Stout Sayings, 1973; Freighters, 1975; H.M.S. Little Fox, 1976; Boston—Brighton, 1977; Old Bosham Bird Watch and Other Stories, 1977, 1978; (with A. Lopez) Wish You Were Here, 1979; All the Wrong Notes, 1981; Faded Ribbons, 1982; (with Richard Caddel) Wine Tales, 1984; Monster Masks, 1986; Rope Boy to the Rescue, 1988; Crossing the Frozen River: Selected Poems, 1988; fiction—Dream Quilt: Thirty Assorted Stories, 1985; Assorted Stories, 1987; translations of the works of Tristan Tzara—A Poem Sequence, 1969, rev. ed. as Cosmic Realities Vanilla Tobacco Drawings, 1975; Destroyed Days, 1971; Selected Poems, 1975; Chanson Dada: Selected Poems, 1987. Add: 21 Belvedere Terr., Norfolk Terr., Brighton BN1 3AF, England.

HARWOOD, Ronald. British, b. 1934. Novels/Short stories, Plays/Screenplays, Biography. *Publs:* All the Same Shadows (in U.S. as George Washington September Sir!), 1961; The Guilt Merchants, 1963; The Girl in Melanie Klein, 1969; Sir Donald Wolfit: His Life and Work in the Unfashionable Theatre, 1971; One Day in the Life of Ivan Denisovich (screenplay), 1971; Articles of Faith, 1973; The Genoa Ferry, 1976; Cesar and Augusta, 1978; One. Interior. Day. Adventures in the Film Trade, 1978; A Family, 1978; (co-ed.) New Stories 3, 1978; The Dresser, 1980; A Night at the Theatre, 1982; After the Lions, 1982; The Ordeal of Gilbert Pinfold, 1983; All the World's a Stage, 1984; Tramway Road, 1984; (ed.) The Ages of Gielgud, 1984; The Deliberate Death of a Polish Priest, 1985; Interpreters, 1985; (ed.) Dear Alec: Guiness at 75, 1989. Add: c/o Judy Daish Assocs., 83 Eastbourne Mews, London W2 6LQ, England.

HASKELL, Francis (James Herbert). British, b. 1928. Art. Prof. of History of Art, Oxford Univ., since 1967. Fellow, King's Coll., Cambridge 1954–67; Librarian of Fine Arts Faculty, Cambridge Univ., 1962–67. *Publs:* Patrons and Painters: A Study of Italian Art and Society in the Age of the Baroque, 1963; Rediscoveries in Art, 1975; L'Arte e il linguaggio della politica, 1978; (with N. Penny) Taste and the Antique, 1981; Past and Present in Art and Taste, 1987; The Painful Birth of the Art Book, 1987. Add: Trinity Coll., Oxford, England.

HASKINS, George Lee. American, b. 1915. History, Law, Politics/Government, Biography. Biddle Prof. of Law, Univ. of Pennsylvania, Philadelphia, since 1974 (Asst. Prof. 1946–48; Assoc. Prof., 1948–49; Prof., 1949–74). Counsel, Law Firm of Curtis, Thayter, Portland, Maine, since 1988. Consulting Counsel, Penn. Railroad and Penn.-Central Railroad, 1951–71; Member of panel preparing official History of U.S. Supreme Court. Former Asst. State Reporter, Superior and Supreme Courts of Pennsylvania. *Publs:* The Statute of York and the Interest of the Commons, 1935; The Beginnings of English Representative Government, 1948; (co-author) American Law of Property, 1952; (with M.P. Smith) Pennsylvania Fiduciary Guide, 1957, 1962; Law and Authority in Colonial Massachusetts, 1960, 1968, 1977; (co-author) A History of the Town of Hancock, Maine 1828-1978, 1978; John Marshall: Foundations of Power, part I of vol. I of History of U.S. Supreme Court, 1981. Add: 3400 Chestnut St., Philadelphia, Pa. 19104, U.S.A.

HASKINS, Jim. American, b. 1941. Children's non-fiction, Social commentary/phenomena, Biography. Prof. of English, Univ. of Florida, since 1977. Asst. Prof., Experimental Coll., Staten Island Community Coll., City Univ. of New York, 1970–77. *Publs:* Diary of a Harlem Schoolteacher, 1969; Resistance: Profiles in Nonviolence, 1970; The War and the Protest: Vietnam, 1971; Revolutionaries: Agents of Change, 1971; Profiles in Black Power, 1972; From Lew Alcind or to Kareem Abdul Jabbar, 1972; (with Hugh F. Butts) The Psychology of Black Language, 1973; Religions, 1973; (ed. and contrib.) Black Manifesto for Education,

1973; (ed.) Jokes From Black Folks, 1973; Deep Like the Rivers: Biography of Langston Hughes, 1973; Pinckney Benton Stewart Pinchback (biography), 1973; Jobs in Business and Office, 1974; Witchcraft, Mysticism and Magic in the Black World, 1974; Adam Clayton Powell: Portrait of a Marching Black, 1974; Street Gangs: Yesterday and Today, 1974; Ralph Bunche: A Most Reluctant Hero, 1974; Babe Ruth and Hank Aaron: The Home Run Kings, 1974; Snow Sculpture and Ice Carving, 1974; The Creoles of Color of New Orleans, 1975; Fighting Shirley Chisholm, 1975; The Consumer Movement, 1975; The Picture Life of Malcolm X, 1975; Dr. J: A Biography of Julius Erving, 1975; Your Rights: Past and Present, 1975; New Kind of Joy: The Story of the Special Olympics, 1976; Teenage Alcoholism, 1976; The Story of Stevie Wonder, 1976; The Long Struggle: The History of American Labor, 1976; Pele: A Biography, 1976; Scott Joplin: The Man Who Made Ragtime, 1976; The Life and Death of Martin Luther King, Jr., 1977; Barbara Jordan, 1977; The Cotton Club, 1977; Who Are the Handicapped?, 1978; Voodoo and Hoodoo: Their Tradition and Craft, 1978; George McGinnis: Basketball Superstar, 1978; The Stevie Wonder Scrapbook, 1978; Bob McAdoo, Superstar, 1978; James Van Der Zee: The Picture Takin' Man, 1979; Andrew Young: Man with a Mission, 1979; Gambling: Who Really Wins?, 1979; The New Americans: Vietnamese Boat People, 1980; I'm Gonna Make You Love Me: The Story of Diana Ross, 1980; Werewolves, 1981; Magic: A Biography of Earvin Johnson, 1982; The Child Abuse Help Book, 1982; The New Americans: Cuban Boat People, 1982; Sugar Ray Leonard, 1982; Black Theater in America, 1982; Katherine Dunham, 1982; Lena: A Personal and Professional Biography of Lena Horne, 1983; Bricktop, 1983; (ed.) The Filipino Nation, 3 vols., 1982; Richard Pryor, 1984; Space Challenger: The Story of Guion Bluford, 1984; Nat King Cole, 1984; About Michael Jackson, 1985; Leaders of the Middle East, 1985; Breakdancing, 1985; Diana Ross: Star Supreme, 1985; The Statue of Liberty: America's Proud Lady, 1986; Black Music in America, 1987; Queen of the Blues: A Biography of Dinah Washington, 1987; Count Your Way Through the Arab World/China/Japan/Russia (4 vols.), 1987; Mabel Mercer: A Life, 1988; Corazon Aquino: Leader of the Philippines, 1988; Winnie Mandela: Life of Struggle, 1988; Bill Cosby: America's Most Famous Father, 1988; Shirley Temple Black: Actress to Ambassador, 1988; (with N.R. Mitgang) Mr. Bojangles: The Biography of Bill Robinson, 1988; (with Kathleen Benson) The Sixties Reader, 1988. Add: 325 West End Ave., Apt. 7D, New York, N.Y. 10023, U.S.A.

HASLAM, Gerald William. American, b. 1937. Novels/Short stories, Language/Linguistics, Literature. Prof. of English, California State Coll., Sonoma, since 1967. Ed., ECOLIT, Environmental Awareness in the English Class, since 1972; Ed.-in-Chief, Western Writers Series, Everett/Edwards Inc., since 1973; Assoc. Ed., Sonoma Review, since 1974; Assoc. Ed., Valley Grapevine, since 1978; Member, Editorial Bd., Literary History of the American West, since 1978. Production Ed., ETC.: A Review of Gen. Semantics, 1968–70. *Publs:* (ed.) Forgotten Pages of American Literature, 1970; William Eastlake, 1970; The Language of the Oil Fields, 1972; OKIES: Selected Stories, 1973; Afro-American Oral Literature, 1974; (ed.) Western Writing, 1974; Jack Schaefer, 1976; Masks: A Novel, 1976; (ed.) California Heartland, 1978; The Wages of Sin, 1980; Hawk Flights: Visions of the West, 1983; Snapshots: Glimpses of the Other California, 1985; Voices of a Place, 1987; The Man Who Cultivated Fire, 1987. Add: P.O. Box 969, Penngrove, Calif. 94951, U.S.A.

HASLEGRAVE, Herbert Leslie. British, b. 1902. Education. Chmn., Loughborough Recreational Planning Consultants, Leics.; Member, Court, Loughborough Univ. of Technology. Principal, St. Helens Technical Coll., Lancs., 1938–43, Barnsley Technical Coll., Yorks 1943–46, Leicester Coll. of Technology, 1947–53, and Loughborough Coll. of Technology, 1953–66; Vice Chancellor, Loughborough Univ. of Technology, 1966–67. Member of the Council, Instn. of Electrical Engineers, 1955–57; Member, National Advisory Council on Education for Industry and Commerce, 1956–66; Joint Hon. Secty., Assn. of Technical Instns., 1966–68; Member of Council, Instn. of Mechanical Engineers, 1965–66; Chmn., National Cttee. on Technician Courses and Examinations, 1967–69; Pres., Whitworth Soc., 1972–73. *Publs:* Journal Bearing Tests, 1937; Post-War Engineering Apprenticeship, 1942; Fifty Years of Progress, 1947; The Contribution of British Technical Colleges to Engineering Education, 1951; Engineering Education and Training, 1954; Halls of Residence in Technical Colleges, 1959; The Evolution of Education and Training for Engineering in a Changing Environment, 1971; Education and Training of Technician Engineers and Technicians, 1977. Add: 1 Woodland View, Southwell, Nottinghamshire, England.

HASLUCK, Nicholas. Australian, b. 1942. Novels/Short stories, Poetry. Lawyer: admitted to the Supreme Court of Western Australia

as barrister and solicitor, 1968. Deputy Chmn., Australia Council, 1978–82. *Publs:* Anchor and Other Poems, 1976; The Hat on the Letter O and Other Stories, 1978; Quarantine (novel), 1978; The Blue Guitar (novel), 1980; (with William Grono) On the Edge (poetry), 1980; The Hand That Feeds You (novel), 1982; The Bellarmine Jug (novel), 1984; (with C.J. Koch) Chinese Journey (poetry), 1985; Truant State (novel), 1987; Collage (essays), 1988. Add: 14 Reserve St., Claremont, W.A. 6010, Australia.

HASLUCK, (Sir) Paul (Meernaa Caedwalla). Australian, b. 1905. Poetry, History, Autobiography/Memoirs/Personal. Member, Literary Staff, The West Australian, 1922–38; Lectr. in Australian History, 1939, and Lectr. in History, 1940, Univ. of Western Australia, Perth; with Australian Dept. of External Affairs, 1941–47: Counsellor in charge of Australian Mission to U.N., and Gen. Assembly, NYC, 1946; Acting Representative, Security Council, Atomic Energy Commn., and Conventional Arms Commn., 1946–47; Reader in History, Univ. of Western Australia, 1948; Liberal Member of Parliament (Aus.) for Curtin, W.A., 1949–69: Minister for Territories, 1951–63; Minister for Defence 1963–64; Minister for External Affairs, 1964–69; Gov.-Gen. of Australia, 1969–74. Leader of Delegations to Economic Commn. for Asia and the Far East (ECAFE) conferences in Wellington, Manila, New Delhi, Tokyo and Canberra, of Colombo Plan conferences in London and Rangoon, of SEATO conferences in London, Washington, Canberra and Wellington, of Asia and Pacific Council (ASPAC) meetings in Seoul, Bangkok and Canberra, and of Five-Power Defence Meeting, Kuala Lumpur, 1964–68; Leader of Australian Delegations to Gen. Assembly of U.N., 1964, 1966 and 1967; Chmn., SEATO Ministerial Council and ANZUS Ministerial Council, 1966, and of ECAFE and ASPAC, 1968. *Publs:* Our Southern Half-Castes, 1938; Into the Desert, 1939; Black Australians, 1942; Workshop of Security, 1948; The Government and the People 1939–41 and 1942–45, 2 vols., Australian Official war history, 1951, 1970; Native Welfare in Australia, 1953; Collected Verse, 1969; An Open Go, 1971; The Poet in Australia, 1975; A Time for Building: Australian Administration in Papua New Guinea, 1975; Mucking About (autobiography), 1977; The Office of Governor-General, 1980; Diplomatic Witness, Australian Foreign Affairs 1941–47, 1980; Dark Cottage (poems), 1984; Shades of Darkness: Aboriginal Affairs, 1925–65, 1988. Add: 2 Adams Rd., Dalkeith, W.A. 6009, Australia.

HASS, Robert. American, b. 1941. Poetry, Translations. Has taught at the State Univ. of New York at Buffalo, Univ. of Virginia, Charlottesville, St. Mary's Coll., Moraga, Calif., and Goddard Coll., Plainfield, Vt.; Poet-in-Residence, The Frost Place, Franconia, N.H., 1978. *Publs:* Field Guide, 1973; Winter Morning in Charlottesville, 1977; Praise, 1979; (with others) Five American Poets, 1979; Twentieth-Century Pleasures: Prose on Poetry, 1984; (co-trans.) The Separate Notebooks, by Czeslaw Milosz, 1984; (trans.) Unattainable Earth, 1986; (ed.) The Selected Poems of Tomas Transtromer, 1987; (ed.) Poems of Robinson Jeffers, 1987; Human Wishes, 1989. Add: c/o Ecco Press, 26 W. 17th St., New York, N.Y. 10011, U.S.A.

HASSALL, William Owen. British, b. 1912. History. Senior Asst. Librarian, Western Manuscripts Dept., Bodleian Library, Oxford, 1938–80, retired; Librarian of the Earl of Leicester at Holkham, 1937–83. Vice-Pres., Oxfordshire Record Soc. (Hon. Secty., 1946–77). *Publs:* Cartulary of St. Mary, Clerkenwell, 1949; Catalogue of Library of Sir E. Coke, 1950; Holkham Bible Picture Book, 1954; Wheatley Records 956-1956; They Saw It Happen 55BC-AD1485, vol. I, 1957; Who's Who in History, vol. I, British Isles 55BC-AD1485, 1960; (with Averil G. Hassall) Douce Apocalypse, 1961; How They Lived, vol. I, Before 1485, 1962; Index of Persons in Oxfordshire Deeds Acquired by the Bodleian Library 1878-1963, 1966; History Through Surnames, 1967; The Holkham Library Illuminations from the Library of the Earl of Leicester, 1970; (with Averil G. Hassall) Treasures from the Bodleian, 1976. Add: Manor House, Wheatley, Oxford, England.

HASSAN, Ihab (Habib). American (born Egyptian), b. 1925. Literature, Autobiography. Vilas Research Prof. of English and Comparative Literature, Univ. of Wisconsin at Milwaukee, since 1970. Instr. of English, Rensselaer Polytechnic Inst., Troy, N.Y., 1952–54; Asst. Prof., 1954–58, Assoc. Prof., 1958–62, Prof., 1962–63, Benjamin L. Waite Prof. of English, 1963–70, Chmn. of the Dept. of English, 1961–62, 1968–69, Dir. of the Coll. of Letters, 1964–66, and Dir. of the Center for the Humanities, 1969–70, Wesleyan Univ., Middletown, Conn.; Tutor, Salzburg Seminar in American Studies, 1965, 1975; Fulbright Lectr., Grenoble, France, 1966–67, and Nice, 1974–75; Dir., NEH Summer Seminars, 1982, 1984, and 1989; Fellow, Research Humanities Inst., Univ. of California, Irvine, 1990; Fellow, Humanities Research Center, National

Australian Univ. Canberra, 1990. *Publs:* Radical Innocence: Studies in the Contemporary American Novel, 1961; Crise du Heros dans le Roman Americain Contemporain 1963; The Literature of Silence: Henry Miller and Samuel Beckett, 1967; The Dismemberment of Orpheus: Toward a Post-modern Literature, 1971, 1982; (ed.) Liberations: New Essays on the Humanities in Revolution, 1971; Contemporary American Literature: An Introduction, 1973; Paracriticisms: Seven Speculations of the Times, 1975; The Right Promethean Fire: Imagination, Science, and Cultural Change, 1980; (ed. with S. Hassan) Innovation/Renovation: New Perspectives on the Humanities, 1983; Out of Egypt: Scenes and Fragments of an Autobiography, 1986; The Postmodern Turn: Essays in Postmodern Theory and Culture, 1987; Selves at Risk: Patterns of Quest in Contemporary American Letters, 1989. Add: 2137 N. Terrace Ave., Milwaukee, Wisc. 53202, U.S.A.

HASSLER, Donald M(ackey). American, b. 1937. Poetry, Literature. Prof. of English, Kent State Univ., since 1977, and coordinator of Writing Certificate Program, since 1986, Kent, Ohio (Instr. through Assoc. Prof. of English, 1965–77; Dir. of Experimental Progs., 1973–83). Advisory Ed., Hellas, since 1988. Writer, Crowell-Collier Encyclopedia, NYC, 1960; Instr. of English, Univ. of Montreal, 1961–65; co-ed., Extrapolation, since 1986. *Publs:* The Comedian as Letter D: Erasmus Darwin's Comic Materialism, 1973; (co-author) On Weighing a Pound of Flesh (verse), 1973; Erasmus Darwin, 1974; Comic Tones in Science Fiction, 1982; Hal Clement, 1982; Patterns of the Fantastic, 1983; Patterns of the Fantastic II, 1984; (co-ed.) Death and the Serpent! Immortality in Science Fiction and Fantasy, 1985; Isaac Asimov, 1987. Add: 1226 Woodhill Dr., Kent, Ohio 44240, U.S.A.

HASTINGS, Beverly. *See* **BARKIN,** Carol and **JAMES,** Elizabeth.

HASTINGS, Brooke. Pseud. for Deborah Hannes Gordon. American, b. 1946. Historical/Romance. Research asst., Columbia Univ., NYC, 1968–70; Secretary, The Huron Inst. and Working Papers magazine, Cambridge, Mass., 1971–73; Researcher and Writer, CARD Consultants, Sacramento, Calif., 1979. *Publs:* Desert Fire, 1980; Innocent Fire, 1980; Playing for Keeps, 1980; Island Conquest, 1981; Winner Take All, 1981; A Matter of Time, 1982; Intimate Strangers, 1982; Rough Diamond, 1982; An Act of Love, 1983; Interested Parties, 1984; Reasonable Doubts, 1984; Tell Me No Lies, 1984; Hard to Handle, 1985; As Time Goes By, 1986; Double Jeopardy, 1986; Forward Pass, 1986; Too Close for Comfort, 1987; Forbidden Fruit, 1987; Both Sides Now, 1988; Catch a Falling Star, 1988; So Sweet a Sin, 1989. Add: 1240 Noonan Dr., Sacramento, Calif. 95822, U.S.A.

HASTINGS, Graham. *See* **JEFFRIES,** Roderic.

HASTINGS, Max M(acdonald). British, b. 1945. History, Military/Defence, Biography, Documentaries/Reportage. Ed., The Daily Telegraph, since 1986. Freelance writer, broadcaster and journalist, London, since 1973. Contrib., Sunday Times, London. Researcher, BBC-TV, 1963–64; Reporter, Evening Standard newspaper, London, 1965–67, 1968–70; Fellow, World Press Inst., St. Paul, Minn., 1967–68; Roving Correspondent, BBC-TV, 1970–73. Somerset Maugham Prize, 1979; Journalist of the Year, 1982; Granada TV Reporter of the Year, 1982. *Publs:* America 1968: The Fire This Time, 1968; Ulster 1969: The Struggle for Civil Rights in Northern Ireland, 1970; Montrose, The King's Champion, 1977; Yoni, Hero of Entebbe, 1979; Bomber Command, 1979; (with others) The Battle of Britain, 1980; Das Reich, 1981; (with Simon Jenkins) The Battle for The Falklands, 1983; Overlord, 1984; (ed.) The Oxford Book of Military Anecdotes, 1985; The Korean War, 1987; Outside Days, 1989. Add: c/o The Daily Telegraph, 181 Marsh Wall, London E14.

HASTINGS, Michael. British, b. 1938. Novels/Short stories, Plays/Screenplays, Poetry, Biography. *Publs:* novels—The Game, 1957; The Frauds, 1960; Tussy Is Me, 1970; The Nightcomers, 1972; And In the Forest the Indians, 1975; other—Love Me, Lambeth (poems), 1961; Three Plays, 1966; Rupert Brooke: The Handsomest Young Man in England, 1967; Bart's Mornings and Other Tales of Modern Brazil, 1975; Sir Richard Burton, 1978; Three Plays, 1980; Two Plays, 1981; Tom and Viv (play), 1985; Three Political Plays, 1988. Add: 2 Helix Gardens, London SW2, England.

HASTINGS, Phyllis (Dora Hodge). Has also written as Julia Mayfield. British, b. 1904. Historical/Romance/Gothic, Recreation/Leisure/Hobbies. Ballet dancer as a child; later operator of a dairy farm and an antique business. *Publs:* As Long as You Live, 1951; Far from Jupiter, 1952; Crowning Glory, 1952; Rapture in My Rags, 1954, 2nd U.K. ed.

as Scarecrow Lover, 1960, 3rd ed. as Rapture, 1966; Dust in My Pillow, 1955; The Field of Roses, 1955, in U.S. as Her French Husband, 1956; The Black Virgin of the Gold Mountain, 1956; The Signpost Has Four Arms, 1957; (as Julia Mayfield) The Forest of Stone, 1957; The Happy Man, 1958; Golden Apollo, 1958; The Fountain of Youth, 1959; Sandals for My Feet, 1960; Long Barnaby, 1961, as Hot Day in High Summer, 1962; The Night the Roof Blew Off, 1962; Their Flowers Were Always Black (in U.K. paperback as The Harlot's Daughter), 1967; The Swan River Story, 1968; The Sussex Saga: All Earth to Love, 1968, Day of the Dancing Sun, 1971; An Act of Darkness, 1969, in U.S. as The House on Malador Street, 1970; The Stars Are My Children, 1970; The Temporary Boy, 1971; When the Gallows Is High, 1971; The Conservatory, 1973; The Gates of Morning, 1973; Bartholomew Fair, 1974, House of the Twelve Caesars, 1975; The Image-Maker, 1976; The Candles of Night, 1977; The Death-Scented Flower, 1977; Field of the Forty Footsteps, 1978; Stratford Affair, 1978; The Feast of the Peacock, 1978; Running Thursday, 1980; Buttercup Joe, 1980; Tiger's Heaven, 1981; The Overlooker, 1982; Blackberry Summer, 1982; The Lion at the Door, 1983; The Free Traders, 1984; My Four Uncles, 1984; The Women Barbers of Drury Lane, 1985; The Julian Maze, 1986; Naked Runner, 1987. Add: The Abbot's Cottage, Upper Lake, Battle, E. Sussex TN33 0AN, England.

HASTINGS, Robert Paul. British, b. 1933. History, Medicine/Health, Transportation. Kent County Inspector for History, since 1980. Ed., Durham County Local History Soc. Bulletin, since 1972. History Master, Birmingham Comprehensive Sch., 1956–66; Lectr., Hereford Coll. of Education, 1966–68; Principal Lectr. and Head of the Dept. of History, St. George Coll. of Education, 1968–77; Headmaster, Hurworth Comprehensive Sch., County Durham, 1977–80. *Publs:* (with V.H.T. Skipp) Discovering Bickenhill, 1963; Between the Wars 1968; The Cold War, 1969; Railroads: An International History, 1972; Medicine: An International History, 1974; Essays in North Riding History, 1981; Poverty and the Poor Laws in the North Riding of Yorkshire, 1982; More Essays in North Riding History, 1984; War and Medicine, 1988. Add: Mid-Kent Area Education Office, Astley House, Hastings Rd., Maidstone, Kent, England.

HASWELL, Chetwynd John Drake. Also writes as Jock Haswell and George Foster. British, b. 1919. Novels/Short stories, History, Military/Defence. Regular Officer, Queen's Royal Regiment, 1938–60; Author for Service Intelligence, 1966–84. *Publs:* (as George Foster) Indian File (novel), 1960; (as George Foster) Soldier on Loan (novel), 1961; The Queen's Royal Regiment, 1967; The First Respectable Spy: Lt. Col. Colquhoun Grant, 1969; James II, Soldier and Sailor, 1972; British Military Intelligence, 1973; Citizen Armies, 1973; The Battle for Empire, 1975; The British Army: A Concise History, 1975; The Ardent Queen: Margaret of Anjou, 1976; Spies and Spymasters: A Concise History of Intelligence, 1977; The Intelligence and Deception of the D-Day Landings, 1979; The Tangled Web: The Art of Tactical and Strategic Deception, 1985; Spies and Spying, 1986. Add: The Grey House, Lyminge, Folkestone, Kent CT18 8ED, England.

HASWELL, Jock. *See* **HASWELL,** Chetwynd John Drake.

HATCH OF LUSBY, Lord; John (Charles) Hatch. British, b. 1917. History. Lectr. in Commonwealth Studies, Univ. of Glasgow, 1948–53; Commonwealth Secty. for the Labour Party (U.K.), 1954–61; Dir. of Extra-Mural Studies, Univ. of Sierra Leone, 1961–62; Dir., Houston Inter-University African Studies Prog., Tex., 1964–70; Dir., Inst. of Human Relations, Zambia, 1980–82. *Publs:* The Dilemma of South Africa, 1952; New From Africa, 1956; Everyman's Africa, 1959; Africa Today and Tomorrow, 1960; A History of Post War Africa, 1965; Africa, the Re-Birth of Self-Rule, 1967; The History of Britain in Africa, 1969; Nigeria, 1970; Tanzania, 1972; Africa Emergent, 1974; Two African Statesmen, 1976. Add: House of Lords, Westminster, London SW1A 0PW, England.

HATCH, Denison. American, b. 1935. Novels, Humor/Satire. Ed. and Publ., Who's Mailing What!, Newsletter and archive service, since 1984; Pres., Denison Hatch Assocs., since 1976. Sales Mgr., Franklin Watts Inc., publrs. 1960–63; Dir. of New Projects, Grolier Enterprises, 1964–66; Book Club Dir., Macmillan Book Clubs, 1966–68, and Meredith Corp., 1969–70; Vice-Pres., Walter Weintz & Co., 1972–76, all in NYC. *Publs:* Statuary Rape (humor), 1959; Statues of Limitations (humor), 1961; Cedarhurst Alley, 1970; The Fingered City, 1973; The Stork, 1977. Add: 210 Red Fox Rd., Stamford, Conn. 06903, U.S.A.

HATCHER, (Melvyn) John. British, b. 1942. Crafts, History. University Reader in Economic and Social History, and Fellow of Corpus

Christi Coll., Cambridge, since 1976. Lectr., 1967–74, and Sr. Lectr., 1974–76, Univ. of Kent, Canterbury. *Publs:* Rural Economy and Society in the Duchy of Cornwall 1300-1500, 1970; English Tin Production and Trade Before 1550, 1973; (with T.C. Barker) A History of British Pewter, 1974; Plague, Population and the English Economy 1348-1530, 1977; (with E. Miller) Medieval England: Rural Society and Economic Change 1086-1348, 1978. Add: Corpus Christi Coll., Cambridge, England.

HATCHER, William S. American, b. 1935. Mathematics/Statistics, Philosophy, Sciences, Theology/Religion. Prof. of Mathematics, Univ. Laval, Quebec, since 1972 (Assoc. Prof., 1968–72). Lectr. in Mathematics, Univ. of Neuchatel, Switzerland, 1965 (Research Assoc., 1962–64); Assoc. Prof. of Mathematics, Univ. of Toledo, Ohio, 1965–68; Guest Prof., Ecole Polytechnique Federale, Lausanne, Switzerland, 1972–73. *Publs:* Foundations of Mathematics, 1976; The Science of Religion, 1977; (with Stephen Whitney) Absolute Algebra, 1978; The Logical Foundations of Mathematics, 1982; (with J. Douglas Martin) The Baha'i Faith: The Emerging Global Religion, 1985. Add: 1060 Brown Ave., Quebec City G1S 2Z9, Canada.

HATTERSLEY, Roy (Sydney George). British, b. 1932. Autobiography/Memoirs/Personal, Biography. Labour Member of Parliament (U.K.) for Sparkbrook div. of Birmingham since 1964, Deputy Leader of the Labour Party since 1983, and Opposition Spokesman on Home Affairs since 1987. (Parliamentary Private Secty., Minister of Pensions and National Insurance 1964–67; Parliamentary Secty., Ministry of Labour, 1967–68, and Dept. of Employment and Productivity, 1968–69; Minister of Defence for Admin., 1969–70; Labour Party Spokesman on Defence, 1972, and on Education, 1972–74; Minister of State, Foreign and Commonwealth Office, 1974–76; Secty. of State for Prices and Consumer Protection, 1976–79; Opposition Spokesman on Home Affairs, 1980–83, and on Treasury Affairs, 1983–87). Columnist for the Guardian, since 1981, Lustie, 1980–81, 1988 to present, and for Punch, 1982–88. Journalist and Health Service Exec., 1956–64; Member of City Council, Sheffield, 1957–65; Dir., Campaign for a European Political Community, 1966–67. *Publs:* Nelson: A Biography, 1974; Goodbye to Yorkshire, 1976; Politics Apart, 1982; A Yorkshire Boyhood, 1983; Press Gang, 1983; Endpiece Revisited, 1984; Choose Freedom, 1987. Add: House of Commons, London SW1, England.

HATTON, Ragnhild (Marie). British, b. 1913. History. Prof. of Intnl. History, Univ. of London, 1968–80, now Emeritus (Reader, 1958–68). *Publs:* Charles XII of Sweden, 1968; (ed. with J.S. Bromley) William III and Louis XIV: Essays 1680-1720, by and for Mark A. Thomson, 1968; War and Peace 1680-1720, 1969; Europe in the Age of Louis XIV, 1969, 1979; (ed. with M.S. Anderson) Essays in Diplomatic History in Memory of David Bayne Horn, 1970; Louis XIV and His World, 1972; (ed.) History of European Ideas, 1973; Charles XII, 1974; (ed.) Louis XIV and Absolutism, 1976; (ed.) Louis XIV and Europe, 1976; George I, Elector and King, 1978. Add: 49 Campden St., London W8, England.

HAUGAARD, Erik (Christian). Danish, b. 1923. Children's fiction. *Publs:* Hakon of Rogen's Saga, 1963; A Slave's Tale, 1965; Orphans of the Wind, 1966; The Little Fishes, 1967; The Rider and His Horse, 1968; The Untold Tale, 1971; (trans.) The Complete Fairy Tales and Stories of Hans Anderson, 1974; A Messenger for Parliament, 1976; Cromwell's Boy, 1978; Chase Me, Catch Nobody, 1980; Leif the Unlucky, 1982; A Boy's Will, 1983; The Samurai's Tale, 1984; Prince Boghole, 1987; Princess Horrid, 1989. Add: Toad Hall, Ballydehob, Co. Cork, Ireland.

HAUGEN, Einar (Ingvald). American, b. 1906. Language/Linguistics. Literature, Translations. Prof. Emeritus, Harvard Univ., Cambridge, Mass., since 1975 (Victor S. Thomas Prof. of Scandinavian and Linguistics, 1964–75). Asst. Prof., 1931–36, Assoc. Prof., 1936–38, Thompson Prof. of Scandinavian Languages, 1938–84, and Vilas Prof., 1962–64, Univ. of Wisconsin, Madison. *Publs:* Beginning Norwegian, 1937, 1961, 1974; Norsk i Amerika, 1939; Reading Norwegian, 1940; Norwegian Word Studies, 1941; Voyages to Vinland, 1941, 1942; Spoken Norwegian, 1946, (with K. Chapman) 1964, 3rd ed. 1982; (ed.) First Grammatical Treatise, 1950, 1972; Norwegian Language in America: A Study in Bilingual Behavior, 1953, 1970; Bilingualism in the Americas, 1956, 3rd ed. 1968; (trans.) History of Norwegian Literature, by H. Beyer, 1956; (trans.) Driving Forces in History, by H. Koht, 1964; (ed.-in-chief) Norwegian-English Dictionary, 1965; Language Conflict and Language Behavior, 1966; The Norwegians in America, 1967; (trans.) Fire and Ice, 1967; Rikssprak og folkemal, 1968; The Ecology of Language, 1972; (with T.L. Markey) The Scandinavian Languages, 1972; Studies in Einar Haugen, 1972; (ed.-in-chief) A Bibliography of Scandinavian Languages and Linguistics, 1974; History of the Scandinavian Languages, 1976; Vocabulary

of Björnson's Literary Works, 1978; (trans.) Norway to America, by Ingrid Semmingsen, 1979; (with Eva L. Haugen) Land of the Free: Björnson's America Letters 1880-1881, 1979; Ibsen's Drama: Author to Audience, 1979; Oppdalsmalet, 1982; Scandinavian Language Structures, 1982; O.E. Rolvaag, 1983; (ed. with J. Buckley) Han Ola og han Per, 1984; Blessings of Babel, 1987. Add: 45 Larch Circle, Belmont, Mass. 02178, U.S.A.

HAUGHTON, Rosemary (Elena Konradin). British, b. 1927. Novels/Short stories, Children's non-fiction, Mythology/Folklore, Theology/Religion. *Publs:* Jesus With Me, 1950; Therese Martin: The Story of St. Therese of Lisieux, 1957; The Family Book, 1959; The Children: Heirs to the Kingdom, 1961; Six Saints for Parents, 1962; The Family God Chose, 1964; The Young St. Mark, 1964; A Home for God's Family, 1965; The Carpenter's Son, 1965; The Boy from the Lake, 1965; Beginning Life in Christ: The Gospel in Christian Education, 1966; On Trying to be Human, 1966; The Young Moses, 1966; The Young Thomas More, 1966; (with A.M. Cocagnac) Bible for Young Christians: The Old Testament, 1966; The Transformation of Man, 1967; (with Cardinal Heenan) Dialogue: The State of the Church Today, 1968; Why Be a Christian?, 1968; Elizabeth's Greeting, 1968; Matthew's Good News of Jesus, 1968; John's Good News of Jesus, 1968; Act of Love, 1969; Holiness of Sex, 1969; Why the Epistles Were Written, 1972; The Theology of Experience (in U.K. as The Knife-Edge of Experience), 1972; Love, 1973; In Search of Tomorrow, 1973; Tales From Eternity, 1974; The Liberated Heart, 1975; The Gospel Where It Hits Us, 1975; The Drama of Salvation, 1976; Feminine Spirituality, 1977; The Catholic Thing, 1980; The Passionate God, 1980; The Re-Creation of Eve, 1985. Add: Lothlorien, Corsock, Castle Douglas, Galloway, Scotland.

HAU'OFA, Epeli. Tongan, b. 1939. Short stories, Sociology. Reader in Sociology, Univ. of the South Pacific, since 1983. Sr. Tutor, Univ. of Papua New Guinea, Port Moresby, 1968–70; Research Fellow, Univ. of the South Pacific, Suva, 1975–77; Visiting Fellow, Univ. of New South Wales, Sydney, 1977; Deputy Private Secty. to the King of Tonga, 1978–81; Dir., Univ. of the South Pacific Rural Development Centre, Tonga, 1981–83. *Publs:* (with Randy Thaman) Our Crowded Islands, 1977; Corned Beef and Tapioca: A Report on the Food Distribution Systems in Tonga, 1979; Tales of the Tikongs (short stories), 1983. Add: Sch. of Social and Economic Development, Univ. of the South Pacific, P.O. Box 1168, Suva, Fiji.

HAUPTMANN, William (Thornton). American, b. 1942. Plays/Screenplays. *Publs:* Heat, 1977; Domino Courts, and Comanche Cafe, 1977; Gillette, 1985; Big River, 1986. Add: 240 Warwick St., Apt. E, Brooklyn, N.Y. 11201, U.S.A.

HAUSER, Marianne. American, b. 1910. Novels/Short stories. Lectr., Queens Coll., City Univ. of New York, NYC, 1965–79. *Publs:* Monique, 1935; Indian Phantom Play, 1937; Dark Dominion, 1947; The Living Shall Praise Thee, 1957; The Choir Invisible, 1958; Prince Ishmael, 1963; A Lesson in Music (short stories), 1964; The Talking Room (novel), 1976; The Memoirs of the Late Mr. Ashley (novel), 1986. Add: 2 Washington Sq. Village, New York, N.Y. 10012, U.S.A.

HAUSER, Philip M. American, b. 1909. Sociology. Lucy Flower Prof. Emeritus of Urban Sociology, and Dir. Emeritus, Population Research Center, Univ. of Chicago (joined faculty, 1932; Chmn., Dept. of Sociology, 1956–65). Consultant on Asian Manpower, The Asia Foundn.; Member, Exec. Council, Council for Asian Manpower Studies; Trustee, Population Reference Bureau; Member, Bd. of Dirs., Selected American Shares, Selected Special Shares, and Family of Mutual Funds—Selected Shares. Deputy Dir., 1938–47, and Acting Dir., 1949–50, U.S. Bureau of the Census, Washington; Asst. to the Scty. of Commerce, 1945–47; U.S. Rep., Population Commn., U.N., 1947–51. Pres., Population Assn. of America, 1950; Member. Bd. of Govs., Metropolitan Housing and Planning Council, Chicago, 1958–70; Vice-Pres., Section K: Social and Economic Sciences, American Assn. for the Advancement of Science, 1959; Chmn., Technical Advisory Cttee. for Population Statistics, U.S. Bureau of the Census, 1960–72; Pres., Sociological Research Assn., 1962; Pres., 1962, and Chmn. of the Census Advisory Cttee., 1967–71, American Statistical Assn.; Chmn., Advisory Panel on Integration of Public Schools, Chicago Bd. of Education, 1963–64; Member of the Council, National Inst. of Child Health and Human Development, 1965–69; Member of Bd., U.N. Inst. for Research in Social Development, Geneva, 1966–72; Pres., American Sociological Assn., 1967–68; Member of Exec. Cttee., and Chmn. of Population Seminar, Southeast Asia Development Advisory Group, 1968–71; Member, Science Development Advisory Panel, National Science Foundn., 1969–70; Chmn., Cttee. to Evaluate National Center of Health Statistics, U.S. Dept. of Health, Education and Welfare, 1971–

72; Pres., National Conference on Social Welfare, 1972–74. *Publs:* (with H. Blumen) Movies, Delinquency and Crime, 1933; Workers on Relief in the U.S., 2 vols., 1939; (ed. with V. Leonard) Government Statistics for Business Use, 1946, 1956; (ed.) Population and World Politics, 1958; (ed.) Urbanization in Asia and the Far East, 1958; (ed. with Duncan) The Study of Population: An Inventory and Appraisal, 1959; (with Duncan) Housing a Metropolis: Chicago, 1960; (ed.) Urbanization in Latin America, 1961; Population Perspectives, 1961; (ed. with L. Schnore) The Study of Urbanization, 1965; (ed.) Handbook for Social Research in Urban Areas, 1965; (with P. Hodge) The Challenge of America's Metropolitan Population Outlook 1960–1985, 1968; (ed.) The Population Dilemma, 1963, 1969; (with E. Kitagawa) Differential Mortality in the United States: A Study in Socioeconomic Epidemiology, 1973; Social Statistics in Use, 1976; World Population and Development, 1979; (with others) Population and the Urban Future, 1983; (ed.) Urbanization and Migration in Asian Development, 1985. Add: 1440 N. State Parkway, Chicago, Ill. 60610, U.S.A.

HAUSMANN, Winifred Wilkinson. Also writes as Winifred Wilkinson. American, b. 1922. Theology/Religion. Minister Emeritus, Unity Center of Cleveland, since 1988 (Ministry, 1958–87). Ministry, Unity Church, Little Rock, Ark., 1957–58. Member, Bd. of Dirs., Assn. of Unity Churches, 1964–66. *Publs:* Focus on Living, 1967; Miracle Power for Today, 1969; Your God-Given Potential, 1978; How to Live Life Victoriously, 1982; Dealing with Stress Through Spiritual Methods, 1985; A Guide to Love-Powered Living, 1986. Add: 327 Katey Rose Lane, Euclid, Ohio 44143-2429, U.S.A.

HAUTZIG, Esther. Has also written as Esther Rudomin. American, b. 1930. Children's fiction, Children's non-fiction, Autobiography/Memoirs/Personal. *Publs:* (as Esther Rudomin) Let's Cook Without Cooking, 1955; Let's Make Presents, 1961; Redecorating Your Room for Practically Nothing, 1967; The Endless Steppe, 1968; In the Park, 1968; At Home, 1969; In School, 1971; Let's Make More Presents, 1973; Cool Cooking, 1974; (trans. and adaptor) I.L. Peretz: The Case Against the Wind and Other Stories, 1975; Life with Working Parents, 1976; A Gift for Mama, 1981; Holiday Treats, 1983; (trans. and adaptor) I.L. Peretz: The Seven Good Years and Other Stories, 1984; Make It Special, 1986; Riches, 1990. Add: 505 West End Ave., New York, N.Y. 10024, U.S.A.

HAVARD, Cyril (William Holmes). British, b. 1925. Medicine/Health. Consultant Physician, Royal Free Hosp., and Royal Northern Hosp., London. Casualty Physician, St. Bartholomews Hosp., London., 1964–66. *Publs:* (ed. and contrib.) Frontiers in Medicine, 1973; (ed. and contrib.) Current Medical Treatment, 5th ed., 1983; The Laboratory Investigations of Endocrine Diseases, 1979, 1983. Add: 121 Harley St., London W1, England.

HAVEMAN, Robert Henry. American, b. 1936. Economics. Prof. of Economics, Univ. of Wisconsin, Madison, since 1970 (Dir., Inst. for Research on Poverty, 1971–76). Chmn., Dept. of Economics, Grinnell Coll., Iowa, 1966–68; Sr. Economist, Subcttee. on Economy in Govt., U.S. Congress, 1968–69; Research Assoc., Resources for the Future Inc., 1969–70. *Publs:* Water Resource Investment and the Public Interest, 1965; (with K. Knopf) The Market System, 1966, 4th ed. 1981; (with J.V. Krutilla) Unemployment, Idle Capacity and the Evaluation of Public Expenditures, 1968; The Economics of the Public Sector, 1970, 1977; (ed. with J. Margolis) Public Expenditures and Policy Analysis, 1970, 3rd ed. 1982; The Economic Performance of Public Investments, 1972; (co-ed.) Benefit-Cost Annual—1971, 1972; (ed. with R. Hamrin) The Political Economy of Federal Policy, 1973; (with A.M. Freeman and A.V. Kneese) The Economics of Environmental Policy, 1973; (co-ed.) Benefit-Cost and Policy Analysis—1972, 1973, and 1974, 3 vols., 1973–75; (with F. Golladay) The Economic Impacts of Tax-Transfer Policy: Regional and Distributional Effects, 1977; A Decade of Federal Anti-Poverty Programs: Achievements, Failures, and Lessons, 1977; (with I. Garfinkel) Earnings Capacity, Poverty, and Inequality, 1978; (ed. with B. Zellner) Policy Studies Review Annual, 1979; (with Burkhauser) Disability Policy in the United States: Structure, Growth, and Economic Impacts, 1982; (ed. with J. Palmer) Jobs for Disadvantaged Workers, 1982; (ed. with K. Hollenbeck) Microeconomic Simulation Models for Public Policy Analysis, 2 vols., 1982; (ed.) Public Finance and Public Employment, 1982; (with R. Burkhauser and V. Halberstadt) Public Policy Toward Disabled Workers, 1985; Poverty Policy and Poverty Research, 1987; Starting Even: An Equal Opportunity Program to Combat the Nation's New Poverty, 1988. Add: Dept. of Economics, Univ. of Wisconsin, 1180 Observatory Dr., Madison, Wisc. 53706, U.S.A.

HAVIARAS, Stratis. American (b. Greek), b. 1935. Novels, Poetry, Art, Translations. Curator of the Poetry Collection, Woodberry Poetry Room, Harvard Univ. Library, Cambridge, since 1974 (Acquisitions Specialist, Head of the Acquisitions Section, and Head of the Gifts and Exchange Div., Harvard Coll. Library, 1968–74). Ed., Arion's Dolphin poetry quarterly, 1971–76. *Publs:* in Greek—Lady with a Compass (verse), 1963; Berlin (verse), 1965; Night of the Stiltwalker (verse), 1967; Apparent Death (verse), 1972; in English—(trans.) 35 Post-War Greek Poets, 1972; (with Paul Hannigan and John Batki) Kiss: A Collaboration (art), 1976; Crossing the River Twice (verse), 1976; (ed.) The Poet's Voice: T.S. Eliot, Ezra Pound, William Carlos Williams and others reading and commenting upon their works (audio cassettes), 1978; When the Tree Sings (novel), 1979; The Heroic Age (novel), 1985; (with Michael Milburn) Vladimir Nabokov at Harvard (audio cassettes), 1988. Add: Poetry Room, Harvard Univ. Library, Cambridge, Mass. 02138, U.S.A.

HAVIGHURST, Alfred F. American, b. 1904. History, Biography. Prof. Emeritus, Dept. of History, Amherst Coll., Mass., (Prof., 1931–70). *Publs:* Twentieth Century Britain, 1962, 1966, as Britain in Transition: The Twentieth Century, 1979, 1985; (ed.) The Pirenne Thesis: Analysis, Criticism and Revision, 1969, 1976; Radical Journalist: H.W. Massingham 1860-1924, 1974; (ed.) Modern England 1901–1970 (bibliographic handbook), 1976, 2nd ed., 1900–1984, 1988. Add: 11 Blake Field, Amherst, Mass. 01002, U.S.A.

HAVIL, Anthony. *See* **PHILIPP,** Eliot Elias.

HAVRAN, Martin Joseph. Canadian, b. 1929. History, Biography. Prof. of History, Univ. of Virginia, Charlottesville, since 1972 (Assoc. Prof. of History, 1968–72; Chmn., 1974–79; Dir., Self-Study Program, 1984–86). Asst. Prof., then Assoc. Prof., Kent State Univ., Ohio, 1957–67. Visiting Prof., Univ. of Alberta, 1965, and Northwestern Univ., 1967–68. Member, Bd. of Overseers, Case Western Reserve Univ., 1976–79; Vice-Pres., 1978–79, and Pres., 1979–81, North American Conference on British Studies; Pres., American Catholic Historical Assn., 1982. *Publs:* Catholics in Caroline England, 1962; (ed. with A.B. Erickson) Readings in English History, 1967; (with A.B. Erickson) England: Prehistory to the Present, 1968; Caroline Courtier: The Life of Lord Cottington, 1973. Add: Corcoran Dept. of History, Randall Hall, Univ. of Virginia, Charlottesville, Va. 22903, U.S.A.

HAWES, Judy. American, b. 1913. Children's fiction, Children's non-fiction. Retired teacher of the handicapped. *Publs:* Fire Flies in the Night, 1963; Bees and Beelines, 1964; Watch Honey Bees With Me, 1964; Shrimps, 1966; Ladybug, Ladybug Fly Away Home, 1967; Why Frogs Are Wet, 1968; What I Like About Toads, 1969; The Goats Who Killed the Leopard (A Story of Ethiopia), 1970; My Daddylonglegs, 1972; Spring Peepers, 1975. Add: 79 Abbington Terr., Glen Rock, N.J. 07452, U.S.A.

HAWK, Alex. *See* **GARFIELD,** Brian.

HAWK, Alex. *See* **KELTON,** Elmer.

HAWK, Alex. *See* **LUTZ,** Giles.

HAWKE, Gary Richard. New Zealander, b. 1942. Economics. Prof. of Economic History, Victoria Univ. of Wellington, since 1974 (Lectr. 1968–70; Reader 1971–73). Ed., New Zealand Economic Papers, 1973–77. *Publs:* Railways and Economic Growth in England and Wales, 1840-1870, 1970; The Development of the British Economy, 1870-1914, 1970; Between Governments and Banks: A History of the Reserve Bank of New Zealand, 1973; The Evolution of the New Zealand Economy, 1977; Economics for Historians, 1980; The Making of New Zealand, 1985. Add: Dept. of Economics, Victoria Univ. of Wellington, Private Bag, Wellington, New Zealand.

HAWKE, Simon. *See* **YERMAKOV,** Nicholas.

HAWKES, Jacquetta. British, b. 1910. Novel/Short stories, Science fiction/Fantasy, Archaeology/Antiquities, History, Biography. Vice-Pres., Council for British Archaeology, 1949–52; Gov., British Film Inst., London, 1950–55; Member, Culture Advisory Cttee., Unesco, 1964–79; Pres., Stratford upon Avon Soc., 1978. *Publs:* Archaeology of Jersey, 1939; (with Christopher Hawkes) Prehistoric Britain, 1944; Early Britain, 1945; Symbols and Speculations (poetry), 1948; A Land, 1951; Guide to Prehistoric and Roman Monuments in England and Wales, 1953; Fables, 1955; (with J.B. Priestley) Journey Down a Rainbow, 1959; Providence Island (novel), 1962; Man and the Sun, 1963; Unesco History of Mankind, vol. I, part I, The World of the Past, 1963; King of the

Two Lands (novel), 1966; The Dawn of the Gods, 1968; The First Great Civilizations, 1973; (ed.) Atlas of Ancient Archaeology, 1975; Atlas of Early Man, 1977; A Quest of Love, 1980; Mortimer Wheeler (biography) 1982; The Shell Guide to British Archaeology, 1986. Add: Littlecote, Leysbourne, Chipping Campden, Glos., England.

HAWKES, John (Clendennin Burne, Jr.). American, b. 1925. Novels/Short stories, Plays. Prof. of English Emeritus, Brown Univ., Providence, R.I. (Asst. Prof., 1958–62; Assoc. Prof., 1962–67; Prof., 1967–88). Asst. to Production Mgr., Harvard Univ. Press, Cambridge, Mass., 1949–55; Visiting Lectr. in English, 1955–56, and Instr. in English, 1956–58, Harvard Univ.; Visiting Lectr., Stanford Univ., Calif., 1966–67; Visiting Distinguished Prof. of Creative Writing, City Coll., City Univ. of New York, 1971–72. *Publs:* The Cannibal, 1949; The Beetle Leg, 1951; The Goose on the Grave, and The Owl: Two Short Novels, 1954; The Lime Twig, 1961; Second Skin, 1964; (co-ed.) The Personal Voice: A Contemporary Prose Reader, 1964; The Innocent Party: Four Short Plays, 1966; (co-ed.) The American Literary Anthology 1: The First Annual Collection of the Best from the Literary Magazines, 1968; Lunar Landscapes: Stories and Short Novels 1949–1963, 1969; The Blood Oranges, 1971; Death, Sleep and the Traveler, 1974; Travesty, 1976; The Passion Artist, 1979; Virginie: Her Two Lives, 1982; Humors of Blood and Skin: A John Hawkes Reader, 1984; Adventures in the Alaskan Skin Trade, 1985; Innocence in Extremis, 1985; Whistlejacket, 1988. Add: 18 Everett Ave., Providence, R.I. 02906, U.S.A.

HAWKESWORTH, Eric (William). British, b. 1921. Recreation/Leisure/Hobbies. Professional entertainer. *Publs:* Practical Lessons in Magic, 1967; Making a Shadowgraph Show, 1969; The Art of Paper Tearing, 1970; Conjuring, 1971; Puppet Shows to Make, 1972; A Magic Variety Show, 1973; Rag Picture Shows, 1974; Pleated Paper Folding: Methods and Routines for the Amateur Performer, 1975; Paper Cutting, 1976. Add: c/o Faber & Faber, 3 Queen Sq., London WC1N 3AU, England.

HAWKING, Stephen W(illiam). British, b. 1942. Physics. Fellow, Gonville and Caius Coll., Cambridge, since 1965, and Lucasian Prof. of Mathematics, Cambridge Univ., since 1979 (Member, Inst. of Theoretical Astronomy, 1968–72; Research Asst., Inst. of Astronomy, 1972–73; Research Asst., Dept. of Applied Mathematics and Theoretical Physics, 1973–75; Reader, 1975–77; Prof. of Gravitational Physics, 1977–79). *Publs:* (with G. Ellis) The Large Scale Structure of Space-Time, 1973; (ed. with W. Israel) General Relativity: An Einstein Centenary Survey, 1979; (ed. with M. Rocek) Superspace and Supergravity, 1981; A Brief History of Time, 1988. Add: Dept. of Applied Mathematics and Theoretical Physics, Cambridge, England.

HAWKINS, Gerald Stanley. American, b. 1928. Antiquities, Astronomy. Ed., U.S. Information Agency, since 1975. Prof. of Astronomy, and Chmn. of Dept., Boston Univ., 1957–69; Dean, Dickinson Coll., Pa., 1969–71; Astronomer, Smithsonian Astrophysics Observatory, Washington, D.C., 1962–74. *Publs:* Splendor in the Sky, 1961; (with John B. White) Stonehenge Decoded, 1965; Beyond Stonehenge, 1973; (with Julia M. Dobson) Conversations in English, 1979; Mindsteps to the Cosmos, 1983; (with W.M. Flinders Petrie) Stonehenge Update, 1989. Add: 2400 Virginia Ave., Washington, D.C. 20037, U.S.A.

HAWLEY, Richard A. American, b. 1945. Novels, Education, Poetry, Social commentary, Autobiography/Memoirs, Essays. Dir. of Upper Sch., Chagrin Falls, Ohio, since 1980 (Teacher, 1968–86; Dean of Students, 1973–79). *Publs:* Aspects of Vision, 1976; With Love to My Survivors, 1982; (ed.) Coming Through School, 1982; Purposes of Pleasure, 1983; The Headmaster's Papers, 1983; A School Answers Back, 1984; (with Robert Peterson and Margaret Mason) Building Drug-Free Schools, 1987; St. Julian, 1987; Seeing Things: A Chronicle of Surprises, 1987; The Big Issues in the Passage to Adulthood, 1988; Drugs and Society: Responding to an Epidemic, 1988. Add: c/o University Sch., Chagrin Falls, Ohio 44022, U.S.A.

HAWTHORNE, Jennie. British, b. 1916. Children's fiction, Money/Finance. Lectr. in Monetary Theory, South West London Coll., since 1972. Lectr. in Creative Writing, Adult Education, Borough of Sutton, 1969–72. *Publs:* The Mystery of the Blue Tomatoes, 1958; David and the Penny Red, 1962; All About Money, 1970; Successful Writing: A Beginner's Guide, 1972; Theory and Practice of Money, 1981; Questions and Answers in Monetary Economics, 1984. Add: South West London Coll., Tooting Broadway, London SW17, England.

HAY, Denys. British, b. 1915. History. Prof. Emeritus of Medieval

History, Univ. of Edinburgh, since 1980 (Prof., 1954–80; Vice-Principal, 1971–75). Literary Dir., Royal Historical Soc., 1954–57; Ed., English Historical Review, 1957–64. *Publs:* (trans.) Anglic Historia of Polydore Vergil, 1950; Polydore Vergil, 1952; From Roman Empire to Renaissance Europe, 1953, rev. ed. as The Medieval Centuries, 1964; (ed.) R.K. Hannay's Letters of James V, 1954; Europe: The Emergence of an Idea, 1957, 1968; Italian Renaissance in its Historical Background, 1961; (with J.D. Scott and M.M. Postan) Design and Development of Weapons, 1964; Europe in the 14th and 15th Centuries, 1966, 2nd ed., 1989; (ed. with W.K. Smith) Aeneas Silvius Piccolomini's De Gestis Basiliensis, 1967; (ed.) The Age of the Renaissance, 1967; The Italian Church in the Fifteenth Century, 1977; Annalists and Historians, 1979; Renaissance Essays, 1988. Add: 31 Fountainhall Rd., Edinburgh EH9 2LN, Scotland.

HAYASHI, Tetsumaro. American, b. 1929. Literature. Prof. of English, Ball State Univ., Muncie, Ind., since 1977 (Asst. Prof., 1968–72; Assoc. Prof., 1972–77). Ed.-in-Chief, Steinbeck Quarterly; Pres., Steinbeck Soc., 1977–83 (Exec. Dir., 1966–77); Pres., Intnl. John Steinbeck Society, since 1983. *Publs:* Sketches of American Culture, 1960; John Steinbeck: A Concise Bibliography, 1967; Arthur Miller Criticism, 1969, 1976; (ed.) A Looking Glass for London and England, by T. Lodge and R. Greene, 1970; (ed. with Richard Astro) Steinbeck: The Man and His Work, 1971; Robert Greene Criticism, 1971; Shakespeare's Sonnets: A Record of 20th Century Criticism, 1972; (ed.) Steinbeck's Literary Dimension, 1973; (compiler) A New Steinbeck Bibliography (1929–1971), 1973, (1971–81), 1983; (ed.) A Study Guide to Steinbeck's The Long Valley, 1976; A Study Guide to Steinbeck: A Handbook to His Major Works, 1974, Pt. II, 1979; (ed.) Steinbeck and Hemingway [William Faulkner, Arthur Miller and Tennessee Williams, Eugene O'Neill, James Joyce]: Research Opportunities and Dissertation Abstracts, 5 vols., 1980–85; John Steinbeck and the Vietnam War (Part I), 1986; (ed.) John Steinbeck: From Salinas to the World, 1986; Steinbeck on Writing, 1988. Add: 1405 N. Kimberly Lane, Muncie, Ind. 47306, U.S.A.

HAYCRAFT, Anna. *See* **ELLIS,** Alice Thomas.

HAYDEN, Donald E. American, b. 1915. Language/Linguistics, Literature. Prof. Emeritus of English, Univ. of Tulsa, Okla., since 1985 (Asst. Prof. of English, 1947–56; Prof., 1956–85; Dean of Liberal Arts, 1956–70). Instr., Syracuse Univ., N.Y., 1937–42; Head of English, Westbrook Junior Coll., Portland, Me., 1942–47. *Publs:* After Conflict, Quiet—A Study of Wordsworth, 1951; (with E.P. Alworth) A Semantics Workbook, 1956; (ed.) Classics in Semantics, 1965; (co-author) Classics in Linguistics, 1967; (ed.) His Firm Estate, 1967; (ed.) Classics in Composition, 1969; Introspection—The Artist Looks at Himself, 1971; Literary Studies: The Poetic Process, 1978; Wordsworth's Walking Tour of 1790, 1983; Wordsworth's Travels in Scotland, Wales and Ireland, Europe, 4 vols., 1985–88. Add: 3626 S. Birmingham Ave., Tulsa, Okla. 74105, U.S.A.

HAYDEN, Eric William. British, b. 1919. Children's fiction, Theology/Religion. Baptist Minister. *Publs:* Church Publicity, 1952; Faith's Glorious Achievement, 1958; Spurgeon on Revival, 1962; History of Spurgeons Tabernacle, 1962; Preaching Through the Bible, 2 vols., 1964, 1966; Everyday Yoga for Christians, 1966; Bible Object Lessons, 3 vols., 1968; When God Takes Over, 1969; Miracle of Time, 1970; Searchlight on Spurgeon, 1973; Jimmy in Space, 1973; Jimmy Plays Cricket, 1974; Sermon Outlines series, 6 vols., 1974–80; Joshua Thomas, 1976; Just the Girl You Want and Other Stories, 1977; Meditation, 1978; Praying for Revival, 1978; The Adventures of Bobby Wildgoose, 1980; Learning to Cope with Agoraphobia, 1983; Letting the Lion Loose, 1984; God's Answer for Fear, 1985; God's Answer for Pressure, 1987. Add: 7 Nanfan and Dobyn Place, Newent, Glos. GL18 1TF, England.

HAYDEN, Tom. (Thomas Emmet Hayden). American, b. 1939. Autobiography/Memoirs, Essays, Politics. Political activist. Founder and Chmn., Campaign for Economic Democracy, since 1977; Member of California State Assembly, since 1982. Co-Founder, Economic Research and Action Program, 1964; Dir., Newark Community Union Project, N.J., 1965–67; National Coordinator, Indochina Peace Campaign, 1973–75. *Publs:* Radical Nomad: Essays on C. Wright Mills and His Times, 1964; (with Staughton Lynd) The Other Side, 1966; Rebellion in Newark: Official Violence and Ghetto Response, 1967; Rebellion and Repression: Testimony by Tom Hayden Before the National Commission on the Causes and Prevention of Violence and the House and the House Un-American Activities Committee, 1969; (contrib.) The Conspiracy, 1969; Trial, 1970; The Love of Possession is a Disease with Them, 1972; Vietnam: The Struggle for Peace 1972-73, 1973; The American Future: New Visions Beyond Old Frontiers, 1980; Reunion: A Memoir, 1988.

Add: Campaign for Economic Democracy, 2506 Santa Monica Blvd., Santa Monica, Calif. 90404, U.S.A.

HAYEK, Friedrich August von. British, b. 1899. Economics, Philosophy, Politics/Government. Prof. Emeritus, Univs. of Chicago and Freiburg, W. Germany. Tooke Prof. of Economic Science and Statistics, London Sch. of Economics, Univ. of London, 1931–50. *Publs:* Prices and Production, 1931; Monetary Theory and the Trade Cycle, 1933; Monetary Nationalism and International Stability, 1935; Profit, Interest and Investment, 1939; The Pure Theory of Capital, 1941; The Road to Serfdom, 1944; Individualism and Economic Order, 1949; John Stuart Mill and Harriet Taylor, 1951; The Sensory Order, 1952; The Counter-Revolution of Science, 1952; The Political Ideal of the Rule of Law, 1955; The Constitution of Liberty, 1960; Studies in Philosophy, Politics and Economics, 1967; Law, Legislation and Liberty, 3 vols., 1973–79; De-Nationalisation of Money, 1976; New Studies in Philosophy, Politics, Economics, and the History of Ideas, 1978. Add: Urachstrasse 27, D-7800 Freiburg, Germany.

HAYES, John (Trevor). British, b. 1929. Art. Dir., National Portrait Gallery, London, since 1974. Asst. Keeper, 1954–70, and Dir., 1970–74, London Museum. *Publs:* London: A Pictorial History, 1969; The Drawings of Thomas Gainsborough, 1970; Catalogue of Oil Paintings in the London Museum, 1970; Gainsborough as Printmaker, 1971; Rowlandson: Watercolours and Drawings, 1972; Gainsborough: Paintings and Drawings, 1975; The Art of Graham Sutherland, 1980; The Landscape Paintings of Thomas Gainsborough, 1982. Add: National Portrait Gallery, St. Martin's Place, London WC2H 0HE, England.

HAYES, Joseph (Arnold). Also writes as Joseph H. Arnold. American, b. 1918. Novels/Short stories, Plays/Screenplays. Partner, Erskine & Hayes, theatrical producers, NYC, since 1954. Asst. Ed., Samuel French Inc., publrs., NYC, 1941–43. *Publs:* (with Marijane Hayes) And Came the Spring, 1942; Christmas at Home, 1943; The Thompsons, 1943; The Bridegroom Waits, 1943; (as Joseph H. Arnold) Sneak Date, 1944; (with M. Hayes) Come Rain or Shine, 1944; (with M. Hayes) Life of the Party, 1945; (with M. Hayes) Ask for Me Tomorrow, 1946; (as Joseph H. Arnold) Where's Laurie, 1946; (with M. Hayes) Come Over to Our House, 1946; Home for Christmas, 1946; A Woman's Privilege, 1947; (with M. Hayes) Quiet Summer, 1947; (with M. Hayes) Change of Heart, 1948; Leaf and Bough, 1949; (with M. Hayes) Too Many Dates, 1950; (with M. Hayes) Curtain Going Up, 1950; (with M. Hayes) Turn Back the Clock, 1950; (with M. Hayes) June Wedding, 1951; (with M. Hayes) Once in Every Family, 1951; Too Young, Too Old, 1952; (with M. Hayes) Mister Peepers, 1952; (with M. Hayes) Head in the Clouds, 1952; The Desperate Hours (novel), 1954, screenplay and play, 1955; (with M. Hayes) Bon Voyage (novel), 1957; The Hours After Midnight (novel), 1958; Don't Go Away Mad (novel), 1962; Calculated Risk, 1962; The Young Doctors (screenplay), 1962; The Third Day (novel), 1964; The Deep End (novel), 1967; Is Anyone Listening?, 1970; Like Any Other Fugitive (novel), 1971; Missing and Presumed Dead (novel), 1974; The Long Dark Night (novel), 1974; Island on Fire, 1978; Winner's Circle (novel), 1980; No Escape (novel), 1982; The Ways of Darkness (novel), 1985. Add: 1168 Westway, Sarasota, Fla. 34236, U.S.A.

HAYES, Paul Martin. British, b. 1942. History, International relations/Current affairs, Biography. Fellow and Tutor in Modern History and Politics, Keble Coll., Oxford Univ., since 1965. *Publs:* The Career and Political Ideas of Vidkun Quisling, 1971; Fascism, 1973; A. and C. Black Modern British Foreign Policy Series: The Nineteenth Century 1814-80, 1975, and the The Twentieth Century 1880-1939, 1978. Add: Keble Coll., Oxford OX1 3PG, England.

HAYES, Samuel Perkins. American, b. 1910. International relations/Current affairs, Social sciences (general). Consultant to World Bank and Development Alternatives, Inc., since 1976. Bd. of Directors, Amateur Chamber Music Players, NYC. Assoc. Dir., Marketing and Research Service, Dun and Bradstreet Inc., NYC, 1945–48; held various positions with the U.S. Govt., 1942–45, 1948–53; Dir., Foundn. for Research on Human Behavior, 1953–60, and Prof. of Economics, 1959–62, Univ. of Michigan, Ann Arbor; Pres., Foreign Policy Assn., NYC, 1962–74; Dir., New York Region, The Campaign for Yale, NYC, 1974–76. *Publs:* (co-ed.) Some Applications of Behavioral Research, 1957; Measuring the Result of Development Projects, 1959; An International Peace Corps, 1961; Evaluating Development Projects, 1966; The Beginning of American Aid to Southeast Asia, 1971. Add: 2122 California St. N.W., Apt. 652, Washington, D.C. 20008, U.S.A.

HAYMAN, Carol Bessent. American, b. 1927. Poetry, Theol-ogy/Religion. Instr. in Creative Writing, Carteret Co. Community Coll. since 1985. *Publs:* Keepsake, 1962; These Lovely Days, 1971; A Collection of Writings, 1972; What is Christmas?, 1974; (ed.) The Bessent Story, 1978. Add: 618 Ann St., Beaufort, N.C. 28516, U.S.A.

HAYMAN, David. American, b. 1927. Literature. Prof. of Comparative Literature, Univ. of Wisconsin, Madison, since 1973. Prof. of English, Univ. of Texas, Austin, 1955–65, and Univ. of Iowa, Iowa City, 1965–73; Prof. of English and American Literature, Univ. de Paris, 1972–73; Prof of English and Am. Literature, Goethe Univ., Frankfurt, Germany, 1984–85. *Publs:* Joyce et Mallarmé, 1956; A First-Draft Version of Finnegan's Wake, 1963; Louis Ferdinand Celine, 1965; Ulysses: The Mechanics of Meaning, 1970, 1982; (with E. Rabkin) Form in Fiction, 1973; (with C. Hart) Ulysses: Critical Essays, 1974; (ed. with others) The James Joyce Archive, 1978; (ed.) In the Wake of the Wake, 1978; (ed.) Philippe Sollers, Writing and the Experience of Limits, 1983; Re-Forming the Narrative: Toward a Mechanics of Modernist Fiction, 1987. Add: Dept. of Comparative Literature, Univ. of Wisconsin, Madison, Wisc. 53706, U.S.A.

HAYMAN, Ronald. British, b. 1932. Literature, Theatre, Autobiography, Biography. Asst. Producer, Northampton Repertory Co., 1962–63. *Publs:* Harold Pinter, 1968; Samuel Beckett, 1968; John Osborne, 1968; John Arden, 1968; Robert Bolt, 1969; John Whiting, 1969; (ed.) Collected Plays of John Whiting, 2 vols., 1969; Techniques of Acting, 1969; (ed.) The Art of the Dramatist and Other Pieces, by John Whiting, 1970; Arthur Miller, 1970; Tolstoy, 1970; Arnold Wesker, 1970; John Gielgud, 1971; Edward Albee, 1971; Eugène Ionesco, 1972; Playback, 1973; The Set-Up, 1974; Playback 2, 1974; The First Thrust, 1975; (ed.) The German Theatre, 1975; The Novel Today 1967–1975, 1976; Leavis, 1976; (ed.) My Cambridge, 1977; Tom Stoppard, 1977; How to Read a Play, 1977; Artaud and After, 1977; De Sade, 1978; Theatre and Anti-Theatre, 1979; British Theatre since 1955: A Reassessment, 1979; Nietzsche: A Critical Life, 1980; K: A Biography of Kafka, 1981; Brecht: A Biography, 1983; Fassbinder, Film Maker, 1984; Brecht: The Plays, 1984; Günter Grass, 1985; Secrets: Boyhood in a Jewish Hotel 1932–54, 1985; Writing Against: A Biography of Sartre, 1986. Add: 25 Church Row, London NW3 6UP, England.

HAYMAN, Walter Kurt. British, b. 1926. Mathematics/Statistics. Prof. of Mathematics, Univ. of York, since 1985. Lectr. 1947–53, and Reader 1953–56, Univ. of Exeter; Prof. of Pure Mathematics, Imperial Coll., Univ. of London, 1956–85. *Publs:* Multivalent Functions, 1958; Meromorphic Functions, 1964; Research Problems in Function Theory, 1967; (with P.B. Kennedy) Subharmonic Functions 1, 1976. Add: Dept. of Mathematics, Univ. of York, Heslington, York YO1 5DD, England.

HAYNES, Dorothy K. Pseudonym for Dorothy Kate Gray. British, b. 1918. Novels/Short stories. *Publs:* Winter's Traces, 1947; Robin Ritchie, 1949; Thou Shalt Not Suffer a Witch, 1949; Haste Ye Back, 1973; Peacocks and Pagodas, 1982; The Gay Goshawk, 1986. Add: 14 Quarryknowe, Lanark ML11 7AH, Scotland.

HAYNES, Renée Oriana. (Mrs. Jerrard Tickell). British. Novels, Theology/Religion, Paranormal, Biography, Literary criticism/history. Dir., Book Reviews Dept., British Council, London, 1945–63; Ed., Journal and Proceedings, Soc. for Psychical Research, London, 1970–81. *Publs:* Neapolitan Ice, 1928; Immortal John, 1932; The Holy Hunger, 1935; Pan, Caesar and God, 1938; Hilaire Belloc, 1953; (ed. and contrib.) The Lawyer, a Conversation Piece, 1951; (trans.) Psychical Phenomena, 1959; The Hidden Springs, 1961; Philosopher King: Benedict XIV, 1970; The Seeing Eye, The Seeing I, 1976; The Society for Psychical Research 1882-1982: A History, 1982. Add: The Garden Flat, 41 Springfield Rd., London NW8 0QJ, England.

HAYNES, Sybille (Edith). British, b. 1926. Archaeology/Antiquities, Travel/Exploration/Adventure. Voluntary Asst., Greek and Roman Dept., British Museum, London, 1951–76. *Publs:* Land of the Chimaera, 1974; Etruscan Sculpture, 1971; Etruscan Bronze Utensils, 1974; Die Tochter der Augurs, 1981; Etruscan Bronzes, 1985; The Augur's Daughter, 1987. Add: Flat 17, Murray Ct., 80 Banbury Rd., Oxford OX2 6LQ, England.

HAYS, Peter L. American, b. 1938. Literature. Prof. of English, Univ. of California, Davis, since 1977 (joined faculty, 1966; Coordinator of Undergrad. Studies, 1973–74; Chmn., Dept. of English, 1974–77). *Publs:* The Limping Hero, 1971. Add: English Dept., Univ. of California-Davis, Calif. 95616, U.S.A.

HAYS, Wilma Pitchford. American, b. 1909. Children's fiction, Children's non-fiction. Former elementary sch. teacher; teacher of juvenile writing, Cape Cod Writer's Conference, 1963–64, 1973, 1974. *Publs:* Pilgrim Thanksgiving, 1955; Christmas on the Mayflower, 1956; Story of Valentine, 1956; Freedom, 1958; Fourth of July Raid, 1959; Easter Fires, 1959; Drummer Boy for Montcalm, 1959; Little Horse That Raced a Train, 1959; Little Lone Coyote, 1961; The Hawaiian Way, 1961; Abe Lincoln's Birthday, 1961; Highland Halloween, 1962; George Washington's Birthdays, 1963; The Pup That Became a Police Dog, 1963; Little Hawaiian Horse, 1963; The Scarlet Badge, 1963; Cape Cod Adventure, 1964; Pontiac (biography), 1965; The French Are Coming, 1965; Little Hurricane Happy, 1965; Eli Whitney, Founder of Industry, 1965; Samuel Morse and the Electronic Age, 1966; The Goose Who Was a Watchdog, 1967; Noko Captive of Columbus, 1967; May Day for Samoset, 1968; Mary's Star, 1968; The Apricot Tree, 1968; Naughty Little Pilgrim, 1969; Rebel Pilgrim (biography), 1969; The Burro Who Ran Away, 1969; Circus Girl Without a Name, 1970; Patrick of Ireland, 1970; The Open Gate, 1970; The Long Blond Wig, 1971; Pilgrim to the Rescue, 1971; Meriwether Lewis Mystery (biography), 1971; For Ma and Pa, 1972; Little Yellow Fur, 1973; (with R.V. Hays) Foods the Indians Gave Us, 1973; Siege, 1976; Monsters and Oil Wells Don't Mix, 1976; Trouble at Otter Creek, 1978; Ghost at Penniman House, 1979; Yellow Fur and Little Hawk, 1980; Rex the Hero Dog, 1986. Add: 1660 La Gorce Dr., Venice, Fla. 34293, U.S.A.

HAYTER, Alethea (Catharine). British, b. 1911. Literature, Biography. On editorial staff, Country Life, 1933–38; with British Council, London, Athens, Paris, Brussels, 1945–71. *Publs:* Mrs. Browning: A Poet's Work and Its Setting, 1962; A Sultry Month: Scenes of London Literary Life in 1846, 1965; Elizabeth Barrett Browning, 1965; Opium and the Romantic Imagination, 1968; (ed.) Confessions of an English Opium Eater, by Thomas de Quincey, 1971; Horatio's Version (fiction), 1972; A Voyage in Vain: Coleridge's Journey to Malta in 1804, 1973; (ed.) Melmoth the Wanderer, 1977; (ed.) FitzGerald to His Friends: Selected Letters of Edward FitzGerald, 1979. Add: 22 Aldebert Terr., London SW8 1BJ, England.

HAYTER, Teresa. British. International relations/Current affairs, Third World problems, Autobiography/Memoirs/Personal. *Publs:* (with A. Moyes) World War III, 1964; French Aid, 1966; Aid as Imperialism, 2nd ed. 1971; Hayter on the Bourgeoisie, 1972; Creation of World Poverty, 1981; (with C. Watson) Aid: Rhetoric and Reality, 1985. Add: c/o Sidgwick & Jackson Ltd., Tavistock Chambers, Bloomsbury Way, London WC1A 2SG, England.

HAYTER, (Sir) William (Goodenough). British, b. 1906. International relations/Current affairs, Biography. Member, H.M. Diplomatic Service, 1930–58; Ambassador in Moscow, 1953–57; Deputy Under-Secty., Foreign Office, 1957–58; Warden of New Coll., Oxford., 1958–76. *Publs:* The Diplomacy of the Great Powers, 1960; The Kremlin and the Embassy, 1966; Russia and the World, 1970; William of Wykeham: Patron of the Arts, 1970; A Double Life, 1974; Spooner: A Biography, 1977. Add: Bassetts House, Stanton St. John, Oxford, England.

HAYTHORNE, George Vickers. Canadian, b. 1909. Economics. Adviser, Canadian Intnl. Development Agency, and Commonwealth Secretariat, London. Secty., Nova Scotia Economic Council, 1938–42; Deputy Minister, Canada Dept. of Labour, Ottawa, 1961–68; Commnr., Prices and Incomes Cmmn., Ottawa, 1969–72; Dir., Inst. of Development Mgmt., Botswana, Lesotho, and Swaziland, 1974–79. *Publs:* Reports of the Nova Scotia Economic Council, vols. 3-7, 1938–43; Land and Labour, 1941; Labor in Canadian Agriculture, 1960; Construction and Inflation, 1973. Add: 2190 Alta Vista Dr., Ottawa K1H 7MI, Canada.

HAYTHORNTHWAITE, Philip John. British, b. 1951. Military/Defence. Company Dir., H. Gerrard Ltd., since 1970. *Publs:* Uniforms of the Napoleonic Wars, 1973; Uniforms of Waterloo, 1974; Uniforms of the American Civil War, 1975; World Uniforms and Battles 1815-50, 1976; Uniforms of the Retreat from Moscow 1812, 1976; Uniforms of the Peninsular War 1807-14, 1978; Weapons and Equipment of the Napoleonic Wars, 1979; Uniforms of the French Revolutionary Wars 1789-1802, 1981; The English Civil War, 1982; Napoleon's Line Infantry, 1982; Uniforms of 1812, 1982; Napoleon's Light Infantry, 1983; Napoleon's Guard Infantry, 2 vols., 1984–85; Civil War Soldiers, 1985; The Alamo and War of Texan Independence, 1986; Austrian Army of the Napoleonic Wars, 2 vols., 1986; Russian Army of the Napoleonic Wars, 2 vols., 1987; Uniforms Illustrated: The Boer War, 1987; British Infantry of the Napoleonic Wars, 1987; Uniforms Illustrated: The Victorian Colonial Wars, 1988; Napoleon's Military Machine, 1988; Napoleon's

Specialist Troops, 1988; Wellington's Specialist Troops, 1988; Wellington's Military Machine, 1989; Austrian Specialist Troops of the Napoleonic Wars, 1989; Fotofax: 1914, 1989; Gustavus Adolphus, 1989; Marlborough, 1989; Frederick the Great, 1989; Wellington, 1989; Fotofax: 1915, 1989–90; Fotofax: 1916, 1990. Add: Park Hill, Parrock Rd., Barrowford, Nelson, Lancs. BB9 6QF, England.

HAYWOOD, Carolyn. American, b. 1898. Children's fiction. Taught at the Friends Central Sch., Philadelphia; Asst. in the studio of Violet Oakley; Portrait painter and mural artist. *Publs:* (illustrated by the author): When I Grow Up, 1931; Betsy series: 12 vols., 1939–78; Two and Two are Four, 1940; Primrose Day, 1942; Here's a Penny, 1944; Penny and Peter, 1946; Eddie series, 14 vols., 1947–78; Penny Goes to Camp, 1948; The Mixed-Up Twins, 1952; Here Comes the Bus!, 1963; Robert Rows the River, 1965; Taffy and Melissa Molasses, 1969; A Christmas Fantasy, illustrated by Glenys and Victor Ambrus, 1972; Away Went the Balloons, 1973; "C" is for Cupcake, 1974; A Valentine Fantasy, 1976; The King's Monster, 1980; Halloween Treats, 1981; Santa Claus Forever!, 1983; Happy Birthday from Carolyn Haywood, 1984; How the Reindeer Saved Santa Claus, 1986; Merry Christmas from Eddie, 1986; Summer Fun, 1986; Hello, Star, 1987. Add: c/o William Morrow & Co., Inc., 105 Madison Ave., New York, N.Y. 10016, U.S.A.

HAYWOOD, Charles. American, b. 1904. Music, Mythology/Folklore, Biography, Translations. Prof. of Music Emeritus, Queens Coll., City Univ. of New York, since 1978 (Prof. since 1939). Lectr., Juilliard Sch. of Music, NYC, 1939–52; Visiting Prof., Hunter Coll., City Univ. of New York, 1958–59, and Univ. of California, Los Angeles 1962–63. Opera singer, concert artist soloist in symphony orchestras, also radio and television appearances, since 1930. *Publs:* James A. Bland, 1946; (ed.) James A. Bland and Negro Minstrelsy, 1947; Cervantes and Music, 1948; (ed.) Modern Russian Art Songs, 1948; A Bibliography of North American Folklore and Folksong, 1951, rev. ed. in 2 vols., 1961; (ed.) Sacred Art Songs, 1958; Negro Minstrelsy and Shakespearean Burlesque, 1966; Folk Songs of the World: A Comparative Study, 1966; (ed.) Maretzek: Life of an Opera Impresario in 19th Century America, 1968; (ed.) George Bernard Shaw on Shakespearian Music and the Actor, 1969; (ed.) Ralph Vaughan Williams and Maud Karpeles: A Correspondence, 1972; Pablo Casals and Catalan Folk Music, 1973; Charles Dickens and His Burlesque: O'Thello, with the Music, 1977. Add: 145 East 92nd St., New York, N.Y. 10128, U.S.A.

HAYWOOD, Richard Mowbray. American, b. 1933. History. Assoc. Prof. of History, Purdue Univ., W. Lafayette, Ind., since 1969. *Publs:* The Beginnings of Railway Development in Russia in the Reign of Nicholas I, 1835-1842, 1969. Add: Dept. of History, Purdue Univ., W. Lafayette, Ind. 47907, U.S.A.

HAZARD, Jack. *See* **BOOTH**, Edwin.

HAZARD, John Newbold. American, b. 1909. Law. Prof. Emeritus of Law, Columbia Univ., NYC, since 1977 (Prof. of Public Law, 1946–77). *Publs:* Soviet Housing Law, 1939; Law and Social Change in the U.S.S.R., 1953; Soviet System of Government, 1957; Settling Disputes in Soviet Society, 1960; (with I. Shapiro) Soviet Legal System, 1962; Communists and Their Law, 1969; Managing Change in the U.S.S.R., 1983; Recollections of a Pioneering Sovietologist, 1983, enlarged ed., 1986; (with W.E. Butler and P.B. Maggs) The Soviet Legal System, 1984. Add: 20 East 94th St., New York, N.Y. 10128, U.S.A.

HAZLEHURST, Cameron. British, b. 1941. History, Politics/Government, Biography. Fellow, Nuffield Coll. 1968–70, and The Queen's Coll. 1970–72, and Lectr. in Politics, University Coll. 1969–72, Oxford Univ.; Sr. Fellow, Inst. of Advanced Studies, Australian National Univ., Canberra, 1972–88; Australian National Campaign Dir., AIDS Education and Information, 1988–89. Asst. Secty., Australian Dept. of Urban and Regional Development, 1974–75. First Asst. Secty., Commonwealth Dept. of Communications, 1984–86. Historical Adviser, Jonathan Cape Ltd., London, 1968–72; Series Research Consultant, BBC television British Empire Series, 1969–72; Contrib. Ed., The Times Higher Education Supplement, London, 1971–72; Research Consultant, ABC-TV Mastermind Series, 1977–82. *Publs:* (ed.) Winston S. Churchill, The People's Rights, 1970; Politicians at War, July 1914 to May 1915, 1971; (ed.) The Lloyd George Liberal Magazine, 1974; (with Christine Woodland) A Guide to the Papers of British Cabinet Ministers 1900–1951, 1974; (ed.) The History of the Ministry of Munitions, 1974; (ed., with J.R. Nethercote) Reforming Australian Government, 1977; Menzies Observed, 1979; (ed.) Australian Conservatism: Essays in Twentieth Century Political History, 1979; (ed.) The Mastermind Book, 1979; (ed.) The Mastermind General Knowledge Book, 1982; Gordon Chalk: A Political Life, 1987; (with Colin Forster) Australian Statisticians and the Development of Official Statistics, 1988. Add: 8 Hunter St., Yarralumla, A.C.T. 2600, Australia.

HAZLITT, Henry. American, b. 1894. Economics, Money/Finance, Sociology. Financial Ed., New York Evening Mail, 1921–23; Editorial Writer, New York Herald, 1923–24; Editorial Writer, 1924–25, and Literary Ed., 1925–29, The Sun, NYC; Literary Ed., The Nation, NYC, 1930–33; Ed., American Mercury, 1933–34; Member of editorial staff, New York Times, 1934–46; Assoc., Newsweek mag., and Columnist, Business Tides, 1946–66; Co-Founder and Co-Ed., 1950–52, and Ed.-in-Chief, 1953, The Freeman; Columnist, Los Angeles Times Syndicate, 1966–69. *Publs:* Thinking as a Science, 1916, 1969; (ed.) A Practical Programme for America, 1932; Instead of Dictatorship, 1933; The Anatomy of Criticism, 1933; A New Constitution Now, 1942, 1974; Economics in One Lesson, 1946; Will Dollars Save the World?, 1947; Time Will Run Back, 1951, 1966; What You Should Know About Inflation, 1960, 1965; The Free Man's Library, 1956; The Failure of the New Economics: An Analysis of the Keynesian Fallacies, 1959, 1984; (ed.) The Critics of Keynesian Economics, 1960; The Foundations of Morality, 1964, 1972; Man vs. the Welfare State, 1969; The Conquest of Poverty, 1973; The Inflation Crisis and How to Resolve It, 1978; From Bretton Woods to World Inflation, 1984. Add: 59 Courtland Ave., Stamford, Conn. 06902, U.S.A.

HAZO, Samuel (John). American, b. 1928. Novels/Short stories, Poetry, Literature, Memoirs. Prof. of English, Duquesne Univ., Pittsburgh, since 1965 (joined faculty, 1955; Dean, Coll. of Arts and Sciences, 1961–66). Dir., Intnl. Poetry Forum, Pittsburgh, since 1966. *Publs:* Discovery and Other Poems, 1959; The Quiet Wars (verse), 1962; Hart Crane: An Introduction and Interpretation, 1963, as Smithereened Apart: A Critique of Hart Crane, 1978; (ed.) The Christian Intellectual: Studies in the Relation of Catholicism to the Human Sciences, 1963; (ed.) A Selection of Contemporary Religious Poetry, 1963; Listen with the Eye (verse), 1964; My Sons in God: Selected and New Poems, 1965; Blood Rights (verse), 1968; (with Ali Ahmed Said) The Blood of Adonis (verse), 1971; (with George Nama) Twelve Poems, 1972; Seascript: A Mediterranean Logbook (fiction), 1972; Once for the Last Bandit: New and Previous Poems, 1972; Quartered (verse), 1974; Inscripts (fiction), 1975; The Very Fall of the Sun (novel), 1978; To Paris (verse), 1981; The Wanton Summer Air (novel), 1982; Thank a Bored Angel (verse), 1983; The Feast of Icarus (essays), 1984; The Color of Reluctance (verse), 1986; The Pittsburgh that Starts Within You (memoir), 1986; Nightwords (verse), 1987; Silence Spoken Here (verse), 1988; Stills (fiction), 1989; The Rest is Prose (essays), 1989. Add: 785 Somerville Dr., Pittsburgh, Pa. 15243, U.S.A.

HAZZARD, Shirley. Australian, b. 1931. Novels/Short stories, International relations/Current affairs. Member of staff, Gen. Service Category, U.N. Headquarters, NYC, 1951–61. *Publs:* Cliffs of Fall, 1963; The Evening of the Holiday, 1966; People in Glass Houses, 1967; The Bay of Noon, 1970; Defeat of an Ideal (intnl. affairs), 1973; The Transit of Venus, 1980. Add: 200 East 66th St., New York, N.Y. 10021, U.S.A.

HEADINGTON, Christopher (John Magenis). British, b. 1930. Music. Tutor in Music, Oxford Univ. Dept. for External Studies, since 1965. Record Critic, Country Life, and Audio Mag. Music Master, Trinity Coll., Glenalmond, Perthshire, 1951–54; Deputy Dir. of Music, Lancing Coll., Sussex, 1954–64; Sr. Asst., Music Presentation, BBC, London, 1964–65. *Publs:* The Orchestra and Its Instruments, 1965; The Bodley Head History of Western Music, 1974; (ed.) Illustrated Dictionary of Musical Terms, 1980; Britten, 1981; The Musician, 1981; Listener's Guide to Chamber Music, 1981; Opera: A History, 1987. Add: c/o Blandford Press, Link House, West St., Poole BH15 1LL, England.

HEADSTROM, Richard (Birger). American, b. 1902. Animals/Pets, Botany, History, Zoology. Teacher, private and public schools in Massachusetts, 1942–64; Associate Curator of Botany, New England Museum of Natural History, 1939–42; Curator of Entomology, Worcester (Mass.) Museums of Science and Industry, 1944–64; now retired. Columnist, The Boston Transcript, 1940–41, The Boston Globe, 1941–45, The Worcester Telegram, 1964–67, and The State, Columbia, S.C., 1965–67. *Publs:* The Origin of Man, 1921; The Story of Russia, 1933; Adventures with a Microscope, 1941; Birds' Nests, 1949; The Living Year, 1950; Birds' Nests of the West, 1951; Garden Friends and Foes, 1954; Adventures with a Hand Lens, 1962; Adventures with Insects, 1963; Adventures with Freshwater Animals, 1964; Nature in Miniature, 1968; A Complete

Field Guide to Nests in the United States, 1970; Lizards as Pets, 1971; Whose Track Is It, 1971; Frogs, Toads and Salamanders as Pets, 1972; Spiders of the United States, 1973; Your Insect Pet, 1973; The Beetles of America, 1977; Your Reptile Pet, 1978; The Families of Flowering Plants, 1978; Lobsters, Crab, Shrimps and Their Relatives, 1979; The Weird and Beautiful, 1982; Identifying Animal Tracks: Mammals, Birds and Other Animals of the Eastern United States, 1983; Suburban Geology [Wildflowers, Wildlife], 3 vols., 1984–85; Memories from a Naturalist's Yearbook, 1986; Nature Science Adventures, 2 vols., 1986. Add: 124 Waterloo St., Aiken, S.C. 29801, U.S.A.

HEADY, Harold F(ranklin). American, b. 1916. Children's non-fiction, Environmental science/Ecology. Prof. Emeritus of Range Mgmt. and Plant Ecology, and Asst. Vice-Pres., Agriculture and Univ. Services and Assoc. Dir., Agricultural Experiment Station, 1977–80, Univ. of California, Berkeley (Assoc. Dean, Coll. of Natural Resources, 1974–77). Asst. Prof. Montana State Univ., Bozeman, 1942–47; Assoc. Prof., Texas Univ., College Station, 1947–51. *Publs:* (with Eleanor B. Heady) High Meadow, 1970; Range Management, 1975. Add: 1864 Capistrano Ave., Berkeley, Calif. 94707, U.S.A.

HEALD, Tim(othy Villiers). Also writes as David Lancaster in U.K. British, b. 1944. Mystery/Crime/Suspense, Biography. Freelance journalist, since 1978. Reporter, Atticus column, The Sunday Times, London, 1965–67; Feature Ed., Town mag., London, 1967; Feature Writer, Daily Express, London, 1967–72; freelance journalist, London, 1972–77; Assoc. Ed., Weekend Mag., Toronto, 1977–78. *Publs:* It's a Dog's Life, 1971; Unbecoming Habits (mystery novel), 1973; Blue Blood Will Out (mystery novel), 1974; Deadline (mystery novel), 1975; Let Sleeping Dogs Die (mystery novel), 1976; The Making of Space 1999, 1976; John Steed: An Authorized Biography, 1977; Just Desserts (mystery novel), 1977; (with Mayo Mohs) H.R.H.: The Man Who Will be King, 1979; Murder at Moose Jaw (mystery novel), 1981; (as David Lancaster in U.K.) Caroline R. (novel), 1981; Masterstroke (mystery novel), 1982; Networks, 1983; Class Distinctions (novel), 1984; Red Herrings (mystery novel), 1985; The Character of Cricket, 1986; Brought to Book (mystery novel), 1988; (ed.) The Newest London Spy, 1988. Add: 305 Sheen Rd., Richmond, Surrey TW10 5AW, England.

HEALEY, Ben(jamin James). Also writes as Jeremy Sturrock and (for Sturrock books, in the U.S.) as J.G. Jeffreys. British, b. 1908. Novels/Short stories, Mystery/Crime/Suspense, Horticulture. Scenic artist and stage designer, Birmingham Repertory Theatre, 1926–31; Art Designer, Decorative Crafts, Birmingham, 1935–40; Scenic Artist, Denham Film Studios, London, 1946–47; Scenic Artist and Art Dir., Riverside Film Studios, London, 1947–50; free-lance scenic artist/art dir. for various film companies, 1951–67. *Publs:* mystery novels—Waiting for a Tiger, 1965; The Millstone Men, 1966; Death in Three Masks (in U.S. as The Terrible Pictures), 1967; Murder Without Crime, 1968; The Trouble with Penelope, 1972; The Vespucci Papers, 1972; (as Jeremy Sturrock) The Village of Rogues (in U.S. as The Thieftaker), 1972; The Stone Baby, 1973; (as Jeremy Sturrock) A Wicked Way to Die, 1973; The Horstmann Inheritance, 1975; (as Jeremy Sturrock) The Wilful Lady, 1975; The Blanket of the Dark, 1976; (as Jeremy Sturrock) A Conspiracy of Poisons, 1977; The Snapdragon Murders, 1978; (as Jeremy Sturrock) Suicide Most Foul, 1981; Last Ferry from the Lido (in U.S. as Last Ferry to Venice), 1982; (as Jeremy Sturrock) Captain Bolton's Corpse, 1982; (as Jeremy Sturrock) The Pangersbourne Murders, 1983; other—The Red Head Herring (novel), 1969; A Gardener's Guide to Plant Names, 1972; The Plant Hunters, 1975; Captain Havoc (novel), 1977; Havoc in the Indies (novel), 1979. Add: 19 Granard Ave., Putney, London SW15 6HH, England.

HEALEY, Denis (Winston). British, b. 1917. Economics, International relations/Current affairs, Politics/Government. Labour M.P. for Leeds East since 1955 (M.P. for S.E. Leeds, 1952–55; Secty. of State for Defence, 1964–70; Shadow Foreign Secty., 1970–74, 1980; Chancellor of the Exchequer, 1974–79). Member, Labour Party National Exec. Cttee. Secty., Labour Party Intnl. Dept., 1946–52. Member of Council, Royal Inst. of Intnl. Affairs, London, 1948–60; Member of the Exec., Fabian Soc., 1954–61; Member of the Council, Inst. of Strategic Studies, London, 1958–61. *Publs:* The Curtain Falls, 1951; New Fabian Essays, 1952; Neutralism, 1955; Fabian International Essays, 1956; A Neutral Belt in Europe, 1958; NATO and American Security, 1959; The Race Against the H Bomb, 1960; Labour Britain and the World, 1963; Managing the Economy, 1979; Healey's Eye, 1980; Labour and World Society, 1985; Beyond Nuclear Deterrence, 1986. Add: House of Commons, London S.W.1, England.

HEALY, David Frank. American, b. 1926. History, International relations/Current affairs. Prof. of History, Univ. of Wisconsin, Milwaukee, since 1971 (Assoc. Prof., 1966–71). Asst. Prof. of History, Illinois Coll., Jacksonville, 1960–64, and Univ. of Delaware, Newark, 1964–66. *Publs:* The United States in Cuba 1898-1902, 1963; U.S. Expansion: The Imperialist Urge in the 1890s, 1970; Gunboat Diplomacy in the Wilson Era: The U.S. Navy in Haiti 1915-1916, 1976; Drive to Hegemony: the U.S. in the Caribbean 1898-1917, 1988. Add: Dept. of History, Univ. of Wisconsin-Milwaukee, Milwaukee, Wisc. 53201, U.S.A.

HEANEY, Seamus. Irish, b. 1939. Poetry, Literature. Boylston Prof. of Rhetoric and Oratory, Harvard Univ., Cambridge, Mass., since 1985 (Visiting Prof., 1982–85). Secondary sch. teacher, 1962–63; Lectr., St. Joseph's Coll. of Education, Belfast, 1963–66; Lectr. in English, Queen's Univ., Belfast, 1966–72, and Carysfort Training Coll., Dublin, 1975–81. *Publs:* Eleven Poems, 1965; Death of a Naturalist, 1966; (with D. Hammond and M. Longley) Room to Rhyme, 1968; A Lough Neagh Sequence, 1969; Door into the Dark, 1969; Night Drive: Poems, 1970; Boy Driving His Father to Confession, 1970; Land, 1971; (ed. with Alan Brownjohn and Jon Stallworthy) New Poems 1970–71, 1971; Wintering Out, 1972; (ed.) Soundings 2, 1974; North, 1975; The Fire i' the Flint: Reflections on the Poetry of Gerard Manley Hopkins, 1975; Bog Poems, 1975; Stations, 1975; Robert Lowell: A Memorial Lecture and an Eulogy, 1978; Field Work, 1979; Selected Poems, 1980; Preoccupations: Selected Prose, 1980; An Open Letter, 1983; Sweeney Astray: A Version from the Irish, 1983; Station Island, 1984; The Haw Lantern, 1987; The Government of the Tongue, 1988. Add: c/o Faber, 3 Queen Sq., London WC1N 3AV, England.

HEAP, (Sir) Desmond. British, b. 1907. Law, Regional/Urban planning. Solicitor, since 1933. Member of Editorial Bd., Journal of Planning Law, since 1948. Comptroller and City Solicitor, Corp. of London, 1947–73. Member of Colonial Office Housing and Town Planning Advisory Panel, 1953–65; Pres., Royal Town Planning Inst., 1955–56; Pres., Law Soc., 1972–73. Assoc., Royal Inst. of Chartered Surveyors; Hon. Member, American Bar Assoc.; Hon. Life Member, Council of the Intnl. Bar Assoc.; Gold Medalist, Royal Town Planning Inst., 1983; Gold Medalist, Lincoln Inst. of Land Policy, USA, 1983. *Publs:* Planning Law for Town and Country, 1938; Planning and the Law of Interim Development, 1944; The Town and Country Planning Act 1944, 1945; An Outline of Planning Law 1943 to 1945, 1945; The New Towns Act 1946, 1947; Introducing the Town and Country Planning Act 1947, 1947; Encyclopaedia of Planning, Compulsory Purchase and Compensation, vol. I, 1949; Heap on the Town and Country Planning Act 1954, 1955; (ed.) Encyclopaedia of Planning Law and Practice, 4 vols., 1960; Introducing the Land Commission Act 1967, 1967; Encyclopaedia of Betterment Levy, 1967; The New Town Planning Procedures, 1969; The Land and the Development; or, The Turmoil and the Torment (4 Hamlyn lectures), 1975; An Outline of Planning Law, 9th ed. 1987. Add: The Atheneum, Pall Mall, London SW1Y 5ER, England.

HEARNE, John. With Morris Cargill, writes as John Morris. Jamaican, b. 1926. Novels/Short stories, Plays/Screenplays. Head of Creative Arts Centre, Univ. of West Indies, Kingston, since 1968 (Resident Tutor, Dept. of Extra-Mural Studies, 1962–67). Teacher in London and Jamaica, 1950–59. *Publs:* Voices Under the Window, 1955; Stranger at the Gate, 1956; The Faces of Love (in U.S. as The Eye of the Storm), 1957; Autumn Equinox, 1959; Land of the Living, 1961; The Golden Savage (play), 1965; (with Morris Cargill as John Morris) Fever Grass, 1969; (with Morris Cargill as John Morris) The Candywine Development, 1970; The Sure Salvation, 1981. Add: c/o Creative Arts Centre, Univ. of the West Indies, Kingston 7, Jamaica.

HEARNE, Reginald. British, b. 1929. Plays/Screenplays. Freelance actor and writer, since 1948; Film Producer, Columbia Films, since 1961. Involved in production admin., Play Fare Productions Ltd. *Publs:* Serena: Echo of Diana; The Little Crime; The Sicians; The Colonel's Ride; Bank Raid; Tangle; The Web; Over My Shoulder; The Practice. Add: Lion Cottage, 14 Greys Rd., Henley-on-Thames, Oxon, England.

HEATER, Derek Benjamin. British, b. 1931. Education, History, International relations/Current affairs, Politics/Government. Education Officer, R.A.F., 1954–57; Asst. Master in secondary schs., 1957–62; Lectr. in History, 1962–66, and Head of the Dept. of History, 1966–76, Brighton Coll. of Education; Dean of the Faculty of Social and Cultural Studies, 1976–79, and Head of the Humanities Dept., 1976–83, Brighton Polytechnic. Chmn., Politics Assn., 1969–73; Ed., Teaching Politics, 1973–79. *Publs:* Political Ideas in the Modern World, 1960; Order and Rebellion: A History of Europe in the Eighteenth Century, 1964; The Cold War, 1964; (ed.) The Teaching of Politics, 1969; (with Gwyneth Owen) World

Affairs, 1972; Contemporary Political Ideas, 1974; Britain and the Outside World, 1976; (with Bernard Crick) Essays on Political Education, 1977; Peace and War, 1978; Essays on Contemporary Studies, 1979; World Studies: Education for International Understanding in Britain, 1980; (ed. with J. Gillespie) Political Education in Flux, 1981; Our World This Century, 1982; Peace Through Education: The Contribution of CEWC, 1984; Our World Today, 1985; Reform and Revolution, 1987; Refugees, 1988; Case Studies in Twentieth-Century World History, 1989. Add: 3 The Rotyngs, Rottingdean, Brighton BN2 7DX, England.

HEATH, Catherine. British, b. 1924. Novels/Short stories. Sr. Lectr., Carshalton Coll. of Further Education, Surrey, since 1970 (Lectr., 1964–70). Asst. Lectr., Univ. of Wales, 1948–50. *Publs:* Stone Walls, 1973; The Vulture, 1974; Joseph and the Goths, 1975; Lady on the Burning Deck, 1978; Behaving Badly, 1984. Add: 17 Penarth Ct., Devonshire Ave., Sutton, Surrey, England.

HEATH, Dwight B. American, b. 1930. Anthropology/Ethnology, History, Sociology. Prof. of Anthropology, Brown Univ., Providence, R.I., since 1959. Consultant in Mental Health, World Health Org., since 1973. *Publs:* A Journal of the Pilgrims at Plymouth: Mourt's Relation, 1963, 1986; Contemporary Cultures and Societies of Latin America: A Reader in the Social Anthropology of Middle and South America and the Caribbean, (ed. with R.N. Adams) 1965, (sole ed.) 1974, 1988; (with C.J Erasmus and H.C. Buechler) Land Reform and Social Revolution in Bolivia, 1969; Historical Dictionary of Bolivia, 1972; (ed. with M.W. Everett and J.O. Waddell) Cross-Cultural Approaches in the Study of Alcohol, 1976; (with A.M. Cooper) Alcohol Use in World Cultures, 1981; (ed. with J.O. Waddell and M.D. Topper) Cultural Factors in Alcohol Research and Treatment of Drinking Problems, 1981. Add: Box 1921, Dept. of Anthropology, Brown Univ., Providence, R.I. 02912, U.S.A.

HEATH, Edward (Richard George). British, b. 1916. Music, Politics/Government, Sports/Physical education/Keeping fit, Autobiography/Memoirs/Personal. Conservative Member of Parliament (U.K.) for Old Bexley and Sidcup, since 1983 (M.P. for Bexley, 1950–74, for Bexley-Sidcup, 1974–83; Asst. Conservative Whip, 1951; Lord Commnr. of the Treasury, 1951; Joint Deputy Govt. Chief Whip, 1952, and Deputy Govt. Chief Whip, 1953–55; Parliamentary Secty. to the Treasury and Govt. Chief Whip, 1955–59; Minister of Labour, 1959–60; Lord Privy Seal, 1960–63; Secty. of State for Industry, Trade, and Regional Development, and Pres. of the Bd. of Trade, 1963–64; Leader of the Opposition, 1965–70; Prime Minister and First Lord of the Treasury, 1970–74; Leader of the Opposition, 1974–75). Pres., Fedn. of Univ. Conservative and Unionist Assns., since 1959; Chmn., of Commonwealth Parliamentary Assn., since 1970; Vice Pres., Bach Choir, since 1970; Member, Brandt Independent Commn. on Intnl. Development Issues, since 1977. Pres., Oxford Univ. Conservative Assn., 1937; Chmn., Fedn. of Univ. Conservative Assns., 1938; Pres., Oxford Union, 1939; served in the Admin. Civil Service, 1946–47. Member of Council, Royal Coll. of Music, London, 1961–70; Chmn., London Symphony Orch. Trust, 1963–70. *Publs:* (with others) One Nation: A Tory Approach to Social Problems, 1950; One World, New Horizons (Godkin Lectures), 1970; Sailing: A Course of My Life, 1975; Music, A Joy for Life, 1976; Travels: Peoples and Places in My Life, 1977; Carols: The Joy of Christmas, 1977. Add: House of Commons, London SW1, England.

HEATH, G. Louis. American, b. 1944. Education, Race relations, Assoc. Prof. of Education, Illinois State Univ., Normal. Consultant, Illinois Commn. on Human Relations; Contrib. Ed., Interracial Review. *Publs:* The High School Rebel, 1969; Red. Brown, and Black Demands for Better Education, 1972; The New Teacher: Changing Patterns of Authority and Responsibility in the American Schools, 1973; The Hot Campus: The Politics That Impede Change in the Technoversity, 1973; Vandals in the Bomb Factory: The History and Literature of the Students for a Democratic Society, 1976; Off the Pigs! The History and Literature of the Black Panther Party, 1976; Mutiny Does Not Happen Lightly: The Literature of the American Resistance to the Vietnam War, 1976. Add: c/o Scarecrow Press, 52 Liberty St., Box 4167, Metuchen, N.J. 08840, U.S.A.

HEATH, Roy A.K. Guyanese, b. 1926. Novels/Short stories. Teacher in London since 1959; barrister since 1964. *Publs:* A Man Come Home, 1974; The Murderer, 1978; From the Heat of the Day, 1979; One Generation, 1980; Genetha, 1981; Kwaku, 1982; Orealla, 1984; The Shadow Bride, 1988. Add: c/o Allison and Busby, 6A Noel St., London W1V 3RB, England.

HEATH, Sandra. *See* **WILSON,** Sandra.

HEATH, Veronica. Pseud. of Veronica Heath Blackett. British, b. 1927. Children's fiction, Animals/Pets, Children's non-fiction. Freelance journalist and Northumberland Country Diarist for The Guardian newspaper, London. *Publs:* Susan's Riding School, 1956; Ponies in the Heather, 1959; Come Riding with Me, 1964; Come Show Jumping with Me, 1966; Ponies and Pony Management, 1966; Come Pony Trekking with Me, 1966; Ponies, 1969; Beginner's Guide to Riding, 1971; The Family Dog, 1972; So You Want to Be a Showjumper, 1974; So You Want to Own a Pony, 1974; Riding for Beginners, 1978; Perfect Cooking with Game, 1983; A Dog at Heel, 1987. Add: Seven Stars House, Whalton, Morpeth, Northumberland NE61 3XA, England.

HEATH, William W(ebster). American, b. 1929. Literature. Prof. of English, Amherst Coll., Massachusetts, since 1969 (Instr., 1956–59; Asst. Prof., 1959–64; Assoc. Prof., 1964–69). *Publs:* Elizabeth Bowen: An Introduction to Her Novels, 1961; (ed.) Discussions of Jane Austen, 1961; Wordsworth and Coleridge: A Study of Their Literary Relations in 1801-1802, 1970; (ed.) Major British Poets of the Romantic Period, 1972. Add: Dept. of English, Amherst Coll., Amherst, Mass. 01002, U.S.A.

HEATHCOTT, Mary. *See* **KEEGAN,** Mary.

HEATH-STUBBS, John (Francis Alexander), OBE. British, b. 1918. Plays/Screenplays, Poetry, Literature, Translations. English teacher, Hall Sch., Hampstead, London, 1944–45; Editorial Asst. Hutchinson & Co., publrs., London, 1945–46; Gregory Fellow in Poetry, Leeds Univ., 1952–55; Visiting Prof. of English, Univ. of Alexandria, Egypt, 1955–58, and Univ. of Michigan, Ann Arbor, 1960–61; Lectr. in English, Coll. of St. Mark and St. John, London, 1963–72. *Publs:* Wounded Thammuz, 1942; Beauty and the Beast, 1943; (trans.) Poems from Giocomo Leopardi, 1946; The Divided Ways, 1947; (ed.) Selected Poems of Shelley, 1947; (ed.) Selected Poems of Tennyson, 1947; (ed.) Selected Poems of Swift, 1947; The Charity of the Stars, 1949; The Swarming of the Bees, 1950; The Darkling Plain: A Study of the Later Fortunes of Romanticism in English Poetry from George Darley to W.B. Yeats, 1950; (ed. with D. Wright) The Forsaken Garden: An Anthology of Poetry 1824-1909, 1950; (trans.) Aphrodite's Garland, 1952; (ed.) Images of Tomorrow: An Anthology of Recent Poetry, 1953; (ed. with D. Wright) The Faber Book of Twentieth Century Verse: An Anthology of Verse in Britain 1900–1950, 1953, 1975; The Talking Ass (play), 1953; A Charm Against the Toothache, 1954; Charles Williams, 1955; (trans.) With P. Avery Thirty Poems of Hafiz of Shiraz, 1955; The Triumph of the Muse and Other Poems, 1958; Helen in Egypt and Other Plays, 1958; The Blue-Fly in His Head: Poems, 1962; (ed.) Selected Poems of Alexander Pope, 1964; Selected Poems, 1965; (trans. with I. Origo) Selected Poetry and Prose, by Giacomo Leopardi, 1966; Satires and Epigrams, 1968; The Verse Satire, 1969; The Ode,1969; The Pastoral, 1969; (trans.) The Horn/Le Cor, by Aldred de Vigny, 1969; Artorius, 1970; (with F.T. Prince and Stephen Spender) Penguin Modern Poets 20, 1971; (ed. with M. Green) Homage to George Barker on His 60th Birthday, 1973; Indifferent Weather: Occasional Poems, 1975; A Parliament of Birds, 1975; (ed. with David Wright) The Faber Book of Twentieth Century Verse, 1975; The Watchman's Flute, 1978; The Mouse, the Bird and the Sausage, 1978; (trans. with Peter Avery) The Ruba'iyat of Omar Khayyam, 1979; (trans. with Carole Whiteside) Anyte, 1979; Birds Reconvened, 1980; Buzz Buzz, 1981; Naming the Beasts, 1982; (ed. with Phillips Salman) Poems of Science, 1984; The Immolation of Aleph, 1986; Cats Parnassus, 1988; Time Pieces, 1988; A Partridge in a Pear Tree, 1988; Collected Poems, 1988. Add: 35 Sutherland Pl., London W2, England.

HEATON, Charles H(uddleston). American, b. 1928. Music. Organist and Choir Dir., East Liberty Presbyterian Church, Pittsburgh, Pa., since 1972. Book Reviewer, The American Organist mag., since 1969. Minister of Music, Second Presbyterian Church, St. Louis, Mo., 1956–72; Ed. of Church Music Dept., Clavier Mag., 1962–69. Contrib. Ed., Journal of Church Music, 1978–84. *Publs:* How to Build a Church Choir, 1958; A Guidebook to Worship Services of Sacred Music, 1962; (ed.) Hymnbook for Christian Worship, 1970. Add: 5436 Plainfield St., Pittsburgh, Pa. 15217, U.S.A.

HEATON, Eric William. British, b. 1920. Theology/Religion. Dean of Christ Church, Oxford, since 1979. Chaplain 1945–46, Dean and Fellow, 1946–53, and Tutor 1951–53, Gonville and Caius Coll., Cambridge; Canon Residentiary 1953–60 and Chancellor 1956–60, Salisbury Cathedral; Official Fellow, Tutor in Theology and Chaplain 1960–74, Sr. Tutor, 1967–73, St. John's Coll., Oxford; Dean of Durham, 1974–79. *Publs:* His Servants the Prophets, 1949, rev. ed. as The Old Testament Prophets, 1977; Everyday Life in Old Testament Times, 1956; The Book of Daniel, 1956; Commentary on the Sunday Lessons, 1959; The Hebrew

Kingdoms,1968; Solomon's New Men, 1974. Add: The Deanery, Christ Church, Oxford OX1 1DP, England.

HEATON-WARD, William Alan. British, b. 1919. Psychiatry. Lord Chancellor's Medical Visitor, since 1978. Vice-Pres., Fortune Riding Centre for the Disabled, since 1980. Surgeon Lt. Comdr. and Neuropsychiatrist, Nore Command, Royal Navy, 1946–48; Consultant Psychiatrist Stoke Park Hosp. Group, Bristol, and Clinical Teacher in Mental Health, Univ. of Bristol, 1954–78. Chmn. of the South Western Div., 1970–75, Chmn. of the Mental Deficiency Section, 1972–75, and Vice-Pres., 1976–78, Royal Coll., of Psychiatrists; Pres., British Soc. for the Study of Mental Subnormality, 1978–80. *Publs:* (co-author) Notes on Mental Deficiency, 1953, 3rd ed. 1955; Mental Subnormality, 1960, 5th ed. as Mental Handicap (co-author), 1984; Left Behind, 1977. Add: Flat 2, 38 Apsley Rd., Clifton, Bristol BS8 2SS, England.

HEAVEN, Constance. Also writes as Constance Fecher and Christina Merlin. British, b. 1911. Historical/Romance/Gothic, Children's fiction, Children's non-fiction, Biography. Actress, 1939–66; Tutor in Creative Writing and Seventeenth Century Life and Manners, City Literary Inst., London, 1967–74. *Publs:* (as Constance Fecher) Queen's Delight, 1966, in U.S. as Queen's Favorite, 1974; (as Constance Fecher) Traitor's Son, 1967; (as Constance Fecher) King's Legacy, 1967; (as Constance Fecher) Player Queen, 1968, in U.S. as The Lovely Wanton, 1977; (as Constance Fecher) Venture for a Crown (juvenile), 1968; (as Constance Fecher) Lion of Trevarrock, 1969; (as Constance Fecher) Heir to Pendarrow (juvenile), 1969; (as Constance Fecher) Bright Star (juvenile), 1970; (as Constance Fecher) The Link Boys (juvenile), 1971; (as Constance Fecher) Night of the Wolf, 1972; The House of Kuvagin, 1972; (as Constance Fecher) The Last Elizabethan: A Portrait of Sir Walter Raleigh (juvenile), 1972; (as Constance Fecher) The Leopard Dagger (juvenile), 1973; The Astrov Inheritance, 1973; Castle of Eastle, 1974; The Place of Stones, 1975; The Fires of Glenlochy, 1976; The Queen and the Gypsy, 1977; Lord of Ravensley, 1978; Heir to Kuragin, 1979; (as Christina Merlin) The Spy Concerto, 1980; The Wildcliffe Bird, 1981; The Ravensley Touch, 1982; (as Christina Merlin) Sword of Mithras, 1982; Daughter of Marignac, 1983; Castle of Doves, 1984; (as Constance Fecher) By the Light of the Moon, 1985; Larksghyll, 1986; The Raging Fire, 1987; The Fire Still Burns, 1989. Add: 37 Teddington Park Rd., Teddington, Middx. TW11 8NB, England.

HEBBLETHWAITE, Peter. British, b. 1930. Theology/Religion. Vatican Affairs Writer, The National Catholic Reporter, Kansas City, since 1979. Lectr. in French Language and Literature, Wadham Coll., Oxford, 1976–79; Ed., The Month, 1967–73. *Publs:* Georges Bernanos, 1965; The Council Fathers and Atheism, 1966; Understanding the Synod, 1968; Theology of the Church, 1969; (trans.) Breaking Through to God by Ladislaus Boros, 1974; The Runaway Church, 1975, 1978; Christian-Marxist Dialogue and Beyond, 1977; The Year of Three Popes, 1978; (trans.) Cosmas or the Love of God, by Pierre de Calan, 1980; Papal Year, 1981; Introducing John Paul II, 1982; John XXIII, Pope of the Council, 1984; Synod Extraordinary, 1986; In the Vatican, 1986, 1987. Add: 45 Marston St., Oxford OX4 1JU, England.

HEBDEN, Mark. *See* **HARRIS,** John.

HECHINGER, Fred M.B.E. American, b.1920. Education. Pres., New York Times Company Foundn. Inc., NYC, since 1977, and Education Columnist, New York Times, since 1978 (Education Ed., 1959–69; Member, Editorial Bd., 1969–77; Asst. Ed., Editorial Page, 1976). Member of the Bd., and Vice-Chmn., Carnegie Corp. of N.Y., Foreign Policy Assn., and Academy for Educational Development. Foreign Corresp., Overseas News Agency, 1947–50; U.S. Corresp., The Times Educational Supplement, London, 1949–52; Education Ed., New York Herald Tribune, NYC, 1950–56; Assoc. Publr. and Exec. Ed., Bridgeport Herald, Conn., 1956–59. *Publs:* An Adventure in Education, 1956; The Big Red Schoolhouse, 1959; (with Grace Hechinger) Teen-Age Tyranny, 1963; (ed.) Pre-School Education Today, 1966; (with Grace Hechinger) The New York Times Guide to New York City Private Schools, 1968; (with G. Hechinger) Growing Up in America, 1975; A Better Start, 1986. Add: 229 West 43rd St., New York, N.Y. 10036, U.S.A.

HECHT, Anthony (Evan). American, b. 1923. Poetry. Prof. of English, Georgetown Univ., Washington, D.C., since 1985. Member of faculty, Smith Coll., Northampton, Mass., 1956–59, and Bard Coll., Annandale-on-Hudson, N.Y., 1962–67; Member of English Dept., State Univ. of New York, Rochester, 1967–84. Poetry Consultant, Library of Congress, Washington, D.C., 1982–84. *Publs:* A Summoning of Stones, 1954; The Seven Deadly Sins: Poems, 1958; Struwwelpeter, 1958; The

Hard Hours: Poems, 1967; Aesopic: Twenty Four Couplets, 1967; (ed. with J. Hollander) Jiggery-Pokery: A Compendium of Double Dactyls, 1967; (trans. with H. Bacon) Seven Against Thebes, by Aeschylus, 1973; Millions of Strange Shadows, 1977; The Venetian Vespers, 1979; Obbligati: Essays in Criticism, 1985. Add: 4256 Nebraska Ave., N.W., Washington, D.C. 20016, U.S.A.

HECHTER, Michael. American, b. 1943. Sociology. Prof. of Sociology, Univ. of Washington, since 1980 (Asst. Prof., 1970–73; Assoc. Prof., 1973–80). *Publs:* Internal Colonialism: The Celtic Fringe in British National Development 1536-1966, 1975; (ed.) The Microfoundations of Macrosociology, 1983; Principles of Group Solidarity, 1987. Add: Dept. of Sociology, Univ. of Washington, Seattle, Wash. 98195, U.S.A.

HECKELMANN, Charles N(ewman). Also writes as Charles Lawton. American, b. 1913. Western/Adventure, Children's fiction, Writing/Journalism. Editorial Consultant, Valueback Publishing, Palm Beach Gardens, Fla., 1981–83. Sports writer, Brooklyn Eagle, 1934–37; Ed.-in-Chief, Cupples and Leon, 1937–41; Ed-in-Chief, 1941–58, and Vice-Pres., 1953–58, Popular Library; Ed.-in-Chief, and Pres., Monarch Books, 1958–65; Managing Ed., David McKay, 1965–68; Sr. Ed., Cowles Book Co., 1968–71; Sr. Ed., 1971–72, and Ed.-in-Chief, and Vice-Pres., 1972–75, Hawthorn Books; Book Ed., National Enquirer, 1975–78—all NYC. Pres., Catholic Writers Guild of America, 1949–52; Vice-Pres., 1955–57, and Pres., 1964–65, Western Writers of America. *Publs:* western novels—Vengeance Trail, 1944; Lawless Range, 1945; Six-Gun Outcast, 1946; Deputy Marshal, 1947; Guns of Arizona, 1949; Outlaw Valley, 1950; Danger Rides the Range, 1950; Two-Bit Rancher, 1950; Let the Guns Roar!, 1950; Fighting Ramrod, 1951; Hell in His Holsters, 1952; The Rawhider, 1952; Hard Man with a Gun, 1954; Bullet Law, 1955; Trumpets in the Dawn, 1958; The Big Valley, 1966; The Glory Riders, 1967; Stranger from Durango, 1980; Return to Arapahoe, 1980; Wagons to Wind River, 1982; children's fiction, as Charles Lawton—Clarkville's Battery, or Baseball Versus Gangsters, 1937; Ros Hackney, Halfback, or, How Clarkville's Captain Made Good, 1937; The Winning Forward Pass, or, Onward to the Orange Bowl Game, 1940; Home Run Hennessey, or, Winning the All-Star Game, 1941; Touchdown to Victory, or, The Touchdown Express Makes Good, 1942; other—Jungle Menance (novelization of screenplay), 1937; Writing Fiction for Profit, 1968; (ed.) With Guidons Flying: Tales of the U.S. Cavalry in the Old West by Members of the Western Writers of America, 1970. Add: 10634 Green Trail Dr. S., Boynton Beach, Fla. 33436, U.S.A.

HECKSCHER, William (Sebastian). Canadian, b. 1904. Art. Emeritus Benjamin Duke Prof. of Art History, and Dir., Univ. Museum of Art, Duke Univ., Durham, since 1974 (Prof., 1966–74); Prof. Emeritus, Utrecht Univ., Netherlands (Prof., 1955–66); Consultant, Dept. of Rare Books, Princeton Univ. Library, since 1976. Member, Advisory Bd., The Journal of Medieval and Renaissance Studies. Prof., State Univ., of Iowa, Iowa City, 1947–55. Kress Prof. in Residence, National Gallery of Art, Washington, D.C., 1979–80. *Publs:* Renaissance Emblems, 1954; Rembrandt's Anatomy of Dr. N. Tulp, 1956; Discussions with Albert Einstein, 1961; Ancient Art and Its Echoes in Post-Classical Times, 1963; Genesis of Iconology, 1964; Holbein's Portrait of Erasmus at Longford Castle, 1967; Shakespeare and The Visual Arts, 1973; Art and Literature, 1985; The Princeton Alciati Companion: Latin Words and Phrases Used in the Sixteenth Century, 1989. Add: Dept. of Rare Books, Princeton Library, Princeton, N.Y. 08540, U.S.A.

HEDDERWICK, Mairi. British, b. 1939. Children's fiction, Local history/Rural topics. *Publs:* Views of Scotland, 1981; Katie Morag Delivers the Mail, 1984; Katie Morag and the Two Grandmothers, 1985; Katie Morag and the Tiresome Ted, 1986; Katie Morag and the Big Boy Cousins, 1987; Peedie Peebles' Summer or Winter Book (in U.S.A. as P.D. Peebles' Summer or Winter Book), 1989; An Eye on the Hebrides, 1989. Add: 15 Ardconnel Ter., Inverness IV2 3HE, Scotland.

HEDGES, Joseph. See **GILMAN,** George G.

HEDLEY, (Gladys) Olwen. British, b. 1912. History, Travel, Biography. Women's Page Ed., and Member of Editorial Staff, Windsor, Slough and Eton Express, 1932–39; with Voluntary Aid Detachment, Casualty and Out-Patient's Dept., then Main Operating Theatres, King Edward VII Hosp., Windsor, during World War II; Asst., Royal Library, Windsor Castle, 1948–64. FRS2, 1975. *Publs:* Round and About Windsor and District, 1948, rev. ed. 1949; Windsor Castle, 1967, 1972; Buckingham Palace/City of London/Hampton Court Palace/Prisoners in the Tower, Princes of Wales—all in Pride of Britain and Treasures of Britain series published since 1968; Royal Palaces, 1972; Queen Charlotte, 1975; The Queen's Silver Jubilee, 1977; A Child's Guide to Windsor Castle, 1979; The Royal Foundation of Saint Catherine, 1984. Add: 15 Denny Cres., London SE11 4UY, England.

HEDRICK, Floyd (Dudley). American, b. 1927. Administration/Management. Chief, Procurement and Supply Div., Library of Congress, Washington, D.C., since 1973; Adjunct Prof. of Business, American Univ., Washington, D.C., and Univ. of Virginia, N. Va. campus. Chmn., Org. and Planning Cttee., National Assn. of Purchasing Mgmt. (Vice-Pres., NAPM, 1972–73; Member, Purchasing Council, American Mgmt. Assn. *Publs:* Purchasing Management in the Smaller Company, 1971; (co-ed.) Purchasing Handbook, 3rd ed. 1971, 4th ed. 1982; Purchasing for Owners of Small Plants, 1976, 1979; (co-ed.) American Management Assn. Management Handbook, 1981. Add: 3824 King Arthur Rd., Annandale, Va., 22003, U.S.A.

HEER, David MacAlpine. American, b. 1930. Demography, Sociology. Prof. of Sociology, Univ. of Southern California, Los Angeles, since 1972. Statistician, U.S. Bureau of the Census, 1957–61; Lectr. and Asst. Research Sociologist, Univ. of California at Berkeley, 1961–64; Asst. Prof. to Assoc. Prof. of Demography, Harvard Univ. Sch. of Public Health, Cambridge, Mass., 1964–72. *Publs:* After Nuclear Attack: A Demographic Inquiry, 1965; Society and Population, 1968, 1975; (ed.) Readings on Population, 1968, (ed.) Social Statistics and the City, 1968; Undocumented Mexicans: America's Legal Underclass?, 1989. Add: Population Research Lab., Univ. of Southern California, Los Angeles, Calif. 90007, U.S.A.

HEERWAGEN, Paul K. American, b. 1895. Children's fiction. Owner and Mgr., Heerwagen Acoustic Co., Fayetteville, Ark. 1946–59. *Publs:* Snowball, 1957, 1985; Indian Scout, Western Painter, 1969. Add: Univ. of Arkansas, Carlson Terrace, Apt. B-105, Fayetteville, Ark. 72701, U.S.A.

HEFFRON, Dorris. Canadian, b. 1944. Novels/Short stories. Lectr. in Literature, Oxford Univ., 1969–79. *Publs:* A Nice Fire and Some Moonpennies, 1971; Crusty Crossed, 1976; Rain and I, 1982. Add: 202 Riverside Dr., Toronto, Ont., Canada.

HEGELER, Sten. Danish, b. 1923. Children's fiction, Recreation/Leisure/Hobbies, Sex. Psychologist and psychoanalyst in private practice. Lectr. in Sexology, Copenhagen Univ., 1969–82. *Publs:* Peter and Caroline; Fem sma matroser; Peter og Marianne i Skole; Jorn pa kostskole; Lise i pension. Henrik og Hannibal; Choosing Toys for Children; (with Inge Hegeler) ABZ of Love; Ask Inge and Sten; World's Best Slimming Diet; On Loneliness; XYZ of Love; Living Is Loving; In Spite of AIDS; On Sélen, 1988. Add: Frederiksberg Alle 25, DK-1820 Frederiksberg C, Denmark.

HEGEMAN, (Sister) Mary Theodore. (Sister Mary Theodore). American, b. 1907. Education. Principal, 1947–64, Supt., 1964–70, and Dir. of Public Relations, 1970–87, St. Coletta Sch., Jefferson, Wisc. *Publs:* The Challenge of the Retarded Child, 1959, 3rd ed. 1969; Development Disability—A Family Challenge; A Short Life of Saint Coletta, 1987. Add: St. Coletta Sch., Jefferson, Wisc. 53549, U.S.A.

HEIDE, Florence Parry. Has also written as Alex B. Allen and Jamie McDonald. American, b. 1919. Children's fiction. Full-time writer. Formerly worked for RKO and in public relations and advertising, New York; former public relations dir., Pittsburgh Playhouse. *Publs:* Benjamin Budge and Barnaby Ball, 1967; (with Sylvia W. Van Clief) Maximilian, 1967; (with Sylvia W. Van Clief) The Day It Snowed in Summer, 1968; (with Sylvia W. Van Clief) How Big Am I?, 1968; (with Sylvia W. Van Clief) It Never Is Dark, 1968; (with Sylvia W. Van Clief) Sebastian, 1968; (with Sylvia W. Van Clief) That's What Friends Are For, 1968; (as Jamie McDonald; with Anne and Walter Theiss) Hannibal, 1968; Maximilian Becomes Famous, 1969; (with Sylvia W. Van Clief) The New Neighbor, 1970; Alphabet Zoop, 1970; Giants Are Very Brave People, 1970; The Little One, 1970; Sound of Sunshine, Sound of Rain, 1970; Look! Look! A Story Book, 1971; The Key, 1971; The Shrinking of Treehorn, 1971; Some Things Are Scary, 1971; Who Needs Me?, 1971; Songs to Sing about Things You Think About (songs), 1971; Christmas Bells and Snowflakes (songs), 1971; Holidays! Holidays! (songs), 1971; My Castle, 1972; (with Sylvia W. Van Clief) The Mystery of the Missing Suitcase, 1972; (with Sylvia W. Van Clief) The Mystery of the Silver Tag, 1972; (as Alex B. Allen; with Sylvia W. Van Clief) Basketball Toss Up, 1972; (as Alex B. Allen; with Sylvia W. Van Clief) No Place for Baseball, 1973; (with Sylvia W. Van Clief) The Hidden Box Mystery,

1973; (with Sylvia W. Van Clief) Mystery at MacAdoo Zoo, 1973; (with Roxanne Heide) Lost! (textbook), 1973; (with Roxanne Heide) I See America Smiling (textbook), 1973; (with Sylvia W. Van Clief) Mystery of the Whispering Voice, 1974; (with Roxanne Heide) Mystery of the Melting Snowman, 1974; (with David Fisher Parry) No Roads for the Wind (textbook), 1974; (with Sylvia W. Van Clief) Who Can? (reader), 1974; (with Sylvia W. Van Clief) Lost and Found (reader), 1974; (with Sylvia W. Van Clief) Hats and Bears (reader), 1974; (with Roxanne Heide) Tell about Someone You Love (textbook), 1974; (as Alex B. Allen; with Sylvia W. Van Clief) Danger on Broken Arrow Trail, 1974 (as Alex B. Allen; with Sylvia W. Van Clief) Fifth Down, 1974; (as Alex B. Allen; with Sylvia W. Van Clief and David Heide) The Tennis Menace, 1975; God and Me (non-fiction), 1975; You and Me (non-fiction), 1975; (with Roxanne Heide) Mystery of the Vanishing Visitor, 1975; (with Roxanne Heide) Mystery of the Bewitched Bookmobile, 1975; When the Sad One Comes to Stay, 1975; Growing Anyway Up, 1976; (with Roxanne Heide) Mystery of the Lonely Lantern, 1976; (with Roxanne Heide) Mystery at Keyhole Carnival, 1977; (with Roxanne Heide) Brillstone Break-In, 1977; (with Roxanne Heide) Mystery of the Midnight Message, 1977 (with Sylvia W. Van Clief) Fables You Shouldn't Pay Any Attention To, 1978; Banana Twist, 1978; Secret Dreamer, Secret Dreams, 1978; (with Roxanne Heide) Fear at Brillstone, 1978; (with Roxanne Heide) Mystery at Southport Cinema, 1978; (with Roxanne Heide) I Love Every-People, 1978; Changes (non-fiction), 1978; Who Taught Me? Was It You, God? (non-fiction), 1978; By the Time You Count to Ten (non-fiction), 1979; (with Roxanne Heide) Face at the Brillstone Window, 1979; (with Roxanne Heide) Mystery of the Mummy's Mask, 1979; (with Roxanne Heide) Body in the Brillstone Garage, 1980; (with Roxanne Heide) Mystery of the Forgotten Island, 1980; (with Roxanne Heide) A Monster Is Coming! A Monster Is Coming!, 1980; (with Roxanne Heide) Black Magic at Brillstone, 1981; Treehorn's Treasure, 1981; Time's Up!, 1982; The Problem with Pulcifer, 1982; The Wendy Puzzle, 1982; (with Roxanne Heide) Time Bomb at Brillstone, 1982; (with Roxanne Heide) Mystery On Danger Road, 1983; Banana Blitz, 1983; Treehorn's Wish, 1984; Time Flies, 1984; Tales for the Perfect Child, 1985; (with Judith Heide Gilliland) The Butagaz Boy, 1990; Grim and Ghastly Goings On in Grubsville, 1990. Add: 6910 Third Ave., Kenosha, Wisc. 53140, U.S.A.

HEIFETZ, Harold. American, b. 1919. Novels/Short stories, Plays/Screenplays. *Publs:* Jeremiah Thunder (novel), 1968; Mama and Her Soldiers (play), 1969; The Hard Charger (novel), 1971; Harry Kelly (play), 1974; Billy God (play), 1975; Hungry Mother Mountain (play), 1977; Zen and Hasidism (non-fiction), 1978. Add: 12142 Emelita St., North Hollywood, Calif. 91607, U.S.A.

HEILBRONER, Robert L. American. Economics. Norman Thomas Prof., New Sch. for Social Research, NYC, since 1972. Vice Pres., American Economic Assn., 1984. *Publs:* The Future as History, 1960; The Making of Economic Society, 1962; The Great Ascent, 1963; The Limits of American Capitalism, 1966; Between Capitalism and Socialism, 1970; The Economic Problem, 1971, (with James K. Galbraith) 8th ed. 1989; The Worldly Philosophers, 1972, latest ed., 1986; Inquiry into the Human Prospect, 1973, 2nd ed., 1980; Marxism: For and Against, 1980; The Nature and Logic of Capitalism, 1986; Behind the Veil of Economics, 1988. Add: New Sch. for Social Research, 66 W. 12th St., New York, N.Y. 10011, U.S.A.

HEILBRUN, Carolyn G(old). Writes mystery novels as Amanda Cross. American, b. 1926. Mystery/Crime/Suspense, Literature. Prof. of English, Columbia Univ., NYC, since 1972 (joined faculty, 1960); Humanities Prof., Avalon Foundn., since 1986. *Publs:* The Garnett Family, 1961; (as Amanda Cross) In the Last Analysis, 1964; (as Amanda Cross) The James Joyce Murder, 1967; Christopher Isherwood, 1970; (as Amanda Cross) Poetic Justice, 1970; (as Amanda Cross) The Theban Mysteries, 1971; Towards a Recognition of Androgyny: Aspects of Male and Female in Literature (in U.K. as Towards Androgyny), 1973; (ed.) Lady Ottoline's Album, 1976; (as Amanda Cross) The Question of Max, 1976; Reinventing Womanhood, 1979; (as Amanda Cross) Death in a Tenured Position, 1981; (as Amanda Cross) Sweet Death, Kind Death, 1984; No Word From Winnifred, 1986; Writing a Woman's Life, 1988; A Trap for Fools, 1989. Add: 615 Philosophy Hall, Columbia Univ., New York, N.Y. 10027, U.S.A.

HEILMAN, Robert B. American, b. 1906. Literature. Staff member, Ohio Univ., Athens, 1928–30, Univ. of Maine, 1931–35, and Louisiana State Univ., Baton Rouge, 1935–48; Prof. of English, 1948–76, now Emeritus, and Chmn. of the Dept., 1948–71, Univ. of Washington, Seattle; Arnold Prof., Whitman Coll., Walla Walla, Wash., 1977. Pres., Philologi-

cal Assn. of Pacific Coast, 1959; Member, Exec. Council, American Assn. of Univ. Profs., 1963–65, and Modern Language Assn. of America, 1966–70. Senator, Phi Beta Kappa, 1967–85. *Publs:* America in English Fiction 1760-1800, 1937; (ed. with C. Brooks) Understanding Drama, 1948; This Great Stage: Image and Structure in King Lear, 1948; (ed.) Modern Short Stories, 1950; Magic in the Web: Action and Language in Othello, 1956; (ed.) Conrad's Lord Jim, 1957; (ed.) English Drama Before Shakespeare, 1962; (ed.) Hardy's Mayor of Casterbridge, 1962; (ed.) Eliot's Silas Marner, 1962; (ed.) Shakespeare's Cymbeline, 1964; (ed.) Euripides' Alcestis, 1965; (ed.) Hardy's Jude the Obscure, 1966; (ed.) Shakespeare's The Taming of the Shrew, 1966; Tragedy and Melodrama: Versions of Experience, 1968; (ed.) Hardy's Tess of the d'Urbervilles, 1971; The Iceman, the Arsonist, and the Troubled Agent: Tragedy and Melodrama on the Modern Stage, 1973; The Charliad, 1973; The Ghost on the Ramparts, and Other Essays in the Humanities, 1974; The Ways of the World: Comedy and Society, 1978; (ed.) Shakespeare: The Tragedies, 1984. Add: c/o Dept. of English, Univ. of Washington, Seattle, Wash. 98195, U.S.A.

HEIM, Alice W(inifred). British, b. 1913. Animals/Pets, Psychology. Fellow, Clare Hall, Cambridge, since 1972. Member of the Medical Research Council's Scientific Staff, Cambridge, 1936–78; Dir. of Studies in Psychology, Newnham Coll., Cambridge, 1946–78. *Publs:* The Appraisal of Intelligence, 1954, 1970; Intelligence and Personality, 1970; Psychological Testing, 1975; Teaching and Learning in Higher Education, 1976; Barking Up the Right Tree, 1980; Thicker Than Water?, 1983; Understanding Your Dog's Behaviour, 1984. Add: 8 Bateman St., Cambridge CB2 1NB, England.

HEIN, Lucille Eleanor. American, b. 1915. Children's fiction, Children's non-fiction, Sociology, Theology/Religion. Instr. in English Literature, Wagner Coll., NYC, 1940–44; Prog. Specialist, National Staff, Camp Fire Girls Inc., 1945–50. *Publs:* Enjoy Your Children, 1959; One Small Circle, 1962; Enjoying the Outdoors with Children, 1966; We Talk with God, 1968; (compiler) Thinking of You, 1969; I Can Make My Own Prayers, 1971; Entertaining Your Child, 1971; Prayer Gifts for Christmas, 1972; Walking in God's World, 1972; A Tree I Can Call My Own, 1974; My Very Special Friend, 1974; From Sea to Shining Sea, 1975; That Wonderful Summer, 1978; Thank You, God, 1981. Add: 33 Central Ave., Staten Island, N.Y. 10301, U.S.A.

HEINEMANN, Larry C(urtiss). American, b. 1944. Novels/Short stories. Instr. in writing, Columbia Coll., Chicago. *Publs:* Close Quarters, 1977; Paco's Story, 1986 (National Book Award). Add: English Dept., Columbia Coll., 600 S. Michigan Ave., Chicago, Ill. 60605, U.S.A.

HEINSOHN, George Edwin. American, b. 1933. Natural history. Sr. Lectr. on Zoology, James Cook Univ. of North Queensland, Townsville, since 1968. Asst. Prof. of Biology, Lewis and Clark Coll., Portland, Ore., 1963–66; Lectr. in Zoology, Univ. of Western Australia, Nedlands, 1966–68. *Publs:* Ecology and Reproduction of the Tasmanian Bandicoots, 1966. Add: Dept. of Zoology, James Cook Univ. of North Queensland, Townsville, Qld. 4811, Australia.

HEINZ, W(ilfred) C(harles). American, b. 1915. Novels/Short stories, Sports/Physical education, Writing/Journalism. Freelance writer and journalist. Reporter, and subsequently, feature writer, war corresp., and sports columnist, New York Sun, 1937–50. *Publs:* The Professional (novel), 1958; (ed.) The Fireside Book of Boxing, 1961; The Surgeon (novel), 1963; (with Vince Lombardi) Run to Daylight! (sport), 1963; (with H. Richard Hornberger, M.D., nom de plume Richard Hooker) MASH (novel), 1968; Emergency (novel), 1974; Once They Heard the Cheers (sport), 1979; American Mirror (journalism), 1982. Add: c/o William Morris Agency Inc., 1350 Ave. of the Americas, New York, N.Y. 10019, U.S.A.

HEISER, Charles B(ixler), Jr. American, b. 1920. Botany. Distinguished Prof. Emeritus of Botany, Indiana Univ., Bloomington, since 1979 (Asst. Prof. to Prof., 1947–79). Pres., American Soc. of Plant Taxonomists, 1967, Soc. for the Study of Evolution, 1975, Soc. for Economic Botany, 1978, Botanical Soc. of America, 1980, and National Academy of Sciences, 1987. *Publs:* Nightshades, The Paradoxical Plants, 1969; Seed to Civilization: The Story of Man's Food, 1973, 1981; The Sunflower, 1976; The Gourd Book, 1979; Of Plants and People, 1985. Add: Dept. of Biology, Indiana Univ., Bloomington, Ind. 47405, U.S.A.

HEITNER, Robert R. American, b. 1920. Literature. Prof. Emeritus, Univ. of Illinois at Chicago Circle, since 1984 (Head, Dept. of German,

1966–76). Chmn., Germanic Languages, Univ. of California, Los Angeles, 1961–64; Prof. of German, Univ. of Texas, Austin, 1964–66. Ed., German Quarterly, 1967–70; Pres., Lessing Soc., 1977–80. *Publs:* German Tragedy in the Age of Enlightenment, 1963; (ed.) The Contemporary Novel in German, 1967; (ed.) A.A. Von Haugwitz: Schuldige Unschuld oder Maria Stuarda, 1964; (trans.) Poetry and Truth, by Goethe, 1987; (trans.) The Italian Journey, by Goethe, 1989. Add: 1555 Astor St., 32 W, Chicago, Ill. 60610, U.S.A.

HEJINIAN, Lyn. American, b. 1941. Poetry. Ed., Tuumba Press and Poetics Journal, both Berkeley. *Publs:* A Thought Is the Bride of What Thinking (poetry), 1976; A Mask of Motion (poetry), 1977; Writing Is an Aid to Memory (poetry), 1978; Gesualdo (poetry), 1978; My Life (prose), 1980, expanded version, 1988; The Guard (poetry), 1984; Redo (poetry), 1984; Individuals (poetry), 1988. Add: c/o Tuumba Press, 2369 Russell St., Berkeley, Calif. 94705, U.S.A.

HELD, Peter. *see* VANCE, Jack.

HELD, Virginia P. American, b. 1929. Economics, Philosophy, Politics/Government. Prof. of Philosophy, Grad. Sch., and Hunter Coll., City Univ. of New York, since 1977 (Asst. Prof., 1969–72; Assoc. Prof., 1973–76). *Publs:* The Public Interest and Individual Interests, 1970; (ed. with K. Nielsen and C. Parsons, and contrib.) Philosophy and Political Action, 1972; (ed. with S. Morgenbesser and T. Nagel) Philosophy, Morality, and International Affairs, 1974; (ed.) Property, Profits, and Economic Justice, 1980; Rights and Goods, 1984. Add: City Univ. of New York, 33 West 42nd St., New York, N.Y. 10036, U.S.A.

HELFMAN, Elizabeth S. American, b. 1911. Children's non-fiction. Teacher, Brooklyn Community Sch., N.Y., 1942–46; Teaching Guide Ed., News Time, NYC, 1959–66. *Publs:* Water for the World, 1960; Land, People, and History, 1962; Rivers and Watersheds in America's Future, 1965; (co-author) Strings on Your Fingers, 1965; Signs and Symbols Around the World, 1967; Wheels, Scoops and Buckets, 1968; Celebrating Nature, 1969; This Hungry World, 1970; The Bushmen and Their Stories, 1971; Our Fragile Earth, 1972; Maypoles and Wood Demons: The Meaning of Trees, 1972; Signs and Symbols of the Sun, 1974; Apples, Apples, Apples, 1977; Blissymbolics: Speaking Without Speech, 1981. Add: 461-A Heritage Village, Southbury, Conn. 06488, U.S.A.

HELFMAN, Harry Carmozin. American, b. 1910. Children's non-fiction. Artist-teacher, Woodward Sch., Brooklyn, N.Y., 1937–65, Emerson Sch., NYC, 1949–50, and Queens Sch., NYC, 1950–51. *Publs:* Origami: The Oriental Art of Paper Folding, 1960; (with E.S. Helfman) Strings on Your Fingers, 1965; Tricks with Your Fingers, 1967; Fun with Your Fingers, 1968; Making Pictures Move, 1969; Making Your Own Movies, 1970; Making Your Own Sculpture, 1971; Making Pictures Without Paint, 1973; Making Designs by Chance, 1974; Creating Things That Move, 1975. Add: 461-A Heritage Village, Southbury, Conn. 06488, U.S.A.

HELLER, Erich. British, b. 1911. Literature. Avalon Prof. Emeritus in the Humanities, Northwestern Univ., Evanston (Prof. since 1960). Dir. of Studies in Modern Languages and Lectr. in German, Peterhouse, Cambridge, 1945–48; Prof. of German, Univ. Coll. Swansea, Wales, 1948–60. *Publs:* The Disinherited Mind, 1952 (Kulturpreis der Deutschen Industrie); Hazard of Modern Poetry, 1953; Thomas Mann: The Ironic German, 1958; The Artist's Journey into the Interior, 1965; Essays über Goethe, 1970; Franz Kafka, 1974; Versuche über Rilke, 1975; The Poet's Self and the Poem, 1976; Die Wiederkehr der Unschuld und andere Essays, 1977; In the Age of Prose, 1984; The Importance of Nietzsche: Ten Essays, 1989. Add: Dept. of German, Northwestern Univ., Evanston, Ill. 60201, U.S.A.

HELLER, Joseph. American, b. 1923. Novels/Short stories, Plays/Screenplays. Instr. in English, Pennsylvania State Univ., University Park, 1950–52; Advertising Writer, Time mag., NYC, 1952–56, and Look mag., NYC, 1956–58; Promotion Mgr., McCall's mag., NYC, 1958–61. *Publs:* Catch-22, 1961, play, 1971; We Bombed in New Haven (play), 1967; Something Happened, 1974; Clevinger's Trial (play), 1974; Good as Gold, 1979; God Knows (novel), 1984; (with Speed Vogal) No Laughing Matter, 1986; Picture This (novel), 1988. Add: Simon and Schuster, 1230 Ave. of the Americas, New York, N.Y. 10020, U.S.A.

HELLER, Mark. British, b. 1914. Sports/Physical education/Keeping fit. Winter Sports Corresp., The Guardian, London. *Publs:* (ed. with Malcolm N.H. Milne) Book of European Skiing, 1966; (with Malcolm N.H. Milne) Teach Yourself Skiing, 1968; Ski, 1969; All About Skiing, 1969; Ski Guide to Austria, 1973; Skiing, 1975; World Ski Atlas, 1978;

The Young Skier, 1979; (with D. Godlington) Complete Skiing Handbook, 1979; Skiing School, 1987. Add: 26 Prenton Lane, Birkenhead, Merseyside L42 8LB, England.

HELLER, Michael D. American, b. 1937. Poetry, Literature. Member of the Faculty, now Master Teacher, American Language Inst., New York Univ., since 1967; Member of Advisory Bd., and Teacher with the New York State Poetry in the Schools Prog., since 1970. *Publs:* Two Poems, 1970; Accidental Center, 1972; Figures of Speaking, 1977; Knowledge, 1979; Conviction's Net of Branches: Essays on the Objectivist Poets and Poetry, 1985; In the Builded Place (poetry), 1989; (ed.) Carl Rakosi: Man and Poet, 1991. Add: P.O. Box 981, Stuyvesant Station, New York, N.Y. 10009, U.S.A.

HELLIE, Richard. American, b. 1937. History. Prof. of Russian History, Univ. of Chicago, since 1980 (Asst. Prof., 1966–71; Assoc. Prof., 1971–80; Chmn., Russian Civilization course, since 1967, and Undergraduate Studies in Russian Civilization, since 1970). Editor, Russian History, since 1988. Asst. Prof., Rutgers Univ., N.J., 1965–66. Member of Editorial Bd., Slavic Review, 1979–82. *Publs:* (author, ed. and trans.) Muscovite Society, 1967, 1970; Enserfment and Military Change in Muscovy, 1971; Slavery in Russia, 1450-1725, 1982, 2nd ed., 1984; (ed.) The Plow, the Hammer, and the Knout: Essays in Eighteenth-Century Russian Economic History by Arcadius Kahan, 1985; (trans.) Ulozhenie: The Law Code of 1649, 1987; (ed.) Ivan the Terrible, 1987; Many scholarly articles, many entries contributed to The Modern Encyclopedia of Russian and Soviet History. Add: 1126 East 59th St., Box 78, Chicago, Ill. 60637, U.S.A.

HELLMAN, Hal. American, b. 1927. Engineering/Technology, Sciences (general). Freelance writer since 1966. Technical Information Mgr., Gen. Precision Inc., Little Falls, N.J., 1956–66. *Publs:* Navigation—Land, Sea and Sky, 1966; The Art and Science of Color, 1967; Controlled Guidance Systems, 1967; Light and Electricity in the Atmosphere, 1968; The Right Size, 1968; Transportation in the World of the Future, 1968, 1974; High Energy Physics, 1968; Communications in the World of the Future, 1969, 1975; Defense Mechanisms, from Virus to Man, 1969; The City in the World of the Future, 1970; Helicopters and Other VTOLs, 1970; Energy and Inertia, 1970; Biology in the World of the Future, 1971; (co-author) The Kinds of Mankind: An Introduction to Race and Racism, 1971; The Lever and the Pulley, 1971; Feeding the World of the Future, 1972; Population, 1972; Energy in the World of the Future, 1973; (ed.) Epidemiological Aspects of Carcinogenesis, 1973; Technophobia: Getting Out of the Technology Trap, 1976; (co-author) Understanding Physics, 1978; Deadly Bugs and Killer Insects, 1978; Computer Basics, 1983; Industrial Sensors—A Report on Leading Edge Technology, 1985; Intelligent Sensors—The Merging of Electronics and Sensing, 1988. Add: 100 High St., Leonia, N.J. 07605, U.S.A.

HELLMANN, Ellen. South African, b. 1908. Race relations, Sociology. Pres., South African Inst. of Race Relations, 1954–56. *Publs:* Problems of Urban Bantu Youth, 1940; Rooiyard: A Sociological Survey of an Urban Native Slum Yard, 1948; (ed.) Handbook on Race Relations in South Africa, 1949; Sellgoods: A Sociological Survey of an African Commerical Labour Force, 1953; (ed.) Conflict and Progress, 1979; (co-ed.) Race Relations in South Africa 1929–79, 1980. Add: 14 First Ave., Lower Houghton, Johannesburg 2196, South Africa.

HELLSTROM, Ward. American, b. 1930. Literature. Dean of Arts and Humanities, Western Kentucky Univ., Bowling Green. Formerly Asst. Prof. to Prof. of English, Univ. of Florida, Gainesville, from 1961. *Publs:* On the Poems of Tennyson, 1972. Add: FAC 200, Western Kentucky Univ., Bowling Green, Ky. 42101, U.S.A.

HELLYER, Arthur George Lee. British, b. 1902. Homes/Gardens, Horticulture. Horticultural Corresp., Financial Times, London, since 1959. Ed., Amateur Gardening mag., 1946–67, and Gardening Illustrated mag., 1947–56. *Publs:* The Amateur Gardening Pocket Guide, 1941; The Amateur Gardener, 1948; The Encyclopedia of Garden Work and Terms, 1954; Flowers in Colour, 1955; Garden Plants in Colour, 1958; Shrubs in Colour, 1965; Garden Pests and Diseases, 1966; Starting with Roses, 1966; Find Out About Gardening, 1967; Gardens to Visit in Britain, 1970; Carter's Book for Gardeners, 1970; All-Colour Gardening Book, 1972; All-Colour Book of Indoor and Greenhouse Plants, 1973; Picture Dictionary of Popular Flowering Plants, 1973; Collingridge Encyclopaedia of Gardening, 1975; (co-author) The Financial Times Book of Garden Design, 1975; The Shell Guide to Gardens, 1977; Gardens of Genius, 1980; The Dobies Book of Greenhouses, 1981; Gardening Through the Year, 1981; Garden Shrubs, 1982. Add: Orchard Cottage, Rowfant,

Crawley, Sussex RH10 4NJ, England.

HELLYER, Jill. Australian, b. 1925. Novels/Short stories, Poetry. Exec. Secty., Australian Soc. of Authors, 1963–71. *Publs:* The Exile (verse) 1969; Not Enough Savages (novel), 1975; Song of the Humpback Whales (verse), 1981. Add: 25 Berowra Rd., Mount Colah, N.S.W. 2079, Australia.

HELLYER, Paul T. Canadian, b. 1923. Politics/Government. Member of Parliament (Canada), 1949–57, 1958–74: Parliamentary Asst. to Minister of National Defence 1956–57; Assoc. Minister 1957; Minister of National Defence 1963–67; Minister of Transport 1967–69; Acting Prime Minister 1968–69. Syndicated columnist, Toronto Sun, 1974–84. *Publs:* Agenda: A Plan for Action, 1971; Exit Inflation, 1981; Jobs for All: Capitalism on Trial, 1984. Add: 506, 65 Harbour Sq., Toronto, Ont. M5J 2L4, Canada.

HELMKER, Judith A. American, b. 1940. Recreation/Leisure/Hobbies, Sports/Physical education/Keeping fit. Health and Physical Education Teacher, Owosso Public Schs., Michigan, since 1961. *Publs:* The Organization and Administration of High School Girl's Athletic Association, 1968; A Manual of Snowmobiling, 1971, 1975; All Terrain Vehicles, 1974; The Autobiography of Pain, 1976; The Complete Guide to Aerobic Exercise, 1986. Add: 2300 Wellington Dr., Owosso, Mich. 48867, U.S.A.

HELMREICH, Ernst Christian. American, b. 1902. History, Theology/Religion. Prof. Emeritus of History and Govt., Bowdoin Coll., Brunswick, Me., since 1972 (Instr., 1931–32; Asst. Prof., 1932–40; Assoc. Prof., 1940–46; Prof., 1946–72). Instr., Purdue Univ., Lafayette, Ind., 1924–26; Asst., Radcliffe Coll., Cambridge, Mass., 1927–29, 1930–31. *Publs:* The Diplomacy of the Balkan Wars 1912–1913, 1938, 1969; (with C.E. Black) Twentieth Century Europe: A History, 1950, 4th ed. 1972; (ed.) Hungary, 1957; Religious Education in German Schools: An Historical Approach, 1959 (German ed., 1966); Religion and the Maine Schools: An Historical Approach, 1960; (ed.) A Free Church in a Free State? The Catholic Church, Italy, Germany, France 1864-1914, 1964, as Church and State in Europe 1864-1914, 1979; The German Churches under Hitler: Background, Struggle, Epilogue, 1979; Religion at Bowdoin College: A History, 1981. Add: 6 Boody St., Brunswick, Me. 04011, U.S.A.

HELMS, Randel. American, b. 1942. Literature. Prof. of English, Arizona State Univ., Tempe. Formerly, Asst. Prof. of English, Univ. of California, Los Angeles. *Publs:* Tolkien's World, 1974; Tolkien and the Silmarils, 1981; Gospel Fictions, 1988. Add: Dept. of English, Arizona State Univ., Tempe, Ariz. 85287, U.S.A.

HELPRIN, Mark. American, b. 1947. Novels/Short stories. *Publs:* A Dove of the East and Other Stories, 1975; Refiner's Fire, 1977; Ellis Island and Other Stories, 1980; Winter's Tale, 1983; (ed. with Shannon Ravenel) Best American Short Stories 1988, 1988. Add: c/o Julian Bach Literary Agency, 747 Third Ave., New York, N.Y. 10017, U.S.A.

HELWIG, David (Gordon). Canadian, b. 1938. Novels/Short stories, Poetry. Member of the faculty of English, Queen's Univ., Kingston, Ont., 1962–80. *Publs:* Figures in a Landscape, 1967; A Time in Winter (play), 1967; The Sign of the Gunman, 1969; The Streets of Summer (short stories), 1969; The Day Before Tomorrow (novel), 1971; (ed. with T. Marshall) Fourteen Stories High: Best Canadian Stories of 71, 1971; The Best Name of Silence, 1972; A Book about Billie, 1972; (ed. with J. Harcourt) 72, 73 and 74; New Canadian Stories, 3 vols., 1972–74; The Glass Knight (novel), 1976; (ed.) The Human Elements, 1978; A Book of the Hours (poetry), 1979; Jennifer (novel), 1979; The King's Evil (novel), 1981; It Is Always Summer (novel), 1982; The Rain Falls Like Rain (verse), 1982; Catchpenny Poems, 1983; A Sound Like Laughter (novel), 1983; The Only Son (novel), 1984; The Bishop, 1986; A Postcard From Rome (novel), 1988; The Hundred Old Names (poetry), 1988. Add: 106 Montreal St., Kingston, Ont. K7K 3E8, Canada.

HEMINWAY, John Hylan, Jr. American, b. 1944. Sciences, Travel/Exploration/Adventure, Biography. Writer, dir., producer for The Search for Mind, WNET/13, NYC; Exec. Producer of "Travels", since 1988. Contributing Ed., Traveler mag., New York. Field producer and documentary writer, A.B.C., 1970–73; Writer/Producer, Survival, Anglia Ltd., 1973–76; Co-Producer, D.L. Sage Productions, NYC, 1976–77; Writer, Producer and Dir. for "The Brain", 1982–84. *Publs:* The Imminent Rains: A Visit Among the Last Pioneers of Africa, 1968; No Man's Land: The Last of White Africa, 1983. Add: 36 East 70th St., New York,

N.Y. 10021, U.S.A.

HEMLOW, Joyce. Canadian, b. 1906. Biography. Greenshields Prof. Emerita of English Language and Literature, McGill Univ., Montreal (faculty member since 1945). *Publs:* The History of Fanny Burney, 1958; (ed.) The Journals and Letters of Fanny Burney (Madame d'-Arblay), 12 vols., 1972–84. Add: Liscomb, Guysboro Co., N.S., Canada.

HEMMING, John Henry. Canadian, b. 1935. Anthropology/Ethnology, History. Joint Chmn., Hemming Publishing Ltd., London; Chmn., Newman Books Ltd., Brintex Ltd., London. Dir. and Secty., Royal Geographical Soc., since 1975. *Publs:* The Conquest of the Incas, 1970; (with Edwin Brooks, René Fuerst and Francis Huxley) Tribes of the Amazon Basin, Brazil, 1973; Red Gold: The Conquest of the Brazilian Indians, 1978; The Search for El Dorado, 1978; Machu Picchu, 1981; Monuments of the Incas, 1982; Change in the Amazon Basin, 2 vols., 1985; Amazon Frontier: The Defeat of the Brazilian Indians, 1987; (with James Ratter and Angelo dos Santos) Maraca, 1988. Add: Hemming Publishing Ltd., 178 Great Portland St., London W1N 6NH, England.

HEMPHILL, Paul (James). American, b. 1930. Social commentary/phenomena, Autobiography/Memoirs/Personal. Sports writer and gen. columnist for newspapers in the American South, 1958–69. *Publs:* The Nashville Sound, 1970; (with Ivan Allen) Mayor: Notes on the Sixties, 1970; The Good Old Boys, 1974; Long Gone, 1979; Too Old to Cry, 1981; The Six Killer Chronicles, 1985; Me and the Boy, 1986. Add: Sterling Lord Literistic, Inc., One Madison Ave., New York, N.Y. 10010, U.S.A.

HÉNAULT, Marie. American, b. 1921. Literature, Film. Prof. of English, St. Michael's Coll., Winooski, Vt., since 1962 (Chmn., English Dept., 1969–72 and 1984–85), currently on leave. Instr. in English, Univ. of Utah, Salt Lake City 1946–49, Univ. of Maryland, College Park 1950–52, and St. Joseph Coll., Emmitsburg, Md. 1961–62. *Publs:* Peter Viereck, 1969; Guide to Erza Pound, 1970; Checklist of Ezra Pound, 1970; (ed.) The Merrill Studies in the Cantos, 1971; Stanley Kunitz, 1980. Add: 235 S. Oakdale, No. 504, Medford, Ore. 97501, U.S.A.

HENBEST, Nigel. British, b. 1951. Astronomy, Children's non-fiction. Ed., British Astronomical Assn. Journal, since 1985. Consultant, New Scientist, London. Former Broadcaster for BBC World Service and British Radio. *Publs:* (with Heather Couper) Space Frontiers, 1978; (with Lloyd Mots) The Night Sky, 1979; (with H. Couper) The Restless Universe, 1982; (with Michael Marten) The New Astronomy, 1983; (with H. Couper) Astronomy, 1983; (with H. Couper) Physics, 1983; (ed.) The Planets, 1985; (with H. Couper) The Sun, 1986; (with H. Couper) New Worlds: In Search of Planets, 1986; (with H. Couper) The Moon, 1987; (with H. Couper) Spaceprobes and Satellites, 1987; (with H. Couper) Telescopes and Observatories, 1987. Add: 55 Colomb St., London SE10 9EZ, England.

HENDERSHOT, Carl H. American. Education, Information science/Computers. Instructional Designer and Ed. of Industrial Training, Hendershot Programmed Learning Consultants, Bay City, Mich. *Publs:* (compiler) Programmed Learning and Individually Paced Instruction Bibliography, 5th ed., 2 vols. with supplements 1-6, 1985; Individually Paced or Self Teaching Instruction Source Book, vol. 1, 1985. Add: 4114 Ridgewood Dr., Bay City, Mich. 48706, U.S.A.

HENDERSON, Dan Fenno. American, b. 1921. History, Law. Prof. of Law, and Dir., Asian Law Prog., Univ. of Washington Sch. of Law, Seattle, since 1962. *Publs:* Conciliation and Japanese Law: Tokugawa and Modern, 2 vols., 1965; The Constitution of Japan: The First Twenty Years, 1969; Foreign Enterprise in Japan: Law and Policies, 1973; Village Contracts in Tokugawa, Japan, 1975; Law and Legal Process in Japan, 1978; Civil Procedure in Japan, 1982, 1985. Add: 632 36th Ave. East, Seattle, Wash. 98112, U.S.A.

HENDERSON, F(rancis) M(artin). New Zealander, b. 1921. Engineering/Technology. Prof. of Civil Engineering, Univ. of Newcastle, N.S.W., 1968–1982, Emeritus Prof. since 1982. Sr. Lectr., 1952–63, and Prof., 1964–68, Univ. of Canterbury, Christchurch. *Publs:* Elliptic Functions with Complex Arguments, 1960; Open Channel Flow, 1966. Add: 35 Woodward St., Merewether, N.S.W. 2291, Australia.

HENDERSON, George Patrick. British, b. 1915. Philosophy. Lectr. in Logic and Metaphysics, 1945–53, Sr. Lectr., 1953–59, and Prof. of Philosophy, 1959–67, Univ. of St. Andrews; Prof. of Philosophy, Univ. of Dundee, 1967–80. Ed., The Philosophical Quarterly, 1962–72.

Publs: The Revival of Greek Thought 1620-1830, 1970; E.P. Papanoutsos, 1983; The Ionian Academy, 1988.   Add: The Pendicle, Invergowrie, Dundee, DD2 5DQ, Scotland.

HENDERSON, Hamish.   British, b. 1919.   Poetry, Translations.   Lectr. and Research Fellow. Sch. of Scottish Studies, Edinburgh Univ., since 1951. *Publs:* (ed. and contrib.) Ballads of World War II Collected by Seumas Mor Maceanruig, 1947; Elegies for the Dead in Cyrenaica, 1948; (trans.) Prison Letters, by Gramsci, 1988.   Add: Sch. of Scottish Studies, Edinburgh Univ., Edinburgh EH8 9LD, Scotland.

HENDERSON, James.   Canadian, b. 1934.   Novels/Short stories, Language/Linguistics, Literature.   Co-ordinator, Language Study Centre, Toronto Bd. of Education, since 1973.   Asst. Co-ordinator, Language Arts, Halton County Bd. of Education, Ont., 1969–73. *Publs:* The Time of Your Life, 1967, 1977; Discussion and Debate, 1971; Writers in Conflict, 1972; Copperhead (novel), 1972; (with R.T. Shepard) Language Moves, 1973; (with Shepard) Language Matters, 1974; Electric English, 1976; Mediascan, 1976; The Language Box, 1977; A Canadian Handbook of English, 1980; An Inquiry Program into Literature, 1980; Living Language, 1982.   Add: c/o Toronto Bd. of Education, 155 College St., Toronto, Ont., Canada.

HENDERSON, Laurence.   British, b. 1928.   Novels/Short stories. *Publs:* With Intent, 1968; Sitting Target, 1970; Cage Until Tame, 1972; Major Enquiry, 1977; The Patriot Game, 1985.   Add: 57 Crown Hill, Rayleigh, Essex, England.

HENDERSON, Patrick (David).   British, b. 1927.   Economics.   Head of the Dept. of Economics and Statistics, OECD, Paris, since 1984. Fellow and Tutor in Economics, Lincoln Coll., Oxford, 1948–65; Univ. Lectr. in Economics, Oxford, 1950–65; Economic Adviser, H.M. Treasury, London, 1957–58; Chief Economist, U.K. Ministry of Aviation, 1965–67; Adviser, Harvard Development Advisory Service, Cambridge, Mass., 1967–68; Visiting Lectr., Economic Development Inst., World Bank, Washington, 1968–69; Economist, World Bank, Washington, 1969–75; Prof. of Political Economy, University Coll., London, 1975–83. *Publs:* (co-author) Nyasaland: The Economics of Federation, 1960; (ed. and contrib.) Economic Growth in Britain, 1965; India: The Energy Sector, 1975. Add: OECD, 2 rue André-Pascal, 75775 Paris, Cedex 16, France.

HENDERSON, Richard.   American, b. 1924.   Recreation/Leisure/Hobbies, Travel/Exploration/Adventure.   Freelance writer and illustrator. Member, Seaworthiness Project Technical Cttee., American Boat and Yacht Council, since 1973.   Former member, Bd. of Advisors, The Telltale Compass, yachtsman's newsletter. *Publs:* First Sail for Skipper, 1960; Hand, Reef and Steer, 1965; (ed. and contrib.) Dangerous Voyages of Captain Andrews, 1966; Single-handed Sailing: The Experiences and Techniques of the Lone Voyager, 1967, 2nd ed., 1988; Sail and Power, 1967–73, 1979; The Racing-Cruiser, 1970; Sea Sense, 1972, 1979; The Cruiser's Compendium, 1973; Better Sailing, 1977; East to the Azores, 1978; Choice Yacht Designs, 1979; Philip L. Rhodes and His Yacht Designs, 1981; (with Robert W. Carrick) John G. Alden and His Yacht Designs, 1983; (with William J. Kotsch) Heavy Weather Guide, 2nd ed. 1984; 53 Boats You Can Build, 1985; Understanding Rigs and Rigging, 1985; Sailing at Night, 1987; Sailing in Windy Weather, 1987.   Add: Gibson Island, Md. 21056, U.S.A.

HENDERSON, William L.   American, b. 1927.   Economics, Money/Finance.   Visiting Prof., Ohio State Univ., Newark campus, since 1987.   Dir. of Development and Planning, Wabash Coll., Crawfordsville, Ind., 1973–75; Asst. to the Pres., 1970–73, and John E. Harris Prof. of Economics, 1975–85, Denison Univ., Granville, Ohio; Dir., Institutional Research, Rollins Coll., Winter Park, Fla., 1985–87. *Publs:* Tax Revision Alternatives for the State of Ohio, 1962; (ed. with Helen A. Cameron) Readings in Public Finance, 1966; (with Cameron) The Public Economy: An Introduction to Government Finance, 1969; (with Larry Ledebur) Economic Disparity: Problems and Strategy for Black America, 1970; (with Ledebur) Urban Economics: Processes and Problems, 1972.   Add: 1277 Lakewood Rd., Columbus, Ohio 43209, U.S.A.

HENDERSON, William Otto.   British, b. 1904.   Economics, Geography, International relations/Current affairs.   Reader in Intl. Economic History, Univ. of Manchester, 1948–72. *Publs:* The Lancashire Cotton Famine 1861-1865, 1934, 1969; The Zollverein, 1939; Britain and Industrial Europe 1750-1870, 1954, 1965; The State and the Industrial Revolution in Prussia 1740-1870, 1958; The Industrial Revolution on the Continent 1800-1914, 1961,1967; The Genesis of the Common Market, 1962; Studies in German Colonial History, 1962; Studies in the Economic

Policy of Frederick the Great, 1963; J.C. Fischer and His Diary of Industrial England 1814-1851, 1966; (ed.) Engels: Selected Writings, 1967; Industrial Britain Under the Regency: The Diaries of Escher, Bodmer, May, and de Gollois 1814-1818, 1968; The Industrialisation of Europe 1790-1914, 1969; (with S. de Vries and T. Luykx) An Atlas of World History, 1965; The Rise of German Industrial Power 1834-1914, 1975; The Life of Friedrich Engels, 2 vols., 1976; Friedrich List, 1983; Manufactories in Germany, 1985; Marx and Engels and the English Workers and Other Essays, 1989.   Add: 21 Roydon Ct., Hemel Hempstead, Herts., England.

HENDERSON-HOWAT, Gerald.   *See* **HOWAT,** Gerald Malcolm David.

HENDERSON SMITH, Stephen Lane.   British, b. 1919.   Poetry.   Gen. Medical Clinical Asst., Accident Dept., Huddersfield Royal Infirmary. Medical Missionary, China and Congo, 1943–55. *Publs:* Four Minutes and Other Verses, 1967; Snow Children, 1968; Beyond the City, 1971; Intimations, 1972; Celebrations, 1973; Glimmerings, 1975; Filterings, 1977; Transparencies, 1980; Soundings, 1982; Foundlings, 1984.   Add: 55 New Hey Rd., Lindley, Huddersfield, Yorks. HD3 4AL, England.

HENDRICKS, George David, Sr.   American, b. 1913.   History, Mythology/Folklore.   Prof. of English, North Texas State Univ., Denton, since 1951. *Publs:* The Bad Man of the West, 1941, 4th ed. 1970; Mirrors, Mice, and Mustaches, 1966; Rooster, Rhymes, and Railroad Tracks, 1978. Add: 1819 Panhandle, Denton, Tex. 76201, U.S.A.

HENDRICKSON, James E. Canadian, b. 1932.   History, Politics/Government.   Assoc. Prof. of History, Univ. of Victoria, B.C., since 1967 (Lectr., 1964–65; Asst. Prof., 1965–67; Head of Dept., 1969–74). *Publs:* Joe Lane of Oregon: Machine Politics and the Sectional Crisis, 1849-1861; (ed.) Journals of the Colonial Legislatures of Vancouver Island and British Columbia 1851-1871, 5 vols.   Add: 2511 Sinclair Rd., Victoria, B.C. V8N 1B5, Canada.

HENDRICKSON, Robert A.   American, b. 1923.   Economics, Law, Biography.   Counsel, Citibank, N.A., since 1986.   Dir., St. Martin's Press, NYC, since 1960, Grove's Dictionaries of Music Inc., since 1977; Chmn., since 1983 and Dir., since 1977, Carl Duisberg Foundn.   Partner, Eaton and Van Winkle, NYC, since 1987.   Partner, Coudert Bros. (lawyers), NYC, 1978–86. Pres., American Foreign Law Assoc., 1983–86. *Publs:* Interstate and International Estate Planning, 1968; Estate Planning for the Migrant Executive, 1969; The Future of Money, 1970; The Cashless Society, 1972; Hamilton I 1757-1789, 1976; Hamilton II 1789-1804, 1976; The Rise and Fall of Alexander Hamilton, 1981; (with William K. Stevens) Current Legal Aspects of International Estate Planning, 1981; (with Neal R. Silverman) Changing the Situs of a Trust, 1981.   Add: Eaton and Van Winkle, 600 Lexington Ave., New York, N.Y. 10022, U.S.A.

HENDRIKS, A(rthur) L(emière).   Jamaican, b. 1922.   Poetry.   Freelance writer since 1971.   Clerk, Arthur Hendriks Furniture Co., Jamaica, 1940–50; Sales Mgr., Radio Jamaica Ltd., 1950–60; Gen. Mgr., Jamaica Broadcasting Corp., 1961–64; Caribbean Dir., Thomson Television Ltd., London, 1964–71. *Publs:* (ed. with C. Lindo) The Independence Anthology of Jamaican Literature, 1962; On This Mountain and Other Poems, 1965; These Green Islands, 1971; Muet, 1971; Madonna of the Unknown Nation, 1974; The Islanders and Other Poems, 1983; Archie and the Princess and the Everythingest Horse (for children), 1983; The Naked Ghost and Other Poems, 1984; Great Families of Jamaica, 1984; To Speak Slowly: Selected Poems, 1986; (with A.L. Hendricks) Check, 1988.   Add: Box 265, Constant Spring, Kingston 8, Jamaica.

HENDRY, Thomas.   Canadian, b. 1929.   Novels/Short stories, Plays/Screenplays, Theatre.   Founding Dir., Toronto Free Theatre, since 1971. Owner, Thomas Hendry, C.A., 1956–58, and Partner, Hendry and Evans, 1958–61, Winnipeg; Founder and Partner, Theatre 77, Winnipeg, 1957–58; Mgr. and Producer, Manitoba Theatre Centre, Winnipeg, 1958–63; Secty. Gen. Canadian Theatre Centre, Toronto, 1964–69; Ed., The Stage in Canada, Toronto, 1965–69; Literary Mgr., Stratford Festival, Ontario, 1969 and 1970; Founding Dir., Playwrights Co-op, 1971–79. *Publs:* 15 Miles of Broken Glass, 1968, 1972; The Canadians (on English-Canadian theatre), 1967; That Boy—Call Him Back, 1972; You Smell Good to Me, and Séance, 1972; The Missionary Position, 1972; (with S. Jack) Grave Diggers of 1942 (musical), 1973; Lady Byron Vindicated, 1976; Naked at the Opera, 1976; Farr Away (novel), 1978; Cultural Capital: The Care and Feeding of Toronto's Artistic Assets, 1983.   Add: 34 Elgin Ave., Toronto Ont. M5R 1G6, Canada.

HENKEL, Steve. American, b. 1933. Children's non-fiction, Recreation, Travel (consumer product evaluations: boats, cars, engines, electronics, optical products, personal gear, etc.; interviews). Freelance writer, photographer and illustrator; Pres., Henkel Creative Services, Darien, Conn., since 1986. Contrib. Ed., Small Boat Journal, since 1986. Engineer and Admin., M.W. Kellogg Co., NYC, 1955–65; Exec. in planning, marketing, and finance, Esso Chemical Co., NYC, 1965–72; Mgr. of Business Analysis, NL Industries, NYC, 1972–79; Mgr. of Planning, Chicago Pneumatic Tool Co., NYC, 1979–81; Dir. of Operations, Flakt Inc., 1981–82; Pres., Henkel Mgmt. Systems, Darien, Ct., 1982–84; Partner, Sailor Publ., East Norwalk, Conn., 1984–86; General Mgr. and Ed.-at-Large, Sailor mag., 1984–86. Contrib. Ed., Yacht mag., 1986–88. Contrib., Yacht Racing/Cruising mag., since 1981; and Sail, Small Boat Journal, Nautical Quarterly, Boating Digest, Oceans, Yachting mags, since 1986. *Publs:* Bikes, 1972; Boating for Less, 1988. Add: 4 Woodland Dr., Darien, Conn. 06820, U.S.A.

HENKES, Robert. American, b. 1922. Art. Instr. in Art, Portage Public Schs., and Kalamazoo Inst. of Arts, Michigan, since 1958. Instr. in Art, Decorah, Iowa, 1948–50; Art Consultant, Kalamazoo, 1951–65; Prof. of Art, Nazareth Coll., Kalamazoo, 1966–72. *Publs:* Orientation to Drawing and Painting, 1965; Notes on Art and Art Education, 1969; Eight American Women Painters, 1977; The Crucifixion in American Painting, 1978; Insights in Art Education, 1978; 300 Lessons in Art, 1981; World Art History, 1982; Activities for the Study of American Art, 1983; New Vision in Drawing and Painting, 1985; Art and the Community, 1986; Sports in Art, 1986; filmstrips—Open Your Eyes To Art, 1981; 20th Century American Painting, 1983; Hispanic Art, 1985. Add: 1124 Bretton Dr., Kalamazoo, Mich., U.S.A.

HENKIN, Louis. American, b. 1917. International relations/Current affairs, Law. Prof. since 1962, and Univ. Prof. since 1979, Columbia Univ., NYC, and Co-Dir., Center for Study of Human Rights (Assoc. Dir., Legislative Drafting and Research Fund, and Lectr. in Law, 1956–57). Member, Bd. of Eds. since 1967, American Journal of Intnl. Law (Co-Editor-in-Chief, 1978–84). Pres., U.S. Instn. of Human Rights, since 1969. Prof. of Law, Univ. of Pennsylvania Law Sch., Philadelphia, 1957–62. Pres., American Soc. of Political and Legal Philosophy, 1985–87. *Publs:* Arms Control and Inspection in American Law, 1958; The Berlin Crisis and the United Nations, 1959; (ed.) Arms Control: Issues for the Public, 1961; Law for the Sea's Mineral Resources, 1968; How Nations Behave: Law and Foreign Policy, 1968, 1979; Foreign Affairs and the Constitution, 1972; (ed.) World Politics and the Jewish Condition, 1973; (ed. with W. Friedman and O. Lissitzyn) Transnational Law in a Changing Society, 1974; The Rights of Man Today, 1978; (co-ed.) International Law: Cases and Materials, 1980, 1987; (ed.) The International Bill of Rights, 1981. Add: Columbia Univ., New York, N.Y. 10027, U.S.A.

HENLEY, Arthur. American. Medicine/Health, Psychology, Sociology. Former Keynote Speaker, National Assn. of Mental Health, and Creative Writing teacher, New York Univ. *Publs:* Demon in My View, 1966; Make Up Your Mind, 1967; (with R.L. Wolk) Yes Power, 1969; (with R.L. Wolk) The Right to Lie, 1970; (with A.J. Montanari) The Montanari Book, 1971; Schizophrenia, 1971, 1987; (with M. Weisinger) The Complete Alibi Handbook, 1972; (with A.J. Montanari) What Other Child Care Books Won't Tell You, 1973; (with A.J. Montanari) The Difficult Child, 1973; Human Resources and Population Policies, 1974; (with D. Brooks) Don't Be Afraid of Cataracts, 1978, rev. ed. 1983; Phobias: The Crippling Fears, 1987, rev. ed., 1988. Add: 73-37 Austin St., Forest Hills, N.Y. 11375, U.S.A.

HENLEY, Beth. (Elizabeth Becker Henley). American, b. 1952. Plays/Screenplays. Actress from 1972; teacher, Dallas Minority Repertory Theatre, 1974–75. *Publs:* Crimes of the Heart, 1982, as screenplay 1986; Am I Blue?, 1982; The Wake of Jamey Foster, 1983; The Miss Firecracker Contest, 1985, as screenplay 1988; The Lucky Spot, 1987. Add: c/o Gilbert Parker, William Morris Agency, 1350 Ave. of the Americas, New York, N.Y. 10019, U.S.A.

HENNESSY, Max. *See* **HARRIS,** John.

HENNESSY, Peter. British, b. 1947. History, Politics/Government. Writer, The Times, London, since 1984 (Reporter, 1974–76; Whitehall Correspondent, 1976–82; Lead Writer, 1982–84). Visiting Fellow, Policies Studies Inst., London, since 1985. Presenter of Granada Television Series "Under Fire", 1985–87; Author and Presenter of Brook Prod. Television "All the Prime Minister's Men", 1986; Author and Presenter, B.B.C. Radio 3's prog. "A Canal Too Far,170, 1987. *Publs:* (with Colin Bennett) A Consumer's Guide to Open Government, 1980; (with Keith Jeffery) States of Emergency: British Governments and Strikebreaking since 1919, 1983; (with Andrew Arends) Mr. Attlee's Engine Room, 1983; (with Michael Cockerell and David Walker) Sources Close to the Prime Minister: Inside the Hidden World of the News Manipulators, 1984; (with Susan Morrison and Richard Townsend) Routine Punctuated by Orgies: The Central Policy Review Staff, 1970–83, 1985; (with Sir Douglas Hague) How Adolph Hitler Reformed Whitehall, 1985; What the Papers Never Said, 1985; Cabinet, 1986; The Great and the Good: An Inquiry Into the British Establishment, 1986; (ed. with Anthony Seldon) Ruling Performance: British Governments from Attlee to Thatcher, 1987; Whitehall, 1986. Add: 26 Merton Rd., London E17 9DE, England.

HENREY, Madeleine. (Mrs. Robert Henrey.) British, b. 1906. Novels/Short stories. *Publs:* The Madeleine Books—The Little Madeleine, 1951; Paloma, 1951; An Exile in Soho, 1952; Madeleine Grown Up, 1952; Madeleine's Journal, 1953; Madeleine Young Wife, 1954; A Month in Paris, 1954; Milou's Daughter, 1955; Mistress of Myself, 1959; Her April Days, 1963; Wednesday at Four, 1964; Winter Wild, 1966; She Who Pays, 1969; The Golden Visit, 1969; London Under Fire 1940–45, 1969; Julia, 1971; A Girl at Twenty, 1974; Green Leaves, 1976; other books—London, 1940; The King of Brentford, 1946; Bloomsbury Fair, 1955; This Feminine World, 1956; A Daughter for a Fortnight, 1957; The Virgin of Aldermanbury, 1958; The Dream Makers, 1961; Spring in a Soho Street, 1962. Add: c/o J.M. Dent & Sons, Publrs. 91 Clapham High St., London SW4 7TA, England.

HENRI, Adrian (Maurice). British, b. 1932. Novels/Short stories, Children's fiction, Poetry, Art. Freelance writer, singer and painter, since 1970. Lectr., Manchester Coll. of Art and Design, 1961–64, and Liverpool Coll. of Art, 1964–68; Member, Liverpool Scene poetry-rock group, 1968–70; Pres., Liverpool Academy of Arts, 1972–81. *Publs:* (with Roger McGough and Brian Patten) The Mersey Sound: Penguin Modern Poets 10, 1967, 1974; Tonight at Noon, 1968; (with M. Kustow) I Wonder: A Guillaume Apollinaire Show (play), 1968; City, 1969; Talking after Christmas Blue, 1969; Poems for Wales and Six Landscapes for Susan, 1970; Autobiography, 1971; America, 1972; (with Nell Dunn) I Want (novel), 1972; Yesterday's Girl (TV play), 1973; Environments and Happenings (in U.S. as Total Art: Environments, Happenings, and Performances), 1974; The Best of Henri (poems), 1975; City Hedges (poems 1970–76), 1977; Words Without a Story (verse), 1979; From the Loveless Motel (poems), 1980; Eric the Punk Cat (for children), 1982; Harbour (poems), 1982; Penny Arcade: Poems 1978–1982, 1983; (with Roger McGough and Brian Patten) New Volume, 1983; Holiday Snaps, 1985; Collected Poems, 1986; The Phantom Lollipop Lady (poems for children), 1986; Eric and Frankie in Las Vegas (for children), 1987; The Wakefield Mysteries (plays), 1988; Rhinestone Rhino (poems for children), 1989. Add: 21 Mount St., Liverpool L1 9HD, England.

HENRY, Marguerite. American. Children's fiction. *Publs:* Auno and Tauno, 1940; Dilly Dally Sally, 1940; Eight Pictured Geographies, 1941; Geraldine Belinda, 1942; Birds at Home, 1942; (with B. True) Their First Igloo, 1943; A Boy and A Dog, 1944; Justin Morgan Had a Horse, 1945, 1954; Robert Fulton, Boy Craftsman, 1945; The Little Fellow, 1945; Eight Pictured Geographies, 1946; Benjamin West and His Cat Grimalkin, 1947; Always Reddy, 1947; Misty of Chincoteague, 1947; King of Wind, 1948; Little or Nothing from Nottingham, 1949; Sea Star: Orphan of Chincoteague, 1949; Born to Trot, 1950; Album of Horses, 1951; Portfolio of Horses, 1952; Brighty of the Grand Canyon, 1953; Wagging Tales, 1955; Cinnabar, The One O'Clock Fox, 1956; Black Gold, 1957; Gaudenzia: Pride of the Palio, 1961, now titled The Wildest Horse Race in the World; Five O'Clock Charlie, 1962; All about Horses, 1962; Stormy, Misty's Foal, 1963; White Stallion of Lipizza, 1964; Mustang, Wild, Spirit of the West, 1966; Dear Readers and Riders, 1969; Album of Dogs, 1970; San Domingo, The Medicine Hat Stallion, 1972; The Little Fellow, 1975; A Pictorial Life Story of Misty, 1976; One Man's Horse, 1977; The Illustrated Marguerite Henry, 1980; Our First Pony, 1984. Add: c/o Rand McNally and Co., P.O. Box 7600, Chicago, Ill. 60680, U.S.A.

HENRY, Will. *See* **ALLEN,** Henry Wilson.

HENSCHEL, Elizabeth Georgie. British. Plays/Screenplays, Animals/Pets, Sports/Physical education/Keeping fit. BBC Overseas Announcer, 1940–46; Lectr. for the British Council in Scandinavia, Finland, Switzerland and Holland, 1946–52. *Publs:* The Well-Dressed Woman; Thomas; Careers with Horses; Murder After Dinner (radio play); Kingfisher Guide to Horses and Ponies; Basic Riding Explained; Illustrated Guide to Horses and Ponies; All About Your Pony. Add: Ballintean,

Kineraig, Kingussie, Inverness-shire, Scotland.

HENSHALL, Audrey Shore. British, b. 1927. Archaeology. Asst. Keeper, National Museum of Antiquities of Scotland, 1960–71; Asst. Secty., Soc. of Antiquaries of Scotland, Edinburgh, 1977–86. *Publs:* The Chambered Tombs of Scotland, 2 vols., 1963, 1972; (with J.L. Davidson) The Chambered Cairns of Orkney: An Inventory of the Structures and Their Contents, 1987. Add: 46 Findhorn Place, Edinburgh, Scotland.

HENSHAW, James Ene. Nigerian, b. 1924. Plays/Screenplays. *Publs:* This Is Our Chance: Plays from West Africa, 1957; Children of the Goddess and Other Plays, 1964; Medicine for Love, 1964; Dinner for Promotion, 1967; Enough Is Enough, 1976; A Song to Mary Charles (Irish Sister of Charity), 1985. Add: Itiaba House, Calabar Rd., Calabar, Nigeria.

HENSLEY, Joe L. American, b. 1926. Mystery/Crime/Suspense, Science fiction/Fantasy. Freelance writer, mainly of SF short stories. Partner, Metford and Hensley, 1955–72, and Hensley, Todd and Castor, 1972–75, Madison; Judge Pro-Tempore, 80th Judicial Circuit, Versailles, Ind., 1975–76. Judge, 5th Judicial Circuit, Madison, Ind., 1971–88. *Publs:* The Color of Hate, 1960; Deliver Us to Evil, 1971; Legislative Body, 1972; The Poison Summer, 1974; Song of Corpus Juris, 1974; The Black Roads (SF novel), 1976; Rivertown Risk, 1977; A Killing in Gold, 1978; Minor Murders, 1979; Outcasts, 1981; Final Doors (short stories), 1981; Robak's Cross, 1985; Robak's Fire, 1987; Robak's Firm (short stories), 1987; Color Him Guilty, 1987. Add: 2315 Blackmore, Madison, Ind. 47250, U.S.A.

HENTOFF, Nat(han Irving). American. Novels/Short stories, Children's fiction, Civil liberties/Human rights, Music, Social commentary/phenomena. Staff Writer, The New Yorker, since 1960; Columnist, Village Voice, NYC; Columnist, Washington Post. Assoc. Ed., Down Beat Mag., NYC, 1953–57. *Publs:* (ed. with N. Shapiro) Hear Me Talkin' to Ya, 1955; (ed.) The Jazz Makers, 1957; (ed. with A. McCarthy) Jazz, 1959; The Jazz Life, 1961; The Peace Agitator, 1963; The New Equality, 1964; Jazz Country, 1965; Call the Keeper, 1966; (ed.) The Collected Essays of A.J. Muste, 1966; Our Children Are Dying, 1966; Onwards, 1967; A Doctor Among the Addicts, 1967; I'm Really Dragged But Nothing Gets Me Down, 1967; Journey Into Jazz, 1968; A Political Life: The Education of John V. Lindsay, 1969; In the Country of Ourselves, 1971; (with others) State Secrets: Police Surveillance in America, 1973; This School Is Driving Me Crazy, 1976; Jazz Is, 1976; Does Anybody Give a Damn, 1977; The First Freedom, 1979; Does This School Have Capital Punishment?, 1981; Blues for Charlie Darwin, 1982; The Day They Came to Arrest the Book, 1982; The Man from Internal Affairs, 1983; Boston Boy: A Memoir, 1986; American Heroes: In and Out of School, 1987; John Cardinal O'Connor: At the Storm Center of a Changing American Catholic Church, 1988. Add: 25 Fifth Ave., New York, N.Y. 10003, U.S.A.

HEPBURN, Ronald William. British, b. 1927. Philosophy. Prof. of Moral Philosophy, Univ. of Edinburgh, since 1975 (Prof. of Philosophy, 1964–75). Prof., Univ. of Nottingham, 1960–64. *Publs:* Christianity and Paradox: Critical Studies in Twentieth-Century Theology, 1958; "Wonder" and Other Essays in Aesthetics and Neighbouring Fields, 1984. Add: Dept. of Philosophy, Univ. of Edinburgh, David Hume Tower, George Sq., Edinburgh EH8 9JX, Scotland.

HEPPENHEIMER, Thomas A. American, b. 1947. Air/Space topics, Physics, Technology. Pres., Center for Space Science, Fountain Valley, Calif., since 1974. Book Review Ed., Journal of the Astronautical Sciences, since 1979. Instr., Univ. of California, Irvine, since 1988. Scientist, Science Applications Inc., Schiller Park, Ill., 1972–73; Member, Technical Staff, Rockwell Intnl. Corp., Downey, Calif., 1973–74; Research Fellow in Planetary Science, California Inst. of Technology, Pasadena, 1974–75; Alexander von Humboldt Fellow, Max-Planck-Institut, Heidelberg, 1976–78. *Publs:* Colonies in Space, 1977; Toward Distant Suns, 1979; The Real Future, 1983; The Man-Made Sun, 1984; The Coming Quake, 1988; Anti Submarine Warfare, 1989; Hypersonic Technologies and the National Aerospace Plane, 1989. Add: 11040 Blue Allium Ave., Fountain Valley, Calif. 92708, U.S.A.

HEPWORTH, Mike. (James Michael Hepworth). British, b. 1938. Criminology/Law Enforcement/Prisons, Sociology. Sr. Lectr. in Sociology, Univ. of Aberdeen, since 1980 (Lectr., 1972–80). Asst. Lectr. in Social Studies, Monkwearmouth Coll. of Further Education, Sunderland, 1965–66; Lectr. in Sociology, Teesside Polytechnic, Middlesbrough, 1967–71; Sr. Lectr. in Sociology, Lanchester Polytechnic, Coventry, 1971.

Publs: Blackmail: Privacy and Secrecy in Everyday Life, 1975; (with M. Featherstone) Surviving Middle Age, 1982; (with B.S. Turner) Confession: Studies in Deviance and Religion, 1982. Add: Rose Cottage, Whiterashes, Aberdeen AB5 0QP, Scotland.

HEPWORTH, Noel P. British, b. 1934. Money/Finance, Politics/Government. Dir., Chartered Inst. of Public Finance and Accountancy, since 1980. Asst. City Treasurer, Manchester, 1968–72; Dir. of Finance, London Borough of Croydon, 1972–80. *Publs:* Local Government Finance, 1970, 7th ed., 1983; (with J. Odling-Smee and A. Grey) Housing Rents, Costs, and Subsidies, 1978, 1981; The Reform of Local Government, 1985; What Future for Local Government, 1988. Add: 2-3 Robert St., London WC2N 6BH, England.

HERBERT, Gilbert. Israeli, b. 1924. Architecture. Mary Hill Swope Prof. of Architecture, Technion, Haifa, since 1974 (Assoc. Prof., 1968; Prof., 1972; Dean of the Faculty of Architecture and Town Planning, 1973–74). Lectr. in Architecture, Univ. of the Witwatersrand, Johannesburg, 1947–61; Reader in Architecture and Town Planning, Univ. of Adelaide, 1961–68; Part-time Prof., Bezalel Academy of Art and Design, Jerusalem, 1970–72, and 1976–78. Assoc. Ed., South African Architectural Record, Johannesburg, 1949–60. *Publs:* The Synthetic Vision of Walter Gropius, 1959; Martienssen and the International Style, 1975; Pioneers of Prefabrication, 1978; The Dream of the Factory-Made House: Walter Gropius and Konrad Wachsmann, 1984. Add: Faculty of Architecture and Town Planning, Technion: Israel Inst. of Technology, Haifa, Israel.

HERBERT, Ivor. British, b. 1925. Novels/Short stories, Plays/Screenplays, Sports/Physical education/Keeping fit, Biography. Racehorse trainer, 1953–60 and 1964–68; Feature Writer, and Columnist, London Evening News, 1954–70. *Publs:* Eastern Windows, 1953; Point to Point, 1964; Arkle: The Story of a Champion, 1966, 1975; The Great St. Trinian's Train Robbery (screenplay), 1966; The Queen Mother's Horses, 1967; (with P. Smyly) The Winter Kings, 1968; The Way to the Top, 1969; (co-author) Night of the Blue Demands (play), 1971; Over Our Dead Bodies, 1972; The Diamond Diggers, 1972; (with J. Cusack) Scarlet Fever, 1972; Winter's Tale, 1974; Red Rum: Story of a Horse of Courage, 1974; The Ferret (screenplay); Hyperion: The Millionaire Horse (television script); Odds Against? (television script); The Queens Horses (television script); The Filly (novel), 1977; Six at the Top, 1977; Spot the Winner, 1978; Longacre, 1978; (ed.) Horse Racing, 1980; (with J. O'Brien) Vincent O'Brien's Great Horses, 1984; Revolting Behaviour, 1987; Herbert's Travels, 1987. Add: c/o David Higham Assoc. Ltd., 5-8 Lower John St., London W1R 4HA, England.

HERBERT, James (John). British, b. 1943. Novels/Short stories, Science fiction/Fantasy. Art Dir. in advertising, 1962–77. *Publs:* The Rats, 1974; The Fog, 1975; The Survivor, 1976; Fluke, 1977; The Spear, 1978; Lair, 1979; The Dark, 1980; The Jonah, 1981; Shrine, 1983; Domain, 1984; Moon, 1985; The Magic Cottage, 1986; Sepulchre, 1987; Haunted, 1988. Add: c/o Bruce Hunter, David Higham Assocs., 5-8 Lower John St., London W1R 4HA, England.

HERBERT, John. Pseud. for John Herbert Brundage. Canadian, b. 1926. Plays/Screenplays. Actor, set and costume designer, stage and house mgr., New Play Soc., Toronto; dancer with Garbut Roberts' Dance Drama Co. Artistic Dir., Adventure Theatre, Toronto, 1960–62, and New Venture Players, Toronto, 1962–65; Artistic Dir. and Producer, Garret Theatre Co., Toronto, 1965–70. *Publs:* Fortune and Men's Eyes, 1967; Some Angry Summer Songs, 1976. Add: 1050 Yonge St., Apt. 1A, Toronto, Ont., Canada.

HERBST, Jurgen. American, b. 1928. Education, History. Prof. of Educational Policy Studies and of History, Univ. of Wisconsin, Madison, since 1966. Assoc. Prof., Wesleyan Univ., Middletown, Conn. 1958–66. *Publs:* (ed.) Josiah Strong, Our Country, 1963; The German Historical School in American Scholarship, 1965, 1972; The History of American Education, 1973; From Crisis to Crisis: American College Government, 1639-1819, 1982; And Sadly Teach: Teacher Education and Professionalization in American Culture, 1989. Add: Dept. of Educational Policy Studies, Univ. of Wisconsin, Madison, Wisc. 53706, U.S.A.

HEREN, Louis. British, b. 1919. History, International relations/Current affairs, Autobiography/Memoirs/Personal. Deputy Ed., The Times, London, 1973–81 (Foreign Corresp. of The Times in India/Pakistan, 1947–48, Middle East, 1948–50, Korean War, 1950, Southeast Asia, 1951–53, India/Pakistan, 1953–55, and Germany, 1956–60; American Ed. and Chief Corresp. in the U.S., 1960–70; Co-Deputy Ed., 1970–73).

Publs: The New American Commonwealth, 1968; No Hail, No Farewell, 1970; Growing Up Poor in London, 1973; Story of America, 1976; Growing Up on The Times, 1978; Alas, Alas for England, 1981; The Power of the Press?, 1985; Memories of Times Past, 1988. Add: Fleet House, Vale of Health, London NW3 1AZ, England.

HERLIHY, James Leo. American, b. 1927. Novels/Short stories, Plays. Teacher of playwriting, City Coll. of New York, 1967–68, and Univ. of Arkansas, 1983. *Publs:* (with William Noble) Blue Denim, 1958; The Sleep of Baby Filbertson and Other Stories, 1959; All Fall Down (novel), 1960; Midnight Cowboy (novel), 1965; A Story That Ends with a Scream and Eight Others, 1967; Bad Bad Jo-Jo, 1968; Laughs, 1968; Stop, You're Killing Me, 1970; The Season of the Witch (novel), 1971. Add: c/o Jay Garon-Brooke Assocs. Inc., 415 Central Park West, New York, N.Y. 10025, U.S.A.

HERMAN, George Richard. American, b. 1925. Novels/Short stories, Children's non-fiction, Language/Linguistics. Assoc. Prof. of English, Arizona State Univ., Tempe, since 1967 (Instr., 1956–60; Asst. Prof., 1960–67; Coordinator of Teacher Training in English, 1960–62; Dir. of Freshman English, 1967–68). *Publs:* Let's Go Logging, 1962; (with D.A. Conlin) Modern Grammar and Composition, vol. I, 1965, vol. II, 1967, vol. III, 1971; (with D.A. Conlin) Resources for Modern Grammar and Composition, 1965, 3rd ed. 1971; (with L.M. Myers) Guide to American English, 4th ed. 1968; (with D.A. Conlin and J. Martin) Our Language Today, vol. 7, 1966, vol. 8, 1971. Add: Dept. of English, Arizona State Univ., Tempe, Ariz. 85287, U.S.A.

HERNTON, Calvin C. American, b. 1933. Novels/Short stories, Plays/Screenplays, Poetry, Race relations. Prof. of Black Studies, Oberlin Coll., Ohio. Instr. in Sociology, Benedict Coll., Columbus, S.C., 1956–57, Alabama Agricultural and Mechanical Coll., Huntsville, 1957–58, Edward Waters Coll., Jacksonville, Fla., 1958–59, and Southern Univ., Baton Rouge, La., 1959–60; Social Investigator, Dept. of Welfare, NYC, 1961–62; Co-Founder, Umbra mag., NYC, 1963. *Publs:* Glad to be Dead (play), 1958; Flame (play), 1958; The Coming of Chronos to the House of Nightsong: An Epical Narrative of the South (poetry), 1964; Sex and Racism in America (in U.K. as Sex and Racism), 1965; White Papers for White Americans, 1966; Coming Together: Black Power, White Hatred, and Sexual Hangups, 1971; The Place (play), 1972; Scarecrow (novel), 1974; (with Joseph Berke) The Cannabis Experience: A Study of the Effects of Marijuana and Hashish, 1974; Medicine Man: Collected Poems, 1976; The Sexual Mountain and Black Women Writers: Adventures in Sex, Literature, and Real Life, 1987. Add: 35 N. Prospect St., Oberlin, Ohio 44074, U.S.A.

HERON, Patrick. British, b. 1920. Art. Art Critic, New English Weekly, 1945–47, and New Statesman and Nation, London, 1947–50; London Correspondent, Arts mag., NYC, 1955–58. *Exhibitions:* one-man shows—Redfern Gallery, London, 1947, 1948, 1950, 1951, 1954, 1956, 1958; Waddington Galleries, London, 1959, 1960, 1963, 1964, 1965, 1967, 1968, 1970, 1973, 1975, 1977, 1979, 1983, 1987; Bertha Schaefer Gallery, NYC, 1960, 1962, 1965; Galerie Charles Lienhard, Zurich, 1963; Traverse Theatre Gallery, Edinburgh, 1965; Sao Paulo Bienal, Brazil, 1953, 1965; Rio de Janeiro, Buenos Aires, Santiago, Lima and Caracas, 1965–67; Dawson Gallery, Dublin, 1967; Waddington Fine Arts, Montreal, 1970; Rudy Komon Gallery, Sydney, 1970; Crossley Gallery, Melbourne, 1970; Mazelow Gallery, Toronto, 1970; Harrogate Festival, Yorkshire, 1970; Whitechapel Art Gallery, London, 1972; Hester Van Royen Gallery, London, 1973; Bonython Gallery, Sydney, 1973; Skinner Gallery, Perth, 1973; Prints on Prince St., NYC, 1974; Rutland Gallery, London, 1975; Festival of Bath, 1975; Galerie Balcon des Arts, Paris, 1977; Riverside Studios, London, 1981; Abbot Hall Art Gall., Kendal, 1984; Castlefield Gall., Manchester, 1985; retrospectives—Wakefield City Art Gallery (and tour), 1952; Richard Demarco Gallery, Edinburgh, 1967; Museum of Modern Art, Oxford, 1968; Univ. of Texas at Austin, 1978; Oriel Gallery, Cardiff, 1979; The Barbican, 1985. *Publs:* Space in Colour, 1953; The Changing Forms of Art, 1955; Braque, 1958; The Ascendancy of London in the Sixties, 1966; Colour in My Painting, 1969; The Shape of Colour, 1973; The British Influence on New York, 1974; The Colour of Colour, 1978. Add: Eagles Nest, Zennor, nr. St. Ives, Cornwall, England.

HERRICK, William. American, b. 1915. Novels/Short stories. *Publs:* The Itinerant, 1967; Strayhorn (in U.K. as Strayhorn, A Corrupt Among Mortals), 1968; Hermanos!, 1969; The Last to Die, 1971; Golcz, 1976; Shadows and Wolves, 1980; Love and Terror, 1981; Kill Memory, 1983; That's Life, 1985. Add: Riders Mill Rd., Old Chatham, N.Y. 12136, U.S.A.

HERRIOT, James (James Alfred Wight). British. Animals/Pets, Country life/Rural societies, Medicine/Health, Autobiography/Memoirs/Personal. Partner, Sinclair & Wight, veterinary surgeons, Thirsk, Yorks., since 1939; Veterinary Inspector, Ministry of Agriculture, Fisheries and Food, (U.K.), since 1939. *Publs:* If Only They Could Talk, 1970; It Shouldn't Happen to a Vet, 1972; All Creatures Great and Small, 1972; Vet in Harness, 1974; All Things Bright and Beautiful, 1974; Let Sleeping Vets Lie, 1974; Vets Might Fly, 1976; Vet in a Spin, 1977; All Things Wise and Wonderful, 1977; James Herriot's Yorkshire, 1979; The Lord God Made Them All, 1981; The Best of James Herriot, 1982; Moses the Kitten, 1984; Only One Woof, 1985; Dog Stories, 1986; Christmas Day Kitten, 1986; Bonny's Big Day, 1987; Blossom Comes Home, 1988. Add: c/o Michael Joseph Ltd., 27 Wrights Lane, London W8 5TZ, England.

HERRMANN, Luke John. British, b. 1932. Art. Prof. of the History of Art, Univ. of Leicester, 1973–88, now Emeritus (Paul Mellon Foundn. Lectr., 1967–70; Sr. Lectr. and Head of Dept., 1970–73). Asst. Ed., The Illustrated London News, 1955–58; Asst. Keeper and Sr. Asst. Keeper, Dept. of Western Art, Ashmolean Museum, Oxford, 1958–67. *Publs:* J.M.W. Turner, 1963; Ruskin and Turner, 1968; British Landscape Painting of the 18th Century, 1973; Turner: Paintings, Watercolours, Drawings and Prints, 1975, 1986; Paul and Thomas Sandby, 1986. Add: c/o History of Art Dept., Univ. of Leicester, Leicester, England.

HERRMANNS, Ralph. Swedish, b. 1933. Novels/Biography. Children's fiction, Plays/Screenplays, Art, Biography. Former Foreign Corresp., Bonnier Group, Stockholm, and Travelling Corresp., Time-Life Inc., NYC. *Publs:* Picasso and His Friends (screenplay); Lee Lan Flies the Dragon Kite, 1961; Our Car Julia, 1963; Children of the North Pole, 1964; River Boy, 1965; Flickan som hade bråttom, 1967; Den förtrollade låan, 1968; The Abominable Snowman, 1969; The World's Most Beautiful Painting, 1970; Natten och drömmen, 1972; Joan Miró, 1972; Sweden 1850 (screenplay), 1973; Posters by Miró, 1974; Goya's Witches (TV) 1974; The Enchanted Forest (screenplay), 1974; Carl Gustaf von Rosen: A Biography, 1975; Stockholm's Royal Palace, 1978; A World of Islands, 1980; En fest för ögat, 1980; Och solen gick ned över profeterna, 1981; Gösta Werner, A Biography, 1981; Den ens bröd, 1982; Jenny Nyström's Art, 1982; Desprez and the Swedish Theatre (TV), 1982; Why New York?, 1982; Israel talar, 1982; Tänk på de dagar, 1984; Slott och herremanshus, 1985; Lögnens triumf, 1985; Blott döden, blott döden, 1986; Hunden: Konsten, 1987; Tàpies (TV), 1988. Add: Brännkyrkagatan 77, 117 23 Stockholm, Sweden.

HERRNSTEIN, Barbara. *See* **SMITH,** Barbara Herrnstein.

HERRON, Orley Rufus. American, b. 1933. Education, Theology/Religion. Pres., National Coll. of Education, Evanston, Ill., since 1977. Asst. to the Pres., Indiana State Univ., Terre Haute, 1968–70; Pres., Greenville Coll., Illinois, since 1970–77. *Publs:* Role of the Trustee, 1969; (co-author) INPUT/OUTPUT: Some Thoughts for Today, 1970; (ed. and contrib.) New Dimensions in Student Personnel Administration, 1970; A Christian Executive in a Secular World, 1979; Who Controls Your Child?, 1980. Add: National College of Education, 2840 Sheridan Rd., Evanston, Ill. 60201, U.S.A.

HERRON, Shaun. Canadian, b. 1912. Novels/Short stories, Mystery/Crime/Suspense. Ed., British Weekly, 1950–58; Sr. Leader Writer, Winnipeg Free Press, 1964–76. *Publs:* Miro, 1968; The Hound and The Fox and The Harper, 1970; Through the Dark and Hairy Wood, 1972; The Whore-Mother, 1973; The Bird in Last Year's Nest, 1974; The MacDonnell (also as The Ruling Passion), 1978; Aladale, 1979; The Blacksmith's Daughter, 1985; One's Absurd, 1986. Add: c/o Curtis Brown Ltd., 10 Astor Pl., New York, N.Y. 10003, U.S.A.

HERRON, William. American, b. 1933. Novels/Short stories, Psychology. Practising psychotherapist and psychoanalyst, since 1962; Prof., St. John's Univ., Jamaica, N.Y., since 1965. Assoc. Prof. and Chmn., Dept. of Psychology, St. Bonaventure Univ., N.Y., 1959–65. *Publs:* (with R.E. Kantor) Reactive and Process Schizophrenia, 1966; (with M. Green, M. Guild, A. Smith and R.E. Kantor) Contemporary School Psychology, 1970, 1984; F. Quantmeyer Hose No. 7 (novel), 1972; (with M. Herron and J. Handron) School Psychology: A Challenge for Change, 1980; (with S. Rouslin) Issues in Psychotherapy, 1982. Add: 5 Pascack Rd., Woodcliff Lake, N.J. 07675, U.S.A.

HERSEY, John (Richard). American, b. 1914. Novels/Short stories, History, Social commentary/phenomena. Adjunct Prof. Emeritus, Yale Univ., New Haven, Conn. (Fellow, Berkeley Coll., 1950–65; Member,

Council on the Humanities, 1951–56; Member, 1959–64, and Chmn., 1964–69, Council Cttee. on Yale Coll.; Master, Pierson Coll., 1965–70; Lectr., Yale Univ., 1971–76; Adjunct Prof. from 1977). Member since 1953, Secty. 1961–76, and Chancellor, 1981–84, American Academy of Arts and Letters. Writer and Corresp. in China, Japan, the South Pacific, Mediterranean, and U.S.S.R., for Time, NYC, 1937–45, Life, NYC, 1944–46, and The New Yorker, 1945–46; Member of Council, 1946–71, Vice-Pres., 1949–55, and Pres., 1975–80, Authors League of America; Ed. and Dir., '47 writers' cooperative mag., 1947–48; Writer-in-Residence, American Academy in Rome, 1970–71. *Publs:* Men on Bataan, 1942; Into the Valley: Skirmish of the Marines, 1943; A Bell for Adano, 1944; Hiroshima, 1946; The Wall, 1950; The Marmot Drive, 1953; A Single Pebble, 1956; The War Lover, 1958; The Child Buyer: A Novel in the Form of Hearings Before the Standing Committee on Education Welfare and Public Morality of a Certain State Senate Investigating the Conspiracy of Mr. Wissey Jones, with Others, to Purchase a Male Child, 1960; Here to Stay: Studies in Human Tenacity, 1962; White Lotus, 1965; Too Far to Walk, 1966; Under the Eye of the Storm, 1967; The Algiers Motel Incident, 1968; (with others) Robert Capa, 1969; Letter to the Alumni, 1970; The Conspiracy, 1972; (ed.) Ralph Ellison: A Collection of Critical Essays, 1973; (ed.) The Writer's Craft, 1974; My Petition for More Space, 1974; The President, 1975; The Walnut Door, 1977; Aspects of the Presidency, 1980; The Call, 1985; Blues, 1987; Life Sketches, 1989. Add: 719 Windsor Lane, Key West, Fla. 33040, U.S.A.

HERWIG, Rob. Dutch, b. 1935. Homes/Gardens, Horticulture. *Publs:* 120 Houseplants You Can Grow, 1972; 120 Houseplants More You Can Grow, 1974; 120 Flowering Bulbs You Can Grow, 1975; 120 Garden Plants You Can Grow, 1975; (with Roger Grounds) Simple Gardening in Pictures; (with Nicolas Arden) Family Circle Book of Houseplants; House Plants in Colour; The Complete Book of Houseplants, 1975; Ideas for Your Garden in Colour, 1975; 201 Indoor Plants in Colour, 1976; Your Flower Garden, 1979; How to Grow Healthy House Plants, 1979; Pocket Guide to House Plants, 1981; Gardener's Guide to Flowers, Trees, and Shrubs, 1982; Encyclopedia of House Plants, 1984; (with W.M. Schubert) The Treasury of Houseplants, 1984; Hamlyn Dictionary of House and Garden Plants, 1985; The Edible Garden, 1986; Trees, Shrubs, and Conifers, 1986; Macmillan Book of Houseplants, 1986. Add: Hofstede Nieuw-Zeggelaar, Lunteren, Netherlands.

HERZBERG, Gerhard. Canadian, b. 1904. Chemistry, Physics. Distinguished Research Scientist, National Research Council of Canada, Ottawa, since 1969 (Principal Research Officer, 1948–49 and Dir., 1949–55, Div. of Physics; Dir., Div. of Pure Physics 1955–69). Lectr. in Physics, Darmstadt Inst. of Technology, Germany, 1930–35; Research Prof. of Physics, Univ. of Saskatchewan, Saskatoon, 1935–45; Prof. of Spectroscopy, Yerkes Observatory of the Univ. of Chicago, 1945–48. *Publs:* Atomic Spectra and Atomic Structure, 1937, 1944; Molecular Spectra and Molecular Structure I: Spectra of Diatomic Molecules, 1939, 1950; Molecular Spectra and Molecular Structure II: Infrared and Raman Spectra of Polyatomic Molecules, 1945; Molecular Spectra and Molecular Structure III: Electronic Spectra and Electronic Structure of Polyatomic Molecules, 1966; The Spectra and Structures of Simple Free Radicals: An Introduction to Molecular Spectroscopy, 1971; (with K. Huber) Molecular Spectra and Molecular Structure IV: Constants of Diatomic Molecules, 1979. Add: National Research Council of Canada, Ottawa, Ont. K1A 0R6, Canada.

HERZOG, Arthur. American, b. 1927. Novels, International relations/Current affairs, Politics/Government, Theology/Religion. *Publs:* Smoking and the Public Interest, 1963; The War-Peace Establishment, 1965; The Church Trap, 1968; McCarthy for President, 1969; The B.S. Factor (social satire), 1973; The Swarm (novel), 1974; Earthsound, 1975; Orca, 1976; Heat, 1977, 1989; I.Q. 83, 1978; Make Us Happy, 1978; Glad to Be Here, 1979; Aries Rising, 1980; The Craving, 1982; L*S*I*T*T*, (reissued as Takeover), 1984; Vesco, 1987; How To Write Almost Anything Better, 1987; The Woodchipper Murder, 1989. Add: 484 W. 43rd St., Apt. 44H, New York, N.Y. 10036, U.S.A.

HESKETH, Phoebe. British, b. 1909. Poetry, Autobiography, Biography. Woman's Page Editor, Bolton Evening News, 1942–45; Lectr., Bolton Women's Coll., 1967–69; Teacher of Creative Writing, Bolton Sch., 1976–78. *Publs:* Poems, 1939; Lean Forward, Spring!, 1948; No Time for Cowards, 1952; Out of the Dark; New Poems, 1954; Between Wheels and Stars, 1956; The Buttercup Children, 1958; Prayer for Sun, 1966; My Aunt Edith (biography of Edith Rigby), 1966; Rivington: The Story of a Village, 1972; A Song of Sunlight (for children), 1974; Preparing to Leave, 1977; The Eighth Day: Selected Poems, 1980; What Can the Matter Be (memoirs), 1985; Over the Brook (poems), 1986; Netting

the Sun: New and Collected Poems, 1989. Add: 10 The Green, Heath Charnock, Chorley, Lancs. PR6 9JH, England.

HESLEP, Robert Durham. American, b. 1930. Education, Philosophy. Prof., Philosophy and Education, Univ. of Georgia, Coll. of Education, Athens, since 1972 (Asst. Prof., 1965–67; Assoc. Prof., 1967–72). Instr. of Philosophy of Education, Pestalozzi-Froebel Teachers Coll., Chicago, 1959–61; Assoc. Prof. of Educational Foundns. and Philosophy, Edinboro State Coll., Pa., 1963–65. Pres., Philosophy of Education Soc., 1976–77. *Publs:* Thomas Jefferson and Education, 1969; (ed.) Philosophy of Education, 1971; (ed. with W. Blackstone) Social Justice and Preferential Treatment, 1977; The Mental in Education: A Philosophical Study, 1981; Professional Ethics and the Georgia Public School Administrator, 1988; Education in Democracy: The Moral Role of Education in the Democratic State, 1989. Add: Coll. of Education, Univ. of Georgia, Athens, Ga. 30602, U.S.A.

HESS, Gary R. American, b. 1937. International relations/Current affairs, Biography. Prof. of History since 1964, and Chmn., History Dept., since 1985 (1973–81), Bowling Green State Univ., Ohio (Acting Dean of College of Arts and Sciences, 1981–82). Exec. Secty.-Treas., Soc. for Historians of American Foreign Relations, 1979–82. *Publs:* Sam Higginbottom of Allahabad: Pioneer of Point IV to India, 1967; America Encounters India, 1941–47, 1971; (ed.) America and Russia: Cold War Confrontation to Coexistence, 1973; The United States at War 1941–45, 1985; The United States' Emergence as a Southeast Asian Power 1940–1950, 1987. Add: Dept. of History, Bowling Green State Univ., Bowling Green, Ohio 43403, U.S.A.

HESS, Robert L. American, b. 1932. History. Pres., Brooklyn Coll., NYC, since 1979. Instr., and subsequently Asst. Prof., Carnegie Inst. of Technology, 1958–61; Asst. Prof., Mount Holyoke Coll., South Hadley, Mass. 1961–64, and Northwestern Univ., Evanston, Ill. 1964–65; Assoc. Prof., 1966–71, Prof. of History, 1971–79, Assoc. Dean of Liberal Arts and Sciences, 1970–72, and Assoc. Vice-Chancellor for Academic Affairs, 1972–79, Univ. of Illinois at Chicago Circle. *Publs:* Italian Colonialism in Somalia, 1966; Ethiopia: The Modernization of Autocracy, 1960; (with Dalvan M. Coger) Semper Ex Africa: A Bibliography of Primary Sources for Nineteenth-Century Tropical Africa, 1972; (ed.) Encyclopaedia Africana: Dictionary of African Biography, vol. I: Ethiopia-Ghana, 1977; (ed.) Proceedings of the Fifth International Conference of Ethiopian Studies, 1979. Add: Office of the Pres., Brooklyn Coll., Brooklyn, N.Y. 11210, U.S.A.

HESSE, Mary Brenda. British, b. 1924. Sciences. Reader, 1968–75, and Prof. of Philosophy of Science, 1975–85, Univ. of Cambridge. *Publs:* Science and the Human Imagination, 1954; Forces and Fields, 1961; Models and Analogies in Science, 1963; The Structure of Scientific Inference, 1974; Revolutions and Reconstructions in the Philosophy of Science, 1980; (with M.A. Arbib) The Construction of Reality, 1987. Add: Dept. of History and Philosophy of Science, Univ. of Cambridge, Cambridge, England.

HESSERT, Paul. American, b. 1925. Theology/Religion. Minister, Francesville Methodist Church, 1951–54; Prof. of Religion and Philosophy, Adrian Coll., Mich., 1954–56; Dir. of Religious Activities and Prof. of Religion, 1956–58, and Chmn., Dept. of Religion, and Head, Div. of the Humanities, 1958–62, Illinois-Wesleyan Univ.; Prof. of Historical Theology, 1962–67, and of Systematic Theology, 1967–82, Garrett-Evangelical Theological Seminary, Evanston, Ill.; Ed., Explor, 1975–80. *Publs:* Introduction to Christianity, 1958; Christian Life, 1967. Add: R.R.2, Box 58, Kingsley, Pa. 18826, U.S.A.

HETZRON, Robert. American (b. Hungarian), b. 1937. Language/Linguistics. Prof. of Hebrew, Univ. of California at Santa Barbara, since 1974 (Asst. Prof., 1966–69; Assoc. Prof., 1969–74). Ed., Journal of Afroasiatic Languages, since 1987. Ed., Afroasiatic Linguistics, 1979–84. *Publs:* The Verbal System of Southern Agaw, 1969; Ethiopian Semitic: Studies in Classification, 1972; Surfacing: From Dependency Relations to Linearity, 1975; The Gunnän-Gurage Languages, 1977; Legszebb verseim, 1988. Add: 1346 San Rafael Ave., Santa Barbara, Calif. 93109, U.S.A.

HEWETT, Dorothy (Coade). Australian, b. 1923. Novels/Short stories, Plays/Screenplays, Poetry. Member, Editorial Cttee., Overland mag., Melbourne, since 1970; Ed. and Dir., Big Smoke Books, and Review Ed., New Poetry, Sydney, since 1979. Chmn., Australian Playwrights Conference, Sydney, since 1975. Millworker, 1950–52; Advertising Copywriter, Sydney, 1956–58; Sr. Tutor in English, Univ. of Western

Australia, Perth, 1964–73; Poetry Ed., Westerly mag., Perth, 1972–73; Writer in Residence, Monash Univ., Melbourne, 1975. *Publs:* Bobbin' Up (novel), 1959; (with Merv Lilly) What about the People (poetry), 1962; The Australians Have a Word for It (stories), 1964; This Old Man Comes Rolling Home, 1968; Windmill Country (poetry), 1968; The Hidden Journey (poetry), 1969; Late Night Bulletin (poetry), 1970; The Chapel Perilous; or, The Perilous Adventures of Sally Bonner, 1971; (ed.) Sandgropers: A Western Australian Anthology, 1973; Rapunzel in Suburbia (poetry), 1975; Miss Hewett's Shenanigans, 1975; Bon-Bons and Roses for Dolly, and The Tatty Hollow Story, 1976; Greenhouse (poetry), 1979; The Man from Mukinupin (play), 1979; Susannah's Dreaming, and The Golden Oldies (plays), 1981; Joan, 1984; Golden Valley, Song of the Seals, 1985. Add: 195 Bourke St., Darlinghurst, N.S.W. 2011, Australia.

HEWITT, (Lady) Alison Hope. British/Australian, b. 1915. Literature. Member of English Dept., Australian National Univ., A.C.T., 1948–80, now retired. Part-time journalist, Canberra Times, and other publications. Former Deputy Chmn., National Literature Bd. of Review. *Publs:* Coming to Terms with Poetry, 1965; Poems for Gardeners and Others, 1987; Canberra's First Schoolhouse, 1987. Add: 9 Torres St., Red Hill, Canberra, A.C.T. 2603, Australia.

HEWITT, Geof. American, b. 1943. Poetry. Founding Ed., The Kumquat Press, Montclair, N.J., later Enosburg, Vt., since 1966. Asst. Ed., Epoch Mag., Ithaca, N.Y., 1964–66; Ed.-in-Chief, The Trojan Horse mag., Ithaca, N.Y., 1965–66; Gilman Teaching Fellow, Johns Hopkins Univ., Baltimore, Md., 1966–67; Teaching Asst., Univ. of Iowa, Iowa City, 1967–69; Instr., Univ. of Hawaii, Honolulu, 1969–70. Contrib. Ed., Cornell Alumni News, Ithaca, N.Y., 1970–75, and New Letters, Kansas City, Mo., 1971–75. *Publs:* Poem and Other Poems, 1966; Waking Up Still Pickled, 1967; (ed.) Quickly Aging Here: Some Poets of the 1970s, 1969; (ed.) Selected Poems of Alfred Starr Hamilton, 1969; (ed.) Living in Whales: Stories and Poems from Vermont Public Schools, 1972; Stone Soup, 1974; I Think They'll Lay My Egg Tomorrow, 1976; Passing Thru, 1989. Add: Calais, Vt. 05648, U.S.A.

HEWLETT, Sylvia Ann. American (born British), b. 1946. Economics, International relations/Current affairs. Vice-Pres. for Economic Studies, and Exec. Dir. of the Economic Policy Council, U.N. Assn. of U.S.A., NYC, since 1981. Asst. Prof. of Economics, Barnard Coll., NYC, 1974–81. *Publs:* The Cruel Dilemma of Development: 20th Century Brazil, 1980; (ed. with Richard S. Weinert) Brazil and Mexico: Patterns in Late Development, 1982; The Global Repercussions of U.S. Monetary and Fiscal Policy, 1984; A Lesser Life: The Myth of Women's Liberation in America, 1986; (ed. with others) Family and Work: Bridging the Gap, 1986. Add: c/o Economics Policy Council, U.N. Assn. of U.S.A., 300 E. 42nd St., New York, N.Y. 10017, U.S.A.

HEWSON, John. Canadian, b. 1930. Language/Linguistics. Prof. of Linguistics, Memorial Univ. of Newfoundland, since 1968 (Asst. Prof. of French, 1960–64; Assoc. Prof. of French 1964–68). *Publs:* Oral French Pattern Practice, 1963; La Pratique du français, 1965; Article and Noun in English, 1972; Beothuk Vocabularies, 1978. Add: Dept. of Linguistics, Memorial Univ., St. John's, Nfld. A1B 3X9, Canada.

HEYDRON, Vicki Ann. (Mrs Randall Garrett). American, b. 1945. Science fiction/Fantasy. Systems analyst and freelance writer. *Publs:* Gandalara cycle (with Randall Garrett)—The Steel of Raithskar, 1981; The Glass of Dyskornis, 1982; The Bronze of Eddarta, 1983; The Well of Darkness, 1983; The Search for Ka, 1984; Return to Eddarta, 1985; The River Wall, 1986; (compiler and contrib.) Takeoff, Too, 1986. Add: c/o Bantam Books, 666 Fifth Ave., New York, N.Y. 10019, U.S.A.

HEYEN, William. American, b. 1940. Poetry. Member of the English Dept., currently Prof., State Univ. of New York at Brockport, since 1967; Visiting Prof., English Dept., Univ. of Hawaii, 1985. English Teacher, Springville High Sch., New York, 1961–62; Instr. in English, State Univ. of New York at Cortland, 1963–65. *Publs:* Depth of Field, 1970; (ed.) Profile of Theodore Roethke, 1971; Noise in the Trees: Poems and a Memoir, 1974; (ed.) American Poets in 1976, 1976; The Swastika Poems, 1977; Long Island Light: Poems and a Memoir, 1979; The City Parables, 1979; Lord Dragonfly: Five Sequences, 1981; Erika: Poems of the Holocaust, 1984; (ed.) The Generation of 2000: Contemporary American Poets, 1984; Vic Holyfield and the Class of 1957: A Romance, 1986; The Chestnut Rain, 1987; Brockport, New York: Beginning with"And", 1988. Add: 142 Frazier St., Brockport, N.Y. 14420, U.S.A.

HEYER, Paul. British, b. 1936. Architecture. Architect in private

practice NYC, since 1961; Head of Paul Heyer Architects, NYC, since 1965. Prof. of Architecture, and Dean, Sch. of Architecture, Pratt Inst., Brooklyn, New York, since 1968. *Publs:* Architects on Architecture: New Directions in America, 1966, 1977; Mexican Architecture: The Work of Abraham Zabludovsky and Teodoro Gonzalez de Leon, 1978. Add: Paul Heyer Assocs., 317 W. 84th St., New York, N.Y. 10024, U.S.A.

HEYERDAHL, Thor. Norwegian, b. 1914. Anthropology/Ethnology, Archaeology, Travel/Exploration/Adventure. Vice-Pres., World Assn. of Federalists; Member, Norwegian Academy of Sciences, and Bd. of Kon-Tiki Museum, Oslo. Expeditions include: Polynesia, 1937–38; Northwest America, 1940–41; Kon-Tiki Expedition, 1947; Galapagos Islands, 1952; Easter Island, 1955–56; Ra Expedition, 1969–70; Tigris Expedition, 1977–78, Maldive Islands, 1982–84, Easter Island, 1986–87. *Publs:* Paa Jakt efter Paradiset, 1938; The Kon-Tiki Expedition, 1952; Aku-aku: The Secret of Easter Island, 1957; Sea Routes to Polynesia, 1967; The Ra Expeditions, 1970; Fatu-Hiva: Back to Nature, 1975; The Art of Easter Island, 1975; Early Man and the Ocean, 1978; The Tigris Expedition, 1980; The Maldive Mystery, 1986. Add: Kon-Tiki Museum, Bygdoynesveien 36, 0275-Oslo 2, Norway.

HEYMAN, Abigail. American, b. 1942. Women, Autobiography/Memoirs/Personal. Freelance photo-journalist. Freelance photographer for UNILDF, since 1973; Teacher of Photography, New Sch. for Social Research, NYC, since 1974. Dir., The Public Gallery, NYC, 1972–74. *Publs:* Growing Up Female: A Personal Photo-Journal, 1974; Butcher, Baker, Cabinet-Maker: Photographs of Women at Work, 1978; Dreams and Schemes: Love and Marriage in Modern Times, 1987. Add: c/o Aperture, 20 E. 23rd St., New York, N.Y. 10010, U.S.A.

HEYMAN, Jacques. British, b. 1925. Architecture, Engineering. Fellow, Peterhouse, Cambridge, 1949–51 and since 1955; Prof. of Engineering, since 1971, and Head of Dept., since 1983, Cambridge Univ. (Sr. Bursar, Peterhouse, 1962–64; Demonstrator, 1951, Lectr., 1954, and Reader, 1968, Cambridge Univ.). Consultant Engineer, Ely Cathedral, since 1972, St. Albans Cathedral, since 1978, and Lichfield and Worcester Cathedrals, since 1986; Member, Architectural Advisory Panel, Westminster Abbey, since 1973, and Cathedrals Advisory Commn. for England, since 1981. Member of the Council, Instn. of Civil Engineers, 1960–63, 1975–78. *Publs:* (with Lord Baker and M.R. Horne) The Steel Skeleton, vol. 2, 1956; Plastic Design of Portal Frames, 1957; Beams and Framed Structures, 1964, 1974; Plastic Design of Frames, 2 vols., 1969–71; Coulomb's Memoir on Statics, 1972; Equilibrium of Shell Structures, 1977; Elements of Stress Analysis, 1982; The Masonry Arch, 1982. Add: Engineering Lab., Trumpington St., Cambridge, England.

HEYWOOD THOMAS, John. British, b. 1926. Philosophy, Theology/Religion. Prof. of Theology, Univ. of Nottingham, since 1974 (Pro-Vice-Chancellor, 1979–84; Dean of Arts, 1985–88). Lectr. in Philosophy of Religion, Univ. of Manchester, 1957–65; Reader in Divinity, Univ. of Durham, 1965–74. *Publs:* Subjectivity and Paradox, 1957; Paul Tillich: An Appraisal, 1963; Paul Tillich, 1965. Add: 5 Manor Ct., Bramcote, Nottingham, England.

HIBBERD, Jack. Australian, b. 1940. Plays/Screenplays. Practising physician. *Publs:* White with Wire Wheels, 1967; Dimboola: A Wedding Reception Play, 1969; A Stretch of the Imagination, 1971; Three Popular Plays, 1976; The Overcoat, Sin, 1981; (with Garrie Hutchinson) The Barracker's Bible: A Dictionary of Sporting Slang, 1983; Squibs, 1984; A Country Quinella, 1984; Captain Midnight V.C., 1984. Add: c/o Almost Managing, P.O. Box 34, Carlton, Vic 3053, Australia.

HIBBERT, Christopher. British, b. 1924. History, Biography. Freelance writer. *Publs:* The Road to Tyburn, 1957; King Mob, 1958; Wolfe at Quebec, 1959; The Destruction of Lord Raglan, 1961; Corunna, 1961; Benito Mussolini, 1962; The Battle of Arnhem, 1962; The Roots of Evil, 1963; The Court at Windsor, 1964; Agincourt, 1964; Garibaldi and His Enemies, 1965; The Making of Charles Dickens, 1967; Charles I, 1968; The Grand Tour, 1969; London: Biography of a City, 1969; The Dragon Wakes, 1970; The Personal History of Samuel Johnson, 1971; George IV: Prince of Wales, 1972; George IV: Regent and King, 1973; The Rise and Fall of the House of Medici, 1974; The Illustrated London News: Social History of Victorian Britain, 1975; (ed.) A Soldier of the Seventy First, 1975; Daily Life in Victorian England, 1975; Edward VII, 1976; The Great Mutiny: India 1857, 1978; Disraeli and His World, 1979; The Court of St. James's, 1979; The French Revolution, 1980; Africa Explored, 1982; (ed. with Ben Weinreb) The London Encyclopaedia, 1983; Queen Victoria in Her Letters and Journals, 1984; Rome: Biography of a City, 1985; Cities and Civilization, 1986; The English: A Social History, 1066-1945, 1987; (ed.) The Encyclopaedia of Oxford, 1988; Venice: The Biography of a City, 1988. Add: 6 Albion Place, West St., Henley-on-Thames RG9 2DT, England.

HIBBERT, Eleanor Alice Burford. *See* **HOLT,** Victoria.

HIBBETT, Howard (Scott). American, b. 1920. Literature, Translations. Prof. of Japanese Literature since 1963, and Chmn. of the Council on East Asian Studies since 1980, Harvard Univ., Cambridge (Assoc. Prof., 1958–63; Chmn., Dept. of Far Eastern Languages, 1965–70; Member, Bd. of Syndics, Harvard Univ. Press, 1974–78); retired, 1986. Instr. in Oriental Languages, 1952–54, and Asst. Prof., 1954–58, Univ. of California at Los Angeles. *Publs:* The Floating World in Japanese Fiction, 1959; (trans.) The Key by Tanizaki Jun'ichiro (novel), 1961; (trans.) Diary of a Mad Old Man by Tanizaki (novel), 1965; (with Gen. Itasaka) Modern Japanese: A Basic Reader, 1965; (trans.) The Harp of Burma by Takeyama Michio (novel), 1966; (trans.) Beauty and Sadness by Kawabata Yasunari (novel), 1974; (trans. and ed.) Contemporary Japanese Literature: An Anthology of Fiction, Film, and Other Writings since 1945, 1977. Add: Coolidge Hall, Harvard Univ., 1737 Cambridge St., Cambridge, Mass. 02138, U.S.A.

HIBBS, John. Writes poetry as John Blyth. British, b. 1925. Poetry, Transport. Prof. since 1987, and Dir. of Transport Studies, City of Birmingham Polytechnic, since 1982 (Principal Lectr., 1973–82). Personal Asst. to Managing Dir., Premier Travel Ltd., 1950–52; Joint Managing Dir., Corona Coaches Ltd., 1956–60; Traffic Survey Officer and Market Research Officer, British Railways Eastern Region, 1961–67; Sr. Lectr. and Principal Lectr. in Transport, City of London Polytechnic, 1967–73. *Publs:* Transport for Passengers, 1963, 1971; (as John Blyth) New Found Land, 1965; (as John Blyth) Being a Patient, 1967; The History of British Bus Services, 1968, 1989; Transport Studies: An Introduction, 1970, 1988; (ed.) The Omnibus, 1971; How to Run the Buses, 1972; People and Transport, 1973; The Bus and Coach Industry: Its Economics and Organization, 1975; Transport Without Politics . . . ?, 1982; Bus and Coach Management, 1985; Regulation: An International Study of Bus and Coach Licensing, 1985; The Country Bus, 1986; The Country Chapel, 1987; The Bus and Coach Operator's Handbook, 1987; Marketing Management in the Bus and Coach Industry, 1989. Add: 134 Wood End Rd., Erdington, Birmingham B24 8BN, England.

HIBDON, James E. American, b. 1924. Economics. Prof. of Economics since 1961, Prof. of Health Admin., Health Sciences Center, since 1968, and Dir., The Leadership Prog., Coll. of Business Admin., Univ. of Oklahoma, Norman. Asst. Prof., 1954–57, and Assoc. Prof. of Economics, 1957–59, Georgia State Univ., Atlanta; Assoc. Prof. of Economics, Texas A & M Univ., College Station, 1959–61; Ed., Review of Regional Economics and Business, 1975–87. Pres., Southwestern Economics Assoc., 1977–78. *Publs:* Price and Welfare Theory, 1969. Add: Div. of Economics, Univ. of Oklahoma, Norman, Okla. 73019, U.S.A.

HICK, John (Harwood). British, b. 1922. Theology/Religion. Danforth Prof. of Religion, Claremont Grad. Sch., California, since 1980. Asst. Prof. of Philosophy, Cornell Univ., Ithaca, N.Y., 1956–59; Stuart Prof. of Christian Philosophy, Princeton Theological Seminary, N.J., 1959–64; Lectr. in Divinity, Cambridge Univ., 1964–67; H.G. Wood Prof. of Theology, Univ. of Birmingham, 1967–82. *Publs:* Faith and Knowledge, 1957, 1966; Philosophy of Religion, 1963, 3rd ed. 1983; (ed.) The Existence of God, 1964; (ed.) Faith and the Philosophers, 1964; (ed.) Classical and Contemporary Readings in the Philosophy of Religion, 1964, 1970; Evil and the God of Love, 1966, 1977; Christianity at the Centre, 1968, 1977; Arguments for the Existence of God, 1971; God and the Universe of Faiths, 1973; (ed.) Truth and Dialogue, 1974; Death and Eternal Life, 1976; (ed.) The Myth of God Incarnate, 1977; (ed. with Brian Hebblethwaite) Christianity and Other Religions, 1980; God Has Many Names, 1980; (with Michael Goulder) Why Believe in God?, 1983; The Second Christianity, 1983; Problems of Religious Pluralism, 1985; (ed. with Hasan Askari) The Experience of Religious Diversity, 1985; An Interpretation of Religion, 1988. Add: Dept. of Religion, Claremont Graduate Sch., Claremont, Calif. 91711, U.S.A.

HICKEN, Victor. American, b. 1921. History, Military/Defence. Distinguished Prof. of History, Western Illinois Univ., Macomb, since 1976 (Instr., 1947–50, Prof., 1950–76, Chmn. of Dept., 1967–69). Chief Researcher, Carnegie Foundn. Grant, American Assn. for the Advancement of Science. *Publs:* Illinois in the Civil War, 1966; The Settlement of Western Illinois, 1966; Western Illinois Factbook, 1968; Illinois at War, 1968; The American Fighting Man, 1969; The Purple and the Gold, 1971;

The World Is Coming to an End, 1975; Gallery of American Heroes, 3 vols., 1976; Between the Rivers, Vols. I-III, 1981–83; Illinois: Its History and Legacy, 1983. Add: 615 Lincoln Dr., Macomb, Ill. 61455, U.S.A.

HICKIN, Norman (Ernest). British, b. 1910. Biology, Natural history, Autobiography/Memoirs/Personal. Scientific Consultant, Rentokil Labs., East Grinstead, Surrey, since 1972 (Scientific Dir., 1950–72). Scientific Fellow, Zoological Soc. of London; Fellow, Royal Entomological Soc. of London (Treas. 1952–60), Inst. of Wood Science. *Publs:* Caddis: Field Study Books, 1952; Woodworm: Its Biology and Extermination, 1954; The Insect Factor in Wood Decay, 1963, 1968; The Woodworm Problem, 1963, 1972; The Dry Rot Problem, 1963, 1972; Household Insect Pests, 1963, 1974; Forest Refreshed, 1965; The Conservation of Building Timbers, 1967; Caddis Larvae, 1967; African Notebook, 1969; Termites: A World Problem, 1971; Bird Nest-Boxing, 1971; Wood Preservation: A Guide to the Meaning of Terms, 1971; Natural History of an English Forest, 1971; Beachcombing for Beginners, 1975; Irish Nature, 1980; Pest-Animals in Buildings: World Review, 1985; Bookworms: Insect Pests of Books, 1985; (ed.) Macroeconomic Impacts of Energy Shocks, 1987; (ed.) Macroeconomic Impacts of Energy Shocks: Contributions from Participating Modelers, 1987. Add: Kateshill, Bewdley, Worcs., England.

HICKINBOTHAM, James. British, b. 1914. Theology/Religion. Prof. of Theology, Univ. Coll. of the Gold Coast (now Ghana), 1950–54; Principal, St. John's Coll., Univ. of Durham, 1954–70; Principal, Wycliffe Hall, Oxford, 1970–79. *Publs:* Conditions of Fellowship, 1948; The Open Table, 1965. Add: 23 St. George's View, Cullompton, Devon EX15 1BA, England.

HICKMAN, Bert G(eorge), Jr. American, b. 1924. Economics. Prof. of Economics, Stanford Univ., California. Sr. Staff, Council of Economic Advisors, Washington, D.C., 1954–56; Sr. Staff, Brookings Inst., Washington, D.C., 1956–66. *Publs:* Growth and Stability of Post War Economy, 1960; Investment Demand and U.S. Economic Growth, 1965; (ed.) Quantitative Planning of Economic Policy, 1965; (ed.) Econometric Models of Cyclical Behavior, 1972; (with Robert M. Coen) Annual Growth Model of the United States Economy, 1976; (ed.) Global Intnl. Economic Models, 1983; (ed.) Global Econometrics, 1983; (ed.) International Monetary Stabilization and the Foreign Debt Problem, 1984; (ed.) Macroeconomic Impacts of Energy Shocks, 1987; (ed.) Macroeconomic Impacts of Energy Shocks: Contributions from Participating Modelers, 1987. Add: Dept. of Economics, Stanford Univ., Stanford, Calif., U.S.A.

HICKS, Eleanor. *See* **COERR,** Eleanor Beatrice.

HICKS, (Sir) John (Richard). British, b. 1904. Economics. Fellow, All Souls Coll., Oxford, since 1952 (Official Fellow, Nuffield Coll., 1946–52, and Drummond Prof. of Political Economy, 1952–65 Oxford Univ.). Lectr., London Sch. of Economics, 1926–35; Fellow, Gonville and Caius Coll., Cambridge, 1935–38; Prof. of Political Economy, Univ. of Manchester, 1938–46. *Publs:* The Theory of Wages, 1932, 1963; Value and Capital, 1939; (with U.K. Hicks and L. Rostas) Taxation of War Wealth, 1941; The Social Framework, 1942; (with U.K. Hicks) Standards of Local Expenditure, 1943; (with U.K. Hicks and C.E.V. Leser) The Problem of Valuation for Rating, 1944; (with U.K. Hicks) The Incidence of Local Rates in Great Britain, 1945; The Problem of Valuation for Rating, 1944; (with U.K. Hicks) The Incidence of Local Rates in Great Britain, 1945; The Problem of Budgeting Reform, 1948; A Contribution to the Theory of the Trade Cycle, 1950; (with U.K. Hicks) Report on Finance and Taxation in Jamaica, 1955; A Revision of Demand Theory, 1956; Essays in World Economics, 1960; Capital and Growth, 1965; Critical Essays in Monetary Theory, 1967; A Theory of Economic History, 1969; Capital and Time, 1973; The Crisis in Keynesian Economics, 1974; Causality in Economics, 1979; Collected Essays on Economic Thought, 2 vols., 1982–83; The Economics of John Hicks, 1984; Methods of Dynamic Economics, 1985. Add: All Souls Coll., Oxford, England.

HIDDEN, (Frederick) Norman. British, b. 1913. Poetry, Literature, Autobiography/Memoirs/Personal. Founding Ed., Workshop New Poetry, London, 1967–81. Vice-Pres., The Poetry Soc., London, since 1974. Member, Exec. Cttee., The English Assn., 1967–81. *Publs:* These Images Claw, 1966; (ed.) A National Anthology of Student Poetry, 1968; (ed.) Say It Aloud, 1972; Dr. Kink and His Old Style Boarding School: Fragments of Autobiography, 1973; A Study Guide to "Under Milk Wood", 1973; (ed.) Over to You (verse anthology), 1975; A Study Guide to Twelfth Night, 1978; (ed., with A. Hollins) Many People, Many Voices, 1978; How To Be Your Own Publisher, 1979; How to Get Your

Poems Accepted, 1981; For My Friends, 1981. Add: 2 Culham Ct., Granville Rd., London N4 4JB, England.

HIEATT, Constance B(artlett). American and Canadian, b. 1928. Children's non-fiction, Literature, Translations. Prof. of English, Univ. of Western Ontario, London, since 1968. Member of faculty, City Coll., 1959-60, and Queensborough Community Coll., 1960-65, City Univ. of New York; Prof. of English, St. John's Univ., Jamaica, N.Y., 1965-68. *Publs:* (co-ed., trans. and adapter) The Canterbury Tales of Geoffrey Chaucer, 1961; (co-ed. and trans.) The Canterbury Tales of Geoffrey Chaucer, 1964, 1971; (adapter) Sir Gawain and the Green Knight, 1967; The Realism of Dream Vision: The Poetic Exploitation of the Dream Experience in Chaucer and His Contemporaries, 1967; (trans.) Beowulf and Other Old English Poems, 1967, 1983; Essentials of Old English: Readings with Keyed Grammar, 1970; (ed.) The Miller's Tale of Geoffrey Chaucer, 1970; (co-ed.) Edmund Spenser: Selected Poetry, 1970; (adapter) The Joy of the Court, 1971; (adapter) The Sword and the Grail, 1972; (adapter) The Castle of Ladies, 1973; (adapter) The Minstrel Knight, 1974; (trans.) Karlamagnus Saga: The Saga of Charlemagne and His Heroes, I, parts 1-3, II, part 4, 1975, and III, part 5-10, 1980; (co-author) Pleyn Delit: Medieval Cookery for Modern Cooks, 1976; (co-ed.) Curye on Inglysch, 1985; An Ordinance of Pottage, 1988. Add: 304 River Rd., Deep River, CT 064717, U.S.A.

HIEBERT, D(avid) Edmond. American, b. 1910. Theology/Religion. Prof. of Greek and New Testament, Mennonite Brethren Biblical Seminary, Fresno, Calif., 1955-75, now Emeritus. Prof. of New Testament, Tabor Coll., Hillsboro, Kans., 1942-55; Ed., The Adult Quarterly, M.B. Publishing House, Hillsboro, Kans., 1958-70. *Publs:* Working by Prayer, 1953; Introduction to the Pauline Epistles, 1954; Titus and Philemon, 1957; First Timothy, 1957; Second Timothy, 1958; Introduction to the Non-Pauline Epistles, 1962; The Thessalonian Epistles, 1971; (compiler) Wayside Wells, 1972; Personalities Around Paul, 1973; Mark: A Portrait of the Servant, 1974; Introduction to the Gospels and Acts, 1975; James: Tests of a Living Faith, 1979; First Peter, 1984; Working with God: Scriptural Studies in Intercession, 1987; Second Peter and Jude, 1989; The Johannine Epistles, 1990. Add: 4864 E. Townsend, Fresno, Calif. 93727, U.S.A.

HIGDON, Hal. American, b. 1931. Children's fiction, Children's non-fiction, Sports/Physical education/Keeping fit. Sr. Ed., Runner's World. Asst. Ed., The Kiwanis mag., 1957-59. *Publs:* The Union vs. Dr. Mudd, 1964; Heroes of the Olympics, 1965; Pro Football U.S.A., 1967; The Horse That Played Center Field, 1967; The Business Healers, 1968; Stars of the Tennis Courts, 1969; 30 Days in May, 1969; The Electronic Olympics, 1969; On the Run from Dogs and People, 1969; Finding the Groove, 1973; Find the Key Man, 1974; The Last Series, 1974; Six Seconds to Glory, 1974; The Crime of the Century, 1976; Summer of Triumph, 1977; Fitness after Forty, 1977; Complete Diet Guide: For Runners and Other Athletes, 1978; Beginner's Running Guide, 1978; Runner's Cookbook, 1979; Johnny Rutherford, 1980; The Marathoners, 1980; The Team That Played in the Space Bowl, 1981. Add: 2815 Lake Shore Dr., Michigan City, Ind. 46360, U.S.A.

HIGGINBOTHAM, Jay. American, b. 1937. Novels/Short stories, History, Travel/Exploration/Adventure, Autobiography/Memoirs/Personal. Dir., Mobile Municipal Archives, since 1983 and Research Consultant, since 1980, Mobile Public Library, Ala. (Head, Dept. of Local History, 1973-78; Acting Head, Special Collections Dept., 1979-80). Asst. Clerk, Mississippi House of Reps., 1955-60; Teacher, Mobile County Public Schs., 1962-72. *Publs:* The Mobile Indians, 1966; Family Biographies, 1967; The Pascagoula Indians, 1967; Pascagoula: Singing River City, 1968; Mobile: City by the Bay, 1968; (trans.) The Journal of Sauvole, 1969; The Birth of Louisiana, 1969; Brother Holyfield (novel), 1972; (with F. Escoffier) A Voyage to Dauphin Island, 1974; Old Mobile: Fort Louis de la Louisiane 1702-1711, 1977; Fast Train Russia (reminiscences), 1981; Autumn in Petrischevo (travel), 1985; The Vital Alliance (speeches and essays), 1988. Add: 60 N. Monterey, Mobile, Ala. 36604, U.S.A.

HIGGINS, Aidan. Irish, b. 1927. Novels/Short stories, Autobiography/Memoirs/Personal. Puppet-operator, John Wright's Marionettes in Europe, South Africa and Rhodesia, 1958-60; Scriptwriter, Filmlets, advertising films, Johannesburg, 1960-61. *Publs:* Felo de Se (in U.S. as Killachter Meadow), 1960; Langrishe, Go Down, 1966; Images of Africa, 1971; Balcony of Europe, 1972; (ed.) A Century of Short Stories, 1977; Scenes from a Receding Past, 1977; (ed.) Colossal Gongorr and the Turkes of Mars, 1979; Bornholm Night Ferry, 1983; Helsingor Station, 1987; The Ronda Gorge, 1987. Add: c/o Allison and Busby Ltd., 44 Hill St.,

London W1X 8LB, England.

HIGGINS, Dick. (Richard Carter Higgins). American, b. 1938. Plays/Screenplays, Poetry, Literature, Translations. Founder, Something Else Press, 1964, and Unpublished Eds., 1972; Teacher, California Inst. of the Arts, 1970-71. *Publs:* What Are Legends, 1960; Jefferson's Birthday/Postface, 1964; A Book About Love and War and Death: Canto One, 1965, Cantos Two and Three, 1969, complete ed., 1972; Towards the 1970s, 1969; FOEW & OMB-WHNW, 1969; (ed. with W. Vostell) Pop Architektur, 1969; Die Fabelhafte Geträume von Taifun-Willi, 1969; Computers for the Arts, 1970; (ed. with W. Vostell) Fantastic Architecture, 1971; Amigo, 1972; The Ladder to the Moon, 1973; For Eugene in Germany, 1973; Gesehen, Gehört and Verstanden, 1973; Le Petit Cirque au Fin du Monde: Un Opéra Arabasque, 1973; Spring Game, 1973; City with All the Angles, 1974; Modular Poems, 1975; Classic Plays, 1976; Legends and Fishnets, 1976; Cat Alley, 1976; The Epitaphs/Gli Epitaphi, 1977; Everyone Has Sher Favorite (His or Hers), 1977; George Herbert's Pattern Poems: In Their Tradition, 1977; The Epickall Quest of the Brothers Dichtung and Other Outrages, 1978; A Dialectic of Centuries: Notes Toward a Theory of the New Arts, 1978; (trans.) Hymns to the Night, by Novalis, 1978; Some Recent Snowflakes (And Other Things), 1979; Piano Album: Short Pieces 1962-1984, 1980; Of Celebration of Morning, 1980; Ten Ways of Looking at a Bird, 1981; 26 Mountains for Viewing the Sunset From, 1981; Sonata for Prepared Piano, 1981; Variation on a Natural Theme, for Orchestra, 1981; Selected Early Works, 1982; 1959/60, 1982; Song for Any Voice(s) and Instrument(s), 1983; Sonata No. 2 for Piano, 1983; Horizons: The Poetics and Theory of the Intermedia, 1983; Intermedia, 1985; Poems, Plain & Fancy, 1986; Pattern Poems: Guide to an Unknown Literature, 1987. Add: P.O. Box 27, Barrytown, N.Y. 12507, U.S.A.

HIGGINS, George V(incent). American, b. 1939. Novels/Short stories, Mystery/Crime/Suspense. Lawyer. Partner, Griffin and Higgins, Boston, since 1978. Reporter, Providence Journal and Evening Bulletin, R.I., 1962-63; Bureau Corresp., Springfield, Mass., 1963-64, and Newsman, Boston, Mass., 1964, Associated Press; Researcher, Guterman, Horvitz & Rubin, Boston, Mass., 1966-67; Legal Asst., Dept. of Attorney Gen., Boston, Mass., 1967; Deputy Asst. Attorney Gen. and Asst. Attorney Gen., Commonwealth of Mass., 1967-70; Instr., Dept. of Law Enforcement Progs., Northeastern Univ., Boston, Mass., 1969-71; Consultant, National Inst. of Law Enforcement and Criminal Justice, Washington, D.C., 1970-71; Asst. U.S. Attorney, District of Mass., 1970-73; Pres., George V. Higgins Inc., Boston, 1973-78. *Publs:* The Friends of Eddie Coyle, 1972; The Digger's Game, 1973; Cogan's Trade, 1974; A City on a Hill, 1975; The Friends of Richard Nixon, 1975; The Judgement of Deke Hunter, 1976; Dreamland, 1977; A Year or So with Edgar, 1979; Kennedy for the Defense, 1980; The Rat on Fire, 1981; The Patriot Game, 1982; A Choice of Enemies, 1984; Penance for Jerry Kennedy, 1985; Imposters, 1986; Outlaws, 1987; The Sins of Their Fathers, 1988; Wonderful Years, Wonderful Years, 1988; Progress of the Seasons: Forty Years of Baseball in Our Town, 1989. Add: 15 Brush Hill Lane, Milton, Mass. 02186, U.S.A.

HIGGINS, Jack. *See* **PATTERSON,** Henry.

HIGGINS, Reynold Alleyne. British, b. 1916. Archaeology/Antiquities, Art. Asst. Keeper, 1947-65, and Deputy Keeper of Greek and Roman Antiquities, 1965-77, British Museum, London. *Publs:* Catalogue of Terracottas in the British Museum, 2 vols., 1954, 1959; Greek and Roman Jewellery, 1961, 1980; Greek Terracotta Figures, 1963; Jewellery from Classical Lands, 1965; Greek Terracottas, 1967; Minoan and Mycenaean Art, 1967, 1981; The Greek Bronze Age, 1970; The Archaeology of Minoan Crete, 1973; The Aegina Treasure: An Archaeological Mystery, 1979; Tanagra and the Figurines, 1986. Add: Hillside Cottage, Dunsfold, nr. Godalming, Surrey GU8 4PB, England.

HIGGINS, Rosalyn. British, b. 1937. International relations/Current affairs, Law. Prof. of Intnl. Law, London Sch. of Economics, since 1981 (Visiting Fellow, 1974-78). Research Specialist in Intnl. Law and U.N. Affairs, Royal Inst. of Intnl. Affairs, 1963-74; Prof., Univ. of Kent, Canterbury, 1978-81. *Publs:* The Development of International Law through the Political Organs of the United Nations, 1963; Conflict of Interests: International law in a Divided World, 1965; The Administration of United Kingdom Foreign Policy through the United Nations, 1966; United Nations Peacekeeping: Documents and Commentary, vol. I, The Middle East, 1969, vol. II, Asia, 1971, vol. III, Africa, 1980, vol. IV, Europe, 1981; (ed. with J. Fawcett) Law in Movement: Essays in Honour of John McMahon, 1974; (ed. with M. Flory) Liberté de Circulation des Personnes en Droit International, 1989. Add: London Sch. of

Economics, Houghton St., London EC4, England.

HIGGINS, Thomas Joseph. American, b. 1899. Theology/Religion. Prof. of Ethics, Loyola Coll., Baltimore, Md., since 1939; Judge, Archdiocese of Baltimore, since 1970. Pres., St. Joseph's Coll., Philadelphia, Pa., and Pastor, Church of Gesu, Philadelphia, 1933–39. *Publs:* Man As Man, 1949, 1958; Perfection Is For You, 1953; Helps and Hindrances To Perfection, 1955; Dogma for the Layman, 1961; Ethical Theories in Conflict, 1967; Basic Ethics, 1968; Judicial Review Unmasked, 1981; Preaching the Sunday and Holy Day Scriptures, 1986. Add: 4501 N. Charles St., Baltimore, Md., 21210, U.S.A.

HIGH, Philip E(mpson). British, b. 1914. Science fiction/Fantasy. Freelance writer, mainly of SF short stories. Has worked as a salesman, reporter, insurance agent, and bus driver; now retired. *Publs:* The Prodigal Sun, 1964; No Truce with Terra, 1964; The Mad Metropolis, 1966, in U.K. as Double Illusion, 1970; These Savage Futurians, 1967; Twin Planets, 1967; Reality Forbidden, 1967; Invader on My Back, 1968; The Time Mercenaries, 1968; Butterfly Planet, 1971; Sold—For a Spaceship, 1973; Come Hunt an Earthman, 1973; Speaking of Dinosaurs, 1974; Fugitive from Time, 1978; Blindfold from the Stars, 1979. Add: 34 King St., Canterbury, Kent CT1 2AJ, England.

HIGHAM, Charles. British, b. 1931. Poetry, Film, Biography. Regular Contributor, New York Times, NYC, since 1980 (Hollywood Correspondent, 1971–80). Film Critic, Nation, Sydney, 1961–63; Literary Ed., The Bulletin, Sydney, 1963–68; former Book and Film Critic, Morning Herald, Sydney, and Australian Corresp., Sight and Sound, London, and Hudson Review, NYC. *Publs:* A Distant Star, 1951; Spring and Death, 1953; The Earthbound and Other Poems, 1959; (ed. with A. Brissenden) They Came to Australia: An Anthology, 1961; Noonday Country: Poems 1954–1965, 1966; (ed. with M. Wilding) Australians Abroad: An Anthology, 1967; (ed.) Australian Writing Today, 1968; (ed. with J. Greenberg) The Celluloid Muse: Hollywood Directors Speak, 1969; (with J. Greenberg) Hollywood in the Forties, 1969; The Films of Orson Welles, 1970; Hollywood Cameramen: Sources of Light, 1970; The Voyage to Brindisi and Other Poems 1966–1969, 1970; Ziegfield, 1972; Hollywood at Sunset, 1972; Cecil B. DeMille, 1973; The Art of the American Film 1900–1971, 1973; Ava, 1974; Kate: The Life of Katharine Hepburn, 1975; Warner Brothers, 1975; Charles Laughton: An Intimate Biography, 1976; The Adventures of Conan Doyle: The Life of the Creator of Sherlock Holmes, 1976; Marlene: The Life of Marlene Dietrich, 1977; Celebrity Circus (interviews), 1979; Errol Flynn: The Untold Story, 1980; Star Maker: The Autobiography of Hal B. Wallis, 1980; Bette: The Life of Bette Davis, 1981; Trading with the Enemy: An Exposé of the Nazi-American Money Plot 1933–1949, 1983; (with Roy Moseley) Princess Merle (in U.K. as Merle: A Biography of Merle Oberon), 1983; Sisters: The Story of Olivia de Havilland and Joan Fontaine (in U.K. as Olivia and Joan), 1984; Audrey: The Life of Audrey Hepburn, 1984; American Swastika, 1985; Orson Welles, 1986; (with Baron C. de Massy) Palace: My Life in the Royal Family of Monaco, 1986; Brando: The Unauthorized Biography, 1987; Wallis: The Secret Lives of the Duchess of Windsor, 1988; (with Roy Moseley) Cary Grant: The Lonely Heart, 1989. Add: c/o Barbara Lowenstein, 250 W. 57th St., New York, N.Y. 10019, U.S.A.

HIGHAM, Robert R.A. British, b. 1935. Business/Trade/Industry. Managing Dir., UXCO Ltd., since 1971. Formerly Ed., European Board Markets, and Editorial Dir., Bettendorf Publs. Inc.; Joint Managing Dir., Mags for Industry Inc., 1964–70; Marketing Mgr., Business Intelligence Services, 1970–71. *Publs:* A Handbook of Papermaking, 1963, 1968; A Handbook of Paper and Board, 2 vols., 1970, 1971; The Pulp, Paper and Board Industry: Its Profits, Future and Investment Risk, 1977, 1984. Add: Deepdene Wood, Dorking, Surrey RH5 4BH, England.

HIGHAM, Robin. American, b. 1925. History, Military/Defence. Prof. of History, Kansas State Univ., Manhattan, since 1963. Ed. Emeritus, Military Affairs, (Ed., 1968–88), and Aerospace Historian, (Ed., 1970–88); Ed., Journal of the West, since 1977; Founder and Pres., Sunflower Univ. Press, since 1977. *Publs:* Britain's Imperial Air Routes, 1960; The British Rigid Airship, 1908–1931, 1961; Armed Forces in Peacetime, 1963; The Military Intellectuals, 1966; (with D. Zook) A Short History of Warfare, 1966; (ed.) Bayonets in the Streets, 1969; (ed.) Official Histories, 1970; (ed.) Civil Wars in the Twentieth Century, 1972; (ed.) Guide to the Sources of British Military History, 1972; Air Power, 1972, 1984, 1988; (ed.) Intervention or Abstention, 1974; (ed.) Guide to the Sources of U.S. Military History, 1975; The Compleat Academic, 1975; (ed. with Abigail T. Siddall) Flying Combat Aircraft I, 1978; (ed. with Jacob W. Kipp) Soviet Aviation and Air Power, 1978; (ed. with Jacob W. Kipp) Garland Bibliographies in International Military History, 1978. (with

Donald J. Mrozek and Jeanne Louise Allen Newell) The Martin Marauder and the Franklin Allens: A Wartime Love Story, 1980; (with Carol Williams) Flying Combat Aircraft II, 1978, and III, 1981; (with Donald J. Mrozek) Supplement I to A Guide to the Sources of U.S. Military History, 1981, Supplement II, 1985; Diary of a Disaster, 1986. Add: 2961 Nevada St., Manhattan, Kans. 66506, U.S.A.

HIGHAM, Roger Stephen. British. History, Travel/Exploration/Adventure. History Master, Junior King's Sch., Canterbury, since 1973. *Publs:* Island Road to Africa, 1968; Provencal Sunshine, 1969; Road to the Pyrenees, 1971; The South Country, 1972; (co-author) Sturry: The Changing Scene, 1972; Kent, 1974; Fordwich: The Lost Port, 1975; Berkshire, 1977; South-East England and East Anglia, 1983; The Pyrenées, 1988. Add: 39 High St., Sturry, Canterbury, Kent, England.

HIGHET, John. British, b. 1918. Education, Sociology, Theology/Religion. Head, Sch. of Social Studies, Robert Gordon's Inst. of Technology, Aberdeen, 1968–81, now retired. Lectr. in Sociology, 1948–63, and in Applied Sociology, 1963–68, Univ. of Glasgow. *Publs:* The Churches in Scotland Today, 1950; Dumfries Speaks Out, 1951; Youth at Leisure, 1956; The Scottish Churches, 1960; A School of One's Choice, 1969. Add: 319 Albert Dr., Glasgow G41 5EA, Scotland.

HIGHLAND, Dora. See **AVALLONE,** Michael.

HIGHLAND, Monica. See **SEE,** Carolyn.

HIGHSMITH, (Mary) Patricia. American, b. 1921. Novels/Short stories, Mystery/Crime/Suspense. Writing/Journalism. *Publs:* Strangers on a Train, 1950; The Blunderer, 1954; The Talented Mr. Ripley, 1955; Deep Water, 1957; (with Doris Sanders) Miranda the Panda Is on the Veranda (juvenile), 1958; A Game for the Living, 1958; This Sweet Sickness, 1960; The Cry of the Owl, 1962; The Two Faces of January, 1964; The Glass Cell, 1964; The Story-Teller (in U.K. as A Suspension of Mercy), 1965; Plotting and Writing Suspense Fiction, 1966; Those Who Walk Away, 1967; The Tremor of Forgery, 1969; The Snail-Watcher and Other Stories (in U.K. as Eleven), 1970; Ripley Under Ground, 1970; A Dog's Ransom, 1972; Ripley's Game, 1974; Little Tales of Misogyny, 1977; Edith's Diary, 1977; Slowly, Slowly in the Wind (stories), 1979; The Boy Who Followed Ripley, 1980; The Black House (stories), 1981; People Who Knock on the Door, 1983; Mermaids on the Golf Course (stories), 1985; Found in the Street, 1986; Tales of Natural and Unnatural Catastrophes, 1987. Add: c/o Diogenes Verlag, Sprecherstrasse 8, 8032 Zurich, Switzerland.

HIGHWATER, Jamake. American Indian, b. 1942. Novels/Short stories, Children's fiction, Art, Children's non-fiction, Cultural/Ethnic topics, History. Asst. Prof., Grad. Sch. of Architecture, Columbia Univ., NYC, since 1984. Founding Pres., Native Land Foundn, since 1984. *Publs:* Indian America: A Cultural and Travel Guide, 1975; Song from the Earth: American Indian Painting, 1976; Ritual of the Wind, 1976; Anpao: An American Indian Odyssey, 1977; Many Smokes, Many Moons, 1978; Dance: Rituals of Experience, 1978; Journey to the Sky: The Rediscovery of the Maya World, 1978; The Sweet Grass Lives On: 50 Contemporary North American Indian Artists, 1981; The Sun, He Dies: The End of the Aztec World, 1981; Moonsong Lullaby, 1981; The Primal Mind, 1981; Eyes of Darkness, 1983; Arts of the Indian Americas, 1983; (ed.) Words in the Blood: Contemporary Indian Writers of North and South America, 1984; Legend Days, 1984; The Ceremony of Innocence, 1985; Eyes of Darkness, 1985; I Wear the Morning Star, 1986; Native Land, 1986; Shadow Show: An Autobiographical Insinuation, 1986. Add: c/o Native Land Foundn., P.O. Box 2026, Canal St. Station, New York, N.Y. 10013, U.S.A.

HIGNETT, Sean. British, b. 1934. Novels/Short stories, Plays/Screenplays. *Publs:* A Picture to Hang on the Wall, 1966; Allotment (short story, television play and stage play), 1969, 1970; (ed.) Curious Hieroglyphick Bible (1789), 1970; A Cut Loaf, 1971; The Crezz (novel), 1976; Brett, 1985. Add: c/o A.D. Peters & Co., 10 Buckingham St., London WC2N 6BU, England.

HIGSON, Philip (John Willoughby). Also writes as Philip Willoughby-Higson. British, b. 1933. Poetry, History, Translations. Sr. Lectr. in History, Chester College of Higher Education, since 1972. Ed. and Contributor, Chester Poets Anthologies, since 1974. Head of the History Dept., Rosebank High Sch., County Durham, 1959–62; Research Fellow in Modern History, University of Liverpool, 1963–65. *Publs:* The Bizarre Barons of Rivington, 1965; Poems of Protest and the Pilgrimage, 1966; To Make Love's Harbour . . ., 1966; The Riposte and Other Poems,

1971; Burlando's Mistress and Other Poems, 1974; (trans. with Elliot R. Ashe) Baudelaire: The Flowers of Evil and All Other Authenticated Poems, 1975; Against the Grain, 1976; Sonnets to My Goddess, 1983; (trans.) Les Névroses, by Maurice Rollinat, 1986; Poems on the Dee, 1987. Add: Sr. Common Room, Chester Coll. of Higher Education, Cheyney Road, Chester CH1 4BJ, England.

HILBERG, Raul. American, b. 1926. History. Prof. of Political Science, Univ. of Vermont, Burlington. *Publs:* The Destruction of European Jews, 1961, 1985; (ed. and trans.) Documents of Destruction, 1971, 1973; (ed. with S.J. Staron and Josef Kermisz) The Warsaw Diary of Adam Czerniakow, 1979; Luke Karamazov, 1987. Add: 236 Prospect Parkway, Burlington, Vt. 05401, U.S.A.

HILBERRY, Conrad Arthur. American, b. 1928. Poetry. English teacher, Kalamazoo Coll., Mich., since 1962. *Publs:* (ed.) The Poems of John Collop, 1962; Encounter on Burrows Hill and Other Poems, 1968; (ed. with M. Keeton) Struggle and Promise: A Future for Colleges, 1968; Rust (poetry), 1974; (ed. with H. Scott and J. Tipton) The Third Coast: Contemporary Michigan Poets, 1976; Man in the Attic (poetry), 1980; Housemarks (poetry), 1980; The Moon Seen as a Slice of Pineapple (poetry), 1984; Luke Karamazov (case study), 1987; (ed. with Michael Delp and Herbert Scott) Contemporary Michigan Poetry: Poems From the Third Coast, 1988. Add: Kalamazoo Coll., Kalamazoo, Mich. 49007, U.S.A.

HILDEBRAND, Verna. American, b. 1924. Education. Prof., Dept. of Family and Child Ecology, Michigan State Univ., East Lansing, since 1967. Instr., Kansas State Univ., Manhattan, 1953–54 and 1959; Instr., Oklahoma State Univ., Stillwater, 1955–56; Asst. Prof. of Home and Family Life, Texas Technological Univ., Lubbock, 1962–67. *Publs:* Introduction to Early Childhood Education, 1971; A Laboratory Workbook for Introduction to Early Childhood Education, 1971, 4th ed. 1986; Guiding Young Children, 1975, 3rd ed. 1985, 1990; Parenting and Teaching Young Children, 1981, 1985, 1990; (with John R. Hildebrand) China's Families: Experiment in Societal Change, 1981; Managemnet of Child Development Centers, 1984, 1990. Add: 308 Michigan, No. 8, East Lansing, Mich. 48823, U.S.A.

HILDICK, E(mund) W(allace). Writes mystery fiction as Wallace Hildick. British, b. 1925. Novels/Short stories, Mystery/Crime/Suspense, Children's fiction, Literature. Jr. Asst., Dewsbury Public Library, 1941–42; clerk, truck repair depot, Leeds, 1942–43; Lab. Asst., Admiralty Signals Establishment, Haslemere and Sowerby Bridge, 1943–46; Teacher, Dewsbury Secondary Modern Sch., 1950–54; Visiting Critic and Assoc. Ed., Kenyon Review, Kenyon Coll., Gambier, Ohio, 1966–67. *Publs:* Jim Starling series, 7 vols., 1958–63; The Boy at the Window, 1960; Bed and Work, 1962; A Town on the Never, 1963; Meet Lemon Kelly (in U.S. as Lemon Kelly), 1963; Birdy Jones, 1963; Mapper Mundy's Treasure Hunt, 1963; Lemon Kelly Digs Deep, 1964; Lunch with Ashurbanipal, 1965; Word for Word: A Study of Authors' Alterations, with Exercises, 1965, abridged ed. as Word for Word: The Rewriting of Fiction, 1966; Louie's Lot, 1965; The Questers, 1966; A Close Look at Newspapers (Magazines and Comics, Television and Sound Broadcasting, Advertising), 4 vols., 1966–69; Calling Questers Four, 1967; The Questers and the Whispering Spy, 1967; Lucky Les: The Adventures of a Cat of Five Tales, 1967; Writing with Care: 200 Problems in the Use of English, 1967; Lemon Kelly and the Home-Made Boy, 1968; Louie's S.O.S., 1968; Birdy and the Group, 1968; Here Comes Parren, 1968; Back with Parren, 1968; Thirteen Types of Narrative, 1968; Birdy Swings North, 1969; Manhattan Is Missing, 1969; Top Boy at Twisters Creek, 1969; Monte Carlo or Bust! (in U.S. as Those Daring Young Men in Their Jaunty Jalopies), 1969; Children and Fiction, 1970; Birdy in Amsterdam, 1970; Ten Thousand Golden Cockerels, 1970; The Dragon That Lived under Manhattan, 1970; The Secret Winners, 1970; Cokerheaton (storypack), 1971; Rushbrook (storypack), 1971; Storypack Teachers Book, 1971; The Secret Spenders, 1971; The Prisoners of Gridling Gap: A Report, With Expert Comments from Doctor Ranulf Quitch, 1971; My Kid Sister, 1971; The Doughnut Dropout, 1972; Kids Commune, 1972; The Active-Enzyme Lemon-Freshened Junior High School, 1973; The Nose Knows, 1973; Only The Best: Six Qualities of Excellence, 1973; Birdy Jones and the New York Heads, 1974; Dolls in Danger (in U.S. as Deadline for McGurk), 1974; Louie's Snowstorm, 1974; The Menaced Midget, 1975; The Case of the Condemned Cat, 1975; Bracknell's Law, 1975; The Weirdown Experiment, 1976; Time Explorers Inc., 1976; A Cat Called Amnesia, 1976; The Case of the Nervous Newsboy, 1976; The Great Rabbit Robbery (in U.S. as The Great Rabbit Rip-Off), 1976; The Top Flight Fully-Automated Junior High School Girl Detective, 1977; Vandals, 1977; The Loop, 1977; The Case of the Invisible Dog, 1977; Louie's Ransom, 1978;

The Case of the Secret Scribbler, 1978; The Case of the Phantom Frog, 1979; The Case of the Treetop Treasure, 1980; The Case of the Snowbound Spy, 1980 The Case of the Bashful Bank Robber, 1981; The Case of the Four Flying Fingers, 1981; McGurk Gets Good and Mad, 1982; The Case of the Felon's Fiddle, 1982; The Case of the Slingshot Sniper, 1983; The Ghost Squad Breaks Through Flies Concorde, and the Halloween Conspiracy, and the Ghoul of Grunberg, 4 vols., 1984–86; The Case of the Vanishing Ventriloquist, 1985; The Case of the Muttering Mummy, 1986; The Ghost Squad and the Prowling Hermits, 1987; The Case of the Wandering Weathervanes, 1988; The Ghost Squad and the Menace of the Malevs, 1988; The Memory Tap, 1989. Add: c/o Coutts and Co. Ltd., 59 The Strand, London WC2, England.

HILGARD, Ernest (Ropiequet). American, b. 1904. Psychology. Prof. Emeritus, Stanford Univ., California, since 1969 (Asst. Prof. to Prof. of Psychology, 1933–69; Dean of the Graduate Division, 1951–55). Instructor in Psychology, Yale Univ., 1928–33. President, American Psychological Association, 1948–49. *Publs:* (with Richard H. Edwards) Student Counseling, 1928; Conditioned Eyelid Reactions to a Light Stimulus, Based on the Reflex Wink to Sound, 1931; (with Donald G. Marquis) Conditioning and Learning, 1940; Theories of Learning, 1948, 1959; (with others) Psychoanalysis as a Science: The Hixon Lectures on the Scientific Status of Psychoanalysis, 1952; Introduction to Psychology, 1953, 9th ed., with others, 1987; Unconscious Processes and Man's Rationality, 1958; (with André Weitzenhoffer) Stanford Hypnotic Susceptibility Scale, Forms A and B, 1959; (with others) The Distribution of Suggestibility to Hypnosis in a Student Population, 1961; (ed., with others) Theories of Learning and Instruction, 1964; Hypnotic Susceptibility, 1965; A Basic Reference Shelf on Learning Theory, 1967; (with Josephine R. Hilgard) The Experience of Hypnosis, 1968; (with Josephine R. Hilgard) Hypnosis in the Relief of Pain, 1975; Divided Consciousness: Multiple Controls in Human Thought and Action, 1977; (ed.) American Psychology in Perspective: Addresses of the Presidents of the American Psychological Association 1892-1977, 1978; Psychology in America: A Historical Survey, 1987. Add: Dept of Psychology, Stanford Univ., Stanford, Calif. 94305, U.S.A.

HILL, Alexis. *See* **CRAIG**, Mary.

HILL, Carol. American, b. 1942. Novels/Short stories, Plays/Screenplays, Social commentary/phenomena. Former actress; Publicist, Crown Publrs., NYC, 1965–67, and Bernard Geis Assocs., NYC, 1967–69; Publicist, 1969–71, and Ed., 1971–73, Pantheon Books, NYC; Publicity Mgr., Random House Inc., publrs., NYC, 1973–74; Sr. Ed., William Morrow & Co., 1974–76. Sr. Ed., Harcourt Brace, NYC, 1976–79. *Publs:* Mother Loves (play), 1967; Jeremiah 8:20, 1970; Subsistence U.S.A., 1973; Let's Fall in Love, 1974; An Unmarried Woman (novelization of screenplay), 1978; The Eleven Million Mile High Dancer, 1985. Add: 2 Fifth Ave., Apt. 19U, New York, N.Y. 10011, U.S.A.

HILL, (John Edward) Christopher. Has also written as K.E. Holme. British, b. 1912. History, Biography. Fellow and Tutor in Modern History, 1938–65, and Master, 1965–78, Balliol Coll., Oxford; Visiting Prof., Open Univ., 1978–80. *Publs:* (ed. and contrib.) The English Revolution 1640, 1940; (as K.E. Holme) Two Commonwealths, 1945; Lenin and the Russian Revolution, 1947; (ed. with E. Dell) The Good Old Cause, 1949; Economic Problems of the Church, 1956; Puritanism and Revolution, 1958; The Century of Revolution, 1961; Society and Puritanism, 1964; Intellectual Origins of the English Revolution, 1965; Reformation to Industrial Revolution, 1967; God's Englishman, 1970; Antichrist in Seventeenth Century England, 1971; The World Turned Upside Down, 1972; (ed.) The Law of Freedom and Other Writings by Gerrard Winstanley, 1973; Change and Continuity in Seventeenth Century England, 1975; Milton and the English Revolution, 1978; Some Intellectual Consequences of the English Revolution, 1980; The Experience of Defeat, 1983; Writing and Revolution, 1985; Religion and Politics in 17th Century England, 1986; People and Ideas in 17th Century England, 1986; A Turbulent, Seditious, and Fractious People: John Bunyan and His Church, 1988. Add: Woodway House, Sibford Ferris, Oxon, England.

HILL, Douglas. Canadian, b. 1935. Children's fiction, History, Literature, Supernatural/Occult topics. Ed., Aldus Books, London, 1962–64; Literary Ed., Tribune, London, 1971–84. *Publs:* (with Pat Williams) The Supernatural, 1965; The Opening of the Canadian West, 1967; (ed.) Window on the Future, 1967; (ed.) The Devil His Due, 1968; John Keats, 1968; Regency London, 1969; Magic and Superstition, 1969; Georgian London, 1970; Fortune Telling, 1970; Return From the Dead, 1970, in the U.S. as the History of Ghosts, Vampires, and Werewolves, 1973; (ed.) Warlocks and Warriors, 1971; The Scots to Canada, 1972; The Comet,

1973; The English to New England, 1974; (with others) Witchcraft, Magic, and the Supernatural, 1974; (with Gail Robinson) Coyote the Trickster, 1975; Tribune 40, 1977; (ed.) The Shape of Sex to Come, 1978; The Exploits of Hercules, 1978; Galactic Warlord, 1979; Deathwing Over Veynaa, 1980; Day of the Starwind, 1981; Planet of the Warlord, 1981; (ed.) Alien Worlds, 1981; The Huntsman, 1982; Young Legionary: The Earlier Adventures of Keill Randor, 1982; Warriors of the Wasteland, 1983; Have Your Own Extraterrestial Adventure, 1983; Alien Citadel, 1984; Exiles of ColSec, 1984; The Caves of Klydor, 1984; The Moon Monsters, 1984; ColSec Rebellion, 1985; (ed.) Planetfall, 1986; How Jennifer (ands Speckle) Saved the Earth, 1986; Blade of the Poisoner, 1987; Master of the Fiends, 1988; Goblin Party, 1988. Add: c/o Gollancz, 14 Henrietta St., London WC2E 8QJ, England.

HILL, Elizabeth Starr. American, b. 1925. Children's fiction. Freelance writer. *Publs:* The Wonderful Visit to Miss Liberty, 1961; The Window Tulip, 1964; Evan's Corner, 1967; Master Mike and the Miracle Maid, 1967; Pardon My Fangs, 1969; Bells: A Book To Begin On, 1970; Ever-After Island, 1977; Fangs Aren't Everything, 1985; When Christmas Comes, 1989. Add: c/o Harold Ober Assocs. Inc., 40 East 49th St., New York, N.Y. 10017, U.S.A.

HILL, Errol (Gaston). Trinidadian, b. 1921. Plays/Screenplays, Theatre. Willard Prof. of Drama and Oratory, Drama Dept., Dartmouth Coll., Hanover, N.H., since 1969 (Assoc. Prof. 1968–69). Drama Tutor, 1952–58, Ed., Caribbean Plays series, 1954–65, Creative Arts Tutor, 1958–65, Univ. of West Indies, Kingston, Jamaica, and Trinidad; Teaching Fellow in Drama, Univ. of Ibadan, Nigeria, 1965–67; Assoc. Prof. of Drama, City Univ. of New York, 1967–68. Ed., ATA Bulletin of Black Theatre, 1971–77. *Publs:* Oily Portraits (produced as Brittle and the City Fathers), 1948; Square Peg, 1949; The Ping Pong: A Backyard Comedy-Drama, 1950; Dilemma, 1953; Broken Melody, 1954; Wey-Wey, 1957; Strictly Matrimony, 1959; Man Better Man, 1960; (ed.) The Artist in West Indian Society: A Symposium, 1964; Dance Bongo, 1965; The Trinidad Carnival: Mandate for a National Theatre, 1972; (with P. Greer) Why Pretend?, 1973; (ed.) A Time and A Season: Eight Caribbean Plays, 1976; (ed.) Three Caribbean Plays, 1979; (ed.) The Theatre of Black Americans, 2 vols, 1980; Shakespeare in Sable: A History of Black Shakespearean Actors, 1984; (ed.) Plays for Today, 1985. Add: Hopkins Center, Dartmouth Coll., Hanover, N.H. 03755, U.S.A.

HILL, Geoffrey. British, b. 1932. Poetry. Fellow, Emmanuel Coll., and Lectr. in English, Cambridge Univ., since 1981. Former Prof. of English, Univ. of Leeds. *Publs:* (Poems), 1952; For the Unfallen 1952–58, 1959; Preghiere, 1964; (with Edwin Brock and S. Smith) Penguin Modern Poets 8, 1966; King Log, 1968; Mercian Hymns, 1971; Somewhere Is Such a Kingdom: Poems 1952–1971, 1975; Tenebrae, 1978; (adaptor) Brand, by Ibsen, 1978; The Mystery of the Charity of Charles Péguy, 1983; The Lords of Limit: Essays on Literature and Ideas, 1984; Collected Poems, 1985. Add: Emmanuel Coll., Cambridge CB2 3AP, England.

HILL, John. See **KOONTZ**, Dean R.

HILL, L. Draper. American, b. 1935. Art, Design. Editorial Cartoonist, The Commercial Appeal, Memphis, since 1971. First Vice pres., Assn. of American Editorial Cartoonists. *Publs:* Cartoon and Caricature from Hogarth to Hoffnung (exhibition catalogue), 1962; The Crane Library, 1962; Bert Thomas, 1965, 1974; Mr. Gillray the Caricaturist, 1965; Fashionable Contrasts, 1966; Illingworth on Target, 1970; The Lively Art of J.P. Alley, 1973; Hugh Haynie: Perspective, 1974; The Satirical Etchings of James Gillray, 1976. Add: c/o Dover, 180 Varick St., New York, N.Y. 10014, U.S.A.

HILL, Lorna. British, b. 1902. Children's fiction, Biography. *Publs:* Sadler's Wells Ballet series; Dancing Peel series; Marjorie books; Patience books; The Vicarage Children; More About Mandy; The Vicarage Children in Skye; La Sylphide: The Life of Marie Taglioni; The Other Miss Perkin, 1978; The Scent of Rosemary, 1978. Add: Brockleside, Keswick, Cumbria, England.

HILL, Michael J. British, b. 1943. Theology/Religion. Regional/Urban Planning, Sociology. Lectr. in Sociology, London Sch. of Economics, since 1967. Ed., A Sociological Yearbook of Religion in Britain, since 1971. *Publs:* A Sociology of Religion, 1973; The Religious Order, 1973; Understanding Social Policy, 1983; Housing Benefit Implementation: From Unified Ideal to Complex Reality, 1984; (with G. Bramley) Analyzing Social Policy, 1986. Add: c/o Martin Robertson and Co., Blackwell, 108 Cowley Rd., Oxford OX4 1JF, England.

HILL, Pamela. Also writes as Sharon Fiske. British, b. 1920. Historical/Romance/Gothic. *Publs:* Flaming Janet (in U.S. as King's Vixen), 1954; Shadow of Palaces (in U.S. as Crown and the Shadow), 1955; Marjory of Scotland, 1956; Here Lies Margot, 1957; Maddalena, 1963; Forget Not Ariadne, 1965; Julia, 1967; The Devil of Aske, 1972; The Malvie Inheritance, 1973; The Incumbent, 1974, in U.S. as The Heatherton Heritage, 1976; Whitton's Folly, 1975; Norah Stroyan, 1976; The Green Salamander, 1977; Tsar's Woman, 1978; Strangers' Forest, 1978; Daneclere, 1978; Homage to a Rose, 1979; Daughter of Midnight, 1979; Fire Opal, 1980; A Place of Ravens, 1980; (as Sharon Fiske) Summer Cyprus, 1981; The House of Cray, 1982; The Fairest One of All, 1982; Duchess Cain, 1983; The Copper-Haired Marshal, 1983; Bride of Ae, 1983; Children of Lucifer, 1984; Still Blooms the Rose, 1984; The Governess, 1985; Sable for the Count, 1985; My Lady Glamis, 1985; Digby, 1987; Fen fallow, 1987; The Sutburys, 1988; Jeannie Urquahart, 1988; The Woman in the Cloak, 1988. Add: c/o Hale, 45-47 Clerkenwell Green, London EC1R 0HT, England.

HILL, Reginald (Charles). Also writes as Dick Morland, Patrick Ruell, and Charles Underhill. British, b. 1936. Novels/Short stories, Mystery/Crime/Suspense, Plays/Screenplays. Full-time writer since 1980. Teacher/Lectr., 1960–80. *Publs:* A Clubbable Woman, 1970; Fell of Dark, 1971; (as Patrick Ruell) The Castle of the Demon, 1971; An Advancement of Learning, 1972; A Fairly Dangerous Thing, 1972; (as Patrick Ruell) Red Christmas, 1972; An Affair of Honour (play), 1972; Ruling Passion, 1973; (as Dick Morland) Heart Clock, 1973; A Very Good Hater, 1974; (as Dick Morland) Albion! Albion!, 1974; (as Patrick Ruell) Death Takes the Low Road, 1974; An April Shroud, 1975; (as Patrick Ruell) Urn Burial, 1976; Another Death in Venice, 1976; (as Charles Underhill) Captain Fantom, 1978; A Pinch of Snuff, 1978; (as Charles Underhill) The Forging of Fantom, 1979; Pascoe's Ghost (stories), 1979; A Killing Kindness, 1980; The Spy's Wife, 1980; Who Guards a Prince, 1981; Ordinary Levels (radio play), 1982; Traitor's Blood, 1983; Deadheads, 1983; Exit Lines, 1984; No Man's Land, 1985; (as Patrick Ruell) The Long Kill, 1986; Child's Play, 1987; (as Patrick Ruell) Death of a Dormouse, 1987; The Collaborators, 1987; There Are No Ghosts In the Soviet Union (stories), 1987; Underworld, 1988. Add:"Oakbank", Broad Oak, Ravenglass, Cumbria, England.

HILL, Rosalind Mary Theodosia. British, b. 1908. History. Prof. Emeritus of History, Univ. of London, since 1976 (Lectr., 1937–56; Reader, 1956–71; Prof., 1971–76). *Publs:* (ed.) The Rolls and Register of Bishop Oliver Sutton, 8 vols., 1947–86; Both Great and Small Beasts, 1955; (ed. and trans.) Anonymi Gesta Francorum, 1956; The Labourer in the Vineyard, 1969; Unfashionable History, 1972; (ed.) The Register of Archbishop William Melton, 2 vols., 1977–89; The Scale of Perfection, 1983. Add: 7 Loom Lane, Radlett, Herts., WD7 8AA, England.

HILL, Susan (Elizabeth). British, b. 1942. Novels/Short stories, Children's fiction, Plays. Novelist, playwright and critic, since 1960. *Publs:* The Enclosure, 1961; Do Me a Favour, 1963; Gentleman & Ladies, 1969; A Change for the Better, 1969; I'm the King of the Castle, 1970; Strange Meeting, 1971; The Albatross (short stories) (in U.S. as The Albatross and Other Stories), 1971; The Bird of Night, 1972; A Bit of Singing and Dancing (short stories), 1973; In the Springtime of the Year, 1974; The Cold Country and Other Plays for Radio, 1975; (ed.) The Distracted Preacher and Other Stories, by Hardy, 1979; The Magic Apple Tree, 1982; The Woman in Black, 1983; Through the Kitchen Window, 1984; One Night at a Time (for children), 1984; (ed.) Ghost Stories, 1984; Through the Garden Gate, 1986; Mother's Magic (for children), 1986; Shakespeare Country, 1987; The Lighting of the Lamps, 1987; Lanterns Across the Snow (novella), 1988; The Spirit of the Cotswolds, 1988; Can It Be True (for children), 1988; Family (autobiography), 1989; Suzie's Shoes (for children), 1989. Add: c/o Michael Joseph Ltd., 24 Wrights Lane, London W8 5TZ, England.

HILL, William Joseph. American, b. 1924. Theology/Religion. Prof. Emeritus of Systematic Theology, Catholic Univ. of America. Prof. of Theology, 1953–71, and Faculty Vice Pres., 1966–70, Pontifical Faculty of Theology, Dominican House of Studies, Washington, D.C. Ed., the Thomist, journal of philosophy and theology, Washington, D.C., 1975–83 (Assoc. Ed., 1957–75); Vice-Pres., 1978–79, and Pres., 1979–80, Catholic Theological Soc. of America; Member of Editorial Bd., New Catholic Encyclopedia, 1973–79. *Publs:* Proper Relations to Indwelling Divine Persons, 1955; (trans. and ed.) Hope—a critical edition and translation from Thomas Aquinas Summa Theologiae II-II, q. 17-22, 1966; Knowing the Unknown God, 1971; The Three-Personed God, 1982. Add: Catholic

Univ. of America, Washington, D.C. 20064, U.S.A.

HILLABY, John. British, b. 1917. Travel/Exploration/Adventure. Mag. contrib. and broadcaster, since 1944. In local journalism up to 1939; Zoological Corresp., Manchester Guardian, 1949; European Science Writer, New York Times, 1951; Biological Consultant, New Scientist, London, 1953. Woodward Lectr., Yale Univ., 1973. *Publs:* Within The Streams, 1949; Nature and Man, 1960; Journey to the Jade Sea, 1964; Journey Through Britain, 1968; Journey Through Europe, 1972; Journey Through Love, 1976; Journey Home, 1983; John Hillaby's Yorkshire: The Moors and Dales, 1986; John Hillaby's London, 1987. Add: 85 Cholmley Gardens, London NW6, England.

HILLARY, (Sir) Edmund (Percival). New Zealander, b. 1919. Travel/Exploration/Adventure, Autobiography/Memoirs/Personal. New Zealand High Commissioner in India, since 1984. Has conducted many expeditions including reaching summit of Mount Everest with Sherpa Tenzing, 1953; first journey overland with vehicles to the South Pole, 1958; first journey up the Ganges River by jet boats, 1977. *Publs:* High Adventure, 1955; (with G. Lowe) East of Everest, 1956; (with V. Fuchs) The Crossing of Antarctica, 1958; No Latitude for Error, 1961; (with D. Doig) High in the Thin Cold Air, 1963; School House in the Clouds, 1965; Nothing Venture, Nothing Win, 1975; From the Ocean to the Sky, 1979; Two Generations, 1983. Add: 278a Remuera Rd., Auckland SE2, New Zealand.

HILLER, Lejaren. American, b. 1924. Chemistry, Music. Birge-Carey Prof. of Music, State Univ. of New York, Buffalo, since 1981 (Prof. since 1968). Asst. Prof. of Chemistry, 1952–58, and Prof. of Music, 1958–68, Univ. of Illinois, Urbana. *Publs:* (with L.M. Isaacson) Experimental Music, 1959; (with R.H. Herber) Principles of Chemistry, 1960; Informationstheorie und Computermusik, 1964. Add: Dept. of Music, State Univ. of New York, Buffalo, N.Y. 14260, U.S.A.

HILLERMAN, Tony. American, b. 1925. Mystery/Crime/Suspense, Children's fiction. Prof. and Chmn. of Journalism since 1966, Univ. of New Mexico, Albuquerque (Assoc. Prof., 1965–66; Asst. to the Pres., 1975–80); retired, 1985. Reporter, News Herald, Borger, Texas, 1948; News Ed., Morning Press, Lawton, Okla., 1949, and City Ed., Constitution, Lawton, 1950; Political Reporter, United Press, Oklahoma City, 1952; Bureau Mgr., United Press, Santa Fe, New Mex., 1953; Exec. Ed., The New Mexican, Santa Fe, 1954. *Publs:* The Great Taos Bank Robbery and Other Affairs of Indian Country (essays), 1970; The Blessing Way (mystery), 1970; The Fly on the Wall (mystery), 1971; The Boy Who Made Dragonfly (juvenile), 1972; Dance Hall of the Dead (mystery), 1973; New Mexico, 1975; Rio Grande, 1976; (ed.) The Spell of New Mexico, 1977; The Listening Woman (mystery), 1978; People of Darkness (mystery), 1980; The Dark Wind (mystery), 1982; The Ghostway (mystery), 1985; Skinwalkers (mystery), 1986; A Thief of Time, 1988. Add: 2729 Texas N.E., Albuquerque, N.M. 87110, U.S.A.

HILLGARTH, J(ocelyn) N(igel). British, b. 1929. History. Prof. of History, Univ. of Toronto and Pontifical Inst. of Mediaeval Studies, Toronto, since 1977. Sr. Research Fellow, Warburg Inst., London, 1959–62; Fellow, Inst. for Advanced Studies, Princeton, N.J., 1963–64; Asst. Prof. of History, Harvard Univ., Cambridge, Mass., 1965–70; Assoc. Prof., 1970–73, and Prof. of History, 1973–77, Boston Coll. *Publs:* (ed.) The Conversion of Western Europe 350-750, 1969; Ramon Lull and Lullism in 14th Century France, 1971; The Spanish Kingdoms, 2 vols., 1976–78; (with Mary Hillgarth) Pere III of Catalonia, Chronicle, 2 vols., 1980; Visigothic Spain, Byzantium and the Irish, 1985; (ed.) Christianity and Paganism 350-750: The Conversion of Western Europe, 1985. Add: 17 Olive Ave., Toronto, Ont. M6G IT7, Canada.

HILLIARD, Noel (Harvey). New Zealander, b. 1929. Novels/Short stories. Sub-Ed., Wellington Evening Post, since 1977. Journalist, Southern Cross, Wellington, 1946–50; Teacher, Khandallah Sch., Wellington, 1955–56, and District High Sch., Mangakino, 1956–64; Chief Sub-Ed., New Zealand Listener, Wellington, 1965–70; Robert Burns Fellow, Univ. of Otago, Dunedin, 1971–72; Deputy Ed., New Zealand's Heritage, New Zealand Today, New Zealand's Nature Heritage, 1972–74. *Publs:* Maori Girl, 1960; A Piece of Land, 1963; Power of Joy, 1965; A Night at Green River, 1969; We Live by a Lake, 1972; Maori Woman, 1974; Wellington: City Alive, 1976; Send Somebody Nice, 1976; Selected Stories, 1977; The Glory and the Dream, 1978; Mahitahi (Work Together): Some Peoples of the Soviet Union, 1989. Add: 28 Richard St., Titahi Bay, Wellington, New Zealand.

HILLIER, Bevis. British, b. 1940. Antiques/Furnishings, Art. Assoc. Ed., Los Angeles Times, since 1984. Ed., British Museum Soc. Bulletin, 1968–70; Antiques Correspondent, 1970–84, and Deputy Literary Ed., 1981–84, The Times, London; Ed., The Connoisseur, 1973–76. *Publs:* Master Potters of the Industrial Revolution, 1965; Pottery and Porcelain, 1700-1914, 1968; Art Deco of the 1920's and 1930's, 1968; Posters, 1969; Cartoons and Caricatures, 1970; The World of Art Deco, 1971; 100 Years of Posters, 1972; Austerity/Binge, 1975; (co-ed.) A Tonic to the Nation: The Festival of Britain, 1976; The New Antiques, 1977; Greetings from Christmas Past, 1982; The Style of the Century 1900–1980, 1983; John Betjeman: A Life in Pictures, 1984; Young Betjeman, 1988. Add: Los Angeles Times, Times-Mirror Sq., Los Angeles, Calif. 90053, U.S.A.

HILLIER, Jack Ronald. British, b. 1912. Art. *Publs:* Japanese Masters of the Colour-Print, 1954; Hokusai: Paintings, Drawings and Woodcuts, 1956; The Japanese Print: A New Approach, 1960; Landscape Prints of Old Japan, 1960; Utamaro, 1961; Japanese Drawings from the Seventeenth to the End of the Nineteenth Century, 1965; Hokusai Drawings, 1966; Japanese Colour Prints, 1966; Japanese Emblems and Design, 1970; Catalogue of the Gale Collection of Japanese Paintings and Prints, 1970; Catalogue of the Harari Collection of Japanese Paintings and Drawings, 1973; Suzuki Harunobu, 1970; The Uninhibited Brush: Japanese Art in the Shijo Style, 1974; The Japanese Print: A New Approach, 1975; Japanese Prints and Drawings from the Vever Collection, 1976; The Art of Hokusai, 1980; The Art of Hokusai in Book Illustration, 1980; Japanese Drawings of the 18th and 19th Centuries, 1980; The Art of the Japanese Book, 1987. Add: 27 Whitepost Hill, Redhill, Surrey, England.

HILLIER, Jim. British, b. 1941. Film. Sr. Lectr. in Film Studies, Univ. of Reading, formerly Bulmershe Coll. of Higher Education, Reading, since 1979. Member of Editorial Bd., Movie, since 1971. Teacher/Adviser, 1969–73, and Deputy Head of the Educational Advisory Service, 1974–78, British Film Inst., London. *Publs:* (ed.) New Cinema Finland, 1972; (with Alan Lovell) Studies in Documentary, 1972; (ed.) Cinema in Finland, 1975; (with Aaron Lipstadt) Roger Corman's New World, 1981; (ed.) Cahiers du Cinema, vol. I: The 1950's, 1985, vol. 2, The 1960s, 1986. Add: 122 Southampton Row, Apt. 20, London WC1B 5AE, England.

HILLIS, Dick (Charles Richard). American, b. 1913. Theology/Religion, Autobiography/Memoirs/Personal. Founder, Overseas Crusades, Inc., Santa Clara, Calif., 1950. Ed., Cable mag. Missionary to China, China Inland Mission, 1933–49; Dir. of Practical Work Dept. and Prof. of Missions, Biola Coll., La Mirada, Calif., 1943–46. *Publs:* Shall We Forfeit Formosa?, 1954; Dare We Recognize Red China?, 1956; Are the Heathen Really Lost?, 1961; Unlock the Heavens, 1963; Inhale the Incense, 1964; Strange Gods, 1965; Born to Climb, 1967; China Assignment, 1967; Sayings of Mao, of Jesus, 1972; Not Made for Quitting, 1973; Listen to the Spirit, 1973; Is There Really Only One Way?, 1974; How Is God Populating Heaven?, 1978; The Spirit Speaks, 1980. Add: c/o Bethany House Publishers, Div. of Bethany Fellowship, Inc., 6820 Auto Club Rd., Minneapolis, Minn. 55438, U.S.A.

HILLMAN, Barry (Leslie). British, b. 1942. Plays, Poetry. Local Govt. Officer, Northamptonshire County Council, since 1974. *Publs:* Endymion Rampant (poetry), 1964; Happy Returns, 1970; Partly Furnished, 1971; Roly-Poly, 1973; Two Can Play at That Game, 1975; The Dispossessed, 1975; Face the Music, 1975; (with Robert Newton) Bibs and Bobs, 1975; Six for the Charleston, 1976; (with Robert Newton) Odds and Sods, 1977; The Queen and the Axe, 1978; The Guests, 1978; (with Robert Newton) A Few Minor Dischords, 1978; These Little Songs (poetry), 1979; Never the Blushing Bride, 1981; The Establishment at Arles, 1982; Beyond Necessity, 1981; Three's a Crowd, 1982; The Amazing Dancing Bear (play), 1985. Add: "Lynry," 48 Louise Rd., Northampton, England.

HILLS, Denis (Cecil). British, b. 1913. Politics/Government, Travel/Exploration/Adventure. Journalist in Germany and Central Europe, 1935–39; Officer, British Army and Allied Central Commn. Germany, 1940–50; Lectr. in English and British Economic History, Univ. of Mainz, 1951–54; Teacher and Lectr., Ankara Coll., Middle East Technical Univ., and Zonguldak Coll., Turkey, 1955–63; Lectr. in English, Makerere Coll., 1963–65, and National Teachers' Coll., 1966–74, Kampala, Uganda, and Gwelo Teacher Training Coll., Rhodesia, 1976–78; Teacher, Uganda and Nairobi schs., 1980–84. *Publs:* My Travels in Turkey, 1964; Man With A Lobelia Flute, 1970; The White Pumpkin (on Uganda), 1975; Rebel People, 1978; The Last Days of White Rhodesia, 1981; The Rock of the Wind: A Return to Africa, 1984; Return to Poland, 1988. Add: The Laurels, Station Rd., Broadway, Worcs., England.

HILLS, George. British, b. 1918. History, Biography. Member, BBC staff, London, 1946–77. *Publs:* Franco: The Man and His Nation, 1967; Spain, 1970; Rock of Contention: A History of Gibraltar, 1974; The Battle for Madrid, 1977; Los Informativos en Radiotelevision, 1981. Add: 67 Bodley Rd., New Malden, Surrey KT3 5QJ, England.

HILLS, Philip James. British, b. 1933. Education, Sciences. Lectr. in Educational Technology, Inst. for Educational Technology, Univ. of Surrey, Guildford, since 1972 (Leverhulme Research Fellow, 1969–72). Sr. Science Master and Head of the Chemistry Dept., Netherthorpe Grammar Sch., Stargley, 1959–64; Lectr. in Education and Science, Inst. of Education, Univ. of Sheffield, 1964–69. *Publs:* Small Scale Physical Chemistry, 1966; Chemical Equilibria, 1969; (with J. Leisten) Studies in Atomic Structure, 1969; (ed. with L.J. Hayness, C.R. Palmer and D.S. Trickey) Alternatives to the Lecture, 1974; The Self-Teaching Process in Higher Education, 1976; (ed. with J. Gilbert) Aspects of Educational Technology, vol. II, 1977; Study Courses and Counselling, 1979; The Future of the Printed Word: Teaching and Learning as a Communications Process, 1979; (with H. Barlow) Effective Study Skills, 1980; (ed.) Trends in Information Transfer, 1981; (ed.) Dictionary of Education, 1984; Teaching, Learning, and Communication, 1986; Educating for a Computer Age, 1986; (with M. McLaren) Communication Skills, 1986; (with McLaren) Teaching Communication Skills, 1986; (with McLaren) Communication Skills: A International Review, 2 vols., 1987; Educational Futures, 1987. Add: c/o Croom Helm, 25 North St., Bromley, Kent BR1 1SD, England.

HILSMAN, Roger. American, b. 1919. International relations/Current affairs, Politics/Government. Prof. of Government, Columbia Univ., New York City. Research Assoc., Center of Intnl. Studies, Princeton, N.J., 1953–56; Chief, Foreign Affairs Div., 1956–58, Deputy Dir. for Research, Legislative Reference Service, 1958–61, Library of Congress, Washington, D.C.; Dir. of Intelligence and Research, U.S. Dept. of State, Washington, 1961–63; Asst. Secty. of State for Far Eastern Affairs, 1963–64. *Publs:* Strategic Intelligence and National Decisions, 1956; (co-author) Military Policy and National Security, 1956; (co-author) NATO and American Security, 1958; (co-author) Alliance Policy in the Cold War, 1958; (co-author) The Guerrilla and How to Fight Him, 1960; (with Good) Foreign Policy in the Sixties, 1965; To Move a Nation, 1967; The Politics of Policy Making in Defense and Foreign Affairs, 1971; The Crouching Future, 1975; To Govern America, 1979; The Politics of Governing America, 1985; Politics of Policy Making: Conceptual Models, 1987. Add: 448 Riverside Dr., New York, N.Y. 10027, U.S.A.

HILTON, George Woodman. American, b. 1925. Transportation. Prof. of Economics, Univ. of California, Los Angeles, since 1966 (Lectr., 1962–63; Assoc. Prof., 1963–66). Instr., Univ. of Maryland, College Park, 1949–51 and 1954–55; Asst. Prof., Stanford Univ., Calif., 1955–60; Lectr., Univ. of California, Berkeley, 1961–62. *Publs:* (with J.F. Due) The Electric Interurban Railways in America, 1960; The Truck System, 1960; The Great Lakes Car Ferries, 1962; The Ma & Pa, 1963; The Night Boat, 1968; The Transportation Act of 1958, 1969; The Cable Car in America, 1971; Monon Route, 1978; American Narrow Gauge Railroads, 1989. Add: Dept. of Economics, Univ. of California, Los Angeles, Calif. 90024, U.S.A.

HILTON, Margery. British. Historical/Romance. *Publs:* A Man Without Mercy, 1950; The Flower of Eternity, 1951; Girl Crusoe, 1952; The Dutch Uncle, 1966; Young Ellis, 1966; Darling Rhadamanthus!, 1966; The Grotto of Jade, 1968; Interlude in Arcady, 1970; Bitter Masquerade, 1970; The Whispering Grove, 1971; Trust in Tomorrow, 1971; Dear Conquistador, 1972; The House of the Amulet, 1972; The Spell of the Enchanter, 1972; Frail Sanctuary, 1973; The Inshine Girl, 1973; Miranda's Marriage, 1974; The Beach of Sweet Returns, 1976; The Dark Side of Marriage, 1978; The House of Strange Music, 1978; Snow Bride, 1979; The Velvet Touch, 1979; Way of a Man, 1981. Add: Harlequin Cottage, South St., Scalby, Scarborough, Yorks, YO13 0QR, England.

HILTON, Peter (John). British, b. 1923. Mathematics. Distinguished Prof. of Mathematics, State Univ. of New York at Binghamton, since 1983. Asst. Lectr., 1948–51, and Lectr., 1951–52, Manchester Univ.; Lectr., Cambridge Univ., 1952–55; Sr. Lectr., Manchester Univ., 1956–58; Mason Prof. of Pure Mathematics, Univ. of Birmingham, 1958–62; Prof. of Mathematics, Cornell Univ., Ithaca, N.Y., 1962–71, and Univ. of Washington, Seattle, 1971–73; Beaumont Univ. Prof., Case Western Reserve Univ., Cleveland, 1972–82. Chmn., U.S. Commn. on Mathematical Instruction, 1971–74. *Publs:* Introduction to Homotopy Theory, 1953; Differential Calculus, 1958; (with S. Wylie) Homology Theory, 1960; Partial Derivatives, 1960; Homotopy Theory and Duality, 1965; (with H.B. Griffiths) Classical Mathematics, 1970; General Cohomology Theory and K-Theory,

1971; (with U. Stammbach) Course in Homological Algebra, 1971; (with Y.-C. Wu) Course in Modern Algebra, 1974; (with G. Mislin and J. Roitberg) Localization of Nilpotent Groups and Spaces, 1975; (with J. Pedersen) Fear No More, 1982; Nilpotente Gruppen und nilpotente Räume, 1984; (with J. Pedersen) Build Your Own Polyhedra, 1987. Add: Dept. of Mathematics, State Univ. of New York, Binghamton, N.Y. 13901, U.S.A.

HILTON, Ronald. American, b. 1911. History (cultural), International relations/Current affairs. Prof., Stanford Univ., Calif., since 1941. Pres., California Inst. of Intnl. Studies, since 1965, and Ed., World Affairs Report, since 1970. Ed., Who's Who in Latin America, Stanford Univ. Press, 1946–51. Ed., Hispanic American Report, 1948–64. *Publs:* Campoamor, Spain and the World, 1940; (ed.) Handbook of Hispanic Source Materials in the United States, 1942, 1956; Four Studies in Franco-Spanish Relations, 1943; (ed. and trans.) Life of Joaquim Nabuco, 1950; (ed.) Ulises Criollo, 1960; (ed.) Movement Toward Latin American Unity, 1969; Scientific Institutions of Latin America, 1970; La América Latina de Ayer de Hoy, 1970; The Latin Americans: Their Heritage and Their Destiny, 1973; A Bibliography of Latin America and the Caribbean, 1980. Add: 766 Santa Ynez, Stanford, Calif. 94305, U.S.A.

HILTON, Suzanne. American, b. 1922. Children's non-fiction. Public Relations Adviser for Jenkintown Sch. District, Pennsylvania, 1970–84. *Publs:* How Do They Get Rid of It?, 1970; How Do They Cope With It?, 1970; It's Smart to Use a Dummy, 1971; It's A Model World, 1972; Beat It, Burn It, and Drown It, 1973; The Way It Was—1876, 1975; Who Do You Think You Are?: Digging for Your Family Roots, 1976; Here Today and Gone Tomorrow: The Story of America's World's Fairs, 1978; Getting There: Frontier Travel Without Power, 1980; We the People: The Way We Were 1783 to 1793, 1981; Faster Than a Horse: Moving West with Engine Power, 1983; (ed. and contr.) Montgomery County, The Second Hundred Years 1880-1980, 1983; The World of Young Tom Jefferson, George Washington, Herbert Hoover [Andrew Jackson], 4 vols., 1986–88. Add: 301 Runnymede Ave., Jenkintown, Pa. 19046, U.S.A.

HIMELSTEIN, Morgan Y. American, b. 1926. Literature, Translations. Prof. of English, Adelphi Univ., Garden City, N.Y., since 1968 (Instr., 1957–60; Asst. Prof., 1960–64; Assoc. Prof., 1964–68; Dir of Grad. Studies in English, 1965–74). Instr. in English, Univ. of Rochester, N.Y., 1948–50; Book Reviewer, American Quarterly, 1968–70. *Publs:* Drama Was a Weapon: The Left-Wing Theatre in New York, 1929–1941, 1963; (trans.) Offenbach: La Grande Duchesse de Gérolstein (opera), 1977; (trans.) Offenbach: La Périchole (opera), 1982; (trans.) Offenbach: Orphé aux Enfers (opera), 1985. Add: 37 Maxwell Rd., Garden City, N.Y. 11530, U.S.A.

HIMMELFARB, Gertrude. American, b. 1922. History, Intellectual history. Prof. Emeritus of History, the Grad. Sch. of the City Univ. of New York, since 1965. Trustee, National Humanities Center, since 1976; Trustee, Woodrow Wilson Center, since 1985; Member, Council of Scholars, Library of Congress, since 1984. Bd. of Dirs., British Inst. of the U.S., since 1985; Bd. of Dirs., Inst. for Contemporary Studies, since 1986; Council of Academic Advisors, American Enterprise Inst., since 1987. *Publs:* (ed.) Essays on Freedom and Power, by Acton, 1948; Lord Acton: A Study in Conscience and Politics, 1952; Darwin and the Darwinian Revolution, 1959; (ed.) On Population, by Malthus, 1960; (ed.) Essays on Politics and Culture, 1962; Victorian Minds, 1968; On Liberty and Liberalism: The Case of John Stuart Mill, 1974; (ed.) On Liberty, by J.S. Mill, 1974; The Idea of Poverty, 1984; Marriage and Morals among the Victorians, 1986; The New History and the Old, 1987. Add: The City Univ. of New York, 33 W. 42nd St., New York, N.Y. 10036, U.S.A.

HIMMELFARB, Milton. American, b. 1918. Theology/Religion, Cultural/Ethnic topics (Judaism, Jewish affairs). member, U.S. Holocaust Memorial Council, since 1986. Dir. of Information and Research, American Jewish Cttee., NYC, 1955–86; Ed., American Jewish Year Book, NYC, 1959–86; Contributing Ed., Commentary mag., NYC, 1960–86; Visiting Prof., Jewish Theological Seminary, NYC, 1967–68, and 1971–72; Visiting Lectr., Yale Univ., 1971; Visiting Prof., Reconstructionist Rabbinical Coll., Philadelphia, 1972–73. *Publs:* The Jews of Modernity, 1973. Add: 165 E. 56th St., New York, N.Y. 10022, U.S.A.

HINCHLIFF, Peter Bingham. South African, b. 1929. Theology/Religion. Fellow and Chaplain, Balliol Coll., Oxford, since 1972. Prof. of Ecclesiastical History, Rhodes Univ., Grahamstown, S. Africa, 1960–69; Secty., Church of England Missionary and Ecumenical Council, London, 1969–72. *Publs:* The South African Liturgy, 1959; The Anglican Church in South Africa, 1963; John William Colenso, 1964;

The One-Sided Reciprocity, 1966; (ed.) Calendar of Cape Missionary Correspondence, 1967; The Church in South Africa, 1968; (ed.) The Journal of John Ayliff, 1971; Cyprian of Carthage, 1974; (with D. Young) The Human Potential, 1981; Holiness and Politics, 1982; Benjamin Jowett and the Christian Religion, 1987. Add: Balliol Coll., Oxford OX1 3BJ, England.

HINCKLEY, Helen. Also writes as Helen Jones. American, b. 1903. Novels/Short stories, Children's fiction, Children's non-fiction, Travel/Exploration/Adventure, Writing/Journalism, Biography. Former teacher of writing for publ., Pasadena City Coll., Calif. *Publs:* The Mountains Are Mine (novel), 1946; (with Najmeh Najafi) Persia is My Heart, 1953; (with N. Najafi) Reveille for a Persian Village, 1958; (as Helen Jones) Over the Mormon Trail, 1963; Land and People of Iran, 1964, 1972; (with Najmeh Najafi) A Wall and Three Willows, 1967; Rails from the West: A Biography of Theodore Judah, 1969; Noah, 1970; Joseph, 1970; Eleven Who Dared, 1971; Who's Afraid, 1971; The Opossum's Table. 1973; Jackson's Big Ache, 1974; How to Write and Publish: A Step at a Time, 1980; Israel: Enchantment of the World, 1987. Add: 1191 East Mendocino, Altadena, Calif. 91001, U.S.A.

HINDE, Thomas. Pseud. for Sir Thomas Willes Chitty. British, b. 1926. Novels, Travel, Autobiography. With Inland Revenue, London, 1951–53, and Shell Petroleum Co., in England, 1953–58, and Nairobi, 1958–60. *Publs:* Mr. Nicholas, 1952; Happy as Larry, 1957; For the Good of the Company, 1961; A Place Like Home, 1962; The Cage, 1962; Spain: A Personal Anthology, 1963; Ninety Double Martinis, 1963; The Day the Call Came, 1964; Games of Chance: The Interviewer and the Investigator, 1965; The Village, 1966; High, 1968; Bird, 1970; Generally a Virgin, 1972; Agent, 1974; Our Father, 1975; (with Susan Hinde) On Next to Nothing, 1975; (with Susan Chitty) The Great Donkey Walk, 1977; The Cottage Book, 1979; Sir Henry and Sons: A Memoir, 1981; Daymare, 1981; Field Guide to the Country Parson, 1982; Stately Gardens of Britain, 1983; Forests of Britain, 1985; Courtiers, 1986; Tales from the Pumproom: An Informal History of Bath, 1988. Add: Bow Cottage, West Hoathly, nr. East Grinstead, Sussex RH19 4QF, England.

HINDE, Wendy. British, b. 1919. Biography. Member, Ed. Staff, The Economist, London, 1950–71; Ed., Intnl. Affairs, Royal Inst. of Intnl. Affairs, London, 1971–79. *Publs:* George Canning, 1973; Castlereagh, 1981; Richard Cobden: A Victorian Outsider, 1987. Add: 31 Clarendon St., Cambridge CB1 1JX, England.

HINDS, (Evelyn) Margery. Canadian. Anthropology/Ethnology, Travel/Exploration/Adventure. Engaged in education and welfare of the Eskimos for the Govt. of Canada, 1948–62; former Arctic Corresp. with the CBC. *Publs:* Nothing Venture, 1941; Victorious Venture, 1948; Schoolhouse in the Arctic, 1958; Kanayu, the Young Hunter, 1965; High Arctic Venture, 1968; Makpa: The Story of an Eskimo-Canadian Boy, 1971. Add: 207-1035 Pendergast St., Victoria, B.C. V8V 2W9, Canada.

HINDUS, Milton. American, b. 1916. Poetry, Literature. Asst. Prof. of Humanities, Univ. of Chicago, 1946–48. Prof. of English, Brandeis Univ., Waltham, Mass., 1948–88. *Publs:* The Crippled Giant, 1950, 1986; The Proustian Vision, 1954; (ed.) Leaves of Grass: One Hundred Years After, 1954; A Reader's Guide to Marcel Proust, 1962; F. Scott Fitzgerald, 1967; (ed.) The Old East Side, 1969; (ed.) Walt Whitman: The Critical Heritage, 1971; A World at Twilight, 1971; Charles Reznikoff: A Critical Essay, 1977; The Worlds of Maurice Samuel, 1977; The Broken Music Box: Selected Poems, 1980; Charles Reznikoff: Man and Poet, 1984; Essays Personal and Impersonal, 1988. Add: c/o Black Sparrow Press, 24 10th St., Santa Rosa, Calif. 95401, U.S.A.

HINE, Daryl. Canadian, b. 1936. Novels/Short stories, Plays/Screenplays, Poetry, Travel/Exploration/Adventure, Translations. Asst. Prof. of English, Univ. of Chicago, 1967–69; Ed., Poetry, Chicago, 1968–78. *Publs:* Five Poems, 1955; The Carnal and the Crane, 1957; The Devil's Picture Book: Poems, 1960; The Prince of Darkness and Company (novel), 1961; Heroics: Five Poems, 1961; Polish Subtitles: Impressions of a Journey, 1962; The Wooden Horse: Poems, 1965; Minutes: Poems, 1968; The Death of Seneca (play), 1968; (trans.) The Homeric Hymns and the Battle of the Frogs and the Mice, 1972; Resident Alien: Poems, 1975; In and Out: Poems, 1975; Daylight Saving: Poems, 1978; (ed. with Joseph Parisi) The "Poetry" Anthology 1912–1977, 1978; Selected Poems, 1981; (trans.) Theocritus: Idylls and Epigrams, 1982; Academic Festival Overtures, 1985. Add: 2740 Ridge Ave., Evanston, Ill. 60201, U.S.A.

HINE, Robert V. American, b. 1921. History. Prof. of History, Univ. of California, Riverside (faculty member, since 1954). *Publs:* California's Utopian Colonies, 1953, 1973; (ed.) William Andrew Spalding, Los Angeles Newspaperman: An Autobiographical Account, 1961; Edward Kern and American Expansion, 1962; (reviser) The Irvine Ranch, by Robert Glass Cleland, 1962; (ed. with Edwin R. Bingham) The Frontier Experience: Readings in the Trans-Mississippi West, 1963, expanded and rev. as The American Frontier: Readings and Documents, 1972; Bartlett's West: Drawing the Mexican Boundary, 1968; (ed. with S. Lottinville) Soldier in the West: Letters of Theodore Talbot during his Services in California, Mexico, and Oregon, 1845-53, 1972; The American West: An Interpretive History, 1973, 2nd ed. 1984; Community on the American Frontier: Separate but Not Alone, 1980; California Utopianism: Contemplations of Eden, 1981. Add: Dept. of History, Univ. of California, Riverside, Calif. 92521, U.S.A.

HINES, (Melvin) Barry. British, b. 1939. Novels/Short stories, Plays/Screenplays. Teacher with L.C.C., 1960–62, and Barnsley Education Authority, Yorks., 1963–68; Yorkshire Arts Assn. Fellow, Univ. of Sheffield, 1972–74; East Midlands Arts Fellow in Creative Writing, Matlock Coll. of Education, 1975–77; Fellow in Creative Writing, Univ. of Wollongong, Australia, 1979. *Publs:* Billy's Last Stand, 1965; The Blinder, 1966; Continental Size Six, 1966; A Kestrel for a Knave, 1968; (with T. Garnett and Ken Loach) Kes (screenplay), 1968; First Signs, 1972; Speech Day, 1973; Gamekeeper, 1975; Two Men from Derby, 1976; The Price of Coal (two films), 1977; The Price of Coal (novel), 1979; Looks and Smiles (novel), 1981; Looks and Smiles (screenplay), 1981; Unfinished Business (novel), 1983; Threads (TV play), 1984. Add: 323 Fulwood Rd., Sheffield S10 3BJ, England.

HINES, Robert S. American, b. 1926. Music. Prof. of Music, since 1972, and Dean, Faculty of Arts and Humanities, since 1984, Univ. of Hawaii, Honolulu (Chmn. of Dept., 1980–84). Asst. Prof., Southern Illinois Univ., 1957–61; Prof., Wichita State Univ., Kans., 1961–71; Visiting Prof., Univ. of Miami, Fla., 1971–72. *Publs:* (ed.) The Composer's Point of View: Essays on 20th Century Choral Music, 1963; (ed.) The Orchestral Composer's Point of View: Essays on 20th Century Music, 1970; Singer's Manual of Latin Diction and Phonetics, 1975; (with A.R. Trubitt) Ear Training and Sight Singing: An Integrated Approach, vol. I 1979, vol. II 1980. Add: Univ. of Hawaii at Manoa, Hawaii Hall 103, Honolulu, Hawaii 96822, U.S.A.

HINSLEY, Sir (Francis) Harry. British, b. 1918. History, International relations. Master, St. John's Coll., Cambridge, 1979–89 (Fellow, 1944–79, and Pres., 1975–79, St. John's Coll.; Lectr., 1949–65, Reader, 1965–69, Prof. of Intnl. Relations, 1969–83, Chmn. of the Faculty Bd. of History, 1970–72, and Vice-Chancellor, 1981–83, Cambridge Univ.). Ed., Historical Journal, 1960–71. *Publs:* Command of the Sea, 1950; Hitler's Strategy, 1951; (ed.) New Cambridge Modern History, vol. II, 1962; Power and the Pursuit of Peace, 1963; Sovereignty, 1966; Nationalism and the International System, 1973; (ed.) British Foreign Policy under Sir Edward Grey, 1977; (co-author) British Intelligence in the Second World War, 4 vols., 1979–87. Add: The Master's Lodge, St. John's Coll., Cambridge, England.

HINSON, E. Glenn. American, b. 1931. Theology/Religion. Prof. of Church History, Southern Baptist Theological Seminary, Louisville, Ky., since 1962 (Instr. in New Testament, 1959–60, and in Church History, 1960–62); Prof. of Religion, Wake Forest Univ., 1982–84. Pastor, First Baptist Church, Eminence, Ind., 1957–59. *Publs:* The Church: Design for Survival, 1967; (co-author) Glossolalia, 1967; Seekers After Mature Faith, 1968; I and II Timothy and Titus, 1971; A Serious Call to a Contemplative Life Style, 1974; Soul Liberty, 1975; Jesus Christ, 1977; The Integrity of the Church, 1978; (ed.) Doubleday Devotional Classics, 3 vols., 1978; A History of Baptists in Arkansas, 1979; (ed.) The Early Church Fathers, 1980; The Evangelization of the Roman Empire, 1981; Are Southern Baptists Evangelicals?, 1982; Understandings of the Church, 1986. Add: Southern Baptist Theological Seminary, 2825 Lexington Rd., Louisville, Ky. 40206, U.S.A.

HINTIKKA, (Kaarlo) Jaakko (Juhani). Finnish, b. 1929. Philosophy. Prof. of Philosophy, Florida State Univ., since 1978, and Prof. of Computer Science, since 1986. Prof. of Philosophy, Univ. of Helsinki, 1959–70; Research Prof., Academy of Finland, 1970–81. Part-time Prof. of Philosophy, Stanford Univ., Calif., 1964–81. *Publs:* Distributive Normal Forms, 1953; Two Papers on Symbolic Logic, 1955; Knowledge and Belief, 1962; (ed. with P. Suppes) Aspects of Inductive Logic, 1966; Models for Modalities, 1969; Tieto on valtaa, 1969; (ed. with D. Davidson) Words and Objections, 1969; (ed.) Philosophy of Mathematics, 1969; (ed. with P. Suppes) Information and Inference, 1970; Logic, Language-

Games, and Information, 1973; Time and Necessity, 1973; (ed. with J. Moravcsik and P. Suppes) Approaches to Natural Language, 1973; Knowledge and the Known, 1974; (with U. Remes) The Method of Analysis, 1974; Induzione, accettazione, informazione, 1974; The Intentions of Intentionality, 1975; (ed.) Rudolph Carnap: Logical Empiricist, 1976; (ed. with others) Essays on Wittgenstein in Honor of G.H. von Wright, 1976; The Semantics of Questions and the Questions of Semantics, 1976; (ed. with R. Butts) Proceedings of the Fifth Intnl. Congress on Logic, Methodology and Philosophy of Science, 4 vols., 1977; Aristotle on Modality and Determinism, 1977; (co-ed.) Essays on Mathematical and Philosophical Logic, 1978; Kieli ja mieli, 1982; The Game of Language, 1983; (ed. with L. Vaina) Cognitive Constraints on Communication 1984; (with Jack Kulas) Anaphora and Definite Descriptions, 1985; (with Merrill B. Hintikka) Investigating Wittgenstein, 1986; (ed. with S. Knuuttila) The Logic of Being, 1986; (ed. with F. Vandamme) Logic of Discovery and Logic of Discourse, 1986; (ed. with L. Haarparanta) Frege Synthesized, 1987. Add: Dept. of Philosophy, Florida State University, Tallahassee, Fla. 33206, U.S.A.

HINTON, S(usan) E(loise). American, b. 1948. Children's fiction. *Publs:* The Outsiders, 1967; That Was Then, This Is Now, 1971; Rumble Fish, 1975; Tex, 1979; Taming the Star Runner, 1988. Add: c/o Delacorte Press, 1 Dag Hammarskjold Plaza, New York, N.Y. 10017, U.S.A.

HINTZE, Naomi A. American, b. 1909. Mystery/Crime/Suspense, Historical/Romance/Gothic, Children's fiction, Supernatural/Occult topics. *Publs:* Buried Treasure Waits for You (juvenile), 1962; You'll Like My Mother, 1969, in U.K. as The House with the Watching Eyes, 1970; The Stone Carnation, 1971; Aloha Means Goodbye, 1972, in U.K. as Hawaii for Danger, 1973; Listen, Please Listen, 1974; (with J.G. Pratt) The Psychic Realm: What Can You Believe, 1975; Cry Witch, 1975; (with Peter van der Linde) Time Bomb, 1976; The Ghost Child, 1983. Add: c/o McIntosh and Otis Inc., 310 Madison Ave., New York, N.Y. 10017, U.S.A.

HIRO, Dilip. Indian. Novels/Short stories, Plays/Screenplays, Poetry, International relations/Current affairs, Race relations. *Publs:* A Triangular View (novel), 1969; Black British, White British, 1971; To Anchor a Cloud (play), 1972; The Untouchables of India, 1975; Inside India Today, 1976; Apply, Apply, No Reply, and A Clean Break (plays), 1978; Interior, Exchange, Exterior (verse), 1980; Inside the Middle East, 1982; Iran under the Ayatollahs, 1985; Three Plays, 1987; Iran: The Revolution Within, 1988; Islamic Fundamentalism, 1988; The Longest War, 1989. Add: 31 Waldegrave Rd., Ealing, London W5 3HT, England.

HIRONS, Montague (John David). British, b. 1916. Biology, Botany, Natural history, Zoology. Sr. Lectr. in Biology and Environmental Studies, Berkshire Coll. of Education, Woodley, Reading, since 1968. *Publs:* (with G.A. Perry) Flowers of Common Trees, 1965; (with G.A. Perry) Fruits of Common Trees, 1965; (with G.A. Perry) Spring Flowers of Wood and Copses, 1965; (with G.A. Perry) Spring Flowers of Hedgerow and Roadside, 1965; (with G.A. Perry) Common Wild Flowers and Fruits, 1965; Insect Life of Farm and Garden, 1966; Progressive Biology: Books 1–3, 1967–70; (with A. Darlington) Pocket Encyclopedia of Plant Galls, 1968; (with G.J.M. Hirons) Farne Islands: The Problems of Soil Erosion, vol. 4, 1972. Add: Betula House, Bloxham, Banbury, Oxon, England.

HIRSCH, E(ric) D(onald), Jr. American, b. 1928. Literature. Kenan Prof. of English, since 1973, Univ. of Virginia, Charlottesville, (Prof., 1966–73, Chmn. of Dept., 1968–71, 1981–83). Served in the U.S. Navy, 1950–52; Instr. in English, 1956–60, Asst. Prof., 1960–63, and Assoc. Prof., 1963–66, Yale Univ., New Haven, Conn. Pres., Cultural Literacy Foundn., since 1987. *Publs:* Wordsworth and Schelling: A Typological Study of Romanticism, 1960, 1971; Innocence and Experience; an Introduction to Blake, 1964; Validity in Interpretation, 1966; The Aims of Interpretation, 1976; The Philosophy of Composition, 1977; Cultural Literacy: What Every American Needs to Know, 1987. Add: 2006 Pine Top Rd., Charlottesville, Va. 22903, U.S.A.

HIRSCH, S. Carl. American, b. 1913. Children's non-fiction. *Publs:* The Globe for the Space Age, 1963; This is Automation, 1964; Fourscore ... and More, 1965; The Living Community: A Venture in Ecology, 1966; Printing from Stone, 1967; On Course!, Navigating in Sea, Air, and Space, 1967, 1970; Cities are People, 1968; Mapmakers of America, 1969; Guardians of Tomorrow, 1971; Stilts, 1971; Meter Means Measure, 1972; The Riddle of Racism, 1973; Famous American Indians of the Plains, 1974; Famous American Heroes of the Revolution, 1975; Theatre of the Night, 1976; He and She, 1976. Add: 820-B Dodge Ave., Evanston, Ill. 60202,

U.S.A.

HIRSCH, Seev. Israeli, b. 1931. Business/Trade/Industry, Economics. Jaffee Prof., Tel-Aviv Univ., since 1981 (joined faculty 1965; Sr. Lectr., 1976–71; Head, Dept. of Accounting, 1966–68; Dean, Leon Recanati Grad. Sch. of Business Admin., 1970–73; Assoc. Prof., 1971–78; Prof., 1978–81). *Publs:* Location of Industry and International Competitiveness, 1967; Identification and Exploitation of the Export Potential of Industrial Firms in Israel, 1969; The Export Performance of Six Manufacturing Industries: A Comparative Study of Denmark, Holland and Israel, 1971; (with R.L. Ankum, H.C.C. Dekker, M.F. Koster and O. Wiberg) Profiles of Six Export Oriented Industries A & B, 1973; Rich Man's, Poor Man's, and Every Man's Goods, 1977; (with R. Arad and A. Tovias) The Economics of Peacemaking: Focus on the Egyptian-Israeli Situation, 1983. Add: Leon Recanati Grad. Sch. of Business Admin, Tel Aviv Univ., Tel Aviv, Israel.

HIRSCH, Werner Z. American, b. 1920. Economics, Mathematics/Statistics, Regional/Urban planning. Prof. of Economics, Univ. of California, Los Angeles, since 1963 (Dir., Inst. of Govt. and Public Affairs, 1963–73). Consultant, Rand Corp., since 1958; Member, Bd. of Dirs., California Council for Environmental and Economic Balance, since 1973. Fiscal Affairs Officer, U.N., 1951–52; Economist, Brookings Instn., Washington, D.C., 1952–53; Asst. Research Dir., St. Louis Metropolitan Survey, 1956–57; Economist, Resources for the Future Inc., Washington, D.C., 1958–59. Pres., Town Hall West, 1978. *Publs:* Introduction to Modern Statistics, 1957; (ed. and contrib.) Urban Life and Form, 1963; (ed.) Elements of Regional Accounts, 1964; (ed. and contrib. with R. Baisden) California's Future Economic Growth, 1965; (ed. and contrib.) Regional Accounts for Policy Decisions, 1966; (ed. and contrib.) Inventing Education for the Future, 1967; (with J.L. Kunen, L.J. Duhl and R. Park) Universities and Foundations Search for Relevance, 1968; (with E.W. Segelhorst and M.J. Marcus) Spillover on Public Education Costs and Benefits, 2nd ed. 1969; (ed. with S. Hale) Agenda for the Los Angeles Area in 1970, 1969; The Economics of State and Local Government, 1970; (with S. Sonenblum) Selecting Regional Information for Government Planning and Decision Making, 1970; (with P.E. Vincent, H.S. Terrell, D.C. Shoup and A. Rosett) Fiscal Pressures on the Central City: The Impact of Commuters, Nonwhites, and Overlapping Governments, 1971; (ed. and contrib.) Los Angeles: Viability and Prospects for Metropolitan Leadership, 1971; (with M.J. Marcus and R.M. Gay) Program Budgeting for Primary and Secondary Public Education, 1972; (ed. and contrib. with S. Sonenblum) Governing Urban America in the 1970s, 1973; Financing Public First-Level and Second-Level Education in the U.S., 1973; Urban Economic Analysis, 1973; (with S. Sonenblum and R. Teoples) Local Government Program Budgeting: Theory and Practice, 1974; Recent Experience with National Planning in the United Kingdom, 1977; Law and Economics: An Introductory Analysis, 1979; (with Robert Ferber) Social Experimentation and Economic Policy, 1982; Urban Economics, 1984. Add: 11601 Bellagio Rd., Los Angeles, Calif. 90049, U.S.A.

HIRSCHHORN, Clive. South African, b. 1940. Film, Biography. Drama Critic, Sunday Express, London, since 1969 (Film Critic, 1966–69). Story Ed., ABC-TV, 1963–64; Pop Columnist, Daily Mail, London, 1964–65. *Publs:* Gene Kelly, 1974, 1984; The Films of James Mason, 1975; The Warner Bros. Story, 1979; The Hollywood Musical, 1981; The Universal Story, 1983. Add: 42D South Audley St., Mayfair, London W1, England.

HIRSCHMAN, Jack. American, b. 1933. Poetry, Translations. Painter and collage-maker. Instr., Dartmouth Coll., Hanover, N.H., 1959–61; Asst. Prof., Univ. of California, Los Angeles, 1961–66. *Publs:* Fragments, 1952; A Correspondence of Americans, 1960; Two, 1963; Interchange, 1964; Kline Sky, 1965; (ed.) Artaud Anthology, 1965; Yod, 1966; London Seen Directly, 1967; Wasn't It Like This in the Woodcut, 1967; William Blake, 1967; (with Asa Benveniste) A Word in Your Season, 1967; Ltd. Interchangeable in Eternity: Poems of Jackruthdavidcelia Hirschman, 1967; Jerusalem: A Three Part Poem, 1968; Aleph, Benoni and Zaddick, 1968; Jerusalem, Ltd., 1968; Shekinah, 1969; Broadside Golem, 1969; Black Alephs: Poems 1960–68, 1969; NHR, 1970; Scintilla, 1970; (trans. with V. Erlich) Electric Iron, by Vladimir Mayakovsky, 1970; Soledeth, 1971; DT, 1971; The Burning of Los Angeles, 1971; HNYC, 1971; (trans.) Love Is a Tree, by Antonin Artaud, 1972; (trans.) A Rainbow for the Christian West, by René Depestre, 1972; Les Vidanges, 1972; The R of the Ari's Raziel, 1972; Adamnan, 1972; (trans.) The Exiled Angel, by Luisa Pasamanik, 1973; (trans.) Igitur, by Stéphane Mallarmé, 1973; (trans.) Wail for the Arat Beggars of the Casbah, by Ait Djafer, 1973; Aur Sea, 1973; Cantillations, 1973; Djackson,

1974; Cockroach Street, 1975; The Cool Boyetz Cycle, 1975; Kashtaninyah Segodnyah, 1976; Lyripol, 1976; The Arcanes of Le Compte de St. Germain, 1977; The Jonestown Arcane, 1979; The Cagliostro Arcane, 1981; The David Arcane, 1982; Kallatumba, 1984; The Necessary Is, 1984; The Bottom Line, 1988. Add: P.O. Box 26517, San Francisco, Calif. 94126, U.S.A.

HIRST, Paul Quentin. British, b. 1946. Sociology. Prof. of Social Theory, Birkbeck Coll., Univ. of London, since 1986 (Lectr. in Sociology, 1969–78; Reader in Social Theory, 1978–86). *Publs:* Durkheim, Bernard and Epistemology, 1975; (with B. Hindess) Pre-Capitalist Modes of Production, 1975; Social Evolution and Sociological Categories, 1976; (with B. Hindess) Mode of Production and Social Formations, 1977; (with others) Marx's Capital and Capitalism Today, 2 vols., 1977–78; (with P. Woolley) Social Relations and Human Attributes, 1982; Marxism and Historical Writing, 1985; Law, Socialism, and Democracy, 1986. Add: Dept. of Politics and Sociology, Birkbeck Coll., Univ. of London, Malet St., London WC1, England.

HISCOCKS, (Charles) Richard. British, b. 1907. International relations/Current affairs, Politics/Government. Emeritus Prof., Univ. of Sussex, Brighton, since 1972 (Prof. of Intnl. Relations, 1964–72). Vice-Pres., U.N. Assn. of the U.K. Prof. of Political Science and Intnl. Relations, Univ. of Manitoba, Winnipeg, 1950–64; U.K. Member, U.N. Sub-Commn. on Discrimination and Minorities, 1952–62. *Publs:* The Rebirth of Austria, 1953; Democracy in Western Germany, 1957; (with E. McInnis and R. Spencer) The Shaping of Post-War Germany, 1960; Poland: Bridge for the Abyss?, 1963; Germany Revived, 1966; The Work of the United Nations for the Prevention of Discrimination in "Die moderne Demokatie und ihr Recht", 1966; The Security Council: A Study in Adolescence, 1973. Add: Dickers, Hunworth, Melton Constable, Norfolk, England.

HITCHCOCK, George (Parks). American, b. 1914. Novels/Short stories, Plays/Screenplays, Poetry. Lectr. in Literature, Univ. of California, Santa Cruz. Ed. and Publr., Kayak mag. and Kayak Books, San Francisco, later Santa Cruz. *Publs:* (with Mel Fowler) Poems and Prints, 1962; The Busy Martyr (play), 1962; Tactics of Survival and Other Poems, 1964; The Dolphin with the Revolver in Its Teeth, 1967; The One Whose Approach I Cannot Evade, 1967; Two Poems, 1967; (with R. Peters) Pioneers of Modern Poetry, 1967; A Ship of Bells: Poems, 1968; (ed.) Losers Weepers: Poems Found Practically Anywhere, 1969; Twelve Stanzas in Praise of the Holy Chariot, 1969; The Rococo Eye, 1970; Another Shore (novel), 1972; The Counterfeit Rose (play), 1975; Lessons in Alchemy, 1976; The Piano Beneath the Skin, 1978; Five Plays, 1981; The Wounded Alphabet, 1983; October at the Lighthouse, 1984; Cloud Taxis, 1985. Add: 325 Ocean View, Santa Cruz, Calif. 95062, U.S.A.

HITCHCOCK, Raymond John. British, b. 1922. Novels, TV Plays. *Publs:* Percy, 1969; Gilt-Edged Boy, 1971; Venus 13, 1972; Attack the Lusitania, 1979; Sea Wrack, 1980; Archangel 006, 1984; The Tunnellers, 1986; Checkmate Budapest, 1988. Add: Abbots Worthy Mill, Winchester, Hants, England.

HIVNOR, Robert. American, b. 1916. Plays/Screenplays. Political cartoonist and commercial artist, 1934–38; Instr., Univ. of Minnesota, Minneapolis, 1946–48; Instr., Reed Coll., Portland, Ore., 1945–55; Asst. Prof., Bard Coll., Annandale-on-Hudson, N.Y., 1956–59. *Publs:* Too Many Thumbs, 1948; The Ticklish Acrobat, 1954; The Assault upon Charles Sumner, 1964; Love Reconciled to War, 1968. Add: 420 East 84th St., New York, N.Y. 10028, U.S.A.

HJORTSBERG, William. American, b. 1941. Novels/Short stories. *Publs:* Alp, 1969; Gray Matters, 1971; Symbiography (novella), 1973; Toro! Toro! Toro!, 1974; Falling Angel, 1978; Tales and Fables (short stories), 1985. Add: Main Boulder Rte., McLeod, Mont. 59052, U.S.A.

HOAGLAND, Edward. American, b. 1932. Novels, Travel, Essays. Part-time teacher, Rutgers Univ., New Brunswick, N.J., Sarah Lawrence, Bronxville, N.Y., City Coll. of New York, New Sch. for Social Research, NYC, Columbia Univ., NYC, Univ. of Iowa, Iowa City, Brown Univ., Providence, RI, and Bennington Coll., Vermont, since 1963. *Publs:* Cat Man, 1956; The Circle Home, 1960; The Peacock's Tail, 1965; Notes from the Century Before: A Journal from British Columbia, 1969; The Courage of Turtles (essays), 1971; Walking the Dead Diamond River, 1973; The Moose on the Wall: Field Notes from the Vermont Wilderness, 1974; Red Wolves and Black Bears, 1976; African Calliope: A Journey to the Sudan, 1979; The Edward Hoagland Reader, 1979; The Tugman's Passage (essays), 1982; Seven Rivers West (novel), 1986; City Tales

(stories), 1986; Hearts Desire (essays), 1988. Add: P.O. Box 51, Barton, VT 05822, U.S.A.

HOARE, Merval Hannah. New Zealander, b. 1914. Poetry, History. *Publs:* Twelve Poems, 1943; Twenty-Eight Poems, 1951; Norfolk Island Poems, 1951; Rambler's Guide to Norfolk Island, 1965, 7th ed., 1982; Norfolk Island: An Outline of Its History, 1969, 4th ed. 1988; The Discovery of Norfolk Island, 1974; Norfolk Island: A History Through Illustration 1774-1974, 1979; The Winds of Change: Norfolk Island 1950–1982, 1983. Add: New Cascade Rd., Norfolk Island, South Pacific.

HOBAN, Russell. American, b. 1925. Novels/Short stories, Science fiction, Children's fiction. Freelance writer and illustrator. *Publs:* What Does It Do and How Does It Work, 1959; The Atomic Submarine, 1960; Bedtime for Frances, 1960; Herman the Loser, 1961; London Men and English Men, 1962; The Song in My Drum, 1962; Some Snow Said Hello, 1963; The Sorely Trying Day, 1964; A Baby Sister for Frances, 1964; Nothing to Do, 1964; Bread and Jam for Frances, 1964; Tom and the Two Handles, 1965; The Story of Hester Mouse, 1965; What Happened When Jack and Daisy Tried to Fool the Tooth Fairies, 1966; Goodnight, 1966; Henry and the Monstrous Din, 1966; The Little Brute Family, 1966; Save My Place, 1967; Charlie the Tramp, 1967; The Mouse and His Child, 1967; Birthday for Frances, 1968; The Pedaling Man and Other Poems, 1968; The Stone Doll of Sister Brute, 1968; Harvey's Hideout, 1969; (with S. Selig) Ten What? 1974; How to Beat Captain Najork and His Hired Sportsmen, 1974; Kleinzeit (adult novel), 1974; Turtle Diary (adult novel), 1975; Dinner at Alberta's, 1975; (with Quentin Blake) A Near Thing for Captain Najork, 1975; (with S. Selig) Crocodile and Pierrot, 1975; The Dancing Tigers, 1978; Arthur's New Power, 1978; The Twenty-Elephant Restaurant, 1978; La Corona and the Tin Frog, 1979; Riddley Walker (adult novel), 1980; Flat Cat, 1980; Ace Dragon Ltd., 1980; The Serpent Tower, 1981; The Great Fruit Gum Robbery, 1981; They Came from Aargh!, 1981; The Battle of Zormla, 1982; The Flight of Bembel Rudzuk, 1982; Pilgermann (adult novel), 1983; Ponders, 4 vols., 1983–84; The Rain Door, 1986; The Marzipan Pig, 1986; The Medusa Frequency (adult novel), 1987. Add: c/o David Higham Assocs., 5-8 Lower John St., London W1R 4HA, England.

HOBBS, Cecil. American, b. 1907. History, Travel/Exploration/Adventure. Consultant on Southeast Asia, Library of Congress, Washington, D.C. since 1972 (Head, Southern Asia Section, and Specialist on Southeast Asia, 1943–72). Member, Bd. of Contributing Consultants, Intnl. Library Review, since 1968, and Member, Intnl. Advisory Bd., Southeast Asia Quarterly, since 1969. Chmn., Cttee. of American Library Resources on Southeast Asia, 1965–70; Assoc. Dir., Conference on Access to Southeast Asia Research Materials, 1969–70; Consultant to Vietnamese Studies, Southern Illinois Univ., 1969–72; Consultant on Southeast Asia, Australian National Univ. Library, Canberra, 1972–73; Consultant on Southeast Asia Studies, National Library of Australia, 1973. *Publs:* Southeast Asia 1935–45, 1946; Report on a Field Trip in Southeast Asia, 1948; (co-author) Indochina: A Bibliography of the Land and People, 1950; An Account of an Acquisition Trip in the Countries of Southeast Asia, 1952; The Burmese Family: An Inquiry into Its History, Customs and Traditions, 1952; Southeast Asia: An Annotated Bibliography, 1952; Account of a Trip to the Countries of Southeast Asia 1952-53, 1953; Channels of Procurement of Publications in Southeast Asia, 1957; Southeast Asia Publication Sources, 1958–59, 1960; Southeast Asia: An Annotated Bibliography of Selected References Sources, 1964; Understanding the Peoples of Southern Asia, 1967; Account of a Trip to the Countries of Southeast Asia, 1965, 1967; (ed.) Conference on Access to Southeast Asia Field Trip for the Library of Congress, 1970–71, 1972; (ed.) Southeast Asia Subject Catalog, 6 vols., 1972; Southeast Asia Materials in the Australian National University Library: A Programme for Development and Use, 1975; Southeast Asian Area Studies and the Library of Congress: Selected Recollections, 1977; Southeast Asia: A Bibliography of Writings 1942–1978, 1980. Add: Hobbs Knob, 5100 Backlick Rd., Annandale, Va. 22003, U.S.A.

HOBBS, Herschel H. American, b. 1907. Theology/Religion. Pastor, First Baptist Church, Oklahoma City, Okla., 1949–73, now Emeritus. Preacher, Intnl. Baptist Hour (radio), 1958–76. Pres., Southern Baptist Convention 1961–63; Vice-Pres., Baptist World Alliance 1965–70. *Publs:* has published more than 121 books since 1951, the most recent of which are: The Cosmic Drama, 1971; The Gospel of Mark, a Study Guide, 1971; The Baptist Faith and Message, 1971; How to Follow Jesus, 1971; (ed. with H. Franklin Paschall) The Teacher's Bible Commentary, 1972; Showers of Blessings, 1973; New Men in Christ, 1974; Studying Adult Life and Work Lessons, 79 vols., 1968–88. Add: 2509 N.W. 120th

St., Oklahoma City, Okla, 73120, U.S.A.

HOBHOUSE, Hermione. British, b. 1934. Architecture. Freelance journalist, reviewer and lectr.; Gen. Ed., Survey of London, since 1983. Researcher and Scriptwriter, Associated-Rediffusion Television, 1956–58, and Granada Television, 1958–63; Part-time Tutor, Architectural Assn. Sch., London, 1973–79. *Publs:* The Ward of Cheap in the City of London: A Short History, 1963; Thomas Cubitt: Master Builder, 1971; Lost London, 1971; History of Regent Street, 1975; Oxford and Cambridge, 1980; Prince Albert: His Life and Work, 1983; Survey of London, Vol. XLII: Southern Kensington, 1986. Add: 61 St. Dunstan's Rd., London W6 8RE, England.

HOBLEY, Leonard Frank. British, b. 1903. Children's non-fiction, Geography, History, Travel/Exploration/Adventure. Schoolmaster, Brighton, Sussex, 1929–63. *Publs:* (with P. Leyden) Story Path to Reading, 1952; Early Explorers, 1954; Opening Africa, 1955; Exploring America, 1955; Exploring the Pacific, 1957; A City in Peril, 1958; Roman or Briton, 1959; Friends Divided, 1960; Britain's Place in the World, 1960; (with G.R. Davis) How to Use an Atlas, 1960; Active Geographies: The British Isles, 1964; Living and Working: An Economic History, 1964; Geography Through Maps, 1965; The Fire Service, 1968; The Early Twentieth Century, 1968; The Story of the Police, 1969; The Trade Union Story, 1969; Working Class and Democratic Movements, 1970; Introducing Earth, 9 vols., 1970–71; The First World War, 1971; The Second World War, 1971; The Town Councillor, 1972; The Farmer, 1972; The Monarchy, 1972; Customs and Excise Men, 1974; Ancient Greece, 1975; The Stuarts, 1975; The Eighteenth Century, 1975; The Nineteenth Century, 1975; 1900–1939, 1976; Since 1945, 1977; Doubts and Affirmations, 1978; Moslems and Islam, 1979; Christians and Christianity, 1979; Jews and Judaism, 1979; Steps in History, books 1-3, 1982–83. Add: 45 Orchard Gardens, Hove, Sussex BN3 7BH, England.

HOBSBAUM, Philip (Dennis). British, b. 1932. Poetry, Literature. Titular Prof. of English Literature, Univ. of Glasgow, since 1985 (Lectr., 1966–72; Sr. Lectr., 1972–79; Reader, 1979–85). Ed., Delta, Cambridge, 1954–55; Co-Ed., Poetry from Sheffield, 1959–61; Lectr. in English, Queen's Univ., Belfast, 1962–66. *Publs:* (ed. with Edward Lucie-Smith) A Group Anthology, 1963; The Place's Fault and Other Poems, 1964; Snapshots, 1965; In Retreat and Other Poems, 1966; (ed.) Ten Elizabethan Poets, 1969; Coming Out Fighting, 1969; Some Lovely Glorious Nothing, 1969; A Theory of Communication: A Study of Value in Literature (in U.S. as Theory of Criticism), 1970; Women and Animals, 1972; A Reader's Guide to Charles Dickens, 1973; Tradition and Experiment in English Poetry, 1979; A Reader's Guide to D.H. Lawrence, 1981; Essentials of Literary Criticism, 1983; A Reader's Guide to Robert Lowell, 1988; (ed.) Wordsworth: Selected Poetry and Prose, 1989. Add: Dept. of English, Univ. of Glasgow, Glasgow, Scotland.

HOBSBAWM, Eric (John Ernest). Also writes as Francis Newton. British, b. 1917. History, Music. Emeritus Prof. of Economic and Social History, Birkbeck Coll., Univ. of London. Fellow, King's Coll., Cambridge, 1949–55. *Publs:* Labour's Turning Point, 1948; Primitive Rebels, 1959; (as Francis Newton) The Jazz Scene, 1959; The Age of Revolution, 1962; Labouring Men, 1964; (ed.) Karl Marx, Precapitalist Economic Formations, 1964; Industry and Empire, 1968; Bandits, 1969; (with G. Rudé) Captain Swing: A Social History of the Great English Uprising, 1969; Revolutionaries, 1973; The Age of Capital, 1975; Worlds of Labour, 1984; The Age of Empire, 1987. Add: Birkbeck Coll., Univ. of London, Malet St., London WC1, England.

HOBSON, Anthony Robert Alwyn. British, b. 1921. Crafts, Librarianship. Dir., 1949–71, and Assoc., 1971–77, Sotheby and Co., London; Sandars Reader in Bibliography, Univ. of Cambridge, 1973–74. *Publs:* French and Italian Collectors and Their Bindings, 1953; Great Libraries, 1970; Apollo and Pegasus (history of the library of G.B. Grimaldi), 1975. Add: The Glebe House, Whitsbury, Fordingbridge, Hants., England.

HOBSON, Fred Colby (Jr). American, b. 1943. Literature. Prof. of English, and Co-Ed. of Southern Review, Louisiana State Univ., Baton Rouge, since 1986. Assoc. Prof. to Prof. of English, Univ. of Alabama, Tuscaloosa, 1972–86. Former Editorial Writer, Journal and Sentinel, Winston-Salem, N.C. Co-Recipient, Pulitzer Prize, 1970*Publs:* Serpent in Eden: H.L. Mencken and the South, 1974; Southern Mythmaking: The Savage and the Ideal, 1978; (co-ed.) Literature at the Barricades: The American Writer in the 1930's, 1982; (ed.) South-Watching: Selected Essays of Gerald W. Johnson, 1982; Tell About the South: The Southern Rage to Explain, 1983. Add: Dept. of English, Louisiana State Univ., Baton Rouge, La. 70803, U.S.A.

HOBSON, (Sir) Harold. British, b. 1904. Novels/Short stories, Theatre, Autobiography/Memoirs/Personal. Special Writer, The Sunday Times, London, since 1976 (Drama Critic, 1947–76). TV Critic, The Listener, London, 1947–51. *Publs:* The First Three Years of the War, 1942; The Devil in Woodford Wells (novel), 1946; Theatre, 1948; Theatre II, 1950; Verdict at Midnight, 1952; The Theatre Now, 1953; The French Theatre of Today, 1953; (ed.) The International Theatre Annual, 1956–60; Ralph Richardson, 1958; (co-author) The Pearl of Days: An Intimate Memoir of the Sunday Times, 1972; The French Theatre from 1830 Onwards, 1977; Indirect Journey (autobiography), 1978; Theatre in Britain, 1984. Add: Nyton House, Nyton Rd., Westergate, Chichester, W. Sussex, England.

HOBSON, Mary. British, b. 1926. Novels/Short stories. *Publs:* This Place Is a Madhouse, 1980; Oh Lily, 1981; Poor Tom, 1982. Add: 63 Horniman Dr., Forest Hill, London SE23, England.

HOBSON, Polly. *See* EVANS, Julia.

HOCH, Edward D. American, b. 1930. Mystery/Crime/Suspense. With Pocket Books Inc., NYC, 1952–54; Copy Writer, Hutchins Advertising Co., Rochester, N.Y., 1954–68. Pres., Mystery Writers of America, 1982. *Publs:* The Shattered Raven, 1969; The Judges of Hades (stories), 1971; The Transvection Machine, 1971; The Spy and the Thief (stories), 1972; City of Brass, 1972; (ed.) Dear Dead Days, 1972; The Fellowship of the Hand, 1973; The Frankenstein Factory, 1975; (ed.) Best Detective Stories of the Year, 6 vols., 1976–81; The Thefts of Nick Velvet (stories), 1978; (ed.) Year's Best Mystery and Suspense Stories, 9 vols., 1982–89; (ed.) All But Impossible, 1981; The Quests of Simon Ark, 1984; Leopold's Way, 1985. Add: 2941 Lake Ave., Rochester, N.Y. 14612, U.S.A.

HOCHMAN, Sandra. American, b. 1936. Novels/Short stories, Children's fiction, Plays/Screenplays, Poetry. Actress. *Publs:* Voyage Home: Poems, 1960; Manhattan Pastures, 1963; The World of Gunter Grass (play), 1966; The Vaudeville Marriage: Poems, 1966; Love Poems, 1966; Love Letters from Asia: Poems, 1968; Earthworks: Poems 1960–70, 1971; Walking Papers (novel), 1971; The Magic Convention (children's fiction), 1971; Year of the Woman (screenplay), 1973; Futures: New Poems, 1974; Happiness Is Too Much Trouble (novel), 1976; Explosion of Loneliness (play), 1977; Endangered Species (novel), 1977; Streams: Life-Secrets for Writing Poems and Songs, 1978; Jogging (novel), 1979; Playing Tahoe (novel), 1981. Add: c/o Yale Univ. Press, 302 Temple St., New Haven, Conn. 06520, U.S.A.

HOCHWALD, Werner. American, b. 1910. Economics. Tileston Prof. of Political Economy, Washington Univ., St. Louis, since 1958 (Instr. in Economics, 1945–47; Asst. Prof., 1947–49; Assoc. Prof., 1949–50; Prof., 1950–58; Chmn. of Dept. 1950–63). Project Dir., National Planning Assn., 1955–58; Kennedy Distinguished Prof. of Economics, Univ. of the South, 1980–81. Pres., Southern Economic Assn., 1966–67. *Publs:* (co-author) Local Impact of Foreign Trade, 1960; (ed.) Design of Regional Accounts, 1961; An Economist's Image of History, 1968; The Rationality Concept in Economic Analysis, 1971; The Idea of Progress, 1973; (with others) Encyclopedia of Economics, 1981. Add: 6910 Cornell Ave., University City, Mo. 63130, U.S.A.

HOCKETT, Charles F(rancis). American, b. 1916. Anthropology/Ethnology, Language/Linguistics. Goldwin Smith Prof. Emeritus of Linguistics and Anthropology, Cornell Univ., Ithaca, N.Y., since 1982 (joined faculty, 1946). Pres., Linguistic Soc. of America, 1964. Pres., Linguistic Assn. of Canada and the United States, 1982. *Publs:* (with C. Fang) Spoken Chinese, 1944; (ed. with C. Fang) Dictionary of Spoken Chinese, 1946; A Manual of Phonology, 1955; A Course in Modern Linguistics, 1958; (with R.L. Pittenger and J.J. Danehy) The First Five Minutes: An Example of Microscopic Interview Analysis, 1960; The State of the Art, 1967; Man's Place in Nature, 1973; (composer and co-librettist) Doña Rosita (opera), 1973; Refurbishing Our Foundations, 1986. Add: 145 N. Sunset Dr., Ithaca, N.Y. 14850, U.S.A.

HOCKING, Anthony. British, b. 1938. Economics, Marketing (Market research). Reader in Economics, Univ. of Tasmania, Hobart, since 1978 (Lectr., 1962–69; Sr. Lectr., 1970–77). Member, Tasmanian Consumer Affairs Council, 1971–88. Chmn., Tasmanian Apple and Pear Marketing Advisory Cttee., 1978–79. *Publs:* (co-author) Economics Institutions and Policy, 1969; Outcome of Income: Economics and Society, 1972; United Kingdom Demand for Southern Hemisphere Apples, 1971; Investigating Economics, 1975, 1980; (co-author) Teaching Economics: A Guide to Investigating Economics, 1975; Shaping the Apple Industry, 1979; (co-author) Investigation Economics, 1984; (co-author) Economics,

1989; (co-author) Micro Economics, 1989. Add: Economics Dept., Univ. of Tasmania, Hobart, Tasmania, Australia.

HOCKING, Mary (Eunice). British, b. 1921. Novels/Short stories. Local Govt. Officer, 1946–70. *Publs:* The Winter City, 1961; Visitors to the Crescent, 1962; The Sparrow, 1964; The Young Spaniard, 1965; Ask No Question, 1967; A Time of War, 1968; Checkmate, 1969; The Hopeful Traveller, 1970; The Climbing Frame, 1971; Family Circle, 1972; Daniel Come to Judgement, 1974; The Bright Day, 1975; The Mind Has Mountains, 1976; Look Stranger, 1979; He Who Plays the King, 1980; March House, 1981; Good Daughters, 1984; Indifferent Heroes, 1985; Welcome Strangers, 1986; An Irrelevant Woman, 1987. Add: 3 Church Row, Lewes, Sussex, England.

HOCKNEY, David. British, b. 1937. Art. *Exhibitions:* one-man shows—Kasmin Ltd., London, 1963, 1965, 1966, 1968, 1969, 1970, 1972, 1976; Alan Gallery, NYC, 1964–67; Stedlijk Museum, Amsterdam, 1966; Whitworth Gallery, Manchester, 1969; Whitechapel Art Gallery, London (retrospective), 1970; Emmerich Gallery, NYC, 1970, 1972; Galerie Springer, Berlin, 1970; Kunsthalle Bielefeld, 1971; Musée des Arts Decoratifs, Paris, 1974; Michael Walls Gallery, NYC, 1974; Galerie Claude Bernard, Paris, 1975; "Paper Pools," Andre Emmerich Gallery, NYC, and Warehouse Gallery, London, 1979; "Travels with Pen, Pencil, and Ink," touring U.S.A., 1978–80, and Tate Gallery, London, 1980; Hayward Gallery (retrospective), 1983. *Publs:* (ed. and illustrator) 14 Poems of C.P. Cavafy, 1967; (illustrator) Six Fairy Tales of the Brothers Grimm, 1969; Hockney on Hockney, 1976; (illustrator) The Blue Guitar, 1977; Travels with Pen, Pencil, and Ink, 1978; Paper Pools, 1980; (with Stephen Spender) China Diary, 1982; Hockney Paints the Stage, 1983; David Hockney: Cameraworks, 1984; David Hockney: A Retrospective, 1988. Add: c/o 7506 Santa Monica Blvd., Los Angeles, Calif. 90046, U.S.A.

HODDER-WILLIAMS, (John) Christopher (Glazebrook). Also writes as James Brogan. British, b. 1926. Mystery/Crime/Suspense, Science fiction/Fantasy. Worked in Africa after World War II; worked in England for film, television, and recording companies; also composer. *Publs:* (as James Brogan) The Cummings Report (suspense), 1958; Chain Reaction, 1959; Final Approach (suspense), 1960; Turbulence (suspense), 1961; The Higher They Fly (suspense), 1963; The Main Experiment, 1964; The Egg-Shaped Thing, 1967; Fistful of Digits, 1968; 98.4, 1969; Panic O'Clock, 1973; The Prayer Machine, 1976; The Silent Voice, 1977; The Thinktank That Leaked, 1979; The Chromosome Game, 1984. Add: c/o Weidenfeld and Nicolson Ltd., 91 Clapham High St., London SW4, England.

HODDINOTT, R(alph) F(ield). British, b. 1913. Archaeology/Antiquities, Architecture, Art, History. Worked for the British Council, Athens, 1939–41, UNRRA, 1945–47, Intnl. Refugee Org., 1947–52, and in government, 1955–67; now retired. *Publs:* Early Byzantine Churches in Macedonia and Southern Serbia, 1963; Bulgaria in Antiquity, 1975; The Thracians, 1981; (co-author) The New Thracian Treasure from Rogozen, Bulgaria, 1986. Add: 11 Sydney House, Woodstock Rd., Bedford Park, London W4 1DP, England.

HODEMART, Peter. *See* **AUDEMARS,** Pierre.

HODGART, Matthew (John Caldwell). British, b. 1916. Novel/Short stories, Literature, Biography. Fellow, Pembroke Coll., Cambridge, and Lectr. in English, Univ. of Cambridge, 1949–64; Prof. of English, Univ. of Sussex, Brighton, 1964–70; Prof. of English, Concordia Univ., Montreal, 1970–77, La Trobe Univ., Melbourne, 1979–80, and Johns Hopkins Univ., Baltimore, 1981. *Publs:* The Ballads, 1950; (with M. Worthington) Song in the Works of James Joyce, 1959; Samuel Johnson, 1962; (ed.) Horace Walpole: Memoirs, 1963; (ed.) Faber Book of Ballads, 1965; Satire, 1969; A New Voyage (fiction), 1969; (ed.) John Ruskin: Selections, 1972; James Joyce: Students' Guide, 1978. Add: 13 Montpelier Villas, Brighton BN1 3DG, England.

HODGE, Francis. American, b. 1915. Theatre. Prof. Emeritus, Dept. of Drama, Univ. of Texas, Austin, since 1979 (Asst. Prof., 1949–55; Assoc. Prof., 1955–62; Prof., 1962–79). Instr. Carroll Coll., Waukesha, Wisc., 1940–42; Instr., Cornell Univ., Ithaca, N.Y., 1946–48; Asst. Prof., Univ. of Iowa, Iowa City, 1948–49; Summer Instr., Univ. of Colorado, 1961, Banff Sch. of Fine Art, 1962–68, Univ. of British Columbia, 1963. Ed., Educational Theatre Journal, Washington, D.C. 1966–68. *Publs:* Yankee Theatre, 1964; Play Directing, 1971, 3rd ed., 1988; (ed.) Innovations in Stage and Theatre Design, 1972. Add: 1109 Bluebonnet Lane, Austin, Tex. 78704, U.S.A.

HODGE, Jane Aiken. British, b. 1917. Historical/Romance/Gothic, Biography. Member, British Bd. of Trade, British Supply Council, North America, 1942–44; with Time Inc., NYC, 1944–47, and Life mag., London, 1947–48. *Publs:* Maulever Hall, 1964; The Adventures, 1965; Watch the Wall, My Darling, 1966; Here Comes a Candle, 1967, in U.S. as The Master of Penrose, 1968; The Winding Stair, 1968; Marry in Haste, 1969; Greek Wedding, 1970; Savannah Purchase, 1971; Only a Novel: The Double Life of Jane Austen, 1972; Strangers in Company, 1973; Shadow of a Lady, 1973; One Way to Venice, 1974; Runaway Bride, 1975; Rebel Heiress, 1975; Judas Flowering, 1976; Red Sky at Night, 1977; Last Act, 1979; Wide Is the Water, 1981; The Lost Garden, 1982; The Private World of Georgette Heyer, 1984; Secret Island, 1985; Polonaise, 1987; First Night, 1989. Add: 23 Eastport Lane, Lewes, Sussex BN7 1TL, England.

HODGE, Paul William. American, b. 1934. Astronomy, Physics. Prof., Univ. of Washington, since 1965. Lectr., Harvard Univ., Cambridge, Mass., 1960–61; Asst. Prof., Univ. of California, Berkeley, 1961–65. *Publs:* (with J.C. Brandt) Solar System Astrophysics, 1963; Galaxies and Cosmology, 1965; (with F.W. Wright) The Large Magellanic Cloud, 1966; An Atlas and Catalog of HII Regions in Galaxies, 1966; Concepts of the Universe, 1967; The Revolution in Astronomy, 1969; Slides for Astronomy, 1971; Concepts of Contemporary Astronomy, 1974; (with F.W. Wright) The Small Magellanic Cloud, 1978; An Atlas of the Andromeda Galaxy, 1981; Interplanetary Dust, 1981; (with R.C. Kennicutt) HII Regions in Galaxies, 1982; (ed.) Galaxies and the Universe, 1984; Galaxies, 1986; The Andromeda Galaxy, 1989. Add: Dept. of Astronomy, Univ. of Washington, Seattle, Wash. 98195, U.S.A.

HODGES, C(yril) Walter. British, b. 1909. Historical novels, Children's fiction, Theatre. Stage and exhibition designer, mural painter, and freelance book, mag. and advertisement illustrator, since 1931. *Publs:* Columbus Sails, 1939; The Flying House: A Story of High Adventure (in U.S. as Sky High: The Story of a House That Flew), 1947; Shakespeare and the Players, 1948; The Globe Restored: A Study of the Elizabethan Theatre, 1953, 1968; The Globe Playhouse 1599-1613, 1969; The Namesake, 1964; Shakespeare's Theatre, 1964; The Norman Conquest, 1966; Magna Carta, 1966; The Spanish Armada, 1967; The Marsh King, 1967; The Overland Launch, 1969; The English Civil War (in U.S. as The Puritan Revolution), 1972; Shakespeare's Second Globe: The Missing Monument, 1973; Playhouse Tales, 1974; The Emperor's Elephant, 1975; Plain Lane Christmas, 1978; The Battlement Garden, 1979; (co-ed.) The Third Globe, 1981. Add: 36 Southover High St., Lewes, Sussex, England.

HODGES, Donald Clark. American, b. 1923. History, Politics/Government, Sociology. Prof. of Philosophy, since 1964, and Dir. of Latin American and Caribbean Studies, since 1987, Florida State Univ., Tallahassee, (Chmn., Dept. of Philosophy, 1964–69; Dir., Center for Grad. and Postgrad. Studies in Social Philosophy, 1967–71). Assoc. Prof. of Philosophy, Univ. of Missouri, 1957–63; Prof. of Philosophy, Univ. of South Florida, Tampa, 1963–64; Prof. of Sociology, Univ. of Buenos Aires, 1974–75. *Publs:* (ed. with K.T. Fann) Readings in U.S. Imperialism, 1971; (ed. with A. Shanab) National Liberation Fronts 1960–1970; 1972; (ed. and trans.) Philosophy of the Urban Guerrilla, 1973; Socialist Humanism: The Outcome of Classical European Morality, 1974; The Latin American Revolution, 1974; Argentina, 1943–1976: The National Revolution and Resistance, 1976; (ed.) The Legacy of Che Guevara, 1977; (with R. Grandy) El destino de la Revolución Mexicana, 1977; (with A. Guillén) Revaloración de la guerrilla urbana, 1977; Marxismo y Revolución en el Siglo XX, 1978; (with R. Gandy) Mexico 1910–1976: Reform or Revolution?, 1979; The Bureaucratization of Socialism, 1981; (with R. Gandy) Mexico 1910–82: Reform or Revolution?, 1983; (with R. Gandy) i Todos los Revolucionarios van al Infierno!, 1984; Intellectual Foundations of the Nicaraguan Revolution, 1987; The Argentine National Revolution and Resistance, 1988. Add: Rte. 7, Box MLC-50, Tallahassee, Fla. 32308, U.S.A.

HODGES, Doris M. Also writes as Charlotte Hunt. British, b. 1915. Novels/Short stories. Secty./Librarian, Education Authority, Bristol, since 1970. Tutor in Creative Writing, Somerset and Bristol Education Authorities, since 1969. Secty./Librarian, Univ. of Bristol, 1946–70. Secty., West Country Writers Assn., 1977–79. *Publs:* (as Charlotte Hunt) Gilded Sarcophagus, 1967; (as Charlotte Hunt) Cup of Thanatos, 1968; (as Charlotte Hunt) Lotus Vellum, 1970; (as Charlotte Hunt) Thirteenth Treasure, 1971; (as Charlotte Hunt) Geminie Revenged, 1972; Healing Gems, 1972; (as Charlotte Hunt) A Touch of Myrrh, 1973; (as Charlotte Hunt) Tremayne's Wife, 1974; (as Charlotte Hunt) A Wreath for Jenny's Grave, 1975; The Chambered Tomb, 1975; The Story of Hymns, 1979;

(as Charlotte Hunt) Physician in Pompiaa, 1979; Writing for Profit, 1979; (as Charlotte Hunt) Treworran Water, 1980; (as Charlotte Hunt) Heart's Journey, 1980; Talismans and Amulets, 1981; Cross Fire (play), 1982. Add: c/o State Mutual Bk. and Periodical Service, Ltd., 521 5th Ave., 17th Flr., New York, N.Y. 10175, U.S.A.

HODGES, Margaret. American, b. 1911. Children's fiction, Children's non-fiction, Mythology/Folklore. Prof. Emeritus, Sch. of Library and Information Science, Univ. of Pittsburgh, Pa., since 1977 (Visiting Lectr., 1964–68; Asst. Prof., 1968–72; Assoc. Prof., 1972–75; Prof., 1975–77). Storyteller, WQED-TV Schs. Services Dept. series, Tell Me a Story, since 1965. Radio and Television Storyteller, 1953–64, and Children's Librarian, 1958–64, Carnegie Library of Pittsburgh, Pa.; Story Specialist, Pittsburgh Public Schs., Pa., 1964–68. *Publs:* One Little Drum, 1958; (co-ed.) Stories to Tell to Children, 1960; What's for Lunch, Charley?, 1961; A Club Against Keats, 1962; (ed.) Tell It Again, Great Tales from Around the World, 1963; Secret in the Woods, 1963; The Wave, 1964; Tell Me a Story (teacher's manual), 1966; Hatching of Joshua Cobb, 1967; (ed.) Constellation, a Shakespearean Anthology, 1968; Sing Out, Charley!, 1968; Lady Queen Anne, a Biography of Queen Anne of England, 1969; Making of Joshua Cobb, 1971; Gorgon's Head, 1972; Hopkins of the Mayflower, Portrait of a Dissenter, 1972; Fire Bringer, 1972; Persephone and the Springtime, 1973; Other World, Myths of the Celts, 1973; Baldur and the Mistletoe, 1974; Freewheeling of Joshua Cobb, 1974; Knight Prisoner: The Tale of Sir Thomas Malory and His King Arthur, 1976; The High Riders, 1980; The Little Humpbacked Horse, 1980; (co-ed.) Elva Smith's History of Children's Literature, 1980; The Avenger, 1982; Saint George and the Dragon, 1984; Making a Difference: The Story of an American Family, 1989; The Voice of the Great Bell, 1989. Add: 5812 Kentucky Ave., Pittsburgh, Pa. 15232, U.S.A.

HODGETTS, Richard M(ichael). American, b. 1942. Administration/Management. Prof. of Management, Business College, Florida Intnl. Univ., Miami, since 1976. Prof. of Management, Univ. of Nebraska, 1966–76. Chmn., History Div., Academy of Management, 1979–80. *Publs:* Management: Theory, Process and Practice, 1979, 1986; (with Max Wortman) Administrative Policy: Text and Cases in The Strategic Management, 2nd ed. 1980; (with Fred Luthans and Kenneth A. Thompson) Social Issues in Business, 1984, 1987; Introduction to Business, 1977, 1985; American Business: Social Challenge, Social Response, 1977; (with Terry Smart) The American Free Enterprise System, 1978; (with Steve Altman and Enzo Valenzi) Organizational Behavior, 1985; Human Relations, 1984, 1987; Management Fundamentals, 1981; Effective Small Business Management, 1982, 1989; (with Terry Smart) Economics and the Free Enterprise System, 1982, 1987; (with Dorothy Cascio) Modern Health Care Management, 1983; Personal Finance, 1983; Management, 1985, 1989; Effective Supervision, 1987. Add: 3930 Durango, Coral Gables, Fla. 33134, U.S.A.

HODGINS, Jack. (John Stanley Hodgins). Canadian, b. 1939. Novels/Short stories. Prof. of Creative Writing, Univ. of Victoria, B.C., since 1985 (Visiting Prof., 1983–85). Teacher, Nanaimo District Sr. Secondary Sch., B.C., 1961–80; Visiting Prof., Univ. of Ottawa, 1981–83; Writer-in-Residence, Simon Fraser Univ., Burnaby, B.C., 1977, and Univ. of Ottawa, 1979. *Publs:* (ed. with W.H. New) Voice and Vision, 1972; (ed.) The Frontier Experience, 1975; (ed.) The West Coast Experience, 1976; Spit Delaney's Island: Selected Stories, 1976; The Invention of the World (novel), 1977; (with Bruce Nesbitt) Teachers' Resource Book to Transition II: Short Fiction, 1978; The Resurrection of Joseph Bourne (novel), 1979; (with Bruce Nesbitt) Teaching Short Fiction, 1981; The Barclay Family Theatre (short stories), 1981; Beginnings (short stories), 1983; The Honorary Patron (novel), 1987; Left Behind in Squabble Bay (children's novel), 1988. Add: Creative Writing Dept., Univ. of Victoria, Box 1700, Victoria, B.C. V8W 2Y2, Canada.

HODGKIN, Robin A. (Robert Allason Hodgkin). British, b. 1916. Education, Geography. Principal, Bakht Er Ruda: The Sudan Inst. of Education, 1949–55; Headmaster, Abbotsholme Sch., 1956–67; Lectr., Dept. of Educational Studies, Oxford Univ., 1969–77. *Publs:* Sudan Geography, 1951; Education and Change, 1957; Reconnaissance on an Education Frontier, 1970; Born Curious, 1976; Playing and Exploring, 1985. Add: Bareppa House, Falmouth, Cornwall TR11 5EG, England.

HODGKISS, Alan Geoffrey. British, b. 1921. Geography. Experimental Officer, Univ. of Liverpool, 1946–83. Ed., Soc. of Univ. Cartographers Bulletin, 1964–73. Contributing Ed., Canadian Cartographer, 1965–75 *Publs:* Maps for Books and Theses, 1970; (ed. with J.A. Patmore) Merseyside in Maps, 1970; Discovering Antique Maps, 1970; Understanding Maps, 1981; (ed. with W.T.S. Gould) Resources of

Merseyside, 1982; (with J.J. Bagley) Lancashire: A History of the County Palatine in Early Maps, 1985; (with A.F. Tatham) Keyguide to Information Sources: Cartography, 1986. Add: 25 Burnham Rd., Allerton, Liverpool L18 6JU, England.

HODGSON, John Syner. Canadian, b. 1917. Public/Social administration. With Canadian Central Mortgage and Housing Corp., 1946–58; National Supvr. of Emergency Shelter, 1946; Quebec Regional Supvr., 1947–53; Dir. of Development, 1955–57; Exec. Dir., 1957–58; Asst. Secty. to the Cabinet, 1959–63; Asst. Deputy Minister of National Defence, 1963; Principal Secty. to the Prime Minister, and Dir., Special Secretariat on Bilingualism, 1966–68; Deputy Minister of Veterans Affairs, 1968–75; Deputy Minister of Revenue, Taxation Div., 1975–77. *Publs:* Public Administration, 1969. Add: Higher Neopardy, Yeoford, Devon EX17 5ES, England.

HODGSON, Peter C. American, b. 1934. Theology/Religion. Prof. of Theology, Vanderbilt Univ., Nashville, since 1973 (Asst. Prof., 1965–69; Assoc. Prof. 1969–73, Chmn. of the Grad. Dept. of Religion, 1975–80). Asst. Prof. of Religion, Trinity Univ., San Antonio, Tex., 1963–65. *Publs:* The Formation of Historical Theology: A Study of F.C. Baur, 1966; (ed. and translator) Ferdinand Christian Baur on the Writing of Church History, 1968; Jesus Word and Presence: An Essay in Christology, 1971; (ed.) The Life of Jesus Critically Examined, by D.F. Strauss, 1972; Children of Freedom: Black Liberation in Christian Perspective, 1974; New Birth of Freedom: A Theology of Bondage and Liberation, 1976; (ed. and trans.) The Christian Religion, by G.W.F. Hegel, 1979; (co-ed.) Christian Theology, 1985; (co-ed.) Readings in Christian Theology, 1985; (ed. and trans.) Lectures on the Philosophy of Religion, vol. 1, 1984, vol. 2, 1987, vol. 3, 1985 (one-volume ed. as The Lectures of 1827, 1988); Revisioning the Church: Ecclesial Freedom in the New Paradigm, 1988; God in History: Shapes of Freedom, 1989. Add: Vanderbilt Divinity Sch., Nashville, Tenn. 37240, U.S.A.

HODGSON, Peter Edward. British, b. 1928. Physics. Lectr. in Nuclear Physics, Oxford Univ., since 1967; Sr. Research Fellow, Corpus Christi Coll., Oxford. *Publs:* Optical Model of Elastic Scattering, 1963; Nuclear Reactions and Nuclear Structure, 1971; Nuclear Heavy-Ion Reactions, 1978; Growth Points in Nuclear Physics, 3 vols., 1980–81; Our Nuclear Future? Add: Nuclear Physics Lab., Oxford, England.

HODIN, Josef Paul. British, b. 1905. Art, Crafts. Dir., Intnl. Relations, Studio International: Journal of Modern Art, London. Hon. Member, Editorial Council, Journal of Aesthetics and Art Criticism; Member, Exec. Cttee. and Editorial Consultative Cttee., British Soc. of Aesthetics. Press Attaché to the Norwegian Govt. in London, 1944–45; Dir. of Studies and Librarian, Inst. of Contemporary Arts, London, 1949–54; Co-Ed., Prisme des Arts, Paris, 1956–59; Co-ed., Quadram, Brussels, 1956–66. *Publs:* Sven Erixson, 1940; Ernst Josephson, 1942; Edvard Munch, 1948; Isaac Grünewald, 1949; Art and Criticism, 1944; J.A. Comenius and Our Time, 1944; The Dilemma of Being Modern, 1956; Henry Moore, 1956; Ben Nicholson, 1957; Barbara Hepworth, 1961; Lynn Chadwick, 1961; Alan Reynolds, 1962; Bekenntnis zu Kokoschka, 1963; Kokoschka: The Artist and His Work, 1966; Der Maler Walter Kern, 1966; The Painter Ruszkowski, 1967; Bernard Leach: A Potter's Work, 1967; Kafka und Goethe, 1968; Die Brühlsche Terrasse, 1969; Emilio Greco: His Life and Work, 1970; The Painter Alfred Manessier, 1972; Edvard Munch, 1972; Bernard Stern: Paintings and Drawings, 1972; Modern Art and the Modern Mind, 1972; Ludwig Meidner, 1973; Hilde Goldschmidt, 1973; Kokoschka und Hellas, 1973; Paul Berger-Bergner, 1974; Die Leute von Elverdingen, 1974; John Milne, Sculptor: Life and Work, 1977; Else Meidner, 1979; Elizabeth Frink, 1979; Douglas Portway, 1979; Franz Luby, 1980; Mary Newcomb, 1985. Add: 12 Eton Ave., London NW3, England.

HODSON, Henry Vincent. British, b. 1906. Economics, International relations/Current affairs. Proprietor, Hodson Consultants, London, since 1971; Consultant Ed., The Intnl. Foundation Directory. Ed., The Round Table, 1933–39; Constitutional Adviser to the Viceroy of India, 1941–42; Ed., The Sunday Times, London, 1950–61; Provost, The Ditchley Foundn., Oxford, 1961–71; Ed., The Annual Register of World Events, London, 1973–88. *Publs:* Economics of a Changing World, 1933; (co-author) The Empire in the World, 1934; Slump and Recovery 1929–37, 1939; (ed.) The British Commonwealth and the Future, 1939; Twentieth Century Empire, 1948; The Great Divide: Britain-India-Pakistan, 1969; The Diseconomics of Growth, 1972. Add: Flat 1, 105 Lexham Gardens, London W8 6JN, England.

HOEHNER, Harold W. American, b. 1935. Theology/Religion. Chmn.

and Prof. of New Testament Literature and Exegesis, since 1977, and Dir. of Th.D. Studies, since 1975, Dallas Theological Seminary (Instr., 1968; Asst. Prof., 1968–73; Assoc. Prof., 1973–77). Assoc. Ed., Bibliotheca Sacra, 1969–74. *Publs:* Herod Antipas, 1972; Chronological Aspects of the Life of Christ, 1977. Add: Dallas Theological Seminary, 3909 Swiss Ave., Dallas, Tex. 75204, U.S.A.

HOENIG, J. Canadian, b. 1916. Psychiatry. Prof. in Psychiatry, Univ. of Toronto. Member of Editorial Bd. of Canadian Journal of Psychiatry, since 1973, and Bd. of Assessors of the British Journal of Psychiatry. Consultant, WHO, Bangalore, India, 1954–56; Reader, Dept. of Psychiatry, Manchester Univ., 1960–68. *Publs:* (ed. with M. Hamilton) The Nature of Psychotherapy, 1963; (ed. with M. Hamilton) General Psychopathology, 1963; (with M. Hamilton) The Desegregation of the Mentally Ill, 1969. Add: Clarke Inst. of Psychiatry, 250 College, Toronto, Ont., Canada.

HOENIGSWALD, Henry M. American, b. 1915. Language/Linguistics. Prof., Univ. of Pennsylvania, Philadelphia, 1959–85, now Emeritus (Lectr., 1943–44; Assoc. Prof., 1948–59). Lectr., Research Asst., and Instr., Yale Univ., New Haven, Conn., 1939–42, 1945–46; Staff member, Foreign Service Inst., Dept. of State, U.S. Govt., 1946–47; Assoc. Prof., Univ. of Texas, Austin, 1947–48; Ed., American Oriental Series, American Oriental Soc., 1954–58. *Publs:* Language Change and Linguistic Reconstruction, 1960–63; (ed. with G. Cardona and A. Senn) Indo-European and Indo-Europeans, 1970; Studies in Formal Historical Linguistics, XI, 1973; (ed. with T.A. Sebeok and R. Longacre) Current Trends in Linguistics, 1973; (ed.) The European Background of American Linguistics, 1979; (ed. with L.F. Wiener) Biological Metaphor and Cladistic Classification, 1987. Add: 619 Williams Hall, Univ. of Pennsylvania, Philadelphia, Pa. 19104, U.S.A.

HOFF, Harry Summerfield. *See* **COOPER,** William.

HOFF, Syd(ney). American, b. 1912. Children's fiction, Plays/Screenplays, Humor/Satire. Daily Cartoonist ("Laugh It Off"), King Features Syndicate, 1957–71. *Publs:* Muscles and Brains, 1940; Military Secrets, 1943; Feeling No Pain: An Album of Cartoons, 1944; Tales of Hoff (television play series), 1947; Oops! Wrong Party (cartoons), 1951; It's Fun Learning Cartooning, 1952; Oops! Wrong Stateroom! (cartoons), 1953; Out of Gas! (cartoons), 1954; Eight Little Artists, 1954; Patty's Pet, 1955; Okay–You Can Look Now (cartoons), 1955; Danny and the Dinosaur, 1958; Sammy, The Seal, 1959; Julius, 1959; Ogluk, The Eskimo, 1960; Where's Prancer?, 1960; Oliver, 1960; Who Will Be My Friends?, 1960; Little Chief, 1961; Albert The Albatross, 1961; Chester, 1961; The Better Hoff (cartoons), 1961; Upstream, Downstream, and Out of My Mind, 1961; Twixt the Cup of the Lipton, 1962; So This Is Matrimony (cartoons), 1962; Stanley, 1962; Grizzwold, 1963; Hunting, Anyone? (cartoons), 1963; From Bed to Nurse; or, What a Way to Die (cartoons), 1963; Lengthy, 1964; Learning to Cartoon, 1966; Mrs. Switch, 1967; Irving and Me, 1967; Wanda's Wand, 1968; The Witch, The Cat, and The Baseball Bat, 1968; Slithers, 1968; Baseball Mouse, 1969; Jeffrey at Camp, 1969; Mahatma, 1969; Roberto and the Bull, 1969; Herschel the Hero, 1969; The Horse in Harry's Room, 1970; The Litter Knight, 1970; Palace Bug, 1970; Siegfried, Dog of the Alps, 1970; Wilfrid the Lion, 1970; The Mule Who Struck It Rich, 1971; Thunderhoof, 1971; When Will It Snow?, 1971; Ida the Bareback Rider, 1972; My Aunt Rose, 1972; Pedro and the Bananas, 1972; Syd Hoff's Joke Book, 1972; The Art of Cartooning, 1973; A Walk Past Ellen's House, 1973; Giants and Other Plays for Kids, 1973; Amy's Dinosaur, 1974; Kip Van Winkle, 1974; Jokes to Enjoy, Draw and Tell, 1974; Dinosaur Do's and Dont's, 1975; Katy's Kitten, 1975; Pete's Pup, 1975; Barkley, 1975; The Littlest Leaguer, 1976; Editorial and Political Cartooning: From the Earliest Times to the Present . . ., 1976; Walpole, 1977; Slugger Sal's Slump, 1979; Santa's Moose, 1979; Scarface Al and His Uncle Sam, 1980; Soft Skull Sam, 1981; How to Draw Dinosaurs, 1981; The Man Who Loved Animals, 1982; The Young Cartoonist: The ABC's of Cartooning, 1983; Syd Hoff's Animal Jokes, 1985; Barney's Horse, 1987; Mrs. Brice's Mice, 1988. Add: c/o G.P. Putnam's Sons, 200 Madison Ave., New York, N.Y. 10016, U.S.A.

HOFFMAN, Alice. American, b. 1952. Novels. Freelance writer. *Publs:* Property Of, 1977; The Drowning Season, 1979; Angel Landing, 1980; White Horses, 1982; Fortune's Daughter, 1985; Illumination Night, 1987; At Risk, 1988. Add: c/o Putnam, 200 Madison Ave., New York, N.Y. 10016, U.S.A.

HOFFMAN, Arthur W(olf). American, b. 1921. Literature. Prof. of English, Syracuse Univ., N.Y., since 1963 (Asst. Prof., 1953–57; Assoc. Prof., 1957–63; Dir. of Grad. Studies in English, 1971–74; Chmn. of the English Dept., 1974–79). *Publs:* John Dryden's Imagery, 1962; (with F.B. Millett and D.R. Clark) Reading Poetry, 1968. Add: Dept. of English, Syracuse Univ., Syracuse, N.Y. 13242, U.S.A.

HOFFMAN, Daniel. American, b. 1923. Poetry, Literature, Mythology/Folklore. Schelling Prof. of English, since 1983, and Poet-in-Residence, since 1978, Univ. of Pennsylvania, Philadelphia (Prof. of English, 1966–83). Chancellor, Academy of American Poets, since 1974. Faculty member, Columbia Univ., NYC, 1952–56, Faculté des Lettres, Dijon, France, 1956–57, and Swarthmore Coll., Pa., 1957–66. Consultant in Poetry, Library of Congress, 1973–74. *Publs:* Paul Bunyan, Last of the Frontier Demigods, 1952; An Armada of Thirty Whales, 1954; The Poetry of Stephen Crane, 1957; (ed.) The Red Badge of Courage and Other Stories, 1957; A Little Geste, 1960; Form and Fable in American Fiction, 1961; American Poetry and Poetics, 1962; The City of Satisfactions, 1963; (ed. with S. Hynes) English Literary Criticism: Romantic and Victorian, 1963; Barbarous Knowledge, 1967; Striking the Stones, 1968; Broken Laws, 1970; Poe Poe Poe Poe Poe Poe Poe, 1972; The Center of Attention, 1974; Able Was I Ere I Saw Elba: Selected Poems, 1977; (ed.) The Harvard Guide to Contemporary American Writing, 1979; Brotherly Love, 1981; (ed.) Ezra Pound and William Carlos Williams, 1983; Hang-Gliding from Helicon: New and Selected Poems 1948–1988, 1988; How to Tell a Story: Folklore, Form and Fable in Faulkner's Fiction, 1989. Add: Dept. of English, Univ. of Pennsylvania, Philadelphia, Pa. 19104, U.S.A.

HOFFMAN, Lee. Also writes as Georgia York. American, b. 1932. Westerns/Adventure, Science fiction/Fantasy, Historical/Romance. Freelance writer since 1966. Formerly in printing production; Asst. Ed., Infinity, and Science Fiction Adventures, both 1956–58. *Publs:* Gunfight at Laramie, 1966; The Legend of Blackjack Sam, 1966; Bred to Kill, 1967; The Valdez Horses, 1967; Telepower (science fiction), 1967; Dead Man's Gold, 1968; The Yarborough Brand, 1968; Wilde Riders, 1969; Loco, 1969; Return to Broken Crossing, 1969; West of Cheyenne, 1969; The Caves of Karst (science fiction), 1972; Always the Black Knight (science fiction), 1970; Change Song (science fiction), 1972; Wiley's Move, 1975; The Truth about the Cannonball Kid, 1975; Fox, 1976; Nothing but a Drifter, 1976; Trouble Valley, 1976; The Sheriff of Jack Hollow, 1977; The Land Killer, 1978; (as Georgia York) Savage Key, 1979; Savannah Grey, 1981; In and Out of the Quandry (stories), 1982; Savage Conquest, 1983. Add: 401 Sunrise Trail N.W., Port Charlotte, Fla. 33952, U.S.A.

HOFFMAN, Michael A(llen). American, b. 1944. Anthropology/Ethnology, Archaeology/Antiquites. Prof., Earth Sciences and Resources Inst., Univ. of South Carolina, since 1982. Director of the Hierakonpolis Expedition. Asst. Prof., Dept. of Anthropology, 1972–77, and Sch. of Architecture, 1977–79, Univ. of Virginia; Assoc. Prof. of Anthropology, Western Illinois Univ., Macomb, 1980–82. *Publs:* Egypt Before the Pharaohs, 1979; The Predynastic of Hierakonpolis, 1982. Add: 216 Colonial Ave., Colonial Beach, Va. 22443, U.S.A.

HOFFMAN, Michael J. American, b. 1939. Novels/Short stories, Literature. Prof. of English since 1975, and Dir. of Humanities Inst., since 1986, Univ. of California, Davis (Grad. Chmn., 1971–72; Dept. Chmn., 1984–89). Instr. of English, Washington Coll., Chestertown, Md., 1962–64; Asst. Prof. of English, Univ. of Pennsylvania, Philadelphia 1964–67. *Publs:* The Development of Abstractionism in the Writings of Gertrude Stein, 1965; The Buddy System (novel), 1973; The Subversive Vision: American Romanticism in Literature, 1973; Gertrude Stein, 1976; (ed.) Critical Essays on Gertrude Stein, 1986; (ed.) Essentials of the Theory of Fiction, 1988. Add: Dept. of English, Univ. of California, Davis, Calif. 95616, U.S.A.

HOFFMAN, Robert Louis. American, b. 1937. History, Politics/Government. Assoc. Prof. of History since 1974, and Fellow of the Inst. of Humanistic Studies since 1978, State Univ. of New York at Albany (Asst. Prof., 1968–74). Instr., Univ. of Vermont, Burlington, 1964–65; Instr. of History and Political Science, Rensselaer Polytechnic Inst., Troy, N.Y., 1965–68. *Publs:* (ed.) Anarchism, 1970, 1973; Revolutionary Justice: The Social and Political Theory of P.J. Proudhon, 1972; More Than a Trial: The Struggle over Captain Dreyfus, 1980. Add: Dept. of History, State Univ. of New York at Albany, Albany, N.Y. 12222, U.S.A.

HOFFMAN, William M. American, b. 1939. Play/Screenplays. Ed., New American Play series, Hill & Wang publrs., NYC, since 1968 (Drama Ed., 1961–68). Playwright-in-Residence, La Mama Theatre, NYC,

1978–79. Star Prof., Hofstra Univ., Hempstead, N.Y., 1980. *Publs:* The Cloisters (lyrics), 1968; Thank You, Miss Victoria, 1970; (ed.) New American Plays 2, 3, 4, 3 vols., 1968–71; (ed.) Gay Plays: The First Collection, 1979; As Is, 1985. Add: c/o Mitch Douglas, ICM, 40 W. 57th St., New York, N.Y. 10019, U.S.A.

HOFFMANN, Ann Marie. British, b. 1930. History, Travel, Writing/Journalism. Secty. to Book Production Mgr., Architectural Press Ltd., London, 1948–50; Secty., World Health Org., Geneva, 1952, and Intnl. Court of Justice, The Hague, 1953–57; Private Secty. to Legal Adviser, Org. for European Economic Cooperation (OEEC), Paris, 1957–58; Admin. Asst., Intnl. Court of Justice, 1958–59, and Conference Services Ltd., London, 1963–66; Private Secty/Researcher to author Robert Henriques, 1959–62; with Authors' Research Services, 1966–87. *Publs:* The Dutch: How They Live and Work, 1971, 1973; Research: A Handbook for Writers and Journalists, 1975, 1979; Bocking Deanery (local history), 1976; Lives of the Tudor Age, 1977; Majorca, 1978; Research for Writers, 1986. Add: Baixada del Rei 8, Carretera de las Curvas, Capdepera, Mallorca, Spain.

HOFFMANN, Donald. American, b. 1933. Architecture. Art Critic, Kansas City Star, since 1965 (gen. assignment reporter, 1956–65). Asst. Ed., Journal of the Soc. of Architectural Historians, 1970–71. *Publs:* (ed.) The Meanings of Architecture: Buildings and Writings by John Wellborn Root, 1967; The Architecture of John Wellborn Root, 1973; Frank Lloyd Wright's Fallingwater, 1978; Frank Lloyd Wright's Robie House, 1984; Frank Lloyd Wright: Architecture and Nature, 1986. Add: 6441 Holmes, Kansas City, Mo. 64131, U.S.A.

HOFFMANN, Malcolm A(rthur). American, b. 1912. Law, Autobiography/Memoirs/Personal. Sr. Partner, Malcolm A. Hoffmann, attorneys-at-law, NYC, since 1959. *Publs:* Government Lawyer, 1956; Hoffmann's Antitrust Laws and Techniques, 1963; (with M.L. Ernst) Back and Forth (essays), 1969; The Teacher. Add: 309 E. 49th St., New York, N.Y. 10017, U.S.A.

HOFFMANN, Peggy. (Margaret Jones Hoffmann). American, b. 1910. Novels/Short stories, Children's fiction, Children's non-fiction, Music. Teacher, Poetry-in-the Schs. prog., since 1974; Instr., Creative Writing Seminar, Meredith Coll., Raleigh, since 1977. *Publs:* Miss B's First Cookbook, 1950; Sew Easy!; (compiler) Sacred Songs, Jr. Choir, 1954; (compiler) Sacred Songs SAB, 1956; (compiler) Select Union Anthems, 1957; Sew Far, Sew Good!, 1958; The Wild Rocket, 1960; (compiler) 22 Chorales (Bach), 1960; (compiler) 10 Select Anthems, 1961; (compiler) Chorales from the Passion (Bach), 1964; (compiler) Everywhere a Folk Song, 1964; (compiler) Year Round Anthem Book, 1964; (compiler) God's Son Is Born (Christmas cantata), 1964, 1970; Shift to High!, 1965; A Forest of Feathers, 1966; (compiler) Funeral Music, 1966; (compiler) The Cross Shines Forth (Easter cantata), 1966; (compiler) Grasshoppers 3, 1966; (compiler) Praise for the Year, 1969; (with G. Biro) The Money Hat, 1969; My Dear Cousin, 1970; (with S. Maas) The Sea Wedding, 1975; (with F. Watson) Been There and Back, 1977; (with Gerald R. Hunter) Bake a Snake, 1981; (compiler) No Pedals (for organ), 1987. Add: 1013 Gardner St., Raleigh, N.C. 27607, U.S.A.

HOFFMANN, Peter (Conrad Werner). Canadian (born German), b. 1930. History. Kingsford Prof. of History, McGill Univ., Montreal, since 1970. Asst. Prof., 1965–68, and Assoc. Prof., 1968–70, Univ. of Northern Iowa, Cedar Falls. *Publs:* Die diplomatischen Beziehungen zwischen Württemberg und Bayern im Krimkrieg und bis zum Beginn der italienischen Krise 1853-1858, 1963; (trans.) John J. McCloy II: Die Verschwörung gegen Hitler: Ein Geschenk an die deutsche Zukunft, 1963; Widerstand, Staatsstreich, Attentat: Der Kampf der Opposition gegen Hitler, 1969; Die Sicherheit des Diktators: Hitlers Leibwachen, Schutzmassnahmen, Residenzen, Hauptquartiere, 1975; The History of the German Resistance 1933-1945, 1977; Hitler's Personal Security, 1979; Widerstand gegen Hitler, 1979; German Resistance to Hitler, 1988. Add: Dept. of History, McGill Univ., 855 Sherbrooke St. W., Montreal, Que. H3A 2T7, Canada.

HOFFMANN, Stanley. American and French, b. 1928. International relations/Current affairs, Politics/Government. Douglas Dillon Prof. of the Civilization of France, Harvard Univ., Cambridge. *Publs:* Organisations internationales et pouvoirs politiques des Etats, 1954; Le Mouvement Poujade, 1956; Contemporary Theory in International Relations, 1963; The State of War, 1963; (ed.) Conditions of World Order, 1968; Gulliver's Troubles, 1968; Decline or Renewal?, 1974; Primacy or World Order, 1978; Duties Beyond Borders, 1981; Dead Ends, 1983; Janus and Minerva, 1986. Add: Center for European Studies, 5 Bryant St., Harvard Univ., Cambridge, Mass. 02138, U.S.A.

HOFFMEISTER, Donald Frederick. American, b. 1916. Natural history, Zoology. Assoc. Curator, Museum of Natural History, Univ. of Kansas, Lawrence, 1944–46. Dir., Museum of Natural History, 1946–84, and Prof. of Zoology, 1959–84, Univ. of Illinois, Urbana. *Publs:* (with Zim) Mammals, 1955; (with Mohr) Fieldbook of Illinois Mammals, 1957; Mammals, 1963; Zoo Animals. 1967; Mammals of Grand Canyon, 1971; Mammals of Arizona, 1986. Add: Museum of Natural History, Univ. of Illinois, Urbana, Ill. 61801, U.S.A.

HOFMANN, Michael. German, b. 1957. Poetry. Freelance writer, London, since 1983. *Publs:* Nights in the Iron Hotel, 1983; Acrimony, 1986. Add: c/o Faber and Faber, 3 Queen St., London WC1N 3AU, England.

HOFSTADTER, Douglas (Richard). American, b. 1945. Information science/Computers (cognitive science), Philosophy. Prof. of Cognitive Science and Dir. of the Center for Research on Concepts and Cognition, Indiana Univ., Bloomington, since 1988. Prof. of Psychology, Univ. of Michigan, Ann Arbor, 1984–1988. Assoc. Prof. of Computer Science, Indiana Univ., Bloomington, 1977–84. Former columnist, Scientific American. *Publs:* Gödel, Escher, Bach: an Eternal Golden Braid, 1979; (with Daniel Debnnett) The Mind's I, 1981; Metamagical Themas, 1985. Add: Indiana University, 510-512 North Fess St., Bloomington, Ind. 47408, U.S.A.

HOFSTETTER, Henry W. American, b. 1914. Medicine/Health (vision). Rudy Prof. Emeritus of Optometry, Indiana Univ., Bloomington (Dir., Div. of Optometry, 1952–70). Ed., Newsletter of the Optometric Historical Soc., since 1970; Chmn., Ed. Cttee. for Intnl. Glossary of Optometric Terms. Faculty member, Ohio State Univ., Columbus, 1942–48; Dean, Los Angeles Coll. of Optometry, 1948–52. *Publs:* Optometry: Professional, Legal, and Economic Aspects, 1948, 1967; (ed.) Manual of Ocular Tests, 2nd ed. 1948; Industrial Vision, 1956; (co-ed.) Dictionary of Visual Science, 1960, 1968, 1980, 1989. Add: 2615 Windermere Woods Dr., Bloomington, Ind. 47401, U.S.A.

HOGAN, Desmond. Irish, b. 1950. Novels/Short stories. Freelance writer. Writer and actor with Children's T. Company theatre group, Dublin, 1975–77; moved to London, 1977; teacher, 1978–79. *Publs:* The Ikon Maker (novel), 1976; The Diamonds at the Bottom of the Sea and Other Stories, 1979; The Leaves on Grey (novel), 1980; Children of Lir: Stories from Ireland, 1981; Stories, 1982; A Curious Street (novel), 1984; A New Shirt (novel), 1986; Lehanon Lodge (stories), 1988; A Link With the River (collected stories), 1989; also plays for radio, television, and the stage. Add: 6 Stanstead Grove, London SE6, England.

HOGAN, James P(atrick). British, b. 1941. Science fiction/Fantasy. Full-time writer, since 1979. Engineer, Solarton Electronics, Farnborough, 1961–62, and Racal Electronics, Bracknell, Berks., 1962–64; Sales Engineer, 1964–66, and Sales Mgr., 1966–68, Intnl. Telephone and Telegraph Co., Harlow, Herts.; Computer Sales Exec., Honeywell, London, 1968–70, and Leeds, 1970–72; Insurance Salesman, 1974–77, and Sales Training Consultant in Maynard, Mass., 1977–79, Digital Equipment Corp., Leeds. *Publs:* Inherit the Stars, 1977; The Genesis Machine, 1977; The Gentle Giants of Ganymede, 1978; The Two Faces of Tomorrow, 1979; Thrice upon a Time, 1980; Giants' Star, 1981; Voyage From Yesteryear, 1982; Lode of the Lifemaker, 1983; The Proteus Operation, 1985; Minds, Machines and No-Nuke Neanderthals (short stories), 1986; Endgame Enigma, 1987; The Mirrow Maze, 1989. Add: 69 S. Washington, Sonora, Calif. 95370, U.S.A.

HOGAN, (Robert) Ray. Also writes as Clay Ringold. American, b. 1908. Westerns/Adventure. Freelance writer. Former Ed., New Mexico Sportsman, 1954–57, and sports columnist, Albuquerque Tribune. *Publs:* Ex-Marshal, 1956; The Friendless One, 1957; Walk a Lonely Trail, 1957; Land of the Strangers, 1957; Longhorn Law, 1957; Marked Man, 1958; Hangman's Valley, 1959; Wanted Alive!, 1959; Marshal Without a Badge, 1959; Outlaw Marshal, 1959; Guns Against the Sun, 1960; Lead Reckoning, 1960; The Ghost Raider, 1960; The Shotgunner, 1960; The Hasty Hangman, 1960; Raider's Revenge, 1960; Rebel Raid, 1961; The Life and Death of Clay Allison, 1961; The Ridge-Runner, 1961; Ride to the Gun, 1961; Ambush at Riflestock, 1961; Track the Man Down, 1961; Marshal for Lawless, 1961; The Jim Hendren Story, 1962; Rebel in Yankee Blue, 1962; Hell to Hallelujah, 1962; New Gun for Kingdom City, and The Shotgunner, 1962; Stranger in Apache Basin, 1963; The Outside Gun, 1963; The Life and Death of Johnny Ringo, 1963, in U.K. as Johnny Ringo, Gentleman Outlaw, 1964, in U.K. paperback as Tombstone Outlaw,

1966; Trail of the Fresno Kid, 1963; Last Gun at Cabresto, 1963; Hoodoo Guns, 1964; Man from Barranca Negra, 1964; The Trackers, 1964; Night Raider, 1964; Rebel Ghost, 1964; Mosby's Last Raid, 1966; Panhandle Pistolero, 1966; Killer's Gun, 1966; Dead Man on a Black Horse, 1966; The Hellsfire Lawman, 1966; Outlaw Mountain, 1967; Legacy of the Slash M, 1967; Border Bandit, 1967; The Wolver, 1967; Devil's Butte, 1967; Texas Lawman, 1967; The Moon-Lighters, 1968; Trouble at Tenkiller, 1968; The Gunmaster, 1968; The Hell Road, 1968; Killer on Warbucket, 1968; (as Clay Ringold) Return to Rio Fuego, 1968; (as Clay Ringold) Reckoning in Fire Valley, 1969; (as Clay Ringold) The Hooded Gun, 1969; The Man Who Killed the Marshal, 1969; The Trail to Tucson, 1969; The Hooded Gun, 1969; Bloodrock Valley War, 1969; Texas Guns, 1969; The Rimrocker, 1970; The Searching Guns, 1970; Guns along the Jicarilla, 1970; Jackman's Wolf, 1970; The Outlawed, 1970; Three Cross, 1970; Deputy of Violence, 1971; Duel in Lagrima Valley, 1971; A Bullet for Mr. Texas, 1971; Marshal of Babylon, 1971; Brandon's Posse, 1971; A Man Called Ryker, 1971; The Devil's Gunhand, 1972; New Gun for Kingdom City, 1972; The Night Hell's Corner Died, 1972; Passage to Dodge City, 1972; The Hangman of San Sabal, 1972; The Hell Merchant, 1972; Lawman for Slaughter Valley, 1972, as Lawman for the Slaughter, 1980; Showdown at Texas Flat, 1972; Conger's Woman, 1973; The Guns of Stingaree, 1973; Highroller's Man, 1973; Skull Gold, 1973; The Vengeance Gun, 1973; Day of Reckoning, 1973; Man Without a Gun, 1974; The Texas Brigade, 1974; Wolf Lawman, 1974; The Jenner Guns, 1974; The Scorpion Killers, 1974; The Tombstone Trail, 1974; The Doomsday Marshal, 1975; Honeymaker's Son, 1975; Betrayal in Tombstone, 1975; The Proving Gun, 1975; Day of the Hangman, 1975; The Last Comanchero, 1975; Roxie Raker, 1975; The Vigilante, 1975; The Yesterday Rider, 1976; High Green Gun, 1976; The Regulator: Bill Thompson, 1976; The Shotgun Rider, 1976; The Iron Jehu, 1976; The Doomsday Posse, 1977; Tall Man Riding, 1977; Omaha Crossing, 1977; Bounty Hunter's Moon, 1977; A Gun for Silver Rose, 1977; The Peace Keeper, 1978; The Glory Trail, 1978; Adam Gann, Outlaw, 1978; Gun Trap at Arabella, 1978; The Raptors, 1979; The Doomsday Trail, 1979; The Hellborn, 1979; Overkill at Saddle Rock, 1979; Brandon's Posse and the Hell Merchant, 1979; Lawman's Choice, 1980; Pilgrim, 1980; Ragan's Law, 1980; The Dead Gun, 1980; The Hell Raiser, 1980; Outlaw's Pledge, 1981; The Doomsday Bullet, 1981; Decision at Doubtful Canyon, 1981; Renegade Gun, 1982; The Renegades, 1982; Fortuna West, Lawman, 1983; The Law and Lynchburg, 1983; The Copper Dun Stud, 1983; Doomsday Canyon, 1983; Agony Ridge, 1984; The Cornudas Guns, 1985; The Rawhiders, 1985; Apache Mountain Justice, 1985; Outlaws' Empire, 1986; Wyoming Drifter, 1986; Doomsday Marshal and the Hanging Judge, 1986; Guns along the Mora, 1987; Solitude's Lawman, 1987; The Crosshatch Men, 1988; Doomsday Marshal & the Comancheros, 1989. Add: 700 Stagecoach Rd. S.E., Albuquerque, N.M. 87123, U.S.A.

HOGAN, Robert (Goode). American, b. 1930. Plays/Screenplays, Literature. Prof. of English, Univ. of Delaware, Newark, since 1970. Publr., Proscenium Press, since 1964; Ed., Journal of Irish Literature, since 1972, and George Spelvin's Theatre Book, since 1978. *Publs:* Experiments of Sean O'Casey, 1960; (ed.) Feathers from the Green Crow, 1962; (ed. with S. Molin) Drama: The Major Genres, 1962; Arthur Miller, 1964; Independence of Elmer Rice, 1965; (ed. with M.J. O'Neill) Joseph Holloway's Abbey Theatre, 1967; (with H. Bogart) The Plain Style, 1967; After the Irish Renaissance, 1967; (ed.) Seven Irish Plays, 1967; (ed. with M.J. O'Neill) Joseph Holloway's Irish Theatre, 3 vols., 1968–70; Dion Boucicault, 1969; The Fan Club, 1969; Betty and the Beast, 1969; (with J. Kilroy) Lost Plays of the Irish Renaissance, 1970; (ed.) Crows of Mephistopheles, 1970; (ed.) Towards a National Theatre, 1970; Eimar O'Duffy, 1972; Mervyn Wall, 1972; (with E. Young-Bruehl) Conor Cruise O'Brien, 1974; (with J. Kilroy) History of the Modern Irish Drama, vol. I, The Irish Literary Theatre, 1975, vol. II, Laying the Foundation, 1976, vol. III, The Abbey Theatre 1905–09, 1978, vol. IV (with R. Burnham and D.P. Poteet) The Rise of the Realists 1910–1915, 1979, and vol. V (with R. Burnham) The Art of the Amateur 1916–1920, 1984; (ed.) The Dictionary of Irish Literature, 1979; Since O'Casey, 1983; (ed. with J.C. Beasley) The Plays of Frances Sheridan, 1984. Add: P.O. Box 361, Newark, Del. 19711, U.S.A.

HOGARTH, Grace. Also writes as Grace Allen, Amelia Gay, and Allen Weston. American, b. 1905. Novels/Short stories, Children's fiction. Staff Artist, later Children's Books Ed., Oxford Univ. Press, NYC and London, 1929–38, Chatto and Windus, London, 1938–39, and Houghton Mifflin, Boston, 1940–43; English rep. for Houghton Mifflin, 1943–47, and other publishers, 1947–56; Children's Book Ed., 1956–63, Managing Dir., 1963–66, Chmn. and Managing Dir., 1966–72, Constable, later Longman Young Books, London; Ed., Lifetime Library, 1968–70. Gov., North London and Camden Schs. for Girls' 1963–71; Member of the Exec.

Cttee., Assn. of Governing Bodies of Girls' Public Day Schs. Trust, 1969–71. *Publs:* Australia: The Island Continent, 1943; (as Grace Allen) This to Be Love, 1949; (as Amelia Gay in U.K., and as Grace Hogarth in U.S.) Lucy's League, 1950; The End of Summer, 1951; (as Amelia Gay in U.K., and Grace Hogarth in U.S.) John's Journey, 1952; Children of This World, 1953; (as Allen Weston, with André Norton) Murders for Sale, 1954; The Funny Guy, 1955; (ed. with Caroline Hogarth) American Cooking for English Kitchens, 1957; As a May Morning, 1958; A Sister for Helen, 1976. Add: 24 Nuffield Lodge, 22 Shepherds Hill, London N6 5AH, England.

HOGBIN, Herbert Ian (Priestley). Australian, b. 1904. Anthropology/Ethnology. Lectr., 1936–48, and Reader in Anthropology, 1948–69, Univ. of Sydney; Professorial Fellow, Macquarie Univ., 1970–79. *Publs:* Law and Order in Polynesia, 1934; Experiments in Civilization, 1939; People of the Southwest Pacific, 1946; Transformation Scene, 1951; Social Change, 1958; Kinship and Marriage in a New Guinea Village, 1963; A Guadalcanal Society, 1964; (co-ed) Studies in Australian and Pacific Anthropology, 1966; (with P. Lawrence) Studies in New Guinea Land Tenure, 1967; Island of Menstruating Men, 1970; (ed.) Anthropology in Papua New Guinea, 1973; The Leaders and the Led, 1978. Add: c/o Terry Beavan, 4 Katrina Pl., Lakeman, N.S.W. 2195, Australia.

HOGENDORN, Jan Stafford. American, b. 1937. Economics. Grossman Prof. of Economics, Colby Coll., Waterville, Me., since 1977 (Asst. Prof., 1966–69; Assoc. Prof., 1969–76; Prof., 1976–77). Instr. of Economics, Boston Univ., Mass., 1963–64. *Publs:* Managing the Modern Economy, 1972, 1975; Markets in the Modern Economy, 1974; Modern Economics, 1975; Nigerian Groundnut Exports, 1978; The Uncommon Market, 1979; The New International Economics, 1979; The Grossman Lectures at Colby College 1977–1983, 1984; The Shell Money of the Slave Trade, 1986; Economic Development, 1987. Add: Dept. of Economics, Colby Coll., Waterville, Me. 04901, U.S.A.

HOGG, Quintin (McGarel); Lord Hailsham of St. Marylebone. British, b. 1907. Law, Politics/Government. Member of the House of Lords, London, since 1970, and Lord Chancellor since 1979 (Conservative M.P. for Oxford, 1938–50; Member, as Viscount Hailsham, House of Lords, 1950 until he disclaimed title, 1963; M.P. for St. Marylebone, London, 1963–70; First Lord of the Admiralty, 1956–57; Minister of Education, 1957; Deputy Leader, 1957–60, and Leader, 1960–63, House of Lords; Lord Pres. of the Council, 1957–59, 1960–64; Lord Privy Seal, 1959–60; Minister for Science and Technology, 1959–64; Secty. of State for Education and Science, 1964; Opposition Spokesman on Education and Science, 1964–66, on Home Affairs, 1966–70; Lord Chancellor, 1970–74). Called to the Bar, Lincoln's Inn, London, 1932; Queen's Counsel, 1953; Bencher, Lincoln's Inn, 1956. Chmn., Conservative Party Org., 1957–59; Rector, Univ. of Glasgow, 1959–62; Pres., Classical Assn., 1960–61. *Publs:* The Law of Arbitration, 1935; One Year's Work, 1944; The Law and Employer's Liability, 1944; The Times We Live In, 1944; Making Peace, 1945; The Left Was Never Right, 1945; The Purpose of Parliament, 1946; The Case for Conservatism, 1947; The Law of Monopolies, Restrictive Practices and Resale Price Maintenance, 1956; The Conservative Case, 1959; Science and Politics, 1963; The Devil's Own Song (verse), 1968; The Door Wherein I Went, 1975; Elective Dictatorship, 1976; The Dilemma of Democracy, 1978. Add: House of Lords, London SW1 0PW, England.

HOGGARD, James. American, b. 1941. Novels/Short stories, Plays/Screenplays, Poetry. Prof., Midwestern State Univ., Wichita Falls, Tex., since 1977 (Instr., 1966–68; Asst. Prof., 1968–72; Assoc. Prof., 1972–77). *Publs:* Isometrics and the Towel; Property; Sunrise; Swinger; Conspiracy; Morganatic Marriage; (with B. Voss) Beau-Bo; Eyesigns, 1977; Trotter Ross (novel), 1981; The Shaper Poems, 1983; Elevator Man (non-fiction), 1983; Two Gulls, One Hawk (poetry), 1983; Breaking an Indelicate Statue (poetry), 1986; The Art of Dying, 1988. Add: 2414 N. Leighton, Wichita Falls, Tex. 76309, U.S.A.

HOGGART, Richard. British, b. 1918. Communications Media, Literature. Chmn., Broadcasting Research Unit. Sr. Staff Tutor, Univ. of Hull, 1957–59; Sr. Lectr., Univ. of Leicester, 1959–62; Dir., Centre for Contemporary Cultural Studies, 1964–73, and Prof. of English, 1962–73, Univ. of Birmingham; an Asst. Dir.-Gen., Unesco, 1970–75; Warden, Goldsmith's Coll., Univ. of London, 1976–84. *Publs:* Auden, 1951; The Uses of Literacy, 1957; W.H. Auden, 1957; (ed.) W.H. Auden: A Selection, 1961; Teaching Literature, 1963; Speaking to Each Other, 2 vols., 1970; Only Connect (Reith Lectures), 1972; An Idea and Its Servants, 1978; An English Temper, 1982; (with Douglas Johnson) An Idea of Europe, 1987; A Local Habitation, 1988. Add: Mortonsfield, Beavers Hill,

Farnham, Surrey GU9 7DF, England.

HOGNER, Dorothy Childs. American. Children's fiction, Children's non-fiction, Cookery/Gastronomy/Wine, Homes/Gardens, Travel/Exploration/Adventure. Owner, Hemlock Hill Herb Farm, Litchfield, Conn., since 1950. Chmn., Childrens Book Cttee., Authors Guild, Authors League of America, 1954–56. *Publs:* Navajo Winter Nights, 1935; South to Padre, 1936; Santa to Padre, 1936; Santa Fe Caravans, 1937; Westward, High, Low and Dry, 1938; Summer Roads to Gaspe, 1939; Old Hank Weatherbee, 1939; Children of Mexico, 1942; The Animal Book, 1942; The Bible Story, 1943; Reward for Brownie, 1944; Our American Horse, 1944; Unexpected Journey, 1945; Farm Animals, 1945; Winky, King of the Gardens, 1946; Blue Swamp, 1947; Barnyard Family, 1948; Daisy, a Farm Fable, 1949; Wild Little Honker, 1951; (with Lilo Hess) Odd Pets, 1951; Snowflake, 1952; Herbs from the Garden to the Table, 1953; Earthworms, 1953; The Horse Family, 1953; Wide River, 1954; The Dog Family, 1954; The Cat Family, 1956; Frogs and Pollywogs, 1956; Snails, 1958; Conservation in America, 1958; Grasshoppers and Crickets, 1960; Water Over the Dam, 1960; A Fresh Herb Platter, 1961; Butterflies, 1962; Water Beetles, 1963; Gardening and Cooking on Terrace and Patio, 1964; Moths, 1964; Weeds, 1968; Birds of Prey, 1969; Good Bugs in Your Garden: Back Yard Ecology, 1974; Water Plants, 1977; Endangered Plants, 1977; Sea Mammals, 1979. Add: Hemlock Hill Herb Farm, Litchfield, Conn. 06759, U.S.A.

HOHENBERG, John. American, b. 1906. Communications Media, History, International relations/Current affairs. Journalist in New York, Washington and abroad, 1924–50; Prof. of Journalism, Columbia Univ., NYC, 1950–74; Admin., Pulitzer Prizes, 1954–76; Prof. of Journalism, Univ. of Tennessee, Knoxville, 1976–77, 1978–81, 1987; Prof., Univ. of Kansas, Lawrence, 1977–78; Univ. of Florida, Gainesville, 1981–82; Univ. of Miami, Coral Gables, 1982–83; Syracuse Univ., New York, 1983–85. *Publs:* (ed.) The Pulitzer Prize Story, 1959; The Professional Journalist, 1960, 5th ed. 1983; Foreign Correspondence: The Great Reporters and Their Times, 1963; (ed.) The New Front Page, 1965; The News Media, 1966; Between Two Worlds: Press, Policy and Public Opinion in Asian-American Relations, 1967; Free Press/Free People, 1971; New Era in the Pacific, 1972; The Pulitzer Prizes 1917–1974, 1974; A Crisis for the American Press, 1978; (ed.) The Pulitzer Prize Story II, 1959–80, 1980; America in Our Time, 1986; The Parisian Girl (novel), 1986; Concise Newswriting, 1987. Add: 6212 Pleasant Ridge Rd., Knoxville, Tenn. 37912, U.S.A.

HOHL, Joan M. *See* **LORIN,** Amii.

HOHNEN, David. British, b. 1925. Literature, Translations. *Publs:* 3-Mal Skandinavien, 1962; A Portrait of Denmark, 1966; (ed.) English-Danish/Danish-English Dictionary, 1966; (reviser and trans.) Knut Hanneborg: The Study of Literature, 1967; also translator of more than 45 books from Danish to English. Add: Nyhavn 14, Copenhagen K, Denmark.

HOLBIK, Karel. American, b. 1920. Economics. Prof. of Economics Emeritus, Boston Univ., Mass., since 1986 (joined faculty 1958); Visiting Faculty, Harvard Univ., Cambridge, Mass., since 1973. Chief, Section for Development of Financial Instns., United Nations, NYC, 1976–79; Fulbright Scholar, Univ. of Tunis, 1983–84. *Publs:* Italy in International Cooperation, 1959; (co-author) Postwar Trade in Divided Germany, 1964; (co-author) West German Foreign Aid 1956–66, 1968; The United States, The Soviet Union and the Third World, 1968; (co-author) American–East European Trade, 1969; (co-author) Trade and Industrialization in the Central American Common Market, 1971; (ed.) Monetary Policy in Twelve Industrial Countries, 1973; (co-author) Industrialization and Employment in Puerto Rico, 1974. Add: 313 Country Club Rd., Newton, Mass. 02159, U.S.A.

HOLBO, Paul Sothe. American, b. 1929. History, International relations/Current affairs. Prof. of History and Vice Provost for Acad. Affairs, Univ. of Oregon, Eugene. Founder-Ed., Diplomatic History journal, 1977. *Publs:* (ed.) Isolationism and Interventionism, 1932–41, 1967; United States Policies Toward China, 1970; (ed. with R. Sellen) The Eisenhower Era, 1974; Tarnished Expansion, 1983. Add: 2090 Broadview, Eugene, Ore. 97405, U.S.A.

HOLBROOK, David (Kenneth). British, b. 1923. Novels/Short stories, Poetry, Songs, lyrics and libretti, Education, Literary criticism/History, Philosophy. Asst. Ed., Our Time mag., 1947–48, and Bureau of Current Affairs, 1948–51, both London; Tutor in Adult Education, 1951–61, and at Bassingbourn Village Coll., Cambs., 1954–61; Fel-

low, King's Coll., Cambridge, 1961–65; part-time Lectr. in English, Jesus Coll., Cambridge, 1968–70; Writer-in-Residence, Dartington Hall, Devon, 1970–72; Asst. Dir. of English Studies, 1973–74, Dir., 1981–88, now Emeritus Fellow, Downing Coll., Cambridge (Leverhulme Emeritus Research Fellow, 1988–90). *Publs:* Children's Games, 1957; The Borderline, 1959; Imaginings, 1961; English for Maturity, 1961; (ed.) Iron Honey Gold, 1961; (ed.) People and Diamonds, 1962; Llareggub Revisited, 1962; Lights in the Sky Country, 1962; Against the Cruel Frost, 1963; (co-author) Penguin Modern Poets, 4, 1963; (ed.) Thieves and Angels, 1963; (ed.) Visions of Life, 1964; The Secret Places: Essays on Imaginative Work in English Teaching and on the Culture of the Child, 1964; English for the Rejected, 1964; The Quest for Love, 1964; Flesh Wounds (novel), 1966; I've Got to Use Words, 1966; The Flowers Shake Themselves Free, 1966; (ed. with E. Poston) The Cambridge Hymnal, 1967; The Exploring Word, 1967; Children's Writing, 1967; Object Relations, 1967; (ed.) Plucking the Rushes, 1968; Old World, New World, 1969; Human Hope and the Death Instinct, 1971; The Masks of Hate: The Problem of False Solutions in the Culture of an Acquisitive Society, 1972; Sex and Dehumanisation in Art, Thought and Life in Our Time, 1972; Dylan Thomas and the Code of Night, 1972; The Pseudo-Revolution: A Critical Study of Extremist Liberation in Sex, 1972; English in Australia Now, 1972; (ed.) The Case Against Pornography, 1972; Gustav Mahler and the Courage to Be, 1975; Sylvia Plath: Poetry and Existence, 1976; Lost Bearings in English Poetry, 1977; Education, Nihilism and Survival, 1977; A Play of Passion (novel), 1978; Chance of a Lifetime, 1978; Moments in Italy, 1978; English for Meaning, 1980; Selected Poems, 1980; Evolution and the Humanities, 1987; Nothing Larger Than Life (novel), 1987; The Novel and Authenticity, 1987; Education and Philosophical Anthropology, 1987; Further Studies in Philosophical Anthropology, 1987; World's Apart (novel); Images of Woman in Literature, 1989. Add: Denmore Lodge, Brunswick Gardens, Cambridge, England.

HOLCK, Manfred, Jr. American, b. 1930. Money/Finance, Theology/Religion. Publisher, The Clergy Journal, Hopkins, Minn., 1975–80, and in Austin, Tex., since 1980. Pastor, St. Martin's Lutheran Church, Houston, Tex., 1956–64; Vice-Pres. for Business Affairs, Wittenberg Univ., Springfield, Ohio, 1965–74; Controller, Texas Lutheran Coll., Seguin, 1974; Controller, Bd. of Pensions, Lutheran Church in America, 1975–80. *Publs:* Accounting Methods for the Small Church, 1961; Money Management for Ministers, 1966; Pre-Parish Planner, 1974; Making It on a Pastor's Pay, 1974; Money and Your Church, 1974; How to Pay Your Pastor More, 1976; Complete Handbook of Church Accounting, 1978; Annual Budgeting, 1978; Cash Management, 1978; Church Finance in a Complex Economy, 1983; Dedication Services for Every Occasion, 1984; Clergy Desk Book, 1985; (ed. with Lois Holck) The Minister's Annual Manual 1987-1988: Preaching and Worship Planning, 1987. Add: P.O. Box 162527, Austin, Tex., 78716, U.S.A.

HOLDEN, Anthony (Ivan). British, b. 1947. Biography, Translations. Freelance journalist. General Reporter, 1973–77, and Columnist ("Atticus"), 1977–79, Sunday Times newspaper, London; Washington Correspondent, The Observer newspaper, London, and Columnist ("Transatlantic Cables"), Punch mag., London, 1979–81; Features Ed., The Times newspaper, London, 1981–82. Presenter, In the Air, BBC Radio 4, 1982–84; Columnist, Sunday Express Magazine, 1982–85; Exec. Ed., Sunday Today, 1985–86. *Publs:* (ed. and trans.) Agamemnon, 1969; (ed. and trans.) Greek Pastoral Poetry, 1974; The St. Albans Poisoner, 1974; Charles, Prince of Wales, 1979; Their Royal Highnesses, 1981; Royal Quiz, 1983; Of Presidents, Prime Ministers, and Princes, 1984; The Queen Mother, 1985; (trans. with Amanda Holden) Don Giovanni, 1987; Olivier, 1988; Charles, 1988. Add: c/o A.P. Watt Ltd., 26-28 Bedford Row, London WC1R 4HL, England.

HOLDEN, Elizabeth Rhoda. *See* **LAWRENCE,** Louise.

HOLDEN, J(ames) Milnes. British, b. 1918. Law, Money/Finance. Prof. of Business Law, Univ. of Stirling, 1974–86, now Emeritus (Sr. Lectr., 1972–73; Reader, 1973–74). Legal Consultant to the Inter-Bank Research Org., London, 1969–72. *Publs:* (ed.) Payne's Carriage of Goods by Sea, 6th ed. 1954; History of Negotiable Instruments in English Law, 1955; (ed. with C. Drover) Chalmers' Marine Insurance Act 1906, 5th ed. 1956; Law and Practice of Banking, vol. I, 4th ed., 1986, vol. II, 7th ed., 1986; (ed.) Jones and Holden's Studies in Practical Banking, 6th ed. 1971. Add: Univ. of Stirling, Stirling FK9 4LA, Scotland.

HOLDEN, Joan. American, b. 1939. Plays/Screenplays. Playwright, San Francisco Mime Troupe, since 1967 (Publicist, 1967–69; Business Mgr., 1978–79). Waitress, Claremont Hotel, Berkeley, Calif., 1960–62; Copywriter, Librarie Larousse, Paris, 1964–66; Research Asst., Univ. of

California at Berkeley, 1966–67; Ed., Pacific News Service, 1973–75; Instr. in Playwriting, Univ. of California at Davis, 1975, 1977, 1979, 1981, 1983, 1985. *Publs:* By Popular Demand: Plays and Other Works by the San Francisco Mime Troupe (includes False Promises/Nos Engañaron); (with others) San Fran Scandals; (with others) The Dragon Lady's Revenge: The Independent Female, or, A Man Has His Pride; (with others) Frijoles, or, Beans to You; (with Richard Benetar and Dan Chumley) Frozen Wages, 1980. Add: c/o San Francisco Mime Troupe, 855 Treat St., San Francisco, Calif. 94110, U.S.A.

HOLDEN, Matthew, Jr. American, b. 1931. Politics/Government, Public/Social administration, Race relations. Henry L. and Grace M. Doherty Prof. of Govt. and Foreign Affairs, Univ. of Virginia, Charlottesville, since 1981. Formerly Prof. of Political Science, Univ. of Wisconsin, Madison, from 1969; Commissioner, Public Service Cttee. of Wisc., 1975–77; Commnr., Federal Energy Regulatory Commn., Washington, D.C., 1977–81. *Publs:* County Government in Ohio, 1958; Inter-Governmental Agreements in Cleveland and Metropolitan Area, 1958; Pollution Control as a Bargaining Process, 1966; (ed.) Varieties of Political Conservatism, 1973; The Politics of Poor Relief: A Study in Ambiguities, 1973; The Divisible Republic, 1973; The Politics of the Black "Nation", 1973; The White Man's Burden, 1973; (ed. with D. Dresang) Yearbook of Politics and Public Policy, 1974; (ed. with D. Dresang) What Government Does, 1975; The Centrality of Administration to Politics, 1984; Cabinet Departments with Domestic Responsibilities, 1984; (with others) Congress and the Afro-American 1902 to 1948: A Tabulation of Legislation Proposals, 1984. Add: 232 Cabell Hall, Univ. of Virginia, Charlottesville, Va. 22905, U.S.A.

HOLDGATE, Martin W. British, b. 1931. Biology, Environmental science/Ecology, History. Dir.-Gen., Intnl. Union for Conservation of Nature and Natural Resources, since 1988. Univ. Lectr., Durham Univ., 1957–60; Asst. Dir. of Research, Scott Polar Research Inst., Cambridge, 1960–63; Chief Biologist, British Antarctic Survey, 1963–66; Deputy Dir. (Research), Nature Conservancy, London, 1966–70; Dir., Central Unit of Environmental Pollution, Dept. of the Environment, London, 1970–74; Dir., Inst. of Terrestrial Ecology, Natural Environment Research Council, 1974–76; Chief Scientist, Depts. of the Environment and Transport, London, 1976–88. *Publs:* History of Appleby, County Town of Westmorland, 1956, 1971; Mountains in the Sea—The Story of the Gough Island Expedition, 1958; (jt. ed.) Biologie Antartique—Antarctic Biology, 1966; (jt. ed.) Antarctic Ecology, 1970; (ed.) The Restoration of Damaged Ecosystems, 1976; (jt. ed.) Environmental Issues, 1977; A Perspective of Environmental Pollution, 1979; (jt. ed.) The World Environment 1972–82, 1982. Add: Pré de la Ferme 13, CH1261 Gingins, Switzerland.

HOLDHEIM, William (Wolfgang). American, b. 1926. Literature, Translations. Prof. of Comparative Literature, and Frederic J. Whiton Prof. of Liberal Studies, Cornell Univ., Ithaca, N.Y., since 1969. Instr. of French, Ohio State Univ., 1955–57; Instr. of European Languages and Literature, 1957–58, Asst. Prof., 1958–61, and Assoc. Prof., 1961–64, Brandeis Univ., Waltham, Mass.; Prof. of French and Comparative Literature, Washington Univ., 1964–69. *Publs:* Benjamin Constant, 1961; (trans.) Ressentiment, by Max Scheler, 1961; Theory and Practice of the Novel, 1968; Der Justizirrtum als literarische Problematik, 1969; Die Suche nach dem Epos, 1978; The Hermeneutic Mode, 1984. Add: 706 Cayuga Heights Rd., Ithaca, N.Y. 14850, U.S.A.

HOLDSTOCK, Robert. British, b. 1948. Science fiction/Fantasy, Astronomy. Freelance writer. *Publs:* Eye among the Blind, 1976; Earthwind, 1977; Necromancer, 1978; (ed.) Octopus Encyclopaedia of Science Fiction, 1978; (ed. with Christopher Priest) Stars of Albion (anthology), 1979; (with Malcolm Edwards) Alien Landscapes (non-fiction), 1979; (with Malcolm Edwards) Tour of the Universe (non-fiction), 1980; Where Time Winds Blow, 1981; In the Valley of the Statues (stories), 1982; (with Malcolm Edwards) Realms of Fantasy (non-fiction), 1983; (with Malcolm Edwards) Lost Realms (non-fiction), 1984; Mythago Wood, 1984; Bulman, 1984; The Emerald Forest (novelization of screenplay), 1985; One of Our Pigeons Is Missing, 1985; The Labyrinth, 1987; (ed. with Christopher Evans) Other Edens, 1987; Lavondyss, 1988. Add: 54 Raleigh Rd., London N8, England.

HOLFORD, Ingrid. British, b. 1920. Meteorology. *Publs:* A Century of Sailing on the Thames, 1968; Interpreting the Weather, 1973; British Weather Disasters, 1976; Guinness Book of Weather Facts and Feats, 1978, 1982; The Yachtsman's Weather Guide, 1979, 1988; Looking at Weather, 1985; The Air Pilots Weather Guide, 1988. Add: 5 Oberfield Rd., Brockenhurst, Hants SO42 7QF, England.

HOLLAND, Cecelia (Anastasia). American, b. 1943. Novels/Short stories, Science fiction/Fantasy, Children's fiction. *Publs:* The Firedrake, 1966; Rakossy, 1967; Kings in Winter, 1968; Until the Sun Falls, 1969; Ghost on the Steppe, 1969; The King's Road, 1970; Cold Iron, 1970; Antichrist, 1970; Wonder of the World, 1970; The Earl, 1971; The Death of Attila, 1973; The Great Maria, 1975; Floating Worlds, 1976; Two Ravens, 1977; The Earl, 1979; Home Ground, 1981; The Sea Beggars, 1982; The Belt of Gold, 1984; Pillar of the Sky, 1985; The Lords of Vaumartin 1988. Add: c/o Houghton Mifflin, 2 Park St., Boston, Mass. O2108, U.S.A.

HOLLAND, Elizabeth Anne. British, b. 1928. Novels/Short stories, Literature. Dir., Survey of Old Bath; Ed., New Tolkien Newsletter, The Road. *Publs:* A Separate Person, 1962; The House in the North, 1963; The House by the Sea, 1965; The Adding Up, 1968; (with R. Giddings) J.R.R. Tolkien: The Shores of Middle-Earth, 1981; Citizens of Bath, 1988. Add: 16 Prior Park Bldgs., Bath, Avon BA2 4NP, England.

HOLLAND, Francis (Ross), Jr. American. History. Historian and Exec. with National Park Service, 1958–83; Dir., Restoration and Preservation, Statue of Liberty, Ellis Island Foundation, 1983–86. *Publs:* American Lighthouses, 1972; Arkansas Pass Light Station, 1976; The Old Point Loma Lighthouse, 1978; Guide to Great American Lighthouses, 1989. Add: 13709 Mills Ave., Silver Spring. Md. 20904, U.S.A.

HOLLAND, Isabelle. Also writes as Francesca Hunt. American, b. 1920. Historical/Romance/Gothic, Children's fiction. Publicity Dir., Lippincott, Dell, and Putnam publishing cos., NYC, 1960–68. *Publs:* Cecily, 1967; Amanda's Choice, 1970; The Man Without a Face, 1972; (as Francesca Hunt) The Mystery of Castle Renaldi, 1972; Heads You Win, Tails I Lose, 1973; Kilgaren (romance), 1974; Trelawny (romance), in U.K. as Trelawny's Fell, 1976; Moncrieff (romance), 1975, in U.K. as The Standish Place, 1976; Of Love and Death and Other Journeys, 1975; Journey for Three, 1975; Darcourt (romance), 1976; Grenelle (romance), 1976; Alan and the Animal Kingdom, 1977; Hitchhike, 1977; The de Maury Papers (romance), 1977; Dinah and the Green Fat Kingdom, 1978; Ask No Questions, 1978; Tower Abbey (romance), 1978; The Marchington Inheritance (romance), 1979; Counterpoint (romance), 1980; Now Is Not Too Late, 1980; Summer of My First Love, 1981; The Lost Madonna (romance), 1981; A House Named Peaceable, 1982; Abbie's God Book, 1982; Perdita, 1983; God, Mrs. Musket and Aunt Dot, 1983; The Empty House, 1983; Kevin's Hut, 1984; Green Andrew Green, 1984; A Death at St. Anselm's, 1984; Flight of the Archangel, 1985; The Island, 1985; Jennie Kiss'd Me, 1985; Love Scorned, 1986; Henry and Grudge, 1986; Toby the Splendid, 1987; Love and the Genetic Factor, 1987; The Christmas Cat, 1987. Add: c/o Elaine Markson Literary Agency, 44 Greenwich Ave., New York, N.Y. 10014, U.S.A.

HOLLAND, James R. Also writes as J.H. Rand. American, b. 1944. Music, Travel/Exploration/Adventure, Biography. Real estate developer, since 1976. Photographer Trainee, 1966, and Contract Photographer, 1967–68, National Geographic Mag., Washington, D.C.; Film Producer, Christian Science Center, Boston, 1969–75. *Publs:* The Amazon, 1971; Mr. Pops, 1972; Tanglewood, 1973. Add: 63 Commonwealth Ave., Boston, Mass. 02116, U.S.A.

HOLLAND, Leslie Arthur. British, b. 1921. Physics (applied). Consultant, chartered engineer, and physicist. Member, Editorial Bd., Surface Coatings and Technology, and Microelectronics and Reliability; Assoc. Ed., Vacuum; Ed., Plasma Technology series. Assoc. Reader in Physics, Brunel Univ., Uxbridge, Middx., 1963–77; Dir. of Research, Central Research Lab., Edwards High Vacuum Intnl. Ltd., Crawley, 1966–73; Visiting Lectr., Sch. of Production Studies, Cranfield Inst. of Technology, 1973–77; Whitworth Fellow, 1975–76; Prof., Sch. of Mathematical and Physical Sciences, Univ. of Sussex, 1976–85. Pres., Intnl. Union of Vacuum Science and Technology, 1977–80. *Publs:* The Vacuum Deposition of Thin Films, 1956; The Properties of Glass Surfaces, 1964; (advisory ed.) Thin Solid Films, pub. by Elsevier Seuoia, 1967–85; (with W. Steckelmacher and J. Yarwood) Vacuum Manual, 1974; (ed.) Thin Film Microelectronics, 1974. Add: Hazelwood, Balcombe Rd., Pound Hill, Crawley, Sussex RH10 3NZ, England.

HOLLAND, Norman N. American, b. 1927. Literature, Psychology. Marston-Milbauer Prof., Univ. of Florida, Gainesville, since 1983. Instr. to Assoc. Prof., Massachusett Inst. of Technology, Cambridge, 1955–66; Prof., 1966–79, McNulty Prof., 1979–83, and Chmn. of the English Dept., 1966–68, State Univ. of New York at Buffalo. *Publs:* The First Modern Comedies, 1959, 1967; The Shakespearean Imagination, 1964, 1968; Psychoanalysis and Shakespeare, 1966, 1975; The Dynamics of Literary

Response, 1968, 1989; Poems in Persons, 1973, 1989; 5 Readers Reading, 1975; Laughing, 1982; The I, 1985; The Brain of Robert Frost, 1988. Add: Dept. of English, Univ. of Florida Gainesville, Fla. 32611, U.S.A.

HOLLAND, Sheila (née Coates). Also writes as Sheila Coates, Laura Hardy, Charlotte Lamb and Sheila Lancaster. British, b. 1937. Historical/Romance/Gothic. Secty., Bank of England, London. 1954–56, and BBC, London, 1956–58. *Publs:* novels, as Sheila Holland—Love in a Mist, 1971; Prisoner of the Heart, 1972; A Lantern in the Night, 1973; Falcon on the Hill, 1974; Shadows at Dawn, 1975; The Growing Season, 1975; The Gold of Apollo, 1976; The Caring Kind, 1976; The Devil and Miss Hay, 1977; Eleanor of Aquitaine, 1978; Maiden Castle, 1978; Love's Bright Flame, 1978; Dancing Hill, 1978; Folly by Candlelight, 1978, in U.S. as The Notorious Gentleman, 1980; Sophia, 1979; The Masque, 1979; The Merchant's Daughter, 1980; Miss Charlotte's Fancy, 1980; Secrets to Keep, 1980; Secrets, 1984; A Woman of Iron, 1985; as Sheila Coates—A Crown Usurped, 1972; The Queen's Letter, 1973; The Flight of the Swan, 1973; The Bells of the City, 1975; as Charlotte Lamb— Follow a Stranger, 1973; Carnival Coast, 1973; Family Affair, 1974; Star-Crossed, 1976; Sweet Sanctuary, 1976; Festival Summer, 1977; Florentine Spring, 1977; Hawk in a Blue Sky, 1977; Kingfisher Morning, 1977; Master of Comus, 1977; Call Back Yesterday, 1978; Desert Barbarian, 1978; Disturbing Stranger, 1978; Autumn Conquest, 1978; The Long Surrender, 1978; The Cruel Flame, 1978; Duel of Desire, 1978; The Devil's Arms, 1978; Pagan Encounter, 1978; Forbidden Fire, 1979; The Silent Trap, 1979; Dark Dominion, 1979; Fever, 1979; Dark Master, 1979; Temptation, 1979; Twist of Fate, 1979; Possession, 1979; Love Is a Frenzy, 1979; Frustration, 1979; Sensation, 1979; Compulsion, 1980; Crescendo, 1980; Stranger in the Night, 1980; Storm Centre, 1980; Seduction, 1980; Savage Surrender, 1980; A Frozen Fire, 1980; Man's World, 1980; Night Music, 1980; Obsession, 1980; Retribution, 1981; Illusion, 1981; Heartbreaker, 1981; Desire, 1981; Dangerous, 1981; Abduction, 1981; A Violation, 1983; Infatuation, 1984; Scandalous, 1989; For Adults Only, 1984; Man Hunt, 1985; Heat of the Night, 1986; Hide and Seek, 1987; Kiss of Fire, 1987; You Can Love a Stranger, 1988; Seductive Stranger, 1989; as Sheila Lancaster—Dark Sweet Wanton, 1979; The Tilthammer, 1980; Mistress of Fortune, 1982; as Laura Hardy—Burning Memories, 1981; Playing with Fire, 1981; Dream Master, 1982; Tears and Red Roses, 1982. Add: Applegate, Port St. Mary, Isle of Man, U.K.

HOLLANDER, John. American, b. 1929. Children's fiction, Poetry, Literature. Prof. of English, Yale Univ., New Haven, Conn., since 1977 (Instr., 1959–61; Asst. Prof., 1961–63; Assoc. Prof., 1963–66). Editorial Bd., Ravitan, since 1981. Lectr., Connecticut Coll., New London, 1957– 59; Prof. of English, Hunter Coll., City Univ. of New York, 1966–77. Member, Poetry Bd., Wesleyan Univ., N.J., 1959–62; Editorial Asst. for Poetry, Partisan Review, New Brunswick, N.J., 1959–66; Overseas Fellow, Churchill Coll., Cambridge, 1967–68; Contrib. Ed., Harper's mag., NYC, 1969–71. *Publs:* A Crackling of Thorns (poetry, 1500-1700), 1961; (ed.) Selected Poems, by Ben Jonson, 1961; (ed. with H. Bloom) The Wind and the Rain: An Anthology of Poems for Young People, 1961; Movie-Going and Other Poems, 1962; A Beach Vision (poetry), 1962; A Book of Various Owls (children's poetry), 1962; Visions from the Ramble (poetry), 1965; The Quest of the Gole (children's poetry), 1966; (ed. with Anthony Hecht) Jiggery-Pokery: A Compendium of Double Dactyls, 1967; (ed.) Poems of Our Moment, 1968; Philomel (poetry), 1968; Types of Shape: Poems, 1969; An Entertainment for Elizabeth, Being a Masque of the Seven Motions: or, Terpsichore Unchained (play), 1969; Images of Voice, 1969; The Night Mirror: Poems, 1971; Town and Country Matters: Erotica and Satirica (poetry), 1972; The Immense Parade on Supererogation Day (children's fiction), 1972; Selected Poems, 1973; (co-ed.) The Oxford Anthology of English Literature, 2 vols., 1973; (ed. with Reuben Brower and Helen Vendler) I.A. Richards: Essays in His Honor, 1973; The Head of the Bed (poetry), 1974; Tales Told of the Fathers (poetry), 1975; Vision and Resonance: Two Senses of Poetic Form, 1975; Reflections on Espionage, 1976; Spectral Emanations: New and Selected Poems, 1978; In Place, 1978; Blue Wine and Other Poems, 1979; (ed. with D. Bromwich) Literature as Experience, 1979; Rhyme's Reason, 1981; The Figure of Echo, 1981; Powers of Thirteen, 1983; In Time and Place, 1986; Harp Lake, 1988; Melodious Guile, 1988. Add: Dept. of English, Yale Univ., Box 3545 Yale Station, New Haven, Conn. 06520, U.S.A.

HOLLANDER, Samuel. British and Canadian, b. 1937. Economics. Prof. of Economics since 1970, and Univ. Prof. since 1984, Univ. of Toronto (Asst. Prof., 1963–67; Assoc. Prof., 1967–70). Asst., Princeton Univ., New Jersey, 1962–63. *Publs:* The Sources of Increased Efficiency: A Study of DuPont Rayon Plants, 1965; The Economics of Adam Smith, 1973; The Economics of David Ricardo, 1979; The Economics

of John Stuart Mill, 1985; Classical Economics, 1987. Add: Dept. of Economics, Univ. of Toronto, 150 St. George St., Toronto, Ont. M5S 1A1, Canada.

HOLLANDER, Stanley C(harles). American, b. 1919. Administration/Management, Business/Trade/Industry. Prof. of Marketing, Michigan State Univ., Grad. Sch. of Business, East Lansing, since 1959 (Assoc. Prof., 1958–59). Instr., Univ. of Buffalo, N.Y., 1947–49; Instr. 1949–54, and Assoc. Prof., 1956–58, Univ. of Pennsylvania, Philadelphia; Asst. Prof., Univ. of Minnesota, Minneapolis, 1954–56. *Publs:* (ed.) Explorations in Retailing, 1959; (ed.) Management Consultants and Clients, 1963; Restraints Upon Retail Competition, 1965; (ed.) Passenger Transportation, 1968; (ed. with R. Moyer) Markets and Marketing in Economic Development, 1968; Multinational Retailing, 1970; (ed.) Business Consultants and Clients, 1972; (ed. with J.J. Boddewyn) Public Policy toward Retailing, 1972; (with D.J. Duncan and C. Phillips) Modern Retailing Management, 8th ed. 1972, (with D.J. Duncan and R. Javitt) 10th ed. 1983. Add: Dept. of Marketing, Michigan State Univ., East Lansing, Mich. 48824, U.S.A.

HOLLANDS, Roy (Derrick). British, b. 1924. Mathematics/Statistics. Mathematics teacher, Altrincham Grammar School, 1952–57, Normanton Grammar School, 1957–61, and Firth Park Comprehensive School, Sheffield, 1961–66; Lectr., Totley Hall Coll. of Education, 1966–71, and Dundee Coll. of Education, 1971–80; now free-lance writer. *Publs:* Mathematical Games and Activities for First Schools, 1971; Modern Mathematics for Parents and Teachers, 1971; The Unconscious Humour of Children, 1973; Mathematics Enrichment Cards, 1975; Maths Games and Activities, 1977; Practice Maths Sheets, 1978; A Dictionary of Mathematics, 1980; Foundation Arithmetic, 1980–81; Basic Arithmetic, 1981; also co-author of other mathematics texts. Add: 48 Grimbald Road, Knaresborough, N. Yorkshire HG5 8HD, England.

HOLLES, Robert. British, b. 1926. Novels/Short stories, Plays/Screenplays, Humour. Artist-in-Residence, Central State Univ. of Oklahoma, 1981–82. *Publs:* Now Thrive the Armourers, 1952; The Bribe Scorners, 1956; Captain Cat, 1960; The Siege of Battersea, 1962; Religion and Davey Peach, 1964; The Nature of the Beast, 1965; Guns at Batasi (screenplay), 1965; Spawn, 1978; I'll Walk Beside You, 1979; Sun Blight, 1982; The Guide to Real Village Cricket, 1983; The Guide to Real Subversive Soldiering, 1985. Add: Ware House, Stebbing, Essex, England.

HOLLEY, Edward Gailon. American, b. 1927. Librarianship, Biography. Prof., Sch. of Info., and Library Science, Univ. of North Carolina, Chapel Hill, since 1985 (Dean, 1972–85). Trustee, OCLC, Inc., since 1985. Chmn., Bd. of Governors, UNC Press, since 1989. Education, Philosophy and Psychology Librarian, Univ. of Illinois, Urbana, 1957–62; Dir. of Libraries, Univ. of Houston, Tex., 1962–71. Pres., American Library Assn., 1974–75. *Publs:* Charles Evans: American Bibliographer, 1963; (compiler) Raking the Historic Coals: The ALA Scrapbook of 1876, 1967; (with D.D. Hendricks) Resources of Texas Libraries, 1968; (with others) Resources of South Carolina Libraries,1976; (with Robert F. Shremser) Library Services and Construction Act, 1983. Add: 1508 Ephesus Church Rd., Chapel Hill, N.C. 27514, U.S.A.

HOLLEY, Irving Brinton, Jr. American, b. 1919. History, Military/Defence. Prof. of History, Duke Univ., Durham, N.C., since 1961 (Instr., 1947–50; Asst. Prof., 1950–54; Assoc. Prof., 1954–61); Prof. Emeritus of Military History, Air War College. Member of faculty, Industrial Coll. of the Armed Forces, 1945–47, and U.S. Military Academy, 1974–75; member, Adv. Comm. on History, Natl. Aeronautical and Space Admin., 1974–81; Chmn., Adv. Comm. on Air Force Historical Program, 1970–79; Visiting Prof., Natl. Defense Univ., Washington, 1978–79; Chmn., Ed. Comm. for Society for History of Technology, 1979–81. *Publs:* Ideas and Weapons, 1953, 3rd ed. 1983; Buying Aircraft: Air Materiel Procurement for the Army Air Forces, 1964; (ed. with C.D.W. Goodwin) The Transfer of Ideas, 1968; General John M. Palmer, Citizen Soldiers, and the Army of a Democracy (biography), 1982. Add: Dept. of History, Duke Univ., Durham, N.C. 27706, U.S.A.

HOLLI, Melvin George. American, b. 1933. Cultural/Ethnic topics, History, Biography. Assoc. Prof. to Prof. of History, Univ. of Illinois, Chicago, since 1965. Research Asst. and Curator of Manuscripts, Historical Collection, and Research and Teaching Fellow, Univ. of Michigan, Ann Arbor, 1961–64. *Publs:* Reform in Detroit, 1969; Detroit: Fur Trading Post to Industrial Metropolis, 1975; (ed. with P. Jones) The Ethnic Frontiers, 1977; (with P. Jones) Ethnic Chicago, 1981; (ed.) Biographical Dictionary of American Mayors 1820-1980, 1982; The Making of the

Mayor, Chicago 1983, 1984; (with P.M. Green) The Mayors: The Chicago Political Tradition, 1987; (with P. M. Green) Bashing Chicago Traditions: Harold Washington's Last Campaign, 1989. Add: 1311 Ashland Ave., River Forest, Ill. 60305, U.S.A.

HOLLINDALE, Peter. British, b. 1936. Literature. Lectr. in English and Education, Univ. of York, since 1965: Sr. Lectr. since 1975. Asst. Master in English, Clifton Coll., Bristol, 1962–65. *Publs:* A Critical Commentary on Shakespeare's King Henry IV, Part Two, 1971; (ed.) Shakespeare: As You Like It, 1974; Choosing Books for Children, 1974; (ed.) Shakespeare: King Henry IV, Part One, 1975; (ed.) Lord Jim, by Conrad, 1982; (ed.) Volpone, by Jonson, 1985; Ideology and the Children's Book, 1988. Add: Dept. of English and Related Literature, Univ. of York, York YO1 5DD, England.

HOLLINGDALE, Reginald John. British, b. 1930. Literature, Philosophy, Translations. Sub-Ed., The Guardian newspaper, London, since 1968. *Publs:* (trans.) Thus Spoke Zarathustra, by Nietzsche, 1961, 1969; (trans.) One Summer on Majorca, by Marielis Hoberg, 1961; (trans.) The Voyage to Africa, by Hoberg, 1964; Nietzsche: The Man and His Philosophy, 1965; Western Philosophy: An Introduction, 1966, 1979; (trans. with Walter Kaufmann) The Will to Power, by Nietzsche, 1967; (trans. with Kaufmann) On the Genealogy of Morals, by Nietzsche, 1967; (trans.) Twilight of the Idols and the Anti-Christ, by Nietzsche, 1968; (trans. and ed.) Essays and Aphorisms of Schopenhauer, 1970; (trans.) Elective Affinities, by Goethe, 1971; Thomas Mann: A Critical Study, 1971; (trans.) Beyond Good and Evil, by Nietzsche, 1973; Nietzsche (critical study), 1973; (trans.) Tangram, by Joost Effers, 1976; (ed. and trans.) A Nietzsche Reader, 1977; (trans.) Ecce Homo by Nietzsche, 1979; (trans.) Otto Dix, by Fritz Loeffler, 1981; (trans.) Daybreak, by Nietzsche, 1982; (ed. and trans.) Tales of Hoffmann, 1982; (trans.) Untimely Meditations, by Nietzsche, 1983; (ed. and trans.) Dithyrambs of Dionysus, by Nietzsche, 1984; (ed. and trans.) Before the Storm, by Fontane, 1985; (trans.) Human, All Too Human, by Nietzsche, 1987; (trans.) Between Literature and Science, by Wolf Lepenier, 1988. Add: 32 Warrington Cres., London W9, England.

HOLLINGSHEAD, (Ronald) Kyle. American, b. 1941. Novels/Short stories. Partner in 4th St. Coin Laundry, Lubbock, Tex. *Publs:* Echo of Texas Rifle, 1967; The Franklin Raid, 1968; Ransome's Debt, 1970; Ransome's Move, 1971; Ransome's Army, 1974; The Man on the Blood Bay, 1977; Across the Border, 1978. Add: 4225 53rd St., Lubbock, Tex. 79413, U.S.A.

HOLLINGSWORTH, Margaret. Canadian (born British), b. 1940. Plays/Screenplays. Free-lance writer since 1972. Journalist, librarian, and teacher in England, 1960–68; librarian, Fort William Public Library, Ont., 1968–72; Asst. Prof., David Thompson Univ. Centre, Nelson, B.C., 1981–83. *Publs:* Dance for My Father, 1976; Alli Alli Oh, 1979; Mother Country, 1980; Bushed, and Operators, 1981; Ever Loving, 1981; Islands, 1983; Willful Acts (collection), 1985; Endangered Species (collection), 1988. Add: c/o Playwrights Union of Canada, 8 York St., Toronto, Ont. M5J 1R2, Canada.

HOLLINGSWORTH, Paul M. American, b. 1932. Education. Prof. of Elementary Education, Brigham Young Univ., since 1985. Dir., Sierra Reading Council of the Intnl. Reading Assn., 1969–85; Prof. and Dir., Reading Center, Coll. of Education, Univ. of Nevada, Reno, 1970–85, and Dir., Div. of Curriculum and Instruction, 1982–85 (Assoc. Prof., 1966–70). *Publs:* (with G.M. Chronister) A Longitudinal View of Development, 1965; (with J. Patrick Kelly) Basic Reading Instruction, 1969; (with Kenneth H. Hoover) Learning and Teaching in the Elementary School, 1970, 1978; (with Kenneth H. Hoover) A Handbook for Elementary School Teachers, 1973, 1978, 1982; Individualized Reading Skills, 1973, 1978; Teaching Reading in the Middle and Upper Grades, 1977; (with S. Templeton and K. Johns) Back to Basics: How To Help Your Child Be a Success in School, 1986. Add: Education Dept., Brigham Young Univ., Provo, Utah 84602, U.S.A.

HOLLIS, Helen Rice. American. Music. Specialist (retired), Div. of Musical Instruments, Smithsonian Instn., Washington, D.C. *Publs:* Pianos in the Smithsonian Institution, 1973; The Piano: A Pictorial Account of Its Ancestry and Development, 1975, rev. ed. 1984; The Musical Instruments of Joseph Haydn: An Introduction, 1977. Add: 3329 Fairmount Blvd., Cleveland, Ohio 44118, U.S.A.

HOLLIS, Jim. *See* SUMMERS, Hollis.

HOLLO, Anselm (Paul Alexis). Finnish, b. 1934. Poetry, Translations.

Assoc., New Coll. of California, San Francisco, since 1981. Prog. Asst. and Coordinator, BBC, London, 1958–66; Visiting Lectr., 1968–69, Lectr. in English and Music, 1970–71, and Head, Translation Workshop, 1971–72, Univ. of Iowa, Iowa City; Poetry Ed., Iowa Review, Iowa City, 1971–72; Assoc. and Visiting Prof., Bowling Green Univ., Ohio, 1972–73; Poet-in-Residence, Hobart and William Smith Coll., Geneva, N.Y., 1973–74; Writer-in-Residence, Sweet Briar Coll., Va., 1978–80. *Publs:* Sateiden Valilla, 1956; St. Texts and Finnpoems, 1961; Loverman, 1961; (ed. and trans.) Kaddisch, by Allen Ginsberg, 1962; (ed. and trans.) Red Cats: Selection from the Russian Poets, 1962; (ed.) Jazz Poems, 1963; (ed. and trans.) In der Flüchtigen Hand der Zeit, by Gregory Corso, 1963; (ed. and trans.) Huuto ja Muita Runoja, by Allen Ginsberg, 1963; (ed. and trans.) Kuolema van Goghin Korvalle, by Allen Ginsberg, 1963; (ed. and trans. with Markku Lahtela) Idan da Lannen Runot, 1963; We Just Wanted to Tell You, 1963; And What Else Is New, 1963; History, 1964; Trobar: Loytaa (poetry), 1964; (ed.) Negro Verse, 1964; (ed. and trans.) Selected Poems by Andre Voznesensky, 1964; (ed. and trans.) Nain Ihminen Vastaa, 1964; (ed. and trans.) Five Feet Two, by Rolf-Gunter Dienst, 1965; (ed. and trans.) Word from the North: New Poetry from Finland, 1965; Here We Go, 1965; The Claim, 1966; The Going-On Poem, 1966; Poems/Runoja (bilingual ed.), 1967; Isadora and Other Poems, 1967; Leaf Times, 1967; (ed. and trans.) Helsinki: Selected Poems, by Pentti Saarikoski, 1967; (ed. and trans.) Selected Poems, by Paavo Haavikko, 1968; The Man in the Tree-Top Hat, 1968; The Coherences, 1968; Tumbleweed: Poems, 1968; (with John Esam and Tom Raworth) Haiku, 1968; Waiting for a Beautiful Bather: Ten Poems, 1969; Maya: Works, 1959–69, 1970; America del Norte and Other Peace Herb Poems, 1970; Message, 1970; (ed. and trans.) The Twelve and Other Poems, by Aleksandr Blok, 1971; (with Jack Marshall and Sam Hamod) Surviving in America, 1972; Sensation 27, 1972; Some Worlds, 1974; Lingering Tangos, 1976; Sojourner Microcosms: New and Selected Poems 1959–1977, 1977; Heavy Jars, 1977; Curious Data, 1978; (ed. and trans. with Gunnar Harding) Recent Swedish Poetry in Translation, 1979; With Ruth in Mind, 1979; Finite Continued, 1980; No Complaints, 1983; (ed. and trans.) Pentti Saarikoski: Poems 1958–80, 1984; Pick Up the House, 1986; (trans.) Au Revoir les Enfants, by Louis Malle, 1988. Add: c/o Blue Wind Press, Box 7175, Berkeley, Calif. 94707, U.S.A.

HOLLOWAY, David. British, b. 1924. History, Biography, Humour. Member, Editorial Staff, Daily Sketch, London, 1941–42, and Daily Mirror, London, 1949; Member, Editorial Staff, 1950–60, Asst. Literary Ed., 1953–58, and Book Page Ed., 1958–60, News Chronicle, London; Deputy Literary Ed., 1960–68, and Literary Ed., 1968–88, Daily Telegraph, London. Chmn., Soc. of Bookmen, 1968–71; Chmn., Judging Panel, Booker Prize, 1969–70. *Publs:* John Galsworthy; Lewis and Clark and the Crossing of America; Derby Day (history); (ed.) Telegraph Year 1-3, 1977–79; Playing the Empire (biography), 1979; (with Michael Geare) Nothing So Became Them . . . (humour), 1986. Add: 95 Lonsdale Rd., London SW13.

HOLLOWAY, (Percival) Geoffrey. British, b. 1918. Poetry. Library Asst., Shropshire County Council, Shrewsbury, 1935–39, 1946; Social Worker, Hatton Psychiatric Hospital, Warwick, 1946–48; Officer, Prisoner's Aid Soc., Lincoln, 1950–51; Hospital Porter, Lincoln Sanatorium, 1951–53; Mental Health Worker, Westmorland County Council, Kendal, 1953–74; Social Worker, Cumbria County Council, Kendal, 1974–83. *Publs:* To Have Eyes, 1972; Rhine Jump, 1974; (ed.) Trio 2, 1977; All I Can Say, 1978; Salt, Roses, Vinegar, 1985; The Crones of Aphrodite, 1986; My Ghost in Your Eye, 1988. Add: 4 Gowan Cres., Staveley, nr. Kendal, Cumbria LA8 9NF, England.

HOLLOWAY, Harry (Albert). American, b. 1925. Politics/Government. Prof. of Political Science, Univ. of Oklahoma, Norman, since 1962. With Dept. of Govt., Univ. of Texas, Austin, 1957–62. *Publs:* (co-author) Party and Factional Division in Texas, 1964; The Politics of the Southern Negro, 1969; (co-author) Public Opinion: Coalitions, Elites, and Masses, 1979, 1986. Add: 455 W. Lindsey, Rm. 205, Dept of Political Science, Univ. of Oklahoma, Norman, Okla. 73019, U.S.A.

HOLLOWAY, John. British, b. 1920. Poetry, Literature, Autobiography. Prof. of Modern English, Cambridge Univ., 1972–82 (Univ. Lectr. in English, 1954–66; Fellow of Queens Coll., 1955; Reader in Modern English, 1966–72). Fellow, All Souls Coll., 1946–60, and John Locke Scholar, 1947, Oxford; Lectr. in English, Aberdeen Univ., 1949–54. Byron Prof., Univ. of Athens, 1961–63; Alexander White Prof., Univ. of Chicago, 1965. *Publs:* Language and Intelligence, 1951; The Victorian Sage: Studies in Argument, 1953; The Minute and Longer Poems, 1956; (ed.) Poems of the Mid-Century, 1957; (ed.) Selected Poems, by Percy Bysshe Shelley, 1959; The Fugue and Shorter Pieces (poetry), 1960; The

Charted Mirror: Literary and Critical Essays, 1960; The Story of the Night: Studies in Shakespeare's Major Tragedies, 1961; The Landfallers: A Poem in Twelve Parts, 1962; The Colours of Clarity: Essays on Contemporary Literature and Education, 1964; The Lion Hunt: A Pursuit of Poetry and Reality, 1964; Wood and Windfall (poetry), 1965; Widening Horizons in English Verse, 1966; A London Childhood (autobiography), 1966; (ed.) Little Dorrit, by Charles Dickens, 1967; Blake: The Lyric Poetry, 1968; New Poems, 1970; (ed. with J. Black) Later English Broadside Ballads, 2 vols., 1974–79; The Proud Knowledge: Poetry, Insight, and Self 1620-1920, 1977; Planet of Winds (poetry), 1977; Narrative and Structure: Exploratory Essays, 1979; The Slumber of Apollo: Reflections on Recent Art, Literature, Language, and the Individual Consciousness, 1983; Oxford Book of Local Verses, 1987. Add: Queens' Coll., Cambridge CB3 9ET, England.

HOLLOWAY, Mark. British, b. 1917. Poetry, History, Biography. *Publs:* Heavens on Earth: A History of Utopian Communities in the United States of America, 1951, rev. ed. 1966; Poems, 1956; William Harvey 1578-1659, 1957; Ten Poems, 1969; Norman Douglas 1868-1952, 1976. Add: c/o A.M. Heath & Co., 40-42 William IV St., London WC2N 4DD, England.

HOLLY, J. Hunter. Pseudonym for Joan Carol Holly. American, b. 1932. Science fiction. Has worked as a photographer, clerk, and ballet teacher. *Publs:* Encounter, 1959; The Green Planet, 1960; The Dark Planet, 1962; The Flying Eyes, 1962; The Running Man, 1963, The Gray Aliens, 1963; The Time Twisters, 1964; The Dark Enemy, 1965; The Mind Traders, 1966; Keeper, 1976; Death Dolls of Lyra, 1977; Shepherd, 1977. Add: c/o Avon Books, 105 Madison Ave., New York, N.Y. 10016, U.S.A.

HOLMAN, Felice. American, b. 1919. Novels/Short stories, Children's fiction, Poetry. *Publs:* Elisabeth the Birdwatcher, 1963; Elisabeth the Treasure Hunter, 1964; Silently the Cat, and Miss Theodosia, 1965; Elisabeth and the Marsh Mystery, 1966; Victoria's Castle, 1966; The Witch on the Corner, 1966; Professor Diggin's Dragons, 1966; The Cricket Winter, 1967; The Blackmail Machine, 1968; A Year to Grow, 1968; The Holiday Rat and the Utmost Mouse, 1969; At the Top of My Voice and Other Poems, 1970; The Future of Hooper Toote, 1972; I Hear You Smiling and Other Poems, 1973; The Escape of the Giant Hogstalk, 1974; Slake's Limbo, 1974; (with N. Valen) The Drac, 1975; The Murderer, 1978; The Wild Children, 1983; The Song in My Head, 1985. Add: c/o Charles Scribner's Sons, 866 Third Ave., New York, N.Y. 10022, U.S.A.

HOLMAN, Robert. British, b. 1936. Sociology. Child Care Officer, Herts. County Council, 1962–64; Lectr. in Social Work, Univ. of Birmingham, 1964–72; Sr. Lectr. in Social Administration, Univ. of Glasgow, 1972–74; Prof. of Social Administration, Univ. of Bath, 1974–76; Leader of Southdown Community Project, 1976–86. *Publs:* Trading in Children, 1973; (ed. with E. Butterworth) Social Welfare in Modern Britain, 1975; Inequality in Child Care, 1976; Poverty, 1978; Kids at the Door, 1981; Resourceful Friends, 1983; (as B. Laken) More Than a Friend, 1984; Putting Families First, 1988. Add: Flat 2/1, 18 Finlarig St., Easterhouse, Glasgow G34, Scotland.

HOLME, K.E. *See* **HILL,** Christopher.

HOLMER, Paul L. American, b. 1916. Philosophy, Theology/Religion. Prof. of Theology, Yale Univ., New Haven, Conn., since 1960 (Instr. in Philosophy, 1945–46). Instr., 1946–48, Asst. Prof., 1948–50, Assoc. Prof., 1950–55, and Prof. of Philosophy, 1955–60, Univ. of Minnesota, Minneapolis. *Publs:* Philosophy and the Common Life, 1959; Theology and the Scientific Study of Religion, 1961; Doubt and Frustration, 1967; (ed.) Kierkegaard's Edifying Discourses, 1967; (co–author) The Theology and Philosophy of Andrew Nygoen, 1971; C.S. Lewis: The Shape of His Faith and Thought, 1976; The Grammar of Faith, 1978; Making Christian Sense, 1984. Add: 43 Swarthmore St., Hamden, Conn. 06517, U.S.A.

HOLMES, Arthur F(rank). American, b. 1924. Philosophy, Theology/Religion. Prof. of Philosophy, Wheaton Coll., Ill., since 1951. *Publs:* Christianity and Philosophy, 1960; Christian Philosophy in the Twentieth Century, 1969; Faith Seeks Understanding, 1971; The Idea of a Christian College, 1975, 1987; (ed.) War and Christian Ethics, 1975; All Truth Is God's Truth, 1977; Contours of a World View, 1983; The Making of a Christian Mind, 1984; Ethics: Approaching Moral Decisions, 1985. Add: 911 N. Washington, Wheaton, Ill. 60187, U.S.A.

HOLMES, Edward M(orris). American, b. 1910. Novels/Short stories, Literature, Memoirs. Prof. Emeritus in English, and Lectr. in Honors,

Univ. of Maine at Orono, since 1977 (Instr., 1956–62; Asst. Prof., 1962–65; Assoc. Prof.rozen Wages, 1980. Add: c/o San Francisco Mime Troupe, 855 Treat St., San Francisco, Calif. 94110, U.S.A.

HOLDEN, Matthew, Jr. American, b. 1931. Politics/Government, Public/Social administration, Race relations. Henry L. and Grace M. D L. and Grace M. Doherty Prof. of Govt. an Aid Soc., Lincoln, 1950–51; Hospital Porter, Lincoln Sanatorium, 1951–53; Mental Health Worker, Westmorland County Council, Kendal, 1953–74; Social Worker, Cumbria County Council, Kendal, 1974–83. *Publs:* To Have Eyes, 1972; Rhine Jump, 1974; (ed.) Trio 2, 1977; All I Can Say, 1978; Salt, Roses, Vinegar, 1985; The Crones of Aphrodite, 1986; My Ghost in Your Eye, 1988. Add: 4 Gowan Cres., Staveley, nr. Kendal, Cumbria LA8 9NF, England.

HOLLOWAY, Harry (Albert). American, b. 1925. Politics/GovernmenPolitics/Government. Prof. of Political Science, Univ. of Oklahoma, Norman, since 1962. Withf Tustan England, 1982; (Gen. Ed.) Foundations of Modern Britain, 1983; (ed. with C. Jones) The London Diaries of William Nicolson, Bishop of Carlisle 1702–1718, 1985; Politics, Religion and Society in England 1679–1742, 1985; (co–author) Stuart England, 1986. Add: Tatham House, Burton–in–Lonsdale, Carnforth, Lancs., England.

HOLMES, Jay. (Joseph Everett Holmes). American, b. 1922. History, Sciences (general). Dir., Bldg. Services Research Div., U.S. Dept. of Energy; with U.S. Conservation and Renewable Energy Program, since 1972. Ed., Associated Press, N.Y., 1954–58; Sloan–Rockefeller Fellow in Science Writing, Columbia Univ., NYC, 1958–59; Assoc. Ed., Missiles and Rockets Mag., 1959–61; with National Aeronautics and Space Admin., 1961–72, Atomic Energy Commn., 1972, and National Science Foundn., 1972–75. *Publs:* America on the Moon (in U.K. as The Race for the Moon), 1962; (ed.) Energy, Environment, Productivity, 1974. Add: 1948 Martha's Rd., Alexandria, Va. 22307, U.S.A.

HOLMES, John. *See* **SOUSTER,** Raymond.

HOLMES, John. British, b. 1913. Animals/Pets. Animal trainer, farmer, and horse breeder. *Publs:* (with MacDonald Daly) Obedient Dogs and How to Have One, 1954; The Family Dog: Its Choice and Training, 1957; The Farmer's Dog, 1960; Obedience Training for Dogs, 1961; The Obedient Dog: Training for Obedience Classes and Working Trials, 1975; (with Mary Holmes) The Colourful World of Dogs, 1976; (with Mary Holmes) Looking After Your Dog, 1981. Add: Formakin Animal Centre, Cranborne, Dorset BH21 5QY, England.

HOLMES, Lowell D. American, b. 1925. Anthropology/Ethnology, Music. Prof. of Anthropology, since 1959, and Chmn. of Dept., Wichita State Univ., Kans. Asst. Prof. of Anthropology, Missouri Valley Coll., Marshall, 1956–58. *Publs:* Ta'u, Stability and Change in a Samoan Village, 1958; Anthropology, An Introduction, 1965, 4th ed. 1987; The Story of Samoa, 1967; (ed.) Readings in General Anthropology, 1971; (ed. with D.O. Cowgill) Aging and Modernisation, 1972; Samoan Village, 1974; (ed.) The Anthropology of Modern Life, 1975; (ed.) The American Tribe, 1978; Other Cultures, Elder Years, 1982; Samoan Islands Bibliography, 1984; Jazz Greats, Getting Better with Age, 1986; Quest For the Real Samoa: The Mead–Freeman Controversy and Beyond, 1987. Add: Dept. of Anthropology, Wichita State Univ., Wichita, Kans. 67208, U.S.A.

HOLMES, Marjorie. American, b. 1910. Novels/Short stories, Human relations, Religion, Writing. Columnist, Washington Star–News, 1954–74, and Woman's Day, 1971–74. *Publs:* World by the Tail, 1943; Ten O'Clock Scholar, 1947; Saturday Night, 1959; Cherry Blossom Princess, 1960; Follow Your Dream, 1961; Senior Trip, 1962; Love Is a Hopscotch Thing, 1963; Love and Laughter, 1967; I've Got To Talk To Somebody, God, 1969; Writing the Creative Article, 1971; Who Am I, God?, 1971; To Treasure Our Days, 1971; Two From Galilee, 1972; Nobody Else Will Listen, 1973; You and I and Yesterday, 1973; As Tall As My Heart, 1974; How Can I Find You, God?, 1975; Beauty in Your Own Backyard, 1976; Hold Me Up a Little Longer, 1977; Lord, Let Me Love, 1978; God and Vitamins, 1980; To Help You Through the Hurting, 1982; Three from Galilee: The Young Man from Nazareth, 1985; Writing the Creative Article Today, 1986; The Messiah, 1987; Marjorie Holmes' Secrets of Health, Energy, and Staying Young, 1987. Add: 637 E. McMurray Rd., McMurray, Pa. 15317, U.S.A.

HOLMES, Martin (Rivington). British, b. 1905. Plays/Screenplays, History, Theatre. Member of Carl Rosa Trust, since 1957. Town Councillor, Appleby–in–Westmorland, since 1974 (Borough Councillor, 1965–74). Member of Staff, London Museum, 1932–65. *Publs:* Medieval

England, 1934; Crichton the Scholar (play), 1936; The Road to Run-nymede (play), 1946; From a Fair Lady (play), 1948, as Dragon's Deathbed, 1955; The Waiting Lady (play), 1949; Sword of Justice (play), 1949; The Last Burgundian (play), 1949; Fotheringhay (play), 1950; The Golden Unicorn (play), 1951; The Master of the Horse (play), 1951; King's Work (play), 1952, as Royal Portrait, 1966; The Smiling Angel (play), 1953; The Crown Jewels, 1953; Personalia, 1957; Arms and Armour in Tudor and Stuart London, 1957, 1970; The London of Elizabeth I, 1959; They Call It Treason (play), 1959; The London of Charles II, 1960; Shakespeare's Public: The Touchstone of His Genius, 1960, 1964; A Man Called Dante (play), 1961; The Heavy Crown (play), 1961; Moorfields in 1559, 1963; The Guns of Elsinore, 1964; Duke of the English (play), 1966; The Parish Churches of Appleby, 1967; Stage Costume and Accessories in the London Museum, 1968; Elizabethan London, 1969; Shakespeare and His Players, 1972; (with H.D.W. Sitwell) The English Regalia, 1972; Appleby and the Crown, 1974; Proud Northern Lady, 1975; Shakespeare and Burbage, 1978. Add: Castle Bank, Appleby-in-Westmorland, Cumbria CA16 6SN, England.

HOLMES, Raymond. *See* **SOUSTER**, Raymond.

HOLMES, Robert Lewis. British, b. 1926. Biology. Prof. of Anatomy, Univ. of Leeds, 1965–83, now Emeritus (Lectr., 1951–52, 1954–58). House Surgeon, Leeds Gen. Infirmary, 1951; Sr. Lectr. in Anatomy, 1958–63, and Reader in Neuroanatomy, 1963–65, Univ. of Birmingham; Ed., Journal of Anatomy, London, 1968–70. *Publs:* Living Tissues, 1965; Reproduction and Environment, 1968; (with J.A. Sharp) The Human Nervous System, 1970; (with J.N. Ball) The Pituitary Gland, 1974; (with C.A. Fox) Control of Human Reproduction, 1979; Anatomy, 1986. Add: 2 Linden Court, Hollin Lane, Leeds LS16 5NB, England.

HOLMSTROM, Lynda Lytle. American, b. 1939. Medicine/Health, Social sciences. Prof. of Sociology, Boston Coll., since 1979 (Instr., 1969–70; Asst. Prof., 1970–74, Assoc. Prof., 1974–79). *Publs:* (asst. ed.) Medical Care, 1966; Two-Career Family, 1972; (with Ann Wolbert Burgess) Rape: Victims of Crisis, 1974; The Victim of Rape: Institutional Reactions, 1978; (with Jeanne Guillemin) Mixed Blessings: Intensive Care for Newborns, 1986. Add: Dept. of Sociology, Boston Coll., Chestnut Hill, Mass. 02167, U.S.A.

HOLROYD, Michael. British, b. 1935. Literature, Biography. Chmn., Soc. of Authors, London, 1973–74; Chmn., National Book League, 1976–78; Member, BBC Archives Cttee., 1976–79. Pres., English PEN, 1985–88. *Publs:* Hugh Kingsmill: A Biography, 1964; Lytton Strachey, 2 vols., 1967–68, rev. ed. 1971; A Dog's Life, 1969; (ed.) The Best of Hugh Kingsmill, 1970; (ed.) Lytton Strachey by Himself, 1971; Unreceived Opinions, 1973; Augustus John, 2 vols., 1974–75, 1976; (with M. Easton) The Art of Augustus John, 1974; (ed.) The Genius of Shaw, 1979; (ed. with Paul Levy) The Shorter Strachey, 1980; (ed. with R. Skidelsky) God's Fifth Column, by William Gerhardie, 1981; (ed.) Essays by Divers Hands, XLII, 1982; Bernard Shaw, 1988–89. Add: c/o A.P. Watt Ltd., 20 John St., London WC1N 2DR, England.

HOLSTI, Kalevi J. Canadian, b. 1935. International relations/Current ffairs. Prof. of Political Science, Univ. of British Columbia, Vancouver, since 1970 (Acting Dir., Inst. of Intnl. Relations, 1970–71). Co-Ed., Canadian Journal of Political Science, 1978–82. Pres., Intnl. Studies Assn., 1986–87. *Publs:* Suomen Ulkopolitiikka Suuntaansa Etsimässä, 1963; International Politics: A Framework for Analysis, 1967, 5th ed. 1987; Why Nations Realign: Foreign Policy Restructuring, 1982; The Dividing Discipline: Hegemony and Pluralism in International Theory, 1985. Add: 207–2080 Maple St., Vancouver, B.C. V6J 4P9, Canada.

HOLSTI, Ole Rudolf. American, (born Finnish), b. 1933. International relations/Current affairs, Politics/Government. George V. Allen Prof. of Political Science, Duke Univ., Durham, N.C., since 1974 (Chmn., Dept. of Political Science, 1978–83). Assoc. Ed., Intnl. Studies Quarterly, and Western Political Quarterly, both since 1970; Corresp. and Contributing Ed., Racing South, and Running Journal mags; Editorial Bd., Duke Univ. Press, since 1984, Univ. Press of America, since 1980, and International Interaction, since 1984. Instr., 1962–65, Asst. Prof., 1965–67, and Research Coordinator and Assoc. Dir., Studies in Intnl. Conflict and Integration, 1962–67, Stanford Univ., Calif.; Assoc. Ed., Journal of Conflict Resolution, 1967–72; Assoc. Prof., 1967–71, and Prof., 1971–74, Univ. of British Columbia, Vancouver. Pres., Intnl. Studies Assn., 1979–80. *Publs:* (co-author) Content Analysis: A Handbook with Application for the Study of International Crisis, 1963; (co-author) Enemies in Politics, 1967; Content Analysis for the Social Sciences and Humanities, 1969;

(co-author and co-ed.) The Analysis of Communication Content: Developments in Scientific Theories and Computer Techniques, 1969; Crisis Escalation War, 1972; (co-author) Unity and Disintegration in International Alliances: Comparative Studies, 1973; (co-author and co-ed.) Change in the International System, 1980; (co-author) American Leadership in World Affairs: Vietnam and the Breakdown of Consensus, 1984. Add: 608 Croom Ct., Chapel Hill, N.C. 27514, U.S.A.

HOLT, James Clarke. British, b. 1922. History. Hon Fellow, Emmanuel Coll. Cambridge, since 1985 (Professorial Fellow, Emmanuel Coll., 1978–81; Prof. of Medieval History, Cambridge Univ., 1978–88; Master of Fitzwilliam College, Cambridge, 1981–88). Asst. Lectr., 1949–51, Lectr., 1951–61, Sr. Lectr., 1961–62, and Prof. of Medieval History, 1962, Univ. of Nottingham; Prof. of History, 1966–78, and Dean, Faculty of Letters and Social Sciences, 1972–76, Univ. of Reading. Member, Advisory Council on Public Records, 1974–81; Pres., Royal Historical Soc., 1980–84. *Publs:* The Northerners: A Study in the Reign of King John, 1961; Praestita Roll 14–18 John, 1964; Magna Carta, 1965; The Making of Magna Carta, 1966; Magna Carta and the Idea of Liberty, 1972; The University of Reading: The First Fifty Years, 1977; Robin Hood, 1982; (ed. with John Gillingham) War and Government in the Middle Ages, 1984; Magna Carta and Medieval Government 1985; (with Richard Mortimer) Handlist of the Acta of Henry II and Richard I, 1986. Add: 5 Holben Close, Barton, Cambridgeshire, England.

HOLT, Michael (Paul). British, b. 1929. Children's fiction, Recreation/Leisure/Hobbies. Sr. Science and Mathematics Ed., Ginn and Co. Ltd., London, 1965–67; Sr. Lectr. in Mathematics, Goldsmiths Coll., Univ. of London, 1967–70; Chmn., Educational Writers Group, Soc. of Authors, London, 1971–73. *Publs:* (with D.T.E. Marjoram) Mathematics Through Experience, 7 books, 1966–75; Exercises, 4 books, 1972; What Is the New Maths?, 1968; Science Happenings, 6 books, 1969; Mathematics in Art, 1971; (with R. Ridout) Joe's Trip to the Moon, 1971; (with R. Ridout) The Train Thief, 1971; (with Z.P. Dienes) Zoo, 1972; (with R. Ridout) The Big Book of Puzzles, 3 vols., 1972–79; (with Z.P. Dienes) Let's Play Maths, 1973; (with D.T.E. Marjoram) Mathematics in a Changing World, 1973; Inner Ring Maths, 1973; Maths, 6 books, 1973–74; (with R. Ridout) All Round English, 1974; (with R. Ridout) Life Cycle Books, 4 books, 1974; Monkey Puzzle Books, 6 books, 1974; Ready for Science, 6 books, 1974; Maps, Tracks, and the Bridges of Konigsberg, 1975; Fun with Numbers, 1976; Math Puzzles and Games, 1977; More Math Puzzles and Games, 1978; Figure it Out Books, 4 vols., 1978–81; (with A. Rothery) Mathsworks, books, 1979; The Puma Puzzle Book, 1980; Basic Skills in Maths, 1981; Answer Me This, 1981; Holt Counting Board, 1981; The Bumper Quiz Book, 1981; (with A. Rothery) Maths Alive, 1982; The Amazing Invisible Ink Puzzle Books, 1982; (with A. Ward) Wide Range Science Story Books 1–2, 1982; The Amazing Invisible Ink Puzzle Books, 1983; Basic Arithmetic Puzzles: Adding and Subtracting, Multiplying and Dividing, 1983; The Dr. Who Quiz Book of Dinosaurs Magic, Science, 3 vols., 1983; (with A. Ward) Wide Range Science Story Books 3–4, 1984; The Dr. Who Book of Space, 1984; Now I Can . . . Count to 3 . . . Count to 5, 1984; Basic Arithmetic Puzzles: Fractions, Decimals, 1984; Now I Can . . . Count to 10, 1985; Dr. Who Book of Puzzles, 1985; The Pan Pocket Puzzler, 1985; Crisis in Space, 1986; Getting on with . . ., 6 vols., 1986; The Great Spy Race, 1987; The Riddle of the Sphinx, 1987. Add: Highley, Whitbourne, Worcester, England.

HOLT, Victoria. Pseud. for Eleanor Alice Burford Hibbert; also writes as Eleanor Burford, Philippa Carr, Elbur Ford, Kathleen Kellow, Jean Plaidy, and Ellalice Tate. British, b. 1906. Mystery/Crime/Suspense, Historical/Romance/Gothic, Children's non-fiction, History, Biography. *Publs:* (as Eleanor Burford) Daughter of Anna, 1941; (as Eleanor Burford) Passionate Witness, 1941; (as Eleanor Burford) The Married Lover, 1942; (as Eleanor Burford) When All the World Is Young, 1943; (as Eleanor Burford) So the Dreams Depart, 1944; (as Eleanor Burford) Not in Our Stars, 1945; (as Jean Plaidy) Together They Ride, 1945; (as Eleanor Burford) Dear Chance, 1947; (as Jean Plaidy) Beyond the Blue Mountains, 1947; (as Eleanor Burford) Alexa, 1948; (as Eleanor Burford) The House at Cupid's Cross, 1949; (as Jean Plaidy) Murder Most Royal (in U.S. as The King's Pleasure), 1949; (as Eleanor Burford) Believe the Heart, 1950; (as Eleanor Burford) The Love Child, 1950; (as Jean Plaidy) The Goldsmith's Wife, 1950, in U.S. paperback as The King's Mistress, 1952; (as Elbur Ford) Poison in Pimlico, 1950; (as Elbur Ford) Flesh and the Devil, 1950; (as Eleanor Burford) Saint or Sinner?, 1951; (as Jean Plaidy) Madame Serpent, 1951, The Italian Woman, 1952, Queen Jezebel, 1953 (trilogy), in 1 vol. as Catherine de'Medici, 1969; (as Eleanor Burford) Dear Delusion, 1952; (as Eleanor Burford) Bright Tomorrow, 1952; (as Jean Plaidy) Daughter of Satan, 1952, in Can. as The Unholy Woman, 1954; (as Elbur Ford) The Bed Disturbed, 1952; (as Kathleen Kellow)

Danse Macabre, 1952; (as Eleanor Burford) Leave Me My Love, 1953; (as Eleanor Burford) When We Are Married, 1953; (as Jean Plaidy) The Sixth Wife, 1953; (as Elbur Ford) Such Bitter Business, 1953, in U.S. as Evil in the House, 1954; (as Kathleen Kellow) Rooms at Mrs. Oliver's, 1953; (as Eleanor Burford) Castles in Spain, 1954; (as Eleanor Burford) Heart's Afire, 1954; (as Jean Plaidy) The Spanish Bridegroom, 1954; (as Jean Plaidy) St. Thomas's Eve, 1954; (as Kathleen Kellow) Lilith, 1954; (as Eleanor Burford) When Other Hearts, 1955; (as Eleanor Burford) Two Loves in Her Life, 1955; (as Jean Plaidy) Gay Lord Robert, 1955; (as Jean Plaidy) Royal Road to Fotheringay, 1955; (as Kathleen Kellow) It Began in Vauxhall Gardens, 1955; (as Eleanor Burford) Begin to Live, 1956; (as Eleanor Burford) Married in Haste, 1956; (as Jean Plaidy) The Wandering Prince, 1956, A Health unto His Majesty, 1956, Here Lies Our Sovereign Lord, 1957 (trilogy), in 1 vol. as Charles II, 1972; (as Kathleen Kellow) Call of the Blood, 1956; (as Ellalice Tate) Defenders of the Faith, 1956; (as Eleanor Burford) To Meet a Stranger, 1957; (as Jean Plaidy) Flaunting Extravagant Queen (Marie Antoinette), 1957; (as Kathleen Kellow) Rochester, the Mad Earl, 1957; (as Ellalice Tate) The Scarlet Cloak, 1957; (as Jean Plaidy) Madonna of the Seven Hills, 1958, Light on Lucrezia, 1958, in 1 vol. as Lucrezia Borgia, 1976; (as Eleanor Burford) Pride of the Morning, 1958; (as Eleanor Burford) Blaze of Noon, 1958; (as Ellalice Tate) The Queen of Diamonds, 1958; (as Jean Plaidy) A Triptych of Poisoners (non–fiction), 1958; (as Jean Plaidy) Louis, The Well–Beloved, 1959; (as Jean Plaidy) The Road to Compiègne, 1959; (as Eleanor Burford) The Dawn Chorus, 1959; (as Eleanor Burford) Red Sky at Night, 1959; (as Kathleen Kellow) Milady Charlotte, 1959; (as Ellalice Tate) Madame du Barry, 1959; The Rise of the Spanish Inquisition, The Growth of the Spanish Inquisition, The End of the Spanish Inquisition (non–fiction), 3 vols., 1959–61, in U.S. in 1 vol. as The Spanish Inquisition: Its Rise, Growth, and End, 1967; Mistress of Mellyn, 1960; (as Eleanor Burford) Night of Stars, 1960; (as Jean Plaidy) Castile for Isabella, 1960, Spain for Sovereigns, 1960, Daughters of Spain, 1961 (trilogy), in 1 vol. as Isabella and Ferdinand, 1970; (as Kathleen Kellow) The World's a Stage, 1960; (as Eleanor Burford) Now That April's Gone, 1961; (as Jean Plaidy) Katharine, The Virgin Widow, 1961, The Shadow of the Pomegranate, 1962, The King's Secret Matter, 1962 (trilogy), in 1 vol. as Katharine of Aragon, 1968; (as Eleanor Burford) Who's Calling, 1962; (as Ellalice Tate) This Was a Man, 1961; (as Jean Plaidy) The Young Elizabeth (juvenile), 1961; (as Jean Plaidy) Meg Roper, Daughter of Sir Thomas More (juvenile), 1961; Kirkland Revels, 1962; (as Jean Plaidy) The Young Mary Queen of Scots (juvenile), 1962; Bride of Pendorric, 1963; (as Jean Plaidy) The Captive Queen of Scots, 1963; (as Jean Plaidy) The Thistle and the Rose, 1963; (as Jean Plaidy) Mary, Queen of France, 1964; (as Jean Plaidy) The Murder in the Tower, 1965; The Legend of the Seventh Virgin, 1965; (as Jean Plaidy) Evergreen Gallant, 1965; (as Jean Plaidy) The Three Crowns, 1965, The Haunted Sisters, 1966, The Queen's Favourites, 1966 (trilogy), in vol. as The Last of the Stuarts, 1977; Menfreya (in U.S. as Menfreya in the Morning), 1966; The King of the Castle, 1967; (as Jean Plaidy) Georgian Saga: Queen in Waiting, 1967, The Princess of Celle, 1967, The Prince and the Quakeress, 1968, Caroline, The Queen, 1968, The Third George, 1969, Perdita's Prince, 1969, Sweet Lass of Richmond Hill, 1970, Indiscretions of the Queen, 1970, The Regent's Daughter, 1971; Goddess of the Green Room, 1971, 10 vols.; The Queen's Confession, 1968; The Shivering Sands, 1969; The Secret Woman, 1970; The Shadow of the Lynx, 1971; On the Night of the Seventh Moon, 1972; (as Philippa Carr) The Miracle at St. Bruno's, 1972; (as Jean Plaidy) Victorian Saga: The Captive of Kensington Palace, 1972, Victoria in the Wings, 1972, The Queen and the Lord M., 1973, the Queen's Husband, 1973, The Widow of Windsor, 1974, 5 vols.; The Curse of the Kings, 1973; The House of a Thousand Lanterns, 1974; (as Philippa Carr) The Lion Triumphant, 1974; (as Jean Plaidy) Norman Trilogy: The Bastard King, 1974, The Lion of Justice, 1975, the Passionate Enemies, 1976; Lord of the Far Island, 1975; (as Philippa Carr) The Witch from the Sea, 1975; (as Jean Plaidy) Mary, Queen of Scots, The Fair Devil of Scotland (non–fiction), 1975; The Pride of the Peacock, 1976; (as Jean Plaidy) Plantagenet Saga: The Plantagenet Prelude, 1976, The Revolt of the Eaglets, 1977, The Heart of the Lion, 1977, The Prince of Darkness, 1978, The Battle of the Queens, 1978, The Queen from Provence, 1979, Edward Longshanks, 1979, The Follies of the King, 1980, The Vow on the Heron, 1980, Passage to Pontefract, 1981, The Star of Lancaster, 1981, Epitaph for Three Women, 1981, Red Rose of Anjou, 1982, The Sun in Splendour, 1982, 14 vols.; (as Philippa Carr) Saraband for Two Sisters, 1976; The Devil on Horseback, 1977; (as Philippa Carr) Lament for a Lost Lover, 1977; My Enemy the Queen, 1978 (as Philippa Carr) The Love–Child, 1978; The Spring of the Tiger, 1979; The Mask of the Enchantress, 1980; (as Philippa Carr) The Song of the Siren, 1980; The Judas Kiss, 1981; (as Jean Plaidy) Hammer of the Scots, 1981; (as Philippa Carr) The Drop of the Dice, 1981; (as Philippa Carr) Will You Love Me in September, 1981; (as Philippa Carr) The Adultress, 1982;

The Demon Lover, 1982; (as Jean Plaidy) My Self, My Enemy, 1983; The Time of the Hunter's Moon, 1983; (as Philippa Carr) Zipperah's Daughter, 1983; (as Philippa Carr) Knave of Hearts, 1983; The Landowner Legacy, 1984; (as Philippa Carr) Voices in a Haunted Room, 1984; The Road to Paradise Island, 1985; (as Philippa Carr) Midsummer's Eve, 1986; (as Jean Plaidy) Victoria, Victorious, 1986; (as Jean Plaidy) The Lady in the Tower, 1986; Silk for a Nightingale, 1986; The Silk Vendetta, 1987; (as Jean Plaidy) The Courts of Love, 1987; (as Philippa Carr) The Pool of St. Branok, 1987; (as Jean Plaidy) In the Shadow of the Crown, 1988; The Indian Fan, 1988; The Captive, 1989. Add: c/o A.M. Heath Ltd., 40 William IV St., London WC2N 4DD, England.

HOLTBY, Robert Tinsley. British, b. 1921. History, Theology/Religion, Biography. Dean of Chichester since 1977. Canon Residentiary and Diocesan Dir. of Education, Carlisle, 1959–67; Gen. Secty., National Soc. and Church of England Bd. of Education, 1967–77. *Publs:* Daniel Waterland: A Study in Eighteenth Century Orthodoxy, 1966; Eric Graham: Principal of Cuddesdon and Bishop of Brechin, 1967; Carlisle Cathedral, 1971; Partners in Education: The Role of the Diocese, 1970; Chichester Cathedral, 1981; Robert Wright Stopford, 1988. Add: The Deanery, Chichester, Sussex PO19 1PX, England.

HOLTTUM, Richard Eric. British, b. 1895. Botany, Horticulture. Hon. Research Worker, Royal Botanical Gardens, Kew. Asst. Dir., 1922–25, and Dir., 1925–49, Botanic Gardens, Singapore; Prof. of Botany, Univ. of Singapore, 1949–54. *Publs:* Orchids of Malaya, 1953; Gardening in the Lowlands of Malaya, 1953; Ferns of Malaya, 1954; Plant Life in Malaya, 1954; (co–ed. and part author) Flora Malesiana Series II, Pteridophyta vol. I, parts 1–5. Add: 50 Gloucester Ct., Kew Rd., Richmond, Surrey TW9 3EA, England.

HOLTZMAN, Abraham. American, b. 1921. Politics/Government. Prof. of Political Science, North Carolina State Univ., Raleigh, since 1962 (Asst. Prof., 1955–57; Assoc. Prof., 1957–62); Teaching Asst., University of California, Los Angeles, 1945–47; Election Examiner, National Labor Relations Bd., 1950; Teaching Fellow and Tutor, Harvard Univ., Cambridge, Mass., 1950–52; Instr., Dartmouth Coll., Hanover, N.H., 1952–53; Staff Asst. to Chmn., Democratic National Cttee., 1954; Advisor to Rules Cttee., Democratic National Convention, 1960. *Publs:* Los Angeles County Chief Administrative Officer: Ten Years Experience, 1948; The Loyalty Pledge Controversy in the Democratic Party, 1960; Interest Groups and Lobbying, 1966; Legislative Liaison: Executive Leadership in Congress, 1970; The Townsend Movement, A Political Study, 1970; American Government: Ideals and Reality, 1980, 1984. Add: 3606 Alamance Dr., Raleigh, N.C. 27609, U.S.A.

HOLTZMAN, Wayne Harold. American, b. 1923. Education, Psychology. Pres., Hogg Foundn. for Mental Health, since 1970, and Prof. of Psychology since 1959, Univ. of Texas, Austin (Asst. Prof., 1949–53; Assoc. Prof., 1953–59; Assoc. Dir., Hogg Foundn., 1955–64; Dean, Coll. of Education, 1964–70). *Publs:* (with W.F. Brown) Survey of Study Habits and Attitudes, 1953; (with J.S. Thorpe, J.D. Swartz and E.W. Herron) Inkblot Perception and Personality, 1961; (with B.M. Moore) Tomorrow's Parents, 1965; (with J.F. Santos, S. Bouquet and P. Barth) The Peace Corps in Brazil, 1966; Computer–Assisted Instruction, Testing and Guidance, 1971; (with W.F. Brown) A Guide to College Survival, 1972, 1987; (with R. Diaz–Guerrero and J.D. Swartz) Personality Development in Two Cultures, 1975; Introduction to Psychology, 1978; (with I. Reyes) Impact of Educational Television on Young Children, 1981; (with K.A. Heller and S. Messick) Placing Children in Special Education, 1982; American Families and Social Policies for Services to Children, 1983; Texas Universities and Mexico, 1984; Beyond the Rorschach, 1988. Add: 3300 Foothill Dr., Austin, Tex., U.S.A.

HOLYER, Ernie. (Erna M. Holyer). American, b. 1925. Children's Fiction, Natural history, Biography. Creative Writing Teacher, San Jose Metropolitan Adult Education Prog., since 1968. *Publs:* Rescue at Sunrise and Other Stories, 1965; Steve's Night of Silence and Other Stories, 1966; A Cow for Hansel, 1967; At the Forest's Edge, 1969; Song of Courage (biography), 1970; Lone Brown Gull and Other Stories, 1971; Shoes for Daniel, 1974; Sigis's Fire Helmet, 1975; The Southern Sea Otter, 1975; Reservoir Road Adventure, 1982. Add: 1314 Rimrock Dr., San Jose, Calif. 95120, U.S.A.

HOLZMAN, Franklyn D(unn). American, b. 1918. Economics. Prof., Dept. of Economics since 1961, and Prof., Fletcher Sch. of Law and Diplomacy, since 1963, Tufts Univ., Medford, Mass; Fellow, Russian Research Center, Harvard Univ., Cambridge, Mass., since 1961. Consultant to U.N., U.S. Arms Control and Disarmament Agency, U.S. Congress Joint

Economic Cttee., U.S. Commn. on Trade Investment Policy, U.S. Dept. of Commerce, and the Brookings Inst. Economist, 1948–49, and Consultant, 1949–52, U.S. Dept. of the Treasury, Washington, D.C.; Asst. Prof., 1952–54, Assoc. Prof., 1954–58, and Prof. of Economics, 1958–61, Univ. of Washington, Seattle; Visiting Prof., Univ. of California at Los Angeles, 1956, Stanford Univ., 1957, Columbia Univ., 1962, and Massachusetts Inst. of Technology, 1963. *Publs:* Soviet Taxation: The Fiscal and Monetary Problems of a Planned Economy, 1955; (ed.) Readings on Soviet Economy, 1962; Foreign Trade under Central Planning, 1974; Financial Checks on Soviet Defense Expenditures, 1975; Foreign Trade under Communism: Politics and Economics, 1976; The Soviet Economy: Past, Present and Future, 1982; The Economics of Soviet Bloc Trade and Finance, 1987. Add: 33 Peacock Farm Rd., Lexington, Mass. 02173, U.S.A.

HOMANS, Peter. American, b. 1930. Psychology, Social Sciences, Religion. Prof. of Religion and Psychological Studies, Univ. of Chicago, since 1978 (Asst. Prof., 1965–68; Assoc. Prof., 1968–78). Lectr., Univ. of Toronto, 1962–64; Asst. Prof., Hartford Seminary Foundn., 1964–65. *Publs:* (ed.) The Dialogue Between Psychology and Theology, 1968; Theology After Freud: An Interpretive Inquiry, 1970; (ed. and contrib.) Childhood and Selfhood: Essays on Tradition, Religion and Modernity in the Psychology of Erik H. Erikson; Jung in Context: Modernity and the Making of a Psychology, 1979; The Ability to Mourn: Dissillusion-ment and the Social Origins of Psychoanalysis, 1989. Add: Swift Hall, Univ. of Chicago, Chicago, Ill. 60637, U.S.A.

HOMBERGER, Eric (Ross). American, b. 1942. Literature. Lectr. in American Literature, Univ. of East Anglia, Norwich, since 1970. *Publs:* (ed., with William Janeway and Simon Schama) The Cambridge Mind: Ninety Years of the "Cambridge Review" 1879–1969, 1970; (ed.) Ezra Pound: The Critical Heritage; The Art of the Real: Poetry in England and America since 1939, 1977; (ed. with H. Klein and J. Flower) The Second World War in Fiction, 1984; American Writers and Radical Politics 1900–1939: Equivocal Commitments, 1986; John le Carré, 1986; (ed. with J. Charmley) The Troubled Face of Biography, 1987. Add: 74 Clarendon Rd., Norwich NR2 2PN, England.

HOME, Alex(ander Frederick) Douglas. (Baron Home of The Hirsel). British, b. 1903. Autobiography/Memoirs/Personal. Member, House of Lords, London, since 1974 (Conservative M.P. for S. Lanark, 1931–45, and for Lanark, 1950–51; Member, House of Lords, as Earl of Home, 1951 until he disclaimed peerages for life, 1963; M.P. for Kinross and W. Perthshire, 1963 until created Life Peer, 1974; Parliamentary Private Secty. to Neville Chamberlain, 1935–40; Jt. Under–Secty. of State for Foreign Affairs, 1945; Minister of State, Scottish Office, 1951–55; Secty. of State for Commonwealth Relations, 1955–60; Leader of the House of Lords and Lord Pres. of the Council, 1957–60; Secty. of State for Foreign Affairs, 1960–63; Prime Minister and First Lord of the Treasury, 1963–64; Leader of the Opposition, 1964–65; Opposition Spokesman on Foreign Affairs, 1965–70; Secty. of State for Foreign and Commonwealth Affairs, 1970–74). Chancellor, Heriot–Watt Univ., Edinburgh, 1966–77. *Publs:* The Way the Wind Blows, 1976; Border Reflections, 1979; Letters to a Grandson, 1984. Add: The Hirsel, Coldstream, Berwickshire, Scotland.

HOME, William Douglas–. British, b. 1912. Plays, Poetry, Autobiography/Memoirs/Personal. *Publs:* Home Truths (poetry), 1939; Now, Barabbas, 1947; The Chiltern Hundreds (in U.S. as Yes, M'Lord), 1947; Master of Arts, 1949; The Bad Samaritan, 1952; The Manor of Northstead, 1954; Half–Term Report: An Autobiography, 1954; The Reluctant Debutante, 1955; The Iron Duchess, 1957; The Plays of William Douglas Home, 1958; Aunt Edwina, 1959; The Bad Soldier Smith, 1961; The Reluctant Peer, 1964; A Friend Indeed, 1965; Betzi, 1965; The Secretary Bird, 1968; The Bishop and the Actress, 1968; The Jockey Club Stakes, 1970; Lloyd George Knew My Father, 1972; The Dame of Sark, 1974; In the Red, 1977; The Kingfisher, 1977; The Editor Regrets, 1978; Mr. Home Pronounced Hume: An Autobiography, 1979; The Golf Umbrella, 1984; Sins of Commission (World War 2 memoirs), 1985; (ed.) The Prime Ministers, 1985. Add: Derry House, Kilmeston, Hants., England.

HOMER, William Innes. American, b. 1929. Art, Photography. Prof., Dept. of Art History, since 1966, and Chmn. of Dept., 1966–81 and since 1986, Univ. of Delaware, Newark. Member of Editorial Bd., American Art Journal, since 1970; Member of Advisory Council, Dunlap Soc., since 1975; Member, Editorial Bd., Winterthur Portfolio, 1978–1980. Member, Delaware State Arts Council, 1969–70. *Publs:* Seurat and the Science of Painting, 1964; Robert Henri and His Circle, 1969; (ed.) Avant–Garde Painting and Sculpture in America 1910–1925, 1975; Alfred Stieglitz and the American Avant–Garde, 1977; The Photographs

of Gertrude Käsebier, 1979; Alfred Stieglitz and the Photo–Secession, 1983; Albert Pinkham Ryder: Painter of Dreams, 1989. Add: Dept. of Art History, Univ. of Delaware, Newark, Del. 19716, U.S.A.

HONAN, Park. American, b. 1928. Literature, Biography. Reader in English, Univ. of Birmingham, since 1976 (Lectr., 1968–72; Sr. Lectr., 1968–76). British Ed., Novel: A Forum on Fiction; Co–ed., Ohio Univ. Press Browning Ed. Assoc. Prof., Brown Univ., Providence, R.I., 1963–68. *Publs:* Browning's Characters: A Study in Poetic Technique, 1961; (ed.) Shelley, 1963; (ed.) Bulwer Lytton's Falkland, 1967; (co–ed.) The Complete Works of Robert Browning, 4 vols., 1969–73; (co–author) The Book, The Ring, and The Poet: A Biography of Robert Browning, 1975; Matthew Arnold: A Life, 1981; (ed.) The Beats, 1987; Jane Austen: Her Life, 1988. Add: 35 Prospect Rd., Birmingham B13 9TB, England.

HONDERICH, Ted. British, b. 1933. Philosophy, Politics/Government. Grote Prof. of the Philosophy of Mind and Logic, Univ. Coll., Univ. of London, since 1988 (Lectr., 1964–72; Reader, 1972–83; Prof. of Philosophy, 1983–88). Ed., Intnl. Library of Philosophy and Scientific Method, The Arguments of the Philosophers and The Problems of Philosophy: Their Past and Present (Routledge). Lectr. in Philosophy, Univ. of Sussex, 1962–64. *Publs:* Punishment: The Supposed Justification, 1969, rev. ed. 1971; (ed. and contrib.) Essays on Freedom of Action, 1973; (ed.) Social Ends and Political Means, 1975; Three Essays on Political Violence, 1977; (ed.) Philosophy As It Is, 1979; Violence for Equality: Inquiries in Political Philosophy, 1979; (ed.) Philosophy Through Its Past, 1984; (ed.) Morality and Objectivity, 1985; A Theory of Determinism: The Mind, Neuroscience, and Life–Hopes, 1988. Add: Dept. of Philosophy, Univ. Coll., Gower St., London WC1, England.

HONE, Joseph. Irish, b. 1937. Mystery/Crime/Suspense, Travel/Exploration/Adventure. Freelance writer and broadcaster since 1968. Part–time Ed. for Hamish Hamilton, publrs., London. Radio Producer, BBC, 1963–67; Information Officer, Radio and Television, U.N. Secretariat, NYC, 1967–68. *Publs:* The Private Sector, 1971; The Sixth Directorate, 1975; The Dancing Waiters: Collected Travels, 1975; The Paris Trap, 1977; The Flowers of the Forest (in U.S. as The Oxford Gambit), 1980; Gone Tomorrow: Some More Collected Travels, 1981; The Valley of the Fox, 1982; Children of the Country: Coast to Coast Across Africa, 1986; Duck Soup in the Black Sea: Further Collected Travels, 1988. Add: Manor Cottage, Shutford, Banbury, Oxon, England.

HONEYCOMBE, Gordon. British, b. 1936. Novels, Plays/Screenplays, Biography, Documentaries/Reportage. Radio Announcer with Radio Hong Kong, 1956–57; Announcer with the Scottish Home Service, 1958; Actor with Royal Shakespeare Co., Stratford and London, 1962–63; Newscaster with Independent Television News, London, 1965–77; News Presenter with TV–am (Good Morning Britain), 1984–89. *Publs:* The Redemption (play), 1964; (co–author) The Golden Vision (TV play), 1968; Neither the Sea nor the Sand (novel), 1969; Dragon Under the Hill (novel), 1972; Adam's Tale, Paradise Lost (dramatisation), 1974; Time and Again (TV play), 1974; Red Watch, 1976; God Save the Queen (dramatisation), 1977; A King Shall Have a Kingdom (dramatisation), 1977; Lancelot and Guinevere (dramatisation), 1978; Family History (TV series), 1979; Waltz of My Heart (musical), 1980; The Edge of Heaven (novel), 1981; Nagasaki 1945, 1981; Royal Wedding, 1981; The Murders of the Black Museum, 1982; The Year of the Princess, 1982; Selfridges, 1984; The Thirteenth Day of Christmas (TV play), 1985; TV–am's Celebration of the Royal Wedding, 1986. Add: c/o Peters Fraser and Dunlop, The Chambers, Chelsea Harbour, Lots Road, London SW10 0XF, England.

HONEYMAN, Brenda. *See* **CLARKE,** Brenda.

HONG, Howard V. American, b. 1912. Philosophy, Theology/Religion, Translations. Prof. of Philosophy, St. Olaf Coll., Northfield, Minn., since 1938. Dir., Kierkegaard Library, St. Olaf Coll., and Gen. Ed., Kierkegaard's Writings (Princeton Univ. Pr., N.J.) Field Secty., U.S.A. and Germany, War Prisoners Aid, World YMCA, 1943–46; Sr. Rep., Service to Refugees, Lutheran World Fedn., Germany, 1947–49. *Publs:* (trans. with Edna H. Hong) For Self–Examination, by Kierkegaard, 1940; (with E.H. Hong) Muskego Boy, 1944; (with Hong) The Boy Who Fought with Kings, 1946; This World and the Church, 1955; (ed.) Integration and the Christian Liberal Arts College, 1956; (co–ed.) Christian Faith and the Liberal Arts, 1960; (re–trans.) Philosophical Fragments, by Kierkegaard, 1962; (ed. and trans. with E.H. Hong) Works of Love, by Kierkegaard, 1962; (ed. and trans. with E.H. Hong) Soren Kierkegaard's Journals and Papers, vol. I, 1967, vol. II, 1970, vols. III–IV, 1975, vols. V–VII, 1978; (ed. and trans. with E.H. Hong) Armed Neutrality and An

Open Letter, by Kierkegaard, 1968, (ed. and trans. with E.H. Hong) Kierkegaard's Thought, by Gregor Malantschuk, 1971; (ed. and trans. with E.H. Hong) Two Ages, by Kierkegaard, 1978; (ed. and trans.) The Sickness unto Death, by Kierkegaard, 1980; (ed. and trans.) The Corsair Affair, by Kierkegaard, 1982; (ed. and trans.) Fear and Trembling and Repetition, by Kierkegaard, 1983; (ed. and trans.) Philosophical Fragments and Johannes Climacus, or De amnibus dubitandum est, by Kierkegaard, 1985; (ed. and trans.) Either/Or, by Kierkegaard, 1987; (ed. and trans.) Stages on Life's Way, by Kierkegaard, 1988. Add: 5174 E. Old Dutch Rd., Northfield, Minn. 55057, U.S.A.

HONIG, Edwin. American, b. 1919. Plays/Screenplays, Poetry, Literature, Translations. Prof. of English Emeritus, Brown Univ., Providence, R.I., since 1982 (Assoc. Prof., 1957–60; Prof., 1960–82; Prof. of Comparative Literature, 1962–82; Chmn., 1968–69). Library Asst., Library of Congress, Washington, D.C. 1941–42; Instr., Purdue Univ., Lafayette, Ind., 1942–43, New York Univ. and Illinois Inst. of Technology, Chicago, 1946–47, and Univ. of New Mexico, Albuquerque, 1947–49; Instr., 1949–52, and Briggs Copeland Asst. Prof., 1952–57, Harvard Univ., Cambridge, Mass. Member, Exec. Bd., Poetry Soc. of America, 1979. *Publs:* García Lorca, 1944, 1962; The Moral Circus: Poems, 1955; The Gazabos: Forty–One Poems, 1959, augmented ed. as The Gazabos: Forty–One Poems, and The Widow, 1961; Dark Conceit: The Making of Allegory, 1959, 3rd ed. 1973; (trans.) The Cave of Salamanca, by Cervantes, 1960; (ed. with O. Williams) The Mentor Book of Major American Poets, 1961; (trans.) Caldéron: Four Plays, 1961; Poems for Charlotte, 1963; (trans.) Cervantes: Eight Interludes, 1964; Survivals: Poems, 1965; Spring Journal: Poems, 1968; (ed. with O. Williams) The Major Metaphysical Poets, 1968; (ed.) Spenser, 1968; (trans.) Caldéron: Life Is a Dream 1970; (trans.) Selected Poems of Fernando Pessoa, 1971; Calisto and Melibea, 1972; Caldéron and the Seizures of Honor, 1972; Four Springs (poems), 1972; (trans.) Divan and Other Writings, by Garca Lorca, 1974; Shake a Spear with Me, John Berryman: New Poems, 1974; At Sixes, 1974; The Afffinities of Orpheus, 1977; The Selected Poems of Edwin Honig 1955–1976, 1979; The Foibles and Fables of an Abstract Man, 1979; Interrupted Praise: New and Selected Poems, 1983; Ends of the World and Other Plays, 1982; Gifts of Light: A Poem, 1983; (trans. with A. Trueblood) Lope de Vega: La Dorotea, 1985; The Poet's Other Voice: Conversations on Literary Translation, 1985; (trans. with S.M. Brown) Poems of Fernando Pessoa, 1986; (trans. with S.M. Brown) The Keeper of Sheep, by Fernando Pessoa, 1986; (trans.) Fernando Pessoa: Always Astonished (selected prose), 1988. Add: English Dept., Brown Univ., Providence, R.I. 02912, U.S.A.

HONORÉ, Tony. (Antony Maurice Honoré). British, b. 1921. Law. Fellow, All Souls Coll., Oxford, and Regius Prof. of Civil Law, Oxford Univ., since 1971 (Fellow, Queen's Coll., 1949–64, and New Coll., 1964–71; Rhodes Reader in Roman–Dutch Law, 1957–71); Acting Warden, All Souls Coll., 1987–89. Lectr., Nottingham Univ., 1948. *Publs:* (with H.L.A. Hart) Causation in the Law, 1959; Gaius, 1962; The South African Law of Trusts, 2nd ed., 1976; Tribonian, 1978; Sex Law, 1978; (with J. Menner) Concordance to the Digest Jurists, 1980; Emperors and Lawyers, 1981; The Quest for Security, 1982; Ulpian, 1982; Making Law Bind, 1987. Add: 94c Banbury Rd., Oxford OX2 6JT, England.

HONOUR, Hugh. British, b. 1927. Art, History, Architecture, Travel. Asst. Dir. of Leeds City Art Gallery and Temple Newsan House, 1953–54; Italian correspondent for Connoisseur mag., 1956–61. *Publs:* Horace Walpole, 1957, 1970; Chinoiserie: The Vision of Cathay, 1961; The Companion Guide to Venice, 1965, as Fodor's Venice: A Companion Guide, 1971; (with Nelly Schargo Hoyt) An Exhibition of Chinoiserie, 1965; (with John Fleming and Nikolas Pevsner) The Penguin Dictionary of Architecture, 1966, as A Dictionary of Architecture, 1969; Neo-Classicism, 1968; Cabinet Makers and Furniture Designers, 1969; Canova's Theseus and the Minotaur, 1969; (with Fleming) A Heritage of Images: A Selection of Lectures, 1970; Goldsmiths and Silversmiths, 1971; The European Vision of America: A Special Exhibition to Honor the Bicentennial of the United States, 1975; The New Golden Land: European Images of America from Discovery to the Present Time, 1975; (with Fleming) Dictionary of the Decorative Arts (in U.K. as The Penguin Dictionary of the Arts), 1977; Romanticism, 1978; (with Fleming) The Visual Art: A History, 1986; The Image of the Black in Western Art, 1989. Add: Villa Marchio, Tofori, Lucca, Italy.

HONRI, Peter. British, b. 1929. Actor, since 1948. *Publs:* Working the Halls, 1973; John Wilton's Music Hall, 1985. Add: c/o Laurence Pollinger Ltd., 18 Maddox St., London WIR 0EU, England.

HOOD, Christopher. British, b. 1943. Novels/Short stories,

Plays/Screenplays. Painter and decorator. Drama teacher, Burgess Hill Sch., Barnet, Herts., 1961–62. *Publs:* The Mullenthorpe Thing (novel), 1971; The White Citroen (ghost story), 1973; (with John Ottewell) Hot on the Hoof (screenplay), 1979; The Other Side of the Mountain (novel), 1979; Contact with Maldonia, 1982; Banana Cat, 1985. Add: Albatross Cottage, 1 Jones St., Treherbert, Rhondda, Glamorgan, Wales.

HOOD, Hugh (John Blagdon). Canadian, b. 1928. Novels/Short stories. Prof. Titulaire, Univ. of Montreal, since 1961. Teaching Fellow, Univ. of Toronto, 1951–55; Assoc. Prof., St. Joseph Coll., West Hartford, Conn., 1955–61. *Publs:* Flying a Red Kite (short stories), 1962; White Figure, White Ground, 1964; The Camera Always Lies, 1967; Around the Mountain: Scenes from Montreal Life, 1967; A Game of Touch, 1970; Strength Down Centre: The Jean Beliveau Story, 1970; The Fruit Man, The Meat Man, and the Manager, 1971; You Can't Get There From Here, 1972; The Governor's Bridge Is Closed, 1973; The Swing in the Garden, 1975; Dark Glasses, 1976; A New Athens, 1977; Selected Stories, 1978; Reservoir Ravine, 1979; (with S. Segal) Scoring, 1979; None Genuine Without This Signature, 1980; Black and White Keys, 1982; Trusting the Tale, 1983; The Scenic Art, 1984, August Nights, 1985; The Motor Boys in Ottawa, 1986; Five New Facts about Giorgione, 1987; Tony's Book, 1988. Add: 4242 Hampton Ave., Montreal, Que. H4A 2K9, Canada.

HOOD, Martin Sinclair Frankland. British, b. 1917. Archaeology/Antiquities. Dir., British Sch. of Archaeology, Athens, 1954–61. *Publs:* The Home of the Heroes: The Aegean Before the Greeks, 1967; The Minoans: Crete in the Bronze Age, 1971; The Arts in Prehistoric Greece, 1978. Add: The Old Vicarage, Great Milton, Oxford OX9 7PB, England.

HOOKER, Jeremy. British, b. 1941. Poetry, Literature. Lectr. in English, Univ. Coll. of Wales, Aberystwyth, 1965–84. *Publs:* The Elements, 1972; John Cowper Powys, 1973; Soliloquies of a Chalk Giant, 1974; David Jones: An Exploratory Study, 1975; Solent Shore, 1978; Landscape of the Daylight Moon, 1978; John Cowper Powys and David Jones, 1979; Englishman's Road, 1980; (ed. with Gweno Lewis) Selected Poems of Alun Lewis, 1981; Poetry of Place: Essays and Reviews 1970–1981, 1982; A View from the Source: Selected Poems, 1982; Itchen Water, 1982; (ed.) Select, 1965–68; Francis Bellerby, 1986; The Presence of the Past, 1987; Master of the Leaping Figures, 1987. Add: c/o Bath Coll. of Higher Educational, Newton Park, Newton St. Loe, Bath BA2 9BN, England.

HOOKER, John (Williamson). New Zealander, b. 1932. Novels/Short stories, Military history. Full–time writer since 1983. Publisher, Penguin Books Australia, Melbourne, 1969–79, and William Collins Australia, Melbourne, 1979–83. *Publs:* Jacob's Season, 1973; The Bush Soldiers, 1984; Standing Orders, 1986; Captain James Cook, 1988; Australians at War—Korea, 1989. Add: 96 Gipps St., Port Fairy, Vic. 3284, Australia.

HOOKER, Morna Dorothy. British, b. 1931. Theology. Lady Margaret's Prof. of Divinity, Cambridge Univ., since 1976; Fellow, Robinson Coll., Cambridge. Jt. Ed., Journal of Theological Studies, since 1985. Lectr., King's Coll., London, 1961–70; Lectr., Oxford Univ., and Fellow, Linacre Coll., Oxford, 1970–76, Lectr., Keble Coll., Oxford, 1972–76. *Publs:* Jesus and the Servant, 1959; The Son of Man in Mark, 1967; (co-ed.) What about the New Testament?, 1975; Pauline Pieces, 1979; Studying the New Testament, 1979; (co-ed.) Paul and Paulinism, 1982; The Message of Mark, 1983; Continuity and Discontinuity, 1986. Add: Divinity School, St. John's St., Cambridge, England.

HOOPER, Kay. Also writes as Kay Robbins. American. Historical/Romance novels. *Publs:* Lady Thief, 1981; Breathless Summer, 1982; Mask of Passion, 1982; Breathless Surrender, 1982; (as Kay Robbins) Return Engagement, 1982; On the Wings of Magic, 1983; (as Kay Robbins) Elusive Dawn, 1983; (as Kay Robbins) Kissed by Magic, 1983; (as Kay Robbins) Taken by Storm, 1983; C.J.'s Fate, 1984; If There Be Dragons, 1984; Pepper's Way, 1984; Something Different, 1984; (as Kay Robbins) Moonlight Rhapsody, 1984; Illegal Possession, 1985; (as Kay Robbins) Eye of the Beholder, 1985; Rafe, The Maverick, 1986; Rebel Waltz, 1986; Time after Time, 1986; Larger than Life, 1986; (as Kay Robbins) Belonging to Taylor, 1986; (as Kay Robbins) On Her Doorstep, 1986; Adelaide, The Enchantress, 1987; In Serena's Web, 1987; Rafferty's Wife, 1987; Zach's Law, 1987; Raven on the Wing, 1987; (with Iris Johansen) Matilda, The Adventuress, 1987; (with Iris Johansen) Sydney, The Temptress, 1987; Velvet Lightning, 1988; Captain's Paradise, 1988; Outlaw Derek, 1988; Summer of the Unicorn, 1988; Shades of Grey, 1988; The Fall of Lucas Kendrick, 1988; Unmasking Kelsey, 1988; (with Iris

Johansen) Copper Fire, 1988; (with Iris Johansen) Golden Flames, 1988; It Takes a Thief, 1989; Aces High, 1989. Add: c/o Dell Publishing, 666 Fifth Ave., New York, N.Y. 10103, U.S.A.

HOOPER, Meredith Jean. Australian, b. 1939. Children's fiction, Air/Space topics, Children's non-fiction, Engineering/Technology, History. *Publs:* Land of the Free: The United States of America, 1968; The Gold Rush in Australia, 1969; Everyday Inventions, 1972; The Story of Australia, 1974; More Everyday Inventions, 1976; Doctor Hunger and Captain Thirst, 1982; Seven Eggs, 1985; Kangaroo Route, 1985; God 'Elp All of Us: Three Great Flights, 1986; Cleared for Take-Off, 1986; History of Australia, 1988; The Journal of Watkin Stench, 1988. Add: 4 Western Rd., London N2 9HX, England.

HOOPER, Peter. Pseud. for Hedley Colwill Hooper. New Zealander, b. 1919. Novels/Short stories, Poetry. Worked as a teacher and bookseller; Deputy Principal, Westland High Sch., Hokitika, 1966–77. *Publs:* Map of Morning and Other Poems, 1964; Journey Towards an Elegy and Other Poems, 1969; The Mind of Bones (poetry), 1971; Earth Marriage (poetry), 1972; (ed. with Barry J. Smithson) Greymouth High School Golden Jubilee 1923–1973, 1973; Profiles in Monochrome (poetry), 1974; Selected Poems, 1977; A Song in the Forest (novel), 1979; The Goat Paddock and Other Stories, 1981; Our Forests Ourselves, 1981; (ed.) Winter Skies, 1983; (ed.) Saturday Afternoons, 1984; People of the Long Water (novel), 1985; Time and the Forest (novel), 1986; (ed.) Levity Brevity Bite, 1986; (ed.) Some Must Die, 1987. Add: Manuka St., Ahaura, via Greymouth, New Zealand.

HOOVER, Dwight Wesley. American, b. 1926. History. Prof. of History, since 1967, and Dir., Center for Middletown Studies, Ball State Univ., Muncie, Ind., (Asst. Prof., 1959–63; Assoc. Prof., 1964–67). Prof. of Historical Sociology, Univ. of Virginia, Charlottesville, 1977–79. Consultant, Middletown Film Project, 1976–81. Senior Fulbright Lectr. in American History, Budapest, 1988. *Publs:* (ed.) Understanding Negro History, 1968; Henry James, Sr., and the Religion of Community, 1969; (co-ed.) American Society in the 20th Century, 1972; (co-ed.) Conspectus of History: Focus on Biography (Issues in World Diplomacy, Revolution, Cities, Family History, Science and History), 6 vols., 1975–81; The Red and the Black, 1976; Cities, 1976; A Pictorial History of Indiana, 1980; (contr.) All Faithful People, 1983; Magic Middletown, 1986; Middletown: An Annotated Bibliography, 1988. Add: 705 N. Forest, Muncie, Ind. 47304, U.S.A.

HOOVER, H(elen) M(ary). American, b. 1935. Science fiction. *Publs:* science fiction for children—Children of Morrow, 1973; The Lion's Cub (historical fiction), 1974; Treasures of Morrow, 1976; The Delikon, 1977; The Rains of Eridan, 1977; The Lost Star, 1979; Return to Earth, 1980; This Time of Darkness, 1980; Another Heaven, Another Earth, 1981; The Bell Tree, 1982; The Shepherd Moon, 1984; Orvis, 1987; The Dawn Palace: The Story of Medea, 1988; Away Is a Strange Place to Be, 1989. Add: 9405 Ulysses Ct., Burke, VA, U.S.A.

HOPCRAFT, Arthur. British, b. 1932. Novels, Screenplays, Sports, Third World problems, Autobiography/Memoirs/Personal. Reporter, The Daily Mirror, 1956–59, The Guardian, 1959–64. *Publs:* Born to Hunger, 1968; The Football Man, 1968; The Great Apple Raid, 1970; (ed. and contrib. with H. McIlvanney) World Cup 70, 1970; (with Kathleen Tynan) Agatha (screenplay), 1979; Mid–Century Men, 1982; televison plays— The Mosedale Horseshoe, 1971; The Panel, 1971; The Birthday Run, 1972; Buggins Ermine, 1972; The Reporters, 1972; Said the Preacher, 1972; Jingle Bells, 1973; Katapult, 1973; The Nearly Man, 1974; Humbug, Finger or Thumb?, 1974; Journey to London, 1974; Baa, Baa, Blacksheep, 1974; Wednesday Love, 1975; Nightingale's Boys, 1975; The Nearly Man (series), 1976; Hannah, 1976; Hard Times (serial), 1977; Tinker, Tailor, Soldier, Spy (serial), 1979; Bleak House (serial), 1985; A Perfect Spy, 1987; A Tale of Two Cities, 1988. Add: c/o A.P. Watt Ltd., 20 John St., London WC1H 2DL, England.

HOPE, A(lec) D(erwent). Australian, b. 1907. Poetry, Literature. English Teacher, N.S.W. Dept. of Education, 1933–36; Lectr. in English and Education, Sydney Teachers Coll., 1937–45; Lectr. in English, Melbourne Univ. 1945–50; Prof. of English, 1950–69, and Library Fellow, 1969–72, Canberra Univ. Coll., later Australian Nat. Univ.; now retired. *Publs:* The Wandering Islands, 1955; Poems, 1960; (ed.) Australian Poetry 1960, 1960; (Poems), 1963; Australian Literature 1950–1962, 1963; The Cave and the Spring: Essays on Poetry, 1965; Collected Poems 1930–1965, 1966; New Poems, 1965–69, 1969; A Midsummer Eve's Dream: Variations on a Theme by William Dunbar, 1970; Dunciad Minor, 1970; Collected Poems 1930–1970, 1972; Selected Poems, 1973; Judith Wright,

1975; Native Companions (essays), 1974; A Late Picking: Poems 1965–1974, 1975; A Book of Answers, 1978; The New Cratylus, 1979; The Pack of Autolycus, 1979; Antechinus: Poems 1975–1980, 1981; The Age of Reason, 1984; Selected Poems, 1986; Ladies from the Sea, 1987. Add: 66 Arthur Circle, Forrest, A.C.T. 2603, Australia.

HOPE, Bob. American (born British), b. 1903. Autobiography/Memoirs/Personal. Actor and comedian. *Publs:* I Never Left Home, 1944; So This Is Peace, 1946; This Is on Me, 1954; I Owe Russia 1200 Dollars, 1963; Five Women I Love, 1967; The Last Christmas Show, 1974; The Road to Hollywood, 1977; Confessions of a Hooker, 1985. Add: 3808 Riverside Dr., Suite 100, Burbank, Calif. 91505, U.S.A.

HOPE, Christopher (David Tully). South African, b. 1944. Novels/Short stories, Children's fiction, Poetry. Underwriter, South British Insurance, Johannesberg, 1966; Ed., Nasionale Pers, publishers, Cape Town, 1966–67; Reviewer, Durban Sunday Tribune, 1968–69; Copywriter, Lintas, Durban, 1967–69, and Durban and Johannesburg, 1973–75; Copywriter, Lindsay Smithers, Durban, 1971; English teacher, Halesowen Secondary Modern Sch., 1972; Ed., Bolt, Durban, 1972–73; Writer–in–Residence, Gordonstoun Sch., Elgin, Scotland, 1978. *Publs:* (with Mike Kirkwood) Whitewashes (poetry), 1971; Cape Drives (poetry), 1974; A Separate Development (novel), 1980; In the Country of the Black Pig and Other Poems, 1981; Private Parts and Other Tales, 1981; (with Yehudi Menuhin) The King, The Cat, and the Fiddle (for children), 1983; Kruger's Alp (novel), 1984; The Dragon Wore Pink (for children), 1985; Englishmen (poetry), 1985; The Hottentot Room (novel), 1986; Black Swan (novella), 1987; White Boy Running (Memoir), 1988. Add: c/o A.P. Watt Ltd., 20 John St., London WC1N 2DR, England.

HOPE, Margaret. *See* KNIGHT, Alanna.

HOPE, Marjorie (Cecilia). American, b. 1923. International relations, Politics, Sociology. Prof. of Sociology, Wilmington Coll., since 1975. Prof. of Sociology, East Stroudsburg State Coll., Pennsylvania, 1973–75. Member, Intnl. Rescue Cttee., 1960–63, and East Orange Head Start, New Jersey, 1970–72. *Publs:* Youth Against the World, 1971; (with J. Young) The Struggle for Humanity, 1977; (with J. Young) The South African Churches in a Revolutionary Situation, 1981; (with J. Young) The Faces of Homelessness, 1986. Add: 1941 Ogden Rd., Wilmington, Ohio 45177, U.S.A.

HOPE, Ronald. British, b. 1921. Geography, History, Travel/Exploration/Adventure. Fellow, Brasenose Coll., Oxford, 1945–47; Dir., Seafarers Education Service, London, 1947–76; Dir., The Marine Soc., 1976–86. *Publs:* Spare Time at Sea, 1954, rev. ed. 1974; Economic Geography, 1956, 5th ed. 1969; Dick Small in the Half–Deck (novel), 1958; Ships, 1958; The British Shipping Industry, 1959; (ed.) The Harrap Book of Sea Verse, 1960; The Shoregoer's Guide to World Ports, 1963; (ed.) Seamen and the Sea, 1965; Introduction to the Merchant Navy, 1965, 4th ed. 1973; (ed.) Retirement from the Sea, 1967; In Cabined Ships at Sea, 1969; (ed.) Voices from the Sea, 1977; (ed.) John Masefield: The Sea Poems, 1978; (ed.) Twenty Singing Seamen, 1979; The Merchant Navy, 1980; (ed.) The Seaman's World, 1982; (ed.) Sea Pie, 1984. Add: Kilmadock House, Doune FK16 6AA, Scotland.

HOPE–SIMPSON, Jacynth (Ann). Also writes as Helen Dudley. British, b. 1930. Novels/Short stories, Children's fiction. *Publs:* Anne Young, Swimmer, 1959; The Stranger in the Train, 1960; The Bishop of Kenelminster, 1961; Young Netball Player, 1961; The Man Who Came Back, 1962; Danger on the Line, 1962; The Bishop's Picture, 1962; The Unravished Bride, 1963; The Witch's Cave, 1964; The Ninepenny, 1964; Hamish Hamilton Book of Myths and Legends, 1965; The Ice Fair, 1965; The High Toby, 1966; The Edge of the World, 1966; Hamish Hamilton Book of Witches, 1966; Escape to the Castle, 1967; The Unknown Island, 1968; They Sailed from Plymouth, 1970; Elizabeth I, 1971; (ed.) Tales in School, 1971; The Gunner's Boy, 1973; Save Tarranmoor!, 1974; Always on the Move, 1975; The Hijacked Hovercraft, 1975; Black Madonna, 1976; Vote for Victoria, 1976; The Making of the Machine Age, 1978; (as Helen Dudley) The Hooded Falcon, 1979; Island of Perfumes, 1985; Cottage Dreams, 1986. Add: Franchise Cottage, Newtown, Milborne Port, Sherborne, Dorset, England.

HOPKINS, Antony. British, b. 1921. Music, Autobiography/Memoirs/Personal. Presenter, Talking about Music, BBC. Former Prof., Royal Coll. of Music, London, and Gresham Prof. of Music, City Univ., London. *Publs:* Talking about Symphonies, 1961; Talking about Concertos, 1964; Music All Around Me, 1967; (with A. Previn) Music Face to Face, 1971; Talking about Sonatas, 1971; Downbeat Guide,

1977; Understanding Music, 1979; The Nine Symphonies of Beethoven, 1980; Songs for Swinging Golfers, 1981; Sounds of Music, 1982; Beating Time (autobiography), 1982; Musicamusings, 1983; Pathway to Music, 1983; The Concertgoer's Companion, vol. I, 1984, vol. II, 1985. Add: Woodyard, Ashridge, Berkhamsted, Herts., England.

HOPKINS, George Emil. American, b. 1937. Air/Space topics, Industrial relations. Prof. of History, Western Illinois Univ., Macomb, since 1968. *Publs:* The Airline Pilots: A Study in Elite Unionization, 1971; Flying the Line, 1982. Add: 1825 E. Maple Ridge, Peoria, Ill. 61614, U.S.A.

HOPKINS, Harry. British, b. 1913. International relations/Current affairs, Sociology, Travel/Exploration/Adventure. Feature writer, John Bull Mag., 1947–60. *Publs:* New World Arising: A Journey Through the Few Nations of Southeast Asia, 1952; England Is Rich, 1957; The New Look: A Social History of the 40s and 50s in Britain, 1963; Egypt, the Crucible: The Unfinished Revolution of the Arab World, 1969; The Numbers Game: The Bland Totalitarianism, 1973; The Strange Death of Private White, 1977; The Long Affray: The Poaching Wars in Britain, 1985. Add: 61 Clifton Hill, St. John's Wood, London NW8 0JN, England.

HOPKINS, Jasper. American, b. 1936. Philosophy, Theology/Religion, Translations. Prof. of Philosophy, Univ. of Minnesota, Minneapolis, since 1974 (Assoc. Prof., 1970–74). Asst. Prof., Case Western Reserve Univ., Cleveland, Ohio, 1963–68; Assoc. Prof., Univ. of Massachusetts, Boston, 1969–70. *Publs:* (co-ed. and trans.) Truth, Freedom, and Evil: Three Philosophical Dialogues by Anselm of Canterbury, 1967; (co-ed. and trans.) Trinity, Incarnation, and Redemption: Theological Treatises by Anselm of Canterbury, 1970; A Companion to the Study of St. Anselm, 1972; (ed. and trans. with Herbert Richardson) Anselm of Canterbury, 3 vols., 1974–76; Hermeneutical and Textual Problems in the Complete Treatises of St. Anselm, 1976; A Concise Introduction to the Philosophy of Nicholas of Cusa, 1978, 1980, 1986; Nicholas of Cusa on God as Not-other: A Translation and an Appraisal of De Li Non Aliud, 1979, 1983, 1987; Nicholas of Cusa on Learned Ignorance: A Translation and an Appraisal of De Docta Ignorantia, 1981, 1985, 1988; Nicholas of Cusa's Debate with John Wenck: A Translation and an Appraisal of De Ignota Litteratura and Apologia Doctae Ignorantiae, 1981, 1984, 1988; Nicholas of Cusa's Metaphysic of Contraction, 1983; Nicholas of Cusa's Dialectical Mysticism: Text, Translation and Interpretive Study of De Visione Dei, 1985, 1988; A New, Interpretive Translation of St. Anselm's Monologion and Proslogion, 1986. Add: Philosophy Dept., Univ. of Minnesota, Minneapolis, Minn. 55455, U.S.A.

HOPKINS, John (Richard). British, b. 1931. Plays/Screenplays. Worked as television studio mgr. and television producer; Writer for BBC Television, 1962–64. *Publs:* Talking to a Stranger: Four Television Plays, 1967; This Story of Yours, 1969; Find Your Way Home, 1971; Losing Time, 1983. Add: Hazelnut Farm, R.F.D.1, Fairfield, Conn. 06430, U.S.A.

HOPKINS, Lee Bennett. American, b. 1938. Novels/Short stories, Children's fiction, Poetry, Children's non-fiction. Freelance writer and educational consultant. *Publs:* (with A.F. Shapiro) Creative Activities for the Gifted Child, 1968; Books Are By People: Interviews with 104 Authors and Illustrators of Books for Young Children, 1969; Let Them Be Themselves: Language Arts for Children in Elementary Schools, 1969, rev. ed. 1974; (ed.) Don't You Turn Back: Poems by Langston Hughes, 1969; (ed.) I Think I Saw a Snail, 1969; Important Dates in Afro-American History, 1969; (ed.) City Spreads Its Wings, 1970; (ed.) City Talk, 1970; (ed.) Me!: A Book of Poems, 1970; This Street's For Me!, 1970; (ed. with M. Arenstein) Faces and Places, 1971; (ed.) Zoo!, 1971; (with M. Arenstein) Partners in Learning: A Child-Centered Approach to Teaching the Social Studies, 1971; Pass the Poetry, Please!, 1972, 1987; (ed.) Girls Can Too!: A Book of Poems, 1972; Charlie's World: A Book of Poems, 1972; Pick a Peck o' Poems, 1972; (ed. with M. Arenstein) Time to Shout, 1973; (ed.) On Our Way: Poems of Pride and Love, 1974; (ed.) Hey-How for Halloween, 1974; (ed.) Poetry on Wheels, 1974; Kim's Place and Other Poems, 1974; (ed.) Take Hold!, 1974; (with S. Rasch) I Really Want to Feel Good about Myself, 1974; More Books by More People: Interviews with 65 Authors of Books for Children, 1974; Meet Madeleine L'Engle, 1974; (ed.) Sing Hey for Christmas Day, 1975; (with M. Arenstein) Do You Know What Day Tomorrow Is?: A Teacher's Almanac, 1975, 1990; I Loved Rose Ann, 1976; (ed. with M. Arenstein) Potato Chips and a Slice of Moon, 1976; (ed. with M. Arenstein) Thread One to a Star, 1976; (ed.) Good Morning to You, Valentine, 1976; Mama (novel), 1977; (ed.) Beat the Drum! Independence Day Has Come, 1977; (ed.) A-Haunting We Will Go, 1977; (ed.) Monsters, Ghoulies and Creepy

Creatures, 1977; (ed.) Witching Time, 1977; Poetry to Hear, Read, Write and Love, 1978; (ed.) To Look at Any Thing, 1978; (ed.) Merrily Comes Our Harvest In, 1978; (ed.) Kits, Cats, Lions and Tigers, 1978; (ed.) Go to Bed, 1979; Wonder Wheels (novel), 1979; (ed.) Merely Players, 1979; (ed.) Easter Buds Are Springing, 1979; (ed.) My Mane Catches the Wind: Poems about Horses, 1979; (ed.) Pups, Dogs, Foxes and Wolves, 1979; (ed.) Elves, Fairies and Gnomes: A Book of Poems, 1980; The Best of Book Bonanza, 1980; (ed.) Moments: Poems about the Seasons, 1980; (ed.) By Myself, 1980; (ed.) Morning, Noon and Nightime, Too!, 1980; Mama and Her Boys (novel), 1981; (ed.) And God Bless Me: Prayers, Lullabies and Dream-Poems, 1982; (ed.) Circus! Circus!, 1982; (ed.) Rainbows Are Made: Poems by Carl Sandburg, 1982; (ed.) The Sky Is Full of Song, 1983; (ed.) A Song in Stone, 1983; (ed.) A Dog's Life, 1983; (ed.) Crickets and Bullfrogs and Whispers of Thunder: Poems by Harry Behn, 1984; (ed.) Surprises: An I Can Read Book, 1984; (ed.) Creatures, 1985; (ed.) Munching: Poems About Food and Eating, 1985; (ed.) Love and Kisses, 1984; (ed.) Best Friends, 1986; (ed.) The Sea Is Calling Me, 1986; (ed.) Dinosaurs, 1987; (ed.) Click, Rumble, Roar: Poems about Machines, 1987; (ed.) More Surprises, 1987; (ed.) Voyages: Poems by Walt Whitman, 1988; Side by Side: Poems to Read Together, 1988; Still as a Star: Nighttime Poems, 1989; People from Mother Goose, 1989; Animals From Mother Goose, 1989. Add: Kemeys Cove, (3–7), Scarborough, N.Y. 10510, U.S.A.

HOPKINS, Lyman. *See* **FOLSOM,** Franklin Brewster.

HOPKINSON, (Sir Henry) Thomas. Writes as Tom Hopkinson. British, b. 1905. Novels/Short stories, History, Literature, Photography, Writing/Journalism, Autobiography/Memoirs/Personal. Ed., Picture Post mag., London, 1940–50; Ed.-in-Chief, Drum mag., South Africa, 1958–61; Dir. for Africa, Intnl. Press Inst., Nairobi, Kenya, 1963–66; Sr. Fellow, Univ. of Sussex, 1967–69; Dir. of Journalism Studies, University Coll., Cardiff, 1970–75. Chmn., National Press Awards, 1968–77; Past Pres., Photographers Gallery, London. *Publs:* A Wise Man Foolish, 1930; (as Vindicator) A Strong Hand at the Helm, 1933; Fascists at Olympia: A Record of Eye-Witnesses and Victims, 1934; (with Mileson Horton as Thomas Pembroke) Photocrimes, 1936; The Man Below, 1939; Mist in the Tagus, 1946; The Transitory Venus, 1948; Down the Long Slide, 1949; Love's Apprentice, 1953; George Orwell, 1953; The Lady and the Cut-Throat, 1958; In the Fiery Continent, 1962; South Africa, 1964; (ed. with D. Hopkinson) Much Silence: The Life and Work of Meher Baba, 1974; Bert Hardy, Photojournalist, 1975; Treasures of the Royal Photographic Society, 1980; Of This Our Time (autobiography), 1982; Under the Tropic (autobiography), 1984; Shady City, 1987. Add: 26 Boulter St., Oxford OX4 1AX, England.

HOPKINSON, Tom. *See* **HOPKINSON,** Thomas.

HOPPE, Arthur (Watterson). American, b. 1925. Novels/Short stories, Humor/Satire. Columnist, San Francisco Chronicle, since 1960 (Reporter, 1949–59). *Publs:* The Love Everybody Crusade, 1960; Dreamboat, 1964; The Perfect Solution to Absolutely Everything, 1968; Mr. Nixon and My Other Problems, 1971; Miss Lollipop and the Doom Machine, 1973; The Tiddling Tennis Theorem, 1977; The Marital Arts, 1985. Add: San Francisco Chronicle, 5th & Mission, San Francisco, Calif. 94119, U.S.A.

HOPPOCK, Robert. American, b. 1901. Education, Sociology. Emeritus Prof. of Counselor Education, New York Univ., NYC, since 1972 (Prof., 1939–72). Asst. Dir., National Occupational Conference, 1933–39. *Publs:* Job Satisfaction, 1935; Group Guidance, 1949; Occupational Information, 1957, 4th ed. 1976. Add: 104 Webster Ave., Manhasset, N.Y. 11030, U.S.A.

HORADAM, Alwyn Francis. Australian, b. 1923. Mathematics. Assoc. Prof. of Mathematics, Univ. of New England, Armidale, 1964–87 (Lectr. 1947–58; Sr. Lectr. 1958–62; Dean of the Faculty of Science, 1966–68; Univ. Ombudsman, 1984; Head, Dept of Mathematics, 1985–87). *Publs:* Outline Course of Pure Mathematics, 1969; Guide to Undergraduate Projective Geometry, 1970; (with M.E. Dunkley and I.W. Stewart) New Horizons in Mathematics, Book I, 1970, Book II, 1972; (with M.E. Dunkley and I.W. Stewart) Teacher's Manual to New Horizons in Mathematics, Book I, 1970, Book II, 1972; (ed. with W.D. Wallis) Combinatorial Mathematics VI: Proceedings, Armidale, August 1978, 1979; (ed. with A.N. Philippou and G.E. Bergum) Fibonacci Numbers and Their Applications: Proceedings, Patras, August 1984, 1986; (co-ed.) Applications of Fibonacci Numbers, 1988. Add: Dept. of Mathematics, Statistics and Computing Science, Univ. of New England, Armidale, N.S.W. 2351, Australia.

HORDER, Mervyn. British, b. 1910. Music. Composer. Ed., G. Duckworth & Co. Ltd., London, 1938–68. *Publs:* (ed.) In Praise of Cambridge, 1952; (ed.) In Praise of Oxford, 1955; (ed.) The Orange Carol Book, 1962, 1973; The Little Genius, 1966; Six Betjeman Songs, 1967; (ed.) Book of Love Songs, 1969; (ed.) Ronald Firbank: Memoirs and Critiques, 1977; A Shropshire Lad (songs), 1980; (ed.) The Easter Carol Book, 1982; Seven Shakespeare Songs, 1988; On Their Own: Shipwrecks and Survivals, 1988; (ed.) In Praise of Norfolk, 1988. Add: c/o G. Duckworth & Co. Ltd., 43 Gloucester Cres., London NW1 7DY, England.

HORECKY, Paul L. American, b. 1913. Librarianship. Trial Attorney, Office of Chief of Counsel, Nuremberg Military Tribunals, 1947–49; Research Asst., Russian Research Center, Harvard Univ., Cambridge, Mass., 1949–51; Slavic Research Analyst, East European Specialist, Asst. Chief and East European Specialist, and Acting Chief, 1951–72, and Chief, Slavic and Central European Div., 1972–77, Library of Congress, Washington, D.C.; Sr. Research Fellow, Inst. for Sino–Soviet Studies, George Washington Univ., Washington, D.C., 1978–79; Visiting Prof., Slavic Research Center, Hokkaido Univ., Sapporo, Japan, 1979–80. *Publs:* (co–ed.) Trials of War Criminals Before the Nuremberg Military Tribunal, vols. and XI, 1950–51; Libraries and Bibliographic Centers in the Soviet Union, 1959; (chief ed. and contrib.) Basic Russian Publications: A Selected and Annotated Bibliography on Russia and the Soviet Union, 1962; (chief ed. and contrib.) Russia and the Soviet Union: A Bibliographic Guide to Western Language Publications, 1965; (chief ed. and contrib.) Southeastern Europe: A Guide to Basic Publications, 1969; (chief ed. and contrib.) East Central Europe: A Guide to Basic Publications, 1969; (chief ed.) A Guide to Yugoslav Libraries and Archives, 1975; (chief ed.) East Central and South–eastern Europe: A Handbook of Library and Archival Resources in North America, 1976. Add: 7116 Fort Hunt Rd., No. 189, Alexandria, Va. 22307, U.S.A.

HORGAN, Paul. American, b. 1903. Novels/Short stories, Children's fiction, Plays, History, Theology/Religion, Biography. Assoc. Fellow, Saybrook Coll., Yale Univ., New Haven, Conn., since 1967; Author–in–Residence since 1967, and Prof. Emeritus since 1971, Wesleyan Univ., Middletown, Conn. (Sr. Fellow, 1959–61, and Dir., 1962–67, Center for Advanced Studies). Member of Production Staff, Eastern Theater, Rochester, N.Y., 1923–26; Librarian, 1926–42, and Asst. to the Pres., 1947, New Mexico Military Inst., Roswell; Pres., Roswell Museum, N.M., 1946–52; Chmn. of the Bd., Santa Fe Opera, N.M., 1958–62. *Publs:* Men of Arms, 1931; The Fault of Angels, 1933; No Quarter Given, 1935; Main Line West, 1936; The Return of the Weed (in U.K. as Lingering Walls) (short stories), 1936; From the Royal City of the Holy Faith of Saint Francis of Assisi: Being Five Accounts of Life in that Place, 1936; (ed. with M.G. Fulton) New Mexico's Own Chronicle: Three Races in the Writings of Four Hundred Years, 1937; A Lamp on the Plains, 1937; Far from Cibola, 1938; The Habit of Empire, 1938; Figures on a Landscape (short stories), 1940; The Common Heart, 1942; A Tree on the Plains: A Music Play for Americans, 1942; Yours, A. Lincoln (play), 1942, (co–author) Look at America: The Southwest, 1947; The Devil in the Desert: A Legend of Life and Death on the Rio Grande, 1952; One Red Rose for Christmas, 1952; Great River: The Rio Grande in North American History, 2 vols., 1954; Humble Powers: Three Novelettes, 1954; The Saintmaker's Christmas Eve, 1955; The Centuries of Santa Fe, 1956; Rome Eternal, 1957; Give Me Possession, 1957; A Distant Trumpet, 1960; Citizen of New Salem (in U.K. as Abraham Lincoln: Citizen of New Salem), 1961; Toby and the Nighttime, 1962; Mountain Standard Time (trilogy), 1962; Conquistadors in North American History (in U.K. as Conquistadors in American History), 1963; Things as They Are, 1964; Peter Hurd: A Portrait Sketch from Life, 1965; Songs After Lincoln, 1965; Memories of the Future, 1966; The Peach Stone: Stories from Four Decades, 1967; Everything to Live For, 1968; Whitewater, 1970; The Heroic Triad: Essays in the Social Energies of Three Southwestern Cultures, 1970; (ed.) Maurice Baring Restored: Selections from His Work, 1970; Encounters with Stravinsky: A Personal Record, 1972; Approaches to Writing, 1973; Lamy of Santa Fe, 1975; The Thin Mountain Air, 1977; Mexico Bay, 1982; Of America East and West, 1984; Under the Sangre de Cristo, 1985; The Clerihews of Paul Horgan, 1985; A Certain Climate: Essays on History, Art and Letters, 1988. Add: 77 Pearl St., Middletown, Conn. 06457, U.S.A.

HORLOCK, John Harold. British, b. 1928. Engineering. Vice–Chancellor, Open Univ., since 1981. Harrison Prof. of Mechanical Engineering, Univ. of Liverpool, 1958–66; Prof. of Engineering, Univ. of Cambridge, 1967–74; Vice–Chancellor, Univ. of Salford, 1974–80. *Publs:* Axial–Flow Compressors, 1958; Axial–Flow Turbines, 1966; Actuator Disk Theory, 1978; (ed.) Thermodynamics and Gas Dynamics of I.C. Engines, 2 vols., 1982–86; Cogeneration: Combined Heat and Power,

1987. Add: Open Univ., Walton Hall, Milton Keynes MK7 6AA, England.

HORN, Siegfried H(erbert). American, b. 1908. Archaeology/Antiquities. Prof. of Archaeology and History of Antiquity, Andrews Univ., Berrien Springs, Mich., 1951–76, now retired. *Publs:* Light from the Dust Heaps, 1955; The Spade Confirms the Book, 1957; Seventh–Day Adventist Bible Dictionary, 1960, 1979; Records of the Past Illuminate the Bible, 1963; (with L.H. Wood) The Chronology of Ezra 7, 1953, 1970; (with R.S. Boraas) Heshbon 1968; The First Campaign at Tell Heshbon, 1969; (with R.S. Boraas) Heshbon 1971; The Second Campaign at Tell Heshbon, 1973; (with R.S. Boraas) Heshbon 1973; The Third Campaign at Tell Heshbon, 1975; Biblical Archaeology: A Generation of Discovery, 1985. Add: 379 Ridge View Dr., Pleasant Hill, Calif. 94523, U.S.A.

HORN, (John) Stephen. American, b. 1931. Politics/Government. Trustee Prof. of Political Science since 1988, California State Univ., Long Beach (Pres., 1970–88). Administrative Asst., Secty. of Labor James P. Mitchell, Washington, D.C., 1959–60; Legislative Asst. to U.S. Sen. Thomas H. Kuchel, Washington, D.C., 1960–66; Sr. Fellow, The Brookings Instn., Washington, D.C., 1966–69; Dean, Grad. Studies and Research, American Univ., Washington, D.C., 1969–70. *Publs:* The Cabinet and the Congress, 1960; Unused Power: The Work of the Senate Committee on Appropriations, 1970; (co–author) Congressional Ethics: The View from the House, 1975. Add: 3944 Pine Ave., Long Beach, Calif. 90807, U.S.A.

HORNE, Alistair (Allan). British, b. 1925. History, Politics/Government, Social commentary/Phenomena, Biography. Sr. Assoc. Fellow, St. Antony's Coll., Oxford. Member of Cttee. of Mgmt., Royal Literary Fund, since 1969. Foreign Corresp., Daily Telegraph, London, 1952–55. *Publs:* Back into Power, 1955; Return to Power, 1956; The Land Is Bright, 1958; Canada and the Canadians, 1961; The Price of Glory, Verdun 1916, 1962; The Fall of Paris, The Siege and the Commune 1870–71, 1976; To Lose a Battle, France 1940, 1969; Death of a Generation, 1970; The Terrible Year, 1971; Small Earthquake in Chile, 1972; A Savage War of Peace: Algeria 1954–62, 1977; Napoleon, Master of Europe 1805–07, 1979; The French Army and Politics, 1870–1970, 1984; Macmillan, 2 vols., 1988–89. Add: 21 St. Petersburgh Pl., London W2, England.

HORNE, Donald Richmond. Australian, b. 1921. Novels, History, Social commentary/Phenomena, Autobiography/Memoirs/Personal. Prof. Emeritus, Univ. of New South Wales. Chmn., The Australia Council, since 1985. Ed., The Observer, Sydney, 1958–61, and The Bulletin, Sydney, 1960–62 and 1967–72; Co–Ed., Quadrant, 1964–66; Contrib. Ed., Newsweek Intnl., 1973–76; Pres., Australian Soc. of Authors, 1984–85. *Publs:* The Lucky Country, 1964; The Permit (novel), 1965; The Education of Young Donald (autobiography), 1967; (with Beal) Southern Exposure, 1967; God Is an Englishman, 1969; The Next Australia, 1970; But What If There Are No Pelicans? (novel), 1971; The Australian People, 1972; Death of the Lucky Country, 1976; Money Made Us, 1976; His Excellency's Pleasure (novel), 1977; Right Way, Don't Go Back, 1977; In Search of Billy Hughes, 1978; Time of Hope, 1980; Winner Take All, 1981; The Great Museum, 1984; The Story of the Australian People, 1985; Confessions of a New Boy (autobiography), 1985; The Public Culture, 1986; The Lucky Country Revisited, 1987; Portrait of an Optimist (autobiography), 1988. Add: 53 Grosvenor St., Woollahra, N.S.W. 2025, Australia.

HORNE, R(alph) A(lbert). American, b. 1929. Chemistry, Environmental science/Ecology, Marine science/Oceanography. Senior Scientist, Radio Corp. of America, Needham, Mass., 1957–58, and Joseph Kaye & Co., Cambridge, Mass., 1958–60; Scientific Staff, Arthur D. Little Inc., Cambridge, Mass., 1960–69, 1972–78; Assoc. Scientist, Woods Hole Oceanographic Inst., 1970–71; Principal Scientist, JBF Scientific Corp., Lexington, Mass., 1971–72; Senior Scientist, GCA/Technology Div., Burlington, Mass., 1978–80. *Publs:* Marine Chemistry, 1969; Water and Aqueous Solutions, 1972; The Chemistry of Our Environment, 1978. Add: R.F.D. 3, Raymond, N.H. 03077, U.S.A.

HORNSBY, Alton, Jr. American, b. 1940. History, Race relations. Prof., and Chmn., Dept. of History, Morehouse Coll., Atlanta, since 1968. Ed., Journal of Negro History, since 1976. Instr., Tuskegee Inst., Ala., 1962–65. *Publs:* (ed.) In The Cage: Eyewitness Accounts of the Freed Negro in Southern Society, 1877–1929, 1971; The Black Almanac, 1972, 1973, 1975, 1977; The Negro in Revolutionary Georgia, 1977. Add: Dept. of History, Morehouse Coll., Atlanta, Ga. 30314, U.S.A.

HOROVITZ, Israel (Arthur). American, b. 1939. Novels/Short stories, Plays/Screenplays, Poetry. Artistic Dir., N.Y. Playwrights Laboratory, NYC, since 1977, and Gloucester Stage Co., Mass., since 1980. Regular Contrib., Village Voice, NYC, since 1968; Columnist, Words from New York, Mag. Litteraire, Paris, since 1971. Prof. of Playwriting, New York Univ., NYC, 1967–69; Playwright–in–Residence, City Coll., City Univ. of New York, 1969–74; Fannie Hurst Visiting Prof., Brandeis Univ., Waltham, Mass., 1974–75. *Publs:* First Season: Line, The Indian Wants the Bronx, It's Called the Sugar Plum, Rats, 1968; Leader, with Play for Trees, 1970; Acrobats, 1971; The Honest to God Schnozzola, 1971; Shooting Gallery, with Plays for Germs, 1973; Dr. Hero, 1973; Cappella (novel), 1973; Spider Poems and Other Writings, 1973; Alfred the Great, 1974; The Primary English Class, 1976; Uncle Snake: An Independence Day Pageant, 1976; Nobody Loves Me (novel), 1976; Hopscotch, with The 75th, 1977; (adaptor) Man with Bags, 1977; Mackerel, 1979; (adaptor) A Christmas Carol, by Dickens, 1979; The Wakefield Plays, 1979; The Good Parts, 1983. Add: c/o Jonathan Sand, Writers and Artists Agency, 162 W. 56th St., New York, N.Y. 10019, U.S.A.

HOROVITZ, Michael. British, b. 1935. Poetry, Literature, Translations. Ed. and Publr., New Departures intnl. review, since 1959. *Publs:* (trans.) Europa, 1961; Alan Davie, 1963; Declaration, 1965; Strangers: Fauve Poems, 1965; Poetry for the People: A Verse Essay in Bop Prose, 1966; Bank Holiday: A New Testament for the Love Generation, 1967; (ed.) Children of Albion, 1969; The Wolverhampton Wanderer: An Epic of Football, Fate and Fun, 1970; Love Poems, 1971; A Contemplation, 1978; Growing Up: Selected Poems and Pictures 1951–1979, 1979; (trans.) The Egghead Republic, 1979; (ed.) Poetry Olympics Anthology, 3 vols., 1980–83; (ed.) A Celebration of and for Francis Horovitz (1938–1983), 1984; Midsummer Morning Jog Log, 1986. Add: New Departures, Mullions, Bisley, Stroud, Glos. GL6 7BU, England.

HOROWITZ, Irving Louis. American, b. 1929. Education, Politics/government, Sociology. Prof. of Sociology, since 1969, and Hannah Arendt Prof. of Social and Political Theory since 1979, Rutgers Univ., New Brunswick, New Jersey (Chmn., Dept. of Sociology, Livingston Coll. at Rutgers, 1969–73). Pres. and Ed.–in–Chief, Transaction, New Brunswick. Chmn., Dept. of Sociology, Hobart and William Smith Colls., 1960–63; Assoc. Prof., then Prof. of Sociology, Washington Univ., St. Louis, 1963–69. *Publs:* Idea of War and Peace in Contemporary Philosophy, 1957, 2nd ed. as War and Peace in Contemporary Social and Philosophy Theory, 1973; Philosophy, Science, and the Sociology of Knowledge, 1961; Radicalism and the Revolt Against Reason: The Social Theories of Georges Sorel, 1961; The War Game: Studies of the New Civilian Militarists, 1963; (ed.) Power, Politics and People: The Collected Essays of C. Wright Mills, 1963; (trans.) Outlines of Sociology by Gumplowicz, 1963; (ed.) Historia y Elementos de la Sociologia del Conocimiento, 2 vols., 1964; Revolution in Brazil: Politics and Society in a Developing Nation, 1964; (ed.) The New Sociology: Essays in Social Science and Social Values in Honor of C. Wright Mills, 1964; (ed.) Sociology and Pragmatism: A Study in American Higher Learning, by Mills, 1964; Three Worlds of Development: The Theory and Practice of International Stratification, 1966, 1972; (ed.) The Rise and Fall of Project Camelot, 1967; Professing Sociology: Studies in the Life Cycle of Social Science, 1968; (ed. with Josue de Castro and John Gerassi) Latin American Radicalism, 1969; Sociological Self–Images: A Collective Portrait, 1969; (ed.) Cuban Communism, 1970, 5th ed. 1984; The Struggle Is the Message: The Organization and Ideology of the Anti–War Movement, 1970; (with William H. Friedland) The Knowledge Factory: Student Power and Academic Politics in America, 1970; (ed.) Masses in Latin America, 1970; (ed.) The Use and Abuse of Social Science: Behavioral Science and Policymaking, 1971; (ed. with Mary Symons Strong) Sociological Realities: A Guide to the Study of Society, 1971; (ed.) The Troubled Conscience: American Social Issues, 1971; Foundations of Political Sociology, 1972; Israeli Ecstasies/Jewish Agonies, 1974; (with James Everett Katz) Social Science and Public Policy in the United States, 1975; (ed. with Charles Nanry) Sociological Realities II: A Guide to the Study of Society, 1975; Genocide: State Power and Mass Murder, 1976, as Taking Lives: Genocide and State Power, 1980; (ed.) Equity, Income, and Policy: Comparative Studies in Three Worlds of Development, 1977; Ideology and Utopia in the United States 1956–1976,1977; (ed.) Science, Sin and Scholarship, 1978; (with Seymour Martin Lipset) Dialogues on American Politics, 1978; (ed.) Constructing Policy: Dialogues with Social Scientists in the National Political Arena, 1979; (ed. with John C. Leggett and Martin Oppenheimer) The American Working Class: Prospects for the 1980's, 1979; El Comunismo Cubano 1959–1979, 1979; (ed.) Policy Studies Review Annual: Volume Five, 1981; Beyond Empire and Revolution: Militarization and Consolidation in the Third World, 1982; C. Wright Mills: An American Utopian, 1983; Winners and Losers: Social and Politi-

cal Polarities in Present–Day America, 1984; Communicating Ideas: The Crisis of Publishing in a Post–Industrial Society, 1986; Persuasions and Prejudices, 1989. Add: 1247 State Road (Route 206), Blawenburg Rd./Rocky Hill Intersection, Princeton, N.J. 08540, U.S.A.

HORSLEY, David. *See* **BINGLEY**, David Ernest.

HORSMAN, Reginald. American, b. 1931. History. Distinguished Prof. of History, Univ. of Wisconsin at Milwaukee, since 1972 (Instr., 1958–59; Asst. Prof., 1959–62; Assoc. Prof., 1962–64; Prof., since 1964). *Publs:* The Causes of the War of 1812, 1962; Matthew Elliott: British Indian Agent, 1964; Expansion and American Indian Policy 1783–1812, 1967; The War of 1812, 1969; Napoleon's Europe, 1970; The Frontier in the Formative Years 1783–1815, 1970; Race and Manifest Destiny, 1981; The Diplomacy of the New Republic 1776–1815, 1985; Dr. Nott of Mobile: Southerner, Physician, and Racial Theorist, 1987. Add: Dept. of History, Univ. of Wisconsin, Milwaukee, Wisc. 53201, U.S.A.

HORTON, Felix Lee. *See* **FLOREN**, Lee.

HORTON, Frank E. American, b. 1939. Transportation, Urban studies. Prof. of Higher Education, Univ. of Toledo, Ohio, since 1989. Asst. Prof. of Geography, 1966–68, Assoc. Prof., 1968–70, Dir. of the Inst. of Urban and Regional Research, 1968–71, Prof of Geography, 1970–75, and Dean for Advanced Studies, 1971–75, Univ. of Iowa, Iowa City; Vice–Pres. for Academic Affairs and Research, Southern Illinois Univ., Carbondale, 1975–80; Chancellor and Prof. of Geography and Urban Affairs, Univ. of Wisconsin, Milwaukee, 1980–85; Pres. and Prof. of Geography, Univ. of Oklahoma, Norman, 1985–88. *Publs:* (ed.) Geographic Research in Urban Transportation and Network Analysis, 1968; (with Brian Joe Lobley Berry) Geographic Perspectives on Urban Studies, 1970; (ed.) Geographic Perspectives on Contemporary Urban Problems, 1973; (with Brian Joe Lobley Berry) Urban Environmental Management: Planning for Pollution Control, 1974. Add: Univ. of Oklahoma, Norman, Okla. 73109, U.S.A.

HORTON, Paul B. American, b. 1916. Sociology. Prof. Emeritus of Sociology, Western Michigan Univ., Kalamazoo (faculty member since 1945). Asst. Prof., Butler Univ., Indianapolis, Ind., 1943–45. *Publs:* (with G. Leslie) Sociology of Social Problems, 1955, 9th ed. 1988; Sociology and the Health Sciences, 1965; (with C. Hunt) Sociology, 1964, 6th ed. 1984; (ed. with G. Leslie) Studies in the Sociology of Social Problems, 1971, 1974; Introductory Sociology, 3rd ed., 1983. Add: 1740 Waite Ave., Kalamazoo, Mich. 49008, U.S.A.

HORVATH, Betty. American, b. 1927. Children's fiction. *Publs:* Hooray for Jasper, 1966; Jasper Makes Music, 1967; Will the Real Tommy Wilson Please Stand Up, 1969; The Cheerful Quiet, 1969; Be Nice to Josephine, 1970; Not Enough Indians, 1971; Small Paul and the Bully of Morgan Court, 1971; Jasper and the Hero Business, 1977. Add: 2340 Waite Ave., Kalamazoo, Mich. 49008, U.S.A.

HOSIER, Peter. *See* **CLARK**, Douglas.

HOSKINS, Robert. Also writes as Grace Corren, John Gregory, Susan Jennifer, and Michael Kerr. American, b. 1933. Historical/Romance/Gothic, Science fiction/Fantasy. Freelance writer since 1972. Worked in family business, 1952–64; Attendant, Wassaic State Sch. for the Retarded, NYC, 1964–66; House Parent, Brooklyn Home for Children, 1966–68; Sub–Agent, Scott Meredith Literary Agency, NYC, 1967–68; Sr. Ed., Lancer Books, NYC, 1969–72. *Publs:* (ed.) First Step Outward, 1969; (as Grace Corren) The Darkest Room, 1969; (ed.) Infinity 1–5, 5 vols., 1970–73; (ed.) The Stars Around Us, 1970; (ed.) Swords Against Tomorrow, 1970; (ed.) Tomorrow 1, 1971; (ed.) The Far–Out People, 1971; (as Grace Corren) A Place on Dark Island, 1971; (ed.) Wondermakers 1–2, 2 vols., 1972–74; (ed.) Strange Tomorrows, 1972; (as Grace Corren) Evil in the Family (science fiction), 1972; (as Susan Jennifer) The House of Counted Hatreds, 1973; (as Grace Corren) Mansions of Deadly Dreams, 1973; (ed.) The Edge of Never, 1973; (ed.) The Liberated Future, 1974; The Shattered People (science fiction), 1975; (as Susan Jennifer) Country of the Kind, 1975; Master of the Stars (science fiction), 1976; To Control the Stars (science fiction), 1977; Tomorrow's Son (science fiction), 1977; (as Grace Corren) Dark Threshold, 1977; (ed.) The Future Now, 1977; Jack–in–the–Box Planet (science fiction), 1978; To Escape the Stars (science fiction), 1978; (as John Gregory) Legacy of the Stars (science fiction), 1979; (as Michael Kerr) The Gemini Run, 1979; (as Grace Corren) The Attic Child, 1979; (as Grace Corren) Survival Run (novelization of screenplay), 1979; (ed.) Against Tomorrow, 1979; The Fury Bombs, 1983. Add: c/o Harlequin, 225 Duncan Mill

Rd., Don Mills, Ont. M3B 3K9, Canada.

HOSTROP, Richard W. American, b. 1925. Education, Librarianship. Publr., ETC Publs., since 1972. Pres., Prairie State Coll., Chicago Heights, Ill., 1967–70; Ed., Linnet Books, Hamden, Conn., 1970–72. *Publs:* Teaching and the Community College Library, 1968; Orientation to the Two–Year College, 1970; Handbook for Achieving Academic Success, 1970; (co–ed.) Learning C.O.D.—Can the Schools Buy Success? 1972; (co–ed.) Accountability for Educational Results, 1972; (ed. with J. Mecklenburger) Education Vouchers: From Theory to Alum Rock, 1972; Learning Inside the Library Media Center, 1972; (ed.) Foundations of Futurology in Education, 1973; (ed.) Education Beyond Tomorrow, 1975; Managing Education for Results, 1983. Add: 700 E. Verde del Sur, Palm Springs, Calif. 92262, U.S.A.

HOTCHNER, A(aron) E(dward). American, b. 1920. Plays/Screenplays, Biography. Admitted to the Missouri Bar, 1941; practised law in St. Louis, 1941–42; Articles Ed., Cosmopolitan mag., 1948–50. *Publs:* The Dangerous American, 1958; (adaptor) For Whom The Bell Tolls, by Hemingway (television play), 1958; (adaptor) The Killers, by Hemingway (television play), 1959; Adventures of a Young Man, by Hemingway (screenplay), 1961; The White House (play), 1964; Papa Hemingway: A Personal Memoir, 1966; The Hemingway Hero (play), 1967; Treasure, 1970; Do You Take This Man? (play), 1970; King of the Hill, 1972; Looking for Miracles, 1974; Doris Day: Her Own Story, 1976; Sophia: Living and Loving, 1979; Sweet Prince (play), 1980; The Man Who Lived at the Ritz, 1982; Choice People, 1984; Welcome to the Club (musical comedy), 1988. Add: 14 Hillandale Rd., Westport, Conn. 06880, U.S.A.

HOTSON, John Hargrove. American, b. 1930. Economics. Prof. of Economics, Univ. of Waterloo, Ont., since 1969. Exec. Dir., Cttee. on Monetary and Economic Reform (Comer). Instr., Wilkes Coll., Wilkes Barre, Pa., 1957–60; Asst. Prof., The Colorado Coll., Colorado Springs, 1963–68; Assoc. Prof., Univ., of South Florida, Tampa, 1968–69. *Publs:* International Comparisons of Money Velocity and Wage Mark–ups, 1968; Stagflation and the Bastard Keynesians, 1976. Add: Dept. of Economics, Univ. of Waterloo, Waterloo, Ont. N22–3G1,Canada.

HOUÉDARD, dom (Pierre)–Sylvester. British, b. 1924. Poetry. Benedictine Monk, Prinknash Abbey, Gloucester, since 1949. Founding Member and Vice–Pres., Assn. of Little Presses, since 1965. Librarian, Farnborough Abbey, 1959–61. *Publs:* Yes–No, 1963; Thalamus–Sol, 1964; Rock Sand Tide, 1964; Frog–Pond–Plop, 1965; Atom, 1965; Kinkon, 1965, rev. ed. as Op and Kinkon Poems and Some Non–Kinkon, 1965; Worm–Wood/Womb–Word, 1966; A Book of Chakras (8 Yantrics): Studies Towards Mechanical Fingers by dsh for Inner Moon Pointing, 1966; To Catch a Whiteman by His Manifesto, 1967; Tantric Poems, Perhaps, 1967; Book of 12 Mudras, 1967; Book of Mazes and Troytowns, 1967; Easter Frog Toy for Pesach–Skipover, 1967; Eros A–Gape, 1967; Semaine Euclidienne, 1968; Poster for the Breakdown of Nations 4th–World Conference, 1968; Deus–Snap, 1968; Miniposters, 1968; The Sun–Cheese Wheel–Ode: A Double–Rolling–Gloster Memorial for Ken Cox, 1969; A Snow Mouse, 1969; En Trance, 1969; 12 Nauhuatl Dance–poems from the Cosmic Typewriter, 1969; Texts, 1969; Streets Go Both Crazy Ways at Once, 1969; Book of Battledores, 1969; Book of Onomastikons, 1969; Splendid Weeping, 1969; Successful Cube Tranceplant in Honor of Chairman Mao, 1970; Ode to the Colonels, 1970; Grove–Sings: Reflecting Poem for ihf, 1970; Auto–de–Chakra–Struction, 1971; (trans.) Office of Our Lady, 1962; Main Calm Line, 1972; Like Contemplation, 1972; Begin Again: A Book of Reflections and Reversals, 1975. Add: Prinknash Abbey, Gloucester GL4 8EX, England.

HOUGH, Charlotte. British, b. 1924. Children's fiction, Children's non-fiction. *Publs:* Jim Tiger, 1956; Morton's Pony, 1957; The Home–makers, 1957; The Hampshire Pig, 1958; The Story of Mr. Pinks, 1958; The Animal Game, 1959; The Trackers, 1960; Algernon, 1961; 3 Little Funny Ones, 1962; Anna and Minnie, 1962; The Owl in the Barn, 1964; More Funny Ones, 1965; Red Biddy, 1966; Sir Frog, 1968; Educating Flora, 1968; My Aunt's Alphabet, 1969; Queer Customer, 1972; Wonky Donkey, 1974; Bad Cat, 1975; Pink Pig, 1975; Charlotte Hough's Holiday Book, 1975; The Mixture as Before, 1976; Verse and Various (miscellany), 1979; The Bassington Murder (adult fiction), 1980. Add: 1A Ivor St., London NW1 9PL, England.

HOUGH, Graham (Goulder). British, b. 1908. Literature. Lectr. in English, Raffles Coll., Singapore, 1930; Prof. of English, Univ. of Malaya, 1946; Visiting Lectr., Johns Hopkins Univ., Baltimore, 1950; Visiting Prof., Cornell Univ., Ithaca, N.Y., 1958; Fellow, 1950–66, and Tutor, 1955–60 of Christ's Coll., and Praelector and Fellow of Darwin Coll., 1966–75, Univ. Reader in English, 1965–66, and Prof. of English, 1966–75, Cambridge Univ. *Publs:* The Last Romantics, 1949; The Romantic Poets, 1953; Two Exiles: Lord Byron and D.H. Lawrence, 1956; The Dark Sun: A Study of D.H. Lawrence, 1956; Image and Experience: Studies in a Literary Revolution, 1960; Legends and Pastorals: Poems, 1961; A Preface to "The Faerie Queene," 1962; (ed.) Orlando Furioso, by Ariosto, 1962; (ed.) Selected Poems of George Meredith, 1962; (ed.) Poems of Samuel Taylor Coleridge, 1963; The Dream and the Task: Literature and Morals in the Culture of Today, 1963; An Essay on Criticism, 1966; Style and Stylistics, 1969; (ed.) Edmund Spenser: The Faerie Queene 1596, 2 vols., 1976; Selected Essays, 1978; The Mystery Religion of W.B. Yeats, 1984. Add: The White Cottage, Grantchester, Cambridge, England.

HOUGH, Richard (Alexander). Also writes as Bruce Carter, Elizabeth Churchill, and Pat Strong. British, b. 1922. Novels/Short stories, Children's fiction, History, Biography. Gen. Mgr. and Children's Books Ed., The Bodley Head, London, 1947–55; Managing Dir., Hamish Hamilton Books for Children, London, 1955–70. Chmn., Auxiliary Hosps. Cttee., King Edwards Hosp. Fund, 1975. *Publs:* (as Bruce Carter) The Perilous Descent to a Strange Lost World (in U.S. as Into a Strange Lost World), 1952; (as Bruce Carter) Speed Six!, 1953; (as Bruce Carter) Peril on the Iron Road, 1953; (as Bruce Carter) Gunpowder Tunnel, 1955; (with Michael Frostick) Motor Racing: A Guide for the Younger Enthusiast, 1955; The Wright Brothers, 1955; Neville Duke, 1955; Six Great Railwaymen: Stephenson, Hudson, Denison, Huish, Stephen, Gresley, 1955; (as Bruce Carter) Target Island, 1956, 1967; (as Elizabeth Churchill) Juliet in Publishing, 1956; (as Bruce Carter) Tricycle Tim, 1957; Tim Baker, Motor Mechanic: A Career Book, 1957; Tourist Trophy: The History of Britain's Greatest Motor Race, 1957; (as Bruce Carter) The Kidnapping of Kensington (in U.K. as The Children Who Stayed Behind), 1958; (with Walter Owen Bentley) W.O.: An Autobiography, 1958; The Fleet That Had To Die, 1958; British Grand Prix: A History, 1958; Admirals in Collision, 1959; (as Bruce Carter) Four Wheel Drift, 1959, 1973; (as Bruce Carter) The Night of the Flood, 1959; (as Bruce Carter) Ballooning Boy, 1960; (ed.) Great Motor Races (in U.S. as Great Auto Races), 1960; B.P. Book of the Racing Campbells, 1960; The Potemkin Mutiny, 1960; (with L.J.K. Setright) A History of the World's Motorcycles, 1960, 1973; (with Geoffrey de Havilland) Sky Fever, 1961; (with Michael Frostick) A History of the World's Sports Cars, 1961; (as Bruce Carter) The Motorway Chase, 1961; (as Pat Strong) The Plane Wreckers, 1961; (as Bruce Carter) Fast Circuit, 1962; The Fighter (novel), 1963; (ed.) First and Fastest: A Collection of the World's Great Motor Races, 1963; (ed.) The Enzo Ferrari Memoirs: My Terrible Joys, by Enzo Ferrari, 1963; (with Michael Frostick) A History of the World's Classic Cars, 1963; The Hunting of Force Z (in U.S. as Death of the Battleship), 1963; Dreadnought: A History of the Modern Battleship, 1964, 1975; (as Bruce Carter) The Playground, 1964; The Battle of Jutland, 1964; (with Michael Frostick) A History of the World's Racing Cars, 1965; (as Bruce Carter) The Airfield Man, 1965; (ed.) The Motor Car Lover's Companion, 1965; (with Michael Frostick) Rover Memories: An Illustrated Survey of the Rover Car, 1966; The Big Battleship; or, The Curious Career of the H.M.S. Agincourt, 1966; (as Bruce Carter) The Gannet's Nest, 1966; Racing Cars, 1967 (with Michael Frostick) A History of the World's High Performance Cars, 1967; Nuvolari and the Alfa Romeo, 1968; Jimmy Murphy and the White Dusenberg, 1968; Fighting Ships, 1969; First Sea Lord: An Authorised Biography of Admiral Lord Fisher, 1969, 1977; The Pursuit of Admiral von Spee (in U.S. as the Long Pursuit), 1969; (as Bruce Carter) B Flight, 1970; The Battle of Midway, 1970; The Battle of Britain, 1971; The Blind Horn's Hate, 1971; Captain Bligh and Mr. Christian: The Men and the Mutiny, 1972, as The Bounty, 1984; (as Bruce Carter) Upley United, 1972; Louis and Victoria: The First Mountbatten (in U.S. as the Mountbattens), 1974; The Bike Racers (reader), 1974; Galapagos: The Enchanted Island, 1975; One Boy's War: Per Astra Ad Ardua (autobiography), 1975; (ed.) Advice to a Granddaughter: Letters from Queen Victoria to Princess Victoria of Hesse, 1975; (as Bruce Carter) The Deadly Freeze, 1976; (as Bruce Carter) Buzzbugs, 1977; Great Admirals, 1977; (as Bruce Carter) Miaow!, 1978; Angels One–Five (novel), 1978; The Murder of Captain James Cook, 1979; The Fight of the Few (novel), 1979; Man o' War: The Fighting Ship in History, 1979; The Fight to the Finish (novel), 1979; The Bike Racers, 1979; Mountbatten, Hero of Our Time, 1980; Nelson, 1980; Buller's Guns (novel), 1981; Razor Eyes (novel), 1981; Buller's Dreadnought (novel), 1982; Edwina: Countess Mountbatten of Burma (biography), 1982; The Great War at Sea 1914–1918, 1983; Buller's Victory (novel), 1984; Former Naval Person: Churchill, Roosevelt and the Wars at Sea, 1985; The Longest Battle: The War at Sea, 1939–1945, 1986; The Ace of Clubs: A History of the Garrick, 1986; Born Royal: The Lives and Loves of the Young Windsors, 1988. Add: 31 Meadowbank, Primrose Hill Rd., London NW3 1AY, England.

HOUGH, S(tanley) B(ennett). Also writes as Rex Gordon and Bennett Stanley. British, b. 1917. Mystery/Crime/Suspense, Westerns/Adventure, Science fiction/Fantasy, Travel/Exploration/Adventure. Radio Operator, Marconi Radio Co., 1936–38; Radio Officer, Intnl. Marine Radio Co., 1939–45; mgr. of a yachting firm, 1946–51. *Publs:* Frontier Incident, 1951; Moment of Decision, 1952; Mission in Guemo, 1953; The Seas South, 1953; (as Bennett Stanley) Sea Struck, 1953, in U.K. as Sea to Eden, 1954; (as Bennett Stanley) The Alscott Experiment, 1954; The Primitives, 1954; (as Rex Gordon) Utopia 239 (science fiction), 1955; Extinction Bomber (science fiction) 1956; (as Rex Gordon) No Man Friday, 1956, in U.S as First on Mars, 1957; (as Bennett Stanley) Government Contract, 1956; A Pound a Day Inclusive: The Modern Way to Holiday Travel, 1957; (as Rex Gordon) First to the Stars (science fiction), 1959, in U.K. as The Worlds of Eclos, 1961; The Bronze Perseus, 1959, in U.S. as The Tender Killer, 1963; Expedition Everyman: Your Way on Your Income to All the Desirable Places of Europe, 1959; Beyond the Eleventh Hour (science fiction), 1961; (as Rex Gordon) First Through Time (science fiction), 1962, in U.K. as The Time Factor, 1964; Expedition Everyman 1964, 1964; Where? An Independent Report on Holiday Resorts in Britain and the Continent, 1964; Dear Daughter Dead, 1965; (as Rex Gordon) Utopia Minus X (science fiction), 1966, in U.K. as The Paw of God, 1967; Sweet Sister Seduced, 1968; (as Rex Gordon) The Yellow Fraction (science fiction), 1969; Fear Fortune, Father, 1974; Creative Writing, 1983. Add: 21 St. Michael's Rd., Ponsanooth, Truro, Cornwall, England.

HOUGHTON, Eric. British, b. 1930. Children's fiction. Full–time writer since 1985. History teacher, Newham Co. Borough, 1953–64; teacher, Hastings, Sussex, 1965–85. *Publs:* The White Wall, 1961; They Marched with Spartacus, 1963; Summer Silver, 1963; The Mouse and the Magician, 1970; A Giant Can Do Anything, 1975; (as Hugo Rice) The Remarkable Feat of King Caboodle, 1978; Steps out of Time, 1979; Time–Piece, 1981; Gates of Glass, 1987; Walter's Wand, 1989. Add: 42 Collier Rd., Hastings, Sussex TN34 3JR, England.

HOULE, Cyril O. American, b. 1913. Education, Librarianship. Instr. 1939–42, Asst. Prof., 1942–45, Assoc. Prof. and Dean of Univ. Coll., 1945–52, and Prof. of Education, 1952–78, Univ. of Chicago. W.W. Kellog Foundn., since 1976. *Publs:* (with F.W. Reeves and T. Fansler) Adult Education, 1938; (with E.W. Burr, T.H. Hamilton and J.R. Yale) The Armed Services and Adult Education, 1947; Libraries in Adult and Fundamental Education, 1951; (with C.A. Nelson) The Citizen and World Affairs, 1956; The Effective Board, 1961; The Inquiring Mind, 1962; Continuing Your Education, 1964; Residential Continuing Education, 1969; The External Degree, 1975; The Design of Education, 1976; Continuing Learning in the Professions, 1980; Patterns of Learning, 1984; Governing Boards, 1989. Add: 5510 Woodlawn Ave., Chicago, Ill. 60637, U.S.A.

HOUN, Franklin W. American, b. 1920. History, Politics/Government. Prof. of Political Science, Univ. of Massachusetts, Amherst, since 1968 (assoc. Prof., 1963–68). Exec. Dir., Chinese Assn. of Social Sciences, 1947–48; Asst. Prof., Michigan State Univ., East Lansing, 1957–59; Assoc. Prof., Univ. of Nebraska, Lincoln, 1960–63; Research Assoc., The Hoover Instn., Stamford Univ., Calif., 1965–66. *Publs:* Central Government of China 1912–1928, 1957; To Change a Nation: Propaganda and Indoctrination in Communist China, 1961; Chinese Political Traditions, 1965; A Short History of Chinese Communism, 1967; A Short History of Chinese Communism, Completely Updated, 1973. Add: 222 Glendale Rd., Amherst, Mass. 01002, U.S.A.

HOUSEHOLD, Humphrey (George West). British, b. 1906. Transportation. Schoolmaster, Swanage, Dorset, 1930–37; Sr. Master, Clayesmore Preparatory Sch., Dorset, 1937–45, Wycliffe Jr. Sch., 1945–48, Westbrook House Sch., Folkestone, Kent, 1949–68, and Ardvreck Sch., Crieff, Perthshire, 1968–73. *Publs:* The Thames and Severn Canal, 1969, 1983; Gloucestershire Railways in the Twenties, 1984; With the LNER in the Twenties, 1985; Narrow Gauge Railways: Wales and The Western Front, 1988; Narrow Gauge Railways: England and the 15–inch, 1989. Add: 44 Earls Ave., Folkestone, Kent, England.

HOUSTON, James A(rchibald). Canadian, b. 1921. Novels/Short stories, Children's fiction, Anthropology/Ethnology. Artist: Assoc. Designer, Steuben Glass, since 1972 (Assoc. Dir., 1962–72). Govt. administrator, West Baffin, 1953–62. *Publs:* Tikta–liktak, 1965; Eagle Mask, 1966; The White Archer, 1967; Eskimo Prints, 1967; Akavak, 1968; Wolf Run, 1971; The White Dawn (for adults), 1971; Ghost Paddle, 1972; Ojibwa Summer, 1972; Kiviok's Magic Journey, 1973; Frozen Fire, 1977; Ghost Fox (for adults), 1977; River Runners, 1979; Spirit Wrestler (for adults), 1980; Long Claws, 1981; Black Diamonds, 1982; Eagle Song,

1983; Ice Swords, 1985; The Falcon Bow, 1986; Whiteout, 1988. Add: 24 Main St., Stonington, Conn. 06378, U.S.A.

HOUSTON, James D. American, b. 1933. Novels/Short stories, Biography. Visiting Prof. in Creative Writing, Univ. of California at Santa Cruz, since 1969. Wallace Stegner Creative Writing Fellow, Stanford Univ., Calif., 1966–67; Gilliland Chair in Telecommunications, San Jose State Univ., Calif., 1985. Member, California Council for Humanities, 1982; Dist. Visiting Writer, Univ. of Hawaii, 1983. *Publs:* Between Battles, 1968; Gig, 1969; A Native Son of the Golden West, 1971; (with J.W. Houston) Farewell to Manzanar (biography), 1973; (with J. Brodie) Open Field (sport biography), 1974; Three Songs for My Father, 1974; Continental Drift, 1978; (co–ed.) California Heartland, 1978; (ed.) West Coast Fiction, 1979; Gasoline: The Automotive Adventures of Charlie Bates, 1980; Californians: Searching for the Golden State, 1982; Love Life (novel), 1985; The Men In My Life, 1987. Add: 2–1130 E. Cliff Dr., Santa Cruz, Calif. 95062, U.S.A.

HOUSTON, R.B. *See* RAE, Hugh C.

HOUSTON, W. Robert. American, b. 1928. Education, Mathematics. Prof. of Education since 1970, and Assoc. Dean since 1973, Univ. of Houston, Tex. Prof. of Education, 1961–70, and Project Dir., Model Elementary Teacher Education Prog., 1968–70, Michigan State Univ., East Lansing. *Publs:* (co–author) Sir Isaac Newton, 1960; (co–author) Extending Mathematics Understanding, 1961; (co–author) Professional Growth Through Student Teaching, 1965; (co–author) Teaching in the Modern Elementary School, 1967; (co–author) Exploring Regions of Latin America and Canada, 1968; (co–author) Extending Understandings of Mathematics, 1969; (co–author) Understanding the Number System, 1969; (co–author) The Elementary School Curriculum, 1970; (co–author) Elementary Education in the Seventies, 1970; Strategies and Resources for Developing Competency–Based Teacher Education Program, 1972; (co–ed.) Competency–Based Teacher Education: Progress, Problems, Prospects, 1972; (co–author) Acquiring Competencies to Teach Mathematics in Elementary Schools, 1973; Competency–Based Instructional Design, 1973; Resources for Performance–Based Education, 1973; (ed.) Exploring Competency–Based Education, 1974; Competency Assessment, Research, and Evaluation, 1975; Modern Elementary Education Teaching and Learning, 1976; Exploring World Regions, 1977; Assessing School/College/Community Needs, 1978; Emerging Professional Roles in Teacher Education, 1978; Focus on the Future Implications for Education, 1978; Designing Short–Term Instructional Programs, 1979; Staff Development and Educational Change, 1980; (co–author) Adult Learners: A Research Report, 1981; Mirrors of Excellence: Reflections for Teacher Education From Training Programs in Ten Corporations and Agencies, 1986; (co–author) Touch the Future: Teach!, 1988. Add: Coll. of Education, Univ. of Houston, Houston, Tex. 77204, U.S.A.

HOVANNISIAN, Richard G. American, b. 1932. History. Prof. of Armenian and Near Eastern History since 1969, and Dir. of the Near Eastern Center since 1982, Univ. of California, Los Angeles (Lectr. in Armenian Studies, 1962–69; Assoc. Dir. of Near Eastern Center, 1979–82). Member of Editorial Bd., Armenian Review, Intnl. Journal of Middle East Studies, Ararat, and Haigazian Armenological Review, Beirut. Prof. of History, Mount Saint Mary Coll., Los Angeles, Calif., 1965–69. Chmn., Soc. for Armenian Studies, 1974–75, 1976–77. *Publs:* Armenia on the Road to Independence, 1967, 4th ed. 1984; The Republic of Armenia, vol. I, 1971, 3rd ed. 1984, vol. II, 1982; The Armenian Holocaust, 1978, 1980; The Armenian Image in History and Literature, 1982; (ed. with S. Vryonis, Jr.) Islam's Understanding of Itself, 1983; Ethics in Islam, 1985; The Armenian Genocide in Perspective, 1986. Add: Dept. of History, Univ. of California, Los Angeles, Calif. 90024, U.S.A.

HOVEY, E. Paul. American, b. 1908. Theology/Religion. Contrib. Ed. and Editorial Assoc., New Pulpit Digest and Pulpit Preaching, since 1958. Contrib., The Ministers Manual, 1969–82. *Publs:* Man who Entertained a King (play), 1946; Doors, 1950; (ed.) Treasury of Inspirational Anecdotes, 1959; (ed.) Treasury for Special Days and Occasions, 1961; Presbyterian Yesterdays in North Idaho, 1964; Christmas Ideals, 1965; Presbyterian Yesterdays in Idaho, 1963; Faith That Come to Idaho, 1972; Genuine Good News Today, 1972; Mark the Road, 1973; One Gift Often Unclaimed, 1974; Treasury of Story Sermons for Children, 1975; (ed.) Pioneer Preacher in Idaho, 1981; Lewiston's First Presbyterian Church, 1982; Perrin B. Whitman—Interpreter, 1984; Presbyterians in Oregon, 1989. Add: 1712 N.E. 125th Ave., Portland, Ore. 97230, U.S.A.

HOWARD, A(rthur) E(llsworth) Dick. American, b. 1933. History, Law, Politics/Government. White Burkett Miller Prof. of Law and Public

Affairs, Univ. of Virginia, Charlottesville, since 1976. Fellow, Woodrow Wilson Intnl. Center for Scholars, 1974–75, 1976–77. *Publs:* Magna Carta: Text and Commentary, 1965; The Road from Runnymede, 1968; (with Barnes, Mashaw and Grosnick) Virginia's Urban Corridor, 1970; Commentaries on the Constitution of Virginia, 1974; State Aid to Private Higher Eduction, 1977; (with Baker and Derr) Church, State, and Politics, 1982. Add: Sch. of Law, Univ. of Virginia, Charlottesville, Va. 22901, U.S.A.

HOWARD, Clark. American, b. 1934. Novels/Short stories, Mystery/Crime/Suspense, Criminology/Law enforcement/Prisons. *Publs:* novel—The Arm, 1967; mystery novels—A Movement Toward Eden, 1969; The Doomsday Squad, 1970; The Killings, 1973; Last Contract, 1973; Summit Kill, 1975; Mark the Sparrow, 1975; The Hunters, 1976; The Last Great Death Stunt, 1977; other—Six Against the Rock, 1977; The Wardens, 1979; Zebra: The True Account of the 179 Days of Terror in San Francisco, 1979, in U.K. as The Zebra Killings, 1980; American Saturday, 1981; Brothers in Blood, 1983; Dirt Rich, 1986; Quick Silver, 1988. Add: c/o Roslyn Targ Agency, 105 W. 13th St., New York, N.Y. 10011, U.S.A.

HOWARD, Constance (Mildred). British, b. 1910. Crafts. Free-lance lecturer and writer. Member, Advisory Cttee. of London Coll. of Fashion, Council of Society of Designer Craftsmen, and Art Workers Guild. Part–time Lectr., 1946–59, Full–time Sr. Lectr., 1959–73, and Principal Lectr., 1973–75, Goldsmiths Sch. of Art, Univ. of London. *Publs:* Design for Embroidery from Traditional English Sources, 1956; Inspiration for Embroidery, 1966; Embroidery and Colour, 1976; (ed.) Textile Crafts, 1978; Constance Howard Book of Stitches, 1979; Twentieth Century Embroidery in Great Britain, 4 vols., 1981–86. Add: 43 Cambridge Rd. S., London W4 3DA, England.

HOWARD, David M. American, b. 1928. Theology/Religion. Intnl. Dir., World Evangelical Fellowship, since 1982. Asst. Gen. Dir., Latin American Mission, serving in Costa Rica, 1953–57,and Colombia, 1958–68; Campus staff member, 1949–51, Missions Dir., 1969–76, and Asst. to the Pres., 1977, Inter–Varsity Christian Fellowship. *Publs:* Hammered as Gold, 1969, reissued in paperback as The Costly Harvest, 1975; Student Power in the World Evangelism, 1970, as Student Power in World Missions, 1979; How Come, God?, 1972; By the Power of the Holy Spirit, 1973; (ed.) Jesus Christ: Lord of the Universe, Hope of the World, 1974; Words of Fire, Rivers of Tears, 1975; The Great Commission for Today, 1976; (ed.) Declare His Glory, 1977; The Dream That Would Not Die, 1986; What Makes a Missionary, 1987. Add: 1 Sophia Rd., 07–09 Peace Centre, Singapore 1025.

HOWARD, Elizabeth Jane. British, b. 1923. Novels/Short stories, Plays/Screenplays. Secty., Inland Waterways Assn., London, 1947–50; Ed., Chatto & Windus Ltd., publrs., 1953–56, and Weidenfeld & Nicolson Ltd., publrs., 1957, both London; Book Critic, Queen Mag., London, 1957–60. Has written 14 plays for TV. *Publs:* The Beautiful Visit, 1950; (with Robert Aickman) We Are for the Dark: Six Ghost Stories, 1951; The Long View, 1956; (with Arthur Helps) Bettina: A Portrait, 1957; The Sea Change, 1959; After Julius, 1965; Something in Disguise, 1969; Odd Girl Out, 1972; Mr. Wrong: Short stories, 1975; (ed.) The Lover's Companion, 1978; Getting It Right, 1982; (with Fay Maschler), Howard and Maschler on Food, 1987. Add: c/o Jonathan Clowes, 22 Prince Albert Rd., London NW1 7ST, England.

HOWARD, Helen Addison (Mrs. Helen Overland). American, b. 1904. Cultural/Ethnic topics, History. Book reviewer, Journal of the West, since 1969 (Member, Editorial Advisory Bd., 1978–88). *Publs:* War Chief Joseph, 1941, 1964; (contrib. ed.) Frontier Omnibus, 1962; Northwest Trail Blazers, 1963; Saga of Chief Joseph, 1965, 2nd ed. 1978; American Indian Poetry, 1979, 1980; (contrib.) Dictionary of Indian Tribes of the Americas, 4 vols., 1980; American Frontier Tales, 1982. Add: 410 S. Lamer St., Burbank, Calif. 91506, U.S.A.

HOWARD, J. Woodford, Jr. American, b. 1931. Politics/Government, Biography. Thomas P. Stran Prof., Johns Hopkins Univ., since 1975 (Assoc. Prof., 1967–69; Prof., 1969–75). Instr., Lafayette Coll., Easton, Pa., 1958–59; Asst. Prof., 1962–66 and Assoc. Prof., 1966–67, Duke Univ., Durham. N.C. *Publs:* Mr. Justice Murphy: A Political Biography, 1968; Courts of Appeals in the Federal Judicial System: A Study of the Second, Fifth, and District of Columbia Circuits, 1981. Add: Dept. of Political Science, Johns Hopkins Univ., Baltimore, Md. 21218, U.S.A.

HOWARD, Jane (Temple). American, b. 1935. Social commentary/phenomena. Book Reviewer, Mademoiselle mag., Washington Post, NY Times Book Review and Contrib., Esquire, Life, and other periodicals. Staff writer, Life mag., NYC, 1966–72; Visiting teacher in writing, Iowa Writers' Workshop 1974, Univ. of Georgia School of Journalism 1975, Yale Univ. 1976, and Southampton Coll. 1984. James Thurber Writer–in–Residence, Ohio State Univ., Columbus, 1986. *Publs:* Please Touch: A Guided Tour of the Human Potential Movement, 1970; A Different Woman, 1973; Families, 1978; Margaret Mead: A Life, 1984. Add: ICM Artists Ltd., 40 W. 57th St., New York, N.Y. 10019, U.S.A.

HOWARD, Linda. Pseud. for Linda S. Howington. American, b. 1950. Historical/Romance. Secretary, Bowman Transportation, Gadsden, Ala., 1969–86. *Publs:* All That Glitters, 1982; An Independent Wife, 1982; Against the Rules, 1983; Come Lie with Me, 1984; Tears of the Renegade, 1985; Sarah's Child, 1985; The Cutting Edge, 1985; Midnight Rainbow, 1986; Almost Forever, 1986; Diamond Bay, 1987; Bluebird Winter, 1987; Heartbreaker, 1987; White Lies, 1988; MacKenzie's Mountain, 1989. Add: 116 Louise Ave., Gadsden, Ala. 35903, U.S.A.

HOWARD, Mary. Also writes as Josephine Edgar. British, b. 1907. Historical/Romance/Gothic. Past Chmn. of Soc. of Women Writers and Journalists, London. *Publs:* Windier Skies, 1930; Dark Morality, 1932; Partners for Playtime, 1938; Strangers in Love, 1939; It Was Romance, 1939; The Untamed Heart, 1940; Far Blue Horizons, 1940; Uncharted Romance, 1941; Devil in My Heart, 1941; Tomorrow's Hero, 1941; Reef of Dreams, 1942; Gay Is Life, 1943; Have Courage, My Heart, 1943; Anna Heritage, 1944; The Wise Forget, 1944; Family Orchestra, 1945; Return to Love, 1946; The Man from Singapore, 1946; Weave Me Some Wings, 1947; The Clouded Moon, 1948; Strange Paths, 1948; Star–Crossed, 1949; First Star, 1949; There Will I Follow, 1949; The Young Lady (in U.K. as Bow to the Storm), 1950; Mist on the Hills, 1950; Sixpence in Her Shoe, 1950; Two Loves Have I, 1950; Promise of Delight, 1952; The Gate Leads Nowhere, 1953; Fool's Haven, 1954; Sew a Fine Seam, 1954; Before I Kissed, 1955; The Grafton Girls, 1956; A Lady Fell in Love, 1956; Shadows in the Sun, 1957; Man of Stone, 1958; The Intruder, 1959; The House of Lies (in U.S as The Crystal Villa), 1960; More Than Friendship, 1960 (Major Award, Romantic Novelists Assn.); Surgeon's Dilemma, 1961; The Pretenders, 1962; (as Josephine Edgar) My Sister Sophie, 1964; The Big Man, 1965; (as Josephine Edgar) Dark Tower, 1966; The Interloper, 1967; The Repeating Pattern, 1968; The Bachelor Girls, 1968; (as Josephine Edgar) Time of Dreaming, 1968; (as Josephine Edgar) The Dancer's Daughter, 1969; Home to My Country, 1971; A Right Grand Girl, 1972; The Cottager's Daughter, 1972; (as Josephine Edgar) The Devil's Innocents, 1972; Soldiers and Lovers, 1973; (as Josephine Edgar) The Stranger at the Gate, 1973; (as Josephine Edgar) The Lady of Wildersley, 1975; Who Knows Sammy Halliday, 1976; (as Josephine Edgar) Duchess, 1976; The Spanish Summer, 1977; (as Josephine Edgar) Countess, 1978; Mr. Rodriguez, 1979; (as Josephine Edgar) Margaret Normanby, 1983; Success Story, 1984; (as Josephine Edgar) Bright Young Things, 1986. Add: 30 Oxford Ct., Oxford Rd., London SW15 2LQ, England.

HOWARD, Maureen. American, b. 1930. Novels/Short stories, Autobiography. Member of the English Dept., Columbia Univ., NYC. Worked in advertising and publishing, 1953–54; Lectr. in English, New Sch. for Social Research, NYC, 1967–68, 1970–71, and since 1974, and at the Univ. of California at Santa Barbara, 1968–69, Amherst Coll., Massachusetts, and Brooklyn Coll. *Publs:* Not a Word about Nightingales (novel), 1960; Bridgeport Bus (novel), 1965; Before My Time (novel), 1975; Facts of Life (autobiography), 1978; Grace Abounding (novel), 1982; Expensive Habits (novel), 1986. Add: c/o Summit Books, Simon and Schuster, 1230 Sixth Avenue, New York, N.Y. 10020, U.S.A.

HOWARD, (Sir) Michael (Eliot). British, b. 1922. History, Military/Defence. Lovett Prof. of History, Yale Univ., New Haven, Conn. Pres., Intl. Inst. for Strategic Studies. Lectr. in History, 1947–53, Lectr. in War Studies, 1953–63, and Prof. of War Studies, 1963–68, King's Coll., Univ. of London; Dean, Faculty of Arts, 1964–68, and Member of Senate, 1966–68, Univ. of London. Fellow, All Souls Coll., Oxford, 1968–80, and Regius Prof. of Modern History, Oxford Univ., 1980–89. *Publs:* (with J. Sparrow) The Coldstream Guards 1920–1946, 1951; Disengagement in Europe, 1958; (ed.) Wellingtonian Studies, 1959; The Franco–Prussian War, 1961; (ed.) The Theory and Practice of War, 1965; The Mediterranean Strategy in the Second World War, 1967; Studies in War and Peace, 1970; The Continental Commitment, 1972; Grand Strategy Vol. IV: 1942–43 (U.K. Official History of Second World War, Military Series) 1972; (with P. Paret) Clausewitz on War; War in European History, 1976; War and the Liberal Conscience, 1978; Causes of Wars, 1983. Add: Dept. of History, Yale Univ., New Haven, Conn., U.S.A.

HOWARD, Patricia. British, b. 1937. Music. Lectr. in Music, Open Univ. *Publs:* Gluck and the Birth of Modern Opera, 1963; The Operas of Benjamin Britten: An Introduction, 1969; Haydn in London, 1980; Mozart's Marriage of Figaro, 1980; Haydn's String Quartets, 1984; Beethoven's Eroica Symphony, 1984; Benjamin Britten: "The Turn of the Screw," 1985; Christoph Willibald Gluck: A Guide to Research, 1987; Music in Vienna 1790–1800, 1988; Beethoven's "Fidelio", 1988. Add: Stepping Stones, Gomshall, Surrey, England.

HOWARD, Philip (Nicholas Charles). British, b. 1933. Language/Linguistics, Military/Defence, Travel/Exploration/Adventure. Literary Ed., The Times, London, since 1978 (Columnist since 1964). Parliamentary Corresp., Glasgow Herald, 1960–64. *Publs:* The Black Watch, 1968; The Royal Palaces, 1970; London's River, 1975; The British Monarchy, 1977; New Words for Old, 1977; Weasel Words, 1978; U and Non–U Revisited, 1978; Words Fail Me, 1980; A Word in Your Ear, 1983; The State of the Language: English Observed, 1984; We Thundered Out: 200 Years of The Times 1785–1985, 1985; Winged Words, 1988; Word–Watching, 1988. Add: Flat 1, 47 Ladbroke Grove, London W11, England.

HOWARD, Richard. American, b. 1929. Poetry, Translations. Poetry Ed., Shenandoah, Lexington, Va.; Dir., Braziller Poetry Series. Freelance literary and art critic and translator. *Publs:* Quantities: Poems, 1962; The Damages: Poems, 1967; Untitled Subjects: Poems, 1969; Alone with America: Essays on the Art of Poetry in the United States since 1950, 1969; Findings: Poems, 1971; Two–Part Inventions: Poems, 1974; (ed.) Preferences: 51 American Poets Choose Poems from Their Own Work and from the Past, 1974; Fellow Feelings (poetry), 1976; Misgivings (poetry), 1979; Lining Up (poetry), 1984; No Traveller (poetry), 1986; also numerous translations of contemporary French writers. Add: c/o Atheneum, 866 Third Ave., New York, N.Y. 10022, U.S.A.

HOWARD, Roger. British, b. 1938. Novels/Short stories, Plays/Screenplays, Poetry, Politics/Government. Lectr. and Founding Dir., Theatre Underground, since 1979, and Ed., New Plays series, since 1980, Univ. of Essex. Teacher, Nankai Univ., Tientsin, China, 1965–67; Lectr., Univ. of Peking, 1972–74; Fellow in Creative Writing, Univ. of York, 1976–78; Writing Fellow, Univ. of East Anglia, 1979. *Publs:* A Phantastic Satire (novel), 1960; From the Life of a Patient (novel), 1961; To the People . . . (poetry), 1966; Praise Songs (poetry), 1966; The Technique of the Struggle Meeting, 1968; The Use of Wall Newspapers, 1968; New Plays 1, 1968; Fin's Doubts, 1968; The Hooligan's Handbook, 1971; Method for Revolutionary Writing, 1972; (ed.) Culture and Agitation: Theatre Documents, 1972; Episodes from the Fighting in the East, 1971; Slaughter Night and Other Plays, 1971; Contemporary Chinese Theatre, 1977; Mao Tse–tung and the Chinese People, 1978; The Society of Poets, 1979; A Break in Berlin, 1980; The Siege, 1981; Partisans, 1983; Ancient Rivers, 1984; The Speechifier, 1984; Contradictory Theatres, 1985; (trans.) Sappa, 1985; The Tragedy of Mao and Other Plays, 1989. Add: Dept. of Literature, Univ. of Essex, Wivenhoe Park, Colchester, Essex, CO4 3SQ, England.

HOWARD–WILLIAMS, Jeremy. British, b. 1922. Sports. Worked in yachting industry, 1959–73; Ed., Adlard Coles Ltd., publrs., 1974–82. *Publs:* Teach Your Child About Sailing, 1963; Sails, 1967; Dinghy Sails, 1971; Offshore Crew, 1973; Night Intruder, 1975; Care and Repair of Sails, 1976; Practical Pilotage for Yachtsmen, 1977; The Complete Crossword Companion, 1984; Small Boat Sails, 1987; Canvas Work, 1989. Add: 17 Havelock Rd., Warsash, Southampton S03 6FX, England.

HOWARTH, David. British, b. 1912. Novels/Short stories, Children's non-fiction, Military/Defence, Autobiography, Biography. BBC Talks Asst., 1934–39. *Publs:* The Shetland Bus, 1951; Group Flashing Two, 1952; One Night in Styria, 1953; We Die Alone, 1955 (also as Escape Alone); The Sledge Patrol, 1957; Heroes of Nowadays (for children), 1957; Dawn of D–Day, 1959; The Shadow of the Dam, 1961; (ed.) My Land and My People, by the Dalai Lama, 1962; The Desert King: A Biography of Ibn Saud, 1964; The Golden Isthmus, 1966; A Near Run Thing: The Day of Waterloo, (in U.S. as Waterloo: A Near Run Thing), 1968; Trafalgar: The Nelson Touch, 1969; Great Escapes (for children), 1969; Sovereign of the Seas, 1974; The Greek Adventure, 1976; 1066, The Year of the Conquest, 1977; The Voyage of the Armada, 1981; Tahiti, 1983; Pursued by a Bear (autobiography), 1986. Add: Wildings Wood, Blackboys, Sussex, England.

HOWARTH, Donald. British, b. 1931. Plays/Screenplays. Stage mgr., and actor in various repertory companies, 1951–56; Literary Mgr., English Stage Co., Royal Court Theatre, London, 1974–75. *Publs:* All Good Children, 1965; A Lily in Little India, 1966; Three Months Gone, 1970. Add: c/o Margaret Ramsay, 14a Goodwin's Court, London WC2, England.

HOWARTH, Patrick (John Fielding). Also writes as C.D.E. Francis. British, 1916. Novels/Short stories, Poetry, History, Biography. Ed., Baltic and Scandinavian Countries, 1938–39; served in Special Operations Exec., 1941–45; Press Attaché, British Embassy, Warsaw, 1945–47; with Civil Service, London, 1948–53; Public Relations Officer, Royal National Life–Boat Instn., London, 1953–79. *Publs:* The Year Is 1851, 1951; The Dying Ukrainian (novel), 1953; A Matter of Minutes (novel), 1953; (ed.) Special Operations, 1955; Questions in the House, 1956; The Life–Boat Story, 1957; How Men are Rescued from the Sea, 1961; Squire: Most Generous of Men (biography), 1963; Play Up and Play the Game, 1973; Lifeboats and Lifeboat People, 1974; When the Riviera Was Ours, 1977; Undercover, 1980; Lifeboat: In Danger's Hour, 1981; Intelligence Chief Extraordinary, 1986; King George VI, 1987. Add: Special Forces Club, 8 Herbert Cresc., London SW1 8EZ, England.

HOWARTH, William (Louis). American, b. 1940. Literature, Natural history and journalism. Prof. of English, Princeton Univ., N.J., since 1981 (Instr. 1966–68; Asst. Prof. 1968–73; Assoc. Prof., 1973–81). Ed.–in–Chief, the Writings of Henry D. Thoreau, 1972–80; Pres., Thoreau Soc., 1974–75. *Publs:* (ed.) A Thoreau Gazetteer, 1970; (ed.) Twentieth-Century Interpretations of Poe's Tales, 1971; The Literary Manuscripts of Henry David Thoreau, 1974; (ed.) The John McPhee Reader, 1977; (ed.) A Week on the Concord and Merrimack Rivers, 1980; (ed.) Walden and Other Writings, 1980; The Book of Concord: Thoreau's Life as a Writer, 1982; Thoreau in the Mountains, 1982; (contr.) Great Rivers of the World, 1984; (contr.) America's Wild Woodlands, 1985; (contr.) Window on America, 1987; Traveling the Trans–Canada, 1987; (contr.) Essays on the Essay: Redefining the Essay, 1989; (contr.) Located Lives: Place & Perspective in Southern Autobiography, 1989; (ed.) Clarence King, Mountaineering in the Sierra Nevada, 1989. Add: Dept. of English, Mc-Cosh 22, Princeton Univ., Princeton, N.J. 08540, U.S.A.

HOWAT, Gerald (Malcolm David). Also writes as Gerald Henderson–Howat. British, b. 1928. Education, History, Sports, Biography. Principal Lectr. Emeritus, Culham Coll. of Education, Oxon, since 1984. Head, Dept. of History, Kelly Coll., Tavistock, 1955–60, Culham Coll. of Education, Oxon, 1960–73, and Radley Coll., Oxon, 1973–77; Sr. Tutor, Lord William's Sch., Thame, Oxon., 1977–86; Visiting Prof., Univ. of Western Kentucky; Visiting Lectr., Univ. of Flinders, S.A., and Univ. of New South Wales. Chief Examiner in History, Oxford and Cambridge Schs. Examination Bd., 1962–88. *Publs:* From Chatham to Churchill, 1966; (ed.) Essays to a Young Teacher, 1966; (with A. Howat) The Story of Health, 1967; The Teaching of Empire and Commonwealth History, 1967; (ed.) Dictionary of World History, 1973; Documents in European History 1789–1970, 1974; Stuart and Cromwellian Foreign Policy, 1974; The Oxford and Cambridge Examination Board 1873–1973, 1974; (ed.) Who Did What, 1975; Learie Constantine, 1975; Village Cricket, 1980; Cricketer Militant, 1980; (with L.G.R. Naylor) Culham College: A History, 1982; Walter Hammond, 1984; Plum Warner, 1987; Len Hutton, 1988; Cricket's Second Golden Age, 1989; Sherriff of Journey's End, 1991. Add: Old School House, North Moreton, Didcot, Oxon., England.

HOWATCH, Susan. British, b. 1940. Historical/Romance/Gothic. *Publs:* The Dark Shore, 1965; The Waiting Sands, 1966; Call in the Night, 1967; The Shrouded Walls, 1968; April's Grave, 1969; The Devil on Lammas Night, 1970; Penmarric, 1971; Cashelmara, 1974; The Rich are Different, 1977; Sins of the Fathers, 1980; The Wheel of Fortune, 1984; Glittering Images, 1987; Glamorous Powers, 1988. Add: c/o Harold Ober Assocs., 40 East 49th St., New York, N.Y. 10017, U.S.A.

HOWE, Doris (Kathleen). Also writes as Mary Munro, and, with Muriel Howe, as Newlyn Nash. British. Romance. *Publs:* 47 novels, the latest being This Girl Is Mine, 1978. Add: Skelwith Bridge, Ambleside, Cumbria LA22 9BW, England.

HOWE, Fanny. American, b. 1940. Novels/Short stories, Children's fiction, Poetry. Visiting writer, Massachusetts Inst. of Technology, Cambridge, since 1978. Lectr. in Creative Writing, Tufts Univ., Medford, Mass., 1968–72, Emerson Coll., Boston, 1973–74, and Columbia Univ., NYC, 1974–77. *Publs:* Forty Whacks, 1969; Eggs, 1970; First Marriage, 1974; Bronte Wilde, 1976; The Amerindian Coastline Poem, 1976; Holy Smoke, 1979; Poems From a Single Pallet, 1980; The White Slave, 1980; The Blue Hills, 1981; Alsace-Lorraine, 1982; Yeah, 1982; In the Middle of Nowhere, 1984; Radio City, 1984; For Erato: The Meaning of Life, 1984; Taking Care, 1985; The Race of the Radical, 1985; Robeson Street, 1985; Introduction to the World, 1986; The Lives of a

Spirit, 1986; The Vineyard, 1988. Add: 195 Winthrop Rd., Brookline, Mass. 02146, U.S.A.

HOWE, Irving. American, b. 1920. History, Literature. Prof. of English since 1963, and Distinguished Prof. since 1970, Hunter Coll., City Univ. of New York, now retired. Taught at Brandeis Univ., Waltham, Mass., 1953–61, and Stanford Univ., Calif., 1961–63. Christian Gauss Prof., Princeton Univ., 1954. *Publs:* Sherwood Anderson: A Critical Biography, 1952; William Faulkner: A Critical Study, 1952; (ed., with E. Greenberg) Treasury of Yiddish Stories, 1954; Politics and the Novel, 1957; (ed.) Modern Literary Criticism, 1958; (with L. Coser) The American Communist Party: A Critical History, 1958; (ed.) New Grub Street, by Gissing, 1962; Edith Wharton: A Collection of Critical Essays, 1962; (ed.) Basic Writings, by Tolstoy, 1963; A World More Attractive: A View of Modern Literature and Politics, 1963; (ed.) 1984, by Orwell, 1963; (co–author) The Radical Papers, 1966; Steady Work, 1966; Thomas Hardy, 1967; The Decline of the New, 1969; (ed.) Essential Works of Socialism, 1971; (co–ed.) A Treasury of Yiddish Poetry, 1971; The Critical Point, 1973; (with Kenneth Libo) World of Our Fathers, 1976; Leon Trotsky, 1978; Celebrations and Attacks, 1979; Margin of Hope, 1982; The American Newness, 1986; (ed.) The Penguin Book of Yiddish Verse, 1987. Add: Graduate Center, CUNY, New York, N.Y. 10036, U.S.A.

HOWE, James. American, b. 1946. Children's fiction, Children's non–fiction, Biography. Freelance actor and director, 1971–75; Literary agent, Lucy Kroll Agency, NYC, 1976–81. *Publs:* (with Deborah Howe) Bunnicula: A Rabbit Tale of Mystery, 1979; Teddy Bear's Scrapbook, 1980; The Hospital Book, 1981; Annie Joins the Circus, 1982; Howliday Inn, 1982; The Case of the Missing Mother, 1983; The Celery Stalks at Midnight, 1983; A Night Without Stars, 1983; The Day the Teacher Went Bananas, 1984; The Muppet Guide to Magnificent Manners, 1984; How the Ewoks Saved the Trees, 1984; Morgan's Zoo, 1984; Mister Tinker in Oz, 1985; What Eric Knew, 1985; Eat Your Poison, Dear, 1986; When You Go to Kindergarten, 1986; Babes in Toyland (retelling), 1986; A Love Note for Baby Piggy, 1986; Stage Fright, 1986; There's a Monster under My Bed, 1986; I Wish I Were a Butterfly, 1987; Carol Burnett: The Sound of Laughter, 1987; The Secret Garden (retelling), 1987; Nighty–Night, 1987; The Fright before Christmas, 1988; Scared Silly, 1989. Add: c/o Amy Berkower, Writers House Inc., 21 W. 26th St., New York, N.Y. 10010, U.S.A.

HOWE, Muriel. Also writes as Barbara Redmayne and, with Doris Howe, as Newlyn Nash. British. Historical/Romance/Gothic. *Publs:* House of Character; Affair at Falconers; Still They Come, Winter Tariff; Master of Skelgale; Stairs of Sand; Pendragon; Private Road to Beyond First Affections; Heatherling. Add: Skelwith Bridge, Ambleside, Cumbria LA22 9BW, England.

HOWE, Robin. British, b. 1908. Cookery/Gastronomy/Wine. *Publs:* (with P. Espir) Sultan's Pleasure, 1952; German Coooking, 1953; Italian Cooking, 1953; Cooking from the Commonwealth, 1958; A Cook's Tour, 1958; Rice Cooking, 1959; Greek Cooking, 1960; Making Your Own Preserves, 1963; Russian Cooking, 1964; French Cooking, 1964; Balkan Cooking, 1965; Soups, 1967; Far Eastern Cookery, 1969; Poultry and Game, 1970; (with André L. Simon) A Dictionary of Gastronomy, 1970; (ed.) Mrs. Groundes–Peace's Old Cookery Notebook, 1971; Regional Italian Cookery, 1972; Traditional Home Cooking, 1973; Cooking from the Heart of Europe, 1975; Pasta Cooking, 1975; Middle Eastern Cookery, 1978; (with Roger Grounds and Brenda Sanctuary) Fresh from the Garden, 1979; Italian Cooking, 1979; International Cooking, 1980; The Mediterranean Diet, 1985. Add: Villa Stoppani, via Delle Valli 10/3, 18100 Imperia, Italy.

HOWE, Tina. American, b. 1937. Plays. Adjunct Prof., New York Univ., since 1983. *Publs:* Birth and After Birth (in The New Women's Theatre), 1977; Museum, 1979; The Art of Dining, 1980; Painting Churches, 1984; Three Plays by Tina Howe, 1984; Coastal Disturbances, 1988 (as Coastal Disturbances: Four Plays by Tina Howe, 1989). Add: c/o Flora Roberts, 157 W. 57th St., New York, N.Y. 10019, U.S.A.

HOWELL, Anthony. British, b. 1945. Novels, Poetry. Ed., Softly Loudly Books, London. Dancer with the Royal Ballet, London, 1966; Lectr. in Creative Writing, Grenoble Univ., 1969–70. *Publs:* Sergei de Diaghileff (1929) (poetry), 1968; Inside the Castle: Poems, 1969; Imruil: A Naturalized Version of His First Ode–Book (pre–Islamic Arabic) 1970; (ed.) Erotic Lyrics, 1970; Femina Deserta, 1971; Anchovy, 1973; The Mekon, 1976; (ed. with Fiona Templeton) Elements of Performance Art, 1977; Notions of a Mirror: Poems Previously Uncollected 1964–1982,

1983; Why I May Never See the Walls of China (poems), 1986; In the Company of Others (novel), 1986. Add: 21 Augusta St., Adamsdown, Cardiff CF2 1EN, Wales.

HOWELL, David (Arthur Russell). British, b. 1936. Politics/Government. Conservative M.P. for Guildford, Surrey, since 1966 (a Lord Commissioner of the Treasury and Parliamentary Secty., Civil Service Dept., 1970–72; Parliamentary Under–Secty. for Northern Ireland, 1972; Minister of State for Northern Ireland, 1972–74; Minister of State, Dept. of Energy, 1974; Secty. of State for Energy, 1979–81; Secty. of State for Transport, 1981–83). Dir., Savory Milln Ltd., since 1985. Member, Intl. Advisory Council, Swiss Bank Corp., since 1988. Journalist and economic consultant. Trustee, Federal Trust for Education and Research, London. Served in the Economic Section of the Treasury, 1959; Leader–Writer and Special Correspondent, The Daily Telegraph newspaper, London, 1960–64; Dir., Conservative Political Centre, London, 1964–66. Chmn., Bow Group, 1961–62, and Ed., Crossbow, 1962–64; Joint Secty., British Council of the European Movement, 1969–70. *Publs:* (co–author) Principles in Practice, 1960; (ed.) Report of the Chatham House Conference on International Trade, 1964; The Conservative Opportunity, 1965; A New Style of Government, 1970; Time to Move on, 1976; Freedom and Capital, 1981; The People's Business, 1983; Blind Victory: A Study in Income, Wealth and Power, 1986. Add: House of Commons, London SW1, England.

HOWELL, F(rancis) Clark. American, b. 1925. Anthropology (Physical anthropology). Prof. of Anthropology, Univ. of California, Berkeley, since 1970. Instr., Washington Univ., St. Louis, Mo., 1953–55; Asst. Prof., 1955–59, Assoc. Prof., 1959–62, and Prof. of Anthropology, 1962–70, Univ. of Chicago. *Publs:* (ed.) Early Man and Pleistocene Stratigraphy in the Circum–Mediterranean Regions, 1960; (ed.) African Ecology and Human Evolution, 1963; Early Man, 1965, 1980; (ed.) Earliest Man and Environments in the Rudolf Basin, East Africa, 1976. Add: 1994 San Antonio Rd., Berkeley, Calif. 94707, U.S.A.

HOWELL, John Christian. American, b. 1924. Human relations, Sex. Prof. of Christian Ethics, Midwestern Baptist Theological Seminary, Kansas City, since 1960 (Academic Dean, 1975–82). Pastor, First Baptist Church, Crowley, Tex., 1950–56; Fellow, Southwestern Baptist Theological Seminary, Fort Worth, Tex., 1954–56; Chaplain–Counselor, Volunteers of America Maternity Home, Fort Worth, Tex., 1954–56; Pastor, West Bradenton Baptist Church, Fla., 1956–60. *Publs:* Teaching About Sex—A Christian Approach, 1966; Growing in Oneness, 1972; Teaching Your Children About Sex, 1973; Equality and Submission in Christian Marriage, 1979; Senior Adult Family Life, 1979; Christian Marriage: Growing in Oneness, 1983; Church and Family Growing Together, 1984; Transitions in Mature Marriage, 1989. Add: 5001 N. Oak St. Trafficway, Kansas City, Mo. 64118, U.S.A.

HOWELL, Roger, Jr. American, b. 1936. History, Biography. Prof. of History, Bowdoin Coll., Brunswick, Me., since 1968 (Asst. Prof., 1964–66; Assoc. Prof., 1966–68; Pres., 1969–78; Chmn., 1967–68, 1982–85). Jr. Instr., Johns Hopkins Univ., Baltimore, Md., 1960–61; Jr. Research Fellow, St. John's Coll., Oxford, 1961–64. *Publs:* (ed.) Prescott: The Conquest of Mexico, The Conquest of Peru, and Other Writings, 1966; Newcastle upon Tyne and the Puritan Revolution, 1967; Sir Philip Sidney: The Shepherd Knight, 1968; The Origins of the English Revolution, 1975; Cromwell, 1977; (ed.) Monopoly on the Tyne 1650–58: Papers Relating to Ralph Gardner, 1978; Puritans and Radicals in North England, 1984; (with E.W. Baker) Maine in the Age of Discovery, 1988. Add: Dept. of History, Bowdoin Coll., Brunswick, Me. 04011, U.S.A.

HOWELL, Virginia Tier. *See* **ELLISON**, Virginia Howell.

HOWELLS, John Gwilym. British, b. 1918. Psychiatry, Psychology, Sociology. Ed., Intnl. Journal of Family Psychiatry, since 1980. Formerly, Dir., Inst. of Family Psychiatry. *Publs:* Family Psychiatry, 1963; (ed.) Modern Perspectives in Psychiatry Series, since 1965; (co–author) Family Relations Indicator, 1967; Theory and Practice of Family Psychiatry, 1968; Remember Maria, 1974; (ed.) World History of Psychiatry, 1974; Principles of Family Psychiatry, 1975; (ed.) Advances in Family Psychiatry, 2 vols., 1979–80; Integral Clinical Investigation, 1982; (with Osborne) A Reference Companion to the History of Abnormal Psychology, 2 vols., 1984; (co–author) The Family and Schizophrenia, 1985; (co–author) Family Diagnosis, 1986. Add: c/o Intl. Journal of Family Psychiatry, Higham, Colchester CO7 6LD, England.

HOWELLS, William White. American, b. 1908. Anthropology/Ethnology, Biology. Prof. of Anthropology Emeritus, Harvard Univ.,

Cambridge, Mass., since 1974 (Prof., 1954–74). Prof. of Anthropology, Univ. of Wisconsin, Madison, 1939–54. *Publs:* Mankind So Far, 1944; The Heathens, 1948; Back of History (in U.K. as Man in the Beginning), 1954; Mankind in the Making, 1959, rev. ed. 1967; (ed.) Ideas of Human Evolution, 1962; The Pacific Islanders, 1973; Evolution of the Genus Homo, 1973; Cranial Variation in Man, 1973. Add: Kittery Point, Me. 03905, U.S.A.

HOWES, Barbara. American, b. 1914. Poetry. Ed., Chimera literary quarterly, NYC, 1943–47. *Publs:* The Undersea Farmer, 1948; In the Cold Country, 1954; Light and Dark, 1959; (ed.) 23 Modern Stories, 1963; (ed.) From the Green Antilles: Writings of the Caribbean, 1966; Looking up at Leaves, 1966; (ed. with G.J. Smith) The Sea–Green Horse, 1970; The Blue Garden, 1972; (ed.) The Eye of the Heart: Stories from Latin America, 1973; Private Signal: Poems New and Selected, 1977; Moving (poetry), 1983; The Road Commissioner and Other Stories, 1983. Add: Brook House, North Pownal, Vt. 05260, U.S.A.

HOWES, Jane. *See* **SHIRAS,** Wilmar H.

HOWINGTON, Linda S. *See* **HOWARD,** Linda

HOWLETT, Duncan. American, b. 1906. Theology/Religion. Minister, Second Church in Salem, Mass., 1935–38, First Unitarian Church, New Bedford, Mass., 1938–46, First Church in Boston, Mass., 1946–58, and All Souls Church (Unitarian), Washington, D.C., 1958–68; Acting Dean of Chapel and Lectr. in Religion, Mount Holyoke Coll., South Hadley, Mass., 1972–73; now retired. Founder and first Pres., Small Woodland Owners Assn. of Maine. *Publs:* Man Against the Church, 1954; The Essenes and Christianity, 1957; The Fourth American Faith, 1964; No Greater Love, 1966; The Critical Way in Religion, 1980. Add: Eastman Hill Rd., Lovell Center, Me. 04016, U.S.A.

HOWLETT, John (Reginald). British, b. 1940. Novels/Short stories, Plays/Screenplays, Biography. *Publs:* (with D. Sherwin) If . . . (screenplay), 1969; James Dean, 1975; Christmas Spy (novel), 1975; Tango November (novel), 1976; Frank Sinatra, 1980; Maximum Credible Accident (novel), 1980; Orange (novel), 1985; Murder of a Moderate Man (novel/TV series), 1985. Add: Orchard House, Stone in Oxney, Tenterden, Kent, England.

HOWSE, Ernest Marshall. Canadian, b. 1902. Literature, Theology/Religion. Co–Pres., Continuing Cttee. on Muslim–Christian Cooperation, 1955–64; Moderator, United Church of Canada, 1964–66; Columnist, Toronto Star, 1970–79. *Publs:* Saints in Politics, 1952, 3rd ed. 1971; The Lively Oracles, 1956; Spiritual Values in Shakespeare, 1956; Roses in December (autobiography), 1982. Add: 31 Eastbourne Ave., Toronto, Ont. M5P 2E8, Canada.

HOY, David Couzens. American, b. 1944. Philosophy. Prof. of Philosophy, Univ. of California, Santa Cruz, since 1981. Instr., Yale Univ., New Haven, Conn., 1969–70; Asst. Prof., Princeton Univ., N.J., 1970–76; Asst. Prof. in Residence, Univ. of California, Los Angeles, 1976–77; Assoc. Prof., Barnard Coll., Columbia Univ., New York, 1977–81; Sr. Mellon Fellow in Humanities and Sr. Lectr. in Philosophy, Columbia Univ., New York, 1981–82. *Publs:* The Critical Circle: Literature, History, and Philosophical Hermeneutics, 1978, 1982; (ed.) Foucault: A Critical Reader, 1986. Add: Dept. of Philosophy, Univ. of California, Santa Cruz, Calif. 95064, U.S.A.

HOYEM, Andrew. American, b. 1935. Poetry, Translations. Book Designer and Publr., The Arion Press, since 1974. Partner, Auerhahn Press, San Francisco, 1961–64, and Grabhorn–Hoyem, Printers, San Francisco, 1966–73. *Publs:* The Wake, 1963; The Music Room, 1965; (trans. and author) Chimeras, by Nerval, 1966; (trans. and author with John Crawford) The Pearl, 1967; Articles, Poems 1960–67, 1969; Picture/Poems, 1975; The First Poet Travels to the Moon, 1975; What If, 1987. Add: 460 Bryant St., San Francisco, Calif. 94107, U.S.A.

HOYLAND, Michael (David). British, b. 1925. Novels, Poetry, Art, Children's non–fiction. Sch. teacher, 1951–63; Lectr., 1963–65, and Sr. Lectr. in Art, Kesteven Coll. of Education, Stoke Rochford, Lincs. *Publs:* (co–author) Introduction Three, 1967; Art for Children, 1970; Variations: An Integrated Approach to Art, 1975; A Love Affair with War (novel), 1981; The Bright Way In (poetry), 1984. Add: c/o Macmillan Ltd., Little Essex St., London WC2R 3LF, England

HOYLE, (Sir) Fred. British, b. 1915. Science fiction/Fantasy, Astronomy, Physics, Autobiography. Hon. Fellow, St. John's Coll.,

Cambridge, since 1973 (Fellow, 1939–72), and Emmanuel Coll., Cambridge, since 1984. Lectr. in Mathematics, 1945–58, Plumian Prof. of Astronomy and Experimental Philosophy, 1958–72, and Dir., Inst. of Theoretical Astronomy, 1966–72, Cambridge Univ.; Staff member, Mt. Wilson and Palomar Observatories, Calif., 1956–62; Prof. of Astronomy, Royal Instn., London, 1969–72; White Prof., Cornell Univ., Ithaca, N.Y., 1972–78. *Publs:* Some Recent Researchers in Solar Physics, 1949; The Nature of the Universe, 1950, rev. ed. 1960; A Decade of Decision, 1953; Frontiers of Astronomy, 1955; Man and Materialism, 1956; The Black Cloud, 1957; Ossian's Ride, 1959; (with John Elliot) A for Andromeda: A Novel for Tomorrow, 1962; Astronomy, 1962; (with Geoffrey Hoyle) Fifth Planet, 1963; (with John Elliot) Andromeda Breakthrough: A Novel of Tomorrow's Universe, 1964; Of Men and Galaxies, 1964; Galaxies, Nuclei, and Quasars, 1965; Encounter with the Future, 1965; (with W.A. Fowler) Nucleosynthesis in Massive Stars and Supernovae, 1965; Man in the Universe, 1966; October the First Is Too Late, 1966; Element 79, 1967; (with Geoffrey Hoyle) Rockets in Ursa Major, 1969; (with Geoffrey Hoyle) Seven Steps to the Sun, 1970; (with Geoffrey Hoyle) The Molecule Men: Two Short Novels, 1971; (with Geoffrey Hoyle) The Inferno, 1972; From Stonehenge to Modern Cosmology, 1972; Nicolaus Copernicus, 1973; (with J.V. Narlikar) Action at a Distance in Physics and Cosmology, 1974; Astronomy Today, 1975; Astronomy and Cosmology, 1975; Astronomy Illustrated: Highlights in Astronomy, 1976; (with Geoffrey Hoyle) Into Deepest Space, 1976; (with Geoffrey Hoyle) The Incandescent Ones, 1977; Ten Faces of the Universe, 1977; On Stonehenge, 1977; (with N.C. Wickramasinghe) Lifecloud, 1978; (with Geoffrey Hoyle) The Westminster Disaster, 1978; The Cosmogony of the Solar System, 1978; (with Chandra Wickramasinghe) Diseases from Space, 1979; (with Geoffrey Hoyle) Commonsense in Nuclear Energy, 1979; (with J.V. Narlikar) The Physics–Astronomy Frontier, 1980; Ice, 1981; (with C. Wickramasinghe) Evolution from Space, 1981; (with C. Wickramasinghe) Space Travellers, The Bringers of Life, 1981; Facts and Dogmas in Cosmology and Elsewhere (Rede Lecture), 1982: (with Geoffrey Hoyle) The Energy Pirate (for children), 1982; (with Geoffrey Hoyle) The Giants of Universal Park (for children), 1982; (with Geoffrey Hoyle) The Frozen Planet of Azuron (for children), 1982; (with Geoffrey Hoyle) The Planet of Death (for children), 1982; The Intelligent Universe: A New View of Creation and Evolution, 1983; Comet Halley (novel), 1985; The Small World of Fred Hoyle (autobiog.), 1986; (with N.C. Wickramasinghe) Cosmic Life Force, 1987. Add: St. John's Coll., Cambridge, England.

HOYLE, Geoffrey. British, b. 1942. Science fiction/Fantasy, Children's fiction, Children's non–fiction. Worked in documentary films, 1963–67. *Publs:* (with Fred Hoyle) Fifth Planet, 1963; (with Fred Hoyle) Rockets in Ursa Major, 1969; (with Fred Hoyle) Seven Steps to the Sun, 1970; (with Fred Hoyle) Molecule Men, 1971; 2010, 1972; (with Fred Hoyle) The Inferno, 1973; Disasters, 1975; (with Fred Hoyle) Into Deepest Space, 1976; (with Fred Hoyle) The Incandescent Ones, 1977: (with Fred Hoyle) The Westminster Disaster, 1978; (with Fred Hoyle) Commonsense in Nuclear Energy, 1979; (with Fred Hoyle) The Energy Pirate (for children), 1982; (with Fred Hoyle) The Giants of Universal Park (for children), 1982; (with Fred Hoyle) The Frozen Planet of Azuron (for children), 1982; (with Fred Hoyle) The Planet of Death (for children), 1982; Flight, 1984. Add: 8 Milner Rd., Bournemouth BH4 8AD, England.

HOYLE, Trevor. British, b. 1940. Novels/Short stories, Science fiction, Plays. *Publs:* novels—The Relatively Constant Copywriter, 1972; Rule of Night, 1975; The Sexless Spy, 1977; The Svengali Plot, 1978; The Man Who Travelled on Motorways, 1979; The Stigma, 1980; (as Joseph Rance) Bullet Train, 1980; Vail, 1984; (as Larry Milne) Ghostbusters, 1985; (as Larry Milne) Biggles, 1986; (as Larry Milne) Hearts of Fire, 1987; K.I.D.S., 1987; science–fiction—Q: Seeking the Mythical Future, 1977; Q: Through the Eye of Time, 1977; Blake's Seven, 1977; Q: The Gods Look Down, 1978; Blake's Seven: Project Avalon, 1979; Earth Cult (in U.S. as This Sentient Earth), 1979; Blake's Seven: Scorpio Attack, 1981; The Last Gasp, 1983; for TV—Blake's Seven: Ultraworld; Whatever Happened to the Heroes. Add: 34 Cedar Lane, Newhay, Rochdale, Lancs. OL16 4LQ, England.

HOYLES, J(ames) Arthur. British, b. 1908. Criminology/Law enforcement/Prisons, Theology/Religion. Methodist Minister, since 1931. Supervisor, Methodist Prison cttee., London, 1964–76. Member, Penal Reform Cttee., British Council of Churches. *Publs:* Treatment of the Young Delinquent, 1952; Religion in Prison, 1953; The Pastor's Dilemma, 1954; The Church and the Criminal, 1964; I Was in Prison, 1969; Christ Alive in Prison, 1971; Sent to Prison, 1980; Punishment in the Bible, 1986. Add: 49 Marcliff Grove, Heaton Mersey, Stockport, Cheshire SK4 2AB, England.

HOYT, Richard. American, b. 1941. Mystery/Crime/Suspense. Freelance writer since 1983. Reporter, Honolulu Star–Bulletin, 1968–69; Reporter, later Asst. City Ed., Honolulu Advertiser, 1969–72; Correspondent, Newsweek, 1969–72; Asst. Prof. of Journalism, Univ. of Maryland, College Park, 1972–76; Asst. Prof., later Assoc. Prof. of Communications, Lewis and Clark Coll., Portland, Ore., 1976–83. *Publs:* Decoys, 1980; 30 for a Harry, 1981; The Manna Enzyme, 1982; Trotsky's Run, 1982; The Siskiyou Two–Step, 1983, rev. ed. as Siskiyou, 1984; Cool Runnings, 1984; Fish Story, 1985; Head of State, 1985; The Dragon Portfolio, 1986. Add: 13120 S.W. Cavalier Ct., Beaverton, Ore. 97005, U.S.A.

HSIAO, Hsia. *See* LIU, Wu–chi.

HUBBARD, Robert Hamilton. Canadian, b. 1916. Art, History. Hon. Historian to the Gov.–Gen. of Canada, since 1981 (Cultural Adviser, 1975–81). Teaching posts in art history, 1941–46; Canadian Art Curator, 1947–54, and Chief Curator, 1954–78, National Gallery of Canada, Ottawa. *Publs:* European Paintings in Canadian Collections, 2 vols., 1956–62; National Gallery of Canada Catalogue of Paintings and Sculpture, 3 vols., 1957–60; An Anthology of Canadian Art, 1960; The Development of Canadian Art, 1963; Canadian Painting (Tate Gallery catalogue), 1964; Victorian Artists, 1965; (with J.–R. Ostiguy) 300 Years of Canadian Art, 1967; (ed.) Scholarship in Canada: Achievement and Outlook, 1968; Three Centuries of Scottish Painting, 1968; The Vincent Massey Bequest: The Canadian Paintings, 1969; Two Quebec Painters, A. Plamondon and T. Hamel, 1970; Thomas Davies, 1972; Thomas Davies in Early Canada, 1972; Cathedral in the Capital, A Short History of Christ Church Cathedral, 1972; The Artist and the Land: Landscape Painting in Canada, 1973; Painters of Quebec: Collection of Maurice Corbeil, 1973; Rideau Hall: An Illustrated History of Government House, Ottawa, 1977; Index to Translations of the Royal Society of Canada 1882–1982, 1985. Add: Rideau Hall, Ottawa K1A 0A1, Canada.

HUBBELL, Richard Whittaker. American, b. 1914. Media. Pres. and Chmn., World Wide Information Services Inc., NYC, since 1958. News Dir., CBS–TV, NYC, 1939–43; Television Officer, U.S. Dept. of State, Washington, D.C. 1951–53. *Publs:* 4000 Years of Television, 1942; Television Programming and Production, 1945, 3rd ed. 1956. Add: 360 First Ave., Apt. MH, New York, N.Y. 10010, U.S.A.

HUBER, Jack T. American. Psychology. Prof. Emeritus, Hunter Coll., City Univ. of New York, since 1967. Prof. of Clinical Psychology, Adelphi Univ., Garden City, N.Y., 1955–67. *Publs:* Report Writing in Psychology and Psychiatry, 1958; Through an Eastern Window (in U.K. as Psychotherapy and Meditation), 1963; (co–ed.) Goals and Behavior in Psychotherapy and Counseling, 1972; (co–author) The Human Personality, 1977; (co–ed.) Therapies for Adults, 1982. Add: 310 E. 55th St., New York, N.Y. 10022, U.S.A.

HUBER, Richard Miller. American, b. 1922. History, Biography. Pres., Richard M. Huber Assocs., Washington, D.C., since 1985. Prof., Dept. of History, 1946–47, and Depts. of History, Politics, English, and American Civilization Prog., 1950–54, Princeton Univ., N.J.; Trustee, Historical Soc. of Princeton, 1955; Asst. Secty., Soc. of American Historians, 1956–58; Pres., Princeton Manor Construction Co., 1958–62; Co-Ed., New Jersey Historical Series, 1963–67; Producer and Moderator, WHWH public affairs radio prog., Princeton, N.J., 1965–67; Moderator, Channel 13 television, NYC, 1967–68; Oral History Project, Princeton, N.J., 1969–71; Dean, Sch. of Gen. Studies, 1971–77, and Exec. Dir., Div. of Continuing Education, Hunter Coll., City Univ. of New York, 1977–82; Asst. Dir. for TV and Radio, 1983–84, and Special Asst. to the Chmn., 1984–85, National Endowment for the Humanities; Pres., Productions-in-Progress, Inc., 1986–89. *Publs:* Big All the Way Through: The Life of Van Santvoord Merle–Smith, 1952; (ed. with W.J. Lane) The New Jersey Historical Series, 31 vols., 1964–65; The American Idea of Success, 1971, 1987. Add: 2950 Van Ness St. N.W., No. 926, Washington, D.C., 20008, U.S.A.

HUBLER, Richard G(ibson). American, b. 1912. Novels/Short stories, Plays/Screenplays, Poetry, Biography. Assoc. Book Reviewer, Los Angeles Times, Calif., since 1960. Public Relations Consultant, NYC, and Los Angeles, 1938–60; former Teacher, Ventura Coll., Univ. of California at Santa Barbara, and Asst. to Pres., San Fernando Valley State Coll., Los Angeles (now California State Univ., San Francisco), 1964. *Publs:* Lou Gehrig, 1941; (with R. Leonard) I Flew for China, 1942; (with J. DeChant) Flying Leathernecks, 1944; I've Got Mine, 1945; The Quiet Kingdom, 1948; The Brass God, 1952; The Chase, 1952; In Darkest Childhood, 1954; The Pass, 1955; Man in the Sky, 1956; SAC: Strategic

Air Command, 1958; (with H. Traubel) St. Louis Woman, 1959; The Shattering of the Image, 1959; True Love, True Love, 1959; Big Eight, 1960; Straight Up: History of the Helicopter, 1961; The Blue–and–Gold Man, 1961; (ed.) The World's Shortest Stories, 1961; (with L. Morrison) Trial and Triumph, 1965; (with Ronald Reagan) Where's the Rest of Me, 1965; The Cole Porter Story, 1965; South of the Moon, 1966; Soldier and Sage, 1966; The Christianis, 1966; Wheeler, 3 vols., 1967; In All His Glory, 1968; The Earthmother Drinks Blood, 1975. Add: Box 793, Ojai, Calif., U.S.A.

HUBY, Pamela Margaret. British, b. 1922. Philosophy. Reader in Philosophy, Univ. of Liverpool, 1983–87 (Asst. Lectr., 1949–52; Lectr.,1952–71; Sr. Lectr., 1971–83). Asst. Lectr., Dept. of Classics, Univ. of Reading, 1944–45; Lectr. in Philosophy, St. Anne's Soc., Oxford, 1947–49. *Publs:* (co–author) Critical History of Western Philosophy, 1964; Greek Ethics, 1967; Plato and Modern Morality, 1972; (co–author) Philosophy and Psychical Research, 1976; (co–author) Stoic and Peripatetic Ethics, 1983; (co–author) Aristotle on Nature and Living Things, 1986; (co–author) The Criterion of Truth, 1989. Add: 9 Princes St., Tunbridge Wells, Kent, England.

HUCK, Arthur. Australian, b. 1926. International relations/Current affairs, Politics/Government. Sr. Associate in Political Science, Univ. of Melbourne, since 1989 (joined faculty, 1958; Dean, Faculty of Arts, 1976–81). *Publs:* The Chinese in Australia, 1968; The Security of China, 1970. Add: Dept. of Political Science, Univ. of Melbourne, Parkville, Vic. 3052, Australia.

HUDDLESTON, Trevor. British, b. 1913. Theology/Religion. Anglican Priest: Chmn., Intnl. Defence and Aid Fund for Southern Africa, since 1983. Ordained, 1937; Prior and Priest–in–Charge, Sophiatown and Orlando Missions, Diocese of Johannesburg, 1943–49; Bishop of Massai, Tanzania, 1960–68; Bishop of Stepney, 1968–78; Bishop of Mauritius and Archbishop of the Province of the Indian Ocean, 1978–83. *Publs:* Naught for Your Comfort, 1956; The True and Living God, 1964; God's World, 1966; I Believe, 1988. Add: House of the Resurrection, Mirfield, W. Yorks. WF14 0BN, England.

HUDNUT, Robert K. American, b. 1934. Theology/Religion. Pastor, Winnetka Presbyterian Church, Ill., since 1975. Trustee, Princeton Univ., N.J., since 1972; Trustee, Asheville Sch., N.C., since 1978. Pastor, St. Luke Presbyterian Church, Wayzata, Minn., 1962–73; Exec. Dir., Minnesota Public Interest Research Group, 1973–75. *Publs:* Surprised by God: What It Means to Be a Minister in Middle–Class America Today, 1967; A Sensitive Man and the Christ, 1969; An Active Man and the Christ, 1971; A Thinking Man and the Christ, 1971; The Sleeping Giant: Arousing Church Power in America, 1971; Arousing the Sleeping Giant: How to Organise Your Church for Action, 1973; Church Growth Is Not the Point, 1975; The Bootstrap Fallacy: What the Self–Help Books Don't Tell You, 1978; This People, This Parish, 1986. Add: 1078 Elm St., Winnetka, Ill. 60093, U.S.A.

HUDSON, Charles. American, b. 1932. Anthropology/Ethnology, History. Prof. of Anthropology, Univ. of Georgia, Athens, since 1977 (Asst. Prof., 1964–68; Assoc. Prof., 1968–77). *Publs:* The Catawaba Nation, 1970; (ed.) Red, White, and Black: Symposium on Indians in the Old South, 1971; (ed.) Four Centuries of Southern Indians, 1974; The Southeastern Indians, 1976; (ed.) Black Drink: A Native American Tea, 1978; Elements of Southeastern Indian Religion, 1984; (ed.) Ethnology of the Southeastern Indians: A Sourcebook, 1985. Add: Dept. of Anthropology and Linguistics, Univ. of Georgia, Athens, Ga. 30602, U.S.A.

HUDSON, Derek. British, b. 1911. Art, History, Literature, Biography. Member, Editorial Staff., The Times, London, 1939–49; Literary Ed., The Spectator, 1949–53; Member, Editorial Staff, OUP, 1955–65. *Publs:* A Poet in Parliament: W.M. Praed, 1939; Thomas Barnes of "The Times," 1943, 1973; British Journalists and Newspapers, 1945; Norman O'Neill: A Life of Music, 1945; Charles Keene, 1947; Martin Tupper: His Rise and Fall, 1949; James Pryde, 1949; Lewis Carroll, 1954, 1976; (with K.W. Luckhurst) The Royal Society of Arts 1754–1954, 1954; (ed.) Modern English Short Stories 1930–1955, 1956; (ed.) English Critical Essays, Twentieth Century, 1958; Sir Joshua Reynolds, 1958; Arthur Rackham: His Life and Work, 1960, 1974; The Forgotten King, 1960; (ed.) Essays and Studies, 1961; Writing Between the Lines, 1965; Holland House in Kensington, 1967; (ed.) The Diary of Henry Crabb Robinson: An Abridgement, 1967; Talks with Fuddy, 1968; Kensington Palace, 1968; Munby: Man of Two Worlds, 1972; For Love of Painting: Sir Gerald Kelly, 1975. Add: 33 Beacon Hill Ct., Hindhead, Surrey, England.

HUDSON, Jan. *See* **SMITH,** George H.

HUDSON, Helen. Pseud. for Helen Lane. American, b. 1920. Novels/Short stories. *Publs:* Tell the Time to None, 1986; Meyer Meyer, 1967; The Listener and Other Stories, 1968; Farnsbee South, 1971; Criminal Trespass, 1985; A Temporary Residence, 1987. Add: 558 Chapel St., New Haven, Conn. 06511, U.S.A.

HUDSON, Jeffrey. *See* **CRICHTON,** Michael.

HUDSON, Liam. British, b. 1933. Novels, Psychology, Autobiography/Memoirs/Personal. Fellow, King's College, Cambridge, 1966–68; Prof. of Educational Sciences, Univ. of Edinburgh, 1968–77; Member, Inst. for Advanced Study, Princeton, N.J., 1974–75; Prof. of Psychology, Brunel Univ., 1977–87. *Publs:* Contrary Imaginations, 1966; Frames of Mind, 1968; (ed.) The Ecology of Human Intelligence, 1970; The Cult of the Fact, 1972; Human Beings: An Introduction to the Psychology of Human Experience, 1975; The Nympholepts, 1978; Bodies of Knowledge, 1982; Night Life, 1985. Add: 34 N. Park, Gerrards Cross, Bucks., England.

HUDSON, Wilma Jones. (Mrs. Wilma Hudson Black). American, b. 1916. Biography. Librarian–Audio–Visual Dir., Zionsville Middle Sch., Indiana, 1968–82, now retired. English Teacher, Edwardsville High Sch., Ill., 1937–42, Shortridge High Sch., Indianapolis, Ind., 1943–47, and 1963–65, and Northview Jr. High Sch., Washington Township, Indianapolis, 1965–66; Librarian and Audio–Visual Dir., Zionsville Elementary Sch., 1966–68. *Publs:* Dwight D. Eisenhower: Young Military Leader, 1970; J.C. Penny: Golden Rule Boy, 1972; Harry S. Truman: Missouri Farm Boy, 1973. Add: 10550 Zionsville Rd., Zionsville, Ind. 46077, U.S.A.

HUDSON, Winthrop S. American, b. 1911. Theology/Religion, Biography. Adjunct Prof., Univ. of North Carolina, Chapel Hill, since 1980. Asst. Prof., Univ. of Chicago, 1944–47; Prof. of History of Christianity, Colgate Rochester Divinity Sch., 1947–77; Prof. of History, Univ. of Rochester, 1970–77; Distinguished Seminary Prof., Colgate Rochester Divinity Sch., 1977–80. *Publs:* John Ponet (1516–56); Advocate of Limited Monarchy, 1942; The Great Tradition of the American Churches, 1953, 1963; Understanding Roman Catholicism, 1959; American Protestantism, 1961; Religion in America, 1965, 4th ed. 1987; Nationalism and Religion in America, 1970; Baptists in Transition, 1979; The Cambridge Connection and the Elizabethan Settlement of 1559, 1980; Walter Rauschenbusch: Selected Writings, 1984. Add: 1403 The Oaks, Chapel Hill, N.C. 27514, U.S.A.

HUFANA, Alejandrino G. Filipino, b. 1926. Plays/Screenplays, Poetry, Literature. Prof. of English and Comparative Literature since 1975, and Principal Researcher in Iloko Literature since 1972, Univ. of the Philippines (Research Asst. in Social Science, 1954–56; joined English Dept., 1956). Co-Founding Ed., Signatures mag., 1955, Comment mag., 1956–62, Heritage mag., 1967–68, and Univ. Coll. Journal (later Gen. Education Journal), 1961–72; Ed., Panorama mag., 1959–61; Managing Ed., Univ. of the Philippines Press, 1965–66; Dir. of the Library, 1970–86, and Ed., Pamana mag., 1971–85, Cultural Center of the Philippines, Manila. *Publs:* 13 Kalisud (poetry), 1955; Man in the Moon (play), 1956, 1972; Sickle Season: Poems of a First Decade 1948–58, 1959; Poro Point: An Anthology of Lives: Poems 1955–1960, 1961; Mena Pecson Crisologo and Iloko Drama, 1963; Curtain–Raisers: First Five Plays, 1964; (ed.) Aspects of Philippine Literature, 1967; (ed.) A Philippine Cultural Miscellany, parts I and II, 1970; The Wife of Lot and Other New Poems, 1971; The Unicorn (play), 1971; Salidom–ay (play), 1971; Notes on Poetry, 1973; Seig Heil: An Epic on the Third Reich, 1975; I.R. Marcos: A Tonal Epic, 1975; Obligations: Poems on Cheers of Conscience, 1976; (ed) Philippine Writing: Poems, Stories and Essays, 1977; Shining On (poetry), 1985. Add: English Dept., Univ. of the Philippines, Diliman, Quezon City, Philippines.

HUFF, Robert. American, b. 1924. Poetry. Prof., Western Washington, Bellingham, since 1967 (Assoc. Prof., 1964–66). Asst. Instr. in Humanities and Counselor, Coll. of Liberal Arts, 1950–52 and 1957–58, Wayne State Univ., Detroit, Mich.; Instr., Univ. of Oregon, Eugene, 1952–55, Fresno State Coll., Calif., 1953–55, and Oregon State Univ., Corvallis, 1955–57 and 1958–60; Poet–in–Residence and Assoc. Prof., Univ. of Delaware, Newark, 1960–64; Writer–in–Residence, Univ. of Arkansas, Fayetteville, 1966–67. *Publs:* Colonel Johnson's Ride, 1959; The Course, 1966; The Ventriloquist, 1977; Shore Guide to Flocking Names, 1985. Add: Dept. of English, Western Washington Univ., Bellingham, Wash. 98225, U.S.A.

HUFFAKER, Clair. American, b. 1928. Novels/Short stories, Westerns/Adventure, Children's non-fiction, Autobiography/Memoirs/Personal. *Publs:* Badge for a Gunfighter, 1957; Rider from Thunder Mountain, 1957; Cowboy (novelization of screenplay), 1958; Guns of Rio Conchos, 1958, as Rio Conchos, 1975; Posse from Hell, 1958; Badman, 1958, in U.K. as The War Wagon, 1974; Flaming Lance, 1958; Seven Ways from Sundown, 1960; Good Lord, You're Upside Down! (novel), 1963; Nobody Loves a Drunken Indian, 1967; The Cowboy and the Cossack, 1973; One Time, I Saw Morning Come Home: A Remembrance, 1974; Guns from Thunder Mountain, 1975; Clair Huffaker's Profiles of the American West (juvenile), 1976. Add: c/o Thorndike Press, P.O. Box 159, Thorndike, Me. 04986, U.S.A.

HUGGETT, Frank Edward. British, b. 1924. Plays/Screenplays, Country life/Rural societies, History, Travel/Exploration/Adventure. Sub-Ed., Daily Telegraph, 1951–53; Ed., Look and Listen, 1956–57; Visiting Lectr., Polytechnic of Central London, 1957–65, and Ministry of Defence, 1965–72. *Publs:* South of Lisbon, 1960; Farming, 1963, 3rd ed. 1975; The Newspapers, 1969, 1972; Modern Belgium, 1969; A Short History of Farming, 1970; Nineteenth Century Reformers, 1971; How It Happened, 1971; Nineteenth Century Statesmen, 1972; Travel and Communications, 1972; A Day in the Life of a Victorian Farm Worker, 1972; The Modern Netherlands, 1972; The Battle for Reform 1815–32, 1973; A Day in the Life of a Victorian Factory Worker, 1973; Factory Life and Work, 1973; The Dutch Today, 2nd ed. 1974; History Not So Long Ago (radio drama), 1974–75; A Dictionary of British History 1815–1973, 1975; The Land Question and European Society, 1975; Life and Work at Sea, 1975; Slavery and the Slave Trade, 1975; Life Below Stairs, 1977; Victorian England as Seen by Punch, 1978; Goodnight Sweetheart, 1979; Carriages at Eight, 1979; Cartoonists at War, 1981; The Dutch Connection, 1982; Teachers, 1986. Add: Flat 6, 40 Shepherds Hill, London N6, England.

HUGGETT, Richard. British, b. 1929. Plays/Screenplays, Theatre, Biography, Humour/Satire. Actor. *Publs:* The First Night of Pygmalion (play), 1970; The Truth About Pygmalion, 1970; The Wit of the Catholics, 1971; The Wit and Humour of Sex, 1975; The Curse of Macbeth, 1981; The Bedside Sex, 1985; Pontius the Pilate, 1986; The Wit of Publishing, 1986; Binkie Beaumont: A Biography, 1988. Add: Arts Theatre Club, Great Newport St., London WC2, England.

HUGHES, Brenda. *See* **COLLOMS,** Brenda.

HUGHES, Colin Anfield. Australian, b. 1930. Politics/Government. Electoral Commissioner since 1984. Prof. of Political Science, Univ. of Queensland, St. Lucia, 1965–75; Professorial Fellow in Political Science, Australian National Univ., Canberra, 1975–84. *Publs:* (ed. with D.G. Bettison and P.W. van der Veur) The Papua New Guinea Elections 1964, 1965; (with J.S. Western) The Prime Minister's Policy Speech: A Case Study in Televised Politics, 1966; (ed.) Readings in Australian Government, 1968; (ed. with B.D. Graham) A Handbook of Australian Government and Politics 1890–1964, 1968; Images and Issues: The Queensland State Elections of 1963 and 1966, 1969; (ed. with D.J. Murphy and R.B. Joyce) Prelude to Power: The Rise of the Labour Party in Queensland 1885–1915, 1970; (ed. with I.F. Nicolson) Pacific Policies, 1972; (with J.S. Western) The Mass Media in Australia: Use and Evaluation, 1972, 1982; (ed. with B.D. Graham) Voting for the Australian House of Representatives 1901–1964, 1974; (ed. with B.D. Graham) Voting for the Queensland Legislative Assembly 1890–1964, 1974; (ed. with B.D. Graham) Voting for the New South Wales Legislative Assembly 1890–1964, 1975; (ed. with B.D. Graham) Voting for the Victoria Legislative Assembly 1890–1964, 1975; (ed. with B.D. Graham) Voting for the South Australian, Western Australian and Tasmanian Lower Houses 1890–1964, 1976; Mr. Prime Minister: Australian Prime Ministers 1901–1972, 1976; (ed.) A Handbook of Australian Government and Politics 1965–74, 1977; (ed. with D.J. Murphy and R.B. Joyce) Labor in Power: The Labor Party in Queensland 1915–1957, 1980; The Government of Queensland, 1980; (ed.) Voting for the Australian State Lower Houses, 2 vols., 1981–87; Race and Politics in the Bahamas, 1981; (ed. with B.J. Costar) Labor to Office: The Victorian State Election 1982, 1983; (ed. with D. Aitkin) Voting for the Australian State Upper Houses 1890–1984, 1986; (ed.) A Handbook of Australian Government and Politics 1975–84, 1987. Add: P.O. Box 161, Jamison Centre, A.C.T. 2614, Australia.

HUGHES, David (John). British, b. 1930. Novels/Short stories. Asst. Ed., London Mag., 1953–54; Ed., Town mag., London, 1960–61; film writer in Sweden, 1961–68; lived in France, 1970–74; Ed., New Fiction Soc., London, 1975–77, 1981–82; Film Critic, Sunday Times newspaper, London, 1982–83. *Publs:* novels—A Feeling in the Air (in U.S. as Man

Off Beat), 1957; Sealed with a Loving Kiss, 1959; The Horsehair Sofa, 1961; The Major, 1964; The Man Who Invented Tomorrow, 1968; Memories of Dying, 1976; A Genoese Fancy, 1979; The Imperial German Dinner Service, 1983; The Pork Butcher, 1984; But for Bunter, 1985, in U.S. as The Joke of the Century, 1987; other—J.B. Priestley: An Informal Study of His Work, 1958; The Road to Stockholm and Lapland, 1964; (with Mai Zetterling) The Cat's Tale (for children), 1965; The Seven Ages of England, 1966; Flickorna (screenplay), 1968; The Rosewater Revolution: Notes on a Change of Attitude, 1971; (ed.) Evergreens, 1977; (ed.) Winter's Tales 1, 1985; (ed.) The Stories of Ernest Hemingway, 1986. Add: c/o Anthony Sheil Assocs., 43 Doughty St., London WC1N 2LF, England.

HUGHES, Dorothy B(elle). American, b. 1904. Mystery/Crime/Suspense, Poetry, Biography. Former Crime Reviewer for the Los Angeles Times, Albuquerque Tribune, New York Herald–Tribune and various magazines. *Publs:* mystery novels—The So Blue Marble, 1940; The Cross–Eyed Bear, 1940; The Bamboo Blonde, 1941; The Fallen Sparrow, 1942; The Blackbirders, 1943; The Delicate Ape, 1944; Johnnie, 1944; Dread Journey, 1945; Ride the Pink Horse, 1946; The Scarlet Imperial, 1946, as Kiss for a Killer, 1954; In a Lonely Place, 1947; The Candy Kid, 1950; The Davidian Report, 1952 (in U.S. paperback, The Body on the Bench, 1955); The Expendable Man, 1963; other—Dark Certainty (verse), 1931; Pueblo on the Mesa: The First Fifty Years of the University of New Mexico, 1939; The Big Barbecue (novel), 1949; Erle Stanley Gardner: The Case of the Real Perry Mason, 1978. Add: 788 Pennsylvania Ave., Ashland, Ore. 97520, U.S.A.

HUGHES, Dusty. British, b. 1947. Plays/Screenplays. Theatre dir., Birmingham, 1970–71; ed., Time Out, London, 1973–76; artistic dir., Bush Theatre, London, 1976–79; script ed., Play for Today series, BBC Television, 1982–84. *Publs:* Molière, or The Union of Hypocrites, 1983; Philistines, 1985; Futurists, and Commitments, 1986; Jenkin's Ear, 1987. Add: c/o Margaret Ramsay Ltd., 14–A Goodwin's Ct., London WC2N 4LL, England.

HUGHES, Edward Stuart Reginald. Australian, b. 1919. Medicine/Health. Emeritus Prof., Monash Univ., since 1985 (Prof. of Surgery, 1973–85). Chmn., Menzies Foundn., since 1978. Surgeon, Royal Melbourne Hosp., 1954–74. Past Pres., Royal Australasian Coll. of Surgeons. *Publs:* (with John Turner) The Management of the Colostomy, 1956; The Surgery of the Anus, Anal Canal and Rectum, 1957; The Surgery of the Colon, 1959; All About an Ileostomy, 1959, 4th ed., 1972; (with A.M. Cuthbertson and K.J. Hardy) Stoma and Fistula Management: A Practical Guide, 1976; (with A.M. Cuthbertson and M. Killingback) Colorectal Surgery, 1980; (with A Buzzard, G.L. Hughes, and D. Wells) Medicine and Surgery for Lawyers, 1986. Add: Suite 20, Cabrini Medical Centre, Isabella St., Malvern, Vic., Australia.

HUGHES, Elizabeth. See ZACHARY, Hugh.

HUGHES, Glyn. British, b. 1935. Novels/Short stories, Poetry. Art teacher in secondary schs. in Lancashire and Yorkshire, 1956–65, and in H.M. Prison, Manchester, 1969–71; Extra–Mural Lectr. in Art, Univ. of Manchester, 1971–73. *Publs:* The Stanedge Bull, 1966; Almost–Love Poems, 1968; Love on the Moor: Poems 1965–1968, 1969; Neighbours: Poems 1965–1969, 1970; Presence, 1971; Toward the Sun: Poems and Photographs, 1971; Rest the Poor Struggler: Poems 1969–1971, 1972; Millstone Grit, 1975; Fair Prospects: Journeys in Greece, 1976; Alibis and Convictions (poems), 1978; The Yorkshire Women (radio verse play), 1978; Dreamers (radio play), 1979; Best of Neighbours: New and Selected Poems, 1979; (ed.) Selected Poems of Samuel Laycock, 1981; Where I Used to Play on the Green (novel), 1981; The Hawthorn Goddess (novel), 1984; Glyn Hughes's Yorkshire, 1985; The Rape of the Rose (novel), 1987. Add: 28 Lower Millbank, Sowerby Bridge, Yorks. HX6 3ED, England.

HUGHES, H. Stuart. American, b. 1916. History. Prof. of History, Univ. of California at San Diego, 1975–86, now Emeritus. Chief, Div. of Research for Europe, Dept. of State, Washington, D.C., 1946–48; Prof. of History, Stanford Univ., California, 1955–56; Asst. Prof. of History, 1948–52, Prof. of History, 1957–69, and Gurney Prof. of History and Political Science, 1969–75, Harvard Univ., Cambridge, Mass. *Publs:* An Essay for Our Times, 1950; Oswald Spengler: A Critical Estimate, 1952, 1962; The United States and Italy, 1953, 3rd ed. 1979; Consciousness and Society, 1958, 1977; Contemporary Europe: A History, 1961, 5th ed. 1981; An Approach to Peace, 1962; History as Art and as Science, 1964; The Obstructed Path, 1968; The Sea Change, 1975; Prisoners of Hope, 1983; Sophisticated Rebels, 1988. Add: 8531 Avenida de la Ondas, La Jolla, Calif. 92037, U.S.A.

HUGHES, John A(nthony). British, b. 1941. Sociology. Reader, Dept. of Sociology, Univ. of Lancaster, since 1987 (Sr. Lectr., 1970–87). Lectr., Univ. of Exeter, 1965–70. *Publs:* (with R.E. Dowse) Political Sociology, 1972; Sociological Analysis: Methods of Discovery, 1976; The Philosophy of Social Research, 1980; (with S.A. Ackroyd) Data Collection in Context, 1981; (with Anderson and Sharrock) The Sociology Game, 1985; Philosophy and the Human Sciences, 1986. Add: Dept. of Sociology, Cartmel Coll., Univ. of Lancaster, Bailrigg, Lancaster, England.

HUGHES, Judith M. American, b. 1941. History. Prof. of History, Univ. of California at San Diego, since 1984 (Assoc. Prof., 1975–84). Asst. Prof. of Social Studies, Harvard Univ., Cambridge, Mass., 1970–75. *Publs:* To the Maginot Line: The Politics of French Military Preparation in the 1920s, 1971; Emotion and High Politics: Personal Relations at the Summit in Late Nineteenth–Century Britain and Germany, 1983; Reshaping the Psychoanalytic Domain: The Work of Melanie Klein, W.R.D. Fairbairn and D.W. Winnicott, 1989. Add: 8531 Avenida de las Ondas, La Jolla, Calif. 92037, U.S.A.

HUGHES, Matilda. See MacLEOD, Charlotte.

HUGHES, Monica. Canadian, b. 1925. Children's fiction. Lab technician, National Research Council, Ottawa, 1952–57. *Publs:* Gold–Fever Trail, 1974; Crisis on Conshelf Ten, 1975; Earthdark, 1977; The Tomorrow City, 1978; The Ghost Dance Caper, 1978; Beyond the Dark River, 1979; The Keeper of the Isis Light, 1980; The Guardian of Isis, 1981; Hunter in the Dark, 1982; Ring–Rise, Ring–Set, 1982; The Isis Pedlar,1982; The Beckoning Lights, 1982; The Treasure of the Long Sault, 1982; Space Trap, 1983; My Name Is Paula Popowich, 1983; Devil on My Back, 1984; Sandwriter, 1985; The Dream Catcher, 1986; Blaine's Way, 1986; Log Jam (in U.K. as Spirit River), 1987. Add: 13816–110A Avenue, Edmonton, Alta. T5M 2M9, Canada.

HUGHES, Philip E(dgcumbe). British, b. 1915. Theology/Religion. Visiting Prof. of New Testament Studies, Westminster Theological Seminary, Philadelphia, Pa., since 1970. Ed., Canterbury Press, since 1977. Vice–Principal, Tyndale Hall, Bristol, England, 1947–52; Exec. Secty., Church Soc., London, 1953–56; Lectr.–in–charge, Mortlake Parish Church, London, 1957–59; Ed., the Churchman, 1959–67; Guest Prof. of New Testament Studies, Columbia Theological Seminary, Decatur, Ga., 1964–68; Prof. of Historical Theology, Conwell Sch. of Theology, Philadelphia, Pa., 1968–79. *Publs:* Revive Us Again, 1947; The Divine Plan for Jew and Gentile, 1949; (trans.) Pierre Marcel: Baptism, 1953; Scripture and Myth, 1956; (co–trans.) Vocabulary of the Bible (in U.S. as Companion to the Bible), 1958; (ed.) Litton: Introduction to Dogmatic Theology, 1960; Commentary on 2 Corinthians, 1962; Christianity and the Problem of Origins, 1963; But for the Grace of God, 1964; (ed.) Christian Foundations Series, 1964–67; Theology of the English Reformers, 1965, 1980; (ed. and trans.) The Register of the Company of Pastors of Geneva in the Time of Calvin, 1966; (ed.) Churchmen Speak, 1966; (ed. and contrib.) Creative Minds in Contemporary Theology, 1966; The Control of Human Life, 1971; Confirmation in the Church Today, 1973; Interpreting Prophecy, 1976; Hope for a Despairing World, 1977; Commentary on Hebrews, 1978; Faith and Works: Cranmer and Hooker on Justification, 1982; Christian Ethics in Secular Society, 1983; LeFèvre: Pioneer of Ecclesiastical Renewal in France, 1984.; The True Image: Christ as the Origin and Destiny of Man, 1988 Add: Rydal Mount, Cherry Lane, Rydal, Pa. 19046, U.S.A.

HUGHES, Phillip William. Australian, b. 1926. Education, Mathematics/Statistics. Prof. of Education, Univ. of Tasmania, since 1981. Principal, Hobart Teachers Coll., Tasmania, 1963–65; Deputy Dir. Gen., Education Dept., Tas., 1965–69; Head, Sch. of Education, Canberra Coll. of Advanced Education, A.C.T., 1970–80. *Publs:*Academic Achievement at the University, 1960; Statistics of Academic Progress 1950–59, 1960; (with J.A. Pitman) An Introduction to Calculus, 1963; Mathematics for 20th Century Schools, 1964; (with K.A. Wilson) Explorations in Mathematics, 1965; An Introduction to Sets: A Basis for Elementary Mathematics, 1966; (with K.A. Wilson) The World of Mathematics 1–4, 1966–67; The Teacher's Role in Curriculum Design, 1973; A Design for the Governance and Organisation of Education in the Australian Capital Territory, 1973; (with W. Mulford) The Development of an Independent Education Authority: Retrospect and Prospect in the Australian Capital Territory, 1978; (with C. Collins) Where Junior Secondary Schools Are Heading; Better Teachers for Better Schools, 1988; Quality in Education, 1988. Add: 171 Acton Drive, Cambridge, Tas. 7170, Australia.

HUGHES, (James) Quentin. British, b. 1920. Architecture, Travel/Exploration/Adventure. Univ. Reader, Univ. of Liverpool, since 1967. Ed., Fort mag. Dean of the Faculty of Engineering and Architecture, and Prof. of Architecture, Royal Univ. of Malta, 1968–72. *Publs:* The Building of Malta, 1956; (with N. Lynton) Renaissance Architecture, 1962; Seaport: Architecture and Townscape in Liverpool, 1964; Fortress, 1966; (ed.) Le Fabbriche e i Desegni di Andrea Palladio, by Ottavio Bertotti Scamozzi, 1968; Liverpool, 1970; Malta, 1972; Military Architecture, 1974; Britain in the Mediterranean and the Defence of Her Naval Stations, 1981. Add: 10A Fullwood Park, Liverpool L17 5AH, England.

HUGHES, R. John. American, b. 1930. International relations/Current affairs. Syndicated Columnist, The Christian Science Monitor, since 1985 (Africa Corresp., 1955–61; Far East Corresp., 1964–70; Managing Ed., 1970; Ed., 1970–79). Pres. and Publr., Hughes Newspapers, Inc., Orleans, Mass., 1979–81 and 1985. Pres., American Soc. of Newspaper Eds., 1978–79; Dir., Voice of America, 1982; Asst. Sect. of State, 1982–84. *Publs:* The New Face of Africa, 1961; Indonesian Upheaval (in Australia & U.K. as The Fall of Sukarno), 1967. Add: Box 1053, Orleans, Mass. 02653, U.S.A.

HUGHES, Robert (Studley Forrest). Australian, b. 1938. Art, History. Sr. Writer (Art Critic) for Time mag., NYC, since 1970; also, writer and narrator of art documentaries for BBC-TV, since 1974 (Rubens, Bernini, The Shock of the New, etc.). Freelance writer, in Australia, Italy, and London, 1958–70. *Publs:* The Art of Australia, 1966; Heaven and Hell in Western Art, 1969; The Shock of the New, 1980; The Fatal Shore, 1986. Add: c/o Time, Time–Life Bldg., Rockefeller Center, New York, N.Y. 10020, U.S.A.

HUGHES, Shirley. British, b. 1927. Children's fiction. *Publs:* Lucy and Tom series, 6 vols., 1960–87; The Trouble with Jack, 1970; Sally's Secret, 1973; Helpers, 1975; It's Too Frightening for Me, 1977; Dogger, 1977; Moving Molly, 1978; Up and Up, 1979; Here Comes Charlie Moon, 1980; Alfie Gets in First, 1981; Alfie's Feet, 1982; Charlie Moon and the Big Bonanza Bust–Up, 1982; Alfie Gives a Hand, 1983; An Evening at Alfie's, 1984; The Nursery Collection, 6 vols., 1985–86; Another Helping of Chips, 1986; Out and About, 1988; The Big Alfie and Annie Rose Story Book, 1988. Add: c/o Bodley Head, 32 Bedford Sq., London WC1B 3EL, England.

HUGHES, Ted. British, b. 1930. Children's fiction, Plays/Screenplays, Poetry, Literature. Ed., Modern Poetry in Trans. mag., London, 1964–71. Poet Laureate, 1984. *Publs:* The Hawk in the Rain (poetry), 1957; Lupercal (poetry), 1960; The Calm (play), 1961; Meet My Folks!, 1961; (with Thom Gunn) Selected Poems, 1962; The Wound (play), 1962; (ed. with Patricia Beer and Vernon Scannell) New Poems 1962, 1962; The Earth–Owl and Other Moon–People, 1963; How the Whale Became, 1963; (ed. with Thom Gunn) Five American Poets, 1963; (ed.) Here Today, 1963; Nessie the Mannerless Monster (in U.S. as Nessie the Monster), 1964; (ed.) Selected Poems, by Keith Douglas, 1964; The Burning of the Brothel (poetry), 1966; Recklings (poetry), 1966; Scapegoats and Rabies: A Poem in Five Parts, 1967; Wodwo, 1967; (ed.) Poetry in the Making, 1967; Animal Poems, 1967; Five Autumn Songs for Children's Voices (poetry), 1968; Seneca's Oedipus (play), 1968; Beauty and the Beast (play), 1968; The Iron Man: A Story in Five Parts (in U.S. as The Iron Giant: A Story in Five Parts), 1968; The Martyrdom of Bishop Farrer (poetry), 1970; A Crow Hymn, 1970; A Few Crows (poetry), 1970; Crow: From the Life and Songs of the Crow (poetry), 1970, 1972; The Coming of the King and Other Plays, 1970, augmented ed. as The Tiger's Bones and Other Plays for Children, 1973; Poetry Is, 1970; Crow Wakes: Poems, 1971; (with Ruth Fainlight and Alan Sillitoe) Poems, 1971; Sean, The Fool, The Devil and the Cats (play), 1971; Orghast (play), 1971; (ed.) A Choice of Emily Dickinson's Verse, 1971; (ed.) A Choice of Shakespeare's Verse (in U.S. as Poems: With Fairest Flowers While Summer Lasts: Poems from Shakespeare), 1971; (ed.) Selected Poems, by Yehuda Amichai, 1971; (ed.) Crossing the Water, by Sylvia Plath (in U.S. as Crossing the Water: Transitional Poems), 1971; Eat Crow (poetry), 1972; Selected Poems 1957–1967, 1972; In the Little Girl's Angel Gaze (poetry), 1972; The Iron Man (play), 1972; The Story of Vasco (play), 1974; Season Songs, 1975; Cave Birds (poetry), 1975; Earth–Moon: Poems, 1976; Gaudete, 1977; Moon–Bells (for children), 1978; Sunstruck, 1977; Chiasmadon, 1977; Moortown Elegies, 1978; A Solstice, 1978; Orts, 1978; Adam and the Sacred Nine, 1979; Moortown, 1979; Remains of Elmet, 1979; Henry Williamson, 1979; (ed.) Collected Poems, by Sylvia Plath, 1981; Under the North Star (verse for children), 1981; Selected Poems 1957–1981 (in U.S. as New Selected Poems), 1982; (ed. with Frances McCullough) The Journals

of Sylvia Plath, 1982; (ed. with Seamus Heaney) The Rattle Bag: An Anthology, 1982; River (verse; photographs by Peter Keen), 1983; What Is Truth? (verse for children), 1984; (ed.) Selected Poems, by Sylvia Plath, 1985; Flowers and Insects (poetry), 1986; Tales of the Early World (for children), 1988; The Cat and the Cuckoo (verse), 1988. Add: c/o Faber & Faber Ltd., 3 Queen Sq., London WC1N 3AU, England.

HUGHES, William (Taylor). American, b. 1936. Physics. Prof. of Physics, Bowdoin Coll., Brunswick, since 1967. *Publs:* Aspects of Biophysics, 1979, 1981; (with C.T. Settlemire) Microbiology, 1978. Add: Dept. of Physics, Bowdoin Coll., Brunswick, Me. 04011, U.S.A.

HUGHES, Zach. *See* **ZACHARY,** Hugh.

HUGILL, Stan(ley James). British, b. 1906. Music, Mythology/Folklore. Former seaman. *Publs:* Shanties From the Seven Seas, 1961, 3rd ed. 1980; Sailortown, 2nd ed. 1968; Shanties and Sailor Songs, 1969; Songs of the Sea, 1977; Sea Shanties, 1977; Shanties from Seven Seas, 1984. Add: 34 Copperhill St., Aberdovey, Gwynedd, Wales.

HULL, David Stewart. American, b. 1938. Film. Pres., Hull House Literary Agency, since 1987. East Coast Story Ed., Universal Pictures, 1966–69; Ed., Coward–McCann Inc., NYC, 1970; Vice–Pres., James Brown Assocs. Inc., NYC, 1971–81; Literary Agent, Peter Lampack Agency, 1981–87. *Publs:* Film in the Third Reich, 1969, 1973; James Henry Cafferty, 1986. Add: 240 E. 82nd St., New York, N.Y. 10028, U.S.A.

HULL, Eleanor. American, b. 1913. Children's fiction, History, Biography. Social Worker, New York City Dept., of Social Services, 1964–69. *Publs:* Tumbleweed Boy, 1949; The Third Wish, 1950; Papi, 1953; The Turquoise Horse, 1955; Suddenly the Sun, 1957; In the Time of the Condor, 1961; The Sling and the Swallow, 1963; Through the Secret Door, 1963; Everybody's Somebody, 1964; Noncho and the Dukes, 1964; The Church Not Made with Hands, 1965; A Trainful of Strangers, 1969; The Second Heart, 1973; Women Who Carried the Good News, 1975; Alice with Golden Hair, 1981; (contrib. ed.) Baptist Life and Thought 1600–1980, 1983; The Summer People, 1984. Add: c/o Macmillan, 866 Third Ave., New York, N.Y. 10022, U.S.A.

HULL, William D. American, b. 1918. Poetry, Literature, Translations. Prof. of English, Hofstra Univ., Hempstead, N.Y., since 1946. *Publs:* Saul at Ednor, 1954; Selected Poems 1942–52; Dandy Brown, 1959; The Catullus of William Hull, 1960, rev. ed. 1968; 19 Poems and 2 nP, 1962; The Other Side of Silence, 1964; The Mastery of Love, 1966; A Canon of the Critical Writings of Edgar Allen Poe, 1966; Collected Poems: 1942–68, 1970; Visions of Handy Hopper: Book I Flood, 1970, Book II Churn, 1971, Book III Park, 1972, Book IV Post, 1973, Book V Hinge, 1974, Book VI Breach, 1975, Book VII, Lock, 1976, Book VIII Rock, 1977, Book IX Knot, 1978, Book X Float, 1979; Index: Voices in Visions, 1980; The Hull Alliterative Beowulf, 1981. Add: 5 First Ave., Merrick, N.Y. 11566, U.S.A.

HULL, William E(dward). American, b. 1930. Theology/Religion. Provost and University Prof., Samford Univ., Birmingham, since 1987. Pastor, First Baptist Church, Shreveport, La., 1975–87. Fellow, 1954–55, Instr., 1955–58, Asst. Prof., 1958–61, Assoc. Prof., 1961–67, Prof., 1967–75, Dir. of Grad. Studies, 1968–70, Dean of the Sch. of Theology, 1969–75, and Provost, 1972–75; Southern Baptist Theological Seminary, Louisville, Ky. Pres., Assn. of Baptist Profs. of Religion, 1967–68. *Publs:* The Gospel of John, 1964; The Bible, 1974; Beyond the Barriers, 1981; Love in Four Dimensions, 1982; The Christian Experience of Salvation, 1987. Add: The Provost, Samford Univ., Birmingham, Ala. 35229, U.S.A.

HULME, Keri. New Zealander, b. 1947. Novels/Short stories, Poetry. Formerly, senior postwoman, Greymouth, and director for New Zealand television; Writer–in–Residence, Canterbury Univ., 1985. *Publs:* The Silences Between (poetry), 1982; The Bone People (novel), 1983; Lost Possessions (novella), 1985; The Windeater/Te Kaihau (short stories), 1986. Add: Okarito, Westland, New Zealand.

HULSE, James Warren. American, b. 1930. History. Prof. of History, Univ of Nevada, Reno, since 1962. Journalist, Nevada State Journal, 1954–59; Asst. Prof., Central Washington State Coll., Ellensburg, 1961–62. *Publs:* The Forming of the Communist International, 1964; The Nevada Adventure: A History, 1965, 5th ed. 1981; Revolutionists in London: A Study of Five Unorthodox Socialists, 1970; The University of Nevada: A Centennial History, 1974; Forty Years in the Wilderness, 1986. Add: Dept. of History, Univ. of Nevada, Reno, Nev. 89557, U.S.A.

HULTENG, John L(inne). American, b. 1921. Media, Writing/Journalism. Prof. of Communications, Stanford Univ., Calif., 1977–86, now Emeritus. Prof. of Journalism, Univ. of Oregon, Eugene, 1961–77 (joined faculty, 1955). Editorial Writer, 1947–53, and Editorial Page Ed., 1953–55, Providence Journal and Evening Bulletin, Rhode Island; Asst. Dir., East–West Communications Inst., East–West Center, Honolulu, 1974–75. Pres., American Assn. of Schools and Dept. of Journalism, 1966–67. *Publs:* (with R. Nelson) The Fourth Estate, 1971, 1983; The Opinion Function, 1973; Messenger's Motives: Ethical Problems of the News Media, 1975, 1985; The News Media: What Makes them Tick? 1979; Playing It Straight, 1981. Add: W. 1224 Riverside, No 184, Spokane, Wash., U.S.A.

HUME, John Robert. British, b. 1939. Archaeology/Antiquities, Business/Trade/Industry. Sr. Lectr. in History, Univ. of Strathclyde, Glasgow, since 1982 (Lectr., 1964–82); on assignment to Historic Buildings and Monuments Commn., since 1984. Member, Inland Waterways Amenity Advisory Council, since 1974. Chmn., Scottish Railway Preservation Soc., 1966–75; Treas., 1968–71, and Ed., 1971–79, Scottish Soc. for Industrial Archaeology, 1968–71; Dir., Scottish Industrial Archaeology Survey, 1978–85. *Publs:* (with J. Butt & I.L. Donnachie) Industrial History in Pictures: Scotland, 1968; The Industrial Archaeology of Glasgow, 1974; (with Michael Moss) Glasgow As It Was, 3 vols., 1975–76; (with Michael Moss) A Plumber's Pastime (photographs), 1975; The Industrial Archaeology of Scotland: The Lowlands and the Borders, 1976; (with Michael Moss) The Workshop of the British Empire, 1977; The Industrial Archaeology of Scotland; The Highlands and Islands, 1977; (with Michael Moss) Beardmore: History of a Scottish Industrial Giant, 1979; (with Michael Moss) The Making of Scotch Whisky, 1981; (with Michael Moss) A Bed of Nails, 1983; (with G. Douglas & M. Oglethorpe) Scottish Windmills, 1984; (with others) Scottish Brickmarks, 1985; (with Michael Moss) Shipbuilders to the World: A History of Harland Wolff, Belfast, 1986. Add: Dept. of History, Univ. of Strathclyde, Glasgow G1, Scotland.

HUME, Robert D. American, b. 1944. Literature. Prof. of English, Pennsylvania State Univ., since 1977. Asst., then Assoc. Prof. of English, Cornell Univ., Ithaca, N.Y., 1969–77. *Publs:* Dryden's Criticism, 1970; The Development of English Drama in the Late Seventeenth Century, 1976; The London Theatre World 1660–1800, 1980; Vice Chamberlain Coke's Theatrical Papers 1906–1715, 1982; The Rakish Stage, 1983; Producible Interpretation, 1985; Henry Fielding and the London Theatre, 1988. Add: Dept. of English, Pennsylvania State Univ., University Park, Pa. 16802, U.S.A.

HUMPHREY, James. American, b. 1939. Poetry, Literature. Poetry writing teacher, National Endowment for the Arts, since 1969, and for Poets Who Teach, since 1974. *Publs:* Argument for Love, 1970; The Visitor, 1972; An Homage: The End of Some More Land, 1972; Looking at Love: Poem for the Experimental Theatre, 1975; Concepts in Imagery, 1975; The Relearning, 1976; After I'm Dead, Will My Life Begin?, 1986; The Athlete, 1988. Add: c/o Poets Alive Press, P.O. Box 999, Harrisburg, N.C. 28075, U.S.A.

HUMPHREY, William. American, b. 1924. Novels/Short stories, Autobiography/Memoirs/Personal. *Publs:* The Last Husband and Other Stories, 1953; Home from the Hill, 1958; The Ordways, 1965; A Time and a Place: Stories (in U.K. as A Time and a Place: Stories of the Red River Country), 1968; The Spawning Run: A Fable, 1970; Proud Flesh, 1973; Farther Off from Heaven (autobiography), 1977; My Moby Dick (autobiography), 1978; Hostages of Fortune, 1984; The Collected Stories of William Humphrey, 1985; Open Season: Sporting Adventures, 1986; No Resting Place, 1989. Add: c/o Delacorte, 1 Dag Hammarskjold Plaza, New York, N.Y. 10017, U.S.A.

HUMPHREYS, B.V. See **SCHNEIDER,** B.V.H.

HUMPHREYS, Emyr (Owen). British, b. 1919. Novels/Short stories, Plays/Screenplays, Poetry. Teacher, Wimbledon Technical Coll., London, 1948–50, and Pwllheli Grammar Sch., N. Wales, 1951–54; Producer, BBC Radio, Cardiff, 1955–58; Drama Producer, BBC Television, 1958–62; Freelance writer and dir., 1962–65; First Lectr. in Drama, University Coll. of North Wales, Bangor, 1965–72. *Publs:* The Little Kingdom, 1947; The Voice of a Stranger, 1949; A Change of Heart, 1951; Hear and Forgive, 1952; A Man's Estate, 1955; The Italian Wife, 1957; Y Tri Llais, 1958; A Toy Epic, 1959; King's Daughter, 1959, televised as Siwan, 1960; The Gift, 1962; Outside the House of Baal, 1965; Natives, 1968; Roman Dream, 1968; An Apple Tree and a Pig, 1969; (with W.S. Jones) Dinas, 1970; Ancestor Worship: A Cycle of 18 Poems, 1970; National

Winner, 1971; Flesh and Blood, 1974; Landscapes, 1976; The Best of Friends, 1978; Penguin Modern Poets 17, 1978; The Anchor Tree, 1980; Miscellany Two, 1981; The Taliesin Tradition, 1983; Jones: a Novel, 1984; Salt of the Earth, 1985; An Absolute Hero, 1986; Open Secrets, 1988; The Triple Net, 1988. Add: Llinon, Pen y Berth, Llanfairpwll Gwyngyll, Gwynedd LL61 5YT, Wales.

HUMPHREYS, Laud. American, b. 1930. Sex, Sociology. Prof. of Sociology, Pitzer Coll., Claremont, Calif., and Prof. of Criminal Justice, Claremont Grad. Sch., since 1972. Chmn. of the Bd., Inst. for the Study of Human Resources, since 1978. Asst. Prof. of Sociology, Southern Illinois Univ., Edwardsville, 1968–70; Assoc. Prof. of Criminal Justice, State Univ. of New York at Albany, 1970–72. *Publs:* Tearoom Trade: Impersonal Sex in Public Places, 1970, 1975; Out of the Closets: The Sociology of Homosexual Liberation, 1972. Add: Pitzer Coll., Claremont, Calif. 91711, U.S.A.

HUMPHRYS, Geoffrey. See **HUMPHREYS,** Leslie George.

HUMPHRYS, Leslie George. Also writes as Geoffrey Humphrys. British, b. 1921. Children's non-fiction. Freelance journalist. Headmaster, North Walsham County Primary Sch., Norfolk, 1959–81. *Publs:* (as Geoffrey Humphrys) Time to Live, 1959; Wonders of Life (Books 1–4), 1959; Weather in Britain, 1963; Your Body at Work, 1963; Men Learn to Fly, 1966; Life is Exciting, 1966; Science Through Experience (Books 1–3), 1967; Fruit and Fruit Growing, 1969; Drinks, 1970; Men Travel in Space, 1971; Glass and Glass Making, 1971; Tools, 1974; Motion and Power, 1974; Machines, 1976. Add: 27 Litester Close, North Walsham, Norfolk, England.

HUNDLEY, Norris C., Jr. American. History. Prof. of History, Univ. of California, Los Angeles, since 1973 (Asst. Prof., 1965–69; Assoc. Prof., 1969–73); Chmn., UCLA Program on Mexico, since 1981. Managing Ed., Pacific Historical Review, since 1968; Member, Editorial Bd., Journal of San Diego History, since 1970; Chmn., Exec. Cttee., Inst. of American Cultures, since 1977; Co-Ed., Golden State series, since 1978. Instr., Univ. of Houston, Tex., 1963–64. *Publs:* John Walton Caughey, Historian, 1961; Dividing the Waters: A Century of Controversy Between the United States and Mexico, 1966; (ed. with John Schutz) The American West: Frontier and Region, 1969; California History: A Teacher's Manual, 1970; (ed.) The American Indian, 1974; Water and the West: The Colorado River Compact and the Politics of Water in the American West, 1975; (ed.) The Chicano, 1975; (ed.) The Asian American, 1976; (with John Caughey) California: History of a Remarkable State, 1982. Add: Dept. of History, Univ. of California, Los Angeles, Calif. 90024, U.S.A.

HUNKER, Henry L. American, b. 1924. Geography, Urban topics (Administration). Prof. of Geography and Public Policy and Management, Ohio State Univ., Columbus (faculty member since 1949, Asst. Dean, Coll. of Commerce and Admin., 1966–68; Dir., Center for Community Analysis, 1968–70). Battelle Fellow, Battelle Memorial Inst., Columbus, Ohio, 1972–73. *Publs:* Industrial Evolution of Columbus, Ohio, 1958; Ohio, 1960; (with A.J. Wright) Factors of Industrial Location in Ohio, 1963; (ed.) Introduction to World Resources, 1964; Industrial Development: Concepts and Principles, 1974; The Teaching and Study of Geography, 1980. Add: 88 West Royal Forest Blvd., Columbus, Ohio 43214, U.S.A.

HUNKIN, Tim(othy) Mark Trelawney. British, b. 1950. Children's fiction, Children's non-fiction. Exhibit designer, Science Museum, London. Cartoonist, The Observer, London, 1973–87. *Publs:* Mrs Gronkwonk and the Post Office Tower; Rudiments of Wisdom, 1974; Almost Everything There Is to Know, 1988. Add: Bulcamp House, Blythburgh, Suffolk IP19 9LG, England.

HUNNINGS, (Thomas) Neville March. British, b. 1929. Film, Law. Ed., Common Market Law Reports, since 1964; European Law Ed., Journal of Business Law, since 1974; Ed., European Commercial Cases, since 1978. Practised at English Bar, 1955–58; Information Officer, Central Office of Information, London, 1958–62; Ed., Cinema Studies, 1960–67, and Bulletin of Legal Developments, 1965–72; Sr. Research Officer, British Inst. of Intnl. and Comparative Law, 1964–72. *Publs:* Film Censors and the Law, 1967; (co-ed.) Legal Problems of an Enlarged European Community, 1972; Gazetteer of European Law, 1983. Add: 11 Russell Hill, Purley, Surrey CR2 2JB, England.

HUNT, Bernice Kohn. American, b. 1920. Children's fiction, Children's non-fiction, Human relations. Psychotherapist in private practice. Ed.-in-Chief, Dandelion Press, Inc., 1978–81. *Publs:* Our

Tiny Servants: Molds and Yeasts, 1962; Computers at Your Service, 1962; The Peaceful Atom, 1963; Everything Has a Shape, 1964; Everything Has a Size, 1964; The Marvelous Mammals: Monotremes and Marsupials, 1964; The Scientific Method, 1964; Light, 1965; Echoes, 1965; One Day It Rained Cats and Dogs, 1965; Koalas, 1965; Light You Cannot See, 1965; Fireflies, 1966; Telephones, 1967; Levers, 1967; The Bat Books, 1967; Racoons, 1968; Secret Codes and Ciphers, 1968; All Kinds of Seals, 1968; The Look–It–Up Book of Transportation, 1968; Ferns: Plants Without Flowers, 1969; Ramps, 1969; (with D. Weinick) A First Look at Psychology, 1969; Talking Leaves: The Story of Sequoyah, 1969; The Beachcomber's Book, 1970; Chipmunks, 1970; The Amistad Mutiny, 1971; How High Is Up?, 1971; Out of the Cauldron: A Short History of Witchcraft, 1972; The Busy Honeybee, 1972; One Sad Day, 1972; The Organic Living Book, 1972; The Gypsies, 1972; What a Funny Thing to Say!, 1974; The Spirit and the Letter: The Struggle for Rights in America, 1974; (with M. Hunt) Prime Time: A Guide to the Pleasures and Opportunities of the New Middle Age, 1975; Marriage, 1976; Great Bread!, 1977; The Divorce Experience, 1977; (with C. Sager) Intimate Partners, 1979. Add: 15 Kingstown Ave., East Hampton, N.Y. 11937, U.S.A.

HUNT, Charlotte. *See* **HODGES**, Doris M.

HUNT, (Sir) David (Wathen Stather). British, b. 1913. International relations/Current affairs, Autobiography/Memoirs/Personal. Dir., Observer Newspapers Ltd., since 1982. Pres., Soc. for the Promotion of Hellenic Studies, since 1986. Fellow, Magdalen Coll., Oxford, 1936–47; entered U.K. Diplomatic Service, 1947: First Secty., Pretoria, S. Africa, 1948–50; Private Secty. to the Prime Minister, 1950–52; Asst. Secty., 1952; Deputy High Commnr., Pakistan, 1954–56; Head, Central African Dept., 1956–59, and Asst. Under Secty. of State, 1959–60, Commonwealth Relations Office; Deputy High Commnr., 1960–62, and High Commnr., 1967–69, Nigeria; High Commnr., Uganda, 1962–65, Cyprus, 1965–66; Ambassador to Brazil, 1969–73. Chmn. of Govs., Commonwealth Inst., 1974–84. Montague Burton Visiting Prof. of Intnl. Relations, Univ. of Edinburgh, 1980. *Publs:* A Don at War, 1966; On the Spot, 1975; The Times Yearbook of World Affairs, 1978, 1979–80; Footprints in Cyprus, 1982; Gothic Art and the Renaissance in Cyprus, 1987; Caterina Cornaro, Queen of Cyprus, 1989. Add: Old Place, Lindfield, Sussex RH16 2HU, England.

HUNT, Edgar Hubert. British, b. 1909. Music. Prof. of Recorder and Flute, Trinity Coll. of Music, London, 1935–84. Ed., The Recorder and Music mag., London, since 1974. Co–Ed., The Amateur Musician, 1936–40; Ed., The English Harpsichord mag., 1973–86. *Publs:* The Recorder and Its Music, 1962; Robert Lucas Pearsall: The 'Compleat Gentleman' and His Music 1795–1856, 1977. Add: Rose Cottage, 8 Bois Lane, Chesham Bois, Amersham, Bucks. HP6 6BP, England.

HUNT, Edward H. British, b. 1939. History, Industrial relations. Sr. Lectr. in Economic History, London School of Economics, since 1969. Asst. Lectr. in Economic History, Queen's Univ. of Belfast, 1966–69. Book Review Ed., Economic History Review, 1981–86. *Publs:* Regional Wage Variations in Britain 1850–1914, 1973; British Labour History 1815–1914, 1981. Add: London School of Economics, Houghton St., London WC2A 2AE, England.

HUNT, E(verette) Howard. Also writes as John Baxter, Gordon Davis, Robert Dietrich and David St. John. American, b. 1918. Novels/Short stories, Mystery/Crime/Suspense. Scriptwriter and Ed., March of Time newsreel series, 1942–43; War Correspondent, Life mag., 1943; screenwriter, 1947–48; Attaché, American Embassy, Paris, 1948–49, Vienna, 1949–50, and Mexico City, 1950–53; Political Officer, Far East Command, Tokyo, 1954–56; First Secty., American Embassy, Montevideo, 1957–60; Consultant, Dept. of Defense, Washington, D.C., 1960–65; with Dept. of State, Washington, 1965–70; Vice–Pres. and Creative Dir., Robert R. Mullen, public relations firm, 1970–72; Consultant to President Richard M. Nixon, 1971–72 (served terms in federal prison for his role in Watergate scandal, 1973–74, 1975–77). *Publs:* novels—East of Farewell, 1942; Limit of Darkness, 1944; Stranger in Town, 1947; novels as John Baxter—A Foreign Affair, 1954; Unfaithful, 1955; A Gift for Gomala, 1962; mystery novels—Maelstrom, 1948, in paperback as Cruel Is the Night, 1955; Bimini Run, 1949; The Violent Ones, 1950; Dark Encounter, 1950; The Judas Hour, 1951; Whisper Her Name, 1952; Lovers Are Losers, 1953; The Berlin Ending, 1973; The Hargrave Deception, 1980; The Gaza Intercept, 1981; The Kremlin Conspiracy, 1985; Cozumel, 1985; mystery novels as Gordon Davis—I Came to Kill, 1953; House Dick, 1961, as Washington Payoff (as E. Howard Hunt), 1975; Counterfeit Kill, 1963; Ring Around Rosy, 1964; Where Murder Waits, 1965; mystery

novels as Robert Dietrich—One for the Road, 1954; The Cheat, 1954; Be My Victim, 1956; Murder on the Rocks, 1957; The House on Q Street, 1959; End of a Stripper, 1959; Mistress to Murder, 1960; Murder on Her Mind, 1960; Angel Eyes, 1961; Steve Bentley's Calypso Caper, 1961; Curtains for a Lover, 1961; My Body, 1962; mystery novels as David St. John—On Hazardous Duty, 1965; Return from Vorkuta, 1965; The Towers of Silence, 1966; Festival for Spies, 1966; The Venus Probe, 1966; One of Our Agents is Missing, 1967; The Mongol Mask, 1968; The Sorcerers, 1969; Diabolus, 1971; The Coven, 1972; other—Give Us This Day, 1973; Undercover: Memoirs of an American Secret Agent, 1974. Add: 1245 N.E. 85th St., Miami, Fla. 33138, U.S.A.

HUNT, Francesca. *See* **HOLLAND**, Isabelle.

HUNT, Gill. *See* **TUBB**, E.C.

HUNT, Gladys M. American, b. 1926. Human relations, Theology/Religion. *Publs:* Does Anyone Here Know God?, 1967; Honey for a Child's Heart, 1969; Listen to Me, 1969; Focus on Family Life, 1970, and as Family Secrets, 1985; The Christian Way of Death, 1971, as Living and Dying, 1981; John: Eyewitness, 1971; The God Who Understands Me: The Sermon on the Mount, 1971; It's Alive, 1971; Ms Means Myself, 1972; Revelation: The Lamb Who is the Lion, 1972; Hebrews: From Shadows to Reality, 1979; Romans: Made Righteous by Faith, 1980; Relationships, 1983; Stories Jesus Told, 1985; (with Keith L. Hunt) Not Alone: The Necessity of Relationships, 1985; Luke: A Daily Dialogue with God, 1986. Add: c/o Shaw Publishing, R.R. 3, Box 1000E, LaBelle, Fla. 33935, U.S.A.

HUNT, Irene. American, b. 1907. Children's fiction. English teacher, Oak Park public schs., Illinois, 1930–45; Instr. in Psychology, Univ. of South Dakota, Vermillion, 1946–50; Teacher, 1950–65, and Dir. of Language Art, 1965–69, Cicero public schs., Illinois. *Publs:* Across Five Aprils, 1964; Up a Road Slowly, 1966; Trail of Apple Blossom, 1968; No Promises in the Wind, 1970; The Lottery Rose, 1976; William, 1977; Claws of a Young Century, 1980; The Everlasting Hills, 1985. Add: 2591 Countryside Bvd., Clearwater, Fla. 33519, U.S.A.

HUNT, J(oseph) McVicker. American, b. 1906. Education, Psychology. Prof. Emeritus of Psychology and of Early Education, Univ. of Illinois, Urbana, since 1974 (Prof. of Psychology, 1951–74; Prof. of Early Education, 1967–74). Instr., and subsequently Assoc. Prof. of Psychology, Brown Univ., Providence, R.I., 1936–46; Dir., Inst. of Welfare Research, Community Service Soc. of New York, NYC, 1946–51. *Publs:* (ed., and co–author with N.S. Endler) Personality and the Behavioral Disorders, 2 vols., 1944, 1984; (with L.S. Kogan) Measuring Results in Social Casework: A Manual on Judging Movement, 1950; (with Kogan and Margaret Blenkner) Testing Results in Social Casework: A Field Test of the Movement Scale, 1953; (with Kogan and Phyllis F. Bartelme) A Follow–Up Study of the Results of Social Casework, 1953; Intelligence and Experience, 1961; The Challenge of Incompetence and Poverty: Papers on the Role of Early Education, 1969; (ed. and contrib.) Human Intelligence, 1972; (with Ina C. Uzgiris) Assessment in Infancy: Ordinal Scales of Psychological Development, 1975; Early Psychological Development and Experience, 1980 (with Ina C. Uzgiris) Infant Performance and Experience: New Findings with the Ordinal Scales, 1987. Add: 1807 Pleasant Circle, Urbana, Ill. 61801, U.S.A.

HUNT, Patricia Joan. British. Children's fiction, Children's non–fiction, Theology/Religion. Town and Country Planning Asst., Cheshire County Council, 1948–73, and Macclesfield Borough Council, 1974–79. *Publs:* First Steps in Teaching, 1966; Puffin the Vicarage Cat, 1966; Sunday School Single Handed, 1967; In and Around the Church, 1969; The History of Our Bible, 1971; What to Look for Inside a Church, 1972; What to Look for Outside a Church, 1972; A First Look at Churches and Chapels, 1974; A First Look at Temples and Other Places of Worship, 1975; A First Look at Water, 1977; St. Michael All–Colour Book of Bible Stories, 1978; Bible Stories, 1981, also published in 5 vols., 1983–84; Bible Alphabet Puzzlers, 1985, and 3 puzzle/quiz books, 1986; 8 children's bible story books, 1985; Let the Children Come, 1989. Add: 54 Bexton Rd., Knutsford, Cheshire WA16 0DS, England.

HUNT, Peter (Leonard). British, b. 1945. Children's fiction, Literary criticism. Sr. Lectr. in English, Univ. of Wales, Cardiff, since 1988. Lectr. in English, Univ. of Wales Inst. of Science and Technology, Cardiff, 1968–87; Visiting Prof., Univ. of Michigan, Ann Arbor, 1977; Visiting Lectr., Massachusetts Inst. of Technology, Cambridge, 1982. *Publs:* Children's Book Research in Britain, 1977, 1982; (ed.) Further Approaches to Research in Children's Literature, 1982; The Maps of Time,

1983; A Step Off the Path, 1985; Backtrack, 1986; (ed.) Bevis, 1989; (ed.) Critical Approaches to Children's Literature, 1989; Sue and the Honey Machine, 1989; Fay Cow and the Mystery of the Missing Milk, 1989; Going Up, 1989. Add: W. Sundial Cottage, Downend, Horsley, Stroud, Glos. GL6 0PF, England.

HUNT, Robert (William Gainer). British, b. 1923. Photography. Visiting Prof. of Physiological Optics, City Univ., London, since 1968. Asst. Dir. of Research, Kodak Ltd., Harrow, 1947–82. Served in the U.K. Ministry of Supply, 1943–46. *Publs:* The Reproduction of Colour, 1957, 4th ed. 1987; (trans.) Light, Colour, and Vision, 1957, 1968; Measuring Colour, 1987. Add: Kewferry House, 10 Kewferry Rd., Northwood, Middx., England.

HUNT, Sam. New Zealander, b. 1946. Poetry. *Publs:* Between Islands, 1964; A Fat Flat Blues (When Morning Comes), 1969; Selected Poems 1965–1969, 1970; A Song about Her, 1970; Postcard of a Cabbage Tree, 1970; Bracken Country, 1971; Letter to Jerusalem, 1971; Bottle Creek Blues, 1971; Bottle Creek, 1972; Beware the Man, 1972; Birth on Bottle Creek, 1972; South into Winter, 1973; Roadsong Paekakariki, 1973; Time to Ride, 1976; Drunkard's Garden, 1978; Collected Poems 1963–80, 1980; Three Poems of Separation, 1981; Running Scared, 1982; Approaches to Paremata, 1985; Selected Poems, 1987. Add: P.O. Box 1, Mana, Wellington, New Zealand.

HUNTER, Alan (James Herbert). British, b. 1922. Mystery/Crime/Suspense. Fiction Critic, Eastern Daily Press, Norwich, 1955–75. *Publs:* The Norwich Poems, 1945; Gently Does It, 1955; Gently by the Shore, 1956; Gently down the Stream, 1957; Landed Gently, 1957; Gently Through the Mill, 1958; Gently in the Sun, 1959; Gently with the Painters, 1960; Gently to the Summit, 1961; Gently Go Man, 1961; Gently Where the Roads Go, 1962; Gently Floating, 1963; Gently Sahib, 1964; Gently with the Ladies, 1965; Gently North–West, 1967 (in U.S. as Gently in the Highlands, 1975); Gently Continental, 1967; Gently Coloured, 1969; Gently with the Innocents, 1970; Gently at a Gallop, 1971; Vivienne: Gently Where She Lay, 1972; Gently French, 1973; Gently in Trees, 1974 (in U.S. as Gently Through the Woods, 1975); Gently with Love, 1975; Gently Where the Birds Are, 1976; Gently Instrumental, 1977; Gently to Sleep, 1978; The Honfleur Decision, 1980; Gabrielle's Way (in U.S. as The Scottish Decision), 1981; Fields of Heather (in U.S. as Death on the Heath), 1981; Gently Between Tides, 1982; Amorous Leander, 1983 (in U.S. as Death on the Broadlands), 1984; The Unhung Man, 1983; Once a Prostitute . . ., 1984; The Chelsea Ghost, 1985; Goodnight, Sweet Prince, 1986; Strangling Man, 1987; Traitor's End, 1988. Add: 3 St. Laurence Ave., Brundall, Norwich NR13 5QH, England.

HUNTER, Archibald MacBride. British, b. 1906. Theology/Religion. Prof. of New Testament Emeritus, and Master Emeritus of Christ's Coll., Univ. of Aberdeen, since 1971. *Publs:* Paul and His Predecessors, 1940; The Unity of the New Testament, 1943; Introducing the New Testament, 1945; The Gospel According to St. Mark, 1949; The Work and Words of Jesus, 1950; Interpreting the New Testament, 1951; Design for Life, 1953; Interpreting Paul's Gospel, 1954; The Epistle to the Romans, 1955; Introducing New Testament Theology, 1957; The Layman's Bible Commentary: vol. 22, 1959; Interpreting the Parables, 1960; Teaching and Preaching the New Testament, 1963; The Gospel According to John, 1965; The Gospel According to St. Paul, 1966; According to John 1968; Bible and Gospel, 1969; Exploring the New Testament, 1971; The Parables Then and Now, 1971; The New Testament for Today, 1974; Jesus Lord and Saviour, 1976; The Gospel Then and Now, 1978; Christ and the Kingdom, 1980; The Fifth Evangelist, 1980; Preaching the New Testament, 1981. Add: 32 Gartconnell Rd., Bearsden, Glasgow G61 3BP, Scotland.

HUNTER, Elizabeth. *See* **CHACE,** Isobel.

HUNTER, Eric J. British, b. 1930. Librarianship. Sr. Lectr., Liverpool Polytechnic, since 1976 (Lectr., 1969–76). Previous appointments in public libraries in Bootle, 1948–65, Warrington, 1965–68, and Liverpool, 1968–69. *Publs:* Appreciation of the Career of John J. Ogle, 1966; Anglo–American Cataloguing Rules 1967: An Introduction, 1972; Examples Illustrating Anglo–American Cataloguing Rules, 1973, 3rd ed. 1989; Cataloguing: A Guidebook, 1974; Display for Librarians, 1975; AACR 2: An Introduction, 1979, 1989; (with K.G.B. Bakewell) Cataloguing, 1979, 1983; The ABC of BASIC: An Introduction to Programming for Librarians, 1982; Computerized Cataloguing, 1985; Classification Made Simple, 1988. Add: 44 Cornwall Way, Ainsdale, Southport, Merseyside PR8 3SH, England.

HUNTER, Evan. Also writes as Ed McBain, Richard Marsten, Ezra Hannon, and Hunt Collins. American, b. 1926. Novel/Short stories, Mystery/Crime/Suspense, Science fiction/Fantasy, Children's fiction, Plays/Screenplays. *Publs:* Find the Feathered Serpent (juvenile), 1952; (as Richard Marsten) Rocket to Luna (juvenile), 1953; (as Richard Marsten) Danger: Dinosaurs (juvenile), 1953; (as Hunt Collins) Cut Me In, 1954; The Blackboard Jungle, 1954; (as Richard Marsten) The Spiked Heel, 1956; (as Hunt Collins) Tomorrow's World, 1956; Second Ending, 1956; (as Ed McBain) Cop Hater, 1956; (as Ed McBain) The Mugger, 1956; (as Ed McBain) The Pusher, 1956; The Jungle Kids (short stories), 1956, in U.K. as The Last Spin, 1960; (as Richard Marsten) Vanishing Ladies, 1957; (as Ed McBain) The Con Man, 1957; Strangers When We Meet, 1958, screenplay, 1960; (as Ed McBain) Killer's Choice, 1958; (as Ed McBain) Killer's Payoff, 1958; (as Ed McBain with Craig Rice) April Robin Murders, 1958; (as Ed McBain) Lady Killer, 1958; (as Ed McBain) Killer's Wedge, 1959; A Matter of Conviction, 1959; (as Ed McBain) 'Til Death, 1959; (as Ed McBain) King's Ransom, 1959; (as Ed McBain) Give the Boys a Great Big Hand, 1960; (as Ed McBain) The Heckler, 1960; (as Ed McBain) The Heckler, 1960; (as Ed McBain) See Them Die, 1960; Mothers and Daughters, 1961; (as Ed McBain) Lady, Lady, I Did it!, 1961; The Remarkable Harry (juvenile), 1961; The Wonderful Button (juvenile), 1961; (as Ed McBain) Like Love, 1962; (as Ed McBain) The Empty Hours (short stories), 1962; The Birds (screenplay), 1962; (as Ed McBain) Ten Plus One, 1963; Happy New Year, Herbie (short stories), 1963; Buddwing, 1964; (as Ed McBain) Ax, 1964; The Easter Man (in U.S. as A Race of Hairy Men) (play), 1964; (as Ed McBain) The Sentries, 1965; (as Ed McBain) He Who Hesitates, 1965; (as Ed McBain) Doll, 1965; The Paper Dragon, 1966; (as Ed McBain) Eighty Million Eyes, 1966; A Horse's Head, 1967; Last Summer, 1968; (as Ed McBain) Fuzz, 1968; Sons, 1969; (as Ed McBain) Shotgun, 1969; The Conjuror (play), 1969; (as Ed McBain) Jigsaw, 1970; (as Ed McBain) Hail, Hail, The Gang's All Here!, 1971; Nobody Knew They Were There, 1971; The Beheading and Other Stories, 1971; Every Little Crook and Nanny, 1972; (as Ed McBain) Sadie When She Died, 1972; (as Ed McBain) Let's Hear It for the Deaf Man, 1972; The Easter Man: A Play and Six Stories, 1972; Seven, 1972; Come Winter, 1973; (as Ed McBain) Hail to the Chief, 1973; (as Ed McBain) Bread, 1974; Streets of Gold, 1974; (as Ed McBain) A Second 87th Precinct Omnibus, 1975; (as Ed McBain) Where There's Smoke, 1975; (as Ed McBain) Blood Relatives, 1975; (as Ezra Hannon) Doors, 1975; (as Ed McBain) Guns, 1976; (as Ed McBain) So Long as You Both Shall Live, 1976; The Chisholms, 1976; Me and Mr. Stenner (juvenile), 1976; (as Ed McBain) Long Time No See, 1977; (as Ed McBain) Goldilocks, 1978; (as Ed McBain) Calypso, 1979; Walk Proud, 1979; (as Ed McBain) Ghosts, 1980; Love, Dad, 1981; (as Ed McBain) Heat, Rumpelstilskin, 1981; (as Ed McBain) The McBain Brief (stories), 1982; (as Ed McBain) Beauty and the Beast, 1982; (as Ed McBain) Ice, 1983; Far from the Sea, 1983; Lizzie, 1984; (as Ed McBain) Snow White and Rose Red, 1985; (as Ed McBain) Eight Black Horses, 1985; (as Ed McBain) Cinderella, 1986; (as Ed McBain) Another Part of the City, 1986; (as Ed McBain) Poison, 1987; (as Ed McBain) After Poison, 1987; (as Ed McBain) Puss in Boots, 1987; (as Ed McBain) Tricks, 1987; (as Ed McBain) McBain's Ladies, 1988; (as Ed McBain) The House That Jack Built, 1988; (as Ed McBain) Lullaby, 1989. Add: c/o John Farquharson Ltd., 250 W. 57th St., New York, N.Y. 10107, U.S.A.

HUNTER, Jack D(ayton). American, b. 1921. Mystery/Crime/Suspense. Pres., Jack D. Hunter Creative Services Inc., Newark, Del., since 1978; Writing Coach, St. Augustine Record, St. Augustine, Fla., since 1983, and Florida Times–Union and Jacksonville Journal, Jacksonville, Fla., since 1981. Reporter, Chester, Pa. Times, 1939–40; served in the U.S. Army, 1941–46; Reporter, Wilmington, Del. Journal, 1947–50; Exec. Secty., U.S. House of Representatives, Washington, D.C., 1950–52; Advertising and Public Relations Exec., E.I. duPont de Nemours Inc., 1952–75; Columnist, Wilmington, Del. Sunday Journal, 1975–77; Special Counsel, U.S. Senate, Washington, D.C., 1977–79; Adjunct Prof., Flagler Coll., St. Augustine, Fla., 1980–83. *Publs:* The Blue Mas, 1964; The Expendable Spy, 1965; One of Us Works for Them, 1967; Spies Inc., 1969; Word of Life (biography), 1973; The Blood Order, 1979; The Terror Alliance, 1980; The Tin Cravat, 1981; Florida Is Closed Today, 1982; Signs of Evil Times, 1985; Judgment in Blood, 1986; The Flying Cross, 1987. Add: 218 Raintree Trail, St. Augustine, Fla. 32086, U.S.A.

HUNTER, J(ames) Paul. American, b. 1934. Literary criticism/history. Prof. of English, Univ. of Chicago, since 1987. Instr., Univ. of Florida, 1957–59; Instr., Williams Coll., Williamstown, Mass., 1962–64; Asst. Prof., Univ. of California, Riverside, 1964–66; Assoc. Prof., 1966–68; Prof. of English, 1968–80, and Chmn. of English, 1973–79, Emory Univ., Atlanta; Dean, Coll. of Arts and Sciences, Univ. of Rochester, N.Y., 1981–86. *Publs:* The Reluctant Pilgrim, 1966; (ed.) Moll Flanders: A

Critical Edition, 1970; (ed.) Norton Introduction to Poetry, 1973, 3rd ed., 1986; (co–ed.) Norton Introduction to Literature, 1973, 4th ed., 1985; Occasional Form, 1975; (ed.) The Plays of Edward Moore, 1982. Add: Dept. of English, Univ. of Chicago, Chicago, Ill. 60637, U.S.A.

HUNTER, Jim. British, b. 1939. Novels/Short stories, Literature. Sr. Lectr., Christ Church Coll., Canterbury, Kent, since 1986. Asst. English Master, Bradford Grammar Sch., Yorks., 1962–66; Sr. English Master, Bristol Grammar Sch., 1966–75; Asst. Headmaster, Broadoak Sch., Weston–Super–Mare, 1975–78; Headmaster, Weymouth Grammar Sch., Dorset, 1978–81; Headmaster, Leighton Park Sch., Reading, 1981–86. *Publs:* The Sun in the Morning, 1961; Sally Cray, 1963; Earth and Stone (in U.S. as A Place of Stone), 1963; (ed.) Modern Short Stories, 1964; The Metaphysical Poets, 1965; The Flame, 1966; Gerard Manley Hopkins, 1966; (ed.) The Modern Novel in English, 1966; (ed.) Modern Poets, 5 vols., 1968–81; (ed.) Henry IV, part I, 1969; Walking in the Painted Sunshine, 1970; (ed.) The Human Animal: Short Stories for Schools, 1973; Percival and the Presence of God, 1978; Top Stoppard's Plays, 1982. Add: c/o Faber, 3 Queen Sq., London WC1N 3AU, England.

HUNTER, Kristin. American, b. 1931. Novels/Short stories, Children's fiction, Plays/Screenplays. Sr. Lectr. in English, Univ. of Pennsylvania, Philadelphia, since 1983 (Lectr. in Creative Writing, 1972–79; Adjunct Prof. of English, 1980–83). Copywriter, Lavenson Bureau of Advertising, Philadelphia, Pa., 1952–59; Research Asst., Sch. of Social Work, Univ. of Pennsylvania, Philadelphia, 1961–62; Copywriter, Wermen Schorr, Philadelphia, 1962–63; Information Officer, City of Philadelphia, 1963–64 and 1965–66. *Publs:* God Bless the Child, 1964; The Double Edge (play), 1965; The Landlord, 1966; The Soul Brothers and Sister Lou, 1968; Boss Cat, 1971; The Pool Table War, 1972; Uncle Daniel and the Racoon, 1972; Guests in the Promised Land: Stories, 1973; The Survivors, 1975; The Lakestown Rebellion, 1978; Lou in the Limelight, 1981. Add: c/o Don Congdon Assocs., 156 Fifth Ave., Suite 625 New York, N.Y. 10010, U.S.A.

HUNTER, Michael (Cyril William). British, b. 1949. Intellectual history, Biography. Reader in History, Birkbeck Coll., Univ. of London, since 1984 (Lectr., 1976–84). Research Fellow, Worcester Coll., Oxford, 1972–75, and Univ. of Reading, 1975–76. *Publs:* John Aubrey and the Realm of Learning, 1975; Science and Society in Restoration England, 1981; The Royal Society and Its Fellows 1660–1700, 1982; (with Annabel Gregory) An Astrological Diary of the 17th Century, 1988. Add: Dept. of History, Birkbeck coll., Malet St., London WC1E 7HX, England.

HUNTER, Mollie. Scottish, b. 1922. Children's fiction, Plays/Screenplays. *Publs:* A Love–Song for My Lady (play), 1961; Stay for an Answer (play), 1961: Patrick Kentigern Keenan (in U.S. as The Smartest Man in Ireland), 1963; Hi Johnny, 1963; The Kelpie's Pearls, 1964; The Spanish Letters, 1964; A Pistol in Greenyards, 1965; The Ghosts of Glencoe, 1966; Thomas and the Warlock, 1967; The Ferlie, 1968, as The Enchanted Whistle, 1986; the Bodach (in U.S. as The Walking Stones), 1970; The Lothian Run, 1970; The 13th Member, 1971; The Haunted Mountain, 1972; A Sound of Chariots, 1972; The Stronghold, 1974; A Stranger Came Ashore, 1975; Talent Is Not Enough: Writing for Children, 1976; The Wicked One, 1977; A Furl of Fairy Wind, 1977; The Third Eye, 1979; You Never Knew Her As I Did, 1981; The Dragonfly Years (in U.S. as Hold on to Love), 1983; The Knight of the Golden Plain, 1983; I'll Go My Own Way, in U.S. as Cat, Herself, 1985; The Mermaid Summer, 1988. Add: The Shieling, Milton, by Drumnadrochit, Inverness–shire, Scotland.

HUNTER, Norman (George Lorimer). British, b. 1899. Children's fiction, Recreation/Leisure/Hobbies. Sr. Copywriter, S.H. Benson Ltd., London, 1938–49; Chief Copywriter, P.N. Barrett & Co., 1949–59, and Central Advertising, 1959–70, both in Johannesburg, South Africa. *Publs:* Simplified Conjuring, 1923. Advertising Through the Press, 1924; New and Easy Magic, 1925; Hey Presto, 1931; Professor Branestawm series, 22 vols., 1933–83; New Conjuring Without Skill, 1935; The Dribblesome Teapot, 1938; Bad Barons of Crashbania, 1940; Jingle Tales, 1949; Successful Conjuring, 1951; The Puffin Book of Majic, 1968; The Home Made Dragon, 1971; Wizards Are a Nuisance, 1973; Dust–Up at the Royal Disco and Other Incredible Stories, 1975; Vanishing Ladies and Other Magic, 1978; Cound Bakwerdz on the Carpet, 1978; Sneeze and Be Slain, 1980. Add: 23 St. Olave's Close, Staines, Middx. TW18 2LH, England.

HUNTER, Sam. American, b. 1923. Art. Prof. of Art History, Princeton Univ., New Jersey, since 1969. Taught at the Univ. of California at Los Angeles, 1955–57, and at Brandeis Univ., Waltham, Mass., 1963–65; Dir., Minneapolis Inst. of the Arts, 1958–60, Rose Art Museum, 1960–65, and Jewish Museum, 1965–68. *Publs:* Masters of Twentieth–Century Art, 1980; The Apocalyptic Vision, 1983; New Image, 1983; George Segal, 1983; The Museum of Modern Art, 1984; Painting and Sculpture since 1940: An American Renaissance, 1985. Add: 146 Mercer St., Princeton, N.J. 08540, U.S.A.

HUNTINGTON, Samuel Phillips. American, b. 1927. Military/Defence, Politics/Government. Eaton Prof. of Science of Government, Harvard Univ., Cambridge., since 1982 (joined faculty, 1950; Dillon Prof. of Intnl. Affairs, 1981–82); Dir., Center for Intnl. Affairs, Harvard Univ., since 1978. Vice–Pres., 1984–85, and Pres., 1986–87, American Political Science Assoc. Asst. Dir., 1958–59, Assoc. Dir., 1959–62, Inst. of War and Peace Studies, and Assoc. Prof. of Government, 1959–62, Columbia Univ., NYC. Member of Council, American Political Science Assn., 1969–71; Member, Presidential Task Force on Intnl. Development, 1969–70; Member, Commn. on U.S./Latin American Relations, 1974/75; Coord. of Security Planning, Natl. Security Council, 1977–78. Co–ed., Foreign Policy journal, 1970–77. *Publs:* The Soldier and the State: The Theory and Politics of Civil–Military Relations, 1957; The Common Defense: Strategic Programs in National Politics, 1961; (ed.) Changing Patterns of Military Politics, 1962; (co–author) Political Power: USA/USSR, 1964; Political order in Changing Societies, 1968; (co–ed.) Authoritarian Politics in Modern Society: The Dynamics of Established One–Party Systems, 1970 (co–author) The Crisis of Democracy, 1975; (with J.M. Nelson) No Easy Choice: Political Participation in Developing Countries, 1976; American Politics: The Promise of Disharmony, 1981; (ed.) The Strategic Imperative: New Policies for American Security, 1982; (co–author) Living with Nuclear Weapons, 1983; (co–ed.) Global Dilemmas, 1985; (co–ed.) Reorganizing America's Defense, 1985; (co–ed.) Understanding Political Development, 1987. Add: 1737 Cambridge St., Cambridge, Mass. 02138, U.S.A.

HUNTLEY, James Robert. American, b. 1923. International relations/Current affairs. Independent Consultant on Intnl. Affairs, Bainbridge Island, Wash. With Govt. of State of Washington, 1949–51, and U.S. Foreign Service, 1952–60; Program Assoc., Intnl. Affairs Div., Ford Foundn., NYC, 1965–67; Secty.–Gen., Council of Atlantic Colleges, London, 1967–68; freelance writer and lectr., England, 1968–74; Research Fellow, Battelle Memorial Inst., Seattle, 1974–83; Pres., Atlantic Council of the U.S., 1983–85. *Publs:* (co–ed.) The Atlantic Community, A Force for Peace, 1963; The NATO Story, 1965, 1969; (with W.R. Burgess) Europe and America—The Next Ten Years, 1970; (ed.) Teaching about the American Impact on Europe, 1970; Toward New Transatlantic Education Relationships, 1970; Man's Environment and the Atlantic Alliance, 1971, 1972; (ed.) Teaching about Collective Security and Conflict, 1972; Uniting the Democracies: Institutions of the Atlantic–Pacific System, 1980. Add: 1811 Eagle Harbor Lane N.E., Bainbridge Island, Wash. 98110, U.S.A.

HUNTON, Richard Edwin. American, b. 1924. Medicine/Health. Physician, Scurry Clinic, Greenwood, S.C., since 1954; Clinical Asst. Prof. of Family Medicine, Medical Univ. of South Carolina. Resident Physician, Spartanburg Gen. Hosp., S.C., 1953–54. Book reviewer, Broadman Press, 1973–75. *Publs:* Formula for Fitness, 1966. Add: Wendover Rd., Forest Hills, Greenwood, S.C. 29649, U.S.A.

HUPPE, Bernard F. American, b. 1911. Language/Linguistics, Literature. Emeritus Distinguished Service Prof. of English, State Univ. of New York at Binghamton. Asst. Prof., Princeton Univ., N.J., 1946–50. *Publs:* (with D.W. Robertson) Piers Plowman and Scriptural Tradition, 1951; (with J. Kaminsky) Logic and Language, 1956; Doctrine and Poetry, 1959; (with D.W. Robertson) Fruyt and Chaff: A Study in Chaucer's Allegory, 1963: A Reading of the Canterbury Tales, 1964; Web of Words, 1969; (with P. Szarmach) The O.E. Homily, 1978; The Hero in the Earthly City: A Study and Translation of Beowulf, 1983; Beowulf: A Translation, 1987; (librettist and composer) Captain Coram's Kids, 1988; (librettist and composer) Prodigal, 1989. Add: Box 406, Castine, Maine 04421, U.S.A.

HURD, Edith Thacher. American. Children's fiction, Children's nonfiction, Natural history. *Publs:* Hurry, Hurry, 1960; Stop, Stop, 1961; Come and Have Fun, 1962; The SooSo Cat, 1963; Johnny Lion's Book, 1965, 1978; Who Will Be Mine?, 1966; The Day the Sun Danced, 1966; What Whale Where?, 1966; Little Dog Dreaming, 1967; The Blue Heron Tree, 1968; Johnny Lion's Bad Day, 1970; Catfish, 1970; The White Horse, 1970; Come with Me to Nursery School, 1970; The Mother Beaver, 1971; The Mother Deer, 1972; Wilson's World (in U.K. as Wilkie's World), 1971; Johnny Lion's Rubber Boots, 1972; The Mother Whale,

1973; The Mother Owl, 1974; The Mother Kangaroo, 1976; Look for a Bird, 1977; The Mother Chimpanzee, 1978; Dinosaur My Darling, 1978; Under the Lemon Tree, 1980; The Black Dog Who Went into the Woods, 1980; I Dance in My Red Pyjamas, 1982; The Song of the Sea Otter, 1983. Add: 1635 Green St., San Francisco, Calif. 94123, U.S.A.

HURD, Michael John. British, b. 1928. Songs, lyrics and libretti, Music, Biography. Freelance composer, writer, and lectr. on music. Prof. of Theory, Royal Marines Sch. of Music, 1953–59. *Publs:* Immortal Hour: The Life and Period of Rutland Boughton, 1962; Young Person's Guide to Concerts, 1962; Young Person's Guide to Opera, 1963; Young Person's Guide to English Music, 1965; Sailor's Songs and Shanties, 1965; (librettist and composer) Little Billy, 1966; (librettist and composer) Jonah-Man Jazz, 1966; Soldiers Songs and Marches, 1966; Benjamin Britten, 1966; The Composer, 1968; An Outline History of European Music, 1969; Elgar, 1969; Vaughan Williams, 1970; Mendelssohn, 1970; (librettist and composer) Mr. Punch, 1970; (librettist with D. Hughes, and composer) The Widow of Ephesus, 1972; (librettist and composer) Swingin' Samson, 1974; (librettist and composer) Rooster Rag, 1976; (librettist and composer) Pilgrim, 1978; The Ordeal of Ivor Gurney, 1978; Tippett, 1978; The Oxford Junior Companion to Music, 1979; The Orchestra, 1980; Vincent Novello—and Company, 1981; (librettist and composer) Adam-in-Eden, 1982; (librettist and composer) Mrs. Beeton's Book, 1983; (librettist and composer) A New Nowell, 1987; (librettist and composer) Capitain Corern's Kids, 1988; (librettist and composer) Prodigal, 1989. Add: 4 Church St., West Liss, Hants., England.

HURLBUT, Cornelius Searle, Jr. American, b. 1906. Earth sciences. Prof. of Mineralogy, Harvard Univ., Cambridge, Mass., 1940–72; Visiting Prof., Boston Coll., 1972–78. *Publs:* (ed.) Minerals and How to Study Them, by E.S. Dana, 1949; (with H.E. Wenden) The Changing Science of Mineralogy, 1964; Minerals and Man, 1968; (with C. Klein) Manual of Mineralogy, 1985; (ed.) The Planet We Live On: An Illustrated Encyclopedia of the Earth Sciences, 1978; (with G.S. Switzer) Gemology, 1979. Add: c/o Dept. of Earth and Planetary Sciences, Harvard Univ., 24 Oxford St., Cambridge, Mass. 02138, U.S.A.

HURLEY, John. American, b. 1928. Plays/Screenplays, Poetry, Literature, Speech/Rhetoric. Prof. of English, Santa Ana Coll., Calif., since 1964. *Publs:* Of Men and Machines, 1968; The Tragic Dr. Jellom, 1969; A Practical Rhetoric, 1970; Untitled, 1970; Madam Liberty, 1973; Mr. Rugglesump, 1973; Twice in Eden: A Musical Play, 1978; Writing Your Way to the Top, 1979; Remedial English Diagnosis Test, 1980; Making Your Language Do What You Want, 1980; Assassination American Style, 1981; (with Jerry Sullivan) Teaching Literature Inductively, 1982; Shakespeare's-XVIII, 1982; Stopping by House on Scary Morning, 1988; Autumn Skies, 1988; First Person: DC Register, 1988. Add: Dept. of English, Rancho Santiago Coll., Santa Ana, Calif. 92706, U.S.A.

HURWITZ, Johanna (née Frank). American, b. 1937. Children's fiction, Children's non-fiction. Children's Librarian, Great Neck Public Library, New York, since 1978. Children's Librarian, New York Public Library, 1959–64; Lectr. in Children's Literature, Queen's Coll., 1965–68; Librarian, Calhoun School, New York, 1968–75; and New Hyde Park school district, New York, 1975–77. *Publs:* Busybody Nora, 1976; Nora and Mrs. Mind-Your-Own-Business, 1977; The Law of Gravity, 1978; Much Ado About Nothing, 1978; Aldo Applesauce, 1979; New Neighbours for Nora, 1979; Once I Was a Plum Tree, 1980; Superduper Teddy, 1980; Aldo Ice Cream, 1981; Baseball Fever, 1981; The Rabbi's Girls, 1982; Tough-Luck Karen, 1982; Rip-Roaring Russell, 1983; DeDe Takes Charge!, 1984; The Hot and Cold Summer, 1984; The Adventures of Ali Baba Berstein, 1985; Russell Rides Again, 1985; Hurricane Elaine, 1986; Yellow Blue Jay, 1986; Class Clown, 1987; Russell Sprouts, 1987; The Cold and Hot Winter, 1988; Teacher's Pet, 1988; Anne Frank: Life in Hiding, 1988; Hurray for Ali Baba Bernstein, 1989. Add: 10 Spruce Pl., Great Neck, N.Y. 11021, U.S.A.

HUSON, Paul. British, b. 1942. Supernatural/Occult topics. Former designer and art director. *Publs:* Mastering Witchcraft: A Practical Guide for Witches, Warlocks and Covens, 1970; The Devil's Picturebook: The Complete Guide to Tarot Cards, 1971; (ed.) The Coffee-Table Book of Witchcraft and Demonology, 1973; Mastering Herbalism, 1974; How to Test and Develop Your E.S.P., 1977; The Keepsake, 1981; The Offering, 1984. Add: c/o Bamberger Business management, 10866 Wilshire Blvd., Suite 1000, Los Angeles, Calif. 40024, U.S.A.

HUSTON, Mervyn J(ames). Canadian, b. 1912. Sciences (general), Sports/Physical education/Keeping fit, Humor/Satire. Prof. Emeritus, Univ. of Alberta (Lectr., 1939–43; Asst. Prof., 1943–46; Acting Dir., Sch.

of Pharmacy, 1946–48; Dir., 1948–55; Dean, Faculty of Pharmacy and Pharmaceutical Sciences, 1955–78). *Publs:* Textbook of Pharmaceutical Arithmetic, 1959; Great Canadian Lover, 1964; Tests and Dictionary of Scientific Words, 1965; Toasts to the Bride, 1969; Canada Eh to Zed, 1973; Great Golf Humor, 1978; Golf and Murphy's Law, 1981; Gophers Don't Pay Taxes, 1981. Add: Faculty of Pharmacy and Pharmaceutical Sciences, Univ. of Alberta, Edmonton, Alta. T6G 2N8, Canada.

HUTCHIN, Kenneth Charles. Also writes as Kenneth Challice, Kenneth Travers, and as A Family Doctor. British, b. 1908. Medicine/Health. Medical Consultant, the Daily Telegraph, London. Staff Surgeon, Herts. Constabulary, 1946–75; Local Treasury Medical Officer, and Gen. Practitioner, National Health Service, 1948–75; Medical Officer, Herts. Soc. for the Blind, 1949–75. Medical Corresp., Sunday Telegraph, London, 1961–65; Member, Attendance Allowance Bd., Dept. of Health and Social Security, 1975–80. *Publs:* Your Diet and Your Health, 1959; Heart Disease and High Blood Pressure, 1960; Allergy, 1961; Coughs, Colds and Bronchitis, 1961; Slipped Discs, 1962; Your Health, 1962; (in U.K. as A Family Doctor) How Not to Kill Your Husband, 1962; The Change of Life, 1963; Diabetes, 1964; (as Kenneth Challice) Family Health and First Aid, 1964; Young Man's Guide to Health, 1964; How Your Body Uses Food, 1965; (in U.K. as A Family Doctor) How Not to Kill Your Wife, 1965; Health of the Businessman, 1966; (in U.K. as A Family Doctor) How Not to Kill Your Children, 1968; Looking Ahead—Health and Sex, 1969; (in U.K. as A Family Doctor) How Not to Kill Yourself, 1973. Add: Wold Cottage, Broad Campden, Chipping Campden, Glos., England.

HUTCHINGS, Arthur (James Bramwell). British, b. 1906. Music, Biography. Emeritus Prof. of Music, University of Durham (Prof., 1947–68) and Univ. of Exeter (Prof., 1968–74). Chmn. of the Corp., Trinity Coll. of Music; Music Advisory Panel, BBC; Editorial Bd., The English Hymnal. *Publs:* Schubert, 1946; A Companion to Mozart's Piano Concertos, 1948; Delius, 1949; The Invention and Composition of Music, 1950; The Baroque Concerto, 1961; Church Music in the Nineteenth Century, 1966; Pelican History of Music, vol. 3, 1967; (contrib.) Music in Britain 1918-1960, 1974; Mozart the Man: The Music, 1976; Purcell (BBC Guides), 1980. Add: Colyton, Devon EX13 6NJ, England.

HUTCHINS, Francis Gilman. Also writes as Frank Madison. American, b. 1939. History, Autobiography/Memoirs/Personal. Historical Consultant, Indian Litigation, since 1977. Asst. Prof., Dept. of Govt., Harvard Univ., 1968–73; Member, Sch. of Social Science, Inst. for Advanced Study, Princeton, N.J. 1973–74; Sr. Research Fellow, Center for the History of the American Indian, Newberry Library, Chicago, 1976–77. *Publs:* The Illusion of Permanence: British Imperialism in India, 1967; (as Frank Madison) A View from the Floor: The Journal of a U.S. Senate Page Boy, 1967; India's Revolution: Gandhi and the Quit India Movement, 1973; Mashpee: The Story of Cape Cod's Indian Town, 1979; Young Krishna, 1980; (trans.) Animal Fables of India, 1985. Add: P.O. Box 723, Wellesley, Mass. 02181, U.S.A.

HUTCHINS, Hazel J. Canadian, b. 1952. Novels/Short stories, Children's fiction. *Publs:* The Three and Many Wishes of Jason Reid, 1983; Anastasia Morningstar and the Crystal Butterfly, 1984; Leanna Builds a Genie Trap, 1986; Ben's Snow Song: A Winter Picnic, 1987. Add: Box 185, Canmore, Alta. T0L 0M0, Canada.

HUTCHINS, Pat. British, b. 1942. Children's fiction. Freelance writer and illustrator. Art Dir., J. Walter Thompson Ltd., advertising agency, London, 1963–66. *Publs:* Rosie's Walk, 1968; Tom and Sam, 1968; The Surprise Party, 1969; Clocks and More Clocks, 1970; Changes, Changes, 1971; Titch, 1971; Good–Night, Owl, 1972; The Wind Blew, 1974; The Silver Christmas Tree, 1974; Don't Forget the Bacon, 1975; The House That Sailed Away, 1976; Follow That Bus, 1977; Happy Birthday Sam, 1978; The Best Train Set Ever, 1978; One Eyed Jake, 1979; The Tale of Thomas Mead, 1979; The Mona Lisa Mystery, 1980; One Hunter, 1981; You'll Soon Grow into Them, Titch!, 1983; The Curse of the Egyptian Mummy, 1983; King Henry's Palace, 1983; The Very Worst Monster, 1985; The Doorbell Rang, 1986; Where's the Baby, 1987. Add: 75 Flask Walk, London NW3, England.

HUTCHINSON, (William Patrick Henry) Pearse. Irish, b. 1927. Poetry, Translations. Trans., Intnl. Labor Org., Geneva, Switz., 1951–53; Drama Critic, Radio Eireann, 1957–61, and Telefis Eireann, 1968; Gregory Fellow in Poetry, Univ. of Leeds, 1971–73. *Publs:* (trans.) Poems, by Josep Carner, 1962; Tongue Without Hands, 1963; Faoustin Bhacach (Imperfect Confession), 1968; Expansions, 1969; (trans.) Friend Songs: Medieval Love–Songs from Galaico–Portuguese, 1970; Watching the Morning Grow, 1973; Frost Is All Over, 1975; Selected Poems, 1982.

Add: c/o Gallery Press, 19 Oakdown Rd., Dublin 14, Ireland.

HUTCHINSON, Ron. British. Plays/Screenplays. Resident Writer, Royal Shakespeare Co., London, 1978–79. *Publs:* Says I, Says He, 1980; Rat in the Skull, 1984; Connie (novelization of television series), 1985. Add: c/o Judy Daish Assocs., 83 Eastbourne Mews, London W2 6LQ, England.

HUTCHISON, Henry. British, b. 1923. Education, Theology/Religion. Minister, Carmunnock Parish Church, since 1977. Minister, Erskine Church, Saltcoats, Ayrshire, 1948–53, Crosshill–Victoria Church, Glasgow, 1953–57, and St. Paul's Church, Peterborough, Ont., 1957–60; Principal, Stanstead Coll., Que., 1960–63; Asst. Prof. of Education, Brandon Univ., Man., 1965–67; Lectr. in Education, Glasgow Univ., 1967–77. *Publs:* The Church and Spiritual Healing, 1955; A Faith to Live By, 1959; The Beatitudes and Modern Life, 1960; Scottish Public Educational Documents, 1973; Kirk Life in Old Carmunnock, 1978; Carmunnock Church 1854–1947, 1979; God Believes in You!, 1980; Well I'm Blessed!, 1981; Have a Word with God, 1981; Healing Through Worship, 1981; A Faith That Conquers, 1982. Add: 161 Waterside Rd., Carmunnock, by Glasgow G76 9AJ, Scotland.

HUTCHISON, Sidney Charles. British, b. 1912. Institutions/Organizations. Secty., Royal Academy of Arts, London, 1968–82, now Hon. Archivist (joined staff, 1929; Librarian, 1949–68; Secty. of Loan Exhibitions, 1955–68). *Publs:* The Homes of the Royal Academy, 1956; The History of the Royal Academy 1768–1968, 1968, and new ed. 1768–1986, 1986. Add: 60 Belmont Close, Mt. Pleasant, Cockfosters, Herts. EN4 9LT, England.

HUTHMACHER, J. Joseph. American, b. 1929. History. Richards Prof. of History, Univ. of Delaware, Newark, since 1970. Gen. Co–Ed., The American Forum Series, Schenkman Publishing Co., since 1972. Instr., Ohio State Univ., Columbus, 1956–57; Assoc. Prof., Georgetown Univ., Washington, D.C., 1957–66; Prof., Rutgers Univ., New Brunswick, N.J., 1966–70. *Publs:* Massachusetts People and Politics 1919–1933, 1959; (author and designer) American History (overhead projection transparencies), 1966; (ed.) Twentieth–Century America: An Interpretation with Readings, 1966; (ed. with B. Labaree and V.P. de Santis) America Past and Present, 2 vols., 1967; A Nation of Newcomers: Ethnic Minority Groups in American History, 1967; Senator Robert F. Wagner and the Rise of Urban Liberalism, 1968; (gen. ed.) From Colony to Global Power: A History of the United States, 6 vols., 1972–73; (ed.) The Truman Years: The Reconstruction of Postwar America, 1972; Trial by War and Depression: The United States 1917–1941, 1973; (ed. with W. Susman) Herbert Hoover and the Crisis of American Capitalism, 1973. Add: c/o Atheneum, 115 Fifth Ave., New York, N.Y. 10003, U.S.A.

HUTTON, John (Harwood). British, b. 1928. Novels/Short stories. Sr. Lectr. in English, Cartrefle Coll., North East Wales Inst., Wrexham, since 1967; retired, 1985. Supply teacher, West Bromwich Education Authority, 1953; Asst. Lectr. in English, University Coll., Bangor, 1953–54; Lectr., Wigan and District Mining and Technical Coll., 1954–58; Head of the English Dept., Ruabon Girls' Grammar Sch., 1959–67. *Publs:* 29 Herriott Street, 1979; Accidental Crimes, 1983. Add: Gwylfa, Old Holyhead Rd., Berwyn, Llangollen, Clwyd, Wales.

HUTTON, Warwick. British, b. 1939. Crafts. Illustrator, painter and glass engraver. Sr. Lectr., Cambridgeshire Coll. of Arts and Technology. Visiting Lectr., Morley Coll., 1973–75. *Publs:* Making Woodcuts, 1974; Noah and the Great Flood, 1978; The Sleeping Beauty, 1979; Nose Tree, 1981; Beauty and the Beast, 1985; Moses in the Bulrushes, 1986; Jonah and the Great Fish, 1986; Adam and Eve, 1987; The Tinderbox, 1988; Theseus and the Minotaur, 1989. Add: 52 Warkworth Terr., Cambridge CB1 1EE, England.

HUXLEY, Anthony Julian. British, b. 1920. Botany, Horticulture, Geography. Freelance writer, photographer, and editorial consultant. Scientific Officer, Operational Research, RAF and Ministry of Aircraft Production, 1941–46; Economic Research Officer, British Overseas Aircraft Corp., 1947–48; on staff 1949–67, and Ed. 1967–71, Amateur Gardening. Pres., The Horticultural Club, London, 1975; Member of the Council, Royal Horticultural Soc., 1979. *Publs:* Cacti and Succulents, 1953; House Plants, 1954; (trans.) Exotic Plants of the World, 1955; (trans.) Beauty in the Garden, 1957; Indoor Plants, 1957; Cacti and Succulents, 1960; (trans.) Orchids of Europe, 1961; Wild Flowers of the Countryside, 1962; Garden Terms Simplified, 1962; (gen. ed.) Standard Encyclopedia of the World's Mountains, 1962; (gen. ed.) Standard Encyclopedia of the World's Oceans and Islands, 1962; (ed. with R. Kay Gresswell) Standard Encyclopedia of the World's Rivers and Lakes, 1965; (with Oleg Polunin) Flowers of the Mediterranean, 1965, 1973; Mountain Flowers, 1967, 1986; Flowers in Greece: An Outline of the Flora, 1967, 1972; (ed.) Garden Perennials and Water Plants, 1971; (ed.) Garden Annuals and Bulbs, 1971; (ed.) Evergreen Garden Trees, and Shrubs, 1973; (ed.) Deciduous Garden Trees and Shrubs, 1973; Plant and Planet, 1974, 1987; (ed.) The Financial Times Book of Garden Design, 1975; (ed.) Encyclopedia of the Plant Kingdom, 1977; (with William Taylor) Flowers of Greece and the Aegean, 1977; (with Alyson Huxley) Huxley's House of Plants, 1978; An Illustrated History of Gardening, 1979; (gen. ed.) Success with House Plants, 1979; Penguin Encyclopedia of Gardening, 1981; (with P. and J. Davies) Wild Orchids of Britain and Europe, 1983; (ed.) The Macmillan World Guide to Houseplants, 1983; Green Inheritance, 1984; The Painted Garden, 1988. Add: 50 Villiers Ave., Surbiton, Surrey KT5 8BD, England.

HUXLEY, Elspeth (Josceline). British, b. 1907. Novels, Mystery/Crime/Suspense, Travel/Exploration/Adventure, Autobiography/Memoirs/Personal. *Publs:* White Man's Country: Lord Delamere and the Making of Kenya, 2 vols., 1935; Red Strangers, 1939; Murder at Government House, 1939; Murder on Safari, 1940; Death of an Aryan, 1941; (with M. Perham) Race and Politics in Kenya, 1944; The Walled City, 1948; The Sorcerer's Apprentice, 1948; I Don't Mind If I Do, 1951; Four Guineas, 1954; A Thing to Love, 1954; The Red Rock Wilderness, 1957; No Easy Way, 1957; The Flame Trees of Thika, 1959; A New Earth, 1960; The Mottled Lizard, 1962; The Merry Hippo, 1963; Forks and Hope, 1964; A Man From Nowhere, 1964; Back Street New Worlds, 1965; Brave New Victuals, 1965; Their Shining Eldorado: A Journey Through Australia, 1967; Love Among the Daughters, 1968; The Challenge of Africa, 1971; (ed.) The Kingsleys: An Anthology, 1973; Livingstone and His African Journeys, 1974; Florence Nightingale, 1975; Gallipot Eyes: A Wiltshire Diary, 1976; Scott of the Antarctic, 1977; Nellie: Letters from Africa, 1980; The Prince Buys the Manor, 1982; Last Days in Eden, 1984; Out in the Midday Sun: My Kenya, 1985. Add: Green End, Oaksey, Malmesbury, Wilts., England.

HUXLEY, George Leonard. British, b. 1932. History, Literature. Dir., Gennadius Library, American Sch. of Classical Studies at Athens, since 1986; Hon. Research Assoc., Trinity Coll., Dublin, since 1983. Fellow, All Souls Coll., Oxford, 1955–61; Prof. of Greek, Queen's Univ. of Belfast, 1962–83. *Publs:* Achaeans and Hittites, 1960; Early Sparta, 1962; The Early Ionians, 1966; Greek Epic Poetry from Eumelos to Panyassis, 1969; (ed. with J.N. Coldstream) Excavations and Studies in Kythera, 1972; Pindar's Vision of the Past, 1975; On Aristotle and Greek Society, 1979; Why Did the Byzantine Empire Not Fall to the Arabs? (lecture), 1986; Homer and the Travellers, 1988. Add: c/o Royal Irish Academy, 19 Dawson St., Dublin 2, Ireland.

HUXTABLE, Ada Louise. American, b. 1921. Architecture, Art. Architecture Critic and Member of the Editorial Bd., The New York Times, 1963–82. Asst. Curator, Museum of Modern Art, NYC, 1946–50; art and architecture critic, 1950–63. *Publs:* Pier Luigi Nervi, 1960; Classic New York, 1964; Will They Ever Finish Bruckner Boulevard?, 1970; Kicked a Building Lately?, 1976; The Tall Building Artistically Reconsidered, 1985; Goodbye History, Hello Hamburger, 1986; Architecture Anyone?, 1986. Add: 969 Park Avenue, New York, N.Y. 10028, U.S.A.

HUXTABLE, (William) John (Fairchild). British, b. 1912. Theology/Religion. Member, Joint Cttee. of Translation of New English Bible, since 1948, and Central Cttee., World Council of Churches, since 1968. Congregational Church Minister, Newton Abbot, Devon, 1937–42, and Palmers Green, London, 1942–54; Principal, New Coll., Univ. of London, 1953–64; Minister Secty., Congregational Church in England and Wales, 1966–72. Moderator of the United Reformed Church, 1972–73; Moderator of the Free Church Federal Council, 1976–77. *Publs:* John Owen's True Nature of a Gospel Church; (co–ed.) A Book of Public Worship; The Promise of the Father; The Bible Says; The Preacher's Integrity; Christian Unity; A New Hope for Church Unity, 1977. Add: Manor Cottage, East Ogwell, Newton Abbot, Devon.

HWANG, David Henry. American, b. 1957. Plays. *Publs:* Broken Promises: Four Plays, 1983; The Sound of a Voice (acting edition), 1984; The Dance and the Railroad and Family Devotions (acting ed.), 1989; FOB and the House of Sleeping Beauties (acting ed.), 1989; M. Butterfly, 1989; FOB and Other Plays, 1989. Add: c/o Paul Yamamoto/William Craver, Writers and Artists Agency, 70 W. 36th St., New York, N.Y. 10018, U.S.A.

HYAM, Ronald. British, b. 1936. History. Lectr. in History since

1960, Fellow and Librarian since 1962, Magdalene Coll., Cambridge; Univ. Lectr. since 1965, Cambridge Univ. *Publs:* Elgin and Churchill at the Colonial Office 1905–1908, 1968; A History of Isleworth Grammar School, 1969; The Failure of South African Expansion 1908–1948, 1972; (with G.W. Martin) Reappraisals in British Imperial History, 1975; Britain's Imperial Century 1815–1914; A Study of Empire and Expansion, 1976; Empire and Sexuality: The British Experience, 1990. Add: Magdalene Coll., Cambridge CB3 0AG, England.

HYAMS, Joe. American, b. 1923. Novels/Short stories, Screenplays, Recreation/Leisure/Hobbies, Sports/Fitness, Biography. Ed., reporter, and columnist. *Publs:* (with W. Wagner) My Life with Cleopatra, 1963; (with M. Riddle) A Weekend Gambler's Handbook, 1963; (with E. Head) How to Dress for Success, 1966; (with P. Sellers) Seller's Market, 1966; Bogie, 1966; A Field of Buttercups, 1968; (with T. Murton) Accomplices to the Crime, 1969; (with T. Trabert) Winning Tactics for Weekend Tennis, 1972; Mislaid in Hollywood, 1973; (with P. Gonzales) Winning Tactics for Singles, 1973; (with Billie Jean King) Billie Jean King's Secrets of Winning Tennis, 1974; Bogart and Bacall; A Love Story, 1975; The Pool (novel), 1978; Zen in the Martial Arts, 1978; The Last Award, 1981; Murder at the Academy Awards, 1981; Playboy Guide to Self-Defense, 1981; (with Chuck Norris) Secrets of Inner Strength, 1987; (with Michael Reagan) On the Outside Looking In, 1987. Add: 540 N. Beverly Glen Blvd., West Los Angeles, Calif. 90024, U.S.A.

HYDE, Dayton O. American, b. 1925. Novels, Natural history. Cattle rancher, since 1950. *Publs:* Sandy, 1968; Yamsi, 1971; Cranes in My Corral, 1972; Brand of a Boy, 1972; The Last Free Man, 1974; (ed.) Raising Wild Waterfowl in Captivity, 1974; Strange Companions, 1975; Island of the Loons, 1984; The Major, the Poacher and the Wonderful One–Trout River, 1985; One Summer in Montana, 1985; Thunder Down the Track, 1986; Don Coyote, 1987; Wilderness Ranch, 1988. Add: Box 234, Chiloquin, Ore., U.S.A.

HYDE, Eleanor. *See* **COWEN,** Frances.

HYDE, H(arford) Montgomery. British, b. 1907. Criminology/Law enforcement/Prisons, History, Law, Sociology, Biography. Barrister–at–Law, since 1934. Ulster Unionist Member of Parliament (U.K.) for North Belfast, 1950–59; Prof. of History, Punjab Univ., Lahore, Pakistan, 1959–62. *Publs:* The Rise of Castlereagh, 1933; (ed. with Marchioness of Londonderry) The Russian Journals of Martha and Catherine Wilmot, 1934; (ed. with Marchioness of Londonderry) More Letters from Martha Wilmot: Impressions of Vienna, 1935; The Empress Catherine and Princess Dashkov, 1935; (with G.R. Falkiner Nuttall) Air Defence and the Civil Population, 1937; Princess Lieven, 1937; Londonderry House and Its Pictures, 1937; Judge Jeffreys, 1940, 1948; Mexican Empire, 1946; Privacy and the Press, 1947; A Victorian Historian: Letters of W.E.H. Lecky, 1947; John Law, 1948, 1969; (ed.) The Trials of Oscar Wilde, 1948, 4th ed. 1973; Cases that Changed the Law, 1951; (ed.) The Romantic 90s, by Richard Le Gallienne, 1951; Mr. and Mrs. Beeton, 1951; Carson, 1953, 1974; (ed.) Trial of Craig and Bentley, 1954; United in Crime, 1954; (ed.) Mr. and Mrs. Daventry, by Frank Harris, 1956; The Strange Death of Lord Castlereagh, 1959; (ed.) Trial of Sir Roger Casement, 1960, 1964; Sir Patrick Hastings, 1960; Recent Developments in Historical Method and Interpretation, 1960; Simla and the Simla Hill States under British Protection, 1815–1835, 1961; An International Casebook of Crime, 1962; The Quiet Canadian, 1962; Room 3603, 1963; Oscar Wilde: The Aftermath, 1963; Norman Birkett, 1964; A History of Pornography, 1964; Cynthia, 1965; The Story of Lamb House, Rye, 1966; Lord Reading, 1967; Strong for Service: Life of Lord Nathan, 1968; Henry James at Home, 1969; Their Good Names, 1970; The Love that Dared Not Speak its Name (in U.K. as The Other Love), 1970; Stalin, 1971; Baldwin, 1973; Oscar Wilde, 1974; The Cleveland Street Scandal, 1976; Neville Chamberlain, 1976; British Air Policy Between the Wars 1918–39, 1976; Crime Has Its Heroes, 1976; Solitary in the Ranks, 1977; The Londonderrys, 1979; The Atom Bomb Spies, 1980; Secret Intelligence Agent, 1982; (ed.) The Annotated Oscar Wilde, 1982; Lord Alfred Douglas, 1984; A Tangled Web, 1986; George Blake: Superspy, 1987; (ed.) Oscar Wilde: The Complete Plays, 1988; (ed.) J.F. Bloxam: The Priest and the Acolyte, 1988; Christopher Millard (Stuart Mason), 1988. Add: Westwell House, Tenterden, Kent, England.

HYDE, Janet S. American, b. 1948. Psychology, Sex. Prof. of Psychology, Denison Univ., Ohio, since 1979. Assoc. Prof. of Psychology, Bowling Green State Univ., Ohio, 1972–79. *Publs:* Half the Human Experience: The Psychology of Women, 1976, 1985; Understanding

Human Sexuality, 1979, 3rd ed. 1986; (co–ed.) The Psychology of Gender, 1986. Add: c/o Johns Hopkins Univ. Press, 701 W. 40th St., Suite 275, Baltimore, Md. 21211, U.S.A.

HYDE, Michael. British, b. 1908. Children's fiction, Travel/Exploration/Adventure. Contrib., BBC Schs. Broadcasts, since 1950, and Gardening Column, The Guardian, London, since 1968. Former primary and secondary sch. teacher. *Publs:* Arctic Whaling Adventures, 1955; Nootka, 1968; What Do They Do? (Macmillan Educational Series), 1971. Add: 63 Kingtree Ave., Cottingham, North Humberside, England.

HYLAND, Ann. Also writes magazine articles as Laurence Ross and Trailrider. British, b. 1936. Sports/Physical education/Keeping fit. Author of Ross's Roundup for Horse World mag. under the name Laurence Ross. *Publs:* Beginners Guide to Western Riding, 1971; Beginners Guide to Endurance Riding, 1974; Endurance Riding, 1976; Foal to Five Years, 1980. Add: c/o 4 Blacksmiths Lane, Rainham, Essex, England.

HYLAND, (Henry) Stanley. British, b. 1914. Mystery/Crime/Suspense, History. Research Librarian, House of Commons, London; Producer, BBC–TV, London; Founder and now Consultant, Hy Vision Ltd., London. *Publs:* (ed.) King and Parliament: A Selected List of Books, 1951; Curiosities from Parliament, 1955; Who Goes Hang? (mystery novel), 1958; Green Grow the Tresses–O (mystery novel), 1967; Top Bloody Secret (mystery novel), 1969. Add: Cage Cottage, Gt. Bardfield, Essex, England.

HYMAN, Harold M(elvin). American, b. 1924. History. William P. Hobby Prof. of History, Rice Univ., Houston, Tex., since 1968 (Chmn. of Dept., 1968–70). Member, Bd. of Eds., Reviews in American History, since 1964, Ulysses S. Grant Assn., since 1968, and The American Journal of Legal History, since 1970. Asst. Prof. of History, Earlham Coll., Richmond, Ind., 1952–55; Visiting Prof., 1955–56, and Prof. of History, 1957–63, Univ. of California, Los Angeles; Assoc. Prof., Arizona State Univ., Tempe, 1956–57; Member, Bd. of Eds., Journal of American History, 1970–74. *Publs:* Era of the Oath: Northern Loyalty Tests during the Civil War and Reconstruction, 1954; To Try Men's Souls: Loyalty Tests in American History, 1959; (with B.P. Thomas) Stanton: The Life and Times of Lincoln's Secretary of War, 1962; Soldiers and Spruce: Origins of the Loyal Legion of Loggers and Lumbermen: The Army's Labor Union of World War I, 1963; (ed.) The Radical Republicans and Reconstruction, 1861–1870, 1966; (ed.) New Frontiers of the American Reconstruction, 1967; (ed. with L.W. Levy) Freedom and Reform: Essays in Honor of Henry Steele Commager, 1967; (ed.) Carleton Paker: The Casual Laborer and Other Essays, 1972; (ed.) Heard 'Round the World: The Impact of the Civil War and Reconstruction, 1968; (ed. with F.B. Hyman) The Circuit Court Opinions of Salmon Portland Chase, 1972; (ed.) Sidney George Fisher: The Trial of the Constitution, 1972; (ed. with H.L. Trefousse) The Political History of the United States of America During the Great Rebellion, 1860–1865, The Political History of the United States of America During the Period of Reconstruction, April 15, 1865–July 1865–July 15, 1870, and the Handbook of Politics, 6 vols., 1972–73; A More Perfect Union: The Impact of the Civil War and Reconstruction on the Constitution, 1973; Crisis and Confidence: 1860–1870, 1975; (with W. Wiecek) Equal Justice under Law: Constitutional Development, 1835–1875, 1982; Quiet Past and Stormy Present: War Powers in American History, 1986; American Singularity, 1987. Add: Dept. of History, Rice Univ., Houston, Tex. 77251, U.S.A.

HYMAN, Ronald T(erry). American, b. 1933. Education. Prof. of Education, Rutgers Univ., New Brunswick, N.J., since 1974 (Assoc. Prof., 1966–74). Research Asst. Columbia Univ., NYC, 1962–64; Asst. Prof., Queens Coll., City Univ. of New York, 1964–66. Lawyer, practising in New Jersey. *Publs:* The Principles of Contemporary Education, 1966; (with A.A. Bellack, H.M. Kliebard and F.L. Smith) The Language of the Classroom, 1966; (ed.) Teaching: Vantage Points for Study, 1968, rev. ed. 1974; Ways of Teaching, 1970, rev. ed. 1974; (ed.) Contemporary Thought on Teaching, 1971; (ed. with M. Hillson) Change and Innovation in Elementary and Secondary Organization, 2nd ed. 1971; (ed.) Approaches in Curriculum, 1973; (ed. with S.L. Baily and contrib.) Perspectives on Latin America, 1974; School Administrator's Handbook of Teacher Supervision and Evaluation Methods, 1975; (with A. Teplitsky) Walk in My Shoes, 1976; Paper, Pencils, and Pennies: Games for Learning and Having Fun, 1977; (with A. Pessin) The Securities Industry, 1977; (with K. Goldstein–Jackson and N. Rudnick) Experiments with Everyday Objects: Science Activities for Children, Parents, and Teachers, 1978;

Stimulation Gaming for Values Education: The Prisoner's Dilemma, 1978; Strategic Questioning, 1979; Improving Discussion Leadership, 1980; Administrator's Faculty Supervision Handbook, 1986; Administrator's Staff Development Activities Manual, 1986. Add: Grad. Sch. of Education, Rutgers Univ., New Brunswick, N.J. 08903, U.S.A

HYNES, Samuel. American, b. 1924. Literature. Prof. of English since 1976, and Woodrow Wilson Prof. of Literature since 1978, Princeton Univ., New Jersey. Member of Faculty, 1949–68, and Prof. of English Literature, 1965–68, Swarthmore Coll.; Prof. of English, Northwestern Univ., Evanston, Ill., 1968–76. *Publs:* (ed.) Further Speculations, by T.E. Hulme, 1955; The Pattern of Hardy's Poetry, 1961; (ed.) English Literary Criticism: Restoration and Eighteenth Century, 1963; William Golding, 1964; (ed.) The Author's Craft and Other Critical Writings of Arnold Bennett, 1968; The Edwardian Turn of Mind, 1968; (ed.) Romance and Realism, 1970; Edwardian Occasions, 1972; The Auden Generation: Literature and Politics in England in the 1930's, 1976; (ed.) Complete Poetical Works of Thomas Hardy, 3 vols., 1982–85; (ed.) Thomas Hardy, 1984; Flights of Passage: Reflections of a World War II Aviator, 1988. Add: Dept. of English, Princeton Univ., Princeton, N.J. 08544, U.S.A.

I

IACOCCA, Lee (Lido Anthony). American, b. 1924. Autobiography/Memoirs. Chmn. of the Bd. and Chief Exec. Officer, Chrysler Corp., Detroit, since 1979 (Pres. and Chief Operating Officer, 1978–79). Pres., Ford Motor Co., Detroit, 1970–78 (Exec. Vice-Pres., 1967–69). *Publs:* (with William Novak) Iacocca: An Autobiography, 1984; (with N.R. Kleinfeld) Talking Straight, 1988. Add: Chrysler Corp., 12000 Chrysler Dr., Highland Park, Mich. 48288, U.S.A.

IAMS, Jack (Samuel H. Iams, Jr.). American, b. 1910. Novels/Short stories, Mystery/Crime/Suspense. Freelance writer since 1945. Formerly a journalist with the London Daily Mail, Baltimore News–Post, Pittsburgh Press, and the New York Daily News. *Publs:* novels—Nowhere with Music, 1938; Table for Four, 1939; The Countess to Boot, 1941; Prophet by Experience, 1943; Prematurely Gay, 1948; mystery novels—The Body Missed the Boat, 1947; Girl Meets Body, 1947; Death Draws the Line, 1949; Do Not Murder Before Christmas, 1949; A Shot of Murder, 1950; What Rhymes with Murder?, 1950; Into Thin Air, 1952; A Corpse of the Old School, 1955. Add: c/o Gollancz, 14 Henrietta St., London WC2E 8QJ, England.

IANNUZZI, John Nicholas. American, b. 1935. Mystery/-Crime/Suspense, Law. Lawyer in New York City; Adjunct Prof. of Law, Fordham Univ. Sch. of Law. *Publs:* What's Happening?, 1963; Part 35, 1970; Sicilian Defense, 1972; Courthouse, 1975; J.T., 1982; Cross Examination: The Mosaic Art, 1983. Add: Iannuzzi and Iannuzzi, 233 Broadway, New York, N.Y. 10279, U.S.A.

IBBOTSON, Eva (Maria Charlotte Michele, née Wiesner). British, b. 1925. Children's fiction, Historical/Romance, Plays/Screenplays. *Publs:* The Great Ghost Rescue, 1975; Which Witch, 1979; A Countess Below Stairs, 1981; Magic Flute, 1982; The Worm and the Toffee Nosed Princess, 1983; A Glove Shop in Vienna, 1984; A Company of Swans, 1985; The Haunting of Hiram C. Hopgood, 1987; Madensky Square, 1988. Add: 2 Collingwood Terr., Jesmond, Newcastle upon Tyne NE2 2JP, England.

ICE, Jackson Lee. American, b. 1925. Philosophy, Theology/Religion. Prof., Florida State Univ., Tallahassee, since 1973 (Asst. Prof., 1955–63; Assoc. Prof., 1963–73). Teaching Fellow, Harvard Univ., Cambridge, Mass., 1952–54. *Publs:* (with John Carey) The Death of God Debate, 1967; (with John Carey) Dass Gott Auferstehe, 1970; Schweitzer: Prophet of Radical Theology, 1971. Add: 1005 Gardenia Dr., Tallahassee, Fla. 32312, U.S.A.

IGGERS, Georg G(erson). American, b. 1926. History. Prof. of History, State Univ. of New York, Buffalo, since 1965, and Distinguished Prof. since 1978. Member of faculty, Univ. of Akron, Ohio, 1948–50, Philander Smith Coll., Little Rock, Ark., 1950–56, Univ. of Arkansas, Fayetteville, 1956–57, Dillard Univ., New Orleans, La., 1957–63, Tulane Univ., New Orleans, 1958–60 and 1963, and Roosevelt Univ., Chicago, 1963–65. *Publs:* The Cult of Authority: The Political Philosophy of the Saint–Simonians, 1958, 1970; The German Conception of History, 1968; (trans. and ed.) The Doctrine of Saint–Simon: An Exposition, 1972; (ed. with K. von Moltke) Leopold von Ranke: The Theory and Practice of History, 1973; New Directions in European Historiography: Four Essays, 1975; (ed. with Harold T. Parker) International Handbook of Historical Studies, 1979. The Social History of Politics, 1986. Add: 100 Ivyhurst Rd., Buffalo, N.Y. 14226, U.S.A.

IGGULDEN, John Manners. Australian, b. 1917. Novels/Short stories. Chmn., Planet Lighting Group Pty. Ltd. and other companies. *Publs:* Breakthrough, 1960; The Storms of Summer, 1960; The Clouded Sky, 1963; Dark Stranger, 1965; (ed.) Summer's Tales 3, 1966; The Promised Land Papers, vol. 1: The Revolution of the Good, 1986, vol. 2: How Things Are Wrong and How to Fix Them, 1989. Add: Promised Land, Via Bellingen, N.S.W. 2454, Australia.

IGNATOW, David. American, b. 1914. Poetry, Autobiography/Memoirs/Personal. Prof. Emeritus, City Univ. of New York; Lectr., Columbia Univ., NYC, since 1977 (Adjunct Prof., Sch. of the Arts, 1969–76); Pres. Emeritus, Poetry Soc. of America. Co-Ed., Beloit Poetry Journal, 1949–59; Poetry Ed., The Nation, 1962–63; Instr., New Sch. for Social Research, 1964–65; Poet–in–Residence, Univ. of Kentucky, Lexington, 1965–66, Univ. of Kansas, Lawrence, 1966–67, and Vassar Coll., Poughkeepsie, N.Y., 1967–68; Co–Ed., Chelsea Mag., 1967–73; Ed.–at–Large, American Poetry Review, 1973–77; Visiting Prof., New York Univ., 1985. *Publs:* Poems, 1948; The Gentle Weight Lifter, 1955; Say Pardon, 1962; Figures of the Human, 1964; Rescue the Dead, 1968; Earth Hard, 1968; Poems: 1934–69, 1970; The Notebooks of David Ignatow, 1974; Facing the Tree, 1975; Selected Poems, 1975; Tread the Dark, 1978; Open Between Us, 1979; Whisper to the Earth, 1982; Leaving the Door Open, 1984; New and Collected Poems: 1975–85, 1986; The One in the Many: A Poet's Memoirs, 1988. Add: P.O. Box 1458, East Hampton, N.Y. 11937, U.S.A.

IGO, John (N., Jr.) American, b. 1927. Poetry, Literature, Mythology/Folklore. Prof. of English, San Antonio Coll., Tex., since 1953; Staff Reviewer, Choice mag., since 1964. Member of English Faculty, and acquisitions Librarian, Trinity Univ., San Antonio, Tex., 1952–53. *Publs:* Gods of Gardens, 1962; (compiler and ed.) Yanaguana: A Chapbook of College Poetry, 1963; A Chamber Faust, 1964; Igo on Poetry, 1965; The Tempted Monk, 1967; (author and compiler) Los Pastores: A Triple Tradition, 1967; No Harbor, Else, 1972; Golgotha, 1973; Day of Elegies, 1974; Alien, 1977; Tropic of Gemini, 1981; Coven, 1984; The Mitotes, 1989. Add: 12505 Woller Rd., San Antonio, Tex. 78249, U.S.A.

IHDE, Don. American, b. 1934. Philosophy. Prof. of Philosophy, State Univ. of New York at Stony Brook, since 1969. *Publs:* Hermeneutic Phenomenology, 1971; (co–ed.) Phenomenology and Existentialism, 1973; Sense and Significance, 1973; Listening and Voice, 1976; Experimental Phenomenology, 1977; Technics and Praxis, 1979; Existential Technics, 1983; Consequences of Phenomenology, 1986. Add: Dept. of Philosophy, State Univ. of New York, Stony Brook, N.Y. 11794, U.S.A.

IHIMAERA, Witi. New Zealander, b. 1944. Novels/Short stories. Member, Te Whanau A Kai, Maori tribe. Journalist, Post Office Headquarters, Wellington, 1968–72; Information Officer, Ministry of Foreign Affairs, Wellington, 1973–74; Robert Burns Fellow, Otago Univ., 1975; Third Secty., Ministry of Foreign Affairs, Wellington, 1976–77; Second Secty., New Zealand High Commnr., Canberra, 1978; First Secty., Ministry of Foreign Affairs, 1979–85; New Zealand Consul, NYC, 1986–88; Counsellor, Public Affairs, New Zealand Embassy, Washington, 1989. *Publs:* Pounamu, Pounamu (short stories), 1972; Tangi, 1973; Whanau, 1974; Maori, 1975; The New Net Goes Fishing, 1977; (co–ed.) Into the World of Light, 1980; The Matriarch, 1986; The Whale Rider, 1987; Dear Miss Mansfield, 1989. Add: c/o Ministry of Foreign Affairs, Private Bag, Wellington 1, New Zealand.

IKERMAN, Ruth C. American, b. 1910. Theology/Religion. Former Secty., Real Gold Orange Distributors, Redlands, Calif., and Baptist Headquarters, Los Angeles, and Reporter, Brawley News, and Journal of Commerce, Los Angeles, both Calif.; Co–Owner, Larry's Paint House, Redlands, Calif., 1955–71. *Publs:* Devotional Programs for Every Month, 1956; Devotional Programs for the Changing Seasons, 1958; Devotional Programs about People and Places, 1960; Cooking by Heart, 1962; The Disciplined Heart, 1964; Women's Programs for Special Occasions; Devotional Thoughts from the Holy Land; Golden Words for Every Day; Calendar of Faith and Flowers; Meditations for Bird Lovers; On Morning Trails; Prayers of a Homemaker; Devotional Alphabet; Devotional Calendar; God's World of Wonders; A Little Book of Comfort, 1976; Let Prayer Help You, 1980; A Heart–Trimmed Christmas, 1984; Blessings for Church Occasions, 1987. Add: 11 Panorama Dr., Redlands, Calif. 92374, U.S.A.

IKLE, Fred C(harles). American, b. 1924. International relations/Current affairs, Politics/Government. Distinguished Scholar, Center for Strategic and Intnl. Studies, Washington, D.C., since 1988. Chmn., Conservation Management Corp., since 1988. Head, Social Science Dept., Rand Corp., Santa Monica, Calif.; Prof. of Political Science, Massachusetts Inst. of Technology, and Research Assoc., Harvard Univ., Cambridge, Mass.; Dir., U.S. Arms Control and Disarmament Agency, Washington, 1973–77; Chmn., Conservation Management Corp., 1978–81; Under–Secty. for Policy, U.S. Dept. of Defense, 1981–88. *Publs:* The Social Impact of Bomb Destruction, 1958; How Nations Negotiate, 1964; Every War Must End, 1971. Add: CSIS, 1800 K St. N.W., Suite 810, Washington, D.C. 20006, U.S.A.

ILERSIC, Alfred Roman. British, b. 1920. Economics. Prof. Emeritus of Social Studies, Bedford Coll., Univ. of London, since 1984 (Prof. 1965–84). *Publs:* Government Finance and Fiscal Policy, 1955; Parliament of Commerce, 1860–1960, 1960; Taxation of Capital Gains, 1962; Statistics, 1964; Rate Equalisation in London, 1968; Local Government Finance in Northern Ireland, 1969. Add: National Liberal Club, London W1, England.

ILES, Bert. *See* **ROSS,** Zola.

ILIE, Paul. American, b. 1932. Literature, Philosophy. Prof. of Spanish and Comparative Literature, Univ. of Southern California, Los Angeles, since 1982. Instr., 1959–62, Asst. Prof., 1962–65; Assoc. Prof., 1965–68, and Prof., 1968–82, Depts. of Spanish and Comparative Literature, Univ. of Michigan, Ann Arbor. *Publs:* La novelistica de Camilo José Cela, 1963; 3rd ed. 1978; Unamuno: An Existential View of Self and Society, 1967; The Surrealistic Mode in Spanish Literature, 1968; (ed.) Documents of the Spanish Vanguard, 1969; Los surrealistas espanoles, 1974; Literature and Inner Exile, 1981. Add: Dept. of Spanish, Univ. of Southern California, Los Angeles 90087, U.S.A.

ILLICH, Ivan. American, b. 1926. Engineering/Technology, Sociology. Prof. of History, Marburg Univ., Germany; Prof. of Philosophy, Humanities and Sciences, Pennsylvania State Univ. and Univ. of California, Berkeley. Former Vice–Pres., Univ. of Puerto Rico; Co–Founder, Center for Intercultural Documentation (CIDOC), Cuernavaca, Mexico. *Publs:* Celebration of Awareness, 1969; De–Schooling Society, 1971; Energy and Equity, 1973; Tools for Conviviality, 1973; Medical Nemesis: The Expropriation of Health, 1976; (with others) Disabling Professions, 1978; A History of Needs, 1978; Shadow Work, 1981; Vernacular Gender, 1982; H2O and the Waters of Forgetfulness, 1984; (with Barry Sanders) ABC: The Alphabetization of the Popular Mind, 1988. Add: STS Program, 128 Willard Bldg., Pennsylvania State Univ., University Park, Pa. 16802, U.S.A.

ILLINGWORTH, Ronald Stanley. British, b. 1909. Medicine/Health. Emeritus Prof. of Child Health, and Paediatrician, Children's Hosp., Univ. of Sheffield. *Publs:* The Normal Child, 1953, 9th ed. 1987; (with C.M. Illingworth) Babies and Young Children, 1954, 7th ed. 1984; Development of the Young Child, Normal and Abnormal, 1960; 9th ed. 1987; The Normal School Child, 1964; (with C.M. Illingworth) Lessons from Childhood: Some Aspects of the Early Life of Unusual Men and Women, 1966; Common Symptoms of Disease in Children, 1967, 9th ed. 1988; The Treatment of the Child at Home: A Guide for Family Doctors, 1971; Basic Developmental Screening, 1973, 4th ed. 1988; The Child at School: A Paediatrician's Manual for Teachers, 1974; Infections and Immunisation of Your Child, 1981; Your Child's Development in the First Five Years, 1981. Add: 8 Harley Rd., Sheffield 11, Yorks., England.

ILSLEY, Velma E(lizabeth). American, b. 1918. Children's fiction. Freelance writer, illustrator, painter and sculptor. *Publs:* The Pink Hat, 1956; A Busy Day for Chris, 1957; The Long Stocking, 1959; M Is for Moving, 1966. Add: 59 E. Shore Rd., Huntington, L.I., N.Y. 11743, U.S.A.

INBAU, Fred E(dward). American, b. 1909. Law. John Henry Wigmore Prof. Emeritus of Law, Northwestern Univ., Chicago, since 1977 (Prof., 1974–77). Pres. Emeritus, Americans for Effective Law Enforcement, since 1981 (Pres., 1966–79; Chmn., 1979–81). Admitted to Louisiana and Illinois Bar, 1933, 1936; Research Asst., 1933–38, Dir., 1938–41, Chicago Police Scientific Crime Detection Lab; Trial Attorney, firm of Lord, Bissell and Kadyk, 1941–45; Ed.–in–Chief, Journal of Police Science and Administration, 1973–78. *Publs:* Self–Incrimination, 1950; Lie Detection and Criminal Interrogation, 3rd ed. 1953; Criminal Justice in Our Time, 1965; Truth and Deception, 1966, 1977; Criminal Interrogation and Confessions, 3rd ed. 1986; Cases and Comments on Criminal Justice, 3rd ed. 1968; Criminal Law for the Police, 1969; Criminal Law and Its Administration, 1970, 4th ed. 1984; Criminal Law for the Layman, 1970, 1977; Medical Jurisprudence, 1971; Evidence Law for the Police, 1972; Scientific Police Investigation, 1972; Scientific Evidence in Criminal Cases, 1973, 3rd ed., 1986; Cases and Comments on Criminal Law, 1973, 3rd ed. 1983; Cases and Comments on Criminal Procedure, 1974, 1980. Add: 222 E. Pearson St., Chicago, Ill. 60611, U.S.A.

INCH, Morris Alton. American, b. 1925. Theology/Religion. Prof. of Theology 1962–86, and of Holy Land Studies since 1986, Wheaton Coll., Illinois (Chmn., Dept of Religious Studies, 1969–84). Assoc. Prof. of Christian Education, 1955–62, Academic Dean, 1959–60 and 1961–62, and Dean of Students, 1960–61, Gordon Coll., Wenham, Mass. *Publs:* Psychology in the Psalms, 1969; Christianity Without Walls, 1972; Paced by God, 1973; Celebrating Jesus as Lord, 1974; (ed. with Samuel J. Schultz) Interpreting the Word of God, 1976; Understanding Bible Prophecy, 1977; The Evangelical Challenge, 1978; My Servant Job, 1979; (gen. ed.) The Literature and Meaning of Scripture, 1981; Doing Theology Across Cultures, 1982; Saga of the Spirit: A Biblical, Systematic and Historical Theology of the Holy Spirit, 1985; Making the Gospel Relevant, 1986. Add: 348 Fairview Ave., W. Chicago, Ill. 60185, U.S.A.

INCLEDON, Philip. *See* **WORNER,** Philip.

INEZ, Colette. American (b. Belgian), b. 1931. Poetry. Lectr. in Comparative Literature, Columbia Univ., NYC, since 1983. Poetry Reviewer, Parnassus Mag., Prairie Schooner, Greenfield Review, etc. Member of staff, Recreation Mag., Intnl. Theatre Mag., and Le Figaro (NYC), 1959–63; Instr., Adult Education, New York Univ., 1962–63; Teacher, Federal Title III Anti–Poverty Progs., NYC, 1964–70; Beck Lectr., Denison Univ., Granville, Ohio, 1974; Instr., Poetry Workshop, New Sch. for Social Research, NYC, 1974–83. Lectr., Poetry Workshop, State Univ. of New York at Stony Brook, 1975–76; Poet–in–Residence, Kalamazoo Coll., Michigan, 1976, 1978, 1981, 1985. Dir., Poetry Soc. of America, 1979–80. *Publs:* The Woman Who Loved Worms, 1972; Alive and Taking Names, 1977; Eight Minutes from the Sun, 1983; Family Life, 1988. Add: 5 West 86th St., New York, N.Y. 10024, U.S.A.

ING, Dean. American, b. 1931. Science fiction. Freelance writer since 1977. Engineer, Aerojet–General, Sacramento, Calif., 1957–62, and Lockheed, San Jose, Calif., 1962, 1965–70; Asst. Prof. of Speech, Missouri State Univ., Maryville, 1974–77. *Publs:* Soft Targets (novel), 1979; Anasazi (short stories), 1980; Systemic Shock (novel), 1981; High Tension (short stories), 1982; Pulling Through (novel), 1983; (ed.) The Lagrangists, by Mack Reynolds, 1983; Single Combat (novel), 1983; (ed.) Home Sweet Home 2010 A.D., by Mack Reynolds, 1984; (ed.) Eternity, by Mack Reynolds, 1984; (ed.) The Other Time, by Mack Reynolds, 1984; Wild Country (novel), 1985; (ed.) Trojan Orbit, by Mack Reynolds, 1985; (ed.) Deathwish World, by Mark Reynolds, 1986; Blood of Eagles (novel), 1987; Firefight 2000 (collection), 1987; The Chernobyl Syndrome (collection), 1987; The Big Lifters (novel), 1988; The Ransom of Black Stealth One (novel), 1989; Cathouse (novel), 1989. Add: 1105 Ivy Lane, Ashland, Ore. 97520, U.S.A.

INGALLS, Jeremy. American, b. 1911. Novels/Short stories, Poetry, Literature, Theology/Religion, Translations. Asst. Prof. of American Literature, Western Coll., Oxford, Ohio, 1941–43; Republic of China Fellow in Classical Chinese, Univ. of Chicago, 1945–47; Resident Poet, Chmn. of Div. of Arts, Prof. of English and Asian Studies, Chmn. of English Dept., and Dir. of Asian Studies, Rockford Coll., Ill., 1947–60. *Publs:* A Book of Legends (short stories), 1941; The Metaphysical Sword (poetry), 1941; Tahl (poetry), 1945; The Galilean Way, 1953; (ed. and trans. with S.Y. Teng) Li Chien–nung's A Political History of China, 1842 to 1928, 1956; The Woman from the Island (poetry), 1958; These Islands Also (poetry), 1959; The Epic Tradition, 1964; (ed. and trans.) The Malice of Empire, by Yao Hsin–nung, 1970; (author and trans.) Nakagawa's Tenno Yugao, 1975; A Summer Liturgy (verse/play), 1976, 1985; This Stubborn Quantum (poetry), 1983; The Epic Tradition and Related Essays, 1989. Add: 6269 East Rosewood, Tucson, Ariz. 85711, U.S.A.

INGALLS, Rachel. American, b. 1941. Novels/Short stories. *Publs:* Theft, 1970; The Man Who Was Left Behind, 1974; Mrs. Caliban, 1982; Binstead's Safari, 1983; Three of a Kind (in U.S.A. as I See a Long Journey), 1985; The Pearlkillers, 1986; Something to Write Home About, 1988. Add: 3 Shepards Hill, London N6, England.

INGATE, Mary. British, b. 1912. Mystery/Crime/Suspense. Self employed farmer and writer. *Publs:* The Sound of the Weir, 1974; This Water Laps Gently, 1977; A Tomb of Flowers, 1979. Add: Chapel Farm, Chedison, Halesworth, Suffolk, England.

INGE, M. Thomas. American, b. 1936. Humanities, Literature. Blackwell Prof. of Humanities, Randolph–Macon Coll., Ashland, Va., since 1984. Gen. Ed., Greenwood Pr. reference series on American popular culture, since 1976. Instr. of English, Vanderbilt Univ., Nashville, 1962–64; Asst. Prof. to Assoc. Prof. of American Thought and Language, Michigan State Univ., East Lansing, 1964–69; Assoc. Prof. to Prof. of English and Chair, Virginia Commonwealth Univ., Richmond, 1969–80; Prof. of English and Head of Dept., Clemson Univ., S.C., 1980–82; Resident Scholar in American Studies, U.S. Information Agency, Washington, D.C., 1982–84. Pres., American Humor Studies Assn., 1978, 1988, South Atlantic Modern Language Assn., 1988–89, and Popular Culture Assn. in the South, 1988–89. *Publs:* (with Thomas Daniel Young) Donald Davidson: An Essay and a Bibliography, 1965; (ed.) Publications of the Faculty of the University College: A Bibliography, 1966; (ed.) Sut Lovingood's Yarns, by George Washington Harris, 1966; (ed.) High Times and Hard Times: Sketches and Tales, by George Washington Harris, 1967; (ed.) Agrarianism in American Literature, 1969; (ed.) August Baldwin Longstreet: A Study of the Development of Culture in the South, by John Donald Wade, 1969; (ed.) Honors College Essays 1967–68, 1969; (ed., with others) The Black Experience: Readings in Afro–American History and Culture from Colonial Times Through the Nineteenth Century, 1969; (ed.) Faulkner: A Rose for Emily, 1970; (ed.) William Byrd of Westover, by Richmond Croom Beatty, 1970; (ed.) Studies in Light in August, 1971; (with Thomas Daniel Young) Donald Davidson, 1971; (ed.) Virginia Commonwealth University Self–Study, 1972; (ed.) The Frontier Humorists: Critical Views, 1975; (ed.) Ellen Glasgow: Centennial Essays, 1976; (ed., with Maurice Duke and Jackson R. Bryer) Black American Writers: Bibliographical Essays, 2 vols., 1978; (ed.) Bartleby the Inscrutable (collection of commentary on the Melville story), 1979; (ed.) Concise Histories of American Popular Culture, 1982; (ed. with Edgar E. MacDonald) James Branch Cabell: Centennial Essays, 1983; (ed. with Maurice Duke and Jackson R. Bryer) American Women Writers: Bibliographic Essays, 1983; (ed.) Huck Finn Among the Critics: A Centennial Selection, 1985; The American Comic Book, 1985; (ed.) Truman Capote: Conversations, 1987; (ed.) Sut Lovingood Yarns, 1987; (ed.) Handbook of American Popular Literature, 1988; (ed.) Naming the Rose: Essays on Eco's The Name of the Rose, 1988; (ed.) A Nineteenth–Century American Reader, 1988; (ed.) Handbook of American Popular Culture, 3 vols., 1978–81, 1989; Comics as Culture: Essays on Comic Art, 1989. Add: Blackwell Chair in the Humanities, Randolph–Macon Coll., Ashland, Va. 23005, U.S.A.

INGHAM, Daniel. See **LAMBOT,** Isobel Mary.

INGHAM, Kenneth. British, b. 1921. History. Emeritus Prof. of History, Univ. of Bristol, since 1986 (Prof., 1967–86). Lectr., 1950–56, and Prof. of History, 1956–62, Makerere Univ., Uganda; Dir. of Studies, Royal Military Academy, Sandhurst, 1962–67. *Publs:* Europe and Africa, 1953; Reformers in India 1793–1833, 1956, 1973; The Making of Modern Uganda, 1958, 1983; A History of East Africa, 1962; (ed.) Foreign Relations of African States, 1974; The Kingdom of Toro in Uganda, 1975; Jan Smuts: The Conscience of a South African, 1986. Add: The Woodlands, 94 West Town Lane, Bristol BS4 5DZ, England.

INGHAM, R(ichard) A(rnison). British, b. 1935. Poetry, Speech/Rhetoric. Lectr. in English and Communications, Chippenham Technological Coll. *Publs:* Yoris, 1974; (with J.M. Buffton) Making Contact, 2 vols., 1980–81; Fifteen from Twenty–Two (verse), 1979. Add: 26 Devonshire Buildings, Bath, Avon, England.

INGILBY, Joan Alicia. British, b. 1911. Country life/Rural societies, History. *Publs:* all with Marie Hartley—The Old Hand–Knitters of the Dales, 1951; Yorkshire Village, 1953; The Yorkshire Dales, 1956; The Wonders of Yorkshire, 1959; Yorkshire Portraits, 1961; Getting to Know Yorkshire, 1964; Life and Tradition in the Yorkshire Dales, 1968; Life in the Moorlands of North East Yorkshire, 1972; Life and Tradition in West Yorkshire, 1976; A Dales Heritage, 1982; Dales Memories, 1986; Yorkshire Album, 1988. Add: Coleshouse, Askrigg, Leyburn, N. Yorks., England.

INGLIS, Brian. Irish, b. 1916. History, Medicine/Health, Sociology. Journalist, TV commentator, and freelance writer. Ed., Spectator, London, 1959–62. *Publs:* The Freedom of the Press in Ireland, 1954; The Story of Ireland, 1956; Revolution in Medicine, 1958; West Briton, 1962; Fringe Medicine, 1964; Private Conscience, Public Morality, 1964; Drugs, Doctors, and Disease, 1965; A History of Medicine, 1965; Abdication, 1966; Poverty and the Industrial Revolution, 1971; Roger Casement, 1973; The Forbidden Game: A Social History of Drugs, 1975; The Opium War, 1976; Natural and Supernatural, 1978; The Book of the Back, 1978; Natural Medicine, 1979; The Diseases of Civilization, 1981; An Alternative Health Guide, 1983; Science and Parascience, 1984; The Paranormal, 1985; The Hidden Power, 1986; The Unknown Guest, 1987; The Power of Dreams, 1987. Add: 23 Lambolle Rd., London NW3, England.

INGMAN, Nicholas. British, b. 1948. Children's non-fiction, Music. Freelance musical arranger; composer and conductor for television, films, and radio; recording artist. Arranger and producer, Norrie Paramor's Independent Record Co., London, 1969–75. *Publs:* The Story of Music, 1972; What Instrument Shall I Play?, 1975; Gifted Children of Music: The Young Lives of the Great Musicians, 1978. Add: 10 The Gardens, E. Dulwich, London, England.

INGRAM, Derek Thynne. British, b. 1925. Politics/Government. Ed., Gemini News Service, London, since 1967. Pres., Commonwealth Journalists Assn., since 1983; Deputy–Chmn., Royal Commonwealth Society, since 1986 (also 1979–82). Member, Editorial Bd., Round Table; Deputy Ed., Daily Mail, London, 1963–66; Pres., Diplomatic and Commonwealth Writers Assn. of Britain, 1972–74; Gov., Commonwealth Inst., 1972–88; Deputy–Chmn., Royal Commonwealth Soc., 1979–82; Ed., Commonwealth Journal, 1983–86. *Publs:* Partners in Adventure, 1960; The Commonwealth Challenge, 1962; Commonwealth for a Colour–Blind World, 1965; The Commonwealth at Work, 1969; The Imperfect Commonwealth, 1977. Add: 5 Wyndham Mews, London W1H 1RS, England.

INGRAM, Hunter. See **LUTZ,** Giles A.

INGRAM, Vernon Martin. British, b. 1924. Biology, Medicine/Health. Prof. of Biochemistry, Massachusetts Inst. of Technology, Cambridge, since 1961 (Visiting Assoc. Prof., 1958–59; Assoc. Prof., 1959–61). Lecture Demonstrator in Chemistry, 1945–47 and Asst. Lectr., 1947–50, Birkbeck Coll., Univ. of London; Member, Scientific Staff, Medical Research Council, Cavendish Labs., Cambridge, England, 1952–58; Lectr. in Medicine, Columbia Univ., NYC, 1961–72. *Publs:* Haemoglobin and Its Abnormalities, 1961; The Hemoglobins in Genetics and Evolution, 1963; The Biosynthesis of Macromolecules, 1965, 1972. Add: 56–601, Massachusetts Inst. of Technology, Cambridge, Mass. 02139, U.S.A.

INGRAMS, Doreen (Constance). British, b. 1906. History, Travel/Exploration/Adventure. Sr. Asst., BBC Arabic Service, 1956–68. Member, Exec. Cttee., Council for the Advancement of Arab–British Understanding, 1967–82. *Publs:* A Survey of Social and Economic Conditions of the Aden Protectorate, 1949; A Time in Arabia, 1970; Palestine Papers 1917–1922: Seeds of Conflict, 1973; Educational Books on Islam and the Arab World, 1975; The Awakened: Women of Iraq, 1983. Add: 3 Westfield House, Tenderden, Kent, England.

INGRAMS, Richard. British, b. 1937. Geography, Humour/Satire. Ed., Private Eye Mag., London, 1963–85. *Publs:* (with J. Wells) Mrs Wilson's Second Diary, 1966; (ed.) What the Papers Never Meant to Say, 1968; (with R. Steadman) Tale of Driver Grope, 1969; (with B. Fantoni) Bible for Motorists, 1970; (ed.) The Life and Times of Private Eye 1961–1971, 1972; (ed.) Private Eye Anatomy of Neasden, 1972; (ed.) Private Eye Book of Pseuds, 1973; (ed.) Private Eye's Bumper Book of Boobs, 1973; (ed.) Private Eye: A Load of Rubbish, 1974; (ed.) Cobbett's Country Book, 1974; (ed.) Beachcomber: The Best of J.B. Morton, 1974; Lord Gnome of the Rings, 1976; (with Michael Heath) Book of Bores, 1976; (ed.) Psecond Book of Pseuds, 1977; God's Apology: A Chronicle of Three Friends, 1977; Goldenballs, 1979; Romney Marsh and the Royal Military

Canal, 1980; (with J. Wells) Dear Bill, 1980; The Other Half, 1981; One for the Road, 1982; (with John Piper) Piper's Places, 1983; (ed.) The Penguin Book of Private Eye Cartoons, 1983; (ed.) Dr. Johnson By Mrs. Thrale, 1984; (ed.) Bumper Book of Covers, 1984; (with J. Wells) Bottoms Up!, 1984; (with J. Wells) Down the Hatch, 1985; (with J. Wells) Just the One, 1986; (with J. Wells) The Best of "Dear Bill", 1986; John Stewart Collis, 1986; (with J. Wells) Mud in Your Eye, 1987; The Ridgeway, 1988; You Might as Well Be Dead, 1988; England: An Anthology, 1989. Add: Private Eye, 34 Greek St., London W1, England.

INMAN, Robert (Anthony). American, b. 1931. Novels/Short stories. Instr. in Germanics, 1957–59, and Ed. and Admin. Asst., 1960–62, Univ. of Washington, Seattle; Head Librarian, Denver Post, Colo., 1964–71; Managing Ed., Journals, AIAA, New York, 1983–87. *Publs:* The Torturer's Horse, 1965; The Blood Endures, 1981. Add: 396 Colony Rd., Geyserville, Calif. 95441, U.S.A.

INNAURATO, Albert. American, b. 1948. Plays/Screenplays. *Publs:* (with Christopher Durang) The Idiots Karamazov, 1974, 1981; The Transfiguration of Benno Blimpie, 1976; Gemini, 1977; Ulysses in Traction, 1978; Bizarre Behavior; Six Plays, 1980; Passione, 1981; Coming of Age in Soho, 1985. Add: 325 W. 22nd St., New York, N.Y. 10011, U.S.A.

INNES, Hammond. *See* **HAMMOND INNES**, Ralph.

INNES, Jean. *See* **SAUNDERS**, Jean.

INNES, Michael. *See* **STEWART**, J.I.M.

IONESCU, Ghita. British, b. 1913. International relations/Current affairs, Politics/Government. Emeritus Prof. of Govt., Univ. of Manchester. Ed., Govt. and Opposition, London Sch. of Economics. *Publs:* Communism in Rumania, 1964; Breakdown of Soviet Empire in Eastern Europe, 1965; The Politics of European Communist States, 1965; (with E. Gellner) Populism, 1967; (ed.) New Politics of European Integration, 1972; Comparative Communist Politics, 1973; (with I. de Madariaga) Opposition, 1974; Between Sovereignty and Integration, 1974; Centripetal Politics, 1975; The Political Thought of Saint-Simon, 1976; (ed.) The European Alternatives, 1977; Politics and the Pursuit of Happiness, 1984. Add: 36 Sandileigh Ave., Manchester M20 9LW, England.

IPSEN, D.C. American, b. 1921. Children's non-fiction, Sciences (general). *Publs:* Units, Dimensions, and Dimensionless Numbers (engineering), 1960; The Riddle of the Stegosaurus, 1969; Rattlesnakes and Scientists, 1970; What Does a Bee See?, 1971; The Elusive Zebra, 1971; Eye of the Whirlwind: The Story of John Scopes, 1973; Isaac Newton: Reluctant Genius, 1985; Archimedes: Greatest Scientist of the Ancient World, 1989. Add: 655 Vistamont Ave., Berkeley, Calif. 94708, U.S.A.

IRBY, Kenneth. American, b. 1936. Poetry. Contr. Ed., Conjunctions mag., NYC. *Publs:* The Roadrunner, 1964; Kansas–New Mexico, 1965; Movements/Sequences, 1965; The Flower of Having Passed Through Paradise in a Dream: Poems 1967, 1968; Relation: Poems 1965–1966, 1970; To Max Douglas, 1971; The Snow Queen, 1973; Archipelago, 1976; Catalpa, 1977; In Excelsis Borealis, 1976; Some Etudes, 1978; Orexis, 1981; A Set, 1983. Add: N–311 Regency Place, Lawrence, Kans. 66044, U.S.A.

IRELAND, David. Australian, b. 1927. Novels/Short stories, Plays/Screenplays. Freelance writer. *Publs:* Image of Clay (play), 1962; The Chantic Bird, 1968; The Unknown Industrial Prisoner, 1971; The Flesheaters, 1972; Burn, 1975; The Glass Canoe, 1976; A Woman of the Future, 1979; City of Woman, 1981; Archimedes and the Seagle, 1984; Bloodfather, 1988. Add: Box 101, Darlinghurst, N.S.W. 2010, Australia.

IRELAND, Kevin (Mark). New Zealander, b. 1933. Poetry. Founding Ed., Mate mag., Auckland. Writer–in–Residence, Canterbury Univ., 1986. *Publs:* Face to Face: Poems, 1963; Educating the Body: Poems, 1968; A Letter from Amsterdam: Poems, 1972; Orchids, Hummingbirds, and Other Poems, 1974; A Grammar of Dreams, 1975; Literary Cartoons, 1978; The Dangers of Art: Poems 1975–1980, 1981; Practice Night in the Drill Hall, 1985; Selected Poems, 1987. Add: 1 Anne St., Devonport, New Zealand.

IREMONGER, Lucille (d'Oyen). British. Novels/Short stories, History, Travel/Exploration/Adventure, Biography. Member, London County Council, 1961–65. *Publs:* It's A Bigger Life (travel), 1948; Creole

(novel), 1950; The Young Traveller in the South Seas, 1952; The Cannibals (novel), 1952; The Young Traveller in the West Indies, 1955; West Indian Folk Tales, 1956; The Ghosts of Versailles, 1957; Love and the Princess, 1958; And His Charming Lady, 1961; Yes, My Darling Daughter (autobiography), 1964; The Fiery Chariot, 1970; How Do I Love Thee, 1976; Lord Aberdeen (biography), 1978; My Sister, My Love, 1981; Orphans of the Heart, 1983. Add: 34 Cheyne Row, London SW3 5HL, England.

IRION, Mary Jean. American, b. 1922. Poetry, Theology/Religion. Visiting Lectr. in Theology and Literature, Lancaster Theological Seminary, Pa., since 1983; Founder and Coordinator, Countermeasure poets workshop, Lancaster, Pa., since 1974; Founder and Dir., Chautauqua Writers' Center, Chautauqua Instn., New York, since 1988. Teacher of English Literature, Lancaster Country Day School, 1968–74, 1980–81. Teacher of Modern Poetry, Chautauqua Instn. Summer Sch., 1983–86. *Publs:* From the Ashes of Christianity, 1968; Yes, World, 1970; Holding On, 1984. Add: 149 Kready Ave., Millersville, Pa. 17551, U.S.A.

IRVINE, Keith. American (born British), b. 1924. History. Pres., Reference Publs. Inc., Algonac, Mich., since 1975; Gen. Ed., Encyclopedia Africana: Dictionary of African Biography, since 1975. Ed., Africa Today, American Cttee. of Africa 1954–56; Research Dir., Ghana Mission to the U.N., New York, 1958–69; Principal Ed. for Geography, Encyclopedia Britannica, Chicago, 1969–73. *Publs:* The Rise of the Colored Races, 1970. Add: 218 St. Clair Dr., Box 344, Algonac, Mich. 48001, U.S.A.

IRVING, Clifford. America, b. 1930. Novels/Screenplays. Corresp., NBC TV, Middle East, 1956. *Publs:* On a Darkling Plain, 1966; The Losers, 1957; The Valley, 1962; The 38th Floor, 1964; (with H. Burkholz) Spy, 1969; The Battle of Jerusalem, 1970; Fake!, 1970; Global Village Idiot: Extracts from Nixon, 1973; Project Octavio, 1978; The Death Freak, 1979; The Hoax, 1981; Tom Mix and Pancho Villa, 1982; The Sleeping Spy, 1983; The Angel of Zin, 1984; Daddy's Girl, 1988. Add: c/o Frank Cooper, 10100 Santa Monica Blvd., Los Angeles, CA 90067, U.S.A.

IRVING, John (Winslow). American, b. 1942. Novels/Short stories. Assistant Professor of English, Mount Holyoke College, South Hadley, Mass., 1967–72, 1975–78. Writer–in–Residence, University of Iowa, Iowa City, 1972–75. *Publs:* Setting Free the Bears, 1969; The Water-Method Man, 1972; The 158–Pound Marriage, 1974; The World According to Garp, 1978; The Hotel New Hampshire, 1981; The Cider House Rules, 1985; A Prayer for Owen Meany, 1989. Add: c/o William Morrow Inc., 105 Madison Ave., New York, N.Y. 10016, U.S.A.

IRWIN, Constance. Also writes as C.H. Frick. American, b. 1913. Historical, Children's fiction. Archaeology/Antiquities, History, Literature. Librarian, Reitz High Sch., Evansville, Ind., 1937–42 and 1947–54; Book Ed., Columbia Univ. Press, NYC, 1947–50; Asst. Prof. of Library Science, Univ. of Iowa, Iowa City, 1961–67. *Publs:* (as Constance Frick) The Dramatic Criticism of George Jean Nathan, 1943; (as C.H. Frick) Tourney Team, 1954; (as C.H. Frick) Five Against the Odds, 1955; (as C.H. Frick) Patch, 1957; Jonathan D., 1958; (as C.H. Frick) The Comeback Guy, 1961; Fair Gods and Stone Faces, 1963; Gudrid's Saga (novel), 1974; Strange Footprints on the Land: Vikings in America, 1980. Add: 415 Lee St., Iowa City, Iowa 52246, U.S.A.

IRWIN, David George. British, b. 1933. Art. Prof. and Head, Dept. of the History of Art, Univ. of Aberdeen, since 1970. Lectr. in the History of Fine Art, Univ. of Glasgow, 1959–70; Member of Cttee., Council of Europe, Age of Neoclassicism, 1969–72; Pres., British Soc. of Eighteenth Century Studies, 1973–77. *Publs:* English Neoclassical Art, 1966; Visual Arts, Taste and Criticism, 1968; Paul Klee, 1969; Winckelmann: Writings on Art, 1972; (ed.) Winckelmann: Arte del Bello, 1973; (ed.) Beunat: Receuil de decorations, 1974; (with F. Irwin) Scottish Painters: At Home and Abroad 1700–1900, 1975; John Flaxman, 1979. Add: Dept. of the History of Art, King's Coll., Univ. of Aberdeen, Aberdeen AB9 2UB, Scotland.

IRWIN, Grace Lilian. Canadian, b. 1907. Novels/Short stories. Pastor, Emmanuel Congregational Church, Toronto, since 1974. Teacher of Classics, 1931–42, and Head of Dept., 1942–69, Humberside Collegiate Inst., Toronto. *Publs:* Least of All Saints, 1952; Andrew Connington, 1954; (ed.) H. Harold Kent: An Architect Preaches, 1957; In Little Place, 1959; Servant of Slaves, 1961; (ed.) H. Harold Kent: The House of Christmas, 1964; (ed.) H. Harold Kent: Job Our Contemporary, 1967, 1973; Contend with Horses, 1968; The Seventh Earl, 1976; (ed.) H. Harold Kent: The Unveiling of Jesus Christ, 1978; Three Lives in Mine,

1986. Add: 33 Glenwood Ave., Toronto, Ont. M6P 3C7, Canada.

IRWIN, John Conran. British, b. 1917. Art, Crafts. Visiting Prof., Univ. of Michigan, Ann Arbor; engaged in research of cosmogenic myth and its relation to origins of monumental art. Keeper, Oriental Dept., Victoria and Albert Museum, London, 1970–78 (Asst. Keeper, 1949–70; Keeper, Indian Section, 1959–70). Unesco expert on museum planning, Indonesia and Malaya, 1956–62. *Publs:* Jamini Roy, 1944; Indian Art, 1947; The Art of India and Pakistan, 1951; Shawls, 1955; Origins of Chintz, 1970; (with M. Hall) Indian Painted and Printed Fabrics, 1971; (with M. Hall) Indian Embroideries, 1973. Add: Apt. 6, Park Ct., Park Rd., Petersfield, Hants. GU32 3DL, England.

IRWIN, Peter George. Australian, b. 1925. Geography. Assoc. Prof., Dept. of Geography, Univ. of Newcastle, N.S.W., 1974–85 (Sr. Lectr., 1966–74). Member of Staff, Newcastle Teachers Coll., 1959–65. *Publs:* (with D.A.M. Lea) New Guinea: The Territory and Its People, 1967; Equatorial and Tropical Rainforest, 1968; The Monsoon Asia, 1968; The Tropical Savanna, 1969; Human Geography, 1970; Cotton Systems of the Namoi Valley, 1972; Systems in Human Geography, 1973; (with J.C.R. Camm) Space, People, Place, 1979; (with J.C.R. Camm) Land, Man, Region, 1982; (with E. and J.C.R. Camm) Skills for Senior School Geography, 1985; (with E. and J.C.R. Camm) Australians in Their Environment, 1987; (with E. and J.C.R. Camm) Resources, Settlement, Livelihood: Perspectives on a Changing World, 1989. Add: 2 Mahogany Drive, New Lambton, N.S.W. 2305, Australia.

ISAAC, Peter Charles Gerald. British, b. 1921. Engineering, Librarianship. Emeritus Prof. of Civil and Public Health Engineering, Univ. of Newcastle upon Tyne; partner, Watson Hawksley, consulting civil engineers, 1973–83. *Publs:* (with W.B. Dobie) Electric Resistance Strain Gauges, 1948; (with R.E.A. Allan) Scientific Survey of Northeast England, 1949; Public Health Engineering, 1953; (ed.) Trade Wastes, 1957; (ed.) Waste Treatment, 1960; (ed.) River Management, 1967; Biography of William Davison of Alnwick, Pharmacist and Printer, 1968; (ed.) Farm Wastes, 1970; (ed.) Civil Engineering: The University Contribution, 1970; (ed.) Management in Civil Engineering, 1971; Davison's Halfpenny Chapbooks, 1971; The Burman Alnwick Collection, 1973. Add: 10 Woodcroft Rd., Wylam, Northumberland NE41 8DJ, England.

ISAACS, Alan. Also writes as Alec Valentine. British, b. 1925. Sciences. Chmn., Market House Books, since 1981. Former research scientist. *Publs:* Introducing Science, 1963; (with E.B. Uvarov) Penguin Dictionary of Science, 1964; Survival of God in the Scientific Age, 1966; (with V. Pitt) Physics, 1971; (co–ed.) Hamlyn World Dictionary, 1971; (ed. with V. Pitt and J. Daintith) Hamlyn Junior Science Encyclopedia, 1972; (ed. with H.J. Gray) Longman's New Dictionary of Physics, 1974; (series ed.) Dictionary of Economics and Commerce, 1976; (series ed.) Dictionary of Philosophy, 1979; (science ed.) Collins English Dictionary, 1979; (ed.) Macmillan Encyclopedia, 1981; (ed. with E. Martin) Hamlyn Dictionary of Music, 1982; (ed. with J. Daintith and E. Martin) Oxford Concise Science Dictionary, 1984; (ed. with E. Martin) Longman Dictionary of 20th Century Biography, 1985; (ed. with J. Monk) Cambridge Illustrated Dictionary of British Heritage, 1986. Add: Market House, Market Sq., Aylesbury, Bucks., England.

ISAACS, Bernard. British, b. 1924. Medicine/Health. Charles Hayward Prof. of Geriatric Medicine, Univ. of Birmingham, since 1975. Member of Editorial Bd., Age and Aging; Chmn., Stroke Cttee., Chest, Heart and Stroke Assn.; Member, Advisory Council, Centre for Policy on Ageing: Scientific Adviser, Dept. of Health and Social Security. Held various jr. appointments in medical subjects and in general practice, 1947–50; Consultant Physician, Foresthall Hosp., Glasgow, 1961–64; Consultant Physician, Dept. of Geriatric Medicine, Glasgow Royal Infirmary, 1964–74. Member of Health Services Research Cttee., Chief Scientists Org., Scotland, 1973–75; Pres., West of Scotland Branch, Chartered Soc. of Physiotherapists, 1973–75; Chmn. Working Party on Geriatrics, Scottish Health Services Research Cttee., 1974. *Publs:* (ed. with W. Anderson) Current Achievements in Geriatrics, 1963; An Introduction to Geriatrics, 1964; (co–author) Survival of the Unfittest, 1972; (co–author) Geriatrics in Modern Practical Nursing, 1974; (ed.) Recent Advances in Geriatric Medicine, 3 vols., 1978–85; (co–author) Care of the Elderly Mentally Infirm, 1979; (co–author) Innovations in the Care of the Elderly, 1984. Add: 33 Greville Dr., Birmingham B15 2UU, England.

ISAACS, Susan. American, b. 1943. Novels/Short stories, Mystery/Crime/Suspense, Plays/Screenplays. Ed., Seventeen Mag., 1966–70; freelance writer, 1970–76. *Publs:* Compromising Positions, 1978; Close Relations, 1980; (with Elkan Abramowitz) A Federal Case

(screenplay), 1980; Almost Paradise, 1984; Compromising Positions (screenplays), 1985; Hello Again (screenplay), 1987; Shining Through, 1988. Add: c/o Harper and Row, 10 E. 53rd St., New York, N.Y. 10022, U.S.A.

ISENBERG, Seymour. American, b. 1930. Crafts, Medicine/Health. In private practice as an osteopathic physician, Northvale, N.J., since 1959; Ed., Glass Workship mag. Ed., Shakespeare Bulletin, 1982–84; Ed., Stages, The National Theatre Mag., 1984–85. *Publs:* (ghostwriter) How to Multiply Your Real Estate Sales, by Eugene F. Di Paola, 1963; (with Anita Isenberg) How to Work in Stained Glass, 1972; (with A. Isenberg) Stained Glass Lamps, 1972; (with A. Isenberg) Stained Glass: Advanced Techniques, 1973; (with A. Isenberg) Stained Glass Painting, 1975; The Consumer's Guide to Successful Surgery, 1975; (with L. Melvin Elting) You Can Be Fat Free Forever, 1975; The 9 Day Wonder Diet, 1978; (with A. Isenberg) Crafting in Glass, 1980; The Executive's Miracle Shape–Up Guide, 1981; (with A. Isenberg) How to Work in Beveled Glass, 1982; Keep Your Kids Thin, 1982; (with A. Isenberg) Anita Isenberg's Patterns to Work in Stained Glass, 1983; (with A. Isenberg) Engraving: The Stone–Wheel Method, 1986. Add: P.O. Box 244, Norwood, N.J. 07648, U.S.A.

ISHIGURO, Hide. Japanese, b. 1934. Philosophy. Prof. of Philosophy, Barnard Coll., NYC, since 1982. Asst. Lectr., 1961–62, and Lectr. in Philosophy, 1962–64, Univ. of Leeds; Lectr., 1964–73, and Reader in Philosophy, 1973–82, University Coll., London. *Publs:* Leibniz's Philosophy of Logic and Language, 1972; Pre–Established Harmony Versus Constant Conjunction, 1978. Add: Dept. of Philosophy, Barnard Coll., New York, N.Y. 10027, U.S.A.

ISHIGURO, Kazuo. British (b. Japanese), b. 1954. Novels/Short stories. Full–time writer since 1982. Grouse-Beater for the Queen Mother, Balmoral, Scotland, 1973–76; community worker, Glasgow, 1976–79; residential social worker, London, 1979–81. *Publs:* (with others) Introduction 7: Stories by New Writers, 1981; A Pale View of Hills, 1982; An Artist of the Floating World, 1986; The Remains of the Day, 1989. Add: c/o Faber and Faber, 3 Queen Sq., London WC1N 3AU, England.

ISHWARAN, K. Canadian, b. 1922. Anthropology/Ethnology, Sociology. Prof., Dept. of Sociology, York Univ., Downsview, Ont., since 1965. Ed., Intnl. Journal of Comparative Sociology, since 1960, Journal of Asian and African Studies, since 1965, and Journal for Developing Societies, since 1975. Lectr., J.G. Coll. of Commerce and S.K. Arts Coll., Hubli, India, 1947–52; Principal, Sangameshwar Coll., Sholapur, India, 1953–54; Research Fellow, Netherlands Foundn. for Intnl. Cooperation, The Hague, 1956–59; Reader, 1959–62, Chmn., Dept. of Grad. Studies in Social Anthropology, 1959–64, and Prof., 1962–64, Karnatak Univ., Dharwar, India; Visiting Prof., Memorial Univ. of Newfoundland, St. John's 1964–65. *Publs:* Family Life in the Netherlands, 1959, rev. ed. 1974; (with Nels Anderson) Urban Sociology, 1965; Tradition and Economy in Village India, 1966, 1968; (ed.) Politics and Change, 1967; Shivapur—A South Indian Village, 1968; (ed.) Change and Continuity in India's Villages, 1970; (ed.) The Canadian Family, 1971, 3rd ed. 1982; Family, Kinship and Community, 1977; A Populistic Community and Modernization in India, 1977; (ed.) Childhood and Adolescence in Canada, 1979; (ed.) Canadian Families: Ethnic Variations, 1980; Religion and Society Among the Lingayats of South India, 1983; Basava and the Lingayat Religion, 1988. Add: Dept. of Sociology, York Univ., Downsview, Ont., M3J 1P3, Canada.

ISRAEL, Charles (Edward). American, b. 1920. Novels/Short stories, Plays/Screenplays, Biography. Radio playwright in Canada, since 1953 (in Hollywood, Calif., 1950–53). Deputy Chief of Repatriation, then Deputy Chief of Voluntary Socs. Div., U.N. Relief and Rehabilitation Admin., Intnl. Refugee Org., Munich, Heidelberg and Bad Kissingen, Germany, 1946–50; Member of Exec. Bd., 1957–59, and of Bd. of Dirs., 1965–66, Assn. of Canadian Radio and Television Artist. *Publs:* How Many Angels, 1956; (with T.C. Fairley) The True North: The Story of Captain Joseph Bernier, 1957; The Mark, 1958; Rizpah, 1961; Who Was Then the Gentleman?, 1963; The Labyrinth: A Play for Television, 1964; Shadows on a Wall, 1965; The Hostages, 1966; Five Ships West: The Story of Magellan, 1966; The Newcomers: Inhabiting a New Land, 1979. Add: c/o Simon and Schuster, 1230 Sixth Ave., New York, N.Y. 10020, U.S.A.

ISRAEL, John (Warren). American, b. 1935. History. Prof. of History, Univ. of Virginia, Charlottesville, since 1984 (Assoc. Prof., 1968–84). Asst. Prof. of History, Claremont Men's Coll., Calif., 1963–68.

Publs: Student Nationalism in China, 1927–1937, 1966; (with Donald W. Klein) Rebels and Bureaucrats: China's December 9ers, 1976. Add: Dept. of History, Randall Hall, Univ. of Virginia, Charlottesville, Va. 22903, U.S.A.

ITZKOFF, Seymour William. American. Education, Biography. Prof., Smith Coll., since 1965 (Dir. of Campus Sch., 1968–71). Faculty member, Herbert Lehman Coll., NYC, 1960–65. *Publs:* Cultural Pluralism and American Education, 1969; Ernst Cassirer: Scientific Knowledge and the Concept of Man, 1971; A New Public Education, 1976; Ernst Cassirer, Philosopher of Culture, 1977; Emanuel Feuermann: Virtuoso, 1979; The Form of Man, 1983; Triumph of the Intelligent, 1985; How We Learn To Read, 1986; Why Humans Vary in Intelligence, 1987. Add: Smith Coll., Dept. of Education and Child Study, Northampton, Mass. 01063, U.S.A.

IVAMY, Edward (Richard Hardy). British, b. 1920. Law. Prof. of Law, Univ. Coll., Univ. of London, 1960–86, now Emeritus (Asst. Lectr., 1947–50; Lectr., 1950–56; Reader, 1956–60). Member, Ed. Bd., Lloyd's Maritime and Commercial Law Quarterly, since 1974. Secty., Soc. of Public Teachers of Law, 1960–63. *Publs:* Show Business and the Law, 1955; (ed.) Payne and Ivamy's Carriage of Goods by Sea, 7th–13th eds. 1963–85; Hire–Purchase Legislation in England and Wales, 1965; Casebook on Carriage by Sea, 1965, 6th ed. 1985; (ed.) Chalmers' Marine Insurance Act 1906, 6th–9th eds. 1966–83; General Principles of Insurance Law, 1966, 5th ed. 1986; Casebook on Sale of Goods, 1966, 5th ed. 1987; (ed.) Topham and Ivamy's Company Law, 13th–16th eds. 1967–78; Casebook on Commercial Law, 1967, 3rd ed. 1979; Fire and Motor Insurance, 1968, 4th ed. 1984; Marine Insurance, 1969, 4th ed. 1985; Casebook on Insurance Law, 1969, 4th ed. 1984; Casebook on Agency, 1970, 3rd ed., 1987; Casebook on Shipping Law, 1970, 4th ed. 1987; Casebook on Partnership, 1971, 1982; Personal Accident, Life, and Other Insurances, 1973, 1980; (ed.) Underhill's Law of Partnership, 12th ed. 1986; Dictionary of Insurance Law, 1981; Dictionary of Company Law, 1983, 1985; Dictionary of Shipping Law, 1984; Encyclopedia of Shipping Law Sources (UK), 1985; Encyclopedia of Oil and Natural Gas Law, 1986; Encyclopedia of Carriage Law Sources, 1987; (ed.) Mozley and Whiteley's Law Dictionary, 10th ed., 1988. Add: 7 Egliston Mews, London SW15, England.

IVENS, Michael William. British, b. 1924. Poetry, Business/Trade/Industry, Economics. Dir., Aims of Industry, since 1971. Dir. and Founder, Foundn. for Business Responsibilities, since 1968. Ed., Twentieth Century mag., 1967–73; Vice Pres., Jr. Hosp. Doctors Assn., 1969–73; Dir., Standard Telephones, 1970–71. *Publs:* Practice of Industrial Communication, 1963; Another Sky, 1963; Last Waltz, 1964; (ed. with R. Dunstan) The Case for Capitalism, 1967; (ed.) Industry and Values, 1970; (ed. with C. Bradley) Which Way: 13 Choices for Britain, 1973; Private and Public; Born Early, 1975; (ed.) Prophets of Free Enterprise, 1975; (ed.) Backman Book of Freedom Quotations, 1978; No Woman Is an Island, 1983. Add: 40 Doughty St., London WC1N 2LF, England.

IVES, Morgan. *See* **BRADLEY,** Marion Zimmer.

IWATA, Masakazu. American, b. 1917. Biography. Prof. Emeritus of History since 1983, and Consultant, Japanese–American History Project, since 1966, Biola Univ., La Mirada, Calif. (Asst. Prof., 1961–64; Assoc. Prof., 1964–67; Prof., 1967–82; Chmn., Dept. of History, 1968–77; Chmn., Div. of Social Sciences/Business, 1977–78; Dean of the Coll., 1978–80). *Publs:* Okubo Toshimichi: Bismarck of Japan, 1964; Planted in Good Soil: The History of Japanese Immigrants in United States Agriculture, 1989. Add: 879 North Vail Ave., Montebello, Calif. 90640, U.S.A.

J

JACK, Ian (Robert James). British, b. 1923. Literature. Fellow, Pembroke Coll., Cambridge, since 1961 (Librarian, 1965–75), and Prof. of English Literature, Cambridge Univ. since 1976 (Lectr. in English, 1961–73, Reader in English, 1973–76). Lectr., then Fellow, Brasenose Coll., Oxford, 1950–61; Visiting Prof., Univ. of Alexandria, 1960; de Carle Lectr., Univ. of Otago, N.Z., 1964; Warton Lectr., British Academy, 1967; Visiting Prof., Univ. of Chicago, 1968–69, Univ. of Calif., Berkeley, 1968–69, Univ. of B.C., 1975, Univ. of Va., 1980–81, Tsuda Coll., Tokyo, 1981, and New York Univ., 1989. *Publs:* Augustan Satire, 1952; English Literature 1815–1832 (Oxford History of English Literature), 1963; Keats and the Mirror of Art, 1967; Browning's Major Poetry, 1973; (gen. ed.) Brontë's novels, Clarendon Ed.; (ed. with H. Marsden) E. Brontë's Wuthering Heights, 1976; (ed.) Oxford English Texts Ed. of Brownings Poetical Works, 1983–; The Poet and His Audience, 1984. Add: Highfield House, High St., Fen Ditton, Cambs. CB5 8ST, England.

JACKER, Corinne. American, b. 1933. Plays/Screenplays, Biology, Children's non–fiction, Information science/Computers, Politics/Government. Freelance writer. *Publs:* Man, Memory, and Machines: An Introduction to Cybernetics, 1964; Window on the Unknown: A History of the Microscope, 1966; The Black Flag of Anarchy: Antistatism in America, 1968; A Little History of Cocoa, 1968; 1868, 1968; The Biological Revolution, 1971; Bits and Pieces (play), 1975; Harry Outside (play), 1975; Night Thoughts, and Terminal (plays), 1977; Later (play), 1979; Domestic Issues (play), 1981; In Place, 1982; Let's Dance, 1985. Add: 110 West 86th St., New York, N.Y. 10024, U.S.A.

JACKMAN, Stuart (Brooke). British, b. 1922. Plays/ Screenplays, Mystery/Crime/Suspense, Theology/Religion. Congregational minister, serving in Barnstaple, Devon, 1948–52, Pretoria, South Africa, 1952–55, Caterham, Surrey, 1955–61, Auckland, 1961–65, Upminster, Essex, 1965–67, and Oxted, Surrey, since 1969. Ed., Council for World Mission, London, 1967–71. *Publs:* mystery novels—Portrait in Two Colours, 1948; The Daybreak Boys, 1961; The Davidson Affair, 1966; The Golden Orphans, 1968; Guns Covered with Flowers, 1973; Slingshot, 1975; The Burning Men, 1976; Operation Catcher, 1980; A Game of Soldiers, 1981; other—But They Won't Lie Down: Three Plays, 1954; The Numbered Days, 1954; Angels Unawares (play), 1956; One Finger for God, 1957; My Friend, My Brother (play), 1958; The Waters of Dinyanti, 1959; The Lazy T.V. and Other Stories (juvenile), 1961; This Desirable Property, 1966; The Davidson File, 1981. Add: c/o Curtis Brown, 162–168 Regent St., London W1R 5TB, England.

JACKMAN, Sydney Wayne. Canadian, b. 1925. History, Politics/Government, Travel/Exploration/Adventure, Biography. Prof. of History, Univ. of Victoria, B.C., since 1964. *Publs:* Galloping Head, 1958; (ed.) Frederick Marryat: A Diary in America, 1962; (ed.) With Burgoyne from Quebec, 1963; (ed.) The English Reform Tradition, 1965; (ed.) The Idea of a Patriot King, 1965; Man of Mercury, 1965; (co–ed.) American Voyageur, 1969; (ed.) Romanov Relations, 1969; Portraits of the Premiers, 1969; (ed.) A Middle Passage, 1970; The Men at Cary Castle, 1971; Vancouver Island, 1972; Tasmania, 1974; Nicholas Cardinal Wiseman, 1977; (ed.) The Journal of William Sturgis, 1978; (ed.) Acton in America, 1979; (ed.) A Curious Cage, 1981; (ed.) At Sea and By Land, 1984; A People's Princess, 1984; (with Hella Haase) Een Ureemdelinge in den Haag, 1984. Add: 1065 Deal St., Victoria, B.C., V85 5G6, Canada.

JACKS, Oliver. *See* **ROYCE,** Kenneth.

JACKSON, Anthony. Canadian, b. 1926. Architecture. Prof., Technical Univ. of Nova Scotia, Halifax, since 1973 (Assoc. Prof., 1963–73). Designer, Design Research Unit, London, 1950–51; Asst. Lectr., Sch. of Architecture, Southend–on–Sea, Essex, 1951–56; Designer, Canadian Govt. Exhibition Commn., Ottawa, 1957–59; Technical Ed., 1959–61, and Managing Ed., 1961–62, The Canadian Architect, Toronto. *Publs:* The Politics of Architecture: A History of Modern Architecture in Britain, 1970; A Place Called Home: A History of Low–Cost Housing in Manhattan, 1976; The Democratization of Canadian Architecture, 1978; The Future of Canadian Architecture, 1979; Space in Canadian Architecture, 1981. Add: Faculty of Architecture, Technical Univ. of Nova Scotia, Box 1000, Halifax, N.S. B3J 2X4, Canada.

JACKSON, Barbara Ann Garvey Seagrave. Wrote as Barbara Ann Garvey Seagrave until 1969. American, b. 1929. Music. Prof. of Music, Univ. of Arkansas, Fayetteville, 1954–56 and since 1961. Founder and Ed., ClarNan Editions, publisher of historic music by women composers, since 1984. Special music teacher, Los Angeles Public Schs., Calif., 1956–57; faculty member, Arkansas Polytechnic Coll., Russellville, 1957–61. *Publs:* (as Seagrave with Benward) Practical Beginning Theory, 1963, as Jackson with Benward, 6th ed. 1987; (as Seagrave with Thomas) Songs of the Minnesingers, 1965; (with Berman and Sarch) The A.S.T.A. Dictionary of String Bowing Terms, 1969, 3rd ed. 1987; (as Seagrave with Thomas) The Songs of the Minnesinger Wizlaw of Rugen, 1969; The Violin Sonatas of Giovanni Antonio Piani (Paris, 1712), 1974; (ed.) Isabella Leonarda's Sonata Duodecima from Op. 16 (1693) for Violin and Continuo, 1983. Add: 235 Baxter Lane, Fayetteville, Ark. 72701, U.S.A.

JACKSON, Clyde O(wen). American, b. 1928. Music, Race relations. Field Mgr., U.S. Postal Service, since 1973 (station Supt., 1972). Member of staff, Music Dept., 1961–68, and Information Officer, 1968–71, Texas Southern Univ., Houston; Ed., The Informer Group of Newspapers, 1969–72. *Publs:* The Songs of Our Years (music history), 1968; Before The Darkness Covers Us (race relations), 1969; In Old Hollywood, 1977; In This Evening Light, 1979; Come Like the Benediction, 1981; Let the Record Show, 1983; We Shall Never Sleep, 1985. Add: 10863 Fairland Dr., Houston, Tex. 77051, U.S.A.

JACKSON, David Cooper. British, b. 1931. Law. Vice–Pres., Immigration Appeal Tribunal, since 1984. Sir John Latham Prof. of Law, Monash Univ., Clayton, Vic., 1965–70; Prof. of Law, Univ. of Southampton, 1971–83. *Publs:* Principles of Property Law, 1967; The "Conflicts" Process, 1975; Enforcement of Maritime Claims, 1985; Maritime Claims: Jurisdiction and Judgement, 1987. Add: Dept of Law, Univ. of Southampton, Southampton, England.

JACKSON, E.F. *See* **TUBB,** E.C.

JACKSON, Elaine. *See* **FREEMAN,** Gillian.

JACKSON, Everatt. *See* **MUGGESON,** Margaret Elizabeth.

JACKSON, Gordon Noel. British, b. 1913. Sports/Physical education/Keeping fit. Farmer and horse breeder. Entered H.M. Diplomatic Service, 1947; Ambassador to Kuwait, 1963–67, and Ecuador, 1967 until retirement in 1970. *Publs:* Effective Horsemanship, 1967, 4th ed. 1980; (ed. with C.E.G. Hope and W. Steinkraus) International Encyclopedia of the Horse, 1973. Add: Lowbarrow House, Leafield, Oxon, England.

JACKSON, John N. Canadian, b. 1925. Geography, Regional/Urban planning. Prof. of Applied Geography, Brock Univ., St. Catharines, Ont., since 1965. Lectr., Manchester Univ., England, 1956–65. *Publs:* Surveys for Town and Country Planning, 1963; Recreational Development and the Lake Erie Shore, 1967; The Industrial Structure of the Niagara Peninsula, 1971; The Urban Future, 1972; The Canadian City: Space, Form, Quality, 1973; Practical Geography: Strategies for Study, 1974; Welland and the Welland Canal: The Welland Canal By–Pass, 1975; (co–author) Railways in the Niagara Peninsula, 1978; (co–author) The Welland Canals: A Comprehensive Guide, 1982; (co–author) The Welland Cannals: The Growth of Mr. Merritt's Ditch, 1988; (co–author) The Four Welland Canals, 1988. Add: Dept. of Geography, Brock Univ., St. Catharines, Ont., Canada.

JACKSON, Kenneth T(erry). American, b. 1939. History, Regional/Urban planning, Urban studies. Prof. of History since 1976, and Mellon Prof. since 1987, Columbia Univ., NYC (Asst. Prof. of History, 1968–71; Dir. of Urban Studies, 1970–77; Assoc. Prof., 1971–76). Exec. Secty., Soc. of American Historians Inc., since 1970; Gen. Ed., Columbia History of Urban Life series, since 1980. Assoc. Dir. of Research, Sch. of Systems and Logistics, U.S. Air Force Inst. of Technology, Ohio, 1965–68. Chmn. Bradley Commn. on History in Schools, 1987–89. *Publs:* The Ku Klux Klan in the City, 1915–1930, 1967; (ed. with L. Dinnerstein) American Vistas, 2 vols., 1971, 5th ed. 1987; (ed. with S.K. Schultz) Cities in American History, 1972; Atlas of American History, 1978; Crabgrass Frontier: The Suburbanization of the United States, 1985; (ed.) The New York City Encyclopaedia, 1989; Silent Cities: The Evolution of American Cemeteries, 1989. Add: Dept. of History, Columbia Univ., New York, N.Y. 10027, U.S.A.

JACKSON, Laura. *See* **RIDING**, Laura.

JACKSON, Neville. *See* **GLASKIN**, G.M.

JACKSON, Peter (William Russell). New Zealander, b. 1926. Education, Finance. Head of Commercial Dept., Mount Roskill Grammar Sch., Auckland, 1961–66; Chief Examiner, Sch. Certificate Bookkeeping, 1967; Deputy Principal, Upper Hutt Coll., 1966–67; Principal, Kaipara Coll. Helensville, 1968–74; Principal, Waitakere Coll., Henderson, Auckland, 1974–87. Chmn., National Recruitment Cttee. of N.Z. Soc. of Accountants, 1970–84; Chmn., Auckland Principals' Assn., 1980–81; Chmn., National Secondary Schools Principals' Conference, 1984–85. *Publs:* Accounting for Seniors. Add: 4 Nuimana Pl., Auckland 8, New Zealand.

JACKSON, Robert J. Canadian, b. 1936. Politics/Government. Prof., Dept. of Political Science, Carleton Univ., Ottawa, since 1974 (Asst. Prof., 1965'68; Assoc. Prof. and Supvr. of Grad. Studies, 1970–71). Assoc. Prof., McGill Univ., Montreal, 1968–70; Legislative Adviser and Dir. of Research, Office of the Pres. of the Privy Council, Ottawa, 1971–73; Sr. Policy Advisor, Leader of the Opposition, House of Commons, 1987–89. *Publs:* Rebels and Whips: Dissensions, Discipline, and Cohesion in British Parties, 1968; (with M. Stein) Issues in Comparative Politics, 1971; Canadian Legislative System: Politicians and Policy-Making, 1974, 1980; Continuity and Discord: Crises and Responses in the Altantic Community, 1985; Politics in Canada, 1985; The Politicization of Business in Western Europe, 1987; Contemporary Canadian Politics, 1987. Add: Dept. of Political Science, Carleton Univ., Ottawa 1, Ont., Canada.

JACKSON, Rosemary Elizabeth. (Rosemary Elizabeth Innes). British, b. 1917. Children's fiction. Art teacher, 1951–58. *Publs:* The Witch of Castlekerry, 1965; The Poltergeist, 1968; Aunt Eleanor, 1969; The Ashwood Train, 1970; The Street of Mars, 1971; The Wheel of the Funfolk, 1972. Add: Learney, Torphins, Aberdeenshire AB3 4NB, Scotland.

JACKSON, (Sir) William (Godfrey Fothergill). History, Military/Defence. British, b. 1917. Gen., British Army (commissioned, Royal Engineers, 1937; served in Norway, 1940, Tunisia, 1942–43, Italy, 1943–44, and the Far East, 1945; Gen. Staff Officer, Headquarters, Allied Land Forces, South East Asia, 1945–48; Instr., Staff Coll., Camberley Surrey, 1948–50, Royal Military Academy Sandhurst, 1951–53; Comdr., Gurkha Engineers, 1958–60; Col., Gen. Staff, Minley Div. of Staff Coll., Camberley, 1961–62; Deputy Dir. of Staff Duties, War Office, London, 1962–64; Imperial Defence Coll., London, 1965; Dir., Chief of Defence Staff—'s Unison Planning Staff, 1966–68; Asst. Chief of the Gen. Staff for Operational Requirements, Ministry of Defence, London, 1968–70; Gen. Officer Comdg.-in-Chief, Northern Command, 1970–72; Quartermaster Gen., 1973–77; Gov. and Comdr.-in-Chief, Gibraltar, 1978–82); Official Historian, Cabinet Officve, since 1983. *Publs:* Attack in the

West, 1953; Seven Roads to Moscow, 1957; The Battle for Italy, 1967; The Battle for Rome, 1969; Alexander of Tunis, 1971; North African Campaigns, 1975; Overlord: Normandy 1944, 1978; British Official History of 2nd World War: Mediterranean and Middle East, vol. VI, Part I, 1985, Part II, 1987, Part III, 1988; Withdrawal from Empire: A Military View, 1986; The Alternative Third World War, 1987; Rock of the Gibraltarians, 1988; The Off-Shore Island, 1989. Add: West Stowell Place, Oare, Marlborough, Wilts., England.

JACKSON, William (Peter Uprichard). British, b. 1918. Botany, Medicine/Health. Emeritus Prof., Dept. of Medicine, Univ. of Cape Town and Groote Schuur Hosp. *Publs:* On Diabetes Mellitus, 1964; Dieting for Overweight and Diabetes, 1965; Calcium Metabolism and Bone Disease, 1967; Diabetes Mellitus, Clinical and Metabolic, 1977; Wild Flowers of Table Mountain, 1977; Wild Flowers of the Fairest Cape, 1980; Origins and Meanings of South African Plane Genera, part 1, 1987. Add: White Lodge, Orange Rd., Newlands, Cape, South Africa.

JACKSON, William Keith. British, b. 1928. Politics/Government. Prof. of Political Science, Univ. of Canterbury, Christchurch, since 1968. *Publs:* (with A. Mitchell and R. Chapman) New Zealand Politics in Action, 1963; (with J. Harré) New Zealand, 1969; (ed.) Fight for Life: New Zealand, Britain and the European Economic Community, 1972; The New Zealand Legislative Council, 1972; New Zealand: Politics of Change, 1973; (co-ed.) Beyond New Zealand: The Foreign Policy of a Small State, 1980; The Dilemma of Parliament, 1987. Add: Dept. of Political Science, Univ. of Canterbury, Christchurch, New Zealand.

JACO, E(gbert) Gartly. American, b. 1923. Medicine/Health, Sociology. Prof. of Sociology, Univ. of California, Riverside, since 1966 (Chmn. of Dept., 1966–70); Prof., Div. of Sociomedical Sciences, Dept. of Preventive Medicine and Public Health, Univ. of Texas Medical Branch, Galveston, since 1978. Exec. Ed., Cap and Gown Press Inc., Houston, Tex., since 1981. Dir., and Assoc. Prof., Div. of Medical Sociology, Univ. of Texas Medical Branch, Galveston, 1955–59; Dir., Lab of Socio-Environmental Studies, Cleveland Psychiatric Inst., Ohio, 1959–61; Assoc. Prof., Western Reserve Univ., 1959–62; Prof., Sch. of Public Health, and Dept. of Sociology, Univ. of Minnesota, Minneapolis, 1962–66. *Publs:* The Social Epidemiology of Mental Disorders, 1960, 1989; (ed.) Patients, Physicians and Illness, 2nd ed. 1972, 3rd ed. 1979. Add: Dept. of Preventive Medicine, Univ. of Texas Medical Branch, Galveston, Tex. 77550, U.S.A.

JACOBS, Arthur David. British, b. 1922. Music, Translations. Member, Editorial Bd., since 1972 (Deputy Ed., 1962–71); Critic and Columnist, Hi Fi News and Record Review, since 1964; Opera Record Reviewer, Sunday Times, London, since 1964; Ed., British Music Yearbook, 1971–79; Prof., Royal Academy of Music, London, 1964–79; Professor and Head of the Dept. of Music, Huddersfield Polytechnic, 1979–84. *Publs:* Gilbert and Sullivan, 1951; A New Dictionary of Music, 1958; (ed. and contrib.) Choral Music, 1963; (with Stanley Sadie) Pan Book of Opera (in U.S. as Great Operas in Synopsis), 1966, reissued as The Opera Guide: A Short History of Western Music, 1972; (ed.) Music Education Handbook, 1976; Arthur Sullivan: A Victorian Musician, 1984; Pan Book of Orchestral Music, 1987. Add: 10 Oldbury Close, Sevenoaks, Kent TN15 9DJ, England.

JACOBS, Clyde (Edward). American, b. 1925. Politics/Government. Prof. Emeritus of Political Science, Univ. of California, Davis. *Publs:* Law Writers, 1954; Justice Frankfurter, 1960; (co-author) California Government, 1965, 1970; (co-author) The Selective Service Act, 1967; The Eleventh Amendment, 1972. Add: 2708 Cadiz St., Davis, Calif. 95616, U.S.A.

JACOBS, Dan(iel) N(orman). American, b. 1924. Politics/Government. Prof. of Political Science, Miami Univ., Oxford, Ohio, since 1965 (Asst. Prof., 1959–62; Assoc. Prof., 1962–65). *Publs:* (ed.) The New Communist Manifesto, 1961, 3rd. ed. 1965; The Masks of Communism, 1963; (ed. with H.H. Baerwald) Chinese Communism, 1963; (contrib. ed.) Dictionary of Political Science, 1964; (contrib.) Handbook of Historical Concepts, 1967; The New Communisms, 1969; (co-author) Ideologies and Modern Politics, 1972, 1976, 1981; From Marx to Mao and Marchais, 1979; Borodin: Stalin's Man in China, 1981; (co-author) Studies of the Third Wave: Recent Migration of Soviet Jews to the United States, 1981; Comparative Politics, 1983. Add: 211 Beechpoint Dr., Oxford, Ohio, U.S.A.

JACOBS, Francis G(eoffrey). British, b. 1939. Law. Advocate-Gen., Court of Justice of the European Communities, since 1988. Lectr. in

Jurisprudence, Univ. of Glasgow, 1963–65; Lectr. in Law, London Sch. of Economics and Political Science, 1965–69; Member of the Secretariat, European Commn. of Human Righgts, and of the Legal Directorate, Council of Europe, Strasbourg, 1969–72; Law Clerk, Court of Justice of the Eueopean Communities, Luxembourg, 1972–74; Prof. of European Law, Univ. of London, 1974–88. Ed., Yearbook of European Law, 1981–88. *Publs:* Criminal Responsibility, 1971; (with Andrew Durand) References to the European Court: Practice and Procedure, 1975; The European Convention on Human Rights, 1975; (ed.) European Law and the Individual, 1976; (with L. Neville Brown) The Court of Justice of the European Communities, 1977, 3rd ed. 1989; The European Union Treaty, 1986. Add: Court of Justice of the European Communities, L2920 Luxembourg.

JACOBS, Helen Hull. American, b. 1908. Novels/Short stories, Children's fiction, Sports/Physical education/Keeping fit, Autobiography/Memoirs/Personal. Comdr., U.S. Naval Reserve (Ret.); Sr. Ed., Grolier Council for Educational Research, NYC, 1961–65. *Publs:* Modern Tennis, 1932; Beyond the Game (autobiography), 1936; Improve Your Tennis, 1936; Barry Court, 1938; Tennis, 1941; By Your Leave, Sir: Story of a WAVE, 1944; Storm Against the Wind, 1944; Laurel for Judy, 1944; Adventure in Bluejeans, 1945; Gallery of Champions, 1949; Center Court, 1952; Judy, Tennis Ace, 1952; Proudly She Serves, 1953; (co–author) Golf, Tennis, Swimming, 1961; Young Sportsman Guide to Tennis, 1961; Better Physical Fitness for Girls, 1964; Famous American Women Athletes, 1964; Courage to Conquer, 1967; The Tennis Machine, 1972; Famous Modern American Woman Athletes, 1974; Beginner's Guide to Winning Tennis, 1975; The Savage Ally, 1975. Add: 26 Joanne Lane, Weston, Conn. 06883, U.S.A.

JACOBS, Jane. Canadian, b. 1916. Economics, Urban Studies. *Publs:* The Death and Life of Great American Cities, 1961; The Economy of Cities, 1969; The Question of Separatism, 1980; Cities and the Wealth of Nations, 1985; The Girl on the Hat (children's book), 1989. Add: c/o Random House, 201 E. 50th St., New York, N.Y. 10022, U.S.A.

JACOBS, John (Arthur). Canadian, b. 1916. Earth sciences. Prof. of Geophysics, Cambridge Univ., since 1974; Professorial Fellow, University Coll. of Wales, Aberystwyth, since 1988. Lectr. in Applied Mathematics, Univ. of London, 1946–51; Assoc. Prof. of Applied Mathematics, 1951–54, and of Geophysics, 1954–57, Univ. of Toronto; Dir., Inst. of Earth Science, Univ. of British Columbia, Vancouver , 1957–67; Killam Memorial Prof. of Science, and Dir., Inst. of Earth and Planetary Physics, Univ. of Alberta, Edmonton, 1967–74; Chmn., Canadian National Cttee. for the Intnl. Union of Geodesy and Geophysics, 1971–75; Assoc. Ed., Physics of the Earth and Planetary Interiors. *Publs:* (with R.D. Russell and J.T. Wilson) Physics and Geology, 1959, 1974; The Earth's Core and Geomagnetism, 1963; Geomagnetic Micropulsations, 1970; A Text Book on Geonomy, 1974; The Earth's Core, 1975, 1987; Reversals of the Earth's Magnetic Field, 1984. Add: Inst. of Earth Studies, University Coll. of Wales, Aberystwyth SY23 3DB, England.

JACOBS, Leah. *See* **GELLIS,** Roberta.

JACOBS, Louis. British, b. 1920. Theology/Religion, Autobiography. Rabbi, New London Synagogue, London, since 1963. *Publs:* Jewish Values, 1960; Studies in Talmudic Logic, 1961; Jewish Prayer, 3rd ed. 1962; Principles of the Jewish Faith, 1964; We Have Reason to Believe, 3rd ed. 1965; Chain of Tradition, 4 vols., 1968–73; Hasidic Prayer, 1972; A Jewish Theology, 1973; What Does Judaism Say About . . .?, 1974; Jewish Mystical Testimonies, 1977; A Tree of Life, 1984; The Talmudic Argument, 1984; The Book of Jewish Belief, 1984; Helping with Inquiries: An Autobiography, 1989. Add: 27 Clifton Hill, London NW8, England.

JACOBS, Walter Darnell. American, b. 1922. International relations/Current affairs, Politics/Government. Prof. of Govt. and Politics, Univ. of Maryland, College Park, 1961–78; Pres., Free Ukraine, 1965; Co–Chmn., American–African Affairs Assn., 1967–80. Dir., Defense Orientation Conference Assn., 1971–74. *Publs:* (co–author) Modern Governments, 3rd ed. 1966; Frunze, 1969; South Africa Looks Outward, 1970; Rhodesia Going on Eight, 1973; (co–author) Terrorism in Southern Africa, 1973; (co–author) At the Sharp Edge in Africa, 1975; Rhodesia to Zimbabwe, 1980. Add: 101 Rutledge Ave., Charleston, S.C. 29401, U.S.A.

JACOBS, Wilbur R(ipley). American, b. 1918. History. Prof. of History, Univ. of California, Santa Barbara, since 1949 (Chmn., Dept. of History, 1955–59). Member, Editorial Bd., ABC Clio Press, Western Historical Quarterly, American West Mag., American Indian Quarterly,

Public Historian, and papers of Will Rogers. *Publs:* (ed.) Letters of Francis Parkman, 2 vols., 1960; Wilderness Politics and Indian Gifts, 1967; (ed.) Frederick Jackson Turner's Legacy, 1969; The Historical World of Frederick Jackson Turner, 1970; (ed.) Benjamin Franklin: Statesman, Philosopher or Materialist?, 1972; Dispossessing the American Indian, 1972, 1985; (with others) Turner, Bolton and Webb: Three Historians of the American Frontier, 1979; (ed.) Indians as Ecologists, 1980. Add: Dept. of History, Univ. of California, Santa Barbara, Calif. 93106, U.S.A.

JACOBSEN, Josephine. Canadian, b. 1908. Novels/Short stories, Poetry, Literature. Hon. Consultant in American Letters, Library of Congress, Washington, D.C., since 1973 (Poetry Consultant, 1971–73); Vice-Pres., Poetry Soc. of America, since 1979. Member of Literature Panel, National Endowment for the Arts, 1980–84. Add: Let Each Man Remember, 1940; For the Unlost, 1946; The Human Climate, 1953; (with W. Mueller) The Testament of Samuel Beckett, 1964; The Animal Inside: Poems, 1966; (with W.R. Mueller) Ionesco and Genet: Playwrights of Silence, 1968; From Anne to Marianne: Some American Women Poets, 1973; The Instant of Knowing (lecture), 1974; The Shade–Seller: New and Selected Poems, 1974; A Walk with Raschid and Other Stories, 1979; The Chinese Insomniacs, 1981; Mr. Morley: 13 Short Stories, 1986; The Sisters: New and Selected Poems, 1987; On the Island: New and Selected Stories, 1989. Add: 220 Stony Ford Rd., Baltimore, Md. 21210, U.S.A.

JACOBSON, Dan. British, b. 1929. Novels/Short stories, Literature. Prof. of English University Coll., London since 1988 (Lectr., 1976–80; Reader, 1980–88). Fellow in Creative Writing, Stanford Univ., Calif. 1956–57; Visiting Prof., Syracuse Univ., N.Y., 1965–66; Visiting Fellow, State Univ. of New York at Buffalo, 1972; Visiting Fellow, Australia National Univ., Canberra, 1981. *Publs:* The Trap, 1955; A Dance in the Sun, 1956; The Price of Diamonds, 1957; A Long Way from London, 1958; The Zulu and the Zeide, 1959; No Further West, 1959; Evidence of Love, 1960; Time of Arrival, 1962; Beggar My Neighbour, 1964; The Beginners, 1966; Through the Wilderness, 1968; The Rape of Tamar, 1970; Inklings, 1973; The Wonder Worker, 1973; The Confessions of Josef Baisz, 1977; The Story of the Stories, 1982; Time and Time Again, 1985; Her Story, 1987; Adult Pleasures, 1988. Add: c/o A.M. Heath & Co., 79 St. Martin's Lane, London WC2, England.

JACOBSON, Jon. American, b. 1938. History, International relations/Current affairs. Assoc. Prof. of History, Univ. of California, Irvine, since 1971 (Asst. Prof., 1965–71). *Publs:* Locarno Diplomacy: Germany and the West 1925–1929, 1972. Add: Dept. of History, Univ. of California, Irvine, Calif. 92717, U.S.A.

JACOBUS, Lee A. American, b. 1935. Poetry, Education, Literature. Prof. of English, Univ. of Connecticut, Storrs, since 1976 (Asst. Prof., 1968–71; Assoc. Prof., 1971–76). Faculty member, Western Connecticut State Coll., 1960–68. *Publs:* Improving College Reading, 1967, 5th ed. 1988; Aesthetics and the Arts, 1968; Issues and Response 1968, rev. ed. 1972; Developing College Reading, 1970, 1979; (ed.) 17 from Everywhere: Short stories from Around the World, 1971; Poetry in Context, 1974; John Cleveland, 1975; Humanities Through the Arts, 1974, 3rd ed. 1983; Sudden Apprehension: Aspects of Knowledge in "Paradise Lost", 1976; The Paragraph and Essay Book, 1977; The Sentence Book, 1980; (ed.) Longman Anthology of American Drama, 1982; Shakespeare and the Quest for Certainty, 1983; Significances: A Rhetoric Reader of Ideas, 1983; Humanities: The Evolution of Values, 1984; Writing as Thinking, 1989. Add: c/o Harcourt Brace Jovanovich, 1250 Sixth Ave., San Diego, Calif. 92101, U.S.A.

JACOBUS, Mary. British, b. 1944. Literature. Prof., Dept. of English, Cornell Univ. Ithaca, since 1982 (Assoc. Prof., 1980–82). Lectr., Dept. of English, Manchester Univ., 1970–71; Fellow and Tutor in English, Lady Margaret Hall, and Lectr. in English, Oxford Univ., 1971–80. *Publs:* Tradition and Experiment in Wordsworth's Lyrical Ballads (1798), 1976; (ed.) Woman Writing and Writing about Women, 1979; Reading Woman, 1986. Add: Dept. of English, Cornell Univ., Ithaca, N.Y. 14853, U.S.A.

JAEGER, Harry Kenneth. British, b. 1922. Business/Trade/Industry, Money/Finance. Sr. Lectr., North East London Polytechnic, Barking, Essex, 1966–81. Company Secty. and Accountant, 1954–66. *Publs:* The Structure of Consolidated Accounting, 1976, 1984. Add: 35 Paget Rd., Ilford, Essex IG1 2HP, England.

JAFFA, George. Pseud. for George Wallace–Clarke. British, b. 1916. Law. Freelance Writer. Land Agent, Canterbury, Ministry of Defence, 1966–78, now retired (Asst. Surveyor of Lands, Admiralty, 1946–49;

Lands Officer, Air Ministry, 1952–56). *Publs:* Your Rights as a Ratepayer, 1973. Add: Sanston, Grasmere Rd., Chestfield, Whitstable, Kent, England.

JAFFÉ, (Andrew) Michael. British, b. 1923. Art. Fellow, King's College, Cambridge, since 1952, Prof. of the History of Western Art, Cambridge Univ., since 1973, and Dir. of the Fitzwilliam Museum, Cambridge, since 1973 (Asst. Lectr., 1956–61, Lectr., 1961–68, Reader, 1968–73, and Head of Dept. of History of Art, 1970–73, Cambridge Univ.; a Syndic, Fitzwilliam Museum, 1971–73). Prof. of Renaissance Art, Washington Univ., St. Louis, 1960–61. *Publs:* Van Dyck's Antwerp Sketchbook, 1966; Rubens, 1967; Jordaens, 1968; Rubens and Italy, 1977. Add: Grove Lodge, Trumpington St., Cambridge, England.

JAFFE, Rona. American. Novels/Short stories, Children's fiction. Freelance writer, and television personality. *Publs:* The Best of Everything, 1958; Away from Home, 1960; The Last of the Wizards, 1961; Mr. Right is Dead, 1965; The Cherry in the Martini, 1966; The Fame Game, 1969; The Other Woman, 1972; Family Secrets, 1974; The Last Chance, 1976; Class Reunion, 1979; Mazes and Monsters, 1981; After the Reunion, 1985. Add: c/o Delacorte Press, 1 Dag Hammarskjold Plaza, New York, N.Y. 10017, U.S.A.

JAFFIN, David. American, b. 1937. Poetry, Theology. Minister, Lutheran Church of Württemberg, Germany, since 1974. Lectr. in European History, Univ. of Maryland, European Division, 1966–70. *Publs:* Conformed to Stone, 1968; Emptied Spaces, 1972; At the Gate, 1974; In the Glass of Winter, 1975; As One, 1975; The Half of a Circle, 1977; Space Of, 1978; Perceptions, 1979; INRI, 1980; Die Welt und der Weltlüberwinder, 1981; The Density for Color, 1982; For the Finger's Want of Sound, 1982; Selected Poems, 1982; Der Bringt Viel Frucht, 1983; Die Heiligkeit Gottes in Jesus Christus, 1984; Jesus Mein Herr und Befreier, 1985; Warum Brauchen Wir das Alte Testament, 1986; Der Auferstandene Christus Als Unsere Seelsorger, 1986; Israel am Ende der Tage, 1987; Malmsheimer Predigten, 1988; Josua, Die Landnahme, 1989; Wastl, Die Geschichte eines Pfarrdackels, 1989; Salomo, Israel am Scheideweg, 1989. Add: Merklinger Strasse 22, 7253 Renningen 2 (Malmsheim), Germany.

JAGER, Martin Otto. Australian, b. 1925. Law, Finance. Emeritus Prof. and Hon. Assoc. in Commerce, since 1985 (Prof., 1966–85), Univ. of Newcastle, N.S.W.. Lectr., then Sr. Lectr., Univ. of Melbourne, 1959–64; Prof. of Accounting, Victoria Univ. of Wellington, N.Z., 1964–66. *Publs:* (with A.G. Topp) Guide to the Companies Act, 1962; (with W.E. Paterson and H.H. Ednie) Australian Company Law, 1962; (with T.R. Johnston) The Law and Practice of Company Accounting in Australia, 1963, 6th ed. (with T.R. Johnston and R.B. Taylor) 1987; (with A.A. Fitzgerald, G.E. Fitzgerald and L.C. Voumand) Form and Contents of Financial Statements, 3rd ed. 1964; (with H.H. Ednie) Australian Company Law Service, 1966–71; (contrib.) Fitzgeralds' Accounting, 5th ed. 1967; (consultant ed. with W.E. Paterson and H.H. Ednie) Australian Company Law, 6 vols., 1971–87; (with R.B. Taylor and R.J. Craig) Financial Statements: Form and Content, 1975; (with K.M. Graham and R.B. Taylor) Company Accounting Procedures, 1984, 3rd ed. 1988. Add: 61 Woodward St., Mercarther Heights, N.S.W. 2291, Australia.

JAGGER, Peter (John). British, b. 1938. History, Theology/Religion, Biography. Warden and Chief Librarian, St. Deiniol's Library, Hawarden, Deeside, Clwyd, since 1977; Member of British Library National Preservation Advisory Cttee. and the Royal Historical Society. Dir., Self Supporting Ministry, N. Wales; Regional Rep., Lambeth Diploma Cttee.; Member, Theological Coll. Principals Conference. Curate of All Saints, Leeds, 1968–71; Vicar of Bolton cum Redmire, Diocese of Ripon, Yorks., 1971–77. *Publs:* Christian Initiation 1552–1969: Rites of Baptism and Confirmation Since the Reformation Period, 1970; (ed.) Being the Church Today: A Collection of Sermons and Addresses by Bishop Henry de Candole, 1974; Bishop Henry de Candole: His Life and Times 1895–1971, 1975; The Alcuin Club and Its Publications 1897–1974, 1975; A History of the Parish and People Movement, 1978; (contr.) A Social History of the Diocese of Newcastle, 1981; Clouded Witness: Initiation in the Church of England in the Mid–Victorian Period, 1850–1875, 1982; Gladstone: Politics and Religion—A Collection of Founder's Day Lectures delivered at St. Deiniol's Library, Hawarden 1967–1983, 1984. Add: St. Deiniol's Library, Hawarden, Deeside, Clwyd CH5 3DF, N. Wales.

JAKES, John. Has also written as Alan Payne and Jay Scotland. American, b. 1932. Novels/Short stories, Mystery/Crime/Suspense, Historical/Romance/Gothic, Westerns/Adventure, Science fiction/Fantasy. Freelance writer since 1971. Formerly worked in advertising. Held various advertising/marketing posts, 1954–70. *Publs:* The Texans Ride North (juvenile), 1952; Wear a Fast Gun, 1956; A Night for Treason, 1956; The Devil Has Four Faces, 1958; (as Alan Payne) This'll Slay You, 1958; (as Alan Payne) Murder He Says, 1958; (as Jay Scotland) The Seventh Man, 1958; (as Jay Scotland) I, Barbarian, 1959; The Imposter, 1959; Johnny Havoc, 1960; (as Jay Scotland) Strike the Black Flag, 1961; (as Jay Scotland) Sir Scoundrel, 1962; (as Jay Scotland) Veils of Salome, 1962; Johnny Havoc Meets Zelda, 1962; (as Jay Scotland) Arena, 1963; (as Jay Scotland) Traitors' Legion, 1963; Johnny Havoc and the Doll Who Had "It," 1963; G.I. Girls, 1963; Tiros: Weather Eye in Space (non–fiction), 1966; Famous Firsts in Sports (non–fiction), 1967; When the Star Kings Die, 1967; Making It Big, 1968; Great War Correspondents (non–fiction), 1968; Brak the Barbarian (short stories), 1968; Great Women Reporters (non–fiction), 1969; The Asylum World, 1969; Brak Versus the Mark of the Demons, 1969, in U.K. as Brak the Barbarian: The Mark of the Demons, 1970; Brak the Barbarian Versus the Sorceress, 1969, in U.K. as Brak the Barbarian: The Sorceress, 1970; The Hybrid, 1969; The Last Magicians, 1969; The Planet Wizard, 1969; Secrets of Stardeep (juvenile), 1969; Tonight We Steal the Stars, 1969; Black in Time, 1970; Mask of Chaos, 1970; Master of the Dark Gate, 1970; Monte Cristo 99, 1970; Six–Gun Planet, 1970; Mention My Name in Atlantis, 1972; Time Gate (juvenile), 1972; Witch of the Dark Gate, 1972; Conquest of the Planet of the Apes (novelization of screenplay), 1972; On Wheels, 1973; Kent Family Chronicles: The Bastard, 1974, The Rebels, 1975, The Seekers, 1975, The Furies, 1976, The Titans, 1976, The Warriors, 1977, The Lawless, 1978, and the Americans, 1980; The Best of John Jakes (short stories), 1977; King's Crusader, 1977; (as Jay Scotland) The Man from Cannae, 1977; When Idols Walked, 1978; Excalibur, 1980; The Bastard Photostory (non–fiction), 1980; The North and South Trilogy, 1982; Love and War, 1984; Heaven and Hell, 1987; California Gold, 1989. Add: c/o Rembar and Curtis, 19 W. 44th St., New York, N.Y. 10036, U.S.A.

JAMES, Alan. British, b. 1943. Children's non–fiction, Biography. Deputy Head, Runnymede First Sch., Ponteland, Northumberland, since 1979. Form Master, Jr. Sch., Royal Grammar Sch., Newcastle upon Tyne, 1968–78. *Publs:* Animals, 1969; Hospitals, 1969; The Post, 1970; Living Light, Book One, 1970; Buses and Coaches, 1971; Tunnels, 1972; Sir Rowland Hill and the Post Office, 1972; Living Light, Book Two, 1972; Money, 1973; Collecting Stamps, 1973; Submarines, 1973; Amphibians and Reptiles, 1973; Clocks and Watches, 1974; Zoos, 1974; Keeping Pets, 1975; Newspapers, 1975; Buildings, 1975; Living Light, Book Five, 1975; Spiders and Scorpions, 1976; Newspapers and the Times in the Nineteenth Century, 1976; The Telephone Operator, 1976; The Vet, 1976; Stocks and Shares, 1977; Circuses, 1978; Let's Visit Finland, 1979; Let's Visit Austria, 1984; Let's Visit Denmark, 1984; Lapps: Reindeer Herders of Lapland, 1986; Homes in Hot Places, 1987; Homes in Cold Places, 1987; Homes on Water, 1988; Castles and Mansions, 1988; Gilbert and Sullivan: Their Lives and Times, 1989. Add: The Stable, Market Sq., Holy Island, Northumberland, TD15 2RU, England.

JAMES, Bill. *See* **TUCKER,** James.

JAMES, Clive (Vivian Leopold). Australian, b. 1939. Poetry, Literature, Autobiography/Memoirs/Personal, Humor/Satire. Feature Writer, The Observer newspaper, London, since 1972 (TV Critic, 1972–82). *Publs:* The Metropolitan Critic, 1974; The Fate of Felicity Fark in the Land of the Media, 1975; Peregrine Prykke's Pilgrimage Through the London World, 1976; Britannia Bright's Bewilderment in the Wilderness of Westminster, 1976; Visions Before Midnight, 1977; Fan–Mail, 1977; At the Pillars of Hercules, 1979; Unreliable Memoirs, 1980; The Crystal Bucket, 1981; Charles Charming's Challenges on the Pathway to the Throne, 1981; From the Land of Shadows, 1982; Glued to the Box, 1982; Brilliant Creatures, 1983; Poem of the Year, 1983; Flying Visits, 1984; Falling Towards England: Unreliable Memoirs II, 1985; Other Passports, 1986; The Remake, 1987; Snakecharmers in Texas, 1988. Add: c/o A.D. Peters and Co., The Chambers, Chelsea Harbour, Lots Rd., London SW10 0XF, England.

JAMES, David Edward. British, b. 1937. Education, Psychology. Prof. of Educational Studies, Univ. of Surrey, Guildford, since 1969 (Lectr. in Human Biology, 1965–69). Head of Biology Section, City of Bath Technical Coll., 1961–63; Head of Educational Psychology, St. Mary's Coll. of Education, Newcastle upon Tyne, 1963–65. *Publs:* A Students Guide to Efficient Study, 1966; Introduction to Psychology, 1968, 1969. Add: Dept. of Educational Studies, Univ. of Surrey, Guildford, Surrey, England.

JAMES, David Geraint. Also writes as AERYNOG. British, b. 1922.

Medicine/Health. Consultant Physician since 1959, and Dean since 1968, Royal Northern Hosp., London. Ed.–in–Chief, The Sarcoidosis Journal. Prof. of Medicine, Univ. of Miami, Fla.; Consulting Ophthalmic Physician, St. Thomas Hosp., London; Consulting Physician, Royal Navy; Hon. Consultant Physician, Sydney Hosp. *Publs:* The Diagnosis and Treatment of Infections, 1957; Circulation of the Blood, 1978; A Colour Atlas of Respiratory Diseases, 1981; Sarcoidosis and Other Granulomatous Disorders, 1985. Add: 149 Harley St., London W1, England.

JAMES, Elizabeth. Also writes with Carol Barkin under joint pseudonym Elizabeth Carroll. American, b. 1942. Novels, Children's non-fiction. *Publs:* with Carol Barkin as Elizabeth Carroll—How To Keep a Secret: Writing and Talking in Code, 1978; What Do You Mean by "Average"?: Means, Medians, and Modes, 1978; How to Write a Term Paper, 1980; A Place of Your Own, 1981; How to Write a Great School Report, 1983; How to be School Smart: Secrets of Successful Schoolwork, 1988; other—(with Malka Drucker) Series TV: How a Show Is Made, 1983; Life Class (novel), 1987. Add: c/o Lothrop, Lee and Shepard Books, 105 Madison Ave., New York, N.Y. 10016, U.S.A.

JAMES, John Ivor Pulsford. British, b. 1913. Medicine/Health. Orthopaedic Surgeon, Royal National Orthopaedic Hosp., London, 1946–58; Asst. Dir., Inst. of Orthopaedics, London, 1948–58; Prof. of Orthopaedic Surgery, Univ. of Edinburgh, 1958–79; Head of Orthopaedic Services, Kuwait, 1979–83. *Publs:* Scoliosis, 1967, 1975; Poliomyelitis, 1987. Add: Abbey Farm, The Vatch, Slad Valley, Gloucester GL6 7LE, England.

JAMES, (William) Louis (Gabriel). British, b. 1933. History, Literature. Prof. in English and Americn Studies, Univ. of Kent, Canterbury, since 1966. Assoc. Ed. Victorian Periodicals Review. Member of faculty, Univ. of Hull, 1958–63, and Univ. of the West Indies, 1963–66. *Publs:* Fiction for the Working Man, 1830–50, 1963; (ed.) The Islands in Between, 1968; (ed.) Print and the People 1815–1851, 1976; Jean Rhys, 1979; (ed.) Performance and Politics in Popular Theatre, 1980. Add: 27 Norman Road, Canterbury, Kent, England.

JAMES, Matthew. See **LUCEY,** James D.

JAMES, Noel David Glaves. British, b. 1911. Agriculture/Forestry, Botany. Gen. practice as a land agent, 1933–39; Bursar, Corpus Christi Coll., Oxford, 1946–51; Land Agent, Oxford Univ., and Fellow of Brasenose Coll., Oxford, 1951–61; Land Agent for Lord Clinton and Clinton Devon Estates, 1961–76. *Publs:* Working Plans for Estate Woodlands, 1948; Notes on Estate Forestry, 1949; An Experiment in Forestry, 1951; The Forester's Companion, 1955, 4th ed. 1989; The Trees of Bicton, 1969; The Arboriculturalist's Companion, 1972; (ed.) A Book of Trees, 1973; Before the Echoes Die Away, 1980; A History of English Forestry, 1981; A Forestry Centenary, 1982; Gunners at Larkhill, 1983; Plain Soldiering, 1987. Add: Blakemore House, Kersbrook, Budleigh Salterton, Devon EX9 7AB, England.

JAMES, Philip Seaforth. British, b. 1914. Law. Prof. Emeritus of English Law, University Coll., Buckingham, since 1989 (Prof. and Head of the Dept. of Law, 1975–81). Fellow and Tutor, Exeter Coll., Oxford, 1946–49, Prof. and Head of the Dept. of Law, Univ. of Leeds, 1952–75. *Publs:* An Introduction to English Law, 1949, 9th ed. 1976; The General Principles of the Law of Torts, 1959; A Shorter Introduction to English Law, 1965; Six Lectures on the Law of Torts, 1980. Add: Chestnut View, Mill Lane, Whitfield, nr. Brackley NN13 5TQ, England.

JAMES, P(hyllis) D(orothy). Pseud. for Phyllis Dorothy White. British, b. 1920. Mystery/Crime/Suspense. Assoc. Fellow, Downing Coll., Cambridge. Member of the Arts Council, and Chmm. of its Literature Panel. Principal Administrative Asst., N.W. Metropolitan Regional Hosp. Bd., London, 1949–68; Principal, Police Dept. and Criminal Policy Dept., 1969–79. Chmn., Soc. of Authors, 1985–87. *Publs:* Cover Her Face, 1962; A Mind to Murder, 1963; Unnatural Causes, 1967; Shroud for a Nightingale, 1971; (with T.A. Critchley) The Maul and the Pear Tree (non–fiction), 1971; An Unsuitable Job for a Woman, 1972; The Black Tower, 1975; Death of an Expert Witness, 1977; Innocent Blood, 1980; The Skull Beneath the Skin, 1982; A Taste for Death, 1986. Add: c/o Elaine Green, Ltd., 31 Newington Green, London N16 9PU, England.

JAMES, R(obert) V(idal) Rhodes. British, b. 1933. History, Biography. Conservative Member of Parliament (U.K.) for Cambridge since 1976. Asst. Clerk, 1955–61, and Sr. Clerk, 1961–64, House of Commons, London; Fellow, All Souls Coll., Oxford, 1963–69, 1979–81; Kratter Prof. of European History, Stanford Univ., California, 1968; Dir., Inst.

for the Study of Intnl. Org., Univ. of Sussex, Brighton, 1968–73; Principal Officer, Exec. Office of the Secty.–Gen. of the U.N., NYC, 1973–76. *Publs:* Lord Randolph Churchill, 1959; An Introduction to the House of Commons, 1961; Rosebery, 1963; Gallipoli, 1965; (ed.) Chips: The Diaries of Sir Henry Channon, 1967; (ed.) Memoirs of a Conservative: The Memoirs and Papers of J.C.C. Davidson, 1968; (ed.) The Czechoslovak Crisis 1968, 1969; Churchill: A Study in Failure 1900–1939, 1970; Britain's Role in the United Nations, 1970; Ambitions and Realities: British Politics 1964–1970, 1971; (ed.) Complete Speeches of Sir Winston Churchill 1897–1963, 8 vols., 1974; Victor Cazalet: A Portrait, 1976; The British Revolution 1880–1939, vol. I, 1976, vol. II, 1977; Albert, Prince Consort, 1983; Anthony Eden, 1986. Add: House of Commons, London SW1A 0AA, England.

JAMES, Stephanie. See **KRENTZ,** Jayne.

JAMES, Sydney V. American, b. 1929. History. Prof. of History, Univ. of Iowa, Iowa City, since 1967 (Assoc. Prof., 1965–67; Chmn., 1970–74). Asst. Prof., Brown Univ., Providence, R.I. 1959–62; Asst. Prof., Univ. of Oregon, Eugene, 1962–65. *Publs:* A People Among Peoples: Quaker Benevolence in Eighteenth–Century America, 1963; (ed.) Three Visitors to Early Plymouth, 1963; (ed.) The New England Puritans, 1967; Colonial Rhode Island: A History, 1976. Add: Dept. of History, Univ. of Iowa, Iowa City, Iowa 52242, U.S.A.

JAMES, Theodore, Jr. American, b. 1934. Architecture, Art, Cookery/Gastronomy/Wine, Homes/Gardens, Recreation/Leisure/Hobbies, Travel/Exploration/Adventure. Freelance writer. Columnist, Women's Wear Daily, 1963–66. *Publs:* (with Rosaline Cole) The Waldorf–Astoria Cookbook, 1969; (with Prince Alexis Obolensky) Backgammon: The Action Game, 1969; Fifth Ave., 1971; The Empire State Building, 1975; How to Select and Grow African Violets and Other Gesneriads, 1983; How to Grow Fruit, Berries and Nuts in the Midwest and East, 1983; Landscaping: A Five-Year Plan, 1988; The Potpourri Gardener, 1990. Add: RR–3, 1415 Indian Neck Lane, Peconic, N.Y. 11958, U.S.A.

JAMES, William, M. See **GILMAN,** George G.; also see **HARVEY,** John B.

JAMESON, Eric. See **TRIMMER,** Eric J.

JANES, J(oseph) Robert. Canadian, b. 1935. Novels/Short stories, Children's fiction, Plays/Screenplays, Children's non-fiction, Earth sciences, Natural history. Full-time writer since 1970; consulting field geologist. Research Engineer in Minerals Benefication, 1959–64, and Field Researcher in Geology, Ontario Research Foundn. Toronto, 1966; Lectr. in Geology, Brock Univ., St. Catharines, Ont., 1966–67 and 1968–70. *Publs:* Rocks, Minerals, and Fossils, 1974; Earth Science, 1974; Geology and the New Global Tectonics, 1976; The Odd-Lot Boys and Tree-Fort War, 1976; (with C. Hopkins and J.D. Hoyes) Searching for Structure, vols. I and II, 1977; The Great Canadian Outback, 1978; Theft of Gold, 1980; The Toy Shop, 1981; Danger on the River, 1982; The Watcher, 1982; The Third Story, 1983; The Hiding Place, 1984; (with J.D.Mollard) Airphoto Interpretation and the Canadian Landscape, 1984; Spies for Dinner, 1984; Murder in the Market, 1985. Add: c/o Stan Colbert, 303 Davenport Rd., Toronto, Ont. M5R 1K5, Canada.

JANET, Lillian. See **O'DANIEL,** Janet.

JANEWAY, Eliot. American, b. 1913. Economics, Money/Finance. Pres., and Dir., Janeway Publishing and Research Corp., and Janeway Ventures Inc., and Publr., Janeway Service, NYC. Former Business Ed., Time Mag., NYC. *Publs:* The Struggle for Survival, 1951; The Economics of Crisis, 1968; What Shall I Do with My Money?, 1970; You and Your Money, 1972; Musing on Money, 1976; Prescriptions for Prosperity, 1983; The Economics of Chaos: On Revitalizing the American Economy, 1989. Add: 15 East 80th St., New York, N.Y. 10021, U.S.A.

JANGER, Allen R. American, b. 1932. Administration/Management. Sr. Research Assoc., The Conference Board, since 1986 (Research Specialist, Research Analyst and Research Asst., 1960–65; Dir. of Information Services, 1965–68; Sr. Specialist, Org. Development Research, 1968–75; Sr. Research Assoc., Mgmt. Research, 1975–81; Dir., Mgmt Research, 1981–82; Exec. Dir., Mgmt. System Programs, 1982–86). *Publs:* (with Harold Stieglitz) Top Management Organization in Divisionalized Companies, 1965; Personnel Administration: Changing Concept and Organization, 1966; (co–author) Programs to Employ the Disadvantaged, 1969; Managing Programs to Employ the Disadvantaged, 1970; Employing the Disadvantaged: An Employer Perspective, 1972; Corporate Organization Structure: Manufacturing, 1973; Corporate Organization Structures: Financial Companies, 1974; The Personnel Function: Changing Objectives and Organization, 1977; Corporate Organization Structures: Service Companies, 1977; Matrix Organization of Complex Businesses, 1979; Organization of International Joint Ventures, 1980; (with Ronald Berenheim) External Challenges to Management Decisionmaking: A Growing International Problem, 1981; (with Ruth Shaeffer) Who Is Top Management?, 1982; Management Outlook (series), 1983. Add: The Conference Board, 845 Third Ave., New York, N.Y. 10016, U.S.A.

JANIFER, Laurence M. Pseud. for Laurence Mark Harris; also writes romance and mystery novels as Larry Mark Harris, Alfred Blake, Andrew Blake, Barbara Wilson, and science fiction novels with Randall Garrett under joint pseud. Mark Phillips. American, b. 1933. Mystery/Crime/Suspense, Historical/Romance/Gothic, Science fiction/Fantasy. Professional comedian since 1957. Ed., Scott–Meredith, Inc., since 1985. Pianist and arranger, NYC, 1950–59; Ed., Scott Meredith Literary Agency, NYC, 1952–57; ed. and art dir., detective and science–fiction mags., 1953–57; Carnival fire–eater, 1960–69. Publs: (ghostwriter) Ken Murray's Giant Joke Book, 1957; (ghostwriter) The Henry Morgan Joke Book, 1958; (ghostwriter) The Foot in My Mouth, by Jeff Harris, 1958; (ghostwriter and ed.) Yes, I'm Here with Someone, by Thomas Sutton, 1958; (as Larry Mark Harris, with Randall Garrett) Pagan Passions (science fiction), 1959; (as Larry Mark Harris) The Pickled Poodles, 1960; (as Larry Mark Harris) The Protector, 1961; (as Mark Phillips) Brain Twister, 1962; (as Alfred Blake) The Bed and I, 1962; (as Andrew Blake) I Deal in Desire, 1962; Slave Planet (science fiction), 1963; (as Mark Phillips) The Impossibles, 1963; (as Mark Phillips) Supermind, 1963; (as Alfred Blake) Faithful for 8 Hours, 1963; (as Andrew Blake) Sex Swinger, 1963; (as Andrew Blake) Love Hostess, 1963; The Wonder War (science fiction), 1964; (as Barbara Wilson) The Pleasure We Know, 1964; You Sane Men (science fiction), 1964, as Bloodworld, 1968; (as Barbara Wilson) The Velvet Embrace, 1965; The Woman Without Name, 1966; (ed.) Masters' Choice, 1966, as 18 Great Science Fiction Stories, 1971; The Final Fear, 1967; You Can't Escape, 1967; A Piece of Martin Cann (science fiction), 1968; (with S.J. Treibich) Target: Terra (science fiction), 1968; Impossible? (SF short stories), 1968; (with S.J. Treibich) The High Sex (science fiction), 1969; (with S.J. Treibich) The Wagered World (science fiction), 1969; (ghostwriter) Tracer!, by Ed Goldfader, 1970; Power (science fiction), 1974; Survivor (science fiction), 1977; Knave in Hand, 1979; Reel, 1983. Add: c/o Doubleday, 666 Fifth Ave., New York, N.Y. 10103, U.S.A.

JANOWITZ, Tama. American, b. 1957. Novels/Short stories, Poetry. Freelance journalist, since 1985. Contributing writer/columnist, Interview mag., NYC, since 1985. Publs: American Dad, 1981; Slaves of New York, 1986; A Cannibal in Manhattan, 1987. Add: c/o Phyllis Janowitz, One Lodge Way, Ithaca, N.Y. 14850, U.S.A.

JANOWSKI, Thaddeus–Marian. American, b. 1923. Architecture, Art. Consulting architect; Prof. of Architecture, Syracuse Univ., N.Y., since 1971. Pres., Inst. for 3–Dimensional Perception, Inc., since 1985.Former Chief Consultant, Cttee. for Urban Affairs and Architecture, Warsaw, Poland; Assoc. Prof., Univ. of Manitoba, Winnipeg, 1962–65, and Iowa State Univ., Ames, 1965–71. Publs: Sacred Art in Poland, 1956; The Urban Scale, 1969; Architectural Graphics and Three Dimensional Communications, 1976. Add: 5903 Balao Way, St. Petersburg Beach, Fla. 33706, U.S.A.

JANOWSKY, Oscar I(saiah). American, b. 1900. Civil liberties/Human rights, History. Prof. of History, 1924–66, and Dir. of Grad. Studies, 1951–57, City Univ. of New York; Distinguished Visiting Prof., Brandeis Univ., Waltham, Mass., 1966–67. Publs: The Jews and Minority Rights, 1933; (with M. Fagen) International Aspects of German Racial Policies, 1937; People at Bay, 1938; (ed.) The American Jew: A Composite Portrait, 1942; Nationalists and National Minorities, 1945; The JWB Survey, 1948; Foundations of Israel, 1959; (ed.) The American Jew: A Reappraisal, 1964; (ed.) The Education of American Jewish Teachers, 1967; Jewish Community Center: Two Essays on Basic Purpose, 1974. Add: 247–C Mayflower Way, Rossmoor–Jamesburg, N.J. 08831, U.S.A.

JANSEN, Jared. See CEBULASH, Mel.

JAQUES, Elliott. British, b. 1917. Sociology. Prof., Emeritus, Brunel Univ., Uxbridge (Head, Sch. of Social Sciences, 1965–71; Dir. of the Inst. of Social and Organizational Studies, 1970–1986). Social Science Consultant, Glacier Metal Co. Ltd. Founder Staff Member,

Tavistock Inst. of Human Relations, London, 1946–51; Consultant on Org., Dept. of Health and Social Security, London, 1952–79. Publs: Changing Culture of a Factory, 1951; Measurement of Responsibility, 1956; Equitable Payment, 1961; (with W. Brown) Product Analysis Pricing, 1964; Time–Span Handbook, 1964; (with W. Brown) Glacier Project Papers, 1965; Progression Handbook, 1968; Work: Creativity and Social Justice, 1970; A General Theory of Bureaucracy, 1976; Levels of Abstraction in Logic and Human Action, 1978; Health Services, 1978; The Form of Time, 1982; Free Enterprise, Fair Employment, 1982; Requisite Organisation, 1988. Add: 1101 S. Arlington Pl., Ridge Rd., Arlington, VA 22202, U.S.A.

JAQUES, Louis Barker. Canadian, b. 1911. Medicine/Health, Theology/Religion. Emeritus Prof. of Physiology, Univ. of Saskatchewan, Saskatoon (Prof. and Head of Dept. of Physiology and Pharmacology, 1946–71). Publs: The Prayer Book Companion, 1963; Anticoagulant Therapy, 1965. Add: 682 University Dr., Saskatoon, Sask, S7N 0J2, Canada.

JARES, Joe. American, b. 1937. Sports/Physical education/Keeping fit. Sports Columnist, Los Angeles Daily News, since 1985. Staff Writer, U.P.I., Los Angeles, 1959; Sports Writer, Los Angeles Herald–Express, 1959–60; Staff Writer, Los Angeles Times, 1961–65, and Sports Illustrated mag., NYC, 1965–80; Sports Ed., Los Angeles Daily News, 1982–85. Publs: (co–author) White House Sportsmen, 1964; (co–author) Clyde, 1970; Basketball, The American Game, 1971; Whatever Happened to Gorgeous George? The Blood and Ballyhoo of Professional Wrestling, 1974; (co–author) Conquest: A Cavalcade of USC Football, 1981; (co–author) The Athlete's Body, 1981. Add: 9701 Cresta Dr., Los Angeles, Calif. 90035, U.S.A.

JARMAN, Rosemary (Josephine) Hawley (née Smith). British, b. 1935. Historical/Romance. Publs: We Speak No Treason, 1971; The King's Grey Mare, 1973, in U.S.A. as Crown of Glory, 1987; Crown in Candlelight, 1978; Crispin's Day, The Courts of Illusion, 1983. Add: Llanungar Cottage, Whitchurch, Solva, Haverfordwest, Dyfed SA62 6UD, Wales.

JARMAN, Thomas Leckie. British, b. 1907. Education, History, Politics/Government. Staff Tutor, Adult Education, Univ. of Nottingham, 1931–34; Lectr. in Education, 1934–62, Reader in the History of Education, 1962–72, Tutor in Modern European History, Univ. of Bristol, 1972–85. Publs: William Marshal, 1930; Through Soviet Russia, 1933; Turkey, 1935; (with T.K. Derry) The European World 1870–1945, 1950, 1977; Landmarks in the History of Education, 1951; The Rise and Fall of Nazi Germany, 1955; (with T.K. Derry) The Making of Modern Britain, 1956; (with T.K. Derry and C.H.C. Blount) Great Britain, 1960; Democracy and World Conflict: British History 1868–1962, 1963; Socialism in Britain, 1972; (with T.K. Derry) Modern Britain, 1979. Add: 6 Tyndall's Court, 48 Tyndall's Park Rd., Bristol BS8 1PW, England.

JARRETT, Derek. British, b. 1928. History, Biography. Ed., Yale Edition of Horace Walpole's Memoirs. Former Principal Lectr. and Head of History Dept., Goldsmiths' Coll., Univ. of London (Lectr., 1964–65; Sr. Lectr., 1965–73). Sr. History Master, Sherborne Sch., 1956–64. Publs: Britain 1688–1815, 1965; The Begetters of Revolution: England's Involvement with France 1759–1789, 1973; Pitt the Younger, 1974; England in the Age of Hogarth, 1974, 1986; The Ingenious Mr. Hogarth, 1976; The Sleep of Reason: Fantasy and Reality from the Victorian Age to the First World War, 1988; Three Faces of Revolution: Paris, London and New York in 1989, 1989. Add: Withiel House, Withiel, Cornwall PL30 5NN, England.

JARVIS, Frederick G.H. Also writes as Fritz Gordon. American, b. 1930. Mystery/Crime/Suspense, Sports/Physical education/Keeping fit, Biography. Ed., since 1960, and Publr. since 1970, New York A.C. Mag., NYC (joined form as columnist, 1956). Music critic, FM Stereo Review, After Dark, and Variety Arts. Publs: (as Fritz Gordon) The Flight of the Bamboo Saucer, 1967; (as Fritz Gordon) Tonight They Die to Mendelssohn, 1968; (with Bob Considine) The First Hundred Years (history of New York Athletic Club), 1969; Murder at the Met, 1971; (with R. Merrill) The Divas, 1978. Add: 190 Riverside Dr., New York, N.Y. 10024, U.S.A.

JASON, Jerry. See SMITH, George H.

JASON, Stuart. See FLOREN, Lee.

JASON, Veronica. See JOHNSTON, Velda.

JASTROW, Robert. American, b. 1925. Air/Space topics, Astronomy. Dir., Goddard Inst. for Space Studies, NASA, since 1961. Adjunct Prof. of Earth Sciences, Dartmouth Coll., Hanover, N.H., since 1973. Adjunct Prof. of Astronomy and Geology, Columbia Univ., NYC, 1961–81. *Publs:* (ed.) Exporation of Space, 1960; (ed. with A.G.W. Cameron) Origin of the Solar System, 1963; Red Giants and White Dwarfs: The Evolution of Stars, Planets and Life, 1967, 1969; (ed. with S.I. Rasool) The Venus Atmosphere, 1969; (with M. Thompson) Astronomy: Fundamentals and Frontiers, 1972; Until the Sun Dies, 1977; God and the Astronomers, 1978; How to Make Nuclear Weapons Obsolete, 1985. Add: Box 191, Hanover, N.H. D3755, U.S.A.

JAUSS, Anne Marie. American, b. 1907. Children's fiction, Children's non–fiction. Freelance writer and illustrator. *Publs:* Wise and Otherwise, 1953; Legends of Saints and Beasts, 1954; Discovering Nature the Year Round, 1955; The River's Journey, 1957; Under a Green Roof, 1960; The Pasture, 1968; (with P.T. Lowe) The Little Horse of Seven Colors, 1970. Add: R.R. 1, 312 Stockholm Vernon Rd., Stockholm, N.J. 07460, U.S.A.

JAY, Antony (Rupert). British, b. 1930. Administration/Management, Business/Trade/Industry, Speech/Rhetoric. Chmn., Video Arts Ltd. Ed., Tonight prog., 1962–63, and Head of Talks Features, 1963–64, BBC, London. Member, Annan Cttee. on Future Broadcasting, 1974–77. *Publs:* (ed.) The Pick of the Rhubarb, 1965; (with D. Frost) To England with Love, 1967; Management and Machiavelli, 1967, 1987; Effective Presentation, 1970; Corporation Man, 1972; The Householder's Guide to Community Defence Against Bureaucratic Aggression, 1972; (with J. Lynn) Yes, Minister (television series), 1980–82, (book versions), 3 vols., 1981–83; The Complete Yes, Minister, 1984, Yes, Prime Minister (television series), 1986, 1987; (book version), vol. I, 1986, vol. II, 1989. Add: c/o Video Arts Ltd., 68 Oxford St., London W1, England.

JAY, Charlotte. *See* **JAY,** Geraldine Mary.

JAY, Eric George. British, b. 1907. Language/Linguistics, Theology/Religion. Prof. Emeritus, Faculty of Divinity, McGill Univ., since 1977 (Prof. of Historical Theology, 1958–75). Lectr. in Theology, King's Coll., Univ. of London, 1934–48; Dean of Nassau, Bahamas, 1948–51; Sr. Chaplain to Archbishop of Canterbury, 1951–58; Prof. of Historical Theology, 1958–75, and Dean of the Faculty of Divinity, 1963–70, McGill Univ., Montreal. *Publs:* The Existence of God, 1946; (trans.) Origen's Treatise on Prayer, 1954; Friendship with God, 1958; New Testament Greek: An Introductory Grammar, 1958; Son of Man, Son of God, 1965; The Church: Its Changing Image Through Twenty Centuries, 2 vols., 1977–78. Add: 3421 Durocher St., Apt. 406, Montreal, P.Q. H2X 2C6, Canada.

JAY, Geraldine Mary. Writes novels as Geraldine Halls, and mystery novels as Charlotte Jay. Australian, b. 1919. Novels/Short stories, Mystery/Crime/Suspense. With her husband operates an oriental antiques business in Adelaide, since 1971 (in Somerset, England, 1958–71). *Publs:* novels, as Geraldine Halls—The Silk Project, 1956; The Cats of Benares, 1967; The Cobra Kite, 1971; The Last of the Men Shortage, 1976; The Felling of Thawle, 1979, in U.S. as The Last Inheritor, 1980; Talking to Strangers, 1982; mystery novels as Charlotte Jay—The Knife is Feminine, 1951; Beat Not the Bones, 1952; The Fugitive Eye, 1953; The Yellow Turban, 1955; (as G.M. Jay) The Feast of the Dead, 1956 (in U.S. as Charlotte Jay, as The Brink of Silence, 1957); The Man Who Walked Away (in U.S. as The Stepfather), 1958; Arms for Adonis, 1960; A Hank of Hair, 1964; (as Geraldine Halls) The Voice of the Crab, 1974. Add: 21 Commercial Rd., Hyde Park, S.A. 5061, Australia.

JAY, Marion. *See* **SPALDING,** Ruth.

JAY, Mel. *See* **FANTHORPE,** R. Lionel.

JAY Peter. British, b. 1937. Economics, International relations/Current affairs. Chief of Staff to Robert Maxwell, Publisher of Mirror Group Newspapers and Chmn. of BPCC and Pergamon, since 1986. Principal, Treasury, London, 1964–67; Economics Ed., The Times, London, 1967–77, and Assoc. Ed., Times Business News, 1969–77; Presenter, Weekend World, TV programme, 1972–77; British Ambassador to the United States, 1977–79; Dir., Economist Intelligence Unit, London, 1979–83; Chmn., National Council for Voluntary Organisations, 1981–86; Sr. Editorial Consultant, 1983–84, and Ed., 1984–86, Banking World, London. *Publs:* The Budget, 1972; (with others) America and the World 1979, 1980; The Crisis for Western Political Economy and Other Essays, 1984; (with Michael Stewart) Apocalypse 2000, 1987. Add: 39 Castlebar Rd., London W5

2DJ, England.

JAY, Peter (Anthony Charles). British, b. 1945. Poetry, Translations. Publr., Anvil Press Poetry, London. Ed., New Measure mag., Oxford, 1965–69. *Publs:* Adonis and Venus (poetry), 1968; (ed.) The Greek Anthology, 1973; (trans.) The Song of Songs, 1975; (trans. with Petru Popescu) The Still Unborn About the Dead, by Nichita Stanescus, 1975; (trans. with Peter Whigham) The Poems of Meleager, 1975; (trans. with V. Nemoianu) Alibi, by Stefan Aug. Doinas, 1975; Lifelines, 1977; (trans.) Crater, by Janos Pilinszky, 1978; Shifting Frontiers: Poems 1962–1977, 1980; (trans.) The Chimeras of Gérard de Nerval, 1985. Add: c/o Anvil Press Poetry, 69 King George St., London SE10 8PX, England.

JEAL, (John Julian) Tim(othy). British, b. 1945. Novels/Short stories, Bioigraphy. Novelist and Biographer. *Publs:* For Love or Money, 1967; Somewhere Beyond Reproach, 1968; Livingstone, 1973; Cushings Crusade, 1974; Until the Colours Fade, 1976; A Marriage of Convenience, 1979; Carnforth's Creation 1983; Baden–Powell, 1989. Add: 29 Willow Rd., London NW3, England.

JEEVES, Malcolm. British, b. 1926. Psychology, Theology/Religion. Prof. of Psychology, since 1969, and Vice–Principal, 1981–85. Univ. of St. Andrews, Fife. Prof. and Head, Dept. of Psychology, Univ. of Adelaide, S.A. 1959–69. *Publs:* (co–author) Where Science and Faith Meet, 1955; Scientific Psychology and Christian Belief, 1965; (with Z.P. Dienes) Thinking in Structures, 1965; (with Z.P. Dienes) The Effects of Structural Relations on Transfer, 1968; The Scientific Enterprise and Christian Faith, 1968; Experimental Psychology: An Introduction for Biologists, 1974; Psychology and Christianity: The View Both Ways, 1976; Psychology Survey No. 3, 1980; (co–author) Analysis of Structural Learning, 1983; Behavioral Sciences: A Christian Perspective, 1983; (co–author) Psychology: Through the Eyes of Faith, 1987. Add: Psychology Lab, Univ. of St. Andrews, St. Andrews, Fife, Scotland.

JEFFARES, A(lexander) Norman. British, b. 1920. Literature, Biography. Lectr. in Classics, Univ. of Dublin, 1943–44; Lectr. in English, Univ. of Groningen, 1946–48; Lectr. in English, Univ. of Edinburgh, 1949–51; Jury Prof. of English, Univ. of Adelaide, 1951–56; Prof. of Englsh, Univ. of Leeds, 1957–74; Prof. of English Studies, Univ. of Stirling, 1974–86. Chmn., Book Trust (Scotland) 1985–89; Vice–Pres., Royal Soc. of Edinburgh, 1988. *Publs:* W.B. Yeats: Man and Poet, 1949, 1962; Seven Centuries of Poetry, 1955, 1960; Oliver Goldsmith, 1959; Language, Literature and Science, 1959; The Poetry of W.B. Yeats, 1961; Selected Plays of W.B. Yeats, 1964; Selected Prose of W.B. Yeats, 1964; (ed. with G.F. Cross) In Excited Reverie: A Centenary Tribute to W.B. Yeats, 1965; Selected Poetry and Prose of Whitman, 1965; Fair Liberty Was All His Cry: A Tercentenary Tribute to Jonathan Swift 1667–1743, 1967; A Commentary on the Collected Poems of W.B. Yeats, 1969; The Circus Animals, 1970; Farquhar's The Beaux Stratagem, 1972; Farquhar's The Recruiting Officer, 1973; (ed.) Restoration Comedy, 1974; (with A.S. Knowland) A Commentary on the Collected Plays of W.B. Yeats, 1975; (ed.) Yeats: The Critical Reception, 1977; Anglo–Irish Literature, 1982; A New Commentary on the Poems of Yeats, 1984; The Poems of Yeats: A New Selection, 1984; Brought Up in Dublin, 1986; Brought Up to Leave, 1986; (ed. with Antony Kamm) An Irish Childhood, 1986; (ed. with Antony Kamm) A Jewish Childhood, 1988; W.B. Yeats: A New Biography, 1988. Add: Craighead Cottage, Fife Ness, Crail, Scotland.

JEFFCOATE, (Sir) (Thomas) Norman (Arthur). British, b. 1907. Medicine/Health. Emeritus Prof. of Obstetrics and Gynaecology, Univ. of Liverpool, since 1972 (Prof. of Obstetrics and Gynaecology, 1945–72). Obstetrical and Gynaecological Surgeon, Liverpool United Teaching Hosp. and Liverpool Regional Hosp. Bd., 1936–72; Vice–Pres., 1967–69, and Pres., 1969–72, Royal Coll. of Obstetricians and Gynaecologists. *Publs:* Principles of Gynaecology, 1957, 4th ed. 1975. Add: 6 Riversdale Rd., Liverpool L19 3QW, England.

JEFFERSON, Alan. British, b. 1921. Military/Defence, Music. Prof. of Vocal Interpretation, Guildhall Sch. of Music and Drama, London, 1967–74. Admin., London Symphony Orchestra, 1967–68; Manager, Concert Orchestra, BBC, London, 1968–73. *Publs:* The Operas of Richard Strauss in Great Britain 1910–1963; The Lieder of Richard Strauss, 1971; Delius, 1972; The Life of Richard Strauss, 1973; Inside the Orchestra, 1974; Strauss, the Musician, 1975; The Glory of the Opera, 1976; The Complete Gilbert and Sullivan Opera Guide, 1984; Richard Strauss: Der Rosenkavalier, 1986. Add: Deviock Farm House, Deviock, Torpoint, Cornwall PL11 3DL, England

JEFFORD, Bat. *See* **BINGLEY,** David Ernest.

JEFFREY, Graham. Also writes as Brother Graham. British, b. 1935. Children's fiction, Religion, Autobiography/Memoirs/Personal, Humor/Satire. Rector, Edmonton and Pyecombe, Sussex. *Publs:* as Brother Graham—Barnabas series, 9 vols., 1966–76; as Graham Jeffery—Bush Brother, 1970; Well Done, Son, 1981; Very Well, Lord, 1981; A Funny Way to Say Hello, 1981; Follow Me, 1981; Thank You for Coming, 1982; Message from the King, 1983; Graham and Grandad, 1985; Britain Revisited, 1987; Thomas the Tortoise, 1988. Add: Poynings Rectory, Brighton, Sussex, England.

JEFFREYS, J.G. *See* **HEALEY,** Ben.

JEFFRIES, Roderic. Also writes as Peter Alding, Jeffrey Ashford, Hastings Draper, Roderic Graeme, and Graham Hastings. British, b. 1926. Novels/Short stories, Mystery/Crime/Suspense, Children's fiction. Full–time writer. Formerly, barrister in London. *Publs:* novels, as Hastings Draper—Wiggery Pokery, 1956; Wigged and Gowned, 1958; Brief Help, 1961; mystery novels—(as Roderic Graeme) Blackshirt series, 20 vols., 1952–69; (as Graham Hastings) Twice Checked, 1959; (as Jeffrey Ashford) Counsel for the Defence, 1960; (as Graham Hastings) Deadly Game, 1961; Evidence of the Accused, 1961; (as Jeffrey Ashford) Investigations Are Proceeding, 1961 (in U.S. as The D.I., 1962); Exhibit No. Thirteen, 1962; (as Jeffrey Ashford) The Burden of Proof, 1962; The Benefits of Death, 1963; (as Jeffrey Ashford) Will Anyone Who Saw the Accident . . . , 1963 (as U.K. paperback, Hit and Run, 1966); An Embarrassing Death, 1964; (as Jeffrey Ashford) Enquiries Are Continuing, 1964 (in U.S. as The Superintendent's Room, 1965); Dead Against the Lawyers, 1965; (as Jeffrey Ashford) The Hands of Innocence, 1965; Death in The Coverts, 1966; (as Jeffrey Ashford) Forget What You Saw, 1967; (as Peter Alding) The C.I.D. Room (in U.S. as All Leads Negative), 1967; A Traitor's Crime, 1968; (as Peter Alding) Circle of Danger, 1968; (as Jeffrey Ashford) Prisoner at the Bar, 1969; (as Peter Alding) Murder among Thieves, 1969; Dead Man's Bluff, 1970; (as Jeffrey Ashford) To Protect the Guilty, 1970; (as Peter Alding) Guilt Without Proof, 1970; (as Jeffrey Ashford) Bent Cooper, 1971; (as Peter Alding) Despite the Evidence, 1971; (as Jeffrey Ashford) A Man Will Be Kidnapped Tomorrow, 1972; (as Peter Alding) Call Back to Crime, 1972; (as Jeffrey Ashford) The Double Run, 1973; (as Peter Alding) Field of Fire, 1973; Mistakenly in Mallorca, 1974; (as Jeffrey Ashford) The Colour of Violence, 1974; (as Peter Alding) The Murder Line, 1974; (as Jeffrey Ashford) Three Layers of Guilt, 1975; (as Peter Alding) Six Days to Death, 1975; Two–Faced Death, 1976; (as Jeffrey Ashford) Slow Down World, 1976; Troubled Deaths, 1977; (as Jeffrey Ashford) Hostage to Death, 1977; (as Peter Alding) Murder is Suspected, 1977; (as Jeffrey Ashford) The Anger of Fear, 1978; Murder Begets Murder, 1979; (as Peter Alding) Ransom Town, 1979; Just Deserts, 1980; (as Jeffrey Ashford) A Recipe for Murder, 1980; Unseemly End, 1981; (as Jeffrey Ashford) The Loss of the Culion, 1981; (as Peter Alding) A Man Condemned, 1981; (as Jeffrey Ashford) Guilt with Honour, 1982; (as Peter Alding) Betrayed by Death, 1982; Deadly Petard, 1983; (as Jeffrey Ashford) A Sense of Loyalty, 1983; Three and One Make Five, 1984; (as Jeffrey Ashford) Presumption of Guilt, 1984; (as Jeffrey Ashford) An Ideal Crime, 1985; Layers of Deceit, 1985; Almost Murder, 1986; (as Jeffrey Ashford) A Question of Principle, 1986; Relatively Dangerous, 1987; (as Jeffrey Ashford) A Crime Remembered, 1987; Death Tricks, 11988; (as Jeffrey Ashford) The Honourable Detective, 1988; Dead Clever, 1989; for children—(as Roderic Graeme) Brandy Ahoy!, 1951; (as Roderic Grame) Where's Brandy?, 1953; (as Roderic Graeme) Brandy Goes a Cruising, 1954; Police and Detection, 1962 (in U.S. as Against Time!, 1964); Police Dog, 1965; Police Car (in U.S. as Patrol Car), 1967; (as Jeffrey Ashford) Grand Prix Monaco, 1968; River Patrol, 1969; (as Jeffrey Ashford) Grand Prix Germany, 1970; (as Jeffrey Ashford) Grand Prix United States, 1971; Police Patrol Boat, 1971; Trapped, 1972; (as Jeffrey Ashford) Grand Prix Britain, 1973; (as Jeffrey Ashford) Dick Knox at Le Mans, 1974; The Riddle of the Parchment, 1976; The Boy Who Knew Too Much, 1977; Eighteen Desperate Hours, 1979; The Missing Man, 1980; Voyage into Danger, 1981; Peril at Sea, 1983; Sunken Danger, 1985; Meeting Trouble, 1986; The Man Who Couldn't Be, 1987. Add: Ca Na Paiaia, Pollensa, Majorca, Spain.

JEFFS, Julian. British, b. 1931. Cookery/Gastronomy/Wine, Law. Barrister. Gen. Ed., Faber's Wine Series, since 1966. Ed., Wine and Food, London, 1965–67. *Publs:* Sherry, 1961, 3rd ed. 1982; (ed. with R. Harling) Wine, 1966; (contributing ed.) Clerk and Lindsell on Torts, 13th ed., 1969, 15th ed. 1982; The Wines of Europe, 1971; Little Dictionary of Drink, 1973; (with others) Encyclopedia of United Kingdom and European Patent Law, 1977. Recipient of Glenfiddich Award, 1976 and 1978. Add: Church Farm House, East Ilsley, Newbury, Berks, England.

JEFFS, Rae. Pseud. for Frances Rae Sebley. British, b. 1921. Biog-

raphy. Publisher's Reader, Hutchinson and Co., London, since 1964 (Publicity Mgr. for the Hutchinson Group, 1957–64). Copy Writer, Heron Books, London, 1966–69. *Publs:* (ed.) Brendan Behan's Island, 1962; (ed.) Hold Your Hour and Have Another, 1963; (ed.) Brendan Behan's New York, 1964; (with Brendan Behan) Confessions of An Irish Rebel, 1965; (ed.) The Scarperer, 1966; Brendan Behan: Man and Showman, 1966. Add: Rotherfield Farmhouse, Newick, Lewes, Sussex, England.

JEFKINS, Frank William. British, b. 1920. Novels, Advertising/Public relations, Marketing, Media. Principal, Frank Jefkins Sch. of Public Relations, Croydon, Surrey, since 1968. Group Copywriter Exec., Intnl. Publ. Corp., 1952–59; Public Relations Mgr., Rentokil Ltd., 1959–63; Dir. and Mgr., Scientific Public Relations Ltd., 1963–68. *Publs:* Copywriting and Its Presentation; Wanted on Holiday; Public Relations in World Marketing; Press Relations Practice; Planned Public Relations Advertising Today; Dictionary of Marketing and Communication; Advertising Made Simple; Marketing and Public Relations Media Planning; Advertisement Writing; Effective Press Relations; Planned Press and Public Relations, 2nd ed., 1986; Public Relations for Marketing Management; Effective PR Planning; Public Relations Made Simple; Modern Marketing; 1983; Effective Publicity Writing; Effective Marketing Strategy; Advertising, 1985; Public Relations, 2nd ed., 1983; Public Relations for Management Success, 1984; Introduction to Marketing; Advertising and Public Relations Communications in Industrializing Countries; International Dictionary of Marketing and Communication; Public Relations Techniques; Public Relations Is Your Business. Add: 84 Ballards Way, South Croydon, Surrey CR2 7LA, England.

JEKEL, Pamela Lee. American, b. 1948. Novels. *Publs:* The Perfect Crime and How to Commit It (non–fiction), 1980; Seastar fiction), 1983; Columbia, 1986, 1987; Thomas Hardy: A Chorus of Heroines, 1986. Add: Roslyn Targ Agency, 105 W. 13th St., Suite 15–E, New York, N.Y. 10011, U.S.A.

JELLICOE, Ann. British, b. 1927. Plays/Screenplays, Travel/Exploration/Adventure. Founding Dir., Colway Theatre Trust, since 1979. Actress, stage mgr., dir., in London and the provinces, 1947–51; Founding Dir., Cockpit Theatre Club, London, 1950–53; Lectr. and Dir., Central Sch. of Speech and Drama, London, 1953–55. Literary Adviser, Royal Court Theatre, London, 1973–75. *Publs:* Rosmersholm, 1960; The Knack, 1962; Two Plays: The Knack, and The Sport of My Mad Mother, 1964; Shelley: or, The Idealist, 1966; Some Unconscious Influences in the Theatre, 1967; The Giveaway, 1970; (with Roger Mayne) Shell Guide to Devon, 1975; 3 Jelliplays, 1975; Community Plays: How to Put Them On, 1987. Add: c/o Margaret Ramsey, 14a Goodwin's Court, London WC2, England.

JELLICOE, (Sir) Geoffrey (Alan). British, b. 1900. Architecture. Partner, with J.C. Shepherd, Shepherd and Jellicoe, London, 1925–31; Principal, G.A. Jellicoe, London, 1931–38; Sr. Partner, with Russell Page and Richard Wilson, Jellicoe, Page and Wilson, London, 1938–39; Principal, G.A. Jellicoe, London, 1939–58; Sr. Partner, with Alan Ballantyne and Francis Coleridge, Jellicoe, Ballantyne and Coleridge, London, 1958–64; Sr. Partner, Jellicoe and Coleridge, London, 1964–73. Studio Master, 1929–34, and Principal, 1932–42, Architectural Assn. Sch., London; Founder Member, 1929, and Pres., 1939–49, Inst. of Landscape Architects; Founder Pres., 1948–54, and now Hon. Life Pres., Intnl. Fedn. of Landscape Architects; Trustee, Tate Gallery, London, 1967–74. *Publs:* (with J.C. Shepherd) Italian Gardens of the Renaissance, 1925; (with J.C. Shepherd) Garden and Designs, 1927; Baroque Gardens of Austria, 1932; Garden Decoration and Ornament, 1936; Gardens of Europe, 1937; Conurbation:Report for the West Midland Group on Post–War Reconstruction and Planning, 1948; Motorways: Their Landscaping, Design and Appearance, 1958; Studies in Landscape Design, 3 vols., 1960–70; Motopia, 1961; (with Susan Jellicoe) Modern Private Gardens, 1968; L'Architettura del Paesaggio, 1969; (with Susan Jellicoe) Water: The Use of Water in Landscape Architecture, 1971; (with Susan Jellicoe) The Landscape of Man, 1975; The Guelph Lectures on Landscape, 1983. Add: 14 Highpoint, North Hill, London N6, England.

JENCKS, Charles (Alexander). American, b. 1939. Architecture. *Publs:* (with George Baird) Meaning in Architecture, 1969; Architecture 2000, 1971; (with Nathan Silver) Adhocism, 1972; Modern Movements in Architecture, 1973; Le Corbusier and the Tragic View of Architecture, 1974; The Language of Post–Modern Architecture, 1977, 5th ed. 1988; The Daydream House of Los Angeles, 1978; Bizarre Architecture, 1979; (ed. with G. Broadbent) Signs, Symbols and Architecture, 1980; Skyscrapers—Skycities, 1980; Late–Modern Architecture: Selected Essays, 1980; Post–Modern Classicism, 1981; Free Style Classicism, 1982; Current Architecture, 1982, and in U.S. as Architecture Today; Abstract Representation, 1983; Kings of Infinite Space, 1983, 1985; Towards a Symbolic Architecture, 1985; What Is Post–Modernism?, 1986; Post–Modernism: The New Classicism in Art and Architecture, 1987; (with T. Farrell) Designing a House: An Architectural Design Profile, 1987; The Prince, the Architects and New Wave Architecture, 1988; (ed.) The Archictecture of Democracy, 1988. Add: c/o Architectural Assn., 36 Bedford Sq., London WC1, England.

JENKIN, Len. (Leonard Jenkin). American, b. 1941. Novels, Plays/Screenplays. Assoc. Prof., Tisch Sch. of the Arts, New York Univ., since 1980; assoc. artistic dir., River Arts Repertory Co., Woodstock, N.Y., since 1983. English teacher, Manhattan Community Coll., 1967–79. Publs: (co–ed.) Survival Printout, 1973; plays—Dark Ride, 1982; Candide, or Optimism, 1982; Limbo Tales, 1982; My Uncle Sam, 1984; Five of Us, 1986; Gogol (in Theatre of Wonders), 1986; novel—New Jerusalem, 1986. Add: c/o Flora Roberts Inc., 157 W. 57th St., New York, N.Y. 10019, U.S.A.

JENKINS, Alan. British, b. 1914. Novels/Short stories, Plays/Screenplays, Business/Trade/Industry, History. Features Ed., Leader Mag., 1949–50; Asst. Ed., Lilliput Mag., 1950–51; Public Relations Dir., Ogilvy Benson & Mather Ltd., London, 1954–70. Publs: Absent Without Leave (novel), 1949; The Swimming Pool (novel), 1951; Our Mr. Dundas (radio play), 1950, television play, 1955; The Burning Secret (radio play), 1951; The Venus of Bainville (radio play), 1951, television play, 1952; (with Paul Tabori) Silent Night (play); The Young Mozart, 1961; Drinka Pinta: History of the Dairy Industry, 1970; On Site: History of Taylor Woodrow Ltd., 1971; The Stock Exchange Story, 1973; London's City, 1973; The Twenties, 1974; The Thirties, 1976; The Forties, 1977; The Rich Rich, 1978; Stephen Potter, 1980; The Book of the Thames, 1983; Men of Property: Knight, Frank & Rutley, 1986. Add: 7 Beech Close, Effingham, Surrey KT4 5PQ, England.

JENKINS, Elizabeth. British. Novels/Short stories, Biography. Publs: The Winters, 1931; Lady Caroline Lamb: A Biography, 1932; Harriet, 1934; The Phoenix' Nest, 1936; Jane Austen: A Biography, 1938; Robert and Helen, 1944; Young Enthusiasts, 1946; Henry Fielding (The English Novelists Series), 1947; Six Criminal Women, 1949; The Tortoise and the Hare, 1954; Ten Fascinating Women, 1955; Elizabeth the Great, 1958; Elizabeth and Leicester, 1961; Brightness, 1963; Honey, 1968; Dr. Gully, 1972; The Mystery of King Arthur, 1975; The Princes in the Tower, 1978; The Shadow and the Light: A Defence of Daniel Home the Medium, 1982. Add: 8 Downshire Hill, London NW3, England.

JENKINS, Harold. British, b. 1909. Literature. Prof. of English, Westfield Coll., Univ. of London, 1954–67; Regius Prof. of Rhetoric and English Literature, Univ. of Edinburgh, 1967–71. Gen. Ed., Arden Ed. of Shakespeare's works, 1958–82. Publs: The Life and Work of Henry Chettle, 1934; (ed.) The Tragedy of Hoffman, 1951; Edward Benlowes: Biography of a Minor Poet, 1952; (ed.) Sir Thomas More, 1954; The Structural Problem in Shakespeare's Henry IV, 1956; Hamlet and Ophelia, 1963; The Catastrophe in Shakespearean Tragedy, 1969; (ed.) Hamlet, 1982. Add: 22 North Crescent, London N3 3LL, England.

JENKINS, John Geraint. British, b. 1929. Business/Trade/Industry, Country life/rural societies, Crafts, History. Curator, Welsh Folk Museum, since 1987. Asst., Leicester City Museums, 1952–53; Asst. Keeper, Univ. of Reading Museum of English Rural Life, 1953–60; Keeper of Material Collections, Welsh Folk Museum, Cardiff, 1960–79; Curator, Welsh Industrial and Maritime Museum, Cardiff, 1979–87. Publs: Agricultural Transport in Wales, 1962; Traditional Country Craftsmen, 1965; Studies in Folk Life, 1969; The Welsh Woollen Industry, 1969; The Wool Textile Industry in Great Britain, 1971; Crefftwyr Gwledig, 1971; The English Farm Wagon, 1972; The Craft Industries, 1972; Nets and Coracles, 1974; Life and Traditions in Rural Wales, 1976; Exploring County Crafts, 1977; Maritime Heritage, 1983; Cockles and Mussels, 1984; The Flannel Makers, 1985; The Coracle, 1987. Add: The Gardens House, St. Fagans, Cardiff, Wales.

JENKINS, Lord. See JENKINS, Roy.

JENKINS, Michael (Romilly Heald). British, b. 1936. Biography. British Ambassador to the Netherlands, since 1988 (entered U.K. Diplomatic Service, 1959; Deputy Secty.–Gen., Commn. of the European Communities, Brussels, 1981–83; Asst. Under–Secty. of State, Foreign and Commonwealth Office, London, 1983–85; Minister, British Embassy, Washington, 1985–87). Publs: Arakcheev, Grand Vizir of the Russian Empire, 1969. Add: c/o Foreign and Commonwealth Office, London SW1, England.

JENKINS, Ray(mond Leonard). British, b. 1935. Children's non–fiction. Freelance television dramatist. Chmn., Writers Guild of Great Britain, 1976–77. Lectr., City of Leicester Coll. of Education, 1963–65; Extra–Mural Lectr., Univ. of London, 1967–68. Publs: Julian, 1968; Five Green Bottles, 1968; The Lawbreakers, 1969; The World of Col. Kelly, 1977; Incident, 1979. Add: 187 Pitshanger Lane, London W5 1RQ, England.

JENKINS, (John) Robin. British, b. 1912. Novels/Short stories. Teacher, Ghazi Coll., Khabul, 1957–59; British Inst., Barcelona, 1959–61; Gaya Sch., Sabah, 1963–68. Publs: Go Gaily Sings the Lark, 1951; Happy for the Child, 1953; The Thistle and the Grail, 1954; The Cone–Gatherers, 1955; Guests of War, 1956; The Missionaries, 1957; The Changeling, 1958; Love is a Fervent Fire, 1959; Some Kind of Grace, 1960; Dust on the Paw, 1961; The Tiger of Gold, 1962; A Love of Innocence, 1963; The Sardana Dancers, 1964; A Very Scotch Affair, 1968; The Holly Tree, 1969; The Expatriates, 1971; A Toast to the Lord, 1972; A Figure of Fun, 1974; A Would–Be–Saint, 1978; Fergus Lamont, 1979; The Awakening of George Darroch, 1985; Poverty Castle, 1986; Just Duffy, 1988. Add: Fairhaven, Toward, by Dunoon, Argyll, Scotland.

JENKINS, Roy (Harris). (Lord Jenkins of Hillhead). British, b. 1920. History, Politics/Government, Biography. Member, House of Lords, since 1987. Labour Member of Parliament (U.K.) for Central Southwark, 1948–50, for the Stechford Div. of Birmingham, 1950–76; Minister of Aviation, 1964–65; Home Secty., 1965–67; Chancellor of the Exchequer, 1967–70; Deputy Leader, Labour Party, 1970–72; Home Secty, 1974–76; Pres., Commn. of the European Communities, 1977–81; Social Democratic Member of Parliament for Hillhead, div. of Glasgow, 1982–87. Publs: (ed.) Purpose and Policy, 1947; Mr. Attlee: An Interim Biography, 1948; Pursuit of Progress, 1953; Mr. Balfour's Poodle, 1954; Sir Charles Dilke: A Victorian Tragedy, 1958; The Labour Case, 1959; Asquith, 1964; Essays and Speeches, 1967; Afternoon on the Potomac, 1972; What Matters Now, 1972; Nine Men of Power, 1974; Partnership of Principle, 1985; Truman, 1986; Baldwin, 1987; Gallery of 20th Century Portraits, 1988; European Diary 1977-81, 1989. Add: St. Amands House, E. Hendred, Oxon., England.

JENKINS, Simon. British, b. 1943. Environmental science/Ecology, Urban studies, Writing/Journalism. Columnist, Sunday Times, London, since 1986. News Ed., Times Educational Supplement, 1966–68; joined Evening Standard, 1968, and ed., 1976–78; Insight Ed., Sunday Times, 1974–75; Political Ed., The Economist, London, 1979–86. Publs: City at Risk, 1971; Landlord to London, 1974; (ed.) Insight on Portugal, 1975; Newspapers: The Power and the Money, 1979; Companion Guide to Outer London, 1981; The Battle for the Falklands, 1983; Images of Hampstead, 1983; With Respect, Ambassador, 1985; The Market for Glory, 1986. Add: 174 Regent's Park Rd., London NW1, England.

JENNIFER, Susan. See HOSKINS, Robert.

JENNINGS, Dean. See FRAZEE, Steve.

JENNINGS, Elizabeth (Joan). British, b. 1926. Poetry, Literature, Translations. English Language and Literature Asst., Oxford City Library, 1950–58; Reader, Chatto & Windus Ltd. Publrs., London, 1958–60. Publs: Poems, 1953; A Way of Looking: Poems, 1955; (ed. with Dannie Abse and Stephen Spender) New Poems, 1956; A P.E.N. Anthology, 1956; The Child and the Seashell, 1957; (ed.) The Batsford Book of Children's Verse, 1958; Let's Have Some Poetry, 1960; Every Changing Shape, 1961; Poetry Today, 1957–60, 1961; (ed.) An Anthology of Modern Verse 1940–1960, 1961; (trans.) The Sonnets of Michelangelo, 1961, Song for a Birth or a Death and Other Poems, 1961; (with Lawrence Durrell and R.S. Thomas) Penguin Modern Poets I, 1962; Recoveries: Poems, 1964; Frost, 1964; Christianity and Poetry (in U.S. as Christian Poetry), 1965; The Mind Has Mountains, 1966; The Secret Brother and Other Poems for Children, 1966; Collected Poems 1967, 1967; The Animals' Arrival, 1969; (ed.) A Choice of Christina Rossetti's Verse, 1970; Lucidities, 1970; Hurt, 1970; Relationships, 1972; Growing Points: New Poems, 1975; Seven Men of Vision: An Appreciation, 1976; Consequently I Rejoice, 1977; After the Ark, 1978; Moments of Grace: New Poems, 1979; Selected Poems, 1979; (ed.) The Batsford Book of Religious Verse, 1981; Celebrations and Elegies: Poems, 1982; (ed.) In Praise of Our Lady, 1982; Extending the Territory (poetry). 1985; A Quintet for Children, 1985; Collected Poems, 1953–86; 1986. Add: c/o David Higham Assocs., 5–8 Lower John St., London W1R 4HA, England.

JENKINS, Gary. Also writes as Gabriel Quyth. American, b. 1928. Novels, Historical/Romance, Children's fiction, Language. *Publs:* March of the Robots (children's fiction), 1962; The Movie Book (children's non-fiction), 1963; Black Magic, White Magic, 1964; Personalities of Language, 1965, as World of Words, 1984; Parades! (children's non-fiction), 1966; The Killer Storms (children's non-fiction), 1970; The Teenager's Realistic Guide to Astrology (chilren's non-fiction), 1971; The Shrinking Outdoors (children's non-fiction), 1972; The Treasure of the Superstition Mountains, 1973; The Earth Book (children's non-fiction), 1974; March of the Heroes, 1975; The Terrible Teague Bunch, 1975; Sow the Seeds of Hemp, 1976; The Rope in the Jungle, 1976; March of the Gods, 1976; March of the Demons, 1977; Aztec, 1980; The Journeyer, 1984; Spangle, 1987; (as Gabriel Quyth) The Lively Lives of Quentin Mobey, 1988. Add: P.O. Box 1371, Lexington, Va. 24450, U.S.A.

JENNINGS, Paul. British, b. 1918. Novels/Short stories, Children's fiction, Humour/Satire. Humour Columnist, The Observer, London, 1949–66. *Publs:* Oddly Enough, 1950; Even Oddlier, 1952; Oddly Bodlikins, 1953; Next to Oddliness, 1955; Model Oddlies, 1956; Gladly Oddly, 1958; Idly Oddly, 1959; I Said Oddly, Diddle I?, 1961; Oodles of Oddlies, 1963; The Jenguin Pennings, 1963; The Hopping Basket (children's fiction), 1964; Oddly Ad Lib, 1965; The Great Jelly of London (children's fiction), 1967; I Was Joking of Course, 1968; The Living Village: A Report on Rural Life in England and Wales, 1968; Just a Few Lines, 1969; It's An Odd Thing But, 1971; The Train to Yesterday (children's fiction), 1974; Britain As She Is Visit, 1976; I Must Have Imagined It, 1977; And Now For Something Exactly The Same (novel), 1977; (ed.) The Book of Nonsense, 1977; The Paul Jennings Companion to Britain, 1981; (ed.) A Feast of Days, 1982; (ed.) My Favourite Railway Stories, 1982; Golden Oddlies, 1983; East Anglia, 1986. Add: 25 High St., Orford, Woodbridge, Suffolk IP12 2NW, England.

JENSEN, Arthur Robert. American, b. 1923. Education, Psychology. Prof. of Educational Psychology, since 1958, and Research Psychologist, Inst. of Human Learning, since 1962, Univ. of California, Berkeley. Research Fellow, Inst. of Psychiatry, Univ. of London, 1956–58. *Publs:* (with P.M. Symonds) From Adolescent to Adult, 1961; (ed. with M. Deutsch and I. Katz) Social Class, Race, and Psychological Development, 1968; Genetics and Education, 1973; Educability and Group Differences, 1973; Educational Differences, 1973; Bias in Mental Testing, 1980; Straight Talk about Mental Tests, 1981. Add: Sch. of Education, Univ. of California, Berkeley, Calif. 94720, U.S.A.

JENSEN, Clayne. American, b. 1930. Recreation/Leisure/Hobbies, Sports/Physical education/Keeping fit. Dean, Coll. of Physical Education/Athletics, Brigham Young Univ., Provo, Utah, since 1974 (Prof. and Asst. Dean, 1968–74). *Publs:* (with K. Tucker) Skiing, 1968, 4th ed. 1982; (co-author) To Improve Body Form and Function, 1968, 3rd ed. 1977; (co-author) Applied Kinesiology, 1970, 3rd ed. 1982; Outdoor Recreation in America, 1970, 4th ed. 1982; (co-author) Scientific Basis of Athletic Conditioning, 1972, 1978; (co-author) Measurement and Statistics in Physical Education, 1972, 3rd ed. 1989; (with C. Thorstenson) Issues in Outdoor Recreation, 1972, 1979; (with M.B. Jensen) Square Dance, 1973; (with M.B. Jensen) Folk Dance, 1973; (with C. Robison) Modern Track and Field Coaching Technique, 1974; Administrative Management of Physical Education and Athletics, 1982, 1988. Add: Coll. of Physical Education, Brigham Young Univ., 212 Richards Bldg., Provo, Utah 84602, U.S.A.

JENSEN, De Lamar. American, b. 1925. History, International relations/Current affairs. Prof. of History, Brigham Young Univ., Provo, Utah, since 1957. Instr. in History, New York Univ., NYC, 1954–57. *Publs:* (compiler and ed.) Machiavelli: Cynic, Patriot, or Political Scientist?, 1960; Diplomacy and Dogmatism: Bernardino de Mendoza and the French Catholic League, 1964; (compiler and ed.) The Expansion of Europe: Motives, Methods and Meanings, 1967; The World of Europe: The Sixteenth Century, 1973; Confrontation at Worms: Martin Luther and the Diet of Worms, 1973; Renaissance Europe, 1980; Reformation Europe, 1981. Add: 1079 Briar Ave., Provo, Utah 84601, U.S.A.

JENSEN, Richard. American, b. 1941. Mathematics/Statistics, Politics/Government. Prof. of History, Univ. of Illinois, Chicago, since 1970. Prof. of History, Washington Univ., St. Louis, 1966–70; Sr. Staff Assoc., President's Commn. on Campus Unrest, 1970; Dir., Family and Community History Center, Newberry Library, Chicago, 1971–82. *Publs:* The Winning of the Midwest 1888–1896, 1971; (with C. Dollar) Historian's Guide to Statistics, 1971; Illinois, 1978. Add: 400 E. Randolph St., No. 3406, Chicago, Ill. 60601, U.S.A.

JEPPSON, J. (Janet Asimov.) American, b. 1926. Novels/Short stories, children's fiction, Writing. Physician since 1952. Training and Supervising Analyst, W.A. White Psychoanalytic Inst., since 1969 (Dir. of Training, 1974–82). Assoc. Ed., Contemporary Psychoanalysis, since 1970. *Publs:* The Second Experiment, 1974; The Last Immortal, 1980; (ed. with Isaac Asimov) Laughing Space, 1982; (with Isaac Asimov) Norby, The Mixed–Up Robot, 1983; (with Isaac Asimov) Norby's Other Secret, 1984; (with Isaac Asimov) Norby and the Lost Princess, 1985; The Mysterious Cure and Other Stories of Pshrinks Anonymous, 1985; (with Isaac Asimov) Norby and the Invaders, 1985; (with Isaac Asimov) Norby and the Queen's Necklade, 1986; (with Isaac Asimov) Norby Finds A Villain, 1987; (with Isaac Asimov) How To Enjoy Writing, 1987; Mind Transfer, 1988. Add: 10 W. 66th St., New York, N.Y. 10023, U.S.A.

JEROME, Joseph. *See* **SEWELL**, Brocard.

JEROME, Judson (Blair). American, b. 1927. Novels/Short stories, Poetry, Literature, Social commentary/phenomena. Poetry columnist, Writer's Digest, since 1960. Prof. of Literature, Antioch Coll., Yellow Springs, Ohio, 1953–73. *Publs:* Light in the West, 1962; The Poet and the Poem, 1963, 3rd ed. 1980; The Ocean's Warning to the Skin Diver, 1964; The Fell of Dark (novel), 1966; Serenade, 1968; Poetry: Premeditated Art, 1968; Plays for an Imaginary Theater, 1970; Culture Out of Anarchy, 1971; Never Saw . . . , 1974; Families of Eden: Communes and the New Anarchism, 1974; Publishing Poetry, 1976; Public Domain, 1977; The Poet's Handbook, 1980; On Being A Poet, 1984; Poet's Market, 1985; Where and How to Publish Your Poetry (annual), 1985–; The Village: New and Selected Poems, 1987. Add: Box 740, Yellow Springs, Oh. 45387, U.S.A.

JESSUP, Frank W(illiam). British, b. 1909. History, Politics/Government. Fellow, Wolfson Coll, Oxford, Since 1964. Deputy County Education Officer for Kent, 1945–52; Dir., Dept. for External Studies, Oxford Univ. 1952–76. *Publs:* Problems of Local Government, 1949; (with R.F. Jessup) The Cinque Ports, 1952; Sir Roger Twysden 1597–1672, 1965; Kent History Illustrated, 1966; (ed.) Background to the English Civil War, 1966; (ed.) Lifelong Learning, 1969; A History of Kent, 1974; Wolfson College, Oxford: The Early Years, 1979. Add: Striblehills, Thame, Oxon, England.

JETER, K.W. American, b. 1950. Novels/Short stories, Science fiction. *Publs:* science–fiction—Seeklight, 1975; The Dreamfields, 1976; Morlock Night, 1979; Dr. Adder, 1984; The Glass Hammer, 1985; Infernal Devices, 1987; Mantis, 1987; Farewell Horizontal, 1989; other novels—Soul Eater, 1983; Night Vision, 1985. Add: c/o St. Martin's Press, 175 Fifth Ave., New York, N.Y. 10010, U.S.A.

JETT, Stephen Clinton. American, b. 1938. Anthropology/Ethnology, Geography. Prof. of Geography, Univ. of California, Davis, since 1979 (Asst. Prof., 1964–72; Assoc. Prof., 1972–79; Chmn., 1978–82, 1987–89). Instr., Ohio State Univ., Columbus, 1963–64. *Publs:* Tourism in the Navajo Country: Resources and Planning, 1967; Navajo Wildlands: As Long as the Rivers Shall Run, 1967; House of Three Turkeys: Anasazi Redoubt, 1977; Navajo Architecture: Forms, History, Distributions, 1981. Add: Dept. of Geography, Univ. of California, Davis, Calif. 95616, U.S.A.

JHA, Akhillshwar. Indian, b. 1932. Novels/Short stories, History. Proprietor, Chanakya Publications, Delhi, since 1980. Lectr. in English, Patna Univ. 1955–66; Lectr. in English, Ramjas Coll., Univ. of Delhi, 1966–86. *Publs:* Janpath Kiss (novel), 1976; Intellectuals at the Crossroads: The Indian Situation, 1977; Modernization and the Hindu Socio–Culture, 1978; Sexual Designs in Indian Culture, 1979; The Imprisoned Mind: Guru–Shisya Tradition in Indian Culture, 1980; Lessons in Love (novel), 1988. Add: F10/14 Model Town, Delhi 110 009, India.

JHABVALA, R(uth) Prawer. American, b. 1927. Novels/Short stories, Plays/Screenplays. *Publs:* To Whom She Will (in U.S. as Amrita), 1955; The Nature of Passion, 1956; Esmond in India, 1957; The Householder, 1960, screenplay 1963; Get Ready for Battle, 1962; Like Birds, Like Fishes and Other Stories, 1963; A Backward Place, 1965; Shakespeare Wallah (screenplay), 1965; A Stronger Climate: 9 Stories, 1968; An Experience of India, 1971; Heat and Dust, 1975; (co–author) Autobiography of a Princess (screenplay), 1975; How I Became A Holy Mother and Other Stories, 1976; In Search of Love and Beauty, 1983; Out of India: Selected Stories, 1986; Three Continents, 1987. Add: 400 E. 52nd St., New York, N.Y. 10022, U.S.A.

JOHANSON, Donal C(arl). American, b. 1943. Anthropology. Dir., Inst. of Human Origins, Berkeley, Calif., since 1982; Prof. of Anthropology, Stanford Univ., California, since 1983. Asst. to Adjunct Prof. of Anthropology, Case Western Reserve Univ., Cleveland, 1972–81; Assoc. Curator of Physical Anthropology, 1972–73, Curator, 1972–82, and former Dir. of Scientific Research, Cleveland Museum of Natural History. *Publs:* (with Maitland A. Edey) Lucy: The Beginnings of Humankind, 1981; (with Maitland A. Edey) Blueprint: Solving the Mystery of Evolution, 1989. Add: Inst. of Human Origins, 2453 Ridge Rd., Berkeley, Calif. 94709, U.S.A.

JOHN, Nancy. *See* **SAWYER,** John and **SAWYER,** Nancy.

JOHN, Robert. British–American. International relations. *Publs:* (with S. Hadawi) The Palestine Diary, 2 vols., 1970, 3rd ed. 1972; Behind the Balfour Declaration: The Hidden Origins of Today's Mid-East Crisis, 1988. Add: 1080 Park Ave., New York, N.Y. 10128, U.S.A.

JOHNS, Avery. *See* **COUSINS,** Margaret.

JOHNS, Marston. *See* **FANTHORPE,** R. Lionel.

JOHNS, Richard A. American, b. 1929. Novels/Short stories, Plays/Screenplays, Theology/Religion. Commercial artist and freelance writer. *Publs:* The Legacy (teleplay), 1965; Thirteenth Apostle, 1966; Garden of the Okapi, 1968; Return to Heroism, 1969; (co–author) Everyday, Five Minutes with God, 1969; Quails, Partridges and Francolins of the World, 1987; North American Owls: Biology and Natural History, 1988. Add: 3324 Teakwood, Tyler, Tex. 75701, U.S.A.

JOHNS, Veronica Parker. American, b. 1907. Mystery/Crime/Suspense. Owner, Seashells Unlimited, since 1964. Pres., New York Shell Club, 1975. *Publs:* Hush, Gabriel, 1941; Shady Doings, 1941; The Singing Widow, 1941; Murder by the Day, 1953; Servant's Problem, 1958; She Sells Sea Shells (non-fiction), 1968. Add: 155 E. 38th St., New York, N.Y. 10016, U.S.A.

JOHNSGARD, Paul A. American, b. 1931. Biology, Environmental science/Ecology, Zoology. Foundn. Prof. of Life Sciences, Univ. of Nebraska, Lincoln, since 1968 (Instr., 1961–62; Asst. Prof., 1962–63; Assoc. Prof., 1964–68). Postdoctoral Fellow, Univ. of Bristol, England, 1959–61. *Publs:* Handbook of Waterfowl Behavior, 1965; Animal Behavior, 1967; Waterfowl: Their Biology and Natural History, 1968; Grouse and Quails of North America, 1973; Song of the North Wind: A Story of the Snow Goose, 1974; Waterfowl of North America, 1975; North American Game Birds of Upland Shoreline, 1975; The Bird Decoy: An American Art Form, 1976; Ducks, Geese and Swans of the World, 1978; A Guide to North American Waterfowl, 1979; Birds of the Great Plains: Breeding Species and Their Distribution, 1979; The Plovers, Sandpipers and Snipes of the World, 1981; Those of the Gray Wind: The Sandhill Cranes, 1981; Teton Wildlife: Observations by a Naturalist, 1982; (with Karin L. Johnsgard) The Natural History of Dragons and Unicorns, 1982; Grouse of the World, 1983; Cranes of the World, 1983; The Platte: Channels in Time, 1984; Prairie Children, Mountain Dreams, 1985; The Pheasants of the World, 1986; Quails, Partridges and Francolins of the World, 1987; North American Owls: Biology and Natural History, 1988. Add: Sch. of Life Sciences, Univ. of Nebraska, Lincoln, Nebr. 68588, U.S.A.

JOHNSON, A.E. *See* **JOHNSON,** Annabel.

JOHNSON, A. Ross. American, b. 1939. International relations/Current affairs, Politics/Government. Sr. Social Scientist, The Rand Corp., Santa Monica, Calif., since 1969. Policy Asst. Radio Free Europe, Munich, 1966–69. *Publs:* The Transformation of Communist Ideology: The Yugoslav Case 1945–53, 1972; Yugoslavia: In the Twilight of Tito, 1974; (with Arnold L. Horelick and John D. Steinbruner) The Study of Soviet Foreign Policy: Decision–Theory–Related Approaches, 1975; (with Robert Dean and Alexander Alexieo) East European Military Establishments: The Warsaw Pact Northern Tier, 1982. Add: 359 23rd St., Santa Monica, Calif. 90402, U.S.A.

JOHNSON, Annabel (Jones). Also writes as A.E. Johnson. American, b. 1921. Children's fiction. *Publs:* As A Speckled Bird, 1956; with Edgar Johnson—The Big Rock Candy, 1957; The Black Symbol, 1959; Torrie, 1960; The Bearcat, 1960; The Rescued Heart, 1961; (as A.E. Johnson) The Secret Gift, 1961; Pickpocket Run, 1961; Wilderness Bride, 1962; A Golden Touch, 1963; The Grizzly, 1964; A Peculiar Magic, 1965; The Burning Glass, 1966; Count Me Gone, 1968; (as A.E. Johnson) A Blues Can Whistle, 1969; The Last Knife, 1971; Finders Keepers, 1981; An Alien Music, 1982; The Danger Quotient, 1984; Prisoner of PSI, 1985;

A Memory of Dragons, 1986. Add: 2925 S. Teller, Denver, Colo. 80227, U.S.A.

JOHNSON, Barbara Ferry. American, b. 1923. Historical/Romance/Gothic. Member of the English Dept., Columbia Coll., South Carolina, since 1964. Assoc. Ed., American Lumberman mag., Chicago, 1945–48; high school English teacher, Myrtle Beach, S.C., 1960–62. *Publs:* Lionors, 1975; Delta Blood, 1977; Tara's Song, 1978; Homeward Winds the River, 1979; The Heirs of Love, 1980; Echoes from the Hills, 1983. Add: c/o Warner Books, 666 Fifth Ave., New York, N.Y. 10103, U.S.A.

JOHNSON, Colin. Also known as Mudrooroo Narogin. Australian, b. 1938. Novels/Short stories, Poetry, Anthropology; Lectr. in Black Australian Literature, Univ. of Queensland, Brisbane. *Publs:* Wild Cat Falling, 1965; Long Live Sandawara, 1979; (with Colin Bourke and Isobel White) Before the Invasion: Aboriginal Life to 1788 (non–fiction), 1980; Doctor Wooreddy's Prescription for Enduring the Ending of the World, 1983; The Song Cycle of Jacky and Selected Poems, 1986; Doin' Wildcat: A Novel Koori Script, 1988; Dalwurra (poem cycle), 1988. Add: c/o English Dept., Univ. of Queensland, Brisbane, Qld. 4067, Australia.

JOHNSON, D(avid) Gale. American, b. 1916. Agriculture/Forestry, Economics. Prof. of Economics since 1954, and Chmn. of Economics since 1980, Univ. of Chicago (Asst. Prof. of Economics, 1944–54; Assoc. Dean, 1957–60, and Dean, 1960–70, Div. of Social Sciences; Acting Dr., Univ. of Chicago Library, 1971–72; Chmn., Dept. of Economics, 1971–75, 1980–84; Vice Pres., Dean of Faculties and Provost, 1975–80); Economist, Council of Intnl. Economic Policy, since 1972. Economist, Office of Price Admin., 1942, Dept. of State, 1946, Dept. of the Army, 1948, and Agency for Intnl. Development, 1961–62; Economist, Rand Corp., 1954–70, and Office of the President's Special Rep. for Trade Negotiations, 1963–65. Dir., U.S. Social Science Research Council, 1954–57; Pres., American Farm Economic Assn., 1964–65; Member, President's National Advisory Commn. on Food and Fiber, 1965–67; Adviser, Policy Planning Council, Dept. of State, 1966–69; Member, National Commn. of Population Growth and the American Future, 1970–72. *Publs:* Forward Prices for Agriculture, 1947; Trade and Agriculture, 1950; Grain Yields and the American Food Supply, 1963; The Struggle Against World Hunger, 1967; World Agriculture in Disarray, 1973, 1989; Farm Commodity Programs: An Opportunity for Change, 1973; World Food Problems and Prospects, 1975; (ed. with J.A. Schnittker) United States Agriculture in a World Context, 1975; Progress of Economic Reform in the People's Republic of China, 1982; (with Karen Brooks) Prospects for Soviet Agriculture in the 1980's, 1983; The World Grain Economy and Climate Change to the Year 2000: Implications for Policy, 1983; (with Kenzo Hemm; and Pierre Lardinois) Agricultural Policy and Trade: Adjusting Domestic Programs in an International Framework, 1985. Add: Dept. of Economics, Univ. of Chicago, Chicago, Ill. 60637, U.S.A.

JOHNSON, David Lawrence. British, b. 1943. Mathematics/Statistics. Lectr. in Mathematics, Univ. of Nottingham. Formerly, Visiting Lectr. in Mathematics, Univ. of Illinois, Urbana; Visiting Prof. of Mathematics, Busan National Univ. *Publs:* Presentations of Groups, 1976; Topics in the Theory of Group Presentations, 1980; (ed. and co–trans.) The Kourovka Notebook, 1983; Presentation of Groups, 1989. Add: Dept. of Mathematics, Univ. Park, Univ. of Nottingham, Nottingham, England.

JOHNSON, Denis. American, b. 1949. Novels/Short stories, Poetry. *Publs:* The Man among the Seals (poetry), 1969; Inner Weather (poetry), 1976; The Incognito Lounge and Other Poems, 1982; Angels (novel), 1983; Fiskadoro (novel), 1985; The Stars at Noon, 1986; The Veil (poetry), 1987. Add: c/o Knopf Inc., 201 E. 50th St., New York, N.Y. 10022, U.S.A.

JOHNSON, Diane. American, b. 1934. Novels/Short stories, Biography. *Publs:* Fair Game, 1965; Loving Hands at Home, 1965; Burning, 1970; Lesser Lives (biography), 1972; The Shadow Knows, 1974; Lying Low, 1978; Terrorists and Novelists, 1983; Dashiell Hammett, 1985; Persian Nights, 1987. Add: 24 Edith, San Francisco, Calif. 94133, U.S.A.

JOHNSON, Elmer Hubert. American, b. 1917. Criminology/Prisons, Sociology. DistinguishedProf. of Sociology and Criminal Justice, Center for Study of Crime, Delinquency and Corrections, Southern Illinois Univ., Carbondale, since 1966. Asst. Prof., then Prof., Dept. of Sociology and Anthropology, North Carolina State Univ., Raleigh, 1949–66; Asst. Dir., North Carolina Prison Dept., Raleigh, 1958–60. *Publs:* Crime, Correction and Society, 4th ed. 1978; Social Problems of Urban Man, 1973; Intnl. Handbook on Contemporary Development in Criminology, 2 vols.,

1984; Handbook on Crime and Delinquency Prevention, 1987. Add: Center for Study of Crime, Delinquency and Corrections, Southern Illinois Univ., Carbondale, Ill. 62901, U.S.A.

JOHNSON, E(mil) Richard. American, b. 1937. Mystery/Crime/ Suspense, Natural History. Inmate at Stillwater, Minnesota State Prison, since 1964. *Publs:* Silver Street, 1968 (in U.K. as The Silver Street Killer, 1969); The Inside Man, 1969; Mongo's Back in Town, 1969; Cage Five Is Going To Break, 1970; The God Keepers, 1970; Case Load—Maximum, 1971; The Judas, 1971; The Cardinalli Contract, 1975; Blind Man's Bluff, 1987; Fur: Food and Survival (non–fiction), 1987; The Hands of Eddy Loyd, 1988. Add: Box 55, Stillwater, Minn., U.S.A.

JOHNSON, Eric W(arner). American, b. 1918. Education, Human relations, Language/Linguistics, Sex. Teacher of English and sex education, Germantown Friends Sch., Philadelphia, Pa., 1946–77. *Publs:* Improve Your Own Spelling, 1956, 4th ed. 1977; (with Dawson, Zollinger and Elwell) Language for Daily Use, 1956, 5th ed. 1978; How to Live Through Junior High School, 1959, 1975; (with Jennings) Four Famous Adventures, 1962; Love and Sex in Plain Language, 1965, 4th ed. 1988; Love and Sex and Growing Up, 1970, 1978; Sex: Telling It Straight, 1970, 1979; How to Achieve Competence in English, 1976, 1982; Venereal Disease, 1978; Teaching School, 1979, 3rd ed. 1987; (with M.S. Calderone) The Family Book about Sexuality, 1981; You Are the Editor: 61 Editing Lessons That Improve Writing Skills, 1981; An Introduction to Jesus of Nazareth, 1981; Trustee Handbook, 5th ed. 1984; Evaluating the Performance of Trustees and School Heads, 1983; Raising Children to Achieve, 1984; (with David McClelland) Learning to Achieve, 1984; People, Love, Sex and Families, 1985; Older and Wiser: Wit, Wisdom and Spirited Advice from the Older Generation, 1986; How to Live with Parents and Teachers, 1986. Add: Fox Cottage, Middle Barton, Oxford OX5 4BS, England.

JOHNSON, Falk S(immons). American, b. 1913. Language/Linguistics, Writing/Journalism. Prof. Emeritus of Linguistics, Univ. of Illinois at Chicago since 1984 (Instr. in English, 1949–56; Asst. Prof. of English, 1956–60; Assoc. Prof. of English, 1960–66; Prof. of English, 1966–73; Prof. of Linguistics, 1973–84). *Publs:* A Spelling Guide and Workbook, 1959; How to Organize What You Write, 1964; Improving What You Write, 1965; A Self–Improvement Guide to Spelling, 1965; Improving Your Spelling, 3rd ed. 1979. Add: 7624 Maple St., Morton Grove, Ill. 60053, U.S.A.

JOHNSON, George (Laclede). American, b. 1952. Information science/Computers, Social commentary, Politics/Government. Ed., The Week in Review, in The New York Times, since 1986. Staff Writer and Copy Ed., Albuquerque Journal, N.M., 1976–78; Staff Writer, Minneapolis Star, 1979–82. *Publs:* Architects of Fear: Conspiracy Theories and Paranoia in American Politics, 1984; Machinery of the Mind: Inside the New Science of Artificial Intelligence, 1986. Add: c/o Esther Newberg, Intnl. Creative Management, 40 W. 57th St., New York, N.Y. 10019, U.S.A.

JOHNSON, H(erbert) Webster. American, b. 1906. Administration/Management, Marketing. Asst. Prof. of Marketing, Western Reserve Univ., Cleveland, 1947–51; Economist, Office of Price Stabilization, U.S. Govt., 1951–52; Prof. of Marketing, Univ. of Detroit, 1952–57; Prof. of Marketing, Wayne State Univ., Detroit, 1957–76. *Publs:* (with W.G. Savage) Administrative Office Management, 1968; Selecting, Training and Supervising Office Personnel, 1969; How to Use the Business Library with Sources of Business Information, 4th ed. 1972, 5th ed. (with A.J. Faria and Ernest Maier), 1983; Creative Selling, 2nd ed. 1974, 4th ed. (with A.J. Faria), 1987; Sales Management, 1976. Add: Sch. of Business Admin., Wayne State Univ., Detroit, Mich. 48202, U.S.A.

JOHNSON, James Henry. British, b. 1930. Geography, Urban studies. Prof. of Geography, since 1974, and Dean of Graduate Studies since 1986, Univ. of Lancaster. Asst. Lectr., 1954–57, Lectr. in Geography, 1957–65, and Reader in Geography, 1965–74, Univ. Coll., Univ. of London. *Publs:* (with B. Mac Aodha) An Agricultural Atlas of County Galway, 1966; Urban Geography, 1967; (ed. with R.U. Cooke) Trends in Geography, 1969; (co–author) An Advanced Geography of the British Isles, 1974; (with J. Salt and P. Wood) Housing and Geographical Mobility of Labour in England and Wales, 1974; (ed.) Suburban Growth, 1974; Urbanisation, 1980; (ed. with C.G. Pooley) The Structure of Nineteenth Century Cities, 1982; (ed.) Aspects of Geography series; (ed.) Geography and Regional Planning, 1983; (ed.) Geography Applied to Practical Problems, 1985; (ed. with J. Salt) Studies in Labour Migration, 1989. Add: Dept. of Geography, Univ. of Lancaster, Bailrigg, Lancaster, England.

JOHNSON, James Ralph. American, b. 1922. Children's fiction, Children's non–fiction, Natural history, Recreation/Leisure/Hobbies. Freelance artist since 1970. With U.S. Marine Corps, 1943–64; freelance writer, 1964–70. *Publs:* Mountain Bobcat, 1953; Lost on Hawk Mountain, 1954; The Last Passenger, 1956; Big Cypress Buck, 1957; Horsemen Blue and Gray, 1960; Wild Venture, 1961; Anyone Can Live Off the Land, 1961; Best Photos of the Civil War, 1962; Utah Lion, 1962; Camels West, 1964; Anyone Can Camp in Comfort, 1964; (with B.B. Johnson) American Wild Horses, 1964; (with B.B. Johnson) American Bears, 1965; Anyone Can Backpack in Comfort, 1965; Wolf Cub, 1966; Advanced Camping Techniques, 1967; Pepper, 1967; Blackie, the Gorilla, 1968; Ringtail, 1968; Moses' Band of Chimpanzees, 1969; Animal Paradise, 1969; Everglades Adventure, 1970; The Southern Swamps of America, 1970; Photography for Young People, 1971; Zoos of Today, 1971; Animals and Their Food, 1972. Add: Box 5295, Santa Fe, N.M. 87501, U.S.A.

JOHNSON, Jesse J. American, b. 1914. Military/Defence, Race relations. Writer, U.S. Army Aviation, since 1967. Served in the U.S. Army, 1942–62 (retiring as Lt. Col.). *Publs:* Ebony Brass; The Black Soldier; A Pictorial History of the Black Soldier in the United States (1619–1969) in Peace and War; A Pictorial History of Black Servicemen (Air Force, Army, Navy, Marines); Black Armed Forces Officers (1736–1971): A Documented Pictorial History; Black Women in the Armed Forces: A Pictorial History; Roots of Two Black Marine Sergeants Major. Add: 41 Cornelius Dr., Hampton, Va. 23666, U.S.A.

JOHNSON,. Joan J. American, b. 1942. Children's non-fiction. English Teacher for Gifted and Talented Students, Darien High School, Connecticut, since 1979. *Publs:* The Cult Movement, 1984; Justice, 1985. Add: c/o Franklin Watts, Inc., 387 Park Ave. South, New York, N.Y. 10016, U.S.A.

JOHNSON, Josephine (Winslow). American, b. 1910. Novels/Short stories, Poetry, Autobiography/Memoirs/Personal. *Publs:* Now in November, 1934; Winter Orchard and Other Stories, 1935; Jordanstown, 1937; Year's End (poetry), 1937; Paulina: The Story of an Apple–Butter Jar, 1939; Wildwood, 1946; The Dark Traveler, 1963; The Sorcerer's Son and Other Stories, 1965; The Inland Island (essays), 1969; Seven Houses: A Memoir of Times and Places, 1973; Circle of Seasons, 1974.

JOHNSON, Mel. *See* MALZBERG, Barry.

JOHNSON, Mike. *See* SHARKEY, Jack.

JOHNSON, Nicholas. American, b. 1934. Media, Politics/Government. Prof. of Law, Univ. Iowa Coll., since 1981. Chmn., National Citizens Communications Lobby, Washington, D.C., since 1975. Law Clerk to U.S. Appeals Judge, 1958–59, and to Supreme Court Justice Hugo L. Black, 1959–60; Acting. Prof. of Law, Univ. of California Law Sch., Berkeley, 1960–63; Law Assoc., Covington and Burling, Washington, D.C., 1963–64; Admin., U.S. Maritime Admin., U.S. Dept. of Commerce, 1964–66; Commnr., Federal Communications Commn., 1966–73; Adjunct Prof. of Law, Georgetown Univ., Washington, bD.C., 1971–73; Chmn., National Citizens Cttee. for Broadcasting, Washinguston, D.C., 1974–78; Commentator, National Public Radio, 1975–77, and WRC–AM Radio, Washington, D.C., 1977; Presidential Adviser, White House Conference on Libraries and Information Services, 1979; Commentator, WSUI–AM Radio, Iowa City, Iowa, 1982; Visiting Prof., California State Univ., Los Angeles, and Western Behavioral Science Inst., La Jolla, Calif., 1986; Syndicated Columnist, King Features, 1986. *Publs:* Cases and Materials on Oil and Gas Law, 1962; How to Talk Back to Your Television Set, 1970; Life Before Death in the Corporate State, 1971; Test Pattern for Living, 1972; Broadcasting in America, 1973; Cases and Materials on Communications Law and Policy, 1981 (and later eds.). Add: P.O. Box 1876, Iowa City, Iowa 52244, U.S.A.

JOHNSON, Paul (Bede). British, b. 1928. Architecture, History, Travel/Exploration/Adventure. Member of editorial staff, New Statesman, London, 1955 (Ed., 1965–70). Asst. Exec. Ed., Realities mag., 1952–55. *Publs:* The Suez War, 1957; Journey into Chaos, 1958; Left of Centre, 1960; Merrie England, 1964; Statesmen and Nations, 1971; The Offshore Islanders, 1972; (with G. Gale) The Highland Jaunt, 1973; A Place in History, 1974; The Life and Times of Edward III, 1974; Elizabeth I, 1974; Pope John XXIII, 1975; A History of Christianity, 1976; Enemies of Society, 1977; The National Trust Book of British Castles, 1978; The Recovery of Freedom, 1980; British Cathedrals, 1980; Ireland, 1980; Pope John Paul II and the Catholic Restoration, 1982; A History of the modern world from 1917 to the 1980's, 1983; The Pick of Paul Johnson, 1985; Oxford Book of Political Anecdotes, 1986; A History of the Jews, 1987. Add: 29 Newton Rd., London W2 5JR, England.

JOHNSON, Sir Peter (Colpoys Paley), Bt. British, b. 1930. Boating/Yachting. Ed., yachting books, Haynes Publishing Group, since 1987. Joined Royal Artillery, 1949; retired as Capt., 1961; Dir., Sea Sure Ltd., 1965–73; Dir. and Ed., Nautical Publishing Co. Ltd., 1970–81. Publishing Dir., Nautical Books, Macmillan London Ltd., 1981–86. *Publs:* Ocean Racing and Offshore Yachts, 1970, 1972; Boating Britain, 1973; Guinness Book of Yachting Facts and Feats, 1975; Guinness Guide to Sailing, 1981; This Is Fast Cruising, 1985; Encyclopedia of Yachting, 1989. Add: Dene End, Buckland Dene, Lymington, Hants. S041 9DT, England.

JOHNSON, Robert Clyde. American, b. 1919. Theology, Religion. Prof. Yale Univ. Divinity Sch., New Haven, Conn., since 1963. Fellow, Ezra Stiles Coll., Yale Univ. Prof. of Systematic Theology, Pittsburgh Theological Seminary, Pa., 1957–63. *Publs:* The Meaning of Christ, 1958; Authority in Protestant Theology, 1959; (ed. and contrib.) The Church and Its Changing Ministry, 1962. Add: 141 Garfield Ave., North Haven, Conn. 06473, U.S.A.

JOHNSON, Robert E(rwin). American, b. 1923. History, Biography. Prof. of History, Univ. of Alabama, since 1967 (Asst. Prof., 1956–63; Assoc. Prof., 1963–67). *Publs:* Thence Round Cape Horn: The Story of U.S. Naval Forces on Pacific Station 1818–1923, 1963; Rear Admiral John Rodgers, 1812–1882, 1967; Far China Station: The U.S. Navy in Asian Waters 1800–1898, 1979; Guardians of the Sea: History of the U.S. Coast Guard 1915 to the Present, 1987. Add: Dept. of History, Box 870212, Univ. of Alabama, Tuscaloosa, AL 35487, U.S.A.

JOHNSON, R(obert) V(incent). Australian, b. 1927. Literature. Reader in English, Univ. of Adelaide, 1971–88 (Lectr. 1958–63; Sr. Lectr. 1963–70). Lectr. in English, Univ. of New England, Armidale, 1954–58. *Publs:* Walter Pater: A Study of His Critical Outlook and Achievement, 1961; Aestheticism, 1969; Caught on the Hop (poetry), 1984. Add: 42 Royal Ave., Burnside, S.A. 5066, Australia.

JOHNSON, Robert W(illard). American, b. 1921. Money/Finance. Prof. of Mgmt. since 1964, and Exec. Dir., Credit Research Centre, since 1974, Purdue Univ., West Lafayette, Ind. Asst. Prof., Southwestern Univ., Memphis, 1948–50; Asst. Prof., Assoc. Prof., and Prof., Univ. of Buffalo, N.Y., 1950–59; Prof., Michigan State Univ., East Lansing, 1959–60. *Publs:* Capital Budgeting, 1970, 1977; (with R.I. Robinson) Self–Correcting Problems in Finance, 1970, 1976; Financial Management, 4th ed., 1971, (with R.W. Melicher) 5th ed. 1982. Add: Grad. Sch. of Mgmt., Krannert Bldg., Purdue Univ., West Lafayette, Ind. 47907, U.S.A.

JOHNSON, Ronald. American, b. 1935. Poetry, Cookery/ Gastronomy/Wine, Translations. Writer–in–Residence, Univ. of Kentucky, Lexington, 1970–71; Roethke Prof. of Poetry, Univ. of Washington, Seattle, 1973. *Publs:* A Line of Poetry, A Row of Tres, 1964; (trans.) Sports and Divertissments, 1965, 1969; Rousseau: Assorted Jungles, 1966; Gorse/Goose/Rose, 1966; Book of the Green Man, 1967; Sun Flowers, 1967; Io and the Ox–Eye Daisy, 1967; The Round Earth on Flat Paper, 1968; Reading 1, Reading 2, 1968; The Aficionado's Southwestern Cooking, 1969; Valley of the Many–Colored Grasses, 1969; Balloons for Moonless Nights, 1969; (trans.) The Spirit Walks, The Rocks Will Talk, 1969; Songs of the Earth, 1970; MAZE/MANE/WANE, 1973; Eyes and Objects, 1975; RADIOS, 1977; ARK: The Foundations, 1980; The American Table, 1984; ARK 50, 1984; Southwestern Cooking: New and Old, 1985; Simple Fare, 1989. Add: 73 Elgin Park, San Francisco, Calif. 94103, U.S.A.

JOHNSON, (John) Stephen. British, b. 1947. Archaeology/Antiquities, History. Inspector of Ancient Monuments, Historic Buildings and Monuments Commission for England, since 1973. *Publs:* The Roman Forts of the Saxon Shore, 1976, 1979; Later Roman Britain, 1980; Late Roman Fortifications, 1983. Add: 50 Holmdere Ave., London SE24 9LF, England.

JOHNSON, Stowers. British. Poetry, Art, Travel/Exploration/Adventure. Principal, Dagenham Literary Inst., 1936–39; Headmaster, Aveley Sch., 1939–68; Ed., Anglo–Soviet Journal, 1966–68; Hon. Art Curator, National Liberal Club, London, 1974–79. *Publs:* Branches Green and Branches Black, 1944; London Saga, 1946; The Mundane Tree, 1947; Mountains and No Mules, 1949; Sonnets, They Say, 1949; Before and After Puck, 1953; When Fountains Fall, 1961; Gay Bulgaria, 1964; Yugos-

lav Summer, 1967; Turkish Panorama, 1969; Collector's Luck, 1968; The Two Faces of Russia, 1969; Agents Extraordinary, 1975; Headmastering Man, 1986; Hearthstones in the Hills, 1987; Collector's World, 1989. Add: Corbière, 45 Rayleigh Rd., Hutton, Brentwood, Essex, England.

JOHNSON, Susan (M). American, b. 1939. Historical/Romance. Seized by Love, 1979; Lovestorm, 1981; Sweet Love, Survive, 1985; Blaze, 1986; The Play, 1987; Silver Flame, 1988. Add: Route 2, Box 85, North Branch. Minn. 55056, U.S.A.

JOHNSON, Terry. British, b. 1955. Plays/Screenplays. Actor and director. *Publs:* Insignificance, 1982; Cries from the Mammal House, 1984; Unsuitable for Adults, 1985, (with Kate Lock) Tuesday's Child, 1987. Add: c/o Phil Kelvin, Goodwin Assocs., 12 Rabbit Row, London W8 4DX, England.

JOHNSON, Virginia. (Mrs. William H. Masters). American, b. 1925. Sex. Co–Chmn., Bd. of Dir., Masters and Johnson Inst., St. Louis, since 1981 (Research Assoc., 1964–69, and Asst. Dir., 1969–73, Co–Dir., 1973–80, Dir., 1981–86); Lectr. in Human Sexuality in Psychiatry, Washington Univ. Sch. of Medicine, St. Louis, Mo., since 1981 (Member of Research Staff, 1957–64, Research Asst., 1960–62, and Research Instr., 1962–64, Div. of Reproductive Biology, Dept. of Obstetrics and Gynecology). Member, Advisory Bd., Homosexual Community Counseling Center; Member, Advisory Cttee., Pastoral Psychology Journal. With Missouri State Insurance Dept., Missouri State Legislature, 1942–44; Reporter and Admin. Secty., St. Louis Daily Record, 1947–50; with Advertising Dept., Columbia Broadcasting System (KMOX), St. Louis, 1950–51. *Publs:* (with William H. Masters) Human Sexual Response, 1966; (with William H. Masters) Human Sexual Inadequacy, 1970; (with William H. Masters) The Pleasure Bond, 1975; (with others) Textbook of Human Sexuality for Nurses, 1979; (with William H. Masters) Homosexuality in Perspective, 1979; (with William H. Masters and R.C. Kolodny) Textbook of Sexual Medicine, 1979; Human Sexuality, 1982; Sex and Human Loving, 1982; (with Masters) Heterosexual Behavior in the Age of AIDS, 1988. Add: 24 S. Kingshighway, St. Louis, Mo. 63108, U.S.A.

JOHNSON, Warren A. American, b 1937. Economics, Environmental science/Ecology. Prof. of Geography since 1975, San Diego State Univ., California (Asst. Prof. 1969–71; Assoc. Prof., 1971–75; Dept. Chmn., 1976–79). Civil Engineer, National Park Service, 1960–67. *Publs:* Public Parks on Private Land in England and Wales, 1971; (co–ed.) Economic Growth vs. the Environment, 1971; Muddling Toward Frugality, 1978; The Future is Not What It Used to Be, 1985. Add: Dept. of Geography, San Diego State Univ., San Diego, Cal. 92182, U.S.A.

JOHNSON, Wendell Stacy. American, b. 1927. Literature. Prof. of English Literature, City Univ. of New York, since 1962. Lectr. in English Literature, Smith Coll., Northampton, Mass., 1952–62. *Publs:* The Voices of Matthew Arnold, 1961; (with M.K. Danziger) An Introduction to Literary Criticism, 1962; Gerard Manley Hopkins: The Poet as Victorian, 1968; (with M.K. Danziger) A Poetry Anthology, 1968; Words, Things and Celebrations, 1972; Sex and Marriage in Victorian Poetry, 1975; Living in Sin: The Victorian Sexual Revolution, 1979; (ed.) Charles Dickens: New Perspectives, 1982; Sons and Fathers: The Generation Link in Literature, 1985; W. H. Auden, 1989. Add: 65 Hampton St., Southampton, N.Y. 11968, U.S.A.

JOHNSON, William Weber. American, b. 1909. Children's non- fiction, History, Travel/Exploration/Adventure, Biography. Prof. Emeritus of Journalism, Univ. of California, Los Angeles, since 1971 (Prof. and Chmn., Grad. Dept. of Journalism, 1961–71). Writer and Corresp. for Time Inc., Los Angeles, Calif., Boston, Mass., Dallas, Tex., Buenos Aires, Argentina, Mexico City, London, and NYC, 1941–61. *Publs:* Sam Houston, The Tallest Texan, 1953; The Birth of Texas, 1960; Captain Corté Conquers Mexico, 1960; Kelly Blue, 1960; Mexico, 1961; The Andean Republics, 1965; Heroic Mexico, 1968; Baja California, 1972; The Story of Sea Otters, 1973; The Forty Niners, 1974; Cortés, 1975. Add: 850 State St., No. 320, San Diego, Calif. 92101, U.S.A.

JOHNSTON, Alan (William). British, b. 1942. Archaeology/Antiquities. Lectr., Dept. of Classical Archaeology, University Coll., London, since 1972. Asst. Lectr., Dept. of Classics, University Coll., Dublin, Ireland, 1969–72. Member of Council, Soc. for the Promotion of Hellenic Studies, 1976–79, 1983–86, and since 1989. *Publs:* The Emergence of Greece, 1976; Trademarks on Greek Vases, 1980. Add: Dept. of Classical Archaeology, University Coll., Gower St., London WC1E 6BT, England.

JOHNSTON, George (Benson). Canadian, b. 1913. Poetry, Translations. Retired Prof. of English, Carleton Univ., Ottawa (joined faculty, 1950). Asst. Prof. of English, Mount Allison Univ., Sackville, N.B., 1946–48. *Publs:* The Cruising Auk, 1959; (trans.) The Saga of Gisli, 1963; Home Free, 1966; Happy Enough, 1972; (trans.) The Faroe Islander's Saga, 1975; (trans.) The Greenlander's Saga, 1976; Between, 1977; Taking a Grip, 1978; (trans.) Rocky Shores, 1981; Auk Redivivus, 1981; (trans.) Wind Over Romsdal, 1982; Ask Again, 1984; (trans.) Pastor Bodvar's Letter, 1985; Carl: Portrait of a Painter, 1986; (trans.) Seeing and Remembering, 1988; (trans.) Bee-Buzz, Salmon-Leap, 1988. Add: R.R. 1, Athelstan, Quebec JOS 1AO, Canada.

JOHNSTON, Jennifer (Prudence). Irish, b. 1930. Novels/Short stories, Plays. *Publs:* The Captains and the Kings, 1972; The Gates, 1973; How Many Miles to Babylon?, 1974; Shadows on Our Skin, 1977; The Old Jest, 1979; The Christmas Tree, 1981; The Nightingale and Not the Lark (play), 1981; The Railway Station Man, 1984; Fool's Sanctuary, 1987; The Invisible Man (play) 1987; Tryptich (play), 1988. Add: Brook Hall, Culmore Rd., Derry BT48 8JE, Northern Ireland.

JOHNSTON, Jill. American, b. 1929 in England. Women, Autobiography/Memoirs/Personal. Columnist and Contributor, Village Voice, NYC, 1959–75; Contributor, Art News, NYC 1959–65; Critic, Art In America, NYC, 1983–87. *Publs:* Marmalade Me, 1971; Lesbian Nation, 1973; Gullibles Travels, 1974; Mother Bound, 1983; Paper Daughter, 1985. Add: c/o Knopf, 201 E. 50th St., New York, N.Y. 10022, U.S.A.

JOHNSTON, Norma. *See* **ST. JOHN**, Nicole.

JOHNSTON, Ronald. British, b. 1926. Novels/Short stories. Council Member, Scottish Arts Council, since 1973; Vice-Pres., Scottish PEN, since 1974; Member, Mgmt., Cttee., Soc. of Authors, since 1975. Assoc., Chartered Insurance Inst.; with Manufacturers Life Insurance of Canada, 1947–51; Salesman, Gen. Mgr. then Dir., Anglo-Dutch Cigar Co. Ltd., 1959–68. *Publs:* Disaster at Dungeness (in U.S. as Collision Ahead), 1964; Red Sky in the Morning (in U.S. as Danger at Bravo Key), 1965; The Stowaway, 1966; The Wrecking of Offshore Five, 1967; The Angry Ocean, 1968; The Black Camels (in U.S. as The Black Camels of Qahran), 1969; Paradise Smith, 1972; The Eye of the Needle, 1975; Flying Dutchman, 1983; Sea Story, 1980. Add: c/o Macdonald, 66-73 Shoe Lane, London EC4P 4AP, England.

JOHNSTON, R(onald) J(ohn). British, b. 1941. Geography. Prof. of Geography, Univ. of Sheffield, since 1974. Ed., Environment and Planning, and Progress in Human Geography. Teaching Fellow, 1964, Sr. Teaching Fellow, 1965, and Lectr., 1966, Monash Univ., Australia; Lectr., 1967–69, Sr. Lectr., 1969–72, and Reader, 1972–74, Univ.of Canterbury, New Zealand; Secty., Inst. of British Geographers, 1982–85. *Publs:* (co-author) Retailing in Melbourne, 1969; Urban Residential Patterns, 1971; (ed.) Urbanization in New Zealand, 1973; Spatial Structures, 1973; (ed.) Society and Environment in New Zealand, 1974; The World Trade System, 1976; The New Zealanders, 1976; (co-ed.) Social Areas in Cities, 3 vols., 1976–78; (co-author) Geography and Inequality, 1977; Multivariate Statistical Analysis in Geography, 1978; (co-ed.) Geography and the Urban Environment (annual), 1978; (with P.J. Taylor) Geography of Elections, 1979; Political, Electoral and Spatial Systems, 1979; Geography and Geographers, 1979, 3rd ed. 1987; City and Society, 1980, 1984; The American Urban System, 1982; Geography and the State, 1982; Philosophy and Human Geography, 1983; Residential Segregation: The State and Constitutional Conflict in American Urban Areas, 1984. 1986; The Geography of English Politics, 1985; On Human Geography, 1986; Bellringing: The English Art of Change Ringing, 1986; A Nation Dividing, 1988. Add: Dept. of Geography, Univ. of Sheffield, Sheffield S10 2TN, England.

JOHNSTON, (Sir) (David) Russell. Scottish, b. 1932. Politics/-Government. Liberal M.P. for Inverness, 1964–83, and for Inverness, Nairn and Lochaber since 1983 (Social and Liberal Democrat since 1988); Deputy Leader, Social and Liberal Democrats, and Spokesman on Foreign and Commonwealth Affairs and European Community Affairs, since 1988 (Liberal Spokesman on Foreign Affairs and Defence, 1974–86). Leader, Scottish Liberal Party, 1974–88; Pres., Scottish Social and Liberal Democrats, since 1988. Teacher, Liberton Secondary Sch., 1961–63; Research Asst. Scottish Liberal Party, 1963–64. Member, Royal Commn. on Local Govt. in Scotland, 1966–69; Member, European Parliament, 1973–75, 1976–79. *Publs:* Highland Development, 1964; To Be a Liberal, 1972; Scottish Liberal Party Conference Speeches, 1979. Add: 35 Southside Rd., Inverness IV2 4XA, Scotland.

JOHNSTON, Velda. Also writes as Veronica Jason. American. Mystery/Crime/Suspense. *Publs:* Along a Dark Path, 1967; House above Hollywood, 1968; A Howling in the Woods, 1968; I Came to the Castle, 1969, in U.K. as Castle Perilous, 1971; The Light in the Swamp, 1970; The Phantom Cottage, 1970; The Face in the Shadows, 1971; The People on the Hill, 1971, in U.K. as Circle of Evil, 1972; The Mourning Trees, 1972; The Late Mrs. Fonsell, 1972; The White Pavilion, 1973; Masquerade in Venice, 1973; I Came to the Highlands, 1974; The House on the Left Bank, 1975; A Room with Dark Mirrors, 1975; Deveron Hall, 1976; The Frenchman, 1976; The Etruscan Smile, 1977; The Hour Before Midnight, 1978; The Silver Dolphin, 1979; The People from the Sea, 1979; A Presence in an Empty Room, 1980; The Stone Maiden, 1980; The Fateful Summer, 1981; (as Veronica Jason) So Wild a Heart, 1981; The Other Karen, 1983; Voices in the Night, 1984; Shadow Behind the Curtain, 1985; The Crystal Cat, 1985; Fatal Affair, 1986; The House on Bostwick Square, 1987; The Girl on the Beach, 1987; The Man at Windmere, 1988. Add: c/o Dodd Mead, 71 Fifth Ave, New York, N.Y. 10003, U.S.A.

JOHNSTON, William. Irish, b. 1925. Theology/Religion; Translations. Ordained Catholic Priest, 1957, and member of Soc. of Jesus. Prof. of Theology, Sophia Univ., Tokyo, since 1960. *Publs:* The Mysticism of 'The Cloud of Unknowing', 1967, 1975; (trans.) Silence, by S. Endo, 1969; The Still Point: On Zen and Christian Mysticism, 1970; Christian/Zen, 1971; (ed.) The Cloud of Unknowing and the Book of Privy Counselling, 1973; Silent Music: The Science of Meditation: The Inner Eye of Love: Mysticism and Religion, 1978; The Mirror Mind: Spirituality and Transformation, 1981; The Wounded Stag, 1984; (trans.) The Bells of Nagasaki, by T. Nagai, 1984; Being in Love, 1988. Add: Sophia Univ., 7 Kioi-Cho, Chiyodaku, Tokyo 102, Japan.

JOHNSTON, William Murray. American, b. 1936. History. Prof. of History, Univ. of Massachusetts, Amherst, since 1975 (Asst. Prof., 1965–70; Assoc. Prof., 1970–75). *Publs:* The Formative Years of R.G. Collingwood, 1967; The Austrian Mind: An Intellectual and Social History 1848-1938, 1972; Vienna, Vienna, 1981; In Search of Italy: Foreign Writers in Northern Italy since 1800, 1987. Add: 104 Shays St., Amherst, Mass. 01002, U.S.A.

JOHNSTONE, Keith. British. Plays/Screenplays, Theatre. Dir., Loose Moose Theatre Co., Calgary, since 1977, and at Calgary Univ. Worked at the Royal Court Theatre, London, in various capacities: Dir., Theatre Studio, 1965–66; Assoc. Dir., 1966; Dir. of Theatre Machine Improvisational Group; Taught at the Royal Academy of Dramatic Art, London. *Publs:* Impro: Improvisation and the Theatre, 1979, 1981; The Last Bird, 1981. Add: c/o Dept. of Drama, Univ. of Calgary, Calgary, Alta. T2N 1N4, Canada.

JOLL, James. British, b. 1918. History. Stevenson Prof. of Intnl. History, London Sch. of Economics, 1967–81, now Emeritus. Fellow and Tutor in Modern History and Politics, New Coll., Oxford, 1946–50; Fellow and Sub-Warden of St. Antony's Coll., Oxford, and Lectr. in Modern History, Oxford Univ., 1951–67; Visiting Member, Inst. for Advanced Study, Princeton, N.J., 1953, 1971. *Publs:* (ed.) Britain and Europe from Pitt to Churchill, 1950, 1961; The Second International 1889-1914, 1955, 1975; (ed.) The Decline of the Third Republic, 1959; Three Intellectuals in Politics, 1960; The Anarchists, 1964, 1979; (ed. with D. Apter) Anarchism Today, 1971; Europe since 1870, 1973, 1983; Gramsci, 1977; The Origins of the First World War, 1984. Add: 24 Ashchurch Park Villas, London W.12, England.

JOLLEY, (Monica) Elizabeth. Australian (born British), b. 1923. Novels/Short stories. Part-time Tutor in English, Fremantle Arts Centre, Western Australia, since 1974; Writer-in-Residence, Western Australian Institute of Technology, Bentley, since 1982. *Publs:* Five Acre Virgin and Other Stories, 1976; The Travelling Entertainer and Other Stories, 1979; Palomino (novel), 1980; The Newspaper of Claremont Street (novel), 1981; Mr. Scobie's Riddle (novel), 1983; Woman in a Lampshade (short story), 1983; Miss Peabody's Inheritance (novel), 1983; Milk and Honey (novel), 1984; Stories, 1984; Foxybaby, 1985; The Well (novel), 1986; The Sugar Mother (novel), 1988; My Father's Moon (novel), 1989. Add: 28 Agett Rd., Claremont, W.A. 6010, Australia.

JOLLY, W(illiam) P(ercy). British, b. 1922. Administration/Management, Engineering/Technology, Biography. Freelance scientific and mgmt. consultant; Visiting Teacher, Dept. of Electronic and Electrical Engineering, King's Coll., Univ. of London, since 1969. Lectr. to Asst. Prof., Dept. of Physics and Electrical Engineering, Royal Naval Coll., Greenwich, London, 1949–60. *Publs:* Physics for Electrical Engineers,

1961; (co-author) Examples in Advanced Electrical Engineering, 1962; (co-author) Operational Research in Management, 1962; Low Noise Electronics, 1967; Cryoelectronics, 1972; Marconi, 1972; Electronics, 1972, 3rd ed. 1983; Sir Oliver Lodge, 1974; Lord Leverhulme, 1976; Jumbo, 1977. Add: 31 The Plantation, Blackheath, London SE3, England.

JOLOWICZ, J(ohn) A(nthony). British, b. 1926. Law. Fellow, Trinity Coll., Cambridge, since 1952, and Prof. of Comparative Law, Cambridge Univ., since 1976 (Asst. Lectr, 1955–59, Lectr., 1959–72, and Reader, 1972–76). Ed., Journal of Soc. of Public Teachers of Law, 1962–80. *Publs:* (ed.) H.F. Jolowicz's Lectures on Jurisprudence, 1963; Winfield and Jolowicz on Tort, 1971, 11th ed., 1979; (with M. Cappelletti) Public Interest Parties and the Active Role of the Judge, 1975; (with others) Droit Anglais, 1986. Add: Trinity College, Cambridge CB2 1TQ, England.

JONAS, George. Canadian, b. 1935. Plays/Screenplays, Poetry, Criminology/Law enforcement/Prisons. Television Drama Producer, CBC, Toronto, since 1970 (Script Ed., 1962–67; Chief Story Ed., 1968–70). *Publs:* The European Lover (play), 1966; The Absolute Smile, 1967; The Happy Hungry Man, 1970; Cities, 1973; The Glove (play), 1974; (co-author) By Persons Unknown, 1977 (Edgar Allan Poe Award); Pushkin (play), 1977; Final Decree (novel), 1981; The Scales of Justice (anthology of radio documentaries), 1983; Vengeance: The True Story of an Israeli Counter-Terrorist Team, 1984; Crocodiles In the Bathtub (selected journalism), 1987; Greenspan: The Case for the Defence (biog.), 1987. Add: c/o The Colbert Agency, 303 Davenport Rd., Toronto, Ont., Canada.

JONAS, Manfred. American, b. 1927. International relations/Current affairs. John Bigelow Prof. of History, Union Coll., Schenectady, N.Y., since 1986 (Asst. to Assoc. Prof., 1963–67; Prof., 1967–81; Washington Irving Prof. in Modern Literacy and Historical Studies, 1981–86). Dr. Otto Salgo Visiting Prof. of American studies, Eötvös Lorand Univ., Budapest, 1983–84. Visiting Prof. in American History, Freie Univ., Berlin, 1959–62; Assoc. Prof. of History, Pennsylvania Military Coll., Chester, 1962–63. *Publs:* (ed.) Die Unabhängigkeitserklärung der Vereinigten Staaten, 1965; Isolationism in America, 1935–1951, 1966; (ed.) American Foreign Relations in the Twentieth Century, 1967; (ed. with F.L. Loewenheim and H.D. Langley) Roosevelt and Churchill: Their Secret Wartime Correspondence, 1975; (co- ed. with R.V. Wells) New Opportunities in a New Nation: The Development of New York after the Revolution, 1982; The United States and Germany: A Diplomatic History, 1984. Add: Dept. of History, Union Coll., Schenectady, N.Y. 12308, U.S.A.

JONES, Adrienne. American, b. 1915. Novels/Short stories, Children's fiction. *Publs:* Thunderbird Pass., 1952; Where Eagles Fly, 1957; Ride the Far Wind, 1964; Wild Voyageur: Story of a Canada Goose, 1966; Sail, Calypso!, 1968; Another Place, Another Spring, 1971; The Mural Master, 1974; So, Nothing is Forever, 1974; The Hawks of Chelney, 1978; The Beckoner, 1980; Whistle Down a Dark Lane, 1982; A Matter of Spunk, 1983; Street Family, 1987. Add: 24491 Los Serranos Dr., Laguna Niguel, Calif. 92677, U.S.A.

JONES, Alan Griffith. British, b. 1943. Language/Linguistics, Travel/Exploration/Adventure. Head of the German Centre, Hatfield Polytechnic, since 1973, and Principal Lectr., since 1985 (Lectr., 1968–72; Sr. Lectr., 1973–82). Hon. Ed., Treffpunkt, 1977–86. *Publs:* (ed.) Anglo-German Songbook, 1968; The Germans: An Englishman's Notebook, 1968; (co-ed.) Deutsche Schüler in England, 1972; (co-ed.) British Teenagers on the Rhine, 1975; (co-ed.) A Handbook of Information for Teachers of German, 1979; This Is Germany, 1980; (co-ed.)German in the Classroom, 1984. Add: 51 Roe Green Close, Hatfield, Herts. AL10 9PF, England.

JONES, Aubrey. British, b. 1911. Economics, Politics/Government. Member, Foreign and Editorial Staff, The Times Newspaper, London, 1937–39, 1947–48; served with Army Intelligence Staff, War Office and Mediterranean, 1940–46; Member of Staff, 1949–55, Economic Dir., 1954, and Gen. Dir., 1955, British Iron and Steel Fedn.; Conservative M.P. for Birmingham Hall Green, 1950–65; Minister of Fuel and Power, 1955–57, and Minister of Supply, 1957–59; Dir., Courtaulds Ltd., 1960–63, Guest Keen and Nettlefolds Steel Co. Ltd., 1960–65; Dir., 1962–65, and Chmn., 1964–65, Staveley Industries Ltd.; Chmn., National Bd. for Prices and Incomes, 1965–70; Chmn., Laporte Industries Ltd., 1970–72; Leading Adviser to Nigerian Public Service Review Commn., 1973–74, and to Iranian Govt., 1974–78; Dir., Cornhill Insurance Co. Ltd., 1971–81 (Chmn., 1972–74), Thomas Tilling Ltd., 1971–81, and Black and Decker

Ltd., 1974–81. *Publs:* The Pendulum of Politics, 1946; Industrial Order, 1950; The New Inflation: The Politics of Prices and Incomes, 1973; (ed.) Economics and Equality, 1976; Oil: The Missed Opportunity, 1981; Britain's Economy: The Root Causes of Stagnation, 1985. Add: 120 Limmer Lane, Felpham, Bognor Regis, PO22 7LP, England.

JONES, Billy Mac. American, b. 1925. Business/Trade/Industry, History, Biography. Pres., Sunflower Heritage Enterprises, Inc. of Kansas, since 1983; Chairholder, Center for Entrepreneurship, Wichita State Univ., Kansas, since 1980. Instr./Coach, Hillsboro High School, Nashville, 1950–54; Instr./Coach, Middle Tennessee State Univ., 1954–58; Asst. Coach, Texas A & M Univ., 1958–59; Dean and Dept. Head, Angelo State Univ., Texas, 1959–69; Pres., Southwest Texas State Univ., 1969–73; Dir./Regent, American Council on Education, 1972–79; Pres., Memphis State Univ., 1973–80; Dir., Memphis School of Banking, 1975–80; Vice- Pres., Memphis Public Television Corp., 1975–80. Pres., Texas State Historical Assn., 1976. *Publs:* Search for Maturity: Saga of Texas 1870-1900, 1965; Health Seekers in the Southwest, 1817-1900, 1967; (with Billy Brunson) Texans All: The People of Texas, 1973; (with Odie Faulk) Miracle of the Wilderness, 1977; (ed.) Heroes of Tennessee, 1978; L.E. Phillips: Banker, Oilman, Civic Leader, 1981; J.A. Mull, Jr.: Independent Oilman, 1982; (ed. with Ron Christy) Complete Information Bank for Entrepreneurs and Small Business Managers, 1982; Dane Gray Hansen: Titan of Northwest Kansas, 1983; The Chandlers of Kansas: A Banking Family, 1983; (with Odie Faulk) Fort Smith: An Illustrated History, 1984; (with Odie Faulk) Tahlequah, NSU, and the Cherokees, 1984; (with Odie Faulk) The Cherokees: An Illustrated History, 1984; Magic with Sand: History of AFG Industries, 1984; Henry A. Bubb: Capitol Federal Savings and Loan Association, 1985. Add: c/o Center for Entrepreneurship and Small Business Management, Wichita State Univ., P.O. Box 48, Wichita, Kans. 67208, U.S.A.

JONES, Bob, Jr. American, b. 1911. Novels/Short stories, Plays/Screenplays, Poetry, Theology/Religion. Chmn., Bd. of Trustees, since 1964, and Chancellor, since 1971, Bob Jones Univ. (Acting Pres., 1932–47; Pres., 1947–71). *Publs:* All Fulness Dwells, 1942; How to Improve Your Preaching, 1945; As the Small Rain, 1945; (compiler) Inspirational and Devotional Verse, 1946; Wine of Morning, 1950; Showers Upon the Grass, 1951; Ancient Truths for Modern Days, 1963; Revealed Religion: Paintings by Benjamin West, 1963; Fundamentals of Faith, 1964; Prologue: A Drama of Jon Hus, 1968; (with B. Jones, Sr. and B. Jones III) Heritage of Faith, 1973; Old Testament Sermons, 4 vols., 1973; Daniel of Babylon, 1984; Cornbread and Caviar, 1985. Add: Bob Jones Univ., Greenville, South Carolina 29614, U.S.A.

JONES, Brian. British, b. 1938. Poetry. *Publs:* The Lady with a Little Dog (radio play), 1962; Poems, 1966; A Family Album, 1968; Interior, 1969; The Mantis Hand and Other Poems, 1970; For Mad Mary, 1974; The Spitfire on the Northern Line, 1975; The Island Normal, 1980; Children of Separation, 1985. Add: c/o Carcanet Press, 208 Corn Exchange Bldgs., Manchester M4 3BQ, England.

JONES, Brian Kinsey.   *See* **BALL,** Brian N.

JONES, Charles W(illiams). American, b. 1905. Literature, Writing/Journalism, Translations. Prof. of English Emeritus, Univ. of California, Berkeley, since 1973 (Prof., 1954–73). Field Rep., Allyn & Bacon, publrs., Boston, Mass., 1926–29; Prof. and Dean Grad. Sch., Cornell Univ., Ithaca, N.Y., 1936–54. *Publs:* The Library Paper, 1938; Bedae Pseudepigrapha, 1939; (with Tresidder and Schubert) Writing and Speaking, 1943; (ed. and contrib.) Bedae Opera de Temporibus, 1943; Saints' Lives and Chronicles, 1947; (ed. and trans.) Medieval Literature in Translation, 1950; The St. Nicholas Liturgy, 1963; (ed.) Bedae Opera Exegetica in Genesim, 1967; (ed.) Bedae Opera Didascalica (3 vols.), 1975, 3rd ed. 1980; (with Horn and Crocker) Carolingian Aesthetics, 1976; St. Nicholas of Myra, Bari, and Manhattan, 1978. Add: Dept. of English, Univ. of California, Berkeley, Calif. 94720, U.S.A.

JONES, (Abbot) Christopher. American, b. 1937. Theology/Religion, Autobiography/Memoirs/Personal. Founder and Spiritual Father, Transfiguration Retreat, Anglican monastic retreat, Pulaski, Wisc., since 1968. *Publs:* Listen, Pilgrim, 1968; Look Around, Pilgrim, 1968; Scott, 1978. Add: Transfiguration Retreat, RFD 1, Box 63A, Pulaski, Wisc. 4162, U.S.A.

JONES, Clifford M. British, b. 1902. Theology/Religion. Former Sr. Lectr. in Religious Education, Inst. of Education, Univ. of Leeds. *Publs:* Beginner's Chemistry, 1933; Chemical Calculations, 1937; The Methods of Christian Educatin, 1950; Bible Study Exercises, 1956; Teaching the

Bible Today, 1963; The Bible Today, 1964; New Testament Illustrations, 1966; Worship in the Secondary School, 1969; Old Testament Illustrations, 1971. Add: 21 Stockhill St., Dewsbury, West Yorks. WF13 2JD, England.

JONES, D(ennis) F(eltham). British. Science fiction/Fantasy. Has worked as a bricklayer and market gardener. *Publs:* Colossus, 1966; Implosion, 1967; Don't Pick the Flowers (in U.S. as Denver Is Missing), 1971; The Fall of Colossus, 1974; Earth Has Been Found (in U.K. as Xenos), 1979. Add: c/o Sedgwick and Jackson Ltd., 1 Tavistock Chambers, Bloomsbury Way, London WC1A 2SG, England.

JONES, Diana Wynne. British, b. 1934. Novels/Short stories, Children's fiction, Plays/Screenplays. *Publs:* The Batterpool Business (play), 1965; The King's Things (play), 1968; The Terrible Fisk Machine (play), 1969; Changeover (fiction), 1970; Wilkins' Tooth (fiction) (in U.S. as Witch's Business), 1973; The Ogre Downstairs (fiction), 1974; Eight Days of Luke (fiction), 1975; Cart and Cwidder (fiction), 1975; Dogsbody (fiction), 1975; Power of Three (fiction), 1976; Charmed Life (fiction), 1977; Drowned Ammet (fiction), 1977; Who Got Rid of Angus Flint? (fiction), 1978; The Spellcoats (fiction), 1979; The Magicians of Caprona (fiction), 1980; The Four Grannies, 1980; The Homeward Bounders, 1981; The Time of the Ghost, 1981; Witch Week, 1982; The Skiver's Guide, 1984; Archer's Goon, 1984; Warlock at the Wheel, 1984; Fire and Hemlock, 1985; Howl's Moving Castle, 1986; A Tale of Time City, 1987; The Lives of Christopher Chant, 1988; Chair Person, 1989; (ed.) Hidden Turnings, 1989. Add: 9 The Polygon, Clifton, Bristol 8, England.

JONES, Douglas C. American, b. 1924. Westerns/Adventure, History. With U.S. Army, from 1943; retired as Chief of the News Branch, Dept. of Defense, The Pentagon, 1968. Member of Faculty, Sch. of Journalism and Mass Communication, Univ. of Wisconsin, Madison, 1968–74. *Publs:* The Treaty of Medicine Lodge, 1966; The Court Martial of George Armstrong Custer, 1976; Arrest Sitting Bull, 1977; A Creek Called Wounded Knee, 1978; Winding Stair, 1979; Elkhorn Tavern, 1980; Weedy Rough, 1981; The Barefoot Brigade, 1982; Season of Yellow Leaf, 1983; Gone the Dreams and Dancing, 1984; Roman, 1986; Hickory Cured, 1987. Add: 1987 Greenview Dr., Fayetteville, Ark. 72710, U.S.A.

JONES, D(ouglas) G(ordon). Canadian, b. 1929. Poetry, Literature, Translations. Prof. Titulaire, English Dept., Univ. of Sherbrooke, Que. (joined faculty, 1963). *Publs:* Frost on the Sun, 1957; Sun is Axeman, 1961; Phrases from Orpheus, 1967; Butterfly on Rock: A Study of Themes and Images in Canadian Literature, 1970; (trans.) The Terror of the Snows, by P.M. Lapointe, 1976; Under the Thunder, the Flowers Light Up the Earth, 1977; A Throw of Particles, 1983; Balthazar and Other Poems, 1988. Add: P.O. Box 356, North Hatley, Que. J0B 2C0, Canada.

JONES, Emrys. British, b. 1920. Geography, Regional/Urban planning, Social sciences (general). Lectr. in Geography, Queen's Univ., Belfast, 1950–59. Prof. of Geography, Univ. of London, 1960–84. *Publs:* (ed.) Belfast in its Regional Setting, 1952; Social Geography of Belfast, 1960; Introduction to Human Geography, 1964; Towns and Cities, 1965; (with D.J. Sinclair) Atlas of London and the London Region, 1970; (ed. with R. Buchanan and D. McCourt) Man and His Habitat, 1971; (with E. van Zandt) Cities, 1974; (ed.) Readings in Social Geography, 1974; (with J. Eyles) Introduction to Social Geography, 1977; (ed.) Encyclopedia of the World and Its People, 1978. Add: 2 Pine Close, North Rd., Berkhamsted, England.

JONES, Eric Lionel. British, b. 1936. Agriculture, Economics, History. Prof. of Economics, La Trobe Univ., Melbourne, since 1975. Research Fellow, Nuffield Coll., Oxford, 1963–67; Research Dir., Inst. of Agricultural History, Univ. of Reading, Berks., 1967–70; Prof. of Economics, Northwestern Univ., Evanston, Ill., 1970–75. *Publs:* Seasons and Prices, 1964; (ed. with G.E. Mingay and contrib.) Land, Labour and Population in the Industrial Revolution, 1967; (ed. and contrib.) Agriculture and Economic Growth in England, 1967; The Development of English Agriculture, 1968; (ed. with S.J. Woolf and contrib.) Agrarian Change and Economic Development 1969; Agriculture and the Industrial Revolution, 1974; (ed. with W.N. Parker and contrib.) European Peasants and Their Markets, 1975; The European Miracle, 1981; Agricoltura e Rivoluzione Industriale, 1982; (with S. Porter and M. Turner) A Gazetteer of English Urban Fire Disasters 1500-1900, 1984; Growth Recurring, 1988. Add: Sch. of Economics, La Trobe Univ., Bundoora, Vic. 3083, Australia.

JONES, Evan (Lloyd). Australian, b. 1931. Poetry, Literature, Biography. Sr. Lectr. in English, Univ. of Melbourne, since 1965 (Tutor, and Sr. Tutor in History, 1955–58; Lectr., 1964). Lectr. in English, Australian National Univ., Canberra, 1960–63. *Publs:* Inside the Whale: Poems, 1960; Understandings: Poems, 1967; Kenneth Mackenzie, 1969; (ed. with G. Little) The Poems of Kenneth Mackenzie, 1972; Recognitions: Poems, 1978; Left at the Post, 1984. Add: Dept. of English, Univ. of Melbourne, Parkville, Vic. 3052, Australia.

JONES, Frank Lancaster. Australian, b. 1937. Race relations, Sociology. Prof. and Head Dept. of Sociology, Australian National Univ., Canberra, since 1972 (Research Asst. in Demography), 1958; Research Scholar in Demography, 1959–62; Research Fellow in Sociology, 1963–66; Fellow in Sociology, 1966–69; Sr. Fellow in Sociology, 1969–72; Acting Head, Dept. of Sociology, 1970–72). Research Officer, Australian Inst. of Aboriginal Studies, Canberra, 1962; Exec. Member, Sociological Assn. of Australia and New Zealand, 1965, 1970–73; Ed., Australian and New Zealand Journal of Sociology, 1970–72. *Publs:* A Demographic Survey of the Aboriginal Population of the Northern Territory, with Special Reference to Bathurst Island Mission, 1963; Dimensions of Urban Social Structure: The Social Areas of Melbourne, 1969; (with L. Broom) A Blanket a Year, 1973; (with Broom) Opportunity and Attainment in Australia, 1976; (co-author) Investigating Social Mobility, 1977; (co-author) The Inheritance of Inequality, 1980. Add: Dept. of Sociology, Australian National Univ., P.O. Box 4, Canberra, A.C.T., Australia 2600.

JONES, Gareth (Hywel). British, b. 1930. Law. Queen's Counsel; Fellow, Trinity Coll., Cambridge, since 1961, Downing Prof. of the Laws of England, since 1973, and Vice-Master, Trinity Coll., since 1986, Cambridge Univ. (Lectr. 1961–74, Tutor, 1967, and Sr. Tutor, 1972, Trinity Coll.; Lectr., 1961–74, and Chmn., Faculty of Law, 1978–81, Cambridge Univ.). Lectr., Oriel and Exeter colls., Oxford Univ., 1956–58. *Publs:* (with Hon. Lord Goff) The Law of Restitution, 1966, 3rd ed. 1986; The History of the Law of Charity 1532-1827, 1969; The Sovereignty of the Law, 1973. Add: Trinity College, Cambridge CB1 1TQ, England.

JONES, Gayl. American, b. 1949. Novels/Short stories, Plays, Poetry. Member of the English Dept., Univ. of Michigan, Ann Arbor, 1975–83. *Publs:* Corregidora (novel), 1975; Chile Woman (play), 1975; Eva's Man (novel), 1976; White Rat (short stories), 1977; Song for Anninho (poetry), 1981; The Hermit-Woman (poetry), 1983; Xarque (poetry), 1985. Add: Lives in Europe.

JONES, Glyn. British, b. 1905. Novels/Short stories, Poetry, Literature, Translations. Formerly schoolmaster in Glamorgan, now retired. *Publs:* The Blue Bed, 1937; Poems, 1939; The Water Music, 1944; The Dream of Jake Hopkins, 1954; (trans. with T.J. Morgan) The Saga of Llywarch the Old, 1955; The Valley, The City, The Village, 1956; The Learning Lark, 1960; The Island of Apples, 1965; The Dragon Has Two Tongues, 1968; Selected Short Stories, 1971; The Beach at Falesa, 1973; Selected Poems, 1975; Welsh Heirs, 1978; (with John Rowlands) Profiles: A Visitor's Guide to Writing in Twentieth-Century Wales, 1980; Setting Out: Memoir of Literary Life in Wales, 1982; Random Entrances to Gwyn Thomas, 1982; When the Thorn-bush Brings Forth Apples, 1982; Honeydew on the Wormwood, 1984; Selected Poems, Fragments, and Fictions, 1988. Add: 158 Manor Way, Whitchurch, Cardiff CF4 1RN, Wales.

JONES, Gwyn. British, b. 1907. Novels/Short stories, History, Mythology/Folklore. Schoolmaster, 1929–35; Lectr., 1935–40, and Prof. of English Language and Literature, 1965–75, University Coll., Cardiff; Ed., Welsh Review, Cardiff and Aberystwyth, 1939–48; Dir., Penmark Press, Cardiff, 1939–60; Prof. of English Language and Literature, University Coll. of Wales, Aberystwyth, 1940–65; Pres., Viking Soc. for Northern Research, 1951–52; Chmn., Welsh Arts Council, 1957–67; Visiting Prof., Univ. of Iowa, 1982. *Publs:* Richard Savage, 1935; (ed. with E.M. Silvanus) Narrative Poems for Schools, 3 vols., 1935; Times Like These, 1936; The Nine Days' Wonder, 1937; A Garland of Bays, 1938; (ed.) Welsh Short Stories, 1940; (ed. with Gweno Lewis) Letters from India, by Alun Lewis, 1946; The Buttercup Field, 1945; The Green Island, 1946; The Still Waters and Other Stories, 1948; A Prospect of Wales, 1948; (trans. with Thomas Jones) The Mabinogion, 1948, 3rd ed. 1989; (ed.) Salmacis and Hermaphroditus, 1951; Sir Gawain and the Green Knight, 1952; The Flowers Beneath the Scythe, 1952; Shepherd's Hey and Other Stories, 1953; (ed.) Circe and Ulysses: The Inner Temple Masque, by William Browne, 1954; Welsh Legends and Folk Tales: Retold, 1955; Scandinavian Legends and Folk Tales: Retold, 1956; The First Forty Years: Some Notes on Anglo-Welsh Literature, 1957; (ed.) Welsh Short Stories, 1956; (ed.) Songs and Poems of John Dryden, 1957; (ed.) The Metamorphosis of Publius Ovidus Naso, 1958; (ed.) The Songs and Sonnets of Shakespeare, 1960; Egil's Saga, 1960; Eirik the Red's Sage, 1961; The Walk Home, 1963; The Norse Atlantic Saga: Being the Norse Voyages of Discovery and Settlement to Iceland, Greenland, America, 1964, rev. ed. 1986; The Legendary History of Olaf Tryggvason, 1968; A History of the Vikings, 1968, rev. ed. 1985; (ed. with I.F. Ellis) Twenty-Five Welsh Short Stories, 1971; Kings, Beasts and Heroes, 1972; Selected Short Stories, 1974; (ed.) The Oxford Book of Welsh Verse in English, 1977; Being and Belonging, 1977; Babel and the Dragon's Tongue, 1981; Fountains of Praise, 1983. Add: Castle Cottage, Seaview Place, Aberystwyth, Dyfed, Wales.

JONES, Gwyn Owain. British, b. 1917. Novels/Short stories, Physics. Prof. of Physics, and Head, Dept. of Physics, Queen Mary Coll., Univ. of London, 1953–68; Dir., National Museum of Wales, Cardiff, 1968–77. Chmn., English Language Section, Yr Academi Gymreig, 1978–81. *Publs:* Glass, 1956, 1971; (with J. Rotblat and G.J. Whitrow) Atoms and the Universe, 1956, 3rd ed. 1973; The Catalyst (novel), 1960; Personal File (novel), 1962; Now (novel), 1965; The Conjuring Show, 1981. Add: 12 Squitchey Lane, Summertown, Oxford, OX2 7LB, England.

JONES, Gwyneth A. *See* **HALAM,** Ann.

JONES, Helen. *See* **HINCKLEY,** Helen.

JONES, Jacqueline. American, b. 1948. Cultural/Ethnic topics, History, Race relations. Assoc. Prof. of American History since 1981, and Chmn. of History Dept. since 1985, Wellesley Coll., Massachusetts. *Publs:* Soldiers of Light and Love: Northern Teachers and Georgia Blacks 1865-1873, 1980; Labor of Love, Labor of Sorrow: Black Women, Work and the Family from Slavery to the Present, 1985. Add: Dept. of History, Wellesley Coll., Wellesley, Mass. 02181, U.S.A.

JONES, Joanna. *See* **BURKE,** John.

JONES, (Henry) John (Franklin). British, b. 1924. Literature. Fellow and Tutor in Jurisprudence, 1949–62, and Fellow and Tutor in English Literature, from 1962, Merton College, Oxford; Prof. of Poetry, Oxford Univ., 1979–84. Football Corresp., The Observer, London, 1956–59. *Publs:* The Egotistical Sublime, 1954; On Aristotle and Greek Tragedy, 1962; (ed.) The Study of Good Letters, by H.W. Garrod, 1963; John Keats's Dream of Truth, 1969; The Same God, 1971; Dostoevsky, 1983, 1985. Add: Holywell Cottage, Oxford, England.

JONES, Julia. British, b. 1923. Plays/Screenplays. *Publs:* The Navigators; Take Three Girls (Golden Prague T.V. Drama Award), 1970; Still Waters; Back of Beyond, 1974; Dutchess of Duke Street, 1977; Quiet As A Nun (dramatisation), 1978; Light a Penny Candle (dramatisation), 1985; Country Ways, 1983; Ladies In Charge, 1986; The Cuckoo Sister (dramatisation), 1986; Echoes, 1987; The Navigators, 1987; The Snow Spider, 1988; Tom's Midnight Garden, 1989. Add: c/o Jill Foster Ltd., 19A Queensgate Terr., London SW7 5PR, England.

JONES, Kaylie (Ann). French, b. 1960. Novels/Short stories. Grants coordinator, 1983–84, Free-lance Worker, 1984–85, and Asst. to Development Dir., 1985–86, Poets and Writers, Inc., NYC. *Publs:* As Soon as It Rains, 1986; Quite the Other Way, 1988. Add: Sterling Lord Literistic Inc., One Madison Ave., New York, N.Y. 10010, U.S.A.

JONES, Landon Y(oung). American, b. 1943. Demography, History. Managing Ed., Money Mag., NYC. Contributing Ed., Time mag., NYC, 1966–69; Ed., Princeton Alumni Weekly, Princeton Univ., New Jersey, 1969–74; Sr. Ed., People Mag., NYC, 1974–84. *Publs:* Great Expectations: America and the Baby Boom Generation, 1980. Add: c/o Money Mag., Room 33-38, 1271 Sixth Ave., New York, N.Y. 10020, U.S.A.

JONES, Langdon. British, b. 1942. Science fiction/Fantasy. Freelance writer and musician. Former Staff Member, New Worlds mag., London. *Publs:* (ed.) The New SF: An Original Anthology of Speculative Fiction, 1969; (ed. with Michael Moorcock) The Nature of the Catastrophe, 1971; The Eye of the Lens (short stories), 1972. Add: c/o Century Hutchinson, 62-65 Chandos Pl., London WC2N 4NW, England.

JONES, (Everett) LeRoi. Also writes as Imamu Amiri Baraka. American, b. 1934. Novels/Short stories, Plays/Screenplays, Poetry, Music, Race relations. Founding Dir., Spirit House, Newark, N.J., since 1966. Prof. of African Studies, State Univ. of New York at Stony Brook, since 1986 (Asst. Prof., 1980–86). Founder, Yugen mag. and Totem Press, NYC, 1958; Co-Ed., Floating Bar mag., NYC, 1961–63; member of faculty, New Sch. for Social Research, NYC, 1961–64; Founding Dir.,

Black Arts Repertory Theatre, Harlem, NYC, 1964–66. *Publs:* Spring and Soforth, 1960; Preface to a Twenty Volume Suicide Note, 1961; (ed.) Four Young Lady Poets, 1962; Blues People: Negro Music in White America, 1963; The Dead Lecturer (poetry), 1964; (ed.) The Moderns: New Fiction in America, 1964; Dutchman, and The Slave, 1964; The System of Dante's Hell (novel), 1965; Jello, 1965; Black Art (poetry), 1966; Home: Social Essays, 1966; Tales, 1967; Black Music, 1967; Arm Yourself and Harm Yourself, 1967; The Baptism, and The Toilet, 1967; Slave Ship, 1967; (ed. with Larry Neal) Black Fire: An Anthology of Afro-American Writing, 1968; Black Magic: Poetry 1961–67, 1969; Four Black Revolutionary Plays, 1969; It's Nationtime (poetry), 1970; In Our Terribleness, 1970; A Black Value System, 1970; Poem for Black Hearts, 1970; (as Imamu Amiri Baraka) Raise Race Rays Raze: Essays since 1965, 1971; Spirit Reach (poetry), 1972; (ed.) African Congress: A Documentary of the First Modern Pan-African Congress, 1972; African Revolution (poetry), 1973; The Creation of the New Ark, 1974; Hard Facts (poetry), 1976; The Motion of History and Other Plays, 1978; Selected Plays and Prose, 1979; Selected Poetry, 1979; AM/TRAK (poetry), 1979; Spring Song, 1979; Reggae or Not, 1981; The Autobiography of LeRoi Jones, 1984. Add: c/o William Morrow, 105 Madison Ave., New York, N.Y. 10016, U.S.A.

JONES, Madison (Percy, Jr.). American, b. 1925. Novels/Short stories. University Writer-in-Residence Emeritus, Auburn Univ., Alabama, (joined faculty 1956; Writer-in-Residence, 1967–87; Prof. of English, 1968–87). Instr. in English, Miami Univ, Oxford, Ohio, 1953–54, and the Univ. of Tennessee, Knoxville, 1955–56. *Publs:* The Innocent, 1957; Forest of the Night, 1960; A Buried Land, 1963; An Exile, 1967; A Cry of Absence, 1971; Passage Through Gehenna, 1978; Season of the Strangler, 1982; Last Things, 1989. Add: 800 Kuderna Acres, Auburn, Ala. 36830, U.S.A.

JONES, Malcolm V(ince). British, b. 1940. Literature. Prof. of Slavonic Studies, Univ. of Nottingham, since 1980, and Pro-Vice-Chancellor, since 1987 (Lectr., 1967–73; Sr. Lectr., 1973–80; Vice Dean, Faculty of Arts, 1976–79; Dean of Faculty of Arts, 1982–85). Hon. Vice-Pres., Intnl. Dostoevsky Soc.; Member, Editorial Bd., Birmingham Slavonic Monographs; General Ed., Cambridge Studies in Russian Literature; Vice-Pres. British Assn. for Soviet, Slavonic and East European Studies, since 1988. Asst. Lectr. in Russian, Sch. of European Studies, Univ. of Sussex, 1965–67; Pres., British Univs. Assn. of Slavists, 1986–88. *Publs:* Dostoyevsky: The Novel of Discord, 1976; (ed.) New Essays on Tolstoy, 1978; New Essays on Dostoyevsky, 1983. Add: Dept. of Slavonic Studies, Univ. of Nottingham, Nottingham NG7 2RD, England.

JONES, Margaret E.W. American, b. 1938. Literature. Prof. of Spanish, Univ. of Kentucky, since 1975 (Asst. Prof., 1967–70; Assoc. Prof., 1970–75). *Publs:* The Literary World of Ana Marie Matute, 1970; Spanish Literature, 1974; Dolores Medio, 1974; The Spanish Novel 1939-1975, 1985. Add: Dept. of Spanish, Univ. of Kentucky, Lexington, Ky. 40506, U.S.A.

JONES, Marion (Patrick). Trinidadian. Novels/Short stories. *Publs:* Pan Beat, 1973; J'Ouvert Morning, 1976. Add: c/o Columbus Publrs., 64 Independence Sq., Port of Spain, Trinidad.

JONES, Mary Voell. American, b. 1933. Children's fiction. *Publs:* Captain Kangaroo's Picnic, 1959; Huckleberry Hound Helps a Pal, 1960; Tick Tock Trouble, 1961; Yogi Bear's Secret, 1963; (with N.R. Knoche) What Do Mothers Do?, 1966; First Songs, 1976; Let's Make Music Today, 1977. Add: 2167 Mohawk Trail, Maitland, Fla. 32751, U.S.A.

JONES, Mervyn. British, b. 1922. Novels/Short stories, Social commentary/phenomena. Asst. Ed., 1955–60, and Drama Critic, 1958–66, Tribune, London; Asst. Ed., New Statesman, London, 1966–68. *Publs:* No Time to Be Young, 1952; The New Town, 1953; The Last Barricade, 1953; Helen Blake, 1955; (with Michael Foot) Guilty Men, 1957; Suez and Cyprus, 1957; On the Last Day, 1958; Potbank, 1961; Big Two (in U.S. as The Antagonists), 1962; Two Ears of Corn: Oxfam in Action (in U.S. as In Famine's Shadow: A Private War on Hunger), 1965; A Set of Wives, 1965; John and Mary, 1966; A Survivor, 1968; Joseph, 1970; Mr. Armitage Isn't Back Yet, 1971; Rhodesia: The White Judge's Burden, 1972; Life on the Dole, 1972; Holding On (in U.S. as Twilight of the Day), 1973; The Revolving Door, 1973; Lord Richard's Passion, 1974; Strangers, 1974; (ed.) Privacy, 1974; (trans.) K.S. Karol: The Second Chinese Revolution, 1974; The Pursuit of Happiness, 1975; (with Fay Godwin) The Oil Rush, 1976; Scenes from Bourgeois Life, 1976; Nobody's Fault, 1977; Today the Struggle, 1978; The Beautiful Words,

1979; A Short Time to Live, 1980; Two Women and Their Man, 1982; Joanna's Luck, 1985; Coming Home, 1986; Chances, 1987; That Year in Paris, 1988. Add: 10 Waterside Pl., Princess Rd., London NW1, England.

JONES, Neil R(onald). American, b. 1909. Science fiction/Fantasy. Formerly stamp dealer, bookkeeper, cost analysis specialist, office mgr., game manufacturer, and insurance claims examiner. *Publs:* short stories—The Planet of the Double Sun, 1967; The Sunless World, 1967; Space War, 1967; Twin Worlds, 1967; Doomsday on Ajiat, 1968. Add: 1028 Fay St., Fulton, N.Y. 13069, U.S.A.

JONES, Owen Rogers. British. Philosophy. Guest Lectr., St. Olaf Coll., Northfield, Minn., 1964–65; Asst. Lectr. to Sr. Lectr., 1957–76, and Reader in Philosophy, 1976–83, University Coll. of Wales, Aberystwyth. *Publs:* The Concept of Holiness, 1961; (ed.) The Private Language Argument, 1971; (with Peter Smith) The Philosophy of Mind, 1986. Add: Cilan, Cae Melyn, Aberystwyth SY23 2HA, Wales.

JONES, Peter (Austin). British, b. 1929. Poetry, Literature. Managing Dir., Carcanet Press Ltd., Manchester, 1970–86. Member of the English Faculty, Christ's Hosp., Horsham, Sussex, 1954–69. *Publs:* Rain, 1970; Seagarden for Julius, 1971; (ed.) Tribute to Freud, by Hilda Doolittle, 1971; The Peace and The Hook, 1972; (ed.) Imagist Poetry, 1972; (ed.) Shakespeare—The Sonnets: A Casebook, 1977; The Garden End: New and Selected Poems, 1977; An Introduction to Fifty American Poets: Critical Essays, 1979; (ed.) British Poetry since 1970: A Critical Survey, 1980. Add: 11 Bancroft Ave., Cheadle Hulme, Cheshire SK8 5BA, England.

JONES, Raymond F. American, b. 1915. Science fiction/Fantasy, Children's fiction, Children's non-fiction, Sciences. Radio engineer, then full-time writer. *Publs:* The Toymaker (short stories), 1951; Renaissance, 1951, as Man of Two Worlds, 1963; The Alien, 1951; This Island Earth, 1952; Son of the Stars (juvenile), 1952; Planet of Light (juvenile), 1953; The Secret People, 1956, as The Deviates, 1959; The Year When Stardust Fell (juvenile), 1958; The World of Weather (juvenile non-fiction), 1961; The Cybernetic Brains, 1962; The Non-Statistical Man (short stories), 1964; Voyage to the Bottom of the Sea (juvenile), 1965; Animals of Long Ago (juvenile non-fiction), 1965; Ice Formation on Aircraft (non-fiction), 1968; Syn, 1969; Physicians of Tomorrow (juvenile non-fiction), 1971; Moonbase One (juvenile), 1971; Radar: How It Works (juvenile non-fiction), 1972; Renegades of Time, 1975; The King of Eolim, 1975; The River and the Dream, 1977; (with Lester del Rey) Weeping May Tarry, 1978. Add: c/o Pinnacle, 1430 Broadway, New York, N.Y. 10018, U.S.A.

JONES, Richard. British, b. 1926. Novels/Short stories. *Publs:* Age of Wonder (in U.S. as The Three Suitors), 1967; The Toy Crusaders (in U.S. as Supper with the Borgias), 1968; A Way Out, 1969; The Tower is Everywhere, 1971; Living in the 25th Hour, 1978. Add: 120 Clapham Common West Side, London SW4 9BB, England.

JONES, Richard Allan. Canadian, b. 1943. History. Prof. of History, Univ. Laval. Quebec, since 1970. *Publs:* Community in Crisis: French-Canadian Nationalism in Perspective, 1967, 1972; L'Idéologie de "L'-Action catholique", 1974; Histoire du Québec, 1976; Vers une hégémonie libérale: Aperçu de la politique canadienne de Laurier à King, 1980; Duplessis and the Union Nationale Administration, 1983; Origins, 1988; Destinies, 1988. Add: St. Cyrille-de-L'Islet, Quebec, Canada, G0R 2W0.

JONES, Richard Benjamin. British, b. 1933. History. Dir. of Studies, Goole Sch., Yorks. Former Head of Arts Faculty, Oakham Sch., Rutland. *Publs:* The French Revolution; Social and Economic History, 1770-1977; The Hanoverians; The Victorians; Napoleon: Man and Myth; New Approaches to the New History; The Making of Contemporary Europe, 1980; The Challenge of Greatness: British History 1760-1914, 1986. Add: Yew Court, 93 Stockton Lane, York, England.

JONES, Richard Granville. British, b. 1926. Theology/Religion. Lectr., Faculty of Theology, Univ. of Manchester; Former Methodist Minister in Sheffield and Birkenhead; Principal, Hartley Victoria Coll., Manchester, 1973–82. *Publs:*a (ed.) Worship for Today, 1968; (co-author) Towards a Radical Church, 1969; How Goes Christian Marriage?, 1978; Groundwork of Worship and Preaching, 1980; Groundwork of Christian Ethics, 1984. Add: 24 Townshend Rd., Norwich NR4 6R6, England.

JONES, Sally Roberts. Has written as Sally Roberts. British, b. 1935.

Poetry, History. Publisher of Alun Books, since 1977. Sr. Asst., Reference Library, London Borough of Havering, 1964,19667; Refernce Librarian, Borough of Port Talbot, 1967–70. *Publs:* (as Sally Roberts) Turning Away, 1969; (as Sally Roberts) Romford in the Nineteenth Century, 1969; (compiler) About Welsh Literature, 1970; Elen and the Goblin, 1977; Strangers and Brothers, 1977; The Forgotten Country, 1977; Books of Welsh Interest: A Bibliography, 1977; Allen Raine, 1979; (ed.) Margam Through the Ages, 1979; Welcome to Town, 1980; Relative Values, 1985. Add: 3 Crown St., Port Talbot, Wales.

JONES, Stanley Bruce. Australian, b. 1927. Mathematics/Statistics. Master in charge of mathematics, Balgowlah High Sch., N.S.W., 1955–70. *Publs:* General Mathematics II, 1959; (co-author) General Mathematics III, 1960; Modern Mathematics, 4 vols., 1963–68; (co-author) Geometry for First Form 1963; (co-author) Level Three Mathematics V and VI, 1967; Betty and Jim Mentals III-VI, 1968; Let's Explore Mathematics III-VI, 1970; Understanding Computer Programming, 1971; New Series Modern Mathematics I-IV, 1971–74; Daily Mathematics Quick Questions, 4 vols., 1977–79; Supplementary and Enrichment Mathematics, books 1 and 2, 1978; Modern Mathematics Core and Lobe, 4 vols., 1982. Add: 19 Alma St., Clontarf, Sydney, N.S.W. 2093, Australia.

JONES, Trevor (Arthur). British, b. 1936. History. Sr. Lectr., Dept. of History, Univ. of Keele, since 1964. Teaching Asst., Univ. of Washington, Seattle, 1959–60; Research Student, London Sch. of Economics, 1960; Asst. Principal, Commonwealth Relations Office, 1960–62; Lectr., Univ. of Ghana, 1962–64.*Publs:* Ghana's First Republic 1960–1966, 1976. Add: Dept. of History, Univ. of Keele, Staffs. ST5 5BG, England.

JONES, Tristan. British, b. 1924. Novels/Short stories, Cookery/Gastronomy/Wine, Autobiography/Memoirs/Personal. Pres., The Atlantis Soc., NYC, since 1980. Able Seaman, Royal Navy, in the Arctic, 1941–44, Far East 1944–46, West Indies, 1946–48, Indian Ocean, 1948–50, and Far East, 1950–52. *Publs:*a The Incredible Voyage (autobiography), 1977; Ice! (autobiography), 1978; Saga of a Wayward Sailor (autobiography), 1979; Dutch Treat: A Novel of World War II, 1979, 1980; Adrift (autobiography), 1980; AKA: A Tale of Dolphins (novel), 1981; A Steady Trade (autobiography), 1981; Catch 'em 'n Cook 'em (fishing and small craft cookery), 1981; (with J. Doyle) Purity (stage play), 1981; One Hand For Yourself, One For the Boat, 1983; Yarns, 1984; Heart of Oak, 1984; A Star to Steer Her By, 1985; The Improbable Voyage of the Yacht "Outward Leg", 1986; Ship Me Somewheres East of Suez, 1988. Add: 246 W. 10th St., Apt. 31G, New York, N.Y. 10014, U.S.A.

JONES, Wilbur Devereux. American, b. 1916. History, International relations/Current affairs. Instr. in History, Western Reserve Univ. (now Case Western Reserve Univ.), Cleveland, 1948–49; Prof. of History, Univ. of Georgia, Athens, 1962–82 (joined staff in 1949). *Publs:* Lord Derby and Victorian Conservatism, 1956; Lord Aberdeen and the Americas, 1958; (with H. Montgomery) Civilization Through the Centuries, 1960; Confederate Rams at Birkenhead, 1961; Prosperity Robinson: The Life of Viscount Goderich 1782-1859, 1967; (with A.B. Erickson) The Peelites, 1846-1857, 1972; The American Problem in British Diplomacy 1841-1861, 1974; Venus and Sothis: How the Ancient Near East was Rediscovered, 1982. Add: 420 South Milledge Ave., Athens, Ga. 30605, U.S.A.

JONES, W(illiam) T(homas). American, b. 1910. Philosophy. Prof. Emeritus of Philosophy, California Inst. of Technology, since 1985. *Publs:* Morality and Freedom in the Philosophy of Kant, 1941; Machiavelli to Bentham, 1947; A History of Western Philosophy, 1952, 3rd ed. in 5 vols., 1976; The Romantic Syndrome, 1962, 1974; The Sciences and the Humanities, 1965; (co-author) Approaches to Ethics, 1967. Add: 920 W. Harrison, Claremont, Calif. 91711, U.S.A.

JONES-EVANS, Eric (John Llewellyn). British, b. 1898. Plays/-Screenplays, Autobiography/Memoirs/Personal. Actor-mgr., playwright, broadcaster, and theatre historian, since 1919. *Publs:* Character Sketches from Dickens, 1947; In the Footsteps of Barnaby Rudge, 1947; John Jasper's Secret, 1951; Suicide Isn't Murder, 1951; Death on the Line, 1954, radio version, 1971; The Black Bag, 1957; Lucky Venture, 1961; Death of a Lawyer, 1962; Scrooge the Miser, 1962; The Haunted Man, 1962; The Weaver of Raveloe, 1963; The Murder of Nancy, 1963; The Jackal, 1964; The Blue Cockade, 1964; Mr. Crummles Presents, 1966; David Copperfield, 1970; Footlight Fever; The Dream Woman, 1973; Markheim, 1973; The Body-Snatchers, 1973; Henry Irving and "The Bells", 1980; The Denville Players: Touring with Dickens, 1982; These Were Actors, 1983; More Theatre Memories, 1984; The Shelley Theatre:

Bournemouth, 1984; The Critics, 1985. Add: The Treshams, Fawley, nr. Southampton, Hants., England.

JONG, Erica. American, b. 1942. Novels/Short stories, Poetry. Lectr. in English, City Coll. of New York, 1964–66, and Univ. of Maryland European Extension, Heidelberg, W. Germany, 1967–68; Instr. in English, Manhattan Community Coll., NYC, 1969–70; Instr. in Poetry, YM-YWHA Poetry Center, NYC, 1971–73. *Publs:* Fruits and Vegetables, 1971; Half-Lives, 1973; Fear of Flying (novel), 1973; Loveroot, 1975; Here Comes and Other Poems, 1975; How to Save Your Own Life (novel), 1977; Selected Poems, 1977; At the Edge of the Body (poems), 1979; Fanny (novel), 1980; Witches (poetry/non-fiction), 1980; Ordinary Miracles (poetry), 1983; Parachutes and Kisses, 1984; Megan's Book of Divorce (children's non-fiction), 1984; Serenissima (novel), 1987. Add: c/o Morton L. Janklow Assocs., 598 Madison Ave., New York, N.Y. 10022, U.S.A..

JOOSE, Barbara M(onnot). American, b. 1949. Children's fiction. *Publs:* The Thinking Place, 1982; Spiders in the Fruit Cellars, 1983; Fourth of July, 1985; Jam Day, 1987; Anna, The One and Only, 1988; Better Than Two, 1988; Dinah's Mad, Bad Wishes, 1989. Add: 2953 Kettle Moraine Dr., Hartford, Wisc. 35027, U.S.A.

JORDAN, Alma Theodora. Trinidadian, b. 1929. Librarianship. Univ. Librarian, Univ. of West Indies, Port-of-Spain, since 1966 (Sr. Asst. Librarian, 1960–66).*Publs:* The Development of Library Service in the West Indies Through Inter-Library Cooperation, 1980; (ed.) Research Library Cooperation in the Caribbean, 1973; The English-speaking Caribbean: A Bibliography of Bibliographies, 1984. Add: 28 Gilwell Rd., Valsayn Park, Trinidad and Tobago.

JORDAN, John E(mory). American, b. 1919. Literature. Prof. of English, Dept. of English, Univ. of California, Berkeley, since 1947 (Academic Asst. to Chancellor, 1962–65; Chmn., English Dept., 1969–73; Academic Asst. to Vice Pres. for Academic Affairs, 1974–75). *Publs:* Thomas De Quincey: Literary Critic, 1952; (ed.) Robert Louis Stevenson's Silverado Journal, 1954; (ed.) Thomas De Quincey's Confessions of an English Opium Eater, 1960; (ed.) Thomas De Quincey's English Mail Coach, 1960; (ed.) Thomas De Quincey's Reminiscences of English Lake Poets, 1961; (author and ed.) De Quincey to Wordsworth: Biography of a Relationship with Letters, 1962, 1968; Using Rhetoric, 1965; (ed.) A Defense of Poetry and Four Ages of Poetry, 1965; (ed. with N. Frye and J. Logan) Some British Romantics, 1966; (co-author) English Language Framework for California Public Schools, 1968; (ed.) Questions of Rhetoric, 1971; (ed.) De Quincey as Critic, 1973; (ed.) Flame in Sunlight: Life and Works of Thomas De Quincey, by E. Sackville West, 1974; Why the Lyrical Ballads?, 1976; (ed.) Wordsworth's Peter Bell, 1985. Add: 834 Santa Barbara Rd., Berkeley, Calif. 94707, U.S.A.

JORDAN, June. Has also written as June Meyer. American, b. 1936. Novels/Short stories, Children's fiction, Poetry, Biography. Prof. of English, since 1981, Dir. of The Poetry Center, since 1986, and Dir. of Creative Writing Prog., since 1986, State Univ. of New York at Stony Brook. Columnist, The Black Poet Speaks of Poetry, American Poetry Review, since 1974. Instr., City Coll., City Univ. of New York, 1967–69, and Sarah Lawrence Coll., Bronxville, N.Y., 1969–70 and 1973–74. *Publs:* Who Look at Me (poetry), 1969; (ed.) Soulscript, 1971; Some Changes (poetry), 1971; His Own Where, 1971; (co-ed.) The Voice of the Children, 1971; Dry Victories, 1972; Fannie Lou Hamer, 1972; New Days (poetry), 1974; I Love You (poetry), 1975; New Life: New Room, 1975; Things I Do in the Dark: Selected Poetry, 1977; Passion: New Poems, 1980; Civil Wars (essays), 1981; Kimako's Story, 1981; Living Room (poetry), 1985; On Call (essays), 1986; Lyrical Campaigns: Selected Poems, 1989; Moving Towards Home: Political Essays, 1989. Add: Dept. of English, State Univ. of New York, Stony Brook, N.Y. 11790, U.S.A.

JORDAN, Laura. *See* **BROWN,** Sandra.

JORDAN, Neil. Irish, b. 1950. Novels/Short stories, Plays/-Screenplays. Co-Founder, Irish Writers Co-operative, 1974. *Publs:* Night in Tunisia and Other Stories, 1976; The Past (novel), 1980; The Dream of a Beast (novel), 1983; (with David Leland) Mona Lisa (screenplay), 1986; High Spirits (screenplay), 1988. Add: c/o Palace Productions, 16-17 Wardour Mews, London W1, England.

JORDAN, Nell. *See* **BARKER,** E.M.

JORDAN, Robert Smith. American, b. 1929. Institutions/Organiza-

tions, International relations/Current affairs, Politics/Government. Prof. of Political Science Univ. of New Orleans, since 1980. Asst. Dir., Army War Coll. Center, 1960–61, Dir., Air Univ. Center, 1961–62, Assoc. Prof. of Political Science and Intnl. Affairs, 1962–70, Asst. to the Pres., 1962–64, Assoc. Dir., Intnl. Org. and Intnl. Security Studies, Prog. of Policy Studies, 1964–65, and Dir., Foreign Affairs Intern Prog., Sch. of Public and Intnl. Affairs, 1968–70, George Washington Univ., Washington, D.C.; Dean, Faculty of Economics and Social Studies, and Head, Dept. of Political Science, Univ. of Sierra Leone, 1965–67; Prof. of Political Science, 1970–76, and Dept. Chmn., 1970–74, State Univ. of New York at Binghamton; Sr. Research Specialist and Dir. of Research, U.N. Inst. for Training and Research, NYC, 1974–80; Adjunct Prof. of Political Science, Columbia Univ., NYC, 1978–80. *Publs:* The NATO International Staff/Secretariat, 1952–57: A Study in International Administration, 1967; Government and Power in West Africa, 1969; (ed. with H. Gibbs and A. Gyorgy) Problems in International Relations, 3rd ed. 1970; (ed. and contrib.) Europe and the Superpowers: Perceptions of European International Politics, 1971; (ed. and contrib.) International Administration: Its Evolution and Contemporary Applications, 1971; (ed.) Multinational Cooperation: Economic, Social, and Scientific Development, 1972; (ed. with P. Toma and A. Gyorgy) Basic Issues in International Relations, 2nd ed. 1974; (with T. Weiss) The World Food Conference and Global Problem-Solving, 1975; Political Leadership in NATO: A Study in Multinational Diplomacy, 1979; (with Norman Graham) The International Civil Service: Changing Role and Concepts, 1980; (ed. and contrib.) Dag Hammarskjold Revisited: The U.N. Secretary-General as a Force in World Politics, 1982; (with Werner Feld) International Organizations: A Comparative Approach, 1983, 1988; (ed.) The U.S. and Multilateral Resource Management, 1985; (with Werner Feld) Europe in the Balance: The Changing Context of European International Politics, 1987; (ed.) Maritime Strategy and the Balance of Power: Britain and America in the Twentieth Century, 1989. Add: Dept. of Political Science, Univ. of New Orleans, New Orleans, La. 70148, U.S.A.

JORDAN, Ruth. British. Biography, Documentaries, Translations. Lectr., Spiro Inst. for Adult Education. Feature Writer, Drama Producer, and Commentator, BBC, London, 1950–67. *Publs:* translator of novels, short stories, and plays into Hebrew, 1960–65; Aspects of Bernard Shaw (radio documentary), 1968; Royal Romances (radio documentaries), 1969; Sophie Dorothea, 1971; Berenice, 1974; George Sand, 1976; Nocturne: A Life of Chopin, 1978; Daughter of the Waves (autobiography), 1983. Add: 63 Peterborough Rd., London SW6 3BT, England.

JORDY, William H. American, b. 1917. Architecture. Henry Ledyard Goddard University Prof. Emeritus of Art, Brown University, Providence (joined faculty, 1955). Instr. and Asst. Prof. of the History of Art and American Studies, Yale Univ., New Haven, Conn., 1948–55. *Publs:* Henry Adams: Scientific Historian, 1952; (ed. with Ralph Coe) American Architecture and Other Writings, by Montgomery Schuyler, 2 vols., 1961; American Buildings and Their Architects, 2 vols.: Progressive and Academic Ideals at the Turn of the Twentieth Century, and The Impact of European Modernism in the Mid-Twentieth century, 1972; Buildings on Paper: Rhode Island Architectural Drawings, 1825-1945, 1982; (with others) The Function of Ornament, 1986. Add: Art Dept., Brown Univ., Providence, R.I. 02912, U.S.A.

JORGENSEN, Ivar. *See* **SILVERBERG,** Robert.

JORGENSEN, Paul A(lfred). American, b. 1916. Literature. Prof. of English, Univ. of California, Los Angeles, 1960–81, now Emeritus (Instr., 1947–49; Asst. prof., 1949–55; Assoc. prof., 1955–60). *Publs:* (ed. with F.B. Shroyer) A College Treasury, 1956, rev. ed. 1967; Shakespeare's Military World, 1956, 1973; (ed. with F.B. Shroyer) The Informal Essay, 1961; Redeeming Shakespeare's Words, 1962, 1985; (ed.) The Comedy of Errors, 1964, 1972; Othello: An Outline-Guide to the Play, 1964; (ed. with F.B. Shroyer) The Art of Prose, 1965; Lear's Self-Discovery, 1967; Our Naked Frailties: Sensational Art and Meaning in Macbeth, 1971; William Shakespeare: The Tragedies, 1985. Add: 234 Tavistock Ave., Los Angeles, Calif. 90049, U.S.A.

JOSEPH, Stephen M. American, b. 1938. Novels/Short stories, Poetry, Education. Writer-in-Residence, New York State-New Jersey State Arts Council. Lectr., Wyoming State Arts Council, since 1973. Teacher, NYC Bd. of Education, 1960–70; Lectr., The Cooper Union, NYC, and New York Univ., 1970–71. *Publs:* (ed.) The Me Nobody Knows, 1969; The Shark Bites Back, 1970; (ed.) Meditations, 1970; Children in Fear, 1974; Mommy, Daddy, I'm Afraid, 1979. Add: 270 First Ave., New York, N.Y. 10009, U.S.A.

JOSEPHS, Ray. American, b. 1912. History, Psychology. Consultant, Business Council for Intnl. Understanding, NYC. Former journalist, corresp., and consultant on Latin American affairs, and Japanese-U.S. economic developments; Chmn., Ray Josephs-/ David E. Levy Inc., and Intnl. Public Relations Co., 1961–86. *Publs:* Spies and Saboteurs in Argentina, 1943; Argentine Diary, 1944; Latin America: Continent in Crisis, 1948; (with James Bruce) Those Perplexing Argentines, 1952; How to Make Money from Your Ideas, 1954; How to Gain an Extra Hour Every Day, 1955; (with D. Kemp) Memoirs of a Live Wire, 1956; Streamlining Your Executive Workload, 1958; (with Oscar Steiner) Our Housing Jungle and Your Pocketbook, 1960; (with Stanley Arnold) The Magic Power of Putting Yourself Over with People, 1962. Add: 860 United Nations Plaza, New York, N.Y. 10017, U.S.A.

JOSEPHY, Alvin M., Jr. American, b. 1915. Business/Trade/Industry, Cultural/Ethnic topics, History. Dir., and Sr. Ed., American Heritage Publishing Co. Inc., NYC, 1960–79. *Publs:* The Long and Short and the Tall, 1946; The Patriot Chiefs, 1961; (ed.) The American Heritage Book of Indians, 1961; (ed.) The American Heritage Book of Natural Wonders, 1963; Chief Joseph's People and Their War, 1964; (ed.) The American Heritage History of the Great West, 1965; The Nez Perce Indians and the Opening of the Northwest, 1965; (ed.) RFK: His Life and Death, 1968; The Indian Heritage of America, 1968; The Artist was a Young Man, 1970; Red Power, 1971; (ed.) The Horizon History of Africa, 1971; (ed.) American Heritage History of Business and Industry, 1972; (reviser) The Pictorial History of the American Indians, by Oliver La Farge, 1974; (ed.) The Law in America, 1974; History of the U.S. Congress, 1975; Black Hills, White Sky, 1978; On the Hill: A History of the American Congress, 1979; Now That the Buffalo's Gone, 1982; War on the Frontier, 1986. Add: 4 Kinsman Lane, Greenwich, Conn. 06830, U.S.A.

JOSIPOVICI, Gabriel (David). British, b. 1940. Novels/Short stories, Plays, Literature. Part-time Prof. Univ. of Sussex, Brighton, since 1984 (Lectr., 1963–74; Reader 1974–84). *Publs:* The Inventory, 1968; Words, 1971; The World and the Book: A Study of Modern Fiction, 1971; Mobius the Stripper (plays and short stories), 1974; The Present, 1975; (ed.) The Modern English Novel: The Reader, The Writer, The Work, 1976; Migrations, 1977; The Lessons of Modernism and Other Essays, 1977; Four Stories, 1977; The Echo Chamber, 1980; The Air We Breathe, 1981; Vergil Dying (play), 1981; Writing and the Body, 1982; Conversations in Another Room, 1984; Contre-Jour, 1986; In the Fertile Land (stories), 1987; The Book of God: A Response to the Bible, 1988. Add: Dept. of English, Univ. of Sussex, Falmer, Brighton, Sussex BN1 9RH, England.

JOSLIN, Sesyle. Also writes as Josephine Gibson and G.B. Kirtland. American, b. 1929. Novels/Short stories, Children's fiction, Poetry. Editorial Asst., Holiday mag., 1947–49, Asst. Fiction Ed., Westminster Press, 1950–52, and Book Ed., Country Gentleman mag., 1950–52, all in Philadelphia; production asst. on Peter Brook's film "Lord of the Flies," Puerto Rico, 1963. *Publs:* What Do You Say, Dear?, 1958; Brave Baby Elephant, 1960; Baby Elephant's Trunk, 1961; What Do You Do, Dear?, 1961; There Is a Dragon in My Bed (French primer), 1961; (with Al Hine, as G.B. Kirtland) One Day in Elizabethan England, 1962; Dear Dragon . . . and Other Useful Letter Forms for Young Ladies and Gentlemen Engaged in Everyday Correspondence, 1962; Senōr Baby Elephant, The Pirate, 1962; Baby Elephant and the Secret Wishes, 1962; Baby Elephant Goes to China, 1963; (with Al Hine, as G.B. Kirtland) One Day in Aztec Mexico, 1963; La Petite Famille (reader), 1964; Baby Elephant's Baby Book, 1964; Please Share That Peanut!, 1965; Spaghetti for Breakfast (Italian primer), 1965; (with Al Hine, as Josephine Gibson) Is There a Mouse in the House? (verse), 1965; There Is a Bull on My Balcony (Spanish primer), 1966; Pinkety, Pinkety: A Practical Guide to Wishing, 1966; La Fiesta (reader), 1967; The Night They Stole the Alphabet, 1968; Doctor George Owl, 1970; The Spy Lady and the Muffin Man, 1971; Last Summer's Smugglers, 1973; The Gentle Savages, 1979; The Piper's Song, 1987. Add: c/o Harcourt Brace Jovanovich, Inc., 1250 Sixth Ave., San Diego, Calif. 92101, U.S.A.

JOY, David (Anthony Welton). British, b. 1942. Transportation. Ed., Dalesman Publishing Co. Ltd., since 1988 (Editorial Asst., 1965–70; Books Ed., 1970–88). Gen. Reporter, Yorkshire Post Newspapers, 1962–65. *Publs:* (with W.R. Mitchell) Settle-Carlisle Railway, 1966; Main Line Over Shap, 1967; Cumbrian Coast Railways, 1968; Whitby- Pickering Railway, 1969; Railways in the North, 1970; Traction Engines in the North, 1970; (with A.J. Peacock) George Hudson of York, 1971; Railways of the Lake Counties, 1973; Regional History of the Railways of Great Britain: South and West Yorkshire, 1975; Railways in Lancashire, 1975; Settle-Carlisle Centenary, 1975; Railways of Yorkshire: The West

Riding, 1976; (with P. Williams) North Yorkshire Moors Railway, 1977; Steam on the North York Moors, 1978; (with A. Haigh) Yorkshire Railways, 1979; Steam on the Settle and Carlisle, 1981; Yorkshire Dales Railway, 1983; Settle-Carlisle in Colour, 1983; Regional History of the Railways of Great Britain: The Lake Counties, 1984; Portrait of the Settle-Carlisle, 1985. Add: Hole Bottom, Hebden, Skipton, N. Yorks, England.

JOY, Donald Marvin. American, b. 1928. Theology/Religion. Prof. of Human Development and Christian Education, Asbury Theological Seminary, Wilmore, Ky., since 1971. Exec. Ed., Free Methodist Publishing House, Winona Lake, Ind., 1958–72. *Publs:* The Holy Spirit and You, 1965; Meaningful Learning in the Church, 1969; (ed.) Moral Development Foundations: Theological Alternatives to Piaget and Kohlberg, 1983; Bonding: Relationships in the Image of God, 1985; Re-Bonding: Preventing and Restoring Broken Relationships, 1986; (with Robbie Joy) Lovers: Whatever Happened to Eden?, 1987; Parents: Launching Children in an Age of Promiscuity, 1988. Add: 600 N. Lexington Ave., Wilmore, Ky. 40390, U.S.A.

JOY, Thomas Alfred. British, b. 1904. Business/Trade/Industry, Librarianship, Autobiography/Memoirs/Personal. Pres., Hatchards Ltd., London, since 1985 (Managing Dir., 1965–85). Mgr., Harrods Library and Book Dept., London, 1936–45; Mgr. of Books, later Deputy Managing Dir., Army and Navy Stores Ltd., London, 1945–69; Pres., Book Trade Benevolent Soc., 1974–86. *Publs:* The Right Way to Run a Library Business, 1949; Bookselling, 1953; The Truth about Bookselling, 1964; Mostly Joy (autobiography), 1971; The Bookselling Business, 1974. Add: 13 Cole Park Gardens, Twickenham, Middx. TW1 1JB, England.

JUDAH, Aaron. British, b. 1923. Novels/Short stories, Children's fiction. *Publs:* Tommy with Hole in His Shoe, 1957; Tales of Teddy Bear, 1958; The Adventures of Henrietta Hen, 1958; Miss Hare and Mr. Tortoise, 1959; The Pot of Gold and Two Other Tales, 1959; God and Mr. Sourpuss, 1959; Basil Chimpy Isn't Bright, 1959; Henrietta in the Snow, 1960; Basil Chimpy's Comic Light, 1960; Anna Anaconda: The Swallowing Wonder, 1960; Henrietta In Love, 1961; The Proud Duck, 1961; The Elf's New House, 1962; Ex-King Max Forever!, 1963; The Careless Cuckoos, 1963; Clown of Bombay, 1963; The Fabulous Haircut, 1964; Clown on Fire, 1965; On the Feast of Stephen, 1965; Cobweb Pennant, 1968; Lillian's Dam, 1970. Add: 6 Lower Denmark Rd., Ashford, Kent TN23 1SU, England

JUDD, Cyril. *See* **MERRIL,** Judith.

JUDD, Denis. British, b. 1938. Novels, History, Biography. Principal Lectr. since 1972, and Head of History, since 1988, Polytechnic of North London (Lectr., 1964–68; Sr. Lectr., 1968–72). *Publs:* Balfour and The British Empire, 1968; The Victorian Empire, 1970; Posters of World War Two, 1972; The British Raj, 1972; Livingstone in Africa, 1973; George V, 1973; Someone Has Blundered, 1973; The House of Windsor, 1973; Edward VII, 1975; Palmerston, 1957; The Crimean War, 1975; Eclipse of Kings, 1976; The Adventures of Long John Silver, 1977; Radical Joe: A Life of Joseph Chamberlain, 1977; The Boer War, 1977; Return to Treasure Island, 1978; Prince Philip, 1980; Lord Reading: A Biography of Rufus Isaacs, 1982; (with P. Slinn) The Evolution of the Modern Commonwealth, 1982; George VI, 1982; Alison Uttley: The Life of a Country Child, 1986; More Tales of Little Grey Rabbit, 1989. Add: 20 Mount Pleasant Rd., London NW10 3EL, England.

JUDD, Frank (Ashcroft). British, b. 1935. International affairs, Politics/Government. Dir., Oxfam, since 1985; Chmn., Intnl. Council of Voluntary Agencies, since 1985. Member of Parliament for Portsmouth West div. of Hampshire, 1966–74, and for the Portsmouth North div., 1974–79; Parliamentary Private Secty. to the Minister of Housing, 1967–70; Parliamentary Private Secty. to the Leader of the Opposition, 1970–72; Opposition Front Bench Spokesman on Defence, with Special Responsibility for Naval, Admin. and Personnel Affairs, 1972–74; Parliamentary Under-Secty. of State for Defence for the Royal Navy, 1974–76; Minister for Overseas Development, 1976–77; Minister of State, Foreign and Commonwealth Office, 1977–79. Dir., Voluntary Service Overseas, 1980–85. *Publs:* (co-author) Radical Future, 1967; (co-author) Fabian International Essays, 1970; Purpose in Socialism, 1973. Add: Belmont, 21 Mill Lane, Old Marston, Oxford OX3 0PY, England.

JUDD, Harrison. *See* **DANIELS,** Norman A.

JUDGE, Harry George. British, b. 1928. Education, History. Fellow Brasenose Coll., Oxford, since 1973. Head Master, Banbury Grammar

Sch., 1962–67, and Principal, Banbury Sch, 1967–73; Dir., Dept of Educational Studies, Oxford Univ., 1973–88. *Publs:* Louis XIV, 1965; School is Not Yet Dead, 1974; Graduate Schools of Education in the United States: A View from Abroad, 1982; A Generation of Schooling: English Secondary Education since 1944, 1984. Add: Univ. of Oxford, Dept. of Educational Studies, 15 Norham Gardens, Oxford OX2 6PY, England.

JUDSON, John. American, b. 1930. Plays/Screenplays, Poetry, Autobiography. Prof. of English, Univ. of Wisconsin, La Crosse (joined faculty 1965). Ed., Juniper Press, and Northeast/Juniper Books, literary mag. and chapbook series, since 1962. *Publs:* (co-author) Two from Where It Snows, 1963; Surreal Songs, 1968; Within Seasons, 1970; (ed.) Voyages to the Inland Sea, 6 vols., 1971–76; Finding Worlds in Winter, 1973; West of Burnam, South of Troy (radio play), 1973; Ash Is the Candle's Wick, 1974; Roots from the Onion's Dark, 1978; A Purple Tale, 1978; North of Athens, 1980; Letters to Jirac, II, 1980; Reasons Why I Am Not Perfect, 1982; The Carrabassett, Street William, Was My River (autobiog.), 1982. Add: 1310 Shorewood Dr., La Crosse, Wisc. 54601, U.S.A.

JUERGENSEN, Hans. American, b. 1919. Poetry. Prof. of Humanities, Univ. of South Florida, Tampa, since 1968 (Asst. Prof., 1961–63; Assoc. Prof., 1963–68). Ed., Gryphon (Univ. of South Florida), since 1975; Member, Bd. of Editors, South and West, Arkansas, since 1977; Special Consultant to U.S. Holocaust Memorial Council, since 1981. Instr. in German, Univ. of Kansas, Lawrence, 1951–53; Asst. Prof., Assoc. Prof., and Chmn..of English, Quinnipiac Coll., Conn., 1953–61; Acting Dean and Lectr. in Humanities, Silvermine Sch. of Art, 1958–61. *Publs:* I Fed You from My Cup, 1958; In Need of Names, 1961; Existential Canon, 1965; Florida Montage, 1966; Sermons from the Ammunition Hatch of the Ship of Fools, 1968; From the Divide, 1970, 1972; Hebraic Modes, 1972; Journey Toward the Roots, 1976; (trans.) The Broken Jug, 1977; The Autobiography of a Pretender, 1977; California Frescoes, 1980; Major-General George H. Homas: A Summary in Perspective, 1980; The Record of a Green Planet, 1982; Fire-tested, 1983; Beachheads and Mountains, 1984; The Ambivalent Journey, 1986; ROMA, 1987; Testimony, 1989. Add: 7815 Pine Hill Dr., Tampa, Fla. 33617, U.S.A.

JUHASZ, Anne McCreary. Canadian, b. 1922. Education, Sociology. Prof. of Educational Psychology, Loyola Univ. of Chicago, since 1970 (Assoc. Prof., 1967–70). Assoc. Prof. of Education, Univ. of British Columbia, Vancouver, 1962–67. *Publs:* Effective Study, 1968; (with G. Szasz) Adolescents in Society, 1969; (with E.A. Thorn, A.C. Smith and K.D. Munroe) The Gage Language Experience Reading Program, rev. ed. 1970; (with A. Ornstein and H. Talmage) A Handbook for Paraprofessionals, 1975. Add: Loyola Univ. of Chicago, 820 N. Michigan Ave., Chicago, Ill. 60611, U.S.A.

JUKES, Geoffrey. British, b. 1928. History, International relations/Current affairs. Sr. Fellow, Inst. of Advanced Studies, Australian National Univ., Canberra, since 1972 (Fellow, 1967–71). With U.K. Foreign Office, 1953–56 and 1965–67, and U.K. Ministry of Defence, 1956–65. *Publs:* The Strategic Situation in the 1980s, 1968; Stalingrad: The Turning Point, 1968; Kursk: The Clash of Armour, 1969; The Defence of Moscow, 1970; Carpathian Disaster, 1971; The Development of Soviet Strategic Thinking since 1945, 1972; The Indian Ocean in Soviet Naval Policy, 1972; The Soviet Union in Asia, 1973; (co-author) China and the World Community (Soviet Views of China), 1973; Hitler's Stalingrad Decisions, 1985; (co-author) Gorbachev at the Helm, 1987; (co-author) In Defence of National Interests, 1988; (co-author) The Soviet Withdrawal from Afganistan, 1989. Add: Inst. of Advanced Studies, Australian National Univ., Canberra, A.C.T., Australia.

JUNKINS, Donald (Arthur). American, b. 1931. Poetry. Prof. of English, Univ. of Massachusetts, Amherst, since 1974 (Asst. Prof.,1966–69; Assoc. Prof., 1969–74; Dir., Master of Fine Arts Program in English, 1970–78). Asst. Prof., Emerson Coll., Boston, 1961; Asst. Prof., California State Coll., Chico, 1963–66. *Publs:* The Sunfish and the Partridge, 1965; The Graves of Scotland Parish, 1968; Walden, 100 Years After Thoreau, 1968; And Sandpipers She Said, 1970; (ed.) The Contemporary World Poets, 1976; The Uncle Harry Poems and Other Maine Reminiscences, 1977; Crossing by Ferry, 1978; The Agamenticus Poems, 1984. Add: Hawks Rd., Deerfield, Mass. 01342, U.S.A.

JUSTER, Norton. American, b. 1929. Children's fiction, Women. Architect, Juster-Pope Assocs., Shelburne Falls, Mass., since 1969; Prof. of Design, Hampshire Coll., Amherst, Mass., since 1970. Architect, Juster and Gugliotta, N.Y., 1960–68; Instr., Pratt Inst., NYC, 1960–70. *Publs:* The Phantom Tollbooth, 1961; The Dot and the Line: A Romance in Lower Mathematics, 1963; Alberic the Wise and Other Journeys, 1965; Stark Naked: A Paranomastic Odyssey, 1969; So Sweet to Labor: Rural Women in America 1865-1895, 1980; Otter Nonsense, 1982; As: A Surfeit of Similes, 1989. Add: 259 Lincoln Ave., Amherst, Mass. 01002, U.S.A.

JUSTICE, Donald (Rodney). American, b. 1925. Poetry. Prof. of English, Univ. of Florida, Gainesville, since 1982. Asst. Prof., Hamline Univ., St. Paul, Minn., 1956–57; Lectr., 1957–59; Asst. Prof., 1959–63; Assoc. Prof., 1963–66, and Prof., 1971–82, English Dept., Univ. of Iowa, Iowa City. *Publs:* The Summer Anniversaries, 1960; (ed.) The Collected Poems of Weldon Kees, 1960; (ed. with Paul Engle and Henri Coulette) Midland, 1961; A Local Storm, 1963; (ed. with A. Aspel) Contemporary French Poetry, 1965; Night Light, 1967; (ed.) Syracuse Poems 1968, 1968; Sixteen Poems, 1970; From a Notebook, 1972; Departures, 1973; Selected Poems, 1979; Platonic Scripts, 1984; The Sunset Maker, 1987. Add: Dept. of English, Univ. of Florida, Gainesville, Fla. 32611, U.S.A.

K

KABAT, Elvin Abraham. American, b. 1914. Biology, Medicine/Health. Higgins Prof. Emeritus, Columbia Univ. Coll. of Physicians and Surgeons, NYC, since 1985 (Research Assoc. in Biochemistry, 1941–46; member of Scientific Staff, Div. of War Research, 1943–45; Asst. Prof. of Bacteriology, 1946–48; Assoc. Prof. of Bacteriology, 1948–52; Prof. of Microbiology, 1953–84). Micro-biologist, Presbyterian Hosp., NYC. Pres., Harvey Soc., 1976–77. *Publs:* (with M.M. Mayer) Experimental Immunochemistry, 1948, 1961, Blood Group Substances: Their Chemistry and Immunochemistry, 1956; Structural Concepts in Immunology and Immunochemistry, 1968, 1976; Sequences of Proteins of Immunological Interest, 4th ed., 1987. Add: Dept. of Microbiology, 701 West 168th St., New York, N.Y. 10032, U.S.A.

KADUSHIN, Alfred. American, b. 1916. Sociology. Prof. of Social Work, Sch. of Social Work, Univ. of Wisconsin, Madison, since 1958 (Asst. Prof., 1950–55; Assoc. Prof., 1955–58). *Publs:* (with Judith Martin) Child Welfare Services, 1967, 4th ed., 1987; Child Welfare Services: A Research Source Book, 1969; Adopting Older Children, 1971; The Social Work Interview, 1972, 1983; Supervision in Social Work, 1976, 1985; Consultation in Social Work, 1977; (with Judith Martin) Child Abuse: An Interactional Event, 1981. Add: 4933 Marathon Dr., Madison, Wisc. 53705, U.S.A.

KAEL, Pauline. American, b. 1919. Film. Movie Critic, The New Yorker mag., since 1968. *Publs:* I Lost it at the Movies, 1965; Kiss Kiss Bang Bang, 1968; Going Steady, 1970; The Citizen Kane Book, 1971; Deeper into Movies, 1973; Reeling, 1976; When the Lights Go Down, 1980; 5001 Nights at the Movies, 1982; Taking It All In, 1984; State of the Art, 1985; Hooked, 1989. Add: c/o The New Yorker, 25 West 43rd St., New York, N.Y. 10036, U.S.A.

KAGAN, Jerome. American, b. 1929. Psychology. Prof. of Psychology, Dept. of Psychology, Harvard Univ., Cambridge, since 1964. *Publs:* (with Howard Moss) Birth to Maturity, 1962; Change and Continuity in Infancy, 1971; (with Richard Kearsley and Philip Zelazo) Infancy, 1978; The Second Year, 1981; The Nature of the Child, 1984; (with Paul Mussen, John Conger and Aletha Huston) Child Development and Personality (text), 6th ed., 1984; (with Julius Segal) Psychology: An Introduction (text), 6th ed., 1988. Add: Dept. of Psychology, Harvard Univ., Cambridge, Mass. 02138, U.S.A.

KAHN, David. American, b. 1930. Military/Defence. Asst. Viewpoints Ed., Newsday, Garden City, N.Y., since 1979. Co-Ed., Cryptologia, since 1977. Reporter, Newsday, 1955–63; Deskman, Herald Tribune, Paris, 1965–67; Sr. Assoc. Member, St. Antony's Coll., Oxford, 1972–74; Assoc. Prof. of Journalism, New York Univ., NYC., 1975–79. *Publs:* The Codebreakers, 1967; Hitler's Spies, 1978; Kahn on Codes, 1983. Add: 120 Wooleys Lane, Great Neck, N.Y. 11023, U.S.A.

KAHN, James. American, b. 1947. Novels/Short stories, Science fiction, Poetry. Physician: emergency room physician, Rancho Encino Hospital, Los Angeles, since 1976. Resident, Los Angeles County Hospital, 1976–77, and Univ. of California at Los Angeles, 1978–79. *Publs:* science-fiction—World Enough and Time, 1982; Time's Dark Laughter, 1982; Poltergeist (novelization of screenplay), 1982; Return of the Jedi (novelization of screenplay), 1983; Indiana Jones and the Temple of Doom (novelization of screenplay), 1984; Timefall, 1986; Poltergeist II (novelization of screenplay), 1986; other novels—Diagnosis Murder, 1978; Goonies (novelization of screenplay), 1985; poetry—(with Jerome

McGann) Nerves in Patterns, 1978. Add: c/o Jane Jordan Browne, 410 S. Michigan Ave., Suite 724, Chicago, Ill. 60605, U.S.A.

KAHN, Sy M. American, b. 1924. Poetry, Literature. Prof. of English and Drama, Univ. of the Pacific, Stockton, Calif., 1963–86, now Emeritus. Fulbright Prof. of American Literature, Univ. of Salonika, Greece, 1958–59, Univ. of Warsaw, Poland, 1966–67, Univ. of Vienna, Austria, 1970–71, and Univ. of Porto, Portugal, 1985–86. *Publs:* Our Separate Darkness, 1963, 3rd ed. 1968; Triptych, 1964; A Later Sun, 1966; The Fight is with Phantoms, 1966; Another Time, 1968; (ed. with M. Raetz) Interculture, 1975; Facing Mirrors, 1980; (ed.) Devour the Fire: Selected Poems of Harry Crosby. Add: 3725 Monitor Circle N., Stockton, CA 95209, U.S.A.

KAIM-CAUDLE, Peter (Robert). British, b. 1916. Medicine/Health, Sociology. Prof. Emeritus of Social Policy, Univ. of Durham, since 1982 (Staff Tutor in Extra Mural Studies, 1950–63; Lectr., 1963–68; Sr. Lectr., 1968–75; Prof. of Social Admin., 1975–79; Prof. of Social Policy, 1979–82). Head of Dept. of Economic Studies, Univ. Coll. of Sierra Leone, 1954–55 and 1961; Research Prof., Economic and Social Research Inst., Dublin, 1968–70. Visiting appointments at Univ. Coll. Cork, Univ. of Calgary, Univ. of Monash, Australian National Univ., and Chung Hsing Univ., Taipei. *Publs* include: Social Policy in the Irish Republic, 1967; Comparative Social Policy and Social Security, 1973; (with G. Marsh) Team Care in General Practice, 1976. Add: Beechwood, Princes St., Durham DH1 4RP, England.

KAIN, John F(orrest). American, b. 1935. Economics, Urban studies. Prof. of Economics since 1969, and Chmn. of the Dept. of Economics since 1986, Harvard Univ., Cambridge, Mass. (Asst. Prof., 1966–67; Assoc. Prof., 1968–69). Assoc. Prof. of Economics, U.S. Air Force Academy, Colorado Springs, 1962–65; Consultant, Dept. of Housing and Urban Development, Washington, D.C., 1966–68, Dept. of Health, Education and Welfare and U.S. Commission on Civil Rights, 1968. *Publs:* (with John R. Meyer and Martin Wohl) The Urban Transportation Problem, 1965; (ed.) Race and Poverty: The Economics of Discrimination, 1969; (ed. with John R. Meyer) Essays in Regional Economics, 1971; (with others) Empirical Models of Urban Land Use, 1971; (with Gregory K. Ingram and J. Royce Ginn) The Detroit Prototype of the NBER Urban Simulation Model, 1972; (with John M. Quigley) Housing Markets and Racial Discrimination, 1975; Essays on Urban Spatial Structure, 1975; (with W.C. Apgar, Jr.) Housing and Neighbourhood Dynamics, 1985. Add: Dept. of City and Regional Planning, Harvard Univ., Cambridge, Mass. 02138, U.S.A.

KAIN, Richard Morgan. American, b. 1908. Literature. Prof. Emeritus of English, Univ. of Louisville, Ky. (Prof. since 1947). *Publs:* Fabulous Voyager: James Joyce's "Ulysses", 1947, 1959; (co-author) Joyce: The Man, the Work, the Reputation, 1956; Dublin in the Age of W.B. Yeats and James Joyce, 1962; (co-author) The Workshop of Daedalus, 1965; Susan L. Mitchell, 1972; (co-author) AE: George William Russell, 1975. Add: 1400 Willow, Louisville, Ky. 40204, U.S.A.

KAINS, Josephine. *See* **GOULART**, Ron.

KAISER, Ward L(ouis). Canadian-American, b. 1923. Education, Geography, Social commentary/phenomena, Theology/Religion. Sr. Ed. and Exec. Dir., Friendship Press, National Council of Churches of Christ in the U.S.A., 1978–86 (Assoc. 1957–59, and Ed., 1960–69, Youth Publs;

Sr. Ed. 1969–86). Minister, United Church of Canada, in Ont., 1949–57; syndicated columnist, 1963–66. *Publs:* Focus: The Changing City, 1963; (with J.L.S. Shearman) Canada: A Study-Action Manual, 1966; Intersection: Where School and Faith Meet (student text and teacher's manual), 1969; The Challenge of a Closer Moon, 1969; Launching Pad: Literacy, 1970; (with C.P. Lutz) You and the Nation's Priorities, 1971; (gen. ed.) People and Systems, 1975; (with others) Forum: Religious Faith Speaks to American Issues, 1976; (trans.) The New Cartography, 1983; (trans.) Space and Time, 1984; A New View of the World: A Handbook to the World Map: Peters Projection, 1987; Live by Faith, Live by Risk, 1989. Add: 251 Diane Pl., Paramus, N.J. 07652, U.S.A.

KALCHEIM, Lee. American, b. 1938. Plays/Screenplays. *Publs:* Match Play (in New Theatre in America), 1965; . . . And the Boy Who Came to Leave (in Playwrights for Tomorrow 2), 1966; Win with Wheeler, 1984; Breakfast with Les and Bess, 1984. Add: c/o ICM, 40 W. 57th St., New York, N.Y. 10019, U.S.A.

KALLEN, Lucille (née Chernos). American. Novels/Short stories, Mystery/Crime/Suspense, Plays/Screenplays. Freelance writer since 1954. Writer, Your Show of Shows television program, N.B.C., NYC, 1949–54. *Publs:* (with Mel Tolkin) Maybe Tuesday (play), 1958; Out There, Somewhere (novel), 1964, in U.K. as Gentlemen Prefer Slaves, 1973; Introducing C.B. Greenfield (mystery), 1979; The Tanglewood Murder, 1980; No Lady in the House (mystery), 1982; The Piano Bird (mystery), 1984; A Little Madness, 1986. Add: c/o Arnold Goodman Assocs., 500 West End Ave., New York, N.Y. 10024, U.S.A.

KALLICH, Martin (Irvin). American. Literature. Prof. of English, Northern Illinois Univ., DeKalb, 1958–79, now retired. Member of faculty, Johns Hopkins Univ., Baltimore, Md., 1943–44, Wayne State Univ., Detroit, Mich., 1945–49, and South Dakota State Coll., Brookings, 1949–58. *Publs:* The Psychological Milieu of Lytton Strachey, 1961; (co-author) The American Revolution Through British Eyes, 1962; Heav'n's First Law, Rhetoric and Order in Pope's Essay on Man, 1967; (co-author) Oedipus: Myth and Drama, 1968; The Other End of the Egg: Religious Satire in Swift's Gulliver's Travels, 1970; The Association of Ideas and Critical Theory in 18th Century England, 1970; Horace Walpole, 1971; (co-author) A Book of the Sonnet, 1972; British Poety and the American Revolution: A Bibliographical Survey of Pamphlets, Journals, Newspapers, Prints, 1988. Add: English Dept., Northern Illinois Univ., DeKalb, Ill. 60115, U.S.A.

KAMEN, Henry (Arthur). British, b. 1936. History, Translations. Reader in History, Univ. of Warwick, Coventry, since 1973 (Lectr., 1966–71; Sr. Lectr., 1971–73). *Publs:* (trans.) In the Interlude: Poems by Boris Pasternak 1945–1960, 1962; The Spanish Inquisition, 1965; The Rise of Toleration, 1967; The War of Succession in Spain 1700-1715, 1969; The Iron Century: Social Change in Europe 1550-1660, 1971; A Concise History of Spain, 1974; Spain in the Later Seventeenth Century 1665-1700, 1980; A Society in Conflict: Spain 1469-1714, 1983; European Society, 1500-1700, 1984; Inquisition and Society in Spain, 1985. Add: 4 Bertie Terr., Leamington Spa, Warwick, England.

KAMENKA, Eugene. Australian, b. 1928. Philosophy, Politics/Government. Professor and Head, History of Ideas Unit, Inst. of Advanced Studies, Australian National Univ., since 1974 (Research Fellow in Philosophy, then Research Fellow, Sr. Research Fellow and Professional Fellow in History of Ideas, 1961–74). Lectr. in Philosophy, Univ. of Malaya in Singapore, 1958–59. *Publs:* The Ethical Foundations of Marxism, 1962, 1972; Marxism and Ethics, 1969; The Philosophy of Ludwig Feuerbach, 1970; (ed.) A World in Revolution?, 1970; Paradigm for Revolution—The Paris Commune 1871-1971, 1972; Nationalism: The Nature and Evolution of an Idea, 1973; (ed. with R.S. Neale) Feudalism, Capitalism and Beyond, 1975; (ed. with R. Brown and A.E.S. Tay) Law and Society, 1978; (ed. with A.E.S. Tay) Human Rights, 1978; (ed. with M. Kuygier) Bureaucracy, 1979; (ed. with F.C. Hutley and A.E.S. Tay) Law and the Future of Society, 1979; (ed. with A.E.S. Tay) Justice, 1979; (ed. with F.B. Smith) Intellectuals and Revolution, 1979; (ed. with A.E.S. Tay) Law-Making in Australia, 1980; (ed. with A.E.S. Tay) Law and Social Control, 1980; (ed.) Community as a Social Ideal, 1982; (ed.) The Portable Karl Marx, 1983; (ed. with R.S. Summers and W.L. Twining) Sociological Jurisprudence and Realist Theories of Law, 1986; (ed.) Utopias, 1987; Bureaucracy, 1989. Add: History of Ideas Unit, Research Sch. of Social Sciences, Australian National Univ., P.O. Box 4, Canberra, A.C.T., Australia 2600.

KAMINSKY, Alice R. American. Literature, Philosophy. Prof. of English, State Univ. of New York Coll. at Cortland, since 1968 (Asst. Prof., 1963–64; Assoc. Prof., 1964–68). *Publs:* (author and ed.) Literary Criticism of George Henry Lewes, 1964; George Henry Lewes as Literary Critic, 1968; (with Jack Kaminsky) Logic: A Philosophical Introduction, 1974; Chaucer's Troilus and Criseyde and the Critics, 1980; The Victim's Song, 1985. Add: Dept. of English, State Univ. of New York at Cortland, Cortland, N.Y. 13045, U.S.A.

KAMINSKY, Jack. American, b. 1922. Philosophy. Prof. of Philosophy, State Univ. of New York at Binghamton, since 1961 (Asst. Prof., 1953–57; Chmn. Philosophy Dept. 1953–61; Assoc. Prof., 1957–61). *Publs:* (with B.F. Huppe) Logic and Language 1956; Hegel on Art, 1962; Language and Ontology, 1969; (with Alice Kaminsky) Logic: A Philosophical Introduction 1974; Essays in Linguistic Ontology, 1982. Add: Dept. of Philosophy, State Univ. of New York at Binghamton, Dept. of Philosophy, Binghamton, N.Y. 13901, U.S.A.

KAMINSKY, Stuart. American, b. 1934. Mystery/Crime/Suspense, Film, Biography. Prof. of Radio, Television and Film, Northwestern Univ., Evanston, Ill. (joined faculty, 1972). Science Writer, Univ. of Illinois, Champaign, 1962–64; Ed., News Service, Univ. of Michigan, Ann Anbor, 1965–66; Dir. of Public Relations and Asst. to the Vice-Pres. for Public Affairs, Univ. of Chicago, 1969. *Publs:* Don Siegel: Director, 1973; Clint Eastwood, 1974; American Film Genres: Approaches to a Critical Theory of Popular Film, 1974; (ed. with Joseph Hill) Ingmar Bergman: Essays in Criticsm, 1975; John Huston: Maker of Magic, 1978; Bullet for a Star (novel), 1977; Murder on the Yellow Brick Road (novel), 1978; You Bet Your Life (novel), 1979 The Howard Hughes Affair (novel), 1979; Never Cross a Vampire (novel), 1980; Coop: The Life and Legend of Gary Cooper, 1980; (with Dana Hodgdon) Basic Filmaking, 1981; Death of a Dissident (novel), 1981; High Midnight (novel), 1981; Catch a Falling Clown (novel), 1982; He Done Her Wrong (novel), 1983; When the Dark Man Calls (novel), 1983; Black Knight on Red Square (novel), 1983; (with Jeffrey Mahan) American Genres (textbook), 1984; Down for the Count (novel), 1985; Red Chameleon (novel), 1985; Exercise in Terror (novel), 1985; Smart Moves (novel), 1987; A Fine Red Rain (novel), 1987; Think Fast, Mr. Peters (novel), 1988; A Cold Red Sunrise (novel) 1988; Writing for Television, 1988; Buried Caesars (novel), 1989. Add: Sch. of Speech, Northwestern Univ., Evanston, Ill. 60201, U.S.A.

KAMM, Dorinda. American, b. 1952. Novels/Short stories. *Publs:* Cliffs Head, 1971; Devil's Doorstep, 1972; The Marly Stones, 1976; Drearloch, 1977; Shadow Game, 1979; Kingsroads Legacy, 1981; The Winteredge Whispers, 1982. Add: 82 New Hyde Park Rd., Franklin Square, N.Y. 11010, U.S.A.

KAMM, Jacob Oswald. American, b. 1918. Economics, Money/Finance. Freelance writer, lectr., and consultant. Asst. in Economics, Brown Univ., Providence, R.I., 1940–41; Prof. of Economics and Dir., Sch. of Commerce, Baldwin-Wallace Coll., Berea, Ohio, 1943–53; Instr. in Economics, Ohio State Univ., Columbus, 1945–46; Columnist, An Economist's View, Cleveland Plain Dealer, Ohio, 1964–68. *Publs:* Decentralization of Securities Exchanges, 1942; An Outline of Socialism, 1944; Principles of Investment, 1944; An Outline of the History of Economic Thought, 1945, 1949; An Outline of Money and Banking, 1946; An Outline of Corporate Finance, 1947; An Outline of the Stock Market, 1947, 1950; Economics of Investment, 1951; (co-author) Introduction to Modern Economics, 1952; Making Profits in the Stock Market, 1952, 4th ed. 1966; (co-author) Essays on Finance, 1953; Investor's Handbook, 1959; (contrib. ed.) Webster's New World Dictionary of the American Language, 1968. Add: Box 718, Sanibel, Fla. 33957, U.S.A.

KAMM, Josephine. British, b. 1905. Children's fiction, Children's non-fiction, History, Biography. With Ministry of Information, ending as Sr. Exec. Officer, 1939–45; Member of Exec. Cttee. and National Council, National Book League, London, 1961–69; Member, Cttee. of Management, Fawcett Library, London, 1961–75; Member, Exec. Cttee., London Centre Intnl. PEN, 1965–69. *Publs:* He Went with Captain Cook, 1952; They Served the People, 1952; Janet Carr: Journalist, 1953; Student Almoner, 1955; Return to Freedom, 1955 (Isaac Siegel Memorial Juvenile Award); Daughter of the Desert: A Biograpy of Gertrude Bell, 1956; Men Who Served Africa, 1957; How Different from Us: A Biography of Miss Buss and Miss Beale, 1958; Leaders of the People, 1959; Emmeline Pankhurst, 1961; Out of Step, 1962; Sir Moses Montefiore, 1962; Malaria Ross, 1963; Malaya and Singapore, 1963; A New Look at the Old Testament (in U.S. as Kings, Prophets and History), 1965; Hope Deferred: Girls' Education in English History, 1965; Young Mother, 1965; Rapiers and Battleaxes: The Women's Movement and its Aftermath, 1966; The

Story of Fanny Burney, 1966; The Hebrew People, 1967; Joseph Paxton and the Crystal Palace, 1967; No Strangers Here, 1968; First Job, 1969; Explorers into Africa, 1970; Indicative Past: A Hundred Years of the Girls' Public Day School Trust, 1971; Where Do We Go From Here?, 1972; Starting Point, 1975; John Stuart Mill in Love, 1977; Runaways, 1978; The Slave Trade, 1980. Add: 39/67 Elm Park Gardens, London SW10 9QE, England.

KAMMEN, Michael. American, b. 1936. History. Newton C. Farr Prof. of American History and Culture, Cornell Univ., Ithaca, N.Y., since 1973 (Asst. Prof., 1965–67; Assoc. Prof., 1967–69; Prof., 1969–73; Chmn., Dept. of History, 1974–76). Chmn., Advisory Bd., and Consultant for Our Story, Children's Television Workshop, NYC, 1974–76. *Publs:* Operational History of the Flying Boat: Open Sea and Seadrome Aspects, Atlantic Theatre, World War II, 1960; (co-ed.) The Glorious Revolution in America: Documents on the Colonial Crisis of 1689, 1964, 1972; (ed.). Politics and Society in Colonial America: Democracy or Deference?, 1967, 1973; A Rope of Sand: The Colonial Agents, British Politics, and the American Revolution, 1968; Deputyes and Libertyes: The Origins of Representative Government in Colonial America, 1969; Empire and Interest: The American Colonies and the Politics of Mercantilism, 1970; (ed.) The Contrapuntal Civilization, 1971; (ed.) The History of the Province of New-York, by William Smith, Jr., 2 vols., 1972; People of Paradox: An Inquiry Concerning the Origins of American Civilization, 1972; What Is the Good of History? Selected Letters of Carl L. Becker 1900–1945, 1973; Colonial New York: A History, 1975; (with J.P. Greene and R.L. Bushman) Society, Freedom, and Conscience: The Coming of the Revolution in Virginia, Massachusetts, and New York, 1976; (with K.E. Boulding and S.M. Lipset) From Abundance to Scarcity: Implications for the American Tradition, 1978; A Season of Youth: The American Revolution and the Historical Imagination, 1978; (ed.) The Past Before Us: Contemporary Historical Writing in the United States, 1980, Spheres of Liberty: Changing Perceptions of Liberty in American Culture, 1986; A Machine That Would Go Of Itself: The Constitution in American Culture, 1986; (ed.) The Origins of the American Constitution: A Documentary History, 1986; Selvages and Biases: The Fabric of History in American Culture, 1987; Sovereignty and Liberty: Constitutional Discourse in American Culture, 1988. Add: Dept. of History, Cornell Univ., Ithaca, N.Y. 14853, U.S.A.

KANDEL, Lenore. American. Poetry. *Publs:* A Passing Dragon, 1959; A Passing Dragon Seen Again, 1959; The Exquisite Navel, 1959 The Love Book, 1966; Word Alchemy, 1967. Add: 925 Sanchez St., San Francisco, Calif. 94114, U.S.A.

KANE, Henry. Also writes as Anthony McCall, Kenneth R. McKay, Mario J. Sagola, and Katherine Stapleton. American, b. 1918. Mystery/Crime/Suspense. Full-time writer. Formerly practiced as a lawyer. *Publs:* A Halo for Nobody, 1947 (in U.S. paperback, Martinis and Murder, 1956); Armchair in Hell, 1958; Report for a Corpse (short stories), 1948 (in U.S. paperback, Murder of the Park Avenue Playgirl, 1957); Hang by Your Neck, 1949; Edge of Panic, 1950; A Corpse for Christmas, 1951 (in U.S. paperback, Homicide at Yuletide, 1966); Until You are Dead, 1951; Laughter Came Screaming, 1953 (in U.S. paperback, Mask for Murder, 1957); My Business is Murder, 1950; Trilogy in Jeopardy, 1955; Trinity in Violence, 1955; Too French and Too Deadly, 1955 (in U.K. as The Narrowing Lust, 1956); The Case of the Murdered Madam (short stories), 1955 (in U.K. as Triple Terror, 1958); Who Killed Sweet Sue?, 1956 (in U.K. as Sweet Charlie, 1957); The Deadly Finger (in U.K. as The Finger), 1957; Death on the Double, 1957; Death for Sale, 1957 (in U.K. as Sleep Without Dreams, 1958); The Name is Chambers (short stories), 1957; Fistful of Death, 1958 (in U.K. as The Dangling Man, 1959); Death is the Last Lover (in U.K. as Nirvana Can Also Mean Death), 1959; The Deadly Doll, 1959; The Private Eyeful, 1959; Peter Gunn (novelization of TV play), 1960; Run for Doom, 1960; The Crumpled Cup, 1961; Death of a Flack, 1961; My Darlin' Evangeline (in U.K. as Perfect Crime), 1961; Dead in Bed, 1961; Death of a Hooker, 1961; Kisses of Death (in U.K. as Killer's Kiss), 1962; Death of a Dastard, 1962; Never Give a Millionaire an Even Break, 1963 (in U.K. as Murder for the Millions, 1964); Nobody Loves a Loser, 1963 (in U.S. paperback, Who Dies There?, 1969); Snatch an Eye, 1963; Two Must Die, 1963; Dirty Gertie, 1963 (as To Die or Not to Die, 1964); Frenzy of Evil, 1963; The Midnight Man (in U.K. as Other Sins Only Speak), 1965; Prey by Dawn, 1965; Conceal and Disguise, 1966; The Devil to Pay, 1966 (in U.S. paperback, Unholy Trio, 1967, and Better Wed Than Dead, 1970); (as Anthony McCall) Operation Delta, 1966; (as Anthony McCall) Holocaust, 1967; Laughter in the Alehouse, 1968; Don't Call Me Madame, 1969; The Schack Job, 1969; The Bomb Job, 1970; Don't Go Away Dead, 1970; Kiss! Kiss! Kill! Kill!, 1970; The Glow Job, 1971; The Moonlighter, 1971;

The Tail Job, 1971; The Virility Factor (non-mystery novel), 1971; Come Kill with Me, 1972; The Escort Job, 1972; Kill for the Millions, 1972; Decision, 1973; A Kind of Rape, 1974; The Violator, 1974; The Avenger, 1975; Lust of Power, 1975; The Tripoli Documents, 1976; (as Mario J. Sagola) The Manacle, 1978; (as Kenneth R. McKay) Shadow of the Knife, 1978; (as Katherine Stapleton) Without Sin among You, 1979; (as Mario J. Sagola) The Naked Bishop, 1980; (as Kenneth R. McKay), Indecent Relations, 1982; The Little Red Phone, 1982. Add: c/o Arbor House, 105 Madison Ave., New York, N.Y. 10016, U.S.A.

KANE, Jim. See CORD, Barry.

KANIN, Garson. American, b. 1912. Novels/Short stories, Plays/Screenplays, Film, Autobiography/Memoirs/Personal, Biography. Freelance dir. and producer since 1938. Asst. to George Abbott 1935–37; on Production Staff, Samuel Goldwyn Productions, Hollywood, Calif., 1937–38. *Publs:* Born Yesterday, 1946; (with Ruth Gordon) Adam's Rib (screenplay), 1949; The Smile of the World, 1949; The Rat Race, 1949, novel, 1960; The Live Wire, 1950; (adaptor) Fledermaus (libretto), 1950; Do Re Mi (novel), 1955, play, 1960; (adaptor) A Gift of Time, 1962; Come on Strong, 1962; Remembering Mr Maugham (book and play), 1966; Where It's At (novel and screenplay), 1969; Cast of Characters: Stories of Broadway and Hollywood, 1969; Tracy and Hepburn: An Intimate Memoir, 1971; A Thousand Summers, 1973; Hollywood, 1974; One Hell of An Actor, 1977; It Takes a Long Time to Become Young, 1978; Moviola, 1979; Smash, 1980; Together Again: Hollywood's Great Movie Teams, 1981; Cordelia?, 1982; Tom, Dick, and Harry (screenplay), 1985. Add: 200 W. 57th St., New York, N.Y. 10019, U.S.A.

KANTO, Peter. See ZACHARY, Hugh.

KANTONEN, T(aito) A(lmar). American, b. 1900. Theology/Religion. Prof. of Systematic Theology Emeritus, Trinity Lutheran Seminary, Columbus Ohio, of Wittenberg Univ., Ohio, since 1968 (Prof., 1932–68). Pastor of Lutheran Churches in Minnesota and Massachusetts, 1920–32. *Publs:* The Message of the Church to the World of Today, 1941; Resurgence of the Gospel, 1948; Risti ja Tähtilippu, 1950; Theology of Evangelism, 1954; The Christian Hope, 1954; Theology for Christian Stewardship, 1956; Life after Death, 1962; (trans.) Divine Humanness, by Aarne Siirala, 1968; Man in the Eyes of God, 1972; Christian Faith Today, 1974; Good News for All Seasons, 1976; To Live Is Christ, 1977; Predicamos a Cristo, 1986. Add: 816 Snowhill Blvd., Springfield, Ohio 45504, U.S.A.

KAPELRUD, Arvid Schou. Norwegian, b. 1912. Archaeology/Antiquities, History, Theology/Religion. Co-Ed., Temenos, since 1965, and Ed., Studia Theologica, 1966–88, Oslo Univ. Press. Prof., Univ. of Oslo, 1954–82 (Asst. Librarian, Univ. Library, 1935–46; Librarian, 1946–52; Assoc. Prof. 1952–54). *Publs:* The Code of Hammurapi, 1943; The Question of Authorship in the Ezra-Narrative, 1944; Joel Studies, 1948; Baal in the Ras Shamra Texts, 1952; Central Ideas in Amos, 1956, 1971; Dödehavsrullene, 1956, 1971; The Ras Shamra Discoveries and the Old Testament, 1963; Israel, 1966; The Violent Goddess, 1969; Vor konge er Baal, 1973; The Message of the Prophet Zephaniah, 1975; Job og hans problem, 1976; God and His Friends in the Old Testament, 1979; Han var ikke i Stormen, 1984. Add: Univ. of Oslo, Blindern, p.b. 1023, Oslo 3, Norway.

KAPLAN, Johanna. American, b. 1942. Novels/Short stories. Teacher of emotionally disturbed children in New York City public schools and at Mt. Sinai Hospital, NYC, since 1966. *Publs:* Other People's Lives (short stories), 1975; O My America! (novel), 1980. Add: 411 West End Ave., New York, N.Y. 10024, U.S.A.

KAPLAN, Justin. American, b. 1925. Literature, Biography. Lectr., Harvard Univ., Cambridge, Mass., 1969–70, 1972–73, 1976, 1978. *Publs:* Mr. Clemens and Mark Twain, 1966; Lincoln Steffens: A Biography, 1974; Mark Twain and His World, 1974; Walt Whitman: A Life, 1980. Add: 16 Francis Ave., Cambridge, Mass. 02138, U.S.A.

KAPLAN, Morton A. American, b. 1921. International relations/Current affairs, Politics/Government. Pres., Professors World Peace Academy, since 1984; Advisory Bd., Washington Times, since 1983; Prof. of Political Science, Univ. of Chicago, since 1965 (Asst. Prof., 1955–61; Assoc. Prof., 1961–65; Chmn., Cttee. on Intnl. Relations, 1959–85; Dir., Ford Workshops Prgs. in Intnl. Relations, 1961–71; Dir., Center of Strategic and Foreign Policy Studies, 1970–85). Ed. and Publr., The World and I. Assoc. Ed., Journal of Conflict Resolution, 1961–81. *Publs:* United States Foreign Policy 1945–1955, 1956; System and

Process in International Politics, 1957, 1965; (with Katzenbach) Political Foundations of International Law, 1961; (ed. and contrib.) New Approaches to International Relations, 1968; Macropolitics: Essays on the Philosophy and Science of Politics, 1969; (ed. and contrib.) Great Issues of International Politics, 1970, 1974; Dissent and the State in Peace and War: An Essay on the Grounds of Public Morality, 1970; On Historical and Political Knowing: An Inquiry into Some Problems of Universal Law and Human Freedom, 1971; (ed. and contrib.) SALT: Problems and Prospects, 1973; On Freedom and Human Dignity: The Importance of the Sacred in Politics, 1973; (ed. and contrib.) Strategic Thinking and Its Moral Implications, 1973; The Rationale for NATO: European Collective Security—Past and Future, 1973; (ed. and contrib.) NATO and Dissuasion, 1974; (ed. and contrib.) The Many Faces of Communism, 1978; Towards Professionalism in International Theory: Macrosystem Analysis, 1979; Global Policy, Challenge of the '80s, 1984; Science, Language and the Human Condition, 1984, 1989; (ed.) Consolidating Peace in Europe: A Dialogue Between East and West, 1987; (co-ed.) The Soviet Union and the Challenge of the Future, 4 vols., 1988–89. Add: Univ. of Chicago, 5828 S. University Ave., Chicago, Ill. 60637, U.S.A.

KAPLAN, Robert B. American, b. 1929. Language/Linguistics, Speech/Rhetoric. Prof. of Applied Linguistics, since 1972, and Dir. of American Language Inst., since 1986, Univ. of Southern California, Los Angeles, (Coordinator, English Communication Prog. for Foreign Students, 1961–65; Asst. Prof. of English, 1963–65; Assoc. Prof., Chmn., Linguistics Dept., and Dir., English Communication, 1965–72; Assoc. Dean, Continuing Education, 1973–76). Field Service consultant, National Assn. for Foreign Student Affairs, since 1966 (Pres., 1983); Gen. Ed., Annual Review of Applied Linguistics, since 1981. Pres., Assn. of Teachers of English as a Second Language, 1968. *Publs:* (ed.) Reading and Rhetoric, 1963; (co-author) Transformational Grammar: A Guide for Teachers, 1968; (co-author) English at Your Fingertips, 1969, 1976; The Anatomy of Rhetoric: Prolegomena to a Functional Theory of Rhetoric, 1971; (ed.) On the Scope of Applied Linguistics, 1980; Migrants in the Workplace: Language, Culture, Attitude, 1980; (co-author) Exploring Academic Discourses, 1983. Add: 30303 Ganado Dr., Rancho Palos Verdes, Calif. 90274, U.S.A.

KAPLANSKY, Irving. American, b. 1917. Mathematics/Statistics. Dir., Mathematical Sciences Research Inst., since 1984. Prof., Dept. of Mathematics, Univ. of Chicago, 1956–84 (member of faculty, 1945–84; Asst. to Assoc. Prof., 1947–56; Chmn., Dept. of Mathematics, 1962–67). *Publs:* Commutative Rings, 1970; Fields and Rings, 1972; Set Theory and Metric Spaces, 1972. Add: c/o Mathematical Sciences Research Inst., 1000 Centennial Dr., Berkeley, Calif. 94720, U.S.A.

KAPP, Colin. British, b. 1928(?). Science fiction/Fantasy. Formerly electrical technician. *Publs:* Transfinite Man, 1964, in U.K. as The Dark Mind, 1965; The Patterns of Chaos, 1972; The Wizard of Anharitte, 1975; The Survival Game, 1976; The Chaos Weapon, 1977; Manalone, 1977; The Ion War, 1978; The Unorthodox Engineers (short stories), 1979; The Timewinders, 1980; Search for the Sun, 1981; The Lost World of Cronus, 1982; The Tyrant of Hades, 1982. Add: c/o Carnell Literary Agency, Danescroft, Goose Lane, Little Hallingbury, Herts. CM22 7RG, England.

KARANIKAS, Alexander. American, b. 1916. Poetry, Literature. Emeritus Prof. of English, Univ. of Illinois at Chicago Circle, since 1982 (joined faculty, 1954). Instr. in English, Kendall Coll., 1952–53, and Northwestern Univ. 1953–54, Evanston, Ill. *Publs:* When a Youth Gets Poetic (Poetry), 1934; In Praise of Heroes (poetry), 1945; Tillers of a Myth: The Southern Agrarians as Social and Literary Critics, 1966; (with Helen Karanikas) Elias Venezis (literary criticism), 1969; Hellenes and Hellions: Modern Greek Characters in American Literature, 1981. Add: 618 North Harvey Ave., Oak Park, Ill. 60302, U.S.A.

KARASZ, Arthur. American, b. 1907. Economics, Third World problems. Member of Bd., Siemens, and Royal Bank of Canada, France, since 1975. With National Bank of Hungary, 1932–46: Pres., 1945–46; Prof. in Central Banking, Univ. of Budapest, 1946–48; Lectr., New Sch. for Social Research, NYC, 1948–49; Prof. in Monetary Policy, De Paul Univ., Chicago, 1949–52; U.N. Adviser on Monetary Matters to Bolivia, 1952–56; joined the Intnl. Bank for Reconstruction and Development, 1956; Dir., European Office, Paris and London, 1968–73; UN Consultant, Lebanon, 1974; Adviser to Akbank, Istanbul, 1974–75. *Publs:* L'Ecole des Totalitaires, 1948; Inflacion, Estabilizacion, 1955; Bolivia: An Experiment in Development, 1957; The World Bank and the Third World, 1970; Intermission: The Smithsonian Agreement of 1971, 1972; Reforming the World Economy, 1977. Add: Coumessas, 30140 St. Félix de Pallières, France.

KARGER, Delmar William. American, b. 1913. Administration/Management, Business/Trade/Industry, Engineering/Technology. Mgmt. and Industrial Engineering Consultant, since 1959; Corporate Dir., Information Systems, since 1981. Former Corporate Dir. of New York Stock Exchange and OTC listed firms. Formerly industrial and electrical engineer, working for Intnl. Harvester, Westinghouse, Pa. Electric Coil Corp., RCA, and Magnavox Co., 1935–59; Prof. and Head of the Dept. of Mgmt. Engineering, 1959–63, Dean of the Sch. of Mgmt., 1963–70, and Ford Foundn. Prof. of Management, 1970–78, Rensselaer Polytechnic Inst., Troy, N.Y.; Corporate Dir. and Pres., Randac Systems, 1961–63; Corporate Dir., Fibre Glass Industries, 1961–82, Golub Corp., 1968–73, Bunker Ramo Corp., 1974–81, and Scott Fetzer, 1976–82. *Publs:* (with F. Bayha) Engineered Work Measurement, 1957, 4th ed. 1985; The New Product, 1960; (with R.G. Murdick) Managing Engineering and Research, 1963, 3rd ed. 1980; (with A.B. Jack) Problems of Small Business in Developing and Exploiting New Products, 1963; (with R.G. Murdick) New Product Venture Management, 1972; How to Choose a Career and Be Happy, 1978; (with W. Hancock) Advanced Work Measurement, 1982; (with F.E. James) The Technical Approach to the Market, 1989; (with T. Triocari) The Management of Research and Engineering, 1990. Add: 506 Circle Dr., De Funiak Springs, Fla. 32433, U.S.A.

KARIEL, Henry S. American, b. 1924. Politics/Government. Prof. of Political Science, Univ. of Hawaii, Honolulu. *Publs:* The Decline of American Pluralism, 1961; In Search of Authority, 1964; The Promise of Politics, 1966; Open Systems, 1969; (ed.) The Political Order, 1970; (ed.) Frontiers of Democratic Theory, 1970; Saving Appearances, 1972; Beyond Liberalism, Where Relations Grow, 1977; The Desperate Politics of Postmodernism, 1989. Add: Dept. of Political Science, Univ. of Hawaii, Honolulu, Hawaii, U.S.A.

KARL, Frederick (Robert). American, b. 1927. Novel/short stories, Intellectual history, Literature, Biography. Prof. of English, New York Univ., NYC. *Publs:* A Reader's Guide to Joseph Conrad, 1960, 1969; The Quest (novel), 1961; The Contemporary English Novel, 1962, 1972; An Age of Fiction, 1964, 1972; The Adversary Literature, 1974; (ed.) Joseph Conrad: A Collection of Criticism, 1975; Joseph Conrad: The Three Lives: Biography, 1979; (co-ed.) Letters of Joseph Conrad, 3 vols., 1983, 1986, 1988; American Fictions 1940–1980, 1983; Modern and Modernism: The Sovereignty of the Artist 1885-1925, 1985; William Faulkner: American Writer, 1989. Add: Dept. of English, New York Univ., New York, N.Y. 10003, U.S.A.

KARMEL, Peter Henry. Australian, b. 1922. Economics, Education. Pres., Australian Council for Educational Research, since 1979; Pres., Academy of the Social Sciences in Australia, since 1987; Chmn., Australian Inst. of Health, since 1987; Exec. Chmn., Canberra Inst. of the Arts, since 1988; Chmn., Australian National Council on AIDS, since 1988. Prof. of Economics, Univ. of Adelaide, 1950–62; Vice-Chancellor, Flinders Univ. of South Australia, 1966–71; Chmn., Interim Council, 1965–69, and Chancellor, 1966–71, Univ. of Papua and New Guinea, Port Moresby; Chmn., Australian Univ. Commn., 1971–77; Vice-Chancellor, Australian National Univ., Canberra, 1982–87. Chmn., Australia Council, 1974–76; Chmn., Commonwealth Tertiary Education Commn. 1977–82; Chmn., Commonwealth Govt. Quality of Education Review Cttee., 1984–85. *Publs:* Applied Statistics for Economists, 1957, 1962, with M. Polasek 1970, 1978; (with M. Brunt) Structure of the Australian Economy, 1962, 3rd ed. 1966; (with G.C. Harcourt and R.H. Wallace) Economic Activity, 1967. Add: 4/127 Hopetown Circuit, Yarralumla, A.C.T. 2600, Australia.

KARNIEWSKI, Janus. *See* **WITTLIN,** Thaddeus.

KAROL, Alexander. *See* **KENT,** Arthur.

KARP, Abraham J. American, b. 1921. History, Theology/Religion. Bernstein Prof. of Jewish Studies, and Prof. of History and Religious Studies, Univ. of Rochester, N.Y., since 1972. Member, Inst. of Contemporary Jewry, Hebrew Univ., Jerusalem; Pres., American Jewish Historical Soc. Former Rabbi, Congregation Beth El, Rochester, N.Y. *Publs:* New York Chooses a Chief Rabbi, 1955; The Jewish Way of Life, 1962; (ed.) Conservative Judaism: The Heritage of Solomon Schechter, 1963; A History of the United Synagogues of America 1913–1963, 1967; (ed.) The Jewish Experience in America, 5 vols., 1969; (ed. with M. Davis) Texts and Studies in American Jewish History, 1971; Beginnings, 1975; Golden Door to America, 1976; The Jewish Way of Life and Thought, 1980; To Give Life, 1980; American Judaism, 1984; Haven and Home: A History of the Jews in America, 1985; Mordecai Manuel Noah: First American Jew, 1988. Add: Dept. of History, Univ. of Rochester,

Rochester, N.Y. 14627, U.S.A.

KARP, David. Also writes as Adam Singer and Wallace Ware. American, b. 1922. Novels/Short stories, Science fiction/Fantasy, Plays/Screenplays, Biography. Pres. of Leda Productions Inc., Los Angeles, since 1968. Trustee Producer, Writers Guild of America Pension Plan, since 1969 (Chmn., 1976, 1988); Trustee, Writers Guild Industry Health Fund, since 1973 (Chmn., 1976, 1988). Continuity Dir., Radio Station WNYC, NYC, 1948–49; member, Editorial Bd., Television Quarterly, 1966–71. Member, Exec. Council, Eastern Branch, 1963–66, and West Branch, 1967–74, Writers Guild of America, also Pres., TV-Radio Branch, 1969–71. *Publs:* The Big Feeling, 1952; The Brotherhood of Velvet, 1952; Cry, Flesh, 1953, reissued as The Girl on Crown Street, 1967; Hardman, 1953; (as Adam Singer) Platoon, 1953; One, 1953; (as Wallace Ware) The Charka Memorial, 1954; The Day of the Monkey, 1955; All Honorable Men, 1956; Leave Me Alone, 1957; (with M.D. Lincoln) Vice- President in Charge of Revolution (biography), 1960; Enter, Sleeping (in U.K. as the Sleep-Walkers), 1960; The Last Believers, 1964; Cafe Univers (play), 1967; Sol Madrid (screenplay), 1967; Che! (screenplay), 1968; Tender Loving Care (screenplay), 1972. Add: 300 E. 56th St., #3C, New York, N.Y. 10022, U.S.A.

KARPAT, Kemal H. Turkish, b. 1925. History, International relations/Current affairs, Sociology. Distinguished Prof. of History, since 1967, and Chmn., Middle East Studies Prog., Univ. of Wisconsin, Madison. Ed., Intnl. Journal of Turkish Studies; Gov., Inst. of Turkish Studies, Wash. D.C., since 1983; Pres., Assoc. of Central Asian Studies, since 1985. Member of faculty, Montana State Univ., Missoula, 1957–61, Middle East Technical Univ., Ankara, 1958–59, and New York, Univ., NYC, 1962–67. *Publs:* Turkey's Politics, 1959; (ed. and contrib.) Political and Social Thought in the Contemporary Middle East, 1968, 1982; Social Change and Politics in Turkey, 1973; An Inquiry into the Social Foundations of Nationlism in the Ottoman State, 1973; (ed.) The Ottoman State and Its Place in World History, 1974; Turkey's Foreign Policy in Transition, 1950–1974, 1975; The Gecekondu: Rural Migration and Urbanization, 1976; The Ottoman Population 1830-1914, 1985. Add: 412L Humanities Bldg., Univ. of Wisconsin, Madison, Wisc. 53706, U.S.A.

KARPLUS, Walter J. American, b. 1927. Information science/Computers. Prof. since 1955, Computer Science Dept., Univ. of California, Los Angeles (Chmn. of Dept., 1972–79). *Publs:* Analog Simulation: Solution of Field Problems, 1958; (with W. Soroka) Analog Methods: Computations and Simulation, 1959; (with R. Tomovic) High Speed Analog Computers, 1962; (ed.) On-Line Computing, 1966; (with J. Girerd) Traitment des Equations Differentielles sur Calculateurs Electroniques, 1968; (with G. Bekey) Hybrid Computation, 1968; Digital Computer Treatment of Partial Differential Equations, 1981. Add: Computer Science Dept., 3732 Boelter Hall, Univ. of California, Los Angeles, Calif. 90024, U.S.A.

KASER, Michael Charles. British, b. 1926. Area Studies, Economics. Professorial Fellow, St. Antony's Coll., since 1972 and Dir. of the Inst. for Russian, Soviet and East European Studies since 1988. Reader in Economics, since 1972, Oxford Univ. (Faculty Fellow, 1963,19672; Lectr. in Soviet Economics, 1963–72; Latin Preacher, 1982). Staff, H.M. Foreign Service, London and Moscow, 1947–51; Staff member, U.N. Secretariat, Geneva, 1951–63. *Publs:* (ed.) Economic Development for Eastern Europe, 1958; Comecon, 1965, 1967; (ed.) Soviet Affairs No. 4, 1966; Soviet Economics, 1970; (with J. Zielinski) Planning in East Europe, 1970; (ed. with R. Portes) Planning and Market Relations, 1971; (ed. with H. Hohmann and K. Thalheim) The New Economic Systems of East Europe, 1975; (ed. with A. Brown) The Soviet Union since the Fall of Khrushchev, 1975; Health Care in the Soviet Union and Eastern Europe, 1976; (Gen. Ed.) Economic History of Eastern Europe 1919–1975, vols., 1985; (co-ed.) The Cambridge Encyclopedia of Russia and the Soviet Union, 1982; (ed. with A. Brown) Soviet Policy for the 1980s, 1982. Add: St. Antony's Coll., Oxford OX2 6JF, England.

KASH, Don E. American, b. 1934. Politics/Government, Public/Social Administration, Sciences (general), Technology. George Lynn Cross Research Prof. of Political Science, and Research Fellow in Science and Public Policy, Univ. of Oklahoma, Norman, since 1970. Dir., Prog. in Science and Public Policy, and Assoc. Prof. of Political Science, Purdue Univ., Lafayette, Ind., 1966–70; Dir., Program in Science and Public Policy, Univ. of Oklahoma, Norman, 1970–78. *Publs:* The Politics of Space Cooperation, 1967; (co-author) North Sea Oil and Gas: Implications for Future United States Development, 1973; Energy under the Oceans, 1973; Energy Alternatives, 1975; Our Energy Future, 1976; U.S. Energy Policy: Crisis and Complacency, 1984; Perpetual Innovation: The New World of Competition, 1989. Add: Science and Public Policy Prog., Univ. of Oklahoma, Rm. 432, 601 Elm St., Norman, Okla. 73019, U.S.A.

KASPERSON, Roger E. American, b. 1938. Geography, Urban studies. Prof. of Govt. and Geography since 1975, and Dir. of the Center for Technology, Environment and Development, since 1978, Clark Univ., Worcester (Asst. Prof., 1968–69; Assoc. Prof., 1969–75; Dean of the Coll., 1971–74). Instr., Univ. of Connecticut, Storrs, 1964–66; Asst. Prof. of Geography, Michigan State Univ., East Lansing, 1966–68. *Publs:* The Dodecanese: Diversity and Unity in Island Politics, 1966; (ed. with J.V. Minghi) The Structure of Political Geography, 1969; (ed. with J.X. Kasperson) Water Re-Use and the Cities, 1977; (ed. with M. Berberian) Equity Issues in Radioactive Waste Management, 1983; (with others) Corporate Management of Health and Safety Hazards: A Comparison of Current Practice, 1988. Add: Center for Technology, Environment and Development, Clark Univ., 950 Main St., Worcester, Mass. 01610, U.S.A.

KASTNER, Joseph. American, b. 1907. Botany, Natural history, Biography. With Time mag., 1924–25, New York World, 1925–29, The New Yorker, 1930, Fortune, 1930–36, and Life mag., 1936–69. *Publs:* (with James Crockett) Evergreens, 1974; Berlioz, 1975; A Species of Eternity (in U.K. as A World of Naturalists), 1977; A World of Watchers, 1986; The Bird Illustrated, 1989. Add: 199 River Rd., Grandview-on-Hudson, N.Y. 10960, U.S.A.

KATCHMER, George Andrew. American, b. 1916. Sports/Physical education/Keeping fit. Writer, Classic Images movie mag. Baseball Coach, 1954–58, Football Coach, 1954–69, and Former Prof., Millersville State Coll. (now Millersville Univ.), Pa. Former writer, Screen Thrills mag. *Publs:* How to Finance Your Athletic Program, 1953; Simplified Multiple Defense, 1958; How to Organize and Conduct Football Practice, 1962; Pre-Game Football Preparation and Strategy, 1965. Add: 27 Blue Rock Rd., Millersville, Pa. 17551, U.S.A.

KATO, Shuichi. Japanese, b. 1919. Art, Literature. Prof. of Asian Studies, Univ. of British Columbia, Vancouver, 1960–69; Prof. of Japanology, Freie Universitaet, Berlin, 1969–73; Prof. of Japanese Studies, Sophia Univ., Tokyo, 1976–85. Visiting Lectr., Yale Univ., New Haven, Conn., 1974–76; Visiting Prof., Cambridge Univ., 1983, Universita degli Studio Venice, 1983–84. *Publs:* Hitsuji No Uta (Song of a Sheep), 1968; Form, Style, Tradition: Reflexions on Japanese Art and Society, 1971; Genso Bara Toshi (Roses and Cities), 1973; Nihon Bungakushi Josetsu (Introduction to Intellectual History of Japan Through Literature), 1974; The Japan-China Phenomenon, 1974; Six Lives Six Deaths: Portraits from Modern Japan, 1979; A History of Japanese Literature, 3 vols., 1979–83; Chosakushu (Collected Works) in 15 vols., 1978–79. Add: Setagaya-Ku, Kaminoge 1-8-16, Tokyo, Japan.

KATZ, Bobbi. Also writes as Peggy Kahn, Ali Reich, Don E. Plumme, Della Maison, Barbara Gail, and Emily George. American, b. 1933. Children's fiction, Poetry. Ed. Random House Books for Young Readers, NYC. Former Creative Writing Consultant, Cornwall Sch. Systems, N.Y.; former Poetry Consultant, Harper and Row Sch. Dept., NYC. *Publs:* Nothing But a Dog, 1972; I'll Build My Friend a Mountain, 1972; Upside Down and Inside Out: Poems for All Your Pockets, 1973; The Manifesto and Me—Meg, 1974; Rod and Reel Trouble, 1974; 1001 Words, 1975; Snow Bunny: Action on the Ice, 1976; Volleyball Jinx, 1977; (with others) The Cousteau Almanac, 1980. Add: 65 W. 96th St., No. 21H, New York, N.Y. 10025, U.S.A.

KATZ, Ephraim. American, b. 1932. Film, Documentaries/Reportage. Film producer and director. *Publs:* (with Q. Reynolds and Z. Aldouby) Minister of Death, 1960; The Film Encyclopedia (in U.K. as the International Film Encyclopedia), 1979; also author of television and film plays. Add: 229 E. 79th St., New York, N.Y. 10021, U.S.A.

KATZ, Martin. American, b. 1929. Biography. Assoc. Prof. of History, Univ. of Alberta, Edmonton, since 1969. *Publs:* Mikhail N. Katkov: Political Biography 1818-1887, 1966. Add: Dept. of History, Univ. of Alberta, Edmonton, Alta., Canada.

KATZ, Menke. American (b. Lithuanian), b. 1906. Pseudonyms: Elchik Hiat and Menke Badanes. Poetry. Ed.-in-Chief, Bitterroot poetry mag., NYC, since 1962; teacher and lectr., on Poetry and Jewish studies. Ed., MIR Yiddish mag., 1944,19647. *Publs:* in Yiddish—Three Sisters, 1932; Dawning Man, 1935; Burning Village I, and Burning Village II, 1938; My Grandma Myrna, 1939; To Happier Days, 1941; The Simple

Dream, 1947; Midday, 1954; Safad, 1979, in English—Land of Manna, 1965; Aspects of Modern Poetry: A Symposiu, 1967; Rock Rose, 1969; Princes of Pig Street, 1969; Burning Village, 1972; World of Old Abe, 1974; Forever and Ever and Wednesday, 1980; (with Harry Smith) Two Friends, vol. 1, 1981, vol. 2, 1988; A Chair for Elijah, 1985; Yiddish Folksong and Poetry, 1985; This Little Land, 1989. Add: Box 489, Spring Glen, N.Y. 12483, U.S.A.

KATZ, Michael Ray. American, b. 1944. Literature, Translations. Prof. of Russian and Chmn. of Slavic Languages Dept., Univ. of Texas, Austin, since 1984. Asst. to Assoc. Prof. of Russian, Williams Coll., Williamstown, Mass., 1972–84. *Publs:* The Literary Ballad in Early Nineteenth Century Russian Literature, 1976; Dreams and the Unconscious in 19th Century Russian Literature, 1984 (trans.) Who Is To Blame?, by Alexander Herzen, 1984; (trans.) What Is To Be Done, by Nikolai Chernyshevsky, 1989; (trans.) Notes from the Underground, by Dostoevsky, 1989. Add: Dept. of Slavic Lang., Univ. of Texas, Austin, Texas, U.S.A.

KATZ, Sanford N. American, b. 1933. Law. Prof. of Law, Boston Coll. Law Sch., Newton Centre, Mass., since 1968. Instr., 1959–60, Asst. Prof., 1960–64, and Assoc. Prof. of Law, 1963–64, Catholic Univ. of America, Washington, D.C.; Prof. of Law, Univ. of Florida, Gainesville, 1964–68; Dir., Law and Child Protection, U.S. Dept. of Health, Education and Welfare, 1973–75. Ed.-in-Chief, Family Law Quarterly, 1971–84. *Publs:* When Parents Fail: The Law's Response to Family Breakdown, 1971; (ed.) The Youngest Minority: Lawyers in Defense of Children, 1974; (with Eekelaar) Family Violence, 1978; (with Meezan and Reisso) Adoptions Without Agencies, 1978; (with Eekelaar) Marriage and Cohabitation, 1980; American Family Law in Transition, 1983; (with Eekelaar) The Resolution of Family Conflict, 1984; Negotiating to Settlement in Divorces, 1987. Add: Boston Coll. Law Sch., Newton Centre, Mass. 02159, U.S.A.

KATZ, Steve. American, b. 1935. Novels/Short stories, Poetry. Assoc. Prof. of English, Univ. of Colorado, Boulder, since 1978 (Dir. of Creative Writing, 1978–81). Staff Member, English Language Inst., Lecce, Italy, 1960; faculty member, Univ. of Maryland Overseas, Lecce, 1961–62; Asst. Prof. of English, Cornell Univ., Ithaca, N.Y., 1962–67; Lectr. in Fiction, Univ. of Iowa, Iowa City, 1969–70; Writer-in-residence, Brooklyn Coll., 1970–71; Asst. Prof. of English, Queens Coll., NYC, 1971–75; Assoc. Prof. of English, Notre Dame Univ., Indiana, 1976–78. *Publs:* The Lestriad (novel), 1962; The Weight of Antony (poetry), 1964; The Exaggerations of Peter Prince, 1968; Creamy and Delicious: Eat My Words (in Other Words) (short stories), 1970; (as Stephanie Gatos) Posh (novel), 1971; Saw (novel), 1972; Cheyenne River Wild Track (poetry), 1973; Moving Parts (novel), 1977; Wier and Pouce (novel), 1984; Stolen Stories, 1985; Florry of Washington Heights (novel), 1987. Add: 3060 8th St., Boulder, Colo. 80302, U.S.A.

KATZ, Welwyn (née Wilton). Canadian, b. 1948. Children's fiction. *Publs:* The Prophecy of Tau Ridoo, 1982; Witchery Hill, 1984; Sun God, Moon Witch, 1986; False Face, 1987; The Third Magic, 1988. Add: 103 Windsor Ave., London, Ont. N6C 1Z8, Canada.

KATZ, William Loren. American, b. 1927. Cultural/Ethnic topics. History. Pres., Ethrac Publications Inc., NYC, since 1972; Columnist, Daily Challenge, NYC, since 1986. Member, Advisory Bd., National Emergency Civil Liberties Cttee., since 1981. Prof., New Sch. for Social Research, NYC, 1978–83. Member, Editorial Bd., Journal of Black Studies, 1971–73. *Publs:* Eyewitness: The Negro in American History; (gen. ed.) The American Negro: His History and Literature; Teacher's Guide to American Negro History; (ed.) Five Slave Narratives, 1970; (co-author) American Majorities and Minorities, 1970; The Black West, 1971, 1987; A History of Black America, 1973; An Album of the Civil War, 1974; An Album of Reconstruction, 1974; Minorities in American History, 6 vols., 1975; (with Jacqueline Hunt) Making Our Way, 1975; Black People Who Made the Old West, 1977; An Album of the Great Depression, 1979; An Album of Nazism, 1980; (gen. ed.) Vital Sources in American History, 1980; (co-ed.) The Antislavery Crusade in America; Black Indians: A Hidden Heritage, 1986; The Invisible Empire: The KKK Impact on History, 1986. Add: 231 W. 13th St., New York, N.Y. 10011, U.S.A.

KAUFELT, David A(llan). American, b. 1939. Novels/Short stories. Former advertising copywriter. *Publs:* Six Months with an Older Woman, 1973; The Bradley Beach Rumba, 1974; Spare Parts, 1978; Late Bloomer, 1979; Midnight Movies, 1980; Three Brothers, 1981; Silver Rose, 1982; The Wine and the Music, 1982; Souvenir, 1983; American Tropic, 1987. Add: c/o Dell, 245 East 47th St., New York, N.Y. 10017,

U.S.A.

KAUFFMAN, Janet. American, b. 1945. Novels/Short stories, Poetry. Prof., Jackson Community Coll., Mich., since 1976. Visiting Prof. of English, Univ. of Michigan, Ann Arbor, 1984–85. *Publs:* (with Jerome McCann) Writing Home (poetry), 1978; The Weather Book (poetry), 1981; Places in the World a Woman Could Walk (short stories), 1984; Collaborators (novel), 1986. Add: c/o Jackson Community Coll., Jackson, Mich, 49201, U.S.A.

KAUFFMANN, Stanley. American, b. 1916. Novels/Short stories. Plays/Screenplays, Film, Literature, Autobiography/Memoirs/Personal. New York Film Critic, New Republic mag., Washington, D.C., since 1967 (Film Critic, 1958–65; Assoc. Literary Ed., 1966–67; Theatre Critic, 1969–79); Visiting Prof., Grad. Center, City Univ., NYC, since 1977 (Distinguished Prof., 1973–76); Theatre Critic, Saturday Review mag., 1979–85. Compere, The Art of Film prog., 1963–67; Theatre Critic, New York Times, 1966. Visiting Prof., Yale Univ. Sch. of Drama, New Haven, Conn., 1967–73 and 1977–86. *Publs:* The Hidden Hero, 1949; The Tightrope, 1952; The Philanderer, 1953; A Change of Climate, 1954; Man of the World, 1956; If it be Love, 1960; A World on Film, 1966; Figures of Light, 1971; (ed. with B. Henstell) American Film Criticism: From the Beginnings to Citizen Kane, 1973; Living Images, 1975; Persons of the Drama, 1976; Before My Eyes, 1980; Albums of Early Life, 1980; Theater Criticisms, 1984; Field of View, 1985. Add: 10 W. 15th St., New York, N.Y. 10011, U.S.A.

KAUFMAN, Bel. American. Novels/Short stories. Member, P.E.N. American Center, Authors League Council; Commn. on Performing Arts; Bd., Sholom Aleichem Foundn. and Phi Delta Kappa; Member, Advisory Council, Town Hall Foundation, NYC. Former Lectr., New Sch. for Social Research, NYC, English teacher in NYC high schs., and Asst. Prof., City Univ. of New York. *Publs:* Up the Down Staircase, 1965; Love, etc., 1979. Add: 1020 Park Ave., New York, N.Y. 10028, U.S.A.

KAUFMAN, Gerald (Bernard). British, b. 1930. Politics/Government, Humour/Satire. Labour M.P. (U.K.) for Gorton Div. of Manchester, since 1983, and for Ardwick Div., 1970–83; Member of Parliamentary Cttee., since 1980 (Under-Secty. of State, Dept. of the Environment, 1974–75, and Dept. of Industry, 1975; Minister of State, Dept. of Industry, 1975–79). On political staff, Daily Mirror, London, 1955–64; Political Corresp., New Statesman, London, 1964–65; Parliamentary Press Liaison Officer, Labour Party, 1965–70. *Publs:* (with David Frost, Christopher Booker and Herb Sargent) How to Live Under Labour, 1964; (ed.) The Left, 1966; To Build the Promised Land, 1973; How to Be a Minister, 1980; (ed.) Renewal, 1983; My Life in the Silver Screen, 1985; Inside the Promised Land, 1986 Add: 87 Charlbert Ct., Eamont St., London NW8 7DA, England.

KAUFMANN, Myron (Stuart). American, b. 1921. Novels. With Associated Press, 1947–60. *Publs:* Remember Me to God, 1957; Thy Daughter's Nakedness, 1968; The Coming Destruction of Israel (non-fiction), 1970; The Love of Elspeth Baker, 1982. Add: 111 Pond St., Sharon, Mass. 02067, U.S.A.

KAUFMANN, William J. American, b. 1942. Astronomy. Adjunct Prof., Dept. of Physics, San Diego State Univ., since 1976. Dir., Griffith Observatory, Los Angeles, 1970–75; Visiting Faculty, Dept. of Physics, 1974–75, and Visiting Scholar, Jet Propulsion Lab., 1976, California Inst. of Technology, Pasadena. *Publs:* Relativity and Cosmology, 1973, 1977; Astronomy: The Structure of the Universe, 1977; The Cosmic Frontiers of General Relativity, 1977; The Cosmic Frontiers of General Relativity, 1977; Exploration of the Solar System, 1978; Stars and Nebulas, 1978; Planets and Moons, 1979; Galaxies and Quasars, 1979; Black Holes and Warped Spacetime, 1979; (ed.) Particles and Fields, 1980; Universe, 1985. Add: 385 Paraiso Dr., Danville, Calif. 94526, U.S.A.

KAVALER, Rebecca. American, b. 1933. Novels/Short stories. *Publs:* Further Adventures of Brunhild (short stories), 1978; Doubting Castle (novel), 1984; Tigers in the Wood (short stories), 1986. Add: 425 Riverside Dr., New York, N.Y. 10025, U.S.A.

KAVANAGH, Dan. *See* **BARNES**, Julian.

KAVANAGH, P(atrick) J(oseph). British, b. 1931. Novels/Short stories, Children's fiction, Screenplays, Poetry, Autobiography/memoirs/Personal. Former Lectr., Univ. of Indonesia, Djarkarta. *Publs:* One and One: Poems, 1959; The Perfect Stranger (autobiography), 1966; On the Way to the Depot (verse), 1967; A Song and Dance (novel),

1968; About Time (verse), 1970; A Happy Man (novel), 1972; Edward Thomas in Heaven (verse), 1974; Scarf Jack (juvenile), 1978; People and Weather (novel), 1978; Life Before Death (verse), 1979; The Irish Captain (juvenile), 1979, in U.K. as Rebel for Good, 1980; Selected Poems, 1982; (ed.) Collected Poems of Ivor Gurney, 1982; (ed. with James Michie) The Oxford Book of Short Poems, 1984; (ed.) The Essential G.K. Chesterton, 1985; Only By Mistake (novel), 1986; Presences (verse), 1987; Peoples and Places (essays), 1988. Add: c/o Chatto & Windus Ltd., 40-42 William IV St., London WC2N 4DF, England.

KAVANAGH, Paul. *See* **BLOCK,** Lawrence.

KAVANAUGH, Cynthia. *See* **DANIELS,** Dorothy.

KAVANAUGH, Ian. *See* **WEBB,** Jean Francis.

KAVANAUGH, James. American, b. 1932. Poetry, Children's non-fiction, Theology/religion. *Publs:* Man in Search of God, 1966; A Modern Priest Looks at His Outdated Church, 1967; The Birth of God, 1968; There Are Men Too Gentle to Live Among Wolves (poetry), 1969; Will You Be My Friend (poetry), 1970; Crooked Angel (children's poetry), 1971; (with E. Shostrom) Between Men and Women, 1972; Celebrate the Sun, 1973; Faces in the City (poetry), 1974; Sunshine Days and Foggy Nights (poetry), 1975; Winter Has Lasted Too Long (poetry), 1977; Walk Easy on the Earth, 1979; A Fable, 1980; Maybe If I Loved You More, 1982; Laughing Down Lonely Caverns, 1984; Search, 1985; The Celibates, 1986; From Loneliness to Love, 1986; Outrageous, 1988. Add: c/o E.P. Dutton, 2 Park Ave., New York, N.Y. 10016, U.S.A.

KAVENAGH, W. Keith. American, b. 1926. History. Lawyer, New York State, since 1978. Asst. Prof. of History, Dowling Coll., Oakdale, N.Y., 1960–66; Documents Collector and Lectr., 1966–71, and Asst. Prof. of History, 1971–74, State Univ. of New York at Stony Brook. *Publs:* Foundations of Colonial America, 3 vols., 1973; Vanishing Tide Lands: Land Use and the Law in Suffolk County, New York, 1640-Present, 1980. Add: 215 South Gillette Ave., Bayport, N.Y. 11705, U.S.A.

KAVIC, Lorne John. Canadian, b. 1936. International Relations/Current Affairs. Pres., Coquitlam College, since 1982; Pres., Pacific Basin Educational Service Inc., since 1980. Pres., Pacific Basin Educational Services (Australia) PL since 1988. Principal, U.S.-Canada Cakuen, since 1988. Instr. in History, Political Science, and Economics, 1966–78, and Principal, 1978–82, Columbia Coll., Vancouver. Visiting Lectr. in Political Science, 1970–71, Visiting Assoc. Prof., 1971–72, and Sessional Lectr., 1972–73, Univ. of British Columbia, Vancouver. *Publs:* India's Quest for Security: Defence Policies 1947–1965, 1967; (co-author) The 1200 Days: A Shattered Dream—Dave Barrett and the N.D.P. in B.C. 1972–75, 1978; (co-ed. and contrib.) Canada and Southeast Asia: Perspectives and Evolution of Public Policies, 1981. Add: 1340 Willow Way, Coquitlam, B.C., V3J 5M3, Canada.

KAWIN, Bruce F. American, b. 1945. Poetry, Film, Literature. Prof. of English and Film, Univ. of Colorado, Boulder, since 1975. Teacher of Comparative Religion, Emanuel Temple Center, Beverly Hills, Calif., 1960–63; Prof. and Anchorman, Literary Workshop, WKCR-FM, NYC, 1964–66; Ed., Columbia Review, NYC, 1966–67; Teaching Fellow, Cornell Univ., Ithaca, N.Y., 1967–70; Part-time Instr., 1969–70, Asst. Prof. of English and Dir. of Film Prog., 1970–73, Dir., Creative Writing Prog. 1971–73, Wells Coll., Aurora, N.Y.; Lectr. in English and Film, Univ. of California at Riverside, 1973–75; Specialist in Film Analysis, Center for Advanced Film Studies, AFI, Beverly Hills, CA, 1974. *Publs:* Slides (poetry), 1970; Telling It Again and Again: Repetition in Literature and Film, 1972; Faulkner and Film, 1977; Mindscreen: Bergman, Godard, and First-Person Film, 1978; To Have and Have Not, 1980; The Mind of the Novel: Reflexive Fiction and the Ineffable, 1982; Faulkner's MGM Screenplays, 1982; How Movies Work, 1987. Add: 915 15th St., Boulder, Colo. 80302, U.S.A.

KAY, Geoffrey. British, b. 1938. Economics, History. Lectr. in Economics, City Univ., London, since 1966. Research Asst., Agricultural Economics Research Inst., Univ. of Oxford, 1960–61; Lectr. in Economics, Univ. of Leeds, 1961–62, and Univ. of Ghana, 1962–65. *Publs:* (ed. with Stephen Hymer) The Political Economy of Colonialism in Ghana, 1972; Development and Underdevelopment: A Marxist Analysis, 1975; The Economic Theory of the Working Class, 1979; (with James Mott) Political Order and the Law of Labor, 1983. Add: Dept. of Social Science, The City Univ., St. Johns St., London EC1V 4PB, England.

KAY, George. British, b. 1936. Geography. Prof. and Head of Geography and Recreation Studies, Staffordshire Polytechnic, Stoke-on-Trent, since 1976. Research Officer, Rhodes-Livingstone Inst., Zambia, 1959–62; Leverhulme Fellow in Commonwealth Studies and Lectr. in Geography, Univ. of Hill, 1962–68; Prof. of Geography, Univ. of Zimbabwe, 1968–74. *Publs:* A Social Geography of Zambia, 1967; Rhodesia: A Human Geography, 1970; (with M. Smout) Salisbury: A Geographical Survey of the Capital of Rhodesia. Add: Dept. of Geography and Recreation Studies, Staffordshire Polytechnic, Stoke-on-Trent ST4 2DF, England.

KAY, Mara. American. Children's fiction. Formerly Sr. Copywriter, Montgomery Ward, NYC. *Publs:* In Place of Katia, 1963; The Burning Candle, 1966; Masha, 1968; The Youngest Lady-in-Waiting; A Circling Star, 1973; Storm Warning, 1976; In Face of Danger, 1977; Restless Shadows, 1980; Lolo, 1981; One Small Clue, 1982. Add: 2 Lent Ave., Hempstead, N.Y. 11550, U.S.A.

KAY, Robin Langford. New Zealander, b. 1919. History. Research Officer, Historical Publs. Branch, Dept. of Internal Affairs, Wellington, since 1966 (Research Officer, War History Branch, 1947–66, Historical Publs. Branch, 1966–77; Historian, 1977–79). Asst. Archivist, Army Headquarters, Wellington, 1944–47. *Publs:* Long Range Desert Group in Libya 1940–41, 1949; Long Range Desert Group in the Mediterranean, 1950; (co-author) The Other Side of the Hill, 1952; 27 Machine Gun Battalion, 1958; Italy, Vol. II, From Cassino to Trieste, 1967; Chronology: New Zealand in the War 1939–1946, 1968; (ed.) The Australian-New Zealand Agreement 1944, 1972; (ed.) The Surrender and Occupation of Japan, 1982; (co-author) Portrait of a Century, The History of the New Zealand Academy of Fine Arts 1882-1982, 1983; (ed.) The ANZUS Pact and the Treaty of Peace with Japan, 1985. Add: Kerehoma, Muri Rd., Pukerua Bay, Wellington, New Zealand.

KAYE, Barrington. Also writes as Tom Kaye and Henry Cooper. British, b. 1924. Novels/Short stories, Poetry, Education, Sociology. Prof. of Education, Univ. of the S. Pacific, Fiji, since 1983 (Reader, 1980–83). Lectr. in Education, 1951–54, and Social Research Fellow, 1955–56, Univ. of Malaya; Sr. Lectr. in Education, Univ. of the Gold Coast (now Univ. of Ghana), 1956–62; Head, Dept. of Education, Redland Coll., Bristol, 1962–72; Chief Technical Adviser, Unesco, Paris, 1972–75; Head, Dept. of Education Studies, Bristol Polytechnic, 1975–80. *Publs:* The Song of my Beloved and Other Poems, 1951; (as Tom Kaye) It Had Been a Mild, Delicate Night (novel), 1957; Bugis Street Blues (poetry), 1960; The Development of the Architectural Profession in Britain, 1960; Upper Nankin Street, Singapore, 1960; (as Tom Kaye) David, From Where He Was Lying (novel), 1962; Bringing Up Children in Ghana, 1962; (with I. Rogers) Group Work in Secondary Schools, 1968; Participation in Learning, 1970; Tom Kaye's Love Poems, 1983; (as Henry Cooper) Upcountry (novel), 1985; Tom Kaye's Other Love Poems, 1988. Add: Dept. of Education, University of the South Pacific, P.O. Box 1168, Suva, Fiji.

KAYE, Geraldine. British, b. 1925. Children's fiction. *Publs:* Obodai and the Tomatoes, 1959; Kwaku and the Bush Baby, 1961; Kwaku Goes Shopping, 1971; Kwasi and the Parrot, 1961; Susie and Sophie, 1961; The Creek near Kwami's Village, 1961; Nii-Ofrong and his Garden, 1961; Kwabena and the Leopard, 1961; Yaa Goes South, 1961; Annan and the Grass Village, 1965; Chik and the Bottle-House, 1965; Tail of the Siamese Cat. 1965; Jin-Bee Leaves Home, 1966; Hamid and the Fisherman, 1966; Ian Gets a Job, 1966; The Sea Monkey; The Blue Rabbit, 1967; Koto and the Lagoon, 1967; Tawno, Gypsy Boy, 1968; Bonfire Night, 1969; Eight Days to Christmas, 1970; Nowhere to Go, 1971; Runaway Boy, 1971; In the Park, 1971; Rainbow Shirt, 1971; Nowhere to Stop, 1972; Kassim Goes Fishing, 1972; The Ginger One, 1972; To Catch a Thief, 1973; The London Adventure, 1973; Kofi and the Eagle, 1973; Marie Alone, 1973; The Rotten Old Car, 1973; Tim and the Red Indian Head-dress, 1973; The Raffle Pony, 1974; Pegs and Flowers, 1974; The Yellow Pom-Pom Hat, 1974; Goodbye, Ruby Red, 1974; Joanna All Alone, 1974; Billy-Boy, 1974; Children of the Turnpike, 1975; A Different Sort of Christmas, 1976; Penny Black, 1977; Joey's Room, 1978; Week Out, 1979; King of the Knockdown Gingers, 1979; The Beautiful Take-Away Palace, 1980; The Day after Yesterday, 1981; The Plum Tree Party, 1982; The Sky-Blue Dragon, 1983; The Donkey Strike, 1984; Comfort Herself, 1984; The Biggest Bonfire in the World, 1985; The Call of the Wild Wood, 1986; The School Pool Gang, 1986; A Breath of Fresh Air, 1987; The Rabbit Minders, 1987; The Donkey Christmas, 1988; Great Comfort, 1988. Add: 39 High Kingsdown, Bristol BS2 8EW, England.

KAYE, Marvin. American, b. 1938. Novels/Short stories, Plays/-Screenplays, Recreation/Leisure/Hobbies. New York Corresp, GRIT newspaper, since 1970 (Reporter, 1963–65). Sr. Ed., Toys Mag., 1966–70. *Publs:* The Histrionic Holmes, 1971; A Lively Game of Death, 1972; A Toy Is Born, 1973; The Stein & Day Handbook of Magic, 1973; The Grand Ole Opry Murders, 1974; Bertrand Russell's Guided Tour of Intellectual Rubbish (drama), 1974; (ed. and contrib.) Fiends and Creatures, 1974; (ed. and contrib.) Brother Theodore's Chamber of Horrors, 1974; The Handbook of Mental Magic, 1975; Bullets for Macbeth, 1976; Catalog of Magic, 1977; My Son, the Druggist, 1977; The Laurel and Hardy Murders, 1978; (with P. Godwin) The Masters of Solitude, 1978; The Incredible Umbrella, 1979; My Brother, the Druggist, 1979; Avon Calling (drama), 1980; The Possession of Immanual Wolf and Other Improbable Tales, 1981; The Amorous Umbrella, 1981; (with P. Godwin) Wintermind, 1981; (ed. and contrib.) Ghosts, 1981; The Soap Opera Slaughters, 1982; (with P. Godwin) Cold Blue Light, 1983; (ed.) Masterpieces of Terror and the Supernatural, 1985; Ghosts of Night and Morning, 1987; (ed.) Devils and Demons, 1987; (ed.) Weird Tales, the Magazine that Never Dies. Add: c/o William Morris Agency, 1350 Ave. of the Americas, New York, NY 10019, U.S.A.

KAYE, M(ary) M(argaret). British, b. 1908. Novels/Short stories, Mystery/Crime/Suspense. *Publs:* Six Bars at Seven, 1940; Death Walks in Kashmir, 1955, as Death in Kashmir, 1984; Death Walks in Berlin, 1955; Death walks in Cyprus, 1956, as Death in Cypress, 1984; Shadow of the Moon, 1957, rev. ed. 1979; Later Than You Think, 1958, as Death in Kenya, 1983; House of Shade, 1959, as Death in Zanzibar, 1983; Night on the Island, 1960, as Death in the Andamans, 1985; Trade Wind, 1963, rev. ed. 1981; The Far Pavilions, 1978; The Ordinary Princess (for children), 1980; (ed.) The Golden Calm, 1980; Thistledown (for children), 1981; (ed.) Moon of Other Days: M.M. Kaye's Kipling, Favourite Verses, 1988. Add: David Higham Assocs. Ltd., 5-8 Lower John St., Golden Square, London W1R 4HA, England.

KAYE, Tom. *See* **KAYE,** Barrington.

KAZAN, Elia. American, b. 1909. Novels/Short stories. Film Dir. and Producer. *Publs:* America America, 1962; The Arrangement, 1967; The Assassins, 1972; The Understudy, 1974; Acts of Love, 1978; The Anatolian, 1982; Elia Kazan: A Life, 1988. Add: c/o Alfred Knopf, 201 E. 50th Street, New York, N.Y. 10022, U.S.A.

KAZEMZADEH, Firuz. American, b. 1924. International relations/Current affairs. Prof. of History since 1967, Yale Univ., New Haven, Conn. (Instr., 1956–57; Asst. Prof., 1957–61; Assoc. Prof., 1961–67; Master of Davenport Coll., 1976–81). Ed., World Order, Baha'i mag., since 1966. *Publs:* The Struggle for Transcaucasia, 1917–1921, 1951; Russia and Britain in Persia, 1864-1914: A Study in Imperialism, 1968. Add: Dept. of History, Hall of Grad. Studies, Yale Univ., New Haven, Conn. 06520, U.S.A.

KAZIN, Alfred. American, b. 1915. Literature, Autobiography/Memoirs/Personal. Tutor in Literature, City Coll. of New York, 1937–42; Literary Ed., 1942–43, and Contributing Ed., 1943–45, The New Republic, NYC; Conributing Ed., Fortune, NYC, 1943–44; Lectr., Black Mountain Coll., North Carolina, 1944; Visiting Prof., Univ. of Minnesota, Minneapolis, 1946, 1950; Fulbright Lectr., Cambridge Univ., 1952; Lectr., Harvard Univ., Cambridge, Mass., 1953; William Allan Neilson Research Prof., Smith Coll., Northampton, Mass., 1954–55; Prof. of American Studies, Amherst Coll., Massachusetts, 1955–58; Berg Prof. of Literature, City Coll. of New York, 1957; Visiting Prof., Univ. of Puerto Rico, Rio Piedras, 1959; Christian Gauss Lectr., Princeton Univ., New Jersey, 1961; Buell Gallagher Prof., City Coll. of New York, 1962; Beckman Prof., Univ. of California, Berkeley, 1963; White Prof. of English, Univ. of Notre Dame, Ind., 1978–79; Distinguished Prof. of English, City Univ. of New York, 1973–85. *Publs:* On Native Grounds: An Interpretation of Modern American Prose Literature, 1942; (ed.) The Portable Blake (in U.K. as the Essential Blake), 1948; (ed.) F. Scott Fitzgerald: The Man and His Work, 1951; A Walker in the City (autobiography), 1951; (ed. with Charles Shapiro) The Stature of Theodore Dreiser: A Critical Study of the Man and His Work, 1955; The Inmost Leaf: A Selection of Essays, 1955; (ed.) Moby Dick, by Herman Melville, 1956; (ed. with Ann Birstein) The Works of Anne Frank, 1959; (ed. with Daniel Aaron) Emerson: A Modern Antholoy, 1959; (ed.) Sister Carrie, by Theodore Dreiser, 1960; (ed.) The Financier, by Theodore Dreiser, 1961; (ed.) The Open Form: Essays for Our Time, 1961; Contemporaries, 1962; Starting Out in the Thirties (autobiography), 1965; (ed.) Selected Short Stories, by Nathaniel Hawthorne, 1966; (ed.) Writers at Work: The Paris Review Interviews, Third Series,1967; (ed.) The Ambassadors, by Henry James, 1969; Bright Book of Life: American Novelists and Storytellers from Hemingway to Mailer, 1973; New York Jew, 1978; An American Proces-

sion, 1984; A Writer's America, 1988; (with David Final) Our New York, 1989. Add: English Dept., City Univ. Grad. Center, 33 W. 42nd St., New York, N.Y. 10036, U.S.A.

KEALEY, Edward J. American, b. 1936. History, Technology, Biography. Prof. of History, Coll. of the Holy Cross, Worcester, Mass., since 1973 (Asst. Prof., 1962–66; Advisor for Grad. Studies, 1964–69; Assoc. Prof., 1966–73; Chmn. of Dept., 1980–83). Lectr., Univ. of Massachusetts Labor Relations Research Center, Worcester, 1969–75. *Publs:* Roger of Salisbury, Viceroy of England, 1972; Medieval Medicus: A Social History of Anglo-Norman Medicine, 1981; Harvesting the Air: Windmill Pioneers in Twelfth Century England, 1987. Add: 5639 186th St., Fresh Meadows, N.Y. 11365, U.S.A.

KEANE, John B(rendan). Irish, b. 1928. Plays/Screenplays, Humour/Satire. Currently, pub owner and operator in Listowel, since 1955, and weekly columnist for the Limerick Leader and the Dublin Evening Herald, since 1973. Pres., Irish P.E.N., 1973–74. *Publs:* Sive, 1959; Sharon's Grave, 1960; The Highest House on the Mountain, 1961; Many Young Men of Twenty, 1961; The Street and Other Poems (verse), 1961; Hut 42, 1963; The Man from Clare, 1963; Strong Tea, 1963; The Year of the Hiker, 1964; Self-Portrait, 1964; The Field, 1965; The Rain at the End of the Summer, 1967; Letters of Successful T.D., 1967; Big Maggie, 1969; The Change in Mame Fadden, 1971; Moll, 1971; Letters of an Irish Parish Priest, 1972; Letters of an Irish Publican, 1973; Values, 1973; The Crazy Wall, 1973; The Gentle Art of Matchmaking, 1973; Letters of a Love-Hungry Farmer, 1974; Letters of a Matchmaker, 1975; Death Be Not Proud (stories), 1976; Letters of a Civic Guard, 1976; Is the Holy Ghost Really a Kerryman, 1976; The Good Thing (play), 1976; Letters of a Country Postman, 1977; Unlawful Sex and Other Testy Matters, 1977; The Buds of Ballybunion, 1979; Stories from a Kerry Fireside, 1980; The Chastitute, 1981; More Irish Short Stories, 1981; Letters of an Irish Minister of State, 1982; Man of the Triple Name, 1984; Owl Sandwiches, 1985; The Bodhrán Makers, (novel) 1986. Add: 37 William St., Listowel, Co. Kerry, Ireland.

KEARNS, Lionel (John). Canadian, b. 1937. Poetry. Consultant in educational technology. *Publs:* Songs of Circumstance, 1963; Listen George, 1965; Pointing, 1967; By the Light of the Silvery McLune: Media Parables, Poems, Signs, Gestures, and Other Assults on the Interface, 1969; About Time, 1974; The Birth of God (film poem), 1974; Negotiating a New Canadian Constitution (film poem), 1975; Poems for a Manitoulin Canada Day, 1976; Practicing Up to Be Human, 1978; Ignoring the Bomb: Poems New and Selected, 1982; Convergences, 1984; Universe, and Other Poems for the Screen, 1988. Add: 1616 Charles St., Vancouver, B.C. V5L 2T3, Canada.

KEATING, Bern. American, b. 1915. Children's non-fiction, History. *Publs:* The Mosquito Fleet, 1963; The Grand Banks, 1968; Alaska!, 1969; Famous American Explorers: Northwest Passage, 1970; Mighty Mississippi, 1971; Florida, 1972; Gulf of Mexico, 1973; Famous American Cowboys, 1977; The Flamboyant Mr. Colt and His Deadly Six- Shooter, 1978; Mississippi, 1984; Legend of the Delta Queen, 1986. Add: 141 Bayou Rd., Greenville, Miss, 38701, U.S.A.

KEATING, H(enry) R(eymond) F(itzwalter). British, b. 1926. Novels/Short stories, Mystery/Crime/Suspense, Literature, Writing. Sub-Ed., Daily Telegraph, London, 1956–58, and The Times, London, 1958–60. Chmn., Crime Writers Assn., London, 1970–71; Chmn., Soc. of Authors, 1983–84; Pres., Detection Club. 1986. *Publs:* Death and the Visiting Firemen, 1959; Zen There Was Murder, 1960; A Rush on the Ultimate, 1961; The Dog It Was That Died, 1962; Death of a Fat God, 1963; The Perfect Murder, 1964; Is Skin-Deep, Is Fatal, 1965; Inspector Ghote series, 11 vols., 1966–81; The Strong Man, 1971; (ed. and contrib.) Blood on My Mind, 1972; The Underside, 1974; A Remarkable Case of Burglary, 1975; Murder Must Appetize, 1975; (ed.) Agatha Christie: First Lady of Crime, 1977; A Long Walk to Wimbledon, 1978; (ed.) Crime Writers, 1978; The World of Sherlock Holmes, 1979; The Murder of the Maharajah, 1980; The Marks and Spencer Book of Great Crimes, 1982; (ed.) Whodunit, 1982; The Lucky Alphonse, 1982; The Sheriff of Bombay, 1984; Mrs. Craggs, Crimes Cleaned Up, 1985; Under A Monsoon Cloud, 1986; Writing Crime Fiction, 1986; The Body in the Billiard Room, 1987; Dead on Time. 1988. Add: 35 Northumberland Pl., London W2 5AS, England.

KEATING, L(ouis) Clark. American, b. 1907. Language/Linguistics, Literature, Translations. Chmn., Dept. of Romance Languages, George Washington Univ., Washington, D.C., 1946–57, and Univ. of Cincinnati, Ohio, 1957–60; Prof. of French, Univ. of Kentucky, Lexington, 1962–74;

Publs: Studies on the Literary Salon in France, 1550-1615, 1941; (with C.C. Gullette and C.P. Viens) Teaching a Modern Language, 1942; (ed. with J. Flores) El Gaucho y la Pampa, 1943; (with H.V. Besso) Conversational French for Army Air Forces, 1944; (with R.L. Grismer) Spanish Conversation for Beginners, 1946; (with C.. Choquette) Short Review of French Grammar, 1948; (with C.D. Eldridge) Souvenirs de la France, 1949; (ed. with J. Swain) Mauriac's Les Chemins de la mer, 1953; (with W.O. Clubb) Journal parisien, 1955; (with M.I. Moraud) Audubon-Lafayette-Lafitte-Les Dupont, 1958–59; Carnet de Voyage, 1959; (with M.I. Moraud) Moliere-Voltaire-Hugo, 1961–69; Critic of Civilization: Georges Duhamel, 1965; Tierra de los Incas, 1966; (trans.) Extirpation of Idolatry in Peru, 1968; (trans. with R.O. Evans) Borges: Introduction to American Literature, 1971; (co-ed.) Impressions d'Amerique, 1971; Joachim du Bellay, 1971; Etienne Pasquier, 1972; (ed. with M.I. Moraud) Selections de Moliere-Voltaire-Hugo, 1972; (trans. with R.O. Evans) Borges: Introduction to English Literature, 1974; Audubon: The Kentucky Years, 1976; (with J.E. Keller) The Book of Count Patronio, 1977. Add: 608 Raintree Rd., Lexington, Ky. 40502, U.S.A.

KEAY, John. British, b. 1941. Travel/Exploration/Adventure. *Publs:* Into India, 1973; When Men and Mountains Meet, 1977; The Gilgit Game, 1979; India Discovered, 1981; Eccentric Travellers, 1982; Highland Drove, 1984; Explorers Extraordinary, 1985. Add: Succoth, Dalmally, Argyll, Scotland.

KEDOURIE, Elie. British, b. 1926. History, Politics/Government. Prof. of Politics, London Univ., since 1965 (Reader, 1961–65). Ed., Middle Eastern Studies, since 1964. Lectr. in Politics Science, London School of Economics, 1953–61. *Publs:* England and the Middle East, 1956; Nationalism, 1960; Afghani and Abduh, 1966; The Chatham House Version, 1970; Nationalism in Asia and Africa, 1971; Arabic Political Memoirs, 1974; In the Anglo-Arab Labyrinth, 1976; (ed.) The Middle Eastern Economy, 1978; (ed.) The Jewish World, 1979; (co-ed.) Towards a Modern Iran, 1980; (co-ed.) Modern Egypt, 1980; Islam in the Modern World, 1980; (co-ed.) Palestine and Israel in the Nineteenth and Twentieth Centuries, 1982; (co-ed.) Zionism and Arabism in Palestine and Israel, 1982; The Crossman Confessions, 1984; (co-ed) Essays in the Economic History of the Middle East, 1988; Diamonds into Glass, 1988. Add: London School of Economics, Houghton St., London WC2A 2AE, England.

KEDZIE, Daniel Peter. American, b. 1930. Money/Finance. Exec. Vice Pres., Mgmt. Progs. Inc., Glen Ellyn, Ill., since 1969. Asst. Prof. of Finance and Insurance, Marquette Univ., Milwaukee, Wisc, 1957–58; Vice Pres., CNA Financial Corp., Chicago, 1968–69; Co-Columnist, Best's Review, 1969–73. *Publs:* Consumer Credit Insurance, 1957; (consulting ed.) Property and Casualty Handbook, 1964; (co-author) Your Future in Insurance, 1965. Add: 200 E. Willow, No. 303A, Wheaton, Ill. 60187, U.S.A.

KEE, Robert. British, b. 1919. Novels/Short stories, History, Autobiography/Memoirs/Personal. Television and radio broadcaster in U.K. *Publs:* A Crowd is not Company, 1947; The Impossible Shore, 1949; A Sign of the Times, 1955; Broadstrop in Season, 1959; Refugee World, 1959; The Green Flag: A History of Irish Nationalism, 1972; Ireland: A History, 1980; The World We Left Behind, 1984; The World We Fought For, 1985; Trial and Error, 1986. Add: c/o Lloyds Bank, 112 Kensington High St., London W8, England.

KEEFFE, Barrie. British, b. 1945. Novels/Short stories, Plays/Screenplays. Member of the Council, National Youth Theatre, since 1977; Member of the Bd. of Dirs., Soho Poly Theatre, London, since 1978. Former Reporter for the Stratford Express, to 1969; Actor, Theatre Royal, Stratford, 1964; Resident Writer, National Youth Theatre, London (Thames TV Playwright scheme), 1977, and Royal Shakespeare Co., 1978. *Publs:* Gadabout (novel), 1969; Gimme Shelter: Gem, Gotcha, Getaway (trilogy), 1977; A Mad World, My Masters, 1977; Frozen Assets, 1978; Barbarians: A Trilogy: Killing Time, Abide with Me, In the City, 1978; Here Comes the Sun, 1978; Sus, 1979; Heaven Sent, 1980; Bastard Angel, 1980; The Long Good Friday (screenplay), 1981; No Excuses (novel), 1983; Better Times, 1985; King of England, 1988. Add: c/o Harvey Unna and Stephen Durbridge Ltd., 24 Pottery Lane, Holland Park, London W11 4LZ, England.

KEEGAN, John (Desmond Patrick). British, b. 1934. History, Military/Defence. Defence Ed., The Daily Telegraph, London, since 1986. Deputy Head of Dept. of War Studies, Royal Military Academy, Sandhurst 1960–86. *Publs:* The Face of Battle, 1976; (with Andrew Wheatcroft) Who's Who in Military History, 1976; (ed.) World Armies, 1979, 1982; Six Armies in Normandy, 1982; (with Andrew Wheatcroft)

Zones of Conflict, 1986; The Mask of Command, 1987; The Price of Admiralty, 1988. Add: c/o Cape, 32 Bedford Sq., London WC1B 3EL, England.

KEEGAN, Mary. Also writes as Mary Heathcott and Mary Raymond. British, b. 1914. Novels/Short stories. Has held editorial appointments with London Evening News, 1934–40, Straits Times and Singapore Free Press, 1940–42, MOI All-India Radio, 1944, Time and Tide, 1945, and John Herling's Labor Letter, 1951–54. *Publs:* If Today Be Sweet, 1956; Island of the Heart, 1957; Love Be Wary, 1958; Her Part of the House, 1960; Hide My Heart, 1961; Thief of My Heart, 1962; Never Doubt Me, 1963; Shadow of a Star, 1963; Take-Over, 1965; Girl in a Mask, 1965; The Divided House, 1966; The Long Journey Home, 1967; I Have Three Sons, 1968; That Summer, 1970; Surety for a Stranger, 1971; The Pimpernel Project, 1972; The Silver Girl, 1973; Villa of Flowers, 1976; April Promise, 1980; Grandma Tyson's Legacy, 1982. Add: Cockenskell, Blawith, Ulverston, Cumbria, England.

KEELEY, Edmund LeRoy. American, b. 1928. Novels/Short stories, Literature, Translations. Prof. of English, and Creative Writing, Princeton Univ., N.J. (joined faculty, 1954). Member, Exec. Cttee., PEN American Center, since 1981. Pres., Modern Greek Studies Assn., 1969–73, 1980–81; Vice-Pres., Poetry Soc. of America, 1977–78, 1981–82. *Publs:* The Libation, 1958; (trans. with P. Sherrard) Six Poets of Modern Greece, 1960; The Gold-Hatted Lover, 1961; (trans. with M. Keeley) The Plant, The Well, The Angel, by V. Vassilikos, 1964; (trans. with P. Sherrard) Four Greek Poets, 1966; (trans. with P. Sherrard) George Seferis: Collected Poems, 1967; The Imposter, 1970; (trans. with G. Savidis) C.P. Cavafy: Passions and Ancient Days, 1971; (ed. with P. Bein) Modern Greek Writers, 1972; Voyage to a Dark Island, 1972; (trans. with P. Sherrard) C.P. Cavafy: Selected Poems, 1972; (trans. with G. Savidis) Odysseus Elytis: The Axion Esti, 1974; (trans. with P. Sherrard) C.P. Cavafy: Collected Poems, 1975; Cavafy's Alexandria, 1976; Ritsos in Parentheses, 1979; (trans. with P. Sherrard) Angelos Sikelianos: Selected Poems, 1979; (ed. with P. Sherrard) Odysseus Elytis: Selected Poems, 1981; (trans. with P. Sherrard) The Dark Crystal: Voices of Modern Greece, 1982; Modern Greek Poetry: Voice and Myth, 1983; A Wilderness Called Peace, 1985; Yannis Ritsos: Exile and Return, Selected Poems 1967–1974, 1985; (co-ed.) The Legacy of R.P. Blackmur: Essays, Memoirs, Texts, 1987; The Salonika Bay Murder: Cold War Politics and the Polk Affair, 1989. Add: 185 Nassau St., Princeton, N.J. 08544, U.S.A.

KEEN, Ernest. American, b. 1937. Psychology. Prof., Bucknell Univ., Lewisburg, since 1974 (Asst. Prof., 1964–69; Assoc. Prof., 1969–74). *Publs:* Three Faces of Being: Toward an Existential Clinical Psychology, 1970; Psychology and the New Consciousness, 1972; Primer in Phenomenological Psychology, 1975; Emotion, 1977. Add: Dept. of Psychology, Bucknell Univ., Lewisburg, Pa., U.S.A.

KEEN, Martin Léon. American, b. 1913. Sciences. Former Sr. Science Ed., Collier's Encyclopedia. *Publs:* How and Why Wonder Book of the Human Body, 1961; How and Why Book of the Microscope, 1961; How and Why Book of Chemistry, 1961; How and Why Wonder Book of Wild Animals, 1962; How and Why Wonder Book of Science Experiments, 1962; How and Why Wonder Book of Sounds, 1962; How and Why Wonder Book of Prehistoric Mammals, 1962; How and Why Wonder Book of Magnets and Magnetism, 1963; The Wonders of the Human Body, 1966; The Wonders of Space: Rockets, Missiles, and Spacecraft, 1967; Let's Experiment, 1968; How and Why Wonder Book of Air and Water, 1969; How and Why Wonder Book of Electronics, 1969; Lightning and Thunder, 1969; Hunting Fossils, 1970; How It Works I, 1972; How It Works II, 1974; World at Our Feet: Soil, 1974; Be a Rockhound, 1979. Add: c/o Messner, 1230 Ave. of the Americas, New York, New York, N.Y. 10020, U.S.A.

KEENE, Donald. American, b. 1922. Area Studies, Literature, Translations. Shincho Prof. of Japanese, Columbia Univ., NYC; Guest Ed., Asahi Shimbun, Tokyo. Lectr., Cambridge Univ., 1948–53. Dir., Japan Soc., New York, 1979–82. *Publs:* The Battles of Coxinga, 1951; The Japanese Discovery of Europe, 1952, 1969; Japanese Literature: An Introduction for Western Readers, 1953; (ed.) Anthology of Japanese Literature, 1955; (ed.) Modern Japanese Literature, 1956; (trans.) The Setting Sun, 1956; Living Japan, 1957; (trans.) Five Modern No Plays, 1957; (trans.) No Longer Human, 1958; (ed.) Sources of Japanese Tradition, 1958; (trans.) Major Plays of Chikamatsu, 1961; (trans.) The Old Woman, the Wife and the Archer, 1961; (trans.) After the Banquet, 1965; Bunraku, the Puppet Theatre of Japan, 1965; No: The Classical Theatre of Japan, 1966; (trans.) Essays in Idleness, 1967; (trans.) Madame de Sade, 1967; (trans.) Friends, 1969; (ed.) Twenty Plays of the No Theatre, 1970;

Landscapes and Portraits, 1971; (trans.) The Man Who Turned into a Stick, 1972; Some Japanese Portraits, 1978; World Within Walls, 1978; Meeting with Japan, 1978; Travels in Japan, 1981; Dawn to the West, 1984; The Pleasures of Japanese Literature, 1988. Add: 407 Kent Hall, Columbia Univ., New York, N.Y. 10027, U.S.A.

KEENLEYSIDE, Hugh L(lewellyn). Canadian, b. 1898. Education. History, International relations/Current affairs. Consultant in economic and resource development problems, Victoria, B.C. Canadian Ambassador, Mexico, 1944–47; Deputy Minister, Mines and Resources, Ottawa, 1947–50; Dir.-Gen., U.N. Technical Assistance Admin., 1950–59; Chmn., B.C. Hydro and Power Authority, 1959–69; Chancellor, Notre Dame Univ. of Nelson, B.C., 1969–77. Hon. Chmn., National Cttee. for the U.N. Conference on Human Settlements, 1974–76. *Publs:* Canada and the United States, 1929, 1952; (with A.F. Thomas) History of Japanese Education, 1937; International Aid, 1966; Memoirs; Hammer the Golden Day (Vol. I), On the Bridge of Time (Vol. II). Add: 3470 Mayfair Dr., Victoria, B.C. V8P 1PG, Canada.

KEESING, Nancy (Florence). Australian, b. 1923. Children's fiction, Poetry, Literature. Vice-Pres., English Assn., Sydney; Member, Council of Kuring-Gai Coll. of Advanced Education; Council Member, Australian Soc. of Authors Ltd., since 1987; Ed., The Australian Author, 1971–73; Chmn., Literature Bd., Australia Council, 1974–77. *Publs:* Imminent Summer (verse), 1951; Three Men and Sydney (verse), 1955; (ed. with Douglas Stewart) Australian Bush Ballads, 1955; (ed. with Douglas Stewart) Old Bush Songs, 1957; By Gravel and Gum (children's novel), 1963; Elsie Carew: Australian Primitive Poet, 1965; Douglas Stewart, 1965, 1969; (ed. with Douglas Stewart) Pacific Book of Bush Ballads, 1967, as Bush Songs, Ballads and Other Verses, 1968, as Favourite Bush Ballads, 1977; (compiler) Gold Fever, 1967, as A History of the Australian Gold Rushes, 1976; Showground Sketchbook (verse), 1968; (compiler) Transition: An Australian Society of Authors Anthology, 1970; The Golden Dream (children's novel), 1974; Garden Island People (memoirs), 1975; (compiler) The Kelly Gang, 1975; (compiler) The White Chrysanthemum, 1977, as Dear Mum, 1985; Hails and Farewells (verse), 1977; (compiler) Henry Lawson: Favourite Verse, 1978; (compiler) Shalom: Australian Jewish Short Stories, 1978; John Lang and "The Forger's Wife" (biography), 1979; Lily on the Dustbin: Slang of Australian Women and Families, 1982; Just Look Out the Window, 1985. Add: c/o Australian Soc. of Authors, 24 Alfred St., Milson's Point, N.S.W. 2061, Australia.

KEESING, Roger M(artin). American, b. 1935. Anthropology/Ethnology. Prof. of Anthropology, Inst. of Advanced Studies, Australian National Univ., Canberra, since 1974. Assoc. Prof., and Acting Dir. of the Center for South Pacific Studies, Univ. of California at Santa Cruz, 1965–74. *Publs:* (with F.M. Keesing) New Perspectives in Cultural Anthropology, 1971; Kin Groups and Social Structure, 1975; Kwaio Dictionary, 1975; Cultural Anthropology: A Contemporary Perspective, 1976; (ed. and trans.) Elota's Story: The Life and Times of a Solomon Islands Big Man, 1978; (with Peter Corris) Lightning Meets the West Wind: The Maaita Massacre, 1980; Kwaio Religion:The Living and the Dead in a Solomon Island Society, 1982; Kwaio Grammar, 1985; Melanesian Pidgin and the Oceanic Substrate, 1988. Add: Dept. of Anthropology, RSPACS, Australian National Univ., Box 4, Canberra, A.C.T. 2600, Australia.

KEETON, George Williams. British, b. 1902. History, International relations/Current affairs, Law. Pres., London Inst. of World Affairs, since 1938. Reader in Law and Politics, Hong Kong Univ., 1924–27; Sr. Lectr. in Law, Univ. of Manchester, 1928–31; Reader in English Law, 1931–37, Prof. of English Law, 1937–69, Dean of the Faculty of Laws, 1939–54, and Vice-Provost, 1966–69, Univ. Coll., Univ. of London; Prof. of Law, Brunel Univ., Uxbridge, Middx., 1969–76. *Publs:* The Development of Extraterritoriality in China, 1928; (with R. Eastwood) The Austinian Theories of Law and Sovereignty, 1929; Elementary Principles of Jurisprudence, 1930; 1939; Shakespeare and His Legal Problems, 1930; The Problem of the Moscow Trial, 1933; The Law of Trusts, 1934, 9th ed. 1967; An Introduction to Equity, 1938, 5th ed., 1960; The Speedy Return, 1938; National Sovereignty and International Order, 1939; (with G. Schwarzenberger) Making International Law Work, 1939, 1946; Mutiny in the Caribbean, 1940; The Case for an International University, 1941; (with R. Schlesinger) Russia and her Western Neighbours, 1942; China, The Far East, and the Future, 1942; 1949; A Liberal Attorney General, 1949; The Passing of Parliament, 1952; Social Change in the Law of Trusts, 1958: Case Book of Equity and Trusts, 1958; Trial for Treason, 1959; Trial by Tribunal, 1960; Guilty But Insane, 1961; The Modern Law of Charities, 1962, 1983; The Investment and Taxation of Trust Funds, 1964; Lord Chancellor Jeffreys, 1964; The Norman Conquest

and the Common Law, 1966; Shakespeare's Legal and Political Background, 1967; Government in Action, 1970; Modern Developments in the Law of Trusts, 1971; The Football Revolution, 1972; English Law: The Judicial Contribution, 1974; (with L.A. Sheridan) The Comparative Law of Trusts, 1976; Harvey the Hasty, 1978. Add: Picts Close, Picts Lane, Princes Risborough, Bucks., England.

KEETON, Morris Teuton. American, b. 1917. Education, Philosophy. Exec. Dir., Council for the Advancement of Experimental Learning, since 1977 (Co-ed., CAEL Sourcebooks, 1978–83). Prof. of Philosophy and Religion, 1956–77, and Vice Pres. and Provost, 1972–77, Antioch Coll., Yellow Springs, Ohio. Pres., American Assn. for Higher Education, 1972–73. *Publs:* The Philosophy of Edmund Montgomery, 1950; Values Men Live By, 1960; Journey Through a Wall, 1964; (with H. Titus) Ethics for Today, 4th ed. 1966, 5th ed. 1973; (with C. Hilberry) Struggle and Promise: Future for Colleges, 1969; Models and Mavericks: A Profile of Private Liberal Arts Colleges, 1971; Shared Authority on Campus, 1971; (co-author and ed.) Experiential Learning: Rationale, Characteristics, Assessment, 1977; (co-author and ed.) Learning by Experience: Who, What, How?, 1978; (co-author and co-ed.) Defining and Assuring Quality in Experiential Education, 1980. Add: 10989 Swansfield Rd., Columbia, Md. 21044, U.S.A.

KEILLOR, Garrison (Edward). American, b. 1942. Fiction, Humor. With Minnesota Public Radio from 1968: began A Prairie Home Companion radio show, 1974, broadcast nationally from 1980. *Publs:* Happy to Be Here, 1983; Lake Wobegon Days: Recollection of a Small American Town, 1985; Leaving Home, 1987; We Are Still Married: Stories and Letters, 1989. Add: American Humor Inst., 80 Eighth Ave., No. 1216, New York, N.Y. 10011, U.S.A.

KEITH, Carlton. *See* **ROBERTSON**, Keith.

KEITH, David. *See* **STEEGMULLER**, Francis.

KEITH, Harold (Verne). American, b. 1903. Westerns/Adventure, Children's fiction, Sports/Physical education/Keeping fit. Elementary sch. teacher, Amorita, Okla., 1922–23; Sports Corresp., Daily Oklahoman, Oklahoma City, Tulsa World, Kansas City Star, and Omaha World-Herald, 1922–29; Asst. Grain Buyer, Red Star Milling Co., Hutchinson, Kans., 1929–30; Sports Publicity Dir., Univ. of Oklahoma, 1930–69. Pres., Coll. Sports Information Directors, 1964–65. *Publs:* Boys' Life of Will Rogers, 1937; Sports and Games, 1941; Oklahoma Kickoff (on football), 1958; Shotgun Shaw: A Baseball Story, 1949; A Pair of Captains, 1951; Rifles for Watie, 1957; Komantcia, 1965; Brief Garland, 1971; The Runt of Rogers School, 1971; Go, Red, Go!, 1972; The Bluejay Boarders, 1972; Susy's Scoundrel, 1974; The Obstinate Lane, 1977; Forty-seven Straight, 1984. Add: 2318 Ravenwood, Norman, Okla. 73071, U.S.A.

KEITH-LUCAS, Bryan. British, b. 1912. History, Politics/Government. Fellow, Nuffield Coll., Oxford, 1950–65; Chmn., National Assn. of Parish Councils, 1964–70; Prof. of Government, 1965–77, and Master of Darwin Coll., 1970–74, Univ. of Kent, Canterbury. *Publs:* (with S. Lloyd Jones and M.A.L. Cripps) Cripps on Compulsory Purchase of Land, 2 vols., 1950; The English Local Government Franchise, 1952; (co-author) F.W. Hirst, by his Friends, 1958; (co-author) What are the Problems of Parliamentary Government in West Africa?, 1958; (co-author) Africa: The Political Pattern, 1961; (ed.) The History of Local Government in England, 2nd ed. 1958, 3rd ed. 1970; (with P.G. Richards) A History of Local Government in the 20th Century, 1978; The Unreformed Local Government System, 1980; (co-author) Studies in Modern Kentish History, 1983; The Hansard Society: The First Forty Years, 1984; Parish Affairs: The Government of Kent under George III, 1986. Add: 7 Church St., Wye, Kent, England.

KELEN, Stephen. Australian (b. Hungarian), b. 1912. Novels/Short stories, Travel/Exploration/Adventure, Biography. Freelance journalist, 1929–42, 1949–60; Tokyo Chief, British Commonwealth Occupation News, 1948–49; Managing Ed., Goodyear Tyre and Rubber Co., Sydney, 1960–77; Pres., Intnl. P.E.N., Sydney Centre, 1975–85. *Publs:* Success at Table Tennis, 1936; I Was There, 1941; Jackals in the Jungle, 1942; Camp Happy, 1944; Heed McGlarity, 1945; Goshu, 1965; Uphill All the Way, 1974; I Remember Hiroshima, 1983. Add: 1 Sussex Rd., St. Ives, N.S.W., Australia 2075.

KELL, Joseph. *See* **BURGESS**, Anthony.

KELL, Richard (Alexander). Irish, b. 1927. Poetry. Asst. Librarian, Luton Public Library, Beds., 1954–56, and Brunel Coll. of Technology (now Brunel Univ.), Uxbridge, Middx., 1956–59; Asst. Lectr., 1960–65, and Lectr. in English, 1966–70, Isleworth Polytechnic, London; Sr. Lectr., Newcastle upon Tyne Polytechnic, 1970–83. *Publs:* (Poems), 1957; Control Tower, 1962; (with others) Six Irish Poets, 1962; Differences, 1969; Heartwood, 1978; Humours, 1978; The Broken Circle, 1981; In Praise of Warmth, 1987. Add: 18 Rectory Grove, Gosforth, Newcastle upon Tyne NE3 1AL, England.

KELLAWAY, George Percival. British, b. 1909. Education, Geography. Principal, Weymouth Coll. of Education, Dorset, 1947–50; Head, Dept. of Education, Fourah Bay Coll., Sierra Leone, 1950–56, and Nigerian Coll. of Arts, Science and Technology, 1956–63; Education Admin., Co. Borough of Wigan Education Cttee., Lancs., 1964–74. *Publs:* A Background of Physical Geography, 1945; Map Projections, 1946; Purposeful Education, 1958; Education for Living, 1967. Add: Brown Fold, Blackrod, Bolton BL6 5LN, Lancs., England.

KELLEHER, Victor (Michael Kitchener). Australian (b. British), b. 1939. Novels/Short Stories, Children's fiction. Assoc. Prof. of English, Univ. of New England, Armidale, New South Wales, 1984–87 (Sr. Lectr., 1976–84). Lectr. in English, Massey Univ., Palmerston North, New Zealand, 1973–76; Lectr., then Sr. Lectr., in English, Univ. of S. Africa, 1970–73; Jr. Lectr. in English, Univ. of Witwatersrand, 1969. *Publs:* Forbidden Paths of Thual (children's fiction), 1979; Voices from the River (novel), 1979; The Hunting of Shadroth (children's fiction), 1981; Master of the Grove (children's fiction), 1982; Africa and After (short stories), 1983, as The Traveller, 1987; Papio (children's fiction), 1984; The Beast of Heaven (novel), 1984; The Green Piper (children's fiction), 1984; Taronga (children's fiction), 1986; The Makers (children's fiction), 1987; EM's Story (novel), 1987; EM's Story (novel), 1988; Baily's Bones (children's fiction), 1988. Add: c/o Curtis Brown, P.O. Box 19, Paddington, N.S.W. 2021, Australia.

KELLETT, Arnold. British, b. 1926. Poetry, History, Language/Linguistics, Theology/Religion, Travel/Exploration/Adventure, Translations. Mayor of Knaresborough, 1979–80 and 1984–85; Former Head of Modern Languages Dept., King James's Sch., Knaresborough, N. Yorks. *Publs:* Isms and Ologies, 1965; (ed.) Maupassant: Contes du Surnaturel, 1969; (trans. and ed.) Tales of Supernatural Terror, 1972; The Knaresborough Story, 1972; Héros de France, 1973; Le Prisonnier en Pyjama, 1974; (trans. and ed.) The Diary of a Madman and Other Tales of Horror, 1975; French for Science Students, 1975; Basic French, 1977; Harrogate, 1978; The Queen's Church, 1978; Know Your Yorkshire, 1980; Countryside Walks in the Harrogate District, 1983; Knaresborough in Old Picture Postcards, 1984; Exploring Knaresborough, 1985; Kellett's Christmas (poetry), 1988. Add: 22 Aspin Oval, Knaresborough, N. Yorks., England.

KELLEY, Leo P(atrick). American, b. 1928. Novels/Short stories, Science fiction/Fantasy, Western/Adventure, Children's fiction. Freelance writer of short stories and novels, since 1969. *Publs:* The Counterfeits, 1967; Odyssey to Earthdeath, 1968; The Accidental Earth, 1968; Time Rogue, 1970; The Coins of Murph, 1971; Brother John (novelization of screenplay), 1971; Mindmix, 1972; Time: 110100, 1972, in U.K. as The Man from Maybe, 1974; (ed.) Themes in Science Fiction: A Journey into Wonder, 1972; (ed.) The Supernatural in Fiction, 1973; (ed.) Fantasy: The Literature of the Marvellous, 1974; Deadlocked! (novel), 1973; Mythmaster, 1973; The Earth Tripper, 1973; science fiction novels for children—The Time Trap, 1977; Backward in Time, 1979; Death Sentence, 1979; Earth Two, 1979; Prison Satellite, 1979; Sunworld, 1979; Worlds Apart, 1979; Dead Moon, 1979; King of the Stars, 1979; On the Red World, 1979; Night of Fire and Blood, 1979; Where No Sun Shines, 1979; Vacation in Space, 1979; Star Gold, 1979; Good-bye to Earth, 1979; Johnny Tall Dog, 1981; The Last Cowboy, 1988; western novels—Luke Sutton series, 8 vols., 1981–88; Cimarron series, 19 vols., 1983–86; Morgan, 1986; A Man Named Dundee, 1988; Thunder Gods' Gold, 1988. Add: 702 Lincoln Blvd., Long Beach, N.Y. 11561, U.S.A.

KELLEY, Robert (Lloyd). American, b. 1925. History. Prof. of History, Univ. of California, Santa Barbara, since 1955 (Asst. to Chancellor, 1960–62; Chmn., Academic Senate, 1973–75). Member, California Commn. for Teacher Preparation and Licensing, 1973–74. Guggenheim fellow, 1982–83. *Publs:* Gold vs. Grain: The Hydraulic Mining Controversy in California's Sacramento Valley, 1959; The Transatlantic Persuasion: The Liberal Democratic Mind in the Age of Gladstone, 1969; The Shaping of the American Past, 1975, 4th ed., 1986; (ed.) The Sounds of Controversy: Crucial Arguments in the American Past, 1975; The Cultural Pattern in American Politics: the First Century, 1979. Add: 2851 Vista Elevada, Santa Barbara, Calif. 93105, U.S.A.

KELLEY, William Melvin. American, b. 1937. Novels/Short stories, Science fiction/Fantasy. *Publs:* A Different Drummer, 1962; Dancers on the Shore (short stories), 1964; A Drop of Patience, 1965; Dem, 1967; Dunsfords Travels Everywhere, 1970. Add: c/o Doubleday, 666 Fifth Ave., New York, N.Y. 10103, U.S.A.

KELLING, Hans-Wilhelm. American, b. 1932. Literature. Prof. of Germanic Languages, since 1962 and Dir. of Foreign Language Housing and Summer Language Inst., since 1985, Brigham Young Univ., Provo, (Chmn. of Dept., 1977–84). Pres., German South Mission, Church of Jesus Christ of Latter-Day Saints, Munich, 1973–76. *Publs:* Deutsche Aufsatzhilfe, 1967; The Idolatry of Poetic Genius in German Goethe Criticism, 1970; Deutsch—Wie man's sagt und schreibt, 1972; Deutsche Kulturgeschichte, 1974. Add: 4084 JKHB, Brigham Young Univ., Provo, Utah 84602, U.S.A.

KELLNER, Bruce. American, b. 1930. Literature, Biography. Prof. of English, Millersville Univ., Pennsylvania, since 1969. Taught at Coe Coll., 1956–60, and Hartwick Coll., 1960–69. *Publs:* Carl Van Vechten and the Irreverent Decades, 1969; (ed.) Keep a-Inchin' Along: Selected Writings About Black Arts and Letters, 1979; (compiler) A Bibliography of the Work of Carl Van Vechten, 1980; Friends and Mentors: Richmond's Carl Van Vechten and Mark Lutz, 1980; (with others) American Literature: Second Supplement to the University of Minnesota Monographs, 1981; The Harlem Renaissance: A Historical Dictionary For the Era, 1984; Letters of Carl Van Vechten, 1987; A Gertrude Stein Companion: Content with the Example, 1988. Add: 514 N. School Lane, Lancaster, Pa. 17603, U.S.A.

KELLOGG, Steven. American, b. 1941. Children's fiction. *Publs:* The Wicked Kings of Bloon, 1970; Can I Keep Him?, 1971; The Mystery Beast of Ostergeest, 1971; The Orchard Cat, 1972; Won't Somebody Play With Me?, 1972; The Island of the Skog, 1973; The Mystery of the Missing Red Mitten, 1974; There Was an Old Woman, 1974; Much Bigger than Martin, 1976; Steven Kellogg's Yankee Doodle, 1976; The Mysterious Tadpole, 1977; The Mystery of the Magic Green Ball, 1978; Pinkerton Behave, 1979; The Mystery of the Flying Orange Pumpkin, 1980; A Rose for Pinkerton, 1981; The Mystery of the Stolen Blue Paint, 1982; Tallyho Pinkerton, 1982; Ralph's Secret Weapon, 1983; Paul Bunyan, 1984; Chicken Little, 1985; Best Friends, 1986; Pecos Bill, 1986; Aster Aardvark's Alphabet Adventures, 1987; Prehistoric Pinkerton, 1987; Johnny Appleseed, 1988; If You Made a Million, 1989. Add: Bennett's Bridge Rd., Sandy Hook, Conn. 06482. U.S.A.

KELLOW, Kathleen. *See* **HOLT**, Victoria.

KELLY, Linda. British, b. 1936. Literature. Theatre. Biography, Travel Ed., Vogue mag., 1960–63. *Publs:* The Marvellous Boy: The Life and Myth of Thomas Chatterton, 1971; The Young Romantics: Paris 1827-1837, 1976; The Kemble Era: John Philip Kemble, Sarah Siddons and the London Stage, 1980; Women of the French Revolution, 1987; (ed. with Christopher Bland) Feasts, 1987; (with Laurence Kelly) Proposals, 1989. Add: 44 Ladbroke Grove, London W11 2PA, England.

KELLY, Louis Gerard. New Zealander/Canadian, b. 1935. Language/Linguistics, Literature, Translations. Prof. of Linguistics and Classics, Univ. of Ottawa, since 1978 (Asst. Prof. 1967–68; Assoc. Prof., 1969–78). Research Assoc., Royal Commn. on Bilingualism and Biculturalism 1965–67; former Lectr. in Phonetics and English, Univ. Laval, Quebec. *Publs:* Twenty-Five Centuries of Language Teaching, 1969; (ed.) Descriptions and Measurement of Bilingualism, 1969; The True Interpreter, 1979; Prorsus Taliter: The Latin Text of Kipling's Just-So Stories. Add: 308 Cherry Hinton Rd., Cambridge CB1 4AU, England.

KELLY, (Lady) Marie-Noële. British, b. 1907. Travel/Exploration/Adventure, Autobiography/Memoirs/Personal. Vice Pres., British Atlantic Cttee. *Publs:* Turkish Delights; Mirrors to Russia; Country Life Book of Russia; Portugal: This Delicious Land; Dawn to Dusk (memoirs). Add: 27 Carlyle St., London SW3, England.

KELLY, Mary (Theresa). British, b. 1927. Mystery/Crime/Suspense. *Publs:* A Cold Coming, 1956; Dead Man's Riddle, 1957; The Christmas Egg, 1958; The Spoilt Kill, 1961; Due to a Death, 1962 (in U.S. as The Dead of Summer, 1963); March to the Gallows, 1964; Dead Corse, 1966; Write on Both Sides of the Paper, 1969; The Twenty-Fifth Hour, 1971; That Girl in the Alley, 1974. Add: c/o Curtis Brown Ltd., 162-168 Regent St., London W1R 5TA, England.

KELLY, Maurice. Australian, b. 1919. Classics, History. Hon. Fellow, and Hon. Curator of the Museum of Antiquities, Univ. of New England, Armidale, since 1980 (Lectr., 1954–60; Sr. Lectr., 1960–65; Assoc. Prof., 1965–79). *Publs:* View From Olympus: A History of Greece, 1964, 1985; (ed.) For Service to Classical Studies: Essays in Honour of Francis Letters, 1966; View From the Forum: A History of Rome to AD410, 1969, 1989. Add: P.O. Box 25, Armidale, N.S.W., Australia 2350.

KELLY, Nora Hickson. Canadian, b. 1910. Criminology/Law enforcement. *Publs:* The Men of the Mounted: A History of the Royal Canadian Mounted Police, 1949; (with W. Kelly) The Royal Canadian Mounted Police: A Century of History, 1973; (with W. Kelly) Policing in Canada, 1976; (with W. Kelly) The Horses of the Royal Canadian Mounted Police: A Pictorial History, 1984. Add: 2079 Woodcrest Rd., Ottawa, Ont. K1H 6H9, Canada.

KELLY, Richard. American, b. 1937. Literature. Prof. of English, Univ. of Tennessee, Knoxville, since 1974 (Asst. Prof., 1965–74). Instr. in English, Univ. of North Carolina, Chapel Hill, 1964–65. Chmn.. of the 19-20th Century Section, 1976, and of the Advanced Composition Section, 1980, South Atlantic Modern Language Assn. *Publs:* (ed.) The Best of Mr. Punch: The Humorous Writings of Douglas Jerrold, 1970; Douglas Jerrold, 1972; Lewis Carroll, 1977; George du Maurier, 1982; (co-ed.) Cartoons from 19th Century Punch, 1982; The Story of "The Andy Griffith Show," 1982; Graham Greene, 1984; The Andy Griffith Show, revised and expanded, 1984; Daphne du Maurier, 1987. Add: Dept. of English, Univ. of Tennessee, Knoxville, Tenn. 37996, U.S.A.

KELLY, Robert. American, b. 1935. Novels/Short stories, Plays, Poetry. Co-Dir. of the Writing Program, Milton Avery Graduate School and Asher B. Edelman Prof. of Literature, Bard Coll., Annandale-on-Hudson, N.Y., (Instr. in German, 1961–62; Instr. in English, 1962–64; Asst. Prof., 1964–69; Assoc. Prof., 1969–74). Ed. Matter mag. and Matter publishing co., NYC, later Annandale-on-Hudson, N.Y., since 1963. Ed., Chelsea Review, NYC, 1958–60; Founding Ed., Trobar mag., 1960–64, and Trobar Books, 1962–64; Contrib. Ed., Caterpillar, NYC, 1969–73; Poet-in-Residence, California Inst. of Technology, 1971–72, Univ. of Kansas, Lawrence, 1975, and Dickinson Coll., Carlisle, Pa., 1976; Contrib. Ed., Sulfur mag., Los Angeles, 1980–81. *Publs:* Armed Descent, 1961; Her Body Against Time, 1963; Round Dances, 1964; Tabula, 1964; Enstasy, 1964; Matter/Fact/Sheet/1, 1964; Matter/Fact/Sheet/2, 1964; The Well Wherein a Deer's Head Bleeds (play), 1964; Lunes, 1964; Lectiones, 1965; (ed. with P. Leary) A Controversy of Poets: An Anthology of Contemporary American Poetry, 1965; Words in Service, 1966; Weeks, 1966; Songs XXIV, 1967; Twenty Poems, 1967; Devotions, 1967; Axon Dendron Tree, 1967; Crooked Bridge Love Society, 1967; A Joining: A Sequence for H.D., 1967; The Scorpions (novel), 1967, 1985; Alpha, 1968; Finding the Measure, 1968; Songs I-XXX, 1968; Sonnets, 1968; From the Common Shore, Book 5, 1968; Statement, 1968; We Are the Arbiters of Beast Desire, 1969; A California Journal, 1969; The Common Shore, Books I-V: A Long Poems about American in Time, 1969; Kali Yuga, 1970; In time (essays), 1971; Eros and Psyche (chamber opera), 1971; Cities (novels), 1971; Flesh: Dream: Book, 1971; Ralegh, 1972; The Pastorals, 1972; Reading Her Notes, 1972; Sulphur, 1972; The Tears of Edmund Burke, 1973; Whaler Frigate Clippership, 1973; The Mill of Particulars, 1973; A Line of Sight, 1974; The Loom, 1975; Sixteen Odes, 1976; The Lady of, 1977; The Convections, 1978; Wheres, 1978; The Book of Persephone, 1978; The Cruise of the Pnyx, 1978; Kill the Messenger Who Brings Bad News, 1979; Sentence, 1980; Spiritual Exercises, 1981; The Alchemist to Mercury, 1982; Russian Tales, 1982; Mulberry Women, 1982; Under Words, 1983; Thor's Thrush, 1984; A Transparent Tree (short stories), 1985; Not This Island Music (poetry), 1987; The Flowers of Unceasing Coincidence (long poem), 1988; Doctor of Silence (short stories), 1988; Oahu (travel notation poems), 1988. Add: Dept. of English, Bard Coll., Annandale-on-Hudson, N.Y. 12504, U.S.A.

KELLY, Thomas. British, b. 1909. Education, Librarianship. Dir. of Extension Studies, 1948–75, and Prof. of Adult Education, 1967–75, Liverpool Univ. Ed., Studies in Adult Education journal, 1969–74. *Publs:* History of King Edward VI Grammar School, Totnes, 1947; Griffith Jones, Llanddowror, 1950; Outside the Walls, 1950; (ed.) Select Bibliography of Adult Education in Great Britain, 1952, 3rd ed. 1974; (ed. with Edith Kelly) A Schoolmaster's Notebook, 1957; George Birkbeck, 1957; History of Adult Education in Great Britain, 1962, 1970; Early Public Libraries, 1966; History of Public Libraries in Great Britain, 1973, 1977; (ed.) European Bibliography of Adult Education, 1975; (with Edith Kelly) Books for the People, 1977; For Advancement of Learning (Centenary History of Liverpool Univ.), 1981. Add: Oak Leaf House,

Ambleside Rd., Keswick, Cumbria, CA12 4DL, England.

KELLY, Tim. Has also written as R.H. Bibolet. American, b. 1937. Novels/Short stories, Plays/Screenplays. *Publs:* Widow's Walk, 1963; Not Far from the Gioconda Tree, 1964; The Burning Man, 1963; Ride of Fury (novel), 1964; (adaptor) King of the Golden River, 1966; Bluebeard Had a Wife, 1967; How to Get Rid of a House-Mother, 1967; While Shakespeare Slept, 1967; (adaptor) Late Flowers, 1967; (adaptor) The Marvelous Playbill, 1967; Two Fools Who Gained a Measure of Wisdom, 1968; The Timid Dragon, 1968; The Natives Are Restless, 1969; The Eskimos Have Landed, 1969; If Sherlock Holmes Were a Woman, 1969; Up the Rent, 1970; The Silk Shirt, 1970; It's a Bird! It's a Plane! It's Chickenman, 1970; Last of Sherlock Holmes, 1970; Always Marry a Bachelor, 1970; Second Best Bed, 1970; (adaptor) The Deceitful Marriage, 1971; The Mouse and the Raven, 1971; Ladies of the Tower, 1971; West of Pecos, 1971; Alias Smedley Pewtree, 1971; Cry of the Banshee (screenplay), 1972; Merry Murders at Montmarie, 1972; The Keeping Place, 1972; The Witch Who Wouldn't Hang, 1972; Lemonade Joe Rides Again, 1972; No Opera at the Op'ry House Tonight, 1972; (as R.H. Bibolet) Barrel of Monkeys, 1973; W.C. Fieldworthy, 1973; (as R.H. Bibolet) Navajo House, 1973; The Brothers O'Toole (screenplay), 1973; The Remarkable Susan, 1973; (adaptor) M*A*S*H, 1973; The Yankee Doodle, 1973; The Gift and the Giving, 1973; Tap Dancing in Molasses, 1973; Seven Wives for Dracula, 1973; Memorial, 1974; (adaptor) Silent Snow, Secret Snow, 1974; Sugar Hill (screenplay), 1974; (adaptor) Frankenstein, 1974; Frankenstein Slept Here, 1974; Reunion on Gallows Hill, 1974; Monster Soup, 1974; Virtue Victorious, 1974; Our Indian Heritage, 1974; Bogard (screenplay), 1975; Get Fisk (screenplay), 1975; (adaptor) Egad, The Woman in White, 1975; Young Dracula, 1975; Sherlock Meets the Phantom, 1975; Happily Never After, 1975; Sherlock Holmes' First Case, 1976; (adaptor) The Canterville Ghost, 1976; Marsha, 1976; Bride of Frankenstein, 1976; (adaptor) Hawk-Shaw the Detective, 1976; (adaptor) Hound of the Baskervilles, 1976; Beau Johnny, 1976; The Cave, 1977; (adaptor from screenplay) Cry of the Banshee, 1977; (adaptor) Wonderful Wizard of Oz, 1977; Mark Twain in the Garden of Eden, 1977; (adaptor) Sherlock Holmes, 1977; (adaptor) The Invisible Man, 1977; Lizzie Borden of Fall River, 1977; Tale That Wagged the Dog, 1977; The Convertible Teacher, 1977; Country Gothic, 1977; (adaptor) Case of the Curious Moonstone, 1977; Jocko, 1977; Dirty Work in High Places, 1977; The Butler Did It, 1977; Crazy, Mixed-Up Island of Dr. Moreau, 1977; Loco-Motion, Commotion, Dr. Gorilla and Me, 1977; Saratoga, 1978; (adaptor) The Time Machine, 1978; It's Bigfoot, 1978; (adaptor) Alice's Adventures in Wonderland, 1978; The Marriage Proposal—Out West, 1978; Nashville Jamboree, 1978; Whatever This Is, We're All in It Together, 1978; (adaptor) Dracula, 1978; (adaptor) Sweeney Todd, 1978; Enter Pharoah Nussbaum, 1978; Great All-American Musical Disaster, 1978; Capt. Fantastic, 1978; Victoria at Eighteen, 1978; Captain Nemo and His Magical Marvellous Submarine Machine, 1979; Pecos Bill and Slue-Foot Sue Meet the Dirty Dan Gang, 1979; Toga, Toga, Toga, 1979; Fall of the House of Usher, 1979; The Soapy Murder Case, 1979; (adaptor) The Uninvited, 1979; Incredible Bulk, 1980; Lady Dracula, 1980; Krazy Kamp, 1980; The Frankensteins Are Back in Town, 1980; Murder in the Magnolias, 1980; Lantern in the Wind, 1980; A-Haunting We Will Go, 1980; Unidentified Flying High School, 1980; The Green Archer, 1980; Terror by Gaslight, 1981; Dark Deeds at Swan's Place, 1981; The Adventures of the Clouded Crystal, 1981; The Shame of Tombstone, 1981; Under Jekyll's Hyde, 1981; Airline, 1981; Toby Tyler, 1981; (adaptor) The Ratcatcher's Daughter, 1981; Nicholas Nickleby, 1981; (adaptor) Nicholas Nickleby, Schoolmaster, 1981; Lumberjacks and Wedding Belles (musical), 1981; The Lalapalooza Bird, 1981; Bloody Jack, 1981; (adaptor) The Adventure of the Speckled Band, 1981; Love is Murder, 1982; (adaptor) Tumbleweeds, 1982; Oliver Twisted, 1982; (adaptor) Mrs. Wiggs of the Cabbage Patch, 1982; Don't Rock the Boat, 1982; First on the Rope, 1982; (adaptor) Little Miss Christie, 1982; The Mystery of the Black Abbot, 1982; Horror High, 1982; Lucky Lucky Hudson, 1982; The 12th Street Gang, 1982; Charming Sally, 1982; Zorro's Back In Town, 1983; Hospital, 1983; The Clods of Hopper, 1983; (adaptor) Tom Sawyer 1983; Videomania, 1983; The Zombie, 1983; The Omelet Murder Case, 1983; What's News At The Zoo, 1983; (adaptor) Alice's Adventures in Wonderland, 1983; The Comedian, 1984; Murder Takes A Holiday, 1984; Beast of the Baskervilles, 1984; (adaptor) A Connecticut Yankee in King Arthur's Court, 1984; Squad Room, 1984; Never Trust a City Slicker, 1984; Laffing Room Only, 1984; How Santa Got His Christmas Tree, 1985; Destiny, 1985; Money, Power, Murder, Lust, Revenge, and Marvelous Clothes (musical), 1985; Murder By Natural Causes, 1985; Life On the Bowery, 1985; Great All-American Disaster Musical, 1985; The Secret of Skull Island, 1986; The Ghostchasers, 1986; Belle of Bisbee, 1986; The Butler Did It, Singing (musical), 1986; Murder Game, 1986; The Face on the Barroom Floor, 1986; The Dracula Kidds,

1986; Hurricane Smith and the Garden of the Golden Monkey, 1986; Hurricane Smith—The Musical, 1986; Tied to the Tracks, 1986; Slambo, 1986; The Woman in White (musical), 1987; Who Walks in the Dark, 1987; Dog Eat Dog, 1987; The 3 Musketeers (musical), 1987 Sherlock Holmes and the Giant Rat of Sumatra, 1987; (adaptor) Les Miserables, 1987; 18 Nervous Gumshoes, 1987; Incredible Day Christmas Disappeared from Evergreen Town, 1987; Time After Time (musical), 1987; It Was A Dark And Stormy Night, 1988; The Vampyre, 1988; Perils of Pumpernickle Pass, 1988; Help! I'm Trapped in a High School, 1988; Victor Hugo .... In Rehearsal, 1989; My Gypsy Robe, 1989; Robin Hood, 1989; Those Wedding Bells Shall Not Ring Out, 1989; Luncheonette of Terror, 1989; The Phantom of the Op'ry, 1989. Add: 8730 Lookout Mountain Ave., Hollywood, Calif. 90046, U.S.A.

KELMAN, Herbert Chanoch. American, b. 1927. International relations/Current affairs, Psychology. Richard Clarke Cabot Prof. of Social Ethics, Harvard Univ., Cambridge, Mass., since 1968 (Lectr. on Social Psychology, 1957–62). Research Psychologist, National Inst. of Mental Health, Bethesda, Md., 1955–57; Prof. of Psychology, and Research Psychologist, Center for Research on Conflict Resolution, Univ. of Michigan, 1962–69. Pres., Intnl. Soc. for Political Psychology, 1985–86. *Publs:* (ed. and contrib.) International Behavior: A Social Psychological Analysis, 1965; A Time to Speak: On Human Values and Social Research, 1968; (with R.S. Ezekiel) Cross-National Encounters, 1970; (ed. with G. Bermant and D.P. Warwick) The Ethics of Social Intervention, 1978; (with V.L. Hamilton) Crimes of Obedience: Toward a Social Psychology of Authority and Responsibility, 1989. Add: Dept. of Psychology, William James Hall, Harvard Univ., Cambridge, Mass. 02138, U.S.A.

KELSEY, Morton T(rippe). American, b. 1917. Theology/Religion. Assoc. Prof., Univ. of Notre Dame, Ind., 1969–82, now Emeritus. Canon, Trinity Cathedral, Phoenix, Ariz., 1946–50; Rector, St. Luke's Episcopal Church, Monrovia, Calif., 1950–69. *Publs:* Tongue Speaking, 1964; Dreams: The Dark Speech of the Spirit, 1968; God, Dreams and Revelation, 1972; Encounter with God, 1972; Healing and Christianity, 1973; Myth, History and Faith, 1974; The Hinge; Dreams: A Way to Listen to God; Discernment: A Study in Ecstasy and Evil; The Christian and the Supernatural; The Other Side of Silence; Afterlife; The Age of Miracles; Tales to Tell; Adventure Inward; Reaching for the Real; Caring; Transcend; Prophetic Ministry; Christo-Psychology; Companions on the Inner Way; Resurrection, 1985; Christianity as Psychology, 1986; Sacrament of Sexuality, 1986; Psychology, Medicine and Christian Healing, 1988. Add: P.O. Box 617, Gualala, Calif. 95445, U.S.A.

KELTON, Elmer. Also writes as Lee McElroy, and Alex Hawk. American, b. 1926. Westerns/Adventure, History. Assoc. Ed., West Texas Livestock Weekly, since 1968. Agricultural Ed., Standard-Times, San Angelo, Tex., 1948–63; Ed., Ranch Mag., 1963–68. *Publs:* Hot Iron, 1955; Buffalo Wagons, 1956; Barbed Wire, 1957; Shadow of a Star, 1959; The Texas Rifles, 1960; Donovan, 1961; Bitter Trail, 1962; Horsehead Crossing, 1963; Massacre at Goliad, 1965; Llano River, 1966; After the Bugles, 1967; Captain's Rangers, 1968; Hanging Judge, 1969; (as Alex Hawk) Shotgun Settlement, 1969; Bowie's Mine, 1971; The Day the Cowboys Quit, 1971; Wagontongue, 1972; The Time It Never Rained, 1973; (as Lee McElroy) Joe Pepper, 1975; (as Lee McElroy) Long Way to Texas, 1976; The Good Old Boys, 1978; The Wolf and the Buffalo, 1980; (as Lee McElroy) Eyes of the Hawk, 1981; Stand Proud, 1984; Dark Thicket, 1985; The Man Who Rode Midnight, 1987. Add: 2460 Oxford, San Angelo, Tex. 76904, U.S.A.

KEMELMAN, Harry. American, b. 1908. Mystery/Crime/Suspense. *Publs:* Friday the Rabbi Slept Late, 1964; Saturday the Rabbi Went Hungry, 1966; Nine Mile Walk (stories), 1967; Sunday the Rabbi Stayed Home, 1969; Commonsense in Education, 1970; Monday the Rabbi Tookff, 1972; Tuesday the Rabbi Saw Red, 1974; Wednesday the Rabbi Got Wet, 1976; Thursday the Rabbi Walked Out, 1978; Conversations with Rabbi Small, 1981; Someday, the Rabbi Will Leave, 1985; One Fine Day, The Rabbi Bought a Cross, 1986. Add: P.O. Box 674, Marblehead, Mass. 01945, U.S.A.

KEMENY, John G(eorge). American, b. 1926. Mathematics/Computers. Prof. of Mathematics and Computer Science, since 1981, Dartmouth Coll., Hanover, N.H. (Prof. of Mathematics, 1953–70; Chmn., Mathematics Dept., 1955–67; Albert Bradley Third Century Prof., 1969–72; Pres., 1970–81; Adjunct Prof. of Mathematics, 1972–81); Chmn., True BASIC, Inc.; Ed. Bd., Abacus, since 1983. Asst. to Albert Einstein, Inst. for Advanced Study, 1948–49, Fine Instr. in Mathematics, 1949–51, and Asst. Prof. of Philosophy, 1951–53, Princeton Univ., N.J. Charter Commnr., National Commn. of Libraries and Information Sys-

tems, 1971–73; Chmn., President's Commn. on the Accident at Three Mile Island, 1979. *Publs:* (co-author) Universal Mathematics, Part II, 1955; (with J.L. Snell and G.L. Thompson) Introduction to Finite Mathematics, 1957, 3rd ed., 1974; (co-author) Modern Mathematical Science, 1959; (with J.L. Snell, H. Mirkil and G.L. Thompson) Finite Mathematical Structures, 1959; (with J.L. Snell) Finite Markov Chains, 1960; (with J.L. Snell) Mathematical Models in the Social Sciences, 1962; (with J.L. Snell, A. Schleifer and G.L. Thompson) Finite Mathematics with Business Applications, 1962, 1972; Random Essays, 1962; (co-author) Denumerable Markov Chains, 1966; (with T.E. Kurtz) BASIC Programming, 1967; Man and the Computer: A New Symbiosis, 1972; (co-author) Back to BASIC, 1984; (with others) Computing for a Course in Finite Mathematics, 1985; (co-author) Structured BASIC Programming, 1987. Add: Dept. of Math, Bradley Hall, Dartmouth Coll., Hanover, N.H. 03755, U.S.A.

KEMP, Betty. British, b. 1916. History. Fellow and Tutor in Modern History, St. Hugh's Coll., Oxford, 1946–78, now Emeritus Fellow. With H.M. Treasury, 1940–45; Lectr., Univ. of Manchester, 1945–46. *Publs:* King and Commons, 1660–1832, 1957; Sir Francis Dashwood, an 18th Century Independent, 1967; Votes and Standing Orders: The Beginning, 1971; (ed. and contrib.) Dictionary of World History, 1750–1914, 1973; Sir Robert Walpole, 1976. Add: St. Hugh's Coll., Oxford, England.

KEMP, Gene. British, b. 1926. Children's fiction. Teacher, St. Sidwell's Sch., Exeter, 1962–74; Lectr., Rolle Coll., 1963–79. *Publs:* Tamworth Pig series, 4 vols., 1972–78; The Turbulent Term of Tyke Tiler, 1977; Gowie Corby Plays Chicken, 1979; (ed.) Ducks and Dragons, 1980; Dog Days and Cat Naps, 1980; The Clock Tower Ghost, 1981; No Place Like, 1983; Charlie Lewis Plays for Time, 1984; The Well, 1984; Jason Bodger and the Priory Ghost, 1985; McMagus Is Waiting For You, 1986; Juniper, 1986; I Can't Stand Losing, 1987; Room with No Windows, 1989. Add: c/o Lawrence Pollinger Ltd., 18 Maddox St., London W1R 0EU, England.

KEMP, (Bernard) Peter. British, b. 1942. Literature. Sr. Lectr. in English, Middlesex Polytechnic, 1968–88. *Publs:* Muriel Spark, 1974; H.G. Wells and the Culminating Ape, 1982. Add: 61 Princes Ave., Finchley, London N3 2DA, England.

KEMPINSKI, Tom. British, b. 1938. Plays/Screenplays. Actor, 1960–71. *Publs:* Duet for One, 1981; Separation, 1989. Add: c/o Anthony Sheil Assocs., 43 Doughty St., London WC1N 2LF, England.

KENDALL, Aubyn. American, b. 1919. Archaeology/Antiquities, Art. Former Curator of Collections, Fort Worth Museum of Science and History. *Publs:* The Art of Pre-Columbian Mexico: An Annotated Bibliography of Works in English, 1973; The Art of Archaeology of Pre-Columbian Middle America, 1977. Add: P.O. Box 1125, Glen Rose, Tex. 76043, U.S.A.

KENDALL, Carol. American, b. 1917. Novels/Short stories, Children's fiction. *Publs:* The Black Seven, 1946; The Baby-Snatcher, 1952; The Other Side of the Tunnel, 1956; The Gammage Cup (in U.K. as The Minnipins), 1959; The Big Splash, 1960; The Whisper of Glocken, 1965; (with Yao-wen Li) Sweet and Sour: Tales from China, 1979; The Firelings, 1982; Haunting Tales from Japan, 1985; The Wedding of the Rat Family, 1988. Add: 928 Holiday Dr., Lawrence, Kans. 66046, U.S.A.

KENDREW, (Sir) John (Cowdery). British, b. 1917. Biology, Chemistry. Hon. Fellow, Trinity Coll., Cambridge, since 1972, and Peterhouse, Cambridge, since 1976. Fellow of Peterhouse, Cambridge, 1947–75; Dept. Chmn., Medical Research Council Lab. for Molecular Biology, Cambridge, 1947–75; Reader, Davy-Faraday Laboratory, Royal Instn., London, 1954–68; Dir.-Gen., European Molecular Biology Lab., 1975–82. Pres., St. John's College, Oxford, 1981–87. Ed.-in-Chief, Journal of Molecular Biology, 1959–87. Member, 1965–72, and Vice-Chmn., 1970–72, Council for Scientific Policy. Recipient, Nobel Prize for Chemistry, with Max Perutz, 1962. *Publs:* (ed. with F.J.W. Roughton) Haemoglobin: A Symposium Based on a Conference held at Cambridge in June 1948 In Memory of Sir John Barcroft, 1949; The Thread of Life: An Introduction to Molecular Biology, 1963, 1966. Add: The Old Guildhall, 4 Church Lane, Linton, Cambridge CB1 6JX, England.

KENEALLY, Thomas (Michael). Australian, b. 1935. Novels/Short stories, Children's fiction, Plays/Screenplays, Journalism. High sch. teacher, Sydney, 1960–64; Lectr. in Drama, Univ. of New England, N.S.W., 1968–70; Writer-in-Residence, Univ. of California, Irvine, 1985.

Publs: The Place at Whitton, 1964; The Fear, 1965; Bring Larks and Heroes, 1967; Three Cheers for the Paraclete, 1968; The Survivor, 1969; A Dutiful Daughter, 1971; The Chant of Jimmie Blacksmith, 1972; Blood Red, Sister Rose, 1974; Moses: The Lawgiver, 1975; Gossip from the Forest, 1975; Season in Purgatory, 1976; Victim of the Aurora, 1977; Ned Kelly and the City of Bees (children's fiction), 1968; Passenger, 1979; Confederates, 1979; The Cut-Rate Kingdom, 1980; Bullie's House (play), 1981; Schindler's Ark (in U.S. as Schindler's List), 1982; Outback, 1983; A Family Madness, 1985; The Playmaker, 1987; Asmara, 1988. c/o Tessa Sayle Agency, 11 Jubilee Pl., London SW3 3TE, England.

KENKEL, William (Francis). American, b. 1925. Sociology. Prof. of Sociology, Univ. of Kentucky, Lexington. Pres., National Council on Family Relations, 1967–68; Vice-Pres., North Central Sociological Assn., 1980–81; Pres., Mid-South Sociological Assn., 1988–89. *Publs:* (with John F. Cuber) Social Stratification in the United States, 1954; (with John F. Cuber and Robert Harper) Problems of American Society, 2nd ed., 1964; The Family in Perspective, 5th ed. 1985; Society in Action (with Ellen Voland) 1975, sole author, 1980. Add: Dept. of Sociology, Univ. of Kentucky, Lexington, Ky. 40506, U.S.A.

KENNA, Peter (Joseph). Australian, b. 1930. Plays/Screenplays. Radio actor and singer. Formerly, member of the Australian Elizabethan Theatre Trust. *Publs:* The Slaughter of St. Teresa's Day, 1959; A Hard God, 1973; Talk to the Moon, Listen Closely, Trespassers Will Be Prosecuted, 1977; The Cassidy Album: A Hard God, Furtive Love, An Eager Hope, 1978. Add: c/o Curtis Brown, 27 Union St., Paddington, N.S.W. 2021, Australia.

KENNAN, George (Frost). American, b. 1904. History, International relations/Current affairs. Prof. Emeritus, Inst. for Advanced Study, Princeton. Joined U.S. Foreign Service, 1927; Vice Consul, Hamburg, 1927; Tallin, U.S.S.R., 1928; Third Secty., Riga Kovno and Tallin, U.S.S.R., 1929; Language Officer Berlin, 1929; Third Secty., Riga, 1931, Moscow, 1934; Consul, then Second Secty., Vienna, 1935; Second Secty., Moscow, 1935; with Dept. of State, Washington, 1937; Second Secty., 1938; and Consul, 1939, Prague, Second Secty., 1939, and First Secty, 1940, Berlin; Counsellor, Lisbon, 1942; Counsellor to U.S. Delegation, European Advisory Cttee., London, 1944; Minister-Counsellor, Moscow, 1945; Deputy for Foreign Affairs, National War Coll., Washington, 1946; Member, Policy Planning Staff, Dept. of State, 1949–50; Chief, Policy Planning Staff, Dept. of State, on leave at Inst. for Advanced Study, Princeton, 1950–51; Ambassador to the U.S.S.R. 1952 until retirement, 1963; numerous visiting professorships, 1954–60; Ambassador to Yugoslavia, 1961–63; Prof., Princeton Univ., 1964–66; Univ. Fellow in History and Slavic Civilizations, Harvard Univ., Cambridge, Mass., 1966–70; Fellow, All Souls Coll., Oxford, 1969. Pres., National Inst. of Arts and Letters, 1965–68, and American Academy of Arts and Letters, 1967–71. *Publs:* American Diplomacy 1900–1950, 1951; Das Amerikanisch-Russische Verhaltnis, 1954; Realities of American Foreign Policy, 1954; Soviet-American Relations, 1917–1920, vol. 1, Russia Leaves the War, 1956, vol. 2, The Decision to Intervene, 1958; Russia, The Atom and the West (Reith Lectures), 1958; Soviet Foreign Policy, 1917–1945, 1960; Russia and the West (Reith Lectures), 1958; Soviet Foreign Policy, 1917–1945, 1960; Russia and the West under Lenin and Stalin, 1961; On Dealing with the Communist World, 1963; Memoirs 1925–50, 1967; Democracy and the Student left, 1968; From Prague after Munich: Diplomatic Papers 1938–40, 1968; The Marquis de Custine and His Russia in 1839, 1971; Memoirs 1950–63, 1972; Cloud of Danger, 1978; The Decline of Bismarck's European Order: Franco-Russian Relations 1875-1890, 1979; The Nuclear Delusion, 1982; The Fateful Alliance, 1984; Sketches from a Life, 1989. Add: 146 Hodge Rd., Princeton, N.J. 08540, U.S.A.

KENNAN, Kent Wheeler. American, b. 1913. Music. Emeritus Prof. of Music Theory and Composition, Univ. of Texas at Austin (joined faculty, 1940). Teacher, Kent State Univ., Ohio, 1939–40, Ohio State Univ., Columbus, 1947–49. *Publs:* The Technique of Orchestration, 1952, 3rd ed., with Donald Grantham, 1983; Counterpoint, 1959, 3rd ed., 1987. Add: 1513 Westover Rd., Austin, Tex. 78703, U.S.A.

KENNEDY, Adrienne. American, b. 1931. Plays/Screenplays. Lectr. in Playwriting, Yale Univ., New Haven, Conn., 1972–73. *Publs:* Funnyhouse of a Negro, 1964; (with John Lennon and Victor Spinetti) The Lennon Play: In His Own Write, 1967, rev. versions, 1968; Cities of Bezique: 2 One-Act Plays: The Owl Answers and A Beast's Story, 1969; People Who Led to My Plays (memoirs), 1987; Adrienne Kennedy in One Act, 1988. Add: 325 W. 89th St., New York, N.Y. 10024, U.S.A.

KENNEDY, David Michael. American, b. 1941. History. William Robertson Coe. Prof. of History and American Studies, Stanford Univ., Calif., since 1980 (Asst. Prof., 1967–72; Assoc. Prof., 1972–80). *Publs:* Birth Control in America: The Career of Margaret Sanger, 1970; (ed. with Paul A. Robinson) Social Thought in America and Europe, 1970; (ed.) Progressivism: The Critical Issues, 1971; (with Thomas A. Bailey) The American Pageant, 7th ed. 1983, 8th ed., 1987; Over Here: The First World War and American Society, 1980; Power and Responsibility: Case Studies in American Leadership, 1986. Add: Dept. of History, Stanford Univ., Stanford. Calif. 94305, U.S.A.

KENNEDY, Edward ("Ted"). American, b. 1932. International relations/Current affairs, Politics/Government. United States Senator (Democrat) from Massachusetts since 1963 (Senate Majority Whip, 1969–71; Chmn., Judiciary Cttee., 1979–81; Ranking Democrat, Labor and Human Resources Cttee., since 1981; also Member, Senate Armed Forces Cttee., Senate Joint Economic Cttee.). Pres., Joseph P. Kennedy Jr. Foundn., since 1961; Trustee, John F. Kennedy Library, Boston, and John F. Kennedy Center for the Performing Arts, Washington, D.C. Member of the Massachusetts Bar, 1959; Asst. District Attorney, Suffolk County, Massachusetts, 1961–62. *Publs:* Decisions for a Decade, 1968; In Critical Condition, 1972; Our Day and Generation, 1979; (with Mark Hatfield) Freeze: How You Can Help Prevent Nuclear War, 1982. Add: 113 Russell Senate Office Bldg., Washington, D.C. 20510, U.S.A.

KENNEDY, Gavin. Scottish, b. 1940. Economics, International relations/Current affairs, Mathematics/Statistics. Prof. of Defence Finance, Heriot-Watt Univ., since 1985. Part-time Lectr. in Economics, National Defence Coll., Latimer. Lectr. in Economics, Brunel Univ., Uxbridge, 1972–74; Sr. Lectr. in Economics, Univ. of Strathclyde, 1974–85. *Publs:* The Military in the Third World, 1974; The Economics of Defence, 1975; (ed.) The Radical Approach, 1976; The Death of Captain Cook, 1978; (ed.) R.T. Gould's Captain Cook, 1978; Bligh, 1978; Burden Sharing in NATO, 1979; (co-author) Managing Negotiations, 1980; (ed.) Sir John Barrow's Mutiny of the Bounty, 1980; (ed.) A Book of the Bounty, 1981; Mathematics for Innumerate Economists, 1982; Everything is Negotiable!, 1982; Defense Economics, 1982; Invitation to Statistics, 1983; Negotiate Anywhere, 1985; Superdeal, 1986; Macroeconomics, 1987; The Pocket Negotiator, 1987; Captain Bligh: The Man and His Mutinies, 1989; Beyond Selling, 1989. Add: 22 Braid Ave., Edinburgh EH10 6EE, Scotland.

KENNEDY, Joseph. British, b. 1923. History. Adult Education Tutor, Univ. of Liverpool, since 1984. Research Fellow, Southampton Univ., 1951–53; Sr. Lectr. in History, Malayan Teachers' Coll., Kirkby, Liverpool, 1954–62; Head of History Dept., Madeley Coll. of Education. Staffs. 1963–78; Head of Faculty of Education, North Staffs. Polytechnic, 1978–84. *Publs:* A History of Malaya, 1962, rev. ed. 1970; Asian Nationalism in the Twentieth Century, 1968; (ed.) Madeley: A History of Staffordshire Parish, 1970; (ed.) Biddulph, Staffordshire: A Local History, 1978; (ed.) Newcastle under Lyme, A Town Portrait, 1984; British Civilians and the Japanese War in Malaya and Singapore 1941–45, 1987; When Singapore Fell: Evacuations and Escapes 1941–42, 1989. Add: 14 Poolfield Ave., Newcastle under Lyme, Staffs. ST5 2NL, England.

KENNEDY, Kieran A. Irish, b. 1935. Economics. Dir., The Economic and Social Research Inst., Dublin, since 1971 (Sr. Research Officer, 1968–70). Council Member, Statistical and Social Inquiry Soc. of Ireland, since 1973. Exec. Officer, Office of the Comptroller and Auditor Gen., Dublin, 1954–55, and the Dept. of Industry and Commerce, Dublin, 1955–58; Administrative Officer, 1958–65, and Asst. Principal Officer, 1965–68, Dept. of Finance, Dublin; Economic Consultant, Central Bank of Ireland, Dublin, 1970–71; Founder Member and Council Member, Irish Council of the European League for Economic Co-operation, 1971–83; Member, National Economic and Social Council, 1973–77; Chmn., Royal Irish Academy National Cttee. for Economics and Social Sciences, 1984–88; . *Publs:* Productivity and Industrial Growth: The Irish Experience, 1971; (with R. Bruton) The Irish Economy, 1975; (with B.R. Dowling) Economic Growth in Ireland: The Experience since 1947, 1975; (ed. with D. Conniffe) Employment and Unemployment Policy for Ireland, 1984; (co-author) The Economic Development of Ireland in the Twentieth Century, 1988. Add: 12 Richelieu Park, Sydney Parade Ave., Dublin 4, Ireland.

KENNEDY, Leigh. American, b. 1951. Novels/Short stories. *Publs:* Faces, 1986; The Journal of Nicholas the American, 1986. Add: 78 High St., Pewsey, Wiltshire SN9 5AQ, England.

KENNEDY, Ludovic (Henry Coverley). British, b. 1919. Criminology/Law enforcement/Prisons, History, International relations/Current affairs. Television and radio journalist, since 1955. *Publs:* Sub-Lieutenant, 1942; Nelson's Band of Brothers, 1951; One Man's Meat, 1953; Ten Rillington Place, 1961; Murder Story (with essay on Capital Punishment); The Trial of Stephen Ward, 1964; Very Lovely People, 1969; Pursuit: Sinking of the Bismark, 1974; A Presumption of Innocence, 1976; The Portland Spy Case, 1978; Menace: The Life and Death of Tirpitz, 1979; (ed.) A Book of Railway (Sea, Air) Journeys, 3 vols., 1980–82; Wicked Beyond Belief, 1980; The Airman and the Carpenter, 1985; On My Way to the Club, 1989. Add: c/o Rogers, Coleridge and White, 20 Powis Mews, London W11, England.

KENNEDY, Michael. British, b. 1926. Music, Biography. Music Critic, Daily Telegraph, London, since 1950 (Asst. Northern Ed., 1958–60; Northern Ed., 1960–86). *Publs:* The Hallé Tradition, 1960; The Works of Ralph Vaughan Williams, 1964, 1980; Portrait of Elgar, 1968, 3rd ed., 1987; Portrait of Manchester, 1970; History of the Royal Manchester College of Music, 1971; Barbirolli, 1971; (ed.) Autobiography of Charles Hallé; Mahler, 1974; Richard Strauss, 1976; (ed.) Concise Oxford Dictionary of Music, 1980; Britten, 1981; (ed.) Oxford Dictionary of Music, 1985; Adrian Boult, 1987. Add: 3 Moorwood Dr., Sale, Cheshire M33 4QA, England.

KENNEDY, Moorhead. American, b. 1930. International relations (terrorism), Autobiography/Memoirs. Exec. Dir., Council for Intl. Understanding, Myrin Inst., NYC, since 1983. Diplomat in Yemen, Greece, Lebanon, Chile, and Iran, and Founder and Dir., Office of Investment Affairs, U.S. Foreign Service, Dept. of State, Washington D.C., 1971–74; U.S. Hostage in Iran, 1979–81; Exec. Dir., Cathedral of Peace Inst., Episcopal Cathedral of St. John the Divine, NYC, 1981–83. *Publs:* The Ayatollah in the Cathedral: Reflections of a Hostage, 1986; (with Terrell E. Arnold) Terrorism: Responding to the New Warfare, 1987. Add: 55 Liberty St., New York, N.Y. 10005, U.S.A.

KENNEDY, Paul Michael. British, b. 1945. History. Dilworth Prof. of History, Yale Univ., New Haven, Conn., since 1983. Theodor Heuss Research Fellow, Univ. of Oxford, 1968–69; Lectr., 1970–75, and Reader in History, 1975–83, Univ. of East Anglia, Norwich. *Publs:* Pacific Onslaught, 1972; Pacific Victory, 1973; The Samoan Tangle: A Study in Anglo-German-American Relations 1878-1900, 1974; The Rise and Fall of British Naval Mastery, 1976; (ed.) The War Plans of the Great Powers 1880-1914, 1979; The Rise of Anglo-German Antagonism 1860-1914, 1980; The Realities Behind Diplomacy, 1981; (ed.) Nationalist and Racialist Movements in Britain and Germany Before 1914, 1981; The Rise and Fall of the Great Powers, 1988. Add: Dept. of History, Yale Univ., New Haven, Conn., U.S.A.

KENNEDY, Peter (Elliott). Canadian, b. 1943. Economics. Prof. of Economics, Simon Fraser Univ., Burnaby, since 1978 (Asst. Prof., 1968–70; Assoc. Prof., 1970–78). *Publs:* Macroeconomics, 1975, 3rd ed. 1984; (with G. Dorosh) Dateline Canada, 1978, 3rd ed. 1987; A Guide to Econometrics, 1979, 1985. Add: Economics Dept., Simon Fraser Univ., Burnaby, B.C. V5A 1S6, Canada.

KENNEDY, Richard (Jerome). American, b. 1932. Children's fiction. Full-time Writer. Has worked as a bookseller, teacher, cab driver, woodcutter, and janitor. *Publs:* The Parrot and the Thief, 1974; The Contests and Cowlick, 1975; The Blue Stone, 1976; Come Again in the Spring, 1976; The Porcelain Man, 1976; Oliver Hyde's Dishcloth Concert, 1977; The Dark Princess, 1978; The Rise and Fall of Ben Gizzard, 1978; The Leprechaun's Story, 1979; The Lost Kingdom of Karnica, 1979; The Mouse God, 1979; Inside My Feet: The Story of a Giant, 1979; Delta Baby and Two Sea Songs (verse), 1979; Crazy in Love, 1980; Song of the Horse, 1981; The Boxcar at the Center of the Universe, 1982; Amy's Eyes, 1985; Collected Stories, 1987. Add: c/o Harper and Row, 10 E. 53rd St., New York, N.Y. 10022, U.S.A.

KENNEDY, William (Joseph). American, b. 1928. Novels/Short Stories. Prof. of English, State Univ. of New York at Albany, since 1983 (Lectr., 1974–82). Founder, New York State Writers Institute. Reporter, Albany Times-Union, 1952–56; Asst. Managing Ed., Puerto Rico World Journal, San Juan, 1956; Reporter, Miami Herald, 1957; Correspondent, Time-Life Publications in Puerto Rico, and Reporter, Knight Newspapers, 1957–59; Founding Managing Ed., San Juan Star, 1959–61; Special Writer, Albany Times-Union, 1963–70. *Publs:* The Ink Truck, 1969; Legs, 1975; Billy Phelan's Greatest Game, 1978; Ironweed, 1983; O Albany! (non-fiction), 1983; (with Francis Ford Coppola) The Cotton Club (screenplay), 1983; (with Brendan Kennedy) Charlie Malarkey and the Belley Button Machine (children's book), 1986; Ironweed (screenplay), 1987; Quinn's Book, 1988. Add: N.Y.S. Writers Institute, State Univ.

of New York, Albany, N.Y. 12222, U.S.A.

KENNEDY, X.J. Pseud. for Joseph Charles Kennedy. American, b. 1929. Poetry, Literature. Asst. Prof., 1963–67, Assoc. Prof., 1967–73, and Prof. of English, 1973–79, Tufts Univ., Medford, Mass. Poetry Ed., The Paris Review, 1962–64; Co-ed, Counter/Measures, 1972–74. *Publs:* Nude Descending a Staircase, 1961; (ed. with J.E. Camp) Mark Twain's Frontier, 1963; An Introduction to Poetry, 1966, 7th ed. 1990; Growing into Love, 1969; (ed. with J.E. Camp and K. Waldrop) Pegasus Descending: A Book of Bad Verse, 1971; Breaking and Entering, 1972; (ed.) Messages: A Thematic Anthology of Poetry, 1973; Emily Dickinson in Southern California, 1974; One Winter Night in August: Nonsense Jingles, 1975; (with J.E. Camp and K. Waldrop) Three Tenors, One Vehicle, 1975; An Introduction to Fiction, 1976, 4th ed., 1987; Literature, 1976, 4th ed., 1987; The Phantom Ice Cream Man, 1979 (ed.) Tygers of Wrath: Poems of Hate, Anger, and Invective, 1981; (ed. with Dorothy M. Kennedy) The Bedford Reader, 1982, 3rd ed., 1988; Did Adam Name the Vinegarroon?, 1982; (with Dorothy M. Kennedy) Knock at a Star: A Child's Introduction to Poetry, 1982; French Leave: Translations, 1984; Hangover Mass, 1984; The Forgetful Wishing Well: Poems for Young People, 1985; Cross Ties: Selected Poems, 1985; Brats, 1986; (with Dorothy M. Kennedy) The Bedford Guide for College Writers, 1987; Ghastlies, Goops and Pinchushions, 1989. Add: 4 Fern Way, Bedford, Mass. 01730, U.S.A.

KENNELLY, (Timothy) Brendan. Irish, b. 1936. Novels/Short stories, Poetry. Prof. of Modern Literature, Trinity Coll., Dublin, since 1973 (Jr. Lectr., 1963–66; Lectr., 1966–69; Assoc. Prof., 1969–73; Chmn., English Dept., 1973–76). *Publs:* (with R. Holzapfel) Cast a Cold Eye, 1959; (with R. Holzapfel) The Rain, The Moon, 1961; (with R. Holzapfel) The Dark about Our Loves, 1962; (with R. Holzapfel) Green Townlands: Poems, 1963; Let Fall No Burning Leaf, 1963; The Crooked Cross (novel), 1963; My Dark Fathers, 1964; Up and At It, 1965; Collection One: Getting Up Early, 1966; Good Souls to Survive: Poems, 1967; The Florentines (novel), 1967; Dream of a Black Fox, 1968; Selected Poems, 1969; A Drinking Cup: Poems from the Irish, 1970; (ed.) The Penguin Book of Irish Verse, 1970, 1972, 1981; Bread, 1971; Love-Cry, 1972; Salvation, The Stranger, 1972; The Voices, 1973; Shelley in Dublin, 1974; A Kind of Trust, 1975; New and Selected Poems, 1976, 1978; Islandman, 1977; The Visitor, 1978; A Small Light, 1979; In Spite of the Wise, 1979; The Boats Are Home, 1980; The House That Jack Didn't Build, 1982; Cromwell, 1983; Selected Poems, 1985; (ed.) Ireland Past and Present, 1986; Real Ireland, 1988; (ed.) Landmarks of Irish Drama, 1988. Add: Trinity Coll., Dublin, Ireland.

KENNEMORE, Tim. British, b. 1957. Children's fiction. *Publs:* The Middle of the Sandwich, 1981; The Fortunate Few, 1981; Wall of Words, 1982; Here Tomorrow, Gone Today (short stories), 1983; Changing Times, 1984. Add: c/o Faber and Faber, 3 Queen Sq., London WC1N 3AU, England.

KENNER, (William) Hugh. Canadian, b. 1923. Literature. Mellon Prof. in Humanities, Johns Hopkins Univ., Baltimore, since 1975 (Prof. of English, 1973–75). Asst. Prof., Assumption Coll., Windsor, Ont., 1946–48; Instr., 1950–51, Asst. Prof., 1951–56, Chmn. of the Dept., 1956–62, Assoc. Prof., 1956–58, and Prof. of English, 1958–73, Univ. of California at Santa Barbara. *Publs:* Paradox in Chesterton, 1947; The Poetry of Ezra Pound, 1951; Wyndham Lewis, 1954; Dublin's Joyce, 1955; Gnomon: Essays on Contemporary Literature, 1958; The Invisible Poet: T.S. Eliot, 1959; (ed.) The Art of Poetry, 1959; The Stoic Comedians: Flaubert, Joyce, and Beckett, 1962; (ed.) T.S. Eliot: A Collection of Critical Essays, 1962; (ed.) Seventeenth Century Poetry: The Schools of Donne and Jonson, 1964; (ed.) Studies in Change: A Book of the Short Story, 1965; The Counterfeiters: An Historical Comedy, 1968; The Pound Era, 1971; A Reader's Guide to Samuel Beckett, 1973; Bucky: Guided Tour of Buckminster Fuller, 1973; A Homemade World: The American Modernist Writers, 1975; Geodesic Math and How to Use It, 1976; Joyce's Voices, 1978, Ulysses, 1980, 1987; A Colder Eye, 1983; The Mechanic Muse, 1986; A Sinking Island: The Modern English Writers, 1988; Mazes: Sixty-Four Essays: 1989. Add: 103 Edgevale Rd., Baltimore, Md. 21210, U.S.A.

KENNY, Anthony (John Patrick). British, b. 1931. Philosophy. Fellow, since 1964, and Master since 1978, Balliol Coll., Oxford (Wilde Lectr. on Natural Religion, 1969–72). *Publs:* Action, Emotion & Will, 1963; (ed. and trans.) Blackfriars Edition of Aquinas' Summa Theologiae, 1964; Descartes, 1968; (ed.) Aquinas, A Collection of Critical Essays, 1969; The Five Ways, 1969; (trans.) Descartes: Philosophical Letters, 1969; (with C. Longuet-Higgins) The Nature of the Mind, 1972; Wittgenstein, 1973; Will, Freedom, and Power, 1975; The Aristotelian Ethics,

1978; Aristotle's Theory of the Will, 1979; The God of the Philosophers, 1979; Aquinas, 1980; Thomas More, 1982; Wyclif, 1985; The Legacy of Wittgenstein, 1984; The Ivory Tower, 1985; (ed.) Wyclif in His Times, 1986; The Road to Hillsborough, 1986; Reason and Religion, 1987; The Heritage of Wisdom, 1987; God and Two Poets, 1988. Add: Balliol Coll., Oxford, England.

KENRICK, Tony. Australian, b. 1935. Mystery/Crime/Suspense. Worked as an advertising copywriter in Sydney, Toronto, NYC, San Francisco, and London, 1953–72. *Publs:* The Only Good Body's a Dead One, 1970; A Tough One to Lose, 1972; Two for the Price of One, 1974; Stealing Lillian, 1975 (in U.K. paperback, The Kidnap Kid, 1976); The Seven Day Soldiers, 1976; The Chicago Girl, 1976; Two Lucky People, 1978; The Nighttime Guy, 1979; The 81st Site, 1980; Faraday's Flowers, 1985; China White, 1986; Shanghai Surprise, 1986; Neon Tough, 1988. Add: c/o Putnam, 200 Madison Ave., New York, N.Y. 10016, U.S.A.

KENSINGER, George. *See* **FICHTER,** George S.

KENT, Alexander. *See* **REEMAN,** Douglas.

KENT, Arthur (William Charles). Also writes as James Bradwell, M. Dubois, Paul Granados, Alexander Karol, Alex Stamper, and Bret Vane. British, b. 1925. Novels/Short stories, Mystery/Crime/Suspense. Journalist with News Chronicle, London, 1943–46, Australian Daily Mirror, 1947–53, Beaverbrook Newspapers, U.K., 1957–69, and BBC, London, 1970–71. *Publs:* (as Bret Vane) Sunny, 1953; (as Bret Vane) Gardenia, 1953; (as Paul Granados) Broadway Contraband, 1954; (as M. Dubois) El Tafile, 1954; (as M. Dubois) Legion Etrangere, 1954; (as M. Dubois) March and Die, 1954; (as Alex Stamper) Revolt at Zaluig, 1954; Inclining to Crime, 1957; Special Edition Murder, 1957; Kansas Fast Gun, 1958; Stairway to Murder, 1958; Wake Up Screaming, 1958; (with G. Thomas) The Camp on Blood Island, 1958; Last Action, 1959; Broken Doll, 1961; Action of the Tiger, 1961; The Weak and the Strong, 1962; The Counterfeiters, 1962; Long Horn, Long Grass, 1964; Black Sunday, 1965; Corpse to Cuba; Plant Poppies on My Grave, 1966; Red Red Red, 1966; (with I. Simson) Fall of Singapore, 1970; (as James Bradwell) The Mean City, 1971; (with Z. de. Tyras) A Life in the Wind, 1971; (as Alexander Karol) Sword of Vengeance, 1973; (as Alexander Karol) Dark Lady, 1974; (as Alexander Karol) The King's Witchfinder, 1975; The Death Doctors; Maverick Squadron, 1975; The Nowhere War, 1975. Add: 26 Verulam Ave., London E17, England.

KENT, Dale Vivienne. Australian, b. 1942. History. Reader in History, La Trobe Univ., Bundoora, Vic. Fellow, Harvard Univ., Cambridge, Mass., 1977–78; Visiting Scholar, Harvard Univ. Center for Italian Renaissance Studies, 1982. *Publs:* The Rise of the Medici: Faction in Florence 1426-1434, 1978; (with F.W. Kent) Neighbours and Neighbourhood in Renaissance Florence, 1982. Add: c/o History Dept., La Trobe Univ., Bundoora, Vic. 3083, Australia.

KENT, Helen. *See* **POLLEY,** Judith Anne.

KENT, Homer Austin, Jr. American, b. 1926. Theology/Religion. Prof., Grace Theological Seminary and Grace Coll., Winona Lake, Ind., since 1951 (Dean, 1962–76; Pres., 1976–86). Consultant trans. of New Intnl. Version of the New Testament, 1968–73. *Publs:* The Pastoral Epistles, 1958; Ephesians: The Glory of the Church, 1971; Jerusalem to Rome, 1972; Epistle to the Hebrews: An Expository Commentary, 1972; Light in the Darkness, 1974; The Freedom of God's Sons, 1976; Treasures of Wisdom, 1978; A Heart Opened Wide, 1982; Faith That Works, 1986. Add: 305 6th St., Winona Lake, Ind., U.S.A.

KENT, Pamela. *See* **BARRIE,** Susan.

KENTON, Maxwell. *See* **SOUTHERN,** Terry.

KENTON, Warren. Also writes as Zev ben Shimon Halevi. British, b. 1933. Novels, Occult topics, Theology/Religion. Freelance writer and lectr. Tutor, Architectural Assn. London, 1966–71; Lectr. Royal Academy of Dramatic Art, London, 1963–81. *Publs:* Stage Properties, 1964; As Above So Below, 1969; The Play Begins (novel), 1971; (as Zev ben Shimon Halevi) Tree of Life, 1972; Astrology, 1974; Adam and the Kabbalistic Tree, 1974; Way of Kabbalah, 1976; Kabbalistic Universe, 1977; Anatomy of Fate, 1978; Kabbalah: Tradition of Hidden Knowledge, 1979; Kabbalah and Exodus, 1979; Work of the Kabbalist, 1984; School of Kabbalah, 1985; Kabbalah and Psychology, 1986; The Anointed (novel), 1987. Add: Gateway Books, Wellow, Bath, BA2 8QJ, England.

KENWARD, Jean. Pseud. for Jean Chesterman. British, b. 1f920. Children's fiction, Poetry. Part-time Lectr. in Creative Writing, Harrow Sch. of Art, Middlesex, since 1969. *Publs:* A Book of Rhymes; Rain: A Flight of Words; The Forest; Old Mister Hotch Potch; (with B. Roe) Sing for Christmas; Ragdolly Anna Stories, 1979; Clutterby Hogg, 1980; Theme and Variations, 1981; Three Cheers for Ragdolly Anna, 1985; (adaptor) Aesop's Fables, 1986; The Hotchpotch Horse, 1987; Ragdolly Anna's Circus, 1987; The Odd Job Man and the Thousand Mile Boots, 1988; A Kettle Full of Magic, 1988; Seasons, 1989; Ragdolly Anna's Treasure Hunt, 1989. Add: 15 Shire Lane, Chorley Wood, Herts., England.

KENWORTHY, Brian J(ohn). British, b. 1920. Literature, Translations. Sr. Lectr. in German, Univ. of Aberdeen, 1968–81 (Asst. Lectr., 1947–52; Lectr., 1952–68). Teacher of Modern Languages, Cotham Grammar Sch., Bristol, 1943–46. *Publs:* George Kaiser, 1957; (co-trans.) The Drama of the Atom, 1958; (co-author) A Manual of German Prose Composition for Advanced Students, 1966; (ed.) George Kaiser: Die Koralle, Gas I and II, 1968 (also trans., 1971); (ed.) Hermann Sudermann: Litauische Geschichten, 1971; (ed.) George Kaiser: Plays, vol. 2, 1982. Add: 22 Upper Cranbrook Rd., Redland, Bristol BS6 7UN, England.

KENYON, John (Philipps). British, b. 1927. History. Joyce and Elizabeth Hall Distinguished Prof. in British History, Univ. of Kansas, Lawrence, since 1987. Fellow, Christ's Coll., Cambridge, 1954–62. and Lectr., Cambridge Univ., 1955–62; G.F. Grant Prof. of History, Univ. of Hull, 1962–81; Prof. of Modern History, Univ. of St. Andrews, 1981–88. *Publs:* Robert Spencer, Earl of Sunderland, 1958; The Stuarts, 1958, 1970; The Stuart Constitution, 1966; The Popish Plot, 1972; Revolution Principles, 1977; Stuart England, 1978; The History Men, 1983; The Civil Wars of England, 1988. Add: 2722 Missouri St., Lawrence, KS 66046, U.S.A.

KENYON, Michael. Also writes as Daniel Forbes. British, b. 1931. Novels/Short stories, Mystery/Crime/Suspense. Regular contributor, Gourmet mag., NYC. Reporter, Manchester Guardian, 1960–64. *Publs:* May You Die in Ireland, 1965; The Whole Hog (in U.S. as Trouble with Series Three), 1967; Out of Season, 1968; Green Grass, 1969; The 100,000 Welcomes, 1970; The Shooting of Dan McGrew, 1971; A Sorry State, 1973; Mr. Big, 1975; Brainbox and Bull (juvenile), 1975; The Rapist, 1977; Deep Pocket (in U.S. as The Molehill File), 1978; The Elgar Variation, 1981 (in U.S. as Daniel Forbes); Zigzag, 1981; The God Squad Bod (in U.S. as the Man at the Wheel), 1982; A Free-Range Wife, 1983; A Healthy Way to Die, 1986; Peckover Holds the Baby, 1988. Add: c/o Richard Scott Simon Ltd., 32 College Cross, London N1, England.

KEPHART, William M. American, b. 1921. Plays/Screenplays, Sociology. Prof. of Sociology, Univ. of Pennsylvania, Philadelphia, since 1964 (Asst. Prof., 1952–56, and Assoc. Prof., 1957–63). Pres. Pennsylvania Sociological Soc., 1965–67. *Publs:* All-American Ape (play), 1941; Service Club (play), 1942; Divorce, 1961; Nursing Dynamics, 1962; Racial Factors and Law Enforcement, 1965; Liberal Education and Business, 1968; Family, Society, and Individual, 1981, 6th ed., 1987; Extraordinary Groups, 1982. Add: Dept. of Sociology, Univ. of Pennsylvania, Philadelphia, Pa. 19104, U.S.A.

KEPPEL, Charlotte. *See* **BLACKSTOCK,** Charity.

KEPPEL-JONES, Arthur (Mervyn). Canadian (b. in South Africa), b. 1909. Science fiction/Fantasy, Area studies. Emeritus Prof. of History, Queen's Univ., Kingston, Ont., since 1976 (Visiting Lectr., 1953–54, and Prof., 1959–76). Lectr., 1933–34, 1936–44, and Sr. Lectr., 1945–53; Univ. of Witwatersrand, Johannesburg; Lectr., 1935, and Prof. of History, 1954–59, Univ. of Natal, Pietermaritzburg. *Publs:* Do We Govern Ourselves?, 1945; When Smuts Goes: A History of South Africa from 1952 to 2010, First Published in 2015 (science fiction), 1947; South Africa: A Short History, 1949, 5th ed., 1975; Friends or Foes?, 1950; (ed.) Thomas Philipps, 1820 Settler: His Letters, 1960; Rhodes and Rhodesia: The White Conquest of Zimbabwe 1884-1902, 1983. Add: 1, College St., Kingston, Ontario, Canada.

KERBY, Susan. *See* **BURTON,** Elizabeth.

KERENSKY, Oleg. British, b. 1930. Dance/Ballet, Literature, Biography. New York Correspondent for The Stage and Music and Musicians, London. Former Ballet Critic, Daily Mail, London, and New Statesman, London, 1968–78. *Publs:* Ballet Scene, 1970; The World of Ballet, 1970; Anna Pavlova, 1973; The New British Drama, 1977; The Guinness Guide to Ballet, 1981.   Add: 210 Bank St., New York, N.Y. 10014, U.S.A.

KERESZTY, Roch A.   American, b. 1933.   Theology/Religion.   Chmn. of Theology Dept., Cistercian Preparatory Sch., Irving, Tex., since 1972 (teacher since 1969); Adjunct Prof. of Theology, Univ. of Dallas, Tex., since 1978) (Lectr. in Theology, 1963–65; Asst. Prof. of Theology, 1965–70; Chaplain, 1963–65; Assoc. Prof., 1970–78).   *Publs:* God Seekers for a New Age: From Crisis Theology to Christian Atheism, 1970; Krisztus, 1977.   Add: Cistercian Abbey, One Cistercian Rd., Irving, Tex. 75039, U.S.A.

KERMAN, Joseph.   American, b. 1924.   Music.   Prof. of Music, Univ. of California, Berkeley, since 1952.   Ed., 19th-Century Music, since 1976.   Heather Prof. of Music, Oxford Univ., 1971–73.   *Publs:* Opera as Drama, 1956, 1988; The Elizabethan Madrigal, 1962; The Beethoven Quartets, 1967; (with H.W. Janson) A History of Art and Music, 1968; (ed.) Beethoven: Autograph Miscellany (the Kafka Sketchbook), 1970; (with V. Kerman) Listen, 1972; The Masses and Motets of William Byrd, 1981; (with A. Tyson) The New Grove Beethoven, 1983 Musicology, 1985; Contemplating Music, 1986.   Add: Music Dept., Univ. of Calif., Berkeley, Calif., U.S.A.

KERMODE, (John) Frank.   British, b. 1919.   Literature.   Fellow of King's Coll., Cambridge, since 1974.   Gen. Ed., Modern Masters, Master-guides series, and Oxford Authors.   John Edward Taylor Prof. of English, Manchester Univ., 1958–65; Winterstoke Prof. of English Literature, Bristol Univ., 1965–67; Lord Northcliffe Prof. of Modern English Literature, Univ. Coll. London, 1967–74; King Edward VII Prof. of English Literature, Cambridge Univ., 1974–82.   *Publs:* (ed.) English Pastoral Poetry, 1952; (ed.) Shakespeare: The Tempest, 1954; Romantic Image, 1957; (ed. and contrib.) The Living Milton, 1960; Wallace Stevens, 1960; (ed.) Discussions of John Donne, 1962; Puzzles and Epiphanies, 1962; (ed.) Edmund Spenser, 1964; (ed.) Four Centuries of Shakespearean Criticism, 1965; The Sense of an Ending, 1967; (ed.) Selected Poetry of Andrew Marvell, 1967; Continuities, 1968; (ed.) The Metaphysical Poets, 1969; (ed.) King Lear: A Casebook, 1970; (ed.) Poems of John Donne, 1970; (ed. with R. Poirier) The Oxford Reader, 1971; Shakespeare, Spenser, Donne, 1971; Modern Essays, 1971; D.H. Lawrence, 1973; (gen. ed. with J. Hollander) Oxford Anthology of English Literature, 1973; The Classic, 1975; (ed.) Selected Prose of T.S. Eliot, 1975; The Genesis of Secrecy, 1979; The Art of Telling (essays), 1983; Forms of Attention, 1985; (ed. with Robert Alter) The Literary Guide to the Bible, 1987; History and Value, 1988.   Add: King's Coll., Cambridge CB2 1ST, England.

KERN, Gregory.   *See* **TUBB,** E.C.

KERNER, Fred.   Also writes as Frederick Kerr and as M.N. Thaler, Canadian, b. 1921.   Cookery/Gastronomy/Wine, Medicine/Health, Psychology.   Ed. Emeritus, Harlequin Enterprises Ltd., since 1985 (Vice-Pres. of Publishing, 1975–85).   Trustee, Canadian Authors Assn. Awards, since 1974.   Ed.-in-Chief, Fawcett Books, NYC, 1959–64; Pres. and Ed.-in-Chief, Hawthorn Books, NYC, 1964–69; Editorial Dir., Book and Educational Divs. Reader's Digest Assn. (Canada) Ltd., Montreal, 1969–75.   Pres., Montreal Branch, 1973–75, National Vice-Pres., 1975–79, and Pres., 1982–83, Canadian Authors Assn.   *Publs:* (with L. Kotkin) Eat, Think and Be Slender, 1954; (with W. Germain) The Magic Power of Your Mind, 1956; (with Joyce Brothers) Ten Days to a Successful Memory, 1957; (anthologist) Love is a Man's Affair, 1958; Stress and Your Heart, 1961; (as Frederick Kerr) Watch Your Weight Go Down, 1962; (with W. Germain) Secrets of Your Supraconscious, 1965; (compiler) A Treasury of Lincoln Quotations, 1965; (with D. Goodman) What's Best for Your Child . . . and You, 1966; (with J. Reid) Buy High, Sell Higher!, 1966; (as M.N. Thaler) It's Fun to Fondue, 1968; (with Ion Grumenza) Nadia, 1976; (ed.) The Canadian Writer's Guide, 1985, 1988.   Add: 25 Farmview Cresc., Willowdale, Ont. M2J 1G5, Canada.

KERNODLE, Rigdon Wayne.   American, b. 1919.   Sociology.   Heritage Prof. and Chmn., Dept. of Sociology, Coll. of William and Mary, Williamsburg (Asst. Prof., Assoc. Prof., and Prof., 1949–72).   Instr. Coll. of William and Mary, 1945–47; Lectr., Univ. of North Carolina, 1947–49.   *Publs:* (with C.F. Marsh) Hampton Roads Communities in World War II, 1951; Last of the Rugged Individualists, 1960; Unsolved Issues in American Society, 1960; (ed.) The Sixth Decade of Our Century, 1959; (ed.) Values, Decisions, and the American Economy, 1961; (ed.) Non-medical Leaves from a Mental Hospital, 1966; (ed.) Three Family Placement Programs in Belgium and the Netherlands, 1972; (ed.) Commentary on Why People Fall in and Out of Romantic Love, 1972; A Comparison of the Social Networks of Black and White Elderly in a Southern Border State, 1981; Remembrance of the Homeplace, 1986; Religion, Supersti-

tion, Magic, and Sports in an Hawaiian Community, 1986; Sex Roles and Sports Knowledge, 1987; Selection of a Retirement Community, 1989.   Add: 108 Governors Dr., Williamsburg, Va. 23185, U.S.A.

KERR, Alexander McBride.   Australian, b. 1921.   Economics.   Deputy-Chmn., Challenge Bank Ltd; Dir., Vincent Corp.   *Publs:* Personal Income of Western Australia, 1949; Northwestern Australia, 1962; Regional Income Estimation—Theory and Practice, 1963; The South West Region of Western Australia, 1965, 1966; Australia's North West, 1967; The Texas Reef Shell Industry, 1968; (ed.) The Indian Ocean Region, 1981.   Add: 146 Alderbury St., Floreat Park, W.A. 6014, Australia.

KERR, Carole.   *See* **CARR,** Margaret.

KERR, Clark.   American, b. 1911.   Economics, Education, Industrial relations.   Prof. of Industrial Relations, Univ. of California at Berkeley, since 1945, and Pres. Emeritus, since 1974 (Assoc Prof., later Prof. and Dir., Inst. of Industrial Relations, 1945–52; Chancellor, 1952–58, Pres., 1958–67).   Chmn., Armour Automation Cttee., since 1959; Member, Univ. Council, Chinese Univ. of Hong Kong, since 1964; Bd. of Mgrs., Swarthmore Coll., since 1968; Trustee, Intnl. Council for Educational Development, since 1971; Chmn. of Bd., Work in America Inst., since 1975; Member, Bd. of Dirs., Assn. of Governing Beds. of Colls. and Univs., since 1977; Bd. of Dirs., National Univ. Consortium for Telecom-munications in Teaching, since 1980.   Acting Asst. Prof. of Labor Economics, Stanford Univ., Calif., 1939–40; Asst. Prof., later Assoc. Prof., Univ. of Washington, Seattle, 1940–45; with U.S. War Labor Bd., 1942–45.   Contract Arbitrator for Boeing Aircraft Co. and Intnl. Assn. of Machinists, 1944–45, Armour and Co., and United Packinghouse Workers, 1945–47, 1949–52, Waterfront Employers' Assn. and Intnl. Longshoremen's and Warehousemen's Union, 1946–47, etc.; First Vice-Chmn., American Council on Education, 1954; Member, Advisory Panel on Social Science Research, National Science Foundn., 1953–57; Member, Bd. of Dirs., Center for Advanced Study in the Behavioral Sciences, 1953–61; Trustee, Carnegie Foundn. for Advancement of Teaching, 1958–60, 1972–80; Rockefeller Foundn, 1960–76; Dir., Carnegie Commn. on the Future of Higher Education, 1967–73; Chmn, Carnegie Council on Policy Studies in Higher Education, 1974–79; Trustee, Educational Testing Service, 1977–80; National Advisory Bd., Inst. for the Study of Educational Policy, Howard Univ., 1974–85; Chmn., Global Perspectives in Education, Inc., 1976–85.   *Publs:* (with E. Wight Bakke) Unions, Management and the Public, 1948, 3rd ed. 1967; (with others) Industrialism and Industrial Man, 1960, 3rd ed. 1967; The Uses of the University, 1963, 3rd ed. 1982; Labor and Management in Industrial Society, 1964; Marshall, Marx and Modern Times, 1969; (with others) Industrialism and Industrial Man Reconsidered, 1975; Labor Markets and Wage Determination, 1977; Education and National Development, 1979; The Future of Industrial Societies: Are They Becoming Alike? 1982; (with Marvin L. Gade) The Many Lives of Academic Presidents: Time, Place, and Character, 1986; (co-ed. with Paul D. Staudohar) Industrial Relations in a New Age, 1986; Economics of Labor in Industrial Society, 1986.   Add: 8300 Buckingham Dr., El Cerrito, Calif. 94530, U.S.A.

KERR, Elizabeth M(argaret).   American, b. 1905.   Literature.   Prof. of English Emeritus, Univ. of Wisconsin-Milwaukee, since 1970 (joined faculty, 1945).   *Publs:* Bibliography of the Sequence Novel, 1950, 1973; (ed. with Ralph Aderman) Aspects of American English, 1963, 1971; Yoknapatawpha: Faulkner's "Little Postage Stamp of Native Soil", 1969; William Faulkner's Gothic Domain, 1978; William Faulkner's Yoknapatawpha: "A Kind of Keystone in the Universe", 1982, 1985.   Add: 435 Starin Rd., Whitewater, Wisc. 53190, U.S.A.

KERR, Frederick.   *See* **KERNER,** Fred.

KERR, Graham.   British, b. 1934.   Cookery/Gastronomy/Wine.   Past Mgr., Royal Ascot Hotel, London; Chief Catering Adviser, Royal New Zealand Air Force; Presenter, The Galloping Gourmet television series and Take Kerr television series.   *Publs:* Graham Kerr Cookbook by the Galloping Gourmet, 1970; Cooking with Graham Kerr, The Galloping Gourmet; The Galloping Gourmet's Kitchen Diary; The New Seasoning, 1976; The Love Feast, 1978; The Graham Kerr Step by Step Cookbook, 1982.   Add: Wilbur Freifeld, 1175 York Ave., New York, N.Y. 10021, U.S.A.

KERR, Jean.   American, b. 1923.   Plays/Screenplays, Autobiography/Memoirs/Personal.   *Publs:* (adaptor with Walter Kerr) The Song of Bernadette, 1944; (adaptor) Our Hearts Were Young and Gay, 1946; The Big Help, 1947; Jenny Kissed Me, 1949; (with E. Brooke) King of Hearts, 1954; Please Don't Eat the Daisies, 1957; (with W. Kerr) Goldilocks, 1958; The Snake Has All the Lines, 1960; Mary, Mary, 1961; Poor Richard, 1964; Penny Candy, 1970; Finishing Touches, 1973; How I Got to Be Perfect, 1978; Lunch Hour, 1980. Add: 1 Beach Ave., Larchmont, N.Y., U.S.A.

KERR, (Anne) Judith. British (b. German), b. 1923. Children's fiction. Secty., Red Cross, London, 1941–45; Teacher and Textile Designer, 1948–53; Script Ed., and Script Writer, BBC-TV, London, 1953–58. *Publs:* The Tiger Who Came to Tea, 1968; Mog the Forgetful Cat, 1970; When Hitler Stole Pink Rabbit, 1971; When Willy Went to the Wedding, 1972; The Other Way Round, 1975; Mog's Christmas, 1976; A Small Person Far Away, 1978; Mog and the Baby, 1980; Mog in the Dark, 1983; Mog and Me, 1984; Mog's Family of Cats, 1985; Mog's Amazing Birthday Caper, 1986; Mog and Bunny, 1988. Add: c/o William Collins Sons & Co. Ltd., 8 Grafton St., London W1X 3LA, England.

KERR, K. Austin. American. History. Prof. of History, Ohio State Univ., Columbus, since 1984 (Instr., 1965–68; Asst. Prof., 1968–71; Assoc. Prof., 1971–84). *Publs:* American Railroad Politics, 1914–1920, 1968; (ed.) The Politics of Moral Behavior, 1973; Organized for Prohibition: A New History of the Anti-Saloon League, 1985; (with Mansel Blackford) Business Enterprise in American History, 1986, 1990; (with Amos Loveday and Mansel Blackford) Local Businesses: Exploring Their History, 1989. Add: Dept. of History, Ohio State Univ., Columbus, Ohio 43210, U.S.A.

KERR, M.E. Pseud. for Marijane Meaker. American, b. 1927. Children's fiction. *Publs:* Dinky Hocker Shoots Smack!, 1972; If I Love You, Am I Trapped Forever?, 1973; The Son of Someone Famous, 1974; Is That You, Miss Blue?, 1975; Love Is a Missing Person, 1975; I'll Love You When You're More Like Me, 1977; Gentlehands, 1978; Little, Little, 1980; What I Really Think of You, 1982; Me Me Me Me Me, 1983; Him She Loves, 1984; I Stay Near You, 1985; Night Kites, 1986; Fell, 1987; Fell Back, 1989. Add: 12 Deep Six Dr., East Hampton, N.Y. 11937, U.S.A.

KERR, Michael. *See* HOSKINS, Robert.

KERR, Walter (Francis). American, b. 1913. Plays/Screenplays, Literature, Theatre. Instr. in Speech and Drama, 1938–45, and Assoc. Prof. of Drama, 1945–49, Catholic Univ. of America, Washington, D.C.; Drama Critic, Commonweal, NYC, 1950–52, and New York Herald Tribune, 1952–66; Drama Critic, New York Times, 1966–83. *Publs:* Murder in Reverse, 1935; (adaptor) Washington Irving's Rip Van Winkle, 1937; From Julia to Joe, 1937; (adaptor) Oliver Goldsmith's The Vicar of Wakefield, 1938; Hyacinth on Wheels, 1939; Christmas Incorporated, 1939; (adaptor) Molière's The Miser, 1942; Stardust, 1946; Sing Out Sweet Land, 1949; (adaptor with Jean Kerr) The Song of Bernadette, 1946; (adaptor) Aristophanes' The Birds, 1952; How Not to Write a Play, 1955; Criticism and Censorship, 1956; Pieces at Eight, 1957; (with J. Kerr) Goldilocks, 1958; The Decline of Pleasure, 1962; The Theatre in Spite of Itself, 1963; (with V. Louise Higgins) Five World Plays, 1964; Harold Pinter, 1967; Tragedy and Comedy, 1967; Thirty Plays Hath November, 1969; God on the Gymnasium Floor, 1970; The Silent Clowns, 1975; Journey to the Center of the Theatre, 1979. Add: 1 Beach Ave., Larchmont, N.Y., U.S.A.

KERSH, Cyril. British, b. 1925. Novels/Short stories. Former Managing Ed., Sunday Mirror, London, and Ed. of Reveille, and Men Only, London. *Publs:* The Aggravations of Minnie Ashe, 1970; The Diabolical Liberties of Uncle Max, 1973; The Soho Summer of Mr. Green, 1974; The Shepherds Bush Connection, 1976; Minnie Ashe at War, 1979. Add: 14 Ossington St., London W2 4LZ, England.

KERSHAW, H(arry) V. British, b. 1918. Novels, Plays/Screenplays. Freelance scriptwriter. Writer and Ed., 1957–62, Producer, 1962–66, and Exec. Producer, 1966–73, Coronation Street, Granada T.V. Ltd. *Publs:* Coronation Street: Early Days, 1976; Coronation Street: Trouble at the Rover's, 1976; Coronation Street: Elsie Tanner Strikes Back, 1977; The Street Where I Live, 1981. Add: Abergele, Clwyd, N. Wales.

KERSHAW, Peter. *See* LUCIE-SMITH, Edward.

KESEY, Ken (Elton). American, b. 1935. Novels/Short stories, Social commentary/phenomena. Publr., Spit in the Ocean mag., Eugene, Ore. *Publs:* One Flew Over the Cuckoo's Nest, 1962; Sometimes a Great Notion, 1966; Kesey's Garage Sale, 1973; Demon Box, 1986. Add: 85829 Ridgeway Rd., Pleasant Hill, Ore. 97455, U.S.A.

KESSEL, John Howard. American, b. 1928. Politics/Government. Prof. of Political Science, Ohio State Univ., Columbus, since 1970. Asst. Prof. of Political Science, Univ. of Washington, Seattle, 1961–65; Arthur E. Braun Prof. of Political Science, Allegheny Coll., Meadville, Pa., 1965–70. Co-Ed., Political Science Annual, 1970–75; Ed., American Journal of Political Science, 1974–76; Pres., Midwest Political Science Assn., 1978–79. *Publs:* The Goldwater Coalition: Republican Strategies in 1964, 1968; (ed. with G. Cole and R. Seddig) Micropolitics, 1970; The Domestic Presidency, 1975; Presidential Campaign Politics: Coalition Strategies and Citizen Response, 1980, 3rd ed. 1988; Presidential Parties, 1984; (co-ed.) Theory Building and Data Analysis in the Social Sciences, 1984. Add: Dept. of Political Science, Ohio State Univ., Columbus, Ohio 43210, U.S.A.

KESSELMAN, Wendy (Ann). American. Children's Fiction, Plays. *Publs:* children's fiction—Franz Tovey and the Rare Animals, 1968; Angelita, 1970; Slash: An Alligator's Story, 1971; Joey, 1982; Time for Jody, 1975; Emma, 1980; There's a Train Going by My Window, 1982; Flick, 1983; plays—My Sister in This House, 1982; The Juniper Tree, 1985. Add: P.O. Box 680, Wellfleet, Mass. 02667, U.S.A.

KESSEN, William. American, b. 1925. Psychology. Prof. of Psychology, Yale Univ., New Haven, Conn., since 1965 (joined faculty, 1954). *Publs:* (co-author) The Language of Psychology, 1959; The Child, 1965; (ed.) Childhood in China, 1975; (co-author) Psychological Development from Infancy, 1979; (ed.) History, Theories, and Methods Handbook of Child Psychology, 1983. Add: Dept. of Psychology, Yale Univ., New Haven, Conn. 06520, U.S.A.

KESSLER, Jascha (Frederick). American, b. 1929. Novels/Short stories, Plays/Screenplays, Poetry, Songs, lyrics and libretti, Translations. Prof. of English, Univ. of California at Los Angeles, since 1970 (Asst. Prof., 1961–64; Assoc. Prof., 1964–70). Instr., Univ. of Michigan, Ann Arbor, 1951–54; Asst. Prof., New York Univ., NYC, 1954–55; Asst. Prof., Hunter Coll., NYC, 1955–56; Asst. Dir., Curriculum Research, Harcourt, Brace and Co. Inc. publrs., NYC, 1956–57; Asst. Prof., Hamilton Coll., Clinton, N.Y., 1957–61. Reviewer, Literature Prog., KUSC-FM, Los Angeles, 1978–85. *Publs:* (ed. and contrib.) American Poems: A Contemporary Collection, 1964, 1972; An Egyptian Bondage and Other Stories, 1967; Whatever Love Declares (poetry), 1969; After the Armies Have Passed (poetry), 1970; In Memory of the Future (poetry), 1976; The Cave (libretto); Bearing Gifts: Two Mythologems, 1979; (trans. with Charlotte Rogers) The Magician's Garden: 24 Stories by Geza Csáth, 1980; Lee Mullican, 1980; (trans. with Amin Banani) Bride of Acacias: The Selected Poems of Forugh Farrokhzad, 1983; Death Comes for the Behaviorist: Four Long Stories, 1983; (trans. with Charlotte Rogers) Opium and Other Stories by Geza Csath, 1983; (trans. with G. Olujic) Rose of Mother-of-Pearl: A Fairytale, 1983; (trans. with Alexander Shurbanov) Time As Seen From Above and Other Poems by Nicolai Kantchev, 1984; (trans.) Under Gemini: The Selected Poems of Miklós Radnóti, 1985; Transmigrations: Eighteen Mythologems, 1985; Classical Illusions: Twenty-Eight Stories, 1985; (trans. with Alexander Shurbanou) Medusa: Selected Poems of Nicolais Kantcheu, 1986; The Face of Creation: Contemporary Hungarian Poetry, 1988; (trans. with Amin Banani) Look! The Guiding Dawn: Selected Poetry of Táheséh, 1989. Add: 218 Sixteenth St., Santa Monica, Cal. 90402, U.S.A.

KESSLER, Milton. American, b. 1930. Poetry. Poet-in-Residence and Assoc. Prof. to Prof. of English, Harpur Coll., State Univ. of New York, Binghamton, since 1965. Co-Ed., Choice mag., Binghamton, since 1972. Instr., Boston Univ., Mass., 1957–58, and Ohio State Univ., Columbus, 1958–63; Lectr. in English, Queens Coll., City Univ. of New York, 1963–65; Visiting Prof., Univ. of the Negev, Israel, 1971–72, Univ. of Hawaii, 1975, Univ. of Haifa, Israel, 1981, Univ. of Antwerp, Belgium, 1985. *Publs:* A Road Came Once, 1963; Called Home, 1967; Woodlawn North: A Book of Poems, 1970; Sailing Too Far, 1973; (with G.E. Kadish and Karl Korte) Pale Is This Good Prince (oratorio), 1973. Add: 25 Lincoln Ave., Binghamton, N.Y. 13905, U.S.A.

KETCHAM, Ralph Louis. American, b. 1927. History, Biography. Prof. of American Studies, Syracuse Univ., N.Y. since 1963. Ed., The Papers of James Madison, Univ. of Chicago, 1956–60; Assoc. Ed., Papers of Benjamin Franklin, Yale Univ., New Haven, Conn., 1961–63. *Publs:* (ed. with W. Hutchinson and W.M.E. Rachal) The Papers of James Madison, vols. I & II, 1962; (ed. with L.W. Labaree) The Papers of Benjamin Franklin, vols. VI & VII, 1963; (ed. with L.W. Labaree) The Autobiography of Benjamin Franklin, 1964; (ed.) The Political Thought of Benjamin Franklin, 1965; Benjamin Franklin, 1965; James Madison: A Biography, 1971; From Colony to Country: The Revolution in American

Thought, 1750-1820, 1974; From Independence to Interdependence, 1975; Presidents Above Party: The First American Presidency 1789-1829, 1984; Antifederalist Papers, 1986; Individualism and Public Life: A Modern Dilemma, 1987. Add: Maxwell Sch., Syracuse Univ., Syracuse, N.Y. 13210, U.S.A.

KETCHUM, Richard M. American, b. 1922. History, Biography. Ed., Blair & Ketchum's Country Journal, 1974–84; Editorial Dir., Book Div., American Heritage Publishing Co., NYC, 1956–74. *Publs:* What is Communism?, 1955; (ed.) What Is Democracy?, 1955; Male Husbandry, 1956; American Heritage Book of Great Historic Places, 1957; (ed.) American Heritage Book of the Revolution, 1958; (ed.) American Heritage Book of the Pioneer Spirit, 1959; (ed.) American Heritage Picture History of the Civil War, 1960; (ed.) The Horizon Book of the Renaissance, 1961; The Battle for Bunker Hill, 1962; (ed.) Four Days, 1964; (ed.) The Original Watercolor Paintings by John James Audubon for the Birds of America; Faces from the Past, 1970; The Secret Life of the Forest, 1970; The Winter Soldiers, 1973; Will Rogers, 1973; George Washington, 1974; Decisive Day, 1974; Second Cutting: Letters from the Country, 1981. Add: Saddlebrook Farm, R.F.D.1, Box 1104, Dorset, Vt. 05251, U.S.A.

KETCHUM, William C. (Jr.). American, b. 1931. Antiques/Furnishings, Crafts. Instr. in Collecting American Antiques, New Sch. of Social Research, NYC, since 1971; Instr. in Art and Art Ed., NY Univ., since 1984; Curator of Special Projects, Museum of American Folk Art, NYC, since 1984; Instr. in Antiques, Marymount Coll., Tarrytown, N.Y., since 1987. *Publs:* Early Potters and Potteries of New York State, 1970, 1987; The Pottery and Porcelain Collectors Handbook, 1971; American Basketry and Woodenware, 1974; A Treasury of American Bottles, 1975; Hooked Rugs, 1976; A Catalog of American Antiques, 1977; The Family Treasury of Antiques, 1978; Early American Crafts, 1979; The Catalog of American Collectibles, 1979; Western Memorabilia, 1980; Furniture II, 1980; The Catalog of World Antiques, 1981; Auction Toys, 1981; Boxes, 1982; American Furniture: Cupboards, Chests and Related Pieces, 1982; Pottery and Porcelain, 1983; American Folk Art of 20th Century, 1983; Collecting American Bottles for Fun and Profit, 1985; Collecting American Toys, 1985; Collecting Sport Memorabilia, 1985; Collecting Items of the 40's and 50's, 1985; All American: Folk Art and Crafts, 1986; American Country Pottery, 1987; Holiday Collectibles, 1989; How to Run an Antiques Businmess, 1990. Add: 241 Grace Church St., Rye, N.Y., U.S.A.

KETTELKAMP, Larry Dale. American, b. 1933. Children's non-fiction. Music, Psychology, Sciences, Supernatural/Occult topics. Freelance writer, ed., music teacher, composer, and lectr.; Instr. of Graphic Design, Rider Coll., Lawrenceville, N.J., since 1986; Dir., Bookarts Assocs., Cranbury, N.J., since 1982. Art Dir., Garrard Publishing Co., Champaign, Ill., 1959–60; Layout and Staff Artist, Highlights for Children mag., Honesdale, Pa., 1962–67; Dir. of Publs., Summy-Birchard Music, Princeton, N.J., 1981–82. *Publs:* Magic Made Easy, 1954, 1981; Spooky Magic, 1955; The Magic of Sound, 1956, 1982; Shadows, 1957; Singing Strings, 1958; Kites, 1959; Drums, Rattles and Bells, 1960; Gliders, 1961; Flutes, Whistles and Reeds, 1962; Puzzle Patterns, 1963; Spirals, 1964; Horns, 1964; Spinning Tops, 1966; Song, Speech and Ventriloquism, 1967; Dreams, 1968; Haunted Houses, 1969; Sixth Sense, 1970; Investigating UFOs, 1971; Religions East and West, 1972; Astrology, Wisdom of the Stars, 1973; Tricks of Eye and Mind, 1976; Hypnosis, 1975; The Dreaming Mind, 1975; A Partnership of Mind and Body: Biofeedback, 1976; Investigating Psychics, 1977; The Healing Arts, 1978; Lasers: The Miracle Light, 1979; Mischievous Ghosts: The Poltergeist and PK, 1980; Your Marvelous Mind, 1980; Electronic Musical Instruments: What They Do, How They Work, 1984; Starter Solos for Classical Guitar, 1984; Intermediate Etudes For Classical Guitar, 1984; The Human Brain, 1986; Modern Sports Science, 1986; Bill Cosby: Family Funny Man, 1987. Add: Wynnewood Dr., Cranbury, N.J. 08512, U.S.A.

KEVE, Paul W(illard). American, b. 1913. Criminology/Law enforcement/Prisons. Prof. Emeritus, Virginia Commonwealth Univ., Richmond, since 1977. Dir. of Court Services, Hennepin County, Minn., 1952–67; Commnr. of Corrections, State of Minnesota, 1967–71; Dir. of Crime Control and Justice Systems, American Technical Assistance Corp., McLean, Va., 1971–73; Dir. of Adult Corrections, State of Delaware, 1973–76. *Publs:* Prison, Probation or Parole?, 1954; The Probation Officer Investigates, 1960; Imaginative Programming in Probation and Parole, 1967; Prison Life and Human Worth, 1975; Corrections, 1981; The McNeil Century: The Life and Times of an Island Prison, 1984; The History of Corrections in Virginia, 1986. Add: 3347 Sherbrook Rd., Richmond, Va. 23235, U.S.A.

KEVLES, Bettyann Holtzmann. American, b. 1938. Animals, Biology,

Natural history. Contributor, Los Angeles Times, since 1981. *Publs:* Watching the Wild Apes: The Primate Studies of Goodall, Fossey, and Galdikas, 1976; Listening In, 1980; Thinking Gorillas, 1981; Females of the Species: Sex and Survival in the Animal Kingdom, 1986. Add: 575 La Loma Rd., Pasadena, Calif. 91108, U.S.A.

KEVLES, Daniel J. American, b. 1939. History. Koepfli Prof. of Humanities, Div. of Humanities and Social Science, California Institute of Technology, Pasadena (joined faculty, 1964). Member, White House Staff, 1964. *Publs:* The Physicists: The History of a Scientific Community in Modern America, 1978; In the Name of Eugenics: Genetics and the Uses of Human Heredity, 1985. Add: Div. of Humanities and Social Sciences, California Inst. of Technology, Pasadena, Calif. 91125, U.S.A.

KEYES, Daniel. American, b. 1927. Novels/Short stories, Science fiction, Psychology. Prof. of English, Ohio Univ., Athens, since 1972 (lectr., 1966–71). Instr. in English, Wayne State Univ., Detroit, Mich., 1961–66. *Publs:* Flowers for Algernon, 1966; The Touch, 1968; The Fifth Sally, 1980; The Minds of Billy Milligan (non-fiction), 1981; Unveiling Claudia (non-fiction), 1986. Add: Dept. of English, Ohio Univ., Athens, Ohio 45701, U.S.A.

KEYFITZ, Nathan. American, b. 1913. Demography, Sociology. Trustee, National Opinion Research Center; Head, Population Program, Intnl. Inst. of Applied Systems Analysis, Austria. Former Sr. Research Statistician, Bureau of Statistics, Ottawa, and Prof. of Sociology, Univ. of Toronto; Prof. of Sociology, Univ. of Chicago, 1963–67; Prof. of Demography, Univ. of California, Berkeley, 1967–72; Andelot Prof. of Sociology and Demography, Harvard Univ., Cambridge, Mass., from 1972, now retired; Lazarus Prof. Emeritus, Ohio State Univ., Columbus; Pres., Population Assn. of America, 1970–71. *Publs:* (with W. Flieger) World Population: An Analysis of Vital Data, 1968; Introduction to the Mathematics of Population, 1968, 1977; (with W. Flieger) Population: Facts and Methods of Demography, 1971; Applied Mathematical Demography, 1977; Population Change and Social Policy, 1982. Add: c/o IIASA, 2361 Laxenburg, Austria.

KEYS, Ancel. American, b. 1904. Medicine/Health. Prof. Emeritus, Sch. of Public Health, Univ. of Minnesota, Minneapolis, since 1972 (Prof. and Dir. of Physiological Hygiene, 1939–40, Prof., 1946–72). *Publs:* The Biology of Human Starvation, 2 vols., 1950; (with M. Keys) Eat Well and Stay Well, 1959, 1963; The Benevolent Bean, 1967, 1972; How to Eat Well and Stay Well the Mediterranean Way, 1975; Seven Countries: A Multivariate Analysis of Death and Coronary Heart Disease, 1980. Add: Div. of Epidemiology, Sch. of Public Health, Univ. of Minnesota, Stadium Gate 27, Minneapolis, Minn. 55455, U.S.A.

KEYS, Thomas Edward. American, b. 1908. Librarianship, Medicine/Health. Prof. of History of Medicine Emeritus, and Librarian Emeritus, Mayo Clinic, Rochester, Minn., since 1972 (Librarian 1946–69; Prof. of History of Medicine, Mayo Grad. Sch., Univ. of Minn., and Sr. Library Consultant, 1969–72). *Publs:* (ed. with F.W. Willius and contrib.) Cardiac Classics, 1941; The History of Surgical Anesthesia, 1945; Applied Medical Library Practice, 1958; (ed. with F.A. Willius and contrib.) Classics of Cardiology, 1961; (ed. with A. Faulconer and contrib.) Foundations of Anesthesiology, 1965; (ed. with J. Key and contrib.) Classics and Other Selected Readings in Medical Librarianship, 1980; (ed. with J. Callahan and J. Key and contrib.) Classics of Cardiology, vol. III, 1983. Add: 4001 N.W. 19th Ave., Apt. 703, Rochester, Minn. 55901, U.S.A.

KEYSERLING, Leon H. American, b. 1908. Economics. Full-time writer and speaker on U.S. national economic performance and policies. Teacher of economics, Columbia Univ., NYC, 1931–33; Legislative Asst. to U.S. Sen. Robert F. Wagner, 1933–37; with various Federal housing agencies, 1937–46; Vice-Chmn., 1946–49, and Chmn., 1949–53, Council of Economic Advisers to the President of the United States; Pres., Conference on Economic Progress, 1954–87; self-employed consulting economist and lawyer until 1987. *Publs:* (with R.G. Tugwell) Redirecting Education, 1934; Toward Full Employment and Full Production, 1954; National Prosperity Program for 1955, 1955; Full Prosperity for Agriculture, 1955; The Gaps in Our Prosperity, 1956; Consumption: Key to Full Prosperity, 1957; Speeding Israel's Progress, 1957; Wages and the Public Interest, 1958; The "Recession": Cause and Cure, 1958; Toward a New Farm program, 1958; Inflation: Cause and Cure, 1959; The Federal Budget and "The General Welfare", 1959; The Economy of Israel, 1959, 1979; Tight Money and Rising Interest Rates, 1960; Food and Freedom, 1960; Jobs and Growth, 1961; (with Benjamin A. Javits) The World

Development Corporation, 1962; Poverty and Deprivation in the U.S., 1962; Key Policies for Full Employment, 1962; The Move Toward Railroad Mergers, 1962; Taxes and the Public Interest, 1963; Two Top-Priority Programs to Reduce Unemployment, 1963; The Toll of Rising Interest Rates, 1964; Progress or Poverty, 1964; Agriculture and the Public Interest, 1965; The Role of Wages in a Great Society, 1966; Goals for Teachers' Salaries in Our Public Schools, 1967; Achieving Nationwide Educational Excellence, 1968; Israel's Economic Progress, 1968; Taxation of Whom and for What, 1969; Growth with Less Inflation or More Inflation Without Growth, 1970; Wages, Prices, and Profits, 1971; The Coming Crisis in Housing, 1972; The Scarcity School of Economics, 1973; Full Employment Without Inflation, 1975; Toward Full Employment Within Three Years, 1976, "Liberal" and "Conservative" Economic Policies and Their Consequences 1919–1979, 1979; Money, Credit, and Interest Rates: Their Gross Mismanagement by the Federal Reserve System, 1980; The Economics of Discrimination, 1981; How to Cut Unemployment to Four Percent, and End Inflation and Deficits, 1983. Add: c/o Conference on Economic Progress, 2101 Conn. Ave., N.W., Washington, D.C. 20008, U.S.A.

KGOSITSILE, Keorapetse (William). South African, b. 1938. Poetry. Lectr. in Literature, Univ. of Nairobi. African Ed.-at-Large, Black Dialogue, San Francisco, Calif. *Publs:* Spirits Unchained, 1969; For Melba, 1970; My Name is Afrika, 1971; (ed.) The Word is Here: Poetry from Modern Africa, 1973; The Present Is a Dangerous Place to Live, 1974; (with others) A Capsule Course in Black Poetry Writing, 1975; Places and Bloodstains: Notes for Ipelang, 1975. Add: Dept. of Literature, Univ. of Nairobi, P.O. Box 30197, Nairobi, Kenya.

KHADDURI, Majid. American, b. 1909. International relations, Law, Political science. Dir., Center for Middle East Studies, since 1949 and Distinguished Research Prof., since 1970, Johns Hopkins Univ. Sch. of Advanced Intnl. Studies, Washington, D.C. Member, Bd. of Govs., since 1960, and Chmn., Publs. Cttee, since 1969, Middle East Inst.; Pres., Shaybani Soc. of Intnl. Law, since 1969. *Publs:* Independent Iraq, 2nd ed. 1961; Islamic Jurisprudence: Shafi'i's Risala, 1961; Modern Libya, 1963; The Islamic Law of Nations: Shaybani's Siyar, 1966; Republican Iraq, 1969; Political Trends in the Arab World, 1970; (ed.) Major Middle Eastern Problems in International Law, 1972; Arab Contemporaries, 1973; Socialist Iraq, 1978; Arab Personalities in Politics, 1981; The Islamic Conception of Justice, 1984; The Gulf War, 1988. Add: 4454 Tindall St. N.W. Washington, D.C. 20016, U.S.A.

KHAN, Ismith (Mohamed). American (b. Trinidadian), b. 1925. Novels/Short stories. Adjunct Lectr. in English, Medgar Evers Coll., Brooklyn, N.Y., since 1986. Research Asst., Dept. of Far Eastern Studies, Cornell Univ., Ithaca, N.Y., 1955–56; Library Asst., N.Y. Public Library, 1956–61; Instr. in Creative Writing, New Sch. for Social Research, NYC, 1959–69; Visiting Prof. of English, Univ. of California at Berkeley, 1970–71; Asst. Prof. of Caribbean and Comparative Literature, Univ. of California at San Diego, 1971–74; Sr. Lectr., Univ. of Southern California, Los Angeles, 1977, and California State Univ., Long Beach, 1978, 1980. *Publs:* The Jumbie Bird, 1961; The Obeah Man, 1964; The Crucifixion, 1987. Add: c/o Nicholson, 41 Eastern Parkway, Apt. 8E, Brooklyn, N.Y. 11238, U.S.A.

KHERDIAN, David. American, b. 1931. Poetry, Literature, Biography. Literary Consultant, Northwestern Univ., Evanston, Ill. 1965; Publisher, Giligia Press, 1967–73; Poetry Judge, Inst. of American Indian Arts, Santa Fe, N.M., 1968; Ed., Ararat mag., 1970; Poet-in-the-Schs., State of New Hampshire, 1971; Dir., Two Rivers Press, 1978–86. *Publs:* David Meltzer: A Sketch from Memory and Descriptive Checklist, 1965; A Bibliography of William Saroyan: 1934–1965, 1965; Gary Snyder: A Biographical Sketch and Descriptive Checklist, 1965; Six Poets of the San Francisco Renaissance: Portraits and Checklist, 1967; (with G. Hausman) Eight Poems, 1968; Six San Francisco Poets, 1969; On the Death of My Father and Other Poems, 1970; (ed. with J. Baloian) Down at the Santa Fe Depot: Twenty Fresno Poets, 1970: Homage to Adana, 1970; Looking Over Hills, 1972; (ed.) Visions of America: By the Poets of Our Time, 1973; A David Kherdian Sampler, 1974; The Nonny Poems, 1974; (ed.) Settling America: The Ethnic Expression of Fourteen Contemporary Poets, 1974; (ed.) Any Day of Your Life, 1975; (ed.) Poems Here and Now, 1976; (ed.) The Dog Writes on the Window with His Nose and Other Poems, 1977; (ed.) Traveling America with Today's Poets, 1977; (ed.) If Dragon Flies Made Honey, 1977; Country Cat, City Cat, 1978; I Remember Root River, 1978; (ed.) I Sing the Song of Myself, 1978; The Road from Home: The Story of an Armenian Girl, 1979; The Farm, 1979; (trans.) The Pearl: Hymn of the Robe of Glory, 1979; It Started with Old Man Bean, 1980; Finding Home, 1981; Beyond Two Rivers, 1981;

Taking the Soundings on Third Avenue, 1981; The Farm: Book Two, 1981; (trans.) Pigs Never See the Stars: Proverbs from the Armenian, 1982; The Song in the Walnut Grove, 1983; The Mystery of the Diamond in the Wood, 1983; Right Now; 1983; The Animal, 1984; Root River Run, 1984; Threads of Light, 1985; Bridger: The Story of a Mountain Man, 1987. Add: 412 First St. N., Charlottesville, VA 22901, U.S.A.

KHOSLA, Gopal Das. Indian, b. 1901. Novels/Short stories, History, Travel/Exploration/Adventure, Biography. Chmn., Netaji Inquiry Commn., Govt. of India, since 1970. Judge, 1943–59, and Chief Justice, 1959–61, High Court, Punjab; Chmn., National Industrial Tribunal, 1965–66, Delhi Police Commn., 1966–67, Film Censorship Inquiry Cttee., 1967–68, Inquiry into National Library, 1968; Cttee. of Inquiry into National Cultural Academics, 1969, and Cttee. of Inquiry into Film and Television Inst. of India, 1971. *Publs:* Stern Reckoning, 1948; Our Judicial System, 1950; Himalayan Circuit, 1956; Price of a Wife, 1958; Horoscope Cannot Lie, 1961; Murder of the Mahatma, 1963; Grim Fairy Tales, 1964; The Last Mughal, 1965; A Way of Loving, 1969; A Taste of India, 1969; Memories and Opinions, 1973; Indira Gandhi, 1974; Last Days of Netaji, 1974; Pornography and Censorship in India, 1976; Know Your Copyright, 1977; Of Mountains and Men, 1980; Never the Twain, 1982; Memory's Gay Chariot, 1985. Add: C-9 Maharani Bagh, New Delhi-65, India.

KHOURI, Fred John. American, b. 1916. International relations/Current affairs. Prof. Emeritus of Political Science, Villanova Univ., Pa., since 1986. Assoc. Ed., The Journal of South Asian and Middle Eastern Studies, since 1977. With Univ. of Tennessee, Knoxville, 1946–47, Univ. of Connecticut 1947–50, and American Univ. of Beirut, 1961–64; Member, Brookings Inst. Middle East Study Group, 1975–76; Sr. Fellow, Middle East Center, Univ. of Pennsylvania, Philadelphia, 1978–79, 1980–81. *Publs:* The Arab States and the U.N., 1954; The Arab-Israeli Dilemma, 1968, 3rd ed. 1985. Add: Villanova Univ., Villanova, Pa., 19085, U.S.A.

KIDDER, Tracy. American, b. 1945. Information science/Computers, Homes. Writer, since 1974. *Publs:* The Road to Yuba City: A Journey into the Juan Corona Murders, 1974; The Soul of a New Machine, 1981 (Pulitzer Prize and American Book Award, 1982); House, 1985. Add: c/o Georges Borchardt Inc., 136 E. 57th St., New York, N.Y. 10022, U.S.A.

KIDWELL, Carol. *See* **MADDISON,** Carol.

KIEFER, Warren (David). Has also written with Harry Middleton under joint pseudonym of Middleton Kiefer. American, b. 1930. Novels/Short stories, Plays/Screenplays. Dir., Intercontinental Mgmt. Assocs. Asst. Mgr. Intnl. Public Relations, Chas Pfizer & Co. Inc., 1954–57; television documentary film writer, 1958–74. *Publs:* (with Harry Middleton as Middleton Kiefer) Pax, 1958; Castle of the Living Dead (screenplay), 1964; The Outrider (screenplay), 1967; Juliette de Sade (screenplay), 1968; Michael Strogonoff (screenplay), 1969; The Last Rebel (screenplay), 1970; The Kidnappers (screenplay), 1971; By Force of Arms (screenplay), 1972; The Lingala Code, 1972; (with Pierre Schoendoerffer) Farwell to the King (screenplay), 1973; Pontius Pilate Papers (novel), 1976; The Snow Queen (novel), 1979. Add: Sarmiento 1881, Buenos Aires, Argentina.

KIELY, Benedict. Irish, b. 1919. Novels/Short stories, History, Literature. Journalist in Dublin, 1939–64. *Publs:* Counties of Contention: Study of the Origins and Implications of the Partition of Ireland, 1945; Land Without Stars, 1946; Poor Scholar: A Study of the Works and Days of William Carleton, 1794-1869, 1947; In a Harbour Green, 1949; Call for a Miracle, 1950; Modern Irish Fiction: A Critique, 1950; Honey Seems Bitter, 1952; The Cards of a Gambler: A Folktale, 1953; There Was an Ancient House, 1955; The Captain with the Whiskers, 1960; A Journey to the Seven Streams: 17 Stories, 1963; Dogs Enjoy the Morning, 1968; A Ball of Malt and Madame Butterfly: Stories, 1973; (ed.) The Various Lives of Keats and Chapman, by Flann O'Brien, 1976; Proxopera, 1977; A Cow in the House and Other Stories, 1978; All the Way to Bantry Bay and Other Irish Journeys, 1978; The State of Ireland, 1980; (ed.) The Penguin Book of Irish Short Stories, 1982; The Small Oxford Book of Dublin, 1983; Nothing Happens in Carmin Cross, 1985; A Letter to Peachtree, 1987; Yeats' Ireland, 1989. Add: c/o the Irish Times, Westmoreland St., Dublin, Ireland.

KIELY, Jerome. Irish, b. 1925. Novels/Short stories, Poetry. Pastor, Parish of Aughadown, Co. Cork, since 1983. Prof. of Preaching Techniques, Catholic Seminary at Carlow, 1950–54; Teacher of English and History,Diocesan Coll., Farranferris, Co. Cork, 1954–67; Curate, Parish of Goleen, Co. Cork, 1967–83. *Publs:* (co-author) New Poets of Ireland, 1963; The Griffon Sings (poetry), 1966; Seven Year Island (novel), 1969; (co-author) Irish Poets 1924–1974, 1975. Add: Priest's House, Lisheen, Skibbereen, Co. Cork, Ireland.

KIENZLE, William X(avier). American, b. 1928. Mystery/Crime/Suspense. Roman Catholic priest: ordained, 1954; archdiocesan priest in five parishes, Detroit, 1954–74; Ed.-in-Chief, Michigan Catholic, Detroit, 1962–74, and MPLS mag., Minneapolis, 1974–77; Assoc. Dir., Center for Contemplative Studies, Western Michigan Univ., Kalamazoo, 1977–78; Dir., Center for Contemplative Studies, Univ. of Dallas, 1978–79. *Publs:* The Rosary Murders, 1979; Death Wears a Red Hat, 1980; Mind over Murder, 1981; Assault with Intent, 1982; Shadow of Death, 1983; Kill and Tell, 1984; Sudden Death, 1985; Deathbed, 1986; Deadline for a Critic, 1987; Marked for Murder, 1988; Eminence, 1989. Add: 22281 Carleton, Southfield, Mich. 48034, U.S.A.

KIERNAN, Brian. Australian, b. 1937. Literature. Assoc. Prof. in English, Univ. of Sydney, since 1972; Member, Cttee. of Mgmt, Australian Soc. of Authors, 1978–82; Pres., Assoc. for the Study of Australian Literature, 1980–83. Free-lance journalist and lectr., in Italy, 1964–68, and Melbourne, 1968–72. *Publs:* Images of Society and Nature: Seven Essays on Australian Novels, 1971; Criticism, 1974; (ed.) The Portable Henry Lawson, 1976, 1980; (ed.) Considerations: New Essays on Kenneth Slessor, Judith Wright and Douglas Stewart, 1977; (ed.) Douglas Stewart, 1977; (ed.) The Most Beautiful Lies, 1977; Patrick White, 1980; (ed.) The Essential Henry Lawson, 1982. Add: English Dept., Univ. of Sydney, Sydney, N.S.W. 2006, Australia.

KIEV, Ari. American, b. 1933. Psychiatry. Clinical Assoc. Prof. of Psychiatry, Cornell Univ. Medical Sch., NYC, since 1967. *Publs:* (ed.) Magic, Faith and Healing, 1964; Curanderismo: Mexican American Folk Psychiatry, 1968; (ed.) Psychiatry in the Communist World, 1968; (ed.) Social Psychiatry, 1969; (with J. Argandona) Mental Health in the Developing World, 1972; Transcultural Psychiatry, 1972; A Strategy for Daily Living, 1973; A Strategy for Handling Executive Stress, 1974; (ed.) Somatic Aspects of Depressive Illness, 1974; The Drug Epidemic, 1975; The Suicidal Patient: Recognition and Management, 1976; A Strategy for Success, 1976; The Courage to Live, 1979; Active Loving, 1979; Riding Through the Downers, 1980; Recovery from Depression, 1982; How to Keep Love Alive, 1982. Add: 150 East 69th St., New York, N.Y. 10021, U.S.A.

KILBOURN, William (Morley). Canadian, b. 1926. History. Prof. of Humanities and History, York Univ., Toronto. Exec. Member, The Canada Council, and Toronto Arts Council. *Publs:* The Firebrand: William Lyon Mackenzie and the Rebellion of Upper Canada, 1960; The Elements Combined: A History of the Steel Company of Canada, 1960; The Making of the Nation: Canada's First Hundred Years, 1967, 1973; Pipeline: Trans-Canada and the Great Debate: A History of Business and Politics, 1970; (ed.) Canada: A Guide to the Peaceable Kingdom, 1970; Toronto Book, 1975; Toronto, 1977; C.D. Howe: A Biography, 1979; Toronto Remembered, 1984; Toronto Observed, 1986. Add: 66 Collier St., Toronto, Ont. M4W 2V5, Canada.

KILBRACKEN, Lord; John Raymond Godley. Irish, b. 1920. Poetry, Art, Natural history, Autobiography/Memoirs, Biography. Freelance writer since 1951, including contracts with Evening Standard (as foreign corresp.), and Tatler; active as Labour Peer in House of Lords; Editorial Dir., Worldwatch Mag., 1984–85. *Publs:* Even for an Hour (poetry), 1940; Tell Me the Next One, 1950; (ed.) Letters from Early New Zealand, 1951; The Master Forger (in U.S. as Master Art Forger), 1951; Living Like a Lord, 1955; A Peer Behind the Curtain (in U.S. as Moscow Gatecrash), 1959; Shamrock and Unicorns (essays), 1962; Van Meegeren, 1967; Bring Back My Stringbag, 1979; The Easy Way to Bird Recognition, 1982; The Easy Way to Tree Recognition, 1983; The Easy Way to Wildflower Recognition, 1984. Add: Killegar, Cavan, Ireland.

KILGORE, James C. American, b. 1928. Poetry. Instr. in English, Langston High Sch., Hot Springs, Ark., 1954–58, A.M. & N. Coll., Pine Buff, Ark., 1958–59, Fair Lawn High Sch., N.J., 1959–60, Central High Sch., Hayti, Mo., 1960–61, and Southwest High Sch., Kansas City, Mo., 1963–66; member, Grad. Sch., Univ. of Missouri, Columbia, and part-time worker at University Hosp., 1961–63; former Prof. of English, Cuyohoga Community Coll., Cleveland, Ohio. *Publs:* The Big Buffalo and Other Poems: A Sampler of the Poetry of James C. Kilgore, 1970; Midnight Blast and Other Poems, 1971; A Time of Black Devotion, 1971; Let It Pass, 1975; A Black Bicentennial, 1976; Until I Met You, 1978; African

Violet: Poems for a Black Woman, 1982. Add: Dept. of English, Eastern Campus, Cuyahoga Community Coll., 25444 Harvard Ave., Warrensville Township, Ohio, 44122, U.S.A.

KILIAN, Crawford. Canadian (b. American), b. 1941. Science fiction. Instr. in English, Capilano Coll., North Vancouver, since 1968. Education Columnist, Vancouver Province, since 1982. *Publs:* science-fiction novels—The Empire of Time, 1978; Icequake, 1979; Eyas, 1982; Tsunami, 1983; Brother Jonathan, 1985; Lifter, 1986; The Fall of the Republic, 1987; Rogue Emperor, 1988; other—Wonders Inc. (for children), 1968; The Last Vikings (for children), 1974; Go Do Some Great Thing: The Black Pioneers of British Columbia, 1978; Exploring British Columbia's Past, 1983; School Wars: The Assault on B.C. Education, 1985. Add: 4635 Cove Cliff Rd., North Vancouver, B.C. V7G 1H7, Canada.

KILLOUGH, (Karen) Lee. American, b. 1942. Science fiction/Fantasy. Radiologic Technologist, Kansas State Univ., Veterinary Hosp., Manhattan, since 1971; also freelance writer of SF short stories. Radiologic Technologist, St. Joseph Hosp., Concordia, Kans., 1964–65, St. Mary Hosp., Manhattan, 1965–67, 1969–71, and Morris Cafritz Mem. Hosp., Washington, D.C., 1967–69. *Publs:* A Voice Out of Ramah, 1979; The Doppelganger Gambit, 1979; The Monitor, the Miners, and the Shree, 1980; Aventine, 1981; Deadly Silents, 1981; Liberty's World, 1985; Spider Play, 1986; Blood Hunt, 1987; The Leopard's Daughter, 1987; Bloodlinks, 1988. Add: Box 422, Manhattan, Kans. 66502, U.S.A.

KILMISTER, Clive William. British, b. 1924. Mathematics, Physics. Gresham Prof. of Geometry, King's Coll., Univ. of London, 1971–88 (Asst. Lectr., 1950–53; Lectr., 1953–59; Reader, 1959–66; Prof. of Mathematics, 1966–84). *Publs:* (with G. Stephenson) Special Relativity for Physicists, 1958; (with B.O.J Tupper) Eddington's Statistical Theory, 1962; Hamiltonian Dynamics, 1964; The Environment in Modern Physics, 1965; (with J.E. Reeve) Rational Mechanics, 1966; Men of Physics: Sir Arthur Eddington, 1966; Language, Logic and Mathematics, 1967; Lagrangian Dynamics, 1967; Special Theory of Relativity, 1970; The Nature of the Universe, 1972; General Theory of Relativity, 1973; Russell, 1984. Add: 11 Vanbrugh Hill, London SE3 7UE, England.

KILPATRICK, James Jackson. American, b. 1920. Law, Politics/Government, Race relations, Travel/Exploration/Adventure, Writing/Journalism. Columnist, Universal Press Syndicate (syndicated columnist since 1964); also, Contributor, National Review; Pres., Op Ed Inc.Reporter, 1941–49, Chief Editorial Writer, 1949–51, and Ed., 1951–66, Richmond News Leader, Virginia. Pres., National Conference of Editorial Writers, 1952–53. *Publs:* (ed. with Louis D. Rubin, Jr.) The Lasting South 1955; The Sovereign States, 1957; The Smut Peddlers, 1960; The Southern Case for School Segregation, 1962; The Foxes' Union, 1977; (with Eugene J. McCarthy) A Political Bestiary, 1978; (with William Bake) The American South: Four Seasons of the Land, 1980, and Towns and Cities, 1982; The Writer's Art, 1984; The Ear Is Human, 1985; A Bestiary of Bridge, 1986. Add: White Walnut Hill, Woodville, Va. 22749, U.S.A.

KILROY, Thomas. Irish, b. 1934. Novels/Short stories, Plays/Screenplays. Prof. of English, University Coll., Galway, since 1977; Headmaster, Stratford Coll., Dublin, 1959–64; Lectr., University Coll., Dublin, 1965–73. *Publs:* The Death and Resurrection of Mr. Roche, 1969; The O'Neill, 1969; The Big Chapel (novel), 1971; (ed.) Sean O'Casey: A Collection of Critical Essays, 1975; Tea and Sex and Shakespeare, 1976; Talbot's Box, 1979; (adaptor) The Seagull, by Chekhov, 1981; Double Cross, 1986; That Man, Bracken, 1986; (adaptor) Ghosts, by Ibsen, 1989. Add: c/o Margaret Ramsay Ltd., 14a Goodwin's Ct., London WC2N 4LL, England.

KILSON, Marion D. de B. American, b. 1936. Anthropology/Ethnology. Dean, Sch. of Arts and Sciences, Salem State Coll., Massachusetts, since 1989. Research Fellow in African Ethnology 1975–81, and Lectr. 1978–80, Harvard Univ., Cambridge, Mass.; Dir., Bunting Inst., Radcliffe Coll., Cambridge, 1977–80; Academic Dean, Emmanuel Coll., Boston, 1980–86; Member, Editorial Staff, Silver Burdett and Ginn, 1987–89. *Publs:* Kpele Lala, 1971; African Urban Kinsmen, 1974; Roal Antelope and Spider, 1976. Add: 4 Eliot Rd., Lexington, Mass. 02173, U.S.A.

KILWORTH, Garry. British, b. 1941. Novels, Children's fiction, Science fiction. Freelance writer since 1982. Served as a Signals Master in the Royal Air Force, 1959–74; Sr. Exec., Cable and Wireless, London and the Caribbean, 1974–82. *Publs:* In Solitary, 1977; The Night of Kadar, 1978; Split Second, 1979; Gemini God, 1981; A Theatre of Timesmiths, 1984; The Songbirds of Pain (short stories), 1984; Witchwater Country, 1986; Spiral Winds, 1987; Cloudrock, 1988; Abandonati, 1988; In the Hollow of the Deep-Sea Wave, 1989. Add: A1/7 Vista Panorama, Rhondda Rd, Kowloon Tong, Hong Kong.

KIM, Richard E. American (born Korean), b. 1932. Novels/Short stories. Adjunct Assoc. Prof. of English, Univ. of Massachusetts, Amherst, since 1969 (Asst. Prof., 1964–68; Assoc. Prof., 1968–69). Instr. of English, California State Coll., Long Beach, 1963–64; Visiting Prof. of English, Syracuse Univ., N.Y., 1970–71; San Diego State Univ., 1975–77. *Publs:* The Martyred, 1964; The Innocent, 1968; Lost Names, 1970; In Search of Lost Years, 1985. Add: Leverett Rd., Shutesbury, Mass. 01072, U.S.A.

KIM, Young (Hum). American, b. 1920. History, International relations/Current affairs. Prof. of History and Political Science, U.S. Intnl. Univ., San Diego, Calif., since 1961 (former Asst. Prof. and Assoc. Prof.). Former Asst. Secty., U.S. Embassy, Seoul, Korea. *Publs:* East Asia's Turbulent Century, 1966; Patterns of Competitive Coexistence: USA vs. USSR, 1966; Twenty Years of Crises: The Cold War Era, 1968; Toward Rational View of China: The Vietnam War in Struggle Against History: U.S. Foreign Policy in an Age of Revolution, 1968; The Central Intelligence Agency: Problems of Secrecy in a Democracy, 1981; America's Frontier Activities in Asia: U.S. Diplomatic History in Asia in the Twentieth Century, 1981; The War of No Return, vol. 1, 1988, vol. 2, 1989. Add: 3001 Conner Way, San Diego, Calif. 92117, U.S.A.

KIMBALL, John (Ward). American, b. 1931. Biology. Instr. in Science, Noble and Greenough Sch., Dedham, Mass., 1953–54; Project Officer, U.S. Air Force, Rome, N.Y., 1954–56; Instr. in Biology, Phillips Academy, Andover, Mass., 1956–69; Special Research Fellow, National Insts. of Health, 1969–72; Asst., then Assoc. Prof. of Biology, Tufts Univ., Medford, Mass., 1972–81; Visiting Lectr., Harvard Univ., Cambridge, Mass., 1982–86. *Publs:* Biology, 1965, 5th ed. 1983; Cell Biology, 1970, 3rd ed. 1984; Man and Nature: Principles of Human and Environmental Biology, 1975; Introduction to Immunology, 1983, 1986. Add: 89 Prospect Rd., Andover, Mass. 01810, U.S.A.

KIMBLE, George (Herbert Tinley). British, b. 1908. Geography. Prof. and Chmn., Dept., of Geography, McGill Univ., Montreal, 1945–50; Dir., American Geographical Soc., 1950–53; Dir., Survey of Tropical Africa, Twentieth Century Fund, NYC, 1953–60; Prof. of Geography, 1957–66, and Chmn. of the Dept., 1957–62, Indiana Univ., Bloomington: Research Dir., U.S. Geography Project, Twentieth Centuiry Fund, NYC, 1962–68. Secty.-Treas., Intnl. Geographical Union, 1949–56. *Publs:* Geography in the Middle Ages, 1938; The World's Open Spaces, 1939; The Shepherd of Banbury, 1941; (co-author) The Weather, 1943, 1951; Military Geography of Canada, 1949; The Way of the World, 1953; Our American Weather, 1955; Tropical Africa, 2 vols., 1960; (with R. Steel) Tropical Africa Today, 1966; Man and His World, 1972; From the Four Winds, 1974; This Is Our World, 1981. Add: 2 Dymock's Manor, Ditchling, E. Sussex BN6 8SX, England.

KIMBRO, Jean. *See* **KIMBROUGH,** Katheryn.

KIMBROUGH, Emily. American, b. 1898. Travel/Exploration/Adventure, Autobiography/Memoirs/Personal, Humor/Satire. *Publs:* (with Cornelia Otis Skinner) Our Hearts Were Young and Gay, 1942; We Followed Our Hearts to Hollywood, 1943; How Dear to My Heart, 1944; It Gives Me Great Pleasure, 1948; The Innocents from Indiana, 1950; Through Charley's Door, 1952; Forty Plus and Fancy Free, 1954; So Near and Yet So Far, 1955; Water Water Everywhere, 1956; A Right Good Crew, 1958; Pleasure by the Busload, 1961; Forever Old, Forever New, 1964; Floating Island, 1968; Time Enough, 1974; Better Than Oceans, 1976. Add: 11 East 73rd St., New York, N.Y. 10021, U.S.A.

KIMBROUGH, Katheryn. Pseud. for John M. Kimbro; also writes as Kym Allyson, Ann Ashton, Charlotte Bramwell, and Jean Kimbro. American, b. 1929. Historical/Romance/Gothic. Stage director, composer, teacher, and actor. *Publs:* The House of Windswept Ridge, 1971; The Twisted Cameo, 1971; The Children of Houndstooth, 1972; Thanesworth House, 1972; The Broken Sphinx, 1972; (as Charlotte Bramwell) Cousin to Terror, 1972; (as Charlotte Bramwell) Stepmother's House, 1972; (as Charlotte Bramwell) Brother Sinister, 1973; Heiress to Wolfskill, 1973; The Phantom Flame of Wind House, 1973; The Three Sisters of Briarwick, 1973; The Specter of Dolphin Cove, 1973; Unseen Torment, 1974; The Shadow over Pheasant Heath, 1974; Phenwick Women series: Augusta, The First, 1975, Jane, The Courageous, 1975, Margaret, The Faithful, 1975, Patricia, The Beautiful, 1975, Rachel, The

Possessed, 1975, Susannah, The Righteous, 1975, Rebecca, The Mysterious, 1975, Joanne, The Unpredictable, 1976, Olivia, The Tormented, 1976, Harriet, The Haunted, 1976, Nancy, The Daring, 1976, Marcia, The Innocent, 1976, Kate, The Curious, 1976, Ilene, The Superstitutious, 1977, Millijoy, The Determined, 1977, Barbara, The Valiant, 1977, Ruth, The Unsuspecting, 1977, Ophelia, The Anxious, 1977, Dorothy, The Terrified, 1977, Ann, The Gentle, 1978, Nellie, The Obvious, 1978, Isabelle, The Frantic, 1978, Evelyn, The Ambitious, 1978, Louise, The Restless, 1978, Polly, The Worried, 1978, Yvonne, The Confident, 1979, Joyce, The Beloved, 1979, Augusta, The Second, 1979, Carol, The Pursued, 1979, Katherine, The Returned, 1980, and Peggy, The Concerned, 1981; A Shriek in the Midnight Tower, 1975; (as Kym Allyson) The Moon Shadow, 1976; (as Jean Kimbro) Twilight Return, 1976; (as John M. Kimbro) Night of Tears, 1976; (as Ann Ashton) The Haunted Portrait, 1976; (as Ann Ashton) The Phantom Reflection, 1978, in U.S. paperback as Reflection, 1979; (as Ann Ashton) Three Cries of Terror, 1980; (as Ann Ashton) Concession, 1981; (as Ann Ashton) Star Eyes, 1983; The Lovely and the Lonely, 1984; (as Ann Ashton) The Right Time to Love, 1986; (as Ann Ashton) If Love Comes, 1987. Add: c/o Doubleday, 666 Fifth Ave., New York, N.Y. 10103, U.S.A.

KIMBROUGH, Robert (Alexander III). American, b. 1929. Literature. Prof. of English, Univ. of Wisconsin, Madison, since 1968 (Instr., to Prof., 1959–68; Integrated Liberal Studies Dept., 1970–75). *Publs:* (ed.) Joseph Conrad, Heart of Darkness: An Authoritative Text, Backgrounds and Sources, Essays in Criticism, 1963, 3rd ed., 1987; Shakespeare's Troilus and Cressida and Its Setting, 1964; (ed.) Henry James, The Turn of the Screw: An Authoritative Text, Backgrounds and Sources, Essays in Criticism, 1966; Troilus and Cressida: A Scene-by-Scene Analysis with Critical Commentary, 1966; Sir Philip Sidney: Selected Prose and Poetry, 1969, 1982; Sir Philip Sidney, 1971, 1983; Christopher Marlowe, 1972; (ed.) The Nigger of the Narcissus, by Joseph Conrad, 1979; (ed.) Youth, by Joseph Conrad, 1984. Add: 3206 Gregory St., Madison, Wisc. 53711, U.S.A.

KIMENYE, Barbara. British. Novels/Short stories, Children's fiction. Social Worker in South London, since 1974. *Publs:* Kalasanda (for adults), 1965; Kalasanda Revisited (for adults), 1966; The Smugglers (reader), 1966; Moses series, 9 vols., 1967–73; The Winged Adventure, 1969; Paulo's Strange Adventure, 1971; Barah and the Boy, 1973; Martha the Millipede, 1973; The Runaways, 1973; The Gemstone Affair (adult novel), 1978; The Scoop (adult novel), 1978. Add: c/o Nelson, Nelson House, Mayfield Rd., Walton-on-Thames, Surrey KT12 5PL, England.

KIMMEL, Eric A. American, b. 1946. Novels/Short stories, Children's fiction. Prof of Education, Portland State Univ., Oregon, since 1978. Asst. Prof. of Education, Indiana Univ., South Bend. 1973–78. Contrib., Horn Book, and Cricket. *Publs:* The Tartar's Sword, 1974; Mishka, Pishka and Fishka, 1976; Why Worry?, 1979; Nicanor's Gate, 1980; Hershel of Ostropol, 1981; (with Rose Zar) In the Mouth of the Wolf, 1983; Anansi and the Moss-Covered Rock, 1988; The Chanukkah Tree, 1988; Charlie Drives the Stage, 1989; Herschel and the Chanukkah Goblins, 1989; I Took My Frog to the Library, 1989. Add: 2525 N.E. 35th Ave., Portland, Ore., U.S.A.

KIMPEL, Benjamin Franklin. American, b. 1905. Philosophy. Emeritus Prof. of Philosophy, Drew Univ., Madison, N.J., since 1973 (Prof. and Chmn. of Dept., 1938–73). Instr. in Bible Literature, 1933–34, Asst. Prof. of Philosophy, 1935–36, and Prof., 1936–67, Kansas Wesleyan Univ., Salina; Minister, Unitarian Fellowship, Amherst, Mass. 1937–38. *Publs:* Principle of Contradiction in Idealistic Metaphysic, 1934; Religious Faith, Language and Knowledge, 1952; Faith and Moral Authority, 1953; Symbols of Religious Faith, 1954; Moral Principles in the Bible, 1956; Language and Religion, 1957; Principles of Moral Philosophy, 1960; Kant's Critical Philosophy, 1964; Hegel's Philosophy of History, 1964; Schopenhauer's Philosophy, 1964; Nietzsche's Beyond Good and Evil, 1965; A Philosophy of Zen Buddhism, 1966; Philosophies of Life of Ancient Greeks and Israelites: An Analysis of Their Parallels, 1980; Emily Dickinson as Philosopher, 1981; A Philosophy of the Religions of Ancient Israelites and Greeks, 1982; Stoic Moral Philosophies: Their Counsel for Today, 1985; Moral Philosophies in Shakespeare's Plays, 1987. Add: West St., North Bennington, Vt. 05257, U.S.A.

KINCAID, Jamaica. American, b. 1949. Novels/Short stories.Contributor, and currently Staff Writer, The New Yorker mag., NYC, since 1974. *Publs:* At the Bottom of the River (short stories), 1984; Annie John (novel), 1985; A Small Place (short stories), 1988. Add: c/o The New Yorker, 25 W. 43rd St., New York, N.Y. 10036, U.S.A.

KINDRED, Wendy. American, b. 1937. Children's fiction. Prof. of Art, Univ. of Maine at Fort Kent. *Publs:* Negatu in the Garden, 1971; Ida's Idea, 1972; Lucky Wilma, 1973; Hank and Fred, 1975. Add: 77 Pleasant St., Fort Kent, Me. 04743, U.S.A.

KING, Anthony. Canadian, b. 1934. Politics/Government. Prof. of Govt., Univ. of Essex, Colchester, since 1969 (Sr. Lectr., and Reader, 1966–69). Adjunct Scholar, American Enterprise Inst.; Co-Ed., British Journal of Political Science. Fellow of Magdalen Coll., Oxford, 1961–65. *Publs:* (with D.E. Butler) British General Election of 1964, 1965; (with D.E. Butler) British General Election of 1966, 1966; (ed.) British Prime Minister: A Reader, 1969, 1985; (with A. Sloman) Westminster and Beyond, 1973; British Members of Parliament: A Self-Portrait, 1974; Britain Says Yes: The 1975 Referendum on the Common Market, 1977; (ed.) The New American Political System, 1978; (ed.) Both Ends of the Avenue: Presidential–Congressional Relations in the 1980s, 1983. Add: Dept. of Govt., Univ. of Essex, Wivenhoe Park, Colchester, Essex CO4 3SQ, England.

KING, Betty (Alice). British, b. 1919. Novels/Short stories, History, Literary Criticism. *Publs:* The Lady Margaret, 1965; The Captive James, 1967; The Lord Jasper, 1967; The King's Mother, 1969; The Rose Both Red and White, 1970; The Beaufort Secretary, 1970; Bright Is the Ring, 1971; Flight of the Merlin, 1972; The Beaufort Bastard, 1973; Margaret of Anjou, 1974; Boadicea, 1975; Emma Hamilton, 1976; Mountains Divide Us, 1977; Owen Tudor, 1977; Nell Gwyn, 1979; Claybourn, 1981; The French Countess, 1982; White Unicorn, 1982; We are Tomorrow's Past, 1984; Women of the Future: The Female Main Character in Science Fiction, 1984. Add: Monkswood Cottage, Camlet Way, Hadley Wood, Herts., England.

KING, Billie Jean. American, b. 1943. Sports/Physical education/Keeping fit, Autobiography/Memoirs/Personal. Professional tennis player since 1967 (amateur tennis player, 1958–67). Publisher, Women Sports, since 1981. *Publs:* (with Kim Chapin) Tennis to Win, 1970; (with Joe Hyams) Billie Jean King's Secret of Winning Tennis, 1974; (with Kim Chapin) Billie Jean, 1974; Tennis Love, 1978; (with Frank Deford) Billie Jean King, 1982. Add: Future Inc., c/o Jorgensen and Rogers, 1990, Bundy Dr. 590 Los Angeles, Calif. 90025, U.S.A.

KING, Bruce (Alvin). American, b. 1933. Intellectual history, Literature. Albert S. Johnston Prof. of Literature, Univ. of No. Alabama, since 1983. Taught at Brooklyn Coll., 1960–61, Univ. of Alberta, Calgary, 1961–62, Univ. of Ibadan, 1962–65, Univ. of Bristol, 1966–67, Univ. of Lagos, 1967–70, Univ. of Windsor, Ontario, 1970–73, Ahmadu Bello Univ., Zaria, Nigeria, 1973–76; Teacher, Univ. of Paris, 1977–78; Rockefeller Found. Humanities Fellow, 1977–78; Univ. of Sterling, Scotland, 1979; Univ. of Canterbury, New Zealand, 1979–83; American Institute of Indian Studies Research Fellowship, 1984; Rockefeller Found. Scholar in Residence, Bellagio Center, 1984. *Publs:* Dryden's Major Plays, 1966; (ed.) Twentieth Century Interpretations of All for Love, 1968; (ed.) Dryden's Mind and Art, 1969; (ed.) Introduction to Nigerian Literature, 1971; (ed.) Literatures of the World in English, 1974; (co-ed.) A Celebration of Black and African Writing, 1976; Marvell's Allegorical Poetry, 1977; (ed.) West Indian Literature, 1979; The New English Literatures, 1980; Ibsen's A Doll's House, 1980; G.B. Shaw's Arms and the Man, 1980; Fielding's Joseph Andrews, 1981; History of Seventeenth-Century English Literature, 1982; (series co-ed.) Modern Dramatists, 1982—; Modern Indian Poetry in English, 1987. Add: c/o Oxford Univ. Press, Inc., 200 Madison Ave., New York, N.Y. 10016, U.S.A.

KING, (David) Clive. British, b. 1924. Children's fiction. Lectr. and Education Officer, British Council, London, 1948–73. *Publs:* Hamid of Aleppo, 1958; The Town That Went South, 1959; Stig of the Dump, 1961; The Twenty-Two Letters, 1964; The Night the Water Came, 1972; Snakes and Snakes, 1975; Me and My Million, 1976; The Devil's Cut, 1978; Ninny's Boat, 1980; The Sound of Propellers, 1986; The Seashore People, 1987. Add: c/o Murray Pollinger, 4 Garrick St., London WC2B 9BH, England.

KING, Cynthia. American, b. 1925. Novels/Short stories. Full-time writer. Assoc. Ed., Hillman Periodicals, NYC, 1945–50; Managing Ed., Fawcett Publs., NYC, 1950–54; Teacher: Creative Writing in public and private schools, Houston, Texas, 1970–75; Coord., Children's Book Art, Cont. Art Museum, Houston, 1975; Resident, Michigan Council for the Arts Creative-Writer-in-the-Schools Program, 1976–84; Coord., Seminars on Book Proposals, 1981, and Writing for Children, 1982; Dir., Short Story Symposium, 1985. *Publs:* In the Morning of Time: The Story of the Norse God Balder, 1970; The Year of Mr. Nobody, 1978; Beggars

and Choosers, 1980; Sailing Home, 1982. Add: 4 Marsh Hen Cove, Fripp Island, S.C. 29920, U.S.A.

KING, Francis (Henry). Has also written as Frank Cauldwell. British, b. 1923. Novels/Short stories, Poetry, Travel/Exploration/Adventure. Literary Reviewer, since 1963, and Theatre Reviewer, 1978–88, Sunday Telegraph, London. Regional Dir., British Council, Kyoto, Japan, 1958–62; Pres., Intnl P.E.N., 1985–89. *Publs:* To the Dark Tower, 1946; Never Again, 1947; An Air That Kills, 1948; The Dividing Stream, 1951; Rod of Incantation, 1952; The Dark Glasses, 1954; (as Frank Cauldwell) The Firewalkers: A Memoir, 1956; The Widow, 1957; (ed.) Introducing Greece, 1957; The Man on the Rock, 1957; So Hurt and Humiliated, 1959; The Custom House, 1961; The Japanese Umbrella, 1964; The Last of the Pleasure Gardens, 1965; The Waves Behind the Boat, 1967; The Brighton Belle, 1968; A Domestic Animal, 1970; Japan, 1970; Flights, 1973; A Game of Patience, 1974; The Needle, 1975; Christopher Isherwood, 1976; Hard Feelings, 1976; Danny Hill, 1977; E.M. Forster and His World, 1978; The Action, 1978; Indirect Method, 1980; Act of Darkness, 1983; Voices in an Empty Room, 1984; One is a Wanderer, 1985; Frozen Music, 1987; The Woman Who Was God, 1988; Punishments, 1989. Add: 19 Gordon Pl., London W8 4JE, England.

KING, Francis P. American, b. 1922. Economics, Education, Money/Finance. Sr. Research Officer, Teachers Insurance and Annuity Assn., NYC, since 1971 (Research Officer, 1954–71). Chmn. of Bd. Tuition Exchange, Allentown, Pa., 1972–88. *Publs:* Financing the College Education of Faculty Children, 1954; (with W.C. Greenough) Retirement and Insurance Plans in American Colleges, 1969; Benefit Plans in Junior Colleges, 1971; (with W.C. Greenough) Pension Plans and Public Policy, 1976; (with Thomas J. Cook) Benefit Plans in Higher Education, 1980. Add: 360 E. 72nd St., New York, N.Y. 10021, U.S.A.

KING, John (Edward). British, b. 1947. Economics, Intellectual History. Lectr. in Economics, Univ. of Lancaster, since 1968. *Publs:* Labour Economics, 1972; (with M.C. Howard) The Political Economy of Marx, 1975, 1985; (ed., with M.C. Howard) The Economics of Marx: Selected Readings, 1976; (with P. Regan) Relative Income Shares, 1976; (ed.) Readings in Labour Economics, 1980; (with H.I. Dutton) Ten Percent and No Surrender: The Preston Strike, 1853-4, 1981; Economic Exiles, 1988. Add: 124 Greaves Rd., Lancaster, England.

KING, Larry L. American, b. 1929. Novels/Short stories, Plays/Screenplays, Politics/Government, Theatre, Autobiography/Memoirs/Personal. Freelance writer. Contributing Ed., Texas Monthly Mag., Austin, since 1974, and Parade, since 1983. Admin. Asst., U.S. Congress, 1954–64; Contributing Ed., Harper's Mag., NYC, 1966–71; Nieman Fellow, Harvard Coll., Cambridge, Mass., 1969–70; Ferris Prof. of Journalism and Political Science, Princeton Univ., New Jersey, 1973–75; Duke Fellow of Communications, Duke Univ., Durham, N.C., 1976. *Publs:* The One-Eyed Man (novel), 1966; . . . And Other Dirty Stories, 1968; Confessions of a White Racist, 1971; The Old Man and Lesser Mortals, 1974; (with Bobby Baker) Wheeling and Dealing: Confessions of a Capitol Hill Operator, 1978; (with Peter Masterson) The Best Little Whorehouse in Texas (play), 1978, as screenplay, 1980; (with Ben Z. Grant) The Kingfish (play), 1979; Of Outlaws, Con Men, Whores, Politicians and Other Artists, 1980; That Terrible Night Santa Got Lost in the Woods, 1981; The Whorehouse Papers, 1982; Warning: Writer at Work, 1985; None But a Blockhead, 1986; Christmas 1933 (play), 1986; The Night Hank Williams Died (play), 1986; The Golden Shadows Old West Museum (play), 1987; Because of Lozo Brown, 1988. Add: c/o The Viking Penguin, 40 W. 23rd St., New York, N.Y. 10010, U.S.A.

KING, Norman A. *See* **TRALINS,** S. Robert.

KING, Paul. *See* **DRACKETT,** Phil.

KING, Robert C(harles). American, b. 1928. Biology. Prof. of Genetics, Northwestern Univ., Evanston, Ill., since 1964 (faculty member since 1956). *Publs:* Genetics, 1962, 1965; Dictionary of Genetics, 1968, 4th ed., with W.D. Stansfield, 1989; Ovarian Development in Drosophila melanogaster, 1970; (ed.) Handbook of Genetics, vols. I-V, 1974–76; (ed. with H. Akai) Insect Ultrastructure, vol. I, 1982, vol. II, 1984. Add: Dept. of Biochemistry, Molecular Biology and Cell Biology, Northwestern University, Evanston, Ill. 60201, U.S.A.

KING, Robert R(ay). American, b. 1942. International relations/Current affairs, Politics/Government. Mgr. of Community and Socioeconomic Planning, Tosco Corp., Boulder, Colo., since 1981. Sr. Analyst. and Asst. Dir., Research and Analysis Dept., Radio Free Europe,

Munich, 1970–77; Member, National Security Council Staff, The White House, 1977–78; Consultant on Intnl. Relations, 1979; Special Asst., Federal Co-Chmn., Appalachian Regional Commn., 1980–81. *Publs:* (with Stephen E. Palmer, Jr.) Yugoslav Communism and the Macedonian Question, 1971; Minorities under Communism: Nationalities as a Source of Tension among Balkan Communist States, 1973; (ed. with Robert W. Dean) East European Perspectives on European Security and Cooperation, 1974; (ed. with J.F. Brown) Eastern Europe's Uncertain Future, 1978; A History of the Romanian Communist Party, 1980. Add: c/o Harvard Univ. Press, 79 Garden St., Cambridge, Mass. 02138, U.S.A.

KING, Ronald. British, b. 1914. Homes/Gardens. Secty., Royal Botanic Gardens, Kew, London, 1959–76. *Publs:* World of Kew, 1976; Botanical Illustration, 1978; Quest for Paradise (history of the world's gardens), 1979; Temple of Flora, 1981; Tresco: England's Island of Flowers, 1985; Royal Kew, 1985. Add: c/o W.H. Smith Publishers, Inc., 112 Madison Ave., New York, N.Y. 10016, U.S.A.

KING, Stephen. American, b. 1947. Novels/Short stories. *Publs:* Carrie, 1974; Salem's Lot, 1975; The Shining, 1977; Night Shift, 1978; The Stand, 1978; The Dead Zone, 1979; Firestarter, 1980; Danse Macabre, 1981; Cujo, 1981; The Dark Tower: The Gunslinger, 1981; Different Seasons, 1982; Christine, 1983; Pet Sematary, 1983; (with Peter Straub) The Talisman, 1984; (as Richard Bachman) Thinner, 1985; It, 1986; The Eyes of the Dragon, 1987; Misery, 1987; The Dark Tower: The Drawing of the Three, 1987; The Tommyknockers, 1987. Add: c/o Viking, 40 W. 23rd St., New York, N.Y. 10010, U.S.A.

KING, Teri. British, b. 1940. History, Recreation/Leisure/Hobbies. Astrologer, Daily Scottish Record, Weekend mag., and Sunday Mirror, London; freelance model, 1956–67. *Publs:* Love, Sex and Astrology, 1974; Business, Success and Astrology, 1974; Astrologers Diet Book, 1977; Your Child and the Zodiac, 1979; Marriage, Divorce, and Astrology, 1980; Further Love, Sex and Astrology, 1985; Sunrise, Sunset, 1988; Hororscopes, 1989. Add: 6 Elm Grove Rd., Barnes, London SW13, England.

KING, Vincent. Pseud. for Rex Thomas Vinson. British, b. 1935. Science fiction/Fantasy. Painter and printmaker; also freelance writer. Art teacher, schs. in London, Bristol, Newcastle upon Tyne, 1963–68, and since 1968 in Redruth. *Publs:* Light a Last Candle, 1969; Another End, 1971; Candy Man, 1971; Time Snake and Superclown, 1976. Add: c/o Pamela Buckmaster, Carnell Literary Agency, Danescroft, Goose Lane, Little Hallingbury, Herts. CM22 7RG, England.

KING, William Richard. American, b. 1938. Administration/Management, Business/Trade/Industry, Information science/Computers. Prof., Univ. of Pittsburgh, Pa., since 1986 (Assoc. Prof., 1967–69; Dir., Doctoral Prog., 1971–74; Prof. of Business Admin., 1969–85; Dir., Strategic Mgmt. Inst., 1980–84). Vice-Pres. and Dir., Cleland-King, Inc., mgmt. consulting and research firm, 1969–86; Assoc. Ed., Management Science, since 1974; Member, Editorial Advisory Bd., OMEGA: The Intnl. Journal of Mgmt. Science, since 1984; Area Ed., International Journal on Policy and Information, since 1981. Asst. Prof. of Operations Research, Case Western Reserve Univ., 1964–65; Asst. Prof. of Statistics and Operations Research, U.S. Air Force Inst. of Technology, 1965–67. Sr. Ed., Management Information Systems Quarterly, 1982–85; Chmn., Intnl. Conference on Information Systems, 1987–88; Pres., Inst. of Management Sciences, 1989–90. *Publs:* Quantitative Analysis for Marketing Management, 1967; Probability for Management Decisions, 1968; (co-author) Systems Analysis and Project Management, 1968, 3rd ed. 1983; (co-ed.) Systems, Organizations, Analysis, Management: A Book of Readings, 1969; (co-author) Management: A Systems Approach, 1972; Marketing Management Information Systems, 1977; (co-author) Strategy Planning and Policy, 78; (co-ed.) Marketing Scientific and Technical Information, 1979; (co-author) The Logic of Strategic Planning, 1982; (co-ed.) Project Management Handbook, 1988; (co-ed.) Strategic Planning and Mgmt. Handbook, 1987; (co-ed.) Management of Information Systems, 1989. Add: Grad. Sch. of Business, Univ. of Pittsburgh, Pittsburgh, Pa. 15260, U.S.A.

KINGDON, John W. American, b. 1940. Politics/Government. Prof. of Political Science, Univ. of Michigan, Ann Arbor, since 1975 (Asst. Prof., 1965–70; Assoc. Prof., 1970–75). *Publs:* Candidates for Office: Beliefs and Strategies, 1968; Congressmen's Voting Decisions, 1973; Agendas, Alternatives and Public Policy, 1984. Add: Dept. of Political Science, Univ. of Michigan, Ann Arbor, Mich. 48109, U.S.A.

KINGDON, Robert McCune. American, b. 1927. History. Prof. of History, Univ. of Wisconsin, Madison, since 1965 (Dir., Inst. for Research

in the Humanities, 1975–87). Instr., and Asst. Prof. of History, Univ. of Massachusetts, Amherst, 1952–57; Asst. Prof., and Prof. of History, Univ. of Iowa, Iowa City, 1957–65. *Publs:* Geneva and the Coming of the Wars of Religion in France, 1956; (ed. with J.-F. Bergier) Registres de la Compagnie des Pasteurs de Genève au temps de Calvin, 2 vols., 1962, 1964; (ed.) William Cecil: Execution of Justice in England, and William Allen: A True, Sincere and Modest Defense of English Catholics, 1965; Geneva and the Consolidation of the French Protestant Movement, 1967; (ed. with R.D. Linder) Calvin and Calvinism: Sources of Democracy?, 1970; (ed.) Théodore de Bèze: Du droit des magistrats, 1971; (ed. and contrib.) Transition and Revolution: Problems and Issues of European Renaissance and Reformation History, 1974; The Political Thought of Peter Martyr Vermigli, 1980; Church and Society in Reformation Europe, 1985; Myths about the St. Bartholomew's Day Massacres, 1988. Add: Inst. for Research in the Humanities, Old Observatory, Univ. of Wisconsin, Madison, Wisc. 53706, U.S.A.

KING-HELE, Desmond. British, b. 1927. Poetry, Air/Space topics, Literature, Sciences, Biography. Ed., Notes and Records of the Royal Soc., since 1989. Deputy Chief Scientific Officer, Royal Aircraft Establishment, Farnborough, 1968–88. *Publs:* Shelley: His Thought and Work, 1960, 3rd ed., 1984; Satellites and Scientific Research, 1960, 1962; Erasmus Darwin, 1963; Theory of Satellite Orbits in an Atmosphere, 1964; Observing Earth Satellites, 1966, 1983; (ed.) Essential Writings of Erasmus Darwin, 1968; The End of the Twentieth Century?, 1970; Poems and Trixies, 1972; Doctor of Revolution, 1977; (ed.) Letters of Erasmus Darwin, 1981; (ed.) The RAE Table of Earth Satellites 1957–82, 1983; Animal Spirits, 1983; Erasmus Darwin and the Romantic Poets, 1986; Satellite Orbits in an Atmosphere, 1987. Add: 3 Tor Rd., Farnham, Surrey, England.

KINGMAN, Sir J(ohn) F(rank) C(harles). British, b. 1939. Mathematics/Statistics. Vice-Chancellor, Univ. of Bristol, since 1985. Fellow, St. Annes's Coll., Oxford, since 1978. Chmn., 1973–76, and Vice-Pres. since 1976, Inst. of Statisticians. Fellow, Pembroke Coll., Cambridge, 1961–65, and Asst. Lectr., 1962–64, and Lectr., 1964–65, Cambridge Univ.; Reader, 1965–66, and Prof., 1966–69, Univ. of Sussex, Brighton; Prof. of Mathematics, Oxford University, 1969–85. Member, Brighton County Borough Council, 1968–71; Vice-Pres., 1977–79, and Pres. 1987–89, Royal Statistical Soc.; Chmn., Science Bd., Science Research Council, 1979–81; Chmn., Science and Engineering Research Council, 1981– 85. *Publs:* (with S.J. Taylor) Introduction to Measure and Probability, 1966; The Algebra of Queues, 1966; Regenerative Phenomena, 1972; Mathematics of Genetic Diversity, 1980. Add: Senate House, Tyndall Ave., Bristol BS8 1TH, England.

KINGMAN, (Mary) Lee. American, b. 1919. Children's fiction, Literature. Freelance writer and ed. Member, Bd. of Dirs., The Horn Book Inc., Boston, Mass. Children's Book Ed., Houghton Mifflin Co., Boston, Mass., 1944–46. *Publs:* Pierre Pidgeon, 1943; Ilenka, 1945; The Rocky Summer, 1948; The Best Christmas, 1949; Philippe's Hill, 1950; The Quarry Adventure (in U.K. as Lauri's Surprising Summer), 1951; Kathy and the Mysterious Statue, 1953; Peter's Long Walk, 1953; Mikko's Fortune, 1955; The Magic Christmas Tree, 1956; The Village Band Mystery, 1956; Flivver, the Heroic Horse, 1958; The House of the Blue Horse, 1960; The Saturday Gang, 1961; Peter's Pony, 1963; Sheep Ahoy!, 1963; Private Eyes, 1964; (ed.) Newbery and Caldecott Medal Books: 1956–1965, 1965; The Year of the Raccoon, 1966; The Secret of the Silver Reindeer, 1968; (ed. with J. Foster and R.G. Lontoft) Illustrators of Children's Books: 1957–1966, 1968; The Peter Pan Bag, 1970; Georgina and the Dragon, 1971; The Meeting Post: A Story of Lapland, 1972; Escape from the Evil Prophecy, 1973; (ed.) Newbery and Caldecott Medal Books 1966–1975, 1975; Break a Leg, Betsy Maybe!, 1976; The Illustrator's Notebook, 1978; Head over Wheels, 1978; (ed. with G. Hogarth and H. Quimby) Illustrators of Children's Books 1967–1976, 1978; The Refiner's Fire, 1981; The Luck of the "Miss L," 1986; (ed.) Newbery and Caldecott Medal Books: 1976–1985, 1986. Add: P.O. Box 7126, Lanesville, Gloucester, Mass. 01930, U.S.A.

KINGSBURY, Donald (MacDonald). Canadian (b. American), b. 1929. Science fiction. Lectr. in Mathematics, McGill Univ., Montreal, 1956–86. *Publs:* Courtship Rite, 1982, in U.K. as Geta, 1984; The Moon Goddess and the Son, 1986. Add: 1563 Ducharme Ave., Montreal, Que. H2V 1G4, Canada.

KINGSLEY, Sidney. American, b. 1906. Plays/Screenplays. Past Pres., Dramatist Guild. *Publs:* Men in White (Pulitzer Prize, 1934), 1933; Dead End, 1935; Ten Million Ghosts, 1936; The World We Make (adaption), 1939; The Patriots, 1943; Detective Story, 1949; Darkness

At Noon (adaptation), 1951; Lunatics and Lovers, 1954; Night Life, 1962. Add: c/o Dramatists Play Service, 440 Park Ave. South, New York, N.Y. 10016, U.S.A.

KING-SMITH, Dick. British, b. 1922. Children's fiction. Freelance writer since 1982. Served in the Grenadier Guards, 1941–46; farmer in Gloucestershire, 1947–67; teacher, Farmborough Primary Sch., Bath, 1975–82. *Publs:* The Fox Busters, 1978; Daggie Dogfoot, 1980, in U.S. as Pigs Might Fly, 1982; The Mouse Butcher, 1981; Magnus Powermouse, 1982; The Queen's Nose, 1983; The Sheep-Pig, 1983, in U.S. as The Gallant Pig, 1985; Harry's Mad, 1984; Lightning Fred, 1985; Saddlebottom, 1985; Noah's Brother, 1986; Dumpling, 1986; Yob, 1986; Pets for Keeps, 1986; E.S.P., 1986; H. Prince, 1986; The Hodgeheg, 1987; Friends and Brothers, 1987; Farmer Bungle Forgets, 1987; Cuckoobush Farm, 1987; Tumbleweed, 1987; Country Watch, 1987; Town Watch, 1987; Water Watch, 1988; George Speaks, 1988; Emily's Legs, 1988; The Jenius, 1988; Sophie's Snail, 1988; Martin's Mice, 1988. Add: Diamond's Cottage, Queen Charlton, near Keynsham, Avon BS18 2SJ, England.

KINGSTON, Frederick Temple. Canadian, b. 1925. Philosophy, Theology/Religion. Principal, Canterbury Coll., since 1965, and Prof. of Philosophy, since 1959, Univ. of Windsor, Ont. Prof. of Theology, Anglican Coll. of British Columbia, Vancouver, 1953–59. *Publs:* French Existentialism: A Christian Critique, 1961, 1968; (ed.) Anglicanism and Principles of Christian Unity, 1972; (ed.) Anglicanism and Contemporary Social Issues, 1973; (ed.) The Church and Industry, 1974; (ed.) The Church and Ethics in Public Life, 1975; On the Importance of Residence Life to Higher Education, 1976; (ed.) The Church and the Arts, 1977; (ed.) Anglicanism and the Essentials of the Faith, 1978; (ed.) Anglicanism and the Lambeth Conference, 1978; (ed.) Living Christian Spirituality, 1979; (ed.) The Reality of God in the Contemporary World, 1982; (ed. with H.P. Cunningham) Friendship and Dialogue Between Ontario and Quebec, 1985; (ed.) The Kingdom of This World and the Kingdom of God, 1986. Add: Canterbury Coll., Univ. of Windsor, Windsor, Ont. N9B 3B9, Canada.

KINGSTON, Maxine Hong. American, b. 1940. Fiction, Autobiography/Memoirs/Personal. Teacher, Sunset High Sch., Hayward, Calif. 1965–67, Kahuku High Sch., Hawaii, 1967–68, Drop-In Sch., Kahaluu, Hawaii 1968–69, Kailua High Sch., Honolulu, 1969, Honolulu Business Coll., 1969–70, Mid-Pacific Inst. Honolulu, 1970–76, Univ. of Hawaii, 1976–77, and Eastern Michigan Univ., 1986. *Publs:* The Woman Warrior: Memoirs of a Girlhood Among Ghosts, 1976; China Men, 1980; Hawai'i One Summer, 1987; Tripmaster Monkey: His False Book, 1988. Add: c/o Alfred A. Knopf Inc., 201 East 50th St., New York, N.Y. 10022, U.S.A.

KINGSTON, Syd. *See* **BINGLEY,** David Ernest.

KINKAID, Matt. *See* **ADAMS,** Clifton.

KINKEAD-WEEKES, Mark. British, b. 1931. Literature. Prof. of English Literature, and Pro Vice-Chancellor, Univ. of Kent, Canterbury, since 1974 (Lectr., then Sr. Lectr., 1965–73). Asst. Prof., then Lectr., Univ. of Edinburgh, 1956–65. *Publs:* (co-ed.) Alexander Pope, 1962; (co-author) William Golding: A Critical Study, 1967, 1984; (ed.) Twentieth Century Interpretations of the Rainbow, 1971; Samuel Richardson: Dramatic Novelist, 1973. Add: Dept. of English, Univ. of Kent, Canterbury, Kent, England.

KINNAMON, Keneth. American, b. 1932. Literature. Ethel Pumphrey Stephens Prof. of English and Chmn. of Dept., Univ. of Arkansas, Fayetteville, since 1982. Asst. Prof., 1966–70, Assoc. Prof., 1970–73, Prof., 1973–82, and Head of English Dept., 1977–82, Univ. of Illinois at Urbana-Champaign. *Publs:* (ed. with Richard K. Barksdale) Black Writers of America: A Comprehensive Anthology, 1972; The Emergence of Richard Wright: A Study in Literature and Society, 1972; (ed.) James Baldwin: A Collection of Critical Essays, 1974; (with Joseph Benson, Michel Fabre and Craig Werner) A Richard Wright Bibliography: Fifty Years of Criticism and Commentary, 1933–82, 1985. Add: Dept. of English, 333 Kimpel Hall, Univ. of Arkansas, Fayetteville, Ark. 72701, U.S.A.

KINNEAR, Michael Steward Read. Canadian, b. 1937. History, Politics/Government. Prof. of History, Univ. of Manitoba, Winnipeg, since 1965. Chmn., Manitoba Ethnic Mosaic Congress, 1970–71. *Publs:* The British Voter: An Atlas and Survey since 1885, 1968, 1981. The Fall of Lloyd George: The Political Crisis of 1922, 1973; (ed.) Glean-ings and Memoranda 1893-1968, 1975. Add: History Dept., Univ. of Manitoba, Winnipeg, Man. R3T 2M8, Canada.

KINNELL, Galway. American, b. 1927. Novels/Short stories, Poetry, Literature, Translations. Dir., Creative Writing Prog., New York Univ., N.Y.C. Former member of faculty, Univ. of Grenoble, France; Poet-in-Residence, Juniata Coll., Huntingdon, Pa., and Univ. of California, Irvine, 1968–69. *Publs:* (with A. Ostroff and W.T. Scott) 3 Self-Evaluations, 1953; (trans.) Bitter Victory, by Rene Hardy, 1956; What a Kingdom It Was, 1960; (trans.) Pre-Columbian Ceramics, by Henri Lehmann, 1962; Flower Herding on Mount Monadnock, 1964; (trans.) The Poems of François Villon, 1965; Black Light (novel), 1966; Poems of Night, 1968; Body Rags, 1968; (trans.) On the Motion and Immobility of Douve, by Yves Bonnefoy, 1968; The Poetics of the Physical World, 1969; (trans.) The Lackawanna Elegy, by Yvan Goll, 1970; The Hen Flower, 1970; First Poems, 1947–1952, 1970; The Book of Nightmares, 1971; The Shoes of Wandering, 1971; The Avenue Bearing the Initial of Christ into the New World: Poems 1946–1964, 1974; (trans.) The Poems of François Villon, 1977; Walking Down Stairs: Selections from Interviews, 1978; Mortal Words, Mortal Acts, 1980; Selected Poems, 1982; How the Alligator Missed Breakfast (for children), 1982; Thoughts Occasioned by the Most Insignificant of Human Events, 1982; The Fundamental Project of Technology, 1983; Remarks on Accepting the National Book Award, 1984; The Past, 1985; (ed.) The Essential Whitman, 1987. Add: Sheffield, Vt. 05866, U.S.A.

KINNEY, Arthur F. American, b. 1933. History, Literature. Thomas W. Copeland Prof. of Literary History, Univ. of Massachusetts, Amherst, since 1986 (Asst. Prof. 1966–68; Assoc. Prof., 1968–73; Prof of English, 1973–86). Affiliate Prof. of English, Clark Univ., Worcester, Mass., since 1971; Ed. English Literary Renaissance, since 1971. Instr., Yale Univ., New Haven, Conn., 1963–66; Founder and Exec. Secty., Northeast Modern Language Assn., 1971–73; Pres., Conference of Editors of Learned Journals, 1971–73, 1981–83; Huntington Library Fellow, 1973–74, 1983; Folger Shakespeare Library Fellow, 1974; Fulbright Fellow, Oxford Univ., England, 1977–78; NEH Senior Fellow, 1977–78, 1983–84; University Research Fellow, 1983–84; Pres., Renaissance English Text Society, 1984; Chancellor's Lectr., 1985–86. *Publs:* (co-ed.) Bear, Man, and God: Seven Approaches to Faulkner's 'The Bear', 1964, 1972; On Seven Shakespearean Tragedies, 1968; On Seven Shakespearean Comedies, 1969; (co-ed.) Symposium, 1969; (co-ed.) Symposium on Love, 1970; (ed.) H.R. Mythomystes, 1972; Titled Elizabethans, 1973; Rogues, Vagabonds and Sturdy Beggars, 1973; Elizabethan Backgrounds, 1974; (ed.) Markets of Bawdry: The Dramatic Criticism of Stephen Gosson, 1974; Faulkner's Narrative Poetics: Style as Vision, 1978; Dorothy Parker, 1978; Rhetoric and Poetic in Thomas More's 'Utopia', 1979; The Compson Family, 1982; Nicholas Hilliard's 'Art of Limning', 1983; Flannery O'Connor's Library: Resources of Being, 1985; The Sartoris Family, 1985; Humanist Poetics: English Thought, Rhetoric and Fiction in the 16th Century, 1986; Essential Articles for the Study of Sir Philip Sidney, 1986; 1576: Sir Philip Sidney and the Making of a Legend, 1986; John Skelton: Priest As Poet, 1987. Add: 25 Hunter Hill Dr., Amherst, Mass. 01002, U.S.A.

KINSELLA, Thomas. Irish, b. 1928. Poetry, Literature, Translations. Prof. of English, Temple Univ., Philadelphia, Pa., since 1970. Dir., Dolmen Press, and Cuala Press, both Dublin; Founder, Peppercanister publrs., Dublin, 1972; Artistic Dir., Lyric Players Theatre, Belfast. Worked in Irish Civil Service, 1946–65; Writer-in-Residence, 1965–67, and Prof. of English, 1967–70, Southern Illinois Univ., Carbondale. *Publs:* The Starlit Eye, 1952; Three Legendary Sonnets, 1952; (trans.) The Breastplate of St. Patrick, 1954, as Faeth Fiadha: The Breastplate of St. Patrick, 1957; (trans.) The Exile and Death of the Sons of Usnech, by Longes Mac n-Usnig, 1954; (trans.) Thirty Three Triads, Translated from the XII Century Irish, 1955; The Death of a Queen, 1956; Poems, 1956; Another September, 1958, rev. ed. 1962; Moralities, 1960; Poems and Translations, 1961; Downstream, 1962; Wormwood, 1966; Nightwalker, 1967; Nightwalker and Other Poems, 1968; (with D. Livingstone and A. Sexton) Poems, 1968; (trans.) The Tain, 1969; Tear, 1969; (with W.B. Yeats) Davis, Mangan, Ferguson: Tradition and the Irish Writer, 1970; Butcher's Dozen, 1972; A Selected Life, 1972; Finistere, 1972; Notes from the Land of the Dead and Other Poems, 1972; New Poems 1973, 1973; Selected Poems 1956–1968, 1973; Vertical Man, 1973; The Good Fight, 1973; One, 1974; A Technical Supplement, 1976; Song of the Night and Other Poems, 1978; The Messenger, 1978; Fifteen Dead, 1979; One and Other Poems, 1979; Peppercanister Poems 1972–1978, 1979; Poems 1956–1973, 1979; One Fond Embrace, 1981; Songs of the Psyche, 1986; Her Vertical Smile, 1986; (ed.) The New Oxford Book of Irish Verse, 1986; Blood and Family, 1988. Add: Dept. of English, Temple Univ., Philadelphia, Pa. 19122,

U.S.A.

KINSELLA, W(illiam) P(atrick). Canadian, b. 1935. Novels/Short stories. Full-time Writer. Asst. Prof., Dept. of English, Univ. of Calgary, 1978–83. *Publs:* Dance Me Outside, 1977; Scars, 1978; Shoeless Joe Jackson Comes to Iowa, 1980; Born Indian, 1981; Shoeless Joe, 1982; The Ballad of the Public Trustee, 1982; The Moccasin Telegraph, 1983; The Thrill of the Grass, 1984; The Iowa Baseball Confederacy, 1985; The Alligator Report, 1985; The Fencepost Chronicles, 1986; Five Stories, 1986; Red Wolf, Red Wolf, 1987; The Further Adventures of Slugger McBatt, 1988; Box Socials, 1989. Add: Box 400, White Rock, B.C. V4B 5G3, Canada.

KINSEY, Elisabeth. *See* **CLYMER,** Eleanor.

KIRBY, David Peter. British, b. 1936. History. Reader in History, Univ. Coll. of Wales, Aberystwyth, since 1973 (Lectr., 1966–69; Sr. Lectr., 1969–73). Asst. Lectr., and Lectr., Univ. of Liverpool, 1962–66. *Publs:* The Making of Early England, 1967; (ed.) St. Wilfrid at Hexham, 1974. Add: Manoravon, Llanon, Dyfed, Wales.

KIRBY, Gilbert Walter. British, b. 1914. Theology/Religion, Biography. Principal, London, Bible Coll., Northwood, Middx., 1966–80; Gen. Secty., 1956–66, and Pres., 1979–83, Evangelical Alliance. *Publs:* The Protestant Churches of Britain, 1963; (ed.) Remember I am Coming Soon, 1964; (ed.) The Question of Healing, 1967; Pastor and Principal: E.F. Kevan, 1968; (ed.) Evangelism Alert, 1972; The Way We Care, 1973; Too Hot to Handle, 1978; Christian Living, 1979; All One in Christ Jesus?, 1984; Why All These Denominations?, 1988. Add: 78 Hallowell Rd., Northwood, Middx. HA6 1DS, England.

KIRK, Donald. American, b. 1938. International relations/Currentffairs. Newspaper corresp., since 1965. *Publs:* Wider War: The Struggle for Cambodia, Thailand and Laos, 1971; Tell It to the Dead, 1975. Add: 4343 davewnport St. N.W., Wash. D.C. 20016, U.S.A.

KIRK, Geoffrey Stephen. British, b. 1921. Classics. Regius Prof. Emeritus of Greek, Cambridge Univ. (Reader, 1958–64; Regius Prof. from 1973). Prof. of Classics, Yale Univ., New Haven, Conn., 1965–71, and Univ. of Bristol 1971–73. *Publs:* (ed.) Heraclitus: The Cosmic Fragments, 1952; (with J.E. Raven) The Presocratic Philosophers, 1956; The Songs of Homer, 1962; (ed.) The Language and Background of Homer, 1964; (ed. and trans.) Euripides: Bacchae, 1970; Myth, 1970; The Nature of Greek Myths, 1974; Homer and the Oral Tradition, 1977; The Iliad: A Commentary, vol. I, 1985, vol. II, 1989. Add: Trinity Coll., Cambridge, England.

KIRK, Russell (Amos). American, b. 1918. Novels/Short stories, Education, History, Politics/Government, Biography. Pres., The Educational Reviewer Inc., educational foundn., since 1960; Ed., The University Bookman quarterly journal, NYC, since 1961; Pres., Marguerite Eyer Wilbur Foundn., since 1979. Former member of faculty, Michigan State Univ., East Lansing, Long Island Univ., N.Y., Los Angeles State Coll., Calif., Pepperdine Univ., Los Angeles, Calif., New Sch. for Social Research, NYC, Hillsdale Coll., Mich., Olivet Coll., Mich., Albion Coll., Mich., Calvin Coll., Mich., Grand Valley State Coll., and Indiana Univ., Bloomington. Ed. Modern Age, 1957–59; Syndicated columnist, Los Angeles Times Syndicate, 1962–75. *Publs:* John Randolph of Roanoke, 1951, 3rd ed. 1978; The Conservative Mind, 1953, 7th ed., 1986; St. Andrews, 1954; Program for Conservatives, 1954, 4th ed., 1987; Academic Freedom, 1955; Beyond the Dreams of Avarice (essays), 1956; The American Cause, 1957; Intelligent Woman's Guide to Conservatism, 1957; Old House of Fear (novel), 1961; The Surly Sullen Bell (short stories), 1962; Confessions of a Bohemian Tory (essays), 1963; The Intemperate Professor (essays), 1965; A Creature of the Twilight (novel), 1966; Edmund Burke, 1967; (with James McClellan) Political Principles of Robert Taft, 1967; Enemies of the Permanent Things (essays), 1969, 1985; Eliot and His Age, 1972, 1985; The Roots of American Order, 1974; Decadence and Renewal in the Higher Learning, 1978; The Princess of All Lands (short stories), 1978; Lord of the Hollow Dark (mystical romance), 1979; The Portable Conservative Reader, 1982; Reclaiming a Patrimony, 1982; Watchers at the Strait Gate (short stories), 1984; The Wise Men Know What Wicked Things Are Written on The Sky, 1987. Add: Piety Hill, Mecosta, Mich. 49332, U.S.A.

KIRKALDY, John Francis. British, b. 1908. Earth sciences. Prof. of Geology, Queen Mary Coll., London, 1962–74, now Emeritus (Reader in Geology, 1947–62). Demonstrator, Geology Dept., Kings Coll., London, 1929–1933; Asst. Lectr., Geology Dept., University Coll., London, 1933–36; Lectr., Geology Dept., King's Coll., London, 1936–47. *Publs:* (with A.K. Wells) Outline of Historical Geology, 1948, 5th ed. 1966; General Principles of Geology, 1954, 5th ed. 1971; The Study of Fossils, 1963; Minerals and Rocks in Colour, 1963, 1968; Fossils in Colour, 1967, 3rd ed. 1972; Geological Time, 1971; (with D.E.B. Bates) Field Geology in Colour, 1976. Add: Stone House, Byfield Rd., Chipping Warden, Banbury, Oxon, England.

KIRKENDALL, Lester A. American, b. 1903. Education, Human relations. Prof. of Family Life Emeritus, Oregon State Univ., Corvallis, since 1969 (Prof., 1949–69). Co-Founder and member, Bd. of Dirs., Sex Information and Education Council of the U.S.; Member, Bd. of Dirs., American Humanist Assn. *Publs:* Sex Adjustments of Young Men, 1940; (with I.R. Kuenzli and F.W. Reeves) Goals for American Education, 1948; Sex Education as Human Relations, 1950; (with C.E. Avery) Progress Report on Oregon Developmental Project in Family Education, 1952; (with F.R. Zeran) Student Councils in Action, 1953; (with C.E. Avery) Oregon Developmental Center, 1955; Premarital Intercourse and Interpersonal Relationships, 1961; (with I. Rubin) Sex in the Adolescent Years; New Directions in Guiding and Teaching Youth, 1968; (with R.F. Osborne) Teacher's Question and Answer Book on Sex Education, 1969; (with I. Rubin) Sex in the Childhood Years, 1970; Kirkendall on Sex: A Collection of Readings, 1970; (ed. with R.N. Whitehurst) The New Sexual Revolution, 1971; (ed. W.J. Adams) The Students' Guide to Marriage and Family Life Literature: An Aid to Individualized Study, 8th ed. 1980; (with Arthur Gravatt) Marriage and the Family in the Year 2020, 1984. Add: 12705 S.E. River Rd., Apt. 703C, Portland, Ore. 97222, U.S.A.

KIRK-GREENE, Anthony (Hamilton Millard). British. History, Politics. Univ. Lectr., and Fellow, St. Antony's Coll., Oxford Univ., since 1967; and Dir. of the Foreign Service Programme since 1986. Gen. Ed., Studies in African History, and Joint Ed., Colonial History Series. H.M. Colonial Service, Nigeria, 1950–57; Sr. Lectr. in Govt., Inst. of Admin., Zaria, Nigeria, 1957–62; Prof. of Govt., Ahmadu Bello Univ., Nigeria, 1962–65; Pres., African Studies Assn. of the U.K., 1988. *Publs:* Adamawa Past and Present, 1958; (with Caroline Sassoon) The Cattle People of Nigeria, 1959; (with Caroline Sassoon) The River Niger, 1961; Barth's Travels in Nigeria, 1962; Principles of Native Administration in Nigeria, 1965; (ed.) The Making of Northern Nigeria, 1965; (with S.J. Hogben) The Emirates of Northern Nigeria, 1966; Hausa Proverbs, 1966; (with Y. Aliyu) A Modern Hausa Reader, 1967; Lugard and the Amalgamation of Nigeria, 1968; (ed.) Language and People of Bornu, 1968; Crisis and Conflict in Nigeria, 1971; (with P. Newman) West African Narratives, 1972; (ed.) Gazetteers of Northern Nigeria, 1972; (with C.H. Kraft) Teach Yourself Hausa, 1973; The Concept of the Good Man in Hausa, 1974; (with Pauline Ryan) Nigeria: Faces North, 1975; (ed.) The Transfer of Power in Africa, 1978; Biographical Dictionary of the British Colonial Governor, 1981; Stand by Your Radios: The Military in Tropical Africa, 1980; (with D. Rimmer) Nigeria since 1970, 1981; The Sudan Political Service: A Profile, 1982; (ed.) Margery Perham: West African Passage, 1983; (with Mahdi Adamu) Pastoralists of the Western Savanna, 1986; (ed.) Margery Perham: Pacific Prelude, 1988. Add: St. Antony's Coll., Oxford, England.

KIRK-GREENE, Christopher (Walter Edward). British, b. 1926. Language/Linguistics. Asst. Master 1949–86, and head of Modern Languages Dept., 1962–78, Eastbourne Coll., Sussex. *Publs:* An Advanced French Vocabulary, 1958; Sixty Modern French Unseens, 1963; Les Mots Amis et Les Faux Amis, 1968; Lisez! Regardez! Répondez!, 1973; A First Book of French Idioms, 1973; Lectures Modernes, 1975; French False Friends, 1981; Modern French Passages for Translation, 1984. Add: 7 South Cliff, Eastbourne, Sussex, England.

KIRKHAM, E. Bruce. American, b. 1938. Literature. Prof. of English, Ball State Univ., Muncie, Ind., since 1980 (Asst. Prof., 1968–74; Assoc. Prof., 1974–80). *Publs:* (ed. with John Fink) Indices to American Literary Annuals and Gift Books, 1825-1865, 1975; The Building of Uncle Tom's Cabin, 1977; A Concordance to the Olney Hymns of John Newton and William Cowper, 1983; A Concordance to the Plymouth Collection of Hymns and Tunes 1885, 1984. Add: Dept. of English, Ball State Univ., Muncie, Ind. 47306, U.S.A.

KIRKHAM, George L. American, b. 1941. Criminology/Law enforcement/Prisons. Assoc. Prof., Sch of Criminology, Florida State Univ., Tallahassee, since 1976 (Asst. Prof., 1971); Editorial Consultant, Educational Media Div., Criminal Justice Series, Harper and Row Publishers, since 1974; Police Officer, City of Tallahassee, Fla., since 1974. Student Professional Asst., California Dept. of Correction, 1964; Correctional

Counselor, California Dept. of Corrections, Soledad, 1965–66; Grad. Intern, Langley-Porter Neuropsychiatric Facility and Mount Zion Hosp. Outpatient Psychiatric Clinic, San Francisco, 1966–67; Juvenile Group Counselor, Santa Clara Co. Juvenile Probation Dept., 1967; Teaching Asst., Sch. of Criminology, Univ. of California at Berkeley, 1967–68; Instr., Dept. of Social Sciences, Asst. Prof. of Sociology, and Research Assoc., The Center for Interdisciplinary Studies, California State Univ. at San Jose, 1968–70; Research Criminologist, Systems Analysis Div., Stanford Research Inst., 1970–71; Police Patrolman, City of Jacksonville, Fla., 1973. *Publs:* Signal Zero, 1976; Introduction to Law Enforcement, 1977. Add: Sch. of Criminology, Florida State Univ., Tallahassee, Fla. 32300, U.S.A.

KIRKMAN, William Patrick. British, b. 1932. International relations/Current affairs. Secty., Cambridge Univ. Careers Service since 1968, Fellow, Wolfson Coll., Cambridge, since 1968 (Vice-Pres., 1980–84); Dir., Press Fellowship Programme, since 1982; Member, U.K. Cttee., Journalists in Europe, since 1985. Member, Editorial Staff, 1957–60, Commonwealth Staff, 1960–64, and Africa Corresp., 1962–64, The Times, London; Asst. Secty., Oxford Univ. Appointments Cttee., 1964–68. Member, Central Council, Royal Commonwealth Soc., London, 1973–75; Chmn., Standing Conference of Univ. Appointments Services, 1971–73. *Publs:* Unscrambling an Empire, 1966; Managing Recruitment, 1988. Add: 19 High St., Willingham, Cambridge CB4 5ES, England.

KIRKPATRICK, Jeane (Duane Jordan). American, b. 1926. Politics/Government. Leavey Prof. in Foundations of American Freedom, Georgetown Univ., Washington, D.C., since 1978 (on leave 1981–85; Asst. Prof. of Political Science, 1967–73; Prof., 1973–78); Sr. Fellow, American Enterprise Inst. for Public Policy Research, since 1977 (on leave 1981–85). Co-Chmn., Task Force on Presidential Elections Process, 20th Century Fund; Member, National Cttee. on Party Structure and Presidential Nomination, Democratic National Cttee., since 1975 (Vice-Chmn., Cttee. on Vice-Presidential Selection, 1972–74). U.S. Representative to the United Nations, and Member of Pres. Reagan's Cabinet, 1981–85. *Publs:* (ed. and contr.) Elections U.S.A., 1956; (ed.) Strategy of Deception, 1963; Foreign Students in the United States: A National Survey, 1966; Mass Behavior in Battle and Captivity, 1968; Leader and Vanguard in Mass Society: The Peronist Movement in Argentina, 1971; Political Woman, 1973; New Presidential Elite: Men and Women in National Politics, 1976; Dismantling the Parties: Reflections on Party Reform and Party Decomposition, 1978; (ed.) The New Class, 1978; (ed.) The New American Political System, 1978; Dictatorships and Doublestandards, 1981; The Reagan Phenomenon, 1983; Force and Freedom, 1987; Legitimacy and Force: State Papers and Current Perspectives 1981-1985, 2 vols., 1987. Add: c/o Dept. of Political Science, Georgetown Univ., Washington,, D.C. 20057, U.S.A.

KIRKUP, James (Falconer). British, b. 1923. Plays/Screenplays, Poetry, Children's non-fiction, Literature, Autobiography/Memoirs/Personal, Translations. Prof. of English, Japan's Woman's Univ., Tokyo, since 1963. Gregory Fellow in Poetry, Leeds Univ., 1950–52; Visiting Poet and Head of Dept. of English, Bath Academy of Art, Corsham, Wilts., 1953–56; Travelling Lectr., Swedish Ministry of Education, Stockholm, 1956–57; Prof. of English, Univ. of Salamanca, Spain, 1957–58, and Tohoku Univ. of Malaya, Kuala Lumpur, 1961–62; Literary Ed., Orient/West Mag., Tokyo, 1963–64; Founder, Poetry Nippon, Japan, 1966; Prof. of English Literature, Nagoya Univ., Japan, 1969–72; Prof. of Comparative Literature, Kyoto Univ. of Foreign Studies, 1976–88. *Publs:* (with J. Ormond and J. Bayliss) Indications, 1942; (with R. Nichols) The Cosmic Shape: An Interpretation of Myth and Legend with Three Poems and Lyrics, 1946; The Drowned Sailor and Other Poems, 1947; The Submerged Village and Other Poems, 1951; The Creation, 1951; A Correct Compassion and Other Poems, 1952; The Spring Journey and Other Poems of 1952–53, 1954; Upon This Rock: A Dramatic Chronicle of Peterborough Cathedral (play), 1955; Masque: The Triumph of Harmony (play), 1955; The True Mystery of the Nativity (play), 1956; (trans.) The Meteor (play), 1956; The Only Child: An Autobiography of Infancy, 1957; The Descent into the Cave and Other Poems, 1957; The Prodigal Son: Poems 1956–1959, 1959; Sorrows, Passions, and Alarms: An Autobiography of Childhood, 1959; The True Mistery of the Passion: Adapted and Translated from the French Medieval Mystery Cycle of Arnoul and Simon Grélan, 1960; These Horned Islands: A Journal of Japan, 1962; Tropic Temper: A Memoir of Malaya, 1962; The Love of Others (novel), 1962; The Refusal to Conform: Last and First Poems, 1963; (trans.) The Physicists (play), 1963; England, Now, 1964; Japan Industrial: Some Impressions of Japanese Industries, 2 vols., 1964, 1965; Japan Marine, 1965; Japan Now, 1966; Frankly Speaking, 1966; Tokyo, 1966; Paper Windows: Poems from Japan, 1968; Filipinescas: Travels Through the Philippine

Islands, 1968; Bangkok, 1968; One Man's Russia, 1968; Japan Physical: A Selection, 1969; (ed.) Shepherding Winds: An Anthology of Poetry from East and West, 1969; Aspects of the Short Story: Six Modern Short Stories with Commentary, 1969; Streets of Asia, 1969; Hong Kong and Macao, 1970; Japan Behind the Fan, 1970; White Shadows, Black Shadows: Poems of Peace and War, 1970; The Body Servant: Poems of Exile, 1971; Broad Daylight, 1971; A Bewick Bestiary, 1971; Transmental Vibrations, 1971; (trans.) Peer Gynt (play), 1972; The Magic Drum (play), 1972; (trans.) Brand, by Ibsen, (play), 1972; Heaven, Hell, and Hari-Kari: The Rise and Fall of the Japanese Superstate, 1974; Zen Gardens, 1975; Ghost Mother (play), 1978; An Actor's Revenge (opera), 1978; Friends in Arms (opera), 1978; (trans.) Modern Japanese Poetry, 1978; Zen Contemplations, 1978; Enlightenment, 1978; Scenes from Sesshu, 1978; Prick Prints, 1978; Steps to the Temple, 1979; Cold Mountain Poems, 1979; Modern Japanese Poetry, 1980; Scenes from Sutcliffe, 1981; Dengonban Messages, 1981; Ecce Homo: My Pasolini, 1982; No More Hiroshimas, 1982; (trans.) To the Unknown God, 1982; (trans.) The Bush Toads, 1982; (trans.) An African in Greenland, 1982; The Damask Drum (opera), 1982; (trans.) Kawabata: Short Stories, 1982; When I Was a Child: A Study of Nursery Rhymes, 1983; To the Ancestral North: Poems for an Autobiography, 1983; The Damask Drum (play), 1984; The Sense of the Visit (poetry), 1985; Fellow Feelings (poetry), 1986; The Mystery and the Magic of Symbols, 1987; I, Of All People: An Autobiography, 1988; The Best of Britain, 1989. Add: BM-Box 2870, London WC1V 6XX, England.

KIRSTEIN, Lincoln. American, b. 1907. Poetry, Dance/Ballet. Founder, 1933, and now Dir., Sch. of American Ballet, NYC; Dir., NYC Ballet Co. Founding Ed., Hound and Horn mag., 1927–34. *Publs:* Dance: A Short History of Theatrical Dancing, 1935; Low Ceiling (verse), 1935; Blast of Ballet, 1938; Ballet Alphabet, 1939; The Classic Ballet, 1952; Rhymes of a Pfc, 1964; Rhymes and More Rhymes of a Pfc, 1966; The Hampton Album, 1966; Movement and Metaphor: Four Centuries of Ballet, 1969; Elie Nadelman, 1973; New York City Ballet, 1973; Lay This Laurel, 1974; Nijinsky Dancing, 1974; Thirty Years: The New York City Ballet, 1978; Bias and Belief: Collected Criticism, 1983; Paul Cadmus, 1984; Portrait of Mr. B: Photographs of George Balanchine with an Essay, 1984; Quarry: A Collection In Lieu of Memoirs, 1987; The Poems of Lincoln Kirstein, 1987. Add: Sch. of American Ballet, 144 W. 66th St., New York, N.Y. 10023, U.S.A.

KIRTLAND, G.B. *See* **JOSLIN,** Sesyle.

KIRTON, James. *See* **BENTON,** Kenneth.

KISH, Leslie. American, b. 1910. Mathematics/Statistics, Sociology. Prof., Sociology Dept., Univ. of Michigan, Ann Arbor, 1960–81, now Emeritus (Lectr., 1951–56; Assoc. Prof., 1956–60). Research Scientist, Inst. for Social Research, Univ. of Michigan, Ann Arbor, since 1973 (Asst. Head, and Head of Sampling, 1951–63; Prog. Dir., 1963–73). Pres., American Statistical Assn., 1977; Pres. Intern. Assoc. Survey Statisticians, 1983–85. *Publs:* Survey Sampling, 1965; (with M.R. Frankel and N. Van Eck) SEPP: Sampling Error Programs Package, 1972; Statistical Design for Research, 1987; Sampling Methods for Agricultural Surveys, 1989. Add: Inst. for Social Research, Univ. of Michigan, Ann Arbor, Mich. 48106, U.S.A.

KISSINGER, Henry (Alfred). American, born German, b. 1923. Government/Politics, History, International relations/Current affairs, Autobiography/Memoirs. Univ. Prof of Diplomacy, Sch. of Foreign Service, and Counselor to the Center for Strategic and Intnl. Studies, Georgetown Univ., Washington, D.C., since 1977. Dir., Harvard Intnl. Seminar, 1951–71; Dir., Defense Studies Prog., 1958–71, and Prof. of Govt., 1962–71, Harvard Univ., Cambridge, Mass.; Asst. to the Pres. of the U.S. for National Security Affairs, 1969–75; U.S. Secty. of State, 1973–77. *Publs:* Nuclear Weapons and Foreign Policy, 1957; A World Restored: Castlereagh, Metternich and the Restoration of Peace, 1812-1822, 1957; The Necessity for Choice: Prospects of American Foreign Policy, 1961; The Troubled Partnership: A Reappraisal of the Atlantic Alliance, 1965; (ed.) Problems of National Security: A Book of Readings, 1965; American Foreign Policy, 1969, 3rd ed. 1977; White House Years (memoirs), 1979; For the Record: Selected Statements 1977-80, 1981; Years of Upheaval (memoirs), 1982; Observations: Selected Speeches and Essays 1982-1984, 1985. Add: Suite 400, 1800 K St. N.W., Washington, D.C. 20006, U.S.A.

KISTNER, Robert William. American, b. 1917. Medicine/Health. Assoc. Prof. of Obstetrics and Gynecology, Harvard Medical Sch., Boston, Mass. (Teaching Fellow, 1950–51 and 1952–53; Asst. in Gynecology,

1953–56; Instr., 1956–58; Assoc., 1958–59; former Asst. Prof.) Assoc. Chief of Staff, Boston Hosp. for Women, Mass, since 1974 (Sr. Gynecologist and Obstetrician, 1968–73). Instr. in Obstetrics and Gynecology, New York State Medical Sch., 1951–52. *Publs:* Principles and Practice of Gynecology, 1964, 4th ed. 1986; Progress in Infertility, 1969, 1975; The Pill—Fact and Fallacy, 1969; The Use of Progestins in Obstetrics and Gynecology, 1969; The Pill, 1970; (with G.W. Patton) Atlas of Infertility Surgery, 1975, 1984. Add: c/o Year Book Medical Publications, 35 E. Wacker Dr., Chicago, Ill., 60601, U.S.A.

KITANO, Harry H.L. American, b. 1926. Race relations, Sociology. Prof. of Social Welfare and Sociology, Univ. of California, Los Angeles, since 1969. *Publs:* Japanese Americans: The Evolution of a Subculture, 1969, 1976; (with Roger Daniels) American Racism: Exploration of the Nature of Prejudice, 1970; Race Relations, 1974, 1985; The Japanese Americans, 1987; (with Roger Daniels) Asian Americans, 1988. Add: Sch. of Social Welfare, Univ. of California, Los Angeles, Calif. 90024, U.S.A.

KITCHEN, Martin. British/Canadian, b. 1936. History. Univ. Prof., Simon Fraser Univ., Burnaby, B.C., since 1966. *Publs:* The German Officer Corps 1890-1914, 1968; A Military History of Germany, 1974; Fascism, 1976; The Silent Dictatorship: The Politics of the German High Command Under Hindenburg and Ludendorf, 1976; The Political Economy of Germany 1815-1914, 1978; The Coming of Austrian Fascism, 1980; Germany in the Age of Total War, 1981; British Policy Towards the Soviet Union During the Second World War, 1986; Europe Between the Wars, 1988. Add: Dept. of History, Simon Fraser Univ., Burnaby, B.C. V5A 1S6, Canada.

KITCHEN, Paddy. British, b. 1934. Novels, Biography. Art Critic, Country Life, since 1986. *Publs:* Lying-in, 1965; A Fleshly School, 1970; Linsey-Woolsey, 1971; Paradise, 1972; A Most Unsettling Person (on Patrick Geddes), 1975; Gerard Manley Hopkins, 1978; A Pillar of Cloud, 1979; Poets' London, 1980; The Golden Veil, 1981; The Way to Write Novels, 1981; Barnwell, 1985; Blue Shoe, 1988. Add: 21 &22, Barnwell PE8 5QB, England.

KITT, Tamara. *See* de REGNIERS, Beatrice Schenk.

KITZINGER, Sheila. British, b. 1929. Medicine/Health, Sex. Social anthropologist and childbirth educator. Lectr., Open Univ. Member, Advisory Bd., National Childbirth Trust, London, since 1958, and Bd. of Consultants, Intnl. Childbirth Education Assn., since 1972. Researcher on race relations in Britain, Univ. of Edinburgh, 1951–53. Chair, Foundn. for Women's Health, Research, and Development; Vice-Chair, Midwives' Information and Resource Service. *Publs:* The Experience of Childbirth, 1962, 4th ed. 1973; Giving Birth—The Parents' Emotions in Childbirth, 1971, 3rd ed. 1979; Education and Counselling for Childbirth, 1977; Women as Mothers, 1978; Birth at Home, 1979; The Good Birth Guide, 1979, 1982; The Experience of Breastfeeding, 1979; The Place of Birth, 1979; Pregnancy and Childbirth, 1980, 1989; Sheila Kitzinger's Birth Book, 1980; Some Women's Experience of Episiotomy, 1981; Episiotomy, 1981; Birth over Thirty, 1982; The New Good Birth Guide, 1983; Woman's Experience of Sex, 1983; Being Born, 1986; Giving Birth: How It Really Feels, 1987; Freedom and Choice in Childbirth, 1987; Some Women's Experiences of Epidurals, 1987; The Midwife Challenge, 1988; The Crying Baby, 1989; Breastfeeding Your Baby, 1989. Add: Standlake Manor, Standlake, nr. Witney, Oxon. OX8 7RH, England.

KITZINGER, Uwe. British, b. 1928. Economics, International relations/Current affairs, Politics/Government. Pres., Templeton Coll., Oxford, since 1984. With Secretariat-Gen., Council of Europe, Strasbourg, France, 1951–58; Founding Ed., Journal of Common Market Studies, 1963; Research Fellow, 1958–62, and Ford Fellow and Investment Bursar, 1962–76, Nuffield Coll., Oxford; Adviser to Sir Christopher Soames, Vice-Pres., Commn. of the European Communities, Brussels, 1973–75; Dean of the European Inst. of Business Admin., Fontainebleau, France, 1976–80; Dir., Oxford Centre for Management Studies, 1980–84. *Publs:* German Electoral Politics, 1960; The Challenge of the Common Market, 1961, 4th ed. 1962, rev. ed. as The Politics and Economics of European Integration, 1963; Britain, Europe and Beyond, 1964; The European Common Market and Community, 1967; Commitment and Identity, 1968; The Second Try, 1969; Diplomacy and Persuasion: How Britain Joined the EEC, 1973; Europe's Wider Horizon, 1975; (with David Butler) The 1975 Referendum, 1976. Add: Standlake Manor, nr. Witney, Oxon, OX8 7RH, England.

KIZER, Carolyn. American, b. 1925. Poetry. Prof. of Poetry, Stanford Univ., Calif., since 1986. Founding Ed., Poetry Northwest, Seattle 1959–65; Dir. of Literary Programs, National Endowment for the Arts 1966–70; Prof., Univ. of N.C., Chapel Hill, 1970–74; Prof., Univ. of Maryland, College Park, 1976–77; Visiting Prof., Barnard Coll., Columbia Univ., Washington Univ., Univ. of Iona and others. *Publs:* The Ungrateful Garden, 1961; Knock upon Silence, 1965; Midnight Was My Cry: New and Selected Poems, 1971; YIN: New Poems, 1984; Mermaids in the Basement: Poems for Women, 1984; Carrying Over: Translations from Various Tongues, 1985; The Nearness of You, 1986; Carrying Over, 1988. Add: 1401 LeRoy Ave., Berkeley, Calif. 94708, U.S.A.

KLAMKIN, Marian. American, b. 1926. Antiques/Furnishings, Crafts, History. Instr., Mannatuck Community Coll., since 1981. Instr. Univ. of Connecticut, Storrs, 1970–72. *Publs:* Flower Arrangements that Last, 1968; Flower Arranging for Period Decoration, 1968; The Collector's Book of Boxes, 1970; The Collector's Book of Wedgwood, 1971: The Collector's Book of Art Nouveau, 1971; The Collector's Book of Bottles, 1971; Hands to Work: Shaker Folk Art and Industries, 1972; White House China, 1972; American Patriotic and Political China, 1973; The Collector's Guide to Depression Glass, 1973; Picture Postcards, 1974; (with C. Klamkin) Wood Carving: North American Folk Sculpture, 1974; The Return of Lafayette, 1824-1825, 1974; Marine Antiques, 1975; Collectibles: A Compendium, 1981. Add: 141 Colonial Rd., Watertown, Conn. 06795, U.S.A.

KLAPPERT, Peter. American, b. 1942. Poetry. Assoc. Prof., since 1981, and Dir., Writing Prog., 1985–88 (and 1979–80), George Mason Univ., Fairfax (Asst. Prof., 1978–81). Instr., Rollins Coll., Winter Park, Fla., 1968–71; Briggs-Copeland Lectr. on English, Harvard Univ., Cambridge, Mass., 1971–74; Lectr., New Coll., Fla., 1972; Writer-in-Residence, 1976–77, and Asst. Prof., 1977–78, Coll. of William and Mary, Williamsburg, Va. *Publs:* Lugging Vegetables to Nantucket, 1971; Circular Stairs, Distress in the Mirrors, 1975; Non Sequitur O'Connor, 1977; The Idiot Princess of the Last Dynasty, 1984; '52 Pick-Up: Scenes from the Conspiracy, A Documentary, 1984; Internal Foreigner, 1984; Minor Constellations, 1989. Add: Dept. of English, George Mason Univ., Fairfax, Va. 22030, U.S.A.

KLARE, George Roger. American, b. 1922. Language/Linguistics, Mathematics/Statistics, Psychology. Distinguished Prof. of Psychology, Ohio Univ., Athens, since 1954 (Chmn., Dept. of Psychology, 1959–63; Dean, Coll.of Arts and Sciences, 1965–71; Acting Dean, Coll. of Arts and Sciences, 1984–85; Acting Assoc. Provost for Graduate and Research Progs., 1986–87). Research Assoc. and Language Prog. Dir., Computer-Aided Instructional Lab., Harvard Univ., Cambridge, Mass., 1968–69. *Publs:* (with B. Buck) Know Your Reader, 1954; The Measurement of Readability, 1963; (with P.A. Games) Elementary Statistics: Data Analysis for the Behavioral Sciences, 1967, instructors' manual, 1967; (with L.R. Campbell) Measuring the Readability of High School Newspapers, Parts I II, 1967; A Manual for Readable Writing, 1975, 4th ed. 1980; How to Write Readable English, 1984. Add: Dept. of Psychology, Ohio Univ., Athens, Ohio 45701, U.S.A.

KLARE, Hugh J. British, b. 1916. Criminology/Law enforcement/Prisons. Member, Parole Bd. for England and Wales, and Probation and After Care Cttee. for Gloucestershire. Secty., Howard League for Penal Reform, 1950–71; Head, Div. of Crime Problems, Council of Europe, 1971–73. *Publs:* Anatomy of Prison, 1960, 1962; (ed.) Changing Concepts of Crime and Its Treatment, 1966; (ed. with Haxby) Frontiers of Criminology, 1967; People in Prison, 1973. Add: 34 Harriots Ct., St. George's Cres., Droitwich Spa, Worcs., England.

KLASS, Sheila Solomon. American, b. 1927. Novels/Short stories, Autobiography/Memoirs/Personal. Prof. of English, Borough of Manhattan Community Coll., City Univ. of New York, since 1982 (Lectr., 1965–67; Instr. 1967–68; Asst. Prof., 1968–73; Assoc. Prof., 1973–82). *Publs:* Come Back on Monday, 1960; Everyone in This House Makes Babies, 1964; Bahadur Means Hero, 1969; A Perpetual Surprise, 1981; Nobody Knows Me in Miami, 1981; To See My Mother Dance, 1981; Alive and Starting Over, 1983; The Bennington Stitch, 1985; Page Four, 1986; Credit Card Carole, 1987. Add: 330 Sylvan Ave., Leonia, N.J. 07605, U.S.A.

KLAYMAN, Maxwell Irving. American, b. 1917. Economics, Third World problems. Dir., Sturtleff House, Oberlin Coll., Ohio, since 1979; Staff member, Campaign for U.N. Reform, since 1984. Staff member, Food and Agriculture Org. of the U.N., Rome, 1951–68, State Univ. of New York at New Paltz, 1968–70, and Univ. of Akron, Ohio, 1970–73;

Dir. of Economics, American Coll. of Switzerland, 1977–79; Development Economist, Novaklhot, Mauretania, 1980; Prof. of Economics and Business, Rockford Coll., 1981–82; Marketing Specialist, Seoul, South Korea, 1983–84. *Publs:* The Mosnav in Israel, 1970; Data Needs for Sector and Project Analyses, 1971. Add: 115 Melbourne Ave., Akron, Ohio 44313, U.S.A.

KLEHR, Harvey. American, b. 1945. History, Politics/Government. Prof. of Political Science, Emory Univ., Atlanta, since 1971. Pres., Historians of American Communism, 1985–87. *Publs:* Communist Cadre: The Social Background of the American Communist Party Elite, 1978; The Heyday of American Communism: The Depression Decade, 1984; Far Left of Center: The American Radical Left Today, 1988. Add: Dept. of Political Science, Emory Univ., Atlanta, Ga. 30322, U.S.A.

KLEIN, Alexander. American (born Hungarian), b. 1923. Novels/Short stories, Plays/Screenplays, Social commentary/phenomena. Consultant, Theatre for Ideas, and Common Cause; Co-Founder, Arden House Annual Convocations on Foreign Policy, since 1947. Adjunct Prof. of History, Political Science and Sociology, Fordham Univ., NYC, 1970–77. Dir. of Public Relations, CARE World Headquarters, NYC, 1972–82. *Publs:* Armies for Peace, 1950; Courage Is the Key, 1953; The Empire City, 1955; Grand Deception, 1955; The Counterfeit Traitor, 1958; The Double Dealers, 1959; The Fabulous Rogues, 1960; The Magnificent Scoundrels, 1961; Rebels, Rogues, Rascals, 1962; That Pellett Woman!, 1965; Natural Enemies?: Youth and the Clash of Generations, 1969; Dissent, Power and Confrontation, 1972; (co-author) Black Banana (screenplay), 1974, filmed as Shalom, Baby!, 1975; The Savage (screenplay), 1975. Add: 75 Bank St., Apt. 3A, New York, N.Y. 10014, U.S.A.

KLEIN, Frederic Shriver. American, b. 1904. History. Assoc. Ed., Historical Times Inc., since 1967. Secty., National Historical Soc., since 1969. Prof. of History, Franklin and Marshall Coll., Lancaster, Pa., 1928–70. *Publs:* Educational Background of Franklin and Marshall College, 1939; Lancaster County since 1841, 1941; (ed.) Just South of Gettysburg, 1963; Old Lancaster: Historic Pennsylvania Community, 1964; (ed. with J. Carrill) The Diary of Henry Kyd Douglas, 1973; (ed.) Fighting the Battles, 1975. Add: c/o Sutter House, 77 Main St., P.O. Box 212, Lititz, Pa. 17543, U.S.A.

KLEIN, Josephine (F.H.). British, b. 1926. Sociology. Asst. Lectr., and Lectr. in Social Psychology, Univ. of Birmingham, 1949–62; Research Fellow, Nuffield Coll., Oxford, 1962–65; Reader in Social Relations, Univ. of Sussex, 1965–70; Dir., Community and Youth Work Training, Goldsmiths' Coll., Univ. of London, 1970–74; now retired. *Publs:* The Study of Groups, 1956; Working with Groups, 1961; Samples from English Cultures, 1965; Our Need for Others and Its Roots in Infancy, 1987. Add: 58 Roupell St., London SE1, England.

KLEIN, Lawrence R(obert). American, b. 1920. Business/Trade/Industry, Economics. Univ. Prof. since 1964, and Benjamin Franklin Prof. since 1968, Univ. of Pennsylvania, Philadelphia (Prof., 1958–64). Consultant, Congressional Budget Office, since 1977 (Canadian Government, 1947; UNCTAD, 1966, 1967, 1975, 1977, 1980; Federal Reserves Board, 1973; UNIDO, 1973–75; Council of Economic Advisors, 1977–80). Assoc. Ed., International Econometric Review, since 1965 (Editor, 1959–65). Recipient, Nobel Prize for Economics, 1980. *Publs:* The Keynesian Revolution, 1947, 1949; Economic Fluctuations in the United States 1921–1941, 1950; A Textbook of Econometrics, 1953; (ed.) Contributions of Survey Methods to Economics, 1954; (with A.S. Goldberger) An Econometric Model of the United States 1929–1952, 1955; (with others) An Econometric Model of the United Kingdom, 1961; An Introduction to Econometrics, 1962; (with R.S. Preston) Stochastic Nonlinear Models, 1965; (ed. with J. Duesenberry, G. Fromm and E. Kuh) The Brookings Quarterly Econometric Model of the United States, 1965; (ed.) Readings in Business Cycles, 1965, 1966; (with Michael K. Evans) The Wharton Econometric Forecasting Model, 1967; (with Robert Summers) The Wharton Index of Capacity Utilization, 1967; (ed.) Economic Growth, 1968; An Essay on the Theory of Economic Prediction, 1968, 1971; (compiler with M.K. Evans and M. Hartley) Econometric Gaming: A Kit for Computer Analysis of Macroeconomic Models, 1969; Expanding the Benefits of Manpower Research, 1973; (ed. with G. Fromm) The Brookings Model: Perspective and Recent Developments, 1975; (with Stefan Schleicher) Techniques of Model Building for Developing Economies, 1975; (ed. with Edwin Burmeister) Econometric Model Performance: Comparative Simulation Studies of the U.S. Economy, 1976; (ed. with M. Nerlove and S.C. Tsiang) Quantitative Economics and Development: Essays in Memory of Tachung Lui, 1980; (with Richard M. Young) An Introduction to Econometric Forecasting and Forecasting Models, 1980: Econometric Models as Guides for Decision-Making, 1981; The Economics of Supply and Demand, 1983; Economic Theory and Econometrics, 1985. Add: Dept. of Economics, Univ. of Pennsylvania, Philadelphia, Pa. 19104, U.S.A.

KLEIN, Robin (née McMaugh). Australian, b. 1936. Children's fiction. *Publs:* The Giraffe in Pepperell, 1978; Honoured Guest, 1979; Sprung!, 1982; Things, 1982; Junk Castle, 1983; Oodoolay, 1983; People Might Hear You, 19867; Brock and the Dragon, 1984; Hating Alison Ashley, 1984; Penny Pollard's Letters, 1984; Ratbags and Rascals, 1984; Thalia the Failure, 1984; Thingnapped!, 1984; The Tomb Comb, 1984; Annabel's Ghost (stories), 1985; Good for Something (audio book), 1985; Snakes and ladders, 1985; Serve Him Right! (audio book), 1985; You're On Your Own, (audio book), 1985; The Enemies, 1985; Halfway Across the Galaxy and Turn Left, 1986; Separate Places, 1985; Boss of the Pool, 1986; Games . . ., 1986; Penny Pollard in Print, 1986; The Princess Who Hated It, 1986; Birk the Berserker, 1987; Get Lost, 1987; Christmas, 1987; Crookbook, 1987; Don't Tell Lucy, 1987; I Shot an Arrow, 1987; The Last Pirate, 1987; (with Max Dann) The Lonely Hearts Club, 1987; Parker-Hamilton, 1987; Laurie Loved Me Best, 1988; Dear Robin: Letters to Robin Klein, 1988; Penny Pollard's Passport, 1988; Against the Odds, 1989. Add: c/o Tim Curnow, Curtis Brown Ltd., P.O. Box 19, Paddington, New South Wales 2021, Australia.

KLEIN, Marcus. American, b. 1928. Literature. Prof. of English, State Univ. of New York, Buffalo, since 1965. *Publs:* After Alienation: American Novels in Mid-Century, 1964; (ed. with R. Pack) Innocence and Experience, 1966; (ed. with R. Pack) Short Stories: Classic, Modern, Contemporary, 1967; (ed.) The American Novel since World War II, 1969; Foreigners: The Making of Modern American Literature 1900–1940, 1981. Add: 90 Lyman Rd., Buffalo, N.Y. 14226, U.S.A.

KLEIN, Philip Alexander. American, b. 1927. Economics. Prof. of Economics, Pennsylvania State Univ., University Park, since 1968 (Instr., 1955–58; Asst. Prof., 1958–61; Assoc. Prof., 1961–68). Research Assoc., Center for Intnl. Business Cycle Research, Columbia Univ., Newark, N.J. Member, Research Staff, National Bureau of Economic Research, NYC, 1955–70, and 1973–78; Academic Visitor, London Sch. of Economics, 1973–74. *Publs:* Financial Adjustments to Unemployment, 1965; (with G.H. Moore) The Quality of Consumer Instalment Credit, 1967; (with R.L. Gordon) The Steel Industry and U.S. Business Cycles, 1971; The Cyclical Timing of Consumer Credit, 1920–1927, 1971; The Management of Market-Oriented Economics, 1973; (with G.H. Moore) Monitoring Business Cycles in Market-Oriented Economics, 1985. Add: Dept. of Economics, Pennsylvania State Univ., 516 Kern Grad. Bldg., University Park, Pa. 16802, U.S.A.

KLEINE-AHLBRANDT, William Laird. American, b. 1932. History. Assoc. Prof. of European History, Purdue Univ., Lafayette, Ind., since 1969 (Asst. Prof., 1963–69). *Publs:* The Policy of Simmering: A Study of British Policy during the Spanish Civil War 1936–39, 1963; (ed.) The Appeasement of the Dictators, 1970; Victorien Sardou: La Tosca, The Life and Times of a Well-Made Thriller, 1989. Add: Dept. of History, Purdue Univ., West Lafayette, Ind., U.S.A.

KLEMENT, Frank L. American, b. 1908. History, Biography. Emeritus Prof. of History, Marquette Univ., Milwaukee (joined faculty, 1948). Visiting Prof. of American History, Univ. of Sussex, Brighton, 1975–76. Intnl. Pres., Phi Alpha Theta, intnl. hon. historical soc., 1973–75. *Publs:* Copperheads in the Middle West, 1960; Wisconsin and the Civil War, 1963; The Limits of Dissent: Clement L. Vallardigham and the Civil War, 1970; Dark Lanterns: Secret Political Societies, Conspiracies and Treason Trials in the Civil War, 1985. Add: 6627 W. Moltke Ave., Milwaukee, Wisc. 53210, U.S.A.

KLINE, Morris. American, b. 1908. Mathematics/Statistics. Prof. of Mathematics, New York Univ., NYC, 1952–74, now Emeritus (joined faculty, 1930). *Publs:* Mathematics in Western Culture, 1953; Mathematics and the Physical World, 1959; Mathematics, a Cultural Approach, 1962; Electromagnetic Theory and Geometrical Optics, 1965; Mathematics for Liberal Arts, 1967; Calculus, an Intuitive and Physical Approach, 1967, 1977; (ed.) Mathematics in the Modern World, 1968; Mathematical Thought from Ancient to Modern Times, 1972; Why Johnny Can't Add: The Failure of the New Math, 1973; Why the Professor Can't Teach, 1978; Mathematics: The Loss of Certainty, 1980; Mathematics for the Nonmathematician, 1985; Mathematics and the Search for Knowledge, 1985. Add: 1024 East 26th St., Brooklyn, N.Y. 11210, U.S.A.

KLINE, Peter. American, b. 1936. Education, Music, Theatre. Educational Consultant since 1983. Co-Dir., Interlocking Curriculum Sch., since 1973. Teacher: Maret Sch., Washington, D.C., 1958–65, 1972–73; Sandy Spring Friends Sch., Md., 1965–70; Sidwell Friends Sch., Washington, D.C., 1970–72; Co-Dir., Interlocking Curriculum Sch., 1973–83. *Publs:* The Theatre Student: Scenes to Perform, Playwriting, Physical Movement, Gilbert and Sullivan Production, The Actor's Voice, Diary of a Play Production, 6 vols., 1969–80; Opera, 1977; The Weight Control Survival Kit, 1982; The Everyday Genius, 1988. Add: 24544 Cutsail Dr., Damascus, MD 20872, U.S.A.

KLINGER, Eric. American, b. 1933. Psychology. Prof. of Psychology, Univ. of Minnesota, Morris, since 1969 (Asst. prof., 1962–63; Assoc. prof., 1963–69); Prof. of Psychology, Univ. of Minnesota, Minneapolis, since 1978. Instr. in Psychology, Univ. of Wisconsin, Madison, 1960–62. *Publs:* Structure and Functions of Fantasy, 1971; Meaning and Void: Inner Experience and the Incentives in People's Lives, 1977; (ed.) Imagery: vol. II: Concepts, Results and Applications, 1981. Add: Div. of Social Sciences, Univ. of Minnesota-Morris, Morris, Minn. 56267, U.S.A.

KNAPP-FISHER, Edward George. British, b. 1915. Theology/Religion. Ordained, 1939; Chaplain, Cuddesdon Coll., Oxford, 1946; Chaplain, St. John's Coll., Cambridge, 1949; Vicar of Cuddesdon and Principal, Cuddesdon Theological Coll., Oxford, 1952–60; Bishop of Pretoria, 1960–75; Archdeacon, 1975–87, and Sub-Dean, 1982–87, Westminster Abbey, London. *Publs:* The Churchman's Heritage, 1952; Belief and Prayer, 1964; To Be or Not To Be, 1967; Where the Truth Is Found, 1975; (co-ed.) Towards Unity in Truth, 1982; Eucharist: Many-Sided Mystery, 1988. Add: 2 Vicars' Close, Canon Lane, Chichester, W. Sussex PO19 1PT, England.

KNAPTON, Ernest John. American, b. 1902. History, Biography. Prof. of History, Wheaton Coll., Norton, Mass., 1931–69, now retired. *Publs:* Lady of the Holy Alliance, 1939; France since Versailles, 1952; Europe, 1450-1815, 1958; Empress Josephine, 1963; (with T.K. Derry) Europe, 1815-1914, 1964; (with T.K. Derry) Europe and the World since 1914, 1966; (with T.K. Derry) Europe, 1815 to the Present, 1966; France, an Interpretive History, 1971; Revolutionary and Imperial France, 1972. Add: 779 Fox Hill Rd., Chatham, Mass. 02633, U.S.A.

KNEALE, (Thomas) Nigel. British, b. 1922. Science fiction/Fantasy, Plays/Screenplays. Freelance writer, mainly of screenplays and television plays. Actor, Stratford upon Avon, 1948–49; Staff Member, BBC-TV, London, 1951–55. *Publs:* Tomato Cain and Other Stories, 1949; The Quatermass Experiment, 1959; Quatermass II, 1960; Quatermass and the Pit, 1960; The Year of the Sex Olympics and Other TV Plays (includes The Road, and The Stone Tape), 1976; Quatermass (novel), 1979. Add: c/o Douglas Rae (Mgmt.) Ltd., 28 Charing Cross Rd., London WC2H 0DB, England.

KNEBEL, Fletcher. American, b. 1911. Novels/Short stories. Reporter, 1936, and Washington Corresp., 1937–50, Cleveland Plain Dealer, Ohio; Washington Corresp., Cowles Publs., Washington, D.C., 1950–64; Writer, Look mag., NYC, 1950–71; Columnist, Potomac Fever syndicated column, 1951–64. *Publs:* (with C. Bailey) No High Ground, 1960; (with C. Bailey) Seven Days in May, 1962; (with C. Bailey) Convention, 1964; Night of Camp David, 1965; The Zinzin Road, 1966; Vanished, 1968; Trespass, 1969; Dark Horse, 1972; The Bottom Line, 1974; Dave Sulkin Cares!, 1978; Crossing in Berlin, 1981; Poker Game, 1983; Sabotage, 1986; (with G. Clay) Before You Sue, 1987. Add: 1070 Oilipuu Place, Honolulu, Hawaii 96825, U.S.A.

KNECHT, Robert Jean. British, b. 1926. History. Prof. of French History, Univ. of Birmingham (Lectr., 1959–68; Sr. Lectr., 1968–77; Reader, 1977–85). *Publs:* (ed.) The Voyage of Sir Nicholas Carewe, 1959; Renaissance and Reformation, 1967; Francis I and Absolute Monarchy, 1969; The Fronde, 1975; (co-ed.) Wealth and Power in Tudor England, 1978; Francis I, 1982; French Renaissance Monarchy: Francis I and Henry II, 1984; French Wars of Religion, 1989. Add: Sch. of History, Univ. of Birmingham, P.O. Box 363, Birmingham B15 2TT, England.

KNIGHT, Alanna (née Cleet). Also writes as Margaret Hope. British. Historical Novels, Biography. Fellow, Soc. of Antiquaries. *Publs:* Legend of the Loch, 1969; The October Witch, 1971; This Outward Angel, 1972; Castle Clodha, 1972; Lament for Lost Lovers, 1972; The White Rose, 1973; A Stranger Came By, 1974; The Passionate Kindness, 1974; A Drink for the Bridge, 1976; The Wicked Wynsleys, 1977; (as Margaret Hope) The Queen's Captain, 1978; (as Margaret Hope) Hostage Most Royal, 1979; (as Margaret Hope) The Shadow Queen, 1979; The Black Duchess, 1980; Castle of Foxes, 1981; Colla's Children, 1982; (as Margaret Hope) Perilous Voyage, 1983; The Clan, 1985; Estella, 1986; The Robert Louis Stevenson Treasury, 1986; RLS in the South Seas, 1987; Enter Second Murderer, 1988; Blood Line, 1989. Add: 4 March Hall Cres., Edinburgh, EH16 5HL, Scotland.

KNIGHT, Bernard. Also writes as Bernard Picton. British, b. 1931. Mystery/Crime/Suspense, Plays/Screenplays, Medicine/Health. Prof. and Consultant in Forensic Pathology, Univ. of Wales, Coll. of Medicine, (Lectr., 1962–65; Sr. Lectr., 1965–76; Reader, 1976). Joint Ed., Welsh Medical Gazette, since 1969. Lectr. in Forensic Medicine, Univ. of London, 1959–65; Medical Ed., Medicine, Science and the Law, 1960–63; Sr. Lectr. in Forensic Pathology, Univ. of Newcastle, 1965–68. *Publs:* (as Bernard Picton) The Lately Deceased, 1963; (as Bernard Picton) Thread of Evidence, 1965; (as Bernard Picton) Mistress Murder, 1966; (as Bernard Picton) Russian Roulette, 1968; (as Bernard Picton) Policeman's Progress, 1969; (as Bernard Picton) Tiger at Bay, 1970; Murder, Suicide or Accident, 1971; Deg Y Dragwyddoldeb, 1972; Legal Aspects of Medical Practice, 1972, 3rd ed. 1982; In the Dead, Behold the Quick (television series), 1973; Edfyn Brau, 1973; Discovering the Human Body, 1980; Forensic Radiology, 1981; Lawyer's Guide to Forensic Medicine, 1982; Sudden Death in Infancy, 1983; Coroner's Autopsy, 1983; Post-Modern Technicians Handbook, 1984; Pocket Guide to Forensic Medicine, 1985; (with K. Simpson) Forensic Medicine, 9th ed. 1985. Add: Inst. of Pathology, Royal Infirmary, Cardiff CF2 1SZ, Wales.

KNIGHT, David. See **PRATHER**, Richard Scott.

KNIGHT, D(avid) M(arcus). British. Intellectual History, Natural History, Sciences. Reader in the History of Science, Dept. of Philosophy, Univ. of Durham. Gen. Ed., Blackwell Science Biographies. *Publs:* Atoms and Elements: A Study of Theories of Matter in England in the 19th Century, 1967, 1970; (ed.) Classical Scientific Paper: Chemistry, 1968, and Second Series, 1970; Natural Science Book in English 1600-1900, 1972; Sources for the History of Science 1660-1914, 1975; The Nature of Science: The History of Science in Western Culture since 1600, 1977; Zoological Illustrations: An Essay Towards a History of Printed Zoological Pictures, 1977; The Transcendental Part of Chemistry, 1978; Ordering the World: A History of Classifying Man, 1981; The Age of Science, 1986; A Companion to the Physical Sciences, 1989. Add: Dept. of Philosophy, Univ. of Durham, 50 Old Elvet, Durham DH1 3HN, England.

KNIGHT, Etheridge. American, b. 1931. Poetry. Poet-in- Residence, Lincoln Univ., Jefferson City, Mo., 1970–71; Poetry Ed., Motive, Nashville, Tenn., 1970–71; Co-Ed., Black Box, Washington, D.C., 1971–72. *Publs:* Poems from Prison, 1968; The Idea of Ancestry, 1968; 2 Poems for Black Relocation Centers, 1968; (ed.) Voce negre dal carcere (in U.S. as Black Voices from Prison), 1968; For Black Poets Who Think of Suicide, 1972; A Poem for Brother Man, 1972; Belly Song and Other Poems, 1973; Born of a Woman: New and Selected Poems, 1980; The Essential Etheridge Knight, 1986. Add: c/o Broadside Press, P.O. Box 04257, Detroit, Mich. 48204, U.S.A.

KNIGHT, Frank (Francis Edgar Knight). Also writes as Cedric Slater. British, b. 1905. Novels/Short stories, Children's fiction, History. Apprentice, 1921–25, and successively Third, Second, and First Mate, 1926–30) Merchant Navy; certified Master Mariner, 1928, and Extra Master Mariner, 1929; worked for marine insurance and yacht broking firms, and as a freelance journalist, 1931–39, 1940–70; served as a Navigation Instr. in the Royal Air Force, 1939–45. *Publs:* The Albatross Comes Home, 1949; Four in the Half-Deck, 1950; The Island of the Radiant Pearls, 1950; The Golden Monkey, 1953; Strangers in the Half-Deck, 1953; Acting Third Mate, 1954; Voyage to Bengal, 1954; Clippers to China, 1955; Mudlarks and Mysteries, 1955; A Beginner's Guide to the Sea, 1955; (as Cedric Salter) Two Girls and a Boat, 1956; The Bluenose Pirate, 1956; Family on the Tide, 1956; Please Keep Off the Mud, 1957; The Patrick Steamboat, 1958; He Sailed with Blackbeard, 1958; The Sea Story: Being a Guide to Nautical Reading From Ancient Times to the Close of the Sailing Ship Era, 1958; A Guide to Ocean Navigation, 1959; Captain Anson and the Treasure of Spain, 1959; The Sea Chest: Stories of Adventure at Sea, 1960; Shadows on the Mud, 1960; The Sea's Fool, 1960; Captains of the Calabur, 1961; The Slaver's Apprentice, 1961; The Last of Lallows, 1961; The Young Drake, 1962; John Harrison, The Man Who Made Navigation Safe, 1962; Pekoe Reef, 1962; Clemency Draper, 1963; The Ship That Came Home, 1963; The Young Columbus, 1963; Stories of Famous Ships, 1963; Stories of Famous Sea Fights, 1963; Up, Sea Beggar's, 1964; Stories of Famous Explorers by Sea, 1964; The Young Captain Cook, 1964; (ed.) They Told Mr. Hakluyt (from Hakluyt's

Voyages), 1954; Stories of Famous Explorers by Lane, 1965; Remember Vera Cruz!, 1965; Kit Baxter's War, 1966; Stories of Famous Sea Adventures, 1966; Prince of Cavaliers: The Story of the Life and Campaigns of Rupert of the Rhine, 1967; Rebel Admiral: The Life and Exploits and Admiral Lord Cochrane, Tenth Earl of Dundonald, 1958; (ed.) Captain Cook and the Voyage of the "Endeavour" 1768-1771, 1968; The Hero (on Lord Nelson), 1969; Russia Fights Japan, 1969; Ships Then and Now, 1969; Olaf's Sword, 1969; That Rare Captain: Sir Francis Drake, 1970; Christopher Columbus, 1970; The Dardanelles Campaign, 1970; General-at-Sea: The Life of Admiral Robert Blake, 1971; Ships, 1973; True Stories of the Sea, 1973; True Stories of Exploration, 1973; The Clipper Ship, 1973; True Stories of Spying, 1975; The Golden Age of the Galleon, 1976. Add: c/o A.M. Heath and Co. Ltd., 40-42 William IV St., London WC2N 4DD, England.

KNIGHT, Gareth. *See* **WILBY,** Basil Leslie.

KNIGHT, George A(ngus) F(ulton). British, b. 1909. Theology/Religion. Dir., Scottish Sch., Budapest, Hungary, 1935–40; Minister, Glasgow, 1942–46; Prof. of Old Testament Studies, Knox Coll., Dunedin, N.Z., 1947–58; Lectr. in Old Testament and Semitic Languages, Univ. of St. Andrews, Scotland, 1959–60; Prof. of Old Testament, McCormick Theological Seminary, Chicago, 1960–65; Principal, Pacific Theological Coll., Suva, Fiji, 1965–72; Moderator, Presbyterian Church of New Zealand, 1974–75. *Publs:* From Moses to Paul, 1949; Ruth and Jonah, 1950, 1965; A Biblical Approach to the Doctrine of the Trinity, 1953; Esther, Song of Songs, Lamentations, 1955; (trans.) A History of the Hungarian Reformed Church, 1956; Hosea, 1960; A Christian Theology of the Old Testament, 1960, 1964; Prophets of Israel, vol. I, Isaiah, 1961; Law and Grace, 1965; Deutero-Isaiah: A Theological Commentary, 1965; (ed. and contrib.) Jews and Christians, 1965; Exile and After, 1966; New Zealand Jesus, 1974; Theology as Narration, 1977; Eschatology in the Old Testament, 1978; What Next? (autobiography), 1980; Theology in Pictures, 1981; Leviticus, 1981; The Psalms, 2 vols, 1982–83; I Am: This is My Name, 1983; Servant Theology, 1984; The New Israel, 1985; Song of Songs, 1988. Add: 22 Gladstone Rd., Dunedin, New Zealand.

KNIGHT, Hardwicke. British, b. 1911. History, Photography, Biography. Keeper of the Educational Photographic Collection, Otago Museum, Dunedin, New Zealand, since 1971. Chief Photographer, EMS Plastic Surgery Unit, Gloucester, England, 1941–46; Dir. of Medical Photography, Enfield Group Hospitals, England, 1948–57; Dir. of Medical Photography, Univ. of Otago Medical Sch. and Dunedin Hospital, 1957–78. Pres., New Zealand Inst. of Medical Photographers, and Dunedin Film Soc., 1966–77. *Publs:* Archaeological Recording, 1960; Photography in New Zealand: A Social and Technical Study, 1971; Dunedin Then, 1974; (with Dr. P. Coutts) Matanaka, 1975; History of Broad Bay School, 1977; Princes Street by Gaslight, 1976; Otago Peninsula, 1978, 3rd ed. 1980; (with Dr. S. Greif) Cutten, 1979; Burton Brothers, Photographers, 1980; The Ordeal of William Larnach, 1981; New Zealand Photographers, 1981; Otago Cavalcade, 7 vols., 1982–86; Hardwicke Knight, Photographer, 1983; Dunedin Early Photographs, 2 vols., 1984–85; Otago Early Photographs, 1988; (with N. Wales) Buildings of Dunedin, 1988. Add: Broad Bay, Dunedin, New Zealand.

KNIGHT, James Allen. American, b. 1918. Medicine/Health, Psychiatry, Theology/Religion. Prof. of Psychiatry and Medical Ethics, Louisiana State Sch. of Medicine, New Orleans, since 1978. Asst. in Psychiatry, 1955–57, Instr., 1957–58, Assoc. Dean and Dir. of Admissions, 1964–74, Sch. of Medicine, Assoc. Prof. of Psychiatry and of Preventive Medicine, and Dir. of Section on Community Psychiatry, 1961–63, and Prof. of Psychiatry, 1964–75, Sch. of Medicine and Sch. of Public Health and Tropical Medicine, Tulane Univ., New Orleans, La.; Asst. Prof. of Psychiatry, 1958–61, and Asst. Dean, 1960–61, Baylor Univ. Coll. of Medicine, Houston, Tex.; Dir., Prog. in Psychiatry and Religion, Union Theological Seminary, NYC, 1963–64; Dean of Medicine and Prof. of Psychiatry, Texas A&M Univ., College Station, Tex., 1975–78. *Publs:* (with W.E. Davis) A Manual for the Comprehensive Community Mental Health Clinic, 1964; A Psychiatrist Looks at Religion and Health, 1964; (with M. Bowers, E. Jackson and L. LeShan) Counseling the Dying, 1964; (with J.P. McGovern) Allergy and Human Emotions, 1967; (ed. with R. Slovenko) Motivations in Play, Games, and Sports, 1967; For the Love of Money: Human Behavior and Money, 1968; Conscience and Guilt, 1969; Medical Student: Doctor in the Making, 1973; Doctor-to-Be: Coping with the Trials and Triumphs of Medical School, 1981. Add: 170 Walnut St., Apt. 8F, New Orleans, La. 70118, U.S.A.

KNIGHT, Karl Frederick. American, b. 1930. Literature, Writing. Prof. of English, Old Dominion Univ., Norfolk Va., since 1962. *Publs:*

The Poetry of John Crowe Ransom, 1964; (ed. with F.C. Watkins) Writer to Writer: Discussions of the Craft of Writing, 1966; (with L.H. Moore) A Concise Handbook of English Composition, 1972. Add: Dept. of English, Old Dominion Univ., Norfolk, Va. 23508, U.S.A.

KNIGHT, William Nicholas. American, b. 1939. Literature. Prof. of English and Dir. of Center for Aging Studies, Univ. of Missouri, Rolla, since 1985 (Prof., 1983–84; Dir., 1981–83; Chmn. of Humanities, 1975–81). Asst. Prof. of English, Wesleyan Univ., Middletown, Conn., 1966–75 (Asst. Chmn., English Dept., 1970–71; Fellow of Wesleyan Center for the Humanities, 1971–72). Dean of Faculty and Prof. of Law, Wethersfield Sch. of Law, since 1973. Reader, Inst. of Advanced Legal Studies, Univ. of London, 1969–70; Visiting Prof. of English, Southern Illinois Univ., Carbondale, 1984–85; Bd. of Renaissance Center of Newberry Library, Chicago, 1984, and Center Fellow, 1984. *Publs:* Shakespeare's Hidden Life: Shakespeare at the Law 1585-1595, 1973. Add: Dept. of English, Univ. of Missouri, Rolla-Rolla, Mo. 65401, U.S.A.

KNIGHTLEY, Phillip (George). Australian, b. 1929. History, Biography. Copyboy, The Telegraph, Sydney, 1945–47; Reporter, the Northern Star, Lismore, 1948–49; Copra Trader and Asst. Ed., The Oceania Daily News, Fiji, 1950; Reporter, the Herald, Melbourne, 1952–54; Reporter, 1954–56, and Foreign Corresp., 1956–60, The Daily Mirror, Sydney; Ed., Imprint, Bombay, 1960–62; with ABC, Sydney, 1963; Special Corresp., The Sunday Times, 1965–85. *Publs:* (with Bruce Page and David Leitch) Philby: The Spy Who Betrayed a Generation, 1968; (with Hugh Atkinson) The Games, 1968; (with Colin Simpson) The Secret Lives of Lawrence of Arabia, 1969; The First Casualty: The War Correspondent as Hero Propagandist, and Myth-Maker, Crimea to Vietnam, 1975; Lawrence of Arabia, 1976; (with Stephen Fay) The Death of Venice, 1976; (ed.) Suffer the Children, 1979; The Vestey Affair, 1981; The Second Oldest Profession: The Spy As Bureaucrat, Patriot, Fantasist, and Whore, 1986; (with Caroline Kennedy) An Affair of State: The Profumo Case and the Framing of Stephen Ward, 1987; Philby: KGB Masterspy, 1988. Add: 4 Northumberland Pl., London W2, England.

KNIGHT-PATTERSON, W.M. *See* **KULSKI,** W.W.

KNIGHTS, L(ionel) C(harles). British, b. 1906. Literature. Asst. Lectr., Lectr., and Sr. Lectr. to English, Univ. of Manchester, 1933–34 and 1935–46; Prof. of English, Univ. of Sheffield, 1947–53, and Univ. of Bristol, 1954–64; Fellow, Queens' Coll., Cambridge, and King Edward VII Prof. of English, Cambridge Univ., 1965–73, now Emeritus. Member, Editorial Bd. Scrutiny: A Quarterly Review, 1932–53. *Publs:* Drama and Society in the Age of Jonson, 1937; Explorations: Essays in Criticism, 1946; Some Shakespearean Themes, 1959; An Approach to Hamlet, 1960; (ed. with B. Cottle) Metaphor and Symbol, 1961; Further Explorations, 1965; Public Voices: Literature and Politics with Special Reference to the 17th Century, 1971; Explorations 3, 1977; "Hamlet" and Other Shakespearean Essays, 1979; Selected Essays in Criticism, 1981. Add: 57 Jesus Lane, Cambridge CB5 8BS, England.

KNOEPFLE, John. American, b. 1923. Poetry, Translations. Prof. of Literature, Sangmon State Univ., Springfield, Ill., since 1972. Producer-Dir., WCET Educational Television, Cincinnati, Ohio, 1953–55; Asst. Instr., Ohio State Univ., Columbus, 1956–57; Instr., Southern Illinois Univ., East St. Louis, 1957–61, St. Louis Univ. High Sch., 1961–62, and Mark Twain Inst., Clayton, Mo., Summers 1962–64; Asst. Prof., Maryville Coll., St. Louis, 1962–66; and Washington Univ. Coll., St. Louis, 1963–66; Assoc. Prof., St. Louis Univ., 1966–72; Consultant Project Upward Bound, Washington, D.C., 1967–70. *Publs:* (trans. with R. Bly and J. Wright) Twenty Poems of Cesar Vallejo, 1961; Poets at the Gate, 1965; Rivers into Islands: A Book of Poems, 1965; Songs for Gail Guidry's Guitar, 1969; An Affair of Culture and Other Poems, 1969; After Gray Days and Other Poems, 1969; The Intricate Land: A Book of Poems, 1970; (with L. Mueller and D. Etter) Voyages to the Inland Sea: Essays and Poems, 1971; Dogs and Cats and Things Like That: A Book of Poems for Children, 1971; The Ten-Fifteen Community Poems, 1971; (trans. with R. Bly and J. Wright) Neruda and Vallejo: Selected Poems, 1971; Our Street Feels Good (for children), 1972; Whetstone: A Book of Poems, 1972; Deep Winter Poems, 1972; (with others) Regional Perspectives, 1973; Thinking of Offerings: Poems 1970–1973, 1975; A Gathering of Voices, 1978; (ed. with Dan Jaffe) Frontier Literature: Images of the American West, 1979; A Box of Sandalwood: Love Poems, 1979; Poems for the Hours, 1979; Selected Poems, 1985; Poems from the Sangamon, 1985; (trans. with Wang Shou-yi) Tang Dynasty Poems, 1985; (trans. with Wang Shou-yi), Sung Dynasty Poems, 1985. Add: 1008 West Adams, Auburn, Ill. 62615, U.S.A.

KNOPF, Terry Ann. American. Race relations. TV critic, Patriot Ledger. Curriculum Specialist, Educational Development Corp., 1963–65; Research Coordinator, Senatorial Campaign of Edward W. Brooke, Mass., 1966–67; Research Assoc., Lemberg Center for the Study of Violence, Brandeis Univ., Waltham, Mass., 1967–73; Assoc. Producer, WCVB (ABC) TV, Needham, Mass., 1973–76; TV Writer, The Miami Herald, 1976–78; Daytime TV Critic, The Boston Globe, 1978–82. *Publs:* Youth Patrols: An Experiment in Community Participation, 1969; Rumors, Race and Riots, 1975. Add: 205 Walden St. Apt. 5S, Cambridge, Mass. 02140, U.S.A.

KNORR, Klaus (Eugene). American, b. 1911. International relations/Current affairs. Prof. Emeritus, Princeton Univ., since 1979 (Prof. of Intnl. Affairs since 1957; Assoc. Dir., 1958–62, Dir., 1962–68, Center of Intnl. Studies; William Stewart Tod Prof. of Public Affairs, 1964–79); Ed., World Politics, since 1953. Assoc. Prof., Yale Univ., New Haven, Conn., 1945–51; Member, Sr. Review Panel, Central Intelligence Agency, Washington, D.C., 1979–80. *Publs:* British Colonial Theories 1570-1850, 1944; The War Potential of Nations, 1956; (ed.) NATO and American Security, 1959; (ed. with Verba) The International System: Theoretical Essays, 1961; On the Uses of Military Power in the Nuclear Age, 1966; Military Power and Potential, 1970; Power and Wealth, 1973; NATO: Past, Present, Prospect, 1974; The Power of Nations, 1975; (ed.) Historical Dimensions of National Security Problems, 1976; (co-ed.) Economic Issues and National Security, 1978. Add: 641 Mt. Lucas Rd., Princeton, N.J. 08540, U.S.A.

KNOTT, Bill (William Kilborn Knott). American, b. 1940. Poetry. *Publs:* The Naomi Poems, Book One: Corpse and Beans, 1968; Aurealism: A Study: A Poem, 1970; (with J. Tate) Are You Ready Mary Baker Eddy?, 1970; Auto-Necrophilia: The Bill Knott Poems, Book 2, 1971; Nights of Naomi, 1971; Love Poems to Myself, 1974; Rome in Rome, 1976; Selected and Collected Poems, 1977; (with James Tate) Lucky Daryll (novel), 1977; Becos, 1983; Poems: 1963–88, 1989; Outremer, 1989. Add: c/o Emerson Coll., 148 Beacon St., Boston, Mass. 02116, U.S.A.

KNOTT, Bill. *See* **KNOTT,** William C.

KNOTT, William C(ecil). Also writes as Bill Knott, Bill J. Carol, Will C. Knott, Tabor Evans, Jake Logan, Bryan Swift, Jon Sharpe and Hank Mitchum. American, b. 1927. Mystery, Westerns and Children's fiction, Writing. Prof. Emeritus, State Univ. of New York at Potsdam, since 1982 (Assoc. Prof. of English, 1967–82). Pres., Western Writers of America, 1981–82. *Publs: non-fiction*—The Craft of Fiction, 1974; The Craft of Non-Fiction, 1974; *children's fiction as Bill J. Carol*—Circus Catch, 1963; Backboard Scrambler, 1963; Scatback, 1964; Clutch Single, 1964; Full Court Pirate, 1965; Hit Away, 1965; Long Pass, 1966; Hard Smash to Third, 1966; They Work and Serve, 1967; Inside the Ten, 1967; Lefty's Long Throw, 1967; Lefty Finds A Catcher, 1968; Touchdown Duo, 1968; Lefty's Long Stretch, 1969; Squeeze Play, 1971; Linebacker Blitz, 1971; Double Play Ball, 1972; High Fly To Center, 1972; Sandy Plays Third, 1972; Crazylegs Merrill, 1973; Stop That Pass, 1973; Fullback Fury, 1974; Flare Pass, 1974; Single To Center, 1974; *fiction as Bill Knott*—Junk Pitcher, 1963; Night Pursuit, 1966; The Dwarf on Black Mountain, 1967; Danger AT Half-Moon Lake, 1968; The Secret of the Old Brownstone, 1969; The Serpent of Pirate Cove, 1970; *fiction as William (or Will) C. Knott*—Taste of Vengeance, 1975; Killer's Roost, 1976; Caulder's Badge, 1976; Killer's Canyon, 1977; Kiowa Blood, 1977; Stampede, 1977; The Return of Zach Stuart, 1980; The Golden Mountain, 1980; Red Skies Over Wyoming, 1980; Lyncher's Moon, 1980; The Texan, 1987; *fiction as Will C. Knott*—The Golden Hawk Series: The Golden Hawk, 1986; Blood Hunt, 1986; Grizzly Pass, 1986; Kill Hawk, 1987; Hell's Children, 1987; Scalper's Trail, 1987; Eyes of the Cat, 1988; *fiction as Tabor Evans*—Longarm series, 27 vols., 1978–87; *fiction as Jake Logan*—Slocum and the Cattle Queen, 1983; Slocum and the Lost Dutchman Mine, 1983; *fiction as Bryan Swift*— Mission Code: King's Pawn, 1981; Mission Code: Minotaur, 1981; Mission Code: Springboard, 1982; *fiction as Hank Mitchum*—Cheyenne, 1983; Seattle, 1983; Sonora, 1983; Abilene, 1984; Cimarron, 1984; *fiction as Jon Sharpe*—The Trailsman Series: Hostage Trail, 1984; White Savage, 1984; Apache Gold, 1984; Sharps Justice, 1984; The Badge, 1984; The Lost Patrol, 1985; The Grizzly Man, 1985; The Renegade Command, 1985; Scorpion Trail, 1985; Hell Town, 1985; Blood Oath, 1986; Posse From Hell, 1986; Killer Clan, 1986. Add: R.D. 1, Cottage Rd., Colton, NY13625, U.S.A.

KNOWLES, Dorothy. British, b. 1906. Film, Literature. Hon. Research Fellow, Royal Holloway and Bedford New Coll., Univ. of London, since 1968. Lectr. in French, Univ. of Liverpool, 1934–68. *Publs:* La Réaction idéaliste au théâtre depuis 1890, 1934; The Censor, the Drama and the Film 1900–1934, 1934; French Drama of the Inter-Wars Years 1918-1938, 1967; Armand Gatti in the Theatre: Wild Duck Against the Wind, 1989. Add: 48 Woodside Park Rd., London N12 8RS, England.

KNOWLES, John. American, b. 1926. Novels/Short stories, Travel/Exploration/Adventure. Reporter, Hartford Courant, Conn., 1950–52; Assoc. Ed., Holiday mag., NYC, 1956–60. *Publs:* A Separate Peace, 1959; Morning in Antibes, 1962; Double Vision: American Thoughts Abroad, 1964; Indian Summer, 1966; Phineas: Six Stories, 1968; The Paragon, 1971; Spreading Fires, 1974; A Vein of Riches, 1978; Peace Breaks Out, 1980; A Stolen Past, 1983; The Private Life of Axie Reed, 1986. Add: c/o Dutton, 2 Park Ave., New York, N.Y. 10016, U.S.A.

KNOWLES, Susanne. British, b. 1911. Poetry. Freelance writer. *Publs:* Birth of Venus and Other Poems, 1945; Mediterranean and Other Poems, 1962; (ed.) Chorus: An Anthology of Bird Poems, 1969; The Sea-Bell and Other Poems, 1974. Add: 7 Richmond Park Rd., London SW14 8JU, England.

KNOWLTON, Derrick. British, b. 1921. Natural history, Biography. Local Govt. Administrative Asst., 1948–69. *Publs:* The Naturalist in Central Southern England, 1973; The Naturalist in Scotland, 1974; Discovering Walks in the New Forest, 1976; The Naturalist in the Hebrides, 1977; Walks in Hampshire, 1978; Looking at Nature: A Beginner's Guide, 1978; Looking at Mammals: A Beginner's Guide, 1979; (co-author) Tramp after God: The Story of Willie Mullan, 1979; (co-author) Found by God: The Story of Vijay Menon, 1982. Add: 17 Priestwood Close, Thornhill, Southampton, Hants., England.

KNOX, Bill. *See* **KNOX,** William.

KNOX, Calvin. *See* **SILVERBERG,** Robert.

KNOX, David Broughton. Australian, b. 1916. Theology/Religion. Principal, Whitefield Coll., Kalk Bay, South Africa, since 1989. Tutor, 1947–50, Vice-Principal, 1954–58, and Principal, 1959–85, Moore Theological Coll., Newtown, N.S.W., Australia. *Publs:* The Doctrine of Faith in the Reign of King Henry VIII, 1961; Thirty-Nine Articles, 1967; The Everlasting God, 1982; The Lord's Supper from Wycliffe to Cranmer, 1984. Add: George Whitefield Coll., Quarry Rd., Kalk Bay, Cape 7975, South Africa.

KNOX, Henry Macdonald. British, b. 1916. Education. Prof. of Education, Queen's Univ. of Belfast, 1951–82, now retired. Lectr. in Education, Univ. of Hull, 1946–49, and Univ. of St. Andrews, Scotland, 1949–51; Assessor in Education, Univ. of Strathclyde, Glasgow, 1984–89. *Publs:* Two Hundred and Fifty Years of Scottish Education 1696-1946, 1953; (ed.) John Dury: The Reformed School 1650, 1958; Introduction to Educational Method, 1961; Schools in Europe: Northern Ireland, 1969. Add: 9 Elliot Gardens, Colinton, Edinburgh EH14 1EH, Scotland.

KNOX, John. American, b. 1900. Theology/Religion, Autobiography/Memoirs/Personal. Prof. and Chaplain, Fisk Univ., Nashville, Tenn., 1929–36; Assoc. Prof., and Prof., Univ. of Chicago, 1939–43; Prof., Union Theological Seminary, NYC, 1943–66, and Episcopal Theological Seminary, Austin, Tex., 1966–71. *Publs:* He Whom a Dream Hath Possessed, 1932; Philemon Among the Letters of Paul, 1935; The Man Christ Jesus, 1942; Marcion and the New Testament, 1942; (co- author) The Vitality of the Christian Tradition, 1944; (co-author) The Christian Answer, 1945; (co-author) The Gospel, the Church, and the World, 1946; On the Meaning of Christ, 1947; Chapters in a Life of Paul, 1950; Criticism and Faith, 1952; The Early Church and the Coming Great Church, 1955; (co-author) The Ministry in Historical Perspectives, 1956; The Integrity of Preaching, 1957; The Death of Christ, 1958; Christ the Lord, 1958; Christ and the Hope of Glory, 1960; The Ethic of Jesus in the Teaching of the Church, 1961; Life in Christ Jesus, 1961; The Church and the Reality of Christ, 1962; Myth and Truth, 1964; (co-author) Lux in Lumine, 1966; (co-author) Studies in Luke-Acts, 1966; Humanity and Divinity of Christ, 1967; Limits of Unbelief, 1970; Never Far from Home (autobiography), 1975. Add: 602 Medford Leas, Medford, N.J. 08055, U.S.A.

KNOX, Robert Buick. British, b. 1918. History, Biography. Presbyterian Minister in Ireland, 1942–58; Prof. of Ecclesiastical History, Theological Coll., Aberystwyth, 1958–68; Prof. of Ecclesiastical History, Westminster Coll., Cambridge, 1968–85. *Publs:* James Ussher, Archbishop of Armagh, 1967; Voices from the Past: History of the English Conference of the Presbyterian Church of Wales, 1889-1938, 1969; Wales and Y Goleuad 1869-79, 1969; Reformation, Conformity, and Dissent,

1977; (with others) A History of Christian Doctrine, 1978; Westminster College, Cambridge, 1979. Add: 26 Killicomaine Dr., Portadown, Craigavon, N. Ireland.

KNOX, William. Writes as Michael Kirk, Bill Knox, Robert MacLeod, and Noah Webster. British, b. 1928. Mystery/Crime/Suspense, Adventure, Plays/Screenplays. Reporter to Deputy News Ed., Evening News, Glasgow, 1945–57; Scottish Ed., Empire News, London, 1957–59; News Ed., Scottish Television, 1959–61; Motoring Corresp., Evening Citizen, Glasgow, 1962– 67. *Publs:* Deadline for a Dream (in U.S. as In at the Kill), 1957; Cockatoo Crime, 1958; Death Department, 1959; Leave It to the Hangman, 1960; (with R. Colquhoun) Life Begins at Midnight, 1961; Death Calls the Shots, 1961; Die for Big Betsy, 1961; (with D. Murray) Ecurie Ecosse, 1961; Little Drops of Blood, 1962; Sanctuary Isle (in U.S. as The Grey Sentinels), 1962; The Man in the Bottle (in U.S. as The Killing Game), 1963; The Drum of Ungara (in U.S as Drum of Power), 1963; The Scavengers, 1964; (with J. Glaister) Final Diagnosis, 1964; (as Robert MacLeod) Cave of Bats, 1964; The Taste of Proof., 1965; Devilweed, 1966; The Deep Fall (in U.S. as Robert MacLeod, The Ghost Car), 1966; Kake of Fury (in U.S. as Robert MacLeod, The Iron Sanctuary), 1966; Isle of Gorgons, 1967; Justice on the Rocks, 1967; Court of Murder, 1968; The Klondyker (in U.S. as Figurehead), 1968; (as Robert MacLeod) Place of Mist, 1969; The Tallyman, 1969; Blueback, 1969; (as Robert MacLeod) A Property in Cyprus (in U.S. as Noah Webster, Flickering Death), 1970; Children of the Mist (in U.S as Who Shot the Bull?), 1970; Seafire, 1970; (as Robert MacLeod) Path of Ghosts, 1971; To Kill a Witch, 1971; (in U.K. as Robert MacLeod; in U.S. as Noah Webster) A Killing in Malta, 1972; Stormtide, 1972; (as Robert MacLeod) The Thin Blue Line, 1973; Nest of Vultures, 1973; Drawn Batons, 1973; (in U.K. as Robert MacLeod; in U.S. as Noah Webster) A Burial in Portugal, 1973; (with E. Boyd) The View from Daniel Pike, 1974; Whitewater, 1974; (in U.K. as Robert MacLeod; in U.S as Michael Kirk) All Other Perils, 1974; Rally to Kill, 1975; (in U.K. as Robert MacLeod; in U.S. as Noah Webster) A Witchdance in Bavaria, 1975; Hellspout, 1975; (in U.K. as Robert MacLeod; in U.S. as Michael Kirk) Dragonship, 1976; Pilot Error, 1977; (in U.K. as Robert MacLeod; in U.S. as Noah Webster) A Pay-Off in Switzerland, 1977; Witchrock, 1977; (in U.K. as Robert MacLeod; in U.S. as Michael Kirk) Salvage Job, 1978; (in U.K. as Robert MacLeod; in U.S. as Noah Webster) Incident in Iceland, 1979; Live Bait, 1979; Bombship, 1980; (as Robert MacLeod) Cargo Risk, 1980; A Killing in Antiques, 1981; Bloodtide, 1982; (as Robert MacLeod) A Problem in Prague, 1982; The Hanging Tree, 1983; (as Robert MacLeod) Monday from Malaga, 1983; (as Robert MacLeod) A Wreath from Tenerife, 1984; Wavecrest, 1985; (as Robert MacLeod in UK as Michael Kirk in US) A Cut In Diamonds, 1985; The Crossfire Killings, 1986; (as Robert Macleod in UK, as Noah Webster in US) The Money Mountain, 1987; Dead Man's Moorings, 1987; (as Robert Macleod in the U.K., Michael Kirk in the U.S.) Witchline, 1988; The Interface Man, 1989. Add: Thanemoss, 55 Newtonlea Ave., Newton Mearns, Glasgow G77 5QF, Scotland.

KNOX-JOHNSTON, Robin. (William Robert Patrick Knox- Johnston). British, b. 1939. Sports/Physical education/Keeping fit, Autobiography/Memoirs/Personal. *Publs:* A World of My Own, 1969; Robin Round the World 1970; Sailing, 1976; Last But Not Least, 1978; Twilight of Sail, 1978; Bunk Side Companion, 1982; Seamanship, 1986; The Boc Challenge, 1986; The Cape of Good Hope: A Maritime History, 1989. Add: 24 Sefton St., Putney, London SW15, England.

KNUDSEN, Margrethe June. British, 1934. Children's fiction, Children's non-fiction. Lectr. in English and Education, Catholic Coll. of Education, Sydney, since 1974. Founding Secty., English Speaking Bd., N.S.W.; Past Secty., Sch. Library Assn., N.S.W., member of faculty, William Balmain Coll., Sydney, 1966–73; *Publs:* (co-ed.) Quicksilver, 3 books, 1965; Goldseekers, 1969. Add: 9 Best Rd., Dual, N.S.W. 2158, Australia.

KNUDSON, Danny Alan. New Zealander, b. 1940. Education, History. Principal, Otago Education Bd., since 1978 (Deputy Principal, 1971–78). Ed., New Zealand Educational Inst., Yearbook of Education: The Creative Arts, 1973–74. *Publs:* The Story of Wakatipu, 1968; Goldfields Wonderland, 1974; (ed. with M.E. Fleming and R.H. Jarratt) The Creative Arts, 1975; Goldtown School, 1976; Standard V, 1892, 1982. Add: 79 Centennial Ave., Wakari, Dunedin, New Zealand.

KNUDSON, R(ozanne) R. American, b. 1932. Children's fiction, Education. *Publs:* (with Arnold Lazarus) Selected Objectives in the English Language Arts, 1967; (ed. with P.K. Ebert) Sports Poems, 1971; Zanballer (novel), 1972; Jesus Song (novel), 1973; You Are the Rain (novel), 1974; Fox Running (novel), 1974; Zanbanger (novel), 1977; Zanboomer (novel), 1978; (with F. Columbo) Weight Training for the Young Athlete, 1978; (with F. Columbo) Starbodies, 1978; Rinehart Lifts (novel), 1980; Just Another Love Story (novel), 1982; Speed (novel), 1982; Muscles!, 1982; Punch, 1982; Zan Hagen's Marathon (novel), 1984; Babe Didrikson (biography), 1985; Frankenstein's 10 K (novel), 1985; Martina Navratilova (biog.), 1986; Rinehart Shouts (novel), 1986; Julie Brown (biog.), 1987; (ed. with May Swenson) American Sports Poems, 1987. Add: 73 Boulevard, Sea Cliff, N.Y. 11579, U.S.A.

KNYE, Cassandra. See **DISCH,** Thomas M. and **SLADEK,** John.

KOCH, C(hristopher) J(ohn). Australian, b. 1932. Novels/Short stories. Radio producer, Australian Broadcasting Commn., Sydney, until 1972. *Publs:* The Boys in the Island, 1958, 1987; Across the Sea Wall, 1965, 1981; The Year of Living Dangerously, 1978; The Doubleman, 1985; (with N. Hasluck) Chinese Journey, 1985; Crossing the Gap (essays), 1987. Add: c/o Curtis Brown Ltd., P.O. Box 19, Paddington, N.S.W. 2021, Australia.

KOCH, Kenneth. American, b. 1925. Novels/Short stories, Plays/Screenplays, Poetry, Education, Literature. Prof. of English, Columbia Univ., NYC, since 1970 (joined faculty, 1959). Lectr. in English, Rutgers Univ., New Brunswick, N.J., 1953–54, 1955–56 and 1957–58, and Brooklyn Coll., N.Y., 1957–59; Dir. of Poetry Workshop, New Sch. for Social Research, NYC, 1958–66. *Publs:* Poems, 1953; Ko: or, A Season on Earth (poetry), 1960; Permanently (poetry), 1960; Thank You and Other Poems, 1962; Guinevere: or, The Death of the Kangaroo, 1964; Bertha and Other Plays, 1966; Poems from 1952 and 1953, 1968; When the Sun Tries to Go On (poetry), 1969; Sleeping with Women (poetry), 1969; The Pleasures of Peace and Other Poems, 1969; Wishes, Lies and Dreams: Teaching Children to Write Poetry, 1970; A Change of Hearts: Plays, Films, and Other Dramatic Works, 1951–71, 1973; Rose, Where Did You Get That Red? Teaching Great Poetry to Children, 1973; The Art of Love: Poems, 1975; The Red Robins (novel), 1975, as play 1979; I Never Told Anybody: Teaching Poetry and Writing in a Nursing Home, 1977; The Duplications, 1977; Les Couleurs des Voyelles, 1978; The Burning Mystery of Anna in 1951, 1979; Desideri, Sogni, Bugie, 1980; (ed. with Kate Farrell) Sleeping on the Wing: An Anthology of Modern Poetry, 1981; Days and Nights (poetry), 1982; Selected Poems 1950–1982, 1985; On the Edge (poetry), 1986; One Thousand Avant-Garde Plays, 1988. Add: Dept. of English, Columbia Univ., New York, N.Y. 10027, U.S.A.

KOCHAN, Miriam (Louise). British, b. 1929. History, Translations. Sub-Ed., Reuters Economic Services, London, 1951–54. Gen. Ed., Berg Women's Series. *Publs:* (trans.) Greece, by Jeanne and Georges Roux, 1958; (trans.) Gothic Cathedrals of France, by Marcel Aubert, 1959; (trans.) Maya Cities, by Paul Rivet, 1960; (trans.) The World of Archaeology, by Marcel Brion, 1961; (trans.) Carthage, by Gilbert Picard, 1964; (trans.) The Greek Adventure, by Pierre Leveque, 1968; Life in Russia Under Catherine the Great, 1969; (trans.) Meiji 1868, by Paul Akamatsu, 1972; (trans.) Capitalism and Material Life, by Fernand Braudel, 1973; (trans.) History of Anti-Semitism vol. III, by Leon Poliakov, 1975; Catherine the Great, 1976; The Last Days of Imperial Russia, 1976; (trans.) The Jewish Bankers and The Holy See, by Leon Poliakov, 1977; Prisoners of England, 1980; Britain's Internees in the Second World War, 1983. Add: 237 Woodstock Rd., Oxford, England.

KOEHLER, G. Stanley. American, b. 1915. Poetry. Prof. of English, Univ. of Massachusetts, Amherst, since 1950. Instr., Oklahoma State Coll., Stillwater, 1938–40, Univ. of Kansas, Lawrence, 1946, and Yale Univ., New Haven, Conn., 1946–50. *Publs:* (with L. Barron, D. Clark and R. Tucker) A Curious Quire, 1962; The Fact of Fall, 1969; Contours of Greece, 1984. Add: Dept. of English, Bartlett Hall, Univ. of Massachusetts, Amherst, Mass. 01002, U.S.A.

KOENIGSBERGER, Helmut Georg. British, b. 1918. History. Lectr. in Economic History, Queen's Univ., Belfast, 1948–51; Sr. Lectr., Univ. of Manchester, 1951–60; Prof. of Modern History, Univ. of Nottingham, 1960–66; Prof. of European History, Cornell Univ., Ithaca, N.Y., 1966–73; Prof. of History, Kings Coll., London, 1973–84. *Publs:* The Government of Sicily Under Philip II of Spain, 1951, 1969; (with G.L. Mosse) Europe in the Sixteenth Century, 1968, 1989; Estates and Revolutions, 1971; The Habsburgs and Europe 1516-1660, 1971; (ed.) Luther: A Profile, 1972; Politicians and Virtuosi, 1986; Medieval Europe 400-1500, 1987; Early Modern Europe 1500-1789, 1987; (ed.) Republiken und Republikanismus im Europa der frühen Neuzeit, 1988. Add: 41A, Lancaster Grove, London NW3 4HB, England.

KOERNER, James D. American, b. 1923. Education, Writing/Journalism, Autobiography/Memoirs/Personal. Vice-Pres. Alfred P. Sloan Foundn., NYC, since 1970. *Publs:* (ed.) The Case for Basic Education, 1959; (ed. with D. Colville) The Craft of Writing, 1961; The Miseducation of American Teachers, 1963; Reform in Education: England and the United States, 1968; Who Controls American Education?, 1968; The Parsons College Bubble, 1970; Hoffer's America, 1973. Add: c/o Alfred P. Sloan Foundn., 630 Fifth Ave., New York, N.Y. 10020, U.S.A.

KOFF, Richard M. American, b. 1926. Novels/Short stories, Sciences. Management consultant, since 1977. Design Engineer, American Hydromath Corp., 1949–55; Managing Ed., McGraw-Hill Publishing Co., NYC, 1955–66; Vice-Pres., Asst. Publr. and Business Mgr., Playboy Enterprises, Chicago, 1966–77. *Publs:* (with J.J. Pippinger) Fluid Power Controls, 1958; How Does It Work?, 1961; Home Computers, 1979; The Home Electronics Catalog, 1979; Strategic Planning for Magazine Executives, 1981; Christopher (novel), 1981; Using Small Computers to Make Your Business Strategy Work, 1984; Increasing Your Wealth in Good Times and Bad, 1985; Business Simulation: IBM-PC Version, 1985. Add: 1031 Sheridan Rd., Evanston, Ill. 60202, U.S.A.

KOGAN, Norman. American, b. 1919. History, International relations/Current affairs. Prof. of Political Science, Univ. of Connecticut, Storrs, since 1963, Emeritus since 1988 (Instr., 1949–52; Asst. Prof., 1952–68; Assoc. Prof., 1958–63; Dir., Center for Italian Studies, 1967–75); Faculty Assoc., Columbia Univ., NYC, since 1966. Exec. Secty.-Treas., Soc. for Italian Historical Studies, 1967–76; Pres., Conference Group on Italian Politics, 1975–77. *Publs:* Italy and the Allies, 1956; The Government of Italy, 1962; The Politics of Italian Foreign Policy, 1963; A Political History of Italy: The Postwar Years, 1983. Add: 7 Eastwood Rd., Storrs, Conn. 06268, U.S.A.

KOGAWA, Joy Nozomi. Canadian, b. 1935. Novels/Short stories, Poetry. Writer-in-Residence, Univ. of Ottawa, 1978. *Publs:* The Splintered Moon, 1967; A Choice of Dreams, 1974; Jericho Road, 1977; Obasan (novel), 1981; Woman in the Woods, 1985; Naomi's Road, 1986. Add: 447 Montrose Ave., Toronto, Ont. M6G 3H2, Canada.

KOHLER, Foy David. American, b. 1908. International relations/Current affairs, Politics/Government. With Foreign Service of U.S.A., 1931–67 (Asst. Secty. of State for European Affairs, 1959; Ambassador to Soviet Union, 1962–66; Deputy Under Secty. of State for Political Affairs, 1966–67); Prof. of Intnl. Studies, Center for Advanced Intnl. Studies, Univ. of Miami, 1968–78; Co-Ed., Monthly Soviet World Outlook, 1976–85; Sr. Assoc., Advanced Intnl. Studies Inst., Washington, D.C., 1978–85. *Publs:* Understanding the Russians: A Citizen's Primer, 1970; (with M.L. Harvey and L. Goure) Soviet Strategy for the Seventies, 1973; (with L. Goure and R. Soll) Convergence of Communism and Capitalism, 1973; (with M.L. Harvey and L. Goure) The Role of Nuclear Forces in Current Soviet Strategy, 1974; (with L. Goure and M.L. Harvey) The Soviet Union and the October 1973 Middle East War, 1974; (with M.L. Harvey) The Soviet Union: Yesterday, Today, Tomorrow, 1975; Salt II: How Not to Negotiate with the Russians, 1979. Add: Waterford Tower Apt. #1102, 605 S.U.S. Hway 1, Juno Beach, Fla. 33408, U.S.A.

KOHLER, (Sister) Mary Hortense. American, b. 1892. History. Prof. of Social Sciences, Dominican Coll., Racine, Wisc., 1937–66; now retired. *Publs:* Life and Work of Mother Benedicta Bauer, 1937; Rooted in Hope, 1962; The Equitable Calendar in a Setting of the History of Calendar Reform, 1987. Add: 5635 Erie St., Siena Center, Racine, Wisc. 53402, U.S.A.

KOLATKAR, Arun (Balkrishna). Indian, b. 1932. Poetry. Works as a graphic artist in an advertising agency in Bombay. *Publs:* Jejuri, 1977. Add: c/o Clearing House, Palm Springs, Cusse Parade, Bombay 400 005, India.

KOLINSKY, Martin. British, b. 1936. International relations, Politics. Sr. Lectr. Univ. of Birmingham. Lectr., Hebrew Univ. of Jerusalem, 1970–72. *Publs:* Continuity and Change in European Society, 1974; (ed. with William E. Paterson) Social and Political Movements in Western Europe, 1976; (ed.) Divided Loyalties, 1978; (with Michalina Vaughan and Peta Sheriff) Social Change in France, 1980. Add: 76 Buryfield Rd., Solihull, W. Midlands B91 2DQ, England.

KOLLER, James. American, b. 1936. Novels/Short stories, Poetry. Ed., Coyote Journal and Coyote Books, San Francisco, then New Mexico and Maine, since 1964. *Publs:* Two Hands: Poems 1959–1961, 1965; Brainard and Washington Street Poems, 1965; Some Cows: Poems of Civilization and Domestic Life, 1966; The Dogs and Other Dark Woods, 1966; I Went to See My True Love, 1967; California Poems, 1971; Messages, 1972; Dark Woman, Who Lay with the Sun, 1972; Shannon, Who Was Lost Before (novel), 1975; Bureau Creek, 1975; If You Don't Like Me You Can Leave Me Alone (novel), 1976; Poems for the Blue Sky, 1976; Messages/Botschaften, 1977; (ed. and contrib.) Andiamo: Selected Poems by James Koller, Franco Beltrametti and Harry Hoogstraten, 1978; Didn't He Ramble/O Wäre Er Nicht Umhergezogen, 1981; Back River, 1981; One Day at a Time, 1981; Great Things are Happening, 1984; Give the Dog a Bone, 1986; Working Notes, 1986; Openings, 1987; Fortune, 1987; (with Franco Beltrametti) Graffiti Lyriques, 1987. Add: P.O. Box 629, Brunswick, Me. 04011, U.S.A.

KOLLER, Marvin Robert. American, b. 1919. Sociology. Prof. of Sociology, Kent State Univ., Ohio, since 1949 (Sr. Guest Student Prog. Coordinator, 1974–80). *Publs:* (with O.W. Ritchie) Sociology of Childhood, 1964, 1978; Modern Sociology, 1965, 1969, (with D.C. King), 1974; Social Gerontology, 1968; Families: A Multi-Generational Approach, 1974; (with D.C. King) Foundations of Sociology, 1975; Humor and Society: Explorations in the Sociology of Humor, 1988. Add: Sociology and Anthropology Dept., Kent State Univ., Kent, Ohio 44242, U.S.A.

KOLSEN, Helmut Max. Australian, b. 1926. Economics. Prof. of Economics, Univ. of Queensland, since 1968 (Acting Head of Dept., 1969–70; Head of Dept., 1971–73; Dean, Faculty of Commerce and Economics, 1977–82). Lectr., in Economics, Univ. of New South Wales (formerly New South Wales Univ. of Technology), 1956–58; Lectr., 1958–63, Sr. Lectr., 1963–65, and Assoc. Prof., 1965–68, Univ. of Sydney; Economic Adviser, Dept. of Decentralisation and Development, N.S.W., 1966–68. Member, Transport Industries Advisory Council, 1977–83, and Interstate Commn., 1984–86. *Publs:* The Economics and Control of Road-Rail Competition, 1968; The Price Mechanism: Demand, Supply and Market Structures, 1970. Add: Dept. of Economics, Univ. of Queensland, St. Lucia, Brisbane, Qld., Australia 4067.

KONDOLEON, Harry. American, b. 1955. Novels, Plays, Poetry. Taught playwriting, New Sch. for Social Research, NYC, 1983–84. *Publs:* plays—Slacks and Tops, 1983; Christmas on Mars, 1983; The Vampires, 1984; Self Torture and Strenuous Exercise (in The Best Short Plays 1984), 1984; Linda Her, and The Fairy Garden, 1985; The Cote d'Azur Triangle, 1985; Anteroom, 1985; The Brides (in Wordplays 2), 1986; Andrea Rescued, 1987; poetry—The Death of Understanding, 1986; novel—The Whore of Tjampuan, 1987. Add: c/o George Lane, William Morris Agency, 1350 Ave. of the Americas, New York, N.Y. 10019, U.S.A.

KONIGSBURG, E(laine) L. American, b. 1930. Children's fiction. *Publs:* Jennifer, Hecate, Macbeth and Me, 1967; From the Mixed-Up Files of Mrs. Basil E. Frankweiler, 1968; About the B'nai Bagels, 1969; George, 1970; Altogether, One at a Time, 1971; A Proud Taste for Scarlet and Miniver, 1973; The Dragon in the Ghetto Caper, 1974; The Second Mrs. Giaconda, 1975; Father's Arcane Daughter, 1976; Throwing Shadows, 1979; Journey to an 800 Number, 1982, in U.K. as Journey by First Class Camel, 1983; Up from Jericho Tel, 1986. Add: c/o Atheneum Publrs., 866 3rd Ave., New York, N.Y. 10022, U.S.A.

KONING, Hans. Wrote as Hans Koningsberger prior to 1972. American (born Dutch), b. 1924. Novels/Short stories, Plays/Screenplays, Politics/Government. *Publs:* Aquarel of Holland, 1950; The Golden Keys, 1956; The Blood-Red Café, 1958; The Affair, 1958; An American Romance, 1960; Walk with Love and Death, 1961, film, 1968; The Wind in the Pines (film), 1961; Hermione, 1962; I Know What I'm Doing, 1964; Love and Hate in China, 1966; The Revolutionary, 1967, screenplay, 1970; (as Hans Koning) The World of Vermeer, 1967; Along the Roads of the New Russia, 1968; The Future of Che Guevara, 1971; The Almost World, 1972; Death of Schoolboy, 1974; The Petersburg-Cannes Express, 1975; Columbus: His Enterprise, 1975; A New Yorker in Egypt, 1976; Amsterdam, 1977; America Made Me, 1979; The Kleber Flight, 1981; DeWitt's War, 1983; Nineteen Sixty Eight, 1987; Acts of Faith, 1988; The Iron Age, 1990. Add: c/o Lantz Office, 888 Seventh Ave., New York, N.Y. 10106, U.S.A.

KONINGSBERGER, Hans. *See* **KONING,** Hans.

KONKLE, Janet Everest. American, b. 1917. Children's fiction. Columnist, Ocala Star-Banner, Florida; Corresp., Riverland News, Dunnellon, Fla. Teacher, Grand Rapids Bd. of Education, 1952–79, now retired. Pres., Michigan Assn. for Childhood Education, 1969–71; Pres., Delta Kappa Gamma, intnl. honor soc., 1968–70. *Publs:* Once There

Was a Kitten, 1951; The Kiten and the Parakeet, 1952; Christmas Kitten, 1953; Easter Kitten, 1955; Tabby's Kittens, 1956; J. Hamilton Hamster, 1957; Susie Stock Car, 1961; The Sea Cart, 1961; Schoolroom Bunny, 1965; The Raccoon Twins, 1972. Add: 7193 N. Cricket Dr., Citrus Springs, Florida 32630, U.S.A.

KONVITZ, Jeffrey. American. b. 1944. Novels/Short stories, Plays/Screenplays. Screenwriter and film producer since 1973; Entertainment Attorney, Finley Kumble Wagner, Beverly Hills, Calif., since 1983. Admitted to the Bar of New York, 1969; Attorney and Agent, Creative Mgmt. Assocs., NYC, 1969–70; in private law practice, NYC, 1970–72; Gen. Counsel, Jerry Lewis Theater Chain, 1971–72; Film Exec., Metro-Goldwyn-Mayer, Culver City, Calif., 1972–73. *Publs:* (co-author) Silent Night, Bloody Night (screenplay), 1971; The Sentinel (novel), 1974, screenplay, 1975; The Guardian, 1979; Gorp (screenplay), 1979; Monster: A Tale of Loch Ness, 1982. Add: 12660 Mulholland Dr., Beverly Hills, Calif. 90211, U.S.A.

KONVITZ, Milton R. American, b. 1908. Civil liberties/Human rights, Law, Philosophy. Prof. Emeritus of Industrial and Labor Relations, and Prof. of Law, Cornell Univ., Ithaca, N.Y., since 1973 (Prof., 1946–73). Gen. Counsel, Newark Housing Authority, N.J., 1938–43, and New Jersey State Housing Authority, 1943–46; Lectr., New York Univ., NYC, 1938–46. *Publs:* On the Nature of Value, 1946; The Alien and the Asiatic in American Law, 1946; The Constitution and Civil Rights, 1947; Civil Rights in Immigration, 1953; (ed.) Bill of Rights Reader, 1954; Fundamental Liberties of a Free People: Religion, Speech, Press, Assembly, 1957; (ed.) Liberian Code of Law, 5 vols., 1957–60; (ed.) Liberian Law Reports, 27 vols., 1957–80; (with T. Leskes) A Century of Civil Rights, 1961; (ed.) First Amendment Freedoms, 1963; Expanding Liberties, 1966; Religious Liberty and Conscience, 1968; (ed.) Judaism and Human Rights, 1972; (ed. with S. Hook) Freedom and Experience; (ed. with A.E. Murphy) Essays in Political Theory; (ed.) Law and Social Action: Essays of Alexander H. Pekelis; (ed.) Education for Freedom and Responsibility, by Edmund Ezra Day; (ed. with C. Rossiter) Aspects of Liberty; (ed. with G. Kennedy) American Pragmatists; (ed. with S.E. Whicher) Emerson; A Collection of Critical Essays; (ed.) The Recognition of Ralph Waldo Emerson; Judaism and the American Idea, 1978; (ed.) Legacy of Horace M. Kalen, 1987. Add: 16 The Byway, Forest Home, Ithaca, N.Y. 14850, U.S.A.

KOONTZ, Dean R(ay). Has also written as David Axton, Brian Coffey, Deanna Dwyer, K.R. Dwyer, John Hill, Leigh Nichols, and Owen West. American, b. 1945. Novels/Short stories, Science fiction/Fantasy, Social commentary/phenomena, Writing/Journalism. English teacher, then freelance writer, since 1969. *Publs:* Star Quest, 1968; The Fall of the Dream Machine, 1969; The Dark Symphony, 1970; Hell's Gate, 1970; Dark of the Woods, 1970; Beastchild, 1970; Anti-Man, 1970; Soft Come the Dragons (SF short stories), 1970; (with Gerda Koontz) The Pig Society (non-fiction), 1970; (with Gerda Koontz) The Underground Lifestyles Handbook (non-fiction), 1970; (as Deanna Dwyer) Demon Child, 1971; (as Deanna Dwyer) Legacy of Terror, 1971; The Crimson Witch, 1971; The Flesh in the Furnace, 1972; A Darkness in My Soul, 1972; Time Thieves, 1972; Warlock, 1972; Starblood, 1972; (as K.R. Dwyer) Chase (novel), 1972; (as Deanna Dwyer) Children of the Storm, 1972; (as Deanna Dwyer) The Dark Summer, 1972; (as Deanna Dwyer) Dance with the Devil, 1973; Demon Seed, 1973; A Werewolf among Us, 1973; Hanging On, 1973; The Haunted Earth, 1973; (as Brian Coffey) Blood Risk (novel), 1973; (as K.R. Dwyer) Shattered (novel), 1973; Writing Popular Fiction (non-fiction), 1973; After the Last Race, 1975; (as Brian Coffey) Surrounded (novel), 1974; (as Brian Coffey) The Wall of Masks (novel), 1975; (as John Hill) The Long Sleep, 1975; Nightmare Journey, 1975; (as K.R. Dwyer) Dragonfly (novel), 1975; (as David Axton) Prison of Ice (novel), 1976; Night Chills, 1976; The Vision, 1977; (as Brian Coffey) The Face of Fear, 1977; (as Leigh Nichols) Key to Midnight, 1979; (as Brian Coffey) The Voice of the Night, 1980; Whispers, 1980; (as Owen West) The Funhouse (novelization of screenplay), 1980; (as Leigh Nichols) The Eyes of Darkness, 1981; (as Owen West) The Mask, 1981; (as Leigh Nichols) House of Thunder, 1982; Phantoms, 1983; Darkness Comes (in U.S. as Darkfall), 1984; (as Leigh Nichols) Twilight, 1984; Strangers, 1986; (as Leigh Nichols) Shadow Fires, 1987; Watchers, 1987; Twilight Eyes, 1987; Oddkins, 1988; Servants of Twilight, 1988; Midnight, 1989. Add: c/o G.P. Putnam's Sons, 200 Madison Ave., New York, N.Y. 10016, U.S.A.

KOOSER, Ted (Theodore Kooser). American, b. 1939. Poetry. Sr. Underwriter, 1973–80, and since 1980 Second Vice-Pres., Lincoln Benefit Life. Publisher, Windflower Press., Lincoln, since 1967; Part-Time Instr. in Creative Writing, Univ. of Nebraska, Lincoln, since 1970. High Sch.

teacher, Madrid, Iowa, 1962–63; Correspondent, 1964–65, and Underwriter, 1965–73, Bankers Life Nebraska, Lincoln. *Publs:* Official Entry Blank, 1969; Grass County, 1971; Twenty Poems, 1973; A Local Habitation, and A Name, 1974; Shooting a Farmhouse; So This Is Nebraska, 1973; Not Coming to Be Barked At, 1976; Hatcher, 1978; Old Marriage and New, 1978; (with William Kloefkorn) Cottonwood County, 1979; Sure Signs: New and Selected Poems, 1980; (ed.) The Windflower Home Almanac of Poetry, 1980; The Blizzard Voices, 1985; One World at a Time, 1985. Add: Route 1, Box 10, Garland, Nebraska 68360, U.S.A.

KOPAL, Zdenek. American, b. 1914. Astronomy, Memoirs. Prof. Emeritus of Astronomy, Univ. of Manchester. Member, Lunar-Planetary Cttee., U.S. National Space Bd.; Vice Chmn., Cttee. for Lunar and Planetary Exploration, British National Cttee. for Space Research (Chmn., 1961–64); Pres., Cttee. on Lunar Nomenclature, Intnl. Astronomical Union (Pres., Commn. on Close Binary Systems, 1948–55); Ed.-in-Chief, Astrophysics and Space Science; Managing Ed., The Moon; Assoc. Ed., Astrophysical Letters and Memorie della Societa Astronomica Italiana. Research Assoc. in Astronomy, Harvard Univ., Cambridge, Mass., 1940–46; Assoc. Prof., Massachusetts Inst. of Technology, Cambridge, 1947–51. *Publs:* An Introduction to the Study of Eclipsing Variables, 1946; Tables of Supersonic Flow of Air Around Cones, 3 vols., 1947–49; The Computation of Elements of Eclipsing Binary Systems, 1950; Numerical Analysis, 1955; Astronomical Optics, 1956; Close Binary Systems, 1959; Figures of Equilibrium of Celestial Bodies, 1960; The Moon, 1960, 1969; Physics and Astronomy of the Moon, 1962, 1972; Photographic Atlas of the Moon, 1965; An Introduction to the Study of the Moon, 1966; Telescopes in Space, 1966; The Measure of the Moon, 1967; Exploration of the Moon by Spacecraft, 1968; The Moon, 1969; Widening Horizons, 1970; Man and His Universe, 1971; New Photographic Atlas of the Moon, 1971; The Solar System, 1972; Mapping of the Moon, 1974; The Moon in the Post-Apollo Era, 1974; Dynamics of Close Binary Systems, 1978; Language of the Stars, 1979; (with E.B. Carling) Photometric and Spectroscopic Binary Systems, 1981; (with J. Rahe) Binary and Multiple Stars as Tracers of Stellar Evolution, 1982; (with B. Hidayat and J. Rahe) Double Stars: Physical Properties and Generic Relations, 1984; (with J. Rahe) Astrometric Binaries, 1985; Of Stars and Men (reminiscences), 1986; (with J. Dommanget and E.L. van Dessel) Wide Components in Double and Multiple Systems, 1988; (with others) Plasma and the Universe, 1988; The Roche Problem, 1989. Add: Greenfield, Parkway, Wilmslow, Cheshire, England.

KOPIT, Arthur (Lee). American, b. 1937. Plays/Screenplays. *Publs:* Oh Dad, Poor Dad, Mama's Hung You in the Closet and I'm Feelin' So Sad: A Pseudoclassical Tragifarce in a Bastard French Tradition, 1960; The Day the Whores Came Out to Play Tennis and Other Plays (in U.K. as Chamber Music and Other Plays), 1965; Indians, 1968; An Incident in the Park, 1968; Wings, 1978; Secrets of the Rich, 1978; Good Help Is Hard to Find, 1982; Nine, 1983; Ghosts (adaptation), 1984; End of the World (with a Symposium to Follow), 1984. Add: c/o Luis Sanjurjo, Intnl. Creative Mgmt., 40 W. 57th St., New York, N.Y. 10019, U.S.A.

KOPLIN, H.T. American, b. 1923. Business/Trade/Industry, Sociology. Prof. of Economics, Univ. of Oregon, Eugene, since 1965 (Instr., 1950–53; Asst. Prof., 1953–58; Assoc. Prof., 1959–65; Dir. of Honors Coll. and Asst. Dean of Coll. of Liberal Arts, 1959–61). *Publs:* Microeconomic Analysis: Welfare and Efficiency in Private and Public Sectors, 1971. Add: Dept. of Economics, Univ. of Oregon, Eugene, Ore. 97403, U.S.A.

KOPP, Richard L. American, b. 1934. Literature. Prof. of Modern Languages and Literatures, since 1978; Dir., Univ. Honors Program, since 1983 and Chmn. of the Dept. of Modern Languages and Literatures since 1988, Fairleigh Dickinson Univ., Madison, N.J. (Asst. Prof., 1969–73; Assoc. Prof., 1973–78). Former Exec. Dir., Opera at Florham. *Publs:* Marcel Proust as a Social Critic, 1971; (co-author) Readings in French Literature, 1974; (co-author) The Moralist Tradition in France, 1982. Add: Dept. of Modern Languages and Literatures, Fairleigh Dickinson Univ., Madison, N.J. 07940, U.S.A.

KOPS, Bernard. British, b. 1926. Novels/Short stories, Plays/Screenplays, Poetry, Autobiography/Memoirs/Personal. Freelance writer. *Publs:* Poems, 1955; The Hamlet of Stepney Green, 1957; Awake for Mourning, 1958; Poems and Songs, 1958; An Anemone for Antigone, 1959; The Dream of Peter Mann, 1960; Motorbike, 1962; The World Is a Wedding, 1963; Four Plays, 1964; The Boy Who Wouldn't Play Jesus, 1965; Yes from No Man's Land, 1965; Stray Cats and Empty Bottles, 1967; Erica, I Want to Read You Something, 1967; David It Is Getting Dark, 1969; By the Waters of Whitechapel, 1969; The Passionate Past of Gloria Gaye, 1971; For the Record, 1971; Settle Down Simon Katz, 1973; Partners, 1975; On Margate Sands, 1978; (ed.) Poetry Hounslow, 1981; Neither Your Honey nor Your Sting: An Offbeat History of the Jews, 1985; Barricades in West Hampstead (poetry), 1988. Add: Flat 1, 35 Canfield Gardens, London NW6, England.

KORDA, Michael (Vincent). American, b. 1933. Social commentary/phenomena, Biography. Ed.-in-Chief, Simon and Schuster, publishers, NYC (joined co., 1958). *Publs:* Male Chauvinism: How It Works, 1973; Power: How to Get It, How to Use It, 1975; Charmed Lives (biography of the Korda brothers), 1979; Worldly Goods, 1982; Queenie, 1985; The Fortune, 1989. Add: Simon and Schuster, 1230 Sixth Ave., New York, N.Y. 10022, U.S.A.

KOREN, Henry Joseph. American, b. 1912. Philosophy, Theology/Religion. Instr. and Prof. of Philosophy, 1949–65, Chmn., Dept. of Philosophy, 1954–65, and Chmn., Dept. of Theology, 1960–66, Duquesne Univ., Pittsburgh, Pa.; Prof. of Philosophy, St. Leo Coll., Florida, 1967–77. Philosophical and Theological Ed., Duquesne Univ. Press, 1951–74. *Publs:* De inspiratione Scripturae, 1942; Introduction to Science of Metaphysics, 1955; Introduction to Philosophy of Animate Nature, 1955; (ed.) Readings in the Philosophy of Nature, 1958; The Spiritans, 1958; The Spiritual Writings of Poullart des Places, 1959; Introduction to Philosophy of Nature, 1960; Knaves or Knights?, 1962; Research in Philosophy, 1966; Marx and the Authentic Man, 1968; (with W. Luijpen) A First Introduction to Existential Phenomenology, 1969; (with W. Luijpen) Religion and Atheism, 1971; Chenapans ou Chevaliers?, 1979; To the Ends of the Earth, 1982; A Spiritan Who Was Who in North America and Trinidad 1732-1981, 1983; The Serpent and the Dove, 1985. Add: 6230 Brush Run Rd., Bethel Park, Pa. 15102, U.S.A.

KORFKER, Dena. American, b. 1908. Children's fiction, Children's non-fiction, Biography. Kindergarten teacher, Oakdale Christian Sch., Grand Rapids, Mich., 1927–73. *Publs:* Can You Tell Me?, 1950; Questions Children Ask, 1951; My Bible ABC Book, 1952; Ankie Comes to America, 1954 The Story of Jesus for Boys and Girls, 1954; My Picture-Story Bible, 1960, as My Bible Story Book, 1988; My Favorite Picture-Stories from the Bible, 1961; Mother of Eighty (biography), 1970; Good-Morning, Lord, 1973. Add: 1720 Plymouth Rd. S.E., Grand Rapids, Mich. 49506, U.S.A.

KORG, Jacob. American, b. 1922. Literature, Biography. Prof. of English, Univ. of Washington, Seattle, since 1965 (Asst. and Assoc. Prof., 1955–65). Former staff member, English Dept., Bard Coll., Annandale-on-Hudson, N.Y., Univ. of Maryland, College Park, and City Coll. of New York. *Publs:* (ed. with S.F. Anderson) Westward to Oregon, 1958; (ed. with R.S. Beal) Thought in Prose, 1958, 3rd ed. 1966; An Introduction to Poetry, 1959; (ed.) London in Dickens' Day, 1960; (ed. with R.S. Beal) The Complete Reader, 1961; (ed.) George Gissing's Commonplace Book, 1962; George Gissing: A Critical Biography, 1963; Dylan Thomas, 1965; (author and ed.) The Force of Few Words, 1966; (ed.) Twentieth Century Interpretations of Bleak House, 1968; (ed.) The Poetry of Robert Browning, 1971; (ed.) Thyrza, by George Gissing, 1974; (ed.) The Unclassed, by George Gissing, 1976; (ed. with C. Korg) George Gissing on Fiction, 1978; Language in Modern Literature, 1979; Browning and Italy, 1983. Add: Dept. of English, Univ. of Washington, Seattle, Wash. 98195, U.S.A.

KORMONDY, Edward J(ohn). American, b. 1926. Biology, Environmental science/Ecology. Chancellor, and Prof. of Biology, Univ. of Hawaii, Hilo, and West Oahu Coll., since 1986. Asst. Prof., Assoc. Prof. and Prof. of Biology, Oberlin Coll., Ohio, 1957–68; Dir., Commn. on Undergrad. Education in the Biological Sciences, American Inst. of Biological Sciences, Washington, D.C., 1968–71; Member of the faculty, 1971–79, and Vice-Pres. and Provost, 1973–78, Evergreen State Coll., Olympia, Wash.; Sr. Professorial Assoc., National Science Foundation, 1979; Provost and Prof. of Biology, Univ. of Southern Maine, Portland, 1979–82; Vice-Pres., Academic Affairs, and Prof. of Biology, California State Univ., Los Angeles, 1982–86. *Publs:* Introduction to Genetics, 1964; (ed.) Readings in Ecology, 1965; (ed.) General Biology, 2 vols., 1966; Concepts of Ecology, 1969, 3rd ed. 1984; (ed. with Robert Leisner) Population, 1971; (ed. with R. Leisner) Pollution, 1971; (ed. with R. Leisner) Ecology, 1971; (with T. Sherman) Biology: The Natural History and Integrity of Organisms, 1978; (with F. McCormick) Handbook of Contemporary Developments in World Ecology, 1981; (with B. Nebel) Environmental Science: The Way the World Works, 1981, 1987; (with B. Essenfeld) Biology, 1984, 1988; International Handbook of Pollution Control, 1989. Add: 1053 Olioli Way, Hilo, Hawaii 96720, U.S.A.

KÖRNER, Stephan. British, b. 1913. Philosophy. Prof. of Philosophy, Univ. of Bristol, 1952–79; Ed., Ratio, 1961–79; Prof. of Philosophy, Yale Univ., New Haven, Conn., 1970–83. *Publs:* Kant, 1955; Conceptual Thinking, 1955; Philosophy of Mathematics, 1960; Experience and Theory, 1966; What is Philosophy?, 1969, in paperback as Fundamental Questions in Philosophy, 1971; Categorial Frameworks, 1970; Abstraction in Science and Morals, 1971; (ed.) Observation and Interpretation, 1957; (ed.) Practical Reason, 1973; (ed.) Explanation, 1974; Experience and Conduct, 1976; Metaphysics: Its Structure and Function, 1983. Add: 10 Belgrave Rd., Bristol BS8 2AB, England.

KORNHAUSER, William. American, b. 1925. Politics, Sociology. Prof. of Sociology, Univ. of California, Berkeley, since 1953. Member, Bd. of Eds., Democracy: A Journal of Political Renewal, 1980–83. Member of faculty, Columbia Univ., NYC, 1952–53; Fellow, Center for Advanced Study, Stanford, Calif., 1954–55; Research Assoc., Princeton Univ., N.J., 1961–62; Fellow, Stevenson Inst., Chicago, 1968–69; Principal Investigator, Inst. on Global Conflict and Cooperation, Univ., of California, 1984–86. *Publs:* The Politics of Mass Society, 1959; Scientists in Industry, 1962. Add: Dept. of Sociology, Univ. of California, Berkeley, Calif. 94720, U.S.A.

KORT, Wesley A. American, b. 1935. Literature, Theology/Religion. Prof., Dept. of Religion, and member of Grad. Faculty of Religion, Duke Univ., Durham, N.C., since 1976 (Asst. Prof., 1965–70; Assoc. Prof., 1970–76; Asst. Dean of Grad. Sch., 1970–71; Asst. Provost, 1973–74). Asst. to Perrin Lowry, Humanities Div., 1961–62, and Preston T. Roberts, Divinity Sch., 1962–63, Univ. of Chicago; Instr., Dept. of Religion, Princeton Univ., N.J., 1963–65. *Publs:* Shriven Selves: Religious Problems in Recent American Fiction, 1972; Narrative Elements and Religious Meaning, 1975; Moral Fiber: Character and Belief in Recent American Fiction, 1982; Modern Fiction and Human Time: A Study in Narrative and Belief, 1985; Story, Text, and Scripture: Literary Interests in Biblical Narratives, 1988. Add: 3514 Winding Way, Durham, N.C. 27707, U.S.A.

KOSINSKI, Jerzy. Also writes as Joseph Novak. American, b. 1933. Novels/Short stories, Literature, Social commentary/phenomena. Fellow, Timothy Dwight Coll., Yale Univ., New Haven, Conn., since 1986. Pres., Polish-American Resources Corp., since 1988. Prof. of English, Wesleyan Univ., Middletown, Conn., 1968–69; Lectr. in English, Princeton Univ., N.J., 1969–70; Prof. of English, Yale Univ., New Haven, Conn., 1970–73. Pres., P.E.N. American Center, 1973–75. *Publs:* (as Joseph Novak) The Future is Ours, Comrade, 1960; (as Joseph Novak) No Third Path: Studies in Collective Behavior, 1962; The Painted Bird, 1965; Notes of the Author, 1965; The Art of the Self, 1968; Steps, 1968; Being There, 1971; The Devil Tree, 1973, 1981; Cockpit, 1975; Blind Date, 1977; Passion Play, 1979; Pinball, 1982; The Hermit of 69th Street: Working Papers of Norbert Kosky, 1987. Add: c/o Scientia Factum Inc., Hemisphere House, 60 West 57th St., Dept. 18-K, New York, N.Y. 10019, U.S.A.

KOSKOFF, David E. American, b. 1939. History, Biography. Lawyer since 1965. *Publs:* Joseph P. Kennedy: A Life and Times, 1974; The Mellons: The Chronicle of America's Richest Family, 1978; The Diamond World, 1981. Add: 73 East Main St., Plainville, Conn. 06062, U.S.A.

KOSSOFF, David. British, b. 1919. Theology/Religion. Actor since 1945. Bible storyteller, BBC Radio and TV, since 1964. Former commercial artist, draughtsman, furniture designer, and technical illustrator. *Publs:* Bible Stories Retold, 1968; The Book of Witnesses, 1971; The Three Donkeys, 1972; The Voices of Masada, 1973; The Little Book of Sylvanus, 1975; You Have a Minute, Lord?, 1977; A Small Town Is a World, 1979; Sweet Nutcracker, 1985. Add: c/o William Collins Ltd., 8 Grafton St., London W.1. England.

KOSTELANETZ, Richard (Cory). American, b. 1940. Novels/Short stories, Poetry, Art, Literature, Media, Music. Literary Dir., The Future Press, since 1976; Co-Ed. and Publisher, Precisely, since 1977. Contrib. Ed., Menu Mag. Co-Compiler, Assembling annual book, and Co-Dir., Assembling Press, Brooklyn, N.Y., 1970–82; Prog. Assoc., Thematic Studies, John Jay Coll., City Univ. of New York, 1972–73; Visiting Prof. of American Studies and English, Univ. of Texas at Austin, 1977. *Publs:* (ed.) On Contemporary Literature, 1964, 1969; (ed. and contrib.) The New American Arts, 1965; (ed.) Twelve from the Sixties, 1967; (ed.) The Young American Writers, 1967; Music of Today, 1967; The Theatre of Mixed Means, 1968; (ed.) Beyond Left and Right, 1968; Master Minds, 1969; And So Forth, 1969; (co-ed.) Assembling, 10 vols., 1970–81; Visual Language, 1970; (ed.) Imaged Words and Worded Images, 1970; (ed.) Possibilities of Poetry, 1970; (ed.) Moholy-Nagy, 1970; (ed.) John Cage, 1970; In the Beginning (novel), 1971; (ed.) Social Speculations, 1971;

(ed.) Future's Fictions, 1971; (ed.) Human Alternatives, 1971; (ed.) Seeing Through Shuck, 1972; (ed.) In Youth, 1972; (ed.) Breakthrough Fictioneers, 1973; (ed.) The Edge of Adaptation, 1973; The End of Intelligent Writing, 1974; I Articulations/Short Fictions, 1974; Recyclings: A Literary Autobiography, vol. I, 1974; Number One, 1974; (ed.) Essaying Essays, 1975; Come Here, 1975; Extrapolate, 1975; Modulations, 1975; Word Prints, 1975; Portraits from Memory, 1975; Openings and Closings, 1975; (ed.) Language and Structure, 1975; Rain Rains Rain, 1976; Numbers:Poems and Stories, 1976; (ed.) Younger Critics in North America, 1976; Constructs, 1976; One Night Stood (novel), 1977; Illuminations, 1977; (ed.) Esthetics Contemporary, 1978, 1988; Foreshortenings and Other Stories, 1978; Wordsand, 1978; (ed.) Assembling Assembling, 1978; Constructs Two, 1978; Grants and the Future of Literature, 1978; Tabula Rasa, 1978; Inexistencies, 1978; Twenties in the Sixties: Previously Uncollected Critical Essays, 1979; "The End" Appendix/"The End" Essentials, 1979; (ed.) Visual Lit Crit, 1979; (ed.) Text-Sound Texts, 1980; (ed.) A Critical Assembling, 1979; Metamorphosis in the Arts, 1980; More Short Fictions, 1980; Exhaustive Parallel Intervals, 1980; (ed.) Scenarios, 1980; Autobiographies, 1981; The Old Poetries and the New, 1981; Reincarnations, 1981; (ed.) Aural Literature Criticism, 1981; (ed.) The Avant-Garde Tradition in Literature, 1982; (ed.) American Writing Today, 1982; Turfs/Arenas/Fields/Pitches, 1983; (co-ed.) Pilot Proposals, 1982; (ed.) Epiphanies, 1983; American Imaginations, 1983; Recyclings, 1984; The Old Fictions and the New, 1987; After Texts/Prose Pieces, 1987; The Grants-Fix, 1987; Conversing with Cage, 1988; On Innovative Music(ian)s, 1989; Unfinished Business, 1989; On Innovative Art(ist)s, 1990. Add: 444 Prince St., New York, N.Y. 10012, U.S.A.

KOSTER, Donald Nelson. American, b. 1910. Literature. Emeritus Prof. of English, Adelphi Univ., Garden City, N.Y., since 1978 (Asst. Prof., 1946–54; Assoc. Prof., 1954–59; Prof., 1959–78). Instr. in English, Univ. of Pennsylvania, Philadelphia, 1936–46. *Publs:* Divorce in the American Drama, 1942; (co-author) Modern Journalism, 1962; Transcendentalism in America, 1975; American Literature and Language: A Guide to Information Sources, 1982. Add: Box 33, Rt. 1, Whitney Point, N.Y. 13862, U.S.A.

KOTKER, Norman R. American, b. 1931. Novels/Short stories, History. Former Ed., Charles Scribner's Sons Inc., publrs., NYC, and Horizon Books, American Heritage Publishing Co., NYC. *Publs:* The Holy Land in the Time of Jesus, 1967; The Earthly Jerusalem, 1969; Herzl the King (novel), 1972; Massachusetts: A Pictorial History, 1976; Miss Rhode Island (novel), 1978; New England Past, 1981; Learning About God (novel), 1988. Add: 45 Lyman Rd., Northampton, Mass. 01060, U.S.A.

KOTKER, Zane H. American, b. 1934. Novels/Short stories. Contrib., The New Republic, The National Review, and New York mags. Contrib. Writer, Reader's Digest General Books, 1974–78; Assoc. Prof., Mount Holyoke Coll., South Hadley, Mass., 1982–83; Prof., MFA Program, Univ. of Mass., Amherst, 1983–84. *Publs:* Bodies in Motion, 1972; A Certain Man, 1976; White Rising, 1981. Add: 45 Lyman Rd., Northampton, Mass. 01060, U.S.A.

KOTLER, Philip. American, b. 1931. Marketing. Social sciences. Johnson Distinguished Prof. of Intnl. Marketing, formerly Harold T. Martin Prof. of Marketing, Northwestern Univ., Evanston, Ill., since 1967 (Asst. Prof., 1962–64; Assoc. Prof., 1965–66). Dir., Marketing Science Inst., Cambridge, Mass. *Publs:* Marketing Management: Analysis, Planning and Control, 1967, 6th ed. 1988; Marketing Decision Making: A Model Building Approach, 1971, 1983; (co-ed.) Creating Social Change, 1972; (co-ed.) Simulation in the Social and Administrative Sciences, 1972; (co-ed.) Readings in Marketing Management, 1972; Marketing for Nonprofit Organizations, 1975, 3rd ed., 1987; Principles of Marketing, 1980, 4th ed., 1989; The New Competition, 1985; Marketing Professional Services, 1984; Strategic Marketing for Educational Institutions, 1985; Marketing: An Introduction, 1987; Marketing for Health Care Organizations, 1987; High Visibility, 1987. Add: Grad. Sch. of Mgmt., Northwestern Univ., Evanston, Ill. 60208, U.S.A.

KOTZWINKLE, William. American, b. 1938. Novels/Short stories, Science fiction, Children's fiction. Freelance writer. *Publs:* science fiction—Hermes 3000, 1972; Doctor Rat, 1976; E.T.: The Extra-Terrestrial (novelization of screenplay), 1982; Superman III (novelization of screenplay), 1983; E.T.: The Book of the Green Planet, 1985; novels—The Fan Man, 1974; Night-Book, 1974; Swimmer in the Secret Sea, 1975; Fata Morgana, 1977; Herr Nightingale and the Satin Woman, 1978; Jack in the Box, 1980; Christmas at Fontaine's 1982; Queen of Swords, 1984; for children—The Fireman, 1969; The Ship That Came Down the Gutter,

1970; Elephant Boy: A Story of the Stone Age, 1970; The Day the Gang Got Rich, 1970; The Oldest Man and Other Timeless Stories, 1971; Return of Crazy Horse, 1971; The Supreme, Superb, Exalted, and Delightful, One and Only Magic Building, 1973; Up the Alley with Jack and Joe, 1974; The Leopard's Tooth, 1976; The Ant Who Took Away Time, 1978; Dream of Dark Harbor, 1979; The Nap Master, 1979; The Extra Terrestrial Storybook, 1982; Great World Circus, 1983; Trouble in Bugland: A Collection of Inspector Mantis Mysteries, 1983; Seduction in Berlin, 1985; The Book of the Green Plant, 1985; Hearts of Wood, 1986; The World Is Big and I'm So Small, 1986. Add: c/o Putnam's, 200 Madison Ave., New York, N.Y. 10016, U.S.A.

KOUWENHOVEN, John A(tlee). American, b. 1909. Architecture, Design, Engineering/Technology, History. Prof. Emeritus of English, Barnard Coll., Columbia Univ., NYC, since 1975 (Assoc. Prof., 1946–50; Prof., 1950–75). Master in English, Harvey Sch., 1932–36; Instr., Columbia Coll., NYC, 1936–38; member, Literature Faculty, Bennington Coll., Vt., 1938–41; Asst. Ed., 1941–43, and Assoc. Ed., 1943–46, Harper's Mag., NYC. *Publs:* Adventures of America 1857-1900, 1938; Made in America: The Arts in Modern Civilization, 1948, as The Arts in Modern American Civilization, 1967; (ed.) Walt Whitman: Leaves of Grass and Selected Prose, 1950; The Columbia Historical Portrait of New York, 1953; The Beer Can by the Highway: Essays on What's American about America, 1961; (ed. with J.F. Thaddeus) When Women Look at Men, 1963; (ed. and contrib.) The New York Guidebook, 1964; Partners in Banking: An Historical Portrait of a Great Private Bank, 1968; (co-author) The Shaping of Art and Architecture in Nineteenth Century America, 1972; Half a Truth is Better Than None, 1982. Add: Dorset, Vt. 05251, U.S.A.

KOVEL, Joel. American, b. 1936. Politics, Alger, Psychology, Race relations. Hiss Prof. of Social Studies, Bard Coll., Annandale-on-Hudson, N.Y. Formerly Prof of Psychiatry, Albert Einstein Coll. of Medicine, Bronx, N.Y., and psychoanalyst in private practice. *Publs:* White Racism: A Psychohistory, 1970; A Complete Guide to Therapy, 1976; The Age of Desire, 1982; Against the State of Nuclear Terror, 1984; The Radical Spirit (essays), 1988; In Nicaragua, 1988. Add: Box 50, Willow, N.Y. 12495, U.S.A.

KOVEL, Ralph Mallory. American. Antiques/Furnishings. Columnist, "Kovels: Antiques and Collecting," Kings Features Syndicate, since 1953; Columnist, "Your Collectibles," House Beautiful since 1979; Ed. and Publisher, Kovels' on Antiques and Collectibles. *Publs:* all with Terry Kovel—Dictionary of Marks: Pottery and Porcelain, 1953, now in 32nd printing; A Directory of Silver, Pewter, and Silver Plate, 1958, American Country Furniture, 1780-1875, 1963, Kovels' Know Your Antiques, 1967, 1973, 1981; Kovels' Antiques and Collectibles Price List, annually since 1968; Kovels' Bottles Price List, biennially since 1971, Kovels' Price Guide for Collector Plates, Figurines, Paperweights and Other Limited Editions, 1974, 1978; Kovels' Collector's Guide to American Art Pottery, 1974; Kovels' Organizer for Collectors, 1978, 1983; Kovels' Illustrated Price Guide to Royal Doulton, 1980, 1984; Kovels' Illustrated Price Guide to Depression Glass and American Dinnerware, 1980, 1983; Kovels' Know Your Collectibles, 1981; The Kovels' Book of Antique Labels, 1982; Kovels' Collector's Source Book, 1983; Kovels' New Dictionary of Marks, Pottery and Porcelain, 1850-1985, 1985; Kovels' Advertising Collectibles Price List, 1986; Kovels' Guide to Selling Your Antiques and Collectibles, 1987. Add: 22000 Shaker Blvd., Shaker Heights, Ohio 44122, U.S.A.

KOVEL, Terry Horvitz. American, b. 1928. Antiques/Furnishings. Columnist, "Kovels: Antiques and Collecting," Register & Tribune Syndicate, since 1953; Columnist, "Your Collectibles," House Beautiful, since 1979. Ed. and Publr., Kovels' on Antiques and Collectibles. *Publs:* all with Ralph Kovel—Dictionary of Marks: Pottery and Porcelain, 1953, now in 32nd printing; A Directory of Silver, Pewter, and Silver Plate, 1958, American Country Furniture, 1780-1875, 1963, Kovels' Know Your Antiques, 1967, 1973, 1981; Kovels' Antiques and Collectibles Price List, annually since 1968; Kovels' Bottles Price List, biennially since 1971, Kovels' Price Guide for Collector Plates, Figurines, Paperweights and Other Limited Editions, 1974, 1978; Kovels' Collector's Guide to American Art Pottery, 1974; Kovels' Organizer for Collectors, 1978, 1983; Kovels' Illustrated Price Guide to Royal Doulton, 1980, 1984; Kovels' Illustrated Price Guide to Depression Glass and American Dinnerware, 1980, 1983; Kovels' Know Your Collectibles, 1981; The Kovels' Book of Antique Labels, 1982; Kovels' Collector's Source Book, 1983; Kovels' New Dictionary of Marks, Pottery and Porcelaine, 1850-1985, 1985; Kovels' Advertising Collectibles Price List, 1986; Kovels' Guide to Selling Your Antiques and Collectibles, 1987. Add: P.O. Box 22000,

Beachwood, Ohio 44122, U.S.A.

KOZOL, Jonathan. American, b. 1936. Novels, Education, Social commentary. Substitute teacher, Boston, 1964–65; Consultant, curriculum development, U.S. Office of Education, 1965; Teacher, elementary sch., Newton, Mass., c.1965; began tutorial prog. for underprivileged children, Roxbury, Mass., 1966, project developed into New Sch. for Children; Educational Dir., Storefront Learning Center, Boston area, 1968–71; Visiting Lectr., colls. and univs. in U.S., 1969–75; Intr., Center for Intercultural Documentation, Cuernavaca, Mexico, 1969, 1970, 1974; Fellow, Ford, Rockefeller, and Guggenheim Foundations, 1970–83. *Publs:* The Fume of Poppies (novel), 1958; Death at an Early Age: The Destruction of the Hearts and Minds of Negro Children in the Boston Public Schools, 1967; Free Schools, 1972, rev. ed. as Alternative Schools: A Guide for Educators and Parents, 1982; The Night Is Dark and I am Far From Home, 1975; Children of the Revolution: A Yankee Teacher in the Cuban Schools, 1978; Prisoners of Silence: Breaking the Bonds of Adult Illiteracy in the United States, 1980; On Being a Teacher, 1981; Illiterate America, 1985; Rachel and Her Children: Homeless Families in America, 1988. Add: c/o Janklow and Nesbit, 598 Madison Ave., N.Y., N.Y. 10022, U.S.A.

KRAEHE, Enno Edward. American, b. 1921. History. Corcoran Prof. of History, Univ. of Virginia, Charlottesville, since 1977 (Prof., 1968–77). Prof. of History, Univ. of Kentucky, Lexington, 1963–64, and Univ. of North Carolina, Chapel Hill, 1964–68. *Publs:* (co-author) Collectivization of Agriculture in Eastern Europe, 1958; Metternich's German Policy, vol. I: The Contest with Napoleon, 1799-1814, 1963, Vol. II: The Congress of Vienna 1814-1815, 1983; (co-author, ed. and trans.) The Metternich Controversy, 1971. Add: 130 Bennington Rd., Charlottesville, Va 22901, U.S.A.

KRAFT, Robert A(lan). American, b. 1934. Religion. Prof. of Religious Studies, Univ. of Pennsylvania, since 1976 (Asst. Prof., 1963–68; Assoc. Prof., 1968–76). Asst. Lectr. in New Testament Studies, Univ. of Manchester, England, 1961–63. *Publs:* The Apostolic Fathers: A New Translation and Commentary, vol. III, Barnabas and the Didache, 1965; (with P. Prigent) Epitre de Barnabe, 1971; (trans. and ed. with G. Krodel) W. Bauer and G. Strecker: Orthodoxy and Heresy in Earliest Christianity, 1971; Septuagintal Lexicography, 1972; (with Ann-Elizabeth Purintun) Paraleipomena Jeremiou, 1972; (with others) Testament of Job, 1974; (with G. Nickelsburg) Early Judaism and Its Modern Interpreters, 1986. Add: Univ. of Pennsylvania, Box 36 Coll. Hall, Philadelphia, Pa. 19104, U.S.A.

KRAFT, William F. American, b. 1938. Psychology. Prof of Psychology, Carlow Coll., Pittsburgh, Pa., since 1969. Dir. of Psychological Services, Somerset State Hosp., Pa., 1965–68, and Dixmont State Hosp., Pittsburgh, Pa., 1968–70. *Publs:* The Search for the Holy, 1971; A Psychology of Nothingness, 1974; Normal Modes of Madness, 1978; Sexual Dimensions of the Celibate Life, 1979; Achieving Promises: A Spiritual Guide for the Transitions of Life, 1982; A Psychospiritual Approach Toward Sexuality, 1989. Add: 8072 Brittany Pl., Pittsburgh, Pa. 15237, U.S.A.

KRAMER, Aaron. American, b. 1921. Poetry, Literature, Translations. Prof. of English, Dowling Coll., (formerly Adelphi Univ., Suffolk campus), Oakdale, N.Y., since 1970 (Instr., 1961–63; Asst. Prof., 1963–66; Assoc. Prof., 1966–70). Ed. Bd., Journal of Poetry Therapy, since 1987. Grad. Prof. of English, Adelphi Univ., Garden City, N.Y., 1975–79. Co-Ed., West Hills Review, 1978–85. *Publs:* Till the Grass is Ripe for Dancing, 1943; Thru Our Guns, 1945; The Glass Mountain, 1946; The Thunder of the Grass, 1948; (trans.) The Poetry and Prose of Heinrich Heine, 1948; The Golden Trumpet, 1949; Thru Every Window, 1950; Denmark Vesey, 1952; Roll the Forbidden Drums!, 1954; A Ballad of August Bondi, 1955; (trans. and ed.) The Teardrop Millionaire, 1955; (ed. with S. Lishinsky and contrib.) The Tune of the Calliope, 1958; (trans. and contrib.) Moses, 1962; (trans.) Songs and Ballads: Goethe, Schiller, Heine, 1963; Rumshinsky's Hat: House of Buttons, 1964; (trans.) Rilke: Visions of Christ, 1967; The Prophetic Tradition in American Poetry, 1835-1900, 1968; Henry at the Grating, 1968; (trans.) Poems by Abraham Reisen, 1971; (ed.) Melville's Poetry: Toward the Enlarged Heart, 1972; (ed.) On Freedom's Side: American Poems of Protest, 1972; (ed. with P. Quin) Long Night's Journey Back to Light, 1973; On the Way to Palermo, 1973; O Golden Land! 1976; Carousel Parkway, 1980; (ed. with V. Clemente and G. Everett) Paumanok Rising, 1980; The Burning Bush, 1983; In Wicked Times, 1983; In the Suburbs, 1986. Add: English Dept., Dowling Coll., Oakdale, N.Y. 11769, U.S.A.

KRAMER, Dale. American, b. 1936. Literature. Prof. of English, Univ. of Illinois, Urbana, since 1971 (Asst. Prof., 1965–67; Assoc. Prof., 1967–71). Ed., Journal of English and German Philology. Instr., 1962–63, and Asst. Prof. of English, 1963–65, Ohio Univ., Athens. *Publs:* Charles Maturin, 1973; Thomas Hardy: The Forms of Tragedy, 1975; (ed.) Critical Approaches to the Fiction of Thomas Hardy, 1979; (ed.) The Woodlanders, by Thomas Hardy, 1981, 1985; (ed.) The Mayor of Casterbridge, by Thomas Hardy, 1987. Add: Dept. of English, Univ. of Illinois, Urbana, Ill. 61801, U.S.A.

KRAMER, Hilton. American, b. 1928. Art. Ed., New Criterion Mag., NYC, since 1982; Art Critic, The New York Observer (weekly newspaper), since 1987. Assoc. Ed. and Feature Ed., Arts Digest, 1954–55; Managing Ed., 1955–58, and Ed., 1959–61, Arts Mag.; Art Critic, The Nation, 1962–63; Art Critic and Assoc. Ed., The New Leader, 1964–65; Art News Ed., from 1965, and Chief Art Critic, 1973–82, The New York Times. *Publs:* The Age of the Avant-Garde: An Art Chronicle of 1956–1972, 1973; The Revenge of the Philistines: Art and Culture 1972–84, 1985; (ed.) The New Criterion Reader: The First Five Years, 1988. Add: c/o New Criterion, 850 Seventh Ave., New York, NY 10019, U.S.A.

KRAMER, (Dame) Leonie (Judith). Australian, b. 1924. Literature. Prof. of Australian Literature, Univ. of Sydney, since 1968. Editorial Adviser, Poetry Australia. Lectr. in English, Canberra Univ. Coll., 1954–56; Lectr., Sr. Lectr., and Assoc. Prof., Univ. of New South Wales, 1958–68. *Publs:* Henry Handel Richardson and Some of Her Sources, 1954; (ed.) Australian Poetry 1961, 1962; A Companion to Australia Felix, 1962; (ed.) Coast to Coast 1963–64, 1964; Myself When Laura: Fact and Fiction in Henry Handel Richardson's School Career, 1966; Henry Handel Richardson, 1967; (ed.) Introduction to Hal Porter: Selected Stories, 1971; (ed.) Introduction to Henry Kingsley: The Hillyars and the Burtons, 1973; (ed.) Henry Kendall, Australian Colonial Poets, Book 2, 1973; (with R.D. Eagleson) Language and Literature: A Synthesis, 1976; (with Eagleson) A Guide to Language and Literature, 1977; A.D. Hope, 1979; (ed.) The Oxford History of Australian Literature, 1981; (ed. with Adrian Mitchell) The Oxford Anthology of Australian Literature, 1985; (ed.) My Country: 200 Years of Australian Poetry and Short Stories, 1985; (ed.) James McAuley: Poetry, Essays and Personal Commentary, 1988; (ed.) David Campbell: Collected Poems, 1989. Add: 12 Vaucluse Rd., Vaucluse, N.S.W., Australia 2030.

KRAMER, Paul J(ackson). American, b. 1904. Biology, Botany. James B. Duke Prof. of Botany Emeritus, Duke Univ., Durham, N.C., since 1974 (joined faculty, 1931; Prof., 1954–74). *Publs:* Plant and Soil Water Relationships, 1949; (with T.T. Kozlowski) Physiology of Trees, 1960; Plant and Soil Water Relationships: A Modern Synthesis, 1969; (with T.T. Kozlowski) Physiology of Woody Plants, 1979; (ed. with N.C. Turner) Adaptations of Plants to Water and High Temperature Stress, 1980; (with C.D. Raper, Jr.) Crop Reactions to Water and Temperature Stress in Humid Temperature Climates, 1982; Water Relations of Plants, 1983; A Collection of Lectures on Tree Physiology (publ. in Chinese), 1982. Add: Cat Meadows, V-235, Chapel Hill, N.C. 27514, U.S.A.

KRANTZ, Hazel. American, b. 1920. Novels/Short stories, Children's fiction, Children's non-fiction. Elementary sch. teacher, Nassau County Schs., N.Y., 1957–68; Ed., True Frontier mag., 1969–71; Copy Ed., Sound Engineering Mag., 1973–78. *Publs:* 100 Pounds of Popcorn, 1960; Freestyle for Michael, 1964; The Secret Raft, 1965; Tippy, 1968; A Pad of Your Own, 1973; The Complete Guide to Happiness and Success, 1980; Pink and White Striped Summer, 1982; None But the Brave, 1986; Daughter of My People: Henrietta Szold and Hadassah, 1987. Add: 1306 Stoney Hill Dr., Ft. Collins, CO., 80525, U.S.A.

KRANTZ, Judith. American. Novels/Short stories. Contrib., Good Housekeeping, 1948–54, McCalls, 1954–59, and Ladies Home Journal. 1959–71; Contributing Ed., Cosmopolitan, 1971–79. *Publs:* Scruples, 1978; Princess Daisy, 1980; Mistral's Daughter, 1982; I'll Take Manhattan, 1986; Till We Meet Again, 1988. Add: c/o Warner Books, 666 Fifth Ave., New York, N.Y. 10103, U.S.A.

KRANZBERG, Melvin. American, b. 1917. Engineering/Technology, History. Callaway Prof. of the History of Technology, Georgia Inst. of Technology, Atlanta, 1972–88. Vice-Pres. of the Intnl. Co-operation in History and Technology Cttee., since 1968; Founder, Society for the History of Technology. Member of faculty, Stevens Inst. of Technology, Hoboken, N.J., 1946–47, Amherst Coll., Mass., 1947–52, and Case Western Reserve Univ., Cleveland, Ohio, 1952–72. National Pres., Sigma Xi, 1979–80; former Ed.-in-Chief, Technology and Culture. *Publs:* The Siege of Paris 1870-1871, 1950, 1970; (ed.) 1848: A Turning

Point?, 1959, 1971; (ed. with C.W. Pursell and co-author) Technology in Western Civilization, 2 vols., 1967; (ed.) with W.H. Davenport) Technology and Culture: An Anthology, 1972; (with J. Geis) By the Sweat of Thy Brow: Men, Women, and Work in the Western World, 1975; (with P. Kelly) Technological Innovation: A Critical Review of Current Knowledge, 1978; (ed. with Timothy Hall) Energy and the Way We Live, 1980; (ed.) Ethics in an Age of Persuasive Technology, 1980; (ed. with Margaret Latimer and Brook Hindle) Bridge to the Future: A Centennial Celebration of the Brooklyn Bridge, 1987; (ed.) Technological Education—Technological Style, 1986. Add: School of Social Sciences, Georgia Inst. of Technology, Atlanta, Ga. 30332, U.S.A.

KRASILOVSKY, Phyllis. American, b. 1926. Children's fiction, Travel/Exploration/Adventure. *Publs:* The Man Who Didn't Wash His Dishes, 1950; The Very Little Girl, 1953; The Cow Who Fell in the Canal, 1957; Scaredy Cat, 1959; Benny's Flag, 1960; The Very Little Boy, 1961; Susan Sometimes, 1962; The Girl Who Was a Cowboy, 1965; The Very Tall Little Girl, 1969; The Shy Little Girl, 1970; The Popular Girls Club, 1972; L.C. Is the Greatest, 1975; The Man Who Tried to Save Time, 1979; The Man Who Entered a Contest, 1980; The First Tulips in Holland, 1982; The Man Who Cooked for Himself, 1982; The Happy Times Story Book, 1987. Add: 1177 Hardscrabble Rd., Chappaqua, N.Y. 10514, U.S.A.

KRASNER, William. American, b. 1917. Novels/Short stories, Plays/Screenplays, Medicine/Health, Social sciences. Freelance writer and ed., since 1946. TV producer and writer, KMOX-TV (CBS), St. Louis, Mo., 1958; Co-Founder, Articles Ed., and Chief Writer, Trans-Action Mag., 1963–69; Sr. Assoc. Ed., Psychiatric Reporter, Philadelphia, 1969; Editorial Consultant, Univ. of Pennsylvania, Philadelphia, 1969–73. *Publs:* Walk the Dark Streets, 1949; The Gambler, 1950; North of Welfare, 1954; The Stag Party, 1957; Salem Village (radio play and later staged), 1959; Drug-Trip Abroad, 1973; Francis Parkman: Dakota Legend, 1982; Death of a Minor Poet, 1984; Resort to Murder, 1985. Add: 538 Berwyn Ave., Berwyn, Pa., 19312, U.S.A.

KRAUS, Joanna Halpert. American, b. 1937. Children's fiction, Plays. Prof., of Theatre Arts, since 1986, and Coordinator, Arts for Children, since 1981, State Univ. of New York at Brockport (Assoc. Prof., 1979–86). Theatre Critic for Quarante mag. since 1985. Assoc. Dir., Baltimore Children's Theatre, 1960–61; Asst. Dir., Clark Center for Performing Arts, NYC, 1963–65; Instr., NYC Community Coll., 1966–69, Columbia Univ. Teachers Coll., NYC, 1970–71, and State Univ. of New York at Purchase, 1970–72; Asst. Prof., State Univ. of New York at New Paltz, 1972–79. Secty., Children's Theatre Assn. of America, 1982–84. *Publs:* The Ice Wolf (play), 1964; Vasalisa (play), 1968; Mean to Be Free (play), 1968; Seven Sound and Motion Stories, 1971, 1980; The Great American Train Ride, 1975; Two Plays from the Far East, 1977; Circus Home (play), 1978; The Last Baron of Arizona (play), 1986; Kimchi Kid (play), 1987; The Shaggy Dog Murder Trial (play), 1987. Add: Dept. of Theatre, State Univ. of New York Coll., Brockport, N.Y. 14420, U.S.A.

KRAUS, Robert. American, b. 1925. Children's fiction, Children's non-fiction. Cartoonist and illustrator. Founding Pres., Windmill Books, since 1966, and Springfellow Books, since 1972. *Publs:* Junior, The Spoiled Cat, 1955; All the Mice Came, 1955; Ladybug, Ladybug!, 1957; I, Mouse, 1958; Mouse at Sea, 1959; The Littlest Rabbit, 1961; The Trouble with Spider, 1962; Miranda's Beautiful Dream, 1964; Penguin's Pal, 1964; The Bunny's Nutshell Library, 4 vols., 1965; Amanda Remembers, 1965; My Son, The Mouse, 1966; The Little Giant, 1967; Unidentified Flying Elephant, 1968; The Children Who Got Married, 1969; Hello, Hippopotamus, 1969; Rumple Nose-Dimple and the Three Horrible Snaps, 1969; Animal Etiquette, 1969; Don't Talk to Strange Bears, 1969; The Rabbit Brothers, 1969; Vip's Mistake Book, 1970; How Spider Saved Christmas, 1970; Whose Mouse Are You?, 1970; Bunya the Witch, 1971; Shaggy Fur Face, 1971; The Tail Who Wagged the Dog, 1971; Ludwig, The Dog Who Snored Symphonies, 1971; Pip Squeak, Mouse in Shining Armor, 1971; Lillian, Morgan, and Teddy, 1971; Leo the Late Bloomer, 1971; The Tree That Stayed Up until Next Christmas, 1972; Good Night, Little A.B.C., 1972; Good Night, Little One, 1972; Good Night, Richard Rabbit, 1972; Milton the Early Riser, 1972; Big Brother, 1973; How Spider Saved Halloween, 1973; Poor Mister Splinterfitzi, 1973; Herman the Helper, 1974; The Night-Lite Story Book, 1974; Rebecca Hatpin, 1974; Owliver, 1974; Pinchpenny Mouse, 1974; I'm a Monkey, 1975; Three Friends, 1975; The Gondolier of Venice, 1976; Kittens for Nothing, 1976; Boris Bad Enough, 1976; The Good Mousekeeper, 1977; The Detective of London, 1977; Noel the Coward, 1977; Springfellow, 1978; Another Mouse to Feed, 1979; Meet the Blunt, 1980; Box of Brownies, 1980; How Spider Saved Turkey, 1981; The King's Trousers,

1981; See the Christmas Lights, 1981; Tubby Books, 6 vols., 1981–82; Leo the Late Bloomer Takes a Bath, 1981; Herman the Helper Cleans Up, 1981; Squeaky Books, 2 vols., 1982; Tony the Tow Truck, 1985; Freddy the Fire Engine, 1985; How Spider Saved Valentine's Day, 1986; Mrs. Elmo of Elephant House, 1986; Where Are You Going Little Mouse? 1986; Come Out and Play, Little Mouse, 1987; Babytown Board Books, 4 vols., 1987; The Hoodwinking of Mrs. Elmo, 1987; Spider's First Day at School, 1987; How Spider Saved Easter, 1988; Spider's Hometown, 1988; Mummy Dearest Creepy Hollow Whooooooodunit Series, 4 vols., 1988; Creepy Hollow Ghostly Glowing Haunted House, 1988; Screamy Mimi, 1988; Phil the Ventriloquist, 1989. Add: c/o Greenwillow Books, 105 Madison Ave., New York, N.Y. 10016, U.S.A.

KRAUSHAAR, Otto F. American, b. 1901. Education. Self-employed educational consultant. Pres. Emeritus, Goucher Coll., Towson, Md., since 1967 (Pres., 1948–67). Prof. of Philosophy, Smith Coll., Northampton, Mass., 1933–48; Research Assoc., Harvard Univ. Grad. Sch. of Education, 1967–71. *Publs:* (co-author) Classic American Philosophers, 1951; American Nonpublic Schools: Patterns of Diversity, 1972; Private Schools: From the Puritans to the Present, 1976; Schools in a Changing City: An Overview of Baltimore's Private Schools, 1976; Baltimore's Adopt-a-School Program, 1978; (with others) Utopias: The American Experience, 1980. Add: 830 W. 40th St., Apt. 1012, Baltimore, Md. 21211, U.S.A.

KRAUSHAR, Peter Maximilian. British, b. 1934. Marketing. Chmn., KAE Group Ltd., since 1969. Chmn., Marketing Soc. Managing Dir., D.F. Marketing Development Ltd., London, 1966–69. *Publs:* New Products and Diversification, 1969, 1977; Practical Business Development: What Works, What Does Not?, 1985. Add: 2 Lauradale Rd., London N2 9LU, England.

KRAUSKOPF, Konrad (Bates). American, b. 1910. Earth sciences. Prof. of Geochemistry Emeritus, Geology Dept., Stanford Univ., since 1976 (Acting Instr. in Physical Science, 1935–39, Asst. Prof. of Geology, 1939–42, Assoc. Prof., 1942–50, and Prof. of Geochemistry, 1950–76). Geologist, U.S. Geological Survey, Menlo Park, Calif., 1944–88. Instr. in Chemistry, Univ. of California, 1934–35; Chief Geographic Section, Gen. Headquarters, U.S. Army Far East Command, Tokyo, 1947–48. Pres., American Geological Inst., 1964, Geological Soc. of America, 1967, and Geochemical Soc., 1970. *Publs:* Fundamentals of Physical Science, 1941, 6th ed. (with A. Beiser), 1971; (with A. Beiser) The Physical Universe, 1960, 5th ed., 1986; (with A. Beiser) Introduction to Physics and Chemistry, 1964, 1969; Introduction to Geochemistry, 1967, 1979; The Third Planet, 1974; (with A. Beiser) Introduction to Earth Science, 1975; Radioactive Waste Disposal and Geology, 1988. Add: 806 La Mesa Dr., Menlo Park, Calif. 94025, U.S.A.

KRAUSS, Ruth. American, b. 1911. Children's fiction, Plays/Screenplays. *Publs:* A Good Man and His Good Wife, 1944, 1962; The Great Duffy, 1945; The Carrot Seed, 1946; The Growing Story, 1947; Bears, 1948; The Happy Day, 1949; The Backward Day, 1950; The Bundle Book, 1951; Hole is to Dig: A First Book of First Definitions, 1952; I Can Fly, 1952; The Big World and the Little House, 1952; A Very Special House, 1953; I'll Be You and You Be Me, 1954; The Birthday Party, 1955; Charlotte and the White Horse, 1955; How to Make an Earthquake, 1956; I Want to Paint My Bathroom Blue, 1956; Monkey Day, 1957; Is This You?, 1958; Moon or a Button, 1959; Somebody Else's Nut Tree, 1959; Open House for Butterflies, 1960; "Mama, I Wish I Was Snow" "Child, You'd Be Very Cold", 1962; A Bouquet of Littles, 1963; Eye Nose Fingers Toes, 1964; The Cantilever Rainbow (play), 1965; The Little King, The Little Queen, The Little Monster, 1967; Everything Under a Mushroom, 1967; This Thumbprint, 1967; There's a Little Ambiguity Over There among the Bluebells and Other Theatre Poems, 1968; If Only (play), 1969; Under Twenty (poems), 1970; I Write It, 1970; Love and the Invention of Punctuation (play), 1973; This Breast Gothic (poems), 1973; Under 13 (poems), 1976; When I Walk I Change the Earth (poem), 1978; Somebody Spilled the Sky (poems), 1979; Minestrone, 1981; Re-examination of Freedom, 1981; Love Poems for Children, 1986; Big and Little, 1987. Add: c/o Scholastic Books, 730 Broadway, New York, N.Y. 10003, U.S.A.

KRAUSZ, Ernest. British, b. 1931. Race relations, Social sciences, Sociology. Prof., Chair of Sociology, since 1972, and Rector, since 1986, Bar-Ilan Univ., Ramat-Gan, Israel. Ed., Studies of Israeli Society, since 1980, Lectr., 1967–70, Sr. Lectr., 1970–72, and Reader, 1971–72, The City Univ., London. *Publs:* Sociology in Britain, 1969; Ethnic Minorities in Britain, 1971; (with S.H. Miller) Social Research Design, 1974; Sociological Research: A Philosophy of Science Perspective, 1986.

Add: Dept. of Sociology, Bar-Ilan Univ., Ramat-Gan, Israel.

KREFETZ, Gerald Saul. American, b. 1932. Economics, Money/Finance. Partner, Page Proofs Literary Agency, NYC, since 1962. *Publs:* (with R. Marossi) Investing Abroad: A Guide to Financial Europe, 1965; (with R. Marossi) Money Makes Money and the Money Money Makes Makes Money, 1971; The Dying Dollar, 1972, 1975; The Book of Income, 1982; The Smart Investor's Guide: How to Make Money in the Coming Bull Market, 1982; Jews and Money: The Myths and the Reality, 1982; How to Read and Profit from Financial News, 1984; Leverage: How to Multiply Your Money, 1985; All about Saving, 1987, How to Pay for College, 1988. Add: 463 West St., New York, N.Y. 10014, U.S.A.

KREGEL, J.A. British, b. 1944. Economics. Prof. of Economics, Johns Hopkins, Sch. of Advanced Intnl. Studies, Bologna Center. Formerly, Sr. Lectr. in Economics, Univ. of Southampton; Prof. of Economics, Rutgers Univ., New Jersey, and the Univ. of Groningen. *Publs:* Rate of Profit, Distribution and Growth: Two Views, 1971; The Theory of Economic Growth, 1972; The Reconstruction of Political Economy, 1973, 1975; The Theory of Capital, 1976; (ed.) Distribution, Effective Demand and International Economic Relations, 1983; (ed.) Barriers to Full Employment, 1987; Inflation and Income Distribution in Capitalist Crisis: Essays in Memory of Sidney Weintraub, 1988. Add: via Belmelono 11, 40126 Bologna, Italy.

KREININ, Mordechai. American, b. 1930. Economics. Prof. of Economics, Michigan State Univ., East Lansing, since 1961 (Lectr. and Study Dir., 1956–57; Asst. Prof., 1957–59; Assoc. Prof., 1959–61). Consultant, U.S. State Dept. since 1970, U.N. since 1971, and Brookings Instn., Washington, D.C., since 1972. Special Advisor on Policy and Research, U.N. Conference on Trade and Development, Geneva, Switz., 1971–73. *Publs:* Israel and Africa: A Study in Technical Cooperation, 1964; Alternative Commercial Policies: Their Effects on the American Economy, 1967; International Economics, 1971, 5th ed. 1987; (co-author) The Monetary Approach to the Balance of Payments: A Survey, 1978; Economics, 1983, 1989; Can Australia Adjust?, 1988. Add: Dept. of Economics, Michigan State Univ., East Lansing, Mich. 48824, U.S.A.

KREISEL, Henry. Canadian, b. 1922. Novels/Short stories, Plays/Screenplays. Univ. Prof. of English, Univ. of Alberta, Edmonton, since 1975 (Head, Dept. of English, 1961–67; Assoc. Dean and Acting Dean of Grad. Studies, 1967–70; Academic Vice-Pres., 1970–75). *Publs:* The Rich Man (novel), 1948; He Who Sells His Shadow: A Fable for Radio, 1956; (ed.) Aphrodite and Other Poems by John Heath, 1959; The Betrayal (novel), 1964; (with F. Moher) The Broken Globe (play), 1975; The Almost Meeting and Other Stories, 1981; Another Country, 1985. Add: 12516 66th Ave., Edmonton, Alta., Canada.

KREJCI, Jaroslav. Czechoslovak, b. 1916. International relations/Current affairs, Social sciences (general). Prof. Sch. of European Studies, Univ. of Lancaster, since 1976 (Research Fellow, 1969–70, Visiting Lectr., 1970–72, Lectr., 1972–74, and Sr. Lectr., 1974–76). With State Planning Office, Prague, 1945–50, and State Bank, Prague, 1950–53; political prisoner, Czechoslovakia, 1954–60; Member, Production Cooperative, Prague, 1960–67, and Inst. of Environment, Academy of Sciences, Prague, 1968. Teacher, Graduate Sch. of Political and Social Science, Prague, 1948–50; External Assoc. Prof., Faculty of Economics, Technical Univ., Prague, 1950–52. *Publs:* Social Change and Stratification in Postwar Czechoslovakia, 1972; Social Structure in Divided Germany, 1976; (ed.) Sozialdemokratie und System wandel, 1978; (with V. Velimsky) Ethnic and Political Nations in Europe, 1981; National Income and Outlay in Czechoslovakia, Poland, and Yugoslavia, 1982; Great Revolutions Compared: The Search for a Theory, 1983; The Civilisations of Asia and the Middle East, Before the European Challenge, 1989. Add: Lonsdale Coll., Univ. of Lancaster, Bailrigg, Lancaster, England.

KRENTZ, Edgar Martin. American, b. 1928. Theology/Religion. Prof. of New Testament, Lutheran School of Theology, Chicago, Il, since 1983. Prof. of New Testament, Christ Seminary-Seminex, St. Louis, Mo., 1975–83. Prof. of New Testament, Concordia Seminary, St. Louis, 1969–75 (Instr., 1953–56; Asst. Prof., 1956–63; Assoc. Prof., 1963–69). *Publs:* Biblical Studies Today, 1966; The Historical-Critical Method, 1975; Easter, Series B, Proclamation 3, 1985; Galatians, Augsburg New Testament Commentary, 1985. Add: 5433 S. Ridgewood Ct., Chicago, Il. 60615, U.S.A.

KRENTZ, Jayne Ann. Also writes as Jayne Bentley, Jayne Castle, Amanda Glass, Stephanie James, Jayne Taylor. American, b. 1948.

Historical/Romance. *Publs:* (as Jayne Taylor) Whirlwind Courtship, 1979; (as Jayne Bentley) A Moment Past Midnight, 1979; (as Jayne Bentley) Turning Towards Home, 1979; (as Jayne Bentley) Maiden of the Morning, 1979; Uneasy Alliance, 1984; Call It Destiny, 1984; Ghost of a Chance, 1985; Man with a Past, 1985; Witchcraft, 1985; Legacy, 1985; The Waiting Game, 1985; True Colors, 1986; Ties that Bind, 1986; Between the Lines, 1986; Sweet Starfire, 1986; Crystal Flame, 1986; Twist of Fate, 1986; The Family Way, 1987; The Main Attraction, 1987; A Coral Kiss, 1987; Chance of a Lifetime, 1987; Midnight Jewels, 1987; Test of Time, 1987; Full Bloom, 1988; Joy, 1988; Gift of Gold, 1988; Dreams, 1989; A Woman's Touch, 1989; Lady's Choice, 1989; (as Amanda Glass) Shield's Lady, 1989; as Jayne Castle—Vintage of Surrender, 1979; Queen of Hearts, 1979; The Gentle Pirate, 1980; Bargain with the Devil, 1981; Right of Possession, 1981; Wagered Weekend, 1981; A Man's Protection, 1982; A Negotiated Surrender, 1982; Affair of Risk, 1982; Power Play, 1982; Relentless Adversary, 1982; Spellbound, 1982; Conflict of Interest, 1983; Double Dealing, 1984; Trading Secrets, 1985; The Desperate Game, 1986; The Chilling Deception, 1986; The Sinister Touch, 1986; The Fatal Fortune, 1986; as Stephanie James—A Passionate Business, 1981; The Dangerous Magic, 1982; Stormy Challenge, 1982; Corporate Affair, 1982; Velvet Touch, 1982; Lover in Pursuit, 1982; Renaissance Man, 1982; A Reckless Passion, 1982; The Price of Surrender, 1983; To Tame the Hunter, 1983; Affair of Honor, 1983; Gamesmaster, 1983; The Silver Snare, 1983; Battle Prize, 1983; Bodyguard, 1983; Serpent in Paradise, 1983; Gambler's Woman, 1984; Fabulous Beast, 1984; Devil to Pay, 1984; Night of the Magician, 1984; Nightwalker, 1984; Raven's Prey, 1984; Golden Goddess, 1985; Wizard, 1985; Cautious Lover, 1985; Green Fire, 1986; Second Wife, 1986; Challoner Bride, 1987; Saxon's Lady, 1987. Add: c/o Harlequin Enterprises Ltd., 225 Duncan Mill Rd., Don Mills, Ont. M3B 3K9, Canada.

KRESH, Paul. American, b. 1919. Plays/Screenplays, Music, Politics/Government, Biography. Communications consultant, since 1981. Contrib. Ed., High Fidelity, since 1985; Record Reviewer, New York Times, NYC, 1986–87. Dir., Artists and Repertoire in North America, Listen for Pleasure, Ltd., since 1986. Scriptwriter, WNYC, 1940–42; Publicist, National Jewish Welfare Bd., 1941–45; Publicity Dir., American ORT Fedn., 1945–46; Asst. Publicity Dir., Council of Jewish Fedns., 1946–47; Writer and Publicist, Nathan C. Belth Assocs., 1947–50; Motion Picture Dir., and Assoc. Publicity Dir., National Jewish Appeal, 1950–59; Contrib. Ed., American Record Guide, 1958–61; Public Relations Dir. and Ed., American Judaism, Union of American Hebrew Congregations, 1959–67; Contrib. Ed., Stereo Review, 1961–81; Book Reviewer, Saturday Review, 1961–71; Vice- Pres., Spoken Arts Inc., 1967–70; Projects Ed., Caedmon Records, 1970–71; Public Relations Dir., 1971–74, and Creative Dir., 1974–81, United Jewish Appeal, Fedn. of Jewish Philanthropies of Greater New York. *Publs:* (with Stephen M. Young) Tales Out of Congress, 1966; (ed.) American Judaism Reader, 1967; The Power of the Unknown Citizen, 1970; The Day the Doors Closed (screenplay); Let It Be (screenplay); The Dock (screenplay); Isaac Bashevis Singer: The Magician of West 86th Street: A Biography, 1979; Isaac Bashevis Singer: The Story of a Storyteller, 1984; An American Rhapsody - The Story of George Gershwin, 1988. Add: 1 David Lane, Yonkers, N.Y. 10701, U.S.A.

KRIEGEL, Leonard. American, b. 1933. Novels/Short stories, Autobiography/Memoirs/Personal. Asst. Prof. to Prof. of English, City Coll. of New York, since 1961. *Publs:* The Long Walk Home, 1964; (ed.) Essential Works of the Founding Fathers, 1964; Edmund Wilson, 1971; Working Through, 1972; Notes for the Two-Dollar Window, 1976; (ed.) The Myth of Manhood, 1978; On Men and Manhood, 1979; Quitting Time, 1980. Add: 355 Eighth Ave., New York, N.Y. 10001, U.S.A.

KRIEGER, Leonard. American, b. 1918. History. Prof. of History, Univ. of Chicago, since 1972 (Univ. Prof., 1962–69). Asst. Instr. to Prof. of History, Yale Univ., New Haven, Conn., 1946–62; Prof. of History, Columbia Univ., NYC, 1969–72. *Publs:* The German Idea of Freedom, 1957, 1974; The Politics of Discretion, 1965; (with J. Higham and F. Gilbert) History, 1965; (ed.) The German Revolution, by Friedrich Engels, 1967; (ed. with F. Stern) The Responsibility of Power, 1968, 1969; Kings and Philosophers, 1970; Essay on the Theory of Enlightened Despotism, 1975; Ranke, 1977. Add: Dept. of History, Univ. of Chicago, Chicago, Ill. 60637, U.S.A.

KRIEGER, Murray. American, b. 1923. Literature. Univ. Prof. of English, Univ. of California, Irvine, since 1974 (Prof., 1967–74; Dir., Sch. of Criticism and Theory, 1976–81; Founding Dir., Univ. of California Humanities Research Inst., 1987–89). Asst. Prof., 1952–55, and Assoc. Prof., 1955–58, Univ. of Minnesota, Minneapolis; Prof., Univ. of Illinois,

Urbana, 1958–63; M.F. Carpenter Prof., of Literary Criticism, Univ. of Iowa, Iowa City, 1963–66. *Publs:* (ed. with E. Vivas) The Problems of Aesthetics, 1953; The New Apologists for Poetry, 1956; The Tragic Vision, 1960; A Window to Criticism: Shakespeare's Sonnets and Modern Poetics, 1964; (ed.) Northrop Frye on Modern Criticism, 1966; The Play and Place of Criticism, 1967; The Classic Vision, 1971; Visions of Extremity in Modern Literature (paperback reprints of The Tragic Vision and The Classic Vision), 2 vols., 1973; Theory of Criticism, 1976; (ed. with C. Dembo) Directions for Criticism: Structuralism and Its Alternatives, 1977; Poetic Presence and Illusion, 1979; Arts on the Level: The Fall of the Elite Object, 1981; (ed.) The Aims of Representation: Subject/Text/History, 1987; Words about Words about Words: Theory, Criticism, and the Literary Text, 1988; A Reopening of Closure: Organicism Against Itself, 1989. Add: Dept. of English and Comparative Literature, Univ. of California, Irvine, Calif. 92717, U.S.A.

KRIEGHBAUM, Hillier. American, b. 1902. Education, Social sciences (General), Writing/Journalism. Emeritus Prof. of Journalism, New York Univ., NYC, since 1973 (Prof., 1948–73). With United Press Assn., 1927–38, 1942; member of faculty, Kansas State Coll., Manhattan, 1938–42; with Veterans Assn., 1945–46; member of faculty, Univ. of Oregon, Eugene, 1946–47; with WHO, 1947–48; Visiting Prof., Manhattenville Coll., N.Y., 1973–75, and Temple Univ., Philadelphia, 1977–78. Pres., American Soc. of Journalism, Sch. Admins., 1960–61; Pres., Assn. for Education in Journalism, 1971–72. *Publs:* American Newspaper Reporting of Science News, 1941; Facts in Perspective: The Editorial Page and News Interpretation, 1956; (ed.) When Doctors Meet Reporters, 1957; Science, the News and the Public, 1958; (with E.C. Arnold) The Student Journalist: A Handbook for Staff and Advisor, 1963; Science and the Mass Media, 1967; (with H. Rawson) To Improve Secondary School Science and Mathematics Teaching, 1968; (with H. Rawson) An Investment on Knowledge, 1969; Pressures on the Press, 1972; (with E.C. Arnold) Handbook of Student Journalism, 1976; (with Kay and Katherine L. Krieghbaum, Jr.) Some Things Remembered, 1982. Add: 731 River St., Mamaroneck, N.Y. 10543, U.S.A.

KRIESBERG, Louis. American, b. 1926. International relations/Current affairs, Sociology. Prof. of Sociology, since 1966, and Dir., Prog. on the Analysis and Resolution of Conflicts, since 1986, Syracuse Univ., N.Y. Instr., Dept. of Sociology, Columbia Univ., NYC, 1953–56; Sr. Fellow in Law and the Behavioral Sciences 1957–58, and Research Assoc., Dept. of Sociology, 1958–62, Univ. of Chicago; Sr. Study Dir., National Opinion Research Center, 1958–62. *Publs:* (ed.) Social Processes in International Relations, 1968; Mothers in Poverty: A Study of Fatherless Families, 1970; Social Conflicts, 1973, 1982; (ed.) Research in Social Movements, Conflicts and Change, 11 vols., 1978–89; Social Inequality, 1979; (ed. with S. Thorsen and T. Northrup) Intractable Conflicts, 1989. Add: Dept. of Sociology, 500 University Place, Syracuse Univ., Syracuse, N.Y. 13244, U.S.A.

KRIM, Seymour. American, b. 1922. Autobiography/Memoirs, Reportage. Teacher of Creative Non-fiction, Columbia Univ., NYC, since 1978–86. Teacher of Writing Workshops, Iowa Writers Workshop, New York Univ., NYC, Univ. of Puerto Rico, and Pennsylvania State Univ., University Park, 1970–74. *Publs:* (ed.) Manhattan: Stories from a Great City, 1954; (ed.) The Beats, 1961; Views of a Nearsighted Cannoneer, 1961; Shake It for the World, Smartass, 1970; You and Me, 1974. Died, 1989.

KRIN, Sylvie. *See* **FANTONI,** Barry.

KRIPKE, Saul (Aaron). American, b. 1940. Philosophy. McCosh Prof. of Philosophy, Princeton Univ., N.J., since 1977; White Prof.-at-Large, Cornell Univ., Ithaca, N.Y., since 1977. Soc. of Fellows Lectr., Harvard Univ., Cambridge, Mass., 1963–67; Assoc. Prof., 1968–72, and Prof., 1972–76, Rockefeller Univ., NYC. *Publs:* Naming and Necessity, 1980; Wittgenstein on Rules and Private Language: An Elementary Exposition, 1982. Add: Dept. of Philosophy, Princeton Univ., Princeton, N.J. 08544, U.S.A.

KRISLOV, Samuel. American, b. 1929. Social sciences (general). Prof. of Political Science, since 1964, and Adjunct Prof. of Law, Univ. of Minnesota, Minneapolis. Member of faculty, Univ. of Oklahoma, Norman, 1957–60, and Michigan State Univ., East Lansing, 1960–64. *Publs:* (co-ed.) American Government: The Clash of Issues, 1960, 8th ed. 1984; (ed. with L. Musolf) The Politics of Regulation, 1964; The Supreme Court in the Political Process, 1965; The Negro in the Federal Bureaucracy, 1967; (with R. Dixon, A.S. Miller and L. Huston) Roles of the Attorney General of the U.S., 1968; The Supreme Court and Political General of

the U.S., 1968; The Supreme Court and Political Freedom, 1968; (with M. Feeley and S. White) The Judicial Process and Constitutional Law (lab manual), 1972; (ed. with K. Boyum, R. Schaffer and S. White) Compliance: A Multi-Disciplinary Approach, 1972; Representative Bureaucracy, 1974; (co-ed.) Understanding Crime, 1977; Representative Bureaucracy and the American Political System, 1981; American Constitutional Law, 1984. Add: 1414 Social Sciences Bldg., Univ. of Minnesota, Minneapolis, Minn. 55455, U.S.A.

KRISTOL, Irving. American, b. 1920. International relations/Current affairs, Politics/government, Social commentary/phenomena. Ed., with Nathan Glazer, The Public Interest mag., NYC, since 1965; John M. Olin Prof. of Social Thought, Grad. Sch. of Business Admin., New York Univ., since 1983. Member, Council on Foreign Relations, NYC. Managing Ed., Commentary mag., NYC, 1947–52; Co-Founder and Ed., with Stephen Spender, Encounter mag., London, 1953–58; Ed., The Reporter mag., NYC, 1959–60; Exec. Vice-Pres., Basic Books Inc., NYC, 1961–69. Member, National Council on the Humanities, 1972–77; Member, President's Commn. on White House Fellowships, 1981–84. *Publs:* (ed. with Daniel Bell) Confrontation: The Student Rebellion and the University, 1969; (ed. with Daniel Bell) Capitalism Today, 1971; On the Democratic Idea in America, 1972; (ed. with Nathan Glazer) The American Commonwealth, 1976; (ed. with Paul H. Weaver) The Americans: 1976, 1976; Two Cheers for Capitalism, 1978; (ed. with Daniel Bell) The Crisis in Economic Theory, 1981; Reflections of a Neoconservative, 1983. Add: 10 E. 53rd St., New York, N.Y. 10022, U.S.A.

KROETSCH, Robert (Paul). Canadian, b. 1927. Novels/Short stories, Poetry. Prof. of English, Univ. of Manitoba, Winnipeg. Laborer and Purser, Yellowknife Transportation Co., N.W.T., 1948–50; Information Specialist, U.S. Air Force Base, Goose Bay, Labrador, 1951–54; Prof. of English, State Univ. of New York at Binghamton. *Publs:* But We Are Exiles, 1966; The Words of My Roaring, 1966; Alberta, 1968; The Studhorse Man, 1969 (Gov.-Gen.'s Award); (with J. Bacque and P. Gravel) Creation, 1970; Gone Indian; Badlands, 1975; What the Crow Said, 1978; The Sad Phoenician (verse), 1979; Field Notes (verse), 1981; Alibi, 1983; Advice to My Friends (verse), 1985; The Lovely Treachery of Words (essays), 1989; Completed Field Notes (verse), 1989. Add: Dept. of English, Univ. of Manitoba, Winnipeg, Man. R3T 2N2, Canada.

KROG, Eustace Walter. British, b. 1917. Literature, Sports/Physical education/Keeping fit. Dir., Literature Bureau, Harare, 1959–82. Ed., Journal of the Mountain Club of Zimbabwe, 1970–89. *Publs:* (ed.) African Literature in Rhodesia, 1964; Rock Climbing in Rhodesia, 1970; A Zimbabwean Author's Guide, 1982; Shona Literature of Zimbabwe, 1982. Add: 6 Clairwood Rd., Alexandra Park, Harare, Zimbabwe.

KRONEGGER, Maria Elisabeth. American, b. 1932. Literature. Prof. of French and Comparative Literature, Michigan State Univ., East Lansing, since 1970 (Asst. Prof., 1964–67; Assoc. Prof., 1967–70). Asst. Prof. of French and Humanities, Hollins Coll., Va., 1962–64. *Publs:* James Joyce and Associate Image Makers, 1968; Impressionist Literature, 1973; Phénoménologie et Littérature: l'origine de l'oeuvre d'art, 1987; The Life Significance of Baroque Poetry, 1988. Add: Wells Hall 502, Michigan State Univ., East Lansing, Mich. 48824, U.S.A.

KROPP, Lloyd. American. Novels/Short stories. Teacher Southern Illinois Univ., Edwardsville, since 1975. Teacher, Univ. of North Carolina, Greensboro, 1970–75. *Publs:* The Drift, 1969; Who is Mary Stark?, 1974; One Hundred Times to China, 1979; Greencastle, 1987. Add: 32 S. Meadow Lane, Edwardsville, Ill. 62025, U.S.A.

KÜBLER-ROSS, Elisabeth. American (b. Swiss), b. 1926. Medicine/Health, Psychiatry, Sociology. Pres. and Chmn. of Bd., Shanti Nilaya Growth and Health Center, Escondido, Calif., since 1977. Instr. in Psychiatry, Colorado General Hospital, Univ. of Colorado Medical School, 1962–65; Member of Staff, LaRabida Children's Hospital and Research Center, Chicago, 1965–70 (Chief Consultant and Research Liaison Secretary, 1969–70); Asst. Prof. in Psychiatry, Billings Hospital, Univ. of Chicago, 1965–70; Medical Dir., Family Service and Mental Health Center, Chicago Heights, Ill., 1970–73; Pres., Ross Medical Assos., Flossmoor, Ill., 1973–77. *Publs:* On Death and Dying, 1969; Questions and Answers on Death and Dying, 1974; Death: The Final Stage of Growth, 1975; To Live Until We Say Goodbye, 1978; Working It Through, 1981; Living With Death and Dying, 1981; Remember the Secret, 1981; On Children and Death, 1985; AIDS: The Ultimate Challenge, 1988. Add: Macmillan Publishing Co., Inc., 866 Third Ave., New York, N.Y. 10022, U.S.A.

KUBLY, Herbert (Oswald). American, b. 1915. Novels/Short stories, Plays/Screenplays, Travel/Exploration/Adventure. Prof. Emeritus of English, Univ. of Wisconsin-Parkside, Kenosha, since 1984 (Prof., 1969–84). Reporter and Art Critic, Pittsburgh Sun Telegraph, 1937–42; Reporter and Feature Writer, New York Herald Tribune, 1942–44; Music Critic, Time mag., NYC, 1945–47; Secty., Dramatists Guild of America, 1947–49; Assoc. Prof., Univ. of Illinois, 1949–54; Writer, Holiday and Life mags., 1955–61; Visiting Lectr., Columbia Univ., and The New Sch. of Social Research, NYC, 1962–64; Prof., San Francisco State Coll., 1964–68. *Publs:* Men to the Sea (play), 1944; Inherit the Wind (play), 1948; American in Italy, 1955; Easter in Sicily, 1956; Varieties of Love, 1958; Italy, 1961; The Whistling Zone, 1963; Switzerland, 1964; At Large 1964; Gods and Heroes, 1968; The Virus (play), 1973; Perpetual Care (play), 1974; The Duchess of Glover, 1975; Native's Return, 1981; The Parkside Stories, 1985. Add: W 4970 Kubly Rd., New Glarus, Wisc. 53574, U.S.A.

KUBRICK, Stanley. American, b. 1928. Plays/Screenplays. Film dir. and producer. Staff Photographer, Look mag., 1946–50. *Publs:* (screenplays) Killer's Kiss, 1955; The Killing, 1956; Paths of Glory, 1957; (co-writer) Dr. Strangelove, 1963; 2001: A Space Odyssey, 1969; A Clockwork Orange, 1972; Barry Lyndon, 1975; The Shining, 1979; Full Metal Jacket, 1987. Add: c/o Louis C. Blau, 10100 Santa Monica Blvd, Los Angeles, Calif. 90067, U.S.A.

KUDIAN, Mischa. British. Children's fiction, Poetry, Literature, Translations. Freelance writer, ed., lectr., and painter. *Publs:* (trans.) Scenes from an Armenian Childhood, by Vahan Totovents, 1962, 1980; Three Apples Fell from Heaven, 1969; (ed. and trans.) The Bard of Loree, by Hovannes Toumanian, 1970; (ed. and reteller) The Saga of Sassoun, by Mischa Kudian, 1970; (ed. and trans.) Tell Me, Bella, by Vahan Totovents, 1972; (ed. and trans.) Soviet Armenian Poetry, 1974; (ed. & trans.) The Muse of Sheerak, by Avetik Issahakian, 1975; (trans.) Selected Works by Avetik Issahakian, 1976; (ed. and trans.) Lamentations of Narek, by Grigor Narekatsi, 1977; (ed. and trans.) Honourable Beggars, by Hagop Baronian, 1978; Candy Floss (selected poems), 1980; (ed. and trans.) Retreat Without Song, by Shahan Shahnour, 1982; More Apples Fell from Heaven, 1982; (trans.) Komitas, the Shepherd Songs, by Levon Miridjanian, 1983; Flutterby (satirical poems), 1984; This Day and Age (satirical poems), 1984; Tenpence a Laugh (satirical poems), 1984; Witricks Galore! (collected poems), 1984; (trans.) The Tailor's Visitors, by Shahan Shahnour, 1984; (ed. and trans.) Jonathan Son of Jeremiah, by Vahan Totovents, 1985; Jesus the Son, by Nerses Shnorhali, 1986. Add: c/o Barclays Bank, 15 Langham Pl., London W1, England.

KUEHL, Warren F(rederick). American, b. 1924. History, International relations/Current affairs. Prof. Emeritus, Univ. of Akron, Ohio, since 1986 (Prof. and Head of History, 1964–71; Prof. of History, and Dir., Center for Peace Studies, 1970–86). Gen. Ed., Library of World Peace Studies, Clearwater Publishing Co. Asst. Prof., Rockford Coll., Ill., 1955–58; Assoc. Prof., 1958–61, and Prof., 1961–64, Mississippi State Univ., State College; Pres., Society for Historians of American Foreign Relations, 1985. *Publs:* Blow the Man Down!: A Yankee Seaman's Adventure Under Sail, 1959; Hamilton Holt: Journalist, Internationalist, Educator, 1960; Dissertations in History: An Index of Dissertations Completed in History Departments of the United States and Canadian Universities, 1873-1960, 1969; Seeking World Order: The United States International Organization to 1920, 1969; Dissertations in History: An Index to Dissertations Completed in History Departments of United States and Canadian Universities, 1961–1970, 1972; Biographical Dictionary of Internationalists, 1983; Dissertations in History: An Index to Dissertations Completed in History Departments of the United States and Canada 1970–1980, 1985. Add: 6995 Country Lakes Circle, Sarasota, Fla. 34243, U.S.A.

KUEHNELT-LEDDIHN, Erik (Ritter von). Also writes as Francis Stuart Campbell, O'Leary, and T. Vitezovic. Austrian, b. 1909. Novels/Short stories, Humanities, International relations/Current affairs. Lectr. and Columnist, since 1949; Corresp., The National Review, since 1955. Special Adviser, Brockhaus Encyclopedia, since 1973. *Publs:* (as T. Vitezovic) Die Anderen, 1931; Gates of Hell, 1933; Night Over the East, 1936; Moscow 1979, 1940; (as F.S. Campbell) The Menace of the Herd, 1943; (as O'Leary) Amerikas Gründerväter, 1948; (as O'Leary) Mord im Blaulicht, 1949; (co-author) Born Catholics, 1954; Liberty or Equality, 1954; Black Banners, 1954; (co-author) Realities, 1958; (co-author) Wanderwege, 1961; (co-author) Between Two Cities, 1962; Die Gottlosen, 1962; (co-author) Schicksalsfragen, 1965; (co-author) Moskau-Peking, 1965; Lateinamerika-Geschichte eines Scheiterns, 1967; Seeds of Anarchy, 1969; Amerika—Leitbild im Zwielicht, 1971; (co-author)

Adel in Österreich, 1971; Luftschlösser, Lügen, Legenden, 1972; Leftism, 1974; Das Rätsel Liebe, 1975; Narrenschiff auf Linkskurs, 1977; Intelligent American's Guide to Europe 1979; Rechts, wo das Herz schlägt, 1980; Austria Infelix, 1983; Die falsch gestellten Weichen, 1985; Gleichheit oder Freiheit?, 1985; (co-author) Moral Wisdom in the Allocation of Economic Resources, 1987; (co-author) Modern Age: The First Twenty-Five Years, 1988. Add: A-6072 Lans, Tyrol, Austria.

KUENNE, Robert Eugene. American, b. 1924. Economics, Military/Defence. Prof. of Economics, Princeton Univ., N.J., since 1956; Consultant, Inst. for Defense Analyses, Arlington, Va., since 1968. Visiting Prof. of Military Systems Analysis, U.S. Army War Coll., Carlisle Barracks, Pa., 1967–84. *Publs:* (with G.B. Turner and R.D. Challener) National Security in the Nuclear Age, 1960; The Theory of General Economic Equilibrium, 1963; The Attack Submarine: A Study in Strategy, 1965; The Polaris Missile Strike: A General Economic Systems Analysis, 1966; (ed.) Monopolistic Competition Theory: Studies in Impact, 1967; Microeconomic Theory of the Market Mechanism: A General Equilibrium Approach, 1968; Eugen von Böhm-Bawerk, 1971; Rivalrous Consonance: A Theory of General Oligopolistic Equilibrium, 1986; (co-author) Warranties in Weapon Systems Procurement, 1988. Add: 63 Bainbridge St., Princeton, N.J. 08540, U.S.A.

KUH, Richard H. American, b. 1921. Law. Lawyer, Warshaw Burstein Cohen Schlesinger and Kuh, NYC. District Attorney, New York County, 1974. *Publs:* Foolish Figleaves?: Pornography in, and out of, Court, 1967. Add: 14 Washington Pl., New York, N.Y., U.S.A.

KUHN, Thomas S. American, b. 1922. Intellectual history, Sciences. Prof., Philosophy and History of Science, Massachusetts Inst. of Technology, Cambridge, since 1979. With the radio research lab., Am-British Lab., OSRD, 1943–45; member of faculty, 1948–57, Harvard Univ., Cambridge, Mass., and Univ. of California, Berkeley, 1957–64; Prof., 1964–68, and M. Taylor Pyne Prof. of the History of Science, 1968–79, Princeton Univ., New Jersey, and Member, Inst. for Advanced Study, Princeton, 1972–79. Pres., History of Science Soc., 1968–70. *Publs:* The Copernican Revolution: Planetary Astronomy in the Development of Western Thought, 1957, 1959; The Structure of Scientific Revolutions, 1962, 1970; (with John L. Heilbron, Paul L. Forman, and Lini Allen) Sources for History of Quantum Physics: An Inventory and Report, 1966; The Essential Tension: Selected Studies in Scientific Tradition and Change, 1977; Black-Body Theory and the Quantum Discontinuity 1894-1912, 1978. Add: c/o Univ. of Chicago Press, 5801 Ellis Ave., 4th Flr., Chicago, Ill. 60637, U.S.A.

KULSKI, W(ladyslaw) W(szebor). Has also written as W.W. Coole and W.M. Knight-Patterson. American, b. 1903. International relations/Current affairs, Politics/Government. With Polish Diplomatic Service, 1928–45; Prof. of Political Science, Univ. of Alabama, Birmingham, 1947–51, and Syracuse Univ., N.Y., 1951–64; James B. Duke Prof. of Political Science, Duke Univ., Durham, N.C., 1964–73. *Publs:* Le problème de la securité internationale, 1927; (as W.W. Coole) Thus Spake Germany, 1941; (as W.M. Knight-Patterson) Germany from Defeat to Conquest, 1945; The Soviet Regime, 1954; Peaceful Co-Existence, 1959; De Gaulle and the World, 1966; International Relations in a Revolutionary Age, 1968; The Soviet Union in World Affairs, 1973; Germany and Poland, 1976. Add: c/o Wachovia Bank and Trust Co., P.O. Box 2252, Durham, N.C. 27702, U.S.A.

KULTERMANN, Udo. American (b. German), b. 1927. Architecture, Art. Ruth and Norman Moore Prof. of Architecture, Washington Univ., St. Louis, since 1986 (Prof. of Architecture, 1967–86). Dir., Museum Schloss Morsbroich, Leverkusen, West Germany, 1959–64; Member, Architecture Cttee., Venice Biennale, 1979–82. *Publs:* Architecture of Today, 1958; Hans und Wassili Luckhardt: Bauten und Entwuerfe, 1958; Dynamische Architektur, 1959; New Japanese Architecture, 1960; Der Schluessel zur Architektur von heute, 1963; Junge deutsche Bildhauer, 1963; New Architecture in Africa, 1963; New Architecture in the World, 1965; History of Art History, 1966; Architektur der Gegenwart: Kunst der Welt, 1967; The New Sculpture, 1967; Gabriel Grupello, 1968; The New Painting, 1969; New Directions in African Architecture, 1969; (with Werner Hofmann) Modern Architecture in Color, 1970; Kenzo Tange: Architecture and Urban Design, 1970; Art and Life, 1970; New Realism, 1972; Ernest Trova, 1977; Die Architektur im 20. Jahrhundert, 1978; I Contemporanei (vol. XIV of Storia della Scultura del Mondo), 1979; Architecture in the Seventies, 1980; Architekten der Dritten Welt, 1980; Zeitgenoessische Architektur in Osteuropa, 1985; Kleine Geschichte der Kunsttheorie, 1987; Visible Cities—Invisible Cities, 1988. Add: Sch. of Architecture, Washington Univ., St. Louis, Mo. 63130, U.S.A.

KUMAR, Shiv K(umar). Indian, b. 1921. Novels/Short stories, Poetry, Literature. Lectr., D.A.V. Coll., Lahore, 1945–47, and Hansraj Coll., Delhi, 1948–49; Programme Exec., All India Radio, Delhi, 1949; Sr. Lectr. and Chmn. of the Dept. of English, Government Coll., Chandigarh, 1953–56; Reader in English, Panjab Univ., Hoshiarpur, 1956–59; Prof. and Chmn. of the Dept. of English, Osmania Univ., Hyderabad, 1959–76; Prof. and Chmn. of the Dept. of English, Univ. of Hyderabad, 1976–79. *Publs:* Virginia Woolf and Intuition, 1957; Virginia Woolf and Bergson's Durée, 1957; (ed.) Modern Short Stories, 1958; (ed.) Leaves of Grass, by Walt Whitman, 1962; Bergson and the Stream of Consciousness Novel, 1962; (ed.) Apollo's Lyre, 1962; (with M.M. Maison) Examine Your English, 1964; (ed.) The Red Badge of Courage, by Stephen Crane, 1964; (ed.) British Romantic Poets: Recent Revaluations, 1966; (ed., with Keith McKean) Critical Approaches to Fiction, 1968; (ed.) British Victorian Literature: Recent Revaluations, 1969; (ed.) The Life, Adventures, and Pyracies of the Famous Captain Singleton, by Daniel Defoe, 1969; Articulate Silences (verse), 1970; (ed.) Indian Verse in English 1970, 1971; Cobwebs in the Sun (verse), 1974; The Last Wedding Anniversary (play), 1975; Subterfuges (verse), 1976; Woodpeckers (verse), 1979; The Bone's Prayer (novel), 1979; Beyond Love and Other Stories, 1980; Nude Before God (novel), 1983. Add: 2-F/Kakatiya Nagar, P.O. Jamia Osmania, Hyderabad 500 007, India.

KUMIN, Maxine. American, b. 1925. Novels/Short stories, Children's fiction, Poetry, Literature. Instr. in English, 1958–61, and Lectr., 1965–68, Tufts Univ., Medford, Mass.; Lectr. in English, Newton Coll., Mass., 1971–72; Visiting Lectr. in English, Univ. of Massachusetts, Amherst, 1972; Adjunct Prof. of Writing, Columbia Univ., 1975; Hurst Prof. of Literature, Washington Univ., Nov. 1977, and Brandeis Univ., Fall 1975; Consultant in Poetry, Library of Congress, 1981–82; Visiting Lectr., Princeton Univ., 1981–82 (Spring 1977 and 1979); Poet-in-Residence, Bucknell Univ., Penn., 1983; Visiting Prof., Mass. Inst. of Technology, Spring 1984; Faculty, Salzburg Seminar, June 1985; Visiting Writer, Massachusetts Inst. of Technology, 1986–87. *Publs:* juvenile fiction—Sebastian and the Dragon, 1960; Spring Things, 1961; Summer Story, 1961; Follow the Fall, 1961; A Winter Friend, 1961; Mittens in May, 1962; No One Writes a Letter to the Snail, 1962; Archibald the Traveling Poodle, 1963; Eggs of Things, 1963; (with Anne Sexton) More Eggs of Things, 1963; Speedy Digs Downside Up, 1964; The Beach Before Breakfast, 1964: Paul Bunyon, 1966; (with Anne Sexton) The Wizard Tears, 1975; What Color is Caesar, 1978; adult fiction and non-fiction—Through Dooms of Love (in U.K. as A Daughter and Her Loves), 1965; The Passions of Uxport, 1968; The Abduction, 1971; The Designated Heir, 1974; To Make a Prairie: Essays on Poets, Poetry, and Country Living, 1979; Why Can't We Live Together Like Civilized Human Beings? (short stories), 1982; In Deep: Country Essays, 1987; poetry—Halfway, 1961; The Privilege, 1965; The Nightmare Factory, 1970; Up Country, 1972; House, Bridge, Fountain, Gate, 1975; The Retrieval System, 1978; Our Ground Time Here Will Be Brief: New and Selected Poems, 1982; The Long Approach, 1985; Nurture, 1989. Add: Joppa Rd., Warner, N.H. 03278, U.S.A.

KUNITZ, Stanley (Jasspon). American, b. 1905. Poetry, Literature, Essays. Staff Member, Writing Dept., Fine Arts Work Center, Provincetown, Mass., since 1968. Ed., Wilson Library Bulletin, NYC, 1928–43; member of faculty, Bennington Coll., Vt., 1946–49; Prof. of English, State Univ. of New York, Potsdam, 1949–50; Lectr., New Sch. for Social Research, NYC, 1950–57; Visiting Prof., Univ. of Washington, Seattle, 1955–56, Queens Coll., Flushing, N.Y., 1956–57, and Brandeis Univ., Waltham, Mass., 1958–59; Dir., YM-YWHA Poetry Workshop, NYC, 1958–62; Danforth Visiting Lectr., U.S., 1961–63; Lectr., 1963–67, and Adjunct Prof. of Writing, 1967–85, Columbia Univ., NYC; Ed., Yale Series of Younger Poets, Yale Univ., Press, New Haven, Conn., 1969–77; Visiting Prof., Yale Univ., New Haven, Conn., 1970, and Rutgers Univ., Camden, N.J., 1974; Consultant in Poetry, Library of Congress, Washington, D.C., 1974–75; Visiting Prof. and Sr. Fellow in Humanities, Princeton Univ., N.J., 1978; Visiting Prof., Vassar Coll., Poughkeepsie, N.Y., 1981. *Publs:* Intellectual Things, 1930; (ed. as Dilly Tante) Living Authors: A Book of Biographies, 1931; (ed. with H. Haycraft and W.C. Hadden) Authors Today and Yesterday: A Companion Volume to "Living Authors", 1933; (ed. with H. Haycraft) British Authors of the Nineteenth Century, 1936; (ed. with H. Haycraft) American Authors, 1600-1900: A Biographical Dictionary of American Literature, 1938; (ed. with H. Haycraft) Twentieth Century Authors: A Biographical Dictionary of Modern Literature, 1942; (with V. Colby) First Supplement, 1955; Passport to the War: A Selection of Poems, 1944; (ed. with H. Haycraft) British Authors Before 1800: A Biographical Dictionary, 1952; Selected Poems 1928-1958, 1958; (ed.) Poems, by John Keats, 1964; (ed. with V. Colby) European Authors, 1000-1900: A Biographical Dictionary of

European Literature, 1967; The Testing-Tree: Poems, 1971; (ed. and trans. with M. Hayward) Poems of Akhmatova, 1973; The Terrible Threshold: Selected Poems, 1940–1970, 1974; (trans.) Story under Full Sail, by A. Voznesensky, 1974; A Kind of Order, A Kind of Folly (essays), 1975; (ed. and co-trans.) Orchard Lamps, by Ivan Drach, 1978; The Poems of Stanley Kunitz 1928–1978, 1979; The Wellfleet Whale and Companion Poems, 1983; Next-to-Last Things (poems and essays), 1985; (ed.) The Essential Blake, 1987. Add: 37 West 12th St., New York, N.Y. 10011, U.S.A.

KUNSTLER, William M. American, b. 1919. Law, Autobiography/Memoirs/Personal. Partner, Kunstler & Kunstler, lawyers, NYC, since 1949; Assoc. Prof. of Law, New York Law Sch., NYC, since 1950, and Pace Coll., NYC, since 1951; Lectr., New Sch. for Social Research, NYC, since 1966. *Publs:* Our Pleasant Vices, 1941; The Law of Accidents, 1954; First Degree, 1960; Beyond a Reasonable Doubt, 1961; The Case for Courage, 1962; . . . And Justice for All, 1963; The Minister and the Choir Singer, 1964; Deep in My Heart, 1966; The Hall-Mills Murder Case, 1980; Trials and Tribulations, 1985. Add: 13 Gay St., New York, N.Y. 10014, U.S.A.

KUNTZ, John Kenneth. American, b. 1934. Theology/Religion. Prof. of Religion, Sch. of Religion, Univ. of Iowa, Iowa City, since 1976 (Asst. Prof., 1967–70; Assoc. Prof., 1970–76). Instr. in Biblical History, 1963–65, and Asst. Prof., 1965–67, Wellesley Coll., Mass. *Publs:* The Self-Revelation of God, 1967; The World of the Old Testament, 1968, 1969, 1979, 1988; The World of the New Testament, The People of Ancient Israel: An Introduction to Old Testament Literature, History, and Thought, 1974; Religion and Women: Images of Women in the Bible, 1978, 1984; Biblical Archaeology: Scratching the Surface in the Holy Land, 1982. Add: 321 Koser Ave., Iowa City, Iowa 52246, U.S.A.

KUPER, Adam (Jonathan). British, b. 1941. Anthropology/Ethnology, Social sciences (general). Prof. and Head of Dept. of Human Sciences, Brunel Univ., Uxbridge, Middx.; Ed., Current Anthropology. Lectr., Makerere Univ., Uganda, 1967–70, and University Coll., London, 1970–76; Prof. of African Cultural, Anthropology, Univ. of Leiden, Netherlands, 1976–85. *Publs:* Kalahari Village Politics: An African Democracy, 1970; (co-ed.) Councils in Action, 1971; Anthropologists and Anthropology: The British School 1922–1972, 1973; Changing Jamaica, 1976; (ed.) The Social Anthropology of Radcliffe-Brown, 1977; Wives for Cattle: Bridewealth and Marriage in Southern Africa, 1982; (co-ed.) The Social Science Encyclopaedia, 1985; South Africa and the Anthropologist, 1987; The Invention of Primitive Society: Transformations of an Illusion, 1988. Add: Brunel Univ., Uxbridge, Middx. UB8 3H, England.

KUPER, Leo. American, b. 1908. Race relations, Sociology. Prof. of Sociology, Univ. of California, Los Angeles, since 1961 (Dir., African Studies Center, 1968–72). Secty., National War Memorial Health Foundn., South Africa, 1946–47; Lectr. in Sociology, Univ. of Birmingham, England, 1949–52; Chmn., Dept. of Sociology, Univ. of Natal, South Africa, 1952–61. *Publs:* (ed.) Living in Towns: Selected Research Papers in Urban Sociology, 1953; Passive Resistance in South Africa, 1956; (with H. Watts and R. Davies) Durban: A Study in Racial Ecology, 1958; The College Brew (satire), 1960; (ed. with H. Kuper) African Law: Adaptation and Development, 1965; An African Bourgeoisie: Race, Class, and Politics in South Africa, 1965; (ed. with M.G. Smith) Pluralism in Africa, 1969; Race, Class and Power, 1974; The Pity of It All, 1977; Genocide, 1981; Prevention of Genocide, 1985. Add: 1282 Warner Ave., Los Angeles, Calif. 90024, U.S.A.

KUPFERBERG, Herbert. American, b. 1918. Children's non-fiction, Music, Biography. Sr. Ed., Parade mag., NYC, since 1967. With New York Herald Tribune, 1942–66. *Publs:* Those Fabulous Philadelphians, 1969; The Mendelssohns, 1971; Felix Mendelssohn (juvenile), 1972; A Rainbow of Sound (juvenile), 1973; Opera, 1975; Tanglewood, 1976; Basically Bach, 1985; The Book of Classical Music Lists, 1985; Amadeus: A Mozart Mosaic, 1986. Add: 113-14 72 Rd., Forest Hills, N.Y. 11375, U.S.A.

KUREISHI, Hanif. British, b. 1954. Plays/Screenplays. Resident writer, Royal Court Theatre, London, 1981, 1985–86. *Publs:* Borderline, 1981; Birds of Passage, 1983; Outskirts, The King and Me, Tomorrow—Today! 1983; My Beautiful Launderette (screenplay), 1986; Sammy and Rosie Get Laid (screenplay), 1988. Add: c/o Sheila Lemon, Lemon and Durbridge Ltd., 24 Pottery Lane, London W11 4LZ, England.

KURIEN, Christopher (Thomas). Indian, b. 1931. Economics, Sociology. Prof., Madras Inst. of Development Studies, since 1978 (Dir., 1978–

88). Tutor, 1953–54, Lectr. in Economics, 1954–62, Prof. and Head, Dept. of Economics, 1962–78, and National Fellow in Economics, 1975–77, Madras Christian Coll., India. *Publs:* Our Five Year Plans, 1966; (ed. with S.V. Anantakrishnan, C.T.K. Chari and S. Rajiva) India Today, 1967; Indian Economic Crisis, 1969; A Theoretical Approach to the Indian Economy, 1970; (ed.) A Guide to Research in Economics, 1973; Poverty and Development, 1974; Poverty, Planning and Social Transformation, 1978; (with Josef James) Economic Change in Tamil Nadu, 1979; Dynamics of Rural Transformation, 1981. Add: 79 Second Main Rd., Gandhinagar, Madras 600 020, India.

KURLAND, Michael (Joseph). Also writes as Jennifer Plum. American, b. 1938. Mystery/Crime/Suspense, Science fiction/Fantasy. Ed., Pennyfarthing Press, San Francisco, since 1976. News Ed., KPFK-Radio, Los Angeles, 1966; Teacher of English, Happy Valley Sch., Ojai, Calif., 1967; Ed., Crawdaddy, NYC, 1969; also former play dir., road mgr. for a band, advertising copywriter, and freelance ghostwriter and writer of SF short stories. *Publs:* (with Chester Anderson) Ten Years to Doomsday, 1964; Mission: Third Force (suspense), 1967; Mission: Tank War (suspense), 1968; Mission: Police Action (suspense), 1969; A Plague of Spies (suspense), 1969; The Unicorn Girl, 1969; Transmission Error, 1970; (as Jennifer Plum) The Secret of Benjamin Square (suspense), 1972; The Whenabouts of Burr, 1975; Pluribus, 1975; Tomorrow Knight, 1976; The Princes of Earth (juvenile), 1978; (ed.) The Redward Edward Papers, by Avram Davidson, 1978; (ed.) The Best of Avram Davidson, 1979; The Infernal Device (suspense), 1979; (with S.W. Barton) The Last President, 1980; Psi Hunt, 1980; Death by Gaslight, 1982; Star Griffin, 1987; Ten Little Wizards, 1988. Add: c/o Doubleday, 666 Fifth Ave., New York, N.Y. 10103, U.S.A.

KURTZ, Katherine. American, b. 1944. Novels/Short stories. Full-time writer. *Publs:* Deryni Rising, 1970; Deryni Checkmate, 1972; High Deryni, 1973; Camber of Culdi, 1976; Saint Camber, 1978; Camber the Heretic, 1981 Lammas Night, 1983; The Bishop's Heir, 1984; The King's Justice, 1985; The Quest for Saint Camber, 1986; The Deryni Archives, 1986; The Legacy of Lehr, 1986; The Harrowing of Gwynedd, 1989. Add: Holybrooke Hall, Kilmacanogue, Bray, Co. Wicklow, Ireland.

KURZ, Ron. American, b. 1940. Novels/Short stories. Former Theatre Mgr., Playhouse Theatre, Baltimore, Md. *Publs:* Lethal Gas, 1974; Black Rococo, 1976; Eyes of a Stranger (screenplay), 1981; Friday the 13th II (screenplay), 1981. Add: Box 164, Antrim, N.H. 03440, U.S.A.

KURZMAN, Dan. American, b. 1929. History, Biography, Documentaries/Reportage. Contrib., Washington Star, since 1975, and Independent News Alliance, since 1979. Corresp., Intnl. News Service, Paris, 1948; Feature Writer, Marshall Plan Information Office, Paris, 1948–49; Corresp., National Broadcasting Co., Middle East, 1950–53; Bureau Chief, McGraw Hill World News Service, Tokyo, 1954–59; Corresp., Washington Post, 1962–68. *Publs:* Kishi and Japan: The Search of the Sun (biography), 1960; Subversion of the Innocents, 1963; Santo Domingo: Revolt of the Damned, 1965; Genesis, 1948; The First Arab-Israeli War, 1970; The Race for Rome, 1975; The Bravest Battle: The Twenty Eight Days of the Warsaw Ghetto Uprising, 1976; Miracle of November: Madrid's Epic Stand 1936, 1980; Ben-Gurion: Prophet of Fire, 1983; Day of the Bomb: Countdown to Hiroshima, 1985; A Killing Wind: Inside the Bhopal Catastrophe, 1987. Add: c/o H. Knopf, 187-Blvd., Apt. 9-H, Passaic,N.J. 07055, U.S.A.

KURZWEIL, Erich Zvi. British/Israel, b. 1911. Education. Prof. of Education, Technion-Israel Inst. of Technology, since 1957 (formerly Sr. Lectr., Assoc. Prof., Head, Dept. of Teacher Training and Gen. Studies). Inspector of Jewish Schs., Central Council for Jewish Education, London, 1947–50; Dir. of English Studies, Hugim High Sch., Haifa, Israel, 1950–57. *Publs:* Modern Trends in Jewish Education, 1964; Anxiety and Education, 1968; Education in a Technological Society, 1968; The Educational Thought of Janusz Korczak, 1968; Vorläufer Progressiver Erziehung, 1974; M. Bruber on Education, 1978; Pathways in Jewish Education, 1981; The Modern Impulse of Traditional Judaism, 1985; Hauptströmungen jüdischer Pädagogik in Deutschland, 1987. Add: 4 Aaron Lane, Ahuza, Haifa, Israel.

KUSHNER, Donn. American, b. 1927. Biology, Children's fiction, Novels/Short stories, Sciences. Prof. of Biology, Univ. of Ottawa, since 1987 (Assoc. Prof. 1965–67). North American Ed., Archives of Microbiology, since 1984; Reviewer of Scientific Books for Children, Canadian Children's Literature. Research Scientist, Forest Insect lab., Sault Sainte Marie, Ont., 1954–61; Research Scientist, National Research Council of Canada, Ottawa, 1961–65. Co-Ed., Canadian Journal of Microbiology, 1977–83. *Publs:* (ed.) Microbial Life in Extreme Environments, 1978; The Violin-Maker's Gift, 1980; The Witness and Other Stories, 1980; Uncle Jacob's Ghost Story, 1984; A Book Dragon, 1987. Add: 289 Clemow Ave., Ottawa, Ont. K1S 2B7, Canada.

KUSHNER, Harold S. American, b. 1935. Theology/Religion. Rabbi, Temple Israel of Natick, Mass., since 1966. Pres., New England Region, Rabbinical Assembly, 1972–74; Pres., Clergy Assn. of Natick, Mass., 1976–78; Ed., Conservative Judaism mag., 1980–84. *Publs:* When Children Ask about God, 1971; Commanded to Live (collected sermons), 1973; When Bad Things Happen to Good People, 1981; When All You've Ever Wanted Isn't Enough, 1986. Add: 145 Hartford St., Natick, Mass., 01760, U.S.A.

KUSIN, Vladimir V. British, b. 1929. History, Politics/Government, Translations. Deputy Dir., Research and Analysis Dept., Radio Free Europe, Munich, since 1979. Lectr., trans., abstractor, and journalist in Czechoslovakia, 1953–68; Research Fellow, Comenius Centre, Univ. of Lancaster, 1969; Sr. Ed., Soviet and East European Abstracts Series, 1970–76, and Dir., 1976–79, Intnl. Information Centre for Soviet and East European Studies, Univ. of Glasgow. *Publs:* (trans.) The Life and Death of Harry Oakes, by G. Bocca, 1965; (trans.) Bikini Beach, by G. Bocca, 1967; (trans.) Rosencrantz and Guildenstern are Dead, by T. Stoppard, 1968; The Intellectual Origins of the Prague Spring, 1971; Political Grouping in the Czechoslovak Reform Movement, 1972; (ed.) The Czechoslovak Reform Movement 1968, 1973; (with Z. Hejzlar) Czechoslovakia 1968–69, 1975; From Dubcek to Charter 77, 1978. Add: Elektrastr. 22a, 8000 Munich 81, West Germany.

KUSKIN, Karla. Has also written as Nicholas Charles. American, b. 1932. Children's fiction and verse. *Publs:* Roar and More (verse), 1956; James and the Rain (verse), 1959; In the Middle of the Trees (verse), 1958; The Animals and the Ark (verse), 1958; Just Like Everyone Else (fiction), 1959; Which Horse is William? (fiction), 1959; Square as a House (verse),1960; The Bear Who Saw the Spring (verse), 1961; All Sizes of Noises (verse), 1962; (as Nicholas Charles) How Do You Get from Here to There? (verse), 1962; Alexander Soames: His Poems, 1962; ABCDEFGHIJKLMNOPQRSTUVWXYZ (verse), 1963; The Rose on My Cake (verse), 1964; Sand and Snow (verse), 1965; (as Nicholas Charles) Jane Ann June Spoon and Her Very Adventurous Trip to the Moon (verse), 1966; The Walk the Mouse Girls Took (fiction), 1967; Watson, The Smartest Dog in the U.S.A.(fiction), 1968; In the Flaky Frosty Morning (verse), 1969; Any Me I Want to Be: Poems (verse), 1972; What Did You Bring Me? (fiction), 1973; What Do You Mean by Design? (screenplay), 1973; An Electric Talking Picture (screenplay), 1973; Near the Window Tree: Poems and Notes, 1975; A Boy Had a Mother Who Bought Him a Hat (verse), 1976; A Space Story, 1978; Herbert Hated Being Small (verse), 1979; Dogs and Dragons, Trees and Dreams (poetry collection), 1980; Night Again (verse), 1981; The Philharmonic Gets Dressed (fiction), 1982; Something Sleeping in the Hall (verse), 1985; The Dallas Titans Get Ready for Bed, 1986; Jerusalem, Shining Still, 1987. Add: 96 Joralemon St., Brooklyn, N.Y. 11201, U.S.A.

KUSTOW, Michael (David). British, b. 1929. Theatre, Translations. Commissioning Ed., Channel 4 TV, since 1981. Dir., Inst. of Contemporary Arts, London, 1967–71; Assoc. Dir., National Theatre of Great Britain,1973–81; Lectr. in Dramatic Arts, Harvard Univ., Cambridge, Mass., 1980–82. *Publs:* (ed.) The Book of Us, 1968; (trans.) Jose Triana: Night of the Assassins, 1968; Tank, 1975; Roger Planchon and People's Theatre, 1975; (trans.) Stravinsky: The Soldier's Story, 1980; One in Four, 1987. Add: c/o Channel 4 TV, 60 Charlotte St., London W1, England.

KYGER, Joanne. American, b. 1934. Poetry. Performer and poet in experimental television project, 1967–68. *Publs:* The Tapestry and the Web, 1965; The Fool in April: A Poem, 1966; Places to Go, 1970; Joanne, 1970; Desecheo Notebook, 1971; Trip Out and Fall Back, 1974; All This Every Day, 1975; The Wonderful Focus of You, 1980;Mexico Blondé, 1981; Japan and India Journal, 1981; Going On: Selected Poems 1958–1980, 1983; Phenomenological, 1989. Add: Box 688, Bolinas, Calif. 94924, U.S.A.

KYLE, Duncan. Pseud. for John Broxholme. Also writes as James Meldrum. British. Mystery/Crime/Suspense. *Publs:* A Cage of Ice, 1970; Flight into Fear, 1972; A Raft of Swords, 1974; (as James Meldrum) The Semonov Impulse, 1975; Terror's Cradle, 1975; In Deep, 1976; Black Camelot, 1978; Green River High, 1979; Stalking Point, 1981; The King's Commissar, 1983; The Dancing Men, 1985; The Back of Bourke. Add: c/o William Collins Ltd., 8 Grafton St., London W1X 3LA, England.

L

LaBARRE, Weston. American, b. 1911. Anthropology/Ethnology, Mythology/Folklore, Psychiatry. James B. Duke Prof. of Anthropology, Duke Univ., Durham, N.C., since 1970 (Asst. Prof., 1946–48; Assoc. Prof., 1948–58; Prof., 1958–70). Faculty member, Rutgers Univ., New Brunswick, N.J., 1939–43. *Publs:* The Aymara Indians of the Lake Titicaca Plateau, 1948; The Human Animal, 1954; Materia Medica of the Aymara Indians, 1959; (co-author) Normal Adolescence, 1968; They Shall Take Up Serpents: Psychology of the Southern Snakehandling Cult, 1969; The Peyote Cult, 1969; The Ghost Dance, 1972; Culture in Context: Selected Papers, 1979; Muelos: A Stone Age Superstition About Sexuality. Add: 172 Carol Woods, Chapel Hill, N.C. 27514, U.S.A.

LABERN, Arthur (Joseph). British, b. 1909. Novels/Short stories, Mystery/Crime/Suspense. Former journalist: crime reporter, feature writer, and war correspondent for the Daily Mirror, Evening Standard, and Daily Mail, all London. *Publs:* mystery novels—It Always Rains on Sunday, 1945; Night Darkens the Street, 1947; Paper Orchid, 1948; Pennygreen Street, 1950; The Big-Money Box, 1960; Brighton Belle, 1963; Goodbye Piccadilly, Farewell Leicester Square, 1966 (as Frenzy, 1971); A Nice Class of People, 1969; Nightmare, 1975; other novels—It Was Christmas Every Day, 1952; It Will Be Warmed When It Snows, 1966; Hallelujah!, 1973; The Last Cruise, 1977. Add: Killingan Beg, Churchtown, Lezayre, Isle of Man, U.K.

LACEY, A(lan) R(obert). British, b. 1926. Philosophy. Lectr., subsequently Sr. Lectr., King's Coll., Univ. of London, since 1984. Sr. Lectr., Dept. of Philosophy, Bedford Coll., Univ. of London, 1973–84 (faculty member since 1954). *Publs:* Dictionary of Philosophy, 1976, 1986; Modern Philosophy: An Introduction, 1982. Add: Dept. of Philosophy, King's Coll., Univ. of London, London WC2, England.

LACEY, Robert. British, b. 1944. History, Biography. Asst. Ed., Sunday Times Mag., London 1969–73; Ed., Look! pages, Sunday Times, 1973–74. *Publs:* (author and ed.) The French Revolution, 2 vols., 1968; (author and ed.) The Rise of Napoleon, 1969; (author and ed.) The Peninsular War, 1969; (author and ed.) 1812: The Retreat from Moscow, 1969; Robert, Earl of Essex: An Elizabethan Icarus, 1971; The Life and Times of Henry VIII, 1972; The Queens of the North Atlantic, 1973; Sir Walter Raleigh, 1973; (author and ed.) Sir Francis Drake and the Golden Hinde, 1975; (ed. and contrib.) Heritage of Britain, 1975; Majesty: Elizabeth II and the House of Windsor, 1977; The Kingdom: Arabia and the House of Saud, 1981; Princess, 1982; Aristocrats, 1983; Ford: The Men and the Machine, 1986; God Bless Her: Her Majesty Queen Elizabeth the Queen Mother, 1987. Add: c/o Curtis Brown Ltd., 162-168 Regent St., London W1R 5TA, England.

LACHS, John. American, b. 1934. Philosophy, Poetry. Prof. of Philosophy, Vanderbilt Univ., Nashville, Tenn., since 1967. Asst. Prof., 1959–62; Assoc. Prof., 1962–66, and Prof., 1966–67, Coll. of William and Mary, Williamsburg, Va. *Publs:* Animal Faith and Spiritual Life: Unpublished and Uncollected Works of George Santayana with Critical Essays on His Thought, 1967; Marxist Philosophy: A Bibliographical Guide, 1967; (ed. with S.M. Lachs) Physical Order and Moral Liberty: Previously Unpublished Essays of George Santayana, 1969; (trans. with P. Heath) J.G. Fichte: The Science of Knowledge, 1970; The Ties of Time (poetry), 1970; Intermediate Man, 1981; Mind and Philosophers, 1987; George Santayana, 1988. Add: Box 12, Station B., Vanderbilt Univ., Nashville, Tenn. 37235, U.S.A.

LACY, Creighton Boutelle. American, b. 1919. Politics/Government, Theology/Religion, Biography. Prof. Emeritus of World Christianity, Duke Univ., Durham, N.C., since 1953. Missionary to China, United Methodist Bd. of Missions, 1946–51. *Publs:* Is China a Democracy?, 1943; Christian Community, 1944; Adam, Where Art Thou?, 1956; Christian Responsibility for the United States and New Nations, 1964; Conscience of India, 1965; Christianity Amid Rising Men and Nations, 1965; Frank Mason North, 1967; Indian Insights, 1972; The Word-Carrying Giant, 1977; Coming Home—to China, 1978. Add: 2714 Dogwood Rd, Durham, N.C. 27705, U.S.A.

LaFEBER, Walter Frederick. American, b. 1933. History, International relations/Current affairs. Noll Prof. of History, Cornell Univ., Ithaca, N.Y., since 1968 (Asst. Prof., 1959–63; Assoc. Prof., 1963–67; Prof., 1967–68). Member, Editorial Bd., Political Science Quarterly, Diplomatic History, Intnl. History Review. Member, Advisory Cttee., Foreign Relations of the United States series, U.S. Dept. of State, 1971–75. *Publs:* The New Empire: An Interpretation of American Expansion, 1860-1898, 1963; (ed.) John Q. Adams and American Continental Empire, 1965; America, Russia and the Cold War, 1967, 6th ed. 1989; (ed.) America and Twenty Years Revolution, 1947–1967, 1969; (ed.) Origins of the Cold War, 1941–1947, 1971; (co-author) Creation of the American Empire, 1973, 1976; (co-author) The American Century, 1974, 1986; The Panama Canal: The Crisis in Historical Perspective, 1978, 1979, 1989; The Third Cold War, 1981; Inevitable Revolutions: The U.S. in Central America, 1983, 1988; (co-author) America in Vietnam; The American Age: U.S. Foreign Policy at Home and Abroad from 1750 to Our Own Time, 1989. Add: Dept. of History, McGraw Hall, Cornell Univ., Ithaca, N.Y. 14853, U.S.A.

LAFFAN, Kevin (Barry). British, b. 1922. Plays/Screenplays, Novels. Repertory actor and dir. until 1950; Dir. of Productions, Pendragon Co., Reading, 1950–52, and Everyman Theatre Co., Reading, 1953–58. *Publs:* Zoo Zoo Widershins Zoo, 1969; It's a Two-Foot-Six-Inches-above-the-Ground World, 1970; Two Plays, 1983; (with N. Mitchel) Amos Goes to War (novel), 1988. Add: c/o ACTAC, 16 Cadogan Lane, London SW1, England.

LAFFERTY, R(aphael) A(loysius). American, b. 1914. Historical/Romance/Gothic, Science fiction/Fantasy. Freelance writer since 1971. Civil Servant, Washington, D.C., 1934–35; Clerk, then Buyer, Clark Electrical Supply Co., Tulsa, Okla, 1936–42, 1946–50, and 1952–71. *Publs:* Past Master, 1968; The Reefs of Earth, 1968; Space Chantey, 1968; Fourth Mansions, 1969; Nine Hundred Grandmothers (short stories), 1970; The Devil Is Dead,1971; Arrive at Easterwine, 1971; The Fall of Rome (historical novel), 1971; The Flame is Green (historical novel), 1971; Okla Hannali (historical novel), 1972; Strange Doings (short stories), 1972; Does Anyone Else Have Something Further to Add? (short stories), 1974; Funnyfingers, and Cabrito (short stories), 1976; Horns on Their Heads (short stories), 1976; Not to Mention Camels, 1976; Apocalypses, 1977; Archipelago, 1979; Aurelia, 1982; The Annals of Klepsis, 1983; Golden Gate and Other Stories, 1983; Four Stories, 1983; Heart of Stone Dear and Other Stories, 1983; Snake in His Bosom and Other Stories, 1983; Through Elegant Eyes (stories), 1983; Ringing Changes (stories), 1984; The Man Who Made Models and Other Stories, 1984; Half a Sky, 1984, Slippery and Other Stories, 1985. Add: 1715 S. Trenton Ave., Tulsa, Okla, 74120, U.S.A.

LAFFIN, John. Has also written as Mark Napier and as Dirk Sabre.

Australian/British, b. 1922. Novels/Short stories, Poetry, Area Studies, Geography, Military/Defense, Politics/Government, Biography. Freelance writer, journalist, broadcaster and lectr. Founder, 1983, and Ed., Middle East and Mediterranean Outlook (MEMO). *Publs:* Return to Glory, 1953; One Man's War, 1954; My Brother's Executioner, 1955; Middle East Journey, 1956; Digger: Story of the Australian Soldier, 1958; (as Dirk Sabre) Murder by Bamboo, 1959; The Walking Wounded, 1959; (as Mark Napier) Doorways to Danger, 1961; Scotland the Brave: The Story of the Scottish Soldier, 1963; Swifter than Eagles, 1963; The Face of War, 1964; British Campaign Medals, 1964; Codes and Ciphers, 1964; Jackboot: The Story of the German Soldier, 1965, 1989; Anzacs at War, 1965; Boys in Battle, 1966; Links of Leadership, 1966; The Hunger to Come, 1966; Tommy Atkins: Story of the English Soldier, 1966; Women in Battle, 1967; New Geography, 1966–67, 1967; Jack Tar: Story of the English Seaman, 1968; The Anatomy of Captivity, 1968; New Geography 1968–69, 1969; Surgeons in the Field, 1970; Devil's Goad, 1970; New Geography, 1970–71, 1971; Fedayeen: The Arab-Israeli Dilemma, 1973; Americans in Battle, 1973; Letters from the Front 1914–1918, 1973; The French Foreign Legion, 1974; The Arab Mind, 1975; The Arabs as Master Slavers, 1976; The Israeli Mind, 1979; The Dagger of Islam, 1979; Damn the Dardanelles! The Story of Gallipoli, 1980, 1989; The Australian Army at War, 1982; The Arab Armies of the Middle East Wars 1948–73, 1982; The Israeli Army in the Middle East Wars 1948–73, 1982; The PLO Connections, 1982; Fight for the Falklands! 1982; Stories from the Western Front 1914–1918, 1985; The Man the Nazis Couldn't Catch, 1985; Know the Middle East, 1985; Brassey's Battles: 3500 Years of Battles, Campaigns and Wars, 1986; War Annual, No. 1, 1986, No. 2, 1987, No. 3, 1988, No. 4, 1989; Battlefield Archaeology, 1987; Passion of Poetry, 1986; British Butchers and Bunglers of World War I, 1988; Western Front I, 1916–1917, 1987, II, 1917–1918, 1988; Holy Wars: Islam Fights, 1988; World War I in Postcards, 1988; Greece, Crete and Syria Campaigns, 1941, 1989; Guidebook to Australian Battlefields of the Western Front of World War I, 1990. Add: Oxford House, Church St., Knighton, Powys, Wales.

LaFOREST, Gerard V. (J.). Canadian, b. 1926. Law. Judge, Supreme Court of Canada, since 1985. Assoc. Prof. of Law, 1956–63, and Prof., 1963–68, Univ. of New Brunswick, Fredericton; Dean of Law, Univ. of Alberta, Edmonton, 1968–70; Asst. Deputy Attorney Gen., Dept. of Justice, Ottawa, 1970–74; Commnr., Law Reform Commn. of Can., 1974–79; Prof. of Law, Univ. of Ottawa, 1971–79, McGill Univ., Montreal, 1972, 1977; Judge, New Brunswick Court of Appeal, 1981–85. *Publs:* Disallowance and Reservation of Provincial Legislation, 1955, 1970; Extradition to and from Canada, 1961, 1977; The Allocation of Taxing Power Under the Canadian Constitution, 1967, 1981; Natural Resources and Public Property Under the Canadian Constitution, 1969; (with others) Le Territoire Québécois, 1970; Water Law in Canada, 1973. Add: 170 Minto Pl., Rockcliffe Park, Ottawa, Ont., K1M 0B7, Canada.

LA FORTUNE, Knolly Stephen. Trinidadian, b. 1920. Novels/Short stories, Poetry. Schoolmaster, I.L.E.A., since 1958 (Teacher in Charge, St. Paul's Roman Catholic Sch. Library, 1968–69). Secty., San Juan District Teacher's Assn., 1954–55 and Art Teacher's Assn., 1954–56; Education Officer, Trinidad and Tobago Assn., London, 1967–68. *Publs:* Moments of Inspiration, 1947; Legend of T-Marie, 1968; Anthology of Caribbean Poets, 1969; Caribbean Folk-Lore, 1975–77; The Schoolmaster Remembers: Colonial Trinidad 1930, 1979; Trouble Make Monkey Eat Pepper (novel), 1984. Add: 68 Arthurdon Rd., Brockley, London SE4, England.

LaGRAND, Louis E. American, b. 1935. Education, Human relations. Prof. of Health Science, State Univ. of New York, Potsdam, since 1970 (Asst. Prof., 1962–65; Head Basketball Coach, 1962–70; Assoc. Prof., 1965–70). Instr in Physical Education, Columbia Univ., NYC, 1958–62. *Publs:* Coach's Complete Guide to Winning Basketball, 1967; Discipline in the Secondary School, 1969; Hatha Yoga in Health and Physical Education, 1974; Coping with Separation and Loss as a Young Adult, 1986; Changing Patterns of Human Existence, 1988. Add: Rt. 2, Potsdam, N.Y. 13676, U.S.A.

LaHOOD, Marvin J(ohn). American, b. 1933. Literature. Prof. of English, State Univ. Coll. of New York at Buffalo, since 1978. Academic Dean and Prof. of English, Salem State Coll., Massachusetts, 1972–75; Dean of Faculty and Prof. of English, D'Youville Coll., Buffalo, N.Y., 1975–78. *Publs:* (ed. with A. Rubulis) Latvian Literature, 1964; (ed.) Tender is the Night: Essays in Criticism, 1969; Conrad Richter's America, 1975; State University College at Buffalo: A History 1946–1972, 1980. Add: 93 Parkhaven Dr., Amherst, N.Y. 14150, U.S.A.

LAHR, John (Henry). American, b. 1941. Novels/Short stories, Theatre, Biography. Literary Advisor, Tyrone Guthrie Theatre, Minneapolis, Minn., 1968, and Literary Advisor, Repertory Theatre, Lincoln Center, NYC, 1969–72; Theatre Ed., Grove Press, NYC, 1969–73. *Publs:* Notes on Cowardly Lion, 1969; (ed.) Showcase I, 1969; Up Against the Fourth Wall, 1970; Acting Out America, 1970; (ed. with A. Lahr) Casebook on Harold Pinter's The Homecoming, 1971; Astonish Me, 1973; (with J. Price) Life-Show, 1973; The Autograph Hound, 1973; (ed. with J. Price) The Great American Life Show, 1974; Hot to Trot (novel), 1974; (ed.) Grove Press Modern Drama: Six Plays, 1975; (ed.) The Complete Plays of Joe Orton, 1975; Prick Up Your Ears: The Biography of Joe Orton, 1978; Coward: The Playwright, 1982; Automatic Vaudeville: Essays on Star Turns, 1984; (ed.) The Orton Diaries, 1986. Add: c/o Knopf, Inc., 201 E. 50th St., New York, N.Y. 10022, U.S.A.

LAIDLER, Keith James. Canadian, b. 1916. Chemistry. Prof. of Chemistry, Univ. of Ottawa, Ont., 1955–81, now Emeritus. *Publs:* Chemical Kinetics, 1950, 3rd ed. 1987; Chemical Kinetics of Excited States, 1955; Chemical Kinetics of Enzyme Action, 1958, 2nd ed. with P.S. Bunting, 1973; Reaction Kinetics, 1963; Theories of Chemical Reaction Rates, 1969; The Chemical Elements, 1970; Physical Chemistry with Biological Applications, 1978; (with J. H. Meiser) Physical Chemistry, 1982. Add: Dept. of Chemistry, Univ. of Ottawa, Ottawa, Ont. K1N 9B4, Canada.

LAIT, Robert. British, b. 1921. Novels/Short stories. Lectr. in Criminology, and Social Science, Univ. of Wales, Swansea, since 1962. *Publs:* The Second Yoke, 1960; The Africans, 1961; Massacre, 1963; The Fireworks, 1965; Mrs. Hardwick's Private War, 1966; A Chance to Kill, 1968; Pit, 1970; Switched Out, 1970; Once Too Often, 1980. Add: Dept. of Social Admin., Univ. of Wales, Swansea, Wales.

LAITHWAITE, Eric Roberts. British, b. 1921. Engineering/Technology. Prof. of Heavy Electrical Engineering, Imperial Coll. of Science and Technology, London, since 1964, Emeritus since 1986. Asst. Lectr., 1950–53, Lectr., 1953–57, and Sr. Lectr., 1957–64, Manchester Univ.; Prof. of Applied Electricity, Royal Instn. of Great Britain, 1967–76. *Publs:* Propulsion without Wheels, 1966, 1970; Induction Machines for Special Purposes, 1966; The Engineer in Wonderland, 1967; Linear Electric Motors, 1971; Exciting Electrical Machines, 1974, 1979; (with A. Watson and P.E.S. Whalley) The Dictionary of Butterflies and Moths in Colour, 1975; Why Does a Glow-worm Glow?, 1977; (ed.) Transport Without Wheels, 1977; (with M.W. Thring) How to Invent, 1977; Engineer Through the Looking-Glass, 1980; (with L.L. Freris) Electric Energy: Its Generation, Transmission and Use, 1980; Invitation to Engineering, 1984; A History of Linear Electric Motors, 1987. Add: Dept. of Electrical Engineering, Imperial Coll., London SW7 2BT, England.

LAKE, David (John). Australian (b. British in India), b. 1929. Science fiction/Fantasy, Poetry, Literature. Lectr., Sr. Lectr., and Reader in English, Univ. of Queensland, since 1967. Asst. Master, Sherrardswood Sch., Welwyn Garden City, Herts., 1953–58, and St. Albans Boys Grammer Sch., Herts., 1958–59; Lectr., in English, Saigon Univ., 1959–61, for the Thai Govt., Bankok, 1961–63, and at Chiswick Polytechnic, London, 1963–64; Reader in English, Jadavpur Univ., Calcutta, 1965–67. *Publs:* John Milton: Paradise Lost, 1967; Greek Tragedy, 1969; Hornpipes and Funerals (poetry), 1973; The Canon of Thomas Middleton's Plays: Internal Evidence for the Major Problems of Authorship, 1975; science fiction novels—Walkers on the Sky, 1976, 1978; The Right Hand of Dextra, 1977; The Wildings of Dextra, 1977; The Gods of Xuma, or, Barsoom Revisited, 1978; The Fourth Hemisphere, 1980; The Man Who Loved Morlocks, 1981; The Ring of Truth, 1983; Warlords of Xuma, 1983; fantasy novels—The Changelings of Chaan, 1985; West of the Moon, 1988. Add: Dept. of English, Univ. of Queensland, St. Lucia, Qld. 4067, Australia.

LAKEMAN, Enid. British, b. 1903. Politics/Government. Editorial Consultant, since 1980 (Research Secty., 1945–60, and Dir., 1960–80), Electoral Reform Soc., London. *Publs:* When Labour Fails, 1946; (with J.D. Lambert) Voting in Democracies, 1955, 1959; How Democracies Vote, 1970, 1974; Power to Elect, 1982. Add: Electoral Reform Soc., 6 Chancel St., London SE1 0UU, England.

LAKER, Rosalind. Pseud. for Barbara Ovstedal; has also written as Barbara Douglas and Barbara Paul. British. Historical/Romance/Gothic. *Publs:* Sovereign's Key, 1969; Far Seeks the Heart, 1970; Sail a Jeweled Ship, 1971; The Shripney Lady, 1972; (as Barbara Ovstedal) Norway (non-fiction), 1973; (as Barbara Ovstedal) Valley of the Reindeer, 1973;

(as Barbara Ovstedal) Red Cherry Summer, 1973; (as Barbara Ovstedal) Souvenir from Sweden, 1974; Fair Wind of Love, 1974, in U.S. as Barbara Douglas, 1980; The Smuggler's Bride, 1975; (as Barbara Paul) The Seventeenth Stair, 1975; (as Barbara Paul) The Curse of Halewood (in U.S. as Devil's Fire, Love's Revenge), 1976; (as Barbara Paul) The Frenchwoman, 1977; Ride the Blue Riband, 1977; Warwyck's Woman, 1978, in U.K. as Warwyck's Wife, 1979; (as Barbara Paul) A Wild Cry of Love, 1978; Claudine's Daughter, 1979; (as Barbara Paul) To Love a Stranger, 1979; Warwyck's Choice (in U.K. as The Warwycks of Easthampton), 1980; Banners of Silk, 1981, in U.K. as Banners of Silk, 1982; Gilded Splendour, 1982; Jewelled Path, 1983; What the Heart Keeps, 1984; This Shining Land, 1985; Tree of Gold, 1986; The Silver Touch, 1987; To Dance with Kings, 1988. Add: c/o Laurence Pollinger Ltd., 18 Maddox St., London W1R 0EU, England.

LAL, P. Indian, b. 1929. Poetry, Literature, Translations. Hon. Prof., St. Xavier's Coll., Calcutta, since 1967 (Prof. of English, 1952–67); Prof. of English, Univ. of Calcutta, since 1967; Founder and Secty., Writers Workshop, publrs., and Ed., Writers Workshop Miscellany, Calcutta. Ed. Orient Review and Literary Digest, 1954–58; Visiting Prof., Hofstra Univ., Hempstead, N.Y., 1962–63; Robert L. Morton Visiting Prof., Ohio Univ., Athens, 1973–74. *Publs:* The Art of the Essay, 1951; (ed.) Ohio Merchant of Venice, by William Shakespeare, 1952; (ed. with K.R. Rao) Modern Indo-Anglian Poetry, 1959; The Parrot's Death and Other Poems, 1960; Love's the First: Poems, 1962; "Change!" They Said: New Poems, 1966; Draupadi and Jayadratha and Other Poems, 1967; An Annotated Mahabharata Bibliography, 1967; (ed.) T.S. Eliot: Homage from India: A Commemoration Volume of 55 Essays and Elegies, 1967; (ed.) The First Workshop Story Anthology, 1967; The Concept of an Indian Literature: Six Essays, 1968; Creations and Transcreations: Three Poems, Selected from the Subhasita-Ratna-Kosa, and the First 92 Slokas from the Mahabharata, 1968; Yakshi from Didarganj: Poems, 1969; (ed.) Modern Indian Poetry in English: The Writers Workshop Literary Reader, 1973; The Man of Dharma and the Rasa of Silence, 1974; Nepal: Where the Gods Are Young, 1976; Calcutta, 1977; Collected Poems, 1977; The Alien Insiders: Indian Writing in English, 1979; Personalities: Meetings with Writers, 1979. Add: 162/92 Lake Gardens, Calcutta 45, India.

LAM, Truong Buu. Vietnamese, b. 1933. History. Assoc. Prof. of History, Univ. of Hawaii, Honolulu, since 1971. Dir., Inst. of Historical Research, Saigon, 1957–64; Assoc. Prof. of History, State Univ. of New York, Stony Brook, 1968–71. *Publs:* Patterns of Vietnamese Response to Foreign Intervention, 1967; New Lamps for Old, 1983; Resistance, Rebellion, Revolution in Vietnamese History, 1984. Add: History Dept., Univ. of Hawaii, 2530 Dole St., Honolulu, Hawaii 96822, U.S.A.

LAMANTIA, Philip. American, b. 1927. Poetry. Asst. Ed., View Mag., NYC, 1944. *Publs:* Erotic Poems, 1946; Narcotica: I Demand Extinction of Laws Prohibiting Narcotic Drugs, 1959; (with A. Artaud) Ekstasis, 1959; Destroyed Works: Hypodermic Light, Mantic Notebook, Still Poems, Spansule, 1962; Touch of the Marvelous, 1966; Selected Poems, 1943–1966, 1967; (with Charles Bukowski and Harold Norse) Penguin Modern Poets, 13, 1969; The Blood of the Air, 1970; Becoming Visible, 1981. Add: c/o City Lights Books, 261 Columbus Ave., San Francisco, Calif. 94133, U.S.A.

LAMAR, Howard Roberts. American, b. 1923. History. Prof. of History since 1964, and Dean of Yale Coll. since 1979, Yale Univ., New Haven, Conn. (Instr., 1949–54; Asst. Prof., 1954–59; Assoc. Prof., 1959–64). Instr. in History, Univ. of Massachusetts, Amherst, 1945–46; Asst. in Instruction, Wesleyan Univ., Middletown, Conn., 1948–49. *Publs:* Dakota Territory, 1861-1889: A Study of Frontier Politics, 1956; (ed.) The Cruise of the Portsmouth, 1845-1847: A Sailor's View of the Naval Conquest of California, by Joseph T. Downey, 1958; The Far Southwest, 1850-1912: A Political History of the Territories of Arizona, Colorado, New Mexico and Utah, 1966; (ed.) Reader's Encyclopedia of the American West, 1977; (ed. with Leonard Thompson) The Frontier in History: North America and Southern Africa Compared, 1981. Add: Dept. of History, Yale Univ., New Haven, Conn. 06520, U.S.A.

LAMB, Charlotte. *See* HOLLAND, Sheila.

LAMB, Elizabeth Searle. American, b. 1917. Poetry, Children's non-fiction, Literature. Pres., Haiku Soc. of America, NYC, 1971; Ed., Frogpond, quarterly journal of Haiku, since 1984. *Publs:* (with J. Bailey and P. Markun) The Pelican Tree and Other Panama Adventures, 1953; Today and Every Day, 1971; Inside Me, Outside Me, 1974; In This Blaze of Sun, 1975; Picasso's Bust of Sylvette, 1977; 39 Blossoms, 1982; Casting Into A Cloud, 1985; Lines for my mother, dying, 1988. Add: 970 Acequia Madre, Santa Fe, N.M. 87501, U.S.A.

LAMB, F(rank) Bruce. American, b. 1913. Agriculture/Forestry, Natural history, Travel/Exploration/Adventure. Ed., Caribbean Forester, and Training Officer, Inst. of Tropical Forestry, U.S. Forest Services, Rio Piedras, Puerto Rico, 1958–60; Technical Dir. of Forest Resources, Champion Intnl. Corp., NYC, 1960–75. *Publs:* Mahogany of Tropical America, 1966; (with M. Cordova-Rios) Wizard of the Upper Amazon (in U.K. as Stolen Chief, in W. Germany as Der Weisse Indo von Amazonas, in Brazil as O Feiticeiro Do Alto Amazonas), 1971, 1974; Rio Tigre: Amazon Jungle Medicine of Manuel Cordova, 1985. Add: 970 Acequia Madre, Santa Fe, N.M. 87501, U.S.A.

LAMB, Geoffrey Frederick. Also writes as Balaam. British. Children's non-fiction, Education, History, Recreation/Leisure/Hobbies, Travel/Exploration/Adventure, Biography. Schoolmaster, 1933–46; Lectr. in English, Camden Training Coll., London, 1947–50. *Publs:* (ed.) Valiant Deeds, 1942; (ed.) United States and United Kingdom, 1944; (ed.) Tales of Human Endeavour, 1946; Six Good Samaritans, 1947; (ed.) The English at School, 1950; (as Balaam) Chalk in My Hair, 1953; English for General Certificate, 1954; The Spirit of Modern Adventure, 1955; (as Balaam) Chalk Gets in Your Eyes, 1955; English for Middle Forms, 1956; Franklin—Happy Voyager, 1956; Thrilling Exploits of Modern Adventure, 1957; The South Pole, 1957; (as Balaam) Come Out to Play, 1958; The Happiest Days, 1959; Great Exploits of World War II, 1959; Thrilling Journeys, 1962; Punctuation for Schools, 1962; Look at Schools, 1964; Moden Adventures in Air and Space, 1964; (ed.) Story and Rhythm, 1966; Composition and Comprehension for C.S.E., 1968; The Pegasus Book of Magicians, 1968; Practical Precis and Comprehension, 1969; One Hundred Good Stories, 1969–70; Modern Adventures at Sea, 1970; Book of the Seashore, 1971; Your Book of Card Tricks, 1972; Your Book of Mental Magic, 1973; Your Book of Table Tricks, 1974; More Good Stories, 1975, 1978; Your Book of Secret Writing, 1976; Victorian Magic, 1976; Magic, Witchcraft and the Occult, 1977; Pencil and Paper Tricks, 1977; Illustrated Magic Dictionary, 1979; The Wheaton Book of Magic Stories, 1981; Pocket Companion Quotation Guide, 1983; Animal Quotations, 1985; Apt and Amusing Quotations, 1986; Magic for All the Family, 1987; Funny Quotes for Numerous Occasions, 1988. Add: Penfold, Legion Lane, Kings Worthy, Winchester, Hants, England.

LAMB, Hubert Horace. British, b. 1913. Environmental science/Ecology, Geography, Meteorology/Atmospheric sciences. Founder, Climatic Research Unit, 1972 and Emeritus Prof., Univ. of East Anglia, Norwich, since 1978. With U.K. Meteorological Office, Bracknell, Berks., 1936–39 and 1945–71 (in charge of research on climatic fluctuations, 1957–71). *Publs:* The English Climate, 1964; The Changing Climate, 1966, 3rd ed. 1972; Climate: Present, Past and Future, 2 vols., 1972–77; Climate, History, and the Modern World, 1982; Weather, Climate and Human Affairs, 1988. Add: Climate Research Unit., Sch. of Environmental Sciences, Univ. of East Anglia, Norwich, Norfolk NR4 7TJ, England.

LAMB, Karl A(llen). American, b. 1933. Politics/Government. Academic Dean and Prof. of Political Science, U.S. Naval Acad., Annapolis, Md., since 1985. Faculty member, Univ. of Michigan, Ann Arbor, 1958–63; Asst. Prof., to Prof. of Politics, Univ. of California, Santa Cruz, 1963–85. *Publs:* (with J. Pierce and J.P. White) Apportionment and Representative Institutions: The Michigan Experience, 1963: (with N.C. Thomas) Congress: Politics and Practice, 1964; (with P.A. Smith) Campaign Decision-Making, 1968; (ed.) Democracy, Liberalism and Revolution, 1971; The People, Maybe, 1971, 3rd ed. 1978; As Orange Goes, 1974; The Guardians: Leadership Values and the American Tradition, 1982. Add: 15 Porter Rd., U.S. Naval Acad., Annapolis, Md. 21402, U.S.A.

LAMBERT, Darwin. American, b. 1916. Novels/Short stories, Natural history. Freelance writer. Ed., Travel Lore mag., Luray, Va., 1937–42, Commonwealth Review newspaper, Luray, Va., 1947–49, Ely Daily Times, Nev., 1956–61, and Daily Alaska Empire newspaper, Juneau, 1961–64; Co-Ed., Exploring Earthmans' World, 1970–76. *Publs:* Beautiful Shenandoah, 1937; Illustrated Guide to Shenandoah National Park, 1942; Gold Strike in Hell (novel), 1964; Herbert Hoover's Hideaway, 1971; The Earth-Man Story, 1972; Timberline Ancients, 1972; Administrative History of Shenandoah National Park, 1979; The Undying Past of the Shenandoah National Park, 1989. Add: 444 Rt. 2, Luray, Va. 22835, U.S.A.

LAMBERT, Derek (William). Also writes as Richard Falkirk. British, b. 1929. Novels, Mystery/Crime/Suspense. Journalist, for Devon, Norfolk, Yorkshire and London newspapers, 1950–68. *Publs:* novels—Angels in the Snow, 1969; The Kites of War, 1969; For Infamous Conduct, 1970; Grand Slam, 1971; The Great Land, 1977; The Lottery, 1983; mystery novels—The Red House, 1972; The Yermakov Transfer, 1974; Touch the Lion's Paw, 1975, in U.S. paperback as Rough Cut, 1980; The Saint Peter's Plot, 1978; The Memory Man, 1979; I, Said the Spy, 1980; Trance, 1981; The Red Dove, 1982; The Judas Code, 1983; The Golden Express, 1984; The Man Who Was Saturday, 1985; Chase, 1987; mystery novels as Richard Falkirk—The Chill Factor, 1971; The Twisted Wire, 1971; Blackstone, 1972; Beau Blackstone, 1973; Blackstone's Fancy, 1973; Blackstone and the Scourge of Europe, 1974; Blackstone Underground, 1976; Blackstone on Broadway, 1977; other—The Sheltered Days: Growing Up in the War, 1965; Don't Quote Me—But, 1979; And I Quote, 1980; Unquote, 1981; Just Like the Blitz: A Reporter's Notebook, 1987. Add: c/o Blake Friedmann Literary Agency, 37-41 Gower St., London WC1E 6HH, England.

LAMBERT, Gavin. American, b. 1924. Novels/Short stories, Plays/Screenplays, Film. Ed., Sight and Sound, London, 1950–55. *Publs:* The Slide Area, 1959; (co-author) Sons and Lovers (screenplay), 1960; The Roman Spring of Mrs. Stone (screenplay), 1961; Inside Daisy Clover (novel and screenplay), 1963, 1965; Norman's Letter, 1966; A Case for the Angels, 1968; The Goodby People, 1971; On Cukor, 1972; GWTW: The Making of Gone with the Wind, 1973; The Dangerous Edge, 1976; In the Night All Cats are Grey, 1976; I Never Promised You a Rose Garden (screenplay), 1977; Running Time, 1982. Add: c/o Macmillan, 866 Third Ave., New York, N.Y. 10022, U.S.A.

LAMBERTON, Donald McLean. Australian, b. 1927. Economics, Information science/Computers. Prof. of Economics, Univ. of Queensland, Brisbane, since 1972 (Head, Dept. of Economics, 1974–78). Editor, Prometheus and Information Economics and Policy. Chmn., Pacific Science Assn. Scientific Cttee. for Economics, since 1976. Prof. of Economics, Case Western Reserve Univ., Cleveland, Ohio, 1969–72. *Publs:* The Theory of Profit, 1965; Science, Technology and the Australian Economy, 1970; (ed.) Economics of Information and Knowledge, 1971; (ed.) Industrial Economics, 1972; (ed.) The Information Revolution, 1974; (ed. with M. Jussawalla) Communication Economics and Development, 1982; (ed. with S. Macdonald and T. Mandeville) The Trouble with Technology, 1983. Add: Dept. of Economics, Univ. of Queensland, St. Lucia, Brisbane, Qld., Australia 4067.

LAMBOT, Isobel Mary. Also writes as Daniel Ingham and Mary Turner. British, b. 1926. Novels/Short stories. Tutor in Creative Writing, Lichfield Evening Inst., 1973–1979. *Publs:* Taste of Murder, 1966; Deadly Return, 1966; Dangerous Refuge, 1966; (as Mary Turner) Perilous Love, 1966; Shroud of Canvas, 1967; Danger Merchant, 1968; The Queen Dies First, 1968; Killer's Laughter, 1968; Let the Witness Die, 1969; Point of Death, 1969; Watcher on the Shore, 1972; (as Daniel Ingham) Contract for Death, 1972; Come Back and Die, 1972; Grip of Fear, 1974; (as Mary Turner) The Justice Hunt, 1974; (as Mary Turner) So Bright A Lady, 1977; The Identity Trap, 1978; Past Tense, 1979; (as Mary Turner) Runaway Lady, 1981; Rooney's Gold, 1984; Still Waters Run Deadly, 1987; Blood Ties, 1987. Add: 45 Bridge St., Kington HR5 3DW, England.

LAMIRANDE, Emilien. Canadian, b. 1926. Theology/Religion. Prof., Dept. of Religious Studies, Univ. of Ottawa, since 1970 (Lectr., Asst. Prof., 1954–65). Prof., 1965–70, Chmn., 1972–74, and Dean, 1967–69, Faculty of Theology, St. Paul Univ.; Fellow, Royal Society of Canada, 1984. *Publs:* Un siècle et demi d'études sur l'ecclésiologie de saint Augustin, 1962; What Is the Communion of Saints, 1963; L'Eglise céleste selon saint Augustin, 1963; Dieu chez les hommes—La signification du Pavillon chrétien, 1967; Etudes sur l'Ecclésiologie de saint Augustin, 1969; La situation ecclésiologique des Donatistes chez saint Augustin, 1972; Church, State and Toleration: An Intriguing Change of Mind in Augustine, 1975; Le P.G. Simard: Un disciple de saint Augustin, 1981; Paulin de Milan et la "Vita Ambrosii," 1982. Add: Dept. of Religious Studies, Univ. of Ottawa, 177 Waller St., Ottawa, Ont. K1N 6N5, Canada.

LAMMING, George (Eric). Barbadian, b. 1927. Novels/Short stories. *Publs:* In the Castle of My Skin, 1953; The Emigrants, 1954; Of Age and Innocence, 1958; Season of Adventure, 1960; The Pleasures of Exile, 1960; Natives of My Person, 1971; Water with Berries, 1972; (ed.) Cannon Shot and Glass Beads: Modern Black Writing, 1974. Add: c/o Longman Group Ltd., 5 Bentinck St., London W1M 5RN, England.

LAMONT, Corliss. American, b. 1892. Poetry, Civil liberties/Human rights, International relations/Current affairs, Philosophy. Seminar Assoc., Columbia Univ., NYC, since 1973 (Instr. in Philosophy, 1928–32; with Sch. of Gen. Studies, 1947–59). Instr., New Sch. for Social Re-

search, NYC, 1940–42; Lectr., Cornell Univ. Ithaca, N.Y., 1943, and Harvard Grad. Sch. of Education, 1944. *Publs:* Issues of Immortality, 1932; You Might Like Socialism: A Way of Life for Modern Man, 1939; The Peoples of the Soviet Union, 1946; A Humanist Funeral Service, 1947; Humanism as a Philosophy, 1949, as The Philosophy of Humanism, 1965; The Independent Mind, 1951; (ed.) Man Answers Death: An Anthology of Poetry, rev. ed. 1952; Soviet Civilization, 1952; Freedom Is as Freedom Does: Civil Liberties Today, 1956; (ed.) Dialogue on John Dewey, 1959; (ed.) Dialogue on George Santayana, 1959; (ed.) A Humanist Symposium on Metaphysics, 1960; (ed.) Albert Rhys Williams: In Memoriam, 1962; The Illusion of Immortality, 1965; Freedom of Choice Affirmed, 1967; (ed.) The Trial of Elizabeth Gurley Flynn by the American Civil Liberties Union, 1968; A Humanist Wedding Service, 1970; (ed.) The Thomas Lamonts in America, 1971; Remembering John Masefield, 1971; Lover's Credo (poetry), 1972; Voice in the Wilderness: Collected Essays of Fifty Years, 1974; (with Lansing Lamont) Letters of John Masefield to Florence Lamont, 1979; Yes to Life: Memoirs of Corliss Lamont, 1981; (ed.) Collected Poems of John Reed, 1985; A Lifetime of Dissent, 1988. Add: 315 West 106th St., Apt. 15C, New York, N.Y. 10025, U.S.A.

LAMONT, Marianne. *See* **RUNDLE,** Anne.

LAMONT-BROWN, Raymond. British, b. 1939. History, Mythology/Folklore, Supernatural/Occult topics, Travel/Exploration/Adventure, Biography. Author and Broadcaster. Lectr., Extra-Mural Dept., Univ. of St. Andrews, since 1977; Managing Ed., Writers' Monthly, 1984–86. *Publs:* The History of St. Mark's Church, Dewsbury 1865-1965, 1965; Book of Epitaphs, 1967, 1969; The Rural District of Doncaster Official Guide and Industrial Handbook, 1968; Clarinda: The Intimate Story of Robert Burns and Agnes Maclehose, 1968; Sir Walter Scott's Letters on Demonology and Witchcraft, 1968; Robert Burns's Commonplace Book 1783-85, 1969; A Book of Superstitions, 1970, 1971; A Book of Proverbs, 1970; A Book of Witchcraft, 1971; Charles Kirkpatrick Sharpe's History of Witchcraft in Scotland, 1972; Phantoms, Legends, Customs and Superstitions of the Sea, 1972; General Trade in Berwick on Tweed 1894, 1972; Robert Burns's Tour of the Border, 1972; Robert Burns's Tours of the Highlands and Stirlingshire, 1973; A New Book of Epitaphs, 1974; The Magic Oracles of Japan, 1974; Casebook of Military Mystery, 1974; Epitaph Hunting, 1977; Scottish Epitaphs, 1978; Phantoms of the Theatre, 1978; Growing Up with the Highland Clans, 1979; Lothian and Border Walks for Motorists, 1980; East Anglian Epitaphs, 1980; My Fun Book of Scotland, 1980; Victorian and Edwardian Fife from Old Photographs, 1980; The Victorian and Edwardian Borderland from Rare Photographs, 1980; Victorian and Edwardian Dundee, 1981; Mary, Queen of Scots, 1982; Mysteries and Legends, 1982; A Visitor's Guide to St. Andrews, 1984; St. Andrews: City of Change, 1984; A Book of British Eccentrics, 1984; Victorian and Edwardian Perthshire, 1984; Victorian and Edwardian Angus, 1985; Irish Grave Humour, 1987; Discovering Fife, 1988; The Life and Times of Berwick-upon-Tweed, 1988. Add: 132 North St., St. Andrews KY16 9AF, Scotland.

LAMPLUGH, Lois. British, b. 1921. Children's fiction, Poetry, History, Autobiography. Full-time writer. Member of the editorial staff, Jonathan Cape Ltd., London, England, 1947–57; served in the Auxiliary Territorial Service, 1939–43. *Publs:* The Stream Way (autobiography), 1948; The Pigeongram Puzzle (children's fiction), 1955; Nine Bright Shiners (children's fiction), 1955; Vagabonds' Castle (children's fiction), 1957; Rockets in the Dunes (children's fiction), 1958; The Sixpenny Runner (children's fiction), 1960; Midsummer Mountains (children's fiction), 1961; The Rifle House Friends (children's fiction), 1965; The Linhay on Hunter's Hill (children's fiction), 1966; The Old Navigator 1967; Honeyhill (for television), 1967–70; The Fur Princess and the Fir Prince (children's fiction), 1969; Mandog (adaptation of TV serial for children), 1972; The Quarry Hare (adult verse), 1976; Sean's Leap (children's fiction), 1979; The Winter Donkey (children's fiction), 1980; Barnstaple: Town on the Taw, 1983; Falcon's Tor (children's fiction), 1984; A History of Ilfracombe, 1984; Minehead with Dunster, 1987. Add: Springside, Bydown, Swimbridge, Devon EX32 0QB, England.

LAMPPA, William R. American, b. 1928. Poetry. Social Worker, Hennepin County Community Services, Minneapolis, Minn., 1964–87. *Publs:* The Crucial Point and Other Poems, 1971; In Familiar Fields with Old Friends, 1972; The Ancient Chariot and Other Poems, 1973. Add: P.O. Box 81, Embarrass, Minn. 55732, U.S.A.

LAN, David. South African, b. 1952. Plays/Screenplays, Anthropology. *Publs:* Painting a Wall, 1974; Bird Child, 1974; Homage to Been Soup, 1975; Paradise, 1975; The Winter Dancers, 1977; Red Earth, 1978;

Sergeant Ola and His Followers, 1979; The Sunday Judge (TV film), 1985; Guns and Rain: Spirit Mediums and Guerrillas in Zimbabwe (nonfiction), 1985; (with Caryl Churchill) A Mouthful of Birds, 1986; Flight, 1986; The Crossing (TV film); 1988, Desire, 1989. Add: c/o Judy Daish Assoc., 83 Eastbourne Mews, London W2, England.

LANCASTER, Henry Oliver. Australian, b. 1913. Mathematics/Statistics. Sr. Lectr., Dept. of Preventive Medicine, 1946–59, Assoc. Prof., Medical Statistics, 1959, and Prof. of Mathematical Statistics, 1959–78, Univ. of Sydney. *Publs:* Bibliography of Statistical Bibliographies, 1968; The Chi-Squared Distribution, 1969; An Introduction to Medical Statistics, 1974. Add: 13 Spit Rd., Mosman, N.S.W. 2088, Australia.

LANCASTER, Sheila. *See* HOLLAND, Sheila.

LANCASTER, Vicky. *See* ELSNA, Hebe.

LANCASTER BROWN, Peter. British, b. 1927. Novels/Short stories, Archaeology/Antiquities, Astronomy, Geography, Travel/Exploration/Adventure. *Publs:* Twelve Came Back, 1957; Call of the Outback, 1970; What Star Is That?, 1971; Astronomy in Colour, 1972, 5th ed. 1983; Coast of Coral and Pearl, 1972; The Seas and Oceans in Colour, 1973; Comets, Meteorites and Men, 1973; Star and Planet Spotting, 1974, 1981; (ed. and co-author) The Lore of Sport Fishing, 1974; Megaliths, Myths, and Men, 1976; The Planet Earth, 1976; Megaliths and Masterminds, 1979; Fjord of Silent Men, 1982; Close Encounter Objects, 1983; The High Tatra Affair, 1983; Astronomy (Colour Library of Science), 1984; Halley and His Comet, 1985; Halley's Comet and the Principia, 1986; The Comet Man: Memoirs of Edmond Halley, 1987; The Man I Might Have Been: A Creative Autobiography of Jack Lemon, 1988. Add: 10A St. Peter's Rd., Aldeburgh, Suffolk, England.

LANCE, James Waldo. Australian, b. 1926. Medicine/Health. Neurologist, Prince Henry Hosp., Sydney, N.S.W., since 1961; Prof. of Neurology, Univ. of New South Wales, Sydney, since 1975 (Assoc. Prof. of Medicine, 1964–75). *Publs:* The Mechanism and Management of Headache, 1969, 4th ed. 1982; A Physiological Approach to Clinical Neurology, 1970, 3rd ed. 1981; Headache, 1975; The Golden Trout, 1978; Introductory Neurology, 1984, 1989; Migraine and Other Headaches, 1986. Add: The Prince Henry Hosp., Little Bay, Sydney, N.S.W. 2036, Australia.

LANCE, Leslie. *See* CHARLES, Theresa.

LAND, Jane. *See* BORLAND, Kathryn.

LANDE, Lawrence Montague. Has also written with Thomas Greenwood as Alain Verval. Canadian, b. 1906. Poetry, History, Music, Philosophy. Notary Public, Que., since 1931. Dr., Canadian Writer's Foundn.; Hon. Corresponding Member for Quebec, Royal Soc. of Arts, London, since 1968; Life Fellow, Intercontinental Biographical Assn. Founder, Lawrence Lande Foundn. for Canadian Historical Research, McGill Univ., Montreal; past Pres., P.E.N. Canada Centre. *Publs:* Psalms Intimate and Familiar (poetry), 1945; Toward the Quiet Mind, 1954; The Third Duke of Richmond, 1956; Old Lamps Aglow, 1957; (with Thomas Greenwood as Alain Verval) Experience (poetry); The Lawrence Lande Collection of Canadiana, 1965; L'Accent, 1970; Rare and Unusual Canadiana: First Supplement to the Lande Bibliography, 1971; The Compleat Moralist, 1973; Adventures in Collecting Books and Blake and Buber, 1976; Canadian Historical Documents and Manuscripts, 7 vols., 1977–83; The Rise and Fall of John Law 1716-1720, 1982; The Political Economy of New France, 1983; The Founder of Our Monetary System: John Law, 1984; John Law: The Beginnings of Exploration, Trade, and Paper Money in North America, 1985; John Law: The Influence of His System and Its Lasting Effect on World Economics, 1986; John Law: The Creditability of Land and the Development of Paper Money in North America, 1987; John Law: Early Trade Rivalries Among Nations and The Beginning of Banking in North America, 1988. Add: 2045 Peel St., Mezzanine, Montreal, Que. H3A 1T6, Canada.

LANDECKER, Manfred. American, b. 1929. Politics/Government. Assoc. Prof., Dept. of Political Science, Southern Illinois Univ., since 1969 (Lectr., 1959–65; Assoc. Prof., 1965–69). Research Asst., Bologna Center, Sch. of Advanced Intnl. Studies of the Johns Hopkins Univ., 1956–58). *Publs:* The President and Public Opinion: Leadership in Foreignffairs, 1968. Add: Dept. of Political Science, Southern Illinois Univ., Carbondale, Ill. 62901, U.S.A.

LANDER, Ernest McPherson, Jr. American, b. 1915. History. Prof.

Emeritus of History, Clemson Univ., S.C. (joined faculty, 1941). Fulbright Lectr. in American History, Jadavpur Univ., Calcutta, India, 1966–67, and Univ. of Lagos, Nigeria, 1970–71. *Publs:* A History of South Carolina, 1865-1960, 1960; (ed. with C.M. McGee) A Rebel Came Home: The (Civil War) Diary of Florida Clemson, 1961; The Textile Industry in Antebellum South Carolina, 1969; South Carolina: The Palmetto State, 1970; (ed. with R.K. Ackerman) Perspectives in South Carolina History: The First 300 Years, 1973; (ed. with R.J. Calhoun) Two Decades of Change: The South since the Supreme Court's Desegregation Decision, 1975; Reluctant Imperialists: Calhoun, the South Carolinians, and the Mexican War, 1980; The Calhoun Family and Thomas Green Clemson: The Decline of a Southern Patriarchy, 1983; South Carolina: An Illustrated History of the Palmetto State, 1988. Add: 217 Riggs Dr., Clemson, S.C. 29631, U.S.A.

LANDER, Jack Robert. Canadian (b. British), b. 1921. History. Prof. Emeritus of History, Univ. of Western Ontario, since 1965. Sr. Lectr. in History, Univ. of Ghana, 1950–63; Assoc. Prof., Dalhousie Univ., Halifax, N.S., 1963–65. *Publs:* The Wars of the Roses, 1967; Conflict and Stability in Fifteenth Century England, 1969; Ancient and Medieval England: Beginnings to AD 1509, 1973; Crown and Nobility 1450-1509, 1976; Government and Community: England 1450-1509, 1980. Add: 5 Canonbury Pl., London N1 2NQ, England.

LANDES, Ruth. American, b. 1908. Anthropology/Ethnology. Prof. Emerita of Anthropology, McMaster Univ., Ontario, Canada, since 1984 (and 1965–79). Consultant, Dept. of Social Work and Agencies, Bureau of Mental Hygiene, Dept. of Education, Dept. of Public Health, Medicine and Nursing, and San Francisco Police, all California, since 1957. Social Worker, NYC, 1929–31; Research Fellow, Dept. of Anthropology, Columbia Univ., NYC, 1933–40; Study Dir., Scientific Research Dept., American Jewish Cttee., 1948–51; Lectr., New Sch. for Social Research, NYC, 1953–55, and Claremont Grad. Sch., California, 1960–62; Consultant to IBM, 1963–66; Prof. of Anthropology, McMaster Univ., Hamilton, Ont., Canada, 1965–79. *Publs:* Ojibwa Sociology, 1937, 1969; The Ojibwa Woman, 1938; The City of Women, 1947; Culture in American Education, 1965; The Latin-Americans of the Southwest, 1965; Ojibwa Religion and the Midewiwin, 1968; The Mystic Lake Sioux, 1969; The Prairie Potawatomi, 1970. Add: Dept. of Anthropology, McMaster Univ., 1280 Main St. West, Hamilton, Ont. L8S 4L9, Canada.

LANDIS, J(ames) D(avid). American, b. 1942. Children's fiction. Sr. Vice-Pres. since 1985, and Publisher and Ed.-in-Chief since 1988, William Morrow and Co. Inc., publishers, NYC (joined company, 1967). Asst. Ed., Abelard Schuman, NYC, 1966–67. *Publs:* The Sisters Impossible, 1979; Daddy's Girl, 1984; Love's Detective, 1984; Joey and the Girls, 1987. Add: William Morrow and Co. Inc., 105 Madison Ave., New York, N.Y. 10025, U.S.A.

LANDON, H(oward) C(handler) Robbins. American, b. 1926. Music. John Bird Prof. of Music, Univ. Coll., Cardiff, since 1978. *Publs:* The Symphonies of Joseph Haydn, 1955; (co-ed.) The Mozart Companion, 1956, 1970; The Collected Correspondence and London Notebooks of Joseph Haydn, 1959; (ed.) Complete Symphonies, by Haydn, 1965–68; (co-ed.) Complete String Quartets, by Haydn, 1968–83; Beethoven, 1970; (ed.) Complete Piano Trios, by Haydn, 1970–78; Haydn: Chronicle and Works (biography), 5 vols., 1976–80; Mozart and the Masons, 1982; Handel and his World, 1984; 1791: Mozart's Last Year, 1988; Mozart: The Golden Years, 1989. Add: Foncoussières, 81800 Rabastens (Tarn), France.

LANDON, Lucinda. American, b. 1950. Children's fiction. Writer and Illustrator; Artists, Visualizations, Providence, R.I., since 1978. Advertising Asst., Boston Center for the Arts, 1974–75; special education teacher, Cambridge, Mass., 1975–76. *Publs:* (also illustrator) Meg Mackintosh and the Case of the Missing Babe Ruth Baseball, 1986; Meg Mackintosh and the Case of the Curious Whale Watch, 1987. Add: Tucker Hollow, R.F.D. 2, Box 798, North Scituate, R.I. 02857, U.S.A.

LANE, Carolyn. American, b. 1926. Children's fiction, Plays. *Publs:* Turnabout Night at the Zoo (play), 1967, novel, 1971; The Wayward Clocks (play), 1967; The Last Grad (play), 1969; Uncle Max and the Sea Lion, 1970; The Voices of Greenwillow Pond, 1972; Child of Air (play), 1972; The Winnemah Spirit (novel), 1975; The Runaway Merry-Go-Round (play), 1978; (adaption) Tales of Hans Christian Anderson (play), 1978; Princess (novel), 1979; The World of the Brothers Grimm (play), 1979; The Ransom of Emily Jane (play), 1980; The Scheme of the Driftless Shifter (play), 1981; Echoes in an Empty Room and Other Supernatural Tales, 1981; Princess and Minerva (novel), 1981; Ghost Island (novel), 1985. Add: 40 Skyline Dr., Groton, Conn. 06340, U.S.A.

LANE, David Stuart. British, b. 1933. Economics, Politics, Sociology. Prof. of Sociology, Univ. of Birmingham, since 1981. Lectr., Univ. of Birmingham, 1962–67; Lectr., 1967–71, and Reader in Sociology, 1971–73, Univ. of Essex, Colchester; Lectr. and Fellow, Emmanuel Coll., Cambridge, 1973–80. *Publs:* The Roots of Russian Communism, 1969; Politics and Society in the USSR, 1970; The End of Inequality? Social Stratification Under State Socialism, 1971; (ed. with G. Kolankiewicz) Social Groups in Polish Society, 1973; The Socialist Industrial State, 1976; (with F. O'Dell) The Soviet Industrial Worker, 1978; Leninism: A Sociological Interpretation, 1981; The End of Social Inequality?, 1982; State and Society in the USSR, 1985; Soviet Economy and Society, 1985; (ed. with B. Stratford); Current approaches to Down's Syndrome, 1985; (ed.) Labour and Employment in the U.S.S.R., 1986; Soviet Labour and the Ethic of Communism, 1987; Elites and Political Power in the U.S.S.R., 1988. Add: University of Birmingham, Birmingham 15, England.

LANE, Gary (Martin). American, b. 1943. Literature. Prof. of English and American Literature, Univ. of Miami, since 1974. Instr. in Modern Poetry and Creative Writing, Muhlenburg Coll., Allentown, Pa., 1969–72; Visiting Lectr., Univ. of Michigan, Ann Arbor, 1972–74. *Publs:* (ed.) A Concordance to the Poems of Theodore Roethke, 1971; (ed.) A Concordance to the Poems of Hart Crane, 1972; (ed.) A Concordance to the Poems of Marianne Moore, 1972; (ed.) A Concordance to Personae: The Poems of Ezra Pound, 1972; (ed.) A Word Index to Joyce's Dubliners, 1972; (ed.) A Concordance to the Poems of Sylvia Plath, 1974; I Am: A Study of Cummings' Poems, 1976; A Concordance to the Poems of Dylan Thomas, 1976; (with Maria Stevens) Sylvia Plath: A Bibliography, 1978; (ed.) Sylvia Plath, 1979. Add: Dept. of English, Univ. of Miami, Coral Gables, Fla. 33124, U.S.A.

LANE, Harlan. American, b. 1936. Intellectual History, Language/Linguistics, Psychology. Prof., Dept. of Psychology, Northeastern Univ., Boston, since 1974 (Chmn. of the Dept., 1974–79). Asst. Prof., 1960–64, Assoc. Prof., 1964–67, and Prof. of Psychology, 1967–71, Univ. of Michigan, Ann Arbor; Prof. of Linguistics, Univ. of Paris-Sorbonne, 1969–73. *Publs:* (with D. Bem) A Laboratory Manual for the Control and Analysis of Behavior, 1964; (with G. Capelle) The World's Research in Language Learning, 1969; Introduction à l'étude du langage, 1972; The Wild Boy of Aveyron: A History of the Education of Retarded, Deaf and Hearing Children, 1976; The Wild Boy of Burundi: Psychological Catastrophies of Childhood, 1979; (ed. with F. Grosjean) Current Perspectives on American Sign Language, 1980; (trans. with F. Philip) Major Philosophical Works of Etienne Bonnot de Condillac, 1982; (ed. with F. Philip) The Deaf Experience: Classics in Language and Education, 1984; When the Mind Hears: A History of the Deaf, 1984. Add: Psychology Dept., Northeastern Univ., 125 Nightingale Hall, 360 Huntington, Boston, Mass. 02115, U.S.A.

LANE, Helen. *See* **HUDSON,** Helen

LANE, Mary D. *See* **DELANEY,** Mary Murray.

LANE, Patrick. Canadian, b. 1939. Poetry, Novels. Writer-in-Residence, The Globe Theatre Co., Regina, Saskatchewan, since 1985; Special Lectr., Univ. of Saskatchewan, Saskatoon. Ed., Very Stone House, publishers, Vancouver, 1966–72; Writer-in-Residence, Univ. of Manitoba, Winnipeg, 1978–79, Univ. of Ottawa, 1980, Univ. of Alberta, Edmonton, 1981–82, Saskatoon Public Library, 1982–83, Concordia Univ., 1985. *Publs:* Letters from the Savage Mind, 1966; For Rita—In Asylum, 1969; Calgary City Jail, 1969; Separations, 1969; Sunflower Seeds, 1969; On the Street, 1970; Mountain Oysters, 1971; Hiway 401 Rhapsody, 1972; The Sun Has Begun to Eat the Mountain, 1972; Passing into Storm, 1973; Beware the Months of Fire, 1974; Certs, 1974; Unborn Things: South American Poems, 1975; For Riel in That Gawdam Prison, 1975; Albino Pheasants, 1977; If, 1977; Poems, New and Selected, 1978; (with Lorna Uher) No Longer Two People, 1979; The Measure, 1980; Old Mother, 1982; Woman in the Dust, 1983; A Linen Crow, A Caftan Magpie, 1985; Selected Poems. Add: c/o The Writer's Union, 24 Ryerson Ave., Toronto, Ont. M5T 2P3, Canada.

LANE, Richard. American, b. 1926. Art, Literature, Translations. Reussearch Assoc., Honolulu Academy of Arts, since 1959. Instr., Kyoto Women's Coll., Japan, 1952; Lectr., Columbia Univ., NYC, 1953–54, and Kanto Coll., 1956–57; Instr., Univ. of Maryland Far East Prog., 1957–60. *Publs:* Saikaku: Novelist of the Japanese Renaissance, 1957; (trans and ed.) Japanese Arts and Crafts of the Meiji Era, 1958; Saikaku and Boccaccio: The Novella in Japan and Italy, 1959; Kaigetsudo, 1959;

(with James A. Michener) Japanese Prints: From the Early Masters to the Modern, 1959; Masters of the Japanese Print, 1962; (with Oliver Statler) The Black Ship Scroll, 1963; (technical ed. with Margaret Gentles) The Clarence Buckingham Collection of Japanese Prints, 1965; The Erotic Theme in Japanese Painting and Prints, 1968–70; (with Philip Rawson) Erotic Art of the East, 1968; Shunga Books of the Ukiyo-e School: Moronobu, series I-VI, 1973–82; Hokusai and Hiroshige, 1976; Images from the Floating World, 1978; The Early Shunga Scroll, 1979; Hiroshige: The Road to Kambara, 1985. Add: Koyama, Gobo-no-uchi 53, Yamashina-ku, Kyoto 607, Japan.

LANE, Ronald (James). Australian, b. 1931. Language/Linguistics. Principal, High Sch., Rainbow, Australia, 1968–71, and Girls' Grammar Sch., Rockhampton, Australia, 1971–75; Dir. of Schools, Australian Capital Territory Schs. Authority, since 1988. Principal, Dickson Coll., Canberra, 1975–88. *Publs:* Beginning Precis Writing, 1962; (co-author) Language and Ideas—Books 1-3, 1964–66; Language and Opinions, 1967. Add: A.C.T. Schools Authority, Canberra, A.C.T. 2602, Australia.

LANE, William L(ister). American, b. 1931. Theology/Religion. Prof. usof Religious Studies, Western Kentucky Univ., Bowling Green, since 1974. Prof. of New Testament and Judaic Studies, 1958–73, and Chmn. New Testament Dept., 1972–73, Gordon-Conwell Theological Seminary, South Hamilton, Mass. *Publs:* (co-ed.) The Encyclopedia of Christianity, 1964; (co-ed.) The Encyclopedia of Modern Christian Missions, 1967; (with Glenn W. Barker and J. Ramsey Michaels) The New Testament Speaks, 1969; Ephesians—2 Thessalonians, 1969; Righteousness in Christ, 1973; (co-trans.) New International Version of the New Testament, 1973; The New International Commentary on the Gospel According to Mark, 1974; Righteousness, 1978; Highlights of the Bible: The New Testament, 1980; Call to Committment: Responding to the Message of Hebrews, 1985; World Biblical Commentary, 1986. Add: Dept. of Religious Studies, Western Kentucky Univ., Bowling Green, Ky. 42101, U.S.A.

LANFRANCO, Guido Gaetan. Maltese, b. 1930. Biology. Biology Lectr., Malta, since 1960. Former Lectr., Coll. of Education, Malta. *Publs:* Guide to the Flora of Malta, 1955, 1960; Complete Guide to the Fishes of Malta, 1958, 3rd ed. 1974; Field Guide to the Wild Flowers of Malta, 1969; Maltese Mammals, 1969; Duwa u Semm fil-Hxejjex Maltin, 1975. Add: 78 Trophimus St., Sliema, Malta.

LANG, David Marshall. British, b. 1924. Cultural/Ethnic topics, Literature. Professor Emeritus of Caucasian Studies, since 1985. Fellow of Modern Languages, St. John's Coll., Cambridge, 1946–52; Warden of Connaught Hall, 1955–83 and Prof. of Caucasian Studies, Sch. of Oriental and African Studies, 1964–84, Univ. of London (Lectr. in Georgian, 1949–58; Reader in Caucasian Studies, 1958–64). *Publs:* Studies in the Numismatic History of Georgia in Transcaucasia, 1955; (compiler and trans.) Lives and Legends of the Georgian Saints, 1956; (trans.) The Wisdom of Balahvar, 1957; The First Russian Radical: Alexander Radishchev, 1959: A Modern History of Georgia, 1962; (compiler) Catalogue of the Georgian Books in the British Museum, 1962; The Georgians, 1966; (trans.) The Balavariani, 1966; (co-ed.) Penguin Companion to Literature, vol. 4, 1969; Armenia, Cradle of Civilization, 1970; (with C. Burney) The Peoples of the Hills: Ancient Ararat and Caucasus, 1971; (ed. and compiler) Guide to Eastern Literatures, 1971; The Bulgarians, 1976; The Armenians: A People in Exile, 1981. Add: Sch. of Oriental and African Studies, Univ. of London, London WC1, England.

LANG, (Lt. Gen. Sir) Derek. British, b. 1913. Autobiography/Memoirs/Personal. Officer, Cameron Highlanders, 1933–69, and Comdr. in Scotland, 1966–69, British Army; Secty., Stirling Univ., 1970–73; Assoc. Consultant, PA Managements Consultants, 1975–84. *Publs:* Return to St. Valery, 1974. Add: Templeland, Kirknewton, Midlothian EH27 8JJ, Scotland.

LANG, Gladys Engel. American. Communications media, Sociology. Prof. of Communications, Political Science, and Sociology, Univ. of Washington, Seattle, since 1984. Prof. of Sociology, State Univ. of New York, Stony Brook, 1970–84. *Publs:* (ed.) Mental Health, 1958; (with Kurt Lang) Collective Dynamics, 1961; (ed.) Old Age in America, 1961; (with Kurt Lang) Politics and Television, 1968; (with Kurt Lang) Voting and Non voting, 1968; (with Kurt Lang) The Battle for Public Opinion: The President, The Press, and the Polls During Watergate, 1983; (with Kurt Lang) Politics and Television Re-Viewed, 1984. Add: 1249 20th Ave. E., Seattle, Wash. 98112, U.S.A.

LANG, King. *See* **TUBB,** E.C.

LANG, Kurt. American, b. 1924. Media, Sociology. Dir., School of Communications, Univ. of Washington, since 1984. Research Sociologist, CBC, Ottawa, Ont., 1954–56; Instr., 1956–59; Asst. Prof., 1959–62, and Assoc. Prof. of Sociology and Chmn., 1963–64, Queens Coll. of the City Univ. of New York, NYC; Prof. of Sociology, State Univ. of New York, Stony Brook, 1964–84. *Publs:* (with G.E. Lang) Collective Dynamics, 1961; (with G.E. Lang) Voting and Nonvoting, 1968; (with G.E. Lang) Politics and Television, 1968; Military Institutions and Sociology of War, 1972; (with G.E. Lang) The Battle for Public Opinion, 1983; (with G.E. Lang) Politics and Television Re-Viewed, 1984. Add: 1249 20th Ave. E., Seattle, Wa. 98112, U.S.A.

LANG, William Rawson. Australian, b. 1909. Industry, Technology, Media. Science Lectr., Perth Technical Coll., W.A., 1934–36; Research Physicist, Inst. of Agriculture, Univ. of Western Australia, Nedlands, 1937–38; Head of Textile Coll., 1945–70, and Head of Sch. of Applied Sciences and Deputy Principal, 1970–74, Gordon Inst. of Technology, Geelong, Vic.; Chmn., Victorian Chapter, Australian Coll. of Education, 1969–71. *Publs:* (with A.J. Farnworth) Textile Education in the Union of Burma, 1956–57; (with E.B. Thomas) The Televiewing Habits of Secondary School Children in Geelong, 1965; Sheep and Wool: Industry in Australia, 1967, 1972; Visions and Realities: A History of the Geelong Infirmary and Benevolent Asylum, 1980; James Harrison: Pioneering Genius, 1982; The Boss, 1982; Markers and Memorials at the Geelong Hospital, 1984; Chords of Memory: Biography of Rea James Dickson, 1985; The Kitchener Memorial Saga, 1987. Add: 13 Humble St., Geelong East, Vic., Australia 3219.

LANGBAUM, Robert (Woodrow). American, b. 1924. Literature. James Branch Cabell Prof. of English and American Literature, Univ. of Virginia, Charlottesville, since 1967 (Assoc. Prof., 1960–63, and Prof., 1963–67). Member, Editorial Bd., Victorian Poetry, since 1963, Style, since 1967, New Literary History, since 1969, Bulletin of Research in the Humanities, since 1977, Studies in English Literature, since 1978, Southern Review, since 1979. Instr. in English, 1950–55, and Asst. Prof., 1955–60, Cornell Univ., Ithaca, N.Y. *Publs:* The Poetry of Experience: The Dramatic Monologue in Modern Literary Tradition, 1957, 1986; The Gayety of Vision: A Study of Isak Dinesen's Art, 1964; (ed.) The Tempest, by Shakespeare, 1964; (ed.) The Victorian Age: Essays in History and in Social and Literary Criticism, 1967; The Modern Spirit: Essays on the Continuity of Nineteenth and Twentieth-Century Literature, 1970; Isak Dinesen's Art, 1975; The Mysteries of Identity: A Theme in Modern Literature, 1977; The Word from Below: Essays on Modern Literature and Culture, 1987. Add: Dept. of English, 115 Wilson Hall, Charlottesville, Va. 22903. U.S.A.

LANGBEIN, John Harriss. American, b. 1941. Law. Max Pam Prof. of American and Foreign Law, Univ. of Chicago Law Sch., since 1971. *Publs:* Prosecuting Crime in the Renaissance: England, Germany, France, 1974; Torture and the Law of Proof: Europe and England in the Ancien Régime, 1977; Comparative Criminal Procedure: Germany, 1977; (with Lawrence Waggoner) Selected Statutes on Trusts and Estates, 1987; (with Bruce Wolk) Pension and Employee Benefit Law, 1989. Add: Univ. of Chicago Law Sch., 1111 East 60th St., Chicago, Ill. 60637, U.S.A.

LANGDON, Robert Adrian. Australian, b. 1924. History, Languages/Linguistics, Travel/Exploration/Adventure. Visiting Fellow, Pacific History, Australian National Univ. Canberra, since 1986 (Exec. Officer, Pacific Manuscripts Bureau, 1968–86). Asst. Ed., Pacific Islands Monthly mag., Sydney, N.S.W., 1964–68. *Publs:* Tahiti: Island of Love, 1959, 5th ed. 1979; The Lost Caravel, 1975; (with Darrell Tryon) The Language of Easter Island: Its Development and Eastern Polynesian Relationships, 1983; The Lost Caravel Re-explored, 1988. Add: 15 Darambal St., Aranda, A.C.T., Australia 2614.

LANGE, John. *See* CRICHTON, Michael.

LANGE, Oliver (pseudonym). American, b. 1927. Novels/Short Stories, Westerns/Adventure. *Publs:* Vandenberg, 1971, as Defiance: An American Novel, 1984; Incident at La Junta, 1973; Red Snow, 1978; Next of Kin, 1980; The Land of the Long Shadow, 1981; Pas de Deux, 1982; The Devil at Home, 1986. Add: c/o JET Literary Assocs. Inc., 124 E. 84th St., Suite 4A, New York, N.Y. 10028, U.S.A.

LANGE, Victor. American, b. 1908. Literature. John N. Woodhull Prof. of Modern Languages, Princeton Univ., N.J., since 1957 (Chmn., Dept. of Germanic Languages, 1958–74). Hon. Prof. of German Literature, Free Univ., Berlin, since 1963. Lectr. in German, Univ. of Toronto, 1932–38; Asst. Prof., and subsequently Prof. of German Literature, Cornell Univ., Ithaca, N.Y., 1938–57. *Publs:* Die Lyrik und ihr Publikum im England des 18 Jahrhunderts, 1936; Kulturkritik und Literaturbetrachtung in Amerika, 1938; (ed.) Deutsche Briefe, 1940; Modern German Literature, 1945; (ed.) The Sorrows of Young Werther, 1959; (ed.) Goethe's Faust, 1950; (ed.) Great German Short Stories, 1952; Goethe's Fiction, 1953; Eduard Morike, 1954; Schlegel: Literary Criticism, 1955; Narrative Forms in 18th Century Fiction, 1958; Schiller's Poetik, 1961; (ed.) Lessings Hamburg Dramaturgy, 1962; (ed.) Goethe's Wilhelm Meister, 1962; (ed.) German Classical Drama, 1962; The Close of the 18th Century, 1962; German Expressionism, 1963; Contemporary German Poetry, 1963; (ed.) Goethe: Twentieth Century Views; New Perspectives in German Literary Criticism, 1979; The Classical Age of German Literature, 1982. Add: 343 Jefferson Rd., Princeton, N.J. 08540, U.S.A.

LANGENDOEN, D. Terence. American, b. 1939. Language/Linguistics. Prof. of Linguistics, Univ. of Arizona, Tucson, since 1988. Asst. Prof., 19864–68, and Assoc. Prof., 1968–69, Ohio State Univ., Columbus; Prof., Brooklyn Coll. and Grad. Center, City Univ. of N.Y., 1969–88. Secty.-Treas., Linguistic Soc. of America, 1984–88. *Publs:* The London School of Linguistics, 1968; The Study of Syntax, 1969; Essentials of English Grammar, 1970; (ed. with C.J. Fillmore) Studies in Linguistic Semantics, 1971; (ed. with T.G. Bever and J.J. Katz) An Integrated Theory of Linguistic Ability, 1976; (with P.M. Postal) The Vastness of Natural Language, 1984. Add: Dept. of Linguistics, Univ. of Arizona, Tucson, Ariz. 85721, U.S.A.

LANGFORD, David. British, b. 1953. Science fiction. Freelance writer since 1980; Managing Dir., Ansible Information Ltd., since 1987. Columnist, 8000 Plus, Bath, since 1986, and GM Magazine, since 1988. Weapons physicist, Atomic Research Establishment, 1975–80. *Publs:* science fiction novels—The Space Eater, 1982; The Leaky Establishment, 1984; (with John Grant) Earthdoom!, 1987; other—(with others) The Necronomicon, 1978; War in 2080: The Future of Military Technology, 1979; An Account of a Meeting with Denizens of Another World 1871, 1979; (with Chris Morgan) Facts and Fallacies: A Book of Definitive Mistakes and Misguided Predictions, 1981; (with Peter Nicholls and Brian M. Stableford) The Science in Science Fiction, 1982; (with Charles Platt) Micromania: The Whole Truth about Home Computers (in U.S. as The Whole Truth Home Computer Handbook), 1984; (with Brian M. Stableford) The Third Millennium: The History of the World AD 2000-3000, 1985. Add: c/o A.P. Watt, 20 John St., London WC1N 2DR, England.

LANGFORD, Gary R(aymond). New Zealander, b. 1947. Novels/Short stories, Plays/Screenplays, Poetry. Writer and Lecturer in Theatre, Macarthur Institute of Higher Ed., since 1977 and Ed., Macarthur Literary Review, since 1984; Dir., Playhouse Theatre since 1982. Ed., Ironback, 1977–83; Co-Ed., Edge Literary Mag., 1970–72. *Publs:* (ed.) Superbox, 1971; (ed.) Shard, 1972; The Family (poetry), 1973; Quartet, 1973; Golden Handshake, 1977; Death of the Early Morning Hero (novel), 1976; Lovers, 1977; Getting On, 1977; Reversals, 1978; I Didn't Ask to Grow Old, 1978; The Death of James Dean (stories), 1978; Superman, The True Story, 1979; Players in the Ballgame, 1979; The Adventures of Dreaded Ned (novel), 1980; Four Ships (poetry), 1981; Don't Jump Out That Window—You're Feeling Fine, 1982; Flappers, 1982; Captain Australia, 1983; Doctor Repulsion's Rock 'n' Roll Horror Show, 1983; Soaps, 1984; Reunion, 1984; Who's Killing the Great Actors of Macbeth, 1984; Playing Molière, 1984; Vanities (novel), 1984; The Pest Exterminator's Shakespeare (poetry), 1984; Pillbox (novel), 1986; Another Country (novel), 1988. Add: c/o 36 Dean St., W. Pennant Hills, Sydney, N.S.W., Australia.

LANGFORD, Gerald. American, b. 1911. Novels/Short stories, Literature, Biography. Prof. of English, Univ. of Texas, Austin, since 1962 (Asst. Prof., 1946–50; Assoc. Prof., 1950–62). *Publs:* Alias O. Henry, 1957; The Richard Harding Davis Years, 1961; The Murder of Stanford White, 1962; (ed.) Ingénue Among the Lions, 1965; (ed.) Faulkner's Revision of Absalom, Absalom!, 1971; (ed.) Faulkner's Revision of Sanctuary, 1972; Destination (novel), 1981. Add: English Dept., Univ. of Texas, Austin, Texas 78712, U.S.A.

LANGFORD, James R. Jerome. American, b. 1937. Intellectual history, Sports. Dir., Univ. of Notre Dame Press, South Bend, Ind., since 1974. Ed., Doubleday and Co., 1967–69; Exec. Ed., Univ. of Michigan Press, Ann Arbor, 1969–74. *Publs:* Galileo, Science, and the Church, 1966; (trans.) Apologia pro Galileo by Thomasso Campanella, 1975; The Game is Never Over, 1980; The Cub Fan's Guide to Life, 1984; Run, Hits and Errors, 1987. Add: c/o Univ. of Notre Dame Press, Notre Dame, Ind. 46556, U.S.A.

LANGLAND, Joseph (Thomas). American, b. 1917. Poetry. Instr., Dana Coll., Blair, Nebr., 1941–42; Asst. Prof., then Assoc. Prof., Univ. of Wyoming, Laramie, 1948–59; Prof. of English, Univ. of Massachusetts, 1959–79. Poetry Ed., Massachusetts Review, Amherst, 1960–66. *Publs:* For Harold, 1945; The Green Town, 1956; (ed. with J.B. Hall) The Short Story, 1956; A Little Homily, 1960; (ed. with P. Engle) Poet's Choice, 1962; The Wheel of Summer, 1963; (trans. with T. Aczel and L. Tikos) Russian Underground Poems 1958–1970, 1973; The Sacrifice Poems, 1975; In the Shell of the Ear, 1977; Any Body's Song, 1980; A Dream of Love, 1986; Twelve Poems with Preludes, 1988. Add: 16 Morgan Circle, Amherst, Mass. 01002, U.S.A.

LANGLEY, Bob. British, b. 1938. Novels/Short stories, Travel/Exploration/Adventure. Broadcaster with BBC since 1968. *Publs:* Walking the Scottish Border; Death Stalk (novel); Lobo (personal experiences), 1977; War of the Running Fox (novel), 1978; Warlords (novel), 1979; Traverse of the Gods (novel), 1980; Autumn Tiger (novel), 1981; Hour of the Gaucho (novel), 1983; Conquistadores (novel), 1985; The Churchill Diamonds (novel), 1986; East of Everest (novel), 1987; Avenge the Belgrano (novel), 1988; Blood River (novel), 1989. Add: c/o Michael Shaw, Curtis Brown, 162-168 Regent St., London W1R 5TA, England.

LANGLEY, Lester D(anny). American, b. 1940. History, Politics. *Publs:* The Cuban Policy of the United States: A Brief History, 1968; (ed.) The United States, Cuba and the Cold War: American Failure or Communist Conspiracy, 1970; (co-ed.) The United States and Latin America, 1971; Struggle for the American Mediterranean: United States–European Rivalry in the Gulf Caribbean, 1976; The United States and the Caribbean 1900–1970, 1980, 1985; The Banana Wars: An Inner History of American Empire 1900–1934; Central America: The Real Stakes, 1985; Mex-America: Two Countries, One Future, 1988. Add: Dept. of History, Univ. of Georgia, Athens, Ga. 30603, U.S.A.

LANGTON, Jane. American, b. 1922. Mystery/Crime/Suspense, Children's fiction. *Publs:* The Majesty of Grace, 1961, republished in paperback as Her Majesty, Grace Jones, 1972; The Diamond in the Window, 1962; The Transcendental Murder, 1964; The Swing in the Summer House, 1967; The Astonishing Stereoscope, 1971; The Boyhood of Grace Jones, 1972; Dark Nantucket Noon, 1975; Paper Chains, 1977; The Memorial Hall Murder, 1978; The Fledgling, 1980; Natural Enemy, 1982; Emily Dickinson is Dead, 1984; The Fragile Flag, 1984; The Hedgehog Boy, 1985; Good and Dead, 1986; Murder at the Gardner, 1988. Add: 9 Baker Farm Rd., Lincoln, Mass. 01773, U.S.A.

LANHAM, Richard Alan. American, b. 1936. Literature, Writing/Journalism. Prof. of English since 1972, Univ. of California, Los Angeles (Asst. Prof., 1965–69; Assoc. Prof., 1969–72; Dir., 1979–82, and Exec. Dir., 1982–86, of Writing Progs.). Instr., and Asst. Prof., Dartmouth Coll., Hanover, N.H., 1962–65. *Publs:* Sidney's Old Arcadia, 1965; A Handlist of Rhetorical Terms, 1968; Tristram Shandy: The Games of Pleasure, 1973; Style: An Anti-Textbook, 1974; The Motives of Eloquence, 1976; Revising Prose, 1979; Revising Business Prose, 1981; Analyzing Prose, 1983; Literacy and the Survival of Humanism, 1983. Add: Dept. of English, Univ. of California, Los Angeles, Calif. 90024, U.S.A.

LANIER, Sterling E(dmund). American, b. 1927. Science fiction/Fantasy, Children's fiction. Full-time writer and sculptor since 1967. Research Historian, Winterthur Museum, Delaware, 1958–60; Ed., John C. Winston Co., 1961, Chilton Books, 1961–62, 1965–67, and Macrae-Smith Co., 1963–64. *Publs:* The War for the Lot (juvenile), 1969; The Peculiar Exploits of Brigadier Ffellowes (short stories), 1972; Hiero's Journey, 1973; The Unforsaken Hiero, 1983; Menace under Marwood, 1983; The Curious Quests of Brig. Ffellowes, 1986. Add: c/o Curtis Brown Ltd., 10 Astor Place, New York, N.Y. 10003, U.S.A.

LANTRY, Mike. *See* **TUBB,** E.C.

LANTZ, J(ohn) Edward. American, b. 1911. Plays/Screenplays, Theology/Religion. Chaplain, Georgia Intnl. Trade Assn., since 1975. Assoc. Ed., Youth Publs., Methodist Publishing House, Nashville, Tenn., 1945–51; Assoc. Prof. of Communications and Ecumenics, Interdenominational Center, Atlanta, Ga., 1965–76. Pres., Atlanta Writers Club, 1974–75. *Publs:* (ed.) Best Religious Stories, 1948; (ed.) Stories of Christian Living, 1950; (ed.) Stories to Grow By, 1953; Speaking in the Church, 1954; (with R.C. Lantz) Bible Characters in Action, 1955; Church Councils in the South, 1956; (with R.C. Lantz) Plays for Happier Homes, 1957; Reading the Bible Aloud, 1959. Add: 1040 Springdale Rd., N.E. Atlanta, Ga. 30306, U.S.A.

LAPINE, James (Elliot). American, b. 1949. Plays/Screenplays, Songs/Lyrics/Libretti. Playwright and director. Formerly photographer; graphic designer, Yale Repertory Theatre, New Haven, Conn.; teacher, Yale Sch. of Drama. *Publs:* Table Settings, 1980; Twelve Dreams, 1982; Sunday in the Park with George, 1986; Into the Woods, 1986. Add: c/o George Lane, William Morris Agency, 1350 Ave. of the Americas, New York, N.Y. 10036, U.S.A.

LAPONCE, Jean Antoine. French and Canadian, b. 1925. Politics/Government. Prof. of Political Science, Univ. of British Columbia, Vancouver, since 1966 (Asst. Prof., 1956–61; Assoc. Prof., 1961–66). Former Instr. in Political Science, Univ. of Santa Clara, Calif. *Publs:* The Protection of Minorities, 1961; The Government of France under the Fifth Republic, 1962; People vs. Politics, 1970; (ed. with P. Smoker) Experimentation and Simulation in Political Science, 1971; Left and Right: The Topography of Political Perceptions, 1981; Langue et Territoire, 1984, as Languages and Their Territories, 1987. Add: Dept. of Political Science, Univ. of British Columbia, Vancouver, B.C. V6T 1WS, Canada.

LAPPE, Frances Moore. American, b. 1944. Cookery/Gastronomy, Economics, International relations/Current affairs. *Publs:* Diet for Small Planet, 1971, 1975; Great Meatless Meals, 1976; (with J. Collins) Food First, 1977; (with J. Collins) World Hunger, 1979; (with A. Beccar-Varela) Mozambique and Tanzania, 1980; (co-author) Aid as Obstacle, 1980; (co-author) What Can We Do? A Food, Land, Hunger Action Guide, 1980; (co-author) Casting New Molds, 1980; (co-author) Now We Can Speak, 1983; What Difference Could a Revolution Make? 1983; What to Do After You Turn Off the TV, 1985; (with J. Collins) World Hunger: Twelve Myths, 1986; (co-author) Betraying the National Interest, 1987; Rediscovering America's Values, 1989. Add: c/o Institute for Food and Development Policy, 1885 Mission St., San Francisco, Calif. 94103, U.S.A.

LAPPING, Brian (Michael). British, b. 1937. Politics/Government, Public/Social administration, Social commentary/phenomena. Television Producer, Granada Television Ltd., since 1970: Exec. Producer, World in Action, 1976–78, The State of the Nation, 1978–80, and End of Empire, 1980–85. Reporter, Daily Mirror, London, 1959–61; Reporter and Deputy Commonwealth Corresp., The Guardian, London, 1961–67; Ed., Venture (Fabian Soc. monthly journal), 1965–69; Feature writer, Financial Times, London, 1967–68; Deputy Ed., New Society, London, 1968–70. *Publs:* (co-ed.) More Power to the People, 1968; The Labour Government 1964–70, 1970; (ed.) The State of the Nation: Parliament, 1973; (ed.) The State of the Nation: The Bounds of Freedom, 1980; End of Empire, 1985; Apartheid: A History, 1986. Add: 94 Highgate Hill, London N6, England.

LAQUEUR, Walter. American, b. 1921. History, Politics/Government. Dir., Inst. of Contemporary History, and Wiener Library, London, since 1964. Chmn., Research Council, Center of Strategic and Intnl. Studies, Washington, D.C. *Publs:* Communism and Nationalism in the Middle East, 1956; The Soviet Union and the Middle East, 1959; Young Germany, 1962; Russia and Germany, 1965; The Fate of the Revolution, 1967; The Road to War (in U.S. as The Road to Jerusalem), 1968; The Struggle for the Middle East, 1969; (ed.) The Israel-Arab Reader, 1969, 1984; Europe since Hitler (in U.S. as Rebirth of Europe), 1970, 1982; Out of the Ruins of Europe, 1971; (ed.) A Dictionary of Politics, 1971; (ed.) A Readers Guide to Contemporary History, 1972; A History of Zionism, 1972, Confrontation: The Middle East War and World Politics, 1974; Weimar, 1974; Guerrilla, 1976; Terrorism, 1977; (ed.) Fascism: A Reader's Guide, 1978; Terrible Secret, 1980; The Missing Years, 1980; Farewell to Europe, 1981; Germany Today, 1985. Add: CSIS, 1800 K St., Washington, D.C. 20006, U.S.A.

LARKIN, Maurice (John Milner). British, b. 1932. History. Richard Pares Prof. of History, Univ. of Edinburgh, since 1976. Asst. Lectr., 1958–61, and Lectr. in Modern History, 1961–65, Univ. of Glasgow; Lectr., 1965–68; Sr. Lectr., 1968–75, and Reader in History, 1976, Univ. of Kent. *Publs:* Gathering Pace: Continental Europe 1870 to 1945, 1969; Church and State After the Dreyfus Affair: The Separation Issue in France, 1974; Man and Society in Nineteenth Century Realism: Determinism and Literature, 1977; France since the Popular Front: Government and People 1936–1986, 1988. Add: Dept. of History, Univ. of Edinburgh, Edinburgh EH8 9JY, Scotland.

LARKIN, Rochelle. American, b. 1935. Also writes as Darrell Fairfield. Historical/Romance/Gothic, Medicine/Health, Recreation/Leisure/Hobbies, Social commentary/phenomena. Ed.,

Countrywide Publs., NYC, 1963; Ed., Kanrom Inc., NYC, 1964–70; Ed., Pinnacle Books, NYC, 1971; Ed.-in-Chief, Lancer Books, NYC, 1973–74. *Publs:* Soul Music, 1970; Supermarket Superman, 1970; (with Milburn Smith) Teen Scene, 1971; The Godmother, 1971; Honor Thy Godmother, 1972; For Godmother and Country, 1972; (with M. Smith) 365 Ways to Say I Want to Be Your Friend, 1973; Black Magic, 1974; The Beatles: Yesterday, Today, Tomorrow, 1974; The Greek Goddess, 1975; Call Me Anytime, 1975; International Joke Book, 1975; The Raging Flood, 1976; Hail Columbia, 1976; The First One, 1976; (with Robin Moore) Valency Girl, 1976; Pusher, 1976; Sexual Superstars, 1976; Harvest of Desire, 1976; Kitty, 1977; (with Robin Moore) Mafia Wife, 1977; Mistress of Desire, 1978; (with Pablo Manzoni) Instant Beauty, 1978; (with Robin Moore) Tri, 1978; Torches of Desire, 1979; Glitterball, 1980; (with Julie Davis) Beverly Johnson's Guide to a Life of Health and Beauty, 1981; Only Perfect, 1981; Golden Days, Silver Nights, 1982; (as Darrell Fairfield) Amber series, 6 vols., 1982; The Crystal Heart, 1983; Angels Never Sleep, 1984; A Bed of Roses, 1984. Add: c/o Leisure Books, 276 Fifth Ave., New York, N.Y. 10001, U.S.A.

LARN, Richard James Vincent. British, b. 1930. Archaeology/Antiquities, History. U.K. Rep., Tauchen and Diver. *Publs:* (with C. Carter) Cornish Shipwrecks: The South Coast, 1969; Cornish Shipwrecks: The Isles of Scilly, 1971; Devon Shipwrecks, 1973; Land's End Shipwrecks, 1974; Goodwin Sands Shipwrecks, 1977; Shipwrecks of the British Isles,1980; (with Z. Cowan) Encyclopedia of Diving, 1980; History of Charlestown, 1980; (with P. McBride) Sir Crowdisley Shovell's Disaster; Diver Guide to South Cornwall; Commercial Diving Manual. Add: Longstone Heritage Centre, St. Mary's, Isles of Scilly, Cornwall, England.

LARRICK, Nancy. American, b. 1910. Children's non-fiction, Literature. Ed., Young American Readers, 1945–51; Education Dir., Children's Books, Random House, publrs., NYC, 1952–59; Adjunct Prof. of Education, Lehigh Univ., Bethlehem, Pa., 1963–75. *Publs:* (with D. Melcher) Printing and Promotion Handbook, 1949, 3rd ed. 1966; See for Yourself, 1952; A Parent's Guide to Children's Reading, 1958, 5th ed. 1982; Teacher's Guide to Children's Books, 1960; Rain, Hail, Sleet and Snow, 1961; A Parent's Guide to Children's Education, 1963; (ed.) Piper, Pipe That Song Again, 1965; (ed.) Poetry of Holidays, 1966; (ed.) Green Is Like a Meadow of Grass, 1968; (ed.) Piping Down the Valleys Wild, 1968; (ed.) On City Streets, 1968; (ed.) I Heard a Scream in the Street, 1970; (ed.) More Poetry for Holidays, 1973; (ed. with E. Merriam) Male and Female Under 18: Frank Comments of Young People About Sex Roles Today, 1973; (ed.) Room for Me and a Mountain Lion, 1974; (ed.) Crazy to Be Alive in Such a Strange World, 1977; (ed.) Bring Me All of Your Dreams, 1980; Children's Reading Begins at Home, 1980; (ed.) Tambourines! Tambourines to Glory, 1982; (ed.) When the Dark Comes Dancing, 1983; (ed.) Cats Are Cats, 1988. Add: 330 W. Cecil St., Winchester, Va. 22601, U.S.A.

LARSEN, Egon. British, b. 1904. Children's non-fiction, History, Technology, Sciences, Biography. London Corresp., Bavarian Radio Network, Munich, since 1954; Fellow of English P.E.N. *Publs:* Inventors' Cavalcade, 1944; Inventors' Scrapbook, 1947; Spotlight on Films, 1950; Men Who Changed the World, 1952; Radar Works Like This, 1952; An American in Europe: Count Rumford, 1953; Men Who Shaped the Future, 1954; The Young Traveller in Germany, 1954; The True Book About Inventions, 1954; Men Under the Sea, 1955; The True Book About Firefighting, 1955; Transistors Work Like This, 1957; Progress of Science: Transport, 1957; You'll See: Report from the Future, 1957; Men Who Fought for Freedom, 1958; Atomic Energy: The First Hundred Years, 1958; Sir Vivian Fuchs, 1959; Power from Atoms, 1960; A History of Inventions, 1961; The Atom, 1961; Film Making, 1962; The Cavendish Laboratory: Nursery of Genius, 1962; Atoms and Atomic Energy, 1963; Laughter in a Damp Climate: Anthology of British Humour, 1963; (with Peter Larsen) Young Africa, 1965; The Pegasus Book of Inventions, 1965; The Deceivers: Lives of the Great Impostors, 1966; Munich, 1967; Great Ideas in Engineering, 1967; Great Humorous Stories of the World, 1967; First with the Truth: Newspapermen in Action, 1968; Lasers Work Like This, 1968; One Man Against Napoleon: Carlo-Andra Pozzo Di Borgo, 1968; Hovercraft and Hydrofoils Work Like This, 1970; Strange Sects and Cults, 1971; (with P. Larsen) United Nations At Work, 1972; Radio and Television, 1975; Weimar Eyewitness, 1977; A Flame in Barbed Wire: The Story of Amnesty International, 1978; Wit as a Weapon: The Political Joke in History, 1980. Add: c/o Norton and Co., 500 Fifth Ave., New York, N.Y. 10110, U.S.A.

LARSON, Arthur. American, b. 1910. International relations/Current affairs, Law, Politics/Government. Dir., Rule of Law Research Center, and James B. Duke Prof. of Law, Duke Univ., Durham, N.C., since 1958.

Assoc. Prof. of Law, 1945–48, and Prof., 1948–53, Cornell Law Sch., Ithaca, N.Y.; Dean, Univ. of Pittsburgh Sch. of Law, 1953; Under Secty. of Labor, U.S. Govt., 1954–56; Dir., U.S. Information Agency, 1956–57; Special Asst. to the Pres., 1957–58; Special Consultant to the Pres., 1958–61; Knapp Prof. of Law, Univ. of Wisconsin Law Sch., Madison, 1968–69. *Publs:* (with R.S. Stevens) Cases and Materials on the Law of Corporations, 1947, 1955; The Law of Workmen's Compensation, 10 vols., 1952, 1989; Know Your Social Security, 1955, rev. ed. 1959; A Republican Looks at His Party, 1956; What We Are For, 1959; Design for Research in International Rule of Law, 1961; When Nations Disagree: A Handbook on Peace Through Law, 1961; (ed. and contrib.) A Warless World, 1963; (with J.B. Whitton) Propaganda: Toward Disarmament in the War of Words, 1964; (ed. and contrib.) Sovereignty Within the Law, 1965; (with D.R. Larson) Vietnam and Beyond, 1965; Eisenhower: The President Nobody Knew, 1968; Workmen's Compensation for Occupational Injuries and Death, 3 vols., 1972, 1989; (co-ed. and contrib.) Population and Law: A Study of the Relations Between Population Problems and Law, 1971; The Law of Employment Discrimination, 5 vols., 1975–89; Cases, Materials and Text on Worker's Compensation Law, 1984; Teacher's Guide to Worker's Compensation, 1985. Add: Dept. of History, Univ. of Rochester, Rochester, N.Y. 19627, U.S.A.

LARSON, Charles. American, b. 1922. Mystery/Crime/Suspense. Producer, Columbia Pictures, 20th Century Fox, and QM Productions, Calif., 1964–73; Exec. Producer, Nakia television series, Columbia Pictures Television, 1974; Co-Creator, Hagen television series, CBS, 1979–80. *Publs:* The Chinese Game, 1969; Someone's Death, 1973; Matthew's Hand, 1974; Muir's Blood, 1976; The Portland Murders, 1983. Add: 2422 S.W. Broadway Dr., Portland, Ore. 97201, U.S.A.

LARSON, Muriel Koller. American, b. 1924. Theology/Religion. *Publs:* Devotions for Women's Groups,1967; How to Give a Devotion, 1967; Devotions for Children, 1969; Living Miracles, 1973; It Took a Miracle, 1974; You are What You Think, 1974; God's Fantastic Creation, 1975; The Bible Says: Quiz Book, 1976; Are You Real, God?, 1976; I Give Up, God, 1978; Joy Every Morning, 1979; What Happens When Women Believe, 1979; Living by Faith, 1984; Praise Every Day, 1984; Ways Women Can Witness, 1984; Me and My Pet Peeves, 1988. Add: 10 Vanderbilt Circle, Greenville, S.C. 29609, U.S.A.

LA SALLE, Peter. American, b. 1947. Novels/Short stories. Assoc. Prof. of English, Univ. of Texas at Austin, since 1987 (Asst. Prof., 1980–86). Lectr. in Creative Writing, Johnson State Coll., Vermont, 1974–76; Asst. Prof. of English, Iowa State Univ., Ames, 1977–80. *Publs:* The Graves of Famous Writers and Other Stories, 1980; Strange Sunlight (novel), 1984. Add: Dept. of English, Univ. of Texas at Austin, Austin, Tex. 78712, U.S.A.

LA SALLE, Victor. *See* **FANTHORPE,** R. Lionel.

LASCH, Christopher. American, b. 1932. Politics/Government, Social commentary/phenomena. Watson Prof. of History, Univ. of Rochester, N.Y., since 1979 (Prof., 1970–79). Instr., Williams Coll., Williamstown, Mass., 1956–59; Asst. Prof., Roosevelt Univ., Chicago, 1960–64; Member of Faculty, 1961–66, and Prof. of History, 1965–66, Univ. of Iowa, Iowa City; Prof. of History, Northwestern Univ., Evanston, Ill., 1966–70. *Publs:* The American Liberals and the Russian Revolution, 1962; The New Radicalism in America, 1965; The Agony of the American Left, 1969; The World of Nations, 1973; The Culture of Narcissism, 1979; Haven in a Heartless World, 1979; The Minimal Self, 1984. Add: Dept. of History, Univ. of Rochester, Rochester, N.Y. 14627, U.S.A.

LASH, Jennifer (Anne Mary). British, b. 1938. Novels/Short stories. *Publs:* The Burial, 1961; The Climate of Belief, 1962; Get Down There and Die, 1977; The Dust Collector, 1979; From May to October, 1980. Add: c/o Hamish Hamilton, 27 Wrights Lane, London W8 5TZ, England.

LASH, N(icholas) L(angrishe) A(lleyne). British, b. 1934. Theology/Religion. Norris-Hulse Prof. of Divinity, Cambridge Univ., since 1978, and Fellow of Clare Hall, Cambridge, since 1987 (Fellow, 1969–85, and Dean, 1971–75, St. Edmund's House; Asst. Lectr., 1974–78). Oscott Coll., 1957–63; Asst. Priest, Slough, Bucks., 1963–68. *Publs:* His Presence in the World, 1968; Change in Focus, 1973; Newman on Development, 1975; Voices of Authority, 1976; Theology on Dover Beach, 1979; A Matter of Hope, 1982; Theology on the Way to Emmaus, 1986; Easter in Ordinary, 1988. Add: Faculty of Divinity, St. John's St., Cambridge CB2 1TW, England.

LASKY, Jesse Louis, Jr. American, b. 1910. Novels/Short stories,

Plays/Screenplays, Social commentary/phenomena. Scriptwriter, BBC and ITV Television, London. Vice-Pres., Screen Writers Branch, Writers Guild of America, 1955. *Publs:* Songs from the Heart of a Boy, 1926; Listening to Silence, 1928; Curtain of Life, 1934; Singing in Thunder, 1935; No Angels in Heaven, 1938; Spindrift, 1948; Naked in a Cactus Garden, 1960; Cry the Lonely Flesh; Whatever Happened to Hollywood?, 1973; (with Pat Silver) Men of Mystery (in U.S. as Dark Dimensions), 1978; (with Pat Silver) Love Scene, 1978; (with Pat Silver) The Offer, 1981. Add: c/o Writers' Guild of Great Britain, 430 Edgware Rd., London W2 1EH, England.

LASKY, Victor. American, b. 1918. Politics/Government, Biography. Columnist, "Say It Straight," North American Newspaper Alliance, NYC, 1962–80. *Publs:* (with R. de Toledano) Seeds of Treason, 1950; (ed.) American Legion Reader, 1953; J.F.K.: The Man and the Myth, 1963; The Ugly Russian, 1965; Robert F. Kennedy: The Myth and the Man, 1968; (with George Murphy) Say, Didn't You Used to be George Murphy?, 1970; Arthur J. Goldberg: The Old and the New, 1970; It Didn't Start with Watergate, 1977; Jimmy Carter: The Man and the Myth, 1979; Never Complain, Never Explain: The Story of Henry Ford II, 1981. Add: 3133 Connecticut Ave., N.W., Washington, D.C. 20008, U.S.A.

LASSON, Kenneth. American, b. 1943. Social commentary/phenomena, Biography. Prof., Univ. of Baltimore Sch. of Law. *Publs:* The Workers: Portraits of Nine American Job-holders, 1971; Proudly We Hail: Profiles of Public Citizens in Action, 1975; Private Lives of Public Servants, 1978; Representing Yourself: What You Can Do Without a Lawyer, 1983; Mousetraps and Muffling Cups, 1986. Add: 6320 Wirt Ave., Baltimore, Md. 21215, U.S.A.

LASSWELL, Marcia. American, b. 1927. Human relations, Psychology. Prof. of Psychology, California State Univ., Pomona, since 1976 (joined faculty, 1960); Clinical Prof. in Graduate Prog. Training, Marriage and Family Therapists, and Co-Dir., Human Relations Center, Univ. of Southern California at Los Angeles; in private practice as Marriage and Family Counselor, since 1959. Member, Bd. of Dirs., Omega Foundn., California State Mental Health Authority (Tri-City), Planned Parenthood at San Gabriel Valley, Open-Door Free Clinic, and Pomona Counseling Service; Fellow, American Assn. of Marriage and Family Counselors (Member, Bd. of Dirs., 1970–72); Member, Southern Calif. Assn. of Marriage and Family Counselors (Vice Pres., 1971–72, and Pres., 1972–73). Lectr., 1952–54, and Asst. Prof., 1959–60, Pepperdine Coll., Los Angeles. *Publs:* College Teaching of General Psychology (textbook), 1967; (with Thomas Lasswell) Love, Marriage and Family (textbook), 1973; (with Norman Lobsenz) No-Fault Marriage, 1976; (with Norman Lobsenz) Styles of Loving, 1980; (with Normal Lobsenz) Equal Time, 1983; (with Thomas Lasswell) Love, Marriage and Family, 1983, 1987. Add: 875 Hillcrest Dr., Pomona, Calif. 91768, U.S.A.

LAST, Joan. British, b. 1908. Music. Prof. of Piano, Royal Academy of Music, 1959–83. *Publs:* The Young Pianist, 1954, 1972; Interpretation in Piano Study, 1960, 1975; Freedom in Piano Technique, 1980. Add: 11 St. Mary's Close, Littlehampton, W. Sussex BN17 5PZ, England.

LASZLO, Ervin. American, b. 1932. Philosophy. Prof. of Philosophy since 1969, and Faculty Exchange Scholar since 1974, State Univ. Coll. of New York, Geneseo. Program Dir., UN Inst. Training and Research, since 1981. *Publs:* Essential Society, 1963; Individualism, Collectivism and Political Power, 1963; Beyond Scepticism and Realism, 1966; The Communist Ideology in Hungary, 1966; (ed.) Philosophy in the Soviet Union, 1967; System, Structure and Experience, 1969; La Metaphysique de Whitehead, 1970; (ed. with J.B. Wilbur) Human Values and Natural Science, 1970; (ed. with R. Gotesky) Human Dignity: This Century and the Next, 1970; (ed. with J.B. Wilbur) Human Values and the Mind of Man, 1971; (ed.) The Relevance of General Systems Theory, 1972; The Systems View of the World, 1972; Introduction to Systems Philosophy, 1972, 1973; (ed. with J. Stulman) Emergent Man, 1973; (ed.) The World System, 1973; (ed. with E.B. Sellon) Vistas in Physical Reality; (ed. with J.B. Wilbur) Value Theory in Philosophy and Social Science, 1974; A Strategy for the Future, 1974; (ed. with Emily B. Sellon) Vistas in Physical Reality, 1976; (ed.) Goals in a Global Community, 2 vols., 1977–78; Goals for Mankind, 1978; The Inner Limits of Mankind, 1978; Regional Cooperation among Developing Countries, 1981; Systems Science and World Order, 1982; (ed.) Regional and Interregional Cooperation, 6 vols., 1984; Europe in the Contemporary World, 1986; Evolution: The Grand Synthesis, 1987. Add: Dept. of Philosophy, State Univ. Coll. of New York, Geneseo, N.Y., U.S.A.

LATHAM, Jean Lee. American, b. 1902. Also writes as Janice Gard and Julian Lee. Historical/Romance/Gothic, Children's fiction, Plays/Screenplays, Poetry. Free-lance writer, 1936–41; and since 1945. Head of the English Dept., Upshur County High Sch., West Virginia, 1926–27; Substitute Teacher, West Virginia Wesleyan Coll., 1927; Teacher, Ithaca Coll., New York, 1928–29; Ed. in Chief, Dramatic Publishing Co., Chicago, 1930–36. *Publs:* Thanks Awfully! (adult play), 1929; (as Janice Gard) Lookin' Lovely (adult play), 1930; First Nighter, Grand Central Station, and Skippy Hollywood Theatre (radio plays), 1930–41; The Alien Note (children's play), 1930; The Christmas Party (children's play), 1930; Crinoline and Candlelight (children's play), 1931; (as Julian Lee) Another Washington, (children's play), 1931; (as Julian Lee) The Christmas Carol, (children's play), 1931; (as Julian Lee) A Fiancé for Fanny, (children's play), 1931; (as Julian Lee) I Will! I Won't!, (children's play), 1931; (as Julian Lee) Keeping Kitty's Dates, (children's play), 1931; (as Julian Lee) Washington for All, (chilren's play), 1931; Christopher's Orphans (adult play), 1931; A Sign unto You (adult play), 1931; Lady to See You (adult play), 1931; (as Janice Gard) Listen to Leon (adult play), 1931; (as Janice Gard) Depend on Me (adult play), 1932; The Blue Teapot (adult play), 1932; (as Julian Lee, with Genevieve and Elwyn Swarthout) Thanksgiving for All, 1932; (as Julian Lee) Christmas for All, 1932; (as Julian Lee) Just for Justin, (chilren's play), 1933; (as Julian Lee) Tiny Jim, (children's play), 1933; (as Julian Lee, with Harriette Wilburr and Nellie Meader Linn) The Children's Book, (children's play), 1933; (as Julian Lee) Lincoln Yesterday and Today, (children's play), 1933; Broadway Bound (adult play), 1933; The Giant and the Biscuits, (children's play), 1934; The Prince and the Patters, (children's play), 1934; Tommy Tomorrow, (children's play), 1935 (as Julian Lee), He Landed from London, (children's play), 1935; 555 Pointers for Beginning Actors and Directors, 1935; Master of Solitaire (adult play), 1935; The Bed of Petunias (adult play), 1937; Here She Comes! (adult play), 1937, Just the Girl for Jimmy (adult play), 1937; Have a Heart! (adult play), 1937; What Are You Going to Wear? (adult play), 1937; Talk Is Cheap (adult play), 1937; Smile for the Lady! (adult play), 1937; Well Met by Moonlight (adult play), 1937; And Then What Happened?, (children's play), 1937; All on Account of Kelly, (children's play), 1937; Mickey the Mighty, (children's play), 1937; (as Julian Lee, with Ann Clark) Christmas Programs for the Lower Grades, 1937; (as Julian Lee, with Ann Clark) Thanksgiving Programs for the Lower Grades, 1937; The Ghost of Rhodes Manor, (children's play), 1939; They'll Never Look There! (adult play), 1939; The Arms of the Law (adult play), 1940; Old Doc (adult play), 1940; Nine Radio Plays, 1940; (as Julian Lee) Big Brother Barges In, (children's play), 1940; (as Julian Lee) The Ghost of Lone Cabin, (children's play), 1940; Gray Bread (adult play), 1941; People Don't Change (adult play), 1941; Señor Freedom (adult play), 1941; Minus a Million (adult play), 1941; The House Without a Key (adult play), 1942; The Nightmare (adult play), 1943; The Story of Eli Whitney, 1953; Medals for Morse, Artist and Inventor, 1954; Carry On, Mr. Bowditch, 1955; Trail Blazer of the Seas, 1956; The Dear-Bought Land (children's fiction), 1957; Young Man in a Hurry: The Story of Cyrus W. Field, 1958; On Stage, Mr. Jefferson!, 1958; Drake, the Man they Called a Pirate, 1960; Samuel F.B. Morse, Artist-Inventor, 1961; Aladdin, 1961; Ali Baba, 1961; Nutcracker, 1961; Puss in Boots, 1961; The Magic Fishbone, 1961; Jack the Giant Killer, 1961; Hop o' My Thumb, 1961; (with Bee Lewi) The Dog That Lost His Family, (children's fiction), 1961; (with Bee Lewi) When Homer Honked, (children's fiction), 1961; (with Bee Lewi) The Cuckoo That Couldn't Count, (children's fiction), 1961; (with B. Lewi) The Man Who Never Snoozed, (children's fiction), 1961; (trans.) Wa O'Ka, by Pablo Ramirez, 1961; The Ugly Duckling, Goldilocks and the Three Bears, and The Little Red Hen, 1962; The Brave Little Tailor, Hansel and Gretel, and Jack and the Beanstalk, 1962; Man of the Monitor: The Story of John Ericson, 1962; Eli Whitney, Great Inventor, 1963; The Chagres: Power of the Panama Canal, 1964; Sam Houston, Hero of Texas, 1965; Retreat to Glory: The Story of Sam Houston, 1965; George W. Goethals, Panama Canal Engineer, 1965; The Frightened Hero: A Story of the Siege of Latham House, (children's fiction), 1965; The Columbia, Powerhouse of North America, 1967; David Glasgow Farragut, Our First Admiral, 1967; Anchor's Aweigh: The Story of David Glasgow Farragut, 1968; Far Voyager: The Story of James Cook, 1970; Rachael Carson, Who Loved the Sea, 1973; What Tabbit the Rabbit Found, (children's fiction), 1974; Who Lives Here? (verse), 1974; Elizabeth Blackwell, Pioneer Woman Doctor, 1975. Add: 12 Phoenetia Ave., Coral Gables, Fla. 33134, U.S.A.

LATHAM, Mavis. *See* **CLARKE,** Mavis Thorpe.

LATHEN, Emma. Joint pseudonym for Mary J. Latis and Martha Hennissart; also writes as R.B. Dominic. Americans. Mystery/Crime/Suspense. *Publs:* Banking on Death, 1961; A Place for Murder, 1964; Accounting for Murder, 1965; Murder Makes the Wheels

Go Round, 1966; Death Shall Overcome, 1967; Murder Against the Grain, 1967; A Stitch in Time, 1968; When in Greece, 1969; Come to Dust, 1969; Murder to Go, 1970; Pick Up Sticks, 1971; Ashes to Ashes, 1971; The Longer the Thread, 1972; Murder Without Icing, 1973; Sweet and Low, 1974; By Hook or By Crook, 1975; Double, Double, Oil and Trouble, 1978; Going for the Gold, 1981; Green Grow the Dollars, 1982; as R.B. Dominic—Murder Sunny Side Up, 1968; Murder in High Places, 1969; There Is No Justice (in U.S. as Murder Out of Court), 1971; Epitaph for a Lobbyist, 1974; Murder Out of Commission, 1976; The Attending Physician, 1980; A Flaw in the System, 1983; Unexpected Developments, 1984; Something in the Air, 1989. Add: c/o Simon and Schuster, 1230 Ave. of the Americas, New York, N.Y. 10020, U.S.A.

LA TOURRETTE, Jacqueline. American, b. 1926. Historical and Suspense Novels. *Publs:* The Joseph Stone, 1971; A Matter of Sixpence, 1972; The Madonna Creek Witch, 1973; The Previous Lady, 1974; The Pompeii Scroll, 1975; Shadows in Umbria, 1979; The Wild Harp, 1981; Patarran, 1983; The House on Octavia Street, 1984; The Incense Tree, 1986. Add: c/o Raines and Raines, 71 Park Ave., New York, N.Y. 10016, U.S.A.

LATTA, Richard J. American, b. 1946. Children's non-fiction, Recreation/Leisure/Hobbies. Science Teacher, Forest Park Jr. High Schs., Ill., since 1969. *Publs:* Games for Travel, 6 vols. 1976–83; Art Activities, 1976; Number Graphs, 1976; Practice in Metrics, 1977; Punctuation and Capitalization Flipper Puzzles, 1977; Grammar Puzzles, 1978; Logic Games, 1978; Visualizing Language, 1978; Adjective and Adverb Packet, 1978; Grammar Flipper Puzzles, 1978; Word Lines, 1979; Match the Syllables, 1979; Fill in the Blanks, 1979; Word Study, 1979; Word Find Book, 25 vols., 1980–85; Syllable Puzzles, 1981; Maze Books, 12 vols., 1982; This Little Pig Had a Riddle, 1984. Add: 126 N. Ind. Bound. Rd., Plainfield, Ill. 60544, U.S.A.

LAUGHLIN, Florence. American, b. 1910. Children's fiction. *Publs:* The Little Left-Over Witch, 1960; The Mystery of McGilley Mansion, 1963; Mystery Mountain, 1964; The Seventh Cousin, 1966; The Horse from Topolo, 1966; Skyrockets for the President, 1973. Add: c/o Ruth Cantor Agency, 156 Fifth Ave., New York, N.Y. 10010, U.S.A.

LAUGHLIN, James. American, b. 1914. Poetry. Founding Ed. and Pres., New Directions Publishing Corp., NYC, since 1936. Ed., New Directions in Prose and Poetry Series, since 1937. Member, U.S. National Commn. for Unesco, 1960–63. *Publs:* (ed.) Poems from the Greenberg Manuscripts: A Selection from the Works of Samuel B. Greenberg, 1939; (ed. with A Hayes) A Wreath of Christmas Poems, 1942; Some Natural Things, 1945; (with H. Fischer) Skiing: East and West, 1947; (ed.) Spearhead: Ten Years' Experimental Writing in America, 1947; Report on Visit to Germany (poetry), 1948; A Small Book of Poems, 1948; The Wild Anemone and Other Poems, 1957; Confidential Report and Other Poems (in U.S. as Selected Poems), 1959; Pulsatilla, 1961; (ed. with H. Carruth) A New Directions Reader, 1964; Die Haare auf Grossvaters Kopf, 1966; Quel che la Matita Scrive, 1970; The Pig: Poems, 1970; The Woodpecker, 1971; (ed. with N. Burton and P. Hart) The Asian Journal of Thomas Merton, 1974; In Another Country: Poems 1935–1975, 1978; Selected Poems, 1955–1985, 1985; The House of Light, 1986; The Owl of Minerva, 1987; The Bird of Endless Time, 1989. Add: c/o New Directions Publs., 80 Eighth Ave., New York, N.Y. 10011, U.S.A.

LAUMER, (John) Keith. American, b. 1925. Mystery/Crime/Suspense, Science fiction/Fantasy, Recreation/Leisure/Hobbies. Freelance writer since 1964. Staff Member, Univ. of Illinois, Urbana, 1952; Foreign Service Vice-Consul and Third Secty., Rangoon, 1956–59. *Publs:* How to Design and Build Flying Models, 1960, 1970; Worlds of the Imperium, 1962; Envoy to New Worlds (short stories), 1963; A Trace of Memory, 1963; The Great Time Machine Hoax, 1964; A Plague of Demons, 1965; The Other Side of Time, 1965; Embassy (suspense), 1965; Galactic Diplomat (short stories), 1965; The Time Bender, 1966; Retief's War, 1966; (with Rosel George Brown) Earthblood, 1966; Catastrophe Planet, 1966; The Monitors, 1966; Enemies from Beyond (novelization of TV series), 1966; (with Gordon R. Dickson) Planet Run, 1967; The Invaders (novelization of TV series), 1967, in U.K. as the Meteor Man, 1968; Nine by Laumer (short stories), 1967; Galactic Odyssey, 1967; The Day Before Forever, and Thunderhead, 1968; Assignment in Nowhere, 1968; Retief and the Warlords, 1968; Greylorn (short stories; in U.K. as The Other Sky), 1968; It's a Mad, Mad, Mad Galaxy (short stories), 1968; The Afrit Affair (suspense; novelization of TV series), 1968; The Drowned Queen (suspense; novelization of TV series), 1968; The Gold Bomb (suspense; novelization of TV series), 1968; The Long Twilight, 1969; Retief, Ambassador to Space (short stories), 1969; The World Shuf-

fler, 1970; The House in November, 1970; Time Trap, 1970; (ed.) Five Fates, 1970; Retief's Ransom, 1971; The Star Treasure, 1971; Deadfall, 1971, as Fat Chance, 1975; Dinosaur Beach, 1971; Retief of the CDT (short stories), 1971; Once There Was a Giant (short stories), 1971; The Infinite Cage, 1972; Night of Delusions, 1972; The Shape Changer, 1972; The Big Show (short stories), 1972; Timetracks (short stories), 1972; The Glory Game, 1973; The Undefeated (short stories), 1974; Retief, Emissary to the Stars (short stories), 1975; Bolo: The Annals of the Dinochrome Brigade, 1976; The Best of Keith Laumer (short stories), 1976; The Ultimax Man, 1978; Retief Unbound (short story omnibus), 1979; Retief at Large (short stories), 1979; The Star Colony, 1981; The Breaking Earth (short stories), 1981; Worlds of the Imperium (short stories), 1982; The Other Sky, 1982; Retief to the Rescue (short stories), 1983; The Galaxy Builder (short stories), 1984; The Return of Retief, 1985; Rogue Bolo, 1985; End as a Hero, 1985; Reward for Retief, 1989. Add: Box 972, Brooksville, Fla. 33512, U.S.A.

LAURENCE, Dan H. American, b. 1920. Literary criticsm, Classics, Music, Plays, Biography. Prof. of English, New York Univ., NYC, 1967–70 (Assoc. Prof., 1962–67); Visiting Prof., Univ. of Texas at Austin, 1974–75; Visting Fellow, Inst. for the Arts and Humanistic Studies, Pennsylvania State Univ., 1976; Mellon Prof., Tulane Univ., New Orleans, 1981. *Publs:* (with Leon Edel) A Bibliography of Henry James, 1957, 1982; Robert Nathan: A Bibliography, 1960; (ed.) Uncollected Writings of Bernard Shaw, 1961; How to Become a Musical Critic, 1961; Platform and Pulpit, 1961; (with David Greene) The Matter with Ireland, 1962; (ed.) Collected Letters of Bernard Shaw, vol. 1, 1965, vol. 2, 1972; (ed.) Bodley-Head Shaw: Collected Plays, 7 vols., 1970–74; Shaw, Books, and Libraries, 1976; (ed. with Daniel J. Leary) Flyleaves, 1977; The Fifth Gospel of Bernard Shaw, 1981; (ed.) Shaw's Music: The Complete Musical Criticism, 3 vols., 1981; (general ed.) Early Texts: Play Manuscripts in Facsimile, 12 vols., 1981; Bernard Shaw: A Bibliography, 2 vols., 1982; (ed. with Martin Quinn) Shaw on Dickens, 1982; (ed. with James Rambeau) Agitations: Shaw's Letters to the Press 1875-1950, 1983. Add: c/o Dodd, Mead and Co., 79 Madison Ave., New York, N.Y. 10016, U.S.A.

LAURENTS, Arthur. American, b. 1918. Novels/Short stories, Plays/Screenplays. Member of Council, Dramatists Guild, since 1955. Radio playwright, 1943–45; Dir., Dramatists Play Service, NYC, 1961–66. *Publs:* Home of the Brave (in U.K. as The Way Back), 1945; The Bird Cage, 1950; The Time of the Cuckoo, 1953; A Clearing in the Woods, 1957; West Side Story, 1958; Gypsy, 1959; Invitation to a March, 1961; Anyone Can Whistle, 1965; Do I Hear a Waltz?, 1966; Hallelujah, Baby!, 1967; The Way We Were (novel and screenplay), 1972; The Enclave, 1974; The Turning Point (novel and screenplay), 1977; Scream (play), 1981; A Loss of Memory (play), 1982. Add: c/o Shirley Bernstein, Paramuse Artists, 1414 Sixth Ave., New York, N.Y., U.S.A.

LAURIE, Edward James. American, b. 1925. Information science/Computers. Prof. of Marketing, and Quantitative Studies, Sch. of Business, San Jose State Univ., Calif. (former Prof. of Mgmt., Dept. Chmn., and Assoc. Dean). *Publs:* Computer Applications in the U.S., 1960; Computers and How They Work, 1963; Computer and Computer Languages, 1966; Modern Computer Concepts, 1970; Computer, Automation and Society, 1979. Add: 1287 Pampas Dr., San Jose, Calif. 95120, U.S.A.

LAURIE, Rona. Speech/Rhetoric, Theatre. Former actress, London; Examiner, and Lectr., 1958–85, and Head, Dept. of Drama in Education, 1970–77, Guildhall Sch. of Music and Drama, London. *Publs:* (ed. with M. Cobby) Speaking Together, Books I & II, 1964; (co-ed.) The 8th 11th, 13th, 17th Anthology, 4 vols., 1964–82; (ed.) A Hundred Speeches from the Theatre, 1966, 1973; (ed.) Scenes and Ideas, 1967; (ed. with M. Cobby) Adventures in Group Speaking; Festivals and Adjudication, 1975; Children's Plays from Beatrix Potter (dramatization), 1980; Auditioning, 1985; Mrs. Tiggywinkle and Friends, 1986. Add: 21 New Quebec St., London W1H 7DE, England.

LAUTERSTEIN, Ingeborg. American, b. 1933. Novels. Dir., Boston Author's Club, since 1983. *Publs:* The Water Castle, 1981; Vienna Girl, 1986. Add: 7 Pleasant St., Rockport, Mass. 01966, U.S.A.

LAVERY, Bryony. British, b. 1947. Plays/Screenplays. Artistic dir., Les Oeufs Malades, 1976–78, Extraordinary Productions, 1979–80, and Female Trouble, 1981–83, all London; Resident playwright, Unicorn Theatre for Children, London, 1985–87. *Publs:* Uniforms and Uniformed, and Numerical Man (in Masks and Faces), 1984; Origin of the Species (Plays by Women, vol. 6), 1987; The Wild Bunch, 1989.

Add: c/o Jonathan Clowes, 22 Prince Albert Rd., London NW1 7ST, England.

LAVIN, Mary. Irish, b. 1912. Novels/Short stories, Children's fiction. Pres., P.E.N., Ireland, 1964–65, and Irish Academy of Letters, 1971–73. *Publs:* Tales from Bective Bridge, 1942; The Long Ago and Other Stories, 1944; The House in Clewe Street, 1945; The Becker Wives and Other Stories (in U.S. as At Sallygap and Other Stories), 1946; Mary O'Grady, 1950; A Single Lady and Other Stories, 1951; The Patriot Son and Other Stories, 1957; A Likely Story, 1957; Selected Stories, 1959; The Great Wave and Other Stories, 1961; The Stories of Mary Lavin, 3 vols., 1964–85; In the Middle of the Fields and Other Stories, 1967; Happiness and Other Stories, 1969; Collected Stories, 1971; The Second Best Children in the World, 1972; A Memory and Other Stories, 1972; The Shrine and Other Stories, 1977; A Family Likeness, 1985. Add: The Abbey Farm, Bective, Navan, Co. Meath, Ireland.

LAVINE, Sigmund Arnold. American, b. 1908. Archaeology/Antiquities, Children's non-fiction, Natural history, Zoology, Biography. Staff Feature Writer, 1926–32, and on Literary Staff, 1935–41, Boston Post; member, Literary Staff, Boston Evening Transcript, 1926–34; Educational Admin., Boston Sch. System, 1934–78; Columnist Boston Herald Advertiser, 1939–77; Literary Staff Member, Worcester Telegram-Gazette, 1945–76. *Publs:* Wandering Minstrels We: The Story of Gilbert and Sullivan, 1954; Wonders Series, 38 vols., 1956–87; Steinmetz: Maker of Lightning, 1958; Strange Partners, 1959; Strange Travelers, 1960; Famous Industrialists, 1961; Famous Merchants, 1963; Kettering: Master Inventor, 1963; Allan Pinkerton: America's First Private Eye, 1963; (with M. Casey) Water Since the World Began, 1965; Handmade in America, 1966; Famous American Architects, 1967; Handmade in England, 1968; Evangeline Booth: Daughter of Salvation, 1970; Horses the Indians Rode, 1974; Indian Corn and Other Gifts, 1974; Games the Indians Played, 1974; Beginner's Book of Gardening, 1977. Add: 9 Magnolia Rd., Milton, Mass. 02186, U.S.A.

LAWDEN, Derek Frank. British, b. 1919. Mathematics/Statistics, Physics. Prof. of Mathematics, Univ. of Aston in Birmingham, 1967–83. Head, Dept. of Mathematics, Univ. of Canterbury, N.Z., 1956–67. *Publs:* Mathematics of Engineering Systems, 1954; Course of Applied Mathematics, 2 vols., 1960; Optimal Trajectories for Space Navigation, 1963; Mathematical Principles of Quantum Mechanics, 1967; Analytical Mechanics, 1972; Electromagnetism, 1973; Analytical Methods of Optimization, 1974; Introduction to Tensor Calculus, Relativity and Cosmology, 1982; Elements of Relativity Theory, 1985; Principles of Thermodynamics and Statistical Mechanics, 1986. Add: Newhall, Church Bank, Temple Grafton, Alcester B49 6NU, England.

LAWLER, Lucille. American, b. 1908. Plays/Screenplays, History. Teacher, Gallatin Co. Schs., Illinois. Vice-Pres., Illinois State Historical Soc., 1969; Pres., Illinois Historical Congress, 1969. *Publs:* Gallatin County: Gateway to Illinois, 1968; Ridgway, Our Town, 1971; Westwood Place (play), 1971; Amazing Shawneetown: A Tale of Two Cities, 1985. Add: R.R. 1, Ridgway, Ill. 62979, U.S.A.

LAWLER, Ray(mond Evenor). Australian, b. 1921. Plays/Screenplays. Former actor and producer, National Theatre Co., Melbourne, and Dir., Melbourne Univ. Repertory Co. *Publs:* Summer of the Seventeenth Doll, 1957; The Piccadilly Bushman, 1961; The Doll Trilogy: Kid Stakes, Other Times, Summer of the Seventeenth Doll, 1978. Add: c/o Curtis Brown, 27 Union St., Paddington, N.S.W. 2021, Australia.

LAWLOR, John James. British, b. 1918. Education, Literature. Secty.-Gen., Intnl. Assoc. of Univ. Profs. of English. Ed., English Literature Section and European Literature Section, Hutchinson Univ. Library, and Ideas and Forms in English Literature, Routledge & Kegan Paul, London. Lectr. in English, Brasenose and Trinity Colls., Oxford, 1947–50; Univ. Lectr. in English Literature, Oxford, 1949–50; Prof. of English Language and Literature, Univ. of Keele, 1950–80. *Publs:* The Tragic Sense in Shakespeare, 1960; Piers Plowman: An Essay in Criticism, 1962; (ed.) Patterns of Love and Courtesy: Essays in Memory of C.S. Lewis, 1966; (with W.H. Auden) To Nevill Coghill, from Friends, 1966; Chaucer, 1968; (ed.) The New University, 1968; (ed.) Higher Education: Patterns of Change in the 1970s, 1972; (ed.) Essays and Studies 1973; Elysium Revisited, 1978. Add: Penwithian, Higher Fore St., Marazion, Cornwall TR17 0BQ, England.

LAWRENCE, Berta. British. Novels/Short stories, History, Biography. *Publs:* A Somerset Journal, 1951; Quantock Country, 1952; The Bond of Green Withy, 1954; The Nightingale in the Branches, 1955;

Coleridge and Wordsworth in Somerset, 1970; Somerset Legends, 1973; Discovering the Quantocks, 1974; Exmoor Villages, 1984. Add: 17 Wembdon Hill, Bridgwater, Somerset, England.

LAWRENCE, Jerome. American, b. 1915. Plays/Screenplays, Songs, lyrics and libretti, Biography. Partner, since 1942, and Pres., since 1955, Lawrence and Lee Inc., NYC and Los Angeles. Prof. of Playwriting at Univ. of So. Calif., New York Univ., Baylor Univ., and Ohio State Univ. Member, Bd. of Dirs.: American Conservatory Theatre, National Repertory Theatre, American Playwrights' Theatre, Dramatists Guild, Authors League. *Publs:* (co-author) Look, Ma, I'm Dancin' (musical), 1948; (with Robert E. Lee) Inherit the Wind, 1955; (with Lee) Auntie Mame, 1957; (with Lee) The Gang's All Here, 1960; (with Lee) Only In America, 1960; (with Lee) Checkmate, 1961; (co-author) Mame (musical), 1967; Dear World (musical), 1969; (co-author) Sparks Fly Upward, 1969; (with Lee) The Night Thoreau Spent in Jail, 1970; Live Spelled Backwards, 1970; (with Lee) The Incomparable Max, 1972; (with Lee) The Crocodile Smile, 1972; Actor: The Life and Times of Paul Muni, 1974; (with Lee) Jabberwock, 1974; (with Lee) First Monday in October, 1975; (with Lee and Norman Cousins) Whisper in the Mind, 1989. Add: 21056 Las Flores Mesa Dr., Malibu, Calif. 90265, U.S.A.

LAWRENCE, Lesley. *See* **LEWIS,** Lesley.

LAWRENCE, Louise. Pseud. for Elizabeth Rhoda Holden. British, b. 1943. Children's (Science) Fiction. Fulltime writer. Asst. Librarian, Gloucestershire County Library, 1960–64, and at Forest of Dean branches, 1969–71. *Publs:* Andra, 1971; The Power of Stars, 1972; The Wyndcliffe, 1975; Sing and Scatter Daisies, 1977; Star Lord, 1978; Cat Call, 1980; The Earth Witch, 1982; Calling B for Butterfly, 1982; Dram Road, 1983; Children of the Dust, 1985; Moonwind, 1986; The Warriors of Taan, 1986. Add: 22 Church Rd., Cinderford, Gloucestershire GL14 2ES, England.

LAWRENCE, P. *See* **TUBB,** E.C.

LAWRENCE, Steven C. Pseud. for Lawrence Agustus Murphy; also writes with Charlotte Murphy under joint pseud. C.L. Murphy. American, b. 1924. Westerns/Adventure, Children's fiction. English Teacher and Dept. Chmn., South Jr. High Sch., Brockton, Mass., 1951–85. Pres. and Treas., Steven C. Lawrence Productions, Brockton, Mass. Instr. in Creative Writing, Stonehill Coll., North Easton, Mass., 1967. *Publs:* The Naked Range, 1956; Saddle Justice, 1957; Brand of a Texan, 1958; The Iron Marshal, 1960; Night of the Gunmen, 1960; Gun Fury, 1961; With Blood in Their Eyes, 1961; Slattery, and Bullet Welcome for Slattery, 1961, Slattery published separately as The Lynchers, 1975; Walk a Narrow Trail, and a Noose for Slattery, 1962; Longhorns North, and Slattery's Gun Says No, 1962; A Texan Comes Riding, 1966; (as C.L. Murphy) Buffalo Grass (juvenile), 1966; That Man from Texas, 1972; Edge of the Land, 1974; Six-Gun Junction, 1974; North to Montana, 1975; Slattery Stands Alone, 1976; A Northern Saga: The Account of the North Atlantic-Murmansk, Russia, Convoys, 1976; Trial for Tennihan, 1976; Day of the Comancheros, 1977; Gun Blast, 1977; Slattery Stands Alone, 1979; Through Which We Serve, 1985; The Green Concord Stagecoach, 1988. Add: 30 Mercedes Rd., Brockton, Mass. 02401, U.S.A.

LAWSON, Chet. *See* **TUBB,** E.C.

LAWSON, James. American, b. 1938. Novels/Short stories. Copywriter, McCann-Marschalk Advertising, 1961–62, J. Walker Thompson Advertising, NYC, 1963–64, and Al Paul Lefton Advertising, Philadelphia, 1964–66; Reporter, Aspen Times, Colorado, 1962; Vice-Pres. and Copy Supvr., Doyle Dane Bernbach Advertising, NYC, 1966–78; Sr. Vice-Pres. and Dir. of Creative Services, Doremus and Co., NYC., 1978–80. *Publs:* The Girl Watcher, 1976; The Copley Chronicles, 1980; The Fanatic, 1981; Forgeries of the Heart, 1981. Add: 756 Greenwich St., New York, N.Y. 10014, U.S.A.

LAWSON, Joan. British, b. 1908. Dance/Ballet, Theatre. Teacher of classical and national dance, and of the history of ballet, Royal Ballet Sch., London, 1963–86. Critic, The Dancing Times, 1940–56; Lectr. to H.M. Forces, Advisory Council for Education, 1940–47. *Publs:* European Folk Dance, 1953; Mime, 1957; (with P. Revitt) Dressing for the Ballet, 1958; Classical Ballet: Its Style and Technique, 1960; A History of Ballet, 1964; The Teaching of Classical Ballet, 1973; Teaching Young Dancers, 1975; The Story of Ballet, 1977; Ballet Stories, 1978; Pas de deux, 1978; The Principles of Classical Dance, 1979; Ballet Class, 1984; Character Dance, 1985. Add: c/o Routledge, Chapman and Hall, 11 New Fetter Ln., London EC4P 4EE, England.

LAWSON, Michael. *See* RYDER, M.L.

LAWTON, Charles. *See* HECKELMANN, Charles N.

LAX, Eric. American, b. 1944. Film, Medicine/Health, Biography, Documentaries/Reportage. Freelance writer. *Publs:* On Being Funny: Woody Allen and Comedy, 1975; Life and Death on 10 West, 1984. Add: 609 Trenton Dr., Beverly Hills, Calif. 90210, U.S.A.

LAYTON, Andrea. *See* BANCROFT, Iris.

LAYTON, Irving (Peter). Canadian, b. 1912. Poetry. Prof. of English Literature, York Univ., Toronto, since 1969. Assoc. Ed., First Statement, later Northern Review, Montreal, 1941–43; former Assoc. Ed., Contact mag., Toronto, and Black Mountain Review, N.C.; Lectr., Jewish Public Library, Montreal, 1943–58; high sch. teacher in Montreal, 1954–60; Part-time Lectr., 1949–65, and Poet-in-Residence, 1965–66, Sir George Williams Univ., Montreal; Writer-in-Residence, Univ. of Guelph, Ont., 1968–69; Writer-in-Residence, Univ. of Toronto, 1981. *Publs:* Here and Now, 1945; Now Is the Place: Stories and Poems, 1948; The Black Huntsmen, 1951; (with R. Souster and L. Dudek) Cerberus, 1952; (ed. with L. Dudek) Canadian Poems, 1850-1952, 1952; Love the Conqueror Worm, 1953; In the Midst of My Fever, 1954; The Cold Green Element, 1955; The Blue Propeller, 1955; The Bull Calf and Other Poems, 1956; Music on a Kazoo, 1956; The Improved Binoculars: Selected Poems, 1956; A Laughter in the Mind, 1958; augmented ed. 1959; (ed.) Pan-ic: A Selection of Contemporary Canadian Poems, 1958; A Red Carpet for the Sun: Collected Poems, 1959; The Swinging Flesh, 1961; (ed.) Poems for 27 Cents, 1961; (ed.) Love Where the Nights Are Long: Canadian Love Poems, 1962; The Laughing Rooster, 1964; Collected Poems, 1965; (ed.) Anvil: A Selection of Workshop Poems, 1966; Periods of the Moon: Poems, 1967; The Shattered Plinths, 1968; The Whole Bloody Bird (obs, aphs, and pomes), 1969; Selected Poems, 1969; (ed.) Poems to Colour: A Selection of Workshop Poems, 1970; Collected Poems, 1971; Nail Polish, 1971; Engagements: The Prose of Irving Layton, 1972; Lovers and Lesser Men, 1973; (ed.) Anvil Blood: A Selection of Workshop Poems, 1973; The Pole-Vaulter, 1974; Seventy-Five Greek Poems, 1974; Selected Poems, 2 vols., 1975; For My Brother Jesus, 1976; The Uncollected Poems 1936–59, 1976; The Poems of Irving Layton, 1977; The Covenant, 1977, Taking Sides: The Collected Social and Political Writings, 1977; The Tightrope Dancer, 1978; Droppings from Heaven, 1979; The Love Poems of Irving Layton, 1979; There Were No Signs, 1979; An Unlikely Affair: The Correspondence of Irving Layton and Dorothy Rath, 1979; For My Neighbors in Hell, 1980; Europe and Other Bad News, 1981; A Wild Peculiar Joy, 1982; The Gucci Bag, 1983; The Reverence and Delight: The Love Poems, 1984; A Spider Danced Cozy Jig, 1984. Add: 6879 Monkland Ave., Montreal, Quebec H4B 1J5, Canada.

LAYTON, W(illiam) I(ssac). American, b. 1913. Mathematics/Statistics. Chmn., since 1982 and Prof., since 1979, Dept. of Mathematics, Computer Science, and Physics, Newberry Coll., South Carolina. Prof. and Chmn., Dept. of Mathematics and Statistics, Stephen F. Austin State Univ., Nacogdoches, Texas, 1950–79 (Coordinator, Data Processing Center, 1963–68). *Publs:* College Arithmetic, 1959, 1971; Essential Business Math, 1965, 1977. Add: 2421 Fulmer Ave., Newberry, S.C. 29108, U.S.A.

LAZARUS, A(rnold) L(eslie). American, b. 1914. Poetry, Literature. Prof. of English, Purdue Univ., Lafayette, Ind., 1962–79, now Emeritus. Consultant, Indiana Arts Commn., and Arts in Education Center, both since 1970. Ed., 1962–70, and on Editorial Bd., since 1970, Quartet, Mag. of the Arts. Chief Midwest Judge, Book of the Month Club Writing Fellowships Prog., 1969–71. *Publs:* (with R. Knudson) Selected Objectives, 1967; (with R. Lowell) Adventures in Modern Literature, 6th ed. 1970; Entertainments and Valedictions (poetry), 1970; (with J.N. Hook) Representative Performance Objectives: High School English, 1971; (with Andrew MacLeish) Modern English, 1971; (with H.W. Smith) Glossary of Literature and Composition, 1973; (with B. Mills) A Suit of Four (poetry), 1973; The Indiana Experience, 1977; (with V.H. Jones) Beyond Graustark: George Barr McCutcheon, 1981; The Best of George Ade, 1985; The World of George Barr McCutcheon, 1987. Add: c/o Indiana Univ. Press, Tenth and Morton Sts., Bloomington, Ind. 47405, U.S.A.

LAZARUS, Richard S. American, b. 1922. Psychology. Prof. of Psychology, Univ. of California, Berkeley, since 1959 (Assoc. Prof., 1957–59). Ed., Foundns. of Modern Psychology series, Prentice-Hall Inc., since 1963. Asst. Prof. of Psychology, Johns Hopkins Univ., Baltimore, 1948–53; Assoc. Prof. of Psychology and Dir. of Clinical Training, Clark Univ., Worcester, Mass., 1953–57. *Publs:* (with G.W. Shaffer)

Fundamental Concepts of Clinical Psychology, 1952; Adjustment and Personality, 1961, 3rd ed. 1976; Personality, 1963, 3rd ed. 1979; Psychological Stress and the Coping Process, 1966; (with E.M. Opton) Personality, 1967; The Riddle of Man: An Introduction to Psychology, 1974; (with W.K. Graham) Clues to the Riddle of Man, 1974; (with A. Monat) Stress and Coping, 1977; (with S. Folkman) Stress, Appraisal and Coping, 1984. Add: 3255 Woodview Dr., Lafayette, Calif. 94549, U.S.A.

LAZER, William. American, b. 1924. Administration/Management, Marketing. Prof., Coll. of Business and Public Admin., Atlanta Univ., Boca Raton, Florida, since 1983. Formerly Prof., Grad. Sch. of Business Admin., Michigan State Univ., E. Lansing (member of faculty, 1955–83). *Publs:* Managerial Marketing: Perspectives and Viewpoints, 1958, 3rd ed. 1967; Basic Bibliography on Industrial Marketing, 1958; Mathematical Models and Methods in Marketing, 1961; Marketing Management: A Systems Perspective, 1971; Managerial Marketing: Policies, Strategies and Decisions, 1973; Social Marketing: Perspectives and Viewpoints, 1973; (with J. Culley) Marketing Management: Concepts and Foundations, 1983; Handbook of Demographics for Marketing and Advertising: A Source Book of Consumer Trends, 1987; (co-ed.) Emerging International Frontiers, 1987. Add: Coll. of Business and Public Admin., Florida, Atlanta Univ., Boca Raton, Fla. 33431, U.S.A.

LEA, Tom. American, b. 1907. Westerns/Adventure, Art, History, Biography. Freelance artist and illustrator since 1936, and freelance writer since 1947. Artist and correspondent for Life mag., 1941–45. *Publs:* (with Thomas E. Tallmadge) John W. Norton, American Painter 1876-1934, 1935; George Catlin Westward Bound a Hundred Years Ago, 1939; Randado, 1941; A Grizzly from the Coral Sea (short stories), 1944; Peleliu Landing, 1945; A Calendar of Twelve Travelers Through the Pass of the North, 1946; Bullfight Manual for Spectators, 1949; The Brave Bulls (novel), 1949; The Wonderful Country (novel), 1950; Western Beef Cattle: Series of Eleven Paintings, 1950; Tom Lea: A Portfolio of Six Paintings, 1953; The Stained Glass Designs in McKee Chapel, Church of Saint Clement, El Paso, Texas, 1953; The King Ranch, 1957; The Primal Yoke (novel), 1960; Maud Durlin Sullivan 1872-1944: Pioneer Southwestern Librarian: A Tribute, 1962; The Hands of Cantu (novel), 1964; A Picture Gallery, 1968; In the Crucible of the Sun, 1974. Add: 2401 Savannah St., El Paso, Tex. 79930, U.S.A.

LEAB, Daniel Josef. American, b. 1936. Film, Writing/Journalism. Prof. of History, Seton Hall Univ., South Orange, N.J., since 1974. Managing Ed., Labor History, since 1974. Instr., and Asst. Prof. of History, Columbia Univ., NYC, 1966–74. *Publs:* A Union of Individuals: The Formation of the American Newspaper Guild 1933–36, 1970; From Sambo to Superspade: The Black Motion Picture Experience, 1975; (with Katharine Kyes Leab) The Auction Companion, 1982; (with Maurice Neufield and Dorothy Swanson) American Working Class History: A Representative Bibliography, 1984; The Labor History Reader, 1985. Add: P.O. Box 216, Washington, Conn. 06793, U.S.A.

LEACH, Douglas Edward. American, b. 1920. History. Prof. Emeritus of History, Vanderbilt Univ., Nashville, Tenn., since 1956. Faculty member, Bates Coll., Lewiston, Me., 1950–56. *Publs:* Flintlock and Tomahawk: New England in King Philip's War, 1956; (ed.) A Rhode Islander Reports on King Philip's War: The Second William Harris Letter of August, 1676, 1963; The Northern Colonial Frontier, 1607-1763, 1966; Arms for Empire: Military History of the British Colonies in North America, 1607-1763, 1973; Roots of Conflict: British Armed Forces and Colonial Americans 1677-1763, 1986; Now Hear This: The Memoir of a Junior Naval Officer in the Great Pacific War, 1987. Add: Dept. of History, Vanderbilt Univ., Nashville, Tenn. 37235, U.S.A.

LEACH, Penelope. British, b. 1937. Psychology. Sr. Research Fellow to the International Centre for Child Studies, Bristol, and Research Assoc. to the Dept. of Mental Health, Univ. of Bristol, since 1988. Vice-Pres., Health Visitors' Assn. since 1983. Research Officer, Medical Research Council, Unit for the Study of Child Development, 1965–71; External Medical Editor, Penguin Books, 1970–78; Vice-Pres., Pre-Sch. Playgroups Assn., 1977–83; Dir., Lifetime Productions Intnl., educational video, 1986–88. *Publs:* Babyhood: Infant Development from Birth to Two Years, 1974, 1983; Baby and Child, 1977, 3rd ed. 1988; Who Cares? A New Deal for Mothers and Their Small Children, 1979; The Parents A-Z: A Handbook for Children's Health Growth and Happiness, and in U.S. as Your Growing Child, 1983, 1985; The First Six Months: Coming to Terms with Your Baby, 1986. Add: 3 Tanza Rd., London NW3 2UA, England.

LEAKEY, Mary (Douglas). British, b. 1913. Archaeology/Antiquities,

Autobiography. Dir. of Research, Olduvai Gorge, Tanzania. *Publs:* Olduvai Gorge, volume 3: Excavations in Bed I and II, 1971; Olduvai Gorge: My Search for Early Man, 1979; Africa's Vanishing Act, 1983; Disclosing the Past (autobiography), 1984. Add: P.O. Box 15028, Nairobi, Kenya.

LEAKEY, Richard (Erskine Frere). British, b. 1944. Anthropology, Autobiography. Dir., Natl. Museum of Kenya, Nairobi, since 1974 (Adm. Dir., 1968–74). Leader, E. Turkana (formerly E. Rudolf) Research Project, since 1968. Tour guide and trapper, 1951–65; leader of photographic safaris in E. Africa, 1965–68; co-leader of anthropological expeditions to Lake Natron, 1963–64, Lake Baringo, 1966, Omo River, 1967. *Publs:* (with R. Lewin) Origins, 1978; (with R. Lewin) People of the Lake, 1979; (with Mary Leakey) Koobi Fora Research Project, vol. 1, 1979; The Making of Mankind, 1981; Human Origins, 1982; One Life (autobiography), 1984. Add: P.O. Box 41658, Nairobi, Kenya.

LEANEY, Alfred Robert Clare. British, b. 1909. Children's non-fiction, Theology/Religion, Translations. Army Chaplain, 1939–46; Chaplain and Vice-Principal, Ripon Hall, Oxford, 1952–55; Lectr., 1956–64, Reader, 1964–69. Prof. of New Testament Studies, 1969–70, and Prof. of Christian Theology, 1970–74, Univ. of Nottingham. *Publs:* The Gospel According to St. Luke, 1958; (ed. and contrib.) A Guide to the Scrolls, 1958; The Epistle to Timothy, Titus and Philemon, 1960; From Judaean Caves: The Story of the Scrolls, 1962; The Rule of Qumran and Its Meaning, 1966; I and II Peter and Jude, 1967; (with R. Davidson) Biblical Criticism, 1970; The New Testament, 1972; The Jewish and Christian World 200 BC to 200 AD, 1984. Add: Dunelm, Pulteney Rd., Bath, Avon, England.

LEAR, John. American, b. 1909. Sciences. Ed., Daily Local News, Mechanicsburg, Pa., 1927; News Reporter, The Patriot, Harrisburg, Pa., 1928–34; Staff writer and Ed., Associated Press, 1931–41; Coordinator of Information, Office of the Gov., San Juan, Puerto Rico, 1942–43; Freelance mag. writer, 1944–48; Managing Ed., Steelways, 1948–49; Chief Articles Ed. and Assoc. Ed., Colliers, 1949–53; Editorial Advisor, IBM, NYC, 1953–54; Business Report writer, Research Inst. of America, 1954–55; American Correspondent, The New Scientist, London, 1956–62; Science Ed. and Sr. Ed., Saturday Review, 1956–72; Vice-Pres. for Communications, Bauer Engineering, 1972; Vice-Pres., Secty., and Chief Ed., Bauer, Sheaffer and Lear, 1973–75; Chief Ed., Keefer and Assocs., Chicago, 1975–76; Contrib. Ed., Atlas World Press Review, NYC, 1976–84; Ed. Consultant, The Rockefeller Foundn., NYC, 1977–82. *Publs:* Forgotten Front, 1943; Kepler's Dream, 1965; Recombinant DNA: The Untold Story, 1978. Add: 130 S. Madison St., Harrisburg, Pa. 17109, U.S.A.

LEAR, Martha Weinman. American, b. 1932. Social commentary/phenomena, Autobiography/Memoirs/Personal. Asst. Ed., Collier's mag., NYC, 1951–55; Assoc. Ed., Women's Home Companion, NYC, 1955–56; Writer, NBC, NYC, 1956–57; Ed., The New York Times Sunday Mag., 1957–61. *Publs:* The Child Worshippers, 1964; Heartsounds, 1980. Add: c/o Simon and Schuster, 1230 Ave. of the Americas, New York, N.Y. 10020, U.S.A.

LEAR, Peter. *See* LOVESEY, Peter.

LEARMONTH, Andrew (Thomas Amos). British, b. 1916. Geography. Prof. Emeritus of Geography, The Open Univ. Asst. Lectr., Lectr., and Sr. Lectr., Liverpool Univ., 1949–62; Prof. of Geography, Australian National Univ., Canberra, 1962–69. *Publs:* (ed. with L. Bhat) Mysore State, vol. I, An Atlas of Resources, 1960, and vol. II, A Regional Synthesis, 1962; (with A. Learmonth) The Eastern Lands, 2nd ed., 1963; (with O. Spate) India and Pakistan, 3rd ed., 1967; (with A. Learmonth) Encyclopaedia of Australia, 1968, 1973; (with N. Learmonth) Regional Landscapes of Australia, 1971; Patterns of Disease and Hunger, 1978; (ed.) Geography of Health, 1981; Disease Ecology, 1988. Add: Bryn Rhwydd Penmachno, Betws-y-Coed, Gwynedd. LL24 0AJ, Wales.

LEARY, Edward A. American. b. 1913. History. Freelance writer. Instr., writing for broadcast and film history, Ball State Univ., Muncie, Ind. Retired public relations and advertising consultant, Indianapolis. Former Weekly Columnist on Indiana History, Indianapolis Star. *Publs:* The Nineteenth State, Indiana, 1966; 4th ed. 1978; Indianapolis, The Story of a City, 1970; (ed.) Indiana Almanac and Fact Book, 1978; Indianapolis, A Pictorial History, 1980; Enterprise, 1982; Compassionate Mission, 1985. Add: 7314 Manchester Dr., Apt. A, Indianapolis, Ind. 46260, U.S.A.

LEARY, Lewis. American, b. 1906. Literature. Instr. in English,

American Univ., Beirut, Lebanon, 1928–31; Member of Faculty, 1935–40, and Assoc. Prof., 1938–40, Univ. of Miami, Coral Gables, Fla.; Member of Faculty, 1941–52, and Prof. of American Literature, 1950–52, Duke Univ., Durham, N.C.; Visiting Prof. of English, 1951–52, Prof., 1952–68, and Chmn. of Dept., 1962–68, Columbia Univ., NYC; William Rand Kenan Jr. Prof. of English, Univ. of North Carolina, Chapel Hill, 1968–76. *Publs:* Idiomatic Mistakes in English, 1932; That Rascal Freneau: A Study in Literary Failure, 1941, 1960; (ed.) The Last Poems of Philip Freneau, 1945, 1971; (ed.) Articles on American Literature, 1947, 4th ed. 1974; The Literary Career of Nathaniel Tucker, 1951; (ed.) Method and Motive in the Cantos of Ezra Pound, 1954; (ed.) The Unity of Knowledge, 1955; (ed.) Contemporary Literary Scholarship; A Critical Review, 1958; (ed.) American Literary Essays, 1960; Mark Twain, 1960; Mark Twain's Letters to Mary, 1961; John Greenleaf Whittier, 1962; (ed.) Mark Twain's Wound, 1962; Washington Irving, 1963; (ed.) The Teacher and American Literature, 1965; Norman Douglas, 1967; (ed.) Mark Twain's Correspondence with Henry Huttleston Rogers, 1969; (ed.) Criticism: Some Major American Writers, 1971; Southern Excursions, 1971; William Faulkner of Yoknapatawpha County, 1973; Soundings: Some Early American Writers, 1975; American Literature: A Study and Research Guide, 1976; Ralph Waldo Emerson: An Interpretive Essay, 1980; The Book Peddling Parson, 1984. Add: 2112 Carol Woods, Chapel Hill, N.C. 27514, U.S.A.

LEASOR, (Thomas) James. British, b. 1923. Novels/Short stories, Suspense, History, Biography. Member, Lloyds of London; Dir., Pagoda Films Ltd., since 1959; Dir., Jason Love Ltd., since 1964. Reporter, Kentish Times, Sidcup, 1941–42; Reporter, and Columnist (as William Hickey), Feature Writer and Foreign Correspondent, Daily Express, London, 1948–55; Editorial Adviser and Consultant, George Newnes and C. Arthur Pearson Ltd., London, 1955–69; Dir., Elm Tree Books Ltd., London, 1960–73. *Publs:* novels—Not Such a Bad Day, 1946; The Strong Delusion, 1950; NTR: Nothing to Report, 1955; Follow the Drum, 1972; Mandarin-Gold, 1973; Jade Gate, 1976; The Unknown Warrior, 1980, in U.S. as Code Name Nimrod, 1981; suspense novels—Passport to Oblivion, 1964, Passport to Peril (in U.S. as Spylight), 1966; Passport in Suspense, 1967 (in U.S. as the Yang Meridian, 1968); Passport for a Pilgrim, 1968; They Don't Make Them Like That Any More, 1969; A Week of Love (short stories), 1969; Never Had A Spanner on Her, 1970; Love-All, 1971; Host of Extras, 1973; The Chinese Widow, 1975; Love and the Land Beyond, 1979; Open Secret, 1982; Ship of Gold, 1984; Tank of Serpents, 1986; Frozen Assets, 1989; other—The Monday Story, 1951; Author by Profession, 1952; Wheels of Fortune: A Brief Account of the Life and Times of William Morris, Viscount Nuffield, 1954; The Serjeant Major: A Biography of R.S.M. Ronald Brittain, 1955; The Red Fort: An Account of the Siege of Delhi in 1857, 1956 (in U.K. paperback, Mutiny at the Red Fort, 1959); (with Kendal Burt) The One That Got Away, 1956; The Millionth Chance: The Story of the R.101, 1957; War at the Top (in U.S. as The Clock with Four Hands), 1959; (with Peter Eton) Conspiracy of Silence (in U.S. as Wall of Silence), 1960; The Plague and the Fire, 1961; Rudolf Hess, The Uninvited Envoy (in U.S. as The Uninvited Envoy), 1962; Singapore: The Battle That Changed the World, 1968; Look Where I'm At! (play; adaptation of the novel Rain in the Doorway by Thorne Smith), 1971; Green Beach (on the Dieppe raid), 1975; Boarding Party, 1978; X-Troop, 1980; Who Killed Sir Henry Oakes?, 1983; The Marine from Mandalay, 1988. Add: Swallowcliffe Manor, Salisbury, Wilts. SP3 5PB, England.

LEATHER, George. *See* SWALLOW, Norman.

LEAVER, Ruth. *See* TOMALIN, Ruth.

LEAVITT, David. American, b. 1961. Novels/Short stories. Reader and Educational Asst., Viking-Penguin Inc., NYC, 1983–84. *Publs:* Family Dancing, 1984; The Lost Language of Cranes, 1986; Equal Affections, 1989. Add: c/o Andrew Wylie, 48 W. 75th St., New York, N.Y. 10023, U.S.A.

LeBOEUF, Michael. American, b. 1942. Psychology. Prof. of Management, Univ. of New Orleans. *Publs:* Working Smart: How to Accomplish More in Half the Time, 1979; Imagineering: How to Profit from Your Own Creative Powers, 1980; The Productivity Challenge: How to Make it Work for America and You, 1982; The Greatest Management Principle in the World, 1985; How to Win Customers and Keep Them for Life, 1988. Add: 1328 Homestead Ave., Metairie, La. 70005, U.S.A.

LEBOWITZ, Albert. American, b. 1922. Novels/Short stories, Law. Lawyer; Partner, Murphy & Schlapprizzi, St. Louis, 1969–81; Partner, Murphy, Schlapprizzi & Lebowitz, 1981–86; of Counsel, Donald L.

Schlapprizzi, P.C., since 1986. *Publs:* Laban's Will, 1966; The Man Who Wouldn't Say No, 1969; A Matter of Days, 1989. Add: 743 Yale Ave., University City, Mo. 63130, U.S.A.

LE CARRE John. Pseudonym of David John Moore Cornwell. British, b. 1931. Mystery/Crime/Suspense. Tutor, Eton Coll., Bucks., 1956–58; member, British Foreign Service, 1960–64 (Second Secty., Bonn, 1960–63; Consul, Hamburg, 1963–64). *Publs:* Call for the Dead, 1960; A Murder of Quality, 1962; The Spy Who Came In from the Cold, 1963; The Looking-Glass War, 1965; A Small Town in Germany, 1968; The Naive and Sentimental Lover, 1971; Tinker, Tailor, Soldier, Spy, 1974; The Honourable Schoolboy, 1977; Smiley's People, 1980; The Little Drummer Girl, 1983; A Perfect Spy, 1986; The Russian House, 1989. Add: c/o John Farquharson Ltd., 162-168 Regent St., London W1R 5TB, England.

LECHNER, Robert. American, b. 1918. Philosophy, Theology/Religion. Ed., Philosophy Today, Celina, Ohio, since 1957; Prof. of Philosophy, DePaul Univ., Chicago, since 1967. Prof. and Head of Dept. of Philosophy, St. Joseph's Coll., Rensselaer, Ind., 1950–59; Prof. of Philosophy, St. Charles Seminary, Celina, Ohio, 1959–67. *Publs:* Aesthetic Experience, 1953; Doors to the Sacred, 1963; Gabriel Marcel as Radical Empiricist, 1984. Add: Philosophy Today, Carthagena Station, Celina, Ohio 45822, U.S.A.

LECHT, Leonard A. American, b. 1920. Economics, Education. Consultant, Conference Bd., NYC, since 1980 (Dir., 1974–79). Prof. and Chmn., Dept. of Economics, Long Island Univ., Brooklyn, N.Y., 1954–63; Dir., Priorities Analysis Research, National Planning Assn., Washington, D.C., 1967–74; Member, National Commission on Employment and Unemployment Statutes, 1978. *Publs:* Experience Under Railway Labor Legislation, 1956; Goal, Priorities and Dollars, 1966; Manpower Needs for National Goals in the 1970s, 1969; Dollars for National Goals: Looking Ahead to 1980, 1974; Evaluating Vocational Education: Planning for the 1970s, 1974; (with others) Changes in Occupational Characteristics, 1976; (ed.) Employment and Unemployment, 1977; Occupational Choices and Training Needs, 1977; Vocational Education, 1981; Expenditures for Retirement and Age-Related Programs, 1981; (co-author) A Comprehensive Development Plan for Taos County, Phase I, the Economy, 1988. Add: P.O. Box 3105, Taos, N.M. 87571, U.S.A.

LECLERC, Ivor. British, b. 1915. Philosophy. Emeritus Prof. of Philosophy, Emory Univ., Atlanta, Ga., since 1982 (Visiting Prof., 1963–64; Prof. 1964–80; Fuller E. Callaway Prof. of Metaphysics and Moral Philosophy, 1980–82). Lectr., 1950–62, and Sr. Lectr., 1962–64, Univ. of Glasgow, Scotland, Pres., Metaphysical Soc. of America, 1980–81, and Intnl. Soc. for Metaphysics, 1980–85. *Publs:* Whitehead's Metaphysics, 1958; (ed.) The Relevance of Whitehead, 1961; (trans. with Eva Schaper) Introduction to General Metaphysics, 1961; The Nature of Physical Existence, 1972; (ed.) The Philosophy of Leibniz and the Modern World, 1973; The Philosophy of Nature, 1986. Add: Box 799, Camden, Me. 04843, U.S.A.

LEDER, Lawrence H. American, b. 1927. History, Politics/Government, Biography. Prof., Dept. of History, Lehigh Univ., Bethlehem, Pa., since 1968. Research Assoc., Sleepy Hollow Restorations, Tarrytown, N.Y., 1956–59; Asst. Prof. of History, Brandeis Univ., Waltham, Mass. 1959–62; Prof., Louisiana State Univ., New Orleans, 1962–68. *Publs:* (ed.) The Livingston Indian Records, 1666-1723, 1956; Robert Livingston, 1654-1728, and the Politics of Colonial New York, 1961; (ed.) The Genesis of American Freedom, 1765-1795, 1961; (ed. with M.G. Hall and M.G. Kammen) The Glorious Revolution in America, 1964; Liberty and Authority: Early American Political Ideology, 1689-1763, 1968, 1976; (ed.) Meaning of the American Revolution, 1969; (ed.) The Colonial Legacy, 4 vols., 1971–73; America 1603-1789, 1972, 1978; (ed.) Dimensions of Change, 1972. Add: Dept. of History, Maginnes Hall, Lehigh Univ., Bethlehem, Pa. 18015, U.S.A.

LEDERMANN, Erich. British, b. 1908. Medicine/Health, Psychiatry. Physician and Psychiatrist. *Publs:* Natural Therapy, 1953; Philosophy and Medicine, 1970; Existential Neurosis, 1972; Good Health through Natural Therapy, 1976, 1978; Mental Health and Human Conscience: The True and False Self, 1984; Your Health in Your Hands: A Case for a Natural Medicine, 1989. Add: 97 Harley St., London W1, England.

LEDWITH, Frank. British, b. 1907. Autobiography/Memoirs/Personal. Worked for Thos. Miller & Son, mgrs. of mutual insurance assns. for shipowners, London, 1924–72. *Publs:* Ships That Go Bump in the Night, 1974; Ships Afloat in the City, 1977; The Best of All Possible Worlds, 1987. Add: 168 Bickenhall Mansions, London W1H 3DF, England.

LEE, Alfred McClung. American, b. 1906. Sociology. Prof. Emeritus of Sociology, Brooklyn Coll. and Grad. Center, City Univ. of New York, since 1971 (Prof., 1949–71); Visiting Scholar, Drew Univ., Madison, N.J., since 1975; Bd. member, Sociological Abstracts, and Language Behavior Abstracts, since 1965. Former faculty member, Yale Univ., Univ. of Kansas, New York Univ., Wayne State Univ., and Univ. of Michigan. Co-Organizer, 1950–51, and Pres., 1953–54, Soc. for the Study of Social Problems; Pres., Eastern Sociological Soc. 1954–55; U.S. Delegate, Intnl. Sociological Assn., 1966–70; Vice-Chmn., Public Affairs Pamphlets, 1970–85; Co-Organizer, 1975–76, and Pres., 1975–77, Assn. for Humanist Sociology; Pres., American Sociological Assn., 1975–76. *Publs:* The Daily Newspaper in America: The Evolution of a Social Instrument, 1937, 3rd ed. 1973; (with E.B. Lee) The Fine Art of Propaganda, 1939, 1972; (with N.D. Humphrey) Race Riot, 1943, 1968; (ed. and co-author) Principles of Sociology, 1946, 1971; (with E.B. Lee) Social Problems in America, 1949, 1955; (ed. and co-author) Readings in Sociology, 1951, 1960; How to Understand Propaganda, 1952; (co-ed. and co-author) Public Opinion and Propaganda, 1954; Fraternities Without Brotherhood, 1955; La Sociologia delle Communicazioni, 1960; (with E.B. Lee) Marriage and the Family, 1961, 1967; Che Cos'e' la Propaganda, 1961; Multivalent Man, 1966, 1970; Toward Humanist Sociology, 1973; Sociology for Whom?, 1978, 1986; Human Rights in the Northern Ireland Conflict: 1968–80, 1980; Terrorism in Northern Ireland, 1983; Sociology for People, 1988. Add: 17 Holden Lane, Madison, N.J. 07940-2614, U.S.A.

LEE, Andrew. *See* **AUCHINCLOSS,** Louis.

LEE, Benjamin. British, b. 1921. Children's fiction. Physician: general practitioner in London, since 1949. *Publs:* Paganini Strikes Again, 1970; The Man in Fifteen, 1972; The Frog Report, 1974; It Can't Be Helped, 1976. Add: c/o The Bodley Head, 32 Bedford Sq., London WC1B 3SG, England.

LEE, Dennis (Beynon). Canadian, b. 1939. Poetry, Literature. Ed., House of Anansi Press, Toronto, 1967–73; Dir., Poetry Prog., McClelland and Stewart, publrs., Toronto, 1981–84. *Publs:* (ed. with R.A. Charlesworth) An Anthology of Verse, 1964; (ed. with R.A. Charlesworth) The Second Century Anthologies of Verse, Book 2, 1967; Kingdom of Absence, 1967; Civil Elegies, 1968; (ed. with H. Adelman) The University Game, 1968; (ed.) T.O. Now: The Young Toronto Poets, 1968; Wiggle to the Laundromat (children's poetry), 1970; Civil Elegies and Other Poems, 1972; Alligator Pie (children's poetry), 1974; Nicholas Knock and Other People (children's poetry), 1974; The Death of Harold Ladoo,1976; Garbage Delight (children's poetry), 1977; Savage Fields: An Essay in Literature and Cosmology, 1977; The Gods, 1979; The Ordinary Bath (juvenile), 1979; Jelly Belly (children's poetry), 1983; Lizzie's Lion (children's poetry), 1984; (ed.) The New Canadian Poets, 1970–1985, 1985; The Difficulty of Living on Other Planets, 1987. Add: c/o Macmillan of Canada, 29 Birch Ave., Toronto, Ont. M4V 1E2, Canada.

LEE, Derek. British, b. 1937. Economics. Sr. Lectr. in Economics, Royal Military Academy Sandhurst, Camberley, Surrey, since 1970. General Ed., Studies in the British Economy, since 1968. *Publs:* (with V. Anthony and A. Skuse) Monopoly, 1968; Regional Planning and the Location of Industry, 1969; Control of the Economy, 1974. Add: c/o Heinemann Educational Books, 22 Bedford Sq., London WC1B 3HH, England.

LEE, (Sir Henry) Desmond (Pritchard). British, b. 1908. Classics, Education. Principal, Hughes Hall, Cambridge, 1974–78, now retired (Sr. Research Fellow, University Coll., Cambridge, 1969–73). Fellow of Corpus Christi Coll., Cambridge, 1933–48 (Life Fellow, 1978); Headmaster, Clifton Coll., Bristol, 1948–54, Winchester Coll., Hants., 1954–68. Chmn., Headmaster's Conference, 1959, 1960, 1967. *Publs:* Zeno of Elea: Text and Notes, 1935; Aristotle's Meteorologica, 1952; translations—Plato's Republic, 1955, 1975; Plato's Timaeus, 1965, 1969; Plato's Timaeus and Critias, 1971; Entry and Performance at Oxford and Cambridge 1966–71, 1972; (ed.) Wittgenstein's Lectures, Cambridge 1930–1932, 1979. Add: 8 Barton Close, Cambridge CB3 9LQ, England.

LEE, Don L(uther). American, b. 1942. Poetry, Literature, Race relations. Ed. and Publisher, Third World Press, Chicago, since 1967; Ed., Black Books Bulletin, Chicago, since 1972. Apprentice Curator, DuSable Museum of African American History, Chicago, 1963–67; Stock Dept. Clerk, Montgomery Ward, Chicago, 1963–64; Post Office Clerk, Chicago, 1964–65; Jr. Exec., Spiegels, Chicago, 1965–66; Writer-in-Residence, Cornell Univ., Ithaca, N.Y., 1968–69; Poet-in-Residence,

Northeastern Illinois State Coll., Chicago, 1969–70; Lectr., Univ. of Ill., Chicago, 1969–71; Writer-in-Residence, Howard Univ., Washington, D.C., 1971–75; Writer-in-Residence, Morgan State Coll., Baltimore, Md., 1972–73. *Publs:* Think Black, 1967; Black Pride, 1968; Back Again, Home, 1968; One Sided Shoot-Out, 1968; For Black People (and Negroes Too), 1968; Don't Cry, Scream, 1969; We Walk the Way of the New World, 1970; Dynamite Voices: Black Poets of the 1960s, 1971; (ed. with P.L. Brown and F. Ward) To Gwen with Love, 1971; Directionscore: Selected and New Poems, 1971; Book of Life (poetry), 1973; From Plan to Planet: Life Studies: The Need for Afrikan Minds and Institutions, 1973; Enemies: The Clash of Races, 1978. Add: Third World Press, 7524 S. Cottage Grove, Chicago, Ill. 60619, U.S.A.

LEE, Donald (Lewis). British, b. 1931. Zoology. Prof. of Agricultural Zoology, Univ. of Leeds, since 1971 (Pro-Vice-Chancellor, 1987–89). Research Fellow, 1958–63, and Fellow, 1963–71, Christ's Coll., Cambridge; Head of Parasitology Dept., Houghton Poultry Research Station, 1966–71. Assoc. Sr. Research Fellow, Brunel Univ., Uxbridge, Middx., 1967–70; Pres., 1978–80, British Soc. of Parasitology. *Publs:* The Physiology of Nematodes, 1965, 2nd ed. with H.J. Atkinson, 1976; (ed., with D.H. Jennings) Symbiosis, 1976. Add: Dept. of Pure and Applied Biology, Univ. of Leeds, Leeds LS2 9JT, England.

LEE, Elsie. Also writes as Elsie Cromwell, Norman Daniels, Jane Gordon, and Lee Sheridan. American, b. 1912. Historical/Romance/Gothic, Cookery, Gardening. Full-time writer. Librarian, Waterhouse and Co., NYC, 1937–42; Office Mgr., Reeves Laboratories, NYC, 1942–45; Librarian, Gulf Oil Co., NYC, 1947–51; Exec. Secty., Andrews Clark and Buckley, NYC, 1951–53. *Publs:* novels—The Blood Red Oscar, 1962; (as Norman Daniels) Sam Benedict: Cast the First Stone (novelization of TV series), 1963; A Comedy of Terrors (novelization of screenplay), 1964; The Masque of the Red Death (novelization of screenplay), 1964; Muscle Beach (novelization of screenplay), 1964; Season of Evil, 1965, in U.K., as Jane Gordon, as Two Hearts Apart, 1973; Dark Moon, Lost Lady, 1965; Clouds over Vellanti, 1965; The Curse of Carranca, 1966, in U.K. as The Second Romance, 1974; Mansion of the Golden Windows, 1966; The Drifting Sands, 1966; Sinister Abbey, 1967, in U.K. as Romance on the Rhine, 1974; The Spy at the Villa Miranda, 1967, in U.K. as The Unhappy Parting, 1973; Doctor's Office, 1968; (as Elsie Cromwell) The Governess, 1969, in U.K. as Guardian of Love, 1972; Satan's Coast, 1969, in U.K. as Mystery Castle, 1973; Fulfilment, 1969; Barrow Sinister, 1969, in U.K. as Romantic Assignment, 1974; (as Elsie Cromwell) Ivorstone Manor, 1970; Silence Is Golden, 1971; Wingarden, 1971; The Diplomatic Lover, 1971; Star of Danger, 1971; The Passions of Medora Graeme, 1972; A Prior Betrothal, 1973; The Wicked Guardian, 1973; Second Season, 1973; An Eligible Connection, 1974; Roommates, 1976; The Habob's Widow, 1976; Mistress of Mount Fair, 1977; other—(as Lee Sheridan; with Michael Sheridan) How to Get the Most Out of Your Tape Recording, 1958; (as Lee Sheridan; with Michael Sheridan) More Fun with Your Tape Recorders and Stereo, 1958; The Exciting World of Rocks and Gems, 1959; Easy Gourmet Cooking, 1962; (as Lee Sheridan; with Michael Sheridan) The Bachelor's Cookbook, 1962; At Home with Planets: A Guide to Successful Indoor Gardening, 1966; Second Easy Gourmet Cookbook, 1968; Book of Simple Gourmet Cookery, 1971; Party Cookbook, 1974. Add: c/o Bill Berger Assocs., 444 E. 58th St., New York, N.Y. 10022, U.S.A.

LEE, Harold Newton. American, b. 1899. Philosophy. Emeritus Prof. of Philosophy, Tulane Univ., New Orleans, La., since 1970 (Asst. Prof., 1925–36; Assoc. Prof., 1936–43; Prof., 1943–70). Instr. and Tutor in Philosophy, Harvard Univ., Cambridge, Mass., 1930–31. *Publs:* Perception and Aesthetic Value, 1938, 1967; (ed. and contrib.) Essays on the Theory of Value and Valuation, 1945; Symbolic Logic, 1961; Percepts, Concepts and Theoretic Knowledge, 1973. Add: 801 Broadway, New Orleans, La. 70118, U.S.A.

LEE, Howard. *See* **GOULART,** Ron.

LEE, John. American, b. 1931. Novels/Short stories. Photographer, Fort Worth Star-Telegram, Texas, 1952–57, Denver Post, 1958–60; Prof. of Journalism, American Univ., Washington, D.C., 1965–67, Univ. of Arizona, Tucson, 1967–71, New York Univ., 1971–74, California State Univ. at Long Beach, 1975–76. *Publs:* Caught in the Act, 1968; Diplomatic Persuaders, 1968; Assignation in Algeria, 1971; The Ninth Man, 1976; The Thirteenth Hour, 1978; Lago, 1980; The Unicorn Quest, 1986. Add: c/o Don Congdon Assocs., 156 Fifth Ave., New York, N.Y. 10010, U.S.A.

LEE, Julian. *See* **LATHAM,** Jean Lee.

LEE, Laurie. British, b. 1914. Plays/Screenplays, Poetry, Travel/Exploration/Adventure, Autobiography/Memoirs/Personal, Translations. Scriptwriter, Crown Film Unit, 1942–44; Publs. Ed., Ministry of Information, 1944–46; member of the Green Park Film Unit, 1946–47; Caption Writer-in-Chief, Festival of Britain, 1950–51. *Publs:* (trans.) The Dead Village, by Avigdor Dagan, 1943; The Sun My Monument, 1944; Land at War, 1945; The Voyage of Magellan: A Dramatic Chronicle for Radio, 1946; The Bloom of Candles, 1947; Peasants' Priest: a Play, 1947; (with R. Keene) We Make a Film in Cyprus, 1947; (ed. with C. Hassall and Rex Warner) New Poems 1954, 1954; My Many-Coated Man, 1955; A Rose for Winter: Travels in Andalusia, 1956; Cider with Rosie (in U.S. as The Edge of Day), 1959; Poems, 1960; The Firstborn (essay on childhood), 1964; As I Walked Out One Midsummer Morning (autobiography), 1969; (with Charles Causley) Pergamon Poets 10, 1970; I Can't Stay Long, 1975; Innocence in the Mirror, 1978; Two Women, 1983; Selected Poems, 1983. Add: c/o André Deutsch Ltd., 105 Great Russell St., London WC1B 3LU, England.

LEE, M. Owen. American, b. 1930. Classics, Film, Music. Roman Catholic Priest; Prof. of Classics, Univ. of Toronto, since 1975. Prof. of Classics, Univ. of St. Thomas, Houston, Tex., 1968–72; Assoc. Prof. of Classics, Loyola Univ., Chicago, 1972–75. *Publs:* (ed. with P.E. Sheehan) The New Saint Basil Hymnal, 1958; Word, Sound, and Image in the Odes of Horace, 1969; Top Ten: A Personal Approach to the Movies, 1973; Fathers and Sons in Virgil's Aeneid, 1979; Death and Rebirth in Virgil's Arcadia, 1989. Add: 81 St. Mary St., Toronto, Ont. M5S 1J4, Canada.

LEE, Maryat (Mary Attaway). American. Plays/Screenplays, Theatre. Dir./Playwright, Founder, EcoTheater, since 1975. Member of faculty, New Sch. of Social Research, NYC, 1966–70; Dir., Prison Arts Prog., Federal Reformatory for Women, Alderson, W. VA., 1974–77; Adjunct Instr., West Virginia Coll. of Grad. Studies, 1978. *Publs:* Dope!, 1951, 1957; Four Men and a Monster, 1967; Day to Day, 1969; The Hinton Play, 1985. Add: 343 Church St., Lewisburg W.V. 24901, U.S.A.

LEE, Mildred. American, b. 1908. Novels/Short stories, Children's fiction. *Publs:* The Invisible Sun, 1946; The Rock and the Willow, 1963; Honor Sands, 1966; The Skating Rink, 1969; Fog, 1972; Sycamore Year, 1974; The People Therein, 1980. Add: c/o Clarion Books, 52 Vanderbilt Ave., New York, N.Y. 10017, U.S.A.

LEE, Peter H. American, b. 1929. Literature, Translations. Prof. of Korean and Comparative Literature, Univ. of California, Los Angeles, since 1987. Asst. Prof. to Prof., Univ. of Hawaii, Honolulu, 1962–87. *Publs:* Studies in Old Korean Poetry, 1959; (trans. and ed.) Kranich am Meer, 1959; (trans. and ed.) Anthology of Korean Poetry, 1964; Korean Literature: Topics and Themes, 1965; (trans.) Lives of Eminent Korean Monks, 1969; (trans. and ed.) Poems from Korea, 1974; (ed.) Flowers of Fire, 1974, 1986; Songs of Flying Dragons: A Critical Reading, 1975; Celebration of Continuity: Themes in Classic East Asian Poetry, 1979; The Silence of Love: Twentieth Century Korean Poetry, 1980; Anthology of Korean Literature: From Early Times to the Nineteenth Century, 1981. Add: Dept. of East Asian Languages and Cultures, UCLA, Los Angeles, Calif. 90024, U.S.A.

LEE, Robert E(dwin). American, b. 1918. Plays/Screenplays, Media. Partner, Lawrence & Lee, since 1942, and Vice-Pres., Lawrence & Lee Inc., NYC and Los Angeles, since 1955; Lectr., Univ. of California at Los Angeles, since 1966. Astronomical Observer, Delaware, Ohio, 1936–37; Dir., Radio Station WHK-WCLE, Cleveland, Ohio, 1937–38; Dir., Young Rubicam, NYC and Hollywood, Calif., 1938–42; Prof. of Playwriting, Coll. of Theatre Arts, Pasadena Playhouse, Calif. 1962–43; Co-Founder, American Playwrights Theatre. *Publs:* all with Jerome Lawrence unless otherwise noted—(as sole author) Television: The Revolutionary Industry, 1944; Inherit the Wind, 1955; (with J. Lawrence and James Hilton) Shangri-La, 1956; Auntie Mame, 1956, rev. version as Mame, 1966; The Gang's All Here, 1959; Only in America, 1959; A Call on Kuprin, 1961; Sparks Fly Upward, 1967; The Incomparable Max, 1969; The Night Thoreau Spent in Jail, 1970; 1971; Jabberwock, 1972; The Crocodile Smile, 1972; First Monday in October, 1975; Sounding Brass, 1975. Add: 15725 Royal Oak Rd., Encino, Calif. 91436, U.S.A.

LEE, Sherman Emery. American, b. 1918. Art. Adjunct Prof. of Art, Univ. of North Carolina at Chapel Hill, since 1983. Prof. of Art, Case Western Reserve Univ., Cleveland, Ohio, since 1962. Curator of Far Eastern Art, Detroit Inst. of Art, Mich., 1941–46; Advisor on Collections, Arts and Monuments Div. Section, U.S. Army, Tokyo, 1946–48; Asst. Dir., and Assoc. Dir., Seattle Art Museum, Wash., 1948–52; Curator of

Oriental Art, 1952–83, and Dir., 1958–83, Cleveland Museum of Art, Ohio (Asst. Dir., 1956–57, Assoc. Dir., 1957–58). *Publs:* Chinese Landscape Painting, 1954, 1962; (with Wen Fong) Streams and Mountains Without End, 1955; Rajput Painting, 1960; Japanese Decorative Style, 1961; Tea Taste in Japanese Art, 1963; History of Far Eastern Art, 1963, 1982; (with Wai-Kam Ho) Chinese Art Under the Mongols, 1968; Ancient Cambodian Sculpture, 1968; Asian Art, 1970; The Colors of Ink, 1974; (ed.) On Understanding Art Museums, 1975; Past, Present, East and West, 1983; Reflections of Reality in Japanese Art, 1983; The Sketchbooks of Hiroshige, 2 vols., 1984. Add: c/o George Braziller, 60 Madison Ave., Suite 1001, New York, N.Y. 10010, U.S.A.

LEE, Tanith. British, b. 1947. Novels/Short stories, Science fiction/Fantasy, Children's fiction. Freelance writer of SF novels and short stories, radio plays, and children's fiction. *Publs:* The Betrothed (short stories), 1968; The Dragon Hoard (juvenile), 1971; Princess Hynchatti and Some Other Surprises (juvenile), 1972; Animal Castle (juvenile), 1972; Companions on the Road (juvenile), 1975, in U.S. as Companions on the Road, and the Winter Players, 1977; The Birthgrave, 1975; Don't Bite the Sun, 1976; The Storm Lord, 1976; The Winter Players (juvenile), 1976; East of Midnight (juvenile), 1977; Drinking Sapphire Wine, 1977, in U.K. same title but includes Don't Bite the Sun, 1979; Volkhavaar, 1977; Vazkor, Son of Vazkor, 1978, in U.K. as Shadowfire, 1979; Quest for the White Witch, 1978; Night's Master, 1978; The Castle of Dark (juvenile), 1978; Shon the Taken (juvenile), 1979; Death's Master, 1979; Electric Forest, 1979; Sabella; or, The Blood Stone, 1980; Kill the Dead, 1980; Day by Night, 1980; Delusion's Master, 1981; The Silver Metal Lover, 1982; Cyrion (short stories), 1982; Prince on a White Horse (juvenile), 1982; Sung in Shadow, 1983; Anackire, 1983; Red as Blood; or, Tales from the Sisters Grimmer, 1983; The Dragon Hoard, 1984; The Beautiful Biting Machine (short stories), 1984; Tamastara; or, The Indian Nights (short stories), 1984; Days of Grass, 1985; The Gorgon and Other Beastly Tales, 1985; Dreams of Dark and Light: The Great Short Fiction of Tanith Lee, 1986; Dark Castle, White Horse, 1986; Delirium's Mistress, 1986; Night's Sorceries, 1987; The White Serpent, 1988; The Book of the Beast (short stories), 1988; The Book of the Damned (short stories) 1988; Forests of the Night, 1989; A Heroine of the World, 1989. Add: c/o Macmillan London Ltd., 4 Little Essex St., London WC2R 3LF, England.

LEE, Veronica. *See* **WOODFORD,** Cecile.

LEE, Wayne C. Also writes as Lee Sheldon. American, b. 1917. Westerns/Adventure, History. Rural Mail Carrier, 1951–77. Pres., Western Writers of America, 1970–71, and Nebraska Writers Guild, 1974–76. *Publs:* Prairie Vengeance, 1954; Broken Wheel Ranch, 1956; Slugging Backstop, 1957; His Brother's Guns, 1958; Killer's Range, 1958; Bat Masterson, 1960; Gun Brand, 1961; Blood on the Prairie, 1962; Thunder in the Backfield, 1962; Stranger in Stirrup, 1962; The Gun Tamer, 1963; Devil Wire, 1963; The Hostile Land, 1964; Gun in His Hand, 1964; Warpath West, 1965; Fast Gun, 1965; Brand of a Man, 1966; Mystery of Scorpion Creek, 1966; Trail of the Skulls, 1966; Showdown at Julesburg Station, 1967; Return to Gunpoint, 1967; Only the Brave, 1967; (as Lee Sheldon) Doomed Planet, 1967; Sudden Guns, 1968; Trouble at Flying H, 1969; Stage to Lonesome Butte, 1969; Showdown at Sunrise, 1971; The Buffalo Hunters, 1972; Suicide Trail, 1972; Wind Over Rimfire, 1973; Son of a Gunman, 1973; Scotty Philip, the Man Who Saved the Buffalo, 1975; Law of the Prairie, 1975; Die Hard, 1975; Law of the Lawless, 1977; Skirmish at Fort Phil Kearney, 1977; Gun Country, 1978; Petticoat Wagon Train, 1978; The Violent Man, 1978. Ghost of a Gunfighter, 1980; McQuaid's Gun, 1980; Trails of the Smoky Hill (non-fiction), 1980; Shadow of the Gun, 1981; Guns at Genesis, 1981; Putnam's Ranch War, 1982; Barbed Wire War, 1983; The Violent Trail, 1984; White Butte Guns, 1984; War at Nugget Creek, 1985; Massacre Creek, 1985; The Waiting Gun, 1986; Hawks of Autumn, 1986; Wild Towns of Nebraska (non-fiction), 1988. Add: Lamar, Nebr. 69035, U.S.A.

LEE, William. *See* **BURROUGHS,** William S.

LEE, William Rowland. British. Education, Language/Linguistics. Lectr., English Dept., Caroline Univ., Prague, 1946–51; Lectr. in Teaching of English as a Foreign Language, Univ. of London Inst. of Education, 1952–57 and 1959–62; Language Teaching Adviser, British Council, 1958–59; Founder-Chmn., Intnl. Assn. of Teachers of English as a Foreign Language, 1967–84. Ed., English Language Teaching Journal, 1961–81; Ed., World Language English, 1981–84. *Publs:* English Intonation: A New Approach, 1958; (with Z. Lee) Teach Yourself Czech, 1959; An English Intonation Reader, 1960; Spelling Irregularity and Reading

Progress, 1960, 1972; (with M. Dodderidge) Time for a Song, 1963; (with H. Coppen) Simple Audiovisual Aids to Foreign Language Teaching, 1964, 1968; Language Teaching Games and Contests, 1965, 1986; (with L. Koullis) The Argonauts' English Course, 1965–73; (with A.W.J. Barron) Phonetics Wall Charts, 1966; English at Home, 1966; (ed.) ELT Selections I, 1966; (ed.) ELT Selections, II, 1967; First Songs in English, 1970; The Dolphin English Course, 1970–73; More Songs in English, 1973; (with V. Maddock) Getting Through Trinity College English, 1981; (with B. Haycraft) It Depends How You Say It, 1982; Study Dictionary of Social English, 1983. Add: 16 Alexandra Gardens, Hounslow, Middx. TW3 4HU, England.

LEE, W(illiam) Storrs III. American, b. 1906. Education, Geography, History, Biography. English Instr., Norwich Free Academy, Connecticut, 1929–30; Ed., Middlebury Coll. Press, 1930–41; Dean of Men, Middlebury Coll., 1945–55; Writer and Ed., Marts & Lundy, 1958–59; English Instr., Hawaii Preparatory Academy, 1962–63; Ed., State Literary Chronicles Series, Funk & Wagnalls and Reader's Digest, 1966–73. *Publs:* Father Went to College, 1936; (ed.) Bread Loaf Anthology, 1939; Stagecoach North, 1941; (ed.) Footpath in the Wilderness, 1941; Town Father, 1952; Green Mountains of Vermont, 1955; Yankees of Connecticut, 1957; The Strength to Move a Mountain, 1958; God Bless Our Queer Old Dean, 1959; Canal Across a Continent, 1961; The Sierra, 1962; The Great California Deserts, 1963; The Islands, 1966; (ed.) Hawaii: A Literary Chronicle, 1967; (ed.) Maine: A Literary Chronicle, 1968; (ed.) California: Literary Chronicle, 1968; (ed.) Washington State: A Literary Chronicle, 1969; (ed.) Colorado: A Literary Chronicle, 1970; (ed.) Partridge in a Swamp: Journals of Viola C. White, 1979. Add: 1194 Uluniu Rd., Kihei, Maui, Hawaii 96753, U.S.A.

LEECH, Geoffrey Neil. British, b. 1936. Language/Linguistics. Prof. of Linguistics, Univ. of Lancaster, since 1974 (Reader in English, 1969–74). Lectr., University Coll., London, 1965–69. *Publs:* English in Advertising, 1966; A Linguistic Guide to English Poetry, 1969; Towards a Semantic Description of English, 1969; Meaning and the English Verb, 1971, 1987; (with R. Quirk, S. Greenbaum and J. Svartvik) A Grammar of Contemporary English, 1972; Semantics, 1974, 1981; (with J. Svartvik) A Communicative Grammar of English, 1975; Explorations in Semantics and Pragmatics, 1980; (ed. with S. Greenbaum and J. Svartvik) Studies in English Linguistics, 1980; (with M.H. Short) Style in Fiction, 1981; (with M. Deuchar and R. Hoogenraad) English Grammar for Today, 1982; Principles of Pragmatics, 1983; (with R. Quirk, S. Greenbaum and J. Svartvik) A Comprehensive Grammar of the English Language, 1985; (ed. with C.N. Candlin) Computers in English Language Teaching and Research, 1986; (co-ed.) The Computational Analysis of English: A Corpus-Based Approach, 1987. Add: Univ. of Lancaster, Bailrigg, Lancaster LA1 4YT, England.

LEECH, Kenneth. British, b. 1939. Medicine/Health, Sociology, Theology/Religion. Dir., Runnymede Trust, since 1987. Curate, Holy Trinity, Hoxton, 1964–67, and St. Anne's, Soho, 1967–71, London; Chaplain, St. Augustines Coll., Canterbury, 1971–74; Rector, St. Matthew's Bethnal Green, London, 1974–81; Race Relations Field Officer, Church of England, 1981–87. *Publs:* (with Brenda Jordan) Drugs for Young People: Their Use and Misuse, 1967, 1974; Pastoral Care and the Drug Scene, 1970; Practical Guide to the Drug Scene, 1973, 1974; Keep the Faith Baby, 1973; Youthquake, 1973; Soul Friend, 1977; True Prayer, 1980; Brick Lane 1978, 1980; The Social God, 1981; What Everyone Should Know About Drugs, 1983; True God, 1985; Spirituality and Pastoral Care, 1986; Struggle in Babylon, 1988. Add: 11 Princelet St., London E1, England.

LEED, Jacob. American, b. 1924. Poetry. Prof. of English, Kent State Univ., Ohio, since 1971 (Assoc. Prof., 1963–71). *Publs:* (ed.) The Computer and Literary Style, 1966; Poems, 1966; Poet-Painter, 1967; In Japan, 1978; Chinese Pictures, 1980. Add: 111 Gore St., Cambridge, Mass. 02141, U.S.A.

LEEDS, Barry H. American, b. 1940. Literature. Prof. of English, Central Connecticut State Univ. since 1976 (Asst. Prof., 1968–71; Assoc. Prof., 1971–76). Consultant and Reviewer, Choice Mag., since 1968. Lectr., City Univ. of New York, 1963–64; Instr., Univ. of Texas at El Paso, 1964–65; Drama Critic, El Paso Herald Post, 1965; Teaching Fellow, Ohio Univ., Athens, 1965–67. *Publs:* The Structured Vision of Norman Mailer, 1969; Ken Kesey, 1981. Add: 133 Jerome Ave., Burlington, Conn. 06013, U.S.A.

LEEDS, (Sir) Christopher (Anthony). British, b. 1935. Economics, History, Literature, Politics/Government. Sr. Lectr., Univ. of Nancy II,

France, since 1983 (Lectr., 1982–83). Asst. Master, Merchant Taylors' Sch., Northwood, Middx., 1966–68, Christ's Hospital, Horsham, Sussex, 1972–75, and Stowe Sch., Bucks., 1978–81. *Publs:* Political Studies, 1968, 3rd ed., 1981; European History 1789-1914, 1971, 1980; Italy under Mussolini, 1972; (with R.S. Stainton and C. Jones) Management and Business Studies, 1974, 3rd ed., 1983; Unification of Italy, 1974; Historical Guide to England, 1976; British Government and Politics, 1981; Basic Economics Revision, 1982; Politics in Action, 1986; World History Since 1900, 1987; English Humour, 1989. Add: 7 rue de Turique, 54000 Nancy, France.

LEEDS, Morton Harold. American, b. 1921. Poetry, Psychology, Sociology. Consultant, The Arbor Consulting Group, since 1985; Special Asst. to the Asst. Secty. for Housing, U.S. Dept. of Housing and Urban Development, Washington, D.C., 1962–85. Exec. Dir., Borinstein Home, 1953–62; Exec. Secty., Indiana State Commn. on Aging and the Aged, Indianapolis, 1955–62. *Publs:* (ed.) Aging in Indiana: Readings in Community Organization, 1959; The Aged: The Social Worker and the Community, 1961; (ed. with H. Shore) Geriatric Institutional Management, 1964; (ed.) Washington Colloquium on Science and Society, Second Series, 1967; Jackstones (poetry), 1970; (with G. Murphy) Outgrowing Self-Deception, 1975; (with G. Murphy) The Paranormal and the Normal, 1980; The Federal Job Game, 1988; The Devil's Disciple's Dictionary, 1988; Ben Myer's Tales, 1988. Add: 6219 Lone Oak Dr., Bethesda, Md. 20817, U.S.A.

LEEDY, Paul D. American, b. 1908. Education, Language/Linguistics. Prof. Emeritus of Education, American Univ., Washington, D.C. Member, Bd. of Abstractors, Psychological Abstracts, since 1961. Assoc. Ed., Abingdon-Cokesbury Press, NYC, 1944–47; Prof. of English, Rutgers Univ., Newark, N.J., 1946–50; Sr. Specialist and Chief Consultant, The Reading Inst., New York Univ., NYC, 1950–61; Editorial Consultant, Chilton Co., publrs., 1955–56; Editorial Consultant, McGraw-Hill Book Co., NYC, 1960–75. *Publs:* (with others) The Wonderful World of Books, 1952; Reading Improvement for Adults, 1956; Read with Speed and Precision, 1963; Improve Your Reading, 1963; (ed.) Perspectives in Reading: College-Adult Reading Instruction, 1964; A Key to Better Reading, 1968; Practical Research: Planning and Design, 1974, 4th ed., 1989; How to Read Research and Understand It, 1981. Add: 239 N. 25th St., Camp Hill, Pa. 17011, U.S.A.

LEERBURGER, Benedict A. American, b. 1932. Technology, Biography. Freelance writer, since 1979. Science Ed., Look Mag., NYC, 1964–69; Dir. of Publs., New York Times, MCA, NYC, 1972–74; Ed. and Publr., Kraus-Thomson Org. Ltd., 1974–77; Publr., Film Review Digest, 1975–77; Ed.-in-Chief, McGraw-Hill Book Co., Webster Div., NYC, 1977–79. *Publs:* Josiah Willard Gibbs: American Theoretical Physicist, 1968; Marketing the Library, 1983; The Complete Consumer's Guide to the Latest Telephones, 1985; Insider's Guide to Foreign Study, 1988. Add: 338 Heathcote Rd., Scarsdale, N.Y. 10543, U.S.A.

LEES, Ray. British, b. 1931. Sociology. Freelance writer since 1987. Research Consultant, Gulbenkian Foundn., London, since 1975. Probation Officer, London Probation Service, 1964–66; Lectr. in Govt., Polytechnic of Central London, 1969–71; Sr. Research Fellow, Univ. of York, 1971–75; Head, Applied Social Science, 1975–87, and Prof., 1979–87, Polytechnic of Central London. *Publs:* Politics and Social Work, 1972; Research Strategies for Social Welfare, 1975; (ed. with George Smith) Action Research in Community Development, 1975; (with N. Bailey and M. Mayo) Resourcing Communities, 1981; (with S. Lees and B. Herand) Studies in Community Development, 3 vols.; (with E. Butterworth and P. Arnold) The Challenge of Community Work, 1981; (with M. Mayo) Community Action for Change, 1984. Add: c/o Routledge, Chapman and Hall, 11 New Fetter Ln., London EC4P 4EE, England.

LEES-MILNE, James. British, b. 1908. Novels, Architecture, Travel, Autobiography/Memoirs/Personal, Biography. Private Secty. to Baron Lloyd, 1931–35; staff member, Reuters, 1935–36, and National Trust, 1936–66. *Publs:* (ed.) The National Trust, 1945; The Age of Adam, 1947; National Trust Guide: Buildings, 1948; Tudor Renaissance, 1951; The Age of Inigo Jones, 1953; Roman Mornings, 1956; Baroque in Italy, 1959; Baroque in Spain and Portugal, 1960; Earls of Creation, 1962; Worcestershire: A Shell Guide, 1964; St. Peter's, 1967; English Country Houses: Baroque, 1970; Another Self, 1970; Heretics in Love (novel), 1973; Ancestral Voices, 1975; William Beckford, 1976; Prophesying Peace, 1977; Round the Clock (novel), 1978; Harold Nicolson, 2 vols., 1980–81; The Country House (anthol.), 1982; The Last Stuarts, 1983; Edwardian Enigma, 1986; Some Cotswold Country Houses, 1987; Venetian Evenings, 1988. Add: Essex House, Badminton, Avon GL9

1DD, England.

LEESON, Robert (Arthur). British, b. 1928. Children's fiction, Children's non-fiction, History. Journalist since 1944; freelance ed. and writer since 1969; Literary and Children's Ed., Morning Star, London 1961–84; Chmn., Writers' Guild, 1985–86. *Publs:* United We Stand: An Illustrated Account of Trade Union Emblems, 1971; Strike: A Live History 1887-1971, 1973; Beyond the Dragon Prow, 1973; Maroon Boy, 1974; The Third Class Genie, 1975; Bess, 1975; The Demon Bike Rider, 1976; The White Horse, 1977; Children's Books and Class Society: Past and Present, 1977; Silver's Revenge, 1978; The Cimaroons, 1978; Travelling Brothers: The Six Centuries' Road from Craft Fellowship to Trade Unionism, 1979; Grange Hill series, 4 vols., 1980–82; Harold and Bella, Jammy and Me, 1980; It's My Life, 1980; The Third Class Genie, 1981; Forty Days of Tucker J, 1983; Candy for King, 1983; Genie on the Loose, 1984; Reading and Righting, 1985; Time Rope (serial novel), 4 vols., 1986; Reversible Giant, 1986; Wheel of Danger, 1986; Never Kiss Frogs, 1988; Hey, Robin!, 1989; Jan on Her Own, 1989. Add: 18 McKenzie Rd., Broxbourne, Hertfordshire, England.

LEFEBURE, Molly. British. Novels/Short stories, Criminology/Law enforcement/Prisons, Geography, Biography. *Publs:* Evidence for the Crown, 1955; Murder with a Difference, 1958; The Lake District, 1963; Scratch and Co., 1968; The Hunting of Wilberforce Pike, 1970; Cumberland Heritage, 1971; The Loona Balloona, 1974; Samuel Taylor Coleridge: A Bondage of Opium, 1974; Cumbrian Discovery, 1977; The Bondage of Love: A Life of Mrs. Samuel Taylor Coleridge, 1986; The Illustrated Lake Poets, 1987; Blitz!, 1988. Add: c/o Watson Little Ltd., 26 Charing Cross Rd., Suite 8, London WC2H 0DG, England.

LEFF, Gordon. British, b. 1926. Intellectual history, Philosophy. Prof. of History, Univ. of York, since 1965; freelance writer, lectr. and occasional broadcaster. Fellow, King's Coll., Cambridge, 1955–59; Lectr., then Sr. Lectr., Manchester Univ., 1956–65. *Publs:* Bradwardine and the Pelagians, 1957; Medieval Thought, 1958; Gregory of Rimini, 1961; The Tyranny of Concepts, 1961; Richard Fitzralph, 1963; Heresy in the Later Middle Ages, 2 vols., 1967; Paris and Oxford Universities in 13th and 14th Centuries, 1968; History and Social Theory, 1969; William of Ockham: The Metamorphosis of Scholastic Discourse, 1975; The Dissolution of the Medieval Outlook, 1976. Add: The Sycamores, 12 The Village, Strensall, Yorks, YO3 5XS, England.

LEGAT, Michael (Ronald). Also writes with Robert Haining as Robert Alexander. British, b. 1923. Novels/Short stories, Literature, Writing, Translations. Editorial Dir., Collier Macmillan Ltd., London, since 1973. Worked for the Bodley Head Ltd., London, 1941–50: Production Mgr., 1946–50; Production Mgr. and Editorial Dir., Transworld Publishers Ltd., 1959–73. *Publs:* (trans.) The Secret Game, by Francois Boyer, 1950; (trans.) The Fearless Heart, by Georges Bernanos, 1952; (trans.) Dettina, by Michael Durafour, 1953; (trans.) The Forbidden Mountain, by Fernand Navarra, 1956; Dear Author: Letters from a Working Publisher to Authors, Prospective and Published, 1972; (as Robert Alexander) The Soul Eater, 1979; An Author's Guide to Publishing, 1982; The Silver Foundation, 1982; Mario's Vineyard, 1984; Putting on a Play, 1984; The Shapiro Diamond, 1984; The Silk Maker, 1985; (ed.) The Illustrated Dictionary of Western Literature, 1987. Add: 8 Pollards Hill West, London SW16 4NS, England.

LEGGATT, Alexander. Canadian, b. 1940. Literature. Prof. of English, Univ. Coll., Univ. of Toronto, since 1975 (Lectr., 1965–67; Asst. Prof., 1967–71; Assoc. Prof., 1971–75); Guggenheim Fellowship, 1985–86. *Publs:* Citizen Comedy in the Age of Shakespeare, 1973; Shakespeare's Comedy of Love, 1974; Ben Jonson: His Vision and His Art, 1981; English Drama: Shakespeare to the Restoration 1590-1660, 1988; Shakespeare's Political Drama, 1988; Harvester Twayne New Critical Introductions to Shakespeare: King Lear, 1988. Add: Dept. of English, Univ. Coll., Univ. of Toronto, Ont. M5S 1A1, Canada.

LEGGE, John David. Australian, b. 1921. History, Politics/Government, Biography. Lectr., 1946–54, Sr. Lectr., 1955–59, and Reader in History, 1960, Univ. of Western Australia; Prof. of History, 1960–78, Chmn. of the Centre of Southeast Asian Studies, 1964–86, and Dean, Faculty of Arts, 1978–86, Monash Univ., Victoria. Dir., Inst. of Southeast Asian Studies, Singapore, 1969–70. Pres., Asian Studies Assn. of Australia, 1976–78; Chmn. Victoria State Library/Museum Buildings Advisory Cttee., 1985–88. *Publs:* (with F. Alexander and F.K. Crowley) The Origins of the Eastern Goldfields Water Scheme in Western Australia; Australian Colonial Policy, 1956; Problems of Regional Autonomy in

Contemporary Indonesia, 1957; Britain in Fiji, 1858-1880, 1958; Central Authority and Regional Autonomy in Indonesia, 1961; Indonesia, 1964, 3rd ed. 1980; Sukarno: A Political Biography, 1972, 1984; Intellectuals and Nationalism in Indonesia, 1988. Add: 7 Eileen St., Armadale, Vic. 3143, Australia.

LEGLER, Philip. American, b. 1928. Poetry. Prof. of English, since 1968, and Poet-in-Residence, Northern Michigan Univ., Marquette. Member of faculty, Ohio Univ., 1953–56, Central Missouri State Coll., 1956–59, New Mexico Highlands Univ., 1959–60, Illinois Wesleyan Univ., 1960–63, and Sweet Briar Coll., VA., 1963–66. *Publs:* A Change of View, 1964; The Intruder, 1972; North Country Images, 1988. Add: English Dept., Northern Michigan Univ., Marquette, Mich. 49844, U.S.A.

Le GUIN, Ursula K(roeber). American, b. 1929. Science fiction/Fantasy, Children's fiction, Poetry, Literature. *Publs:* Rocannon's World, 1966; Planet of Exile, 1966; City of Illusion, 1967; A Wizard of Earthsea, 1968; The Left Hand of Darkness, 1969; The Tombs of Atuan, 1971; The Lathe of Heaven, 1971; The Farthest Shore, 1972; The Dispossessed, 1974; The Wind's Twelve Quarters (short stories), 1975; Wild Angels (poetry), 1975; A Very Long Way from Anywhere Else, 1976; The Word for World Is Forest, 1976; Orsinian Tales, 1976; (ed.) Nebula Award Stories 11, 1977; The Language of the Night (criticism), 1978; Leese Webster, 1979; Malafrena, 1979; The Beginning Place (in U.K. as Threshold), 1980; (ed. with Virginia Kidd) Interfaces, 1980; (ed. with Virginia Kidd) Edges, 1981; Hard Words and Other Poems, 1981; The Compass Rose (short stories), 1982; The Eye of the Heron, 1983; In the Red Zone (poetry), 1983; The Visionary, 1984; Always Coming Home, 1985; Buffalo Gals and Other Animal Presences, 1987; A Visit from Dr. Katz, 1988; Catwings, 1988; Fire and Stone, 1989; Catwings Return, 1989; Dancing at the Edge of the World (essays), 1989. Add: c/o Virginia Kidd, Box 278, Milford, Pa. 18337, U.S.A.

LEGUM, Colin. South African, b. 1919. International relations/Current affairs, Politics/Government. Ed., Africa Contemporary Record, since 1969, Middle East Contemporary Survey, since 1977, and Third World Reports, since 1981. Africa and Commonwealth Corresp., The Observer, London, 1949–81. *Publs:* (ed.) Attitude to Africa, 1951; Must We Lose Africa?, 1954; Bandung, Cairo and Accra, 1958; (ed.) Congo Disaster, 1961; (ed.) Africa Handbook, 1961, rev. ed 1969; Pan Africanism, 1962, 1977; (with M. Legum) South Africa: Crisis for the West, 1964; (ed.) Zambia: Independence and After, 1964; (with M. Legum) The Bitter Choice, 1968; (ed.-in-chief) Traveller's Guide to Africa, 1974; After Angola, 1976; Vorster's Gamble for Africa, 1976; The Year of the Whirlwind, 1977; Conflict over the Horn of Africa, 1977; The West's Crisis in Southern Africa, 1978; The Continuing Conflict over the Horn of Africa, 1978; The Battlefronts of Southern Africa, 1987; South Africa on the Rocks, 1989. Add: Wild Acre, Plaw Hatch, Sharpthorne RH19 4SL, England.

LEHMAN, Yvonne. American, b. 1936. Novels/Short stories. Founder, Dir., Blue Ridge Writers Conference, since 1975. *Publs:* Red Like Mine, 1970; Dead Men Don't Cry, 1973; Fashions of the Heart, 1981; In Shady Groves, 1983; Smoky Mountain Sunrise, 1984; Taken By Storm, 1984; More Than A Summer's Love, 1985; In Shady Groves, 1989. Add: P.O. Box 188, Black Mountain, N.C. 28711, U.S.A.

LEHMANN, Geoffrey (John). Australian, b. 1940. Novels/Short stories, Poetry. Qualified as a solicitor in 1963; Principal, C.R. Wilcox and Lehmann, Sydney, since 1969. *Publs:* (with L.A. Murray) The Ilex Tree, 1965; A Voyage of Lions and Other Poems, 1968; Conversation with a Rider, 1972; (ed.) Comic Australian Verse, 1972; From an Australian Country Sequence, 1973; A Spring Day in Autumn (novel), 1974; Australian Primitive Painters, 1977; Ross Poems, 1978; Nero's Poems: Translations of the Public and Private Poems of the Emperor Nero, 1981; (ed. with Robert Gray) The Younger Australian Poets, 1983. Add: 8 Highfield Rd., Lindfield, N.S.W. 2070, Australia.

LEHMANN, Rosamond (Nina). British, b. 1901. Novels/Short stories, Plays/Screenplays, Autobiography/Memoirs/Personal. Past Pres., English Centre, and Intnl. Vice-Pres., Intnl. P.E.N.; former Council Member, Soc. of Authors. *Publs:* Dusty Answer, 1927; A Note in Music, 1930; Invitation to the Waltz, 1932; Letter to a Sister, 1932; The Weather in the Streets, 1936; No More Music (play), 1939; The Ballad and the Source, 1944; The Gipsy's Baby and Other Stories, 1946; (trans) Jacques Lemarchand: Genevieve, 1947; The Echoing Grove, 1953; (trans.) Jean Cocteau: Children of the Game (in U.S. as The Holy Terrors), 1955; (with W. Tudor Pole) A Man Seen Afar, 1965; The Swan in the Evening: Fragments of an Inner Life, 1967; (with C.H. Sandys) Letters from Our

Daughters, 1972; The Sea-Grape Tree, 1976; Rosamond Lehmann's Album, 1985. Add: 30 Clareville Grove, London SW7 5AS, England.

LEHMANN-HAUPT, Christopher. American, b. 1934. Autobiography/Reportage. Senior Daily Book Reviewer, New York Times, since 1969. Editor, A.S. Barnes, NYC, 1961–63; Editor, Holt Rinehart and Winston, NYC, 1963–64; Sr. Editor, Dial Press, NYC, 1964–65; Deskman, New York Sunday Times Book Review, 1965–69. *Publs:* (contributor) The Ultimate Fishing Book, 1981; Me and DiMaggio: A Baseball Fan Goes in Search of His Gods, 1986. Add: 627 W. 247th Street, New York, N.Y. 10471, U.S.A.

LEHMBERG, Stanford Eugene. American, b. 1931. History. Prof. of History, Univ. of Minnesota, Minneapolis, since 1969. Member of history faculty, Univ. of Texas at Austin, 1956–69. *Publs:* Sir Thomas Elyot, Tudor Humanist, 1960; (ed.) Sir Thomas Elyot's Book Named the Governor, 1962; Sir Walter Mildmay and Tudor Government, 1964; The Reformation Parliament, 1529-1536, 1970; The Later Parliaments of Henry VIII 1536-1547, 1977; The Reformation of Cathedrals, 1988. Add: Dept. of History, Univ. of Minnesota, Minneapolis, Minn. 55455, U.S.A.

LEHRER, James (Charles). American, b. 1934. Novels, Memoirs. Co-anchor, The MacNeil/Lehrer NewsHour, PBS affiliates, since 1983; co-partner, MacNeil-Lehrer Productions. Political Reporter, Dallas Morning News, 1959; Court Reporter, 1959–66, Political Columnist, 1966–68, and City Ed., 1968–69, Dallas Times Herald; Consultant, 1970, Exec. Dir. of Public Affairs, 1970–72, ed. and host of nightly news prog., KERA-TV, Dallas; first Public Affairs Coordinator, PBS, Washington, D.C., 1972–73; correspondent, PBS news service, National Public Affairs Center for Television, 1973; Co-anchor, The Robert MacNeil Report, 1975–76, and Co-anchor and Assoc. Ed., The MacNeil/Lehrer Report, 1976–83. *Publs:* Viva Max! (novel), 1966; We Were Dreamers (memoir), 1975; Kick the Can (novel), 1988; Crown Oklahoma (novel), 1989. Add: MacNeil/Lehrer NewsHour, 3620 27th St. S., Arlington, Va. 22206, U.S.A.

LEHRER, Stanley. American, b. 1929. Education, Sociology, Theology/Religion, Biography. Publr. and Editorial Dir., USA Today Mag., since 1978, Newsview, since 1979, Your Health, since 1980, and The World of Science, since 1980. Pres., Soc. for the Advancement of Education, NYC, since 1968. Youth Service Ed., Open Road Mag., NYC, 1950–51; Managing Ed., 1953–68, and Publr., 1968–72, Sch. and Soc. Mag., NYC; Publr., Intellect Mag., 1972–78. *Publs:* (ed.) The Countdown on Segregated Education, 1960; (ed.) Religion, Government, and Education, 1961; (ed.) A Century of Higher Education: Classical Citadel to Collegiate Colossus, 1962; (ed.) John Dewey: Master Educator, 1966; (ed.) Automation, Education, and Human Values, 1966; (ed.) Conflict and Change on the Campus: The Response to Student Hyperactivism, 1970; Leaders, Teachers, and Learners in Academe: Partners in the Educational Process, 1970; (ed.) Education and the Many Faces of the Disadvantaged: Cultural and Historical Perspectives, 1972. Add: 82 Shelbourne Lane, New Hyde Park, N.Y. 11040, U.S.A.

LEIBER, Fritz (Reuter, Jr.). American, b. 1910. Science fiction/Fantasy, Horror, Poetry. Ed., Science Digest, 1944–56. *Publs:* Night's Black Agents, 1947; Gather, Darkness!, 1950; Conjure Wife, 1953; The Green Millennium, 1953; Destiny Times Three, 1957; Two Sought Adventure: Exploits of Fafhrd and the Gray Mouser, 1957; The Big Time, with The Mind Spider and Other Stories, 1961 (Hugo Award); The Silver Eggheads, 1961; Shadows with Eyes (short stories), 1962; The Wanderer, 1964; A Pail of Air (short stories), 1964; Ships to the Stars, 1964; Tarzan and the Valley of Gold, 1966; The Night of the Wolf (short stories), 1966; The Secret Songs (short stories), 1968; Swords Against Wizardry, 1968; Swords in the Mist, 1968; The Swords of Lankhmar, 1968; A Spectre is Haunting Texas, 1969; The Demons of the Upper Air (poetry), 1969; You're All Alone, 1969; Swords Against Death, 1970; Swords and Deviltry, 1971; Night Monsters, 1974; The Best of Fritz Leiber, 1974; The Book of Fritz Leiber (short stories and essays), 1974; The Second Book of Fritz Leiber (stories and essays), 1975; Swords and Ice Magic, 1977; Our Lady of Darkness, 1977; Sonnets to Jonquil and All (poetry), 1978; Heroes and Horrors (short stories), 1978; The Change War, 1978; Ship of Shadows, 1979; (co-ed.) The World Fantasy Awards 2, 1980; The Ghost Light, 1984; The Knight and Knave of Swords, 1988. Add: 565 Geary St., San Francisco, Calif. 94102, U.S.A.

LEIBOLD, Jay. American, b. 1957. Novels/Short stories, Children's fiction. Full-time writer since 1982. Editorial Asst., Farrar Straus and Giroux, NYC, 1981–82. *Publs:* Sabotage, 1984; Spy for George

Washington, 1985; Grand Canyon Odyssey, 1985; The Antimatter Formula, 1986; Beyond the Great Wall, 1987; Secret of the Ninja, 1987. Add: 46 Albion St., San Francisco, Calif. 94103, U.S.A.

LEIGH, Mike. British, b. 1943. Plays/Screenplays. Theatre and film dir., and lectr. *Publs:* Abigail's Party, Goose-Pimples, 1983; Ecstacy, Smelling a Rat, and High Hopes, 1989. Add: c/o A.D. Peters Ltd., The Chambers, Chelsea Harbour, Lots Rd., London SW10 0XF, England.

LEIGH, Roberta. *See* **LINDSAY,** Rachel.

LEIGH, Stephen. American, b. 1951. Science fiction. Musician; vocalist and bassist in various groups, since 1969. *Publs:* Slow Fall to Dawn, 1981; Dance of the Hag, 1983; A Quiet of Stone, 1984; The Bones of God, 1986; Crystal Memory, 1987; Dr. Bones & The Secret of the Lona, 1988; Robots & Aliens #1: Changling, 1989; The Abraxas Marvel Circus, 1989. Add: 121 Nansen St., Cincinnati, Ohio 45216, U.S.A.

LEIGH FERMOR, Patrick (Michael). British. Novels/Short stories, Travel/Exploration/Adventure, Translations. *Publs:* The Traveller's Tree, 1950; (trans.) Julie de Carneilhan and Chance Acquaintances, by Colette, 1951; A Time to Keep Silence, 1953; The Violins of Saint-Jacques, 1953; Mani, 1958; Roumeli, 1966; A Time of Gifts, 1977; Between the Woods and the Water, 1986; The Cretan Runner, 1988. Add: c/o John Murray Ltd., 50 Albemarle St., London W1, England.

LEIGHTON, Albert C(hester). American, b. 1919. History. Lectr. of History, Univ. of Texas at San Antonio, since 1986; Emeritus Prof., State Univ. of New York at Oswego, since 1985 (Prof. of Medieval History, 1964–85). With U.S. Army, 1937 until retirement with rank of Capt. in 1957; Fulbright Research Prof., Univ. of Munich, W. Germany, 1978–79. Originator and coordinator of Intnl. Research in Historical Cryptanalysis. *Publs:* Transport and Communication in Early Medieval Europe, 1972. Add: 8406 Burwell, San Antonio, Tex. 78250, U.S.A.

LEIGHTON, Alexander (Hamilton). American, b. 1908. Psychiatry. Prof. of Psychiatry and Community Health, Dalhousie Univ., Halifax, since 1975. Prof. of Sociology, Anthropology and Psychiatry, Cornell Univ., Ithaca, N.Y., 1948–66; Prof. of Social Psychiatry and Head, Dept. of Behavioral Sciences, Harvard Univ. Sch. of Public Health, Boston, 1966–75. *Publs:* The Navaho Door, 1944; The Governing of Men, 1945; Human Relations in a Changing World, 1949; My Name Is Legion, 1959; An Introduction to Social Psychiatry, 1960; Psychiatric Disorder Among the Yoruba, 1963; Come Near (novel), 1971; Caring for Mentally Ill People, 1982. Add: Dept. of Psychiatry, Dalhousie Univ., Halifax, N.S., Canada.

LEIGHTON, Lee. *See* **OVERHOLSER,** Wayne D.

LEISY, James Franklin. Also writes as Frank Lynn and Julia Ericson. American, b. 1927. Plays/Screenplays, Music. Co-founder, Franklin Beedle and Assocs., since 1985; Dir. and Advisor, Mayfield Publishing Co., since 1985; Co-owner and Advisor, Jones and Bartlett, since 1985; Co-owner Farmer-Leisy Productions, since 1980. Ed., Prentice-Hall, 1949–54, and Allyn and Bacon, 1954–56; Founder, Chmn. of the Bd., and CEO, Wadsworth, 1956–85; Deputy Chmn., Intnl. Thomson Org., 1979–85; Chmn., Intnl. Thomson Books, 1980–85; Founder, and Chmn. of Bd., Science Books Intnl., 1981–83, and of Linguistics Intnl., 1983–85; Co-owner, Stephen Greene Press, 1978–85; former Dir., numerous cos. *Publs:* (ed.) Abingdon Song Kit, 1957; (ed.) Let's All Sing, 1959; (ed. as Frank Lynn) Songs for Swinging Housemothers, 1961, 1963; (ed. as Frank Lynn) Songs for Singing, 1961; (ed.) Songs for Pickin' and Singin', 1962; (ed. as Frank Lynn) The Beer Bust Songbook, 1963; Hootenanny Tonight, 1964; Folk Song Fest: Songs and Ideas for Performance Artistry, 1964; The Folk Song Abecedary, 1966; (ed.) Alpha Kappa Psi Sings, 1967; The Good Times Songbook, 1974; Scrooge: The Christmas Musical, 1978; Alice: A Musical Play, 1980; Cuckoo Clock in a Music Box, 1980; Pinocchio: A Musical Play, 1981; Tiny Tim's Christmas Carol, 1981; The Pied Piper, 1982; (as Julia Ericson) The Nutcracker and Princess Pirlipat, 1982; A Visit from St. Nicholas, 1983; Pandora, 1984; Talkin' 'bout America, 1986; Mouse Country, 1987; The Dingalong Circus Holiday, 1987. Add: 183 Patricia Drive, Atherton, Calif. 94025, U.S.A.

LEITCH, Adelaide. Canadian, b. 1921. Children's fiction, History. Reporter, Midland Free Press, Ontario, 1943–45; Reporter and Feature Writer, Windsor Daily Star, Ontario, 1945–48; Managing Ed., Guardian Press, St. John's Nfld., 1952–53; Ed., Adventures in Huronia, Ont., 1960–67. *Publs:* Flightline North, 1952; The Great Canoe (children's fiction), 1962; Lukey Paul from Labrador (children's fiction), 1964; Canada,

Young Giant of the North, 1964; 1968; Mainstream (children's fiction), 1966; The Visible Past: The Pictorial History of Simcoe County, 1967; The Blue Roan (juvenile fiction), 1971; Into the High Country: The Story of Dufferin, The Last 12,000 Years to 1974, 1975; Floodtides of Fortune: The Story of Stratford, 1980. Add: 169 Hanna Rd., Toronto, Ont. M4G 3N9, Canada.

LEITCH, David Bruce. New Zealander, b. 1940. History, Transportation. Solicitor, Burridge and Co., since 1964. New Zealand Regional Ed., Intnl. Railway Journal (U.K.) since 1975; Hon. Locomotive Supt., Masterton Jaycee Miniature Railway, since 1972. New Zealand News Rep., Railways Transportation, Sydney, 1969–71. *Publs:* A Century of Worship, 1967; Engine Pass: New Zealand Railways, 1967; Railways of New Zealand, 1972; (co-author) New Zealand Railways Corporation's 125th Jubilee History, 1988. Add: 27 Essex St., Masterton, New Zealand.

LEITCH, Maurice. British. Novels/Short stories, Plays/Screenplays. Radio Drama Producer, BBC, London, 1970–79 (Features producer, Belfast, 1962–70). *Publs:* The Liberty Lad, 1965; Poor Lazarus, 1969; Stamping Ground, 1975; Silver's City, 1981; The Hands of Cheryl Boyd, 1987; Chinese Whispers, 1987; Burning Bridges, 1989. Add: c/o Rogers, Coleridge and White, 20 Powis Mews, London W11 1JN, England.

LEITH, Prue. (Prudence Margaret Leith). British, b. 1940. Cookery/Gastronomy/Wine. Cookery Columnist, The Guardian, since 1980. Founded Leith's Good Food, 1965, restaurant, 1969, Sch. of Food and Wine, 1975, and farm, 1976; Cookery Corresp., Daily Mail, 1969–73, and Sunday Express, 1973–80. *Publs:* Leith's All-Party Cook Book, 1969; Parkinson's Pie, 1972; Cooking for Friends, 1978; The Best of Prue Leith, 1979; (with J.B. Reynaud) Leith's Cookery Course, 1979–80; The Cook's Handbook, 1981; Dinner Parties, 1984; (with Caroline Waldegrave) Leith's Cookery School, 1985; (with Polly Tyrer) Entertaining with Style, 1986. Add: 94 Kensington Park Rd., London W11 2PN, England.

LEJEUNE, Anthony. Pseudonym for Edward Anthony Thompson. British, b. 1928. Mystery/Crime/Suspense. Political journalist; Deputy Ed., 1955–57, and Ed., 1957–58, Time and Tide, London; Special Writer, Daily Express, London, 1958–61, and The Sunday Times, London, 1961–63; former Editorial Dir., Tom Stacey Ltd., publishers, London; Columnist, Heritage Syndicate, Washington, D.C. *Publs:* mystery novels—Crowded and Dangerous, 1959; Mr. Diabolo, 1960; News of Murder, 1961; Duel in the Shadows, 1962; Glint of Spears, 1963; The Dark Trade, 1965 (in U.S. paperback, Death of a Pornographer, 1967); Strange and Private War, 1986; Professor in Peril, 1987; Key Without a Door, 1988; other—(ed.) Time and Tide Anthology, 1956; Freedom and the Politicians, 1964; (ed.) Enoch Powell's "Income Tax at 4s. 3d. in the £", 1970; (ed.) The Case for South West Africa, 1971; The Gentlemen's Clubs of London, 1970; (ed.) Drink and Ink 1919–1977, by Dennis Wheatley, 1979. Add: Lane End, Hillside Rd., Pinner Hill, Middlesex, England.

LEKAI, Louis J. American, b. 1916. History. Cistercian Monk of the Abbey of Our Lady of Dallas. Assoc. Prof., 1956–58, and Prof. of History, 1958–82, Univ. of Dallas, Irving, Tex. Editorial Bd. Member, Analecta Cisterciensia, and Cistercian Publications. Asst. Prof. of History, Canisius Coll., Buffalo, N.Y., 1952–56. *Publs:* The White Monks, 1953; The Rise of the Cistercian Strict Observance, 1968; The Cistercians, 1977; Nicolas Cotheret's Annals of Citeaux, 1983. Add: c/o Cistercian Publications, Western Mich. Univ. Sta., Kalamazoo, Mich. 49008, U.S.A.

LELAND Jeremy Francis David. Anglo-Irish, b. 1932. Novels/Short stories. Citizens Advice Bureau worker. *Publs:* A River Decrees, 1969, 1972; The Jonah, 1970; The Tower, 1972; Lirri, 1973; The Last Sandcastle, 1983; Bluff, 1987; Breaking Up, 1987; Tenant's Rights, 1987. Add: c/o Gemma O'Connor, 9 Beaumont Rd., Headington Quarry, Oxford OX3 8JN, England.

LELCHUK, Alan. American, b. 1938. Novels/Short stories. Adjunct Prof., Dartmouth Coll., N.H. since 1985. Assoc. Ed., Modern Occasions literary and cultural quarterly, 1970–72. Writer-in-Residence, Brandeis Univ., Waltham, Mass., 1966–81; Writer-in-Residence, Amherst Coll., Mass., 1982–84. *Publs:* American Mischief, 1973; Miriam at Thirty-Four, 1974; Shrinking, 1978; (ed. with Gershon Shaked) Eight Great Hebrew Short Novels, 1983; Miriam in Her Forties, 1985; On Home Ground, 1987; Brooklyn Boy, 1989. Add: c/o Georges Borchardt Inc., 136 E. 57th St., New York, N.Y. 10022, U.S.A.

LEMARCHAND, Elizabeth (Wharton). British, b. 1906. Mystery/Crime/Suspense. Deputy Headmistress, Godolphin Sch., Salisbury, 1940–60; Headmistress, Lowther Coll., Abergele, Denbighshire, 1960–61. *Publs:* Death of an Old Girl, 1967; The Affacombe Affair, 1968; Alibi for a Corpse, 1969; Death on Doomsday, 1971; Cyanide with Compliments, 1972; Let or Hindrance, 1973 (in U.S. as No Vacation from Murder, 1974); Buried in the Past, 1974; Step in the Dark, 1976; Unhappy Returns, 1977; Suddenly While Gardening, 1978; Change for the Worse, 1980; Nothing to Do with the Case, 1981; Troubled Waters, 1982; The Wheel Turns, 1984; Light Through Glass, 1984; Who Goes Home, 1986; The Glade Manor Murder, 1988. Add: Flat 11, Grove House, Fore St., Topsham, Exeter EX3 0HF, England.

LeMASTER, J.R. American, b. 1934. Poetry. Prof. of English, and Dir. of American Studies, Baylor Univ., Waco, Texas, since 1977. Prof. of English, Defiance Coll., Ohio, 1962–77. *Publs:* (ed.) Poets of the Midwest, 1966; The Heart Is a Gypsy, 1967; (ed. with S. Sternlicht) Symposia Poets, 1969; (ed. with W. Chaney) There Comes a Time, 1971; Children of Adam, 1971; (ed. with C. Perrin) Certain Reconciliations, 1972; (ed. with J. O'Kelley) On Weighing a Pound of Flesh, 1973; (ed. with C. Winzeler) The Poem as Unidentified Flying Object, 1974 ; (ed. with M.W. Clarke) The World of Jesse Stuart, 1975; Weeds and Wildflowers, 1975; (with M.W. Clarke) Jesse Stuart: Essays on His Work, 1977; (ed.) Jesse Stuart: Selected Criticism, 1978; Jesse Stuart: A Reference Guide, 1979; (ed.) The Keeper of Juno's Swans, 1979; (ed.) Making Sense of Grammar, 1980; (ed.) The Builder and the Dream, 1980; Jesse Stuart: Kentucky's Chronicler-Poet, 1980; First Person, Second, 1983; (with E. Hudson Long) The New Mark Twain Handbook, 1985; Purple Bamboo, 1986. Add: Dept. of English, Baylor Univ., Waco, Tex. 76703, U.S.A.

LE MAY, G(odfrey) H(ugh) L(ancelot). British, b. 1920. History, Politics/Government. Fellow and Sr. Tutor, Worcester Coll., Oxford, since 1968. Asst. Ed., The Sudan Star, Khartoum, 1942–44; Sub-Ed., The Star, Johannesburg, 1944–46; Lectr., Rhodes Univ., Grahamstown, S. Africa, 1947–48; Lectr., Balliol Coll., Oxford, 1952–53; Prof., Univ. of the Witwatersrand, Johannesburg, 1953–68. *Publs:* British Government 1914–1953, 1955, 1964; British Supremacy in South Africa 1899-1907, 1965; Black and White in South Africa, 1973; The Victorian Constitution, 1979. Add: Worcester Coll., Oxford, England.

LEMON, Lee Thomas. American, b. 1931. Literature. Prof. of English, Univ. of Nebraska, Lincoln, since 1961. Assoc. Ed., Prairie Schooner, Lincoln, Nebr., since 1966. *Publs:* Partial Critics, 1965; (ed. and co-trans) Russian Formalist Criticism, 1965; Approaches to Literature, 1967; Glossary for the Study of English, 1971; Portrait of the Artist in Contemporary Fiction, 1984. Add: Andrews Hall 224, Dept. of English, Univ. of Nebraska, Lincoln, Nebr. 68588, U.S.A.

LEMONS, James Stanley. American, b. 1938. Cultural topics, History. Prof. of History, Rhode Island Coll., Providence, since 1976 (Asst. Prof., 1967–71; Assoc. Prof., 1971–76). Instr., Ohio State Univ., Columbus, 1965–67. *Publs:* The Woman Citizen: Social Feminism in the 1920s, 1973; (ed.) Aspects of the Black Experience, 1975; (with George Kellner) Rhode Island: The Independent State, 1982; The First Baptist Church in America, 1988. Add: Dept. of History, Rhode Island Coll., Providence, R.I. 02908, U.S.A.

LEMOS, Ramon Marcelino. American, b. 1927. Philosophy. Prof. of Philosophy, Univ. of Miami, Coral Gables, Fla., since 1967 (Instr., 1956–58; Asst. Prof., 1958–62; Assoc. Prof., 1962–67; Chmn., 1971–84). *Publs:* Experience, Mind and Value: Philosophical Essays, 1969; Rousseau's Political Philosophy: An Exposition and Interpretation, 1977; Hobbes and Locke: Power and Consent, 1978; Rights, Goods and Democracy, 1986; Metaphysical Investigations, 1988. Add: Dept. of Philosophy, Univ. of Miami, Coral Gables, Fla. 33124, U.S.A.

LENDVAI, Paul. Austrian, b. 1929. History, Politics/Government, Biography. Ed.-in-Chief, Europaeische Rundschau, Vienna, since 1973, and Dir., since 1987. Former Vienna Corresp., Financial Times, London. *Publs:* Egypt, 1952; Greece, 1954; Eagles in Cobwebs: Nationalism and Communism in the Balkans, 1969; Anti-Semitism Without Jews: Communist Eastern Europe, 1971; (with K.H. Ritschel) Kreisky: Portrait of a Statesman, 1972; The Limits to Change in the Danubian Region, 1977; The Bureaucracy of Truth: How Communist Governments Manage the News, 1981; The Lonely Albania, 1985; Hungary: The Art of Survival, 1988. Add: Ebendorferstrasse 6/4, 1010 Vienna, Austria.

L'ENGLE, Madeleine. American, b. 1918. Novels/Short stories, Science Fiction/Fantasy, Children's fiction, Plays/Screenplays, Poetry, Autobiography/Memoirs/Personal. Teacher, St. Hilda's and St. Hugh's Schs., NYC, since 1960; Writer-in-Residence, Cathedral of St. John the Divine, NYC, since 1965; Council Member, Author's League of America, since 1976; Pres., Author's Guild of America, 1985. *Publs:* The Small Rain, 1945, reissued as Prelude, 1969; Ilsa, 1946; And Both Were Young, 1949; Camilla Dickinson, 1951, as Camilla, 1964; A Winter's Love, 1957; A Wrinkle in Time, 1962; Meet the Austins, 1960; The Moon by Night, 1963; The 24 Days Before Christmas, 1964; The Arm of the Starfish, 1965; The Love Letters, 1966; The Journey with Johah (play), 1967; The Young Unicorns, 1968; Lines Scribbled on an Envelope (poetry), 1969; Dance in the Desert (short story), 1969; The Other Side of the Sun, 1971; A Circle of Quiet (autobiography), 1972; A Wind in the Door, 1973; The Summer of the Great-Grandmother (autobiography), 1974; Dragons in the Waters, 1976; The Irrational Season, 1977; A Swiftly Tilting Planet, 1978; The Weather of the Heart, 1978; A Ring of Endless Light, 1980; Walking on Water, 1981; The Sphinx at Dawn, 1982; A Severed Wasp, 1983; And It Was Good, 1984; House Like a Lotus, 1984; Trailing Clouds of Glory, 1985; A Stone for a Pillow, 1986; Many Waters, 1986; A Cry Like a Bell, 1987; Two Part Invention, 1988. Add: Crosswicks, Goshen, Conn. 06756, U.S.A.

LENGYEL, Cornel (Adam). American, b. 1915. Plays/Screenplays, Poetry, History, Biography. Lectr. in English Literature, Sacramento State Univ., California, since 1962. Mgr., Forty-Niner Theatre, Georgetown, Calif., 1946–49; Visiting Lectr. and Writer-in-Residence, Hamline Univ., St. Paul, Minn. 1968–69; Visiting Lectr., Massachusetts Inst. of Technology, Cambridge, 1970. *Publs:* Thirty Pieces, 1933; The World's My Village, 1935; Jonahs Fugitive, 1936; The Giant's Trap, 1938; First Psalms, 1950; The Atom Clock, 1951; Eden Inc., 1954, as Omega, 1963; American Testament: The Story of a Promised Land, 1956; Four Days in July, 1958; I, Benedict Arnold: The Anatomy of Treason, 1960; Presidents of the U.S.A., 1961; Ethan Allan and the Green Mountain Boys, 1961; Will of Stratford, 1964; Three Plays, 1964; Fifty Poems, 1965; The Declaration of Independence, 1969; Four Dozen Songs, 1970; The Lookout's Letter, 1971; The Creative Self: Aspects of Man's Quest and the Springs of Creativity, 1971; Doctor Franklin, 1976; The Master Plan, 1978; The Case of Jesus, 1980; The Case of the Jews, 1982; The Case of Doktor Mengele, 1986; Manimal's Dilemma: An Appraisal of Man's Evolutionary Past and Future, 1989. Add: Adams Acres West, El Dorado National Forest, Georgetown, Calif. 95634, U.S.A.

LENNOX-SHORT, Alan. South African, b. 1913. Poetry, Language/Linguistics, Literature. Retired. Assoc. Prof. in English, Univ. of Cape Town, since 1978 (Lectr., 1962–66, Sr. Lectr., 1966–75; Assoc. Prof., 1975–78). English Language Ed., Dictionary of South African Biography; Language Adviser, Standard Encyclopaedia of Southern Africa; Ed., UCT, and Elts Occasional Papers, Cape Town. Former Ed., Natal Witness, Pietermaritzburg. *Publs:* Our English, 1964; Language, Literature and Life, 1965; Third Thoughts on English, 1966; (ed. with R.E. Lighton) Stories South African, 1969; Effective Expression: A Course in Communication, 1970; (co-author) The Art of English, 10 vols., 1970–74; Brief Candle, 1971; Airing Your English, 1971; (ed.) Stories from Seven Countries, 1972; (ed.) English and South Africa, 1973; English Prose in Action, 1975; Idiomatic English, 1977; (ed. with D. Welsh) UCT at 150: Reflections, 1979. Add: P.O. Box 313, Claremont, Cape, 7735, South Africa.

LENT, Blair. Also writes as Ernest Small. American, b. 1930. Children's fiction. Freelance writer and illustrator since 1963. *Publs:* Pistachio, 1963; (with M. Hodges) The Wave, 1964; (as Ernest Small) Baba Yaga, 1966; John Tabor's Ride, 1966; From King Boggen's Hall to Nothing-at-All, 1967; (with E. Dayrell) Why the Sun and the Moon Live in the Sky, 1968, as animated film, 1970; The Little Match Girl, by Hans Christian Andersen, 1968; (with A. Mosel) Tikki Tikki Tembo, 1968; (with W. Sleator) The Angry Moon, 1970; (with A. Mosel) The Funny Little Woman, 1972; (with V. Haviland) Tales Told in India, 1973; (with K. Chukovsky) The Telephone, 1977; (with A. Fisher) I Stood Upon a Mountain, 1979; Bayberry Bluff, 1987. Add: 10 Dana St., Cambridge, Mass. 02138, U.S.A.

LENT, John A. American, b. 1936. Media. Dir., Third World Media Assocs., since 1986; Prof. of Communications, Temple Univ., Philadelphia, since 1976 (Assoc. Prof., 1974–76). Instr. in English and Journalism, and Dir. of Public Relations, West Virginia Inst. of Technology, Montgomery, 1960–62 and 1965–66; Lectr., De La Salle Coll., Manila, 1964–65; Asst. Prof. of Journalism, Wisconsin State Univ., Eau Claire, 1966–67; Asst. Prof., Marshall Univ., Huntington, W. Va., 1967–69; Visiting Assoc. Prof., Univ. of Wyoming, Laramie, 1969–70; Teaching Asst., and Assoc. Ed., International Communications Bulletin, Univ. of Iowa, Iowa City, 1970–72; Organizer and first Coordinator, Mass Communications Prog., Universiti Sains Malaysia, Penang, 1972–74. *Publs:* Philippine Mass Communications Bibliography, 1966; Newhouse, Newspapers, Nuisances (biography), 1966; (co-author) Pied Type, A Load of Coal and the Laser Beam (filmstrip), 1969; Philippine Mass Communications: Before 1811, After 1966, 1971; (ed.) Asian Newspapers' Reluctant Revolution, 1971; Asian Mass Communications: A Comprehensive Bibliography, 1975, Supplement, 1978; Third World Mass Media and Their Search for Modernity, 1977; Broadcasting in Asia and the Pacific, 1978; Asian Newspapers, 1982; Comic Art: An International Bibliography, 1987; Global Guide to Communications, 1987. Add: 669 Ferne Blvd., Drexel Hill, Pa. 19026, U.S.A.

LEONARD, Constance. American, b. 1923. Mystery/Crime/Suspense, Children's fiction. *Publs:* The Great Pumpkin Mystery, 1971; The Other Maritha, 1972; Steps to Nowhere, 1974; Hostage in Illyria, 1976; Shadow of Ghost, 1978; The Marina Mystery, 1981; Stowaway, 1983; Aground, 1984; Strange Waters, 1985. Add: Box 126, Francestown, N.H. 03043, U.S.A.

LEONARD, Elmore. American, b. 1925. Novels/Short stories, Mystery/Crime/Suspense, Westerns/Adventure. Full-time writer since 1967. Copywriter, Campbell Ewald advertising agency, Detroit, 1950–61; writer of industrial and educational films, 1961–63; Dir., Elmore Leonard Advertising Co., 1963–66. *Publs:* The Bounty Hunters, 1953; The Law at Randado, 1955; Escape from Five Shadows, 1956; East Stand at Saber River, 1959; in U.K. as Lawless River, 1959, 2nd U.K. ed. as Stand on the Saber, 1960; Hombre, 1961; Valdez Is Coming, 1969; The Big Bounce, 1969; The Moonshine War, 1969; Forty Lashes Less One, 1972; Mr. Majestyk (novelization of his screenplay), 1974; Fifty-Two Pickup, 1974; Swag, 1976, in paperback as Ryan's Rules, 1976; The Hunted, 1977; Unknown Man No. 89, 1977; The Switch, 1978; Gunsights, 1979; City Primeval, 1980; Gold Coast, 1980; Split Images, 1982; Cat Chaser, 1982; Stick, 1983; La Brava, 1983; Glitz, 1985; Bandits, 1987; Touch, 1987 Freaky Deaky, 1988; Killshot, 1989. Add: c/o H.N. Swanson, Inc., 8523 Sunset, Los Angeles, Calif., U.S.A.

LEONARD, Hugh. Pseud. for John Keyes Byrne. Irish, b. 1926. Plays/Screenplays, Autobiography/Memoirs/Personal. Civil Servant, Dublin, 1945–59; Script Ed., Granada TV, Manchester, 1961–63; freelance writer, London, 1963–70. *Publs:* Stephen D (adaptation of A Portrait of the Artist as a Young Man, and Stephen Hero, by James Joyce), 1962; The Poker Session, 1963; The Late Arrival of the Incoming Aircraft, 1964; The Patrick Pearse Motel, 1971; Da, 1973; Summer, 1974; Home Before Night: Memoirs of an Irish Time and Place, 1979; A Life, 1980; Three Plays: Da, A Life, Time Was, 1981; Kill, 1982; Pizzazz, 1983; The Mask of Moriarty, 1985; Out After Dark (autobiography), 1989. Add: Rossaun Pilot View, Dalkey, Co. Dublin, Ireland.

LEONARD, Maurice. British, b. 1939. Biography. Television Producer and journalist. *Publs:* The Medium, 1972; Battling Bertha, 1974; Madame Blavatsky, 1976; Slobodskaya, 1979. Add: c/o Thames Television, 306 Euston Rd., London NW1 3BB, England.

LEONARD, Tom. British, b. 1944. Poetry. *Publs:* Six Glasgow Poems, 1969; A Priest Came On at Merkland Street, 1970; Poems, 1973; Bunnit Husslin, 1975; (with Alex Hamilton and James Kelman) Three Glasgow Writers, 1976; My Name Is Tom, 1978; If Only Bunty Was Here, 1979; Ghostie Men, 1980; Intimate Voices: Writing 1965–83, 1984; Satires and Profanities, 1985; Situations Theoretical and Contemporary, 1986. Add: 56 Eldon St., Glasgow G3 6NJ, Scotland.

LEONARD, William Norris. American, b. 1912. Economics, Transportation. Visiting Prof. of Economics, Univ. of Tampa, since 1979. Prof. of Economics, 1953–74, and Asst. Pres., 1965–66, Hofstra Univ., Hempstead, N.Y.; Consultant, Federal Trade Commn., 1968–69, and Senate Antitrust Subcttee., 1968–73; Prof. of Economics, Herbert Lehmann Coll., City Univ. of New York, 1974–77; Pres., Eastern Economic Assn., 1984–85. *Publs:* Railroad Consolidation, 1946, 1970; Business Size, Market, Power, and Public Policy, 1969. Add: c/o AMS Press, 56 E. 13th St., New York, N.Y. 10003, U.S.A.

LEONTIEF, Wassily (W.) American (born Russian), b. 1906. Economics. Prof. of Economics, New York Univ., since 1975 (Dir., Inst for Economic Analysis, 1978–85). Consultant, Dept. of Commerce, since 1966, Environmental Protection Agency, since 1975, and the United Nations, since 1980 (also, 1961–62). Instr., 1931, Asst. Prof., 1933–39, Assoc. Prof., 1939–46, Prof., 1946–75, Dir. of the Economics Project,

1948–72, and Henry Lee Prof. of Economics, 1973–75, Harvard Univ., Cambridge, Mass. Consultant, Dept. of Labor, 1941–47, and Office of Strategic Studies, 1943–45. Recipient, Nobel Prize in Economics, 1973; Foreign Member, U.S.S.R. Academy of Sciences, 1988. *Publs:* Die Wirtschaft als Krieslauf, 1928; The Structure of American Economy 1919–1929: An Empirical Application of Equilibrium Analysis, 1941, 1960; (with others) Studies in the Structure of the American Economy: Theoretical and Empirical Explorations in Input-Output Analysis, 1953; Essays in Economics: Theories and Theorizing, 1966; Input-Output Economics, 1966; The New Outlook in Economics, 1967; Struktureller Ansatz zur Analyse internationaler ökonomischer Interdependenzen, 1971; The Economic System in an Age of Discontinuity: Long-Range Planning or Market Reliance?, 1976; (with others) The Future of the World Economy, 1977; Essays in Economics: vol. 2: Theories, Facts and Policies, 1977; (with F. Duchin) Military Spending: Facts and Figures, 1983; (with others) The Future of Non-Fuel Minerals in the U.S and World Economy, 1983; (with F. Duchin) The Impact of Automation on Workers, 1985. Add: Inst. of Economic Analysis, New York Univ., Room 203, 269 Mercer Street, New York, N.Y. 10003, U.S.A.

LePAN, Douglas (Valentine). Canadian, b. 1914. Novels/Short stories, Poetry, Autobiography/Memoirs/Personal. Univ. Prof., Univ. of Toronto, since 1970 (Lectr., 1937–38; Principal, Univ. Coll., 1964–70). Instr. and Tutor in Engish Literature, Harvard Univ., Cambridge, Mass, 1938–41; joined Canadian Dept. of External Affairs, 1945; First Secty. on the Staff of the Canadian High Commnr. in London, 1945–48; various appointments in the Dept. of External Affairs, including that of Special Asst. to the Secty. of State, Ottawa, 1949–51; Counsellor and later Minister Counsellor at the Canadian Embassy, Washington, D.C., 1951–55; Secty. and Dir. of Research, Royal Commn. on Canada's Economic Prospects (Gordon Commn.), 1955–58; Asst. Under-Secty. of State for External Affairs, 1958–59; Prof. of English Literature, Queen's Univ., Kingston, Ont., 1959–64. Member, Canada Council, 1964–70. *Publs:* The Wounded Prince and Other Poems, 1948; The Net and the Sword: Poems, 1953; The Deserter (novel), 1964; Bright Glass of Memory (memoirs), 1979; Something Still to Find (poetry), 1982; Weathering It (poetry), 1987. Add: Massey Coll., 4 Devonshire Pl., Toronto, Ont., M5S 2E1, Canada.

LEPORE, Dominick James. American, b. 1911. Poetry. Member of Cttee., Reading Study of Poetry in the Classroom, 1963–69, and Public Relations Rep., 1969–72, National Council of Teachers of English; formerly, Teacher and Chmn., Dept. English, Kosciuszko Jr. High Sch., Enfield, Conn. *Publs:* The Praise and the Praised, 1955; Within His Walls, 1968. Add: 4 Mitchell Dr., Enfield, Conn. 06082, U.S.A.

LE RICHE, William Harding. Canadian, b. 1916. Medicine/Health. Prof. Emeritus of Epidemiology, Dept. of Preventive Medicine and Biostatistics, Univ. of Toronto, since 1984 (Prof., 1962–84, Head of the Dept. of Epidemiology and Biometrics, 1962–75). *Publs:* (with C.E. Balcom and G. van Belle) The Control of Infections in Hospitals, 1966; (with J. Milner) Epidemiology as Medical Ecology, 1971; A Complete Family Guide to Nutrition and Meal Planning, 1976; A Chemical Feast, 1982. Add: 30 Golfdale Rd., Toronto, Ont. M4N 2B6, Canada.

LERMAN, Rhoda. American, b. 1936. Novels/Short stories. *Publs:* Call Me Ishtar, 1972, 1977; Girl That He Marries, 1976; Eleanor: A Novel, 1979; Book of the Night, 1984; That's Why We Dance, 1988. Add: c/o Salem House Publications, 462 Boston St., Topsfield, Mass. 01983, U.S.A.

LERNER, Laurence (David). British, b. 1925. Novels/Short stories, Poetry, Literature. Professorial Fellow, Univ. of Sussex, Brighton, since 1985 (Lectr. then Reader, 1962–70; Prof. of English, 1970–85); Kenan Prof. of English, Vanderbilt Univ., Nashville, since 1985. Schoolmaster, St. George's Grammar Sch., Cape Town, 1946–47; Asst. Lectr. then Lectr. in English, Univ. Coll., of the Gold Coast, Legon, Ghana, 1949–53; Extra-Mural Tutor then Lectr. in English, Queen's Univ. of Belfast, 1953–62. *Publs:* The Englishmen, 1959; Domestic Interior and Other Poems, 1959; The Truest Poetry, 1960; (ed.) Shakespeare's Tragedies: A Selection of Modern Criticism, 1963; The Directions of Memory: Poems 1958–63, 1964; (ed. with John Holmstrom) George Eliot and Her Readers: A Selection of Contemporary Reviews, 1966; (ed.) Shakespeare's Comedies: Selection of Modern Criticism, 1967; The Truthtellers: Jane Austen, George Eliot, and D.H. Lawrence, 1967; (ed. with John Holmstrom) Thomas Hardy and His Readers: A Selection of Contemporary Reviews, 1968; A Free Man, 1968; Selves, 1969; The Uses of Nostalgia, 1972; A.R.T.H.U.R.; The Life and Opinions of a Digital Computer, 1974; An Introduction to English Poetry, 1975; (ed.) The Context of English Literature: The Victorians, 1978; Love and Marriage, 1979; The Man I Killed,

1980; A.R.T.H.U.R. and M.A.R.T.H.A., 1980; The Literary Imagination, 1982; (ed.) Reconstructing Literature, 1983; A Dialogue, 1983; Chapter and Verse: Bible Poems, 1984; Selected Poems, 1984; My Grandfather's Grandfather, 1985; Rembrandt's Mirror, 1987; The Frontiers of Literature, 1988. Add: 50 Compton Ave., Brighton BN1 3PS, England.

LERNER, Max. American, b. 1902. History. Columnist, Los Angeles Times Syndicate, and New York Post; Emeritus Prof. of World Politics and American Civilization, Brandeis Univ., Waltham, Mass. Prof. of Human Behavior, Grad. Sch. of Human Behavior, U.S. Intnl. Univ., San Diego, Calif. Former Welch Prof. of American Studies, Notre Dame Univ., Indiana. *Publs:* The Mind and Faith of Justice Holmes, 1943, 1989; Actions and Passions, 1949; America as a Civilization, 1957, 1987; The Unfinished Country, 1959; Essential Works of John Stuart Mill, 1961; The Age of Overkill, 1962; Education and Radical Humanism, 1962; (co-ed.) Toqueville's Democracy in America, 1966; Toqueville and American Civilization, 1969; Values in Education, 1976; Ted and the Kennedy Legend, 1980. Add: New York Post, 210 South St., New York, N.Y. 10002, U.S.A.

LERNER, Robert E(arl). American, b. 1940. History. Prof. of History, since 1976, Northwestern Univ., Evanston, Ill., (Asst. Prof., 1967–71; Assoc. Prof. 1971–76); Dir. of Humanities, 1981–83). Instr. in History, Princeton Univ., N.J., 1963–64; Asst. Prof. of History, Western Reserve Univ., Cleveland, 1964–67. *Publs:* The Age of Adversity: Europe in the Fourteenth Century, 1968; The Heresy of the Free Spirit in the Later Middle Ages, 1972; (co-author) One Thousand Years: Western Europe in the Middle Ages, 1974; The Powers of Prophecy, 1983; (co-author) World Civilizations, 1986; (co-author) Western Civilizations: Their History and Their Culture, 11th ed. 1988; Add: Dept. of History, Northwestern Univ., Evanston, Ill. 60201, U.S.A.

Le ROI, David. British, b. 1915. Animals/Pets, Children's non-fiction, Natural History, Sciences. Freelance journalist, writer and ed. since 1964; Advisory Science Ed., I.P.C. Pubs., London (Science Ed. and Chief Feature Writer, 1960–64). Assoc. Ed., New Universal Encyclopedia, 1945–49; Exec. Ed., Household Encyclopedia, 1950–51; Asst. Ed., Waverley Technical Pubs., 1952; Exec. Ed., World of Wonder, 1953–54; Science and Technical Ed., Book of Knowledge, 1955–56; Science Ed., Children's Encyclopedia, 1957–59; Ed., Marts Press, 1977. *Publs:* Book of Jets, 1949; Aeronautics, 1950; Things to Make and Do, 1951; Sea, Land and Air Weapons, 1952; Hamsters and Gunea Pigs, 1955; The Aquarium, 1955; Pigeons, 1957; Town Dogs, 1957; Book of Inventions, 1957; Tortoises and Lizards, 1958; Cage Birds, 1958; Book of Flight, 1958; Modern Wonders, 1958; Jets and Rockets, 1959; Nuclear Power, 1959; Radio, Radar and Television, 1959; Modern Agriculture, 1960; Man-Made Materials, 1960; Modern Medicine, 1960; Look at Roads, 1961; How We Get Our Oil, 1962; Aluminium, 1963; Cats, 1963; Science Today and Tomorrow, 1964; Treasure Book of Animals, 1966; Second Treasure Book of Animals, 1967; How it Works, 1967; Book of Wonders of Nature, 1967; Third Treasure Book of Animals, 1968; Second Book of Wonders of Nature, 1968; 1001 Questions and Answers, 1968; Fourth Treasure Book of Animals, 1969; New Ideas for this Modern Age, 1969; Third Book of Wonders of Nature, 1969; The Channel Tunnel, 1969; Book of Firsts, 1973; In the Days of the Dinosaurs, 1974; Rabbits, 1974; Prehistoric Life, 1975; Stars and Planets, 1975; Mice and Gerbils, 1976; Ponies and Donkeys, 1976; Goats, 1977. Add: c/o I.P.C. Magazines, King's Reach Tower, Stamford St., London SE1 9LS, England.

LESCROART, John T. American, b. 1948. Mystery/Crime/Suspense. Word processor for Pettit and Martin, Los Angeles, since 1985. Professional singer and guitarist, Los Angeles and San Francisco, 1972–77; Advertising Dir. for "Guitar Player", Cupertino, Calif., 1977–79; Assoc. Dir., Guardians of the Jewish Homes for the Aging, Los Angeles, 1979–83; Assoc. Consultant, A.T. Kearney Inc., Alexandria, Va., 1982–85. *Publs:* Sunburn, 1982; Son of Holmes, 1986; Rasputin's Revenge, 1987. Add: 8583 Airdrome St., Los Angeles, Calif. 90035, U.S.A.

LeSHAN, Eda J. American, b. 1922. Human relations, Psychology. Contrib. Ed., Woman's Day mag., NYC; Columnist, Newsday, since 1987. Commentator, Newsfront Educational TV prog., NYC, 1968–70; Moderator, How Do Your Children Grow, WNET-TV, NYC, 1970–72; Commentator, Get Along prog., CBS-Radio, 1981–83. *Publs:* How to Survive Parenthood, 1965; The Conspiracy Against Childhood, 1967; Sex and Your Teenager, 1969; Natural Parenthood, 1970; What Makes Me Feel This Way?, 1970; How Do Your Children Grow?, 1972; The Wonderful Crisis of Middle Age, 1973; Understanding Your Feelings, 1974; Learning to Say Goodbye: When a Parent Dies, 1976; What's the Matter with Me?, 1976; What's Going to Happen to Me?, 1978; Winning the Losing Battle: Why I Will Never Be Fat Again, 1979; The Roots of Crime, 1981; Eda LeShan on Living Your Life, 1982; Grandparents: A Special Kind of Love, 1984; When Your Child Drives You Crazy, 1985; Oh to Be Fifty Again!, 1986; When a Parent Is Very Sick, 1987; When Grownups Drive You Crazy, 1988. Add: 263 West End Ave., New York, N.Y. 10023, U.S.A.

Le SIEG, Theo. *See* **SEUSS, Dr.**

LESIKAR, Raymond Vincent. American, b. 1922. Writing/Journalism. Emeritus Prof. of Mgmt., Louisiana State Univ., Baton Rouge, since 1977 (Assoc. Prof., 1954–59; Prof. 1960–77). Prof., Univ. of North Texas, Denton, 1979–87. Asst. Prof., Univ. of Texas, Austin, 1949–54. *Publs:* (with R.D. Hay) Business Report Writing, 1957; (with W.P. Boyd) Productive Business Writing, 1959; Report Writing for Business, 1961, 7th ed. 1986; Business Communication: Theory and Application, 1968, 6th ed. 1989 ; (with W. Perlick) Introduction to Business: A Societal Approach, 1972; 3rd ed. 1979; How to Write a Report, 1974, 1985; Basic Business Communication, 1979, 4th ed. 1988. Add: Rt. 1, Argyle, Tex. 76226, U.S.A.

LESLIE, Aleen. American, b. 1908. Novels/Short stories, Plays/Screenplays. Daily Columnist, Pittsburgh Pres, Pa., 1934–43; film writer, Hollywood, 1937–53. *Publs:* (co-author) The Doctor Takes a Wife, 1940; (co-author) Affectionately Yours (screenplay), 1941; A Date with Judy (radio series), 1941–49, television series, 1943–44, play, 1945; Slightly Married (play), 1943; (co-author) Father Was a Fullback (screenplay), 1951; (co-author) Father is a Bachelor (screenplay), 1951; The Scent of the Roses (novel), 1963, (play), 1966; The Windfall (novel), 1970. Add: 1700 Lexington Rd., Beverly Hills, Calif. 90210, U.S.A.

LESLIE, Desmond. British, b. 1921. Novels/Short stories, Plays/Screenplays, Air/Space topics. Co-Founder, Flying Saucer Review, 1954; Formerly journalist with Picture Post, Illustrated London News, Everybodies, Vogue, and Life mags. *Publs:* Careless Lives, 1945; Pardon My Return, 1946; Angels Weep, 1949; Stranger at My Door (filmscript); (with G. Adamski) Flying Saucers Have Landed, 1953, 1970; Hold Back the Night, 1956; The Amazing Mr. Lutterworth, 1959; (with P. Moore) How Britain Won the Space Race, 1973; The Jesus File, 1974; Find the Croc o' Gold, 1987. Add: Castle Leslie, Glaslough, Co. Monaghan, Ireland.

LESLIE, Robert Franklin. American, b. 1911. Environmental science/Ecology, Natural history, Autobiography/Memoirs/Personal. Former schoolteacher. *Publs:* Read the Wild Water, 1966; High Trails West, 1967; The Bears and I, 1968; Wild Pets, 1970; Wild Burro Rescue, 1973; Wild Courage, 1974; In the Shadow of a Rainbow, 1974; Miracle at Square Top Mountain, 1979; Ringo the Robber Raccoon, 1984; Lorenzo the Magnificent, 1985; Emil of the Lighthouse, 1985; In One of Your Moods Again, Herman?, 1985. Add: 1270 Coe St., Camarillo, Calif. 93010, U.S.A.

LESLIE, Ward S. *See* **WARD,** Elizabeth Honor.

LESLY, Philip. American, b. 1918. Advertising/Public relations, Business/Trade/Industry. Pres. since 1949, and author of bi-monthly commentary, Managing the Human Climate, since 1970, Philip Lesly Co., Chicago. *Publs:* (with T.R. Sills) Public Relations: Principles and Procedures, 1945; (ed.) Public Relations in Action, 1947; (author and ed.) Public Relations Handbook, 1950, 3rd ed., 1967; Everything and the Kitchen Sink (history of industry), 1955; (author and ed.) Lesly's Public Relations Handbook, 1971, 4th ed. 1988; The People Factor: Managing the Human Climate, 1974; How We Discommunicate, 1979; Selections from Managing the Human Climate, 1979; Overcoming Opposition, 1984; Bonanzas and Fool's Gold, 1987. Add: 155 Harbor Dr., Suite 2201, Chicago, Ill. 60601, U.S.A.

LESSER, Milton. *See* **MARLOWE,** Stephen.

LESSING, Doris (May). Has also written as Jane Somers. British, b. 1919. Novels/Short stories, Science fiction/Fantasy, Plays/Screenplays, Poetry. *Publs:* The Grass Is Singing, 1950; This Was the Old Chief's Country: Stories, 1951; Martha Quest, 1952; Retreat to Innocence, 1953; Five: Short Novels, 1953; A Proper Marriage, 1954; The Habit of Loving, 1957; Going Home, 1957; A Ripple from the Storm, 1958; Fourteen Poems, 1959; In Pursuit of the English: Documentary, 1960; The Golden Notebook, 1962; Play with a Tiger, 1962; A Man and Two Women: Stories, 1963; African Stories, 1964; Landlocked, 1965; Particularly Cats, 1967;

Nine African Stories, 1968; The Four-Gated City, 1969; Briefing for a Descent into Hell, 1971; The Story of a Non-Marrying Man and Other Stories, 1972; The Temptation of Jack Orkney and Other Stories, 1972; The Summer Before Dark, 1973; The Memoirs of a Survivor, 1974; A Small Personal Voice: Essays, Reviews, Interviews, 1974; Collected Stories, 2 vols., 1978; Shikasta, 1979; The Marriages Between Zones Three, Four, and Five, 1980; The Sirian Experiments, 1981; The Making of the Representative for Planet 8, 1982; The Sentimental Agents, 1983; (as Jane Somers) The Diary of a Good Neighbour, 1983; (as Jane Somers) If the Old Could, 1984; The Diaries of Jane Somers, 1984; The Good Terrorist, 1985; Prisons We Choose to Live Inside, 1986; (with others) The Wind Blows Away Our Words, 1987; The Fifth Child, 1988; The Doris Lessing Reader, 1989. Add: c/o Jonathan Clowes Ltd., 22 Prince Albert Rd., London NW1 7ST, England.

LESTER, David. British/American, b. 1942. Psychiatry, Psychology. Prof. of Psychology, Stockton State Coll., Pomona, N.J. since 1971. Research Dir., Suicide Prevention and Crisis Service, Buffalo, N.Y., 1969–71. Publs: Explorations in Exploration, 1969; (with G. Lester) Suicide: The Gamble With Death, 1971; Why People Kill Themselves, 1972, 1983; Comparative Psychology, 1973; (ed. with G. Brockopp) Crisis Intervention and Counseling by Telephone, 1973; A Physiological Basis for Personality Traits: A New Theory of Personality, 1974; Unusual Sexual Behavior, 1975; (with G. Lester) Crime of Passion, 1975; The Use of Alternative Modes for Communication in Psychotherapy, 1977; (ed.) Gambling Today, 1979; The Psychological Basis for Handwriting Analysis, 1980; (with B. Sell and K. Sell) Suicide: A Guide to Information Sources, 1980; (ed.) The Elderly Victim of Crime, 1981; Psychotherapy for Offenders, 1981; (with M. Murell) Introduction to Juvenile Delinquency, 1981; The Structure of the Mind, 1982; (with A. Levitt) Insanity and Incompetence, 1984; Gun Control, 1984; The Murderer and His Murder, 1986; The Death Penalty, 1987; Suicide as a Learned Behavior, 1987; (with M. Braswell) Correctional Treatment, 1987; The Biochemical Basis of Suicide, 1988; Suicide from a Psychological Perspective, 1988; Why Women Kill Themselves, 1988; Can We Prevent Suicide?, 1989. Add: Psychology Prog., Stockton State Coll., Pomona, N.J. 08240, U.S.A.

LESTER, G(odfrey) A(llen). British, b. 1943. Archaeology/Antiquities, Language/Linguistics, Literature. Lectr. in English Language, Univ. of Sheffield, since 1967. Publs: Brasses and Brass Rubbing in the Peak District, 1971, 1972; The Anglo-Saxons, 1976; Three Late Medieval Morality Plays, 1981; Sir John Paston's 'Grete Boke', 1984; Index of Middle English Prose, Handlist II, 1985; Chaucer: The Pardoner's Tale, 1987; (ed.) Handbook of Teachers of Medieval English Language and Literature in Great Britain and Ireland, 1987; (ed.) Vegetius, De Re Militari, 1988. Add: Dept. of English Language, The Univ., Sheffield S10 2TN, England.

LESTER, Julius. American, b. 1939. Children's fiction, Poetry, History, Literature, Music, Mythology/Folklore, Autobiography/Memoirs/Personal. Prof. of Judaic Studies, Univ. of Massachusetts, Amherst, since 1971; Musician and Singer. Dir., Newport Folk Festival, Rhode Island, 1966–68; Contrib. Ed., SING OUT, New York, 1964–69; Contrib. Ed., Broadside of New York, 1964–70. Publs: (with Pete Seeger) The 12-String Guitar as Played by Leadbelly: An Instructional Manual, 1965; The Angry Children of Malcolm X, 1966; (ed. with Mary Varela) To Praise Our Bridges: An Autobiography by Fanny Lou Hamer, 1967; (ed. with Mary Varela) Our Folk Tales: High John, The Conqueror, and Other Afro-American Tales, 1967; The Mud of Vietnam: Photographs and Poems (verse), 1967; Revolutionary Notes, 1969; (ed.) Ain't No Ambulances for No Nigguhs Tonight, by Stanley Couch, 1969; Look Out Whitey! Black Power's Gon' Get Your Mama!, 1968; (ed.) To Be a Slave, 1968; Black Folktales, 1969; Search for the New Land: History as Subjective Experience, 1969; (ed.) The Seventh Son: The Thought and Writings of W.E.B. Du Bois, 2 vols., 1971; The Knee-High Man and Other Tales, 1972; Long Journey Home: Stories from Black History, 1972; Two Love Stories, 1972; Who I Am, 1974; All Is Well (autobiography), 1976; This Strange New Feeling (short stories), 1982; Do Lord Remember Me, 1984; The Tales of Uncle Remus: The Adventures of Brer Rabbit, 1987; The Tales of Uncle Remus: Further Adventures of Brer Rabbit, 1988; Lovesong: Becoming a Jew (autobiography), 1988. Add: 600 Station Rd., Amherst, Mass. 01002, U.S.A.

LESTER, Richard (Allen). American, b. 1908. Economics. Prof. of Economics Emeritus, since 1974, and Assoc., Industrial Relations Section, since 1945, Princeton Univ., New Jersey (Prof. 1948–74; Dean of the Faculty, 1968–73). Vice-Pres., American Economic Assn., 1961; Vice Chmn., President's Commn. on the Status of Women, 1962–63; Pres.,

Industrial Relations Research Assn., 1966. Publs: Monetary Experiments, 1939, 1978; Labor and Industrial Relations, 1951; As Unions Mature, 1958; The Economics of Unemployment Compensation, 1962; Economics of Labor, 2nd ed., 1964; Manpower Planning in a Free Society, 1966; Antibias Regulation of Universities, 1974; Reasoning about Discrimination: The Analysis of Professional and Executive Work in Federal Antibias Programs, 1980; Labor Arbitration in State and Local Government, 1984. Add: 32 Maclean Circle, Princeton, N.J. 08540, U.S.A.

L'ESTRANGE, Anna. See **ELLERBECK,** Rosemary.

LETCHFORD, Stanley. British, b. 1924. Mathematics/Statistics. Jr. Lectr., New Coll., Oxford Univ., 1950–52; Dir. of Mathematics Studies, Collier Macmillan Schs., 1962–82. Publs: Modern Arithmetic, 1970, 1975; Business Mathematics and Statistics, 1974, 3rd ed. 1984; The Economic System, 1975; Statistics: A Foundation Course, 1980; Statistics Workbook, 1982; (ed.) Quantitative Methods in Business, by Curwin and Slater, 1985. Add: 21 Gorringe Dr., Lower Willingdon, Eastbourne, Sussex BN20 9ST, England.

LE VAY, David. British, b. 1915. Medicine/Health, Biography, Translations. Consultant Linguistic ed., Excerpta Medica, Amsterdam; Ed. and Trans., Springer Verlag; Consultant Orthopaedic Surgeon, Southeast Metropolitian Regional Hosp. Bd., London, now retired. Publs: A Guide to the National Health Service, 1946; A Synopsis of Orthopedic Surgery, 1947; Anatomy, 1948; Physiology, 1948; Life of Hugh Owen Thomas, 1956; (trans.) Colette: Places, 1970; (trans.) Giono: Ennemonde, 1970; (trans.) Colette: Journey for Myself, 1971; (trans.) Wittig: Les Guerrières, 1971; (trans.) Colette: The Evening Star, 1973; (trans. with M. Crosland) Colette: 1001 Mornings, 1973; (co-ed.) Orthopedic Surgery and Traumatology, 1973; (trans) Colette: Journal à Rebours de ma Fenêtre, 1974; (trans.) Wittig: Le Corps Lesbien, 1974; (trans.) Valentin: History of Orthopedics, 1974; Scenes from Surgical Life, 1976; (trans.) Roth: Flight Without End, 1977; (trans.) Roth: The Silent Prophet, 1979; (trans.) Roth: Weights and Measures, 1982; Human Anatomy and Physiology, 1985; (trans.) Wittig: Virgile, Non, 1987; (trans.) Du Port: La Décade de Medecine, 1988. Add: c/o Coutts and Co., 16 Cavendish Sq., London W1A 1EE, England.

LEVENSON, Christopher. Canadian (born British), b. 1934. Poetry, Translations. Member of the English Dept., Carleton Univ., Ottawa, Ont., since 1968. Ed., Arc, since 1978. Taught at the Intnl. Quaker Sch., Eerde, Holland, 1957–58, Univ. of Munster, W. Germany, 1958–61, and Rodway Technical High Sch., Margotsfield, Glas., 1962–64. Publs: (ed.) Poetry from Cambridge, 1958; (with I. Crichton Smith and K. Gershon) New Poets 1959, 1959; (trans.) Van Gogh, by Abraham M.W.J. Hammacher, 1961; (trans.) The Golden Casket: Chinese Novellas of Two Millenia, 1965; (trans.) The Leavetaking, and Vanishing Point, by Peter Weiss, 1966; Cairns, 1969; Stills, 1972; Into the Open, 1977; The Journey Back, 1978; No-Man's Land, 1980; (trans.) Seeking Hearts Solace, 1981. Add: Dept. of English, Carleton Univ., Ottawa, Ont. K1S 5B6, Canada.

LEVERENCE, John. American, b. 1946. Biography. Awards Dir., Acad. of Television Arts and Sciences, since 1979. Publs: Irving Wallace: Writer's Profile, 1974; (contr.) In Recognition of William Gaddis, 1985; Family Life (dramatic trilogy), 1987. Add: 3500 Olive, No. 700, Burbank, Calif. 91505, U.S.A.

LEVERTOV, Denise. American, b. 1923. Poetry, Essays, Translations. Prof., Stanford Univ., Stanford, Calif., since 1981. Visiting Lectr., Drew Univ., Madison, N.J., 1965, and Univ. of California, Berkeley, 1969; Visiting Prof., Massachusetts Inst. of Technology, Cambridge, 1969–70, and Univ. of Cincinnati, 1973; Prof., Tufts Univ., Medford, Mass., 1973–79; Fannie Hurst Prof. (Poet in Residence), Brandeis Univ., Waltham, Mass., 1981–83; also, Poetry ed., The Nation, N.Y., 1961–62; and Mother Jones, San Francisco, 1976–78. Publs: The Double Image, 1946; Here and Now, 1957; Overland to the Islands, 1958; 5 Poems, 1958; With Eyes at the Back of Our Heads, 1959; The Jacob's Ladder, 1961; O Taste and See: New Poems, 1964; City Psalm, 1964; Psalm Concerning the Castle, 1966; The Sorrow Dance, 1967; (with Kenneth Rexroth and W.C. Williams) Penguin Modern Poets 9, 1967; (ed.) Out of the War Shadow: An Anthology of Current Poetry, 1967; (ed. and trans. with E.C. Dimock) In Praise of Krishna: Songs from the Bengali, 1967; Three Poems, 1968; A Tree Telling of Orpheus, 1968; The Cold Spring and Other Poems, 1968; A Marigold from North Vietnam, 1968; In the Night: A Story, 1968; Embroideries, 1969; (trans.) Selected Poems of Guillevic, 1969; Relearning the Alphabet (poetry), 1970; Summer Poems, 1969, 1970; A New Year's Garland for My Students, MIT 1969–1970; To Stay Alive, 1971; Footprints, 1972; The Poet in the World (essays), 1973; The Freeing of the Dust, 1976; Life in the Forest, 1978; Modulations for Solo Voice, 1978; Collected Earlier Poems, 1979; Wanderer's Daysong, 1981; A Mass for the Day of St. Thomas Didymus, 1982; Candles in Babylon, 1982; Light Up the Cave (prose), 1982; & Poems 1960-1970, 1983; Oblique Prayers, 1984; Selected Poems, 1986; Poems 1968-72, 1987; Breathing the Water, 1987; (trans.) Black Iris, 1988. Add: c/o New Directions Inc., 80 Eighth Ave., New York, N.Y. 10011, U.S.A.

LEVEY, (Sir) Michael (Vincent). British b. 1927. Novels/Short stories, Art, Music. Dir., National Gallery, London, 1973-86 (Asst. Keeper, 1951-66; Deputy Keeper, 1966-68; Keeper, 1968-73). Slade Prof. of Fine Art, Cambridge Univ., 1963-64. *Publs:* Painting in XVIIIth Century Venice, 1959, 1980; From Giotto to Cézanne, 1962; Durer, 1964; Later Italian Pictures in the Collection of H.M. The Queen, 1964; Rococo to Revolution, 1966; Early Renaissance, 1967 (Hawthornden Prize, 1968); The Life and Death of Mozart, 1971; Painting at Court, 1971; (with W.W. Kalnein) Art and Architecture of the 18th Century in France, 1972; High Renaissance, 1974; The World of Ottoman Art, 1976; The Case of Walter Pater, 1978; Sir Thomas Lawrence (exhibition catalogue), 1979; The Painter Depicted, 1982; Tempting Fate, 1982; An Affair on the Appian Way, 1984; Giambattista Tiepolo, 1986; Men at Work, 1989. Add: 3/185 Old Brompton Rd., London SW5 0AN, England.

LEVI, Anthony H.T. British, b. 1929. Humanities, Literature, Philosophy. Formerly, Buchanan Prof. of French Languages and Literature, Univ. of St. Andrews, from 1971. Lectr., Christ Church, and Tutor, Campion Hall, Oxford, 1966-71; Reader 1966-69, and Prof. 1969-71, Univ. of Warwick, Coventry. *Publs:* French Moralists: The Theory of the Passions, 1585-1649, 1964; Religion in Practice, 1966; (ed.) Humanism in France at the End of the Middle Ages and in the Early Renaissance, 1970; (ed.) Erasmus: The Praise of Folly, 1971; (co-ed.) The Writer and the Artist in France, 1975; Pagan Virtue and the Humanism of the Northern Renaissance, 1975; (ed.) Collected Works of Erasmus, vols. 27-28, 1986. Add: c/o Univ. of St. Andrews, St. Andrews, Scotland.

LEVI, Edward H(irsch). American, b. 1911. Law. Glen A. Lloyd Distinguished Service Prof. Emeritus, Univ. of Chicago (Asst. Prof., 1936-40; Dean of Law Sch., 1959-62; Provost, 1962-68; Pres., 1968-75); Attorney-General of the U.S., 1975-77. *Publs:* (ed. with J.W. Moore) Gilbert's Collier on Bankruptcy, 1937; Introduction to Legal Reasoning, 1949, 1962; (ed. with R.S. Steffen) Elements of the Law, 1950; Four Talks on Legal Education, 1952; Point of View, 1969; The Crisis in the Nature of Law, 1969. Add: 1116E. 59th St., Chicago, Ill. 60637, U.S..A

LEVI, Peter (Chad Tigar). British, b. 1931. Novels, Poetry, Travel/Exploration/Adventure, Translations. Fellow, St. Catherine's Coll., Oxford; since 1977; Prof. of Poetry, Oxford Univ., since 1984. Member, Soc. of Jesus, 1948-77. *Publs:* Earthly Paradise, 1958; The Gravel Ponds: Poems, 1960; Beaumont: 1861-1961, 1961; Orpheus Head, 1962; Water, Rock and Sand, 1962; (trans. with R. Milner-Gulland) Selected Poems of Yevtushenko, 1962; The Shearwaters, 1965; Fresh Water, Sea Water: Poems, 1965; Pancakes for the Queen of Babylon: Ten Poems for Nikos Gatsos, 1968; Ruined Abbeys, 1968; Life is a Platform, 1971; Death is a Pulpit, 1971; (trans.) Guide to Greece, by Pausanias, 2 vols., 1971; The Light Garden of the Angel King: Journeys in Afghanistan, 1972; (with Adrian Mitchell and John Fuller) Penguin Modern Poets 22, 1973; (ed.) The English Bible from Wycliff to William Barnes, 1974; (ed.) Pope, 1974; John Clare and Thomas Hardy, 1975; Collected Poems, 1976; (trans.) The Psalms, 1977; The Noise Made by Poems, 1977; Five Ages, 1978; The Head in the Soup (novel), 1979; The Hill of Kronos, 1980; Atlas of the Greek World, 1980; Private Ground, 1981; The Flutes of Autumn, 1983; The Echoing Green: Three Elegies, 1983; Grave Witness (novel), 1984; (trans. with Anne Pennington) Marko the Prince, 1984; The Lamentation of the Dead (lecture), 1984; (trans.) Gospel of John, 1985; Shakespeare's Birthday (elegies), 1985; A History of Greek Literature, 1985; The Frontiers of Paradise: A Study of Monks and Monasteries, 1987; Knit One, Drop One (novel), 1987; To the Goat (novel), 1988; Life and Times of William Shakespeare, 1988; Goodbye to the Art of Poetry (lecture), 1989; Shadow and Bone (poetry), 1989. Add: Austin's Farm, Stonesfield, Oxford, England.

LEVIN, Bernard. British, b. 1928. Social commentary/phenomena. Columnist, The Times, London, since 1971. Former columnist with Daily Mail, London. *Publs:* The Pendulum Years: Britain and the Sixties, 1970; Taking Sides, 1979; Conducted Tour, 1981; Speaking Up, 1982; Enthusiasms, 1983; The Way We Live Now, 1984; To the End of the Rhine, 1987; All Things Considered, 1988. Add: c/o Curtis Brown Ltd., 162-168 Regent St., London W1, England.

LEVIN, Betty (née Lowenthal). American, b. 1927. Children's fiction. Member of the Faculty, Radcliffe Seminars, Cambridge, Mass.; also a sheep farmer. Research Assistant, Museum of Fine Arts, Boston, 1951-52; part-time teaching fellow, Harvard Grad. School of Education, 1953; creative writing fellow, Radcliffe Institute, 1968-70; Massachusetts Coordinator, McCarthy Historical Archive, 1969; Instr., Pine Manor Open College, Chestnut Hill, Mass., 1971-75, and Emmanuel College, Boston, 1975; feature writer, Minute Man Publ., Lexington, Mass., 1972; Adjunct Prof., Simmons Coll., Boston, 1975-87. *Publs:* The Zoo Company, 1973; The Sword of Culann, 1973; A Griffon's Nest, 1975; The Forespoken, 1976; Landfall, 1979; The Beast on the Brink, 1980; The Keeping Room, 1981; A Binding Spell, 1984; Put On My Crown, 1985; The Ice Bear, 1986; Julia MacRae Books, 1987. Add: Old Winter St., Lincoln, Mass. 01773, U.S.A.

LEVIN, Gerald. American, b. 1929. Literature, Speech/Rhetoric, Biography. Prof. Emeritus of English, Univ. of Akron, Ohio, since 1986 (Asst. Prof., 1960-65; Assoc. Prof., 1965-68; Prof., 1969-85). Instr., Univ. of Michigan, Ann Arbor, 1955-56; Instr., Univ. of Colorado, Boulder, 1956-57; Eastern Illinois Univ., Charleston, 1957-60. *Publs:* Prose Models, 1964, 7th ed. 1987; Brief Handbook of Rhetoric, 1966; The Short Story, 1967; (ed.) The Art of Rhetoric, by Francis Connolly, 1968; (with F. Connolly) Rhetoric Case Book, 1969; Styles for Writing, 1971; Sigmund Freud, 1975; Short Essays, 1977, 5th ed. 1989; Richardson the Novelist, 1978; Writing and Logic, 1982; Macmillan College Handbook, 1987; The Educated Reader, 1988. Add: 48 Pilgard, Glastonbury, Conn. 06033, U.S.A.

LEVIN, Harry. American, b. 1912. Literature. Prof. Emeritus, Harvard Univ., Cambridge, Mass., since 1983 (joined faculty 1939; Irving Babbitt, Prof. of Comparative Literature, 1960-83). *Publs:* The Broken Column: A Study in Romantic Hellenism, 1931; (ed.) Ben Jonson, Selected Works, 1938; James Joyce: A Critical Introduction, 1941; (ed.) Rochester, A Satire Against Mankind and Other Poems, 1942; (ed.) The Portable James Joyce, 1945; (ed.) Perspectives of Criticism, 1950; The Overreacher: Study of Christopher Marlowe, 1952; (ed.) William Shakespeare, Coriolanus, 1956; Symbolism and Fiction, 1956; Contexts of Criticism, 1957; The Power of Blackness: Hawthorne, Poe, Melville, 1958; The Question of Hamlet, 1959; (ed.) Nathaniel Hawthorne, The Scarlet Letter, 1960; Irving Babbitt and the Teaching of Literature, 1960; The Gates of Horn: A Study of Five French Realists, 1963; (ed.) William Shakespeare, The Comedy of Errors, 1965; Countercurrents in the Study of English, 1967; Refractions: Essays in Comparative Literature, 1968; Why Literary Criticism Is Not an Exact Science, 1968; The Myth of the Golden Age in the Renaissance, 1969; Grounds for Comparison, 1972; (ed.) Veins of Humor, 1972; Ezra Pound, T.S. Eliot, and the European Horizon, 1975; Shakespeare and the Revolution of the Times, 1976; Memories of the Moderns, 1980; (ed.) Henry James, The Ambassadors, 1986; Playboys and Killjoys: An Essay on the Theory and Practice of Comedy, 1987. Add: 246 Widener Library, Harvard Univ., Cambridge, Mass. 02138, U.S.A.

LEVIN, Ira. American, b. 1929. Novels/Short stories, Plays/Screenplays. *Publs:* A Kiss Before Dying (novel), 1953; (adaptor) No Time for Sergeants (play), 1956; Critic's Choice (play), 1961; Rosemary's Baby (novel), 1967; This Perfect Day (novel), 1970; The Stepford Wives (novel), 1972; Veronica's Room (play), 1974; Break a Leg (play), 1974; The Boys from Brazil (novel), 1976; Deathtrap (play), 1978. Add: Harold Ober Assocs. Inc., 40 East 49th St., New York, N.Y. 10017, U.S.A.

LEVIN, Peter (Hirsch). British, b. 1936. Politics/Government. Lectr. in Social Admin., London Sch. of Economics and Political Science, since 1970 (Sr. Research Officer, 1967-70). With A.E.I. (Woolwich) Ltd., Essex, 1960-61; Standard Telecommunications Labs., Harlow, Essex, 1961-64, and Building Research Station, Watford, Herts., 1964-67. *Publs:* Government and the Planning Process, 1976. Add: London Sch. of Economics, Houghton St., London WC2A 2AE, England.

LEVIN, Richard Louis. American, b. 1922. Literature. Prof. of English, State Univ. of New York, Stony Brook, since 1957 (Dept. Chmn., 1960-63 and 1965-66). Member, Joseph Crabtree Foundn., since 1971; Advisory Cttee. member, Modern Language Assn., and Advisory Bd. member, World Center for Shakespeare Studies, both since 1974; Member, Academic Council, Shakespeare Globe Theater Center, since 1981. Instr., 1949-53, and Asst. Prof., 1953-57, Univ. of Chicago; American Council of Learned Societies Fellowship, 1963-64; Trustee, Shakespeare Assn. of America, 1977-80; National Endowment for the Humanities Senior Fellowship, 1974; Guggenheim Foundation Fellowship, 1978-79;

Fulbright Lectureship, 1984–85. *Publs:* (ed.) Tragedy: Plays, Theory, and Criticism, 1960; (ed.) The Question of Socrates, 1961; (ed.) Tragedy: Alternate Edition, 1965; (ed.) Thomas Middleton's Michaelmas Term, 1966; The Multiple Plot in English Renaissance Drama, 1971; New Readings vs. Old Plays: Recent Trends in the Reinterpretation of English Renaissance Drama, 1979. Add: English Dept., State Univ. of New York, Stony Brook, N.Y. 11794, U.S.A.

LEVINE, Israel E. American, b. 1923. Children's non-fiction. Ed., City College of N.Y. Alumnus Magazine, since 1987. Asst. Dir., 1946–54, and Dir. of Public Relations, 1954–73, City Coll. of New York; Ed., Health Care Week, 1977–79; Ed., William H. White Publications, 1979–81; Dir. of Communications, American Jewish Congress, 1981–87. *Publs:* (with A. Lateiner) The Techniques of Supervision, 1954; The Discoverer of Insulin: Dr. Frederick G. Banting, 1959; Conqueror of Smallpox: Dr. Edward Jenner, 1960; Behind the Silken Curtain: The Story of Townsend Harris, 1961; Inventive Wizard: George Westinghouse, 1962; Champion of World Peace: Dag Hammarskjold, 1962; Miracle Man of Printing: Ottmar Mergenthaler, 1963; Electronics Pioneer: Lee DeForest, 1964; Young Man in the White House: John Fitzgerald Kennedy, 1964; Oliver Cromwell, 1966; Spokesman for the Free World: Adlai Stevenson, 1967; Lenin: The Man Who Made a Revolution, 1969; The Many Faces of Slavery, 1975. Add: 140-41 69th Rd., Flushing, N.Y. 11367, U.S.A.

LEVINE, Mortimer. American, b. 1922. History. Joint Gen. Ed., Archives of British History and Culture, Conference on British Studies, West Virginia Univ., since 1967; Member, Advisory Bd., The Folger Library Ed. of the Works of Richard Hooker, Harvard Univ. Press, since 1969. Lectr. in History, Brooklyn Coll., N.Y., 1954–55; Instr., 1955–57, Asst. Prof., 1957–61, Assoc. Prof., 1961–67, and Prof. of History, 1967–84, West Virginia Univ., Morgantown. *Publs:* The Early Elizabethan Succession Question 1558-1568, 1966; Tudor England 1485-1603 (bibliography), 1968; Tudor Dynastic Problems 1460-1571, 1973. Add: 529 Woodhaven Dr., West Virginia Univ., Morgantown, W. Va. 26505, U.S.A.

LEVINE, (Albert) Norman. Canadian, b. 1924. Novels/Short stories, Poetry, Autobiography/Memoirs/Personal. Employed by Dept. of National Defence, Ottawa, 1940–42; Head of English Dept., Barnstaple Boys Grammar Sch., Devon, 1953–54; resident Writer, Univ. of New Brunswick, Fredericton, 1965–66. *Publs:* The Tightrope Walker (verse), 1950; The Angled Road, 1952; Canada Made Me, 1958, 1979; One Way Ticket, 1961; (ed.) Canadian Winter's Tales, 1968; From a Seaside Town, 1970; I Don't Want to Know Anyone Too Well: 15 Stories, 1971; Selected Stories, 1975; I Walk by the Harbour, 1976; Thin Ice, 1979; Why Do You Live So Far Away?, 1984; Champagne Barn, 1984; Django, KARFunkelstein, and Roses, 1987. Add: 103 Summerhill Ave., Toronto, Ont. M4T 1BI, Canada.

LEVINE, Philip. American, b. 1928. Poetry. Prof. of English, California State Univ., Fresno, since 1958. *Publs:* On the Edge, 1963; Not this Pig, 1968; 5 Detroits, 1970; Thistles, 1970; Pili's Wall, 1971; Red Dust, 1971; They Feed They Lion, 1972; 1933, 1974; The Names of the Lost, 1976; Ashes, 1979; 7 Years from Somewhere, 1979; One for the Rose, 1981; Selected Poems, 1984; Sweet Will, 1985; (ed.) The Essential Keats, 1987; A Walk with Tom Jefferson, 1988. Add: 4549 North Van Ness Ave., Fresno, Calif. 93704, U.S.A.

LEVINE, Stuart George. American, b. 1932. Literature. Prof. of English, Univ. of Kansas, Lawrence, since 1969 (Instr., Asst. Prof., Assoc. Prof., 1958–69; Founding Chmn., Dept. of American Studies, 1965–70). Ed., American Studies mag., since 1959. Member, Exec. Cttee., Mid-America American Studies Assn, since 1983. Chmn., Awards Comm., American Studies Assn, 1984–85. *Publs:* Materials for Technical Writing, 1963; (with N.O. Lurie) The American Indian Today, 1968; (ed.) The Story of American Painting, by Charles Caffin, 1970; Edgar Poe, Seer and Craftsman, 1972; (ed. with Susan Levine) The Short Fiction of Edgar Allan Poe, 1975; (ed. with Susan Levine) The Collected Writings of Edgar Allan Poe: 'Eureka' and the Major Criticism, 1990. Add: 1846 Barker Ave., Lawrence, Kans. 66044, U.S.A.

LEVINSON, Deirdre. British, b. 1931. Novels/Short stories. *Publs:* Five Years, 1966; Modus Vivendi. Add: c/o Penguin, 40 W. 23rd St., New York, N.Y. 10010, U.S.A.

LEVINSON, Harry. American, b. 1922. Administration/Management, Psychology. Pres., The Levinson Inst., since 1968. Prof., Dept. of Psychiatry, Harvard Medical Sch., Boston, since 1986 (Lab. of Community Psychiatry, 1972–85). Dir., Div. of Industrial Mental Health, The Menninger Foundn., Topeka, Kans., 1954–68; Thomas Henry Carroll-Ford

Foundn. Distinguished Visiting Prof., Harvard Business Sch., Cambridge, Mass., 1968–72. *Publs:* (with W.C. Menninger) Human Understanding in Industry, 1956; (ed.) Toward Understanding Men, 2nd ed. 1957; (with C.R. Price, K.J. Munden, H.J. Mandl and C.M. Solley) Men, Management and Mental Health, 1962; Emotional Health: In the World of Work, 1964, 1984; (with P. Tournier, V. Frank, H. Thielicke, P. Lehman and S.H. Miller) Are You Nobody?, 1966; The Exceptional Executive, 1968; Executive Stress, 1969; (with A.G. Spohn and J. Molinari) Organizational Diagnosis, 1972; The Great Jackass Fallacy, 1973; Psychological Man, 1976; (with Cynthia Lang) Executive, 1981; Casebook for Psychological Man, 1982; (with Stuart Rosenthal) CEO: Corporate Leadership in Action, 1984; (ed.) Designing and Managing Your Career, 1988. Add: 225 Brattle St., Cambridge, Mass. 02138, U.S.A.

LEVINSON, Olga May. South African. Art, History. Writer, broadcaster and lecturer. Hon. Life Pres., South African Assn. of Arts (S.W.A.), (Pres., 1958–76), Founding member, S.W.A. Performing Arts Council, S.W.A. Broadcasting Corp. and T.V. Bd.; Founding member, Bushman Foundation. *Publs:* Call Me Master (humour/personal experiences), 1958; The Ageless Land, 1961; Adolph Jentsch, 1973; South West Africa, 1976; Story of Namibia, 1978; Diamonds in the Desert, 1983. Add: Heynitz Castle, P.O. Box 458, Windhoek, Namibia.

LEVIS, Larry (Patrick). American, b. 1946. Poetry. Assoc. Prof. of English, Univ. of Utah, since 1980. Instr., California State Univ., Fresno, 1970; Lectr., California State Univ., Los Angeles, 1970–72; Visiting Lectr., Univ. of Iowa, Iowa City, 1972; Asst. Prof., Univ. of Missouri, Columbia, 1974–80. *Publs:* Wrecking Crew, 1972; The Rain's Witness, 1975; The Afterlife, 1977; The Dollmaker's Ghost, 1981; Winter Stars, 1985. Add: Dept. of English, University of Utah, Salt Lake City, Utah 84112, U.S.A.

LEVITIN, Sonia (née Wolff). Also writes as Sonia Wolff. American, b. 1934. Children's fiction, Novels. Teacher, Writer's Program, Palos Verdes Peninsula, Calif., since 1978 (Creative writing teacher, 1973–76). Elementary sch. teacher, Mill Valley, Calif., 1956–57; Adult education teacher, Daly City, Calif., 1962–64, and Acalanes Adult Center, Lafayette, Calif., 1965–72. *Publs:* Journey to America, 1970; Rita the Weekend Rat, 1971; Roanoke: A Novel of the Lost Colony, 1973; Who Owns the Moon?, 1973; Jason and the Money Tree, 1974; A Single Speckled Egg, 1975; The Mark of Conte, 1976; Beyond Another Door, 1977; Reigning Cats and Dogs (novel), 1978; The No-Return Trail, 1978; A Sound to Remember, 1979; Nobody Stole the Pie, 1980; The Fisherman and the Bird, 1982; All the Cats in the World, 1982; (as Sonia Wolff) What They Did to Miss Lily (novel), 1982; The Year of Sweet Senior Insanity, 1982; Smile Like a Plastic Daisy, 1984; A Season of Unicorns, 1986; The Return, 1987; Incident at Loring Groves, 1988; Silver Days, 1989. Add: 9617 Oak Pass Rd., Beverly Hills, Calif. 90210, U.S.A.

LEVOY, Myron. American, b. 1930. Children's fiction, Novels. *Publs:* A Necktie in Greenwich Village (novel), 1968; Penny Tunes and Princesses, 1972; The Witch of Fourth Street and Other Stories, 1972; Alan and Naomi, 1977; A Shadow Like a Leopard, 1981; Three Friends, 1984; The Hanukkah of Great-Uncle Otto, 1984; Pictures of Adam, 1986; The Magic Hat of Mortimer Wintergreen, 1988. Add: c/o Susan Cohen, Writers House Inc., 21 W. 26th St., New York, N.Y. 10010, U.S.A.

LEVY, Alan. American, b. 1932. Plays/Screenplays, Songs, Lyrics and Libretti, Social commentary/phenomena, Autobiography/Memoirs/Personal, Biography. Foreign Corresp. since 1967 (accredited to Life mag. and Good Housekeeping mag. in Prague, 1967–71); Contrib. Writer, Intnl. Herald Tribune, Paris, ARTnews, NYC, N.Y. Sunday Times, and Reader's Digest in Vienna, since 1971. Reporter, Courier-Journal, Louisville, Ky., 1953–60; Investigator, Carnegie Commn. on Educational Television, 1966–67; Dramaturg, Vienna's English Theatre, Ltd., 1977–82. *Publs:* (with B. Krisher and J. Cox) Draftee's Confidential Guide, 1957, rev. ed. with R. Flaste, 1966; Operation Elvis, 1960; The Elizabeth Taylor Story, 1961; Wanted: Nazi Criminals at Large, 1962; Interpret Your Dreams, 1962, 1975; (with G. Stuart) Kind-Hearted Tiger, 1964; The Culture Vultures, 1968; God Bless You Real Good: My Crusade with Billy Graham, 1969; Rowboat to Prague, 1972; Good Men Still Live!, 1974; The Bluebird of Happiness, 1976; Forever, Sophia, 1979, 1986; So Many Heroes, 1980; The World of Ruth Draper (play), 1982; Just an Accident? (text for symphonic requiem: music by René Staar), 1983; Ezra Pound: The Voice of Silence, 1983; W.H. Auden: In the Autumn of the Age of Anxiety, 1983; Treasures of the Vatican Collections, 1983; Vladimir Nabokov: The Velvet Butterfly, 1984; Ezra Pound: A Jewish View, 1988. Add: c/o June Hall Literary Agency, The Chambers, Chelsea Harbour,

Lots Rds., London SW10 0XF, England.

LEWES, Charles. *See* **DIXON,** Roger.

LEWIN, Michael Z. American, b. 1942. Mystery/Crime/Suspense, Education. High sch. science teacher, USA, 1966–69. *Publs:* How to Beat College Tests: A Guide to Ease the Burden of Useless Courses, 1970; Ask the Right Question, 1971; The Way We Die Now, 1973; The Enemies Within, 1974; Night Cover, 1976; The Silent Salesman, 1978; Outside In, 1980; Missing Woman, 1981; Hard Line, 1982; Out of Time (in U.S. as Out of Season), 1984; Late Payments, 1986; Child Proof (in U.S. as And Baby Will Fall), 1988. Add: 5 Welshmill Rd., Frome, Somerset BA11 2LA, England.

LEWIN, Moshe. French, b. 1921. History, Politics/Government. Prof. of Russian History, Univ. of Pennsylvania, Philadelphia, since 1978. Dir. of Studies, Ecole Pratique des Hautes Etudes, Paris, 1965 and 1966; Sr. Fellow, Russian Inst., Columbia Univ., NYC, 1967–68; Prof. in Soviet History and Politics, Centre for Russian and E. European Studies, Univ. of Birmingham, 1968–78; member, Inst. for Advanced Study, Princeton, N.J., 1972–73. *Publs:* Russian Peasant and Soviet Power, 1928–1930, 1966; Lenin's Last Struggle, 1967; Political Undercurrent in Soviet Economic Debates: From Bukharin to Modern Reformers, 1974; The Making of the Soviet System, 1985; The Gorbachev Phenomenon, 1988. Add: Dept. of History, Coll. Hall/Co. Univ. of Pennsylvania, Philadelphia, Pa. 19704, U.S.A.

LEWIS, (Sir) Arthur. British, b. 1915. Economics, Politics/Government. Prof. Emeritus, Princeton Univ., New Jersey, since 1983 (Prof. of Public and Intnl. Affairs, 1963–68; James Madison Prof. of Political Economy, 1968–82; Distinguished Univ. Prof. of Economics and Intnl. Affairs, 1982–83). Asst. Lectr., and subsequently Lectr., London Sch. of Economics, 1938–48; Prof. of Political Economy, Univ. of Manchester, 1948–58; Vice-Chancellor, Univ. of the West Indies, 1959–63. Pres., American Economic Assn., 1983. Recipient, Nobel Prize, 1979. *Publs:* Economic Problems of Today, 1940; Overhead Costs, 1949; Economic Survey 1919–1939, 1950; Principles of Economic Planning, 1950; The Theory of Economic Growth, 1955; Politics in West Africa, 1965; Development Planning, 1966; Some Aspects of Economic Development, 1969; Aspects of Tropical Trade 1883-1965, 1969; (ed.) Tropical Development 1883-1913, 1971; Growth and Fluctuations 1870-1913, 1978; Racial Conflict and Economic Development, 1985. Add: Woodrow Wilson Sch., Princeton Univ., Princeton, N.J. 08540, U.S.A.

LEWIS, Claudia Louise. American, b. 1907. Children's fiction, Anthropology/Ethnology, Children's non-fiction, Literature. Teacher of creative writing and multi-cultural education, Bank St. Coll. of Education, NYC, since 1943; Teacher of Children's Literature, New Sch. for Social Research, NYC, since 1979. *Publs:* Children of the Cumberland, 1946; Writing for Young Children, 1954; Straps the Cat, 1957; When I Go to the Moon, 1961; The Strange Home, 1964; Poetry of Earth and Space, 1967; Indian Families of the Northwest Coast, 1970; Up and Down the River: Boat Poems, 1979; A Big Bite of the World: Children's Creative Writing, 1979; Long Ago in Oregon, 1987. Add: 610 W. 112th St., New York, N.Y. 10025, U.S.A.

LEWIS, Herbert S. American, b. 1934. Anthropology/Ethnology. Prof. of Anthropology, Univ. of Wisconsin, Madison, since 1973 (Asst. Prof., 1963–67; Assoc. Prof., 1967–73). Instr. in Anthropology and Political Science, Northwestern Univ., Evanston, Ill., 1961–63; Visiting Assoc. Prof., The Hebrew Univ., Jerusalem, Israel, 1969–70. *Publs:* A Galla Monarchy: Jimma Abba Jifar, Ethiopia, 1830-1932, 1965; Leaders and Followers: Some Anthropological Perspectives, 1974; The Yemenites of Israel, 1989. Add: Dept. of Anthropology, Univ. of Wisconsin, Madison, Wisc. 53706, U.S.A.

LEWIS, Hywel David. British, b. 1910. Poetry, Philosophy. Emeritus Prof., Dept. of History and Philosophy of Religion, King's Coll., Univ. of London, since 1977 (Prof. and Dept. Head, 1955–77). Ed., Muirhead Library of Philosophy, since 1947, and Religious Studies, Cambridge Univ. Press, since 1964; Pres., Inst. of Religion and Theology of Great Britain and Ireland, and Intnl. Soc. for Metaphysics; Chmn., Council of Royal Inst. of Philosophy, since 1965. Lectr., 1936–46, Sr. Lectr., 1947, and Prof. of Philosophy, 1947–55, University Coll., Bangor. *Publs:* Morals and the New Theology, 1947; Morals and Revelation, 1951; Our Experience of God, 1959; Freedom and History, 1962; (ed.) Clarity Is Not Enough, 1962; Teach Yourself the Philosophy of Religion, 1965; (with R.L. Slater) World Religions, 1966; Dreaming and Experience, 1968; The Elusive Mind, The Elusive Self (Gifford Lectures), 2 vols.,

1969–82; The Self and Immortality, 1973; Persons and Life After Death, 1977; Jesus in the Faith of Christians, 1980; Freedom and Alienation, 1985. Add: 1 Normandy Park, Normandy, Guildford, Surrey GU3 2AL, England.

LEWIS, Jack Pearl. American, b. 1919. Theology/Religion. Prof. of Bible, Harding Univ. Grad. Sch. of Religion, Memphis, since 1957 (Assoc. Prof., 1954–57). Minister in various churches in Texas, Rhode Island and Kentucky, 1941–54. *Publs:* The Minor Prophets, 1966; The Interpretation of Noah and the Flood in Jewish and Christian Literature, 1968; Historical Backgrounds of Bible History, 1971; (ed.) The Last Things, 1972; Archaeology and the Bible, 1975; The Gospel According to Mathew, 2 vols., 1976; The English Bible from the KJV to the N1V, 1981; Leadership Questions Confronting the Church, 1985; Exegesis of Difficult Passages, 1988. Add: 1132 South Perkins Rd., Memphis, Tenn. 38117, U.S.A.

LEWIS, Janet. (Janet Winters). American, b. 1899. Novels/Short stories, Children's fiction, Poetry, Songs, lyrics and libretti. Lectr. in English, Univ. of California, Berkeley. Formerly Lectr. in Creative Writing and English, Stanford Univ., Calif. *Publs:* The Indians in the Woods (poetry), 1922; The Friendly Adventures of Ollie Ostrich, 1923; The Wheel in Midsummer (poetry), 1927; The Invasion, 1932; The Wife of Martin Guerre, 1941, libretto, 1958; Against a Darkening Sky, 1943; Good-bye Son and Other Stories, 1946; The Earth-Bound (poetry), 1946; The Trial of Soren Quist, 1947; Poems 1924–1944, 1950; The Ghost of Monsieur Scarron, 1959; Keiko's Bubble, 1961; Birthday of the Infanta (libretto), 1978; Poems Old and New, 1981; The Swans (libretto), 1986; The Legend (libretto), 1987; Late Offerings (verse), 1988. Add: 143 West Portola Ave., Los Altos, Calif. 94022, U.S.A.

LEWIS, John N(oël) C(laude). British, b. 1912. Crafts, Design (general), Recreation/Leisure/Hobbies. Freelance writer and book designer since 1948. Typographic and Design Consultant, Univ. of Essex, since 1964. Tutor in Typography, Royal Coll. of Art, 1951–64. *Publs:* A Handbook of Printing Types, 1947; A Ship Modeller's Logbook, 1950; Small Boat Conversion, 1951; (with J. Brinkley) Graphic Design, 1954; A Handbook of Type and Illustration, 1956; Printed Ephemera, 1962; Typography: Basic Principles, 1963; (with B. Gill) Illustration: Aspects and Directions, 1964; The Twentieth-Century Book: Its Illustration and Design, 1967, 1984; A Taste for Sailing, 1969, 1989; (with E. Smith) The Graphic Reproduction and Photography of Works of Art, 1969; Anatomy of Printing, 1970; Small Craft Conversion, 1972; Heath Robinson: Artist and Comic Genius, 1973; Vintage Boats, 1975; Collecting Printed Ephemera, 1976; Repair of Wooden Boats, 1977; Typography: Design and Practice, 1977; John Nash: The Painter as Illustrator, 1978; Rowland Hilder, Painter and Illustrator, 1978; (with Griselda Lewis) Prattware: English and Scottish Relief Decorated and Underglaze Coloured Earthenware 1780-1840, 1984; Rowland Hilder, Painter of the English Landscape, 1987. Add: 6 Doric Pl., Woodbridge, Suffolk, England.

LEWIS, J(ohn) Parry. British, b. 1927. Economics, Regional/Urban planning. Prof. of Economics of Regions and Towns, Univ. of Manchester, 1967–82, now retired. Prof. of Economics, Univ. of Exeter, 1965–67. *Publs:* Introduction to Mathematics for Students of Economics, 1959, 1969; Building Cycles and Britain's Growth, 1965; (with D.F. Medhurst) Urban Decay: An Analysis and a Policy, 1969; A Study of the Cambridge Sub-Region, 1973; Urban Economics, 1979; Development Strategies Reconsidered, 1986; Freedom to Drink, 1985. Add: c/o Inst. for Economic Affairs, 2 Lord North St., London SW1P 3LB, England.

LEWIS, J(ohn) R(oyston). Writes mystery novels as Roy Lewis. British, b. 1933. Mystery/Crime/Suspense, Law. Managing Dir., Felton Press, publishers, Newcastle, since 1974; Principal, Wigan Coll. of Technology, since 1981; Dir., Wigan New Enterprise Ltd., and Templar North Publications Ltd., since 1982. Teacher, Okehampton Secondary Sch., Devon, 1957–59; Lectr., Cannock Chase Secondary Sch., Staffordshire, 1959–61, Cornwall Technical Coll., Redruth, 1961–63, and Plymouth Coll. of Technology, Devon, 1963–67; Inspector of Schools, Newcastle, 1967–75. Intnl. Pres., Chartered Inst. of Secretaries and Administrators, 1988. *Publs:* on law—Cases for Discussion, 1965; Law for the Retailer: An Outline for Students and Business Men, 1964 (as Law for the Retailer), 1974; An Introduction to Business Law, 1965; Law in Action, 1965; Questions and Answers on Civil Procedure, 1966; Building Law, 1966; Democracy: The Theory and the Practice, 1966; Managing Within the Law, 1967; (with John A. Holland) Principles of Registered Land Conveyancing, 1967; Company Law, 1967; Revision Notes for Ordinary Level British Construction, 1967; Civil and Criminal Procedure, 1968; Landlord

An Outline for Students and Business Men, 1964 (as Law for the Retailer), 1974; An Introduction to Business Law, 1965; Law in Action, 1965; Questions and Answers on Civil Procedure, 1966; Building Law, 1966; Democracy: The Theory and the Practice, 1966; Managing Within the Law, 1967; (with John A. Holland) Principles of Registered Land Conveyancing, 1967; Company Law, 1967; Revision Notes for Ordinary Level British Construction, 1967; Civil and Criminal Procedure, 1968; Landlord and Tenant, 1968; Outlines of Equity, 1968; (with Anne Redish) Mercantile and Commercial Law, 1969; (as David Springfield) The Company Executive and the Law, 1970; Law for the Construction Industry, 1976; Administrative Law for the Construction Industry, 1976; The Teaching of Public Administration in Further and Higher Education, 1979; The Victorian Bar 1837-1882, 1980; Certain Private Incidents, 1980; mystery novels—A Lover too Many, 1969; A Wolf by the Ears, 1970; Error of Judgment, 1971; The Fenokee Project, 1971; A Fool for a Client, 1972; The Secret Singing, 1972; Blood Money, 1973; Of Singular Purpose, 1973; A Question of Degree, 1974; Double Take, 1975; A Part of Virtue, 1975; Witness My Death, 1976; Distance Banner, 1976; Nothing but Foxes, 1977; An Uncertain Sound, 1978; An Inevitable Fatality, 1978; A Violent Death, 1979; A Certain Blindness, 1980; Seek for Justice, 1981; A Relative Distance, 1981; Dwell in Danger, 1982; A Gathering of Ghosts, 1982; A Limited Vision, 1983; Once Dying, Twice Dead, 1984; Most Cunning Workmen, 1984; A Blurred Reality, 1985; A Trout in the Milk, 1986; Premium on Death, 1987; Men of Subtle Craft, 1987. Add: c/o William Collins Ltd., 8 Grafton St., London W1X 3AL, England.

LEWIS, Judith Mary. Also writes with Clifford Lewis as Judith Berrisford. British, b. 1921. Novels/Short stories, Children's fiction, Homes/Gardens, Travel/Exploration/Adventure. Gardening Corresp., Good Housekeeping mag., London. *Publs:* Taff, a Welsh Sheepdog; Sue's Circus Horse; Ponies Next Door; Ponies All Summer; Ponies Forest Adventure; Red Rocket; Mystery Horse; Timber; Joker the Foxhound; Trot Home Salley; A Dog Called Scamp; Son of Taff; Trouble at Ponyways; Skipper the Dog from the Sea; Skipper and Headland Four; Skipper's Exciting Summer; The Small Shrub Garden; Gardening on Lime; The Very Small Garden; The Wild Garden; Window-Box and Container Gardening; The Young Gardener; Jackie's Pony Summer Camp; Jackie and the Misfit Pony, 1975; The Small Shrub Garden, 1976; Jackie on Pony Island, 1977; A Show Jumper in the Family, 1978; The Weekend Gardener, 1978. Add: 36 Rheast Mooar Ave., Ramsey, Isle of Man, U.K.

LEWIS, Lesley. Also writes as Lesley Lawrence. British, b. 1909. Art, History. *Publs:* Connoisseurs and Secret Agents in Eighteenth Century Rome, 1961; The Private Life of a Country House 1912-39, 1980. Add: 38 Whitelands House, Cheltenham Terr., London SW3 4QY, England.

LEWIS, Mervyn. *See* FREWER, Glyn.

LEWIS, Norman. American, b. 1912. Language/Linguistics, Speech/Rhetoric. Prof. of English, Rio Hondo Coll., Whittier, Calif., since 1964 (Chmn., Communications Dept., 1964–75). Instr., City Univ. of New York, 1943–52; Assoc. Prof., New York Univ., NYC, 1955–64. *Publs:* (with Wilfred Funk) 30 Days to a More Powerful Vocabulary, 1942, 1970; Power with Words, 1943; How to Read Better and Faster, 1944, 4th ed. 1978; Lewis English Refresher and Vocabulary Builder, 1945; Word Power Made Easy, 1949, 1978; Rapid Vocabulary Builder, 1951, 1980; How to Get More Out of Your Reading, 1951; 20 Days to Better Spelling, 1953; (ed.) New Roget's Thesaurus in Dictionary Form, 1961, 1978; Dictionary of Correct Spelling, 1962; Correct Spelling Made Easy, 1963; Dictionary of Modern Pronunciation, 1963; New Guide to Word Power, 1963; New Power with Words, 1964; Thirty Days to Better English, 1964; How to Become a Better Reader, 1964; Modern Thesaurus of Synonyms, 1965; R.S.V.P.: Reading, Spelling Vocabulary, Pronunciation, books I-III, 1966, enlarged ed., books I and II, 1982, book III, 1983, book A, 1985, book B, 1986; See, Say, and Write: Spelling Texts, books I and II, 1973; Instant Spelling Power, 1973; R.S.V.P. for College English Power, books I-III, 1978; Instant Word Power, 1980; RSVP with Etymology, books I-III, 1980–82; New American Dictionary of Good English, 1987. Add: c/o Dept. of English, Rio Hondo Coll., Whittier, Calif. 90608, U.S.A.

LEWIS, Peter (Elvet). British, b. 1937. Literature, Media. Sr. Lectr. in English, Univ. of Durham, since 1964. Member, Northern Arts Literature Panel, 1965–70, 1982–86. *Publs:* (ed.) The Beggar's Opera, by John Gay, 1973; (ed.) Poems '74, 1974; John Gay: The Beggar's Opera (criticism), 1976; (co-ed.) Implosions, by Deryck Cumming, 1977; (ed.) Papers of the Radio Literature Conference 1977; (ed.) Radio Drama, 1981; John Le Carré, 1985, Fielding's Burlesque Drama, 1987; (co-ed.) John

Gay and the Scriblerians, 1988. Add: Sch. of English, Univ. of Durham, Elvet Riverside I, New Elvet, Durham DH1 3JT, England.

LEWIS, Robert (Arthur). British, b. 1945. Business/Trade/Industry, Economics. Lectr., subsequently Sr. Lectr., in Economic History, Univ. of Exeter, since 1972. Research Assoc., Centre for Russian and East European Studies, Univ. of Birmingham, 1970–72. *Publs:* Science and Industrialisation in the USSR, 1979. Add: Dept. of Economic History, Univ. of Exeter, Exeter EX4 4RJ, England.

LEWIS, Roy. British, b. 1913. Novels/Short stories, History, Sociology. Publr. with the Keepsake Press. Asst. Foreign Ed. and Washington Corresp., The Economist, London, 1952–61; Asst. Foreign Ed., 1961–71, and Leader Writer, until 1981, The Times, London. *Publs:* (co-author) The Colonial Problem, 1939; Shall I Emigrate, 1948; (co-author) The English Middle Classes, 1949; (co-author) The Visitors Book, 1951; (co-author) Professional People, 1952; Sierra Leone, 1954; The Boss, 1958; (co-author) Evolution Man, 1959; The British in Africa, 1971; Force for the Future: The Role of the Police over the Next Ten Years, 1976; Enoch Powell: Principle in Politics, 1979. Add: 2 Park House Gardens, Twickenham, Middx., England.

LEWIS, Roy. *See* LEWIS, J.R.

LEWIS, Shannon. *See* LLYWELYN, Morgan.

LEWIS, Thomas L.T. British, b. 1918. Medicine/Health. Consultant Obstetrician and Gynaecologist, Guy's Hosp., and Queen Charlotte's Hosp., London, since 1948 now Emeritus; also, Emeritus Civilian Consultant in Obstetrics and Gynaecology to British Army; Examiner in Obstetrics and Gynaecology, Univs. of London and Cambridge, and Royal Coll. of Obstetricians and Gynaecologists. Edwin Tooth Prof., Brisbane 1959; Sims-Black Prof. to Australia, New Zealand and Rhodesia, 1970. *Publs:* Progress in Clinical Obstetrics and Gynaecology, 1964; (ed. and contrib.) Gynaecology, 14th ed. 1985; (ed. and contrib.) Obstetrics, 14th ed. 1985; (co-author) French's Index of Differential Diagnosis, 12th ed. 1985. Add: 13 Copse Hill, London SW20 0NB, England.

LEWIS, Thomas P(arker). American, b. 1936. Children's fiction. Pres., Pro/Am Music Resources, White Plains, N.Y., since 1982. Coordinator, Institutional and Corporate Marketing Depts., Harper & Row, Publrs., Inc., NYC, 1964–82. *Publs:* Hill of Fire, 1971; The Dragon Kite, 1974; Clipper Ship, 1978; A Call for Mr. Sniff, 1981; Mr. Sniff's Motel Mystery, 1983; The Blue Rocket Fun Show, 1986; The Pro-Am Guide to U.S. Books About Music, 1987, 1988; Frida Cat, 1989. Add: 63 Prospect St., White Plains, N.Y. 10606, U.S.A.

LEWIS, W(alter) David. American, b. 1931. Business/Trade/Industry, Economics, Engineering/Technology, History. Hudson Prof. of History and Engineering, Auburn Univ., Ala., since 1971. Fellowship Coordinator, Eleutherian Mills-Hagley Foundn., Wilmington, Del., and Lectr. in History, Univ. of Delaware, Newark, both 1959–65; Assoc. Prof. of History, 1965–71, and Prof., 1971, State Univ. of New York, Buffalo. *Publs:* From Newgate to Dannemora: The Rise of the Penitentiary in New York, 1796-1848, 1965; (ed. with D.T. Gilchrist) Economic Change in the Civil War Era, 1965; Iron and Steel in America, 1976; (ed. with B.E. Griessman) The Southern Mystique: Technology and Human Values in a Changing Region, 1977; (with Wesley P. Newton) Delta: The History of an Airline, 1979; (with William F. Trimble) The Airway to Everywhere: A History of All American Aviation 1937–1953, 1987. Add: 7008 Haley Center, Auburn Univ., Auburn, Ala. 36830, U.S.A.

LEWIS, William Russell. British, b. 1926. Economics, International relations/Current affairs, Politics/Government, Biography, Humor/Satire. Leader and Feature Writer, Daily Mail, London, since 1977. Dir., Common Market's Office, London, 1960–65; Sr. Economic Leader, Daily Telegraph, London, 1965–66; Dir., Conservative Political Centre, London, 1966–75. *Publs:* Rome or Brussels, 1971; (with C. Davies) Reactionary Joke Book, 1973; The New Service Society, 1973; Margaret Thatcher: A Personal and Political Biography, 1975, 3rd ed. 1983; The Survival of Capitalism, 1977; Tony Benn: A Critical Biography, 1978; The Official Shop Steward's Joke Book, 1980; (with others) Apartheid, Capitalism or Socialism, 1986; Anti-Racism: A Mania Exposed, 1988. Add: 14 Woodmansterne Rd., Carshalton Beeches, Surrey, England.

LEWIS-SMITH, Anne. British, b. 1925. Poetry. Member of Editorial Bd., Envoi Mag., since 1973, main ed. since 1984; Publisher, Envoi Poets Publications; Ed. for BAFM Yearbook (Brit. Assn. of Friends of Museums) and member of BAFM Council. English Dir., World Poetry

Day, since 1967; Vice Pres., Studie Scambi Intnl., Italy; Pres., Amis des Musé des Ballon. Feature Writer, Women's Page, Stamford Mercury, 1964–70, and Cambridgeshire Life, and Northamptonshire Life, 1967–70. *Publs:* Seventh Bridge, 1964; The Beginning, 1966; Flesh and Flowers, 1967; Dandelion Flavour, 1970; Dinas Head, 1977; Places and Passions, 1986; In the Dawn, 1987. Add: Pen Fford, Newport, Dyfed SA42 0QT, Wales.

LEWTY, Marjorie. British, b. 1906. Historical/Romance/Gothic. *Publs:* Never Call It Loving, 1958; The Million Stars, 1959; The Imperfect Secretary, 1959; The Lucky One, 1961; This Must Be Forever, 1962; Alex Rayner, Dental Nurse, 1965; Dental Nurse at Denley's, 1968; Town Nurse—Country Nurse, 1970; The Extraordinary Engagement, 1972; The Rest Is Magic, 1973; All Made of Wishes, 1974; Flowers in Stony Places, 1975; The Fire in the Diamond, 1976; To Catch a Butterfly, 1977; The Time and the Loving, 1977; The Short Engagement, 1978; A Very Special Man, 1979; A Certain Smile, 1979; Prisoner in Paradise, 1980; Love Is a Dangerous Game, 1980; Beyond the Lagoon, 1981; A Girl Bewitched, 1981; Makeshift Marriage, 1982; Dangerous Male, 1983; One Who Kisses, 1983; Riviera Romance, 1984; A Lake in Kyoto, 1985; Acapulco Moonlight, 1985; Villa in the Sun, 1986; In Love with the Man, 1986; Honeymoon Island, 1987; Falling in Love Again, 1988. Add: The Knapp, Studland, Swanage, Dorset BH19 3AE, England.

LEXAU, Joan M. Also writes as Joan L. Nodset. American. Children's fiction. Editorial Secty., Catholic Digest, St. Paul, 1953–55; Advertising Production Mgr., Glass Packer mag., NYC, 1955–56; Reporter, Catholic News, NYC, 1956–57; Corresp., Religious News Service, NYC, 1957; Children's Books Production Liaison, Harper and Row, Publishers, NYC, 1957–61. *Publs:* Olaf Reads, 1961; Cathy is Company, 1961; Millicent's Ghost, 1962; The Trouble with Terry, 1962; Olaf is Late, 1963; That's Good, That's Bad, 1963; Jose's Christmas Secret, 1963, rev. ed. as The Christmas Secret, 1973; (as Joan L. Nodset) Who Took the Farmer's Hat?, 1963; (as Joan L. Nodset) Go Away, Dog, 1963; Benjie, 1964; Maria, 1964; (as Joan L. Nodset) Where Do You Go When You Run Away?, 1964; (ed.) Convent Life: Catholic Religious Orders for Women in North America, 1964; I Should Have Stayed in Bed!, 1965; More Beautiful Than Flowers, 1966; The Homework Caper, 1966; A Kite over Tenth Avenue, 1967; Finders Keepers, Losers Weepers, 1967; Every Day a Dragon, 1967; Three Wishes for Abner, 1967; Striped Ice Cream!, 1968; The Rooftop Mystery, 1968; A House So Big, 1968; Archimedes Takes a Bath, 1969; Crocodile and Hen, 1969; It All Began with a Drip, Drip, Drip . . . , 1970; Benjie on His Own, 1970; Me Day, 1971; A T for Tommy, 1971; That's Just Fine, and Who-o-o Did It?, 1971; Emily and the Klunky Baby and the Next-Door Dog, 1972; (as Joan L. Nodset) Come Here, Cat, 1973; The Tail of the Mouse, 1974; I'll Tell on You, 1976; Beckie and the Bookworm, 1979; I Hate Red Rover, 1979; The Spider Makes a Web, 1979; Jack and the Beanstalk, 1980; The Poison Ivy Case, 1984; The Dog Food Caper, 1985, Don't Be My Valentine, 1985. Add: P.O. Box 270, Otisville, N.Y. 10963, U.S.A.

LEY, Alice Chetwynd. British, b. 1913. Historical/Romance, Mystery/Crime/Suspense. Tutor in Creative Writing, Harrow Coll. of Further Education, 1963–84. Former Chmn., Romantic Novelists Assn. *Publs:* The Jewelled Snuff Box, 1959; The Georgian Rake, 1960; The Guinea Stamp, 1961, in U.S. as The Courting of Joanna, 1976; Master of Liversedge, 1966, in U.S. as The Master and the Maiden, 1977; Clandestine Betrothal, 1967; Toast of the Town, 1969; Letters for a Spy, 1970, in U.S. as The Sentimental Spy, 1977; A Season at Brighton, 1971; Tenant of Chesdene Manor, 1974, in U.S. as Beloved Diana, 1977; The Beau and the Bluestocking, 1975; At Dark of the Moon, 1977; An Advantageous Marriage, 1977; A Regency Scandal, 1979; A Conformable Wife, 1981; The Intrepid Miss Haydon, 1983; A Reputation Dies, 1984; A Fatal Assignation, 1987; Masquerade of Vengeance, 1989. Add: 42 Cannonbury Ave., Pinner, Middx. HA5 1TS, England.

LEYSER, Karl (Joseph). British, b. 1920. History. Chichele Professor of Medieval History, Oxford Univ., and Fellow of All Souls College, Oxford, 1984–88 (Fellow of Magdalen Coll., Oxford, 1948–84, Emeritus Fellow since 1984). Member of the Council, Max-Planck-Inst. für Geschichte, Gottingen, since 1978. *Publs:* Rule and Conflict in an Early Medieval Society, Ottonian Saxony, 1979; Medieval Germany and Its Neighbors, 1982. Add: Manor House, Islip, Oxford, England.

LEYTON, Sophie. *See* WALSH, Sheila.

L'HEUREUX, John (Clarke). American, b. 1934. Novels/Short stories, Poetry. Prof. of English, Stanford Univ., Calif., since 1973; Contrib. Ed., The Atlantic, Boston, since 1970. Entered the Soc. of Jesus,

1954; ordained a priest, 1966; requested laicization, 1970. *Publs:* Quick as Dandelions: Poems, 1964; Rubrics for a Revolution, 1967; Picnic in Babylon: A Priest's Journal, 1967; One Eye and a Measuring Rod: Poems, 1968; No Place for Hiding: Poems, 1971; Tight White Collar (novel), 1972; The Clang Birds (novel), 1972; Family Affairs (short stories), 1974; Jessica Fayer (novel), 1976; Desires (short stories), 1981; A Woman Run Mad (novel), 1988; Comedians (short stories), 1990. Add: Dept. of English, Stanford Univ., Stanford, Calif. 94305, U.S.A.

LI, Tien-yi. American, b. 1915. History, Literature, Biography. Mershon Prof. of Chinese Literature and History, Ohio State Univ., Columbus, 1969–85, now Emeritus (Chmn., Dept. of East Asian Languages and Literatures, 1971–75). Asst. Prof., 1951–59, Assoc. Prof., 1959–62, Dir. and Ed. of Far Eastern Publs., 1960–69, Prof., 1962–69, Yale Univ., New Haven, Conn.; Ed. and Secty., Tsing Hua Journal of Chinese Studies, 1955– 88. *Publs:* A Study of Thomas Hardy, 1937; (ed. with W.C. Liu and C.T. Chang) Modern English Readers, 1945, 1947; The United States and the Settlement of the Shantung Question, 1946; (ed.) The Dictatorship of the People's Democracy, 1951; Chinese Newspaper Manual, 1952, 1962; Woodrow Wilson's China Policy, 1913–1917, 1952; (ed. with Wu-chi Liu) Readings in Contemporary Chinese Literature, 6 vols., 1953– 1958, rev. ed. 1964–1968; (ed.) Selected Readings in Chinese Communist Literature, 1954, 1967; (ed.) Ku-chin hsiao-shuo, 2 vols., 1958; (ed.) Ching-shih t'ung-yen, 2 vols., 1958; (ed.) Hsing-shih heng-yen, 3 vols., 1959; (ed.) Erh-k'o P'o-an Ching-ch'i, 2 vols., 1960, 1980; (ed.) The Selected Works of George A. Kennedy, 1964; (ed.) On the People's Democratic Dictatorship, 1965; (ed.) P'o-an ching-ch'i, 2 vols., 1967; Chinese Fiction: A Bibliography of Books and Articles in Chinese and English, 1968; The History of Chinese Literature: A Selected Bibliography, 1969; Chinese Historical Literature, 1977. Add: East Asian Languages and Literatures Dept., Ohio State Univ., Columbus, Ohio 43210, U.S.A.

LICHTBLAU, Myron I. American, b. 1925. Literature. Prof. of Spanish, Syracuse Univ., N.Y. since 1968 (Asst. Prof., 1959–63; Assoc. Prof., 1963–68; Chmn., Dept. of Romance Languages, 1968–74; Chmn., Dept. of Foreign Languages and Literature 1986–88). Teacher of Spanish, NYC secondary schs., 1948–57; Instr. of Spanish, Indiana Univ., Bloomington, 1957–59. *Publs:* The Argentine Novel in the Nineteenth Century, 1959; (ed.) Las dos vidas del pobre Napoleon, by Manuel Galvez, 1963; El arte estilítico de Eduardo Mallea, 1967; Manuel Galvez, 1972; A Practical Reference Guide to Reading Spanish, 1977; (ed.) Manuel Pacho, by E. Calderón, 1980; (trans.) History of an Argentine Passion by Eduardo Mallea, 1983; (ed.) Mallea ante la critica, 1985; (ed.) La emigración y el exilio en la literatura hispánica del siglo veinte, 1988; Raguela y la creatividad linguistica, 1989. Add: Dept. of Foreign Languages and Literature, Syracuse Univ., Syracuse, N.Y. 13210, U.S.A.

LICHTENBERG, Jacqueline. American, b. 1942. Science fiction/Fantasy. Policy Advisor, Star Trek Welcommittee. Former Chmn., Science Fiction Writers of America Speakers Bureau. *Publs:* House of Zeor, 1974, 3rd ed. 1981; (with S. Marshak and J. Winston) Star Trek Lives!, 1975; Unto Zeor, Forever, 1978, 1980; (with J. Lorrah) First Channel, 1980, 1981; Mahogany Trinrose, 1981, 1982; Molt Brother, 1982; (with J. Lorrah) Channel's Destiny, 1982, Ren Sime, 1984; City of a Million Legends, 1985; Dushau, 1985; Farfetch, 1985; Outreach, 1986; (with Jean Lorrah) Zelerod's Doom, 1986; Those of My Blood, 1988. Add: 8 Fox Lane, Spring Valley, N.Y. 10977, U.S.A.

LICHTENBERG, Philip. American, b. 1926. Human relations, Psychiatry, Psychology. Prof. Bryn Mawr Coll., Pa., since 1968 (Assoc. Prof., 1961–68). Research Fellow in Clinical Psychology, Harvard Univ., Cambridge, Mass., 1951–52; Research Asst. Prof., New York Univ., NYC, 1952–54; Research Psychologist, Michael Reese Hosp., Chicago, 1954–57; Research Psychologist, New York State Mental Health Research Unit, Syracuse, 1957–61. *Publs:* (with R. Kohrman and H. MacGregor) Motivation for Child Psychiatry Treatment, 1960; Psychoanalysis: Radical and Conservative, 1969; (with D.G. Norton) Cognitive and Mental Development in the First Five Years of Life, 1970; Lectures in Psychoanalysis for Social Workers, 1978; Getting Even: The Equalizing Law of Relationships, 1988. Add: 25 Lowry's Lane, Rosemont, Pa. 19010, U.S.A.

LICHTENSTADTER, Ilse. American, b. 1907. Literature, Sociology, Theology/Religion. Emeritus Lectr. on Arabic, Harvard Univ., Cambridge, Mass., since 1974 (Lectr., 1960–74). General Ed., Library of Classical Arabic Literature, NYC, since 1972. Specialist in Semitic Languages, Oxford Univ. Press, 1935–48; Library Cataloguer, Jewish Theological Seminary, NYC, 1938–45; Asst. Prof., 1942–44, Assoc. Prof.,

1944–45, and Prof. of Arabic Language and Literature and of Classical and Contemporary Islam, 1945–52, Asia Inst., NYC; Lectr. in Contemporary Islam, New York Univ., NYC, 1952–60; Lectr. in History of Islam, Rutgers Univ., New Brunswick, N.J., 1959–60. *Publs:* Women in the Ayyam al-Arab, 1935; (ed.) The Kitab al-Muhabbar, 1942; Islam and the Modern Age, 1958; Introduction to Classical Arabic Literature, 1974. Add: 14 Concord Ave., Cambridge, Mass. 02138, U.S.A.

LICKLIDER, Roy E. American, b. 1941. International relations/Current affairs. Assoc. Prof. of Political Science, Rutgers Univ., New Brunswick, N.J., since 1972 (Asst. Prof., 1968–72). Asst. Prof. of Political Science, Tougaloo Coll., Mississippi, 1967–68; Program Officer, Exxon Education Foundn., 1977–78. *Publs:* The Private Nuclear Strategists, 1974; Political Power and the Arab Oil Weapon: The Experience of Five Industrial Nations, 1988. Add: Dept. of Political Science, Rutgers Univ., New Brunswick, N.J. 08903, U.S.A.

LIDDELL, (John) Robert. British, b. 1908. Novels/Short stories, Literature, Travel, Translations. Sr. Asst., Dept. of Western Manuscripts, Bodleian Library, Oxford, 1933–38; Lectr., Univ. of Helsingfors, Finland, 1939; and Farouk I Univ., Alexandria, 1941–46; Lectr., 1946–51, and Asst. Prof., 1951–52, Fuad I Univ., Cairo; Head of English Dept., Athens Univ., 1963–68. *Publs:* The Almond Tree, 1938; Kind Relations (in U.S. as Take This Child), 1939; The Gantillons, 1940; Watering Place, (stories), 1945; A Treatise on the Novel, 1947; The Last Enchantments, 1948; Unreal City, 1952; Some Principles of Fiction, 1953; Aegean Greece, 1954; The Novels of Ivy Compton-Burnett, 1955; Byzantium and Istanbul, 1956; The Morea, 1958; The Rivers of Babylon, 1959; (trans.) Demetrios Sicilianos: Old and New Athens, 1960; The Novels of Jane Austen, 1963; Mainland Greece, 1965; An Object for a Walk, 1966; The Deep End, 1968; Stepsons, 1969; Cavafy: A Critical Biography, 1974; The Novels of George Eliot, 1977; Elizabeth and Ivy (memoir), 1986; The Aunts, 1987. Add: c/o Barclays Bank, High St., Oxford, England.

LIDDLE, Peter (Hammond). British, b. 1934. History. Keeper, The Liddle Collection, Univ. of Leeds, since 1988. History Teacher, Havelock Sch., Sunderland, 1957; Head, History Dept., Gateacre Comprehensive Sch., Liverpool, 1958–67; Lectr., Notre Dame Coll. of Education, 1967. Lectr., 1967–70, and Sr. Lectr. in History, 1970–87, Sunderland Polytechnic. Chmn., Sunderland Industrial Archaeological Soc., 1969. Vice-Pres., British Audio-Visual Trust. *Publs:* Men of Gallipoli, 1976; World War One: Personal Experience Material for Use in Schools, 1977; Testimony of War 1914–18, 1979; Sailor's War 1914–18, 1985; Gallipoli: Pens, Pencils and Cameras at War, 1985; 1916: Aspects of Conflict, 1985; (ed. and contr.) Home Fires and Foreign Fields, 1985; The Airman's War 1914–18, 1987; The Soldier's War 1914–18, 1988; Voices of War, 1988. Add: Edward Boyle Library, Univ. of Leeds, Leeds LS2 9JT, England.

LIDDY, James. American, b. 1934. Poetry, Literature. Prof. of English, Univ. of Wisconsin, Milwaukee, since 1981 (joined faculty 1976). Staff member, San Francisco State Coll., 1967–69, State Univ. of New York at Binghamton, 1969, Denison Univ., Ohio, 1971–72, Univ. of Wisconsin, Parkside, 1972–73, and University Coll., Galway, 1973–74. *Publs:* A Life of Stephen Dedalus, 1959; A Munster Song of Love and War, 1960; Esau My Kingdom, 1962; In a Blue Smoke, 1964; Blue Mountain, 1968; Patrick Kavanagh, 1973; Baudelaire's Bar Flowers, 1975; Corca Bascinn, 1977; Comyn's Lay, 1979; Chamber Pot Music, 1982; Young Men Go Walking Out (novel), 1986; A White Thought in a White Shade: New and Selected Poems, 1987. Add: 2637 N. Cramer 26, Milwaukee, Wisc. 53211, U.S.A. or Coolgreany, Gorey, Co. Wexford, Ireland.

LIDZ, Theodore. American, b. 1910. Psychiatry, Psychology. Sterling Prof. Emeritus, Yale Univ., New Haven, since 1978 (Prof. of Psychiatry, Yale Univ. Sch. of Medicine, 1951–78). Career Investigator, National Inst. of Mental Health, 1961–78. *Publs:* The Family and Human Adaptation, 1963; (with S. Fleck and A. Cornelison) Schizophrenia and the Family, 1965, rev. ed., with S. Fleck, 1985; The Person, 1968, 1977; (ed. with M. Edelson) Training Tomorrow's Psychiatrist, 1970; The Origin and Treatment of Schizophrenic Disorders, 1973; Hamlet's Enemy, 1975; (with Ruth W. Lidz) Oedipus in the Stone Age, 1989. Add: Dept. of Psychiatry, Yale Univ. Sch. of Medicine, 25 Park St., New Haven, Conn. 06519, U.S.A.

LIEBER, Robert J. American, b. 1941. International relations/Current affairs. Prof. of Govt., Georgetown Univ., Washington, D.C., since 1982. Teaching Fellow, Dept. of Govt., Harvard Univ., Cambridge, Mass., 1966–68; Asst. Prof., 1968–72, Assoc. Prof., 1972–77, Prof. of Political Science, 1977–81, and Chmn. of Dept., 1975–76, 1977–80, Univ. of California,

Davis. *Publs:* British Politics and European Unity: Parties, Elites, and Pressure Groups, 1970; Theory and World Politics, 1972; Oil and the Middle East War: Europe in the Energy Crisis, 1976; (co-author) Contemporary Politics: Europe, 1976; (ed.) Eagle Entangled: U.S. Foreign Policy in a Complex World, 1979; (ed.) Eagle Defiant: U.S. Foreign Policy in the 1980's, 1983; The Oil Decade, 1983; (ed.) Eagle Resurgent? The Reagan Era in American Foreign Policy, 1987; No Common Power: Understanding International Relations, 1988. Add: Dept. of Govt., Georgetown Univ., Washington, D.C. 20057, U.S.A.

LIEBERMAN, Herbert. American, b. 1933. Novels/Short stories, Plays/Screenplays. Managing Ed., Reader's Digest Condensed Books, since 1977 (Sr. Ed., 1969–77). With New York Times, 1959–61, Macmillan Co. Publrs., 1961–63, and American Book Co., 1963–67. *Publs:* Matty and the Moron and Madonna (play), 1965; The Adventures of Dolphin Green, 1967; Crawlspace, 1971; The Eighth Square, 1973; Brilliant Kids, 1975; City of the Dead, 1976; The Climate of Hell, 1978; Night Call From a Distant Time Zone, 1982; Nightbloom, 1984; The Green Train, 1986; Shadow Dancers, 1989. Add: c/o Georges Borchardt Inc., 136 E. 57th St., New York, N.Y. 10017, U.S.A.

LIEBERMAN, Laurence (James). American, b. 1935. Poetry, Literature. Prof. of English, Univ. of Illinois, Urbana, since 1970 (Assoc. Prof. of English, 1968–70); Poetry Ed., Univ. of Illinois Press, Urbana, since 1971. Former Poetry Ed., Orange County Illustrated, and Orange County Sun, Calif.; taught at Orange Coast Coll., Costa Mesa, Calif., 1960–64, and Coll. of the Virgin Islands, St. Thomas, 1964–68. *Publs:* The Unblinding: Poems, 1968; (ed.) The Achievement of James Dickey: A Comprehensive Selection of His Poems with a Critical Introduction, 1968; The Osprey Suicides (poetry), 1973; Unassigned Frequencies: American Poetry in Review 1964–77, 1977; God's Measurements (poetry), 1980; Eros at the World Kite Pageant: Poems 1979–82, 1983; The Mural of Wakeful Sleep (poetry), 1985; The Creole Mephistopheles (poetry), 1989. Add: Dept. of English, 608 S. Wright St., Univ. of Illinois, Urbana, Ill. 61801, U.S.A.

LIEBHAFSKY, Herbert Hugo. American, b. 1919. Economics, Politics/Government. Prof. of Economics, Univ. of Texas, Austin, retired (Asst. Prof., 1956–58; Assoc. Prof., 1958–62). Economist, U.S. Dept. of State, Washington, D.C., 1949–53. *Publs:* The Nature of Price Theory, rev. ed. 1968; Hakekat teori harga, 1970; American Government and Business, 1971. Add: Dept. of Economics, University of Texas, Austin, Tex. 78712, U.S.A.

LIETAER, B(ernard) A. Belgian, b. 1942. Economics, Money/Finance. Independent Consultant, Bernard Lietaer Mgmt., since 1972. Sr. Consultant, Cresap, McCormick & Paget, Inc., NYC, 1969–72. *Publs:* Financial Management of Foreign Exchange, 1971; Europe and Latin America and Multinationals, 1979. Add: c/o Saxon House, Gower House, Croft Rd., Aldershot GU11 3HR, England.

LIEU, Hou-Shun. Chinese, b. 1921. Economics. Prof. and Area Chmn. of Economics, State Univ. of New York at Farmingdale, since 1967; Member of Bd. since 1968, and Chmn. since 1980, Suffolk County, N.Y. Public Employment Relations Bd. Contrib. Ed., The China Economist; Editorial Adviser, Soochow Journal of Literature and Social Studies. Section Head, Economic Analyst, Asst. Div. Chief, Div. Chief, and Economist, Bank of China, 1946–67; Assoc. Prof. of Economics, Taiwan Provincial Coll. of Law and Commerce, 1956–57; Assoc. Prof., then Prof. of Economics, Soochow Univ. Law Sch. at Taipei, 1957–59. Secty., Cttee. A, Economic Stabilization Bd., Taiwan, 1956–57; Alternate Member, Allocations Cttee., Council for U.S. Aid, Taiwan, 1956–57; Member, Southeast Asia Trade Promotion Cttee., Taiwan, 1958–59. Ed., Bi-Monthly Economic Review, 1953–59, and The Commercial Bulletin, 1957; Member, Editorial Bd., Foreign Trade Monthly, 1956–60. *Publs:* The Concept of Economic Homeostasis, 1956; A Draft Plan for an Asian Payments Union and an Asian Development Bank, 1959; International and Inter-Regional Economics, 1960; The Atom—Man—The Universe, 1972; Some Aspects of the Multinational Corporations, 1973; Essays on Linguistics, 1974, 1980; A General Study of the Multinational Corporation, 1975, 4th ed. 1987, Learning Languages by Playing Games, 1979, 1981; Pleasures of Reading and Writing, 1979; The Genesis of Criminology, 1987; Words and Legends, 1987. Add: 28 Marshmallow Dr., Commack, N.Y. 11725, U.S.A.

LIFSHIN, Lyn. American, b. 1948. Poetry. Dir., Albany Public Library Poetry Workshop, New York. English Instr., State Univ. of New York, Albany, 1968; Writing Consultant, New York State Mental Health Dept., 1969, and Empire State Coll., N.Y., 1973; Poet-in-Residence,

Mansfield State Coll., Pa., 1974. *Publs:* Why Is the House Dissolving?, 1968; Black Apples, 1970, 1973; Leaves and Night Things, 1971; Femina Two, 1972; Moving By Touch, 1972; Merchurochrome Sun Poems, 1972; Tentacles, Leaves, 1972; Love Poems, 1972; Museum, 1974; Forty Days, Apple Nights, 1974; The Croton, 1974; Shaker Poems, 1974; The Old House, 1974; Wild Flowers Smoke, 1974; Green Bandages, 1974; All The Women Poets, 1974; Audley End Poems, 1974; Upstate Madonna, 1975; Some Madonna Poems, 1976; Leaning Sout, 1976; Plymouth Women, 1976; North, 1976; (ed.) Tangled Vines: A Collection of Mother and Daughter Poems, 1978; Glass, 1978; Paper Apples, 1978; Offered by Owner, 1979; Crazy Arms, 1979; 35 Sundays, 1980; Colors of Cooper Black, 1981; (ed.) Ariadne's Thread, 1982; Hotel Lifshin, 1982; Mad Girl Poems, 1982; Blue Dust New Mexico, 1982; Reading Lips, 1982; Madonna Who Shifts for Herself, 1982; Want Ads, 1982; In the Dark with Just One Star, 1982; Kiss the Skin Off (winner of Jack Kerouac Award), 1985; Naked Charm, 1984; Blue Horses Nuzzle Thursday, 1985; Raw Opals, 1987; Many More Madonnas, 1988; Red Hair and the Jesuit, 1988; Unsealed Lips, 1989; Rubbed Silk, 1989; Film on Me: Not Made of Glass, 1989. Add: 2142 Appletree Lane, Niskayuna, N.Y. 12307, U.S.A.

LIFTON, Betty Jean. American, b. 1926. Children's fiction, Plays/Screenplays, Autobiography/Memoirs/Personal. *Publs:* Joji and the Dragon, 1957; Mogo the Mynah, 1958; Joji and the Fog, 1959; Kap the Kappa, 1960, play 1974; The Dwarf Pine Tree, 1963; Joji and the Amanojaku, 1965; The Cock and the Ghost Cat, 1965; The Rice-Cake Rabbit, 1966; The Many Lives of Chio and Goro, 1966; Taka-Chan and I: Dog's Journey to Japan, 1967; Kap and the Wicked Monkey, 1968; The Secret Seller, 1968; The One-Legged Ghost, 1968; A Dog's Guide to Tokyo, 1969; Return to Hiroshima, 1970; The Silver Crane, 1971; The Mud Snail Son, 1971; Good Night, Orange Monster, 1972; (with Thomas C. Fox) Children of Vietnam, 1972; (ed.) Contemporary Children's Theater, 1974; Twice Born: Memoirs of an Adopted Daughter, 1975; Jaguar, My Twin, 1976; Lost and Found: The Adoption Experience, 1979; I'm Still Me, 1981; A Place Called Hiroshima, 1985; The King of Children: A Biography of Janusz Korczak, 1988. Add: 300 Central Park W., New York, N.Y. 10024, U.S.A.

LIFTON, Robert Jay. American, b. 1926. Politics/Government, Psychiatry, Psychology, Essays. Member of Faculty, Washington Sch. of Psychiatry, Hong Kong and Washington, D.C., 1954–55; Research Psychiatrist, Walker Reed Army Inst. of Research, 1956; Research Assoc. in Psychiatry, Massachusetts Gen. Hosp., and Assoc. in East Asian Studies, Harvard Univ., Cambridge, 1956–61; Candidate, Boston Psychoanalytic Inst., 1957–60; Research Assoc. in Psychiatry, Tokyo Univ., 1960–61; Assoc. Prof. 1961–67, and Foundations' Fund Research Prof. of Psychiatry, 1967–84, Yale Univ., New Haven, Conn. Consultant, Behavioral Sciences Study Section, National Inst. of Mental Health, 1962–64; Consultant, New York Bar Assn. Cttee. on the Invasion of Privacy, 1963–64; Consultant to Arnold and Porter, concerning 1972 Buffalo Flood Creek disaster, 1973–74. *Publs:* Thought Reform and the Psychology of Totalism: A Study of Brainwashing in China, 1961; (ed.) The Woman in America, 1965; Death in Life: Survivors of Hiroshima, 1968; Revolutionary Immortality: Mao Tse-Tung and the Chinese Cultural Revolution, 1968; History and Human Survival: Essays on the Young and Old, Survivors and the Dead, Peace and War, and on Contemporary Psychohistory, 1970; Boundaries: Psychological man in Revolution, 1970; (ed.) America and the Asian Revolutions, 1970; (ed. with R.A. Falk and G. Kolko) Crimes of War, 1971; Home From the War: Vietnam Veterans—Neither Victims Nor Executioners, 1973, 1974; (with E. Olson) Living and Dying, 1974; (ed. with Eric Olson) Explorations in Psychohistory: The Wellfleet Papers, 1975; The Life of the Self: Towards a New Psychology, 1976; The Broken Connection: On Death and the Continuity of Life, 1979; (with Shuichi Kato and Michael Reich) Six Lives/Six Deaths: Portraits from Modern Japan, 1979; (with Richard A. Falk) Indefensible Weapons: The Political and Psychological Case Against Nuclearism, 1982; (ed. with Eric Chivian, Sally Chivian and John Mack) Last Aid: Medical Dimensions of Nuclear War, 1982; The Nazi Doctors: Medical Killing and the Psychology of Genocide, 1986; The Future of Immortality, 1987. Add: c/o Psychology Dept., John Jay Coll., 444 W. 56th St., New York, N.Y. 10019, U.S.A.

LIFTON, Walter. American, b. 1918. Education, Human relations. Emeritus Prof. of Education, State Univ. of New York, Albany (joined faculty, 1970). Research Psychologist, Coll. of Engineering, New York Univ., 1948–50; Assoc. Prof. of Education, Coll. of Education, Univ. of Illinois, 1950–59; Dir., Guidance Publs. and Services Dept., Science Research Assocs., Inc., Chicago, 1959–64; Interim Dir., Action for a Better Community, Rochester, N.Y., 1964–65; Coordinator of Pupil Personnel Services, City Sch. District, Rochester, N.Y., 1964–70; Pres., Assn. for Specialists in Group Work, 1980–81. *Publs:* (ed.) Keys to Vocational Decisions, 1964; Working with Groups: Group Process and Individual Growth, 1965; (ed.) Education for Tomorrow: The Role of Media, Career Development, and Society, 1970; Groups: Facilitating Individual Growth and Societal Change, 1972. Add: 222 Heritage Rd., Guilderland, N.Y. 12084, U.S.A.

LIGGERO, John (Gerold). American, b. 1921. Education. Private educational counselor and freelance writer. Teacher, 1951–56, High Sch. Guidance Counselor, 1956–73, and High Sch. Guidance Dir., 1973–76, Glen Cove Bd. of Education, New York. *Publs:* A Successful Approach to High School Counseling, 1968. Add: 67 Highwood Rd., Oyster Bay, N.Y. 11771, U.S.A.

LIGGETT, Thomas. American, b. 1918. Children's fiction. Publr., World Peace News, NYC, since 1970. Ed. and Publr., Perris Progress, Calif., 1947–49; City Ed., Daily Midway Driller, Taft, Calif., 1949–52; County News Ed. and Sportswriter, Bakersfield Californian, 1952–57; Ed. and Publr., California Crossroads mag., 1959–66; Information Dir., Leonard Wood Memorial for Medical Research, NYC, 1967–70. *Publs:* Pigeon, Fly Home!, 1956; The Hollow, 1958. Add: 777 United Nations Plaza, 11th Floor, New York, N.Y. 10017, U.S.A.

LILLINGTON, Kenneth (James). British, b. 1916. Novels/Short stories, Children's fiction, Plays/Screenplays, Literature. Lectr. in English Literature, Brooklands Technical Coll., Weybridge, Surrey, now retired. *Publs:* The Devil's Grandson, 1954; Soapy and the Pharoah's Curse, 1957; Conjuror's Alibi, 1960; The Secret Arrow, 1960; Blue Murder, 1960; A Man Called Hughes, 1962; My Proud Beauty, 1963; First (and Second) Book of Classroom Plays, 1967–68; Fourth (and Seventh) Windmill Book of One-Act Plays, 1967–72; Cantaloup Crescent, 1970; Olaf and the Ogre, 1972; (ed.) Nine Lives, 1977; For Better for Worse, 1979; Young Man of Morning, 1979; What Beckoning Ghost, 1983; Selkie, 1985; Full Moon, 1986; An Ash-Blonde Witch, 1987; The Hallowee'n Cat, 1987; Gabrielle, 1988; Jonah's Mirror, 1988; Josephine, 1989. Add: c/o Faber and Faber, 3 Queen Sq., London WC1N 3AU, England.

LIMA, Robert (F. Jr.). American, b. 1935. Plays, Poetry, Literature, Translations. Prof. of Spanish and Comparative Literature, Pennsylvania State Univ., University Park, since 1965 (Chmn., Dept. of Comparative Literature, 1970–75). Lectr. in Romance Literatures, Hunter Coll., City Univ. of New York, 1962–65; Poet-in-Residence, Univ. de San Marcos, Peru; Visiting Prof., Univ. Católica, Peru, 1976–77; Sr. Fulbright Fellow, 1976–77. Editorial Assoc., Modern Intnl. Drama, 1967–81. *Publs:* Episode in Sicily (play), 1959; (co-ed.) Seventh Street Anthology: Poems of "Les Deux Magots", 1961; (co-ed.) Readers Encyclopedia of American Literature, rev. ed. 1962; The Theatre of Garcia Lorca, 1963; (ed. and trans.) Borges the Labyrinth Maker, 1965; (ed. and trans.) Valle-Inclán: Autobiography, Aesthetics, Aphorisms, 1966; Ramon del Valle-Inclán, 1972; An Annotated Bibliography of Ramon del Valle-Inclán, 1972; (ed.) Surrealism: A Celebration, 1975; (co-author) Poems of Exile and Alienation, 1976; Fathoms (poetry), 1981; (co-author) Dos Ensayos Sobre Teatro Español de Los Veinte, 1984; The Olde Ground (poetry), 1985; Valle-Inclán: The Theatre of His Life, 1988; (ed.) Savage Acts: Three Plays by Valle-Inclán, 1988 . Add: N 346 Burrowes Bldg., Pennsylvania State Univ., University Park, Pa., 16802, U.S.A.

LIMBACHER, James L. American, b. 1926. Film, Librarianship, Music. Audiovisual Librarian, Dearborn Dept. of Libraries, Mich., 1955–83; Instr., Speech and Theatre, Wayne State Univ., Detroit, Mich. *Publs:* Four Aspects of the Film, 1966; Using Films, 1967; Feature Films, 8 eds.; A Reference Guide to Audiovisual Information, 1972; The Song List, 1973; Haven't I Seen You Somewhere Before?, 1978; Keeping Score, 1980; Sexuality in World Cinema, 1983; Film and TV Music, 1989. Add: Morley Manor, Apt. 1201, 21800 Morley Ave., Dearborn, Mich. 48124, U.S.A.

LIMBURG, Peter R. American, b. 1929. Marine Science/Oceanography, Natural history. Special Ed., Harper Encyclopedia of Science, 1960–61; Sr. Technology Ed., The New Book of Knowledge, 1961–66; Ed., School Dept., Harcourt, Brace & World, publrs., 1966–69; Co-ordinating Ed., Colliers's Encyclopedia, 1969–70, all NYC. Pres., Forum of Writers for Young People, 1975–76, 1980–81. *Publs:* The First Book of Engines, 1969; The Story of Corn, 1971: What's in the Names of Fruit, 1972; What's in the Names of Antique Weapons, 1973; (with James B. Sweeney) Vessels for Underwater Exploration: A Pictorial History, 1973; Watch Out, It's Poison Ivy!, 1973; What's in the Names of Flowers, 1974; (with James B. Sweeney) 102 Questions and Answers about the Sea, 1975;

What's in the Name of Birds, 1975; Chickens, Chickens, Chickens, 1975; What's in the Names of Stars and Constellations, 1976; Poisonous Plants, 1976; What's in the Names of Wild Animals, 1977; Oceanographic Institutions, 1979; The Story of Your Heart, 1979; Farming the Waters, 1980; Stories Behind Words, 1986. Add: Banksville Rd., Bedford, N.Y. 10506, U.S.A.

LINCOLN, C(harles) Eric. American, b. 1924. Race relations, Sociology, Novels, Biography. Prof. of Religion and Culture, Duke Univ., Durham, N.C., since 1976. Prof., Sociology of Religion, Union Theological Seminary, NYC, 1966–73; Founding Pres., Black Academy of Arts and Letters. Prof. of Sociology and Religion, and Chmn. of the Dept. of Religious Studies, Fisk Univ., Nashville, Tenn., 1973–76; Adjunct Prof. of Religion, Vanderbilt Univ., Nashville, 1973–76. *Publs:* The Black Muslims in 1961, 1961, 1973; My Face is Black, 1964; The Negro Pilgrimage in America, 1967; Sounds of the Struggle, 1967; Is Anybody Listening, 1968; A Profile of Martin Luther King, 1969, 1985; The Coming of Age of the Black Americans, 1969; The New Blacks and the Black Estate, 1970; (ed.) The Black Experience in Religion, 1973; The Black Church since Frazier, 1974; (with Langston Hughes and Milton Metzer) Pictorial History of Black Americans, 1983; Race, Religion and Its Continuing American Dilemma, 1984; The Avenue, Clayton City (novel), 1988. Add: Dept. of Religion, Duke Univ., Durham, N.C. 27706, U.S.A.

LINCOLN, Geoffrey. *See* **MORTIMER,** John.

LINCOLN, Les. *See* **CHARLES,** Theresa.

LIND, Levi Robert. American, b. 1906. Literature, Translations. Univ. Distinguished Prof. of Classics, Univ. of Kansas, Lawrence, since 1940. *Publs:* Medieval Latin Studies: Their Nature and Possibilities, 1941; The Vita Sancti Malchi of Reginald of Canterbury, 1942; (trans.) The Epitome of Andreas Vesalius, 1949; (trans.) Lyric Poetry of the Italian Renaissance, 1954; (trans.) Ten Greek Plays in Contemporary Translations, 1957; (trans.) Latin Poetry in Verse Translation, 1957; (ed. and trans.) Ecclesiale by Alexander of Villa Dei, 1958; (trans.) Berengario da Carpi, A Short Introduction to Anatomy, 1959; (trans.) Vergil's Aeneid, 1963; (trans.) Aldrovandi on Chickens: The Ornithology of Ulisse Aldrovandi (1600), 1963; Epitaph for Poets and Other Poems, 1966; (ed.) Problemata Varia Anatomica: The University of Bologna MS 1165, 1968; Twentieth Century Italian Poetry: A Bilingual Anthology, 1974; (trans.) Johann Wolfgang von Goethe, Roman Elegies and Venetian Epigrams, 1974; (trans.) Studies in Pre-Vesalian Anatomy, 1974; (trans.) Ovid, Tristia, 1975; (trans.) André Chénier, Elegies and Camille, 1978; Gabriele Zerbi, Gerontocomia, and Maximianus: Elegies, 1988. Add: 1714 Indiana St., Lawrence, Kans. 66044, U.S.A.

LINDARS, Barnabas. *See* **LINDARS,** Frederick Chevallier.

LINDARS, Frederick C(hevallier). Also writes as Barnabas Lindars. British, b. 1923. Theology/Religion. Rylands Prof. of Biblical Criticism and Exegesis, Manchester Univ., 1978–90. Anglican priest, since 1948; Member of Soc. of St. Francis, Anglican Franciscan Friars, since 1952. Curate, St. Luke's Pallion, Sunderland, 1948–52; Asst. Lectr. in Divinity, 1961–66, Lectr., 1966–78, Cambridge Univ.; Fellow and Dean, Jesus Coll., Cambridge, 1976–78. *Publs:* New Testament Apologetic, 1961; (ed. with P.R. Ackroyd) Words and Meanings, 1968; Behind the Fourth Gospel, 1971; The Gospel of John, 1972; (ed. with S.S. Smalley) Christ and Spirit in the New Testament, 1973; (with B. Rigaux) Témoignage de l'évangile de Jean, 1974; Jesus Son of Man, 1983; The Theology of Hebrews, 1989. Add: The Friary, Hilfield, Dorchester, DT2 7BE, England.

LINDBECK, (K.) Assar (E.). Swedish, b. 1930. Economics. Prof. of Intnl. Economics, and Dir. of Inst. for Intnl. Economic Studies, Univ. of Stockholm, since 1971 (Lectr., 1959–60, Reader, 1962–63, and Acting Prof. of Economics, 1963). Chmn., Selection Cttee. for the Nobel Prize in Economic Sciences, Swedish Council for Economic Planning; Member, Swedish Govt. Research Council, since 1969. Part-time Employee, 1953–54, and Member of Economic Secretariat, 1955–56, Treasury Dept., Stockholm; Rockefeller Foundn. Fellow at Yale Univ., New Haven, Conn., the Fed. Reserve Bd., Washington, D.C., and at the Univ. of Michigan, Ann Arbor, 1957–59; Prof. of Economics, Stockholm Sch. of Economics, 1964–71; Wesley Clair Mitchell Research Prof., Columbia Univ., NYC, 1968–69; Ford Rotating Research Prof., Univ. of California at Berkeley, 1969; Irving Fisher Visiting Prof., Yale Univ., 1976–77; Visiting scholar, Stanford Univ., 1977; and Simon Fraser Univ., 1980. Expert, Swedish Dept. of Domestic Affairs, 1964–66; Economic Adviser, Swedish Central Bank, 1964–68, 1971–73; Member of expert group on agriculture and

economic growth, 1964–65, expert group on fiscal policy, 1966–68, and expert group on non-inflationary growth, 1976–77, Org. for Economic Co-operation and Development; Consultant, World Bank, 1986–87. *Publs:* The "New" Theory of Credit Control in the United States: An Interpretation and Elaboration, 1959, 1962; A Study of Monetary Analysis, 1963; Monetary-Fiscal Analysis and General Equilibrium, 1967; (with Gulbrandsen) The Economics of the Agriculture Sector, 1971; The Political Economy of the New Left: An Outsider's View, 1971; Swedish Economic Policy, 1972; Inflation: Global, International and National Aspects, 1980. Add: Östermalmsgatan 50, S-11426 Stockholm, Sweden.

LINDBERGH, Anne Morrow. American, b. 1906. Environmental science/Ecology, Autobiography/Memoirs/Personal. Dir., Harcourt Brace Jovanovitch, NYC, since 1975. *Publs:* North to the Orient, 1935; Listen, the Wind, 1938; The Wave of the Future, 1940; The Steep Ascent, 1944; Gift from the Sea, 1955; The Unicorn, 1958; Dearly Beloved, 1963; Earth Shine, 1970; Bring Me a Unicorn, 1972; Hour of Gold, Hour of Lead, 1973; Locked Rooms and Open Doors, 1974; The Flower and the Nettle, 1976; War Within and Without, 1980. Add: c/o Harcourt Brace Jovanovich, 1250 Sixth Ave., San Diego, Calif. 92101, U.S.A.

LINDE, Shirley Motter. American. Medicine/Health. Pres., Pavilion Publishing Co., NYC; Ed., Feeling Better newsletter. *Publs:* (ed.) Radioactivity in Man, 1961; (ed.) Science and the Public, 1962; (ed.) Response of the Nervous System to Ionizing Radiation, 1962; The Big Ditch: Story of the Suez Canal, 1962; Total Rehabilitation of Epileptics, 1962; (ed.) Medical Science in the News, 1965; Heart Attacks That Aren't, 1966; Airline Stewardess Handbook, 1968; Modern Woman's Medical Dictionary, 1968; Cosmetic Surgery: What It Can Do For You, 1971; Emergency Family First Aid Guide, 1971; Sickle Cell: A Complete Guide to Prevention and Treatment, 1972; (with Arthur Michele) Orthotherapy (in U.K. as You Don't Have to Ache: A Guide to Orthotherapy), 1971; (with Howard G. Rapoport) The Complete Allergy Guide; The Sleep Book, 1974; (with Frank A. Finnerty) High Blood Pressure, 1974; (with Gideon Panter) Now That You've Had Your Baby, 1974; The Whole Health Catalogue, 1978; (with Robert Atkins) Dr. Atkins' Superenergy Diet, 1980; How to Beat a Bad Back, 1980; The Joy of Sleep, 1980; (with Robert Allen) Lifegain, 1981; 201 Medical Tests You Can Do at Home, 1984; Directory of Holistic Medicine and Alternate Health Care Services in the U.S., 1986; (with Robert Johnson) The Charleston Program, 1989; (with Peter Harri) How to Fight Insomnia, 1989. Add: 152 1st Ave. N., Tierra Verde, Fla. 33715, U.S.A.

LINDER, Robert D. American, b. 1934. Politics/Government, Theology/Religion. Prof. of History, Kansas State Univ., since 1973 (Asst. Prof., 1965–67; Assoc. Prof., 1967–73). *Publs:* The Political Ideas of Pierre Viret, 1964; (ed. with R.G. Clouse and R.V. Pierard) Protest and Politics: Christianity and Contemporary Affairs, 1968; (ed. with Robert M. Kingdon) Calvin and Calvinism: Sources of Democracy?, 1970; (ed.) God and Caesar: Case Studies in the Relationship of Christianity and the State, 1971; (ed. with Clouse and Pierard) The Cross and the Flag, 1972; (with Pierard) Politics: A Case for Christian Action, 1973; (ed. with others) Eerdman's Handbook to the History of Christianity, 1977; (with Pierard) Twilight of the Saints: Biblical Christianity and Civil Religion in America, 1978; (with Pierard) Civil Religion and the Presidency, 1988. Add: Dept. of History, Kansas State Univ., Manhattan, Kans. 66506, U.S.A.

LINDGREN, Henry Clay. American, b. 1914. Psychology. Prof. Emeritus of Psychology, San Francisco State Univ., Calif., since 1984 (joined faculty, 1947). *Publs:* Educational Psychology in the Classroom, 1956, 7th ed. 1985; (with D. Byrne) Psychology, 1961, 4th ed. 1975; An Introduction to Social Psychology, 1969, 3rd ed. (with J.H. Harvey), 1981; (with L. Fisk) Survival Guide for Teachers, 1973; (with L. Fisk) Learning Centers, 1974; Children's Behavior, 1975; (with L.W. Fisk) Psychology of Personal Development, 1976; How to Live with Yourself and Like It, 1978; (with R.I. Watson) Psychology of the Child, 1979; Great Expectations: The Psychology of Money, 1980; Leadership, Authority, and Power, 1982. Add: 120 Lansdale Ave., San Francisco, Calif. 94127, U.S.A.

LINDHOLM, Richard W(adsworth). American, b. 1913. Economics, Money/Finance. Prof. of Finance, Univ. of Oregon, Eugene, since 1965 (Dean, Coll. of Business Admin., 1958–71, and Grad. Sch. of Mgmt., 1967–71). Fiscal Economist, Bd. of Govs., Federal Reserve System, Washington, D.C., 1950–51 and 1964–65. *Publs:* Introduction to Fiscal Policy, 1948; Public Finance and Fiscal Policy, 1948; (with J. Balles and J. Hunter) Principles of Money and Banking, 1955; (ed. and contrib.) Vietnam; First Five Years, 1959; (ed. and contrib.) Property Taxation:

U.S.A., 1967; Taxation of the Timber Industry, 1973; (ed. and contrib.) Property Taxation and the Finance of Education, 1974; Value Added Tax, 1976; Money Managements and Institutions, 1978; Financing and Managing State and Local Government, 1979; The Economics of VAT, 1980; A New Federal Tax System, 1984. Add: 2520 Fairmount Blvd., Eugene, Ore. 97403, U.S.A.

LINDSAY, Jack. Also writes as Richard Preston. Australian, b. 1900. Novels/Short stories, Art, History, Biography, Translations. Co-Ed., Vision, Sydney, 1923–24; Proprietor and Dir., Fanfrolico Press, London, 1927–30; Co-Ed., London Aphrodite, 1928–29; Ed., Poetry and the People, London, 1938–39; Ed., Anvil, London, 1947; Co-Ed., Arena, London, 1949–51. *Publs:* has written 76 works of fiction, plays, short story collections, volumes of verse, and books on history, art, and autobiography from 1923–1959—The Writing on the Wall: An Account of Pompeii in Its Last Days, 1960; The Roaring Twenties: Literary Life in Sydney, New South Wales, in the Years 1921–26, 1960; The Death of the Hero, 1960; The Revolt of the Sons, 1960; William Morris: Writer, 1961; All on the Never-Never: A Novel of the British Way of Life, 1961; Our Celtic Heritage, 1962; Fanfrolico and After, 1962; The Way the Ball Bounces, 1962; Daily Life in Roman Egypt, 1963; Masks and Faces, 1963; Nine Days Wonder: Wat Tyler, 1964; Choice of Times, 1964; The Clashing Rocks: A Study of Early Greek Religion and Culture, and the Origins of Drama, 1965; Leisure and Pleasure in Roman Egypt, 1965; Our Anglo-Saxon Heritage, 1965; Thunder Underground: A Story of Nero's Rome, 1965; J.M. W. Turner: His Life and Work: A Critical Biography, 1966; Our Roman Heritage, 1967; Meetings with Poets: Memories of Dylan Thomas, Edith Sitwell, Louis Aragon, Paul Eluard, Tristan Tzara, 1968; Men and Gods on the Roman Nile, 1968; The Ancient World: Manners and Morals, 1968; Cézanne: His Life and Art, 1969; The Origins of Alchemy in Graeco-Roman Egypt, 1970; Cleopatra, 1971; The Origins of Astrology, 1971; Gustave Courbet: His Life and Work, 1972; Death of a Spartan King, and two Other Stories of the Ancient World, 1974; The Normans and Their World, 1974; Helen of Troy: Woman and Goddess, 1974; Blast Power and Ballistics: Concepts of Force and Energy in the Ancient World, 1974; William Morris, 1975; The Troubadours and Their World, 1976; Hogarth: His Art and World, 1977; Decay and Renewal (essays), 1977; William Blake, 1978; The Monster City: Defoe's London 1688-1730, 1978; Thomas Gainsborough, 1981; The Crisis in Marxism, 1981; The Blood-Vote, 1985. Add: 56 Maids Causeway, Cambridge, England.

LINDSAY, John (Vliet). American, b. 1921. Politics/Government. Partner, law firm of Webster and Sheffield, NYC. Exec. Asst. to the U.S. Attorney Gen., 1955–57; Member for the 17th District of New York (Republican), U.S. House of Representatives, 86th-89th Congresses, 1959–65; Mayor of New York City, 1966–73. *Publs:* Journey into Politics, 1967; The City, 1970; The Edge, 1976. Add: c/o Norton, 500 Fifth Ave., New York, N.Y. 10110, U.S.A.

LINDSAY, Maurice. British, b. 1918. Short stories, Poetry, Architecture, Biography. Dir., 1967–83, and Consultant since 1983, Scottish Civic Trust; Hon. Secty.-Gen., Europa Nostra, since 1983. Drama Critic, Scottish Daily Mail, Edinburgh, 1946–47; Music Critic, Bulletin, Glasgow, 1946–60; freelance broadcaster, BBC, Glasgow, 1946–61; Prog. Controller, 1961–62, Production Controller, 1962–64, and Features Exec. and Sr. Interviewer, 1964–67, Border Television, Carlisle. *Publs:* The Advancing Day, 1940; Perhaps Tomorrow, 1941; Predicament, 1942; No Crown for Laughter, 1943; (ed.) Sailing Tomorrow's Seas, 1944; Poetry Scotland, vol. I-III and IV, 1945–53; (ed. with F. Urquhart) Modern Scottish Poetry: An Anthology of the Scottish Renaissance 1920–45, 1946; The Enemies of Love, 1946; No Scottish Twilight, 1947; (ed. with H.B. Cruickshank) Selected Poems by Sir Alexander Gray, 1948; Hurlygush, 1948; The Scottish Renaissance, 1949; At the Wood's Edge, 1950; Ode for St. Andrew's Night and Other Poems, 1951; The Lowlands of Scotland: Glasgow and the North, 1953, 1974; Robert Burns: The Man, His Work, The Legend, 1954, 3rd ed. 1980; Dunoon: The Gem of the Clyde Coast, 1954; The Lowlands of Scotland: Edinburgh and the South, 1956; (ed.) Selected Poems by Marion Angus, 1956; The Exiled Heart, 1957; (with D. Somervell) Killochan Castle, 1958; Clyde Waters, 1958; The Burns Encyclopedia, 1959, 3rd ed. 1980; Snow Warning, 1962; By Yon Bonnie Banks, 1962; John Davidson, 1962; One Later Day, 1964; The Discovery of Scotland, 1964; (ed. with E. Morgan and G. Bruce) Scottish Poetry, 1966–72; (consultant ed.) Voice of Our Kind, 1971; This Business of Living, 1971; Comings and Goings, 1971; The Eye Is Delighted: Some Romantic Travellers in Scotland, 1971; Portrait of Glasgow, 1972, 1980; Selected Poems 1942-72, 1973; (ed. with A. Scott and R. Watson) Scottish Poetry, 1974; Scotland: An Anthology, 1974; Robin Philipson, 1975; (ed.) Modern Scottish Poetry: An Anthology, 1976; A History of Scottish

Literature, 1977; Walking Without an Overcoat: Poems 1972–76, 1977; Collected Poems, 1979; Lowland Scottish Villages, 1979; Francis George Scott and the Scottish Renaissance, 1979; (ed.) As I Remember, 1979; (ed.) Scottish Comic Verse 1425-1980, 1980; A Net to Catch the Winds, 1981; (with Anthony F. Kersting) The Buildings of Edinburgh, 1981; Thank You for Having Me (autobiography), 1983; (with Dennis Hardley) Unknown Scotland, 1984; The Castles of Scotland, 1986; The French Mosquitoes Woman, 1987; Count All Men Mortal: The History of the Scottish Provident Institution, 1987; Victorian and Edwardian Glasgow, 1987; Requiem for a Sexual Athlete, 1988; Glasgow, 1989; Glasgow 1837, 1989; (ed. with Alexander Scott) The Comic Poems of William Tennant, 1989; (ed. with Joyce Lindsay) The Scottish Dog, 1989. Add: 7 Milton Hill, Milton, Dunbarton, Scotland.

LINDSAY, Rachel. Also writes as Roberta Leigh and Janey Scott. Historical/Romance/Gothic. *Publs:* (as Roberta Leigh) In Name Only, 1951; (as Roberta Leigh) Dark Inheritance, 1952; (as Roberta Leigh) The Vengeful Heart, 1952; The Widening Stream, 1952; (as Roberta Leigh) Beloved Ballerina, 1953; Alien Corn, 1954; (as Roberta Leigh) And Then Came Love, 1954; Healing Hands, 1955; Mask of Gold, 1956; (as Roberta Leigh) Pretence, 1956; Castle in the Trees, 1958; (as Roberta Leigh), Stacy, 1958; House of Lorraine, 1959; The Taming of Laura, 1959; (as Janey Scott) Memory of Love, 1959; Business Affair, 1960; (as Janey Scott) Melody of Love, 1960; (as Janey Scott) A Time to Love, rev. ed (as Rachel Lindsay) as Unwanted Wife, 1976; Heart of a Rose, 1961; Song in My Heart, 1961; (as Janey Scott) Sara Gay—Model Girl, Sara Gay in Mayfair, Sara Gay in New York, Sara Gay in Monte Carlo, 4 vols., 1961; Lesley Forrest, M.D., 1962; Moonlight and Magic, 1962; Design for Murder, 1964; No Business to Love, 1966; Love and Lucy Granger, 1967; Price of Love, 1967; (as Roberta Leigh) My Heart's a Dancer, 1970; Love and Dr. Forrest, 1971; The Latitude of Love, 1971; A Question of Marriage, 1972; Cage of Gold, 1973; Chateau in Provence, 1973; (as Roberta Leigh) Cinderella in Mink, 1973; Food for Love, 1974; (as Roberta Leigh) If Dreams Came True, 1974; (as Roberta Leigh) Shade of the Palms, 1974; Affair in Venice, 1975; Love in Disguise, 1975; Innocent Deception, 1975; Prince for Sale, 1975; (as Roberta Leigh) Heart of the Lion, 1975; (as Roberta Leigh) Man in a Million, 1975; (as Roberta Leigh) Temporary Wife, 1975; The Marquis Takes a Wife, 1976; Roman Affair, 1976; Secretary Wife, 1976; Tinsel Star, 1976; A Man to Tame, 1976; (as Roberta Leigh) Cupboard Love, 1976; (as Roberta Leigh) To Buy a Bride, 1976; (as Roberta Leigh) The Unwilling Bridegroom, 1976; (as Roberta Leigh) Man Without a Heart, 1976; Forbidden Love, 1977; Prescription for Love, 1977; (as Roberta Leigh) Girl for a Millionaire, 1977; (as Roberta Leigh) Too Young to Love, 1977; Rough Diamond Lover, 1978; An Affair to Forget, 1978; Forgotten Marriage, 1978; Brazilian Affair, 1978; (as Roberta Leigh) Facts of Love, 1978; (as Roberta Leigh) Night of Love, 1978; (as Roberta Leigh) The Savage Aristocrat, 1978; (as Roberta Leigh) Not a Marrying Man, 1978; (as Roberta Leigh) Love in Store, 1978; Man of Ice, 1980; (as Roberta Leigh) Love and No Marriage, 1980; (as Roberta Leigh; in Can. as Rachel Lindsay) Rent a Wife, 1980; (as Roberta Leigh) Wife for a Year, 1980, in Can. (as Rachel Lindsay), 1981; (as Roberta Leigh) Love Match, 1980; Untouched Wife, 1981; (as Roberta Leigh) Confirmed Bachelor, 1981; (as Roberta Leigh) Impossible Man to Love, 1987; (as Roberta Leigh) Too Bad to Be True, 1987; (as Roberta Leigh) Not Without Love, 1989; (as Roberta Leigh) No Man's Mistress, 1989. Add: c/o Mills and Boon Ltd., Eton House, 18-24 Paradise Rd., Richmond, Surrey TW9 1SR, England.

LINDSEY, Hal. American. Theology/Religion. *Publs:* The Late Great Planet Earth, 1973; There's a New World Coming, 1973; The Liberation of Planet Earth, 1974; Satan is Alive and Well on Planet Earth, 1974; The World's Final Hour, 1976; The Terminal Generation, 1977; The Events That Changed My Life, 1977; The Nineteen Eighties, 1981; The Promise, 1982; The Rapture, 1983; A Prophetical Walk Through the Holy Land, 1983; Combat Faith, 1986. Add: P.O. Box 4000, Palos Verdes, Calif. 90274, U.S.A.

LINDSEY, Johanna. American, b. 1952. Historical/Romance. *Publs:* Captive Bride, 1977; A Pirate's Love, 1978; Fires of Winter, 1980; Paradise Wild, 1981; Glorious Angel, 1982; So Speaks the Heart, 1983; Heart of Thunder, 1983; A Gentle Feuding, 1984; Brave the Wild Wind, 1984; Love Only Once, 1985; Tender Is the Storm, 1985; A Heart So Wild, 1986; When Love Awaits, 1986; Hearts Aflame, 1987; Secret Fire, 1987; Tender Rebel, 1988; Silver Angel, 1988; Defy Not the Heart, 1989. Add: c/o Avon Books, 105 Madison Ave., New York, N.Y. 10016, U.S.A.

LINE, David. *See* **DAVIDSON,** Lionel.

LINE, Maurice Bernard. British, b. 1928. Librarianship. Prof.

Assoc., Univ. of Sheffield, since 1977; Visiting Prof., Univ. of Loughborough, since 1986. Sub-Librarian, Univ. of Southampton, 1964–65; Deputy Librarian, Univ. of Newcastle upon Tyne, 1965–68; Librarian, Univ. of Bath, 1968–71; Librarian, National Central Library, London, 1971–73; Dir.-Gen., British Library Lending Div., 1974–85; Dir.-Gen., Science, Technology and Industry, British Library, 1985–88. *Publs:* Bibliography of Russian Fiction in English Translation to 1900 (excluding periodicals), 1963, 1972; The College Student and the Library, 1965; Library Surveys, 1967, 1982; (with K.P. Barr) Essays on Information and Libraries, 1975; (with J. Line) National Libraries, 1979, and National Libraries 2, 1987; (with S. Vickers) Universal Availability of Publications, 1983. Add: 10 Blackthorn Lane, Burn Bridge, Harrogate, N. Yorks, HG3 1NZ, England.

LING, Roger (John). British, b. 1942. Architecture, Art, Classics. Reader in Classical Art and Archaeology, Univ. of Manchester, since 1971. Lectr. in Classics, University Coll., Swansea, Wales, 1967–71; Faculty Member, British School at Rome, 1974–78, and 1981–85. *Publs:* The Greek World, 1976; (with T.C.B. Rasmussen) rev. ed. of A. Boethius: Etruscan and Early Roman Architecture, 1978; (with N. Davey) Wall Painting in Roman Britain, 1982; The Hellenistic World to the Coming of the Romans, 1984; Romano-British Wall Painting, 1985; Rev. ed. of D.E. Strong: Roman Art, 1988. Add: History of Art Dept., Univ. of Manchester, Manchester M13 9PL, England.

LINGARD, Joan (Amelia). British. Novels, Children's fiction, Plays/Screenplays. *Publs:* Liam's Daughter, 1963; The Prevailing Wind, 1964; The Tide Comes In, 1966; The Headmaster, 1968; The Lord on Our Side, 1970; The Twelfth Day of July, 1970; Across the Barricades, 1972; Into Exile, 1973; Frying as Usual, 1973; The Clearance, 1974; A Proper Place, 1974; Hostages to Fortune, 1975; The Resettling, 1975; The Pilgrimage, 1976; The Reunion, 1977; Snake Among the Sunflowers, 1977; The Gooseberry, 1978; The Second Flowering of Emily Mountjoy, 1979; The File on Fraulein Berg, 1980; Greenyards, 1981; Maggie, 3 vols., 1982; Strangers in the House, 1981; The Winter Visitor, 1983; Sisters by Rite, 1984; Reasonable Doubts, 1986; The Freedom Machine, 1986; The Guilty Party, 1987; Rags and Riches, 1988; The Women's House, 1989; Tug of War, 1989. Add: c/o David Higham Assoc., 5-8 Lower John St., London W1R 4HA, England.

LINGEMAN, Richard. American, b. 1931. History, Literature, Medicine/Health. Exec. Ed., The Nation, NYC, since 1978. Member. Bd. of Dirs., Small Town Inst., Ellensburg, Wash., since 1980. Exec. Ed., Monocle, NYC, 1960–66; Asst. Ed., New York Times Book Review, 1969–78. *Publs:* Drugs from A to Z: A Dictionary, 1969, 1974; Don't You Know There's a War On? (history), 1970; Small Town America: A Narrative History 1620 to the Present, 1980; Theodore Dreiser: At the Gates of the City 1871-1907, 1986. Add: c/o The Nation, 72 Fifth Ave., New York, N.Y. 10011, U.S.A.

LINGENFELTER, Richard Emery. American, b. 1934. History, Mythology/Folklore. Research Physicist, Center for Astrophysics, Univ. of California at San Diego, since 1979. Physicist, Lawrence Radiation Lab., Livermore, Calif., 1957–62; Research Geophysicist, Inst. of Geophysics and Planetary Physics, 1962–68, and Prof.-in-Residence, Depts. of Astronomy and Planetary and Space Science, 1969–79, Univ. of California at Los Angeles; Fulbright Research Scholar, Tata Inst. for Fundamental Research, Bombay, India, 1968–69. *Publs:* The Nonpareil Press of T.S. Harris, 1957; First Through the Grand Canyon, 1958; (ed.) The Cement Hunters: A Story of Lost Gold in California's High Sierra, 1960; (ed.) Washoe Rambles, 1963; The Newspapers of Nevada, 1858-1958; (ed. with R. Dwyer and D. Cohen) The Songs of the Gold Rush, 1964; The Rush of '89, 1967; Presses of the Pacific Islands, 1817-1867, 1967; (ed. with R. Dwyer and D. Cohen) Songs of the American West, 1968; The Hardrock Miners: A History of the Mining Labor Movement in the American West, 1863-1893, 1973; Steamboats on the Colorado River, 1978; (with Karen Gash) Newspapers of Nevada 1854-1979, 1984; (with Richard Dwyer) Lying on the Eastern Slope, 1984; (ed. with Richard Dwyer) Death Valley and the Amargosa: A Land of Illusion, 1986; Death Valley Lore: Classic Tales of Fantasy, Adventure, and Mystery, 1988; (with Richard Dwyer) Dan DeQuille—The Washoe Giant: A Biography and Anthology, 1989. Add: Center for Astrophysics, Univ. of California, La Jolla, Calif. 92093, U.S.A.

LINK, Arthur S(tanley). American, b. 1920. History, Biography. George Henry Davis '86 Prof. of American History since 1976, Princeton Univ. (Instr. in History, 1945–48; Asst. Prof., 1948–49; member, Inst. for Advanced Study, 1949; Prof., 1960–65; Edwards Prof. of American History, 1965–76). Assoc. Prof. of History, 1949–54, and Prof., 1954–60, Northwestern Univ., Evanston, Ill. *Publs:* Wilson: The Road to the White House, 1947; (with R.W. Leopold) Problems in American History, 1952, with S. Coben, 1966; Woodrow Wilson and the Progressive Era, 1954; American Epoch: A History of the United States Since the 1890's, 1955, 6th ed. 1986; Wilson: The New Freedom, 1956; Wilson the Diplomatist, 1957; Wilson: The Struggle for Neutrality, 1914–15, 1960; La Politica de los Estados Unidos en América Latina, 1913–1916, 1960; Woodrow Wilson: A Brief Biography, 1963; (with D.S. Muzzey) Our American Republic, 1963; (with D.S. Muzzey) Our Country's History, 1964; Wilson: Confusions and Crises, 1915–1916, 1964; Woodrow Wilson, Pequena Biografia, 1964; Historia Moderna dos Estados Unidos, 3 vols., 1965; Wilson: Campaigns for Progressivism and Peace, 1916–1917, 1965; (ed.) The Papers of Woodrow Wilson, 60 vols. 1966; (ed.) The First Presbyterian Church of Princeton: Two Centuries of History, 1967; (ed. with R.W. Patrick) Writing Southern History: Essays in Historiography in Honor of Fletcher M. Green, 1967; The Growth of American Democracy: An Interpretive History, 1968; Woodrow Wilson: A Profile, 1968; The Impact of World War I, 1969; (with W.M. Leary) The Progressive Era and the Great War, 1896-1920, 1969; (ed. with W.M. Leary) The Diplomacy of World Power: The United States 1889-1920, 1970; The Higher Realism of Woodrow Wilson and Other Essays, 1971; (with S. Coben) The Democratic Heritage: A History of the United States, 1971; Woodrow Wilson: Revolution, War and Peace, 1979; co-author) The American People, 1981, 1987; (ed.) Woodrow Wilson and a Revolutionary World, 1982. Add: c/o Wilson Papers, Firestone Library, Princeton Univ., Princeton, N.J. 08544, U.S.A.

LINK, Frederick M(artin). American, b. 1930. Literature. Prof. of English since 1968, and currently Chmn., Univ. of Nebraska, Lincoln, (Assoc. Profs., 1965–68; Exec. Dir., Univ. of Nebraska Press, 1973–75). Instr., 1957–60, and Asst. Prof., 1960–63, Boston Univ. *Publs:* (ed.) The Fortunes of Nigel, by Walter Scott, 1965; (ed.) The Rover, by Aphra Behn, 1967; (ed.) Aphra Behn, 1968; Aureng-Zebe, by John Dryden, 1971; English Drama 1660-1800: A Guide to Information Sources, 1976; (ed.) The Plays of Hannah Cowley, 2 vols., 1979; (ed.) The Plays of John O' Keeffe, 4 vols., 1981; John O'Keeffe: A Bibliography, 1982. Add: Dept. of English, Univ. of Nebraska, Lincoln, Nebr. 68508, U.S.A.

LINKLETTER, Art(hur Gordon). American, b. 1912. Human relations, Social commentary/phenomena, Autobiography/Memoirs/Personal, Humor/Satire. Television entertainer; Head, Linkletter Enterprises. *Publs:* People are Funny, 1947; Kids Say the Darndest Things, 1957; (with A. Gordon) Secret World of Kids, 1959; (with D. Jennings) Confessions of a Happy Man, 1960; Kids Still Say the Darndest Things, 1961; Kids Sure Rite Funny, 1962; Oops!, 1967; Wish I'd Said That, 1968; Linkletter Down Under, 1968; Drugs at My Doorstep, 1973; How to be a Super Salesman, 1973; Women Are My Favorite People, 1973; Yes, *You* Can!, 1979; I Didn't Do It Alone, 1980; Hobo on the Way to Heaven, 1981; Public Speaking for Private People, 1981; Old Age Is Not for Sissies, 1988. Add: 8500 Wilshire Blvd., Suite 815, Beverly Hills, Calif. 90211, U.S.A.

LINNEY, Romulus. American, b. 1930. Novels, Plays/Screenplays. Actor and dir. in stock for 6 years; Stage Mgr., Actors Studio, NYC, 1960; has taught at the Univ. of North Carolina, Chapel Hill and Raleigh, Univ. of Pennsylvania, Philadelphia, Brooklyn Coll., NYC, Columbia Univ., NYC, Connecticut Coll., New London, Princeton Univ., New Jersey, and Hunter Coll., NYC. *Publs:* (ed. with Norman A. Bailey and Domenick Cascio) Ten Plays for Radio, 1954; (ed. with Norman A. Bailey and Domenick Cascio) Radio Classics, 1956; Heathen Valley (novel), 1963; Slowly, By Thy Hand Unfurled (novel), 1965; The Sorrows of Frederick (play), 1966; Democracy and Esther, and The Love Suicide at Schofield Barracks, 1973; Holy Ghosts, and The Sorrows of Frederick, 1977; Old Man Joseph and His Family, 1978; Jesus Tales (novel), 1980; The Captivity of Pixie Shedman, 1981; Tennessee, 1981; Childe Byron, 1981; The Death of King Philip, 1983; Laughing Stock, 1984; Sand Mountain, 1985; A Woman Without a Name, 1986; Pops, 1987; Heathen Valley, 1988; Juliet, Yancy and April Snow, 1989. Add: Peregrine Whittlesey, 345 E. 80th St., New York, N.Y. 10021, U.S.A.

LINOWES, David Francis. American, b. 1917. Administration/Management, Economics. Boeschenstein Prof. of Political Economy and Public Policy, Univ. of Illinois, Urbana, since 1976 (Distinguished Arthur Young Visiting Prof., 1973–74). Sr. Adviser, Inst. of Govt. and Public Affairs. Member, Advisory Board, Office of Arms Control, Defense and Intnl. Security. Dir., Chris-Craft Industries Inc., Saturday Review/World Mag. Inc., and Work in America Inst. Inc. Consulting Founding Partner, Leopold and Linowes, Washington, D.C., 1946–82; National Partner, Laventhal & Horwath, N.Y.C., 1965–76. Chmn., City Affairs Cttee., N.Y. Chamber of Commerce, 1969–72; Chmn., U.S. Privacy Protection Commn., 1975–77; Chmn., Federal Commn. on Fiscal Accountability of Nation's Energy Resources, 1981–82; Chmn., Pres.'s Commn. on Privatization, 1988–89. *Publs:* Managing Growth Through Acquisition, 1968; Strategies for Survival, 1973; The Corporate Conscience, 1974; Personal Privacy in an Information Society, 1977; (ed.) Impact of the Communication and Computer Revolution on Society, 1986; Socio-economical Management, 1986; Privacy in America, 1989. Add: 803 Fairway Dr., Champaign, IL. 61820, U.S.A.

LINSTRUM, Derek. British, b. 1925. Architecture. Radcliffe Reader and Dir. of Conservation Studies, Univ. of York, since 1971.Architectural Corresp., The Yorkshire Post. Sr. Architect, West Riding Council, Yorks., 1958–66; Sr. Lectr., Dept. of Architectural Studies, Leeds Polytechnic, 1966–71. *Publs:* Historic Architecture of Leeds, 1969; Sir Jeffry Wyatville: Architect to the King, 1972; Catalogue of the Drawings in the Collection of the Royal Institute of British Architects: The Wyatt Family, 1974; West Yorkshire Architects and Architecture, 1978. Add: The King's Manor, York YO1 2EP, England.

LIONEL, Robert. *See* **FANTHORPE,** R. Lionel.

LIONNI, Leo. American (born Dutch), b. 1910. Children's fiction, Design. Freelance designer, 1930–39; Art. Dir., N.W. Ayer and Son Inc., Philadelphia, 1939–47; Design Dir., Olivetti Corp., NYC, 1949–59; Art. Dir., Fortune mag., NYC, 1949–62; Head of the Graphics Design Dept., Parsons Sch. of Design, NYC, 1952–54; Ed., Panorama, Milan, 1964–65. Has held many one-man shows throughout the world. *Publs:* Little Blue and Little Yellow, 1959; Design for the Printed Page, 1960; Inch by Inch, 1961; On My Beach There Are Many Pebbles, 1961; Swimmy, 1963; Tico and the Golden Wings, 1964; Frederick, 1967; The Alphabet Tree, 1968; The Biggest House in the World, 1968; Alexander and the Wind-Up Mouse, 1969; Fish Is Fish, 1971; Il Taccuino di Leo Lionni, 1972; The Greentail Mouse, 1973; In the Rabbit-garden, 1975; A Colour of His Own, 1975; Pezzettino, 1975; La Botanica Parallela, 1976, trans. by Patrick Creagh as The Parallel Botany, 1977; I Want to Stay Here! I Want to Go There! A Flea Story, 1977; Geraldine, The Music Mouse, 1979; Let's Make Rabbits, 1982; Cornelius, 1983; Who? What? Where? When?, 4 vols., 1983; Letters [Numbers, Colors, Words] to Talk About, 4 vols., 1985; Frederick's Fables, 1985; It's Mine!, 1986; Nicholas—Where Have You Been?, 1987; Six Crows, 1988; Tillie and the Wall, 1989. Add: Porcignana, Radda in Chianti, Siena, Italy.

LIPMAN, David. American, b. 1931. Sports/Physical education/Keeping fit. Managing Ed., Post-Dispatch, St. Louis, Mo., since 1979 (Sports Reporter, 1960–66; Asst. Sports Ed., 1966–68; News Ed., 1968–71; Asst. Managing Ed., 1971–78). *Publs:* (ghostwriter) Maybe I'll Pitch Forever, 1962; Mr. Baseball: The Story of Branch Rickey, 1966; Ken Boyer, 1967; Joe Namath: A Football Legend, 1970; (co-author) The Speed King: Bob Hayes of the Dallas Cowboys, 1971; Bob Gibson, Pitching Ace, 1973; Jim Hart, Underrated Quarterback, 1977. Add: c/o St. Louis Post-Dispatch, 900 N. Tucker Blvd., St. Louis, Mo. 63101, U.S.A.

LIPMAN, Matthew. American, b. 1923. Art, Philosophy, Writing/Journalism. Prof. of Philosophy, since 1972, and Dir., Inst. for the Advancement of Philosophy for Children, Montclair State Coll. Upper Montclair, N.J. Ed., Thinking: The Journal of Philosophy for Children, since 1978. Lectr. in Philosophy, Brooklyn Coll., N.Y., 1953; Lectr. to Adjunct Assoc. Prof., City Coll. of New York, 1953–75; Asst. to Assoc. Prof., 1954–67, and Prof., 1967–72, Columbia Univ., NYC. *Publs:* What Happens in Art, 1967; Discovering Philosophy, 1969, 1977; Contemporary Aesthetics, 1973; (with Ann M. Sharp) Harry Stottlemeier's Discovery, 1974; (with Ann M. Sharp) Instructional Manual to Accompany Harry Stottlemeier's Discovery, 1975; Lisa, 1976, 1983; (with Ann M. Sharp and Frederick S. Oscanyan) Ethical Inquiry, 1977, 1985; (with Ann M. Sharp and Frederick S. Oscanyan) Philosophy in the Classroom, 1977, 1980; Suki, 1978; (ed. with Ann M. Sharp) Growing Up with Philosophy, 1978; Mark, 1980; (with Ann M. Sharp) Writing: How and Why, 1980; (with Ann M. Sharp) Social Inquiry, 1980; Pixie, 1981; (with Ann Margaret Sharp) Looking for Meaning, 1982, 1984; Kio and Gus, 1982; (with Ann M. Sharp) Wondering at the World, 1986; Elfie, 1988; (with Ann Gazzard) Getting Our Thoughts Together, 1988; Philosophy Goes to School, 1988. Add: Inst. for Advancement of Philosophy for Children, Montclair State Coll., Upper Montclair, N.J. 07043, U.S.A.

LIPMAN, Vivian David. British, b. 1921. History. Hon. Research Fellow, Univ. Coll., London. Dir. of Ancient Monuments and Historic Bldgs., Dept. of the Environment, London, 1972–78 (joined govt. service, 1947). *Publs:* Local Government Areas, 1949; Social History of the Jews

in England, 1954; A Century of Social Service, 1959; (ed.) Three Centuries of Anglo-Jewish History, 1961; The Jews of Medieval Norwich, 1967; (ed. with Sonia L. Lipman) The Century of Moses Montefiore, 1985. Add: 9 Rotherwick Rd., London NW11 9DG, England.

LIPSCOMB, William Nunn. American, b. 1919. Chemistry. Abbott and James Lawrence Prof. of Chemistry, Harvard Univ., since 1971 (Prof., 1959–71). Asst. Prof., 1946–50, Assoc. Prof., 1950–54, Acting Chief, Physical Chemistry Div., 1952–54, and Prof. and Chief, Physical Chemistry Div., 1954–59, Univ. of Minnesota, Minneapolis. Recipient, Nobel Prize in Chemistry, 1976. *Publs:* Boron Hydrides, 1963; (with G.R. Eaton) Nuclear Magnetic Resonance Studies of Boron and Related Compounds, 1969. Add: Dept. of Chemistry, Harvard Univ., 12 Oxford St., Cambridge, Mass. 02138, U.S.A.

LIPSET, Seymour Martin. American, b. 1922. Politics/Government, Sociology. Munro Prof. of Political Science and Sociology, and Sr. Fellow, The Hoover Instn., Stanford Univ., California, since 1975. Assoc. Prof. of Sociology, Columbia Univ., NYC, 1950–56; Prof. of Sociology, Univ. of Calfornia, Berkeley, 1956–65; George Markham Prof. of Govt. and Sociology, Harvard Univ., Cambridge, Mass., 1965–75. *Publs:* Agrarian Socialism, 1950, 1971; (with M. Trow and J.S. Coleman) Union Democracy, 1956, 1975; (with R. Bendix) Social Mobility in Industrial Society, 1959; Political Man, 1960; The First New Nation, 1963; Revolution and Counter-Revolution, 1965; (with E. Raab) Politics of Unreason, 1970; Rebellion in University, 1972; (with D. Riesman) Education and Politics at Harvard, 1975; (with E.C. Ladd) The Divided Academy; (with I.L. Horowitz) Dialogues of American Politics, 1978; (with W. Schneider) The Confidence Gap, 1983, 1987; Conflict and Consensus, 1985. Add: Hoover Instn., Stanford Univ., Stanford, Calif. 94305, U.S.A.

LIPSITZ, Lou. American, b. 1938. Poetry, Politics/Government. Prof. of Political Science, Univ. of North Carolina, Chapel Hill, since 1975 (Assoc. Profs., 1964–75). Reporter, Daily Standard, Celina, Ohio, 1957–58; Instr., Univ. of Connecticut, Storrs, 1961–64. *Publs:* Cold Water, 1967; (ed.) American Politics: Behavior and Controversy, 1967; (ed.) Essentials of American Government Today, 1975; Reflections on Samson (verse) 1977. Add: 168 Lake Ellen Dr., Chapel Hill, N.C., U.S.A

LIPSTEIN, Kurt. British, b. 1909. Law. Lectr., 1946–62, Reader in Conflict of Laws, 1962–73, and Prof. of Comparative Law, 1973–76, Cambridge Univ.; Visiting Prof., Univ. of Pennsylvania, 1962, and Northwestern Univ., 1966, 1968; Prof. Associé, Univ of Paris I, 1977–78. *Publs:* (ed.) International Encyclopaedia of Comparative Law, vol. III; The Law of the European Economic Community, 1974; (ed.) Harmonization of Private International Law, 1978; Principles of the Conflict of Laws, National and International, 1981. Add: Clare Coll., Cambridge, England.

LIPSYTE, Robert (Michael). American, b. 1938. Children's fiction, Novels, Sports. Host, The Eleventh Hour television program, NYC, since 1989. Sports columnist, New York Times, 1957–71; Columnist, New York Post, 1977; Essayist, CBS News, 1982–86; Corresp. NBC News, 1986–88. *Publs:* Nigger, 1964; The Masculine Mystique, 1966; The Contender, 1967; Assignment: Sports, 1970; (with Steve Cady) Something Going, 1973; Liberty Two, 1974; Sportsworld: An American Dreamland, 1975; One Fat Summer, 1977; Free to Be Muhammed Ali, 1978; Summer Rules, 1981; Jock and Jill, 1982; The Summerboy, 1982. Add: c/o Harper and Row, 10 E. 53rd St., New York, N.Y. 10022, U.S.A.

LIPTON, Dean. American, b. 1919. Criminology/Law enforcement/Prisons. Dir., San Francisco Writers' Workshop, since 1960. Reporter, Los Angeles Daily News, 1946–68; publicist for various political campaigns, 1948–68; Ed. and Publr., Jewish Record, San Francisco, 1953–55; art critic for various mags. and newspapers, 1968–72. *Publs:* Faces of Crime and Genius: The Historical Impact of the Genius-Criminal, 1971; Malpractice: Autobiography of a Victim, 1978; Blue Grass Frontier, 1980. Add: 2348 Cabrillo, San Francisco, Cal. 94121, U.S.A.

LIPTON, Lenny. American, b. 1940. Film, Technical writing. Film Ed., 1964–65, and Contrib., 1979–82, Popular Photography mag.; Film Reviewer, Berkeley Barb, California, 1965–69; Instr. of Filmmaking, San Francisco Art Inst., 1970–72; Columnist, Take One, 1973–74; Columnist, Super 8 Filmmaker, 1974; Pres., Stereographic Corp., 1981–87. *Publs:* Puff the Magic Dragon (song), 1963; Independent Filmmaking, 1972; The Super 8 Book, 1975; Lipton on Filmmaking, 1979; Foundations of the Stereoscopic Cinema, 1982. Add: 15 La Cuesta, Greenbrae, Calif. 94904, U.S.A.

LIPTZIN, Sol. American, b. 1901. Cultural/Ethnic topics, Literature, Biography. Prof., City Univ., NYC, 1923–63, and American Coll., Jerusalem, 1968–74. *Publs:* Shelley in Germany, 1924; The Weavers in German Literature, 1926; Lyric Pioneers of Modern Germany, 1928; (ed.) Heine, 1928; (ed.) From Novalis to Nietzsche, 1929; Arthur Schnitzler, 1932; Historical Survey of German Literature, 1936; Richard Beer-Hofmann, 1936; Germany's Stepchildren, 1945; (trans. and ed.) Peretz, 1946; Eliakum Zunser, 1950; English Legend of Henrich Heine, 1954; Generation of Decision, 1958; Flowering of Yiddish Literature, 1963; The Jew in American Literature, 1966; Maturing of Yiddish Literature, 1970; History of Yiddish Literature, 1972; (co-author) Einführung in die jiddische Literatur, 1978; Biblical Themes in World Literature, 1985. Add: 21 Washington St., Jerusalem, Israel.

LISK, Jill (Rosina Ann). British, b. 1938. History. Asst. History Mistress, Taunton Sch., Somerset. Former History Mistress, Barr's Hill Girls Grammar Sch., Coventry, La Sainte Union Convent Grammar Sch., Bath, and Bridgwater Girls Grammer Sch., Somerset. *Publs:* The Struggle for Supremacy in the Baltic 1600-1725, 1967; Essays in European History 1494-1789, 2 vols., 1988. Add: 26 Northfield, Bridgwater, Somerset, England.

LISS, Sheldon B. American, b. 1936. International relations/Current affairs, Politics/Government. Prof. of History, Univ. of Akron, Ohio, since 1969. (Assoc. Prof., 1967–69). Editorial Consultant, Latin American Inst., since 1965. Asst. Prof., Indiana State Univ., 1964–66; Visiting Prof., Univ. of Notre Dame, Ind., 1966–69. *Publs:* A Century of Disagreement: The Chamizal Conflict, 1864-1964, 1965; The Canal: Aspects of United States-Panamanian Relations, 1967; (ed. with P.K. Liss) Man, State, and Society in Latin American History, 1972; Diplomacy and Dependency: Venezuela, the United States, and the Americas, 1978; Marxist Thought in Latin America, 1984; Roots of Revolution: Radical Thought in Cuba, 1987; Radicalism in Central America: Thought and Praxis, 1990. Add: 6876 Mill Rd., Brecksville, Ohio 44141, U.S.A.

LIST, Ilka (Katherine). American, b. 1935. Children's fiction, Children's non-fiction. Art Teacher, Brooklyn Friends Sch., New York, 1968–71. *Publs:* Let's Explore the Shore, 1962; Questions and Answers about Seashore Life, 1971; Grandma's Beach Surprise (children's novel), 1975; (with Albert List, Jr.) A Walk in the Forest, 1976. Add: c/o Harper and Row, 10 E. 53rd St., New York, N.Y. 10022, U.S.A.

LISTER, Raymond George. British, b. 1919. Art, Crafts. Managing Dir. and Ed., Golden Head Press, Cambridge, 1952–72; Sr. Research Fellow, 1975–85, Fellow, 1985–86, now Emeritus, Wolfson Coll., Cambridge. Pres., Royal Soc.of Miniature Painters, Sculptors, and Engravers, 1970–80, and Private Libraries Assn., 1971–74. *Publs:* The British Miniature, 1951; Silhouettes, 1953; Thomas Gosse, 1953; The Muscovite Peacock: A Study of the Art of Leon Bakst, 1954; Decorated Porcelains of Simon Lissim, 1955; Decorative Wrought Ironwork in Great Britain, 1957; The Loyal Blacksmith, 1957; Decorative Cast Ironwork in Great Britain, 1960; The Craftsman Engineer, 1960; Edward Calvert, 1962; Great Craftsmen, 1962; The Miniature Defined, 1963; Beulah to Byzantium, 1965; How to Identify Old Maps and Globes, 1965; Victorian Narrative Paintings, 1966; The Craftsman in Metal, 1966; Great Works of Craftsmanship, 1967; William Blake, 1968; Samuel Palmer and His Etchings, 1969; Hammer and Hand: An Essay on the Ironwork of Cambridge, 1969; British Romantic Art, 1973; Samuel Palmer, 1974; (ed.) The Letters of Samuel Palmer, 2 vols., 1974; Internal Methods: A Study of Willliam Blake's Art Techniques, 1975; Apollo's Bird, 1975; For Love of Leda, 1977; Great Images of British Printmaking, 1978; Samuel Palmer: A Vision Recaptured, 1978; Samuel Palmer in Palmer Country, 1980; George Richmond, 1981; Bergomask, 1982; There Was a Star Danced, 1983; Prints and Printmaking, 1984; Samuel Palmer and "The Ancients", 1984; The Paintings of Samuel Palmer, 1985; The Paintings of William Blake, 1986; Samuel Palmer: His Life and Art, 1987; Catalogue Raisonné of the Works of Samuel Palmer, 1988. Add: Windmill House, Linton, Cambridge CB1 6NS, England.

LISTER, R(ichard) P(ercival). British, b. 1914. Novels/Short stories, Poetry, Travel/Exploration/Adventure. *Publs:* The Way Backwards, 1950; The Oyster and the Torpedo, 1951; Rebecca Redfern, 1953; The Idle Demon, 1958; The Rhyme and the Reason, 1963; The Questing Beast, 1965; Journey in Lapland (in U.S. as The Hard Way to Haparanda), 1965; Turkey Observed (in U.S. as A Muezzin from the Tower of Darkness Cries), 1967; The Secret History of Genghis Khan (in U.S. as Genghis Khan), 1969; One Short Summer, 1974; Marco Polo's Travels, 1976; The Travels of Herodotus, 1980; The Albatross and Other Poems, 1986. Add: 120 Hatherley Ct., Hatherley Grove, London W2, England.

LITTELL, Robert. American, b. 1935. Mystery/Crime/Suspense. Formerly an editor with Newsweek mag., based in Eastern Europe and the Soviet Union. *Publs:* (with Richard Z. Chesnoff and Edward Klein) If Israel Lost the War (non-fiction), 1969; (ed.) The Czech Black Book, 1969; The Defection of A.J. Lewinter, 1973; Sweet Reason, 1974; The October Circle, 1976; Mother Russia, 1978; The Debriefing, 1979;The Amateur, 1981; The Sisters, 1985; The Revolutionist, 1988. Add: c/o Simon and Schuster, 1230 Sixth Ave., New York, N.Y. 10020, U.S.A.

LITTLE, Bryan (Desmond Greenway). British b. 1913. Architecture, History, Travel/Exploration/Adventure, Biography. Part-time Tutor, Extra-Mural Dept., Bristol Univ. Civil Servant (Administrative Grade) with Admiralty, 1936–45. Pres., Bristol and Gloucestershire Archaeological Soc., 1979–80. *Publs:* The Building of Bath, 1947; Cheltenham, 1952; The Three Choirs Cities, 1952; Exeter, 1953; The City and County of Bristol, 1954; The Life and Work of James Gibbs, 1955; Portrait of Cambridge, 1955; The Monmouth Episode, 1956; Crusoe's Captain, 1960; Cambridge Discovered, 1960; Bath Portrait, 1961; English Historic Architecture, 1964; Catholic Churches Since 1623, 1966; Cheltenham in Pictures, 1967; Portrait of Somerset, 1969; English Cathedrals, 1972; The Colleges of Cambridge, 1973; (co-author) St. Ives in Huntingdonshire, 1974; Sir Christopher Wren, 1975; (with others) Bristol: An Architectural History, 1979; Abbeys and Priories in England and Wales, 1979; Public Buildings and Statues in Bristol, 1982; Portrait of Exeter, 1983; Architecture in Norman Britain, 1985. Add: c/o Lloyds Bank, 58 Queen's Rd., Bristol 8, England.

LITTLE, Ian (Malcolm David). British, b. 1918. Economics. Emeritus Fellow, Nuffield Coll., Oxford, since 1976 (Fellow, All Souls Coll., 1948–50, Trinity Coll., 1950–52, and Nuffield Coll., 1952–76; Investment Bursar, Nuffield Coll., 1958–70; Prof. of Economics of Developing Nations, 1970–76). Deputy Dir., Economic Section, H.M. Treasury, 1953–55; Dir., Investing in Success Ltd., and Foreign Growth Stocks Ltd., 1960–65; Vice-Pres., Org. for Economic Cooperation and Development Centre (O.E.C.D.), Paris, 1965–67; Bd. Member, British Airports Authority, 1969–74; Dir., Gen. Funds Investment Trust Ltd., 1973–76; Special Adviser, Intnl. Bank for Reconstruction and Development, Washington, D.C., 1976–78. *Publs:* A Critique of Welfare Economics, 1950; The Price of Fuel, 1953; (with Rosenstein-Rodan) Nuclear Power and Italy's Energy Position, 1957; (with Evely) Concentration in British Industry, 1960; Aid to Africa, 1964; (with Clifford) International Aid, 1965; (with Rayner) Higgledy-Piggledy Growth Again, 1966, 1978; (with Mirrlees) Manual of Industrial Projects Analysis in Developing Countries, vol. II: Social Cost-Benefit Analysis, 1969; (co-author) Industry and Trade in Some Developing Countries, 1970; (with Mirrlees) Project Appraisal and Planning for Developing Countries, 1974; (with Scott) Using Shadow Prices, 1976; Economic Development: Theory, Policy, and International Relations, 1982; (co-author) Small Manufacturing Enterprises: A Comparative Study of India and Other Economies, 1987. Add: 7 Ethelred Ct., Old Headington, Oxford OX3 9DA, England.

LITTLE, (Flora) Jean. Canadian, b. 1932. Children's fiction, Poetry. Visiting Instr., Florida State Univ., Tallahassee; Specialist Teacher, Beechwood Sch. for Crippled Children, Guelph, Ont. *Publs:* Mine for Keeps, 1962; Home from Far, 1965; Spring Begins in March, 1966; Take Wing, 1968; When the Pie Was Opened: Poems, 1968; One to Grown On, 1969; Look Through My Window, 1971; Kate, 1971; From Anna, 1972; Stand in the Wind, 1975; Listen for the Singing, 1977; Mama's Going to Buy You a Mockingbird, 1985; Lost and Found, 1986; Different Dragons, 1986; Hey, World, Here I am: Poems, 1986; Little By Little, 1987. Add: 198 Glasgow St. N., Guelph, Ont. N1H 4X2, Canada.

LITTLEDALE, Freya (Lota). American. Children's fiction. English teacher, 1952–53; Ed., South Shore Record newspaper, 1953–55; Assoc. Ed., Maco Mag. Corp., 1960–61, and Rutledge Books and Ridge Press, 1961–62; Juvenile Book Ed., Parents' Mag. Press, 1962–65. Writing instr., Fairfield Univ., Conn., 1984, 1986–89. *Publs:* (ed.) A Treasure Chest of Poetry, 1964; (ed.) Fairy Tales, by Hans Christian Andersen, 1964; (ed.) Grimms' Fairy Tales, 1964; (ed.) Andersen's Fairy Tales, 1966; (ed.) 13 Ghostly Tales, 1966; The Magic Fish, 1967; (with H. Littledale) Timothy's Forest, 1969; (ed.) Ghosts and Spirits of Many Lands, 1970; King Fox and Other Old Tales, 1971; (ed.) Stories of Ghosts, Witches, and Demons, 1971; The Magic Tablecloth, the Magic Goat, and Hitting Stick, 1973; (ed.) Thirteen Ghostly Tales, 1974; (ed.) Strange Tales from Many Lands, 1975; Stop That Pancake, 1975; The King and Queen Who Wouldn't Speak, 1975; The Giant's Garden, 1975; The Elves and the Shoemaker, 1975; Seven at One Blow, 1977; The Snow Child, 1978; I Was Thinking, 1979; (adaptor) Pinocchio, 1979; The Magic Plum Tree, 1981; Snow White and the Seven Dwarfs, 1980; (adaptor) The Wizard of Oz, 1982; The Sleeping Beauty, 1984; (adaptor) Frankenstein, 1983; (adaptor) The Little Mermaid, 1986; The Farmer In the Soup, 1987; Peter and the North Wind, 1988; The Twelve Dancing Princesses, 1988. Add: c/o Curtis Brown, 10 Astor Place, New York, N.Y. 10003, U.S.A.

LITVINOFF, Emanuel. British, b. 1915. Novels/Short stories, Plays/Screenplays, Poetry. Dir., Contemporary Jewish Library, London, since 1958. Founder, Jews in Eastern Europe journal, London. *Publs:* Conscripts: A Symphonic Declaration, 1941; The Untried Soldier, 1942; A Crown for Cain, 1948; The Lost Europeans, 1959; The Man Next Door, 1968; Journey Through a Small Planet, 1972; Notes for a Survivor, 1973; A Death Out of Season, 1974; (ed.) Soviet Anti-Semitism: The Paris Trial, 1974; Blood on the Snow, 1975; The Face of Terror, 1978; Falls the Shadow, 1983. Add: c/o David Higham Assocs., 5-8 Lower John St., London W1R 4HA, England.

LITWACK, Leon. American, b. 1929. History, Race relations. Prof. of History, Univ. of California, Berkeley, since 1965. Asst. to Assoc. Prof., Univ. of Wisconsin, Madison, 1958–65. Member, Editorial Bd., Journal of Negro History, 1974–79; Chmn., Nominations Bd., Org. of American Historians, 1976–77. *Publs:* North of Slavery: The Negro in the Free States 1790-1860, 1961; (ed.) The American Labor Movement, 1962; (ed. with Kenneth Stampp) Reconstruction: An Anthology of Revisionist Writings, 1969; (with others) The United States, 4th ed., 1976; Been in the Storm So Long: The Aftermath of Slavery, 1979; (with August Meier) Black Leaders of the Nineteenth Century, 1988. Add: Dept. of History, Univ. of California, Berkeley, Calif. 94720, U.S.A.

LIU, Wu-chi. Also writes as Hsiao Hsia. American, b. 1907. History, Literature, Philosophy, Biography. Emeritus Prof., Dept. of East Asian Languages and Culture, Indiana Univ., Bloomington, since 1976 (Prof., 1961–76; Chmn., 1962–67). Visiting Prof. of Chinese Language and Literature, 1951–53, and Sr. Ed. and Assoc. Dir. of Research, Human Relations Area Files, 1955–60, Yale Univ., New Haven, Conn.; Prof. of Chinese and Dir., Chinese Language and Area Center, Univ. of Pittsburgh, Pa., 1960–61; Visiting Prof. of Chinese Literature, Univ. of California, Berkeley, 1981. Chmn. of Ed. Bd., Tsing Hua Journal of Chinese Studies, 1978–87. *Publs:* (co-ed.) Readings in Contemporary Chinese Literature, 5 vols., 1953–58, rev. ed., 3 vols, 1964–68; A Short History of Confucian Philosophy, 1955; Confucius: His Life and Time, 1955; (ed. as Hsiao Hsia) China: Its People, Its Society, Its Culture, 1960; An Introduction to Chinese Literature, 1966; Su Man-shu, 1972; (co-ed. and trans.) Sunflower Splendor: Three Thousand Years of Chinese Poetry, 1975; (co-ed.) K'uei Yeh Chi, 1976. Add: 2140 Santa Cruz Ave., Menlo Park, Calif. 94025, U.S.A.

LIVELY, Penelope. British, b. 1933. Novels/Short stories, Children's fiction, Plays/Screenplays. *Publs:* Astercote, 1970; The Whispering Knights, 1971; The Wild Hunt of Hagworthy, 1971; The Driftway, 1972; The Ghost of Thomas Kempe, 1973; The House in Norham Gardens, 1974; Going Back, 1975; The Boy Without a Name. 1975; The Presence of the Past: An Introduction to Landscape History, 1975; A Stitch in Time, 1976; Fanny's Sister, 1976; The Stained Glass Window, 1976; The Road to Lichfield, 1977; The Voyage of Qv 66, 1978; Fanny and the Monsters, 1978; Nothing Missing But the Samovar, 1978; Treasures of Time, 1979; Judgement Day, 1980; Fanny and the Battle of Potter's Piece, 1980; The Revenge of Samuel Stokes, 1981; Next to Nature, Art, 1982; Perfect Happiness, 1983; Corruption and Other Stories, 1984; According to Mark, 1984; Uninvited Ghosts and Other Stories, 1984; Dragon Trouble, 1984; Pack of Cards: Stories 1978-86, 1986; Moon Tiger, 1987; A House Inside Out, 1987. Add: c/o Murray Pollinger, 4 Garrick St., London WC2E 9BH, England.

LIVERSIDGE, Henry Douglas. British, b. 1913. Children's non-fiction, History, Travel/Exploration/Adventure, Biography. Former News Ed., Sunday Chronicle, London; Asst. Leader Writer, Daily Mail, London; Corresp. and Staff Writer, Reuters; and Ed., Publications Div., Central Office of Information, London, now retired. *Publs:* White Horizon, 1951; The Last Continent, 1958; The Third Front, 1960; The Whale Killers, 1963; Peter the Great, 1968; Joseph Stalin, 1969; St. Francis of Assisi, 1969; Lenin, 1969; St. Ignatius of Loyola, 1970; The White World, 1972; The Luddites, 1972; The Day the Bastille Fell, 1972; Queen Elizabeth II, 1974; Prince Charles, 1975; Prince Philip, 1976; Queen Elizabeth the Queen Mother, 1977; The Mountbattens, 1978. Add: 56 Love Lane, Pinner, Middx. HA5 3EX, England.

LIVESAY, Dorothy. Canadian, b. 1909. Poetry, Short stories. Social Worker, Englewood, N.J., 1935–36, and Vancouver, 1936–39, 1953–55; Corresp., Toronto Daily Star, 1946–49; Documentary Scriptwriter, CBC,

1950–55; high sch. teacher, Vancouver, 1956–58; Unesco English Specialist, Paris, 1959–60, and Zambia, 1960–63; Lectr. in Creative Writing, Univ. of British Columbia, 1965–66; Writer-in-Residence, Univ. of New Brunswick, Fredericton, 1966–68; Assoc. Prof. of English, Univ. of Alberta, Edmonton, 1968–71; Lectr. in Canadian Literature, Univ. of Victoria, 1971–73; Writer-in-Residence, 1974–75, and Prof., 1975–76, Univ. of Manitoba, Winnipeg; Writer-in-Residence, Univ. of Ottawa, 1977, Simon Fraser Univ., Burnaby, B.C., 1979–80, and Univ. of Toronto, 1983; Adjunct Prof., Woman's Studies, Simon Fraser Univ., Burnaby, B.C., 1986–87. *Publs:* Green Pitcher, 1928; Signpost, 1931; Day and Night: Poems, 1944; Poems for People, 1947; (ed.) The Collected Poems of Raymond Knister, 1949; Call My People Home (play), 1950; New Poems, 1955; Selected Poems, 1926–1956, 1957; The Colour of God's Face, 1965; The Unquiet Bed, 1967; The Documentaries: Selected Longer Poems, 1968; Plainsongs, 1971, 1972; (ed. with S. Mayne) Forty Women Poets of Canada, 1971; Collected Poems: The Two Seasons, 1972; A Winnipeg Childhood (short stories), 1973; Ice Age, 1975; Right Hand Left Hand (autobiography), 1977; The Woman I Am (selected poems), 1978; The Raw Edges, 1981; The Phases of Love, 1983; Feeling the Worlds, 1984; The Self-Completing Tree, 1986; Beginnings (short stories), 1989. Add: 607 Cornwall St., Victoria, B.C. V8V 4L2, Canada.

LIVINGOOD, James Weston. American, b. 1910. History. Retired Guerry Prof. of History, Univ. of Tennessee at Chattanooga, (Dean, Coll. of Arts and Sciences, 1957–66; Dean of Univ., 1966–69). *Publs:* The Philadelphia-Baltimore Trade Rivalry, 1780-1860, 1937; (with G.E. Govan) The University of Chattanooga: Sixty Years, 1947; (with G.E. Govan) The Chattanooga Country: From Tomahawks to TVA, 1952, 3rd ed. 1977; (with G.E. Govan) A Different Valor: The Story of General Joseph E. Johnston C.S.A., 1956; (ed. with G.E. Govan) The Haskell Memoirs: The Personal Narrative of a Confederate Officer, 1960; (with J.L. Raulston) Sequatchie: A Story of the Southern Cumberlands, 1974; Chattanooga: An Illustrated History, 1980; Hamilton County (Tennessee County History Series), 1981; A History of Hamilton County, Tennessee, 1981; Centennial History: Chattanooga and Hamilton County Medical Society, 1983. Add: 395 Shallowford Rd., Chattanooga, Tenn. 37411, U.S.A.

LIVINGS, Henry. British, b. 1929. Short stories, Plays/Screenplays, History. *Publs:* Eh?, 1965; The Little Mrs. Foster Show, 1967; Good Grief!, 1968; Honour and Offer, 1969; The Ffinest Ffamily in the Land, 1970; Pongo Plays 1-6, 1971; This Jockey Drives Late Nights, 1972. 1976; (adaptor) Cinderella, 1976; Six More Pongo Plays, 1974; Jonah, 1975; That the Medals and the Baton Be Put in View: The Story of a Village Band 1875-1975, 1975; Pennine Tales, 1983; Flying Eggs and Things: More Pennine Tales, 1986. Add: 49 Grains Rd., Delph, Oldham OL3 5DS, England.

LIVINGSTON, Myra Cohn. American, b. 1926. Children's fiction, Poetry. Has lectured on poetry and conducted writing workshops throughout the U.S. since 1959; Poet-in-Residence, Beverly Hills Unified Sch. District, 1966–84; Sr. Extension Instr., Univ. of California, Los Angeles, since 1972. Professional French horn player, 1940–48; Asst. Ed., Campus mag., Los Angeles, 1948–50; worked in public relations for movie and musical personalities, 1949–52; Instr. in Creative Writing for Children, Dallas Public Library, 1959–64; Instr., Los Angeles County Museum of Art, 1966–67, Beverly Hills Public Library, 1966–74, and Univ. of California Elementary Sch., Los Angeles, 1972. Pres., Friends of the Beverly Hills Public Library, 1979–81. *Publs:* Whispers and Other Poems, 1958; Wide Awake and Other Poems, 1959; I'm Hiding, 1961; See What I Found, 1962; Talk to Elephants!, 1962; I'm Not Me, 1963; Happy Birthday, 1964; The Moon and a Star and Other Poems, 1965; I'm Waiting, 1966; Old Mrs. Twindlytart and Other Poems, 1967; (ed.) A Tune Beyond Us: A Collection of Poetry, 1968; A Crazy Flight and Other Poems, 1969; (ed.) Speak Roughly to Your Little Boy: A Collection of Parodies and Burlesques, 1971; (ed.) Listen, Children, Listen: An Anthology of Poems for the Very Young, 1972; (ed.) What a Wonderful Bird the Frog Are: An Assortment of Humorous Poetry and Verse, 1973; When You Are Alone/It Keeps You Capone: An Approach to Creative Writing for Children, 1973; (ed.) The Poems of Lewis Carroll, 1973; Come Away, 1974; The Malibu and Other Poems, 1974; The Way Things Are and Other Poems, 1974; (ed.) One Little Roon, An Everywhere: Poems of Love, 1975; 4-Way Stop and Other Poems, 1976; (ed.) O Frabjous Day: Poetry for Holidays and Special Occasions, 1977; (ed.) Callooh! Callay! Holiday Poems for Young Readers, 1978; O Sliver of Liver and Other Poems, 1979; No Way of Knowing: Dallas Poems, 1980; (ed.) Poems of Christmas, 1980; A Circle of Seasons, 1982; How Pleasant to Know Mr. Lear!, 1982; (ed.) Why Am I Grown So Cold, 1982; Sky Songs, 1983; (ed.) Christmas Poems, 1984; A Song I Sang to You and Other Poems,

1984; The Child as Poet: Myth or Reality?, 1984; Monkey Puzzle and Other Poems, 1985; Celebrations, 1985; (ed.) Easter Poems, 1985; A Learical Lexicon, 1985; Worlds I Know and Other Poems, 1985; (ed.) Thanksgiving Poems, 1985; Sea Songs, 1986; Earth Songs, 1986; Poems for Jewish Holidays, 1986; Higgledy-Piggledy, 1986; Valentine Poems, 1987; Cat Poems, 1987; I Like You, If You Like Me, 1987; (ed.) New Year's Poems, 1987; (ed.) These Small Stones, 1987; Space Songs, 1988; (ed.) Poems for Mothers, 1988; There Was a Place, 1988. Add: 9308 Readcrest Dr., Beverly Hills, Calif. 90210, U.S.A.

LIVINGSTONE, Douglas (James). South African, b. 1932. Plays/Screenplays, Poetry. Bacteriologist in charge of marine pollution, National Inst. for Water Research, South Africa, since 1964, National Research Inst. for Oceanology, since 1986, and Earth, Marine, Atmospheric Science, and Technology, since 1988. Officer in charge of Pathological Diagnostic Lab., Kabwe Gen. Hosp., Zambia, 1959–63. *Publs:* The Skull in the Mud, 1960; Sjambok and Other Poems from Africa, 1964; The Sea My Winding Sheet, 1964; (with T. Kinsella and A. Sexton) Poems, 1968; Eyes Closed Against the Sun, 1970; A Rhino for the Boardroom, 1974; A Rosary of Bone, 1975; The Anvil's Undertone, 1978; Selected Poems, 1984; The Semblance of the Real, 1984. Add: P.O. Box 17001, Congella 4013, Natal, South Africa.

LIYONG, Taban lo. Ugandan, b. 1938. Novels/Short stories, Poetry, Cultural/Ethnic topics. Member of the Inst. of Development Studies Cultural Div., since 1968, and Lectr. in English, Univ. of Nairobi. *Publs:* The Last Word: Cultural Synthesism, 1969; Fixions and Other Stories, 1969; Eating Chiefs: Lwo Culture from Lolwe to Malkal, 1970; Meditations in Limbo (novel), 1970; Franz Fanon's Uneven Ribs: With Poems More and More, 1971; The Uniformed Man (short stories), 1971; Another Nigger Dead: Poems, 1972; Popular Culture of East Africa: Oral Literature, 1972; Thirteen Offensives Against Our Enemies, 1973; Ballads of Underdevelopment, 1974; (ed.) Sir Apolo Kagwa Discovers England, 1974; Meditations, 1977; To Still a Passion, 1977; Meditations, 1978. Add: Dept. of English, Univ. of Nairobi, P.O. Box 30197, Nairobi, Kenya.

LLEWELLYN-JONES, (John) Derek. British, b. 1923. Medicine/Health, Sociology. Assoc. Prof. of Obstetrics, Sydney Univ., since 1965. Council Member, Australian Council for Overseas Aid, and Pres., Zero Population Growth. Former Sr., Obstetrician and Gynaecologist, Fedn. of Malaya. *Publs:* Fundamentals of Obstetrics and Gynaecology, 2 vols., 1969, 4th ed., 1986; Every Woman, 1971, 4th ed. 1986; On Trial: Zero Population Growth, 1974; Human Reproduction and Society, 1974; People Populating, 1974; Sex and V.D., 1974; Every Body, 1980; Every Man, 1981, 1987; Breast Feeding, 1983; A to Z of Women's Health, 1983; Herpes, AIDS, and Other Sexually Transmitted Diseases, 1985; Every Girl, 1987. Add: c/o Faber and Faber, 3 Queen Sq., London WC1N 3AU, England.

LLEWELLYN-JONES, Frank. British, b. 1907. Physics. Prof. Emeritus of Physics, Univ. of Wales, Swansea, since 1974 (Prof. and Head of Dept. of Physics, 1945–65; Principal, Univ. Coll. of Swansea, 1965–74; Vice-Chancellor, Univ. of Wales, 1969–71; Univ. Professional Fellow, 1974–86; Leverhulme Emeritus Fellow, 1975–77). Demonstrator, Electrical Dept., Oxford Univ., 1929–32; Sr. Demy, Magdalen Coll., Oxford, 1931; Sr. Scientific Officer, Royal Aircraft Establishment, 1940–45; Wales Fellow, Jesus Coll., 1965–66, 1969–71; part-time Dir., South West Group, British Steel Corp., 1968–70. Chmn., Central Advisory Council for Education, Wales, 1961–64. *Publs:* Fundamental Processes of Electrical Contact Phenomena, 1953; Physics of Electrical Contacts, 1957; Ionization and Breakdown in Gases, 1957, 1966; The Glow Discharge, 1966; Ionization Avalanches and Breakdown, 1967. Add: Dept. of Physics, Univ. of Wales, Singleton Park, Swansea SA2 8PP, Wales.

LLEWELYN OWENS, Joan. British, b. 1919. Children's fiction, Children's non-fiction, Education. Freelance Careers Consultant, Daily Telegraph Careers Information Service, London, 1970–86. *Publs:* Sally Grayson: Wren, 1954; Library Life for Deborah, 1957; Margaret Becomes a Doctor, 1957; Sue Takes Up Physiotherapy, 1958; Diana Seton: Veterinary Student, 1960; Hospital Careers for Girls, 1961; Working with Children, 1962; Travel While You Work, 1963; Working in the Theatre, 1964; Careers in Social Work, 1965; Writing as a Career, 1967; The Graduate's Guide to the Business World, 1973; The Law Courts, 1976. Add: 23 Pennington Rd., Southborough, Tunbridge Wells, Kent TN4 0SS, England.

LLOYD, Dennis. (Baron Lloyd of Hampstead). British, b. 1915. Law. Barrister-at-Law since 1936; Quain Prof. of Jurisprudence, Univ. Coll., Univ. of London, 1956–82, now Emeritus (Reader in English Law,

1947–56). Q.C., 1975. *Publs:* Law of Unincorporated Associations, 1938; Public Policy, 1953; (with John Montgomerie) Rent Control, 2nd ed. 1955; (with G.W. Keeton) United Kingdom: Development of Its Law and Constitution, 1955; (with John Montgomerie) Business Lettings, 1956; The Idea of Law, 1964, 13th ed. 1987; Law (series) 1968; Introduction to Jurisprudence, 5th ed. 1985. Add: Faculty of Laws, Univ. Coll., 4-8 Endsleigh Gardens, London WC1H 0EG, England.

LLOYD, Geoffrey Ernest Richard. British, b. 1933. Philosophy. Prof. of Ancient Philosophy and Science, Cambridge Univ., since 1983; Master of Darwin Coll., Cambridge, since 1989 (Asst. Lectr., 1965–67; Lectr., 1967–74; Reader, 1974–83). Sr. Tutor, King's Coll., Cambridge, 1969–73. *Publs:* Polarity and Analogy: Two Types of Argumentation in Early Greek Thought, 1966; Aristotle: The Growth and Structure of His Thought, 1968; Early Greek Science: Thales to Aristotle, 1970; Greek Science after Aristotle, 1973; (ed.) Hippocratic Writings, 1978; (ed.) Aristotle On Mind and the Senses, 1978; Magic, Reason and Experience, 1979; Science, Folklore and Ideology, 1983; Science and Morality in Greco-Roman Antiquity, 1985; The Revolutions of Wisdom, 1987. Add: Darwin Coll., Cambridge CB3 9EU, England.

LLOYD, Howell Arnold. British, b. 1937. History. Prof. of History, Univ. of Hull, since 1985 (Lectr., 1964–73; Sr. Lectr., 1973–82; Reader, 1982–85). *Publs:* The Gentry of South-West Wales, 1540-1640, 1968; (with G. Connell-Smith) The Relevance of History, 1972; The Rouen Campaign, 1590-1592; Politics, Warfare and the Early-Modern State, 1973; The State, France, and the Sixteenth Century, 1983; La Nascita dello stato moderno nella Francia del Cinquecento, 1986. Add: Dept. of History, Univ. of Hull, Cottingham Rd., Hull HU6 7RX, England.

LLOYD, Levanah. *See* **PETERS,** Maureen.

LLOYD, Marjorie. British, b. 1909. Children's fiction. *Publs:* Fell Farm Holiday; Fell Farm for Christmas; Fell Farm Campers; The Farm in Mallerstang; One Summer Term; The Family at Foxy Beck; River Trail; Fell Trek; Patch the Puppy; One Silver Shilling; Kit; Der Verlorene Silberschilling. Add: East High Green, Great Musgrave, Kirkby Stephen, Cumbria CA17 4DW, England.

LLOYD, Peter Cutt. British, b. 1927. Anthropology/Ethnology, History, Sociology, Third World problems. Prof. of Social Anthropology, Univ. of Sussex, Brighton, since 1978 (Reader, 1967–78). Hon. Dir., Intnl. African Inst., since 1988. Head, Dept. of Sociology, Univ. of Ibadan, Nigeria, 1959–64; Sr. Lectr., then Reader in West African Sociology, Univ. of Birmingham, 1964–67. *Publs:* Yoruba Land Law, 1962; (ed.) The New Elites of Tropical Africa, 1966; (ed. with A. Mabogunje and B. Awe) The City of Ibadan, 1967; Africa in Social Change, 1967; Classes, Crises and Coups, 1971; The Development of Yoruba Kingdoms in the 18th and 19th Centuries, 1971; Power and Independence, 1974; Slums of Hope?, 1979; The "Young Towns" of Lima, 1980; A Third World Proletariat?, 1982. Add: 10 Withdean Rd., Brighton, BN1 5BL, England.

LLOYD, T(revor) O(wen). British, b. 1934. History. Prof., Dept. of History, Univ. of Toronto, since 1971 (Lectr., 1959–63; Asst. Prof., 1963–67; Assoc. Prof., 1967–71). *Publs:* The General Election of 1880, 1968; Canada in World Affairs, 1957–59, 1968; (ed. with J.T. McLeod) Agenda 1970, 1968; Empire to Welfare State: English History 1906–1967, 1970, 3rd ed. (as 1906–85), 1986; Suffragettes International, 1971; The Growth of Parliamentary Democracy in Britain, 1973; The British Empire 1558-1983, 1984. Add: Dept. of History, Univ. of Toronto, Toronto, Ont., Canada.

LLOYD-JONES, Peter Hugh Jefferd. British, b. 1922. Classics. Student of Christ Church, Oxford, and Regius Prof. of Greek, Oxford Univ., 1960–89 (Fellow and E.P. Warren Praelector in Classics, Corpus Christi Coll., Oxford, 1954–60). Fellow of Jesus Coll., Cambridge, 1948–54; Asst. Lectr., 1950–52, and Lectr. in Classics, 1952–54, Cambridge Univ. *Publs:* Appendix to the Loeb edition of Aeschylus, 1957; Menandri Dyscolus, 1960; Greek Studies in Modern Oxford, 1961; (trans.) Greek Metre, by Paul Maas, 1962; (ed.) The Greeks, 1962; Tacitus, 1964; (trans.) Aeschylus: Agamemnon, The Libation-Bearers, and The Eumenides, 1970; The Justice of Zeus, 1971, 1983; (ed.) Maurice Bowra: A Celebration, 1974; Females of the Species: Semonides of Amorgos on Women, 1975; Myths of the Zodiac, 1978; (with Marcelle Quinton) Imaginary Animals, 1980; (with P. J. Parsons) Supplementum Hellenisticum, 1983; Blood for the Ghosts, 1982; Classical Survivals, 1982; (with N.G. Wilson) Sophocles' Fabulae, 1989; (with N. G. Wilson) Sophocles, 1989; Collected Academic Papers, 1989. Add: Christ Church, Oxford, England.

LLYWELYN, Morgan. Also writes as Shannon Lewis. American, b. 1937. Novels/Short Stories, Historical/Romance. Full-time Writer. *Publs:* The Wind from Hastings, 1978; Lion of Ireland: The Legend of Brian Boru, 1980; (as Shannon Lewis) Personal Habits, 1982; The Horse Goddess, 1982; Bard: The Odyssey of the Irish, 1984; Grania, She-King of the Irish Seas, 1986; Xerxes, 1987; Red Branch, 1989; The Isles of the Blest, 1989. Add: c/o Abner Stein, 10 Roland Gardens, London SW7 3PH, England.

LOADES, David Michael. British, b. 1934. History. Prof. of History, University Coll. of North Wales, Bangor, since 1980. Lectr. in Political Science, Univ. of St. Andrews, Scotland, 1961–63; Lectr., 1963–71, Sr. Lectr., 1971–77, and Reader in Modern History, 1977–80, Univ. of Durham. *Publs:* Two Tudor Conspiracies, 1965; (ed.) The Papers of George Wyatt, 1968; The Oxford Martyrs, 1970; Politics and the Nation 1450-1660, 1974, 3rd ed. 1986; The Reign of Mary Tudor, 1979; (ed.) The End of Strife, 1984; The Tudor Court, 1986; (co-ed) Law and Government under the Tudors: Essays Presented to Sir Geoffrey Elton, 1988. Add: Dept. of History, University Coll. of North Wales, Bangor, Wales.

LOBEL, Anita. American (born Polish), b. 1934. Children's fiction. *Publs:* Sven's Bridge, 1965; The Troll Music, 1966; Potatoes, Potatoes, 1967; The Seamstress of Salzburg, 1970; Under a Mushroom, 1970; A Birthday for the Princess, 1973; King Rooster, Queen Hen, 1975; The Pancake, 1978; The Straw Maid, 1983. Add: c/o Greenwillow Books, 105 Madison Ave., New York, N.Y. 10016, U.S.A.

LOCHHEAD, Douglas (Grant). Canadian, b. 1922. Poetry, Literature. Writer-in-Residence, Mount Allison Univ., Sackville, N.B., since 1987. Gen. Ed., Literature of Canada Series: Poetry and Prose in Reprint, since 1972, and Toronto Reprint Library of Canadian Prose and Poetry, since 1973, Univ. of Toronto Press. *Publs:* The Heart Is Fire: Poems, 1959; Poems in Folio, no. and no. 2, 1959, 1963; It is All Around: Poems, 1960; (ed. with Northrup Frye and J.A. Irving) The Stepsure Letters, by Thomas McCulloch, 1960; Poet Talking, 1964; A&B&C&: An Alaphabet, 1969; Millwood Road Poems, 1970; (ed. with Raymond Souster) Made in Canada: An Anthology of Contemporary Canadian Poetry, 1970; (ed.) Bibliography of Canadian Bibliographies, rev. ed. 1972; (ed. with R. Souster) 100 Poems of Nineteenth Century Canada, 1974; Prayers in a Field: Poems, 1974; The Full Furnace: Collected Poems, 1975; High Marsh Road, 1980; Battle Sequence, 1980; A E: A Long Poem, 1980; The Panic Field, 1984; Tiger in the Skull, 1986; Upper Cape Poems, 1989; Dykelands, 1989; Vigils and Mercies, 1989. Add: Canadian Studies Centre, Mount Allison Univ., Sackville, N.B., Canada.

LOCHHEAD, Liz. British, b. 1947. Plays/Screenplays, Poetry. Art Teacher, Bishopbriggs High Sch., Glasgow. *Publs:* Memo for Spring (poetry), 1972; Now and Then (screenplay), 1972; The Grimm Sisters (poetry), 1981; Blood and Ice (play), 1982; Dreaming Frankenstein, and Collected Poems, 1984; Silver Service (play), 1984; True Confessions and New Clichés, 1985. Add: c/o Salamander Press, 18 Anley Rd., London W14 0BY, England.

LOCHMAN, Jan Milic. Czech, b. 1922. Theology/Religion. Prof. of Systematic Theology, Univ. of Basel, since 1969. Prof. of Theology, Comenius Faculty, Prague, 1950–68. *Publs:* The Church in a Marxist Society, 1970; (with H. Marcuse, R. Shaull and J.C. Bennett) Marxism and Radical Religion, 1970; Encountering Marx, 1977; Living Roots of Reformation, 1979; Reconciliation and Liberation, 1980; Signposts to Freedom, 1981; The Theology of Praise, 1982; The Faith We Confess, 1984; Christ and Prometheus?, 1988. Add: Heuberg 33, 4051 Basel, Switzerland.

LOCKE, Elsie (Violet). New Zealander, b. 1912. Children's fiction, Children's non-fiction, History, Biography. *Publs:* The Runaway Settlers, 1965; The End of the Harbour, 1968; The Roots of the Clover, 1971; It's the Same Old Earth, 1974; Maori King and British Queen, 1974; Moko's Hideout and Other Stories, 1976; Look under the Leaves, 1975; Discovering the Morrisons, 1975; (with Ken Dawson) The Boy with the Snowgrass Hair, 1976; Explorer Zach, 1978; The Gaoler, 1978; Student at the Gates, 1981; Journey under Warning, 1984; The Kauri and the Willow, 1984; A Canoe in the Mist, 1984; Two Peoples, One Land: A History of Aotearoa/New Zealand, 1988. Add: 392 Oxford Terr., Christchurch 1, New Zealand.

LOCKE, Hubert G. American, b. 1934. History, Theology/Religion. Dir., William D. Douglas Inst., since 1971. Dean and Prof. of Public Affairs, Univ. of Washington, Seattle, since 1982 (Assoc. Dean, 1976–77; Vice Provost, 1977–82). Dir. of Religious Affairs, 1957–62, Faculty Re-

search Assoc., Center for Urban Studies, and Adjunct Asst. Prof. of Urban Education, 1967–69, and Leo M. Franklin Memorial Prof. of Urban Education, 1967–69, and Leo M. Franklin Memorial Prof. of Human Relations, 1969–70, Wayne State Univ., Detroit; Special Asst. to the Commnr. of Police of Detroit, 1966–67; Dean, Coll. of Public Affairs, Univ. of Nebraska at Omaha, 1972–75. *Publs:* The Detroit Riot of 1967, 1969; The Care and Feeding of White Liberals, 1970; (ed. with Franklin H. Littell) The German Church Struggle and the Holocaust, 1974; The Church Confronts the Nazis, 1984; Exile in the Fatherland, 1987. Add: University of Washington, DP-30, Seattle, Wash. 98195, U.S.A.

LOCKERBIE, D(onald) Bruce. American, b. 1935. Plays/Screenplays, Education, Literature, Theology/Religion. Scholar-in-Residence, Stony Brook Sch., New York, since 1957. Visiting Consultant at American Schs. in Asia and Africa, since 1974. *Publs:* Billy Sunday, 1965; Patriarchs and Prophets, 1969; Hawthorne, 1970; Melville, 1970; Twain, 1970; Major American Authors, 1970; (with L. Westdahl) Success in Writing, 1970; Purposeful Writing, 1972; The Way They Should Go, 1972; The Liberating Word, 1974; The Cosmic Center: The Apostles' Creed, 1977; A Man under Orders: Lt. Gen. William K. Harrison, 1979; Who Educates Your Child?, 1980; The Timeless Moment, 1980; Asking Questions, 1980; Fatherlove, 1981; In Peril on the Sea, 1984; The Christian, The Arts, and Truth, 1985. Add: Stony Brook Sch., Route 25-A, Stony Brook, N.Y. 11790, U.S.A.

LOCKLEY, Ronald Mathias. British, b. 1903. Novels/Short stories, Natural history. Founder, Nature in Wales (Chief Ed., 1955–70); Co-Founder, West Wales Naturalists' Trust, now Dyfed Wildlife Trust. *Publs:* Dream Island, 1930; The Island Dwellers, 1932; Island Days, 1934; Birds of the Green Belt, 1936; The Sea's a Thief, 1936; I Know an Island, 1938; Early Morning Island, 1939; A Pot of Smoke, 1940; The Way to an Island, 1941; Shearwaters, 1942; Dream Island Days, 1943; Inland Farm, 1943; Islands Round Britain, 1945; Birds of the Sea, 1945; The Island Farmers, 1946; Letters from Skokholm, 1947; The Cinnamon Bird, 1948; The Golden Year, 1948; (ed.) White's Natural History of Selborne, 1949, 1976; (with J. Buxton) Island of Skomer, 1950; The Charm of the Channel Islands, 1950; (ed.) The Nature-Lover's Anthology, 1951; Puffins, 1953; Travels with a Tent in Western Europe, 1953; (with R. Russell) Bird-Ringing, 1953; Gilbert White, 1954, 1976; (with J. Fisher) Sea-Birds, 1954; The Seals and the Curragh, 1954; Pembrokeshire, 1957; (ed.) In Praise of Islands, 1957; (ed.) The Bird-Lover's Bedside Book, 1958; The Pan Book of Cage Birds, 1961; Britain in Colour, 1964; The Private Life of the Rabbit, 1964, 1976; Grey Seal, Common Seal, 1966; Wales, 1966; Animal Navigation, 1967; Traveller's Guide to the Channel Islands, 1968; The Book of Bird-Watching, 1968; The Island, 1969; Man Against Nature, 1970; The Naturalist in Wales, 1970; Ocean Wanderers, 1974; Seal Woman, 1974; Orielton, 1977; Myself When Young, 1979; Whales, Dolphins and Porpoises, 1979; (with Noel Cusa) New Zealand Endangered Species, 1980; The House above the Sea, 1980; (with Richard Adams) A Voyage Through the Antarctic, 1982; (with Geoff Moon) New Zealand's Birds, 1982; The Flight of the Storm Petrel, 1983; The Lodge above the Waterfall, 1987; (with Betty Brownlie) Secrets of Natural New Zealand, 1987. Add: 6 Calder Pl., Auckland 6, New Zealand.

LOCKLIN, Gerald Ivan. American, b. 1941. Novels/Short stories, Poetry. Prof. of English, California State Univ., Long Beach, since 1965. Instr., California State Univ., Los Angeles, 1964–65. *Publs:* (with Ronald Koertge and Charles Stetler) Tarzan and Shane Meet the Toad (poetry); Poop and Other Poems, 1972; Son of Poop, 1973; Locked In (short stories), 1973; Toad's Europe, 1973; The Toad Poems, 1974; The Chase: A Novel, 1976; The Criminal Mentality (poems), 1976; The Four-Day Work Week and Other Stories, 1977; Toad's Sabbatical (poetry), 1978; Frisco Epic (poetry), 1978; Pronouncing Borges (poetry), 1978; The Cure: A Novel for Speedreaders, 1979; A Weekend in Canada (short stories), 1979; Two Summer Sequences (poetry and prose), 1979; Two Weeks on Mr. Stanford's Farm (poetry), 1980; The Last Toad (poetry), 1980; Two for the Seesaw and One for the Road (poetry), 1980; Scenes from a Second Adolescence and Other Poems, 1981; By Land, Sea, and Air (poetry), 1982; Why Turn a Perfectly Good Toad into a Prince? (poems & story), 1984; The Case of the Missing Blue Volkswagen (novella), 1985; Gringo and Other Poems, 1985; (with Ray Zepeda) We Love L.A.: The Olympic Boxing Poems, 1985; The Clubford Midget Shoots Pool (poems), 1986; The English Mini-Tour (poems), 1987; A Constituency of Dunces (poems), 1988; The Death of Jean-Paul Sartre and Other Poems, 1988; Children of a Lesser Demagogue, 1988; (with Joyce Shipley, Michael Salinger, Chris Franke, and Mark Weber) Toad Comes to Cleveland (poems), 1988; Return to Ronnie Scott's (long poem), 1988; On the Rack (poems), 1988; The Gold Rush and Other Stories, 1989. Add: English Dept., California State Univ.-Long Beach, Long Beach,

Calif. 90840, U.S.A.

LOCKWOOD, David. British, b. 1929. Sociology. Prof. of Sociology, Univ. of Essex, Colchester, since 1968. Lectr., London Sch. of Economics, 1953–60; Univ. Lectr., Faculty of Economics, and Fellow, St. John's Coll., Cambridge Univ., 1960–68. Member, Social Science Research Council, 1973–76. *Publs:* The Blackcoated Worker: A Study in Class Consciousness, 1958, 1989; (with J.H. Goldthorpe, F. Bechhofer and J. Platt) The Affluent Worker: Industrial Attitudes and Behaviour, 1968; The Affluent Worker: Political Attitudes and Behaviour, 1968; The Affluent Worker in the Class Structure, 1969. Add: 82 High St., Wivenhoe, Essex, England.

LOCKWOOD, W(illiam) B(urley). British, b. 1917. Language/Linguistics. Prof. of Germanic and Indo-European Philology, Univ. of Reading, 1966–82. *Publs:* Introduction to Modern Faroese, 1955, 1964, 1977; The Faroese Bird Names, 1961; An Informal History of the German Language, 1965, 1976; Historical German Syntax, 1968; Indo-European Philology, Historical and Comparative, 1969, 3rd ed. 1977; A Panorama of Indo-European Languages, 1972; Languages of the British Isles Past and Present, 1975; Die Färöischen Sigurdlieder, 1983; The Oxford Book of British Bird Names, 1984; German Today, 1987. Add: Reading Univ., Reading, Berks., England.

LOCKYER, Roger Walter. Also edits as Philip Francis. British, b. 1927. History, Biography. Sr. Lectr. in History, Royal Holloway Coll., Univ. of London, since 1964. *Publs:* (ed.) The Trial of Charles I, 1959; (with J. Thorn and D. Smith) A History of England, 1961; (ed.) Cavendish's Life of Cardinal Wolsey, 1962; (ed. as Philip Francis) A Selection from the Diary of John Evelyn, 1963; Tudor and Stuart Britain 1471-1714, 1964; The Monarchy, 1965; (ed.) A Selection from Clarendon's History of the Great Rebellion, 1967; Henry VII, 1968; (ed.) Bacon's History of the Reign of King Henry VII, 1971; Hapsburg and Bourbon Europe 1470-1720, 1974; Buckingham, 1981. Add: 64 Fielding Rd., London W4 1HL, England.

LODGE, David. British, b. 1935. Novels/Short stories, Plays/Screenplay, Literature. Prof. of Modern English Literature, Univ. of Birmingham, since 1976 (Lectr. in English, 1960-71, Sr. Lectr., 1971-76). Asst., British Council, London, 1959-60. *Publs:* The Picturegoers, 1960; Ginger, You're Barmy, 1962; (with M. Bradbury and J. Duckett) Between These Four Walls (revue), 1963; The British Museum is Falling Down, 1965; Language of Fiction, 1966; (ed.) Graham Greene, 1966; (ed.) Jane Austen's Emma: A Casebook, 1968; Out of the Shelter, 1970; The Novelist at the Crossroads and Other Essays on Fiction and Criticism, 1971; Evelyn Waugh, 1971; (ed.) Jane Austen: Emma, 1971; (ed.) Twentieth Century Criticism: A Reader, 1972; (ed.) Thomas Hardy: The Woodlanders, 1974; Changing Places, 1975; (ed.) George Eliot: Scenes of Clerical Life; The Modes of Modern Writing, 1977; How Far Can You Go?, 1980; Working with Structuralism, 1981; Small World, 1984; Write On, 1986; Henry James: The Spoils of Poyton, 1987; Nice Work, 1988; (ed.) Modern Criticism and Theory 1989. Add: Dept. of English, Univ. of Birmingham B15 2TT, England.

LODGE, (Sir) Thomas. British, b. 1909. Medicine/Health. Emeritus Chmn. of Bd., Modern Medicine. Former Consultant Radiologist, United Sheffield Hosps., and Clinical Lectr. in Radiodiagnosis, Univ. of Sheffield, now retired. *Publs:* Recent Advances in Radiology, 3rd ed. 1955, 6th ed. 1979. Add: 46 Braemore Ct., Kingsway, Hove, E. Sussex BN3 4FG, England.

LOEPER, John J(oseph). American, b. 1929. Children's fiction, Children's non-fiction, History. *Publs:* Understanding Your Child Through Astrology, 1970; Men of Ideas, 1970; Going to School in 1776, 1972; The Flying Machine, 1975; The Shop on High Street, 1976; The Golden Dragon, 1977; Mr. Marley's Main Street Confectionery, 1979; Galloping Gertrude, 1980; By Hook and Ladder, 1981; Away We Go!, 1981; The House on Spruce Street, 1982; Going to School in 1876, 1985; Biography of Henry Bergh, 1990. Add: 110 Kiltie Dr., New Hope, Pa. 18938, U.S.A.

LOETHER, Herman John. American, b. 1930. Sociology. Prof. of Sociology, California State Univ., Dominguez Hills, since 1967 (Asst. Prof., 1957–62, Assoc. Prof., 1962–66, and Prof., 1966–67, C.S.U., Los Angeles). *Publs:* Problems of Aging, 1967, 1975; (with D.G. McTavish) Descriptive Statistics for Sociologists, 1974; (with D.G. McTavish) Inferential Statistics for Sociologists, 1974; (with D.G. McTavish) Statistical Analysis for Sociologists: A Student Manual, 1974; (with D.G. McTavish) Descriptive and Inferential Statistics: An Introduction, 1976,

1980, 1988. Add: 6564 Monero Dr., Rancho Palos Verdes, Calif. 90274, U.S.A.

LOEWENSTEIN, Louis Klee. American, b. 1927. Urban studies. Prof., San Francisco State Coll., Calif., 1968–71; Acting Prof. of Urban Planning, Stanford Univ., California, 1974–76. *Publs:* The Location of Residences and Work Places in Urban Areas, 1965; (co-author) Jobs, People and Land: Bay Area Simulation Study, 1968; (ed.) Urban Studies: An Introductory Reader, 1971, 1977; Streets of San Francisco, 1984. Add: 3858 Jackson St., San Francisco, Calif. 94118, U.S.A.

LOEWINSOHN, Ron(ald William). American, b. 1937. Poetry. Member of the English Dept., Univ. of Calif., Berkeley, since 1970. Taught poetry workshops at San Francisco State Coll., 1960–61; Teaching Fellow, Harvard Univ., 1968–70. *Publs:* Watermelons, 1959; The World of the Lie, 1963; Against the Silences to Come, 1965; L'Autre, 1967; Lying Together, Turning the Head and Shifting the Weight, The Produce District and Other Places, Moving A Spring Poem, 1967; Three Backyard Dramas with Mamas, 1967; The Sea, Around Us, 1968; The Step, 1968; These Worlds Have Always Moved in Harmony, 1968; Meat Air: Poems, 1957-1969, 1970; The Leaves, 1973; (ed.) Embodiment of Knowledge, by William Carlos Williams, 1974; Eight Fairy Tales, 1975; Goat Dances, 1976; Magnetic Field(s) (novel), 1983; Where All the Ladders Start, 1987. Add: Dept. of English, Univ. of California, Berkeley, Calif. 94720, U.S.A.

LOFTON, John M(arion). American, b. 1919. History, Law, Media, Theology/Religion. Editorial Writer, 1952–70, and Ed. of Editorial Page, 1966–70, Pittsburgh Post-Gazette, Pa; Member, Editorial Bd., St. Louis Post-Dispatch, Mo., 1971–85. *Publs:* (with G. Swetnam, W.M. Schutte and D.M. Goodfellow) Pittsburgh's First Unitarian Church, 1961; Insurrection in South Carolina: The Turbulent World of Denmark Vesey, 1964, revised as Denmark Vesey's Revolt, 1983; Justice and the Press, 1966; The Press as Guardian of the First Amendment, 1980. Add: Rt. 1, Box 104, Grantville, Kans. 66429, U.S.A.

LOGAN, Ford. *See* **NEWTON,** D.B.

LOGAN, Jake. *See* **EDMONDSON,** G.C.

LOGAN, Jake. *See* **KNOTT,** William C.

LOGAN, Jake. *See* **SMITH,** Martin Cruz.

LOGAN, Lillian. American, b. 1909. Education. Prof. Emerita of Education, Brandon Univ., Man., since 1978 (Prof., 1965–78). Prof. of Education, Evansville Univ., Ind., 1954–62, and Findlay Coll., Ohio, 1962–65. *Publs:* Teaching the Young Child, 1960; (with V. Logan) Teaching the Elementary School Child, 1961; (with V. Logan) Dynamic Approach to Language Arts, 1967; (with G. Rimmington) Social Studies, 1969; (with V. Logan) Design for Creative Teaching, 1971; (with V. Logan) Creative Communications, 1972; (with V. Logan) Educating Young Children, 1972; (with V. Logan) Estrategias para una Enseñanza Creativa, 1980. Add: 602 15th St., Brandon, Man. R7A 4W5, Canada.

LOGAN, Mark. *See* **NICOLE,** Christopher.

LOGAN, Virgil G. American, b. 1904. Education. Prof. of Speech and English, Brandon Univ., Man., 1965–74, now Emeritus. Member of faculty, Evansville Univ., Ind., 1954–62, and Findlay Coll., Ohio, 1962–65. *Publs:* all with Lillian Logan—Teaching the Elementary School Child, 1961; Dynamic Approach to Language Arts, 1967; Design for Creative Teaching, 1971; Creative Communications, 1972; Educating Young Children, 1974; (with L. Logan) Estrategias para una Enseñanza Creativa, 1980. Add: 602 15th St., Brandon, Man. R7A 4W5, Canada.

LOGUE, Christopher. British, b. 1926. Plays/Screenplays, Poetry, Documentaries/Reportage, Translations. Contrib., Private Eye, London. *Publs:* Wand and Quadrant, 1953; Devil, Maggot, and Son, 1955; (trans.) The Man Who Told His Love: Twenty Poems Based on Pablo Neruda's "Los Cantos d'Amores", 1958; The Trial of Cob and Leach: A News Play, 1959; Songs, 1959; Trials by Logue (Antigone and Cob and Leach), 1960; Songs from "The Lily-White Boys", 1960; Creon (play), 1961; (trans.) Patrocleia, 1962; True Stories, 1966; (trans.) Pax, 1967; The Girls, 1969; New Numbers, 1969; Twelve Cards, 1972; Friday (play), 1972; Savage Messiah (screenplay), 1972; (ed.) True Stories from "Private Eye", 1973; Puss-in-Boots Pop-Up, 1976; Ratsmagic, 1976; The Crocodile, 1976; Abecedary, 1977; (ed.) The Children's Book of Comic Verse, 1978; The Magic Circus (juvenile), 1979; Bumper Book of True Stories, 1980; Ode to the Dodo: Poems 1953-1978, 1981; War Music: An Account of Books

16-19 of the Iliad, 1981; (ed.) London in Verse, 1982; (ed.) Sweet and Sour: An Anthology of Comic Verse, 1983; (ed.) The Oxford Book of Pseuds, 1983; (ed.) The Children's Book of Children's Rhymes, 1987. Add: 18 Denbigh Close, London W11, England.

LOH, Pichon P(ei) Y(ung). American, b. 1928. History, Politics/Government, Biography. Calman Prof. of Political Science and East Asian History, Upsala Coll., East Orange, N.J., since 1965 (Chmn., Social Science Div., 1971–72, Educational Policies Council, 1972–73, and Personnel Policies Council, 1981–82). Seminar Assoc., Modern China Seminar, Columbia Univ., NYC, since 1960. Asst. Prof., Assoc. Prof., Prof., and Chmn., Dept. of History and Political Science, Anderson Univ., Ind., 1956–65; Research Assoc., East Asian Inst., Columbia Univ., NYC, 1967–69. *Publs:* (ed.) The Kuomintang Debacle of 1949: Conquest or Collapse?, 1965; The Early Chiang Kai-shek: A Study of His Personality and Politics, 1887-1924, 1971. Add: 15 Evergreen Pl., Tenafly, N.J. 07670, U.S.A.

LOLLIS, Lorraine. American, b. 1911. History. Secondary sch. teacher of English and Spanish, 1932–34 and 1954–60; Dir. of Voluntary Service, Christian Church (Disciples of Christ), 1971–73. *Publs:* The Shape of Adam's Rib, 1970. Add: 880 Mandalay, Apt. C-403, Clearwater, Fla. 34630, U.S.A.

LOMAS, Peter (Eric Samuel). British, b. 1923. Human relations, Psychology. Psychotherapy in private practice, since 1959. Dir., Mitcham Child Guidance Clinic, Surrey, 1968–69. *Publs:* (ed.) The Predicament of the Family, 1967; True and False Experience, 1973; The Case for a Personal Psychotherapy, 1981; The Limits of Interpretation, 1987. Add: 41 Beaulands, De Freville Ave., Cambridge, England.

LONDON, Herbert I. American, b. 1939. Education, Sociology. Prof. of Social Studies since 1967, and Dean of the Gallatin Div., New York Univ., NYC (formerly Dir. of Univ. Without Walls Prog.). Consultant, Hudson Inst., since 1969. *Publs:* (ed. and contrib.) Education in the Twenty-First Century, 1969; Non-White Immigration and the White Australia Policy, 1970; Fitting In: Crosswise at Generation Gap, 1974; (ed. and contrib.) Social Science Theory, Structure and Application, 1975; The Overheated Decade, 1976; The Seventies: Counterfeit Decade, 1979; Myths That Rule America, 1981; Closing the Circle: A Cultural History of the Rock Revolution, 1984; Why Are They Lying to Our Children?, 1984; Military Doctrine and the American Character, 1984; Armageddon in the Classroom, 1986. Add: 2 Washington Sq. Village, New York, N.Y. 10012, U.S.A.

LONDON, Laura. Joint pseudonym for Sharon Curtis (America, b. 1952) and Thomas Dale Curtis (American, b. 1951). Historical/Romance/ Gothic. *Publs:* A Heart Too Proud, 1978; The Bad Baron's Daughter, 1978; Moonlight Mist, 1979; Love's a Stage, 1980; The Gypsy Heiress, 1981; The Windflower, 1984. Add: P.O. Box 175, Greendale, Wisc. 53129, U.S.A.

LONEY, Glenn Meredith. American, b. 1928. Plays/Screenplays, Literature, Theatre, Travel. Prof. of Theatre, City Univ. of New York, since 1961. Ed., Art Deco News. Prof. of English and Speech, Univ. of Maryland Overseas, 1956–59; Prof. of English and Speech, Hofstra Univ., Hempstead, N.Y., 1959–61. *Publs:* Briefing and Conference Techniques, 1959; (ed.) Dramatic Soundings, 1968; (ed. with R. Corrigan) Tragedy, 1971; (ed. with R. Corrigan) Comedy, 1971; (ed. with R. Corrigan) Forms of Drama, 1972; (ed.) Midsummer Night's Dream, 1974; (with P. McKay) The Shakespeare Complex, 1975; The Young Vic Scapino, 1975; Your Future in the Performing Arts, 1980; The House of Mirth (play), 1981; Twentieth Century Theatre, 1982; California Gold Rush Dramas, 1982; Unsung Genius, 1984; Musical Theatre in America, 1984; Creating Careers in Musical Theatre, 1988; Staging Shakespeare, 1989. Add: Prof. in Theatre, City Univ. Grad. Center, 33 West 42nd St., New York, N.Y. 10036, U.S.A.

LONEY, Martin. British, b. 1944. Race relations, Sociology. Sr. Lectr. in Social Policy, Open Univ., since 1978. Research Dir., World Univ. Service, Geneva, 1971–73; Gen. Secty., National Council for Civil Liberties, London, 1973–74; Asst. Prof., Sch. of Social Work, Carleton Univ., Ottawa, Canada, 1974–76; Sr. Lectr. in Community Work, South Bank Polytechnic, London, 1976–78. *Publs:* Rhodesia: White Racism and Imperial Response, 1975; (ed.) The Crisis of the Inner City, 1979; (ed.) Social and Community Work in a Multi-Racial Society, 1982; (ed.) Community Work and the State, 1982; Community Against Government, 1983; (ed.) Social Policy and Social Welfare, 1983; The Politics of Greed, 1986. Add: Faculty of Social Sciences, The Open Univ., Walton Hall,

Milton Keynes MK7 6AA, England.

LONG, A(nthony) A(rthur). British, b. 1937. Classics, Philosophy. Prof. of Classics, Univ. of California, Berkeley, since 1983. Lectr. and Reader in Greek and Latin, Univ. Coll., London, 1966–73; Prof. of Greek, Univ. of Liverpool, 1973–83; Joint Ed., Classical Quarterly, 1975–81. *Publs:* Language and Thought in Sophocles, 1968; (ed.) Problems in Stoicism, 1971; Hellenistic Philosophy, 1974, 1986; (co-ed.) Theophrastus of Eresus, 1985; (with D.N. Sedley) The Hellenistic Philosophers, 1987. Add: Dept. of Classics, Univ. of California, Berkeley, Calif. 94720, U.S.A.

LONG, Edward Leroy, Jr. American, b. 1924. Theology/Religion. James W. Pearsall Prof. of Christian Ethics and Theology of Culture, Drew Univ., Madison, N.J., 1976–86, now Emeritus. Minister to Students, Blacksburg Presbyterian Church, Va., 1951–54; Assoc. Prof. of Philosophy and Ethics, 1951–54, and Assoc. Prof. and Head of Dept. of Philosophy and Religion, 1955–57, Virginia Polytechnic Inst., Blacksburg; Assoc. Prof., 1957–65, and Prof. of Religion, 1965–76, Oberlin Coll., Ohio. Series Ed., The Haddam House Series on the Christian in His Vocation, Assn. Press Publrs., 1960–64. *Publs:* Science and Christian Faith, 1950; The Christian Response to the Atomic Crisis, 1950; Religious Beliefs of American Scientists, 1952; Conscience and Compromise: An Approach to Protestant Casuistry, 1954; The Role of the Self in Conflicts and Struggle, 1962; A Survey of Christian Ethics, 1967; War and Conscience in America, 1968; (with J.T. Stephens) The Christian as a Doctor, 1960; (ed. with R.T. Handy) Theology and Church in Times of Change: Essays in Honor of John Coleman Bennett, 1970; A Survey of Recent Christian Ethics, 1982; Peace Thinking in a Warring World, 1983; Academic Bonding and Social Concern, 1984. Add: c/o The Theological School, Drew Univ., Madison, N.J. 07940, U.S.A.

LONG, Eugene Thomas. American, b. 1935. Philosophy, Theology/Religion. Prof. Dept. of Philosophy, Univ. of South Carolina, since 1973 (Assoc. Prof., 1970–73; Chmn., 1972–87). Asst. to Prof. of Philosophy, Randolph–Macon Coll., Ashland, Va., 1964–70; Fellow, Duke Univ., Univ. of N.C. Cooperative Program in the Humanities, 1968–69; Secretary–Treasurer, The Metaphysical Soc. of America, 1977–83, and American Philosophical Assn., 1985–91. Pres., Soc. for Philosophy of Religion, 1980–81. *Publs:* Jaspers and Bultmann: A Dialogue Between Philosophy and Theology in the Existentialist Tradition, 1968; (ed. and contrib.) God, Secularization and History: Essays in Memory of Ronald Gregor Smith, 1974; (ed.) Experience, Reason and God, 1980; (co–ed. and contrib.) God and Temporality, 1984; Existence, Being and God, 1985; (co–ed. and contrib.) Being and Truth, 1986. Add: Dept. of Philosophy, Univ. of South Carolina, Columbia, S.C. 29208, U.S.A.

LONG, Frank Belknap. American, b. 1903. Science fiction/Fantasy, Poetry, Supernatural/Occult topics, Biography. Former Assoc. Ed., Mike Shane Mystery Mag., and Satellite Science Fiction. *Publs:* The Hounds of Tindalos, 1946; John Carstairs: Space Detective, 1951; The Horror from the Hills, 1963; The Martian Visitors, 1965; Journey to a Star, 1965; Monster from Out of Time, 1971; Survival World, 1971; The Night of the Wolf, 1972; Rim of the Unknown, 1972; Howard Phillips Lovecraft: Dreamer on the Night Side, 1975; The Early Long, 1975; In Mayan Splendor (poetry), 1977; Rehearsal Night, 1981. Add: 421 West 21st St., New York, N.Y. 10011, U.S.A.

LONG, Freda Margaret. British, b. 1932. Historical/Romance/Gothic. Local Govt. Secty., 1950–58. *Publs:* John Plantagenet, 1965; The Coveted Crown, 1966; The Lion and the Lily, 1965; The Passionate Prince, 1968; The Spanish Tudor, 1968; Bess, 1969; The People's Martyr, 1969; Lords of the Manor, 1970; The Bartered Queens: The Queen's Progress; The Brandon Brood; Three Crowns for Mary; Royal Clown; The Gilded Cage; The Murder of Caroline Matilda; Requiem for Richard; The Hundred Days; An Admirable Woman; For the Love of Albert; The Master of Frinton Park; The Heir of Frinton Park; Mischief at Frinton Park; The Regiment; The Empresses; Haworth Harvest; The Apprentice Monarchs; Louis the Divine; The Austrian Woman; Children of the King; King on the Run; A Husband for Arabella; Duel of the Queens; Return of the King; The King over the Water; The Soldier's Woman; The Road to Moscow, The Dressmaker. Add: 144 Western Rd., Sompting, Lancing, Sussex, England.

LONGAIR, Malcolm (Sim). British, b. 1941. Astronomy. Astronomer Royal for Scotland, Regius Prof. of Astronomy, Univ. of Edinburgh, and Dir., Royal Observatory, Edinburgh, since 1980. Chmn., Space Telescope Advisory Panel, since 1977; Member, European Space Agency Telescope Working Group, since 1977, and NASA Space Telescope Science

Working Group, since 1977. Fellow, 1967–71, and Official Fellow, Clare Hall, Cambridge, and Demonstrator, 1970–75, and Lectr. in Physics, 1970–80, Cambridge Univ. Ed., Monthly Notices of Royal Astronomical Soc., 1974–78. *Publs:* (ed.) Confrontation of Cosmological Theories with Observational Data, 1974; (co–ed.) The Large– Scale Structure of the Universe, 1978; (with J.E. Gunn and M.J. Rees) Observational Cosmology, 1978; (co–ed.) The Scientific Uses of the Space Telescope, 1980; High Energy Astrophysics: An Informal Introduction, 1980; (co–ed.) Astrophysical Cosmology, 1982; Theoretical Concepts in Physics, 1984. Add: Royal Observatory, Blackford Hill, Edinburgh EH9 3HJ, Scotland.

LONGBAUGH, Harry. *See* **GOLDMAN,** William.

LONGFORD, Earl of. (Francis Aungier Pakenham). British, b. 1905. History, Autobiography/Memoirs/Personal, Biography. Dir., Sidgwick Jackson, publrs., London (Chmn., 1970–80). Lectr. in Politics, 1932–34, and Student in Politics, 1934–36 and 1952–64, Christ Church, Oxford; Personal Asst. to Sir William Beveridge, 1941–44; Parliamentary Under Secty. of State, War Office, 1946–47; Chancellor, Duchy of Lancaster, 1947–48; Minister of Civil Aviation, 1948–51; First Lord of the Admiralty, 1951; Chmn., National Bank Ltd., 1955–63; Lord Privy Seal, 1964–65; Leader of the House of Lords, 1964–68; Secty. of State for the Colonies, 1965–66; Lord Privy Seal, 1966–68. *Publs:* Peace by Ordeal: The Anglo–Irish Treaty of 1921, 1935; Born to Believe (autobiography), 1953; (with R. Opie) Causes of Crime, 1958; The Idea of Punishment, 1961; Five Lives, 1964; Humility, 1969; (with T. O'Neill) De Valera, 1970; The Life of Jesus Christ, 1974; The Grain of Wheat, 1974; Abraham Lincoln, 1975; Kennedy, 1976; St. Francis of Assisi, 1978; Nixon, 1980; (with Anne McHardy) Ulster, 1981; Pope John Paul II, 1982; Diary of a Year, 1982; Eleven at No. 10: A Personal View of Prime Ministers, 1984; One Man's Faith, 1984; The Search for Peace, 1985; The Bishops, 1986. Add: Bernhurst, Hurst Green, East Sussex, England.

LONGFORD, Elizabeth. (Countess of Longford, formerly Elizabeth Pakenham). British, b. 1906. History, Biography, Memoirs.Formerly, Trustee, National Portrait Gallery, London, and member of Advisory Bd., Victoria and Albert Museum, London. *Publs:* Jameson's Raid, 1960; Victoria R.I. (in U.S. as Queen Victoria: Born to Succeed), 1964, illustrated, 1973; Wellington: The Years of the Sword, 1969; Wellington: Pillar of State, 1972; Churchill, 1974; The Royal House of Windsor, 1974; Byron's Greece, 1975; Byron, 1976; A Pilgrimage of Passion: The Life of Wilfrid Scawen Blunt, 1979; Louisa, Lady in Waiting, 1979; Images of Chelsea, 1980; The Queen Mother, 1981; Eminent Victorian Women, 1981; Elizabeth R., 1983; The Pebbled Shore: Memoir, 1986. Add: 18 Chesil Ct., Chelsea Manor St., London, SW3, England.

LONGLEY, Michael. Irish, b. 1939. Poetry. Asst. Dir., Arts Council of Northern Ireland, Belfast, since 1970. Asst. Master, Avoca Sch., Blackrock, 1962–63; Belfast High Sch. and Erith Secondary Sch., 1963–64, and Royal Belfast Academical Instn., 1964–69. *Publs:* Ten Poems, 1965; (with Seamus Heaney and D. Hammond) Room to Rhyme, 1968; Secret Marriages: Nine Short Poems, 1968; (with B. Tebb and I. Crichton Smith) Three Regional Voices, 1968; No Continuing City: Poems 1963–68, 1969; (ed.) Causeway: The Arts in Ulster, 1971; (ed.) Under the Moon, Over the Stars: Young People's Writing from Ulster, 1971; Lares, 1972; An Exploded View: Poems, 1968-1972, 1973; Fishing in the Sky, 1975; Man Lying on a Wall, 1976; The Echo Gate: Poems 1975–1978, 1979; Selected Poems, 1963-1980, 1980; Patchwork, 1981; Poems 1963-1983, 1985; (ed.) Selected Poems by Louis MacNeice, 1988. Add: 32 Osborne Gardens, Malone, Belfast 9, Northern Ireland.

LONGMATE, Norman Richard. British, b. 1925. Mystery/Crime/Suspense, Education, History. Admin. Officer, The Electricity Council, London, 1957–82; Fleet Street journalist, 1957–62; Chief Asst., BBC Secretariat, London, 1965–83 (Radio Producer, 1963–65). *Publs:* (ed.) A Socialist Anthology, 1953; Oxford Triumphant, 1955; Death Won't Wash, 1957; A Head for Death, 1958; Strip Death Naked, 1959; Vote for Death, 1960; Death in Office, 1961; Keith in Electricity, 1961; Electricity Supply, 1961; Electricity as a Career, 1964; King Cholera, 1966; (ed.) Writing for the B.B.C., 1966; The Waterdrinkers, 1968; Alive and Well: Medicine and Public Health 1830 to the Present Day, 1970; How We Lived Then, 1971; If Britain Had Fallen, 1972; The Workhouse, 1974; The Real Dad's Army, 1974; The G.I.'s: The Americans in Britain 1942–45, 1975; Milestones in Working Class History, 1975; Air-Raid: The Bombing of Coventry 1940, 1976; When We Won The War: The Story of Victory in Europe 1945, 1977; The Hungry Mills: The Story of the Lancashire Cotton Famine 1862, 1978; (ed.) The Home Front, 1981; The Doodlebugs, 1981; The Bombers, 1982; The Breadstealers: The Fight Against the Corn Laws 1838-1846, 1984; Hitler's Rockets, 1985; Defend-

ing the Island: vol. I, From Caesar to the Armada, 1989. Add: c/o Century Hutchinson, 62–65 Chandos Pl., London WC2 4NW, England.

LONGRIGG, Roger. Also writes as Ivor Drummond, Rosalind Erskine, Domini Taylor, and Frank Parrish. British, b. 1929. Novels/Short stories, Mystery/Crime/Suspense. *Publs:* A High–Pitched Buzz, 1956; Switchboard, 1957; Wrong Number, 1959; Daughters of Mulberry, 1961; (as Rosalind Erskine) The Passion Flower Hotel, 1962; The Papers Boats, 1963; (as Rosalind Erskine) Passion Flowers in Italy, 1963; The Artless Gambler, 1964; (as Rosalind Erskine) Passion Flowers in Business, 1965; Love among the Bottles, 1967; (as Ivor Drummond) The Man with the Tiny Head, 1969; The Sun on the Water, 1969; (as Ivor Drummond) The Priests of the Abomination, 1970; The Desperate Criminals, 1971; (as Ivor Drummond) The Frog in the Moonflower, 1972; The History of Horse Racing, 1972; The Jevington System, 1973; (as Ivor Drummond) The Jaws of the Watchdog, 1973; (as Ivor Drummond) The Power of the Bug, 1974; Their Pleasing Sport, 1975; The Turf, 1975; The History of Foxhunting, 1975; (as Ivor Drummond) The Tank of Sacred Eels, 1976; The Babe in the Wood, 1976; (as Ivor Drummond) The Necklace of Skulls, 1977; (as Frank Parrish) Fire in the Barley, 1977; The English Squire and His Sport, 1977; (as Ivor Drummond) The Stench of Poppies, 1978; (as Frank Parrish) Sting of the Honeybee, 1978; (as Ivor Drummond) The Diamonds of Loreta, 1980; Bad Bet, 1982; (as Frank Parrish) Snare in the Dark, 1982; (as Frank Parrish) Bait on the Hook, 1983; (as Domini Taylor) Mother Love, 1983; (as Domini Taylor) Gemini, 1984; (as Frank Parrish) Face at the Window, 1984; (as Frank Parrish) Fly in the Cobweb, 1986; (as Domini Taylor) Suffer Little Children, 1987; (as Frank Parrish) Caught in the Birdline, 1987; (as Domini Taylor) Praying Mantis, 1988. Add: c/o Curtis Brown, 162–168 Regent St., London W1R 5TA, England.

LONGSTREET, Stephen. Also writes as Thomas Burton, Paul Haggard, David Ormsbee, and Henri Weiner. American, b. 1907. Novels/Short stories, Plays/Screenplays, Art, History, Music, Biography. Freelance writer and painter; Staff Member, Arts and Humanities Dept., Univ. of California, Los Angeles; Member, Bd. of Dirs., Graphic Soc. of Los Angeles County Museum of Art; Trustee, Los Angeles Art Assn. (Pres., 1970–82). As Thomas Burton: Film Critic, Saturday Review, NYC, 1940; Ed., Time Mag., NYC, 1941. Prof. of Modern Writing, Univ. of Southern California, 1975–80. *Publs:* Decade 1929–1939, 1940; The Golden Touch, 1941; Great Grab: An American Novel, 1941; Last Man Around the World, 1941; The Gay Sisters, 1942; The Last Man Comes Home, 1942; The Land I Live, 1943; Nine Lives with Grandfather: The Times and Turmoils of an Early American, 1944; Stallion Road, 1945, screenplay, 1946; The Sisters Liked Them Handsome, 1946; Three Days, 1947; The Crystal Girl, 1948; Gauguin (play), 1948; High Button Shoes: A Period Comedy in Two Acts, 1949; The Pedlocks, a Family, 1951; The Beach House, 1952; A Century on Wheels: The Story of Studebaker 1852–1952, 1952; The Lion at Morning, 1954; The Boy in the Model T: A Journey into the Just–Gone Past, 1956; The Real Jazz, Old and New, 1956; The Promoters, 1957; The Burning Man, 1958; (with E. Longstreet) Man of Montmartre: A Novel Based on the Life of Maurice Utrillo, 1958, screenplay, 1963; (with B. Pearson) Never Look Back: The Autobiography of a Jockey, 1958; (with Mae West) Goodness Had Nothing to Do with It, 1959; The Crime, 1959; (with E. Longstreet) The Politician, 1959; (with E. Longstreet) Geisha, 1960; Eagles Where I Walk, 1961; Gettysburg, 1961; (ed.) A Treasury of the World's Great Prints, 1961; The Flesh Peddlers, 1962; A Few Painted Feathers, 1963; The Figure in Art, 1963; Living High, 1963; The Nylon Island, 1964; The Golden Runaways, 1964; Sportin' House: A History of the New Orleans Sinners and the Birth of Jazz, 1965; War in the Golden Weather, 1965; (with H. Carmichael) Sometimes I Wonder: The Story of Hoagy Carmichael, 1965; Pedlock and Sons, 1966; (with J.J. Godoff) Remember William Kite?, 1966; Masts to Spear the Stars, 1967; The Young Men of Paris, 1967; Senator Silverthorn, 1968; The Wilder Shore: A Gala Social History of San Francisco's Sinners and Spenders 1849–1906, 1968; (with E. Lockstreet) A Salute to American, Cooking, 1968; Pedlock Saint, Pedlock Sinner, 1969; She Walks in Beauty, 1970; War Cries on Horseback, The Stories of the Indian Wars of the Great Plains, 1970; (with E. Longstreet) Yoshiwara: City of the Senses, 1970; The Canvas Falcons: The Story of the Men and Planes of World War I, 1970; (ed.) Nell Kimball: Her Life as an American Madam, 1970; The Pedlock Inheritance, 1972; We All Went to Paris: Americans in the City of Light 1776–1971, 1972; The Divorce, 1974; The General, 1974; City of Two Rivers, 1975; The Bank, 1976; God and Sarah Pedlock, 1976; Strike the Bell Boldly, 1977; All Star Cast, 1977; Win or Lose, 1977; The Pedlocks in Love, 1978; Straw Boss, 1978; Ambassador, 1978; Storm Watch, 1979; The Queen Bees: The Women Who Shaped America, 1979; The Pembroke Colors, 1981; The Dream Seekers, 1981; Wheel of Fortune, 1981; The Golden Touch, 1982; All or Nothing, 1983; Our Father's House, 1985; Storyville to Harlem: Fifty Years in the Jazz Scene,

1986; Sons and Daughers, 1987; screenplays—The Gay Sisters, 1942; The Imposter, 1944; Uncle Harry, 1945; The Jolson Story, 1946; Duel in the Sun, 1946; The Greatest Show on Earth, 1952; Stars and Stripes Forever, 1952; Houdini, 1953: (with D. Freeman) The First Travelling Saleslady, 1956; Untamed Youth, 1957; (with others) The Helen Morgan Story, 1957; Born Reckless, 1959; Wild Harvest, 1961; Rider on a Dead Horse, 1963; The Secret Door, 1964; as Thomas Burton—And So Dedicated, 1940; Bloodbird, 1941; as Paul Haggard—Dead is the Doornail, 1937; Death Talks Shop, 1938; Death Walks on Cat Feet, 1938; Poison from a Wealthy Widow, 1938; as David Ormsbee—The Sound of an American, 1942; Chico Goes to the Wars: A Chronicle . . . 1933–1943, 1943; as Henri Weiner—Crime on the Cuff, 1936; The Case of the Severed Skull, 1940. Add: c/o Putman Publishing, 200 Madison Ave., New York, N.Y. 10016, U.S.A.

LONGWORTH, Philip. British, b. 1933. History. Prof. of History, McGill Univ., Montreal, since 1984. *Publs:* (trans.) A Hero of Our Time, by Lermontov, 1962; The Art of Victory, 1965; The Unending Vigil, 1967, 1985; The Cossacks, 1969; The Three Empresses, 1971; The Rise and Fall of Venice, 1974; Alexis, Tsar of All the Russias, 1984. Add: c/o A.M. Heath and Co., 79 St. Martins Ln., London WC2N 4AA, England.

LONGYEAR, Barry B. American, b. 1942. Science fiction. Freelance writer since 1977. Publisher, Sol III Publications, Philadelphia, 1968–72, and Farmington, Maine, 1972–77. *Publs:* City of Baraboo, 1980; Manifest Destiny (stories), 1980; Circus World (stories), 1980; Elephant Song, 1981; The Tomorrow Testament, 1983; It Came from Schenectady, 1984; Sea of Glass, 1986; Saint Mary Blue, 1988; Naked Came the Robot, 1988; The God Box, 1989; Homecoming, 1989. Add: Box 751, Farmington, Maine 04938, U.S.A.

LOOMES, Brian. British, b. 1938. Crafts, Biography. Antique Dealer, since 1967. Formerly, Professional Genealogist. *Publs:* Yorkshire Clockmakers, 1972; Westmorland Clocks and Clockmakers, 1974; The White Dial Clock, 1974; Lancashire Clocks and Clockmakers, 1975; Country Clocks and their London Origins, 1976; Watch and Clock Makers of the World, vol. II, 1976; Complete British Clocks, 1978; The Early Clockmakers of Great Britain, 1982; Grandfather Clocks and their Cases, 1985. Add: Calf Haugh Farm, Pateley Bridge, Yorks., England.

LOOMIE, Albert Joseph. American, b. 1922. History. Prof. of History, Fordham Univ., since 1968 (member of faculty since 1958). Member of the Jesuit Order since 1939. *Publs:* (with C.M. Lewis) The Spanish Jesuit Mission in Virginia, 1570–72, 1953; Toleration and Diplomacy: The Religious Issue in Anglo–Spanish Relations 1603–1605, 1963; The Spanish Elizabethans: The English Exiles at the Court of Philip II, 1964; Guy Fawkes in Spain, 1971; Spain and the Jacobean Catholics, vol. I, 1973, vol. II, 1978; Ceremonies of Charles I: The Notebooks of John Finet 1628–41, 1987. Add: Dept. of History, Fordham Univ., New York, N.Y. 10458, U.S.A.

LOOMIS, Edward (Warren). American, b. 1924. Novels/Short stories, Literature, Writing/Journalism. Prof. Emeritus of English, Univ. of California at Santa Barbara (Instr., 1959–60; Asst. Prof., 1960–62; Assoc. Prof., 1962–66). *Publs:* End of a War, 1958; The Charcoal Horse, 1959; Heroic Love (short stories), 1960; The Hunter Deep in Summer, 1961; The Mothers, 1962; Men of Principle, 1963; Vedettes: A Collection of Stories, 1964; On Fiction, Critical Essays and Notes, 1966; Four Women (short stories), 1967; Of Bank Burning: A Documentary Novel from Isla Vista, 1970; Creative Writing: The Art of Lying, 1971. Add: Dept. of English, Univ. of California, Santa Barbara, Calif., U.S.A.

LOPREATO, Joseph. American, b. 1928. Sociology. Prof. of Sociology, Univ. of Texas, since 1966 (Chmn., Dept. of Sociology, 1969–72). Asst. Prof. of Sociology, Univ. of Massachusetts, Amherst, 1960–62; Visiting Lectr. of Sociology, Univ. of Rome, 1962–64; Assoc. Prof., Univ. of Connecticut, Storrs, 1964–66. *Publs:* Vilfredo Pareto, 1965; Peasants No More, 1967; Italian Americans, 1970; (with C.E. Hazelrigg) Class, Conflict, and Mobility, 1972; (with L.S. Lewis) Social Stratification: A Reader, 1974; The Sociology of Vilfredo Pareto, 1975; Human Nature and Biocultural Evolution, 1984. Add: Dept. of Sociology, Univ. of Texas, Austin, Tex. 78712, U.S.A.

LORAINE, Philip. *See* ESTRIDGE, Robin.

LORANT, Stefan. American, b. 1901. History, Autobiography/Memoirs/Personal, Biography. Ed., Munchner Illustrierte Presse, Munich, 1928–33; Ed., Weekly Illustrated, 1934, Lilliput, 1937–40, and Picture Post, 1938–40, all London. *Publs:* I Was Hitler's Prisoner, 1935;

Lincoln, His Life in Photographs, 1941; (ed.) The New World, 1946, 1965; FDR, A Pictorial Biography, 1950; The Presidency, 1951; Lincoln, A Picture Story of His Life, 1952, 3rd ed. 1969; The Life of Abraham Lincoln, 1954; The Life and Times of Theodore Roosevelt, 1959; Pittsburgh, The Story of an American City, 1964, 4th ed. 1988; The Glorious Burden: The American Presidency, 1968, 1976; Sieg Heil! An Illustrated History from Bismarck to Hitler, 1974; The Years Before Hitler, 1989. Add: Box 803, Lenox, Mass. 01240, U.S.A.

LORD, Allison. *See* ELLIS, Julie.

LORD, Graham John. British, b. 1943. Novels/Short stories. Book Critic, Sunday Express, London, since 1969 (Reporter, 1965–69). *Publs:* Marshmallow Pie, 1970; A Roof Under Your Feet, 1973; The Spider and the Fly, 1974; God and All His Angels, 1976; The Nostradamus Horoscope, 1981; Time Out of Mind, 1986. Add: Sunday Express, 245 Blackfriars Rd., London SE1 9UX, England.

LORD, Jeffrey. *See* NELSON, Ray.

LORD, John Vernon. British, b. 1939. Children's fiction. Prof. of Illustration, Brighton Polytechnic, since 1986 (Head, Dept. of Visual Communication, 1974–81). Chmn., CNAA Graphic Design Bd., 1981–84. *Publs:* (with J. Burroway) The Truck on the Track, 1970; (with J. Burroway) The Giant Jam Sandwich, 1972; The Runaway Roller Skate, 1973; Mr. Mead and His Garden, 1974; Who's Zoo, 1977; Miserable Aunt Bertha, 1980; Edward Lear's Nonsense Verse, 1984; Doodles and Diaries, 1985; (with J. Michie) Aesop's Fables, 1989; (with Ruth Craft) The Song That Sings the Bird, 1989. Add: Upwell, 4 Orchard Lane, Ditchling, Hassocks, Sussex BN6 8TH, England.

LORD, Nancy. *See* TITUS, Eve.

LORD, Robert. New Zealander, b. 1945. Plays/Screenplays. *Publs:* Moody Tuesday, 1972; Balance of Payments, 1978; Bert and Maisey (play), 1988; Country Cops (play), 1988. Add: c/o Gilbert Parker, William Morris Agency, 1350 Ave. of the Americas, New York, N.Y. 10019, U.S.A.

LORD, Walter. American, b. 1917. History. Member of Bd. of Dirs., Union Settlement, since 1959; Trustee, New York Soc. Library, since 1963, New York Historical Soc., since 1965, and South St., Seaport Museum, since 1980; Member, Ocean Liner Museum, since 1983. Member of Bd. of Dirs., Municipal Art Soc., NYC, 1958–67, and Museum of the City of New York, 1964–72. Member of Council, Author's League, 1972–82; Pres., Soc. of American Historians, 1981–84. *Publs:* (ed.) The Fremantle Diary, 1954; A Night to Remember, 1955; Day of Infamy, 1957; The Good Years, 1960; A Time to Stand, 1961; Peary to the Pole, 1963; The Past That Would Not Die, 1965; Incredible Victory, 1967; The Dawn's Early Light, 1972; Lonely Vigil, 1977; The Miracle of Dunkirk, 1982; The Night Lives On, 1986. Add: 116 E. 68th St., New York, N.Y. 10021, U.S.A.

LORDE, Audre (Geraldin). American, b. 1934. Poetry. Prof. of English, Hunter Coll., NYC, since 1981. Staff member, Mt. Vernon Public Library, NYC, 1961–63; Instr., Town Sch., NYC, 1966–68, City Coll. of New York, 1968–70, and Lehman Coll., NYC, 1969–70; Lectr., John Jay Coll. of Criminal Justice, NYC, 1970–81. *Publs:* The First Cities, 1968; Cables to Rage, 1970; From a Land Where Other People Live, 1973; New York Head Shop and Museum, 1974; Between Our Selves, 1976; Coal, 1976; The Black Unicorn, 1978; The Cancer Journals, 1980; Chosen Poems Old and New, 1982; Zami: A New Spelling of My Name, 1983; Our Dead Behind Us, 1984; Sister In Arms, 1985; A Burst of Light (essays), 1988. Add: 207 St. Paul's Ave., Staten Island, N.Y. 10304, U.S.A.

LORENZ, Sarah. *See* WINSTON, Sarah.

LORIN, Amii. Pseud. for John M. Hohl; also writes as Paula Roberts. American. Historical/Romance. *Publs:* Morning Rose, Evening Savage, 1980, in U.K. as Morning Rose, 1982; The Tawny Gold Man, 1980; Breeze Off the Ocean, 1980; (as Paula Roberts) Come Home to Love, 1980; Morgan Wade's Woman, 1981; The Game is Played, 1981; Snowbound Weekend, 1982; Gambler's Love, 1982; Candleglow, 1983; While the Fire Rages, 1984; Nightstriker, 1985; Power and Seduction, 1985; as John Hohl—Thorne's Way, 1982; Moments Harsh, Moments Gentle, 1984; A Taste for Rich Things, 1984; A Much Needed Holiday, 1986; Texas Gold, 1986; California Copper, 1986; Nevada Silver, 1987; Someone Waiting, 1987; The Scents of Lilacs, 1987; Lady Ice, 1987;

One Tough Hombre, 19876; Falcon's Flight, 1987; Window on Yesterday, 1988; Window on Tomorrow, 1989; The Gentleman Insists, 1989. Add: c/o Silhouette Books, 300 E. 42nd St., New York, N.Y. 10017, U.S.A.

LORRIMER, Claire. Pseud. for Patricia Denise Clark; also writes as Patricia Robins and Susan Patrick. British, b. 1921. Historical/Romance/Gothic, Children's fiction, Poetry, Biography. Sub-Ed., Woman's Illustrated mag., London, 1938–40. *Publs:* novel, as Susan Patrick—Statues of Snow, 1948; novels, as Patricia Robins—To the Stars, 1944; See No Evil, 1945; Three Loves, 1949; Awake My Heart, 1950; Beneath the Moon, 1951; Leave My Heart Alone, 1951; The Fair Deal, 1952; Heart's Desire, 1953; So This Is Love, 1953; Heaven in Our Hearts, 1954; One Who Cares, 1954; Love Cannot Die, 1955; The Foolish Heart, 1956; Give All to Love, 1956; Where Duty Lies, 1957; He Is Mine, 1957; Love Must Wait, 1958; Lonely Quest, 1959; Lady Chatterley's Daughter, 1961; The Last Chance, 1961; The Long Wait, 1962; The Runaways, 1962; Seven Loves, 1962; With All My Love, 1963; The Constant Heart, 1964; Second Love, 1964; The Night Is Thine, 1964; There Is But One, 1965; No More Loving, 1965; Topaz Island, 1965; Love Me Tomorrow, 1966; The Uncertain Joy, 1966; The Man Behind the Mask, 1967; Forbidden, 1967; Sapphire in the Sand, 1968; Return to Love, 1968; Laugh on Friday, 1969; No Stone Unturned, 1969; Cinnabar House, 1970; Under the Sky, 1970; The Crimson Tapestry, 1972; Play Fair with Love, 1972; None But He, 1973; novels, as Claire Lorrimer—A Voice in the Dark, 1967; The Shadow Falls, 1974; Relentless Storm, 1975; The Secret of Quarry House, 1976; Mavreen, 1976; Tamarisk, 1978; Chantal, 1980; The Garden (cameo), 1980; The Chatelaine, 1981; The Wilderling, 1982; Last Year's Nightingale, 1984; Frost in the Sun, 1986; House of Tomorrow (biography), 1987; juvenile, as Patricia Robins —The Adventures of the Three Baby Bunnies, 1934; Tree Fairies, 1945; Sea Magic, 1946; The Heart of a Rose, 1947; The £100 Reward, 1966. Add: Chiswell Barn, Marsh Green, Edenbridge, Kent TN8 5AP, England.

LOSS, Louis. American, b. 1914. Law. William Nelson Cromwell Prof. Emeritus of Law, Harvard Univ., Cambridge, Mass., since 1984 (Prof., 1952–62; William Nelson Cromwell Prof., 1962–84). Reporter, American Law Inst.'s Federal Securities Code, Philadelphia. Assoc. Gen. Counsel, U.S. Securities and Exchange Commn., 1948–52. *Publs:* Securities Regulation, 1st ed., 1 vol., 1951, 2nd ed., 3 vols., 1961, supplement vols. 4–6, 1969; Blue Sky Law, 1958; (ed.) Multinational Approaches—Corporate Insiders, 1976; Fundamentals of Securities Regulation, 1983, 1987; (co-ed.) Japanese Securities Regulation, 1983. Add: Harvard Law Sch., Cambridge, Mass. 02138, U.S.A.

LOTHIAN, (Thomas Robert) Noel. Australian, b. 1915. Horticulture. Sr. Lectr. in Horticulture, Univ. of New Zealand, 1944–47; Dir., Botanic Gardens, Adelaide, 1948–80. *Publs:* Practical Home Gardener; (with I. Holliday) Growing Australian Plants; Commonsense Gardening; Complete Australian Gardener. Add: P.O. Box 27A, Crafers, S.A., Australia 5152.

LOTT, Arnold S. American, b. 1912. History. Gen. Ed., Leeward Publs. Inc., and Leeward Enterprises Inc., Annapolis, since 1974. With U.S. Navy from 1931 until retirement as Lt. Comdr. in 1961. *Publs:* A Long Line of Ships, 1954; Most Dangerous Sea, 1960; Alamanac of Naval Facts, 1962; Brave Ship, Brave Men, 1965; Blue Jacket Manual, 1973; (co-author) North Carolina, 1974; (co-author) Alabama, 1975; (co-author) Pearl Harbor Attack, 1975; (with E. Engle) America's Maritime Heritage, 1975; Yorktown, 1975; Ward, First Shot Ship, 1977; Arizona, 1978; Traditions of the Navy, 1978; Man in Flight, 1979; (co-ed.) Ships Data 1, 1982. Add: c/o Naval Inst. Press, U.S. Naval Inst., Annapolis, Md. 21402, U.S.A.

LOTT, Milton. American, b. 1919. Westerns/Adventure. Welder in a shipyard, 1940–44; millwright 1948–54. *Publs:* The Last Hunt, 1954; Dance Back the Buffalo, 1959; Backtrack, 1965. Add: 1212 Soda Canyon Rd., Napa, Calif. 94558, U.S.A.

LOTTMAN, Herbert. American, b. 1927. Intellectual history, Biography. International Corresp. of Publishers Weekly, NYC. *Publs:* Detours from the Grand Tour, 1970; How Cities are Saved, 1976; Albert Camus: A Biography, 1979; The Left Bank: Writers, Artists and Politics from the Popular Front to the Cold War, 1982; Pétain, Hero or Traitor?, 1985; People's Anger: Justice and Revenge after the Liberation of France, 1986; Flaubert: A Biography, 1988. Add: B.P. 214, 75264 Paris Cedex 06, France.

LOVELACE, Earl. Trinidadian, b. 1935. Novels/Short stories, Agricultural Asst., Jamaican Civil Service. *Publs:* While Gods are Fall-

ing, 1965; The Schoolmaster, 1968; The Dragon Can't Dance, 1979; The Wine of Astonishment, 1982; Jestina's Calypso and Other Plays, 1984. Add: c/o Andre Deutsch, 105 Great Russell St., London WC1B 3LJ. England.

LOVELL, (Sir) (Alfred Charles) Bernard. British, b. 1913. Astronomy. Prof. of Radio Astronomy, and Dir. of Nuffield Radio Astronomy Labs. at Jodrell Bank, Univ. of Manchester, 1951–81. Pres., Royal Astronomical Soc., 1969–71. *Publs:* Science and Civilization, 1939; World Power Resources and Social Development, 1945; (with J.A. Clegg) Radio Astronomy, 1952; Meteor Astronomy, 1954; (with R. Hanbury Brown) The Exploration of Space by Radio, 1957; The Individual and the Universe, 1959; The Exploration of Outer Space, 1962; (with M. Joyce Lovell) Discovering the Universe, 1963; Our Present Knowledge of the Universe, 1967; The Story of Jodrell Bank, 1968; Out of the Zenith: Jodrell Bank, 1957–70, 1973; The Origins and International Economics of Space Exploration, 1973; Man's Relation to the Universe, 1975; P.M.S. Blackett: A Biographical Memoir, 1976; In the Center of Immensities, 1978; Emerging Cosmology, 1981; The Jodrell Bank Telescopes, 1985, Voice of the Universe, 1987; (with F. Graham Smith) Pathways to the Universe, 1988. Add: Jodrell Bank, Macclesfield, Cheshire, England.

LOVELL, Marc. *See* **McSHANE,** Mark.

LOVESEY, Peter (Harmer). Also writes as Peter Lear. British, b. 1936. Mystery/Crime/Suspense, Sports/Physical education/Keeping fit. Head of Gen. Education Dept., Hammersmith and West London Coll., London, 1969–75. *Publs:* The Kings of Distance, 1968; (with Tom McNab) The Guide to British Track and Field Literature, 1275–1968, 1969; Wobble to Death, 1970; The Detective Wore Silk Drawers, 1971; Abracadaver, 1972; Mad Hatter's Holiday, 1973; Invitation to a Dynamite Party (in U.S. as The Tick of Death), 1974; A Case of Spirits, 1975; Swing, Swing Together, 1976; (as Peter Lear) Goldengirl, 1977; Waxwork, 1978; The Official Centenary History of the Amateur Athletic Association, 1979; (as Peter Lear) Spider Girl, 1980; The False Inspector Dew, 1982; Keystone, 1983; Butchers and Other Stories of Crime, 1985; (as Peter Lear) The Secret of Spandau, 1986; Rough Cider, 1986; Bertie and the Tinman, 1987; On the Edge, 1989. Add: c/o John Farquharson Ltd., 162–168 Regent St., London W1R 5TB, England.

LOW, Alfred D. American, b. 1913. History, International relations/Current affairs, Politics/Government. Prof. of History Emeritus, Marquette Univ., Milwaukee, Wisc., since 1983 (Prof., 1965–83); Visiting Lectr., Adult Education, Seattle, since 1986. Asst. Prof., 1946–47, and Assoc. Prof. of History and Political Science, 1947–57, Marietta Coll., Ohio; Assoc. Prof., 1957–60, and Prof. of History and Political Science, 1960–63, Youngstown Univ., Ohio; Prof. of History and Political Science and Chmn. of Dept., Iowa Wesleyan Coll., Mt. Pleasant, 1964–65; Visiting Prof., Univ. of Michigan, Ann Arbor, 1973; Visiting Prof., Univ. of Wisc., Madison, 1976; Visiting Prof., Hebrew Univ. of Jerusalem, 1984. *Publs:* Lenin and the Question of Nationality, 1958; The Soviet Hungarian Republic and the Paris Peace Conference, 1963; The Anschluss Movement, 1918–1919, and the Paris Peace Conference, 1974; The Sino–Soviet Dispute: An Analysis of the Polemics, 1976; Jews in the Eyes of the Germans, 1979; An Annotated Bibliography of the Anschluss Movement 1918–1938, 1984; The Anschluss Movement 1931–1938 and the Great Powers, 1985; The Sino–Soviet Confrontation since Mao–Zedong, 1987; Soviet Jewry and Soviet Policy, 1989. Add: 1840 184th Ave., N.E., Bellevue, Wash. 98007, U.S.A.

LOW, Anthony. American, b. 1935. Literature. Prof. of English, New York Univ., since 1978 (Asst. Prof., 1968–71; Assoc. Prof., 1971–78). Asst. Prof., Seattle Univ., Wash., 1965–68. *Publs:* Augustine Baker, 1970; The Blaze of Noon: A Reading of Samson Agonistes, 1974; Love's Architecture: Devotional Modes in Seventeenth–Century English Poetry, 1978; (ed.) Urbane Milton: The Latin Poems, 1984; The Georgic Revolution, 1985. Add: Dept. of English, New York Univ., 19 University Pl., New York, N.Y. 10003, U.S.A.

LOW, Dorothy Mackie. Pseud. for Lois Dorothea Low when writing romance fiction; also writes romantic suspense as Zoe Cass, and suspense as Lois Paxton. British, b. 1916. Mystery/Crime/Suspense, Historical/Romance/Gothic. Chmn., Romantic Novelists Assn., 1969–71. *Publs:* Isle for a Stranger, 1962; Dear Liar, 1963; A Ripple on the Water, 1964; The Intruder, 1965; A House in the Country, 1968; (as Lois Paxton) The Man Who Died Twice,1969; To Burgundy and Back, 1970; (as Lois Paxton) The Quiet Sound of Fear, 1971; (as Lois Paxton) Who Goes There?, 1972; (as Zoe Cass) Island of the Seven Hills, 1974; (as Zoe Cass) The Silver Leopard, 1976; (as Zoe Cass) A Twist in the Silk, 1980;

(as Lois Paxton) The Man in the Shadows, 1983. Add: 6 Belmont Mews, Abbey Hill, Kenilworth, Warwickshire, CV8 1LU, England.

LOW, Rachael. British. Film. Researcher engaged in a history of British cinema: with British Film Inst., London, 1945–48, and Gulbenkian Research Fellow, Lucy Cavendish Coll., Cambridge, 1968–71; Fellow Commoner of Lucy Cavendish Coll., 1983. *Publs:* History of the British Film, 1896–1906, 1948; (with Roger Manvell), 1906–1914, 1949, 1914–1918, 1950, 1918–1929, 1971, 1929–39, 3 vols., 1979–85. Add: c/o Allen Unwin Ltd., 40 Museum St., London WC1, England.

LOWBURY, Edward (Joseph Lister). British, b. 1913. Poetry, Literature. Physician. Hon. Dir., Hosp. Infection Research Lab., Birmingham, 1960–79; Visiting Prof., Univ. of Aston, Birmingham, 1979–88. *Publs:* Fire: A Symphonic Ode, 1934; Crossing the Line, 1946; Metamorphoses, 1955; (with T. Heywood) Facing North (miscellany), 1960; Time for Sale, 1961; New Poems, 1965; Daylight Astronomy, 1968; Figures of Eight, 1969; (with T. Salter and A. Young) Thomas Campion: Poet, Composer, Physician, 1970; Green Magic, 1972; Two Confessions, 1973; The Night Watchman, 1974; (with J. Press and M. Riviere) Poetry and Paradox, 1976; (ed.) Widening Circles, 1976; Troika, 1977; (ed.) Night Ride and Sunrise, 1978; Selected Poems, 1978; The Ring, 1979; A Letter from Masada, 1982; (ed. with Alison Young) The Poetical Works of Andrew Young, 1985; Birmingham, Birmingham!, 1985; Variations on Aldeburgh, 1987; A Letter from Hampstead, 1987; Apocryphal Letters, 1989. Add: 79 Vernon Rd., Birmingham B16 9SQ, England.

LOWDEN, Desmond Scott. British, b. 1937. Novels/Short stories, Plays/Screenplays. *Publs:* Bandersnatch, 1969; The Boondocks, 1972; Bellman and True, 1975; Boudapesti 3, 1979; Sunspot, 1981; Cry Havoc, 1984. Add: c/o Deborah Rogers Ltd., 20 Powis Mews, London W11 1JN, England.

LOWE, Stephen. British, b. 1947. Plays/Screenplays. Artistic dir., Meeting Ground Theatre Co., Nottingham, since 1984. Actor and dir., Stephen Joseph Theatre–in–the–Round, Scarborough, Yorks., 1975–78; Sr. Lectr., Dartington Coll. of Arts, Devon, 1978–82. *Publs:* Touched, 1977, 1981; The Ragged Trousered Philanthropists, 1978, 1983; Tibetan Inroads, 1981; Cards, 1983; Moving Pictures: Four Plays, 1985; (ed.) Peace Plays, 2 vols., 1985, 1989; Divine Gossip, 1989; (trans.) William Tell, 1989. Add: c/o Goodwin Assocs., 12 Rabbit Row, London W8 4DX, England.

LOWELL, Elizabeth. Pseud. for Ann Elizabeth Maxwell; also writes as A.E. Maxwell. American, b. 1944. Historical/Romance. *Publs:* (as A.E. Maxwell) Golden Empire, 1979; Summer Thunder, 1983; The Danvers Touch, 1983; Forget Me Not, 1984; Lover in the Rough, 1984; Summer Games, 1984; A Woman Without Lies, 1985; The Valley of the Sun, 1985; Traveling Man, 1985; Fires of Eden, 1986; Sequel, 1986; The Fire of Spring, 1986; Too Hot to Handle, 1986; Tell Me No Lies, 1986; Love Song for a Raven, 1987; Sweet Wind, Wild Wind, 1987; (as A.E. Maxwell) Redwood Empire, 1987; Fever, 1988; Chain Lightning, 1988; Dark Fire, 1988; Reckless Love, 1989; as Ann Maxwell—Change, 1975; The Singer Enigma, 1976; A Dead God Dancing, 1979; Name of a Shadow, 1980; The Jaws of Menx, 1981; Fire Dancer, 1982; Dancer's Luck, 1983; Dancer's Illusion, 1983; Timeshadow Rider, 1986; as A.E. Maxwell— (with Evan Maxwell and Ivar Ruud) The Year–Long Day, 1977; (with Evan Maxwell) Steal the Sun, 1981; (with Evan Maxwell) Just Another Day in Paradise, 1985; (with Evan Maxwell) The Frog and the Scorpion, 1986; (with Evan Maxwell) Gatsby's Vineyard, 1987; (with Evan Maxwell) Just Enough Light to Kill, 1988; (with Evan Maxwell) The Art of Survival, 1989. Add: P.O. Box 7857, Laguna Niguel, Calif. 92677, U.S.A.

LOWEN, Alexander. American, b. 1910. Human relations, Psychiatry, Psychology, Sex. Psychiatrist in private practice since 1953; Assoc. Dir., New England Heart Center. Exec. Dir., Inst. for Bioenergetic Analysis, NYC. *Publs:* Physical Dynamics of Character Structure, 1958; Love and Orgasm, 1965; The Betrayal of the Body, 1967; Depression and the Body, 1973; Pleasure, 1975; Bioenergetics, 1975; (with Leslie Lowan) The Way to Vibrant Health, 1977; Fears of Life, 1980; Narcissism, 1983; Love, Sex and Your Heart, 1988. Add: Puddin Hill Rd., New Canaan, Conn., U.S.A.

LOWENTHAL, Leo. American, b. 1900. Literature, Sociology, Autobiography/Memoirs/Personal. Prof. of Sociology Emeritus, Univ. of California, Berkeley, (joined faculty, 1956); also at Univ. of Frankfurt, W. Germany. Sr. Research Assoc., Inst. of Social Research, Frankfurt, 1926–33; Lectr. in Sociology, Columbia Univ., NYC, 1940–54; Dir. of Research, Voice of America, U.S. Dept. of State, 1949–54. *Publs:*

Prophets of Deceit, 1949; Literature and the Image of Man, 1957; (with S.M. Lipset) Culture and Social Character, 1961; Literature, Popular Culture and Society, 1961; Erzaehlkunst und Gesellschaft, 1971; Notizen zur Literatur Soziologie, 1975; Mitmachen wollte ich nie (autobiography), 1980; Schriften (collected writings) 5 vols., 1982–87; Communication in Society, vol. I: Literature and Mass Culture, 1984, vol. II: Literature and the Image of Man, 1986; An Unmastered Past: Autobiographical Reflections, 1987. Add: Dept. of Sociology, 410 Barrows, Univ. of California, Berkeley, Calif. 94720, U.S.A.

LOWING, Anne. *See* GEACH, Christine.

LOWNDES, Robert A(ugustine) W(ard). American, b. 1916. Science fiction/Fantasy, Literature. Production Assoc., Radio Electronics mag., since 1978; Ed., Airmont Classics; also freelance writer of science fiction short stories under various pseuds. Worked for the Civilian Conservation Corps, 1934, 1936–37, 1939; asst. on a squab farm; salesman; porter, Greenwich Hosp. Assn., Conn., 1937–38; Literary Agent, Fantastory Sales Service, 1940–42; Ed., Future Fiction, 1940–42, and Science Fiction Quarterly, 1940–42, 1951–58; Ed. Dir., Columbia mags., 1942–60; Ed., Future Science Fiction, 1950–60, Dynamic Science Fiction, 1952–54, and Science Fiction Stories, 1953–60; Ed., Avalon science–fiction series, Thomas Bouregy, 1955–67; Ed., Famous Science Fiction, 1960–69, Mag. of Horror, 1962–71, Startling Mystery Stories, 1966–71, Weird Terror Tales, 1969–70, and Bizarre Fantasy Fiction, 1970–71; Assoc. Ed., 1971–77, and Managing Ed., 1977–78, Sexology and Luz mags; Production Chief, 1978–81, and Ed. in English, 1982–84, Luz mag. *Publs:* Mystery of the Third Mine (juvenile), 1953; (with James Blish) The Duplicated Man, 1959; The Puzzle Planet, 1961; Believer's World, 1961; Three Faces of Science Fiction, 1973; (ed.) The Best of James Blish, 1979. Add: 717 Willow Ave., Hoboken, N.J. 07030, U.S.A.

LOWRY, Beverly (Fey). American, b. 1938. Novels. Assoc. Prof. of Fiction Writing, Univ. of Houston, since 1976. *Publs:* Come Back, Lolly Ray, 1977; Emma Blue, 1978; Daddy's Girl, 1981; The Perfect Sonya, 1987; Breaking Gentle, 1988. Add: Dept. of History, Univ. of Houston, Houston, Tex. 77004, U.S.A.

LOWRY, Charles W. American, b. 1905. Theology/Religion. Ed., The Blessings of Liberty, since 1956; Columnist, The Pilot, Southern Pines, N.C., since 1979. Member, N.C. Commn. on the Bicentennial of the U.S. Constitution, since 1985. Pres., Foundn. for Religious Action. Episcopal Chaplain, Univ. of California, Berkeley, 1933–34; Prof. of Systematic Theology, Protestant Episcopal Theological Seminary, Alexandria, Va., 1934–43; Rector, All Saints' Episcopal Church, Chevy Chase, Md., 1943–53; Minister, Village Chapel, Pinehurst, N.C., 1966–73. *Publs:* The Trinity and Christian Devotion, 1946; Christianity and Materialism, 1948; Communism and Christ, 1952, 1962; Conflicting Faiths: Christianity vs. communism, 1953; To Pray or Not to Pray!: Hand Book on Church and State in U.S., 1963; The Kingdom of Influence, 1969; William Temple: An Archbishop for All Seasons, 1982; The First Theologians, 1986. Add: Box 1829, Pinehurst, N.C. 28374, U.S.A.

LOWRY, Lois (née Hammersberg). American, b. 1937. Children's fiction, Literary criticism. *Publs:* Black American Literature, 1973; Literature of the American Revolution, 1974; Values and the Family, 1977; A Summer to Die, 1977; Find a Stranger, Say Goodbye, 1978; Here in Kennebunkport, 1978; Anastasia Krupnik, 1979; Autumn Street, 1980, in U.K. as The Woods at the End of Autumn Street, 1987; Anastasia Again!, 1981; Anastasia at Your Service, 1982; The One Hundredth Thing about Caroline, 1983; Taking Care of Terrific, 1983; Anastasaia, Ask Your Analyst, 1984; Us and Uncle Fraud, 1984; Anastasia on Her Own, 1985; Switcharound, 1985; Anastasia Has the Answers, 1986; Anastasia's Chosen Career, 1987; Rabble Starkey, 1987, in U.K. as The Road Ahead, 1988; All About Sam, 1988; Number the Stars, 1989. Add: 34 Hancock St., Boston, Mass. 02114, U.S.A.

LOWRY, Ritchie Peter. American, b. 1926. Sociology. Prof. of Sociology, Boston Coll., Chestnut Hill, Mass., since 1966 (Chmn., Dept. of Sociology, 1967–70). Founder, Pres., Good Money Publications, Inc., Vermont, since 1982. Instr. to Assoc. Prof. of Sociology, California State Univ. at Chico, 1955–64; Sr. Research Scientist and Assoc. Prof. of Research, Special Operations Research Office, American Univ., Washington, D.C., 1964–66. *Publs:* Who's Running This Town? Community Leadership and Social Change, 1965, 1968; (ed.) Problems of Studying Military Roles in Other Cultures: A Working Conference, 1967; (with R.P. Rankin) Sociology: The Science of Society, 1969, rev. ed. 1972; Social Problems: A Critical Analysis of Theory and Public Policy, 1974; (with R.P. Rankin) Sociology: Social Science and Social Concern, 1977; Information Flow in Government Agencies, 1977; Looking Different Ways, 1977; Bridging the Gap: Public, Scientific, and Policy Views of Rape, 1978; A Meta-Analysis of Research Grant Applications Assigned to the NIMH Work and Mental Health Program, 1984. Add: Dept. of Sociology, Boston Coll., Chestnut Hill, Mass., U.S.A.

LOWRY, Robert (James). American, b. 1919. Novels/Short stories. Ed. and Publr., Little Man Press, Cincinnati, 1938–42; Production Mgr. and Ed., New Directions, Publrs., NYC, 1945–46; Book Reviewer, Time Mag., NYC, 1949–50, and New York Times, 1950–56; Staff Writer, American Mercury mag., NYC, 1951–53. *Publs:* Casualty, 1946; Find Me in Fire, 1948; The Wolf That Fed Us, 1949; The Big Cage, 1949; The Violent Wedding, 1953; Happy New Year, Kamerades!, 1954; What's Left of April, 1956; The Last Party, 1956; New York Call Girl, 1958; The Prince of Pride Starring, 1959; That Kind of Woman, 1959; Party of Dreamers, 1962; Dreams, 1976; The Nut, 1976; A Chronology of My Life Since 1952, 1979; Diary, 1979; Fun in Gun, 1984. Add: c/o Greenwood Press, 88 Post Rd., Box 5007, Westport, Conn. 06881, U.S.A.

LOXMITH, John. *See* **BRUNNER,** John.

LUARD, Nicholas. Also writes as James McVean. British, b. 1937. Mystery/Crime/Suspense, Environmental science/Ecology. Worked for NATO and in theatre and publishing. *Publs:* mystery novels—The Warm and Golden War, 1967; The Robespierre Serial, 1975; Travelling Horseman, 1975; The Orion Line, 1976, in U.S. as Double Assignment, 1977; (as James McVean) Bloodspoor, 1977; The Dirty Area (in U.S. as The Shadow Spy), 1979; (as James McVean) Seabird Nine, 1981; (as James McVean) Titan, 1984; Gondar, 1988; other—(with Dominick Elwes) Refer to Drawer, 1964; The Last Wilderness: A Journey Across the Great Kalahari Desert, 1981; Andalucia: A Portrait of Southern Spain, 1983; The Wildlife Parks of Africa, 1985. Add: 6 Fernshaw Rd., London SW10 0TF, England.

LUBAR, Joel F. American, b. 1938. Biology, Psychology. Regional Ed., Intnl. Journal of Physiology and Behavior, since 1969. Prof. of Psychology, Univ. of Tennessee, Knoxville, since 1971 (Assoc. Prof., 1967–71). Asst. Prof., Dept. of Psychology, Univ. of Rochester, N.Y., 1963–67. *Publs:* Biological Foundations of Behavior, 1969; (with R.L. Isaacson, L. Schmaltz and R. Douglas) A Primer of Physiological Psychology, 1971; First Reader in Physiological Psychology, 1972; Biological Foundations of Behavior, 1974; (with W. Deering) Behavioral Approaches to Neurology, 1981; Physiological Bases of Behaviour, 1982. Add: Dept. of Psychology, Univ. of Tennessee, Knoxville, Tenn. 37996, U.S.A.

LUBIN, Bernard. American, b. 1923. Psychology. Prof. of Psychology, Univ. of Missouri, Kansas City, since 1976 (Chmn. of the Dept., 1976–83). Member, Editorial Bd., American Journal of Community Psychology, Journal of Community Psychology, and Intnl. Journal of Group Psychotherapy; Consultant Reader, Psychological Reports. Prof., 1967–74, and Dir. of Psychology Training, 1969–74, Univ. of Missouri Sch. of Medicine, Kansas City; Prof. and Dir. of Clinical Training, Dept. of Psychology, Univ. of Houston, 1974–76. *Publs:* (with M. Zuckerman) Multiple Affect Adjective Check List: Manual, 1965, 1986; (with A.W. Lubin) Group Psychotherapy: A Bibliography of the Literature from 1956 through 1964, 1966; (with E.E. Levitt) The Clinical Psychologist: Background, Roles and Functions, 1967; Depression Adjective Check Lists: Manual, 1967, 1981; (with E.E. Levitts) Depression: Concepts, Controversies and Some New Facts, 1975, 1983; (with L.D. Goodstein and A.W. Lubin) Organizational Change Source Book, vols. I and II, 1979; (with W.A. O'Connor) Ecological Approaches to Clinical and Community Psychology, 1983; (with A.W. Lubin) Comprehensive Index to Group Psychotherapy Writings, 1987; (with R. Gist) Psychological Aspects of Disaster, 1988. Add: Dept. of Psychology, Univ. of Missouri, 5319 Holmes St., Kansas City, Mo. 64110, U.S.A.

LUCAS, Barbara. (Mrs. Bernard Wall). British, b. 1911. Novels/Short stories, Plays/Screenplays, Theology/Religion. *Publs:* Stars Were Born, 1934; The Trembling of the Sea, 1936; Anna Collett, 1946; Growing Up, 1956; Prelude to a Wedding, 1964; (with B. Wall) Thaw at the Vatican, 1964; More Ado About Nothing, 1969; Widows and Widowers, 1979; Poor Wilfred (radio play), 1984. Add: Swan Cottage, Rackham, Pulborough, W. Sussex, England.

LUCAS, Celia. British, b. 1938. Children's fiction, Biography. Dir., with Ian Skidmore, Two's Company, public relations consultancy, since 1986. Editorial Asst., George Rainbird Ltd., London, 1962–65; Art Ed., W.H. Allen Ltd., London, 1965–66; Researcher, 1966–68 and Reporter, 1968–71, Daily Mail, London and Manchester; Partner, 1971–74, and Dir.,

1974–86, Welsh Border News Agency. *Publs:* Prisoners of Santo Tomas, 1974; Steel Town Cats, 1987; (with Ian Skidmore) Glyndwr Country, 1988. Add: Virgin and Child Cottage, Brynsiencyn, Anglesey, North Wales.

LUCAS, Christopher John. American, b. 1940. Education. Prof. of Education, Univ. of Missouri, since 1974 (Asst. Prof., 1967–70; Assoc. Prof., 1970–74). *Publs:* (ed.) What Is Philosophy of Education?, 1969; Our Western Educational Heritage, 1972; (ed.) Challenge and Choice in Contemporary Education, 1976; Yesterday's China, 1982; Foundations of Education, 1984. Add: Coll. of Education, Univ. of Missouri, Columbia, Mo. 65211, U.S.A.

LUCAS, John. British, b. 1937. Poetry, Literature. Prof. of English, Loughborough Univ. Former Reader in English Studies, Univ. of Nottingham. *Publs:* (with J. Goode and D. Howard) Tradition and Tolerance in 19th Century Fiction, 1966; (ed.) Poems of George Crabbe, 1967; The Melancholy Man: A Study of Dickens' Novels, 1970; (ed.) Jane Austen's Mansfield Park, 1971; (ed.) Literature and Politics in the 19th Century, 1971; About Nottingham, 1971; Chinese Sequence, 1972; A Brief Bestiary, 1972; Arnold Bennett: A Study of His Fiction, 1974; (ed.) W.H. Mallock's The New Republic, 1974; Tim and the Quarry Affair, 1974; Egil's Saga, 1975; The Literature of Change, 1977; The 30's: A Challenge to Orthodoxy, 1978; (ed.) Poems of G.S. Fraser, 1981; Romantic to Modern: Essays on Ideas and Culture 1750-1900, 1982; The Days of the Week, 1983; Moderns and Contemporaries, Novelists, Poets, Critics, 1985; (with Basil Haynes) The Trent Bridge Battery, 1985; Modern English Poetry: From Hardy to Hughes, 1986; (ed.) Oliver Goldsmith, 1988; Studying Grosz on the Bus, 1989; Imagining England: Poetry and Nationhood 1688–1900, 1989. Add: 19 Devonshire Ave., Beeston, Nottingham, England.

LUCAS, John Randolph. British, b. 1929. Philosophy. Fellow, Merton Coll., Oxford Univ., since 1960 (Jr. Research Fellow, 1953–56). Fellow, Corpus Christi Coll., Cambridge, 1956–59; member, Archbishop's Commn. on Christian Doctrine, 1967–72. *Publs:* The Principles of Politics, 1966; The Concept of Probability, 1970; The Freedom of the Will, 1970; (co–author) The Nature of Mind, 1972; A Treatise on Time and Space, 1973; (co–author) The Development of Mind, 1974; Democracy and Participation, 1976; Freedom and Grace, 1976; On Justice, 1980; Space, Time and Causality, 1985; The Future, 1989. Add: Merton Coll., Oxford OX1 4JD, England.

LUCE, Gay (Gaer). American, b. 1930. Psychology. Writer, lecturer and workshop leader since 1971; Founder and Member of the Bd., SAGE (Senior Actualization and Growth Explorations), Oakland, Calif., since 1974. Member, President's Scientific Advisory Cttee., 1962–63, and National Inst. of Mental Health, 1963–73; Founder, Holistic Health Council, Berkeley, Calif., 1973; Vice–Pres., Nyingma Inst., Berkeley, 1974–77. *Publs:* Current Research in Sleep and Dreams, 1965; (with Julius Segal) Sleep, 1966; (with Julius Segal) Insomnia, 1970; Biological Rhythms in Psychiatry and Medicine, 1970; Body Time, 1971; Your Second Life, 1979. Add: c/o Delacorte Press, 666 Fifth Ave., New York, N.Y. 10103, U.S.A.

LUCEY, James D. Also writes as Matthew James; name now legally changed to James D. Pierce. American, b. 1923. Westerns/Adventure. Enrolled Agent, representing taxpayers before the Internal Revenue Service. Copywriter, 1956–58, and Account Exec., 1958–61, T.L. Parkhouse Advertising Agency, Glendale, Calif. *Publs:* (as Matthew James) The Adventures of Davy West, 1965; Shackle, 1966. Add: 530 W. Stocker St., Glendale, Calif. 91202, U.S.A.

LUCHINS, Edith Hirsch. American, b. 1921. Mathematics, Psychology. Prof. of Mathematics, Rensselaer Polytechnic Inst., Troy, N.Y., since 1970 (Assoc. Prof., 1962–70). Instr. of Mathematics, Brooklyn Coll., N.Y.,1944–46 and 1948; Research Assoc., Univ. of Oregon, Eugene, 1957–58; Assoc. Prof., Univ. of Miami, Coral Gables, Fla., 1959–62. *Publs:* all with A.S. Luchins—Rigidity of Behavior, 1959; Logical Foundations of Mathematics for Behavioral Scientists, 1965; Wertheimer's Seminars Revisited, Problem Solving and Thinking, Revisiting Wertheimer's Seminars, 4 vols., 1975–81. Add: 53 Fordham Ct., Albany, N.Y. 12209, U.S.A.

LUCIA, Ellis (Joel). American, b. 1922. History, Biography. Ed., The Caxton Printers, since 1984; Review Ed., The Oregonian, 1976–80; Columnist, Times Publications, Tualatin Valley, 1984–85. *Publs:* The Saga of Ben Holladay, 1959; Klondike Kate, 1962; Tough Men, Tough Country, 1963; The Big Blow, 1963; Don't Call It Or–E–Gawn, 1964;

Head Rig, 1965; Wild Water, 1965; Sea Wall, 1966; This Land Around Us, 1969; Mr. Football: Amos Alonzo Stagg, 1970; (ed.) The Gunfighters, 1971; (with Mike Hanley) Owyhee Trails, 1974; The Big Woods, 1975; Cornerstone, 1975; Magic Valley, 1976; (ed.) Oregon's Golden Years, 1976; Seattle's Sisters of Providence, 1978; Tillamook Burn Country, 1983; (ed.) Maverick Writers, by Jean Mead, 1989. Add: P.O. Box 17507, Portland, Ore. 97217, U.S.A.

LUCIE, Doug. British, b. 1953. Plays/Screenplays. Resident writer, Oxford Playhouse, 1979–80, and Univ. of Iowa, Iowa City, 1980. Publs: Progress, and Hard Feelings, 1985; Fashion, 1987. Add: c/o Michael Imison Playwrights Ltd., 28 Almeida St., London N1 1TD, England.

LUCIE–SMITH, (John) Edward (McKenzie). Also writes as Peter Kershaw. British, b. 1933. Poetry, Art, Photography, Translations. Freelance journalist. Education Officer, R.A.F., 1954–56; Co–Founder, Turret Books, London, 1965. Publs: (Poems), 1954; A Tropical Childhood and Other Poems, 1961; (ed.) Rubens, 1961; (ed.) Raphael, 1961; (trans.) Manet, by Robert Rey, 1962; (ed. with Philip Hobsbaum) A Group Anthology, 1963; (with Jack Clemo and George MacBeth) Penguin Modern Poets 6, 1964; Confessions and Histories, 1964; Fir–Tree Song, 1965; Jazz for the N.U.F., 1965; A Game of French and English, 1965; Three Experiments, 1965; Mystery in the Universe: Notes on an Interview with Allen Ginsberg, 1965; (ed.) The Penguin Book of Elizabethan Verse, 1965; Gallipoli—Fifty Years After (poetry), 1966; Cloud Sun Fountain Statue, 1966; Op Art, 1966; What is a Painting?, 1966; Silence, 1967; "Heureux Qui, Comme Ulysse . .", 1967; Borrowed Emblems, 1967; (ed.) The Liverpool Scene, 1967; (ed.) A Choice of Browning's Verse, 1967; (ed.) The Penguin Book of Satirical Verse, 1967; (trans.) Jonah: Selected Poems of Jean–Paul de Dadelsen, 1967; (trans. with P. Claudel) Five Great Odes, 1970; (trans.) The Muses, by P. Claudel, 1967; Towards Silence, 1968; Teeth and Bones, 1968; Six Kinds of Creature, 1968; Thinking about Art: Critical Essays, 1968; (as Peter Kershaw) A Beginner's Guide to Auctions, 1968; Snow Poem, 1969; Egyptian Ode, 1969; Movements in Art since 1945 (in U.S. as Late Modern: The Visual Arts since 1945), 1969; Six More Beasts, 1970; Lovers, 1970; (ed.) Holding Your Eight Hands: A Book of Science Fiction Verse, 1969; (ed. with P. White) Art in Britain, 1969–1970, 1970; (ed.) British Poetry since 1945, 1970; (ed. with S. Watson–Taylor) French Poetry Today: A Bi–Lingual Anthology, 1971; (ed.) Primer of Experimental Poetry, 1870–1922, 1971; The Rhino, 1971; A Girl Surveyed, 1971; The Yak, The Polar Bear, The Dodo, The Goldfish, The Dinosaur, The Parrot, 1971; A Concise History of French Painting, 1971; Eroticism in Western Art, 1972; Symbolist Art, 1972; The First London Catalogue: All the Appurtenances of a Civilised, Amusing and Comfortable Life, 1974; The Well–Wishers, 1974; The Invented Eye: Masterpieces of Photography, 1839–1914, 1975; Joan of Arc, 1976; (with Celeste Dars) How the Rich Lived, 1976; (with Celeste Dars) Work and Struggle, 1977; Art Today, 1977; Fantin–Latour, 1977; The Dark Pageant (novel), 1977; Outcasts of the Sea, 1978; A Concise History of French Painting 1978; Super–Realism, 1979; Furniture: A Concise History, 1979; Cultural Calendar of the Twentieth Century, 1979; The Story of Craft, 1981; The Body, 1981; Bertie and the Big Red Ball (for children), 1982; A History of Industrial Design, 1983; (ed.) Masterpieces from the Pompidou Centre, 1983; Art Terms: An Illustrated Dictionary, 1984; Beasts with Bad Morals (poetry), 1984; Art of the 1930's, 1985; Lives of the Great 20th Century Artists, 1986; Sculpture since 1945, 1987. Add: c/o Rogers, Coleridge and White, 20 Powis Mews, London W11, England.

LUCKEY, T(homas) D(onnell). American, b. 1919. Chemistry. Prof. of Biochemistry, Univ. of Missouri Medical Sch., retired (Chmn. of Dept., 1954–68). Co–Ed., Proceedings of Intnl. Symposium on Intestinal Microecology; Member, Intnl. Bd. of Eds., Thymus Editorial Bd., Microecology and Therapy. Asst. Research Prof., 1946–52, and Assoc. Research Prof., 1952–54, Notre Dame Univ., Ind. Publs: Cram Cards in Biochemistry, 1958; Germfree Research and Gnotobiology, 1963; (ed. and contrib.) Thymic Hormones, 1973; Heavy Metal Toxicity, Safety and Hormology, 1975; Metal Toxicity in Mammals, 2 vols., 1977–78; Hormesis with Ionizing Radiation, 1980. Add: 1009 Sitka Ct., Loveland, Colo. 80537, U.S.A.

LUDBROOK, John. Australian, b. 1929. Medicine/Health. Sr. Principal Research Fellow, Univ. of Melbourne, since 1989. Prof. of Surgery, Univ. of Adelaide, 1969–80, now Emeritus. Sr. Lectr. in Surgery, Univ. of Otago, 1959–63; Prof. of Surgery, Univ. of New South Wales, 1964–68; Dir., Baker Medical Research Inst., Melbourne, 1981–88. Publs: (with G.J. Fraenkel and H.A.F. Dudley) Guide to House Surgeons, 8th ed. 1961–85; (with R. G. Elmslie) Introduction to Surgery: 100 Topics, 1971–77; Analysis of the Venous System, 1972; (with V.C. Morsbole) Clinical

Science for Surgeons, 1988. Add: 349 Canning St., North Carlton, Vic. 3054, Australia.

LUDLOW, Geoffrey. See MEYNELL, Laurence.

LUDLOW, Howard Thomas. American, b. 1921. Administration/Management, Industrial relations. Prof. of Industrial Relations, SetonHall Univ., South Orange, N.J., since 1958 (Instr., 1949–52; Asst. Prof., 1952–56; Assoc. Prof., 1956–58). Publs: Business Management, 1965; Labor Economics, 1966. Add: 22 Martha Blvd., Parlin, N.J. 08859, U.S.A.

LUDLUM, Robert.Also writes as Jonathan Ryder and Michael Shepherd. American, b. 1927. Mystery/Crime/Suspense. Publs: The Scarlatti Inheritance, 1971; The Osterman Weekend, 1972; The Matlock Paper, 1973; (as Jonathan Ryder) Trevayne, 1973; (as Jonathan Ryder) The Cry of the Halidon, 1974; The Rhinemann Exchange, 1974; (as Michael Shepherd) The Road to Gandolfo, 1975; The Gemini Contenders, 1976; The Chancellor Manuscript, 1977; The Matarese Circle, 1979; The Bourne Identity, 1980; The Parsifal Mosaic, 1982; The Aquitaine Progression, 1984; The Bourne Supremacy, 1986; The Holcroft Covenant, 1985; The Icarus Agenda, 1988. Add: c/o Henry Morrison, Inc., P.O. Box 235, Bedford Hills, N.Y. 10507, U.S.A.

LUDWIG, Jack. Canadian, b. 1922. Novels/Short stories, Plays/Screenplays, Literature. Prof. of English, State Univ. of New York at Stony Brook, since 1961. Member of faculty, Williams Coll., Williamstown, Mass., 1949–53, Bard Coll., Annandale–on–Hudson, N.Y., 1953–58, and Univ. of Minnesota, Minneapolis, 1958–61; Chmn., Humanities Group, Harvard Univ. Intnl. Seminar, 1963–66; Writer–in–Residence, Univ. of Toronto, Ont., 1968–69. Publs: (ed. with R. Poirier) Stories British and American, 1953; (ed. with S. Bellow and K. Botsford) The Noble Savage, 1960–62; Recent American Novelists, 1962; Confusions (novel), 1963, 1965; Above Ground (novel), 1968, 1974; Bustout (play), 1969; Ubu Rex (play), 1970; (ed. with A. Wainwright) Soundings: New Canadian Poets, 1970; Hockey Night in Moscow, 1972; A Woman of Her Age (novel), 1973; the Great Hockey Thaw, 1974; Homage to Zolotova (poetry), 1974; Games of Fear and Winning, 1976; The Great American Spectaculars, 1976; Five Ring Circus, 1977. Add: P.O. Box A. Setauket, N.Y. 11733, U.S.A.

LUEBKE, Frederick Carl. American, b. 1927. History. Prof. of History, Univ. of Nebraska, Lincoln, since 1972 (Assoc. Prof. 1968–72; Dir., Center for Great Plains Studies, 1983–88). Assoc. Ed., Great Plains Quarterly, since 1985 (Ed., 1981–84). Asst. Prof. of History, Concordia Coll., Seward, Nebr., 1961–68. Publs: Immigrants and Politics, 1969; (ed.) Ethnic Voters and the Election of Lincoln, 1971; Bonds of Loyalty: German Americans and World War I, 1974; (ed.) The Great Plains: Environment and Culture, 1979; (ed.) Ethnicity on the Great Plains, 1980; (ed.) Vision and Refuge: Essays on the Literature of the Great Plains, 1981; (co–ed.) Mapping the North American Plains, 1987; Germans in Brazil: A Comparative History of Cultural Conflict During World War I, 1987. Add: 3117 Woodsdale Blvd., Lincoln, Nebr. 68502, U.S.A.

LUELLEN, Valentina. See POLLEY, Judith Anne.

LUKAS, J(ay) Anthony. American, b. 1933. Current affairs, Politics. Freelance journalist. With Baltimore Sun, 1958–62; with New York Times, 1962–71: in NYC, Washington, D.C., the Congo (now Zaire), New Delhi, Chicago, 1969–70; staff writer for New York Times Mag., 1970–71; Nieman Fellow, Harvard Univ., Cambridge, Mass, 1968–69; Assoc. Ed., MORE monthly journal, 1971–77; Contributing Ed., New Times, 1973–76; Adjunct Prof. of Journalism, Boston Univ., Mass., 1977–78, and John F. Kennedy Sch. of Government, Harvard Univ., 1979–80. Publs: The Barnyard Epithet and Other Obscenities: Notes on the Chicago Conspiracy, 1970; Don't Shoot—We Are Your Children, 1971; Nightmare: The Underside of the Nixon Years, 1976; Common Ground: A Turbulent Decade in the Lives of Three American Families, 1985. Add: c/o Alfred E. Knopf, 201 East 50th St., New York, N.Y. 10022, U.S.A.

LUKAS, Richard Conrad. American, b. 1937. History. Univ. Prof. of History, Tennessee Technological Univ., Cookeville, since 1983 (Asst. Prof., 1963–66; Assoc. Prof.,1966–69; Prof. since 1969). Research Consultant, U.S. Air Force Historical Archives, 1957–58. Publs: Eagles East: The Army Air Forces and the Soviet Union, 1941–45, 1970; (ed.) From Metternich to the Beatles, 1973; The Strange Allies: The United States and Poland, 1941–45, 1978; Bitter Legacy: Polish–American Relations in the Wake of World War II, 1982; Forgotten Holocaust: The Poles under German Occupation, 1986. Add: Dept. of History, Tennessee

Technological Univ., Cookeville, Tenn. 38501, U.S.A.

LUKE, Peter (Ambrose Cyprian). British, b. 1919. Novels/Short stories, Plays/Screenplays, Autobiography/Memoirs/Personal. Freelance writer, producer and dir. since 1967. Book Critic, Queen mag., London, 1957–58; Story Ed., Armchair Theatre, 1958–60, and Ed., Bookman, ABC–TV, London, 1960–61; Ed., Tempo arts prog., ABC–TV, 1961–62; Drama Producer, BBC television, London, 1963–67. *Publs:* The Play of Hadrian VII (based on works of F. Rolfe "Baron Corvo"), 1968; Sisyphus and Reilly: An Autobiography, 1972; Bloomsbury, 1974; (ed.) Enter Certain Players: Edward MacLiammoir and the Gate 1928–1978, 1979; Paquito and the Wolf (for children), 1981; Telling Tales: Collected Short Stories, 1981; The Other Side of the Hill: A Novel of the Peninsular War, 1984; The Mad Pomegranate and the Praying Mantis: An Andalusian Adventure, 1985; Married Love, 1988. Add: c/o Harvey Uuna Ltd. and Stephen Durbridge, 24 Pottery Lane, Holland Park, London W11 4LZ, England.

LUKE, Thomas. *See* **MASTERTON,** Graham.

LUKER, Kristin. American, b. 1946. Civil Liberties/Human Rights, Sociology, Women. Prof. of Sociology, Univ. of California, Berkeley, since 1985. Asst. Prof. of Sociology, 1975–81, and Assoc. Prof., 1981–85, Univ of California at San Diego. *Publs:* Taking Changes: Abortion and the Decision Not to Contracept, 1975; Abortion and the Politics of Motherhood, 1984. Add: Dept. of Sociology, Univ. of California, Berkeley, Calif. 94720, U.S.A.

LUKES, Steven M. British, b. 1941. Philosophy, Politics/Government, Sociology. Prof. of Social and Political Theory, European Univ. Inst., Flornece, since 1988. Member, Editorial Bd., Archives Européennes de Sociologie; Vice-Pres., Research Cttee. on the History of Sociology, Intnl. Sociological Assn. Research Fellow, Nuffield Coll., Oxford 1964–66; Fellow and Tutor in Sociology and Politics, Balliol Coll., Oxford, 1966–88. *Publs:* (ed. with Anthony Arblaster) The Good Society—A Book of Readings, 1970; Emile Durkheim, His Life and Work, an Historical and Critical Study, 1973; Individualism, 1973; Power: A Radical View, 1974; Essays in Social Theory, 1977; (co-ed.) Durkheim and the Law, 1984; (with I. Galnoor) No Laughing Matter, 1985; Marxism and Morality, 1985. Add: European Univ. Inst., Badia Fiesolana, I-50016 San Domenico di Fiesole, Florence, Italy.

LUNAN, Duncan. British, b. 1945. Science fiction/Fantasy, Air/Space topics, Astronomy. Full-time writer. Science Fiction Critic, The Glasgow Herald; Chmn., Glasgow SF Circle, since 1969; Secty., Assn. in Scotland to Research into Astronautics (ASTRA), since 1985 (Pres., 1966–72, 1978–85; Vice–Pres., 1972–76; Treas., 1977–78). Mgr., Glasgow Parks Dept. Astronomy Project, 1978–79. Vice–Pres., European Space Assn., 1977–79. *Publs:* Man and the Stars, 1974; New Worlds for Old, 1979; Man and the Planets, 1983. Add: c/o Morrow and Co., 105 Madison Ave., New York, N.Y. 10016, U.S.A.

LUND, Gerald N. American, b. 1939. Novels/Short stories, Theology/Religion. Instr., Church Education System, Church of Jesus Christ of Latter–Day Saints (Curriculum writer, 1967–69); Zone Administrator, Inst. of Religion, Salt Lake City, since 1986 (joined staff, 1976). *Publs:* The Coming of the Lord, 1971; This Is Your World, 1973; One in Thine Hand, 1982; The Alliance, 1983; Leverage Point, 1985; The Freedom Factor, 1987. Add: c/o Deseret Books, P.O. Box 30178, Salt Lake City, Utah 84130, U.S.A.

LUNDBERG, Donald E. American, b. 1916. Business/Trade/Industry, Cookery/Gastronomy/Wine. Prof., California State Polytechnic Univ., Ponoma., 1973–84, now Emeritus (Chmn., Dept. of Hotel, Restaurant, and Travel Mgmt., 1973–80). Pacific Ed., Hotels and Restaurants International, since 1982. Asst. Prof. of Hotel Admin., Cornell Univ., Ithaca, N.Y., 1946–49; Dean of Students and Prof. of Psychology, Idaho State Coll., Pocatello, 1949–50; Prof. and Head, Dept. of Hotel and Restaurant Mgmt., Florida State Univ., Tallahassee, 1950–59; Chmn., Dept. of Hotel Admin., Univ. of New Hampshire, Durham, 1959–62; Head, Dept. of Hotel Restaurant and Travel Admin., Univ. of Massachusetts, Amherst, 1963–73. *Publs:* Personnel Practices in Hotels, 1947; (with C. Vernon Kane) Business Management: Hotels, Motels and Restaurants, 1952; (ed.) Motel Management Correspondence Course, 1953; Operating Manual for Navy Messes and Clubs Ashore, 1954; Personnel Management in Hotels and Restaurants, 1955; Inside Innkeeping, 1956; (ed.) Readings in Club Management, 1956; Adventure in Costa Rica, 1960; rev. ed. 1968, (with P. Dukas) How to Operate a Restaurant, 1960; (with J.A. Armatas) The Management of People in Hotels, Restaurants and Clubs, 1964, 1980;

The Logic of Cookery, A Programmed Primer, 1964; (with I.H. Kolschevar) Understanding Cooking, 1964; The Hotel and Restaurant Business, 1970, 3rd ed. 1985; (with J. Amendola) Understanding Baking, 1971; The Tourist Business, 1971, 5th ed. 1985; Front Office Human Relations, 1979; The Restaurant: From Concept to Operation, 1985; (with Carolyn B. Lundberg) International Travel and Tourism, 1985. Add: c/o Van Nostrand Reinhold, 115 Fifth Ave., New York, N.Y. 10003, U.S.A.

LUNDEBERG, Philip (Karl). American, b. 1923. History. Curator of Naval History Emeritus, National Museum of History and Technology, Smithsonian Instn., Washington (Assoc. Curator, 1959–61). Asst. to the Historian of U.S. Naval Operations in World War II, Div. of Naval History, U.S. Navy Dept., 1950–53; Asst. Prof. of History, St. Olaf Coll., Northfield, Minn., 1953–55, and U.S. Naval Academy, Annapolis, Md., 1955–59. Vice Pres., 1968–71, and Pres., 1971–73, American Military Inst.; Chmn., Intnl. Congress of Maritime Museums, 1972–73; Chmn., Council of American Maritime Museums, 1974–76; Vice–Pres., 1974–79, and Pres., 1980–83, U.S. Commn. on Military History; Secty., Intnl. Commn. on Museum Security, 1975–79. *Publs:* German Naval Literature of World War II, 1956; (co–author) Geography and National Power, 1958; (co–author) Sea Power, 1960, 1981; (co–author) The Great Sea War, 1962; The German Naval Critique of the U–Boat Campaign 1915–18, 1963; Undersea Warfare and Allied Strategy in World War I, 1967; (ed.) Bibliographie de l'Histoire des Grandes Routes Maritimes, vol. II: Etats–Unis d'Amerique, 1971; Samuel Colt's Submarine Battery, 1974. Add: National Museum of History and Technology, Smithsonian Instn., Washington, D.C. 20560, U.S.A.

LUNDWALL, Sam J(errie). Swedish, b. 1941. Science fiction, Literature. Publisher, Fakta and Fantasi, Stockholm, since 1980. Ed., Jules Verne–Magasinet, Stockholm, since 1972. Also, singer, musician, illustrator, and television producer. Electronics engineer, L.M. Ericson, Stockholm, 1956–64; Photographer, Christian Fox Amphoux, France, 1968–69; Ed., Askild and Karnekull, Stockholm, 1970–73; Publisher, Delta Forlag, Stockholm, 1973–80. *Publs:* science fiction—No Time for Heroes, 1971; Alice's World, 1971; Bernhard the Conqueror, 1973; 2018; or, The King Kong Blues, 1975; Tio sanger och Alltid Lady Macbeth, 1975; Bernards magiska sommar, 1975; Morkrets furste, 1975; Mardrommen, 1976; Gast i Frankensteins hus, 1976; Fangelsestaden, 1978; Flicka i fonster vid varldens kant, 1980; Crash, 1982; other—Visor i var tid (poetry), 1965; Science Fiction: What It's All About, 1971; Den fantastiska romanen, 4 vols., 1972–74; Biografi over Science Fiction & Fantasy, 1974; Utopia–Dystopia, 1977; Science Fiction: An Illustrated History, 1978. Add: Storskogsvagen 19, 16139 Bromma, Sweden.

LUNN, Janet (Louise, née Swoboda). Canadian, b. 1928. Children's fiction, History. Writer in Residence, Kitchener Public Library, Ontario, since 1988. Children's book consultant, Ginn and Co., Scarborough, Ont., 1968–78; Children's ed., Clarke Irwin, Toronto, 1972–75; Writer-in–Residence, Regina Public Library, Ontario, 1982–83; Chairwoman, Writers Union of Canada, 1984–85. *Publs:* (with Richard Lunn) The County, 1967; Double Spell, 1968, 1985, in U.S. as Twin Spell, 1969; Larger Than Life, 1979; The Twelve Dancing Princesses (retelling), 1979; The Root Cellar, 1983; Shadow in Hawthorn Bay, 1986; Amos's Sweater, 1988; A Hundred Shining Candles, 1989; Duck Cakes for Sale, 1989. Add: R.R. 2, Hillier, Ont., KK 2J, Canada.

LUNT, George (Gordon). British, b. 1943. Bio-Chemistry. Reader in Biochemistry, Bath Univ., since 1971. Deputy Chief Ed., Journal of Neurochemistry. Research Fellow, Univ. of Birmingham, 1967–68, and 1970–71; Wellcome Trust Research Fellow, Inst. of Cell Biology, Univ. of Buenos Aires, 1968–70. *Publs:* (with R. Harrison) Biological Membranes: Their Structure and Function, 1975, 1980; (with R. Marchbanks) The Biochemistry of Muscular Dystrophy and Myasthenia Gravis, 1979; Neurotox '88: Molecular Basis of Drug and Pesticide Action, 1988. Add: Biochemistry Dept., Bath Univ., Bath BA2 7AY, England.

LUNT, James Doiran. British, b. 1917. History, Travel/Exploration/Adventure, Biography. Emeritus Fellow, Wadham Coll., Oxford (Fellow and Domestic Bursar 1973–84). Former Major–Gen., British Army, 1937–72. *Publs:* Charge to Glory; Scarlet Lancer; The Barren Rocks of Aden; Bokhara Burnes; (ed. and author) From Sepoy to Subedar; History of the Duke of Wellington's Regiment; History of the 16th/5th The Queen's Royal Lancers: John Burgoyne of Saratoga; Imperial Sunset, 1981; Glubb Pasha, 1984; A Hell of a Licking: The Retreat from Burma 1941-42, 1986; Hussein of Jordan: A Political Biography, 1989. Add: Hilltop House, Little Milton, Oxon, England.

LUPOFF, Richard A(llen). American, b. 1935. Mystery, Science fiction/Fantasy, Literature. Ed., Canyon Press, since 1986; Contributing Ed., Science Fiction Eye, since 1987. Technical Writer, Sperry Univac, NYC, 1958–63; Ed., Canaveral Press, NYC, 1962–70; Film Producer, IBM, NYC and Poughkeepsie, N.Y., 1963–70; Ed., Xero fan mag., 1963; West Coast Ed., Crawdaddy, 1970–71, and Changes, 1971–72; Ed., Organ, 1972; Book Ed., Algol, 1973–79. *Publs:* (ed.) The Reader's Guide to Barsoom and Amtor, 1963; Edgar Rice Burroughs, Master of Adventure (criticism), 1965, 1968; One Million Centuries, 1967; (ed. with Don Thompson) All in Color for a Dime, 1970; Sacred Locomotive Flies, 1971; Into the Aether, 1974; (ed. with Don Thompson) The Comic–Book Book, 1974; The Crack in the Sky, 1976, in U.K. as Fool's Hill, 1978; Lisa Kane (juvenile), 1976; Sandworld, 1976; The Triune Man, 1976; Barsoom: Edgar Rice Burroughs and the Martian Vision (criticism), 1976; Sword of the Demon, 1977; Space War Blues, 1978; (with Robert E. Howard) The Return of Skull–Face, 1978; Nebogipfel at the End of Time, 1979; The Ova Hamlet Papers (short stories), 1979; (ed.) What If? Stories That Should Have Won The Hugo, 1980; Stroka Prospekt, 1982; Sun's End, 1984; Circumpolar, 1984; Lovecraft's Book, 1985; The Digital Wristwatch of Philip K. Dick, 1985; Countersolar, 1987; Galaxy's End, 1988; The Forever City, 1988; The Black Tower, 1988; The Comic Book Killer, 1988. Add: 3208 Claremont Ave., Berkeley, Calif. 94705, U.S.A.

LURIA, Salvador (Edward). American (born Italian), b. 1912. Biology, Medicine/Health. Non–Resident Fellow, Salk Inst. for Biological Studies, San Diego, Calif., since 1965; Prof. Emeritus, Massachusetts Institute of Technology, Cambridge, (Prof. of Microbiology, 1959–64; Sedgwick Prof., 1964–70). Ed., Virology, since 1955.Instructor to Assoc. Prof., Indiana Univ., Bloomington, 1943–50; Prof. of Bacteriology, Univ. of Illinois, Urbana, 1950–59. Assoc. Ed., Journal of Microbiology, 1950–55. President, American Society for Microbiology, 1967–68. Recipient, Nobel Prize for Medicine (jointly), 1969. *Publs:* (with James E. Darnell, Jr.) General Virology, 1953; Life: The Unfinished Experiment, 1973; 36 Lectures in Biology, 1975. Add: Room 56–423, Dept. of Biology, Massachusetts Inst. of Technology, Cambridge, Mass. 02139, U.S.A.

LURIE, Alison. American, b. 1926. Novels, Children's fiction. Prof. of English, Cornell Univ., Ithaca, N.Y., since 1976 (Lectr. in English, 1969–73). *Publs:* V.R. Lang: A Memoir, 1959; Love and Friendship, 1962; The Nowhere City, 1965; Imaginary Friends, 1967; Real People, 1969; The War Between the Tates, 1974; Only Children, 1979; The Heavenly Zoo (juvenile), 1979; Clever Gretchen (juvenile), 1980; Fabulous Beasts (juvenile), 1981; The Language of Clothes, 1982; Foreign Affairs, 1984; The Truth About Lorin Jones, 1988. Add: c/o Dept. of English, Cornell Univ., Ithaca, N.Y. 14853, U.S.A.

LURIE, Morris. Australian, b. 1938. Novels/Short stories, Children's fiction, Plays, Essays. Full–time writer, Melbourne, since 1973. *Publs:* adult fiction—Rappaport (novel), 1966; The London Jungle Adventures of Charlie Hope (novel), 1968; Happy Times (short stories), 1969; Rappaport's Revenge (novel), 1973; Inside the Wardrobe: 20 Stories, 1975; Flying Home (novel), 1978; Running Nicely (short stories), 1979; Dirty Friends (short stories), 1981; Seven Books for Grossman (novel), 1983; Outrageous Behaviour (short stories), 1984; The Night We Ate the Sparrow: A Memoir and Fourteen Stories, 1985; other—The Twenty–Seventh Annual African Hippopotamus Race (for children), 1969; Arlo the Dandy Lion (for children), 1971; The English in Heat (essays), 1972; Hack Work (essays), 1977; Waterman: Three Plays, 1979; Public Secrets: Blowing the Whistle on Australia, England, France, Japan, the U.S.A., and Places Worse, 1981; Toby's Millions (for children), 1982; The Story of Imelda, Who Was Small (for children), 1984; Snow/Jobs (essays), 1985; Night–Night! (for children), 1986; Whole LIfe (autobiography), 1987; Play Life as a Movie (essays), 1988; Two Brothers, Running (screenplay), 1988 . Add: c/o Penguin Books, P.O. Box 257, Ringwood, Vic. 3134, Australia.

LUST, Peter. Canadian, b. 1911. International relations/Current affairs, Zoology. Canadian Corresp., Der Stern, W. Germany, since 1971. Canadian Corresp., Der Spiegel, W. Germany, 1967–70. *Publs:* Two Germanies, Mirror of an Age, 1966; The Last Seal Pup, 1967; Cuba, Time Bomb at Our Door, 1973. Add: Box 2, Dorval Airport, Dorval, Que, H4Y 1A2, Canada.

LUTTWAK, Edward (Nicolae). American, b. 1942. History, International relations/Current affairs, Politics/Government. Assoc., Center of Strategic and Intnl. Studies, Washington, D.C., since 1978. Visiting Prof., Johns Hopkins Univ., Baltimore, 1974–78, and Georgetown Univ., Washington, D.C., 1978–82. *Publs:* Coup D'Etat, 1968; Dictionary of Modern War, 1971; The Strategic Balance 1972, 1972; The US–USSR

Strategic Balance, 1974; The Political Uses of Sea Power, 1974; (co–author) The Israeli Army, 1975; The Grand Strategy of the Roman Empire, 1977; Strategy and Politics, 1980; The Grand Strategy of the Soviet Union, 1983; The Pentagon and the Art of War, 1985; Strategy and History: Collected Essays, 1985; (co–author) Yearbook of International Politics 1983–84, 1984, 1984–85, 1985; Strategy: The Logic of War and Peace, 1987. Add: CSIS, 1800 K St. N.W., Washington, D.C. 20006, U.S.A.

LUTYENS, Mary. Also writes as Esther Wyndham. British, b. 1908. Historical/Romance/Gothic, Biography. *Publs:* Forthcoming Marriages, 1933; Perchance to Dream, 1935; Rose and Thorn, 1936; Spider's Silk, 1938; Family Colouring, 1940; A Path of Gold, 1941; Together and Alone, 1942; So Near to Heaven, 1943; Julie and the Narrow Valley, 1944; And Now There Is You, 1953; Weekend at Hurtmore, 1954; The Lucian Legend, 1955; Meeting in Venice, 1956; To Be Young, 1959; (ed.) Lady Lytton's Court Diary, 1961; Effie in Venice, 1965; Millais and the Ruskins, 1967; (ed.) Freedom from the Known, by Krishnamurti, 1969; (ed.) The Only Revolution by Krishnamurti, 1970; (ed.) The Urgency of Change, by Krishnamurti, 1971; The Ruskins and the Grays, 1972; Cleo, 1973; Krishnamurti: The Years of Awakening, 1975; The Lyttons in India, 1979; Edwin Lutyens, 1980; Krishnamurti: The Years of Fulfilment, 1982; Krishnamurti: The Open Door, 1988. Add: Elizabeth Close, Randolph Ave., London W9, England.

LUTZ, Giles A(lfred). Also writes as James B. Chaffin, Wade Everett, Alex Hawk, Hunter Ingram, Reese Sullivan, and Gene Thompson. Westerns/Adventure. *Publs:* Fight or Run, 1954; The Golden Bawd, 1956; To Hell—and Texas, 1956; Fury Trail, 1957; Gun the Man Down, 1957; (as Gene Thompson) Six–Guns Wild, 1957; Outcast Gun, 1958; Relentless Gun, 1958; The Homing Bullet, 1959; (as James B. Chaffin) Guns of Abilene, 1959; Law of the Trigger, 1959; The Challenger, 1960; The Honyocker, 1962, in U.K. as Range Feud, 1963; Wild Quarry, 1962; The Long Cold Wind, 1962; Gun Rich, 1962; (as Gene Thompson) Range Law, 1962; Killer's Trail, 1963; Halfway to Hell, 1963; The Golden Land, 1963; (as Gene Thompson) The Branded One, 1964; The Bleeding Land, 1965; (as Hunter Ingram), The Trespassers, 1965; (as Reese Sullivan) Nemesis of Circle A, 1965; (as Reese Sullivan) The Blind Trail, 1965; (as Reese Sullivan) The Demanding Land, 1966; (as Reese Sullivan) Deadly Like a .45, 1966; The Hardy Breed, 1966; (as Hunter Ingram) Man Hunt, 1967; The Magnificent Failure, 1967; (as Gene Thompson) Ambush in Abilene, 1967; (as Gene Thompson) The Outcast, 1968; (as Reese Sullivan) The Trouble Borrower, 1968; (as Reese Sullivan) The Vengeance Ghost, 1968; (as Hunter Ingram) Contested Valley, 1968; Wild Runs the River, 1968; (as Wade Everett) The Whisky Traders, 1968; The Vengeance Ghost, 1968; (as Alex Hawk) Tough Town, 1969; The Deadly Deputy, 1969; (as Hunter Ingram) The Long Search, 1969; Montana Crossing, 1970; (as Hunter Ingram) Forked Tongue, 1970; (as Gene Thompson) Wolf Blood, 1971; The Lonely Ride, 1971; (as Hunter Ingram) Border War, 1972; The Outsider, 1973; The Black Day, 1974; The Grudge, 1974; The Offenders, 1974; Blood Feud, 1974; Stagecoach to Hell, 1975; The Stubborn Breed, 1975; (as Hunter Ingram) Fort Apache, 1975; (as Hunter Ingram) The Forbidden Land, 1975; My Brother's Keeper, 1975; Man on the Run, 1976; Reprisal!, 1976; The Stranger, 1976; A Drifting Man, 1976; Night of the Cattlemen, 1976; The Way Homeward, 1977; A Time for Vengeance, 1977; The Turn Around, 1978; The Shoot Out, 1978; Lure of the Outlaw Trail, 1979; The Echo, 1979; Killer's Trail, 1980; The Great Railroad War, 1981; Thieves' Brand, 1981; The Feud, 1982; Smash the Wild Bunch, 1982; War on the Range, 1982; The Tangled Web, 1983; The Ragged Edge, 1985. Add: 113 Red Bud Ave., Belton, Mo. 64012, U.S.A.

LUTZ, John (Thomas). American, b. 1939. Mystery/Crime/Suspense. Full–time writer since 1975. *Publs:* The Truth of the Matter, 1971; Buyer Beware, 1976; Bonegrinder, 1977; Lazarus Man, 1979; Jericho Man, 1980; The Shadow Man, 1981; (with Bill Pronzini) The Eye, 1984; Nightlines, 1984; The Right to Sing the Blues, 1986; Tropical Heat, 1986; Ride the Lightning, 1987; Scorcher, 1987; Dancer's Debt, 1988; Better Mousetraps (short stories), 1988; Kiss, 1988; Shadowtown, 1988. Add: 880 Providence Ave., Webster Groves. Mo. 63119, U.S.A.

LUTZKER, Edythe. American (b. German), b. 1904. Women, Biography. Founder and Vice–Pres., Waldemar M. Haffkine Intnl. Memorial Cttee. Grantee, National Library of Medicine of U.S. Dept. of Health, Education and Welfare, Washington, D.C., 1966, 1968–71, 1972–74. *Publs:* Medical Education for Women in Great Britain, 1969; Women Gain Place in Medicine, 1969; Edith Pechey–Phipson, M.D., England's and India's Foremost Pioneering Woman Doctor, 1973. Add: 201 W. 89th

St., New York, N.Y. 10024, U.S.A.

LUZBETAK, Louis J(oseph). American, b. 1918. Anthropology/Ethnology, Language/Linguistics, Theology/Religion. Prof. of Cultural Anthropology, Catholic Univ. of America, and Georgetown Univ., Washington, D.C., 1956–65; Exec. Dir., Center for Applied Research in the Apostolate, Washington, D.C. 1965–73; Pres., Divine Word Coll., Epworth, Iowa, 1973–78; Ed., Anthropos: Intnl. Review of Ethnology and Linguistics, 1979–82. *Publs:* Marriage and the Family in Caucasia, 1951; Middle Wahgi Dialects, 1954; Tabare Dialects, 1954; Middle Wahgi Phonology, 1954; The Church and Cultures: An Applied Anthropology for the Religious Worker, 1963, 6th ed., 1984; (ed.) The Church in the Changing City, 1966; Clergy Distribution USA: A Preliminary Survey of Priest Utilization, Availability, and Demand, 1967. Add: 1025 Michigan Ave. N.E., Washington, D.C. 20017, U.S.A.

LYALL, Gavin (Tudor). British, b. 1932. Mystery/Crime/Suspense. Journalist, Picture Post mag., London, 1956–57; television film dir., BBC TV, 1958; Journalist and aviation ed., Sunday Times, London, 1959–63. Chmn., Crime Writers Assn., 1966–67. *Publs:* The Wrong Side of the Sky, 1961; The Most Dangerous Game, 1963; Midnight Plus One, 1965; Shooting Script, 1966; (ed.) The War In the Air 1939–1945: An Anthology of Personal Experiences, 1968; Venus with Pistol, 1969; Blame the Dead, 1973; Judas Country, 1975; Operation Warboard—Wargaming World War II in 20–25mm Scale, 1976; The Secret Servant, 1980; The Conduct of Major Maxim, 1982; The Crocus List, 1985; Uncle Target, 1988. Add: 14 Provost Rd., London NW3 4ST, England.

LYCAN, Gilbert L(ester). American, b. 1909. History, International relations/Current affairs, Politics/Government. Emeritus Prof. of History and Univ. Historian, Stetson Univ., DeLand, Fla., since 1975 (prof., 1946–75). Instr. in History, State Teachers Coll., Valley City, N.D., 1937–42; Drafting Officer, U.S. Dept. of State, 1942–43; Chmn., Dept. of Social Science, Queens Coll., N.C., 1943–45; Chmn., Social Science Div., Missouri State Univ., Maryville, 1945–46. *Publs:* (co-author) Bases of World Order, 1945; (with W.C. Grady) Inside Racing, 1961; Twelve Major Turning Points in American History, 1968; Alexander Hamilton and American Foreign Policy, 1970; Stetson University: The First Hundred Years, 1983. Add: Apt. 216, Highland Farms, Black Mountain, N.C. 28711, U.S.A.

LYDEN, Fremont James. American, b. 1926. Administration/Management, Public/Social administration. Prof. of Public Affairs, and Adjunct Prof. of Political Science, Grad Sch. of Public Affairs, Univ. of Washington, Seattle, since 1975 (Instr., 1956–59; Asst. Prof., 1962–66; Assoc. Prof., 1966–75). Mgmt. Analyst, Position Classifier, U.S. Bureau of Reclamation, 1952–55; Research Assoc., Harvard Medical Sch. and Grad. Sch. of Public Admin., Harvard Univ., 1960–62. *Publs:* The Physician in Society, 1961; (ed. with E.G. Miller) Planning–Programming–Budgeting: A Systems Approach to Management, 1967, 1972; (assoc. ed. and contrib.) Comparative Administrative Theory, 1968; (with O.L. Peterson and H.J. Geiger) The Training of Good Physicians: Career Decisions in Medicine, 1968; (ed. and contrib.) Reader on Policies, Decisions and Organization, 1969; (with E.G. Miller) Public Budgeting: Program Planning and Evaluation, 1978, 1982; (with Marc Lindenberg) Public Budgeting in Theory and Practice, 1983. Add: Grad. Sch. of Public Affairs, Univ. of Washington, Seattle, Wash. 98195, U.S.A.

LYDOLPH, Paul Edward. American, b. 1924. Geography. Prof. of Geography, Univ. of Wisconsin, Milwaukee, since 1959 (Chmn. of Dept., 1962–69 and 1971–72). Assoc. Prof. of Geography, Los Angeles State Coll., Calif., 1952–59; Ford Foundn. Fellow, Berkeley, Calif., 1956–57. *Publs:* Geography of the USSR, 1964, 3rd ed. 1977; The Soviet Union (vol. 7 of World Survey of Climatology); Geography of the USSR: Topical Analysis, 1979; Weather and Climate, 1985; The Climate of the Earth, 1985. Add: Box 323, Rt. 2, Elkhart Lake, Wisc. 53020, U.S.A.

LYKIARD, Alexis. British, b. 1940. Novels/Short stories, Poetry, Translations. Creative Writing Tutor, Arvon Foundn., since 1974. Writer-in-Residence, Sutton Library (Greater London Arts), 1977, Loughborough Art Coll. (Arts Council of GB), 1982–83, and Tavistock (Devon Libraries), 1983–85, H.M. Prison Channings Wood, 1988. *Publs:* Lobsters, 1961; Journey of the Alchemist, 1963; The Summer Ghosts, 1964; (ed.) Wholly Communion, 1965; Zones, 1966; Paros Poems, 1967; A Sleeping Partner, 1967; Robe of Skin, 1969; Strange Alphabet, 1970; (trans.) Lautréamont's Maldoror, 1970; (ed.) Best Horror Stories of J. Sheridan Le Fanu, 1970; Eight Lovesongs, 1972; The Stump, 1973; Greek Images, 1973; Lifelines, 1973; Instrument of Pleasure, 1974; (trans.) The

Piano Ship, 1974; (ed.) The Horror Horn, by E.F. Benson, 1974; Last Throes, 1976; Milesian Fables, 1976; A Morden Tower Reading, 1976; (trans.) Laure, by Emmanuelle Arsan, 1977; The Drive North, 1977; (ed.) New Stories 2, 1977; (trans.) Nea, by Emmanuelle Arsan, 1978; (trans.) Lautréamont: Poésies etc., 1978; (ed.) Man with a Maid, 1982; Scrubbers, 1983; (ed.) The Memoirs of Dolly Morton by Hugues Rebell, 1984; Cat Kin, 1985; Out of Exile, 1986; trans.—Secrets of Emmanuelle, by E. Arsan, 1980; Vanna, by E. Arsan, 1981; Oh Wicked Country!, 1982; Nostradamus: Countdown to Apocalypse, by J–C. de Fontbrune, 1983; Joy, by Joy Laurey, 1983; Indiscreet Memoirs, by Alain Dorval, 1984; Nostradamus 2, by J–C. de Fontbrune, 1984; Florian, by Antoine S., 1986; Violette, by Marquise de Mannoury d'Ectot, 1986; The Exploits of a Young Don Juan, by Apollinaire/Irène, by Aragon, 1986; (ed.) Beat Dreams and Plymouth Sounds, 1987; (trans.) Days and Nights, by Alfred Jarry, 1989; Living Jazz, 1989; Safe Levels, 1990. Add: c/o A.M. Heath and Co. Ltd., 24 St. Martin's Lane, London WC2N 4AA, England.

LYLE–SMYTH, Alan. *See* **CAILLOU,** Alan.

LYNAM, Shevawn. Irish. Novels/Short stories, Communications Media, Biography. Reporter, Marshall Plan Information Service, Paris, 1950–54; Ed.–in–Chief, NATO Letter, 1958–63; Editorial Publicity Officer, Irish Tourist Bd., 1963–71. *Publs:* The Spirit and the Clay, 1954; (with others) Michael/Frank, 1969; Humanity Dick, 1975. Add: Cronroe, Ashford, Co. Wicklow, Ireland.

LYNCH, Eric. *See* **BINGLEY,** David Ernest.

LYNCH, Frances. *See* **COMPTON,** D.G.

LYNCH, John. British, b. 1927. History. Emeritus Prof. of Latin American History and Dir. of Inst. of Latin American Studies, Univ. of London, since 1987 (Lectr., Reader and Prof. of Latin American History, Univ. Coll., 1961–87). Lectr. in History, Univ. of Liverpool, 1954–61. *Publs:* Spanish Colonial Administration, 1782–1810: The Intendant System in the Viceroyalty of the Rio de la Plata, 1958; Spain Under the Habsburgs, 2 vols., 1964–69; (ed. with R.A. Humphreys) The Origins of the Latin American Revolutions 1808–1826, 1965; The Spanish American Revolutions 1808–1826, 1973; Argentine Dictator: Juan Manuel de Rosas 1829–1852, 1981; (with others) The Cambridge History of Latin America, vol. 3, 1985, vol. 4, 1986; Bourbon Spain 1700-1808, 1989. Add: 8 Templars Cres., London N3 3QS, England.

LYNCH, William E(dward). American, b. 1930. Theology/Religion. Counsellor, Lynch Consultants, gen. family consultants, since 1972. *Publs:* The World Dwells Among Us, 1965; Jesus in the Synoptic Gospels, 1967; The Psychology of Jesus, 1977; How to Love, 1978; No-One of God's Children Goes To Hell, 1988. Add: Apt. B–205, 111 Crandon Blvd., Key Biscayne, Fla. 33149, U.S.A.

LYNDS, Dennis. Also writes as Michael Collins, William Arden, John Crowe, Carl Dekker, and Mark Sadler; has also written with others, under house names Maxwell Grant and Nick Carter. American, b. 1924. Novels/Short stories, Mystery/Crime/Suspense, Science fiction/Fantasy, Children's fiction. Full-time writer since 1967. Asst. Ed., Chemical Week, New York, 1951–52; Editorial Dir., American Inst. of Management, NYC, 1952–53; Assoc. Ed., then Managing Ed., Chemical Engineering Progress, NYC, 1954–60. Ed., Chemical Equipment and Laboratory equipment, NYC, 1962–66; Instr., Santa Barbara City Coll. Adult Education Div., California, 1966–67. *Publs:* mystery novels—(as Maxwell Grant) The Shadow Strikes, 1964; (as Maxwell Grant) Shadow Beware, 1965; (as Maxwell Grant) Cry Shadow, 1965; (as Maxwell Grant) The Shadow's Revenge, 1965; (as Maxwell Grant) Mark of the Shadow, 1966; (as Maxwell Grant) Shadow—Go Mad!, 1966; (as Maxwell Grant) The Night of the Shadow, 1966; (as Maxwell Grant) The Shadow—Destination: Moon, 1967; (as Michael Collins) Act of Fear, 1967; (as William Arden) A Dark Power, 1968; (as William Arden) Deal in Violence, 1969; (as Michael Collins) The Brass Rainbow, 1969; (as Michael Collins) Night of the Toads, 1970; (as Mark Sadler) The Falling Man, 1970; (as Michael Collins) Walk a Black Wind, 1971; (as William Arden) The Goliath Scheme, 1971; (as Mark Sadler) Here to Die, 1971; (as William Arden) Die to a Distant Drum, 1972, in U.K. as Murder Underground, 1974; (as Michael Collins) Shadow of a Tiger, 1972; (as Mark Sadler) Mirror Image, 1972; (as John Crowe) Another Way to Die, 1972; (as John Crowe) A Touch of Darkness, 1972; (as Michael Collins) The Silent Scream, 1973; (as Carl Dekker) Woman in Marble, 1973; (as William Arden) Deadly Legacy, 1973; (as Mark Sadler) Circle of Fire, 1973; (as John Crowe) Bloodwater, 1974; (as Nick Carter) The N3 Conspiracy, 1974; (as Dennis Lynds) Charlie Chan Returns (novelization of TV play), 1974; (as Michael

Collins) Blue Death, 1975; (as John Crowe) Crooked Shadows, 1975; (as Dennis Lynds) S.W.A.T.—Crossfire (novelization of TV play), 1975; (as Michael Collins) The Blood–Red Dream, 1976; (as Nick Carter) The Green Wolf Connection, 1976; (as Nick Carter) Triple Cross, 1976; (as John Crowe) When They Kill Your Wife, 1977; (as Michael Collins) The Nightrunners, 1978; (as John Crowe) Close to Death, 1979; (as Michael Collins) The Slasher, 1980; (as Mark Sadler) Touch of Death, 1983; (as Michael Collins) Freak, 1983; (as Mark Sadler) Deadly Innocents, 1986; (as Michael Collins) Minnesota Strip, 1987; (as Michael Collins) Red Rosa, 1988; (as Michael Collins) Castrato, 1989; other—Combat Soldier (novel), 1962; Uptown Downtown (novel), 1963; (as William Arden) The Mystery of the Moaning Cave (Laughing Shadow, Shrinking House, Blue Condor, Dead Man's Riddle, Dancing Devil, Headless Horse, Deadly Double, Purple Pirate, Smashing Glass, Wrecker's Ball) (juvenile), 11 vols., 1968–86; (as Michael Collins) Lukan War (SF novel), 1969; (as Michael Collins) The Planets of Death (SF novel), 1970; (as William Arden) The Secret of the Crooked Cat (juvenile), 1970; (as William Arden) The Secret of the Phantom Lake (juvenile), 1973; (as William Arden) The Secret of the Shark Reef (juvenile), 1979; Why Girls Ride Sidesaddle (short stories), 1980. Add: 12 St. Anne Dr., Santa Barbara, Calif. 93109, U.S.A.

LYNES, Russell. American, b. 1910. Architecture, Art, Design, Social commentary/phenomena. Columnist ("Russell Lynes Observes"), Architectural Digest, since 1974. Joined staff, Harper's Magazine, NYC, 1944: Managing Ed., 1948–67; Contributing Ed., 1967–81. Columnist ("The State of Taste"), Art in America, in the early 1970's. *Publs:* Snobs, 1950; Guests, 1951; The Tastemakers, 1954; A Surfeit of Honey, 1957; Cadwallader: A Diversion, 1959; The Domesticated Americans, 1963; Confessions of a Dilettante, 1966; The Art–Makers of Nineteenth Century America, 1970; Good Old Modern, 1973; More Than Meets the Eye, 1981; The Lively Audience: A Social History of the Visual and the Performing Arts in America 1890–1955, 1985. Add: 427 E. 84th St., New York, N.Y. 10028, U.S.A.

LYNN, Frank. See LEISY, James Franklin.

LYNN, Jonathan. British, b. 1943. Novels/Short stories, Plays/Screenplays. Artistic Dir., Cambridge Theatre Col., 1976–81. *Publs:* (with George Layton) Doctor in Charge, Doctor at Sea, Doctor on the Go (television series), 1971–74; (with George Layton) My Name is Harry Worth (television series), 1973; Pig of the Month (play), 1974; (with Barry Levinson) The Internecine Project (screenplay), 1974; (with George Layton) My Brother's Keeper (2 television series), 1975, 1976; A Proper Man (novel), 1976; (with Antony Jay) Yes Minister (television series), 1980–83, as paperback, 3 vols., 1981–83, as (hardback) The Complete Yes Minister, 1984; Clue (screenplay), 1985. Add: c/o A.D. Peters, The Chambers, Chelsea Harbour, Lots Rd., London SW10 0XF, England.

LYNN, Richard. British, b. 1930. Psychology. Prof. of Psychology, Univ. of Ulster, Coleraine, since 1972. Lectr., Exeter Univ., Devon, 1956–67; Prof. of Psychology, Economic and Social Research Inst., Dublin, 1967–72. *Publs:* Arousal, Attention and the Orientation Reaction, 1966; Personality and National Character, 1971; Introduction to the Study of Personality, 1971; (ed.) The Entrepreneur, 1974; Dimensions of Personality, 1981; Educational Achievement in Japan, 1987. Add: Dunderg House, Coleraine, Co. Londonderry, North Ireland.

LYNNE, James Broom. Also writes as James Quartermain. British, b. 1920. Novels/Short stories, Plays/Screenplays. Freelance graphic designer, specialising in book design. Art Dir., William Larkins Studio, London, 1962–66; Art Ed., Macdonald & Co., London, 1966–69; art sch. lectr., London, 1970–72, and Suffolk Coll. of Higher and Further Education, 1972–78. *Publs:* The Trigon, 1962; Ketch, 1963; Tobey's Wednesday (in U.S. as The Wednesday Visitors), 1967; The Marchioness, 1968; Drag Hunt, 1969; (as James Quartermain) The Diamond Hook, 1970; (as James Quartermain) The Man Who Walked on Diamonds, 1972; (as James Quartermain) Rock of Diamonds, 1972; The Commuters (in U.S. as Collision), 1973; The Colonel's War, 1975; Verdict, 1977; Jet Race, 1978; Rogue Diamond, 1980. Add: Gissings, East Bergholt, Colchester, Essex, England.

LYNTON, Norbert (Casper). British, b. 1927. Art. Prof. of the History of Art, Univ. of Sussex, Brighton, 1975–89 (Dean, Sch. of European Studies, 1985–88). Lectr. in the History of Art and Architecture, Leeds Coll. of Art, 1950–61; Sr. Lectr., then Head of the Dept. of Art History and Gen. Studies, Chelsea Sch. of Art, London, 1961–70; Dir. of Exhibitions, Arts Council of Great Britain, 1970–75. London Correspon-

dent, Art International, 1961–66; Art Critic, The Guardian, London, 1965–70. *Publs:* (with others) Simpson's History of Architectural Development, vol. 4, The Renaissance, 1962; Kenneth Armitage, 1962; Paul Klee, 1964; The Modern World, 1968; The Story of Modern Art, 1980; Looking at Art, 1981; (with others) Looking into Paintings, 1985. Add: 28 Florence Rd., Brighton, Sussex BN1 6DJ, England.

LYON, Elinor. (Elinor Wright). British, b. 1921. Children's fiction. *Publs:* Hilary's Island, 1948; Wishing Watergate, 1949; The House in Hiding, 1950; We Daren't Go A Hunting, 1951; Run Away Home, 1953; Sea Treasure, 1955; Dragon Castle, 1956; The Golden Shore, 1957; Daughters of Aradale, 1957; Riders' Rock, 1958; Cathie Runs Wild, 1960; Carver's Journey (in U.S. as The Secret of Hermit's Bay), 1962; Green Grow the Rushes, 1964; Echo Valley, 1965; The Dream Hunters, 1966; Strangers at the Door, 1967; The Day That Got Lost, 1968; The Wishing Pool, 1970; The King of Grey Corrie, 1974; The Floodmakers, 1976. Add: Bron Meini, Harlech, Wales.

LYONS, Arthur. American, b. 1946. Mystery/Crime/Suspense. Owner of a restaurant, Palm Springs, Calif., since 1967. *Publs:* The Second Coming: Satanism in America (non–fiction), 1970, in U.K. as Satan Wants You: The Cult of Devil Worship, 1971; The Dead Are Discreet, 1974; All God's Children, 1975; The Killing Floor, 1976; Dead Ringers, 1977; Castles Burning, 1980; Hard Trade, 1982; At the Hands of Another, 1983; Three with a Bullet, 1985; Fast Fade, 1987; (with Thomas Noguchi) Unnatural Causes, 1988. Add: c/o Mysterious Press, 129 W. 56th St., New York, N.Y., U.S.A.

LYONS, David (Barry). American, b. 1935. Philosophy. Prof. of Philosophy since 1971, and of Law since 1979, Cornell Univ., Ithaca, N.Y. (Asst. Prof., 1964–67; Assoc. Prof., 1967–71; Chmn. of the Dept. of Philosophy, 1978–84). Co.–Ed., 1968–70, 1973–75, and Managing Ed., 1978–81, The Philosophical Review. *Publs:* Forms and Limits of Utilitarianism, 1965; In the Interest of the Governed: A Study in Bentham's Philosophy of Utility and Law, 1973; (ed.) Rights, 1979; Ethics and the Rule of Law, 1984. Add: Sage Sch. of Philosophy, Goldwin Smith Hall, Cornell Univ., Ithaca, N.Y. 14853, U.S.A.

LYONS, Delphine C. See SMITH, Evelyn, E.

LYONS, Dorothy Marawee. American, b. 1907. Children's fiction. *Publs:* Silver Birch, 1939; Midnight Moon, 1941; Golden Sovereign, 1946; Red Embers, 1948; Harlequin Hullabaloo, 1949; Copper Khan, 1950; Dark Sunshine, 1951; Blue Smoke, 1953; Java Jive, 1955; Bright Wampum, 1958; Smoke Rings, 1960; Pedigree Unknown, 1973; The Devil Made the Small Town, 1984. Add: 900 Calle de los Amigos, C 102, Santa Barbara, Calif. 93105, U.S.A.

LYONS, Elena. See FAIRBURN, Eleanor.

LYONS, Nick. American, b. 1932. Business/Trade/Industry, Literature, Sports/Physical education/Keeping fit. Pres., Nick Lyons Books, since 1978. Prof. of English, Hunter Coll., City Univ. of N.Y., 1961–88; Exec. Ed., Crown Publrs., 1964–74. *Publs:* (ed.) Jones Very: Selected Poems, 1966; Fisherman's Bounty, 1970; The Seasonable Angler, 1970; Fishing Widows, 1974; The Sony Vision, 1976; Bright Rivers, 1978; Locked Jaws, 1979; Confessions of a Fly–Fishing Addict, 1989. Add: 342 W. 84th St., New York, N.Y. 10024, U.S.A.

LYONS, Thomas Tolman. American, b. 1934. Civil liberties/Human rights, History, Race relations. History teacher, Phillips Academy, Andover, Mass., since 1963. History Teacher, Mount Hermon Sch., 1958–63. *Publs:* (ed.) Presidential Power in the Era of the New Deal, 1964; (ed.) Realism and Idealism in Wilson's Peace Program, 1965; (ed.) Reconstruction and the Race Problem, 1968; Black Leadership in American History, 1970; The Supreme Court in Contemporary American Life, 1975; The Expansion of the Federal Union, 1978; After Hiroshima, 1979, 1985; The President: Teacher, Preacher, Salesman, 1984. Add: History Dept., Phillips Academy, Andover, Mass. 01810, U.S.A.

LYONS, W.T. American, b. 1919. Poetry. Staff Advisor to Supply and Fiscal Officer for Supply Mgmt., Financial Mgmt. and Personnel Admin. Industrial Relations Liaison Officer, and Staff Advisor to the Commanding Officer for Civilian Personnel Mgmt., and Admin Asst., Mgmt. Analysis Officer and Head of Admin. and Planning Div., Supply and Fiscal Dept., U.S. Naval Air Station and U.S. Naval Air Facility, 1952–63; Asst. for Manpower Mgmt. and Utilization, Consultant to Naval Bureaus, Offices and Systems Commands, Prog. Admin., and Project Mgr.

for Mgmt. and Industrial Engineering, U.S. Naval Research and Development Lab., 1963–68; Principal Adviser and Staff Asst. to the Asst. Vice Chief of Naval Operations, Mgmt. Analyst, and Manpower Analyst, Office of the Chief of Naval Operations, 1968 until retirement in 1973, all in Washington, D.C. *Publs:* Soul in Solitude, 1970; The Odyssey of Godwin Gipson and Other Poems (Poetry of the Black Experience), 1974; The Heartbeat of Soul, 1975. Add: 4208 E. Capitol St. N.E., No. 204, Washington, D.C. 20019, U.S.A.

LYSAUGHT, Jerome P. American, b. 1930. Education, Medicine/Health. Prof. of Education and Prof. of Pediatrics, Univ. of Rochester, N.Y., since 1969 (Asst. Prof., 1963–66; Assoc. Prof., 1966–69); Ed., Ed. Admin. Qtly., since 1985. Coordinator, Rochester Clearinghouse on Self–Instructional Materials for Health Care Facilities, River Campus Station, Rochester. Asst. Mgr., Educational Microfilm Systems, Eastman Kodak Co., 1954–61; Dir., National Commn. for the Study of Nursing and Nursing Education, 1967–73. *Publs:* (ed.) Programmed Learning: Evolving Principles and Industrial Applications, 1961; (with Clarence M. Williams) A Guide to Programmed Instruction, 1963; (ed.) Programmed Instruction in Medical Education, 1965; (ed. with Hilliard Jason) Self–Instruction in Medical Education, 1968; (ed.) Individualized Instruction in Medical Education, 1968; An Abstract for Action: Report of the National Commission for the Study of Nursing and Nursing Education, 1970, appendices, 1971; (ed.) Instructional Systems for Medical Education, 1971; (ed.) Instructional Technology in Medical Education, 1973; From Abstract into Action: Implementation of the Recommendations of the National Commission for the Study of Nursing and Nursing Education, 1973; (ed.) Action in Nursing: Progress in Professional Purpose, 1974; A Luther Christmas Anthology, 1978; Action in Affirmation: Toward an Unambiguous Profession of Nursing, 1980. Add: 17 Bretton Woods Dr., Rochester, N.Y. 14618, U.S.A.

LYTLE, Andrew (Nelson). American, b. 1902. Novels/Short stories, Literature, Autobiography/Memoirs/Personal, Biography. Prof. of English, Univ. of the South, Sewanee, Tenn. since 1968 (Prof. of History, 1942–43; Lectr. in English, 1961–67). Ed., Sewanee Review, Tenn., since 1961 (Managing Ed., 1942–43). Lectr. in Creative Writing, Univ. of Florida, Gainesville, 1948–61. *Publs:* Bedford Forrest and His Critter Company (in U.K. as Bedford Forrest), 1931, 1960; The Long Night, 1936; At the Moon's End, 1941; A Name for Evil, 1947; The Velvet Horn, 1957; A Novel, A Novella and Four Stories, 1958; The Hero with the Private Parts: Essays, 1966; (ed.) Craft and Vision: The Best Fiction from The Sewanee Review, 1971; A Wake for the Living: A Family Chronicle, 1975; Stories: Alchemy and Others, 1984. Add: Log Cabin, Monteagle, Tenn. 37356, U.S.A.

M

MAAS, Peter. American, b. 1929. Novels/Short stories, Social Commentary/Phenomena, Biography. Assoc. Ed., Collier's mag., 1954–56; Sr. Ed., Look mag., 1959–61; contrib., Saturday Evening Post, 1961–66; consultant, Curtis Publishing Co., 1966–67; contrib., New York mag., 1968–71. *Publs:* The Rescuer, 1967; The Valachi Papers, 1969; Serpico, 1973; King of the Gypsies, 1975; Made in America, 1979; Marie: A True Story, 1983; Pursuit, 1986; Manhunt, 1986. Add: Intnl. Creative Management, 40 W. 57th St., New York, N.Y. 10019, U.S.A.

MABBETT, Ian William. British, b. 1939. History. Reader in History, Monash Univ., Clayton, since 1983 (Lectr., 1965–72; Sr. Lectr. 1972–83). *Publs:* A Short History of India, 1968, 1983; Truth, Myth and Politics in Ancient India, 1972; Modern China, 1985; (ed.) Patterns of Kingship and Authority in Traditional Asia, 1985; Kings and Emperors of Asia, 1985. Add: Dept. of History, Monash Univ., Clayton, Vic., Australia.

MABEE, Carleton. American, b. 1914. History, Biography. Prof. of History, State Univ. of New York, New Paltz, 1965–80, now Emeritus. *Publs:* The American Leonardo: A Life of Samuel F.B. Morse, 1943; The Seaway Story, 1961; Black Freedom: The Nonviolent Abolitionists from 1830 Through the Civil War, 1970; Black Education in New York State: From Colonial to Modern Times, 1979; (ed. with James A. Fletcher) A Quaker Speaks from the Black Experience: The Life and Selected Writings of Barrington Dunbar, 1979. Add: Route 2, Box 1421, Gardiner, N.Y. 12525, U.S.A.

MABEY, Richard Thomas. British, b. 1941. Education, Environmental science/Ecology, Natural history. Lectr. in Liberal Studies, Dacorum Coll. of Further Education, Hemel Hempstead, Herts., 1963–65; Sr. Ed., Penguin Books Educational Div., 1966–73; Leverhulme Research Fellowship, 1983–84. Member, Nature Conservancy Council, 1982–86. *Publs:* (ed.) Class, 1967; Behind the Scene, 1968; The Pop Process, 1969; Children in Primary School, 1972; Food, 1972; Food for Free, 1972; The Unofficial Countryside, 1973; The Pollution Handbook, 1974; The Roadside Wildlife Book, 1974; Street Flowers, 1976; (ed.) The Natural History of Selborne, 1977; The Flowering of Britain, 1980; The Common Ground, 1980; Back to the Roots, 1983; (ed.) Landscape with Figures, 1983; Oak and Company, 1983; Cold Comforts, 1983; In a Green Shade, 1983; (ed.) Second Nature, 1984; The Frampton Flora, 1985; Gilbert White, 1986. Add: c/o Richard Scott Simon, 32 College Cross, London N1 1PR, England.

MacADAMS, Lewis (Perry, Jr.). American, b. 1944. Poetry, Documentaries/Reportage. Dir., Bolinas Community Public Utility District, Calif. Former Switchman, Southern Pacific Railroad. *Publs:* (co-ed.) Where the Girls Are: A Guide to Eastern Women's Colleges, 1966; City Money: Poems, 1966; Water Charms, 1968; The Poetry Room, 1970; A Bolinas Report: Reportage and Exhortation, 1971; Tilth: Interviews, 1972; Dance, 1972; Now Let us Eat of This Pollen and Place Some on Our Heads, For We Are to Eat of It, 1973; The Population Explodes, 1973; Live at the Church, 1977; The Grateful Dead, 1983.

MACAINSH, Noel Leslie. Australian, b. 1926. Poetry, Art. Reader in English, James Cook Univ. of North Queensland, since 1969. Pres., Goethe Soc. of Townsville, since 1972; member, Literature Bd., Arts Council of Australia, since 1974. *Publs:* Clifton Pugh, 1961; Eight by Eight, 1963; Nietzsche in Australia, 1975. Add: Dept. of English, James Cook Univ. of North Queensland, Townsville, Qld., Australia 4810.

MACAULAY, David (Alexander). British, b. 1946. Architecture, Children's non-fiction. Freelance illustrator and writer, since 1979. Instr. in Interior Design, 1969–73, and Instr. in Two-Dimensional Design, 1974–76, Adjunct Faculty, Dept. of Illustration, Rhode Island School of Design, Providence; public school teacher of art in Central Falls, R.I., 1969–72, and Newton, Mass., 1972–74; designer, Morris Nathanson Design, 1969–72. *Publs:* (all self-illustrated): Cathedral: The Story of Its Construction, 1973, 1981; City: A Story of Roman Planning and Construction, 1974; Pyramid, 1975; Underground, 1976; Castle, 1977, 1982; Great Moments in Architecture, 1978; Motel of the Mysteries, 1979; Unbuilding, 1980; Mill, 1983; Why the Chicken Crossed the Road, 1987; The Way Things Work, 1988. Add: 27 Rhode Island Ave., Providence, R.I. 02906, U.S.A.

MACAULAY, John Ure. New Zealander, b. 1925. Hon. Dir., Geography Resource Centre, since 1974. Geography Master, Papakura High Sch., 1954–59; Head of Social Studies Dept., Manurewa High Sch., 1960–68; Review Ed., New Zealand Journal of Geography, 1969–77; Sr. Lectr. in Geography, Christchurch Teacher's Coll., 1969–83 (Lectr. 1968–69). *Publs:* School Certificate Geography Notes, 1957; Lands of Contrast: A Course in School Certificate Geography, 1966, 3rd ed., 1975; Map Outlines at Work, 1970; (ed. with J.M. Renner) Source Book on British Isles Geography, 1974; (co-ed.) Source Book on African Geography, 1977; (co-ed.) Senior Atlas for New Zealand, 1978, 1983. Add: Christchurch Teachers' Coll., Dovedale Ave., Christchurch 4, New Zealand.

MACAULEY, Robie (Mayhew). American, b. 1919. Novels/Short stories, Writing/Journalism. Adjunct Prof. Harvard Univ., Cambridge, MA, since 1988. Instr. in English, Bard Coll., Annandale-on-Hudson, N.Y., 1946–47, and Univ. of Iowa, Iowa City, 1947–50; Asst. Prof., Univ. of North Carolina Women's Coll., Greensboro, 1950–53; Teacher, Kenyon Coll., Gambier, Ohio, 1953–66; Ed., Kenyon Review, 1959–66; Fiction Ed., Playboy mag., Chicago, 1966–77; Exec. Ed., Houghton Mifflin Co., Boston, 1977–88. *Publs:* The Disguises of Love, 1952; The End of Pity and Other Stories, 1957; (with George Lanning) Technique in Fiction, 1964; (ed.) Gallery of Modern Fiction: Stories from the Kenyon Review, 1966; A Secret History of Time to Come, 1979. Add: c/o Roberta Pryor, 24 W. 55th St., New York, NY 10019, U.S.A.

MAC AVOY, Roberta Ann. American, b. 1949. Science fiction/Fantasy. *Publs:* Tea with the Black Dragon, 1983; Damiano, 1983; Damiano's Lute, 1984; Raphael, 1984; (co-author) The Book of Kells, 1985; Twisting the Rope, 1986; The Grey Horse, 1987; The Third Eagle, 1988. Add: Underhill at Nelson Farm, 1669 Nelson Rd., Scotts Valley, Calif. 95066, U.S.A.

MACBEATH, Innis (Stewart). British, b. 1928. Administration/Management, Industrial Relations. Secty, Iona Appeal, since 1984. Staff, Glasgow Herald, 1952–56; with The Times newspaper, London, 1957–73: Labour Ed., 1969–73; Assoc. Sr. Consultant, Inbucon Ltd., 1973–83; Prof. of Industrial Relations, London Grad. Sch. of Business Studies, 1974–81. *Publs:* Votes, Virtues, and Vices, 1969; The Times Guide to the Industrial Relations Act, 1971; The European Approach to Worker-Management Relationships, 1973; Cloth Cap and After, 1974; Power Sharing in Industry, 1975; Workers' Participation in Industrial Decision-Making, 1976; (ed.) Daughters of the Glen, by A. Stewart, 1986; Iona's Million, 1987. Add: Park House, Muthill, Perthshire PH5 2AE, Scotland.

MacBETH, George (Mann). British, b. 1932. Novels, Children's fiction, Plays, Poetry. Ed., Fantasy Poets series, Fantasy Press, Oxford, 1952–54; Producer, Overseas Talks Dept., 1957, and Talks Dept., 1958, Ed., Poet's Voice, 1958–65, New Comment, 1959–64, and Poetry Now, 1965–76, BBC. *Publs:* A Form of Words: Poems, 1954; Lecture to the Trainees, 1962; The Broken Places: Poems, 1963; (ed.) The Penguin Book of Sick Verse, 1963; (with Jack Clemo and Edward Lucie-Smith) Penguin Modern Poets 6, 1964; (with Jack Clemo and Edward Lucie-Smith) Penguin Modern Poets 6, 1964; The Doomsday Show (play), 1964; (ed.) The Penguin Book of Animal Verse, 1965; A Doomsday Book: Poems and Poem-Games, 1965; The Twelve Hotels, 1965; Missile Commander, 1965; The Calf, 1965; The Humming Bird: A Monodrama, 1966; The Castle, 1966; Noah's Journey, 1966; (ed.) Poetry 1900–1965; An Anthology, 1967; The Screens, 1967; The Colour of Blood: Poems, 1967; The Night of Stones: Poems, 1969; A War Quartet, 1969; A Death, 1969; Zoo's Who (poetry), 1969; Jonah and the Lord, 1969; (ed.) The Penguin Book of Victorian Verse: A Critical Anthology, 1969; The Burning Cone, 1970; The Bamboo Nightingale, 1970; Poems, 1970; The Hiroshima Dream, 1970; Two Poems, 1970; (ed.) The Falling Splendour: Poems of Alfred, Lord Tennyson, 1970; A Prayer, Against Revenge, 1971; The Orlando Poems, 1971; Collected Poems 1958–1970, 1971; The Scene-Machine (play), 1971; A Farewell, 1972; Lusus: A Verse Lecture, 1972; A Litany, 1972; My Scotland: Fragments of a State of Mind, 1973; Shrapnel, 1973; Prayers, 1973; The Vision, 1973; A Poet's Year, 1973; Elegy for the Gas Dowsers, 1974; Shrapnel, and a Poet's Year, 1974; The Samurai (novel), 1975; In the Hours Waiting for the Blood to Come (poetry), 1975; The Survivor (novel), 1977; (ed.) The Book of Cats, 1977; The Seven Witches (novel), 1978; Buying a Heart (poetry), 1978; Poems of Love and Death, 1980; The Born Losers (novel), 1981; A Kind of Treason (novel), 1982; The Rectory Mice (juvenile), 1982; Poems from Oby, 1982; The Long Darkness, 1983; Anna's Book (novel), 1983; (ed.) Poetry for Today, 1983; T$e Lion of Pescara (novel), 1984; Dizzy's Woman (novel), 1986; The Cleaver Garden (poetry), 1986; The Book of Daniel (children's poems), 1986; Anatomy of a Divorce, 1988. Add: c/o Anthony Sheil Assoc., 43 Doughty St., London WC1N 2LF, England.

MacCAIG, Norman (Alexander). British, b. 1910. Poetry. Reader in Poetry, Stirling Univ., Scotland, since 1972 (Lectr. in English Studies, 1970–72). Fellow in Creative Writing, Univ. of Edinburgh, 1966–70. *Publs:* Far Cry, 1943; The Inward Eye, 1946; Riding Lights, 1955; The Sinai Sort, 1957; A Common Grace, 1960; A Round of Applause, 1962; Measures, 1965; Surroundings, 1966; Rings on a Tree, 1968; A Man in My Position, 1969; (ed. with Alexander Scott) Contemporary Scottish Verse, 1959–69, 1970; Selected Poems, 1971; Selected Poems, 1972; The White Bird, 1973; The World's Room, 1974; Tree of String, 1977; Old Maps and New: Selected Poems, 1978; The Equal Skies, 1980; A World of Difference, 1983; Collected Poems, 1985; Voice-Over, 1988. Add: 7 Leamington Terr., Edinburgh 10, Scotland.

MACCOBY, Michael. American, b. 1933. Administration/Management, Sociology. Dir., Prog. on Technology, Public Policy, and Human Development, J.F. Kennedy School of Govt., Harvard Univ., since 1978; Pres., The Maccoby Group, Consultants for Strategic Development, since 1989. Faculty Member, Washington Sch. of Psychiatry, Washington, D.C., 1974–87. *Publs:* (with Erich Fromm) Social Character in a Mexican Village, 1970; The Gamesman: The New Corporate Leaders, 1976; The Leader: A New Face for American Management, 1981; Why Work: Leading the New Generation, 1988. Add: 4825 Linnean Ave. N.W., Washington, D.C. 20008, U.S.A.

MacCORMICK, (Donald) Neil. British, b. 1941. Law, Politics. Regius Prof. of Public Law, Univ. of Edinburgh, since 1972 (Dean of Faculty of Law, 1974–76, 1985–88). Lectr., St. Andrews Univ., Scotland (Queen's Coll., Dundee), 1965–67; Fellow and Tutor in Jurisprudence, Balliol Coll., Oxford, 1967–72, and Lectr. in Law, 1968–72, and Pro-Proctor, 1971–72, Oxford Univ. Pres., Assn. for Legal and Social Philosophy, 1974–76; Pres., Soc. of Public Teachers of Law, 1983–84. *Publs:* (ed.) The Scottish Debate: Essays on Scottish Nationalism, 1970; (ed.) Lawyers in Their Social Setting, 1976; Legal Reasoning and Legal Theory, 1978; H.L.A. Hart, 1981; Legal Right and Social Democracy: Essays in Legal and Political Philosophy, 1982; (with O. Weinbergen) An Institutional Theory of Law, 1986. Add: The Old College, Edinburgh, EH8 9YL, Scotland.

MacCRACKEN, Mary. American, b. 1926. Autobiography/Memoirs/Personal. In private practice as a specialist in learning disabilities, Englewood, N.J., since 1973. Teacher of emotionally disturbed children, 1965–70; supplemental teacher, 1970–73; Resource Room Teacher, 1973–79. *Publs:* A Circle of Children, 1973; "Lovey": A Very Special Child, 1976; City Kid, 1980; Turnabout Children, 1986. Add: 325 Morrow Rd., Englewood, N.J. 07631, U.S.A.

MacDONALD, Caroline. New Zealander, b. 1948. Children's fiction. Ed., teaching materials, Deakin Univ., Geelong, Australia, 1984–88. *Publs:* Elephant Rock, 1984; Visitors, 1984; Yellow Boarding House, 1985; Joseph's Boat, 1988; Earthgames, 1988; The Lake at the End of the World, 1988. Add: P.O. Box 4189, Hamilton, New Zealand.

MACDONALD, Ian David. British, b .1932. Plays/Screenplays, Mathematics/Statistics. Foundn. Prof. of Mathematics, Univ. of Newcastle, N.S.W., 1964–68; Sr. Lectr. in Mathematics, Univ. of Stirling, 1970–84. *Publs:* The Theory of Groups, 1968; Alex (play), 1985. Add: 10 Middleton, Menstrie FK11 7HA, Scotland.

MACDONALD, John M(arshall). American, b. 1920. Criminology/Law enforcement/Prisons, Psychiatry. Prof. Emeritus of Psychiatry, Univ. of Colorado Sch. of Medicine, Denver (joined faculty, 1951). *Publs:* Psychiatry and the Criminal, 1958, with L.C. Whitaker, 1969; (with S. Boyd and J. Galvin) The Murderer and His Victim, 1961; (with Margaret Mead) Homicidal Threats, 1968; Rape: Offenders and Their Victims, 1971; (with N.K. Rickles) Indecent Exposure, 1973; Armed Robbery, 1975; Bombers and Firesetters, 1977; Burglary and Theft, 1980; (with Jerry Kennedy) Criminal Investigations of Drug Offenses, 1983; Psychiatry and the Criminal, 1986; (with S. Boyd) The Murderer and His Victim, 1986; (with D. Michaud) The Confession, 1987. Add: 2205 E. Dartmouth Circle, Englewood, Colo. 80110, U.S.A.

MACDONALD, Malcolm. *See* **ROSS-MACDONALD,** Malcolm John.

MACDONALD, Simon Gavin George. British, b. 1923. Biology, Physics. Prof. of Physics, Univ. of Dundee, since 1973–88 (Sr. Lectr., 1967–73; Dean, Faculty of Science, 1970–73; Vice-Principal, 1974–79). Chmn., Bd. of Dirs., Dundee Repertory Theatre, since 1975. Sr. Lectr., Univ. Coll. of the West Indies, Kingston, Jamaica, 1957–62, and Univ. of St. Andrews, Scotland, 1962–67; Convener, Scottish Univs. Council on Entrance, 1977–83. Chmn., Fedn. of Scottish Theatres, 1978–80. *Publs:* Problems and Solutions in General Physics, 1967; (with D.M. Burns) Physics for Biology and Premedical Students, 1970; (with D.M. Burns) Physics for the Life and Health Sciences, 1974. Add: 10 Westerton Ave., Dundee DD5 3NJ, Scotland.

MacDONALD, William L(loyd). American, b. 1921. Archaeology/Antiquities, Architecture. Assoc. Ed., Princeton Encyclopedia of Classical Sites; Advisory Ed., Architectura journal. Instr., 1956–59, Asst. Prof. 1959–63, and Assoc. Prof. of the History of Art, 1963–65, Yale Univ., New Haven, Conn.; A.P. Brown Prof. of History of Art, Smith Coll., Northampton, Mass., 1965–80. *Publs:* Early Christian and Byzantine Architecture, 1962; The Architecture of the Roman Empire, 1965, 1982, vol. 2 1986; The Pantheon: Design, Meaning, and Progeny, 1976; Northampton, Massachusetts Architecture and Buildings, 1976; Piranesi's Caceri: Sources of Invention, 1979. Add: 3811 39th St. NW, Washington D.C. 20016, U.S.A.

MACDOUALL, Robertson. *See* **MAIR,** George Brown.

MacDOWELL, Douglas Maurice. British, b. 1931. Classics. Prof. of Greek, Univ. of Glasgow, since 1971. Asst. Lectr., Lectr., Sr. Lectr., and Reader in Greek and Latin, Univ. of Manchester, 1958–71. *Publs:* (ed.) Andokides: On the Mysteries, 1962; Athenian Homicide Law, 1963; (ed.) Aristophanes: The Wasps, 1971; The Law in Classical Athens, 1978; Spartan Law, 1986. Add: Univ. of Glasgow, Glasgow G12 8QQ, Scotland.

MacEOIN, Gary. American, b. 1909. Civil liberties/Human rights, International relations/Current affairs, Theology/Religion, Autobiography, Biography. Adjunct Prof., World Development Issues, Fordham Univ., NYC, since 1963. Ed., Port-of-Spain Gazette, Trinidad, 1944–47; Information Dir., Caribbean Commn., Trinidad, 1948–49; Ed., La Hacienda mag., NYC, 1950–62; Lectr., Columbia Univ., NYC, 1954–61. *Publs:* Cervantes, 1950; Nothing Is Quite Enough, 1953; (with A. Curtis Wilgus and Hugh Foot) The Caribbean: Contemporary International Relations, 1957; Moreau, Holy Cross Founder, 1962; Latin America: The Eleventh Hour, 1962; No Peaceful Way: The Chilean Struggle for Dignity, 1964; Colombia, Venezuela, Guianas, 1965; New Challenges to American Catholics, 1965; What Happened at Rome?, 1966; All of Which I Saw, Part of Which I Was, 1967; (with F.X. Murphy) Synod '67: A New Sound in Rome, 1968; (ed.) Remi de Roo and Douglas Roche: Man to Man, 1969; (ed. and trans.) José Montserrat-Torrents: The Abandoned Spouse, 1969; Revolution Next Door: Latin America in the 1970s, 1971; Agent for Change, 1973; Northern Ireland, Captive of History, 1974; (trans.) J.M. Diez-Alegra: I Believe in Hope, 1974; Chile under Military Rule, 1974; (ed.) Christians in Search of a Just Society, 2 vols., 1977; (with N. Riley) Puebla: A Church Being Born, 1982; Memoirs and Memories, 1986; Central America's Options: Death or Life, 1988. Add: 64 High St., Nutley, N.J. 07110, U.S.A.

MACE, David (Robert). British, b. 1907. Human relations, Sociology. Prof. Emeritus of Family Sociology, Bowman Gray Sch. of Medicine, Wake Forest Univ., Winston-Salem since 1977 (Prof., 1967–1977); Co-Dir., Marriage Enrichment Training Prog., Dept. of Pastoral Care, N.C. Baptist Hosp., Winston-Salem, since 1977. Methodist Minister in England, 1930–40; Gen Secty., National Marriage Guidance Council of Great Britain, 1942–49; Prof. of Human Relations, Drew Univ., Madison N.J., 1949–59; Assoc. Prof. of Family Study Sch. of Medicine, Univ. of Pennsylvania, Philadelphia, 1959–60; Exec. Dir., American Assn. of Marriage Counselors 1960–67, Pres., National Council on Family Relations (U.S.A.), 1961–62, and Sex Information and Education Council of the U.S., 1966–68; Founder and Pres., Assn. of Couples for Marriage Enrichment, 1973–80. *Publs:* Does Sex Morality Matter?, 1943; Marriage Counselling, 1948; Marriage Crisis, 1948; Marriage: The Art of Lasting Love, 1952; Hebrew Marriage: A Sociological Study, 1953; Whom God Hath Joined, 1953; Success in Marriage, 1958; Youth Looks Toward Marriage, 1958; (with Vera Mace) Marriage East and West, 1960; (with V. Mace) The Soviet Family, 1963; (with Evelyn Duvall and Paul Popenoe) The Churches Look at Family Life, 1964; (trans.) Love and Sexuality, by Robert Grimm, 1964; Sex, Love, and Marriage in the Caribbean, 1965; Youth Considers Marriage, 1966; The Christian Response to the Sexual Revolution, 1970; Getting Ready for Marriage, 1972; Abortion: The Agonizing Decision, 1972; Sexual Difficulties in Marriage, 1972; (with V. Mace) We Can Have Better Marriages, 1974; The Training of Health Professionals in Human Sexuality, 1975; (with V. Mace) Marriage Enrichment in the Church, 1976; Towards Better Marriages, 1976; (with V. Mace) Men, Women, and God, 1976; (with V. Mace) How to Have a Happy Marriage, 1977; (with V. Mace) What's Happening to Clergy Marriages, 1980; Good Companions: Marriage, 1982; Love and Anger in Marriage, 1982; Prevention in Family Services, 1983; Letters to a Retired Couple: Marriage in the Later Years, 1985. Add: Highland Farms, Black Mountain, N.C. 28711, U.S.A.

MACESICH, George. American, b. 1927. Economics. Prof. of Economics since 1963, and Dir. of the Center for Yugoslav-American Studies since 1965, Florida State Univ., Tallahassee (Asst. Prof.,1959–61; Assoc. Prof., 1961–63). Member, U.S.-Yugoslav Economic Council. *Publs:* Yugoslavia: Theory and Practice of Development Planning, 1964; Commercial Banking and Regional Development in the U.S. 1950–60, 1965; Money in a European Common Market Setting, 1972; Financial, Industrial and Regional Development: American Experience with the Small Business Administration 1955–1965, 1972; Monetary and Financial Organization for Growth and Stability: The U.S. and Yugoslavia, 1972; Economic Stability: A Comparative Analysis, 1973; Monetary Theory and Policy: Theoretical and Empirical Issues, 1973; (with D. Dimitrijevic) Money and Finance in Contemporary Yugoslavia, 1973; The Intermaterial Monetary Economy and the Third World, 1981; (with H. Tsai) Money in Economic Systems, 1982; Monetarism: Theory and Policy, 1983; Politics of Monetarism: Its Historical and Institutional Development, 1984; World Banking and Finance: Co-operation Versus Conflict, 1984; (with Dimitrijevic) Money and Finance in Yugoslavia: A Comparative Analysis, 1985; World Crises and Developing Countries, 1985; Economic Nationalism and Stability, 1985; Monetary Policy and Rational Expectations, 1987; Monetary Reform and Co-operation Theory, 1989; (ed. with G. Macesich, R. Lang, and D. Vojnic) Essays on the Yugoslav Economic Model, 1989. Add: Center for Yugoslav-American Studies, 930 W. Park Ave., Florida State Univ., Tallahassee, Fla. 32306, U.S.A.

MacEWAN, J(ohn) W(alter) Grant. Canadian, b. 1902. Agriculture/Forestry, History. Dean, Faculty of Agriculture and Home Economics, Univ. of Manitoba, Winnipeg, 1946–51; Liberal Member for Calgary, Legislative Assembly of Alberta, 1955–59; Leader of the Liberal Party in Alberta, 1958–60; Mayor of Calgary, Alta., 1963–65; Lt. Gov. of Alberta, 1965–74. *Publs:* (co-author) Canadian Animal Husbandry, 1936; (co-author) General Agriculture, 1939; Breeds of Farm Livestock in Canada, 1941; Feeding of Farm Animals, 1945; Sodbusters, 1948; Agriculture on Parade, 1957; Between the Red and the Rockies, 1957; Eye Opener Bob, 1957; Fifty Mighty Men, 1958; Calgary Cavalcade, 1958; Blazing the Old Cattle Trails, 1965; Hoofprints and Hitchingposts, 1967; Tatanga Mani, 1968; Poking into Politics, 1969; West to the Sea, 1969; Harvest of Bread, 1969; Portraits from the Plains, 1971; Power for Prairie Plows, 1971; Sitting Bull, 1973; Battle for the Bay, 1975;

And Mighty Women Too, 1975; Memory Meadows, 1976; Cornerstone Colony, 1977; Rhyming Horseman of the Qu'Appelle, 1979; Pat Burns, Cattle King, 1979; History of Western Canadian Agriculture, 1980; Metis Makers of History, 1981; Highlights of Shorthorn History, 1982. Add: 132 Hallbrook Dr., Calgary, Alta., Canada.

MACFADYEN, Amyan. British, b. 1920. Biology, Environmental science/Ecology. Prof. of Biology, New Univ. of Ulster, Coleraine, since 1967, now Emeritus. Ed., Advances in Ecological Research, since 1974. Lectr., then Reader, Univ. Coll. of Swansea, 1956–65; Pres., British Ecological Soc., 1972–74. Pres., Intnl. Soc. for Ecology, 1974–78. *Publs:* Animal Ecology: Aims and Methods, 1957, 1963, rev. ed. 1965; (with H. Petrusewicz) Productivity of Terrestrial Animals, 1970; (with J.M. Anderson) The Role of Terrestrial and Aquatic Organisms in Decomposition Processes, 1976. Add: 23 Mountsandel Rd., Coleraine, Northern Ireland.

MACFADYEN, Kenneth Alexander. British, b. 1908. Engineering/Technology, Physics. Member, Scientific Staff, Research Labs. of the G.E.C., 1929–45; member, Academic Staff, Univ. of Birmingham, 1945–73. *Publs:* Small Transformers and Inductors, 1953; A Physics Laboratory Handbook for Students, 1963. Add: 28 Kingshill Dr., Birmingham B38 8SA, England.

MACFARLANE, Leslie John. British, b. 1924. Politics/Government. Tutor and Fellow in Politics, St. John's Coll., Oxford, since 1969. Lectr. in Politics, Oxford Univ. Tutor in Politics, Ruskin Coll, Oxford, 1963–69. *Publs:* British Politics 1918–1964, 1965; The British Communist Party: Origin and Development until 1929, 1966; Modern Political Theory, 1970; Political Disobedience, 1971; Violence and the State, 1974; Issues in British Politics since 1945, 1975; The Right to Strike, 1981; The Theory and Practice of Human Rights, 1985. Add: St. John's Coll., Oxford, England.

MacGIBBON, Jean. British, b. 1913. Novels/Short stories, Children's fiction. Editorial Dir., MacGibbon and Kee, publishers, London, 1948–54. *Publs:* When the Weather's Changing, 1945; Peter's Private Army, 1960; Red Sail, White Sail, 1961; (trans.) Women of Islam, by Assia Djébar, 1961; The Red Sledge, 1962; (trans.) Girls of Paris, by Nicole de Buron, 1962; Pam Plays Doubles, 1962; The View-Finder, 1963; A Special Providence, 1964; Liz, 1969; Sandy in Hollow Tree House, 1967; The Tall Ship, 1973; Hal, 1974; Jobs for the Girls, 1975; After the Raft Race, 1976; Three's Company, 1978; I Meant to Marry Him (autobiography), 1985. Add: c/o Victor Gollancz Ltd., 14 Henrietta St., London WC2E 8QJ, England.

MacGREGOR, (John) Geddes. American (b. British), b. 1909. Philosophy, Theology/Religion, Travel/Exploration/Adventure, Biography. Emeritus Distinguished Prof. of Philosophy, Univ. of Southern California, Los Angeles, since 1975 (Dean, Grad. Sch. of Religion, 1960–66; Distinguished Prof. of Philosophy, 1966–75); Hon. Canon of San Diego, since 1987. Asst., Dept. of Logic, Univ. of Edinburgh, 1947–49; first holder of the Rufus Jones Chair in Philosophy and Religion, Bryn Mawr Coll., Pa., 1949–60. *Publs:* Aesthetic Experience in Religion, 1947; Christian Doubt, 1951; Les Frontiè res de la Morale et de la Religion, 1952; From a Christian Ghetto, 1954; The Vatican Revolution, 1957; The Tichborne Impostor, 1957; The Thundering Scot, 1957; The Bible in the Making, 1959; Corpus Christi, 1959; Introduction to Religious Philosophy, 1959; The Coming Reformation, 1960; The Hemlock and the Cross, 1963; God Beyond Doubt, 1966; A Literary History of the Bible, 1968; The Sense of Absence, 1968; So Help Me God, 1970; Philosophical Issues in Religious Thought, 1973; The Rhythm of God, 1974; He Who Lets Us Be, 1975, 1987; Reincarnation in Christianity, 1978; Gnosis, 1979; Scotland Forever Home, 1980, 1985; The Nicene Creed Illumined by Modern Thought, 1980; Reincarnation as a Christian Hope, 1982; The Gospels as a Mandala of Wisdom, 1982; The Christening of Karma, 1984; (ed.) Immortality and Human Destiny, 1985; Apostles Extraordinary, 1986; Angels, 1988. Add: 876 Victoria Ave., Los Angeles, Calif. 90005, U.S.A.

MacGREGOR, James Grierson. Canadian, b. 1905. History, Autobiography/Memoirs/Personal, Biography. Chmn., Alberta Power Commn., Edmonton, 1952–70; former Pres., Historical Soc. of Alberta. *Publs:* Blankets and Beads, 1949; The Land of Twelve-Foot Davis, 1952; Behold the Shining Mountains, 1954 North-West of Sixteen, 1958; Pack Saddles to Tete Jaune Cache, 1962; Edmonton Trader, 1963; Peter Fidler, 1965; Edmonton: A History, 1967; Vilni Zemli: Free Lands, 1969; The Klondike Rush Through Edmonton, 1970; A History of Alberta, 1972; Overland by the Yellowhead, 1974; Paddle Wheels to Bucket-Wheels,

1974; The Battle River Valley, 1976; Senator Hardisty's Prairies, 1977; John Rowand, Czar of the Prairies, 1978; Vision of an Ordered Land, 1981; Grande Prairie, 1983. Add: 1801, 8210-111th St., Edmonton, Alta. T6G 2C7, Canada.

MACGREGOR, James Murdoch. Has also written as J.T. McIntosh. British, b. 1925. Science fiction/Fantasy, Wine, Photography. Sub.-Ed., Thomson Org. Ltd., Aberdeen, 1964–86. *Publs:* (as J.T. McIntosh) World Out of Mind, 1953; (as J.T. McIntosh) Born Leader, 1954; (as J.T. McIntosh) One in 300, 1955; (as J.T. McIntosh) The Fittest, 1955; Glamour in Your Lens, 1958; When the Ship Sank, 1959; Incident Over the Pacific (in U.K. as A Cry to Heaven), 1960; The Iron Rain, 1962; Wine Making for All, 1966; Beer Making for All, 1967; (as J.T. McIntosh) Time for a Change, 1967; (as J.T. McIntosh) Six Gates from Limbo, 1968; (with Peter O'Donnell) Take a Pair of Private Eyes, 1968; (as J.T. McIntosh) A Coat of Blackmail, 1970; (as J.T. McIntosh) Transmigration, 1970; (as J.T. McIntosh) Flight from Rebirth, 1971; (as J.T. McIntosh) The Cosmic Spies, 1972; (as J.T. McIntosh) The Space Sorcerers (in U.S. as The Suiciders), 1972; (as J.T. McIntosh) Galactic Takeover Bid, 1973; (as J.T. McIntosh) This is the Way the World Begins, 1976; (as J.T. McIntosh) Norman Conquest 2066, 1977; (as J.T. McIntosh) A Planet Called Utopia, 1979. Add: 63 Abbotswell Dr., Aberdeen, Scotland.

MacGUIGAN, Mark R. Canadian, b. 1931. Law, Politics/Government. Judge, Fed. Court of Appeal, since 1984. Member, Ontario Bar. Asst. Prof. of Law, 1960–63, and Assoc. Prof., 1963–66, Univ. of Toronto; Prof. of Law, 1966–67, and Visiting Lectr., 1967–68, Osgoode Hall Law Sch., York Univ.; Prof. of Law, 1967–69, and Dean of Law, 1967–68, Univ. of Windsor; Lectr. in Law, Carleton Univ., 1969–70; Member of Parliament (Can.) for Windsor-Walkerville, 1968–84, and Secty. of State for External Affairs, 1980–82; Parliamentary Secty. to Minister of Manpower and Immigration, 1972–74; Parliamentary Secty. to Minister of Labour, 1974–75; Minister of Justice and Attorney General, 1982–84. *Publs:* Jurisprudence: Readings and Cases, 2nd ed. 1966; (with Cohen and others) Report to the Minister of Justice of the Special Committee on Hate Propaganda in Canada, 1966; Cases and Materials on Creditors' Rights, 2nd ed. 1967; (co-author) Third Report of the Special Committee on Statutory Instruments, 1968; (co-author) Final Report of the Special Joint Committee of the Senate and of the House of Commons on the Constitution of Canada, 1972. Add: Supreme Court Bldg., Ottawa K1A 0H9, Ont., Canada.

MacGUIRE, Gregory. American, b. 1954. Children's fiction, Literary criticism. Staff member, 1979–83, and Assoc. Dir. and Asst. Prof., 1983–87, Center for the Study of Children's Literature, Simmons Coll., Boston. *Publs:* The Lightning Time, 1979; The Daughter of the Moon, 1980; Lights on the Lake, 1981; The Dream Stealer, 1983; (ed. with Barbara Harrison) Innocence and Experience: Essays and Conversations on Children's Literature, 1987; I Feel Like the Morning Star, 1989; The Peace and Quiet Diner, 1989. Add: 4 Hubbard St., Jamaica Plain, Mass. 02130, U.S.A.

MACHIN, George Ian Thom. British, b. 1937. History. Reader in Modern History, Univ. of Dundee, since 1982 (Lectr., 1967–75; Sr. Lectr., 1975–82). Asst. Lectr., 1961–63, and Lectr., 1963–64, Univ. of Singapore; Lectr., Queen's Coll., Univ. of St. Andrews, 1964–67. *Publs:* The Catholic Question in English Politics 1820–1830; Politics and the Churches in Great Britain 1832–1868, and 1869–1921. Add: Dept. of Modern History, Univ. of Dundee, Dundee DD1 4HN, Scotland.

MACINTOSH, Joan. New Zealander, b. 1924. History, Autobiography/Memoirs/Personal. *Publs:* The Wreck of the Tararua; Never a Dull Moment; Fortrose; 100 Years in Retrospect; Throw Out the Lifeline; Makarewa, 1979; Colac Bay, 1980; From Waste Lands to Wealth, 1985. Add: 28 Alamein St., Riverton, Southland; or P.O. Box 54, Riverton, New Zealand.

MACINTYRE, Alasdair. British, b. 1929. Philosophy, Theology/Religion. W. Alton Jones Prof. of Philosophy, Vanderbilt Univ., Nashville, since 1982. Fellow, University Coll., Oxford, 1963–66; Prof. of History of Ideas, Brandeis Univ., Waltham, Mass., 1969–71; Univ. Prof. in Philosophy and Political Science, Boston Univ., 1972–80; Luce Prof., Wellesley Coll., Massachusetts, 1980–82. *Publs:* Marxism and Christianity, 1953, 1969; (ed. with A.G.N. Flew) New Essays in Philosophical Theology, 1955; (ed.) Metaphysical Beliefs, 1957; The Unconscious, 1958; Short History of Ethics, 1966; (ed.) Hume's Ethical Writings, 1966; (with Paul Ricoeur) The Religious Significance of Atheism, 1969; Marcuse: An Exposition and a Polemic, 1970; (ed. with Dorothy Emmet) Sociological Theory and Philosophical Analysis, 1970; Against the Self-

Images of the Age: Essays in Ideology and Philosophy, 1971; (ed.) Hegel: A Collection of Critical Essays, 1972; After Virtue, 1981. Add: Dept. of Philosophy, Vanderbilt Univ., Nashville, Tenn. 37235, U.S.A.

MacINTYRE, Elisabeth. Pseud. for Elisabeth Eldershaw. Australian, b. 1916. Children's fiction. Designer, Lever's Advertising Agency, Lintas, 1937–42; freelance artist and feature writer, The Age, Melbourne, Sunday Telegraph, Sydney, Australian Woman's Weekly, and the New South aWales Education Dept. School Magazine; television cartoonist for the ABC. *Publs:* Ambrose Kangaroo: A Story That Never Ends, 1941; The Handsome Duckling, 1944; The Black Lamb, 1944; The Forgetful Elephant, 1944; The Willing Donkey, 1944; Ambrose Kangaroo Has a Busy Day, 1955; Susan, Who Lives in Australia (verse) (in Aust., as Katherine), 1944, 1958; Willie's Woollies: The Story of Australian Wool, 1951; Mr. Koala Bear (verse), 1954; The Riddle of Rum Jungle (radio serial), 1957; Jane Likes Pictures, 1959; The Kings of Corroboree Plains (radio serial), 1960; Ambrose Kangaroo Goes to Town, 1964; Hugh's Zoo, 1964; The Affable, Amiable Bulldozer Man (verse), 1965; Ninji's Magic, 1966; The Purple Mouse, 1975; It Looks Different When You Get There, 1977; A Wonderful Way to Learn the Language, 1982. Add: c/o Jane Eldershaw, 372 Fifth Ave., New York NY 10018, U.S.A.

MACK, Maynard. American, b. 1909. Literature. Sterling Prof. of English, Yale Univ., New Haven, Conn., since 1965 (Prof. of English, 1936–65; Assoc. Dir., Shakespeare Inst., 1953–62; Dir., Div. of Humanities, 1962–64; Chmn., Dept. of English, 1965–68; Dir., National Humanities Inst., 1974–77). Vice-Pres., Intnl. Shakespeare Assn., since 1976. Pres., Modern Language Assn., 1970, Shakespeare Assn. of America, 1975–76, and Modern Humanities Research Assn., 1984. *Publs:* (ed.) Pope: Essay on Man, 1950; (ed.) Alexander Pope: An Essay on Man: The Manuscripts of the Morgan and Houghton Libraries, 1962; King Lear in Our Time, 1965; (ed.) Pope: The Translations of Homer, 1967; The Garden and the City, 1969; Collected in Himself (essays), 1982; (ed. with George D. Lord) Poetic Traditions of the English Renaissance, 1982; The Last and Greatest Art, 1984; Alexander Pope: A Life, 1985. Add: 1314 Yale Station, New Haven, Conn. 06520, U.S.A.

MACKAY, Claire (née Bacchus). Canadian, b. 1930. Children's fiction, Children's non-fiction. Free-lance researcher and writer since 1978. Library Asst., Polysar Corp., Sarnia, Ont., 1952–55; medical social worker, Wascana Hospital, Regina, Sask., 1969–71; research librarian, Steelworkers' Union, Toronto, 1972–78. *Publs:* Mini-Bike Hero, 1974; Mini-Bike Racer, 1976; Exit Barney McGee, 1979; (with Marsha Hewitt) One Proud Summer, 1981; Mini-Bike Rescue, 1982; The Minerva Program, 1984; Pay Cheques and Picket Lines: All About Unions in Canada (non-fiction), 1987. Add: 6 Frank Crescent, Toronto, Ont. M6G 3K5, Canada.

MacKAY, Donald (Iain). British, b. 1937. Economics. Chmn., Pieda, economic consultants. Economic Consultant to the Secty. of State for Scotland, since 1971; Gov. National Inst. of Economic Research, since 1982; Member, Scottish Economic Council, since 1983. Formerly Consultant to British Steel Corporation, Organisation for Economic Cooperation and Development, National Joint Council for Local Authorities, and Confederation of Employee Organisations. With English Electric Co., 1959–62; Lectr., Univ. of Aberdeen, 1962–65, and Univ. of Glasgow, 1965–71; Prof. of Political Economy, Univ. of Aberdeen, 1971–76; Prof. of Economics, Heriot-Watt Univ., Edinburgh, 1976–82. *Publs:* Geographical Mobility and the Brain Drain: A Case Study of Aberdeen University Graduates 1860–1960, 1970; Local Labour Markets and Wage Structures, 1970; Labour Markets Under Different Employment Conditions, 1971; The Political Economy of North Sea Oil, 1975; (ed.) Scotland 1980, 1977. Add: Newfield, 14 Gamekeeper's Rd., Edinburgh EH4 6LU, Scotland.

MACKAY, James Alexander. Also writes as Ian Angus, Bruce Garden, and Peter Whittington, and translates as William Finlay. British, b. 1936. Antiques/Furnishings, History, Recreation/Leisure/Hobbies, Biography, Translations. Columnist, Financial Times, London, since 1967; Ed., The Burns Chronicle, since 1977, The Burnsian, since 1986, and the Postal History Annual, since 1979. Asst. Keeper, British Museum, London, 1961–71; Ed.-in-Chief, New Intnl. Encyclopedia of Stamps, I.P.C., London, 69–72. *Publs:* A Guide to the Uists, 1961; St. Kilda, 1963; The Tapling Collection, 1963; World of Stamps, 1964; Commonwealth Stamp Design, 1965; (with G. Crabb) Tristan da Cunha, 1965; Churchill on Stamps, 1966; The Story of Malta, 1966; (as Bruce Garden) Make Money with Stamps, 1967; Money in Stamps, 1967; Cover Collecting, 1968; The Story of Great Britain, 1968; Value in Coins and Medals, 1968; The Story of Eire, 1969; The Story of East Africa, 1970; Antiques of the Future,

1970; An Introduction to Small Antiques, 1970; Commemorative Medals, 1970; Airmails, 1870–1970, 1971; Commemorative Pottery and Porcelain, 1971; Coin Collecting for Grown-Up Beginners, 1971; Greek and Roman Coins, 1971; (as Peter Whittington) Undiscovered Antiques, 1972; (as Ian Angus) Collecting Antiques, 1972; World of Classic Stamps, 1972; L'Univers des Timbres, 1972; Glass Paperweights, 1973; The Animaliers, 1973; Stamps of the World in Colour, 1973; (as Ian Angus) Stamps, Posts and Postmarks, 1973; (as Ian Angus) Coins and Money Token, 1973; (as Ian Angus) Medals and Decorations, 1973; (English language ed.) New World Encyclopedia, 1973; (trans. as William Finlay) Collecting Postal History, by Prince Dmitry Kandaouroff, 1973; (as Peter Whittington) Kitchen Antiques, 1974; A Source Book of Stamps, 1974; Dictionary of Turn of the Century Antiques, 1974; Collecting Famous Faces, 1974; History of Stamp Design, 1974; Robert Bruce, King of Scots, 1974; An Encyclopaedia of Small Antiques, 1975; The Price Guide to Collectable Antiques, 1975; Rural Crafts in Scotland, 1976; Encyclopaedia of World Stamps 1945–1975, 1976; Orkney, VIII, Shetland, IX, Mull, Iona, Coll and Tiree, X, The Other Argyll Islands, XI, Scottish Islands Catalogue, and XII, The Isle of Wight, 1978–82; Floating Post Offices of the Clyde, 1979; Collectables, 1979; English and Welsh Postmarks since 1840, 1980; Cheque Collecting, 1980; Price Guide to More Collectable Antiques, 1980; The Antique Collectors' Companion, 1980; The St. Michael Book of Stamp Collecting, 1980; Antique Market Values, 1980; British Post Office Numbers 1929–69, Orkney, VIII, Shetland, IX, Mull, Iona, Coll and Tiree, X, The Other Argyll Islands, XI, Scottish Islands Catalogue, and XII, The Isle of Wight, 1978–82; Floating Post Offices of the Clyde, 1979; Collectables, 1979; English and Welsh Postmarks since 1840, 1980; Cheque Collecting, 1980; Price Guide to More Collectable Antiques, 1980; The Antique Collectors' Companion, 1980; The St. Michael Book of Stamp Collecting, 1980; Antique Market Values, 1980; British Post Office Numbers 1929–69, 1981; Telegraphic Codes of the British Isles, 1870–1924, 1981; The Scottish Highland Postal Service, 1981; Numismatics, 1982; The Parcel Post of the British Isles, 1982; Irish Postmarks since 1840, 1982; The Guinness Book of Stamp Facts and Feats, 1982; The History of Modern English Coinage 1485–1982, 1982; Collecting Local History, 1983; Local Collecting, 1983; Registered Mail, 1983; Official Mail, 1984; The Postal History of Glasgow, 1984; British Special Stamps 1971–83, 1984; Surcharged Mail of the British Isles, 1985; The Burns Federation 1885–1985, 1985; Sub Office Rubber Datestamps of England and Wales, 4 vols., 1985–86; The Postal History of Dumfries, 1986; (ed.) The Complete Works of Robert Burns, 1986; Scottish Cancelling Machines, 1986; Philatelic Terms Illustrated, 1987; Numbered Handstamps of Scotland, 1987; (ed.) The Complete Letters of Robert Burns, 1987; Provincial Krag Cancellations of England and Wales, 1987. Burnsiana, 1988; Burns-Lore of Dumfries and Galloway, 1988; Postmarks of England and Wales since 1660, 1988; The Gold Sovereign for Collecting and Investment, 1989. Add: 11 Newall Terr., Dumfries DG1 1LN, Scotland.

MACKELWORTH, R(onald) W(alter). British, b. 1930. Science fiction/ Fantasy. Life insurance marketing mgr., since 1985 (commenced Insurance career, 1950); also freelance writer, mainly of SF short stories. *Publs:* Firemantle, 1968, in U.S. as the Diabols, 1969; Tiltangle, 1970; Starflight 3000, 1972; The Year of the Painted World, 1975; Shakehoue, 1979. Add: 32 Mark Way, Godalming, Surrey, England.

MACKENZIE, Andrew Carr. British, b. 1911. Supernatural/Occult topics, Area Studies. Book Reviewer, Journal of Soc. for Psychical Research, since 1972. London News Ed., Sheffield Morning Telegraph, 1958–76; London Staff Writer, Yorkshire Post, 1971–76. *Publs:* The Unexplained, 1966; Frontiers of the Unknown, 1968; Apparitions and Ghosts, 1971; (ed.) A Gallery of Ghosts, 1972; The Riddle of the Future, 1974; Dracula Country, 1977; Hauntings and Apparitions, 1982; Romanian Journey, 1983; (ed.) A Concise History of Romania, 1985; Archaeology in Romania, 1986; The Seen and the Unseen, 1987. Add: 18 Castlebar Park, London W5 1BX, England.

MacKENZIE, David. American, b. 1927. History, Biography. Prof. of History, Univ. of North Carolina, Greensboro, since 1969. Lectr. in History, Princeton Univ. of N.J. 1959–61; Asst. to Assoc. Prof. of History, Wells Coll., Aurora, N.Y., 1961–68. *Publs:* The Serbs and Russian Pan-Slavism, 1875–1878, 1967; Lion of Tashkent: The Career of General M.G. Cherniaev, 1974; A History of Russia and the Soviet Union, 1977, 3rd ed., 1987; Ilija Garašanin: Balkan Bismarck, 1985; Ilija Garašanin: Drzavnik i diplomata, 1987; A History of the Soviet Union, 1987; Apis: The Congenial Conspirator, 1989. Add: 1000 Fairmont St., Greensboro, N.C. 27401, U.S.A.

MacKENZIE, Donald. Canadian, b. 1918. Mystery/Crime/Suspense,

Autobiography/Memoirs/Personal. Full-time writer since 1948. *Publs:* Occupation Thief (in U.K. as Fugitives; autobiography), 1955; Gentleman at Crime (autobiography), 1956; Nowhere to Go, 1956 (in U.S. as Manhunt, 1957); The Juryman, 1957; Scent of Danger, 1958 (in U.K. paperback, Moment of Danger, 1959); Dangerous Silence, 1960; Knife Edge, 1961; The Genial Stranger, 1962; Double Exposure, 1963 (in U.S. paperback, I Spy, 1964); Cool Sleeps Balaban, 1964; The Lonely Side of the River, 1965; Salute from a Dead Man, 1966; Death Is a Friend, 1967; Three Minus Two (in U.S. as The Quiet Killer), 1968; Dead Straight, 1969; Night Boat from Puerto Vedra, 1970; The Kyle Contract, 1970; Sleep Is for the Rich, 1971 (in U.K. paperback, The Chalice Caper, 1974); Postscript to a Dead Letter, 1973; Zaleski's Percentage, 1974; The Spreewald Collection, 1975; Raven series, 9 vols., 1976–84; Dark, Deep, and Dead, 1978; Nobody Here by That Name, 1986; A Savage State of Grace, 1988. Add: c/o Russell and Volkening Inc., 50 W. 29 St., New York, N.Y. 10001, U.S.A.

MACKENZIE, Lee. *See* **BOWDEN,** Jean.

MACKENZIE, Norman H(ugh). Canadian, b. 1915. Literature. Prof. of English, Queen's Univ., Kingston, since 1966, Emeritus since 1980 (Dir. of Grad. Studies in English, 1967–73; Chmn., Council for Grad. Studies and Research, 1971–73). Prof. and Head of English, Univ. Coll. of Rhodesia, Salisbury, 1955–65, and Laurentian Univ., Ont., 1965–66. *Publs:* South African Travel Literature in the 17th Century, 1955; (ed. with W.H. Gardner) The Poems of Gerard Manley Hopkins, 1967; Hopkins, 1968; (ed.) Poems by G.M. Hopkins, 1974; Reader's Guide to Hopkins, 1981. Add: 416 Windward Pl., Kingston, Ont. K7M 4E4, Canada.

MACKERRAS, Colin Patrick. Australian, b. 1939. History, International relations/Current affairs, Literature. Foundn. Prof., Sch. of Modern Asian Studies, Griffith Univ., Brisbane, since 1974; Co-Dir., Key Centre for Asian Languages and Studies, Brisbane, since 1988. Teacher of English, Peking Foreign Languages Inst., 1964–66; Research Scholar, 1966–69; Research Fellow, 1969–73, Ed., Papers on Far Eastern History, journal, 1970–73, and Sr. Research Fellow, 1973, Dept. of Far Eastern History, Australian National Univ., Canberra. *Publs:* (with Neale Hunter) China Observed 1964–67, 1967; The Uighur Empire According to the T'ang Dynastic Histories, 744-840, 1968, rev. ed. as The Uighur Empire According to the T—'ang Dynastic Histories: A Study in Sino-Uighur Relations, 744-840, 1972; The Rise of the Peking Opera 1770–1870; Social Aspects of the Theatre in Manchu China, 1972; Amateur Theatre in China, 1949–1966, 1973; (ed. with D. Leslie and W. Gungwu) Essays on the Sources for Chinese History, 1973; The Chinese Theatre in Modern Times, 1975; China: The Impact of Revolution, 1976; Musical Cultures of Asia: China, 1980; The Performing Arts in Contemporary China, 1981; Modern China: A Chronology, 1982; Chinese Theater from its Origins to the Present Day, 1983; (with E.S.K. Fung) From Fear to Friendship, 1985; (ed. with Nick Knight) Marxism in Asia, 1985; (ed. with Robert Cribb and Allan Healy) Contemporary Vietnam: Perspectives from Australia, 1988; Western Images of China, 1989. Add: Sch. of Modern Asian Studies, Griffith Univ., Nathan, Qld., Australia 4111.

MACKESY, Piers Gerald. British, b. 1924. History. Fellow, now Emeritus Fellow, Pembroke Coll., Oxford, since 1954; Member, Council of National Army Museum, since 1983, and Council of the Soc. for Army Historical Research, since 1985. Harkness Fellow, Harvard Univ., 1953–54; Visiting Fellow, Inst. for Advanced Study, Princeton, N.J., 1961–62; Visiting Prof., California Inst. of Technology, 1966. *Publs:* The War in the Mediterranean, 1803–1810, 1957; The War for America, 1775–1783, 1964; Statesmen at War: The Strategy of Overthrow, 1798–1799, 1974; The Coward of Minden: The Affair of Lord George Sackville, 1979; War without Victory: The Downfall of Pitt, 1799–1802. Add: Leochel Cushnie House, Cushnie, Alford AB3 8LJ, Scotland.

MACKIE, Alastair (Webster). British, b. 1925. Poetry. English Teacher, Waid Academy, Anstruther, Fife, since 1959. English Teacher, Stromness Academy, Orkney, 1951–59. *Publs:* Soundings, 1966; To Duncan Glen, 1971; Clytach, 1972; At the Heich Kirk-Yaird, 1974; (ed.) Four Gates of Lothian and Other Poems, by Forbes MacGregor, 1979; Ingaitherins: Selected Poems, 1987. Add: 13 St. Adrian's Pl., Anstruther, Fife, Scotland.

MACKIE, Margaret Davidson. Australian, b. 1914. Education. Lectr. in Education, Armidale Coll. of Advanced Education, since 1951. Teacher, N.S.W. secondary schs., 1940–49. *Publs:* Education in the Inquiring Society, 1966; Educative Teaching, 1969; (with G. Kelly) What is Right?, 1971; The Beginning Teacher, 1973; Philosophy and School Administration, 1977. Add: 3 Fitzgerald Ave., Armidale, N.S.W. 2350,

Australia.

MACKINLAY, Leila (Antoinette Sterling). Also writes as Brenda Grey. British, b. 1910. Historical/Romance/Gothic, Theatre. Adjudicator and Teacher of English Literature, I.L.E.A., since 1946; Ed., Romantic Novelists News; music productions critic, Amateur Stage mag., since 1945. Adjudicator, Waterford Intnl. Festival of Light Opera, Ireland, 1959–61. *Publs:* Little Mountebank, 1930; Fame's Fetters, 1931; Madame Juno, 1930; An Exotic Young Lady, 1932; Willed to Wed, 1933; (as Brenda Grey) Modern Micawbers, 1933; The Pro's Daughter, 1934; Shadow Lawn, 1934; Love Goes South, 1935; Into the Net, 1935; Night Bell, 1936; Young Man's Slave, 1936; Doubting Heart, 1937; Apron-Strings, 1937; Caretaker Within, 1938; Theme Song, 1938; Only Her Husband, 1939; The Reluctant Bride, 1939; Man Always Pays, 1940; Woman at the Wheel, 1940; Ridin' High, 1941; None Better Loved, 1941; Time on Her Hands, 1942; The Brave Live On, 1942; Green Limelight, 1943; Lady of the Torch, 1944; Two Walk Together, 1945; Piper's Pool, 1946; Piccadilly Inn, 1946; Blue Shutters, 1947; Echo of Applause, 1948; Peacock Hill, 1948; Restless Dream, 1949; Pilot's Point, 1949; Six Wax Candles, 1950; Spider Dance, 1950; Guilt's Pavilions, 1951; Five Houses, 1952; Unwise Wanderer, 1952; Cuckoo Cottage, 1953; She Married Another, 1953; Midnight Is Mine, 1954; Fiddler's Green, 1954; Vagabond Daughter, 1955; Riddle of a Lady, 1955; Musical Productions (non-fiction), 1955; Man of the Moment, 1956; She Moved to Music, 1956; Divided Duty, 1957; Mantle of Innocence, 1957; Love on a Shoestring, 1958; The Secret of Her Life, 1958; Seven Red Roses, 1959; Uneasy Conquest, 1959; Food of Love, 1960; Spotlight on Susan, 1960; Beauty's Tears, 1961; Spring Rainbow, 1961; Vain Delights, 1962; Broken Armour, 1963; False Relations, 1963; Fool of Virtue, 1964; Practice for Sale, 1964; (as Brenda Grey) Stardust in Her Eyes, 1964; (as Brenda Grey) Girl of His Choice, 1965; Ring of Hope, 1965; No Room for Loneliness, 1965; An Outside Chance, 1966; (as Brenda Grey) How High the Moon, 1966; (as Brenda Grey) Throw Your Bouquet, 1967; (as Brenda Grey) A Very Special Person, 1967; The Third Boat, 1967; Mists of the Moor, 1967; Frost at Dawn, 1968; Homesick for a Dream, 1968; Wanted—Girl Friday, 1968; (as Brenda Grey) Shadow of a Smile, 1968; (as Brenda Grey) Tread Softly on Dreams, 1970; (as Brenda Grey) Son of Summer, 1970; Farewell to Sadness, 1970; The Silken Purse, 1970; Bridal Wreath, 1971; (as Brenda Grey) Mixed Singles, 1971; Husband in Name, 1972; Strange Involvement, 1972; Birds of Silence, 1974; Fortune's Slave, 1975; Twilight Moment, 1976; The Uphill Path, 1979. Add: 4N Portman Mansions, Chiltern St., London W1M 1LF, England.

MACKSEY, K(enneth) J(ohn). British, b. 1923. Historical/Romance/Gothic, History, Military, Biography. Officer, Royal Tank Regiment, British Army, 1941 until retirement with rank of Maj. in 1968; Deputy Ed., History of the Second World War, and History of the First World War, Purnell, London, 1968–70. *Publs:* The Shadow of Vimy Ridge, 1965; To the Green Fields Beyond, 1965; Armoured Crusader: General Sir Percy Hobart, 1967; Afrika Korps, 1968; Panzer Division, 1968; Crucible of Power: The Fight for Tunisia, 1969; Tank Force, 1970; Tank: A History of AFVs, 1970; Tank Warfare, 1971; Beda Fomm, 1971; The Guinness History of Land Sea, Air Warfare, 3 vols., 1973–76; Battle (in U.S. as Anatomy of a Battle) (novel), 1974; The Partisans of Europe in the Second World War, 1975; The Guinness Guide to Feminine Achievements, 1975; Guderian, Panzer General, 1975; The Guinness Book of 1952 1953, 1954, 3 vols., 1977–79; Kesselring, 1978; Rommel's Campaigns and Battles, 1979; The Tanks, vol. III of the History of the Royal Tank Regiment, 1979; Invasion: The German Invasion of England, July, 1940, 1980; The Tank Pioneers, 1981; History of the Royal Armoured Corps, 1914–1975, 1983; Commando Strike, 1985; First Clash, 1985; Technology in War, 1986; Godwin's Saga, 1987; Military Errors of World War 2, 1987; Tank Versus Tank 1988. Add: Whatley Mill, Beaminster, Dorset, England.

MACK SMITH, Denis. British, b. 1920. History. Extraordinary Fellow, Wolfson Coll., Oxford, since 1987. Asst. Master, Clifton Coll., Bristol, 1941–42; Fellow, 1947–62, and Tutor, 1948–58, Peterhouse, and Lectr., 1952–62, Cambridge Univ.; Sr. Research Fellow, All Souls Coll., Oxford, 1962–87. *Publs:* Cavour and Garibaldi 1860, 1954; Garibaldi, 1957; Italy: A Modern History, 1959, rev. ed., 1969; Medieval Sicily, 1968; Modern Sicily, 1968; Da Cavour a Mussolini, 1968; (ed.) The Making of Italy 1796–1870, 1968; (ed.) Garibaldi, 1969; (ed.) Le Rivoluzioni d'Italia, by E. Quinet, 1970; Victor Emanuel, Cavour, and the Risorgimento, 1971; (ed.) Scritti Politici, by G. La Farina, 1972; Mussolini's Roman Empire, 1976; Un Monumento al Duce, 1976; Cento Anni di Vita Italiana Attraverso il Corriere della Sera, 1978; L'Italia del Ventesimo Secolo, 1978; (ed.) I Mille: Da Genova a Capua, 1981; Mussolini, 1981; (ed.) Un Viaggio Elettorale, by F. de Sanctis, 1983; (co-ed.)

Nelson History of England; (co-author) A History of Sicily, 1986; Cavour, 1987. Add: White Lodge, Osler Rd., Oxford, OX3 9BJ, England.

MACKWORTH, Cecily. (Marquise de Chabannes la Palice). French/British. Novels/Short stories, Poetry, Literature, Translations. Middle East Corresp., Paris Presse, 1947–48; Features Writer, L'-Information, 1954; Paris Corresp., Twentieth Century, 1957–61. *Publs:* Eleven Poems, 1938; I Came Out of France, 1941; (ed. and trans.) A Mirror for French Poetry, 1946; François Villon, 1947; The Mouth of the Sword, 1949; The Destiny of Isabelle Eberhardt, 1951; Spring's Green Shadow, 1952; (trans.) The Regent, by Renée Massip, 1957; Guillaume Apollinaire and the Cubist Life, 1961; English Interludes, 1974; Correspondence de Mallarmé et Marras, 1980; Ends of the World, 1987; (co-ed.) Documents Stéphane Mallarmé, 1988. Add: 6 rue de Coutures-Saint-Gervais, 75003 Paris, France.

MacLACHLAN, Patricia. American. Children's fiction. *Publs:* Through Grandpa's Eyes, 1980; Arthur, For the Very First Time, 1980; Moon, Stars, Frogs, and Friends, 1980; Mama One, Mama Two, 1982; Cassie Binegar, 1982; Tomorrow's Wizard, 1982; Seven Kisses in a Row, 1983; Unclaimed Treasures, 1984; Sarah, Plain and Tall, 1985; The Facts and Fictions of Minna Pratt, 1988. Add: c/o Harper and Row, 10 E. 53rd St., New York, N.Y. 10022, U.S.A.

MACLAGAN, Michael. British, b. 1914. Archaeology, Genealogy/-Heraldry, History, Biography. Fellow of Trinity Coll., Oxford, 1939–81; Richmond Herald of Arms, Coll. of Arms, London, 1980–89. Lord Mayor of Oxford, 1970–71. *Publs:* (ed. and trans.) Bede: Ecclesiastical History Books I and II, 1949; Trinity College, 1955; (co-author) The Colour of Heraldry, 1958; (ed.) Richard de Bury: Philobiblon, 1960; Clemency Canning, 1962; City of Constantinople, 1968; (with J. Louda) Lines of Succession, 1981. Add: 20 Northmoor Rd., Oxford OX2 6UR, England.

MacLAINE, Allan H(ugh). American, b. 1924. Literature. Prof. of English, Univ. of Rhode Island, Kingston, since 1962 (Dean of Div. of Univ. Extension, 1967–71). Instr., Brown Univ., Providence, R.I., 1947–50; Instr., Univ. of Massachusetts, Amherst, 1951–54; Asst. Prof., 1954–56, and Assoc. Prof., 1956–62, Texas Christian Univ., Fort Worth. Pres., Coll. English Assn., 1965–66. *Publs:* The Student's Comprehensive Guide to the Canterbury Tales, 1964; Robert Fergusson, 1965; Allan Ramsay, 1985. Add: Dept. of English, Univ. of Rhode Island, Kingston, R.I. 02881, U.S.A.

MacLAINE, Shirley. American, b. 1934. Autobiography/Memoirs, Biography Motion-picture actress. Films include: The Trouble with Harry, 1955; The Matchmaker, 1958; The Apartment, 1960; The Children's Hour, 1962; Irma Ia Douce, 1963; Sweet Charity, 1968; Two Mules for Sister Sara, 1970; The Turning Point, 1977; Terms of Endearment, 1983 (Academy Award: Best Actress); etc. *Publs:* Don't Fall Off the Mountain, 1970; (ed.) McGovern: The Man and his Beliefs, 1972; You Can Get There from Here, 1975; Out on a Limb, 1983; Dancing in the Light, 1985; It's All in the Playing, 1987; Going Within: A Guide for Inner Transformation, 1989. Add: c/o International Creative Management, 8899 Beverly Blvd., Los Angeles, Calif. 90048, U.S.A.

MacLAREN, A. Allan. British, b. 1938. Social Commentary, Sociology, Theology/Religion. Head of Sociology, Univ. of Strathclyde, Glasgow. Lectr., Dept. of Political Economy, Univ. of Aberdeen, 1965–68. *Publs:* Religion and Social Class: The Disruption Years in Aberdeen, 1974; (ed.) Social Class in Scotland, Past and Present, 1976. Add: Sociology Unit, Univ. of Strathclyde, Glasgow 1, Scotland.

MACLEAN, Alasdair. British, b. 1926. Poetry. *Publs:* From the Wilderness, 1973; Waking the Dead, 1976; Night Falls on Ardnamurchan, 1984. Add: c/o Gollancz, 14 Henrietta St., London WC2E 8QJ, England.

MacLEAN, Art. *See* **SHIRREFFS,** Gordon Donald.

MACLEAN, Arthur. *See* **TUBB,** E.C.

MACLEAN, (Sir) Fitzroy. British, b. 1911. History, Travel/Exploration/Adventure, Autobiography/Memoirs/Personal, Biography. Former Conservative M.P.: Under Secty. of State for War, 1954–57. *Publs:* Eastern Approaches, 1949; Disputed Barricade, 1957; A Person from England, 1958; Back to Bokhara, 1959; Jugoslavia, 1969; A Concise History of Scotland, 1970; To the Back of Beyond, 1974; To Caucasus, 1976; Take Nine Spies, 1978; Holy Russia, 1979; Tito, 1980; The Isles of the Sea, 1985; Bonnie Prince Charlie, 1988; Portrait of the Soviet Union,

1988. Add: Strachur, Argyllshire, Scotland.

MacLEAN, Katherine. American, b. 1925. Science fiction/Fantasy, Plays/Screenplays. Research lab. asst., 1943–45; electrocardiograph technician, 1951–56; Lectr., Univ. of Connecticut and Univ. of Maine, 1961–74. *Publs:* (with C. de Vet) Cosmic Checkmate, 1962; The Diploids, 1966, 1974; The Man in the Birdcage, 1971; Missing Man, 1974; Garbage In Garbage Out (radio play), 1974; The Kid in the Computer (radio play), 1974; (with Carl West) Dark Wing, 1979; The Trouble with You Earth People (short stories), 1980. Add: P.O. Box 1563, Biddeford, Me. 04005, U.S.A.

MacLENNAN (John) Hugh. Canadian, b. 1907. Novels/Short stories, Geography, History. Prof. of English, McGill Univ., Montreal, 1965–79, now Emeritus (Assoc. Prof., 1951–63). Classics Master, Lower Canada Coll., Montreal, since 1935. *Publs:* Oxyrhynchus: An Economic and Social Study, 1935; Barometer Rising, 1941; Two Solitudes, 1945; The Precipice, 1948; Cross Country, 1948; Each Man's Son, 1951; Thirty and Three (essays), 1954; The Watch That Ends the Night, 1959; (ed.) McGill: The Story of a University, 1960; Scotchman's Return and Other Essays (in U.K. as Scotsman's Return and Other Essays), 1960; Seven Rivers of Canada (in U.S. as The Rivers of Canada), 1961; The Colour of Canada, 1967; Return of the Sphinx, 1967; The Other Side of Hugh MacLennan, 1979; Voices in Time, 1980; On Being a Maritime Writer, 1984. Add: 1535 Summerhill Ave., Montreal 25, Que., Canada.

MACLEOD, Alison. British, b. 1920. Novels, Plays. *Publs:* Dear Augustine (play), 1958; The Heretics (in U.S. as The Heretic), 1965; The Hireling (in U.K. as The Trusted Servant), 1968; City of Light (in U.K. as No Need of the Sun), 1969; The Muscovite, 1971; The Jesuit (in U.S. as Prisoner of the Queen), 1972; The Portingale, 1976. Add: 63 Muswell Hill Pl., London N10 3RP, England.

MacLEOD, Alistair. Canadian, b. 1936. Novels/Short stories, Poetry. English Prof., Univ. of Windsor, Ont., since 1969. *Publs:* The Lost Salt Gift of Blood, 1976; As Birds Bring Forth the Sun and Other Stories, 1986. Add: 231 Curry Ave., Windsor, Ont., Canada.

MacLEOD, Charlotte (Matilda). Also writes as Alisa Craig and Matilda Hughes. American (b. Canadian), b. 1922. Mystery/Crime/Suspense, Children's fiction, Supernatural/Occult topics. Pres., American Crime Writers League, 1989–91. *Publs:* Mystery of the White Knight, 1964; (as Matilda Hughes) The Food of Love, 1965; Next Door to Danger, 1965; (as Matilda Hughes) Headlines for Caroline, 1967; The Fat Lady's Ghost, 1968; Mouse's Vineyard (juvenile), 1968; Ask Me No Questions, 1971; Brass Pounder (juvenile), 1971; Astrology for Sceptics (non-fiction), 1972; King Devil, 1978; Rest You Merry, 1978; The Family Vault, 1979; The Luck Runs Out, 1979; We Dare Not Go a-Hunting, 1980; The Withdrawing Room, 1980; (as Alisa Craig) A Pint of Murder, 1980; The Palace Guard, 1981; (as Alisa Craig) The Grub-and-Stakers Move a Mountain, 1981; (as Alisa Craig) Murder Goes Mumming, 1981; Wrack and Rune, 1982; Cirak's Daughter (juvenile), 1982; The Bilbao Looking Glass, 1983; The Terrible Tide (as Alisa Craig), 1983; Something the Cat Dragged In, 1983; Maid of Honor (juvenile), 1984; The Convivial Codfish, 1984; The Curse of the Giant Hogweed, 1985; (as Alisa Craig) The Grub and Stakers Quilt a Bee, 1985; The Plain Old Man, 1985; Grab Bag, 1987; The Corpse in Oozak's Pond, 1987; The Recycled Citizen, 1988; The Silver Ghost, 1988; (as Alisa Craig) The Grub and Stakers Pinch a Poke, 1988; Vane Pursuit, 1989; (as Alisa Craig) Trouble in the Brasses, 1989. Add: c/o Jed Mattes Inc., 175 West 73rd St., No. 8H, New York, N.Y. 10023, U.S.A.

MacLEOD, Ellen Jane. Also writes as Ella Anderson. British. Historical/Romance/Gothic, Children's fiction, Plays/Screenplays. *Publs:* The Seven Wise Owls, 1956; Alaska Star, 1957; Adventures of Lazy N, 1957; The Ski Lodge Mystery, 1957; (as Ella Anderson) The Crooked Signpost, 1957; (as Ella Anderson) The Hawaiian Lei, 1958; (as Ella Anderson) Jo-Jo, 1959; Mystery Gorge, 1959; Mystery of Tolling Bell, 1960; (as Ella Anderson) The Vanishing Light, 1961; The Fourth Window, 1961; (as Ella Anderson) The Talking Mountain, 1962; Orchids for a Rose, 1963; One Stormy Night, 1964; Island in the Mist, 1965; Something Fishy, 1966; The Years Between, 1966; Hearts in Conflict, 1967; Stranger in Glen, 1969; The Broken Melody, 1970; Trouble at the Circle 'G', 1971; The Kelpie Ledge, 1972; Isle of Shadows, 1974; From Aunt Jane, with Love, 1974; Wing Home, My Heart, 1975; Those Joyful Days, 1976; Another Time, Another Place, 1977; Till the Day We Meet, 1980; Will Ye No' Come Back Again, 1984. Add: 12 Montgomery Pl., Buchlyvie, Stirlingshire FK8 3NF, Scotland.

MacLEOD, Jean S. Also writes as Catherine Airlie. British, b. 1908. Historical/Romance/Gothic. Secty., British Ministry of Labour, Newcastle upon Tyne, 1930–35. *Publs:* Life for Two, 1936; Human Symphony, 1937; Summer Rain, 1938; Sequel to Youth, 1938; Mist Across the Miles, 1938; Dangerous Obsession, 1938; Run Away from Love, 1939; Return to Spring, 1939; The Rainbow Isle, 1939; The Whim of Fate, 1940; Silent Bondage, 1940; The Lonely Farrow, 1940; Heatherbloom, 1940; The Reckless Pilgrim, 1941; The Shadow of a Vow, 1941; One Way Out, 1941; Forbidden Rapture, 1941; Penalty for Living, 1942; Blind Journey, 1942; Bleak Heritage, 1942; Reluctant Folly, 1942; Unseen To-morrow, 1943; The Rowan Tree, 1943; Flower o' the Broom, 1943; The Circle of Doubt, 1943; Lamont of Ardgoyne, 1944; Two Paths, 1944; Brief Fulfillment, 1945; The Bridge of Years, 1945; This Much to Give, 1945; One Love, 1945; The Tranquil Haven, 1946; Sown in the Wind, 1946; The House of Oliver, 1947; And We in Dreams, 1947; The Chalet in the Sun, 1948; Ravenscrag, 1948; (as Catherine Airlie) The Wild Macraes, 1948; (as Catherine Airlie) From Such a Seed, 1949; Above the Lattice, 1949; To-morrow's Bargain, 1949; Katherine, 1950; The Valley of Palms, 1950; (as Catherine Airlie) The Restless Years, 1950; Roadway to the Past, 1951; Once to Every Heart, 1951; (as Catherine Airlie) Fabric of Dreams, 1951; Cameron of Gare, 1952; Music at Midnight, 1952; (as Catherine Airlie) Strange Recompense, 1952; The Silent Valley, 1953; The Stranger in Their Midst, 1953; (as Catherine Airlie) The Green Rushes, 1953; (as Catherine Airlie) Hidden in the Wind, 1953; Dear Doctor Everett, 1954; The Man in Authority, 1954; (as Catherine Airlie) A Wind Sighing, 1954; (as Catherine Airlie) Nobody's Child, 1954; After Long Journeying, 1955; Master of Glenkeith, 1955; (as Catherine Airlie) The Valley of Desire, 1955; (as Catherine Airlie) The Ways of Love, 1955; The Way in the Dark, 1956; My Heart's in the Highlands, 1956; (as Catherine Airlie) The Mountain of Stars, 1956; (as Catherine Airlie) The Unguarded Hour, 1956; Journey in the Sun, 1957; (as Catherine Airlie) Land of Heart's Desire, 1957; The Prisoner of Love, 1958; (as Catherine Airlie) Red Lotus, 1958; The Gated Road, 1959; Air Ambulance, 1959; (as Catherine Airlie) The Last of the Kintyres, 1959; The Little Doctor, 1960; Nurse Lang, 1960; The White Cockade, 1960; (as Catherine Airlie) Shadow on the Sun, 1960: The Silver Dragon, 1961; (as Catherine Airlie) One Summer's Day, 1961; (as Catherine Airlie) The Country of the Heart, 1961; Slave of the Wind, 1962; The Dark Fortune, 1962; Mountain Clinic, 1962; (as Catherine Airlie) The Unlived Year, 1962; (as Catherine Airlie) Passing Strangers, 1963; Sugar Island, 1964; The Black Cameron, 1964; (as Catherine Airlie) The Wheels of Chance, 1964; Crane Castle, 1965; The Wolf of Heimra, 1965; Doctor's Daughter, 1965; The Tender Glory, 1965; (as Catherine Airlie) The Sea Change, 1965; The Drummer of Corrae, 1966; (as Catherine Airlie) Doctor Overboard, 1966; Lament for a Lover, 1967; The Master of Keills, 1967; The Bride of Mingalay, 1967; (as Catherine Airlie) Nurse Jane in Teneriffe, 1967; The Moonflower, 1967; Summer Island, 1968; The Joshua Tree, 1970; The Fortress, 1970; The Way Through the Valley, 1971; The Scent of Juniper, 1971; Light in the Tower, 1971; Moment of Decision, 1972; Adam's Wife, 1972; The Rainbow Days, 1973; Over the Castle Wall, 1974; Time Suspended, 1974; The Phantom Pipes, 1975; Journey into Spring, 1976; Island Stranger, 1977; Viking Song, 1977; The Ruaig Inheritance, 1978; Search for Yesterday, 1978; Meeting in Madrid, 1979; Brief Enchantment, 1979; Black Sand, White Sand, 1981; Moreton's Kingdom, 1981; Cruel Deception, 1982; Zamora, 1982; A Distant Paradise, 1983; Beyond the Reef, 1983; Valley of the Snows, 1985; The Olive Grove, 1985; The Apollo Man, 1986; After the Hurricane, 1986; The Valley of the Snows, 1987; Call Back the Past, 1988; Legacy of Doubt, 1989; Shadow on the Hills, 1989. Add: "Rose Garth" Thornton-Le-Beans, North Yorkshire, England.

MacLEOD, Robert. *See* **KNOX,** William.

MacLEOD, Robert. American, b. 1906. Westerns/Adventure. Formerly wrote Red Ryder comic strip. *Publs:* The Appaloosa, 1966; The Californio, 1966; The Muleskinner, 1967; Apache Tears, 1974; Feather in the Wind, 1976; Ambush at Junction Rock, 1979; The Running Gun, 1979; Six Guns South, 1979. Add: c/o Fawcett, 666 Fifth Ave., New York, N.Y. 10103, U.S.A.

MacLEOD, Sheila. British, b. 1939. Novels, Science fiction, Literature. *Publs:* The Moving Accident (novel), 1968; The Snow-White Soliloquies (science-fiction), 1970; Letters from the Portuguese (novel), 1971; Xanthe and the Robots (science fiction), 1977; Circuit-Breaker (science fiction), 1978; The Art of Starvation, 1981; Axioms (novel), 1984; D.H. Lawrence's Men and Women, 1985. Add: 39 Parkholme Rd., London E8 3AG, England.

MAC LOW, Jackson. American, b. 1922. Plays/Screenplays, Poetry. Composer of musical and performance works, performer, musician, and, since music teacher, English teacher, trans. and ed., 1950–66; Poetry Ed., Why? (later Resistance) mag., 1950–54, Reference Book Ed., Funk and Wagnalls, publrs., 1957–58, 1961–62, and Unicorn Books, 1958–59, Copy Ed., Alfred A. Knopf Inc., NYC, 1965–66; Instr., American Language Inst., New York Univ., 1966–73; Poetry Ed., WIN mag., NYC, 1966–76; NEA-sponsored Writer-In-Residence, State Univ. of New York at Albany, 1984; Visiting Prof. of Creative Writing, State Univ. of New York at Binghamton, 1989. *Publs:* poetry and plays—The Twin Plays, 1963, 1966; The Pronouns—A Collection of 40 Dances—For the Dancers, 1964, 3rd ed. with new essays 1979; Verdurous Sanguinaria (play), 1967; August Light Poems, 1967; 22 Light Poems, 1968; 23rd Light Poem: For Larry Eigner, 1969; Stanzas for Iris Lezak, 1972; 4 trains, 1974; 36th Light Poem: In Memoriam Buster Keaton, 1975; 21 Matched Asymmetries, 1978; 54th Light Poem: For Ian Tyson, 1978; A Dozen Douzains for Eve Rosenthal, 1978; phone, 1979; Asymmetries 1-260, 1980; "Is That Wool Hat My Hat?", 1982; A Vocabulary for Annie Brigitte Gilles Tardos (portfolio), 1982; From Pearl Harbor Day to FDR's Birthday, 1982; Bloomsday, 1984; French Sonnets, 1984, 1989; The Virginia Woolf Poems, 1985; Representative Works 1938–1985, 1986; Pieces o'Six, 1989; Words Nd Ends from Ez, 1989; verbal performance scores and broadsides—A Vocabulary for Carl Fernbach-Flarsheim, 1968; A Vocabulary for Sharon Belle Mattlin , 1974; A Vocabulary for Vera Regina Lachmann, 1974; Guru-Guru Gatha, 1975; 1st Milarepa Gatha, 1976; 1st Sharon Belle Mattlin Vocabulary Crossword Gatha, 1976; The WBAI Vocabulary Gatha, 1977, 1979; Musicwords (for Phil Niblock), 1978; A Notated Vocabulary for Eve Rosenthal, 1978; A Vocabulary Gatha for Pete Rose, 1978; Homage to Leona Bleiweiss, 1978; Antic Quatrains, 1980; Vocabulary Gatha for Anne Tardos, 1980; Dream Meditation, 1980; expanded 1982; A Vocabulary Gatha for Malcolm Goldstein, 1981; 1st Happy Birthday, Anne, Vocabulary Gatha, 1982; 2nd Happy Birthday, Anne, Vocabulary Gatha, 1982; Nucleus Meditation, 1982; Pauline Meditation, 1982; Two Heterophonies, 1984; Phonemicon from "Hereford Bosons 1," 1984. Add: 42 N. Moore St., New York, N.Y. 10013, U.S.A.

MacMAHON, Bryan Michael. Irish, b. 1909. Novels/Short stories, Children's fiction, Plays/Screenplays, History, Translations. Formerly, Principal Teacher, Scoil Réalta na Maidine 2 (Morning Star No. 2 Sch.), Listowel, Co Kerry (joined faculty, 1942). Pres., Irish P.E.N., 1972–73.; Member of the Irish Academy of Letters. *Publs:* The Lion Tamer and Other Stories, 1948; The Bugle in the Blood (play), 1949; Jackomoora and the King of Ireland's Son, 1950; Children of the Rainbow, 1952; The Red Petticoat and Other Stories, 1955; Song of the Anvil (play), 1960; The Honey Spike (play), 1961, novel, 1967; Brendan of Ireland, 1967; Patsy-O and His Wonderful Pets, 1970; Here's Ireland, 1971; The Gap of Life (play), 1972; (trans.) Peig, 1974; The End of the World, 1976; The Sound of Hooves and Other Stories, 1985. Add: 38 Church St., Listowel, Co. Kerry, Ireland.

MACMASTER, Robert Ellsworth. American, b. 1919. Biography. Prof. of History and Literature, Massachusetts Inst. of Technology, Cambridge, since 1967 (Instr., 1952–53; Asst. Prof., 1953–60; Assoc. Prof., 1960–67). *Publs:* Danilevsky: A Russian Totalitarian Philosopher, 1967. Add: 461 Main St., Hingham, Mass. 02043, U.S.A.

MACMILLAN, John Angus David. British, b. 1934.Sociology.Principal Lectr. in Criminology, Teesside Polytechnic, Middlesbrough, since 1974. Asst. Warden in hostels for offenders, Leeds and London, 1959–64; Research Asst., Univ. of Reading, 1965–69; Lectr. in Criminology, Univ. of Glasgow, 1969–70; Research Officer, Home Office Research Unit, London, 1971–74. *Publs:* Deviant Drivers, 1975. Add: Dept. of Administrative and Social Studies, Teesside Polytechnic, Middlesbrough, Cleveland, England.

MACNAB, P(eter) A(ngus). British, b. 1903. History, Folklore. Branch Mgr., Clydesdale Bank Ltd., Glasgow, 1955–63; now retired. *Publs:* The Isle of Mull, 1970; Tall Tales from an Island, 1984; Mull and Iona, 1987; Highways and Byways in Mull and Iona, 1988. Add: Fairway, Seamill, West Kilbride KA23 9HP, Scotland.

MACNAB, Roy (Martin). South African, b. 1923. Poetry, History, Biography. Cultural Attaché, South African High Commn., London, 1955–59; Counsellor for Cultural and Press Affairs, South African Embassy, Paris, 1959–67; Dir., South Africa Foundn., London, 1968–84. *Publs:* Testament of a South African, 1947; (ed. with M. Starkie) Oxford Poetry 1947, 1947; (ed. with C. Gulston) South African Poetry: A New Anthology, 1948); Towards the Sun: A Miscellany, 1950; South and Central Africa, 1954; (ed.) Poets in South Africa: An Anthology, 1958; The Man of Grass and Other Poems, 1960; Journey into Yesterday: South African Milestones in Europe, 1962; The French Colonel (biography),

1975; The English-Speaking South Africans, 1975; Winged Quagga, 1981; The Story of South Africa House, 1983; Gold Their Touchstone, 1987; For Honour Alone, 1988. Add: c/o Travellers Club, London SW1, England.

MacNEIL, Duncan. *See* **McCUTCHAN,** Philip.

MACNEIL, Ian Roderick. American, b. 1929. Law, Sociology. Wigmore Prof. of Law, Northwestern Univ., Chicago, since 1980. Asst. Prof., 1959–62, Assoc. Prof., 1962–63, Prof., 1963–72, and 1974–76, and Ingersoll Prof. of Law, 1976–80, Cornell Univ., Ithaca, N.Y. Visiting Prof. of Law, Univ. of East Africa, Dar es Salaam, 1965–67; Visiting Prof. of Law, Duke Univ., Durham, N.C., 1971–72; Prof. of Law, and member, Center for Advanced Studies, Univ. of Virginia, Charlottesville, 1972–74; Visiting Fellow, Univ. of Edinburgh, 1978–79, 1987, and Oxford Univ., 1979; Braucher visiting Prof. of Law, Harvard Univ., Cambridge, Mass., 1988–89. *Publs:* Bankruptcy Law in East Africa, 1966; Contracts: Instruments of Social Cooperation: East Africa, 1968; (with R.B. Schlesinger) Formation of Contracts: A Study of the Common Core of Legal Systems, 1968; (with R.S. Morison) Students and Decision Making, 1970; Cases and Materials on Contracts: Exchange Transactions and Relations, 1971, 1978; The New Social Contract, 1980. Add: Northwestern Univ. Sch. of Law, 357 E. Chicago Ave., Chicago, Ill. 60611, U.S.A.

MACPHERSON, (Jean) Jay. Canadian, b. 1931. Poetry, Literature, Mythology/Folklore. Prof. of English, Victoria Coll., Univ. of Toronto, Ont., since 1974 (joined faculty 1957). *Publs:* The Boatman, 1957; Four Ages of Man, 1962; Welcoming Disaster: Poems 1970–1974, 1974; Poems Twice Told., 1981; The Spirit of Solitude: Conventions and Continuities in Late Romance, 1982. Add: Victoria Coll., Toronto, Ont. M5S 1K7, Canada.

MacPHERSON, Margaret. Scottish, b. 1908. Children's fiction. Hon. Secty., Skye Labour Party, since 1960; Member, Consultative Council, Highlands and Islands Development Bd., since 1970. Member, Commn. of Inquiry into Crofting, Inverness, 1951–54. *Publs:* The Shinty Boys, 1963; The Rough Road, 1965; Ponies for Hire, 1967; The New Tenants, 1968; The Battle of the Braes, 1972; The Boy on the Roof, 1974. Add: Ardrannach, Torvaig, Portree, Isle of Skye, Scotland.

MACQUARRIE, John. British, b. 1919. Theology/Religion. Lady Margaret Prof. of Divinity, Oxford Univ., since 1970, now retired.Former Canon of Christ Church, Oxford. Lectr. in Systematic Theology, Univ. of Glasgow, 1953–62; Prof., Union Theological Seminary, NYC, 1962–70. *Publs:* An Existentialist Theology, 1955; The Scope of Demythologizing, 1960; Twentieth Century Religious Thought, 1963; Studies in Christian Existentialism, 1965; Principles of Christian Theology, 1966; God-Talk, 1967; God and Secularity, 1967; (ed.) A Dictionary of Christian Ethics, 1967; (ed.) Contemporary Religious Thinkers, 1968; Martin Heidegger, 1968; Three Issues in Ethics, 1970; Paths in Spirituality, 1972; Existentialism, 1972; The Faith of the People of God, 1972; The Concept of Peace, 1973; Thinking about God, 1975; Christian Unity and Christian Diversity, 1975; The Humility of God, 1978; Christian Hope, 1978; In Search of Humanity, 1982; In Search of Deity, 1984; Theology, Church, and Ministry, 1986. Add: 206 Headley Way, Oxford OX3 7TA, England.

MacQUEEN, John. British, b. 1929. Literature. Endowment Fellow, Univ. of Edinburgh, since 1988 (Lectr. in Medieval English and Scottish Literature, 1959–63; Masson Prof. of Medieval and Renaissance Literature, 1963–72; Dir. of the Sch. of Scottish Studies, 1969–88; Prof. of Scottish Literature and Oral Tradition, 1972–88). *Publs:* St. Nynia, 1961; (with T. Scott) The Oxford Book of Scottish Verse, 1966; Robert Henryson, 1967; Ballattis of Luve, 1970; Allegory, 1970; (ed. with Winifred MacQueen) A Choice of Scottish Verse 1470–1570, 1972; Progress and Poetry, 1982; Numerology, 1985; The Rise of the Historical Novel, 1989. Add: 12 Orchard Toll, Edinburgh EH4 3JF, Scotland.

MacSHANE, Frank (Sutherland). American, b. 1927. Literature, Biography. Prof., Writing Div., Sch. of the Arts, Columbia Univ., NYC, since 1967 (Dean, Sch. of the Arts, 1971–72). Dir., Columbia Trans. Center, NYC; Council Member, Authors Guild. Asst. Prof. of English, Univ. of California, Berkeley, 1959–64; Assoc. Prof., Williams Coll., Williamstown, Mass., 1964–67. *Publs:* (trans.) The Visits of the Queen of Sheba, by Miguel Serrano, 1960; (trans.) The Mysteries, by Miguel Serrano, 1960; Many Golden Ages, 1962; (ed.) Impressions of Latin America, 1963; (trans.) The Serpent of Paradise, by Miguel Serrano, 1963; (ed.) Critical Writings of Ford Madox Ford, 1964; (ed.) The American in Europe, 1965; The Life and Work of Ford Madox Ford, 1965; (trans.)

C.G. Jung and Hermann Hesse: A Record of Two Friendships, by Miguel Serrano, 1966; (trans.) The Ultimate Flower, by Miguel Serrano, 1969; (trans.) El/Ella, by Miguel Serrano, 1972; (ed.) Ford Madox Ford: The Critical Heritage, 1972; (ed. with D. Halpern and N.T. di Giovanni) Borges on Writing, 1973; The Life of Raymond Chandler, 1976; (ed.) The Notebooks of Raymond Chandler, 1976; The Life of John O'Hara, 1981; (ed.) Selected Letters of Raymond Chandler, 1981; (ed.) The Collected Stories of John O'Hara, 1985; Into Eternity: The Life of James Jones, American Writer, 1985. Add: c/o Aaron M. Priest Literary Agency, 122 E. 42nd St., Suite 3902, New York, N.Y. 10168, U.S.A.

MacSWEENEY, Barry. British, b. 1948. Poetry. Dir., Blacksuede Boot Press; Ed., Harvest, and the Blacksede Boot, Barnet, Herts. Former freelance journalist. *Publs:* Poems 1965–68: The Boy from the Green Cabaret Tells of His Mother, 1969; The Last Bud, 1969; (with P. Bland) Joint Effort, 1970; Flames on the Beach at Viareggio: Poems, 1970; Our Mutural Scarlet Boulevard, 1970; Elegy for January: An Essay Commemorating the Bi-Centenary of Chatterton's Death, 1970; The Official Biography of Jim Morrison, Rock Idol (poetry), 1971; Brother Wolf, 1972; 5 Odes, 1972; Dance Steps, 1972; Fog Eye, 1973; 6 Odes, 1973; Pelt Feather Log, 1975; Odes, 1979; Blackbird: Elegy for William Gordon Calvert, Being Book Two of Black Torch, 1980; Ranter, 1986. Add: c/o Pig Press, 7 Cross View Terrace, Melville's Cross, Durham DH1 4JY, England.

MacTHOMAIS, Ruaraidh. *See* **THOMSON,** Derick S.

MACVEAN, Jean. British. Novels/Short stories, Plays/Screenplays, Poetry. Reviewer for The Tablet, Agenda, Temenos. Staff member, British Foreign Office, 1941–51. *Publs:* Ideas of Love, 1954; The Intermediaries, 1965; The Image of Freedom (play), 1981; Flight of the Swan (radio play), 1982; Eros Reflected (poetry), 1988; The Adjacent Kingdom (poetry), 1988. Add: 21 Peel St., London W8 7PA, England.

MACVEY, John Wishart. British, b. 1923. Air/Space topics, Astronomy. Plant Mgr., 1961–62; Asst. Technical Information Officer, 1962–71; Co. Technical Information Officer, Nobel's Explosives Ltd., Div. of I.C.I., 1971–80 (Research Chemist, 1956–61). *Publs:* (with C.P. Snow, B. Lovell, and P. Moore) Speaking of Space, 1962; Alone in the Universe?, 1963; Journey to Alpha Centauri, 1965; How We Will Reach the Stars, 1969; Whispers from Space, 1973; Interstellar Travel, Past, Present and Future, 1977; Space Weapons/Space War, 1979; Where Will We Go When the Sun Dies?, 1980; Colonizing Other Worlds, 1984. Add: Mellendean, 15 Adair Ave., Saltcoats, Ayrshire KA21 5QS, Scotland.

MACVICAR, Angus. British, b. 1908. Novels/Short stories, Children's fiction, Plays/Screenplays, Autobiography/Memoirs/Personal. Ed., Campbeltown Courier, 1931–33. Hon. Sheriff Substitute, Argyll, 1965. *Publs:* The Purple Rock, 1933; Death by the Mistletoe, 1934; The Screaming Gull, 1935; The Temple Falls, 1935; The Ten Green Brothers, 1936; The Cavern, 1936; Flowering Death, 1937; The Crooked Finger, 1937; Crime's Masquerader, 1938; The Singing Spider, 1938; Eleven for Danger, 1939; Strangers from the Sea, 1939; The Crouching Spy, 1940; Death on the Machar, 1946; Greybreak, 1947; Fugitive's Road, 1947; The Crocodile Men, 1947; Escort to Adventure, 1948; The Black Wherry, 1949; Faraway Island, 1950; King Abbie's Adventure, 1951; Stubby Sees It Through, 1951; The Grey Pilot, 1952; Tiger Mountain, 1953; The Lost Planet, 1954; Return to the Lost Planet, 1955; Minister's Monday (play), 1956; Secret of the Lost Planet, 1956; Dinny Smith Comes Home, 1956; Final Proof (play), 1957; The Atom Chasers, 1957; The Atom Chasers in Tibet, 1958; Mercy Flight (play), 1958; Red Fire on the Lost Planet, 1959; Storm Tide (play), 1959; Peril on the Lost Planet, 1961; Under Suspicion (play), 1962; Space Agent and the Isles of Fire, 1962; The Hammers of Fingal, 1962; The Killings on Kersivay, 1963; Kilpatrick, Special Reporter, 1963; Stranger at Christmas (play), 1964; The Grey Shepherds, 1964; The High Cliffs of Kersivay, 1964; Space Agent and the Ancient Peril, 1964; Murder at the Open, 1965; Life-Boat, Green to White, 1966; Let's Visit Scotland, 1966; The Canisbay Conspiracy, 1966; The Kersivay Kraken, 1966; Rescue Call, 1967; Night on the Killer Reef, 1967; The Cave of the Hammers, 1968; Maniac, 1969; Duel in Glenfinnan, 1969; Super Nova and the Rogue Satellite, 1969; Super Nova and the Frozen Man, 1970; Salt in My Porridge, 1971; The Golden Venus Affair, 1972; The Painted Doll Affair, 1973; Heather in My Ears, 1974; Rocks in My Scotch, 1977; Silver in My Sporran, 1979; Bees in My Bonnet, 1982; Golf in My Gallowses, 1983; Gremlins in My Garden, 1985; Capers in My Kirk, 1987. Add: Achnamara, Southend, Campbeltown, Argyll, Scotland.

MADDEN, David. American, b. 1933. Novels/Short stories,

Plays/Screenplays, Poetry, Literature. Writer-in-Residence, Louisiana State Univ., Baton Rouge, since 1968. Asst. Ed., The Kenyon Review, 1964–66. Pres., Popular Culture Assn., 1975–77; Assoc. Ed., Fiction Intnl, 1973–83. *Publs:* The Beautiful Greed, 1961; Wright Morris, 1964; (ed.) Tough Guy Writers of the Thirties, 1968; (ed.) Proletarian Writers of the Thirties, 1968; The Poetic Image in Six Genres, 1969; Cassandra Singing (play), 1957; The Shadow Knows, 1970; (ed.) American Dreams, American Nightmares, 1970; James M. Cain, 1970; (ed.) Rediscoveries, 1971; Brothers in Confidence, 1972; (co-ed.) The Popular Culture Explosion, 2 vols., 1972; (ed.) Nathaniel West, 1973; Bijou, 1974; (ed.) Remembering James Agee, 1974; (ed.) Creative Choices, 1975; The Suicide's Wife, 1978; Pleasure-Dome, 1979; A Primer of the Novel, 1980; On the Big Wind, 1980; The New Orleans of Possibilities (short stories), 1982; Writers' Revisions, 1981; (co-ed.) Studies in the Short Story, 1985; Cain's Craft, 1985; Revising Fiction, 1988, (ed. with Peggy Bach) Rediscoveries II, 1988. Add: 614 Park Blvd., Baton Rouge, La. 70806, U.S.A.

MADDEN-WORK, Betty I. American, b. 1915. Architecture, Art, Crafts. Technical Asst., Art Dept., 1961–63, and Curator of Art, 1963–78, Illinois State Museum, Springfield. *Publs:* Art, Crafts, and Architecture in Early Illinois, 1974. Add: 25 Redwood Lane, Springfield, Ill. 62704, U.S.A.

MADDISON, Angela Mary. *See* **BANNER,** Angela.

MADDISON, Angus. British, b. 1926. Economics. Prof. of Economics, Univ. of Groningen, Netherlands, since 1978. Lectr. in Economics, St. Andrews Univ., Scotland, 1951–52; Dir., Research Project on Developing Countries, Twentieth Century Fund, 1966–69; Harvard Univ., 1969–71; Head, Economics Div., 1958–62, Dir., Development Dept., 1963, and Head, Central Analysis Div., 1974–78, OECD, Paris. *Publs:* (co-author) Problems of Long-Term Economic Projections, 1963; Economic Growth in the West, 1964; Foreign Skills and Technical Assistance in Economic Development, 1965; (with A.D. Stavrianopoulos and B. Higgins) Foreign Skills and Technical Assistance in Greek Development, 1966; (co-author) Technical Assistance and the Needs of Developing Countries, 1968; Economic Growth in Japan and the U.S.S.R., 1969; Economic Progress and Policy in Developing Countries, 1970; Class Structure and Economic Growth: India and Pakistan since the Moghuls, 1972; Economic Performance and Policy in Europe 1913–70, 1974; Phases of Capitalist Development, 1982; Two Crises: Latin America and Asia 1929–38 and 1973–83, 1985. Add: Chevincourt, 60150 France.

MADDISON, Carol (Evelyn Beryl). Also writes as Carol Kidwell. Canadian, b. 1923. Literature. Dean, American Coll. in Paris, 1966–67, now Emeritus (Chmn., Humanities Div., and Prof. of English, 1963–66). Asst. Prof. of Classics, Univ. of New Brunswick, Canada, 1946–49. *Publs:* Apollo and the Nine: A History of the Ode, 1960; Marc Antonio Flaminio—Poet, Humanist and Philosopher, 1964; (as Carol Kidwell) Michael Marullus 1453–1500: Soldier Poet of the Renaissance. Add: Sanderstead House, Rectory Park, Sanderstead, Surrey CR2 9JR, England.

MADDOCK, R(eginald) B(ertram). British, b. 1912. Children's fiction. Headmaster, Evelyn Street Sch., Warrington, 1949–57, and Richard Fairclough Secondary Sch., Warrington, 1957–73. *Publs:* Corrigan and the White Cobra Tomb of Opi, Yellow Peril, Black Riders, Golden Pagoda, Dream-Makers, Blue Crater, Green Tiger, Red Lions, and Little People 10 vols., 1956–63; Rocky and the Lions, 1957; The Time Maze, 1960; The Last Horizon, 1961; The Willow Wand, 1962; The Tall Man from the Sea, 1962; Rocky and the Elephant, 1962; One More River, 1963; The Widgeon Gang, 1964; The Great Bow, 1964; The Pit, 1966; The Dragon in the Garden, 1968; Sell-Out (in U.S. as Danny Rowley), 1969; Northmen's Fury, 1970; Thin Ice, 1971; The Big Ditch, 1971; Home and Away, 1980. Add: 116 Dudlow Green Rd., Appleton, Warrington WA4 5EH, England.

MADDOCKS, Margaret (Kathleen Avern). British, b. 1906. Novels/Short stories, Autobiography/Memoirs/Personal. *Publs:* Come Lasses and Lads, 1944; The Quiet House, 1947; Remembered Spring, 1949; Fair Shines the Day, 1952, as The Open Door, 1980; Piper's Tune, 1954; A Summer Gone, 1957; The Frozen Fountain, 1959; Larksbrook, 1962; The Green Grass, 1963; November Tree, 1964; The Silver Answer, 1965; Dance Barefoot, 1966; Fool's Enchantment, 1968; Thea, 1969; The Weathercock, 1971; A View of the Sea, 1973; The Moon Is Square, 1975; An Unlessoned Girl (autobiography), 1977. Add: 40 Heathfield Green, Midhurst, W. Sussex GU29 9QA, England.

MADDOX, Carl. *See* **TUBB,** E.C.

MADDOX, Robert James. American, b. 1931. History, International relations/Current affairs, Politics/Government. Prof. of History, Pennsylvania State Univ., University Park, since 1973 (Asst. Prof., 1966–68; Assoc. Prof., 1968–73). Instr. of History, Paterson State Coll., Wayne, N.J., 1962–64; Asst. Prof., Michigan State Univ., East Lansing, 1964–66. *Publs:* William E. Borah and American Foreign Policy, 1969; The New Left and American Foreign Policy, 1973; The Unknown War with Russia, 1977; From War to Cold War: The Education of Harry S. Truman, 1988. Add: Dept. of History, Pennsylvania State Univ., University Park, Pa. 16802, U.S.A.

MADDOX, Russell Webber. American, b. 1921. Politics/Government, Public/Social administration. Prof. of Political Science, Oregon State Univ., since 1962 (Asst. Prof., 1950–55; Assoc. Prof., 1955–62). *Publs:* Extraterritorial Powers of Municipalities in the United States, 1955; (with R.F. Fuquary) State and Local Government, 1962, 4th ed. 1981; (ed.) Issues in State and Local Government, 1965. Add: Dept. of Political Science, Oregon State Univ., Corvallis, Ore. 97331, U.S.A.

MADDY, Y(ulisa) A(madu). Sierra Leonean, b. 1936. Novels, Plays/Screenplays. Worked for Sierra Leone Railways; radio producer in Denmark and Britain, early 1960's; drama instructor and/or artistic dir., Univ. of Zambia, 1969–70, Keskidee Arts Centre, London, 1971–73, Ministry of Tourism and Culture, Freetown, 1974–77, Morley Coll., London, 1979–80, Ibadan Univ., Nigeria, 1980–83, Performing Arts Resource Center, Conn., 1983–85, Gbakanda Afrikan Tiata and Leeds Univ., 1986–87. *Publs:* plays—Obasai and Other Plays, 1971; Life Everlasting (in Short African Plays), 1972; Big Breeze Blow, 1984; Big Berrin, 1984; novel—No Past, No Present, 1973. Add: 19 Francis St., Leeds LS7 4BY, England.

MADGE, Charles (Henry). British, b. 1912. Poetry, Politics/Government, Sociology, Third World problems. Reporter, Daily Mirror, London, 1935–36; founded Mass Observation, 1937; staff member, National Inst. of Social and Economic Research, 1940–42; member, research staff, Policy and Economic Planning, 1943; Dir., Pilot Press, London, 1944; Social Development Officer, Stevenage, 1947–50; Prof. of Sociology, Univ. of Birmingham, 1950–70. *Publs:* The Disappearing Castle (poetry), 1937; (with T. Harrisson) Mass Observation, 1937; (ed. with H. Jennings) May the Twelfth: Mass Observation Day-Surveys 1937, by over 200 Observers, 1937; (ed. with T. Harrisson) First Year's Work, 1937–38, by Mass Observation, 1938; (ed. with T. Harrisson) Britain, by Mass Observation, 1938; (ed. with T. Harrisson) War Begins at Home, by Mass Observation, 1940; The Father Found, 1941; War-Time Pattern of Saving and Spending, 1943; (with D. Tyerman) Industry after the War: Who Is Going to Run It?, 1943; (ed.) Target for Tomorrow series, 1943–45; (ed.) Pilot Guide to the General Elections, 1945; (ed.) Pilot Papers: Social Essays and Documents, 1945–47, 1947; Survey Before Development in Thai Villages, 1957; Evaluation and the Technical Assistance Expert: An Operational Analysis, 1961; Society in the Mind: Elements of Social Eidos, 1964; (with B. Weinberger) Art Students Observed, 1973; (with P. Willmott) Inner City Poverty in Paris and London, 1981; (ed. with Mary-Lou Jennings) Pandaemonium, by Humphrey Jennings, 1985; (with Tom Harrison) Britain by Mass-Observation, 1986; (with Humphrey Jennings) May the Twelfth, 1987. Add: 28 Lynmouth Rd., London N2, England.

MADGETT, Naomi Long. American, b. 1923. Poetry, Literary criticism/History, Writing/Journalism. Prof. of English, Eastern Michigan Univ., Ypsilanti, 1973–84, now Emeritus (Assoc. Prof., 1968–73). Publr. and Ed., Lotus Press, since 1974. Staff Writer, Michigan Chronicle, 1946–47; Service Rep., Michigan Bell Telephone Co., 1948–54; teacher, Detroit Public Schs., 1955–65 and 1966–68; Research Assoc., Oakland Univ., Rochester, Mich., 1965–66; Lectr., Univ. of Michigan, Ann Arbor, 1970. *Publs:* Songs to a Phantom Nightingale, 1941; One and the Many, 1956; Star by Star, 1965, 1970; (with E. Tincher and H.B. Maloney) Success in Language and Literature, B, 1967; Pink Ladies in the Afternoon, 1972; Deep Rivers (teachers' guide), 1974; Exits and Entrances, 1978; A Student's Guide to Creative Writing, 1980; Phantom Nightingale: Juvenilia, 1981; (ed.) A Milestone Sampler: 15th Anniversary Anthology, 1988; Octavia and Other Poems, 1988. Add: 16886 Inverness Ave., Detroit, Mich. 48221, U.S.A.

MADISON, Frank. *See* **HUTCHINS,** Francis Gilman.

MAES-JELINEK, Hena. Belgian. Literature. Prof., Univ. of Liège. *Publs:* Criticism of Society in the English Novel Between the Wars, 1970; (ed.) Commonwealth Literature and the Modern World, 1975; The Naked Design, 1976; (ed.) Explorations: Essays by Wilson Harris, 1980; Heart

of Darkness, 1982; Wilson Harris, 1982; (ed.) Multiple worlds, Multiple Words 1987. Add: Résidence Petit Paradis, 1 Quai de Rome, 4000 Liège, Belgium.

MAESTRO, Giulio. American, b. 1942. Children's fiction. Freelance writer, designer, and illustrator, since 1969. Asst. to Art Dir., Design Organization, Inc., NYC, 1965–66; Asst. Art Dir., Warren A. Kass Graphics Inc., NYC, 1966–69. *Publs:* The Tortoise's Tug of War, 1971; The Remarkable Plant in Apartment 4, 1973; One More and One Less, 1974; Leopard Is Sick, 1978; Leopard and the Noisy Monkeys, 1980; A Raft of Riddles, 1982; Riddle Romp, 1983; Just Enough Rosie, 1983; What's a Frank Frank?, 1984; Razzle-Dazzle Riddles, 1985; What's Mite Might?, 1986. Add: c/o Crown Publrs. Inc., 225 Park Ave., S., New York, N.Y. 10003, U.S.A.

MAGEE, Bryan. British, b. 1930. Novels/Short stories, Poetry, Music, Philosophy, Politics/Government, Social commentary/phenomena. Music Critic, Musical Times, since 1969; Theatre Critic, BBC, since 1966; Arts Critic, ITV Television, since 1966. M.P. (U.K.) for Leyton, Labour, 1974–82, S.D.P., 1982–83. *Publs:* Crucifixion and Other Poems, 1951; Go West Young Man, 1958; To Live in Danger, 1960; The New Radicalism, 1962; The Democratic Revolution, 1964; Towards 2000, 1965; One in Twenty, 1966; The Television Interviewer, 1966; Aspects of Wagner, 1968; Modern British Philosophy, 1971; The Philosophy of Karl Popper, 1973; Facing Death, 1977; Men of Ideas, 1978; The Philosophy of Schopenhauer, 1983; The Great Philosophers, 1987. Add: 12 Falkland House, Marloes Rd., London W8 5LF, England.

MAGEE, Wes. British, b. 1939. Children's fiction, Poetry. Headmaster, Brough Sch., Humberside. *Publs:* Postcard from a Long Way Off, 1969; The Radish, 1970; Urban Gorilla, 1972; Proust in a Crowded Store, 1974; Creature of the Bay: A Set of Poems, 1977; Reptile Rhymes (juvenile), 1977; Headland Graffiti, 1978; No Surrender, 1978; The Dream Spectres, 1978; No Man's Land, 1978; The Real Spirit of Christmas (play; juvenile), 1978; Oliver, The Daring Birdman (juvenile), 1978; The Space Beasts (juvenile), 1979; A Dark Age, 1982; (ed.) All Through the Day, 1982; (ed.) Dragon's Smoke (juvenile), 1985; (ed.) A Shooting Star (juvenile), 1985; (ed.) A Calendar of Poems (juvenile), 1986; Story Starters (juvenile), 1986; Don't Do That! (juvenile), 1987; (ed.) A Christmas Stocking, 1988; (ed.) A Big Poetry Book, 1989; (ed.) Read a Poem, Write a Poem, 1989; The Witch's Brew and Other Poems, 1989; Morning Break and Other Poems, 1989; (ed.) Madtail Miniwhale, 1989. Add: Santone House, Low St., Sancton, York, England.

MAGGAL, (Rabbi) Moshe Morris. American, b. 1908. Theology/Religion. Rabbi, and freelance writer, lectr. and journalist; Publr. and Ed., Voice of Judaism, since 1960. Founder and Pres., National Jewish Information Service, since 1960. Ed., Iton Meyuhad, Hebrew weekly, Tel Aviv, Israel, 1940–47; Rabbi, Temple Meyer-David, Claremont, N.H., 1951–52; Temple Beth Aaron, Billings, Mont., 1952–54, Alhambra Jewish Center, Calif., 1955–57, Temple Beth Kodesh, Canoga Park, Calif., 1959–61, and Congregation Ahavath Israel, Hollywood, Calif., 1966–71; Assoc. Ed., Heritage Newspaper, Los Angeles, Calif., 1958–60. *Publs:* Acres of Happiness, 1967; The Secret of Israel's Victories: Past, Present, and Future, 1982. Add: 3761 Decade St., Las Vegas, Nev. 89121, U.S.A.

MAGGS, Colin Gordon. British, b. 1932. Transportation. Deputy Headmaster, Batheaston Church of England Sch., Bath, since 1967. *Publs:* Weston Clevedon and Portishead Railway, 1964; Midland and South Western Junction Railway, 1967; Bristol and Gloucester/Avon and Gloucestershire Railways, 1969; Bath Tramways, 1971; Highbridge in Its Heyday, 1973; Weston Super Mare Tramways, 1974; Bristol Port Railway and Pier, 1975; Newport Tramways, 1977; East Somerset Railway, 1977; Sidmouth, Seaton and Lyme Regis Railway, 1977; Wrington Vale Light Railway, 1978; Barnstaple and Ilfracombe Railway, 1978; Railways to Exmouth, 1980; Taunton to Barnstaple Line, 1980; Rail Centres: Bristol, 1981; Railways of the Cotswolds, 1981; Bath to Weymouth Line, 1982; Rail Centres: Swindon, 1983; The Honeybourne Line, 1985; The Camerton Branch, 1985; Rail Centres: Exeter, 1985; The Birmingham and Gloucester Line, 1986; The Clevedon Branch, 1987; GWR Principal Stations, 1987. Add: 8 Old Newbridge Hill, Bath BA1 3LX, England.

MAGNUS, Samuel Woolf. British, b. 1910. Law. Barrister, England, 1937–59, Barrister, 1959–68, Queen's Counsel, 1964, High Court Judge, 1968–70 and Justice of Appeal, 1971, Zambia; Deputy Circuit Judge, Lord Chancellor's Dept., London, 1971–77; Member, Foreign Compensation Commn., 1977–83. *Publs:* (with M. Estrin) Companies Act 1947, 1947; Companies: Law and Practice, 1948, 5th ed. 1967, supplement, 1981; (with A.M. Lyons) Advertisement Control, 1949; Magnus on Leasehold

Property (Temporary Provisions) Act 1951, 1951; Magnus on Landlord and Tenant Act, 1954, 1954; Magnus on Housing Repairs and Rents Act 1954, 1954; Magnus on the Rent Act 1957, 1957; (with F.E. Price) Knight's Annotated Housing Acts, 1958; (with Tovell) Magnus on Housing Finance, 1960; Companies Act 1967, 1967; Magnus on the Rent Act 1968, 1969; Magnus on Business Tenancies, 1970; Magnus on the Rent Act 1977, 1978; Butterworth's Company Forms Manual, 1988. Add: 33 Apsley House, Finchley Rd., London NW8, England.

MAGNUSSON, Magnus. Icelandic, b. 1929. Archaeology/Antiquities, History, Translations. Presenter of various T.V. progs. for BBC. Chmn., Ancient Monuments Bd. for Scotland, since 1981. Chief Features Writer and Asst. Ed., Scottish Daily Express, 1957–61; Asst. Ed., The Scotsman, 1961–68. Lord Rector, Univ. of Edinburgh, 1975–78; Chmn., Scottish Youth Theatre, 1977–78. *Publs:* (trans. with Hermann Palsson) Njal's Saga, 1960; (trans.) The Atom Station, by Halldor Laxness, 1961; (trans.) Paradise Reclaimed, by Halldor Laxness, 1962; (trans. with Hermann Palsson) The Vinland Sagas, 1965; (trans. with Hermann Palsson) King Harald's Saga, 1966; (trans.) The Fish Can Sing, by Halldor Laxness, 1966; (trans.) Golden Iceland, by Samivel, 1967; (trans. with Hermann Palsson) Laxdaela Saga, 1969; (trans.) World Light, by Halldor Laxness, 1969; Introducing Archaeology, 1972 (Times Educational Supplement Information Book Award); Viking Expansion Westwards, 1973; (trans.) Christianity under Glacier, by Halldor Laxness, 1973; The Clacken and the Slate, 1974; Hammer of the North, 1976, 2nd ed. as Viking Hammer of the North, 1980; B.C.: The Archaeology of the Bible Lands, 1977; Landlord or Tenant?: A View of Irish History, 1978; Iceland, 1979; Vikings!, 1980; Magnus on the Move, 1981; Treasures of Scotland, 1981; Lindisfarne, the Cradle Island, 1984; Iceland Saga, 1987. Add:Blairskaith House, Balmore-Torrance, Glasgow G64 4AX, Scotland.

MAGUIRE, Michael. British, b. 1945. Novels/Short stories. *Publs:* Shot Silk, 1975; Slaughter Horse, 1975; Scratchproof, 1976; Mylor, The Most Powerful Horse in the World, 1977; Mylor: The Kidnap, 1978; Superkids, 1979; Hot Metal, 1982; Scorcher, 1987. Add: W.H. Allen, 175 St. John St., London EC1V 4LL, England.

MAHESHWARI, Shriram. Indian, b. 1931. Politics/Government, Public/Social administration. Prof. of Political Science and Public Admin., Indian Inst. of Public Admin., New Delhi since 1973 (Reader in Public Admin., 1965–73). Pres., Indian Public Admin. Assn., since 1988. Lectr., Agra Coll., 1955–62, St. Stephen's Coll., Delhi, 1962, and Univ. of Rajasthan, Jaipur, 1964. *Publs:* The General Election in India, 1962; The Evolution of Indian Administration, 1970; Local Government in India, 1971; Government Through Consultation, 1972; Administrative Reforms Commission, 1972; (co-author) Public Administration, 14th ed. 1986; Indian Administration, 3rd ed. 1979; (ed.) Study of Public Administration in India, 1974; (ed.) Indian Polity, by George T. Chesney, 1976; President's Rule in India, 1977; State Governments in India, 1979; (ed.) Teaching of Public Administration in India,1979; Administrative Reform in India, 1981; Open Government in India, 1981; Indian Parliamentary System, 1981; Electoral Politics in the National Metropolis, 1982; Comparative Government and Politics, 1983; Political Development in India, 1984; Rural Development in India: A Public Policy Approach, 1985; The Higher Civil Service in Japan, 1987. Add: Dept. of Political Science and Public Admin., Indian Inst. of Public Admin., Indraprastha Estate, New Delhi 110002, India.

MAHON, Derek. British, b. 1941. Poetry. Poetry Ed., New Statesman, London; Dream Critic, The Listener, London. English Teacher, Belfast High Sch., Newtownabbey, Co. Antrim, 1967–68; Lectr. in English, The Language Centre of Ireland, Dublin, 1968–70; Poet-in-Residence, Emerson Coll., Boston, 1976–77, and New Univ. of Ulster, Coleraine, 1977–79. *Publs:* Twelve Poems, 1965; Night-Crossing, 1968; Ecclesiastes, 1970; Beyond Howth Head, 1970; (ed.) Modern Irish Poetry, 1972; Lives, 1972; The Man Who Built His City in Snow, 1972; The Snow Party, 1975; Light Music, 1977; The Sea in Winter, 1979; Poems 1962–1978, 1979; Courtyards in Delft, 1981; (trans.) The Chimeras, by Nerval, 1982; The Hunt by Night, 1982; A Kensington Notebook, 1984; Antarctica, 1986. Add: c/o Deborah Rogers Ltd., 20 Powis Mews, London W11 1JN, England.

MAHON, John K(eith). American, b. 1912. History. Prof. of History, Univ. of Florida, Gainesville, since 1966 (Asst. Prof., 1954–60; Assoc. Prof., 1960–66; Chmn. of Dept., 1966–73). Civilian Military Historian, 1951–54, and Acting Chief, Organizational History and Honors Branch, 1953–54, Office of the Chief of Military History, U.S. Dept. of the Army, Pres., Florida Historical Soc., 1980–82. *Publs:* The American Militia: Decade of Decision, 1789–1800, 1960; (ed.) Reminiscences of the Second Seminole War, by John Bemrose, 1966; History of the Second Seminole War, 1968; The War of 1812, 1972; History of the Militia and the National Guard, 1983. Add: 4129 S.W. 2nd Ave., Gainesville, Fla. 32607, U.S.A.

MAHONEY, Thomas Arthur. American, b. 1928. Administration/Management, Industrial relations. Prof., Owen Grad. Sch. of Mgmt., Vanderbilt Univ., Nashville, Tenn., since 1982. Prof. of Industrial Relations, Grad. Sch. of Business Admin., Univ. of Minnesota, Minneapolis, 1956–82. Education Consultant, State Farm Insurance Co., 1959–82; member, Mgmt. Seminars, National Development and Mgmt. Foundn. of South Africa, 1961–76; Gov.'s Advisory Cttee. on Manpower Development and Training, 1962–65; Dir., 1964–66, and Asst. Dir., 1967–72, Industrial Relations Center; Member, Mgmt. Seminars, Inst. de Admin. Cientifica de las Empresas, Mexico, 1966–78; Chmn., Univ. of Minnesota Civil Service Cttee., 1968–72; Gov., Academy of Management, 1977–79; Ed., Academy of Management Journal, 1982–85. *Publs:* Building the Executive Team: A Guide to Management Development, 1961; (with T. Jerdee and A. Nash) The Identification of Management Potential: A Research Approach to Management Development, 1961; (with T. Jerdee and S. Carroll) Development of Managerial Performance: A Research Approach, 1962; Compensation and Reward Perspectives, 1979. Add: Owen Grad. Sch. of Management Vanderbilt Univ., Nashville, Tenn. 37203, U.S.A.

MAHY, Margaret. New Zealander, b. 1936. Children's fiction, Poetry, History. Full-time writer. Former Librarian, Sch. Library Service, Christchurch; Writer-in-Residence, Canterbury Univ., 1984, and Coll. of Advanced Ed. of W.A., 1985. *Publs:* The Dragon of an Ordinary Family, 1969; A Lion in the Meadow, 1969; Mrs. Discombobulous, 1969; Pillycock's Shop, 1969; The Procession, 1969; The Little Witch, 1970; Sailor Jack and the 20 Orphans, 1970; The Princess and the Clown, 1970; The Boy with Two Shadows, 1971; Seventeen Kings and Forty Two Elephants (verse), 1972; The First Second, Third Margaret Mahy Story Book: Stories and Poems, 3 vols., 1972–75; The Man Whose Mother Was a Pirate, 1972; The Railway Engine and the Hairy Brigands, 1973; Rooms for Rent (in U.K. as Rooms to Let), 1974; The Witch in the Cherry Tree, 1974; Clancy's Cabin, 1974; The Rare Spotted Birthday Party, 1974; Stepmother, 1974; New Zealand: Yesterday and Today, 1975; The Bus under the Leaves, 1975; The Ultra-Violet Catastrophe! or, The Unexpected Walk with Great-Uncle Magnus Pringle, 1975; The Great Millionaire Kidnap, 1975; Leaf Magic, 1975; The Boy Who Was Followed Home, 1975; The Wind Between the Stars, 1976; David's Witch Doctor, 1976; The Pirate Uncle, 1977; Nonstop Nonsense, 1977; The Great Piratical Rumbustification, 1979; Fearsome Robots and Frightened Uncles, 1980; Raging Robots and Unruly Uncles, 1981; The Chewing-Gum Rescue, 1982; The Haunting (Carnegie Medal and Esther Glen Medal), 1983; The Changeover, 1983; The Pirate's Mixed-Up Voyage, 1983; The Birthday Burglar and a Very Wicked Headmistress, 1984; The Catalogue of the Universe, 1985; Jam, 1985; Aliens in the Family, 1986; The Tricksters, 1986; The Downhill Crocodile Whizz and Other Stories, 1986; Memory, 1987; The Horrible Story and Others, 1987; The Door in the Air, 1988; The Blood and Thunder, 1989; Adventures on Hurricane Peak, 1989. Add: R.D. No. 1, Lyttelton, New Zealand.

MAIER, Paul Luther. American, b. 1930. Historical/Romance/Gothic, Theology/Religion, Biography. Prof. of Ancient History, and Campus Chaplain to Lutheran students, Western Michigan Univ., Kalamazoo, since 1958. Member of Advisory Bd., Christian Herald Family Bookshelf, since 1967; Resource Scholar, Christianity Today Institute, since 1985. *Publs:* A Man Spoke, A World Listened: The Story of Walter A. Maier, 1963; Pontius Pilate, (novel), 1968; First Christmas, 1971; First Easter, 1973; First Christians, 1976; (ed.) The Best of Walter A. Maier, 1980; The Flames of Rome (novel), 1981; (assoc. ed.) Josephus—The Jewish War, 1982; (ed.) Josephus: The Essential Writings, 1988. Add: Dept. of History, Western Michigan Univ., Kalamazoo, Mich. 49008, U.S.A.

MAIL, Audrey Maureen. New Zealander, b. 1924. Children's non-fiction. Sr. Mistress, Hawera High Sch., 1973–86 (Sr. Mistress, Hawera Main Sch., 1959–61; Careers Adviser Hawera High Sch., 1970–72). Supvr., Jr. Classes, Turu-turu Sch., 1962–66. *Publs:* Springboard Series, 12 books, 1966; Little Reader, 5 books, 1967. Add: 36 Mawhitiwhiti Rd., Normanby, Taranaki, New Zealand.

MAILER, Norman. American, b. 1923. Novels/Short stories, Plays/Screenplays, Poetry, Social commentary/phenomena, Documentaries/Reportage. Member, Editional Bd., Dissent mag., 1953–63; Columnist, Esquire mag., NYC, 1962–63; Co-Founding Ed., Village Voice newspaper, NYC, 1965. *Publs:* The Naked and the Dead, 1948; Barbary Shore, 1951; The Deer Park, 1955, play, 1967; Advertisements for Myself,

1959; The White Negro, 1959; Deaths for the Ladies and Other Disasters (poetry), 1962; The Presidential Papers, 1963; An American Dream, 1965; Cannibals and Christians, 1966; The Bullfight, 1967; Why Are We in Vietnam? (novel), 1967; Wild 90, (screenplay), 1967; Beyond the Law (screenplay), 1967; The Armies of the Night: History as a Novel, The Novel as History, 1968 (National Book Award Pulitzer Prize); Maidstone (screenplay), 1968, published as Maidstone: A Mystery, 1971; The Idol and the Octopus: Political Writings on the Kennedy and Johnson Administrations, 1968; Miami and the Siege of Chicago: An Informal History of the Republican and Democratic Conventions of 1968, 1969; Of a Fire on the Moon, 1970; The Prisoner of Sex, 1971; The Long Patrol: Twenty-Five Years of Writing from the Works of Norman Mailer, 1971; St. George and the Godfather, 1972; Existential Errands, 1972; Marilyn: A Biography, 1973; The Fight, 1975; Some Honorable Men, 1976; Genius and Lust, 1976; A Transit to Narcissus, 1978; The Executioner's Song, 1979 (Pulitzer Prize); Of Women and Their Elegance, 1980; Pieces and Pontifications, 1982; Ancient Evenings, 1983; Tough Guys Don't Dance, 1984. Add: c/o Rembar, 19 West 44th St., New York, N.Y., U.S.A.

MAIN, Barbara York. Australian, b. 1929. Natural history, Zoology. Freelance writer and professional entomologist. *Publs:* Spiders of Australia, 1964; Between Wodjil and Tor, 1967; Twice Trodden Ground, 1971; Spiders, 1976; (co-ed.) Summerland, 1979. Add: c/o Zoology Dept., Univ. of Western Australia, Nedlands, W.A., Australia.

MAINONE, Robert Franklin. American, b. 1929. Poetry. Naturalist, Kellogg Bird Sanctuary, Michigan State Univ., Augusta, since 1967. *Publs:* An American Naturalist's Haiku, 1964; Parnassus Flowers, 1965; Where Waves Were, 1966; This Boundless Mist, 1968; Shadows, 1971; Young Leaves, 1974; High on the Wind, 1975; Moonlight, 1979; The Journey North, 1984; The Spring Within, 1989. Add: 7431 Pine Lake Rd., Delton, Mich. 49046, U.S.A.

MAIR, (Alexander) Craig. British, b. 1948. History, Travel/Exploration/Adventure, Biography. Principal Teacher of History, Wallace High Sch., Stirling, Scotland. *Publs:* A Time in Turkey, 1973; A Star for Seamen: The Stevenson Family, 1978; The Lighthouse Boy, 1981; Britain at War 1914–1919, 1982; Mercat Cross and Tolbooth, 1988; David Angus: Victorian Railway Engineer, 1989; Stirling: Its People and Their Heritage, 1989. Add: Mornish, 21 Keir St., Bridge of Allan, Stirlingshire FK9 4AY, Scotland.

MAIR, George Brown. Also writes as Robertson Macdouall. British, b. 1914. Mystery/Crime/Suspense, Medicine/Health, Travel/Exploration/Adventure, Autobiography/Memoirs/Personal. Assoc. Prof. of Surgery, Univ. of Durham, 1945–46; Surgeon, Law Hosp., Lanarkshire, 1946–53; Gen. Practitioner, Grangemouth, Scotland, 1954–68; Cosmetic Surgeon, Rotterdam, 1976–80. *Publs:* Surgery of Abdominal Hernia, 1948; (as Robertson Macdouall) Surgeon's Saga, 1949; Doctor Goes East, 1957; Doctor Goes West, 1958; Doctor Goes North, 1958; Destination Moscow, 1960; The Day Khruschev Panicked, 1961; Doctor in Turkey, 1961; Death's Foot Forward, 1963; Miss Turquoise, 1964; Live, Love and Cry, 1965; Kisses from Satan, 1966; The Girl from Peking, 1967; Black Champagne, 1968; Goddesses Never Die, 1969; A Wreath of Camellias, 1970; Crimson Jade, 1971; Paradise Spells Danger, 1973; Confessions of a Surgeon, 1974; Arranging and Enjoying Your Package Holiday, 1975; Escape from Surgery, 1975; How to Die with Dignity, 1980, supplement, 1981. Add: 5 Forglen Rd., Bridge of Allan, Stirlingshire FK9 4BG, Scotland.

MAIROWITZ, David (Zane). American, b. 1943. Novels/Short stories, Plays/Screenplays, Politics/Government. Visiting Prof. in Documentary Theatre, Univ. of California, 1967; Ed., Running Man mag., London, 1968–69; London Drama Critic, Village Voice, NYC, 1968–76; Visiting Prof. of Political Theatre, Stanford Univ., Calif., 1975; Drama Critic, Plays and Players, London, 1975–80. *Publs:* (ed.) Some of IT, 1969; (ed. with P. Stansill) BAMN: Outlaw Manifestos and Ephemera 1965–1970, 1971; The Radical Soap Opera, 1974; (ed.) Inside German Communism, 1976; In the Slipstream (stories), 1977; Reich for Beginners, 1986. Add: 53 rue des Teinturiers, 84000 Avignon, France.

MAITRA, Priyatosh. Indian, b. 1930. Economics. Assoc. Prof. Economics, Univ. of Otago, Dunedin. With the Indian Statistical Inst., Calcutta, 1956–68; Visiting Prof., Univ. of Tokyo, 1973–74, and Univ. of Edinburgh, 1980. *Publs:* Import Substitution Potential in East Africa, 1967; Underdevelopment Revisited, 1977; The Mainspring of Economic Development, 1980; Population, Technology, and Development, 1986; (co-ed.) Technological Change, Development, and Environment, 1988. Add: 41 Prestwick St., Maori Hill, Dunedin, New Zealand.

MAJOR, Clarence. American, b. 1936. Novels/Short stories, Poetry, Language/Linguistics, Literature. Prof. of English, Univ. of Colorado, Boulder, since 1981 (Assoc. Prof., 1977–81). Assoc. Ed., Proof Mag., Chicago, 1959–60; Ed., Coercion Review, Chicago, 1958–65; Assoc. Ed., Caw! mag., 1967–68, and Journal of Black Poetry, 1967–70; taught in the Harlem Education Prog. Writers Workshop, NYC, 1967, and the Teachers and Writers Collaborative, NYC, 1967–72; taught at Sarah Lawrence Coll., Bronxville, N.Y., 1972–75, Howard Univ., Washington, D.C., 1974–75, and Univ. of Washington, Seattle, 1976–77. *Publs:* The Fires That Burn in Heaven, 1954; Love Poems of a Black Man, 1964; Human Juices, 1965; All-Night Visitors (novel), 1969; (ed.) The New Black Poetry, 1969; Swallow the Lake, 1970; Dictionary of Afro-American Slang (in U.K. as Black Slang: A Dictionary of Afro-American Talk), 1970; Symptoms and Madness, 1971; Private Line, 1971; The Cotton Club: New Poems, 1972; NO (novel), 1973; The Syncopated Cakewalk, 1974; The Dark and Feeling: Black American Writers and Their Work, 1974; Reflex and Bone Structure (novel), 1975; Emergency Exit (novel), 1979; Inside Diameter: The France Poems, 1985; My Amputations (novel), 1986. Add: Dept. of English, Univ. of Colorado, Boulder, Colo. 80309, U.S.A.

MAJOR, J(ames) Russell. American, b. 1921. History. Prof. of History, Emory Univ., Atlanta, Ga., since 1949. *Publs:* The Estates General of 1560, 1951; The Deputies to the Estates General of Renaissance France, 1960; Representative Institutions in Renaissance France, 1421–1559, 1960; The Western World: Renaissance to the Present, 1966; The Age of the Renaissance and Reformation, 1970; Bellièvre, Sully and the Assembly of Notables of 1596, 1974; Representative Government in Early Modern France, 1980; The Monarchy, the Estates, and the Aristocracy in Renaissance France, 1988. Add: Dept. of History, Emory Univ., Atlanta, Ga. 30322, U.S.A.

MAJOR, Kevin. Canadian, b. 1949. Children's fiction, Literature. Substitute teacher, Holy Cross Central High School, Eastport, Newfoundland, since 1976. High school teacher in Newfoundland, 1973–76. *Publs:* (ed.) Doryloads (anthology of Newfoundland literature and art), 1974; Hold Fast (children's fiction), 1978; Far From Shore, 1980; Thirty-Six Exposures (children's fiction), 1984; Dear Bruce Springsteen (children's fiction), 1987; Blood Red Ochre, 1989. Add: c/o The Writers' Union of Canada, 24 Ryerson Ave., Toronto, Ontario M5T 2P3, Canada.

MAKANOWITZKY, Barbara. *See* **NORMAN,** Barbara.

MAKINSON, Randell L. American, b. 1932. Architecture, Crafts. Architect in private practice, Los Angeles, 1954–70, and since 1977; Curator, The Gamble House: Greene and Greene Library, Univ. of Southern California, Los Angeles, since 1966 (Lectr., Instr., and Asst. Prof. of Architectural Design, 1956–65). *Publs:* A Guide to the Work of Greene and Greene, 1974; Greene and Greene, vol. I, Architecture as a Fine Art, 1977, and vol. II, Furniture and Related Designs, 1978; (with Esther McCoy) Five California Architects, 2nd ed., 1987. Add: 400 Arroyo Terrace, Pasadena, Calif. 91130, U.S.A.

MALACHY, Frank. *See* **McAULIFFE,** Frank.

MALAND, David. British, b. 1929. Barrister. Sr. History Master, Stamford Sch., Lincs., 1956–66: Headmaster, Cardiff High Sch., Glam., 1966–69; Headmaster, Denstone Coll., Uttoxeter, 1969–78; High Master, Manchester Grammar Sch., 1978–86. *Publs:* Europe in the Seventeenth Century, 1966; (co-trans.) La Guerre de Trente Ans, by G. Pagès, 1970; Culture and Society in Seventeenth Century France, 1971; Europe in the Sixteenth Century, 1973; Europe at War 1600–1650, 1980. Add: Windrush, Underhill Lane, Westmeston, Nr. Hassocks, E. Sussex BN6 8XG, England.

MALCOLM, Norman (Adrian). American, b. 1911. Philosophy. Visiting Prof. of Philosophy, King's Coll., Univ. of London, since 1978. Asst. Prof., 1947–50, Assoc. Prof., 1950–55, Prof., 1955–65, and Susan Linn Sage Prof. of Philosophy, 1965–79, Cornell Univ., Ithaca, New York; Fellow, Center for Advanced Studies in the Behavioral Sciences, Palo Alto, California, 1968–69. *Publs:* Ludwig Wittgenstein: A Memoir, 1958; Dreaming, 1959; Knowledge and Certainty: Essays and Lectures, 1963; (with others) Studies in the Theory of Knowledge, 1970; Problems of Mind: Descartes to Wittgenstein, 1971; Memory and Mind, 1977; Thought and Knowledge, 1977; (with D.M. Armstrong) Consciousness and Causality, 1984; Nothing Is Hidden, 1986. Add: Dept. of Philosophy, King's Coll., Strand, London WC2, England.

MALDÉ Gualtiero. *See* **SERVADIO,** Gaia.

MALEFAKIS, Edward. American, b. 1932. History. Prof. of History, Columbia Univ., NYC, since 1974. Asst. Prof., Wayne State Univ., Detroit, 1963–64, and Columbia Univ., NYC, 1964–68; Instr., 1962–63, and Assoc. Prof., 1968–71, Northwestern Univ., Evanston, Ill; Prof. of History, Univ. of Michigan, Ann Arbor, 1971–74. *Publs:* Agrarian Reform and Peasant Revolution in Spain, 1970; (ed.) Indalecio Prieto: Discursos Fundamentales, 1975; (ed.) La Guerra de Espana 1936–1939, 1986. Add: Dept. of History, Fayerweather Hall, Columbia Univ., New York, N.Y. 10027, U.S.A.

MALEK, James S. American, b. 1941. Literature. Prof. and Chmn., Dept. of English, De Paul Univ., Chicago, since 1981. Prof. of English, 1968–78, Chmn. of the Dept. of English, 1973–76, and Assoc. Dean of the Grad. Sch., 1977–78, Univ. of Idaho, Moscow; Prof. and Chmn., Dept. of English, Wayne State Univ., Detroit, 1987–81. *Publs:* The Arts Compared: An Aspect of Eighteenth-Century British Aesthetics, 1974; (ed.) The Plays of John Home, 1980. Add: Dept. of English, De Paul Univ., 802 W. Belden, Chicago, Ill. 60614, U.S.A.

MALET, (Baldwyn) Hugh (Grenville). British, b. 1928. Archaeology (industrial), History, Travel/Exploration/Adventure, Biography. Univ. Lectr. in Local History, Univ. of Salford, now retired. Former Dir. of Studies, Brasted Theological Training Coll., Kent; in Sudan Political Service, 1950–56. *Publs:* Voyage in a Bowler, 1960, 1985; The Canal Duke, 1961; In the Wake of the Gods, 1970; Bridgewater: The Canal Duke 1736–1803, 1977; Coal, Cotton, and Canals: Collected Essays in Local Canal History, 1981, 1982; O.W. Malet and the Conservation of Taunton Castle, 1988. Add: The Vyne, Blue Anchor, Nr. Minehead, Somerset, TA24 6JX.

MALGONKAR, Manohar (Dattatray). Indian, b. 1913. Novels/Short stories, Plays/Screenplays, History. Self-employed farmer in Jagalbet, since 1959. Professional big-game hunter, 1935–37; Cantonment Exec. Officer, Govt. of India, 1937–42; Owner, Jagalbet Mining Syndicate, 1953–59. *Publs:* Kanhoji Angray, Maratha Admiral: An Account of His Life and His Battles with the English, 1959; Distant Drum, 1960; Combat of Shadows, 1962; Puars of Dewas Senior, 1963; The Princes, 1963; A Bend in the Ganges, 1964; Spy in Amber (screenplay), 1971; The Chhatrapatis of Kolhapur, 1971; The Devil's Wind: Nana Saheb's Story, 1972; Bombay Beware, 1974; A Toast in Warm Wine, 1975; Rumble Tumble, 1976; Dead and Living Cities, 1977; Line of Mars (play), 1977; (with K. Shah) Shalimar, 1978; The Men Who Killed Gandhi, 1978; Cue from the Inner Voice, 1980; The Garland Keepers, 1980; Inside Goa, 1982; Bandicoot Run, 1982; Princess, 1985.. Add: P.O. Burbusa Jagalbet, Londa, Belgaum District, India.

MALIN, Irving. American, b. 1934. Literature. Prof. of English, City Coll. of New York, since 1972 (Instr., 1960–64; Asst. Prof., 1965–68; Assoc. Prof., 1969–71). Advisory Ed., Studies in American Jewish Literature, Twentieth Century Literature, Saul Bellow Newsletter, Review of Contemporary Fiction and Dalkey Archive Press. *Publs:* William Faulkner: An Interpretation, 1957; New American Gothic, 1962; (ed. with I. Stark) Breakthrough, 1964; Jews and Americans, 1965; (ed.) Psychoanalysis and American Fiction, 1965; (ed.) Saul Bellow and the Critics, 1967; (ed.) Truman Capote's In Cold Blood: A Critical Handbook, 1968; Saul Bellow's Fiction, 1969; (ed.) Critical Views of Isaac Bashevis Singer, 1969; (ed. with M.J. Friedman) William Styron's The Confessions of Nat Turner: A Critical Handbook, 1970; Nathanael West's Novels, 1972; Isaac Bashevis Singer, 1972; (ed.) Contemporary American-Jewish Literature: Critical Essays, 1973; (ed. with R.K. Morris) The Achievement of William Styron, 1975; (ed.) Conrad Aiken's Prose, 1982; (co-ed) Paul Bowles, 1986. Add: 96–13 68th Ave., Forest Hills, N.Y. 11375, U.S.A.

MALIN, Peter. *See* **CONNER,** Rearden.

MALING, Arthur (Gordon). American, b. 1923. Mystery/Crime/-Suspense. Reporter, The San Diego Journal, 1945–46; Exec., Maling Brothers Inc., retail shoe chain, Chicago, 1946–72. *Publs:* Decoy, 1969; Go-Between, 1970, in U.K. as Lambert's Son, 1972; Loophole, 1971; The Snowman, 1973; Dingdong, 1974; Bent Man, 1975; Ripoff, 1976; Schroeder's Game, 1977; (ed.) When Last Seen, 1977; Lucky Devil, 1978; (ed.) Mystery Writers' Choice, 1978; The Rheingold Route, 1979; The Koberg Link, 1979; From Thunder Bay, 1981; A Taste of Treason, 1983; Lover and Thief, 1988. Add: 111 E. Chestnut St., Chicago, Ill. 60611, U.S.A.

MALKIEL, Yakov. American, b. 1914. History, Language/Linguistics, Literature. Prof. Emeritus of Linguistics and Romance Philology, Univ. of California, Berkeley, since 1985 (Lectr., 1942–45; Instr., 1945–46; Asst. Prof. of Spanish and Portuguese, 1946–48; Assoc. Prof., 1948–52;

Prof. of Romance Philology, 1952–85, and of Linguistics, 1966–85; Assoc. Dean, Grad. Div., 1963–66). Ed.-in-Chief, Romance Philology quarterly, 1947–82. *Publs:* Essays on Linguistic Themes, 1968; (co-ed. and co-author) Directions for Historical Linguistics: A Symposium, 1968; (co-author) On Four Modern Humanists, 1969; Linguistics and Philology in Spanish America, 1925–70, 1972; Etymological Dictionaries: A Tentative Typology, 1975; From Particular to General Linguistics: Essays 1965–93, 1983; Theory and Practice of Romance Etymology: Studies in Language, Culture and History 1947–1987, 1989. Add: Dept. of Linguistics, Univ. of California, Berkeley, Calif. 94720, U.S.A.

MALLIK, Provash. Indian. Screenplays. Film writer and producer, London; Gen. Mgr., Molliko Films. *Publs:* Detective and Dave, 1978; Boomerang, 1981. Add: Molliko Films (London) Ltd., 16/18 New Bridge St., London EC4V 6AU, England.

MALLIK, Umesh. Indian, b. 1918. Novels/Short stories, Plays/Screenplays, Chmn., Managing Dir., Producer, and Scriptwriter, Molliko Films Ltd., since 1965. Founded Mallicon Film Productions Ltd., 1962. Former Producer and Scriptwriter, Bill and Michael Luckwell Productions Ltd.; Former Promoter and Presenter of Leon Hepner and Sir Peter Daubney, 1950–60. *Publs*, 1962; The Man Who Could Not Walk, 1960; The Beggar Empress; A Guy Called Caesar; Treason and Trumpets, 1963; Kubla Khan; Beethoven and Bonaparte; The Beggar Empress, Monkey God; (with Provash Mallik) The Detective and Dare; (with Janet Bennett) When the Elephants Stampede; These Are Gangsters (TV series); Beethoven—The God and Man (TV series). Add: c/o Molliko Films Ltd., 16/18 New Bridge St., London EC4V 6AU, England.

MALLIN, Jay. America, b. 1927. International relations/Current affairs, Biography, Documentaries/Reportage. News Dir., Radio Marti, since 1985. Stringer Corresp. in Cuba during the 1950's; City Ed., Havana Herald, Cuba 1951–53; Stringer Corresp., Time Mag., NYC, 1956–80; Corresp., Miami News, Fla., 1957–63; Research Scientist, Center for Advanced Intnl. Studies, Univ. of Miami, Fla., 1967–69; Corresp., Copley News Service, 1972–74; Ed., The Net, 1974–85; Latin American corresp., Washington Times, 1982–85. *Publs:* Fortress Cuba, 1965; Caribbean Crisis, 1965; Terror in Viet Nam, 1966; (ed.) "Che" Guevara on Revolution, 1969; (ed.) Strategy for Conquest, 1970; (ed.) Terror and Urban Guerrillas, 1971; Ernesto "Che" Guevara, 1973; General Vo Nguyen Giap, 1973; Fulgencio Batista, 1974; The Great Managua Earthquake, 1974; Merc: American Soldiers of Fortune, 1978. Add: 1444 Rhode Island Ave. N.W., Washington, D.C. 20005, U.S.A.

MALLINSON, Jeremy (John Crosby). Animals/Pets, Environmental science/Ecology, Travel/Exploration/Adventure. Zoological Dir., Jersey Wildlife Preservation Trust, since 1963. *Publs:* Okavango Adventure, 1973; Careers with Animals, 1975; Modern Classic Animal Stories, 1977, in U.S.A. as Such Agreeable Friends, 1978; The Shadow of Extinction, Europe's Threatened Wild Mammals, 1978; The Facts about a Zoo, Featuring the Jersey Wildlife Preservation Trust, 1980; Travels in Search of Endangered Species, 1989. *Publs:* Clos Tranquil, High St., St. Aubin, Jersey, Channel Islands.

MALLINSON, Vernon. British, b. 1910. Education, Language/Linguistics. Prof. Emeritus, Univ. of Reading, since 1975 (Reader in Education, 1960–67; Prof. of Comparative Education, 1967–75; Warden of Whiteknights Hall, 1961–70). *Publs:* Lire et Ecrire, 1938; Ecrire, 1939; Amusons-nous, 1940; Tendances nouvelles dans la littérature anglaise contemporaine, 1946; Extraits de Poil de Carotte, 1947; Creative French I, 1948; Nous les gosses, 1949; (ed.) The Adolescent at School, 1949; Creative French II, 1950; Creative French Ill, 1952; Monsieur Maubenoit, Philatéliste, 1953; Teaching a Modern Language, 1953; None Can Be Called Deformed, 1956; An Introduction to the Study of Comparative Education, 1957; 4th ed., 1975; Choix de poèmes, 1963; Power and Politics in Belgian Education, 1963; Modern Belgian Literature, 1830–1960, 1966; Belgium, 1969; The Western European Idea in Education, 1980; (with others) Educating the Gifted Child, 1980; (co-author) Histoire mondiale de l'éducation, 1981. Add: 23 Palmerston Ct., Walmer, Deal, Kent CT14 7JU, England.

MALLORY, Drew. *See* **GARFIELD,** Brian.

MALONE, Michael. American, b. 1942. Novels. Taught at various U.S. colls., and most recently, Yale Univ., New Haven, Conn. *Publs:* Painting the Roses Red, 1974; The Delectable Mountains, 1976; Psychetypes (non-fiction), 1977; Heroes of Eros (non-fiction), 1979; Dingley Falls, 1980; Uncivil Seasons, 1983; Handling Sin, 1986; Time's Witness, 1989. Add. c/o Peter Matson, Sterling Lord Literistic, One

Madison Ave., New York, N.Y. 10010, U.S.A.

MALOUF, David. Australian, b. 1934. Novels/Short stories, Poetry. Lectr., Univ. of Sydney, 1968–77. *Publs:* (with others) Four Poets, 1962; Bicycle and Other Poems, 1970 (in U.S. as The Year of the Foxes and Other Poems, 1979); (ed., with others) We Took Their Orders and Are Dead: An Anti-War Anthology, 1971; Neighbours in a Thicket, 1974; (ed.) Gesture of Hand (anthology of Australian poetry), 1975; Johnno (novel), 1975; Poems, 1975–76, 1976; An Imaginary Life (novel), 1978; First Things Last (verse), 1981; Child's Play (novel), 1982; Fly Away Peter (in U.S. as The Bread of Time to Come) (novel), 1982; Harland's Half Acre (novel), 1984; Antipodes (short stories), 1985; 12 Edmondstone St., 1985; Voss (opera libretto), 1986; Blood Relations (drama), 1987. Add: 53 Myrtle St., Chippendale, N.S.W. 2008, Australia

MALPASS, Eric (Lawson). British, b. 1910. Novels/Short stories. *Publs:* Beefy Jones, 1957; Operazione Gemelli, 1965; Morning's at Seven, 1965; At the Height of the Moon, 1967; Fortinbras Has Escaped, 1970; Oh My Darling Daughter, 1970; Sweet Will, 1973; The Cleopatra Boy, 1974; A House of Women, 1975; The Long Long Dances, 1978; Summer Awakening, 1978; The Wind Brings Up the Rain, 1978; Liebe Blüht zu allen Zeiten, 1981; Und doch singt die Amsel, 1983; Lampenschein und Sternenlicht (in U.K. as The Lamplight and the Stars), 1985; Of Human Frailty, 1987; Wenn der Tiger schlafen geht, 1989. Add: Broadleaves, 216 Breedon St., Long Eaton, Nottingham, England.

MALZBERG, Barry (Nathaniel). Also writes as Mike Barry, Claudine Dumas, Mel Johnson, Lee W. Mason, Francine de Natale, K.M. O'-Donnell, and Gerrold Watkins. American, b. 1939. Mystery/-Crime/Suspense, Historical/Romance/Gothic, Science fiction/Fantasy. Freelance writer: author of many novels under various pseuds. for Midwood, Oracle, Soft Cover Library, and Traveler's Companion Series. Investigator, NYC Dept. of Welfare, and Reimbursement Agent, N.Y. State Dept. of Mental Hygiene; Ed., Scott Meredith Literary Agency, NYC; Ed., Amazing and Fantastic mags., 1968; Managing Ed., Escapade, 1968. *Publs:* science fiction—Oracle of the Thousand Hands, 1968; (as K.M. O'Donnell) The Empty Rooms, 1969; (as K.M. O'Donnell) Final War and Other Fantasies (short stories), 1969; (as K.M. O'Donnell) Dwellers of the Deep, 1970; The Falling Astronauts, 1971; (as K.M. O'Donnell) Universe Day, 1971; (as K.M. O'Donnell) Gather in the Hall of the Planets, 1971; In the Pocket and Other S-F Stories, 1971; Overlay, 1972; Beyond Apollo, 1972; Revelations, 1972; The Men Inside, 1973; Phase IV, 1973; In the Enclosure, 1973; Herovit's World, 1973; Guernica Night, 1974; On an Alien Planet, 1974; The Day of the Burning, 1974; Tactics of Conquest, 1974; The Sodom and Gomorrah Business, 1974; Underlay, 1974; The Destruction of the Temple, 1974; Out from Ganymede (short stories), 1974; (ed. with Edward L. Ferman) Final Stage, 1974; The Gamesman, 1975; Conversations, 1975; Galaxies, 1975; The Many Worlds of Barry Malzberg (short stories), 1975; Scop, 1976; Down Here in the Dream Quarter (short stories), 1976; (ed. with Edward L. Ferman) Arena: Sports SF, 1976; (ed. with Edward L. Ferman) Graven Images, 1976; The Last Transaction 1977; (ed. with Bill Pronzini) Dark Sins, Dark Dreams: Crime in SF, 1977; Chorale, 1978; (ed. with Bill Pronzini) The End of the Summer: Science Fiction in the Fifties, 1979; (ed. with Bill Pronzini) Shared Tomorrows: Collaboration in SF, 1979; The Man Who Loved the Midnight Lady (stories), 1980; (ed. with Martin Greenberg) Neglected Vision, 1980; (ed. with Martin Greenberg) The Science Fiction of Mark Clifton, 1980; The Cross of Fire, 1982; (ed. with Martin H. Greenberg) The Science Fiction of Kris Neville, 1984; The Remaking of Sigmund Freud, 1985; (ed. with others) Uncollected Stars, 1986; suspense and romance—Screen, 1968; (as Claudine Dumas) Diary of Parisian Chambermaid, 1970; In My Parents' Bedroom, 1970; Confessions of Westchester County, 1971; The Spread, 1971; Horizontal Woman, 1972, as The Social Worker, 1977; The Case for Elizabeth Moore, 1972; The Masochist, 1972, as Everything Happened to Susan, 1978; The Way of the Tiger, The Sign of the Dragon, 1973; (as Mike Barry) Bay Prowler, 1973; (as Mike Barry) Boston Avenger, 1973; (as Mike Barry) Night Raider, 1973; (as Mike Barry) Chicago Slaughter, 1974; (as Mike Barry) Desert Stalker, 1974; (as Mike Barry) Havana Hit, 1974; (as Mike Barry) Los Angeles Holocaust, 1974; (as Mike Barry) Miami Marauder, 1974; (as Mike Barry) Peruvian Nightmare 1974; (as Mike Barry) Detroit Massacre, 1975; (as Mike Barry) Harlem Showdown, 1975; (as Mike Barry) The Killing Run, 1975; (as Mike Barry) Philadelphia Blow-Up, 1975; (as Mike Barry) Phoenix Inferno, 1975; (with Bill Pronzini) The Running of Beasts, 1976; (as Lee W. Mason) Lady of a Thousand Sorrows, 1977; (with Bill Pronzini) Acts of Mercy, 1977; (with Bill Pronzini) Night Screams, 1979; (with Bill Pronzini) Prose Bowl, 1980; (ed. with Bill Pronzini and Martin H. Greenberg) The Arbor House Treasury of Horror and the Supernatural, 1981. Add: Box 61, Teaneck, N.J. 07666, U.S.A.

MAMET, David. American, b. 1947. Children's fiction, Plays/Screenplays. Assoc. Dir., New Theatre Co., Chicago, since 1985. Artist-in-Residence, Goddard Coll., Plainfield, Vt., 1971–73; Founder and Artistic Dir., St. Nicholas Theatre Co., Chicago, 1973–76; Faculty Member, Illinois Arts Council, 1974; Visiting Lectr., Univ. of Chicago, 1975–76; Teaching Fellow, Yale Sch. of Drama, New Haven, Conn., 1976–77; Assoc. Artistic Dir., Goodman Theatre, Chicago, 1978–79. Contrib. Ed., Oui mag., 1975–76. *Publs:* A Life in the Theatre, 1978; American Buffalo, Sexual Perversity in Chicago, Duck Variations: Three Plays, 1978; Sexual Perversity in Chicago, and Duck Variations: Two Plays, 1978; The Water Engine, and Mr. Happiness: Two Plays, 1978; Dark Pony, and Reunion, 1979; The Woods, 1979; Lakeboat, 1981; Edmond, 1983; Warm and Cold (for children), 1984; Glengarry Glen Ross, 1984; Short Plays and Monologues, 1985; Goldberg Street (collection), 1985; The Cherry Orchard (adaptation), 1985; Dramatic Sketches and Monologues, 1985; Three Children's Plays, 1986; The Owl (for children), 1986; Writing in Restaurants (essays), 1986; Three Jewish Plays, 1987; House of Games (screenplay), 1987; Speed-the-Plow, 1988; Things Change (screenplay), 1988; Uncle Vanya (adaptation), 1988. Add: c/o Howard Rosenstone, Rosenstone/Wender, 3 E. 48th St., New York, N.Y. 10017, U.S.A.

MANCHEL, Frank. American, b. 1935. Film, History, Media. Prof. of English, Univ. of Vermont, Burlington; film reviewer and critic-at-large. *Publs:* Movies and How They Are Made, 1968; When Pictures Began to Move, 1968; The Lamancha Project, 1968; La Mancha Plus One, 1969; When Movies Began to Speak, 1969; Terrors of the Screen, 1970; La Mancha Plus Two, 1970; Cameras West, 1971; Yesterday's Clown: The Rise of Film Comedy, 1973; Film Study: A Resource Guide, 1973; An Album of Great Science Fiction Films, 1976; Women on the Hollywood Screen, 1977; The Talking Clowns, 1978; Gangsters on the Screen, 1978; The Box-Office Clowns, 1979; An Album of Great Sports Movies, 1980; An Album of Great Science Fiction Movies, 1982; An Album of Modern Horror Films, 1983. Add: Dept. of English, Univ. of Vermont, Burlington, Vt. 05405, U.S.A.

MANCHESTER, William. American, b. 1922. Novels/Short stories, History, Biography. Fellow, East Coll., since 1968, Writer-in-Residence since 1974, and Adjunct Prof. of History since 1979, Wesleyan Univ., Conn. (Lectr. in English, 1968–69). Hon. Fellow, Yale Univ., New Haven, Conn., since 1989. Reporter, Daily Oklahoman, 1945–46; Reporter, Foreign Corresp., War Corresp., and Assoc. Ed., Baltimore Sun, 1947–55; Managing Ed., Wesleyan Univ. Publs., 1955–56; Fellow, Wesleyan Univ. Center for Advanced Studies, 1959–68. Trustee, 1970–74, and Pres., 1970–72, Friends of Univ. of Massachusetts Library. *Publs:* Disturber of the Peace (in U.K. as The Sage of Baltimore), 1951; The City of Anger, 1953; Shadow of the Monsoon, 1956; Beard the Lion, 1958; A Rockefeller Family Portrait, 1959; The Long Gainer, 1961; Portrait of a President, 1962; The Death of a President, 1967; The Arms of Krupp, 1968; The Glory and the Dream: A Narrative History of America, 1932–1972, 1975; Controversy and Other Essays in Journalism, 1976; American Caesar: Douglas MacArthur, 1978; Goodbye, Darkness, 1980; The Last Lion, vol. I, Visions of Glory, 1983, vol. II, Alone, 1988; One Brief Shining Moment, 1983; Images, 1989. Add: c/o Harold Matson Co., 276 Fifth Ave., New York, N.Y. 10001, U.S.A.

MANDEL, Eli(as Wolf). Canadian, b. 1922. Poetry, Literature. Prof. of English and Humanities, York Univ., since 1967 (Assoc. Prof., 1965–66). Assoc. Prof., 1957–63, and Prof. of English, 1964–65, Univ. of Alberta, Edmonton. *Publs:* (with G. Turnbull and P. Webb) Trio, 1954; Fuseli Poems, 1960; (ed. with Jean-Guy Pilon) Poetry 62, 1961; Black and Secret Man, 1964; Criticism: The Silent Speaking Words, 1966; An Idiot Joy, 1967; Irving Layton, 1969; (ed.) Five Modern Canadian Poets, 1970; (ed. with D. Maxwell) English Poems of the Twentieth Century, 1971; (ed.) Contexts of Canadian Criticism, 1971; (ed.) Poets of Contemporary Canada, 1960–70, 1972; (ed.) Eight More Canadian Poets, 1972; Crusoe: Poems Selected and New, 1973; Stony Plain, 1973; Out of Place, 1977; Another Time (essays), 1977; (ed.) The Poems of Irving Layton, 1977; Dreaming Backwards: Selected Poems, 1981; Life Sentence: Poems and Journals 1976–80, 1981; The Poetry of Irving Layton, 1981. Add: Dept. of English, York Univ., Downsview, Ont. M3J 1P3, Canada.

MANDEL, Ernest. Belgian, b. 1923. Economics, Politics/Government, Sociology. Prof., Free Univ. of Brussels, Flemish Section, since 1970. *Publs:* Marxist Economic Theory, 1962; Formation of the Economic Thought of Karl Marx, 1967; Contradictions of Imperialism: Europe vs. America?, 1971; (ed.) Workers Control, Workers Councils, Workers Self-Management, 1971; Late Capitalism, 1972; The Decline of the Dollar,

1973; From Stalinism to Eurocommunism, 1978; The Second Slump, 1978; Trotsky, 1979; Revolutionary Marxism Today, 1979; The Long Waves of Capitalist Development, 1980; Delightful Murder, 1984; The Meaning of the Second World War, 1986; Beyond Perestroika, 1989. Add: 127 Rue Jos, Impens 1030, Brussels, Belgium.

MANDEL, Oscar. American, b. 1926. Novels/Short stories, Plays/Screenplays, Poetry, Literature, Essays, Translations. Prof. of Humanities, California Inst. of Technology, Pasadena, since 1961. *Publs:* A Definition of Tragedy, 1961; (ed. and trans.) The Theatre of Don Juan: A Collection of Plays and Views (1630–1963), 1963; Chi Po and The Sorcerer, 1964; The Gobble-Up Stories, 1967; The Fatal French Dentist (play), 1967; (ed. and trans.) Seven Comedies of Marivaux, 1968; (ed. and trans.) Five Comedies of Medieval France, 1970; The Collected Plays, 2 vols., 1970–72; (ed. and trans.) Three Classic Don Juan Plays, 1971; Simplicities (poetry), 1974; The Patriots of Nantucket (play), 1976; Amphitryon (play), 1977; (ed. and trans.) The Land of Upside Down, by Ludwig Tieck, 1978; Philoctetes and the Fall of Troy, 1981; Annotations to Vanity Fair, 1981; Collected Lyrics and Epigrams, 1981; Ariadne and French Classical Tragedy, 1982; The Book of Elaborations, 1985; The Kukkurrik Fables, 1987; Sigismund, Prince of Poland (play), 1988; August von Kotzebue: The Comedy, the Man, 1989. Add: Div. of Humanities, California Inst. of Technology, Pasadena, Calif. 91125, U.S.A.

MANFRED, Frederick (Feikema). Also writes as Feike Feikema. American, b. 1912. Novels/Short stories, Westerns/Adventure, Poetry, Autobiography/Memoirs/Personal. Consultant in the Humanities, Augustana Coll., Sioux Falls, South Dakota, since 1984. Reporter, Minneapolis Journal, Minn., 1937–39; Abstract Writer, Modern Medicine, Minneapolis, 1942–43; Writer-in-Residence, Macalester Coll., St. Paul, Minn., 1949–51. *Publs:* (as Feike Feikema) The Golden Bowl, 1944; (as Feike Feikema) Boy Almighty, 1945; (as Feike Feikema) This Is the Year, 1947; (as Feike Feikema) The Chokecherry Tree, 1948, 1961; (as Feike Feikema) World's Wanderer, rev. ed. as Wanderlust, 1962; The Primitive, 1949; The Brother, 1950; The Giant, 1951; Lord Grizzly, 1954; Morning Red: A Romance, 1956; Riders of Judgment, 1957; Conquering Horse, 1959; Arrow of Love, 1961; Scarlet Plume, 1964; The Secret Place, 1965; Winter Count (poetry), 1966; King of Spades, 1966; Eden Prairie, Apples of Paradise, 1968; Conversations with Frederick Manfred, 1974; Milk of Wolves, 1976; The Manly-Hearted Woman, 1976; Green Earth, 1977; The Wind Blows Free (autobiography), 1979; Sons of Adam, 1980; Dinkytown, 1984; Prime Fathers, 1985; Winter Count II (poetry), 1985; Selected Letters of Frederick Manfred 1932-54, 1989; Flowers of Desire, 1989. Add: Roundwind, R.R.3, Luverne, Minn. 56156, U.S.A.

MANGIONE, Jerre (Gerlando). American, b. 1909. Novels/Short stories, History, Sociology, Autobiography/Memoirs/Personal. Prof. of American Literature, and Dir. of Writing Prog., Univ. of Pennsylvania, Philadelphia, since 1968, now Emeritus (Lectr., 1961–63; Assoc. Prof., 1963–68). Book Reviewer, New York Herald Tribune, NYC, 1931–35, and New Republic, NYC, 1931–37; Book Ed., Robert M. McBride Co., NYC, 1934–37; National Coordinating Ed., Federal Writers' Project, 1937–39; Information Specialist, 1940–42, Special Asst. to U.S. Commnr., 1942–48, and Ed.-in-Chief, Monthly Review, 1946–48, Immigration and Naturalization Service, U.S. Dept. of Justice; Advertising and public relations writer, NYC and Philadelphia, 1948–61; Chmn., Literary Arts Cttee., Philadelphia Art Alliance, 1958–61; Ed.-in-Chief, WFLN Philadelphia Guide, 1959–61; National Pres., Friends of Danilo Dolci Inc., NYC, 1969–71. *Publs:* Mount Allegro, 1943, 1989; The Ship and the Flame, 1948; Reunion in Sicily, 1950, 1984; Night Search (in U.K. as To Walk the Night), 1965; Life Sentences for Everybody (fables), 1966; A Passion for Sicilians: The World Around Danilo Dolci, 1968, in paperback as The World Around Danilo Dolci: A Passion for Sicilians, 1972, 1986; America Is Also Italian, 1969; The Dream and the Deal: The Federal Writers' Project, 1935-1943, 1972, 1983; Mussolini's March on Rome, 1975; An Ethnic at Large: A Memoir of America in the Thirties and Forties, 1978, 1983. Add: Dept. of English, Univ. of Pennsylvania, Philadelphia, Pa. 19104, U.S.A.

MANGO, C(yril) A(lexander). British, b. 1928. Art, History, Literature. Bywater and Sotheby Prof. of Byzantine and Modern Greek, Oxford Univ., since 1973. Faculty member, Dumbarton Oaks Byzantine Center, Harvard Univ., Washington, D.C., 1951–63, 1968–73; Koraes Prof., King's Coll., Univ. of London, 1963–68. *Publs:* The Homilies of Photius, 1958; The Brazen House, 1959; The Mosaics of St. Sophia at Istanbul, 1962; The Art of the Byzantine Empire: Sources and Documents, 1972; Architettura bizantina, 1974; Byzantium, 1980; Byzantium and Its Image, 1984; Le Développement Urbain de Constantinople, 1985. Add: Exeter College, Oxford, England.

MANGO, Karin N. British, b. 1936. Children's fiction, Mythology/Folklore. Freelance writer since 1986. Member, Manhattan Exec. Bd. of Self-Help for Hard of Hearing People, Inc., since 1985. Asst. Head of Education Dept., George H. Harrap and Co. Ltd., London, 1958–60; Education Correspondent, McGraw-Hill Book Co., NYC, 1960; Freelance Copy Ed. and Proofreader, R.R. Bowker Co., NYC, 1979–82; Staff Writer, Suzanne Pathy Speak-Up Inst., NYC, 1981–86. *Publs:* Cantering Through, 1951; The Children's Book of Russian Folktales, 1961; The Children's St. Francis, 1963; New York Holiday, 1971; (ed.) Marguerite V. Doggett, Long Island Printing: A Checklist of Imprints, 1979; (ed.) Calendar of Manuscripts of the Revolutionary Period, 1980; Armor: Yesterday and Today, 1980; A Various Journey, 1983; Mapmaking, 1984; Somewhere Green, 1987; Codes, Ciphers and Other Secrets, 1988. Add: 189 Dean St., Brooklyn, N.Y. 11217, U.S.A.

MANHEIM, Jarol B(ruce). American, b. 1946. Politics/Government. Prof. of Communication and Political Science, and Dir. of Political Communication Prog., The George Washington Univ., Washington, D.C., since 1987. Asst. Prof. of Political Science, City Coll., NYC, 1971–75; Assoc. Prof. of Political Science, Virginia Polytechnic Inst. and State Univ., Blacksburg, 1977–87. Assoc. Ed., Journal of Politics, 1978–79; Ed., Longman Professional Studies in Political Communication and Policy, 1979–85; Literature Review Ed., Policy Studies Journal, 1980–82. *Publs:* (ed.) Annual Editions Readings in American Government '74/'75, 1974, '75/'76, 1975, and '76/'77, 1976; The Politics Within: A Primer in Political Attitudes and Behavior, 1975, 1982; (with Melanie Wallace) Political Violence in the United States 1875–1974: A Bibliography, 1975; Déja Vu: American Political Problems in Historical Perspective, 1976; (with Richard C. Rich) Empirical Political Analysis: Research Methods in Political Science, 1986; American Politics Yearbook, 1982; (with Allison Ondrasik) Datamap: Index of Published Tables of Statistical Data, 1983, 4th ed., 1988. Add: 5309 Waneta Rd., Bethesda, Md. 20816, U.S.A.

MANHIRE, Bill. New Zealander, b. 1946. Poetry, Short stories. Reader in English, Victoria Univ., Wellington. Ed., Amphedesma Press, Dunedin, 1971–75. *Publs:* (ed.) New Zealand Universities Arts Festival Yearbook 1969, 1969; Malady, 1970; The Elaboration, 1972; How to Take Off Your Clothes at the Picnic, 1977; (ed.) New Zealand Listener Short Stories, 1977; (ed.) New Zealand Listener Short Stories, Vol. II, 1978; Dawn/Water, 1979; Zoetropes, 1981; Good Looks, 1982; Locating the Beloved and Other Stories, 1983; Zoetropes: Poems 1972–82, 1984; (ed. with M. McLeod) Some Other Country: New Zealand's Best Short Stories, 1984; Maurice Gee, 1986; The Brain of Katherine Mansfield, 1988; (ed.) Six by Six, 1989. Add: Dept. of English, Victoria Univ. of Wellington, Private Bag, Wellington, New Zealand.

MANKOWITZ, Wolf. British, b. 1924. Novels/Short stories, Plays/Screenplays, Poetry, Antiques, Crafts. Film producer since 1955. *Publs:* Make Me an Offer, 1952; The Portland Vase and the Wedgwood Copies, 1952; A Kid for Two Farthings, 1953; The Bespoke Overcoat, 1953; Wedgwood, 1953; Laugh Till You Cry: An Advertisement, 1955; Five One-Act Plays, 1955; My Old Man's a Dustman (in U.S. as Old Soldiers Never Die), 1956; ABC of Show Business, 1956; The Mendelman Fire and Other Stories, 1957; (with R.G. Haggar) A Concise Encyclopedia of Pottery and Porcelain, 1957; (with Julian More) Expresso Bongo, 1958; Expresso Bongo: A Wolf Mankowitz Reader, 1961; Cockatrice, 1963; The Biggest Pig in Barbados: A Fable, 1965; The Penguin Wolf Mankowitz, 1967; Majollika and Company (juvenile), 1967; The Blue Arabian Nights, 1972; The Samson Riddle: An Essay and a Play, with the Text of the Original Story of Samson, 1972; XII Poems, 1972; The Day of the Women and the Night of the Men, 1975; Dickens of London, 1976; The Extraordinary Mr. Poe, 1978; Raspberry Reich, 1979; Abracadabra, 1980; Mazeppa (biography of Adah Issacs Menken), 1981; The Devil in Texas, 1985; Gioconda, 1987; The Magic Cabinet of Prof. Smacker, 1988. Add: The Bridge House, Ahakista, Co. Cork, Ireland.

MANLOVE, Colin (Nicholas). British, b. 1942. Literature. Reader in English Literature, Edinburgh Univ. *Publs:* Modern Fantasy: Five Studies, 1975; Literature and Reality 1600–1800, 1978; The Gap in Shakespeare, 1981; The Impulse of Fantasy Literature, 1983; Science Fiction: Ten Explorations, 1986; C.S. Lewis: His Literary Achievement, 1987; Critical Thinking: A Guide to Interpreting Literary Texts, 1989. Add: Dept. of English Literature, David Hume Tower, George Sq., Edinburgh EH8 9JX, Scotland.

MANN, (Francis) Anthony. British, b. 1914. Novels/Short stories, History, Autobiography/Memoirs/Personal, Biography. Special Corresp. in the Mediterranean, The Daily Telegraph and Telegraph Sunday Mag., since 1973 (joined staff, 1936; Vienna Corresp., 1938; Berlin Corresp., 1938–39; Copenhagen Corresp., 1939–40; Chief Corresp. for Germany, 1946; Chief Corresp. for Southern Europe, Rome, 1952; and subsequently special Corresp. in America, Europe, Africa and Asia; Chief European Corresp., The Sunday Telegraph, 1961; Chief Paris Corresp., 1965–73; and Special Corresp.). Pres., Anglo-American Press Assn., Paris, 1972–73. *Publs:* Where God Laughed: The Sudan Today, 1954; Well-Informed Circles, 1961; Zelezny: Portrait Sculpture 1917–1970, 1970; Tiara, 1973; Comeback: Germany 1945–1952, 1980. Add: c/o Lloyds Bank, Law Courts, 222 Strand, London WC2R 1BB, England.

MANN, Chris(topher Michael Zithulele). South African, b. 1948. Poetry. Dir., Valley Trust, near Durban, since 1980. Teacher, Baring High Sch., Swaziland, 1975–76; Lectr., Rhodes Univ., Grahamstown, 1977–79. *Publs:* First Poems, 1977; (ed.) A New Book of South African Verse in English, 1979; The Sand Labyrinth (verse play), 1980; New Shades, 1982. Add: Box 33, Botha's Hill, Natal 3660, South Africa.

MANN, Emily. American, b. 1952. Plays. Assoc. Dir., Guthrie Theatre, Minneapolis, 1978–79; resident dir., BAM Theatre Co., Brooklyn, 1981–82. *Publs:* Still Life, 1982; Annulla: An Autobiography, 1985; Execution of Justice, 1986. Add: c/o George Lane, William Morris Agency, 1350 Ave. of the Americas, New York, N.Y. 10019, U.S.A.

MANN, James. *See* **HARVEY,** John B.

MANN, Jessica. British. Mystery/Crime/Suspense, Literature. *Publs:* Charitable End, 1971; Mrs. Knox's Profession, 1972; The Only Security, 1973; The Sticking Place, 1974; Captive Audience, 1975; The Eighth Deadly Sin, 1976; The Sting of Death, 1978; Funeral Sites, 1981; Deadlier Than the Male (criticism), 1981; No Man's Island, 1983; Grave Goods, 1984; A Kind of Healthy Grave, 1986; Death Beyond the Nile, 1988. Add: Lambessow, St. Clement, Cornwall, England.

MANN, Josephine. *See* **PULLEIN-THOMPSON,** Josephine.

MANN, Peggy. American. Novels/Short stories, Children's fiction, Children's non-fiction, Travel, Medicine/Health (drug abuse prevention). *Publs:* A Room in Paris (novel), 1955; The Street of the Flower Boxes, 1966; That New Baby, 1967; The Boy with a Billion Pets, 1968; When Carlos Closed the Street, 1969; Clara Barton: Battlefield Nurse, 1969; The Club House, 1969; Amelia Earhart; First Lady of Flight, 1970; The 25 Cent Friend, 1970; The Lost Doll, 1971; Golda: The Life of Israel's Prime Minister, 1971; Whitney Young, Jr.: Crusader for Equality, 1972; William the Watchcat, 1972; How Juan Got Home, 1972; (with R. Kluger) The Last Escape, 1973; The Secret Dog of Little Luis, 1974; My Dad Lives in a Downtown Hotel, 1974; (with J. Houlton) Ghost Boy, 1975; Handwriting: How to Look Inside, 1975; Now Is Now, 1975; Last Road to Safety, 1975; King Lawrence the Alarm Clock, 1975; (with V. Siegal) The Man Who Bought Himself, 1975; A Present for Yanya, 1975; Ralph Bunche: U.N. Peacemaker, 1975; Easter Island: Land of Mysteries, 1976; Lonely Girl, 1976; There Are Two Kinds of Terrible, 1977; The Drop-In, 1979; Twelve Is Too Old, 1980; "Gizelle, Save the Children!", 1980; Marijuana Alert, 1984; Arrive Alive: How to Keep Drunk and Drugged Drivers Off the Road, 1985; Pot Safari, 1987; The Sad Story of Mary Wanna or How Marijuana Harms You, 1988. Add: c/o Curtis Brown Ltd., 10 Astor Pl., New York, N.Y. 10003, U.S.A.

MANN, Peter H(enry). British, b. 1926. Literature, Sociology. Dir., Library and Information Statistics Unit, Loughborough Univ., since 1987 (Dir., Centre for Library and Information Management, 1983–87). Research Worker, Univ. of Liverpool, 1950–52; Research Fellow, Univ. of Nottingham, 1952–54; Lectr., 1954–64, Sr. Lectr., 1964–72, and Reader in Sociology, 1972–83, Univ. of Sheffield. *Publs:* An Approach to Urban Sociology, 1965; Methods of Sociological Enquiry, 1968; (with J.L. Burgoyne) Books and Reading, 1969; Books: Buyers and Borrowers, 1971; Students and Books, 1974; From Author to Reader: A Social Study of Books, 1982; A Readers' Guide to Fiction Authors, 1985. Add: Library and Information Statistics Unit, Loughborough Univ., Leics. LE113TU, England.

MANN, (Anthony) Phillip. British, b. 1942. Science fiction. Lectr., 1969–75, Sr. Lectr. 1975–84, and since 1984 Reader in Drama, Victoria Univ., Wellington. Assoc. Dir., Downstage Theatre, Wellington, since 1984. Lectr. in Drama, Humboldt State Univ., 1967–69; English Ed., Xin Hua News Agency, Beijing, 1978–80. *Publs:* The Eye of the Queen, 1982; Ben's Bed (for children), 1985; Master of Paxwax, 1986; The Fall

of the Families, 1987; Pioneers, 1988. Add: 22 Bruce Ave., Brooklyn, Wellington, New Zealand.

MANN, William (Somervell). British, b. 1924. Music. Radio broadcaster, since 1949; Assoc. Ed., Opera, since 1954. Music Critic, Cambridge Review, 1946–48; Asst. Music Critic, 1948–60, and Music Critic, 1960–82, The Times, London. *Publs:* Introduction to the Music of J.S. Bach, 1950; The Record Guide, 1955; Chamber Music, 1957; (co-ed.) The Analytical Concert Guide, 1957; (with F. Reizenstein) Let's Fake an Opera, 1958; Richard Strauss's Operas, 1964; (trans.) Wagner's The Ring, 1964; (trans.) Wagner's Tristan, 1968; The Operas of Mozart, 1977; Music in Time, 1982. Add: The Old Vicarage, Coleford, Bath BA3 5NG, England.

MANNE, Henry G. American, b. 1928. Economics, Law. Dean and Univ. Prof., George Mason Univ. Sch. of Law, since 1986. Admitted to the Bar of the State of Ill., and of the State of N.Y.; corporate law practice, Chicago, 1953–54; Asst. Prof. of Law, 1956–57, and Assoc. Prof. of Law, 1959–62, St. Louis Univ., Mo.; Assoc. Prof., 1962–64, and Prof. of Law, 1964–68, George Washington Univ., Washington, D.C.; Kenan Prof. of Law, Univ. of Rochester, N.Y., 1968–74; Distinguished Prof. of Law, and Dir., Law and Economics Center, Univ. of Miami, Coral Gables, Fla., 1974–80; Prof. of Law, and Dir., Law and Economics Center, Emory Univ., Atlanta, 1980–86. *Publs:* Insider Trading and the Stock Market, 1966; Supplementary Cases and Material for Business Association II, 1967; (with H.C. Wallich) The Modern Corporation and Social Responsibility, 1973; (ed.) Economic Policy and the Regulation of Corporate Securities, 1969; The Economics of Legal Relationships, 1975; (co-ed) Auto Safety Regulations, 1976; Medical Malpractice Guidebook: Law and Economics, 1985; (ed. with James Dorn) Economic Liberties and the Judiciary, 1987. Add: Sch. of Law, George Mason University, Fairfax, Va. 22030, U.S.A.

MANNERS, Alexandra. *See* **RUNDLE,** Anne.

MANNERS, Gerald. British, b. 1932. Geography. Prof. of Geography, University Coll. London, since 1980 (Reader, 1967–80). Gov., City Parochial Foundn., since 1977; Chmn., Sadler's Wells Foundation, since 1986 (Gov. since 1968). Lectr. in Economic Geography, University Coll. of Swansea, 1957–67. Chmn., Regional Studies Assn., 1981–84. *Publs:* The Geography of Energy, 1964, 1971; (ed. and contrib.) South Wales in the Sixties, 1964; The Changing World Market for Iron Ore, 1950–1980, 1971; (ed. with M. Chisholm) Spatial Policy Problems of the British Economy, 1971; (ed. and contrib.) Regional Development in Britain, 1972, 1980; (with J. McDivitt) Minerals and Men, 1974; Coal in Britain: An Uncertain Future, 1981; (with D. Morris) Office Policy in Britain, 1986. Add: Dept. of Geography, University Coll., London WC1, England.

MANNERS, Miss. *See* **MARTIN,** Judith.

MANNERS, Robert Alan. American, b. 1913. Anthropology/Ethnology. Prof. of Anthropology since 1961, and Levitz Prof. of Anthropology since 1972, Brandeis Univ., Waltham, Mass., now Emeritus (Lectr., 1952; Asst. Prof., 1952–56; Assoc. Prof., 1956–61; Chmn. of Dept. 1963–68). Instr. in Anthropology, Univ. of Rochester, N.Y., 1950–52. Ed.-in-Chief, American Anthropologist, 1973–75; Pres., Northeastern Anthropological Assn., 1978–79. *Publs:* People of Puerto Rico, 1956; (ed. with J. Duffy) Africa Speaks, 1961; (ed.) Process and Pattern in Culture, 1964; Contemporary Change in Traditional Societies, 1967; (ed. with D. Kaplan) Theory in Anthropology: A Sourcebook, 1968; (with D. Kaplan) Culture Theory, 1972; An Ethnological Report on the Hualapai Indians of Arizona, 1974; Havasupai Indians: An Ethnohistorical Report, 1974; Southern Paiute and Chemehuevi: An Ethnohistorical Report, 1974. Add: 134 Sumner St., Newton, Mass. 02159, U.S.A.

MANNING, David (John). British, b. 1938. Philosophy, Politics/Government. Sr. Lectr. in Politics, Univ. of Durham, since 1975. Prof. of Political Philosophy, Univ. of California at Fullerton, 1984–85; Prof. of History, Univ. of Madras, 1986. *Publs:* The Mind of Jeremy Bentham, 1968; Liberalism, 1976; (ed.) The Form of Ideology, 1980; The Place of Ideology in Political Life, 1984. Add: Dept. of Politics, Univ. of Durham, 48 Old Elvet, Durham DH1 3HY, England.

MANNING, Marsha. *See* **GRIMSTEAD,** Hettie.

MANNING, Rosemary. British, b. 1911. Novels/Short stories, Children's fiction, Children's non-fiction. *Publs:* Green Smoke, 1957; Dragon in Danger, 1959; Look Stranger (in U.S. as The Shape of Innocence), 1960; Dragon's Quest, 1961; The Chinese Garden, 1962; Man on a Tower, 1965; Heraldry, 1966; Boney Was a Warrior, 1966; (ed.) A Grain of Sand: Selections from Blake, 1967; The Rocking Horse, 1970; Railways and Railwaymen, 1977; A Dragon in the Harbour, 1980; Down by the Riverside, 1983; A Time and a Time, 1986; A Corridor of Mirrors (autobiography), 1987.   Add: 20 Lyndhurst Gardens, London NW3 5NR, England.

MANNING, S(tanley) A(rthur). British, b. 1921. Environmental science/Ecology, Natural history. Biology and mathematics teacher in various English independent schs., 1948–70; with local Govt. services, Cambridge, 1970–77. *Publs:* The Right Way to Understand the Countryside, 1948; Broadland Naturalist: The Life of Arthur H. Patterson, 1948; Trees and Forests, 1964; Bakers and Bread, 1964; A Ladybird Book of Butterflies, Moths and Other Insects, 1965; Systematic Guide to Flowering Plants of the World, 1965; The Insect World, 1971; The Woodland World, 1972; The Naturalist in South-East England, 1974; Nature in East Anglia, 1976; Portrait of Essex, 1977; Portrait of Cambridgeshire, 1978; Nature in the West Country, 1979; Portrait of Broadland, 1980. Add: 9 Eversley Ct., Cromer, Norfolk NR27 9HR, England.

MANOR, Jason. *See* **HALL,** Oakley.

MANSELL, Darrel (Lee, Jr.). American, b. 1934. Literature. Prof. of English, Dartmouth Coll., Hanover, N.H., since 1974 (Instr., 1962–64, Asst. Prof., 1964–68, and Assoc. Prof., 1968–74). Fulbright Scholar, Oxford Univ., England, 1961–62. *Publs:* The Novels of Jane Austen: An Interpretation, 1973. Add: English Dept., Dartmouth Coll., Hanover, N.H. 03755, U.S.A.

MANSERGH, Nicholas. Irish, b. 1910. History, Politics/Government. Research Prof. of Commonwealth Relations, Chatham House, 1947–53; Smuts Prof. of History of the British Commonwealth, Univ. of Cambridge, 1953–70; Fellow, 1955–69, and since 1979, and Master, 1969–79, St. John's Coll., Cambridge; Ed.-in-Chief, India Office Records, on The Transfer of Power in India, 1967–82. *Publs:* The Irish Free State: Its Government and Politics, 1934; The Government of Northern Ireland, 1936; The Commonwealth and the Nations, 1948; The Coming of the First World War, 1949; Survey of the British Commonwealth Affairs, vol. I, 1931–39, vol. II, 1939–52, 1958; Documents and Speeches on Commonwealth Affairs, 1931–1962, vols., 1953, 1963; South Africa 1906–1961, 1962; The Commonwealth Experience, 1969, 1982; The Irish Question, 3rd ed. 1975. Add: St. John's Coll., Cambridge, England.

MANSFIELD, Bruce Edgar. Australian, b. 1926. History, Biography. Visiting Prof., Univ. of Sydney, since 1986. Lectr., 1951–58, Sr. Lectr., 1958–64, and Assoc. Prof., 1964–65, Univ. of Sydney; Prof. of History, 1965–75, and Deputy Vice-Chancellor, 1976–85, Macquarie Univ., North Ryde, N.S.W. Ed., Journal of Religious History, 1959–87; Pres., Australian Historical Assn., 1977–78. *Publs:* Australian Democrat: The Career of Edward William O'Sullivan 1846–1910, 1965; Knox: A History of Knox Grammar School 1924–1974, 1974; Phoenix of His Age: Interpretations of Erasmus 1550–1750, 1979. Add: Dept. of History, Univ. of Sydney, Sydney, N.S.W. 2006, Australia.

MANSFIELD, Walter Kenneth. British, b. 1921. Engineering, Physics, Translations. Reader in Nuclear Engineering, Queen Mary Coll., Univ. of London, since 1966 (former Lectr., and Sr. Lectr.). *Publs:* Elementary Nuclear Physics, 1958; (trans.) Reactor Physics, by Schulten and Guth, 2 vols., 1967. Add: Queen Mary Coll., Mile End Rd., London E1 4NS, England.

MANSOOR, Menahem. American, b. 1911. History, Language/Linguistics, Biography. Sr. Education Officer, Jerusalem, 1946–49; Asst. Press Attaché, British Foreign Service, Tel Aviv, 1949–54; Research Fellow, Johns Hopkins Oriental Seminary, 1954–55; Prof. and Chmn., Dept. of Hebrew and Semitic Studies, Univ. of Wisconsin, Madison, 1955–77, and Prof. Emeritus since 1982. *Publs:* The Story of Irish Orientalism, 1944; First Semester Hebrew: Modern, 1957, rev. ed. 1972; First Semester Hebrew: Biblical, 1957, rev. ed. 1974; First Semester Arabic, 1959, 2nd rev. ed. 1969; General Survey of Hebrew Literature in Translation: The Biblical Period, 1959, rev. ed. 1966; English-Arabic Dictionary of Political, Diplomatic and Conference Terms, 1961; (ed. and trans.) The Thanksgiving Hymns, 1961; Say It Correctly in Arabic: Conversational Arabic, 1961; Concordance of the Thanksgiving Hymns, 1962; Say It Correctly in Hebrew: Conversational Hebrew, 1962; Biblical Archaeology: The Dead Sea Scrolls, vol. I, 1964; The Dead Sea Scrolls: College Textbook and Guide, 1964; Second Semester Arabic, 1964; Second Semester Hebrew: Modern, rev. ed. 1964; Selections from Exodus and

Leviticus, 1964; Legal and Documentary Arabic Reader, 2 vols., 1965; Selections from Genesis, rev. ed. 1966; Intermediate Modern Hebrew Reader, 1967; Modern Hebrew Conversation, 1967; Readings from the Book of Esther, 1968; Selections from Joshua, 1969; Readings from the Aramaic of Daniel and Ezra, 1971; Advanced Modern Hebrew Literature Readers, 2 vols., 1971; Newspaper Hebrew Reader, vol. I, 1971; Second Semester Hebrew, 1971; Political and Diplomatic History of the Arab World, 1900–1967, with Computerized Index, 7 vols., 1972; Basic Course in Standard Spoken Hebrew, 3 vols., 1973; (trans. and ed.) The Book of Direction to the Duties of the Heart, by Bahya Ibn Pakuda, 1973; The Arab World: Biographical Dictionary of the Arab World 1900–1967, 1975; Contemporary Hebrew, 1975; (ed. with J.N. McGovern and K.N. Schoville) The Book and the Spade, 1975; Jewish Cultural History, 2 vols., 1976; The Arab World: Documentary Study 1900–1967, 8 vols., 1978; Basic Course in Standard Arabic, 1978; Biblical Hebrew Step by Step, 1979; Biblical Hebrew Step by Step II, 1984. Add: 1225 Sweet Briar, Madison, Wisc. 53705, U.S.A.

MANTEL, Samuel J(oseph), Jr. American, b. 1921. Administration/Management. Prof. of Mgmt. and Quantitative Analysis since 1969, and Joseph S. Stern Prof. of Mgmt. since 1973, Univ. of Cincinnati, Ohio. Columnist, Gainsville Morning News, Ga., 1955–56, Asst. and Assoc. Prof. of Economics, 1956–69, and Dir., Economics-in-Action Prof., 1956–68, Case Western Reserve Univ., Cleveland, Ohio. *Publs:* Cases in Managerial Decisions, 1964; Project Management: A Managerial Perspective, 1985, 1989. Add: Dept. of Quantitative Analysis, Coll. of Business Admin., Univ. of Cincinnati, Cincinnati, Ohio 45221, U.S.A.

MAPES, Mary A. *See* **ELLISON,** Virginia Howell.

MAPLE, Eric William. British, b. 1915. Mythology/Folklore, Supernatural/Occult topics. Freelance writer, broadcaster, and lectr. on the occult and folklore. Consultant, Man, Myth and Magic (part-work), 1967–70. *Publs:* The Dark World of Witches, 1962; The Realm of Ghosts, 1964; The Domain of Devils, 1966; Magic, Medicine and Quackery, 1968; Superstition and the Superstitious, 1971; The Magic of Perfume, 1973; Witchcraft—The Story of Man's Quest for Psychic Power, 1973; The Ancient Art of Occult Healing, 1974; Incantations and Words of Power, 1974; Deadly Magic, 1976; Supernatural England, 1977; Ghosts: Monsters (children's book), 1978; The Secret Lore of Plants and Flowers, 1980; Old Wives' Tales, 1981. Add: 52 Buckingham Rd., Wanstead, London E11, England.

MAPLES, Evelyn Palmer. American, b. 1919. Children's fiction, Poetry. Freelance writer and ed., since 1981. Schoolteacher, 1937–38. Proofreader, 1953–63, and Ed., 1963–81, Herald Publishing House, Independence, Mo.; Ed., Independence Press, Mo., 1972–81. *Publs:* Norman Learns About the Sacraments, 1961; What Saith the Scripture?, 1961; Jomo, the Missionary Monkey, 1966; That Ye Love (poetry), 1971; Lehi, Man of God, 1972; The Brass Plates Adventure, 1972; Norman Learns About the Scriptures, 1972; The Many Selves of Ann-Elizabeth, 1973; Big Tree, 1983; What Do You Think of That?, 1983; A Story about You, 1983; The First Christmas, 1983; Jesus, 1983; Mr. Red Ears, 1983; Friends Come to the Door, 1983; Endnotes (poetry), 1989. Add: Rt. 1, Box 137, Niangua, Mo. 65713, U.S.A.

MAPP, Alf Johnson, Jr. American, b. 1925. History, Literature, Biography. Eminent Prof. of Creative Writing, English and American Literature and Journalism, Old Dominion Univ., Norfolk, since 1982 (Lectr., Instr., and Asst. Prof., 1961–73; Assoc. Prof., 1973–79; Prof., 1979–82). Member, Editorial Bd., Jamestown Foundn., since 1967. Editorial Writer, 1945–46, Assoc. Ed., 1946–48, and Editorial Chief, 1948–54, Portsmouth Star, Va.; News Ed., Editorial Writer, and Columnist, Virginian-Pilot, Norfolk, 1954–58. Member, Publs. Bd., Virginia Independence Bicentennial Commn., 1967–81. *Publs:* The Virginia Experiment: The Old Dominion's Role in the Making of America, 1957, 3rd ed., 1987; Frock Coats and Epaulets, 1963, 3rd ed. 1987; America Creates Its Own Literature, 1967; Just One Man, 1968; The Golden Dragon: Alfred the Great and His Times, 1974, 3rd ed. 1980; (co-author) Chesapeake Bay in the American Revolution, 1981; Thomas Jefferson: A Strange Case of Mistaken Identity, 1987; (co-author) Portsmouth: A Pictorial History, 1989; Constitutionalism, 1989. Add: Willow Oaks, 2901 Tanbark Lane, Portsmouth, Va. 23703, U.S.A.

MAPP, Edward. American. Education, Film. Dean of Faculty, Borough of Manhattan Community Coll., City Univ. of New York, since 1977 (Prof. and Chmn. of the Library Dept., 1964–77). Library Asst., New York Public Library, NYC, 1948–55; teacher of Library and English in public schs., Brooklyn, N.Y., 1957–64. *Publs:* (compiler) Books for

Occupational Education Programs: A List for Community Colleges, Technical Institutes and Vocational Schools, 1971; Blacks in American Films: Today and Yesterday, 1972; (ed.) Puerto Rican Perspectives, 1974; (compiler) Directory of Blacks in the Performing Arts, 1978. Add: c/o Scarecrow Press, Inc., 52 Liberty St., Box 4167, Metuchen, N.J. 08840, U.S.A.

MARANDA, Pierre. Canadian, b. 1930. Anthropology/Ethnology, Mythology/Folklore, Language/Linguistics (semiotics, semiography), Information Science/Computers. Prof. of Anthropology, Univ. of British Columbia, Vancouver, (Faculty member since 1969); Research Prof., Univ. Laval, Quebec, since 1975. Research Fellow, Harvard Univ., Cambridge, Mass., 1964–68; Research Dir., Ecole Pratique des Hautes Etudes, Paris, 1968–69. Visiting Prof., College de France, Paris, 1975, and Universidade Federal Rio de Janeiro, 1983. *Publs:* (with E.K. Maranda) Structural Models in Folklore, 1962; (ed. with J. Pouillion) Echanges et Communications, 2 vols., 1970; (ed. with E.K. Maranda) Structural Analysis of Oral Tradition, 1971; (with E.K. Maranda) Structural Models in Folklore and Transformational Essays, 1971; (ed.) Mythology, 1972; Introduction to Anthropology: A Self-Guide, 1972; French Kinship: Structure and History, 1974; (ed.) Soviet Structure Folkloristics, vol. 1, 1974, (ed.) Symbolic Production Symbolique, 1977; (ed.) The Social Appropriation of Logic, 1978; Dialogue conjugal, 1985; Discan: A Computer System for Content and Discourse Analysis, 1987. Add: Dept. d'Anthropologie, Univ. Laval, Quebec G1K 7P4, Canada.

MARCH, Hilary. *See* **PULVERTAFT,** Lalage.

MARCH, N(orman) H(enry). British, b. 1927. Chemistry, Physics. Coulson Prof. of Theoretical Chemistry, and Head of the Dept., Oxford Univ., and Fellow of University Coll., Oxford, since 1977. Consultant, Theoretical Physics Div., Atomic Energy Research Establishment, Harwell, since 1968; Chmn., Solid-State Advisory Cttee., Intnl. Centre for Theoretical Physics, Trieste. Prof. of Physics, Univ. of Sheffield, 1961–71; Prof. of Theoretical Solid-State Physics, Blackett Lab., Imperial Coll., London, 1972–77. Chmn., Solid State Sub-Cttee., Meetings Cttee., Inst. of Physics, 1971–75. *Publs:* (with W.H. Young and S. Sampanthar) The Many-Body Problem in Quantum Mechanics, 1967; Liquid Metals, 1968; (with W. Jones) Theoretical Solid State Physics, 2 vols., 1973; (ed.) Orbital Theories of Molecules and Solids, 1974; Self-Consistent Fields in Atoms, 1975; (with M.P. Tosi) Atomic Dynamics in Liquids, 1976; (with M. Parrinello) Collective Effects in Solids and Liquids, 1983; (with S. Lundqvist) The Theory of Inhomogeneous Gas, 1983; (with M.P. Tosi) Coulomb Liquids, 1983; (with M.P. Tosi) Polymers, Liquid Crystals, and Low Dimensional Solids, 1984; (with R.A. Street and M.P. Tosi) Amorphous Solids and the Liquid State, 1985; Chemical Bonds Outside Metal Surfaces, 1986; (with P.N. Butcher and M.P. Tosi) Crystalline Semiconducting Materials and Devices, 1986; (with B.M. Deb) The Single-Particle Density in Physics and Chemistry, 1987; (with S. Lundquist and M.P. Tosi) Order and Chaos in Nonlinear Physical Systems, 1988; (with J.A. Alonso) Electrons in Metals and Alloys, 1989. Add: Elmstead, 6 Northcroft Rd., Englefield Green, Egham, Surrey, England.

MARCHAND, Leslie A(lexis). American, b. 1900. Literature. Prof. Emeritus, Rutgers Univ., New Brunswick, N.J., since 1966 (Instr. in English, 1937–42; Asst. Prof. of English, 1942–46; Asst. to the Acting Dean of the Coll. of Arts and Sciences, 1944–45; Assoc. Prof. of English, 1946–53; Prof. of English, 1953–66). Member, Bd. of Dirs., Keats-Shelley Assn. of America, since 1951; Vice Pres., Byron Soc. Asst. in English, Univ. of Washington, Seattle, 1920–23; Prof. of English and French, Alaska Agricultural Coll. and Sch. of Mines (now Univ. of Alaska) 1923–27, 1934–35; Taught English in Extension, Columbia Univ., NYC, 1928–34; Lectr. in English, Columbia Coll. of Pharmacy, 1936–37; Night Wire Filing Ed., Associated Press, Newark Bureau, N.J., and miscellaneous editorial work for Encore mag., Pocket Books, and Thomas Y. Crowell, 1943;44. *Publs:* The Athenaeum: A Mirror of Victorian Culture, 1941; (ed.) Letters of Thomas Hood from the Dilke Papers in the British Museum, 1945; (ed.) Selected Poetry of Lord Byron, 1951, 1967; Byron: A Biography, 3 vols., 1957; (ed.) Lord Byron: Don Juan, 1958; Byron's Poetry: A Critical Introduction, 1965; Byron: A Portrait, 1970; Byron's Letters and Journals, 12 vols., 1973–82; Lord Byron: Selected Letters and Journals, 1982. Recipient of Ivan Sandrof Award, National Book Critics Circle, 1982. Add: 1551 Beach Rd., Apt. 301, Englewood, Fla. 34223, U.S.A.

MARCHANT, Catherine. *See* **COOKSON,** Catherine.

MARCHANT, Tony. British, b. 1959. Plays/Screenplays. *Publs:* Thick as Thieves, 1982; Welcome Home, Raspberry, The Lucky Ones,

1983; The Attractions, 1988. Add: c/o Lemon and Durbridge Ltd., 24 Pottery Lane, London W11 4LZ, England.

MARCUS, Frank. British, b. 1928. Plays/Screenplays. Regular contrib. to Plays and Players mag., London, and Dramatists' Guild Quarterly, NYC. Actor, dir., and scenic designer, Unity Theatre, London; Founder, Intnl. Theatre Group; Theatre Critic, The Sunday Telegraph, 1968–78. *Publs:* (adaptor) Merry-Go-Round, 1953; The Formation Dancers, 1964; The Killing of Sister George, 1965; Mrs. Mouse, Are You Within?, 1969; The Window, 1970; Blank Pages, 1972; Blind Date, 1977; Notes on a Love Affair, 1972; Beauty and the Beast, 1976; (adaptor) The Guardsman, 1978; (adaptor) The Weavers, 1980; (adaptor) Anatol, 1982; (adaptor) La Ronde, 1982. Add: 8 Kirlegate, Meare, nr. Glastonbury, Somerset BA6 9TA, England.

MARCUS, Harold G. American, b. 1936. History, International relations/Current affairs. Prof. of History, Michigan State Univ., East Lansing, since 1974 (Assoc. Prof. of History, 1968–74). Asst. Prof. of History, Haile Sellassie I Univ., Addis Ababa, Ethiopia, 1961–63; Asst. Prof. of History, Howard Univ., Washington D,C., 1963–68. *Publs:* The Modern History of Ethiopia and the Horn of Africa, 1972; The Life and Times of Menilek II: Ethiopia 1844–1913, 1974; Ethiopia, Britain and the United States 1941–1977, 1983; Haile Sellassie I, The Formative Years 1892–1936, 1986. Add: Dept. of History, Michigan State Univ., East Lansing, Mich. 48824, U.S.A.

MARCUS, Stanley. American, b. 1905. Autobiography/Memoirs/Personal. Chmn. of Bd. Emeritus, Neiman-Marcus, retail speciality store, Dallas, Tex. since 1977 (Secty., Treas., and Dir., 1926–28; Merchandise Mgr. of the Sport Shop, 1928–29; Merchandise Mgr. of All Apparel Div., 1929–35; Exec. Vice Pres., 1935–50; Pres., 1950–72; Chmn. of the Bd. and Chief Exec. Officer, 1973–74). Past Dir., Dallas Symphony Soc.; Past Pres., Dallas Museum of Art. *Publs:* Minding the Store, 1974; Quest for the Best, 1979; His and Hers, 1983. Add: 1 Nonesuch Rd., Dallas, Tex. 75214, U.S.A.

MARCUSE, Frederick Lawrence. Canadian, b. 1916. Psychology. Prof. of Psychology, Univ. of Manitoba, since 1972. Faculty member, Cornell Univ., Ithaca, N.Y., 1940–50; Prof. of Psychology, and Chmn., Grad. Student Admission and Financial Support, Washinghon State Univ., Pullman, 1950–72. *Publs:* Areas Psychology, 1955; Hypnosis: Fact and Fiction, 1960; Hypnosis Throughout the World, 1968; Humour Is No Laughing Matter, 1988. Add: Dept. of Psychology, Univ. of Manitoba, Winnipeg, Man. R3T 2N2, Canada.

MARDEN, Charles Frederick. American, b. 1902. Sociology. Instr., 1928–35, Asst. Prof., 1935–57, Assoc. Prof., 1957–62, and Prof. of Sociology, 1962–67, Rutgers Univ., New Brunswick, N.J.; Prof. of Sociology, Holy Cross Coll., Worcester, Mass., 1967–70. *Publs:* Rotary and Its Brothers, 1935; Minorities in American Society, 1952, 5th ed. (with Gladys Meyer) 1978. Add: Highwood Easton Ave., Somerset, N.J. 08873, U.S.A.

MARGENAU, Henry. American, b. 1901. Philosophy, Physics. Eugene Higgins Prof. of Physics and Natural Philosophy Emeritus, Yale Univ., New Haven, since 1969; Exec. Dir., Center for Integrative Education, New Rochelle, N.Y., since 1969; Ed., Found. of Physics, since 1969; Consultant to Argonne National Lab., Bureau of Standards, Avco Rand Corp., Social Science Research Council, National Research Council, General Electric Co., and Radiation Weapons Cttee. of the Lockheed Corp. Trustee, Connecticut Coll. Pres., Philosophy of Science Assn., 1954–64; Member, Cttee. Atomic Age, World Council of Churches, 1955–57. *Publs:* Foundations of Physics, 1936; Mathematics and Physics and Chemistry, vol. I, 1943; vol. II, 1964; Physics: Principles and Application, 1949, 1953; The Nature of Physical Reality, 1950; The Nature of Concepts, 1950; Open Vistas, 1961; Ethics and Science, 1964; The Scientist, 1965; Theory of Intermolecular Forces, 1969; Integrative Principles of Modern Thought, 1972; Physics and Philosophy: Selected Essays, 1978; Einstein's Space and Van Gogh's Sky, 1983; The Miracle of Existence, 1984. Add: 173 Westwood Rd., New Haven, Conn. 06515, U.S.A.

MARGOLIN, Victor. American, b. 1941. Art, Architecture, Design. Asst. Prof. of Design History, Univ. of Illinois, Chicago, since 1982. Ed. Bd., Design Issues: A Journal of History, Theory and Criticism, Chicago, since 1987 (Ed., 1983–86). Visiting Lectr., Univ. of Illinois at Champaign-Urbana, 1981–82. *Publs:* American Poster Renaissance: The Great Age of Poster Design 1890–1900; (with Ira and Vivian Brichta) The Promise and the Product: 200 Years of American Advertising Posters; (ed.) Propaganda: The Art of Persuasion, World War II; (ed.) Design Discourse: History, Theory, Criticism. Add: 1207 Leonard, Evanston, Ill. 60201, U.S.A.

MARGOLIS, Diane Rothbard. American, b. 1933. Administration/Management, Public/Social administration, Women. Asst. Prof., Dept. of Sociology, Univ. of Connecticut, Stamford, since 1976. Instr., Dept. of Sociology, Univ. of New Haven, Conn., 1971–72, and Div. of Social Sciences, State Univ. of New York at Purchase, 1973–74. *Publs:* (with Richard J. Margolis) How the Federal Government Builds Ghettos, 1965; (with Richard J. Margolis) Who Shall Wear the Badge?, 1971; The Managers: Corporate Life in America, 1979; Women's Organizations in the Public Service: The Next Decade, 1980. Add: c/o Morrow, 105 Madison Ave., New York, N.Y. 10016, U.S.A.

MARGOLIS, Joseph. American, b. 1924. Art, Philosophy. Prof. of Philosophy, Temple Univ., Philadelphia, Pa., since 1968. Head, Dept. of Philosophy, Univ. of Western Ontario, London, 1965–67; member of faculty, Univ. of Toronto, Ont., 1967–68; Visiting Prof., New York Univ., NYC, 1970–71. Pres., American Soc. of Aesthetics, 1987–89. *Publs:* (ed.) Philosophy Looks at the Arts, 1962, 3rd ed. 1981; The Language of Art and Art Criticism, 1965; Psychotherapy and Morality, 1966; (ed.) Contemporary Ethical Theory, 1966; (ed.) An Introduction to Philosophical Inquiry, 1968, 1978; (ed.) Fact and Existence, 1969; Values and Conduct, 1971; Knowledge and Existence, 1973; Negativities: The Limits of Life, 1975; Persons and Minds, 1978; Art and Philosophy, 1980; Philosophy of Psychology, 1984; Culture and Cultural Entities, 1984; Pragmatism Without Foundations, 1986; Psychology: Designing the Discipline, 1986; Science Without Unity, 1987; Texts without Referents, 1988. Add: Dept. of Philosophy, Temple Univ., Philadelphia, Pa. 19100, U.S.A.

MARIAH, Paul. American, b. 1937. Poetry. Founder and Co-Ed., ManRoot Mag., since 1969; Mental Health Therapist, Baker Places, since 1972. Poetry Ed., Van Guard Mag., 1967–68, and Vector Mag., 1968–69; Teachers' Asst. in English, San Francisco State Coll., 1969–70; Project Scheduler and Research Asst., The New Kinsey Study, Indiana Univ., 1969–70; former Secty. to Kay Boyle, and to Robert Duncan. Member, 1969–70, and Pres., 1972, Council of Religion and the Homosexual, San Francisco. *Publs:* Folio: Diana, 1968; Personae Non Gratae, 1971; The Soon Ring, 1973; Letter to Robert Duncan While Bending the Bow, 1974; (ed.) A Jack Spicer Reader, 1975; Apparitions of a Black Pauper's Suit, 1976; (ed.) New Voices of the Seventies, 1977; (ed.) Collected Poems of Amnesia Glasscock, by John Steinbeck, 1977; (ed.) North of Manhattan: Collected Poems, Ballads, and Songs 1954–1975, by Jack Micheline, 1977; (ed.) Odes for Odd Occasions, by James Broughton, 1977; This Light Will Spread: Selected Poems 1960–1975, 1978; (ed. and co-trans.) Complete Poems of Jean Genet, 1981; (ed. and co-trans.) Appogiatures, by Jean Cocteau, 1983; (with Robert Bertholf—) Robert Duncan: A Complete Bibliography, 1983. Add: c/o Man Root, Box 762, Boyes Hot Springs, Calif. 95416, U.S.A.

MARIN, Alfred. *See* **COPPEL,** Alfred.

MARINO, Susan. *See* **ELLIS,** Julie.

MARK, Jan(et Marjorie). British, b. 1943. Children's fiction. Arts Council Writer Fellow, Oxford Polytechnic, 1982–84. *Publs:* Thunder and Lightening, 1976; Under the Autumn Garden, 1977; The Ennead, 1978; Divide and Rule, 1979; The Short Voyage of the Albert Ross, 1980; Nothing to Be Afraid Of, 1980; Hairs in the Palm of the Hand, 1981; Aquarius, 1982; The Dead Letter Box, 1982; The Long Distance Poet, 1982; Handles, 1983; Feet, 1983; Childermas (adult), 1984; At the Sign of the Dog and Rocket, 1985; Trouble Half-Way, 1985; Frankie's Hat, 1986; Out of the Oven, 1986; Zeno Was Here (adults), 1987; Dream House, 1987; Enough Is Too Much Already, 1988. Add: 98 Howard St., Oxford OX4 3BY, England.

MARKANDAYA, Kamala (Purnalya). Indian, b. 1924. Novels/Short stories. Former journalist. *Publs:* Nectar in a Sieve, 1954; Some Inner Fury, 1955; A Silence of Desire, 1960; Possession, 1963; A Handful of Rice, 1966; The Coffer Dams, 1969; the Nowhere Man, 1972; Two Virgins, 1973; The Golden Honeymoon, 1977; Pleasure City, 1982. Add: Chatto and Windus, 30 Bedford Sq., London WC1B 3RP, England.

MARKFIELD, Wallace (Arthur). American, b. 1926. Novels/Short stories. Film Critic, New Leader, NYC, 1954–55. *Publs:* To an Early Grave, 1964; Teitlebaum's Window, 1970; You Could Live if They Let You, 1974; Multiple Orgasms (short stories), 1977. Add: c/o Alfred A. Knopf Inc., 201 East 50th St., New York, N.Y. 10022, U.S.A.

MARKHAM, Robert. *See* **AMIS,** Kingsley.

MARKO, Katherine D(olores). American, b. 1913. Children's fiction. *Publs:* The Sod Turners, 1970; God, When Will I Ever Belong?, 1979; Whales, Giants of the Sea, 1980; How the Wind Blows, 1981, God, Why Did Dad Lose His Job?, 1982; Away to Fundy Bay, 1985. Add: 471 Franklin Blvd., Elgin, Ill. 60120, U.S.A.

MARKOOSIE, Canadian, b. 1942. Children's fiction. Pilot, Atlas Aviation, Resolute, Can., 1969–75; Translator, Northern Quebec Innuit Assn., Montreal and Port Harrison, 1975–76. *Publs:* Harpoon of the Hunter, 1970. Add: c/o McGill-Queen's Univ. Press, 855 Sherbrooke St. W., Montreal, Que. H3A 2T7, Canada.

MARKOVIC, Vida E. Yugoslavian, b. 1916. Literature. Prof. Emeritus of Modern Literature, Univ. of Belgrade, since 1981 (—joined faculty in 1947; Prof. of English and Head of Dept., 1960–70; Prof. of Mod Literature, 1970–81); Head of English Dept., Univ. of Nis, Yugoslavia, since 1971. Member, Intnl. Assn. of Univ. Professors of English (IAUPE), and on IAUPE Intnl. Consultative Cttee., since 1974; Member of Intnl. Federation of Modern Languages and Literatures; Member, Editors Bd., New Literary History, Charlottesville, Va. Visiting Prof. in Dept. of English at various universities in Yugoslavia, 1961–71, and at Univ. of Novi Sad, 1963–65; Visiting Fellow, Princeton Univ., 1965–66; Lectr., Bryn Mawr Coll. and Simon Frazer Univ., 1966; Visiting Prof., Univ. of Oregon, 1967, 1969; Fellow, Folger Shakespeare Library, 1973. *Publs:* Engleski roman XX, veka, vol. I, 1963, 1968, vol. II, 1965, 1977; Lion in the Garden: Interviews with William Faulkner 1926–62, 1968; The Reputation of Galsworthy in England, 1969; The Changing Face, 1970; Podeljena licnost, 1970; Raskol izmedju reci i igre (Rift Between Word and Play), 1977; Prilog epistemologiji knjizevnosti (Towards an Epistemology of Literature), 1978; Nezaustavljeno vreme (Time Never Stops) (novel), 1989. Add: 29 Laze Simica, 11000 Belgrade, Yugoslavia.

MARKS, Stan(ley). Australian (b. British), b. 1929. Novels/Short stories, Plays/Screenplays, Cultural/Ethnic topics. Former journalist and foreign corresp. for various newspapers in Australia, Canada and England; Supvr. of Publicity, A.B.C., Melbourne, 1958–64; Public Relations Officer, Trans Australian Airlines, 1965–67; Public Relations Mgr., Australian Tourist Commn., Melbourne, 1969–85. *Publs:* God Gave You One Face (novel), 1964; Is She Fair Dinkum?, 1967; Graham Is An Aboriginal Boy, 4th ed. 1969; Moose Who Sailed with Captain Cook, 1970; When A Wife Strikes (television and stage play), 1971; Animal Olympics, 1972; Rarua Lives in Papua New Guinea, 1973; Fifty Years of Achievement, 1974; Katut Lives In Bali, 1977; St. Kilda Sketchbook, 1980; Malvern Sketchbook, 1980; Welcome to Australia, 1985; Out and About in Melbourne, 1988. Add: 348 Bambra Rd., South Caulfield, Melbourne, Vic., Australia 3162.

MARKSON, David M. American, b. 1927. Novels/Short stories, Plays/Screenplays, Literature. Ed., Dell Books, NYC, 1952–53, and Lion Books, NYC, 1954–55; Fellow, Centro Mexicano de Escritores, Mexico, 1960–61; member of faculty, Long Island Univ., Brooklyn, N.Y., 1964–66, and Columbia Univ., NYC, 1979–87. *Publs:* Epitaph for a Tramp, 1959; Epitaph for a Dead Beat, 1961; (ed.) Great Tales of Old Russia, 1963; Miss Doll, Go Home, 1965; The Ballad of Dingus Magee, 1966; Going Down, 1970; Face to the Wind (screenplay), 1974; Springer's Progress, 1977; Malcolm Lowry's Volcano, 1978; Wittgenstein's Mistress, 1988. Add: 215 W. 10th St., N.Y., N.Y. 10014, U.S.A.

MARKSTEIN, George. British, b. 1929. Mystery/Crime/Suspense. Has worked as a military correspondent and feature writer, and in television as a story consultant, script ed. and series writer. *Publs:* The Cooler, 1974; The Man from Yesterday, 1976; Chance Awakening, 1977; The Goering Testament, 1978; Tara Kane (non-mystery novel), 1978; Traitor for a Cause, 1979; Ultimate Issue, 1981; Ferret, 1983; Soul Hunters, 1986. Add: New English Library, Mill Rd., Dunton Green, Sevenoaks, Kent TN13 2YA, England.

MARKUS, Julia. American, b. 1939. Novels/Short stories. Adjunct Prof., Hofstra Univ., New York, since 1981. Asst. Ed., Browning Inst. Studies, since 1973. *Publs:* La Mora (novel), 1976; A Patron of the Arts (novella), 1977; (ed.) Casa Guidi Windows, by Elizabeth Barrett Browning, 1977; Uncle (novel), 1978; American Rose (novel), 1981; Friends along the Way, 1985; Siding with Nola Neitherland, 1989. Add: c/o Houghton Mifflin Co., 2 Park St., Boston, Mass. 02108, U.S.A.

MARLAND, Michael. British, b. 1934. Education. Headmaster, North Westminster Community Sch., London, since 1980. Hon. Prof.

of Education, Univ. of Warwick, Coventry: Member of the Exec., National Book League; Gen. Ed., Student Drama Series, Blackie and Son Ltd., London, since 1966, Imprint Books, Longman Group Ltd., London, since 1967, and Heinemann Organisation in Schs. series, since 1968. Head of the English Dept., 1964–68, and Dir. of Studies, 1968–71, Crown Woods Sch., London; Headmaster, Woodberry Down Comprehensive Sch., London, 1971–79. *Publs:* (ed.) Spotlight, 1966; (compiler) Pictures for Writing, 1967; Following the News, 1967; Towards the New Fifth, 1969; Peter Grimes (play), 1971; (co-ed.) The Practice of English Teaching, 1971; Head of Department, 1971; Pastoral Care, 1974; The Question of Advertising, 1974; Craft of the Classroom, 1975; Language Across the Curriculum, 1977; Minority Experience, 1978; Pressures of Life, 1978; Education for the Inner City, 1980; Departmental Management, 1981; Sex Differentiation and Schooling, 1983; Short Stories For Today, 1984; Meetings and Partings, 1984; School Management Skills, 1985. Add: 22 Compton Terr., London N1 2UN, England.

MARLATT, Daphne (née Buckle). Canadian, b. 1942. Poetry, Literary criticism (Theory), Novels. Member, Tessera feminist editorial collective, since 1983; Contrib. Ed., West Coast Review, since 1988. Instr. in English, Capilano Coll., North Vancouver, 1968, 1973–76; Writer-in-Residence, Univ. of Manitoba, 1982, and Univ. of Alberta, 1985–86; Ruth Wynn Woodward Prof. in Women's Studies, Simon Fraser Univ., Vancouver, 1988–89. Poetry Ed., Capilano Review, Vancouver, 1973–76; Ed., with Paul de Barros, Periodics, Vancouver, 1977–81; Contributing Ed., Island, 1981–84, and Brick, 1985–87. *Publs:* Frames of a Story (poetry), 1968; leaf leaf's (poetry), 1969; Rings (poem narrative), 1971; Vancouver Poems, 1972; Steveston (poetry), 1974, 1984; (ed.) Steveston Recollected: A Japanese-Canadian History, 1975; Our Lives (poetry), 1975, 1979; Zocalo (novel), 1977; The Story, She Said (poetry), 1977; (ed. with Carole Itter) Opening Doors: Vancouver's East End, 1979; Selected Writing: Net Work, 1980; What Matters: Writing 1968–1970, 1980; Here and There (poetry), 1981; How Hug a Stone (poetry), 1983; Touch to My Tongue (poetry and theory), 1984; Ana Historic (novel), 1988; (with Betsy Warland) Double Negative (poetry), 1988. Add: 2533 W. 5th Ave., Vancouver, B.C. V6K 1S9, Canada.

MARLOR, Clark Strang. American, b. 1922. Art, Speech/Rhetoric. Prof., Adelphi Univ., Garden City, N.Y., since 1956, Emeritus since 1984. Instr., Kalamazoo Coll., Mich., 1946–47; Instr., Miami Univ., Oxford, Ohio, 1947–50; Instr., Queens Coll., City Univ. of New York, Flushing, N.Y., 1950–55. *Publs:* (with D. Mulgrave and E.E. Baker) Bibliography of Speech and Allied Areas, 1962; A History of the Brooklyn Art Association with an Index of Exhibitions, 1970; The Society of Independent Artists: The Exhibition Record, 1917–1944, 1984. Add: 295 Sterling Pl., Brooklyn, N.Y. 11238, U.S.A.

MARLOW, Joyce. Pseud. for Joyce Mary Connor. British, b. 1929. Novels/Short stories, Children's fiction, History. Professional actress, 1950–65. *Publs:* The Man with the Glove, 1964; A Time to Die, 1966; Billy Goes to War, 1967; The House on the Cliffs, 1968; The Peterloo Massacre, 1969; The Tolpuddle Martyrs, 1971; Captain Boycott and the Irish, 1973; The Life and Times of George I, 1973; The Uncrowned Queen of Ireland, 1975; Mr. and Mrs. Gladstone, 1977; Kings and Queens of Britain, 1977; Kessie, 1985; Sarah, 1987. Add: 109 St. Albans Rd., Sandridge, St. Albans AL4 9LH, England.

MARLOWE, Derek. British, b. 1938. Novels/Short stories, Mystery/Crime/Suspense, Plays/Screenplays. *Publs:* Scarecrow (play), 1961; A Dandy in Aspic, 1966; The Memoirs of Venus Lackey, 1968; A Single Summer with L.B.: The Summer of 1816, 1969 (in U.S. as A Single Summer with Lord B, 1970); Echoes of Celandine, 1970, as The Disappearance, 1977; Do Your Remember England?, 1972; Somebody's Sister, 1974; Nighshade, 1975; The Rich Boy from Chicago, 1980; Nancy Astor (novelization of TV play), 1982. Add: c/o Fraser & Dunlop Scripts Ltd., The Chambers, Chelsea Harbour, Lots Rd., London SW10 0XD, England.

MARLOWE, Hugh. See **PATTERSON,** Henry.

MARLOWE, Stephen. Has also written as Milton Lesser, Andrew Frazer, Jason Ridgway, and C.H. Thames. American, b. 1928. Mystery/Crime/Suspense, Science fiction/Fantasy. Member, Bd. of Dirs., Mystery Writers of America. *Publs:* mystery novels—Catch the Brass Ring, 1954; Turn Left for Murder, 1955; Model for Murder, 1955; The Second Longest Night, 1955; Dead on Arrival, 1956; Mecca for Murder, 1956, (as C.H. Thames) Violence Is Golden, 1956, Killers Are My Meat, 1957; Murder Is My Dish, 1957; Trouble Is My Name, 1957; (as Jason Ridgway) West Side Jungle, 1958; Violence Is My Business, 1958; Terror Is My Trade, 1958; Blond Bait, 1959; (with Richard S. Prather)

Double in Trouble, 1959; (as Andrew Frazer) Find Eileen Harden—Alive!, 1959; Passport to Peril, 1959; Homicide Is My Game, 1959; (as Jason Ridgway) Adam's Fall, 1969; Danger Is My Line, 1960; Death Is My Comrade, 1960; (as Andrew Frazer) The Fall of Marty Moon, 1960; Peril Is My Pay, 1960; Manhunt Is My Mission, 1961; (as Jason Ridgway) People in Class Houses, 1961; Jeopardy Is My Job, 1962; (as Jason Ridgway) Hardly a Man Is Now Alive, 1962; (as C.H. Thames) Blood of My Brother, 1963; Francesca, 1963; Drum Beat—Berlin, 1964; Drum Beat—Dominique, 1965; Drum Beat—Madrid, 1966; (as Jason Ridgway) The Treasure of the Cosa Nostra, 1966; The Search for Bruno Heidler, 1966; Drum Beat—Erica, 1967; Come Over, Red Rover, 1968; Drum Beat—Marianne, 1968; The Summit, 1970; The Man With No Shadow, 1974; The Cawthorn Journals, 1975, in U.K. paperback as Too Many Chiefs, 1977; Translation, 1976; The Valkyrie Encounter, 1978; 1956, 1981; Deborah's Legacy, 1983; science fiction novels—(as Milton Lesser) Earthbound, 1952; (as Milton Lesser) The Star Seekers, 1953; (as Milton Lesser) Stadium Beyond the Stars, 1960; The Shining, 1963; (as Milton Lesser) Secret of the Black Planet (short stories), 1965; other—(as Milton Lesser) Spacemen Go Home, 1961; (as Milton Lesser) Lost Worlds and the Men Who Found Them (juvenile), 1962; (as Milton Lesser) Walt Disney's Strange Animals of Australia (juvenile), 1963. Add: c/o Campbell Thomson & McLaughlin, 31 Newington Green, London N16 9PU, England.

MARON, Margaret. American. Novels/Short stories, Mystery/Crime/Suspense. *Publs:* One Coffee With, 1981; Death of a Butterfly, 1984; Death in Blue Folders, 1985; Bloody Kin, 1985; The Right Jack, 1987; Baby Doll Games, 1988; Picture Them Dead, 1988. Add: c/o Charlotte Sheedy Agency, 145 W. 86th St., New York, N.Y. 10024, U.S.A.

MAROWITZ, Charles. American, b. 1934. Plays/Screenplays, Theatre. Artistic Dir., Open Space Theatre of Los Angeles, since 1982. Artistic Dir., Open Space Theatre, London, 1968–81. *Publs:* The Method as Means, 1961; (adaptor) The Marowitz Hamlet, 1965; (adaptor) Marlowe: Dr. Faustus, 1965; (ed. and contrib.) Theatre at Work, 1971; (ed. and contrib.) Encore Reader, 1970; A Macbeth, 1973; (ed. and contrib.) Open Space Plays, 1974; Confessions of a Counterfeit Critic, 1974; The Shrew, 1975; Artaud at Rodex, 1976; The Act of Being, 1977; The Marowitz Shakespeare, 1978; New Theatre Voices of the 50's and 60's, 1981; Sex Wars, 1982; Potboilers: Three Black Comedies, 1986; Prospero's Staff: Acting and Directing in the Contemporary Theatre, 1986; Disciples, 1987. Add: c/o Los Angeles Actors Theatre, 1089 N. Oxford Ave., Los Angeles, Calif. 90029, U.S.A.

MARR, David G(eorge). American, b. 1937. History, International relations/Current affairs, Politics/Government. Sr. Fellow, Research Sch. of Pacific Studies, Australian National Univ., Canberra, since 1975. Lectr. in History, Univ. of California, Berkeley, 1968–69; Asst. Prof. of Vietnamese Studies, Cornell Univ., Ithaca, N.Y., 1969–72, Co-dir., Indochina Resource Center, Washington, D.C., and Berkeley, 1971–75. *Publs:* Vietnamese Anticolonialism 1885–1925, 1971; Tradition and Revolution in Vietnam, 1974; (co-ed.) Perception of the Past in Southeast Asia, 1979; Vietnamese Tradition on Trial 1920–1945, 1981; (co-ed) Southeast Asia in the 9th to 14th Centuries, 1986; (co-ed.) Postwar Vietnam: Dilemmas in Socialist Development, 1988. Add: Research Sch. of Pacific Studies, Australian National Univ., P.O. Box 4, Canberra, A.C.T. 2601, Australia.

MARRECO, Anne. See **ACLAND,** Alice.

MARR-JOHNSON, Diana (Julia). British, b. 1908. Novels/Short stories. *Publs:* Rhapsody in Gold; Bella North; Goodnight Pelican; Face of a Stranger, Faces My Fortune; Take a Golden Spoon; Three for a Wedding. Add: Flat 3, 14 Onslow Sq., London SW7, England.

MARSDEN, Peter Richard Valentine. British, b. 1940. Archaeology/Antiquities. Archaeologist, Guildhall Museum, Museum of London, since 1959. Lectr. on panel of Foyles Lecture Agency. *Publs:* A Roman Ship from Blackfriars, London, 1966; Londinium, 1971; The Wreck of the Amsterdam, 1974; Roman London, 1980; The Historic Shipwrecks of South-East England, 1987, The Roman Forum Site in London, 1987. Add: 21 Meadow Lane, Lindfield, W. Sussex RH16 2RJ, England.

MARSH, Derick Rupert Clement. Australian, b. 1928. Literature. Foundn. Prof. of English, La Trobe Univ., Melbourne, 1966–76, and since 1980. Lectr. and Sr. Lectr. in English, Univ. of Natal, S. Africa, 1954–60; Sr. Lectr. in English, Univ. of Sydney, 1961–66; Visiting Prof. of English, Queen's Univ., Kingston, Ont., 1964–65; Visiting Fellow, Wolfson Coll. Cambridge, 1976; Prof. and Head of the Dept. of English, Univ. of

Western Australia, 1976–80. *Publs:* The Recurring Miracle, 1962, 3rd ed. 1980; A Commentary on Shakespeare's Henry IV-Part I, 1964; (with K.G.W. Cross) Poetry: Reading and Understanding, 1966, 1970; Shakespeare's Hamlet, 1970; Passion Lends Them Power: A Study of Shakespeare's Love Tragedies, 1976. Add: English Dept., La Trobe Univ., Bundoora, Vic., Australia 3083.

MARSH, Jean. Pseud. for Evelyn Marshall; has also written as Lesley Bourne.British, b. 1897.Mystery/Crime/Suspense, Historical/Romance/Gothic, Children's fiction, History. Teacher in Halesowen until 1919, then journalist for Thomson and Leng groups until late 1920's; Contract Writer, Amalgamated Press group until 1939; radio broadcaster during World War II; Writer, Children's Hour for BBC-Radio until 1956. *Publs:* The Shore House Mystery, 1931; Murder Next Door, 1933; Death Stalks the Bride, 1943; On the Trail of the Albatross (adaptation of juvenile radio serial), 1950; Secret of the Pygmy Herd (adaptation of juvenile radio serial), 1951; Identity Unwanted, 1951; Death Visits the Circus, 1953; The Pattern Is Murder, 1954; Death among the Stars, 1955; Death at Peak Hour, 1957; (as Lesley Bourne) Trouble for Tembo (juvenile), 1958; Adventure with a Boffin (adaptation of a juvenile radio serial), 1962; The Valley of Silent Sound (adaptation of juvenile radio serial), 1962; Sand Against the Wind, 1973; Loving Partnership, 1978; The Family at Castle Trevissa, 1979; Bewdley, XV Century Sanctuary Town (non-fiction), 1979; All Saint's Centenary (non-fiction), 1980; Sawdust and Dreams, 1980; Mistress of Tanglewood, 1981; Unbidden Dream, 1981; The Rekindled Flame, 1982; This Foolish Love, 1982; The Divided Heart, 1983; Sanctuary for Louise, 1983; Quest for Love, 1984; Destiny at Castle Rock, 1985; Pride of Vallon, 1986; The Golden Parakeet, 1986; Loving Heritage, 1987; Island of Dreams, 1987; Mission to Argana, 1988. Add: The Spinney, Stourport Rd., Bewdley, Worcs. DY12 1BJ, England.

MARSH, John. British, b. 1904. Theology/Religion. Prof. of Christian Theology, Univ. of Nottingham, 1949–53; Chaplain and Tutor,1938–49, and Principal, 1953–70, Mansfield Coll., Oxford. *Publs:* The Living God, 1942; (ed.) Congregationalism Today, 1943; (co-author) Book of Congregational Worship, 1948; (co-ed.) Intercommunion, 1952; The Fulness of Time, 1952; The Significance of Evanston, 1954; (trans.) Stauffer: Theology of the New Testament, 1955; A Year with the Bible, 1957; Amos and Micah, 1969; (trans.) Bultmann: History of the Synoptic Tradition, 1963; Pelican Commentary on St. John, 1967; Jesus in His Lifetime, 1981. Add: 5 Diamond Ct., Moreton Rd., Summertown, Oxford OX2 7AX, England.

MARSH, Norman Stayner. British, b. 1913. Law. Queen's Counsel, 1967; Law Fellow, Univ. Coll., Oxford, 1946–60; Secty.-Gen., Intnl. Commn. of Jurists, Geneva, 1956–58; Dir., British Inst. of Intnl. and Comparative Law, London, 1960–65; Law Commissioner, London, 1965–78. *Publs:* The Rule of Law in a Free Society, 1960; Interpretation in a National and International Context, 1974; Public Access to Government-Held Information, 1987. Add: 13 North Side, Clapham Common, London SW4, England.

MARSH, Peter T. Canadian, b. 1935. History, Politics/Government, Theology/Religion. Prof. of History, Syracuse Univ., N.Y., since 1978 (Assoc. Prof., 1967–78; Chmn., Dept. of History, 1968–70; Dir., Honors Prog., 1978–86). Assoc. Ed., Journal of British Studies, 1978–84; Founder and Assoc. Ed., Canadian Journal of History. Instr., 1962–63, and Asst. Prof. of History, 1963–67, Univ. of Saskatchewan, Saskatoon. National Prog. Chmn., Conference on British Studies, 1975–77. *Publs:* The Victorian Church in Decline: Archbishop Tait and the Church of England 1868–1882, 1969; The Discipline of Popular Government, 1978; (ed.) The Conscience of the Victorian State, 1978; Contesting the Boundaries of Liberal and Professional Education: The Syracuse Experiment, 1988. Add: 917 Madison St., Apt. 116, Syracuse, N.Y. 13210, U.S.A.

MARSH, Robert Mortimer. American, b. 1931. Business/Trade/Industry, Sociology. Prof. of Sociology, Brown Univ., Providence, since 1968 (Assoc. Prof., 1967–68). Foreign Area Fellow, Ford Foundn., 1956–58; Instr. to Asst. Prof., Univ. of Michigan, 1958–61; Asst. Prof. of Sociology and Asian Studies, Cornell Univ., Ithaca, N.Y., 1961–65; Assoc. Prof. of Sociology, Duke Univ., Durham, N.C., 1965–67. *Publs:* The Mandarins: The Circulation of Elites in China, 1600–1900, 1961; Comparative Sociology: A Codification of Cross-Societal Analysis, 1967; (with Hiroshi Mannari) Modernization and the Japanese Factory, 1976;. (ed. with J. Michael Armer) Comparative Sociological Research in the 1960's and 1970's, 1982 ; (with Hiroshi Mannari) Organizational Change in Japanese Factories, 1988. Add: Dept. of Sociology, Brown Univ., Providence, R.I. 02912, U.S.A.

MARSHAK, Robert Eugene. American, b. 1916. Education, Physics, Autobiography/Memoirs/Personal. Univ. Distinguished Prof. of Physics, Virginia Polytechnic Inst., Blacksburg, since 1979. Chmn. and Harris Prof., Dept. of Physics and Astronomy, 1950–64, and Distinguished Univ. Prof., 1964–70, Univ. of Rochester, N.Y.; Pres., City Coll. of New York, 1970–79. *Publs:* (with E.C. Nelson and L.I. Schiff) Our Atomic World, 1946; Meson Physics, 1952; (with E.C.G. Sudarshan) Introduction to Elementary Particle Physics, 1961; (ed.) Perspectives in Modern Physics, 1966; (ed. with R.L. Cool) Advances in Particle Physics, vol. I, 1968; vol. II, 1969; (with Riazuddin and C.P. Ryan) Theory of Weak Interactions in Particle Physics, 1969; Problems and Prospects of an Urban Public University, 1973; Academic Renewal in the 1970's: Memoirs of a City College President, 1982. Add: Dept. of Physics, Virginia Polytechnic Inst., Blacksburg, Va. 24061, U.S.A.

MARSHALL, Donald Stanley. American, b. 1919. Anthropology/Ethnology, Language/Linguistics, Sex. Public Lectr. in Anthropology, U.S. Army, since 1949; Professional Lectr., Dept. of State Foreign Service Inst., since 1951; Owner and General Anthropologist, Far Lands House, Alexandria, Va., since 1959. Lectr. in Anthropology, Auckland Univ. Coll., N.Z., 1951–52; Research Anthropologist for Polynesia, Peabody Museum of Salem, Mass., 1953–58; made expeditions to Polynesia in 1951–53, 1954–55, 1957–59; did field work in Tahiti, 1960, 1961, 1963, 1967, and in other parts of the South Pacific and Southeast Asia, 1965–71. *Publs:* (ed.) Songs and Tales of the Sea Kings, 1957; Ra'ivavae: An Expedition to the Most Fascinating and Mysterious Island in Polynesia (in U.K. as Island of Passion, Ra'ivavae), 1961; (with J.F. Stimson) A Dictionary of Some Tuamotuan Dialects of the Polynesian Language, 1964; (ed.) Comprehensive Army Study on Thailand, 3 vols., 1968; Human Sexual Behavior, 1972. Add: Far Lands House, 3414 Halcyon Dr., Alexandria, Va. 22305, U.S.A.

MARSHALL, Edward. *See* **MARSHALL,** James.

MARSHALL, Elizabeth Margaret. Pseud.: Elizabeth Sutherland. Scottish, b. 1926. Novels/Short stories. Asst. Social Worker, Scottish Episcopal Church Social Service Bd., 1975–80. *Publs:* Lent Term, 1973; Seer of Kintail, 1974; Hannah Hereafter, 1976; The Eye of God, 1977; (ed., as Elizabeth Sutherland) The Prophecies of Brahan Seer, by Alexander MacKenzie, 1977; The Weeping Tree, 1980; Ravens and Black Rain, The Story of Highland Second Sight, 1985; (ed., as Elizabeth Sutherland) The Gold Key and the Green Life, 1986. Add: 17 Mackenzie Terr., Rosemarkie, Fortrose, Ross-shire, Scotland.

MARSHALL, Helen Edith. American, b. 1898. History, Biography. Teacher in public schs. in Kansas, Colorado and New Mexico, 1916–31; Instr., Univ. of New Mexico, Albuquerque, 1930–31; Prof. of History, and Head, Dept. of Social Science, Eastern New Mexico Coll., Portales, 1934–35; faculty member, Illinois State Univ., Normal, 1935 until retirement as Prof. of History in 1967. *Publs:* Dorothea Dix: Forgotten Samaritan, 1937; Grandest of Enterprises (history), 1956; The Eleventh Decade (history), 1967; Mary Adelaide Nutting: Pioneer of Modern Nursing, 1972. Add: 4-300 S. Heather Ridge Circle, Green Valley, Ariz., U.S.A.

MARSHALL, Henry. British, b. 1920. Plays, Songs, lyrics and libretti. Master-at-Arms to the Royal Academy of Dramatic Art, London; Ed., The Fight Director, mag. of the Soc. of British Fight Dirs. Former Pantomime Librettist, Theatre Royal, Windsor, the Alexandra Theatre, Birmingham, and the Playhouse Theatre, Salisbury. *Publs:* A Man Like Me (play), 1962; Stage Swordplay, 1977. Add: 56 Goldhurst Terr., London NW6 3HT, England.

MARSHALL, Jack. American b. 1937. Poetry. *Publs:* The Darkest Continent, 1967; Bearings, 1970; Floats, 1972; Bits of Thirst, 1974; Bits of Thirst and Other Poems and Translations, 1976; Arriving on the Playing Fields of Paradise, 1983; Arabian Nights, 1986. Add: 1056 Treat Ave., San Francisco, Calif. 94110, U.S.A.

MARSHALL, James (Edward). Also writes as Edward Marshall. American, b. 1942. Children's fiction. Freelance writer and illustrator, since 1970. French and Spanish teacher, Cathedral High School, Boston, 1968–70. *Publs:* George and Martha series, 6 vols., 1972–84; 1972; What's the Matter with Carruthers?, 1972; Yummers, 1972; Miss Dog's Christmas Treat, 1973; (with Harry Allard) The Stupids series, 3 vols., 1974–81; Willis, 1974; The Guest, 1975; Eugene, 1975; Sing Out, Irene, 1975; (with Harry Allard) Miss Nelson series, 3 vols., 1977–85; A Summer in the South, 1977; Portly McSwine, 1979; Taking Care of Carruthers, 1981; Rapscallion Jones, 1983; The Cut-Ups, 1984; Three Up a Tree,

1986; Merry Christmas, Space Case, 1986; Wings, 1986; Yummers Too, 1986; The Cut-Ups Cut Loose, 1987; George and Martha Round and Round, 1988; Fox on the Job, 1988; The Cut-Ups At Camp Custer, 1989. As Edward Marshall—Troll Country, 1980; Space Case, 1980; Three by Sea, 1981; Fox series, 6 vols., 1982–85. Add: c/o Sheldon Fogelman, 10 E. 40th St., New York, N.Y. 10016, U.S.A.

MARSHALL, James Vance. *See* **PAYNE,** Donald Gordon.

MARSHALL, Joanne. *See* **RUNDLE,** Anne.

MARSHALL, John. British, b. 1922. Transportation. Lectr. in Railway History, Extra-Mural Dept., Univ. of Manchester, 1970–80. *Publs:* The Lancashire and Yorkshire Railway, 3 vols., 1969–72; Guinness Book of Rail Facts and Feats, 1971, 3rd ed. 1979; Metre Gauge Railways in South and East Switzerland, 1974; Biographical Dictionary of Railway Engineers, 1978; Forgotten Railways: North West England, 1981; The Cromford and High Peak Railway, 1982; Guinness Factbook: Rail, 1985; Guinness Rail: The Records, 1985; The Guinness Railway Book, 1989; The Severn Valley Railway, 1989. Add: 24 Maypole Close, Bewdley, Worcs. DY12 1BZ, England.

MARSHALL, Margaret (Lenore). Also writes as Margaret L. Wiley. American, b. 1908. Intellectual history. Prof. Emeritus of English, City Univ. of New York, Brooklyn Coll., since 1971 (Instr., 1946–52; Asst. Prof., 1952–61; Assoc. Prof., 1961–66; Prof., 1966–71). *Publs:* The Subtle Knot: Creative Scepticism in 17th Century England, 1952; Creative Sceptics, 1966. Add: Fyfield Lodge, Fyfield Rd., Oxford OX2 6QE, England.

MARSHALL, Paule. American, b. 1929. Novels/Short stories. Staff Writer, Our World mag., 1953–56. *Publs:* Brown Girl, Brownstones, 1959; Soul Clap Hands and Sing (short stories), 1961; The Chosen Place, The Timeless People, 1969; Reena and Other Stories, 1983; Praisesong for the Widow, 1983. Add: 407 Central Park West, New York, N.Y. 10025, U.S.A.

MARSHALL, Rosalind Kay. British. History, Biography. Asst. Keeper I, Scottish National Portrait Gallery, since 1973. Assoc. Ed., Review of Scottish Culture, since 1985. *Publs:* The Days of Duchess Anne, 1973; Mary of Guise, 1977; Virgins and Viragos: A History of Women in Scotland 1080–1980, 1983; Queen of Scots, 1986; Bonnie Prince Charlie, 1988; Henrietta Maria, 1990. Add: Scottish National Portrait Gallery, 1 Queen St., Edinburgh, Scotland.

MARSHALL, (Sir) Roy. Barbadian/British, b. 1920. Law. Prof. of Law, Univ. of Sheffield, 1956–59; Vice-Chancellor, Univ. of West Indies, Jamaica, 1969–74; Secty.-Gen., Cttee. of Vice Chancellors and Principals of British Univs., 1974–79; Vice-Chancellor, Univ. of Hull, 1979–85. *Publs:* The Assignment of Choses in Action, 1950; (ed.) Theobald: On Wills, 12th ed., 1963; (with Nathan) A Casebook on Trusts, 1967. Add: Kirk House, Kirk Croft, Cottingham HU16 4AU, England.

MARSHALL, Tom. Canadian, b. 1938. Novels/Short stories, Poetry, Literature. Prof. of English, Queen's Univ., Kingston, Ont., since 1985 (Instr., 1964–66; Lectr., 1966–69; Asst. Prof., 1969–73; Assoc. Prof., 1973–85). Poetry Ed., The Canadian Forum, 1973–78. *Publs:* (with T. Eadie and C. Norman) The Beast with Three Backs (poetry), 1965; The Silences of Fire, 1969; (ed.) A .M. Klein, 1970; The Psychic Mariner: A Reading of the Poems of D.H. Lawrence, 1970; Magic Water, 1971; (ed. with D. Helwig) Fourteen Stories High, 1971; The Earth-Book, 1974; The White City, 1976; Rosemary Goal (novel), 1978; Harsh and Lovely Land: The Major Canadian Poets and the Making of a Canadian Tradition, 1979; The Elements, 1980; Playing with Fire, 1984; Dance of the Prticles, 1984; Glass Houses (short stories), 1985; Adele at the End of the Day (novel), 1987; Voices on the Brink (novel), 1989. Add: Dept. of English, Queen's Univ., Kingston, Ont. K7L 3N6, Canada.

MARSHALL, William (Leonard). Australian, b. 1944. Mystery/Crime/ Suspense. *Publs:* The Fire Circle, 1969; The Age of Death, 1970; The Middle Kingdom, 1971; Yellowthread Street, 1975; Gelignite, 1976; The Hatchet Man, 1976; Thin Air, 1977; Shanghai, 1979; Skulduggery, 1979; Sci Fi, 1981; Perfect End, 1981; War Machine, 1982; The Far Away Man, 1984; Roadshow, 1985; Head First, 1986; Manila Bay, 1986; Frogmouth, 1987; Whisper, 1988. Add: c/o Secker and Warburg, 81 Fulham Rd., London SW3 6RB, England.

MARSTEN, Richard. *See* **HUNTER,** Evan.

MARSZALEK, John F. American, b. 1939. History, Area studies (19th century U.S. and race relations). Prof. of History, Mississippi State Univ., Starkville, since 1980 (Assoc. Prof., 1973–80). Instr., Canisius Coll., Buffalo, N.Y., 1967–68; Asst. Prof., 1968–72, and Assoc. Prof. of History, 1972–73, Gannon Univ., Erie, Pa. *Publs:* Court Martial: A Black Man in America, 1972; A Black Businessman in White Mississippi 1886–1974, 1977; (ed.) The Diary of Miss Emma Holmes 1861–1866, 1979; Sherman's Other War: The General and the Civil War Press, 1981; Black Physician: Bringing Hope in Mississippi, 1985; Grover Cleveland, A Bibliography, 1988. Add: 108 Grand Ridge, Starkville, Miss. 39759, U.S.A.

MARTELL, James. *See* **BINGLEY,** David Ernest.

MARTELLARO, Joseph Alexander. American, b. 1924. Economics. Prof. of Economics, Northern Illinois Univ., DeKalb, since 1967 (Assoc. Dean, Grad Sch., 1969–73; Dean, 1973–74). Member, Intnl. Editorial Bd., Journal of Economics and Intnl. Relations. Chmn. for Economics, Indiana Univ. at South Bend, 1966–67. Special Chair, Prof. of Economics, National Taiwan Univ., 1988. *Publs:* Economic Development in Southern Italy, 1965; Perspectives for Teachers of Latin American Culture, 1970; Economic Reform in China, Hungary, and the USSR, 1989. Add: 1702 Margaret Lane, DeKalb, Ill. 60115, U.S.A.

MARTELLI, George Ansley. British, b. 1903. Novels/Short stories, History, Travel/Exploration/Adventure, Biography. With Royal Navy, 1921–29, and 1943–46; Chief Foreign Corresp., Morning Post, London, 1931–37; Head of Italian Region, Political Warfare Exec., U.K. Foreign Office, 1939–43; public relations consultant, 1950–55. *Publs:* Snotty, 1930; Italy Against the World, 1937; Whose Sea?, 1938; From Such a Seed, 1946; The Elveden Enterprise, 1952; Force Ten, 1958; Leopold to Lumumba, 1962; Agent Extraordinary, 1960; Jemmy Twitcher, 1962; Experiment in World Government, 1966; Livingstone's River, 1969; Robert's People, 1971. Add: Wooth Manor, Bridport, Dorset, England.

MARTIN, Boyd A. American, b. 1911. Politics/Government. William E. Borah Distinguished Prof. of Political Science, since 1970, and Dir., Inst. of Human Behavior, since 1970, Univ. of Idaho, Moscow (Instr. in Political Science, 1938–39; Instr., 1940–43; Asst. Prof., 1943–44; Assoc. Prof., 1944–47; Prof., 1947–70; Dean of Letters and Science, 1955–70). Acting Instr. in Political Science, Stanford Univ., Calif., 1939–40; Chmn., William E. Borah Foundn. on the Outlawry of War, 1947–55. *Publs:* The Direct Primary in Idaho, 1947; (with J.S. Roucek) Introduction to Political Science, 1950; (with F.H. Jonas) Western Politics, 1961, rev. ed. as Politics in the American West, 1969, supplement, 1971; State and Local Government in Idaho: A Reader, 1970; Recent Elections in Idaho: 1964–1970, 1975. Add: 516 Eisenhower, Moscow, Idaho 83843, U.S.A.

MARTIN, David. British, b. 1915. Novels/Short stories, Children's fiction, Poetry, Travel/Exploration/Adventure. Member of the Council, Australian Soc. of Authors. *Publs:* Battlefields and Girls, 1942; Tiger Bay, 1946; The Shoes Men Walk In, 1946; The Shepherd and the Hunter, 1946; The Stones of Bombay, 1949; Poems 1938/58, 1958; Spiegel the Cat, 1961; The Young Wife, 1962; The Hero of Too (in U.S. as The Hero of the Town), 1965; The King Between (in U.S. as The Littlest Neutral), 1966; The Gift, 1966; The Idealist, 1968; Where a Man Belongs, 1969; On the Road to Sydney, 1970; Hughie, 1971; Frank and Francesca, 1972; Gary, 1972; The Chinese Boy, 1974; The Cabby's Daughter, 1975; Mister P and His Remarkable Flight, 1975; The Devilish Mystery of the Flying Mum, 1977; The Man in the Red Turban, 1978; The Mermaid Attack, 1979; Peppino Says Goodbye, 1980; I Rhyme My Time, 1980; Armed Neutrality for Australia, 1984; The Girl Who Didn't Know Kelly, 1985; Fox on My Door, 1987; The Kitten Who Wouldn't Purr, 1987; Clowning Sim, 1988. Add: 28 Wood St., Beechworth, Vic. 3747, Australia.

MARTIN, David Alfred. British, b. 1929. Sociology, Theology/Religion. Prof. of Sociology, London Sch. of Economics, 1971–88 (Lectr., 1962–67; Reader, 1967–71). Univ. Prof. of Human Values, Southern Methodist Univ., Dallas, 1986–88. *Publs:* Pacifism, 1965; A Sociology of English Religion, 1967; (ed.) Anarchy and Culture: The Crisis in the Universities, 1968; The Religious and the Secular, 1969; (ed.) Fifty Key Words in Sociology, 1970; Tracts Against the Times, 1973; A General Theory of Secularization, 1978; The Dilemmas of Contemporary Religion, 1978; The Making and Breaking of the Image, 1978; (ed.) Crisis for Cranmer and King James, 1979; (ed.) No Alternative, 1981; Aspiring Flames, 1989; Divinity in a Grain of Bread, 1989. Add: London Sch. of Economics and Political Science, Aldwych, London WC2, England.

MARTIN, Ernest Walter. British. Country life/Rural societies, History,

Literature, Social Commentary/Phenomena, Sociology. Hon. Research Fellow in Rural Social Studies, Univ. of Exeter, since 1974; Fellow, Royal Historical Soc. *Publs:* (ed.) In Search of Faith, 1944; (ed.) The New Spirit, 1946; (ed.) The Countryman's Chap-Book, 1949; A Wanderer in the West Country, 1951; The Secret People, 1954; Dartmoor, 1958; Where London Ends, 1958; (ed.) Cobbett's Rural Rides, 1958; The Case Against Hunting, 1959; The Tyranny of the Majority, 1961; The Book of the Village, 1962; The Book of the Country Town, 1962; (ed.) Country Life in England, 1965; The Shearers and the Shorn, 1966; (ed.) Comparative Development in Social Welfare, 1972. Add: Editha Cottage, Black Torrington, Beaworthy, Devon, England.

MARTIN, F. David. American, b. 1920. Art, Humanities (general). John Howard Harris Prof. of Philosophy and Chmn., Bucknell Univ., Lewisburg, Pa., since 1968, Emeritus since 1983 (Asst. Prof., 1949–50; Assoc. Prof., 1950–56; Prof., 1956–83). Instr. in Humanities, Univ. of Chicago, 1947–49. *Publs:* Art and the Religious Experience, 1972; (with L.A. Jacobus) The Humanities Through the Arts, 1974, 3rd ed. 1982; Sculpture and Enlivened Space, 1981. Add: Dept. of Philosophy, Bucknell Univ., Lewisburg, Pa. 17837, U.S.A.

MARTIN, F(rancis) X(avier). Irish, b. 1922. History, Biography. Prof. of Medieval History, Univ. Coll., National Univ. of Ireland, Dublin, since 1962 (Asst. Lectr., 1959–62). Chmn., Council of Trustees, National Library of Ireland, since 1977. *Publs:* The Problem of Giles of Viterbo, 1469–1532, 1960; (ed. with J.A. Watt and J.B. Morrall) Medieval Studies presented to Aubrey Gwynn, 1961; Friar Nugent: A Study of Francis Lavalin Nugent, 1569–1635, 1962; (ed.) The Irish Volunteers, 1913–1915, 1963; (ed.) The Howth Gun-running, 1914: Recollections and Documents, 1964; (ed.) 1916 and University College, Dublin, 1966; (ed. with T.W. Moody) The Course of Irish History, 1967, 1984; (ed.) Leaders and Men of the Easter Rising, Dublin 1916, 1967; The 1916 Rising—Myth, Fact and Mystery, 1967; (ed. with F.J. Byrne) The Scholar Revolutionary: Eoin MacNeill, 1867–1945, and the Making of the New Ireland, 1973; (ed. with T.W. Moody and F.J. Byrne) A New History of Ireland, vol. III, 1974, vol. VIII, 1982, vol. IX, 1984, vol. IV, 1986, vol. II, 1987, vol. V, 1989; No Hero in the House: The Coming of the Normans to Ireland, 1977; (ed. with A.B. Scott) The Conquest of Ireland, by Giraldus Cambrensis, 1978; Lambert Simnel: The Crowning of a King at Dublin 24 May 1487, 1988. Add: Dept. of Medieval History, University Coll., Dublin 4; or, Augustinian House of Studies, Ballyboden, Dublin 16, Ireland.

MARTIN, Fredric. *See* **CHRISTOPHER,** Matt F.

MARTIN, Geoffrey Haward. British, b. 1928. History. Hon. Research Fellow, Loughborough Univ. of Technology, and University Coll. London, since 1987. Hon. General Ed., Suffolk Records Soc., since 1957; Chmn., British Records Assn., since 1982; Member, Royal Commn. on Historical Monuments (England), since 1987. Prof. of History, 1973–82, and Pro-Vice Chancellor 1979–82, Univ. of Leicester (Lectr. in History, 1952–66; Reader, 1966–73); Chmn. of the Bd., Leicester Univ. Press, 1975–82; Keeper of Public Records, 1982–88. Visiting Prof. of History, Carleton Univ., Ottawa, 1958–59 and 1967–68. Chmn., Commonwealth Archivists Assn., 1984–88; Vice-Pres., Royal Historical Soc., 1984–88. *Publs:* Early Court Rolls of the Borough of Ipswich, 1954; The Story of Colchester, 1959; The Town, 1961; (ed.) Royal Charters of Grantham, 1463–1688, 1963; (ed. with S. McIntyre) Bibliography of British and Irish Municipal History, 1972; (ed.) Ipswich Recognizance Rolls, 1294–1327, 1973. Add: Dept. of Library and Information Studies, Loughborough Univ., Loughborough, Leics. LE11 3TU, England.

MARTIN, Geoffrey John. British, b. 1934. Geography, Biography. Prof. of Geography, Southern Connecticut State Univ., New Haven, since 1966. Asst. Prof., Eastern Michigan Univ., Ypsilanti, 1959–65, and Wisconsin State Univ., Platteville, 1965–66; Natl. Science Foundation Scholar, 1984–85. *Publs:* Mark Jefferson: Geographer, 1968; Ellsworth Huntington: His Life and Thought, 1973; The Life and Thought of Isaiah Bowman, 1980; (with P.E. James) The Association of American Geographers: The First Seventy-Five Years, 1979; All Possible Worlds, 1981. Add: 189 Banks Rd., Easton, Conn. 06430, U.S.A.

MARTIN, George R(aymond) R(ichard). American, b. 1948. Science fiction/Fantasy. Freelance writer since 1978. Chess Tournament Dir., Continental Chess Assn., Mount Vernon, N.Y., 1973–75; Instr. of Journalism, Clarke Coll., Dubuque, Iowa, 1976–78, *Publs:* A Song for Lya and Other Stories, 1976; Song of Stars and Shadows (short stories), 1977; Dying of the Light, 1977; (ed.) New Voices in Science Fiction, 1-4, 1977–81; (with Lisa Tuttle) Windhaven, 1981; Sandkings, 1981; Fevre Drama,

1982; The Armageddon Rag, 1983; (co-ed.) The Science-Fiction Weight-Loss Book, 1983; Songs the Dead Men Sing, 1983; (ed.) The John W. Campbell Awards 5-6, 1984–86; Nightflyers, 1985; The Voyaging, 1986; (ed.) Night Visions, 1987. Add: 102 San Salvador, Santa Fe, N. Mex. 87501, U.S.A.

MARTIN, George Whitney. American, b. 1926. Institutions/Organizations, Music, Biography. Book Ed., The Opera Quarterly, since 1983. *Publs:* The Opera Companion: A Guide for the Casual Operagoer, 1961, 4th ed. 1988; Battle of the Frogs and Mice: An Homeric Fable, 1962, 1987; Verdi, His Music, Life, and Times, 1963, 3rd ed. 1983; The Red Shirt and the Cross of Savoy: The Story of Italy's Risorgimento, 1748–1871, 1969; Causes and Conflicts: The Centennial History of the Association of the Bar of the City of New York, 1870–1970, 1970; Madam Secretary: Frances Perkins, 1976; The Companion to Twentieth Century Opera, 1979, 2nd ed., 1984; The Damrosch Dynasty: America's First Family of Music, 1983; Aspects of Verdi, 1988. Add: 21 Ingleton Circle, Kennet Square, Penn. 19348, U.S.A.

MARTIN, Judith. Also writes as Miss Manners. American, b. 1938. Novels, Human relations, Humor/Satire. Syndicated columnist, United Feature Syndicate. Reporter and Critic, The Washington Post, 1960–83. *Publs:* The Name on the White House Floor (essays), 1973; Miss Manners' Guide to Excruciatingly Correct Behavior, 1982; Gilbert: A Comedy of Manners (novel), 1982; Miss Manners' Guide to Rearing Perfect Children, 1984; Common Courtesy, 1985; Style and Substance (novel), 1986. Add: c/o United Features Syndicate, 200 Park Ave., New York, N.Y. 10017, U.S.A.

MARTIN, Laurence (Woodward). British, b. 1928. International relations/Current affairs, Military/Defence. Vice–Chancellor, Univ. of Newcastle upon Tyne, since 1978. Member, Research Council, Georgetown Univ., Washington, D.C.; Member of Council, Inst. for the Study of Conflict, London; Dir., European-American Inst. for Security Research. Instr. in Political Science, Yale Univ., New Haven, Conn., 1955–56 Asst. Prof. of Political Science, Massachusetts Inst. of Technology, Cambridge, 1956–61; Assoc. Prof., Sch. of Advanced Intnl. Studies, Johns Hopkins Univ., Washington, D.C., 1961–64; Woodrow Wilson Prof. of Intnl. Politics, Univ. of Wales, 1964–68; Prof. and Head of the Dept. of War Studies, King's Coll., Univ. of London, 1968–77. *Publs:* (with Arnold Wolfers) The Anglo-American Tradition in Foreign Affairs, 1956; Peace Without Victory: Woodrow Wilson and the British Liberals, 1958, 1973; Neutralism and Non-Alignment, 1963; Diplomacy in Modern European History, 1966; The Sea in Modern Strategy, 1967; Ballistic Missile Defense and the Alliance, 1969; (with Robert Osgood) America and the World, 1970; Arms and Strategy, 1973; (co-author) Retreat from Empire: The First Nixon Administration, 1973; Strategy in the Nuclear Age, 1979; The Two-Edged Sword: Armed Force in the Modern World, 1982; Before the Day After, 1986; Armées et Arsenaux en Europe, 1986; The Changing Face of Nuclear Warfare, 1987. Add: Univ. of Newcastle upon Tyne, 6 Kensington Terr., Newcastle upon Tyne NE1 7RU, England.

MARTIN, Marjorie. American, b. 1942. Children's fiction, Poetry, Children's non-fiction. Poetry Ed., Town and Country tabloid, Manila, Ark., since 1971. Brooklyn Dir., American Poets Fellowship Soc., 1967–68; Co-Ed., with E. Martin, Garden of Poets, syndicated column, 1971–74. *Publs:* A Friend Asked Me, 1968; The Span of Dreams, 1971. Add: P.O. Box 1035, F.D.R. Station, New York, N.Y. 10150, U.S.A.

MARTIN, Peter. *See* **MELVILLE,** James.

MARTIN, Ralph (Guy). American, b. 1920. History, Politics/Government, Biography, Documentaries/Reportage. Assoc. Ed., New Republic mag., 1945–48, and Newsweek mag., 1953–55; Exec. Ed., House Beautiful mag., 1955–57. *Publs:* Boy from Nebraska, 1946; The Best Is None Too Good, 1948; (with R. Harrity) Eleanor Roosevelt: Her Life in Pictures, 1958; (with R. Harrity) The Human Side of FDR, 1960; (with E. Plaut) Front Runner, Dark Horse, 1960; (with M. Stone) Money, Money, Money, 1960; (with R. Harrity) Man of Destiny: Charles de Gaulle, 1961; (with R. Harrity) Man of the Century: Winston Churchill, 1961; (with R. Harrity) The Three Lives of Helen Keller, 1962; (with R. Harrity) World War II: From D-Day to VE Day, 1962; The Bosses, 1964; Ballots and Bandwagons, 1964; President from Missouri, 1964; Skin Deep (novel), 1964; World War II: War in the Pacific, 1965; Wizard of Wall Street, 1965; The G.I. War, 1967; Man of the People, 1968; Jennie: The Life of Lady Randolph Churchill, vol. I, The Romantic Years, 1854–1895, 1970, vol. II, The Dramatic Years, 1895–1921, 1971; Lincoln Center for the Performing Arts, 1972; The Woman He Loved: The Story of the Duke and Duchess of Windsor, 1974; Cissy: The Life of Eleanor Medill Patterson, 1979; A Hero for Our Time: An Intimate Story of the Kennedy Years, 1984; Charles and Diana, 1985; Golda, Golda Meir: The Romantic Years, 1988. Add: 135 Harbor Rd., Westport, Conn. 06880, U.S.A.

MARTIN, Rhona. British, b. 1922. Novels/Short stories, Historical/Romance. Full-time writer since 1979. Formerly fashion artist, freelance theatrical designer, cinema mgr., and accounts secty. and office mgr. *Publs:* Gallows Wedding, 1978; Mango Walk, 1981; The Unicorn Summer, 1984; Goodbye, Sally, 1987; Writing Historical Fiction, 1988. Add: c/o John McLaughlin, Campbell Thomson and McLaughlin Ltd., 31 Newington Green, London N16 9PU, England.

MARTIN, Robert Bernard. Also writes as Robert Bernard. American, b. 1918. Novels/Short stories, History, Literature. Prof. of English, Princeton Univ., N.J., Emeritus since 1975; Citizens' Prof. of English, Univ. of Hawaii, Honolulu, since 1984, Emeritus since 1988. *Publs:* (with T.M. Parrott) A Companion to Victorian Literature, 1955; (ed.) Charles Kingsley's American Notes: Letters from a Lecture Tour 1874, 1958; The Dust of Combat: A Life of Charles Kingsley, 1960; Enter Rumor: Four Early Victorian Scandals, 1962; (ed.) Victorian Poetry: Ten Major Poets, 1964; The Accents of Persuasion: Charlotte Bronte's Novels, 1966; (as Robert Bernard) Death Takes a Sabbatical, 1967; (as Robert Bernard) Death Takes the Last Train, 1967; (as Robert Bernard) Deadly Meeting, 1970; (as Robert Bernard) Illegal Entry, 1972; The Triumph of Wit: Victorian Comic Theory, 1974; Tennyson: The Unquiet Heart, 1980; With Friends Possessed: A Life of Edward FitzGerald, 1985. Add: 8 Walton St., Oxford OX1 2HG, England.

MARTIN, Roderick. British, b. 1940. Administration/Management, Industrial relations, Sociology. Fellow, Templeton Coll., Oxford, since 1988. Official Fellow in Politics and Sociology, Trinity Coll. 1969–84, and Univ. Lectr. in Sociology 1966–84, Oxford Univ. (Sr. Research Fellow, Jesus Coll., 1966–69); Prof. of Industrial Sociology, Imperial Coll., London, 1984–88. *Publs:* (ed. with Rev. D.E.H. Whitely) Sociology, Theology and Conflict, 1969; Communism and the British Trade Unions 1924–33, 1969; (with R.H. Fryer) Redundancy and Paternalist Capitalism, 1973; The Sociology of Power, 1977; New Technology and Industrial Relations in Fleet Street, 1981; (with R.Undy) Ballots and Trade Union Democracy, 1984; (with J. Wallace) Working Women in Recession, 1984; (with B. Moore) Management Structures and Techniques, 1985. Add: Templeton Coll., Kennington, Oxford OX1 5NY, England.

MARTIN, Valerie. American, b. 1948. Novels/Short Stories. *Publs:* Set in Motion, 1978; Alexandra, 1979; A Recent Martyr, 1987; The Consolation of Nature and Other Stories, 1988. Add: c/o Doubleday, 666 Fifth Ave., New York, N.Y. 10103, U.S.A.

MARTIN, Victoria Carolyn. British, b. 1945. Novels/Short stories. *Publs:* September Song, 1969; The Windmill Years, 1978; Seeds of the Sun, 1979; Tigers of the Night, 1985; The Opposite House, 1985; Obey the Moon, 1987. Add: Newells Farm House, Lower Beeding, Horsham, Sussex, England.

MARTINDALE, Andrew (Henry Robert). British, b. 1932. Architecture, Art. Prof. of Visual Arts, Univ. of East Anglia, Norwich, since 1974 (Sr. Lectr., 1965–74). Lectr. in History of Art, Courtauld Inst., Univ. of London, 1959–65. *Publs:* Gothic Art, 1967; The Rise of the Artist in the Middle Ages, and Early Renaissance, 1972; The Triumphs of Caesar by Andrea Mantegna, 1979; (co-ed.) The Vanishing Past, 1981; Simone Martini, 1988. Add: Sch. of Art History and Music, Univ. of East Anglia, Norwich NR4 7TJ, England.

MARTINET, André. French, b. 1908. Language/Linguistics. Prof. of Structural Linguistics, Ecole des hautes études, Paris, since 1938. Prof. of Gen. and Comparative Linguistics, Columbia Univ., NYC, 1947–55; Prof. of Linguistics, The Sorbonne, Paris, 1955–77. *Publs:* La gémination consonantique d'origine expressive dans les langues germaniques, 1937; La phonologie du mot en danois, 1937; La prononciation du français contemporain, 1945; Phonology as Functional Phonetics, 1949; (ed. with U. Weinrich) Linguistics Today, 1954; Economie des changements phonétiques, 1944; La description phonologique, 1956; Eléments de linguistique générale, 1960; A Functional View of Language, 1962; La linguistique synchronique, 1965; La français sans fard, 1969; (ed.) Le langage, 1969; La Linguistique, Guide alphabétique, 1970; (with H. Walter) Dictionnaire de la prononciation française dans son usage réel, 1973; Studies in Functional Syntax, 1975; Evolution des langues et reconstruction, 1975; Grammaire fonctionnelle du français, 1979; Syntaxe Générale, 1985; Des steppes aux océans: L'Indo-européen et les "Indo-Européens," 1986. Add: 10 Ave. de la Gare, 92330 Sceaux, France.

MARTINI, Teri. American, b. 1930. Novels/Short stories, Children's fiction, Children's non-fiction. Former teacher, Tenafly, N.J. Bd. of Education. *Publs:* The Fisherman's Ring, 1954; True Book of Indians, 1954; Treasure of the Mohawk, 1956; True Book of Cowboys, 1956; Sandals on the Golden Highway, 1959; What a Frog Can Do, 1962; Mystery of the Hard Luck House, 1965; The Lucky Ghost Shirt, 1971; Patrick Henry, Patriot, 1972; Mystery of the Woman in the Mirror, 1973; John Marshall, 1974; Mystery Writers of Tunbridge Wells, 1975; The Dreamer Lost in Terror, 1976; To Love and Beyond, 1977; Dreams to Give, 1979; The Arrundel Touch, 1980; Cowboys, 1981; Indians, 1982; Love's Lost Melody, 1986. Add: c/o Atheneum Publishers, 866 Third Ave., New York, N.Y. 10022, U.S.A.

MARTLAND, Thomas R(odolphe). American, b. 1926. Philosophy, Religion. Prof. of Philosophy, State Univ. of New York at Albany, since 1966. Member, Editorial Bd., Journal of Comparative Literature and Aesthetics. Guest Ed., Annals of Scholarship, 1982: Coatson Visiting Prof., Syracuse Univ., New York, 1987; Chmn., Steering Cttee., Eastern Div., American Soc. Aesthetics, 1988. Add: Dept. of Philosophy, State Univ. of New York at Albany, Albany, N.Y. 112222, U.S.A.

MARTY, Martin E. American, b. 1928. History, Theology/Religion. Fairfax M. Cone Prof. of Divinity, Univ. of Chicago, since 1963. Sr. Ed., The Christian Century, since 1956; Co-Ed., Church History; Ed., Context fortnightly newsletter. Lutheran pastor, Chicago, 1952–63. *Publs:* The New Shape of American Religion, 1959; A Short History of Christianity, 1959; The Infidel: Free-Thought and American Religion, 1961; The Improper Opinion, 1961; Baptism, 1962; The Hidden Discipline, 1962; Second Chance for American Protestants, 1963; Varieties of Unbelief, 1964; Church Unity and Church Mission, 1964; The Modern Schism, 1969; The Search for a Usable Future, 1969; Righteous Empire, 1970; Protestantism, 1972; You Are Promise, 1973; The Fire We Can Light, 1973; A Nation of Behavers, 1977; Religion, Awakening, and Revolution, 1978; Friendship, 1980; By Way of Response, 1981; The Public Church, 1981; A Cry of Absence, 1983; Pilgrims in Their Own Land, 1984; An Invitation to American Catholic History, 1985; Modern American Religion: The Irony of it All, vol. 1, 1893–1919, 1986; Religion and Republic. The American Circumstance, 1987. Add: Swift Hall, Univ. of Chicago, Chicago, Ill. 60637, U.S.A.

MARTY, Sid. Canadian, b. 1944. Poetry, History. Park warden in national parks in Banff and Jasper, Alberta, and in Yoho, British Columbia, 1966–78. *Publs:* Headwaters, 1973; Tumbleweek Harvest, 1973; Men for the Mountains (on park wardens), 1978; Nobody Danced with Miss Rodeo, 1981; A Grand and Fabulous Notion (history, National Parks), 1984. Add: c/o McClelland and Stewart, 481 University Ave., Toronto, Ont. M5G 2E9, Canada.

MARTYN, Howe. Canadian, b. 1906. Administration/Management, Business/Trade/Industry. Prof. of Intnl. Business, American Univ., Washington, D.C., Emeritus since 1975. Joint Mgr., Intnl. Marketing Div., Unilever, London, 1948–54. *Publs:* International Business: Organization, Management and Social Impact of the Multinational Corporation, 1964; Multinational Business Management, 1970. Add: One Rosedale Rd., Apt. 305, Toronto, Ont. M4W 2Pl, Canada.

MARTZ Louis (Lohr). American, b. 1913. Literature. Sterling Prof. of English, Yale Univ., New Haven, since 1971 (Instr., 1938–44; Asst. Prof., 1944–48; Assoc. Prof., 1948–54; Prof. of English, 1954–57; Chmn. of Dept., 1956–62; Douglas Tracy Smith Prof. of English and American Literature, 1957–71; Dir., Div. of Humanities, 1959–62). Editorial Chmn., Yale Edition of the Works of Thomas More. *Publs:* The Later Career of Tobias Smollett, 1942; (ed.) Pilgrim's Progress, by John Bunyan, 1949; The Poetry of Meditation: A Study in English Religious Literature of the Seventeenth Century, 1954, 1962; (compiler) The Meditative Poem, 1963; The Paradise Within: Studies in Vaughan, Traherne, and Milton, 1964; The Poem of the Mind: Essays on Poetry, English and American, 1966; (ed.) Milton: A Collection of Critical Essays, 1966; (ed. with Richard Sylvester) Thomas More's Prayer Book, 1969; The Wit of Love: Donne, Carew, Crashaw, Marvell, 1969; (compiler) Seventeenth Century Verse, vol. I, 1969; (ed.) Hero and Leander, by Christopher Marlowe, 1972; (ed. with Frank Manley) Thomas More's Dialogue of Comfort, 1976; (ed. with Aubrey Williams) The Author in His Work: Essays on a Problem in Criticism, 1978; Poet of Exile: A Study of Milton's Poetry, 1980; (ed.) H.D.: Collected Poems 1912–1944, 1983; (ed.) George Herbert and Henry Vaughan, 1986; (ed.) H.D.: Selected Poems, 1988. Add: 994 Yale Station, New Haven, Conn. 06520, U.S.A.

MARVIN, Blanche. American, b. 1926. Children's fiction,

Plays/Screenplays, Poetry. Self-employed literary and dramatist's agent. Artistic Dir. and Owner, Cricket Theatre, NYC, 1958–65; former actress. *Publs:* Legend of Scarface and Blue Water; Sleeping Beauty; Chekhov's Two Sisters; Stage by Stage. Add: 21A St. John's Wood High St., London NW8, England.

MARVIN, Julie. *See* **ELLIS**, Julie.

MARVIN, Philip. American, b. 1916. Administration/Management, Business/Trade/Industry. Prof., Univ. of Cincinnati, since 1965 (Dean of Professional Development, 1965–74). Div. Mgr., American Mgmt. Assn., 1955–64; Pres., Clark Cooper Field & Wohl, 1964–65. *Publs:* Top-Management and Research, 1953, 1956; Administrative Management, 1954; Planning New Products, vol. I, 1958, vol. II, 1964; Management Goals: Guidelines and Accountability, 1968; Multiplying Management Effectiveness, 1971; Developing Decisions for Action, 1971; Man in Motion, 1972; Product Planning Simplified, 1972; The Right Man for the Right Job at the Right Time, 1973; Fundamentals of Effective R and D Management, 1973; Managing Your Career, 1974; Managing Your Successful Career, 1978; Executive Time Management, 1980. Add: 11 Canborne Way, Madison, Conn. 06443, U.S.A.

MARWICK, Arthur. British, b. 1936. History. Prof. of History, The Open Univ., since 1969 (Dean of Arts, 1978–84). Asst. Lectr., Univ. of Aberdeen, 1959–60; Lectr., Univ. of Edinburgh, 1960–69. *Publs:* The Explosion of British Society, 1914–1962, 1963, 1971; Clifford Allen: The Open Conspirator, 1964; The Deluge: British Society and the First World War, 1965; Britain in the Century of Total War: War, Peace, and Social Change 1900–1967, 1968; The Nature of History, 1970, 1981; War and Social Change in the Twentieth Century, 1974; The Home Front: The British and the Second World War, 1976; Women at War, 1914–1918, 1977; Class: Image and Reality in Britain, France and the U.S.A. since 1930, 1980; (ed.) Thames and Hudson Illustrated Dictionary of British History, 1980; British Society since 1945, 1982; Britain in Our Century: Images and Controversies, 1984; (ed.) Class in the Twentieth Century, 1986; Beauty in History, 1988; (ed.) Total War and Social Change, 1988. Add: Flat 5, 67 Fitzjohn's Ave., London NW3 6PE, England.

MARWICK, Max(well) Gay. British (South African born, formerly Australian), b. 1916. Anthropology/Ethnology. Lectr., 1950–53, Sr. Lectr. in Sociology, 1953–56, and Acting Dir., Inst. for Social Research, 1955–56, Univ. of Natal, Durban; Prof. and Head, Dept. of Social Anthropology and African Admin., Univ. of the Witwatersrand, Johannesburg, 1957–63; Joint Ed., African Studies, 1957–63; Prof. and Chmn., Dept. of Anthropology and Sociology, Monash Univ., Melbourne, 1963–68; News and Notes Ed., Australian Journal of Sociology, 1964–66; Prof. of Sociology and Head of Dept., Univ. of Stirling, 1969–74; Sr. Lectr., 1975–76, Reader, 1976–81, and Chmn., 1978–79, Sch. of Humanities, Griffith Univ., Brisbane. *Publs:* Sorcery in Its Social Setting: A Study of the Northern Rhodesian Cewa, 1965; (ed. and contrib.) Witchcraft and Sorcery, 1970, 1982. Add: 46 Lewis Rd., Chipping Norton, Oxon. OX7 5JS, England.

MARX, Arthur. American, b. 1921. Novels/Short stories, Plays/Screenplays, Biography, Humor/Satire. Film writer, and TV writer and producer. *Publs:* The Ordeal of Willie Brown, 1951; Life with Groucho, 1954; Not as a Crocodile, 1958; The Impossible Years (play), 1965; Minnie's Boys (play), 1970; Son of Groucho, 1972; Everybody Loves Somebody Sometime, Expecially Himself, 1974; Sugar and Spice (play), 1974; My Daughter's Rated X (play), 1975; Goldwyn, 1976; Red Skelton, 1979; Groucho: A Life in Review (play), 1986; The Nine Lives of Mickey Rooney (biography), 1986; My Life with Groucho (biography), 1988. Add: c/o Scott Meredith, 845 Third Ave., New York, N.Y. 10022, U.S.A.

MARX, Gary T. American, b. 1938. Criminology/Law enforcement, Race relations, Social commentary/phenomena, Sociology. Prof. of Sociology, Massachusetts Inst. of Technology, Cambridge, since 1973. Research Assoc., Survey Research Center, 1965–67, and Lectr. in Sociology, 1966–67, Univ. of California, Berkeley; Asst. Prof. of Social Relations, 1967–69, and Lectr., 1969–73, Harvard Univ., Cambridge, Mass. *Publs:* The Social Basis of the Support of a Depression Era Extremist: Father Coughlin, 1962; Protest and Prejudice, 1967; (co-ed.) Confrontation: Psychology and the Problems of Today, 1970; (ed.) Racial Conflict: Tension and Change in American Society, 1971; (ed.) Muckraking Sociology: Research as Social Criticism, 1972; (co-ed.) Sociology: Classic and Popular Approaches, 1979; Society Today, 1982; Undercover Police: Surveillance in America, 1988. Add: Dept. of Urban Studies and Planning, Massachusetts Inst. of Technology, Cambridge, Mass. 02139, U.S.A.

MARX, Robert (Frank). American, b. 1936. Archaeology/Antiquities (marine archaeology), History (naval and maritime), Travel/Exploration/Adventure. Dir. of Operations, Phoenician Explorations, since 1979. Member, Council of Nautical Archaeology, London, and the Council of Underwater Archaeology. Oceanographic Consultant, Intnl. Minerals and Chemicals, 1959–60; Adventure Ed., Saturday Evening Post mag., 1960–63; Underwater Archaeologist, Jamaica Govt., 1965–68; Underwater Archaeological Consultant, Real Eight Co., Melbourne, Fla., 1968–71; Dir., Salvage for Seafinders Corp., Bahamas, 1971–74; has taught underwater archaeology and maritime history at Scripps Instn. of Oceanography, La Jolla, Calif., and the Univ. of California at San Diego, 1974–75; Consultant, Planet Ocean: Intnl. Oceanographic Foundation, 1974; Pres., Sea World Enterprises, Inc., 1974–76; Contr. Ed., Aquarius mag., 1972–76; Expedition Leader, L.O.S.T., Inc., 1978. *Publs:* Historia de Isla de Cozumel, 1959; Voyage of the Nina II, 1963; Following Columbus, 1964; The Battle of the Spanish Armada 1588, 1965; The Battle of Lepanto 1571, 1966; They Dared the Deep: A History of Diving, 1967; History of the Sunken City of Port Royal, 1967; Always Another Adventure, 1967; Treasure Fleets of the Spanish Main, 1968; Shipwrecks in Florida Waters, 1969; Shipwrecks in Mexican Waters, 1971; Shipwrecks of the Western Hemisphere, 1971; Sea Fever: Famous Underwater Explorers, 1972; Port Royal Rediscovered, 1973; The Lure of Sunken Treasure, 1973; The Underwater Dig, 1975, 1989, Still More Adventures, 1976; Capture of the Spanish Plate Fleet: 1628, 1976; Spanish Treasures in Florida Waters, 1978; Buried Treasures of the United States, 1978, 1987, Into the Deep: A History of Man's Underwater Explorations, 1978; Diving for Adventure, 1979; Quest for Treasure: Discovery of the Galleon Maravillas, 1982; Shipwrecks in Florida Waters: A Billion Dollar Graveyard, 1985. Add: 205 Orlando Blvd., Indialantic, Fla. 32903, U.S.A.

MARZANI, Carl. American, b. 1912. Novels/Short stories, Environmental science/Ecology, History, Documentaries/Reportage. Visiting Prof. of World Politics, Inter-American Univ., San German, Puerto Rico, since 1974. Instr. in Economics, New York Univ., NYC, 1939–41; Member of staff, U.S. office of Strategic Services, Washington, D.C., 1942–45; Deputy Div. Chief, U.S. Dept. of State, Washington, D.C., 1945–46; Educational Dir., UE-CIO, 1951–54; Publ., Marzani and Munsell, 1954–66. *Publs:* We Can Be Friends: The Origins of the Cold War, 1952; (ed. and trans.) The Open Marxism of Antonio Gramsci, 1957; The Survivor, 1958; (with V. Perlo) Dollars and Sense of Disarmament, 1959; (with R. Light) Cuba vs. CIA, 1963; (ed.) The Shelter Hoax, 1965; The Wounded Earth: An Ecological Survey, 1972; The Promise of Eurocommunism, 1980. Add: 260 West 21st St., New York, N.Y. 10011, U.S.A.

MASAO, Maruyama. Japanese, b. 1914. History, Politics/Government. Prof. Emeritus of Political Theory, Univ. of Tokyo, since 1971. *Publs:* Thought and Behavior in Modern Japanese Politics, 1963, 1969; Studies in the Intellectual History of Tokugawa Japan, 1974; Denken in Japan, 1988. Add: 2-44-5 Higashicho, Kichijoji, Musashino-shi, Tokyo, Japan.

MASCALL, Eric Lionel. British, b. 1905. Philosophy, Theology/Religion. Subwarden, Lincoln Theological Coll., 1937–45; Univ. Lectr., in the Philosophy of Religion, Oxford Univ., 1947–62; Prof. of Historical Theology, King's Coll., Univ. of London, 1962–73. *Publs:* He Who Is, 1943; Christ, the Christian and the Church, 1946; Existence and Analogy, 1949; Corpus Christi, 1953, 1965; Christian Theology and Natural Science, 1956; Via Media, 1956; Words and Images, 1957; The Recovery of Unity, 1958; The Importance of Being Human, 1958; Pi in the High, 1959; Grace and Glory, 1961; The Secularisation of Christianity, 1965; The Christian Universe, 1966; Theology and the Future, 1968; The Openness of Being, 1971; Theology and the Gospel of Christ, 1977; Whatever Happened to the Human Mind, 1980; Jesus, Who He Is and How We Know Him, 1985; The Triune God, 1986. Add: St. Mary's Hoose, Kings Mead, East Blatchington, Seaford BN25 2ET, England.

MASEFIELD, Geoffrey (Bussell). British, b. 1911. Poetry, Agriculture/Forestry, History. Fellow of Wolfson Coll., Oxford Univ. (Lectr. in Tropical Agriculture, 1948–76). Agricultural Officer, Uganda, 1935–48; Ed., Tropical Agricultural journal, 1953–65. *Publs:* I Am Not Armed (poetry), 1938; (with S. Wood) This Springing Wilderness (poetry), 1942; The Uganda Farmer, 1948; Handbook of Tropical Agriculture, 1949; Short History of Agriculture in the British Colonies, 1950; Famine: Its Prevention and Relief, 1963; Food and Nutrition Procedures in times of Disaster, 1967; (with S.G. Harrison, M. Wallis and B.E. Nicholson) The Oxford Book of Food Plants, 1969; (with A.N. Duckham) Farming Systems of the World, 1970; History of the Colonial Agricultural Service, 1972. Add: Steepway, Adey's Lane, Wotton-under-Edge, Glos. GL12 7PS,

England.

MASON, Bobbie Ann. American, b. 1940. Novels/Short stories. Full-time Writer. Asst. Prof. of English, Mansfield State Coll., Mansfield, Pa., 1972–79. *Publs:* Nabokov's Garden: A Nature Guide to Ada, 1974; The Girl Sleuth: A Feminist Guide to the Bobbsey Twins, Nancy Drew and Their Sisters, 1975; Shiloh and Other Stories, 1982; In Country, 1985; Spense + Lila, 1988. Add: Amanda Urban, International Creative Management, 40 W. 57th St., New York, N.Y. 10019, U.S.A.

MASON, Douglas Rankine. Also writes as John Rankine and R.M. Douglas. British, b. 1918. Science fiction/Fantasy. Headmaster, St. George's Primary Sch., Wallasey, 1967–79; Merseyside County Councillor, 1981–85. *Publs:* (as John Rankine) The Blockade of Sinitron, 1964; (as John Rankine) Interstellar Two Five, 1966; From Carthage Then I Came, 1966; (as John Rankine) Never the Same Door, 1967; (as John Rankine) One Is One, 1968; (as John Rankine) Moons of Triopus, 1968; Landfall Is a State of Mind, 1968; The Tower of Rizwan, 1968; The Janus Syndrome, 1969; (as John Rankine) Binary Z, 1969; (as John Rankine) The Weizman Experiment, 1969; Matrix, 1970; Satellite 54-0, 1971; Horizon Alpha, 1971; Dilation Effect, 1971; (as John Rankine) The Plantos Affair, 1971; (as John Rankine) The Ring of Garamas, 1972; The Resurrection of Roger Diment, 1972; The Phaeton Condition, 1973; The End Bringers, 1973; (as John Rankine) Operation Umanaq, 1973; (as John Rankine) The Fingalnan Conspiracy, 1973; (as John Rankine) The Bromius Phenomenon, 1973; The Omega Worm, 1974; Pitman's Progress, 1976; Euphor Unfree, 1977; (as John Rankine) The Thorburn Enterprise, 1977; Mission to Pactolus R, 1978; (as John Rankine) The Star of Hesiock, 1979; (as R.M. Douglas) The Darkling Plain, 1979; The Typhon Intervention, 1981. Add: c/o Carnell Literary Agency, Danescroft, Goose Lane, Little Hallingbury, Bishops Stortford, Herts. CM22 7RG, England.

MASON, Edmund (John). British, b. 1911. Archaeology/Antiquities, Recreation/Leisure/Hobbies, Travel/Exploration/Adventure, Translations. Adult Education Lectr., since 1948, and Vice Chmn., Western District, 1965–68 and since 1973, Workers Educational Assn. (District Chmn., Western District, 1969–72). District Estate Surveyor, Dept. of the Environment, 1934–76. Chmn. and Trustee, Steepholm Trust, 1968–74; Trustee, South Brecons Field Study Centre, 1969–84. *Publs:* (with A.W. Coysh and V. Waite) The Mendips, 1954, 4th ed. 1977; (trans.) Caves and Cave Diving, by Guy de Lavaur, 1956; The Story of Wookey Hole, 1963, 3rd ed. 1970; Portrait of the Brecon Beacons, 1975; Caves and Caving in Britain, 1977; (with Dorrien Mason) Avon Villages, 1982; The Wye Valley, 1987. Add: 33 Broadleys Ave., Henleaze Park, Henleaze, Bristol BS9 4LY, England.

MASON, Francis K(enneth). British, b. 1928. Air/Space topics, History, Recreation/Leisure/Hobbies. Aviation Consultant, Aston Publications Ltd., Harvest Hill, Bourne End, Bucks. Archivist and researcher. Ed., Flying Review Intnl., 1963–64; Managing Dir., Profile Publs. Ltd., 1964–67; Managing Ed., Guinness Superlatives Ltd., Enfield, Middx., 1968–71; Managing Dir., Alban Book Services, Watton, Norfolk, 1971–80. *Publs:* Hawker Aircraft since 1920, 1961, 3rd ed. 1989; Hawker Hurricane, 1962; Gloster Gladiator, 1963; (ed.) North American Sabre, 1963; The Hawker Hunter, 1965; The Hawker Sea Hawk, 1966; The Westland Lysander, 1966; The Hawker Siddley Kestrel, 1967; The Hawker Hunter Two-Seater, 1967; The Hawker Tempest, 1967; British Fighters of the Second World War, 1968; Air Facts and Feats, 1969; Battle Over Britain, 1969; (ed.) British Gallantry Awards, 1970; Know Britain, 1972; Know Aviation, 1973; (ed.) Ribbons and Medals, 1974; A Dictionary of Military Biography, 1975; Harrier, 1981; Famous Pilots and Their Planes, 1981; Lockheed Hercules, 1984; Phantom, 1984; War in the Air, 1985; Tornado, 1986; (with M. Turner) Luftewaffe Aircraft, 1986; The Hawker Hurricane, 1987; The Hawker Typhoon and Tempest, 1988; The Auro Lancaster, 1989. Add: Beechwood, Watton, Norfolk, England.

MASON, Haydn Trevor. British, b. 1929. Literature. Prof. of French, Univ. of Bristol, since 1981. Ed., Studies on Voltaire and the Eighteenth Century, since 1977. Instr. in French, Princeton Univ., New Jersey, 1954–57; Lectr., Univ. of Newcastle, 1960–63; Lectr., 1964–65, and Reader, 1965–67, Univ. of Reading; Prof. of European Literature, Univ. of East Anglia, Norwich, 1967–79; Prof. of French Literature, Univ. de Paris III, 1979–81. Chmn., Assn. of Univ. Professors of French, 1981–82; Pres., Soc. for French Studies, 1982–84, and British Soc. for Eighteenth Century Studies, 1984–86. *Publs:* Pierre Bayle and Voltaire, 1963; (ed.) Marivaux: Les Fausses Confidences, 1964; (trans. and ed.) Leibniz-Arnauld Correspondence, 1967; (ed.) Voltaire: Zadig and Other Stories, 1971; Voltaire, 1974; Voltaire: A Life, 1981; French Writers and Their Society 1715–1800, 1982; Cyrano de Bergerac: L'Autre Monde, 1984; (ed.) Myth and its Making in the French Theatre, 1988. Add: Dept. of French, University of Bristol, Bristol, BS8 1TE, England.

MASON, Herbert (Molloy). American, b. 1927. Air/Space topics, History, Travel/Exploration/Adventure. *Publs:* The Lafayette Escadrille, 1964; High Flew the Falcons, 1965; Famous Firsts in Exploration, 1965; The Texas Rangers, 1966; Bold Men, Far Horizons, 1967; The Commandos, 1967; The New Tigers, 1968; Duel for the Sky, 1969; The Great Pursuit, 1970; Death From the Sea, 1972; The Rise of the Luftwaffe, 1973; Missions of Texas, 1974; The Fantastic World of Ants, 1974; Secrets of the Supernatural, 1975; The United States Air Force, 1976; To Kill the Devil, 1979; The Luftwaffe, 1981; Hitler Must Die, 1985. Add: c/o John Hawkins and Assocs., 71 W. 23rd St., N.Y., N.Y. 10010, U.S.A.

MASON, Lee W. *See* **MALZBERG**, Barry.

MASON, Malcolm John. New Zealander, b. 1912. Travel/Exploration/Adventure, Autobiography/Memoirs/Personal. Chartered Accountant, Mason King & Partners, since 1957. Pres., P.E.N., N.Z. Centre, 1960–64. *Publs:* The Way Out, 1946; The Water Flows Uphill, 1964; Why Not Japan?, 1965. Add: 29 Everest St., Khandallah, Wellington, New Zealand.

MASON, Nicholas. British, b. 1938. History, Sports/Physical education/Keeping fit. Deputy Sports Ed., The Guardian newspaper, London, since 1988. Managing Ed., Sunday Times Mag., 1973–77; Deputy Sports Ed., The Sunday Times, London, 1977–86; Sports Ed., London Daily News, 1987. *Publs:* (ed.) The Olympics, 1972; Football!: The Story of All the World's Football Games, 1974; (ed. with G. Perry) Rule Britannia: The Victorian World, 1974; (ed. with J. Lovesey and E. Taylor) The Sunday Times Sports Book, 1979; (with Sebastian Coe) The Olympians, 1984, 1988. Add: 89 Lusted Hall Lane, Tatsfield, Westerham, Kent, England.

MASON, Philip. Also writes as Philip Woodruff. British, b. 1906. Novels/Short stories, Children's fiction, History, Race relations, Autobiography. Served in the Indian Civil Service, 1927–47; Dir. of Studies in Race Relations, Royal Inst. of Intnl. Affairs, London, 1952–58; Dir., Inst of Race Relations, London, 1958–69. *Publs:* (as Philip Woodruff) Call the Next Witness, 1945; (as Philip Woodruff) The Wild Sweet Witch, 1947; (as Philip Woodruff) Whatever Dies, 1948; (as Philip Woodruff) The Sword of Northumbria, 1948; (as Philip Woodruff) The Island of Chamba, 1950; (as Philip Woodruff) Hernshaw Castle, 1950; (as Philip Woodruff) Colonel of Dragoons, 1951; (as Philip Woodruff) The Founders, 1953; (as Philip Woodruff) The Guardians, 1954; An Essay on Racial Tension, 1954; Christianity and Race, 1956; The Birth of a Dilemma, 1958; (ed. and contrib.) Man, Race and Darwin, 1960; Common Sense about Race, 1961; Prospero's Magic, 1962; (ed. and contrib.) Unity and Diversity: India and Ceylon, 1967; Patterns of Dominance, 1970; Race Relations, 1970; How People Differ, 1971; A Matter of Honour, 1974; Kipling: The Glass, The Shadow and the Fire, 1975; The Dove in Harness, 1976; A Shaft of Sunlight, 1978; Skinner of Skinner's Horse, 1979; The English Gentleman, 1982; A Thread of Silk 1984; The Men Who Ruled India, 1985. Add: 4 Mulberry House, Church St., Fordingbridge, Hants. SP6 1BE, England.

MASON, Ronald Charles. British, b. 1912. Novels, Literature, Sports, Recreation/Leisure/Hobbies. Sr. Examiner, Estate Duty Office, Inland Revenue, 1949–69; Staff Tutor in Literature, Extra–Mural Dept., Univ. of London, 1969–79. *Publs:* Timbermills, 1938; The Gold Garland, 1939; Cold Pastoral, 1946; The House of the Living, 1947; The Spirit above the Dust: A Study of Herman Melville, 1951; Batsman's Paradise, 1955; Jack Hobbs, 1960; Walter Hammond, 1962; Sing All a Green Willow, 1967; Plum Warner's Last Season, 1970; Warwick Armstrong's Australians, 1971; (with G. Bush) Songs More Songs from a Summer School, 1975–80; Ashes in the Mouth, 1982. Add: 22 Rosehill Farm Meadow, Park Rd., Banstead, Surrey, England.

MASSEY, James Earl. American, b. 1930. History, Theology/Religion, Biography. Prof. of Religious Studies, and Campus Minister, Anderson Coll., Indiana, 1969–77. Historian, National Assn. of the Church of God since 1957, and member and Vice Chmn., Publ. Bd. of the Church of God since 1962; Feature Writer, Vital Christianity mag., since 1960; member, Editorial Bd., Christian Scholar's Review, since 1970. Contrib. Ed., Gospel Trumpet mag., 1960–69; Editorial Advisor, Tyndale House Publrs., 1968–69. *Publs:* The Growth of the Soul, 1955; An Introduction to the Negro Churches in the Church of God Reformation Movement, 1957; When Thou Prayest, 1960; The Worshipping Church,

1961; Raymond S. Jackson: A Portrait, 1967; The Soul Under Seige, 1970; The Hidden Disciplines, 1972; The Responsible Pulpit (speech/rhetoric), 1974; Howard Thurman: Preacher, The Sermon in Perspective, 1976; Concerning Christian Unity, 1979; Designing the Sermon, 1980; Educating for Service, 1984; Spiritual Disciplines, 1985; Preaching from Hebrews, 1988. Add: c/o Warner Press Publs., 1200 E. Fifth St., Anderson, Ind. 46012, U.S.A.

MASSIALAS, Byron G. American, b. 1929. Education, Politics/-Government, Social sciences (general). Prof. of Education, Dept. of Curriculum and Instruction, Florida State Univ., Tallahassee, since 1970 (Head, Dept. of Social Studies Education, 1970–73). Ed., Addison-Wesley Series in Education: Social Behavioral, and Philosophical Foundations, since 1968. Instr. in Social Studies, Indiana Univ., Bloomington, 1959–61; Asst. Prof. of Education in the Social Sciences, Univ. of Chicago, 1961–65; Assoc. Prof. of Education, 1965–70, and Dir., Social Science Research Training Prog., 1966–70, Univ. of Michigan, Ann Arbor. *Publs:* (ed. with A.M. Kazamias) Crucial Issues in the Teaching of Social Studies, 1964; (with A.M. Kazamias) Tradition and Change in Education: A Comparative Study, 1965; (ed. with F.R. Smith and contrib.) New Challenges in the Social Studies: Implications of Research for Teaching, 1965; (with C. Cox) Inquiry in Social Studies, 1966; (ed. with C. Cox and contrib.) Social Studies in the United States: A Critical Appraisal, 1967; (with J. Zevin) Creative Encounters in the Classroom, 1967; Education and the Political System, 1969; (with J. Zevin) World History Through Inquiry series, 9 vols., 1969–70; (with N. Sprague and J.A. Sweeney) Structure and Process of Inquiry into Social Issues in Secondary Schools, vol. I, 1970; (ed. and contrib.) Political Youth, Traditional Schools: National and International Perspectives, 1972; (co-author) Options: A Study Guide to Population and the American Future, 1973; (with N. Sprague) Social Issues Through Inquiry, 1975; (with J. Hurst) Social Studies in a New Era: The Elementary School as Laboratory, 1978; Education in Greece, 1980; (with Jack Zevin) Teaching Creatively, 1983; (with Samir Jarrar) Education in the Arab World, 1983; (with Samir Jarrar) Arab Education in Transition, 1989. Add: 2402 Killarney Way, Tallahassee, Fla. 32308, U.S.A.

MASSIE, Allan. British, b. 1938. Novels/Short stories. *Publs:* novels—Change and Decay in All Around I See, 1978; The Last Peacock, 1980; The Death of Men, 1981; One Night in Winter, 1984; The Hanging Tree, 1986; Augustus, 1986; other—Muriel Spark, 1979; Ill Met by Gaslight: Five Edinburgh Murders, 1980; The Caesars, 1983; (ed.) Edinburgh and the Borders: In Verse, 1983; Portrait of Scottish Rugby, 1984; Colette, 1986; 101 Great Scots, 1987; Byron's Travels, 1988. Add: c/o Bodley Head, 32 Bedford Sq., London WC1B 3EL, England.

MASSIE, Joseph Logan. American, b. 1921. Administration/Management, Business/Trade/Industry. Joined faculty, 1946, Alumni Prof., and Prof of Business Admin., from 1971, (now retired), Univ. of Kentucky, Lexington. Asst. Prof., Univ. of Chicago, 1955–57. *Publs:* Blazer and Ashland Oil, 1960; (with W.W. Haynes) Management: Analysis, Concept, and Cases, 1961, 3rd ed. 1975; Essentials of Management, 1964, 4th ed., 1987; (ed. with J. Luytjes) Management in an International Concept, 1972; (with J. Douglas) Managing: A Contemporary Introduction, 1973, 4th ed. 1985. Add: 205 Culpepper Rd., Lexington, Ky. 40502, U.S.A.

MASSINGHAM, Harold (William). British, b. 1932. Poetry. Tutor, Extra-Mural Dept., Univ. of Manchester, since 1971. School teacher, Manchester Education Cttee., 1955–70. *Publs:* Black Bull Guarding Apples, 1965; Creation, 1968; The Magician: A Poem Sequence, 1969; Storm, 1970; Snow-Dream, 1971; The Pennine Way, 1971; Frost-Gods, 1971; Doomsday, 1972; Mate in Two (on chess), 1976. Add: Extra-Mural Dept., Univ. of Manchester, Manchester, England.

MASSON, David I(rvine). British, b. 1915. Science fiction/Fantasy, Poetry, Language/Linguistics, Librarianship. Asst. Librarian, Univ. of Leeds, 1938–40, and Univ. of Liverpool, 1944–55; Sub-Librarian, in charge of Brotherton Collection, Univ. of Leeds, 1956–79. *Publs:* Hand List of Incunabula in the University Library, Liverpool, 1948, supplement, 1955; Catalogue of the Romany Collection . . . University of Leeds, 1962; The Caltraps of Time (short stories), 1968; Poetic Sound-Patterning Reconsidered, 1976. Add: c/o Faber and Faber Ltd., 3 Queen Sq., London WC1N 3AU, England.

MASTERS, Roger D. American, b. 1933. Philosophy, Politics/Government, Sociology. Prof. of Govt., Dartmouth Coll., Hanover, N.H., since 1973 (Assoc. Prof., 1967–73). Chmn., Editorial Bd., Biology and Social Life section, Social Science Information, Paris. Instr., and Asst. Prof., Dept. of Political Science, Yale Univ., New Haven,

Conn., 1961–67; Cultural Attaché, U.S. Embassy, Paris, 1969–71. *Publs:* (ed. and co-trans.) Rousseau's First and Second Discourses, 1964; The Nation Is Burdened, 1967; Political Philosophy of Rousseau, 1968; Rousseau's Social Contract, Geneva Manuscript, and Political Economy, 1978; (co-ed.) Ostracism, 1986; The Nature of Politics, 1989. Add: Dept. of Govt., Dartmouth Coll., Hanover, N.H. 03755, U.S.A.

MASTERS, William H. American, b. 1915. Sex. Prof. of Clinical Obstetrics and Gynecology, Washington Univ. Sch. of Medicine, St. Louis, since 1969 (Asst., 1944–47, Instr., 1947–49, Asst. Prof., 1949–51, and Assoc. Prof. of Obstetrics and Gynecology, 1951–64, Assoc. Prof. of Clinical Obstetrics and Gynecology, 1964–69, Dir., Div. of Reproductive Biology, 1960–63); Co-Dir., Masters and Johnson Inst. (formerly Reproductive Biology Research Foundn.), St. Louis, since 1973 (Dir., 1964–73). Asst. Resident Obstetrician and Gynecologist to St. Louis Maternity Hosp., and Barnes Hosp. of St. Louis, 1944 (Resident, 1945–47); Asst. Attending Obstetrician and Gynecologist to Jewish Hosp. of St. Louis; Consulting Gynecologist, St. Louis City Infirmary. *Publs:* (with Virginia Johnson) Human Sexual Response, 1966; (with Virginia Johnson) Human Sexual Inadequacy, 1970; (with Virginia Johnson and Robert J. Levin) The Pleasure Bond, 1975; (ed. with Virginia Johnson and Robert C. Kolodny) Ethical Issues in Sex Therapy and Research, Vol. 1, 1977, vol. 2, 1980; (with Virginia Johnson) Homosexualty in Perspective, 1979; (with Virginia Johnson and Robert C. Kolodny) Textbook of Sexual Medicine, 1979. Add: 4529 Pershing Pl., St. Louis, Mo. 63108, U.S.A.

MASTERSON, J.B. *See*EDMONDSON, G.C.

MASTERSON, Thomas R(obert). American, b. 1915. Personnel management. Founder and Dir., Center for Corporate Policy and Direction. Founder and Pres., Sigma Alpha Nu Honor Soc. Instr., Asst. Prof. and Assoc. Prof., Coll. of Commerce, De Paul Univ., Chicago, 1948–60; Assoc. Prof., 1960–64, and Prof., Grad. Sch. of Business, 1965 until retirement, Emory Univ., Atlanta. Chmn., Planning Cttee., Georgia Conservancy, 1972–74. *Publs:* (ed.) Ethics in Business, 1969; Motivating the Under-Performer, 1969. Add: Grad. Sch. of Business, Emory Univ., 873 N. Superior Ave., Decatur, Ga. 30033, U.S.A.

MASTERSON, Whit. *See*WADE, Robert.

MASTERTON, Graham. Also writes as Thomas Luke. British, b. 1946. Novels/Short stories, Psychology, Sex, Supernatural/Occult topics. Deputy Ed., Mayfair mag., London, 1967–70; Exec. Ed., Penthouse mag., London, 1970–74. *Publs:* Your Erotic Fantasies, 1970; Girls Who Said Yes, 1971; Sex Is Everything, 1972; How a Woman Loves to Be Loved, 1974; Isn't It Time You Did Something Kinky?, 1975; How A Woman Longs to Be Loved, 1975; How to Be the Perfect Lover, 1976; How to Drive Your Man Wild in Bed, 1976; Fireflash Five (novel), 1976; Confessions of a Wanton Waitress, 1976; Confessions of a Racy Receptionist, 1976; The Manitou (novel), 1976; The Djinn (novel), 1977; Plague (novel), 1977; 1001 Erotic Dreams Interpreted, 1977; Women's Erotic Dreams, 1977; The Sphinx (novel), 1977; Charnel House (novel), 1978; The Devils of D-Day (novel), 1978; The Sweetman Curve (novel), 1979; Revenge of the Manitou (novel), 1979; Rich (novel), 1979; (as Thomas Luke) The Hell Candidate, 1980; Heirloom, 1981; Famine, 1981; Railroad (in U.S. as A Man of Destiny), 1981; The Wells of Hell (novel), 1982; The Pariah (novel), 1982; Solitaire (novel), 1982; Maiden Voyage (novel), 1984; Tengu (novel), 1984; Ikon (novel), 1984; Corroboree (novel), 1984; Lady of Fortune (novel), 1985; Condor (novel), 1985; Family Portrait (novel; in U.S. as Picture of Evil), 1986; Death Trance (novel), 1986; Headlines (novel), 1988; Silver (novel), 1988; Night Warriors (novel), 1988; How to Drive Your Woman Wild in Bed, 1988; Mirror (novel), 1988; Death Dream (novel), 1988; Ritual (novel), 1988; Lords of the Air (novel), 1989; Hurry Monster (novelette), 1989; Scare Care (Anthology), 1989. Add: c/o Sphere Books, 27 Wrights Lane, London W8 5TZ, England.

MASTNY, Vojtech. American, b. 1936. History, International relations/Current affairs, Politics/Government. Prof. of Strategy, U.S. Naval War Coll., Newport, R.I., since 1982. Asst. Prof. of History, California State Coll., Long Beach, 1967–68; Asst. Prof. of History, 1968–74 and Acting Dir., Inst. of East Central Europe, 1970–71, Columbia Univ., NYC; Prof. of History, Univ. of Illinois, Urbana, 1974–80; Visiting Prof. of Soviet Studies, Johns Hopkins Sch. of Advanced Intnl. Studies, Washington, D.C., 1977–82. *Publs:* The Czechs Under Nazi Rule: The Failure of National Resistance 1939–42, 1971; (ed.) Disarmament and Nuclear Tests, 1971; (ed.) East European Dissent, 1972; (ed.) Czechoslovakia: Crisis in World Communism, 1972; Russia's Road to the Cold

War: Diplomacy, Warfare, and the Politics of Communism 1941–45, 1979; (ed.) Power and Policy in Transition, 1984; (ed.) Soviet-East European Survey, 1985–86, 1986–87, 2 vols., 1987. Helsinki, Human Rights, and European Security,1986. Add: Duke Univ. Press, Box 6697 College Station, Durham, N.C. 27708, U.S.A.

MASTROSIMONE, William. American, b. 1947. Plays/Screenplays. *Publs:* The Woolgatherer, 1981; Extremities, 1984; Shivaree, 1984; A Tantalizing, 1985; Nanawatai, 1986; Cat's-Paw, 1987. Add: c/o George Lane, William Morris Agency, 1350 Ave. of the Americas, New York, N.Y. 10019, U.S.A.

MASUR, Harold Q. American, b. 1909. Mystery/Crime/Suspense. Lawyer; practiced law in NYC, 1935–42. Past Pres., and currently Gen. Counsel, Mystery Writers of America. *Publs:* Bury Me Deep, 1947; Suddenly a Corpse, 1949; You Can't Live Forever, 1950; So Rich, So Lovely, and So Dead, 1952; The Big Money, 1954; Tall, Dark, and Deadly, 1956; (ed.) Dolls Are Murder, 1957; The Last Gamble (in U.K. as The Last Breath), 1958, in U.S. paperback, Murder on Broadway, 1959; Send Another Hearse, 1960; The Name Is Jordan (short stories), 1962; Make a Killing, 1964; The Legacy Lenders, 1967; (ed.) Murder Most Foul, 1971; The Attorney, 1973; The Broker, 1981; The Mourning After, 1982. Add: 520 E. 20th St., New York, N.Y. 10009, U.S.A.

MATCHETT, William H(enry). American, b. 1923. Poetry. Prof. Emeritus of English, Univ. of Washington, Seattle, since 1983 (Instr., 1954–56; Asst. Prof., 1956–60; Assoc. Prof., 1960–66; Prof. 1966–83). Member, Editorial Bd., Poetry Northwest, Seattle, since 1961. Teaching Fellow, Harvard Univ., Cambridge, Mass., 1953–54; Ed., Modern Language Quarterly, 1963–82. *Publs:* Water Ouzel and Other Poems, 1955; (with J. Beaty) Poetry: From Statement to Meaning, 1965; The Phoenix and the Turtle: Shakespeare's Poem and Chester's "Loues Martyr", 1965; (ed.) The Life and Death of King John, by William Shakespeare, 1966; Fireweed and Other Poems, 1980. Add: 1017 Minor Ave., No. 702, Seattle, Wash. 98104, U.S.A.

MATHER, Anne. Has also written as Caroline Fleming. Historical/Romance/Gothic. *Publs:* Caroline, 1965; Beloved Stranger, 1966; Design for Loving, 1966; Masquerade, 1966; The Arrogance of Love, 1968; (as Caroline Fleming) Dark Venetian, 1969, in Can. (as Anne Mather), 1976; The Enchanted Island, 1969; Dangerous Rhapsody, 1969; Legend of Lexandros, 1969; Dangerous Enchantment, 1969; Tangled Tapestry, 1969; The Arrogant Duke, 1970; Charlotte's Hurricane, 1970; Lord of Zaracus, 1970; Sweet Revenge, 1970; Who Rides the Tiger, 1970; Moon Witch, 1970; Master of Falcon's Head, 1970; The Reluctant Governess, 1971; The Pleasure and the Pain, 1971; The Sanchez Tradition, 1971; Storm in a Rain Barrel, 1971; Dark Enemy, 1971; All the Fire, 1971; The High Valley, 1971; The Autumn of the Witch, 1972; Living with Adam, 1972; A Distant Sound of Thunder, 1972; Monkshood, 1972; Prelude to Enchangement, 1972; The Night of the Bulls, 1972; Jack Howard's Wife, 1973; A Savage Beauty, 1973; Chase a Green Shadow, 1973; White Rose of Winter, 1973; Mask of Scars, 1973; The Waterfalls of the Moon, 1973; The Shrouded Web, 1973; Seen by Candlelight, 1974; Legacy of the Past, 1974; Leopard in the Snow, 1974; The Japanese Screen, 1974; Rachel Trevellyan, 1974; Silver Fruit upon Silver Trees, 1974; Dark Moonless Night, 1974; Witchstone, 1974; No Gentle Possession, 1975; Pale Dawn, Dark Sunset, 1975; Take What You Want, 1975; Come the Vintage, 1975; Dark Castle, 1975; Country of the Falcon, 1975; For the Love of Sara, 1975; Valley Deep, Mountain High, 1976; The Smouldering Flame, 1976; Wild Enchantress, 1976; Beware the Beast, 1976; Devil's Mount, 1976; Forbidden, 1976; Come Running, 1976; Alien Wife, 1977; The Medici Lover, 1977; Born Out of Love, 1977; A Trial Marriage, 1977; Devil in Velvet, 1977; Loren's Baby, 1978; Rooted in Dishonour, 1978; Proud Harvest, 1978; Scorpion's Dance, 1978; Captive Destiny, 1978; Fallen Angel, 1978; Apollo's Seed, 1979; Hell or High Water, 1979; The Judas Trap, 1979; Lure of Eagles, 1979; Melting Fire, 1979; Images of Love, 1980; Sandstorm, 1980; Spirit of Atlantis, 1980; Whisper of Darkness, 1980; Castles of Sand, 1981; Forbidden Flame, 1981; A Haunting Compulsion, 1981; Innocent Obsession, 1981; Edge of Temptation, 1982; Duelling Fire, 1982; Smokescreen, 1982; Season of Mists, 1982; A Passionate Affair, 1982; Stormspell, 1982; Impetuous Masquerade, 1982; Wild Concerto, 1983; Cage of Shadows, 1983; An Elusive Desire, 1983; Green Lightning, 1983; Sirocco, 1983; Moondrift, 1984; Act of Possession, 1985; Pale Orchid, 1985; Stolen Summer, 1985; An All-Consuming Passion, 1985; Hidden in the Flame, 1985; The Longest Pleasure, 1986; Night Heat, 1987; Burning Inheritance, 1987; Dark Mosaic, 1989; A Fever in the Blood, 1989. Add: c/o Mills and Boon, Eton House, 18-24 Paradise Rd., Richmond, Surrey TW9 1SR, England.

MATHER, Berkely. Pseud. for Col. John Evan ("Jasper") Weston-Davies. British. Soldier in the British Army for 30 years: Lt. Col. Chmn., Crime Writers Assn., 1966. Mystery/Crime/Suspense, Plays/Screenplays. *Publs:* The Achilles Affair, 1959; The Pass Beyond Kashmir, 1960; Geth Straker and Other Stories, 1962; The Road and the Star, 1965; The Gold of Malabar, 1967; The Springers (in U.S. as A Spy for a Spy), 1968; The Break in the Line (in U.S. as The Break), 1970; The Terminators, 1971; Snowline, 1973; The White Dacoit, 1974; With Extreme Prejudice, 1975; The Memsahib, 1977; The Pagoda Tree, 1979; The Midnight Gun, 1981; Hour of the Dog, 1982. Add: c/o Curtis Brown Ltd., 162-168 Regent St., London W1R 5TA, England.

MATHER, Leonard (Charles). British, b. 1909. Law, Money/Finance. Dir., Midland Bank plc., London, 1968–85 (joined bank, 1926; Vice-Chmn., 1972–74). Chmn., United Dominions Trust Ltd., 1974–81. *Publs:* The Lending Banker, 1955; Banker and Customer Relationship and the Accounts of Personal Customers, 1956; The Accounts of Limited Company Customers, 1958; Securities Acceptable to the Lending Banker, 1960. Add: Rochester House, Parkfield, Seal, Sevenoaks, Kent, England.

MATHERS, Peter. Australian, b. 1931. Novels/Short stories. *Publs:* Trap, 1966; The Wort Papers, 1972; A Change for the Better (stories), 1984. Add: c/o The Almost Managing Company, 83 Faraday St., Carlton, Victoria, Australia 3053.

MATHESON, Richard (Burton). American, b. 1926. Historical/Romance/Gothic, Science fiction/Fantasy. Freelance writer, especially of screenplays and TV plays. *Publs:* Someone Is Bleeding, 1953; Fury on Sunday, 1954; I Am Legend (SF novel), 1954; Born of Man and Woman (short stories), 1954, as Third from the Sun, 1955; The Shrinking Man (SF novel), 1956; The Shores of Space (short stories), 1957; A Stir of Echoes, 1958; Ride the Nightmare, 1959; The Beardless Warriors, 1960; Shock! (short stories), 1961; Shock II! (short stories), 1964; Shock III! (short stories), 1966; Shock Waves (short stories), 1970; Hell House, 1971; Bid Time Return, 1975; What Dreams May Come, 1978; Shock 4 (short stories), 1980; Scars and Other Distinguishing Marks (short stories), 1987. Add: P.O. Box 81, Woodland Hills, Calif. 91365, U.S.A.

MATHESON, Sylvia A. *See* **SCHOFIELD,** Sylvia Anne.

MATHEW, Ray(mond Frank). Australian, b. 1929. Novels/Short stories, Plays/Screenplays, Poetry, Literature. Schoolteacher in New South Wales, 1949–51; free-lance journalist, 1951–52; staff member, Commonwealth Scientific and Independent Research Org., Sydney, 1952–54; tutor and lectr., Worker's Education Assn., Univ. of Sydney, 1955–60. *Publs:* With Cypress Pine (poetry), 1951; We Fnd the Bunyip, 1955; Song and Dance (poetry), 1956; A Spring Song, 1958; Sing for St. Ned: An Entertainment for the Theatre, 1960; The Life of the Party, 1960; A Bohemian Affair: Short Stories, 1961; South of the Equator (poetry), 1961; Miles Franklin, 1963; Charles Blackman, 1965; (with M. Abdullah) The Time of the Peacock (short stories), 1965; The Joys of Possession (novel), 1967. Add: c/o Currency Press, P.O. Box 452, Paddington, N.S.W. 2021, Australia.

MATHEWS, Russell Lloyd. Australian, b. 1921. Economics. Emeritus Prof., Australian National Univ., Canberra (Asst. to the Vice-Chancellor, 1949–53; Prof. of Accounting and Public Finance, 1965–78; Dir., Centre for Research on Federal Financial Relations, 1972–86). Member, Grants Commn., Australia, since 1972. Reader in Commercial Studies, 1953–57, and Prof. of Commerce, 1958–64, Univ. of Adelaide. Member, Commn. of Inquiry into Land Tenures, 1973–75; Chmn., Cttee. of Inquiry into Inflation and Taxation, 1975; Chmn., Advisory Council for Inter-Govt. Relations, 1977–79. *Publs:* (co-author) Inflation and Company Finance, 1958; Militia Battalion at War, 1961; Accounting for Economists, 1962; Public Investment in Australia, 1967; The Accounting Framework, 1971, 1979; (co-author) Federal Finance, 1972; Australian Federalism, 1980; Fiscal Equalisation in Education, 1983. Add: 22 Cobby St., Campbell, A.C.T. 2601, Australia.

MATHIAS, Peter. British, b. 1928. History. Master, Downing Coll., Cambridge, since 1987. Gen. Ed., Cambridge Economic History of Europe, and Debates in Economic History, Methuen, London, since 1967. Research Fellow, Jesus Coll., Cambridge, 1952–55; Lectr. in History, Cambridge Univ., and Fellow, Tutor and Dir. of Studies in History, Queens' Coll., Cambridge, 1955–68; Chichele Prof. of Economic History and Fellow, All Souls Coll. Oxford Univ., 1969–87. *Publs:* The Brewing Industry in England, 1700–1830, 1959; Retailing Revolution, 1967; The

First Industrial Nation, 1969, 1983; (ed.) Science and Society, 1600–1900, 1972; The Transformation of England, 1979. Add: Downing Coll., Cambridge, England.

MATHIAS, Roland (Glyn). British, b. 1915. Short stories, Poetry, History, Literature. Headmaster, Pembroke Dock Grammar Sch., Wales, 1948–58, The Herbert Strutt Sch., Belper, Derbyshire, 1958–64, and King Edward's Five Ways Sch., Birmingham, 1964–69; Ed., The Anglo-Welsh Review, 1961–76; Chmn., Literature Cttee., Welsh Arts Council, 1976–79. *Publs:* Days Enduring and Other Poems, 1943; Break in Harvest and Other Poems, 1946; The Roses of Tretower, 1952; The Eleven Men of Eppynt and Other Stories, 1956; The Flooded Valley, 1960; Whitsun Riot: An Account of a Commotion Amongst Catholics in Herefordshire and Monmouthshire in 1605, 1963; (ed. with S. Adams) The Shining Pyramid and Other Stories by Welsh Authors, 1970; Absalom in the Tree, 1971; Vernon Watkins, 1974; (ed.) David Jones: Eight Essays on His Work as Writer and Artist, 1976; (co-ed.) The Collected Stories of Geralnt Goodwin, 1976; The Hollowed Out Elder Stalk: John Cowper Powys as Poet, 1978; Snipe's Castle, 1979; Burning Brambles: Selected Poems 1944–1979, 1983; (co-ed.) Anglo-Welsh Poetry 1480–1980, 1984; A Ride Through the Wood: Essays on Anglo-Welsh Literature, 1985; Anglo-Welsh Literature: An Illustrated History, 1987. Add: Deffrobani, Maescelyn, Brecon, Wales.

MATHIESON, Donald Lindsay. New Zealander, b. 1936. Law. Barrister, since 1959; Queen's Counsel, 1986. Lectr. to Prof. of Law, Victoria Univ., Wellington, 1961–71, 1977–81; Crown Counsel, Crown Law Office, Wellington, 1971–76; Sr. Partner, Hogg Gillespie Carter and Oakley, 1981–85. *Publs:* (ed.) Cross on Evidence, New Zealand edition, 1963, 4th ed. 1989; Industrial Law in New Zealand, Vol. I, 1970. Add: 33 Marsden Ave., Karori, Wellington, New Zealand.

MATHIS, Sharon Bell. American, b. 1937. Novels/Short stories, Poetry, Biography. Teacher, Stuart Jr. High Sch., Washington, D.C., since 1965; Librarian, Friendship Educational Center, Washington, since 1976. Columnist, Ebony Jr! mag., since 1973. Writer-in-Residence, Howard Univ., Washington, 1972–74. *Publs:* Brooklyn Story, 1970; Sidewalk Story, 1971; Teacup Full of Roses, 1972; Ray Charles (biography), 1973; Listen for the Fig Tree, 1974; The Hundred Penny Box, 1975; Cartwheels (novel), 1978. Add: c/o Curtis Brown, 10 Astor Pl., New York, N.Y. 10003, U.S.A.

MATILAL, B(imal) K(rishna). Indian, b. 1935. Philosophy, Religion. Fellow, All Souls Coll., Oxford, and Spalding Prof. of Religions and Ethics, Oxford Univ., since 1976. Ed., Journal of Indian Philosophy, since 1971. Lectr., Sanskrit Coll., Calcutta Univ., 1957–65; Asst. Prof., 1965–67, and Assoc. Prof., 1967–71, Univ. of Pennsylvania, Philadelphia; Prof., Univ. of Toronto, 1971–77. *Publs:* The Navya-nyaya Doctrine of Negation, 1968; Epistemology, Logic, and Grammar in Indian Philosophical Analysis, 1971; The Logical Illumination of Indian Mysticism, 1977; The Central Philosophy of Jainism, 1981; Logical and Ethical Issues in Indian Religions, 1982; Logic, Language, and Reality, 1985; (ed.) Analytical Philosophy in Comparative Perspective, 1985; Perception: An Essay on Classical Indian Theories of Knowledge, 1986. Add: Oriental Institute, Oxford University, Oxford, England.

MATSON, Wallace I. American, b. 1921. Philosophy. Prof. of Philosophy, Univ. of California, Berkeley, since 1955. Asst. Prof. of Philosophy, Univ. of Washington, 1950–55. *Publs:* The Existence of God, 1965; A History of Philosophy, 1968; Sentience, 1976; A New History of Philosophy, 1987. Add: Dept. of Philosophy, Univ. of Calif., Berkeley Calif. 94720, U.S.A.

MATSUBA, Moshe. Formerly Avraham Chaim Ben-Yosef. Israeli, b. 1917. Social commentary/phenomena, Sociology. Farmer, Japanese Commune Movement, since 1972. Ed., Commumanity, since 1973. Kibbutz member in Israel, 1956–71. *Publs:* The Purest Democracy in the World, 1963; Ancient History: The Twentieth Century, 1970; (with Kusakari, Zenzo and Steinbach) The Communes of Japan, 1977. Add: Japanese Commune Movement, Kibbutz Akan, Shin Shizen Juku, Nakasetsuri, Tsurui Mura, Akan Gun, Hokkaido 085-12, Japan.

MATTHEW, Christopher C.F. British, b. 1939. Novels/Short stories, Travel/Exploration/Adventure, Humor/Satire. Lectr. in English, La Colline Sch. of Languages, La Tour de Peilz, Switzerland, 1963–64; Advertising Copywriter, London Press Exchange, Ltd., 1964–66; Copywriter, J. Walter Thompson Co. Ltd., 1966–68, Masius, Wynne-Williams, 1968–70, and Thomson Group Marketing, 1970; Ed., The Times Travel Guide,

1973–75. *Publs:* A Different World: Stories of Great Hotels, 1976; Diary of a Somebody, 1978; The Long-Haired Boy, 1980; Loosely Engaged, 1980; The Crisp Report, 1981; Annotated Three Men in a Boat, 1982; How to Survive Middle Age, 1983; The Junket Man, 1983; Family Matters, 1987. Add: c/o Deborah Rogers Ltd., 49 Blenheim Crescent, London, W11, England.

MATTHEWS, Denis. British, b. 1919. Music, Autobiography/Memoirs/Personal. Concert pianist: debut, London, 1939; has given frequent recitals and concerts since 1943; tours: Vienna, 1950; South Africa, 1953–54, 1962; Canada, 1951, 1957, 1960; Poland, 1956, 1960; World Tour, 1964; Latin America, 1968, 1970; Australia, 1977, 1979. Prof. of Music, Univ. of Newcastle upon Tyne, 1971–84; Lectr., Royal Academy of Music and Royal Coll. of Music, London. *Publs:* In Pursuit of Music (autobiography), 1966; Beethoven's Piano Sonatas, 1967; Keyboard Music, 1972; Brahms's Three Phases, 1972; Brahms Piano Music, 1978; Toscanini, 1982; Beethoven, 1985. Add: 6 Reddings Rd., Moseley, Birmingham B13 8LN, England.

MATTHEWS, Ellen. *See* **BACHE,** Ellen.

MATTHEWS, Jack. (John Harold Matthews). American, b. 1925. Novels/Short stories, Poetry. Distinguished Prof. of English, Ohio Univ., Athens, since 1977 (Lectr., 1964–70; Prof., 1971–76). Assoc. Prof., 1959–62, and Prof. of English, 1962–64, Urbana Coll., Ohio; Distinguished Writer-in-Residence, Witchita State Univ., Kans., 1970–71. *Publs:* Bitter Knowledge (short stories), 1964; An Almanac for Twilight (poetry), 1966; Hanger Stout, Awake!, 1967; Beyond the Bridge, 1970; The Tale of Asa Bean, 1971; The Charisma Campaigns, 1972; (ed. with E.G. Hemley) The Writer's Signature: Idea in Story and Essay, 1972; Pictures of the Journey Back, 1973; (ed.) Archetypal Themes in the Modern Story, 1973; Collecting Rare Books for Pleasure and Profit, 1977; Tales of the Ohio Land (short stories), 1979; Dubious Persuasions (short stories), 1981; Sassafras (novel), 1983; Crazy Women (short stories), 1985; Ghostly Populations (short stories), 1987. Add: 24 Briarwood Dr., Athens, Ohio 45701, U.S.A.

MATTHEWS, Patricia. Also writes as P.A. Brisco, Patty Brisco, and Laura Wylie. American, b. 1927. Novels/Short stories, Historical/Romance/Gothic, Children's fiction, Poetry. Member, Bd. of Dirs., Friends of the Theatre, California State Univ., Los Angeles, since 1981. Secty. and admin., California State Univ., 1959–77. *Publs:* (as Patty Brisco) Merry's Treasure (—juvenile), 1969; (as Patty Brisco, with Clayton Matthews) Horror at Gull House (gothic), 1970; (as Patty Brisco) Merry's Treasure (—juvenile), 1970; (as Patty Brisco, with Clayton Matthews) House of Candles (gothic), 1973; (as Patty Brisco, with Clayton Matthews) The Crystal Window (gothic), 1973; (as Patty Brisco) The Carnival Mystery (—juvenile), 1974; (as Patty Brisco, with Clayton Matthews) Mist of Evil (gothic), 1976; Love's Avenging Heart, 1977; Love's Wildest Promise, 1977; Love Forever More, 1977; (as Patty Brisco) The Campus Mystery (—juvenile), 1977; Love's Daring Dream, 1978; Love's Pagan Heart, 1979; Love's Magic Moment, 1979; Love's Golden Destiny, 1979; (as Laura Wylie) The Night Visitor, 1979; (as P.A. Brisco) The Other People (novel), 1979; Love's Many Faces (poetry), 1979; (as Patty Brisco) Raging Rapids (—juvenile), 1979; (as Patty Brisco) Too Much in Love (—juvenile), 1979; Love's Raging Tide, 1980; Love's Bold Journey, 1980; Love's Sweet Agony, 1980; Tides of Love, 1981; (with Clayton Matthews) Midnight Whispers, 1981; Embers of Dawn, 1982; (with Clayton Matthews) Empire, 1982; Flames of Glory, 1983; Gambler in Love, 1985; Tame the Restless Heart, 1986; Enchanted, 1987; Thursday and The Lady, 1987; Love, Forever More, 1988; Mirrors, 1988; Oasis, 1988; The Dreaming Tree, 1989. Lives in San Diego County. Add: c/o Worldwide Library, 225 Duncan Mills Rd., Don Mills, Ont. M3B 3K9, Canada.

MATTHEWS, Peter (Hugoe). British, b. 1934. Language/Linguistics. Fellow, St. John's Coll., Cambridge, and Prof. and Head of Dept. of Linguistics, Cambridge Univ., since 1980. Lectr., University Coll. of N. Wales, 1961–65; Lectr., 1965–69, Reader, 1969–75, and Prof., 1975–80, Univ. of Reading. Ed., Journal of Linguistics, 1970–79. *Publs:* Inflectional Morphology, 1972; Morphology, 1974; Generative Grammar and Linguistic Competence, 1979; Syntax, 1981; Do Languages Obey General Laws?, 1982. Add: 10 Fendon Close, Cambridge CB1 4RU, England.

MATTHEWS, Robert C(harles) O(liver). British, b. 1927. Economics, Hobbies. Master, Clare Coll., Cambridge, since 1975, and Prof. of Political Economy, Cambridge Univ., since 1980 (Asst. Lectr., 1949–51, and Lectr., 1951–65, Cambridge Univ.; Fellow, St. John's Coll., Cambridge, 1950–65). Managing Trustee, Nuffield Foundn., since 1975; Member of

Exec. Cttee., Natl. Inst. of Economic and Social Research, since 1975; Chmn., Bank of England Panel of Academic Consultants, since 1977; Trustee, Urwick Orr and Partners Ltd., since 1978. Lectr., Merton Coll., Oxford, 1948–49, and Fellow, All Souls Coll., Oxford, and Drummond Prof. of Political Economy, 1965–75, Oxford Univ. Member, Central Advisory Council on Science and Technology, 1967–70; Chmn., Social Science Research Council, 1972–75; Member of the Council, British Academy, 1972–75, and Royal Economics Soc., 1973–82. *Publs:* A Study in Trade Cycle History, 1954; The Trade Cycle, 1958; (with M. Lipton and J.M. Rice) Chess Problems, 1963; (with F.H. Hahn) Théorie de la croissance économique, 1972; (ed.) Economic Growth: Trends and Factors, 1981; (with C.H. Feinstein and J.C. Odling-Smee) British Economic Growth 1856–1973, 1982; (co-ed.) The Grants Economy and Collective Consumption, 1982; (ed.) Slower Growth in the Western World, 1982; (co-ed.) Contemporary Problems in Economic Policy, 1983. Add: The Master's Lodge, Clare College, Cambridge, England.

MATTHEWS, Thomas Stanley. American, b. 1901. Novels/Short stories, Poetry, Autobiography/Memoirs/Personal. Member, Editorial Staff, The New Republic, 1925–29; Member, Editorial Bd., 1929–37, Asst. Managing Ed., 1937–42, Managing Ed., 1943–49, and Ed., 1949–53, Time mag., NYC. *Publs:* To the Gallows I Must Go (in paperback as Darling I Hate You), 1931; The Moon's No Fool, 1936; (ed.) Selected Letters of Charles Lamb, 1956; The Sugar Pill, 1957; Name and Address, 1960; O My America!, 1962; The Worst Unsaid, 1962; Great Tom, 1974; Why so Gloomy?, 1976; Jacks or Better (in U.K. as Under the Influence), 1977; Journal to the End of the Day, 1981; Tell Me About It, 1985; Angels Unawares, 1985; Sorry about That, 1986; Mind Your Head!, 1988. Add: Cavendish Hall, Cavendish, Suffolk, England.

MATTHEWS, William. American, b. 1942. Poetry. Prof. of English, City Coll. of the City Univ. of New York, since 1985. Asst. Prof. of English, Cornell Univ., Ithaca, N.Y., 1969–73, and Univ. of Colorado, Boulder, 1974–77; Assoc. Prof. of English, Univ. of Washington, Seattle, 1978–85. *Publs:* Broken Syllable, 1969; Ruining the New Road, 1970; The Cloud, 1971; Sleek for the Long Flight, 1972; An Oar in the Old Water, 1974; Stick and Stones, 1975; Rising and Falling, 1979; Flood, 1982; A Happy Childhood, 1984; Foreseeable Futures, 1987; Curiosities, 1989; Blues If You Want, 1989. Add: 523 W. 121st St., New York, N.Y. 10027, U.S.A.

MATTHIAS, John (Edward). American, b. 1941. Poetry, Literature. Prof. of English, Univ. of Notre Dame, since 1981 (Asst. Prof. of English, 1967–73; Assoc. Prof., 1973–81). *Publs:* Bucyrus, 1970; Other Poems, 1970; (ed.) Contemporary British Poetry, 1971; (ed.) Twenty-Three Modern British Poets, 1971; Herman's Poems, 1974; Turns, 1975; Crossing, 1979; Introducing David Jones, 1979; (ed. and trans. with Goran Printz-Pahlson) Contemporary Swedish Poetry, 1979; (ed.) Five American Poets, 1979; Bathory and Lermontov, 1980; (trans. with Goran Printz-Pahlson) Rainmaker, by Jan Ostergren, 1983; Northern Summer: New and Selected Poems 1963–83, 1984; Places, Poems, 1989: (ed.) David Jones: Man and Poet, 1989. Add: Dept. of English, Univ. of Notre Dame, Notre Dame, Ind. 46556, U.S.A.

MATTHIESSEN, Peter. American, b. 1927. Novels/Short stories, Anthropology/Ethnology, Natural history. Founder, 1952, and Ed., Paris Review, Paris and NYC; has made anthropological and natural history expeditions to Alaska, Canadian N.W.T., Peru, New Guinea, Africa, Australia and Nepal; commercial fisherman, 1954–56. *Publs:* Race Rock (novel), 1954; Partisans (novel), 1955; Wildlife in America, 1959; Raditzer (novel), 1961; The Cloud Forest: A Chronicle of the South American Wilderness, 1961; Under the Mountain Wall: A Chronicle of Two Seasons in the Stone Age, 1962; At Play in the Fields of the Lord (novel), 1965; The Shorebirds of North America, 1967; Oomingmak: The Expedition to the Musk Ox Island in the Bering Sea, 1967; Sal Si Puedes: Cesar Chavez and the New American Revolution, 1970; Blue Meridian: The Search for the Great White Shark, 1971; Everglades: Selections from the Writings of Peter Matthiessen, 1971; Seal Pool, 1972; The Wind Birds, 1973; The Tree Where Man was Born, 1974; Far Tortuga (novel), 1975; The Snow Leopard, 1978; Sand Rivers, 1981; In the Spirit of Crazy Horse, 1983; Indian Country, 1984; Midnight Turning Gray (short stories), 1984, rev. ed. as By the River Styx, 1989; Nine-Headed Dragon River, 1986; Men's Lives, 1986. Add: Bridge Lane, Sagaponack, L.I., N.Y. 11962, U.S.A.

MATTINGLEY, Christobel (Rosemary). Australian, b. 1931.Children's fiction, History. Librarian, Dept. of Immigration, Canberra, 1951, Latrobe Valley Libraries, Victoria, 1953, Prince Alfred Coll., Adelaide, 1956–57, and St. Peter's Girls' Sch., Adelaide, 1966–70; Acquisitions

Librarian, 1971, and Reader Services Librarian, 1972, Wattle Park Teachers' Coll., Adelaide; Reader Services Librarian, Murray Park Coll. of Advanced Education, Adelaide, 1973–74; Scriptwriter, South Australian Film Corp., 1977–79. Chmn., National Book Council, S. Australia Branch, 1979–84. *Publs:* The Picnic Dog, 1970; Windmill at Magpie Creek, 1971; Worm Weather, 1971; Emu Kite, 1972; Queen of the Wheat Castles, 1973; The Battle of the Galah Trees, 1974; Show and Tell, 1974; Tiger's Milk, 1974; The Surprise Mouse, 1974; Lizard Log, 1975; The Great Ballagundi Damper Bake, 1975; The Long Walk, 1976; The Special Present, 1977; New Patches for Old, 1977; The Big Swim, 1977; Budgerigar Blue, 1978; The Jetty, 1978; Black Dog, 1979; Rummage, 1981; Brave with Ben, 1982; Lexl and the Lion Party, 1982; Duck Boy, 1983; The Magic Saddle, 1983; Southerly Buster, 1983; The Angel with a Mouth Organ, 1984; Ghost Sitter, 1984; The Miracle Tree, 1985; McGruer and the Goat, 1987; (ed.) South Australian Sesquicentenary Aboriginal History Volume: Survival in Our Own Land, 1988. Add: Allendale Grove, Stonyfell, S.A. 5066, Australia.

MATURA, Mustapha. Trinidadian, b. 1939. Plays/Screenplays. *Publs:* As Time Goes By, and Black Pieces, 1972; Play Mas, 1976; Nice, Rum an Coca Cola, and Welcome Home Jacko, 1980; Play Mas, Independence, and Meetings, 1982. Add: c/o Judy Daish Assocs., 83 Eastbourne Mews, London W2 6LQ, England.

MAUDE, H(enry) E(vans). British, b. 1906. Anthropology/Ethnology, Geography, History. Visiting Fellow, Australian National Univ., Canberra, since 1972 (Sr. Fellow and Professorial Fellow, 1959–70); Hon. Prof., Univ. of Adelaide, since 1973. With British Colonial Admin. Service, in South Pacific, 1929–45; Resident Commnr., Gilbert and Ellice Islands Colony, 1946–48; Founder, South Pacific Literature Bureau, 1949; Deputy Secty.-Gen. and Exec. Officer for Social Development, South Pacific Commn., 1949–57; Co-Founder and Joint Ed., Journal of Pacific History, 1966–71; Gen. Ed., Pacific History Series, 1968–77, and Pacific Monograph Series, 1969–77. Founder, Pacific Manuscripts Bureau, 1969. *Publs:* (with H. C. Maude) String Figures from the Gilbert Islands; The Evolution of the Gilbertese Boti; Of Islands and Men; The Gilbertese Maneaba, 1980; Slavers in Paradise, 1981. Add: 11 Namatjira Dr., Weston, Canberra, A.C.T., Australia 2611.

MAUGHAN, Anne Margery. British. Historical/Romance/Gothic. Co. Dir., The Witton Park Slag Co. Ltd. *Publs:* Monmouth Harry, 1956; Young Pitt, 1974; The King's Malady, 1978. Add: 2 Ryton Sq., Sunderland, Co. Durham, England.

MAUGHAN, Joyce Bowen. American, b. 1928. Children's non-fiction, Women. Teacher, Manicopa Country Community Coll., since 1973; private therapist for women and Children. Columnist, Thoughts in Passing, Sun Valley Spur Newspaper, 1968–69. *Publs:* Talks for Tots, vols. I & II, 1964, 1967; Talk Themes for Sub-Teens, 1964; Stories That Never Grow Old, 1965; Stories You'll Want to Remember, 1969; Identity Crisis of the Woman Thirty to Fifty Years of Age, 1974; Unicornucopia: Guidebook for Gifted and Talented, 1977. Add: 735 East 3rd St., Mesa, Ariz. 85203, U.S.A.

MAVOR, Elizabeth (Osborne). British, b. 1927. Novel/Short stories, Biography. *Publs:* Summer in the Greenhouse, 1959; The Temple of Flora, 1961; The Virgin Mistress: A Biography of the Duchess of Kingston (in U.S. as The Virgin Mistress: A Study in Survival: The Life of the Duchess of Kingston), 1964; The Redoubt, 1967; The Ladies of Llangollen: Study in Romantic Friendship, 1971; A Green Equinox, 1973; Life with the Ladies of Llangollen, 1984; The Grand Tour of William Beckford, 1986; The White Solitaire, 1988. Add: 11 Gorwell, Watlington, Oxon., England.

MAX, Nicholas. *See* **ASBELL,** Bernard.

MAXWELL, A. E. *See* **LOWELL,** Elizabeth.

MAXWELL, Ann Elizabeth. *See* **LOWELL,** Elizabeth.

MAXWELL, D. E. S. Irish, b. 1925. Literature, Biography. Prof. of English, York Univ., Toronto, since 1967. Lectr., Univ. of Ghana, 1956–61; Asst. Dir. of Examinations, Civil Service Commn., England, 1961–63; Prof. of English and Head of Dept., Univ. of Ibadan, Nigeria, 1963–67. *Publs:* The Poetry of T.S. Eliot, 1952; American Fiction: The Intellectual Background, 1963; Cozzens, 1964; Herman Melville, 1968; (ed. with S.B. Bushrui) W.B. Yeats Centenary Essays, 1965; Poets of the Thirties, 1969; Brian Friel, 1973; Modern Irish Drama, 1984. Add: Dept. of English, York Univ., Downsview, Ont. M3J 1P3, Canada.

MAXWELL, John. *See* FREEMANTLE, Brian.

MAXWELL, Kenneth Robert. British, b. 1941. History, International relations/Current affairs. Sr. Fellow, Research Inst. on Intnl. Change, Columbia Univ., NYC, since 1978 (Prof. of History, 1976–84); Dir., Carnões Center For Portuguese Speaking World, since 1988. Gulbenkian Fellow, Newberry Library, Chicago, 1968–69; Assoc. Prof. of History, Univ. of Kansas, Lawrence, 1969–71; Member, Inst. for Advanced Study, Princeton, N.J., 1971–75. Prog. Dir., The Tinken Foundn., Inc., NYC, 1979–85. *Publs:* Conflicts and Conspiracies: Brazil and Portugal 1750–1808, 1973; The Press and the Rebirth of Iberian Democracy, 1983; Portugal: Ten Years after the Revolution, 1984; Spain's Prospects, 1985; Portugal in the 1980's: The Dilemmas of Democratic Consolidation, 1985; Pombal: Illuminismo, Império e Despotismo, 1985; The Causes and Consequences of the Revolution in Portugal, 1986. Add: Research Inst. on Intnl. Change, Columbia Univ., 420 W. 118th St., New York, N.Y. 10027, U.S.A.

MAXWELL, Patricia Anne. With Carol Albritton writes as Elizabeth Trehearne; also writes as Jennifer Blake, Patricia Ponder, and Maxine Patrick. American, b. 1942. Mystery/Crime/Suspense, Historical/Romance/Gothic. *Publs:* Secret of Mirror House, 1970; Stranger at Plantation Inn, 1971; (with Carol Albritton, as Elizabeth Trehearne) Storm at Midnight, 1973; The Bewitching Grace, 1974; Dark Masquerade, 1974; The Court of the Thorn Tree, 1974; Bride of a Stranger, 1974; The Notorious Angel, 1977; (as Jennifer Blake) Love's Wild Desire, 1977; (as Patricia Ponder) Haven of Fear, 1977; (as Patricia Ponder) Murder for Charity, 1977; Sweet Piracy, 1978; (as Maxine Patrick) The Abducted Heart, 1978; Night of the Candles, 1978; (as Maxine Patrick) Bayou Bride, 1979; (as Jennifer Blake) Tender Betrayal, 1979; (as Maxine Patrick) Snowbound Heart, 1979; (as Jennifer Blake) The Storm and the Splendor, 1979; (as Maxine Patrick) Love at Sea, 1980; (as Jennifer Blake) Golden Fancy, 1980; (as Maxine Patrick) Captive Kisses, 1980; (as Jennifer Blake) Embrace and Conquer, 1981; (as Maxine Patrick) April of Enchantment, 1981; (as Jennifer Blake) Royal Seduction, 1983; (as Jennifer BLake) Surrender in Moonlight, 1984; (as Jennifer BLake) Midnight Waltz, 1985; (as Jennifer Blake) Fierce Eden, 1985; (as Jennifer Blake) Royal Passion, 1986; (as Jennifer Blake) Prisoner of Desire, 1986; (as Jennifer Blake) Southern Rapture, 1987; (as Jennifer Blake) Louisiana Dawn, 1987; (as Jennifer Blake) Perfume of Paradise, 1988; (as Jennifer Blake) Love and Smoke, 1989. Add: Rt. 1, Box 133, Quitman, La. 71268, U.S.A.

MAXWELL, Vicky. *See* WORBOYS, Anne.

MAXWELL, William. American, b., 1908. Novels/Short stories, Autobiography/Memoirs/Personal. Member of English faculty, Univ. of Illinois, Urbana, 1931–33; Member of staff, The New Yorker mag., 1936–76. *Publs:* Bright Center of Heaven, 1934; They Came Like Swallows, 1937; The Folded Leaf, 1945; The Heavenly Tenants, 1946; Time Will Darken It, 1948; The Château, 1961; The Old Man at the Railroad Crossing and Other Tales, 1966; Ancestors, 1971; Over by the River and Other Stories, 1977; So Long, See You Tomorrow, 1980; (ed.) The Garden and the Wilderness, by Charles Pratt, 1980; (ed.) The Letters of Sylvia Townsend Warner, 1982. Add: 544 East 86th St., New York, N.Y. 10028, U.S.A.

MAXWELL, William. *See* ALLAN, Ted.

MAY, Derwent (James). British, b. 1930. Novels/Short stories. Literary and Arts Ed., The Sunday Telegraph, London, since 1986. *Publs:* The Professionals, 1964; Dear Parson, 1969; The Laughter in Djakarta, 1973; A Revenger's Comedy, 1979; Proust, 1983; The Times Nature Diary, 1983; Hannah Arendt, 1986. Add: 201 Albany St., London NW1, England.

MAY, Elaine. American, b. 1932. Plays/Screenplays. Actress, and stage and film dir. *Publs:* An Evening with Mike Nichols and Elaine May, 1960; A Matter of Position, 1962; Not Enough Rope, 1962; Adaptation, 1969; A New Leaf (screenplay), 1971; Mikey and Nicky (screenplay), 1976; (with Warren Beatty) Heaven Can Wait (screenplay), 1978; The Better Part of Valor, 1983; Hotline, 1983; Ishtan (screenplay), 1987. Add: c/o Directors Guild of America, 7950 W. Sunset Blvd., Los Angeles, Calif. 90046, U.S.A.

MAY, Gita. American, b. 1929. Biography, Essays. Prof. of French, since 1968, and Dept. Chmn., since 1983, Columbia Univ., NYC (Lectr., 1953–56; Instr., 1956–58; Asst. Prof., 1958–61; Assoc. Prof., 1961–68). Member, Editorial Bd., Romanic Review, since 1959, and the French

Review, since 1975. Member, Delegate Assembly, 1973–75, Cttee. on Research Activities, 1975–78, and Exec. Council, 1980–83, Modern Language Assn.; Member, Editorial Bd., Eighteenth-Century Studies, 1975–78; Pres., American Society for 18th-Century Studies, 1985. Pres., Northeast American Soc. for 18th Century Studies, 1981. *Publs:* Diderot et Baudelaire: critiques d'Art, 1957, 3rd ed. 1973; (ed. with Otis Fellows) Diderot Studies III, 1961; De Jean-Jacques Rousseau à Madame Roland: Essai sur la sensibilité préromantique et Révolutionnaire, 1964, 1974; Madame Roland and the Age of Revolution, 1970; Stendhal and the Age of Napoleon, 1977; (contr.) European Writers: The Age of Reason and the Enlightenment, 1984; The Romantic Century, 1985. Add: 404 West 116th St., New York, N.Y. 10027, U.S.A.

MAY, Henry F(arnham). American, b. 1915. History. Prof. Emeritus of History, Univ. of California, Berkeley, since 1980 (Assoc. Prof., 1952–56; Prof. of History, 1956–63; Chmn. of Dept., 1964–66). Instr. in History, Lawrence Coll. (now Lawrence Univ.), Appleton, Wisc., 1941–42; Asst. Prof., 1947–48, and Assoc. Prof., 1948–49, Scripps Coll., Claremont, Calif.; Visiting Assoc. Prof., Bowdoin Coll., Brunswick, Me., 1950–51; Fulbright Lectr., Belgian univs., 1959–60; Pitt Prof. of American History Instns., Cambridge Univ., 1971–72. *Publs:* Protestant Churches and Industrial America, 1949, 1967; The End of American Innocence: A Study of the First Years of Our Own Time 1912–1917, 1959; (with Charles G. Sellers, Jr.) A Synopsis of American History, 1963, 1969; (ed.) Oldtown Folks, by Harriet Beecher Stowe, 1966; The Enlightenment in America, 1976; Ideas, Faiths, and Feelings, 1983; Coming to Terms, 1988. Add: Dept. of History, Univ. of California, Berkeley, Calif, 94707, U.S.A.

MAY, Julian. American, b. 1931. Science fiction. Founder, with Ted Dikty, Publication Assocs., Chicago, 1957–74, West Linn, Ore., 1974–80, and Mercer Island, Wash., since 1980. Formerly, Ed., Booz Allen and Hamilton, Chicago; Ed., Consolidated Book Publishers, Chicago, 1954–57. *Publs:* The Saga of Pliocene Exile: The Many-Colored Land, 1981, The Golden Torc, 1981, The Nonborn King, 1983, and The Adversary, 1984; A Pliocene Companion, 1984; Intervention, 1987. Add: P.O. Box 851, Mercer Island, Wash. 98040, U.S.A.

MAY, Robin. (Robert Stephen May). British, b. 1929. History, Music, Theatre. Freelance writer, 1966–70, and since 1976. Actor, 1953–63; commercial artist's agent, 1963–66; Feature Writer, Look and Learn mag., London, 1970–76. *Publs:* Operamania, 1966; Theatremania, 1967; The Wit of the Theatre, 1969; Who's Who in Shakespeare, 1972; A Companion to the Theatre, 1973; (with G.A. Embleton) The American West, 1974; (with G.A. Embleton) Wolfe's Army, 1974; The Gold Rushes, 1977; A Companion to the Opera, 1977; Opera, 1977; (with Joseph G. Rosa) Gunsmoke, 1977, in U.S.A. as, Gun Law: The Story of the Wild West, 1978; (with Joseph G. Rosa) Cowboy, 1980; Behind the Baton, 1981; Indians, 1982; Gunfighters, 1983; William the Conqueror and the Normans, 1984; Canute and the Vikings, 1984; Plains Indians of North America, 1984; History of the American West, 1984; History of the Theatre, 1986; A Guide to the Opera, 1987. Add: 23 Malcolm Rd., London SW19 4AS, England.

MAY, Rollo (Reece). American, b. 1909. Psychology, Psychiatry, Theology. Supervisory and training analyst, William Alanson White Institute of Psychiatry: Psychology and Psychoanalysis, NYC, since 1958 (Asst. Prof. of Psychiatry, 1948–74); in private practice of psychoanalysis in Tiburon, Calif., since 1975. Ordained Congregational minister, 1938; Instr. in English, Anatolia College, Saloniki, Greece, 1930–33; student adviser, Michigan State College of Agriculture and Allied Science (now Michigan State Univ.), East Lansing, 1934–36; minister of Congregational church in Verona, N.J., 1938–40; student adviser, City College (now City College of the City Univ. of New York), 1945; private practice of psychoanalysis in New York City, 1950–75; Lectr. in Psychotherapy, New School for Social Research, NYC, 1955–76; Visiting Prof., Harvard Univ., summer 1964, Princeton Univ., 1967, and Yale Univ., 1972; Distinguished Visiting Prof., Brooklyn College, 1974–75; Dean's Scholar at New York Univ., 1971; Regent's Prof., Univ. of California at Santa Cruz, 1973. *Publs:* The Art of Counseling, 1939, 1989; The Springs of Creative Living: A Study of Human Nature and God, 1940; The Meaning of Anxiety, 1950, 1977; Man's Search for Himself, 1953; (ed. with Ernest Angel and Henri F. Ellenberger) Existence: A New Dimension in Religion and Literature, 1960; Existential Psychology, 1961; Psychology and the Human Dilemma, 1967, 1980; (with Leopold Caliger) Dreams and Symbols, 1968; Love and Will, 1969; Power and Innocence: A Search for the Sources of Violence, 1972; Paulus: Reminiscences of a Friendship, 1973; The Courage to Create, 1975, 1984; Freedom and Destiny, 1981; The Discovery of Being: Writings in Existential Psychology, 1983, 1986;

My Quest for Beauty, 1985; (with others) Politics and Innocence: A Humanistic Debate, 1986; Paulus: The Dimensions of a Teacher, 1988; Paulus: Tillich As Spiritual Teacher, 1988. Add: 98 Sugarloaf Dr., Tiburon, Calif. 94920, U.S.A.

MAY, Wynne. (Winifred Jean May). Historical/Romance/Gothic.*b-Publs:* A Cluster of Palms, 1967; The Highest Peak, 1967; The Valley of Aloes, 1967; Tawny Are the Leaves, 1968; Tamboti Moon, 1969; Where Breezes Falter, 1970; Sun, Sea and Sand, 1970; A Grain of Gold, 1971; The Tide at Full, 1971; A Slither of Silk, 1972; A Bowl of Stars, 1973; Pink Sands, 1974; Plume of Dust, 1975; A Plantation of Vines, 1977; Island of Cyclones, 1979; A Scarf of Flame, 1979; Fire in the Ash, 1984; The Leopard's Lair, 1984; Tomorrow's Sun, 1989. Lives in S. Africa. Add: c/o Mills and Boon Ltd., Eaton House, 18-24 Paradise Rd., Richmond, Surrey TW9 1SR, England.

MAYBURY, Anne. Pseud. for Anne (Arundel) Buxton; also writes as Katherine Troy. British. Historical/Romance/Gothic. Vice-Pres., Soc. of Women Journalists, and Romantic Novelists Assn. *Publs:* The Best Love of All, 1932; The Enchanted Kingdom, 1932; The Love That Is Stronger Than Life, 1932; Love Triumphant, 1932; The Way of Compassion, 1933; The Second Winning, 1933; Farewell to Dreams, 1934; Harness the Winds, 1934; Catch at a Rainbow, 1935; Come Autumn—Come Winter, 1935; The Garden of Wishes, 1935; The Starry Wood, 1935; The Wondrous To-Morrow, 1936; Give Me Back My Dreams, 1936; Lovely Destiny, 1936; The Stars Grow Pale, 1936; This Errant Heart, 1937; This Lovely Hour, 1937; I Dare Not Dream, 1937; Oh, Darling Joy!, 1937; Lady, It Is Spring!, 1938; The Shadow of My Loving, 1938; They Dreamed Too Much, 1938; Chained Eagle, 1939; Gather Up the Years, 1939; Return to Love, 1939; The Barrier Between Us, 1940; Dare to Marry, 1940; I'll Walk with My Love, 1940; Dangerous Living, 1941; The Secret of the Rose, 1941; All Enchantments Die, 1941; To-Day We Live, 1942; Arise, Oh Sun!, 1942; Lady Fell in Love, 1943; Journey into Morning, 1944; Can I Forget You?, 1944; The Valley of Roses, 1945; The Young Invader, 1947; The Winds of Spring, 1948; Storm Heaven, 1949; The Sharon Women, 1950; First, The Dream, 1951; Goodbye, My Love, 1952; The Music of Our House, 1952; Her Name was Eve, 1953; The Heart Is Never Fair, 1954; Prelude to Louise, 1954; Follow Your Hearts, 1955; The Other Juliet, 1955; Forbidden, 1956; Dear Lost Love, 1957; Beloved Enemy, 1957; The Stars Cannot Tell, 1958; My Love Has a Secret, 1958; The Gay of Heart, 1959; The Rebel Heart, 1959; Shadow of a Stranger, 1960; Bridge to the Moon, 1960; Stay Until Tomorrow, 1961; (as Katherine Troy) Someone Waiting, 1961, in U.S. (as Anne Maybury), 1966; (as Katherine Troy) Whisper in the Dark, 1961, in U.S. (as Anne Maybury), 1966; The Night My Enemy, 1962; I am Gabriella!, 1962, as Gabriella, 1979; Green Fire, 1963; (as Katherine Troy) Enchanter's Nightshade, 1963, in U.S. (as Anne Maybury) as The Winds of Night, 1967; My Dearest Elizabeth (in U.S. as the Brides of Bellenmore), 1964; (as Katherine Troy) Falcon's Shadow, 1964, in U.S. (as Anne Maybury), 1967; Pavilion at Monkshood, 1965; Jessica, 1965; (as Katherine Troy; in U.S. as Anne Maybury) The House of Fand, 1966; The Moonlit Door, 1967; (as Katherine Troy) The Night of the Enchantress, 1967; The Minerva Stone, 1968; (as Katherine Troy) Farramonde, 1968; (as Katherine Troy) Storm over Roseheath (in U.S. as Roseheath), 1969; Ride a White Dolphin, 1971; The Terracotta Palace, 1971; Walk in the Paradise Garden, 1972; The Midnight Dancers, 1973; Jessamy Court, 1974; The Jewelled Daughter, 1976; Dark Star, 1977; Radiance, 1979; Invitation to Alannah, 1983. Add: c/o A.M. Heath, 79 St. Martin's Lane, London WC2N 4AA, England.

MAYER, Adrian C. British, b. 1922. Anthropology/Ethnology. Prof. of Asian Anthropology, Univ. of London, since 1966 (Lectr., Sch. of Oriental and African Studies, 1956–64; Reader, 1964–66). Research Fellow, Australian National Univ., 1953–56. *Publs:* Land and Society in Malabar, 1952; Caste and Kinship in Central India, 1960; Peasants in the Pacific, 1961, 1973; Indians in Fiji, 1963; (ed.) Culture and Morality, 1981. Add: Sch. of Oriental and African Studies, Malet St., London WC1, England.

MAYER, Bernadette. American, b. 1945. Poetry. *Publs:* Story, 1968; Moving, 1971; Poetry, 1976; Studying Hunger, 1976; Memory, 1976; The Golden Book of Words, 1978; Midwinter Day, 1982; Utopia, 1984. Add: 172 E. 4th St., New York, N.Y. 10009, U.S.A.

MAYER, Gerda (Kamilla). British, b. 1927. Poetry. *Publs:* Oddments, 1970; Gerda Mayer's Library Folder, 1972; (ed.) Poet Tree Centaur: A Walthamstow Group Anthology, 1973; (with Florence Elon and Daniel Halpern) Treble Poets 2, 1975; The Knockabout Show (juvenile), 1978; Monkey on the Analyst's Couch, 1980; (with Norman Nicholson

and Frank Flynn) The Candy-Floss Tree (for children), 1984; March Postman, 1985; A Heartache of Grass, 1988. Add: 12 Margaret Ave., London E4 7NP, England.

MAYER, Herbert T. American, b. 1922. Theology/Religion. Ordained Lutheran minister. Exec. Dir., Parish Koinonia Ministries, Inc., Venice, Fla. Instr., Concordia Coll., Seward, Nebr., 1949–51; Pastor, Mt. Calvary Lutheran Church, Janesville, Wisc., 1952–57; Prof. of History, Concordia Coll., Milwaukee, Wisc., 1957–59; Prof., Concordia Seminary, St. Louis, Mo., 1959–74. Ed., Concordia Theological Monthly, 1964–74; Founder, Currents in Theology and Mission, 1974; Prof. of Historical Theology, Christ Seminary-Seminex, St. Louis, 1974–83. *Publs:* Interpreting the Holy Scriptures, 1967; Books of the New Testament, 1968; (ed. with Carl S. Meyer) The Caring God, 1972; Pastoral Care: Its Roots and Renewal, 1979; Theology for the Laity, 1979. Add: 2024 Oak Ridge Circle, Venice, Fla. 34293, U.S.A.

MAYER, Raymond (Richard). American, b. 1924. Administration/Management, Money/Finance. Prof. of Mgmt., Loyola Univ. of Chicago, since 1960 (Chmn. of Mgmt., 1960–65 and 1966–68). *Publs:* Production Management, 1962, 1968; Financial Analysis of Investment Alternatives, 1966; Production and Operations Management, 1975, 4th ed. 1982; Capital Expenditure Analysis, 1978. Add: 1619 Jenks St., Evanston, Ill. 60201, U.S.A.

MAYFIELD, Julia. *See* **HASTINGS,** Phyllis.

MAYHAR, Ardath (née Hurst). Also writes as Frank Cannon. American, b. 1930. Science fiction, Children's fiction, Westerns/Adventure. Full-time writer since 1982; Co-Operator, View from Orbit bookstore, Nacogdoches, Tex., since 1984. Dairyman, 1947–57; Operator, East Texas Bookstore, Nacogdoches, 1958–62; Proofreader, Capital Journal, Salem, Ore., 1968–75; chicken farmer, 1976–78; Proofreader, Daily Sentinel, Nacogdoches, 1979–82. *Publs:* How the Gods Wove in Kyrannon, 1979; The Seekers of Shar Nuhn, 1980; Soul-Singer of Tyrnos, 1981; Warlock's Gift, 1982; Khi to Freedom, 1982; Runes of the Lyre, 1982; Golden Dream, 1983; Lords of the Triple Moons, 1983; (with Marylois Dunn) The Absolutely Perfect House, 1983; Exile on Vlahil, 1984; The Saga of Grittel Sundotha, 1985; The World Ends in Hickory Hollow, 1985; Medicine Walk (for children), 1985; Carrots and Miggle (for children), 1986; The Wall, 1987; Makra Choria, 1987; (as Frank Cannon) Feud at Sweetwater Creek, 1987; (with Ron Fortier) Trail of the Seahawks, 1987; (as Frank Cannon) Bloody Texas Trail, 1988; (as Frank Cannon) Texas Gunsmoke, 1988; A Place of Silver Silence, 1988. Add: Rt. 1, Box 146, Chireno, Tex. 75937, U.S.A.

MAYHEW, Christopher (Paget); Lord Mayhew. British, b. 1915. Plays/ Screenplays, Politics/Government, Theology/Religion, Autobiography. Chmn., ANAF Foundn., and Middle East Intnl. Publishers Co. Labour M.P. (U.K.) for Norfolk South, 1945–50; Under-Secty. of State for Foreign Affairs, 1946–50; Minister of Defence, Royal Navy, 1964 until resignation, 1966; Labour M.P. (U.K.) for Woolwich East, London, 1951–74, and for Greenwich, Woolwich East, 1974. *Publs:* Those in Favour (television play), 1951; Man Seeking God, 1955; Britain's Role Tomorrow, 1967; Party Games, 1969; (with Michael Adams) Publish It Not . . . . : The Middle East Cover Up, 1975; The Disillusioned Voter's Guide to Electoral Reform, 1976; Time to Explain (autobiography), 1987. Add: 39 Wool Rd., London SW20, England.

MAYHEW, David Raymond. American, b. 1937.Politics/Government. Alfred Cowles Prof. of Govt., Yale Univ., New Haven, Conn., since 1982 (Asst. Prof., 1968–72; Assoc. Prof., 1972–77; Prof., 1977–82). Instr., 1963–64, then Asst. Prof., 1964–67, Dept of Govt. Univ. of Massachusetts, Amherst. *Publs:* Party Loyalty Among Congressmen, 1966; Congress: The Electoral Connection, 1974; Placing Parties in American Politics, 1986. Add: Dept. of Political Science, Yale Univ., New Haven, Conn. 06520, U.S.A.

MAYNARD, Christopher. Canadian, b. 1949. Children's fiction, Children's non-fiction. Dir., The Strip Ltd., and Maynard and How Publishing, London. Ed. Macdonald Educational, London, 1972–74, and Intercontinental Book Productions, Maidenhead, Berks., 1976–77. *Publs:* Planet Earth, 1974; Prehistoric World, 1974; (with Edward Holmes) Great Men of Science, 1975; The Amazing World of Dinosaurs, 1976; (with others) The Real Cowboy, 1976; The Amazing World of Money, 1977; (ed.) Scimitar Paperbacks, 1977–78; (with others) Economy Guide to Europe, 1978; (with Gail Rebuck) New York, 1978; (with Marianne Gray) Indians and Palefaces, 1978; The Razzmatazz Gang, 1978; Father Christmas and His Friends, 1979; War Vehicles, 1980; The Great

Ice Age, 1987; (with D. Jefferis) The Aces: Pilots and Planes of World War I, 1987; (with D. Jefferis) Air Battles: Air Combat in World War II, 1987; The First Great Kids Catalogue, 1987. Add: 78 Carlton Mansions, Randolph Ave., London W9, England.

MAYNARD, Geoffrey (Walter). British, b. 1921. Economics. Visiting Prof. of Economics, Reading Univ., since 1976 (Prof. of Economics, 1968–76); Economic Consultant, Investcorp International Ltd., since 1986. Ed., Bankers Mag., 1968–72; Deputy Chief Economic Advisor, H.M. Treasury, 1976–77; Dir. of Economics, Europe and Middle East, Chase Manhattan Bank, 1977–86. *Publs:* Economic Development and the Price Level, 1962; (co-author) International Monetary Reform and Latin America, 1966; (co-author) A World of Inflation, 1976; The Economy under Mrs. Thatcher, 1988. Add: Flat 219, Queens Quay, 58 Upper Thames St., London EC4, England.

MAYNARD, Nan(cy Kathleen Brazier). British, b. 1910. Novels/Short stories. Legal Secty., Maidenhead Town Hall, 1965–83. *Publs:* This Is My Street, 1962; Weep Not, My Wanton, 1964; The Bawdy Wind, 1965; Flesh and Blood, 1967; All Sauce for the Gander, 1968; Almost an Affair, 1970; A Fig for Virtue, 1970; When the Devil Drives; Strumpet Voluntary, 1970; Rings for Her Fingers: A Crumb for Every Sparrow; The Wayward Flesh; Leaf in the Wind, 1973; Red Roses Dying, 1974; If You Can't Catch, Don't Throw, 1976; A Grief Ago, 1976; Losers Weepers, 1977; Table 21, 1978; Last Dawn, 1981; One for the Stairs, 1982; Springtime of Tears, 1984; The Distance and the Dark, 1985; Silence and Tears, 1985; Love Is a Green, Green Apple, 1986; Big Girls Don't Cry, 1986; And Then the Rain Stopped, 1986; As Long as the Birds Still Sing, 1987. Add: Morven House, 5 Keble Rd., Maidenhead, Berks., England.

MAYNE, Richard. British, b. 1926. History, Politics/Government. *Publs:* The Community of Europe, 1962; The Institutions of the European Community, 1968; The Recovery of Europe, 1970; The Europeans, 1972; (ed.) Europe Tomorrow, 1972; (ed.) The New Atlantic Challenge, 1975; (trans.) The Memoirs of Jean Monnet, 1978; Postwar: The Dawn of Today's Europe, 1983; (ed.) Western Europe: A Handbook, 1986. Add: Albany Cottage, 24 Park Village East, London NW1, England.

MAYNE, Seymour. Canadian, b. 1944. Poetry, Translations. Prof., Univ. of Ottawa, since 1985 (Asst. Prof., 1973–78; Assoc. Prof., 1978–85). Managing Ed., Very Stone House, Vancouver, 1966–69; Ed., Ingluvin Publs., Montreal, 1970–73; Ed., Mosaic Press/Valley Editions, Oakville, 1973–83. *Publs:* That Monocycle the Moon, 1964; Tiptoeing on the Mount, 1965; From the Portals of Mouseholes, 1966; (co-ed.) Collected Poems of Red Lane, 1968; Manimals, 1969; Mouth, 1970; Face, 1971; (co-ed.) Forty Women Poets of Canada, 1971; (ed.) Engagements: The Prose of Irving Layton, 1972; (ed.) Cutting the Keys, 1974; For Stems of Light, 1974; (co-trans.) Genealogy of Instruments, by J. Harasymowicz, 1974; (ed. and introduction) The A.M. Klein Symposium, 1975; Name, 1975, 1976; (ed.) Splices, 1975; (ed. and introduction) Choice Parts, 1976; Diasporas (poetry), 1977; (ed. and introduction) Irving Layton: The Poet and His Critics, 1978; The Impossible Land: Poems New and Selected, 1981; (trans.) Burnt Pearls: Ghetto Poems of Abraham Sutzkever, 1981; (ed. and co-trans.) Generations: Selected Poems of Rachel Korn, 1982; Vanguard of Dreams: New and Selected Poems, 1984; (ed. and introduction) Essential Words: An Anthology of Jewish Canadian Poetry, 1985; Children of Abel, 1986; Diversions, 1987. Add: Dept. of English, Univ. of Ottawa, Ottawa K1N 6N5, Canada.

MAYNE, William. British, b. 1929. Children's fiction. *Publs:* Follow the Footprints, 1953; The World Upside Down, 1954; A Swarm in May, 1955; The Member for the Marsh, 1956; The Choristers' Cake, 1956; The Blue Boat, 1957; A Grass Rope, 1957; The Long Night, 1957; Underground Alley, 1958; (with R.D. Caesar as Dynely James) The Gobbling Billy, 1959; The Thumbstick, 1959; Thirteen O'Clock, 1959; The Rolling Season, 1960; Cathedral Wednesday, 1960; The Fishing Party, 1960; Summer Visitors, 1961; The Changeling, 1961; The Glass Ball, 1961; The Last Bus, 1962; The Twelve Dancers, 1962; The Man from the North Pole, 1963; On the Stepping Stones, 1963; Words and Music, 1963; Plot Night, 1963; A Parcel of Trees, 1963; Water Boatman, 1964; Whistling Rufus, 1964; (ed. with E. Farjeon) The Hamish Hamilton Book of Kings (in U.S. as A Cavalcade of Kings), 1964; Sand, 1964; A Day Without Wind, 1964; The Big Wheel and the Little Wheel, 1965; (ed. with E. Farjeon) The Hamish Hamilton Book of Queens (in U.S. as A Cavalcade of Queens), 1965; Pig in the Middle, 1965; No More School, 1965; Earthfasts, 1966; Rooftops, 1966; The Old Zion, 1966; The Battlefield, 1967; (compiler) The Hamish Hamilton Book of Heroes (in U.S. as William Mayne's Book of Heroes), 1967; The Big Egg, 1967; Toffee Join, 1968; Over the Hills and Far Away (in U.S. as The Hill Road), 1968;

The Yellow Aeroplane, 1968; The House on Fairmont, 1968; (compiler) The Hamish Hamilton Book of Giants, (in U.S. as William Mayne's Book of Giants), 1968; Ravensgill, 1970; Royal Harry, 1971; A Game of Dark, 1971; (ed.) Ghosts, 1971; The Incline, 1972; Skiffy, 1972; Robin's Real Engine, 1972; Jersey Shore, 1973; A Year and a Day, 1976; Party Pants, 1977; Max's Dream, 1977; It, 1977; While the Bells Ring, 1979; An Egg for Tea, 1979; Salt River Times, 1980; The Mouse and the Egg, 1980; The Patchwork Cat, 1981; All the King's Men, 1982; Winter Quarters, 1982; The Mouldy, 1983; Underground Creatures, 1983; Green, Red, Blue, and Yellow Books of Hob, 1984; Drift, 1985; Corbie, 1986; Come, Come to My Corner, 1986; Tibber, 1986; Barnabas Walks, 1986; The Blemyah Stories, 1987; Kelpie, 1987; Gideon Ahoy!, 1987; Leap Frog, 1987; Mousewing, 1987; Tiger's Railway, 1987; A Horse in Town, 1987; Lamb Shenkin, 1987; Antar and the Eagles, 1989; Netta 1989; Pandora, 1990. Add: c/o David Higham Assoc., 3-5 Lower John St., London W1R 4HA, England.

MAYO, James. *See* **COULTER,** Stephen.

MAYO, Patricia Elton. British, b. 1915. Criminology/Law enforcement/Prisons, Politics/Government, Sociology. Head of Field Research Group, British Inst. of Mgmt., 1947–50; Project Mgr., Trade Union Projects, O.E.E.C. (now O.E.C.D.), 1952–54; Consultant Sociologist, European Cttee. on Crime Problems, 1958–62. *Publs:* Probation and After-Care in Europe, 1963; The Making of a Criminal: A Comparative Case Study of Two Delinquency Areas, 1968; The Roots of Identity: Three National Movements in Contemporary European Politics, 1974; (co-author) The State of the Union of Europe, 1980. Add: Bryn Awel House, Montgomery, Powys SY15 6PU, Wales.

MAYR, Ernst. American, b. 1904. Biology, Zoology. Asst. Curator, Zoological Museum, Univ. of Berlin, 1926–32; Whitney Research Assoc. in Ornithology, 1931–32, Assoc. Curator, 1932–44, and Curator, Whitney-Rothschild Collection, 1944–53, American Museum of Natural History, NYC; Alexander Agassiz Prof. of Zoology from 1953, and Dir., Museum of Comparative Zoology, 1961–70, Harvard Univ., Cambridge, Mass. Founded Soc. for the Study of Evolution, 1946; Founding Editor, Evolution, 1947–49. *Publs:* List of New Guinea Birds, 1941; Systematics and the Origin of Species, 1942; Birds of the Southwest Pacific, 1945; (with Jean Delacour) Birds of the Philippines, 1946; (with E.G. Linsley and R.L. Usinger) Methods and Principles of Systematic Zoology, 1953; Animal Species and Evolution, 1963; Evolution and the Diversity of Life, 1976; The Growth of Biological Thought, 1982; Towards a New Philosophy of Biology, 1988. Add: 11 Chauncy St., Cambridge, Mass. 02138, U.S.A.

MAZER, Norma Fox. American, b. 1931. Children's fiction, Poetry. *Publs:* I, Trissy, 1971; A Figure of Speech, 1973; Saturday, The Twelfth of October, 1975; Dear Bill, Remember Me? and Other Stories, 1976; (with Harry Mazer) The Solid Gold Kid, 1977; Up in Seth's Room, 1979; Mrs. Fish, Ape, and Me, The Dump Queen, 1980; Taking Terri Mueller, 1981; Summer Girls, Love Boys and Other Stories, 1982; When We First Met, 1982; Someone to Love, 1983; Supergirl (novelization of screenplay), 1984; Downtown, 1984; Three Sisters 1986; A, My Name Is Ami, 1986, in U.K. as A for Ami, 1988; B, My Name Is Bunny (in U.K. as A Name Like Bunny), 1988; After the Rain, 1987; Silver, 1988; (with Harry Mazer) Heartbeat, 1989; (ed. with Marjorie Lewis) Waltzing on Water: Poetry by Women, 1989. Add: Brown Gulf Road, Jamesville, N.Y. 13078, U.S.A.

MAZZARO, Jerome. American, b. 1934. Poetry, Literature, Translations. Prof. of Comparative and English Literature, State Univ. of New York, Buffalo, since 1964. Contrib. Ed., Salmagundi, since 1968. Instr. of English, Univ. of Detroit, Mich., 1958–61; Ed., Fresco, 1960–61; Asst. Prof. of English, State Univ. of New York, Cortland, 1962–64. Ed., Modern Poetry Studies, 1970–78. Ed. The Poetry Review, 1985–86. *Publs:* The Achievement of Robert Lowell: 1939–1959, 1960; (trans.) Juvenal's Satires, 1965; The Poetic Themes of Robert Lowell, 1965; Changing the Windows (poetry), 1966; (ed.) Modern American Poetry, 1970; Transformations in the Renaissance English Lyric, 1970; (ed.) Profile of Robert Lowell, 1971; (ed.) Profile of William Carlos Williams, 1971; William Carlos Williams: The Later Poems, 1973; Postmodern American Poetry, 1980; The Figure of Dante, 1981; The Caves of Love (poetry), 1985; Rubbings (poetry), 1985. Add: 147 Capen Blvd., Buffalo, N.Y. 14226, U.S.A.

McALINDON, Thomas. British, b. 1932. Literature. Reader, Dept. of English, Univ. of Hull. *Publs:* Shakespeare and Decorum, 1974; English Renaissance Tragedy, 1986. Add: Dept. of English, Univ. of

Hull, Hull, England.

McALLISTER, Bruce (Hugh). American, b. 1946. Science fiction. Dir. of the Writing Program since 1974 and Prof. of English since 1983, Univ. of Redlands, Calif. (Visiting Instr., 1971–74; Asst. Prof., 1974–79; Assoc. Prof., 1979–83). Consultant, VSP Assoc., Sacramento, since 1982. *Publs:* Humanity Prime (novel), 1971; (ed.) SF Directions, 1972; (ed.) Their Immortal Hearts, 1980; The Faces Outside (short stories)), 1985. Add: 935 Aaron Dr., Redlands, Calif. 92374, U.S.A.

McARTHUR, Harvey King. American, b. 1912. Theology/Religion. Pastor, Blackstone Federated Churches, Mass., 1941–44; U.S. Army Chaplain, 1944–46; Instr., Dept. of Biblical History, Wellesley Coll., Mass., 1947–48; Assoc. Prof., 1948–53, Prof., 1953–60, Hosmer Prof., 1960–76, and Acting Pres., 1976–78, Hartford Seminary Foundn. *Publs:* (ed. and contrib.) New Testament Sidelights, 1960; Understanding the Sermon on the Mount, 1960; The Quest Through the Centuries, 1966; (ed. and contrib.) In Search of the Historical Jesus, 1969. Add: 16 S. Sycamore Knolls, S. Hadley, Mass. 01075, U.S.A.

McAULEY, James J. Irish, b. 1936. Poetry. Prof. of English, Eastern Washington Univ., Cheney since 1978 (Asst. Prof., 1970–73; Assoc. Prof., 1973–78). Journalist, literary critic and lectr., Dublin, 1954–66; Teaching Asst., English Dept., Univ. of Arkansas, Fayetteville, 1966–68; Asst. Prof., and Dir. of Creative Writing, Lycoming Coll., Williamsport, Pa., 1968–70. *Publs:* Observations, 1960; A New Address, 1965; The Revolution (verse satire), 1966; Draft Balance Sheet, 1970; After the Blizzard, 1975; The Exile's Recurring Nightmare, 1975; An Irish Bull, and Praise, 1981; Recital: The Exile's Book of Hours, 1982. Add: Dept. of English, Eastern Washington Univ., Cheney, Wash. 99004, U.S.A.

McAULIFFE, Frank (Malachi). Also writes as Frank Malachy. American, b. 1926. Mystery/Crime/Suspense. *Publs:* (as Frank Malachy) Hot Town (non-mystery novel), 1956; Of All the Bloody Cheek (short stories), 1965; Rather a Vicious Gentleman (short stories), 1968; For Murder I Charge More (short stories), 1971; The Bag Man, 1979. Add: 1828 Swift Blvd., Ventura, Calif. 93003, U.S.A.

McBAIN, Ed. *See* **HUNTER,** Evan.

McBAIN, Laurie (Lee).American, b. 1949. Historical/Romance. *Publs:* Devil's Desire, 1975; Moonstruck Madness, 1977; Tears of Gold, 1979; Chance the Winds of Fortune, 1980; Dark Before the Rising Sun, 1982; Wild Bells to the Wild Sky, 1983; When the Splendor Falls, 1985. Add: c/o Harold Ober Assocs., 40 E. 49th St., New York, N.Y. 10017, U.S.A.

McBRIDE, Robert. British, b. 1941. Literature. Prof. of French, Univ. of Ulster, since 1982. Sr. Lectr. in French, Queen's Univ. of Belfast, 1973–81 (Asst. Lectr., 1965–68; Lectr., 1968–73). *Publs:* The Sceptical Vision of Molière: A Study in Paradox, 1977; Aspects of Seventeenth-Century French Drama and Thought, 1979. Add: Dept. of French, Univ. of Ulster, Coleraine, Northern Ireland.

McBRIEN, Richard P(eter). American, b. 1936. Theology/Religion. Prof. of Theology since 1972, and Dir. of the Inst. of Religious Education and Pastoral Ministry since 1975, Boston Coll., Chestnut Hill, Mass. (Visiting Prof., 1966–70; Assoc. Prof., 1970–72); Crowley-O'Brien-Walter Prof. of Theology, and Chmn. of the Dept. of Theology, Univ. of Notre Dame, Ind., since 1980. Former Chmn., Joint Grad. Prog., Boston Coll. and Andover Newton Theological Sch., Mass., and Pres., Catholic Theological Soc. of America. *Publs:* The Church in the Thought of Bishop John Robinson, 1966; What Do We Really Believe?, 1969; Do We Need the Church?, 1969; Church: The Continuing Quest, 1970; Who Is a Catholic?, 1971; For the Inquiring Catholic, 1973; The Remaking of the Church, 1973; Has the Church Surrendered?, 1974; Roman Catholicism, 1975; In Search of God, 1977; Basic Questions for Christian Educators, 1977; Catholicism, 2 vols., 1980; Caesar's Coin: Religion and Politics in America, 1987; Ministry: A Theological, Pastoral Handbook, 1987. Add: Dept. of Theology, Univ. of Notre Dame, Notre Dame, Ind. 46556, U.S.A.

McCABE, Eugene. Irish, b. 1930. Novels/Short Stories, Children's fiction, Plays/Screenplays. Farmer since 1955. *Publs:* plays—Victims, 1976; The King of the Castle, 1978; Gale Day, and Pull Down a Horseman, 1979; Cancer, 1980; novel—Victims, 1976; short stories—Heritage, 1978; for children—Cyril, 1986. Add: Drumard, Clones, Co. Monoghan, Ireland.

McCABE, John C(harles), III. American, b. 1920. Film, Theatre, Biography. Chmn., Dept. of Dramatic Art, New York Univ., NYC, 1957–67, and Dept. of Drama and Theatre, Mackinac Coll., Mich., 1967–70. *Publs:* Mr. Laurel & Mr. Hardy, 1961; George M. Cohan: The Man Who Owned Broadway, 1973; The Comedy World of Stan Laurel, 1973; Laurel & Hardy, 1975; (with G.B. Harrison) Proclaiming the World, 1975; Charlie Chaplin, 1978; (ghostwriter) Cagney by Cagney, by James Cagney, 1978. Add: Box 363, Mackinac Island, Mich. 49757, U.S.A.

McCAFFERY, Margo. American, b. 1938. Medicine/Health (nursing). Asst. Head Hurse, Surgical Unit, Navarro Co. Memorial Hosp., 1958–69; Instr. in Surgical Nursing, Texas Woman's Univ., Dallas, 1959–60; Asst. Prof. of Nursing of Children and Chmn. of Dept., Vanderbilt Univ., Nashville, Tenn., 1961–62; Instr. in Pediatric Nursing, 1962–65 and Asst. Prof. in Pediatric Nursing, 1965–70, Univ. of California, Los Angeles. *Publs:* Clinical Nursing: Nursing Practice Theories Related to Cognition, Bodily Pain, and Man-Environment Interactions, 1968; Nursing Management of the Patient with Pain, 1972, 1979; Pain: A Nursing Approach to Assessment and Analysis, 1983; Pain: Clinical Manual for Nursing Practice, 1989. Add: 1458 Berkeley St., Apt. 1, Santa Monica, Calif. 90404, U.S.A.

McCAFFREY, Anne (Inez). American, b. 1926. Historical/Romance/Gothic, Science fiction. Copywriter, Liberty Music Shops, 1948–50; Copywriter and Exec. Secty., Helen Rubinstein Inc., 1950–54. *Publs:* Restoree, 1967; Decision at Doona, 1969; Dragonflight, 1968; Ship Who Sang, 1970; (ed.) Alchemy and Academe, 1969; Dragonquest, 1971; The Mark of Merlin, 1971; Ring of Fear, 1971; To Ride Pegasus, 1973; (ed.) Cooking Out of This World, 1973; Kilternan Legacy, 1975; Dragonsong, 1976; Dragonsinger, 1977; Get Off the Unicorn, 1977; The White Dragon, 1978; Dinosaur Planet, 1978; Dragondrums, 1979; The Worlds of Anne McCaffrey (stories), 1981; Crystal Singer, 1982; The Coelura, 1983; Moreta, Dragonlady of Pern, 1983; Dinosaur Planet Survivors, 1984; Stitch in Snow, 1984; Killashandra, 1985; Nerilka's Story, 1986; The Year of the Lucy, 1986; Habit Is an Old Horse, 1986; The Carradyne Touch, 1988; Dragonsdawn, 1988. Add: Dragonhold, Kilaquade, Greystones, Co. Wicklow, Ireland.

McCALL, Anthony. *See* **KANE,** Henry.

McCALL, Edith. American, b. 1911. Children's fiction, Children's non-fiction, History. Teacher in elementary schs., Elmhurst, Ill., 1930–35, and Western Springs, Ill., 1943–47; Reading Consultant, La Grange, Ill., 1947–55. *Publs:* The Button Family Adventures (12 books), 1953–58; Log Fort Adventures, 1958; Steamboats to the West, 1959, 1980; Hunters Blaze the Trails, 1959, 1980; Explorers in a New World, 1960, 1980; Men on Iron Horses, 1960; Settlers on a Strange Shore, 1960, 1980; Wagons over the Mountains, 1961, 1980; Cumberland Gap and Trails West, 1961, 1980; Mail Riders: Paul Revere to Pony Express, 1961, 1980; Pioneers on Early Waterways, 1961, 1980; How We Get Our Mail, 1961; How Airplanes Help Us, 1961; How We Get Our Cloth, 1961; How We Get Our Clothing, 1961; Gold Rush Adventures, 1962, 1980; Heroes of the Western Outposts, 1962, 1980; Pioneer Show Folk, 1963; Pirates and Privateers, 1963, 1980; Cowboys and Cattle Drives, 1964, 1980; Pioneer Traders, 1964, 1980; The Butternut Bill Books, 8 books, 1965–69; Forts in the Wilderness, 1968, 1980; English Village in the Ozarks, 1969, 1985; Stalwart Men of Early Texas, 1970, 1980; Conquering the Rivers: Henry Miller Shreve and the Navigation of America's Inland Waterways (history), 1984; Message from the Mountains, 1985, Mississippi Steamboatman: The Story of Henry M. Shreve, 1985; Better Than a Brother, 1988. Add: P.O. Box 255, Hollister, Mo. 65672, U.S.A.

McCALL, Marsh Howard, Jr. American, b. 1939. Classics. Prof. of Classics since 1981, and Dean of Continuing Studies Program since 1988, Stanford Univ., California (Assoc. Prof., 1976–81; Assoc. Dean of Undergrad. Studies, 1978–80; Chmn., 1977–84). Instr., Dept. of Classics, Harvard Univ., Cambridge, Mass., 1965–68; Fellow, Center for Hellenic Studies, Washington, D.C., 1968–69; Assoc. Prof. of Classics, Johns Hopkins Univ., Baltimore, 1970–75; Visiting Prof. of Classics, Univ. of California, Berkeley, 1975–76. Assoc. Ed., American Journal of Philology, 1970–75. *Publs:* Ancient Rhetorical Theories of Simile and Comparison, 1969; (ed. and contrib.) Aeschylus: A Collection of Critical Essays, 1972. Add: Dept. of Classics, Stanford Univ., Stanford, Calif. 94305, U.S.A.

McCALL, Robert B. American, b. 1940. Psychology. Sr. Scientist and Chief, Perceptual-Cognitive Development Section, Fels Research Inst., Yellow Springs, Ohio, since 1968 (Chmn., Dept. of Psychology, 1968–71). Prof. of Psychology and Dir., Office of Child Development,

Univ. of Pittsburgh, since 1986. National Science Foundn. Postdoctoral Fellow, Harvard Univ., Cambridge, Mass., 1965–66; Asst. Prof. of Psychology, Univ. of North Carolina, Chapel Hill, 1966–68; Executive Asst. to the Dir., and Sr. Scientist and Science Writer, Father Flanagan's Boys Town, 1977–86. *Publs:* Fundamental Statistics for Psychology, 1972, 4th ed. 1986; Infants, 1979. Add: c/o Harvard University Press, 79 Garden St., Cambridge, mass. 02138, U.S.A.

McCALLUM, Phyllis. American, b. 1911. Plays/Screenplays, *Publs:* all plays for children—The Pale Pink Dragon, 1966; The Uniform Unicorn, 1967; The Tough and Tender Troll, 1967; The Grateful Griffin, 1968; The Vanilla Viking, 1969; Hansel and Gretel and the Golden Petticoat, 1973; Crumple, Rumpelstiltskin, 1974; Jack and the Beanstalk, 1976; The Dignified Donkey of New Almaden, 1976; The Twelve Dancing Princesses, 1978; The Swiss Family Robinson (musical), 1978; Christmas with Little Women, 1980. Add: 1187 Clark Way, San Jose, Calif. 95125, U.S.A.

McCANN, Edson. *See* **del REY,** Lester.

McCARRY, Charles. American, b. 1930. Novels/Short stories, Biography. Ed.-at-Large, National Geographic Mag., since 1983. Ed., Lisbon Evening Journal, Ohio, 1952–55; Reporter and Columnist, Ohio Vindicator, Youngstown, 1955–56; Asst. to the Secty. of Labor, Washington, D.C., 1956–58; with Central Intelligence Agency, 1958–60, and 1960–67; freelance journalist and writer, 1967–83. *Publs:* Citizen Nader (biography), 1972; The Miernik Dossier, 1973; The Tears of Autumn, 1975; The Secret Lovers, 1977; Double Eagle, 1979; The Better Angels, 1979; (with others) The Great Southwest, 1981; The Last Supper, 1983; The Bride of the Wilderness, 1988. Add: c/o William Morris Agency, 1350 Ave. of the Americas, New York, N.Y. 10019, U.S.A.

McCARTHY, Eugene (Joseph). American, b. 1916. Poetry, Politics/Government. Member, Bd. of Dirs., Harcourt Brace Jovanovich, Inc., Publrs. Members, U.S. House of Representatives for 4th District of Minnesota, 1949–58; U.S. Senator (Democrat) from Minn., 1958–70; Adlai Stevenson Prof. of Political Science, New Sch. for Social Research, NYC, 1973–74. Candidate for U.S. Presidency, 1976. *Publs:* Frontiers in American Democracy, 1960; Dictionary of American Politics, 1962; A Liberal Answer to the Conservative Challenge, 1964; Limits of Power, 1967; The Year of the People, 1969; Other Things and the Aardvark (poetry), 1970; The Hard Years: A Look at Contemporary America and American Institutions, 1975; (with others) Regulation and Political Campaigns, 1977; Mr. Raccoon and His Friends, 1977; America Revisited, 1978; (with James J. Kilpatrick) A Political Bestiary, 1978; Ground Fog and Night (poetry), 1979; The Ultimate Tyranny, 1980; Gene McCarthy's Minnesota, 1982; Complexities and Cantraries, 1982; The View From Rappahannock, 1984; Up 'til Now, 1987; Required Reading, 1988. Add: Box 22, Woodville, Va. 22749, U.S.A.

McCARTHY, Gary. American, b. 1943. Historical/Romance Westerns/Adventure. Full-time writer since 1979. Labor Economist, State of Nevada, Carson City, 1970–77; Economist, Copley Intnl. Corp., La Jolla, Calif., 1977–79. *Publs:* The Derby Man, 1976; Showdown at Snakegrass Junction, 1978; The First Sheriff, 1979; Mustang Fever, 1980; The Pony Express War, 1980; Winds of Gold, 1980; Silver Shot, 1981; Explosion at Donner Pass, 1981; The Legend of the Lone Ranger (novelization of screenplay), 1981; North Chase, 1982; Rebel of Bodie, 1982; The Rail Warriors, 1983; Silver Winds, 1983; Wind River, 1984; Powder River, 1985; The Last Buffalo Hunt, 1985; Mando, 1986; The Mustangers, 1987; Transcontinental, 1987; Sodbuster, 1988; Blood Brothers, 1989; The Colorado, 1989. Add: 323 Matilija St., No. 204, Ojai, Calif. 93023, U.S.A.

McCARTHY, Mary (Therese). American, b. 1912. Novels/Short stories, Literature, Autobiography/Memoirs/Personal, Essays. Stevenson Chair in Literature, Bard Coll., Annandale-on-Hudson, N.Y., since 1986 (Instr., 1945–46). Ed., Covici Friede Publrs., NYC, 1936–38; Ed., 1937–1938, and Drama Critic, 1937–62, Partisan Review, New Brunswick, N.J.; Instr., Sarah Lawrence Coll., Bronxville, N.Y., 1948. *Publs:* The Company She Keeps, 1942; (trans.) Simone Weil: The Iliad: or, The Poem of Force, 1948; (trans.) Rachel Bespaloff: On the Iliad, 1948; The Oasis (in U.K. as A Source of Embarrassment), 1949; Cast a Cold Eye, 1950; The Groves of Academe, 1952; A Charmed Life, 1955; Sights and Spectacles, 1937–56, 1956, in U.K. as Sights and Spectacles: Theatre Chronicles, 1937–58, 1958, augmented ed. as Mary McCarthy's Theatre Chronicles, 1937–62, 1963; Venice Observed: Comments on Venetian Civilization, 1956; Memories of a Catholic Girlhood, 1957; The Stones of Florence, 1959; On the Contrary, 1961; The Group, 1963; Vietnam,

1967; Hanoi, 1968; The Writing on the Wall, 1970; Birds of America, 1971; Medina, 1972; The Seventeenth Degree, 1974; The Mask of State: Watergate Portraits, 1974; Cannibals and Missionaries, 1979; Ideas and the Novel, 1980; Occasional Prose, 1985; How I Grew, 1987. Recipient of National Book Award and MacDowell Award, 1984. Add: Main St., Castine, Me. 04421, U.S.A.

McCARTHY, Shaun. Writes as Desmond Cory; also writes as Theo Callas. British, b. 1928. Mystery/Crime/Suspense. Assoc. Prof. of English, University Coll., Bahrain, since 1980. Free-lance journalist and translator in Europe, 1951–54; language teacher in Spain and Sweden, 1954–60; Lectr., Univ. of Wales Inst. of Science and Technology, Cardiff, 1960–77; Lectr., Univ. of Qatar, 1977–80. *Publs:* Secret Ministry, 1951 (in U.S. as The Nazi Assassins, 1970); Begin, Murderer!, 1951; This Traitor, Death, 1952 (in U.S. as The Gestapo File, 1971); This Is Jezebel, 1952; Dead Man Falling, 1953 (in U.S. as The Hitler Diamonds, 1979); Lady Lost, 1953; Intrigue, 1954 (in U.S. as Trieste, 1968); The Shaken Leaf, 1955; Height of Day, 1955 (in U.S. as Dead Men Alive, 1969); (as Theo Callas) City of Kites, 1955; The Phoenix Sings, 1955; High Requiem, 1956; Johnny Goes North, 1956 (in U.S. as The Swastika Hunt, 1969); Pilgrim at the Gate, 1957; Johnny Goes East, 1958 (also as Mountainhead, 1966); Johnny Goes West, 1959; Johnny Goes South, 1959 (also as Overload, 1964); Pilgrim on the Island, 1959; (as Theo Callas) Ann and Peter in Southern Spain (juvenile), 1959; Jones on the Belgrade Express (juvenile), 1960; The Head, 1960; Stranglehold, 1961; Undertow, 1962; Hammerhead, 1963 (in U.S. as Shockwave, 1964); The Name of the Game, 1964; Deadfall, 1965; Feramontov, 1966; Timelock, 1967; The Night Hawk, 1969; Sunburst, 1971; Take My Drum to England, 1971 (in U.S. as Even If You Run, 1972); Bit of a Shunt Up the River, 1974; The Circe Complex, 1975; Bennett, 1977; (as Shaun McCarthy) Lucky Ham (non-mystery novel), 1977. Add: c/o George Greenfield, John Farquharson Ltd., 162–168 Regent St., London W1R 5TB, England.

McCARTHY, William E(dward) J(ohn). British, b. 1925. Industrial relations. Fellow, Nuffield Coll. and Centre for Mgmt. Studies, Oxford Univ., since 1968 (Research Fellow of Nuffield Coll., 1959–63; Staff Lectr. and Tutor in Industrial Relations, 1964–65). Dir. of Research, Royal Commn. on Trade Unions and Employers' Assn., London, 1965–68; Sr. Economic Adviser, Dept. of Employment, 1968–70; Special Adviser, European Economic Commn., 1974–75. *Publs:* The Future of the Unions, 1962; The Closed Shop in Britain, 1964; The Role of Shop Stewards in British Industrial Relations: A Survey of Existing Information and Research, 1966; (with Arthur Ivor Marsh) Disputes Procedures in Britain, 1967; (with V.G. Munns) Employers' Associations: The Results of Two Studies, 1967; The Role of Government in Industrial Relations, 1968; Shop Stewards and Workshop Relations: The Results of a Study, 1968; (ed.) Industrial Relations in Britain: A Guide for Management and Unions, 1969; The Reform of Collective Bargaining: A Series of Case Studies, 1971; Trade Unions, 1972, 1985; (with A.I. Collier) Coming to Terms with Trade Unions, 1972; (with N.D. Ellis) Management by Agreement, 1973; (with J.F. O'Brien and V.C. Dowd) Wage Inflation and Wage Leadership, 1975; Making Whitley Work, 1977; (co-author) Change in Trade Unions, 1981; (co-author) Strikes in Post-War Britain, 1984; Freedom At Work, 1985; The Future of Industrial Democracy, 1988; (co-author) A Manual of Employee Relations, 1989. Add: 4 William Orchard Close, Old Headington, Oxford, England.

McCARTY, Clifford. American, b. 1929. Film, Music. Owner and Mgr., Boulevard Bookshop, Los Angeles, 1958–80, and Boulevard Books, Topanga, Calif., since 1980. *Publs:* Film Composers in America: A Checklist of Their Work, 1953, 1972; Bogey: The Films of Humphrey Bogart, 1965; (with T. Thomas and R. Behlmer) The Films of Errol Flynn, 1969; Published Screenplays: A Checklist, 1971; (with G. Ringgold) The Films of Frank Sinatra, 1971; (ed.) Film Music 1, 1989. Add: P.O. Box 89, Topanga, Calif. 90290, U.S.A.

McCASLIN, Nellie. American, b. 1914. Plays, Theatre, Essays. Prof. since 1972, New York Univ., NYC. Teacher of Dramatic Arts, Tudor Hall, Indianapolis, Ind., 1937–44; Instr. in Drama and English, National Coll. of Education, Evanston, Ill., 1944–56; Drama Dir., and Dean of Students, Mills Coll. of Education, NYC, 1957–72; Pres., Children's Theatre Assn. of America, 1973–75. *Publs:* Legends in Action, 1945; More Legends in Action, 1950; Tall Tales and Tall Men, 1956; Pioneers in Petticoats, 1961; Little Snow Girl, 1963; Rabbit Who Wanted Red Wings, 1963; Creative Drama in the Classroom, 1968, 5th ed., 1990; Children's Theatre in the United States; A History, 1971; (ed.) Children and Drama, 1975, 1985; Act Now!, 1975; Puppet Fun, 1977; Theatre for Young Audiences, 1978; Shows on a Shoestring, 1979, 1989; Children's Theatre in America 1903–1985, 1987; Creative Drama Handbooks for

Teachers, Grades 1-3, 4-6, 1987.   Add: 40 East 10th St., New York, N.Y. 10003, U.S.A.

McCAUGHREN, Geraldine (née Jones). British, b. 1951. Novels, Children's fiction, Education (reading textbooks), Translations. *Publs:* Children's fiction—1001 Arabian Nights (retelling), 1982; The Canterbury Tales (retelling), 1984; Seaside Adventure, 1986; (with Chrissie Wells) Tell the Time, 1986; Who's That Knocking on My Door?, by Michel Tilde, 1986; The Story of Noah (retelling), 1987; A Little Lower Than the Angels, 1987; The Story of Christmas (retelling), 1988; A Pack of Lies, 1988; other—Adventure in New York (textbook), 1979; Raise the Titanic (textbook), 1980; Modesty Blaise (textbook), 1981; The Maypole (novel), 1989.   Add: 3 Melton Dr., Didcot, Oxon OX11 7JP, England.

McCAUGHREN, Tom. Irish, b. 1936. Children's fiction. Reporter, 1968–75, Asst. News Ed., 1975–76, and since 1977 Security Corresp., RTE Radio and Television, Dublin. *Publs:* The Legend of the Golden Key, 1983; The Legend of the Phantom Highwayman, 1983; Run with the Wind, 1983; The Legend of the Corrib King, 1984; Run to Earth, 1984; The Children of the Forge, 1985; Run Swift, Run Free, 1986.   Add: c/o The Children's Press, 90 Lower Baggot St., Dublin 2, Ireland.

McCAULEY, Martin. British, b. 1934. History, Politics/Government Sr. Lectr. in Soviet and East European Studies, Sch. Slavonic and East European Studies, Univ. of London, since 1968 (Member of Council, 1976). *Publs:* (ed. and trans.) The Russian Revolution and the Soviet State 1917–1921, 1975, 1980; Khrushchev and the Development of Soviet Agriculture: The Virgin Land Programme 1953–64, 1976; (ed. and co-author) Communist Power in Europe 1944–1949, 1977, 1980; Marxism–Leninism in the German Democratic Republic: The Socialist Unity Party (SED), 1979; The Stalin File, 1979; The Soviet Union Since 1917, 1981; Stalin and Stalinism, 1983; The Origins of the Cold War, 1983; (ed. and contrib.) The Soviet Union since Brezhnev, 1983; The German Democratic Republic since 1945, 1984; Octobrists to Bolsheviks: Imperial Russia 1905–1917, 1984; (ed. and contrib.) Leadership and Succession in the Soviet Union, Eastern Europe and China, 1985; (with Peter Waldron) The Origins of the Modern Russian State 1855–81, 1987; (ed.) The Soviet Union under Gorbachev, 1987.   Add: Sch. of Slavonic and East European Studies, Senate House, Malet St., London WC1E 7HU, England.

McCLATCHY, J(oseph) D(onald). American, b. 1945. Poetry. Poetry Ed., Yale Review, since 1980. Contrib. Ed., American Poetry Review. Asst. Prof., Yale Univ., New Haven, Conn., 1974–81; Lectr., Creative Writing Prog., Princeton Univ., N.J., 1981–87. *Publs:* (ed.) Anne Sexton: The Artist and Her Critics, 1978; Scenes from Another Life, 1981; Stars Principal, 1986; (ed.) Recitative: Prose by James Merrill, 1986; (ed.) Poets on Painters, 1988; White Paper, 1989.   Add: 54 W. 16th St., New York, N.Y. 10011, U.S.A.

McCLELLAND, Charles Edgar. American, b. 1940. History, Intellectual history. Prof. of History, Univ. of New Mexico, Albuquerque, since 1974. Instr. of History, Princeton Univ., N.J., 1966–68; Asst. Prof. of History, Univ. of Pennsylvania, Philadelphia, 1968–74. *Publs:* The German Historians and England, 1971; (with S.P. Scher) Postwar German Culture, 1974; State, Society and University in Germany 1700–1914, 1979.   Add: Dept. of History, Univ. of New Mexico, Albuquerque, N.M. 87131, U.S.A.

McCLELLAND, Ivy Lillian. British, b. 1908. Literature. Former Reader, Glasgow Univ. *Publs:* Origins of the Romantic Movement in Spain, 1937, 1945; Tirso de Molina: Studies in Dramatic Realism, 1946; Jerónimo Benito Feijoo, 1969; Spanish Drama of Pathos, 2 vols., 1970; Ignacio de Luzán, 1973; Diego de Torres Villarroel, 1976; (ed.) Benito Jerónimo Feijoo, 1985; Ideological Hesitancy in Spain: The Early Eighteenth, Century 1990.   Add: c/o Liverpool Univ. Press, P.O. Box 146, Liverpool L69 3BX, England.

McCLELLAND, Vincent Alan. British, b. 1933. History, Theology/Religion. Prof. of Educational Studies at the Univ., and Dir. at the Inst. of Education, Univ. of Hull, since 1978. Lectr. in Education, Univ. of Liverpool, 1964–69; Prof. of Education, National Univ. of Ireland, Cork, 1969–77. *Publs:* Cardinal Manning: His Public Life and Influence 1865–92, 1962; English Roman Catholics and Higher Education 1830–1903, 1973.   Add: Univ. of Hull, Hull, England.

McCLOSKEY, Mark. American, b. 1938. Poetry. Asst. Prof., Glendale Coll., Calif., since 1987. Asst. Ed., Ohio Univ. Press, 1964–66;

Asst. Prof. of English, State Univ. of New York, Cortland, 1966–70; Asst. Prof. of Creative Writing, Univ. of Southern California, Los Angeles, 1970–73; Lectr., 1973–74, and Visiting Asst. Prof., 1974–77, California State Univ., Chico. *Publs:* (ed. and trans. with P.R. Murphy) The Latin Poetry of George Herbert: A Bilingual Edition, 1965; Goodbye, But Listen, 1968; The Sheen in Flywings is What It Comes To, 1972; All That Mattered, 1976; The Secret Documents of America, 1977.   Add: 1525 Dixon, Los Angeles, Calif. 91205, U.,S.A.

McCLOSKEY, (John) Robert. American, b. 1914. Children's fiction, Artist and illustrator. *Publs:* Lentil, 1940; Make Way for Ducklings, 1941; Homer Price, 1943; Blueberries for Sal, 1948; Centerburg Tales, 1951; One Morning in Maine, 1952; Time of Wonder, 1952; Burt Dow, Deep Water Man, 1963.   Add: Little Deer Isle, Maine 04650, U.S.A.

McCLOY, Helen. Also writes as Helen Clarkson. American, b. 1904. Mystery/Crime/Suspense. *Publs:* Dance of Death, 1938; The Man in the Moonlight, 1940; The Deadly Truth, 1941; Who's Calling, 1942; Cue For Murder, 1942; Do Not Disturb, 1943; The Goblin Market, 1943; Panic, 1944; The One That Got Away, 1945; She Walks Alone, 1948; Through a Glass, Darkly, 1949; Alias Basil Willing, 1951; Unfinished Crime, 1954; The Long Body, 1955; Two Thirds of a Ghost, 1956; The Slayer and the Slain, 1957; (as Helen Clarkson) The Last Day, 1959; Before I Die, 1963; The Singing Diamonds (stories), 1965; The Further Side of Fear, 1967; Mr. Splitfoot, 1968; A Question of Time, 1971; A Change of Heart, 1973; The Sleepwalker, 1974; Minotaur Country, 1975; The Changeling Conspiracy, 1976; The Impostor, 1977; The Smoking Mirror, 1979; Burn This, 1980; Hate and Wait, 1986.   Add: 944 Ohayo Mountain Rd., Woodstock, N.Y. 12498, U.S.A.

McCLUNG, Robert Marshall. American, b. 1916. Children's fiction, Children's non-fiction. Member, Curatorial Staff, New York Zoological Park, NYC, 1948–55, and Editorial Staff, National Geographic Mag., Washington, D.C., 1958–62. *Publs:* Wings in the Woods, 1948; Sphinx, 1949; Ruby Throat, 1950; Stripe, 1951; Spike, 1952; Tiger, 1953; Bufo, 1954; Vulcan, 1955; Major, 1956; Green Darner, 1956; Leaper, 1957; Luna, 1957; Buzztail, 1958; Little Burma, 1958; All about Animals and Their Young, 1958; Whooping Crane, 1959; Otus, 1959; Shag, 1960; Whitefoot, 1961; Possum, 1963; Mammals and How They Live, 1963; Screamer, 1964; Spotted Salamander, 1964; Honker, 1965; Caterpillars and How They Live, 1965; The Swift Deer, 1966; Ladybug, 1966; Butterflies and Moths and How They Live, 1966; The Mighty Bears, 1967; Horseshoe Crab, 1967; Black Jack, 1967; Redbird, 1968; Lost Wild America, 1969; Blaze, 1969; Aquatic Insects and How They Live, 1970; Thor, 1971; Bees, Wasps, and Hornets and How They Live, 1971; Scoop, 1972; Samson, 1973; Mice, Moose, and Men, 1973; Gypsy Moth, 1974; Sea Star, 1975; Lost Wild Worlds, 1976; Peeper, First Voice of Spring, 1977; Hunted Mammals of the Sea, 1978; America's Endangered Birds, 1979; Snakes: Their Place in the Sun, 1979; The Amazing Egg, 1980; Vanishing Wildlife of Latin America, 1980; Rajpur, Last of the Bengal Tigers, 1982; Mysteries of Migration, 1983; Gorilla, 1984; The True Adventures of Grizzly Adams, 1985; Whitetail, 1987; Lili, 1988.   Add: 91 Sunset Ave., Amherst, Mass. 01002, U.S.A.

McCLURE, Gillian Mary. British, b. 1948. Children's fiction. Writer and illustrator. *Publs:* The Emperor's Singing Bird, 1974; Prickly Pig, 1976; Fly Home McDoo, 1979; What's the Time Rory Wolf, 1982; What Happened to the Picnic?, 1987; Cat Flap, 1989.   Add: The Hamilton Kerr Institute, Mill Lane, Whittlesford, Cambs., England.

McCLURE, James. British, b. 1939. Mystery/Crime/Suspense. Managing Dir., Sabensa Gakulu Ltd., Oxford, since 1975. Photographer and teacher, Natal, 1958–63; journalist, Natal, Edinburgh, and Oxford, 1963–69; Deputy Ed., Oxford Times Group, 1971–74. *Publs:* The Steam Pig, 1971; The Caterpillar Cop, 1972; Four and Twenty Virgins, 1973; The Gooseberry Fool, 1974; Snake, 1975; Rogue Eagle, 1976; Killers (non fiction), 1976; The Sunday Hangman, 1977; The Blood of an Englishman, 1980; Spike Island: Portrait of a British Police Division, 1980; The Artful Egg, 1984; Copworld, 1985; Imago, 1988.   Add: 14 York Rd., Headington, Oxford OX3 8NW, England.

McCLURE, Michael (Thomas). American, b. 1932. Novels/Short stories, Plays/Screenplays, Poetry. Prof. of Humanities and Sciences, Calforina Coll. of ARts and Crafts, Oakland, since 1977 (Assoc. Prof., 1962–77) **Publs:** Passage, 1956; (ed. with James Harmon) ARt II/Moby I, 1957; Peyote Poem, 1958; For Artaud, 1959; Hymns to St. Geryon and Other Poems, 1959; The Feast, 1960; Pillow 1961; The New Book: A Book of Torture, 1961; Dark Brown, 1961; (ed. with D. Meltzer and Lawrence Ferlinghetti) Journal for the Protection of All Beings, 1961;

Meat Science Essays, 1963, 1967; The Growl, 1964; The Blossom: or Billy the Kid, 1964; Two for Bruce Conner, 1964; Ghost Tantras, 1964; Double Murder! Vahroooooooohr! 1964; Love Lion, Lioness, 1964; 13 Mad Sonnets, 1964; Poisoned Wheat, 1965; Dream Table, 1965; Unto Caesar, 1965; Mandalas, 1965; The Beard, 1965, 1967; The Maze (TV documentary), 1967; The Shell, 1968; Hail Thee Who Play: A Poem 1968; Love Lion Book, 1968; The Sermons of Jean Harlow and the Curses of Billy the Kid, 1969; The Cherub, 1969; The Charbroiled Chinchilla: The Pansy, The Meatball, Spider Rabbit, 1969; Little Odes, Poems, and a Play, The Raptors, 1969; The Surge: A Poem, 1969; Hymns to St. Geryon and Dark Brown, 1969; Lion Fight, 1969; Freewheelin' Frank, Secretary of the Angels, as Told to Michael McClure by Frank Reynolds, 1969; The Brutal Brontosaurus: Spider Rabbit, The Meatball, The Shell, Apple Glove, The Authentic Radio Life of Bruce Conner and Snoutburbler, 1970; The Mad Cub (novel), 1970; The Meatball, 1971; Spider Rabbit, 1971; The Pansy, 1971; Gargoyle Cartoons, 1971; Star, 1971; The Adept (nove), 1971; Polymorphous Pirates: The Pussy, The Button, the Feather, 1972; The Feather, 1972; The Mammals, 1972;99 Theses, 1972; September Blackberries, 1974; Jaguar Skies (poetry), 1975; Gorf (musical play), 1976; Antechamber and Other Poems, 1978; The Grabbing of the Fairy, 1978; Josephine the Mouse Singer, 1980; Fragments of Perseus, 1982; Selected Poems, 1985. Add: 5862 Bolboa Dr., Oakland, Calif. 94611, U.S.A.

McCONICA, James Kelsey. Canadian, b. 1930. History. Pres., Univ. of St. Michael's Coll., Toronto, since 1984; Prof., Pontifical Inst. of Medieval Studies, Toronto, since 1976 (Assoc. Prof., 1967–70); Research Fellow, All Souls Coll., Oxford, since 1978 (Visiting Fellow, 1969–71, 1977). Instr., 1956–57, and Asst. Prof. of History, 1957–62, Univ. of Saskatchewan, Saskatoon; Assoc. Dir., Center for Medieval Studies, 1973–76. *Publs:* English Humanists and Reformation Politics, 1965; (ed.) The Correspondence of Erasmus 1515–1517, vols. III and IV of Collected Works of Erasmus, 1976, 1977; Thomas More: A Short Biography, 1977; The History of the University of Oxford: The Collegiate University, vol. 3, 1986. Add: 81 St. Mary St., Toronto M5S 1J4, Canada.

McCONKEY, James (Rodney). American, b. 1921. Novels/Short stories, Literature, Autobiography/Memoirs/Personal. Goldwin Smith Prof. of English, Cornell Univ., Ithaca, N.Y., since 1987 (Asst. Prof., 1956–62; Assoc. Prof., 1962–65; Prof. of English, 1965–87). Asst. Prof., and Assoc. Prof. of English, Morehead State Coll. (now Morehead State Univ.), Ky., 1950–56. *Publs:* The Novels of E.M. Forster, 1957; (ed.) The Structure of Prose, 1962; Night Stand (short stories), 1965; Crossroads (novel), 1968; A Journey to Sahalin (novel), 1971; The Tree House Confessions (novel), 1979; Court of Memory, 1983; To a Distant Island (novel), 1984; (ed.) Chekhov and Our Age, 1985; Kayo: The Authentic and Annotated Autobiographical Novel from Outer Space (novel), 1987. Add: R.D. 1, Trumansburg, N.Y. 14886, U.S.A.

McCONNELL, Grant. American, b. 1915. Politics/Government. Prof. of Govt., Univ. of California at Santa Cruz, since 1969 (Exec. Vice Chancellor, 1970–71). Consultant on conservation since 1957; Member, Bd. of Dirs., North Cascades Conservation Council. Instr. in Economics, Mt. Holyoke Coll., South Hadley, Mass., 1939–40; with Dept. of Agriculture, and Office of Price Admin., 1940–42; Lectr. in Political Science, 1951–53, and Asst. Prof., 1953–57, Univ. of California at Berkeley; Assoc. Prof. of Political Science, 1957–65, Prof., 1965–69, and Chmn. of Dept., 1967–69, Univ. of Chicago. *Publs:* The Decline of Agrarian Democracy, 1953; The Steel Seizure of 1952, 1960; Steel and the Presidency, 1962, 1963; Private Power and American Democracy, 1965; The Modern Presidency, 1975; Stehekin: A Valley in Time, 1988. Add: c/o The Mountaineers Books, 306 Second Ave., W., Seattle, Wash. 98119, U.S.A.

McCONNELL, J(ames) D(ouglas) R(utherford). Also writes as Douglas Rutherford. British, b. 1915. Mystery/Crime/Suspense, Language/Linguistics. Asst. Master, 1945–59, House Master and Modern Languages Teacher, 1959 until retirement, 1973, Eton Coll., Berks. *Publs:* (as Douglas Rutherford) Comes the Blind Fury, 1950; (as Douglas Rutherford) Telling of Murder, 1951; (as Douglas Rutherford) Meet a Body, 1952; (as Douglas Rutherford) Grand Prix Murder, 1954; (as Douglas Rutherford) The Perilous Sky, 1955; (as Douglas Rutherford) A Shriek of Tyres, 1956; (as Douglas Rutherford) The Long Echo, 1957; (as Douglas Rutherford) Murder is Incidental, 1961; Learn Italian Quickly, 1961; (as Douglas Rutherford) The Creeping Flesh, 1963; (as Douglas Rutherford) The Black Leather Murders, 1965; (ed.) Best Motor Racing Stories, 1965; Learn Spanish Quickly, 1966; Eton: How It Works, 1967; Learn French Quickly, 1968; (as Douglas Rutherford) Skin for Skin, 1968; (as Douglas Rutherford) The Gilt-Edged Cockpit, 1969; (as Douglas Rutherford) Best Underworld Stories, 1969; (as Douglas Rutherford)

Clear the Fast Lane, 1971; (as Douglas Rutherford) The Gunshot Grand Prix, 1972; (as Douglas Rutherford) Killer on the Track, 1973; (as Douglas Rutherford) Rally to the Death, 1974; (as Douglas Rutherford) Race Against the Sun, 1975; (as Douglas Rutherford) Kick Start, 1975; (as Douglas Rutherford) Mystery Tour, 1975; (ed.) Treasures of Eton, 1976; (as Douglas Rutherford) Return Load, 1977; (as Douglas Rutherford) Collision Course, 1978; (as Douglas Rutherford) Turbo, 1980; (as Douglas Rutherford) Porcupine Basin, 1981; The Benedictine Commando, 1981; (as Douglas Rutherford) Stop at Nothing, 1983; English Public Schools, 1985; Battlefield Madonna, 1985; (with Phil Edwards) Healing for You, 1985; (as Douglas Rutherford) A Game of Sudden Death, 1987. Add: Hal's Croft, Monxton, Andover, Hants SP11 8AS, England.

McCONNELL, James Vernon. American, b. 1925. Biology, Psychology, Social sciences, Humor/Satire. Prof. of Psychology, Univ. of Michigan, Ann Arbor, since 1963 (joined faculty, 1956). Pres., Planarian Press, Ann Arbor, since 1964. Editor and Publisher, Women Runner's Digest, and Intnl. Journal of Comparative Psychology, 1959–79; editor, Journal of Biological Psychology, 1966–79. *Publs:* (co-author) Psychology, 1961; (ed.) The Worm Re-Turns: The Best from the Worm Runner's Digest, 1965; (ed.) A Manual of Psychological Experimentation on Planarians, 1965, 1967; (contrib. ed.) Readings in Social Psychology Today, 1970; (ed. with M. Schutjer) Science, Sex and Sacred Cows, 1971; Understanding Human Behavior, 1974, 5th ed., 1986; (with R. Trotter) Psychology, The Human Science, 1978. Add: Dept. of Psychology, Univ. of Michigan, Ann Arbor, Mich. 48109, U.S.A.

McCORD, Anne. British, b. 1942. Children's non-fiction. Asst. Registrar, Univ. of Reading, since 1978. Teacher, 1964–71; Higher Scientific Officer, British Museum of Natural History, London, 1971–78. *Publs:* All About Early Man, 1974; Dinosaurs, 1977; Prehistoric Mammals, 1977; Early Man, 1977; Children's Encyclopaedia of Prehistoric Life, 1980. Add: Sch. of Education, The Univ., London Rd., Reading RG1 5AQ, England.

McCORD, David (Thompson Watson). American, b. 1897. Novels/Short stories, Children's fiction, Poetry, Essays. Assoc. Ed., 1923–25, and Ed., 1940–46, Harvard Alumni Bulletin; Member of the Drama Staff, Boston Evening Transcript, 1923–28; Lectr., Lowell Inst., Boston, 1950; Staff Member, Bread Loaf Writers Conference, Vermont, 1958, 1960, 1962, 1964; Instr. in Creative Writing, Harvard Univ., summers 1963, 1965, 1966; Councilor, Harvard Soc. of Advanced Study and Research, 1967–72. *Publs:* Oddly Enough (essays), 1926; Floodgate (verse), 1927; Stirabout (essays), 1928; (ed.) Once and For All (essays), 1929; Oxford Nearly Visited: Fantasy (verse), 1929; Fiftieth Anniversary Ode (verse), 1930; Alice in Botolphland (play), 1932; The Crows: Poems, 1934; Bay Window Ballads (verse), 1935; H.T.P.: Portrait of a Critic (on Henry Taylor Parker), 1935; Notes on the Harvard Tercentenary, 1936; An Acre for Education, Being Notes on the History of Radcliffe College, 1938; 4th ed. 1963; And What's More (verse), 1941; On Occasion (verse), 1943; Remembrance of Things Passed (verse), 1947; About Boston: Sight, Sound, Flavor, and Inflection, 1948; A Star Aday (verse), 1950; Poet Always Next But One (verse), 1951; Blue Reflections on the Merchants Limited (verse), 1952; The Camp at Lockjaw (story), 1952; Far and Few (verse), 1952; The Old Bateau and Other Poems, 1953; . . . as Built with Second Thoughts, 1953; The Related Man, 1953; Odds Without Ends (verse), 1954; Whereas to Mr. Franklin (verse), 1954; 60 Lines for Three-Score Hatch (verse), 1957; David McCord's Oregon, 1959; On the Frontier of Understanding, 1959; The Language of Request: Fishing with a Barbless Hook (essays), 1961; Take Sky (verse collection), 1962; The Fabrick of Man: Fifty Years of the Peter Bent Brigham Hospital, 1963; In Sight of Sever: Essays from Harvard, 1963; Books Fall Open (verse), 1964; Sonnets to Baedecker, 1965; Observation Tower (verse), 1966; All Day Long (verse), 1966; (co-author) Art and Education, 1966; Children and Poetry (lectr.), 1966; (ed.) Bibliotheca Medica: Physician for Tomorrow, 1966; (ed.) New England Revisited, by Arthur Griffin, 1966; Every Time I Climb a Tree (verse), 1967; Notes from Four Cities 1927–1953, 1969; (ed.) Stow Wengenroth's New England, 1969; For Me to Say (verse), 1970; Poem for the Occasion, 1970; Mr. Bidery's Spidery Garden (verse), 1972; Pen, Paper, and Poem (verse), 1973: Away and Ago (verse), 1974; The Star in the Pail (verse), 1975; One at Time: Collected Poems for the Young, 1977; Sestina for the Queen (verse), 1977; Speak Up, 1980; All Small, 1986. Add: Harvard Club of Boston, 374 Commonwealth Ave., Boston, Mass. 02215, U.S.A.

McCORMACK, Gavan. British, b. 1937. History. Sr. Lectr., La Trobe Univ., Melbourne, since 1977. Former Staff Member, Univ. of Leeds; Dir., Japanese Studies Centre, Melbourne, 1982–83. *Publs:* (co-author) Japanese Imperialism Today, 1973; Chang Tso-lin in Northeast

China 1911-1928, 1977; (co-ed.) Korea North and South, 1977; (ed. and trans.) Twice Victims: The Koreans at Hiroshima, 1981; Cold War Hot War: An Australian Perspective on the Korean War, 1983; (ed. and trans.) The Price of Growth: Dilemmas of Contemporary Japan, by Kidaka Rokuro, 1984; (ed. with Y. Sugimoto) Democracy in Contemporary Japan, 1986; (ed. with Y. Sugimoto) The Japanese Trajectory: Modernization and Beyond, 1989. Add: 26 Sylvan St., Montmorency, Vic. 3094, Australia.

McCORMICK, (George) Donald (King). Also writes as Richard Deacon. British, b. 1911. History, Social commentary/phenomena, Travel/Exploration/Adventure, Biography. N. African Corresp., 1946–49, Commonwealth Corresp., 1949–55, Asst. Foreign Mgr., 1955–63, and Foreign Mgr., 1963–73, Sunday Times, London. *Publs:* The Talkative Muse, 1934; Islands for Sale, 1950; Mr. France, 1955; The Wicked City, 1956; The Hell-Fire Club, 1958; The Mystery of Lord Kitchener's Death, 1959; The Identity of Jack the Ripper, 1959, rev. ed. 1970; The Incredible Mr. Kavanagh, 1960; The Wicked Village, 1960; Blood on the Sea, 1962; Temple of Love, 1962; Mask of Merlin, 1963; The Silent Killer, 1964; Pedlar of Death, 1965; (as Richard Deacon) The Private Life of Mr. Gladstone, 1965; (as Richard Deacon) Madoc and the Discovery of America, 1966; Red Barn Mystery, 1967; (as Richard Deacon) John Dee, 1968; Murder by Witchcraft, 1968; Murder by Perfection, 1970; (as Richard Deacon) A History of the British Secret Service, 1970; (as Richard Deacon) A History of the Russian Secret Service, 1972; One Man's Wars, 1972; How to Buy an Island, 1973; Master Book of Spies, 1973; Islands of England and Wales, 1974; Islands of Scotland, 1974; Islands of Ireland, 1974; (as Richard Deacon) A History of the Chinese Secret Service (in U.S. as The Chinese Secret Service), 1974; Master Book of Escapes, 1975; William Caxton, 1976; Matthew Hopkins: Witchfinder General, 1976; Taken for a Ride, 1976; The Book of Fate, 1976; Who's Who in Spy Fiction, 1977; The Israeli Secret Service, 1977; The Silent War, 1978; The British Connection, 1979 (later withdrawn); Spy!, 1980; (as Richard Deacon) Escape!, 1980; Approaching 1984, 1980; Love in Code, 1980; (as Richard Deacon) A History of the Japanese Secret Service, 1982; With My Little Eye, 1982; Zita, 1983; "C": A Biography of Sir Maurice Oldfield, 1985; The Cambridge Apostles, 1985; The Truth Twisters, 1986; Spycolpaedia, 1987. Add: 8 Barry Ct., 36 Southend Rd., Beckenham, Kent BR3 2AD, England.

McCORMICK, Eric Hall. New Zealander, b. 1906. Art, History, Literature, Biography. Research Fellow in Arts, Univ. of Auckland, 1973–85 (Sr. Lect., 1947–51; Research Fellow and Ed., 1963–64). Secty., National Historical Cttee., 1936–40; Ed., Centennial Publs., 1939–40; Chief War Archivist, 1945–47; Pres. of Honour, P.E.N. (N.Z. Centre), 1976–77. *Publs:* Letters and Art in New Zealand, 1940; Works of Frances Hodgkins in New Zealand, 1954; The Expatriate, 1954; Eric Lee-Johnson, 1956; The Inland Eye, 1959; Tasman and New Zealand, 1959; New Zealand Literature, 1959; The Fascinating Folly, 1961; (ed.) New Zealand or Recollections of It by E. Markham, 1963; (ed.) Narrative of a Residence in New Zealand, by A. Earle, 1966; Alexander Turnbull, 1974; Omai, Pacific Envoy, 1978; Portrait of Frances Hodgkins, 1981. Add: 30 Harrybrook Rd., Green Bay, Auckland 7, New Zealand.

McCORMICK, John O(wen). American, b. 1918. Literature, Sports/Physical education/Keeping fit. Prof. of Comparative Literature, Rutgers Univ., New Brunswick, N.J., since 1959, now Emeritus. Sr. Tutor and Teaching Asst., Harvard Univ., Cambridge, Mass., 1946–51; Lectr., Salzburg Seminar in American Studies, Austria, 1951–52; Prof. of American Studies, Free Univ. of Berlin, 1952–53, 1954–59. *Publs:* Catastrophe and Imagination, 1957; Amerikanische Lyrik, 1957; Der moderne amerikanische Roman, 1960; (ed., with Mairi MacInnes) Versions of Censorship, 1962; (ed.) Syllabus of Comparative Literature, 1963, 1972; (with Mario Sevilla) The Complete Aficionado, 1967; The Middle Distance: A Comparative History of American and European Imaginative Literature 1919–1932, 1971; Fiction as Knowledge: The Modern Post-Romantic Novel, 1975; George Santayana: A Biography, 1987. Add: Hovingham Lodge, Hovingham, York YO6 4NA, England.

McCORQUODALE, Barbara. *See* CARTLAND, Barbara.

McCOURT, James. American, b. 1941. Novels/Short stories. Member, Creative Writing Program, Princeton Univ., New Jersey, 1984; Ezra Stiles Coll., Yale Univ., New Haven, Conn., 1986–88. *Publs:* Mawrdew Czgowchwz, 1975; Kaye Wayfaring in "Avenged," 1984. Add: c/o Elaine Markson, 44 Greenwich Ave., New York, N.Y. 10011, U.S.A.

McCOY, Ralph E. American, b. 1915. Intellectual History, Personnel management, Librarianship. Librarian, Univ. of Illinois, 1948–55; Dean of Library Affairs, Southern Illinois Univ., Carbondale, 1956–76; Interim Dir. of Libraries, Univ. of Georgia, 1978–79; Interim Exec. Dir., Assn. of Research Libraries, 1980; Interim Univ. Librarian, Rutgers Univ., 1985–86. *Publs:* Personnel Administration for Libraries, 1953; Freedom of the Press, 1968; Theodore Schroeder: A Cold Enthusiast, 1973; Freedom of the Press: A Bibliocyclopedia, 1979; (with R.B. Downs) The Finest Freedom Today, 1984. Add: 1902 Chautauqua, Carbondale, Ill. 62901, U.S.A.

McCRAW, Thomas K. American, b. 1940. Administration/Management, History, Politics/Government. Prof. of Business History, Harvard Business Sch., Boston, since 1978 (Visiting Assoc. Prof., 1976–78), Newcomen Research Fellow, Harvard Univ., Cambridge, Mass., 1973–74; Assoc. Prof., Univ. of Texas at Austin, 1974–78. *Publs:* Morgan vs Lilienthal: The Feud Within the TVA, 1970; TVA and the Power Fight 1933–1939, 1971; (ed. and contrib.) Regulation in Perspective: Historical Essays, 1981; Prophets of Regulation, 1984; (ed. and contrib.) America vs. Japan, 1986; (ed.) The Essential Alfred Chandler, 1988. Recipient of Pulitzer Prize for History, 1985. Add: Harvard Business Sch., Soldiers Field, Boston, Mass. 02163, U.S.A.

McCREA, (Sir) William (Hunter). British, b. 1904. Astronomy, History, Mathematics/Statistics, Physics. Emeritus Prof. of Astronomy, Univ. of Sussex, Brighton, since 1972 (Research Prof., 1966–72). Fellow, Royal Soc., since 1952. Prof. of Mathematics, Queen's Univ. of Belfast, N. Ire., 1936–44; Temporary Principal Experimental Officer, Admiralty, London, 1943–45; Prof. of Mathematics, Royal Holloway Coll., Univ. of London, 1944–66. *Publs:* Relativity Physics, 1935; Analytical Geometry of Three Dimensions, 1942; Physics of the Sun and Stars, 1950; (trans.) The New Cosmos, by A. Unsöld, 1969; (co-author) Cosmology Now, 1973; The Royal Greenwich Observatory, 1975; (co-author) History of the Royal Astronomical Society 1920–1980, 1987. Add: 87 Houndean Rise, Lewes, E. Sussex, England.

McCREADY, Jack. *See* POWELL, Talmage.

McCREERY, Charles Anthony Selby. British, b. 1942. Philosophy, Psychology, Sciences. Research Officer, Inst. of Psychophysical Research, Oxford, since 1964. *Publs:* Science, Philosophy and ESP, 1967; Psychical Phenomena and the Physical World, 1973; (with Celia Green) Apparitions, 1975. Add: 118 Banbury Rd., Oxford OX2 6JU, England.

McCUE, Lillian Bueno. *See* de la TORRE, Lillian.

McCULLAGH, Sheila K(athleen). British, b. 1920. Education. Lectr., Univ. of Leeds Inst. of Education, 1949–57, Education Clinic, London, Ont., 1958–60, and Teachers Coll., London, Ont., 1960–63. *Publs:* Pirate Reading Scheme: Griffin Readers, 1959–78; Tales and Adventures, 1960; Dragon Pirate Stories, 1963–74; Sea Hawk Readers and Library Books, 1964; One, Two, Three and Away, 1964–87; Adventures in Space, 1966; Stories to Start With, 1973; Handbook for the Pirate Reading Scheme, 1973, 1976; Into New Worlds, 1974; Flightpath to Reading series, 1974; Hummingbird Books, 1977–85; Whizzbang Adventures, 1977–79; Buccaneers, 1979; Silver Ship, 1980; Journey Through the Strange Land, 1980; Tim Paperbacks, 1983; New Buccaneers, 1984; Early Hummingbirds, 1985; Puddle Lane Reading Programme, 1985–87. Add: 27 Royal Cres., Bath BA1 2LT, England.

McCULLOCH, Alan McLeod. Australian, b. 1907. Art. Dir., Mornington Peninsula Arts Centre, Vic., since 1970. Art Critic, Argus, Melbourne, 1945–47, and Herald, Melbourne, 1951–81. *Publs:* Trial by Tandem, 1951; Highway Forty, 1952; Encyclopedia of Australian Art, 2 vols., 1968–78, 1984; The Golden Age of Australian Painting: Impressionism and the Heidelberg School, 1969; Artists of the Australian Goldrush, 1975. Add: Tucks Rd., Shoreham, Vic., Australia 3916.

McCULLOUGH, Colleen. Australian, b. 1937. Novels, Historical/Romance, Food/Wine. Full-time writer since 1976. Researcher, Sch. of International Medicine, Yale Univ., New Haven, Conn., 1967–76. *Publs:* romance novels—The Thorn Birds, 1977; An Indecent Obsession, 1981; The Ladies of Missalonghi, 1987; other—Tim (novel), 1974; Cooking with Colleen McCullough and Jean Easthope, 1982; A Creed for the Third Millenium (novel), 1987. Add: c/o Harper and Row, 10 E. 53rd St., New York, N.Y. 10022, U.S.A.

McCULLOUGH, Constance M. American, b. 1912. Education. Prof. of Education Emeritus, San Francisco State Univ., since 1973 (Prof., 1947–73). Asst. Prof. of Education and English, Western Reserve Univ., Cleveland, Ohio, 1939–47. Bd. Member, 1969–72, and Pres., 1974–75,

Intnl. Reading Assn.*Publs:* (with D.V. Smith) Essentials of English Tests, 1939; Handbook for Teaching the Language Arts in Elementary Schools, 1939, 1969; (with R. Strang and A. Traxler) Problems in the Improvement of Reading, 1946, 1955; Ginn Basic Readers Series; (with D. Russell) 100 Series, Books 4 and 5, 1951, 1964, (with T. Clymer) 360 Series, Books 4 and 5, 1970, (with T. Clymer) 720 Series, Books 4 and 5, 1982; (with R. Strang and A. Traxler) The Improvement of Reading, 1961, 1967; McCullough Word Analysis Tests, 1961; (with M. Tinker) Teaching Elementary Reading, 1962, 3rd ed. 1975; (with Indian Cttee.) Hindi Readers, 1965; (with Indian Cttee.) Preparation of Textbooks in Mother Tongue, 1969; (ed.) Inchworm, Inchworm: Persistent Problems in Reading Education, 1980. Add: 1925 Cactus Ct., No. 4, Walnut Creek, Calif. 94595, U.S.A.

McCURTIN, Peter. Mystery/Crime/Suspense, Historical/Romance/-Gothic, Westerns/Adventure. *Publs:* Hangtown, 1970, in U.K. as Arizona Hangtown, 1972; The Slavers, 1970; Tough Bullet, 1970; Mafioso, 1970; The Sun Dance Murders, 1970; Cosa Nostra, 1971; Escape from Devil's Island, 1972; Omertà, 1972; The Syndicate, 1972; Screaming on the Wire, 1972; Boston Bust Out, 1973; Death Hunt, 1973; Manhattan Massacre, 1973; New Orleans Holocaust, 1973; Vendetta, 1973; The Pleasure Principle, 1974; The Deadliest Game, 1976; Spoils of War, 1976; The Massacre at Umtali, 1976; Ambush at Derati Wells, 1977; First Blood, 1977; The Guns of Palembang, 1977; Operation Hong Kong, 1977; Body Count, 1977; Battle Pay, 1978; Day of the Halfbreeds, 1979; Death Dance, 1979; Nightriders, 1979; Loanshark, 1979; Minnesota Strip, 1979; The Marauders, 1980.

McCUTCHAN, (Donald) Philip. Also writes as Duncan MacNeil; has also written as T.I.G. Wigg and Robert Conington Galway. British, b. 1920. Novels/Short stories. Chmn., Crime Writers' Assn., 1965–66. *Publs:* Whistle and I'll Come, 1957; The Kid, 1958; (as T.I.G. Wigg) A Job with the Boys, 1958; Storm South, 1959; Gibraltar Road, 1960; (as T.I.G. Wigg) For the Sons of Gentlemen, 1960; (as T.I.G. Wigg) A Rum for the Captain, 1961; Hopkinson and the Devil of Hate, 1961; Redcap, 1961; Bluebolt One, 1962; Leave the Dead Behind Us, 1962; The Man from Moscow, 1963; Marley's Empire, 1963; (as Robert Conington Galway) Assignment series, 10 vols., 1963–70; Warmaster, 1963; Bowering's Breakwater, 1964; Moscow Coach, 1964; Sladd's Evil, 1965; The Dead Line, 1966; A Time for Survival, 1966; Skyprobe, 1966; Poulter's Passage, 1967; The Screaming Dead Balloons, 1968; The Day of the Coastwatch, 1968; The Bright Red Businessmen, 1969; The All-Purpose Bodies, 1969; (as Duncan MacNeil) Drums Along the Khyber, 1969; Man, Let's Go On, 1970; Hartinger's Mouse, 1970; (as Duncan MacNeil) Lieutenant of the Line, 1970; Half a Bag of Stringer, 1971; This Drakotny, 1971; (as Duncan MacNeil) Sadhu on the Mountain Peak, 1971; The German Helmet, 1972; The Oil Bastards, 1972; (as Duncan MacNeil) The Gates of Kunarja, 1972; Pull My String, 1973; (as Duncan MacNeil) The Red Daniel, 1973; Call for Simon Shard, 1974; Coach North, 1974; Beware, Beware the Bight of Benin, 1974; (as Duncan MacNeil) Subaltern's Choice, 1974; A Very Big Bang, 1975; Halfhyde series, 15 vols., 1975–89; (as Duncan MacNeil) By Command of the Viceroy, 1975; Blood Run East, 1976; The Guns of Arrest, 1976; (as Duncan MacNeil) The Mullah from Kashmir, 1976; Tall Ships, the Golden Age of Sail (non-fiction), 1976; The Eros Affair, 1977; (as Duncan MacNeil) Wolf in the Fold, 1977; Blackmail North, 1978; (as Duncan MacNeil) Charge of Cowardice, 1978; Sunstrike, 1979; Great Yachts (non-fiction), 1979; as Duncan MacNeil) The Restless Frontier, 1979; Corpse, 1980; (as Duncan MacNeil) Cunningham's Revenge, 1980; (as Duncan MacNeil) The Train at Bundarbar, 1980; Cameron series, 13 vols., 1980–89; Shard Calls the Tune, 1981; Werewolf, 1982; (as Duncan MacNeil) A Matter for the Regiment, 1982; The Hoof, 1983; Rollerball, 1984; Shard at Bay, 1985; The Executioners, 1986; The Convoy Commodore, 1986; Convoy North, 1987; Greenfly, 1987; Overnight Express, 1988; Convoy South, 1988; Convoy East, 1989; The Boy Who Liked Monsters, 1989; Cholera Convoy, 1990. Add: 107 Portland Rd., Worthing, W. Sussex BN11 1QA, England.

McCUTCHEON, Hugh Davie-Martin. Also writes as Hugh Davie-Martin and Griselda Wilding. British, b. 1909. Novels/Short stories, Mystery/Crime/Suspense. Town Clerk of Renfrew, Scotland, 1945–74. *Publs:* Alamein to Tunis, 1946; The Angel of Light (in U.S. as Murder at the Angel), 1951; None Shall Sleep Tonight, 1954; Prey for the Nightingale, 1954; Cover Her Face, 1955; The Long Night Through, 1956; Comes the Blind Fury, 1957; To Dusty Death, 1960; Yet She Must Die, 1961; The Deadly One, 1962; Suddenly in Vienna, 1963; Treasure of the Sun, 1964; The Black Attendant, 1966; Killers Moon (in U.S. as The Moon Was Full), 1967; The Scorpion's Nest, 1968; A Hot Wind from Hell, 1969; Brand for the Burning, 1970; Something Wicked, 1970; Red Sky at Night, 1972; Instrument of Vengeance, 1975; (as Hugh Davie-Martin) The Girl

in My Grave, 1976; (as Hugh Davie-Martin) The Pearl of Oyster Island, 1977; Night Watch, 1978; (as Hugh Davie-Martin) Spaniard's Leap, 1979; The Cargo of Death, 1980; (as Hugh Davie-Martin) Death's Bright Angel, 1982; (as Griselda Wilding) Promise of Delight, 1988. Add: 19 Bentinck Dr., Troon, Ayrshire, Scotland.

McCUTCHEON, William Alan. British, b. 1934. History, Transportation. Teacher of Geography and French, Royal Belfast Academical Instn., 1956–62; Dir., Survey of Industrial Archaeology, Ministry of Finance, Govt. of Northern Ireland, 1962–68; Dir., Ulster Museum, Belfast, 1977–82 (Keeper of Technology and Local History, 1968–77). *Publs:* The Canals of the North of Ireland, 1965; Railway History in Pictures: Ireland, vols. 1 and 2, 1969, 1971; Wheel and Spindle, 1977; The Industrial Archaeology of Northern Ireland, 1980. Add: 7 Sussex Gardens, Petersfield, Hants, GU31 4JY, England.

McDARRAH, Fred W. American, b. 1926. Arts, Cultural/Ethnic topics, Photography. Photography Reviewer and Picture Ed., Village Voice newspaper, NYC, since 1959; Book Critic, Photo District News, NYC. *Publs:* The Beat Scene, 1960; The Artist's World in Picture, 1961, 2nd ed., 1989; Greenwich Village, 1963; New York, New York, 1964; (with J. Gruen) The New Bohemia, 1966; Sculpture in Environment, 1967; (with J.J. Young) Guide for Ecumenical Discussion, 1970; Museums in New York, 1978, 4th ed., 1984; Photography Marketplace, 1975, 1977; (ed.) Stock Photo and Assignment Source Book, 1977, 1984; Kerouac and Friends: A Beat Generation Album, 1984. Add: 505 La Guardia Pl., Apt. 10D, New York, N.Y. 10012, U.S.A.

McDONALD, Eva Rose. British. Historical/Romance/Gothic.*Publs:* Lazare the Leopard, 1959; Dark Enchantment, 1960; The Rebel Bride, 1960; The Prettiest Jacobite, 1961; The Captive Lady, 1962; The Maids of Taunton, 1963; The Black Glove, 1964; The Reluctant Bridegroom, 1965; The Runaway Countess, 1966; The Gretna Wedding, 1967; The Austrian Bride, 1968; Lord Byron's First Love, 1968; The Lost Lady, 1969; The Wicked Squire,1970; The French Mademoiselle, 1970; Shelley's Springtime Bride, 1971; The White Petticoat, 1971; The Spanish Wedding, 1972; The Lady from Yorktown, 1972; Regency Rake, 1973; The Revengeful Husband, 1974; Lament for Lady Flora, 1974; Lord Rochester's Daughters, 1974; Roman Conqueror, 1975; November Nocturne, 1975; Cromwell's Spy, 1976; King in Jeopardy, 1976; Dearest Ba, 1976. Norman Knight, 1977; The Road to Glencoe, 1977; Cry Treason Thrice, 1977; The Deadly Dagger, 1978; Candlemas Courtship, 1978; Queen Victoria's Prince, 1978; Napoleon's Captain, 1979; John Ruskin's Wife, 1979; Château of Nightingales, 1979; House of Secrets, 1980. Add: Wyldwynds, 105 Bathurst Walk, Iver, Bucks. SL0 9EF, England.

McDONALD, Forrest. American, b. 1927. Business/Trade/Industry, Economics, History, Biography. Prof. of History, Univ. of Alabama, since 1976., Special Researcher, 1953–56, and Exec. Secty. to American History Research Center, 1957–58, State Historical Soc. of Wisconsin; member of faculty, Brown Univ., Providence, R.I., 1963–67; Prof. of History, Wayne State Univ., Detroit, 1967–76. *Publs:* Let There Be Light: The Electric Utility Industry in Wisconsin, 1957; We The People: The Economic Origins of the Constitution, 1958; Insull, 1962; (ed.) Empire and Nation, 1962; E. Pluribus Unum: The Formation of the American Republic, 1965; The Torch is Passed, 1968; (ed.) Confederation and Constitution, 1968; Enough Wise Men, 1970; The Boys Were Men: The American Navy in the Age of Fighting Sail, 1971; (with L. Decker and T. Govan) The Last Best Hope, 3 vols., 1972; The Presidency of George Washington, 1974; Phaeton Ride: The Crisis of American Success, 1974; The Presidency of Thomas Jefferson, 1976; Alexander Hamilton: A Biography, 1979; A Constitutional History of the United States, 1982; Novus Ordo Seclorum: The Intellectual Origins of the Constitution, 1985; Requiem: Variations on Eighteenth-Century Themes, 1988. Add: History Dept., Univ. of Alabama, Tuscaloosa, Ala. 35487, U.S.A.

McDONALD, Gregory. American, b. 1937. Novels/Short stories, Mystery/Crime/Suspense. Full-time writer. Arts and Humanities Ed. and Critic-at-Large, Boston Globe, 1966–73. *Publs:* novels—Running Scared, 1964; Love among the Mashed Potatoes, 1978; mystery novels—Fletch series, 9 vols., 1974–88; Flynn series, 3 vols., 1977–85; Who Took Toby Rinaldi?, 1980; The Education of Gregory McDonald, 1985; Safekeeping, 1985; (ed.) The Last Laugh, 1986; A World Too Wide, 1987. Add: c/o William Morris Agency, 1350 Ave. of the Americas, New York, N.Y. 10019, U.S.A.

McDONALD, Hugh Dermot. British, b. 1910. Philosophy, Theology/-Religion. Prof. and Vice-Principal, London Bible Coll., from 1948, now retired. Visiting Prof., Northern Baptist Theological Seminary, Chicago,

Winona Lake Sch. of Theology, Ind., Trinity Evangelical Divinity Sch., Deerfield, Ill., Regent Coll., Univ. of British Columbia, North Western Baptist Seminary, Vancouver, and Carey Hall, Univ. of British Columbia, Vancouver, Canada. *Publs:* Ideas of Revelation, 1700–1860; Theories of Revelation, 1960–1960; I and He; Jesus Human and Divine; Living Doctrines of the New Testament; The Church and Its Glory; Freedom in Faith; What the Bible Teaches about the Bible; The Christian Doctrine of Man; Forgiveness and Atonement, 1984; The Atonement of the Death of Christ, 1985, The God Who Responds, 1986; Epistle to the Colossians, 1988. Add: 43 The Rough, Newick, Sussex, England.

McDONALD, Jamie. *See* **HEIDE,** Florence Parry.

McDONALD, Lynn. Canadian, b. 1940. Criminology/Law enforcement/Prisons, Sociology. Pres., National Action Cttee. on the Status of Women. Assoc. Prof. of Sociology, McMaster Univ., Hamilton, Ont., 1965–74; Prof. of Sociology, Dalhousie Univ., Halifax, N.S., 1975–77; Member of Parliament (Canada), 1982–88. Acting Ed., Canadian Review of Sociology and Anthropology, 1970–71. *Publs:* Social Class and Delinquency, 1969; The Sociology of Law and Order, 1976; The Party That Changed Canada: The New Democratic Party Then and Now, 1987. Add: 33 Grandview Ave., Toronto M4K 1J1, Canada.

McDONALD, Roger. Australian, b. 1941. Novels, Poetry. Poetry Ed., Univ. of Queensland Press, 1969–76. *Publs:* Citizens of Mist, 1968; (ed.) The First Paperback Poets Anthology, 1974; Airship, 1975; 1915: A Novel, 1979; Slipstream (novel), 1982; Melba: A Novel, 1988; The Australians, 1989; Rough Wallaby (novel), 1989. Add: c/o Hilary Linstead and Assocs., 9 Bronte Rd., Bondi Junction, N.S.W. 2022, Australia.

McDONALD, William Andrew. American (b. Canadian), 1913. Archaeology/Antiquities, Classics, Language/Linguistics. Prof. Emeritus of Classics, Univ. of Minnesota, Minneapolis, since 1980 (Prof. since 1948; Regents Prof., 1973–80). Dir., Minnesota Messenia Expedition, Greece, since 1961, and Center for Ancient Studies. Member of faculty, Lehigh Univ., Bethlehem, Pa., 1939–43, Univ. of Texas, Austin, 1945–46, and Moravian Coll., Bethlehem, Pa., 1946–48. *Publs:* The Political Meeting Places of the Greeks, 1943; Progress into the Past, 1967; (with D.J. Georgacas) The Place Names of Southwestern Peloponnesus, 1969; (ed. with G. Rapp) Minnesota Messenia Expedition: Reconstructing a Bronze Age Regional Environment, 1972; (co-ed.) Excavations at Nichoria in Southwest Greece, vol. 3, 1982. Add: Dept. of Classics, Univ. of Minnesota—Twin Cities, 310 Folwell Hall, Minneapolis, Minn. 55455, U.S.A.

McDONNELL, Kevin Lee. Australian, b. 1932. Education, Sciences. Provincial, Christian Brothers, New South Wales and Papua New Guinea, since 1984. Science Master at secondary schs. in Sydney, 1960–72; Tutor, Macquarie Univ., North Ryde, N.S.W., 1973–77; Lectr., Mt. St. Mary Teachers Coll., Sydney, 1974–79. *Publs:* (with R.G. Cull and G.R. Meyer) Science and the Environment of Man, 1966; (with R.G. Cull and G.R. Meyer) Objective Tests in Science, 1967; (with K.R. Glasson) Graded Exercises in Geological Mapping, 1968; (with D.G. Massey and J.H.S. Tebbutt) Enquiring into the Earth, 1968; (ed. with J.J. Veevers) Phanerozoic Earth History of Australia, 1985. Add: Christian Brothers, 179 Albert Rd., Strathfield, N.S.W. 2135, Australia.

McDONNELL, Lois Eddy. American. Children's fiction. Teacher, Carlisle Area Schs., Pa., 1936–43 and 1958–66; Asst. Prof., Shippensburg Univ., Pennsylvania, 1966–79. Add: Everyone Needs a Church 1951, 1959; Hana's New Home, 1957; The Home and Church: Partners in Christian Education, 1961; Stevie's Other Eyes, 1962; Susan Comes Through the Fire, 1969. Add: 123 Parker St., Carlisle, Pa. 17013, U.S.A.

McDORMAND, Thomas Bruce. Canadian, b. 1904. Theology/-Religion, Autobiography/Memoirs/Personal. Gen. Secty., 1955–59, and Pres., 1970–73, Baptist Fedn. of Canada; Gen. Secty., Baptist Convention, Ont. and Que., 1948–55; Exec. Vice-Pres., Acadia Univ., Wolfville, N.S. 1959–61; Pres., Eastern Baptist Coll. and Theological Seminary, Philadelphia, Pa., 1961–67; Gen. Secty., Atlantic Baptist Convention, 1967–70; Vice-Pres., Baptist World Alliance, 1970–75. *Publs:* The Art of Building Worship Service, vol. 1, 1942, vol. II, 1958; The Christian Must Have an Answer, 1959; Judson Concordance to Hymns, 1965; Unforgettable Encounters, 1975; Understanding the Bible Today, 1976; Hymns and Poems, 1979; No Need to Wait; A Diversified Ministry, 1987. Add: 50 Elmwood Dr., Amherst, N.S., Canada.

McDOWELL, Edwin Stewart. American, b. 1935. Novels, Biography.

Reporter, New York Times, since 1978. Editorial Writer, The Arizona Republic, 1960–72, and the Wall St. Journal, NYC, 1972–78. *Publs:* Portrait of an Arizonan, 1964; Three Cheers and a Tiger, 1966; To Keep Our Honor Clean, 1980; The Lost World, 1988. Add: c/o New York Times, 229 W. 43rd St., New York, N.Y. 10036, U.S.A.

McDOWELL, Frederick P.W. American, b. 1915. Literature. Emeritus Prof. of English, Univ. of Iowa, Iowa City, since 1985 (Instr., 1949–51; Asst. Prof., 1951–58; Assoc. Prof., 1958–63; Prof., 1963–85). *Publs:* Ellen Glasgow and the Ironic Art of Fiction, 1960; Elizabeth Madox Roberts, 1962; Caroline Gordon, 1966; (ed.) The Poet as Critic, 1967; E.M. Forster, 1969, 1982; E.M. Forster: An Annotated Bibliography of Secondary Writings about Him, 1977. Add: Dept. of English, Univ. of Iowa, Iowa City, Iowa 52242, U.S.A.

McDOWELL, John (Henry). British, b. 1942. Classics, Philosophy. Prof. of Philosophy, Univ. of Pittsburgh, since 1986. Fellow and Praelector, University Coll., Oxford, 1966–86, and Lectr. in Philosophy, Oxford Univ., 1967–86. James C. Loeb Research Fellow, Harvard Univ., Cambridge, Mass., 1969; Visiting Prof., Univ. of Michigan, Ann Arbor, 1975, Univ. of California at Los Angeles, 1977; Univ. of Minnesota, 1982, Jadavpur Univ., Calcutta, 1983; Sr. Fellow, Council of the Humanities, Princeton Univ., New Haven, N.J., 1984. *Publs:* (trans.) Plato: Theaetetus, 1973; (ed. with Gareth Evans) Truth and Meaning, 1976; Criteria, Defeasibility, and Knowledge, 1984. Add: Dept. of Philosophy, Univ. of Pittsburgh, Pittsburgh, Pa. 15260, U.S.A.

McDOWELL, Michael. Also writes, with Dennis Schuetz, as Nathan Aldyne and Axel Young. American, b. 1950. Novels/Short stories, Mystery/Crime/Suspense, Historical/Romance/Gothic. *Publs:* The Amulet, 1979; Cold Moon over Babylon, 1980; (with Dennis Schuetz, as Nathan Aldyne) Vermilion, 1980; Gilded Needles, 1980; The Elementals, 1981; (with Dennis Schuetz, as Axel Young) Blood Rubies, 1981; Katie, 1982; Cobalt, 1982; Wicked Stepmother, 1983; Blackwater, 6 vols., 1983; Slate, 1984; Toplin, 1985; Jack and Susan series, 3 vols., 1985–87. Add: c/o The Otte Co., 6 Goden St., Belmont, Mass. 02178, U.S.A.

McELDOWNEY, Richard Dennis. New Zealander, b. 1926. Autobiography/Memoirs/Personal, Biography. Ed., 1966–72, and Managing Ed., 1972–86, Auckland Univ. Press. *Publs:* The World Regained, 1957; Donald Anderson: A Memoir, 1966; (ed.) Tikera, by Sygurd Wisniowski, 1972; Arguing with My Grandmother, 1973; Frank Sargeson in His Time, 1976; Full of the Warm South, 1983 Add: 54a Challenger St., St. Heliers, Auckland, New Zealand.

McELFRESH, (Elizabeth) Adeline. Also writes as John Cleveland, Jane Scott, Elizabeth Wesley and Jennifer Blair. American, b. 1918. Mystery/Crime/Suspense, Historical/Romance/Gothic, Children's fiction. Feature Writer, 1982–83 (Proofreader, 1936–42; Feature Ed., 1943–56; Staff Writer, 1973–75; City Ed., 1975–78; Managing Ed., 1978–82): Sun-Commercial newspaper, Vincennes; Reporter, Daily News, Troy, Ohio, 1942–43; Dir. of Public Relations, Good Samaritan Hosp., Vincennes, Ind., 1966–70. *Publs:* My Heart Went Dead (mystery), 1949; Murder with Roses (mystery), 1950; Keep Back the Dark (mystery), 1951; Charlotte Wade, 1952; Homecoming, 1953; The Old Baxter Place, 1954; Doctor Jane, 1954; (as John Cleveland) Minus One Corpse (mystery), 1954; Ann and the Hoosier Doctor, 1955, as Hill Country Nurse, 1959; (as Elizabeth Wesley) Nora Meade, M.D., 1955; (as Elizabeth Wesley) Ann Foster, Lab Technician, 1956; (as Elizabeth Wesley) Sharon James, Freelance Photographer, 1956; (as Jane Scott) Barbara Owen, Girl Reporter, 1956; (as Jane Scott) Kay Rogers, Copy Writer, 1956; Shattered Halo (mystery), 1956; Young Doctor Randall, 1957; Nurse Kathy, 1957; (as Elizabeth Wesley) Polly's Summer Stock, 1957; as Summer Stock Romance, 1961; Calling Doctor Jane, 1957; Dr. Jane's Mission, 1958; (as Elizabeth Wesley) Doctor Barbara, 1958; (as Elizabeth Wesley) Nurse Judy, 1958; (as Jane Scott) A New Love for Cynthia, 1958; Career for Jenny (juvenile), 1958; Dr. Jane Comes Home, 1959; Kay Mannion, M.D., 1959, in U.K. as Kay Mannion, M.D., 1960; (as Elizabeth Wesley) Jane Ryan, Dietician, 1959; (as Jane Scott) Nurse Nancy, 1959; Wings for Nurse Bennett, 1960; Ann Kenyon, Surgeon, 1960; (as Elizabeth Wesley) Doctor Dee, 1960; (as Jane Scott) A Nurse for Rebel's Run, 1960; Summer Change (juvenile), 1960; Dr. Jane's Choice, 1961; To Each Her Dream, 1961; Night Call, 1961; Hospital Hill, 1961; Romantic Assignment, 1961; Jeff Benton, M.D., 1962; Jill Nolan, Surgical Nurse, 1962; Jill Nolan, R.N., 1962; (as Elizabeth Wesley) Dr. Dee's Choice, 1962; Challenge for Dr. Jane, 1963; Jill Nolan's Choice, 1963; (as Elizabeth Wesley) Dr. Dorothy's Choice, 1963; The Magic Scalpel of Dr. Farrer, 1965; Nurse Nolan's Private Duty, 1966; Dr. Jane, Interne, 1966; Nurse for Mercy's Mission, 1969; Assignment in the Islands, 1970; Nurse in Yucatan, 1970;

Skye Manor, 1971; Flight Nurse, 1971; Ellen Randolph, 1971; Doctor for Blue Hollow, 1971; Patient in 711, 1972; Danger at Olduvai, 1972; Evil Island, 1974; Kanesbrake, 1975; Dangerous Assignment, 1975; Long Shadow, 1976; To Last a Lifetime, 1977; If Dreams Were Wild Horses, 1988. Add: R.R.3, Vincennes, Ind. U.S.A.

McELROY, Colleen J. American, b. 1935. Novels/Short stories, Poetry, Plays. Prof. of English and Dir. of Creative Writing, Univ. of Washington, Seattle, since 1983 (Predoctoral Lectr., 1972–73; Asst. Prof., 1973–79; Assoc. Prof., 1979–82). Member, Editorial Bd., Callaloo literary magazine, since 1984. Ed.-in-chief, Dark Waters literary magazine, Seattle, 1973–78; Trustee, Washington State Commn. for the Humanities, 1980–83. *Publs:* Speech and Language of the Preschool Child (textbook), 1972; The Mules Done Long Since Gone, 1973; Music from Home: Selected Poems, 1976; Winters Without Snow, 1979; Lie and Say You Love Me, 1981; Looking for a Country Under Its Original Name, 1984; Queen of the Ebony Isles, 1984; Jesus and Fat Tuesday (fiction), 1987. Add: 2616 4th Ave. N., No. 406, Seattle, Wash. 98109, U.S.A.

McELROY, Joseph (Prince). American, b. 1930. Novels/Short stories. Prof. of English, Queens Coll., City Univ. of New York, since 1964. *Publs:* A Smuggler's Bible, 1966; Hind's Kidnap, 1969; Ancient History, 1971; Lookout Cartridge, 1974; Plus, 1977; Ship Rock, 1980; Women and Men, 1987; The Letter Left to Me, 1988. Add: c/o Melanie Jackson, 250 W. 57th St., New York, N.Y. 10107, U.S.A.

McELROY, Lee. *See* KELTON, Elmer.

McEVEDY, Colin (Peter). British, b. 1930. History. Consultant Psychiatrist, St. Bernards Hosp., Middx., since 1971. Former Registrar, The Maudsley Hosp., and Sr. Registrar, Dept. of Psychological Medicine, Middlesex Hosp., London. *Publs:* The Penguin Atlas of Medieval History, 1961; The Penguin Atlas of Ancient History, 1967; (with Sarah McEvedy) The Atlas of World History, 3 vols., 1970–73; The Penguin Atlas of Modern History, 1972; (with Richard Jones) Atlas of World Population History, 1980; The Penguin Atlas of African History, 1980; The Penguin Atlas of Recent History (Europe since 1815), 1982; The Century World History Factfinder, 1984; Penguin Atlas of North Americn History, 1988. Add: 7 Caithness Rd., London W14, England.

McEVOY, Marjorie. Writes under own name for Gothic and suspense novels, and as Marjorie Harte for medical background novels. British. Historical/Romance/Gothic. *Publs:* No Castle of Dreams, 1960; A Red, Red Rose, 1960; The Meaning of a Kiss, 1961; (as Marjorie Harte) A Call for the Doctor, 1961; (as Marjorie Harte) Goodbye, Doctor Garland, 1962; (as Marjorie Harte) Nurse in the Orient, 1962; Forever Faithful, 1962; Softly Treads Danger, 1963; Calling Nurse Stewart, 1963; (as Marjorie Harte) Doctors in Conflict, 1963; (as Marjorie Harte) Masquerade for a Nurse (in U.S. as Strange Journey), 1964; (as Marjorie Harte) Doctor Mysterious, 1965; Moon over the Danube, 1966; Who Walks by Moonlight?, 1966; Brazilian Stardust, 1967; Dusky Cactus, 1968; The Grenfell Legacy, 1968; (as Marjorie Harte) Cover Girl, 1968, in U.S. as The Closing Web, 1973; The White Castello, 1969, in U.S. as Castle Doom, 1970; The Hermitage Bell, 1971; (as Marjorie Harte) No Eden for a Nurse, 1971; My Love Johnny (in U.S. as Eaglescliffe), 1971; Peril at Polvellyn, 1973; The Chinese Box, 1973; Ravensmount, 1974; The Wych Stone, 1974; The Queen of Spades, 1975; Echoes From the Past, 1979; Calabrian Summer, 1980; The Sleeping Tiger, 1983; Star of Randevi, 1984; Temple Bells, 1985; Camelot Country, 1986. Add: 54 Miriam Ave., Chesterfield, Derbyshire S40 3NF, England.

McEWAN, Ian. British, b. 1948. Novels/Short stories, Plays/Screenplays. *Publs:* First Love, Last Rites (stories), 1975; In Between the Sheets (stories), 1978; The Cement Garden, 1978; The Imitation Game (television plays), 1981; The Comfort of Strangers, 1981; Or Shall We Die? (libretto), 1982; The Ploughman's Lunch (film), 1982; The Child in Time (novel), 1987; Soursweet (screenplay), 1989. Add: c/o Jonathan Cape, 32 Bedford Sq., London WC1B 3EL, England.

McFADDEN, David. Canadian, b. 1940. Novels/Short stories, Poetry. *Publs:* The Poem Poem, 1967; The Saladmaker, 1968; Letters from the Earth to the Earth, 1968; The Great Canadian Sonnet (novel), 1970; Intense Pleasure, 1972; The Ova Years, 1972; Poems Worth Knowing, 1973; A Knight in Dried Plums, 1975; The Poet's Progress, 1977; On the Road Again, 1978; I Don't Know, 1978; A New Romance, 1978; The Individual Human Being, 1978; A Trip Around Lake Huron (novel), 1980; My Body Was Eaten By Dogs: Selected Poems, 1981; A Trip Around Lake Erie (novel), 1981; Three Stories and Ten Poems, 1982; Country of the Open

Heart, 1982; Animal Spirits: Stories to Live By, 1983; A Pair of Baby Lambs, 1983; The Art of Darkness, 1984. Add: 204-66 Spadina Rd., Toronto, Ont. M5R 2TH, Canada.

McFADDEN, Roy. British, b. 1921. Poetry. Co-Ed., Ulster Voices, 1941–42, Rann: An Ulster Quarterly of Poetry, 1948–53, and Irish Voices, 1953, all in Belfast. *Publs:* A Poem: Russian Summer, 1942; (with Alex Comfort and I. Serraillier) Three New Poets, 1942; Swords and Ploughshares, 1943; Flowers for a Lady, 1945; The Heart's Townland, 1947; Elegy for the Dead of the "Princess Victoria", 1952; The Garryowen, 1972; Verifications, 1977; A Watching Brief, 1979; The Selected Roy McFadden, 1983; Letters to the Hinterland, 1986. Add: 13 Shrewsbury Gardens, Belfast 9, Northern Ireland.

McFADZEAN of Kelvinside, Baron; Francis Scott McFadzean. British, b. 1915. Business/Trade/Industry. Former Dir., Shell Transport and Trading Co. Ltd., and Shell Petroleum Co. Ltd., 1964–86 (joined Royal Dutch/Shell in 1952; served in various posts in U.K., Middle and Far East; Managing Dir., Royal Dutch/Shell group of companies, 1964–76; Chmn., Shell Intnl. Marine Ltd., 1966–76, Shell Canada Ltd., 1970–76, Shell Petroleum Co./, 1972–76, and Shell Transport and Trading Co., 1972–76; Dir., Shell Oil Co., 1972–76); Dir., Beecham Group Ltd., since 1974, and Coats Patons Ltd., since 1979. Formerly a Civil Servant, with the U.K. Bd. of Trade and Treasury; later with Malayan Govt., and the Colonial Development Corp. in the Far East; Dir., Private Investment Co. for Asia, 1969–80; Dir., 1975, and Chmn. and Chief Exec., 1976–79, British Airways; Chmn. and Chief Exec., Rolls Royce Ltd., London, 1980–83. Visiting Prof. of Economics, Strathclyde Univ., 1967–76; Chmn., Trade Policy Research Centre, 1971–82. *Publs:* Galbraith and the Planners, 1968; Energy in the Seventies, 1971; The Operation of a Multi-National Enterprise, 1971; (with others) Towards an Open World Economy, 1972; The Economics of John Kenneth Galbraith, 1977; (with others) Global Strategy for Growth, 1981. Add: House of Lords, London SW1A 0PW, England.

McFARLAND, C.K. American, b. 1934. History, Administration/Management. Prof. of History and Management, Arkansas State Univ., since 1971. Asst. Prof., Univ. of Southwestern Louisiana, Lafayette, 1965–66; Assoc. Prof., Texas Christian Univ., Fort Worth, 1966–71. *Publs:* Roosevelt, Lewis, and the New Deal, 1970; (ed.) Readings in Intellectual History, 1970; (ed.) The Modern American Tradition, 1972. Add: Drawer 1690 State University, Ark. 72467, U.S.A.

McFARLAND, Dalton E(dward). American, b. 1919. Administration/Management. Univ. Prof. Emeritus and Prof. of Business Admin., Univ. of Alabama, Birmingham, since 1972. Member, Review Bd., Journal of Behavioral Economics, since 1977. Prof. and Chmn., Dept. of Mgmt., Michigan State Univ., East Lansing, 1952–72. *Publs:* Management: Principles and Practices, 1958, 5th ed. 1979; Action Strategies for Managerial Achievement, 1977; Management and Society, 1982; The Managerial Imperative: The Age of Macromanagement, 1986. Add: 31 Sherman Ave., Grand Haven, Mich. 49417, U.S.A.

McFARLANE, Bruce John. Australian, b. 1936. Economics. Prof. of Politics, Univ. of Adelaide, since 1976 (Reader, 1973–76) Research Fellow in Economics, 1962–68, and Sr. Lectr. in Politics, 1968–72, Australian National Univ., Canberra. *Publs:* (with M. Gough, H. Hughes and G. Palmer) Queensland: Industrial Enigma; (with E.L. Wheelwright) China's Road to Socialism; (with R. Catley) From Tweedledum to Tweedledee: The New Labor Government in Australia; Economic Policy in Australia; Radical Economics; Australian Capitalism in Boom and Depression; (with P. Limqueco) Neo-Marxian Theories of Growth; (with N. Maxwell) China's Changed Road of Development; (with M. Beresford) A Manual of Political Economy; Radical Economics, 1982; Yugoslavia, 1988. Add: Dept. of Politics, Univ. of Adelaide, North Terr., Adelaide, S.A., Australia.

McFARLANE, James Walter. British, b. 1920. Literature, Translations. Prof. of European Literature, Univ. of East Anglia, Norwich, since 1964, now Emeritus. Ed., Scandinavica (Intnl. Journal of Scandinavian Studies), since 1975; Managing Ed., Norvik Press, since 1985. Lectr. and Sr. Lectr. in German and Scandinavian, Univ. of Newcastle upon Tyne, 1947–63. *Publs:* (trans.) Knut Hamsun: Pan, 1955; Ibsen and the Temper of Norwegian Literature, 1960; (ed. and trans.) The Oxford Ibsen, 8 vols., 1960–77; (ed.) Discussions of Ibsen, 1962; (trans.) Thorkild Hansen: Arabia Felix, 1964; North West to Hudson Bay, 1970; (ed.) Henrik Ibsen: A Critical Anthology, 1970; (co-ed.) Modernism: European Literature 1890–1930, 1976; (trans.) Knut Hamsun: Wayfarers, 1980; (ed.) Slaves of Love and Other Norwegian Short Stories, 1982; Ibsen and

Meaning, 1989. Add: The Croft, Stody, Melton Constable, Norfolk, England.

McGAHERN, John. Irish, b. 1934. Novels/Short stories, Plays/Screenplays. Fellow, Univ. of Reading, Berks., 1968 and 1971; O'Connor Prof. of Literature, Colgate Univ., Hamilton, N.Y., 1969, 1972, 1978; Northern Arts Fellow, 1974–76. *Publs:* The Barracks, 1965; The Dark, 1966; Nightlines, 1971; Sinclair (play), 1971; Swallows (television play), 1974; The Leavetaking, 1975; Getting Through (stories), 1978; The Pornographer, 1979; High Ground and Other Stories, 1985. Add: c/o Faber & Faber, 3 Queen Sq., London WC1N 3AU, England.

McGANNO, Michael. *See* **NAHA,** Ed.

McGARRITY, Mark. Also writes as Bartholomew Gill. American, b. 1943. Novels/Short stories, Mystery/Crime/Suspense. Freelance writer since 1971. *Publs:* novels as Mark McGarrity—Little Augie's Lament, 1973; Lucky Shuffles, 1973; A Passing Advantage, 1980; Neon Caesar, 1989; mystery novels as Bartholomew Gill—McGarr and the Politician's Wife, 1977; McGarr and the Sienese Conspiracy, 1977; McGarr on the Cliffs of Moher, 1978; McGarr at the Dublin Horse Show, 1980; McGarr and the P.M. of Belgrave Square, 1983; McGarr and the Method of Descartes, 1984; McGarr and the Legacy of a Woman Scorned, 1986; Death of a Joyce Scholar, 1989. Add: 159 North Shore Rd., Andover, N.J. 07821, U.S.A.

McGAUGHEY, Florence Helen. American, b. 1904. Poetry, Songs, lyrics and libretti. Prof. Emeritus of English, Indiana State Univ., Terre Haute, since 1970 (Prof., 1946–70). *Publs:* Wind Across the Night, 1938; Music in the Wind, 1941; Spring Is a Blue Kite, 1946; Reaching for the Spring, 1958; Selected Poems, 1961; Shadows, 1965; Petals From a Plum Tree, 1967; The Dispossessed (libretto), 1973; Songs of Sorrow (lyrics), 1974; Written in the Stars (libretto), 1974. Add: 1120 Davis Ave., Apt. A-103, Terre Haute, Ind. 47802, U.S.A.

McGEE, Greg(ory William). New Zealander, b. 1950. Plays/Screenplays. *Publs:* Foreskin's Lament, 1981; Tooth and Claw, 1984; Out in the Cold, 1984. Add: 8 John St., Ponsonby, Auckland 2, New Zealand.

McGEE, Terence Gary. New Zealander, b. 1936. Geography. Dir., Inst. of Asian Research, Univ. of British Columbia, Vancouver. Member, Editorial Bd., Urban Anthropology, Pacific Viewpoint, and Journal of Urban History. Former Prof. of Urban Geography, Univ. of Hong Kong; Sr. Fellow, Australian National Univ., Canberra. *Publs:* The Southeast Asian City, 1967; The Urbanization Process in the Third World, 1971; Hawkers in Hong Kong, 1974; Labor Markets, Urban Systems and the Urbanisation Process in Southeast Asian Countries, 1982; (with W.R. Armstrong) Theatres of Accomlation: Studies in Latin America and Asia, 1985. Add: Inst. of Asian Research, Univ. of British Columbia, Vancouver, B.C. V6T 1WS, Canada.

McGILL, Angus. British. Humour. Columnist since 1962, and scriptwriter for comic strip Augusta, The Evening Standard newspaper. *Publs:* Yea Yea Yea, 1963; Pub: An Anthology, 1969; Clive, 1970; Clive in Love, 1971; Clive and Augusta, 1972; Augusta the Great, 1977; I, Augusta, 1979; (with Kenneth Thomson) Live Wires, 1982. Add: c/o The Evening Standard, 2 Deny St., London W8 5EE, England.

McGINNISS, Joe. American, b. 1942. Politics/Government, Social commentary/phenomena. Newspaper reporter, 1964–68. *Publs:* The Selling of the President, 1968; The Dream Team, 1972; Heroes, 1976; Going to Extremes, 1980; Fatal Vision, 1983; Blind Faith, 1989. Add: c/o Morton L. Janklow, 598 Madison Ave., New York, N.Y. 10022, U.S.A.

McGLASHAN, M(axwell) L(en). British, b. 1924. Chemistry. Prof. and Head of the Dept. of Chemistry, University Coll., London, since 1974. Ed., Journal of Chemical Thermodynamics, since 1969. Asst. Lectr. to Sr. Lectr. in Chemistry, Canterbury University Coll., Christchurch, N.Z., 1945–53; Lectr., then Reader in Chemistry, Univ. of Reading, 1954–64; Prof. of Physical Chemistry, Univ. of Exeter, 1964–74. *Publs:* Physicochemical Quantities and Units, 1968, 1971; (ed.) Manual of Symbols and Terminology for Physicochemical Quantities and Units, 1970; (ed.) Chemical Thermodynamics, 2 vols., 1973–78; Chemical Thermodynamics, 1979. Add: 9 Camden Sq., London NW1 9UP, England.

McGOUGH, Roger. British, b. 1937. Children's fiction, Plays/Screenplays, Poetry. Former Lectr., Liverpool Coll. of Art; Poetry Fellow, Univ. of Loughborough, Leics., 1973–75. *Publs:* (with others) Birds, Marriages and Deaths (play), 1964; The Chauffeur-Driven Rolls (play), 1966; The Commission (play), 1967; (with Adrian Henri and Brian Patten) The Mersey Sound: Penguin Modern Poets 10, 1967; Frinck, A Life in the Day of, and Summer with Monika: Poems, 1967; Watchwords, 1969; The Puny Little Life Show (play), 1969; Stuff (play), 1970; After the Merrymaking, 1971; Out of Sequence, 1973; Gig, 1973; Sporting Relations, 1974; In the Glassroom, 1976; Mr. Noselighter (children's book), 1977; The Lifeswappers (television play), 1977; Holiday on Death Row, 1979; Unlucky for Some, 1980; Waving at Trains, 1982; The Great Smile Robbery (children's book), 1982; (with Adrian Henri and Brian Patten) New Volume, 1983; Sky in the Pie (children's book), 1983; Crocodile Puddles, 1984; The Stowaways (children's book), 1986; Noah's Ark (children's book), 1986; Melting into the Foreground, 1986; Nailing the Shadow (children's book), 1987; A Matter of Chance (dance play), 1988; An Imaginary Menagerie, 1988; Helen Highwater (children's book), 1989; Counting by Numbers (children's book), 1989; Selected Poems, 1989. Add: c/o Peters Fraser and Dunlop, The Chambers, Chelsea Harbour, Lots Rd., London SW10 0XF, England.

McGOVERN, John Phillip. American, b. 1921. Medicine/Health. Prof. of the History and Philosophy of Biomedical Sciences, Univ. of Texas Grad. Sch. of Biomedical Sciences, Houston, since 1981 (Prof. and Chmn., Dept. of the History of Medicine, 1970–81). Clinical Prof. of Pediatrics (Allergy), Baylor College of Medicine, Houston, since 1956; Prof., Dept. of Internal Medicine, Univ. of Texas Medical Sch., Houston, since 1978; Distinguished Adjunct Prof. of Health and Safety Education, Kent State Univ., Ohio, since 1972. Assoc. Prof. of Pediatrics, Tulane Univ. Sch. of Medicine, New Orleans, La., 1954–56. Pres., American Assn. for the Study of Headache, 1963–64, and American Coll. of Allergy & Immunology, 1968–69. *Publs:* (with W. Mandel) Bibliography on Sarcoidosis, 1964; (with J. Knight) Allergy and Human Emotions, 1967; (with C. Roland) William Osler: The Continuing Education, 1969; (with G. Stewart) Penicillin Allergy, 1970; (ed.) Asthma and Hay Fever, 1971; (with C. Burns) Humanism in Medicine, 1973; Chronobiology in Allergy and Immunology, 1977; (co-author) Recent Advances in the Chronobiology of Allergy and Immunology, 1981; (with J. Barondes and C. Roland) The Persisting Osler, 1985; (co-ed.) The Collected Essays of Sir William Osler, vols. 1-3, 1985; (with J. Van Eys) The Doctor as a Person, 1988. Add: 6969 Brompton St., Houston, Tex. 77025, U.S.A.

McGRATH, John (Peter). British, b. 1935. Plays/Screenplays, Theatre, Translations. Stage, television, and film dir. *Publs:* Events While Guarding the Bofors Gun, 1966; (adaptor) Bakke's Night of Fame, 1968; Random Happenings in the Hebrides: or, The Social Democrat and the Stormy Sea, 1970; (trans. with M. Teitelbaum) Rules of the Game, 1970; The Fish in the Sea, 1973; The Cheviot, the Stag, and the Black, Black Oil, 1973; The Game's a Bogey, 1974; Little Red Hen, 1975; Yobbo Nowt, 1975; Joe's Drum, 1979; Two Plays for the Eighties, 1981; Good Night Out: Popular Theatre: Audience, Class, and Form (non-fiction), 1981. Add: c/o Margaret Ramsay, 14a Goodwin's Court, London WC2, England.

McGRATH, Thomas M. American, b. 1916. Novels/Short stories, Children's fiction, Poetry. Prof. Emeritus of English, Moorhead Univ., Minnesota. English Instr., Colby Coll., Waterville, Me., 1940–41; Asst. Prof., Los Angeles State Coll., 1950–54, and C.W. Post Coll., Long Island, N.Y., 1960–61; Assoc. Prof., North Dakota State Univ., Fargo, 1962–67. Founding Ed., Crazy Horse mag., 1960–71. *Publs:* First Manifesto, 1940; (with W. Peterson and J.F. Lewis) Three Young Poets, 1942; The Dialectics of Love, 1944; To Walk a Crooked Mile, 1947; Longshot O'Leary's Garland of Practical Poesie, 1949; Witness to the Times, 1954; Figures from a Double World, 1955; The Gates of Ivory, The Gates of Horn (novel), 1957; About Clouds, 1959; Beautiful Things, 1960; Letter to an Imaginary Friend, 1962, 1970; New and Selected Poems, 1962; The Movie at the End of the World: Collected Poems, 1973; A Sound of One Hand, 1975; Open Songs, 1977; Letters to Tomasito, 1977; Passages Toward the Dark, 1982; Echoes Inside the Labyrinth, 1983; This Coffin Has No Handles (novel), 1985; Letter to An Imaginary Friend, Parts III and IV (conclusion), 1985; Selected Poems 1938-88, 1988. Add: 911 22 Ave. S., No. 160, Minneapolis, Minn. 55404, U.S.A.

McGRATH, Tom. British. Plays/Screenplays. Writer and Resident Dramatist, Dundee Coll. of Art. Dir., Third Eye Centre, Glasgow, 1974–77; Resident Dramatist, Traverse Theatre Club, Edinburgh, 1978; Tutor in Playwrighting, Iowa Univ., 1984. *Publs:* (with Jimmy Boyle) The Hardman, 1977. Add: c/o Michael Imison Playwrights Ltd., 28 Almeida St., London N1 1TD, England.

McGRAW, Eloise Jarvis. American, b. 1915. Novels/Short stories, Children's fiction, Plays. Instr. in Painting, Oklahoma City Univ., 1942–

43; with husband, owned and farmed a filbert orchard, Willamette Valley, Ore., 1952–70; Teacher, Portland State Univ., summers 1971–78. *Publs:* Sawdust in His Shoes, 1950; Crown Fire, 1951; Moccasin Trail, 1952; Mara, Daughter of the Nile, 1953; Pharaoh, 1958; Techniques of Fiction Writing, 1959; The Golden Goblet, 1961; Steady, Stephanie (play), 1962; (with Lauren McGraw) Merry Go Round in Oz, 1963; Greensleeves, 1968; Master Cornhill, 1973; A Really Weird Summer, 1977; Joel and the Great Merlini, 1979; (with Lauren Lynn McGraw) The Forbidden Fountain of Oz, 1980; The Money Room 1982; Hideaway, 1983; The Seventeenth Swap, 1986; The Trouble with Jacob, 1988. Add: 1970 Indian Trail, Lake Oswego, Ore. 97034, U.S.A.

McGREGOR, Iona. British, b. 1929. Novels, Children's fiction, Children's non-fiction. Sub-Ed., Dictionary of the Older Scottish Tongue, Edinburgh Univ. Press, 1951–57; Classics Teacher, Simon Langton Girls' Sch., Canterbury, 1958–62, and Beaverwood Sch., Chislehurst, Kent, 1962–69. *Publs:* An Edinburgh Reel, 1968; The Popinjay, 1969; The Burning Hill, 1970; The Tree of Liberty, 1972; The Snake and the Olive, 1974; Edinburgh and the Eastern Lowlands, 1979; Wall and Bruce, Oliver and Boyd, 1986; Penguin Passnotes: The Importance of Being Earnest, 1987; The Adventures of Huckleberry Finn, 1988; Death Wore a Diadem, 1989. Add: 9 Saxe Coburg St., Edinburgh EH3 5BN, Scotland.

McGREGOR, Malcolm Francis. Canadian, b. 1910. Classics, History. Instr. and subsequently Prof. of Classics and Ancient History, Univ. of Cincinnati, Ohio, 1936–54; Prof. and Head, Dept. of Classics, Univ. of British Columbia, Vancouver, 1954–77; Lectr. in History, Vancouver Community Coll., 1977–88. *Publs:* (with B.D. Meritt and H.T. Wade-Gery) The Athenian Tribute Lists, vol. I, 1939, vol. II, 1949, vol. III, 1950, vol. IV, 1953; Athenian Policy, at Home and Abroad, 1967; (with D.W. Bradeen) Studies in Fifth-Century Attic Epigraphy, 1974; (ed. with D.W. Bradeen) Phoros: Tribute to Benjamin Dean Meritt; The Athenians and Their Empire, 1987. Add: 4495 West Seventh Ave., Vancouver, B.C. V6R 1X1, Canada.

McGUANE, Thomas. American, b. 1939. Novels/Short stories, Westerns. Professional film dir. and screenwriter. *Publs:* The Sporting Club, 1968; The Bushwhacked Piano, 1971; Ninety-Two in the Shade (novel and screenplay), 1974; Panama, 1978; An Outside Chance, 1980; Nobody's Angel, 1981; Something to be Desired, 1983; To Skin a Cat (stories), 1986. Add: c/o Dutton, 2 Park Ave., New York, N.Y. 10016, U.S.A.

McGUCKIAN, Medbh (née McCaughan). Irish, b. 1950. Poetry. English teacher, St. Patrick's Coll., Knock, Belfast, since 1975. Ed., Fortnight magazine. Writer-in-Residence, Queen's Univ., Belfast, 1985–88. *Publs:* Single Ladies: Sixteen Poems, 1980; Portrait of Joanna, 1980; (with Damian Gorman and Douglas Marshall) Trio Poetry, 1981; The Flower Master, 1982; Venus and the Rain, 1984; On Ballycastle Beach, 1988. Add: c/o Oxford Univ. Press, Walton St., Oxford OX2 6DP, England.

McGUIGAN, F. J(oseph). American, b. 1924. Biology, Psychiatry, Psychology. Prof. of Psychology and Dir. of Inst. for Stress Mgmt., United States Intnl. Univ., San Diego, Calif. Pres., Pavlovian Soc., Pres., Intnl. Stress and Tension-Control Soc., and member, Editorial Bd., Journal of Biofeedback and Self-regulation, all since 1974. Prof. of Psychology, Hollins Coll., Va., 1955–76. *Publs:* (with A.D. Calvin) Current Studies in Psychology, 1958; Experimental Psychology, 1960, 5th ed. 1990; (co-author) Psychology, 1961; The Biological Basis of Behavior, 1963; Thinking: Studies of Covert Language Behavior, 1966; (with P.J. Woods) Contemporary Studies in Psychology, 1972; (ed. with R.A. Schoonover) The Psychophysiology of Thinking, 1973; (ed. with D.B. Lumsden) Contemporary Approaches to Conditioning and Learning, 1973; Principle of Covert Behavior: A Study in the Psychophysiology of Thinking, 1975; Cognitive Psychophysiology, 1978; Psychophysiological Measurement of Covert Behavior, 1979; (ed.) Stress and Tension Control, 3 vols., 1980, 1986, 1989; Calm Down, 1981; (ed. with T. Ban) Critical Issues in Psychology, Psychiatry and Physiology, 1985. Add: U.S. Intnl. Univ., 10455 Pomerado Rd., San Diego, Calif. 92131, U.S.A.

McGUIRE, Joseph William. American, b. 1925. Administration/Management, Economics, Sociology. Prof., Univ. of California, Irvine, since 1974 (Vice-Pres., Planning, 1971–74). Prof., Univ. of Washington, 1950–63; Dean and Prof., Univ. of Kansas, Lawrence, 1963–68; Dean and Prof., Univ. of Illinois, Urbana, 1968–71. *Publs:* (ed. and co-author) Interdisciplinary Studies in Business Behavior, 1962; Business and Society, 1963; Theories of Business Behavior, 1964; (with J.S.

Pichler) Inequality: The Poor and the Rich in America, 1969; (ed. and co-author) Contemporary Management: Issues and Viewpoints, 1974. Add: Grad. Sch. of Mgmt., Univ. of California, Irvine, Calif. 92717, U.S.A.

McGURN, Barrett. American, b. 1914. International relations/Current affairs, Theology/Religion, Autobiography/Memoirs/Personal; Pres., Carroll Publishing Co., Washington, D.C., since 1987. Life Member, Bd. of Govs., Overseas Press Club of America (Pres., 1963–65); Member, Bd. of Dirs., Our Sunday Visitor Company, Fort Wayne, Indiana, since 1988. News reporter, 1935–42, 1945–66; Rome Bureau Chief, 1946–52, 1955–62, Paris Bureau Chief, 1952–55, and Moscow Bureau Chief, 1957, New York Herald Tribune; South Pacific War Corresp. and Washington National Bureau Chief, Yank mag., U.S. Army, 1942–45; U.S. Embassy Press Attaché, Rome, 1966–68; U.S. Embassy Counselor for Public Affairs, Saigon, 1968–69; Deputy Spokesman, Dept. of State, Washington, D.C., 1969–72; World Affairs Commentator for the U.S. Information Agency, 1972–73; Spokesman, U.S. Supreme Ct., 1973–82; Dir. of Communications, Archdiocese of Washington, D.C., 1984–87. *Publs:* (co-author) The Best from Yank, 1945; (co-author) Yank: The GI Story of the War, 1946; (co-author) Combat, 1950; (co-author) Highlights from Yank, 1953; Decade in Europe, 1958; A Reporter Looks at the Vatican, 1962; A Reporter Looks at American Catholicism, 1967; (co-author) I Can Tell It Now, 1964; (co-author) How I Got That Story, 1967; (co-author) Heroes for Our Times, 1968; (co-author) Saints for All Seasons, 1978. Add: 5229 Duvall Dr., Westmoreland Hills, Md. 20816, U.S.A.

McHUGH, Heather. American, b. 1948. Poetry. Milliman Writer-in-Residence, Univ. of Washington, Seattle, since 1984. Asst., then Assoc. Prof. of English, State Univ. of New York at Binghamton, 1976–84. Member, Bd. of Dirs., Associated Writing Programs, 1981–83, and Literature Panel, National Endowment for the Arts, 1983–86. *Publs:* Dangers, 1977; World of Difference, 1981; (trans.) D'après tout: Poems, by Jean Follain, 1981; To the Quick, 1987; Shades, 1988; (trans., with Niko Boris) Because the Sea Is Black: Poems by Blaga Dimitrora, 1989. Add: 220 Water St., Eastport, Maine 04631, U.S.A.

McHUGH, John (Francis). British, b. 1927. Theology/Religion, Translations. Sr. Lectr., Univ. of Durham, 1978–88 (Lectr. in Biblical Studies, Ushaw Coll., 1957–76; Dir. of Studies, 1967–72; Lectr. in Theology, Univ. of Durham, 1976). *Publs:* (trans.) Ancient Israel: Its Life and Institutions, by R. de Vaux, 1961; (trans. and ed.) The Gospels and the Jesus of History, by X. Leon-Dufour, 1968; (ed.) The Bible and the Ancient Near East, by R. de Vaux, 1971; The Mother of Jesus in the New Testament, 1975; (contrib.) The Psalms: A New Translation for Worship, 1977. Add: Stamford House, Stamford Rd., Alderley Edge SK9 7NS, England.

McILVANNEY, William. British, b. 1936. Novels/Short stories, Mystery/Crime/Suspense, Poetry. English teacher, Irvine Royal Academy, 1971–72; Fellow in Creative Writing, Univ. of Strathclyde, Glasgow, 1972–73; Asst. Rector, Greenwood Academy, Irvine, 1973–75. *Publs:* Remedy Is None (novel), 1966; A Gift from Nessus (novel), 1968; The Longships in Harbour (poetry), 1970; Landscapes and Figures (poetry), 1973; Docherty (novel), 1975; Laidlaw (mystery novel), 1977; The Papers of Tony Veitch (mystery novel), 1983; Weddings and After (poetry), 1984; The Big Man (mystery novel), 1985; Glasgow 1956–1986, 1986; In Through the Head (poetry), 1988; Walking Wounded (short stories), 1989. Add: c/o George Freenfield, John Farquharson Ltd., 162-168 Regent St., London W1R 5TB, England.

McILWAIN, Henry. British, b. 1912. Medicine/Health, Chemistry. Prof. of Biochemistry, Inst. of Psychiatry, Univ. of London, 1954–80, now Emeritus (Sr. Lectr., 1948–50; Reader, 1950–54); Hon. Sr. Research Fellow, Univ. of Birmingham, since 1987. Member, Scientific Staff, Medical Research Council, London, 1944–48; Visiting Prof., St. Thomas's Hospital Medical Sch., London, 1980–87. *Publs:* Biochemistry and the Central Nervous System, 1955, 5th ed. (with H.S. Bachelard) 1985; (ed. and contrib.) Practical Neurochemistry, 1962, 1975; Chemical Exploration of the Brain, 1963. Add: Dept. of Pharmacology, The Medical Sch., Birmingham B15 2TJ, England.

McINERNY, Jay. American, b. 1955. Novels. Ed., Time-Life. Publs., Japan; reader, Random House, publrs., NYC; fact-checker, New Yorker mag., 1980. *Publs:* Bright Lights, Big City, 1984; Ransom, 1985; Story of My Life, 1988. Add: c/o ICM, 40 W. 57th St., New York, N.Y. 10019, U.S.A.

McINERNY, Ralph (Matthew). American, b. 1929. Novels/Short stories, Philosophy. Prof. of Philosophy, since 1955, and Michael P. Grace Prof. of Medieval Studies, and Dir. of the Jacques Maritain Center, Univ. of Notre Dame, Ind. Ed. The New Scholasticism, 1977–88 (Assoc. Ed., 1966–77); Ed ., Catholicism in Crisis, 1982–87. *Publs:* The Logic of Analogy, 1961; History of Western Philosophy, vol. I, 1963, vol. II, 1969; Thomism in an Age of Renewal, 1966; (ed.) New Themes in Christian Philosophy, 1966; Studies in Analogy, 1967; Jolly Rogerson, 1967; (trans.) Kierkegaard: The Difficulty of Being Christian, 1968; A Narrow Time, 1969; The Priest, 1973; Gate of Heaven, 1975; Rogerson at Bay, 1976; Her Death of Cold, 1976; Spinnaker, 1977; The Seventh Station, 1977; St. Thomas Aquinas, 1977; Romanesque, 1978; Quick as a Dodo, 1978; Bishop as a Pawn, 1978; Lying Three, 1979; Abecedary, 1979; Second Vespers, 1980; Thicker Than Water, 1981; Not a Blessed Thing, 1981; The Frozen Maiden of Calpurnia, 1982; Ethica Thomistica, 1982; Let Us Prey, 1982; Loss of Patients, 1982; Connolly's Life, 1983; The Grass Widow, 1983; History of the Ambrosiana, 1983; Getting a Way with Murder, 1984; And Then There Were Nun, 1984; The Noonday Devil, 1985; Rest in Pieces (novel), 1985; Miracles, 1986; Being and Predication, 1986; Sine Qua Nun, 1986; Cause and Effect (novel), 1987; Leave of Absence, 1987; The Basket Case (novel); Art and Prudence, 1988; Veil of Ignorance (novel), 1988; Abracadaver (novel), 1989. Add: 2158 Portage Ave., South Bend, Ind. 46616, U.S.A.

McINTOSH, Christopher (Angus). British, b. 1943. Intellectual history. Former Asst. Ed. of Country Life mag., London, and of the Illustrated London News. *Publs:* The Astrologers and Their Creed, 1969; Astrology, 1970; Eliphas Lévi and the French Occult Revival, 1972; The Rosy Cross Unveiled, 1980; The Swan King, 1982; The Devil's Bookshelf, 1985. Add: 588 West End Ave., Apt. 3C, New York, NY 10024, U.S.A.

McINTOSH, J. T. *See* **MACGREGOR,** James Murdoch.

McINTOSH, Kinn Hamilton. *See* **AIRD,** Catherine.

McINTOSH, Peter C(hisholm). British, b. 1915. Sports/Physical education/Keeping fit. Deputy Dir. of Physical Education, Univ. of Birmingham, 1946–59; Sr. Inspector of Physical Education, I.L.E.A., 1959–74; member, 1966–74, and Chmn., Information and Research Cttee., 1970–74, The Sports Council; Chmn., Physical Education Cttee., The Schools Council, 1969–74; Prof. and Dir., Sch. of Physical Education, Univ. of Otago, Dunedin, N.Z., 1974–78; Visiting Prof., Calgary and Alberta Universities, 1978–80, and W. London Inst. of Higher Education, 1980–85. *Publs:* Physical Education in England since 1800, 1952, 1968; (with A.D. Munrow and B.N. Knapp) Britain in the World of Sport, 1956; (co-author and ed.) Landmarks in the History of Physical Education, 1957, 1983; Games and Sports: How They Developed, 1962; Sport in Society, 1963, 1987; (ed.) Mass Media: Sport and International Understanding, 1971; Fair Play: Ethics in Sport and Education, 1979; (with V. Charlton) Sport for All in the U.K. and a Way Ahead, 1985; Education Against Violence: The Potential of Fair Play in Sport, 1989. Add: 12 Windmill Dr., Leatherhead, Surrey KT22 8PW, England.

McINTYRE, Vonda N(eel). American, b. 1948. Science fiction/Fantasy. *Publs:* The Exile Waiting, 1975; (ed. with Susan J. Anderson) Aurora: Beyond Equality, 1976; Dreamsnake, 1978; Fireflood and Other Stories, 1979; The Entropy Effect, 1981; Star Trek: The Wrath of Khan, 1982; Superluminal, 1983; Star Trek 3: The Search for Spock, 1984; Enterprise, 1986; Star Trek 4: The Voyage Home, 1986; Barbary, 1986; Starfarers, 1989. Add: P.O. Box 31041, Seattle, Wash. 98103, U.S.A.

McINTYRE, W(illiam) David. British, b. 1932. History, International relations/Current affairs. Prof. of History, Univ. of Canterbury, Christchurch, since 1966. Lectr. in Commonwealth and American History, Univ. of Nottingham, U.K., 1959–65. *Publs:* Colonies into Commonwealth, 1966; The Imperial Frontier in the Tropics 1865–1875, 1967; (with W.J. Gardner) Speeches and Documents on New Zealand History, 1971; The Commonwealth of Nations 1869–1971, 1977; The Rise and Fall of the Singapore Naval Base 1919-1942, 1979; The Journal of Henry Sewell 1853-7, 2 vols., 1980; (with L. Richardson) Provincial Perspectives, 1981; New Zealand Prepares For War 1919–39, 1988. Add: 54A Bryndwr Rd., Christchurch 5, New Zealand.

McKAY, Alexander Gordon. Canadian, b. 1924. Archaeology/Antiquities, Architecture, Classics. Prof. of Classics, McMaster Univ., Hamilton, Ont., since 1961 (Asst. Prof. of Classics, 1957–59; Assoc. Prof., 1959–61; Chmn. Dept. of Classics, 1962–68, and 1976–79; Dean, Faculty of Humanities, 1968–73). Instr., Wells Coll., Aurora, N.Y., 1949–50; Instr., Univ. of Pennsylvania, Philadelphia, 1950–51; Lectr., Univ. of

Manitoba, Winnipeg, 1951–52; Lectr., Mt. Allison Univ., Sackville, N.B., 1952–53; Asst. Prof., 1953–54, and Assoc, Prof. of Classical Philology, 1954–55, Waterloo Coll., Ont.; Asst. Prof., Univ. of Manitoba, 1955–57. Assoc. Ed., Waterloo Review, 1955–58; Secty. 1957–59, Vice-Pres., 1971–73, and Pres., 1978–80, Classical Assn. of Canada; Hon. Ed., 1970–84, and Pres., 1984–87, Royal Soc. of Canada. *Publs:* Naples and Campania: Texts and Illustrations, 1962; Victorian Architecture in Hamilton, 1967; Vergil's Italy, 1970; (with D.M. Shepherd) Roman Lyric Poetry: Catullus and Horace, 1970; Ancient Campania: Vol. I, Cumae and the Phlegraean Fields, 1972, Vol. II, Naples and Coastal Campania, 1972; Houses, Villas and Palaces in the Roman World, 1975; (with D.M. Shepherd) Roman Satire, 1976; Vitruvius, Architect and Engineer, 1978; (ed.) New Perspectives in Canadian Archaeology, 1978; Selected Papers., Royal Society of Canada, 3 vols., 1979; The Written Word, 1980; Roma Antiqua: Latium and Etruria, 1986; Housing for the Spirit: Christ's Church Cathedral, Hamilton, 1988. Add: 1 Turner Ave., Hamilton, Ont. L8P 3K4, Canada.

McKEACHIE, Wilbert J. American, b. 1921. Education, Psychology. Prof. of Psychology, Univ. of Michigan, Ann Arbor, since 1959 (joined faculty 1946; Chmn., Dept. of Psychology, 1961–71). Member, Bd. of Dirs., American Inst. for Research, since 1971. Member, Bd. of Dirs., 1964–82, and Pres., 1976, American Psychological Assn. *Publs:* (co-ed.) Reading in Introductory Psychology, 1951; (ed.) A Review Outline of General Psychology, 1951, 1953; Teaching Tips, 1951, 8th ed, 1986; (co-author) Improving Undergraduate Instruction in Psychology, 1952; (ed.) The Appraisal of Teaching in Large Universities, 1959; (co-author) Undergraduate Curricula in Psychology, 1961; Man in His World: Human Behavior, 1962; (co-author) A Review Outline of Psychology, 1962; (co-author) Psychology, 1966, 3rd ed. 1976; (co-author) Some Thoughts About Teaching the Beginning Course in Psychology, 1968; (co-author) The Importance of Teaching, 1968; Research on College Teaching, A Review, 1970; XIP Readings in Psychology, 1972; (co-author) Psychology: The Short Course, 1972; Improving Undergraduate Education through Faculty Development, 1985. Add: 580 Union Dr., Ann Arbor, Mich. 48109, U.S.A.

McKEAN, J(ohn) M(aule). Scottish, b. 1943. Architecture. Tutor in design, Polytechnic of North London, since 1979. In architectural practice with Fielden and Mawson, Norwich, 1965–66, and with the Greater London Council, 1969–70; Tutor, Univ. of Ceylon, Colombo, 1968–69, London Coll. of Printing, 1976–77, Architectural Association, London, 1975–79, North East London Polytechnic, 1976–80; Head of History of Desin Unit, Polytechnic of N. London, 1981–85. Technical and later News and Features Ed., The Architect's Journal, London, 1971–75; U.K. Correspondent, Architecture, Paris, 1975–77. *Publs:* (co-author) Architecture of the Western World, 1980; Masterpieces of Architectural Drawing, 1982; (co-author) The Principles of Architecture, 1983; The World Crystal, 1984; Archetypal Dwelling, 1986; Learning from Segal/Von Segal Lernen (English/German text), 1988; Places For Peace: A Handbook on Peace Gardens, 1989. Add: 34 Dukes Ave., London N10 2PU, England.

McKEATING, Henry. British, b. 1932. Theology/Religion. Lectr., then Sr. Lectr. in Theology, Univ. of Nottingham, since 1959. *Publs:* (contrib.) Difficulties for Christian Belief, 1967; (contrib.) A Source Book of the Bible for Teachers, 1970; Living With Guilt, 1970; Cambridge Bible Commentary: Amos, Hosea, Micah, 1971; God and the Future, 1974; Studying the Old Testament, 1979; Why Bother with Adam and Eve?, 1982. Add: Wesley Coll., Henbury Rd., Westbury-on-Trym, Bristol BS10 7QD, England.

McKEE, David (John). British. Children's fiction, Plays/Screenplays, Poetry. *Publs:* Bronto's Wings, 1964; Two Can Toucan, 1964; Mr. Benn series, 5 vols., 1967–80; Hans in Luck, 1967; Mark and the Monocycle, 1968; Elmer: The Story of a Patchwork Elephant, 1968; The Magician series, 7 vols., 1970–82; Six Men, 1971; The Man Who Was Going to Mind the House: A Norwegian Folk-Tale, 1972; Lord Rex: The Lion Who Wished, 1973; The Day the Tide Went Out, and Out, and Out..., 1975; Elmer Again and Again, 1975; Two Admirals, 1977; Tusk-Tusk, 1978; King Rollo series, 9 vols., 1979–81; Not Now Bernard, 1980; The Magicians and Double Trouble, 1981; I Hate My Teddy Bear, 1982; King Rollo's Playroom and Other Stories, 1983; The Hill and the Rock, 1984; King Rollo's Letter and Other Stories, 1984; Two Monsters, 1985; King Rollo's Spring, Summer, Autumn and Winter, 4 vols., 1986; The Sad Story of Veronica Who Played the Violin, 1987; The Magician's Apprentice, 1987; Snow Women, 1987; Who's a Clever Baby, Then?, 1988; The Magician and the King's Crown, 1988. Add: c/o Andersen Press, 62-65 Chandos Pl., London WC2N 4NW, England.

McKENNA, Marian Cecilia. American, b. 1926. History, Biography. Prof. of History, Univ. of Calgary, Alta., since 1966. Member of faculty, Hunter Coll., City Univ. of New York, 1953–59, and Manhattanville Coll., Purchase, N.Y., 1959–66. *Publs:* Borah, 1961; Pictorial History of Catholicism, 1962; Myra Hess: A Portrait, 1976; Tapping Reeve and the Litchfield Law School, 1986. Add: 3343 Upton Pl. N.W., Calgary, Alta. T2N 4G9, Canada.

McKENZIE, Barbara. American, b. 1934. Literature. Freelance photographer and writer since 1986. Asst. Prof. of English, Drew Univ., Madison, N.J., 1964–68; Assoc. Prof. of Radio, Television and Film, Univ. of Georgia, Athens, 1968–86. *Publs:* Mary McCarthy, 1966; (ed.) The Process of Fiction: Contemporary Stories and Criticism, 1969, 1974; (ed.) Fiction's Journey: 50 Stories, 1978; Flannery O'Connor's Georgia, 1980. Add: 104 Forest Lane, Tryon, N.C. 28782, U.S.A.

McKENZIE, Paige. *See* **BLOOD**, Marje.

McKEOWN, Tom. American, b. 1937. Poetry. Member of faculty, Alpena Coll., Mich., 1962–64, Wisconsin State Univ., 1964–68, Stephens Coll., Columbia, Mo., 1968–74, Univ. of Wisconsin, Stevens Point, 1976–81, Savannah Coll. of Art and Design, Ga., 1982–83, Univ. of Wisconsin at Oshkosh, 1983–87. *Publs:* Alewife Summer, 1967; Last Thoughts, 1969; The Winds of the Calendar, 1969; Drunk All Afternoon, 1969; The Milk of the Wolf, 1970; The Cloud Keeper, 1972; The Luminous Revolver, 1974; Driving to New Mexico, 1974; The House of Water, 1974; Maya Dreams, 1977; Certain Minutes, 1978; Circle of the Eye, 1982; Invitation of the Mirrors, 1985. Add: P.O. Box 82, Pentwater, Mich. 49449, U.S.A.

McKILLIP, Patricia (Anne). American, b. 1948. Novels, children's fiction. *Publs:* children's fiction—The House on Parchment Street, 1973; The Throme of the Erril of Sherill, 1973; The Forgotten Beasts of Eld, 1974; The Night Gift, 1976; Riddle of Stars, 1979, in U.K. as The Chronicles of Morgan, Prince of Hed, 1981; The Riddle-Master of Hed, Heir of Sea and Fire, and Harpist in the Wind (trilogy), 1976–79; Moon-Flash, 1984; The Moon and the Face, 1985; The Changeling Sea, 1988; novel—Stepping from the Shadows, 1982; Fool's Run, 1987. Add: Howard Morhaim Literary Agency, 174 Fifth Ave., Room 709, New York, N.Y. 10010, U.S.A.

McKINLAY, Brian John. Australian, b. 1933. History, Mathematics/Statistics. Education History Officer, Ministry of Education, Victoria. Former primary and secondary sch. teacher in Victoria; Lectr., State Coll. of Melbourne. Consultant, Focus Social Studies Project, Jacaranda Press, 1970–74. *Publs:* Primary Mathematics, 1965; The First Royal Tour, 1970; Western District Sketchbook, 1971; Diamond Valley Sketchbook, 1973; Carlton Sketchbook, 1974; Collingwood and Fitzroy Sketchbook, 1978; A Documentary History of the Australian Labour Movement 1850–1975, 1978; History at Your Fingertips, 1979; Growing Things, 1979; A.L.P.: A Short History of the Australian Labor Party, 1981; Australia, 1942: End of Innocence, 1985; Schooldays, 1985; Outdoors for Kids, 1987; Australia for Kids, 1988; Sweet and Simple Pleasure, 1988; A Century of Struggle, 1988. Add: 2 De Blonay Cres., Greensborough, Vic., Australia 3088.

McKINLEY, (Jennifer Carolyn) Robin. American, b. 1952. Children's fiction. Full-time writer since 1985. Worked as editorial asst., freelance editor, and teacher, 1972–85. *Publs:* Beauty: A Retelling of the Story of Beauty and the Beast, 1978; The Door in the Hedge, 1981; The Blue Sword, 1982; The Hero and the Crown, 1985; Tales from the Jungle Book, 1985; (ed.) Imaginary Lands, 1985; Black Beauty (retelling), 1986; The Outlaws of Sherwood, 1988; The Light Princess (retelling), 1988. Add: c/o Merrilee Heifetz, Writers House Inc., 21 W. 26th St., New York, N.Y. 10010, U.S.A.

McKNIGHT, Allan (Douglas). Australian, b. 1918. Environmental science/Ecology. Chmn., Disarmament Working Group, United Nations Assn. (U.K.). Deputy Secty., Australian Cabinet, 1951–55; Permanent Secty., Dept. of the Army, Australia, 1955–58; Exec. Commnr., Australian Atomic Energy Commn., 1958–64; Australian Gov. on Bd. of Intnl. Atomic Energy Agency, 1958–64, and Chmn. of Bd., 1961; Inspector Gen., Intnl. Atomic Energy Agency, Vienna, 1964–68; Visiting Fellow, Science Policy Research Unit, Univ. of Sussex (U.K.), 1968–72; Lectr., Civil Service Coll., London, 1972–77. *Publs:* IAEA and Euratom Safeguards for Non-Proliferation, 1970; Atomic Safeguards, 1971; Scientists Abroad, 1971; (ed.) Environmental Pollution Control, 1974; World Disarmament: A Draft Treaty, 1978. Add: 4/13 Clifton Pl., Brighton BN1 3FN, England.

McKNIGHT, Tom Lee. American, b. 1928. Geography. Prof. of Geography, Univ. of California, Los Angeles, since 1956. Instr. in Geography, Southern Methodist Univ., Dallas, Tex., 1953–55; Instr., Univ. of Texas, Austin, 1955–56. *Publs:* Manufacturing in Dallas: A Study of Effects, 1956; Dallas, 1959; Manufacturing in Arizona, 1962; (with E.J. Forcue and C.L. White) Regional Geography of Anglo-America, 3rd ed. 1964, 6th ed., 1985; (with C.L. White and P.F. Griffin) World Economic Geography, 1964; Feral Livestock in Anglo-America, 1964; The Camel in Australia, 1969; Australia's Corner of the World: A Geographical Summation, 1970; Friendly Vermin: A Survey of Feral Livestock in Australia, 1976; The Long Paddock: Australia's Travelling Stock Routes, 1977; Physical Geography: A Landscape Appreciation, 1984, 1987. Add: Dept. of Geography, U.C.L.A., Los Angeles, Calif. 90000, U.S.A.

McKUEN, Rod. American, b. 1933. Poetry. Singer and composer. *Publs:* And Autumn Came, 1954; Stanyan Street and Other Sorrows, 1966; Listen to the Warm, 1967; Twelve Years of Christmas, 1968; Lonesome Cities, 1968; In Someone's Shadow, 1969; With Love, 1970; Caught in the Quiet, 1970; Moment to Moment, 1971; Fields of Wonder, 1971; The Carols of Christmas, 1971; And to Each Season, 1972; Beyond the Boardwalk, 1972; Come to Me in Silence, 1973; A New Book of Lyrics, 1973; The R.M. 1974 Calender, 1973; Caught in the Quiet, 1973; Seasons in the Sun, 1974; Celebrations of the Heart, 1975; Rod McKuen Omnibus, 1975; Alone, 1975; Finding My Father (autobiography), 1976; Hand in Hand, 1976; The Sea Around Me, 1977; Coming Close to the Earth, 1978; Love's Been Good to Me, 1979; We Touch the Sky, 1979; Looking for a Friend, 1980; An Outstretched Hand, 1980; The Power Bright and Shining, 1980; Too Many Midnights, 1981; Book of Days, 1981; The Beautiful Strangers, 1981; The Works of Rod McKuen, vol. I, Poetry, 1950–82; Watch for the Wind, 1982; Rod McKuen: 1984 Book of Days, 1983; The Sound of Solitude, 1983; Suspension Bridge, 1984; Another Beautiful Day, 1984. Add: P.O. Box G, Beverly Hills, Calif. 90213, U.S.A.

McLAGLEN, John J. *See* **HARVEY**, John B.

McLAREN, Ian Francis. Australian, b. 1912. History, Biography. Hon. Bibliographer, Univ. of Melbourne, since 1976. Liberal Member of the Victorian Legislative Assembly for Bennettswood, 1967–79 (Member for Glen Iris, 1945–47, and for Caulfield, 1965–67). Pres., Royal Historical Soc. of Victoria, 1956–59. *Publs:* Local History in Australia, 1954; The Rhur of Australia: A History of the Latrobe Valley, 1955; Como: An Historic Melbourne Home, 1957; All Saints' Church East St. Kilda, 1958; Australian Aviation: A Bibliographical Survey, 1958; All Saints Church of England, East St. Kilda 1858–1958, 1960; The Victorian Exploring Expedition: 1860–1861: The Burke and Wills Tragedy, 1960; C.J. Dennis, His Life and Work, 1961; The McEvoy Gold Mine Disaster 1895, 1962; William John Wills 1834–1861, 1962; Edward Edgar Pescott, 1872–1954, 1965; How Victoria Began: Printed Works on Australia Felix and the Port Phillip District to 1850, 1968; In the Wake of Flinders, 1974; The Library of Ian McLaren, 1974; C.J. Dennis Contributions to Literary Magazines, 1976; Bibliography of C.J. Dennis, 1979; C.J. Dennis in Herald and Weekly Times, 1981; Talking about C.J. Dennis, 1982; Annotated Bibliography of Marcus Clarke, 1982; Whitcombe's Story Books: A Trans-Tasman Survey, 1984; Publisher's Author Advertisements, 1984; The Chinese in Victoria, 1985; John Dunmore Lang, Turbulent Australian Scot: A Comprehensive Bibliography, 1985; Mary Gaunt, A Cosmopolitan Australian: An Annotated Bibliography, 1986; Grace Jennings Carmichael: From Croajingolong to London, 1986; Melbourne Public Library in 1888, 1986; Index to the Weekly Times Annual 1911–1934, 1986; Cabinet Photographs and Postcards Relating to A.L. Gordon, 1986; Adam Lindsay Gordon: A Comprehensive Bibliography, 1986; (ed.) Visit to Geelong and Western District of Victoria, by J.D. Lang, 1987; Henry Kendall: A Comprehensive Bibliography, 1987; Australian Explorers and Explorations, 1987; Book Collecting in Australia, 1987. Add: 237 Waverley Rd., East Malvern, Vic. 3145, Australia.

McLAREN, John. Australian, b. 1932. Education, Literature, Politics/Government. Head, Dept. of Humanities, Footscray Inst. of Technology, since 1976. *Publs:* Our Troubled Schools, 1968; Libraries for the Public, 1969; (ed.) Towards a New Australia, 1972; A Dictionary of Australian Education, 1974; (co-author) Equal but Cheaper, 1977; (ed.) A Nation Apart, 1983; An Introduction to Australian Literature, 1986. Add: c/o FIT, P.O. Box, 64, Footscray, Vic. 3011, Australia.

McLAUGHLIN, Dean (Benjamin, Jr.) American, b. 1931. Science fiction/Fantasy. Buyer, Slater's Inc. bookshop, Ann Arbor, Mich. *Publs:* Dome World, 1962; The Fury from Earth, 1963; The Man Who Wanted Stars, 1965; Hawk among the Sparrows (short stories), 1976. Add: 1214 W. Washington St., Ann Arbor, Mich. 48103, U.S.A.

McLAUGHLIN, Terence Patrick. British, b. 1928. Crafts, Sciences, Social commentary/phenomena. Chemical consultant since 1968. Research Mgr., Unilever Research Lab., 1954–61; Dir., Lever Industrial Ltd., 1961–68. *Publs:* (co-author) Modern Cosmeticology, 1964; The Cleaning, Hygiene and Maintenance Handbook, 1969; Music and Communication, 1970; Coprophilia, or a Peck of Dirt (in U.S. as Dirt), 1971; The Gilded Lily, 1972; Candle-Making, 1973; Papier Mâché Work, 1974; A House for the Future, 1976; Make Your Own Electricity, 1977; Working Toys and Models, 1977; (with Eve McLaughlin) Cost-Effective Self-Sufficiency, 1978; A Diet of Tripe, 1978; The Coward's Weapon, 1980. Add: Varneys, 18 Rudds Lane, Haddenham, Bucks., England.

McLEAN, Allan Campbell. British, b. 1922. Novels/Short stories. *Publs:* The Hill of the Red Fox, 1955; The Islander (in U.S. as The Gates of Eden), 1962; The Glasshouse, 1969; The Year of the Stranger, 1971;The Highlands and Islands of Scotland, 1976; Ribbon of the Fire, 1985; A Sound of Trumpets, 1985. Add: Anerley Cottage, 16 Kingsmills Rd., Inverness IV2 3JS, Scotland.

McLEAN, J. Sloan. *See* **WUNSCH**, Josephine M.

McLEAN, (John David) Ruari. British, b. 1917. Design, History, Biography, Translations. Typographer. Ed. Motif, 1-13 periodical, Shenval Press, London, 1957–68; former Art Ed., The Connoisseur, London and Hon. Typographic Adviser, H.M. Stationery Office, London, 1966–80. *Publs:* George Cruikshank, 1948; Modern Book Design, 1951; 1958; (trans. as David Hardie) Late Spring, by Joe Lederer, 1958; The Wood Engravings of Joan Hassall, 1960; Victorian Book Design, and Colour Printing, 1963, 1972; (ed.) The Reminiscences of Edmund Evans, 1967; (trans.) Asymmetric Typography, by Jan Tschichold, 1967; Magazine Design, 1969; Victorian Publishers' Bookbindings in Cloth and Leather, 1974; Jan Tschichold, Typographer, 1975; Joseph Cundall, A Victorian Publisher, 1976; (ed.) A Book of Cuts, by Edward Bawden, 1979; The Thames and Hudson Manual of Typography, 1980; Victorian Publishers' Bookbindings in Paper, 1982; Benjamin Fawcett, Engraver and Colour Printer, 1988. Add: Pier Cottage, Carsaig, Isle of Mull, Argyll, Scotland.

McLEAN, Sammy. American, b. 1929. Literature. Assoc. Prof., Comparative Literature and Germanics, Univ. of Washington, Seattle, since 1973 (Asst. Prof., 1967–73). Instr., 1961–63, and Asst. Prof., 1963–65, Dartmouth Coll., Hanover, N.H.; Lectr. in German, Univ. of Maryland Overseas Prog., London, 1965–67. *Publs:* The Bänkelsan and the Work of Bertolt Brecht, 1972. Add: Comparative Literature and Germanics, DH-30, Univ. of Washington, Seattle, Wash. 98195, U.S.A.

McLEISH, Kenneth. British, b. 1940. Children's fiction, Art, Children's non-fiction, Classics, Translations. *Publs:* (trans.) Four Greek Plays, 1964; Land of the Eagles, 1969; (trans.) The Frogs, 1970; (ed. with V. McLeish) Aspects of Greek Life Series, 1972; Chicken Licken, 1973; (with Roger Nichols) Through Greek Eyes, 1974; (with Roger Nichols) Through Roman Eyes, 1975; The Robe of Blood, 1975; Odysseus Returns, 1976; Roman Comedy, 1976; The Peace Players, 1977; (with V. McLeish) Composers and their World series, 1978; (with Frederic Raphael) The Poems of Catullus, 1978; (with Frederic Raphael) The Oresteia of Aeschylus, 1979; (trans.) Sophocles, Three Plays, 1979; (trans.) Aristophanes: Three Plays, 1980; The Theatre of Aristophanes, 1980; Hostages (for children), 1980; (with V. McLeish) This Is Music, 1980; (with Frederic Raphael) The List of Books, 1980; (ed. with Brian Redhead) The Anti-Booklist, 1981; The Shining Stars (for children), 1981; (with V. McLeish) The Oxford First Companion to Music, 1982; The Way of the Stars (for children), 1982; (ed. with Brian Redhead) Pieces of Hate, 1982; Children of the Gods, 1983; The Penguin Companion to the Arts in the Twentieth Century, 1985; Shakespeare's People A-Z, 1985; Tales of the Mediterranean, 1986; (with V. McLeish) The Listener's Guide to Classical Music, 1986; The Seven Wonders of the World (for children), 1986; (with V. McLeish) The Longman Guide to Bible Quotations, 1986; Myths and Folk-stories of the British Isles (for children), 1986; Roman Myths and Legends (for children), 1987; Stories from the Bible (for children), 1987; The Longman Book of People (for children), 1987; The Cambridge Junior Companion to Greece and Rome, 1987; The Reader's Guide to Novels, 1988. Add: c/o A.P. Watt Ltd., 26/28 Bedford Row, London WC1R 4HL, England.

McLELLAN, David. British, b. 1940. Intellectual history. Prof. of Political Theory, Univ. of Kent, Canterbury. *Publs:* The Young Hegelians and Karl Marx, 1969; Marx Before Marxism, 1970; (ed.) Karl Marx: The Early Texts, 1971; (ed.) Marx's Grundrisse, 1971; The Thought of Karl Marx, 1971; Karl Marx: His Life and Thought, 1973; Marx, 1971; (ed.) Karl Marx: Selected Writings, 1975; Engels, 1977; Marxism after Marx, 1979; Karl Marx: The Legacy, 1983; Marx: The First Hundred Years, 1983; Ideology, 1985; Marxism and Religion, 1987. Add: 13 Ivy Lane, Canterbury, Kent, England.

McLELLAN, David S. American, b. 1924. History, International relations/Current affairs, Biography. Prof. of Political Science, Miami Univ., Oxford, Ohio, since 1971 (Ed., Miami Univ. Press, 1975–78). Prof. of Political Science, Univ. of California, 1955–71. *Publs:* (with William C. Olson and Fred Sondermann) The Theory and Practice of International Relations, 1960, 6th ed. 1978; The Cold War in Transition, 1965; Dean Acheson: The State Department Years, 1976; (with David C. Acheson) Among Friends: Personal Letters of Dean Acheson, 1980; Cyrus Vance, 1985. Add: Dept. of Political Science, Miami Univ., Oxford, Ohio 45056, U.S.A.

McLEOD, Wallace. Canadian, b. 1931. Archaeology/Antiquities, Classics, History. Prof. of Classics, Victoria Coll., Univ. of Toronto, since 1974 (Asst. Prof. of Classics, 1962–66; Assoc. Prof., 1966–74). Instr. in Classical Languages, Trinity Coll., Hartford, Conn., 1955–56; Instr. in Classics, Univ. of British Columbia, Vancouver, 1959–61; Lectr. Classics, Univ. of Western Ontario, London, 1961–62. Assoc. Ed., 1965–70, Acting Ed., 1973, and Acting Assoc. Ed., 1985, Phoenix mag. *Publs:* Composite Bows from the Tomb of Tutankhamun, 1970; (ed.) Beyond the Pillars: More Light on Freemasonry, 1973; Meeting the Challenge: The Lodge Officer at Work, 1976; The Sufferings of John Coustos: A Facsimile Reprint, 1979; Whence Come We? Freemasonry in Ontario 1764–1980, 1980; Self Bows and Other Archery Tackle from the Tomb of Tutankhamun, 1982; The Old Gothic Constitutions: Facsimile Reprints, 1985. Add: Victoria Coll. 321, Univ. of Toronto, Toronto M5S 1K7, Canada.

McLURE, James. American. Plays *Publs:* Lone Star, 1980; Pvt. Wars, 1980; Laundry and Bourbon, 1981; The Day They Shot John Lennon, 1984; Wild Oats, 1985. Add: c/o Dramatists Play Services, 440 Park Ave. S., New York, N.Y. 10016, U.S.A.

McMANUS, Kay. British, b. 1922. Short stories, Children's fiction, Plays/Screenplays. Radio playwright, 1956–88; contributor to TV: Jackanory, Coronation Street, etc. Contr., BBC series Jackanory; Playhouse Coronation St; Scene. *Publs:* Listen and I'll Talk, 1966; Raven (short stories), 1969; Hattie in a Hurry, 1987; Tolly on Tuesday, 1988. Add: "Farm Cottage", Bow Brickhill, Bucks, MK17 9JT, England.

McMASTER, Juliet (Sylvia). British, b. 1937. Literature. University Prof. of English, Univ. of Alberta, since 1986 (Asst. Prof., 1965–70; Assoc. Prof., 1970–76; Prof., 1976–86). *Publs:* Thackeray: The Major Novels, 1971; (ed.) Jane Austen's Achievement, 1976; Jane Austen on Love, 1978; Trollope's Palliser Novels, 1978; (with R.D. McMaster) The Novel from Sterne to James, 1981; Dickens the Designer, 1987. Add: Dept. of English, Univ. of Alberta, Edmonton, Alta., T6G 2E5, Canada.

McMILLAN, James. Also writes as Coriolanus. Economics, Politics/Government, Social commentary/phenomena. Policy Adviser, Express Newspapers, London, 1976 until retirement, 1986 (Industrial Writer, 1952–53; Asst. Ed., Glasgow Evening Citizen, 1953–57; Leader Writer, 1957–69, Chief Leader Writer, 1969–76, Daily Express London). *Publs:* (as Coriolanus) The Glass Lie, 1965; (with Bernard Harris) The American Take-Over of Britain, 1967; The Honours Game, 1968; Anatomy of Scotland, 1969; The Roots of Corruption, 1972; (with Peter Grosvenor) The British Genius, 1973; The Way We Were 1900–1914, 1978; The Way It Was 1914–1934, 1979; The Way It Happened 1935–1950, 1980; (with Jakob Keston) The Secret of Torgan, 1982; Five Men at Nuremberg, 1984; The Way It Changed 1950–1975, 1987; The Dunlop Story, 1989. Add: Thurleston, Fairmile Park Rd., Cobham, Surrey, England.

McMILLEN, Neil Raymond. American, b. 1939. History. Prof. of History, Univ. of Southern Mississippi, Hattiesburg, since 1978 (Asst. Prof., 1969–70; Assoc. Prof., 1970–78). Asst. Prof. of History, Ball State Univ., Muncie, Ind., 1967–69. *Publs:* The Citizens' Council: Organized Resistance to the Second Reconstruction, 1971; Thomas Jefferson: Philosopher of Freedom, 1973; (with C. Sellers and H. May) A Synopsis of American History, 1984; Dark Journey: Black Mississipians in the Age of Jim Crow, 1989. Add: Dept. of History, Univ. of Southern Mississippi, Hattiesburg, Miss. 39401, U.S.A.

McMULLEN, Jeremy (John). British, b. 1948. Civil liberties/Human rights, Industrial Relations, Law. Barrister. Member, Industrial Law Soc. Exec. Cttee. Attorney, Kelley Drye & Warren, NYC, 1972–73;

General Municipal and Boilermakers Union Legal and Regional Officer, 1973–84. Member, TUC (Trade Union Congress) Working Party on Law Reform, 1976–78. *Publs:* Rights at Work: A Worker's Guide to Employment Law, 1978, 1983; Employment Law under the Tories, 1981; Policing the Miners' Strike, 1985. Add: 15 Old Square, Lincoln's Inn, London WC2A 3HH, England.

McMULLEN, Mary. American, b. 1920. Mystery/Crime/Suspense. *Publs:* Stranglehold, 1951, in U.K. as Death of Miss X, 1952; The Doom Campaign, 1974; A Country Kind of Death, 1975; The Pimlico Plot, 1975; Funny, Jonas, You Don't Look Dead, 1976; A Dangerous Funeral, 1977; Death by Bequest, 1977; Prudence Be Damned, 1978; The Man with Fifty Complaints, 1978; Welcome to the Grave, 1979; But Nellie Was So Nice, 1979; My Cousin Death, 1980; Something of the Night, 1980; The Other Shoe, 1981; Better Off Dead, 1982; Until Death Do Us Part, 1982; A Grave Without Flowers, 1983; The Gift Horse, 1985; The Bad-News Man, 1986. Add: c/o Doubleday and Co. Inc., 666 Fifth Ave. Park Ave., New York, N.Y. 10103, U.S.A.

McMURTRY, Larry (Jeff). American, b. 1936. Novels/Short stories, Westerns, Essays. *Publs:* Horseman Pass By (in U.K. as Hud), 1961; Leaving Cheyenne, 1963; The Last Picture Show, 1966, screenplay with Peter Bogdanovitch, 1971; In a Narrow Grave (essays), 1968; Moving On, 1970; All My Friends Are Going to be Strangers, 1972; It's Always We Rambled (essay), 1974; Terms of Endearment, 1975; Somebody's Darling, 1978; Cadillac Jack, 1982; The Desert Rose, 1983; Lonesome Dove, 1985; Texasville, 1987; Film Flam: Essay on Hollywood, 1987; Anything for Billy, 1988; Some Can Whistle, 1989. Add: c/o Simon and Schuster, 1230 Sixth Ave., New York, N.Y. 10020, U.S.A.

McNAIR, Kate. American, b. 1911. Novels/Short stories, Plays/Screenplays. *Publs:* A Sense of Magic, 1965; The Stock Pot (play), 1965; A Book of Directions, 1970. Add: 3400 Petty Rd., Muncie, Ind. 47304, U.S.A.

McNALLY, Terrence. American, b. 1939. Plays/Screenplays. Stage Mgr., Actors Studio, NYC, 1961; Tutor, 1961–62; Film Critic, The Seventh Art, 1963–65; Asst. Ed., Columbia College Today, NYC, 1965–66. *Publs:* Apple Pie, 1969; Sweet Eros, Next and Other Plays, 1969; Three Plays: Cuba Si!, Bringing It All Back Home, Last Gasps, 1970; Where Has Tommy Flowers Gone?, 1972; Bad Habits: Ravenswood and Dunelawn, 1974; The Ritz and Other Plays, 1976; The Rink, 1985. Add: 218 West 10th St., New York, N.Y. 10014. U.S.A.

McNAMARA, Eugene Joseph. Canadian, b. 1930. Novels/Short stories, Poetry, Literature. Prof., Univ. of Windsor, Ont., since 1959. Ed., Univ. of Windsor Review, since 1965. Ed., Mainline, 1967–74. *Publs:* For The Mean Time, 1965; (ed.) The Interior Landscape: Literary Criticism of Marshall McLuhan, 1969; Outerings, 1970; Love Scenes, 1970; Dillinger Poems, 1971; Hard Words, 1972; Passages, 1972; Diving for the Body, 1974; In Transit, 1974; Salt (stories), 1976; Screens, 1977; The Search for Sarah Grace (stories), 1977; Forcing the Field (poems), 1982; Spectral Evidence (short stories), 1985; The Moving Light (poems), 1986. Add: 166 Randolph Pl., Windsor, Ont., Canada.

McNAMARA, Robert (Strange). American, b. 1916. International relations/Current affairs. Dir., Corning Glass Works, TWA, Royal Dutch Petroleum, The Washington Post, and Bank of America, since 1981. Associated with Ford Motor Co., Detroit, 1946–61; Vice-Pres. and Gen. Mgr., Ford Div., 1955–57; Dir. and Group Vice Pres. of Car Divs., 1957–60; Pres., 1960–61; U.S. Secty. of Defense (Kennedy and Johnson admins.), 1961–68; Pres., Intnl. Bank for Reconstruction and Development, Washington, 1968–81. *Publs:* The Essence of Security: Reflections in Office, 1968; One Hundred Countries, Two Billion People, 1973; The McNamara Years at the World Bank, 1981; Blundering into Disaster, 1986. Add: 2412 Tracy Pl. N.W., Washington, D.C. 20008, U.S.A.

McNAUGHT, Judith. American, b. 1944. Historical/Romance. Exec. Producer, KMOX-CBS Radio, St. Louis, 1970–73; Asst. Dir. and motion picture dir., Moritz Inc., St. Louis, 1973–76; Pres., Pro-Temps, Inc., St. Louis, 1979–85. *Publs:* Tender Triumph, 1983; Double Standards, 1984; Whitney, My Love, 1985; Once and Always, 1987; Something Wonderful, 1988; A Kingdom of Dreams, 1989. Add: c/o Perry Knowlton, Curtis Brown, 10 Astor Pl., New York, N.Y. 10003, U.S.A.

McNAUGHTON, H(oward) D(ouglas). New Zealander, b. 1945. Reader in English, also Chmn. of the Dept., Univ. of Canterbury, Christchurch, since 1978 (Asst. Lectr., 1974; Lectr., 1975–77; Sr. Lectr., 1978–86). Trust Bd. Member, Playmarket Inc., Wellington, since 1974;

Trustee and Trust Secty., Univ. of Canterbury Drama Soc., since 1975; Advisory Ed., Act bulletin, Wellington, since 1975. Asst. Latin Master, Shirley Boys' High Sch., Christchurch 1968–71; Theatre Critic of the Press, Christchurch, 1968–80, and of the New Zealand Listener, Wellington 1974–80. Member, Drama Advisory Council, Queen Elizabeth II Arts Council of New Zealand, 1973–75. *Publs:* (ed.) Contemporary New Zealand Plays, 1974, 1979; New Zealand Drama: A Bibliographical Guide, 1974; (ed.) Landfall: Drama in New Zealand, 1975; Bruce Mason, 1976; The Canterbury Repertory Theatre 1928–1978, 1978; New Zealand Drama, 1980; (ed.) James K. Baxter: Collected Plays, 1982; New Zealand Theatre Annals: Christchurch 1900–1919, 1983. Add: Dept. of English, Univ. of Canterbury, Christchurch, New Zealand.

McNEIL, Florence. Canadian, b. 1940. Poetry, Children's fiction, Plays. Full-time writer since 1976. Instr., Western Washington State Univ., Bellingham, 1965–68; Asst. Prof., Univ. of Calgary, 1968–73, and Univ. of British Columbia, 1973–76. *Publs:* A Silent Green Sky (poetry), 1965; Walhachin (poetry), 1972; The Rim of the Park (poetry), 1972; Emily (poetry), 1975; Ghost Towns (poetry), 1975; A Balancing Act (poetry), 1979; When Is a Poem: Creative Ideas for Teaching Poetry Collected from Canadian Poets, 1980; The Overlanders (poetry), 1982; Miss P and Me (children's fiction), 1982; (ed.) Here Is a Poem (anthology), 1983; Barkerville (poetry), 1984; All Kinds of Magic (children's fiction), 1984; Barkerville (play), 1987; Catriona's Island (young adult novel), 1988; Poems New and Selected, 1989; (ed.) Poems for Children (anthology), 1989; Vancouver: A Social History (non-fiction), 1990. Add: 20 Georgia Wynd, Delta, B.C. V4M 1A5, Canada.

McNEILL, Anthony. Jamaican, b. 1941. Poetry. Civil service clerk, Port Maria and Kingston, 1960–64; journalist, the Gleaner Co., Kingston, 1965–66; scriptwriter, JIS radio, Kingston, 1966–68; trainee mgr., Jamaica Playboy Club-Hotel, Ocho Rios, 1968–69; Editorial Asst., Jamaica Journal, Kingston, 1970; Teaching Asst., Univ. of Massachusetts, Amhurst, 1971–76. *Publs:* Hello Ungod, 1971; Reel from "The Life-Movie", 1972; Credences at the Altar of Cloud, 1979. Add: Inst. of Jamaica, 12-16 East St. Kingston, Jamaica.

McNEILL, Janet. (Mrs. Robert Alexander). British, b. 1907. Novels/Short stories, Children's fiction. *Publs:* fiction for adults—A Child in the House, 1955; Tea at Four o'Clock, 1956; The Other Side of the Wall, 1956; Furnished Room, 1958; Search Party, 1959; As Strangers Here, 1960; The Early Harvest, 1962; The Maiden Dinosaur, 1964 (in U.S. as the Belfast Friends, 1966); Talk to Me, 1965; The Small Widow, 1967; fiction for children—My Friend Specs McCann, 1955; A Pinch of Salt, 1956; A Light Dozen: Eleven More Stories, 1957; Specs Fortissimo, 1958; This Happy Morning, 1959; Special Occasions: Eleven More Stories, 1960; Various Specs, 1961; Try These for Size, 13; The Giant's Birthday, 1964; Tom's Tower, 1965; The Mouse and the Mirage, 1966; The Battle of St. George Without, 1966; I Didn't Invite You to My Party, 1967; The Run-Around Robins, 1967; The Day They Lost Grandad, 1968; Goodbye, Dove Square, 1969; Dragons, Come Home! and Other Stories, 1969; Umbrella Thursday, 1969; Best Specs: His Most Remarkable Adventures, 1970; The Other People, 1970; The Youngest Kite, 1970; The Prisoner in the Park, 1971; Much Too Much Magic, 1971; A Helping Hand, 1971; Wait for It and Other Stories, 1972; A Monster Too Many, 1972; A Snow-Clean Pinny, 1973; A Fairy Called Andy Perks, 1973; We, Three Kings, 1974; Ever After, 1975; The Magic Lollipop, 1975; The Three Crowns of King Hullabaloo, 1975; Just Turn the Key, 1976; The Hermit's Purple Shirts, 1976. Add: St. Monica's, Cote Lane, Westbury-on-Trym, Bristol BS9 3UN, England.

McNEILL, William Hardy. American, b. 1917. History. Prof. of History, Univ. of Chicago, 1957–87, now Emeritus (Instr., 1947–49; Chmn., Coll. History staff, 1948–55; Asst. Prof., 1949–55; Assoc. Prof., 1955–57; Chmn., Dept. of History, 1961–67). Ed., Journal of Modern History, 1971–81. *Publs:* The Greek Dilemma, War and Aftermath, 1947; (with F. Smothers and E.D. McNeill) Report on the Greeks, 1948; History Handbook, 1949, rev. ed. and History Handbook of Western Civilization, 1953; America, Britain and Russia: Their Co-operation and Conflict 1941–46, 1953; Past and Future, 1954; Greece: American Aid in Action 1947–1956, 1957; (with M.R. Buske and W. Roehm) World History in Maps, 1960, 1963; The Rise of the West, 1963; Europe's Steppe Frontier 1500–1800, 1964; A World History, 1967; (ed.) Lord Action, Essays in the Liberal Interpretation of History, 1967; The Contemporary World, 1967, 1975; (co-ed.) Readings in World History, 10 vols., 1968–73; Venice, the Hinge of Europe 1081–1797, 1974; The Shape of European History, 1974; Plagues and People, 1976; (co-ed.) Human Migration, 1978; Metamorphosis of Greece since World War II, 1978; The Human Condition: An Historical and Ecological View, 1980; Pursuit of Power: Technology,

Armed Force, and Society since 1000 A.D.,1982; The Great Frontier: Freedom and Hierarchy in Modern Times, 1983; Mythistory and Other Essays, 1986; Polyethnicity and National Unity in World History, 1986; A History of the Human Community: Prehistory to the Present, 1987. Add: Box 45, Colebrook, Conn. 06021, U.S.A.

McNEISH, James. New Zealander, b. 1931. Novels/Short stories, Plays/Screenplays, Biography. Writer-in-Residence, Berlin Kunstlerprogramm, 1983. *Publs:* Tavern in the Town, 1957; Fire Under the Ashes, 1965; Mackenzie, 1970; The Mackenzie Affair, 1972; (co-author) Larks in a Paradise, 1974; The Glass Zoo, 1976; As for the Godwits (autobiography), 1977; (with Brian Brake) Art of the Pacific, 1980; Belonging: Conversations in Israel, 1980; Joy, 1982; Walking on My Feet, 1983; the Man from Nowhere: A Berlin Diary, 1985; Lovelock, 1986. Add: c/o George Greenfield, John Farquharson Ltd., 162/168 Regent St., London W1R 5TB, England.

McNELLY, Theodore Hart. American, b. 1919. Politics/Government. Prof. of Govt. and Politics, Univ. of Maryland, College Park, since 1967 (Lectr. and Asst. in European Div., 1953–58; Lectr. in Far East Div., 1958–60; Asst. Prof., 1960–62, and Assoc. Prof., 1962–67, College Park). Assoc. Member, Univ. Seminar on Modern East Asia: Japan, Columbia Univ., NYC, since 1966. Taught at Kemper Military Sch., Boonville, Mo., 1942–43; Research Analyst, Washington, D.C., 1943–46, and Tokyo, 1946–48; Instr. in Political Science, Washington Univ., St. Louis, Mo., 1951–53. *Publs:* Contemporary Government of Japan, 1963; (ed.) Sources in Modern East Asian History and Politics, 1967; Politics and Government in Japan, 1972, 3rd ed. 1984; (co-author) Democratizing Japan: The Allied Occupation, 1987; (ed.) Framing the Constitution of Japan 1944–1949: Primary Sources in English (on microfiche), 1989. Add: 14800 Cobblestone Dr., Silver Spring, Md. 20904, U.S.A.

McNULTY, Faith. American, b. 1918. Short stories, Children's fiction, Animals/Pets, Children's non-fiction, Natural history. Staff Writer, The New Yorker mag., since 1953. *Publs:* Arty the Smarty, 1962; (with E. Keiffer) Wholly Cats, 1962; When a Boy Wakes Up in the Morning, 1962; When a Boy Goes to Bed at Night, 1963; The Whooping Crane (for adults), 1966; Must They Die? (for adults), 1971; Prairie Dog Summer, 1972; The Great Whales (for adults), 1974; Woodchuck, 1974; Whales, 1975; Mouse and Tim, 1978; How to Dig a Hole to the Other Side of the World, 1979; The Burning Bed (for adults), 1980; The Wildlife Stories of Faith McNulty (for adults), 1980; Hurricane, 1983; The Lady and the Spider, 1986; Peeping in the Shell, 1986; A Hug from Koko, 1990. Add: c/o the New Yorker, 25 West 43rd St., New York, N.Y. 10036, U.S.A.

McPHEE, John (Angus). American, b. 1931. Essays. Staff Writer, The New Yorker, since 1965; Ferris Prof. of Journalism, Princeton Univ., New Jersey, since 1975. Assoc. Ed., Time mag., NYC, 1957–64. *Publs:* A Sense of Where You Are, 1965; The Headmaster, 1966; Oranges, 1967; The The Crofter and the Laird, 1970; Encounters with the Archdruid, 1971; The Deltoid Pumpkin Seed, 1973; The Curve of Binding Energy, 1974; Pieces of the Frame, 1975; The Survival of the Bark Canoe, 1975; The John McPhee Reader, 1977; Coming into the Country, 1977; Giving Good Weight, 1979; Basin and Range, 1981; In Suspect Terrain, 1982; La Place de la Concorde Suisse, 1984; Table of Contents, 1985; Rising from the Plains, 1986; The Control of Nature, 1989. Add: c/o Farrar Straus, 19 Union Sq. W., New York, N.Y. 10003, U.S.A.

McPHERSON, James A(lan). American, b. 1943. Novels/Short stories, Transportation. Contrib. Ed., Atlantic Monthly, Boston, since 1969. Instr., Univ. of Iowa Law Sch., 1968–69, and Univ. of California at Santa Cruz, 1969–70. *Publs:* Hue and Cry, 1969; (with Miller Williams) Railroad: Trains and Train People in American Culture, 1976; Elbow Room, 1977. Add: c/o Little Brown and Co., 34 Beacon St., Boston, Mass. 02106, U.S.A.

McPHERSON, James Munro. American, b. 1936. History, Race relations. Edwards Prof. of American History, Princeton Univ., N.J., since 1982 (Instr., 1962–65; Asst. Prof., 1965–66; Assoc. Prof., 1966–72; Prof., 1972–82). *Publs:* The Struggle for Equality: Abolitionists and the Negro in the Civil War and Reconstruction, 1964; The Negro's Civil War: How American Negroes Felt and Acted in the War for the Union, 1965; Marching Toward Freedom: The Negro in the Civil War, 1860–1865, 1968; The Abolitionist Legacy: From Reconstruction to the NAACP, 1975; Ordeal by Fire: The Civil War and Reconstruction, 1982; Battle Cry of Freedom: The Era of the Civil War, 1988. Add: 15 Randall Rd., Princeton, N.J. 08540, U.S.A.

McPHERSON, Sandra. American, b. 1943. Poetry. Prof. of English and Dir. Creative Writing Progr., Univ. of California at Davis, since 1985. Ed., California Quarterly, intermittently since 1985. Member of the faculty, Writers Workshop, Univ. of Iowa, Iowa City, 1974–76, 1978–80, and Pacific Northwest Coll. of Art, Oregon Writers Workshop, 1981–85. Poetry Ed., Antioch Review, Yellow Springs, Ohio, 1979–81. *Publs:* Elegies for the Hot Season, 1970; Radiation, 1973; The Year of Our Birth, 1978; Sensing, 1979; Patron Happiness, 1983; Pheasant Flower, 1985. Streamers, 1988. Add: 2052 Calaveras Ave., Davis, Calif. 95616, U.S.A.

McQUAY, Mike. Also writes as Victor Appleton; Susan Claudia; Franklin W. Dixon; Laura Lee Hope; and Carolyn Keene. American, b. 1949. Novels, Children's fiction, Science fiction. Artist-in-Residence, Central State Univ., Edmond, Okla., since 1980. *Publs:* novel—(as Susan Claudia) Cradle to Grave, 1983; science-fiction novels—Lifekeeper, 1980; Escape from New York (novelization of screenplay), 1981; Mathew Swain: Hot Time in Old Town, 1981; Mathew Swain: When Trouble Beckons, 1981; Mathew Swain: Deadliest Show in Town, 1982; Mathew Swain: The Odds Are Murder, 1983; Jitterbug, 1984; Pure Blood, 1985; Motherearth, 1985; My Science Project (novelization of screenplay), 1985; other, for children—(as Victor Appleton) Tom Swift: Crater of Mystery, 1982; (as Victor Appleton) Tom Swift: Planet of Nightmares, 1983; (as Carolyn Keene and Franklin W. Dixon) Nancy Drew/Hardy Boys: Supersleuths II, 1984; (as Carolyn Keene) Nancy Drew: Ghost Stories II, 1985; (as Laura Lee Hope) Bobsey Twins: Haunted House, 1985. Add: 5933 N.W. 81st., Oklahoma City, Okla. 73132, U.S.A.

McQUOWN, Judith H. American, b. 1941. Business/Trade/Industry, Money/Finance. Pres., Judith H. McQuown and Co. Inc., NYC, since 1973; Ed., McQuown's Designer Markdowns weekly newsletter. Chief, Underwriting Div., Municipal Securities, City of New York, 1972–73. *Publs:* Inc. Yourself: How to Profit by Setting Up Your Own Corporation, 1977, 3rd ed. 1981; Tax Shelters That Work for Everyone, 1979; The Fashion Survival Manual: How to Find It, Fix It, Fake It, and Make It on a Budget, 1981; Playing the Takeover Market: How to Profit from Corporate Mergers, Spinoffs, Tender Offers, and Liquidations, 1982; How to Profit After You Incorporate Yourself, 1985; Keep One Suitcase Empty, 1987. Add: c/o Macmillan Publishing Co., Inc., 866 Third Ave., New York N.Y. 10022, U.S.A.

McRAE, Kenneth Douglas. Canadian, b. 1925. History, International relations/Current affairs, Politics/Government. Prof. of Political Science, Carleton Univ., Ottawa, since 1964 (joined faculty, 1955). Research Supvr., Royal Commn. on Bilingualism and Biculturalism, 1964–69; Pres., Canadian Political Science Assn., 1978–79; Hon. Secty., Royal Soc. of Canada, 1980–83. *Publs:* (ed.) Jean Bodin: The Six Bookes of a Commonweale, 1962; (co-author) The Founding of New Societies: Studies in the History of the United States, Latin America, South Africa, Canada and Australia, 1964; Switzerland: Example of Cultural Co-Existence, 1964; (ed. and project dir.) The Federal Capital: Governmental Institutions, 1969; (ed. and co-author) Consociational Democracy: Political Accommodation in Segmented Societies, 1974; Conflict and Compromise in Multilingual Societies, Vol. I, Switzerland, 1983, Vol. II, Belgium, 1986. Add: Dept. of Political Science, Carleton Univ., Ottawa, Ont. K1S 5B6, Canada.

McSHANE, Mark. Also writes as Marc Lovell. British, b. 1929. Novels, Mystery/Crime/Suspense. *Publs:* The Straight and Crooked, 1960; The Passing Evil, 1961; Seance on a Wet Afternoon, 1961; Untimely Ripped, 1962; The Girl Nobody Knows, 1965; Night's Evil, 1966; Way to Knowhere, 1967; (as Marc Lovell) Ghost of Megan, 1968; Crimson Madness of Little Doom, 1968; Ill Met by a Fish Shop on George Street, 1968; Singular Case of the Multiple Dead, 1969; The Man Who Left Well Enough, 1970; (as Marc Lovell) Imitation Thieves, 1971; Seance for Two, 1972; (as Marc Lovell) A Presence in the House, 1973; (as Marc Lovell) An Enquiry into the Existence of Vampires, 1974; The Othello Complex, 1974; The Headless Snowman, 1974; (as Marc Lovell) Dreamers In A Haunted House, 1975; Lashed But Not Leashed, 1976; (as Marc Lovell) The Blind Hypnotist, 1976; (as Marc Lovell) The Second Vanetti Affair, 1977; (as Marc Lovell) The Guardian Spector, 1977; (as Marc Lovell) Fog Sinister, 1977; Lifetime, 1977; (as Marc Lovell) A Voice From the Living, 1978; (as Marc Lovell) And They Say You Can't Buy Happiness, 1979; The Hostage Game, 1979; (as Marc Lovell) Hand over Mind, 1979; (as Marc Lovell) Shadows and Dark Places, 1980; The Spy Game, 1980; The Halcyon Way, 1982; (as Marc Lovell) The Spy with His Head in the Clouds, 1982; (as Marc Lovell) Spy on the Run, 1982; (as Marc Lovell) Apple Spy in the Sky, 1982; (as Marc Lovell) Apple to the Core, 1983; (as Marc Lovell) Looking for Kingford, 1983; (as Marc Lovell) How Green Was My Apple, 1984; (as Marc Lovell) The Only

Good Apple in a Barrel of Spies, 1984; (as Marc Lovell) The Spy Who Got His Feet Wet, 1985; The Spy Who Barked in the Night, 1985; Good Spies Don't Grow on Trees, 1986; That Great Big Trenchcoat in the Sky, 1987; A Face in the Dark, 1987. Add: Can Tumi, La Cabaneta, Majorca, Spain.

McVEAN, James. *See* **LUARD**, Nicholas.

McWHIRTER, George. Canadian, b. 1939. Novels/Short stories, Poetry, Translations. Prof. and Head of Creative Writing, Univ. of British Columbia, Vancouver, since 1970. Asst. Master, Kilkeel Secondary Sch., N. Ire., 1962–64, and Bangor Grammar Sch., N. Ire., 1964–65; English teacher, Univ. of Barcelona, Spain, 1965–66, and Alberni Secondary Sch., Port Alberni, B.C., 1966–68; Advisory Ed., Prism Intnl., Vancouver, 1970–73. *Publs:* Catalan Poems, 1971; Bodyworks (stories), 1974; Columbuscade, 1974; Queen of the Sea, 1976; Twenty-Five, 1978; The Island Man, 1981; God's Eye (stories), 1981; Coming to Grips with Lucy (stories), 1982; Five Before Dark (poetry), 1983; Paula Lake (novel), 1984; Cage (novel), 1987; (trans.) The Selected Poems of José Emilio Pacheco, 1987. Add: 4637 W. 13th Ave., Vancouver 8, B.C., Canada.

McWILLIAMS, Margaret (Ann Edgar). American, b. 1929. Cookery/Gastronomy/Wine, Medicine/Health. Prof. of Home Economics, California State Univ., Los Angeles, since 1968 (Asst. Prof., 1961–66; Assoc. Prof., 1966–68). *Publs:* Food Fundamentals, 1966, 4th ed. 1986; Nutrition for the Growing Years, 1967, 4th ed. 1986; (with L. Kotschevar) Understanding Food, 1969; Illustrated Guide to Food Preparation, 2nd ed. 1970, 5th ed. 1986; (with L. Davis) Food For You, 1971, 1976; (with F.J. Stare) Living Nutrition, 1973, 4th ed. 1984; Meatless Cookbook, 1973; (with F.J. Stare) Nutrition for Good Health, 1974, 1982; Experimental Foods Manual, 1977, 1981; 3rd ed., 1989; (with H. Paine) Modern Food Preservation, 1977; Fundamentals of Meal Management, 1978; (with H. Heller) World of Nutrition, 1984; Parents' Nutrition Book, 1986; Foods: Experimental Perspectives; 1989. Add: Dept. of Family Studies and Consumer Sciences, California State Univ., Los Angeles, Calif. 90032, U.S.A.

MEACHAM, Ellis K(irby). American, b. 1913. Novels/Short stories. Retired Judge, Second Div. of the Municipal Court, Chattanooga, Tenn. Deputy Gov.-Gen., National Soc. of Mayflower Descendants, since 1979 (former Gov., Tenn. Chapter, from 1976). In general civil law practice, 1937–72; Attorney, City of Chattanooga, 1948–72. *Publs:* The East Indiaman, 1968; On the Company's Service, 1971; For King and Company, 1976. Add: 414 S. Crest Rd., Chattanooga, Tenn. 37404, U.S.A.

MEAD, Matthew. British, b. 1924. Poetry, Translations. Ed., Satis mag., Edinburgh, 1960–62. *Publs:* A Poem in Nine Parts, 1960; Identities, 1964; Kleinigkeiten, 1966; Identities and Other Poems, 1967; The Administration of Things, 1970; (with Harry Guest and J. Beeching) Penguin Modern Poets 16, 1970; In the Eyes of the People, 1973; Minusland, 1977; The Midday Muse, 1979; A Roman in Cologne, 1985. Add: c/o Anvil Press, 69 King George St., London SE10 8PX, England.

MEAD, (Edward) Shepherd. American, b. 1914. Novels/Short stories, Essays, Humour/Satire. Dir., Nouvelles Eds. S.A., Lausanne, Switzerland, since 1969. With Benton and Bowles Inc., NYC, 1936–56; Consultant to S.H. Benson, 1958–62. *Publs:* The Magnificent MacInnes, 1949; Tessie, the Hound of Channel One, 1951; How to Succeed in Business Without Really Trying, 1952, musical version 1961; The Big Ball of Wax, 1954; How to Get Rich in TV Without Really Trying, 1956; How to Succeed with Women Without Really Trying, 1957; The Admen, 1958; Readers Digest Book Club, 1959; The Four Window Girl, 1959; "Dudley, There Is No Tomorrow!" "Then How About This Afternoon?", 1963; How to Live Like Lord Without Really Trying, 1964; The Carefully Considered Rape of the World, 1966; How to Succeed at Business Spying by Trying, 1968; 'ER: or, The Brassbound Beauty, the Bearded Bicyclist, and the Gold-Colored Teen-Age Grandfather, 1969; How to Stay Medium-Young Practically Forever Withour Really Trying, 1971; Free the Male Man! The Manifesto of the Men's Liberation Movement, 1972; How to Get to the Future Before It Gets to You, 1974; How to Succeed in Tennis Without Really Trying, 1977; (with Dakin Williams) Tennessee Williams: An Intimate Biography, 1983. Add: 53 Rivermead Ct., Ranelagh Gardens, London SW6 3RY, England.

MEAD, Sidney (Hirini) Moko. New Zealander, b. 1927. Anthropology/Ethnology. Prof. of Maori, Victoria Univ. of Wellington, since 1977. Sr. Lectr. in Maori Studies, Univ. of Auckland, 1970–71; Assoc. Prof., 1971–72 and 1973–77, McMaster Univ., Hamilton, Ont. *Publs:* Taniko

Weaving, 1952; We Speak Maori, 1959; Ko te Tahae Nei Ko Tawhaki, 1960; The Art of Maori Carving, 1961; (with B. Biggs and P. Hohepa) Selected Readings in Maori, 1959; (with B. Biggs) He Kohikohinga Aronui, 1964; The Art of Taniko Weaving, 1968; Traditional Maori Clothing, 1969; The Costume Styles of Classical Maori in New Zealand, 1969; (with Petersen) Portraits of the New Zealand Maori Painted in 1844 by George French Angas, 1972; Material, Culture and Art in the Star Harbour Region, Eastern Solomons, 1973; Lapita Pottery Style of Fiji, 1975. (ed.) Exploring the Visual Art of Oceania, 1979; (with O.E. Phillis) Te One Matua: The Abundant Earth, 1982; (with B. Kernot) Art and Artists of Oceania, 1983; (ed.) Te Maori: Maori Art from New Zealand Collections, 1984. Add: Dept. of Maori, Victoria Univ. of Wellington, Private Bag, Wellington, New Zealand.

MEADE, James (Edward). British, b. 1907. Economics. Fellow and Lectr. in Economics, 1930–37, and Bursar, 1934–37, Hertford Coll., Oxford; Member, Economic Section, League of Nations, Geneva, 1938–40; Economic Asst., 1940–45, and Dir., 1946–47, Economic Section, Cabinet Office, London; Prof. of Commerce, with special reference to Intnl. Trade, London Sch. of Economics, 1947–57; Prof. of Political Economy, 1957–68, and Fellow of Christ's Coll., 1957–74, Cambridge Univ; Nuffield Research Fellow, 1969–74. Member of Council, 1945–62, and Pres., 1964–66, Royal Economic Soc.; Pres., Section F, British Assn. for the Advancement of Science, 1957; Chmn., Economic Survey Mission to Mauritius, 1960. *Publs:* Public Works in their International Aspect, 1933; The Rate of Interest in a Progressive State, 1933; Economic Analysis and Policy, 1936; Consumers' Credits and Unemployment, 1937; The Economic Basis of Durable Peace, 1940; (with R. Stone) National Income and Expenditure, 1944; Planning and the Price Mechanism, 1948; The Theory of International Economic Policy, vol. I, 1951, vol. II, 1955; A Geometry of International Trade, 1952; Problems of Economic Union, 1953; The Theory of Customs Unions, 1955; The Control of Inflation, 1958; A Neo-Classical Theory of Economic Growth, 1960; (co-author) Three Case Studies in European Economic Union, 1962; Efficiency, Equality and the Ownership of Property, 1964; Principles of Political Economy, 3 vols., 1965–72; Theory of Indicative Planning, 1970; Theory of Economic Externalities, 1973; The Intelligent Radical's Guide to Economic Policy, 1975; Stagflation: Wage Fixing, Vol. I, 1982, Demand Management, vol. II, 1983; Alternative Systems of Business Organization and of Workers' Remuneration, 1986. Recipient: Nobel Prize for Economics, 1977. Add: 40 High St., Little Shelford, Cambridge CB2 5ES, England.

MEADOW, Charles T. American, b. 1929. Children's non-fiction, Information science/Computers. Mgr., Customer Services, DIALOG Information Services, since 1982. Ed., Journal of American Soc. for Information Science, since 1977. Consulting Analyst, Gen. Electric Co., 1956–60; Sr. Systems Analyst, IBM Corp., 1960–68; Chief, Systems Development Div., National Bureau of Standards, 1968–71, and Asst. Dir., Div. of Mgmt. Information and Telecommunications, U.S. Atomic Energy Commn. 1971–74, Washington, D.C.; Prof. of Information Science, Drexel Univ., Philadelphia, 1974–82. *Publs:* The Story of Computers (children), 1970; Man-Machine Communication, 1970; The Analysis of Information Systems, 2nd ed. 1973; Sounds and Signals: How We Communicate, 1975; Applied Data Management, 1976; Basics of Online Searching, 1981; (with A.S. Tedesco) Telecommunications for Management, 1984. Add: 4090 Ben Lomond Dr., Palo Alto, Calif. 94306, U.S.A.

MEANS, Gordon Paul. American, b. 1927. Politics/Government. Prof. of Political Science, McMaster Univ., Hamilton, Ont., since 1967. Assoc. Prof. of Political Science, McMaster Univ., Hamilton, Ont., since 1967. Asst. Prof., Willamette Univ., Salem, Ore., 1958–60; Asst. Prof., Gustavus Adolphus Coll., St. Peter, Minn., 1960–65; Assoc. Prof., Univ. of Washington, Seattle, 1966–67.*Publs:* Malaysian Politics, 1970, 1976; Development and Underdevelopment in Southeast Asia, 1977; The Past in Southeast Asia's Present, 1978; (ed.) Senqoi-English, English-Senqoi Dictionary, 1986. Add: 1271 King St. West, Hamilton, Ont., Canada.

MEASHAM, Donald Charles. British, b. 1932. Poetry, Literature. Head of Sch. of Humanities, Derbyshire Coll. of Higher Education, since 1983. Founder Ed., Staple mag., since 1983. Head of English Dept., Hockley Co. Secondary Sch., Essex, 1960–63; Principal Lectr. in English and Head of Dept., Matlock Coll. of Higher Education, Derbyshire, 1969–83. *Publs:* (ed.) Leaving, 1965; English Now and Then, 1965; (ed.) Fourteen, 1965; (ed.) Larger than Life, 1967; (ed.) The Personal Element, 1969; Sentiment and Sentimental Psychology in Jane Austen, 1971; Mid C Dream (play), 1977; (ed.) Lawrence and the Real England, 1985. Add: Tor Cottage, 81 Cavendish Rd., Matlock, Derbyshire DE4 3HD, England.

MEBANE, John Harrison. American, b. 1909. Antiques/Furnishings. Managing Ed., The High Point Enterprise, N.C., 1930–42; Editorial Writer, Atlanta Journal, Ga., 1942–51; Mgr., Atlanta Office, Dudley-Anderson-Yutzy, Ga., 1951–68; Ed., Antiques Journal, 1968–78. *Publs:* Books Relating to the Civil War, 1963; Treasure at Home, 1964; New Horizons in Collecting, 1966; The Coming Collecting Boom, 1968; The Poor Man's Guide to Collecting Antiques, 1969; What's New That's Old, 1970; The Complete Book of Collecting Art Nouveau, 1970; (with D. Cowie) How to Deal in Antiques, 1972; Collecting Nostalgia, 1972; Best Sellers in Antiques, 1974. Add: P.O. Box 338, Mableton, Ga. 30059, U.S.A.

MECH, L(ucyan) David. American, b. 1937. Environmental science/Ecology, Zoology. Wildlife Research Biologist, U.S. Fish and Wildlife Service, St. Paul, Minn., since 1969. Adjunct Prof., Univ. of Minnesota, Minneapolis, since 1978 (research assoc., 1963–66). Asst. Prof. and Research Fellow, Macalester Coll., St. Paul, Minn., 1966–69. *Publs:* The Wolves of Isle Royale, 1966; The Wolf: The Ecology and Behavior of an Endangered Species, 1970; Handbook of Animal Radio-Tracking, 1983. Add: 1704-D Pleasant St., St. Paul, Minn. 55113, U.S.A.

MEDNICK, Murray. American, b. 1939. Plays/Screenplays, Poetry. Founder and Artistic Dir., the Padua Hills Playwrights' Workshop/Festival, Los Angeles, Calif., since 1978. Playwright-in-Residence and Artistic Dir., Theatre Genesis, NYC, 1970–73. *Publs:* (with Tony Barsha) The Hawk: An Improvisational Play, 1968; The Hunter, 1969; The Deer Kill, 1971; Taxes, 1983; The Coyote Cycle, 1984. Add: 2242 Lake Shore Ave., Los Angeles, Calif. 90039, U.S.A.

MEDOFF, Mark (Howard). American, b. 1940. Plays/Screenplays. Dramatist-in-Residence, New Mexico State Univ., Las Cruces, since 1975 (Assoc. Prof. of English, 1966–75; Prof. of Drama and Chmn. of the Dept. 1978–87). Supvr. of Publications, Capital Radio Engineering Inst., Washington, D.C. 1962–64. *Publs:* When You Comin' Back, Red Ryder?, 1974; (with Carleene Johnson) The Odyssey of Jeremy Jack (juvenile), 1974; Four Short Plays, 1974; The Wager: A Play, and Doing a Good One for the Red Man, and The War on Tatem: Two Short Plays, 1975; The Wager, 1975; The Kramer, 1976; Children of a Lesser God, 1980; The Majestic Kid, 1981; The Hands of Its Enemy, 1984; Kringle's Window, 1985; The Homage that Follows, 1986; The Heart Outright; 1986. Add: Box 3585, Las Cruces, N.M. 88003, U.S.A.

MEDVEDEV, Roy (Alexandrovich), Russian, b. 1925. History, Literature, Politics/Government, Sociology, Biography. Sch. Teacher, Sverdlovsk region, U.S.S.R., 1952–54; Sch. Dir., Leningrad region, U.S.S.R.; Deputy Ed.-in-Chief, Prosveshchenie Publishing House, 1957 60; Head of Dept. of Vocational Education, Research Inst. of Education, Moscow, 1961–71. *Publs:* Let History Judge, 1971; (with Zhores A. Medvedev) Questions of Madness, 1971; On Socialist Democracy, 1975; (with Zhores A. Medvedev) Khrushchev: The Years in Power, 1976; Political Essays, 1976; Problems in the Literary Biography of Mikhail Sholokhov, 1977; (ed.) Samizdat Register, 2 vols., 1977–80; The October Revolution, 1979; On Stalin and Stalinism, 1979; On Soviet Dissent, 1980; Nikolai Bukharin: The Last Years, 1980; Leninism and Western Socialism, 1981; All Stalin's Men, 1983; An End to Silence: Uncensored Opinion in the Soviet Union; 1984; China and the Superpowers, 1986. Add: Abonement Post Box 45, Moscow G-19, U.S.S.R.

MEDVEDEV, Zhores (Alexandrovich). British, b. Russian, 1925. Biology, History, Politics/Government, Sociology. Sr. Research Fellow, MRC National Inst. for Medical Research Div. of Genetics, London, since 1973; Assoc. Ed., Experimental Gerontology. Member of Editorial Bd., Mechanism of Ageing and Development, Ireland. Sr. Research Scientists, K. Timiriasev Academy of Agricultural Sciences, Moscow, 1951–62; Head of Lab. of Molecular Radiobiology, Research Inst. of Medical Radiology, Obninsk, Kaluga region, U.S.S.R., 1963–69; Sr. Research Scientist, Lab. of Proteins, Research Inst. of Biochemistry and Physiology of Farm Animals, Borovsk, Kaluga region, U.S.S.R., 1970–72. *Publs:* Protein Biosynthesis, 1966; The Rise and Fall of T.D. Lysenko, 1969; Molecular-Genetic Mechanisms of Development, 1970; (with Roy A. Medvedev) Questions of Madness, 1971; Medvedev Papers, 1971; Ten Years After Ivan Denisovich; (with Roy A. Medvedev) Khrushchev: The Years in Power, 1976; Soviet Science, 1978; Nuclear Disaster in the Urals, 1979; Andropov, 1983; Gorbachev, 1986; Soviet Agriculture, 1987; Legacy of Chernobyl, 1989. Add: National Inst. for Medical Research, Mill Hill, London NW7 1AA, England.

MEDVEI, Victor Cornelius. British, b. 1905. Medical writer. Medical consultant; Examining Physician in London for the U.N. Principal Medical Officer, Treasury Medical Service, responsible for overseas services, 1966–70. *Publs:* The Mental and Physical Effects of Pain, 1949; (ed. with J.L. Thornton) The Royal Hospital of St. Bartholomew 1123–1973, 1974; A History of Endocrinology, 1982. Add: 38 Westmoreland Terr., London SW1, England.

MEEKS, Esther MacBain. American, b. 1921. Children's fiction. *Publs:* Jeff and Mr. James Pond, 1962; Web of Winter, 1967, 5th ed., 1989; Canticles for Christmas, 1969. Add: 2911 Oak St., Terre Haute, Ind. 47803, U.S.A.

MEEKS, Wayne A. American, b. 1932. Intellectual history, Theology/Religion. Prof. of Religious Studies, Yale Univ., New Haven, Conn., since 1973 (Assoc. Prof., 1969–73; Chmn. of Dept. 1972–75, 1978–79, and 1982–83). Instr. in Religion, Darmouth Coll., Hanover, N.H., 1964–65; Asst. Prof., 1966–68, and Assoc. Prof., 1968–69, Indiana Univ., Bloomington; Pres., Society of Biblical Literature, 1985. *Publs:* Go from Your Father's House: A College Student's Introduction to the Christian Faith, 1964; The Prophet-King: Moses Traditions and the Johannine Christology, 1967; (ed.) The Writings of St. Paul, 1972; (ed. with F.O. Francis) Conflict at Colossae, 1972; (ed. with J. Jervell) God's Christ and His People, 1977; (with R.L. Wilken) Jews and Christians in Antioch, 1978; (ed.) Zur Soziologie des Urchristentums, 1979; The First Urban Christians: The Social World of the Apostle Paul, 1983; The Moral World of the First Christians, 1986. Add: Dept. of Religious Studies, Yale Univ., P.O. Box 2160, New Haven, Conn. 06520, U.S.A.

MEGGED, Aharon. Israeli, b. 1920. Novels/Short stories, Plays/Screenplays. Kibbutz member, Sdot-Yam, 1938–50; Ed., Massa bi-weekly, 1952–55; Literary Ed., Lamerchav daily newspaper, 1955–68; Cultural Attaché, Israel Embassy, London, 1968–71; Journalist, Davar Daily, Tel-Aviv, 1971–85. Author-in-Residence, Haifa Univ., 1974, and Oxford Univ., 1978. Pres., Israeli P.E.N. Centre, 1980–88. *Publs:* Spirit of the Seas, 1950; Hedva and I, 1955; Far in the Wasteland (play), 1955; Israeli Folk, 1957; Fortunes of a Fool, 1960; The Escape, 1962; Hanna Senesh (play), 1962; The First Sin (play), 1962; Living on the Dead, 1965; The High Season (play), 1967; The Short Life, 1972; Evyatar's Notebooks, 1973; Mid-day, 1973; Of Trees and Stones, 1974; The Bat, 1976; Heinz, His Son and the Evil Spirit, 1977; Asahel, 1978; Young Love, 1979; Journey in the Month of Av, 1981; The Flying Camel and the Golden Hump, 1982; The Children's Journey to the Promised Land, 1984; The Turbulent Zone, 1985; Indecent Act, 1986; Foiglman, 1987; The Writing Desk (essays), 1989. Add: 26 Rupin St., Tel-Aviv, Israel.

MEGGERS, Betty J. American, b. 1921. Anthropology/Ethnology, Archaeology, Environmental Science/Ecology. Research Assoc., Smithsonian Instn., since 1954. Exec. Secty., American Anthropological Assn., 1959–61. *Publs:* Ecuador, 1966; (trans.) The Civilizational Process, by Darcy Ribeiro, 1968; Amazonia: Man and Culture in a Counterfeit Paradise, 1971; Prehistoric America, 1972; (ed. with E.S. Ayensu and W.D. Duckworth) Tropical Forest Ecosystems in Africa and South America: A Comparative Review, 1973; (trans.) People and Cultures of Ancient Peru, by Luis G. Lumbreras, 1974. Add: Smithsonian Instn., Washington, D.C. 20560, U.S.A.

MEGGITT, Mervyn John. Australian, b. 1924. Anthropology/Ethnology. Prof. of Anthropology, Queens Coll. of City Univ. of New York, since 1967. Lectr. to Sr. Lectr. in Anthropology, Univ. of Sydney, N.S.W., 1955–65; Prof. of Anthropology, Univ. of Michigan, Ann Arbor, 1965–67. *Publs:* Desert People, 1962; The Lineage System of the Mae Enga of New Guinea, 1965; (ed. with P. Lawrence) Gods, Ghosts and Men in Melanesia, 1965; Gadjari Among the Walbiri Aborigines of Central Australia, 1966; (ed. with R.M. Glasse) Pigs, Pearlshells and Women, 1969; Studies in Enga History, 1974; Blood Is Their Argument, 1977; (with R.J. Gordon) Law and Order in the New Guinea Highlands, 1985. Add: 241 Central Park West, New York, N.Y. 10024, U.S.A.

MEGGS, Brown (Moore). American, b. 1930. Novels. Pres., Angel Records, Los Angeles, since 1984. With Capitol Records, Hollywood, 1958–76: Exec. Vice-Pres., Chief Operating Officer, and Member of the Bd. of Directors; Pres., Nanbrook Corp., Pasadena, Calif., 1976–84. *Publs:* Saturday Games, 1974; The Matter of Paradise, 1975; Aria, 1978; The War Train, 1981. Add: 1450 El Mirador Dr., Pasadena, Calif. 91103, U.S.A.

MEHRABIAN, Albert. American, b. 1939. Psychology. Prof. of Psychology, Univ. of California, Los Angeles, since 1976 (Asst. Prof. 1964–70; Assoc. Prof., 1970–76). *Publs:* (with M. Wiener) Language

Within Languages: Immediacy, A Channel in Verbal Communication, 1968; An Analysis of Personality Theories, 1968; Tactics of Social Influence, 1970; Silent Messages, 1971; Nonverbal Communication, 1972; Public Places and Private Spaces, 1976; Basic Behavior Modification, 1978; Basic Dimensions for a General Psychological Theory, 1980; Eating Characteristics and Temperament, 1987. Add: Dept. of Psychology, Univ. of California, Los Angeles, Calif. 90024, U.S.A.

MEHROTRA, Arvind Krishna. Indian, b. 1947. Poetry, Translations. Reader in English, Univ. of Allahabad, since 1978 (Lectr., 1968–77). Visiting Writer, Univ. of Iowa, Iowa City, 1971–73; Lectr. in English, Univ. of Hyderabad, 1977–78. *Publs:* Bharatmata: A Prayer, 1966; Woodcuts on Paper, 1967; Pomes/Poemes/Poemas, 1971; (trans.) Three Poems, by Bogomil Gjuzel, 1973; Nine Enclosures, 1976; Distance in Statute Miles, 1982; Middle Earth, 1984. Add: Dept. of English Studies, Univ. of Allahabad, Allahabad 211 002, India.

MEHROTRA, Sriram. Indian, b. 1931. History, Politics/Government. Prof. of History, Himachal Pradesh Univ., Simla, India, since 1972. Lectr. in South Asian Politics, Sch. of Oriental and African Studies, Univ. of London, 1962–71; Fellow, Indian Inst. of Advanced Study, Simla, 1971–79. *Publs:* India and the Commonwealth 1885–1929, 1965; The Emergence of the Indian National Congress, 1971; The Commonwealth and the Nation, 1978; Towards India's Freedom and Partition, 1979. Add: History Dept., Himachal Pradesh Univ., Simla 171 005, India.

MEHTA, Ved (Parkash). American (born Indian), b. 1934. Novels/Short stories, Area studies, Autobiography/Memoirs/Personal, Biography. Staff Writer, The New Yorker mag., since 1961. *Publs:* Face to Face, 1957; Walking the Indian Streets, 1960, 1971; Fly and the Fly-Bottle, 1963, 1983; The New Theologian, 1966; Delinquent Chacha (novel), 1967; Portrait of India, 1970; John Is Easy to Please, 1971; Daddyji, 1972; Mahatma Gandhi and His Apostles, 1977; The New India, 1978; Mamaji, 1979; The Photographs of Chachaji, 1980; A Family Affair, 1982; Vedi, 1982; The Ledge Between the Streams, 1984; Sound—Shadows of the New World, 1986; Three Stories of the Raj, 1987. Add: 139 East 79th St., New York, N.Y. 10021, U.S.A.

MEINHARDT, Peter. British, b. 1903. Law. Freelance writer and legal consultant, since 1968. Legal Adviser, Intnl. Gen. Electric Co. of N.Y. Ltd., London 1933–48; Co. Secty., Loewy Robertson Engineering Co. Ltd., Bournemouth, 1948–68. *Publs:* Inventions, Patents and Monopoly, 1946, 1950; Inventions, Patents and Trade Marks, 1971; Company Law in Europe, 1975, 3rd ed. 1981; Company Law in Great Britain, 1982; (with K. Havelock) Concise Trade Mark Law and Practice, 1983. Add: 6934 Bioggio, Ticino, Switzerland.

MEINKE, Peter. American, b. 1932. Novels/Short stories, Poetry, Literature. Prof. of Literature and Dir. of Writing Workshop, Eckerd Coll., St. Petersburg, Fla., since 1966 (Dir., Overseas Prog., Univ. of Neuchatel, Switzerland, 1971–72). Fulbright Senior Lectr., Univ. of Warsaw, Poland, 1978–79; Jenny Moore Writer-in-Residence, George Washington Univ., Washington D.C., 1981–82; Thurber Writer-in-Residence, Columbus, Ohio, 1987; McGee Writer-in-Residence, Davidson Coll., N.C., 1989. *Publs:* Howard Nemerov, 1968; The Legend of Larry the Lizard, 1969; Very Seldom Animals, 1970; Lines from Neuchatel (poetry), 1974; The Night Train and the Golden Bird, 1977; The Rat Poems, 1978; Trying to Surprise God (poetry), 1981; The Piano Tuner, 1986; Underneath the Lantern (poetry), 1986; Night Watch on the Chesapeake (poetry), 1987; Far from Home (poetry), 1988. Add: Writing Workshop, Eckerd Coll., St. Petersburg, Fla. 33733, U.S.A.

MELADY, Thomas (Patrick). American, b. 1927. Race relations, Third World problems. Former Asst. Secty., U.S. Dept. of Education. Lectr., Addis Ababa Univ., 1955–56; Prof. and Chmn., Dept. of Asian and Non-Western Studies, Seton Hall Univ., South Orange, N.J., and Pres., Africa Service Inst., 1959–67; Lectr., St. John's Univ., N.Y., and Adjunct Prof. of African History, Fordham Univ., NYC, 1960–67; U.S. Ambassador to Burundi, 1969–72; to Uganda, 1972–73; Prof. of Afro-Asian Affairs, and Dir., Office of Intnl. Studies, Seton Hall Univ., South Orange, N.J., 1973–74; Exec. Vice-Pres., St. Joseph's Coll., Philadelphia, 1974–76; Pres., Sacred Heart Univ., 1976–81 (Prof. of Political Science, 1976–86). *Publs:* Profiles of African Leaders, 1961; White Man's Future in Black Africa, 1962; Faces of Africa, 1964; Kenneth Kuanda of Zambia, 1964; Revolution of Color, 1965; Western Policy and the Third World, 1967; (co-author) House Divided, 1969; Development: Lessons for the Future, 1973; Burundi: The Tragic Years, 1974; (co-author) Uganda: The Asian Exiles, 1975; Idi Amin Dada: Hitler in Africa, 1977. Add: 637 Rock Ridge Rd., Fairfield, Conn. 06430, U.S.A.

MELCHIOR, Ib (Jorgen). American (born Danish), b. 1917. Novels/Short stories, Plays/Screenplays, Translations. Freelance writer, dir., and producer, since 1957. Toured Europe as Actor, Stage Mgr., and Co-Dir., English Players, 1937–39; Stage Mgr., Radio City Music Hall and Center Theatre, NYC, 1941–42; with Office of Strategic Services, 1942–43, and U.S. Military Intelligence, 1943–45; Television Writer, Actor, and Dir., NYC, 1947–50; Dir., Perry Como Show, 1951–54, Eddy Arnold Show, 1952, and T.V.'s Top Tunes, 1953, C.B.S., and of March of Medicine, N.B.C., 1955–56; Assoc. Producer, G-L Enterprises, 1952–53. Member, Advisory Cttee., Narcotics Information Clinic Prog., Los Angeles, Calif., 1971. *Publs:* (trans.) Rosmersholm, by Henrik Ibsen, 1946; (trans.) Hedda Gabler, by Henrik Ibsen, 1947; (trans.) Hour of Vengeance (stage play), 1962; Order of Battle (novel), 1972; Sleeper Agent (novel), 1975; The Haigerloch Project (novel), 1977; The Watchdogs of Abaddon (novel), 1979; The Marcus Device (novel), 1980; The Tombstone Cipher (novel), 1983; Eva (novel), 1984; V-3 (novel), 1985; Code Name: Grand Guignol (novel), 1987. Add: 8228 Marmont Lane, Los Angeles, Calif. 90069, U.S.A.

MELDRUM, James. *See* **KYLE**, Duncan.

MELFI, Leonard. American, b. 1935. Plays/Screenplays. *Publs:* Encounters: 6 One-Act Plays, 1967; Stars and Stripes, 1968; Jack and Jill, 1969; Fantasies at the Frick, 1980; Porno Stars at Home, 1980; Later Encounters: 7 One-Act Plays, 1980; Tales of a New York Playwright, 1985. Add: c/o Helen Harvey, 410 W. 24th St., New York, N.Y. 10011, U.S.A.

MELLANBY, Kenneth. British, b. 1908. Children's fiction, Education, Environmental science/Ecology, Medicine/Health, Natural history. Ed., Environmental Pollution, Elsevier, Amsterdam, and New Naturalist, Collins, London; Environmental Consultant. First Principal, Univ. Coll., Ibadan, Nigeria, 1947–53; Head, Entomology Dept., Rothamsted Experimental Station, Harpenden, Herts., 1955–61; Dir., Monks Wood Experimental Station, Natural Environment Research Council, Huntingdon, 1961–74. *Publs:* Scabies, 1943; Human Guinea-pigs, 1945; The Birth of Nigeria's University, 1958; Pesticides and Pollution, 1967; The Mole, 1971; The Biology of Pollution, 1972; Can Britain Feed Itself, 1975; Talpa: The Story of a Mole (children's fiction), 1976; (with F.H. Perring) The Ecological Effects of Pesticides, 1978; Farming and Wildlife, 1981; (ed.) Air Pollution, Acid Rain, and the Environment, 1988; Waste, Wildlife, and the Countryside, 1989. Add: 38 Warkworth St., Cambridge CB1 1EG, England.

MELLANDER, G(ustavo) A. American, b. 1935. Education, History, International relations/Current affairs. Chancellor, West Valley-Mission Comm. Coll. District, Saratoga, Calif., since 1985. Reporter, The Panama American, 1954–55 and The Star & Herald, 1955–57; Dean of Faculty, Inter-American Univ., San Juan, Puerto Rico 1966–69; Academic Dean, York Coll., 1969–72; Dir., Office of Independent Colleges, New Jersey Dept. of Higher Education, Trenton, 1972–75; Pres., Passaic County Comm. Coll., New Jersey, 1975–85; Pres., Mission Coll., Santa Clara, Calif., 1985. *Publs:* (with C. Barnett) Area Handbook for Cuba, 1961; (with L. Legters) Area Handbook for Panama, 1962; (with B. Maday) Malaysia and Singapore, 1966; (with C. Hatch) The Dispatch Index: The Depression 1930's, 1971; The United States in Panamanian Politics, 1971; (with C. Hatch) York County's Presidential Elections: From Lincoln to Nixon, 1972; (with C. Hatch) The York Dispatch Index: The War Torn 1940's, 1973. Add: c/o Interstate, 19 N. Jackson St., Danville, Ill. 61832, U.S.A.

MELLEN, Joan. American, b. 1941. Film. Assoc. Prof., Temple Univ., Philadelphia, since 1973 (Asst. Prof., 1967–73). *Publs:* A Film Guide to the Battle of Algiers, 1973; Marilyn Monroe, 1973; Women and Their Sexuality in the New Film, 1973; Voices from the Japanese Cinema, 1975; The Waves at Genji's Door: Japan Through Its Cinema, 1976; Big Bad Wolves: Masculinity in the American Film, 1978; (ed.) The World of Luis Bunuel, 1978; Natural Tendencies, 1981; Privelege: The Enigma of Sacha Bruce, 1983; Bob Knight: His Own Man, 1988. Add: 25 Elm Ridge Rd., Pennington, N.J. 08534, U.S.A.

MELLER, Norman. American, b. 1913. Politics/Government. Prof. Emeritus of Political Science, Univ. of Hawaii, Honolulu, since 1977 (Dir., Legislative Reference Bureau, 1947–55; Prof., 1947–77; Dir., Pacific Islands Studies Prog., 1965–75). Admitted to California State Bar, 1936. *Publs:* (with R. Horwitz) Land and Politics in Hawaii, 1963, 3rd ed. 1966; (with J. Anthony) Fiji Goes to the Polls, 1968; Papers on the Papua-New Guinea House of Assembly, 1968; The Congress of Micronesia, 1969; With an Understanding Heart: Constitution Making in Hawaii, 1971; Institutional Adaptability: Legislative Reference in Japan and the United States, 1974; Constitutionalism in Micronesia, 1985. Add: Dept. of Political Science, Univ. of Hawaii, Honolulu, Hawaii 96822, U.S.A.

MELLERS, Wilfrid (Howard). British, b. 1914. Cultural/Ethnic topics, Music. Prof. of Music, Univ. of York, 1964–81, now retired. Staff Tutor in Music, Extra-Mural Dept., Univ. of Birmingham, 1948–59; Mellon Prof. of Music, Univ. of Pittsburgh, 1960–63. *Publs:* Music and Society, 1946; Studies in Contemporary Music, 1948; Music in the Making, 1950; Fran\ois Couperin and the French Classical Tradition, 1950; Man and His Music, 2 vols., 1957–58; Harmonious Meeting: A Study of Music, Poetry and Theatre in England 1600–1900, 1964; Music in a New Found Land: Themes and Developments in the History of American Music, 1964; Caliban Reborn: Renewal in 20th Century Music, 1966; Twilight of the Gods: The Beatles in Retrospect, 1973; Bach and the Dance of God, 1980; Beethoven and the Voice of God, 1981; A Darker Shade of Pale: A Backdrop for Bob Dylan, 1984; The Secret Garden: Homage to Frederio Mompou, 1985; Angels of the Night: Popular Female Singers of Our Time, 1986; The Masks of Orpheus, 1987; François Couperin and the French Classical Tradition, 1987. Add: Oliver Sheldon House, 17 Aldwark, York YO1 2BX, England.

MELLON, Melvin Guy. American, b. 1893. Chemistry. Prof. Emeritus of Analytical Chemistry, Purdue Univ., Lafayette, Ind. (joined faculty, 1919); Section Ed./Advisor, Chemical Abstracts, since 1961. *Publs:* Chemical Publications, 1928, 5th ed. 1982; Methods of Quantitative Chemical Analysis, 1937; Colorimetry for Chemists, 1945; (ed. and contrib.) Analytical Absorption Spectroscopy, 1950; Quantitative Analysis, 1955; Searching the Chemical Literature, 1964. Add: 338 Overlook Dr., West Lafayette, Ind. 47906, U.S.A.

MELLOR, John W(illiams). American, b. 1928. Agriculture/Forestry, Economics. Dir., Intnl. Food Policy Research Inst. Prof., Dept. of Agricultural Economics, Cornell Univ., Ithaca, N.Y. 1965–80 (Lectr., 1952–54; Asst. Prof., 1954–58; Assoc. Prof., 1958–65; Assoc. Dir, 1961–66, and Acting Dir., 1964–65, Center for Intnl. Studies); CECA Visiting Prof., Balwant Rajput Coll., Agra, India, 1959–60; Rockefeller Foundn.Visiting Prof., Indian Agricultural Research Inst., New Delhi, 1964–65. *Publs:* The Economics of Agricultural Development, 1966; (with T.F. Weaver, U.J. Lele and S.R. Simons) Developing Rural India: Plan and Practice, 1968; The New Economics of Growth: A Strategy for India and the Developing World, 1976; India: A Rising Middle Power, 1979; Agricultural Change and Rural Poverty, 1985; (co-ed.) Accelerating Food Production Growth in Sub-Saharan Africa, 1987; Agricultural Price Policy for Developing Countries, 1988. Add: c/o Intnl. Food Policy, 1776 Massachusetts Ave. N.W., Washington, D.C. 20036, U.S.A.

MELLOWN, Elgin W(endell). American, b. 1931. Literature. Assoc. Prof. of English, Duke Univ., Durham, N.C., since 1968 (Asst. Prof., 1965–68). Member of faculty, Univ. of Alabama, 1958–65. *Publs:* Bibliography of the Writings of Edwin Muir, 1964; (with P. Hoy) Checklist of Writings about Edwin Muir, 1971; Descriptive Catalogue of the Bibliographies of 20th Century British Writers, 1972, 1978; Edwin Muir, 1979; Jean Rhys: Descriptive and Annotated Bibliography, 1984. Add: 1004 Minerva Ave., Durham, N.C. 27701, U.S.A.

MELLOWS, Anthony (Roger). British, b. 1936. Law. Sr. Partner, Messrs. Alexanders, solicitors, London, since 1962; Prof. of the Law of Property since 1974, and Fellow since 1980, King's Coll., Univ. of London (Asst. Lectr. in Law, 1962–64, Lectr., 1964–71, Reader, 1971–74). Admitted solicitor, 1960. *Publs:* Local Searches and Enquiries, 1964, 1967; Conveyancing Searches, 1964; The Preservation and Felling of Trees, 1964; The Trustee's Handbook, 1965, 3rd ed. 1975; Land Charges, 1966; (co-author) The Modern Law of Trusts, 1966, 5th ed. 1983; Taxation for Executors and Trustees, 1967, 6th ed. 1984; The Law of Succession, 1970, 4th ed. 1983; Taxation of Land Transactions, 1973, 3rd ed. 1982. Add: Messrs. Alexanders, 203/219 Temple Chambers, Temple Ave., London EC4Y 0EN, England.

MELLY, (Alan) George (Heywood). British, b. 1926. Media, Autobiography/Memoirs/Personal, Humor/Satire. Jazz singer with John Chilton's Feetwarmers since 1974. Jazz singer with Mick Mulligan's Band, 1949–61; Writer, Flook strip cartoon, 1956–71; Pop Music Critic, 1965–67, TV Critic, 1967–71, and Film Critic, 1971–73, Observer newspaper, London; Compere, George, Granada-TV show, 1974. *Publs:* I Flook, 1962; Owning Up, 1965; Revolt into Style, 1970; Flook by Trog, 1970; Rum, Bum, and Concertina, 1977; (with B. Fantoni) Media Mob, 1980; Great Lovers, 1981; Tribe of One, 1981; Mellymobile, 1982; Swans Reflecting Elephants, 1982; Scouse Mouse, 1984; It's All Writ Out for

You: The Life and Work of Scottie Wilson, 1985. Add: 33 St. Lawrence Terr., London W10 5SR, England.

MELONEY, Franken. *See* **FRANKEN,** Rose.

MELTON, David. American, b. 1934. Children's fiction, Poetry, Children's non-fiction, Education, Medicine/Health. Special Audio/Visual Aids Consultant, Aviation Dept., Kansas City, Mo., since 1969, and Swope Ridge Health Care Center, Kansas City, since 1974. Sch. Teacher, Burnt Mills, N.Y., 1956–57; Advisor and Co-ordinator of High School and Coll. Yearbook Dept., and later Sales Rep., Burger-Baird Engraving Co., Kansas City, 1957; from Salesman to Vice Pres. in Charge of Sales, Glenn Printing Co., Kansas City, 1958–69; Graphic Designer, The Ruberoid News, 1959–64. *Publs:* Todd (autobiographical), 1968; I'll Show You the Morning Sun (poems), 1971; Judy: A Remembrance (biography/poetry), 1971; When Children Need Help, 1972; This Man, Jesus (children's book), 1972; Burn the Schools, Save the Children, 1975; (with Raymundo Veras) Children of Dreams, Children of Hope, 1975; A Boy Called Hopeless (children's novel), 1976; Happy Birthday, America! (anthology), 1976; How to Help Your Preschooler Learn More, Faster and Better, 1976; And God Created . . . (poems), 1976; Theodore, 1978; The Survival Kit for Parents and Teenagers, 1979; The One and Only Autobiography of Ralph Miller, 1979; Harry S. Truman, 1980; Promises to Keep, 1984; Written and Illustrated by . . , 1985; The One and Only Second Autobiography of Ralph Miller, 1986; How to Capture Live Authors and Bring them to Your Schools, 1986. Add: 7422 Rosewood Circle, Prairie Village, Kans. 66208, U.S.A.

MELTZER, David. American, b. 1937. Novels/Short stories, Science fiction/Fantasy, Children's fiction, Poetry, Literature, Autobiography/Memoirs/Personal. Ed., Tree, Bolinas, Calif. Ed., Maya Mill Valley, Calif., 1966–71. *Publs:* (with D. Schenker) Poems, 1957; Ragas, 1959; The Clown: A Poem, 1960; (ed. with Michael McClure and Lawrence Ferlinghetti) Journal for the Protection of All Beings, 1961, No. 4, 1978; We All Have Something to Say to Each Other: Being an Essay Entitled "Patchen" and Four Poems, 1962; Introduction to the Outsiders (essay on Beat Poetry), 1962; Bazascope Mother (essay on Robert Alexander), 1964; The Process, 1965; In Hope I Offer A Fire Wheel, 1965; Journal of the Birth, 1967; Nature Poem, 1967; The Agency Trilogy (novel), 1968; Round the Lunch Box: Rustic and Domestic Home Movies for Stan and Jane Brakhage, 1969; Yesod, 1969; From Eden Book, 1969; Isla Vista Notes: Fragmentary, Apocalyptic, Didactic Contradictions, 1970; Greenspeech, 1970; Luna, 1970; Letter and Numbers, 1970; Bronx Lil-Head of Lillin S.A.C., 1970; 32 Beams of Light, 1970; The Brain-Plant Tetralogy: Lovely, Healer, Out, and Glue Factory (novel), 1970; Star (novel), 1970; (ed.) The San Francisco Poets, 1971; Knots, 1971; (ed.) Birth: An Anthology, 1973; Bark: A Polemic, 1973; Hero/Lil, 1973; Tens: Selected Poems 1961–1971, 1973; The Eyes, The Blood, 1973; Bark, 1973; Birth, 1973; The Secret Garden: an Anthology of Texts from the Jewish Mystical Tradition, 1976; French Broom, 1974; Blue Rags, 1974; Six, 1976; Abra (for children), 1976; Two-Way Mirror: A Poetry Notebook (prose), 1977; (ed.) Birth: An Anthology of Ancient Texts, Songs, Prayers, and Stories, 1981; The Art, The Veil (poetry), 1981; The Name: Selected Poems, 1972–82, 1984; (ed.) Death: An Anthology of Ancient Texts, Songs, Prayers, and Stories, 1984; The Book Within the Book: Approaching the Kabbalah, 1988. Add: Box 9005, Berkeley, Calif. 94709, U.S.A.

MELTZER, Morton Franklin. American, b. 1930. Administration/Management, Information science/Computers. Mgr., Technical Information Center, Martin Marietta Corp., Orlando, Fla., since 1959. Prof. of Business Communications, Crummer Sch. of Finance and Business Admin., Rollins Coll., Winter Park, Fla., since 1968. *Publs:* The Information Center: Management's Hidden Asset, 1967; The Information Imperative, 1971; Information: The Ultimate Management Resource, 1981. Add: c/o Books on Demand, Dir. of University Microfilms, Intnl., 300 N. Zeeb Rd., Ann Arbor, Mich. 48106, U.S.A.

MELUCH, R(ebecca) M. American, b. 1956. Science fiction. Full-time writer since 1978; Asst. Instr., Kim's Martial Arts Sch., Fairview Park, Ohio, since 1982. *Publs:* Sovereign, 1979; Wind Dancers, 1981; Wind Child, 1982; Jerusalem Fire, 1985. Add: 29520 Schwartz Rd., Westlake, Ohio 44145, U.S.A.

MELVILLE, Anne. *See* **POTTER,** Margaret.

MELVILLE, James. Pseud. for (Roy) Peter Martin. British, b. 1931. Mystery/Crime/Suspense, Cookery. Local govt. officer, London County Council, 1948–49, 1951–54; schoolteacher, London, 1954–56; Deputy Publicity Officer, Royal Festival Hall, London, 1956–60; British Council

Officer, 1960–83. *Publs:* (as Peter Martin; with Joan Martin) Japanese Cooking, 1970; The Wages of Zen, 1979; The Chrysanthemum Chain, 1980; Sort of Samurai, 1981; The Ninth Netsuke, 1982; Sayonara, Sweet Amaryllis, 1983; Death of a Daimyo, 1984; The Death Ceremony, 1985; The Imperial Way, 1986; Go Gently, Gaijin, 1986; Kimono for a Corpse, 1987; The Reluctant Ronin, 1988; A Haiku for Hanae, 1989; (as Peter Martin) Modern Japan, 1989. Add: Barn Cottage, Hatfield, Leominster, Herefordshire HR6 0SF, England.

MELVILLE, Jennie. *See* **BUTLER,** Gwendoline.

MELVIN, A(rthur) Gordon. American, b. 1894. Education, Natural history, Travel/Exploration/Adventure. Prof. of Education, Coll. of City of New York, 1928–54, now retired. *Publs:* Progressive Teaching, 1932; The Technique of Progressive Teaching, 1932; Education for a New Era, 1933; Building Personality, 1934; The Activity Program, 1936; The New Culture, 1937; Activated Curriculum, 1939; Method for New Schools, 1941; Thinking for Everyman, 1942; Peoples World, 1943; Teaching, 1944; Education, A History, 1946; Adventures on Midsummer Evenings, 1951; General Methods of Teaching, 1952; Mexico Travel Guide, 1956; Gems of World Oceans, 1964; Sea Shells of the World, 1968; Sea Shell Parade, 1973; (with Lorna S. Melvin) 1000 World Sea Shells, 1980. Add: 863 Watertown St., West Newton, Mass. 02165, U.S.A.

MELWOOD, (Eileen) Mary. Pseud. for Eileen Mary Lewis. British. Children's fiction, Plays/Screenplays. *Publs:* plays—It Isn't Enough (radio), 1957; The Tingalary Bird, 1964; Five Minutes to Morning, 1965; Masquerade, 1970; The Small Blue Hoping Stone, 1976; fiction—Nettlewood, 1974; The Watcher Bee, 1982; Reflections in Black Glass, (adult novel), 1987. Add: 5 Hove Lodge Mansions, Hove St., Hove, Sussex BN3 2TS, England.

MELZACK, Ronald. Canadian, b. 1929. Children's fiction, Psychology. Prof. of Psychology, McGill Univ., Montreal, Que., since 1967 (Assoc. Prof., 1963–67). Lectr., Univ. Coll., London, 1957–58; Research Fellow, Univ. of Pisa, Italy, 1958–59; Assoc. Prof., Massachusetts Inst. of Technology, 1959–63. *Publs:* The Day Tuk Became a Hunter and Other Eskimo Stories, 1967; Raven, Creator of the World, 1970; The Puzzle of Pain, 1973; Why the Man in the Moon Is Happy and Other Eskimo Creation Stories, 1977; (with P.D. Wall) The Challenge of Pain, 1982; (ed.) Pain Measurement and Assessment, 1983; (ed. with P.D. Wall) Textbook of Pain, 1984. Add: 51 Banstead Rd., Montreal West, Que., Canada.

MENARD, Orville D. American, b. 1933. Politics/Government. Prof. of Political Science, Univ. of Nebraska at Omaha, since 1974 (Asst. Prof., 1963–68; Assoc. Prof., 1968–73; Asst. Dean, Coll. of Arts and Sciences, 1974–75). Instr., Texas Arts and Industries Univ., Kingsville, 1963–64. *Publs:* The Army and the Fifth Republic, 1967; Political Bossism in Mid-America, 1989. Add: Dept. of Political Science, Univ. of Nebraska, Omaha, Nebr. 68182, U.S.A.

MENDELSOHN, Martin. British, b. 1935. Law, Marketing. Partner, Adlers, Solicitors, London, since 1959. *Publs:* The Guide to Franchising, 1970, 4th ed. 1985; How to Evaluate a Franchise, 1981, 3rd ed. 1987; How to Franchise Your Business, 1981, 1987; International Franchising: An Overview, 1985; Franchise Manual, 1988; The Ethics of Franchising, 1988. Add: 110 Woodcock Hill, Kenton, Harrow, Middx. HAB 0JL; or, 22–26 Paul St., London EC2A 4JH, England.

MENDELSON, Morris. American, b. 1922. Economics, Money/-Finance (capital markets). Prof. of Finance, Wharton Sch., Univ. of Pennsylvania, Philadelphia, since 1973 (Assoc. Prof., 1961–73). Member, Intnl. Faculty for Corporate and Capital Market Law, since 1975. *Publs:* (with R.W. Goldsmith and R.E. Lipsey) Studies in the National Balance Sheets of the United States, vol. II, 1963; (with I. Friend, E. Miller, J.R. Longstreet and A.P. Hess) Investment Banking and the New Issue Market, 1967; From Automated Quotes to Automated Trading, 1972; (with S. Robbins) Investment Analysis and Securities Markets, 1976. Add: Finance Dept., Univ. of Pennsylvania, Philadelphia, Pa. 19104–6367, U.S.A.

MENDENHALL, George Emery. American, b. 1916. History, Theology/Religion. Assoc. Prof., 1952–58, and Prof. of Near Eastern Studies, 1958–86, Univ. of Michigan, Ann Arbor; Dir., American Sch. of Oriental Research, Jerusalem, 1965–66, and American Center of Oriental Research, Amman, Jordan, 1975. *Publs:* Law and Covenant in Israel and the Ancient Near East, 1955; The Tenth Generation: The Origins of the Biblical Tradition, 1973; The Syllabic Inscriptions from Byblos, 1985. Add: Dept. of Near Eastern Studies, Univ. of Michigan, Ann Arbor, Mich. 48109, U.S.A.

MENENDEZ, Albert J. American, b. 1942. Politics/Government, Sociology, Theology/Religion, Biography, Documentaries/Reportage. Asst. Ed., and Dir. of Research, Church and State, Americans United for Separation of Church and State, since 1972. *Publs:* The Bitter Harvest: Church and State in Northern Ireland, 1974; Church-State Relations: An Annotated Bibliography, 1975; The Sherlock Holmes Quiz Book, 1975; The American Political Quiz Book, 1976; Religion at the Polls, 1977; Classics of Religious Liberty, 1978; John F. Kennedy: Catholic and Humanist, 1974; The Dream Lives On, 1982; Christmas in the White House, 1983; Religious Conflict in America, 1985; School Prayer and Other Religious Issues in American Education, 1985; The Subject is Murder, 1985; The Road to Rome, 1986; Religion and the U.S. Presidency, 1986; Civil War Novels: An Annotated Bibliography, 1986; The Catholic Novel, 1987, The December Dilemma; Christmas in American Public Life, 1988. Add: 8120 Fenton St., Silver Spring, Md. 20910, U.S.A.

MENUHIN, (Sir) Yehudi. British (b. American), b. 1916. Music. Founder and Artistic Dir., Gstaad, Switzerland Music Festival, since 1957; Founder and Dir., Yehudi Menuhin Music Sch., Surrey, since 1963; Pres., Trinity Coll. of Music, London, since 1971. Artistic Dir., Bath Festival, 1959–68; Joint Artistic Dir., Festival of Windsor, Berks., 1969–72; Pres., Intnl. Music Council, Unesco, 1969–73. *Appearances:* Debut at the age of 7, with San Francisco Orch.; between the ages of 10 and 15, appeared with the New York Symphony Orch., Berlin Symphony Orch., and with other major orchs. of Europe and America; first world concert tour, 1935; has subsequently toured extensively and performed with most of the world's major orchs. and conductors; during World War II gave more than 500 concerts for Armed Forces and Red Cross; first artist to play in liberated Paris, Brussels, Bucharest, Budapest and Antwerp; gave series of concerts in Moscow in 1945 and Israel, 1950; made first tour of Japan, 1951, and of India, 1952; has also toured in Latin America, South Africa, Australia and New Zealand; records for EMI/Angel. Has introduced many contemporary works: Sonata for Violin Alone, by Bela Bartok, and works by William Walton, Ben-Haim, Georges Enesco, Pizzetti, Ernest Bloch, etc. *Publs:* The Violin: Six Lessons With Yehudi Menuhin, 1971; Theme and Variations, 1972; The Violin, 1976; Unfinished Journey (autobiography), 1977; The Music of Man, 1979; (with C. Hope) The King, the Cat, and the Fiddle (for children), 1983; Life Class, 1986. Add: c/o Anglo Swiss Artists Management, 4 Primrose Mews, Sharpleshall St. London NW1 8YW, England.

MERDINGER, Charles (John). American, b. 1918. Engineering/Technology. Chmn., Bd. of Trustees, Sierra Nevada Coll. Career Officer, U.S. Navy Civil Engineer Corps., 1941–70; Pres., Washington Coll., Chestertown, Md., 1970–73; Vice-Pres., Aspen Inst. for Humanistic Studies, Aspen, Colorado, and NYC, 1973–74; Deputy Dir., Scripps Inst. of Oceanography, La Jolla, Calif., 1974–80; Dir., Avco Corp., 1979–85. *Publs:* A History of Civil Engineering, 1963. Add: P.O. Box 7249, Incline Village, Lake Tahoe, Nev. 98450, U.S.A.

MEREDITH, Scott. American, b. 1923. Writing/Journalism, Biography. Literary agent: Pres., Scott Meredith Literary Agency, NYC, since 1942. *Publs:* Writing to Sell, 1950, 3rd ed. 1987; Writing for the American Market, 1960; The Kaufman Circle: The Life and Times of George S. Kaufman and His Friends, 1974; The Science of Gaming, 1974; Louis B. Mayer and His Enemies, 1986; (ed. with Margaret Truman) The Harry S Truman Memoirs, 1988. Add: 845 Third Ave., New York, N.Y. 10022, U.S.A.

MEREDITH, William (Morris, Jr.). American, b. 1919. Poetry, Songs, lyrics and libretti, Translations. Copyboy and Reporter, The New York Times, 1940–41; Resident Fellow in Creative Writing, Princeton, N.J., 1947–48, 1949–50, 1965–66; Assoc. Prof. of English, Univ. of Hawaii, Honolulu, 1950–51; Opera Critic, Hudson Review, NYC, 1955–56; Member of the Dept. from 1955, and Prof. of English, 1965–83, Connecticut Coll., New London; Dir. of Humanities, Upward Bound Prog., 1964–68; Poetry Consultant, Library of Congress, 1978–80. *Publs:* Love Letter from an Impossible Land, 1944; Ships and Other Figures, 1948; The Open Sea and Other Poems, 1958; The Bottle Imp (libretto), 1958; (ed.) Shelley, 1962; The Wreck of the Thresher and Other Poems, 1964; (trans.) Alcools: Poems 1878–1913, by Guillaume Apollinaire, 1964; (ed.) University and College Poetry Prizes, 1960–66, in Memory of Mrs. Fanny Fay Wood, 1966; (ed. with M. Jarrell) Eighteenth Century Minor Poets, 1968; Earth Walk: New and Selected Poems, 1970; Hazard, The Painter, 1976; The Cheek, 1980; Reasons for Poetry, and The Reason for Criticism (lectures), 1982; Partial Accounts, 1987. Add: 6300 Bradley Blvd., Bethesda, Md, 20817, U.S.A.

MERLIN, Christina. *See* HEAVEN, Constance.

MERLIN, David. *See* MOREAU, David Merlin.

MERNE, Oscar James. Irish, b. 1943. Environmental science/Ecology, Natural history, Zoology. Wildlife Officer with Forest and Wildlife Service, Bray, since 1977. Asst. Producer of Weekly Wildlife Prog., RTE Television, Ireland, 1966–68; Head Warden, Wexford Wildfowl Reserve, North Slob, Ireland, 1968–77. *Publs:* Ducks, Geese and Swans, 1974; The Birds of Wexford, 1974; (with Richard Roche) Saltees: Islands of Birds and Legends, 1977; Wading Birds, 1978. Add: Forest & Wildlife Service, Sidmonton Pl., Bray, Co. Wicklow, Ireland.

MERRIAM, Eve. American, b. 1916. Children's fiction, Plays/Screenplays, Poetry, Biography, Essays. Lectr., since 1970. Copywriter, 1939–42; Radio Writer, 1942–46; Moderator of weekly prog. on poetry, WQXR Radio, NYC, 1942–46; Feature Ed., Deb mag., NYC, 1946; Fashion Copy Ed., Glamour mag., NYC, 1947–48; Member of the Staff, Bank Street Coll. of Education, NYC, 1958–60; Teacher, Coll. of the City of New York, 1966–69 *Publs:* Family Circle (verse), 1946; The Real Book about Franklin D. Roosevelt, 1952; The Real Book of Amazing Birds, 1952; Tomorrow Morning: Poems, 1953; Montgomery, Alabama, Money, Mississippi, and Other Places, 1956; Emma Lazarus: Woman with a Torch, 1956; The Double Bed from the Feminine Side (verse), 1958; The Voice of Liberty: The Story of Emma Lazarus, 1959; The Trouble with Love: Poems, 1960; Figleaf: The Business of Being in Fashion, 1960; A Gaggle of Geese (fiction), 1960; Mommies at Work, 1961; There Is No Rhyme for Silver (verse), 1962; Basics: An I-Can-Read Book for Grownups (verse), 1962; Funny Town (verse), 1963; What's in the Middle of a Riddle?, 1963; After Nora Slammed the Door: American Women in the 1960's: The Unfinished Revolution, 1964; What Can You Do with a Pocket?, (fiction), 1964; It Doesn't Always Have to Rhyme (verse), 1964; The Story of Ben Franklin, 1965; Do You Want to See Something? fiction), 1965; Small Fry (fiction), 1965; Don't Think about a White Bear (verse), 1965; Catch a Little Rhyme (verse), 1966; Miss Tibbett's Typewriter fiction), 1966; Andy All Year Round (fiction), 1967; Epaminondas fiction), 1968; Independent Voices (verse), 1968; Man and Woman: The Human Condition, 1968; (with others) Equality, Identity, and Complementarity: Changing Perspectives of Man and Woman, 1968; The Inner City Mother Goose (verse), 1969; The Nixon Poems, 1970; Finding a Poem, 1970; I Am a Man: Ode to Martin Luther King, Jr., 1971; Project 1-2-3 fiction), 1971; Inner City (play), 1971; (ed.) Growing Up Female in America: Ten Lives, 1971; Boys and Girls, Girls and Boys (fiction), 1972; Bam, Zam, Boom: A Building Book, 1972; Out Loud (verse), 1973; (ed. with Nancy Larrick) Male and Female under 18: Frank Comments by Young People about Their Sex Roles Today, 1973; Out of Our Fathers' House (play), 1975; We the Women (television play), 1975; The Club (play), 1976; A Husband's Notes about Her: Fictions, 1976; Rainbow Writing (verse), 1976; AB to Zogg: A Lexicon for Science Fiction and Fantasy Readers, 1977; The Birthday Cow (verse), 1978; Unhurry Harry (fiction), 1979; The Good Life: Lady Macbeth of Westport (play), 1979; At Her Age (play), 1979; Goodnight to Annie (fiction), 1980; Dialogue for Lovers (play), 1980; A Word or Two with You (verse), 1981; Plagues For Our Time (play), 1982; And I Ain't Finished Yet (play),1983; If Only I Could Tell You: Poems for Young Lovers and Dreamers, 1983; The Christmas Box (fiction), 1985; Blackberry Ink, 1985; Fresh Paint (poetry), 1986; The Birthday Door, (fiction), 1986; Halloween ABC (poetry), 1987; You Be Good and I'll Be Night (poetry), 1988; Chortles: New and Selected Word Play Poems, 1989. Add: 101 W. 12th St., New York, N.Y. 10011, U.S.A.

MERRIL, (Josephine) Judith (Grossman). Also wrote with C.M. Kornbluth under joint pseud. Cyril Judd. Canadian, b. 1923. Science fiction/Fantasy. Freelance writer and lectr. since 1949: Documentary Scriptwriter, Canadian Broadcasting Corp.; Commentator and Performer, Dr. Who TV series, TV-Ontario. Research asst. and ghostwriter, 1943–47; Ed., Bantam Books, NYC, 1947–49; Dir., Milford Science Fiction Writers Conference, 1956–61; Writing Teacher, Adult Education Prog., Port Jervis, N.Y., 1963–64; Book Ed., Fantasy and Science Fiction, 1965–69. *Publs:* Shadow on the Hearth, 1950; (ed.) Shot in the Dark, 1950; (ed.) Beyond Human Ken, 1952; (as Cyril Judd) Gunner Cade, 1952; (as Cyril Judd) Outpost Mars, 1952, as Sin in Space, 1956; (ed.) Beyond the Barriers of Space and Time, 1954; (ed.) Human?, 1954; (ed.) Galaxy of Ghouls, 1955, as Off the Beaten Orbit, 1959; (ed.) S-F: The Year's Greatest Science-Fiction and Fantasy 1-6, continued as The Year's Best S-F, 7th-11th Annual, 12 vols., 1956–68, as SF'57-'59, 3 vols., 1957–59, in U.K. as Annual SF and the Best of Sci-Fi, 5 vols., 1965–70; The Tomorrow People, 1960; Out of Bounds (short stories), 1960; (ed.) SF: The Best of the Best, 1967; Daughters of Earth (short stories), 1968; (ed.)

England Swings SF, 1968, in U.K. abridged ed. as The Space-Time Journal, 1972; Survival Ship and Other Stories, 1973; The Best of Judith Merril (short stories), 1976; (ed.) Tesseracts: Canadian S-F, 1985; Daughters of Earth and Other Stories, 1985. Add: 40 St. George St., Toronto Ont M5S 2E4, Canada.

MERRILL, James (Ingram). American, b. 1926. Novels/Short stories, Plays/Screenplays, Poetry. *Publs:* Jim's Book: A Collection of Poems and Short Stories, 1942; The Black Swan, 1946; First Poems, 1951; The Bait (play), 1953; Short Stories (poetry), 1954; The Immortal Husband (play), 1955; The Seraglio (novel), 1957; The Country of a Thousand Years of Peace and Other Poems, 1959, 1970; Selected Poems, 1961; Water Street: Poems, 1962; The Thousand and Second Night, 1963; Violent Pastoral, 1965; The (Diblos) Notebook (novel), 1965; Nights and Days: Poems, 1966; The Fire Screen: Poems, 1969; Two Poems, 1972; Braving the Elements, 1972; The Yellow Pages, 1974; Divine Comedies, 1976; Mirabell: Books of Number, 1978; Scripts for the Pageant, 1980; From the First Nine, 1982; The Changing Light at Sandover, 1982; Marbled Paper, 1982; Santonini: Stopping the Leak, 1982; From the First Nine: Poems 1947–1976, 1982; Souvenirs, 1984; Bronze, 1984; Late Settings, 1985; Recitative, 1986; The Inner Room 1988; Three Poems 1988. Add: 107 Water St., Stonington, Conn. 06378, U.S.A.

MERRILL, Jean (Fairbanks). American, b. 1923. Children's fiction. Feature Ed., Scholastic Mag., 1947–50; Ed., Literary Cavalcade, 1956–57; Assoc. Ed., Bank St. Coll. of Education Publs. Div., NYC, 1964–65. *Publs:* Henry, The Hand-Painted Mouse, 1951; The Woover, 1952; Boxes, 1953; The Tree-House of Jimmy Domino, 1955; The Travels of Marco, 1956; A Song for Gar, 1957; The Very Nice Things, 1959; Blue's Broken Heart, 1960; Shan's Lucky Knife, 1960; Emily Emerson's Moon, 1960; The Superlative Horse, 1961; Tell about the Cowbarn, Daddy, 1963; The Pushcart War, 1964; High, Wide and Handsome, 1964; The Elephant Who Liked to Smash Small Cars, 1967; Red Riding, 1968; (ed.) A Few Flies and I: Haiku by Issa, 1969; The Black Sheep, 1969; Here I Come, Ready or Not!, 1970; Mary, Come Running, 1970; How Many Kids Are Hiding on My Block?, 1970; Please, Don't Eat My Cabin, 1971; The Second Greatest Clown in the World, 1972; The Jackpot, 1972; The Toothpaste Millionaire, 1972; The Bumper Sticker Book, 1973; Maria's House, 1974. Add: Angel's Ark, 29 S. Main St., Randolph, Vt. 05060, U.S.A.

MERRILL, Thomas F. American, b. 1932. Literature. Prof. of English, Univ. of Delaware, Newark. Asst. Prof., Univ. of California at Los Angeles, 1964–66, and DePauw Univ., Greencastle, Ind., 1967–69, rev. ed., 1988; *Publs:* Williams Perkins, 1966; Allen Ginsberg, 1969; rev. ed. 1988; Christian Criticism, 1976; The Poetry of Charles Olson, 1982; Epic God-Talk, 1986. Add: Dept. of English, Univ. of Delaware, Newark, Del. 19711, U.S.A.

MERTON, Robert K(ing). American, b. 1910. Sciences, Sociology. University Prof., Columbia Univ., New York, 1974–79, now Emeritus (Asst. Prof., 1941–44; Assoc. Dir. of Bureau of Applied Social Research, 1942–71; Assoc. Prof., 1944–47; Prof., 1947–63; Giddings Prof. of Sociology, 1963–74). Adjunct Prof., Rockefeller Univ., NYC, since 1979. President, American Sociological Association, 1957; Delegate, U.S.S.R. Academy of Sciences, 1961. *Publs:* Science, Technology, and Society in Seventeenth-Century England, 1938, 1970; (with Marjorie Fiske and Alberta Curtis) Mass Persuasion: The Social Psychology of a War Bond Drive, 1946, 1971; Social Theory and Social Structure, 1949, 1957, 1968; (ed. with Paul F. Lazarsfeld) Continuities in Social Research: Studies in the Scope and Methods of "The American Soldier," 1950; (with Marjorie Fiske and Patricia L. Kendall) The Focused Interview, 1952; (ed. with others) Freedom to Read: Perspective and Program, 1957; (ed. with George G. Reader and Patricia L. Kendall) The Student-Physician: Introductory Studies in the Sociology of Medical Education, 1957; (ed. with Leonard Broom and Leonard S. Cottrell, Jr.) Sociology Today: Problems and Prospects, 1959; (ed. with Robert A. Nisbet) Contemporary Social Problems: An Introduction to the Sociology of Deviant Behavior and Social Disorganization, 1961, 1966, 1976; On the Shoulders of Giants: A Shandean Postscript, 1965; On Theoretical Sociology: Five Essays, Old and New, 1967, 1985; The Sociology of Science: Theoretical and Empirical Investigations, 1973; Sociological Ambivalence and Other Essays, 1976; (ed. with Jerry Gaston and Adam Podgorecki) The Sociology of Science in Europe, 1977; (ed. with others) Toward a Metric of Science: Thoughts Occasioned by the Advent of Science Indicators, 1978; (ed. with James S. Coleman and Peter H. Rossi) Qualitative and Quantitative Social Research: Essays in Honor of Paul F. Lazarsfeld, 1979; The Sociology of Science: An Episodic Memoir, 1979; (ed. with Thaddeus J. Trenn) Genesis and Development of a Scientific Fact, by Ludwick Fleck, 1979; (ed. with Matilda W. Riley) Sociological Traditions from

Generation to Generation: Glimpses of the American Experience, 1980; (ed. with Peter M. Blau) Continuities in Structural Inquiry, 1981; Social Research and the Practicing Professions, 1982. Add: Fayerweather 415, Columbia Univ., New York, N.Y. 10027, U.S.A.

MERWIN, Sam(uel Kimball), Jr. Also writes romance novels as Elizabeth Deare Bennett. American, b. 1910. Mystery/Crime/Suspense, Historical/Romance/Gothic, Science fiction/Fantasy. Reporter, Boston Evening American, 1932–33; New York Bureau Chief, Philadelphia Inquirer, 1936–37; Staff Writer, Country Home, NYC, 1938–39; Sports and Mystery Ed., Standard Mags., 1941–51, and King Size Publs., 1952–53: Ed., Startling Stories, 1945–51, Fantastic Story Mag., 1950–51, Wonder Stories Annual, 1950–51, and Thrilling Wonder Stories, 1951–54; Ed., Fantastic Universe, 1953; Assoc. Ed., Galaxy, 1953–54; Ed., Renown Publs., 1955–56, 1975–79, and Brandon House, 1966–67; also freelance writer, under various pseuds., of SF short stories, screenplays, and TV plays. *Publs:* Murder in Miniatures, 1940; Death in the Sunday Supplement, 1942; The Big Frame, 1943; (with Leo Margulies) The Flags Were Three, 1945; Message from a Corpse, 1945; Knife in My Back, 1945; A Matter of Policy, 1946; Body and Soul (novelization of screenplay), 1947; The House of Many Worlds (science fiction), 1951; The Creeping Shadow, 1952; Killer to Come (science fiction), 1953; The White Widows, 1953, as The Sex War, 1960; (with Guido Orlando) Confessions of a Scoundrel (non-fiction), 1954; Three Faces of Time (science fiction), 1955; The Time Shifters (science fiction), 1971; (as Elizabeth Deare Bennett) Regatta Summer, 1974; (as Elizabeth Deare Bennett) Gower Court Manner, 1975; Chauvinisto (science fiction), 1976.

MERWIN, W(illiam) S(tanley). American, b. 1927. Plays/Screenplays, Poetry, Translations. Playwright-in-Residence, Poet's Theatre, Cambridge, Mass., 1956–57; Poetry Ed., The Nation, NYC, 1962; Assoc., Theatre de la Cite, Lyons, France, 1964–65. *Publs:* A Mask for Janus, 1952; The Dancing Bears, 1954; Green with Beasts, 1956; Favor Island, 1957; Eufemia, adaptation of play by Lope de Rueda, 1958; The Poem of the Cid, 1956; The Drunk in the Furnace, 1960; (ed.) West Wind: Supplement of American Poetry, 1961; The Gilded West, 1961; Turcaret, adaptation of play by Alain Lesage, 1961; The False Confession, adaptation of play by Marivaux, 1961; The Moving Target: Poems, 1963; Yerma, adaptation of play by Garcia Lorca, 1966; The Lice: Poems, 1967; Three Poems, 1968; Selected Translations 1948–1968, 1968; Animae: Poems, 1969; The Carrier of Ladders, 1970; The Miner's Pale Children, 1970; Signs: A Poem, 1971; Chinese Figures: Second Series, 1971; Japanese Figures, 1971; Asian Figures, 1972; Writings to an Unfinished Accompaniment, 1974; The Compass Flower, 1977; Houses and Travellers: A Book of Prose, 1977; Selected Translations 1968–1978, 1978; Feathers from the Hill, 1978; Unframed Originals: Recollections, 1982; Finding the Islands, 1982; Opening the Hand, 1983; Regions of Memory: Uncollected Prose 1949-1982, 1987. Add: c/o Atheneum Publrs., 866 Third Ave., New York, N.Y. 10022, U.S.A.

MESA-LAGO, Carmelo. American, b. 1934. Area studies, Economics, Public/Social Administration. Prof. of Economics since 1976, and Distinguished Service Prof. of Economics and Latin American Studies since 1980, Univ. of Pittsburgh (Asst. Prof., 1967–70; Assoc. Prof., 1970–76; Dir. of the Center for Latin American Studies, 1974–86). Ed., Cuban Studies; Member, Bd. of Eds., Journal of Interamerican Studies and World Affairs, and Caribbean Review. Asst. Prof., Sch. of Law, Univ. of Madrid, 1961–62; Research Assoc., Univ., of Miami, 1962–65; Visiting Prof., Oxford Univ., Fall 1977; Regional Advisor, U.N. Economic Commn. for Latin America, 1983–84. *Publs:* Planificacion de la Seguridad Social, 1959; The Labor Sector and Socialist Distribution in Cuba, 1968; Revolutionary Change in Cuba, 1971; The Labor Force, Employment, Unemployment and Underemployment in Cuba 1898–1970, 1972; Cuba in the 1970's: Pragmatism and Institutionalization, 1974; Comparative Socialist Systems: Essays on Politics and Economics, 1975; Social Security in Latin America, 1978; (co-author) Latin American Studies in Europe, 1979; (co-ed and contrib.) Cuba in the World, 1979; The Economy of Socialist Cuba, 1981; (co-ed. and contrib.) Cuba in Africa, 1982; (ed. and contrib.) The Crisis of Social Security: Latin American Experiences and Lessons, 1985; El desarrollo de la seguridad social en América Latina, 1985. Add: Dept. of Economics, Univ. of Pittsburgh, Pittsburgh, Pa. 15260, U.S.A.

MESERVE, Walter Joseph, Jr. American, b. 1923. Literary criticism/History, Plays, History, Theatre, Biography. Distinguished Prof. of Theatre and English, Graduate Sch., City Univ. of New York, since 1988. Dir., Inst. for American Theatre Studies, 1983–88. *Publs:* (ed.) The Complete Plays of W.D. Howells, 1960; Outline History of American Drama, 1965; (ed.) Discussions of Modern American Drama, 1966; (co-ed.) American Satiric Comedies, 1969; Robert E. Sherwood, 1970; (co-ed.) Modern Drama from Communist China, 1970; (ed.) The Rise of Silas Lapham, by W.D. Howells, 1971; (ed.) Studies in Death of a Salesman, 1972; (co-ed.) Modern Literature from China, 1974; An Emerging Entertainment: The Drama of the American People to 1828, 1977; (co-author) The Revels History of Drama in English VIII: American Drama, 1977; American Drama to 1900: A Guide to Information Sources, 1980; (with Mollie Ann Meserve) Cry Woolf (play), 1982; Heralds of Promise: The Drama of the American People During the Age of Jackson 1829–1849, 1986. Add: Graduate Sch. City Univ. of New York, 33 West 42nd St., New York, N.Y. 10036, U.S.A.

MESSEL, Harry. Canadian, b. 1922. Physics. Prof. of Physics, Head of the Sch. of Physics, and Dir. of the Science Foundn. for Physics, Univ. of Sydney, 1952–87; now Emeritus. Vice-Chmn., Australian SSC (Survival Service Commn.), IUCN (Intnl. Union for the Conservation of Nature); Member, SSC Steering Cttee., and Deputy Chmn. SSC Crocodile Specialist Group. Member, Australian Atomic Energy Commn., 1974–81. *Publs:* (ed. and co-author) Selected Lectures in Modern Physics for School Science Teachers, 1958; Lecture Notes on an Introductory Course in Modern Physics, 1958; (ed. with S. Butler) From Nucleus to Universe, 1960; (ed. and co-author) A Modern Introduction to Physics, 3 vols., 1960–61; (ed. and co-author with S. Butler) Space and the Atom, 1961; (ed. and co-author with S. Butler) A Journey Through Space and the Atom, 1962; (ed. and co-author with S. Butler) The Universe of Time and Space, 1962; (ed. and co-author with S. Butler) Light and Life in the Universe, 1964; (ed. and co-author) Science for High School Students, 1964; (ed. and author with S. Butler) An Introduction to Modern Physics, 1964; (ed. with S. Butler) Space Physics and Radio Astronomy, 1964; (ed. with S. Butler) The Universe and Its Origin, 1964; (ed. and co-author) Time, 1965; (ed. and co-author) Abridged Science for High School Students, 2 vols., 1965; (ed. and co-author) Senior Science for High School Students, 1965; (ed. with S. Butler) Atoms to Andromeda, 1965; (ed. with S. Butler) Apollo and the Universe, 1967; (ed. with S. Butler) Man in Inner and Outer Space, 1968; (ed. with S. Butler) Nuclear Energy Today and Tomorrow, 1969; (with D. Crawford) Electron-Photon Shower Distribution Function, 1970; (ed. with S. Butler) Pioneering in Space, 1970; (ed. with S. Butler) Molecules to Man, 1971; (ed. with S. Butler) Brain Mechanisms and the Control of Behaviour, 1972; (ed. with S. Butler) Focus on the Stars, 1973; (ed. with S. Butler) Solar Energy, 1974; (ed. with S. Butler) Our Earth, 1975; (principal ed. and co-author) Multistrand Senior Science for High School Students, 1975; (ed. with S. Butler) Australian Animals and Their Environment, 1977; (ed.) Energy for Survival, 1979; (ed. and co-author) Tidal Rivers in Northern Australia and their Crocodile Populations, 20 monographs, 1979–87; (ed.) The Biological Manipulation of Life, 1981; Science Update, 1983; (ed.) The Study of Populations, 1985; (ed. and co-author) Highlights in Sciences, 1987. Add: Sch. of Physics, Univ. of Sydney, Sydney, N.S.W. 2006, Australia.

MESSER, Thomas M. American, b. 1920. Art, Biography. Trustee, Guggenheim Foundn., NYC, since 1980. Dir., Roswell Museum, New Mexico, 1949–52, American Fedn. of Arts, NYC, 1952–56, Inst. of Contemporary Art, Boston, 1956–61, Guggenheim Museum, NYC, 1961–88, and Peggy Guggenheim Collection, 1980–88. Adjunct Prof., Harvard Univ., Cambridge, Mass., 1961; Sr. Fellow, Center for Advanced Studies, Wesleyan Univ., Middletown, Conn., 1966, 1971. Pres., Assn. of Art Museum Directors, 1974–75. *Publs:* The Emergent Decade: Latin American Painters and Painting in the 1960's, 1966; Edvard Munch, 1973; Pablo Picasso, 1974; Sixty Works: The Peggy Guggenheim Collection, 1982; Acquisition Priorities, 1983; Munch, 1986. Add: Guggenheim Foundn., 527 Madison Ave., New York, NY 10022, U.S.A.

METCALF, Donald. Australian, b. 1929. Medicine/Health. Head, Cancer Research Unit, Walter and Eliza Hall Inst., Melbourne, since 1965. Member, Scientific Council, Intnl. Agency for Research on Cancer, Lyons, France, 1965–69. *Publs:* The Thymus, 1966; (with M.A.S. Moore) Haemopoietic Cells, 1971; Hemopoietic Colonies, 1977; The Hemopoietic Colony Stimulating Factors, 1984. Add: 268 Union Rd., Balwyn, Vic. 3103, Australia.

METCALF, John (Wesley). Canadian, b. 1938. Novels/Short stories. Teacher, Rosemount High Sch., Montreal, 1962–63, Royal Canadian Air Force Base, Cold Lake, Alberta, 1964–65, at a Catholic comprehensive sch. in England, 1965, and at schools and universities in Montreal, part-time 1966–71; Writer-in-Residence, Univ. of New Brunswick, Fredericton, 1972–73, Loyola Coll., Montreal, 1976, Univ. of Ottawa, 1977, Concordia Univ., Montreal, 1980–81, and Univ. of Bologna, 1985. *Publs:* (ed. with others) Wordcraft 1-5 (textbooks), 5 vols., 1967–77; (ed.) The Razor's Edge, by Maugham, 1967; (ed.) The Flight of the Phoenix, by Elleston Trevor, 1968; (ed.) Daughter of Time, by Josephine Tey, 1968; (ed. with Gordon Callaghan) Rhyme and Reason, 1969; (with C. J. Newman and D. O. Spettigue) New Canadian Writing 1969, 1969; The Lady Who Sold Furniture (short stories), 1970; (ed. with Gordon Callaghan) Salutation, 1970; (ed.) Sixteen by Twelve, 1970; Going Down Slow (novel), 1972; (ed.) The Narrative Voice, 1972; (ed.) Kaleidoscope, 1972; (ed.) The Speaking Earth: Canadian Poetry, 1973; The Teeth of My Father (short stories), 1975; (ed. with Joan Harcourt) Best Canadian Stories, 2 vols., 1976–77; (with John Newlove) Dreams Surround Us: Fiction and Poetry, 1977; (ed. with Clark Blaise) Here and Now, 1977; Girl in Gingham (novel), 1978, as Private Parts: A Memoir, 1980; (ed. with Clark Blaise) Best Canadian Stories, 3 vols., 1978–80; (ed.) Stories Plus, 1979; (ed.) New Worlds, 1980; General Ludd (novel), 1980; (ed.) First Second, Third Impressions, 3 vols., 1980–82; (ed. with Leon Rooke) Best Canadian Stories, 2 vols., 1981–82; (ed.) Making It New, 1982; Selected Stories, 1982; Kicking Against the Pricks (critical essays), 1982; (ed. with Leon Rooke) The New Press Anthology 1-2, 2 vols., 1984–85; Adult Entertainment (short stories), 1986; (ed.) The Bumper Book (essays), 1987; (ed.) Carry On Bumping, 1988; (ed.) Writers in Aspic, 1988; What Is A Canadian Literature?, 1988; (with Leon Rooke) The Macmillan Anthology, 2 vols., 1988–89. Add: P.O. Box 2700, Station D, Ottawa, Ont. K1P 5W7, Canada.

METGE, Alice Joan. New Zealand, b. 1930. Anthropology/Ethnology. Assoc. Prof. of Anthropology, Victoria Univ. of Wellington, 1968–88 (Sr. Lectr., 1965–68). Lectr., Dept. of Univ. Extension, Univ. of Auckland, 1961–64. *Publs:* A New Maori Migration, 1964; The Maoris of New Zealand, 1967, 1976; (with P. Kinloch) Talking Past Each Other, 1978: In and Out of Touch, 1986. Add: 8 Paisley Terr., Karori, Wellington 5, New Zealand.

METZGER, Bruce M(anning). American, b. 1914. Theology/-Religion. George L. Collord Prof. of New Testament, Princeton Theological Seminary, New Jersey, 1964–84, now Emeritus (Teaching Fellow, 1938–40; Instr. in New Testament, 1940–44; Asst. Prof., 1944–48; Assoc. Prof., 1948–54; Prof., 1954–64). Member since 1952, and Chmn. since 1976, Standard Bible Cttee. Member, United Bible Socs. Greek New Testament Cttee., 1962–84. *Publs:* The Saturday and Sunday Lessons from Luke in the Greek Gospel Lectionary, 1944; Lexical Aids for Students of New Testament Greek, 1946, 1955; A Guide to the Preparation of a Thesis, 1950; (compiler) Index of Articles on the New Testament and the Early Church Published in Festschriften, 1951, supplement 1955; (compiler) Annotated Bibliography of the Textual Criticism of the New Testament, 1955; (with E.E. Flack) The Text, Canon, and Principal Versions of the Bible, 1956; An Introduction to the Apocrypha,1957; (compiler) Lists of Words Occurring Frequently in the Coptic New Testament, 1961; (ed. with H.G. May) The Oxford Annotated Bible, 1962; (compiler with I.M. Metzger) The Oxford Concise Concordance to the Revised Standard Version of the Holy Bible, 1962; The Text of the New Testament, Its Transmission, Corruption, and Restoration, 1964; (ed.) The Oxford Annotated Apocrypha, 1965; The New Testament, Its Background, Growth, and Content, 1965; (compiler) Index to Periodical Literature on Christ and the Gospels, 1966; Historical and Literary Studies: Pagan, Jewish, and Christian, 1968; (compiler) Index to Periodical Literature on the Apostle Paul, 1960, 1970; (ed.) New Testament Tools and Studies, vols. I-XI, 1960–87; (ed. with K. Aland, M. Black, and A. Wikgren) The Greek New Testament, 1966, 3rd ed. 1975; A Textual Commentary on the Greek New Testament, 1971; (ed. with H.G. May) The New Oxford Annotated Bible, 1973; The Early Versions of the New Testament: Their Origin, Transmission, and Limitations, 1977; New Testament Studies: Philological, Versional, and Patristic, 1980; Manuscripts of the Greek Bible, 1981; (gen. ed.) The Reader's Digest Condensed Bible, 1982; the Canon of the New Testament: Its Origin, Development, and Significance, 1987. Add: 20 Cleveland Lane, Princeton, N.J. 08540, U.S.A.

METZGER, Michael M. American, b. 1935. Literature. Prof. of German, State Univ. of New York at Buffalo, since 1971 (Asst. Prof., 1963–67; Assoc. Prof., 1967–71). Instr., Univ. of Illinois, Urbana, 1961–63. *Publs:* Lessing and the Language of Comedy, 1966; (with E.A. Metzger) Clara Schumann, 1967; (with E.A. Metzger) Paul Klee, 1967; (ed. with G.F. Schmidt) Der Hofmeister und die Gouvernante, 1969; (with E.A. Metzger) Stefan George, 1972; (ed. with E.A. Metzger) Aegidius Albertinus: Institutiones Vitae Aulicae oder Hof-Schul, 1975; (ed. with E.A. Metzger) Benjamin Neukirchs Anthologie Herrn von Hoffmannswaldau und Anderer Deutschen: Gedichte, 1981, 1987. Add: Dept. of Modern Languages., State Univ. of New York, Buffalo, N.Y. 14260, U.S.A.

METZGER, Stanley D(avid). American, b. 1916. Business/Trade/Industry, International relations/Current affairs, Law. Prof. of Law, Geor-

getown Univ. Law Center, Washington, D.C., since 1960. Asst. Legal Adviser, Economic Affairs, U.S. Dept. of State, 1946–60. Chmn., U.S. Tariff Commn., 1967–69. *Publs:* International Law, Trade and Finance, 1962; Trade Agreement and the Kennedy Round, 1964; (ed. and contrib.) Law of International Trade, 1965, 3rd ed. 1972. Add: 17628 Camino Ancho, San Diego, Calif. 92128, U.S.A.

MEUDT, Edna (Kritz). American, b. 1906. Plays, Poetry. Member of the Faculty, Poetry Workshop, Rhinelander Sch. of Arts, Univ. of Wisconsin Extension Services, since 1965; Ed., The Country Poet, since 1983. Pres., Wisc. Fellowship of Poets, 1952–54 (and 1962–64); Pres., Natl. Fed. of State Poetry Societies, 1960–62; Vice-Pres. for Letters, Wisconsin Academy of Sciences, Arts and Letters, 1973; Chmn., Creative Writing Panel, Wisconsin Arts Bd., 1974. *Publs:* Round River Canticle, 1960; In No Strange Land, 1965; No One Sings Face Down, 1970; (with Gard and O'Brien) A Case of Semantics (play), 1970; The Ineluctable Sea, 1975; Promised Land (play), 1976; (ed.) An Uplands Reader I, 1979, II, 1981; Plain Chant for a Tree, 1980; (with William Wilkie) Iowa County Perspectives, 1981; The Rose Jar (antobiography), 1989. Add: Route 3, Dodgeville, Wisc. 53533, U.S.A.

MEWSHAW, Michael. American, b. 1943. Novels/Short stories, Literary criticism/History (literary journalism). Assoc. Prof. of Literature, Univ. of Texas at Austin, 1973–83. Writer-in-Residence, American Academy in Rome, 1977–78. *Publs:* Man in Motion, 1970; Walking Slow, 1972; The Toll, 1974; Earthly Bread, 1976; (co-ed.) Intro 9, 1978; Land Without Shadow, 1979; Life for Death, 1980; Short Circuit, 1983; Year of the Gun, 1984; Blackballed, 1986; Money to Burn, 1987; Playing Away, 1988. Add: c/o Owen Laster, William Morris Agency, 1350 Sixth Ave., New York, N.Y. 10019, U.S.A.

MEYENDORFF, John. American, b. 1926. History, Philosophy, Social sciences (general), Theology/Religion. Prof. of Church History and Patristics, and Dean, St. Vladimir's Orthodox Theological Seminary, Tuckahoe, N.Y., since 1959; Lectr. in Orthodox Theology, Union Theological Seminary, NYC, since 1962; Prof. of Byzantine and East European History, Fordham Univ., Bronx, N.Y., since 1967. Corresponding Fellow, British Academy; Advisor and Contrib., The Encyclopedia Britanica. Research Fellow, Centre National de la Recherche Scientique, 1953–56; Dumbarton Oaks Fellow, 1957; former Asst. Prof. of Church History, St. Sergius Orthodox Inst., Paris; Lectr. in Byzantine Theology, Harvard Univ., Dumberton Oaks, Washington, D.C., 1960–67; Adjunct Prof. of Religion, Columbia Univ., NYC, 1961–66; N.E.H. Fellow, 1977–78; Acting Dir. of Studies, Center for Byzantine Studies, Harvard Univ., Dumbarton Oaks, 1978; Guggenheim Fellow, 1981. *Publs:* (ed. and trans.) Gregoire Palamas: Defense des Saints Hesychastes, 2 vols., 1959, 1974; St. Gregory Palamas and Orthodox Spirituality, 1959; A Study of Gregory Palamas, 1959; The Orthodox Church, 1960; (with Afanassieff, Koulomzine and Schmemann) The Primacy of Peter in the Orthodox Church, 1961; Orthodoxy and Catholicity, 1965; (ed.) G.P. Fedotov: The Russian Religious Mind, vol. II, 1966; Christ in Eastern Christian Thought, 1969; Marriage in Orthodox Perspective, 1971, 1975; Byzantine Hesychasm: Historical, Theological and Social Problems, 1974; Byzantine Theology, 1979, 1983; Living Tradition, 1979; Byzantium and the Rise of Russia, 1981; The Byzantine Legacy in the Orthodox Church, 1982; Catholicity and the Church, 1984. Add: 575 Scarsdale Rd., Crestwood, N.Y. 10707, U.S.A.

MEYER, Ben Franklin. American, b. 1927. History, Theology/Religion. Prof. of Religious Studies, McMaster Univ., Hamilton, since 1974 (Assoc. Prof., 1969–73). Asst. Prof. of Religion, Grad. Theological Union, Berkeley, Calif., 1965–68. *Publs:* The Man for Others, 1970; The Church in Three Tenses, 1971; The Aims of Jesus, 1979; Self-Definition in Early Christianity, 1980; The Early Christians: Their World Mission and Self-Discovery, 1986; Critical Realism and the New Testament, 1989. Add: Dept. of Religious Studies, McMaster Univ., Hamilton, Ont. L85 4K1, Canada.

MEYER, Charles Robert. American, b. 1920. History, Theology/Religion. Prof. of Systematic Theology, St. Mary of the Lake Seminary, Mundelein, since 1968 (Asst. Prof., 1949–67; Dean of Theologians, 1954–66; Librarian, 1966–67; Assoc. Prof., 1967–69; Dean of Sch. of Theology, 1977–81). *Publs:* The Thomistic Concept of Justifying Contrition, 1949; A Contemporary Theology of Grace, 1971; The Touch of God: A Theological Analysis of Religious Experience, 1972; Man of God: A Study of the Priesthood, 1974; What a Modern Catholic Believes about the Holy Spirit, 1974; Religious Belief in a Scientific Age, 1983. Add: Univ. of St. Mary of the Lake, Mundelein, Ill. 60060, U.S.A.

MEYER, John R(obert). American, b. 1927. Economics. Prof. of Economics, Harvard Univ., Cambridge, Mass., 1959–68, and since 1973. Pres., National Bureau of Economic Research, NYC, 1967–77; Prof. of Economics, Yale Univ., New Haven, Conn., 1968–73; Vice Chmn., Union Pacific Corp., 1982–83. *Publs:* (with E. Kuh) The Investment Decision, 1957; (with others) The Economics of Competition in the Transportation Industries, 1959; (with A. Conrad) The Economics of Slavery, 1964; (with Kain and Wohl) The Urban Transportation Problem, 1965; (with D. Farrar) Managerial Economics, 1970; (with J.M. Quigley) Local Public Finance and the Fiscal Squeeze, 1977; (with others) The Economics of Competition in the Telecommunications Industry, 1979; (with J. A. Gomez-Ibanez) Autos Transit and Cities, 1981; (with others) Airline Deregulation: The Early Experience, 1981; (with C. V. Oster, Jr.) Deregulation and the New Airline Entrepreneurs, 1984; (with C. V Oster, Jr.) Deregulation and the Future of Intercity Passenger Travel, 1987. Add: Dept. of Economics, Havard Univ., Cambridge, Mass. 02138, U.S.A.

MEYER, June. *See* **JORDAN,** June.

MEYER, Lawrence. American, b. 1941. Mystery/Crime/Suspense, International relations/Current affairs. Journalist with The Washington Post since 1969. *Publs:* A Capitol Crime, 1977; False Front, 1979; Israel Now: Portrait of a Troubled Land, 1982. Add: 3311 Ross Pl. N.W., Washington, D.C. 20008, U.S.A.

MEYER, Leonard B. American, b. 1918. Humanities (general), Music. Benjamin Franklin Prof. of Music and Humanities, Univ. of Pennsylvania, Philadelphia, since 1975, Emeritus since 1988. Instr., 1946–50, Asst. Prof., 1951–56, Assoc. Prof., 1956–61, Prof. and Chmn., 1961–70, and Phyllis Fay Horton Distinguished Service Prof., 1972–75, Univ. of Chicago. *Publs:* Emotion and Meaning in Music, 1956; (co-author) The Rhythmic Structure of Music, 1961; Music, the Arts and Ideas, 1967; Explaining Music: Essays and Explorations, 1973; Style and Music: Theory, History, and Ideology. Add: Dept. of Music, Univ. of Pennsylvania, Philadelphia, Pa. 19104, U.S.A.

MEYER, Michael (Leverson). British, b. 1921. Novels, Plays/-Screenplays, Biography, Autobiography/Memoirs, Translations. Lectr. in English Literature, Uppsala Univ., Sweden, 1947–50; Visiting Prof. of Drama, Dartmouth Coll., N.H., 1978, Univ. of Colorado, 1986. *Publs:* (ed. with Sidney Keyes) Eight Oxford Poets, 1941; (ed.) Collected Poems of Sidney Keyes, 1945; (ed.) Minos of Crete, by Sidney Keyes, 1948; (ed.) The End of the Day, by Keith Foottit and Andrew Tod, 1948; The End of the Corridor (novel), 1951; (trans.) The Long Ships, by Frans G. Bengtsson, 1954; (trans.) Brand, by Ibsen, 1960; (trans.) The Lady from the Sea, 1960; (trans.) John Gabriel Borkman, 1960; (trans.) When We Dead Awaken, 1960; (trans.) The Master Builder, 1961; (trans.) Little Eyolf, 1961; (trans.) The Wild Duck, 1962; (trans.) Hedda Gabler, 1962; (trans.) Ghosts, 1962; (trans.) Peer Gynt, 1963; (trans.) An Enemy of the People, 1963; (trans.) The Pillars of Society, 1963; (trans.) The Pretenders, 1964; (trans.) Strindberg: The Plays, vol. I, 1964; (trans.) A Doll's House, 1965; (trans.) Rosmersholm, 1966; The Ortolan (play), 1967; Henrik Ibsen, vols., 1967–71; (trans.) Strindberg's A Dream Play, 1973; (trans.) Strindberg: The Plays, vol. II, 1975; Lunatic and Lover (play), 1981; (ed.) Summer Days, 1981; Strindberg (biography), 1985; Ibsen on File, 1985; (trans.) Emperor and Galilean, 1986; File on Strindberg, 1986; Not Prince Hamlet (memoirs), 1989. Add: 4 Montagu Sq., London W1H 1RA, England.

MEYER, Nicholas. American, b. 1945. Mystery/Crime/Suspense, Historical/Romance/Gothic. *Publs:* Target Practice, 1974; The Seven Per-Cent Solution, 1974; The West End Horror, 1976; (with Barry J. Kaplan) Black Orchid, 1978; Confessions of a Homing Pigeon, 1981. Add: c/o Bloom and Dekom, 9255 Sunset Blvd., Los Angeles, Calif. 90069, U.S.A.

MEYEROWITZ, Patricia. American (b. British), b. 1933. Short stories, Art, Literature. Self-employed artist. *Publs:* Jewelry and Sculpture Through Unit Construction, 1967; (ed.) Gertrude Stein: Writings and Lectures 1909–1945, 1967; And Little Child: Stories of Anyone, 1982. Add: P.O. Box 8, Easton, Pa. 18044, U.S.A.

MEYERS, Jeffrey. American, b. 1939. Art, Literature. Prof. of English, Univ. of Colorado, Boulder (on staff since 1975). Taught at Univ. of California, Los Angeles, 1963–65, Univ. of Maryland, Overseas Div., 1965–66, Tufts Univ., Boston, 1967–71, Univ. of Kent, Canterbury, 1979–80, and Univ. of Massachusetts, Amherst, 1982–83; in rare books dept., Christie's, London, 1974. *Publs:* Fiction and the Colonial Experience, 1973; The Wounded Spirit: A Study of Seven Pillars of Wisdom, 1973; T.E. Lawrence: Bibliography, 1974; A Reader's Guide to George Orwell, 1975; (ed.) George Orwell: The Critical Heritage, 1975; Painting and the Novel, 1975; Catalogue of the Library of the Late Siegfried Sassoon, 1975; A Fever at the Core, 1976; George Orwell: An Annotated Bibliography of Criticism, 1977; Homosexuality and Literature 1890–1930, 1977; Married to Genius, 1977; Katherine Mansfield: A Biography, 1978; The Enemy: A Biography of Wyndham Lewis, 1980; Wyndham Lewis: A Revaluation, 1980; (ed.) Hemingway: The Critical Heritage, 1982; D.H. Lawrence and the Experience of Italy, 1982; Disease and the Novel 1860–1960, 1984; The Craft of Literary Biography, 1985; D. H. Lawrence and Tradition, 1985; (ed.) Wyndham Lewis, by Roy Campbell, 1985; Hemingway: A Biography, 1985; The Legacy of D. H. Lawrence, 1987; Manic Power: Robert Lowell and His Circle, 1987; Robert Lowell: Interviews and Memoirs, 1988; T.E. Lawrence: Soldier, Writer, Legend, 1989; The Biographer's Art, 1989; Graham Greene: A Revaluation, 1989; The Spirit of Biography, 1989. Add: English Dept., Univ. of Colorado, Boulder, Colo. 80309, U.S.A.

MEYERS, Susan. American, b. 1942. Children's fiction. *Publs:*Melissa Finds a Mystery, 1966; The Cabin on the Fiord, 1968; The Mysterious Bender Bones, 1970; The Truth about Gorillas, 1980; Pearson, A Harbor Seal Pup, 1980; P.J. Clover, Private Eye, 3 vols., 1981–88. Add: c/o Dutton, 2 Park Ave., New York, N.Y. 10016, U.S.A.

MEZEY, Robert. American, b. 1935. Poetry, Translations. Prof. of English and Poet-in-Residence, Pomona Coll., Claremont, Calif., since 1976. Instr., Western Reserve Univ., Cleveland, 1963–64, and Franklin and Marshall Coll., Lancaster, Pa., 1965–66; Asst. Prof., Fresno State Univ., California, 1967–68; Assoc. Prof., Univ. of Utah, Salt Lake City, 1973–76. *Publs:* Berg Goodman Mezey: Poems, 1957; The Wandering Jew, 1960; The Lovemaker: Poems, 1961; White Blossoms: Poems, 1965; (trans.) The Mercy of Sorrow, by Uri Zri Greenberg, 1965; Favors, 1968; (ed. with S. Berg) Naked Poetry: Recent American Poetry in Open Forms, 1969; The Book of Dying: Poems, 1970; Last Words: For John Lawrence Simpson 1896–1969, 1970; The Door Standing Open: New and Selected Poems 1954–1969. 1970; (ed. and trans.) Poems from the Hebrew, 1973; Couplets, 1976; Small Song, 1979; Selected Translations, 1981; Evening Wind (poems), 1987; (trans.) Tungsten, 1988. Add: Dept. of English, Pomona Coll., Claremont, Calif. 91711, U.S.A.

MICHAEL, I(an) D(avid) L(ewis). Also writes as David Serafin. British, b. 1936. Mystery fiction, Literature. Fellow, Exeter Coll., Oxford, and King Alfonso XIII Prof. of Spanish Studies, Oxford Univ., since 1982, Asst. Lectr., 1957–60, Lectr., 1960–69, and Sr. Lectr., 1969–70, Univ. of Manchester; Prof. of Spanish and Head of Dept., 1971–82, and Deputy Dean, Faculty of Arts, 1975–77, 1980–82, Univ. of Southampton. *Publs:* The Treatment of Classical Material in the Libro de Alexandre, 1970; Spanish Literature and Learning to 1474: A Companion to Spanish Studies, 1973, 3rd ed. 1977; The Poem of the Cid, 1975; Poema de Mio Cid, 1976; Gwyn Thomas, 1977; (co-ed.) Medieval and Renaissance Studies in Honour of Robert Brian Tate, 1986; as David Serafin: Saturday At Glory, 1979; Madrid Underground, 1982; Christmas Rising 1982; The Body in Cadiz Bay, 1985; Port of Light, 1987; The Angel of Torremolinos, 1988. Add: Exeter College, Oxford, OX1 3DP, England.

MICHAELS, Barbara. Pseud. for Barbara (Louise) G(ross) Mertz; also writes mystery-romance as Elizabeth Peters. American, b. 1927. Mystery/Crime/Suspense, Historical/Romance/Gothic, Archaeology/Antiquities. Egyptologist. *Publs:* (as Barbara G. Mertz) Temples, Tombs, and Hieroglyphs: The Story of Egyptology, 1964, 1978; (as Barbara G. Mertz) Red Land, Black Land: The World of the Ancient Egyptians, 1966, 1978; The Master of Blacktower, 1966; Sons of the Wolf, 1967; Ammie, Come Home, 1968; (as Elizabeth Peters) The Jackal's Head, 1968; (as Barbara G. Mertz, with Richard Mertz) Two Thousand Years in Rome, 1968; Prince of Darkness, 1969; (as Elizabeth Peters) The Camelot Caper, 1969; The Dark on the Other Side, 1970; (as Elizabeth Peters) The Dead Sea Cipher, 1970; (as Elizabeth Peters) The Night of Four Hundred Rabbits, 1971, in U.K. as Shadows in the Moonlight, 1975; (as Elizabeth Peters) The Seventh Sinner, 1972; Greygallows, 1972; The Crying Child, 1973; Witch, 1973; (as Elizabeth Peters) Borrower of the Night, 1973; House of Many Shadows, 1974; (as Elizabeth Peters) The Murders of Richard III, 1974; The Sea King's Daughter, 1975; (as Elizabeth Peters) Crocodile on the Sandbank, 1975; Patriot's Dream, 1976; (as Elizabeth Peters) Legend in Green Velvet, 1976, in U.K. as Ghost in Green Velvet, 1977; Wings of the Falcon, 1977; (as Elizabeth Peters) Devil-May-Care, 1977; Wait for What Will Come, 1978; (as Elizabeth Peters) Street of the Five Moons, 1978; The Walker in Shadows, 1979; (as Elizabeth Peters) Summer of the Dragon, 1979; (as Elizabeth Peters) The Love Talker, 1980; The Wizard's Daughter, 1980; (as Elizabeth Peters) The Curse of the Pharaohs, 1981; Someone in the House, 1981; (as Elizabeth

Peters) The Copenhagen Connection, 1982; Black Rainbow, 1982; (as Elizabeth Peters) Silhouette in Scarlet, 1983; Here Stay, 1983; (as Elizabeth Peters) Die for Love, 1984; The Grey Beginning, 1984; (as Elizabeth Peters) The Mummy Case, 1985; Be Buried in the Rain, 1985; (as Elizabeth Peters) Lion in the Valley, 1986; Shattered Silk, 1986; Trojan Gold, 1987; (as Elizabeth Peters) Search the Shadows, 1987; Deeds of the Disturber, 1988; (as Elizabeth Peters) Smoke and Mirrors, 1989. Add: c/o Dominick Abel Literary Agency, 498 West End Ave., New York, N.Y. 10024, U.S.A.

MICHAELS, Dale. *See* **RIFKIN**, Shepard.

MICHAELS, Fern. Joint Pseudonym for Roberta Anderson, b. 1942, and Mary Kuczkir, b. 1933. Americans. Novels, Historical/Romance. Free-lance writers. *Publs:* romance novels—Pride and Passion, 1975; Vixen in Velvet, 1976; Captive Passions, 1977; Valentina, 1978; Captive Embraces, 1979; Captive Splendors, 1980; The Delta Ladies, 1980; Golden Lasso, 1980; Sea Gypsy, 1980; Beyond Tomorrow, 1981; Captive Innocence, 1981; Whisper My Name, 1981; Without Warning, 1981; Nightstar, 1982; Paint Me Rainbows, 1982; Wild Honey, 1982; All She Can Be, 1983; Free Spirit, 1983; Tender Warrior, 1983; Cinders to Satin, 1984; Texas Rich, 1985; Ever the Empire, 1986; To Taste the Wine, 1987; Texas Fury, 1989; Texas Heat, 1986; others—Panda Bear Is Critical (novel), 1982; other by Mary Kuczkir—My Dish Towel Flies at Half Mast, 1979. Add: c/o Ballantine Books, Inc., 201 E. 50th St., New York, N.Y. 10022, U.S.A.

MICHAELS, Kristin. *See* **WILLIAMS**, Jeanne.

MICHAELS, Leonard. American, b. 1933. Novels/Short stories. Prof. of English, Univ. of California, Berkeley, since 1970 (Asst. Prof., Univ. of California at Davis, 1967–69). Ed., University Publishing; Corresp. Ed., Partisan Review. *Publs:* Going Places, 1969; I Would Have Saved Them If I Could, 1975; The Men's Club, 1981. Add: 438 Beloit Ave., Kensington, Calif. 94708, U.S.A.

MICHAELS, Steve. *See* **AVALLONE**, Michael.

MICHEL, Milton Scott. American, b. 1916. Novels/Short stories, Mystery/Crime/Suspense, Plays/Screenplays. *Publs:* The X-Ray Murders, 1942; Sweet Murders, 1943; The Black Key, 1945; The Psychiatric Murders, 1946; Dear Dead Harry!, 1947; Angels Kiss Me (play), 1950; Rise by Sin (play), 1952; Sixth Finger in a Five Finger Glove (play), 1959; The Murder of Me (play), 1962; Journey into Limbo, 1962. Add: 80 Broome Ave., Atlantic Beach, N.Y. 11509, U.S.A.

MICHELSON, William Michael. Canadian, b. 1940. Architecture, Geography, Sociology, Urban studies. Prof. of Sociology, Univ. of Toronto, since 1972 (Asst. Prof., 1966–68; Assoc. Prof., 1968–72; Assoc. Dir., Centre for Urban and Community Studies, 1973–80). Instr., 1964–65, and Asst. Prof. of Sociology, 1965–66; Princeton Univ., New Jersey; Prof. of Social Ecology, Univ. of California at Irvine, 1980–84. *Publs:* Man and His Urban Environment: A Sociological Approach, 1970; Behavioral Research Methods in Environmental Design, 1974; Contemporary Topics in Urban Sociology, 1977; Environmental choice, Human Behavior, and Residential Satisfaction, 1977; Public Policy in Temporal Perspective, 1978; The Child in the City, 2 vols., 1979; From Sun to Sun: Daily Obligations and Community Structure in the Lives of Employed Women and their Families, 1985; Methods in Environmental and Behavioral Research, 1987. Add: Center for Urban and Community Studies, Univ. of Toronto, 455 Spadina Ave., Toronto, Ont. M5S 2G8, Canada.

MICHENER, James A(lbert). American, b. 1907. Novels/Short stories, Art, Social commentary/phenomena. Member U.S. Advisory Bd. for Intnl Broadcasting, Washington, D.C., since 1983. Master, Hill Sch., Pottstown, Pa., 1929–31, and George Sch., Newtown, Pa., 1934–36; Prof., Univ. of Northern Colorado, Greeley, 1936–40; Visiting Prof., Harvard Univ., Cambridge, Mass., 1940–41; Assoc. Ed., Macmillan Co. Inc., publrs., NYC, 1941–49; Secty., Pennsylvania Constitution Convention, 1967–68. *Publs:* (ed.) The Future of the Social Sciences: Proposals for an Experimental Social Studies Curriculum, 1939; (with H. Long) The Unit in the Social Sciences, 1940; Tales of the South Pacific, 1947; The Fires of Spring (novel), 1949; Return to Paradise (short stories), 1951; The Voice of Asia, 1951; The Bridge at Toko-Ri (novel), 1953; Sayonara (novel), 1954; The Floating World, 1954; (with A. Grove Day) Rascals in Paradise, 1957; The Bridge at Andau (novel), 1957; Selected Writings, 1957; (ed.) Sketch-Books, by Hokusai, 1958; Japanese Prints from the Early Masters to the Moderns, 1959; Hawaii (novel), 1959; Report of

the County Chairman, 1961; Caravans (novel), 1963; The Source (novel), 1965; Iberia: Spanish Travels and Reflections, 1968; The Modern Japanese Print: An Appreciation, 1968; Presidential Lottery: The Reckless Gamble in Our Electoral System, 1969; The Quality of Life, 1970; Facing East: A Study of the Art of Jack Levine, 1970; The Drifters (novel), 1971; Kent State: What Happened and Why, 1971; (ed.) Firstfruits: A Harvest of Twenty-Five Years of Israeli Writing, 1973; A Michener Miscellany 1950–1970, 1973; Centennial (novel), 1974; About "Centennial": Some Notes on the novel, 1974; Sports in America, 1976; Chesapeake (novel), 1978; The Covenant, 1980; Space, 1982; Poland, 1983; Texas, 1985; Legacy (novel), 1987; Alaska (novel), 1988; Journey (novel), 1989. Add: P.O. Box 125, Pipersville, Pa. 18947, U.S.A.

MICHIE, James. British, b. 1927. Poetry, Translations. Dir., The Bodley Head, publrs., London. Formerly, Lectr. at London Univ. *Publs:* (ed. with Kingsley Amis) Oxford Poetry 1949, 1949; Possible Laughter, 1959; (trans.) The Odes of Horace, 1964; (trans.) The Poems of Catullus: A Bilingual Edition, 1969; (trans.) The Epigrams of Martial, 1973; (ed.) The Bodley Head Book of Longer Short Stories (in U.S. as The Book of Longer Short Stories), 1974; (trans.) Selected Fables, by La Fontaine, 1979; (trans. with Colin Leach) The Helen of Euripides, 1981; New and Selected Poems, 1983. Add: c/o The Bodley Head., 32 Bedford Sq., London WC1B 3EL, England.

MICKEL, Emanuel J., Jr. American, b. 1937. Literature. Prof., Indiana Univ., Bloomington, since 1973 (Assoc. Prof., 1968–73). Asst. Prof., Univ. of Nebraska, Lincoln, 1965–67. *Publs:* The Artificial Paradises in French Literature, vol. I, 1969; (ed. with R.T. Cargo) Studies in Honor of Alfred J. Engstrom, 1972; Marie de France, 1974; (with Jan Nelson) The Old French Crusade Cycle, vol. I, 1977; Eugene Fromentin, 1981. Add: c/o Twayne, 70 Lincoln St., Boston, Mass. 02111, U.S.A.

MICKOLUS, Edward (Francis). American, b. 1950. International relations/Current affairs, Politics/Government. Pres., Vinyard Software, since 1984. Pres. and Chmn. of the Bd. of Dirs., National Collegiate Conference Assn., 1972–74. *Publs:* ITERATE: International Terrorism: Attributes of Terrorist Events (data codebook), 1976; Annotated Bibliography on International and Transnational Terrorism, 1976, 1979; The Literature of Terrorism: A Selectively Annotated Bibliography, 1980; Transnational Terrorism: A Chronology of Events 1968–1979, 1980; Combatting International Terrorism: A Quantitative Analysis, 1981; International Terrorism: Attributes of Terrorist Events 1968–1977: ITERATE II Data Codebook, 1982; (ed. with P.A. Flemming) Terrorism 1980-1987: A Selectively Annotated Bibliography, 1988; (with others) International Terrorism in the 1980's: A Chronology of Events, Vol. I, 1988. Add: c/o Greenwood Press, Inc., 88 Post Rd. W., Box 5007, Westport, Conn. 06887, U.S.A.

MIDDLEBROOK, Martin. British, b. 1932. History. *Publs:* The First Day on the Somme, 1971; The Nuremberg Raid, 1973; Convoy, 1976; Battleship, 1977; The Kaiser's Battle, 1978; (ed.) The Bruckshaw Diaries, 1979; The Battle of Hamburg, 1980; The Peenemünde Raid, 1982; The Schweinfurt-Regensburg Mission, 1983; The Bomber Command War Diaries, 1985; Operation Corporate, 1985; (ed.) The Everlasting Arms, 1988; The Berlin Raids, 1988; The Fight for the "Malvimas," 1989. Add: 48 Linden Way, Boston, Lincs. PE21 9DS, England.

MIDDLETON, (John) Christopher. British, b. 1926. Poetry, Essays, Translations. Prof. of Germanic Languages and Literature, Univ. of Texas at Austin, since 1966. Lectr. in English, Univ. of Zurich, 1952–55; former Sr. Lectr. in German, King's Coll., Univ. of London. *Publs:* Torse 3: Poems 1949–1961, 1962; (ed. and trans. with M. Hamburger) Modern German Poetry 1910–1960: An Anthology with Verse Translations, 1963; (with David Holbrook and David Wevill) Penguin Modern Poets 4, 1963; the Metropolitans (libretto), 1964; Nonsequences: Selfpoems, 1965; (ed. and trans. with W. Burford) the Poet's Vocation: Selections from the Letters of Holderlin, Rimbaud, and Hart Crane, 1967; (ed.) German Writing Today, 1967; (ed.) Selected Poems, by Georg Trakl, 1968; Our Flowers and Nice Bones, 1969; Die Taschenelefant: Satire, 1969; The Fossil Fish: 15 Micro-poems, 1970; Briefcase History: 9 Poems, 1972; Fractions for Another Telemachus, 1974; The Lonely Suppers of W. V. Balloon, 1975; Eight Elementary Inventions, 1976; Pataxanadu and Other Prose, 1977; (co-trans.) In the Egg and Other Poems, by Günter Grass, 1977; Bolshevism in Art and Other Expository Writings, 1978; Carminalenia (stories), 1980; (ed. and trans.) Robert Walser: Selected Poems, 1982; The Pursuit of the Kingfisher (essays), 1983; III Poems, 1983; (ed. and trans.) Goethe, Selected Poems, 1983; Two Horse Wagon Going By, 1986; Selected Writings, 1989. Add: Dept. of German, Univ. of Texas, Austin, Tex. 78712, U.S.A.

MIDDLETON, Drew. American, b. 1913. International relations/Current affairs, Military/Defense, Politics/Government. Military Corr., New York Times, since 1970 (Chief Corresp. to USSR, 1946–47; Germany, 1947–53; London, 1953–63; Paris, 1963–65; and the UN, 1965–68; European Affairs Corr., 1968–70). *Publs:* Our Share of the Night, 1946; The Struggle for Germany, 1949; The Defense of Western Europe, 1952; These Are the British, 1957; The Sky Suspended, 1960; The Supreme Choice, 1963; The Atlantic Community, 1965; Retreat from Victory, 1973; Where Has Last July Gone?, 1974; Can America Win the Next War?, 1975; Submarine, 1976; The Duel of the Giants: China and Russia in Asia, 1978; Crossroads of Modern Warfare, 1983. Add: c/o New York Times, 229 W. 43rd Street, New York, N.Y. 10036, U.S.A.

MIDDLETON, O(sman) E(dward). New Zealander, b. 1925. Novels/Short stories, Children's fiction, Poetry. *Publs:* Six Poems, 1951; Short Stories, 1953; The Stone and Other Stories, 1959; A Walk on the Beach, 1964; From the River to the Tide, 1964; The Loners, 1972; Selected Stories, 1975; Confessions of an Ocelot and Not for a Seagull, 1979. Add: 20 Clifford St., Dunedin, New Zealand.

MIDDLETON, Stanley. British, b. 1919. Novels/Short stories. Head of the Dept. of English, High Pavement Coll., Nottingham, 1958–83; Judith E. Wilson Visiting Fellow, Emmanuel Coll., Cambridge, 1982–83. *Publs:* Short Answer, 1958; Harris's Requiem, 1960; A Serious woman, 1961; The Just Exchange, 1962; Two's Company, 1963; Him They Compelled, 1964; Terms of Reference, 1966; The Golden Evening, 1968; Wages of Virtue, 1969; Apple of the Eye, 1970; Brazen Prison, 1971; Cold Gradations, 1972; Holiday, 1974; Distractions, 1975; Still Waters, 1976; Ends and Means, 1977; Two Brothers, 1978; In a Strange Land, 1979; The Other Side, 1980; Blind Understanding, 1982; Entry into Jerusalem, 1982; The Daysman, 1984; Valley of Decision, 1985; An After Dinner's Sleep, 1986; After a Fashion, 1987; Recovery, 1988; Vacant Places, 1989. Add: 42 Caledon Rd., Sherwood, Nottingham NG5 2NG, England.

MIDWINTER, Eric (Clare). British, b. 1932. Education, Sport, Biography. Ageing Dir., Centre for Policy on Ageing, since 1980. Co-Dir., Advisory Centre for Education, Cambridge; Educational Consultant, Home Office Community Development Projects. Teacher, lectr., and deputy principal in colls. in Manchester, Newcastle, and Liverpool, 1956–68; Dir. of the Liverpool Educational Priority Area Project, 1968–72; Dir. of Priority, Centre for Urban Community Education, Liverpool, 1972–75; Head of the Public Affairs Unit, National Consumer Council, London, 1975–80. *Publs:* Victorian Social Reform, 1968; Social Administration in Lancashire 1830–1860, 1969; Nineteenth Century Education, 1970; Old Liverpool, 1971; Projections: An Education Priority Project at Work, 1972; Social Environment and the Urban School, 1972; Priority Education, 1972; Patterns of Community Education, 1973; Education and the Community, 1975; Education for Sale, 1977; Make 'em Laugh: Famous Comedians and Their World, 1978; Schools in Society, 1980; W.G. Grace: His Life and Times, 1981; Age is Opportunity: Education and Older People, 1982; Mutual Aid Universities, 1984; The Wage of Retirement: The Case for a New Pensions Policy, 1985; Fair Game: Myth and Reality in Sport, 1986; Caring for Cash: The Issue of Private Domiciling, 1986; Polls Apart: Older Voters at the 1987 General Election, 1987; Retired Leisure: Four Ventures in Post-Work Activity, 1987; The Lost Seasons, 1987; New Design for Old: Function, Style and Older People, 1988. Add: Centre for Policy on Ageing, 25/31 Ironmonger Row, London EC1V 3QP, England.

MIEL, Alice Marie. American, b. 1906. Education, Human relations. Prof. of Education, Teachers Coll., Columbia Univ., NYC, 1945–71. *Publs:* (with G.R. Koopman and J.P. Misner) Democracy in School Administration, 1943; Changing the Curriculum: A Social Process, 1946; (ed. with K. Wiles) Toward Better Teaching, 1949; (with P. Brogan) More Than Social Studies, 1957; (ed. and co-author) Creativity in Teaching: Invitations and Instances, 1961; (with A. Lewis) Supervision for Improved Instruction: New Challenges, New Responses, 1972. Add: 1649 N.W. 19th Circle, Gainesville, Fla. 32605, U.S.A.

MIELE, Angelo. American (born Italian), b. 1922. Air/Space topics (aerospace engineering, applied mathematics). Prof. of Aerospace Sciences and Mathematical Sciences, Rice Univ., Houston, since 1964. Assoc. Ed., Journal of the Astronautical Sciences, Optimal Control Application and Methods, and Applied Mathematics and Computation; Ed.-in-Chief, Journal of Optimization Theory and Applications; Ed., Mathematical Concepts in Science and Engineering series, Plenum Publishing Corp., NYC. Research Asst. Prof. of Aeronautical Engineering, Polytechnic Inst. of Brooklyn, N.Y. 1952–55; Prof. of Aeronautical En-

gineering, Purdue Univ., Lafayette, Ind., 1955–59; Dir. of Astrodynamics and Flight Mechanics, Boeing Scientific Research Labs., 1959–64; Visiting Prof. of Aeronautics and Astronautics, Univ. of Washington, Seattle, 1961–64. *Publs:* Flight Mechanics, 1962; (ed.) Theory of Optimum Aerodynamic Shapes, 1965. Add: Dept. of Mechanical Engineering, Rice Univ., Houston, Tex. 77251, U.S.A.

MIERNYK, William Henry. American, b. 1918. Economics. Benedum Prof. of Economics, West Virginia Univ., Morgantown, 1965–87, now Emeritus. Prof. of Economics, Northeastern Univ., Boston, 1952–62, and Univ. of Colorado, Boulder, 1962–65. *Publs:* Inter-Industry Labor Mobility, 1955; Trade Unions in the Age of Affluence, 1962; The Economics of Labor and Collective Bargaining, 1965, 1973; The Elements of Input-Output Analysis, 1965; (co-author) Impact of the Space Program on a Local Economy, 1967; (co-author) Simulating Regional Economic Development, 1970; Economics, 1971; (co-author) Air Pollution Abatement and Regional Economic Development, 1974; (co-author) Regional Impacts of Rising Energy Prices, 1978; Regional Analysis and Regional Policy, 1982; The Illusions of Conventional Economics, 1982. Add: 824 Price St., Morgantown, W. Va. 26505, U.S.A.

MIHANOVICH, Clement Simon. American, b. 1913. Sociology. Prof. of Sociology, St. Louis Univ., 1947–81, now Emeritus (Instr., 1938–42; Dir. of the Dept. of Sociology, 1940–64; Asst. Prof., 1942–45; Assoc. Prof., 1945–47). *Publs:* Principles of Juvenile Delinquency, 1950; Current Social Problems, 1950; (ed. and contrib.) Marriage and the Family, 1952; (ed. and contrib.) Social Theorists, 1953; (ed. and contrib.) Papal Pronouncements on Marriage and the Family: From Leo XIII to Pius XII, 1955; (ed. and contrib.) Glossary of Sociological Terms, 1957; (ed. and contrib.) A Guide to Catholic Marriage, 1963; (ed. and contrib.) Enciclopedia Practica del Matrimonio e della Familia, 1963; (co-ed. and contrib.) International Manual on the European Economic Community, 1963; (ed. and contrib.) Introduction to Futures Studies, 1975. Add: 6214 Devonshire, St. Louis, Mo. 63109, U.S.A.

MIKHAIL, Edward H. Canadian, b. 1928. Literature. Prof. of English Literature, Univ. of Lethbridge, Alta., since 1972 (Assoc. Prof. of English, 1966–72). Lectr. and Asst. Prof., Univ. of Cairo, 1949–66. *Publs:* The Social and Cultural Setting of the 1890's, 1969; John Galsworthy the Dramatist, 1971; Comedy and Tragedy: A Bibliography of Criticism, 1972; Sean O'Casey: A Bibliography of Criticism, 1972; A Bibliography of Modern Irish Drama 1899–1970, 1972; Dissertations on Anglo-Irish Drama, 1973; (co-ed.) The Sting and the Twinkle: Conversations with Sean O'Casey, 1974; J.M. Synge: A Bibliography of Criticism, 1975; Contemporary British Drama 1950–1976; An Annotated Critical Bibliography, 1976; W.B. Yeats: Interviews and Recollections, 1977; J.M. Synge: Interviews and Recollections, 1977; English Drama 1900–1950, 1977; Lady Gregory: Interviews and Recollections, 1977; Oscar Wilde: An Annotated Bibliography of Criticism, 1978; A Research Guide to Modern Irish Dramatists, 1979; Oscar Wilde: Interviews and Recollections, 1979; The Art of Brendan Behan, 1979; Brendan Behan: An Annotated Bibliography of Criticism, 1980; An Annotated Bibliography of Modern Anglo-Irish Drama, 1981; Lady Gregory: An Annotated Bibliography of Criticism, 1982; Brendan Behan: Interviews and Recollections, 1982; Sean O'Casey and His Critics, 1985; The Abbey Theatre, 1988; James Joyce: Interviews and Recollections, 1989. Add: 6 Coachwood Point W., Lethbridge, Alta. T1K 6B9, Canada.

MIKLOWITZ, Gloria D. American, b. 1927. Children's fiction, Children's non-fiction. Vice-Pres., P.E.N., Center USA West; Dir., California Writers Guild; Instr., Writers Digest Sch. *Publs:* Barefoot Boy, 1964; The Zoo That Moved, 1968; (with W.A. Young) The Zoo Was My World, 1969; The Parade Starts at Noon, 1970; The Marshmallow Caper, 1971; Sad Song, Happy Song, 1973; Turning Off, 1973; A Time to Hurt, A Time to Heal, 1974; Harry S. Truman, 1975; Paramedic Emergency, 1977; Nadia Comaneci, 1977; Runaway, 1977; Earthquake, 1977: Unwed Mother, 1977; (with Peter Desberg) Riddles for Scary Nights, 1977; Tracy Austin, 1978; Martin Luther King, Jr., 1978; Save That Raccoon!, 1978; Steve Cauthen, 1978; Did You Hear What Happened to Andrea?, 1979; Roller Skating, 1979; Movie Stunts, 1980; The Love Bombers, 1980; (with Madeleine Yates) Young Tycoons, 1981; Before Love, 1982; Close to the Edge, 1983; Carrie Loves Superman, 1983; The Day the Senior Class Got Married, 1983; The War Between The Classes, 1985; After the Bomb, 1985; Love Story, Take Three, 1986; After the Bomb: Week One, 1987; Secrets Not Meant to Be Kept, 1987; Good-bye Tomorrow, 1987; The Emerson High Vigilantes, 1988; Anything to Win, 1989; Suddenly Super Rich, 1989. Add: 5255 Vista Miguel Dr., La Canada, Calif. 91011, U.S.A.

MILES, Betty. American, b. 1928. Children's fiction, Children's non-fiction, Environmental science/Ecology. *Publs:* A House for Everyone, 1958; The Cooking Book, 1959; What Is the World?, 1959; Having a Friend, 1960; A Day of Summer, 1960; Mr. Turtle's Mystery, 1961; A Day of Winter, 1962; The Feast on Sullivan Street, 1963; (assoc. ed.) The Bank Street Readers, 1965; A Day of Autumn, 1967; Joe Finds a Way, 1969; A Day of Spring, 1970; Just Think!, 1971; Save the Earth!, 1974; The Real Me, 1974; Just the Beginning, 1975; All It Takes Is Practice, 1976; Looking On, 1977; The Trouble with Thirteen, 1979; Maudie and Me and the Dirty Book, 1980; The Secret Life of the Underwear Champ, 1981; I Would If I Could, 1982; Sink or Swim, 1986. Add: 94 Sparkill Ave., Tappan, N.Y. 10983, U.S.A.

MILES, Elton. American, b. 1917. Literature, Mythology/Folklore. Prof. of English, Sul Ross State Univ., Alpine, Tex., 1952–81, now Emeritus (Assoc. Prof., 1949–52; Chmn., Dept. of English, 1949–77; Prof., 1952–81). *Publs:* (ed.) Regional Culture in the Southwest, 1953; (ed.) Lucky Seven: Autobiography of a Cowman, 1957; (ed.) The Way I Heard It, 1959; Southwest Humorists, 1969; Tales of the Big Bend, 1976; H.L. Mencken, 1982; More Tales of the Big Bend, 1988. Add: 505 E. Hendryx, Alpine, Tex. 79830, U.S.A.

MILES, John. *See* **BICKHAM,** Jack M.

MILES, Keith. *See* **TRALINS,**S. Robert.

MILES, Leland. American, b. 1924. Language/Linguistics, Literature, Philosophy, Theology/Religion. Pres., Univ. of Bridgeport, Conn., 1974–87, now Emeritus (Dean, Coll. of Arts and Sciences, 1964–67). Prof. of English, Univ. of Cincinnati, 1960–64; Pres., Alfred Univ., New York, 1967–74. Co-ed., Studies in British History and Culture, 1965–79. *Publs:* Americans Are People, 1956; John Colet and the Platonic Tradition, 1961; Where Do You Stand on Linguistics?, 1964, 1968; (ed.) St. Thomas More's Dialogue of Comfort Against Tribulation, 1966. Add: Tide Mill Landing, Suite 102, 2425 Post Rd., Southport, Conn. 06490, U.S.A.

MILES, (Dame) Margaret. British, b. 1911. Education. Member of the Council, Bedford Coll., Chelsea Coll., Royal Sch. of Art, British Assn. and Inst. of Education. Mistress, Westcliff High Sch., 1935–39, and Badminton Sch., 1939–44; Lectr., Dept. of Education, Univ. of Bristol, 1944–46; Headmistress, Pate's Grammar Sch., Cheltenham, 1946–52, and Mayfield Sch., Putney, London, 1952–73. *Publs:* And Gladly Teach, 1965; Comprehensive Schooling: Problems and Perspectives, 1968. Add: Tanycraig, Pennal, Machynlleth, Powys SY20 9LB, Wales.

MILES, Michael Wade. American, b. 1945. History, Politics/Government. Member, History Dept., Princeton Univ., N.J., since 1979. Member, Faculty of History, Goddard Coll., Plainfield, Vt., 1969–74, and Univ. of North Carolina, Greensboro, 1978–79; Editorial Writer, Greensboro Daily News, 1976–78. *Publs:* The Radical Probe: The Logic of Student Rebellion, 1971; The Odyssey of the American Right, 1980. Add: c/o Oxford University Press, Inc., 200 Madison Ave., New York , N.Y. 10016, U.S.A.

MILFORD, Nancy. American, b. 1938. Biography. Bd. Member, The Author's Guild, since 1972, and Soc. of American Historians, since 1973; Founder-Member, The Writers Room, since 1978. Visiting Appt., Vassar Coll. and Bard Coll., 1983–84. *Publs:* Zelda, 1970. Add: c/o Carl Brandt, 1501 Broadway, New York, N.Y. 10016, U.S.A.

MILGATE, Rodney Armour. Australian, b. 1934. Plays/Screenplays, Poetry, Art. Head, Sch. of Studio Studies, City Art Inst., Sydney. Freelance writer, artist and lecturer. *Publs:* A Refined Look at Existence, 1966; Art Composition: A Contemporary View, 1966; Pictures at an Exhibition (verse), 1980. Add: City Art Institute, P.O. Box 259, Paddington, N.S.W. 2021, Australia.

MILGRAM, Gail Gleason. American, b. 1942. Education. Dir. of Education/Training and Prof., Center of Alcohol Studies, Rutgers Univ., New Brunswick, N.J., since 1971. *Publs:* The Teenager and Smoking, 1972; The Teenager and Sex, 1974; An Annotated Bibliography of Alcohol Education Material, 1975, 1980; Your Career in Education, 1976; Coping with Alcohol, 1980; When and How to Talk with Children About Alcohol and Drugs: A Guide to Parents, 1983; What, When and How to Talk to Students About Alcohol and Other Drugs: A Guide for Teachers, 1986. Add: Center of Alcohol Studies, Rutgers Univ., New Brunswick, N.J. 08903, U.S.A.

MILHAVEN, John Giles. American, b. 1927. Philosophy, Theology/Religion. Prof. of Religious Studies, Brown Univ., Providence, since 1976 (Assoc. Prof., 1970–76). Asst. Prof. of Philosophy, Fordham Univ., NYC, 1961–66; Assoc. Prof. of Pastoral Theology, Woodstock Coll., NYC, 1966–70. *Publs:* Towards a New Catholic Morality, 1970. Add: 20 Penrose Ave., Providence, R.I. 02906, U.S.A.

MILHOUSE, Paul William. American, b. 1910. Theology/Religion, Biography. Bishop, United Methodist Church, since 1960, and Bishop-in-Residence, Oklahoma City Univ., since 1980 (Pastor, 1928–51; Ed., 1951–59; Exec. Secty., 1959–60). *Publs:* Enlisting and Developing Church Leaders, 1946; Come Unto Me, 1946; Except the Lord Build the House, 1949; Doorways to Spiritual Living, 1950; Christian Worship in Symbol and Ritual, 1953; Lift Up Your Eyes, 1955; Laymen in the Church, 1957; At Life's Crossroads, 1959; (ed.) Facing Frontiers, 1960; Philip William Otterbein, Pioneer Preacher, 1968; Nineteen Bishops in the Evangelical United Brethren Church, 1974; Organizing for Effective Ministry, 1980; Theological and Historical Roots of United Methodists, 1980; Oklahoma City University: Miracle at 23rd at Blackwelder, 1984; Detours Into Yesterday, 1984; Turning Dollars into Service, 1987; St. Luke's of Oklahoma City, 1989. Add: 2501 N. Blackwelder, Oklahoma City, Okla. 73106, U.S.A.

MILLAR, George. British, b. 1910. Novels/Short stories, History, Travel/Exploration/Adventure, Autobiography/Memoirs/Personal, Biography. Self-employed farmer since 1962. *Publs:* Maquis (in U.S. as Waiting in the Night), 1945; Horned Pigeon, 1946; My Past Was an Evil River (novel), 1947; Isabel and the Sea, 1948; Through the Unicorn Gates, 1950; A White Boat from England, 1951; Siesta, 1953; Orellana (in U.S. as Crossbowman's Story), 1954; Oyster River, 1963; Horseman, 1970; Bruneval Raid, 1974; Road to Resistance, 1979. Add: Sydling Court, nr. Dorchester, Dorset DT2 9PA, England.

MILLAR, James (Primrose Malcolm). British, b. 1893. Education, History, Public/Social administration. Gen. Secty., National Council of Labour Colleges (Gen. Secty., 1927–66). Ed., Plebs (a Labour monthly), 1947–66. *Publs:* The Trained Mind: Trained for What?, 1925; Education for Emancipation; (with others) We Did Not Fight, 1935; Trade Union Education Today, 1961; The Labour College Movement, 1979. Add: 5 Mount Boone, Dartmouth, Devon, England.

MILLAR, Margaret (Ellis). American, b. 1915. Mystery/Crime/-Suspense, Historical/Romance/Gothic, Autobiography/Memoirs/Personal. Screenwriter, Warner Brothers, Hollywood, Calif., 1945–46. Pres., Mystery Writers of America, 1957–58. *Publs:* The Invisible Worm, 1941; The Weak-Eyed Bat, 1942; The Devil Loves Me, 1942; Wall of Eyes, 1943; Fire Will Freeze, 1944; The Iron Gates, 1945, in U.K. as Taste of Fear, 1950; Experiment in Springtime, 1947; It's All in the Family, 1948; The Cannibal Heart, 1949; Do Evil in Return, 1950; Vanish in an Instant, 1952; Rose's Last Summer, 1952, in U.S. paperback as The Lively Corpse, 1956; Wives and Lovers, 1954; The Beast in View, 1955; An Air That Kills (in U.K. as The Soft Talkers), 1957; The Listening Walls, 1959; A Stranger in My Grave, 1960; How Like an Angel, 1962; The Fiend, 1964; The Birds and Beasts Were There (autobiography), 1968; Beyond This Point Are Monsters, 1970; Ask for Me Tomorrow, 1976; The Murder of Miranda, 1979; Mermaid, 1982; Banshee, 1983; Spider Webs, 1987. Add: 87 Seaview Dr., Santa Barbara, Calif. 93108, U.S.A.

MILLAR, (Sir) Oliver (Nicholas). British, b. 1923. Art. Surveyor of the Queen's Pictures, 1972–88, Emeritus since 1988 (Asst. Surveyor of the King's Pictures, 1947–49, and Deputy Surveyor, 1949–72); Dir. of the Royal Collection, 1987–88. Trustee, National Portrait Gallery, London, since 1972. *Publs:* Gainsborough, 1949; (with M.D. Whinney) English Art 1625–1714, 1957; Rubens's Whitehall Ceiling, 1958; Abraham van der Doort's Catalogue, 1960; Tudor, Stuart, and Early Georgian Pictures in the Collection of HM the Queen, 1963; Zoffany and His Tribuna, 1967; Later Georgian Pictures in the Collection of HM the Queen, 1969; Inventories and Valuations of the King's Goods, 1972; The Queen's Pictures, 1977; and museum exhibition catalogues. Add: Yonder Lodge, Penn, Bucks., England.

MILLAR, (Sir) Ronald (Graeme). British, b. 1919. Plays/Screenplays. Deputy Chmn., Theatre Royal, Haymarket, London, since 1977. *Publs:* Frieda, 1947; Waiting for Gillian (adaptation), 1955; The Bride and the Bachelor, 1958; A Ticklish Business, 1959; The More the Merrier, 1960; The Bride Comes Back, 1960; The Affair (adaptation), 1962; The Affair, The New Men, The Masters: Three Plays Based on the Novels and with a Preface by C.P. Snow, 1964; Robert and Elizabeth (adaptation), 1967; Number 10 (adaptation), 1967; They Don't Grow on Trees, 1969; Abelard and Heloise, 1970; The Case in Question (adaptation), 1975; A Coat of Varnish, 1982. Add: 7 Sheffield Terr., London W8, England.

MILLARD, Alan Ralph. British, b. 1937. Archaeology/Antiquities, Language/Linguistics. Reader in Hebrew and Ancient Semitic Languages, Univ. of Liverpool, since 1985 (Rankin Lectr., 1970–76; Sr. Lectr., 1976–85). Librarian, Tyndale Library for Biblical Research, Cambridge, 1963–70. Ed., Tyndale Bulletin, 1966–80. *Publs:* (reviser) Archaeology Gives Evidence, by A. Rendle Short, 1962; (with W.G. Lambert) Cuneiform Texts from Babylonian Tablets, vol. 46, 1965; Catalogue of the Cuneiform Tablets in the Kouyunijk Collection, Second Supplement, 1968; Atrahasis: The Babylonian Story of the Flood, 1969; (ed.) The Lion Handbook to the Bible, 1973; The Bible B.C.: What Can Archaeology Prove?, 1977; (ed.) The Lion Encyclopaedia of the Bible, 1978, 1986; (with A.A. Assaf and P. Bordreuil) La Statue de Tell Fekherye et son Inscription Bilingue assyro-araméenne, 1983; Treasures from Bible Times, 1985. Add: Sch. of Archaeology and Oriental Studies, Univ. of Liverpool, P.O. Box 147, Liverpool L69 3BX, England.

MILLER, Abraham (H.). American, b. 1940. Law, Politics/Government, Sociology. Prof. of Political Science, Univ. of Cincinnati, since 1971. Asst. Study Dir., Univ. of Michigan Inst. for Social Research, Ann Arbor, 1964–66; Asst. Prof. of Political Science, Univ. of Illinois, Urbana, 1966–68; Asst. Prof. of Sociology, Univ. of California at Davis, 1968–71. *Publs:* (ed. with James McEvoy) Black Power and Student Rebellion, 1969; Terrorism and Hostage Negotiations, 1980; (ed.) Terrorism, the Media and the Law, 1982. Add: Dept. of Political Science, Univ. of Cincinnati, Cincinnati, Ohio 45221-0375, U.S.A.

MILLER, Alan W. American, b. 1926. Theology/Religion. Rabbi, Soc. for the Advancement of Judaism, NYC, since 1961; Psychoanalyst, since 1979. Faculty member, New Sch. for Social Research, NYC, since 1977. Lectr. in Hebrew and Midrash, Leo Baeck Coll., London, 1958–61; Visiting Assoc. Prof. in Professional Skills, Jewish Theological Seminary of America, NYC, 1986–88. *Publs:* God of Daniel S.: In Search of the American Jew, 1969. Add: 15 W. 86th St., New York, N.Y. 10024, U.S.A.

MILLER, Arthur. American, b. 1915. Novels/Short stories, Children's fiction, Plays/Screenplays, Autobiography. Intnl. Pres., P.E.N., London and NYC, 1965–69; Assoc. Prof. of Drama, Univ. of Michigan, Ann Arbor, 1973–74. *Publs:* Situation Normal, 1944; Focus (novel), 1945; All My Sons, 1947; Death of a Salesman, 1949; (adaptor) An Enemy of the People, 1950; The Crucible, 1953; A View from the Bridge, and Memory of Two Mondays: Two One-Act Plays, 1955; Collected Plays, 1957; The Misfits (screenplay and novel), 1961; Jane's Blanket, 1963; After the Fall, 1964; Incident at Vichy, 1961; I Don't Need You Anymore: Stories, 1967; The Price, 1968; (with Inge Morath) In Russia, 1969; The Portable Arthur Miller, 1971; The Creation of the World and Other Business, 1972; Theatre Essays, 1978; (with Inge Morath) Chinese Encounters, 1979; The American Clock, 1980; Collected Plays 2, 1981; (adaptation) Playing For Time, 1981; Two-Way Mirror, 1982; "Salesman" in Beijing, 1984; Danger! Memory!, 1986; Timebends (autobiog.), 1987; Conversations with Arthur Miller, 1987. Add: c/o Kay Brown, ICM, 40 W. 57th St., New York, N.Y. 10019, U.S.A.

MILLER, Charles A. American, b. 1937. Law. Prof., Dept. of Politics, Lake Forest Coll., Illinois, since 1985 (Assoc. Prof., 1974–85). Asst. Prof., Dept. of Social Science, Clark Coll., Atlanta, 1967–70, and Dept. of Politics, Princeton Univ., New Jersey, 1970–74. *Publs:* The Supreme Court and the Uses of History, 1969; A Catawba Assembly, 1973; Isn't That Lewis Carroll?, 1984; Jefferson and Nature: An Interpretation, 1988. Add: Dept. of Politics, Lake Forest Coll., Lake Forest, Ill. 60045, U.S.A.

MILLER, Christian. British, b. 1920. Novels/Short stories. *Publs:* The Champagne Sandwich, 1969; Daisy, Daisy, 1980; A Childhood in Scotland, 1981. Add: The Old Stables, Newtown, Newbury, Berks., England.

MILLER, David. British, b. 1946. Politics/Government. Official Fellow in Social and Political Theory, Nuffield Coll., Oxford, since 1979. Lectr. in Politics, Univ. of Lancaster, 1969–76; Lectr. in Politics, Sch. of Social Studies, Univ. of East Anglia, Norwich, 1976–79. *Publs:* Social Justice, 1976; Philosophy and Ideology in Hume's Political Thought, 1981; (co-ed.) The Nature of Political Theory, 1983; Anarchism, 1984; (ed.) The Blackwell Encyclopaedia of Political Thought, 1987; Market, State and Community: Theoretical Foundations of Market Socialism, 1989. Add: Nuffield Coll., Oxford OX1 1NF, England.

MILLER, Donald George. American, b. 1909. Theology/Religion, Translations. Prof. of New Testament, Union Theological Seminary, Richmond, Va., 1943–62; Pres., Pittsburgh Theological Seminary, 1962–70; Pastor, Laurinburg Presbyterian Church, North Carolina, 1970–74, now retired. *Publs:* The Stone Which the Builders Rejected, 1946; Conqueror in Chains: A Story of the Apostle Paul, 1951; Fire in Thy Mouth, 1954; The Way to Biblical Preaching, 1957; The Nature and Mission of the Church, 1957; (ed. and contrib.) Tools for Bible Study, 1958; The Gospel According to Luke, 1959; (trans.) The Gospel According to Matthew, by S. de Dietrich, 1961; The Gospel According to John and the Johannine Epistles, 1962; Live as Free Men: A Study Guide on Galatians, 1964; The Finality of Jesus Christ, 1968; The Authority of the Bible, 1972; (trans.) Exegesis, 1978; (ed. and contrib.) P.T. Forsyth: The Man, The Preacher's Theologian, Prophet for the 20th Century, 1981; (ed.) The Hermeneutical Quest, 1986. Add: 401 Russell Ave., Apt. 405, Gaithersburg, Md. 20877, U.S.A.

MILLER, Douglas T. American. History. Prof. of History, Michigan State Univ., East Lansing, since 1975 (Assoc. Prof., 1966–75). Asst. Prof. of History, Univ. of Maine, Orono, 1963–66; John Adams Chair in American Civilization, Univ. of Amsterdam, 1987–88. *Publs:* Jacksonian Aristocracy, 1967; The Birth of Modern America, 1970; (ed.) The Nature of Jacksonian America, 1972; Then Was the Future, 1973; (co-author) The Fifties, 1977; Visions of America, 1988; Frederick Douglass, 1988. Add: Dept. of History, Michigan State Univ., East Lansing, Mich. 48824, U.S.A.

MILLER, Frances A. American, b. 1937. Children's fiction, Autobiography/Memoirs, Biography. Writer and public speaker since 1983. Reading tutor and volunteer in public schools, Oakland and San Ramon, Calif., 1966–75. *Publs:* The Truth Trap, 1980; Aren't You the One Who...?, 1983; Losers and Winners, 1986. Add: 50 Deer Meadow Lane, Danville, Calif. 94526, U.S.A.

MILLER, Frederick Walter Gascoyne. New Zealander, b. 1904. History, Autobiography/Memoirs/Personal. Former journalist, Otago Daily Times, Dunedin; The Press, Christchurch; Southland Daily News; and Southland Times (journalist from 1922). *Publs:* Gold in the River, 1946; Golden Days of Lake County, 1949, 5th ed. 1973; Beyond the Blue Mountains, 1954, 1978; West to the Fiords, 1954, 1976; Waikaia: The Golden Century, 1966; Ink on My Fingers, 1967; The Story of the Kingston Flyer, 1976; King of Counties: A History of the Southland County; Hokonui: The School and the People, 1982. Add: 156 Venus St., Invercargill, New Zealand.

MILLER, Helen Hill. American, b. 1899. History, Politics/Government, Travel/Exploration/Adventure, Biography. Corresp., 1940, and American Editorial Rep., 1943–50, The Economist, London; Washington Corresp., Newsweek mag., 1950–52. *Publs:* Greek Horizons, 1961; Sicily and the Western Colonies of Greece, 1965; Greece, 1965; The Case for Liberty, 1965; Bridge to Asia: The Greeks in the Eastern Mediterranean, 1967; The Realms of Arthur, 1969; Greece Through the Ages: As Seen by Travellers from Herodotus to Byron, 1972; Historic Places Around the Outer Banks, 1974; George Mason: Gentleman Revolutionary, 1975; Passage to America: Ralegh's Colonists Take Ship for Roanoke, 1983; Captains From Devon: the great Elizabethan Seafarers who won the oceans for England, 1985. Add: 167 Tall Pine Lane, Kitty Hawk, N.C. 27949, U.S.A.

MILLER, Hugh. British, b. 1937. Novels, Screenplays. Editorial Asst., Scottish ITV, Glasgow, 1958–60; technical and photographic asst. to a forensic pathologist, Univ. of Glasgow, 1960–62; Mgr., 1963–64, and Co-Owner, 1965–70, Unique Studios, London; Ed., Bulletin, 1967–69, and Gen, 1968–71. *Publs:* A Pocketful of Miracles (magic), 1969; Secrets of Gambling (magic), 1970; Professional Presentations (magic), 1971; The Open City, 1973; Levels (documentary filmscript), 1973; Drop Out, 1973; Short Circuit, 1973; Koran's Legacy (magic), 1973; Kingpin, 1974; Double Deal, 1974; Feedback, 1974; Ambulance, 1975; The Dissector, 1976; A Soft Breeze from Hell, 1976; The Saviour, 1977; The Rejuvenators, 1978; Terminal 3, 1978; Olympic Bronze, 1979; Head of State, 1979; District Nurse, 1984; Honour a Physician, 1985; The EastEnders, 10 vols., 1986; Teen EastEnders, 2 vols., 1986; Snow on the Wind, 1987; Heroes, 1988; Beggars and Choosers, 1989. Add: 40 St. John's Ct., Warwick, England.

MILLER, Ian. *See* **MILNE,** John.

MILLER, James Edwin (Jr.). American, b. 1920. Language/Linguistics, Literature. Helen A. Regenstein Prof. of English, Univ. of Chicago

(Faculty member since 1962; (Dept. Chmn., 1978–84). Prof. and Chmn., Dept. of English, Univ. of Nebraska, Lincoln, 1953–62. *Publs:* Critical Guide to Leaves of Grass, 1958; (with B. Slote and Karl Shapiro) Start with the Sun, 1960; Reader's Guide to Herman Melville, 1962; F. Scott Fitzgerald: His Art and Technique, 1964; J.D. Salinger, 1965; Quests Surd and Absurd, 1967; Word, Self, Reality, 1972; Theory of Fiction: Henry James, 1972; T.S. Eliot's Personal Waste Land: Exorcism of the Demons, 1977; The American Quest for a Supreme Fiction: Whitman's Legacy in the Personal Epic, 1979. Add: Dept. of English, Univ. of Chicago, 1050 E. 59th St., Chicago, Ill. 60637, U.S.A.

MILLER, Jason. American, b. 1932. Plays/Screenplays. Stage and film actor. *Publs:* Three One-Act Plays (includes Lou Gehrig Did Not Die of Cancer, Perfect Son, and The Circus Lady), 1970; Nobody Hears a Broken Drum, 1970; That Championship Season, 1973. Add: c/o Screen Actors Guild, 7750 Sunset Blvd., Los Angeles, Calif. 90046, U.S.A.

MILLER, Jim Wayne. American, b. 1936. Novels/Short stories, Poetry, Songs/Lyrics/ Libretti, Translations. Prof. of German Languages and Literature, Western Kentucky Univ., Bowling Green, since 1963. Ed.-in-Chief, Jesse Stuart Foundn., since 1986. Member, Bd. of Dirs., 1972–78, and Pres., 1973–74, Kentucky Humanities Council; Member, Bd. of Dirs., Appalachian Community Service Network, 1980–84; Chmn., Appalachian Studies Conference, 1982–83. *Publs:* Copperhead Cane (poetry), 1964; The More Things Change the More They Stay the Same (ballads), 1971; Dialogue with a Dead Man (poetry), 1974; (trans.) The Figure of Fulfillment, by Emil Lerperger, 1975; The Mountains Have Come Closer, 1980; (ed.) I have a Place, 1981; Vein of Words (poetry,) 1984; Nostalgia for 70 (poetry), 1986; His First, Best Country (fiction), 1987; Brier, His Book (Poetry), 1988; Newfound (novel), 1989. Add: 1512 Eastland Dr., Bowling Green, Ky. 42101, U.S.A.

MILLER, J(ohn) D(onald) Bruce. Australian, b. 1922. International relations/Current affairs, Politics/Government. Prof. of Intnl. Relations, Australian National Univ., Canberra, 1962–87, now Emeritus; Exec. Dir; Academy of the Social Sciences in Australia, since 1989. Prof. of Politics, Univ. of Leicester, 1957–62. *Publs:* Australian Government and Politics, 1954; Richard Jebb and the Problem of Empire, 1956; The Commonwealth in the World, 1958; The Nature of Politics, 1962; (ed. with T.H. Rigby) The Disintegrating Monolith, 1965; Britain and the Old Dominions, 1966; Australia, 1966; The Politics of the Third World, 1966; (ed.) India, Japan, Australia: Partners in Asia?, 1968; Survey of Commonwealth Affairs: Problems of Expansion and Attrition 1953–1969, 1974; The European Economic Community and Australia, 1976; The World of States, 1981; Norman Angell and the Futility of War, 1986; (ed.) Australians and British, 1988. Add: 16 Hutt St., Yarralumla, A.C.T. 2600, Australia.

MILLER, Jonathan (Wolfe). British, b. 1934. Medicine/Health, Biography. Stage and television director; Research Fellow in Neuropsychology, Univ. of Sussex, Brighton; Artistic Dir. Old Vic Theatre, London, since 1988. Co-author and appeared in Beyond the Fringe (revue), London and NYC, 1961–64; Editor of Monitor (BBC TV documentary series), 1965; Research Fellow in the History of Medicine, University Coll., London, 1970–73; Assoc. Dir., National Theatre, London, 1973–75; produced The Body in Question (BBC series), 1978; Exec. Producer, BBC Shakespeare Series, 1979–80. *Publs:* McLuhan, 1971; (ed.) Freud: The Man, His World, His Influence, 1972; The Body in Question, 1978; Darwin for Beginners, 1982; Subsequent Performances, 1986. Add: 63 Gloucester Cres., London NW1, England.

MILLER, Jordan Yale. American, b. 1919. Literature, Theatre. Member of the faculty, Dept of English, Kansas State Univ., Manhattan, 1950–69; Chmn., Dept. of English, Univ. of Rhode Island, Kingston, 1969–80. *Publs:* (ed. and contrib.) American Dramatic Literature, 1961; Eugene O'Neill and the American Critic, 1962, 1973; (ed. and contrib.) Playwright's Progress, 1965; Maxwell Anderson, Gifted Technician, 1967; Eugene O'Neill, 1968; The War Play Comes of Age, 1969; Lorraine Hansberry, 1969; (ed. and contrib.) Twentieth Century Interpretations of A Streetcar Named Desire, 1971; Camino Real, 1970; Expressionism: The Wasteland Enacted, 1974; The Other O'Neill, 1974; (ed. and contrib.) Heath Introduction to Drama, 1976, 3rd ed., 1988; The Three Halves of Tennessee William's World, 1988; (field ed. and contrib.) Twayne Critical History of American Drama Series, 1990. Add: c/o Dept. of English, Univ. of Rhode Island, Kingston, R.I. 02881, U.S.A.

MILLER, J(oseph) Hillis. American, b. 1928. Literature.Distinguished Prof. of English and Comparative Literature, Univ. of California, Irvine, since 1986. Ed., English Literary History, since 1953. Instr., Williams Coll., Williamstown, Mass., 1952–53; Member of the faculty, 1953–72, Prof. of English, 1963–68, Chmn. of the Dept., 1964–68, and Prof. of English and Humanistic Studies, 1968–72, Johns Hopkins Univ., Baltimore; Prof. of English, 1972–86, Prof. of Comparative Literature 1979–86, and Frederick W. Hilles Prof. of English, 1976–86, Yale Univ., New Haven, Conn. Ed., Modern Language Notes, 1953–61; Trustee, Keuka Coll., Keuka Park, N.Y., 1971–80. *Publs:* Charles Dickens: The World of His Novels, 1958; The Disappearance of God: Five Nineteenth-Century Writers, 1963; Poets of Reality: Six Twentieth-Century Writers, 1965; (ed. with Roy Harvey Pearce) The Act of the Mind: Essays on the Poetry of Wallace Stevens, 1965; (ed.) William Carlos Williams: A Collection of Critical Essays, 1966; The Form of Victorian Fiction: Thackeray, Dickens, Trollope, George Eliot, Meredith, and Hardy, 1968; Thomas Hardy: Distance and Desire, 1970; Charles Dickens and George Cruikshank, 1971; (ed.) Aspects of Narrative, 1971; (ed.) The Well-Beloved, by Thomas Hardy, 1976; Fiction and Repetition: Seven English Novels, 1982; The Linguistic Moment: From Wordsworth to Stevens, 1985; The Ethics of Reading, 1987. Add: Dept. of English, Univ. of California, Irvine, Calif. 92717, U.S.A.

MILLER, Karl (Fergus Connor). British, b. 1931. Biography. Lord Northcliffe Prof. of Modern English Literature, University Coll., London, since 1974. Ed., London Review Review of Books, since 1979. Asst. Principal, H.M. Treasury, London 1956–57; Producer, BBC Television, 1957–58; Literary Ed., The Spectator, London, 1958–61, and the New Statesman, London, 1961–67; Ed., The Listener, London, 1967–73. *Publs:*(ed.) Poetry from Cambridge 1952–54, 1955; (ed.) Writing in England Today; The Last Fifteen Years, 1968; (ed.) Memoirs of a Modern Scotland, 1970; (ed.) A Listener Anthology, August 1967-June 1970, 1970; (ed.) A Second Listener Anthology, 1973; Cockburn's Millennium, 1975 (James Tait Black Award); (ed.) Robert Burns, 1981; Doubles: Studies in Literary History, 1985. Add: 26 Limerston St., London SW10, England.

MILLER, K(eith) Bruce. American, b. 1927. Philosophy. Prof. of Philosophy, Averett Coll. since 1986. American Baptist Chaplain, 1958, and Lectr., 1959–71, Univ. of Southern California, Los Angeles; Lectr., Extension Dept., Univ. of California at Los Angeles, 1973; Pres., Luther Rice Coll., Alexandria, Va., 1976–78. *Publs:* Ideology and Moral Philosophy, 1971. Add: 4525 Roberts Rd., Fairfax, Va. 22032, U.S.A.

MILLER, Kenneth E. American, b. 1926. International relations/Current affairs, Politics/Government. Prof. of Political Science since 1967, Rutgers Univ., Newark, N.J. (Instr., Asst. Prof. and Assoc. Prof., 1955–67; Chmn., Political Science Dept., 1962–69, 1977–85; Assoc. Dean, 1969–70). *Publs:* Socialism and Foreign Policy, 1967; Government and Politics in Denmark, 1968; (ed. with N. Samuels) Power and the People, 1973; Denmark, 1987. Add: Dept. of Political Science, Rutgers Univ., Newark, N.J. 07102, U.S.A.

MILLER, Lynn H. American, b. 1937. Plays/Screenplays, Politics/-Government. Prof. of Political Science, Temple Univ., Philadelphia (joined faculty in 1969 as Assoc. Prof.). Asst. Prof., Univ., of California at Los Angeles, 1965–69. *Publs:* Organizing Mankind: Analysis of Contemporary International Organization, 1972; (ed. with Ronald W. Pruessen) Reflections on the Cold War, 1974; The Eye of a Bird (play), 1978; Global Order: Values and Power in International Politics, 1985, 1990; (ed. with Jack H. Schuster) Governing Tomorrow's Campus, 1989. Add: Dept. of Political Science, Temple Univ., Philadelphia, Pa. 19122, U.S.A.

MILLER, Mary. *See* **DURACK**, Dame Mary.

MILLER, (Hanson) Orlo. Canadian, b. 1911. Novels/Short stories, Plays/Screenplays, History. Ordained Anglican priest, 1964; Rector, St. Paul's Church, Point Edward, Ont., 1970–77 (Asst. Curate, St. Paul's Cathedral, London, Ont., 1963–65; Rector, Mitchell, Ont., 1965–69). *Publs:* A Century of Western Ontario, 1949; Raiders of the Mohawk, 1953; The London Club, 1954; (with F. Landon) Up the Proof Line, 1954; This Was London (play), 1955; The Saint, 1955; The Donnellys Must Die, 1962; The Watersavers, 1962; A Sound of Voices, 1965; Gargoyles and Gentlemen, 1967; Cronyn (play), 1973; Death to the Donnellys, 1975; The Day-Spring, 1976; Ship 22, 1977; (with Maridon Miller) Truly Rural, 1977; The Point, 1978; Twenty Mortal Murders, 1978; The London Club Centennial, 1980; The Proudfoot Papers (play), 1982; This Was London: The First Two Centuries, 1988. Add: 183 Gammage St., London, Ont. N5Y 2B4, Canada.

MILLER, Randolph Crump. American, b. 1910. Education, Language/Linguistics, Theology/Religion. Horace Bushnell Prof. of Christian Nurture, Yale Univ., New Haven, 1963–81, now Emeritus (Prof. of Christian Education, 1952–63). Managing Ed., Religious Education, since 1982 (ed., 1958–78). Member of the faculty, Church Divinity Sch. of the Pacific, 1936–52. Exec. Secty., Religious Ed. Assn. of U.S. and Canada, 1982–85. *Publs:* What We Can Believe, 1941; A Guide for Church School Teachers, 1943, 1947; (co-author and co-ed.) Christianity and the Contemporary Scene, 1943; (ed. and co-author) The Church and Organized Movements, 1946; Religion Makes Sense, 1950; The Clue to Christian Education, 1950; The Symphony of the Christian Year, 1954; Education for Christian Living, 1956, 1963; Biblical Theology and Christian Education, 1956; Be Not Anxious, 1957; I Remember Jesus, 1958; Christian Nurture and the Church, 1961; Your Child's Religion, 1962, 1975; Youth Considers Parents as People, 1965; The Language Gap and God, 1970; Living with Anxiety, 1971; Live until You Die, 1973; The American Spirit in Theology, 1974; This We Can Believe, 1976; The Theory of Christian Education Practice, 1980. Add: 21 Autumn St., New Haven, Conn. 06511, U.S.A.

MILLER, Stuart C(reighton). American, b. 1927. History, International relations/Current affairs, Race relations. Prof. of Social Science and History, San Francisco State Univ., since 1971 (Asst. Prof., 1962–66; Assoc. Prof., 1966–71). High sch. teacher of social studies, Garden City, N.Y., 1955–59; Instr. of History, Columbia Univ., NYC, 1959–62. *Publs:* The Unwelcome Immigrant: The American Image of the Chinese, 1969; Ends and Means: The American Missionary Justification of Force in Nineteenth Century China, 1974; Benevolent Assimilation: The American Conquest of the Philippines, 1982. Add: 181 San Carlos Ave., Sausalito, Calif. 94965, U.S.A.

MILLER, Susan. American, b. 1944. Plays/Screenplays. Taught at Pennsylvania State Univ., 1969–73, and Univ. of California, Los Angeles, 1975–76; writer-in-residence, Mark Taper Forum Theatre, Los Angeles, 1975. *Publs:* No One Is Exactly 23 (in Pyramid 1), 1968; Cross Country (in West Coast Plays), 1978; Confessions of a Female Disorder (in Gay Plays), 1979. Add: c/o Flora Roberts Inc., 157 W. 57th St., New York, N.Y. 10019, U.S.A.

MILLER, Vassar (Morrison). American, b. 1924. Poetry. Instr. in Creative Writing, St. John's Sch., Houston, 1975–76. *Publs:* Adam's Footprint, 1956; Wage War on Silence: A Book of Poems, 1960; My Bones Being Water: Poems, 1963; Onions and Roses, 1968; If I Could Sleep Deeply Enough, 1974; Small Change, 1977; Approaching Nada, 1977; Selected and New Poems, 1982; Stuggling to Swim on Concrete, 1984; (ed.) Despite This Flesh: The Disabled in Stories and Poem, 1985. Add: 1615 Vassar St., Houston, Tex. 77006, U.S.A.

MILLER, Wade. *See* **WADE,** Robert.

MILLER, Walter M(ichael), Jr. American, b. 1922. Science fiction/Fantasy. Engineer and freelance writer, mainly of SF short stories and novellas. *Publs:* A Canticle for Leibowitz, 1960; Conditionally Human (short stories), 1962; The View from the Stars (short stories), 1964; The Best of Walter M. Miller, Jr. (short stories), 1980; The Darfstellar and Other Stories, 1982; The Science Fiction Stories of Walter M. Miller, Jr., 1984; (co-ed.) Beyond Armegeddon, 1985. Add: c/o G.K. Hall, 70 Lincoln St., Boston, Mass. 02111, U.S.A.

MILLER, Warren E. American, b. 1924. Politics/Government. Prof. of Political Science, Arizona State Univ., Tempe, since 1982. Adjunct Prof., Univ. of Michigan, Ann Arbor, since 1982 (joined faculty, 1951); Fellow, American Assoc. for the Advancement of Science, 1984. *Publs:* (with W.A. Campbell and G. Gurin) The Voter Decides, 1954; (with others) The American Voter, 1960; (with others) Elections and the Political Order, 1966; (with Teresa E. Levitin) Leadership and Change, 1976; (with others) The American National Election Studies Data Sourcebook, 1952–1978, 5 vols., 1980; (with M.K. Jennings) Parties in Transition, 1986; Without Consent, 1988. Add: Dept. of Political Science, Arizona State University, Tempe, Ariz. 85287, U.S.A.

MILLER, Wilma Hildruth. American, b. 1936. Education. Prof. of Education, Illinois State Univ., Normal, since 1972 (Assoc. Prof., 1968–72). Elementary sch. teacher, Dixon, Ill., 1958–63, and Tucson, Ariz., 1963–64; Asst. Prof., Wisconsin State Univ., Whitewater, 1965–68. *Publs:* Identifying and Correcting Reading Difficulties in Children, 1971; The First R: Elementary Reading Today, 1972, 1983; (ed.) Elementary Reading Today: Selected Articles, 1972; Diagnosis and Correction of Reading Difficulties in Secondary School Students, 1973; Teaching Reading in the Secondary School, 1974; Reading Diagnosis Kit, 1974, 3rd ed., 1986; Reading Correction Kit, 1975, 1982; Corrective Reading Skills Activity File, 1977; The Reading Activities Handbook, 1980; Teaching Elementary Reading Today, 1984; Reading Teacher's Complete Diagnosis and Correction Manual, 1988. Add: Specialized Educational Development Dept., Illinois State Univ., Normal, Ill. 61761, U.S.A.

MILLERSON, Gerald (Edward Thomas). British, b. 1923. Media Consultant. Formerly, Technical Mgr., BBC Television, London. *Publs:* The Technique of Television Production, 1961, 12th ed. 1989; The Technique of Lighting for Television and Motion Pictures, 1972, 1982; Television Camera Operation, 1974, 3rd ed. 1982; Basic Television Staging, 1974, 1982; Television Lighting Methods, 1974, 1982; Effective Television Production, 1976, 1983; Video Camera Techniques, 1983; Video Production Handbook, 1987; TV Scenic Design Handbook, 1988. Add: 328 Hempstead Rd. Watford, Herts. WD1 3NA, England.

MILLETT, John. Australian. Poetry. Ed., then Managing Ed., South Head Press and Poetry Australia, since 1970; also a lawyer. *Publs:* Calendar Adam, 1971; The Silences, 1973; Love Tree of the Coomera, 1975; West of the Cunderand, 1977; (with Grace Perry) Last Bride at Longsleep, 1981; Tail Arse Charlie, 1982; Come Down Cunderang, 1985; Blue Dynamite, 1986. Add: Lytton Rd., Moss Vale, N.S.W. 2577, Australia.

MILLETT, Kate. (Katherine Murray Millett). American, b. 1934. Women. Leader in the Feminist movement. *Publs:* Sexual Politics, 1970; Flying, 1974; The Prostitution Papers, 1976; Sita, 1977; The Basement, 1980; Going to Iran, 1982. Add: c/o Georges Borchardt Inc., 136 E. 57th St., New York, N.Y. 10022, U.S.A.

MILLETT, Mervyn (Richard Oke). Australian, b. 1910. Agriculture/Forestry, Botany. Research Officer, Forestry and Timber Bureau, 1934–50, Sr. Research Officer, Tariff Bd., 1951–60, and Ed., Australian National Antarctic Research Expeditions Scientific Reports, Antarctic Div., Dept. of Science, 1960–74, Australian Public Service; Ed-in-Chief, The Commonwealth Professional, 1974–77. *Publs:* Australian Eucalypts, 1969; Native Trees of Australia, 1971; With Love for Ever, 1983; Paintings by Greta Millett, 1987. Add: 72 McNicol Rd., Tecoma, Vic. 3160, Australia.

MILLGRAM, Abraham E(zra). American, b. 1901. Education, Literature, Theology/Religion. Rabbi, Congregation Beth Israel, Philadelphia, 1930–40; Dir., Hillel Foundn., Univ. of Minnesota, Minneapolis, 1940–45; Educational Dir., United Synagogue of America, NYC, 1945–61. *Publs:* (author and ed.) Sabbath: The Day of Delight, 1944; Handbook for the Congregational School Board Member, 1953; (ed. and trans.) An Anthology of Medieval Hebrew Literature, 1961; (ed.) Great Jewish Ideas, 1964; Jewish Worship, 1971; Jerusalem Curiosities, 1990. Add: 12 Ben-Maimon Ave., Jerusalem, Israel.

MILLHISER, Marlys. American, b. 1938. Mystery/Crime/Suspense, Historical/Romance/Gothic. Jr. high sch. history teacher, 1963–65. *Publs:* Michael's Wife, 1972; Nella Waits, 1974; Willing Hostage, 1976; The Mirror, 1978; Nightmare Country, 1981; The Threshold, 1984. Add: 1743 Orchard Ave., Boulder, Colo. 80304 U.S.A.

MILLIGAN, Spike. (Terence Alan Milligan). Irish, b. 1918. Plays/Screenplays, Poetry, Humor/Satire. Radio and TV personality: The Goon Show, BBC Radio; Show Called Fred, ITV; World of Beachcomber, Q5-Q10, BBC-2 Television; Curry and Chips, BBC; Oh in Colour, BBC; A Milligan for All Seasons, BBC; etc. *Publs:* (with J. Antrobus) The Bed Sitting Room (play); Oblomov (play); Son of Oblomov (play); Silly Verse for Kids, 1959; A Dustbin of Milligan, 1961; Puckoon, 1963; The Little Pot Boiler, 1963; A Book of Bits, 1965; The Bedside Milligan, 1968; Milliganimals, 1968; The Bald Twit Lion, 1970; Milligan's Ark, 1971; Adolf Hitler: My Part in His Downfall, 1971; The Goon Show Scripts, 1972; Small Dreams of a Scorpion, 1972; Rommel? Gunner Who?, 1973; Badjelly the Witch, 1973; More Goon Show Scripts, 1974; Spike Milligan's Transports of Delight, 1974; Dip the Puppy, 1974; The Great McGonagal Scrapbook, 1975; (with Jack Hobbs) The Milligan Book of Records, Games, Cartoons and Commercials, 1975; Monty: His Part in My Victory, 1976; Mussolini: His Part in My Downfall, 1978; A Book of Goblins (verse), 1978; Open Heart University (verse), 1979; Indefinite Articles and Slunthorpe, 1981; The 101 Best and Only Limericks of Spike Milligan, 1982; The Goon Cartoons, 1982; Sir Nobonk and the Terrible Dragon, 1982; The Melting Pot, 1983; More Goon Cartoons, 1983; There's a Lot About, 1983; Further Transports of Delight, 1985; Floored Masterpieces and Worse Verse, 1985; Where Have All the Bullets Gone, 1985; Goodbye Soldier, 1986; The Looney: An Irish Fantasy, 1987; Startling Verse for All the Family, 1987; William McGonagall Meets George Gershwin, 1988. Add: Spike Milligan Productions, 9 Orme Ct., London W2, England.

MILLINGTON, (Terence) Alaric. British, b. 1922. Education, Mathematics. Visiting Lectr. Kings Coll., Univ. of London, since 1985. Unesco Consultant, since 1971; Consultant, Yorkshire Television, and Inner London Education Authority, since 1977, and Manpower Service Commn., since 1987. Asst. Master, Finchley County Grammar Sch., 1949–53; Head of Maths Dept., Haverstock Sch., 1953–57, and Furzedown Coll. of Education, 1957–69; Lectr. in Mathematics Education, Chelsea Coll., Univ. of London, 1969–85. Co-Ed., Education for Teaching Journal, Assn. of Teachers in Colls. and Depts. of Education, 1959–66; British Council Consultant, S.E. Asia, 1974, and Pakistan, 1978. *Publs:* (with W. Millington) Dictionary of Mathematics, 1966, 3rd ed. 1981; Living Mathematics, parts 1-6, 1967–72; (trans. with Jaggers) Guide to Mathematical Films, 1970; Introduction to Sets, 1971; (with Brown and Matthews) Mathematics Through School, 1972; History of Mathematics, 1972; Mathematics and Creativity, 1977; (co-author) Never a Dull Moment, 1982. Add: 10 Creswick Walk, London NW11 6AN, England.

MILLS, A(nthony) R(eginald). British. Sports/Physical education, Travel/Exploration/Adventure, Biography. Publr., with Muller, Nelson, and W.H. Allen, all London, 1961–80, Press Assn. since 1981. Journalist, 1951–60. *Publs:* Middle-Distance Running, 1961; Portrait of Moscow, 1965; (ed.) Two Victorian Girls, 1966; The Halls of Ravenswood, 1967; Portrait of Leningrad, 1967; Two Victorian Ladies, 1969. Add: c/o National Westminster Bank, 358 Oxford St., London W1, England.

MILLS, Edward D(avid). British, b. 1915. Architecture. Architect in private practice, London and Lingfield, Surrey, since 1937. Chmn., Faculty of Architecture, British Sch. in Rome. RIBA Alfred Bossom Research Fellow, 1953; Churchill Fellow, 1969. *Publs:* The Modern Factory, 1951; The Modern Church, 1952; (ed.) Architects Detail Sheets, 5 vols., 1952–61; The New Architecture in Great Britain, 1953; (ed.) Factory Design in Great Britain, 1967; The Changing Work Place, 1972; (ed.) Planning, 10th ed. 1985; (with Harry Kaylor) The Design of Polytechnic Institute Buildings, 1972; Building Maintenance and Preservation, 1980; The National Exhibition Centre, 1976; Design for Holidays and Tourism, 1984. Add: Gate House Farm, Newchapel, Lingfield, Surrey, England.

MILLS, James (Spencer). American, b. 1932. Novels, Documentaries/Reportage. Reporter, Worcester Telegram and Evening Gazette, Massachusetts, 1955, Corpus Christi Caller Times, Texas, 1958, and United Press Intnl., 1959; Reporter, Writer and Ed., Life mag., NYC, 1960–66. *Publs:* The Panic in Needle Park, 1966; The Prosecutor, 1969; Report to the Commissioner, 1972; One Just Man, 1974; On the Edge, 1975; The Seventh Power, 1976; The Truth about Peter Harley, 1979; The Underground Empire, 1986. Add: c/o Lynn Nesbit, Intnl. Creative Mgmt., 40 W. 57th St., New York, N.Y. 10019, U.S.A.

MILLS, Mervyn. British, b. 1906. Novels/Short stories, Plays/Screenplays, History. Publr.'s Asst., Edward Arnold and Co., London, 1924–27; Literary Agent, Agence Litteraire Intnl., Paris, 1927–29; freelance writer for radio and television, 1929–39; Squadron Leader, R.A.F.V.R. (mentioned in despatches), 1941–46; Sr. Air Historian, U.K. Ministry of Defence, 1948–71, now retired. *Publs:* The Long Haul; Tempt Not the Stars; The Winter Wind; Nelson of the Nile (play); The Tree of Heaven (play); Dance Without Music (television play); (adaptor) The Queen of Spades (television play); The Skull (radio play); Peter Simple series (radio plays); The Lost World series (radio plays); Paul Jones (radio play); Mexican Gold (radio play); RAF Operations in Libya, Western Desert and Tunisia, July 1942 to May 1943; RAF Operations from Malta, June 1940 to May 1945. Add: Clover Leys Farm, Burwash Common, East Sussex, England.

MILLS, Paul (Richard). British, b. 1948. Poetry. Fellow in Creative Writing, Univ. of Manchester, since 1976. Teacher, Highgate Sch., Birmingham, 1974–76. *Publs:* North Carriageway, 1976; Third Person, 1978. Add: c/o Carcanet New Press, 330 Corn Exchange Bldgs., Manchester M4 3BG, England.

MILLS, Ralph J(oseph), Jr. American, b. 1931. Poetry, Literature. Prof. of English, Univ. of Illinois at Chicago, since 1967 (Assoc. Prof., 1965–67). Instr. in English, 1959–61, and Asst. Prof. and Assoc. Chmn. of the Cttee. on Social Thought, 1962–65, Univ. of Chicago. *Publs:* Theodore Roethke, 1963; Contemporary American Poetry, 1965; (ed.) On the Poet and His Craft: Selected Prose of Theodore Roethke, 1965; Richard Eberhart, 1966; Edith Sitwell: A Critical Essay, 1966; Kathleen

Raine: A Critical Essay, 1967; (ed.) Selected Letters of Theodore Roethke, 1968; Creation's Very Self: On the Personal Element in Recent American Poetry, 1969; (ed.) The Notebooks of David Ignatow, 1973; Door to the Sun: Poems, 1974; Cry of the Human: Essays on Contemporary American Poetry, 1975; A Man to His Shadow, 1975; Night Road/Poems, 1978; Living with Distance, 1979; With No Answer, 1980; (ed.) Open Between Us: Essays, Reviews and Interviews of David Ignatow, 1980; March Light: Poems, 1983; For a Day: Poems, 1985; Each Branch: Poems 1976–1985, 1986; Awhile: Poems, 1989. Add: Dept. of English, Univ. of Illinois, Chicago, Ill. 60680, U.S.A.

MILLUM, Trevor. British. Novels/Short stories, Poetry. Head of Faculty, Longcroft Sch., Beverley, since 1985. Teacher, Nchelenge Secondary Sch., Luapula, Zambia, 1971–74; Teacher of English, Matthew Humberstone Sch., Cleethorpes, 1975–77; Head of English, Baysgarth Sch., Barton on Humber, 1977–81; Head of Faculty, United World Coll., Singapore, 1981–84. *Publs:* Images of Woman: Visual Communication in Advertising, 1975; Exercises in African History, 1978; Traffic Island and Other Stories, 1984; (ed.) Pigs Is Pigs, 1988; Warning: Too Much Schooling Can Damage Your Health, 1988; Mixing It and Other Stories, 1989; (ed.) Funny Bones, 1989. Add: Fern House, Barrow on Humber, South Humberside, England.

MILLWARD, Eric (Geoffrey William). British, b. 1935. Short stories, Poetry. Staff member, British Airways. Former Poetry Ed., Towards Survival. *Publs:* A Child in the Park, 1969; Dead Letters, 1978; Appropriate Noises, 1987. Add: 2 Victoria Row, Knypersley, Stoke-on-Trent, Staffordshire, England.

MILNE, Christopher Robin. British, b. 1920. Autobiography/Memoirs/Personal. Bookshop proprietor, 1951–81. *Publs:* The Enchanted Places, 1974; The Path Through the Trees, 1979; The Hollow on the Hill, 1982; The Windfall-A Fable, 1985; The Open Garden, 1988. Add: Embridge Forge, Bowden, Dartmouth, Devon, England.

MILNE, John. Also writes as Ian Miller. British, b. 1952. Novels, Mystery. Writer since 1980; playwright for television; journalist, contributing to Time Out, Daily Telegraph, etc. Policeman, 1969–73; manual worker, 1973–76; art student, 1976–80 *Publs:* Tyro, 1982; London Fields, 1983; Out of the Blue, 1985; (as Ian Miller) Wet Wickets and Dusty Balls: The Diary of a Cricketing Year, 1986; Dead Birds, 1986; Shadow Play, in U.S. as The Moody Man, 1987; Daddy's Girl, 1988; Dead Awkward, 1990. Add: c/o A.D. Peters & Co. Ltd., The Chambers, Chelsea Harbour, Lots Rd., London SW10 0XF England.

MILNE, Lorus J(ohnson). American. Biology, Botany, Children's non-fiction, Environmental science/Ecology, Natural history, Zoology. Prof. of Zoology, Univ., of New Hampshire, Durham, since 1948. *Publs:* all with Margery Milne—A Multitude of Living Things, 1947; Famous Naturalists, 1952; The Biotic World of Man, 1952, 3rd ed. 1965; The Mating Instinct, 1954; The World of Night, 1956; Paths Across the Earth, 1958; Animal Life, 1959; Plant Life, 1959; (with R. and M. Buchsbaum) The Lower Animals: Living Invertebrates of the World, 1960; The Balance of Nature, 1960; (with the Editors of Life) The Mountains, 1962; The Senses of Animals and Men, 1962; Because of a Tree, 1963; The Valley: Meadow, Grove and Stream, 1962; Water and Life, 1964; The Crab That Crawled Out of the Past, 1965; Gift from the Sky, 1967; Living Plants of the World, 1967; Patterns of Survival, 1967; The Phoenix Forest, 1968; The Ages of Life: A New Look at the Effects of Time on Mankind and Other Living Things, 1968; The Nature of Animals, 1969; North American Birds, 1969; When the Tide Goes Far Out, 1970; The Nature of Life: Earth, Plants, Animals, Man, and Their Effect on Each Other, 1970; The Nature of Plants, 1971; The Cougar Doesn't Live Here Any More: Does the World Still Have Room for Wildlife?, 1971; The How and Why of Growing, 1972; The Arena of Life: The Dynamics of Ecology, 1972; Invertebrates of North America, 1972; The Animal in Man, 1973; Because of a Flower, 1975; (with F. Russell) The Secret Life of Animals, 1976; Ecology Out of Joint, 1977; A World Alive: The Natural Wonders of a New England River Valley, 1978; Gadabouts and Stick-at-Homes: Wild Animals and Their Habitats, 1980; Insect Worlds: A Guide for Man on Making the Most of the Environment, 1980; The Audubon Society Field Guide to North American Insects and Spiders, 1980; Dreams of a Perfect Earth, 1982; Nature's Clean-up Crew: The Burying Beetles, 1982; (contr.) The Audubon Society Encyclopedia of Animal Life, 1982; (with Les Line) The Audubon Society Book of Insects, 1983; Nature's Great Carbon Cycle, 1983; The Mystery of the Bog Forest, 1984; (with Margery Milne) A Shovelful of Earth, 1987. Add: 1 Garden Lane, Durham, N.H. 03824, U.S.A.

MILNE, Margery (Joan Greene). American. Biology, Botany, Children's non-fiction, Environmental Science/Ecology, Natural history, Zoology. With the Recreation and Parks Prog., Univ. of New Hampshire, Durham. *Publs:* all with Lorus J. Milne—A Multitude of Living Things, 1947; Famous Naturalists, 1952; The Biotic World of Man, 1952, 3rd ed. 1965; The Mating Instinct, 1954; The World of Night, 1956; Paths Across the Earth, 1958; Animal Life, 1959; Plant Life, 1959; (with R. and M. Buchsbaum) The Lower Animals: Living Invertebrates of the World, 1960; The Balance of Nature, 1960; (with the Editors of Life) The Mountains, 1962; The Senses of Animals and Men, 1962; Because of a Tree, 1962; The Valley: Meadow, Grove and Stream, 1963; Water and Life, 1964; The Crab That Crawled Out of the Past, 1965; Gift from the Sky, 1967; Living Plants of the World, 1967; Patterns of Survival, 1967; The Phoenix Forest, 1968; The Ages of Life: A New Look at the Effects of Time on Mankind and Other Living Things, 1968; The Nature of Animals, 1969; North American Birds, 1969; When the Tide Goes Far Out, 1970; The Nature of Life: Earth, Plants, Animals, Man, and Their Effect on Each Other, 1970; The Nature of Plants, 1971; The Cougar Doesn't Live Here Any More: Does the World Still Have Room for Wildlife?, 1971; The How and Why of Growing, 1972; The Arena of Life: The Dynamics of Ecology, 1972; Invertebrates of North America, 1972; The Animal in Man, 1973; Because of a Flower, 1975; (with F. Russell) The Secret Life of Animals, 1976; Ecology Out of Joint, 1977; A World Alive: The Natural Wonders of a New England River Valley, 1978; Gadabouts and Stick-at-Homes: Wild Animals and Their Habitats, 1980; Insect Worlds: A Guide for Man on Making the Most of the Environment, 1980; The Audubon Society Field Guide to North American Insects and Spiders, 1980; Dreams of a Perfect Earth, 1982; Nature's Clean-Up Crew: The Burying Beetles, 1982; (with L. Line) The Audubon Society Book of Insects and Spiders, 1982; (with Lorus Milne) A Shovel-ful of Earth, 1987. Add: 1 Garden Lane, Durham, N.H. 03824, U.S.A.

MILNE, W(illiam) Gordon. American, b. 1921. Literature. Prof. of English since 1964, and Chmn. of American Studies since 1976, Lake Forest Coll., Illinois (joined faculty, 1951; Chmn., Dept. of English, 1964–75). *Publs:* George William Curtis and the Genteel Tradition, 1956; The American Political Novel, 1966; The Sense of Society: A History of the American Novel of Manners, 1977; Stephen Crane at Brede: An Anglo-American Literary Circle of the 1890's, 1980; Ports of Call: A Study of the American Nautical Novel, 1986. Add: Box 273, Rye Beach, N.H. 03871, U.S.A.

MILNER, Esther. American (b. Canadian), b. 1918. Psychology, Sociology. Prof. Emerita, Brooklyn Coll., City Univ. of New York, since 1977 (Asst. Prof., then Assoc. Prof., 1952–57; Prof. 1960–77). Teaching Asst., Univ. of Minnesota, Minneapolis, 1943–44; Civilian Technician, Dept. of National Defence, Ottawa, 1944–45; Research Asst., Commn. on Human Development, Univ. of Chicago, 1946–47; Asst. Prof., then Assoc. Prof., Univ. of Atlanta, 1949–51; Asst. Prof., Univ. of Alberta, 1957–60. *Publs:* The Failure of Success: The American Crisis in Values, 1959, as The Failure of Success: The Middle-Class Crisis, 1968; Human Neural and Behavioral Development: A Relational Inquiry, 1967; (ed.) The Impact of Fertility-Limitation on Women's Life, Career and Personality, 1970. Add: R.D. #4, Box 116A, Hudson, N.Y. 12534, U.S.A.

MILNER, Ian Frank George. New Zealander, b. 1911. Literature, Translations. Assoc. Prof. of English Literature, Charles Univ., Prague, 1964–76, now retired (Lectr., 1951–54; Sr. Lectr., 1955–63). Political Affairs Officer, U.N., NYC, 1947–51. Co-ed., Prague Studies in English, 1973–76. *Publs:* New Zealand's Interests and Policies in the Far East, 1940; (trans. with V. Fried) J. Macek: The Hussite Movement in Bohemia, 1965; (trans. with George Theiner) Selected Poems of Miroslav Holub, 1967; (ed. and trans.) Peter Bezruc: Silesian Songs, 1967; The Structure of Values in George Eliot, 1968; (trans. with Jarmila Milner) Selected Poems of Vladimir Holan, 1971; (trans. with J. Milner) Although, by Miroslav Holub , 1971; (trans. with J. Milner) Notes of a Clay Pigeon, by Miroslav Holub, 1977; (trans.) A Night with Hamlet, by Vladimir Holan, 1980; Milner of Waitaki: Portrait of The Man, 1983; (co-trans.) The Fly and Other Poems, by Miroslav Holub, 1987. Add: Lopatecka 11a, Prague 4, 14700 Czechoslovakia.

MILNER, Marion. Also writes as Joanna Field. British, b. 1900. Art, Psychology, Autobiography/Memoirs/Personal. Psychoanalyst in private practice, London, since 1943. Training Analyst, British Psychoanalytic Soc. *Publs:* (as Joanna Field) A Life of One's Own, 1934; (as Joanna Field) An Experiment in Leisure, 1973; The Human Problem in Schools, 1938; (as Joanna Field) On Not Being Able to Paint, 1950, 2nd ed. (as M. Milner) 1957; The Hands of the Living God, 1969; The Suppressed Madness of Sane Men, 1987; Eternity's Sunrise, 1987. Add: 12 Provost

Rd., London NW3, England.

MILNER, Ron(ald). American, b. 1938. Plays/Screenplays. Founding Dir., Spirit of Shango theatre co., Detroit. Writer-in-Residence, Lincoln Univ., Pennsylvania, 1966–67; member of the faculty, Michigan State Univ., East Lansing, 1971–72. *Publs:* (ed. with Woodie King) Black Drama Anthology, 1971; What the Wine Sellers Buy, 1974. Add: c/o Crossroads Theatre Co., 320 Memorial Parkway, New Brunswick, N.J. 08901, U.S.A.

MILOTTE, Alfred George. American, b. 1904. Children's non-fiction. Former producer of nature films for Walt Disney Productions. *Publs:* The Story of the Platypus, 1959; The Story of a Hippopotamus, 1964; (with Elma Milotte) The Story of an Alaskan Grizzly Bear, 1969, as Toklat, 1987. Add: P.O. Box 7227, Bonney Lake, Sumner, Wash. 98390, U.S.A.

MILSOM, Charles Henry. Also writes as William Weston. British, b. 1926. History, Navigation, Sport. Served in the Royal Navy and Merchant Navy, 1945–55; Reporter, 1955–58, Sub-Ed., 1958–72, Features Ed., 1972–79, and Chief Sub-Ed., 1979–85, Journal of Commerce, Liverpool. *Publs:* Guide to the Merchant Navy, 1968; The Coal Was There for Burning, 1975; The Competitive Swimmers Handbook, 1982; (ed.) Sea Breezes, 1986; Bule Funnels in the Mersey, 1988. Add: 110 Manor Dr., Upton, Wirral, Merseyside L49 4PJ, England.

MILSOM, Stroud Francis Charles. British, b. 1923. Law, History. Prof. of Law, and Fellow of St. John's Coll., Cambridge, since 1976. Fellow, Trinity Coll., Cambridge, 1948–55, and New Coll., Oxford, 1956–64; Prof. of Legal History, Univ. of London, 1965–76. Literary Dir., The Selden Soc., 1964–80. *Publs:* (trans. and ed.) Novae Narrationes, 1963; (ed.) Pollock and Maitland's History of English Law, 1968; Historical Foundations of the Common Law, 1969, 1981; The Legal Framework of English Feudalism, 1976; Studies in the History of the Common Law, 1985; (with J.H. Baker) Sources of English Legal History, 1986. Add: St. John's Coll., Cambridge CB2 1TP, England.

MILTON, John R. American, b. 1924. Novels/Short stories, Poetry, Cultural/Ethnic topics, Literature, Biography. Ed. South Dakota Review, since 1963. Prof. of English since 1963, and Dir. of the Creative Writing Prog. since 1965, Univ. of South Dakota, Vermillion (Chmn. of English Dept., 1963–65). Instr. in English and Philosophy, Augsburg Coll., Minn., 1949–57; Chmn. of English Dept., Jamestown Coll., N.D., 1957–63. *Publs:* The Loving Hawk, 1962; Western Plains, 1964; The Tree of Bones, 1965; This Lonely House, 1968; (ed.) The American Indian Speaks, 1969; (ed.) Three West, 1970; (ed.) American Indian II, 1971; Oscar Howe: The Story of an American Indian, 1972; Conversations with Frank Waters, 1972; (with D.E. Wylder, D. Walker, and M. Westbrook) Interpretative Approaches to Western American Literature, 1972; The Tree of Bones and Other Poems, 1973; Conversations with Frederick Manfred, 1974; Crazy Horse, 1974; The Blue Belly of the World, 1974; The Literature of South Dakota, 1976; Notes to a Bald Buffalo (novel), 1976; South Dakota: A History, 1977; The Novel of the American West, 1980. Add: 630 Thomas, Vermillion, S.D. 57069, U.S.A.

MILTON, Joyce. American, b. 1946. Children's fiction, Children's non-fiction, History, Sciences, Biography. Freelance writer since 1977. Librarian, New York Public Library, 1967–69, and Walden Sch., NYC, 1969–71; Young Adult Ed., Kirkus Review, NYC, 1971–77. *Publs:* Sunrise of Power: Ancient Egypt, Alexander and the World of Hellenism, 1979; (with Rafael Steinberg and Sarah Lewis) Religion at the Crossroads: Byzantium and the Turks, 1979; Tradition and Revolt: Imperial China, Islands of the Rising Sun, 1980; Controversy: Science in Conflict, 1980; A Friend of China, 1980; Here Come the Robots, 1981; (with Jane O'Connor) The Dandee Diamond Mystery, 1983; Save the Loonies, 1983; Ruthie the Robot, 1983; (with Ronald Radosh) The Rosenberg File: A Search for the Truth, 1983; Secrets of the Mummies, 1984; Dinosaur Days, 1985; Don Quixote , 1985; (with Ann L. Bardach) Vicki, 1986; Marching to Freedom: The Story of Martin Luther King Jr., 1987; George Washington, 1988; Christopher Columbus: A Punch-and-Play Storybook, 1988. Add: 60 Plaza St., Brooklyn, N.Y. 11238, U.S.A.

MILWARD, Alan S. British, b. 1935. Economics, History. Prof. of Economic History, Univ. of London, since 1986. Lectr. in Economic History, Univ. of Edinburgh, 1960–65; Lectr. in Economic History, Univ. of East Anglia, Norwich, 1965–67; Assoc. Prof. of Economics, Stanford Univ., California, 1967–71; Prof. of European Studies, Univ. of Manchester Inst. of Science and Technology, 1971–83; Prof. of Contemporary History, European Univ. Inst., Florence, 1983–86. *Publs:* The

German Economy at War, 1965; The New Order and the French Economy, 1970; The Economic Effects of the Two World Wars on Britain, 1970; The Fascist Economy in Norway, 1972; (with S.B. Saul) Economic Development of Continental Europe 1780-1870, 1973; (with S.B. Saul) The Development of the Economies of Continental Europe 1870–1914, 1977; War Economy and Society 1939–1945, 1978; The Reconstruction of Western Europe, 1984. Add: London Sch. of Economics, Aldwych, London WC2, England.

MINARIK, Else H(olmelund). American (born Danish), b. 1920. Children's fiction, Poetry. *Publs:* Little Bear, 1957; No Fighting, No Biting!, 1958; Father Bear Comes Home, 1959; Cat and Dog, 1960; Little Bear's Friend, 1960; Little Bear's Visit, 1961; Little Giant Girl and the Elf Boy, 1963; The Winds That Come from Far Away and Other Poems, 1964; A Kiss for Little Bear, 1968; (trans.) My Grandpa Is a Pirate, by Jan Loof, 1968; What If?, 1987; It's Spring!, 1989; Percy and the Five Houses, 1989. Add: c/o Greenwillow Books, 105 Madison Ave., New York, N.Y. 10016, U.S.A.

MINCHINTON, Walter Edward. British, b. 1921. Economics, History. Prof. of Economic History, Univ. of Exeter, since 1964 now Emeritus (Dept. Head, 1964–84). Asst. Lectr., 1948–50, Lectr., 1950–59, and Sr. Lectr., 1959–64, University Coll., Swansea. *Publs:* The British Tinplate Industry: A History, 1957; (ed.) The Trade of Bristol in the Eighteenth Century, 1957; Politics and the Port of Bristol in the Eighteenth Century, 1963; Essays in Agrarian History, 2 vols., 1969; Industrial Archaeology in Devon, 1969, 1973, 1980; (ed.) Industrial South Wales 1750–1914: Essays in Welsh Economic History, 1969; (ed.) Mercantilism: System or Expediency?, 1969; (ed.) The Growth of English Overseas Trade in the Seventeenth and Eighteenth Centuries, 1969; Wage Regulation in Pre-Industrial England, 1971; Devon at Work: Past and Present, 1974; Windmills of Devon, 1977; (ed.) American Papers in the House of Lords Record Office: A Guide, 1983; A Limekiln Miscellany: The South-West and South Wales, 1984; A Guide to Industrial Archaeology Sites in Britain, 1984; Virginia Slave Trade Statistics 1698–1775, 1984; Devon's Industrial Past: A Guide, 1986; Life to the City: An Illustrated History of Exeter's Water Supply from the Romans to the Present Day, 1987. Add: 53 Homefield Rd., Exeter EX1 2QX, England.

MINEAR, Paul Sevier. American, b. 1906. Theology/Religion. Emeritus Prof. of Biblical Theology, Yale Univ., New Haven, Conn., since 1971 (joined faculty, 1956). Prof. of New Testament, Garrett Theological Coll., 1934–44, and Andover Newton Theological Sch., 1944–56. Dir., Faith and Order Commn., World Council of Churches, 1961–63; Vice-Rector, Ecumenical Inst. for Advanced Theological Study, 1970–72. *Publs:* Introduction to Paul, 1937; And Great Shall Be Your Reward, 1941; Eyes of Faith, 1946; The Choice, 1948; The Kingdom and the Power, 1950; (co-author) Kierkegaard and the Bible, 1952; Christian Hope and the Second Coming: Jesus and His People, 1956; (ed.) The Nature of the Unity We Seek, 1958; Horizons of Christian Community, 1959; Images of the Church in the New Testament, 1960; The Gospel of Mark, 1962; (ed.) Faith and Order Findings, 1963; I Saw a New Earth, 1968; The Obedience of Faith, 1971; Commands of Christ, 1972; I Pledge Allegiance, 1975; To Heal and to Reveal, 1976; To Die and to Live, 1977; New Testament Apocalyptic, 1981; Matthew: The Teacher's Gospel, 1982; John: The Martyr's Gospel, 1985; Death Set to Music, 1986; The God of the Gospels, 1988. Add: c/o Westminster/John Knox Press, 100 Witherspoon St., Louisville, Ky. 40202, U.S.A.

MINEAR, Richard Hoffman. American, b. 1938.History, Translations. Prof. of History, Univ. of Massachusetts, Amherst, since 1975 (Assoc. Prof., 1970–75). Asst. Prof., Ohio State Univ., Columbus, 1967–70. *Publs:* Japanese Tradition and Western Law, 1970; Victors' Justice: Tokyo War Crimes Trial, 1971; (ed.) Through Japanese Eyes (high school readings), 1974, 1982; (trans.) Requiem for Battleship Yamato, by Yoshida Mitsuru, 1985; (ed. and trans.) Hiroshima: Three Witnesses, 1990. Add: Dept. of History, Univ. of Massachusetts, Amherst, Mass. 01003, U.S.A.

MINER, Earl (Roy). American, b. 1927. Literature, Translations. Townsend Martin Class of 1917 Prof. of Comparative Literature, Princeton Univ., New Jersey, since 1975 Stet (Prof. of English, 1972 75). Taught at Williams Coll., Williamstown, Mass., 1953 55, and the Univ. of California, Los Angeles, 1955–72. *Publs:* The Japanese Tradition in British and American Literature, 1958; (with R.H. Brower) Japanese Court Poetry, 1961; Nihon o Utsusu Chiisana Kagami, 1962; (ed.) The Fables of Aesop Paraphras'd in Verse, 1965; Restoration Dramatists, 1967; Dryden's Poetry, 1967; (with R.H. Brower) Fujiwara Teika's Superior Poems of Our Time, 1967; An Introduction to Japanese Court

Poetry, 1968; (trans.) Japanese Poetic Diaries, 1969; (ed.) Selected Poetry and Prose of John Dryden, 1969, 1985; (ed.) The Works of John Dryden, vol. III, 1969; The Metaphysical Mode from Donne to Cowley, 1969; (ed.) Seventeenth-Century Imagery, 1971; The Cavalier Mode from Jonson to Cotton, 1971; (ed.) English Criticism in Japan, 1972; John Dryden, 1973; The Restoration Mode from Milton to Dryden, 1974; (ed.) Illustrious Evidence: Approaches to English Literature of the Early 17th Century, 1975; (ed.) The Works of John Dryden, vol. XV, 1976; (ed.) Literary Uses of Typology from the Late Middle Ages to the Present, 1977; (trans.) Japanese Linked Poetry, 1979; (trans. with Hiroko Odagiri) The Money's Straw Raincoat and Other Poetry of the Basho School, 1982; (ed.) A History of Japanese Literature, 2 vols., 1984–86; Principles of Classical Japanese Literature, 1985; (with Hiroko Odagiri and Robert E. Morrell) The Princeton Companion to Classical Japanese Literature, 1985. Add: 22 McCosh, Princeton Univ., Princeton, N.J. 08544, U.S.A.

MINER, Ward L(ester). American, b. 1916. Literature, Biography. Prof. Emeritus of English, Youngstown State Univ., Ohio, since 1976 (Prof., 1957 76). *Publs:* The World of William Faulkner, 1952; (with T.M. Smith) Transatlantic Migration: The Contemporary American Novel in France, 1955; William Goddard, Newspaperman, 1962. Add: Harborside, Me. 04642, U.S.A.

MINES, Samuel. Also writes as Peter Field. American, b. 1909. Westerns/Adventure, Environmental science/Ecology, Medicine/Health. Book Reviewer, Book World, Washington Post, since 1971. Ed., Collier's Mag., NYC, 1955 56; Staff Writer, American Cyanamid, NYC, 1955 61, and Pfizer Inc., NYC, 1961–74; Contrib. Ed., Ecology Today, 1971– 73. *Publs:* (as Peter Field) Coyote Gulch, 1936; (ed.) The Best from Startling Stories (in U.K. as Startling Stories), 1953; (ed.) Moment Without Time, 1956; The Last Days of Mankind, 1971; The Conquest of Pain, 1974, 1979; Pfizer: An Informal History, 1978; The Melancholy Chord: A Study of Anxiety/Depression, 1978. Add: 881A Heritage Village, Southbury, Conn. 06488, U.S.A.

MINGAY, G(ordon) E(dmund). British, b. 1923. Economics, History. Prof. of Agrarian History, Univ. of Kent, Canterbury, Emeritus since 1985 (Reader in Economic and Social History, 1965 68). Lectr. in Economic History, London Sch. of Economics, 1957 65; Ed., The Agricultural History Review, 1972–84. *Publs:* English Landed Society in the Eighteenth Century, 1963; (with J.D. Chambers) The Agricultural Revolution 1750 1880, 1966; (ed. with E.L. Jones) Land, Labour and Population in the Industrial Revolution, 1967; Enclosure and the Small Farmer in the Age of the Industrial Revolution, 1968; (ed. with P.S. Bagwell) Britain and America: A Study of Economic Change 1850 1939, 1970; Fifteen Years On: The B.E.T. Group 1956-1971, 1973; (ed.) Arthur Young and His Times, 1975; The Gentry, 1976; Georgian London, 1976; Rural Life in Victorian England, 1976; The Agricultural Revolution, 1977; (ed.) The Victorian Countryside, 1981; An Epic of Progress: A History of British Frisian Cattle, 1982; The Transformation of Britain 1930-1939, 1985. Add: c/o Rutherford Coll., Univ. of Kent, Canterbury CT2 7NX, England.

MINGHELLA, Anthony. British, b. 1954. Novels, Plays/Screenplays. Lectr. in drama, Univ. of Hull, 1976 81. *Publs:* novel—On the Line, 1982; plays—Whale Music, 1983; A Little Like Drowning, 1985; Two Planks and a Passion, 1985; Made in Bangkok, 1986; The Story Teller (stories), 1988; Interior: Room, Exterior: City (three plays), 1989. Add: c/o Judy Daish Assocs., 83 Eastbourne Mews, London W2 6LQ, England.

MINHINNICK, Robert. British, b. 1952. Poetry. Has worked as a clerk, postman, salvage worker teacher, journalist, and writer-in-residence. *Publs:* A Thread in the Maze, 1978; Native Ground, 1979; Life Sentences, 1983; The Dinosaur Park, 1985, The Looters, 1989. Add: 11 Park Ave., Porthcawl, Mid-Glamorgan, Wales.

MINIUM, Edward W. American, b. 1917. Mathematics/Statistics (statistical psychology). Emeritus Prof. of Psychology, San Jose State Univ., California, since 1982 (joined faculty, 1948; Chmn. of Dept., 1961 66). *Publs:* Statistical Reasoning in Psychology and Education, 1970, 1978; (with Robert B. Clarke) Elements of Statistical Reasoning, 1982. Add: 2281 Lansford Ave., San Jose, Calif. 95125, U.S.A.

MINOGUE, Kenneth Robert. Australian, b. 1930. Philosophy, Politics/Government. Prof. of Political Science, London Sch. of Economics, since 1984 (Lectr., 1956 70; Reader, 1971 84). *Publs:* The Liberal Mind, 1963; Nationalism, 1967; The Concept of a University, 1973; (ed. with A. de Crespigny) Contemporary Political Philosophers, 1976; Alien Powers: The Pure Theory of Ideology, 1985. Add: 16 Buckland Cres., London NW3 5DX, England.

MINOT, Stephen. American, b. 1927. Novels/Short stories, Literature. Instr., and Asst. Prof., Bowdoin Coll., Maine, 1955–58; Asst. Prof., 1959–68, Assoc. Prof., 1969–77, and Prof., 1977–80, Trinity Coll., Hartford, Conn.,; Writer-in-Residence, Johns Hopkins Univ., Baltimore, 1974–75, and Pitzer Coll., Claremont, Calif., 1989. *Publs:* Chill of Dusk, 1964; Three Genres: The Writing of Fiction, Poetry, and Drama, 1965, 4th ed. 1987; (ed. with R. Wilson) Three Stances of Modern Fiction, 1972; Crossings (short stories), 1975; Ghost Images, 1979; Surviving the Flood, 1981. Add: 69 Hickory Hill Rd., Simsbury, Conn. 06070, U.S.A.

MINOT, Susan. American, b. 1956. Novels/Short stories. Assoc. Ed. Grand Street, NYC, 1982–86; Adjunct Prof., Grad. Writing Prog., New York Univ., 1987, and Columbia Univ., NYC, 1989. *Publs:* Monkeys, 1986; Lust & Other Stories, 1989. Add: c/o Georges Borchardt Inc., 136 E. 57th St., New York, N.Y. 10021, U.S.A.

MINOW, Newton N(orman). American, b. 1926. Media, Politics/Government. Partner, Sidley Austin, attorneys, Chicago, since 1965; Dir., Aetna Life Insurance Co. of Illinois and Aetna Casualty and Surety Co. of Illinois, both since 1973, Foote Cone and Belding, Chicago, since 1980, CBS Inc., since 1983, Encyclopaedia Britannica, since 1983, and Sara Lee Corp., since 1988. Dir., 1965–75 and since 1976, and Chmn., 1970–72, Rand Corp., California; Trustee, Univ. of Notre Dame, Indiana, 1966–77 and since 1983; Dir., Annenberg Washington Program, since 1987. Chmn., Federal Communications Commn., Washington, D.C., 1961–63; Gen. Counsel and Dir., Encyclopaedia Britannica Inc., and Dir., Encyclopaedia Britannica Educational Corp., Chicago, 1963–65; Dir., Chicago Pacific Corp., 1984–89. Trustee, Mayo Foundn., 1973–81; Chmn., Bd. of Govs., Public Broadcasting Service, 1979–80. *Publs:* Equal Time: The Private Broadcaster and the Public Interest, 1964; (with others) Voters' Time, 1969; (with J.B. Martin and L. M. Mitchell) Presidential Television, 1973; For Great Debates, 1987. Add: 179 E. Lake Shore Dr., Apt. 15W, Chicago, Ill. 60611, U.S.A.

MINSHALL, Vera. British, b. 1924. Novels/Short stories. Library Clerk, Stockport Central Reference Library, 1975–82, now retired. *Publs:* Was a Stranger, 1963; The Doctor's Secret, 1966; Call of the High Road, 1967; This Stony Ground, 1969. Add: 17 Fenton Ave., Hazel Grove, Stockport, Cheshire SK7 4AN, England.

MINSHULL, Roger (Michael). British, b. 1935. Geography. Sr. Lectr. in Geography, Bishop Grosseteste Coll., Lincoln, since 1967. Asst. Master in Geography, Rishworth Sch., Halifax, Yorks, 1959–62; Head of the Geography Dept., Broughton High Sch., Salford, 1962–66, and Levenshulme High Sch., Manchester, 1966–67. *Publs:* Regional Geography: Theory and Practice, 1967; Human Geography from the Air, 1968; Landforms from the Air, 1969; The Changing Nature of Geography, 1970; Settlements from the Air, 1971; (co-author) Simulation Games in Geography, 1972; (co-author) Correlation Techniques in Geography, 1972; (co-author) Networks in Geography, 1973; Introduction to Models in Geography, 1975. Add: Dept. of Geography, Bishop Grosseteste Coll., Lincoln, England.

MINSKY, Betty Jane. American, b. 1932. Business/Trade/Industry. Exec. Dir., Clinton Area New Development Organization, since 1988. S. Michigan Corresp., Religious News Service, NYC. Mgr., Cheboygan, Mich. Chamber of Commerce, 1961–65, and St. Johns, Mich. Chamber of Commerce, 1965–67; Staff Writer, Lansing State Journal daily newspaper, Michigan 1967–88. *Publs:* Gimmicks Make Money in Retailing, 1963, 1973. Add: 1738 E. Silvers Rd., Rt. 6, St Johns, Mich. 48879, U.S.A.

MINTER, David Lee. American, b. 1935. Literature. Prof. of English, Dean of Emory Coll., and Vice-Pres. for Arts and Sciences, Emory Univ., Atlanta, since 1981. Universitatslektor, Univ. of Hamburg, 1965–66; Lectr., Yale Univ., New Haven, Conn., 1966–67; Prof. of English, Rice Univ., Houston, 1974–80 (Asst. Prof., 1967–69; Assoc. Prof., 1969–74). *Publs:* The Interpreted Design as a Structural Principle in American Prose, 1969; (ed.) Twentieth Century Interpretations of Light in August, 1969; William Faulkner: His Life and Work, 1980; (co-ed.) The Harper American Literature, 1986; (ed.) The Norton Critical Edition of The Sound and the Fury, 1987; (co-ed.) The Colombia Literary History of the United States, 1987. Add: 300 White Hall, Emory University, Atlanta, Ga. 30322, U.S.A.

MINTZ, Ruth Finer. American, b. 1919. Poetry, Translations. Lectr. in American Poetry, Univ. of Tel Aviv, 1968–69; Lectr. in Modern Hebrew Literature, Univ. of Judaism, Los Angeles, 1975–77. *Publs:* The Darkening Green, 1965; (ed. and trans.) Modern Hebrew Poetry, 1966, 4th ed. 1982; Traveler Through Time, 1970; Jerusalem Poems—Love Songs, 1976; Auguries, Charms, Amulets, 1983. Add: Neve Granot-Rehov Airaham Granot, Block 3 Ent 5, Jerusalem 90376, Israel.

MINTZ, Samuel I(saiah). American, b. 1923. Literature, Philosophy. Prof. of English, City Coll. and Grad. Center, City Univ. of New York (joined faculty, 1948). Visiting Prof., Columbia Univ., NYC, 1969–70; Visiting Fellow, Wolfson Coll., Oxford, 1973. *Publs:* The Hunting of Leviathan: Thomas Hobbes in the Seventeenth Century, 1962; (co-ed.) From Smollett to James, 1981. Add: Dept. of Engligh, City Coll. of New York, New York, N.Y. 10031, U.S.A.

MIRABELLI, Eugene, Jr. American, b. 1931. Novels/Short stories. Assoc. Prof., State Univ. of New York at Albany, since 1969 (Asst. Prof., 1965–69). Instr., Williams Coll., Williamstown, Mass., 1960–64. *Publs:* The Burning Air, 1959; The Way In, 1968; No Resting Place, 1972. Add: 29 Bennett Terr., Delmar, N.Y. 12054, U.S.A.

MIRENBURG, Barry L. American, b. 1952. Philosophy, Social commentary/phenomena. Book Publisher, Barlenmir House Publrs., NYC, since 1970; also, Pres., Barlenmir House of Graphics, since 1970; Barlenmir House of Music, Barlenmir House Foundn. on the Arts, since 1972, and Barlenmir House Theatres Inc., since 1974. Advisory Bd. Member, East Coast Writers. *Publs:* (co-ed.) Barlenmir House Anthology (poetry and short stories); The Joy of Living. Add: 413 City Island Ave., New York, N.Y. 10064, U.S.A.

MIRSKY, Mark (Jay). American, b. 1939. Novels/Short stories, Writing/Journalism. Prof. of English, City Coll. of New York. *Publs:* Thou Worm, Jacob, 1967; Proceedings of the Rabble, 1970; Blue Hill Avenue, 1972; The Secret Table, 1975; My Search for the Messiah, 1977, The Red Adam, 1989. Add: 513 E. 13th St., New York, N.Y. 10009, U.S.A.

MISHAN, E. J. British, b. 1917. Economics, Social commentary/phenomena, Sociology. Prof. in Economics, London Sch. of Economics, 1956–77 (former Lectr. and Reader in Economics). *Publs:* The Cost of Economic Growth, 1967; Twenty-One Popular Economic Fallacies, 1969; Welfare Economics: An Assessment, 1969. Cost-Benefit Analysis, 1971; Making the World Safe for Pornography, 1973; The Economic Growth Debate, 1977; An Introduction to Normative Economics, 1980; Economic Efficiency and Social Welfare, 1980; Pornography, Psychedelics, and Technology, 1981; Introduction to Political Economy, 1982; Economic Myths and the Mythology of Economics, 1986. Add: 22 Gainsborough Gardens, London NW8, England.

MITCHELL, Adrian. British, b. 1932. Novels/Short stories, Plays/Screenplays, Poetry. Ed., Isis mag., Christ Church Oxford, 1954–55; Reporter, Oxford Mail, 1955–57, and Evening Standard, London, 1957–59; Columnist and Reviewer, Daily Mail, Woman's Mirror, The Sun, The Sunday Times, Peace News, The Black Dwarf, and The Guardian, all in London; Instr., Univ. of Iowa, Iowa City, 1963–64; Granada Fellow in the Arts, Univ. of Lancaster, 1967–69; Fellow, Wesleyan Univ. Center for the Humanities, Middletown, Conn., 1971; Resident Writer, Sherman Theatre, Cardiff, 1974–75; Visiting Writer, Billericay Comprehensive Sch., Essex, 1978–80; Judith E. Wilson Fellow, Cambridge Univ., 1980–81. *Publs:* (Poems) 1955; (ed. with Richard Selig) Oxford Poetry 1955, 1955; If You See Me Comin' (novel), 1962; Poems, 1964; The Marat/Sade, adaptation of the play by Peter Weiss, 1965; Peace Is Milk (verse), 1966; (with others) US (play; in U.S. as Tell Me Lies), 1968; Out Loud (verse), 1968; The Body (screenplay commentary), 1969; The Bodyguard (novel), 1970; (ed.) Jump, My Brothers, Jump: Poems from Prison, by Tim Daly, 1970; (ed. with Brian Elliott) Bards in the Wilderness, 1971; Ride the Nightmare: Verse and Prose, 1971; Tyger: A Celebration of the Life and Work of William Blake (play), 1971; Man Friday (television play), 1972; as stage play 1973, as novel 1975; Cease-Fire (verse), 1973; (with John Fuller and Peter Levi) Penguin Modern Poets 22, 1973; Man Friday, and Mind Your Head (plays), 1973; Wartime (novel), 1973; The Apeman Cometh (verse), 1975; Houdini, 1977; Naked in Cheltenham, 1978; For Beauty Douglas: Collected Poems and Songs, 1981; Nothingmas Day (for children), 1983; On the Beach at Cambridge, 1984; (adaptor) The Government Inspector, 1985; The Baron Rides Out (for children), 1985; The Baron on the Island of Cheese (for children), 1986; Leonardo, The Lion from Nowhere (for children), 1986; The Pied Piper (play), 1987; The Baron All at Sea (for children), 1987; Our Mammouth (for children), 1987; Our Mammouth Goes to School (for children), 1988; Woman Overboard (play), 1988; The Patchwork Girl of Oz (play), 1988; Love Songs of World War Three (lyrics), 1989. Add: c/o Fraser and Dunlop Scripts Ltd., 91 Regent St., London W1R 8RU, England.

MITCHELL, Broadus. American, b. 1892. Economics, History, Biography. Lectr. in Economics in various U.S. universities, 1919–68. Member, Columbia Univ. Grad. Seminar in Early American History and Culture, NYC. *Publs:* The Rise of Cotton Mills in the South, 1921; F.L. Olmstead: Critic of the Old South, 1924; (with G.S. Mitchell) The Industrial Revolution in the South, 1930; William Gregg: Factory Master of the Old South, 1930; a Preface to Economics, 1933; (with L.P. Mitchell) Practical Problems in Economics, 1937; (with L.P. Mitchell) American Economic History, 1947; Depression Decade; 1947; American Adventure, 1949; Heritage from Hamilton: Alexander Hamilton, 2 vols., 1957; (with L.P. Mitchell) A Biography of the Constitution of the United States, 1962–1964, 1974; Great Economists in Their Times, 1965; Postscripts to Economic History, 1967; The Road to Yorktown, 1970; Alexander Hamilton: The Revolutionary Years, 1971; The Price of Independence, 1974; Alexander Hamilton: A Concise Biography, 1976. Add: c/o Dyer, 5 Memory Lane, Croton, N.Y. 10520, U.S.A.

MITCHELL, David (John). New Zealander, b. 1940. Poetry. *Publs:* Orange Grove, 1969; Pipe Dreams in Ponsonby, 1972. Add: c/o RKS ART, 41a Victoria St. W., Auckland, New Zealand.

MITCHELL, David (John). British, b. 1924. History, Biography, Staff Journalist, Picture Post, London, 1947–52; Owner-Mgr., Pictorial Press Ltd., London, 1954–57; Picture Ed., Central Office of Information, London, 1957–65. *Publs:* (ed.) Flanders and Other Fields: Memoirs of Baroness de T'Serclaes, 1964; Women on the Warpath: Story of Women of the First World War (in U.S. as Monstrous Regiment), 1966; The Fighting Pankhursts, 1967; The Pankhursts, 1970; 1919 Red Mirage, 1970; The Missionary Impulse, 1973; Bernardo O'Higgins, 1975; Pirates, 1976; Queen Christabel: A Biography of Christabel Pankhurst, 1977; The Jesuits: A History, 1980; The Spanish Civil War, 1982; Here Is Spain, 1988. Add: 20 Mountacre Close, Sydenham Hill, London SE26, England.

MITCHELL, (Sibyl) Elyne (Keith). Australian, b. 1913. Novels/Short stories, Children's fiction, Sports, Travel/Exploration/Adventure, Autobiography/Memoirs/Personal. Works on family cattle station. *Publs:* Australia's Alps, 1942; Speak to the Earth, 1945; Soil and Civilization, 1946; Images in Water, 1947; Flow River Blow Wind, 1953; Black Cockatoos Mean Snow, 1956; Silver Brumby series, 6 vols., 1958–76; Kingfisher Feather, 1962; Winged Skis, 1964; Moon Filly, 1968; Jinki Dingo of the Snows, 1970; Light Horse to Damascus, 1971; The Colt at Taparoo, 1975; Light Horse: The Story of Australia's Mounted Troops (for adults), 1978; The Colt from Snowy River, 1979; The Snowy Mountains (for adults), 1980; Snowy River Brumby, 1980; Brumby Racer, 1981; Man from Snowy River, 1982; Chauvel Country (for adults), 1983; Discoverers of the Snowy Mountains (for adults), 1985; The Light Horse Men (novelization of film), 1987; A Vision of the Snowy Mountains, 1988. Add: Towong Hill, Corryong, Vic., Australia.

MITCHELL, Geoffrey Duncan. British. Sociology. Emeritus Prof. of Sociology, and Research Fellow, Inst. of Population Studies, Univ. of Exeter (Lectr. and Sr. Lectr., 1954–67; Prof., 1967–86). Sr. Research Worker, Univ. of Liverpool, 1950–52; Lectr. in Sociology, Univ. of Birmingham, 1952–54. *Publs:* (with T. Lupton, M.W. Hodges and C.S. Smith) Neighbourhood and Community, 1954; Sociology: The Study of Social Systems, 1959, 1972; (ed. and contrib.) A Dictionary of Sociology, 1968; A Hundred Years of Sociology, 1968; (ed. and contrib.) A New Dictionary of Sociology, 1979; (with R. Snowden) The Artificial Family, 1981; (with R. and E. Snowden) Artificial Reproduction, 1983. Add: 26 West Ave., Exeter, Devon, England.

MITCHELL, George Archibald Grant. British, b. 1906. Biology, Medicine/Health. Emeritus Prof. of Anatomy and Dir. of the Anatomical Labs., Univ. of Manchester (Prof. and Dir., 1946–74; Dean, Medical Sch., 1952–60; Pro-Vice-Chancellor of the Univ., 1960–64). Pres., Anatomical Soc. of Great Britain and Ireland, 1961–63; Hon Secty., 1955–70, and Chmn., 1970–73, Intnl. Anatomical Nomenclature Cttee. *Publs:* (with A.E. Porritt) Penicillin Therapy and Control in 21 Army Group; The Essentials of Neuroanatomy, 1951, 4th ed. (with D. Mayor) 1984; Anatomy of the Autonomic Nervous System, 1953; Basic Anatomy, 1954 3rd ed. 1966; (with E.L. Patterson) Nomina Anatomica, 1955, 1961; Cardiovascular Innervation, 1956. Add: 16 Fellpark Rd., Manchester M23, England.

MITCHELL, James (William). Also writes as James Munro. British, b. 1926. Mystery/Crime/Suspense. Lectr. in English, South Shields Technical Coll., 1950–59; television writer, London, 1959–63; Lectr. in Liberal Studies, Sunderland Coll. of Art, Co. Durham, 1963–64. *Publs:*

Here's a Villain, 1957, in U.S. as The Lady Is Waiting, 1958; A Way Back, 1959, in U.S. as The Way Back, 1960; Steady Boys, Steady, 1960; Among Arabian Sands, 1962; (as James Munro) The Man Who Sold Death, 1964; (as James Munro) Die Rich, Die Happy, 1965; (as James Munro) The Money That Money Can't Buy, 1967; (as James Munro) The Innocent Bystanders, 1969; Magnum for Schneider, 1969, in U.S. as A Red File for Callan, 1971, in U.K. paperback as Callan, 1974; Ilion Like a Mist, 1969, in U.K. paperback as Venus in Plastic, 1970; The Winners, 1970; Russian Roulette, 1973; Death and Bright Water, 1974; Smear Job, 1975; The Evil Ones, 1982; Sometimes You Could Die, 1985; Dead Ernest, 1986. Add: 41 Barons Keep, Gliffon Rd., London WI4 9AU, England.

MITCHELL, Jerome. American, b. 1935. Literature. Prof. of English, Univ. of Georgia, Athens, since 1972 (Assoc. Prof., 1967–72). Assoc. Ed., South Atlantic Bulletin, 1970–76; Fulbright Guest Prof., Univ. of Bonn, 1972–73; Richard Merton Guest Prof., Univ. of Regensburg, 1978–79. *Publs:* Thomas Hoccleve: A Study in Early 15th Century English Poetic, 1968; (reviser with A.I. Doyle) Hoccleve's Works: The Minor Poems, 1970; (ed. with W. Provost) Chaucer the Love Poet, 1973; The Walter Scott Operas, 1977; Scott, Chaucer, and Medieval Romance, 1987. Add: Dept. of English, Univ. of Georgia, Athens, Ga. 30602, U.S.A.

MITCHELL, Joan E. British, b. 1920. Economics, Politics/Government. Prof. of Political Economy, Univ. of Nottingham, 1978–85. Member, National Bd. for Prices and Incomes, 1965–68. *Publs:* Crisis in Britain, 1951, 1963; Groundwork to Economic Planning, 1966; The National Board for Prices and Incomes, 1972; Price Determination and Prices Policy, 1977. Add: 15 Ranmoor Rd., Gedling, Nottingham, England.

MITCHELL, John Howard. American, b. 1921. Writing/Journalism. Prof. of English, Univ. of Massachusetts, Amherst, since 1966 (Asst. Prof., 1954–59; Assoc. Prof., 1959–66). Former communications consultant. *Publs:* Handbook of Technical Communication, 1962; Writing for Technical and Professional Journals, 1968. Add: Dept. of English, Univ. of Massachusetts, Amherst, Mass. 01002, U.S.A.

MITCHELL, John Phillimore. British, b. 1918. Medicine/Health. Consultant Urological Surgeon, now Consultant Emeritus, United Bristol Hosps., and Southmead Gen. Hosp., since 1952; Hon. Prof. of Surgery (Urology), Univ. of Bristol; Member, Court of Examiners, Royal Coll. of Surgeons (England). *Publs:* Urology for Nurses, 1965; (with G.N. Lumb) A Handbook for Surgical Diathermy, 1966; The Principles of Transurethral Resection and Haemostasis, 1972; Endoscopic Operative Urology, 1981; Trauma to the Urinary Tract, 1984. Add: Abbey Cottage, Parry's Close, Bristol BS9 1AW, England.

MITCHELL, Joseph. American, b. 1908. Short stories, Essays. Staff Writer, The New Yorker, NYC since 1938. Reporter, New York Herald Tribune, 1929–31, and New York World Telegram, 1931–38. *Publs:* My Ears Are Bent (newspaper articles), 1938; McSorley's Wonderful Saloon, 1943; Old Mr. Flood, 1948; The Bottom of the Harbor, 1959; Joe Gould's Secret, 1965. Add: c/o The New Yorker, 25 W. 43rd St., New York, N.Y. 10036, U.S.A.

MITCHELL, (Charles) Julian. British, b. 1935. Novels/Short stories, Plays/Screenplays, Biography. Midshipman, Royal Naval Volunteer Reserve, 1953–55. *Publs:* Imaginary Toys, 1961; A Disturbing Influence, 1962; As Far as You Can Go, 1963; The White Father, 1964; (adapter) A Heritage and Its History, 1965; a Circle of Friends, 1966; The Undiscovered Country, 1968; (with Peregrine Churchill) Jennie: Lady Randolph Churchill: A Portrait with Letters, 1974; (adapter) A Family and a Fortune, 1974; Half-Life (play), 1977; The Enemy Within (play), 1980; Another Country (play), 1982, (film), 1984; Francis (play), 1983; After Aida (play), 1985. Add: 2 Castle Rise, Llanvaches, Newport, Gwent NP6 3BS, Wales.

MITCHELL, Juliet. New Zealander, b. 1940. Women. Psychoanalyst: Freelance writer, broadcaster and lectr. since 1971. Lectr. in English, Univ. of Leeds, 1962–63, and Univ. of Reading, 1965–70. *Publs:* Women: The Longest Revolution, 1966; Woman's Estate, 1972; Psychoanalysis and Feminism, 1974; (co-ed.) Rights and Wrongs of Women, 1977; (co-ed.) Feminine Sexuality, 1982; Women: The Longest Revolution, 1984; (with A. Oakley) What is Feminism?, 1986; (ed.) The Selected Writings of Melanie Klein, 1987. Add: c/o Deborah Rogers, 20 Powis Mews, London W11 IJN, England.

MITCHELL, Loften. American, b. 1919. Novels, Plays/Screenplays,

Race relations, Theatre. Ed., NAACP Journal, 1964. *Publs:* A Land Beyond the River, 1957; Tell Pharaoh, 1963; Star of the Morning, 1965; Black Drama: The Story of the American Negro in the Theatre, 1967; The Stubborn Old Lady Who Resisted Change (novel), 1973; (ed.) Voices of the Black Theatre, 1975; Bubbling Brown Sugar, 1984. Add: 15 McNamara Ave., Binghamton, N.Y. 13903, U.S.A.

MITCHELL, Margaretta. American, b. 1935. Poetry, Photography. Vice-Pres., ASMP Northern California Chapter, 1988–89. *Publs:* Gift of Place, 1969; (co-author) To a Cabin, 1973; Recollections: Ten Women of Photography, 1979; (contrib.) Rising Goddess, 1982; Dance For Life, 1985; (with others.) Ruth Bernhard: The Eternal Body, 1986. Add: 280 Hillcrest Rd., Berkeley, Calif. 94705, U.S.A.

MITCHELL, Memory F. American, b. 1924. History, Politics/Government. Instr., Dept. of History, Meredith Coll., Raleigh, N.C., 1949–50; Admin. Asst., North Carolina State Bd. of Public Welfare, Raleigh, 1950–54; Judge, Cabarrus County Domestic Relations Court, Concord, N.C., 1954–55; Asst. State Archivist, 1956–61, and Chief, Historical Publs. Section, 1961–82, Div. of Archives and History, Raleigh, now retired. Chmn., Editorial Bd., American Archivist, 1972–74. *Publs:* Legal Aspects of Conscription and Exemption in North Carolina 1861–1865, 1965; (ed.) Messages, Addresses, and Public Papers of Terry Sanford, Governor of North Carolina 1961–1965, 1966; North Carolina's Signers: Brief Sketches of the Men Who Signed the Declaration of Independence and the Constitution, 1969; (ed.) Messages, Addresses, and Public Papers of Daniel Killian Moore, Governor of North Carolina 1965–69, 1971; (ed.) Addresses and Public Papers of Robert Walter Scott, Governor of North Carolina 1969–1973, 1974; (ed.) Addresses and Public Papers of James Eubert Holshouser, Jr., Governor of North Carolina 1973–77, 1978; (ed.) Addresses and Public Papers of James Baxter Hunt, Jr., Governor of North Carolina 1977–1981, 1982. Add: 2431 Medway Dr., Raleigh, N.C. 27608, U.S.A.

MITCHELL, Robby K. American, b. 1916. Poetry. Real Estate Mgr., Shaunlyn Homes, since 1961. State Councillor, Texas, since 1969. Poet Laureate of Texas, 1970–71. *Publs:* Mockingbird's Song in the Night, 1956; Fire and Frost, 1963; And Burn My Brand, 1969; Splinter of Bone, 1978; (ed.) First Flight, 1980; (ed.) Feathers on The Wind, 1984; (ed.) Wings over Texas, 1987. Add: 405 N. Waddill, McKinney, Tex, 75069, U.S.A.

MITCHELL, Roger. American, b. 1935. Poetry. Assoc. Prof. of English, Marquette Univ., Milwaukee, since 1971 (Asst. Prof., 1968–71). Ed., The Minnesota Review, since 1973. Asst. Prof. and Instr., Univ. of Wisconsin, Madison, 1963–68. *Publs:* Letters from Siberia and Other Poems, 1971; (co-ed.) This Book Has No Title: An Anthology of Milwaukee Poetry, 1971; Edges, 1973; Moving, 1975; Clear Space on a Cold Day, 1986. Add: English Dept., Marquette Univ., Milwaukee, Wisc., U.S.A.

MITCHELL, W(illiam) O(rmond). Canadian, b. 1914. Novels/Short stories, Plays/Screenplays. *Publs:* Who Has Seen the Wind, 1947; The Alien, 1954; Jake and the Kid, 1961; The Kite, 1962; The Black Bonspiel of Wullie MacCrimmon, 1965, as play 1966; The Vanishing Point, 1973; Back to Beulah (play), 1976; How I Spent My Summer Holidays, 1981; The Dramatic W.O. Mitchell (plays), 1982; Since Daisy Creek, 1984. Add: 3031 Roxboro Glen Rd., Calgary, Alta., Canada.

MITCHISON, Naomi (Margaret). British, b. 1897. Novels/Short stories, Children's fiction, Plays/Screenplays, Poetry, Children's non-fiction, History. Member, Argyll County Council, 1945–66, and Highland Panel, 1947–65, Scotland; Member, Highland and Island Advisory Council, Scotland, 1966–76; Tribal Adviser and Mmarona (Mother) to the Bakgatla of Botswana, 1963–73. *Publs:* The Conquered, 1923; When the Bough Breaks and Other Stories, 1924; Cloud Cuckoo Lane, 1925; The Laburnum Branch (poetry), 1926; Black Sparta: Greek Stories, 1928; Anna Comnena, 1928; Barbarian Stories, 1929; Nix-Nought-Nothing: Four Plays for Children, 1929; The Hostages and Other Stories for Boys and Girls, 1930; Comments on Birth Control, 1930; The Corn King and the Spring Queen, 1931; (with L.E. Gielgud) The Price of Freedom, 1931; Boys and Girls and Gods, 1931; The Powers of Light, 1932; The Delicate Fire: Short Stories and Poems, 1933; The Home and a Changing Civilisation, 1934; (with Wyndham Lewis) Beyond This Limit, 1935; We Have Been Warned, 1935; Vienna Diary, 1935; The Fourth Pig, 1936; (with R.H.S. Crossman) Socrates, 1937; An End and a Beginning and Other Plays, 1937; The Moral Basis of Politics, 1938; Kingdom of Heaven, 1939; (with L.E. Gielgud) As It Was in the Beginning, 1939; The Blood of Martyrs, 1939; The Bull Calves, 1947; (with D. Macintosh) Men and

Herring, 1949; The Big House, 1950; (with D. Macintosh) Spindrift, 1951; Lobsters on the Agenda, 1952; Travel Light, 1952; The Swan's Road, 1954; Graeme and the Dragon, 1954; To the Chapel Perilous, 1955; The Land the Ravens Found, 1955; Little Boxes, 1956; The Far Harbour, 1957; Behold Your King, 1957; Five Men and a Swan: Short Stories and Poems, 1958; Other People's Worlds, 1958; Judy and Lakshmi, 1959; The Rib of the Green Umbrella, 1960; The Young Alexander the Great, 1960; Karensgaard: The Story of a Danish Farm, 1961; (with G.W.L. Paterson) A Fishing Village on the Clyde, 1961; Presenting Other People's Children, 1961; Memoirs of a Spacewoman, 1962; The Young Alfred the Great, 1962; The Fairy Who Couldn't Tell a Lie, 1963; Alexander the Great, 1964; Henney and Crispies, 1964; Ketse and the Chief, 1965; When We Become Men, 1965; Return to the Fairy Hill, 1966; Friends and Enemies, 1966; The Big Surprise, 1967; Highland Holiday, 1967; African Heroes, 1968; Don't Look Back, 1969; The Family at Ditlabeng, 1969; The Africans: A History, 1970; Sun and Moon, 1970; Cleopatra's People, 1972; A Danish Teapot, 1973; Sunrise Tomorrow, 1973; Small Talk, 1973; A Life for Africa: The Story of Bram Fischer, 1973; Oil for the Highlands?, 1974; All Change Here, 1976; Snake!, 1976; Solution Three, 1977; The Cleansing of the Knife (poetry), 1979; The Two Magicians, 1979; You May Well Ask, 1979; Images of Africa, 1980; The Vegetable War, 1980; Mucking Around: Five Continents over Fifty Years, 1981; What Do You Think Yourself: Scottish Short Stories, 1982; Not by Bread Alone, 1983; Among You, Taking Notes: The Wartime Diary of Naomi Mitchison 1939–45, 1985; Beyond This Limit, 1986; Early in Orcadia, 1987. Add: Carradale, Campbeltown, Argyll, Scotland.

MITCHISON, Rosalind. British, b. 1919. History, Biography. Prof. of Social History, Univ. of Edinburgh, since 1981, Emeritus since 1986 (Asst. Lectr., 1954–57; Lectr., 1967–76; Reader, 1976–81). *Publs:* Agricultural Sir John (biography), 1962; A History of Scotland, 1970; (ed. with N.T. Phillipson) Scotland in the Age of Improvement, 1970; British Population Change since 1860, 1977; Life in Scotland, 1978; (ed.) The Roots of Nationalism, 1980; Lordship to Patronage: Scotland 1603–1745, 1983; (ed. with Peter Roebuck) Economy and Society in Scotland and Ireland 1500-1939, 1988; (ed. with T.M. Devine) People and Society in Scotland, vol. I, 1988. Add: Dept. of Economic and Social History, Univ. of Edinburgh, Edinburgh, Scotland.

MITCHUM, Hank. *See* **NEWTON,** D.B.

MITFORD, Jessica. American (b. British), b. 1917. Social commentary/phenomena, Autobiography/Memoirs/Personal. *Publs:* Lifeitselfmanship, 1956; Hons and Rebels (in U.S. as Daughters and Rebels), 1960; The American Way of Death, 1963; The Trial of Doctor Spock, 1970; Kind and Usual Punishment (in U.K. as The American Prison Business), 1973; A Fine Old Conflict, 1977; Poison Penmanship: The Gentle Art of Muckraking (in U.K. as The Making of a Muckraker), 1979; Faces of Philip: A Memoir of Philip Toynbee, 1984; Grace Had an English Heart; 1988. Add: 6411 Regent St., Oakland, Calif. 94618, U.S.A.

MITGANG, Herbert. American, b. 1920. Novels/Short stories, Plays/Screenplays, Literature, Biography. Publishing, Cultural Corresp., The New York Times, since 1976 (Member, Editorial Bd., 1963–64, 1967–76); Contributing Ed., Art News, NYC, since 1973; Pres., Authors League Fund, since 1976. Exec. Ed., CBS News, 1964–67; Pres., Authors Guild, 1971–75; Visiting Lectr., Yale Univ., New Haven, Conn., 1975–76. *Publs:* The Man Who Rode the Tiger: The Life and Times of Judge Samuel Seabury, 1963; The Return, 1958; (ed.) The Letters of Carl Sandburg, 1968; (ed.) America at Random, 1969; Working for the Reader, 1970; (ed.) Washington D.C. in Lincoln's Time, 1971; Abraham Lincoln: A Press Portrait, 1971; (ed.) Spectator of America, 1972; Get These Men Out of the Hot Sun, 1972; The Fiery Trial: A Life of Lincoln, 1974; Mister Lincoln (play), 1980; The Montauk Fault, 1982; Kings in the Counting House, 1984; Gur'nor (play), 1987. Add: c/o New York Times, 229 W. 43rd St., New York, N.Y. 10036, U.S.A.

MITSON, Eileen N(ora). British, b. 1930. Novels/Short stories, Autobiography/Memoirs/Personal. ; Columnist, Christian Woman, since 1982. *Publs:* Stairway of Surprises, 1964; The Door in the Wall, 1967; His Bright Designs, 1968; Beyond the Shadows, 1968; Amazon Adventure, 1969; House Full of Strangers, 1970; The Inside Room, 1973; A Kind of Freedom, 1976; Reaching for God, 1978; (co-author) Creativity, 1985. Add: 39 Oaklands, Hamilton Rd., Reading Berks. RG1 5RN, England.

MO, Timothy. British (born Hong Kong), b. 1953. Novels. *Publs:* The Monkey King, 1978; Sour Sweet, 1982; An Insular Possession, 1986. Add: c/o Deutsch, 106 Great Russell St., London WC1B 3LJ, England.

MOAT, John. British, b. 1936. Novels/Short stories, Poetry. *Publs:* 6d per Annum, 1966; Heorot (novel), 1968; A Standard of Verse, 1969; Thunder of Grass, 1970; The Tugen and the Toot (novel), 1973; The Ballad of the Leat, 1974; Bartonwood (juvenile), 1978; Fiesta and the Fox Reviews His Prophecy, 1979; (with John Fairfax) The Way to Write, 1981; Skeleton Key, 1982; Mai's Wedding (novel), 1983; Welcombe Overtures, 1987; The Missing Moon (novel), 1988; The Miraculous Mandarin (poetry), 1989. Add: c/o A.D. Peters and Co., The Chambers, Chelsea Harbour, Lots Rd., London SW10 0XF, England.

MOBERG, David O. American, b. 1922. Sociology, (gerontology),Theology/Religion. Prof. of Sociology, Marquette Univ., Milwaukee, since 1968 (Chmn. of the Dept., 1968–77). Co-Ed., Research in the Social Scientific Study of Religion, since 1986; Assoc. Ed., Review of Religious Research, since 1983 (Ed., 1969–73; Contr. Ed., 1973–77); Member, Editorial Cttee., Social Compass, since 1968; Consulting Ed., Perspectives on Science and Christian Faith, since 1987. Consulting Ed., Eternity mag., 1960–86; Ed., 1962–64, and Consulting Ed., 1964–73, Journal of the American Scientific Affiliation; Assoc. Ed., Sociological Quarterly, 1963–69; Contrib. Ed., The Other Side, 1967–76; Ed., Adris Newsletter, 1971–76; Consulting Ed., California Sociologist, 1982–86. *Publs:* The Church as a Social Institution, 1962, 1984; (with R.M. Gray) The Church and the Older Person, 1962, 1977; Inasmuch: Christian Social Responsibility in the Twentieth Century, 1965; (ed.) International Directory of Religious Information Systems, 1971; The Great Reversal: Evangelism and Social Concern, 1972, 1977; (ed.) Spiritual Well-Being: Sociological Perspectives, 1979; Wholistic Christianity, 1985. Add: Dept. of Social and Cultural Sciences, Marquette Univ., Milwaukee, Wisc. 53233, U.S.A.

b**MOE**, Christian H(ollis). American, b. 1929. Plays/Screenplays, Theatre. Prof. of Theatre since 1968, Dir. of the Playwriting Program since 1969, and Dir. of Graduate Studies in Theatre since 1970, Southern Illinois Univ., Carbondale (Asst. Prof., 1958–63; Assoc. Prof., 1963–68). Chmn., National Playwriting Awards, American College Theatre Festival, 1980–82. *Publs:* (with George McCalmon) Creating Historical Drama, 1965; (ed. with George Plochmann) Introduction to Western Humanities: A Syllabus, vols. I-III, 1966; (with Darwin Payne) The Strolling Players (play), 1971; (ed. with Darwin Payne) Six New Plays for Children, 1971; (with Cameron Garbutt) How Santa Claus Came to Simpson's Crossing (play adaptation), 1975; (ed. with Boyd Butler and Archibald McLeod) America at the Confluence, 1973; (with Cameron Garbutt) Three Rabbits White (play), 1979; (with Cameron Garbutt) Tom Sawyer: An adaptation (play), 1979; (with Cameron Garbutt) Get Your Act Together (play), 1982; The Village That Voted the Earth is Flat (musical), 1987. Add: 603 S. Curtis Pl., Carbondale, Ill. 62901, U.S.A.

MOENSSENS, Andre A. American, b. 1930. Criminology/Law enforcement/Prisons, Law. Prof. of Law, and Dir. of the Inst. for Trial Advocacy, Univ. of Richmond Sch. of Law, since 1973. Consultant in criminal law and scientific evidence. Prof. of Law, Chicago-Kent Coll. of Law, Illinois Inst. of Technology, Chicago, 1967–73. *Publs:* Fingerprints and the Law, 1969; Fingerprint Techniques, 1971; (with Inbau and Vitullo) Scientific Police Investigation, 1971; (with Inbau) Scientific Evidence in Criminal Cases, 1973, 3rd ed. 1982; (with Inbau and Thompson) Cases and Comments on Criminal Law, 1973, 3rd ed. 1982; Cases and Comments on Criminal Procedure, 1979. Add: Univ. of Richmond Sch. of Law, Richmond, Va. 23173, U.S.A.

MOFFAT, Gwen. British, b. 1924. Novels/Short stories, Mystery/Crime/Suspense, Environmental science/Ecology, Recreation/Leisure/Hobbies, Travel/Exploration/Adventure. *Publs:* mystery novels—Lady with a Cool Eye, 1973; Deviant Death, 1973; The Corpse Road, 1974; Miss Pink at the Edge of the World, 1975; Over the Sea to Death, 1976; A Short Time to Live, 1976; Persons Unknown, 1978; Die Like a Dog, 1982; Last Chance Country, 1983; Grizzly Trail, 1984; Snare, 1987; other—Space Below My Feet (autobiography), 1961; Two Star Red: A Book about R.A.F. Mountain Rescue, 1964; On My Home Ground (autobiography), 1968; Survival Count (on conservation), 1972; Hard Option (novel), 1975; Hard Road West, 1981; The Buckskin Girl (western), 1982. Add: c/o A.M. Heath, 79 St. Martin's Lane, London WC2N 4AA, England.

MOFFAT, John Lawrence. New Zealander, b. 1916. Education, Language/Linguistics. Principal Lectr. in Post-Primary Language, Secondary Div., Christchurch Teachers' Coll., 1954–79, now retired. Education Columnist, Learn and Live, Christchurch Star, since 1965. Language Master, Christchurch Boys' High Sch., 1939–53. *Publs:* The Structure of English, 1968; A Guide to Study, 1971. Add: Soul's Repose, 51 London St., Christchurch 1, New Zealand.

MOFFETT, Judith. American, b. 1942. Poetry, Science fiction, Translations. Asst. Prof. of English, Univ. of Pennsylvania, Philadelphia, since 1979 (Visiting Lectr., 1978–79). Asst. Prof., Behrend Coll., Pennsylvania State Univ., Erie, 1971–75; Visiting Lectr., Program in Creative Writing, Univ. of Iowa, Iowa City, 1977–78. *Publs:* Keeping Time (verse), 1976; (trans.) Gentleman, Single, Refined, and Selected Poems 1937–59, by Hjalmar Gullberg, 1979; Whinny Moor Crossing (verse), 1984; James Merrill: An Introduction to the Poetry (criticism), 1984; Pennterra (science fiction), 1987. Add: 39 Rabbit Run, Wallingford, Pa. 19085, U.S.A.

MOFFETT, Samuel Hugh. American, b. 1916. History, Theology/Religion. Prof. of Missions and Ecumenics, Princeton Theological Seminary, N.J., 1981–87, now Emeritus (member of faculty, 1953–55). Missionary of the United Presbyterian Church: to China, 1947–51: member of faculty, Yenching Univ., Peking, 1948–49, Nanking Theological Seminary, 1949–50; to Korea, 1955–81; Principal, Kyongan Hisher Bible Sch., Andong, 1957–59, Prof. of Historical Theology and Church History, 1960–81, Dean of Grad. Sch., 1966–70, and Assoc. Pres., 1970–81, Dir., Asian Center for Theological Studies and Mission, Seoul, 1974–81. *Publs:* Where'er the Sun, 1953; The Christians of Korea, 1962; (with E.F. Moffett) Joy for an Anxious Age, 1966; The Biblical Background of Evangelism, 1968; Asia and Missions (in Korean), 1976; (with P. Underwood and J. Sibley) First Encounters: Korea 1880–1910, 1982. Add: Princeton Theological Seminary, Princeton, N.J. 08542, U.S.A.

MOGGACH, Deborah. British, b. 1948. Novels/Short stories, Plays/Screenplays. Asst. Librarian, Oxford Univ. Press, London, 1971–73. *Publs:* You Must Be Sisters, 1978; Close to Home, 1979; A Quiet Drink, 1980; Hot Water Man, 1982; Porky, 1983; To Have and to Hold, 1986; Smile, 1987; Driving in the Dark, 1988; Stolen, 1989. Add: 24 Ivor St., London NW1, England.

MOHL, Ruth. American, b. 1891. Literature, Biography, Essays. Assoc. Prof. of English Language and Literature, Brooklyn Coll., City Univ. of New York, 1942–62, now retired. *Publs:* The Three Estates in Medieval and Renaissance Literature, 1933; Studies in Spenser, Milton, and the Theory of Monarchy, 1949; (trans. and ed.) John Milton's Commonplace Book, 1953; John Milton and His Commonplace Book, 1969; Edmund Spenser: His Life and Works. 1987. Add: 982 W. California Ave., St. Paul, Minn. 55117, U.S.A.

MOHLER, James Aylward. American, b. 1923. Theology/Religion. Member, Soc. of Jesus, since 1942; ordained to Roman Catholic priesthood, 1955; Prof. of Religious History, John Carroll Univ., Cleveland, since 1974 (Instr., 1960–65; Asst. Prof., 1965–69; Assoc. Prof., 1969–74). Instr., St. Ignatius High Sch., Chicago, 1949–52; Vice-Pres., Univ. of Detroit High Sch., 1958–60. *Publs:* (co-author) Speaking of God, 1967; Man Needs God: An Interpretation of Biblical Faith, 1967; The Beginning of Eternal Life: The Dynamic Faith of Thomas Aquinas, 1968; Dimensions of Faith, Yesterday and Today, 1969; The Origin and Evolution of the Priesthood, 1970; The Heresy of Monasticism: The Christian Monks, Types and Anti-Types, 1971; The School of Jesus: An Overview of Christian Education, Yesterday and Today, 1973; Cosmos, Man, God, Messiah: An Introduction to Religion, 1973; Dimensions of Love: East and West, 1975; Sexual Sublimation and the Sacred, 1978; The Sacrament of Suffering, 1979; Dimensions of Prayer, 1981; Love, Marriage, and the Family, 1982; Paradise: Gardens of the Gods, 1984. Add: John Carroll Univ., Cleveland, Ohio 44118, U.S.A.

MOKASHI-PUNEKAR, Shankar. Indian, b. 1928. Poetry, Literature, Essays, Translations. Prof. of English, Inst. of Kannada Studies, Univ. of Mysore, since 1980. Ed., Jayakar-natak, 1950–51; Asst. Lectr. in English, Lingaraj Coll., Belgaum, 1954–56, and Kishinchand Chellaram Coll., Bombay, 1956–61; Music Critic, The Times of India, Bombay, 1965–67; Principal, Sri Poornapraina Coll., Udipi, 1967–68; Asst. Prof. of English, Indian Inst. of Technology, Bombay, 1969–70. *Publs:* The Captive: Poems, 1965; The Later Phase in the Development of W.B. Yeats: A Study in the Stream of Yeats's Later Thought and Creativity, 1966; (trans.) The Cycle of the Seasons, by Kalidasa, 1966; The Pretender, 1967; P. Lal: An Appreciation, 1968; An Epistle to Professor David McCutchion, 1970; Indo-Anglian Creed and Other Essays, 1972; Interpretations of the Later Poems of W.B. Yeats, 1973; (ed.) Perspectives on Indian Drama in English, 1977; Theoretical and Practical Studies in Indo-English Literature, 1978. Add: Inst. of Kannada Studies, Univ. of Mysore, Manasa Gangotri, Mysore 570 006, India.

MOL, Johannis (Hans) J(acob). American (b. Dutch), b. 1922. Sociology, Theology/Religion. Prof., Dept. of Religion, McMaster Univ., Hamilton, since 1970. Deputy admin., Dutch sugar beet industry, 1946–48; Chaplain to immigrants, Bonegilla, Australia, 1952–54; Pastor, Bethel Presbyterian Church, White Hall, Md., 1956–60; Lectr. in Sociology, Univ. of Canterbury, Christchurch, N.Z., 1961–63; Fellow in Sociology, Inst. of Advanced Studies, Australian National Univ., Canberra, 1963–70. Secty.-Treas., Sociological Assn. of Australia and New Zealand, 1963–69; Member, Bd. of Dirs., Religious Research Assn., 1972–74. *Publs:* Churches and Immigrants, 1961; Race and Religion in New Zealand, 1966; The Breaking of Traditions, 1968; Christianity in Chains, 1969; Religion in Australia, 1971; (ed.) Western Religion, 1972; The Sacralization of Identity, 1975; Identity and the Sacred: A Sketch for a New Social Scientific Theory of Religion, 1976; (ed.) Identity and Religion, 1978; Wholeness and Breakdown: A Model for the Interpretation of Nature and Society, 1978; The Fixed and the Fickle: Religion and Identity in New Zealand, 1982; The Firm and the Formless: Religion and Identity in Aboriginal Australia, 1982; Meaning and Place, 1983; Faith and Fragility: Identity and Religion in Canada, 1985; The Faith of Australians, 1985. Add: Dept. of Religion, McMaster Univ., Hamilton, Ont. L8S 4KI, Canada.

MOLDEA, Dan E. American, b. 1950. Criminology, Politics/Government, Writing/Journalism. Freelance investigative journalist, Washington, D.C., since 1974. Contrib. Ed., Organized Crime Digest, since 1984. Assoc. Fellow, Inst. for Policy Studies, Washington D.C., 1981–84. *Publs:* The Hoffa Wars: Teamsters, Rebels, Politicians, and the Mob, 1978; The Hunting of Cain: A True Story of Money, Greed, and Fratricide, 1983; (with others) First Harvest: The Institute for Policy Studies 1963-1983, 1983; Dark Victory: Ronald Reagan, MCA, and the Mob, 1986. Add: 3921 Fulton St. N.W., Washington, D.C. 20007, U.S.A.

MOLE, John. British, b. 1941. Poetry, Literary criticism. Chmn. of the English Dept., St. Albans Sch., since 1981. Ed., Mandeville Press, Hitchin, Herts. English Teacher, Haberdashers' Aske's Sch., Elstree, Herts., 1964–73; Exchange Teacher, Riverdale Country Sch., NYC, 1969–70; Chmn. of the English Dept., Verulam Sch., Hertfordshire, 1973–81. *Publs:* A Feather for Memory, 1961; The Instruments, 1971; Something about Love, 1972; The Love Horse, 1974; Scenarios, 1975; A Partial Light, 1975; Our Ship, 1977; On the Set, 1978; From the House Opposite, 1979; (with Mary Norman) Once There Were Dragons (juvenile), 1979; Feeding the Lake, 1981; (with Peter Scupham) Christmas Games, 1983; (ed. with Anthony Thwaite) Poetry 1945 to 1980, 1983; In and Out of the Apple, 1984; (with Peter Scupham) Christmas Visits, 1985; Learning the Ropes, 1985; (with Peter Scupham) Winter Emblems, 1986; Homing, 1987; Boo to a Goose, 1987; Passing Judgements (criticism), 1989. Add: 11 Hill St., St. Albans, Herts., England.

MOLLENHOFF, Clark (Raymond). American, b. 1921. Politics/Government, Biography. Prof. of Journalism and Law, Washington and Lee Univ., Lexington, Va., since 1976. Admitted to the Iowa Bar, 1944, also the Washington, D.C. Bar, and the Bar of the U.S. Supreme Court; Reporter, Look, and Minneapolis Star and Tribune, Cowles Publications, Washington Bureau, 1950–69; Special Counsel to President Nixon, 1969–70; Chief of Washington Bureau, Des Moines Register and Tribune, 1970–77. Member, U.S. Advisory Commn. on Information Policy, 1962–65. *Publs:* Washington Cover-Up, 1962; Tentacles of Power, 1965; Despoilers of Democracy, 1965; The Pentagon, 1967; George Romney: Mormon in Politics, 1968; Strike Force, 1972; The Man Who Pardoned Nixon, 1976; Game Plan for Disaster, 1976; The President Who Failed, 1980; Investigative Reporting, 1981, Atanasoff—Forgotten Father of the Computer, 1988. Add: 207 Reid Hall, Washington and Lee Univ., Lexington, Va. 24450, U.S.A.

MOLLENKOTT, Virginia Ramey. American, b. 1932. Education, Literature, Philosophy, Theology/Religion. Prof. of English, William Paterson Coll. of New Jersey, since 1967. Faculty member, Shelton Coll., 1955–63, and Nyack Coll., 1963–67. Asst. Ed., Seventeenth-Century News, 1964–73. *Publs:* Adamant and Stone Chips: A Christian Humanist Approach to Knowledge, 1967; In Search of Balance, 1969; (ed.) Adam Among the Television Trees: An Anthology of Verse by Contemporary Christian Poets, 1971; Women, Men, and the Bible, 1977; (with Letha Scanzoni) Is the Homosexual My Neighbor?, 1978; Speech, Silence, Action!, 1980; (with Catherine Barry) Views from the Intersection, 1983; The Divine Feminine, 1983; Godding: Human Responsibility and the Bible, 1987; (ed.) Women of Faith in Dialogue, 1987. Add: 11 Yearling Trail, Hewitt, N.J. 07421, U.S.A.

MOLLOY, M(ichael) (Joseph). Irish, b. 1917. Plays/Screenplays.

Farmer. *Publs:* The King of Friday's Men, 1954; The Paddy Pedlar, 1954; The Will and the Way, 1957; Old Road, 1961; The Wood of the Whispering, 1961; Daughter from Over the Water, 1963; Petticoat Loose, 1982. Add: Milltown, Tuam, Co. Galway, Ireland.

MOMADAY, N(avarre) Scott. American, b. 1934. Novels/Short stories, Poetry, Autobiography/Memoirs/Personal. Prof. of English and Comparative Literature, Univ. of Arizona, Tucson, since 1980. Formerly taught at the Univ. of California at Santa Barbara and Berkeley, and New Mexico State Univ; Prof. of English, Stanford Univ., California, 1972–80. *Publs:*(ed.) The Complete Poems of Frederick Goddard Tuckerman, 1965; Owl in the Cedar Tree, 1965; House Made of Dawn (novel), 1968; The Journey of Tai-Me: Retold Kiowa Indian Tales, 1968; enlarged ed. as Way to Rainy Mountain, 1969; (ed.) American Indian Authors, 1972; Colorado: Summer/Fall/Winter/Spring, 1973; The Gourd Dancer (verse), 1976; The Names: A Memoir, 1976; A Poem, 1979; The Ancient Child (novel), 1989. Add: Dept. of English, Univ. of Arizona, Tucson, Ariz. 85704, U.S.A.

MONACO, James. American, b. 1942. Communications Media, Film. Publisher, New York Zoetrope Inc., since 1975; Founder and Pres., Baseline Inc., since 1982. Member of the Faculty, New Sch. for Social Research, NYC, since 1967. Formerly Media Commentator, National Public Radio's "Morning Edition." *Publs:* The New Wave: Godard, Truffaut, Chabrol, Rohmer, Rivette, 1976; How to Read a Film: The Art, Technology, Language, History and Theory of Film and Media, 1977, 1981; Celebrity: The Media as Image Makers, 1978; Media Culture: Television, Radio, Records, Books, Newspapers, Movies, 1978; Alain Resnais: The Role of Imagination, 1978; American Film Now: The People, The Power, The Money, The Movies, 1979; Who's Who in American Film Now, 1981, 1987; Connoisseurs Guide to the Movies, 1985. Add: Baselinc Inc., 838 Broadway, New York, N.Y. 10003, U.S.A.

MONET, Jacques. Canadian, b. 1930. History. Prof. of History, Regis Coll., Univ. of Toronto, since 1982 (Pres., 1982–88). *Publs:* The Last Cannon Shot: A Study of French-Canadian Nationalism, 1969; The Canadian Crown, 1979; Jules Léger: A Selection of His Writings on Canada, 1982. Add: Regis College, 15 St. Mary St., Toronto M4Y 2R5, Canada.

MONEY, David Charles. British, b. 1918. Environmental science/Ecology, Geography. Dir., DCM Activities (Bedford) Ltd. Former Head, Dept. of Geography, Bedford Sch. *Publs:* Human Geography; Climate, Soils, and Vegetation; Australia and New Zealand; South America; The Earth's Surface; Patterns of Settlement; Man's Environment; Problems of Development; East Africa; Basic Geography; Western Australia; Man the Homemaker; Environmental Systems (series); China: The Land and the People, 1984; China Today, 1987; The Foundations of Geography, 1987; Climate and Environmental Systems, 1988; Australia Today, 1989. *Publs:* 52 Park Ave., Bedford MK40 2NE, England.

MONEY, Keith. British, b. 1935. Animals, Art, Ballet, Horticulture, Sports, Biography. Freelance writer, artist and photographer. *Publs:* Salute the Horse, 1960; (with P. Smythe) Florian's Farmyard, 1962; The Horseman in Our Midst, 1963; The Equestrian World, 1963; The Art of the Royal Ballet, 1964, 1967; The Art of Margot Fonteyn, 1965, 1975; The Royal Ballet Today, 1968; Fonteyn: The Making of a Legend, 1973; John Curry, 1978; (with Peter Beales) Georgian and Regency Roses, 1978; Early Victorian Roses, 1978; Late Victorial Roses, 1980; Edwardian Roses, 1980; Anna Pavlova: Her Life and Art, 1982; The Bedside Book of Old-Fashioned Roses, 1985; By Some Other Sea: The Story of Rupert Brooke, 1987. Add: Carbrooke Hall Farm, Thetford, Norfolk, England.

MONK, Robert C. American, b. 1930. Theology/Religion. Prof. of Religion, McMurry Coll., Abilene, since 1964. Minister/Dir., Wesley Foundn., Texas A and M Univ., 1954–58; Dir., Texas Methodist Student Movement, 1961–64. *Publs:* John Wesley: His Puritan Heritage, 1966; (with others) Exploring Religious Meaning, 1980, 3rd ed. 1987; Exploring Christianity: An Introduction, 1983; (with others) The Methodist Excitement in Texas, 1984. Add: McMurry Coll., Abilene, Tex. 79605, U.S.A.

MONSARRAT, Ann Whitelaw. British, b. 1937. Cultural/Ethnic topics, Fashion/Costume, Biography. Journalist, West Kent Mercury, 1954–58, and Daily Mail, London, 1958–61; Asst. Ed., Stationery Trade Review, 1961. *Publs:* And the Bride Wore . . . The Story of the White Wedding, 1973; An Uneasy Victorian: Thackeray the Man, 1980. Add: San Lawrenz, Gozo, Malta.

MONTAG, Tom. American, b. 1947. Poetry. Ed. and Publr., Monday

Morning Press, Milwaukee, since 1971, Margins, since 1972, and Margins Books, since 1974. Former Researcher, Center for Venture Mgmt. *Publs:* Wooden Nickel, 1972; Twelve Poems, 1972; Measures, 1972; To Leave/This Place, 1972; Making Hay, 1973; (ed. with F. Stearns) The Urban Ecosystem: A Holistic Approach, 1974; Making Hay and Other Poems, 1975; Ninety Notes Toward Partial Images and Lover Prints, 1976; Concerns: Essays and Reviews, 1977; Letters Home, 1978. Add: c/o Sparrow Press, 103 Waldron St., W. Lafayette, Ind. 47906, U.S.A.

MONTAGU OF BEAULIEU, Lord; Edward John Barrington Douglas-Scott-Montagu. British, b. 1926. Recreation/Leisure/Hobbies, Social commentary/phenomena. Founder Trustee of the National Motor Museum, Beaulieu, Hants. Founder and Publr., Veteran and Vintage Mag., 1956–79. *Publs:* The Motoring Montagus, 1959; Lost Causes of Motoring, 1960; Jaguar: A Biography, 1961; The Gordon Bennett Races, 1963; Rolls of Rolls Royce, 1966; The Gilt and the Gingerbread, 1967; Lost Causes of Motoring in Europe, vol. I, 1969, vol. II, 1971; More Equal Than Others, 1970; (with A. Bird) History of the Steam Car, 1971; Early Days on the Road, 1976; The Horseless Carriage, 1975; Behind the Wheel, 1977; Royalty on the Road, 1980; Home, James, 1982; The British Motorist, 1987; English Heritage, 1987. Add: Palace House, Beaulieu, Brockenhurst, Hants. SO42 7ZN, England.

MONTAGU, Ashley. American (b. British), b. 1905. Anthropology/Ethnology. Res. Assoc., British Museum of Natural History, 1926; Curator, Physical Anthropology, Wellcome Hist. Museum, 1929; Asst. Prof. of Anatomy, New York Univ., 1931–38; Assoc. Prof., Hahnemann Medical Coll., 1938–41; Prof. and Chmn., Dept. of Anthropology, Rutgers Univ., New Brunswick, N.J., 1949–55; Regents Prof., Univ. of California at Santa Barbara, 1962. *Publs:* Coming into Being among the Australian Aborigines, 1937, 1974; Man's Most Dangerous Myth: The Fallacy of Race, 1942; Edward Tyson M.D., F.R.S. 1650–1708, and the Rise of Human and Comparative Anatomy in England, 1943; Introduction to Physical Anthropology, 1945; Adolescent Sterility, 1946; On Being Human, 1950; On Being Intelligent, 1951; Statement on Race, 1952, 1972; Darwin, Competition and Cooperation, 1952; The Natural Superiority of Women, 1953; The Direction of Human Development, 1955; Immortality, 1955; Biosocial Nature of Man, 1956; Anthropology and Human Nature, 1957; Man: His First Million Years, 1957; The Reproductive Development of the Female, 1957; Education and Human Relations, 1958; The Cultured Man, 1958; Human Heredity, 1959; Handbook of Anthropometry, 1960; Man in Process, 1961; Prenatal Influences, 1962; The Humanization of Man, 1962; Race, Science and Humanity, 1963; (with J. Lilly) The Dolphin in History, 1963; Life Before Birth, 1964; The Science of Man, 1964; (with E. Steer) Anatomy and Physiology, 1965; (with C.L. Brace) Man's Evolution, 1965; The Idea of Race, 1965; The Human Revolution, 1965; Up the Ivy, 1966; The American Way of Life, 1967; The Anatomy of Swearing, 1967; (with E. Darling) The Prevalence of Nonsense, 1967; Man Observed, 1968; Man: His First Two Million Years, 1969; Sex, Man and Society, 1969; (with E. Darling) The Ignorance of Certainty, 1970; Immortality, Religion and Morals, 1971; Touching, 1971, 3rd ed. 1986; The Elephant Man, 1971; (with M. Levitan) Textbook of Human Genetics, 1971; (with S.S. Snyder) Man and the Computer, 1972; (ed.) Race and IQ, 1975; The Nature of Human Aggression, 1976; (with C.L. Brace) Human Evolution, 1977; (ed.) Learning Non-Aggression, 1978; (with Floyd Matson) The Human Connection, 1979; (ed.) Sociobiology Examined, 1980; Growing Young, 1981, 1989; (ed.) Science and Creationism, 1982; (with Floyd Matson) The Dehumanization of Man, 1983; What We Know About "Race", 1985; Humanity Speaking to Human Kind, 1986; Living and Loving, 1986; The Peace of the World, 1987; Coming into Being, 1988; The Story of People, 1988. Add: 321 Cherry Hill Rd., Princeton, N.J. 08540, U.S.A.

MONTAGU, Jennifer (Iris Rachel). British, b. 1931. Art. Curator of the Photographic Collection, Warburg Inst., London, since 1971 (Asst. Curator, 1964–71). Asst. Regional Dir., Arts Council of Great Britain, 1953–54; Lectr., Univ. of Reading, 1958–64; Slade Prof., Cambridge, 1980–81. *Publs:* Bronzes, 1963; (with J. Thuillier) Charles Le Brun, 1963; Alessandro Algardi, 1985. Add: 10 Roland Way, London SW7 3RE, England.

MONTAGUE, John (Patrick). Irish, b. 1929. Novels/Short stories, Plays/Screenplays, Poetry. Lectr. in Poetry, University Coll., Cork. Worked for the State Tourist Bd., Dublin, 1956–61. *Publs:* Forms of Exile, 1958; The Old People, 1960; Poisoned Lands and Other Poems, 1961; (ed.) The Dolmen Miscellany of Irish Writing, 1962; Death of a Chieftain and Other Stories, 1964; All Legendary Obstacles, 1966; Patriotic Suite, 1966; (ed. with Liam Miller) A Tribute to Austin Clarke on His Seventieth Birthday, 9 May 1966, 1966; Home Again, 1967; A

Chosen Light, 1967; The Rough Field, 1972; Hymn to the New Omagh Road, 1968; The Bread God: Lecture, with Illustrations in Verse, 1968; A New Siege, 1969; (with J. Hewitt) The Planter and the Gael, 1970; Tides, 1970; Small Secrets, 1972; The Rough Field (play), 1972; A Fair House (translations from Irish), 1973; The Cave of Night, 1974; O'Riada's Farewell, 1964; (ed.) The Faber Book of Irish Verse, 1974; A Slow Dance, 1975; The Great Cloak, 1978; Selected Poems, 1982; The Dead Kingdom, 1984; Mount Eagle, 1989. Add: Dept. of English, University Coll., Cork, Ireland.

MONTELEONE, Thomas F. American, b. 1946. Science fiction/Fantasy. Psychotherapist, C.T. Perkins Hosp., Jessup, Md., 1969–78. Secty., Science Fiction Writers of America, 1976–78; Vice-Pres., Horror Writers of America, Inc., 1988. *Publs:* Seeds of Change, 1975; The Time Connection, 1976; (ed.) The Arts and Beyond: Visions of Man's Aesthetic Future, 1977; The Time-Swept City, 1977; The Secret Sea, 1979; Guardian, 1980; Night Things, 1980; Ozymandias, 1981; Dark Stars and Other Illuminations (short stories), 1981; (with David F. Bischoff) Day of the Dragonstar, 1983; Night Train, 1984; (with David F. Bischoff) Night of the Dragonstar, 1985; R.A.M.: Random Access Messages (anthol.), 1984; Lyrica, 1987; The Magnificent Gallery, 1987; (with John De Chancie) Crooked House, 1987; Fantasma, 1989; (with David F. Bisckoff) Dragonstar Destiny, 1989; Borderlands (anthology), 1990; Fearful Symmetries (short stories), 1990. Add: P.O. Box 5788 Baltimore, Md. 21208, U.S.A.

MONTGOMERY, David Bruce. American, b. 1938. Marketing. Robert A. Magowan Prof. of Marketing, Grad. Sch. of Business, Stanford Univ., California, since 1978 (Assoc. Prof., 1970–73; Prof. of Mgmt., 1973–78). Asst. Prof., 1966–69, and Assoc. Prof., 1969–70, Massachusetts Inst. of Technology, Cambridge. *Publs:* (with G.L. Urban) Management Science in Marketing, 1969; (with W.F. Massy and D.G. Morrison) Stochastic Models of Buying Behavior, 1970; (ed. with G.L. Urban) Applications of Management Science in Marketing, 1970; (ed.) Management Science: Marketing Management Models, 1971; (co-author) Consumer Behavior: Theoretical Sources, 1973; (with G.S. Day, G.J. Eskin and C.B. Weinberg) Cases in Computer and Model Assisted Marketing: Planning, 1973; (with G.J. Eskin) Cases in Computer and Model Assisted Marketing: Data Analysis, 1975; (ed. with D.R. Wittink) Market Measurement and Analysis, 1980. Add: Grad. Sch. of Business, Stanford Univ., Stanford, Calif. 94305, U.S.A.

MONTGOMERY, John D. American, b. 1920. Politics/Government. Ford Foundn. Prof. of Intnl. Studies, Harvard Univ., Cambridge, Mass. *Publs:* The Purge in Occupied Japan: A Study in the Use of Civilian Agencies under Military Government, 1953; The State Versus Socrates: A Case Study in Civic Freedom, 1954; Forced to Be Free: The Artificial Revolution in Germany and Japan, 1957; Cases in Vietnamese Administration, 1959; The Politics of Foreign Aid: American Experience in Southeast Asia, 1962; (with W. Sifflin) Approaches to Development: Politics, Administration and Change, 1966; Foreign Aid in International Politics, 1967; Technology and Civic Life; Making and Implementing Development Decisions, 1974; Policy Sciences and Population, 1975; Patterns of Policy, 1979; International Dimensions of Land Reform, 1984; Aftermath: Tarnished Outcomes of American Foreign Policy, 1985; Bureaucrats and People: Grassroots Participation in Third World Development, 1988. Add: Kennedy Sch. of Govt., Harvard Univ., Cambridge, Mass. 02138, U.S.A.

MONTGOMERY, Marion. American, b. 1925. Novels/Short stories, Poetry, Humanities (general), Literature. Prof. of English Emeritus, Univ. of Georgia, Athens. *Publs:* Dry Lightning, 1960; The Wandering of Desire, 1962, 1963; Darrell, 1964; Stones from the Rubble, 1965; Ye Olde Bluebird, 1967; The Gull and Other Georgia Scenes, 1969; Ezra Pound: A Critical Essay, 1970; T.S. Eliot: An Essay on the American Magus, 1970; The Reflective Journey Toward Order: Essays on Dante, Wordsworth, Eliot, and Others, 1973; Fugitive, 1974; Eliot's Reflective Journey to the Garden, 1978; Why Flannery O'Connor Stayed Home, 1981; Why Poe Drank Liquor, 1982; Why Hawthorne Was Melancholy, 1984; Possum, and Other Receits for the Recovery of "Southern" Being, 1987; The Trouble with You Innerleckchuls, 1988; Virtue and Modern Shadows of Turning, 1989; Words, Words, Words: The Feeding of the Larger Body., 1989. Add: Crawford, Ga. 30630, U.S.A.

MOODIE, Graeme Cochrane. British, b. 1924. Politics/Government. Prof. of Politics, Univ. of York, since 1963. Lectr. in Political Science, Univ. of St. Andrews, 1947–53; Commonwealth Fellow, Princeton Univ., New Jersey, 1949–51; Lectr. and Sr. Lectr., Univ. of Glasgow, 1953–63. *Publs:* (with G. Marshall) Some Problems of the Constitution, 1959, 5th ed. 1971; The Government of Great Britain, 1961, 3rd ed. 1971; (ed. and contrib.) Government Organisation and Economic Development, 1966; (with G. Studdert-Kennedy) Opinions, Publics, and Pressure Groups, 1970; (with R. Eustace) Power and Authority in British Universities, 1974; (ed.) Standards and Criteria in Higher Education, 1986. Add: Dept. of Politics, Univ. of York, Heslington, York YO1 5DD, England.

MOONEY, Christopher Francis. American, b. 1925. Law, Theology/ Religion. Prof. of Religious Studies, Fair Field Univ., Connecticut, since 1980 (Academic Vice-Pres., 1980–87). Member of the Theology Faculty, Canisius Coll., Buffalo, N.Y., and St. Peter's Coll., Jersey City, N.J., 1959–61; Prof. of Theology, 1964–69, and Chmn. of the Dept., 1965–69, Fordham Univ., NYC; Pres., Woodstock Coll., NYC, 1969–74; Asst. Dean, Univ. of Pennsylvania Law Sch., Philadelphia, 1978–80. *Publs:* Teilhard de Chardin and the Mystery of Christ, 1966; (ed.) The Presence and Absence of God, 1969; (ed.) Prayer: The Problem of Dialogue, 1969; The Making of Man, 1971; Man Without Tears, 1975; Religion and the American Dream, 1977; Inequality and the American Conscience, 1983; Public Virtue: Law and the Social Character of Religion, 1986; Boundaries Dimly Perceived: Law, Religion, Education and the Comman Good, 1989. Add: Fairfield Univ., Fairfield, Conn. 06430, U.S.A.

MOONMAN, Eric. British, b. 1929. Management, Politics/Government. Dir., Centre for Contemporary Studies. Human Relations Adviser, British Inst. of Mgmt., 1956–62; Sr. Research Fellow in Mgmt. Sciences, Univ. of Manchester, 1962–66; Labour Member of Parliament (U.K.) for Billericay, Essex, 1966–70, and for Basildon, 1974–79. *Publs:* The Manager and the Organization, 1960; (ed.) European Science and Technology, 1968; Communication in an Expanding Organization, 1969; Reluctant Partnership, 1970; Alternative Government, 1984; (ed.) Violent Society, 1987. Add: 1 Beacon Hill, London N7, England.

MOORCOCK, Michael (John). Has also written as Bill Barclay; Edward P. Bradbury; James Colvin; Desmond Reid. British, b. 1939. Novels/Short stories, Science fiction/Fantasy. Ed., Tarzan Adventures, 1956–58, Sexton Blake Library, 1959–61, and New Worlds, London, 1964–79. *Publs:* The Stealer of Souls and Other Stories, 1961; (as Desmond Reid, with James Cawthorn) Caribbean Crisis, 1962; The Fireclown, 1965, as The Winds of Limbo, 1969; The Sundered Worlds, 1965, as The Blood Red Game, 1970; Stormbringer, 1965; (ed.) The Best of New Worlds, 1965; (as Edward P. Bradbury) Michael Kane series: Warriors of Mars, 1965, as The City of the Beast, 1970, Blades of Mars, 1965, as Lord of the Spiders, 1970, and Barbarians of Mars, 1965, as The Masters of the Pit, 1970; The Twilight Man, 1966, as The Shores of Death, 1970; (as Bill Barclay) Printer's Devil, 1966; (as Bill Barclay) Somewhere in the Night, 1966, as The Chinese Agent, 1970; (as James Colvin) The Deep Fix, 1966; (ghostwriter) The LSD Dossier, by Roger Harris, 1966; (ed.) Best SF Stories from New Worlds 1-8, 1967–74; The Wrecks of Time, 1967, as The Rituals of Infinity, 1971; The Jewel in the Skull, 1967; (ed.) The Traps of Time, 1968; The Final Programme, 1968; Sorcerer's Amulet, 1968, as The Mad God's Amulet, 1969; The Sword of the Dawn, 1968; (ed.) The Inner Landscape, 1969; The Ice Schooner, 1969; Behold the Man, 1969; The Black Corridor, 1969; The Time Dweller, 1969; The Secret of the Runestaff, 1969, as The Runestaff, 1969; The Singing Citadel, 1970; The Eternal Champion, 1970; Phoenix in Obsidian, 1970, as The Silver Warriors, 1973; (ed.) New Worlds Quarterly 1-5, and New Worlds 6, 1971–73; (co-ed.) The Nature of the Catastrophe, 1971; A Cure for Cancer, 1971; The Warlord of the Air, 1971; The Knight Queen, King of the Swords (trilogy), 3 vols., 1971; The Sleeping Sorceress, 1971, as The Vanishing Tower, 1977; An Alien Heat, 1972; Breakfast in the Ruins, 1972; The English Assassin, 1972; Elric of Melniboné, 1972, as The Dreaming City, 1972; The Jade Man's Eyes, 1973; The Bull and the Spear, 1973; The Champion of Garathorm, 1973; Count Brass, 1973; The Oak and the Ram, 1973; Elric: The Return to Melnibone, 1973; The Land Leviathan, 1974; The Hollow Lands, 1974; The Sword and the Stallion, 1974; (ed.) Before Armageddon, 1975; (with Philip James) The Distant Suns, 1975; The Quest for Tanelorn, 1975; The Adventures of Una Persson and Catherine Cornelius in the Twentieth Century, 1976; The End of All Songs, 1976; Moorcock's Book of Martyrs, 1976; The Lives and Times of Jerry Cornelius, 1976; Legends from the End of Time, 1976; The Sailor on the Seas of Fate, 1976; (ed.) England Invaded, 1977; The Transformation of Miss Mavis Ming, 1977, as Messiah at the End of Time, 1978; The Weird of the White Wolf, 1977; The Bane of the Black Sword, 1977; Sojan (for children), 1977; Condition of Muzak, 1977; Gloriana, 1978; Dying for Tomorrow, 1978; The Golden Barge, 1979; My Experiences in the Third World War, 1980; The Russian Intelligence, 1980; The Great Rock 'n' Roll Swindle, 1980; Byzantium Endures, 1981; The Entropy Tango, 1981; The Warhound and the World's

Pain, 1981; The Brothel in Rosenstrasse, 1982; The Dancers at the End of Time (omnibus), 1983; The Retreat from Liberty, 1983; (ed.) New Worlds: An Anthology, 1983; The Laughter of Carthage, 1984; The Opium General and Other Stories, 1984; The Chronicles of Castle Brass, 1985; Letters from Hollywood, 1986; The City in the Autumn Stars, 1986; The Dragon in the Sword, 1986; Wizardry and Wild Romance: A Study in Epic Fantasy, 1987; Fantasy: The 100 Best Books, 1988. Add: c/o Anthony Sheil Assocs., 43 Doughty St., London WC1N 2LF, England.

MOORE, Austin. *See* **MUIR,** Augustus.

MOORE, Barbara. American, b. 1934. Novels/Short stories. Reporter, Fort Worth Star-Telegram, Texas, 1955–57, Denver Post, 1958–60, and San Antonio Light, Texas, 1963–65. *Publs:* Hard on the Road, 1974; The Fever Called Living, 1976; Something on the Wind, 1978; The Doberman Wore Black, 1983; The Wolf Whispered Death, 1986. *Publs:* c/o Harold Matson Co. Inc., 276 Fifth Ave., New York, N.Y. 10001, U.S.A.

MOORE, Brian. Canadian, b. 1921. Novels/Short stories, Plays/Screenplays. Served with the U.N. Relief and Rehabilitation Admin. Mission, Poland, 1946–47; Regents Prof. of English, Univ. of California at Los Angeles, 1974–75. (Prof., 1975–89). *Publs:* Judith Hearne (in U.S. as The Lonely Passion of Judith Hearne), 1955; The Feast of Lupercal, 1957; The Luck of Ginger Coffey, 1960, screenplay, 1963; An Answer from Limbo, 1962; (co-author) Canada, 1963; The Emperor of Ice-Cream, 1965; (with Alfred Hitchcock) Torn Curtain (screenplay), 1966; The Slave (screenplay), 1967; I Am Mary Dunne, 1968; Fergus, 1970; The Revolution Script, 1971; Catholics, (screenplay) 1973, (stageplay), 1976; The Great Victorian Collection, 1975; The Doctor's Wife, 1976; The Mangan Inheritance, 1979; The Temptation of Eileen Hughes, 1981; Cold Heaven, 1983; (with Claude Chabrol) The Blood of Others (screenplay), 1984; Black Robe, 1985; The Colour of Blood, 1987. Add: c/o Perry Knowlton, Curtis-Brown Inc., 10 Astor Pl., New York, N.Y. 10003, U.S.A.

MOORE, Carey Armstrong. American, b. 1930. Theology/Religion, Translations. Prof. of Religion, since 1969, and Chmn. of Dept., since 1982, Gettysburg Coll., Pennsylvania (Asst. Prof., 1959–65; Assoc. Prof., 1966–68). *Publs:* Esther: Introduction, Translation, and Notes, 1971; A Light Unto My Path, 1974; Daniel, Esther, and Jeremiah: The Additions, 1977; (ed.) Studies in the Book of Esther, 1982; (trans.) Judith, 1985. Add: Dept. of Religion, Gettysburg Coll., Gettysburg, Pa. 17325, U.S.A.

MOORE, Carl Leland. American, b. 1921. Business/Trade/Industry. Prof. of Accounting, Lehigh Univ., Bethlehem, Pa., since 1948. *Publs:* Profitable Applications of the Break-Even System, 1971; (with R.K. Jaedicke and Lane K. Anderson) Managerial Accounting, 7th ed. 1988; (with J.B. Hobbs) Financial Accounting, 1974, 1984. Add: Coll. of Business and Economics, Lehigh Univ., Bethlehem, Pa. 18015, U.S.A.

MOORE, Carman. American, b. 1936. Music, Biography. Music Critic, N.Y. Times and The Village Voice, NYC. Former member of the faculty, New York Univ., NYC, Yale Univ., New Haven, Conn., Brooklyn Coll., NYC, and Queens Coll., NYC. *Publs:* Somebody's Angel Child: The Story of Bessie Smith, 1970; Growth of Black Sound in America, 1981. Add: 148 Columbus Ave., New York, N.Y. 10023, U.S.A.

MOORE, C(atherine) L(ucille). Also wrote with Henry Kuttner under joint pseud. Lewis Padgett. American, b. 1911. Mystery/Crime/-Suspense, Science fiction/Fantasy. Staff Member, and later Pres., Fletcher Trust Co., Indianapolis, 1930–40; Instr. of Writing and Literature, Univ. of Southern Calfornia, 1958–61. (Though not always acknowledged, most of her writing from 1940 was written in collaboration with her husband Henry Kuttner, until his death in 1958.) *Publs:* (as Lewis Padgett) The Brass Ring (mystery novel), 1946, as Mystery in Brass, 1947; (as Lewis Padgett) The Day He Died (mystery novel), 1947; (with Henry Kuttner) Fury, 1950, as Destination Infinity, 1958; (as Lewis Padgett) A Gnome There Was (short stories), 1950; (as Lewis Padgett) Tomorrow and Tomorrow, and The Fairy Chessmen, 1951, in U.K. as Tomorrow and Tomorrow and The Far Reality, 2 vols., 1962, The Fairy Chessmen published separately as The Chessboard Planet, 1956; Judgment Night (includes stories), 1952; (as Lewis Padgett) Well of the Worlds, 1953; Shambleau and Others (short stories), 1953; (as Lewis Padgett) Mutant (short stories), 1953; (as Lewis Padgett) Line to Tomorrow (short stories), 1954; Northwest of Earth, 1954; (as Lewis Padgett) Beyond Earth's Gates, 1954; (with Henry Kuttner) No Boundaries (short stories), 1955; Doomsday Morning, 1957; (with Henry Kuttner) Earth's Last Citadel, 1964; (with Henry Kuttner) Valley of the Flame, 1964; (with

Henry Kuttner) The Time Axis, 1965; Jirel of Joiry (short stories), 1969, as Black God's Shadow, 1977; (with Henry Kuttner) The Mask of Circe (mystery novel), 1971; The Best of C.L. Moore (short stories), 1975; (with Henry Kuttner) Clash by Night and Other Stories, 1980; (with Henry Kuttner) Chessboard Planet and Other Stories, 1983. Add: c/o Boyd Correll, 1948 Hanscom Dr., S. Pasadena, Calif. 91030, U.S.A.

MOORE, Charles W(illard). American, b. 1925. Architecture. Partner, Moore Grover Harper, architects, Essex, Conn., since 1975; Prof. of Architecture, Univ. of California at Los Angeles, since 1975; Centennial Prof. of Architecture, Univ. of Texas, Austin, since 1985. Partner, Moore-Lyndon-Turnbull-Whitaker, Berkeley, Calif., 1962–64, and MLTW/Moore Turnbull, Berkeley, 1964–70; Principal Charles W. Moore Assocs., 1970–75. Asst. Prof., Univ. of Utah, Salt Lake City, 1950–52, and Princeton Univ., New Jersey, 1957–59; Assoc. Prof., 1959–65, and Chmn. of the Dept. of Architecture, 1962–65, Univ. of California at Berkeley; Chmn., 1965–69, Dean, 1969–71, and Prof., 1971–75, Yale Univ. Sch. of Architecture, New Haven, Conn.*Publs:* (with G. Allen and D. Lyndon) The Place of Houses, 1974; (with N. Pyle) The Yale Mathematics Building Competition: Architecture for a Time of Questioning, 1974; (with G. Allen) Dimensions, 1976; (with K.C. Bloomer) Body Memory and Architecture, 1977. Add: Moore Grover Harper, 1725A Selby, Los Angeles, Calif. 90024, U.S.A.

MOORE, Elizabeth. *See* **ATKINS,** Meg Elizabeth.

MOORE, E(velyn) Garth. British, b. 1906. Law, Theology/Religion. Fellow, Corpus Christi Coll., Cambridge, since 1947 (former Dir. of Studies); Chancellor, Official Principal and Vicar-Gen. of the Diocese of Southwark, since 1948, Diocese of Durham, since 1954, and Diocese of Gloucester, since 1957. Pres., Churches' Fellowship for Psychical and Spiritual Studies, 1963–83. Called to the Bar, Gray's Inn, London, 1928; ordained priest, 1962. *Publs:* (ed.) Kenny's Cases on Criminal Law, 8th ed. with supplement; (co-ed.) Ecclesiastical Law in Halsbury's Laws of England, 3rd ed.; Introduction to English Canon Law, 1966, (with Timothy Briden) 1985; Believe It or Not, 1977; The Church's Ministry of Healing, 1977; (with Timothy Briden) Macmorran's Handbook for Churchwardens and Parochial Church Councillors, 1986. Add: Corpus Christi Coll., Cambridge, England.

MOORE, Hal G. American, b. 1929. Mathematics. Prof. of Mathematics, since 1971, and Assoc. Dept. Chmn., since 1986, Brigham Young Univ., Provo (Asst. Prof., 1961–67; Assoc. Prof., 1967–71). Chmn., National Lectureships Cttee., Sigma Xi, The Scientific Research Soc., since 1982. Teacher, Salt Lake City Public Schools, 1952–53; Instr., Carbon Jr. Coll., Utah, 1953–55; Mathematician, U.S. Naval Ordnance Test Station, California, 1957; Instr., Purdue Univ., West Lafayette, Ind., 1957–61. *Publs:* Pre-Calculus Mathematics, 1973, 1977; (with John Higgins) University Calculus, 1969; (with Adil Yagub) Elementary Linear Algebra, 1980; College Algebra and Trigonometry, 1984. Add: 288 TMCB, Brigham Young Univ., Provo, Utah 84602, U.S.A.

MOORE, John A(lexander). American, b. 1915. Biology, Zoology. Emeritus Prof. of Biology, Univ. of California at Riverside, since 1982 (Prof., 1969–82). Asst. Prof., Assoc. Prof., and Prof., Columbia Univ., NYC, 1943–69. *Publs:* Principles of Zoology, 1957; The Wonder of Life, 1961; The Frogs of Eastern New South Wales, 1961; Heredity and Development, 1963, 1972; A Guide Book to Washington, 1963; Biological Science: An Inquiry into Life, 1963, 3rd ed. 1973; (ed.) Biology of the Amphibia, 1964; (ed.) Ideas in Modern Biology, 1965; (ed.) Ideas in Evolution and Behavior, 1965; Science for Society: A Bibliography, 1970, 1971; (co-author) Interaction of Man and the Biosphere, 1970, 3rd ed. 1979; Readings in Heredity and Development, 1972; (ed.) Academic Abbreviations and Acronyms, 1981; (co-author) Dobzhansky's Genetics of Natural Populations, 1981; Science as a Way of Knowing: Evolutionary Biology, 1984; Science as a Way of Knowing: Human Ecology, 1985; Science as a Way of Knowing: Genetics, 1986; Science as a Way of Knowing: Developmental Biology, 1987; Science as a Way of Knowing: Form and Function, 1988; (ed.) Great Books in Experimental Biology, 17 titles, 1989. Add: Dept. of Biology, Univ. of California, Riverside, Calif. 92521, U.S.A.

MOORE, John Michael. British, b. 1935. Classics. Headmaster, The King's Sch. Worcester, since 1983. Asst. Master, Winchester Coll., Hampshire, 1960–64; Head of Classics Dept., Director of VI form, Radley Coll., Abingdon, 1964–83. *Publs:* The Manuscript Tradition of Polybius, 1965; (with P.A. Brunt) Res Gestae Divi Augusti, 1967; (with J.J Evans) Variorum, 1969; Timecharts, 1969; Aristotle and Xenophon on Democracy and Oligarchy, 1974, 1983. Add: 9, College Green, Worcester WR1 2LP,

England.

MOORE, John N(orton). American, b. 1937. International relations/Current affairs, Law. Prof. of Law since 1969, and Dir. of Graduate Programs, since 1976, Univ. of Virginia, Charlottesville. Dir., Center for Oceans Law and Policy, and Center for Law and National Security; U.S. Counselor on Intnl. Law, and U.S. Ambassador to Law of the Sea Negotiations. Member, Council on Foreign Relations, since 1975; Chmn., Bd. of Dirs. of the U.S. Inst. of Peace, since 1985. Member, Bd. of Editors, The American Journal of International Law, 1970–88. *Publs:* Law and the Indo-China War, 1972; (ed.) The Arab Israeli Conflict, vols. I-II, 1974; (ed.) Law and Civil War in the Modern World, 1974; (co-ed.) Readings in International Law, 1979; Law and the Granada Mission, 1984; The Secret War in Central America, 1987. Add: University of Virginia School of Law, Charlottesville, Va. 22901, U.S.A.

MOORE, (James) Mavor. Canadian, b. 1919. Plays/Screenplays, Poetry, Literature. Pres., Mavor Moore Production Ltd., Toronto, since 1961; Prof. of Theatre, York Univ., Toronto, since 1970. Member, Bd. of Dirs., Stratford Festival, Ontario, since 1953, and Bd. of Govs., National Theatre Sch., Montreal, since 1958; Member, Canada Council, since 1974. Feature Producer, Toronto, 1941–42, Chief Producer for Intnl. Service, Montreal, and Pacific Region Producer, Vancouver, 1945–46, CBC Radio; Teacher, Academy of Radio Arts, Toronto, 1946–49; Managing Producer, New Play Soc., Toronto, 1946–50, 1954–57; Radio Dir., 1946–50, and Exec. Television Producer, 1954–60, U.N. Information Div., NYC; Chief Producer, CBC Television, Toronto, 1950–54; Chmn., Canadian Theatre Centre, 1957–58; Drama Critic, Toronto Telegram, 1958–60; Stage Dir., Canadian Opera Co., Toronto, 1959–61, 1963; Gen. Dir., Confedn. Centre, Charlottetown, P.E.I., 1963–65; Founder and Artistic Dir., Charlottetown Festival, 1964–67; Gen. Dir., St. Lawrence Centre for the Arts, Toronto, 1965–70. *Publs:* And What Do You Do? A Short Guide to the Trades and Professions (poetry), 1960; (trans.) Yesterday the Children Were Dancing, 1969; (ed.) The Awkward Stage: The Ontario Theatre Study, 1969; Getting In, 1972; Come Away, Come Away, 1973; Four Canadian Playwrights, 1973; (ed.) An Anthology of Canadian Plays, 1973; The Pile, The Store, Inside Out, 1973; Slipping on the Verge: The Performing Arts in Canada with Theatre as a Case Study, 1983. Add: 176 Moore Ave., Toronto, Ont. M4T 1V8, Canada.

MOORE, Nicholas. British, b. 1918. Poetry, Literature. Ed., Seven, 1938–40, and New Poetry, 1944–45. *Publs:* A Wish in Season: Poems, 1941; The Island and the Cattle, 1941; A Book for Priscilla: Poems, 1941; (ed. with J. Bayliss and D. Newton) The Fortune Anthology, 1942; Buzzing Around with a Bee and Other Poems, 1942; The Cabaret, The Dancer, The Gentleman: Poems, 1942; Henry Miller, 1943; The Glass Tower: Poems 1936–43, 1944; (with F. Marnau and W. Gardiner) Three Poems, 1944; Thirty-Five Anonymous Odes, 1944; The War of the Little Jersey Cows: Poems by Guy Kelly, 1945; (ed.) The P L Book of Modern American Short Stories, 1945; (ed. with D. Newton) Atlantic Anthology, 1945; Recollections of the Gala: Selected Poems, 1943–1948, 1950; The Tall Bearded Iris (horticulture), 1956; Identity: Poems, 1969; Resolution and Identity, 1970; Spleen (31 versions of Baudelaire's poem), 1973. Add: 89 Oakdene Rd., St. Mary Cray, Kent BR5 2AL, England.

MOORE, Patrick (Alfred). British, b. 1923. Astronomy, Children's fiction, Children's non-fiction. Freelance writer and television personality. Presenter, The Sky at Night, BBC-TV series, since 1957. Ed., Yearbook of Astronomy, since 1962; Pres., British Astronomical Assn., since 1982. Dir. of the Armagh Planetarium, N. Ire., 1965–68. *Publs:* (trans.) Planet Mars, 1950; Master of the Moon, 1952; A Guide to the Moon, 1953; Suns, Myths and Men, 1954; (with A.L. Helm) Out into Space, 1954; Frozen Planet, 1954; The True Book about the Worlds Around Us, 1956; A Guide to the Planets, 1954, 1960; Destination Luna, 1955; (with H.P. Wilkins) The Moon, 1955; Quest of the Spaceways, 1955; Mission to Mars, 1955; (with I. Geis) Earth Satellite: The New Satellite Projects Explained, 1955; World of Mists, 1956; Domes of Mars, 1956; The Boys' Book of Space, 1956, 6th ed. 1963; Wheel in Space, 1956; The Planet Venus, 1956, 3rd ed. 1961; (with Wilkins) How to Make and Use a Telescope, 1956; True Book about the Earth, 1956; Guide to Mars, 1956, 3rd ed. 1960; Voices of Mars, 1957; The True Book about Earthquakes and Volcanoes, 1957; Isaac Newton, 1957; Science and Fiction, 1957; The Amateur Astronomer, 1957; The Earth Our Home, 1957; Peril on Mars, 1958; Your Book of Astronomy, 1958; The Solar System, 1958; (ed. with Bates) Space Research and Exploration, 1958; The Boys' Book of Astronomy, 1958; (with Wilkins) The Moon, 1958, 1961; The True Book about Man, 1959; Rockets and Earth Satellites, 1959, 1960; Raiders of Mars, 1959; Astronautics, 1960; Captives of the Moon, 1960; Guide to the Stars, 1960, Stars and Space, 1960; (with H. Brinton) Navigation, 1961; Astronomy, 1961; Wanderer in Space, 1961; The Stars, 1962; (with H. Brinton) Exploring Maps, 1962; (with P. Murdin) The Astronomer's Telescope, 1962; (with F.L. Jackson) Life in the Universe, 1962; The Planets, 1962; The Observer's Book of Astronomy, 1962; Crater of Fear, 1962; Telescopes and Observatories, 1962; Invader from Space, 1963; Survey of the Moon, 1963; Space in the Sixties, 1963; Exploring the Moon, 1964; The True Book about Roman Britain, 1964; The Sky at Night, 1965; (with Jackson) Life on Mars, 1965; Against Hunting, 1965; (with H. Brinton) Exploring Other Planets, 1965; Exploring the World, 1966; Exploring the Planetarium, 1966; Legends of the Stars, 1966; Naked-Eye Astronomy, 1966; The New Look of the Universe, 1966; (with P. Cattermole) Craters of the Moon, 1967; Your Book of Astronomy, 1967; Amateur Astronomer's Glossary, 1967; Basic Astronomy, 1967; The Sun, 1968; Space, 1968; (trans.) The Structure, 1968; (ed.) Some Mysteries of the Universe, 1969; The Development of Astronomical Thought, 1969; Moon Flight Atlas, 1969; Planet of Fire, 1969; Seeing Stars, 1970; Atlas of the Universe, 1970; Guide to the Planets, 1971; (with D. Hardy) Challenge of the Stars, 1972; Stories of Science and Invention, 1972; Can You Speak Venusian, 1972; Astronomy of Birr Castle, 1972; Astronomy and Space, 1972; (with Cross) Mars, 1973; Man the Astronomer, 1973; The Comets, 1973; Colour Star Atlas, 1973; Astronomy for O Level, 1973; Astronomical Telescopes and Observatories for Amateurs, 1973; Domes of Mars, 1974; Guide to the Moon, 1976; Guide to the Stars, 1976; Spy in Space, 1976; Watchers of the Stars, 1976; The Southern Stars, 1976; Around the Starlit Sky, 1976; Planet of Fear, 1977; Legends of the Planets, 1977; (with Collins) The Astronomy of Southern Africa, 1977; Guide to Mars, 1977; The A to Z of Astronomy, 1978; Killer Comet, 1978; The Moon Raiders, 1978; Man's Future in Space, 1978; Guide to Comets, 1978; The Sky at Night, vol. VI, 1978; The Voice from the Stars, 1979; Guinness Book of Astronomy Facts and Feats, 1979; Your Book of Astronomy, 1979; Fun-to-Know-About Mysteries of Space (for children), 1979; Terror Star, 1979; The Secret of the Black Hole, 1980; Out of Darkness: The Planet Pluto, 1980; Pocket Guide to Astronomy, 1980, in U.K. as Patrick Moore's Pocket Guide to Astronomy, 1982; (with Magnus Pike) Everyman's Scientific Facts and Feats, 1981; The Moon (atlas), 1981; (with Garry Hunt) Jupiter, 1981; William Herschel, Astronomer and Musician, 1981; The Unfolding Universe, 1982; (with Garry Hunt) Saturn, 1982; What's New in Space (for children), 1982; Countdown! or, How Nigh Is the End, 1983; Travellers in Space and Time, 1983; The Space Shuttle Action Book (for children), 1983; (with John Mason) The Return of Halley's Comet, 1984; (with Peter Cattermole) The Story of the Earth, 1984; Armchair Astronomy, 1984; Stargazing: Astronomy Without a Telescope, 1985; Exploring the Sky at Night with Binoculars, 1986; Man and the Stars, 1986; Television Astronomer, 1987; (with Garry Hunt) Atlas of Uranus, 1987; Astronomy for the Under-Tens, 1987; Space Travel for the Under-Tens, 1988; The Planet Neptune, 1989. Add: 39 West St., Selsey, West Sussex, England.

MOORE, Rayburn Sabatzky. American, b. 1920. Literary criticism/history, History, Biography. Prof. of English since 1965, Chmn. of the American Studies Prog. since 1968, and Chmn. of the Div. of Language and Literature since 1975, Univ. of Georgia, Athens (Chmn., Sophomore English Prog., 1962–64; Dir., Grad. Studies in English, 1964–69; Member, Exec. Cttee. Grad. Sch., 1966–69, and Editorial Bd., Univ. of Georgia Press, 1972–74). Vice-Pres., Interstate Grocer Co., Helena, Ark., 1947–50; Grad. Asst., Duke Univ., 1952–54; Asst. Prof. to Prof., Hendrix Coll. Conway, Ark., 1954–59. Member, Editorial Bd., 1974–82, and Chmn., 1980–82, Georgia Review. *Publs:* Constance F. Woolson, 1963; (ed.) For the Major and Selected Short Fiction of Constance F. Woolson, 1967; Paul Hamilton Hayne, 1972; (ed.) A Man of Letters in the Nineteenth-Century South: Selected Letters of Paul Hamilton Hayne, 1982; (ed.) A History of Southern Literature, 1985; (ed.) Selected Letters of Henry James to Edmund Gosse, 1988. Add: Dept. of English, Univ. of Georgia, Athens, Ga. 30602, U.S.A.

MOORE, Raylyn. American, b. 1928. Novels/Short stories, Biography. Part-Time Instr. in Fiction Writing, Humanities Dept., Monterey Peninsula Coll., California, since 1969. Reporter with various newspapers, 1949–64; ed. of a trade mag., 1965–68. *Publs:* Mock Orange, 1968; Wonderful Wizard, Marvelous Land (critical biography), 1974; What Happened to Emily Goode after the Great Exhibition, 1978. Add: 302 Park St., Pacific Grove, Calif. 93950, U.S.A.

MOORE, Raymond S. American, b. 1915. Education, Psychology, Sciences, Theology/Religion, Biography. Pres., Hewitt Research Foundn., Berrien Springs, since 1964. Pres., Nihon San-iku Gakuin Coll., Chiba-ken, Japan, 1951–56, and Philippine Union Coll., 1956–57; Vice-Pres., Loma Linda Univ., California, 1960–62; Grad. Programs Of-

ficer, U.S. Office of Education, 1964–67. *Publs:* Science Discovers God, 1953; Michibiki, 1956; China Doctor, 1961; Caring for Young Children, 1975; Better Late Than Early, 1975; How to Socialize Little Children, 1976; School Can Wait, 1979; Home Grown Kids, 1981; Home-Spun Schools, 1982; The Abaddon Conspiracy, 1985; Communications Receivers: The Vacuum-Tube Era—50 Glorious Years 1932-1981, 1987. Add: c/o RSM Communications Inc, 116 Walnut St., Walpole, Mass. 02081, U.S.A.

MOORE, Richard. American, b. 1927. Poetry, Songs, lyrics and libretti. Lectr. in Humanities, New England Conservatory of Music, Boston, since 1965. Teacher of English, Boston Univ., 1956–57; Instr. in English, Trinity Coll., Burlington, Vt., 1962–65. *Publs:* A Question of Survival, 1971; Word from the Hills, 1972; Chocorua (libretto), 1972; Empires, 1981; The Education of a Mouse, 1983. Add: 81 Clark St., Belmont, Mass. 02178, U.S.A.

MOORE, Wilbert E(llis). American, b. 1914. Economics, History, Sociology. Prof. of Sociology and Law, Univ. of Denver, 1979–88, now Emeritus. With Pennsylvania State Univ., University Park, 1940–43, Princeton Univ., New Jersey, 1945–64, and Russell Sage Foundn., NYC, 1964–70. *Publs:* Economic Demography of Eastern and Southern Europe, 1945; (ed. with G. Gurvitch) Twentieth Century Sociology, 1945; Industrial Relations and the Social Order, 1946, 1951; Industrialization and Labor, 1951; Economy and Society, 1955; (ed. with S. Kuznets and J.J. Spengler) Economic Growth: Brazil, India, Japan, 1955; (ed. with A.S. Feldman) Labor Commitment and Social Change in Developing Areas, 1960; Conduct of the Corporation, 1962; Social Change, 1962, 1974; Man, Time and Society, 1963; (ed. with B.F. Hoselitz) Industrialization and Society, 1963; The Impact of Industry, 1965; (ed. with R.M. Cook) Readings on Social Change, 1967; Order and Change, 1967; (ed. with E.B. Sheldon) Indicators of Social Change, 1968; (with D.R. Young) Trusteeship and the Management of Foundations, 1969; Professions: Roles and Rules, 1970; American Negro Slavery and Abolition, 1971; (ed.) Technology and Social Change, 1972; World Modernization: The Limits of Convergence, 1981. Add: 7207 S. Vine St., Littleton, Colo. 80122, U.S.A.

MOORE, W(ilfred) G(eorge). British, b. 1907. Geography. Schoolmaster until 1967. *Publs:* The Geography of Capitalism, 1938; (co-author) Complete Self-Educator, 1939; The *orld's Wealth, 1947; (co-author) Younger Children's Encyclopedia, 1949; Penguin Dictionary of Geography, 1949; The Soil We Live On, 1950; (co-author) The World We Live In, 1951; Essential Geography, 4 vols., 1956–58; Children Far and Near, 8 vols., 1956–58; Adventures in Geography, 4 vols., 1957–61; New Visual Geography, 17 vols., 1959–72; Around the World in Colour, 1960; (co-author) Geography, 1961; (co-ed.) Encyclopedia of World Geography: Europe, 1961; A Family in Samoa, 1961; A Family in Greece, 1962; (co-author) A Family in New Zealand, 1963; A Family in Japan, 1964; (co-author) Technology, 1964; More Children Far and Near, 7 vols., 1965–67; Penguin Encyclopedia of Places, 1971; Find the Answer Geography, 1973; Geography (data books), 1974; Man and His World, 3 vols., 1976–77; Fundamental Geography of the British Isles, 1981. Add: Fouroaks, 34 Copsewood Way, Northwood, Middx. HA6 2UA, England.

MOOREHEAD, Caroline. British, b. 1944. Biography, Documentaries/Reportage, Translations. Feature Writer, The Independent Newspaper, London, since 1988. Psychologist, Neuropsychiatric Hosp., Rome, 1966–68; Reporter, Time mag., Rome, 1968–69; Feature Writer, Telegraph Mag., London, 1969–70; Features Ed., Times Educational Supplement, 1970–73; Feature Writer, The Times Newspaper, London, 1973–88. *Publs:* (ed. and trans.) Myths and Legends of Britain, 1968; Helping: A Guide to Voluntary Work, 1975; Fortune's Hostages, 1980; Sidney Bernstein: A Biography, 1973; Freya Stark; A Biography, 1985; Troublesome People: Enemies of War 1916-1986, 1987; (ed.) Over the Rim of the World: The Letters of Freya Stark, 1988. Add: 36 Fitzroy Rd., London NW1, England.

MOORE-RINVOLUCRI, Mina (Josephine). British, b. 1902. Education, Language/Linguistics, Literature. Lectr. in Education, 1938–40, University Coll., Cardiff; Lectr. in French, Univ. of Liverpool, 1943–46; Lectr. in Education, Univ. of Newcastle upon Tyne, 1947–48, and Univ. of Liverpool, 1948–69; Sr. Lectr. in Education, 1969–72, and Dir. of the Limerick Centre until 1974, University Coll., Cork. *Publs:* Bernard Shaw et la France, 1934; (ed.) Charme de province, 1940; Oral Work in Modern Languages, 1954; East Germany, 1973. Add: Cefn Bach, Cyffy Llioe, NR. Ruthin, Clwyd, Wales.

MOOREY, Peter Roger Stuart. British, b. 1937. Archaeology/Antiquities. Keeper, Dept. of Antiquities, Ashmolean Museum, Oxford, since 1983 (Sr. Asst. keeper, 1961–83). Ed., Levant (journal of the British Sch. of Archaeology in Jerusalem), 1968–86. *Publs:* Archaeology, Artefacts and the Bible, 1969; Ancient Egypt, 1970, 1988; Catalogue of the Ancient Persian Bronzes in the Ashmolean Museum, Oxford, 1971; Ancient Persian Bronzes in the Adam Collection, 1974; Ancient Bronzes from Luristan, 1974; Biblical Lands, 1975; Kish Excavations 1923–1933, 1978; Cemeteries of the First Millennium B.C. at Deve Huyuk, 1980; Excavation in Palestine, 1981; (with B. Buchanan) Catalogue of Ancient Near Eastern Seals in the Ashmolean Museum, vols, 2-3, 1984–88; Materials and Manufacture in Ancient Mesopotamia: The Evidence of Art and Archaeology: Metals and Metalwork, Glazed Materials and Glass, 1985. Add: Ashmolean Museum, Oxford, England.

MOORHEAD, Diana. New Zealander (b. British), b. 1940. Children's fiction. Librarian, Massey High Sch., Auckland, 1969–80, Kelston Boys High Sch., 1981–85, and Takapuna City Libraries, since 1986. *Publs:* In Search of Magic, 1971; The Green and the White, 1974; Gull Man's Glory, 1976. Add: 58 Yeovil Rd., Te Atatu, Auckland 8, New Zealand.

MOORHOUSE, Geoffrey. British, b. 1931. History, Sociology, Theology/Religion, Travel/Exploration/Adventure. Chief Features Writer, The Guardian, London, 1963–70. *Publs:* The Other England, 1964; The Press, 1964; Against All Reason, 1969; Calcutta, 1971; The Missionaries, 1973; The Fearful Void, 1974; The Diplomats: The Foreign Office Today, 1977; The Boat and the Town, 1979; The Best Loved Game, 1979; India Britannica, 1983; To the Frontier, 1984. Add: Park House, Gayle, Nr. Hawes, N. Yorks. DL8 3RT, England.

MOOTE, A. Lloyd. American, b. 1931. History. Prof. of History, Univ. of Southern California, Los Angeles, since 1971 (Asst. Prof., 1962–65; Assoc. Prof., 1965–71). Lectr., Univ. of Toronto, 1958–61; Asst. Prof., Univ. of Cincinnati, 1961–62. Pres., Soc. for French Historical Studies, 1985; Member, Inst. for Advanced Study, Princeton, N.J., 1988–89. *Publs:* The Seventeenth Century: Europe in Ferment, 1970; The Revolt of the Judges: The Parlement of Paris and the Fronde 1643–1652, 1971; (co-author) The World of Europe; Louis XIII, The Just, 1989. Add: Dept. of History, Univ. of Southern California, Los Angeles, Calif. 90089-0034, U.S.A.

MORAES, Dom(inic Frank). British, b. 1938. Poetry, Autobiography/Memoirs/Personal. Former Scriptwriter, Granada TV, London; Roving Reporter, New York Times Mag., 1968–71; Managing Ed., Asia Mag., Hong Kong, 1971–73; Chief Literary Consultant, U.N. Fund for Populations, 1973–77. *Publs:* Green Is the Grass (essay on cricket), 1951; A Beginning (verse), 1957; Poems, 1960; Gone Away: An Indian Journal, 1960; Penguin Modern Poetry 2: Kingsley Amis, Dom Moraes, Peter Porter, 1962; 15 Poems for William Shakespeare, 1964; (trans.) The Brass Serpent, by Carmi Charny, 1964; John Nobody (verse), 1965; Bedlam Etcetera (verse), 1966; Poems 1955–1965, 1966; My Son's Father: An Autobiography (in U.S. as My Son's Father: A Poet's Autobiography), 1968; The Tempest Within: An Account of East Pakistan, 1971; From East to West (essays), 1971; The People Time Forgot, 1972; A Matter of People, 1974; (ed.) Voices for Life: Reflections on the Human Condition, 1975; The Open Eyes: A Journey Through Karnataka, 1976; Mrs. Gandhi, 1980; Bombay, 1980; Absences (verse), 1983; Collected Poems 1957-1987, 1988. Add: c/o Curtis Brown, 162-168 Regent St., London W1R 5TA, England.

MORAY WILLIAMS, Ursula. British, b. 1911. Children's fiction. First Life Member, Puffin Club, Puffin Books, London, 1974. Former Justice of the Peace: former Chmn. of the Juvenile Bench, Evesham. *Publs:* Jean Pierre, 1931; For Brownies, 1932; Grandfather (poetry), 1933; The Pettabomination, 1933; The Autumn Sweepers (plays), 1933; Kelpie the Gipsy's Pony, 1934; More for Brownies, 1934; Anders and Marta, 1935; Adventures of Anne, 1935; Tales for the Sixes and Sevens, 1936; The Twins and Their Ponies, 1936; Sandy-on-the-Shore, 1936; (with C.S. John) Adventures of Boss and Dingbatt, 1937; Elaine of La Signe, 1937; Dumpling, 1937; Adventures of the Little Wooden Horse, 1938; Adventures of Puffin, 1940; Pretenders Island, 1940; Peter and the Wanderlust, 1940; A Castle for John Peter, 1941; Gobbolino the Witch's Cat, 1942; The Good Little Christmas Tree, 1943; The Three Toymakers, 1945; The House of Happiness, 1946; Malkins Mountain, 1948; The Story of Laughing Dandino, 1948; Jockin the Jester, 1951; The Bimkelbys at Home, 1951; The Binkelbys on the Farm, 1953; Secrets of the Wood, 1953; Grumpa, 1955; Golden Horse with a Silver Tail, 1957; Hobbie, 1958; The Moonball, 1958; The Noble Hawks, 1959; Nine Lives of Island MacKenzie, 1959; Beware of This Animal, 1963; Johnnie Tigerskin, 1964; O for a Mouseless House!, 1964; High Adventure, 1965; The Cruise of

the Happy Go Gay, 1967; A Crown for a Queen, 1968; The Toymaker's Daughter, 1968; Mog, 1969; Boy in a Barn, 1970; Johnny Golightly and His Crocodile, 1970; Hurricanes, 4 vols., 1971; Castle Merlin, 1972; A Picnic with the Aunts, 1973; Kidnapping of My Grandmother, 1973; Grandpapa's Folly and the Woodworm Bookworm, 1974; The Line, 1974; Beware of This Animal, 1976; Bogwoppit, 1978; Jeffy The Burglar's Cat, 1981; Bellabelinda and the No-Good Angel, 1982; Further Adventures of Gobbolino and the Little Wooden Horse, 1984; Spid, 1985; Paddy on the Island, 1987. Add: Court Farm, Beckford, nr. Tewkesbury, Glos., England.

MORE, Caroline. *See* **CONE,** Molly.

MOREAU, David Merlin. Also writes as David Merlin. British, b. 1927. Novels/Short stories, Administration/Management, Medicine/-Health. Flying Corresp., The Director, since 1970; Publicity Dir., Dewplan Group, since 1981. European Market Controller, Beecham Group, Brentford, Middx., 1956–65; Managing Dir., Syntex Pharmaceutical Ltd., Maidenhead, Berks., 1965–70; Gen. Mgr., 1970–72, and Chmn., 1972–79, Weddel Pharmaceutical Ltd.; Managing Dir., Elga Group, 1972–80; BBC Radio 4 series, More Wrestling than Dancing, 1984–88. *Publs:* (as David Merlin) The Simple Life, 1962; (as David Merlin) The Built-In Urge, 1963; Summer's End, 1966; Look Behind You: An Alphabetical Guide to Executive Survival, 1973. Add: Rowley Cottage, Langley Park, Bucks. SL3 6DT, England.

MORENO, Antonio. Spanish, b. 1918. Psychology, Theology/Religion. Prof. of Philosophy, Grad. Theological Union, Berkeley, since 1966. Ordained Roman Catholic Priest, 1951. Instr. and subsequently Prof. of Philosophy, Notre Dame Univ., Indiana, 1959–61, 1964–66. *Publs:* Jung, God and Modern Man, 1971. Add: 2401 Ridge Rd., Berkeley, Calif. 94709, U.S.A.

MORETON, John. *See* **COHEN,** Morton N.

MOREY, Walt(er Nelson). American, b. 1907. Novels/Short stories, Children's fiction. Filbert farmer since 1937. Construction worker, mill-worker, and theatre mgr. in Oregon and Washington in the 1930's; burner foreman and supt., Kaiser Shipyards, Vancouver, Wash., 1940–45; deep-sea diver and fish trap inspector, Alaska, 1951; Dir., Oregon Nut Cooperative, Newberg, 1960–61. *Publs:* (with Virgil Burford) North to Danger, 1954, 1969; Gentle Ben, 1965; Home Is the North, 1967; Kavik, The Wolf Dog, 1968; Angry Waters, 1969; Gloomy Gus (in U.K. as The Bear at Friday Creek). 1970; Deep Trouble, 1971; Scrub Dog of Alaska, 1971; Canyon Winter, 1972; Runaway Stallion, 1973; Run Far, Run Fast, 1974; Operation Blue Bear, 1975; Year of the Black Pony, 1976; Sandy and the Rock Star, 1979; The Lemon Meringue Dog, 1980. Add: 10830 S.W. Morey Lane, Wilsonville, Ore. 97070, U.S.A.

MORGAN, Alison M. British, b. 1930. Children's fiction. Teacher, 1952–59. *Publs:* Fish, 1971 (in U.S. as A Boy Called Fish, 1973); Pete, 1972; Ruth Crane, 1973; At Willie Tucker's Place, 1975; River Song, 1976; Leaving Home (in U.S. as All Sorts of Prickles), 1979; Paul's Kite, 1981; Brighteye, 1984; Christabel, 1984; The Eyes of the Blind, 1985; Staples for Amos, 1986; The Raft, 1988; The Wild Morgans, 1988; A Walk with Smudge, 1989; Smudge and the Danger Lion, 1989. Add: Talcoed, Llanafan, Builth Wells, Powys, Wales.

MORGAN, Dan. British, b. 1925. Science fiction/Fantasy. Managing Dir., Dan Morgan Ltd. (retail menswear). Former Lectr. on Contemporary Novel, Extra-Mural Dept., Univ. of Nottingham. *Publs:* Guitar, 1965; The New Minds, 1967; The Several Minds, 1969; Mind Trap, 1970; Inside, 1971; (with J. Kippax) Thunder of Stars, 1974; (with J. Kippax) Seed of Stars, 1974; (with J. Kippax) The Neutral Stars, 1975; The Country of the Mind, 1975; The Concrete Horizon, 1976; Spanish Guitar, 1982; Beginning Windsurfing, 1982; (with Nick Penny) You Can Play the Guitar, 1983. Add: 1 Chapel Lane, Spalding, Lincs. PE11 1BP, England.

MORGAN, Dewi. British, b. 1916. History, Literature, Theology/Religion. Rector, St. Bride's Church, London, 1962–84, and Prebendary, St. Paul's Cathedral, 1976–84, now Emeritus. Ed., Glamorgan County Mag., 1948–50; Ed. and Press Secty., Soc. for the Propagation of the Gospel, 1950–62; Ed., St. Martin's Review, 1953–55. *Publs:* Expanding Frontiers, 1957; The Bishops Come to Lambeth, 1957; Lambeth Speaks, 1958; The Undying Fire, 1959; (ed.) They Became Anglicans, 1959; 1662 and All That, 1961; But God Comes First, 1962; Agenda for Anglicans, 1963; Seeds of Peace, 1965; Arising from the Psalms, 1966; (ed.) They Became Christians, 1966; (ed.) Faith in Fleet Street, 1967;

God and Sons, 1967; (with Michael Perry) The Printed Word, 1969; Church in Transition, 1970; Phoenix of Fleet Street, 1973; Where Belonging Begins, 1988. Add: 217 Rosendale Rd., London SE21 8LW, England.

MORGAN, Edwin (George). British, b. 1920. Poetry, Essays, Translations. Titular Prof. of English, Univ. of Glasgow, 1975–80 (Asst. Lectr., 1947–50; Lectr., 1950–65; Sr. Lectr., 1965–71; Reader, 1971–75). Visiting Prof. of English, &iv. of Strathclyde, Glasgow, 1987–90. *Publs:* The Vision of Cathkin Braes, 1952; (trans.) Beowulf, 1952; The Cape of Good Hope, 1955; (trans.) Poems from Eugenio Montale, 1959; (trans.) Sovpoems: Brecht, Neruda, Pasternak, Tsvetayeva, Mayakovsky, Martynov, Yevtushenko, 1961; (ed.) Collins Albatross Book of Longer Poems: English and American Poetry from the Fourteenth Century to the Present Day, 1963; Starryveldt, 1965; Scotch Mist, 1965; Sealwear, 1966; (ed. with G. Bruce and M. Lindsay) Scottish Poetry One to Six, 1966–72; Emergent Poems, 1967; The Second Life, 1968; Gnomes, 1968; Proverbfolder, 1969; (with Alan Bold and Edward Brathwaite) Penguin Modern Poets 15, 1969; The Horseman's Word: A Sequence of Concrete Poems, 1970; Twelve Songs, 1970; (ed.) New English Dramatists 14, 1970; (trans. with David Wevill) Sandor Weores and Ferenc Juhasz: Selected Poems, 1970; The Dolphin's Song, 1971; Glasgow Sonnets, 1972; Instamatic Poems, 1972; (trans.) Wi the Haill Voice: Poems by Mayakovsky, 1972; The Whittrick: A Poem in Eight Dialogues, 1973; From Glasgow to Saturn, 1973; Essays, 1974; (trans.) Fifty Renascence Love-Poems, 1975; Rites of Passage: Selected Translations, 1976; East European Poets, 1976; Hugh MacDiarmid, 1976; The New Divan, 1977; Colour Poems, 1978; (trans.) Platen: Selected Poems, 1978; Star Gate: Science Fiction Poems, 1979; (ed.) Scottish Satirical Verse, 1980; Poems of Thirty Years, 1982; Grafts/Takes, 1983; 4 Glasgow Subway Poems, 1983; Sonnets from Scotland, 1984; Selected Poems, 1985; From the Video Box, 1986; Newspoems, 1987; Tales from Limerick Zoo, 1988; Themes on a Variation, 1988. Add: 19 Whittingehame Ct., Glasgow G12 0BG, Scotland.

MORGAN, Elaine (Neville). British, b. 1920. Biology. *Publs:* The Descent of Woman, 1972, 1985; Falling Apart, 1976; The Aquatic Ape: A Theory of Human Evolution, 1982. Add: 24 Aberffrwd Rd., Mountain Ash., Glam., Wales.

MORGAN, (George) Frederick. American, b. 1922. Poetry. Founder and Ed., The Hudson Review, NYC, since 1947. Chmn. of the Advisory Council, Dept. of Romance Languages and Literatures, Princeton Univ., New Jersey, since 1974. *Publs:* (ed.) The Hudson Review Anthology, 1961; (ed.) The Modern Image: Outstanding Stories from The Hudson Review, 1965; A Book of Change, 1972; Poems of the Two Worlds, 1977; The Tarot of Cornelius Agrippa, 1978; Death Mother and Other Poems, 1979; The River, 1980; Refractions, 1981; Seven Poems by Mallarmé, 1981; Northbook, 1982; Eleven Poems, 1983; The Fountain and Other Fables, 1984; Poems: New and Selected, 1987. Add: The Hudson Review, 684 Park Ave., New York, N.Y. 10021, U.S.A.

MORGAN, Helen (Gertrude Louise). British, b. 1921. Children's fiction, Poetry. *Publs:* The Little Old Lady, 1961; Mary Kate series, 3 vols., 1963–72; Tales of Tigg's Farm, 1963; A Mouthful of Magic, 1963; Two in the Garden, 1964; The Tailor and the Sailor and the Small Black Cat, 1964; Dream of Dragons, 1965; Two in the House, 1965; Satchkin Patchkin, 1966; Two on the Farm, 1966; Two by the Sea, 1967; Mrs. Pinny and the Blowing Day, 1968; Mrs. Pinny and the Sudden Snow, 1969; Mother Farthing's Luck, 1971; Mrs. Pinny and the Salty Sea Day, 1972; The Sketchbook Crime, 1980. Add: c/o Barclays Bank, Calverley Rd., Tunbridge Wells, Kent, England.

MORGAN, H(oward) G(ethin). British, b. 1934. Psychiatry. Norah Cooke Hurle Prof. of Mental Health, Univ. of Bristol; Hon. Consultant Psychiatrist, South Western Regional Health Authority. Formerly, Sr. Registrar, Professorial Unit, The Maudsley Hosp., London. *Publs:* (with B. Cooper) Epidemiological Psychiatry, 1973; (with H.H. Morgan) Aids to Psychiatry, 1979; Death Wishes?, 1979. Add: Dept. of Mental Health, Univ. of Bristol, 41 St. Michael's Hill, Bristol BS2 8DZ, England.

MORGAN, Janet. British, b. 1934. Communications Media, Politics/Government, Biography. Adviser to the Group Bd., Granada Group, London, since 1986. Lectr. in Politics, Exeter Coll., Oxford, 1974–76; Dir. of Studies, St. Hugh's Coll., Oxford, 1975–76, and Lectr. in Politics, 1976–78; Member, Central Policy Review Staff, U.K. Cabinet Office, London, 1978–81; Visiting Fellow, All Souls Coll., Oxford, 1983; Special Adviser to the Dir.-Gen., BBC, London, 1983–86. *Publs:* The House of Lords and the Labour Government 1964–70, 1975; Reinforcing Parliament, 1976; (ed.) The Diaries of a Cabinet Minister 1964–70, by

Richard Crossman, 3 vols., 1975–77; (ed.) Backbench Diaries 1951–63, by Richard Crossman, 1980; (ed. with Richard Hoggart) The Future of Broadcasting, 1982; Agatha Christie: A Biography, 1984. Add: c/o David Higham Associates Ltd., 5-8 Lower John St., London W1R 4HA, England.

MORGAN, Lael. American, b. 1936. Anthropology/Ethnology, Recreation/Leisure/Hobbies, Social commentary/phenomena, Travel/Exploration/Adventure. *Publs:* The Woman's Guide to Boating and Cooking, 1968, 1974; And the Land Provides: Alaskan Natives in a Year of Transition, 1974; Tatting, 1977; Alaska's Native People, 1979; Aleutian Islands, 1980; Kotzebue Basin, 1981; Art and Eskimo Power: The Life and Times of Alaskan Howard Rock, 1988. Add: Box 60529, Fairbanks, Alaska 99706, U.S.A.

MORGAN, Marabel. American. Cookery/Gastronomy/Wine, Human Relations, Women. *Publs:* The Total Woman, 1973; Total Joy, 1976; The Total Woman Cookbook, 1980; The Electric Woman, 1985. Add: c/o Total Woman, 1300 N.W. 167th St., Miami, Fla. 33169, U.S.A.

MORGAN, Marjorie. *See* **CHIBNALL**, Marjorie McCallum.

MORGAN, Mark. *See* **OVERHOLSER**, Wayne D.

MORGAN, Neil. American, b. 1924. Georgraphy, History, Social acommentary/phenomena, Travel/Exploration/Adventure. Columnist and Ed., San Diego Tribune, since 1950; Syndicated Columnist, Assignment West, Copley News Service, since 1958. Columnist, San Diego Daily Journal, 1946–50. *Publs:* My San Diego, 1951; It Began with a Roar, 1953; Know Your Doctor, 1954; Crosstown, 1955; San Diego 1960, 1959; Westward Tilt, 1963; Neil Morgan's San Diego, 1964; The Pacific States, 1967; The California Syndrome, 1969; (with R. Witty) Marines of the Margarita, 1970; The Unconventional City, 1972; (with Tom Blair) Yesterday's San Diego, 1976; This Great Land, 1983. Add: c/o San Diego Tribune, P.O. Box 191, San Diego, Calif. 92112, U.S.A.

MORGAN, Patricia. British, b. 1944. Criminology/Law enforcement/Prisons, Psychology. Teacher, 1967–71; Research Fellow, London Sch. of Economics, 1979–82. *Publs:* Child Care: Sense and Fable, 1975; Delinquent Fantasies, 1978; (co-author) Criminal Welfare on Trial, 1981. Add: c/o Maurice Temple Smith Ltd., Gower House, Croft Rd., Aldershot GU11 3HR, England.

MORGAN, (Colin) Pete(r). British, b. 1939. Plays/Screenplays, Poetry. *Publs:* C'mon Everybody: Poetry of the Dance, 1965; A Big Hat or What?, 1968; Loss of Two Anchors, 1970; Still the Same Old Harry (play), 1972; Gardens by the Sea (documentary film), 1973; Poems for Shortie, 1973; The Grey Mare Being the Better Steed, 1973; I See You on My Arm, 1976; All the Voices Going Away (play), 1979; The Spring Collection, 1979; One Greek Alphabet, 1980; Reporting Back, 1983; A Winter Visitor, 1984; The Pete Morgan Poetry Pack, 1984; The Yorkshire Ridings, 1987. Add: c/o Secker and Warburg, 81 Fulham Rd., London SW3 6RB, England.

MORGAN, Robert. British, b. 1921. Plays/Screenplays, Poetry, Autobiography/Memoirs/Personal. Full-time writer since 1980. Head of Remedial Dept., Cowplain Secondary Sch., 1964–74; Adviser for Special Education, Gosport Education Authority, 1974–80. *Publs:* The Night's Prison, 1967; Rainbow Valley (radio play), 1967; Poems and Extracts, 1968; The Master Miners (play), 1972; The Storm (poetry), 1974; On the Banks of the Cynon (poetry), 1976; The Pass (poetry), 1976; My Lamp Still Burns (autobiography), 1981; Poems and Drawings, 1984; The Miners and Other Stories, 1986; Memoir (poetry), 1987; Landmarks (poetry), 1988. Add: 72 Anmore Rd., Denmead, Hants. PO7 6NT, England.

MORGAN, Ted. American, b. 1932. Biography. Member of staff, Associated Press, NYC, 1958–59, and New York Herald Tribune, in NYC, Paris and Rome, 1959–64. *Publs:* On Becoming American, 1979; Maugham, 1980; Rowing Toward Eden, 1981; Churchill: Young Man in a Hurry 1874–1915, 1982; F.D.R.: A Biography, 1985; Literary Outlaw: The Life and Times of William S. Burroughs, 1988. Add: c/o Henry Holt and Co., 115 W. 18th St., New York, N.Y. 10011, U.S.A.

MORGAN, Theodore. American, b. 1910. Economics. Emeritus Prof. of Economics, Univ. of Wisconsin, Madison, since 1980 (Prof., 1947–80). Deputy-Gov., Central Bank of Ceylon, 1951–53; Consultant to the Ford Foundn., from 1956; Sr. Staff Member, Council of Economic Advisers, Washington, D.C., 1961–62; former Chmn., Regional Development Panel, South East Asia Advisory Group; Adviser to the Ministry of Economic Affairs, Govt. of Thailand, 1970; Teaching, Admin., and Research in Indonesia, 1959–60; Kenya, 1961; Singapore, 1967–69; Philippines, 1983–84. *Publs:* Income and Employment, 1947, 1952; Hawaii: A Century of Economic Change 1778–1876, 1948; Introduction to Economics, 1950; (co-author) The Challenge of Our Times, 1954, 1971; Introduction to Economics, 2nd ed. 1956; (co-author and co-ed.) Readings in Economic Development, 1963; (co-author) The Economic Development of Kenya, 1963; (co-author and co-ed.) Economic Interdependence in Southeast Asia, 1969; (co-author and co-ed.) Economic Development: Readings in Theory and Practice, 1970; (co-author and co-ed.) Exchange Rate Policy in Southeast Asia, 1973; Economic Development: Concept and Strategy, 1975. Add: 3534 Topping Rd., Madison, Wisc. 53705, U.S.A.

MORGAN-GRENVILLE, Gerard (Wyndham). British, b. 1931. Recreation/Leisure/Hobbies, Sciences (general), Travel/Exploration/Adventure, Autobiography/Memoirs/Personal. Chmn., Soc. for Environmental Improvement Ltd., since 1972. Dir., Dexam Intnl. (Holdings) Ltd., Dexam Intnl. Ltd., Dexam Intnl. Sarl, Goodwood Metalcraft Ltd., and Project Finance Ltd.; Chmn., Chargebarge Ltd., Chargebarge Sarl, and Quarry Trading Co. Ltd.; Chmn., Great Scottish and Western Railway Co., 1984. Chmn., National Centre for Alternative Technology; Countryside Commnr. for England, 1983, and for Wales, 1984. *Publs:* Barging into France, 1972; Barging into Southern France, 1973; Holiday Cruising in France, 1973; Cruising the Sahara, 1974; Barging into Burgundy, 1975; Nuclear Power: What It Means to You, 1980. Add: Henbant Fach, Llanbedr Crickhowell, Powys, Wales.

MORGAN-WITTS, Max. British, b. 1931. History, International relations/Current affairs. Producer, Granada Television, London, 1957–63; Producer, 1963–66, and Series Exec. Ed., 1966–72, BBC Television, London. *Publs:* all with Gordon Thomas—The Day Their World Ended, 1969; The San Francisco Earthquake, 1971; The Strange Fate of the Morro Castle, 1972; Voyage of the Damned, 1974; The Day Guernica Died, 1975; Ruin from the Air, 1977; The Day the Bubble Burst, 1979; Trauma, 1981; Pontiff, 1983; The Year of Armageddon, 1984; sole author—The Golden Opportunity of a Thousand Years, 1986. Add: c/o Jonathan Clowes, 22 Prince Albert Rd., London NW1, England.

MORIARTY, Frederick L. American, b. 1913. Theology/Religion. Prof. of Biblical Studies Emeritus, Boston Coll., since 1987 (Prof. of Theology, 1960–78). Prof. of Biblical Studies, Weston Sch. of Theology, Cambridge, Mass., 1950–70; Prof. of Biblical Studies, Gregorian Univ., Rome, 1963–77, Loyola Univ., Chicago, 1979–81 and Gonzaga Univ., Spokane, Wash., 1981–87. *Publs:* Introducing the Old Testament, 1960; Foreword to the Old Testament Books, 2nd ed. 1964. Add: Boston Coll., Chestnut Hill, Mass. 02167, U.S.A.

MORICE, Anne. *See* **SHAW,** Felicity.

MORLAN, George K(olmer). American, b. 1904. Philosophy, Psychology. Mgr. of Literature of Sales Education, 1950–57, and Coordinator of Professional Services, 1957–65, Lederle Labs., Pearl River, N.J.; Assoc. Prof. of Psychology, Michigan Technological Univ., 1965–66. *Publs:* America's Heritage from John Stuart Mill, 1936, 1973; Laymen Speaking, 1938; How to Influence Yourself, 1944; Guide for Young Lovers, 1969. Add: 4611 N.W. 45th St., Tamarac, Fla. 33319, U.S.A.

MORLAND, Dick. *See* **HILL,** Reginald.

MORLEY, David. British, b. 1923. Medicine/Health. Prof. Emeritus of Tropical Child Health, Univ. of London Inst. of Child Health, since 1988 (Reader, 1965–78; Prof, 1978–88). Member, Editorial Bd., Medicine Digest, Postgraduate Doctor, and Journal of Environmental Paediatrics and Tropical Child Health. Lectr., Univ. of Ibadan, Nigeria, 1959–61; Sr. Lectr., Dept. of Human Nutrition, London Sch. of Hygiene and Tropical Medicine, 1961–65. *Publs:* Paediatric Priorities in the Developing World, 1973; (with Margaret Woodland) See How They Grow, 1979; (with J.R. Rohde and G. Williams) Practising Health for All; (with Hermione Lovel) My Name Is Today, 1986. Add: Inst. of Child Health, 30 Guilford St., London WC1N 1EH, England.

MORLEY, Sheridan (Robert). British, b. 1941. Film, Theatre, Biography. London Drama Critic, Intnl. Herald Tribune, Paris, since 1979. Newscaster, ITN television, London, 1964–67; Interviewer, BBC television Late Night Line Up, 1967–73; Deputy Features Ed., The Times, London, 1973–75; Arts Ed. and Drama Critic, Punch, London, 1975–88. *Publs:* A Talent to Amuse (biography of Noel Coward), 1969; (ed.) Theatre '71-'74, 4 vols., (ed.) Adventure and the Cinema, 1973; (ed.)

Romance and the Cinema, 1973; Review Copies, 1974; Oscar Wilde, 1976; Marlene Dietrich, 1977; Sybil Thorndike, 1977; Gladys Cooper, 1979; Noel Coward and His Friends, 1979; (ed.) The Stephen Sondheim Songbook, 1980; (ed.) Punch at the Theatre, 1980; Gertrude Lawrence, 1981; (ed.) The Noel Coward Diaries, 1983; Tales from the Hollywood Raj, 1984; Shooting Stars, 1984; The Theatregoers Quiz Book, 1984; Katharine Hepburn, 1985; The Other Side of the Moon (Biography of David Niven), 1985; (ed.) Bull's Eyes, 1985; Great Stage Stars, 1985; Spread a Little Happiness, 1987; Out in the Midday Sun, 1988; Elizabeth Taylor, 1988; Odd Man Out (biography of James Mason), 1989. Add: c/o Prince of Wales Theatre Offices, Coventry St., London W1, England.

MOROWITZ, Harold J. American. Biology, Intellectual history, Philosophy, Sciences. Prof. of Molecular Biophysics and Biochemistry, Yale Univ., New Haven, since 1955. With the National Bureau of Standards, 1951–53, and the National Institutes of Health, Bethesda, Md., 1953–55. *Publs:* (ed. with H. Quastler) Proceedings of the First National Biophysics Conference, 1959; (ed. with T. Waterman) Theoretical and Mathematical Biology, 1961; Life and the Physical Sciences, 1963; Energy Flow in Biology, 1968; Entropy for Biologists, 1970; (with L. Morowitz) Life on the Planet Earth, 1975; Ego Niches, 1977; Foundations of Bioenergetics, 1978; The Wine of Life, 1979; Mayonnaise and the Origin of Life, 1982; Cosmic Joy and Local Pain, 1987. Add: 56 Ox Bow Lane, Woodbridge, Conn. 06525, U.S.A.

MORPURGO, J(ack) E(ric). British, b. 1918. History, Literature, Travel/Exploration. Prof. of American Literature, Univ. of Leeds, 1969–83, now Emeritus. Ed., Penguin Parade, 1947–59; Gen. Ed., Penguin Histories, 1949–72; Dir.-Gen., National Book League, London, 1954–69; Prof. of American Studies, Univ. of Geneva, 1967–69. *Publs:* Charles Lamb and Elia, 1949; (ed.) Leigh Hunt: Autobiography, 1949; American Excursion, 1949; (ed.) Lewis Carroll: Humorous Verse, 1950; (ed.) Marlowe: Edward II, 1952; (ed.) E.J. Trelawny: The Last Days of Shelley and Byron, 1952; (ed.) Keats: Poems, 1953; (ed. with Edmund Blunden) Christ's Hospital Book, 1953, 1954; (with R.B. Nye) History of the United States, 1955, 1970; (ed. with Kenneth Pelmear) Rugby Football: An Anthology, 1958; The Road to Athens, 1963; (with Martin Hurlimann) Venice, 1964; (ed.) Cobbett: A Year's Residence n the U.S.A., 1968; (ed.) Cooper: The Spy, 1968; Barnes Wallis: A Biography, 1970, 1971; Treason at West Point, 1976; Their Majesties' Royall Colledge: William and Mary in the XVII and XVIII Centuries, 1976; Allen Lane: King Penguin, 1979; Verses Humorous and Post-Humorous, 1981; (ed.) Cobbett's America, 1985. Add: 12 Laurence Mews, London W12 9AT, England.

MORRESSY, John. American, b. 1930. Novels/Short stories, Science fiction, Children's fiction. Prof. of English, Franklin Pierce Coll., Rindge, N.H., since 1968. *Publs:* The Blackboard Cavalier, 1966; The Addison Tradition, 1968; Starbrat, 1972; Nail Down the Stars, 1973; A Long Communion, 1974; The Humans of Ziax II, 1974; The Windows of Forever, 1975; Under a Calculating Star, 1975; A Law for the Stars, 1976; The Extraterritorial, 1977; Frostworld and Dreamfire, 1977; Drought on Ziax II, 1978; Ironbrand, 1980; Graymantle, 1981; Kingsbane, 1982; The Mansions of Space, 1983; Other Stories, 1983; The Time of the Annihilator, 1985; A Voice for Princess, 1986; The Questing of Kedrigern, 1987; Kedrigern in Wanderland, 1988. Add: Apple Hill Rd., East Sullivan, N.H. 03445, U.S.A.

MORRIS, Benjamin Stephen. British, b. 1910. Education. Sr. Psychologist, WOSB, 1945–46; Sr. Staff Member, Tavistock Inst. of Human Relations, London, 1946–50; Dir., National Foundn. for Educational Research in England and Wales, 1950–56; Prof. of Education, 1956–75, Dir. of the Inst. of Education, 1956–68, and Dean of the Faculty of Education, 1971–74, Univ. of Bristol; Visiting Prof., Harvard Univ., Cambridge, Mass., 1969–70. *Publs:* Objectives and Perspectives in Education: Studies in Educational Theory 1955–70, 1972; Some Aspects of Professional Freedom of Teachers, 1977. Add: 13 Park View, Leyburn, N. Yorks. DL8 5HN, England.

MORRIS, Bruce P. American, b. 1909. Economics. Prof. of Economics, Univ. of Massachusetts, Amherst, since 1948 (Assoc. Prof., 1948–50; Dean, Sch. of Home Economics, 1970–71). Asst. Prof., Hiram Coll., 1937–39; Asst. Prof., Jefferson Coll., Washington, 1939–42; Branch Chief, Office of Price Admin., U.S. Govt., 1942–46; Asst. Prof., Amherst Coll., Massachusetts, 1946–48. Add: Problems of American Economic Growth, 1961; (with C.W. King) Economic Growth and Development, 1967; The Economics of the Special Taxation of Chain Stores, 1981. Add: 3231 Stansberry Dr., Port Richey, Fla. 33568, U.S.A.

MORRIS, Charles (William). American, b. 1901. Language/Linguistics, Philosophy. Prof. Emeritus, Univ. of Florida, Gainesville, since 1971 (Lecturer, 1947–58; Research Prof., 1958–71). Instr. in Philosophy, Rice Univ., Houston, 1925–30; Assoc. Prof., Univ. of Chicago, 1931–47. President, Western Division, American Philosophical Assn., 1937. *Publs:* Six Theories of Mind, 1932; Pragmatism and the Crisis of Democracy, 1934; (ed.) Mind, Self, and Society from the Standpoint of a Social Behaviorist, 1934; Logical Positivism, Pragmatism, and Scientific Empiricism, 1937; Foundations of the Theory of Signs, 1938; (ed. with others) The Philosophy of the Act, 1938; Paths of Life: Preface to a World Religion, 1942; Signs, Language, and Behavior, 1946; The Open Self, 1948; Varieties of Human Value, 1956; Signification and Significance: A Study of the Relations of Signs and Values, 1964; Festival (poems), 1966; The Pragmatic Movement in American Philosophy, 1970; Writings on the General Theory of Signs, 1971; Symbolism and Reality: A Study in the Nature of Mind, 1987. Add: c/o Benjamins, John, North America, Inc., 1 Buttonwood Sq. Philadelphia, Pa. 19130, U.S.A.

MORRIS, Christopher Hugh. British, b. 1938. International relations/Current affairs. Special Corresp. BBC TV News, since 1980. Reporter, Daily Sketch, London, 1958–62; Corresp. in Spain for the Daily Express and Independent Television News, London, 1962–67, and for the Daily Mail, BBC TV and Radio, NBC, Australian Broadcasting, and Canadian Broadcasting, 1967–72; Reporter BBC News, Radio and TV, 1972–80. *Publs:* The Day They Lost the H Bomb, 1966; The Big Catch, 1966. Add: 1 Howards Wood Dr., Gerrards Cross, Bucks. SL9 7HR, England.

MORRIS, Desmond. British, b. 1928. Novels/Short stories, Anthropology/Ethnology, Biology, Zoology. Researcher, Oxford Univ., 1951–56; Head of Granada TV and Film Unit at the Zoological Soc. of London, 1956–59; Curator of Mammals, Zoological Soc. of London, 1959–67; Dir., Inst. of Contemporary Arts, London, 1967–68; Research Fellow, Wolfson Coll., Oxford, 1973–81. *Publs:* The Biology of Art, 1962; The Mammals, 1965; (with Ramona Morris) Men and Snakes, 1965; (with R. Morris) Men and Apes, 1966; (with R. Morris) Men and Pandas, 1966; (ed.) Primate Ethology, 1967; The Naked Ape, 1967; The Human Zoo, 1969; Patterns of Reproductive Behaviour, 1970; Intimate Behaviour, 1971; Manwatching, 1977; (co-author) Gestures, 1979; Animals Days (autobiography), 1979; The Soccer Tribe, 1981; Inrock (fiction), 1983; The Book of Ages, 1983; The Art of Ancient Cyprus, 1985; Bodywatching, 1985; The Illustrated Naked Ape, 1986; Catwatching, 1986; Dogwatching, 1986; The Secret Surrealist, 1987; Cat Lore, 1987; The Animals Roadshow, 1988; The Human Nestbuilers, 1988; Horsewatching, 1988. Add: c/o Jonathan Cape, 32 Bedford Sq., London WC1B 3EL, England.

MORRIS, Edmund. American, b. 1940. Biography. *Publs:* The Rise of Theodore Roosevelt (Pulitzer Prize), 1979. Add: 240 Central Park S., New York, N.Y. 10019, U.S.A.

MORRIS, (Clifford) Eric. British, b. 1940. Military/Defence. Political/Defence Analyst and Consultant since 1986. Lectr. and Deputy Head, Dept. of War Studies and Intnl. Affairs, Royal Military Academy, Sandhurst, 1970–84; Military/Defence Dir., Special Projects Div., Pacific Intnl. Ltd., Winchester, 1984–86. *Publs:* Blockade: Berlin and the Cold War, 1973; Tanks: An Illustrated History, 1975; Weapons and Warfare of the Twentieth Century, 1976; The Russian Navy: Myth and Reality, 1977; War in Peace: An Illustrated History of Conflict since 1945, 1981; Corregidor, 1982; Salerno, 1983; Churchill's Private Armies, 1986; Terrorism: Threat and Response, 1988; Guerillas in Uniform, 1989. Add: 23 Marine Dr., Barry, S. Glamorgan CF6 8QP, Wales.

MORRIS, George E(dward, Sr.). American, b. 1937. Engineering/Technology. Owner, Scientific Illustrators, Champaign, since 1974; Instr. in Mathematics, Parkland Coll., Champaign, since 1977. Machine Designer, Caterpillar Tractor Co., Peoria, Ill., 1957–60; Tool Designer, Eureka Williams Co., Bloomington, Ill., 1960–61; Electro-Mechanical Designer, Electrical Engineering Dept., 1961–70, and Admin. Asst., Mechanical Engineering Dept., 1970–74, Univ. of Illinois, Urbana. *Publs:* Technical Illustrating, 1975; Engineering: A Decision-Making Process, 1977. Add: Box 1677, Champaign, Ill. 61824, U.S.A.

MORRIS, Harry. American, b. 1924. Poetry, Literature. Prof. of English, Florida State Univ., Tallahassee, since 1967 (Asst. Prof., 1961–63; Assoc. Prof., 1963–67). *Publs:* (with I. Ribner) Poetry: A Critical and Historical Introduction, 1962; Richard Barnfield: Colin's Child, 1963; The Sorrowful City, 1966; Birth and Copulation and Death, 1969; The Snake Hunter, 1970; Last Things in Shakespeare, 1985. Add: Dept. of English, Florida State Univ., Tallahassee, Fla. 32306, U.S.A.

MORRIS, Helen. British, b. 1909. Literature. Principal Lectr. and Head of the English Dept., Homerton Coll., Cambridge, 1960–75. *Publs:* Portrait of a Chef, 1938; Elizabethan Literature, 1958; Notes on Shakespeare's King Lear, 1965; Notes on Shakespeare's Richard II, 1966; Where's That Poem? (bibliography), 1967, 1974; Notes on Shakespeare's Antony and Cleopatra, 1968; Notes on Shakespeare's Romeo and Juliet, 1970; Love (anthology), 1978; Animals (anthology), 1980; The New Where's that Poem, 1985; Macmillan Master Guides: Romeo and Juliet, Henry IV Part I. Add: 5 Merton St., Cambridge, England.

MORRIS, James. *See* **MORRIS,** Jan.

MORRIS, Jan. (Formerly James Morris). British, b. 1926. Novels, History, Travel/Exploration/Adventure, Autobiography/Memoirs/Personal. Member, Editorial Staff, The Times newspaper, London, 1951–56, and The Guardian newspaper, London, 1957–62. *Publs:* Coast to Coast, 1956; Sultan in Oman, 1957; The Market of Seleukia, 1957; Coronation Everest, 1958; South African Winter, 1958; The Hashemite Kings, 1959; Venice, 1960; The Upstairs Donkey, 1962; The World Bank, 1963; Cities, 1963; The Presence of Spain, 1964; Oxford, 1965; Pax Britannica, 1968; The Great Port, 1970; Places, 1972; Heaven's Command, 1973; Conundrum, 1974; Travels, 1976; The Oxford Book of Oxford, 1978; Farewell the Trumpets, 1978; Spain, 1979; Destinations, 1980; My Favourite Stories of Wales, 1980; The Venetian Empire, 1980; (ed.) Wales: An Anthology, 1982; The Spectacle of Empire, 1982; Wales, The First Place, 1982; A Venetian Bestiary, 1982; (with Simon Winchester) Stones of Empire, 1983; The Matter of Wales, 1985; Last Letters from Hav, 1985; Among the Cities, 1985; Scotland, The Place of Visions, 1986; Manhattan '45, 1987; Hong Kong, 1988; Pleasures of a Tangled Life (autobiography), 1989. Add: Trefan Morys, Llanystumdwy, Gwynedd, Wales.

MORRIS, Janet E(llen). American, b. 1946. Historical/Romance/Gothic, Science fiction/Fantasy. Songwriter and recording artist. Lighting Designer, Chip Monck Enterprises, NYC, 1963–64; Bass Player, Christopher Morris Band, 1975, 1977. *Publs:* High Couch on Silistra 1977; The Golden Sword, 1977; Wind from the Abyss, 1978; The Carnellian Throne, 1979; I, The Sun (historical novel), 1980; Dream Dancer, 1980; Cruiser Dreams, 1981; Earth Dreams, 1982; (with Chris Morris) The Forty-Minute War, 1984; (with David A. Drake) Active Measures, 1985; Beyond Sanctuary, 1985; (ed.) Afterwar, 1985; (ed.) Heroes Rebels, Crusaders, Angels in Hell, 4 vols., 1986–87; Beyond the Veil, 1986; Beyond Wizardwall, 1986; (with Chris Morris) Medusa, 1986; (with C.J. Cherryh) Gates of Hell, 1986; Tempus, 1987; Warlord!, 1987; (with C.J. Cherryh) Kings in Hell, 1987. Add: Box 1073, Mashpee, Mass. 02649, U.S.A.

MORRIS, (Margaret) Jean. Also writes as Kenneth O'Hara. British, b. 1924. Novels/Short stories, Children's fiction, Plays/Screenplays, History, Translations. Full-time writer. *Publs:* Man and Two Gods (novel), 1953; Island of Gulls (play), 1956; Half of a Story (novel), 1957; (as Kenneth O'Hara) A View to a Death (novel), 1958; The Adversary (novel), 1959; (as Kenneth O'Hara) Sleeping Dogs Lying (novel), 1960; (as Kenneth O'Hara) Double Cross Purposes (novel), 1962; The Blackamoor's Urn (novel), 1962; A Dream of Fair Children, 1966; (as Kenneth O'Hara) Unknown Man, Seen in Profile (novel), 1967; (with Radost Pridham) The Peach Thief and Other Bulgarian Stories (trans.), 1968; (as Kenneth O'Hara) The Bird-Cage (novel), 1969; (as Kenneth O'Hara) The Company of St. George (novel), 1972; The Six Wives of Henry VIII (play), 1972; The Monarchs of England, 1975; (as Kenneth O'Hara) The Delta Knife (novel), 1976; (as Kenneth O'Hara) The Ghost of Thomas Penry (novel), 1977; (as Kenneth O'Hara) The Searchers of the Dead (novel), 1979; The Path of the Dragons (children's fiction), 1980; Twist of Eight (children's fiction), 1981; (as Kenneth O'Hara) Nightmare's Nest (novel), 1982; The Donkey's Crusade (children's fiction), 1983; The Song under the Water (children's fiction), 1985; The Troy Game (children's fiction), 1987; The Paper Canoe (children's fiction), 1988. Add: Flat 1, 56 Pevensey Rd., Eastbourne BN21 3HT, England.

MORRIS, John. *See* **HEARNE,** John.

MORRIS, John W(esley). American, b. 1907. Geography. Prof. Emeritus of Geography and Assoc. Dir. Emeritus of Regional and City Planning, Univ. of Oklahoma, Norman (member of the faculty since 1947). Secty., 1955–58, and Pres., 1960–61, National Council for Geographic Education; Pres., Southwestern Social Science Assn., 1965–66. *Publs:* Oklahoma Geography, 1952, 1962; (ed.) Texas Today: A Geography, 1953, 1963; (ed.) Tennessee Geography, 1954, 1964; (ed.) Louisiana Geography, 1957; (with Otis Freeman) World Geography, 1958,

3rd ed. 1972; (ed.) Geography of Kansas, 1959; (with E.A. McReynolds) Historical Atlas of Oklahoma, 1965, 1976; (ed.) Methods of Geographic Instruction, 1968; The Southwestern United States, 1970; (ed.) Geography of Oklahoma, 1977; Ghost Towns of Oklahoma, 1977; (ed.) Cities of Oklahoma, 1979; (with Charles R. Goins) Oklahoma Homes: Past and Present, 1980; (ed.) Boundaries of Oklahoma, 1980; (ed.) Drill Bits, Picks, and Shovels, 1982. Add: 833 McCall Dr., Norman, Okla. 73069, U.S.A.

MORRIS, Julian. *See* **WEST,** Morris.

MORRIS, Katharine. British. Novels. *Publs:* New Harrowing, 1933; The Vixen's Cub, 1951; Country Dance, 1953; The House by the Water, 1957; The Long Meadow, 1958. Add: Bleasby, Nottingham, England.

MORRIS, Leon Lamb. Australian, b. 1914. Theology/Religion. Priest-in-Charge, Minnipa Mission, South Australia, 1940–45; Vice-Principal, Ridley Coll., Melbourne, 1945–59; Warden, Tydale House, Cambridge, England, 1961–63; Principal, Ridley Coll., 1964–79. *Publs:* The Apostolic Preaching of the Cross, 1955; The Wages of Sin, 1955; Tyndale Commentary on I, II Thessalonians, 1955; The Story of the Cross, 1956; Tyndale Commentary on I Corinthians, 1957; The Lord from Heaven, 1958; New International Commentary on I, II Thessalonians, 1958; Spirit of the Living God, 1959; The Story of the Christ Child, 1960; The Biblical Doctrine of Judgment, 1960; The Dead Sea Scrolls and St. John's Gospel, 1960; Ministers of God, 1964; The Abolition of Religion, 1964; The New Testament and the Jewish Lectionaries, 1964; The Cross in the New Testament, 1965; Glory in the Cross, 1965; Tyndale Commentary on Ruth, 1968; Tyndale Commentary on Revelation, 1969; Bible Study Books: I Timothy-James, 1969; Studies in the Fourth Gospel, 1969; This Is the Testimony, 1970; New International Commentary on John, 1971; Apocalyptic, 1972; (with E.M. Blaiklock) Bible Characters and Doctrines: The Holy Spirit, 1974; Tyndale Commentary on Luke, 1974; I Believe in Revelation, 1976; Expositor's Bible Commentary on Hebrews, 1981; Testaments of Love, 1981; What's a Nice Church Like Ours Doing in a World Like This?, 1983; The Atonement, 1983; Bible Study Commentary on Hebrews, 1983; The Word Was Made Flesh, 1986; New Testament Theology, 1986; The Bread of Life, 1987; The Cross of Jesus, 1988; Commentary on Romans, 1988; The True Vine, 1988; Crucified and Risen, 1988. Add: 17 Queen's Ave., Doncaster, Vic. 3108, Australia.

MORRIS, Michael (Spence Lowdell). South African, b. 1940. Novels/Short stories, Poetry, International relations/Current affairs. Freelance writer, and independent researcher into armed conflict in South Africa. Chmn., Good Hope Comforts Fund, Cape Town, and Ed., Poetry South gen. collections. *Publs:* The Sweetness and the Sadness, 1964; A Passion for Home, 1965; Dreams of War, 1967; Now That I'm Dead, 1968; Redfive, 1969; Phoenix, 1970; Requiem, 1971; Terrorism, 1971; Fuzzversus, 1973; Armed Conflict in Southern Africa, 1974; The Crises of Godson Darker, 1974; Ant in a Stream, 1975; The Art of Conflict in Southern Africa, 1975; Battlelines: A Survey of the Effect of Conflict in South Africa, 1975; The Spirit of Michael Webfoot (novel), 1977. Add: P.O. Box 1464, Cape Town 8000, South Africa.

MORRIS, Robert K. American, b. 1933. Literature. Prof. of English, City Coll. of the City Univ of New York, since 1974. *Publs:* The Novels of Anthony Powell, 1968; Continuance and Change, 1972; The Consolations of Ambiguity, 1972; (ed. with Irving Malin) The Achievement of William Styron, 1974, 1981; Paradoxes of Order, 1975; Old Lines, New Forces, 1977; Fables, 1985. Add: Rt. 1, Box 263, South Rd., Denmark, Me. 04022, U.S.A.

MORRIS, Sara. *See* **BURKE,** John.

MORRIS, Stephen. British, b. 1935. Poetry. Sr. Lectr., Faculty of Art, The Polytechnic, Wolverhampton, since 1972 (Asst. Lectr., 1967–69; Lectr., 1969–72). *Publs:* Alien Poets, 1965; (with Peter Finch) Wanted for Writing Poetry, 1968; Penny Farthing Madness, 1969; Born Under Leo, 1972; The Revolutionary, 1972; The Kingfisher Catcher, 1974; Death of a Clown, 1976; Widening Circles, 1977; The Moment of Truth, 1978; Too Long at the Circus, 1980; The Umbrellas of Mr. Parapluie, 1985; Rolling Dice, 1986. Add: Rue Las Cours, Aspiran 34800, Herault, France.

MORRIS, William Otis. American, b. 1922. Economics, Human relations, Law. Prof. of Law, West Virginia Univ., since 1958. Member of the faculty, Coll. of Commerce, Univ. of Illinois, 1946–55; Assoc. Prof. of Law, Stetson Univ. Coll. of Law, St. Petersburg, Fla., 1955–58; Visiting

Prof. and Distinguished Lectr., Cumberland Coll. of Law, Samford Univ. 1985. *Publs:* Dental Litigation, 1972, 1978; The Law of Domestic Relations, 1973, supplement, 1983; Statutes and Cases on Domestic Relations in West Virginia, 1973; Veterinarian in Litigation, 1974; Revocation of License by the Administrative Process, 1984. Add: 644 Bellaire Dr., Morgantown, W. Va. 26505, U.S.A.

MORRIS, Willie. American, b. 1934. Novels/Short stories, Social commentary/phenomena. Ed.-in-Chief, The Texas Observer, 1960–62; Exec. Ed., 1965–67, and Ed.-in-Chief, 1967–71, Harper's Mag., NYC. *Publs:* North Toward Home, 1967; Yazoo: Integration in a Deep Southern Town, 1971; Good Old Boy, 1972; The Last of the Southern Girls, 1973; James Jones, 1978; Terrains of the Heart, 1981; The Courting of Marcus Dupree, 1983; Always Stand in Against the Curve, 1984; Homecomings, 1989; Taps, 1989. Add: c/o Doubledaym 245 Park Ave. New York, N.Y. 10167, U.S.A.

MORRIS, Wright (Marion). American, b. 1910. Novel/Stories, Autobiography, Essays. Prof. of English, San Francisco State Coll., 1962–75; also a photographer. *Publs:* My Uncle Dudley, 1942; The Man Who Was There, 1945; The Inhabitants (photo-text), 1946; The Home Place (photo-text), 1948; The World in the Attic, 1949; Man and Boy, 1951; The Works of Love, 1952; The Deep Sleep, 1953; The Huge Season, 1954; The Field of Vision, 1956; Love among the Cannibals, 1957; The Territory Ahead (essays), 1958; Ceremony in Lone Tree, 1960; (ed.) The Mississippi River Reader, 1962; What a Way to Go, 1962; Cause for Wonder, 1963; One Day, 1965; In Orbit, 1967; A Bill of Rites, A Bill of Wrongs, A Bill of Goods (essays), 1967; God's Country and My People (photo-text), 1968; Wright Morris: A Reader, 1970; Green Grass, Bly Sky, White House (short stories), 1970; Fire Sermon, 1971; War Games, 1972; Love Affair: A Venetian Journal, 1972; A Life (novel), 1973; Here Is Einbaum (short stories), 1973; About Fiction, 1975; Real Losses, Imaginary Gains, 1976; The Fork River Space Project, 1977; Earthly Delights, Unearthly Adornments, 1978; Plains Song, 1980; Will's Boy, 1981; Photographs and Words, 1982; Solo, 1983; A Cloak of Light (memoirs), 1985; Collected Stories 1948–1986, 1986. Add: c/o Harper & Row, 10 E. 53rd St., New York, N.Y. 10022, U.S.A.

MORRISH, Ivor. British, b. 1914. Education, Race relations, Sociology, Theology/Religion. Sr. Lectr. in Divinity, and Librarian, Bognor Regis Coll. of Education, Sussex, 1961–67; Principal Lectr., La Sainte Union Coll. of Education, Southampton, 1967–74. Academic Ed., Allen and Unwin Ltd., London, 1970–78. *Publs:* Disciplines of Education, 1967, 4th ed. 1971; Education since 1800, 1970, 3rd ed. 1973; The Background of Immigrant Children, 1971; The Sociology of Education: An Introduction, 1972, 1978; Aspects of Educational Change, 1976; The Dark Twin, 1980; Obeah, Christ and Rastaman, 1982. Add: Starboard, Victoria Rd. S., Bognor Regis, West Sussex PO21 2NA, England.

MORRIS-JONES, Wyndraeth Humphreys. British, b. 1918. Politics/Government. Asst. Lectr. and subsequently Lectr., London Sch. of Economics, 1946–55; Prof. of Political Theory and Institutions, Durham Univ., 1955–65; Dir., Inst. of Commonwealth Studies and Prof. of Commonwealth Affairs, Univ. of London, 1966–83. *Publs:* Parliament in India, 1957; The Government and Politics of India, 1964, 3rd ed. 1971; (ed.) The Making of Politicians: Studies from Africa and Asia, 1976; Politics Mainly Indian, 1979; (ed. with A.F. Madden) Australia and Britain: Studies in a Changing Relationship, 1980; (ed.) From Rhodesia to Zimbabwe: Behind and Beyond Lancaster House, 1980; (ed. with Georges Fischer) Decolonisation and After: The British and French Experience, 1980. Add: 95 Ridgway, London SW19 4SX, England.

MORRISON, Arnold. British, b. 1928. Education. Prof. Emeritus of Education, Univ. of Stirling, since 1975. Member, Education Subcttee., Univ. Grants Cttee., since 1978; Member, Gen. Teaching Council for Scotland, since 1978. Lectr. in Education, Moray House Coll. of Education, Edinburgh, 1962–66; Lectr. in Psychology, Univ. of Edinburgh, 1966–70; Sr. Lectr. in Education, Univ. of Dundee, 1970–75. Member, Bd. of Mgmt., Dundee Northern Hosps., 1970–74; Gov., Dundee Educational Trust, 1971–74; Member, National Panel of Assessors, Scottish Nursing Staffs Cttee., Edinburgh, 1972–74. *Publs:* (with D. McIntyre) Teacher and Teaching, 1969, 1973; (with D. McIntyre) Schools and Socialization, 1971; (ed. with D. McIntyre) Social Psychology of Teaching, 1972. Add: 4 Victoria Pl., Stirling, Scotland.

MORRISON, Bill. Irish, b. 1940. Plays/Screenplays. Member of the Bd., Merseyside Young People's Theatre, since 1978, and Playhouse Theatre, since 1981, both Liverpool. Actor from 1963; resident writer, Victoria Theatre, Stoke-on-Trent, 1969–71; radio producer, BBC, Belfast,

1975–76; resident writer, Everyman Theatre, 1977–78; Lectr., C.F. Mott Coll., 1977–78; drama producer, Radio City, 1979–81; assoc. dir. 1981–83, and artistic dir., 1983–85, Playhouse Theatre. *Publs:* Sam Slade Is Missing (in The Best Short Plays of 1973), 1973; Flying Blind, 1978; Tess of the d'Urbervilles (adaptation), 1980. Add: c/o Michael Imison Playwrights Ltd., 28 Almeida St., London N1 1TD, England.

MORRISON, (Philip) Blake. British, b. 1950. Poetry, Literature. Literary Ed., The Observer, London, since 1987 (Deputy Literary Ed., 1981–86). Part-time Lectr., Goldsmiths' Coll., London, and Open Univ., 1976–80; Poetry and Fiction Ed., Times Literary Supplement, 1978–81. *Publs:* The Movement: English Poetry and Fiction of the 1950's, 1980; (with others) Poetry Introduction 5, 1982; Seamus Heaney, 1982; (ed. with Andrew Motion) The Penguin Book of Contemporary British Poetry, 1982; Dark Glasses, 1984; The Ballad of the Yorkshire Ripper, 1987; The Yellow House, 1987. Add: 4 Macartney House, Chesdrfield Walk, London SE10, England.

MORRISON, James Frederic. American. History, International relations/Current affairs, Politics/Government. Assoc. Prof. of Political Science, Univ. of Florida, Gainesville, since 1966. Visiting Prof., Univ. of Poznan, Poland, 1974–75, 1981–82. *Publs:* The Polish People's Republic, 1968; (with K.R. Legg) Politics and the International System, 1971. Add: Political Science Dept., Univ. of Florida, Gainesville, Fla. 32611, U.S.A.

MORRISON, Kristin Diane. American, b. 1934. Literature, Theatre. Prof. of English, Boston Coll., since 1984 (Asst. Prof. of English, 1969–71; Assoc. Prof., 1971–84). Asst. Prof. of English, New York Univ., NYC, 1967–69; Academic Dean and Prof. of English, Newton Coll., Massachusetts, 1972–74. *Publs:* (with M. Anderson, J. Guicharnaud and J.D. Zipes) Crowell's Handbook of Contemporary Drama, 1971; Handbook of Contemporary Drama, 1972; In Black and White, 1972; Canters and Chronicles: The Use of Narrative in the Plays of Samuel Beckett and Harold Pinter, 1983. Add: Dept. of English, Boston Coll., Chestnut Hill, Mass. 02167, U.S.A.

MORRISON, Robert Haywood. American, b. 1927. Writing/Journalism. Self-employed realtor since 1959; Pres., Investors Corp. of South Carolina, Charlotte, since 1961. Asst. in Business English, Univ. of Illinois, Urbana, 1947–48; Head of Business Communication, and Secty. of the Faculty, Univ. of Kansas, Lawrence, 1948–51; Ed., Daily News-Enterprise, Newton, N.C., 1952–54; Prof. of Journalism, Winthrop Coll., Rock Hill, S.C., 1955–59. *Publs:* A Guide to Bank Correspondence, 1949; Problems and Cases in Business Writing, 1951; Better Letters for Hotels and Restaurants, 1952; (with J. Montgomery) Profit-Making Letters, 1959; (with T. Sundberg) Bank Correspondence Handbook, 1964. Add: 1333 Queens Rd., Charlotte, N.C. 28207, U.S.A.

MORRISON, Roberta. *See* **WEBB,** Jean Francis.

MORRISON, Theodore. American, b. 1901. Novels/Short stories, Poetry, Literature. Prof. Emeritus of English, Harvard Univ., Cambridge, since 1972. Member, Editorial Staff, Atlantic Monthly, 1925–30; Dir., Bread Loaf Writers Conference, Middlebury Coll., Vermont, 1932–55. *Publs:* The Serpent in the Cloud, 1931; Notes of Death and Life, 1935; The Devious Way, 1944; (trans.) The Portable Chaucer, 1949; The Dream of Alcestis, 1950; The Stones of the House, 1953; To Make a World, 1957; The Whole Creation, 1962; Chautauqua, 1974; Middlebury College Breadloaf Writers' Conference: The First Thirty Years, 1976; Leave of Absence, 1981. Add: 164 Red Gate Lane, Amherst, Mass. 01002, U.S.A.

MORRISON, Toni. (Chloe Anthony Wofford Morrison). American, b. 1931. Novels/Short stories. Schweitzer Prof. of the Humanities, State Univ. of New York au Albany, since 1984. Instr. in English, Texas Southern Univ., Houston, 1955–57, and Howard Univ., Washington, D.C. 1957–65; Sr. Ed., Random House, Publrs., NYC, 1965–84; Bard Coll., Annandale-on-Hudson, N.Y., 1975–77; Distinguished Visting Prof., Yale Univ., New Haven, Conn., 1979–80, and Rutgers Univ., New Brunswick, N.J., 1983–84. Regents Lectr., Univ. of California, Berkeley, 1987; Santagata Lectr., Bowdoin Coll., 1987. *Publs:* The Bluest Eye, 1970; Sula, 1974; Song of Solomon, 1977; Tar Baby, 1981; Beloved, 1987 (Pulitzer Prize). Add: HU355, State Univ. of New York, Albany, N.Y. 12222, U.S.A.

MORRISON, Tony. (Anthony James Morrison). British, b. 1936. Natural history, Travel/Exploration/Adventure. Co-Dir. and Television Film Producer, South American Pictures, and Nonesuch Expeditions Ltd., London, since 1961. *Publs:* (co-author) Steps to a Fortune, 1967; Animal

Migration, 1973; Land above the Clouds, 1974; The Andes, 1976; Pathways to the Gods, 1978; (co-ed.) Lizzie: A Victorian Lady's Amazon Adventure, 1985; The Mystery of the Nasca Lines, 1986; (ed.) Margaret Mee: In Search of Flowers of the Amazon Forests, 1988. Add: England.

MORRISON, Wilbur H(oward). American, b. 1915. History, Military/Defence. Lt. Col., U.S.A.F. Reserve, now retired. Radio announcer and news commentator, New York, 1935–41 and 1946–54; public relations exec. with aerospace firms, 1954–70. *Publs:* Hellbirds: The Story of the B29's in Combat, 1960; The Incredible 305th: The "Can Do" Bombers of World War II, 1962; Wings Over the Seven Seas: U.S. Naval Aviation's Fight for Survival, 1975; Point of No Return: The Story of the Twentieth Air Force, 1979; Fortress Without a Roof: The Allied Bombing of the Third Reich, 1982; Above and Beyond: 1941–1945, 1983. Add: 2036 E. Alvarado St., Fallbrook, Calif. 92028, U.S.A.

MORRISS, Frank. American, b. 1923. Children's fiction, Theology/Religion. Freelance writer, lectr. and teacher. Pres., Colorado Catholic Academy. Contributing Ed., The Wanderer, St. Paul, Minn.; Exec. Dir., WANDERER Forum, Foundation Affiliates. *Publs:* Boy of Philadelphia, 1955; Adventures of Broken Hand, 1957; Alfred of Wessex, 1959; Submarine Pioneer, 1961; Saints for the Small, 1965; The Forgotten Revelation, 1966; The Conservative Imperative, 1970; The Divine Epic, 1974; A Neglected Glory, 1976; (co-author) Abortion, 1979; The Catholic as Citizen, 1980; A Christmas Celebration, 1983. Add: 3505 Owens St., Wheat Ridge, Colo. 80033, U.S.A.

MORRITT, Hope. Canadian, b. 1930. Novels/Short stories, History, Autobiography/Memoirs/Personal, Biography. Feature Writer, Sarnia Observer, Ontario, 1969–73. *Publs:* Sarah, 1974; (with N.W. Linder) Nahanni, 1975; (with N.W. Linder) Pauline (biography), 1979; Pyramid (poetry), 1980; Land ofthe Fireweed (memoir), 1987; Bohunk Road (novel), 1987. Add: 15 Albert St., Point Edward, Ont. N7V 1P7, Canada.

MORSE, Carol. *See* **HALL,** Marjory.

MORSE, Donald E. American, b. 1936. Literature. Prof. of English, Oakland Univ., Rochester, Mich., since 1974 (Asst. Prof., 1967–69; Assoc. Prof., 1969–74); Chmn. and Prof, of Rhetoric, Communications and Journalism, 1980–86). Asst. Prof. of Literature, Babson Coll., Wellesley, Mass., 1963–67. Ed., CEA Critic, 1976–78, and CEA Forum, 1976–77. *Publs:* The Choices of Fiction, 1974; The Fantastic in World Literature and the Arts, 1987. Add: Dept. of English, Oakland Univ., Rochester, Mich. 48309, U.S.A.

MORSE, J. Mitchell. American, b. 1912. Education, Literature, Writing/Journalism. Prof. of English, Temple Univ., Philadelphia, 1967–79, now retired. Instr. to Prof., Pennsylvania State Univ., University Park, 1948–67. *Publs:* The Sympathetic Alien: James Joyce and Catholicism, 1959; Matters of Style, 1968; The Irrelevant English Teacher, 1972; Prejudice and Literature, 1976. Add: Park Plaza 15S, 3900 Ford Rd., Philadelphia, Pa. 19131, U.S.A.

MORSE, Richard McGee. American, b. 1922. History. Secretary, Latin America Program, The Wilson Center, since 1984. Lectr., Instr. and Asst. Prof. of History, Columbia Univ., NYC, 1949–58; Dir., Inst. of Caribbean Studies, Univ. of Puerto Rico, 1958–61; Prof. of History and Dept. Chmn., State Univ. of New York, Long Island Center, 1961–62; Assoc. Prof., 1962–63, and Prof., 1963–78, Yale Univ., New Haven, Conn.; Social Science Prog. Adviser, Ford Foundn., Brazil Office, 1973–75; William H. Bonsall Prof. of History, Stanford Univ., Calif., 1978–84. *Publs:* The Narrowest Street (play), 1945; From Community to Metropolis: A Biography of Sao Paulo, Brazil, 1958, 1974; (ed.) The Bandeirantes: The Historical Role of the Brazilian Pathfinders, 1965; La investigacion urbana: tendencias y planteos, 1971; Las ciudades de America Latina: antecedentes y desarrollo historico, 2 vols., 1973; (ed.) Joaquin Capelo: Lima en 1900, estudio critico y antologia, 1973; El Espejo de Prospero, 1982; New World Soundings: Culture and Ideology in the Americas, 1989, Add: 4412 Volta Pl. NW, Washington, D.C., 20007, U.S.A.

MORTIMER, Chapman. *See* **CHAPMAN-MORTIMER,** William.

MORTIMER, James Edward. British, b. 1921. Industrial relations. National Official, Draughtsmen's and Allied Technicians' Assn., 1948–68; Dir., London Co-operative Soc., 1967–70; Member, National Bd. for Prices and Incomes, 1968–71, London Transport Exec., 1971–74, Wilberforce Enquiry into Electricity Supply Dispute, 1971, Armed Forces Pay Review Body, 1971–74, and E.D.C. Chemicals, 1972–74; Chmn., Advisory Bd., Conciliation and Arbitration Service, 1974–81; Gen. Secty., Labour Party, 1982–85. *Publs:* A History of the Association of Engineering and Shipbuilding Draughtsmen, 1959; (with C. Jenkins) British Trade Unions Today; (with C. Jenkins) The Kind of Laws the Unions Ought to Want; Industrial Relations; Trade Unions and Technological Change; History of the Boilermakers' Society, vol. I, 1834–1906, vol. II, 1906–39; (with Valerie Ellis) A Professional Union: The Evolution of the Institution of Professional Civil Servants, 1980. Add: 31 Charleston St., London SE17 1NG, England.

MORTIMER, John (Clifford). Has also written as Geoffrey Lincoln. British, b. 1923. Novels/Short stories, Mystery/Crime/Suspense, Plays/Screenplays, Travel/Exploration/Adventure. Practising barrister: called to the Bar, 1948; Queen's Counsel, 1966. Chmn., League of Dramatists. Has served as Drama Critic for the New Statesman, Evening Standard, The Observer, all London. *Publs:* Charade, 1947; Rumming Park, 1948; Answer Yes or No (in U.S. as The Silver Hook), 1950; Like Men Betrayed, 1953; The Narrowing Stream, 1954; Three Winters, 1956; (as Geoffrey Lincoln) No Moaning at the Bar, 1957; (with Penelope Mortimer) With Love and Lizards (travel), 1957; Three Plays: The Dock Brief, What Shall We Tell Carolina?, I Spy, 1958; The Wrong Side of the Park, 1960; Lunch Hour, 1960, screenplay 1963; Lunch Hour and Other Plays, 1960; Two Stars for Comfort, 1962; A Voyage Round My Father, 1963; (adaptor) A Flea in Her Ear, 1966, screenplay 1967; The Judge, 1967; (adaptor) Cat Among the Pigeons, 1969; Come As You Are: Four Short Plays, 1970; Five Plays, 1970; (adaptor) The Captain of Kopenick, 1971; Knightsbridge, 1973; Collaborators, 1973; The Fear of Heaven, 1976; Heaven and Hell: The Fear of Heaven, and The Prince of Darkness, 1977; (adaptor) The Lady from Maxim's, 1977; Will Shakespeare, 1978; Rumpole of the Bailey, 1978; The Trials of Rumpole, 1979; Rumpole's Return, 1981; Regina vs. Rumpole, 1981; Rumpole and the Golden Thread, 1983; Paradise Postponed, 1985; In Character, 1985; Character Parts, 1986; The Trials of Rumpole, 1987; Summer's Lease, 1988; Rumpole and the Age of Miracles, 1988. Add: c/o A.D. Peters, 10 Buckingham St., London WC2N 6BU, England.

MORTIMER, Penelope (Ruth). Has also written as Penelope Dimont. British, b. 1918. Novels/Short stories, Travel/Exploration/Adventure, Autobiography/Memoirs/Personal. Film Critic, The Observer, London, 1967–70. *Publs:* (as Penelope Dimont) Johanna, 1947; A Villa in Summer, 1954; The Bright Prison, 1956; (with John Mortimer) With Love and Lizards (travel), 1957; Daddy's Gone A-Hunting (in U.S. as Cave of Ice), 1958; Saturday Lunch with the Brownings, 1960; The Pumpkin Eater, 1962; My Friend Says It's Bullet-Proof, 1967; The Home, 1971; Long Distance, 1974; About Time: An Aspect of Autobiography, 1979; The Handyman, 1983; Queen Elizabeth: A Life of the Queen Mother, 1986. Add: The Old Post Office, Chastleton, Moreton-in-Marsh, Glos., England.

MORTON, Brenda. British. Crafts, Recreation/Leisure/Hobbies. *Publs:* Make Your Own Soft Toys, 1957; Hobbies for the Housebound, 1961; Brownie Handwork, 1964; Needlework Puppets, 1964; Mascot Toys, 1969; Floppy Toys, 1971; The Woodland Book for Guides and Brownies, 1972; Toys with Gussets (in U.S. as Soft Toys Made Easy), 1972; Your Book of Knitted Toys, 1973; Do-It-Yourself Dinosaurs, 1973; Cuddly Dolls, 1976; Sleeve Puppets, 1978; Toys from Knitted Squares, 1982. Add: 11 Chisholm Ave., Dunblane FK15 0BP, Scotland.

MORTON, Bruce Rutherfurd. New Zealander, b. 1926. Mathematics. Prof. of Applied Mathematics, Monash Univ., Clayton, Vic., since 1967. Asst. Lectr., University Coll., London, 1955–56; Lectr. and Sr. Lectr., Univ. of Manchester, 1956–66. *Publs:* Numerical Approximation, 1964. Add: Dept. of Mathematics, Monash Univ., Clayton, Vic. 3168, Australia.

MORTON, Henry W. American, b. 1929. Politics/Government, Sociology. Prof. of Political Science, Queens Coll., City Univ. of New York, since 1970 (joined faculty, 1960). *Publs:* Soviet Sport: Mirror of Soviet Society, 1963; (with others) Soviet Policy-Making, 1967; The Soviet Union and Eastern Europe, 1971; (with others) Soviet Policy and Society in the 1970's, 1974; (co-author) The Contemporary Soviet City, 1984. Add: 12 Francis Terr., Glen Cove, N.Y. 11542, U.S.A.

MORTON, Richard Everett. British, b. 1930. Literature, Theatre. Prof. of English since 1970, and Chmn. of the Dept. since 1976, McMaster Univ., Hamilton (Asst. Prof., 1965–66; Assoc. Prof., 1966–70). Lectr. in English, Univ. of the Witwatersrand, Johannesburg, 1955–60; Prof. of English, Lake Erie Coll., Painesville, Ohio, 1960–62. *Publs:* (ed. with W.M. Peterson) Three Hours after Marriage, by John Gay, 1961; (ed.) Lutrin Made English, by Boileau, 1967; (ed.) Poems by Anne Killigrew,

1967; The Works of Dylan Thomas, 1970; The Poetry of W.B. Yeats, 1971; (ed.) Poems of Sir Aston Cokayne, 1978. Add: Dept. of English, McMaster Univ., Hamilton, Ont., Canada.

MORTON, Robert Steel. British, b. 1917. Medicine/Health. Retired consultant venereologist. *Publs:* Venereal Diseases, 1966, 1972; VD and Diseases Transmitted Sexually, 1968, 5th ed. 1976; Sexual Freedom and Venereal Disease, 1971; (contrib. and ed. with J.R.W. Harris) Recent Advances in Sexually Transmitted Diseases, 1974; Gonorrhea, 1977. Add: 9 Cortworth Rd., Sheffield S11 9LM, England.

MORTON, Stanley. *See* **FREEGOOD**, Morton.

MOSEL, Tad. American, b. 1922. Plays/Screenplays, Biography. Visiting Critic in Television Writing, Yale Univ. Drama Sch., New Haven, Conn., 1957–58; Adj. Prof., Dramatic Wrting, Univ. of Penn., Univ. of N. Carolina, Syracuse Univ., New York Univ. Recipient of Pulitzer Prize and New York Drama Critics Circle Award, 1961. *Publs:* Other People's Houses: Six Television Plays, 1956; The Five-Dollar Bill, 1958; (adapter) All the Way Home, 1961; Impromptu, 1961; That's Where the Town's Going, 1962; (with Gertrude Macy) Leading Lady: The World and Theatre of Katharine Cornell, 1978. Add: 400 E. 57th St., New York, N.Y. 10022, U.S.A.

MOSES, Elbert Raymond, Jr. American, b. 1908. Speech/Rhetoric. Prof. Emeritus and Past Chmn., Dept. of Speech and Dramatic Arts, Clarion State Univ., Pennsylvania (joined faculty, 1959). Instr. in Speech, Woman's Coll., Univ. of North Carolina, 1936–38, Ohio State Univ., Columbus, 1938–46, East Illinois State Univ., Charleston, 1946–56, and Michigan State Univ., East Lansing, 1956–59; Fulbright Lectr., Philippines, 1955–56. *Publs:* A Guide to Effective Speaking, 1956; Phonetics: History and Interpretation, 1964; Three Attributes of God, 1983; Adventures in Reasoning, 1988. Add: 2001 Rocky Dells Dr., Prescott, Ariz. 86303, U.S.A.

MOSKOW, Michael H. American, b. 1938. Economics, Industrial relations, Politics/Government, Public/Social administration. Vice-Pres., Strategy and Business Development, Premark Intnl., Chicago, since 1977, and Vice-Pres., Premark Intnl., since 1986. Instr. in English and History, Eastside High Sch., Paterson, N.J., 1960–61; Instr. in Economics, Lafayette Coll., Easton, Pa., 1964–65; Asst. Prof. of Mgmt., 1966–67, Drexel Inst. of Technology, Philadelphia; Dir., Bureau of Economic and Business Research, and Assoc. Prof. of Economics, 1967–69, Temple Univ., Philadelphia; Sr. Staff Economist, Council of Economic Advisers, 1969–71; Exec. Dir., Construction Industry Collective Bargaining Commn., 1970–72; Deputy Under-Secty., 1971–72, and Asst. Secty., 1972–73, Dept. of Labor; Asst. Secty., Dept. of Housing and Urban Development, 1973–75; Dir., Council on Wage and Price Stability, 1975–76; Under-Secty., Dept. of Labor, 1976–77; Dir., Vice-Pres., Esmark Inc., Chicago, 1977–82; Pres., Velsicol Chemical Corp., Chicago, 1982–84; Vice-Pres., Dart and Kraft Inc., Chicago, 1985–86. *Publs:* Teachers and Unions, 1966; (with M. Lieberman) Collective Negotiations for Teachers; (ed. with S. Elam and M. Lieberman) Readings on Collective Negotiations in Public Education, 1967; (ed. with S. Elam) Employment Relations in Higher Education, 1969; (with J.J. Loewenberg and E. Koziara) Collective Bargaining in Public Employment, 1970; Labor Relations in the Performing Arts: An Introductory Survey, 1970; (ed. with J.J. Loewenberg) Collective Bargaining in Government: Readings and Cases, 1972; Strategic Planning in Business and Government, 1978. Add: 400 Sheridan Rd., Winnetka, Ill. 60093, U.S.A.

MOSLEY, Leonard. British, b. 1913. Novels/Short stories, Film, History, Biography. Former Drama and Film Critic, Daily Express, London. *Publs:* Backs to the Wall; On Borrowed Time; Hirohito; Curzon; Gideon Goes to War; The Last Days of the British Raj; Faces from the Fire; Power Play, 1973; Reich Marshal: A Biography of Herman Goering, 1974; Charles Lindbergh, 1976; The Battle of Britain, 1977; Dulles, 1978; The Druid, 1982; Zanuck: The Rise and Fall of Hollywood's Last Tycoon, 1984; The Real Walt Disney, 1986. Add: c/o Weidenfeld and Nicolson Ltd., 91 Clapham High St., London SW4, England.

MOSLEY, Nicholas. (Lord Ravensdale). British, b. 1923. Novels/Short stories, History, Theology/Religion, Travel/Exploration/Adventure. *Publs:* Spaces of the Dark, 1951; The Rainbearers, 1955; Corruption, 1957; African Switchback, 1958; The Life of Raymond Raynes, 1961; Meeting Place, 1962; Accident, 1965; Experience and Religion: A Lay Essay in Theology, 1965; Assassins, 1966; Impossible Object, 1968; Natalie, Natalia, 1971; The Assassination of Trotsky, 1972, screenplay 1973; Impossible Object (screenplay), 1975; Julian Grenfell:

His Life and the Times of His Death 1888–1915, 1976; Catastrophe Practice, 1979; Imago Bird, 1980; Serpent, 1981; Rules of the Game: Sir Oswald and Lady Cynthia Mosley 1869–1933, 1982; Beyond the Pale: Sir Oswald Mosley and Family 1933–1980, 1983; Judith, 1986. Add: 21a Heath St., London NW3, England.

MOSS, Barbara. British, b. 1946. Information science/Computers, Math. Independent consultant since 1987. Lectr. in Mathematics, Univ. of Salford, 1968–80; Member, Computer Dept., The Economist Group, London, 1982–85; Head of Computing, Graham Bannock and Partners, London, 1985–87. *Publs:* (with David Hopkin) Automata, 1976; (with Graham Flegg and Cynthia Hay) Nicholas Chuquet, Renaissance Mathematician, 1984. Add: 36 Haroldstone Rd., London E17 7AW, England.

MOSS, Cynthia J(ane). American, b. 1940. Biology, Zoology. *Publs:* Portraits in the Wild: Behavior Studies of East African Mammals, 1975, 1982; Elephant Memories: Thirteen Years in the Life of an Elephant, 1988. Add: c/o Univ. of Chicago Press, 5801 Ellis Dr., 4th floor, Chicago, Ill. 69637, U.S.A.

MOSS, Leonard. American, b. 1931. Literature. Prof. of Comparative Literature, State Univ. of New York at Geneseo, since 1971 (Asst. Prof., 1960–68; Assoc. Prof., 1968–71). Instr., Indiana Univ., Bloomington, 1958–60. *Publs:* Arthur Miller, 1967, 1980. Add: English Dept., State Univ. of New York, Geneseo, N.Y. 14454, U.S.A.

MOSS, Nancy. *See* **MOSS**, Robert.

MOSS, (Victor) Peter (Cannings). British. Children's fiction, History, Literature. Lectr., Lewes Technical Coll., Sussex, until 1974. *Publs:* Our Own Homes Through the Ages, 1956; Meals Through the Ages, 1958; Sports and Pastimes Through the Ages, 1962; Tombstone Treasure, 1965; Hermit's Hoard, 1965; History Alive, 5 vols., 1967–71; Today's English, 2 vols., 1968; Town Life Through the Ages, 1973; The Media, 1974; Crime and Punishment, 1974; Medicine and Morality, 1974; Statistics Alive, 1975; People and Politics, 1976; Prejudice and Discrimination, 1976; Ghosts over Britain, 1977; Work and Leisure, 1978; Family and Friends, 1978; History Scene, I, II and III, 1978–80; Modern World History 1900–1977, 1978; Encounters with the Past, 1979; Commerce in Action, 1981; The Private Past, 1983; (with S. Lamont) Religion and the Supernatural, 1985; History Scene IV, 1985; History Scene: Into the Modern World, 1987. Add: Brook Cottage, Ripe, Lewes, Sussex, England.

MOSS, Robert. Pseudonyms: Nancy Moss, Roberta Moss, and Naunton Lane. British. Children's fiction. Clerk, Engall, Cox and Co., estate agents, Cheltenham, 1920–25; Guide Book Writer, Edward J. Burrow and Co. Ltd., Cheltenham, 1925–37; freelance writer, 1937–38; Cost Office Clerk, Boulton-Paul Aircraft Co. Ltd., Wolverhampton, 1938–45; Ed., Juvenile Productions Ltd., London, 1945–50; Ed., Purnell Books, London, 1950–68. *Publs:* The House of the Hundred Heads, 1939; (as Roberta Moss) Jenny of the Fourth, 1953; (as Roberta Moss) Jenny's Exciting Term, 1954; (as Nancy Moss) School on the Precipice, 1954; (as Nancy Moss) Susan's Stormy Term, 1955; (as Nancy Moss) Strange Quest at Cliff House, 1956; (as Roberta Moss) Shy Girl at Southdown, 1957; (as Roberta Moss) Mystery at Gull's Nest, 1957; (as Nancy Moss) The Cliff House Monster, 1957; (as Nancy Moss) The Riddle of Cliff House, 1957; (ed.) The Girl Guide Annual, 1957–1981; (ed.) The Brownie Annual, 1957–81; (ed.) The Scout's Pathfinder Annual, 1958–77; (ed.) The Sixer Annual for Cub Scouts, 1958–77; ABC in Real-Life Pictures, 1960; The Golden Bar Book of Brownie Stories, 1961; The Golden Ladder Book of Brownie Stories, 1963; (ed.) The Arrow Book of Cub Scout Stories, 1968; The Challenge Book of Brownie Stories, 1968, 2nd book, 1982; (ed.) The Challenge Book of Girl Guide Stories, 1969; (ed.) The Venture Book of Brownie Stories, 1969; The Pathfinder Book of Scout Stories, 1969; The Wild White Pony and Other Girl Guide Stories, 1973, 1976. Add: Green Acres, Kidnappers' Lane, Cheltenham, Glos. GL53 0NP, England.

MOSS, Robert (John). Australian, b. 1946. International relations/Current affairs, Politics/Government. Ed., Foreign Report, The Economist, London, since 1974 (Leader Writer, 1970–74). Dir., National Assn. for Freedom, since 1975; Council Member, Foreign Affairs Research Inst., since 1976. Lectr. in History, Australian National Univ., Canberra, 1968–69; Leader-Writer, The Canberra Times, 1967–69. *Publs:* Urban Guerrillas, 1972; Chile's Marxist Experiment, 1973; (ed.) The Ulster Debate, 1973; Revolutionary Challenges in Spain, 1974; (ed.) The Stability of the Caribbean, 1974; The Collapse of Democracy, 1976.

Add: c/o The Economist, 25 St. James's St., London SW1, England.

MOSS, Roberta. *See* **MOSS**, Robert.

MOSS, Rose. American, b. 1937. Novels/Short stories, Business/Trade/Industry. Freelance writer and Management Consultant. Lectr., University Coll. of Pius XII, Basutoland, 1957–59; Lectr., Univ. of Natal, South Africa, 1960; Lectr., Univ. of South Africa, Pretoria, 1961–63; Instr., Univ. of Massachusetts, Boston, 1968–69; Lectr. in English, Wellesley Coll., Massachusetts, 1972–82. *Publs:* The Family Reunion, 1974; The Terrorist, 1979, as The Schoolmaster, 1981. Add: 580 Walnut St., Newtonville, Mass. 02160, U.S.A.

MOSS, Stanley. American, b. 1935. Poetry. Pres., Stanley Moss and Co., art dealers, NYC, since 1959. Publisher, Sheep Meadow Press, NYC, since 1977. Founding member, Haleyon, Cambridge, Mass. Formerly, Poetry Ed., New American Review, NYC.*Publs:* The Wrong Angel, 1966, 1969; Skull of Adam, 1978; The Intelligence of Clouds, 1989. Add: c/o Horcourt Bruce Jovanovich, 111 Fifth Ave., New York, N.Y. 10003, U.S.A.

MOSS, Stirling. British, b. 1929. Recreation/Leisure/Hobbies, Sport/Physical education/Keeping fit. Managing Dir., Stirling Moss Ltd., London, since 1954. Motoring Ed., Harper's/Queen mag., London. Former professional racing driver. *Publs:* (ed.) My Favourite Car Stories, 1960; A Turn at the Wheel, 1961; (with Ken Purdy) All But My Life, 1963; (with Laurence Pomeroy) The Design and Behaviour of the Racing Car, 1964; How to Watch Motor Racing, 1975; (with Mike Hailwood) Racing and All That, 1980; (with Doug Nye) My Cars, My Career, 1987. Add: Stirling Moss Ltd., 46 Shepherd St., London W1Y 8JN, England.

MOSSE, George L. American, b. 1918. History. Basom Prof. of History, Univ. of Wisconsin, Madison, since 1955; Prof., Hebrew Univ., Jerusalem, since 1969. Co-Ed., Journal of Contemporary History, since 1966. Prof., Univ. of Iowa, Iowa City, 1944–55. *Publs:* Struggle for Sovereignty in England, 1950; The Reformation, 1950, 3rd ed. 1963; (ed. with others) Europe in Review, 1957; The Holy Pretence, 1957; The Culture of Western Europe, 1961, 3rd ed. 1988; Crisis of German Ideology, 1964; Nazi Culture, 1966; (with H.G. Konigsberger) Europe in the Sixteenth Century, 1968, 1989; Germans and Jews, 1970; Nationalisation of the Masses, 1974; (ed. with B. Vago) Jews and Non-Jews in East-Central Europe, 1974; (ed.) Police Forces in History, 1975; Nazism, 1975; Towards the Final Solution, 1978; (ed.) International Fascism, 1979; Masses and Man, 1980; Nationalism and Sexuality, 1985; German Jews Beyond Judaism, 1985. Add: Dept. of History, Univ. of Wisconsin, Madison, Wisc. 53706, U.S.A.

MOSSOP, Irene. *See* **CHARLES**, Theresa.

MOSTERT, P(aul) S(tallings). American, b. 1927. Mathematics/Statistics. Prof. of Mathematics, Univ. of Kansas, Lawrence, since 1970 (Chmn. of the Dept., 1970–73); Pres., Equix Biomechanics Corp., since 1989. Asst. Prof., 1954–57, Assoc. Prof., 1957–62 and Prof., 1962–70 (Chmn. of Dept., 1968–70). Tulane Univ., New Orleans; Visiting Prof., Univ. of Tubingen, W. Germany, and Member, Inst. for Advanced Study, Princeton, N.J., 1967–68. Managing Ed., 1968–87, and Exec. Ed., 1970–85, Semigroup Forum; Pres., Equix, Inc., 1984–85; Pres., Pennfield Biomechanics Corp., 1985–89. *Publs:* Analytic Trigonometry, 1960; (with K.H. Hoffmann) Splitting in Topological Groups, 1963; (with K.H. Hoffmann) Elements of Compact Semigroups, 1967; (ed.) The Proceedings of the Conference on Transformation Groups, 1968; (with K.H. Hoffmann) The Cohomology Ring of Finite and Compact Abelian Groups, 1973. Add: 184 Park Ave., #2, Lexington, Ky. 40508, U.S.A.

MOTION, Andrew. British. Poetry, Literature. Poetry Ed., Chatto and Windus, publishers, London, since 1982. Lectr. in English, Univ. of Hull, 1977–80; Ed., Poetry Review, London, 1980–82. *Publs:* The Pleasure Steamers, 1978; The Poetry of Edward Thomas, 1980; Independence, 1981; Philip Larkin, 1982; (ed. with Blake Morrison) The New Penguin Book of Contemporary British Poetry, 1982; Secret Narratives, 1983; Dangerous Play: Poems 1974–1984, 1984; The Lamberts, 1986; Natural Causes, 1987. Add: Chatto and Windus, 30 Bedford Sq., London WC1B 3RP, England.

MOTLEY, Annette. Historical/Romance/Gothic. *Publs:* My Lady's Crusade, 1977; The Sins of the Lion, 1979; The Quickenberry Tree, 1983; Green Dragon, White Tiger, 1986; Men on White Horses, 1988. Add: c/o Macdonald, Greater London House, Hampstead Rd., London NW1

7QX, England.

MOULD, Daphne (Desiree Charlotte Pochin). British, b. 1920. History, Theology/Religion, Travel/Exploration/Adventure, Autobiography/Memoirs/Personal. *Publs:* The Road from the Isles, 1950; Scotland of the Saints, 1953; The Rock of Truth, 1953; The Mountains of Ireland, 1955; Irish Pilgrimage, 1955; The Celtic Saints, 1956; The Irish Dominicans, 1957; Peter's Boat, 1959; The Angels of God, 1961; The Irish Saints, 1963; Saint Brigid, 1965; The Aran Islands, 1972; Ireland from the Air, 1972; Murder Is No Navigator (radio play), 1972; Irish Monasteries, 1976; Valentia Island, 1978; Discovering Cork, 1987. Add: Aherla House, Aherla, Co. Cork, Ireland.

MOULE, Charles Francis Digby. British, b. 1908. Theology/Religion. Clerk in Holy Orders, since 1933 (Canon Theologian of Leicester Cathedral, 1955–76). Fellow, Clare Coll., Cambridge, since 1944; Hon Fellow, Emmanuel Coll., Cambridge, since 1972 (Vice-Principal, Ridley Hall, Cambridge, 1936–44; Dean, Clare Coll., 1944–51; Asst. Lectr. in Divinity, 1944–47, Lectr., 1947–51, and Lady Margaret's Prof., 1951–76, Cambridge Univ). *Publs:* An Idiom Book of New Testament Greek, 1953, 1959; The Meaning of Hope, 1953; The Sacrifice of Christ, 1956; The Epistles of Paul the Apostle to the Colossians and to Philemon, 1957; Worship in the New Testament, 1960; The Birth of the New Testament, 1962, 3rd ed. 1981; (ed.) Miracles: Cambridge Studies in Their Philosophy and History, 1965; The Gospel According to Mark, 1965, 1969; (co-ed.) Christian History and Interpretation: Studies Presented to John Knox, 1967; The Phenomenon of the New Testament, 1967; (ed.) The Significance of the Message of the Resurrection for Faith in Jesus Christ, 1968; The Origin of Christology, 1977; The Holy Spirit, 1978; Essays in New Testament Interpretation, 1982; (co-ed.) Jesus and the Politics of His Day, 1984. Add: 1 King's Houses, Pevensey, East Sussex, England.

MOULTON, James Louis. British, b. 1906. History. Contrib., Navy Intnl., 1965–69, and since 1973. Regular Officer, Royal Marines, commissioned 1924, retired as Maj.-Gen., 1961; Contrib., 1962–73, Naval Ed., 1964–68, and Ed., 1969–73, Brassey's Annual, London; Defence Corresp., Glasgow Herald, 1966–67. *Publs:* Haste to the Battle, 1963; Defence in a Changing World, 1964; The Norwegian Campaign of 1940, 1966; The Royal Marines, 1972, 1981; Battle for Antwerp, 1978. Add: Fairmile, Woodham Rd., Woking, Surrey GU21 4DN, England.

MOULY, George Joseph. American, b. 1915. Psychology. Prof. of Educational Psychology, Univ. of Miami, since 1949. Instr. of Mathematics, Univ. of Saskatchewan, Saskatoon, 1946–47; Research Asst., Univ. of Minnesota, Minneapolis, 1947–49. *Publs:* Psychology for Effective Teaching, 1960, 3rd ed. 1973; (with Walton) Test Items in Education, 1962; The Science of Educational Research, 1963, 1970; (ed.) Readings in Educational Psychology, 1971; The Art and Science of Investigation, 1978; Educational Research, 1978; Psychology for Teaching, 1982. Add: Dept. of Psychology, Univ. of Miami, Coral Ga'Des, Fla. 33143, U.S.A.

MOUNTFIELD, David. *See* **GRANT,** Neil.

MOURANT, A(rthur) E(rnest). British, b. 1904. Archaeology/Antiquities, Biology, Earth sciences. Dir., Blood Group Reference Lab., Medical Research Council, 1946–65; Dir., Serological Population Genetics Lab., Medical Research Council, London, 1965–71, and St. Bartholomew's Hosp., London, 1971–78; Hon. Sr. Lectr. in Haematology, Medical Coll. of St. Bartholomew's Hosp., London, 1965–78; Visiting Prof., Columbia Univ., NYC, 1953, and Collège de France, Paris, 1980. *Publs:* Earthquakes in the Channel Islands, 1932; (with P.L. Mollison and R.R. Race) The Rh Blood Groups and Their Clinical Effects, 1948, 1952; The Distribution of the Human Blood Groups, 1954, as co-author 1976; (with A.C. Kopec and K. Domaniewska-Sobczak) The ABO Blood Groups: Comprehensive Tables and Maps of World Distribution, 1958; (ed. with F.E. Zeuner) Man and Cattle, 1963; Jersey Archaeological Sites, 1966; (with A.C. Kopec and K. Domaniewska-Sobczak) Blood Groups and Diseases, 1978; (with A.C. Kopec and K. Domaniewska-Sobczak) The Genetics of the Jews, 1978; John Ranulph de la Haule Marett: Pioneer Biological Anthropologist, 1981; Blood Relations, 1983. Add: The Dower House, Maison de Haut, Longueville, St. Saviour, Jersey, Channel Islands.

MOWAT, David. British, b. 1943. Plays/Screenplays. *Publs:* Anna-Luse and Other Plays, 1970; The Normal Woman, and Tyyppi, 1970; The Others, 1970; (with others) New Writers II, 1974. Add: 8 Folly Bridge Ct., Oxford OX1 1SW, England.

MOWAT, Farley (McGill). Canadian, b. 1921. Children's fiction, Anthropology/Ethnology, History, Natural history, Travel/Exploration/Adventure, Humor/Satire. Arctic explorer, 1947–49. *Publs:* People of the Deer, 1952; The Regiment, 1955; Lost in the Barrens, 1956; The Dog Who Wouldn't Be, 1957; Coppermine Journey, 1958; The Grey Seas Under, 1958; The Desperate People, 1959; Ordeal by Ice, 1960; Owls in the Family, 1961; The Serpents Coil, 1961; The Black Joke, 1962; Never Cry Wolf, 1963; Westviking, 1965; Curse of the Viking Grave, 1966; Canada North, 1967; The Polar Passion, 1967; This Rock Within the Sea, 1968; The Boat Who Wouldn't Float, 1969; Sibir, 1970; A Whale for the Killing, 1972; Tundra, 1973; Wake of the Great Sealers, 1975; The Snow Walker, 1975; Canada North Now, 1976; And No Birds Sang, 1979; The World of Farley Mowat, 1980; Sea of Slaughter, 1984; My Discovery of America, 1985; Woman in the Mists, 1987. Add: c/o McClelland and Stewart Ltd., 481 University Ave., Toronto, Ont. M5G 2E9, Canada.

MOWRER, Lilian T(homson). American. International relations/Current affairs, Autobiography/Memoirs/Personal, Biography, Documentaries/Reportage. Emeritus Pres., UMANO Foundn. Inc., since 1980; Corresp., Town and Country, U.S.A., and Referee, London, 1925–31; Washington, D.C. Chmn., Women's Action Cttee. for Lasting Peace, 1943–49. *Publs:* Journalist's Wife, 1937; Arrest and Exile, 1940; Riptide of Aggression, 1942; Concerning France, 1944; The U.S.A. and World Relations, 1950; John Scott of Long Island, 1960; I've Seen It Happen Twice, 1968; (with Edgar A. Mowrer) UMANO—and Price of Lasting Peace, 1973. Add: Wonalancet, N.H. 03897, U.S.A.

MOXON, Roland James. British, b. 1920. History, Travel/Exploration/Adventure. Chmn. and Managing Dir., Moxon Paperbacks Ltd., Accra, since 1967. Dir., Gold Coast (Ghana) Information Services, 1948–60; Adviser, Ghana Ministry of Information, 1960–67. *Publs:* Volta: Man's Greatest Lake, 1969, 1984; The Baden Powell Ashanti Diaries 1895-96, 1986; Leo Cooper, 1989. Add: Moxon Paperbacks Ltd., P.O. Box M160, Accra, Ghana.

MOYER, K. E. American, b. 1919. Psychology. Prof., Carnegie-Mellon Univ., Pittsburgh, since 1961 (Instr., 1949–50; Asst. Prof., 1950–54; Assoc. Prof., 1954–61). Instr. in Psychology and Physical Education, Pearl River Jr. Coll., Poplarville, Miss., 1946–47; Veterans Counselor and Instr. in Psychology, Washington Univ., St. Louis, 1947–49. *Publs:* The Physiology of Hostility, 1971; You and Your Child, 1974; (ed.) The Physiology of Aggression and Implications for Control, 1976; The Psychobiology of Aggression, 1976; (with J.M. Crabtre) Bibliography of Aggressive Behavior, 1977; Neuroanatomy, 2 vols., 1980–81; Violence and Aggression: A New Perspective, 1987. Add: 252 Gates Dr. Munhall, PA 15120 U.S.A.

MOYES, Patricia. British, b. 1923. Mystery/Crime/Suspense, Translations. Aide to Peter Ustinov, 1946–54; Asst. Ed., Vogue mag., London, 1954–58. *Publs:* (trans.) Time Remembered, by Jean Anouilh, 1955; Dead Men Don't Ski, 1959; Down Among the Dead Men (in U.K. as The Sunken Sailor), 1961; Death on the Agenda, 1962; Murder a la Mode, 1963; Falling Star, 1964; Johnny Under Ground, 1965; Murder by 3's, 1965; Murder Fantastical, 1967; Death and the Dutch Uncle, 1968; Helter-Shelter, 1968; Many Deadly Returns (in U.K. as Who Saw Her Die?), 1970; Season of Snows and Sins, 1971; The Curious Affair of the Third Dog, 1973; After All, They're Only Cats, 1973; Black Widower, 1975; The Coconut Killings, 1977; Who Is Simon Warwick?, 1978; How to Talk to Your Cat, 1978; Angel Death, 1980; A Six-Letter Word for Death, 1983; Night Ferry to Death, 1985; Black Girl, White Girl, 1989. Add: P.O. Box 1, Virgin Gorda, British Virgin Islands, West Indies.

MOYNAHAN, Julian (Lane). American, b. 1925. Novels, Literary criticism/history. Distinguished Prof. of English, Rutgers Univ., New Brunswick, N.J., since 1974 (Prof., 1966–74). Member of the faculty, Amherst Coll., Massachusetts, 1953–55; Princeton Univ., New Jersey, 1955–63, and University Coll., Dublin, 1963–64. *Publs:* Sisters and Brothers, 1960; The Deed of Life: The Novels and Tales of D.H. Lawrence, 1963; (ed.) Sons and Lovers: Text, Background and Criticism, 1968; Pairing Off, 1969; Vladimir Nabokov, 1970; Garden State, 1973; (ed.) The Portable Thomas Hardy, 1977; Where the Land and Water Meet, 1979. Add: 3439 Lawrenceville Rd., Princeton, N.J. 08540, U.S.A.

MOYNIHAN, Daniel Patrick. American, b. 1927. Social sciences. U.S. Senator from New York since 1977. Asst. to Secty., Asst. Secty., and Acting Secty. to Governor of New York State, 1955–58; Dir., New York State Govt. Research Project, Syracuse Univ., New York, 1959–61; Special Asst. to the U.S. Secty. of Labor, 1961–62; Exec. Asst. to the

Secty. of Labor, 1962–63; Asst. Secty. of Labor, 1963–65; Prof. of Education and Urban Politics, Harvard Univ., Cambridge, Mass., and Dir., Massachusetts Inst. of Technology/Harvard Univ. Joint Center for Urban Studies, 1966–69; Counsellor to the U.S. President, 1969–70; U.S. Rep. to 26th Session of U.N. Gen. Assembly, 1971; Consultant to the Pres. of the U.S., 1971–73; Prof. of Govt., Harvard Univ., Cambridge, Mass., 1972–76. U.S. Ambassador to India, 1973–75, and to the U.N. 1975–76. *Publs:* (with Nathan Glazer) Beyond the Melting Pot, 1963; (ed.) Defenses of Freedom: The Public Papers of Arthur J. Goldberg, 1966; (with others) Equal Educational Opportunity, 1969; Maximum Feasible Misunderstanding: Community Action in the War on Poverty, 1969; (ed.) On Understanding Poverty: Perspectives from the Social Sciences, 1969; (ed.) Toward a National Urban Policy, 1970; The Politics of a Guaranteed Income, 1973; Coping, 1973; (ed. with Nathan Glazer) Ethnicity: Theory and Experience, 1975; (with S.A. Weaver) A Dangerous Place, 1978; Counting Our Blessings: Reflections on the Future of America, 1980; Loyalties, 1984; Family and Nation, 1986; Come the Revolution, 1988. Add: United States Senate, Washington, D.C. 20510, U.S.A.

MOYNIHAN, John Dominic. British, b. 1932. Sports/Physical education/Keeping fit, Autobiography/Memoirs/Personal. Sports Writer and Book Reviewer, Sunday Telegraph, London, since 1966 (Asst. Literary Ed., 1968–72). Jr. Reporter, Bromley Mercury, 1953–54; Reporter, Feature Writer, Columnist, and Diarist, Evening Standard, London, 1954–63; Feature Writer, Daily Express, London, 1963–64; Diarist, The Sun, London, 1964–65. *Publs:* The Soccer Syndrome, 1966; Not All a Ball, 1970; Park Football, 1970; (ed.) Football Fever, 1974; Soccer, 1974; The Chelsea Story, 1982; The West Ham Story, 1985. Add: c/o Sunday Telegraph, 181 Marsh Wall, London E14 9SR, England.

MOYNIHAN, Maurice (Gerard). Irish, b. 1902. Money/Finance. Admin. Officer, 1925–32, and Asst. Principal Officer, 1932–37, Dept. of Finance; Secty. to the Irish Govt., 1937–60; Civil Service Commnr., 1937–53; Dir., 1953–60, and Gov., 1961–69, Central Bank of Ireland; Commnr. of Charitable Donations and Bequests for Ireland, Dublin, 1961–79; Dir., Trinity Bank Ltd., Dublin, 1972–80. *Publs:* Currency and Central Banking in Ireland 1922–60, 1975; (ed.) Speeches and Statements by Eamon de Valera 1917–73, 1980. Add: 48 Castle Ave., Clontarf, Dublin 3, Ireland.

MPHAHLELE, Ezekiel (Es'kia Mphahlele). South African, b. 1919. Novels/Short stories, Autobiography/Memoirs/Personal, Essays. Prof. of African Literature, Univ. of the Witwatersrand, Johannesburg, since 1979, Emeritus since 1988. Teacher of English and Afrikaans, Orlando High Sch., Johannesburg, 1945–52; Fiction Ed., Drum mag., Johannesburg, 1955–57; Lectr. in English Literature, Univ. of Ibadan, Nigeria, 1957–61; Dir. of African Progs., Intnl. Assn. for Cultural Freedom, Paris, 1961–63; Dir. of Chem-chemi Creative Centre, Nairobi, Kenya, 1963–65; Lectr., University Coll., Nairobi, 1965–66, Univ. of Denver, 1966–74, and Univ. of Pennsylvania, Philadelphia, 1974–77. *Publs:* Man Must Live and Other Stories, 1947; Down Second Avenue (autobiography), 1959; The Living Dead and Other Stories, 1961; The African Image (essays), 1962, 1974; (ed. with E. Komey) Modern African Stories, 1964; (ed.) African Writing Today, 1967; In Corner B and Other Stories, 1967; The Wanderers (novel), 1971; Voices in the Whirlwind and Other Essays, 1972; Chirundu (novel), 1979; The Unbroken Song, 1981; Bury Me at the Marketplace, 1984; Father Come Home, 1984; Afrika My Music: An Autobiography 1957–1983, 1986. Add: African Studies Inst., Univ. of the Witwatersrand, Johannesburg 2001, South Africa.

MRAZEK, James E(dward). American, b. 1914. History, Military/Defence, Sports/Physical education/Keeping fit. Federal Disaster Reporting Officer, U.S. Federal Disaster Assistance Admin. With U.S. Army, 1938–58, retiring as Col.; Research Assoc. in Washington, D.C., for the Univ. of Pittsburgh, 1961–66; Technical Writer, Goddard Space Flight Center, Radio Corp. of America, Beltsville, Md., 1966–68. *Publs:* The Art of Winning Wars, 1968, 1970; The Fall of Eben Emael, 1970, 1972; Sailplanes and Soaring, 1973; The Glider War, 1973; Fighting Gliders of World War II, 1973; Hang Gliding and Soaring, 1976, 1981; Ultralights, 1982. Add: c/o St. Martin's Press, 175 Fifth Ave., New York, N.Y. 10010, U.S.A.

MTSHALI, Oswald (Joseph). South African, b. 1940. Poetry. Deputy Headmaster, Pace Commercial Coll., Jabulani, Soweto. *Publs:* Sounds of Cowhide Drum, 1971; Fireflames, 1980. Add: 5803 Zone 5, Pimville 1808, Soweto, South Africa.

MUCHA, Jiri. Czechoslovakian, b. 1915. Novels/Short stories, Plays/Screenplays, Poetry, Autobiography/Memoirs/Personal, Biography,

Translations. *Publs:* The Bridge, 1945; Problems of Lieutenant Knap, 1945; Fire Braves Fire, 1947; Scorched Crop, 1949; The War Continues, 1949; A Probable Face, 1963; Black and White New York, 1965; Alphonse Mucha, 1966; Living and Partly Living (memoirs), 1968; Marieta by Night, 1968; Mucha Posters and Photographs, 1971; The Graphic Work of Alphonse Mucha, 1973; Lloyd's Head, 1987; Strange Loves, 1987; plays—The Golden Age, 1948; The Fireflies, 1962; December 18 A.D., 1967; screenplays—The Rift, 1955; The Flood, 1956; The First and the Last, 1957; The King of Kings, 1959; 39 in the Shade, 1962; The Dreambook, 1987. Add: 9 rue Boulard, 75014 Paris, France.

MUDD, Emily H(artshorne). American, b. 1898. Human relations, Psychology. Emeritus Prof. of Family Study in Psychiatry since 1967, and Consultant in Behavioral Sciences, Div. of Human Reproduction, Dept. of Obstetrics, since 1970, Sch. of Medicine, Univ. of Pennsylvania, Philadelphia (Asst. Prof., 1952–56; Dir., Div. of Family Study in Psychiatry, 1952–67; Prof., 1956–67). Member Advisory Cttee., Physicians for Social Responsibility, since 1986. Research Asst., Dept. of Microbiology, Univ. of Pennsylvania, 1925–32; Dir., Marriage Council of Philadelphia, 1932–67; Faculty, Veterans Admin., For Training in Manage Counseling for Neuropsychiatric Residents, Philadelphia, 1947–64; Vice-Pres., Interprofessional Commission on Marriage and Divorce Laws and Family Courts, American Bar Assoc., 1950–60; Assoc., Dept. of Psychiatry, Pennsylvania Div., Philadelphia Gen. Hosp., 1967–74. Chmn., Awards Cttee., World Academy of Art and Science, 1976–85. *Publs:* The Practice of Marriage Counseling, 1951; (with A.H. Olsen and H.A. Bourdeau) Readings on Marriage and Family Relations, 1953; (with A. Krich) Man and Wife: A Sourcebook of Family Attitudes, Sexual Behavior and Marriage Conseling, 1957; (with A. Stone, M.J. Karpf and J.F. Nelson) Marriage Counseling: A Casebook, 1958; (with R.C. Leslie) Professional Growth for Clergymen Through Supervised Training in Marriage Counseling and Family Problems, 1970. Add: 734 Millbrook Lane, Haverford, Pa. 19041, U.S.A.

MUEHL, Lois Baker American. b. 1920. Children's fiction. retired Dir., Reading Lab., Rhetoric Prog., Univ. of Iowa, Iowa City, 1965–85. Reading Specialist, Johnson C. Smith Univ., Charlotte, N.C. 1967–69; EFL Teacher, refugees in Thailand, 1980, 1982, in Korea, 1985, and in China, 1987–88. *Publs:*My Name Is . . . 1959; Worst Room in the School, 1961; One Very Happy Family (play), 1964; Hidden Year of Devlin Bates, 1967; Winter Holiday Brain Teasers, 1979; A Reading Approach to Rhetoric, 1983; (with Siegmar Muehl) Hermann, Missouri 1852: News and Voice, 1987. Add:430 Crest View Ave., Iowa City, Iowa 52245, U.S.A.

MUELLER, David L. American, b. 1929. Theology/Religion. Prof. of Theology, Southern Baptist Theological Seminary, Louisville. *Publs:* An Introduction to the Theology of Albrecht Ritschl, 1969; Makers of the Modern Theological Mind: Karl Barth, 1972. Add: 4908 Crofton Rd., Louisville, Ky. 40207, U.S.A.

MUELLER, Lisel. American, b. 1924. Poetry. Instructor, M.F.A. Writing Program, Goddard Coll., Vermont, since 1977. Instructor in Poetry, Elmhurst Coll., 1969–77. *Publs:* Dependencies, 1965; Life of a Queen, 1970; The Private Life, 1976; Voices from the Forest, 1977; The Need to Hold Still, 1980; Second Language: Poems, 1986. Add: M.F.A. Writing Program, Goddard Coll., Plainsfield, Vt. 05667, U.S.A.

MUELLER, Robert Emmett. American, b. 1925. Novels/Short stories, Poetry, Essays. *Publs:* Inventivity, 1963, 1967; Inventor's Notebook, 1964; Eyes in Space, 1965; The Science of Art, 1967; Abracadabra (fiction), 1970; Rainbows Always Recede (fiction), 1975; Cyberthetics, 1982; Flutestruck, 1983; Shadows on the Nile, 1989. Add: Britton House, Roosevelt, N.J. 08555, U.S.A.

MUELLER, William R(andolph). American, b. 1916. Literature, Theology/Religion, Essays. Dir., William Mueller Assoc., since 1985. Lectr., Johns Hopkins Sch. of Health Services. Member, Dept. of English, Williams Coll., Williamstown, Mass. 1946–48, Santa Barbara Coll., Univ. of California, 1948–51, Univ. of North Carolina at Greensboro, 1951–59, and Goucher Coll., Baltimore, 1959–72; Dir., The Humanities Inst., 1972–84. *Publs:* The Anatomy of Robert Burton's England, 1952; (ed. with D.C. Allen) That Soueraine Light: Essays in Honor of Edmund Spenser 1552–1952, 1952; (ed.) Spenser's Critics: Changing Currents in Literary Taste, 1959; The Prophetic Voice in Modern Fiction, 1959; John Donne: Preacher, 1962; (with J. Jacobsen) The Testament of Samuel Beckett, 1964; (with J. Jacobsen) Ionesco and Genet: Playwrights of Silence, 1968; Celebration of Life: Studies in Modern Fiction, 1972; Apology for the Life of William Mueller: The

Growth of an Existentialist, 1984. Add: 1108 Bellemore Rd., Baltimore, Md. 21210, U.S.A.

MUGGERIDGE, Malcolm. British, b. 1903. Social commentary/phenomena, Theology/Religion, Autobiography/Memoirs/Personal, Biography. Lectr., Egyptian Univ., Cairo, 1927–30; Member, Editorial Staff, 1930–32, and Moscow Corresp., 1932–33, Manchester Guardian; Asst. Ed., Calcutta Statesman, 1934–35; Member, Editorial Staff, Evening Standard, London, 1935–36; Washington Corresp., 1946–47, and Deputy Ed., 1950–52, Daily Telegraph, London; Ed., Punch, London 1953–57. Rector, Univ. of Edinburgh, 1967–68. *Publs:* Three Flats, 1931; Autumnal Face, 1931; Winter in Moscow, 1933; The Ernest Atheist: A Life of Samuel Butler, 1936; In a Valley of This Restless Mind, 1938; The Thirties, 1940; (ed.) Ciano's Diary, 1947; Ciano's Papers, 1948; Affairs of the Heart, 1949; Tread Softly, For You Tread on My Jokes, 1966; (with P. Hogarth) London a la Mode, 1966; Muggeridge Through the Microphone, 1967; Jesus Rediscovered, 1969; Something Beautiful for God, 1971; Paul: Envoy Extraordinary, 1972; Chronicles of Wasted Time, vol. I, 1972, vol. II, 1973; Malcolm's Choice, 1972; Jesus: The Man Who Lives, 1975; A Third Testament, 1973; A Twentieth-Century Testimony, 1979; Like It Was (diaries), 1981; Picture Palace, 1987; My Life in Pictures, 1987; Conversion: A Spiritual Journey, 1988. Add: Park Cottage, Robertsbridge, Sussex, England.

MUGGESON, Margaret Elizabeth. Writes as Margaret Dickinson and Everatt Jackson. British, b. 1942. Novels/Short stories. Local Govt. Officer, Skegness District Education Office, 1963–70. *Publs:* Pride of the Courtneys, 1968; Brackenbeck, 1969; Portrait of Jonathan, 1970; (as Everatt Jackson) The Road to Hell, 1975; The Abbeyford Trilogy: Sarah, Adelina, and Carrie, 1981; Lifeboat!, 1983; Beloved Enemy, 1984. Add: 17 Seacroft Dr., Skegness, Lincs. PE25 3AP, England.

MUIR, (Charles) Augustus. Has also written as Austin Moore. British. Novels/Short stories, History, Travel/Exploration/Adventure, Biography. Former Ed., The World, and The Passing Show, London. *Publs:* The Third Warning, 1925; The Black Pavilion (in U.S. as The Ace of Danger), 1926; The Blue Bonnet, 1926; The Shadow on the Left, 1928; The Silent Partner, 1929; (as Austin Moore) Birds of the Night, 1930; Beginning the Adventure (in U.S. as The Dark Adventure), 1932; (as Austin Moore) The House of Lies, 1932; The Green Lantern, 1933; The Riddle of Garth, 1933; Scotland's Road of Romance: Travels in the Footsteps of Prince Charlie, 1934; Raphael MD, 1935; The Crimson Crescent, 1935; Saytr Mask, 1936; The Bronze Door, 1936; The Red Carnation, 1937; The Man Who Stole the Crown Jewels, 1937; Castles in the Air, 1938; The Sands of Fear, 1940; The Intimate Thoughts of John Baxter, Bookseller, 1942; Joey and the Greenwings, 1943; Heather-Track and High Road (travels), 1944; (ed.) The Saintsbury Memorial Volume (in U.S. as Saintsbury Miscellany), 1945; Scottish Portrait (history), 1948; (ed.) A Last Vintage: Essays by George Saintsbury, 1950; The Story of Jesus, 1953; The Fife Coal Company: A History, 1953; (ed.) How to Choose and Enjoy Wine, 1953; The History of the Shotts Iron Company, 1954; Candlelight in Avalon: A Spiritual Pilgrimage, 1954; Nairns of Kirkcaldy, 1956; 75 Years of Progress: Smith's Stamping Works and Smith-Clayton Forge, 1958; Biography of Dr. John White, C.H., 1958; The First of Foot: The History of the Royal Scots, 1961; Blyth, Greene, Jourdain, 1961; Churchill and Sim, Timber Brokers, 1963; Andersons of Islington, 1963; The Kenyon Tradition, 1964; The History of Baker Perkins Ltd., 1968; In Blackburne Valley: The History of Bowers Mills, 1969; The British Paper and Board Makers Association 1872–1972, 1972; The Vintner of Nazareth: A Study of Palestine in the Early Days of Christ, 1972; (with Mair Davies) A Victorian Shipowner: A Portrait of Sir Charles Cayzer, Baronet, of Gartmore, 1978. Add: 26 Bentfield Rd., Stansted, Essex CM24 8HW, England.

MUIR, Dexter. *See* **GRIBBLE**, Leonard.

MUIR, Frank. British, b. 1920. Social commentary/phenomena, Humor/Satire. Freelance writer and broadcaster. Member of the panel, My Word and Call My Bluff, BBC television. Asst. Head of BBC Light Entertainment Group, London 1964–67; Head of Entertainment, London Weekend Television, 1967–69. *Publs:* (with Patrick Campbell) Call My Bluff, 1972; (with Denis Norden) You Can't Have Your Kayak and Heat It, 1973; (with D. Norden) Upon My Word, 1974; Christmas Customs and Traditions, 1975; The Frank Muir Book (in U.S. as An Irreverent and Thoroughly Incomplete Social History of Almost Everything), 1976; What-a-Mess series, 15 vols., 1977–88; (with Simon Brett) Frank Muir Goes into . , 4 vols., 1978–81; (with D. Norden) Take My Word for It, 1978; (with D. Norden) The Glums, 1979; (with S. Brett) Frank Muir on Children, 1980; (with D. Norden) Oh, My Word!, 1980; (with P. Muir)

The Big Dipper, 1981. Add: Anners, Thorpe, Egham, Surrey TW20 8UE, England.

MUIR, Kenneth (Arthur). British, b. 1907. Literature, Biography, Translations. King Alfred Prof. of English Literature, Univ. of Liverpool, 1951–74, now Emeritus. Ed., Shakespeare Survey, 1965–79. *Publs:* (ed.) Collected Poems of Sir Thomas Wyatt, 1949; Elizabethan Lyrics, 1953; John Milton, 1955; (ed.) The Pelican Book of English Prose, 1, 1956; Shakespeare's Sources, 1957; (ed. with F. Wilson) The Life and Death of Jack Straw, 1957; (ed.) John Keats, 1958; Shakespeare and the Tragic Pattern, 1959; (trans.) Five Plays of Jean Racine, 1960; Shakespeare as a Collaborator, 1960; (ed.) Unpublished Poems of Sir Thomas Wyatt, 1961; Last Periods, 1961; Life and Letters of Sir Thomas Wyatt, 1963; Introduction to Elizabethan Literature, 1967; New Companion to Shakespeare Studies, 1971; Shakespeare's Tragic Sequence, 1972; Shakespeare the Professional, 1973; (ed.) Three Plays of Thomas Middleton, 1975; The Singularity of Shakespeare, 1977; The Sources of Shakespeare's Plays, 1977; Shakespeare's Comic Sequence, 1979; (trans.) Four Comedies of Calderon, 1980; (ed.) Troilus and Cressida, by Shakespeare, 1982; (ed.) Interpretations of Shakespeare, 1985; Shakespeare, Contrasts and Controversies, 1985; King Lear, 1986; Antony and Cleopatra, 1987; Negative Capability and the Art of the Dramatist, 1987. Add: 6 Chetwynd Rd., Oxton, Birkenhead, Merseyside, L43 2JJ, England.

MUIR, Richard. British, b. 1943. Country Life/Rural Societies. Full-time writer since 1980. Lectr. in Geography, Trinity Coll., Dublin, 1970–71; Sr. Lectr. in Geography, CCAT, Cambridge, 1971–80. *Publs:* Modern Political Geography, 1975, 1980; The English Village, 1980; (co-author) Politics, Geography and Behaviour, 1980; Riddles in the British Landscape, 1981; Reading the Landscape, 1981; The Lost Villages of Britain, 1982; Traveller's History of Britain and Ireland, 1983; (co-author) Visions of the Past, 1983; (co-author) The National Trust Guide to Prehistoric and Roman Britain, 1983; History from the Air, 1983; (co-author) The Shell Countryside Book, 1984; (co-author) East Anglian Landscapes, 1984; Shell Guide to Reading the Celtic Landscapes, 1985; The National Trust Guide to Dark Age and Medieval Britain, 1985; Landscape and Nature Photography, 1986; The Stones of Britain, 1986; (co-author) The National Trust Guide to Rivers of Britain, 1986; (co-author) Hedgerows: Their History and Wildlife, 1987; Old Yorkshire, 1987; The Countryside Encyclopaedia, 1988; Portraits of the Past, 1989; Barleybridge, 1989. Add: Waterfall Close, Birstwith, Harrogate, N. Yorks., England.

MUIRDEN, Bruce Wallace. Australian, b. 1928. Politics/Government. Press Secty. to Minister of Transport, South Australia, since 1983. Ed., Australian Humanist, since 1966, and Labor Herald, since 1971. Features Ed., The News, Adelaide, 1968–70. *Publs:* (ed.) Austroverse, 1952; The Puzzled Patriots, 1968; When Power Went Public, 1978. Add: 219 Kensington Rd., Kensington, S.A. 5068, Australia.

MUKHERJEE, Bharati. Canadian, b. 1940. Novels/Short stories. Assoc. Prof., Dept. of English, McGill Univ., Montreal, since 1966. *Publs:* Tiger's Daughter, 1972; Wife, 1975; Kautilya's Concept of Diplomacy, 1976; (with Clark Blaise) Days and Nights in Calcutta, 1977; Darkness, 1985; The Middleman and Other Stories, 1989. Add: Dept. of English, McGill Univ., Montreal, Que., Canada.

MULDOON, Paul. Irish, b. 1951. Poetry. Radio producer, BBC, Northern Ireland. *Publs:* Knowing My Place, 1971; New Weather, 1973; Spirit of Dawn, 1975; Mules, 1977; Names and Addresses, 1978; Why Brownlee Left, 1980; Immram, 1980; Quoof, 1983; The Wishbone, 1984; Selected Poems 1968-1983, 1986; (ed.) The Faber Book of Contemporary Irish Poetry, 1986; Meeting the British, 1987; (ed.) The Essential Byron, 1989. Add: c/o Faber and Faber, 3 Queen Sq., London WC1N 3AU, England.

MULLAN, Bob. British, b. 1947. Philosophy, Social commentary, Sociology, Biography. Freelance television producer since 1986. Lectr. in Sociology, Univ. of East Anglia, Norwich, 1978–86. *Publs:* Stevenage Ltd.: Aspects of the Planning and Politics of Stevenage New Town 1946-1978, 1980; (with E. Ellis Cashmore) Approaching Social Theory, 1983; Life as Laughter: Following Bhagwan Shree Rajneesh, 1983; The Mating Trade, 1984; (with Laurie Taylor) Uninvited Guests: The Intimate Secrets of Television and Radio, 1986; Sociologists on Sociology, 1987; The Enid Blyton Story, 1987; Are Mothers Really Necessary?, 1988. Add: 2 Trix Rd., Norwich NR2 2HB, England.

MULLARD, Chris(topher Paul). British, b. 1944. Politics/Government, Race relations, Sociology. Regional Secty., Tyneside Campaign

Against Racial Discrimination, 1967–69; Community Relations Officer, Tyne and Wear Community Relations Council, 1969–73. *Publs:* Black Britain, 1973; Racism in Society and Schools, 1980; Race, Power, and Resistance, 1985. Add: c/o Routledge, Chapman and Hall Inc., 24 W. 35th St., New York, N.Y. 10001, U.S.A.

MULLENIX, Dennis (Eugene). American, b. 1941. Antiques/Furnishings. Principal, Dennis Mullenix and Assocs., literary agents, Peoria, since 1978; also, Engineer with Affolter and Bettler, Pekin, Ill., since 1978. Engineer with the Illinois Dept. of Transportation, 1966–70, and with Daily and Assocs., Peoria, 1970–78. *Publs:* Antiques: A Browser's Handbook, 1977. Add: 4210 N. University, Peoria, Ill. 61614, U.S.A.

MULLER, John E. *See* **FANTHORPE,** R. Lionel.

MULLER, Marcia. American, b. 1944. Mystery/Crime/Suspense. Full-time writer since 1983. Merchandising Supvrs., Sunset mag., Menlo Park, Calif., 1967–69; interviewer in San Francisco for the Univ. of Michigan Inst. of Social Research, 1971–73; held various part-time jobs until 1979; Partner, Invisible Ink, San Francisco, 1979–83. *Publs:* Edwin of the Iron Shoes, 1977; Ask the Cards a Question, 1982; The Cheshire Cat's Eye, 1983; The Tree of Death, 1983; (ed. with Bill Pronzini) The Web She Weaves, 1983; Games to Keep the Dark Away, 1984; (ed. with Bill Pronzini) Child's Ploy, 1984; (ed. with Bill Pronzini) Witches' Brew, 1984; Leave a Message for Willie, 1984; (with Bill Pronzini) Double, 1984; (ed. with Bill Pronzini) Dark Lessons: Crime and Detection on Campus, 1985; (ed. with Bill Pronzini) She Won the West: An Anthology of Western and Frontier Stories by Women, 1985; The Legend of the Slain Soldiers, 1985; There's Nothing to Be Afraid of, 1985; (ed. with Bill Pronzini) Chapter and Hearse, 1985; (ed. with Bill Pronzini) Kill or Cure, 1985; (ed. with Bill Pronzini) The Wickedest Show on Earth, 1985; (ed. with Bill Pronzini) The Deadly Arts, 1985; The Cavalier in White, 1986; (with Bill Pronzini) Beyond the Grave, 1986; (ed. with Bill Pronzini) 1001 Midnights, 1986; (with Bill Pronzini) The Lighthouse, 1987; Eye of the Storm, 1988; There Hangs the Knife, 1988; (with Bill Pronzini and Martin H. Greenberg) Lady on the Case, 1988; There's Something in a Sunday, 1989; Dark Star, 1989; The Shape of Dread, 1989. Add: P.O. Box 1349, Sonoma, Calif. 95476, U.S.A.

MULLER, Robert. British, b. 1925. Novels/Short stories, Plays/Screenplays. Drama Critic, The Daily Mail, London, 1960–62. *Publs:* novels—Cinderella Nightingale; The World That Summer; The Shores of Night; The Lost Diaries of Albert Smith; After All, This Is England; Lovelife; Virginities; (ed.) The Television Dramatist; The World That Summer (film); plays—Night Conspirators; Die Unberatenen; Cut-Throat; television plays—Fall of Eagles; The Explorers; Afternoon of a Nymph; The Paradise Suite; Easier in the Dark; A Cold Peace; Man of Straw; The Legacy; Exil; Bel Ami; Nana; Vienna 1900; Youth under Hitler; Albert Schweitzer. Add: 2 Camden Sq., London NW1, England.

MULLETT, John St. Hilary. British, b. 1925. Music, Theology/Religion. Rector of Ashwell, Church of England, since 1977. Rector of Que Que, Matabeleland, Central Africa, 1952–60; Vicar of Bollington, Cheshire, 1961–69, and Oxton, Cheshire, 1969–77. *Publs:* One People, One Church, One Song, 1968; Oxton St. Saviour Guide, 1977; They Took Them to Church, 1979; To Love and to Cherish, 1982; A Church Service Following a Second Marriage, 1983. Add: 13 Church Lane, Madingley, Cambridge CB3 8AF, England.

MULLIGAN, Raymond A. American, b. 1914. Public/Social administration, Sociology. Prof. Emeritus, Univ. of Arizona, Tucson, since 1984 (Assoc. Prof., 1953–59; Prof. 1959–84; former Head of Dept. of Public Admin., and former Acting Head of Dept. of Sociology). Asst. Instr., Indiana Univ., 1941–42, 1945–47; Prof., DePauw Univ., Greencastle, Ind., 1947–53. *Publs:* Welfare Policies and Administration in Arizona, 1963; (with H. Fredericksen) The Child and His Welfare, 3rd ed. 1972. Add: 6901 Big Bear Dr., Tucson, Ariz. 85715, U.S.A.

MULLINS, Edwin. British, b. 1933. Novels, Art, History. *Publs:* Souza, 1962; Alfred Wallis, 1967; Josef Herman, 1967; Braque, 1969; Elisabeth Frink, 1972; The Pilgrimage to Santiago, 1974; Angels on the Point of a Pin, 1979; Great Paintings, 1981; Sirens, 1983; The Arts of Britain, 1983; The Painted Witch, 1985; A Love Affair With Nature, 1985; The Golden Bird, 1987; The Lands of the Sea, 1988. Add: 7 Lower Common South, London SW15 1BP, England.

MULLINS, Helene. American, b. 1899. Novels/Short stories, Poetry. *Publs:* (with Marie Gallagher) Paulus Fry (novel), 1924; Earthbound (poetry), 1929; Balm in Gilead (poetry), 1929; Convent Girl (novel),

1929; Streams from the Source (poetry), 1938; The Mirrored Walls (poetry), 1970. Add: 16 W. 16th St., New York, N.Y. 10011, U.S.A.

MUMFORD, Lewis. American, b. 1895. Architecture, Regional/Urban planning, Social commentary/phenomena. Lectr., New School for Social Research, NYC, 1925, and Geneva School of International Studies, 1925, 1929; Visiting Prof., Dartmouth College, Hanover, N.H., 1929–35; Lectr., Columbia Univ., NYC, 1931–35; Prof., Stanford Univ., California, 1942–44; Prof. of City Planning, 1951–56, and Ford Prof., 1959–61, Univ. of Pennsylvania, Philadelphia; Visiting Prof., Massachusetts Institute of Technology, Cambridge, 1957–61, and Univ. of California, Berkeley, 1961–62; Visiting Lectr., 1973–74, and Charles Abrams Prof., 1975, Massachusetts Institute of Technology. Assoc. Ed., Fortnightly Dial, 1919; Acting Ed., Sociological Review, London, 1920; Contributing Ed., New Republic, 1927–40; Columnist ("The Sky Line"), The New Yorker, 1932. Recipient, National Book Award, 1962; National Medal for Literature, 1972. *Publs:* The Story of Utopias, 1922, 1923; Sticks and Stones: A Study of American Architecture and Civilization, 1924; Aesthetics: A Dialogue, 1925; The Golden Day: A Study in American Experience and Culture, 1926, as The Golden Day: A Study in American Literature and Culture, 1933; Architecture, 1926; (ed. with others) The American Caravan: A Yearbook of American Literature (and, The Second, and The New American Caravan, American Caravan IV, and The New Caravan) 5 vols., 1927–36; American Taste, 1929; Herman Melville, 1929, as Herman Melville: A Study of His Life and Vision, 1962, 1963; The Brown Decades: A Study of the Arts in America 1865–1895, 1931; Technics and Civilization, 1934; (ed. with others) America and Alfred Stieglitz: A Collective Portrait, 1934; Whither Honolulu?, 1938; The Culture of Cities, 1938; Men Must Act, 1939; Regional Planning in the Pacific Northwest: A Memorandum, 1939; Faith for Living, 1940, 1941; The South in Architecture, 1941; (with Herbert Agar and Frank Kingdon) World-Wide Civil War, 1942; The School of Humanities: A Description, 1942; (with Henry A. Wallace and Jay Allen) New World Theme, 1943; The Social Foundations of Post-War Building, 1943; The Condition of Man, 1944; Thomas Beer, Aristocrat of Letters, 1944; The Plan of London County, 1945; City Development: Studies in Disintegration and Renewal, 1945, 1946; Values for Survival: Essays, Addresses, and Letters on Politics and Education, 1946; Atomic War—The Way Out, 1948; Man as Interpreter, 1950; The Conduct of Life, 1951; Art and Technics, 1952; Towards a Free World: Long-Range Planning Under Democratic Control, 1952; (ed.) Roots of Contemporary American Architecture, 1952; In the Name of Sanity, 1954; The Human Prospect, 1955; From the Ground Up: Observations on Contemporary Architecture, Housing, Highway Building, and Civic Design, 1956; The Transformations of Man, 1956, 1957; The Human Way Out, 1958, 1962; The Role of the Creative Arts in Contemporary Society, 1958; The City in History: Its Origins, Its Transformations, and Its Prospects, 1961; Social Responsibility in the Business Community, 1961; The Highway and the City, 1964; Myth of the Machine: Technics and Human Development, 1967; The Urban Prospect, 1968; (ed.) Essays and Journals, by Ralph Waldo Emerson, 1968; Myth of the Machine: The Pentagon of Power, 1970, 1971; (ed.) The Ecological Basis of Planning, by Arthur Glikson, 1971; The Letters of Lewis Mumford and Frederic J. Osborn: A Transatlantic Dialogue, 1971, as Lewis Mumford and Frederic J. Osborn: A Transatlantic Dialogue, 1972; Interpretations and Forecasts 1922–1972: Studies in Literature, History, Biography, Technics, and Contemporary Society, 1973; Architecture as a Home for Man: Essays for "Architectural Record", 1975; Findings and Keepings 1914–1936 (Analects for an Autobiography), 1975; My Works and Days: A Personal Chronicle 1895–1975, 1979; Sketches from Life: The Early Years, 1982. Add: R.D. 1, Amenia, N.Y. 12501, U.S.A.

MUMFORD, Ruth. *See* **DALLAS,** Ruth.

MUNDEL, Marvin Everett. American, b. 1916. Administration/Management, Engineering/Technology, Business/Trade/Industry, Information science/computers, Politics/Government. Principal, M.E. Mundel and Assocs., 1953–63 and since 1965. Prof. and Chmn. of Industrial Engineering, Purdue Univ., Lafayette, Ind., 1950–53; Dir., U.S. Army Mgmt. Engineering Training Agency, 1952–53; Principal Staff Officer, Industrial Engineering and Work Measurement, Bureau of the Budget, Washington, D.C., 1963–65. *Publs:* A Conceptual Framework for the Management Sciences, 1967; Motion and Time Study, 6th ed. 1985; Toward the Improvement of Government, 1970; Measuring and Enhancing Productivity in the Government and Service Organizations, 1975; Improving Productivity and Effectiveness, 1983; BASIC-A Personal Computer Language, 1986; Measuring the Productivity of Commercial Banks: Algorithms and PC Programs, 1987; Measuring Total Productivity in Manufacturing Organization: Algorithms and PC programs, 1987. Add:

821 Loxford Terr., Silver Spring, Md. 20901, U.S.A.

MUNDIS, Hester (Jane). American, b. 1938. Novels/Short stories, Animals/Pets. Asst. Copy Dir., Fawcett Publications, NYC, 1961–63; Assoc. Ed., Macfadden-Bartell Corp., NYC, 1963–64; Copy Chief and Assoc. Ed., Dell Books and Delacorte Press, NYC, 1964–67; Exec. Ed., Popular Library, NYC, 1967–70; Sr. Ed., Avon Books, NYC, 1970–71. *Publs:* Jessica's Wife, 1975; No He's Not a Monkey, He's an Ape and He's My Son, 1976; Separate Ways, 1978; Working Girl, 1981; Powerman, 1984; Out on a Broken Limb: 101 Ways to Avoid Reincarnation, 1989. Add: Moonshaw Rd., West Shokan, N.Y. 12494, U.S.A.

MUNDY, Max. *See* **SCHOFIELD**, Sylvia Anne.

MUNFORD, William Arthur. British, b. 1911. History, Librarianship, Biography. Librarian Emeritus, National Library for the Blind. *Publs:* Penny Rate: Aspects of British Public Library History 1850–1950, 1951; William Ewart, M.P., 1960; Edward Edwards, 1963; (with W.G. Fry) Louis Stanley Jast, 1966; James Duff Brown, 1968; A History of the Library Association, 1976; (with S. Godbolt) The Incomparable Mac: A Biographical Study of Sir J.Y.W. MacAlister, 1983; Who Was Who in British Librarianship 1800-1985, 1987. Add: 11 Manor Ct., Grange Rd., Cambridge CB3 9BE, England.

MUNONYE, John. Nigerian, b. 1929. Novels/Short stories. Civil Servant, Ministry of Education, Nigeria, now retired. *Publs:* The Only Son, 1966; Obi, 1969; Oil Man of Obange, 1971; A Wreath for the Maidens, 1973; A Dancer of Fortune, 1974; Bridge to a Wedding, 1978. Add: P.O. Box 23, Akokwa, Orlu, Imo State, Nigeria.

MUNRO, Alice. Canadian, b. 1931. Novels/Short stories. *Publs:* Lives of Girls and Women (novel), 1971; Dance of the Happy Shades (short stories), 1968; Something I've Been Meaning to Tell You (short stories), 1974; Who Do You Think You Are? (in U.S. as The Beggar Maid), 1979; The Moons of Jupiter, 1982; Progress of Love, 1986. Add: 1648 Rockland, Victoria, B.C., Canada.

MUNRO, James. *See* **MITCHELL**, James.

MUNRO, John M(urchison). British, b. 1932. History, Literature. Prof. of English, American Univ. of Beirut, since 1965. Instr. in English, Washington Univ., St. Louis, 1956–60, and Univ. of North Carolina, Chapel Hill, 1960–63; Asst. Prof. of English, Univ. of Toronto, 1963–65. *Publs:* (with T.Y. Greet and Charles Edge) The Worlds of Fiction, 1964; (ed.) English Poetry in Transition, 1968; Arthur Symons, 1969; The Decadent Poetry of the 1890's, 1970; Images and Memories, 1970; The Royal Aquarium: Failure of a Victorian Compromise, 1971; (ed.) Selected Poems of Theo. Marzials, 1974; James Elroy Flecker, 1976; A Mutual Concern (history of education), 1977; The Nairn Way (social history of Syria), 1980; Cyprus: Between Venus and Mars (political history), 1984. Add: Dept. of English, American Univ. Beirut, Lebanon.

MUNRO, Mary. *See* **HOWE**, Doris.

MUNRO, Ronald Eadie. *See* **GLEN**, Duncan.

MUNSCH, Robert. Canadian, b. 1945. Children's fiction. Full-time writer. Teacher, Bay Area Childcare, Coos Bay, Oregon, 1973–75; Asst. Prof. of Early Childhood Education, Univ. of Guelph, 1975–84. *Publs:* Mud Puddle, 1979; The Dark, 1979; The Paper Bag Princess, 1980; Jonathan Cleaned Up, Then He Heard a Sound, 1981; The Boy in the Drawer, 1982; Murmel, Murmel, Murmel, 1982; Angela's Airplane, 1983; Fire Station, 1983; David's Father, 1983; Millicent and the Wind, 1984; Thomas' Snowsuit, 1985; Mortimer, 1985; 50 Below Zero, 1985; I Have to Go, 1986; Love You Forever, 1986, 1986; Moira's Birthday, 1987; A Promise Is a Promise, 1987; Pigs, 1989. Add: c/o Writers' Union of Canada, 24 Ryerson Ave., Toronto, Ontario, M5T 2P3, Canada.

MUNSON, Thomas Nolan. American, b. 1924. Philosophy, Theology/Religion. Prof. of Philosophy, DePaul Univ., Chicago, since 1966, Emeritus since 1989. Prof., West Baden Coll., Indiana, 1959–61; Prof., Loyola Univ., Chicago, 1961–65. *Publs:* The Essential Wisdom of George Santayana, 1962; Reflective Theology: Philosophical Orientations in Religion, 1968; Religious Consciousness and Experience, 1975; The Challenge of Religion: Philosophical Approach, 1985. Add: 16098 Country Club, Dolores, Colo. 81323, U.S.A.

MUNZ, Peter. New Zealander, b. 1921. History, Philosophy, Theology/Religion, Biography. Prof. of History, Victoria Univ. of Wellington,

since 1966, Emeritus since 1987 (Sr. Lectr., 1948–61; Assoc. Prof., 1961–66). *Publs:* The Place of Hooker in the History of Thought, 1952; (trans.) The Carolingian Empire, 1956; Problems of Religious Knowledge, 1959; The Origin of the Carolingian Empire, 1960; Relationship and Solitude, 1964; (trans.) Italian Humanism, 1965; Frederick Barbarossa, 1969; Life in the Age of Charlemagne, 1969; (trans.) Science and Civic Life in the Italian Renaissance, 1969; (ed.) The Feel of Truth, 1969; The Concept of the Middle Ages as a Sociological Category, 1969; Reflections on the Theory of the Revolution in France, 1972; When the Golden Bough Breaks, 1973; (with G. Ellis) Boso's Life of Pope Alexander III, 1973; The Shapes of Time, 1977; Our Knowledge of the Growth of Knowledge, 1985. Add: 128 Ohiro Rd., Wellington, New Zealand.

MUNZER, Martha E. American, b. 1899. Regional/Urban studies. Freelance writer, lectr. and teacher. Chemistry teacher, 1930–54; Researcher and Writer, Conservation Foundn., NYC, 1954–68; with Wave Hill Center for Environmental Studies, Riverdale, N.Y., 1968–72. *Publs:* Unusual Careers, 1962; Planning Our Town, 1964; Pockets of Hope: Studies of Land and People, 1967; Valley of Vision: The TVA Years, 1969; (with H.W. Vogel) Block by Block: Rebuilding City Neighborhoods, 1973; (with J. Vogel, Jr.) New Towns: Building Cities from Scratch, 1974; Full Circle: Rounding Out a Life, 1978; The Three R's of Ecology: An Anthology, 1986. Add: 4411 Tradewinds Ave. E., Lauderdale by the Sea, Fla. 33308, U.S.A.

MURCHIE, Guy. American, b. 1907. Natural history, Philosophy. Feature Writer and War Corresp., Chicago Tribune, 1934–42. *Publs:* Men on the Horizon, 1932; Mutiny of the Bounty, 1937; Soldiers of Darkness, 1937; Song of the Sky, 1954, abridged ed. as The World Aloft, 1970; Music of the Spheres, 1961; The Seven Mysteries of Life, 1978. Add: 333 Old Mill Rd. No. 215 Santa Barbara, Calif. 93110, U.S.A.

MURDOCH, (Dame) Iris. British, b. 1919. Novels/Short stories, Plays/Screenplays, Poetry, Philosophy. Hon. Fellow, St. Anne's Coll., Oxford, since 1963 (Fellow and Univ. Lectr. in Philosophy, 1948–63). Asst. Principal in the Treasury, London, 1942–44; Admin. Officer, U.N. Relief and Rehabilitation Admin., London, Belgium and Austria, 1944–46; Lectr., Royal Coll. of Art, London, 1963–67. *Publs:* Sartre: Romantic Rationalist, 1953; Under the Net, 1954; The Flight from the Enchanter, 1956; The Sandcastle, 1957; The Bell, 1958; A Severed Head, 1961, play with J.B. Priestley, 1963; An Unofficial Rose, 1962; The Unicorn, 1963; The Italian Girl, 1964, play with J. Saunders, 1967; The Red and the Green, 1965; The Time of the Angels, 1966; The Nice and the Good, 1968; Bruno's Dream, 1969; A Fairly Honourable Defeat, 1970; An Accidental Man, 1971; The Sovereignty of Good, 1971; The Black Prince, 1972; The Three Arrows, and The Servants in the Snow: Two Plays, 1973; The Sacred and Profane Love Machine, 1974; A Word Child, 1975; Henry and Cato, 1977; The Fire and the Sun: Why Plato Banned the Artists, 1977; The Sea, The Sea, 1978; Nuns and Soldiers, 1980; The Philosopher's Pupil, 1982; The Good Apprentice, 1985; Acastos: Two Platonic Dialogues, 1986; The Book and the Brotherhood, 1987. Add: c/o Ed Victor Ltd., 162 Wardour St., London W1V 4AT, England.

MURDOCK, Eugene C. American, b. 1921. History. Chmn., Dept. of Social Science, Rio Grande Coll., Ohio, 1952–56; Asst. Prof., Assoc. Prof., and Prof. of History, Marietta Coll., Ohio, 1956–86; Member of Ed. Bd.: Ohio History, 1964–74; Pro Football Digest, 1967–69; Journal of Sport History, 1973–78. *Publs:* Ohio's Bounty System in the Civil War, 1963; Patriotism Limited 1862–1865, 1967; One Million Men, 1971; (co-author) Fenton Glass, 3 vols., 1978, 1980, 1989; Ban Johnson: Czar of Baseball, 1982; Mighty Casey: All-American, 1984; The Civil War/North: An Annotated, Selective Bibliography, 1986; Buckeye Empire: An Illustrated History of Ohio Enterprise, 1988; Bernard P. McDonough: The Man and His Work, 1989. Add: 415 Columbia Ave., Williamstown, W. Va. 26187, U.S.A.

MURDY, Louise Baughan. American, b. 1935. Literature. Assoc. Prof. of English, Winthrop Coll., Rock Hill, since 1970 (Asst. Prof., 1963–70). Instr. in Humanities and English, Florida State Univ., Tallahassee, 1962–63. *Publs:* Sound and Sense in Dylan Thomas's Poetry, 1966. Add: 659 Guilford Rd., Rock Hill, S.C. 29730, U.S.A.

MURIE, Margaret E(lizabeth). American, b. 1902. Cultural/Ethnic topics, Autobiography/Memoirs/Personal. Member of the Council, The Wilderness Soc.; Member of the Bd., Teton Science Sch., Jackson Hole, Wyo. Consultant, National Park Service, 1975. *Publs:* Two in the Far North, 1962; (with Olaus J. Murie) Wapiti Wilderness, 1965; (ed.) Journeys to the Far North, by Olaus J. Murie, 1973; Island Between, 1978; (ed.) The Alaskan Bird Sketches of Olaus Murie, 1979. Add: Box 70,

Moose, Wyo. 83012, U.S.A.

MURNANE, Gerald. Australian, b. 1939. Science fiction. *Publs:* Tamarisk Row, 1974; A Lifetime on Clouds, 1976; The Plains, 1982; Landscape with Landscape, 1985; Inland, 1988. Add: 22 Falcon St., Macleod, Vic. 3085, Australia.

MURPHEY, Rhoads. American, b. 1919. Geography, History. Prof. of History, Univ. of Michigan, Ann Arbor, since 1982 (Prof. of Asian Studies and Geography, and Dir., Center for Chinese Studies, 1968–75). Member, Bd. of Dirs., 1959–70 and since 1973, Exec. Secty. since 1976, and Pres., 1987, Assn. for Asian Studies. Asst. Prof. to Prof. of Geography, Univ. of Washington, Seattle, 1952–64. Ed. Journal of Asian Studies, 1959–65. *Publs:* Shanghai: Key to Modern China, 1953; An Introduction to Geography, 1961, 4th ed. 1978; (co-author) A New China Policy, 1965; (co-ed.) Approaches to Modern Chinese History, 1967; The Scope of Geography, 1969, 3rd ed. 1981; The Treaty Ports, 1970; (co-author) Experiment Without Precedent: The New China, 1972; The Mozartian Historian, 1977; The Outsiders: Westerners in Asia, 1977; The Fading of the Maoist Vision, 1980; (co-author) The Chinese, 1986. Add: Center for Chinese Studies, Univ. of Michigan, Ann Arbor, Mich. 48109, U.S.A.

MURPHY, Dervla Mary. Irish, b. 1931. Politics, Travel/Exploration/Adventure. *Publs:* Full Tilt, 1965; Tibetan Foothold, 1966; The Waiting Land, 1967; In Ethiopia with a Mule, 1968; On a Shoestring to Coorg, 1976; Where the Indus Is Young, 1977; A Place Apart, 1978; Wheels Within Wheels, 1979; Race to the Finish?, 1981; Eight Feet in the Andes, 1983; Muddling through in Madagascar, 1985; Ireland, 1985; Tales from the Two Cities, 1987; Cameroon with Egbert, 1989. Add: The Old Market, Lismore, Co. Waterford, Ireland.

MURPHY, E. Jefferson. American, b. 1926. Area studies. Coordinator, Five Colleges Inc., Amherst, Mass., since 1975. Formerly with the Afro-American Inst., NYC, 1954–71: Exec. Vice-Pres., 1965–71; Consultant, Carnegie Corp. of New York, 1973–75. *Publs:* Understanding Africa, 1969, 1978; History of African Civilization, 1972; (with H. Stein) Teaching Africa Today, 1973; The Bantu Civilization of Southern Africa, 1974; Creative Philanthropy: Carnegie Corporation and Africa 1953–74, 1975. Add: c/o I.N. Thut World Education Center, Univ. of Connecticut, Sch. of Education, Box 4-32, Storrs, Conn. 06268, U.S.A.

MURPHY, Gordon J. American. Engineering/Technology, Information science/Computers. Prof. of Electrical Engineering and Computer Science, Northwestern Univ., Evanston, Ill., since 1960 and Dir., The Laboratory for the Design of Electronic Systems, since 1987 (Assoc. Prof., 1957–60; Chmn., Dept. of Electrical Engineering, 1960–69). Engineering consultant since 1959. Asst. Prof., Milwaukee Sch., of Engineering, 1949–51, and Univ. of Minnesota, Minneapolis, 1956–57; Project Engineer, AC Electronics Div., Gen. Motors Corp., 1951–52. *Publs:* Basic Automatic Control Theory, 1957, 1966; Control Engineering, 1959. Add: 638 Garden Ct., Glenview, Ill. 60025, U.S.A.

MURPHY, Jill (Frances). British, b. 1949. Children's fiction. Freelance writer and illustrator. Worked in a children's home for four years, and as a nanny for one year. *Publs:* The Worst Witch, 1974; The Worst Witch Strikes Again, 1980; Peace at Last, 1981; A Bad Spell for the Worst Witch, 1982; On the Way Home, 1982; Whatever Next!, 1983; Five Minutes' Peace, 1986; All in One Piece, 1987; Worlds Apart, 1988. Add: c/o A.P. Watt Ltd., 26-28 Bedford Row, London WC1R 4HL, England.

MURPHY, Richard. Irish, b. 1927. Poetry. Compton Lectr. in Poetry, Univ. of Hull, 1969; O'Connor Prof. of Literature, Colgate Univ., Hamilton, N.Y., 1971; Visiting Prof. of Poetry or Writer, Bard Coll., Annandale-on-Hudson, N.Y., 1972–74, Princeton Univ., New Jersey, 1974–75, Univ. of Iowa, Iowa City, 1976–77, Syracuse Univ., N.Y., 1977–78, Catholic Univ. of American, Washington, D.C., 1983, Pacific Lutheran Univ., Tacoma, Wash., 1985, and Wichita State Univ., Kans., 1987. *Publs:* Sailing to an Island, 1963; The Battle of Aughrim, 1968; High Island (in U.S. as High Island: New and Selected Poems), 1974; Selected Poems, 1979; The Price of Stone, 1985; The Mirror Wall, 1989. Add: Knockbrack, Glenalua Rd., Killiney, Co. Dublin, Ireland.

MURPHY, Richard Thomas. American, b. 1908. Archaeology/Antiquities, History, Theology/Religion, Translations. Member, Dominican Fathers, since 1935. Parish Priest, St. Dominic's Roman Catholic Church, New Orleans, since 1974. Prof. in Dominican houses of study, Washington, D.C., 1939–44, and River Forest, Ill., 1944–48; Prof., Aquinas Inst., Dubuque, Iowa, 1951–66, and King's and Brescia colleges,

Univ. of Western Ontario, London, 1966–74. *Publs:* (trans. with J. Della Penta) Ricciotti: History of Israel, 2 vols., 1955; (trans.) Chardon: The Cross of Jesus, 1957; The Sunday Gospels, 1960; The Sunday Epistles, 1961; The Work of Père Lagrange, 1963; (trans.) Summa Theologiae: The Passion of Christ, vol. 54, 1965; Background to the Bible, 1978; Days of Glory: The Passion, Death and Resurrection of Jesus Christ, 1980. Add: 775 Harrison Ave., New Orleans, La. 70124, U.S.A.

MURPHY, Roland Edmund. American, b. 1917. Theology/Religion. George Washington Ivey Prof. of Biblical Studies Emeritus, Duke Univ. Divinity Sch., Durham, N.C., (joined faculty as Prof. of Old Testament, 1971). Teacher, Catholic Univ. of America, Washington, D.C., 1948–70. *Publs:* Seven Books of Wisdom, 1960; The Dead Sea Scrolls and the Bible, 1966; (co-ed. and contrib.) The Jerome Biblical Commentary, 1968; (ed.) Theology, Exegesis and Proclamation, 1971; The Psalms and Job, 1978; Wisdom Literature, 1981; Wisdom Literature and Psalms: Interpreting Biblical Texts, 1983; Ecclesiastes and Song of Songs, 1987. Add: 1600 Webster St. N.E., Washington, D.C. 20017, U.S.A.

MURPHY, Shirley R(ousseau). American, b. 1928. Children's fiction. Painter and sculptor, 1954–71. *Publs:* White Ghost Summer, 1967; The Sand Ponies, 1967; Elmo Doolan and the Search for the Golden Mouse, 1970; (with P.J. Murphy) Carlos Charles, 1971; Poor Jenny Bright as a Penny, 1974; The Grass Tower, 1976; Silver Woven in My Hair, 1977; The Flight of Fox, 1978; The Pig Who Could Conjure the Wind, 1978; The Ring of Fire, 1979; Soonie and the Dragon, 1979; The Wolf Bell, 1979; Caves of Fire and Ice, 1980; The Castle of Hape, 1980; The Joining of the Stone, 1981; Tattie's River Journey, 1983; Nightpool, 1985; Valentine for a Dragon, 1986; The Ivory Lyre, 1987; The Dragonbirds, (with Welsh Suggs) Medallion of the Black Hound, 1989. Add: U.S.A.

MURPHY, Sylvia. British, b. 1937. Novels, Education. Asst. Teacher, Inner London Education Authority, 1969–74; Deputy Head Teacher, N. Devon, 1974–77; Publicity Officer, Beaford Arts Centre, N. Devon, 1977–79; Asst. Teacher, Exeter, 1979–81; Head of Careers and Social Education, Sidmouth Coll., Devon, 1981–87. *Publs:* The Complete Knowledge of Sally Fry (novel), 1984; Learning to Work Together: Journal of Moral Education, 1984; The Life and Times of Barley Beach (novel), 1987. Add: 54 Camperdown Terr., Exmouth, Devon EX8 1EQ, England.

MURPHY, Thomas. Irish, b. 1935. Plays/Screenplays. Engineering teacher, Vocational Sch., Mountbellow, 1957–62. Member, Intnl. Cttee. on English in the Liturgy, 1972–75; Member, Bd. of Directors, 1972–83, and Writer-in-Assn., 1986–88, Irish National Theatre, Abbey Theatre; Founding Member, Moli Productions, 1974; Dir. and Writer-in-Assn., Druid Theatre Co., Galway, 1983–85. *Publs:* A Whistle in the Dark, 1961; Famine, 1966; The Orphans, 1968; Epitaph under Ether, 1968; On the Outside, 1969; The Fooleen: A Crucial Week in the Life of a Grocer's Assistant, 1969; The Morning after Optimism, 1971; The Whitehouse, 1973; On the Inside, 1974; The Vicar of Wakefield (adaption), 1974; The Sanctuary Lamp, 1975; The J. Arthur Maginnis Story, 1976; The Informer (adaption), 1981; She Stoops to Conquer (adpation), 1982; The Gigli Concern, 1983; Conversations on a Homecoming, 1985; Bailegangaire, 1985; A Thief of a Christmas, 1985. Add: c/o Fraser and Dunlop, The Chambers, Chelsea Harbour, Lots Rd., London SW10 0XF, England.

MURPHY, Walter Francis. American, b. 1929. Novels/Short stories, Law, Politics/Government. McCormick Prof. of Jurisprudence, Princeton Univ., New Jersey, since 1968 (Asst. Prof., 1958–61; Assoc. Prof., 1961–65; Prof., 1965–68; Chmn. of the Dept. of Politics, 1966–69). Book Review Articles Ed., World Politics, 1972–78. *Publs:* (co-ed.) Courts, Judges, and Politics, 1961, 4th ed. 1986; Congress and the Court, 1962; Elements of Judicial Strategy, 1964; Wiretapping on Trial, 1965; (co-ed.) Modern American Democracy, 1969; (co-author) The Study of Public Law, 1972; (co-author) American Democracy, 10th ed. 1983; (co-author) Public Opinion and Constitutional Courts, 1974; Comparative Constitutional Law, 1978; The Vicar of Christ (novel), 1979; (co-ed.) Basic Cases in Constitutional Law, 1980, 1987; The Roman Enigma (novel), 1981; (co-author) American Constitutional Interpretation, 1986; Upon This Rock (novel), 1987. Add: Dept. of Politics, Princeton Univ., Princeton, N.J. 08544, U.S.A.

MURPHY, William Francis. American, b. 1906. Psychiatry. In private practice of psychoanalysis since 1946, retired in 1984. Consultant, U.S. Naval Hosp., Chelsea, Mass., since 1946, and Boston Veterans Admin. Hosp., since 1958; member of the faculty, Boston Psychoanalytic Inst., since 1955 (Instr. in Psychosomatic Medicine, 1951–56). Instr. in Psychiatry, 1946–55, Clinical Assoc., 1955–68, and Asst. Clinical Prof.

of Psychiatry 1968–74, Harvard Medical Sch.; Asst. Prof. of Psychiatry, Boston Univ. Sch. of Medicine, 1953–55. *Publs:* (with F. Deutsch) The Clinical Interview, 2 vols., 1955; The Tactics of Psychotherapy, 1965. Add: 1 Concord Rd., Lincoln, Mass. 01773, U.S.A.

MURRAY, Albert. American, b. 1916. Novels/Short stories. Instr. in Literature, Tuskegee Inst., 1940–43, 1946–51; Instr., Grad. Sch. of Journalism, Columbia Univ., NYC, 1968; O'Connor Prof. of Literature, Colgate Univ., 1970; Paul Anthony Brick Lectr., Univ. of Missouri, 1972; Writer-in-Residence, Emory Univ., 1978; Prof. of Humanities, Colgate Univ., 1982; Woodrow Wilson Fellow, Drew Univ., 1983. *Publs:* The Omni-Americans, 1970; South to a Very Old Place, 1972; The Hero and the Blues, 1973; Train Whistle Guitar, 1974; Stomping the Blues, 1976; Good Morning Blues; The Autobiography of Count Basie, 1985. Add: 45 W. 132nd St., New York, N.Y. 10037, U.S.A.

MURRAY, Beatrice. *See* **POSNER,** Richard.

MURRAY, Charles (Alan). American, b. 1943. Social policy. Sr. Research Fellow, Manhattan Inst. for Policy Research. Research Scientist, 1974–79, and Chief Scientist, 1979–81, American Insts. for Research. *Publs:* (with Louis A. Cox) Beyond Probation, 1979; Losing Ground: American Social Policy 1950-80, 1984; In Pursuit: Of Happiness and Good Government, 1988; (With Catherine Bly Cox) Apollo: The Race to the Moon, 1989. Add: Manhattan Inst. for Policy Research, 42 East 71st St., New York, N.Y. 10021, U.S.A.

MURRAY, Frances. Pseud. for Rosemary Booth, née Sutherland. British, b. 1928. Romance, Children's fiction. Principal teacher of history, Guernsey Ladies' Coll., St. Peter Port, since 1976. History teacher, Perth Academy, Scotland, 1966–72, and Linlathen High Sch., Dundee, 1972–76. *Publs:* The Dear Colleague, 1972; The Burning Lamp, 1973; Ponies on the Heather (for children), 1973; The Heroine's Sister, 1975; Ponies and Parachutes (for children), 1975; Red Rowan Berry, 1976; Castaway, 1978; White Hope (for children), 1978; Payment for the Piper (in U.S. as Brave Kingdom), 1983; The Belchamber Scandal, 1985; Shadow over the Islands, 1986. Add: c/o David Higham Assocs., 5—8 Lower John St., London W1R 4HA, England.

MURRAY, John Joseph. American, b. 1915. History, Humanities (general). Henrietta Arnold Prof. of History Emeritus, Coe Coll., Cedar Rapids, since 1982 (Henrietta Arnold Prof., 1954–82). Asst. Prof., 1946–49, and Assoc. Prof., 1946–54, Indiana Univ., Bloomington; Fulbright Research Scholar, Univ. of Leiden, The Netherlands, 1951–52; Instr. in History, Northwestern Univ., Evanston, Ill., 1954–56; Social Science Fellow to England, 1960–61; Guggenheim Fellow, 1968–69. *Publs:* (ed.) Essays in Modern European History, 1952; An Honest Diplomat at The Hague, 1956; (ed.) The Heritage of the Middle West, 1958; A Student Guidebook to English History, 1964; Amsterdam in the Age of Rembrandt, 1967; George I, the Baltic and the Whig Split, 1969; Antwerp in the Age of Plantin, 1970; The Pilgrim's Story (TV script); Christmas Through the Eyes of Washington Irving and Dickens (TV script); The Origin of Christmas Customs (TV script); Rubens 400 Years (TV script), 1977; An Olde Flemish Christmas (TV script), 1978; It Took All of Us: 100 Years, Iowa Light and Power Co., 1982; England and Flanders: The Influence of the Low Countries on Tudor-Stuart England, 1985. Add: 1508 Circa del Lago, B-211, Lake San Marcos, Calif. 92069, U.S.A.

MURRAY, Les(lie) A(llan). Australian, b. 1938. Poetry. Scientific and Technical Translator, Australian National Univ., Canberra, 1963–67; Co-Ed., Poetry Australia, 1973–80. *Publs:* (with Geoffrey Lehmann) The Ilex Tree, 1965; The Weatherboard Cathedral, 1969; Poems Against Economics, 1972; Lunch and Counter Lunch, 1974; Selected Poems: The Vernacular Republic, 1976; 1982; Ethnic Radio, 1978; The Peasant Mandarin (prose), 1978; The Boys Who Stole the Funeral, 1980; The Vernacular Republic: Poems 1961–1981, 1982; Equanimities, 1982; The People's Otherworld, 1983; Persistence in Folly, 1984; (with Peter Solness) The Australian Year, 1986; Selected Poems, 1986; The Daylight Moon and Other Poems, 1988. Add: 27 Edgar, St., Chatswood, N.S.W. 2067, Australia.

MURRAY, Linda. Novels, Art. Taught in the Extramural Dept., Univ. of London. *Publs:* (with Peter Murray) The Penguin Dictionary of Art and Artists, 1959, 6th ed. 1988; (with Peter Murray) The Art of the Renaissance, 1963; The High Renaissance and Mannerism, 1967, 1977; The Dark Fire (novel), 1977; Michelangelo, 1980; Michelangelo: His Life, Work, and Times, 1984. Add: The Old Rectory, Farnborough, Banbury OX17 1DZ, England.

MURRAY, Peter (John). British, b. 1920. Architecture, Art. Prof. of the History of Art, Birkbeck Coll., Univ. of London, 1967–80, now Emeritus. Pres., Soc. of Architectural Historians, 1969–72. *Publs:* Watteau, 1948; Index of Attributions...Before Vasari, 1959; (with Linda Murray) The Penguin Dictionary of Art and Artists, 1959, 6th ed. 1988; (with P. Kidson) History of English Architecture, 1962, 1965; (with Linda Murray) The Art of the Renaissance, 1963; The Architecture of the Italian Renaissance, 1963, 3rd ed. 1986; Renaissance Architecture, 1971; The Dulwich Picture Gallery: A Catalogue, 1980; (ed.) Jacob Burckhardt: The Architecture of the Italian Renaissance, 1985. Add: The Old Rectory, Farnborough, Banbury OX17 1DZ, England.

MURRAY, Robert Allen. American, b. 1929. Anthropology/Ethnology, Archaeology/Antiquities, History. Interpretive Planner and Historian, Western Interpretive Services. Member, National Special Advisory Panel on Historic Properties, since 1973. Consultant, ABC-TV, 1965, World Film Services Ltd., 1967–68, Learning Corp. of America, 1969, Time-Life Books, 1973, BBC-TV, 1977, and National Geographic Soc., 1978; Member, Bd. of Dirs., Council on Abandoned Military Posts, 1968–70. *Publs:* Pipestone: History, 1964; Fort Laramie's Historic Buildings: An Illustrated Guide, 1965; Military Posts in the Powder River Country of Wyoming 1865–1894, 1968; (ed.) E.S. Topping's Chronicles of the Yellowstone, 1968; Pipes on the Plains (anthropology/archaeology), 1968; The Army on Powder River, 1969; Citadel on the Santa Fe Trail, 1970; Researching the Frontier Military Posts, 1971; Miner's Delight, Investor's Despair (history), 1973; (author and ed.) Fort Laramie: Visions of a Grand Old Post, 1974; Fort Fred Steele: Desert Outpost on the Union Pacific, 1974; Military Posts of Wyoming, 1974, 1975; Johnson County, Wyoming: 175 Years of History at the Foot of the Big Horn Mountains, 1981; The Army Moves West, 1981; The Bozeman Trail: Highway of History, 1988. Add: P.O. Box 6467, Sheridan, Wyo. 82801, U.S.A.

MURRAY, Rona. Canadian, b. 1924. Short Stories, Poetry, Plays. Special Instr., Univ. of Victoria, 1961–62; Head of the English Dept., Rockland Sch., Victoria, 1962–63; Teaching Asst./Lectr., Univ. of British Columbia, 1963–66; Assoc. Lectr., Selkirk Coll., Castlegar, B.C., 1968–74; Instr., Douglas Coll., Surrey, B.C., 1974–76; Visiting Lectr. in Creative Writing, 1977–79, and in English, 1981–83, Univ. of Victoria. *Publs:* The Enchanted Adder, 1965; The Power of the Dog and Other Poems, 1968; Oootischenie, 1974; Selected Poems, 1974; The Art of the Earth (anthology), 1979; From an Autumn Journal, 1980; Journey, 1981; Adam and Eve in Middle Age, 1984; The Indigo Dress and Other Stories, 1986; also, the plays, Blue Ducks' Feather and Eagledown, produced 1958; One, Two, Three Alary, produced 1970; and Creatures, produced 1980. Add: 3825 Duke Rd., R.R. 1, Victoria, B.C. V8X 3W9, Canada.

MURRAY, William Hutchison. British, b. 1913. Novels/Short stories, Natural history, Recreation/Leisure/Hobbies, Travel/Exploration/Adventure. Member, Countryside Commn. for Scotland, Perth, 1968–80. *Publs:* Mountaineering in Scotland, 1947; Undiscovered Scotland, 1951; Scottish Himalayan Expedition, 1951; The Story of Everest, 1953; Five Frontiers (in U.S. as Appointment in Tibet), 1959; The Spurs of Troodos, 1960; Maelstrom, 1962; Highland Landscape, 1962; Dark Rose the Phoenix, 1965; The Hebrides, 1966; The West Highlands of Scotland, 1968; The Real MacKay, 1969; The Islands of Western Scotland, 1973; The Scottish Highlands, 1976; The Curling Companion, 1981; Rob Roy MacGregor, 1982; Scotland's Mountains, 1987. Add: Lochwood, Loch Goil, Argyll, Scotland.

MURRAY-SMITH, Stephen. Australian, b. 1922. History, Literature, Biography. Reader in Education, Univ. of Melbourne, since 1975 (Nuffield Research Fellow, 1961–65; Lectr. in Education, 1966–74). Ed., Overland, since 1954. National Organising Secty., Australian Peace Council, 1952–58; Ed. and Research Officer, Victoria Teachers' Union, 1958–61; Ed., Melbourne Studies in Education, 1973–82; Chmn., Natl. Book Council, 1981–83. *Publs:* (ed.) The Tracks We Travel, 1953; Henry Lawson, 1963, 1975; (ed.) An Overland Muster, 1965; (ed.) His Natural Life, by Marcus Clarke, 1970; (ed. with Judah Waten) Classic Australian Short Stories, 1974; Mission to the Islands, 1979; Indirections, 1981; (ed.) The Dictionary of Australian Quotations, 1984; (with A.J. Dane) The Tech, 1986; Right Words, 1986. Add: Ti-tree Lane, Mt. Eliza, Vic. 3930, Australia.

MURRELL, John. Canadian, b. 1945. Plays. Schoolteacher; assoc. dir., Stratford Festival, Ont., 1978. *Publs:* Metamorphosis, 1970; Memoir, 1978; Uncle Vanya (adaptation), 1978; Watching for the Parade, 1980; New World, Farther West, 1985. Add: c/o Talonbooks, 201-1019 E. Cordova, Vancouver, B.C. V6A 1M8, Canada.

MURRY, Colin Middleton. Also writes as Richard Cowper. British, b. 1926. Novels/Short stories, Science fiction/Fantasy. Head of the English Dept., Whittingehame Coll., Brighton, Sussex, 1960–67, and Atlantic Coll., Glamorgan, Wales, 1967–70. *Publs:* The Golden Valley, 1958; Recollections of a Ghost, 1960; A Path to the Sea, 1961; Taj Mahal by Candlelight (play), 1966; Private View, 1972; One Hand Clapping, 1975; I at the Keyhole, 1975; Shadows on the Grass, 1977; as Richard Cowper—Breakthrough, 1967; Phoenix, 1968; Domino, 1970; Kuldesak, 1972; Clone, 1972; Time Out of Mind, 1973; The Twilight of Briareus, 1973; Worlds Apart, 1974; The Custodians, 1976; The Road to Corlay, 1978; Profundis, 1979; The Web of the Magi, 1980; A Dream of Kinship, 1981; A Tapestry of Time, 1982; The Tithonian Factor, 1984; Shades of Darkness, 1986. Add: Landscott, Lower St., Dittisham, nr. Dartmouth, Devon, England.

MUSAPHIA, Joseph. New Zealander, b. 1935. Plays/Screenplays. Columnist, The Dominion, and The Sunday Times, Wellington, since 1974; freelance radio and television writer. Shop Asst., Ballintyne's, Christchurch, 1950–51; Motor Mechanic, David Crozier's, Christchurch, 1951–54; Commercial Artist, Stuart Wearn, Christchurch, 1954–55, Wood and Braddock, Wellington, 1955, John Haddon, London, England, 1956–57, and for agencies in Wellington, 1958–60; Cartoonist, The New Zealand Listener, Wellington, 1958–60; fish and chip shop owner, Wellington, 1971–73; Writers Fellow, Victoria Univ. of Wellington, 1979. *Publs:* The Guerrilla, 1976; Mothers and Fathers, 1978; Shotgun Wedding, 1981. Add: 75 Monro St., Wellington 3, New Zealand.

MUSE, Benjamin. American, b. 1898. History, Race relations. In the U.S. Diplomatic Service, 1920–34; Virginia State Senator, 1936; Member, President's Cttee. on Equal Opportunity in the Armed Forces, 1962–64. *Publs:* Virginia's Massive Resistance, 1961; Tarheel Tommy Atkins, 1963; Ten Years of Prelude, 1964; The American Negro Revolution, 1968; The Twentieth Century as I Saw It, 1982. Add: Heron House, Reston, Va. 22090, U.S.A.

MUSGRAVE, Susan. Canadian, b. 1951. Novels, Children's fiction, Poetry. Writer-in-Residence, Univ. of Waterloo, Ont., 1983–85. *Publs:* Songs of the Sea-Witch, 1970; Mindscapes, 1971; Entrance of the Celebrant, 1973; Grave-Dirt and Selected Strawberries, 1973; Gullband, 1974; The Impstone, 1976; (with Sean Virgo) Kistkatinaw Songs, 1977; Selected Strawberries and Other Poems, 1977; Becky Swan's Book, 1978; A Man to Marry, A Man to Bury, 1978; The Charcoal Burner (novel), 1980; Hag Head (for children), 1981; Tarts and Muggers: Poems New and Selected, 1982; Cocktails at the Mausoleum, 1985; The Dancing Chicken (novel), 1987. Add: Box 2421, Sidney, B.C. V8L 3Y3, Canada.

MUSGROVE, Frank. British, b. 1922. Education, Sociology. Sarah Fielden Prof. of Education, Univ. of Manchester, 1970–82, now Emeritus (Ed., Research in Education, 1971–76; Dean, Faculty of Education, 1976–78). Prof. of Research in Education, Univ. of Bradford, 1965–70. *Publs:* The Migratory Elite, 1963; Youth and the Social Order, 1964; The Family, Education and Society, 1966; (with P.H. Taylor) Society and the Teacher's Role, 1969; Patterns of Power and Authority in English Education, 1971; Ecstasy and Holiness, 1974; Margins of the Mind, 1977; School and the Social Order, 1979; Education and Anthropology, 1982. Add: Dibscar, The Cedar Grove, Beverley, N. Humberside HU17 7EP, England.

MUSIKER, Reuben. South African, b. 1931. Librarianship. Univ. Librarian and Prof. of Librarianship since 1975, Univ. of the Witwatersrand, Johannesburg. Deputy Univ. Librarian, Rhodes Univ., Grahamstown, 1962–72. *Publs:* South African Bibliography, 1970, 1980; Special Libraries, 1970; Guide to South African Reference Books, 1971; Guide to Cape of Good Hope Official Publications 1854–1910, 1976; South Africa (bibliography), 1979; Companion to South African Libraries, 1986. Add: The Library, Univ. of the Witwatersrand, Jan Smuts Ave., Johannesburg 2001, South Africa.

MUSOLF, Lloyd D(aryl). American, b. 1919. Administration/Management, Politics/Government, Public/Social administration. Prof. Emeritus of Political Science, Univ. of California at Davis, since 1987 (Prof. 1963–87). Instr., 1949–50, Asst. Prof., 1950–55, and Assoc. Prof., 1955–59, Vassar Coll., Poughkeepsie, N.Y.; Assoc. Prof., 1959–61, and Prof., 1961–63, Michigan State Univ., East Lansing. *Publs:* Federal Examiners and the Conflict of Law and Administration, 1953; Public Ownership and Accountability: The Canadian Experience, 1959; (co-ed.) The Politics of Regulation, 1964; Promoting the General Welfare: Government and the Economy, 1965; (ed.) Communication Satellites in Political Orbit, 1968; (co-ed. and contrib.) Legislatures in Developmental Perspective, 1970;

(co-author) American National Government: Policies and Politics, 1971; Mixed Enterprise: A Developmental Perspective, 1972; Legislatures, Environment Protection, Development Goals: British Columbia and California, 1975; (co-author) Malaysia's Parliamentary System, 1979; (co-ed. and contrib.) Legislatures in Development: Dynamics of Change in New and Old States, 1979; Uncle Sam's Private, Profitseeking Corporations: Comsat, Fannie Mae, Amtrak, and Conrail, 1982. Add: 844 Lake Blvd., Davis, Calif. 95616, U.S.A.

MUSSER, Joe. American, b. 1936. Novels/Short stories, Plays/Screenplays. Pres., Four Most Productions Inc., Wheaton, Ill., since 1973 (Dir. of Creative Services, 1966–73). *Publs:* The Centurian (radio play), 1963; Dawn at Checkpoint Alpha (radio play), 1966; Behold, a Pale Horse, 1970; (co-author) Doctor in a Strange Land, 1968; Road to Spain (screenplay), 1971; The Rapture (screenplay), 1972; (with Joni Eareckson) Joni, 1976; Josh, 1981; The Coming World Earthquake, 1982; A Skeptic's Quest, 1984. Add: c/o Tyndale House, 336 Gundersen Drive, Wheaton, Ill. 60187, U.S.A.

MUSSEY, Virginia T.H. *See* **ELLISON,** Virginia Howel.

MUSTO, Barry. Also writes as Robert Simon. British, b. 1930. Novels/ Short stories. *Publs:* The Lawrence Barclay File, 1969; Storm Centre, 1970; (as Robert Simon) The Sunless Land; The Fatal Flaw, 1974; Code Name, Bastille; No Way Out; The Weighted Scales; The Lebanese Partner, 1984. Add: Thistles, Little Addington, Kettering, Northants., England.

MUTH, Richard F(erris). American, b. 1927. Economics, Urban studies. Fuller E. Callaway Prof. and Chair, Dept. of Economics, Emory Univ., Atlanta, since 1983. Assoc. Prof., Grad. Sch. of Business, Univ. of Chicago, 1959–64; Economist, Inst. for Defense Analyses, Washington, D.C., 1964–66; Prof. of Economics, Washington Univ., St. Louis, 1966–70, and Stanford Univ., Calif., 1970–83. *Publs:* (with H.S. Perloff, E.S. Dunn and E. Lampard) Regions, Resources and Economic Growth, 1960; Cities and Housing, 1969; Urban Economic Problems, 1974. Add: Dept. of Economics, Emory Univ., Atlanta, Ga. 30322, U.S.A.

MUUSS, Rolf Eduard. German, b. 1924. Education, Psychology. Prof. of Education since 1964, and Dir. of the Special Education Prog. since 1977, Goucher Coll., Towson, Md. (Assoc. Prof. of Education and Child Development, 1959–64); Elizabeth C. Todd Distinguished Prof., 1980–84; Chmn., Dept. of Sociology and Anthropology, 1980–83). Teaching Assoc., Sheppard and Enoch Pratt Hosp., Towson, since 1969. Research Asst. Prof., Child Welfare Research Station, Univ. of Iowa, Iowa City, 1957–59; Research Assoc. in Education, Johns Hopkins Univ., Baltimore, 1962–63. *Publs:* First Aid for Classroom Discipline Problems, 1962; Theories of Adolescence, 1962, 4th ed. 1982; Adolescent Behavior and Society: A Book of Readings, 1971, 3rd ed. 1980; Grundlagen der Jugendpsychologie, 1982. Add: Dept. of Education, Goucher Coll., Towson, Md. 21204, U.S.A.

MYERS, Elisabeth P. American, b. 1918. Children's non-fiction, Biography. *Publs:* Katharine Lee Bates, 1961; F.W. Woolworth, 1962; George Pullman, 1963; Singer of Six Thousand Songs, 1965; America's Prima Ballerina, 1966; Edward Bok, 1967; Jenny Lind, 1968; Angel of Appalachia, 1968; Rutherford B. Hayes, 1969; Benjamin Harrison, 1969; South America's Yankee Genius, 1969; Frederick Douglass, 1970; Langston Hughes: Poet of His People, 1970; William Howard Taft, 1970; Andrew Jackson, 1970; Mary Cassatt, 1971; Madam Secretary, 1972; David Sarnoff, 1972; John D. Rockefeller, 1973; Pearl Buck, 1974; Thomas Paine, 1976. Add: 1165 E. Regency Dr., Bloomington, Ind. 47401, U.S.A.

MYERS, Jack (Elliott). American, b. 1941. Poetry. Prof. of English, Southern Methodist Univ., Dallas, since 1975. *Publs:* Black Sun Abraxas, 1970; (co-author) Will It Burn, 1974; The Family War, 1977; I'm Amazed That You're Still Singing, 1981; (ed.) A Trout in Milk, 1982; (ed. with Roger Weingarten) New American Poets of the 80s, 1984; Coming to the Surface, 1984; (ed. with Michael Simms) The Longman Dictionary and Handbook of Poetry, 1985; As Long As You're Happy, 1986. Add: Dept. of English, southern Methodist Univ., Dallas, Tex. 75275, U.S.A.

MYERS, Jacob M(artin). American, b. 1904. Theology/Religion. Prof. of Old Testament, Lutheran Theological Seminary, Gettysburg, since 1942 (Lectr. in New Testament, 1937–40; Instr. in Old Testament, 1940–42). Pastor, Grace Lutheran Parish, Gettysburg, 1930–50. *Publs:* Linguistic and Literary Form of the Book of Ruth, 1955; The Layman's Bible Commentary: Hosea to Jonah, 1959; Anchor Bible: I Chronicles, II

Chronicles, and Ezra-Nehemiah, all 1965; Invitation to the Old Testament, 1966; The World of the Restoration, 1968; Anchor Apocrypha: I-II Esdras, 1974; Grace and Torah, 1975. Add: 141 Seminary Ave., Gettysburg, Pa. 17325, U.S.A.

MYERS, John Myers. American, b. 1906. Novels/Short stories, Westerns/Adventure, Poetry, History, Essays. Freelance writer. Former advertising copywriter, newspaperman, and farmer. Assembled Western Americana collection for Arizona State Univ. Library, Tempe. *Publs:* The Harp and the Blade (novel), 1941; Out on Any Limb (novel), 1942; The Wild Yazoo (novel), 1947; The Alamo, 1948; Silverlock (novel), 1949; The Last Chance: Tombstone's Early Years, 1950; Doc Holliday, 1955; Dead Warrior (novel), 1956; I, Jack Swilling, Founder of Phoenix, Arizona (novel), 1961; Maverick Zone (verse tales), 1961; The Deaths of the Bravos, 1962; (ed.) Building a State in Apache Land, 1963; Pirate, Pawnee, and Mountain Man: The Saga of Hugh Glass, 1963, as The Saga of Hugh Glass, 1976; San Francisco's Reign of Terror, 1966; The Chaparral Cock (poetry), 1967–68; Print in a Wild Land, 1967; (ed.) The Westerners: A Roundup of Pioneer Reminiscences, 1969; The Border Wardens, 1971; The Moon's Fire-Eating Daughter (novel), 1980. Add: 6515 E. Hermonsa Vista Dr., Mesa, Ariz. 85205, U.S.A.

MYERS, Paul. British, b. 1932. Mystery/Crime/Suspense. Classical Production Mgr., Decca Intnl., London, since 1980. Album Annotator and Producer, Kapp Records, NYC, 1959–62; Artists and Repertoire Dept., CBS Masterworks, NYC, 1962–68 (Vice-Pres. in London, 1974–80). *Publs:* (with Ned Sherrin) A Night on the Town, 1984; Deadly Variations, 1985; Deadly Cadenza, 1986; Deadly Aria, 1987; Deadly Sonata, 1987. Add: 23 Chandos Rd., London N2 9AR, England.

MYERS, Robert Manson. American, b. 1921. Novels/Short stories, Literature, Music. Prof. of English, Emeritus, Univ. of Maryland, College Park, since 1986 (Asst. Prof., 1959–63; Assoc. Prof., 1963–68; Prof., 1968–86). Instr. in English, Yale Univ., New Haven, Conn., 1945–47; Asst. Prof. of English, Tulane Univ., New Orleans, 1948–53. *Publs:* Handel's Messiah: A Touchstone of Taste, 1948; From Beowulf to Virginia Woolf, 1952; Handel, Dryden and Milton, 1956; Restoration Comedy, 1961; The Children of Pride (novel), 1972; A Georgian at Princeton, 1976.

Add: Dept. of English, Univ. of Maryland, College Park, Md. 20742, U.S.A.

MYERS, Walter Dean. Has also written as Walter M. Myers. American, b. 1937. Children's fiction, Business (vocational guidance). Free-lance Writer since 1977. Employment Supervisor, New York State Dept. of Labor, Brooklyn, 1966–69; Senior Ed., Bobbs Merrill Publishers, NYC, 1970–77; teacher of creative writing and Black history, NYC, 1974–75. *Publs:* children's fiction—(as Walter M. Myers) Where Does the Day Go?, 1969; The Dragon Takes a Wife, 1972; Fly, Jimmy, Fly!, 1974; Fast Sam, Cool Clyde, and Stuff, 1975; Brainstorm, 1977; Mojo and the Russians, 1977; Victory for Jamie, 1977; It Ain't All for Nothin', 1978; The Young Landlords, 1979; The Black Pearl and the Ghost, 1980; The Golden Serpent, 1980; Hoops, 1981; The Legend of Tarik, 1981; Won't Know Till I Get There, 1982; The Nicholas Factor, 1983; Tales of a Dead King, 1983; Motown and Didi: A Love Story, 1984; Mr. Monkey and the Gotcha Bird, 1984; The Outside Shot, 1984; Adventure in Granada, 1985; The Hidden Shrine, 1985; Duel in the Desert, 1986; Ambush in the Amazon, 1986; Crystal, 1987; Shadow of the Red Moon, 1987; Sweet Illusions, 1987; Fallen Angles, 1988; Me, Mop, and the Moondance Kid, 1988; Scorpions, 1988; other—The World of Work: A Guide to Choosing a Career, 1975; Social Welfare: A First Book, 1976. Add: 2543 Kennedy Blvd., Jersey City, N.J. 07304, U.S.A.

MYERS, Walter M. *See* **MYERS,** Walter Dean.

MYLES, Symon. *See* **FOLLETT,** Ken.

MYRICK, David. American. History. Staff Member, 1944–73, and Asst. to the Vice-Pres., 1973–77, Treasury Dept., Southern Pacific Transportation Co. Ed. and Publr., Telegraph Hill Bulletin, San Francisco, 1956–60; Vice-Pres. and Dir., The Dakota Farmer Co., 1961–67. *Publs:* Railroads of Nevada and Eastern California, vol. I, 1962, vol. II, 1963; New Mexico's Railroads: A Historical Survey, 1970; San Francisco's Telegraph Hill, 1972; Rails Around the Bohemian Grove, 1973; Railroads of Arizona, vol. I, 1975, vol. II, 1980; Montecito and Santa Barbara, 1988. Add: c/o Interurban Press, P.O. Box 6444, Glendale, Calif. 91205, U.S.A.

N

NABOKOV, Peter (Francis). Has also written as Peter Towne. American, b. 1940. Architecture, Children's non-fiction, History, Race relations, Biography. Staff reporter, New Mexican newspaper, Santa Fe, N.M., 1967–68; Instr. in American Indian Studies, Monterey Penisula Coll., California, 1970–73, 1977–1978; Research Assoc., Human Resources Research Organization, Carmel, Calif., 1972–75; Instr., Univ. of Californian, Berkeley, 1979, 1982. *Publs:* Two Leggings: The Making of a Crow Warrior, 1967; Tijerina and the Courthouse Raid, 1970; (as Peter Towne) George Washington Carver, 1975; (ed.) Native American Testimony: An Anthology of Indian and White Relations: First Encounter to Dispossession, 1978; Indian Running, 1981; Architecture of Acoma Pueblo: The 1934 Historic American Buildings Survey Project, 1986; India Running: Native American History and Tradition, 1987; (with Robert Easton) Native American Architecture, 1988. Add: c/o Oxford Univ. Press, 200 Madison Ave., New York, N.Y. 10016, U.S.A.

NADER, G(eorge) A(lbert). Canadian, b. 1940. Geography, Urban studies. Prof. of Geography, Trent Univ., Peterborough, since 1970. Asst. Prof. of Geography, Univ. of Saskatchewan, Saskatoon, 1967–70. *Publs:* Cities of Canada, vol. I, Theoretical, Historical and Planning Perspectives, 1975, and vol. II, Profiles of Fifteen Metropolitan Centres, 1976. Add: Dept. of Geography, Trent Univ., Peterborough, Ont. K9J 7B8, Canada.

NADER, Ralph. American, b. 1934. Social commentary/phenomena. Lawyer: has practiced law in Hartford, Conn., since 1959; consumer protection activist. Lectr. in History and Govt., Univ. of Hartford, 1961–63; Lectr., Princeton Univ., New Jersey, 1967–68. *Publs:* Unsafe at Any Speed: the Designed-In Dangers of the American Automobile, 1965, 1972; (ed.) The Consumer and Corporate Accountability, 1973; (co-ed.) Taming the Giant Corporation, 1976; (ed.) Who's Poisoning America, 1981; (co-ed.) Eating Clean: Food Safety and the Chemical Harvest, 1982; (with W. Taylor) The Big Boys: Styles of Corporate Power, 1986; Nader on Australia, 1986. Add: P.O. Box 19367, Washington, D.C. 20036, U.S.A.

NAGEL, Paul C. American, b. 1926. History. Distinguished Lee Scholar, R.E. Lee Memorial Foundn., since 1986. Prof. of History, 1964–69, and Dean, Coll. of Arts and Sciences, 1965–69, Univ. of Kentucky, Lexington; Prof. of History, 1969–78, and Vice-Pres. for Academic Affairs, 1970–74, Univ. of Missouri, Columbia; Prof. of History and Head of Dept., Univ. of Georgia, Athens, 1978–81; Dir., Virginia Historical Soc., 1981–85. *Publs:* One Nation Indivisible: The Union in American Thought 1776–1861, 1964; This Sacred Trust: American Nationality 1798–1898, 1971; Missouri: A History, 1977; Descent from Glory: Four Generations of the John Adams Family, 1983; (co-author) Extraordinary Lives: The Art and Craft of American Biography, 1986; The Adams Women, 1987; (co-author) George Caleb Bingham, 1989. Add: 612 W. Franklin, Apt. 8-B, Richmond, Va. 23220, U.S.A.

NAGEL, Stuart. American, b. 1934. Civil liberties/Human rights, Law, Politics/Government, Public/Social administration. Prof. of Political Science, Univ. of Illinois, Urbana, since 1969 (Asst. Prof., 1962–65; Assoc. Prof., 1966–68). Fellow, Center for Advanced Study in the Behavioral Sciences, Palo Alto, Calif., 1964–65; Sr. Scholar, East-West Center, Honolulu, 1965; Asst. Counsel, U.S. Senate Subcttee. on Admin. Practice and Procedure, 1966; Russell Sage Fellow in Law and Social Science, Yale Law Sch., New Haven, Conn., 1970–71; Visiting Fellow, National Inst. for Law Enforcement and Criminal Justice, U.S. Dept. of Justice, 1974–75. *Publs:* The Legal Process from a Behavioral Perspective, 1969; (ed.) The Rights of the Accused in the Law and Action, 1972;

(ed.) Law and Social Change, 1973; (ed.) Environmental Politics, 1974; Improving the Legal Process: Effects of Alternatives, 1975; (ed.) Policy Studies in America and Elsewhere, 1975; (ed.) Policy Studies and the Social Sciences, 1975; (ed.) Modeling the Criminal Justice System, 1977; (with others) Legal Policy Analysis: Finding an Optimum Level or Mix, 1977; (with others) The Legal Process: Modeling the System, 1977; (ed.) Policy Studies Review Annual, 1977; (with others) Policy Analysis and Social Science Research, 1979; (with others) Decision Theory and the Legal Process, 1979; (ed.) Improving Policy Analysis, 1980; (ed.) Policy Studies Handbook, 1980; Policy Evaluation: Making Optimum Decisions, 1982; (ed.) The Political Science of Criminal Justice, 1982; (ed.) Encyclopedia of Policy Studies, 1982; (ed.) The Policy Studies Field: Its Basic Literature, 1984; (ed.) Productivity and Public Policy, 1984; Contemporary Public Policy Analysis, 1984; Public Policy: Goals, Means and Methods, 1984; Public Policy Analysis and Management, 1986; Causation, Production, and Legal Analysis, 1986; Law Policy and Optimizing Analysis, 1986; (ed.) Law and Policy Studies, 1987; Microcomputers as Decision Aids in Law Practice, 1987; Higher Coals for America: Doing Better than the Best, 1988; Policy Studies: Integration and Evaluation, 1988, (ed.) Law and Policy Studies, 1988. Add: 361 Lincoln Hall, Political Science Dept., Univ. of Illinois, Urbana, Ill. 61801, U.S.A.

NAHA, Ed. Also writes as D.B. Drumm and Michael McGann. American, b. 1950. Mystery, Science Fiction/Fantasy, Film, Music. East Coast Publicity Mgr., 1972–75, and Assoc. Producer of East coast Artists and Repertory, 1975–77, CBS Records, NYC; Columnist, Starlog, NYC; 1977–84, New York Post, 1980–87, and Heavy Metal, 1983–86. *Publs:* science fiction/fantasy—Wanted (short stories), 1980; The Paradise Plot (novel), 1980; The Suicide Plague (novel), 1982; (as D.B. Drumm) First, You Fight (novel), 1984; (as D.B. Drumm) The Road Ghost (novel), 1985; (as D.B. Drumm) The Stalking Time (novel), 1986; (as D.B. Drumm) Hell on Earth (novel), 1986; (as D.B. Drumm) The Children's Crusade (novel), 1987; Robo-Cop (novelization), 1987; (as D.B. Drumm) The Prey (novel), 1987; (as D.B. Drumm) Ghost Dancers, 1988; Breakdown (fantasy novel), 1988; (as Michael McGann) The Marauders (novel), 1988; (as Michael McGann) Blood Kin (novel), 1989; Ghostbusters II (novelization), 1989; Orphans (fantasy novel), 1989; Mystery novel—The Con Game (novel) 1986; On Edge (novel), 1989; Dead Bang (noveliation), 1989; Razzle-Dazzle (novel), 1990. other—Horrors: From Screen to Scream, 1975; Science Fiction Aliens (for children), 1977; Lillian Roxon's Rock Encyclopedia, 1978; The Rock Encyclopedia, 1978; The Science Fictionary: An A-Z Guide to the World of SF Authors, Films, and TV Shows, 1980; The Films of Roger Corman: Brilliance on a Budget, 1982; The Making of "Dune," 1984. Add: c/o Harvey Klinger Agency, 301 W. 53rd St., New York, N.Y. 10019, U.S.A.

NAHAL, Chaman. Indian, b. 1927. Novels/Short stories, Literature, Philosophy. Member, Dept. of English, Delhi Univ., since 1963. Columnist, Talking about Books, The Indian Express newspaper, 1966–73; Assoc. Prof. of English, Long Island Univ., New York, 1968–70. *Publs:* The Weird Dance (short stories), 1965; A Conversation with J. Krishnamurti, 1965; D.H. Lawrence: An Eastern View, 1970; (ed.) Drugs and the Other Self; 1971; The Narrative Pattern in Ernest Hemingway's Fiction, 1971; My True Faces (novel), 1973; Azadi (novel), 1975; Into Another Dawn (novel), 1977; The English Queens (novel), 1979; The Crown and the Loincloth (novel), 1982; The New Literatures in English, 1985; The Bhagavad-Gita: A New Rendering, 1987; Sunrise in Fiji (novel), 1988. Add: 2/1 Kalkaji Extension, New Delhi 110019, India.

NAHAS, Gabriel G(eorges). French, b. 1920. Biology, Medicine/Health, Sociology. Research Prof. of Anesthesiology, Columbia Univ. Coll. of Physicians and Surgeons, NYC, since 1962 (Assoc. Prof. and Dir. of Research, 1959–62). Consultant, United Nations Commission on Narcotics; Attending Anesthesiologist, Presbyterian Hosp., NYC, since 1967; Adjunct Prof., Inst. d'Anesthesiologie, Univ. de Paris Faculte de Medecine, since 1968. Dir. of Research, INSERM, Paris, since 1973. *Publs:* (ed.) In Vitro and in Vivo: Effects of Amine Buffers, 1961; (ed.) Regulation of Respiration, 1963; (ed. with D.V. Bates) Respiratory Failure, 1965; (ed.) Current Concepts of Acid-Base Measurement, 1966; (ed. with C.F. Fox) Body Fluid Replacement, 1970; Marihuana: Deceptive Weed, 1973; (ed. with H. Peters) Hashish and Mental Illness, by J.J. Moreau, 1973; (ed. with K. Schaefer) Carbon Dioxide and Metabolic Regulations, 1974; Keep Off the Grass, 1976, 1985; (ed. with W.D.M. Paton) Marihuana: Chemistry, Biochemistry and Cellular Effects, 1976; Hashish, Cannabis, Marijuana, 1976; Histoire d'H, 1977, (ed. with W.D.M. Paton) Cannabis: Biological effects, 1979; (ed. with H. Brill) Drug Abuse in the Modern World: A Perspective for the Eighties, 1980; (ed.) Drogue et Civilisation, 1982; Histoire du Hash, 1983; La Filière du Rail, 1983; Marihuana in Science and Medicine, 1984; Une Epidémie d'amour, 1985; Les Guerres de la Cocaine, 1987; Abrégé de Toxicomanie, 1988; America's Great White Plague, 1989. Add: Columbia Univ. Coll. of Physicians and Surgeons, 630 W. 168th St., New York, N.Y. 10032, U.S.A.

NAHM, Milton C. American, b. 1903. Art, Philosophy, Autobiography/Memoirs/Personal. Prof. Emeritus, Bryn Mawr Coll., Pennsylvania, since 1972 (Member, Philosophy Dept., 1930–46; Prof. and Chmn. of Dept., 1946–72; Leslie Clark Prof. in the Humanities, 1970–72). Sr. Fellow, National Endowment for the Humanities, 1972–73. *Publs:* (ed. and contrib.) Selections from Early Greek Philosophy, 1934, 4th ed. 1964; (ed.) John Wilson's The Cheats, 1935; (ed. with F.P. Clarke) Philosophical Essays in Honor of Edgar A. Singer, Jr., 1942; Aesthetic Experience and Its Presuppositions, 1946; (ed.) Aristotle's On the Art of Poetry and Music, 1948, 1956; (ed. with L. Strauss) Philosophical Essays, by Isaac Husik, 1952; The Artist as Creator, 1956, reprinted as Genius and Creativity, 1965; Las Vegas and Uncle Joe: The New Mexico I Remember, 1964; (ed. and contrib.) Readings in Philosophy of Art and Aesthetics, 1975. Add: 1102 Old Gulph Rd., Rosemont, Pa. 19010, U.S.A.

NAIDEN, James. American, b. 1943. Poetry, Literature, Plays. Ed., The North Stone Review/Tendon Press, since 1971; Poetry Critic, Minneapolis Star and Tribune, 1970–85; news reporter, KFAI-FM, Minneapolis. *Publs:* The Orange Notebook, 1973; Asphyxiations/1-40, 1986. *Publs:* c/o The North Stone Review, D Station, Box 14098, Minneapolis, Minn. 55414, U.S.A.

NAIPAUL, V(idiadhar) S(urajprasad). British, b. 1932. Novels/Short stories, History, Social commentary/phenomena, Autobiography/Memoirs/Personal. Freelance writer. Ed., Caribbean Voices, BBC, London, 1954–56; Reviewer, New Statesman, London, 1957–61. *Publs:* The Mystic Masseur, 1957; The Suffrage of Elvira, 1958; Miguel Street, 1959; A House for Mr. Biswas, 1961; The Middle Passage: Impressions of Five Societies—British, French and Dutch—in the West Indies and South America, 1962; Mr. Stone and the Knights Companion, 1963; An Area of Darkness: An Experience of India, 1964; A Flag on the Island, 1967; The Mimic Men, 1967; The Loss of El Dorado: A History, 1969; In a Free State, 1971; The Overcrowded Barracoon: Selected Articles 1958–1972, 1972; Guerrillas, 1975; India: A Wounded Civilization, 1977; A Bend in the River, 1979; The Return of Eva Peron, 1980; Among the Believers: An Islamic Journey, 1981; Finding the Centre: Two Narratives, 1984; The Enigma of Arrival, 1987; A Turn in the South, 1989. Add: c/o Aitken and Stone Ltd., 29 Fernshaw Rd., London SW10 0TG, England.

NAISBITT, John. American, b. 1929. Business, Social commentary. Pres., Naisbitt Group, Washington, D.C., since 1982 (periodicals include Trend Report, Bellwether Report, John Naisbitt's Trend Letter; also the Year Ahead annual). Gov.-at-Large, National Assn. of Security Dealers; Dir., CRS/Sirrine architecture/engineering Group, Houston. Special Asst. to U.S. Commnr. of Education, then Aide to Secty. of U.S. Dept. of Health, Education, and Welfare, also for a time Special Asst. to Pres. Lyndon B. Johnson, mid-1960s; Asst. to the Pres., Science Research Assocs., c.1966–68; Pres., Urban Research Corp., Chicago, 1968–c.1975 (periodicals include NewsBank, Urban Crisis Monitor, Urban Reporter, and Trend Report); established Center for Policy Research, Washington, D.C., c. 1975. *Publs:* (with Maryl Levine) Right On! A Documentary on Student Protest, 1970; Megatrends: Ten New Directions Transforming Our Lives, 1982; (with Patricia Aburdine) Reinventing the Corporation: Transforming Your Job and Your Company for the New Information Society, 1985. Add: Naisbitt Group, Suite 301, 1101 30th St. N.W., Washington, D.C. 20007, U.S.A.

NAJARIAN, Peter. American. Novels/Short stories, Poetry. *Publs:* Voyages, 1971; Wash Me on Home, Mama, 1978; Daughters of Memory, 1986. Add: c/o Ararat Press, 585 Saddle River Rd., Saddle Brook, N.J. 07662, U.S.A.

NAKAYAMA, Shigeru. Japanese, b. 1928. Astronomy, Sciences, Translations. Prof. Kanagawa Univ. Editorial Consultant, Dictionary of Scientific Biography, Charles Scribners' Sons, NYC, since 1967; Advisory Ed., Journal for the History of Astronomy, since 1970, and Fundamenta Scientiae, since 1980, and the Scientists, since 1987. Ed., Heibonsha, 1951–55. *Publs:* (trans.) Modern Scientific Readers, 1955; (trans.) Mathematics in Western Culture, by M. Kline, 1956, 1962; (ed. with W. Yuasa) Chronology of Modern Science and Technology, 1961; (trans.) Origin of the Earth, by Smart, 1962; Astrology, 1964; (co-ed.) Earth and Space Sciences, 1965; (trans.) Science and Nation, by Dupre and Lakoff, 1965; (with W. Sugimoto) History of Science, 1967; (ed.) International Relations (history of science), 1968; History of Japanese Astronomy, 1969; (ed. with W. Hirose) Modern Scientific Thought, 1971; (trans.) Structure of Scientific Revolution, by Kuhn, 1971; (trans.) Cosmology, by Charon, 1971; (ed. with W. Hirose) Western Learning (history of science), 1972; (trans.) Science and Change, by Kearney, 1972; Japanese Astronomy, 1972; (ed. with W. Sivin) Chinese Science, 1973; (ed. with W. Swain and Yagi) Science and Society in Modern Japan, 1974; Academic Traditions, 1974; Japanese Views of Science, 1977; Characteristics of Scientific Development in Japan, 1977; Hideyo Noguchi, 1978; The Birth of the Imperial University, 1978; Environmentalist's Cosmology, 1980; The View of Science at the Crossroad, 1980; Contemporary History of Science and Society, 1981; (ed.) The History of Astronomy, 1982; (ed.) Biographical Dictionary of Astronomers, 1983; (ed.) Western Learning in Mid-nineteenth century Japan, 1984; History of the Science of the Heavens, 1984; Science Studies for Citizens, 1984; (trans.) Copernicus in China, by N. Sivin, 1984; Academic and Scientific Traditions in China, Japan and the West, 1984; (ed.) Rethinking of Paradigms, 1984; Thoughts on the 21st Century, 1986; (ed.) Technological Capacity of Japan, 1986; (trans.) The Third Mellenium, by Stableford and Langford, 1987; Research Guide to the History of Science, 1987; A Trip To American Universities, 1988; Naozo Ichinoke, 1989. Add: 3-7-11 Chuo, Nakano, Tokyo, Japan.

NAKHNIKIAN, George. American, b. 1920. Philosophy. Prof. Emeritus of Philosophy, Indiana Univ., Bloomington, since 1988 (Chmn., Dept. of Philosophy, 1968–72; Prof., 1968–88). Joined Dept. of Philosophy as Instr., 1949, subsequently Prof., 1961–68, and Chmn., 1956–68, Wayne State Univ., Detroit. *Publs:* (ed.) J.S. Mill: Nature and Utility of Religion, 1958; (ed. with H.N. Castaneda) Morality and the Language of Conduct, 1963; (ed. with W.P. Alston) Readings in 20th Century Philosophy, 1963; (trans. with W.P. Alston) Edmund Husserl: The Idea of Phenomenology, 1964; An Introduction to Philosophy, 1967; (ed.) Bertrand Russell's Philosophy, 1974. Add: 2213 Queens Way, Bloomington, Ind. 47401, U.S.A.

NAMIAS, Jerome. American, b. 1910. Meteorology/Atmospheric sciences. Research Meteorologist, Scripps Instn. of Oceanography, Univ. of California at San Diego, since 1968. Research Assoc., Massachusetts Inst. of Technology, Cambridge, 1936–41; Chief, Extended Forecast Div., U.S. Weather Bureau, 1941–71. *Publs:* Subsidence Within the Atmosphere, 1934; Extended Forecasting by Mean Circulation Methods, 1947; 30-Day Forecasting: A Review of a Ten-Year Experiment, 1953; Short Period Climatic Variations: Collected Works of J. Namias 1934–1974, 1975, and 1975–82, 1983. Add: Scripps Instn. of Oceanography, Univ. of California at San Diego, La Jolla, Calif. 92093 U.S.A.

NANDA, Bal Ram. Indian, b. 1917. History, Biography. Dir., Nehru Memorial Museum and Library, New Delhi, 1965–79; National Fellow, Indian Council of Social Science Research, 1979–82. *Publs:* Mahatma Gandhi: A Biography, 1958; The Nehrus: Motilal and Jawaharlal, 1962; (ed.) Nehru and the Modern World, 1967; (ed.) Socialism in India, 1972; (ed. with V.C. Joshi) Studies in Modern Indian History, 1973; Gokhale, Gandhi and the Nehrus, 1974; (ed.) Indian Foreign Policy; The Nehru Years, 1976; Gokhale, The Indian Moderates, and the British Raj, 1977; (ed.) Science and Technology in India, 1977; (ed.) Essays in Modern Indian History, 1980; Jawaharlal Nehru: A Pictorial Biography, 1980; Gandhi and His Critics, 1985; Gandhi, Pan-Islamism, Imperialism, and Nationalism in India, 1989. Add: S-174 Panch Shila Park, New Delhi 110017, India.

NANDY, Pritish. Indian, b. 1947. Poetry, Translations. Ed., Dialogue Calcutta, later Dialogue India, since 1968. *Publs:* Of Gods and Olives: 21 Poems, 1967; I Hand You in Turn My Nebbuk Wreath: Early Poems, 1968; On Either Side of Arrogance, 1968; (ed.) Getting Rid of Blue Plastic: Poems Old and New, by Magaret Randall, 1968; (ed.) Some Modern Cuban Poems, 1968; Rites for a Plebeian Statue: An Experiment in Verse Drama, 1969; From the Outer Bank of the Brahmaputra, 1969; (ed.) Selected Poems of Subhas Mukhopadhyay, 1969; (ed.) Selected Poems of Parvez Shadedi, 1969; (ed.) Selected Poems of G. Sankara Kurup, 1969; (ed.) Selected Poems of Agyeya, 1969; (trans.) Ravana's Lament: A Selection from the Abhiseka Swarga of the Meghnad-Badh Kavya of Michael Madhusudhan Datta, 1969; Masks to Be Interpreted as Messages, 1970; (ed. and trans.) The Complete Poems of Samar Sen, 1970; (ed.) Selected Poems of Amrita Pritam, 1970; Collected Poems, 1973; (ed.) Indian Poetry in English Today, 1973; (ed.) Modern Indian Poetry, 1974; (ed.) Bengali Poetry Today, 1974; Riding the Midnight River: Selected Poems, 1975; Lone Song Street, 1975; Stranger Called I, 1976; In Secret Anarchy, 1976; Nowhere Man, 1978; Anywhere Is Another Place, 1979; Tonight This Savage Rite: The Love Poetry of Kamala Das and Pritish Nandy, 1979; The Rainbow Last Night, 1981; Some Friends, 1983. Add: 5 Pearl Rd., Calcutta 17, India.

NAPIER, John Russell. Writes technical books as J.R. Napier, and popular books as John Napier. Died.

NAPIER, Mark. *See* **LAFFIN,** John.

NAPIER, Mary. *See* **WRIGHT,** Patricia.

NARANG, Gopi Chand. Indian, b. 1931. Language/Linguistics. Prof. of Urdu, Univ. of Delhi, since 1986. Member, Linguistic Panel, Urdu Development Bd., Govt. of India, since 1971; Member, Advisory Cttee., All India Radio and Television, since 1972; Member, Urdu Advisory Bd., National Academy of Letters, National Book Trust, India; Chmn., Urdu Cttee., National Council for Education and Research. Lectr., 1958–61, Reader, 1961–74, and Prof. and Head, Dept. of Urdu, 1974–86, Jamia Millia Univ., New Delhi. Visiting Prof., Univ. of Wisc., 1963–65, 1968–70. *Publs:* Urdu Romances Based on Indian Folk Tales, 1961; Karkhandari Dialect of Delhi Urdu, 1961; Readings in Literary Urdu Prose, 1967; A Linguistic Study of Karbal Katha, 1970; Urdu Orthography, 1974; Tales from Puranas, 1974; (ed.) Anthology of Urdu Short Stories, 1978; Anis Shanasi, 1980; Urdu Afsanah, 1981; Indian Poetry Today, 1982; Safar Ashna, 1983; Iqbal Ka Fan, 1984; Usloobiyate-Meer, 1985; Sanihah-e-Karbala bataur Sheri Istiarah, 1986; Nai Urdu Kitab, 1987; Naya Urdu Afsana, 1988. Add: D-252 Sarvodaya Enclave, New Delhi-17, India.

NARAYAN, R(asipuran) K(rishnaswami). Indian, b. 1907. Novels/Short stories, Travel/Exploration/Adventure, Autobiography/Memoirs/Personal. *Publs:* Cyclone and Other Stories; Swami and Friends: A Novel of Malgudi, 1935; The Bachelor of Arts, 1937; The Dark Room, 1938; Malgudi Days, 1943; Mysore, 1944; The English Teacher (in U.S. as Grateful to Life and Death), 1945; An Astrologer's Day and Other Stories, 1947; Mr. Sampath (in U.S. as The Printer of Malgudi), 1949; Dodu and Other Stories, 1950; The Financial Expert, 1952; Waiting for Mahatma, 1955; Lawley Road, 1956; The Guide, 1958; My Dateless Diary, 1960; The Man-Eater of Malgudi, 1961; Gods, Demons and Others, 1964; The Vendor of Sweets (in U.K. as The Sweet Vendor), 1967; A Horse and Two Goats, 1970; My Days: A Memoir, 1974; Reluctant Guru (essays), 1974; The Painter of Signs, 1976; The Mahabharata, 1978; A Tiger for Malgudi, 1983; Under the Banyan Tree and Other Stories, 1985; Talkative Man, 1986. Add: 15 Vivekananda Rd., Yadavagiri, Mysore 2, India.

NASATIR, A(braham) P(hineas). American, b. 1904. History. Research Prof. of History Emeritus, San Diego State Univ. (joined faculty, 1928). *Publs:* (trans. and ed.) Inside Story of Gold Rush, 1934; French Activities in California, 1942; Before Lewis and Clark, 2 vols., 1952; (with H.M. Bailey) Latin America: Development of Its Civilization, 1960, 3rd ed. 1974; (ed.) James: Three Years Among Indians and Mexicans, 1962; (trans. and ed.) Derbec: French Journalist in Gold Rush, 1964; (ed. and co-author) Douglas: Manuel Lisa, 1964; (with N. Loomis) Pedro Vial and the Roads to Santa Fe, 1967; (with J. Mills) Commerce and Contraband Trade at New Orleans, 1967; Spanish War Vessels on the Mississippi, 1968; (co-author) Calendar of the British Archives Relating to California and the Pacific Coast, 1969; Borderlands in Retreat, 1975; (with G.C. Din) Imperial Osage, 1984. Add: 3340 N. Mountain View Dr., San Diego, Calif. 92116, U.S.A.

NASH, Gary B. American, b. 1933. History. Prof. of History, Univ.

of California at Los Angeles, since 1966. Asst. Prof. of History, Princeton Univ., New Jersey, 1964–66. *Publs:* Quakers and Politics: Pennsylvania 1681-1726, 1968; Class and Society in Early America, 1970; (ed. with Richard Weiss) The Great Fear: Race in the Mind of America, 1970; Red, White, and Black: The Peoples of Early America, 1974, 1982; The Urban Crucible: Social Change, Political Consciousness, and the Origins of the American Revolution, 1979; (ed. with David Sweet) Struggle and Survival in Colonial America, 1980; (co-ed.) The Private Side of American History, 2 vols., 1983; (with J.R. Jeffrey) The American People, 2 vols., 1985; Retracing the Past, 2 vols., 1985; Race, Class, and Politics, 1986; Forging Freedom: The Formation of Philadelphia's Black Community 1720-1840, 1988. Add: 16174 Alcima Ave., Pacific Palisades, Calif. 90272, U.S.A.

NASH, Gerald D(avid). American, b. 1928. History. Prof. of History, Univ. of New Mexico, Albuquerque, since 1961. Asst. Prof., Stanford Univ., California, 1957–60; Ed., The Historian, 1974–84. *Publs:* State Government and Economic Development: California 1849–1933, 1964; (ed.) Issues in American Economic History, 1964, 3rd ed. 1980; (ed.) F.D. Roosevelt, 1967; United States Oil Policy 1890–1964, 1968; Perspectives on Administration: History, 1969; The Great Transition: United States in Twentieth Century, 1971; The American West in Twentieth Century, 1973; (with E. Hawley and J. Huthmacher) Herbert Hoover and Crisis of American Liberalism, 1973; The Great Depression and World War II, 1979; The West Transformed: The Impact of World War II, 1985; (ed. with Noel Pugach and Richard Tomasson) Social Security: The First Fifty Years, 1988; (ed. with Richard Etulain) The 20th Century West: Historical Interpretations, 1989; World War II and the West: Reshaping the Economy, 1990. Add: Dept. of History, Univ. of New Mexico, Albuquerque, N.M. 87131, U.S.A.

NASH, Newlyn. *See* **HOWE,** Doris and **HOWE,** Muriel.

NASH, Patrick Gerard. Australian, b. 1933. Law. Barrister, Victoria, since 1980; Queen's Counsel, 1987. Legal Ed., The Australian Accountant since 1962. Legal Officer, Australian Attorney-Gen.'s Dept., 1956–57; Lectr. in Law, Univ. of Tasmania, 1957–59; Barrister, 1959–62; Lectr., Univ. of Melbourne, 1962–64; Lectr., Prof., and Dean of Law, Monash Univ., Clayton, Vic., 1964–66, 1970–80; Foundn. Prof. and Dean of Law, Univ. of Papua New Guinea, 1966–70. *Publs:* Paul's Justices of the Peace, 2nd ed. 1965; Some Problems of Administering Law in the Territory of Papua New Guinea, 1967; Nash on Magistrates' Courts, 1975; Civil Procedure Cases and Text, 1976; (Victorian) Justices Manual, 1978; Bourke's Criminal Law, 3rd ed., 1981; Ward and Kelly, Summary Justice, Victorian Commentary, 1984; (with C.K.J. Rao) Homicide: The Law and the Proofs, 1986. Add: Owen Dixon Chambers West, 525 Lonsdale St., Melbourne, Vic. 3000, Australia.

NASH, Paul. American, b. 1924. Art, Education, Human relations. Vice-Pres. for Academic Affairs, Rhode Island School of Design. Prof. of Education, Boston Univ., 1962–84. *Publs:* The Educated Man, 1965; Authority and Freedom in Education, 1966; Culture and the State, 1966; Models of Man, 1968; History and Education, 1970; A Humanistic Approach to Performance Based Teacher Education, 1973; The Consultant's Handbook, 1981. Add: Rhode Island School of Design, 2 College St., Providence, R.I. 02903, U.S.A.

NASH, Roderick. American, b. 1939. Environmental science/Ecology, History, Biography. Prof. of History and Environmental Studies, and Chmn. of Environmental Studies, Univ. of California, Santa Barbara (joined faculty, 1966). *Publs:* (with M. Curti) Philanthropy in the Shaping of American Higher Education, 1965; Wilderness and the American Mind, 1967, 3rd. ed. 1982; (ed.) The American Environment: Readings in the History of Conservation, 1968, 1973; (with M. Borden, O. Graham and R. Oglesby) The American Profile, 1970, as Portrait of a Nation, 2 vols., 1972; (ed.) The American Culture: The Call of the Wild 1900–1916, 1970; The Nervous Generation: American Thought 1917–1930, 1970; (ed. and co-author) Grand Canyon of the Living Colorado, 1970; (ed.) Environment and Americans: The Problem of Priorities, 1972; From These Beginnings: A Biographical Approach to American History, 1973, 3rd ed. 1984; The Big Drops: Ten Legendary Rapids, 1978; The Rights of Nature: A History of Environmental Ethics, 1989. Add: Dept. of History, Univ. of California, Santa Barbara, Calif. 93106, U.S.A.

NASH, William George. British, b. 1920. Engineering/Technology. Head, Dept. of Construction, Southampton Technical Coll., 1969–80, now retired. (Lectr., 1947–64; Principle Lectr., 1964–69). *Publs:* Brickwork, 3 vols., 1969; Brickwork Bonding Problems and Solutions, 1977; Brickwork Repair and Restoration, 1986. Add: Deepdene, 1c Coopers

Close, West End, Southampton, Hants. SO3 3DE, England.

NASR, Seyyed Hossein. Iranian, b. 1933. Philosophy, Sciences (general), Theology/Religion. Prof. of Islamic Studies, George Wash. Univ., Wash. D.C., since 1984. Prof. of the History of Science and Philosophy, Tehran Univ., since 1958 (Dean of the Faculty of Art and Letters, 1968–72; Vice Chancellor, 1970–71); Chancellor, Aryamehr Univ, Tehran, 1972–75; Pres., Imperial Iranian Academy of Philosophy, 1974–79; Prof. of Religion, Temple Univ., Philadelphia, 1979–84. *Publs:* Three Muslim Sages, 1964; An Introduction to Islamic Cosmological Doctrines, 1964; (with H. Corbin and O. Yahya) Histoire de la Philosophie Islamique, 1964; Ideals and Realities of Islam, 1966, 1975; Islamic Studies, 1967; Science and Civilization in Islam, 1968; The Encounter of Man and Nature: The Spiritual Crisis of Modern Man, 1968; Sufi Essays, 1972; Islamic Science, 1976; Sacred Art in Persian Culture, 1976; Islam and the Plight of Modern Man, 1976; Islamic Life and Thought, 1981; Knowledge and the Sacred, 1982; Islamic Art and Spirituality, 1986; Traditional Islam in the Modern World, 1987; The Soviet Union and Arab Nationalism, 1987; (with others) Expectations of the Millennium: Shi'ism in History, 1988; Shi'ism; Doctrines, Thought and Spirituality, 1988. Add: 712 Gelman Library, George Washington Univ., Washington, D.C. 20052, U.S.A.

NASSAR, Eugene Paul. American, b. 1935. Literature. Prof. of English, Utica Coll. of Syracuse Univ., since 1971 (Asst. Prof., 1964–66; Assoc. Prof., 1966–71). Instr. in English, Hamilton Coll, Clinton, N.Y., 1962–64. *Publs:* Wallace Stevens: An Anatomy of Figuration, 1965, 1968; The Rape of Cinderella: Essays in Literary Continuity, 1970; The Cantos of Ezra Pound: The Lyric Mode, 1975; Wind of the Land, 1979, Essays: Critical and Metacritical, 1983. Add: 704 Lansing St., Utica, N.Y., U.S.A.

NASSAUER, Rudolf. British, b. 1924. Novels/Short stories, Poetry. *Publs:* Poems, 1947; The Hooligan, 1959; The Cuckoo, 1962; The Examination, 1973; The Unveiling, 1975; The Agents of Love, 1976; Midlife Feasts, 1977; Reparations, 1981; Kramer's Goats, 1986. Add: 51 St. James's Gardens, London W11, England.

NATANSON, Maurice (Alexander). American, b. 1924. Literature, Philosophy, Social sciences (general). Prof. of Philosophy, Yale Univ., New Haven, Conn., since 1976. Instr. in Philosophy, Univ. of Nebraska, Lincoln, 1950–51; Lectr. in Philosophy, Grad. Faculty, New Sch. for Social Research, NYC, 1952–53; Asst. Prof. to Assoc. Prof., Univ. of Houston, 1953–57; Assoc. Prof. to Prof., Univ. of North Carolina, Chapel Hill, 1957–65; Visiting Prof., Univ. of California, Berkeley, 1964–65; Prof., Cowell Coll., Univ. of California, Santa Cruz, 1965–76; Guest Prof., Univ. of Konstanz, 1974. *Publs:* A Critique of Jean-Paul Sartre's Ontology, 1951; The Social Dynamics of George H. Mead, 1956; Literature, Philosophy, and the Social Sciences, 1962; (ed.) The Problem of Social Reality, by Alfred Schutz, 1962; (ed.) Philosophy of the Social Sciences, 1963; (ed. with H. W. Johnstone) Philosophy, Rhetoric, and Argumentation, 1965; (ed.) Essays in Phenomenology, 1966; (ed.) Psychiatry and Philosophy, 1969; (ed.) Phenomenology and Social Reality, 1970; the Journeying Self, 1970; (ed.) Phenomenology and the Social Sciences, 2 vols., 1973; Edmund Husserl, 1973; Phenomenology, Role, and Reason, 1974; Anonymity, 1986. Add: Dept. of Philosophy, Yale Univ., New Haven, Conn. 06520, U.S.A.

NATCHEZ, Gladys. American, b. 1915. Psychology. Prof. Emerita, City Coll., City Univ. of New York (joined faculty, 1956). *Publs:* Personality Patterns and Oral Reading, 1959; (with F. Roswell) Reading Disability: Diagnosis and Treatment, 1964, 1971; (ed.) Children with Reading Problems: Classic and Contemporary Issues, 1968; Gideon: A Boy Who Hates Learning in School, 1975; Reading Disability: A Human Approach to Learning, 1977. Add: 263 West End Ave., New York, N.Y. 10023, U.S.A.

NATH, Shiv Kumar. Indian, b. 1936. Economics. Sr. Lectr., Univ. of Warwick, Coventry, since 1969 (Lectr., 1965–69). *Publs:* A Reappraisal of Welfare Economics, 1969; A Perspective of Welfare Economics, 1974; (with W. Grant) Politics of Economic Policy. Add: Brookfields, Swerford, Oxon. OX7 4BG, England.

NATHAN, David. British, b. 1926. Novels, Plays/Screenplays, Theatre, Biography. Theatre Critic since 1970, and Deputy Ed. since 1988, Jewish Chronicle, London. Reporter, feature writer, and theatre critic on Daily Herald, London, and The Sun, London, 1955–69. *Publs:* (with Freddie Hancock) Hancock, 1969; The Freeloader, 1970; The Laughtermakers: A Quest for Comedy, 1971; A Good Human Story

(television play), 1977; The Belman of London (radio play), 1982; The Bohemians (radio play), 1982; Glenda Jackson, 1984; John Hurt: An Actor's Progress, 1986; The Story So Far (novel), 1986. Add: 16 Augustus Close, Brentford Dock, Brentford, Middx., England.

NATHAN, Hans. American, b. 1910. Music. *Publs:* (co-author) A History of Song, 1960; (ed.) The Continental Harmony, by William Billings, 1961; Dan Emmett and the Rise of Early Negro Minstrelsy, 1962, 1977; William Billings: Data and Documents, 1975. Add: c/o Univ. of Oklahoma Press, 1005 Asp Ave., Norman, Okla. 73019, U.S.A.

NATHAN, Leonard. American, b. 1924. Poetry, Literature. Prof. of Rhetoric, Univ. of California, Berkeley, since 1961 (Chmn., Dept. of Rhetoric, 1969–73). *Publs:* Western Reaches, 1958; Tragic Drama of W.B. Yeats, 1963; Glad and Sorry Seasons, 1963; Matchmaker's Lament, 1967; The Day the Perfect Speakers Left, 1969; Flight Plan, 1971; Without Wishing, 1973; The Likeness, 1975; Returning Your Call, 1975; (trans.) The Transport of Love, 1976; The Teachings of Grandfather Fox, 1976; Lost Distance, 1978; Dear Blood, 1980; Holding Patterns, 1982; (trans.) Songs of Something Else, 1982; (trans.) Grace and Mercy in Her Wild Hair, 1982; (trans.) Happy as a Dog's Tail, 1985; Carrying On: New and Selected Poems, 1985. Add: 40 Beverley Rd., Kingston, Calif. 94707, U.S.A.

NATHAN, Norman. American, b. 1915. Novels/Short stories, Poetry, Literature, Writing/Journalism. Prof. of English, Florida Atlantic Univ., Boca Raton, since 1968. Instr., City Coll. of New York, 1946–49; Prof. of English, Utica Coll., Syracuse Univ., 1949–68. *Publs:* Though Night Remain, 1959; Judging Poetry, 1961; The Right Word, 1962; Writing Sentences, 1964; Short Stories, 1969; Prince William B., 1975. Add: 1189 S.W. Tamarind Way, Boca Raton, Fla. 33486, U.S.A.

NATHAN, Peter. British, b. 1914. Psychology, Medicine. *Publs:* The Psychology of Fascism, 1943; Retreat from Reason: An Essay on the Intellectual Life of Our Time, 1955; The Nervous System, 1969, 3rd ed. 1988. Add: 85 Ladbroke Rd., London W11 3PJ, England.

NATUSCH, Sheila. New Zealander, b. 1926. History, Natural history, Biography. *Publs:* (with N.S. Seaward) Stewart Island, 1951; Native Plants, 1956; Native Rock, 1959; Animals of New Zealand, 1967; A Bunch of Wild Orchids, 1968; New Zealand Mosses, 1969; Brother Wohlers: A Biography, 1969; On the Edge of the Bush: Women in Early Southland, 1976; Hell and High Water: A German Occupation of the Chatham Islands 1843–1910, 1977; The Cruise of the Acheron: Her Majesty's Steam Vessel on Survey in New Zealand Waters 1848–51, 1978; The Roaring Forties, 1978; Fortnight in Iceland, 1979; Wild Fare for Wilderness Foragers, 1979; Wellington with S.N., 1982; A Pocketful of Pebbles, 1983; Stewart Island: A Souvenir, 1983; Southward Ho! The Search for a Southern Edinburgh, 1844, 1985; (with Lois Chambers) Granny Gurton's Garden, 1987; William Swainson: The Anatomy of a Nineteenth-Century Naturalist, 1987. Add: 46 Ohiro Bay Parade, Wellington 2, New Zealand.

NATWAR-SINGH, K. Indian, b. 1931. Autobiography/Memoirs/Personal, Essays. Minister of State for Steel, Govt. of India, since 1984 (Member of Staff, Indian Embassy, Peking, 1956–58, and Permanent Indian Mission to the U.N., NYC, 1961–66; Indian Rep., Exec. Bd., Unicef, 1962–66; Alternate Indian Delegate, U.N. Gen. Assembly, 1963; Rapporteur, U.N. Cttee. on Decolonization, 1963–66, and U.N. Trusteeship Cttee., 1965; Deputy Secty., and Joint Secty., Prime Minister's Secretariat, New Delhi, 1966–71; Indian Ambassador to Poland, 1971–73; Member, Indian Delegation, U.N. General Assembly, 1971; Deputy High Commissioner, London, 1973–77; attended meeting of Commonwealth Heads of State and Govt., Kingston, Jamaica, 1975; High Commissioner in Zambia, 1977–80; Ambassador to Pakistan, 1980–82; Secty., Ministry of External Affairs, 1982–84). *Publs:* E.M. Forster: A Tribute, 1964; The Legacy of Nehury, 1965; Tales from Modern India, 1966; Stories from India, 1971; Maharaja Suraj Mal 1707–63; Curtain Raisers, 1984. Add: c/o Ministry of Steel, Udyog Bhavan, New Delhi 110 011, India.

NAUGHTON, Bill. British, b. 1910. Novels/Short stories, Children's fiction, Plays/Screenplays, Autobiography/Memoirs/Personal. He worked as a lorry driver, weaver, and coal-bagger. *Publs:* A Roof over Your Head, 1945; Rafe Granite, 1947; One Small Boy, 1957; Late Night in Watling Street and Other Stories, 1959; The Goalkeeper's Revenge, 1961; Alfie (play), 1963; novel, 1966; All in Good Time, 1963; Spring and Port Wine (in U.S. as Keep It in the Family), 1965; Pony Boy, 1966; Alfie Darling, 1970; A Dog Called Nelson, 1976; The Bees Have Stopped Working and Other Stories, 1976; My Pal Spadger, 1977; On the Pig's Back: An Autobiographical Excursion, 1987. Add: Kempis, Orrisale Rd.,

Ballasalla, Isle of Man, United Kingdom.

NAVASKY, Victor. American, b. 1932. Politics. Ed., The Nation, NYC, since 1978. Co-Ed., Monocle political satire mag., and Outsider's Newsletter, NYC, from 1961; Consultant, U.S. Civil Rights Commission, 1961; Manuscript Editor, 1970–72, and writer, 1973–77, In Cold Print column, New York Times Mag.; Adjunct Prof., New York Univ., 1972–73; managed former U.S. Attorney Gen. Ramsey Clarke's campaign for U.S. Senate, 1974; Ferris Visiting Prof. of Journalism, Princeton Univ., N.J., 1976–77. *Publs:* Kennedy Justice, 1971; Naming Names, 1980; (with Christopher Cerf) The Experts Speak, 1984. Add: c/o The Nation, 72 Fifth Ave., New York, N.Y. 10011, U.S.A.

NAYLOR, Gloria. American, b. 1950. Novels. Missionary for the Jehovah's Witnesses, N.Y., N.C., and Fla., 1968–75; telephone operator, NYC hotels, 1975–81; Writer-in-Residence, Commington Community of the Arts, Mass., 1983; Visiting Prof., George Washington Univ., Washington, D.C., 1983–84; Visiting Writer, New York Univ., 1986; Columnist, New York Times, 1986. *Publs:* The Women of Brewster Place: A Novel in Seven Stories, 1982; Linden Hills, 1985; Mama Day, 1988. Add: c/o Ticknor and Fields, 52 Vanderbilt Ave., New York, N.Y. 10017, U.S.A.

NAYLOR, Phyllis Reynolds. American, b. 1933. Novels/Short stories, Children's fiction, Children's non-fiction. Pres., Children's Book Guild, Washington, D.C., 1974–75 (and 1983–84). *Publs:* The Galloping Goat, 1965; Grasshoppers in the Soup, 1965; What the Gulls Were Singing, 1967; To Shake a Shadow, 1967; The New Schoolmaster, 1967; A New Year's Surprise, 1967; Knee Deep in Ice Cream, 1967; Jennifer Jean, the Cross-Eyed Queen, 1967; When Rivers Meet, 1968; Dark Side of the Moon, 1969; Meet Murdock, 1969; The Private I, 1969; To Make a Wee Moon, 1969; Making It Happen, 1970; Ships in the Night, 1970; Wrestle the Mountain, 1971; No Easy Circle, 1972; How to Find Your Wonderful Someone, 1972; To Walk the Sky Path, 1973; An Amish Family, 1974; Witch's Sister, 1975; Getting Along in Your Family, 1976; Walking Through the Dark, 1976; Witch Water, 1977; Crazy Love: An Autobiographical Account of Marriage and Madness, 1977; The Witch Herself, 1978; How I Came To Be Writer, 1978; In Small Doses, 1979; Revelations, 1979; Getting Along with Your Friends, 1979; How Lazy Can You Get?, 1979; Change in the Wind, 1979; Eddie, Incorporated, 1980; Shadows on the Wall, 1980; Getting Along with Your Teachers, 1981; All Because I'm Older, 1981; Faces in the Water, 1981; Footprints at the Window, 1981; The Boy with the Helium Head, 1982; Never Born a Hero, 1982; String of Chances, 1982; The Solomon System, 1983; The Mad Gasser of Bessledorf Street, 1983; A Triangle Has Four Sides, 1983; Night Cry, 1984; Old Sadie and the Christmas Bear, 1984; The Dark of the Tunnel, 1985; The Agony of Alice, 1985; The Keeper, 1986; The Bodies in the Bessledorf Hotel, 1986; Unexpected Pleasures, 1986; The Year of the Gopher, 1987; Beetles, Lightly Toasted, 1987; The Body, the Bed, and the Rose, 1987; Maudie in the Middle, 1988; One of the Third Grade Thonkers, 1988; Alice in Rapture, Sort of, 1989; Keeping a Christmas Secret, 1989; The Craft of Writing the Novel, 1989; Bernie and the Bessledorf Ghost, 1990; Send No Blessings, 1990; King of the Playground, 1991; The Witch's Eye, 1991; Shiloh, 1991. Add: 9910 Holmhurst Rd., Bethesda, Md. 20817, U.S.A.

NEAGLEY, Ross (L.). American, b. 1907. Education. Prof. of Education Admin. Emeritus, Temple Univ., Philadelphia (Dir., Evening Sch., and Grad. Program, Dept. of Elementary Education, 1949–58, Dir., Dept. of Educational Admin., 1958–65, Prof. until retirement in 1973). Teacher, Science and Instrumental Music, Darby, Pa., 1929–31; Media, Pa., 1931–41; Supervising Principal, Newtown Boro Schools, Pa., 1941–44; Supt., Mt. Pleasant Special Sch. District, Wilmington, Del., 1944–49. *Publs:* (co-author) Planning Facilities for Higher Education, 1960; Elementary School Administration, 1964, 1967; Handbook for Effective Supervision of Instruction, 1964, 3rd ed. 1980; Handbook for Effective Curriculum Development, 1967; The Administrator and Learning Resources, 1972; Planning and Developing Innovative Community Colleges, 1972. Add: 524 Sch. Lane, Rehoboth Beach, Del. 19971, U.S.A.

NEAL, Ernest Gordon. British, b. 1911. Natural history. Vice-Pres. Somerset Nature Conservation. Former schoolmaster; Head of the Science Dept., Taunton Sch., 1946–71; Former Pres., Mammal Soc. *Publs:* Exploring Nature with a Camera, 1946; The Badger, 1948; Woodland Ecology, 1953; Topsy and Turvey: My Two Otters, 1971; Uganda Quest, 1971; (with K. Neal) Biology for Today, 2 vols., 1974; Badgers, 1977; Badgers in Close-up, 1984; The Natural History of Badgers, 1986. Add: 42 Park Ave., Bedford, England.

NEAL, Frank. British, b. 1932. Economics, Mathematics/Statistics. Sr. Lectr. in Economics and Social Statistics, Univ. of Salford, Lancs., since 1974. Work Study Engineer, British Insulated Callender's Cables Ltd., Prescot, Lancs., 1952–55; Asst. Lectr. in Economics, Southport Technical Coll., Lancashire, 1959–61; Research Asst., Dept. of Economics, Univ. of Liverpool, 1962–63; Principal Lectr. in Economics, Chelmer Inst. of Higher Education, Chelmsford, Essex, 1963–69, and Sheffield Polytechnic, 1969–74. *Publs:* Investment in Liverpool Shipping During the Industrial Revolution; (with R.W. Quincy) Using Mathematics in Economics, 1973; (with R. Shone) Economic Model Building, 1976; (with E. Rick) The Environment of Business, 1983; Sectarian Violence: The Liverpool Experience, 1988. Add: 74 South Dr., Chorltonville, Manchester M21 2FB, England.

NEAL, Fred Warner. American, b. 1915. History, International relations/Current affairs, Politics/Government. Prof. of Intnl. Relations and Govt., Claremont Grad. Sch., California, since 1957. Exec. Vice-Pres., American Cttee. on U.S.-Soviet Relations (Formerly Cttee. on East-West Accord) since 1974. Consultant on Russian Affairs, Dept. of State, Washington, D.C., 1945–49; Assoc., American Univs. Field Staff, 1954–55; Fellow, Twentieth Century Fund, 1958–61. Assoc. and Consultant on Intnl. Relations, Center for the Study of Democratic Instns., 1964–80. *Publs:* Titoism in Action, 1958; U.S. Foreign Policy and the Soviet Union, 1962; (with G. Hoffman) Yugoslavia and the New Communism, 1962; War and Peace in Germany, 1963; (ed.) Small States in a World of Big Nations, 1966; (ed. with M. Harvey) Pacem in Terris III, 1974; (ed.) American Foreign Policy at Home and Abroad, 1976; Survey of Detente: Past, Present, Future, 1977; (ed.) Detente or Debacle, 1979. Add: 210 E. Foothill, Claremont, Calif. 91711, U.S.A.

NEAL, Harry Edward. American, b. 1906. History, Politics/Government, Social sciences (general), Writing/Journalism. Freelance writer since 1957. Member, U.S. Secret Service, 1926–57, retired as Asst. Chief. *Publs:* Writing and Selling Fact and Fiction, 1949; The Story of the Kite, 1954; Nature's Guardians: Your Career in Conservation, 1956; Pathfinders: U.S.A., 1957; The Telescope, 1958; Skyblazers, 1958; Six Against Crime, 1959; Disease Detectives, 1959; (co-author) The United States Secret Service, 1960; Communication: From Stone Age to Space Age, 1960; Engineers Unlimited, 1960; Treasures by the Millions, 1961; Money Masters, 1961; The Hallelujah Army, 1961; Diary of Democracy, 1962, 1970; Your Career in Electronics, 1963; From Spinning Wheel to Spacecraft, 1964; Nonfiction: From Idea to Published Book, 1964; Your Career in Foreign Service, 1965; The Mystery of Time, 1966; Money, 1967; The Pennsylvania Colony, 1967; The Protectors, 1968; The Virginia Colony, 1969; Oil, 1970; Of Maps and Men, 1970; The People's Giant, 1970; The Story of the Secret Service, 1971; The Story of Offshore Oil, 1977; The Secret Service in Action, 1980; Before Columbus: Who Discovered America?, 1981. Add: 210 Spring St., Culpeper, Va. 22701, U.S.A.

NEAL, Hilary. *See* **NORWAY**, Kate.

NEAL, (Sister) Marie Augusta. American, b. 1921. Sociology, Theology/Religion. Prof., Sociology Dept., Emmanuel Coll., Boston, since 1953, and Chmn. since 1989 (Chmn., 1963–73). Visiting Prof. in Sociology of Religion, Univ. of California, Berkeley, 1968, and Harvard Divinity Sch., Cambridge, Mass., 1973–75. Vice-Pres., 1979–81, and Pres., 1982–84, Soc. for Scientific Study of Religion. *Publs:* Values and Interests in Social Change, 1965; A Sociotheology of Letting Go, 1977; Catholic Sisters in Transition From the 1960's to the 1980's, 1984; The Just Demands of the Poor, 1987; From Nuns to Sisters: an expanding vocation, 1989. Add: 400 The Fenway, Boston, Mass. 02115, U.S.A.

NEALE, Walter Castle. American, b. 1925. Economics. Prof. of Economics, Univ. of Tennessee, Knoxville, since 1968, and chair, Asian Studies, since 1986. Instr. in Economics, Yale Univ., New Haven, Conn., 1953–55; Research Assoc. in Maharashtra and Punjab, India, for Center for Intnl. Studies, Massachusetts Inst. of Technology, Cambridge, 1955–56; Instr. in Economics, Yale Univ., 1956–58; Asst. Prof. Economics, 1958–62, Assoc. Prof., 1962–64, and Prof., 1965–68, Univ. of Texas at Austin; Sr. Fulbright Lectr., Dept. of Economics, Panjab Univ., Chandigarh, India, 1960–61; Fulbright-Hays Faculty Research Fellow, Planning Research and Action Inst., Lucknow, India, 1964–65; Ford Foundation Faculty Research Fellow, 1967–68. *Publs:* Economic Change in Rural India: Land Tenure and Land Reform in Uttar Pradesh 1800–1955, 1962; India: The Search for Unity, Democracy and Progress, 1965, 2nd ed., with John Adams, 1976; Monies in Societies, 1976; Developing Rural India: Policies, Politics and Progress, 1988. Add: Dept. of Economics, Univ. of Tennessee, Knoxville, Tenn. 37996, U.S.A.

NEAME, Alan John. British, b. 1924. Novels/Short stories, Poetry, Theology/Religion, Translations. Consultant to the Intnl. Commn. for the Use of English in the Roman Liturgy. Head of Modern Languages, Cheltenham Coll., Gloucestershire, 1948–52; Lectr. in English, Univ. of Baghdad, 1952–56. *Publs:* The Adventures of Maude Noakes, 1959; (ed.) Stanley's Diaries, 1961; (ed.) Jerusalem Bible, 1966; Maude Noakes, Guerilla, 1966; The Happening at Lourdes, 1967; (trans.) The Psalms, 1969; The Holy Maid of Kent, 1971; (trans.) Life of Jeanne Jugan, 1975; (trans.) Concerning Religious Life, 1975; (trans.) Summoned by Love, 1977; (trans.) Face to Face with God, 1977; (trans.) The Hermitage Within, 1977; (trans.) Follow Me, 1978; (trans.) Made in Heaven, 1978; (trans.) The Little Way, 1979; (trans.) Life of Jeanne Jugan, by Milcent, 1980; (trans.) A Thousand Reasons for Living, 1980; (ed.) The Foreigner and The Palestinians, by Desmond Stewart, 2 vols.; (trans.) I, Francis, by Carretto, 1982; (trans.) I Sought and I Found, 1984; (trans.) Why, Lord?, 1985; (ed. and trans.) New Jerusalem Bible, 1985; (trans.) The Gospel with Dom Helder Camara, 1986; (trans.) Journey Without End, 1987; Monumental Inscriptions of St. Mary, Selling, 1984; Brief Guide to the Church of St. Mary the Virgin, Selling, Kent, 1985; Brief Guide to the Church of St. Peter, Molash, Kent, 1987; (trans.) God Saw That It Was Good, 1989. Add: Trafalgar House, Selling, nr. Faversham, Kent, England.

NECKER, Claire. American, b. 1917. Animals/Pets. Museum Curator of Zoology, 1938–40; Physicist, 1944–49; Chemist, 1949–52; Partner, antiquarian book business, 1942–59; former Librarian, Lake County Public Library, Merrillville, Ind. *Publs:* (compiler and ed.) Cats and Dogs, 1969; The Natural History of Cats, 1970; Four Centuries of Cat Books, 1972; (ed. and contrib.) Supernatural Cats (anthology), 1972; The Cat's Got Our Tongue, 1973. Add: c/o Scarecrow Press, 52 Liberty St., Metuchen, N.J. 08840, U.S.A.

NEEDLE, Jan. British, b. 1943. Children's fiction, Literature. *Publs:* Albeson and the Germans, 1977; My Mate Shofiq, 1978; A Fine Boy for Killing, 1979; The Size Spies, 1979; Rottenteeth, 1980; The Bee Rustlers, 1980; A Sense of Shame, 1980; Wild Wood, 1981; Losers Weepers, 1981; Another Fine Mess, 1981; (with Peter Thomson) Brecht, 1981; Piggy in the Middle, 1982; Going Out, 1983; A Game of Soldiers (TV serial), 1983, and book, 1985; A Pitiful Place, 1984; Great Days at Grange Hill, 1984; Tucker's Luck, 1984; Behind the Bike Sheds, 1985; Tucker in Control, 1985; Behind the Bike Sheds, (TV series), 1985; Wagstaffe, The Wind-Up Boy, 1987; Uncle in the Attic, 1987; Skeleton at School, 1987; Soft Soap (TV play), 1987; Truckers (TV series), 1987; In the Doghouse, 1988; The Sleeping Party, 1988; The Thief (novel, TV play), 1989. Add: c/o Rochelle Stevens and Co., 15-17 Islington High St., London N1 1LQ, England.

NEELS, Betty. British. Historical/Romance/Gothic. Former nurse in the Netherlands and England. *Publs:* Amazon in an Apron, 1969; Blow Hot, Blow Cold, 1969, in Can. as Surgeon from Holland, 1970; Sister Peters in Amsterdam, 1969; Nurse in Holland, 1970; Fate Is Remarkable, 1970; Nurse Harriet Goes to Holland, 1970; Damsel in Green, 1970; The Fifth Day of Christmas, 1971; Tangled Autumn, 1971; Tulips for Augusta, 1971; Uncertain Summer, 1972; Victory for Victoria, 1972; Saturday's Child, 1972; Tabitha in Moonlight, 1972; Wish with the Candles, 1972; Three for a Wedding, 1973; Winter of Change, 1973; Enchanting Samantha, 1973; Cassandra by Chance, 1973; Stars Through the Mist, 1973; Cruise to a Wedding, 1974; The End of a Rainbow, 1974; The Gemel Ring, 1974; The Magic of Living, 1974; Henrietta's Own Castle, 1975; A Small Slice of Summer, 1975; Heaven Is Gentle, 1975; Tempestuous April, 1975; Cobweb Morning, 1975; Roses for Christmas, 1975; A Star Looks Down, 1975; The Edge of Winter, 1976; The Moon for Lavinia, 1976; Gem of a Girl, 1976; Esmeralda, 1976; The Hasty Marriage, 1977; A Matter of Chance, 1977; Grasp a Nettle, 1977; The Little Dragon, 1977; Britannia All at Sea, 1978; Never While the Grass Grows, 1978; Philomela's Miracle, 1978; Ring in a Teacup, 1978; Pineapple Girl, 1978; Midnight Sun's Magic, 1979; The Promise of Happiness, 1979; Sun and Candlelight, 1979; Winter Wedding, 1980; Hannah, 1980; Caroline's Waterloo, 1980; Last April Fair, 1980; The Silver Thaw, 1980; When May Follows, 1980; Heaven Round the Corner, 1981; An Apple for Eve, 1981; Not Once but Twice, 1981; A Girl to Love, 1982; All Else Confusion, 1982; A Dream Come True, 1982; Judith, 1982; Midsummer Star, 1983; Roses and Champagne, 1983; Never Say Goodbye, 1983; Never Too Late, 1983; Polly, 1984; Once for All Time, 1984; Year's Happy Ending, 1984; Heidelburg Wedding, 1984; A Summer Idyll, 1984; At the End of the Day, 1985; Magic in Vienna, 1985; Never the Time and the Place, 1985; A Girl Called Rose, 1986; Two Weeks to Remember, 1986; The Secret Pool, 1986; Stormy Springtime, 1987; The Doubtful Marriage, 1987; When Two Paths Meet, 1988; No Need to Say Goodbye, 1989. Add:

Lawn House, 50 Bell St., Shaftesbury, Dorset, England.

NEELY, Martina. American, b. 1939. Cookery/Gastronomy/Wine. *Publs:* The Greenbrier Hotel Cookbook, 1975; The Italian Heritage Festival Cookbook, 1980; (with William J. Neely) The Official Chili Cookbook, 1981. Add: P.O. Box 25, Jane-Lew, W. Va. 26378, U.S.A.

NEELY, Richard. American. Mystery/Crime/Suspense. Full-time writer. Formerly an advertising executive. *Publs:* Death to My Beloved, 1969; The Plastic Nightmare, 1969; While Love Lay Sleeping, 1969; The Walter Syndrome, 1970; The Damned Innocents, 1971, in U.S. paperback as Dirty Hands, 1976; The Japanese Mistress, 1972; The Sexton Women, 1972; The Smith Conspiracy, 1972; The Ridgway Women, 1975; A Madness of the Heart, 1976; Lies, 1978; No Certain Life, 1978; The Obligation, 1979; An Accident Woman, 1981; Shadows from the Past, 1983. Add: c/o Delacorte Press, 1 Dag Hammarskjold Plaza, New York, N.Y. 10017, U.S.A.

NEELY, William J. American, b. 1930. Novels/Short stories, Recreation/Leisure/Hobbies, Travel, Biography. Mgr., Racing Public Relations, Goodyear Tire and Rubber Co., Akron, Ohio, 1961–66; Public Relations Mgr., Humble Oil Co., Memphis, Tenn., 1966–70. *Publs:* Spirit of America, 1970; Grand National, 1971; A Closer Walk, 1971; Stand on It, 1973; Country Gentlemen, 1974; Drag Racing, 1974; Cars to Remember, 1975; Daytona USA, 1979; The Playboy Book of Sports Car Racing, Driving and Rallying, 1980; (with Martina Neely) The Official Chili Cookbook, 1981; A.J., 1984; Cale, 1986; King Richard I, 1986; Alone In The Crowd, 1988. Add: Quail Ridge Farm, Jane Lew, W. Va. 26378, U.S.A.

NEGANDHI, Anant. Indian, b. 1929. Administration/Management, Business/Trade/Industry, Economics. Member of the faculty, Univ. of Illinois, Urbana. Member, Advisory Bd., Quarterly Journal of Mgmt. Development, since 1970; Ed., Org. and Administrative Sciences, since 1974. Asst. Prof. of Business, Univ. of California at Los Angeles, 1964–67; Assoc. Prof., 1967–70, Prof. of Admin. Sciences, 1970–79, and Dir. of the Center for Business and Economic Research, 1971–75, Kent State Univ., Ohio. *Publs:* Private Foreign Investment Climate in India, 1965; (with R.F. Gonzalez) The United States Overseas Executive: His Orientations and Career Patterns, 1967; (with S.B. Prasad) Managerialism for Economic Development, 1968; (ed. with A.J. Melcher and J.P. Schwitter) Comparative Administration and Management: Conceptual Schemes and Research Findings, 1969; (ed. with J.P. Schwitter) Organizational Behavior Models, 1970; Comparative Management, 1971; Environmental Settings in Organizational Functioning, 1971; Organization Theory in an Inter-organizational Perspective, 1971; Management and Economic Development in Taiwan, 1972; Conflict and Power in Complex Organizations, 1973; Organization Theory in an Open System, 1975; Frightening Angels, 1975; Quest for Survival and Growth: A Comparative Study, 1979; Beyond Theory Z:A Comparative Study of American, German, and Japanese Multinationals, 1984; International Management, 1987. Add: Sch. of Business Admin., Univ. of Illinois, Champagne, Ill. 61820, U.S.A.

NEHRT, Lee C(harles). American, b. 1926. Business/Trade/Industry, Economics, International relations/Current affairs. Curator, Intnl. Museum of Blacksmithing, Nashville, Indiana, since 1989. Consultant, World Bank, U.N. and private industries; Pres., Academy of Intnl. Business. Former Prof. of Intnl. Business, Indiana Univ., Consultant to U.S. Treasury, and Adviser to the Govt. of Tunisia and Univ. of Dacca; Clinton Prof. of Intnl. Mgmt., Wichita State Univ., 1974–78; Dir., World Trade Inst., NYC, 1978–81; Owens-Illinois Prof. of Intnl. Mgmt., Ohio State Univ., Columbus, 1981–86; Adviser, Govt. of Indonesia, 1986–89. *Publs:* Foreign Marketing of Nuclear Power Plants, 1965; Financing Capital Equipment Exports, 1966; (ed.) International Finance for Multinational Business, 1967, 1972; (with F. Truitt and R. Wright) International Business: Past, Present and Future, 1969; The Political Climate for Private Investment in North Africa, 1970; (with Ali El Salmi) Managerial Policy and Strategy for the Arab World, 1973; (with Lamp Li and Gano Evans) Managerial Policy, Strategy and Planning for South East Asia, 1974; (with Emanuel Soriano) Business Policy in an Asian Context, 1977, 1984; Business and International Education, 1977; The Internationalization of the Business School Curriculum, 1979; Case Studies of Internationalization of the Business School Curriculum, 1981. Add: 550 Birdie Galyan Rd., Bloomington, In 47401, U.S.A.

NEIGHBOUR, Ralph W(ebster, Sr). American, b. 1906. Novels/Short stories, Theology/Religion. Producer, Morning Sunshine Radio Program, and Pres., Ralph Neighbour Evangelistic Assn. Inc., since 1950. Pastor, Church of the Open Door, Elyria, Ohio, 1950–71. *Publs:* Dare to Decide, 1941; A Voice from Heaven, 1958; The Shining Light, 1960; Thine Enemy, 1962; The Searching Heart, 1964; Promise, Provision and Pardon, 1966; Golden Nuggets, 1969; The Drama of Redemption, 1971; (with G. Stover) Planet Earth on the Brink of Eternity, 1974; Health, Wealth and Happiness, 1974; Morning Sunshine, 1979; Morning Dawns, 1979; Eyewitness of His Majesty (novel), 1987. Add: 1306 Forest Home, Houston, Tex. 77077, U.S.A.

NEIL, J. Meredith. American, b. 1937. Architecture, Cultural/Ethnic topics. Freelance writer and consultant. Asst. Prof., 1967–71, and Assoc. Prof., 1971–72, Dept. of American Studies, Univ. of Hawaii, Honolulu; Exec. Dir., Idaho Bicentennial Commn., 1972–76; Visiting Lectr., Dept. of History in Art, Univ. of Victoria, B.C., 1976–77; City Conservator, Seattle, 1978–81; Visiting Prof. of American Studies, Univ. of Wyoming, Laramie, 1982. Publs: Paradise Improved: Environmental Design in Hawaii, 1972; (ed. with Marshall Fishwick) Architecture and Popular Culture, 1972; Towards a National Taste: America's Quest for Aesthetic Independence, 1975; Saints and Oddfellows: A Bicentennial Sampler of Idaho Architecture, 1976; The Sights of Seattle: Growth of the City, 1983. Add: 2512 33rd Ave., S., Seattle, Wash. 98144, U.S.A.

NEILAN, Sarah. Historical/Romance/Gothic. Publs: (ed.) Ann and Peter (children's travel book series); The Braganza Pursuit, 1976; An Air of Glory, 1977; Paradise, 1981. Add: c/o Hodder and Stoughton Ltd., 47 Bedford Sq., London WC1B 3DP, England.

NEILSON, James Warren. American, b. 1933. History, Biography. Prof. of History, and Chmn. of the Dept. of Social Science, Mayville State Coll., North Dakota, since 1958. Publs: Shelby M. Cullom: Prairie State Republican, 1962; From Protest to Preservation: What Republicans Have Believed, 1968; The School of Personal Service: A History of Mayville State College, 1980. Add: Mayville State Coll., Mayville, N.D. 58257, U.S.A.

NELSON, Cordner. American, b. 1918. Novels/Short stories, Sports/Physical Education/Keeping fit, Biography. Ed., Track and Field News, 1948–71. Publs: The Jim Ryun Story, 1967, 1968; The Miler (novel), 1969; Track and Field: The Great Ones, 1970; (with Roberto L. Quercetani) Runners and Races: 1500/Mile, 1973; The Advanced Running Book, 1984; Excelling in Sports/How to Train, 1985; (with Roberto L. Quercetani) The Milers, 1985; Track's Greatest Champions, 1986. Add: Box 6476, Carmel, Calif. 93921, U.S.A.

NELSON, Daniel. American, b. 1941. Administration/Management, History. Prof. of History, Univ. of Akron, Ohio, since 1975 (Assoc. Prof., 1970–75). Specialist in Industrial Collections, Eleutherian Mills Historical Library, 1967–69; Coordinator, Hagley Fellowship Prog., 1969–70. Publs: Unemployment Insurance: The American Experience 1915-35, 1969; Managers and Workers: Origins of the New Factory System in the U.S. 1880-1920, 1975; Frederick W. Taylor and the Rise of Scientific Management, 1980; American Rubber Workers and Organized Labor 1900-1941, 1988. Add: Dept. of History, Univ. of Akron, Akron, Ohio 44325, U.S.A.

NELSON, Geoffrey Kenneth. British, b. 1923. Poetry, Sociology, Religion. Country Life and Natural History Wildlife Corresp., Worcestershire—The County Magazine, since 1988. Principal Lectr. in Sociology, City of Birmingham Polytechnic, 1977–88, Hon. Research Fellow since 1988. Hon. Secty., Sociology Section, British Assn., 1972–77. Publs: Spiritualism and Society, 1969; (with R.A. Clews) Mobility and Religious Commitment, 1971; A Poet's Reading, 1980; Butterfly's Eye, 1980; (with C. Hill et al.) Video—Violence and Children, 1983; Cults, New Religions, and Religious Creativity, 1987. Add: 32 Clun Rd., Northfield, Birmingham B31 1NU, England.

NELSON, Harry William. American, b. 1908. Poetry, Songs, lyrics and libretti. Teacher, Robert E. Fitch Sr. High Sch., Groton, Conn., 1934–64; Founder and First Pres., Indian and Colonial Research Center, Old Mystic Conn., 1965–70. Publs: Startled Flight, 1930; Impelling Reminiscence, 1940; Ours Is the Work, 1942; The Years of the Whirlwind, 1943; The Moon Is Near, 1944; Never to Forget This, 1944; The Fever in the Drum, 1945; From Moon-Filled Sky (lyrics), 1947; The Winter Tree, 1972; Not of This Star Dust, 1973; Blame the Skulk of Night, 1974; Wolf Stone, Wolf Stone, 1976; Encounter at the Aquarium, 1978; Command Performance and Other Poems, 1980; A Catch of Creation, 1984. Add: 213 Pleasant Valley Rd., Groton, Conn. 06340, U.S.A.

NELSON, J. Bryan. British, b. 1932. Biology, Environmental science/Ecology, Natural history. Reader in Zoology, Univ. of Aberdeen,

from 1980, now retired (Visiting Research Fellow, 1966–67; Lectr. and Sr. Lectr., 1967–80). Publs: Galapagos: Islands of Birds, 1968; Azraq Desert Oasis, 1974; The Sulidae: Gannets and Boobies, 1978; The Gannet, 1978; Seabirds: Their Biology and Ecology, 1980; Living with Seabirds, 1986; The Gannet, 1989. Add: Balkirk, Glenlochar, Castle Douglas DG7 2LU, Scotland.

NELSON, J. Robert. American, b. 1920. Theology/Religion. Prof. Emeritus of Systematic Theology, Boston Univ. Sch. of Theology, (Dean, 1972–74). Exec. Secty., Commn. on Faith and Order, World Council of Churches, Geneva, 1953–57; Dean and Prof. of Theology, Vanderbilt Divinity Sch., Nashville, Tenn., 1957–60; Prof. of Theology, Oberlin Grad. Sch. of Theology, Ohio, 1962–65. Publs: The Realm of Redemption, 1951; (ed. and contrib.) Christian Unity in North America, 1958; One Lord, One Church, 1958; Criterion for the Church, 1963; Church Union in Focus, 1968; Crisis in Unity and Witness, 1968; (ed. and contrib.) No Man Is Alien, 1971; Doctrines of the Future, 1979; Science and Our Troubled Conscience, 1980; Human Life, 1984. Add: c/o Inst. of Religion, Texas Medical Center, Box 20569, Houston, Tex. 77025, U.S.A.

NELSON, Jack Lee. American, b. 1932. Education, Sex, Social sciences, Sociology. Prof., Grad. Sch. of Education, Rutgers Univ., New Brunswick, N.J., since 1968. Editorial Consultant, Education Books, Random House and Alfred Knopf publs; Series Ed., Hayden American Values Series, Hayden Book Co.; Advisory Council Member, Webster's New World Dictionary. Instr. in Sociology and Psychology, Citrus Coll., Azusa, and Asst. Prof. of Education, California State Univ., Los Angeles, both 1958–63; Assoc. Prof. of Education, State Univ. of New York, 1963–68. Publs: (ed. with T. Linton) Patterns of Power: Social Foundations of Education, 1968, 1974; (with F. Besag) Sociology Perspectives in Education, 1970; Teaching Elementary Social Studies thru Inquiry, 1970; (ed.) Teenagers and Sex, 1970; (ed.) Population and Survival, 1972; (ed. with K. Carlson and T. Linton) Radical Ideas and the Schools, 1972; Introduction to Value Inquiry, 1974; Values and Society, 1975; Population and Progress, 1977; Values, Rights, and the New Morality, 1977; (with J. Michaelis) Secondary Social Studies, 1980; (ed. with V. Green) International Human Rights: Contemporary Issues, 1980; (with F. Besag) Foundations of Education: Stasis and Change, 1984; (with S. Palonsky and K. Carlson) Critical Issues in Education, 1990. Add: Dept. of Educational Theory, Policy and Admin., Grad. Sch. of Education, Rutgers Univ., New Brunswick, N.J. 08903, U.S.A.

NELSON, James Graham. American, b. 1929. Literature, Biography. Prof. of English Literature, Univ. of Wisconsin, Madison, since 1961. Lectr. in English, Columbia Univ., NYC, 1958–61. Publs: The Sublime Puritan: Milton and the Victorians, 1963; Sir William Watson, 1966; The Early Nineties: A View from the Bodley Head, 1971; Elkin Mathews, Publisher to Yeats, Joyce, Pound, 1989. Add: Dept. of English, Univ. of Wisconsin, Madison, Wisc. 53706, U.S.A.

NELSON, Lowry, Jr. American, b. 1926. Literature, Translations. Prof. of Comparative Literature, Yale Univ., New Haven, Conn., since 1970 (Assoc. Prof., 1964–70). Member, Soc. of Fellows, 1951–54, and Instr., 1954–56, Harvard Univ., Cambridge, Mass.; Asst. Prof., 1956–59, and Assoc. Prof. of English, 1960–64, Univ. of Calif., Los Angeles. Publs: (trans. with R. Wellek) Franz Kafka and Prague, by Pavel Eisner, 1950; Baroque Lyric Poetry, 1961; (ed. with P. Demetz and T. Greene) The Disciplines of Criticism: Essays in Literary Theory, Interpretation, and History, 1968; (ed.) Cervantes: A Collection of Critical Essays, 1969; The Poetry of Guido Cavalcanti, 1986; (co-ed.) Vyacheslav Ivanov: Poet, Critic, and Philosopher, 1986. Add: Dept. of Comparative Literature, Yale Univ., New Haven, Conn. 06520, U.S.A.

NELSON, Marguerite. See **FLOREN,** Lee.

NELSON, Martha. American, b. 1923. Women, Theology/Religion. Publs: The Christian Woman in the Working World, 1970; A Woman's Search for Serenity, 1972; On Being A Deacon's Wife, 1973; (with Pat James) Police Wife: How to Live with the Law and Like It, 1974; This Call We Share, 1977; (with Carl Nelson) The Ministering Couple: A Plus For Any Church, 1983; See How You Are Loved, 1988. Add: Rt. 5, Box 692, Blanchard, Okla. 73010, U.S.A.

NELSON, Ray. (Radell Faraday Nelson). Also writes as R.N. Elson and Jeffrey Lord. American, b. 1931. Novels/Short stories, Science fiction/Fantasy. Freelance writer and artist since 1962. Founder, Microcosm Fiction Workshop, later Ramona Street Regulars, 1967; Teaching Asst., Adams Jr. High Sch., El Cerrito, Calif., since 1968. Formerly artist, sign maker, painter, translator, and computer programmer; Co-Dir., Berkeley Free Univ., 1967–68. Pres., Calif. Writers Club, 1977–78, 1987–89. *Publs:* (with Philip K. Dick) The Ganymede Takeover (science fiction), 1967; The Agony of Love, 1969; Girl with the Hungry Eyes, 1969; (as R.N. Elson) How to Do It, 1970; (as R.N. Elson) Black Pussy, 1970; (as R.N. Elson) Sex Happy Hippy, 1970; (as R.N. Elson) The DA's Wife, 1970; Blake's Progress (science fiction), 1975; Then Beggars Could Ride (science fiction), 1976; The Ecolog (science fiction), 1977; The Revolt of the Unemployables (science fiction), 1978; (as Jeffrey Lord) Dimension of Horror (science fiction), 1979; The Prometheus Man (science fiction), 1982; Time Quest (fantasy), 1985. Add: 333 Ramona Ave., El Cerrito, Calif. 94530, U.S.A.

NELSON, Richard. American, b. 1950. Plays/Screenplays. Literary mgr., BAM Theatre Co., Brooklyn, 1979–81; assoc. dir., Goodman Theatre, Chicago, 1980–83; dramaturg, Guthrie Theatre, Minneapolis, 1981–82. *Publs:* The Vienna Notes (in Word Plays 1), 1980; Il Campiello (adaptation), 1981; An American Comedy and Other Plays, 1984; Between East and West (in New Plays USA 3), 1986; Principia Scriptoriae, 1986; (ed.) Strictly Dishonorable and Other Lost American Plays, 1986; Rip Van Winkle, 1986; Jungle Coup (in Plays from Playwrights Horizons), 1987; Accidental Death of an Anarchist (adaptation), 1987; Sensibility and Sense, 1989; Some Americans Abroad, 1989. Add: 32 South St., Rhinebeck, N.Y. 12572, U.S.A.

NELSON, Roy P(aul). American, b. 1923. Design (general), Writing/Journalism. Prof. of Journalism, Sch. of Journalism, Univ. of Oregon (—joined staff, 1955). *Publs:* Fell's Guide to the Art of Cartooning, 1962; (with B. Ferris) Fell's Guide to Commercial Art, 1966; The Design of Advertising, 1967, 6th ed. 1989; (with J.L. Hulteng) The Fourth Estate, 1971, 1983; Publication Design, 1972, 4th ed. 1987; Cartooning, 1975; Articles and Features, 1978; Comic Art and Caricature, 1978; (with R. Copperud) Editing the News, 1983; Humorous Illustration and Cartooning, 1984. Add: Sch. of Journalism, Univ. of Oregon, Eugene, Ore. 97403, U.S.A.

NELSON-HUMPHRIES, Tessa. Also writes as Tessa Nelson Unthank. British. Biography. Prof. of English Literature, Cumberland Coll., Williamsburg, Ky., since 1964. Columnist, The British Vegetarian (formerly Alive mag.), London, since 1973. Head of English Dept., Richard Thomas Sch. for Girls, Walsall, Staffs., U.K., 1957–58; Dir. of English Studies, Windsor Coll., Buenos Aires, 1958–60; Lectr. in English, Univ. of New Mexico, Carlsbad, 1960–63. *Publs:* Maria Edgeworth 1767-1849, 1971. Add: English Dept., C.C. Station, Williamsburg, Ky. 40769, U.S.A.

NEMEROV, Howard. American, b. 1920. Novels/Short stories, Poetry, Literature. Edward Mallinckrodt Distinguished Univ. Prof. of English, Washington Univ., St. Louis, Mo., since 1976 (Prof., 1969–76). Instr. in English, Hamilton Coll., Clinton, N.Y., 1946–48; Assoc. Ed., Furioso, Madison, Conn., later Northfield, Minn., 1946–51; member of Literature Faculty, Bennington Coll., Vt., 1948–66; Visiting Lectr., Univ. of Minnesota, Minneapolis, 1958–59; Writer-in-Residence, Hollins Coll., Va., 1962–64; Consultant in Poetry, Library of Congress, Washington, D.C., 1963–64; Prof. of English, Brandeis Univ., Waltham, Mass., 1966–69. *Publs:* The Image and the Law, 1947; The Melodramatists (novel), 1949; Guide to the Ruins, 1950; Federigo: or, The Power of Love (novel), 1954; The Salt Garden, 1955; The Homecoming Game (novel), 1957; Mirrors and Windows, 1958; A Commodity of Dreams and Other Stories, 1959; New and Selected Poems, 1960; The Next Room of the Dream: Poems and Two Plays, 1962; (with others) Five American Poets, 1963; Poetry and Fiction: Essays, 1963; Journal of Fictive Life, 1965; (ed.) Poets on Poetry, 1965; The Blue Swallows, 1967; The Winter Lightning: Selected Poems, 1968; Stories, Fables and Other Diversions, 1971; Gnomes and Occasions: Poems, 1972; Reflexions on Poetry and Poetics, 1972; The Western Approaches (poetry), 1975; The Collected Poems, 1977; Figures of Thought (essays), 1978; Sentences (poetry), 1980; Inside the Onion (poetry), 1984; New and Selected Essays, 1985; The Oak in the Acorn: On Remembrance of Things Past and Teaching Proust, Who Will Never Learn, 1987; War Stories: Poems About Long Ago and Now, 1987. Add: Dept. of English, Washington Univ., St. Louis, Mo. 63130, U.S.A.

NERLICH, Graham C. Australian, b. 1929. Philosophy. Hughes Prof. of Philosophy, Univ. of Adelaide. *Publs:* The Shape of Space, 1976. Add: Dept. of Philosophy, Univ. of Adelaide, Adelaide, S.A. 5001, Australia.

NESBIT, Troy. *See* **FOLSOM,** Franklin Brewster.

NETTLER, Gwynne. Canadian, b. 1913. Criminology/Law enforcement/Prisons, Philosophy, Psychology, Sociology. Prof. Emeritus of Sociology, Univ. of Alberta, Edmonton (joined faculty, 1963). Assoc., Dando, S.A., Industrial Psychology, Mexico City, 1959–61; Sr. Clinical Psychologist, Nevada State Dept. of Health, 1961–63. *Publs:* Explanations, 1970; Explaining Crime, 1974, 3rd ed. 1984; Social Concerns, 1976; Criminal Careers, 4 vols, 1982. Add: 12862 Circulo Dardo, San Diego, Calif. 92128, U.S.A.

NEUFELD, Peter Lorenz. Canadian, b. 1931. Animals/Pets, History. Developer of new domestic animal breeds; former school trustee and Exec. Table Officer of Manitoba Assn. of School Trustees. Sch. teacher in Manitoba, 1952–67. *Publs:* Aurora, 1968; The Invincible White Shepherd, 1970. Add: P.O. Box 81, Minnedosa, Man. R0J 1E0, Canada.

NEUGEBOREN, Jay. American, b. 1938. Novels/Short stories, Autobiography/Memoirs/Personal. Prof. and Resident Writer, Univ. of Massachusetts, Amherst, since 1971. Preceptor, Columbia Univ., NYC, 1964–66; Lectr., Stanford Univ., Calif., 1966–67; Asst. Prof., State Univ. of New York, Old Westbury, 1969–70. *Publs:* Big Man, 1966; Listen Ruben Fontanez, 1968; Corky's Brother, 1969; Parentheses: An Autobiographical Journey, 1970; Sam's Legacy, 1974; An Orphan's Tale, 1976; (ed.) The Story of Story Magazine by Martha Foley, 1980; The Stolen Jew, 1981; Before My Life Began, 1985; Poli: A Mexican Boy in Early Texas, 1989. Add: English Dept., Univ. of Mass., Amherst, Ma. 01003, U.S.A.

NEUHAUS, Richard J(ohn). American, b. 1936. Theology/Religion. Dir., The Rockford Inst. Center on Religion and Society, since 1984. Ed., Forum Letter, and The Religion and Society Report; Ed.-in-Chief, This World; Ed., Encounter Series, Eerdmans publishers, since 1986. *Publs:* The Lutherans, 1969; (ed.) Theology and the Kingdom of God, 1970; (with Peter Berger) Movement and Revolution, 1970; In Defense of People, 1971; The American Revelation, 1974; Time Toward Home, 1975; Christian Faith and Public Policy, 1976; (ed.) Against the World For the World, 1976; (with Peter Berger) To Empower People, 1977; Freedom for Ministry, 1979; The Naked Public Square, 1984; Dispensations: The Future of South Africa as South Africans See It, 1986; The Catholic Moment, 1987. Add: Center on Religion and Society, 152 Madison Ave., New York, NY 10016, U.S.A.

NEUMEYER, Peter. American, b. 1929. Children's fiction, Poetry, Children's non-fiction, Education, Literature. Prof. of English and Comparative Literature, San Diego State Univ., California, since 1978. Assoc. in English, Univ. of California, Berkeley, 1962–63; Asst. Prof. of Education, Harvard Univ., Cambridge, Mass., 1963–69; Assoc. Prof. of English, State Univ. of New York at Stony Brook, 1969–75; Prof. and Chmn. of English, West Virginia Univ., 1975–78. *Publs:* (ed.) Kafka's The Castle (essays), 1969; Donald and the . . ., 1969; Donald Has a Difficulty, 1970; Why We Have Day and Night, 1970; The Faithful Fish, 1971; (with Jack Carpenter) Elements of Fiction: An Introduction to the Short Story, 1974; Homage to John Clare, 1979; Dream Cat, 1982; The Phantom of the Opera, 1988. Add: 7968 Windsor Dr., La Mesa, Calif. 92041, U.S.A.

NEUSNER, Jacob. American, b. 1932. History, Theology/Religion, Translations. Univ. Prof. of Religious Studies, and Ungerleider Distinguished Scholar of Judaic Studies, Brown Univ., Providence, R.I., since 1975 (Prof. 1968–75). Pres., Max Richter Foundn., since 1969; Member, Advisory Bd., Trinity Univ. Monograph Series in Religion, since 1973; Ed., Studies in Judaism in Late Antiquity monograph series, since 1973; Ed., Studies in Judaism in Modern Times monograph series, since 1976; Member, Intnl. Advisory Cttee., Jewish Quarterly Review, since 1979; Ed., Chicago Studies in the History of Judaism Series, since 1980; Member, Editorial Bd., The Second Century, since 1980; Ed., Basic Jewish Ideas series, since 1981; Member, Bd. of Dirs., Jewish Spectator, since 1982. Instr. of Religion, Columbia Univ., NYC, 1960–61; Asst. Prof. of Hebrew, Univ. of Wisconsin, Milwaukee, 1961–62; Research Assoc., Brandeis Univ., Waltham, Mass, 1962–64; Asst. Prof., 1964–66, and Assoc. Prof. of Religion, 1966–68, Dartmouth Coll., Hanover, N.H. *Publs:* A Life of Yohanan ben Zakkai, 1962, 1970; Fellowship in Judaism: The First Century and Today (essays), 1963; History and Torah: Essays on Jewish Learning, 1965; A History of the Jews in Babylonia, 5 vols., 1965-70; (ed.) Religions in Antiquity: Essays in Memory of Erwin Ramsdell Goodenough, 1968, 1972; Judaism in the Secular Age: Essays on Fellowship, Community and Freedom, 1970; Development of a Legend: Studies on the Traditions Concerning Yohanan ben Zakkai, 1970; (ed.) Formation of the Babylonian Talmud: Studies in the Achievements of Late Nineteenth and Twentieth Century Historical and Literary Critical

Research, 1970; The Way of Torah: An Introduction to Judaism, 1970, 4th ed. 1978; Aphrahat and Judaism: The Christian-Jewish Argument in Fourth Century Iran, 1971; The Rabbinic Traditions about the Pharisees before 70, 3 vols., 1971; There We Sat Down: Talmudic Judaism in the Making, 1972; 1978; American Judaism: Adventure in Modernity, 1972, 3rd ed. 1978; (ed.) Contemporary Judaic Fellowship in Theory and Practice, 1972; Eliezer ben Hyrcanus: The Tradition and the Man, 2 vols., 1973; The Idea of Purity in Ancient Judaism, 1973; (ed.) The Modern Study of the Mishnah, 1973; (ed.) Soviet Views of Talmudic Judaism: Five Papers by Yu A. Solodukho, 1973; From Politics to Piety: The Emergence of Pharisaic Judaism, 1973, 1978; Invitation to the Talmud: A Teaching Book, 1973, 1975; (ed.) Understanding Jewish Theology: Classical Themes and Modern Perspectives, 1973, 1976; A History of Mishnaic Law of Purities, 22 vols., 1974-77; (ed.) The Life of Torah, 1974; (ed.) Understanding Rabbinic Judaism, 1974, 1977; (ed.) Christianity, Judaism and Other Greco-Roman Cults: Studies for Morton Smith at Sixty, 4 vols., 1975; First-Century Judaism in Crisis: Yohanan ben Zakkai and the Renaissance of Torah, 1975; Torah and Messiah: The Essentials of Judaism, 1975; (ed.) Understanding American Judaism, 2 vols., 1975; The Academic Study of Judaism: Essays on Reflections, 1975, 1982, 2nd series, 1977, 3rd series, 1980; Early Rabbinic Judaism: Historical Studies in Religion, Literature and Art, 1975; Talmudic Judaism in Sasanian Babylonia (essays), 1976; Between Time and Eternity: The Essentials of Judaism, 1976; (trans.) The Tosefta, 5 vols., 1977-80; Learn Mishnah (for children), 1978; The Glory of God Is Intelligence, 1978; History of the Mishnaic Law of Holy Things, 6 vols., 1978-79; A History of the Mishnaic Law of Women, 5 vols., 1979-80; Learn Talmud (for children), 1979; Method and Meaning in Ancient Judaism (essays), 1979, 2nd series, 1980, 3rd series, 1980; Meet Our Sages (for children), 1980; Form-Analysis and Exegesis: A Fresh Approach to the Interpretation of Mishnah, 1980; (trans. and ed. with Martin Hengel and Peter Schaefer) Uebersetzung des Talmud Yerushalmi, 1980; Stranger at Home: Essays on Zionism, "The Holocaust", and American Judaism, 1980; Mitzvah (for children), 1981; Judaism in the American Humanities (essays), 1981; Judaism: The Evidence of the Mishnah, 1981; (ed.) The Study of Ancient Judaism, 2 vols., 1981; A History of Mishnaic Law of Appointed Times, 5 vols., 1981-83; (ed.) Take Judaism, for Example: Studies Toward the Comparison of Religions, 1982; Judaism: The Evidence of the Yerushalmi: Toward the Natural History of a Religion, 1982; Israel after Catastrophe: The Religious World-View of the Mishnah (lectures), 1983; (trans.) The Palestinian Talmud: A Preliminary Translation and Explanation, 35 vols., 1982-; (trans.) The Mishnah: A New American Translation, 1983; (ed.) From Yeshiva to University: University Doctoral Studies in Jewish Learning: The Disciplinary Aspect, 1983; Judaism: The First Two Centuries, 1983; The Foundations of Judaism: Method, Teleology, and Doctrine, 1982; Judaism in Society: The Evidence of the Yerushalmi, 1983; The Talmud of the Land of Israel: A Preliminary Translation and Explanation, 4 vols., 1983-89; (ed.) In the Margins of the Yerushalmi: Notes on the English Translation, 1983; (ed.) The New Humanities and Academic Disciplines: The Case of Jewish Studies, 1984; The Talmud of Babylonia: An American Translation, 6 vols., 1984-85; Judaism and Scripture: The Evidence of Leviticus Rabbah, 1985; (ed. with Richard S. Sarason) The Tosefta: Translated from the Hebrew, 1985; Genesis Rabbah: The Judaic Commentary on Genesis, 3 vols., 1985; The Oral Torah: The Sacred Books of Judaism, 1985; The Integrity of Leviticus Rabbah: The Problem of the Autonomy of a Rabbinic Document, 1985; Constancy and Change in the Formation of Judaism, 1986; Judaism: The Classical Statement, 1986; (ed. with B.A. Levine and E.S. Frerichs) New Perspectives on Ancient Judaism, vols., 1987; (ed.) Religion and Society in Ancient Times: Essays in Honor of Howard Clark Kee, 1987; Vanquished Nation, Broken Spirit: The Virtues of the Heart in Formative Judaism, 1987; The Enchantments of Judaism, 1987; Israel: Judaism and Its Social Metaphors, 1988; Judaism Without Christianity: An Introduction to the System of the Mishnah, 1989. Add: c/o Dept. of Judaic Studies, Brown Univ., Providence, R.I. 02906, U.S.A.

NEUSTADT, Richard E. American, b. 1919. Politics/Government. Douglas Dillon Prof. of Government, Harvard Univ., Cambridge, Mass., since 1987 (Assoc. Dean of Kennedy Sch. of Govt., 1965-75; Dir., Inst. of Politics, 1966-71; Lucius Littauer Prof., 1975-86). Economist, Office of Price Admin., Washington, D.C., 1942; Staff Member, Bureau of the Budget, 1946-50; Member, White House Staff, 1950-53; Prof. of Govt., Columbia Univ., NYC, 1954-65. Special Consultant, Subcttee. on National Policy Machinery, U.S. Senate, Washington, D.C., 1959-61; Member, Advisory Bd., Commn. on Money and Credit, 1960-61; Special Consultant to President Kennedy, 1961-63; Bureau of the Budget, 1961-70, Dept. of State, 1963, and to President Johnson, 1964-66; Member, Council on Foreign Relations, 1963. *Publs:* Presidential Power, 1960, 1980; Alliance Politics, 1970; (with H.V. Finiberg) The Swine Flu Affair,

1978; The Epidemic That Never Was, 1982; (with E.R. May) Thinking in Time, 1986. Add: 1010 Memorial Dr., Cambridge, Mass. 02138, U.S.A.

NEVILLE, Emily Cheney. American, b. 1919. Children's fiction. Office worker, 1940-41, and Feature Writer, 1941-44, New York Daily Mirror; admitted to the New York Bar, 1977. *Publs:* It's Like This, Cat, 1963; Berries Goodman, 1965; The Seventeenth Street Gang, 1966; Traveler from Small Kingdom, 1968; Fogarty, 1969; Garden of Broken Glass, 1975; The Bridge, 1988. Add: Keene Valley, N.Y. 12943, U.S.A.

NEVILLE, Robert C(ummings). American, b. 1939. Philosophy, Theology/Religion. Prof. of Religion, Philosophy, and Theology, since 1987, and Dean of the Sch. of Theology Boston Univ. since 1988. Instr. Yale Univ., New Haven, Conn., 1963-65; Asst. Prof., 1965-68, and Assoc. Prof., 1968-71, Fordham Univ., NYC; Assoc. for Behavioral Sciences, Inst. of Soc., Ethics and the Life Sciences, Hastings, N.Y., 1971-73; Assoc. Prof., 1971-74, and Prof., 1974-77, State Univ. of New York at Purchase; Prof. of Philosophy and Religious Studies, State Univ. of New York at Stony Brook, 1978-87. *Publs:* God the Creator, 1968; The Cosmology of Freedom, 1974; (ed. with W. Gaylin and G. Meister) Operating on the Mind, 1975; Soldier, Sage, Saint, 1978; Creativity and God, 1980; Reconstruction of Thinking, 1981; The Tao and the Daimon, 1982; (ed.) New Essays in Metaphysics, 1987; The Puritan Smile, 1987; Recovery of the Measure, 1989. Add: Sch. of Theology, Boston Univ., Boston, Mass. 02215, U.S.A.

NEVIN, Edward Thomas. British, b. 1925. Economics. Prof. of Economics, University of Swansea, since 1968. Gov., National Inst. of Economic and Social Research; Economic Adviser, Police Fedn. of England and Wales. Lectr., 1952-63, and Prof. of Economics, 1963-68, University Coll. of Wales, Aberystwyth; Chmn., Assn. of Univ. Teachers of Economics, 1972-74. *Publs:* The Problem of the National Debt, 1954; The Mechanism of Cheap Money, 1955; Textbook of Economic Analysis, 1958, 5th ed. 1981; Capital Funds in Underdeveloped Countries, 1961; A Workbook of Economic Analysis, 1966, 1969; (with E.W. Davis) The London Clearing Banks, 1970; An Introduction to Micro-Economics, 1973; (ed.) The Economics of Devolution, 1978. Add: Dept. of Management Science, University Coll. of Swansea, Swansea SA2 8PP, Wales.

NEVIN, Evelyn C. Pseud. for Evelyn Ferguson. American, b. 1910. Children's fiction. Assoc. Ed., Curtis Publishing Co., Philadelphia, 1945; Ed., Westminster Pres. Philadelphia, 1950-61. *Publs:* The Lost Children of the Shoshones, 1946; The Sign of the Anchor, 1947; Underground Escape, 1949; Captive of the Delawares, 1952; The River Spirit and the Mountain Demons, 1965; The Extraordinary Adventures of Chee Chee McNerney, 1971; An Extraordinary Journey, 1972; Auf Heimlichen Pfaden, 1973. Add: 432 N. Avenida Felicidad, Tucson, Ariz. 85705, U.S.A.

NEVINS, Francis M(ichael), Jr. American, b. 1943. Mystery/Crime/Suspense, Literature. Prof., St. Louis Univ. Sch. of Law, since 1978 (Asst. Prof., 1971-75; Assoc. Prof., 1975-78). Admitted to the New Jersey Bar, 1967; Asst. to the Ed.-in-Chief, Clark Boardman Co., law publishers, NYC, 1967; served in the U.S. Army, 1968-69; Staff Attorney, Middlesex County Legal Services Corp., New Brunswick, N.J., 1970-71. *Publs:* mystery novels—Publish and Perish, 1975; Corrupt and Ensnare, 1978; The 120-Hour Clock, 1986; The Ninety Million Dollar Mouse, 1987; other—(ed.) The Mystery Writer's Art, 1970; (with others) Detectionary, 1971, 1977; (ed.) Nightwebs: Stories by Cornell Woolrich, 1972; (ed.) Multiplying Villainies: Selected Mystery Criticism of Anthony Boucher, 1973; Royal Bloodline: Ellery Queen, Author and Detective, 1974; (ed. with M. H. Greenberg and J. & W. Shine) The Good Old Stuff: Stories by John D. MacDonald, 1982; (with R. Stanich) The Sound of Detection: Ellery Queen's Adventures in Radio, 1983; (ed. with M. H. Greenberg) Exeunt Murderers: The Best Mystery Stories of Anthony Boucher, 1983; (ed. with M. H. Greenberg) Buffet for Unwelcome Guests: The Best Short Mystery Stories of Christianna Brand, 1983; Missouri Probate: Intestary, Wills and Basic Administration, 1983; (ed. with M. H. Greenberg and J. & W. Shine) More Good Stuff: Stories by John D. MacDonald, 1984; (ed. with M. H. Greenberg) Carnival of Crime: The Best Mystery Stories of Fredric Brown, 1985; (ed. with M. H. Greenberg) The Best of Ellery Queen, 1985; (ed. with M. H. Greenberg) Leopold's Way: Detective Stories by Edward D. Hoch, 1985; (ed. with M. H. Greenberg) Darkness at Dawn: Early Suspense Classics by Cornell Woolrich, 1985; (ed. with M. H. Greenberg) Hitchcock in Prime Time, 1985 (ed. with M. H. Greenberg) The Adventures of Henry Turnbuckle: Detective Comedies by Jack Ritchie, 1987; (ed.) Better Mousetraps: The Best Short Stories of John Lutz, 1988; Cornell Woolrich: First You Dream,

Then You Die, 1988; (ed. with M. H. Greenberg) Mr. President—Private Eye, 1988; The Films of Hopalong Cassidy, 1988. Add: 7045 Cornell, University City, Mo. 63130, U.S.A.

NEW, Anthony (Sherwood Brooks). British, b. 1924. Architecture, Hobbies. Architect in private practice, London, since 1958. *Publs:* The Observer's Book of Postage Stamps, 1967; The Observer's Book of Cathedrals, 1972; A Guide to the Cathedrals of Britain, 1980; Property Services Agency Historic Buildings Register (London), 1983; A Guide to the Abbeys of England and Wales, 1985; The New Observer's Book of Stamp Collecting, 1987; A Guide to the Abbeys of Scotland, 1988. Add: 26 Somerset Rd., New Barnet, Herts., England.

NEWALL, Venetia June. British, b. 1935. Mythology/Folklore. Hon. Research Fellow in Folklore, Dept. of English, Univ. of London, since 1971. Gen. Ed., The Folklore of the British Isles series, Batsford Ltd., London, 1972–78. *Publs:* An Egg at Easter: A Folklore Study, 1971; The Folklore of Birds and Beasts, 1971; (ed. and author with C. Blacker et al.) The Witch Figure, 1973; (with Russell Ash et al.) Folklore Myths and Legends of Britain, 1973; Encyclopaedia of Witchcraft and Magic, 1974; (ed.) Folklore Studies in the Twentieth Century, 1980. Add: Univ. Women's Club, 2 Audley Sq., South Audley St., London W1Y 6DB, England.

NEWBY, Eric. British, b. 1919. Travel/Exploration/Adventure, Autobiography/Memoirs/Personal. Mgr., Worth-Paquin, 1955–56; with Secker & Warburg Ltd., publrs., 1956–59; Model Dress Buyer, John Lewis Partnership, 1959–63; Travel Ed., The Observer Newspaper, London, and Gen. Ed., Time Off Books, 1963–73. *Publs:* The Last Grain Race, 1956; A Short Walk in the Hindu Kush, 1958; Something Wholesale, 1962, 1985; Time Off Guide to Southern Italy, 1966; Slowly Down the Ganges, 1966; My Favourite Stories of Travel, 1967; Grain Race (in U.S. as Windjammer), 1968; (with D. Petry) Wonders of Britain, 1968; Wonders of Ireland, 1969; Love and War in the Apennines (in U.S. as When the Snow Comes They Will Take You Away), 1971; Ganga, 1973; World Atlas of Exploration, 1975; Great Ascents, 1977; The Big Red Train Ride, 1978; A Traveller's Life, 1982; On the Shores of the Mediterranean, 1984; A Book of Travellers' Tales, 1986; Round Ireland in Low Gear, 1987. Add: West Bucknowle House, Wareham, Dorset BH20 5PQ, England.

NEWBY, P(ercy) H(oward). British, b. 1918. Novels/Short stories, Children's fiction, History, Literature. Producer, Talks Dept, 1949–58, Controller, Third Prog., 1958–70, and Radio 3, 1970–71, Director of Programmes, 1971–75, and Managing Dir., 1975–78, BBC Radio, London. Lectr. in English Language and Literature, Fuad I Univ., Cairo, 1942–46; freelance writer and journalist, 1946–49. *Publs:* A Journey to the Interior, 1945; Agents and Witnesses, 1947; The Spirit of Jem, 1947; Mariner Dances, 1948; The Loot Runners, 1949; The Snow Pasture, 1949; Maria Edgeworth, 1950; The Young May Moon, 1950; The Novel 1945-1950, 1951; A Season in England, 1951; A Step to Silence, 1952; The Retreat, 1953; The Picnic at Sakkara, 1955; Revolution and Roses, 1957; Ten Miles from Anywhere and Other Stories, 1958; A Guest and His Going, 1959; The Barbary Light, 1962; One of the Founders, 1965; (ed.) Tales from the Arabian Nights, 1967; Something to Answer For, 1969 (Booker Prize); A Lot to Ask, 1973; Kith, 1977; The Egypt Story, 1979; Warrior Pharaohs, 1980; Feelings Have Changed, 1981; Saladin in His Time, 1983; Leaning in the Wind, 1986. Add: Garsington House, Garsington, Oxford OX9 9AB, England.

NEWCOMER, James W. American, b. 1912. Poetry, Literature. Vice-Chancellor Emeritus, Trustees Prof. of English and Dir., Texas Christian Univ. Press, Fort Worth, since 1973 (Vice-Chancellor, 1965–73). Dean of Coll., Olivet Coll., Mich., 1952–60; Dean of Faculty, Dean of Grad. Studies, Texas Woman's Univ., Denton, 1960–65. *Publs:* (with Earl J. McGrath and Kevin Bennell) Liberal Education and Pharmacy, 1960; Maria Edgeworth the Novelist, 1967, Maria Edgeworth, 1973; Celebration (poetry), 1973; The Merton Barn Poems, 1981; Maria Edgeworth, The Grand Duchy of Luxemburg, 1984; The Resonance of Grace (poetry), 1984; The Nationhood of Luxembourg, 1989; Lady Morgan the Novelist, 1989. Add: 1100 Elizabeth Blvd., Fort Worth, Texas 76110, U.S.A.

NEWELL, Crosby. *See* **BONSALL,** Crosby.

NEWELL, William H. New Zealander, b. 1922. Anthropology/Ethnology, Sociology. Assoc. Prof. of Anthropology, Univ. of Sydney, since 1969. Head of Dept. of Sociology, Intnl. Christian Univ., Tokyo, 1960–69; Corresp., Economic and Political Weekly, Bombay, 1959–68. *Publs:* Scheduled Castes and Tribes of Himachel Pradesh, 1961; Treacherous

River, 1962; (ed. with K. Morioka) Sociology of Japanese Religion, 1968; (ed.) Ancestors, 1974; (ed.) Japan in Asia 1939-1942, 1980. Add: 4 Fort St., Petersham, N.S.W. 2049, Australia.

NEWELL, William T. American, b. 1929. Business/Trade/Industry. Prof. since 1960, Grad. Sch. of Business Admin., Univ. of Washington, Seattle (Chmn., Dept. of Mgmt., 1976–82). Instr., Coll. of Business Admin., Univ. of Texas, Austin, 1956–60. *Publs:* Long Range Planning Practices and Policies, 1963; (with A.N. Schrieber) Cases in Manufacturing Management, 1965; (with R.C. Meier) Simulation in Business and Economics, 1969; (with R.A. Johnson and R.C. Vergin) Operations Management: A Systems Concept, 1972; (with Johnson and Vergin) Production and Operations Management: A Systems Concept, 1974; (with R.C. Meier) Cases in Production and Operations Management, 1982. Add: Grad. Sch. of Business Admin., Univ. of Washington, Seattle, Wash. 98195, U.S.A.

NEWHALL, Beaumont. American, b. 1908. Art, Photography. Fellow of the John D. and Catherine T. MacArthur Foundn., Chicago, since 1984. Member, Photography Cttee., Museum of Modern Art, NYC, since 1964; Honorary Trustee, Intnl. Museum of Photography, George Eastman House, Rochester, N.Y., since 1980. Librarian, 1935–42, and Curator of Photography, 1940–45, Museum of Modern Art, NYC; Curator, 1948–58, and Dir., 1958–71, International Museum of Photography, George Eastman House, Rochester, N.Y.; Prof. of Art, State Univ. of New York at Buffalo, 1968–71; Assoc. Curator, Photography Collection, Exchange National Bank, Chicago, 1968–71; Prof. of Art, Univ. of New Mexico, Albuquerque, 1971–84. *Publs:* The History of Photography (first ed. published as Photography 1839-1937; second ed. published as Photography: A Short Critical History), 1937, 5th ed. 1982; (with Lincoln Kirstein) The Photographs of Henri Cartier-Bresson, 1947, as Photographs by Cartier-Bresson, 1963; On Photography: A Source Book of Photo History in Facsimile, 1956 abridged student ed. as The Art and Science of Photography, 1956; (with Nancy Newhall) Masters of Photography, 1958; The Daguerreotype in America, 1961, 3rd ed. 1976; Frederick H. Evans, 1964, 1975; (with Nancy Newhall) T.H. O'Sullivan, Photographer, 1966; Latent Image: The Discovery of Photograpy, 1967; Airborne Camera: The World from the Air and Outer Space, 1958; (with Diana Edkins) William Henry Jackson, 1974; Photography: Essays and Images, 1980; Photography and the Book, 1980; In Plain Sight, 1983; (with Amy Conger) Edward Weston Omnibus, 1983; Supreme Instants: The Photography of Edward Weston, 1986. Add: Route 7, Box 126-C, Santa Fe, N. Mex. 87505, U.S.A.

NEWILL, Robert (George Douglass). British, b. 1921. Medicine/Health. Physician, University Coll. Hosp., London, since 1970. *Publs:* Infertile Marriage, 1975; (co-author) Fertility Handbook, 1986. Add: 39 Park Rd., Aldeburgh, Suffolk IP15 5ET, England.

NEWLIN, Margaret Rudd. Also writes as Margaret Rudd. American, b. 1925. Poetry, Literature. Teacher, Bryn Mawr Coll., Pa., 1953–54, and Washington Coll., Chestertown, Md., 1955–56. *Publs:* (as Margaret Rudd) Divided Image: A Study of Yeats and Blake, 1953; Organiz'd Innocence: The Story of Blake's Prophetic Books, 1956; The Fragile Immigrants, 1971; Day of Sirens, 1973; The Snow Falls Upward: Collected Poems, 1976; The Book of Mourning, 1982; Collected Poems 1963-1985, 1986. Add: Shipley Farm, Secane, Pa. 19018, U.S.A.

NEWLOVE, John (Herbert). Canadian, b. 1938. Poetry. Formerly, Sr. Ed., McClelland and Stewart Ltd., publrs., Toronto. *Publs:* Grave Sirs: Poems, 1962; Elephants, Mothers and Others, 1963; Moving in Alone, 1965; Notebook Pages, 1966; Four Poems, 1967; What They Say, 1967; Black Night Window, 1968; The Cave, 1970; Lies, 1972; (ed.) Canadian Poetry: The Modern Era, 1977; The Fat Man: Selected Poems 1962-1972, 1977; (with John Metcalf) Dreams Surround Us, 1977; The Green Plain, 1981; (ed.) The Collected Poems of F.R. Scott, 1981; The Night the Dog Smiled, 1986. Add: 568 Gladstone Ave., Ottawa, Ont. K1R 5B3, Canada.

NEWMAN, Andrea. British, b. 1938. Novels/Short stories. *Publs:* A Share of the World, 1964; Mirage, 1965; The Cage, 1966; Three into Two Won't Go, 1967; Alexa (in U.S. as The City Lover), 1968, and TV serial, 1982; A Bouquet of Barbed Wire, 1969, and TV serial, 1975; An Evil Streak, 1977; Another Bouquet (TV serial), 1977, and book 1978; Mackenzie (TV series and novel), 1980; A Sense of Guilt, 1988, as TV serial, 1989. Add: c/o A.D. Peters, 10 Buckingham St., London WC2N 6BU, England.

NEWMAN, Aubrey N. British, b. 1927. History, Biography. Prof. of

History, Univ. of Leicester; Hon. Research Fellow, University Coll. London. Research Fellow, Bedford Coll., Univ. of London, 1954–55. Pres., Jewish Historical Soc. of England, 1977–79. *Publs:* The Parliamentary Diary of Sir Edward Knatchbull 1722-1730, 1963; The Stanhopes of Chevening: A Family Biography, 1969; (compiler, with Helen Miller) A Bibliography of English History 1485-1760; (ed.) Migration and Settlement, 1971; (ed.) Provincial Jewry in Victorian Britain, 1975; The United Synagogue 1870-1970, 1977; The Jewish East End 1840-1939, 1981; (ed.) Public Finance: The Collected Essays of Dame Lucy Sutherland, 1984; The Board of Deputies 1760-1985, 1987. Add: Dept. of History, Univ. of Leicester, Leicester LE1 7RH, England.

NEWMAN, Charles (Hamilton). American, b. 1938. Novels/Short stories, Literature, Humor/Satire. Dir., American P.E.N., since 1976. Advisory Ed., The TriQuarterly Review, since 1975 (Founder and Ed., 1964–75). Instr. of English, 1964–65, Asst. Prof., 1965–68, Assoc. Prof., 1968–73, and Prof., 1974–75, Northwestern Univ., Evanston, Ill; Prof. and Chmn., The Writing Seminars, Johns Hopkins Univ., Baltimore, 1975–77. *Publs:* New Axis; or, The Little Ed Stories: An Exhibition, 1966; (ed. with G. Gomori) New Writing from East Europe, 1968; (ed.) The Art of Sylvia Plath, 1970; (ed. with W. Henkin) New American Writers Under Thirty, 1970; (ed. with A. Appel) Nabokov: Criticisms and Reminiscences, Translations and Tributes, 1970; The Promise-keeper: A Tephramancy, 1971; (ed. with G.A. White) Literature in Revolution, 1972; A Child's History of America: Some Ribs and Riffs for the Sixties, 1973; (ed. with M. Kinzie) Prose for Borges, 1974; There Must Be More to Love Than Death, 1976; White Jazz, 1984; The Post-Modern Aura, 1985. Add: c/o Georges Borchardt Inc., 136 E. 57th St., New York, N.Y. 10022, U.S.A.

NEWMAN, C(oleman) J. Canadian, b. 1935. Novels/Short stories, Plays/Screenplays. Member of the faculty, Univ. of British Columbia, Vancouver, since 1972. Former member of faculty, Sir George Williams Univ., MacDonald Coll., and McGill Univ., all Montreal. *Publs:* We Always Take Care of Our Own, 1965; (with others) New Canadian Writing 1969, 1969; A Russian Novel, 1972; radio plays—All the State Children; The Jam on Gerry's Rocks; A Work of Art (also television play); and The Haunted House of Capuscins; television plays—The Birth of a Salesman; and A Bottle of Milk for Mother. Add: Dept. of Creative Writing, Univ. of British Columbia, Vancouver, B.C., Canada.

NEWMAN, Daisy. American. Novels/Short stories, Children's fiction, History, Autobiography. Head Resident, 1957–62, and Dir., Music Center, 1960–62, Radcliffe Coll., Cambridge, Mass. *Publs:* Timothy Travels (children), 1928; Sperli the Clockmaker (children), 1932; Now That April's There (novel), 1945; Diligence in Love (novel), 1951; The Autumn's Brightness (in U.K. as Dilly), 1955; Mount Joy (children), 1968; A Procession of Friends (history), 1972; I Take Thee, Serenity (novel), 1975; Indian Summer of the Heart (novel), 1982; A Golden String (autobiog.), 1987. Add: c/o Houghton Mifflin, 2 Park St., Boston, Mass. 02108, U.S.A.

NEWMAN, Edwin (Harold). American, b. 1919. Novels, Language/ Linguistics. Television commentator in NYC, since 1961. Reporter, United Press, Washington, D.C., 1941–42, 1945–56; Writer for evening news, CBS, Washington, D.C., 1947–49; freelance journalist and broadcaster in London, 1956–57, in Rome, 1957–58, and in Paris, 1958–61. *Publs:* Strictly Speaking: Will America Be the Death of English?, 1974; A Civil Tongue, 1976; Sunday Punch, 1979; Edwin Newman on Language, 1980; I Must Say, 1988. Add: c/o Warner Books, 666 Fifth Ave., New York, N.Y. 10103, U.S.A.

NEWMAN, G(ordon) F. British, b. 1945. Novels, Mystery, Plays/ Screenplays. Film producer and screenwriter. *Publs:* novels—Sir, You Bastard, 1970, in U.S. paperback as Rogue Cop, 1973; Billy: A Family Tragedy, 1972; The Abduction, 1972; The Player and the Guest, 1972; You Nice Bastard, 1972; Three Professional Ladies, 1973; The Split, 1973; You Flash Bastard, 1974; The Streetfighter, 1975; A Detective's Tale, 1977; The Guvnor, 1977, in U.S. as Trade-Off, 1979; A Prisoner's Tale, 1977; A Villain's Tale, 1977; The List, 1979; The Obsession, 1980; Charlie and Joanna, 1981; The Men with the Guns, 1982; Law and Order, 1983; The Nation's Health, 1984; Set a Thief, 1986; The Testing Ground, 1987; also numerous plays and screenplays. Add: Wessington Court, Woolhope, Herefordshire HR1 4QN, England.

NEWMAN, Margaret. *See* **POTTER,** Margaret.

NEWMAN, Oscar. American, b. 1935. Architecture, Psychology. Principal, Oscar Newman and Assocs., architects and city planners, NYC,

since 1968; Pres., Inst. for Community Design Analysis, NYC, since 1972. Asst. Prof. of Architecture, Nova Scotia Technical Coll., Halifax, 1961–63, and Univ. of Montreal, 1963–64; Assoc. Prof. of Architecture, Washington Univ., St. Louis, 1964–68, and Columbia Univ., NYC, 1968–70; Assoc. Prof. of City Planning, New York Univ., NYC, 1970–73. *Publs:* (ed) CIAM '59 in Otterlo, 1961; Defensible Space, 1972; Architectural Design for Crime Prevention, 1973; Design Guidelines for Achieving Defensible Space, 1976; Community of Interest, 1980; Unmasking a King, 1981; Review and Analysis of the Chicago Housing Authority, 1982; Express to Brighton Beach, 1983. Add: c/o Macmillan Publishing Co., 866 Third Ave., New York, N.Y. 10022, U.S.A.

NEWMAN, P(aul) B(aker). American, b. 1919. Poetry. Prof. of English, Queens Coll., Charlotte, N.C., since 1967 (Assoc. Prof. of English, 1963–67). Lectr. in English, Univ. of Puerto Rico, Mayaguez, 1956–58; Asst. Prof. of English, Kansas State Univ., Manhattan, 1959–62. *Publs:* The Cheetah and the Fountain, 1968; Dust of the Sun, 1969; The Ladder of Love, 1970; Paula, 1975; The House on the Saco, 1978; The Light of the Red Horse, 1981; The G. Washington Poems, 1986. Add: 2215 Hassell Pl., Charlotte, N.C. 28209, U.S.A.

NEWMAN, Peter (Charles). Canadian, b. 1929. International relations/Current affairs, Politics/Government. Asst. Ed., 1951–54, Montreal Ed., 1954–55, and Production Ed., 1955–56, Financial Post, Toronto; Asst. Ed., 1956–60, Ottawa Ed., 1960–63, National Affairs Ed., 1963–64, Ed., 1971–83, Maclean's mag., Toronto; Ottawa Ed., 1964–69, and Ed.-in-Chief, 1969–71, Toronto Daily Star. *Publs:* Flame of Power, 1959; Renegade in Power: The Diefenbaker Years, 1963; Distemper of Our Times: Canadian Politics in Transition, 1968; Home Country: People, Places and Power Politics, 1973; The Canadian Establishment, vol. I, 1975; Bronfman Dynasty, 1978; The Acquistors, 1981; The Establishment Man, 1982; True North—Not Strong and Free, 1983; Debrett's Illustrated Guide to the Canadian Establishment, 1983; Company of Adventurers, 1985; Caesars of the Wilderness, 1987; Sometimes a Great Nation, 1988. Add: 4855 Major Rd., Victoria, B.C. V84 2L8, Canada.

NEWMAN, Sharan (née Hill). American, b. 1949. Historical/ Romance, Children's fiction. Instr. in English, Temple Univ., Philadelphia, 1976, and Oxnard Coll., California, 1977–79; Dir. and teacher, Asian Refugee Comm., Thousand Oaks, Calif., 1980. *Publs:* The Daga's Harp, 1977, Guinevere, 1981; The Chessboard Queen, 1983; Guinevere Evermore, 1985. Add: c/o Don Cogdon, Matson Co., 276 Fifth Ave., New York, N.Y. 10001, U.S.A.

NEWMAN, William S. American, b. 1912. Music. Alumni Distinguished Prof. of Music Emeritus, Univ. of North Carolina, Chapel Hill, since 1977 (joined faculty as Asst. Prof., 1945; Prof., 1955–62; Alumni Distinguished Prof. and Dir. of Grad. Studies in Music, 1962–77). Concert pianist; American Rep., Directorium, Intnl. Musicological Soc. *Publs:* The Pianist's Problems, 1950, 4th ed. 1984; Understanding Music, 1953, 1967; A History of the Sonata Idea, vol. I, The Sonata in the Baroque Era, 1959, 4th ed. 1983, vol. II, The Sonata in the Classic Era, 1963, 3rd ed. 1983, and vol. III, The Sonata since Beethoven, 1969, 3rd ed. 1983; Performance Practices in Beethoven's Piano Sonatas: An Introduction, 1971; Beethoven on Beethoven: Playing His Piano Music His Way, 1988. Add: Music Dept., Hill Hall, Univ. of North Carolina, Chapel Hill, N.C. 27514, U.S.A.

NEWMARK, Leonard. American, b. 1929. Language/Linguistics. Prof. of Linguistics, Univ. of California, San Diego, since 1963. Asst. Prof. of English, Ohio State Univ., Columbus, 1954–62; Assoc. Prof. of Linguistics, Indiana Univ., Bloomington, 1962–63. *Publs:* Structural Grammar of Albanian, 1957; (with M. Bloomfield) A Linguistic Introduction to the History of English, 1964; (with J. Hinely and J. Mintz) Using American English, 1964; (with others) Spoken Albanian, 1980; (with P. Prifti and P. Hubbard) Standard Albanian: A Reference Grammar, 1982. Add: 2643 St. Tropez Pl., La Jolla, Calif. 92037, U.S.A.

NEWSOME, David Hay. British, b. 1929. History, Theology/Religion, Biography. Lectr. in Ecclesiastical History, Cambridge Univ., 1960–70 (Fellow, 1959–70 and Sr. Tutor, 1965–70, Emmanuel Coll.; Birkbeck Lectr. in Ecclesiastical History, 1972); Headmaster, Christ's Hosp., Horsham, Sussex, 1970–79; Master, Wellington Coll., Crowthorne, Berks., 1980–89. *Publs:* A History of Wellington College 1859-1959, 1959; Godliness and Good Learning, 1961; The Parting of Friends: A Study of the Wilberforces and Henry Manning, 1966; Bishop Westcott and the Platonic Tradition, 1969; Two Classes of Men: Platonism in English Romantic Thought, 1974; On the Edge of Paradise: A.C. Benson the Diarist, 1980; Edwardian Excursions from the Diaries of A.C. Benson,

1980. Add: The Retreat, Thornthwaite, Keswick, Cumbria, England.

NEWTON, D(wight) B(ennett). Also writes as Dwight Bennett, Clement Hardin, Ford Logan, Hank Mitchum, and Dan Temple. American, b. 1916. Westerns/Adventure. Freelance writer since 1946. Story consultant and staff writer for TV series Wagon Train, 1957, Death Valley Days, 1958, and Tales of Wells Fargo. Founding Member, 1953, and Secty.-Treas., 1953–58, 1967–71, Western Writers of America. *Publs:* Guns of the Rimrock, 1946; The Gunmaster of Saddleback, 1948; Range Boss (in U.K. as The Trail Beyond Boothill), 1949; Shotgun Guard, 1950, in U.K. as Stagecoach Guard, 1951; Six-Gun Gamble, 1951; Guns along the Wickiup, 1953; Rainbow Rider, 1954, in U.S. paperback as Triple Trouble, 1978; (as Ford Logan) Fire in the Desert, 1954; The Outlaw Breed, 1955; Maverick Brand, 1962; On the Dodge, 1962; Guns of Warbonnet, 1963; The Savage Hills, 1964; Bullets in the Wind, 1964; Fury at Three Forks, 1964; The Manhunters, 1966; Hideout Valley, 1967; The Tabbart Brand, 1967; Shotgun Freighter, 1968; The Wolf Pack, 1968; The Judas Horse, 1969; Syndicate Gun, 1972; Massacre Valley, 1973; Range Tramp, 1973; Trail of the Bear, 1975; The Land Grabbers, 1975; Bounty on Bannister, 1975; Broken Spur, 1977; as Dwight Bennett—Stormy Range, 1951, in U.K. (as D.B. Newton) Range Feud, 1953; Lost Wolf River, 1954; Border Graze, 1952; Top Hand, 1955; The Avenger, 1956; Cherokee Outlet, 1961; The Oregon Rifles, 1962; Rebel Trail, 1963; Crooked River Canyon, 1966; Legend in the Dust, 1970; The Big Land, 1972; The Guns of Ellsworth, 1973; Hangman's Knot, 1975; The Cheyenne Encounter, 1976; West of Railhead, 1977; The Texans, 1979; Disaster Creek, 1981; as Clement Hardin—Hellbent for a Hangrope, 1954; Cross Me in Gunsmoke, 1957; The Lurking Gun, 1961; The Badge Shooters, 1962; Outcast of Ute Bend, 1965; The Ruthless Breed, 1966; The Paxman Feud, 1967; The Oxbow Deed, 1967; Ambush Reckoning, 1968; Sheriff of Sentinel, 1969; Colt Wages 1970; Stage Line to Rincon, 1971; as Dan Temple—Outlaw River, 1955; The Man from Idaho, 1956; Bullet Lease, 1957; The Love Goddess, 1962; Gun and Star, 1964; as Hank Mitchum—Station 1: Dodge City, 1982; Station 2: Laredo, 1982; Station 3: Tombstone, 1983; Station 6: Santa Fe, 1983; Station 11: Deadwood, 1984; Station 13: Carson City, 1984; Station 20: Leadville, 1985; Station 26: Tulsa, 1986. Add: 11 N.W. Kansas Ave., Bend, Ore. 97701, U.S.A.

NEWTON, Kenneth. British, b. 1940. Education, Sociology, and urban Affairs. Prof. of Political Science, Univ. of Dundee, since 1978. Research Fellow, Nuffield Coll., Oxford, 1974–78. Lectr., Univ. of Birmingham, 1965–74. *Publs:* (ed. and contrib. with S. Abrams) Opportunities After O Level, 1965; The Sociology of Communism, 1969; Second City Politics, 1976; Balancing the Books, 1980; (ed.) Urban Political Economy, 1980; (with L.J. Sharpe) Does Politics Matter?, 1984; (with T. Karrau) Politics of Local Expenditure, 1985. Add: Dept. of Political Science, The University, Dundee DD1 4HN, England.

NEWTON, Norman Lewis. Canadian, b. 1929. Novels/Short stories, Plays/Screenplays, Poetry, History. Radio Producer (Music and Drama), CBC, since 1962. *Publs:* The House of Gods, 1961; The One True Man, 1963; The Big Stuffed Hand of Friendship, 1969; Thomas Gage in Spanish America, 1969; Fire in the Raven's Nest, 1973; On the Broken Mountain, 1979; plays—The Abdication, 1955; The Lion and the Unicorn, 1958; (trans.) Le Misanthrope of Molière; The Sharing of Glycera; The Death of the Hawk; Listen to What I Say; Orphens in the Underworld; Seabird Island (opera libretto), 1977. Add: 1236 W. 27th Ave., Vancouver 9, B.C., Canada.

NEWTON, Robert R(ussell). American, b. 1918. Astronomy, Physics. Retired in 1984 from the Applied Physics Lab. of Johns Hopkins Univ. (Member of Principal Staff, 1957–84 and Supervisor of Space Sciences Branch, 1960–84). Asst. Prof. of Physics, Univ. of Tennessee, Knoxville, 1948–54; Prof. of Physics, Tulane Univ., New Orleans, 1954–57. *Publs:* (with J.B. Rosser and G.L. Gross) Mathematical Theory of Rocket Flight, 1948; Ancient Astronomical Observations and the Accelerations of the Earth and Moon, 1970; Medieval Chronicles and the Rotation of the Earth, 1972; Ancient Planetary Observations and the Validity of Ephemeris Time, 1976; The Crime of Claudius Ptolemy (history of astronomy), 1977; The Moon's Acceleration and Its Physical Origins, 2 vols., 1979-84. Add: Applied Physics Lab., Johns Hopkins Rd., Laurel, Md. 20707, U.S.A.

NEWTON, Suzanne. American, b. 1936. Children's fiction. Consultant in creative writing in North Carolina public schs., since 1972. Freelance writer. Writer-in-Residence, Peace Jr. Coll. for Women, 1974–75, and Meredith Coll., Raleigh, N.C., 1982–83. *Publs:* Purro and the Prattleberries, 1971; c/o Arnold's Corners, 1974; What Are You Up To,

William Thomas, 1977; Reubella and the Old Focus Home, 1978; M.V. Sexton Speaking, 1981; I Will Call It Georgie's Blues, 1983; An End to Perfect, 1984; A Place Between, 1986. Add: 841-A Barringer Dr., Raleigh, N.C. 27606, U.S.A.

NGUGI, J(ames) T. Also writes as Ngugi Wa Thiong'o. Kenyan, b. 1938. Novels/Short stories, Plays/Screenplays, Literature, Politics/Government. Literary and political journalist; Contrib., Sunday Nation, Nairobi. Former Ed., Penpoint mag., Kampala. *Publs:* The Black Hermit (play), 1962; This Time Tomorrow (play), 1964; Weep Not, Child, 1964; The River Between, 1965; A Grain of Wheat, 1967; Homecoming: Essays on African and Caribbean Literature, Culture and Politics, 1972; Secret Lives, 1974; Petals of Blood, 1977; (with M.G. Mugo) The Trial of Dedan Kimathi, 1977; Writers in Politics, 1980; Devil on the Cross, 1981; Detained: A Writer's Prison Diary, 1981; Education for a National Culture, 1981; I Will Marry When I Want (play), 1982; Barrel of a Pen: Resistance to Repression in Neo-Colonial Kenya, 1983; Matigari, 1989. Add: c/o Heinemann International, Halley Ct., Jordan Hill, Oxford OX2 8EJ, England.

NIBLETT, William Roy. British. Education, Humanities (general). Emeritus Prof., Univ. of London, since 1973 (Dean, Inst. of Education, 1960–68; Prof. of Higher Education, 1968–73). Prof. of Education, Univ. Coll. of Hull, 1945–47; Prof. of Education, Univ. of Leeds, 1947–59. *Publs:* Essential Education, 1947; Education and the Modern Mind, 1954; Education: The Lost Dimension, 1955; Christian Education in a Secular Society, 1960; (ed.) The Expanding University, 1962; (ed.) Moral Education in a Changing Society, 1963; (ed.) How and Why Do We Learn?, 1965; (ed.) Higher Education Demand and Response, 1969; (ed. with J. Freeman Butts) World Yearbook of Education 1972-73, 1972; Universities Between Two Worlds, 1974; (ed.) The Sciences, the Humanities, and the Technological Threat, 1975; (with D. Humphreys) The University Connection, 1975; (with others) Studies in Education, 1980. Add: 7 Blenheim Rd., Bristol, BS6 7JL, England.

NICHOLAS, David M(ansfield). American, b. 1939. Architecture, History, Sociology. Assoc. Prof. of History, Univ. of Nebraska, Lincoln, since 1971 (Asst. Prof., 1967–71). *Publs:* Town and Countryside: Social, Economic, and Political Tension in Fourteenth Century Flanders, 1971; Stad en Platteland in de Middeleeuwen, 1971; The Medieval West: A Preindustrial Civilization, 1973; The Domestic Life of a Medieval City: Women, Children, and the Family in Fourteenth Century Ghent, 1985; The Metamorphosis of a Medieval City: Ghent in the Age of the Arteveldes, 1987; The Van Arteveldes of Ghent: The Varieties of Vendetta and the Hero in History, 1988. Add: c/o Cornell Univ. Press, Box 250, 124 Roberts Pl., Ithaca, N.Y. 14851, U.S.A.

NICHOLAS, Herbert George. British, b. 1911. History, Politics/Government. Fellow, New Coll., since 1951, and Rhodes Prof. of American History and Instns., 1968–78, Oxford Univ. (Nuffield Reader in the Comparative Study of Instns., 1956–68). *Publs:* The American Union, 1948; The British General Election of 1950, 1951; (ed.) To the Hustings, 1956; The United Nations as a Political Institution, 1959, 5th ed. 1975; Britain and the United States, 1963; The United States and Britain, 1975; The Nature of American Politics, 1980, 1986; (ed.) Washington Despatches, 1941-45, 1981. Add: New Coll., Oxford, England.

NICHOLS, Jack. American, b. 1938. Human relations, Sex. Asst. to Bureau Chief, New York Post, Washington, D.C., 1961; Ed., Companion, Strange Unknown, Duke, Buccaneer, Jaguar, and Stud mags., Countryside Publications, NYC, 1968–69; Managing Ed., Screw mag., Milky Way Productions, NYC, 1969–70; former ed. of Gay mag., NYC. *Publs:* (with Lige Clarke) I Have More Fun With You Than Anybody, 1972; (with Lige Clarke) Roommates Can't Always Be Lovers, 1975; Men's Liberation, 1975; Welcome To Fire Island, 1976. Add c/o Penguin Books, 40 W. 23rd St., New York, N.Y. 10010, U.S.A.

NICHOLS, John. American, b. 1940. Novels/Short stories, Westerns, Autobiography/Memoirs/Personal. Freelance writer and photographer. *Publs:* The Sterile Cuckoo, 1965; The Wizard of Loneliness, 1966; The Milagro Beanfield War, 1974, The Magic Journey, 1978, The Nirvana Blues, 1981 (New Mexico trilogy); A Ghost in the Music, 1979; If Mountains Die, 1979; The Last Beautiful Days of Autumn, 1982; On the Mesa, 1986; American Blood, 1987; A Fragile Beauty, 1987. Add: Box 1165, Taos, N.M. 87571, U.S.A.

NICHOLS, John Gordon. British, b. 1930. Poetry, Literature. Principal Lectr. in English, since 1966, Notre Dame Coll., Liverpool (Sr.

Lectr., 1964–66; Head of English Dept., 1970–80). Head of English Dept., King David Sch., Liverpool, 1957–62; Lectr., Edge Hill Coll. of Education, 1962–64. *Publs:* The Flighty Horse, 1968; (ed. with T. Pey) The Poet's Purpose, 1969; The Poetry of Ben Jonson, 1969; The Poetry of Sir Philip Sidney, 1974; The Colloquies of Guido Gozzano with a Selection from his Letters, 1987; Gabriele d'Annunzio: Halcyon, 1988. Add: 43 Warren Dr., Wallasey, Merseyside, England.

NICHOLS, Leigh. *See* **KOONTZ,** Dean R.

NICHOLS, Peter (Richard). British, b. 1927. Plays/Screenplays, Autobiography. Gov., Greenwich Theatre, London, since 1970. Member, Arts Council Drama Panel, 1972–75. Visiting Playwright, Guthrie Theatre, Minneapolis, 1976. Recipient: Evening Standard Award, 1967, 1969, 1977; John Whiting Award, 1969. *Publs:* A Day in the Death of Joe Egg (in U.S. as Joe Egg), 1967; The National Health; or, Nurse Norton's Affair, 1969; Forget-Me-Not-Lane, 1971; Chez Nous, 1974; The Free-way, 1974; Privates on Parade, 1977; Born in the Garden, 1979; Passion Play, 1980; Poppy, 1982; Feeling You're Behind: An Autobiography, 1984; A Piece of My Mind, 1987. Add: c/o Margaret Ramsay Ltd., 14 Goodwin's Court, London WC2, England.

NICHOLS, R. Eugene. American, b. 1914. Psychology. Sr. Minister, Unity on the Parkway, Denver, since 1987. Founder, Inst. of Mental Cybernetics, 1970. Minister-Dir., Church of Religious Science, Riverside, Calif., 1953–59; Dir., Science of Mind Church, Denver, 1959–87. *Publs:* The Science of Mental Cybernetics, 1970; The Science of Higher Sense Perception, 1972; Esoteric Keys to Personal Power, 1977; Picture Yourself a Winner, 1978. Add: 6394 E. Floyd Dr., Denver, Colo. 80222, U.S.A.

NICHOLS, Roger. British, b. 1939. Music. Part-time Lectr. in Music, Univ. of Birmingham, 1978–80. *Publs:* Debussy, 1973; Messiaen, 1975; Ravel, 1977; Ravel Remembered, 1987; (ed. and trans.) Debussy: Letters, 1987; (with Richard Langham Smith) Pelléas et Mélisande, 1989. Add: West End Cottage, Docklow, Leominster, Herefordshire, England.

NICHOLS, Ruth. Canadian, b. 1948. Novels/Short stories, Historical/Romance/Gothic, Children's fiction. *Publs:* A Walk Out of the World, 1969; Ceremony of Innocence, 1969; The Marrow of the World, 1972; Song of the Pearl, 1976; The Left-Handed Spirit, 1978. Add: c/o Gage Educational Publishing, 164 Commander Blvd., Agincourt, Ont. M1S 3C7, Canada.

NICHOLSON, Christina. *See* **NICOLE,** Christopher.

NICHOLSON, E(rnest) W(ilson). British, b. 1938. Religion. Fellow, Oriel Coll., Oxford, and Oriel Prof. of the Interpretation of Holy Scripture, Oxford Univ., since 1979. Lectr. in Hebrew and Semitic Languages, Trinity College, Dublin, 1962–67; Fellow, University Coll. (now Wolfson Coll.), Cambridge, 1967–69, and Fellow, 1969–79, Chaplain, 1969–73 and Dean, 1973–79, Pembroke Coll., Cambridge, and Lectr. in Divinity, Cambridge Univ., 1967–79. *Publs:* Deuteronomy and Tradition, 1967; Preaching to the Exiles, 1971; Exodus and Sinai in History and Tradition, 1973; (with J. Baker) The Commentary of Rabbi David Kimhi on Psalms 120-150, 1973; Commentary on Jeremiah, 2 vols., 1973-75; God and His People: Covenant and Theology in the Old Testament, 1986. Add: Oriel College, Oxford OX1 4EW, England.

NICHOLSON, Geoffrey. British, b. 1929. Sports/Physical education/Keeping fit. Sports Ed., The Observer, London, 1976–78; Rugby Corresp., The Independent, 1986–88. *Publs:* (with W. John Morgan) Report on Rugby (social history), 1959; The Professionals, 1964; (ed.) Touchdown, 1970; (ed.) Motor Racing (children), 1973; (ed.) Football (children), 1974; The Great Bike Race, 1977; (with C. Thomas) The Crowning Years, 1980; Eamonn McCabe, Sports Photographer, 1982. Add: Aber-Rhaeadr Farmhouse, Llanrhaeadr-ym-Mochnant, Powys SY10 0AX, Wales.

NICHOLSON, Hubert. Has also written as Elliott Selby. British, b. 1908. Novels/Short stories, Poetry, Autobiography/Memoirs/Personal. *Publs:* Face Your Lover, 1935; Date, 1935; Half My Days and Nights, 1941; New Spring Song, 1943; Here Where the World is Quiet, 1944; No Cloud of Glory, 1946; A Voyage to Wonderland, 1947; The Sacred Afternoon, 1949; Little Heyday, 1954; The Mirage in the South, 1955; Sunk Island, 1956; (as Elliott Selby with John Gee) The Triumph of Tchaikovsky, 1959; Mr. Hill and Friends, 1960; Patterns of Three and Four, 1965; Duckling in Capri, 1966; The Lemon Tree, 1970; Dead Man's Life, 1971; Ella, 1973; Ventriloquists and Dolls, 1978; Selected Poems 1930-80, 1981; Late Light, 1987. Add: Kertch Cottage, 3 Albert Rd., Epsom, Surrey, England.

NICHOLSON, Ranald. British, b. 1931. History. Prof. of History, Univ. of Guelph, Ont., 1967–78. *Publs:* Edward III and the Scots: The Formative Years of a Military Career 1327-1335, 1965; Scotland: The Later Middle Ages, 1973; (ed. with Peter McNeill) Historical Atlas of Scotland, 1975; Port St. Mary: A Memory of the Present, 1986. Add: Rock View, Marine Parade, Peel, Isle of Man.

NICOL, Abioseh. (Davidson Sylvester Hector Willoughby Nicol). Sierra Leonean, b. 1924. Novels/Short stories, History. Hon. Fellow, Christ's Coll., Cambridge, since 1972. House Physician and Research Asst., London Hosp. Medical Coll., Univ. of London, 1950–52; Univ. Lectr., The Medical Sch., Ibadan, 1952–54; Fellow and Suprv. in Natural Sciences and Medicine, Christ's Coll., Cambridge, 1957–59; Sr. Pathologist, Sierra Leone Govt., 1958–60; Principal, Fourah Bay Coll., 1960–67, and Vice-Chancellor, 1966–68, Univ. of Sierra Leone, Freetown; Danforth Lectr., Assn. of American Colls., 1968–70; Ambassador of Sierra Leone to the U.N., 1968–71, and to Denmark, Norway, Sweden, and Finland, 1971–72; Under Secty.-Gen. of the United Nations, 1972–82; Pres., World Fedn. of United Nations Assns., 1983–87. *Publs:* Alienation: An Essay, 1960; Africa: A Subjective View, 1964; The Truly Married Woman and Other Stories, 1965; Two African Tales, 1965; Africanus Horton: The Dawn of Nationalism in Modern Africa (in U.S. as Black Nationalism in Africa, 1867), 1969; New and Modern Roles for Commonwealth and Empire, 1976; The United Nations and Decision Making, 1978; Nigeria and the Future of Africa, 1980; Paths to Peace, 1981; The United Nations Security Council, 1981; Creative Women, 1982. Add: Christ's Coll., Cambridge, England.

NICOL, Donald MacGillivray. British, b. 1923. History. Emeritus Prof. of Modern Greek and Byzantine History, Language and Literature, Univ. of London (joined faculty, 1970). Lectr. in Classics, University Coll., Dublin, 1952–64; Visiting Fellow, Dumbarton Oaks, Washington D.C., 1964–65; Visiting Prof. of Byzantine History, Indiana Univ., Bloomington, 1965–66; Sr. Lectr. and Reader in Byzantine History, Univ. of Edinburgh, 1966–70. *Publs:* The Despotate of Epiros, 1957; Meteora: The Rock Monasteries of Thessaly, 1963, 1975; The Byzantine Family of Kantakouzenos 1100-1460, 1968; The Last Centuries of Byzantium 1261-1453, 1972; Byzantium: Its Ecclesiastical History and Relations with the Western World, 1972; Church and Society in the Last Centuries of Byzantium, 1979; The End of the Byzantine Empire, 1979; The Despotate of Epiros 1267-1479: A Contribution to the History of Greece in the Middle Ages, 1984; Studies in Late Byzantine History and Prosopography, 1986; Byzantium and Venice: A Study in Diplomatic and Cultural Relations, 1988. Add: c/o American Sch. of Classical Studies, Souedias 54, Athens 10676, Greece.

NICOLAEFF, Ariadne. Also writes as Nicholas Moore. British, b. 1915. Plays/Screenplays, Translations. Radio Producer, BBC, London, 1947–63. *Publs:* Poems, 1937; (as Nicholas Moore) Lock and Key, 1956; (co-trans.) Chekov: Ivanov; (trans.) Chekov: The Bear, The Cherry Orchard, Three Sisters, Uncle Vanya, 1964–72; (trans.) A. Arbuzov: The Promise, 1967, Confession at Night, 1971, and the Twelfth Hour: The Third Wife, 1973; (trans.) J. Edliss: Abel, Where's Your Brother, 1974; (trans.) Turgenev: A Month in the Country, 1974; (trans.) A. Arbuzov: Once Upon Time, 1976, Evening Light, 1976, Old-World, 1976, and Cruel Games, 1980; (trans.) Selected Plays of Aleiksei Arbuzov, 1982; Chance Visitor, 1984. Add: 27 Gt. Livermere, Bury St. Edmunds, Suffolk, England.

NICOLAYSEN, (F.) Bruce. American, b. 1934. Novels/Short stories, Plays/Screenplays. Copy Chief, Carson/Roberts Advertising, Los Angeles, 1966–70; Creative Dir., Ogilvy and Mather, Los Angeles, 1970–74. *Publs:* Perilous Passage (novel; in U.K. as The Passage), 1977, as The Passage (screenplay), 1978; Tiger Ten (screenplay), 1978; (co-author) The Brinks Job (screenplay), 1979; From Distant Shores (novel), 1980, On Maiden Lane (novel), 1981; Beekman Place (novel), 1982; The Pirate of Gramercy Park (novel), 1983; Gracie Square (novel), 1984. Add: Apple Hill Rd., Bennington, Vt. 05201, U.S.A.

NICOLE, Christopher. Also writes as Robin Cade, Peter Grange, Mark Logan, Christina Nicholson, and Andrew York. British, b. 1930, Novels/Short stories, Mystery/Crime/Suspense, Historical/Romance/Gothic, History, Sports/Physical education/Keeping fit. Clerk, Royal Bank of Canada, in the West Indies, 1947–56. *Publs:* West Indian Cricket, 1957; Off White, 1959; Shadows in the Jungle, 1961;

Ratoon, 1962; Dark Noon, 1963; Amyot's Cay, 1964; Blood Amyot, 1964; The Amyot Crime, 1965; The West Indies: Their People and History, 1965; White Boy, 1966; The Self-Lovers, 1968; The Thunder and the Shouting, 1969; The Longest Pleasure, 1970; Heroes, 1972; The Face of Evil, 1972; Lord of the Golden Fan, 1973; Caribee, 1974; The Devil's Own, 1975; Mistress of Darkness, 1976; Black Dawn, 1977; Sunset, 1978; The Secret Memoirs of Lord Byron, 1978; Haggard, 1980; (as C.R. Nicholson), This Friday Spy, 1980, in U.S. (as Robin Nicholson) as A Passion for Treason, 1981; Haggard's Inheritance (in U.S. as The Inheritors), 1981; The New Americas, 2 vols., 1982; The Young Haggards, 1982; The Crimson Pagoda, 1983; The Anderson Line, 1984; The Sun Rises, 1984; The Sun and the Dragon, 1985; The Sun in Flames, 1985; The Scarlet Princess, 1984; Red Dawn, 1985; Black Majesty, 1986; The Sea and the Sand, 1986; Old Glory, 1986; The Ship with No Name, 1987; Iron Ships, Iron Men, 1987; The Wind of Destiny, 1987; Raging Sea, Searing Sky, 1988; The Passion and the Glory, 1988; The High Country, 1988; Pearl of the Orient, 1988; The Regiment, 1988; The Happy Valley, 1989; as Andrew York—The Eliminator, 1966; The Co-Ordinator, 1967; The Predator, 1968; The Deviator, 1969; The Doom Fisherman (in U.S. as Operation Destruct), 1969; The Dominator, 1969; Manhunt for a General (in U.S. as Operation Manhunt), 1970; The Infiltrator, 1971; Where the Cavern Ends, 1971; The Expurgator, 1972; Appointment in Kiltone (in U.S. as Operation Neptune), 1972; The Captivators, 1974; The Fascinator, 1975; Dark Passage, 1976; Tallant for Trouble, 1977; Tallant for Disaster, 1978; The Combination, 1983; as Peter Grange—King Creole, 1966; The Devil's Emissary, 1968; The Tumult at the Gate, 1970; The Golden Goddess, 1973; as Robin Cade—The Fear Dealers, 1974; as Mark Logan—Tricolour, 1976; Guillotine, 1976; Brumaire, 1978; as Christina Nicholson—The Power and the Passion, 1977; The Savage Sands, 1978. Add: c/o John Farquharson Ltd., 162–168 Regent St., London W1R 5TB, England.

NICOLL, Helen. British, b. 1937. Children's fiction. Producer and director of children's television programs, since 1975. *Publs:* Meg and Dog, 1972; Meg's Eggs, 1972; Meg at Sea, 1973; Meg on the Moon, 1973; Meg's Car, 1975; Meg's Castle, 1975; Meg's Veg, 1976; Mog's Mumps, 1976; Quest for the Gloop: The Exploits of Murfy and PHIX, 1980; Mog at the Zoo, 1982; (ed.) Poems for Seven Year Olds and Under, 1983; Mog in the Fog, 1984; Owl at School, 1984; Mog's Box, 1987. Add: c/o Heinemann Ltd., 81 Fulham Rd., London SW3 6RB, England.

NICOLSON, Ian. British, b. 1928. Recreation/Leisure/Hobbies, Travel/Exploration/Adventure. Partner, A. Mylne and Co., Dunbartonshire, since 1959. Founder and Partner, Nicolson Hughes Sails. *Publs:* Sea Saint, 1958; Log of the Maken, 1960; Dinghy Cruising, 1961; Building the St. Mary, 1962; Outboard Boats and Engines, 1963; Guide to Boatbuying, 1964; Designer's Notebook, 1967, 1988; Small Steel Craft, 1971; Surveying Small Craft, 1974; Marinize Your Boat, 1975; Boat Data Book, 1977; Build Your Own Boat, 1982; Cold Moulded and Strip Plank Wood Boatbuilding, 1983; Yacht Designer's Sketchbook, 1983; Improve Your Own Boat, 1984; The Ian Nicolson Omnibus, 1986; Comfort in the Cruising Yacht, 1986; Build a Simple Dinghy, 1987; Roving in Open Boats, 1988; Race Winner!, 1989. Add: Linnfield Cove, Dunbartonshire, Scotland.

NICOLSON, Nigel. British, b. 1917. History, Biography. Dir., Weidenfeld and Nicolson Ltd., publrs., London, since 1947. Conservative Member of Parliament (U.K.), 1952–59; Chmn., U.N. Assn., 1960–67. *Publs:* The Grenadier Guards 1939-45, 1949; People and Parliament, 1958;, Lord of the Isles, 1960; Great Houses of Britain, 1965, 1978; (ed.) Harold Nicolson: Diaries and Letters, 3 vols., 1966-68; Great Houses, 1968; Alex, 1973; Portrait of a Marriage, 1973; (ed. with J. Trautmann) The Letters of Virginia Woolf, 6 vols., 1975-80; Mary Curzon, 1977; Napoleon 1812, 1985; (with Adam Nicolson) Two Roads to Dodge City, 1986; Kent, 1988. Add: Sissinghurst Castle, Cranbrook, Kent, England.

NIEBURG, H(arold) L(eonard). American, b. 1927. International relations/Current affairs, Military/Defence, Politics/Government. Prof. of Political Science, State Univ. of New York at Binghamton, since 1970. Faculty Member, Univ. of Wisconsin, Milwaukee, 1963–70. *Publs:* Nuclear Secrecy and Foreign Policy, 1964; In the Name of Science, 1966; Political Violence: The Behavioral Process, 1969; Culture Storm: Politics and the Ritual Order, 1973; Public Opinion/Tracking and Targeting, 1983. Add: R.D. 2, Rockwell Rd., Vestal, N.Y. 13850, U.S.A.

NIELSEN, Helen (Berniece). American, b. 1918. Mystery/Crime/Suspense. *Publs:* The Kind Man, 1951; Gold Coast Nocturne, 1951, in U.K. as Murder by Proxy, 1952, in U.S. paperback, Dead on the Level, 1954; Obit Delayed, 1952; Detour, 1953, in U.S. paperback, Detour to

Death, 1955; The Woman on the Roof, 1954; Stranger in the Dark, 1955; The Crime Is Murder, 1956; Borrow the Night, 1957, in U.S. paperback, Seven Days Before Dying, 1958; The Fifth Caller, 1959; False Witness, 1959; Sing Me a Murder, 1960; Woman Missing and Other Stories, 1961; Verdict Suspended, 1964; After Midnight, 1966; A Killer in the Street, 1967; Darkest Hour, 1969; Shot on Location, 1971; The Severed Key, 1973; The Brink of Murder, 1976; Line of Fire, 1987. Add: 3621-66 Vista Campana S., Oceanside, CA 92056, U.S.A.

NIELSEN, Niels Christian, Jr. American, b. 1921. Theology/Religion. J. Newton Rayzor Prof. of Philosophy and Religious Thought, and Chmn. of the Dept. of Religious Studies, Rice Univ., Houston (joined faculty, 1951). Secty., American Soc. for the Study of Religion, since 1976. Ordained Elder, Methodist Church. Instr. in Religion, Yale Coll., New Haven, Conn., 1948–51. *Publs:* Philosophy and Religion in Post-War Japan, 1957; (co-trans.) Geistige Landerkunde, USA, 1960; A Layman Looks at World Religions, 1962; God in Education, 1966; Solzhenitsyn's Religion, 1975; The Religion of President Carter, 1977; The Crisis of Human Rights, 1978; (ed.) Religions of the World, 1983. Add: Dept. of Religious Studies, Rice Univ., Houston, Tex. 77001, U.S.A.

NIERENBERG, Gerard I. American, b. 1923. Business/Trade/Industry, Language/Linguistics. Partner, law firm of Nierenberg Zeif and Weinstein, NYC, since 1947. *Publs:* Art of Negotiating, 1968; Creative Business Negotiating, 1971; (with H. Calero) How to Read a Person Like a Book, 1971; Fundamentals of Negotiating, 1973; (with H. Calero) Meta-Talk, 1973; How to Give and Receive Advice, 1975; The Art of Creative Thinking, 1982; The Complete Negotiator, 1986; How to Give Yourself Good Advice, 1986; Workable Ethics, 1987. Add: c/o Nierenberg, Zeif & Weinstein, 230 Park Ave., New York, N.Y. 10169, U.S.A.

NIGRO, Felix A(nthony). American, b. 1914. Public/Social administration. Prof. Emeritus of Political Science, Univ. of Georgia, Athens, since 1982 (Prof., 1969–82). Lectr., U.N. Central American Advanced Sch. of Public Admin., 1956–57; Prof. of Political Science, Southern Illinois Univ., Carbondale, 1957–61, and San Diego State Univ., California, 1961–65; Charles P. Messick Prof. of Admin., Univ. of Delaware, 1965–69. *Publs:* (ed.) Public Administration: Readings and Documents, 1951; Public Personnel Administration, 1959; Management-Employee Relations in the Public Service, 1969; (with Lloyd G. Nigro) Modern Public Administration, 7th ed. 1989; (with Lloyd G. Nigro) The New Public Personnel Administration, 1976, 3rd ed. 1986. Add: 199 West View Dr., Athens, Ga. 30606, U.S.A.

NIKLAUS, Robert. British, b. 1910. Literature. Prof. of French and Head of the Dept. of French and Italian, Univ. of Exeter, 1952–75, now Emeritus (Dean, Faculty of Arts, 1959–62; Deputy Vice-Chancellor, 1965–67). Visiting Prof., Univ. of British Columbia, Vancouver, 1975–76; Head of the Dept. of Languages, Univ. of Nigeria, 1977–78, Gen. Ed., Textes Français Classiques et Modernes, Hodder and Stoughton. *Publs:* Jean Moreas: Poete Lyrique, 1936; (with J.S. Wood) French Prose Composition, 1936; The Year's Work in Modern Language Studies, vol.s VII-XIII, 1937-52; (with J.S. Wood) French Unseens, 1940; Les Pensees philosophiques de Diderot, 1941, 3rd ed. 1957; (ed.) Les Reveries du Promeneur Solitaire, by Rousseau, 1942, 4th ed. 1961; (ed.) Lettre sur les Aveugles, 1951, 1963; Diderot and Drama, 1952; (with C.E. Loveman) Modern Method French Course, vols. IV-V, 1958; (ed. with Thelma Niklaus) Marivaux: Arlequin poli par l'amour; Beaumarchais: Le Barbier de Seville, 1968; Literary History of France: The 18th Century, 1970; Beaumarchais: Le mariage de Figaro, 1982. Add: Dept. of French and Italian, Univ. of Exeter, Queen's Bldg., The Queen's Dr., Exeter EX4 4QH, England.

NILE, Dorothea. *See* **AVALLONE,** Michael.

NILSON, (Amabel Rhoda) Bee. British, b. 1908. Cookery/Gastronomy/Wine, Medicine/Health. Head, Experimental Kitchens, Ministry of Food, London, 1943–46; Principal Lectr. in Nutrition, Polytechnic of North London, 1948–68. *Publs:* The Penguin Cookery Book, 1952; The Book of Meat Cookery, 1962; Cooking for Special Diets, 1964; Pears Family Cookbook, 1964; The Career Woman's Cookbook, 1966; Deep Freeze Cooking, 1969; (ed.) The Coeliac Handbook, 1970; Bee's Blender Book, 1971; Pears Book of Meats and Accompaniments, 1971; Pears Book of Cakes and Puddings, 1971; Pears Book of Light Meals, 1972; Bee Nilson's Book of Kitchen Management and Kitchen Handbook, 1972; Fondue, Flambe and Side Table Cooking, 1972; (ed.) Annie's Edwardian Cookery Book, 1972; Cooking with Yogurt, Cultured Cream and Soft Cheese, 1973; Making Ice-Cream and Other Cold Sweets, 1973; Herb Cookery, 1974; (ed.) The Women's Institute Diamond Jubilee Cookbook, 1975; The Best of Bee Nilson, 1975. Add: 27 Betjeman Close, Pinner Rd., Pinner, Middx. HA5 5SA, England.

NIMMO, Jenny. British, b. 1944. Children's fiction. *Publs:* The Bronze Trumpeter, 1975; Tatty Apple, 1984; The Snow Spider, 1986; Emlyn's Moon, 1987, in U.S. as Orchard of the Cresant Moon, 1989; The Red Secret, 1989; The Chestnut Soldier, 1989. Add: Henllan Mill, Llangynyw, Welshpool, Powys SW21 9EN, Wales.

NIMS, John Frederick. American, b. 1913. Poetry, Literature, Translations. Taught at the Univ. of Notre Dame, Ind. 1939–45, 1946–52, 1954–58, Univ. of Toronto, 1945–46, Bocconi Univ., Milan, 1952–53, Univ. of Florence, 1953–54, Univ. of Madrid, 1958–60, Univ. of Illinois, Urbana, 1961–1965, Harvard Univ., 1964, 1968–69, Univ. of Florida, Gainesville, 1973–77; Prof. of English, Univ. of Illinois, Chicago, 1965–73, 1977–85. Ed., 1945–48, 1978–84, and Guest Ed., 1960–61, Poetry, Chicago. *Publs:* The Iron Pastoral, 1947; A Fountain in Kentucky and Other Poems, 1950; (trans.) The Poems of St. John of the Cross, 1959, 3rd ed. 1979; (trans.) Andromache, 1959; Knowledge of the Evening: Poems, 1950-1960, 1960; (ed.) Ovid's Metamorphoses: The Arthur Golding Translation, 1965; Of Flesh and Bone, 1967; (trans.) Sappho to Valery: Poems in Translation, 1971, 1980; Western Wind: An Introduction to Poetry, 1974, 1982; The Harper Anthology of Poetry, 1982; The Kiss: A Jambalaya, 1982; Selected Poems, 1982; A Local Habitation: Essays on Poetry, 1985. Add: 3920 Lake Shore Dr., Chicago Ill. 60613, U.S.A.

NINEHAM, Dennis Eric. British, b. 1921. Theology/Religion. Hon. Fellow, Keble Coll., Oxford, since 1980 (Warden, 1969–79). Fellow, Queen's Coll., Oxford, 1945–54; Prof. of Divinity, London Univ., 1954–64; Regius Prof. of Divinity, Cambridge Univ., 1964–69; Prof. of Theology, Univ. of Bristol, 1980–86. *Publs:* (ed.) Studies in the Gospels 1955; (ed.) On the Authority of the Bible, 1960; A new Way of Looking at the Gospels, 1961; The Gospel of St. Mark, 1963; (ed.) The Church's Use of the Bible, 1965; (ed.) New English Bible Reviewed, 1965; The Use and Abuse of the Bible, 1976; Explorations in Theology, 1977; 1977; (contrib.) Myth of God Incarnate, 1977; (contrib.) Imagination and the Future, 1980. Add: 4 Wootten Dr., Iffley Turn, Oxford OX4 4DS, England.

NISBET, Stanley Donald. British, b. 1912. Institutions/Organizations. Assoc. Ed., World Yearbook of Education since 1981. Prof. of Education, Queen's Univ. of Belfast, 1946–51; Prof. of Education, Univ. of Glasgow, 1951–78. *Publs:* Purpose in the Curriculum, 1957; (with B.L. Napier) Promise and Progress: A Study of Glasgow University Students in the 1960's, 1970. Add: 6 Victoria Park Corner, Glasgow G14 9NZ, Scotland.

NISH, Ian Hill. British, b. 1926. History, International relations/Current affairs. Prof. of History, London Sch. of Economics, since 1980 (Sr. Lectr., 1963–72; Reader, 1972–80). Lectr. in History, Univ. of Sydney, 1958–62. *Publs:* The Anglo-Japanese Alliance, 1962, 1985; The Story of Japan (in U.S. as Short History of Japan), 1968; Alliance in Decline, 1973; Japanese Foreign Policy, 1869-1942, 1977; The Origins of the Russo-Japanese War, 1985. Add: Oakdene, Charlwood Dr., Oxshott, Surrey KT22 0HB, England.

NISSENSON, Hugh. American, b. 1933. Novels/Short stories. *Publs:* A Pile of Stones, 1965; Notes from the Frontier, 1968; In the Reign of Peace, 1972; My Own Ground, 1976; The Tree of Life, 1985; The Elephant and My Jewish Problem, 1988. Add: 411 West End Ave., New York, N.Y. 10024, U.S.A.

NISSMAN, Albert. American, b. 1930. Poetry, Education. Prof. of Education, Div. of Grad. Studies, Rider Coll., Lawrenceville, N.J., since 1974 (Asst. Prof. of English and Education, and Dir. of Professional Lab. Experiences, 1966–70; Assoc. Prof. of Education, 1970–74). Teacher in public schs., Philadelphia, 1952–53; Teacher of English and Social Studies, 1953–63, and District English Chmn. and Reading Consultant, Bristol Township Sch. District, Pennsylvania. *Publs:* Student Teacher: A Dress Rehearsal for a Career, 1967; Readings: Seminar in Student Teaching, 1967; Fragments/Figments (poetry), 1967; (with Jack Lutz) Organizing and Developing a Summer Professional Workshop, 1972; Operation Classroom: A Direct Experience Approach, 1975; Shirim: Songs of My Jewishness (poetry), 1985. Add: 24 Needlepoint Lane, Garfield Park North, Willingboro, N.J. 08046, U.S.A.

NISSMAN, Blossom S. American, b. 1928. Children's non-fiction, Education. Exec. Dir., Central Burlington Co. Region, New Jersey, since 1972; Superintendent, Long Beach Island Sch., Ship Bottom, N.J., since

1988. Weekly Columnist, Beach Haven Times. Learning Disabilities Consultant, Willingboro Sch. District, New Jersey, 1970–72. *Publs:* Counselor's Handbook, 1955; Alphabet Land, 1970; Ask Counselor, 1970; New Dimensions in Elementary Guidance, 1971; Your Child and Drugs: A Preventive Approach, 1973; What You Always Wanted to Know About Tests But Were Afraid to Ask!, 1973; Practical Guidance for Space Age Children, 1979; Improving Middle School Guidance, 1980; Mainstreaming: Who? Why? When? How?, 1980; Career Assessment Guidelines for Middle and High School Students with Special Needs, 1980; Job Preparation, Selection, Performance, Retention, 1981; Tips for Teachers, 1981; Teacher Tested Alternatives for Use in Classroom Management, 1981; Answers to Questions Most Frequently Asked about Classfied Students, 1981; Searching for Teaching Excellence, 1982; Burlington County Job File, 1983. Add: 14 Tahoe Lane, Manahawkin, N.J. 08050, U.S.A.

NITCHIE, George Wilson. American, b. 1921. Poetry, Literature. Prof. of English, Simmons Coll., Boston, since 1966, Emeritus since 1986 (Instr., 1947–50; Asst. Prof., 1950–59; Assoc. Prof., 1959–66). *Publs:* Seven Poems by George W. Nitchie, 1959; Human Values in the Poetry of Robert Frost, 1960; Marianne Moore: An Introduction to the Poetry, 1969. Add: 50 Pleasantview Ave., Weymouth, Mass. 02188, U.S.A.

NITSKE, W. Robert. American, b. 1909. History, Biography. Feature Ed., Mercedes-Benz Star. National Secty.-Treas., Mercedes-Benz Club of America. Former columnist for Motor-racing and reporter on intnl. races. *Publs:* The Complete Mercedes Story, 1955; The Amazing Porsche and Volkswagen Story, 1958; (co-author) Rudolf Diesel: Pioneer of the Age of Power, 1965; Life of Wilhelm Conrad Rontgen: Discoverer of the X-Ray, 1971; (trans. and ed.) Travels in North America 1822-24 by Duke Paul Wilhelm of Wurttemberg, 1973; Mercedes-Benz 300 SL, 1974; The Zeppelin Story, 1977; Mercedes-Benz Production Models 1946-1975, 1977, 1946-86, 1986; Mercedes-Benz: A History, 1978; Mercedes-Benz Diesel Automobiles, 1981. Add: 2426 Tucana St., Tucson, Ariz. 85745, U.S.A.

NIVEN, Alastair (Neil Robertson). British, b. 1944. Literature. Dir. of Literature, Arts Council of Great Britain, since 1987. Co-Ed., Journal of Commonwealth Literature, since 1979; Hon. Fellow, Univ, of Warwick, since 1988. Lectr., Univs. of Ghana, 1968–69, Leeds, 1969–70, and Stirling, 1970–78; Dir.-Gen., Africa Centre, London, 1978–84; Special Asst. to the Secty.-Gen., Assn. of Commonwealth Universities, 1985–87; Chapman Fellow, Inst. of Commonwealth Univs., Univ. of London, 1984–85; Visiting Fellow, Australian Studies Centre, Univ. of London, 1985. *Publs:* (ed.) The Commonwealth Writer Overseas, 1976; D.H. Lawrence: The Novels, 1978; The Yoke of Pity: The Fictional Writings of Mulk Raj Anand, 1978; D.H. Lawrence, 1980; (ed.) Under Another Sky: The Commonwealth Poetry Prize Anthology, 1987; (with Sir Hugh Springer) The Commonwealth of Universities, 1987; Truth into Fiction: Raja Rao, 1988. Add: Eden House, 28 Weathercock Lane, Woburn Sands, Bucks. MK17 8NT, England.

NIVEN, Larry (Laurence Van Cott). American, b. 1938. Science fiction/Fantasy. *Publs:* World of Ptavvs, 1966; Gift from Earth, 1968; Neutron Star, 1968; The Shape of Space, 1969; Ringworld, 1970; (with David Gerold) The Flying Sorcerer, 1971; Protector, 1973; The Flight of the Horse, 1973; Three Trips in Time and Space, 1973; A Hole in Space, 1974; (with Jerry Pournelle) A Mote in God's Eye, 1974; Tales of Known Space, 1975; The Long Arm of Gil Hamilton, 1976; (with Jerry Pournelle) Inferno, 1976; A World Out of Time, 1977; (with Jerry Pournelle) Lucifer's Hammer, 1977; The Magic Goes Away, 1978; Convergent Series, 1979; The Ringworld Engineers, 1980; The Patchwork Girl, 1980; (with Steven Barnes) Dream Park, 1981; (ed.) The Magic May Return, 1981; (with Jerry Pournelle) Oath of Fealty, 1981; (with Steven Barnes) The Descent of Anansi, 1982; The Integral Trees, 1983; (ed.) More Magic, 1984; The Time of the Warlock, 1984; (with Jerry Pournelle) Footfall, 1985; Limits: Collected Stories, 1985; The Smoke Ring, 1987; (with Jerry Pournelle) The Legacy of Heorot, 1987. Add: 3961 Vanalden, Tarzana, Calif., U.S.A.

NIVEN, (Sir) (Cecil) Rex. British, b. 1898. Area studies, Travel/Exploration/Adventure. With Nigerian Admin. Service, 1921–54; Speaker, Northern House of Assembly, Nigeria, 1952–60. *Publs:* Short History of Nigeria, 1937; Nigeria's Story, 1939; Nigeria—Outline of a Colony, 1946; How Nigeria is Governed, 1950; West Africa, 1958; Short History of the Yoruba Peoples, 1958; You and Your Government, 1958; (with Sardauna of Sokoto) My Life, 1962; Nine Great Africans, 1964; Nigeria (Nations of the Modern World), 1967; War of Nigerian Unity, 1970; A Nigerian Kaleidoscope, 1982. Add: 12 Archery Sq., Walmer, Kent, England.

NIXON, Joan Lowery. American, b. 1927. Children's fiction, Children's non-fiction. Elementary sch. teacher, Los Angeles, 1947–50; Creative writing instr., Midland Col., Texas, 1971, and Univ. of Houston, 1974–78. *Publs:* Mystery of Hurricane Castle, 1964; Mystery of the Grinning Idol, 1965; Mystery of the Hidden Cockatoo, 1966; Mystery of the Haunted Woods, 1967; Mystery of the Secret Stowaway, 1968; Delbert: The Plainclothes Detective, 1971; The Alligator under the Bed, 1974; The Mysterious Red Tape Gang, 1974; The Secret Box Mystery, 1974; The Mysterious Prowler, 1976; Who Is My Neighbor?, 1976; Five Loaves and Two Fishes, 1976; (with Hershell Nixon) Oil and Gas: From Fossils to Fuel, 1977; The Son Who Came Home Again, 1977; Writing Mysteries for Young People, 1977; (with Hershell Nixon) Volcanoes: Nature's Fireworks, 1978; When God Listens, 1978; When God Speaks, 1978; The Boy Who Could Find Anything, 1978; Danger in Dinosaur Valley, 1978; Muffie Mouse and the Busy Birthday, 1978; Bigfoot Makes a Move, 1979; The Grandmother's Book, 1979; The Kidnapping of Christina Lattimore, 1979; The Butterfly Tree, 1979; The New Year's [Valentine's, Halloween, April Fool, Happy Birthday, Thanksgiving, Christmas Eve, Easter] Mystery, 8 vols., 1979–81; Before You Were Born, 1980; (with Hershell Nixon) Glaciers: Nature's Frozen Rivers, 1980; Gloria Chipmunk, Star!, 1980; Casey and the Great Idea, 1980; If You Say So, Claude, 1980; The Seance, 1980; Kidnapped on Astarr, 1981; (with Hershell Nixon) Earthquakes: Nature in Motion, 1981; Mysterious Queen of Magic, 1981; Mystery Dolls from Planet Urd, 1981; The Spectre, 1982; Days of Fear, 1983; The Gift, 1983; A Deadly Game of Magic, 1983; Magnolia's Mixed-Up Magic, 1983; The Ghosts of Now, 1984; (with Hershell Nixon) Land under the Sea, 1985; The House on Hackman's Hill, 1985; Maggie, Too, 1985; The Stalker, 1985; And Maggie Makes Three, 1986; Beats Me, Claude, 1986; The Other Side of Dark, 1986; The Dark and Deadly Pools, 1987; A Family Apart, 1987; Fat Chance, Claude, 1987; Haunted Island, 1987; Maggie Forevermore, 1987; Caught in the Act, 1988; In the Face of Danger, 1988; Secret, Silent Screams, 1988; If You Were a Writer, 1988; Island of Dangerous Dreams, 1989; A Place to Belong, 1989; You Bet Your Britches, Claude, 1989; Star Baby, 1989; Whispers from the Dead, 1989. Add: 10215 Cedar Creek Dr., Houston, Tex. 77042, U.S.A.

NIXON, Richard (Milhous). American, b. 1913. Politics/Governments. In law practice, Whittier, Calif., 1937–42; Attorney, Office of Price Admin., Washington, 1942; Member for the 12th district of California (Republican). U.S. Congress, 1947–51; served as Member, House Cttee. of Education and Labor, and House Cttee. on Un-American Activities; Senator from California, U.S. Senate, 1951–53; Vice Pres. of the U.S., Eisenhower Admin., 1953–61; Republican Candidate for President of the U.S. (against John F. Kennedy), 1960; Member, law firm of Adams, Duque and Hazeltine, Los Angeles, 1961–63; Republican Candidate for Gov. of the State of Calfornia, 1962; Member, law firm of Mudge, Stern, Baldwin and Todd, NYC, 1963–64, Partner, law firm of Nixon, Mudge, Rose, Guthrie and Alexander, 1964–67; and Nixon, Rose, Guthrie, Alexander and Mitchell, NYC, 1967–68; President of the United States, 1969–74. *Publs:* Six Crises, 1962; Memoirs, 1978; The Real War, 1980; Leaders, 1982; Real Peace: A Strategy for the West, 1983; No More Vietnams, 1985; 1999; Victory Without War, 1988. Add: 26 Federal Plaza, New York, N.Y. 10278, U.S.A.

NIXSON, Frederick Ian. British, b. 1943. Business/Trade/Industry, Economics, Third World problems. Sr. Lectr. in Economics, Univ. of Manchester, since 1979 (Lectr., 1971–79). Lectr. in Economics, Makerere Univ., Kampala, Uganda, 1968–71. *Publs:* Economic Integration and Industrial Location: An East African Case Study, 1973; (with D. Colman) Economics of Change in Less Developed Countries, 1978, 1986; (ed. with C.H. Kirkpatrick) The Industrialisation of Less Developed Countries, 1983; (with C.H. Kirkpatrick and N. Lee) Industrial Structure and Policy in Less Developed Countries, 1984; (with R.R. Jordan) Language for Economics: Integrated Study Skills and Advanced Language Practice, 1986. Add: Dept. of Economics, Univ. of Manchester, Manchester M13 9PL, England.

NKOSI, Lewis. British (b. South African), b. 1936. Novels, Plays/Screenplays, Essays. Prof. of English, Univ. of Zambia, Lusaka. Staff Member, Ilange Lase Natal (Zulu newspaper), Durban, South Africa, 1955–56, Drum mag. and Golden City Post, Johannesburg, 1956–60, South African Information Bulletin, Paris, 1962–68; Radio Producer, BBC Transcription Centre, London, 1962–64; Literary Ed., New African mag., London, 1965–68. *Publs:* The Rhythm of Violence, 1964; Home and Exile (essays), 1965; The Transplanted Heart: Essays on South Africa, 1975; Tasks and Masks: Themes and Styles of African Literature, 1981; Mating Birds (novel), 1986. Add: Dept. of English, Univ. of Zambia, P.O. Box 31338, Lusaka, Zambia.

NOAH, Harold J. British, b. 1925. Economics, Education. Gardner Cowles Prof. of Economics and Education, Teachers Coll., Columbia Univ., NYC, since 1969 (Instr. in Comparative Education, 1962–64; Asst. Prof. of Economics and Education, 1964–66; Assoc. Prof., 1966–69; Assoc. Chmn., 1967–71, and Acting Chmn., 1971–72, Dept. of Philosophy and the Social Sciences; Dean, 1976–81). Ed., Comparative Educational Review, 1966–71, and Soviet Education, 1970–79. *Publs:* Financing Soviet Schools, 1967; (trans. and ed.) The Economics of Education in the U.S.S.R., 1969; (with Max A. Ecksteir) Toward a Science of Comparative Education, 1969; (with Eckstein) Scientific Investigations in Comparative Education, 1969; Reviews of National Policies for Education: Germany, 1972, and Canada, 1976; (with Eckstein and others) The National Case Study: An Empirical Comparative Study of Twenty-One Educational Systems, 1976; Educational Financing and Policy Goals for Primary Schools: General Report, 1979. Add: Box 169, Teachers Coll., Columbia Univ., 525 W. 120th St., New York, N.Y. 10027, U.S.A.

NOAKES, Michael. British, b. 1933. Art. Portrait and landscape painter. Pres., Royal Inst. of Oil Painters, 1972–78. *Publs:* A Professional Approach to Oil Painting, 1968. Add: 146 Hamilton Terr., London NW8 9UX, England.

NOAKES, Vivien. British, b. 1937. Novels, Biography. *Publs:* Edward Lear: The Life of a Wanderer, 1968, 3rd ed. 1985; (with Charles Lewsen) For Lovers of Cats (Birds, Flowers and Gardens, Food and Drink), 4 vols., 1978; The Victorian Country Book (Town Book, Country Book, Workaday Book, Soldiers and Sailors Book), 4 vols., 1979; Edward Lear, 1812–1888, at the Royal Academy of Arts, 1985; (ed.) The Selected Letters of Edward Lear, 1988. Add: 146 Hamilton Terr., London NW8 9UX, England.

NOBEL, Phil, *See* **FANTHORPE,** R. Lionel.

NOBLE, Charles. *See* **PAWLEY,** Martin.

NOBLE, William Charles. British, b. 1935. Biology, Environmental science/Ecology, Medicine/Health, Biography. Head, Dept. of Bacteriology, St. John's Hosp. for Diseases of the Skin, since 1964; Prof. of Microbiology, Univ. of London, since 1980. Asst. Ed., British Journal of Dermatology, since 1972; Ed., Journal of Hygiene, since 1980. Staff Member, Medical Research Council, Air Hygiene Unit, 1957–61; Boots Research Fellow, St. Mary's Hosp. Medical Sch., London, 1961–64; Consultant in Hosp. Epidemiology, Leiden, Netherlands, 1970–80; Hon. Lectr. in Microbiology, Middx. Hosp. Medical Sch., London, 1971–82. *Publs:* Coli: Great Healer of Men, 1974; Microbiology of Human Skin, 1974, 1981; (with Jay Naidoo) Micro-organisms and Man, 1979; Prevent Infection, 1983; Microbial Skin Disease, Its Epidemiology, 1983. Add: Dept. of Microbial Diseases, Inst. of Dermatology, Lambeth Hospital, London SE11 4TH, England.

NOCHLIN, Linda Weinberg. American, b. 1931. Architecture, Art, Essays. Mary Conover Mellon Prof. of Art, Vassar Coll., Poughkeepsie, N.Y. (Asst. Prof. of Art History, 1952). *Publs:* Mathis at Colmar: A Visual Confrontation, 1963; (ed.) Impressionism and Post-Impressionism 1874-1904, 1966; Realism, 1971; (ed. with Thomas Hess) Woman as Sex Object: Studies in Erotic Art 1730-1970, 1972; Gustave Courbert: A Study of Style and Society, 1976; (with Ann Harris) Women Artists 1550-1950, 1977; (ed. with Henry Millon) Art and Architecture in the Service of Politics, 1978; Women, Art, and Power, and Other Essays, 1988. Add: c/o Harper and Row, 10 E. 53rd St., New York, N.Y. 10022, U.S.A.

NOCK, O(swald) S(tevens). British, b. 1905. Engineering/Technology, History, Transportation, Travel/Exploration/Adventure. With Westinghouse Brake and Signal Co. Ltd., 1925–70; retired as Chief Mechanical Engineer, Signal Div. *Publs:* London and North Western Railway; Caledonian Railway; Highland Railway; Great Northern Railway; Lancashire and Yorkshire Railway; Great Western Railway in the Nineteenth Century; Great Western Railway in the Twentieth Century; London and South Western Railway; South Eastern and Chatham Railway; History of the Great Western Railway, 3 vols.; Locomotives of R.E.L. Maunsell; Locomotives of Sir Nigel Gresley; Locomotives of the North Eastern Railway; Premier Line; Locos of the London and North Western Railway; Kings and Castles of the Great Western Railway; Locomotive Monographs (series of 12); Historical Steam Locomotives; The British Railway Steam Locomotive 1925-1965; Steam Locomotive Engine 6000; Southern Steam; London North Eastern Railway; LMS Steam; Great Western Railway Steam; Railways of Britain; British Trains, Past and Present; Branch Lines; Scottish Railways; British Railways in Action; British Railways in Transition; Main Lines Across the Border; The Railway Encyclopaedia; British Steam Railways; Steam Railways in Retrospect; The Golden Age of Steam; British Locomotives at Work; British Locomotives from the Footplate; 4000 Miles on the Footplate; British Steam Locomotives at Work; Fifty Years of Western Express Running; Sixty Years of Western Express Running; Rail, Steam and Speed; Speed Records on British Railways; The Railway Race to the North; Britain's New Railway; Electric, Euston to Glasgow; Underground Railways of the World; Fifty Years of Railway Signalling; British Railway Signalling; The Railway Engineers; William Stanier: An Engineering Biography; The Blandford Series of Railway Colour Books; Single Line Railways; Continental Main Lines; Railway Holiday in Austria; Railways of the World Series, 5 vols.; Railways Then and Now; "Out the Line"; Encyclopaedia of Railways; Last Ten Years of British Steam; World Atlas of Railways; Sixty Years of West Coast Express Running; Pictorial History of Trains; 150 Years of Main Line Railways; Rocket-150; Two Miles a Minute; Railway Signalling; Reminiscences of the Inter-War Years; History of the LMS; Railway Archaeology; Line Clear Ahead; On Steam; Irish Steam; British Locomotives of the 20th Century, 3 vols., 1983–85; From the Footplate, 1984; Great British Trains, 1985; Great Locomotives of the Southern Railway (LNER, LMS), 3 vols., 1987–89. Add: Twenty Eight, High Bannerdoiwn, Batheaston, Bath BA1 7JY, England.

NODSET, Joan L. *See* **LEXAU**, Joan M.

NOEL, John. *See* **BIRD**, Dennis Leslie.

NOEL-HUME, Ivor. British, b. 1927. Novels/Short stories, Antiques/Furnishings, Archaeology/Antiquities, Natural history. Archaeological Dir., Colonial Williamsburg Foundn., Williamsburg, Va., since 1957. Bd. member, Jamestown-Yorktown Foundn., since 1987. Research Assoc., Smithsonian Instn., since 1959. Vice-Pres., Soc. for Post-Medieval Archaeology, U.K., 1967–76; Council Member, Inst. of Early American History and Culture, 1974–76. *Publs:* Archaeology in Britain, 1953; (co-author) Tortoises, Terrapins and Turtles, 1954; Treasure in the Thames, 1956; Great Moments in Archaeology, 1957; Here Lies Virginia, 1963; 1775: Another Part of the Field, 1966; Historical Archaeology, 1969; Artifacts of Colonial America, 1970; All the Best Rubbish, 1974; Early English Delftware from London and Virginia, 1976; Martin's Hundred, 1982. Add: P.O. Box 1711, Williamsburg, Va. 23187, U.S.A.

NOGEE, Joseph L(ippman). American, b. 1929. Politics/Government. Prof. of Political Science, Univ. of Houston, since 1966 (Asst. Prof., 1958–61; Assoc. Prof., 1961–66). Instr., Yale Univ., New Haven, Conn., 1956–57. *Publs:* Soviet Policy Toward International Control of Atomic Energy, 1961; (with J. Spanier) The Politics of Disarmament, 1962; (ed.) Man, State and Society in the Soviet Union, 1972; (with R. Donaldson) Soviet Foreign Policy since World War II; (ed. with J. Spanier) Congress, The Presidency, and American Foreign Policy; (ed.) Soviet Politics, Russia after Brezhnev; (with J. Spanier) Peace Impossible—War Unlikely, 1988. Add: 8735 Link Terr, Houston, Tex. 77025, U.S.A.

NOLAN, Christopher. Irish, b. 1965. Stories, Poetry, Autobiography. *Publs:* Dam-Burst of Dreams, 1981; Under the Life of the Clock: The Life Story of Christopher Nolan, 1987. Add: 158 Vernon Ave., Clontarf, Dublin 3, Ireland.

NOLAN, Frederick. *See* **CHRISTIAN**, Frederick H.

NOLAN, Paul T. American, b. 1919. Plays/Screenplays, Literature. Dupre Prof. of Humanities, Univ. of Southwestern Louisiana, Lafayette, since 1966 (Prof. of English, 1955–66). *Publs:* Round the World Plays, 1961, 1969; Three Plays of John W. Crawford, 1966; Writing the One-Act Play for the Amateur, 1966; Provincial Drama in America, 1967; Marc Connelly, 1970; Drama Workshop Plays, 1971; Other Great Plays, 1971; Describing People, 1972; The Loneliest Game, 1973; (with J. Burke) Between Hisses, 1973; John Wallace Crawford, 1981; Folk Tale Plays, Around the World, 1982; Directing the Amateur Stage, 1985. Add: Dept. of English, Univ. of Southwestern Louisiana, Lafayette, La. 70501, U.S.A.

NOLAN, William F(rancis). American, b. 1928. Novels/Short stories, Mystery/Crime/Suspense, Science fiction/Fantasy, Westerns, Poetry, Film, Literature, Sports, Biography. *Publs:* (ed.) Ray Bradbury Review, 1952; (ed. with C. Beaumont) Omnibus of Speed, 1958; (with J. Fitch) Adventure on Wheels, 1959; Barney Oldfield, 1961; Phil Hill: Yankee Champion, 1962; (ghost ed. with Charls Beaumont) The Fiend in You, 1962; Impact 20 (stories), 1963; (ed. with C. Beaumont) When Engines Roar, 1964; Men of Thunder, 1964; John Huston: King Rebel, 1965; (ed.) Man Against Tomorrow, 1965; (ed.) The Pseudo-People, 1965; Sinners

and Supermen, 1965; (ghost ed.) Il Meglio della Fantascienza, 1967; (with G.C. Johnson) Logan's Run, 1967; (ed.) 3 to the Highest Power, 1968; Death Is for Losers, 1968; The White Cad Cross-Up, 1969; (ed.) A Wilderness of Stars, 1969; Dashiell Hammett: A Casebook, 1969; (ed.) A Sea of Space, 1970; (ed.) The Future Is Now, 1970; (ed.) The Human Equation, 1971; (ghost ed.) The Edge of Forever, 1971; Space for Hire, 1971; Steve McQueen: Star on Wheels, 1972; Carnival of Speed, 1973; Alien Horizons (stories), 1974; Hemingway: Last Days of the Lion, 1974; The Ray Bradbury Companion, 1975; Wonderworlds (stories) 1977; Logan's World, 1977; Logan's Search, 1980; (ed. with M. Greenberg) Science Fiction Origins, 1980; (ed.) Max Brand's Best Western Stories, 3 vols., 1981–87; Hammett: A Life at the Edge, 1983; McQueen, 1984; Things Beyond Midnight (stories), 1984; Look Out for Space, 1985; The Black Mask Boys, 1985; The Work of Charles Beaumont (bibliography), 1986; Dark Encounters (poetry), 1986; (ed.) Max Brand: Western Giant, 1986; Logan: A Trilogy, 1986; (with Boden Clarke) The Work of William F. Nolan (bibliography), 1988; (as Terence Duncan) Rio Renegades. 1989. Add: c/o Peekner Agency, 3418 Shelton Ave., Bethlehem, PA 18017, U.S.A.

NOLEN, Claude. American, b. 1921. History. Prof. of History, St. Edward's Univ., Austin, since 1956. History Teacher, Marked Tree, Arkansas High Sch., 1949–52; Grade Sch. Teacher, Scruggs Sch., St. Louis, 1952–55; History Teacher, Coll. and Academy of the Sacred Heart, Grand Coteau, La., 1955–56. *Publs:* The Negro's Image in the South: Anatomy of White Supremacy, 1967. Add: 410 W. Alpine, Austin, Tex. 78704, U.S.A.

NOLTINGK, Bernard Edward. British, b. 1918. Administration/Management, Technology. Consultant. Head, Electronics Dept., Motor Industry R.A., 1941–47; Head, Ultrasonics Dept., Mullard Research Labs., 1947–52; Head of Strata Control Group, Mining Research Establishment, National Coal Bd., 1952–55; Head of Electronics and Ultrasonics, Tube Investments Research Labs., 1955–60; Head, Instrumentation Section, Central Electricity Research Labs., Leatherhead, Surrey, 1960–81. *Publs:* The Human Element in Research Management, 1959; The Art of Research: A Guide for the Graduate, 1965; (ed.) Instrument Technology, 4 vols., 1985–87; (ed.) Instrumentation Reference Book, 1988. Add: Windwhistle, Nutcombe Lane, Dorking, Surrey, England.

NOONAN, John Ford. American, b. 1943. Plays/Screenplays. Stagehand, Fillmore East Rock Theatre, NYC, 1969–71; Stockbroker, E.F. Hutton Co., NYC, 1971–72; Prof. of Drama, Villanova Univ., Pennsylvania, 1972–73. *Publs:* The Year Boston Won the Pennant, 1970; A Coupla White Chicks Sitting Around Talking, 1981; Some Men Need Help, 1983. Add: 484 W. 43rd St., New York, N.Y. 10036, U.S.A.

NOONAN, Lowell G. American, b. 1922. Politics/Government. Prof. of Political Science, California State Univ. at Northridge, since 1960. Instr., subsequently Asst. Prof. and Assoc. Prof. of Political Science, Univ. of Southern California, Los Angeles, 1949–60. *Publs:* (co-author) European Politics and Government: A Comparative Approach, 1962; France: The Politics of Continuity in Change, 1970; (co-author) Western European Political Party System, 1980. Add: Dept. of Political Science, California State Univ., 18111 Nordhoff St., Northridge, Calif. 91330, U.S.A.

NOONE, Edwina. *See* **AVALLONE**, Michael.

NORBECK, Edward. American, b. 1915. Anthropology/Ethnology, Social sciences. Prof. of Anthropology, Rice Univ., Houston, since 1962 (Assoc. Prof., 1960–62; Dean of Humanities and Social Sciences, 1965–67; Chmn., Dept. of Anthropology and Sociology, 1960–71; Dir., Grad. Prog. in Behavioral Science, 1969–80). Vice-Pres. and Ed., Tourmaline Press, Houston, since 1970. Asst. Prof., Univ. of Utah, Salt Lake City, 1952–54, and Univ. of California, Berkeley, 1954–60. *Publs:* Takashima, A Japanese Fishing Community, 1954; Pineapple Town—Hawaii, 1959; Religion in Primitive Society, 1961; (ed. with J.D. Jennings) Prehistoric Man in the New World, 1964; Changing Japan, 1965, 1976; (ed. with D. Price-Williams and W.M. McCord) The Study of Personality: An Interdisciplinary Appraisal, 1968; Religion and Society in Modern Japan: Continuity and Change, 1970; (ed. with S. Parman) The Study of Japan in the Behavioral Sciences, 1970; Religion in Human Life: Anthropological Views, 1974; (ed.) The Anthropological Study of Human Play, 1974; Country to City: The Urbanization of a Japanese Hamlet, 1978; (ed.) Forms of Play of Native North Americans, 1979; (ed.) Health, Illness and Medical Care in Japan, 1987. Add: Dept. of Anthropology, Rice Univ., Houston, Tex. 77001, U.S.A.

NORCROSS, Lisabet. *See* **GLADSTONE**, Arthur M.

NORDEN, Charles. *See* **DURRELL**, Lawrence.

NORLING, Bernard. American, b. 1924. History. Prof. of History, Notre Dame Univ., Indiana, since 1950, now Emeritus (Asst. Chmn., Dept. of History, 1964–76; Acting Chmn., 1967–68, 1978). *Publs:* Towards a Better Understanding of History, 1960; Timeless Problems in History, 1970; (with Charles Poinsatte) Understanding History Through the American Experience, 1976; (with Samuel C. Grashio) Return to Freedom: The War Memoirs of Col. Samuel C. Grashio, 1982; (with Ray Hunt) Behind Japanese Lines: An American Guerrilla in the Philippines, 1986. Add: 504 E. Pokagon, South Bend, Ind. 46617, U.S.A.

NORMAN, Barbara. Also translates under the name of Barbara Makanowitzky. American, b. 1927. Cookery/Gastronomy/Wine, History, Translations. Freelance translator, 1959–63. *Publs:* (trans. as Barbara Makanowitzky) Fathers and Sons, 1959; The Short Stories of Leo Tolstoi, 1960; Seven Short Novels by Chekhov, 1963, 1971; The Spanish Cookbook, 1966; The Russian Cookbook, 1967; Tales of the Table, 1972; Requiem for Spanish Village, 1972; (trans.) Sparrow in the Snow, 1973; Napoleon and Talleyrand: The Last Two Weeks, 1976. Add: c/o Stein and Day, Scarborough House, Briarcliff Manor, N.Y. 10510, U.S.A.

NORMAN, Bruce (Anthony John). British, b. 1936. Plays/Screenplays, Archaeology, Communications media/Broadcasting, History. Head, BBC Archaeology and History Dept., since 1976 (ed., Horizon series, 1972–74, Chronicle series, 1977–82 and since 1989). *Publs:* Secret Warfare (on codes and ciphers), 1973; The Inventing of America, 1976; The Birth of Television, 1984; Footsteps: Pioneers of Archaeology, 1987; Discoveries under Water, 1988; The Armada, 1988; television plays—Lancashire Night Out, The Appointment, Coronation Street, Chatterton, Case of the Midwife Toad, Charles Dickens, The Rat Man, The Crime of Captain Colthurst. Add: 14 The Ryde, Old Hatfield, Herts., England.

NORMAN, John. American, b. 1912. History, Politics/Government, Biography. Prof. of History and Govt., Pace Univ., Westchester, Pleasantville, N.Y., since 1966. Asst. Prof. of History and Culture, Univ. of Syracuse, N.Y., 1943–44; Field Rep., Office of Strategic Services, 1944–45; attached to the U.S. Delegation to the U.N. at the San Francisco Conference, 1945; Asst. Prof. of History, Carnegie Inst. of Technology, Pittsburgh, 1946; Assoc. Prof. and Chmn., Dept. of Political Science, Chatham Coll., Pittsburgh, 1946–49; Head of the Italian Section, 1949, and Historian, 1950–53, Office of Intelligence Research, U.S. Dept. of State, Washington, D.C.; Assoc. Prof., 1953–58, and Prof., 1958–66, Dept. of History and Govt., Fairfield Univ., Connecticut. *Publs:* Edward Gibbon Wakefield: A Political Reappraisal, 1963; Labor and Politics in Libya and Arab Africa, 1965. Add: Dept. of History and Govt., Pace Univ., Westchester, Pleasantville, N.Y. 10570, U.S.A.

NORMAN, John. Pseud. for John (Frederick) Lange (Jr.). American, b. 1931. Science fiction/Fantasy, Philosophy, Sex. Prof. of Philosophy, Queens Coll., City Univ. of New York, since 1974 (joined faculty 1964). Formerly radio writer; Story Analyst for Warner Brothers; film writer, Univ. of Nebraska; and Technical Writer, Rocketdyne (North American Aviation). *Publs:* Tarnsman of Gor, 1966; Outlaw of Gor, 1967; Priest-Kings of Gor, 1968; (ed. as John Lange) Values and Imperatives: Studies in Ethics, by C.I. Lewis, 1969; Nomads of Gor, 1969; Assassin of Gor, 1970; Ghost Dance, 1970; (as John Lange) The Cognitivity Paradox: An Inquiry Concerning the Claims of Philosophy, 1970; Raiders of Gor, 1971; Captive of Gor, 1972; Hunters of Gor, 1974; Imaginative Sex, 1974; Marauders of Gor, 1975; Time Slave, 1975; Tribesmen of Gor, 1976; Slave Girl of Gor, 1977; Beasts of Gor, 1978; Explorers of Gor, 1979; Fighting Slave of Gor, 1980; Rogue of Gor, 1981; Guardsman of Gor, 1981; Savages of Gor, 1982; Blood Brothers of Gor, 1982; Kajira of Gor, 1983; Players of Gor, 1984; Mercenaries of Gor, 1985;Dancers of Gor, 1985; Renegades of Gor, 1986; Vagabonds of Gor, 1987. Add: Dept. of Philosophy, Queens Coll., Flushing, N.Y. 11367, U.S.A.

NORMAN, Lilith. Australian, b. 1927. Children's fiction, Plays/Screenplays, History. Library Asst., Newtown Library, Sydney, 1947–49; Telephonist, Bonnington Hotel, London, 1950–51; Sales Asst., Angus and Robertson Books, Sydney, 1952–53; Nurse, Balmain District Hosp., and Ed., 1975–78, New South Wales Dept. of Education School Magazine. *Publs:* The City of Sydney: Official Guide, 1959; Facts about Sydney, 1959; Asia: A Select Reading List, 1959; Some Notes on the Early Land Grants at Potts Point, 1959; A History of the City of Sydney Public Library, 1960; Notes on the Glebe, 1960; Historical Notes on Pad-

dington, 1961; Historical Notes on Newtown, 1962; Climb a Lonely Hill, 1970; The Shape of Three, 1971; The Flame Takers, 1973; Catch Kandy (television series), 1973; Mockingbird-Man (reader), 1977; A Dream of Seas, 1978; My Simple Little Brother, 1979; The Brown and Yellow: Sydney Girls' High School 1883-1983, 1983; The Laurel and Hardy Kids, 1989; The Hex, 1989. Add: c/o Curtis Brown (Aust.) Pty. Ltd., P.O. Box 19, Paddington, N.S.W. 2021, Australia.

NORMAN, Marsha. American, b. 1947. Novels, Plays/Screenplays. Worked with disturbed children, Kentucky Central State Hospital, 1969–71; teacher, Brown Sch., Louisville, and book reviewer, Louisville Times, mid-1970's; resident writer, Actors Theatre, Louisville, 1977–80. *Publs:* plays—Getting Out, 1977; Third and Oak: The Laundromat, The Pool Hall, 2 vols., 1980–85; 'Night, Mother, 1983 (Pulitzer Prize); The Holdup, 1987; Traveler in the Dark, 1988; Four Plays by Marsha Norman, 1988; novel—The Fortune Teller, 1987. Add: c/o John Breglio, Paul, Weiss, Rifkin, Wharton and Garrison, 1285 Ave. of the Americas, New York, N.Y. 10019, U.S.A.

NORRIS, Geoffrey. British, b. 1947. Music. Music Critic, Daily Telegraph, London, since 1983. Lectr. in Music History, Royal Northern Coll. of Music, Manchester, 1975–77; Supervising and Commissioning Ed., The New Oxford Companion to Music, 1977–83. *Publs:* Rakhmaninov, 1976; (with R. Threlfall) A Catalogue of the Compositions of S. Rachmaninoff, 1982; (with C. Norris) Shastakovich: The Man and His Music, 1982. Add: D44 Du Cane Ct., London SW17 7JH, England.

NORRIS, Leslie. British, b. 1921. Poetry, Literature. Teacher, Grass Royal Sch., Yeovil, Somerset, 1948–52; Deputy Head, Southdown Sch., Bath, 1952–55; Head Teacher, Aldingbourne Sch., Chichester, 1956–58; Principal Lectr. in Degree Studies, Coll. of Education, Bognor Regis, Sussex, 1958–73; Visiting Prof. of English, Univ. of Seattle, 1973, 1980. *Publs:* Tongue of Beauty, 1941; Poems, 1946; The Ballad of Billy Rose, 1964; The Loud Winter, 1967; Finding Gold, 1967; Curlew, 1969; Ransoms, 1970; (ed.) Vernon Watkins 1906-1967, 1970; His Last Autumn, 1972; Mountains, Polecats, Pheasants and Other Elegies, 1973; Stone and Fern, 1973; Wthan Moonfields, 1973; The Dove and the Tree, 1973; Glyn Jones, 1973; Sliding and Other Stories, 1976; Islands off Maine, 1977; Merlin and the Snake's Egg, 1978; (ed.) Tributes to Andrew Young, 1978; Winter Voices, 1980; Walking the White Fields, 1980; The Girl from Cardigan, 1988; Sequences, 1988. Add: Plas Nant, Northfields Lane, Aldingbourne, Chichester, Sussex, England.

NORRIS, Phyllis Irene. British, b. 1909. Novels/Short stories, Children's fiction. *Publs:* The Mystery of the White Ties, 1936; The Harlands Go Hunting, 1938; The Nasturtium Club, 1939; The Duffer's Brigade, 1939; Meet the Kilburys, 1940; The House of the Lady-Bird, 1946; The Polkemin Mystery, 1949; The Cranstons at Sandly Bay, 1949. Add: Rooftree, 49 Hulse Rd., Salisbury, Wilts., England.

NORSE, Harold. American, b. 1916. Novels, Poetry. Ed., Bastard Angel mag., San Francisco. *Publs:* The Undersea Mountain: Poems, 1953; The Roman Sonnets of G.G. Belli, 1960; The Dancing Beasts, 1962; Karma Circuit: 20 Poems and a Preface, 1967; (with Charles Bukowski and Philip Lamantia) Penguin Modern Poets 13, 1969; Hotel Nirvana, 1974; I See America Daily, 1974; Beat Hotel (novel), 1975; Carnivorous Saint: Gay Poems, 1977; Mysteries of Magritte, 1984; The Love Poems, 1986. Add: 157 Albion St., San Francisco, Calif. 94110, U.S.A.

NORTH, Andrew. *See* **NORTON**, Andre.

NORTH, Colin. *See* **BINGLEY**, David Ernest.

NORTH, Elizabeth (Stewart). British, b. 1932. Novels/Short stories, Plays/Screenplays. Teacher of Creative Writing. Writer-in-Residence, Bretton Hall Coll. of Higher Education, 1984–85. *Publs:* Make Thee an Ark (radio play), 1969; Wife Swopping (radio play), 1969; The Least and Vilest Things (novel), 1971; Pelican Rising (novel), 1975; Enough Blue Sky (novel), 1977; Everything in the Garden (novel), 1978; Florence Avenue (novel), 1979; Dames (novel), 1981; Ancient Enemies (novel), 1982; The Real Tess (radio feature), 1984; Jude the Obscure (adaptation for radio), 1985. Add: 8 Huby Park, Huby, Leeds, England.

NORTH, Gil. *See* **HORNE**, Geoffrey.

NORTH, Joan Marian. British, b. 1920. Children's fiction. *Publs:* Emperor of the Moon, 1956; The Cloud Forest, 1965; The Whirling Shapes, 1968; The Light Maze, 1971. Add: 8 Grey Close, London NW11 6QG, England.

NORTH, Robert. American, b. 1916. Archaeology/Antiquities, Theology/Religion. Prof. of Biblical Archaeology, Pontifical Biblical Inst., Rome, since 1951 (Dir., Jerusalem Branch, 1956–59). Assoc. Ed., Theology Digest; Ed., Elenchus (Bibliographicus) of Biblica. *Publs:* The General Who Rebuilt the Jesuits, 1944; Sociology of the Biblical Jubilee, 1954; Guide to Biblical Iran, 1956; Teilhard and the Creation of the Soul, 1967; Archeo-Biblical Egypt, 1967; Stratigraphia geobiblica, 1970; Reges: Introduction, 1971; In Search of the Human Jesus, 1971; A History of Biblical Map Making, 1979. Add: via Pilotta 25, 00187 Rome, Italy.

NORTHCOTT, Douglas (Geoffrey). British, b. 1916. Mathematics. Asst. Lectr., 1949–51, and Lectr., 1951–52, Cambridge Univ.; Town Trust Prof., Univ. of Sheffield, 1952–82. *Publs:* Ideal Theory, 1952; An Introduction to Homological Algebra, 1960; Lessons on Rings, Modules and Multiplicities, 1968; A First Course of Homological Algebra, 1973; Finite Free Resolutions, 1976; Affine Sets and Affine Groups, 1980; Multilinear Algebra, 1984. Add: Dept. of Pure Mathematics, Univ. of Sheffield, Sheffield S10 2TN, England.

NORTON, Andre (Alice). Has also written as Andrew North. American, b. 1912. Science fiction/Fantasy, Children's fiction. Former Librarian, Children's Dept., Cleveland Public Library. *Publs:* Prince Commands, 1934; Ralestone Luck, 1948; Follow the Drum, 1942; The Sword Is Drawn, 1944; Rogue Reynard (juvenile), 1947; Scarface, 1948; The Sword in Sheath, 1949; Huon of the Horn (juvenile), 1951; (ed.) Bullard of Space, 1951; Star Man's Son, 1952; (ed.) Space Service, 1952; Star Rangers, 1953; At Sword's Points, 1954; (ed.) Space Pioneers, 1954; The Stars Are Ours!, 1954; (co-author) Murders for Sale, 1954; Yankee Privateer, 1955; (as Andrew North) Sargasso of Space, 1955; Star Guard, 1955; Stand to Horse, 1956; (ed.) Space Police, 1956; (as Andrew North) Plague Ship, 1956; Crossroads of Time, 1956; Star Born, 1957; Sea Siege, 1957; Time Traders, 1958; (as Andrew North) Voodoo Planet, 1959; The Secret of Lost Race, 1959; The Star Gate, 1959; Beast Master, 1959; Galactic Derelict, 1959; Sioux Spacemen, 1960; Storm over Warlock, 1960; Shadow Hawk, 1960; Ride Proud, Rebel!, 1960; Catseye, 1961; Lord of Thunder, 1962; Eye of Monster, 1962; Rebel Spurs, 1962; Defiant Agents, 1962; Judgment on Janus, 1963; Witch World, 1963; Key out of Time, 1963; Ordeal in Otherwhere, 1964; Night of Masks, 1964; Web of Witch World, 1964; X Factor, 1965; Quest Crosstime, 1965; Three Against Witch World, 1965; Year of the Unicorn, 1965; Steel Magic, 1965; Victory on Janus, 1966; Moon of Three Rings, 1966; Octagon Magic, 1967; Warlock of Witch World, 1967; Operation Time Search, 1967; Zero Stone, 1968; Dark Piper, 1968; Sorceress of Witch World, 1968; Fur Magic, 1968; Uncharted Stars, 1969; Postmarked the Stars, 1969; (co-author) Bertie and May, 1969; High Sorcery (short stories), 1970; Ice Crown, 1970; Dread Companion, 1970; Exiles of the Stars, 1971; Android at Arms, 1971; Dragon Magic, 1972; Spell of Witch World (short stories), 1972; Breed to Come, 1972; Crystal Gryphon, 1972; Garan the Eternal (short stories), 1973; (ed.) Gates to Tomorrow, 1973; Forerunner Foray, 1973; Here Abide Monsters, 1973; Lavender-Green Magic, 1974; Jargoon Pard, 1974; (co-author) Many Worlds of Andre Norton, 1974; Iron Cage, 1974; (ed.) Small Shadows Creep, 1974; (co-author) Day of the Ness, 1975; Outside, 1975; White Jade Fox, 1975; Merlin's Mirrow, 1975; No Night Without Stars, 1975; Knave of Dreams, 1975; Perilous Dreams, 1976; (with Dorothy Madlee) Star Ka'at, 1976; Wraiths of Time, 1976; Red Hart Magic, 1976; Velvet Shadows, 1977; Opal-Eyed Fan, 1977; Trey of Swords (short stories), 1977; Quag Keep, 1978; (with Dorothy Madlee) Star Ka'at World, 1978; Yurth Burden, 1978; (with Dorothy Madlee) Star Ka'ats and the Plant People, 1979; Zarathor's Bane, 1979; (with Phyllis Miller) Seven Spells to Sunday, 1979; Snow Shadow, 1979; Iron Butterflies, 1980; Voorloper, 1980; Lore of Witchworld (short stories), 1980; Gryphon in Glory, 1981; Forerunner, 1981; Horn Crown, 1981; Ten Mile Treasure, 1981; (with Dorothy Madlee) Star Ka'ats and Winged Warriors, 1981; Moon Called, 1982; (with Enid Cushing) Caroline, 1982; Wheel of Stars, 1983; Ware Hawk, 1983; Stand and Deliver, 1984; (with Phyllis Miller) House of Shadows, 1984; (with A.C. Crispin) Gryphon's Eyrie, 1984; Werewrath, 1984; Flight in Yiktor, 1986; Magic in Yiktor, vols. 3-4, 1986–87; Tales of Witch World, vols. 1-2, 1987–88; Serpents's Tooth, 1988; Moon Mirror, 1988; Four from Witch World, 1989. Add: 1600 Spruce Ave., Winter Park, Fla. 32789, U.S.A.

NORTON, Augustus Richard. American, b. 1946. International relations/Current affairs, Third world problems. Permanent Assoc. Prof. of Comparative Politics, Dept. of Social Sciences, U.S. Military Academy, West Point, since 1984 (formerly, Asst. Prof. of Intnl. Relations). Regional Dir., Inter-University Seminar on Armed Forces and Society, since 1982. Adjunct Asst. Prof. of Political Science, Univ. of Illinois, Chicago, 1975–77; Adjunct Asst. Prof. of Political Science, Old Dominion Univ., Norfolk, Va., 1979. *Publs:* Moscow and the Palestinians, 1974;

(ed. with Martin M. Greenberg) Studies in Nuclear Terrorism, 1979; (ed. with Greenberg) International Terrorism: An Annotated Bibliography and Research Guide, 1980; (ed. with others) NATO: A Bibliography and Resource Guide, 1984; (with others) The Emergence of a New Lebanon: Fantasy or Reality?, 1984; (ed. with Greenberg) Touring Nam: The Vietnam War Reader, 1985; Amal and the Shi'a Struggle for the Soul of Lebanon, 1987; (ed. with Greenberg) The International Relations of the PLO, 1989. Add: Dept. of Social Sciences, USMA, West Point, N.Y. 10996, U.S.A.

NORTON, Bess. *See* **NORWAY**, Kate.

NORTON, Mary. British, b. 1903. Children's fiction. *Publs:* The Magic Bed-Knob, 1945; Bonfires and Broomsticks, 1947; The Borrowers, 1952; The Borrowers Afield, 1955; Bed-knob and Broomstick (rev. version of The Magic Bed-Knob and Bonfires and Broomsticks), 1957; The Borrowers Afloat, 1959; The Borrowers Aloft, 1961; Poor Stainless, 1971; Are All the Giants Dead?, 1975; The Borrowers Avenged, 1982. Add: The Old Rectory, Kilcoe, Aughadown, Ballydehob, West Cork, Ireland.

NORTON, Olive. *See* **NORWAY**, Kate.

NORTON, Philip. British, b. 1951. History, Politics/Government. Prof. of Government, Univ. of Hull, since 1986 (Lectr., 1977–82; Sr. Lectr., 1982–84; Reader, 1984–86). Lectr., Univ. of Sheffield, 1975–76, and Wroxton Coll., Fairleigh Dickinson Univ., Rutherford, N.J., 1977. *Publs:* Dissension in the House of Commons 1945-74, 1975; Conservative Dissidents, 1978; Dissension in the House of Commons 1974-79, 1980; The Commons in Perspective, 1981; (with A. Aughey) Conservatives and Conservatism, 1981; The Constitution in Flux, 1982; The British Polity, 1984; (ed.) Law and Order and British Politics, 1984; (ed. with J. Hayward) The Political Science of British Politics, 1986; Parliament in Perspective, 1987; (ed.) Legislatures, 1989. Add: Dept. of Politics, Univ. of Hull, Hull HU6 7RX, England.

NORWAY, Kate. Pseud. for Olive (Marion Claydon) Norton; also writes as Hilary Neal and Bess Norton. British, b. 1913. Mystery/Crime/Suspense, Historical/Romance/Gothic, Children's fiction. Counsellor, Citizens Advice Bureau. Nurse, 1930–36; Columnist, Birmingham News, 1954–59. *Publs:* Sister Brookes of Bynd's 1957, in Can. as Nurse Brookes, 1958; The Morning Star, 1959; Junior Pro, 1959; (as Bess Norton) The Quiet One, 1959; Norse Elliot's Diary, 1960; (as Bess Norton) Night Duty at Duke's, 1960; (as Bess Norton) The Red Chalet, 1960; Waterfront Hospital, 1961; The White Jacket, 1961; (as Bess Norton) The Summer Change, 1961; (as Bess Norton) The Waiting Room, 1961; (as Hilary Neal) Factory Nurse, 1961; (as Olive Norton) Bob-a-Job Pony (juvenile), 1961; Goodbye, Johnny, 1962; (as Bess Norton) A Nurse Is Born, 1962; (as Hilary Neal) Tread Softly, Nurse, 1962; The Night People, 1963; Nurse in Print, 1963; (as Bess Norton) The Green Light, 1963; (as Bess Norton) The Monday Man, 1963; (as Hilary Neal) Star Patient, 1963; (as Hilary Neal) Love Letter, 1963; The Seven Sleepers, 1964; A Professional Secret, 1964; (as Bess Norton) St. Luke's Little Summer, 1964; (as Hilary Neal) Houseman's Sister, 1964; (as Hilary Neal) Nurse Off Camera, 1964; The Lambs, 1965; (as Bess Norton) A Miracle at Joe's 1965; (as Bess Norton) St. Julian's Day, 1965; (as Hilary Neal) Mr. Sister, 1965; (as Hilary Neal) The Team, 1965; (as Hilary Neal) Charge Nurse, 1965; The Nightingale Touch, 1966; Be My Guest, 1966, as Journey in the Dark, 1973; Merlin's Keep, 1966; (as Bess Norton) What We're Here For, 1966; (as Bess Norton) Night's Daughters, 1966; (as Hilary Neal) A Simple Duty, 1966; (as Hilary Neal) Nurse Meg's Decision, 1966; (as Olive Norton) A School of Liars (crime), 1966; A Nourishing Life, 1967; (as Bess Norton) The Night Is Kind, 1967; (as Olive Norton) Now Lying Dead (crime), 1967; The Faithful Failure, 1968; (as Olive Norton) The Speight Street Angle, 1968; Dedication Jones, 1969; To Care Always, 1970; Reluctant Nightingale, 1970; Paper Halo, 1970; (as Olive Norton) Dead on Prediction (crime), 1970; The Bedside Manner, 1971; Casualty Speaking, 1971; (as Olive Norton) The Corpse-Bird Cries (crime), 1971; The Gingham Year, 1973; Voices in the Night, 1973. Add: 1 Holly Lane, Four Oaks, Warwicks., England.

NORWICH, John Julius (Cooper). (Viscount Norwich). British, b. 1929. History, Literature, Travel/Exploration/Adventure. With H.M. Foreign Service, 1952–64: served in Belgrade, Beirut, and Geneva; First Secty., Foreign Office, London, 1961–64. *Publs:* (with R. Sitwell) Mount Athos, 1966; The Normans in the South (in U.S. as The Other Conquest), 1967; Sahara, 1968; The Kingdom in the Sun, 1970; (ed.) Great Architecture of the World, 1975; Venice: The Rise to Empire, 1977; Christmas Crackers, 1980; Venice: The Splendour and the Fall, 1981; The Architecture of Southern England, 1985; Glyndebourne, 1985; Byzantium: The Early Centuries, 1988.   Add: 24 Blomfield Rd., London W9, England.

NORWOOD, Warren.   American, b. 1945.   Science fiction.   Asst. Mgr., Univ. Bookstore, Univ. of Texas, Arlington, 1973–76; Mgr., Century Bookstore, Ft. Worth, 1976–77; publisher's rep. in Fort Worth, 1978–83; taught creative writing, Tarrant Co. Jr. Coll., 1983–83.   *Publs:* The Windhover Tapes, comprising An Image of Voices, 1982, Flexing the Warp, 1983, Fize of the Gabriel Ratchets, 1983, and a Planet of Flowers, 1984; (with Ralph Mylius) The Seren Cenacles, 1983; Double Spiral War, comprising Midway Between, 1984, Polar Fleet, 1985, and Final Command, 1986; True Jaguar, 1988.   Add: 2428 Las Brisas, Ft. Worth, Tex. 76116, U.S.A.

NOSSAL, (Sir) Gustav (Joseph Victor).   Australian, b. 1931. Medicine/Health.   Dir., Walter and Eliza Hall Inst. of Medical Research, Melbourne, since 1965 (Research Fellow, 1957–59; Deputy Dir., 1961– 65); Prof. of Medical Biology, Univ. of Melbourne, since 1965.   Asst. Prof., Dept. of Genetics, Stanford Univ. Sch. of Medicine, California, 1959–61.   *Publs:* Antibodies and Immunity, 1968, 1977; Antigens, Lymphoid Cells and the Immune Reponse, 1971; Medical Science and Human Goals, 1975; Nature's Defences, 1978; Reshaping Life: Key Issues in Genetic Engineering, 1984.   Add: 46 Fellows St., Kew, Vic 3101, Australia.

NOSTRAND, Howard Lee.   American, b. 1910.   Language/Linguistics, Literature.   Prof. of Romance Languages and Literature, Univ. of Washington, Seattle, 1939–81, now Emeritus (Chmn. of Dept., 1939–64). Former member of faculty, Univ. of Buffalo, U.S. Naval Academy at Annapolis, Md., and Brown Univ., Providence, R.I.   Romance Ed., Modern Language Quarterly, 1940–44; Cultural Attaché, U.S. Embassy, Peru, 1944–47; Visiting Prof., Collège de France, 1975, and Simon Fraser Univ., 1982.   *Publs:* Le Theatre antique, 1934; (trans. and ed.) Ortega y Gasset: Mission of the University, 1944, 1966; The Cultural Attaché, 1947; Research on Language Teaching: Bibliography, 1962, 1965; (co-author) Film-Recital of French Poems and Cultural Commentary, 1964; Background Data for the Teaching of French, 1967; (co-ed.) La France en Mutation, 1979; (co-author) Savoir vivre en français, 1988.   Add: GN-60, Univ. of Washington, Seattle, Wash. 98195, U.S.A.

NOTLEY, Alice.   American, b. 1945.   Poetry, Autobiography.   Full-time writer.   *Publs:* 165 Meeting House Lane, 1971; Phoebe Light, 1973; Incidentals in the Day World, 1973; For Frank O'Hara's Birthday, 1976; Alice Ordered Me to Be Made: Poems 1975, 1976; A Diamond Necklace, 1977; Songs for the Unborn Second Baby, 1979; When I Was Alive, 1980; Waltzing Matilda, 1981; Tell Me Again (autobiography), 1981; How Spring Comes, 1981; (with Andrei Codrescu) Three Zero, Turning Thirty, 1982; Sorrento, 1984; Margaret and Dusty, 1985; At Night the States, 1988.   Add: 101 St. Mark's Pl., New York, N.Y. 10009, U.S.A.

NOTT, Kathleen (Cecilia).   British.   Novels/Short stories, Poetry, Philosophy.   Ed., PEN Intnl., London, since 1960 (Pres., British Centre, Intnl. PEN, 1974–75).   Pres., Progressive League, London, 1958–60. *Publs:* Mile End, 1938; The Dry Deluge, 1947; Landscapes and Departures, 1947; The Emperor's Crrey TW9 1UB, England.

NOURSE, Alan E(dward).   American, b. 1928.   Novels/Short stories, Science fiction/Fantasy, Children's fiction, Children's non-fiction, Sciences.   Freelance writer, 1956–58, and since 1964.   Owner, Chamberlain Press, 1953–55; Intern, Virginia Mason Hosp., Seattle, Wash., 1955–56; in private medical practice, North Bend, Wash., 1958–64.   Pres., Science Fiction Writers of America, 1968–69.   *Publs:* science fiction—Trouble on Titan (juvenile), 1954; A Man Obsessed, 1955, as The Mercy Men, 1968; Rocket to Limbo (juvenile), 1957; (with J.A. Meyer) The Invaders Are Coming, 1959; Scavengers in Space (juvenile), 1959; Star Surgeon (juvenile), 1960; Tiger by the Tail (juvenile short stories), 1961, in U.K. as Beyond Infinity, 1964; Raiders from the Rings (juvenile), 1962; The Counterfeit Man (juvenile short stories), 1963; The Universe Between (juvenile), 1965; Psi High and Others (short stories), 1968; Rx for Tomorrow (juvenile short stories), 1971; The Bladerunner, 1974; The Fourth Horseman, 1983; other—Junior Intern (novel), 1955; So You Want to Be a Doctor Lawyer, Scientist, (with Eleanore Halliday) Nurse, (with James C. Webbert) Engineer, Physicist, (with James C. Webbert) Chemist, Surgeon, (with Carl Meinhardt) Architect (juvenile), 9 vols., 1957–69; Nine Planets, 1960, 1970; (with Geoffrey Marks) The Management of a Medical Practice, 1963; The Body, 1964; Universe, Earth, and Atom: The Story of Physics, 1969; Virginia Mason Medical Center: The First Fifty Years, 1970; Venus and Mercury (juvenile), 1972; Ladies' Home Journal Family Medical Guide, 1973; The Backyard Astromomer, 1973; The Giant

Planets (juvenile), 1974; The Outdoorsman's Medical Guide, 1974; The Asteroids (juvenile), 1974; Clear Skin, Healthy Skin (juvenile), 1976; Lumps, Bumps, and Rashes (juvenile), 1976; Viruses (juvenile), 1976; The Tooth Book (juvenile), 1977; Vitamins (juvenile), 1977; Fractures, Dislocations, and Sprains (juvenile), 1978; The Practice (novel), 1978; Hormones (juvenile), 1979; Patient: Inside the Mayo Clinic, 1979; Menstruation: Just Plain Talk (juvenile), 1980; Your Immune System (juvenile), 1980; Herpes (juvenile), 1985; (with Dr. Janice Phelps) The Hidden Addiction and How to Get Free, 1986; AIDS (juvenile), 1986; The Elk Hunt, 1986; Birth Control (juvenile), 1986.   Add: Route 1, Box 173, Thorp, Wash. 98946, U.S.A.

NOUWEN, Henri J(osef Machiel).   Dutch, b. 1932 (came to U.S. in 1964).   Psychology, Theology/Religion.   Prof. of Pastoral Theology, Yale Univ., New Haven, Conn., since 1977 (Assoc. Prof., 1971–77).   Ordained Roman Catholic priest, 1957; Visiting Prof. of Psychology, Univ. of Notre Dame, Ind., 1966–68; Faculty member and Chmn. of Dept. of Behavorial Sciences, Catholic Theological Inst., 1969–70.   *Publs:* Intimacy: Pastoral Psychological Essays, 1969; Bidden om het leven: Het contemplatief engagement van Thomas Merton, 1970; Creative Ministry, 1971; With Open Hands, 1972; The Wounded Healer: Ministry in Contemporary Society, 1972; (with Walter J. Gaffney) Aging, 1974; Out of Solitude: Three Meditations on the Christian Life, 1974; Reaching Out: The Three Movements of the Spiritual Life, 1975; The Genesee Diary: Report from a Trappist Monastery, 1976; The Living Reminder: Service and Prayer in Memory of Jesus Christ, 1977; Clowning in Rome: Reflection on Solitude, Celibacy, and Contemplation, 1979; Behold the Beauty of the Lord: Praying with Icons, 1987.   Add: c/o Ave., Maria Press, Notre Dame, Ind. 46556, U.S.A.

NOVACK, George.   American, b. 1905.   Philosophy, Politics/Government.   Ed., Intnl. Socialist Review.   *Publs:* The Logic of Marxism, 1942; The Law of Uneven and Combined Development, 1958; The Long View of History, 1960; Moscow Versus Peking, 1963; The Age of Permanent Revolution, 1964; The Origins of Materialism, 1965; Existentialism Versus Marxism, 1966; Empiricism and Its Evolution, 1969; Democracy and Revolution, 1970; Understanding History, 1972, 1980; Humanism and Socialism, 1973; Pragmatism Versus Marxism, 1975; America's Revolutionary Heritage, 1976; Polemics in Marxist Philosophy, 1978.   Add: c/o Pathfinders Press, 410 West St., New York, N.Y. 10014, U.S.A.

NOVAK, Joseph.   *See* **KOSINSKI,** Jerzy.

NOVAK, Maximillian Erwin.   American, b. 1930.   Intellectual History, Literature.   Prof. of English, Univ. of California at Los Angeles, since 1969 (Asst. Prof., 1962–67; Assoc. Prof., 1965–68).   Assoc. Ed., Augustan Reprint Soc.   Instr., 1958–61, and Asst. Prof. 1961–62, Univ. of Michigan.   *Publs:* Economics and the Fiction of Daniel Defoe, 1962; Defoe and the Nature of Man, 1963; (with Herbert Davis) The Uses of Irony, 1966; Congreve, 1971; (with Aubrey Williams) Congreve Considered, 1971; (ed. with Edward Dudley) The Wild Man Within, 1972; (ed.) Thomas Southerne: Oroonoko, 1976; (ed.) English Literature in the Age of Disguise, 1977; Realism, Myth and History in Defoe's Fiction, 1983; English Literature in the Eighteenth Century, 1983; (ed.) California Edition of the Works of John Dryden, vol. X, 1970, vol. XIII, 1984.   Add: Dept. of English, Univ. of California, Los Angeles, Calif. 90024, U.S.A.

NOVAK, Michael.   American, b. 1933.   Novels/Short stories, Philosophy, Social commentary/phenomena, Theology/Religion.   Holder of George Frederick Jewett Chair in Religion and Public Policy and Resident Scholar, American Enterprise Inst., Washington, D.C., since 1977; appointed to the Board for Intnl. Broadcasting, (governing Radio Free Europe and Radio Liberty), since 1984.   Publr., The Novak Report on the New Ethnicity (monthly).   Asst. Prof., Stanford Univ., California, 1965–68; Assoc. Prof., State Univ. of New York at Old Westbury, 1968– 71; Assoc. Dir., Humanities Prog., Rockefeller Foundn., 1973–74; Ledden-Watson Distinguished Prof. of Religion, Syracuse Univ., New York, 1977–79; U.S. Rep. and Chief of U.S. Delegation, U.N. Human Rights Commn., 1981–82.   *Publs:* The Tiber Was Silver (novel), 1961; A New Generation: American and Catholic, 1964; The Open Church: Vatican I: Act II, 1964; The Experience of Marriage, 1964; Belief and Unbelief, 1965, 1986; A Time to Build, 1967; American Philosophy and the Future: Essays for a New Generation, 1968; A Theology for Radical Politics, 1969; Naked I Leave (novel), 1970; The Experience of Nothingness, 1970; All the Catholic People, 1971; Ascent of the Mountain, Flight of the Dove, 1971; Politics: Realism and Imagination, 1971; (with K.L. Novak) A Book of Elements, 1972; The Rise of the Unmeltable Ethnics, 1972; Choosing Our King, 1974; The Joy of Sports, 1976; The Guns of Lattimer, 1978; The American Vision, 1979; The Spirit of Democratic Capitalism, 1982;

Confession of a Catholic, 1983; Freedom with Justice: Catholic Social Thought and Literal Institutions, 1984; Human Rights and the New Realism, 1986; Character and Crime, 1986; Will it Liberate?: Questions about Liberation Theology, 1986; Taking Glasnost Seriously, 1988. Add: 1150 17th St. N.W., Washington, D.C. 20036, U.S.A.

NOVE, Alec. British, b. 1915. Economics, Intellectual history. Emeritus Prof. of Economics, Univ. of Glasgow, since 1982 (Prof., 1963–82). Member of Civil Service, 1946–58; Reader in Russian Social and Economic Studies, Univ. of London, 1958–63. *Publs:* The Soviet Economy, 1961, 3rd ed. 1968; Was Stalin Really Necessary?, 1964; (with J.A. Newth) The Soviet Middle East, 1967; An Economic History of the U.S.S.R., 1969; (ed., with D.M. Nuti) Socialist Economics, 1972; Efficiency Criteria for Nationalised Industries, 1973; Stalinism and After, 1975; The Soviet Economic System, 1977; Political Economy and Soviet Socialism, 1979; The Economics of Feasible Socialism, 1983; Socialism, Economics, and Development, 1986. Add: 55 Hamilton Dr., Glasgow G12 8DP, Scotland.

NOWRA, Louis. Australian, b. 1950. Novels/Short stories, Plays/Screenplays. Writer-in-Residence, Univ. of Queensland, Brisbane, 1979; Assoc. Artistic Dir., Sydney Theatre Co., 1980. *Publs:* The Misery of Beauty: The Loves of Frogman (novel), 1976; Inner Voices, 1978; (ed.) The Cheated, 1979; Visions, 1980; Inside the Island, 1981; The Precious Woman, 1981; Sunrise, 1983; The Golden Age, 1985. Add: c/o Hilary Linstead and Assocs., 223 Commonwealth St., Surry Hills, N.S.W. 2010, Australia.

NOYES, Stanley. American, b. 1924. Novels/Short stories, Poetry. Literary Arts Coordinator, New Mexico Arts Div., Santa Fe, N.M., 1977 until retirement, 1986 (Dir., Poetry in Schools, 1972–77). Instr., Extension Div., Univ. of California, Berkeley, 1954–55; Asst. Prof. of Humanities, California Coll. of Arts and Crafts, Oakland, 1954–61; Lectr., Coll. of Santa Fe, N.M., 1965–71. Poetry Ed., New Mexico Mag., 1973–77. *Publs:* No Flowers for a Clown, 1961; Shadowbox, 1970; Faces and Spirits (poetry), 1974; (ed. with Gene Frumkin) The Indian Rio Grande: Recent Poems from 3 Cultures, 1977; Beyond the Mountains, Beyond the Mountains (poetry), 1979; The Commander of Dead Leaves: A Dream Collection (poetry), 1984. Add: 634 E. Garcia, Santa Fe, N.M. 87501, U.S.A.

NUGENT, Walter T.K. American, b. 1935. History. Tackes Prof. of History, Notre Dame Univ., Ind., since 1984. Prof. of History, Indiana Univ., Bloomington, 1968–84 (Asst. Prof., 1963–64; Assoc. Prof, 1964–68; Assoc. Dean, Coll. of Arts and Sciences, 1967–71; Acting Chmn., Near East Language and Literature Dept., 1969–70; Assoc. Dean of Overseas Study, 1972–76; Chmn., History Dept., 1974–77). *Publs:* The Tolerant Populists, 1963; Creative History: An Introduction to Historical Method, 1967, 1973; The Money Question During Reconstruction, 1967; Money and American Society 1865-1880, 1968; Modern American, 1973; From Centennial to World War: American Society 1876-1917, 1977; Structures of American Social History, 1981. Add: Dept. of History, Notre Dame Univ., Notre Dame, Ind. 46556, U.S.A.

NUNIS, Doyce B(lackman), Jr. American, b. 1924. History. Prof. of History, Univ. of Southern California, Los Angeles, 1968–88 (Assoc. Prof., 1965–68). Ed., Southern Californian Quarterly, since 1962; Pres., Bd. of Trustees, Mission Santa Barbara Archive, since 1971. Historian, El Pueblo de Los Angeles State Historic Park, 1971–80; Sheriff, Los Angeles Corral of Westerners, 1973; Pres., Zamorano Club, 1975–76. *Publs:* Andrew Sublette: Rocky Mountain Prince 1808-1853, 1960; (ed.) The Golden Frontier: Recollections of Herman Francis Rinehart 1851-1860, 1962; (ed.) Josiah Belden: 1841 California Overland Pioneer, 1962; (ed.) California Diary of Faxon Dean Atherton 1836-39, 1964; (ed.) A Youthful Goldseeker: The Letters of Jasper Smith Hill 1850-52, 1964; (ed.) Journey of James H. Bull, Baja, California 1843, 1965; (trans. with L. Jay Oliva) A California Medical Journey, by Pierre Garnier, M.D., 1967; Trials of Issac Graham, 1968; Past Is Prologue: Centennial Profile of Pacific Mutual Life Insurance Co., 1968; (ed.) Hudson's Bay Company's First Fur Brigade to the Sacramento Valley: Alexander McLeod's 1829 Hunt, 1968; (ed.) Sketches of a Journey on the Two Oceans, by Abbe Henri-J.-A. Alric, 1971; (ed.) San Francisco Vigilance Committee of 1856: Three Views, 1971; (ed.) The Drawing of Ignacio Tirsch, S.J., 1972; (ed.) Los Angeles and Its Environs in the Twentieth Century: A Bibliography of a Metropolis, 1973; A History of American Political Thought, 2 vols., 1975; The Mexican War in Baja, California, 1977; (ed.) A Frontier Doctor, by Henry F. Hoyt, 1979; (ed.) Los Angeles from the Days of the Pueblo, 1981; (ed.) The Letters of Jacob Baegart 1749-1761: Jesuit Missionary in Baja California, 1982; (ed.) The 1769

Transit of Venus: The First Planned Scientific Expedition in Baja California, 1982; Men, Medicine, and Water: The Building of the Los Angeles Aqueduct 1908-1913, 1982; (ed.) Frontier Fighter by George W. Coe, 1984; (ed.) Southern California Historical Anthology, 1984; (ed.) The Life of Tom Horn, by Tom Horn, 1987. Add: Dept. of History, Univ. of Southern California, Los Angeles, Calif. 90089, U.S.A.

NUNN, Frederick McKinley. American, b. 1937. History, Politics/Government. Prof. of History, since 1972, and Assoc. Dean, Coll. of Liberal Arts and Sciences, since 1983, Portland State Univ., Ore. (Asst. Prof., 1965–67; Assoc. Prof. 1967–72; Asst. Dir., Pacific Rim Studies Center, 1972–73; Head of Dept., 1980–82; Asst. Dean, 1982–83). Member, Editorial Advisory Bd., Military Affairs, 1973–78; Bd. of Ed., Latin American Research Review, 1984–85. *Publs:* Chilean Politics, 1920-31: The Honorable Mission of the Armed Forces, 1970; The Military in Chilean History: Essays on Civil-Military Relations 1810-1973, 1976; Yesterdays Soldiers: European Military Professionalism in South America 1890-1940, 1983. Add: Dept. of History, Portland State Univ., P.O. Box 751, Portland, Ore. 97207, U.S.A.

NUNN, G. Raymond. British, b. 1918. Librarianship. Prof. of History and Asian Studies, Univ. of Hawaii, Honolulu, since 1961 (Dir., East-West Center Library, 1961–64). Head, Asia Library, Univ. of Michigan, 1951–61. *Publs:* Chinese Publishing Statistics, 1949-59, 1961; Chinese Periodicals, International Holdings 1949-1960, 1961; Resources for Research on Asia at the University of Hawaii and in Honolulu, 1965; Modern Japanese Book Publishing, 1965; Publishing in Mainland China, 1966; South and Southeast Asia: A Bibliography of Bibliographies, 1967; Asia, an Annotated and Selected Guide to Reference Works, 1971; Indonesian Newspapers, an International Union List, 1972; Vietnamese, Cambodian and Laotian Newspapers, an International Union List, 1972; Thai and Burmese Newspapers, an International Union List, 1972; Buku Referensi Indonesia, 1972; Asia, a Core Collection, 1973; Asian Libraries and Librarianship, an Annotated Bibliography, 1973; South-east Asian Periodicals: An International Union List, 1977; Japanese Periodicals and Newspapers in Western Language: An International Union List, 1980; Asia, Reference Works: A Select Annotated Guide, 1980; Asia and Oceania: A Guide to Archival and Manuscript Sources in the United States, 1985. Add: 2631 Ferdinand Ave., Honolulu, Hawaii 96822, U.S.A.

NUNN, John. British, b. 1955. Recreation/Leisure/Hobbies. Chess grandmaster, 1978. *Publs:* The Pirc for the Tournament Player, 1980; Tactical Chess Endings, 1981; (with M. Stean) Sicilian Defence Najdorf Variation, 1982; The Benoni for the Tournament Player, 1982; Beating the Sicilian, 1984; Solving in Style, 1985; Secrets of Grandmaster Play, 1987; Najdorf for the Tournament Player, 1988. Add: 228 Dover House Rd., London SW15 5AH, England.

NUNN, William Curtis. Also writes as Will Curtis and as Ananias Twist. American, b. 1908. Poetry, History, Biography, Humor/Satire. Emeritus Prof. of History, Texas Christian Univ., Fort Worth, since 1976 (Assoc. Prof. 1946–51; Prof. 1951–76). Assoc. Prof. of History, Southwest Texas State Teachers Coll., San Marcos, 1941–44, and Univ. of Houston, Tex., 1945–46. *Publs:* (co-author) Texas: The Story of the Lone Star State, 1948; Escape from Reconstruction, 1956; (co-author as Ananias Twist) Snide Lights on Texas History, 1959; Texas Under the Carpetbaggers, 1962; (co-author) Frontier Forts of Texas, 1966; (ed.) Ten Texans in Gray, 1968; (co-author) Capitals of Texas, 1968; (as Will Curtis) Peace Unto You (poetry), 1970; (co-author) Indians of Texas, 1971; (co-author) Women of Texas, 1972; Somervell: Story of a Texas County, 1975; (ed.) Ten More Texans in Gray, 1980; Marguerite Clark: America's Darling of Broadway and the Silent Screen, 1981. Add: 300 Huguley Blvd., Apt. 320, Burleson, TX 76028, U.S.A.

NURNBERG, Walter. British, b. 1907. Photography. Professional photographer since 1933, specialising in industrial photography since 1947. Contrib. Ed., British Journal of Photography. Head, Sch. of Photography, West Surrey Coll. of Art and Design, Guildford, 1968–74. *Publs:* Advert Photography; Baby, the Camera and You; Lighting for Photography; Lighting for Portraiture. Add: 18 Cornwood Close, London N2 0HP, England.

NURSTEN, Jean Patricia (Frobisher). British. Education, Sociology. Consultant in social work since 1984. Psychiatric social worker, 1950–64; Sr. Lectr. in Applied Social Studies, Univ. of Bradford, Yorks., 1964–76; Sr. Consultant in Social Work, Berks. Social Services, 1976–79; Sr. Lectr. in Social Work, London Sch. of Economics, 1979–84. *Publs:* (with J.H. Kahn) Unwillingly to School, 1964, 3rd ed. 1980; (ed.) Social

Work Series (Pergamon), 24 vols., 1965–; Process of Casework, 1974. Add: 3 Cintra Ave., Reading, Berks., England.

NUTTALL, Jeff. British, b. 1933. Novels/Short series, Plays/ Screenplays, Poetry. Lectr., Foundation Studies Dept., Bradford Coll. of Art, Yorks., 1968–70; Lectr. in Fine Arts, Leeds Polytechnic, 1970–80; Head of Fine Arts, Liverpool Polytechnic, 1981–85. former Ed., My Own Mag. *Publs:* (with K. Musgrove) The Limbless Virtuoso, 1963; Songs Sacred and Secular, 1964; Poems I Want to Forget, 1965; Pieces of Poetry, 1965; Come Back Sweet Prince: A Novelette, 1966; Isabel, 1967; The Case of Isabel and the Bleeding Foetus (novel), 1967; Journals, 1968; (with Alan Jackson and William Wantling) Penguin Modern Poets 12, 1968; Mr. Watkins Got Drunk and Had to Be Carried Home (novel), 1968; Oscar Christ and the Immaculate Conception (novel), 1968; Bomb Culture (social criticism), 1969; Love Poems, 1969; Pig (novel), 1969; Selected Poems, 1970; Poems 1962-1969, 1970; Barrow Boys (play), 1972; Snipe's Spinster (novel), 1974; Foxes' Lair (novelette), 1974; Objects, 1976; (with Rodick Carmichael) Common Factors/Vulgar Factions, 1977; The Gold Hole (novel), 1978; King Twist: A Portrait of Frank Randle, 1978; What Happened to Jackson (novel), 1978; The Patriarchs (novel), 1978; Performance Art, 2 vols., 1980; Grape Notes, Apple Music, 1980; Muscle (novel), 1983; Scenes and Dubs (poems), 1987; Mad with Music (poems), 1987; The Pleasures of Necessity (polemic), 1988. Add: 71 White Hart Lane, London SW13 0PP, England.

NUTTING, (Sir) Anthony. British, b. 1920. History, International relations/Current affairs, Biography. Conservative M.P. (U.K.) for Melton Div. of Leicester, 1945 until resignation in 1956: Parliamentary Under-Secty. of State for Foreign Affairs, 1951–54, and Minister of State for Foreign Affairs and U.K. Delegate to U.N. Gen. Assembly, 1954–56. *Publs:* I Saw for Myself, 1958; Disarmament, 1959; Europe Will Not Wait, 1960; Lawrence of Arabia, 1961; The Arabs, 1964; Gordon: Martyr and Misfit, 1966; No End of a Lesson, 1967; Scramble for Africa, 1970; Nasser, 1972. Add: 2 Douro Pl., London W8, England.

NUWER, Hank. American, b. 1946. Novels/Short stories, Mystery/ Crime/Suspense, Sports/Fitness. Freelance writer since 1969; Head, Magazine Div., Dept. of Journalism, Ball State Univ., Muncie, Ind., since 1985. *Publs:* (with William Boyles) The Deadliest Profession, 1980; (with William Boyles) A Killing Trade, 1981; (with William Boyles) The Wild Ride, 1981; (with William Boyles) Bold Mountain, 1982; (with Carole Shaw) Come Out, Come Out, Wherever You Are, 1982; Strategies of the Great Football Coaches, 1987; Strategies of the Great Baseball Managers, 1988; Rendezvousing with Contemporary Authors, 1988. Add: c/o Dept. of Journalism, Ball State Univ., Muncie, Ind. 47306, U.S.A.

NWAPA, Flora. Nigerian, b. 1931. Novels/Short stories, children's fiction and non-fiction. Managing Dir., Tana Press Ltd. and Flora Nwapa Books Ltd., Enugu, since 1978. Women's Education Officer, Calabar, 1958; teacher, Queen's School, Enugu, 1959–62; Asst. and Registrar (public relations), Univ. of Lagos, 1962–67; Commissioner and Member of Executive Council, East Central State, 1970–75; with ministries of Health and Social Welfare; Lands Survey and Urban Development; and Establishments. *Publs:* Efuru (novel), 1966; Idu (novel), 1970; This Is Lagos and Other Stories (short stories), 1971; Emeka, Driver's Guard (children's fiction), 1972; Never Again (novel), 1974; Mammywater (children's fiction), 1979; My Tana Colouring Book (chilren's non-fiction), 1979; Wives at War and Other Stories (short stories), 1980; Journey to Space (children's fiction), 1980; The Miracle Kittens (children's fiction), 1980; The Adventures of Deke (children's fiction), 1980; My Animal Number Book (children's non-fiction), 1981; One Is Enough (novel), 1982; Women Are Different (novel), 1986; Cassava Song and Rice Song (poetry), 1986. Add: c/o Tana Press Ltd., 2A Menkiti Lane, Ogui, Enugu, Nigeria.

NYANAPONIKA, (Reverend). Lay name is Siegmund Feniger. German, b. 1901. Philosophy, Religion, Translations. Buddhist Monk, since 1936. Ed., The Wheel, since 1958; Co-founder, Ed., and Secty., since 1958, and Pres., since 1973, Buddhist Publ. Soc., Kandy, Sri Lanka. *Publs:* The Heart of Buddhist Meditation, 1962; Abhidhamma Studies: Researches in Buddhist Psychology, 1965; The Life of Sariputta, 1966; (ed.) Pathways of Buddhist Thought, 1971; The Vision of Dhamma, 1986. Add: Forest Hermitage, Kandy, Sri Lanka.

NYE, Harold G. *See* **HARDING,** Lee.

NYE, Joseph S(amuel), Jr. American, b. 1937. Institutions/Organizations, International relations/Current affairs, Politics/Government. Prof.

of International Security and Dir. of the Center for Science and Intnl. Affairs, Harvard Univ., Cambridge, Mass., since 1971 (Instr., 1964–66; Asst. Prof., 1966–69; Assoc. Prof. 1969–71). Exec. Cttee, Member, Center for Intnl. Affairs, Harvard Univ. Deputy to Under-Secty. of State for Security Assistance, Science and Technology, 1977–79. *Publs:* Pan-Africanism and East African Integration, 1965; (ed.) International Regionalism, 1968; Peace in Parts: Integration and Conflict in Regional Organization, 1971; (with E.B. Haas and R.L. Butterworth) Conflict Management by International Organizations, 1972; (author and ed. with R.O. Keohane) Transnational Relations and World Politics, 1972; Power and Independence, 1977; (ed. with David Deese) Energy and Security, 1980; Living with Nuclear Weapons, 1983; (ed.) The Making of America's Soviet Policy, 1984; (ed. with Samuel P. Huntington) Global Dilemmas, 1985; (co-author) Hawks, Doves, and Owls, 1985; Nuclear Ethics, 1986; Fateful Visions, 1988. Add: Center for Science and Intnl. Affairs, Kennedy Sch. of Govt., 79 John F. Kennedy St., Cambridge, Mass. 02138, U.S.A.

NYE, Nelson (Coral). Also writes as Clem Colt and Drake C. Denver. American, b. 1907. Westerns/Adventure, Animals/Pets, Recreation/Leisure/Hobbies. Freelance writer since 1935. Former publicity writer and reviewer for Buffalo and Cincinnati newspapers, ranch hand in Calif. and Tex., rancher and breeder of quarter horses in Arizona. Founding Member, 1953, and Pres., 1953, 1960–61, Western Writers of America. *Publs:* Two Fisted Cowpoke, 1936, in U.S. paperback as The No-Gun Fighter, 1956; The Killer of Cibecue, 1936, in U.K. as The Sheriff of Navajo County, 1937, in U.S. paperback as Trouble on the Tonto Rim, 1961; The Leather Slapper, 1937; Quick-Fire Hombre, 1937, in U.S. paperback as Gunfighter Brand, 1958; The Star-Packers, 1937, in U.K. as Drake C. Denver, 1938; The Waddy from Roarin' Fork, 1938, in U.S. (as Clem Colt) as Fiddle-Back Ranch, 1944, in U.S. paperback as Tornado on Horseback, 1955; G Stands for Gun, 1938; Prairie Dust, 1938; The Bandit of Bloody Run, 1939; Smoke-Wagon Kid, in U.S. as Clem Colt, 1943; Pistols for Hire, 1941, in U.S. paperback as A Bullet for Billy the Kid, 1950; Gunfighter Breed, 1942; Salt River Ranny, 1942, in paperback as Gunshot Trail, 1955; Come A-Smokin', 1943; Beneath the Belt, 1943; Gunslick Mountain, 1944, in U.S. as Clem Colt, 1945; Cartridge Case Law, 1944; Wild Horse Shorty, 1944; Blood of Kings, 1946; The Barber of Tubac, 1947, in U.S. paperback as The Gun-Wolf of Tubac, 1949, as Arizona Dead-Shot, 1957, as The Gun Wolf, 1980; Gunman, Gunman, 1949, in U.K. (as Drake C. Denver) as Long Rope, 1949, in U.S. paperback as Plunder Valley, 1952; Riders by Night, 1950, in U.K. as Rustlers of K.C. Ranch, 1950; Caliban's Colt, 1950; Horses Is Fine People, 1950; Thief River, 1951; Born to Trouble, 1951; Wide Loop, 1952, in U.K. as The Crazy K, 1953; Desert of the Damned, 1952; Hired Hand, 1954; The Red Sombrero, 1954; The Lonely Grass (in U.K. as Clem Colt), 1955; The Parson of Gunbarrel Basin, 1955; Blood Sky, 1956, in U.S. as Horses, Women and Guns, 1959, in U.S. paperback as Arizona Renegade, 1969; Bandido, 1957, as Boss Gun, 1969; South Fork, 1957, in U.S. as Maverick Marshal, 1958; The Overlanders, 1959; Long Run, 1959, in U.K. as River of Horns, 1960; Ride the Wild Plains, 1959, in U.S. as The Last Bullet, 1960, in paperback as Loco, 1969; The Wolf That Rode (in U.K. as Johnny Get Your Gun), 1960; Gunfight at the OK Corral (novelization of screenplay), 1960; Not Grass Alone, 1961; The Irreverent Scout, 1961, in U.S. paperback as Frontier Scout, 1982; Rafe, 1962; Hideout Mountain, 1962; Death Comes Riding, 1962, in U.S. as The Seven Six-Gunners, 1963; Death Valley Slim, The Kid from Lincoln County, 1963; Bancroft's Banco (in U.K. as Wild River), 1963; Treasure Trail from Tucson (in U.K. as Weeping Widow Mine), 1964; Sudden Country, 1964; Gun Feud at Tiedown, Rogue's Rendezvous, 1964; Ambush at Yuma's Chimney, 1965; The Bravo Brand, 1965; The Marshal of Pioche, 1966; Iron Hand, 1966; Single Action, 1967; The Trail of Lost Skulls, 1967; The Rider on the Roan, 1967; A Lost Mine Named Salvation, 1968; The Trouble at Pen Blanca, 1969; Wolftrap, 1969; Gringo, 1969; The Texas Gun, 1970; Trouble at Quinn's Crossing, 1971; Hellbound for Ballarat, 1971; Kelly, 1971, in U.K. as The Palominas Pistolero, 1980; The Clifton Contract, 1972; The Lost Padre, 1988; No Place to Hide, 1988; Mule Man, 1988; The Fight At Four Corners, 1989; Pantalones, 1989; The Outside Man, 1989; Buffalo Jones, 1990; The Man from Goose Flats, 1990; The White Chip, 1990; The Crying Wolf, 1991; Bend of the River, 1991; The Deadly Gun, 1991; as Clem Colt—Gun-Smoke (in U.K. as Nelson Nye), 1938; The Shootin' Sheriff, 1938; The Bar Nothing Brand (in U.K. as Drake C. Denver as No Wire Range), 1939; Center-Fire Smith, 1939; Hair-Trigger Realm, 1940; Trigger-Finger Law, 1940; The Five Diamond Brand, 1941; Triggers for Six, 1941; The Sure-Fire Kid, 1942; Trigger Talk, 1942; Rustlers' Roost, 1943, in U.S. paperback (as Nelson Nye) as The Texas Tornado, 1955; Guns of Horse Prairie, 1943; Maverick Canyon, 1944; Once in the Saddle, 1946, (as Nelson Nye) as The One-Shot Kid, 1954, (as Nelson Nye) as Gun-Hunt for the Sundance Kid, 1962; Coyote Song,

1947, in U.K. as Nelson Nye, 1949, in U.S. paperback (as Nelson Nye) as Ranger's Revenge, 1956; Saddle Bow Slim, 1948; Tough Company, 1952; Strawberry Roan, 1953; No Tomorrow, 1953; Smoke Talk (in U.K. as Nelson Nye; in U.S. paperback as Six-Gun Buckaroo), 1954; Quick Trigger Country (in U.K. as Nelson Nye), 1955; as Drake C. Denver— Turbulent Guns, 1940, in U.S (as Clem Colt) as The Renegade Cowboy), 1944; The Feud at Sleepy Cat, 1940; Tinbadge, 1941, in U.S. paperback (as Nelson Nye) as Shotgun Law, 1967; Wildcats of Tonto Basin, 1941; Gun Quick, 1942; The Desert Desperadoes, 1942; Lost Water, 1942; Breed of the Chaparral, 1946, in U.K. as Clem Colt, 1949, in U.S. paperback (as Nelson Nye) as Guns of Arizona, 1958, as Ramrod Vengeance, 1969; non-fiction as Nelson Nye—Outstanding Modern Quarter Horse Sires, 1948; Champions of the Quarter Tracks, 1950; (ed.) Western Roundup, 1961; (ed.) They Won Their Spurs, 1962; Your Western Horse: His Ways and His Rider, 1963; The Complete Book of the Quarter Horse, 1964; Speed and the Quarter Horse: A Payload of Sprinters, 1973; Great Moments in Quarter Racing History, 1983; Deadly Companions, 1987; Horse Thieves, 1987. Add: 3290 W. Ironwood Ridge Dr., Tucson, Ariz. 85745, U.S.A.

NYE, Robert. British, b. 1939. Novels/Short stories, Children's fiction, Plays/Screenplays, Poetry. Poetry Ed., The Scotsman, since 1967; Poetry Critic, The Times, London, since 1971. *Publs:* Juvenilia 1, 1961; Juvenilia 2, 1963; Taliesin, 1966; March Has Horse's Ears, 1966; Doubtfire, 1967; (trans.) Beowulf, 1968; Tales I Told My Mother, 1969; (with William Watson) Sawney Bean, 1969; Sisters, 1969; Darker Ends, 1969; Wishing Gold, 1970; Fugue (screenplay), 1971; Poor Pumpkin, 1971; Cricket, 1972; (ed.) A Choice of Sir Walter Raleigh's Verse, 1972; The Mathematical Princess and Other Stories, 1972; (ed.) A Choice of Swinburne's Verse, 1973; (ed.) The Faber Book of Sonnets, 1976; Falstaff (novel), 1976; Penthesilia, 1976; (ed.) The English Sermon 1750-1850, 1976; Divisions on a Ground, 1976; Out of the World and Back Again (juvenile), 1977; Merlin (novel), 1978; The Bird of the Golden Land (juvenile), 1980; Faust (novel), 1980; Harry Pay the Pirate (juvenile), 1981; The Voyage of The Destiny (novel), 1982; The Facts of Life and Other Fictions, 1983; Three Tales (for children), 1983; (ed.) PEN New Poetry 1, 1986; The Memoirs of Lord Byron (novel), 1989; A Collection of Poems 1955-1988, 1989. Add: c/o Anthony Sheil Assocs., 43 Doughty St., London WC1N 2LF, England.

NYE, Russel (Blaine). American, b. 1913. History, Biography. Distinguished Prof. of English, Michigan State Univ., East Lansing, since 1963, now Emeritus (joined faculty, 1940). Pres., American Studies Assn., 1955–56, and Popular Culture Assn., 1969–72. *Publs:* George Bancroft, Brahmin Rebel, 1944; Civil Liberty and Slavery, 1948; Midwestern Progressive Politics, 1951; (with J.E. Morpurgo) The History of the United States, 1955, 1970; A Baker's Dozen, 1956; Cultural Life of the New Nation, 1960; This Almost Chosen People, 1966; The Unembarrassed Muse, 1970. Add: 301 Oxford Rd., East Lansing, Mich. 48823, U.S.A.

O

OAKES, James. American, b. 1953. History. Prof. of History, Northwestern Univ., Eranston, Ill., since 1986. Asst. Prof. of History, Purdue Univ., Lafayette, Ind., 1981–82, and Princeton Univ., N.J., 1982–86. *Publs:* The Ruling Race: A History of American Slaveholders, 1982. Add: Dept. of History, Northwestern Univ., Evanston, Ill. 60208, U.S.A.

OAKES, Philip. British, b. 1928. Novels/Short stories, Plays/Screenplays, Poetry, Autobiography/Memoirs/Personal, Biography. Scriptwriter for Granada TV and BBC, London, 1958–62; Film Critic, The Sunday Telegraph, London, 1963–65; Asst. Ed., Magazine, 1965–67, and Arts Columnist, 1969–80, Sunday Times, London. *Publs:* Unlucky Jonah: Twenty Poems, 1954; (with Tony Hancock) The Punch and Judy Man (screenplay), 1962; Exactly What We Want (novel), 1962; In the Affirmative, 1968; The God Botherers (in U.S. as Miracles: Genuine Cases Contact Box 340; novel), 1969; Married/Singular, 1973; Experiment at Proto (novel), 1973; Tony Hancock: A Biography, 1975; (ed.) The Entertainers, 1975; A Cast of Thousands (novel), 1976; (ed.) The Film Addict's Archive, 1977; From Middle England (memoirs), 1980; Dwellers All in Time and Space (memoirs), 1982; Selected Poems, 1982; At the Jazz Band Ball: A Memory of the 1950's, 1983. Add: c/o Elaine Greene Ltd., 31 Newington Green, London N16 9PU, England.

OAKLEY, Ann. British, b. 1944. Anthropology/Ethnology, Sociology, Women. Deputy Dir., Thomas Coram Research Unit, Inst. of Education, London Univ. Formerly Research Officer, Bedford Coll., Univ. of London. *Publs:* Sex, Gender and Society, 1972; Housewife, 1974; The Sociology of Housework, 1974; (ed. with J. Mitchell) The Rights and Wrongs of Women, 1976; Becoming a Mother, 1979; Women Confined, 1980; Subject Women, 1981; (with A. McPherson and H. Roberts) Miscarriage, 1984; Taking it Like a Woman, 1984; The Captured Womb, 1984; (ed. with J. Mitchell) What Is Feminism?, 1986; The Men's Room, 1987. Add: c/o Rogers, Coleridge and White, 20 Powis Mews, London W11 1JN, England.

OAKLEY, Charles Allen. British, b. 1900. History, Business/Trade/Industry. Lectr., Univ. of Glasgow, since 1920. Chmn., Scottish Film Council, since 1939; Ed., Glasgow Chamber of Commerce Monthly Journal, since 1953 (Glasgow Corp. Annual Industrial Guide, 1958–75). Scottish Controller, Ministry of Aircraft Production, 1939–45; Scottish Controller, Bd. of Trade, 1945–53; Pres., Glasgow Chamber of Commerce, 1965–66; Pres., Scottish Council of Chambers of Commerce, 1967–68. *Publs:* Men at Work, 1945; The Second City, 1946; (ed.) Scottish Industry, 1953; Where We Came In, 1964; History of a Faculty, 1973; Dear Old Glasgow Town, 1974; Our Illustrious Forbears, 1978; Those Were the Years (autobiography), 1984. Add: 10 Kirklee Circus, Glasgow G12, Scotland.

OAKLEY, Graham. British, b. 1929. Children's fiction. Scenic artist in theatres, and at the Royal Opera House, 2 years; Designer, BBC TV, 15 years, until 1977. *Publs:* The Church Mouse, 1972; The Church Cat Abroad, 1973; The Church Mice series, 1974; Magical Changes, 1979; Hetty and Harriet, 1981; Henry's Quest, 1986. Add: c/o Macmillan Children's Books, 4 Little Essex St., London WC2R 3LF, England.

OAKLEY, Stewart Philip. British, b. 1931. History. Sr. Lectr. in European History, Univ. of East Anglia, Norwich, since 1973 (Lectr., 1969–73). Lectr. in Modern History, Univ. of Edinburgh, 1960–69. *Publs:* The Story of Sweden, 1966; A Short History of Sweden, 1966; The Story of Denmark, 1972; A Short History of Denmark, 1972; Scandinavian History 1520-1970: A List of Books and Articles in English, 1984; William III and the Northern Crowns During the Nine Years War 1689-1697, 1987. Add: 16 College Rd., Norwich NR2 3JJ, England.

OAKS, Dallin H. American, b. 1932. Law. Church official and Member of Council of Twelve, Church of Jesus Christ of Latter–Day Saints. Law Clerk to U.S. Supreme Court Chief Justice Earl Warren, 1957–58; private practice of law, Kirkland and Ellis, 1958–61; Prof. of Law, Univ. of Chicago Law Sch., 1961–71; Pres., Brigham Young Univ., Provo, Utah, 1971–80; Utah Supreme Court Justice, 1981–84. *Publs:* (with G. Bogert) Cases on the Law of Trusts, 4th ed. 1967, 5th ed. 1978; (with W. Lehman) A Criminal Justice System and the Indigent: A Study of Chicago and Cook County, 1968; The Criminal Justice Act in the Federal District Courts, 1969; (ed.) The Wall Between Church and State, 1973; (with M. Hill) Carthage Conspiracy: The Trial of the Accused Assassins of Joseph Smith, 1975; Trust Doctrines in Church Controversies, 1984; Pure in Heart, 1988. Add: 47 E. South Temple, Salt Lake City, Utah 84150, U.S.A.

OAKSEY, Lord; John Geoffrey Tristram Lawrence. British, b. 1929. Sports. Racing Correspondent, Daily Telegraph, London, since 1957, and Racing Post, since 1989; Commentator, Independent Television, London, since 1970. *Publs:* (with Michael Seth-Smith, Peter Willett and Roger Mortimer) History of Steeplechasing, 1967; The Story of Mill Reef, 1974. Add: Hill Farm, Oaksey, Malmesbury, Wilts., England.

OATES, Joyce Carol. American, b. 1938. Novels/Short stories, Plays/Screenplays, Poetry, Literature. Assoc. Prof. of English, Univ. of Windsor, Ont., since 1967; Instr. in English, 1961–65, and Asst. Prof., 1965–67, Univ. of Detroit; Writer-in-Residence, Princeton Univ., New Jersey, 1978–81. *Publs:* By the North Gate (short stories), 1963; With Shuddering Fall, 1964; Upon the Sweeping Flood and Other Stories, 1966; A Garden of Earthly Delights, 1967; Expensive People, 1968; Anonymous Sins and Other Poems, 1969; Them, 1969; The Wheel of Love (short stories), 1970; Love and Its Derangements (poetry), 1970; Cupid and Psyche, 1970; Wonderland, 1971; The Edge of Possibility: Tragic Forms in Literature, 1972; Marriage and Infidelities (short stories), 1972; Do With Me What You Will, 1973; The Hostile Sun: The Poetry of D.H. Lawrence, 1973; Angel Fire: Poems, 1973; New Heaven, New Earth: Visionary Experience in Literature, 1974; Miracle Play, 1974; The Hungry Ghosts: Seven Allusive Comedies, 1974; The Goddess and Other Women (short stories), 1974; Where Are You Going, Where Have You Been: Stories of Young America, 1974; The Poisoned Kiss and Other Stories from the Portuguese, 1975; The Seduction and Other Stories, 1975; The Assassins: A Book of Hours, 1975; The Fabulous Beasts (poetry), 1975; Childwold, 1976; Crossing the Border (short stories), 1976; The Triumph of the Spider Monkey, 1976; Night-Side (short stories), 1977; Son of the Morning, 1978; Women Whose Lives Are Food, Men Whose Lives Are Money (poetry), 1978; Unholy Loves, 1979; Cybele, 1979; (co-ed.) The Best American Short Stories 1979, 1979; The Step-Father, 1979; Bellefleur, 1980; Three Plays, 1980; Angel of Light, 1981; Sentimental Education, 1981; Contraries: Essays, 1981; A Bloodsmoor Romance, 1982; The Profane Ant: Essays and Reviews, 1983; Mysteries of Winterthurn, 1984; Last Days, 1984; Solstice, 1985; Marya: A Life, 1986; Raven's Wing (short stories), 1986; On Boxing (non-fiction), 1987; You Must Remember This, 1987; The Assignation (short stories), 1988; American Appetites, 1989; The Time Traveller: Poems 1983-1989, 1989. Add: c/o Dept. of English, Univ. of Windsor, Windsor, Ont., Canada.

OATES, Stephen B(aery). American, b. 1936. History, Biography. Prof. of History and Adjunct Prof. of English, Univ. of Massachusetts, Amherst, since 1971 (Asst. Prof., 1968–69; Assoc. Prof., 1969–70). Instr. to Asst. Prof., Univ. of Texas, Arlington, 1964–68. *Publs:* Confederate Cavalry West of the River, 1961; (ed.) Rip Ford's Texas, 1963, 1987; (ed.) The Republic of Texas, 1968; Visions of Glory: Texans on the Southwestern Frontier, 1970; To Purge This Land with Blood: A Biography of John Brown, 1970, 1984; (ed.) Portrait of America: From the Cliff Dwellers to the End of Reconstruction, 1973, 1987; (ed.) Portrait of America: From Reconstruction to the Present, 1973, 1987; The Fires of Jubilee: Nat Turner's Fierce Rebellion, 1975; With Malice Toward None: The Life of Abraham Lincoln, 1977; Our Fiery Trial: Abraham Lincoln, John Brown, and the Civil War Era, 1979; Let the Trumpet Sound: The Life of Martin Luther King, Jr., 1982; Abraham Lincoln: The Man Behind the Myths, 1984; (ed.) Biography as High Adventure, 1986; William Faulkner, The Man and the Artist, 1987. Add: 10 Bride Path, Amherst, Mass. 01002, U.S.A.

OATES, Wallace Eugene. American, b. 1937. Economics, Environmental science/Ecology. Prof. of Economics, Univ. of Maryland, College Park, since 1979. Prof. of Economics, Princeton Univ., New Jersey, 1965–79. *Publs:* Fiscal Federalism, 1972; (with Harry Kelejian) Introduction to Econometrics: Principles and Applications, 1974, 3rd ed. 1989; (with William Baumol) The Theory of Environmental Policy, 1975, 1988; (with William Baumol) Economics, Environmental Policy, and the Quality of Life, 1979. Add: Dept. of Economics, Univ. of Maryland, College Park, Md. 20742, U.S.A.

OATTS, Lewis Balfour. British, b. 1902. History, Autobiography/Memoirs/Personal. Regular British Army Officer, Highland Light Infantry, 1922–48. *Publs:* Proud Heritage, vol. I, 1952, vol. II, 1959, vol. III, 1961, vol. IV, 1963; Jungle in Arms, 1964; I Serve: History of the 3rd Carabiniers, 1966; The Highland Light Infantry, 1969; Emperor's Chambermaids: History of 14/20th King's Hussars, 1973. Add: Arbury Hall, Nuneaton, Warwicks., England.

O'BALLANCE, Edgar. British, b. 1918. History, International relations/Current affairs. Freelance writer and journalist. *Publs:* The Arab-Israeli War 1948, 1956; The Sinai Campaign 1956, 1959; The Story of the French Foreign Legion, 1961; The Red Army of China, 1962; The Indo-China War 1945-54, 1964; The Red Army of Russia, 1964; The Greek Civil War 1944-49, 1966; Malaya: The Communist Insurgent War 1948-1960, 1966; The Algerian Insurrection 1954-1962, 1967; Korea 1950-53, 1969; War in the Yemen 1962-1967, 1971; The Third Arab-Israeli War 1967, 1972; The Kurdish Revolt 1961-70, 1973; Arab Guerilla Power, 1974; The Electronic War in the Middle East 1968-70, 1974; The Wars in Vietnam 1954-72, 1975; The Secret War in the Sudan 1955-72, 1977; No Victor, No Vanquished, 1978; The Language of Violence, 1979; Terror in Ireland, 1979; The Bloodstained Cedars of Lebanon, 1980; The Tracks of the Bear, 1982; The Gulf War 1980-1987, 1987. Add: Wakebridge Cottage, Wakebridge, Matlock, Derbyshire, England.

O'BRIAN, Frank. *See* GARFIELD, Brian.

O'BRIANT, Walter H(erbert). American, b. 1937. History, Philosophy. Assoc. Prof. of Philosophy, Univ. of Georgia, Athens, since 1969 (Asst. Prof., 1965–69). Vice Pres., American Leibniz Soc., 1977–88. *Publs:* Introduction to Philosophy, 1968, 3rd ed. 1982; Gottfried Wilhelm Leibniz's General Investigations Concerning the Analysis of Concepts and Truths, 1968. Add: Dept. of Philosophy, Univ. of Georgia, Athens, Ga. 30602, U.S.A.

O'BRIEN, Anne Sibley. American, b. 1952. Children's fiction. Writer and illustrator since 1982. Visual Aids Designer for Health Education, Kojedo Community Health Project, Kodejo Island, Korea, 1976–77; Teacher and Asst. Dir., Community SEED Center, Shelburne Falls, Mass., 1977–88; freelance illustrator, 1978–80; Dir., Community "Interainment" Agency, Portland, Maine, 1980–82. *Publs:* (all self-illustrated) Come Play with Us, 1985; I'm Not Tired, 1985; Where's My Truck?, 1985; I Want That!, 1985; I Don't Want to Go, 1986; It's Hard to Wait, 1986; It Hurts, 1986; Don't Say No, 1986. Add: c/o Henry Holt and Co., 521 Fifth Ave., New York, N.Y. 10175, U.S.A.

O'BRIEN, Conor Cruise. Irish, b. 1917. History, Literature, Politics/Government, Third World problems. Consultant Ed., The Observer newspaper, London, since 1981 (Ed., 1978–81). Pro-Chancellor, Dublin Univ., since 1973. Joined Dept. of External Affairs, Ireland, 1944: Counsellor, Paris, 1955–56; Member, Irish Delegation to the U.N., NYC, 1956–60; Asst. Secty., Dept. of External Affairs, Dublin, 1960; and Rep. of the Secty.-Gen. of the U.N. in Katanga, 1961; Vice-Chancellor, Univ. of Ghana, Legon, 1962–65; Albert Schweitzer Prof. of Humanities, New York Univ., NYC, 1965–69; Labour Member of the Dail Eireann (Irish Parliament) for Dublin North East, 1969–77, and Minister of Posts and Telegraphs, 1973–77. *Publs:* Maria Cross, 1952; Parnell and His Party, 1957; (ed.) The Shaping of Modern Ireland, 1959; To Katanga and Back, 1962; Conflicting Concepts for the U.N., 1964; Writers and Politics, 1965; The United Nations: Sacred Drama, 1967; Murderous Angels (play), 1968; Power and Consciousness, 1969; Albert Camus, 1969; (ed.) Edmund Burke: Reflections of the Revolution in France, 1969; Conor Cruise O'-Brien Introduces Ireland, 1969; (with M. Cruise O'Brien) The Suspecting Glance, 1970; A Concise History of Ireland, 1971; States of Ireland, 1972; King Herod Advises (play), 1973; Neighbours, 1980; The Siege: The Saga of Israel and Zionism, 1986; Passion and Cunning and Other Essays, 1988; God Land: Reflections on Religion and Nationalism, 1988. Add: Whitewater, Howth Summit, Dublin, Ireland.

O'BRIEN, Edna. Irish, b. 1932. Novels/Short stories, Plays/Screenplays, Children's fiction. *Publs:* The Country Girls, 1960; A Nice Bunch of Flowers (play), 1962; The Lonely Girl, 1962; The Girl with Green Eyes (screenplay), 1964; Girls in Their Married Bliss, 1964; August Is A Wicked Month, 1965; Casualties of Peace, 1966; The Love Object (stories), 1968; Three Into Two Won't Go (screenplay), 1968; A Pagan Place, 1970, as play, 1972; Zee and Co. (screenplay), 1971; Night, 1972; A Scandalous Woman and Other Stories, 1974; Mother Ireland, 1976; Johnny I Hardly Knew You, 1977; Arabian Days, 1977; The Collected Edna O'Brien, 1978; Mrs. Reinhardt and Other Stories (in U.S. as A Rose in the Heart), 1978; (ed.) Some Irish Loving, 1979; Virginia (play), 1981; The Dazzle, 1981; James and Nora, 1981; A Christmas Treat, 1982; Returning, 1982; The Rescue, 1983; A Fanatic Heart, 1984; Vanishing Ireland, 1986; Tales for the Telling, 1986; The High Road, 1989. Add: Duncan Heath Assocs., 162-170 Wardour St., London W1, England.

O'BRIEN, Elmer. American, b. 1911. Intellectual history, Philosophy, Theology/Religion. Writer-in-Residence, Ignatius Coll., Guelph, Ont., since 1973. Assoc. Prof. of Theology, Regis Coll., Toronto, 1951–60; Visiting Prof., Fordham Univ. Grad. Sch., Bronx, N.Y., 1952–53 and 1954–58; Prof. Loyola Coll., Concordia Univ., Montreal, 1962–73. *Publs:* The Essential Plotinus, 1964; Varieties of Mystic Experience, 1964; (ed.) Theology in Transition, 1965; (ed.) The Convergence of Traditions, 1967. Add: Ignatius Coll., P.O. Box 1238, Guelph, Ont. N1H 6N6, Canada.

O'BRIEN, Katharine E. American, b. 1901. Poetry, Mathematics. Chmn., Dept. of Mathematics, Coll. of New Rochelle, N.Y., 1925–36; Head, Dept. of Mathematics, Deering High Sch., Portland, Maine, 1940–71; Lectr. in Mathematics, Univ. of Maine, Portland, 1962–73; Lectr. in Mathematics, Brown Univ., Summer Sessions, 1962–65, 1967. *Publs:* Sequences, 1966; Excavation and Other Verse, 1967. Add: 130 Hartley St., Portland, Me. 04103, U.S.A.

O'BRIEN, Lawrence F(rancis). American, b. 1917. Politics/Government, International relations/Current affairs, Autobiography/Memoirs/Personal. Sr. Adviser, National Basketball Assn., 1984–89 (Commnr., 1975–84). With O'Brien Realty Co., Springfield, Mass., 1942–52; Pres. of Bd. and Business Mgr., Western Massachusetts Hotel and Restaurant Health Fund, 1952–58; State Dir. of Org., campaigns of John F. Kennedy for U.S. Senate, 1952 and 1958; involved in public relations work, Springfield, Mass., 1958–60; National Dir. of Org., 1960, and Chmn., 1968–69 and 1970–72, Democratic National Cttee.; National Dir. of Org. for Kennedy-Johnson campaign, 1960; Special Asst. to the U.S. President for Congressional Relations, 1961–65; Postmaster Gen. of the U.S., 1965–68; Democratic Party Campaign Mgr. for Presidential Election, 1968; Pres., McDonnell and Co., NYC, 1969; Pres., O'Brien Assocs., management consultants, Washington, D.C., 1969, 1973–75; Chmn., Democratic National Convention, 1972; Pres., Intnl. Basketball Hall of Fame, 1985–87. *Publs:* O'Brien Manual 1960, 4th ed. 1972; No Final Victories, 1974. Add: 860 United Nations Plaza, New York, N.Y. 10017, U.S.A.

O'BRIEN, Patrick. British, b. 1932. Economics, History, Transportation. Fellow of St. Antony's Coll., Oxford, and Lectr. in Economic History, Oxford Univ., since 1970. Lectr., Sch. of Oriental and African Studies, Univ. of London, 1960–67. *Publs:* The Revolution in Egypt's Economic System, 1966; The New Economic History of Railways, 1977; Railways and the Economic Development of Western Europe 1830-1914, 1983; Economic Effects on the American Civil War, 1988. Add: St. Antony's Coll., Oxford, England.

O'BRIEN, Tim. American, b. 1946. Novels/Short stories. Writer. National affairs reporter for the Washington Post. *Publs:* If I Die in a Combat Zone, 1973; Northern Lights, 1974; Going After Cacciato, 1978 (National Book Award); The Nuclear Age, 1985. Add: c/o Lynn Nesbit, I.C.M., 40 W. 57th St., New York, N.Y. 10019, U.S.A.

O'BROIN, Leon. Irish, b. 1902. History, Biography. Secty., and Permanent Head, Dept. of Posts and Telegraphs, Ireland, 1947–67. *Publs:* The Unfortunate Mr. Emmet, 1958; Dublin Castle and the 1916 Rising: The Story of Sir Matthew Nathan, 1966; Charles Gavan Duffy: Patriot and Statesman, 1967; The Chief Secretary: Augustine Birrell in Ireland, 1969; Fenian Fever, 1971; The Prime Informer: A Suppressed Scandal, 1971; Revolutionary Underground: The Story of the Irish Republic Brotherhood 1858-1924, 1976; Michael Collins, 1980; No Man's Man: Joseph Brennan, 1982; Frank Duff, 1982; In Great Haste: The Letters of Michael Collins and Kitty Kiernon, 1983; Just Like Yesterday (autobiography), 1986. Add: St. Raphael, 128 Stillorgan Rd., Donnybrook, Dublin 4, Ireland.

O'CASEY, Brenda. *See* **ELLIS**, Alice Thomas.

O'COLLINS, Gerald Glynn. Australian, b. 1931. Theology/Religion, Biography. Prof. of Fundamental Theology since 1974, and Dean of Faculty since 1985, Gregorian Univ., Rome (Visiting Prof., 1973). Research Fellow, Pembroke Coll., Cambridge, 1967–69; Lectr. in Theology, Corpus Christi Coll. and Jesuit Theological Coll., Melbourne, 1969–73. *Publs:* Patrick McMahon Glynn, 1965; Theology and Revelation, 1968; Man and His New Hopes, 1969; Foundations of Theology, 1971; The Easter Jesus, 1973; The Theology of Secularity, 1974; Faith Under Fire, 1974; (ed.) Patrick McMahon Glynn: Letters to His Family, 1974; Has Dogma a Future?, 1975; The Calvary Christ, 1977; What Are They Saying about Jesus?, 1977; What Are They Saying about the Resurrection?, 1978; A Month with Jesus, 1978; The Second Journey, 1978; Fundamental Theology, 1981; Finding Jesus, 1983; Interpreting Jesus, 1983; Jesus Today, 1986; Jesus Risen, 1987; Interpreting the Resurrection, 1988; Friends in Faith, 1989. Add: Pontificia Universita Gregoriana, Piazza della Pilotta 4, 00187 Rome, Italy.

O'CONNELL, Jeremiah J. American, b. 1932. Administration/Management, Business/Trade/Industry. Prof., Bentley Coll., Waltham, Mass., since 1988 (Dean, Grad. Sch., 1978–88). Assoc. Prof., Wharton Sch., Univ. of Pennsylvania, Philadelphia, 1964–70; Asst. Dir., 1970–74, and Assoc. Dir., 1974–78, Centre d'Etudes Industrielles (CEI), Geneva. *Publs:* (with C.E. Summer) The Managerial Mind: Science and Theory on Policy Decisions, 1964, 4th ed. 1978; Managing Organizational Innovation, 1968; (co-ed.) Inflation, 1974; (co-ed.) The Petroleum Industry in Western Europe, 1975; (co-author) Scanning the International Environment, 1980. Add: Bentley Coll. Graduate Sch., Waltham, Mass. 02254, U.S.A.

O'CONNOR, Anthony Michael. British, b. 1939. Geography. Reader in Geography, University Coll., Univ. of London, since 1985 (Lectr., 1967–85). Lectr., Makerere Univ., Kampala, Uganda, 1963–67; Prof. of Geography, Fourah Bay Coll., 1974–75. *Publs:* Railways and Development in Uganda, 1965; An Economic Geography of East Africa, 1966, 1971; The Geography of Tropical African Development, 1971, 1978; Urbanization in Tropical Africa, 1981; The African City, 1983. Add: 42 Crossways, Sutton, Surrey SM2 5LB, England.

O'CONNOR, Francis V(alentine). American, b. 1937. Poetry, Art, History. Asst. Prof., Univ. of Maryland, College Park, 1964–70; Sr. Visiting Research Assoc., National Collection of Fine Arts, Smithsonian Instn., Washington, D.C., 1970–72; Ed., Federal Art Patronage Notes, 1974–86; Robert Sterling Clark Visiting Prof. of Art History, Williams Coll., Williamstown, Mass., 1990. *Publs:* Federal Art Patronage 1933-1943, 1966; Jackson Pollock, 1967; Federal Support for the Visual Arts: The New Deal and Now, 1969, 1971; (ed.) The New Deal Art Projects: An Anthology of Memoirs, 1972; (ed.) Art for the Millions, 1973; (ed. with E.V. Thaw) Jackson Pollock: A Catalogue Raisonne of Paintings, Drawings and Other Works, 1978. Add: Apt. 11C, 250 E. 73rd St., New York, N.Y. 10021, U.S.A.

O'CONNOR, Patricia W. American, b. 1931. Literature, Theatre. Prof. of Romance Languages and Literatures, Univ. of Cincinnati, since 1972 (Instr., 1962–63; Asst. Prof., 1963–66; Assoc. Prof., 1966–72). Ed., Estreno mag. *Publs:* Women in the Theatre of Gregorio Martinez Sierra, 1967; Gregorio and Maria Martinez Sierra, 1977; (ed. with Anthony M. Pasquariello) El traguluz, 1977; (ed. with Anthony M. Pasquariello) Contemporary Spanish Theater, 1980; Plays of Protest from the Franco Era, 1981; Contemporary Spanish Theatre: The Social Comedies of the Sixties, 1983; Gregorio and Malia Martinez Sierra: Cronica de una Colaboracion, 1987; Dramaturgas españolas de hoy: Una introducción, 1989. Add: Dept. of Romance Languages and Literatures, Univ. of Cincinnati, Cincinnati, Ohio 45221, U.S.A.

O'CONNOR, Raymond G(ish). American, b. 1915. History, Military/Defence. With U.S. Navy, 1935–55; member of the faculty, Stanford Univ., California, 1955–59, Univ. of Kansas, Lawrence, 1959–65, and Temple Univ., Philadelphia, 1965–69; Prof. and Chmn., Dept. of History, Univ. of Miami, 1969–80. *Publs:* Perilous Equilibrium, 1962; (co-ed.) Readings in 20th Century American History, 1963; (ed. and co-author) American Defense Policy in Perspective, 1965; (co-author) History of American Military Affairs, 1968; (ed.) The Japanese Navy in World War II, 1969, 1986; Diplomacy for Victory, 1971; Force and Diplomacy, 1972; War, Diplomacy and History, 1979. Add: 212 Claudius Dr., Aptos, Calif. 95003, U.S.A.

O'CONNOR, William E. American, b. 1922. Air/Space topics, Economics, Politics/Government. Foreign Affairs Officer, Dept. of State, Washington, D.C., 1944–50; Foreign Affairs Analyst, 1951–54, and Asst. Div. Chief, 1955–71, Civil Aeronautics Bd., Washington, D.C.; Asst. Prof., 1972–75, and Assoc. Prof., 1975–78, Embry-Riddle Aeronautical Univ., Daytona Beach, Fla. *Publs:* Economic Regulation of the World's Airlines: A Political Analysis, 1971; An Introduction to Airline Economics, 1978, 4th ed. 1989. Add: Sandy Park Apts. No. 619, 1049 Brentwood Dr., Daytona Beach, Fla. 32017, U.S.A.

ODAGA, Asenath (Bole). Kenyan, b. 1938. Novels/Short stories, Children's fiction, Plays/Screenplays, Mythology/Folklore. Free-lance writer since 1982; Founding Member and Secretary, Writers Assn. of Kenya; Chmn., Children's Literature Assn. of Kenya, since 1988. Tutor, Church Missionary Soc. Teacher Training Coll., Ngiya, 1957–58; teacher, Butere Girls Sch., 1959–60; Headmistress, Nyakach Girls Sch., 1961–63; Asst. Secty., Kenya Dairy Bd., Nairobi, 1965–67; Secty., Kenya Library Services, Nairobi, 1968; Advertising Asst., East African Standard newspaper and Kerr Downey and Selby Safaris, both Nairobi, 1969–70; Asst. Dir., curriculum development program, Christian Churches Educational Assn., Nairobi, 1974–75; research fellow, Institute of African Studies, Univ. of Nairobi, 1976–81. *Publs:* Jande's Ambition (children's fiction), 1966; The Secret of the Monkey Rock (children's fiction), 1966; The Diamond Ring (children's fiction), 1967; The Angry Flames (children's fiction), 1968; The Hare's Blanket and Other Tales (folktales), 1967; Sweets and Sugar Cane (children's fiction), 1969; The Villager's Son (children's fiction), 1971; Kip on the Farm (children's fiction), 1972; Kip on the Coast (children's fiction), 1977; Nyathini Koa e Nyuolne Nyaka Higni Adek, (in Luo: Your Child from Birth to Age Three (nonfiction), 1976; Kip Goes to the City (children's fiction), 1977; Poko Nyar Mugumba (Poko Mugumba's Daughter; folktale), 1978; (ed., with David Kirui and David Crippen) God, Myself, and Others (Christian stories), 1976; Thu Tinda: Stories from Kenya (folktales), 1980; The Two Friends (folktales), 1981; Miaha (in Luo: The Bride; play), 1981; Simbi Nyaima (The Sunken Village; play), 1982; Oral Literature: A School Certificate Course (children's non-fiction), 1982; Ange ok Tel (Regret Never Comes First; children's fiction), 1982; Kenyan Folk Tales, 1982; Sigendini gi Timbe Luo Moko (Stories and Some Customs of the Luo), 1982; A Reed on the Roof, Block Ten, With Other Stories, 1982; My Home (reader), 1983; The Shade Changes (fiction), 1984; Yesterday's Today: The Study of Oral Literature, 1984; Literature for Children and Young People in Kenya, 1985; The Storm (fiction), 1986; Nyamgondho the Son of Ombare and Other Luo Stories, 1986; Between the Years (fiction), 1987; The Rag Ball (children's fiction), 1987; A Bridge in Time (fiction), 1987; Riana (fiction), 1989. Add: P.O. Box 1743, Kisumu, Kenya, Africa.

O'DANIEL, Janet. Has written with Lillian Ressler as Lillian Janet, and with Amy Midgley as Evelyn Claire and Amanda Clark. American. Novels/Short stories, Children's fiction. *Publs:* (with L. Ressler) Touchstone (novel), 1947; (with L. Ressler) City Beyond Devil's Gate, 1950; O Genesee, 1958; The Cliff Hangers, 1961; Garrett's Crossing (children), 1969; A Part for Addie (children), 1974; (as Evelyn Claire)— Storm Remembered, 1984; No More Heartache, 1986; Prescription for Love, 1987; as Amanda Clark—Flower of the Sea, 1985. Add: 211 Birchwood Ave., Upper Nyack, N.Y. 10960, U.S.A.

ODD, Gilbert. British, b. 1902. Sports/Physical education/Keeping fit. Ed., Boxing News, 1941–43 and 1947–57; Hon. Member, National Sporting Club, 1948–68; Steward, British Boxing Bd. of Control, 1960–68. *Publs:* Ring Battles of the Century, 1948; Was the Referee Right?, 1953; Debatable Decisions, 1953; Heavyweight Boxing, 1973; Cruisers to

Mighty Atoms, 1974; Ali, The Fighting Prophet, 1975; Boxing: The Great Champions, 1976; The Fighting Blacksmith: Bob Fitzsimmons, 1976; Len Harvey, Prince of Boxers, 1977; Boxing: The Inside Story, 1977; (ed.) In the Ring and Out (on Jack Johnson), 1978; The Woman in the Corner, 1978; (ed.) John L. Sullivan's Autobiography, 1979; Encyclopedia of Boxing, 1983, 1989; King of the Ring: 100 Years of World Heavyweight Boxing 1885-1985, 1985; Battling for Belts: History of the Lord Lonsdale Challenge Belts, 1989. Add: Little Court, Northiam, Sussex TN31 6NA, England.

ODELL, Peter R(andon). British, b. 1930. Earth sciences, Economics, Geography, International relations. Dir., Center for Intnl. Energy Studies, Erasmus Univ., Rotterdam, since 1981 (Prof. of Economic Geography, 1968–81). Economist, Shell Intnl., 1958–61; Lectr. in Economic Geography, London Sch. of Economics, 1961–68. *Publs:* An Economic Geography of Oil, 1963; Oil: The New Commanding Height, 1966; Natural Gas in Western Europe: A Case Study in the Economic Geography of Energy Resources, 1969; Oil and World Power: A Geographical Interpretation, 1970, 8th ed. 1986; (with D.A. Preston) Economies and Societies in Latin America: A Geographical Interpretation, 1973, 1978; Energy Needs and Resources, 1974, 1978; (with K.E. Rosing) The North Sea Oil Province, 1975; The West European Energy Economy: The Case for Self-Sufficiency, 1976; (with Rosing) Optimal Developments of North Sea Oilfields, 1976; (with L. Vallenilla) The Pressures of Oil: A Strategy for Economic Revival, 1978; British Offshore Oil Policy: A Radical Alternative, 1980; (with Rosing) The Future of Oil, 1980, 1982; (with J.A. van Reyn) Energie: Geen Probleem?, 1981; (co-ed.) The International Oil Industry: An Inter-disciplinary Perspective, 1986. Add: Postbus 4002, 3006 AA Rotterdam, Netherlands.

ODELL, Robin Ian. British, b. 1935. Criminology/Law enforcement/ Prisons, Philosophy. Ed., Water Research Centre., Buckinghamshire, since 1968. Technical Demonstrator, Sch. of Education, Univ. of Southampton, 1961–68. *Publs:* Jack the Ripper in Fact and Fiction, 1965; (co-author) Humanist Glossary, 1967; Crime and Punishment, 1975; Exhumation of a Murder, 1975; (co-author) Murderers' Who's Who, 1979, 1989; (co-author) Lady Killers, 1980; (co-author) Lady Killers 2, 1981; (co-author) Murder-Whatdunit, 1982; Murder Whereabouts, 1986; (co-author) Jack the Ripper, 1987. Add: 11 Red House Dr., Sonning Common, Reading, Berks. RG4 9NT, England.

O'DELL, Scott. American, b. 1898. Novels/Short stories, Children's fiction. Film cameraman in the 1920's; Book Ed. of a Los Angeles newspaper in the 1940's. *Publs:* Representative Photoplays Analyzed, 1924; Woman of Spain (adult novel), 1934; Hill of the Hawk (adult novel), 1953; (with William Doyle) Man Alone, 1953, in U.K. as Lifer, 1954; Country of the Sun: Southern California: An Informal History and Guide, 1957; The Sea Is Red (adult novel), 1958; Island of the Blue Dolphins, 1960; The King's Fifth, 1966; The Black Pearl, 1967; (with Rhoda Kellogg) The Psychology of Children's Art, 1967; The Dark Canoe, 1968; Journey to Jericho, 1969; Sing Down the Moon, 1970; The Treasure of Topo-el-Bampo, 1972; The Cruise of the Arctic Star, 1973; Child of Fire, 1974; The Hawk That Dare Not Hunt by Day, 1975; The 290, 1976; Zia, 1976; Carlota, 1977, in U.K. as Daughter of Don Saturnino, 1979; Kathleen, Please Come Home, 1978; The Captive, 1979; Sarah Bishop, 1980; The Feathered Serpent, 1981; The Spanish Smile, 1982; The Amethyst Ring, 1983; The Castle in the Sea, 1983; Alexandria, 1984; The Road to Damietta, 1985; Streams to the River, River to the Sea, 1986; The Serpent Never Sleeps, 1987; Back Star, Bright Dawn, 1988; My Name Is Not Angelica, 1989. Add: c/o Houghton Mifflin Co., 2 Park St., Boston, Mass. 02107, U.S.A.

O'DOHERTY, Eamonn (Feichin). Irish, b. 1918.Education, Language/ Linguistics, Psychology, Theology/Religion. Prof. of Logic and Psychology, University Coll. Dublin, since 1949 (Lectr., 1945–49). *Publs:* (with D.J. McGrath) The Priest and Mental Health, 1962; Religion and Personality Problems, 1965; Helping the Disturbed Religious: Vocation, Formation, Consecration and Vows, 1971; The Psychology of Vocation, 1972; The Religious Formation of the Elementary School Child, 1973; The Religious Formation of the Adolescent, 1973; Human Psychology, vols. I-III, 1976-77; Religion and Psychology, 1978; The I.R.A. at War: An Illustrated History, 1916 to the Present, 1986. Add: 33 Louvain St., Dublin 14, Ireland.

O'DONNELL, K.M. *See* **MALZBERG,** Barry.

O'DONNELL, Kevin, Jr. American, b. 1950. Science fiction. Asst. Lectr. in English, Hong Kong Baptist Coll., 1972–73, and American English Language Inst., Taipei, 1973–74; Managing Ed., 1979–81, and

Publisher, 1983–83, Empire, New Haven, Conn. *Publs:* Bander Snatch, 1979; Mayflies, 1979; Caverns, 1981; Reefs, 1981; War of Omission, 1982; Lava, 1982; ORA:CLE, 1984; (with the Haven Group) The Electronic Money Book (non-fiction), 1984; Cliffs, 1986; (with Mary Kittredge) The Shelter, 1987; Fire on the Border, 1990. Add: c/o Howard Morhaim Literary Agency, 175 Fifth Ave., New York, N.Y. 10010, U.S.A.

O'DONNELL, Lillian. American, b. 1926. Mystery/Crime/Suspense. Actress in Broadway and television productions, and Stage Mgr. and Dir., Schubert Org., NYC, 1944–54. *Publs:* Death on the Grass, 1960; Death Blanks the Screen, 1961; Death Schuss, 1963; Murder under the Sun, 1964; Death of a Player, 1964; Babes in the Woods, 1965; The Sleeping Beauty Murders, 1967; The Face of the Crime, 1968; The Tachi Tree (nonmystery novel), 1968; Dive into Darkness (non-mystery novel), 1971; The Phone Calls, 1972; Don't Wear Your Wedding Ring, 1973; Dail 577 R-A-P-E, 1974; The Baby Merchants, 1975; Leisure Dying, 1976; Aftershock, 1977; No Business Being a Cop, 1979; Falling Star, 1979; Wicked Designs, 1980; The Children's Zoo, 1981; Cop With a Shield, 1983; Lady Killer, 1984; Casual Affairs, 1985; The Other Side of the Door, 1987; A Good Night to Kill, 1988. Add: c/o Putnam, 200 Madison Ave., New York, N.Y. 10016, U.S.A.

O'DONNELL, Peter. British, b. 1920. Mystery/Crime/Suspense. . Writer of the strip cartoons, Garth, 1953–66, Tug Transom, 1954–66, Romeo Brown, 1956–62, and Modesty Blaise, since 1963. *Publs:* Modesty Blaise, 1965; Sabre-Tooth, 1966; I, Lucifer, 1967; A Taste for Death, 1969; The Impossible Virgin, 1971; Pieces of Modesty (short stories), 1972; The Silver Mistress, 1973; Murder Most Logical (play), 1974; Last Day in Limbo, 1976; Dragon's Claw, 1978; The Xanadu Talisman, 1981; The Night of Morningstar, 1982; Dead Man's Handle, 1985. Add: 49 Sussex Sq., Brighton BN2 1GE, England.

O'DONOVAN, Joan Mary. British, b. 1914. Novels/Short stories. Adviser for Secondary Education, Oxfordshire County Council, 1965–77. Fiction Reviewer, Oxford Mail, 1970–77. *Publs:* Dangerous Worlds, 1958; The Visited (in U.S. as A Singular Passion), 1959; Shadows on the Wall, 1960; The Middle Tree, 1961; The Niceties of Life, 1964; She, Alas!, 1965; Little Brown Jesus, 1970; Argument with an East Wind, 1986. Add: 98B Banbury Rd., Oxford OX2 6JT, England.

OESTERREICHER, John M. American, b. 1904. Theology/Religion. Dir., Inst. of Judaeo-Christian Studies since 1953, and Distinguished Univ. Prof. Emeritus, Seton Hall Univ., South Orange, N.J. Prof. of Religion, Waehringer Maedchen Realgymnasium Vienna, 1935–38; Research Prof. of Sacred Theology, Manhattan Coll. of the Sacred Heart, NYC, 1944–53. Member, Secretariat for Promotion of Christian Unity, Second Vatican Council, 1961–67; appointed papal chamberlain with title of monsignor, 1961; appointed honorary prelate, 1967. *Publs:* Racisme-Antisémitisme-Antichristianisme, 1943; Walls Are Crumbling (in paperback as Five in Search of Wisdom), 1952; The Israel of God, 1963; (ed.) The Bridge, 5 vols., 1961, 1970; (ed.) Jerusalem, 1974; Anatomy of Contempt, 1975; The Unfinished Dialogue: Martin Buber and the Christian Way, 1980; The New Encounter (Between Christians and Jews), 1985. Add: Seton Hall Univ., South Orange, N.J. 07079, U.S.A.

O'FAOLAIN, Julia. Irish. Novels/Short stories, Women, Translations. *Publs:* (trans.) Two Memoirs of Renaissance Florence, 1967; (trans.) A Man of Parts, by Piero Chiara, 1968; We Might See Sights!, 1968; Three Lovers, 1971; (ed. with Lauro Martines) Not in God's Image, 1973; Man in the Cellar, 1974; Women in the Wall, 1975; No Country for Young Men, 1980; The Obedient Wife, 1982; Daughters of Passion, 1982; The Irish Signorina, 1984. Add: c/o Rogers, Coleridge and White, 20 Powis Mews, London W11 1JN, England.

O'FAOLAIN, Sean. Irish, b. 1900. Novels/Short stories, Plays/Screenplays, History, Literature, Travel/Exploration/Adventure, Autobiography/Memoirs/Personal, Biography. Lectr. in English, Boston Coll., 1929, and St. Mary's Coll., Strawberry Hill, Middx., 1929–33; former Ed., The Bell, Dublin; Dir., Arts Council of Ireland, 1957–59. *Publs:* (ed.) Lyrics and Satires of Tom Moore, 1929; Midsummer Night Madness and Other Stories, 1932; A Nest of Simple Folk, 1933; The Life of Eamon de Valera, 1933; Constance Markievicz; or, The Average Revolutionary, 1934; There's Birdie in the Cage, 1935; Bird Alone, 1936; A Born Genius, 1936; A Purse of Coppers: Short Stories, 1937; She Had to Do Something (play), 1937; (ed.) Autobiography, by Theobald Wolfe Tone, 1937; King of the Beggars: Life of Daniel O'Connell, 1938; (ed.) The Silver Branch: A Collection of the Best Old Irish Lyrics, 1938; Come Back to Erin, 1940; An Irish Journey, 1940; The Great O'Neill: A Biography of Hugh O'Neill, Earl of Tyrone 1550-1616, 1942; The Story of

Ireland, 1943; Teresa and Other Stories (in U.S. as The Man Who Invented Sin and Other Stories), 1947; The Irish: A Character Study, 1947, 1970; The Short Story, 1948; Summer in Italy, 1949; Newman's Way: The Odyssey of John Henry Newman, 1952; South to Sicily (in U.S. as Autumn in Italy), 1953; The Vanishing Hero: Studies of the Hero in the Modern Novel, 1956; The Finest Stories of Sean O'Faolain (in U.K. as The Stories of Sean O'Faolain), 1957; I Remember! I Remember!, 1961; (ed.) Short Stories: A Study in Pleasure, 1961; Vive Moi!, 1964; The Heat of the Day: Stories and Tales, 1966; The Talking Trees, 1970; Foreign Affairs, and Other Stories, 1976; Selected Stories, 1978; And Again?, 1979; The Collected Stories of Sean O'Faolain, 3 vols., 1980–82. Add: 17 Rosmeen Park, Dunlaoire, Dublin, Ireland.

O'FARRELL, Padraic. Irish, b. 1932. Poetry, Area studies. *Publs:* Superstitions of Irish Country People, 1978; Folktales of the Irish Coast, 1978; Irish Records, 1978; How the Irish Speak English, 1980; Who's Who in the Irish War of Independence, 1980; Gems of Irish Wisdom, 1980; The Sean Mac Eoin Story, 1982; The Bedside Book of the West of Ireland, 1981; The Ernie O'Malley Story, 1983; Shannon Through Her Literature, 1984; Fore: The Fact and the Fantasy, 1984; Life Train (poetry), 1986; Tell Me, Sean O'Farrell: The Story of an Irish Schoolmaster, 1986; The Wit and Humour of Dail Eireann, 1987; The Book of Mullingar, 1987. Add: Lynn Ave., Mullingar, Co. Westmeath, Ireland.

O'FARRELL, Patrick (James). New Zealander, b. 1933. History, Biography. Prof. of History, Univ. of New South Wales, Sydney, since 1972. Visiting Prof. of History, University Coll., Dublin, 1965–66 and 1972–73, and Trinity Coll., Dublin, 1972–73. *Publs:* Harry Holland: Militant Socialist, 1964; The Catholic Church in Australia: A Short History 1788-1967, 1968; (ed.) Documents in Australian Catholic History, vol. I, 1788-1884, vol. II, 1884-1968, 1969; Ireland's English Question, 1971; England and Ireland since 1800, 1975; The Catholic Church and Community in Australia: A History, 1977, 1985; Letters from Irish Australia 1825-1929, 1984; The Irish in Australia, 1987. Add: Sch. of History, Univ. of New South Wales, P.O. Box 1, Kensington, N.S.W. 2033, Australia.

OFFUTT, Andrew J(efferson V.). American, b. 1934(?). Science fiction/Fantasy. Sales Agent, Proctor and Gamble, 1957–62; Agency Mgr., Coastal States Life Insurance Co., Lexington, Ky., 1963–68; Insurance Agent, Andrew Offutt Assocs., 1968–71. *Publs:* Author of over 100 works, including—Evil is Live Spelled Backwards, 1970; The Great 24-Hour Thing, 1971; The Castle Keeps, 1972; Messenger of Zhuvastou, 1973; Ardor on Aros, 1973; The Galactic Rejects (juvenile), 1973; Operation: Super Ms., 1974; Sword of the Gael, 1975; (with D. Bruce Berry) The Genetic Bomb, 1975; Chieftain of Andor, 1976, in U.K. as Clansman of Andor, 1978; The Undying Wizard, 1976; (with Richard K. Lyon) Demon in the Mirror, 1977; Sign of the Moonbow, 1977; The Mists of Doom, 1977; My Lord Barbarian, 1977; (ed.) Swords Against Darkness 1-5, 5 vols., 1977–79; Conan and the Sorcerer, 1978; The Sword of Skelos, 1979; The Iron Lords, 1979; Shadows Out of Hell, 1979; King Dragon, 1980; (with Keith Taylor) When Death Birds Fly, 1980; (with Keith Taylor) The Tower of Death, 1980; (with Richard K. Lyon) The Eyes of Sarsis, 1980; Conan the Mercenary, 1980; (with Richard K. Lyon) Web of the Spider, 1981; (with Keith Taylor) The Tower of Death, 1982; The Lady of the Snowmist, 1983; Shadowspawn, 1987. Add: Funny Farm, Haldeman, Ky. 40329, U.S.A.

O'FLAHERTY, James Carneal. American, b. 1914. Literature, Philosophy, Theology/Religion, Translations. Prof. Emeritus of German, Wake Forest Univ., since 1984 (Prof. 1947–84). Instr. in Religion and Social Sciences, Georgetown Coll., Kentucky, 1939–41; Teacher, Pleasureville High Sch., 1941–42; Pastor, Normal Park Baptist Church, 1942–47. *Publs:* Unity and Language: A Study in the Philosophy of Hamann, 1952, 1966; (trans.) Hamann's Socratic Memorabilia: Translation and Commentary, 1967; (co-author and trans.) Raabe's Else von der Tanne: Translation and Commentary, 1972; (ed. with T. Sellner and R.M. Helm) Nietzsche and the Classical Tradition, 1975, 1979; Johann Georg Hamann, 1979; (ed. with T. Sellner and R.M. Helm) Nietzsche and the Judaeo-Christian Tradition, 1985; The Quarrel of Reason with Itself: Essays on Hamann, Nietzsche, Lessing and Michaelis, 1988; Johan Georg Hamann: Einführung in sein Leben und Werk, 1989. Add: 2164 Faculty Dr., Winston-Salem, N.C. 27106, U.S.A.

OGAWA, Dennis. American, b. 1943. Cultural/Ethnic topics. Prof., American Studies Dept., Univ. of Hawaii, Honolulu, since 1969. *Publs:* From Japs to Japanese: Evolution of Japanese-American Stereotypes, 1971; Jan Ken Po: The World of Hawaii's Japanese Americans, 1973; Kodomo No Tame Ni, 1978; Ellison Onizuka: A Remembrance, 1987.

Add: American Studies Dept., Univ. of Hawaii, Honolulu, Hawaii 96822, U.S.A.

OGBURN, Charlton. American, b. 1911. Environmental science/Ecology, History, Natural history, Biography. Publicity Writer, Viking Press, NYC, 1932–33; Writer, Alfred P. Sloan Foundn., NYC, 1937–39; Book Reviewer, Book of the Month Club, NYC, 1940–41; with U.S. Army, to Captain, 1941–45; with Div. of Southeast Asian Affairs, Dept. of State, Washington, D.C., 1946–50; Political Adviser, and Acting U.S. Rep. for Cttee. of Good Offices on Indonesia, U.N. Security Council, 1947–48; Policy Planning Adviser, Bureau of Far East Affairs, 1952–54; Chief of Div. for Research on Near East, South Asia, and Africa, 1954–57. *Publs:* The White Falcon, 1955; The Bridge, 1957; Big Caesar, 1958; The Marauders, 1959; U.S. Army, 1960; (with Dorothy Ogburn) Shakespeare: The Man Behind the Name, 1962; The Gold of the River Sea, 1965; The Winter Beach, 1966; Down, Boy, Down, Blast You!, 1967; The Forging of Our Continent, 1968; The Continent in Our Hands, 1971; Winespring Mountain, 1973; The Southern Appalachians, 1974; The Adventure of Birds, 1976; Railroads: The Great American Adventure, 1977; The Mysterious William Shakespeare: The Myth and the Reality, 1984. Add: 403 Hancock St., Beaufort, S.C. 29902, U.S.A.

OGILVIE, Elisabeth (May). American, b. 1917. Mystery/Crime/Suspense, Historical/Romance/Gothic, Children's fiction, Autobiography/Memoirs/Personal. *Publs:* High Tide at Noon, 1944; Storm Tide, 1945; Honeymoon (novelization of screenplay), 1947; The Ebbing Tide, 1947; Rowan Head, 1949; My World Is an Island (reminiscences), 1950; The Dawning of the Day, 1954; Whistle for a Wind: Maine 1820 (juvenile), 1954; No Evil Angel, 1956; Blueberry Summer (juvenile), 1956; The Fabulous Year (juvenile), 1958; The Witch Door, 1959; How Wide the Heart (juvenile), 1959; The Young Islanders (juvenile), 1960; Becky's Island (juvenile), 1961; Call Home the Heart, 1962; Turn Around Twice (juvenile), 1962, as Mystery on Hopkins Island, 1966; Ceiling of Amber (juvenile), 1964; Masquerade at Sea House (juvenile), 1965; There May Be Heaven, 1966; The Seasons Hereafter, 1966; The Pigeon Pair (juvenile), 1967; Waters on a Starry Night, 1968; Come Aboard and Bring Your Dory (juvenile), 1969, in U.K. as Nobody Knows about Tomorrow, 1971; Bellwood, 1969; The Face of Innocence, 1970; A Theme for Reason, 1970; Weep and Know Why, 1972; Strawberries in the Sea, 1973; Image of a Lover, 1974; Where the Lost Aprils Are, 1975; The Dreaming Swimmer, 1976; An Answer in the Tide, 1978; A Dancer in Yellow, 1979; The Devil in Tartan, 1980; The Silent Ones, 1981; Too Young to Know (juvenile), 1983; The Road to Nowhere, 1983; Jennie About to Be, 1984; The World of Jenny G, 1986; The Summer of the Osprey, 1987; When the Music Stopped, 1989. Add: c/o McGraw-Hill Inc., 1221 Ave. of the Americas, New York, N.Y. 10020, U.S.A.

OGILVY, C. Stanley. American, b. 1913. Mathematics/Statistics, Sports. Prof. Emeritus, Hamilton Coll., Clinton, N.Y., since 1974 (joined faculty, 1953; Chmn. and Prof., Dept. of Mathematics, 1969–74). *Publs:* Successful Yacht Racing, 1951; Through the Mathescope, 1956; Thoughts on Small Boat Racing, 1957, 1966; Tomorrow's Math: Unsolved Problems for the Amateur, 1962, 1972; (with J.T. Anderson) Excursions in Number Theory, 1966; A Calculus Notebook, 1968; (with R. Breusch) Calculus and Analytic Geometry with Applications, 1969; Excursions in Geometry, 1969; (co-ed.) Selected Papers on Calculus, 1969; Win More Sailboat Races, 1976. Add: 943 Greacen Point Rd, Mamaroneck, N.Y. 10543, U.S.A.

OGLETREE, Thomas Warren. American, b. 1933. Philosophy, Theology/Religion. Prof. of Theological Ethics, and Dean of the Theological Sch., Drew Univ., Madison, N.J., since 1981. Assoc. Ed., Journal of Religious Ethics. Asst. Prof. of Philosophy and Religion, Birmingham-Southern Coll., Alabama, 1963–65; Assoc. Prof. of Constructive Theology, Chicago Theological Seminary, 1965–70; Prof. of Theological Ethics, 1970–81, and Chmn., Grad. Dept. of Religion, 1980, Vanderbilt Univ., Nashville. Ed., Soundings, 1975–80; Pres., Soc. of Christian Ethics, 1983–84. *Publs:* Christian Faith and History: A Critical Comparison of Ernst Troeltsch and Karl Barth, 1965; The Death of God Controversy, 1966; (ed.) Openings for Marxist-Christian Dialogue, 1968; (with H. Aptheker and S. Bliss) From Hope to Liberation: Toward a New Marxist-Christian Dialogue, 1974; (ed. with George Lucas, Jr.) Lifeboat Ethics: The Moral Dilemmas of World Hunger, 1976; The Use of the Bible in Christian aEthics, 1983; Hospitality to the Stranger: Dimensions of Moral Understanding, 1985. Add: Office of the Dean, Drew Univ. Theological Sch., Madison, N.J. 07940, U.S.A.

O'GORMAN, Ned. (Edward Charles O'Gorman). American, b. 1929. Children's fiction, Poetry, Education. Dir., Addie MacCollins Library and Storefront Sch., NYC, since 1966. Ed., Jubilee mag., NYC, 1962–65. *Publs:* The Night of the Hammer: Poems, 1959; Adam Before His Mirror, 1961; The Buzzard and the Peacock, 1964; The Harvesters' Vase, 1969; (ed.) Prophetic Voices: Essays and Words in Revolution, 1969; The Storefront: A Community of Children on Madison Avenue and 129th Street, 1970; The Blue Butterfly, 1971; The Wilderness and the Laurel Tree: Guide to Parents and Teachers on the Observation of Children, 1972; The Flag the Hawk Flies, 1972; The Children Are Dying, 1978; (ed.) Perfected Crystal, Terrible Steel: An Unconventional Source Book of Spiritual Readings in Prose and Poetry, 1981; How to Put Out a Fire, 1984. Add: 2 Lincoln Sq., New York, N.Y. 10023, U.S.A.

O'GRADY, Desmond (James Bernard). Irish, b. 1935. Poetry, Translations. Teacher: has taught in Paris, Rome, Cairo, Alexandria, and Boston. *Publs:* Chords and Orchestrations, 1956; Reilly, 1961; Professor Kelleher and the Charles River, 1964; Separazioni, 1965; The Dark Edge of Europe: Poems, 1967; The Dying Gaul, 1968; (trans.) Off Licence: Translations from Irish, Italian and Armenian Poetry, 1968; Hellas, 1971; Separations, 1973; Stations, 1976; Sing Me Creation, 1977; The Gododdin (translation from the Welsh), 1977; Limerick Rake (translation from the Irish), 1978; Headgear of the Tribe, 1979; His Skaldcrane's Nest, 1979; Grecian Glances (translations from the Greek Classical Anthology), 1981. Add: Kinsale, Co. Cork, Ireland.

O'GRADY, Rohan. Pseud. for June O'Grady Skinner; also writes as A. Carleon. Canadian, b. 1922. Historical/Romance/Gothic. Freelance writer. Formerly newspaper librarian. *Publs:* O'Houlihan's Jest: A Lament for the Irish, 1961; Pippin's Journal; or, Rosemary Is for Remembrance, 1962, in U.S. paperback as Master of Montrolfe Hall, 1965, as Curse of the Montrolfes, 1983; Let's Kill Uncle, 1963; Bleak November, 1970; (as A. Carleon) The May Spoon, 1981; The Curse of the Montrolfes, 1983. Add: 2373 Marine Dr., West Vancouver, B.C. V7V 1K9, Canada.

O'HARA, Kenneth. *See* **MORRIS,** Jean.

O'HIGGINS, Paul. Irish, b. 1927. Civil liberties/Human rights, Law. Fellow, Christ's Coll., Cambridge Univ., since 1959 (Univ. Asst. Lectr. in Law, 1961–66; Univ. Reader in Labour Law, 1979–1984). Regius Prof. of Law, Trinity Coll., Dublin, 1984–87; Prof. of Law, King's Coll., London. *Publs:* (with B.A. Hepple) Public Employee Trade Unionism in the U.K.: The Legal Framework, 1971; (with Hepple) Individual Employment Law, 1971, 4th ed. 1983; (gen. ed. with Hepple) Encyclopaedia of Labour Relations Law, 1972; Censorship in Britain, 1972; (contrib. and ed.) Encyclopaedia of Personnel Management, 1974; Workers' Rights, 1976, 1985; Civil Liberty: Cases and Materials, 1981; (with M.T. Partington) Social Security Law, 1986; Bibliographies on Labour Law, 1972, 3rd ed. 1986, Social Security Law, 1986, and Irish Trials, 1986; (co-author) Fairness at Work, 1986. Add: Christ's Coll., Cambridge CB2 3BU, England.

OINAS, Felix J(ohannes). American, b. 1911. Education, Humanities (general), Language/Linguistics, Mythology/Folklore. Instr. in Finno-Ugric Languages, Univ. of Budapest, 1938–40; Lectr. in Estonian Language, Baltic Univ., Hamburg, 1946–48; Prof. of Slavic and Finno-Ugric Languages, Indiana Univ., Bloomington, 1965–81, now Emeritus (Lectr., 1951–52, Instr., 1952–55, Asst. Prof., 1955–61, Assoc. Prof., 1961–65). *Publs:* Petofi, 1939; (ed. with Karl Inno) Eesti, 1949; The Development of Postpositional Cases in Balto-Finnic Languages, 1961; (compiler) Estonian General Reader, 1963, 1972; Basic Course in Estonian, 1966, 4th ed. 1979; Studies in Finnic-Slavic Folklore Relations, 1967; (ed. with S. Soudakoff) The Study of Russian Folklore, 1975; (ed.) Folklore, Nationalism, and Politics, 1978; (ed.) Heroic Epic and Saga: An Introduction to the World's Great Epics, 1978; Kalevipoeg in Fetters and Other Essays on Folklore, Mythology, and Literature, 1979; (ed.) European Folklore, 1981; The Study of Finnic Folklore: Homage to Kalevala, 1985; Essays on Russian Folklore and Mythology, 1985. Add: 2513 E. 8th St., Bloomington, Ind. 47401, U.S.A.

OJA, Carol J. American, b. 1953. Music. Instr., Conservatory of Music, Brooklyn Coll. of the City Univ. of New York, since 1984 (Research Asst., Inst. for Studies in American Music, 1980–84). *Publs:* Stravinsky in "Modern Music", 1982; (ed.) American Music Recordings: A Discography of 20th Century U.S. Composers, 1982. Add: 560 Riverside Dr., Apt. 12-L, New York N.Y. 10027, U.S.A.

OKAI, John. Ghanaian. Poetry. Lectr. in Russian, Univ. of Ghana, Legon. *Publs:* Flowerfall, 1969; The Oath of Fontomirom and Other Poems, 1971; Lorgorligi: Logarithms and Other Poems, 1974. Add:

Dept. of Modern Languages, Univ. of Ghana, P.O. Box 25, Legon, Ghana.

OKARA, Gabriel (Immomotime Obainbaing). Nigerian, b. 1921. Novels/Short stories, Poetry. Dir. of the Rivers State Publishing House, Port Harcourt, since 1972. *Publs:* The Voice (novel), 1964; The Fisherman's Invocation (verse), 1978. Add: c/o Heinemann, 22 Bedford Sq., London WC1B 3HH, England.

O'KELLY, Elizabeth. British, b. 1915. Human relations, International relations/Current affairs, Third World problems. Freelance lectr. and consultant. Principal Community Development Officer, H.M. Overseas Civil Service, Cameroons, 1950–61; Adviser to the Govt. of Sarawak on Women's Insts., 1962–65; Acting Dir., Asian Christian Service, Viet Nam, 1967–69; Gen. Secty., Associated Country Women of the World, 1969–72. *Publs:* Aid and Self Help, 1973; Rural Women: Their Integration in Development Programmes, 1978; Water and Sanitation for All, 1982; Processing and Storage of Food Grains by Rural Families, 1983. Add: 2 Downash House, Rosemary Lane, Flimwell, E. Sussex TN5 7PS, England.

OKORO, Anezi. Nigerian, b. 1929. Children's fiction, Medicine. Prof. of Medicine, Univ. of Nigeria, Nsukka, since 1975. Pres., African Assoc. for Dermatology, since 1986. House surgeon, Univ. Coll. Hospital, Ibadan, 1959–57; Medical Officer, 1957–64, and Consultant Dermatologist, 1965–66, Ministry of Health, Lagos; Assoc. Lectr., Coll. of Medicine, Univ. of Lagos, 1964–66; Consultant dermatologist, Ministry of Health, Enugu, 1966–74; Dir., Nigerian National Petroleum Corp., Lagos, 1977–81; Visiting Prof., Medical Coll. of Georgia, Augusta, 1987, and Univ. of Minnesota, Minneapolis, 1988. *Publs:* The Village School, 1966; The Village Headmaster, 1967; Febechi down the Niger, 1971; Febechi in Cave Adventure, 1971; One Week in Trouble, 1973; (also illustrator) Dr. Amadi's Postings, 1975; Pictorial Handbook of Common Skin Diseases, 1981; Education Is Great, 1986; Je Je Kule, 1989; Double Trouble, 1989. Add: Skin Clinic, Univ. of Nigeria Teaching Hospital, P.M.B. 01129, Enugu, Nigeria.

OKPAKU, Joseph (Ohiomogben). Nigerian, b. 1943. Plays/Screenplays, History. Pres. and Publr., The Third Press, Joseph Okpaku Publishing Co. Inc., NYC, since 1969. Member, Exec. Bd., African Studies Assn., since 1971. *Publs:* Born Astride the Grave (play), 1966; The Virtues of Adultery (radio play), 1967; Verdict!: The Exclusive Picture Story of the Trial of the Chicago 8, 1970; (ed.) New African Literature and the Arts, vols. I and II, 1970, vol. III, 1973; (ed.) Nigeria-Biafra: Dilemma of Nationhood, 1971; Superfight No. II, 1974. Add: 444 Central Park W., New York, N.Y. 10025, U.S.A.

O'LAOGHAIRE, Liam. *See* **O'LEARY,** Liam.

OLDFIELD, Jenny. British, b. 1949. Children's fiction, Literature. Teacher of English, Edgbaston High Sch., Birmingham, 1972–74; Lectr. in English, Wroxton Coll., Fairleigh Dickinson Univ., Banbury, Oxon., 1976; Teacher of English, King Edward's High Sch. for Girls, Edgbaston, Birmingham, 1977. *Publs:* Tomorrow Shall Be My Dancing Day, 1974; Mr. Hardisty's Kind Offer, 1975; Secret of the Seasons, 1976; Jane Eyre and Wuthering Heights: A Study Guide, 1976; The True Loves of Tannockburn, 1980; Terrible Pet, 1980; Fancy That, 1980; Going Soft, 1980; Yours Truly, 1980; Rough Remedies, 1981; Smile, Please, 1981; Said the Blind Man, 1986. Add: The Shakespeare Inst., Univ. of Birmingham, Edgbaston, Birmingham 15, England.

OLDFIELD, Pamela. British, b. 1931. Historical/Romance, Children's fiction. *Publs:* for children—Melanie Brown Goes to School, 1970; Melanie Brown Climbs a Tree, 1972; The Adventures of Sarah and Theodore Bodgitt, 1974; Melanie Brown and the Jar of Sweets, 1974; The Halloween Pumpkin, 1976; Simon's Extra Gran, 1976; A Witch in the House, 1976; The Terribly Plain Princess and Other Stories, 1977; The Adventures of the Gumby Gang, 1978; The Gumby Gang Again, 1978; Katy and Dom, 1978; More About the Gumby Gang, 1979; The Princess Well-May-I, 1979; Children of the Plague, 1979; The Gumby Gang Strikes Again, 1980; The Rising of the Wain, 1980; The Riverside Cat, 1980; Cloppity, 1981; The Willerbys and the Burglar [Haunted Mill, Old Castle, Sad Clown, Bank Robbers, Mystery Man] 6 vols., 1981–84; Parkin's Storm, 1982; The Gumby Gang on Holiday, 1983; (ed.) Helter-Skelter: Stories for Six-Year-Olds, 1983; Tommy Dobbie and the Witch-Next-Door, 1983; (ed.) Hurdy-Gurdy, 1984, in U.S. as Merry-Go-Round: Stories for Seven-Year-Olds, 1985; Ghost Stories, 1984; Barnaby and Bell and the Lost Button, 1985; Barnaby and Bell and the Birthday Cake, 1985; The Christmas Ghost, 1985; (ed.) Roller Coaster, 1986; Ginger's Nine Lives, 1986; The Return of the Gumby Gang, 1986; Toby and the Donkey,

1986; The Ghosts of Bellering Oast, 1987; Spine Chillers, 1987; (ed.) Stories from Ancient Greece (retellings), 1988; Sam, Sue and Cinderella, 1989; Bomb Alert, 1989; Secret Persuader, 1989; novels—The Rich Earth, 1980; This Ravished Land, 1980; After the Storm, 1981; White Water, 1982; Green Harvest, 1983; Summer Song, 1984; Golden Tally, 1985; The Gooding Girl, 1985; The Stationmaster's Daughter, 1986; Lily Golightly, 1987; Turn of the Tide, 1988; A Dutiful Wife, 1989. Add: c/o Blackie Children's Books, 7 Leicester Place, London WC2H 7BP England.

OLDHAM, Frank. British, b. 1903. Physics, Biography. Asst. Master, Manchester Grammar Sch., 1927–33; Headmaster, Hinckley Grammar Sch., Leicester, 1933–63; Chmn., Education Group, Inst. of Physics, London, 1963–66. *Publs:* Thomas Young, Philosopher and Physician, 1933; (with E. Langton) General Physics, 1939; (with A. Wood) Thomas Young, Natural Philosopher, 1954; (with E. Langton) Physics for Today, 1962. Add: 2 Cae'r Gelach, Llandegfan, Menai Bridge, LL59 5UF, Wales.

OLDSEY, Bernard S. American, b. 1923. Novels/Short stories, Literature, Writing/Journalism, Essays. Prof. of English, West Chester Univ., Pennsylvania, since 1969. Ed., College Literature journal, since 1973. Assoc. Prof. of English and Comparative Literature, Pennsylvania State Univ., University Park, 1950–69. *Publs:* (with H.F. Graves) From Fact to Judgment, 1957, 1963; (with A.O. Lewis) Visions and Revisions in Modern American Literary Criticism, 1962; (with S. Weintraub) The Art of William Golding, 1965; The Spanish Season (novel), 1970; Hemingway's Hidden Craft, 1979; Ernest Hemingway: The Papers of a Writer, 1981; British Novelists 1930-1960, 1983. Add: 1003 Woodview Lane, West Chester, Pa. 19380, U.S.A.

O'LEARY. *See* **KUEHNELT-LEDDIHN**, Erik.

O'LEARY, Liam. Also writes as Liam O'Laoghaire. Irish, b. 1910. Film. Founder, Liam O'Leary Film Archives, 1976. Acquisitions Officer, National Film Archive, London, 1953–66; Film Acceptance Officer, Radio Telefis Eireann, 1967–86. *Publs:* (as Liam O'Laoghaire) Invitation to the Film, 1945; The Silent Cinema, 1965; Rex Ingram, Master of the Silent Cinema, 1980. Add: 2 Otranto Pl., Sandycove, Co. Dublin, Ireland.

OLECK, Howard L. American, b. 1911. Novels/Short stories, History, Law. Prof. of Law, Stetson Univ., St. Petersburg, 1978–81, now Emeritus. Ed., National Insurance Laws Service, since 1963; syndicated columnist ("Law for the Living"), 1959–78, and since 1980. Historian, U.S. Army, 1945–58; Distinguished Prof. of Law, Cleveland State Univ., 1956–74; Prof. of Law, Wake Forest Univ., Winston-Salem, N.C., 1974–78. Ed., Negligence and Compensation Service, 1956–65; Pres., SCRIBES, U.S. Law Writers Society, 1972–73. *Publs:* History of Allied Planning of Operations: European Theatre of Operations 1939-45, 1945; Creditors' Rights and Remedies, 1949; Negligence Investigation Manual, 1953; Debtor-Creditor Law, 1953, supplement 1959; (ed.) Organizing Corporate and Other Business Enterprises, 1953; Negligence Forms of Pleading, 1954, supplement 1957; New York Corporations, 1954; (ed.) Directors' and Officers' Encyclopedic Dictionary, 1955; Damages to Persons and Property, 1955; Non-Profit Corporations, Organizations, and Associations, 1956, 5th ed. 1988; Markham's Negligence Counsel: Law Digest Section, 1956; Modern Corporation Law, 6 vols., 1960, supplement 1978; (ed.) Connecticut Insurance Laws, 1962; (ed.) New Jersey Insurance Laws, 1962; Cases on Damages, 1962; Heroic Battles of World War II, 1962; (ed.) Encyclopedia of Negligence, 2 vols., 1962; Eyewitness Battles of World War II, 1963; Law for Living, 1967; A Singular Fury (novel), 1968; Primer on Legal Writing, 1969, 1979; Law for Everyone, 1971; The Lion of Islam (novel), 1977; Parliamentary Law for Nonprofit Organizations, 1979; Oleck's Tort Law Practice Manual, 1982. Add: 5940 Pelican Bay Plaza, #301, St. Petersburg, Fla. 33707, U.S.A.

OLIVA, L. Jay. American, b. 1933. History, Translations. Prof. of History since 1960, and Chancellor since 1983, New York Univ. (Acting Dean, University Coll. of Arts and Sciences, 1971–73). *Publs:* Misalliance: Study of French Policy in Russia During the Seven Years' War, 1964; Russia and the West from Peter to Khrushchev, 1965; (trans. with Doyce B. Nunis) A Medical Journey to California, 1967; Russia in the Era of Peter the Great, 1969; (ed.) Peter the Great, 1970; (ed.) Catherine the Great, 1971; (ed.) Report of the Commission on Undergraduate Education, 1971. Add: 1221 Bobst Library, New York Univ., New York, N.Y. 10003, U.S.A.

OLIVER, (Symmes) Chad(wick). American, b. 1928. Westerns/Ad-

venture, Science fiction/Fantasy, Anthropology/Ethnology. Prof. of Anthropology, since 1968, and Dept. Chmn., since 1980, Univ. of Texas at Austin, (Instr., 1955–59; Asst. Prof., 1959–62; Assoc. Prof., 1963–68; and Dept. Chmn., 1967–71). *Publs:* Shadows in the Sun, 1954; Mists of Dawn (juvenile fiction), 1952; Another Kind (short stories), 1955; The Winds of Time, 1957; Unearthly Neighbors, 1960; Ecology and Cultural Continuity as Contributing Factors in the Social Organization of the Plains Indians, 1962; The Wolf Is My Brother (western novel), 1967; The Shores of Another Sea, 1971; The Edge of Forever, ed. by William F. Nolan (short stories), 1971; Giants in the Dust, 1976; Cultural Anthropology: The Discovery of Humanity, 1980. Add: 301 Eanes Rd., Austin, Tex. 78746, U.S.A.

OLIVER, Egbert S(amuel). American, b. 1902. History, Literature, Autobiography/Memoirs/Personal. Emeritus Prof. of English, Portland State Univ. (faculty member, 1950–67; Head, Dept. of English, 1961–67). Prof., English Dept., Willamette Univ., Salem, Ore., 1929–50. *Publs:* (ed.) Readings for Ideas and Form, 1935; (ed.) Giving Form to Ideas, 1946; (ed.) Melville's Piazza Tales, 1948; Studies in American Literature, 1965; (ed.) American Literature 1890-1965: An Anthology, 1967; (ed.) The Tarbells of Yankton, 1978; The Shaping of a Family: A Memoir, 1979; The Columbia County Tarbells, 1980; Homes in the Oregon Forest: Settling Columbia County, Oregon 1870-1920, 1983; Thomas Condon of Oregon: A Man With a Mission, 1984; Saints and Sinners, 1987; Obed Dickinson's War Against Sin in Salem 1853-1867, 1987. Add: 1220 N.E. 17th Ave., Portland, Ore. 97232, U.S.A.

OLIVER, Francis Richard. British, b. 1932. Economics, Mathematics/Statistics. Reader in Statistics and Econometrics, Univ. of Exeter, since 1970 (Lectr., 1958–69; Sr. Lectr., 1969–70). *Publs:* The Control of Hire Purchase, 1961; What Do Statistics Show, 1964. Add: Dept. of Economics, Univ. of Exeter, Exeter EX4 4RJ, England.

OLIVER, John E(dward). American, b. 1933. Geography. Prof, Indiana State Univ., Terre Haute, since 1988 (Assoc. Prof., 1973–81; Prof., 1981–87). Asst. Prof. and subsequently Assoc. Prof., Columbia Univ., NYC, 1969–73. *Publs:* (with J. Wreford Watson) A Geography of Bermuda, 1964; What We Find When We Look at Maps, 1970; Climate and Man's Environment, 1973; Perspectives on Applied Physical Geography, 1977; Physical Geography: Principles and Applications, 1979; Climatology: Selected Applications, 1981; (with J. Hidore) Climatology: An Introduction, 1982; (with R. Fairbridge) Encyclopedia of Climatology, 1986. Add: Dept. of Geography, Indiana State Univ., Terre Haute, Ind. 47809, U.S.A.

OLIVER, Kenneth A(rthur). American, b. 1912. Poetry, Language/Linguistics, Literature, Translations. Prof. Emeritus of English and Comparative Literature, Occidental Coll., Los Angeles, since 1977 (Prof., 1948–77; Chmn., Dept. of English and Comparative Literature, 1949–66; Chmn., Div. of Humanities and Fine Arts, 1962–67). Head, English and Foreign Language Depts., West Linn High Sch., Oregon, 1935–41; Instr. of Comparative Literature, Univ. of Wisconsin, 1947–48; Fulbright Lectr., Salonica, Greece, 1956–57. *Publs:* (ed.) The Road and the Stars, by Theodore Parker, 1957; (trans;) Impromptu: The Courtship of Brunhild, 1961; (trans. and contrib.) An Anthology of Medieval Lyrics, 1962; (trans. and contrib.) Laurel Masterpieces of World Literature: Medieval Age, 1963; (ed.) Walk the Rugged Earth; Perhaps a 'Darned' Word, 1969; (trans. and contrib.) Styx and The Peacock, by Christoph Meckel, 1974; Words Every College Student Should Know, 1974, 3rd ed. 1983; A Sound Curriculum in English Grammar: Guidelines for Teachers and Parents, 1975, 1976; (assoc. ed.) A Guide to the Teaching of World Literature, 1980; My Privilege to Live: Some Glimpses Across a Life, 1985. Add: 677 Wipwood Dr. S.E., Salem, OR 97306, U.S.A.

OLIVER, Leslie Claremont. British, b. 1909. Medicine/Health. In private practice as neurosurgeon. Consulting Neurosurgeon, Charing Cross, Westminster and Royal Northern hospitals, London, since 1947. Resident Surgeon, West London Hosp., 1937–38 and 1944–45; First Asst., Dept. of Neurosurgery, London Hosp., 1938–39; Founder, Neurosurgical Center, Old Church Hosp., Romford, Essex, 1945–74. *Publs:* Essentials of Neurosurgery, 1952; Parkinson's Disease and Its Surgical Treatment, 1953; (ed. and contrib.) Basic Surgery, 1958; Parkinson's Disease, 1967; Removable Intracranial Tumours, 1969; Le Francais Pratique, 1979. Add: 20 Harley St., London W1N 1AF, England.

OLIVER, Mark. *See* **TYLER-WHITTLE**, Michael.

OLIVER, Mary. American, b. 1935. Poetry. *Publs:* No Voyage and Other Poems, 1963, enlarged ed. 1965; The River Styx, Ohio and Other

Poems, 1972; The Night Traveler, 1978; Twelve Moons, 1979; American Primitive, 1983; Dream Work, 1986. Recipient of Pulitzer Prize, 1984. Add: c/o Molly Malone Cook Literary Agency, Box 338, Provincetown, Mass. 02657, U.S.A.

OLIVER, Paul. British, b. 1927. Architecture, Music. Head, Dept. of Arts and History, 1966–71, and the Grad. Sch., 1971–73, Architectural Assn. Sch. of Architecture, London; Dir. of Art and Design, Dartington Coll. of Arts, Totnes, Devon, 1973–78; Assoc. Head, Dept. of Architecture, Oxford Polytechnic, 1978–87. Ed., Blues Paperbacks series, Studio Vista Publrs., London, 1970–73. *Publs:* Bessie Smith, 1959; Blues Fell This Morning, 1960 (Prix d'Etrangers); Conversation with the Blues, 1965; Screening the Blues (in U.S. as Aspects of the Blues Tradition), 1968; Shelter and Society, 1969; The Story of the Blues, 1969; Savannah Syncopators: African Retentions in the Blues, 1970; (co-author) Jazz on Record, 1968; (ed.) Shelter in Africa, 1971; (ed. with O. Doumanis) Shelter in Greece, 1971; (ed.) Shelter Sign and Symbol, 1975; (co-author) Dunroamin: The Suburban Semi and Its Enemies, 1981; Early Blues Songbook, 1982; Songsters and Saints: Vocal Traditions on Race Records, 1984; Blues the Record: Thirty Years of Blues Commentary, 1984; Dwellings: The House Across the World, 1987; (with Max Harrison) The Grove Book of Gospel, Blues, and Jazz, 1987; (ed.) The Blackwell Guide to Blues Records, 1989; Paul Oliver and Richard Hayward, Architecture: An Invitation, 1990; (ed.) Black Music in Britain, 1990. Add: Parrotts, Wootton by Woodstock, Oxon., England.

OLIVER, Robert Tarbell. American, b. 1909. Cultural/Ethnic topics, History, Speech/Rhetoric. Research Prof. Emeritus of Intnl. Speech, Pennsylvania State Univ., University Park, since 1970 (Prof., 1949–70; Head, Dept. of Speech, 1949–65). Adviser on Intnl. Relations to Pres. Syngman Rhee, Korea, 1942–60, and to Korean delegations to the U.N., 1947–60. *Publs:* Training for Effective Speech, 1939; Effective Speech Notebook, 1940; Psychology of Persuasive Speech, 1942; (with H.W. Robbins) Developing Ideas, 1943; Korea: Forgotten Nation, 1944; Four Who Spoke Out, 1946; (with D. Dickey and H. Zelko) Essentials of Communicative Speech, 1949; Why War Came in Korea, 1950; Persuasive Speaking, 1950; The Truth about Korea, 1951; Verdict in Korea, 1952; Syngman Rhee: The Man Behind the Myth, 1954; Effective Speech for Democratic Living, 1959; Culture and Communication, 1962; (with D.A. Barbara) The Healthy Mind, 1962; Becoming an Informed Citizen, 1964; History of Public Speaking in America, 1965, 1974; (with H.P. Zelko and P. Holtzman) Communicative Speaking and Listening, 1968; Communication and Culture in Ancient India and China, 1970; Syngman Rhee and American Involvement in Korea 1942-1960: A Personal Narrative, 1978; The Influence of Rhetoric in the Shaping of Great Britain, 1986; Public Speaking in the Reshaping of Great Britain, 1987; Leadership in Asia: Persuasive Communication in the Making of Nations 1850-1950, 1989. Add: 10 Byford Ct., Chestertown, Md. 21620, U.S.A.

OLIVER, Roland Anthony. British, b. 1923. Area studies, History. Prof. of African History, Sch. of Oriental and African Studies, Univ. of London, 1963–86 (Lectr., 1948–58; Reader, 1958–63). Co-Ed., with J.D. Fage, Journal of African History and Cambridge History of Africa. *Publs:* The Missionary Factor in East Africa, 1952; Sir Harry Johnston and the Scramble for Africa, 1957; (ed.) The Dawn of African History, 1958; (ed. with G. Mathew) A History of East Africa, 1961; (with J.D. Fage) A Short History of Africa, 1961; (ed.) The Middle Age of African History, 1967; (with A. Atmore) Africa since 1800, 1967; (ed. with J.D. Fage) Papers in African Prehistory, 1970; (with B.M. Fagan) Africa in the Iron Age, 1975; (with A. Atmore) The African Middle Ages 1400-1800, 1980. Add: Frilsham Woodhouse, Newbury, Berks., England.

OLLARD, Richard. British, b. 1923. History, Biography. Lectr. and Sr. Lectr. in History and English, Royal Naval Coll., Greenwich, 1948–59; Ed., William Collins and Sons, London, 1960–83. *Publs:* (ed. with H.E. Bell) Historical Essays 1600-1750, 1963; The Escape of Charles II, 1967; Man of War: Sir Robert Holmes and the Restoration Navy, 1969; Pepys, 1974; This War Without an Enemy: A History of the English Civil Wars, 1976; The Image of the King: Charles I and Charles II, 1979; An English Education: A Perspective of Eton, 1982; (ed. with Pamela Tudor-Craig) For Veronica Wedgwood These: Studies in 17th Century History, 1986; Clarendon and His Friends, 1987; (ed.) Clarendon's Four Portraits, 1989. Add: c/o Curtis Brown Ltd., 162 Regent St., London W1, England.

OLLERENSHAW,(Dame) Kathleen. British, b. 1912. Education, Mathematics/Statistics. Chmn. of the Court, Royal Northern Coll. of Music, since 1968; Alderman, 1974–80, and Hon. Alderman, since 1980, Manchester; Vice-Pres., Univ. of Manchester Inst. of Technology, since 1977; Deputy Pro-Chancellor, Univ. of Lancaster, since 1979; Pro-Chancellor, Univ. of Salford, since 1984. Member 1956–80, and Leader of the Conservative Opposition 1977–79, Manchester City Council (Lord Mayor, 1975–76); Pres., Inst. of Mathematics and Its Applications, 1979. *Publs:* Education of Girls, 1961; The Girls' Schools, 1966; Returning to Teaching, 1974; The Lord Mayor's Party, 1976; First Citizen, 1977. Add: 2 Pine Rd., Didsbury, Manchester M20 0UY, England.

OLLIER, Cliff(ord) David. British, b. 1931. Earth sciences, Geography. Prof. of Geography, Univ. of New England, Armidale, N.S.W., since 1979. Soil Scientist, Dept. of Agriculture, Entebbe, Uganda, 1956–58; Sr. Lectr. in Geology, Univ. of Melbourne, 1959–66; Head, Geology Dept., Univ. of Papua New Guinea, Boroko, 1967–69, and Canberra Coll. of Advanced Education, 1969–75; Research Fellow, Research Sch. of Pacific Studies, Australian National Univ., Canberra, 1975–79. Past Chmn., Geological Soc. of Australia. *Publs:* Weathering, 1969, 1984; Volcanoes, 1970, 1988; Earth History in Maps and Diagrams, 1973; Weathering and Landforms, 1974, 1987; Tectonics and Landforms, 1981. Add: 207 Erskine St., Armidale, N.S.W., Australia.

OLMSTED, Robert W(alsh). American, b. 1936. Children's fiction, Poetry. Teacher of High Sch. English, Grand Rapids, Minn., since 1972. Publr., Northwoods Press, Bigfork, Minn. *Publs:* Northern Lights, 1969; (ed.) New England Voices, 1972; (ed.) Summertime, 1972; (ed.) Man: When Born of Fire, 1972; The First Christmas Ever, 1973; (ed.) Spring Songs, 1973; The Diesel Years, 1975; (ed.) Rendevous with the Sea, 1976; Shadows on Cassiopeia, 1976; (ed.) Poems for Coffee Breaking, 1976; (ed.) Two Hundred Years to Here, 1976; (ed.) Showcase 1976, 1977; Wild Strawberries at 3000 Feet, 1986. Add: c/o American History Press, P.O. Box 123, S. Thomaston, Me. 04861, U.S.A.

OLNEY, Ross R(obert). American, b. 1929. Children's non-fiction, Recreation/Leisure/Hobbies, Sports-Physical education/Keeping fit, Biography. *Publs:* The Young Sportsman's Guide to Surfing, 1965; Americans in Space, 1966, 1971; The Young Sportsman's Guide to Water Safety, 1966; Daredevils of the Speedway, 1966; Light Motorcycle Riding, 1967; The Inquiring Mind: Astronomy, 1967; Sound All Around, 1967; The Story of Traffic Control, 1968; Let's Go Sailing, 1968; King of the Drag Strip, 1968; Internal Combustion Engines, 1969; The Inquiring Mind: Oceanography, 1969; Men Against the Sea, 1969; Tales of Time and Space, 1969; Great Moments in Speed, 1970; Kings of Motor Speed, 1970; Kings of the Surf, 1970; Great Dragging Wagons, 1970; The Incredible A.J. Foyt, 1970; The Indianapolis 500, 1970; Simple Gasoline Engine Repair, 1972; Air Traffic Control, 1972; Shudders, 1972; Drag Strip Danger, 1972; How To Keep Your Car Running, Your Money in Your Pocket, and Your Mind Intact!, 1973; Simple Bicycle Repair and Maintenance, 1974; (with R. Grable) The Racing Bugs: Formula Vee and Super Vee, 1974; Driving: How to Get a License and keep It, 1974; Motorcycles, 1974; (with P. Olney) Quick and Easy Magic Fun, 1974; Light Motorcycle Repair, 1975; Motorcycling, 1975; Photographing Action Sports, 1976; Simple Appliance Repair, 1976; Superstars of Auto-Racing, 1976; Gymnastics, 1976; Hang Gliding, 1976; How to Understand Soccer, 1976; Auto Racing's Young Lions, 1977; (with Chan Bush) Better Skateboarding for Boys and Girls, 1977; (with Mary Ann Duganne) How to Make Your Car Run Better, 1977; This Game Called Hockey, 1978; The Young Runner, 1978; A.J. Foyt, 1978; Illustrated Auto Racing Dictionary for Young People, 1978; Janet Guthrie, 1978; Modern Auto-Racing Superstars, 1978; Modern Racing Cars, 1978; (with Chan Bush) Roller Skating, 1979; Tricky Discs, 1979; How to Understand Auto Racing, 1979; (with Pat Olney) Magic, 1979; Out to Launch: Model Rockets, 1979; Modern Motorcycle Superstars, 1980; Auto Racing: Micro Style, 1980; (with Chan Bush) Better Kite Flying for Boys and Girls, 1980; The Amazing Yo-Yo, 1980; Model Airplanes, R/C Style, 1980; The Young Bicyclist, 1980; Listen to Your Car, 1981; Farm Giants, 1982; Modern Speed Record Superstars, 1982; Windsurfing, 1982; Winners, 1982; Construction Giants, 1983; (with Pat Olney) Time, How to have More of It, 1983; (with Pat Olney) How Long?, 1984; The Farm Combine, 1984; Super-Champions of Auto Racing, 1984; Ocean-Going Giants, 1985; Car of the Future, 1986; The Shell Auto Car Guide, 1986; (with Ross D. Olney) The Amazing Transistor, 1986; (with Pat Olney) Imagining, 1987; (with Pat Olney) Up Against the Law, 1987. Add: Larry Sternig Literary Agency, 742 Robertson, Milwaukee, Wisc. 53213, U.S.A.

OLSEN, Otto H. American, b. 1925. History, Humanities, Race relations, Social sciences (general). Prof. of American History and Dept. Chmn., Northern Illinois Univ., DeKalb, since 1967. Instr. in World History, Univ. of North Carolina, Chapel Hill, 1957–60; Asst. Prof. of American History, Old Dominion Coll., Norfolk, Va., 1960–64; Assoc. Prof. of American History, Morgan State Coll., Baltimore, 1964–67; Visiting Prof., Univ. of Wisconsin, 1966–67. *Publs:* Carpetbagger's Crusade:

The Life of Albion W. Tourgee, 1965; (ed.) The Thin Disguise: Turning Point in Negro History – Plessey vs. Ferguson, 1967; (ed) The Negro Question: From Slavery to Caste 1863-1910, 1971; The Reconstruction and Redemption of the South, 1979; (ed.) The Invisible Empire, 1988. Add: 565 Garden Rd., DeKalb, Ill. 60115, U.S.A.

OLSEN, T(heodore) V(ictor). Also writes as Christopher Storm, Joshua Stark, and Cass Willoughby. American, b. 1932. Historical/Romance/Gothic, Westerns/Adventure. *Publs:* Haven of the Hunted, 1956; The Man from Nowhere, 1959; McGivern, 1960; High Lawless, 1960; Gunswift, 1960; Ramrod Rider, 1961; Brand of the Star, 1961; Brothers of the Sword, 1962; Savage Sierra, 1962; (as Christopher Storm) The Young Duke, 1964; (as Joshua Stark) Break the Young Land, 1964; (as Christopher Storm) The Sex Rebels, 1964; A Man Called Brazos, 1964; Canyon of the Gun, 1965; (as Christopher Storm) Campus Motel, 1965; The Stalking Moon, 1965; The Hard Men, 1966; (as Cass Willoughby) Autumn Passion, 1966; Bitter Grass, 1967; (as Joshua Stark) The Lockhart Breed, 1967; Blizzard Pass, 1968; Arrow in the Sun, 1969; (as Joshua Stark) Keno, 1970; A Man Named Yuma, 1971; Eye of the Wolf, 1971; There Was a Season, 1972; Summer of the Drums, 1972; Starbuck's Brand, 1973; Mission in the West, 1973; Run to the Mountain, 1974; Track the Man Down, 1975; Day of the Buzzard, 1976; Westward They Rode, 1976; Bonner's Stallion, 1977; Rattlesnake, 1979; Roots of the North, 1979; Allegories for One Man's Moods, 1979; Our First Hundred Years, 1981; Blood of the Breed, 1982; Birth of a City, 1983; Red is the River, 1983; Lazlo's Strike, 1983; Lonesome Gun, 1985; Blood Rage, 1987; A Killer is Waiting, 1988; Under the Gun, 1989. Add: P.O. Box 856, Rhinelander, Wisc. 54501, U.S.A.

OLSEN, Tillie. American, b. 1913. Novels/Short stories, Biography, Essays. Writer-in-Residence, Amherst Coll., Mass., 1967–70, and Masschusetts Inst. of Technology, 1973–74;n Visiting Prof., Stanford Univ., Calif. 1972, and Univ. of Massachusetts, Boston, 1974. *Publs:* Tell Me A Riddle (short fiction), 1962 (O'Henry Award); (ed.) Life in the Iron Mills, by Rebecca Harding Davis, 1972; Tonnondio, from the Thirties, 1974; Silences, 1978; Mother to Daughter, Daughter to Mother: Mothers on Mothering, 1984. Add: 1435 Laguna, San Francisco, Calif. 94115, U.S.A.

OLSON, David Richard. Canadian, b. 1935. Education, Psychology. Prof. of Applied Psychology, Ontario Inst. for Studies in Education, Toronto, since 1971 (Assoc. Prof., 1966–71). *Publs:* Cognitive Development:The Child's Acquisition of Diagonality, 1970; (ed.) Media and Symbols: The Forms of Expression Communication and Education, 1974; (ed.) Social Foundations of Language and Thought: Essays in Honor of J.S. Bruner, 1980; (with Ellen Bialystok) Spatial Cognition: The Mental Representation of Spatial, 1982; (ed.) with N. Torrance and A. Hildyard) Literary, Language and Learning: The Nature and Consequences of Reading and Writing, 1985; (ed. with F. Holthoon) Common Sense: A Foundation for the Social Sciences, 1987; (co-ed.) Developing Theories of Mind, 1988. Add: 252 Bloor St. West, Toronto, Ont., Canada.

OLSON, Elder (James). American, b. 1909. Plays/Screenplays, Poetry, Literature. Distinguished Prof. of English, Univ. of Chicago, 1954–77, now Emeritus (Asst. Prof., 1942–48; Assoc. Prof., 1948–53). Instr., Armour Inst. of Technology, Chicago, 1938–42. *Publs:* Thing of Sorrow: Poems, 1934; General Prosody, Rhythmic, Metric, Harmonics, 1938; The Cock of Heaven, 1940; (with others) Critics and Criticism, 1952; The Poetry of Dylan Thomas, 1954; The Scarecrow Christ and Other Poems, 1954; Poems and Plays 1948-1958, 1958; A Crack in the Universe (play), 1962; Tragedy and the Theory of Drama, 1961; Collected Poems, 1963; The Abstract Tragedy: A Comedy of Masks, 1963; (ed.) American Lyric Poems: From Colonial Days to the Present, 1963; (ed.) Aristotle's "Poetics" and English Literature: A Collection of Critical Essays, 1965; The Theory of Comedy, 1968; Olson's Penny Arcade (poetry), 1975; On Value Judgments in the Arts and Other Essays, 1976; Last Poems, 1984. Add: 1501 Los Alamos Ave., Albuquerque, N.M. 87104, U.S.A.

OLSON, James Clifton. American, b. 1917. History, Biography. Pres. Emeritus, Univ. of Missouri System, since 1984 (Chancellor, Univ. of Missouri-Kansas City, 1968–76; Interim Pres., Univ. of Missouri System, 1976–77; Pres., 1977–84). Dir., Nebraska State Historical Soc., 1946–56; Prof. and Chmn., Dept. of History, 1956–68, and Vice-Chancellor for Grad. Studies and Research, 1968, Univ. of Nebraska, Lincoln. *Publs:* J. Sterling Morton, 1942; (with G.E. Condra and R. Knapp) The Nebraska Story, 1951; (with J.L. Cate and W.F. Craven) The Army Air Forces in World War II, vol. IV, 1951, vol. V, 1953; History of Nebraska, 1955, 1966; (with Vera F. Olson) Nebraska Is My Home, 1956, 1965; (with Vera F. Olson) This Is Nebraska, 1960, 1968; Red Cloud and the Sioux Problem, 1965; (with Vera F. Olson) The University of Missouri: An Illustrated History, 1988. Add: Univ. of Missouri-Kansas City, 5100 Rockhill Rd., Kansas City, Mo. 64110, U.S.A.

OLSON, Toby. (Merle Theodore Olson). American, b. 1937. Novels/Short stories, Poetry. Prof., Temple Univ., Philadelphia, since 1975. Assoc. Dir., Aspen Writers Workshop, Colorado, 1964–67; Asst. Prof., Long Island Univ., 1966–74; Member of the Faculty, The New Sch., NYC, 1967–75; Poet-in-Residence, State Univ. of New York at Cortland, 1972, and Friends Seminary, NYC, 1974–75. *Publs:* The Brand: A Five-Part Poem, 1969; Worms into Nails, 1969; The Hawk-Foot Poems, 1969; Maps, 1969; Pig's Book, 1970; Cold House, 1970; Poems, 1970; Tools, 1971; Shooting Pigeons, 1971; Vectors, 1972; Home, 1972; Fishing, 1973; The Wrestlers and Other Poems, 1974; City, 1974; A Kind of Psychology, 1974; Changing Appearance: Poems 1965-70, 1975; A Moral Proposition, 1975; Priorities, 1975; Seeds, 1975; Standard-4, 1975; Home, 1976; Three and One, 1976; The Life of Jesus (novel), 1976; Doctor Miriam: Five Poems by Her Admiring Husband, 1977; Aesthetics, 1978; The Florence Poems, 1978; Seaview (novel), 1982; We Are the Fire, 1984; The Woman Who Escaped from Shame (novel), 1986; Utah (novel), 1987. Add: 329 S. Juniper St., Philadelphia, Pa. 19107, U.S.A.

O'MALLEY, Frank. *See* **O'ROURKE,** Frank.

O'MALLEY, Mary. British, b. 1941. Plays/Screenplays. *Publs:* Once A Catholic, 1978; Look Out... Here Comes Trouble, 1979. Add: c/o William Morris Agency, 31–32 Soho Sq., London W1V 6AP, England.

O'MALLEY, Patrick. *See* **O'ROURKE,** Frank.

OMARI, T. Peter. Ghanaian, b. 1930. Mathematics/Statistics, Sociology, Biography. Exec. Dir., African Centre for Applied Research and Training in Social Development, Tripoli, Libya, since 1982. Consultant, Dag Hammarskjold Foundn., Uppsala, Sweden, and Swedish Intnl. Development Authority, Stockholm, since 1968. Research Assoc., Univ. of Wisconsin, Madison, 1955–56; Mass Education Officer, Dept. of Social Welfare and Community Development, Ghana, 1956–58; Lectr. in Sociology, 1958–62; and Sr. Lectr., 1962–63, Univ. of Ghana, Accra; Chief, Social Development Section, U.N. Economic Cttee. for Africa, Addis Ababa, 1973–82 (Social Affairs Officer and Head, Social Development Division, 1963–69; Social Affairs Officer, Regional and Community Development Section, U.N. Headquarters, NYC, 1969–70; Asst. to Exec. Secty., 1971–73). *Publs:* Socialized Medicine for Ghana: A Report to the Ghana Medical Association, 1962; Marriage Guidance for Young Ghanaians, 1962; A Basic Course in Statistics for Sociologists, 1962; Kwame Nkrumah: The Anatomy of an African Dictatorship, 1970. Add: Economic Commn. for Africa, P.O. Box 3005, Addis Ababa, Ethiopia.

O'MEARA, John Joseph. Irish, b. 1915. Classics, Humanities (general), Philosophy, Biography. Prof. Emeritus of Latin, Univ. Coll., Dublin (joined faculty, 1945); Dir. of Eriugenian Studies, Royal Irish Academy, since 1984. Member of the Governing Body, University Coll., 1956–59, 1962–65; member of the Senate of the National Univ. of Ireland, Dublin, 1964–72; Vice-Pres., Royal Irish Academy, 1967–70. *Publs:* (trans.) Against the Academics, by St. Augustine, 1950; (trans.) Topography of Ireland, by Giraldus Cambrensis, 1951; (trans.) On Prayer and Exhortation to Martyrdom, by Origen, 1954; The Young Augustine: The Growth of St. Augustine's Mind Up to His Conversion, 1954; (with Courcelle and Mohrmann) Recherches Augustiniennes, 1958; Porphyry's Philosophy from Oracles in St. Augustine, 1959; Charter of Christendom: The Significance of St. Augustine's City of God, 1962; Porphyry's Philosophy from Oracles in Eusebius's Praeparatio Evangelica and Augustine's Dialogues of Cassiciacum, 1969; Eriugena, 1969; (with L. Bieler) The Mind of Eriugena, 1973; An Augustine Reader, 1973; (trans.) Navigatio Sancti Brendani Abbatis, 1976; (ed. with B. Naumann) Latin Script and Letters A.D. 400-900, 1976; The Creation of Man in De Genesi ad Litteram, 1980; (trans. with I.P. Sheldon-Williams) Eriugena's Periphyseon, 1987; Eriugena, 1988. Add: 15 Maple Rd., Dublin 14, Ireland.

ONDAATJE, Michael. Canadian, b. 1943. Novels, Plays/Screenplays, Poetry, Literature. Member of Dept. of English, Glendon Coll., York Univ., Toronto, since 1971. Ed., Mongrel Broadsides. Taught at the Univ. of Western Ontario, London, 1967–71. *Publs:* The Dainty Monsters, 1967; The Man with Seven Toes, 1969; The Left-Handed Poems: Collected Works of Billy the Kid, 1970, play, 1973; Leonard Cohen, 1970; (ed.) The Broken Ark, 1971; Rat Jelly, 1973; Eliminating Dance, 1978; Coming Through Slaughter (novel), 1979; Rat Jelly and Other Poems, 1979; (ed.) The Long Poem Anthology, 1979; Running in the Family, 1983; Secular Love (poems), 1985; In the Skin of a Lion (novel), 1987. Add: Dept. of English, Glendon Coll., York Univ., 2275 Bayview Ave., Toronto, Ont., Canada.

ONEAL, Elizabeth. Also writes as Zibby Oneal. American, b. 1934. Children's Fiction, Children's non-fiction. Lectr., Residential Coll., Univ. of Michigan, Ann Arbor. *Publs:* War Work, 1970; The Improbable Adventures of Marvelous O'Hara Soapstone, 1971; The Language of Goldfish, 1980; A Formal Feeling, 1982; In Summer Light, 1985; Grandma Moses, Painter of Rural American, 1986. Add: 501 Onondaga St., Ann Arbor, Mich. 48104, U.S.A.

O'NEILL, Judith (née Lyall). Australian, b. 1930. Children's fiction, Literary criticism. Tutor in English, Univ. of Melbourne, 1954–56 and 1960–62; Tutor, Open Univ., Cambridge, England, 1971–72; English teacher, St. Mary's Sch., Cambridge, 1973–82. *Publs:* (ed.) Critics on Keats, 1967; (ed.) Critics on Charlotte and Emily Brontë, 1968; (ed.) Critics on Pope, 1968; (ed.) Critics on Jane Austin, 1969; (ed.) Critics on Marlowe, 1969; (ed.) Critics on Blake, 1970; Martin Luther, 1975; Transported to Van Diemen's Land, 1977; Jess and the River Kids, 1984; Stringybark Summer, 1985; Deepwater, 1987; The Message, 1989. Add: 9 Lonsdale Terr., Edinburgh EH3 9HN, Scotland.

O'NEILL, Patrick Geoffrey. British, b. 1924. Language/Linguistics, Theatre, Translations. Emeritus Prof. of Japanese, Univ. of London, since 1986 (Lectr., 1949–67; Prof., 1968–86). *Publs:* A Guide to No, 1953; Early No Drama, 1958; An Introduction to Written Japanese, 1963; Respect Language in Modern Japanese, 1966; Japanese Kana Workbook, 1967; A Programmed Introduction to Literary-Style Japanese, 1968; Japanese Names, 1972; Essential Kanji: 2000 Japanese Characters, 1973; (ed.) Tradition and Modern Japan, 1982; A Reader of Handwritten Japanese, 1984. Add: Sch. of Oriental and African Studies, Univ. of London, Malet St., London WC1E 7HP, England.

O'NEILL, Robert John. Australian, b. 1936. History, Biography, Defence. hichele Prof. of the History of War and Fellow of All Souls Coll., Oxford, since 1987. Section Ed., Australian Dictionary of Biography. Officer, Australian Regular Army, 1958–68; Historical researcher, German univs. and archives, 1964–65; Sr. Lectr. in History, Royal Military Coll., Duntroon, 1967–69; Sr. Fellow, 1969–77, Head of the Strategic and Defence Studies Centre, 1971–82, Prof. Fellow, 1977–82, in Intnl. Relations, Australian Natl. Univ; Australian Official Historian for the Korean War, 1970–82; Dir., Intnl. Inst. for Strategic Studies, London, 1982–87. Editorial Bd. Member, Australian Documents on Foreign Policy, 1971–82. *Publs:* The German Army and the Nazi Party 1933-39, 1966; Vietnam Task, 1968; Indo-China Tragedy, 1969; General Giap: Politician and Strategist, 1969; (ed.) The Strategic Nuclear Balance, 1975; (ed.) The Defence of Australia: Fundamental New Aspects, 1977; (ed.) Insecurity! The Spread of Weapons in Indian and Pacific Oceans, 1978; (with Jean Fielding) A Select Bibliography of Australian Military History 1891-1939, 1978; Australia in the Korean War 1950-53, 2 vols., 1980–85; (ed. with D.M. Horner) New Directions in Strategic Thinking, 1981; (ed.) The Conduct of East-West Relations in the 1980's, 1985; (ed.) New Technology and Western Security Policy, 1985; (ed.) Doctrine, the Alliance, and Arms Control, 1986; (ed. with David Schwartz) Hedley Bull on Arms Control, 1987; (ed.) East Asia, the West, and International Security, 1987; (ed.) Security in the Mediterranean, 1988. Add: All Souls Coll., Oxford, England.

O'NEILL, William L. American, b. 1935. History. Prof. of History, Rutgers Univ., New Brunswick, N.J., since 1971. Asst., then Assoc. Prof., Univ. of Wisconsin, Madison, 1966–71. *Publs:* (ed.) Echoes of Revolt, 1966; Divorce in the Progressive Era, 1967; Everyone Was Brave, 1969; (ed.) The Woman Movement, 1969; (ed.) American Society since 1945, 1969; Coming Apart: An Informal History of America in the 1960's, 1971; (ed.) Women at Work, 1972; (ed.) The American Sexual Dilemma, 1972; (ed.) Insights and Parallels, 1973; (co-author) Looking Backward: A Reintroduction to American History, 1974; The Progressive Years, 1975; The Last Romantic: A Life of Max Eastman, 1978; A Better World: The Great Schism—Stalinism and the American Intellectuals, 1982; American High: The Years of Confidence, 1945-1960, 1986. Add: Dept. of History, Rutgers Univ., New Brunswick, N.J. 08903, U.S.A.

ONG, Walter J(ackson). American, b. 1912. Cultural/Ethnic topics, Humanities, Intellectual history, Language/Linguistics. Prof. of English since 1959, Prof. of Humanities in Psychiatry since 1970, and Univ. Prof. of Humanities since 1981, St. Louis Univ. (Instr., 1953–54, Asst. Prof., 1954–57, and Assoc. Prof., 1957–59, Dept. of English). Terry Lectr., Yale Univ., New Haven, Conn., 1963–74, and Lincoln Lectr., Central and

West Africa, 1974; Messenger Lectr., Cornell Univ., Ithaca, N.Y., 1979–80. *Publs:* Frontiers in American Catholicism, 1957; Ramus, Method and the Decay of Dialogue, 1958; Ramus and Talon Inventory, 1958; American Catholic Crossroads, 1959; (ed. and co-author) Darwin's Vision and Christian Perspectives, 1960; The Barbarian Within, 1962; In the Human Grain, 1967; The Presence of the Word, 1967; (ed. and co-author) Knowledge and the Future of Man, 1968; (ed.) Petrus Ramus and Audomarus Talaeus: Collectaneae Praefationes Epistolae Orationes, 1969; (ed.) Petrus Ramus: Scholae in Liberales Artes, 1970; Rhetoric, Romance and Technology, 1971; Why Talk?, 1973; Interfaces of the Word, 1977; Fighting for Life: Contest, Sexuality, and Consciousness, 1981; Orality and Literacy, 1982; Hopkins, the Self, and God, 1986. Add: Dept. of English, St. Louis Univ., St. Louis, Mo. 63103, U.S.A.

ONYEAMA, Dillibe. Nigerian, b. 1951. Novels, Race relations, Autobiography/Memoirs/Personal. Sub-Ed., Drum Publs., London, since 1974. *Publs:* Nigger at Eton; John Bull's Nigger; (compiler) I'm the Greatest: The Humour of Muhammad Ali; Book of Black Man's Humour, 1975; Sex Is a Nigger's Game, 1976; Juju, 1977; Secret Society, 1978; Return, 1978; Female Target, 1979; Revenge of the Medicine Man, 1980; Rules of the Game, 1981; Night Demon, 1982; Chief Onyeama, 1982; Godfathers of Voodoo, 1985. Add: c/o Sphere Books, 27 Wright's Lane, London W8 5TZ, England.

OPIE, Iona. British, b. 1923. Children's fiction, Language/Linguistics, Literature, Mythology/Folklore. *Publs:* all with Peter Opie—(ed.) The Oxford Dictionary of Nursery Rhymes, 1951; (ed.) The Oxford Nursery Rhyme Book, 1955; The Lore and Language of Schoolchildren, 1959; Puffin Book of Nursery Rhymes, 1963; A Family Book of Nursery Rhymes, 1964; Children's Games in Street and Playground, 1969; (ed.) The Oxford Book of Children's Verse, 1973; Three Centuries of Nursery Rhymes and Poetry for Children, 1973; (ed.) The Classic Fairy Tales, 1974; A Nursery Companion, 1980; The Oxford Book of Narrative Verse, 1983; The Singing Game, 1985; Tail Feathers from Mother Goose: The Opic Rhyme Book, 1988. Add: Westerfield House, West Liss, Hants., England.

OPIE, June. British, b. 1926. Novels/Short stories, Art, Documentaries/Reportage. Ed., Assn. for Disabled Professionals Quarterly. Formerly, psychologist at H.M. prison and cerebral palsy research unit. *Publs:* Over My Dead Body, 1957; Portrait of a Painter; Mokau; Come and Listen to the Stars Singing, 1988. Add: 264 A Annandale St., Annandale, N.S.W. 2038, Australia.

OPPENHEIM, Felix E. American, b. 1913. Philosophy, Politics/Government. Prof. of Political Science Emeritus, Univ. of Massachusetts, Amherst. *Publs:* Dimensions of Freedom, 1961; Moral Principles in Political Philosophy, 1968; Political Concepts: A Reconstruction, 1981. Add: 41 Arnold Rd., Amherst, Mass. 01002, U.S.A.

ORAM, Clifton (Albert). New Zealander, b. 1917. Public/Social administration. Sr. Inspector, State Services Commn., 1960–63; Part-time Lectr. on Social Policy and Admin., Victoria Univ. of Wellington, 1967–70. Member, 1968–77, and Deputy Chmn., 1970–77, Social Security Commn.; Member, Social Development Council, 1971–77, and Legal Aid Bd., 1971–77; Chmn., Welfare Services Distribution Cttee., 1978–82; Secty.-Mgr., New Zealand Artificial Limb Bd., 1978–86. *Publs:* Social Policy and Administration in New Zealand, 1969. Add: 25 Melrose St., Upper Hutt, New Zealand.

ORCHARD, Dennis Frank. British, b. 1912. Engineering/Technology. Emeritus Prof. of Highway Engineering, Univ. of New South Wales, Sydney. Sr. Planning Engineer, Harlow Development Corp., England, 1950–53; Consultant to the U.N., 1966–67. *Publs:* Concrete Technology, vol. I, 1957, vol. II, 1961, vol. III, 1975. Add: 1 Jenkins St., Chatswood, N.S.W. 2067, Australia.

ORD-HUME, Arthur W.J.G. British. Engineering/Technology, Recreation/Leisure/Hobbies. Head of Design, Agricultural Aviation Co. Ltd.; Chief Designer, Southern Aircraft; Managing Dir. and Chief of Design, Phoenix Aircraft Ltd.; Dir., Light Aviation Supplies; Technical Ed., Flying Review Intnl; Ed., Aerospace Review, The Music Box, Independent Electrical Retailer, and Music and Automata. *Publs:* Aircraft Design and Construction for Amateurs; Personal Flying; Build Your Own Light Aircraft; Collecting Musical Boxes and How to Repair Them; Player Piano; The History of the Mechanical Piano and How to Repair It; Clockwork Music; Mechanical Music; Barrel Organ: The History of the Mechanical Organ and Its Repair; Perpetual Motion; Musical Box; Restoring Musical Boxes; Joseph Haydn and the Mechanical Organ; Pianola:

The History of the Self-Playing Piano; Restoring Pianolas; George Frederik Handel and Mr. Clay's Musical Clocks; The Harmonium, 1986. Add: c/o Unwin Hyman Ltd., 37/39 Queen Elizabeth St., London SE1 2QB, England.

ORDISH, George. British, b. 1906. Novels/Short stories, Agriculture/Forestry, Business/Trade/Industry, History. Ed., Tropical Science, London, 1962–72. *Publs:* Untaken Harvest, 1952; Wine Growing in England, 1953; Garden Pests, 1954; The Living House, 1956, 1985; (with E. Hyams) The Last of the Incas, 1960; (with P. Binder) Pigeons and People, 1965; Biological Methods of Crop Pest Control, 1967; (with P. Binder) Ladies Only, 1968; The Great Wine Blight, 1972, 1987; John Curtis, Pioneer of Pest Control, 1974; The Year of the Butterfly, 1975; Vineyards in England and Wales, 1977; The Year of the Ant, 1978; The American Living House, 1981; The Living Garden, 1985. Add: c/o Mrs D. Owen Assocs., 78 Narrow St., Limehouse, London E14 8BP, England.

ORDWAY, Frederick I., III. American, b. 1927. Air/Space topics. Special Asst. to the Dir., Saturn Systems Office, Army Ballistic Missile Agency, 1957–60; Chief, Space Systems Information Branch, Marshall Space Flight Center, NASA, 1960–65; Scientific and Technical Consultant, MGM cinerama film 2001, 1965–66; Sr. Research Assoc., Research Inst., 1967–69, and Prof. of Science and Technology Applications and Evaluations, Sch. of Grad. Studies and Research, 1967–73, Univ. of Alabama, Huntsville; Special Asst. to the Administration, Energy Research and Development Administration, 1975–77, and policy and intnl. affairs positions, U.S. Dept. of Energy, since 1977. *Publs:*(co-author) Space Flight, 1958; (ed.) Advances in Space Science and Technology, vols. I-XI, and 2 supplements, 1959–67; (co-author) International Missile and Spacecraft Guide, 1960; Annotated Bibliography of Space Science and Technology, 1962; (co-author) Basic Astronautics: An Introduction to Space Sciences, Engineering and Medicine, 1962; (co-author) Careers in Astronautics and Rocketry, 1962; (co-author) From Peenemunde to Outer Space, 1962; (co-ed.) Astronautical Engineering and Science, 1963; (co-author) Applied Astronautics: An Introduction to Space Flight, 1963; (co-author) Conquering the Sun's Empire, 1963; Life in Other Solar Systems, 1965; (co-author) Intelligence in the Universe, 1966; (co-author) History of Rocketry and Space Travel, 1966, 3rd ed. 1975; (co-author) Histoire Mondiale de l'Astonautique, 1968; (co-author) Dividends from Space, 1971; (co-author) Antares Space Filmstrips, 1972; (co-author) Pictorial Guide to the Earth, 1974; (co-author) The Rocket's Glare, 1976; (co-author) New Worlds: Discoveries from Our Solar System, 1979; (co-author) The Rocket Team, 1979; (co-author) Space Travel: A History, 1985. Add: c/o M.I.T. Press, 55 Hayward St., Cambridge, Mass. 02142, U.S.A.

OREL, Harold. American, b. 1926. Literature. Univ. Distinguished Prof. of English, Univ. of Kansas, Lawrence, since 1974 (Prof. since 1957). Instr. in English, Univ. of Maryland, College Park, 1952–56. *Publs:* (ed.) The World of Victorian Humor, 1961; (ed. with G.J. Worth) Six Essays in Nineteenth-Century English Literature and Thought, 1962; Thomas Hardy's Epic-Drama: A Study of The Dynasts, 1963; (ed.) Thomas Hardy's Personal Writings: Prefaces, Literary Opinions, Reminiscences, 1966; The Development of William Butler Yeats 1885-1900, 1968; (ed. with P. Wiley) British Poetry 1880-1920: Edwardian Voices, 1969; (ed. with G.J. Worth) The Nineteenth-Century Writer and His Audience, 1969; English Romantic Poets and the Enlightenment, 1973; (ed.) Irish History and Culture: Aspects of a People's Heritage, 1975; The Final Years of Thomas Hardy 1912-1928, 1976; (ed.) Thomas Hardy's The Dynasts, 1978; The Scottish World, 1981; Rudyard Kipling: Interviews and Recollections, vols., 1983; Victorian Literary Critics, 1984; The Literary Achievement of Rebecca West, 1985; The Victorian Short Story, 1986; The Unknown Thomas Hardy, 1987; (ed.) Victorian Short Stories: An Anthology, 1987. Add: 713 Schwarz Rd., Lawrence, Kans. 66049, U.S.A.

OREM, Reginald. American, b. 1931. Education. Education Specialist, District of Columbia Govt., Washington, D.C., since 1970. Reading Consultant, Reading Technics, 1961–63; Employee Development Officer, District of Columbia Children's Center, 1964–66; Professional Assoc., Planning Research Corp., 1966–68. *Publs:* (ed.) A Montessori Handbook, 1965; (with William Amos) Managing Student Behavior, 1967; (ed.) Montessori for the Disadvantaged, 1967; (with George L. Stevens) The Case for Early Reading, 1968; (ed.) Montessori and the Special Child, 1969; (ed. with Ken Edelson) Children's House Parent-Teacher Guide to Montessori, 1970; (with George L. Stevens) American Montessori Manual, 1970; (ed.) Learning to See and Seeing to Learn, 1971; Montessori Today, 1971; Montessori: Her Method and the Movement, 1974; Development Vision for Lifelong Learning, 1977; (with Marjorie Coburn)

Montessori: Prescription for Children with Learning Disabilities, 1978; Maria Montessori: Methods, Schools, Materials, 1978. Add: Box 379, College Park, Md. 20740, U.S.A.

ORGAN, Troy Wilson. American, b. 1912. Philosophy. Prof. of Philosophy, Ohio Univ., Athens, since 1954. Teacher of Philosophy, Parsons Coll., Fairfield, Iowa, 1941–45, Univ. of Akron, 1945–46, and Chatham Coll., Pittsburgh, 1946–54. *Publs:* An Index to Aristotle, 1949; The Examined Life, 1956; The Self in Indian Philosophy, 1964; The Art of Critical Thinking, 1965; The Hindu Quest for the Perfection of Man, 1970, 1980; Hinduism, 1974; Western Approaches to Eastern Philosophy, 1975; Third Eye Philosophy, 1987; Philosophy and the Self: East and West, 1987; The Self in Its Worlds: East and West, 1988. Add: 65 Second St., Athens, Ohio 45701, U.S.A.

ORGANSKI, A(bramo) F(imo) K(enneth). American, b. 1923. Demography, International relations/Current affairs, Military/Defence. Prof. of Political Science since 1965, and Prog. Dir., Center for Political Studies, Inst. for Social Research, since 1970, Univ. of Michigan, Ann Arbor. Prof., Brooklyn Coll., City Coll. of New York, 1960–64; Visiting Assoc Prof, Columbia Univ., 1961; Visiting Prof., Fletcher Sch. of Law and Diplomacy, Tufts and Harvard Univs., 1963–67. *Publs:* World Politics, 1958, 1968; (with K. Organski) Population and World Power, 1961; The Stages of Political Development, 1965; (with J. Kugler) The War Ledger, 1980; (with J. Kugler, V. Cohen and T. Johnson) Births, Deaths and Taxes: The Demographic and Political Transitions, 1984; The $36 Billion Bargain: Why Does the U.S. Give Aid to Israel?, 1989. Add: Inst. for Social Research, Room 4046, Ann Arbor, Mich. 48106, U.S.A.

ORGEL, Doris. Also writes as Doris Adelberg. American, b. 1929. Children's fiction, Children's non-fiction. *Publs:* Dwarf Long-Nose, 1960; The Tale of Gockel, Hinkel, and Gackeliah, 1961; Schoolmaster Whackwell's Wonderful Sons, 1962; (as Doris Adelberg) Grandma's Holidays, 1963; Sarah's Room, 1963; (as Doris Adelberg) Lizzie's Twins, 1964; The Heart of Stone, 1964; Cindy's Snowdrops, 1966; The Goodbyes of Magnus Marmalade, 1966; The Story of Lohengrin, 1966; Cindy's Sad and Happy Tree, 1967; In a Forgotten Place, 1967; Whose Turtle?, 1968; On the Sand Dune, 1968; Phoebe and the Prince, 1969; Merry, Rose, and Christmas-Tree June, 1969; Next Door to Xanadu, 1969; A Monkey's Uncle, 1969; The Uproar, 1970; The Mulberry Music, 1971; Baron Munchausen, 1971; The Child from Far Away, 1971; Little John, 1972; Bartholomew, We Love You!, 1973; A Certain Magic, 1976; Merry, Merry FIBruary, 1977; The Devil in Vienna, 1978; Risking Love, 1984; My War with Mrs. Galloway, 1985; Whiskers Once and Always, 1986; Midnight Soup and a Witch's Hat, 1987. Add: c/o Writers House, 21 W. 26th St., New York, N.Y. 10010, U.S.A.

ORLANS, Harold. American, b. 1921. Education. Staff member, National Science Foundn., 1954–59; Sr. Fellow, Brookings Instn., 1960–73; Sr. Research Assoc., National Academy of Public Admin., Washington, D.C., 1973–83; Consultant, Gallaudet Research Inst., 1983–84; Special Asst., U.S. Commn. on Civil Rights, 1984–86. *Publs:* Stevenage (Utopia Ltd.), 1952; The Effects of Federal Programs on Higher Education, 1962; Contracting for Atoms, 1967; (ed.) Science Policy and the University, 1968; The Nonprofit Research Institute, 1972; Contracting for Knowledge, 1973; Private Accreditation and Public Eligibility, 1975; (with others) GI Course Approvals, 1979; (ed.) Nonprofit Organizations, 1980; (ed.) Human Services Coordination, 1982; (ed.) Adjustment to Adult Hearing Loss, 1985. Add: 3314 Brooklawn Terr., Chevy Chase, Md. 20815, U.S.A.

ORMEROD, Roger. British. Mystery/Crime/Suspense. *Publs:* Time to Kill, 1974; The Silence of the Night, 1974; Full Fury, 1975; A Spoonful of Luger, 1975; Sealed with a Loving Kill, 1976; The Colour of Fear, 1976; A Glimpse of Death, 1976; Too Late for the Funeral, 1977; This Murder Come to Mind, 1977; A Dip into Murder, 1978; The Weight of Evidence, 1978; The Bright Face of Danger, 1979; The Amnesia Trap, 1979; Cart Before the Hearse, 1979; More Dead than Alive, 1980; Double Take, 1980; One Breathless Hour, 1981; Face Value, 1983; Seeing Red, 1984; The Hanging Doll Murder, 1984; Dead Ringer, 1985; Still Life with Pistol, 1986; A Death to Remember, 1986; An Alibi Too Soon, 1987; The Second Jeopardy, 1987; An Open Window, 1988; By Death Possessed, 1988; Guilt on the Lily, 1989. Add: c/o Constable, 10 Orange St., London WC2H 7EG, England.

ORMOND, John. British, b. 1923. Poetry. BBC Documentary Film-Maker, Cardiff, since 1957 (TV News Asst., 1955–57). Staff Writer, Picture Post, London, 1945–49; Sub-Ed., South Wales Evening Post, Swansea, 1949–55. *Publs:* (with James Kirkup and John Bayliss) Indications, 1942; Requiem and Celebration, 1969; Definition of a Waterfall, 1973; (with Emyr Humphreys and John Tripp) Penguin Modern Poets, 1979; In Place of Empty Heaven: The Poetry of Wallace Stevens (lecture), 1983; Selected Poems, 1987. Add: 15 Conway Rd., Cardiff, Wales.

ORMONDROYD, Edward. American, b. 1925. Children's fiction. Retired Technical Services Librarian, Finger Lakes Library System, Ithaca, N.Y. Has worked as a merchant seaman, bookstore clerk, paper factory machine operator. *Publs:* David and the Phoenix, 1957; The Tale of Alain, 1960; Time at the Top, 1963; Jonathan Frederick Aloysius Brown (verse), 1964; Theodore, 1966; Michael, The Upstairs Dog, 1967; Broderick, 1969; Theodore's Rival, 1971; Castaways on Long Ago, 1973; Imagination Greene, 1973; All in Good Time, 1975; Johnny Castleseed, 1985. Add: 425 Butternut Dr., Newfield, N.Y. 14867, U.S.A.

ORMSBEE, David. *See* **LONGSTREET,** Stephen.

ORMSBY, Frank. Irish, b. 1947. Poetry. Ed., Honest Ulsterman mag., Belfast, since 1969; English teacher, Royal Belfast Academical Instn., since 1971. *Publs:* Ripe for Company, 1971; Business as Usual, 1973; A Store of Candles, 1977; Being Walked by a Dog, 1978; (ed.) Poets from the North of Ireland, 1979; A Northern Spring, 1986; (ed.) Northern Windows, 1987. Add: 70 Eglantine Ave., Belfast BT9 6DY, Northern Ireland.

ORNSTEIN, Robert. American, b. 1925. Plays/Screenplays, Literature. Oviatt Prof. of English, Case Western Reserve Univ., Cleveland, since 1974 (Chmn., Dept. of English, 1966–68; Prof., 1966–74). Pres., Shakespeare Assn. of America, 1977. *Publs:* The Moral Vision of Jacobean Tragedy, 1960; (ed.) Discussion of Shakespeare's Problem Comedies, 1961; (ed. with H. Spencer) Elizabethan and Jacobean Tragedy, 1964; (ed. with H. Spencer) Elizabethan and Jacobean Comedy, 1964; A Kingdom for a Stage: The Achievement of Shakespeare's History Plays, 1972; A Poet's World (film script), 1973; Sidewalks and Similes (film script), 1973; Dead Ends and New Dreams (film script), 1973; Harpsichord Building in America (film script), 1977; The Staging of Shakespeare (film script), 1977; The Poetry of Robert Frost (film script), 1977; Multimind, 1986; Shakespeare's Comedies, 1986. Add: 3122 Woodbury Rd., Cleveland, Ohio 44120, U.S.A.

O'ROURKE, Frank. Also writes as Kevin Connor, Frank O'Malley, and Patrick O'Malley. American, b. 1916. Novels/Short stories, Mystery/Crime/Suspense, Westerns/Adventure. *Publs:* "E" Company, 1945; Flashing Spikes, 1948; Action at Three Peaks, 1948; Thunder on the Buckhorn, 1949; The Team, 1949; (as Frank O'Malley) The Best Go First, 1950; Bonus Rookie, 1950; The Greatest Victory and Other Baseball Stories, 1950; Blackwater, 1950; The Gun, 1951, in U.S. paperback as Warbonnet Law, 1952; The Football Gravy Train, 1951; Never Come Back, 1952; Nine Good Men, 1952; Concannon, 1952, in U.K. as by Frank O'Malley, 1956; The Heavenly World Series and Other Baseball Stories, 1952; Gold under Skull Peak, 1952; Gunsmoke over Big Muddy, 1952; Violence at Sundown, 1953; Latigo, 1953; Gun Hand, 1953; Ride West (short stories), 1953; The Catcher, and The Manager: Two Baseball Fables, 1953; Thunder in the Sun, 1954; High Vengeance, 1954; High Dive, 1954; The Big Fifty, 1955; Dakota Rifle, 1955; Car Deal!, 1955; The Last Round, 1956; The Diamond Hitch, 1956; Hard Men (short stories), 1956; Battle Royal, 1956; The Last Chance, 1956; Segundo, 1956; The Man Who Found His Way, 1957; Legend in the Dust, 1957; The Bravados, 1957; A Texan Came Riding, 1958; The Last Ride, 1958; The Far Mountains, 1959; Ambuscade, 1959; Desperate Rider, 1959; Violent Country, 1959; The Bride Stealer, 1960; Window in the Dark, 1960; The Springtime Fancy, 1961; The Great Bank Robbery, 1961; (as Patrick O'Malley) The Affair of the Red Mosaic (Swan Lake, Jolie Madame, Chief Strongheart, John Donne, Blue Pig, Bumbling Briton), 7 vols., 1961–65; Gunlaw Hill, 1961; Bandoleer Crossing, 1961; (as Kevin Connor) New Departure, 1962; The Bright Morning, 1963; A Private Anger, and Flight and Pursuit, 1963; Instant Gold, 1964; A Mule for the Marquesa, 1964, in U.K. as The Professionals, 1967; The Duchess Says No, 1965; P's Progress, 1966; The Swift Runner, 1969; The Abduction of Virginia Lee, 1970; The Shotgun Man, 1976; Badger, 1977. Add: c/o Carlson and Nichols, 311 E. 50th St., 5H, New York, N.Y. 10022, U.S.A.

O'ROURKE, William. American, b. 1945. Novels/Short stories, Civil liberties/Human rights, Social commentary/phenomena. Assoc. Prof., Univ. of Notre Dame, Ind., since 1981. Asst. Prof., Rutgers Univ., Newark, 1975–78; Asst. Prof., Mt. Holyoke Coll., Hadley, Mass., 1978–81. *Publs:* The Harrisburg 7 and the New Catholic Left, 1972; The Meekness of Isaac (novel), 1974; On the Job: Fiction about Work, 1977; Idle Hands (novel), 1981; Criminal Tendencies (novel), 1987. Add:

Dept. of English, Univ. of Notre Dame, Notre Dame, Ind. 46556, U.S.A.

ORR, Clyde. American, b. 1921. Earth sciences, Engineering/Technology. Prof. of Chemical Engineering, Georgia Inst. of Technology, Atlanta, retired (joined faculty, 1948). *Publs:* (with J.M. Dalla Valle) Fine Particle Measurement, 1959; Between Earth and Space, 1959; Particulate Technology, 1966; (ed.) Filtration, 2 vols., 1977–79. Add: 5091 Hidden Branches Circle, Dunwoody, Ga. 30338, U.S.A.

ORR, Gregory (Simpson). American, b. 1947. Poetry, Literature. Assoc. Prof. of English, Univ. of Virginia, Charlottesville, since 1980 (Asst. Prof., 1975–80). Poetry Consultant, Virginia Quarterly Review, Charlottesville, since 1976. *Publs:* Burning the Empty Nests, 1973; Gathering the Bones Together, 1975; Salt Wings, 1980; The Red House, 1980; Stanley Kunitz: An Introduction to the Poetry, 1985; We Must Make a Kingdom, 1986; New and Selected Poems, 1987. Add: Dept. of English, Univ. of Virginia, Charlottesville, Va. 22903, U.S.A.

ORR, Robert Richmond. New Zealander, b. 1930. Philosophy. Sr. Lectr. in Govt., London Sch. of Economics, since 1964. *Publs:* Reason and Authority, 1966. Add: London Sch. of Economics, Aldwych, London WC2, England.

ORTIZ, Alfonso A. American, b. 1939. Anthropology/Ethnology. Prof. of Anthropology, Univ. of New Mexico, Albuquerque, since 1974. Chmn., National Advisory Council, Center for the History of the American Indian, Newberry Library, Chicago, since 1978. Asst. Prof., 1967–70, and Assoc. Prof. of Anthropology, 1970–74, Princeton Univ., New Jersey. *Publs:* The Tewa World: Space, Time, Being and Becoming in a Pueblo Society, 1969; (ed.) New Perspectives on the Pueblos, 1972; (ed.) Handbook of North American Indians, vol. 9, 1980; (co-compiler) To Carry Forth the Vine: An Anthology of Traditional Native North American Poetry, 1981; American Indian Myths and Legends, 1984; Comparative Study of Infant Mortality in the Texas-Mexico Border Area of Loredo-Nuevo Laredo, 1984. Add: 830 E. Zia Rd., Santa Fe, N. Mex. 87505, U.S.A.

ORTIZ, Simon J. American, b. 1941. Short stories, Poetry. Consultant Ed., Pueblo of Acoma Press, since 1982. Public Relations Consultant, Rough Rock Demonstration Sch., Arizona, 1969–70, and National Indian Youth Council, Albuquerque, 1970–73; teacher, San Diego State Univ., California, 1974, Inst. of American Arts, Santa Fe, New Mexico, 1974, Navajo Community Coll., Tsaile, Ariz., 1975–77, and Coll. of Marin, Kentfield, Calif., 1976–79. Ed., Quetzal, Chinle, Ariz., 1970–73. *Publs:* Naked in the Wind, 1970; Going for the Rain, 1976; A Good Journey, 1977; The People Shall Continue 1977; Howbah Indians (short stories), 1978; Song, Poetry, Language, 1978; Fightback, 1980; From Sand Creek, 1981; A Poem Is a Journey, 1981; Blue and Red (for children), 1982; The Importance of Childhood, 1982; Fightin': New and Collected Stories, 1983. Add: 308 Sesame S.W., Albuquerque, N. Mex. 87105, U.S.A.

OSBORN, Eric Francis. Australian, b. 1922. Classics, Philosophy, Theology/Religion. Prof. of New Testament and Early Christianity, United Faculty of Theology, Queen's Coll., Univ. of Melbourne, 1958–87. Ed., Australian Biblical Review, 1959–85. *Publs:* The Philosophy of Clement of Alexandria, 1957; Word and History, 1967; The Bible: The Word in the World, 1969; Justin Martyr, 1973; Ethical Patterns in Early Christian Thought, 1976; The Beginning of Christian Philosophy, 1981; La Morale dans la Pensée Chrétienne Primitive, 1985; Anfänge christlichen Denkens, 1986. Add: Queen's Coll., Univ. of Melbourne, Parkville, Vic. 3052, Australia.

OSBORN, Ronald Edwin. American, b. 1917. Theology/Religion, Biography. Prof., American Church History, Sch. of Theology at Claremont, Calif., since 1973 (Visiting Prof., 1970–72). Prof., Christian Theological Seminary, Indianapolis, 1950–73 (Dean, 1959–70). *Publs:* Ely Vaughn Zollars, 1947; The Spirit of American Christianity, 1958; (ed. with W.B. Blakemore) The Reformation of Tradition, 1963; A Church for These Times, 1965; In Christ's Place: Christian Ministry in Today's World, 1967; Experiment in Liberty, 1978; The Faith We Affirm, 1979; (ed.) Seeking God's Peace in a Nuclear Age, 1985. Add: c/o C.B.P., P.O. Box 179, St Louis, Mo. 63166, U.S.A.

OSBORNE, Charles. British, b. 1927. Poetry, Literature, Music. Drama Critic, Daily Telegraph, London; Opera Critic, Jewish Chronicle, London. Member of the Editorial Bds., Opera and Annual Register. Asst. Ed., London Mag., 1958–66; Asst. Dir., 1966–71, and Literature Dir., 1971–86, Arts Council of Great Britain. *Publs:* (ed.) Australian

Dir., 1971–86, Arts Council of Great Britain. *Publs:* (ed.) Australian Stories of Today, 1961; (ed.) Opera 66, 1966; (with Brigid Brophy and Michael Levey) Fifty Works of English Literature We Could Do Without, 1967; Kafka, 1967; Swansong, 1968; The Complete Operas of Verdi, 1969; Ned Kelly, 1970; (ed.) Australia and New Zealand, 1970; (ed. and trans.) Letters of Verdi, 1971; The Concert Song Companion, 1974; Wagner and His World, 1977; (ed.) The Dictionary of Composers, 1977; Verdi, 1978; The Complete Operas of Mozart, 1978; W.H. Auden: The Life of a Poet, 1979; The Complete Operas of Puccini, 1981; The Round Dance and Other Plays, by Schnitzler (trans.), 1982; The Life and Crimes of Agatha Christie, 1982; The World Theatre of Wagner, 1982; The Dictionary of Opera, 1983; Letter to W.H. Auden and Other Poems, 1984; Schubert and His Vienna, 1985; Giving It Away, 1986; Verdi: A Life in the Theatre, 1987; The Complete Operas of Richard Strauss, 1988. Add: c/o Aitken and Stone Ltd., 29 Fernshaw Rd., London SW10 0TG, England.

OSBORNE, David. *See* **SILVERBERG, Robert.**

OSBORNE, John (James). British, b. 1929. Plays/Screenplays, Autobiography/Memoirs/Personal. *Publs:* Look Back in Anger, 1956; The Entertainer 1958, screenplay 1960; (with A. Creighton) Epitaph for George Dillon, 1957; The World of Paul Slickey, 1959; A Subject for Scandal and Concern, 1961; Luther, 1961; Plays for England: The Blood of the Bambers, Under Plain Cover, 1963; Tom Jones (screenplay), 1964; Inadmissible Evidence, 1965; (adaptor) A Bond Honoured, 1966; A Patriot for Me, 1966; Time Present, and The Hotel in Amsterdam, 1968; The Right Prospectus: A Play for Television, 1969; Very Like a Whale, 1970; West of Suez, 1971; (adaptor) Hedda Gabler, 1972; The Gift of Friendship, 1972; A Sense of Detachment, 1972; A Place Calling Itself Rome, 1973; (adaptor) The Picture of Dorian Gray, 1973; The End of Me Old Cigar, 1975; Watch It Come Down, 1975; You're Not Watching Me, Mummy, and Try a Little Tenderness, 1978; A Better Class of Person (autobiography), 1981; Too Young to Fight, Too Old to Forget, 1985; A Better Class of Person, and God Rot Turnbridge Wells, 1985; (adaptor) The Father, 1988. Add: c/o Fraser and Dunlop, The Chambers, Chelsea Harbour, Lots Rd., London SW10 0XF, England.

OSBORNE, Milton (Edgeworth). Australian, b. 1936. Area studies, History, Politics/Government. Sr. Research Fellow, Dept. of Intnl. Relations, Australian National Univ., Canberra, since 1979. Member, Australian Foreign Service, 1958–62; Temporary Lectr., Univ. of Sydney, 1962–63; Sr. Lectr., then Assoc. Prof. of History, Monash Univ., Melbourne, 1967–71; Assoc. Prof. of History, The American Univ., Washington, D.C.., 1972–74; Dir., British Inst. in South-East Asia, Singapore, 1975–79. *Publs:* The French Presence in Cochinchina and Cambodia: Rule and Response 1859-1905, 1969; Region of Revolt: Focus on Southeast Asia, 1970, 1971; Politics and Power: The Sihanouk Years, 1973; River Road to China: The Mekong River Expedition 1866-73, 1975; Southeast Asia: An Introductory History, 1979, 3rd ed. 1985; Before Kampuchea: Preludes to Tragedy, 1979; (ed.) Ho Chi Minh, 1982. Add: Dept. of Intnl. Relations, Australian National Univ., P.O. Box 4, Canberra, A.C.T. 2600, Australia.

OSBOURNE, Ivor (Livingstone). Jamaican, b. 1951. Novels/Short stories. Managing Dir., Antilles Book Co. and Antilles Media Productions Ltd., Kingston, since 1977. *Publs:* The Mercenary, 1977; The Mango Season, 1979; The Prodigal, 1985. Add: c/o Akira Press, P.O. Box 409, London E2 7EU, England.

OSGOOD, Charles E(gerton). American, b. 1916. Language/Linguistics, Psychology. Prof. of Psychology and Communications since 1952, and Dir. of the Center for Advanced Study since 1965, Univ. of Illinois, Urbana (Assoc. Prof., 1949–52; Dir. of the Institute of Communications Research, 1957–65). Asst. Prof. of Psychology, Univ. of Connecticut, Storrs, 1946–49. President, American Psychological Assn., 1961. *Publs:* Method and Theory in Experimental Psychology, 1953; (ed. with Thomas A. Sebeok) Psycholinguistics: A Survey of Theory and Research Problems, 1954; (with others) The Measurement of Meaning, 1957; (ed. with James G. Snider) Semantic Differential Technique: A Sourcebook, 1958; Graduated Reciprocation in Tension-Reduction: A Key to Initiative in Foreign Policy, 1960; The Human Side of Policy in a Nuclear Age, 1961; (with Kellogg V. Wilson) Some Terms and Associated Measures for Talking about Human Communications, 1961; Studies on the Generality of Affective Meaning Systems, 1961; An Alternative to War or Surrender, 1962; (ed. with M.S. Miron) Approaches to the Study of Aphasia, 1963; Perspective in Foreign Policy, 1966; Conservative Words and Radical Sentences in the Semantics of International Politics, 1968; Interpersonal Verbs and Interpersonal Behavior, 1968; (with others) Cross-Cultural Universals of Affective Meaning, 1975; Focus on Mean-

ing, 1980; Lectures on Language Performance, 1980. Add: 304 E. Mumford Drive, Urbana, Ill. 61801, U.S.A.

O'SHEA, Sean. *See* **TRALINS, S. Robert.**

O'SHEA, Pat (née Shiels). Irish, b. 1931. Children's fiction. *Publs:* The Hounds of the Morrigan, 1985; Finn MacCool and the Small Men of Deeds (retelling), 1987. Add: c/o Oxford Univ. Press, Walton St., Oxford OX2 6DP, England.

OSOFISAN, Femi. (Babafemi Adeyemi Osofisan). Nigerian, b. 1946. Novels, Plays/Screenplays, Literature. Faculty member, Univ. of Ibadan, since 1973; Ed., Opinfa: Ibadan Poetry Chapbooks. Founding member of bd., Guardian, Ibadan, 1984–85. *Publs:* plays—A Restless Run of Locusts, 1975; The Chattering and the Song, 1977; Who's Afraid of Solarin?, 1978; Once upon Four Robbers, 1972; Morountodun and Other Plays, 1982; Farewell to a Cannibal Rage, 1986; Two Short Plays, 1986; Midnight Hotel, 1986; Esu and the Vagabond Minstrels, 1987; novel— Kolera Kolej, 1975; other—Beyond Translation, 1986; The Orality of Prose: A Comparatist Look at the Works of Rabelais, Joyce and Tutuola, 1986. Add: Dept. of Theatre Arts, Univ. of Ibadan, Ibadan, Nigeria.

OSTERBROCK, Donald E. American, b. 1924. Astronomy. Prof. of Astronomy, Univ. of California, Santa Cruz, since 1973 (Dir. of Lick Observatory, 1973–81). Instructor, 1953–55, and Asst. Prof. of Astronomy, 1955–58, California Inst. of Technology, Pasadena; Asst. Prof., 1958–59, Assoc. Prof., 1959–61, Prof. of Astronomy, 1961–73, and Chmn. of the Dept. of Astronomy, 1969–72, Univ. of Wisconsin, Madison. Councillor, 1970–73, Vice-Pres., 1975–77, and Pres., 1988–90, American Astronomical Soc.; Chmn., 1971–74, Astronomy Section, and Secty., 1980–83, and Chmn., 1983–85, Class of Physical and Mathematical Sciences, National Academy of Sciences; Letters Ed., Astrophysical Journal, 1971–73. *Publs:* (ed. with C. O'Dell) Planetary Nebulae, 1968; Astrophysics of Gaseous Nebulae, 1974; James E. Keeler, Pioneer American Astrophysicist, and the Early Development of American Astrophysics, 1984; (with J.R. Gustafson and W.J. Shiloh Unruh) Eye on the Sky: Lick Observatory's First Century, 1988; (ed. with P.H. Raven) Origins and Extinctions, 1988; Astrophysics of Gaseous Nebulae and Active Galactic Nuclei, 1989; (ed. with J.S. Miller) Active Galatic Nuclei, 1989. Add: 120 Woodside Ave., Santa Cruz, Calif. 95060, U.S.A.

O'SULLIVAN, Timothy. British, b. 1945. Biography. Part-Time Ed., Routledge and Kegan Paul, publrs., London, 1973–80. *Publs:* Thomas Hardy: An Illustrated Biography, 1975; Julian Hodge: A Biography, 1981; Royal Marriages (biographical sketches), 1981. Add: 12 Buccleuch Rd., Datchet, Berks. SL3 9BP, England.

O'SULLIVAN, Vincent (Gerard). New Zealander, b. 1937. Novels/Short stories, Plays/Screenplays, Poetry, Literature. Sr. Lectr., Waikato Univ., Hamilton. Formerly, Lectr., Victoria Univ., Wellington. Ed., Comment, Wellington, 1963–66. *Publs:* Our Burning Time, 1965; Revenants, 1969; (ed.) An Anthology of Twenieth-Century New Zealand Poetry, 1970; Bearings, 1973; Miracle: A Romance (novel), 1976; James K. Baxter, 1976; Butcher & Co., 1977; Brother Jonathan, Brother Kafka, 1979; Dandy Edison for Lunch, 1981; (ed.) Katherine Mansfield's The Aloe, 1982; The Butcher Papers, 1982; The Rose Ballroom, 1982; (ed.) New Zealand Writing since 1945, 1983; (ed. with Margaret Scott) The Collected Letters of Katherine Mansfield, vol. I, 1903-1917, 1984, vol. 2, 1918-1919, 1986; Shuriken (play), 1984; The Pilate Tapes, 1987. Add: c/o John McIndoe Ltd., 51 Crawford St., Dunedin, New Zealand.

O'TOOLE, Rex. *See* **TRALINS, S. Robert.**

OTTENBERG, Simon. American, b. 1923. Anthropology/Ethnology. Prof. of Anthropology, Univ. of Washington, Seattle, since 1955. *Publs:* (ed. with Phoebe V. Ottenberg) Cultures and Societies of Africa, 1960; Double Descent in an African Society: The Afikpo Village Group, 1968; Leadership and Authority in an African Society: The Afikpo Village Group, 1971; Anthropology and African Aesthetics, 1972; Masked Rituals of Afikpo, 1975; (ed.) African Religious Groups and Beliefs, 1982; Boyhood Rituals in an African Society, 1989. Add: Dept. of Anthropology, Univ. of Washington, Seattle, Wash. 98195, U.S.A.

OVARD, Glen F. American, b. 1928. Children's fiction, Poetry, Administration/Management, Economics, Education. Prof. of Education, Brigham Young Univ., Provo, since 1963 (Asst. Prof. and Assoc. Prof., 1959–63; Coordinator, Education Experiment Progs., 1964–69). Curriculum Consultant and Sr. High Sch. Supvr., Alpine Sch. District, American Fork, Utah, 1963–64; Prog. Dir., Prog. in Individualizing Instruction, Rocky Mountain Educational Lab., Denver, 1966–67; Education Consultant, Progs. on Individualizing Learning, Kettering Foundn., IDEA Materials Center, Dayton, Ohio, 1967–70; Pres., Individualized Instruction and Learning—World Wide Assn., 1969–78; Consultant, Hawaii State Dept. of Education, 1970–71; Visiting Prof., Monash Univ., Melbourne, 1977; Visiting Scholar, Univ. of London, 1983. *Publs:* (ed.) On Planning Academic Classrooms: A Guide for Secondary School Planners, 1962; Administration of the Changing Secondary School, 1966; Change and Secondary School Administration: A Book of Readings, 1968; (with J. Kenneth Davies) Economics in the American System, 1970; (with Philip Kapfer) Preparing and Using Individualized Learning Packages for Ungraded, Continuous Progress Education, 1971; Talofa Alii, 1979. Add: 2948 N. Chippewa Way, Provo, Utah 84604, U.S.A.

OVEREND, William George. British, b. 1921. Chemistry. Ed., Chemical Science Texts Series, English Univs. Press., since 1960. Asst. Lectr. in Chemistry, University Coll., Nottingham, 1946–47; Research Chemist, Dunlop Rubber Co. Ltd., and British Rubber Producers' Research Assn., 1947–49; Hon. Research Fellow, 1947–49, and Lectr. in Chemistry, 1949–55, Univ. of Birmingham; Reader in Organic Chemistry, 1955–57, Prof. of Chemistry, 1957–87, and Master of Birkbeck Coll., 1979–87, Univ. of London. *Publs:* The Use of Tracer Elements in Biology, 1951; (ed.) Programmes in Organic Chemistry, vols. I-VIII. Add: The Retreat, Nightingales Lane, Chalfont St. Giles, Bucks. HP8 4SR, England.

OVERHOLSER, Wayne D. Also writes as John S. Daniels, Lee Leighton, Mark Morgan, Wayne Roberts, Dan J. Stevens, and Joseph Wayne. American, b. 1906. Westerns/Adventure, History. Freelance writer since 1945. Former teacher and high sch. principal. Member, Bd. of Dirs., Western Writers of America, 1953–54, 1957–58. *Publs:* Buckaroo's Code, 1947; West of the Rimrock, 1949; Gun Crazy, 1950; Draw or Drag, 1950; Steel to the South, 1951; Fabulous Gunman, 1952; (as Mark Morgan) Fighting Man, 1953; Valley of Guns, 1953; The Violent Land, 1954; Tough Hand, 1954; (with William M. Raine) High Grass Valley, 1955; A Long Shadow, 1955; Gunlock, 1956; (as Wayne Roberts, with Robert G. Athearn) Silent River, 1956; The Lone Deputy, 1957; Desperate Man, 1957; Hearn's Valley, 1958; War in Sandoval County, 1960; The Judas Gun, 1960; Standoff at the River, 1961; The Killer Marshal, 1961; The Bitter Night, 1961; The Trial of Billy Peale, 1962; A Gun for Johnny Deere, 1963; To the Far Mountains, 1963; Day of Judgment, 1965, in U.K. as Colorado Incident, 1966; Brand 99, 1966; Ride into Danger, 1967; Summer of the Sioux, 1967; North to Deadwood, 1968; Buckskin Man, 1969; (with Lewis B. Patten) The Meeker Massacre (nonfiction), 1969; The Long Trail North, 1972; The Noose, 1972; Sun on the Wall, 1973; Red Snow, 1976; The Mason County War, 1976; The Dry Gulcher, 1977; The Trouble Kid, 1978; The Diablo Ghost, 1978; The Cattle Queen Feud, 1979; Nightmare in Broken Bow, 1980; Revenge in Crow City, 1980; Danger Patrol, 1982; Best Western Stories, 1984; as Dan J. Stevens—Oregon Trunk, 1950; Wild Horse Range, 1951; Blood Money, 1956; Hangman's Mesa, 1959; Gun Trap at Bright Water, 1963; Land Beyond the Law, 1964; Stage to Durango, 1977; Deadline, 1966; Killer from Owl Creek, 1967; Stranger in Rampart, 1968; The Dry Fork Incident, 1969; Hunter's Moon, 1973; as Joseph Wayne—The Sweet and Bitter Land, 1950, in U.S. paperback as Gunplay Valley, 1951; The Snake Stomper, 1951; By Gun and Spur, 1952, as The Colt Slinger, 1954; The Long Wind, 1953, in U.K. as Guns at Lariat, 1955; Bunch Grass, 1954; The Return of the Kid, 1955; (with Lewis B. Patten) Showdown at Stony Creek, 1957; Pistol Johnny, 1960; (with Lewis B. Patten) The Gun and the Law, 1961; Land of Promises, 1962; The Bad Man, 1962; Proud Journey, 1963; Deadman Junction, 1964; Red Is the Valley, 1967; as John S. Daniels—Gunflame, 1952; The Nester, 1953; The Land Grabbers, 1955; The Man from Yesterday, 1957; Smoke of the Gun, 1958; Ute Country, 1959; The Gunfighters, 1961; The Crossing, 1963; Trail's End, 1964; The Hunted, 1965; War Party, 1966; The Day the Killers Came, 1968; The Three Sons of Adam Jones, 1969; as Lee Leighton—Law Man, 1953; Beyond the Pass, 1956; (with Lewis B. Patten) Tomahawk, 1958; (with Chad Merriman) Colorado Gold, 1958; Fight for the Valley, 1960; Gut Shot, 1962; Big Ugly, 1966; Hanging at Pulpit Rock, 1967; Bitter Journey, 1969; Killer Gun, 1969; You'll Never Hang Me, 1971; Cassidy, 1973; Greenhorn Marshal, 1974. Add: 500 Mohawk Dr., Apt. 406, Boulder, Colo. 80303, U.S.A.

OVERTON, Jenny (Margaret Mary). British, b. 1942. Children's fiction. Freelance publishing ed. *Publs:* Creed Country, 1969; The Thirteen Days of Christmas, 1972; The Nightwatch Winter, 1973; The Ship from Simnel Street, 1985. Add: c/o Crest Hill, Peaslake, Guildford, Surrey, England.

OVERY, Paul (Vivian). British, b. 1940. Architecture, Art, Design. Art Critic, The Listener, London, 1966–68, The Financial Times, London, 1968–70, and The Times, London, 1973–78; Literary Ed., New Society, London, 1970–71. *Publs:* Edouard Manet, 1967; De Stijl, 1969; Kandinsky: The Language of the Eye, 1969; Paul Neagu: A Generative Context, 1981; (co-author) The Rietveld Schröder House, 1988. Add: 92 South Hill Park, London NW3, England.

OWEN, Alun (Davies). British, b. 1925. Plays/Screenplays. Worked as stage mgr., dir. and actor, 1942–59. *Publs:* The Rough and Ready Lot, 1960; Three TV Plays, 1961; Progress to the Park, 1962; Anatomy of a T.V. Play: The Rose Affair, 1962; Dare to Be a Daniel, 1965; A Little Winter Love, 1965; Shelter, 1968; George's Room, 1968; Norma, 1970; Doreen 1971; The Wake, 1972; The Male of the Species, 1972; A Hard Day's Night, 1972; Passing Through, 1977. Add: c/o Blake Friedmann Agency, 37-41 Gower St., London WC1E 6HH, England.

OWEN, Charles. British, b. 1915. Administration/Management, History, Military/Defence, Travel/Exploration. Mgmt. consultant. *Publs:* Independent Traveller, 1966; Britons Abroad, 1968; The Maltese Islands, 1969; The Opaque Society, 1969; (contrib.) Great Trains, 1974; No More Heroes, 1975; The Grand Days of Travel, 1979; Just Across the Channel, 1982. Add: 25 Montagu St., London W1H 1TB, England.

OWEN, David (Anthony Llewellyn). British, b. 1938. Medicine/Health, Politics/Government. Co-Founder, Social Democratic Party, 1981 and Leader, 1983–87. Physician; Member of Parliament (U.K.) for the Devonport div. of Plymouth since 1974 (Member for the Sutton div. of Plymouth, 1966–74; Parliamentary Under-Secty. of State for Defence for the Royal Navy, 1968–70; Parliamentary Under-Secty. of State for Health, 1974; Minister of State, Dept. of Health and Social Security, 1975–77; Secty. of State for Foreign and Commonwealth Affairs, 1977–79). Research Fellow, Medical Unit, St. Thomas's Hosp., London, 1966–67. *Publs:* A Unified Health Service, 1968; The Politics of Defence, 1972; In Sickness and in Health, 1976; Human Rights, 1978; Face the Future, 1981; A Future that Will Work, 1984; A United Kingdom, 1986; Our NHS, 1988. Add: 78 Narrow St., Limehouse, London E14, England.

OWEN, Derwyn (Randulph Grier). Canadian, b. 1914. Theology/Religion. Prof. Emeritus of Religious Studies, Trinity Coll., Univ. of Toronto (Provost and Vice-Chancellor, 1957–72). *Publs:* Scientism, Man and Religion, 1952; Body and Soul, 1956. Add: 350 Lonsdale Ave., Toronto, Ont. M5P 1R6, Canada.

OWEN, Douglas David Roy. British, b. 1922. Literature, Mythology/Folklore, Translations. Emeritus Prof. of French, Univ. of St. Andrews (joined faculty, 1951). Gen. Ed., Forum for Modern Language Studies, since 1965. *Publs:* (ed. with R.C. Johnston) Fabliaux, 1957; The Evolution of the Grail Legend, 1968; The Vision of Hell, 1970; (ed.) Arthurian Romance: Seven Essays, 1970; (trans.) The Song of Roland, 1972; (ed. with R.C. Johnston) Two Old French Gauvain Romances, 1972; The Legend of Roland, 1973; Noble Lovers, 1975; (trans.) Chrétien de Troyes: Arthurian Romances, 1987. Add: 7 West Acres, St. Andrews KY16 9UD, Scotland.

OWEN, (John) Gareth. British, b. 1936. Children's fiction, Poetry. Teacher, Downshall Secondary Modern Sch., Ilford, Essex, 1961–65; Lectr. and Sr. Lectr., Bordesley Coll. of Education, Birmingham, 1965–82; owner and mgr. of an independent record co., 1976–83. *Publs:* Nineteen Fragments, 1974; Salford Road, 1976; Song of the City, 1985; The Final Test, 1985; Bright Lights Blaze Out, 1986; The Man with Eyes like Windows, 1987; Douglas the Drummer, 1989; Ruby and the Dragon, 1989; Saving Grace, 1989. Add: c/o Rogers Coleridge and White, 20 Powis Mews, London W11 1JN, England.

OWEN, Roderic. British, b. 1921. Novels/Short stories, Plays/Screenplays, History, Travel/Exploration/Adventure, Biography. Company Dir., G.K. Sales (London) Ltd. *Publs:* The Desert Air Force, 1948; The Flesh Is Willing; (with Bridget Chetwynd) Love for Money (play); Where the Poor Are Happy; Tedder; Easier for a Camel; Green Heart of Heaven; Worse Than Wanton; Lepard & Smiths 1757-1957; The Golden Bubble; Away to Eden; Roddy Owen's Africa; (with Tristan de Vere Cole) Beautiful and Beloved, 1972; The Fate of Franklin, 1977; Great Explorers, 1979. Add: 22 Gilston Rd., London SW10 9SR, England.

OWEN, Warwick (Jack Burgoyne). New Zealander, b. 1916. Literature. Prof. of English, McMaster Univ., Hamilton, since 1965. Asst. Lectr., Lectr., and Sr. Lectr. in English, University Coll. of North Wales, Bangor, 1946–65. *Publs:* (ed.) Wordsworth's Preface to Lyrical Ballads,

1957; (ed.) Wordsworth and Coleridge: Lyrical Ballads 1798, 1967, 1969; Wordsworth as Critic, 1969, 1971; (ed. with J.W. Smyser) Prose Works of William Wordsworth, 3 vols., 1974; (ed.) Wordsworth's Literary Criticism, 1974; (ed.) William Wordsworth: The Fourteen-Book Prelude, 1985. Add: Dept. of English, McMaster Univ., Hamilton, Ont. L8S AL9, Canada.

OWENS, Joseph. Canadian, b. 1908. Philosophy. Roman Catholic priest since 1933; Prof. of Philosophy, Pontifical Inst. of Mediaeval Studies, Toronto, since 1960. Member, Editorial Bd., The Monist, since 1961, and Ancient Philosophy, since 1981. Parish Asst., St. Joseph's Church, Moose Jaw, Sask., 1934–35, St. Patrick's, Toronto, 1935–36, and Maria-Hilf Church, Tomslake, 1940–44; Instr. of Philosophy, St. Alphonsus Seminary, Woodstock, 1936–40, 1948–51, 1953; Instr. of Mediaeval Moral Doctrine, Accademia Alfonsiana, Rome, 1952–53. *Publs:* The Doctrine of Being in the Aristotelian Metaphysics, 1951, 3rd ed. 1978; St. Thomas and the Future of Metaphysics, 1957; A History of Ancient Western Philosophy, 1959; An Elementary Christian Metaphysics, 1963; An Interpretation of Existence, 1968; The Wisdom and Ideas of St. Thomas Aquinas, 1968; The Philosophical Tradition of St. Michael's College, Toronto, 1979; St. Thomas Aquinas on the Existence of God, ed. by John R. Catan, 1980; Aquinas on Being and Thing, 1981; Aristotle, ed. by John R. Catan, 1981; Human Destiny, 1985. Add: Pontifical Inst. of Mediaeval Studies, 59 Queen's Park Cres., Toronto, Ont. M5S 2C4, Canada.

OWENS, Rochelle. American, b. 1936. Short stories, Plays/ Screenplays, Poetry. Founding Member, New York Theatre Strategy. Distinguished Writer in Residence, Brown Univ., Providence, RI, 1989. *Publs:* Futz, 1961; Not Be Essence That Cannot Be (poetry), 1961; (co-author) Four Young Lady Poets, 1962; The Girl on the Garage Wall (short stories), 1962; The Obscenities of Reva Cigarnik (short stories), 1963; Salt and Core (poetry), 1968; Futz and What Came After, 1968; Futz (film), 1969; I Am the Babe of Joseph Stalin's Daughter (poetry), 1972; (ed.) Spontaneous Combustion: Eight New American Plays, 1972; The Karl Marx Play and Others, 1974; The Joe 82 Creation Poems, 1974; Poems, 1974; The Widow and the Colonel (play), 1977; Mountain Rites (play), 1978; The Joe Chronicles II, 1978; Shemuel (poetry), 1979; Chucky's Hunch (play), 1982; Who Do You Want, Peire Vidal (play), 1983; French Light (poetry), 1984; Constructs, 1985; W.C. Fields in French Light, 1986; How Much Paint Does the Painting Need (poetry), 1988. Add: 1401 Magnolia, Norman, Okla. 73069, U.S.A.

OXLEY, William. British, b. 1939. Poetry, Literature, Travel. Freelance writer. Articled clerk, Manchester, 1957–64; Chartered Accountant, Deloitte and Co., London, 1964–68, and Lazard Bros. and Co., London, 1968–76. *Publs:* The Dark Structures, 1967; New Workings, 1969; Passages from Time: Poems from a Life, 1971; The Icon Poems, 1972; Sixteen Days in Autumn (travel), 1972; Opera Vetera, 1973; Mirrors of the Sea, 1973; Eve Free, 1974; Mundane Shell, 1975; Superficies, 1976; The Exile, 1979; The Notebook of Hephaestus and Other Poems, 1981; (trans.) Poems of a Black Orpheus, 1981; The Synopthegms of a Prophet (aphorisms), 1981; The Idea and Its Imminence, 1982; Of Human Consciousness, 1982; The Cauldron of Inspiration, 1983; A Map of Time, 1984; The Triviad and Other Satires, 1984; The Inner Tapestry, 1985; Vitalism and Celebration (essays), 1987; The Mansands Trilogy, 1988; Mad Tom on Tower Hill, 1988. Add: 6 The Mount, Furzeham, Brixham, South Devon TQ5 8QY, England.

OZ, Amos. Israeli, b. 1939. Novels/Short stories, Historical/ Romance/Gothic. Formerly, Member of kibbutz, teacher and farmer, in Israel. *Publs:* Where the Jackals Howl, 1965; Elsewhere, Perhaps, 1966; My Michael, 1968; Unto Death, 1971; Touch the Water, Touch the Wind, 1973; The Hill of Evil Counsel, 1976; Soumchi, 1978; Under This Blazing Light, 1979; In the Land of Israel, 1983; A Perfect Peace, 1984; Black Box, 1987; To Know a Woman, 1989. Add: c/o Deborah Owen Ltd., 78 Narrow St., London E14, England.

OZICK, Cynthia. American, b. 1928. Novels/Short stories, Essays. *Publs:* Trust (novel), 1966; The Pagan Rabbi and Other Stories, 1971; Bloodshed and Three Novellas, 1976; Levitation: Five Fictions, 1981; The Cannibal Galaxy, 1983; Art & Ardor (essays), 1983; The Messiah of Stockholm, 1987; Metaphor & Memory (essays), 1989; The Shawl, 1989. Add: c/o Alfred A. Knopf Inc., 201 E. 50th Street, New York, N.Y. 10022, U.S.A.

OZMON, Howard. American, b. 1935. Philosophy. Prof. of Philosophy and Education, Virginia Commonwealth Univ., Richmond. Asst. Prof. of Education, Univ. of Virginia, Charlottesville, 1964–67; Prof. of Philosophy and Education, Chicago State Coll., 1967–70. *Publs:* The Philosophical Development of Educational Thought, 1963; The Philosophy of John Dewey, 1964; Challenging Ideas in Education, 1967; Twelve Great Philosophers, 1968; Utopias and Education, 1969; Contemporary Critics of Education, 1970; Dialogue in the Philosophy of Education, 1971; Kaltran, 1972; (with Sam Craver) Busing: A Moral Issue, 1972; Jennifer's Birthday Present, 1974; Philosophical Foundations of Education, 1976, 3rd ed. 1986. Add: Sch. of Education, Virginia Commonwealth Univ., Richmond, Va 23225, U.S.A.

P

PACE, Eric. American, b. 1936. Novels/Short stories, Mystery/Crime/Suspense. Reporter, New York Times, since 1973 (Reporter and Foreign Corresp., New York, Saigon, Cairo, Paris and Beirut, 1965–71). Reporter and Staff Foreign Corresp., Time and Life mags., New York, Bonn, Paris and Hong Kong, 1959–65. *Publs:* Saberless, 1969; Any War Will Do, 1973; Nightingale, 1979. Add: c/o New York Times, 229 W. 43rd St., New York, N.Y. 10036, U.S.A.

PACIFICO, Carl. American, b. 1921. Administration/Management, Marketing, Psychology. Mgmt. Consultant, Management Supplements, Columbia, Md., since 1966. *Publs:* Creative Thinking in Practice, 1967; Effective Profit Techniques for Managers, 1969; Performance Chemicals, 1971; Practical Industrial Management, 1980; Think Better, Feel Better, 1989. Add: 5121 W. Penfield Rd., Columbia, Md. 21045, U.S.A.

PACK, Robert. American, b. 1929. Children's fiction, Poetry, Literature. Ed., Discovery, NYC. Taught at Barnard Coll., NYC, 1957–64, and at Middlebury Coll., Vermont, 1964–78; Dir., Bread Loaf Writers Conference, 1973–78. *Publs:* The Irony of Joy, 1955; (ed. with D. Hall and L. Simpson) New Poets of England and America, 1957; Wallace Stevens: An Approach to His Poetry and Thought, 1958; A Stranger's Privilege, 1959; The Forgotten Secret, 1959; What Did You Do?, 1961; (ed. and trans. with M. Lelach) Mozart's Librettos, 1961; (ed. with D. Hall) New Poets of England and America: Second Selection, 1962; Guarded by Women, 1963; Selected Poems, 1964; How to Catch a Crocodile, 1964; (ed. with T. Driver) Poems of Doubt and Belief: An Anthology of Modern Religious Poetry, 1964; (ed. with M. Klein) Literature for Composition on the Theme of Innocence and Experience, 1966; (ed. with M. Klein) Short Stories: Classic, Modern, Contemporary, 1967; Home from the Cemetery, 1969; Nothing But Light, 1972; Keeping Watch, 1976; Waking to My Name: New and Selected Poems, 1980; Faces in a Single Tree: A Cycle of Monologues, 1984; Affirming Limits: Essays on Mortality, Choice and Poetic Form, 1985; Clayfield Rejoices, Clayfield Laments: A Sequence of Poems, 1986; Before It Vanishes: Poems, 1989. Add: c/o David R. Godine, Publisher, 300 Massachusetts Ave., Boston, Mass. 021151, U.S.A.

PACK, Roger A(mbrose). American, b. 1907. Classics. Prof. Emeritus of Greek and Latin, Univ. of Michigan, Ann Arbor, since 1975 (Instr., 1938–46; Asst. Prof., 1946–57; Assoc. Prof. 1957–65; Prof., 1965–75). *Publs:* The Greek and Latin Literary Texts from Greco-Roman Egypt, 1952, 1965; Artemidori Daldiani Onirocritica, 1963. Add: 400 Maynard, Ann Arbor, Mich. 48104, U.S.A.

PACKARD, Vance. American, b. 1914. Social commentary/phenomena. Writer and Ed., Associated Press Feature Service, NYC, 1938–42; Ed. and Staff Writer, American Mag., 1942–56; Lectr., Columbia Univ., NYC, 1942–44, and New York Univ., 1946–57. *Publs:* (with C.R. Adams) How to Pick a Mate: The Guide to a Happy Marriage, 1946; Animal IQ: The Human Side of Animals, 1950, rev. ed. as The Human Side of Animals, 1961; The Hidden Persuaders, 1957, 1981; The Status Seekers, 1959; The Waste Makers, 1960; The Pyramid Climbers, 1962; The Naked Society, 1964; The Sexual Wilderness, 1968; A Nation of Strangers, 1972; The People Shapers, 1977; Our Endangered Children, 1983. Add: 87 Mill Rd., New Canaan, Conn. 06840, U.S.A.

PACKER, James Innell. British, b. 1926. Theology/Religion. Prof. of Theology, Regent Coll., Vancouver, since 1979. Warden, Latimer House, Oxford, 1961–69; Principal, Tyndale Hall Theological Coll., 1969–71; Assoc. Principal, Trinity Coll., Bristol, 1971–79. *Publs:* Fundamentalism and the Word of God, 1958; (with O.R. Johnston) Luther's Bondage of the Will, 1958; Evangelism and the Sovereignty of God, 1961; (ed. with J.D. Douglas, R.V.G. Tasker, F.F. Bruce and D.J. Wiseman) New Bible Dictionary, 1962; Our Lord's Understanding of the Law of God, 1962; Keep Yourselves from Idols, 1963; (ed. and contrib.) The Church of England and the Methodist Church, 1963; God Has Spoken, 1965; (ed. and contrib.) All in Each Place, 1965; Tomorrow's Worship, 1966; (with A.M. Stibbs) The Spirit Within You, 1967; (ed. and contrib.) Guidelines, 1967; (ed. and contrib.) Fellowship in the Gospel, 1968; (with C.O. Buchanan, E.L. Mascall and G. Leonard) Growing into Union, 1970; Knowing God, 1973; I Want to Be a Christian, 1977; For Man's Sake, 1978; (with R.T. Beckwith and G.E. Duffield) Across the Divide, 1978; The Evangelical Anglican Identity Problem, 1978; Beyond the Battle for the Bible, 1980; A Kind of Noah's Ark?, 1981; God's Words, 1981; Freedom, Authority and Scripture, 1982; The Apostles Creed, 1983; (with R.T. Beckwith) The 39 Articles, 1984; Keep in Step with the Spirit, 1984; (with Thomas Howard) Christianity, the True Humanism, 1985; (ed.) The Best in Theology, vol. I, 1986, vol. II, 1987; Through the Year with Jesus, 1986; Your Father Loves You, 1986; God in Our Midst, 1987; Hot Tub Religion, 1987; Here We Stand: Justification by Faith Today, 1988. Add: Regent Coll., 2130 Wesbrook Mall, Vancouver, B.C. V6T 1W6, Canada.

PACKETT, Charles Neville. British, b. 1922. Business/Trade/Industry, History/Exploration/Adventure. Managing Dir., Sydney Packett and Sons Ltd., insurance brokers, Bradford, since 1971 (Dir., 1941–71). Gov., Ashville Coll., Harrogate, Yorks. *Publs:* Guide to the Republic of San Marino, 1958, 1964; History of the Greek Order of St. Dennis of Zante, 1962; City of Bradford Local Savings Committee Year Book, 1962; Guide to Tongatapu Island, Kingdom of Tonga, 1969, 4th ed. 1981; The Orders of Knighthood of the Most Serene Republic of San Marino, 1970; Guide to the Republic of Nauru, 1971, 1978; (ed.) A Short History of the Republic of San Marino, 1972; A History and A to Z of Her Majesty's Lieutenancy of Counties with Particular Reference to the West Riding of Yorkshire 1547-1972, 1973; The County Lieutenancy in the U.K. 1547-1975, 1975; Association of Lieutenants of Counties and Custodes Rotulorum: A Brief History 1907-1977, 1977; Diamond Jubilee History (1920-1980) of Sydney Packett and Sons Ltd., 1980; The Texas Navy: A Brief History, 1983; A History of the Bradford Club, 1986; A History of the Lieutenancy of the City of London, 1987. Add: Lloyds Bank Chambers, Hustlergate, Bradford, Yorks. BD1 1PA, England.

PADFIELD, Peter. British, b. 1932. Novels, History, Autobiography/Memoirs/Personal, Biography. *Publs:* The Sea Is a Magic Carpet (autobiography), 1959; The Titanic and The Californian, 1965; An Agony of Collisions (history), 1966; Aim Straight (biography), 1967; Broke and the Shannon (biography), 1969; The Battleship Era, 1972; Guns at Sea, 1973; The Great Naval Race, 1974; Nelson's War, 1975; The Lion's Claw (novel), 1978; Tide of Empires, 2 vols., 1979–82; The Unquiet Gods (novel), 1980; Rule Britannia: The Victorian and Edwardian Navy, 1981; Beneath the Houseflag of the P & O, 1982; Gold Chains of Empire (novel), 1982; Donitz, The Last Fuhrer, 1983; Salt and Steel (novel), 1986; Armada, 1988. Add: Drybridge Hill, Woodbridge, Suffolk, England.

PADGETT, Lewis. *See* **MOORE,** C.L.

PADGETT, Ron. American, b. 1942. Novels/Short stories, Plays, Poetry, Translations. Has taught poetry workshops at the Poetry Project at St. Mark's in-the-Bowery, NYC, and poetry writing in NYC public schools, since 1968; Dir. of Publications, Teachers and Writers Collaborative, NYC, since 1982. Founding Ed., Full Court Press, NYC, 1973–88. *Publs:* In Advance of the Broken Arm: Poems, 1964; (with Ted Berrigan) Seventeen: Collected Plays, 1965; 2/2 Stories for Andy Warhol, 1965; Sky: An Opener, 1966; (with Ted Berrigan) Bean Spasms: Poems and Prose, 1967; Tone Arm, 1967; (with J. Brainard) 100,000 Fleeing Hilda, 1967; (with T. Clark) Bun, 1968; (with Ted Berrigan and J. Brainard) Some Thing, 1968; (trans.) The Poet Assassinated, by Apollinaire, 1968; Great Balls of Fire, 1969; (with J. Dine) The Adventures of Mr. and Mrs. Jim and Ron, 1970; (ed. with D. Shapiro) An Anthology of New York Poets, 1970; (trans.) Entretiens avec Marcel Duchamp/Dialogues with Marcel Duchamp, 1970; Sweet Pea, 1971; Poetry Collection, 1971; (with Ted Berrigan and T. Clark) Back in Boston Again, 1972; Antlers in the Treetops, 1973; (trans. with B. Zavatsky) The Poems of A.O. Barnabooth, by Valery Larbaud, 1974; Toujours l'amour, 1976; (with George Schneeman) Arrive by Pullman, 1978; Tulsa Kid, 1979; Triangles in the Afternoon, 1979; (with Trevor Winkfield) How to Be a Woodpecker, 1983; (with Trevor Winkfield) How to Be Modern Art, 1984; (trans.) The Poet Assassinated and Other Stories, by Apollinaire, 1984; (ed.) The Complete Poems of Edwin Denby, 1986; (ed.) Handbook of Poetic Forms, 1987; Among the Blacks, 1988. Add: 342 E. 13th St., New York, N.Y. 10003, U.S.A.

PADOVANO, Anthony T. American, b. 1934. Theology/Religion. Ordained Catholic Priest, 1959; Prof. of American Literature, Ramapo Coll., Mahwah, N.J., since 1971. Feature Writer, National Catholic Reporter, since 1971. Ed.-in-Chief, Roman Echoes, 1959; Prof. of Systematic Theology, Darlington Seminary, Mahwah, N.J., 1962–74; Parish Asst., St. Catharine's Glen Rock, N.J., 1963–74; Member, Editorial Bd., The Advocat, 1966–73. *Publs:* The Estranged God, 1966; Who Is Christ?, 1967; Belief in Human Life, 1969; American Culture and the Quest for Christ, 1970; Dawn Without Darkness, 1971; Free to Be Faithful, 1972; Eden and Easter, 1974; Presence and Structure, 1975; A Case for Worship, 1976; America: Its People, Its Promise, 1976; The Human Journey: Thomas Merton, Symbol of a Century, 1981; Trilogy, 1982; Contemplation and Compassion, 1984; Winter Rain, 1984; His Name Is John, 1985; Christmas to Calvary, 1987; Love and Destiny, 1987; Summer Lightning, 1988; Conscience and Conflict, 1988. Add: 9 Millstone Dr., Morris Plains, N.J. 07950, U.S.A.

PAETRO, Maxine. American, b. 1946. Novels/Short stories, Business/Trade/Industry. Vice-Pres. and Dir. of Creative Operations, DFS/Dorland Worldwide advertising agency, NYC, since 1981. Formerly: Mgr. of Creative Dept., Ogilvy and Mather, NYC; Vice-Pres. and Assoc. Mgr. of Creative Services, Young and Rubicam, NYC; Vice-Pres. and Mgr. of Creative Dept., Foote, Cone and Belding Communications Inc., NYC. *Publs:* How to Put Your Book Together and Get a Job in Advertising, 1979; Manshare, 1986; Babydreams, 1988. Add: c/o Elaine Markson Literary Agency Inc., 44 Greenwich Ave., New York, N.Y. 10011, U.S.A.

PAFFARD, Michael (Kenneth). British, b. 1928. Language/Linguistics, Literature. Fellow of Univ. of Keele, since 1983 (Lectr. and Sr. Lectr., 1953–83). *Publs:* Inglorious Wordsworths, 1973; The Unattended Moment, 1976; Thinking about English, 1978. Add: 3 Church Bank, Keele, Staffs, ST5 5AT, England.

PAFFORD, John Henry Pyle. British, b. 1900. Librarianship. Goldsmiths' Librarian, Univ. of London, 1945–67; Joint Ed., Somerset and Dorset Notes and Queries, 1971–83. *Publs:* (ed.) Bale's King John (play), 1931; Library Co-operation in Europe, 1935; (ed.) The Sodder'd Citizen (play), 1936; (ed.) Parliamentary Garrisons in Wiltshire 1645-46, 1940; Books and Army Education, 1946; American Libraries, 1949; W.P. Ker: A Bibliography, 1950; (ed.) Mundy's Chruso-thriambos (play), 1962; (ed.) The Winter's Tale (Arden Shakespeare), 1963; (ed.) Watts' Divine Songs for Children (poetry), 1971; (ed.) L Bryskett's Works, 1972. Add: Hillside, Allington Park, Bridport, Dorset DT6 5DD, England.

PAGE, Charles H. American, b. 1909. Sociology, Sports. Robert MacIver Prof. of Sociology, Univ. of Massachusetts, Amherst, since 1973. Prof. and Chmn., Sociology and Anthropology, Smith Coll., Northampton, Mass., 1946–52 and 1953–60; Prof. and Chmn., Sociology and Anthropology, City Coll. of New York, 1952–53; Advisory Ed., Random House-Knopf Inc., NYC, 1954–80; Prof. and Chmn., Sociology and Anthropology, Princeton Univ., New Jersey, 1960–65; Provost, Adlai E. Stevenson Coll., Univ. of California at Santa Cruz, 1965–68. Ed., Doubleday and Co. Inc., 1952–54; Ed., American Sociological Review, 1958–60. *Publs:* Class and American Sociology, 1940, 1969; (with R.

MacIver) Society: An Introductory Analysis, 1949; (ed. with M. Berger and T. Abel) Freedom and Control in Modern Society, 1954; 1964; (ed. and co-author) Sociology and General Education, 1963; (with J. Talamini) Sport and Society, 1973; Fifty Years in the Sociological Enterprise: A Lucky Journey, 1982. Add: 7 Hampton Terr., Northampton, Mass. 01060, U.S.A.

PAGE, Emma. Pseud. for Honoria Tirbutt. British. Mystery/Crime/Suspense, Radio plays. *Publs:* In Loving Memory, 1970; Family and Friends, 1972; A Fortnight by the Sea (in U.S. as Add a Pinch of Cyanide), 1973; Element of Chance, 1975; Every Second Thursday, 1981; Last Walk Home, 1982; Cold Light of Day, 1983; Scent of Death, 1985; Final Moments, 1987; A Violent End, 1988. Add: c/o Collins Ltd., 8 Grafton St., London W1X 3LA, England.

PAGE, Geoff(rey Donald). Australian, b. 1940. Novels/Short stories, Poetry. Sr. English Teacher, Narrabundah Coll., Canberra, since 1974. English and history teacher, Canberra high schools, 1964–74. *Publs:* (with Philip Roberts) Two Poets, 1971; Smalltown Memorials (poetry), 1975; Collecting the Weather (poetry), 1978; Cassandra Paddocks (poetry), 1980; Clairvoyant in Autumn (poetry), 1983; (ed.) Shadows from the Wire: Poems and Photographs of Australians in the Great War, 1983; Benton's Conviction (novel), 1985; (trans. with Wendy Coutts) Century of Clouds: Poems of Guillaume Apollinaire, 1985; Collected Lives (poetry), 1986; Smiling in English, Smoking in French (poetry), 1987; Footwork (poetry), 1988; Winter Vision (novel), 1989; Invisible Histories (stories), 1990. Add: 8 Morehead St., Curtin, A.C.T. 2605, Australia.

PAGE, Kathy. British, b. 1958. Novels/Short stories. Carpenter, London Borough of Lambeth, 1983–86; Tutor in Creative Writing, Univ. of London, 1986–87. *Publs:* (ed.) Eve Before the Holocaust, 1985; Back in the First Person, 1986; The Unborn Dreams of Clara Riley, 1987; Island Paradise, 1989. Add: 53 Melrose Rd., Norwich NR4 7PN, England.

PAGE, Louise. British, b. 1955. Plays/Screenplays. Resident writer, Royal Court Theatre, London, 1982–83. *Publs:* Tissue (in Plays by Women 1), 1982; Salonika, 1983; Real Estate, 1985; Golden Girls, 1985; Beauty and the Beast, 1986. Add: c/o Phil Kelvin, Goodwin Assocs., 12 Rabbit Row, London W8 4DX, England.

PAGE, Norman. British, b. 1930. Literature, Biography. Prof. of Modern English Literature, and Head of English Studies, Univ. of Nottingham, since 1985. Head of English Dept., Ripon Coll., 1960–69; Asst. Prof. to Prof., Univ. of Alberta, Edmonton, 1969–85. Gen. Ed., Macmillan Modern Novelists and Macmillan Author Chronologies series. *Publs:* The Language of Jane Austen, 1972; Speech in the English Novel, 1973, 1987; (ed.) Wilkie Collins: The Critical Heritage, 1974; Thomas Hardy, 1977; E.M. Forster's Posthumous Fiction, 1977; (ed.) Hardy's Jude the Obscure, 1978, 1980; (ed.) Thomas Hardy: The Writer and His Background, 1980; (ed.) D.H. Lawrence: Interviews and Recollections, 1981; (ed.) Nabokov: The Critical Heritage, 1982; (ed.) A Thomas Hardy Annual, 5 vols., 1982–87; (ed.) Tennyson: Interviews and Recollections, 1983; A.E. Housman: A Critical Biography, 1983; A Dickens Companion, 1984; (ed.) Henry James: Interviews and Recollections, 1984; A Kipling Companion, 1984; (ed.) The Language of Literature, 1984; (ed.) William Golding: Novels 1954-67, 1985; (ed.) Byron: Interviews and Recollections, 1985; A Conrad Companion, 1986; (ed.) Dr. Johnson: Interviews and Recollections, 1987; E.M. Forster, 1987; A Dickens Chronology, 1988; A Byron Chronology, 1988. Add: Dept. of English, Univ. of Nottingham, Nottingham NG7 2RD, England.

PAGE, P. K. Also writes as Judith Cape. Canadian, b. 1916. Poetry. Worked as a sales clerk and radio actress in St. John, N.B., and filing clerk and historical researcher in Montreal: Scriptwriter, National Film Bd., Ottawa, 1946–50. *Publs:* The Sun and the Moon, 1944; As Ten as Twenty, 1946; The Metal and the Flower, 1954; Cry Ararat! Poems New and Selected, 1967; The Sun and The Moon and Other Fictions, 1973; Poems Selected and New, 1974; (ed.) To Say the Least: Canadian Poets from A to Z, 1979; Evening Dance of the Grey Flies, 1981; The Glass Air, 1985; Brazilian Journal, 1987. Add: 3260 Exeter Rd., Victoria, B.C. V8R 6H6, Canada.

PAGE, Robin. British, b. 1943. Country life/Rural societies, Natural history, Politics/Government. Partner, Birds Farm Publications. Member, South Cambridgeshire District Council, since 1970. With Dept. of Health and Social Security, 1964–69. *Publs:* (contrib.) Down with the Poor, 1971; The Benefits Racket, 1972; Down among the Dossers, 1973; The Decline of an English Village, 1974; The Hunter and the Hunted, 1977; Weather Forecasting: The Country Way, 1977; Cures and Remedies:

The Country Way, 1978; Weeds: The Country Way, 1979; Animal Cures: The Country Way, 1979; The Journal of a Country Parish, 1980; Journeys into Britain, 1982; The Country Way of Love, 1983; The Wildlife of the Royal Estates, 1984; Count One to Ten, 1986; The Fox's Tale, 1986; (contrib.) The Duchy of Cornwall, 1987; The Fox and the Orchid, 1987. Add: Bird's Farm, Barton, Cambs., England.

PAGELS, Elaine. American. Theology/Religion. Prof. of Religion, Princeton Univ., since 1982. Asst. to Prof., Barnard Coll., Columbia Univ., NYC, 1970–82. *Publs:* The Johannine Gospel in Gnostic Exegesis, 1973; The Gnostic Paul: Gnostic Exegesis of the Pauline Letters, 1975; The Gnostic Gospels, 1979; Adam, Eve, and the Serpent, 1988. Add: Dept. of Religion, Princeton Univ., Princeton, N.J. 08544, U.S.A.

PAGET, Julian (Tolver). British, b. 1921. History. Regular Army Officer, Coldstream Guards, 1940–66. *Publs:* Counter-Insurgency Campaigning (in U.S. as Counter-Insurgency Operations), 1967; Last Post: Aden 1964-67, 1969; Story of the Guards, 1976; The Pageantry of Britain, 1979; The Yeomen of the Guard, 1985; Wellington's Peninsular War: The Battles and Battlefields, 1989; Discovering London's Ceremonial and Traditions, 1989. Add: 4 Trevor St., London SW7, England.

PAINTER, Charlotte. American. Novels/Short stories. Prof., San Francisco State Univ., since 1975. Lectr., Stanford Univ., California, 1966–69, Univ. of Calfornia, Berkeley, 1972–73, and the Univ. of California at Davis, 1977–80. *Publs:* Who Made the Lamb, 1965; Confession from the Malaga Madhouse, 1971 (ed. with Mary Jane Moffat) Revelations: Diaries of Women, 1974; Seeing Things, 1976; Gifts of Age, 1985, 1989. Add: P.O. Box 372-635F, Oakland, Calif. 94618, U.S.A.

PAINTER, Helen (Welch). American, b. 1913. Education, Literature. Prof. of Elementary Education and English, Kent State Univ., Ohio, since 1967. Faculty member, Univ. of Akron, Ohio, 1945–67. *Publs:* Poetry and Children, 1970; (ed.) Reaching Children and Young People Through Literature (essays), 1971. Add: 88 Monroe Ave., Cuyahoga Falls, Ohio 44221, U.S.A.

PAINTER, John. Australian, b. 1935. History, Theology/Religion. Sr. Lectr., La Trobe Univ., Bundoora, Vic., since 1977. Formerly: Staff Member, Univ. of Cape Town, South Africa, and the Univ. of Durham, England. *Publs:* John: Witness and Theologian, 1975, 1978; Reading John's Gospel Today, 1979; Theology as Hermeneutics, 1984. Add: c/o History Dept., La Trobe Univ., Bundoora, Vic. 3083, Australia.

PAKENHAM, Thomas (Frank Dermot). Irish, b. 1933. History. Treas., British Irish Assn., since 1973; Secty., Christopher Ewart-Biggs Memorial Trust, since 1976. Worked for the Times Educational Supplement, 1959–61, the Sunday Telegraph, 1961, and The Observer, 1961–64—all London. *Publs:* The Mountains of Rasselas: An Ethiopian Adventure, 1959; The Year of Liberty: The Story of the Irish Rebellion of 1798, 1969; The Boer War, 1979; (ed. with V. Pakenham) Dublin: A Travellers' Companion, 1988. Add: Tullynally, Castle Pollard, Westmeath, Ireland.

PAL, Pratapaditya. Indian, b. 1935. Art. Sr. Curator of Indian and Islamic Art, Los Angeles County Museum of Art, since 1970; Prof. of Fine Arts, Univ. of Southern California, Los Angeles, since 1970. Keeper of the Indian Collection, Museum of Fine Arts, Boston, 1967–70. *Publs:* Ragamala Paintings in the Museum of Fine Arts, Boston, 1967; (with D. Bhattacaryya) The Astral Divinities of Nepal, 1968; The Art of Tibet, 1969; (with H.C. Tseng) Lamaist Art, 1969; (with J. Fontein) Oriental Art, 1969; Vaishnava Iconology in Nepal, 1970; Indo-Asian Art: The John G. Ford Collection, 1971; (ed.) Aspects of Indian Art, 1972; Krishna: The Cowherd King, 1972; (ed. and co-author) Islamic Art: The Nasli M. Heeramaneck Collection, 1973; The Art of Nepal, vol. I, Sculpture, 1974; Buddhist Art in Licchavi Nepal, 1974; Bronzes of Kashmir, 1975; The Sensuous Immortals, 1977; The Divine Presence, 1978; The Ideal Image, 1978; The Art of Nepal, vol. II, Painting, 1978; The Classical Tradition in Rajput Painting, 1978; Elephants and Ivories, 1981; Hindu Religion and Iconology, 1981; Indian Paintings in Los Angeles Museums, 1982; A Buddhist Paradise, 1982; Art of Tibet, 1983; Court Paintings of India, 1983; Light of Asia, 1984; Art of Nepal, 1985; From Merchants to Emperors, 1986; Indian Sculpture, vol. 1, 1986; Icons of Piety, Images of Whimsy, 1987. Add: Los Angeles County Museum of Art, 5905 Wilshire Blvd., Los Angeles, Calif. 90036, U.S.A.

PALEY, Grace. American, b. 1922. Novels/Short stories. Member of the faculty, Sarah Lawrence Coll., Bronxville, N.Y. *Publs:* The Little Disturbances of Man: Stories of Women and Men at Love, 1959; Enor-

mous Changes at the Last Minute, 1974; Later the Same Day, 1985; Leaning Forward, 1985. Add: 126 W. 11th St., New York, N.Y. 10011, U.S.A.

PALMER, Alan Warwick. British, b. 1926. History, Biography. Head of the History Dept., Highgate Sch., London, 1953–69. *Publs:* (with C.A. Macartney) Independent Eastern Europe, 1962; Dictionary of Modern History 1789-1945, 1962; Yugoslavia, 1964; Gardeners of Salonika, 1965; Napoleon in Russia, 1967; The Lands Between, 1970; Metternich, 1972; Life and Times of George IV, 1972; Russia in War and Peace, 1972; Alexander I, 1974; Frederick the Great, 1974; Bismarck, 1976; (with Veronica Palmer) Quotations in History, 1976; Kings and Queens of England, 1976; The Kaiser, 1978; Dictionary of Twentieth Century History, 1979; Princes of Wales, 1979; Who's Who in Modern History, 1980; (with Veronica Palmer) Who's Who in Shakespeare's England, 1981; The Chancelleries of Europe, 1983; (with Veronica Palmer) Royal England, 1983; Napoleon's Europe, 1984; Crowned Cousins, 1985; The Banner of Battle, 1987; (with Veronica Palmer) Who's Who in Bloomsbury, 1988; The East End, 1989. Add: 4 Farm End, Woodstock, Oxford OX7 1XN, England.

PALMER, (John) Carey (Bowden). British, b. 1943. Novels/Short stories, Education. Founder and Principal, Richmond Tutorial Coll., since 1975. History Tutor and Lectr., 1966–74. *Publs:* Decline and Fail, 1970; Crammers, 1977. Add: Richmond Tutorial Coll., 105 Kew Rd., Richmond, Surrey, England.

PALMER, Cedric King. British, b. 1913. Music. Freelance composer and conductor, and teacher of piano and theory. *Publs:* Music, 1944, 5th ed. 1986; Compose Music, 1947; (with C. Turfery) The Musical Production, 1953; The Piano, 1957, 3rd ed., 1986; Orchestration, 1964; (with S. Rhys) ABC of Church Music, 1969. Add: Clovelly Lodge, 2 Popes Grove, Twickenham, Middx. TW2 5TA, England.

PALMER, C(yril) Everard. Canadian, b. 1930. Novels/Short stories, Children's fiction. *Publs:* A Broken Vessel, 1960; The Cloud with the Silver Lining, 1966; Big Doc Bitterroot, 1968; The Sun Salutes You, 1970; The Hummingbird People, 1971; A Cow Called Boy, 1972; The Wooing of Beppo Tate, 1972; Baba and Mr. Big, 1972; My Father Sun-Sun Johnson, 1974; A Dog Called Houdini 1978; Beppo Tate and Roy Penner, 1980; Houdini Come Home, 1981. Add: 2590 Angyle Rd., No. 1109, Mississauga, Ont. L5B 1V3, Canada.

PALMER, Diana. Pseud. for Susan (Eloise Spaeth) Kyle; also writes as Susan Kyle, Diana Blayne, and Katy Currie. American, b. 1946. Novels, Historical/Romance. Reporter, The Times, Gainesville, 1969–85, and Tri-County Advertiser, Clarkesville, Georgia, 1972–82; free-lance journalist, 1986. *Publs:* Romance novels—Now and Forever, 1979; Storm Over the Lake, 1979; To Have and to Hold, 1979; Sweet Enemy, 1979; Bound By a Promise, 1979; To Love and to Cherish, 1979; Dream's End, 1979; If Winter Comes, 1979; At Winter's End, 1979; The Cowboy and the Lady, 1982; September Morning, 1982; Heather's Song, 1982; (as Diana Blayne) A Waiting Game, 1982; Darling Enemy, 1983; Friends and Lovers, 1983; Fire and Ice, 1983; Snow Kisses, 1983; (as Diana Blayne) A Loving Arrangement, 1983; (as Diana Blayne) White Sand, Wild Sea, 1983; (as Diana Blayne) Dark Surrender, 1983; Diamond Girl, 1984; Lady Love, 1984; Roomful of Roses, 1984; Heart of Ice, 1984; Passion Flower, 1984; The Rawhide Man, 1984; (as Katy Currie) Blind Promises, 1984; (as Diana Blayne) Color Love Blue, 1984; The Cattleman's Choice, 1985; Love by Proxy, 1985; The Tender Stranger, 1985; Soldier of Fortune, 1985; The Australian, 1985; Loveplay, 1986; Eye of the Tiger, 1986; After the Music, 1986; Champagne Girl, 1986; Unlikely Lover, 1986; (as Diana Blayne) Tangled Destinies, 1986; Betrayed by Love, 1987; Rage of Passion, 1987; Rawhide and Lace, 1987; Fit for a King, 1987; Enamored, 1988; Calhoun, 1988; Justin, 1988; Tyler, 1988; (as Susan Kyle) The Diamond Spur, 1988; Hoodwinked, 1989; (as Susan Kyle) Fire Brand, 1989; Reluctant Father, 1989; other—The Morcai Battalion (novel), 1980. Add: P.O. Box 844, Cornelia, Ga. 30531, U.S.A.

PALMER, Frank Robert. British, b. 1922. Language/Linguistics. Prof. of Linguistic Science, Univ. of Reading, 1965–87. Member of the Council, Philological Soc., 1962–67, 1969–74, 1978–82, and since 1984; Chmn., Linguistic Assn., 1965–68; Ed., Journal of Linguistics, 1969–78. *Publs:* Morphology of the Tigre Noun, 1962; Linguistic Study of the English Verb, 1965; (ed.) Selected Papers of J.R. Firth 1951–1958, 1968; (ed.) Prosodic Analysis, 1970; Grammar, 1971, 1984; The English Verb, 1974, 1987; Semantics, 1976; Modality and the English Modals, 1979, 1989; Mood and Modality, 1986. Add: Dept. of Linguistic Science, Univ. of Reading, Whiteknights, Reading RG6 2AA, England.

PALMER, Juliette. British, b. 1930. Children's non-fiction. Freelance author and illustrator. *Publs:* Cockles and Shrimps, 1973; Mountain Wool, 1974; Swan Upping, 1974; Stow House Fair, 1976; Barley Sow, Barley Grow, 1978; Barley Ripe, Barley Reap, 1979. Add: Melmott Lodge, The Pound, Cookham, Berks. SL6 9QD, England.

PALMER, Madelyn. Also writes as Geoffrey Peters. Australian, b. 1910. Mystery/Crime/Suspense. Clerical Officer, Office of Population Censuses and Surveys, Titchfield, Hants., now retired. *Publs:* Dead Fellah, 1961; The Claw of a Cat, 1964; The Eye of a Serpent, 1964; The Whirl of a Bird, 1965; The Twist of a Stick, 1966; The Flick of a Fin, 1967; The Mark of a Buoy, 1967; The Chill of a Corpse, 1968; Fareham Creek, 1974; The Scottish Barbarian, 1976; The Monk of Falconsway, 1977; Quite by Chance, 1978. Add: 14 Park Lane, Fareham, Hants., England.

PALMER, Michael. American, b. 1943. Poetry. Ed., Joglars mag., Providence, R.I., 1964–66. *Publs:* Plan of the City of O, 1971; Blake's Newton, 1972; C's Songs, 1973; Six Poems, 1973; The Circular Gates, 1974; (trans.) Relativity of Spring, 1976; Without Music, 1977; Alogon, 1980; Transparency of the Mirror, 1980; Notes for Echo Lake, 1981; (ed.) Code of Signals: Recent Writings in Poetics, 1983; First Figure (poetry), 1984; Sun (poetry), 1988. Add: 265 Jersey St., San Francisco, Calif. 94114, U.S.A.

PALMER, Michael Denison. British, b. 1933. History, Social sciences. Headmaster, De Burgh Sch., Tadworth, Surrey, since 1977. Deputy Headmaster, The Littlehampton Sch., Sussex, 1972–77. *Publs:* Government, 1970; Cities, 1971; Ships and Shipping, 1971; Henry VIII, 1971, 1984; Warfare, 1972; World Population, 1973; Resources and Energy, 1974; Elizabeth I, 1988. Add: 13 Denham Rd., Epsom, Surrey, England.

PALMER, Norman D. American, b. 1909. International relations/Current affairs, Third World problems. Prof. of Political Science, Univ. of Pennsylvania, Philadelphia, 1951–79, now Emeritus (Assoc. Prof., 1947–51). Instr., then Assoc. Prof. and Chmn., Dept. of History and Govt., Colby Coll., Waterville, Me., 1933–42 and 1946–47; with the U.S. Navy, 1942–46. Pres., Intnl. Studies Assn., 1970–71. *Publs:* The Irish Land League Crisis, 1940; (with H. Perkins) International Relations: The World Community in Transition, 1953, 3rd ed. 1969; (with S. Leng) Sun Yat-sen and Communism, 1958; The Indian Political System, 1961, 1971; South Asia and United States Policy, 1966; (ed.) Design for International Relations Research, 1970; Elections and Political Development: The South Asian Experience, 1975; The United States and India, 1984; (with others) The Art and Science of Politics, 1985. Add: 958 Terrace Dr., Friday Harbor, Wash. 98250, U.S.A.

PALMER, Peter John. Australian, b. 1932. Geography, History. Member of faculty, Ouyen High Sch., 1954–57, Alexandra High Sch., 1958–63, Burwood High Sch., 1964–68, Ashwood High Sch., 1969, and Waverley High Sch., 1970–76; Deputy Principal, Koonung High Sch., 1977–80; Principal, Preston East High Sch., 1981–88. *Publs:* The Past and Us, 1957; The Twentieth Century, 1964; (ed. and co-author) Confrontation, 1971; (ed. and co-author) Interaction, 1973; (ed. and co-author) Expansion, 1974; (ed. and co-author) Survival, 1975; (ed. and co-author) Three Worlds, 1977; (ed. and co-author) Earth and Man, 1980; (ed. and co-author) Man on the Land, 1981; (exec. ed.) Macmillan Australian Atlas, 1983; (ed. and co-author) Man and Machines, 1983; (ed. and co-author) Challenge, 1985. Add: 34 Ardgower Ct., Lower Templestowe, Vic. 3107, Australia.

PALSSON, Hermann. Icelandic, b. 1921. History, Literature, Translations. Prof., Univ. of Edinburgh (Lectr., 1954–63; Sr. Lectr., 1963–66). Gen. Ed., The New Saga Library, since 1972. *Publs:* (trans. with M. Magnusson) Njal's Saga, 1960; (trans. with M. Magnusson) The Vinland Sagas, 1965; (trans. with M. Magnusson) King Harald's Saga, 1966; (trans. with P. Edwards) Gautrek's Saga and Other Medieval Tales, 1968; (trans. with M. Magnusson) Laxdaela Saga, 1969; (trans. with P. Edwards) Arrow-Odd: A Medieval Novel, 1970; (with P. Edwards) Legendary Fiction in Medieval Iceland, 1970; (ed. with A.J. Aitkin and A. McIntosh) Edinburgh Studies in English and Scots, 1971; Art and Ethics in Hrafnkel's Saga, 1971; (trans. with P. Edwards) The Book of Settlements, 1972; (trans.) Hrafnkel's Saga, 1972; (trans. with P. Edwards) Hrolf Gautreksson, 1972; (trans. with P. Edwards) Eyrbyggja Saga, 1973; (trans. with D. Fox) Grettir's Saga, 1974; (trans.) The Confederates, 1974; (trans. with P. Edwards) Orkneyinga Saga, 1978; (trans. with P. Edwards) Gongo-Hrolf's Saga, 1980; (ed. with A. Fenton) The Northern and Western Isles in the Viking World, 1984; (trans. with P. Edwards) Seven Viking Romances, 1985; (trans. with P. Edwards) Knytlinga Saga, 1986. Add: 13 Royal

Terrace Mews, Edinburgh 7, Scotland.

PALUMBO, Dennis. American, b. 1929. Politics/Government. Prof., City Univ. of New York/Brooklyn Coll., since 1966. Instr., Michigan State Univ., East Lansing, 1960–62; Asst. Prof., Univ. of Hawaii, Honolulu, 1962–63; Asst. Prof., Univ. of Pennsylvania, Philadelphia, 1963–66. *Publs:* (co-ed.) Major Problems of Government in the U.S., 1962; Statistics in Political and Behavioral Science, 1969, 1977; American Politics, 1973; Cities, 1979; (co-ed.) Urban Policy, 1979; (ed.) Evaluating and Optimizing Public Policy, 1980; (with M.A. Harder) Implementing Public Policy, 1981. Add: Dept. of Political Science, City Univ. of New York, Brooklyn, N.Y., U.S.A.

PAMA, Cornelis. Dutch, b. 1916. Genealogy/Heraldry, History. Ed., Nederlandse Post, since 1975. Hon. Ed., Familia Journal of the Genealogical Soc. of South Africa, since 1963, and Arma Journal of the Heraldry Soc. of South Africa. Mgr., Bailliere Tindall and Cox Ltd., London, 1948–55; Gen. Mgr., W. and G. Foyle, Cape Town, 1955–67; Dir., A.A. Balkema Publs., Cape Town, 1967–72; Ed., Tafelberg Publs., Cape Town, 1972–77. *Publs:* Lions and Virgins; (ed.) The South African Library 1818-1968; Genealogies of Old South African Families; Heraldry of South African Families; Vintage Cape Town; Regency Cape Town; Bowler's Cape Town; Heraldiek and Genealogie; The Wine Estates of South Africa; Historic Wine Farms of the Cape. Add: P.O. Box 4839, Cape Town 8000, South Africa.

PANICHAS, George A(ndrew). American, b. 1930. Cultural/Ethnic topics, Literature, Philosophy. Prof. of English, Univ. of Maryland, College Park, since 1968 (Instr., 1962–63; Asst. Prof., 1963–66; Assoc. Prof., 1966–68). Member, Editorial Bd., since 1971, and Ed., since 1984 (Assoc. Ed., 1978–84), Modern Age. *Publs:* Adventure in Consciousness: The Meaning of D.H. Lawrence's Religious Quest, 1964; (ed. with George R. Hibbard and Allan Rodway) Renaissance and Modern Essays, 1966; Epicurus, 1967; (ed.) Mansions of the Spirit: Essays in Literature and Religion, 1967; (ed.) Promise of Greatness: The War of 1914-1918, 1968; (ed.) The Politics of 20th Century Novelists, 1971; The Reverent Discipline: Essays in Literary Criticism and Culture, 1974; The Burden of Vision: Dostoyevsky's Spiritual Art, 1977; (ed.) The Simone Weil Reader, 1977; (ed.) Irving Babbitt: Representative Writings, 1981; The Courage of Judgment: Essays in Criticism, Culture, and Society, 1982; (co-ed.) Irving Babbitt in Our Time, 1986; (ed.) Modern Age: The First Twenty-Five Years, 1988. Add: Apt. 402, 4313 Knox Rd., College Park, Md. 20740, U.S.A.

PANITCH, Leo (Victor). Canadian, b. 1945. Economics, Politics/Government. Prof. of Political Science, York Univ., Toronto, since 1984. Co-Ed., The Socialist Register (annual). Assoc. Prof. to Prof. of Political Science, Carleton Univ., Ottawa, 1972–84. *Publs:* Social Democracy and Industrial Militancy: The Labour Party, the Trade Unions and Incomes Policy 1945-1974, 1976; The Canadian State: Political Economy and Political Power, 1977; Working Class Politics in Crisis, 1986; The Assault on Trade Union Freedoms, 1988. Add: Dept. of Political Science, York Univ., Toronto M6G 2P4, Canada.

PANKHURST, Richard (Keir Pethick). British, b. 1927. History, Travel/Exploration/Adventure. Librarian, Royal Asiatic Society, London, since 1980. Prof. and Dir., Inst. of Ethiopian Studies, Haile Sellassie Univ., Addis Ababa, 1963–80. *Publs:* (with E. Sylvia Pankhurst) Ethiopia and Eritrea, 1953; William Thompson: Britain's Pioneer Socialist, Feminist and Co-operator, 1954; Kenya: The History of Two Nations, 1954; The Saint Simonians, Mill and Carlyle, 1956; An Introduction to the Economic History of Ethiopia, 1961; Travellers in Ethiopia, 1965; State and Land in Ethiopian History, 1966; The Ehtiopian Royal Chronicles, 1967; An Introduction to the History of the Ethiopian Army, 1967; Primitive Money: Money and Banking in Ethiopia, 1967; Economic History of Ethiopia, 1968; (with Geoffrey Last) A History of Ethiopia in Pictures, 1969; History of Ethiopia, 1970; (ed.) Tax Records and Inventories of Emperor Tweodros of Ethiopia, 1979; History of Ethiopian Towns, 2 vols., 1983–85; (with Graham Hancock) Under Ethiopian Skies, 1983; (with David Appleyard) Letters from Ethiopian Rulers, 1985; History of Ethiopian Terms: From the Middle Ages to 1935, 2 vols., 1989. Add: 22 Lawn Rd., London NW3 2XR, England.

PANSHIN, Alexei. American, b. 1940. Science fiction/Fantasy, Literature. Librarian, Brooklyn Public Library, 1966–67. *Publs:* Rite of Passage, 1968; Star Well, 1968; The Thurb Revolution, 1968; Heinlein in Dimension: A Critical Analysis, 1968; Masque World, 1969; Farewell to Yesterday's Tomorrow (short stories), 1975, 1976; (with Cory Panshin) SF in Dimension: A Book of Explorations, 1976; (with Cory Panshin)

Mondi Interiori (in Italian), 1978; (with Cory Panshin) Earth Magic, 1978; Transmutations: A Book of Personal Alchemy (miscellany), 1982; (with Cory Panshin) The World Beyond the Hill, 1989. Add: R.D. 1, Box 168, Riegelsville, Pa. 18077, U.S.A.

PAPAS, William. British (born South African), b. 1927. Children's fiction, Humour/Satire.Book Illustrator, Painter and Print Maker. Formerly Cartoonist, The Guardian and The Sunday Times newspapers, and Punch mag. *Publs:* The Press, 1964; The Story of Mr. Nero, 1965; The Church, 1965; Parliament, 1966; Freddy the Fell-Engine, 1966; The Law, 1967; Tasso, 1967; No Mules, 1967; Taresh, the Tea Planter, 1968; A Letter from India, 1968; A Letter from Israel, 1968; Theodore; or, The Mouse Who Wanted to Fly, 1969; Elias the Fisherman, 1970; The Monk and the Goat, 1971; (ed.) American Folk Tales and Legends, 1972; The Long-Haired Donkey, 1972; The Most Beautiful Child, 1973; The Zoo, 1974; People of Old Jerusalem, 1980. Add: c/o Oxford University Press, Children's Books, Walton St., Oxford OX2 6DP, England.

PARADIS, Adrian Alexis. American, b. 1912. Business, Children's non-fiction. Ed., Phoenix Publishing Co., Sugar Hill, N.H., since 1972. Asst. Secty., American Airlines Inc., 1942–68; Exec. Secty., 1969–73, and Chmn., 1974–75, Ottauquechee Regional Planning and Development Commn., Woodstock, Vt. *Publs:* Seventy-Five Ways for Boys to Earn Money, 1950; Never Too Young to Earn, 1954; For Immediate Release: Careers in Public Relations, 1955; From High School to a Job, 1956; Americans at Work, 1958; Dollars for You: 150 Ways for Boys to Earn Money, 1958; Librarians Wanted: Careers in Library Service, 1959; The New Look in Banking, 1961; Business in Action, 1962; (with B. Burke) Life You Save, 1962; Labor in Action, 1963; The Problem Solvers, 1964; Gail Borden, 1964; You and the Next Decade, 1965; Government in Action, 1965; (with G. Paradis) Grow in Grace: The Reference Handbook, 1966; Toward a Better World, 1966; The Bulls and the Bears, 1967; Economics in Action Today, 1967; The Hungry Years, 1967; (with G. Paradis) Your Life: Make It Count, 1968; Harvey Firestone, 1968; Henry Ford, 1968; Jobs to Take You Places, Here and Abroad, 1968; Trade: The World's Lifeblood, 1969; Two Hundred Million Miles a Day, 1969; Job Opportunities for Young Negroes, 1969; Economics Reference Book, 1970; Gold: King of Metals, 1970; From Trails to Superhighways, 1971; How Money Works: The Federal Reserve System, 1972; Labor Reference Book, 1972; International Trade in Action, 1973; Inflation in Action, 1974; (with R.H. Wood) Social Security in Action, 1975; Opportunities in Banking, 1980; Opportunities in Aviation, 1980; Opportunities in Transportation, 1983; The Labor Almanac, 1983; Planning Your Military Career, 1984; Opportunities in Your Own Service Business, 1985; Ida Tarbell, 1985; Planning Your Career of Tomorrow, 1986; Opportunities in Part-Time and Summer Jobs, 1987; Small Business Information Source Book, 1987; Planning Your Vocational/Technical Career, 1987; Opportunities in Military Careers, 1989. Add: Sugar Hill, N.H. 03585, U.S.A.

PARDOE, M(argot Mary). British, b. 1902. Children's fiction. Proprietor, Crossacres Hotel, Selworthy, Somerset, 1937–47. *Publs:* The Far Island, 1936; Four Plus Bunkle, 1939; Bunkle Began It Butts In, Bought It, Breaks Away, and Belinda Baffles Them, Went For Six, Gets Busy, 8 vols., 1942–51; The Ghost Boat, 1951; Bunkle's Brainwave, 1952; Bunkle Scents a Clue, 1953; The Boat Seekers, 1953; Charles Arriving, 1954; The Dutch Boat, 1955; May Madrigal, 1955; Argle's Mist, 1956, in U.S. as Curtain of Mist, 1957; The Nameless Boat, 1957; Argle's Causeway, 1958; Argle's Oracle, 1959; The Greek Boat Mystery, 1960; Bunkle Brings It Off, 1961. Add: 25 Wodehouse Rd., Old Hunstanton, Norfolk, England.

PARFITT, Tudor (Vernon). Welsh, b. 1944. History, Theology/Religion. Lectr. in Hebrew and Jewish Studies, Sch. of Oriental and African Studies, Univ. of London, since 1974. Lectr., Univ. of Toronto, 1972–74; Parkes Fellow, Univ. of Southampton, 1977. *Publs:* (trans. with Glenda Abramson) Great Tranquillity, by Yehuda Amichai, 1982; (with Glenda Abramson) The Great Transition, 1985; Operation Moses, 1985; The Thirteenth Gate, 1987; The Jews in Palestine 1800-1882, 1987. Add: c/o Dept. of Near and Middle East Studies, Sch. of Oriental and African Studies, Univ. of London, London WC1 7HP, England.

PARGETER, Edith. Also writes mystery novels as Ellis Peters. British, b. 1913.Mystery/Crime/Suspense, Historical/Romance/Gothic, Translations. *Publs:* Hortensius, Friend of Nero, 1936; Iron-Bound, 1936; The City Lies Foursquare, 1939; Ordinary People, 1941; She Goes to War, 1942; The Eighth Champion of Christendom, 1945; Reluctant Odyssey, 1946; Warfare Accomplished, 1947; By Firelight (in U.S. as By This Strange Fire), 1948; The Fair Young Phoenix, 1948; The Coast of Bohemia (non-fiction), 1950; Lost Children, 1951; Fallen into the Pit,

1951; Holiday with Violence, 1952; This Rough Magic, 1953; Most Loving Mere Folly, 1953; The Soldier at the Door, 1954; A Means of Grace, 1956; The Assize of the Dying (short stories), 1958; (as Ellis Peters) Death Mask, 1959; (as Ellis Peters) The Will and the Deed, 1960; The Heaven Tree, 1960; (as Ellis Peters) Death and the Joyful Woman, 1961; (as Ellis Peters) Funeral of Figaro, 1962; The Green Branch, 1962; The Scarlet Seed, 1963; (as Ellis Peters) Flight of a Witch, 1964; The Lily Hand (short stories), 1965; (as Ellis Peters) A Nice Derangement of Epitaphs (in U.S. as Who Lies Here?), 1965; (as Ellis Peters) The Piper on the Mountian, 1966; (as Ellis Peters) Black Is the Colour of My True Love's Heart, 1967; (as Ellis Peters) The Grass Widow's Tale, 1968; (as Ellis Peters) The House of Green Turf, 1969; (as Ellis Peters) Mourning Raga, 1969; (as Ellis Peters) The Knocker on Death's Door, 1970; (as Ellis Peters) Death to the Landlords, 1972; A Bloody Field by Shrewsbury, 1972; (as Ellis Peters) City of Gold and Shadows, 1973; (as Ellis Peters) The Horn of Roland, 1974; Sunrise in the West, 1974; The Dragon at Noonday, 1975; The Hounds of Sunset, 1976; (as Ellis Peters) Never Pick Up Hitch-Hikers!, 1976; (as Ellis Peters) A Morbid Taste for Bones, 1977; Afterglow and Nightfall, 1977; (as Ellis Peters) Rainbow's End, 1978; The Marriage of Meggotta, 1979; (as Ellis Peters) One Corpse Too Many, 1979; (as Ellis Peters) Monk's-Hood, 1980; (as Ellis Peters) Saint Peter's Fair, 1981; (as Ellis Peters) The Leper of Saint Giles, 1981; (as Ellis Peters) The Virgin in the Ice, 1982; (as Ellis Peters) The Sanctuary Sparrow, 1983; (as Ellis Peters) The Devil's Novice, 1983; (as Ellis Peters) Dead Man's Ransom, 1984; (as Ellis Peters) The Pilgrim of Hate, 1984; (as Ellis Peters) An Excellent Mystery, 1985; (as Ellis Peters) The Raven in the Foregate, 1986; (as Ellis Peters) The Rose Rent, 1986; (as Ellis Peters) The Hermit of Eyton Forest, 1987; (as Ellis Peters) The Confession of Brother Halvin, 1988. Translations—Tales of the Little Quarter: Stories, by Jan Neruda, 1957; The Sorrowful and Heroic Life of John Amos Comenius, by Frantisek Kosik, 1958; A Handful of Linden Leaves: An Anthology of Czech Poetry, 1958; Don Juan, by Josef Toman, 1958; The Abortionists, by Valja Styblova, 1961; Granny, by Bozena Nemcova, 1962; (with others) The Linden Tree (anthology), 1962; The Terezin Requiem, by Josef Bor, 1963; Legends of Old Bohemia, by Alois Jirasek, 1963; May, by Karel Hynek Macha, 1965; The End of the Old Times, by Vladislav Vancura, 1965; A Close Watch on the Trains, by Bohumil Hrabal, 1968; Report on My Husband, by Josef Slaska, 1969; A Ship Named Hope, by Ivan Klima, 1970; Mozart in Prague, by Jaroslav Seifert, 1970. Add: 14 Park Lane, Madeley, Telford, Salop. TF7 5HE, England.

PARHAM, William Thomas. British, 1913. Travel/Exploration/Adventure, Biography. *Publs:* Von Tempsky, Adventurer, 1969; Island Volcano, 1973; Men at Arms, 1977; Away from It All, 1977; John Roberts: Man in His Time, 1983; John Francis Fulloon: A Man of Two Cultures, 1985; (with T.J. Ryan) The Colonial New Zealand Wars, 1986; (with H. Parham) Along Life's Path, 1987. Add: 19 Lincoln Ave., Tawa, Wellington, New Zealand.

PARIS, Bernard Jay. American, 1931. Literature. Prof. of English, since 1981, and Dir., Inst. for Psychological Study of the Arts, since 1985, Univ. of Florida, Gainesville. Instr., Lehigh Univ., Bethlehem, Pa., 1956–60; Asst. Prof. to Prof., Michigan State Univ., E. Lansing, 1960–81. *Publs:* Experiments in Life: George Eliot's Quest for Values, 1965; A Psychological Approach to Fiction: Studies in Thackeray, Stendhal, George Eliot, Dostoevsky and Conrad, 1974; Character and Conflict in Jane Ausen's Novels: A Psychological Approach, 1978; (ed.) Third Force Psychology and the Study of Literature, 1986 (ed. with Norman Holland and Sidney Homan) Shakespeare's Personality, 1989. Add: Dept. of English, Univ. of Florida, Gainesville, Fla. 32611, U.S.A.

PARISH, James (Robert). American, b. 1944. Film, media. Self-employed marketing consultant, since 1988. Pres., Entertainment Copyright Research Co. Inc., NYC, 1965–68; Reviewer-Interviewer, Variety, NYC, 1968–69; Exec., MCRB, N. Hollywood, 1977–78, 1981–87, and at Homeowners Marketing Services, N. Hollywood, 1987–88. *Publs:* (ed. with P. Michael) American Movies Reference Book, 1969; (ed. with L. Maltin) Television Movies, 1969; (with P. Michael) The Emmy Awards: A Pictorial History, 1970; The Great Movie Series, 1971; The Fox Girls, 1971; (with A.H. Maril) The Cinema of Edward G. Robinson, 1972; The Paramount Pretties, 1972; (with R.L. Bowers) The MGM Stock Company, 1973; The Slapstick Queens, 1973; Actors Television Credits, 1973, supplements 1978, 1982; (with M.R. Pitts) The Great Spy Pictures, 1974; (with S. Whitney) The George Raft File, 1974; (with S. Whitney) Vincent Price Unmasked, 1974; (with M.R. Pitts) Film Directors Guide: United States, 1974; The RKO Gals, 1974; Hollywood's Great Love Teams, 1974; The Great Movie Heroes, 1974; Good Dames, 1974; (with D.E. Stanke) The Glamour Girls, 1975; (with D.E. Stanke) The Debonairs, 1975; (with L. DeCarl) Hollywood Players: The 40's, 1975;

(with J. Ano) Liza!: Liza Minnelli Story, 1975; (with M.R. Pitts) The Great Gangster Pictures, 1975; (co-author) Film Directors Guide: Western Europe, 1975; The Elvis Presley Scrapbook, 1975; Great Western Stars, 1976; The 30's, 1976; The Tough Guys, 1976; (with M.R. Pitts) The Great Science Fiction Pictures, 1976; (with M.R. Pitts) The Great Western Pictures, 1976; (with Don E. Stanke) The Swashbucklers, 1976; Film Actors Guide: Western Europe, 1977; (with Don E. Stanke) The All-Americans, 1977; (with Don E. Stanke) The Leading Ladies, 1977; Hollywood Character Actors, 1978; (with others) The Hollywood Beauties, 1978; (with M.R. Pitts) Hollywood on Hollywood, 1978; (with W.T. Leonard) The Funsters, 1979; (with D. Stake) The Forties Gals, 1979; (as Frances Maugham) Hollywood Happiness, 1979; (with G. Mark) The Hollywood Regulars, 1980; (with G. Mark) The Best of MGM, 1980; (with Mark A. Trost) Actors TV Credits: Supplement I, 1980; (with Vincent A. Terrace) Actors TV Credits: Supplement II, 1982; (with Vincent A. Terrace) Actors TV Credits: Supplement III, 1986; (with Michael R. Pitts) Great Spy Pictures II, 1986; (with Michael R. Pitts) Great Gangster Pictures II, 1987; (with Michael R. Pitts) Great Western Pictures II, 1988; Add: 4338 Gentry Ave. No. 1, Studio City, Calif. 91604, U.S.A.

PARK, (Rosina) Ruth (Lucia). Australian. Novels/Short stories, Children's fiction, Plays/Screenplays. *Publs:* The Uninvited Guest (play), 1948; The Harp in the South, 1948; Poor Man's Orange (in U.S. as 12 Plymouth Street), 1949; The Witch's Thorn, 1951; A Power of Roses, 1953; Pink Flannel, 1955; (with D'Arcy Niland) The Drums Go Bang (autobiographical), 1956; One-a-Pecker, Two-a-Pecker (in U.S. as Frost and the Fire), 1957; The Good-Looking Women (in U.S. as Serpent's Delight), 1961; The Hole in the Hill (in U.S. as The Secret of the Maori Cave), 1961; The Ship's Cat, 1961; Uncle Matt's Mountain, 1962; The Road to Christmas, 1962; The Road under the Sea, 1962; The Muddle-Headed Wombat series, 11 vols., 1962–76; Shaky Island, 1962; Airlift for Grandee, 1964; Ring for the Sorcerer, 1967; The Sixpenny Island (in U.S. as Ten-Cent Island), 1968; Nuki and the Sea Serpent, 1969; The Companion Guide to Sydney, 1973; Callie's Castle, 1974; The Gigantic Balloon, 1975; Swords and Crowns and Rings, 1977; Come Danger, Come Darkness, 1978; Playing Beatie Bow, 1980; When the Wind Changed, 1980; The Big Brass Key, 1983; The Sydney We Love, 1983; Missus, 1985; My Sister Sif, 1986; The Tasmania We Love, 1987; Roger Bandy, 1988; Callie's Family, 1988; Things in Corners, 1989. Add: c/o Curtis Brown Pty. Ltd., P.O. Box 19, Paddington, N.S.W. 2021, Australia.

PARKER, Barrett. American, b. 1908. Poetry, History, Biography. Consultant, Lectr. and Ed., U.S. Army, 1942–46, and U.S. Foreign Service, 1947–70; Asst. to the U.S. Ambassador, London, 1950–53; Cultural Attaché, U.S. Embassy, Tehran, 1955–57; Dir., U.S. Information Services, U.S. Embassy, Ottawa, 1965–68; Lectr. in English, American Univ., Washington, D.C., 1970–73. Donor, St. Croix Island as Intnl. Park, 1982; Chmn., Episcopal Diocesan (Me.), World Peace Commn., 1982–84; Special Asst. to the Bishop, Episcopal Diocesc of Maine, 1986–88. *Publs:* A Yank in England, 1944; (ed.) A Selection of American Documents, 1945; Other Poems, 1946; Collects and Prayers in Wartime, 1950; (ed.) Famous British Generals, 1952; William Belmont Parker: A Memoir, 1954; (ed.) U.S. and Vietnam, 3 vols., 1966–67; (ed.) Canadian-American Relations 1867-1967, 3 vols., 1968; (ed. with Ahmed Javid) A Collection of Afghan Legends, 1971; Poems, 1972; Selected Poems 1944-1974, 1974; On the Making of a Bibliography, 1974; (ed. with Sylvia Sherman) In Commemoration of Joshua Lawrence Chamberlain: A Guide/Bibliography, 1978; The Role of the Elderly in Tomorrow's World,. 1980; Can World Leaders Avert a Nuclear Holocaust?, 1980; Samuel de Champlain: A Monograph, 1983; The Model Sailboat, 1985; Verse and Other Trivia, 1986; Letters to the Editor, 1987; Twelve Poems for a Birthday, 1988; Poems for Christmas, 1989. Add: 43 Spring St., Brunswick, Me. 04011, U.S.A.

PARKER, Derek. British, b. 1932. Poetry, Dance/Ballet, Literature, Media, Psychology, Supernatural/Occult topics, Travel/Exploration/Adventure, Biography. Registrar, Royal Literary Fund, London; Chmn., Management Cttee., Soc. of Authors, London. Ed., Poetry Review, London, 1966–71. *Publs:* The Fall of Phaeton, 1954; Company of Two, 1955; Byron and His World, 1968; (ed. with J. Lehmann) Selected Letters of Edith Sitwell, 1970; The Question of Astrology, 1970; Astrology in the Modern World, 1970; (with J. Parker) The Compleat Astrologer, 1971; (with J. Parker) The Compleat Lover, 1972; (with J. Parker) The Compleat Astrologers' Sunsign Guide, 1973; (with J. Parker) Love Signs, 1974; The West Country, 1974; John Donne and His World, 1974; Familiar to All: The Biography of William Lilly, 1974; (ed.) Sacheverell Sitwell, 1975; (with J. Parker) The Natural History of the Chorus Girl, 1975; Radio: The Great Years, 1976; (with J. Parker) How Do You Know Who You Are, 1980; (ed.) An Anthology of Erotic Poetry, 1980; The West

Country and the Coast, 1980; (ed.) An Anthology of Erotic Prose, 1981; (with J. Parker) The Do-It-Yourself Health Book, 1982; (with J. Parker) The New Compleat Astrologer, 1984; (with J. Parker) The Compleat Book of Dreaming, 1985; (with J. Parker) Life Signs, 1986; (with J. Parker) Travellers' Guide to Egypt, 1987. Add: 37 Campden Hill Towers, London W11 3QW, England.

PARKER, Franklin. American, b. 1921. Education, Biography.Assoc. Prof., State Univ. of New York at New Paltz, 1956–57, and Univ. of Texas at Austin, 1957–64; Prof., Univ. of Oklahoma, Norman, 1964–68; Benedum Prof. of Education, West Virginia Univ., Morgantown, 1968–86. *Publs:* African Development and Education in Southern Rhodesia, 1960; Africa South of the Sahara, 1966; George Peabody: A Biography, 1971; (co-ed. with B.J. Parker) American Dissertations on Foreign Education: A Bibliography with Abstracts (series): Canada, 1971, India, 1972, Japan, 1972, Africa, 1973, Scandinavia, 1974, China, 2 vols., 1975, Korea, 1976, Mexico, 1976, South America, 1977, Central America, 1979, Pakistan and Bangladesh, 1980, Iran and Iraq, 1980, and Israel, 1980, The Middle East (Arab Education, Bahrain, Jordan, Kuwait, Lebanon, Saudi Arabia, Syria), 1981, Thailand, 1983, Asia, 1985, Pacific, 1986, Philippines, 1986, and Australia and New Zealand, 1988; The Battle of the Books: Kanawha County, 1975; What Can We Learn from the Schools of China?, 1977; (co-ed. with B.J. Parker) Education in Puerto Rico and of Puerto Ricans in the U.S.A.: Abstracts of American Doctoral Dissertations, 1978; (co-ed. with B.J. Parker) Women's Education—A World View: American Doctoral Dissertations, 1979; British Schools and Ours, 1979; Women's Education—A World View: Annotated Bibliography of Books and Reports, 1980; U.S. Higher Education: Guide to Information Sources, 1980; Education in People's Republic of China, 1986. Add: c/o Coll. of Education and Psychology, Western Carolina Univ., Cullowhee, NC 28723, U.S.A.

PARKER, Gordon. British, b. 1940. Novels/Short stories, Plays/Screenplays. Book Reviewer, BBC Radio and ITV. *Publs:* The Darkness of the Morning, 1975; Lightning in May, 1976; The Pool, 1978; Action of the Tiger, 1981; radio plays—The Seance, 1978; God Protect the Lonely Widow, 1982. Add: 14 Thornhill Close, Seaton Delaval, Northumberland, England.

PARKER, Nancy W(inslow). American, b. 1930. Children's fiction, Children's non-fiction. Freelance artist and painter. Art Dir., Appleton-Century-Crofts Inc., publrs., 1968–70; Graphic Designer, Holt Rinehart and Winston Inc., publrs., NYC, 1970–72. *Publs:* The Man with the Take-Apart Head, 1974; The Party at the Old Farm, 1975; Mrs. Wilson Wanders Off, 1976; Love from Uncle Clyde, 1977; The Crocodile under Louis Finnesberg's Bed, 1978; The President's Cabinet (non-fiction), 1978; The Ordeal of Byron B. Blackbear, 1979; Paddums, The Cathcarts' Orange Cat, 1980; Poofy Loves Company, 1980; The Spotted Dog, 1980; Cooper, The McNallys' Big Black Dog, 1981; The President's Car (non-fiction), 1981; Love from Aunt Betty, 1983; The Christmas Camel, 1983; The United Nations from A to Z, 1985; (with J.R. Wright) Bugs, 1987. Add: 51 E. 74th St., New York, N.Y. 10021, U.S.A.

PARKER, Richard. British, b. 1915. Novels/Short stories, Children's fiction. *Publs:* Three Pebbles, 1954; Sword of Ganelon, 1957; Lion at Large, 1959; Valley Full of Pipers, 1962; House That Guilda Drew, 1963; Boy Who Wasn't Lonely, 1964; Boy on a Chain, 1964; Perversity of Pipers, 1964; Private Beach, 1964; M for Mischief, 1965; Hendon Fungus, 1967; Spell Seven, 1971; Paul and Etta, 1972; Old Powder Line, 1972; Keeping Time, 1973; One Green Bottle, 1973; Time to Choose, 1973; He Is Your Brother, 1974; Snatched, 1974; Fire Curse, 1975; Quarter Boy, 1976; In and Out the Window, 1976. Add: 36 Central Parade, Herne Bay, Kent, England.

PARKER, Robert B(rown). American, b. 1932. Novels/Short stories, Mystery/Crime/Suspense. Technical writer and Group Leader, Raytheon Co., 1957–59; Copywriter and Ed., Prudential Insurance Co., Boston, 1959–62; Partner, Parker Farman Co., advertising agency, Boston, 1960–62; Teaching Fellow and Lectr., Boston Univ., 1962–64; Instr., Massachusetts State Coll., Lowell, 1964–66; Lectr., Suffolk Univ., Boston, 1965–66; Instr., Massachusetts State Coll., Bridgewater, 1964–68; Asst. Prof., 1968–74, Assoc. Prof., 1974–77, and Prof., 1977–79, Northeastern Univ., Boston. *Publs:* fiction—The Godwulf Manuscript, 1973; God Save the Child, 1974; Mortal Stakes, 1975; Promised Land, 1976; The Judas Goat, 1978; Wilderness, 1979; Looking for Rachel Wallace, 1980; Early Autumn, 1981; A Savage Place, 1981; Surrogate, 1982; Ceremony, 1982; The Widening Gyre, 1983; Love and Glory, 1983; Valediction, 1984; A Catskill Eagle, 1985; Taming a Sea Horse, 1986; Pale Kings and Princes, 1987; Crimson Joy, 1988; Playmates, 1989; (with Raymond Chandler) Poodle Springs, 1989; other—(ed.) The Personal Response to

Literature, 1971; (ed.) Order and Diversity, 1973; Sports Illustrated Training with Weights, 1974; (with Joan H. Parker) Three Weeks in Spring, 1978. Add: Helen Brann Agency, 94 Curtis Rd., Bridgewater, Conn. 06752, U.S.A.

PARKER, Robert Stewart. Australian, b. 1915. Politics/Government, Public/Social administration. Social Science Research Fellow, 1947–48, Reader in Public Admin., 1954–60, Reader in Political Science, 1961–62, and Prof. of Political Science, 1963–78, Australian National Univ., Canberra. Prof. of Political Science and Public Admin., Victoria Univ. Coll., New Zealand, 1949–53. *Publs:* Public Service Recruitment in Australia, 1942; (ed.) Economic Stability in New Zealand, 1953; Highlights of NSW Local Government Legislation over the Last Fifty Years, 1956; (co-author) The Government of the Australian States, 1960; (co-ed.) The Politics of Dependence, 1971; Papua New Guinea as an Emergent State, 1972; (co-author) Politics of Urban Growth, 1972; (co-ed.) The Emergence of the Australian Party System, 1977; The Government of New South Wales, 1978. Add: 54 Munro St., Curtin, A.C.T. 2605, Australia.

PARKER, Stanley R. British, b. 1927. Politics, Sociology. Principal Social Survey Officer, Office of Population Censuses and Surveys, London, from 1973, now retired. Visiting Assoc. Prof., Univ. of Waterloo, Ontario, 1974; Visiting Research Fellow, Flinders Univ. of South Australia, 1986–87. *Publs:* (with L. Moss) The Local Government Councillor, 1967; (with R. Brown, J. Child and M. Smith) The Sociology of Industry, 1967, 4th ed. 1981; (with M. Thomas) Workplace Industrial Relations, 1968; (with C. Thomas, N. Ellis and W. McCarthy) Effects of the Redundancy Payments Act, 1971; The Future of Work and Leisure, 1971; (ed. with M. Smith and C. Smith) Leisure and Society in Britain, 1973; Workplace Industrial Relations 1972, 1974; The Sociology of Leisure, 1976; Work and Retirement, 1982; Leisure and Work, 1983; (with Alan Graefe) Recreation and Leisure: An Introductory Handbook, 1987. Add: 46 Hurstwood Rd., London NW11 0AT, England.

PARKER, Thomas (Henry Louis). British, b. 1916. Theology/Religion. Vicar of Brothertoft, Lincs., 1948–55; Rector of Great and Little Ponton, Lincs., 1955–61; Vicar of Oakington, Cambridge, 1961–71; Lectr. in Theology, 1971–75, and Reader, 1975–81, Univ. of Durham. *Publs:* Oracles of God, 1947; Doctrine of Knowledge of God, 1952, rev. ed. as Calvin's Doctrine of Knowledge of God, 1970; Portrait of Calvin, 1954; (ed. and trans.) Calvin's Sermons on Isaiah 53, 1956; (ed.) Essays in Christology for Karl Barth, 1956; (trans.) Barth's Church Dogmatics, 1957; (trans.) Calvin's Commentary on John, vol. I, 1959, vol. II, 1961; (trans. with D. Cairns) Brunner's Commentary on Galatians, 1965; (ed.) English Reformers, 1966; (ed. with J.I. McCord) Service in Christ, 1966; Karl Barth, 1970; Calvin's New Testament Commentaries, 1971; (trans.) Calvin's Commentary on Gospels, vol. II, 1973; John Calvin, 1975; (ed.) Calvini Commentarius in Epistolam ad Romanos, 1981; Calvin's Old Testament Commentaries, 1986; Romans 1532-1542, 1986. Add: 72 Windsor Rd., Cambridge, England.

PARKER, W. Dale. American, b. 1925. Philosophy, Politics/Government, Social sciences. Freelance writer, lectr., and designer. *Publs:* The Philosophy of Genius, 1971; Gutless America, 1973. Add: P.O. Box 1441, Titusville, Fla. 32780, U.S.A.

PARKER, W(illiam) H(enry). Canadian, b. 1912. Geography, International relations/Current affairs, Translations. Sr. Lectr., Royal Military Academy, Sandhurst, 1947–52; Asst. Prof., McMaster Univ., Hamilton, Ont., 1952–56; Assoc. Prof., Univ. of Manitoba, Winnipeg, 1956–60; Lectr. in the Geography of the Soviet Union, 1964–79; Student, Christ Church, Oxford, 1975–79. *Publs:* Canada, 1955; (trans.) France, 1956; (trans.) Moscow and Leningrad, 1958; Anglo-America, 1962; An Historical Geography of Russia, 1968; The Soviet Union, 1969; The Superpowers: The United States and the Soviet Union Compared, 1972; The Russians: How They Live and Work, 1973; Motor Transport in the Soviet Union, 1979; Mackinder: Geography as an Aid to Statecraft, 1982; The Priapea: Poems for a Phallic God, 1988. Add: Stowe Grange, St. Briavels, Glos. GL15 6QH, England.

PARKES, Roger Graham. British, b. 1933. Novels/Short stories. With Beaverbrook Newspapers, London, 1959–64; Story Ed., BBC-TV, London, 1964–71. *Publs:* Deathmask, 1970; Line of Fire, 1971; The Guardians, 1973; (with Edward Boyd) The Dark Number, 1973; The Fourth Monkey, 1978; Alice Ray Morton's Cookham, 1981; Them and Us, 1985; Riot, 1986; Y-E-S, We'll Crack it, 1987; Y-E-S, We'll Help, 1987; An Abuse of Justice, 1988. Add: Cartlands Cottage, Kings Lane, Cookham Dean, Berks. SL6 9AY, England.

PARKIN, Molly. British, b. 1932. Novels/Short stories. Former Fashion Ed., Nova mag., Harper's Bazaar mag., and The Sunday Times newspaper, London. *Publs:* Love All, 1974; Uptight, 1975; Full Up, 1976; Write Up, 1977; Switchback, 1978; Good Golly, Ms. Molly, 1978; Fast and Loose, 1979; Molly Parkin's Purple Passages, 1979; Up and Coming, 1980; Bite of the Apple, 1981; Love Bites, 1982; Breast Stroke, 1983; Cock-a-Hoop, 1985. Add: c/o St. Martin's Press, 175 Fifth Ave., New York, N.Y. 10010, U.S.A.

PARKINSON, Cyril Northcote. British, b. 1909. Administration/Management, History, Politics/Government, Biography. Former Sr. History Master, Blundell's Sch., Tiverton; Master, Royal Naval Coll., Dartmouth; Lectr., Univ. of Liverpool; Raffles Prof. of History, Univ. of Malaya, 1950–58; Prof. Emeritus, Troy State Univ., Alabama; Fellow of Emmanuel Coll., Cambridge. *Publs:* Edward Pellew, Viscount Exmouth, 1934; Trade in the Eastern Seas, 1937; (ed.) The Trade Winds, 1948; The Rise of the Port of Liverpool, 1952; War in the Eastern Seas, 1954; Britain in the Far East, 1955; Parkinson's Law: The Pursuit of Progress, 1958; The Evolution of Political Thought, 1958; British Intervention in Malaya 1867-1877, 1960; The Law and the Profits, 1960; East and West, 1963; Ponies Plot, 1965; A Law unto Themselves, 1966; Left Luggage, 1967; Mrs. Parkinson's Law, 1968; The Life and Times of Horatio Hornblower, 1970; The Law of Delay, 1971; The Fur-Lined Mousetrap, 1972; Devil to Pay, 1973; Industrial Disruption, 1973; Big Business, 1974; The Fireship, 1975; Gunpowder, Treason, and Plot, 1975; The Rise of Big Business, 1977; Touch and Go, 1977; Britannia Rules, 1977; (with Nigel Rowe) Communicate, 1977; Dead Reckoning, 1978; Jeeves: A Gentleman's Personal Gentleman, 1979; The Law of Longer Life, 1980; So Near So Far, 1981; The Guernseyman, 1982; The Fur-Lined Moustrap, 1984; The Management Jungle, 1984. Add: 36 Harkness Dr., Canterbury CT2 7RP, England.

PARKINSON, Michael. British. Sports/Physical education/Keeping fit, Biography. Television personality and talk show compere. *Publs:* Football Daft, 1968; Cricket Mad, 1969; (with Willis Hall) A to Z of Soccer, 1970; (with Clyde Jeavons) Pictorial History of Westerns, 1972; Sporting Fever, 1974; Best: A Biography of George Best, 1975; Parkinson, 1975; (with Willis Hall) Football Final, 1975; Bats in the Pavilion, 1977; The Woofits, 1980; Parkinson's Lore, 1981; The Best of Parkinson, 1982. Add: The Pier House, Strand on the Green, London W4 3NN, England.

PARKINSON, Thomas (Francis). American, b. 1920. Plays/Screenplays, Poetry, Literatue. Prof. of English, Univ. of California, Berkeley (joined faculty, 1948). *Publs:* W.B. Yeats, Self-Critic: A Study of His Early Verse, 1951; Men, Women, Vines, 1959; (ed.) A Casebook on the Beat, 1961; (ed.) Masterworks of Prose, 1962; W.B. Yeats: The Later Poetry, 1964; Thanatos: Earth Poems, 1965, 1976; (ed.) Robert Lowell: A Collection of Critical Essays, 1968; Protect the Earth (includes essays), 1970; Homage to Jack Spicer and Other Poems: Poems 1965-1969, 1970; Twenty-Five Years of the Endless War (play), 1973; The Canters of T.P., Chiefly Concerning John Wayne, 1978; Hart Crane and Ivor Winters: Their Literary Correspondence, 1978; Poets, Poems, Movements, 1987. Add: 1001 Cragmont, Berkeley, Calif. 94708, U.S.A.

PARKS, Edna Dorintha. American, b. 1910. Music. Prof. Emeritus of Music, Wheaton Coll., Norton, Mass., since 1976 (Asst. Prof., 1957–61; Assoc. Prof., 1961–64; Prof. 1964–76). *Publs:* The Hymns and Hymn Tunes Found in the English Metrical Psalters, 1966; (compiler) Early English Hymns: An Index, 1972. Add: 81 Essex Ct., Bedford, Mass. 01730, U.S.A.

PARKS, Gordon (Alexander Buchanan). American, b. 1912. Novels/Short stories, Poetry, Photography, Autobiography/Memoirs/Personal. Film Dir.; Photographer and writer for Life mag., 1949–70; Editorial Dir., Essence mag., NYC, 1970–73. *Publs:* The Learning Tree, 1963, screenplay 1969; A Choice of Weapons, 1966; A Poet and His Camera, 1968; Whispers of Intimate Things, 1971; Born Black, 1971; In Love, 1971; Moments Without Proper Names (poetry), 1975; Flavio, 1978; To Smile in Autumn, 1979; Shannon, 1981. Add: 860 United Nations Plaza, New York, N.Y., U.S.A.

PARKS, Tim. British, b. 1954. Novels, Translations. *Publs:* Tongues of Flame, 1985; (trans.) Erotic Tales, by Alberto Moravia, 1985; Loving Roger, 1986; (trans.) The Voyeur, by Alberto Moravia, 1986; Home Thoughts (novel), 1987; (trans.) Indian Nocturne, By Antonio Tabucchi, 1988; Family Planning (novel), 1989. Add: London SW10 0TG, England.

PARMET, Herbert S. American, b. 1929. History, Biography. Distinguished Prof. of History, Queensborough Community Coll., and the Grad. Sch. of City Univ. of New York, since 1968. *Publs:* (with M. Hecht) Aaron Burr: Portrait of an Ambitious Man, 1967; (with M. Hecht) Never Again: A President Runs for a Third Term, 1968; Eisenhower and the American Crusades, 1972; The Democrats, 1976; Jack: The Struggles of John F. Kennedy, 1980; JFK: The Presidency of John F. Kennedy, 1983; The Age of Nixon, 1990. Add: R.D.1, Hillsdale, N.Y. 12529, U.S.A.

PAROTTI, Philip. American, b. 1941. Novels/Short stories. Prof. of English, Sam Houston State Univ., Huntsville, Tex., since 1972.Commissioned Officer, U.S. Navy, 1963–67, and U.S. Naval Reserve, 1967 until retirement, 1983. *Publs:* The Greek Generals Talk, 1986; The Trojan Generals Talk, 1988. Add: English Dept., Sam Houston State Univ., Huntsville, Tex. 77341, U.S.A.

PARRISH, Frank. *See* **LONGRIGG**, Roger.

PARRISH, Patt. *See* **BUCHEISTER**, Patt.

PARRISH, William E. American, b. 1931. History, Biography. Prof. of History, Mississippi State Univ., since 1978. Member of the Faculty, 1955–78, Harry S. Truman Prof. of American History, 1971–78, and Dean of the Coll., 1973–75, Westminster Coll., Fulton, Mo. Gen. Ed., Sesquicentennial History of Missouri; Member, State Historical Records Advisory Bd., since 1980. *Publs:* David Rice Atchison of Missouri: Border Politician, 1961; Turbulent Partnership: Missouri and the Union 1861-1865, 1963; Missouri under Radical Rule 1865-1870, 1965; (ed.) The Civil War: A Second American Revolution?, 1970; Westminster College: An Informal History 1851-1961, 1971; A History of Missouri 1860-1875, 1973; (with Charles T. Jones and Lawrence O. Christensen) Missouri: The Heart of the Nation, 1980. Add: Dept. of History, Mississippi State Univ., Mississippi State, Miss. 39762, U.S.A.

PARROTT, Ian. British, b. 1916. Music. Vice-Pres., Elgar Soc. and Warlock Soc. Asst. Dir. of Music, Malvern Coll., 1937; Lectr. in Music, Univ. of Birmingham, 1947–50; Gregynog Prof. of Music, University Coll. of Wales, Aberystwyth, 1950–83. *Publs:* Pathways to Modern Music, 1947; A Guide to Musical Thought, 1955; Method in Orchestration, 1957; The Spiritual Pilgrims, 1969; Elgar, 1971; Second Impression, 1977; The Music of Rosemary Brown, 1978. Add: Henblas, Abermad, nr. Aberystwyth, Wales.

PARRY, Albert. American, b. 1901. History, International relations/Current affairs, Politics/Government, Sciences (general), Biography, Translations. Prof. of Russian Civilization and Language Emeritus, Colgate Univ., Hamilton, N.Y., since 1969 (Prof., 1947–69). Prof., Case Western Reserve Univ., Cleveland, 1969–71. *Publs:* Garrets and Pretenders: A History of Bohemianism in America, 1933, 1960; Tattoo, 1933, 1971; Whistler's Father, 1939; (with W. Williams) Riddle of the Reich, 1941; Russian Cavalcade, 1944; (trans.) Building Lenin's Russia, by Simon Liberman, 1945; Russia's Rockets and Missiles, 1960; The New Class Divided: Science and Technology Versus Communism, 1966; America Learns Russian: A History of the Teaching of the Russian Language in the United States, 1967; (trans.) Peter Kapitsa on Life and Science, 1968; (trans.) The Moscow Puzzles: 359 Mathematical Recreations by Boris A. Kordemsky, 1972; The Russian Scientist, 1973; (with H.T. Moore) Twentieth-Century Russian Literature, 1974; Terrorism: From Robespierre to Arafat, 1976; (with V.A. Nikolaev) The Loves of Catherine the Great, 1982; Full Steam Ahead: The True Story of Peter Demens, 1987. Add: 6919 Place de la Paix, St. Petersburg, Fla. 33707, U.S.A.

PARRY, Ellwood C., III. American, b. 1941. Art. Assoc. Prof. of Art History, Univ. of Iowa, Iowa City, since 1976. Asst. Prof. of Art History, Columbia Univ., NYC, 1969–75. *Publs:* The Image of the Indian and the Black Man in American Art 1590-1900, 1974; Reflections of 1776: The Colonies Revisited, 1974; The Art of Thomas Cole: Ambition and Imagination, 1988. Add: c/o Univ. of Delaware Press, Associated University Presses, Inc., 440 Forsgate Dr., Cranbury, N.J. 08512. U.S.A.

PARRY, Hugh Jones. Writes fiction as James Cross. American, b. 1916. Novels/Short stories, Mystery/Crime/Suspense, Social sciences. Assoc. Dir. and Research Prof. of Sociology, Social Research Group, George Washington Univ., D.C., since 1966. Assoc. Dir. and Dir., Opinion Research Center, Univ. of Denver, 1947–49; Dir., Troop Attitude Research Branch. U.S. Armed Forces, Europe, 1950–52; Project Officer, Research Dir., and Dir. of Research, U.S. Information Agency, 1955–65. *Publs:* (with Leo P. Crispi) Public Opinion in Westren Europe, 1953; as James Cross—Root of Evil, 1957; The Dark Road, 1959; The Grave of

Heros, 1961; To Hell for Half a Crown, 1967. Add: 4814 Falstone Ave., Chevy Chase, Md. 20815, U.S.A.

PARRY, Wilfrid Hocking. British, b. 1924. Medicine/Health. Consultant Physician in genito-urinary medicine, Trent Regional Health Authority, since 1982. Consultant in Smallpox, Trent Regional Health Authority, and Dept. of Health and Social Services, London, since 1969. Principal Medical Officer, City of Liverpool, 1955–62; Deputy Medical Officer of Health and Deputy Principal Sch. Medical Officer, Sheffield, 1965–69; Special Lectr. in Medical Admin. and Community Health, Univ. of Nottingham, and Medical Officer of Health, City of Nottingham, 1969–74; Area Medical Officer, Sheffield, 1974–82; Hon. Clinical Lectr. in Community Medicine, Univ. of Sheffield, 1976–82. *Publs:* Communicable Diseases, 1969, 3rd ed. 1979. Add: 135 Dore Rd., Dore, Sheffield S17 3NF, England.

PARSONS, C(hristopher) J(ames). British, b. 1941. Education, Language/Linguistics, Writing/Journalism. Principal Lectr., Hammersmith and West London Coll., since 1974. Lectr., Kidderminster Coll. of Further Education, 1963–64, Canterbury Technical Coll., 1964–67, and Merton Technical Coll., London, 1967–74. *Publs:* Theses and Project Work, 1973; Library Use in Further Education, 1973; How to Study Effectively, 1976; Problems in Business Communication, 1977; Communication for Business Students, 1978; Communication Skills Library, 1980; Assignments in Communications, 1982. Add: 12 Berber Rd., London SW11 6RZ, England.

PARSONS, Coleman O. American, b. 1905. Literature. Emeritus Prof. of English, Grad. Sch., City Univ. of New York, since 1976 (Grad. Prof. of English, 1963–76). Adviser in Scottish Literature, Yale Univ., New Haven, Conn., since 1973. Instr. to Prof. of English, Long Island Univ., Brooklyn, N.Y., 1931–32 and 1937–41; faculty member, Vassar Coll., Poughkeepsie, N.Y., 1933–34, American Univ., Washington, D.C. 1934–35, and City Coll. of New York, 1941–72; Supvr. of English, City Coll. of New York, 1956–61. Founder, Parsons Collection of Scottish Literature, Columbia Univ., NYC, 1976. *Publs:* Witchcraft and Demonology in Scott's Fiction, 1964; (ed.) Joseph Glanvill's Saducismus Triumphatus, 1966; (ed.) George Sinclair's Satan's Invisible World Discovered, 1969; (ed.) Sir Walter Scott's The Two Drovers, 1971. Add: Grad. Sch., City Univ. of New York, 33 W. 42nd St., New York, N.Y. 10036, U.S.A.

PARSONS, Jack. British, b. 1920. Demography, Social sciences (general). Visiting Lectr., Univ. Coll., Cardiff, since 1982. Advisory Ed., Population and Environment Mag., since 1986. Research Assoc., 1959–61, and Lectr. in Social Instns., 1961–74, Brunel Univ., Uxbridge, Middx.; Sr. Lectr. in Population Studies, and Deputy Dir., David Owen Centre for Population Growth Studies, University Coll., Cardiff, 1975–81. *Publs:* The Blackhill Campaign (documentary film), 1964; Population Versus Liberty, 1971; (co-author) Changing Directions, 1974; The Economic Transition, 1975; (co-author) Environment and the Industrial Society, 1976; Population Fallacies 1977; (co-author) Britain's Crisis in Sociological Perspective, 1977; (co-author) Human Fertility Control, 1979. Add: Treferig Cottage Farm, Llantrisant, Mid-Glam CF7 8LQ, Wales.

PARSONS, Peter Angas. Australian, b. 1933. Biology. Prof. of Genetics, La Trobe Univ., Bundoora, since 1966. Member, Editorial Bd., Behavior Genetics, since 1972, and Journal of Biogeography, since 1978. Fellow, St. John's Coll., Cambridge, 1959–62; Reader in Human Genetics, Univ. of Melbourne, 1962–66. Vice-Pres., 1973–74, and Pres., 1975–76., Australian Inst. of Nuclear Science and Engineering. *Publs:* The Genetic Analysis of Behaviour, 1967; Behavioural and Ecological Genetics: Study in Drosophla, 1973; (with L. Ehrman) The Genetics of Behaviour, 1976; (with L. Ehrman) Behaviour Genetics and Evolution, 1981; The Evolutionary Biology of Colonizing Species, 1983. Add: Dept. of Genetics and Human Variation, La Trobe Univ., Bundoora, Vic. 3083, Australia.

PARTHASARATHY, R(ajagopal). Indian, b. 1934. Poetry. Asst. Prof. of English and of Asian Studies, Skidmore Coll., Saratoga Springs, N.Y., since 1986. Lectr. in English, Ismail Yusuf Coll., Bombay, 1959–62, and Mithibai Coll., Bombay, 1962–65; Lectr. in English Language Teaching, British Council, Bombay, 1965–66; Asst. Prof. of English, Presidency Coll., Madras, 1966–67; Lectr. in English, South Indian Education Soc. Coll., Bombay, 1967–71; Regional Ed., Madras, 1971–78, and Ed., 1978–82, Oxford University Press, Delhi; Member, Intnl. Writing Program, Univ. of Iowa, Iowa City, 1978–79; Asst. Instn. in English, Univ. of Texas at Austin, 1982–86. *Publs:* (ed. with J.J. Healy) Poetry from Leeds, 1968; (ed.) Twentieth-Century Indian Poets, 1976; Rough Passage (verse), 1977.   Add: Dept. of English, Skidmore Coll., Saratoga Springs, N.Y. 12866, U.S.A..

PARTRIDGE, Astley Cooper.   South African, b. 1901.   Language/Linguistics, Literature, Biography.   Prof. Emeritus, Dept. of English, Univ. of the Witwatersrand, Johannesburg, since 1966 (joined faculty, 1954). *Publs:* Readings in South African English Prose, 1941, 3rd ed. 1954; The Problem of Henry VIII Re-opened: Some Linguistic Criteria for the Two Styles Apparent in the Play, 1949; (with F.P. Wilson) Gentleness and Nobility, 1950; The Accidence of Ben Jonson's Plays, Masques and Entertainments, 1953; Studies in the Syntax of Ben Jonson's Plays, 1953; Orthography in Shakespeare and Elizabethan Drama, 1964; Modern Prose, 1964; The Tribe of Ben, 1966; The Story of Our South African Flag, 1966; Thus the Bowl Should Run, 1969; Scenes fom South African Life, 1969; Tudor to Augustan English, 1969; Lives, Letters and Diaries, 1971; The Language of Renaissance Poetry: Spenser, Shakespeare, Donne, and Milton, 1971; Landmarks in the History of English Scholarship, 1972; The Foundations of English Criticism, 1972; English Biblical Translation, 1972; Folklore of Southern Africa, 1974; The Language of Modern Poetry: Yeats, Eliot, Auden, 1975; A Substantive Grammar of Shakespeare's Non-Dramatic Texts, 1976; John Donne: Language and Style, 1978; A Companion to Old and Middle English Studies, 1982; Language and Society in Anglo-Irish Literature, 1984.   Add: 12 Cluny Rd., Forest Town, Johannesburg, South Africa.

PARTRIDGE, James W.   British, b. 1936.   Medicine/Health.   Consultant Paediatrician, Warwick Hosp., West Midlands Area Health Authority, since 1972.   Consultant Paediatrician, Charles Burns Child Guidance Unit, Birmingham.   *Publs:* The Baby's First Days, 1974, as Caring for Your Baby, 1975.   Add: 85 Willes Rd., Leamington Spa, Warwicks., England.

PARTRIDGE, Jenny (Lilian).   British, b. 1947.   Children's fiction. Founder, Romany Studio Workshop, since 1972.   *Publs:* (all self-illustrated) Mr. Squint, 1980; Colonel Grunt, 1980; Peterkin Pollensnuff, 1980; Hopfellow, 1980; Grandma Snuffles, 1981; Dominic Sly, 1981; Harriet Plume, 1981; Lop-Ear, 1981; Oakapple Wood Stories, 1982; A Tale of Oakapple Wood, 1983; Four Friends in Oakapple Wood, 1984; Jack Flax, 1986; Rafferty's Return, 1986; Rifkins, 1986; Clara Quince, 1986. Add: c/o Christopher Shepheard-Walwyn, 51 Vineyard Hill Rd., London SW19, England.

PARVIN, Betty.   British, b. 1917.   Poetry.   Pres., Nottingham Poetry Soc., 1979–88.   Member, Advisory Panel, East Midlands Arts Assn., 1970–74.   *Publs:* A Stone My Star, 1961; The Bird with the Luck, 1968; Sketchbook from Mercia, 1969; (ed.) Poetry Nottingham, 1970; Sarnia's Gift, 1972; A Birchtree with Finches, 1974; Country Matters, 1979; The Book of Daniel, 1980; Prospect, 1981; The Book of Oliver, 1983; (ed.) It's All Ours, 1985.   Add: Bamboo, Bunny Hill Top, Costock, nr. Loughborough, Leics., England.

PASCAL, Francine.   American, b. 1938.   Novels/Short stories, Historical/ Romance, Children's fiction, Plays/Screenplays, Biography.   Writer and lecturer; co-author, with John Pascal, of the soap opera "The Young Marrieds," ABC-TV.   *Publs:* (with John Pascal and Michael Stewart) George M, 1968, TV adaptation 1970; (with John Pascal) The Strange Case of Patty Hearst, 1974; Hangin' Out with Cici, 1977; My First Love and Other Disasters, 1970; The Hand-Me-Down-Kid, 1980; Save Johana!, 1981; About Face, 1984; Dangerous Love, 1984; Dear Sister, 1984; Deceptions, 1984; Heartbreaker 1984; Kidnapped!, 1984; Love on the Run, 1984; Power Play, 1984; Racing Hearts, 1984; Too Good to Be True, 1984; Wrong Kind of Girl, 1984; Love and Betray and Hold the Mayo!, 1985; Crash Landing, 1985; Jats Off to Katzoff, 1985; Caitlin, 1985; Head over Heels, 1985; Love Letters, 1985; Memories, 1985; Say Goodbye, 1985; Promises, 1985; Rags to Riches, 1985; Showdown, 1985; Loving Caitlin, 1985; Perfect Summer, 1985; Runaway, 1985; Special Christmas, 1985; Too Much in Love, 1985; Lost Love, 1985; Sweet Valley Higher Super Edition: Spring Break, 1986; Sweet Valley High Super Edition: Winter Carnival, 1986; Alone in the Crowd, 1986; The New Jessica, 1986; Nowhere to Run, 1986; Promises Broken, 1986; Choosing Sides, 1986; Taking Sides, 1986; Tender Promises, 1986; Best Friends, 1986; Bitter Rivals, 1986; Haunted House, 1986; Jealous Lies, 1986; Lovestruck, 1986; Malibu Summer, 1986; Teacher's Pet, 1986; Keeping Secrets, 1987; Against the Rules, 1987; Tug of War, 1987; Leaving Home High, 1987; Stretching the Truth, 1987; On the Edge, 1987; Buried Treasure, 1987; Double Jeopardy, 1987; Forbidden Love, 1987; Last Chance, 1987; The New Girl, 1987; A New Promise, 1987; One of the Gang, 1987; Out of Control, 1987; Outcast, 1987; Rumors, 1987; Spring Fever, 1987; Starting Over, 1987; Sweet Valley Twins, 1987; Leaving Home, 1988; Secret Ad-

mirer, 1988; Sweet Valley High, no. 47, 1988; Sweet Valley High, no. 48, 1988; Sweet Valley Twins: Center of Attention, 1988; Sweet Valley Twins: Super Book, 1988; Together Forever, 1988; Troublemaker, 1988; The Bully, 1988; Caught in the Middle, 1988; Class Trip, 1988; Dreams of Forever, 1988; Family Secrets, 1988; Forever and Always, 1988; Hard Choices, 1988; The Older Boy, 1988; On the Run, 1988.   Add: c/o Amy Berkower, Writers House, 21 W. 26th St., New York, N.Y. 10010, U.S.A.

PASCALE, Richard Tanner.   American, b. 1938.   Administration/ Management, Politics/Government.   Lectr., Grad. Sch. of Business, Stanford Univ., California, since 1974.   *Publs:* Managing the White House: An Intimate Study of the Presidency, 1974; The Art of Japanese Management, 1981.   Add: Grad. Sch. of Business, Stanford Univ., Stanford, Calif. 94305, U.S.A.

PASCARELLA, Perry.   American, b. 1934.   Business/Trade/Industry. Ed.-in-Chief, Industry Week, Cleveland, since 1986 (Exec. Ed., 1971–86). Asst., Assoc., and Business Ed., 1961–69, and Managing Ed., 1969–70, Steel mag.; Managing Ed., Industry Week mag., 1970–71.   *Publs:* Technology: Fire in a Dark World, 1979; Human Management in the Future Corporation, 1980; The New Achievers, 1984.   Add: 30413 Winsor Dr., Bay Village, Ohio 44140, U.S.A.

PASEWARK, William Robert.   American, b. 1924.   Administration/ Management, Business/Trade/Industry, Education.   Owner, Office Management Consultants, since 1977.   Instr. in Business Education, New York Univ., 1949–51; Assoc. Prof. of Business Education, Meredith Coll., Raleigh, N.C., 1951–52; Asst. Prof., Michigan State Univ., E. Lansing, 1952–56; Prof. of Business Education, Texas Tech Univ., Lubbock, 1956–83.   *Publs:* (with P.L. Agnew) Key-Driven Calculator Course, 1962; (with P.L. Agnew) Rotary Calculator Course, 1962; (with P.L. Agnew) Full-Keyboard Adding Listing Machine Course, 1963; (with N. Cornelia) Office Machines Course, 1971, 5th ed. 1979; Duplicating Machine Processes, 1971; (with J. Meehan and M.E. Oliverio) Secretarial Office Procedures, 1972, 8th ed. (with M.E. Oliverio) 1982; (with J. Meehan and M.E. Oliverio) Clerical Office Procedures, 5th ed. 1973, 6th ed. 1978; (ed. with D. Kilchenstein) Individualized Instruction in Business and Office Education, 1973; (with N. Cornelia) Ten-Key Adding-Listing Machine Course, 1974, as sole author, 1981; Electronic and Mechanical Printing Calculator Course, 1974, 2nd ed. as Electronic Printing Calculator, 1982; Electronic Display Calculator, 1975, 1984; Machine Transcription Word Processing, 1979, 1987; Calculating Machines Simulation, 1982; Procedures for the Modern Office, 1983; Electronic Display/Printing Calculator, 1983; Reprographics, 1984; (with J. Willis) SuperCalc 3, 1986; (with J. Willis) Working with SuperCalc 4, 1987; Electronic Office Machine, 6th ed., 1987; (with M.E. Oliverio) The Office: Procedures and Technology, 1988; Electronic Printing Calculator, 1990.   Add: 4403 W. 11th St., Lubbock, Tex. 79416, U.S.A.

PASK, Raymond Frank.   Australian, b. 1944.   Geography.   Teacher, Ministry of Education, Victoria, since 1982.   Teacher, Inner London Education Authority, 1969–81.   *Publs:* People and Places: Case Studies in Australian Geography, 1969, 1974; Develop the Pilbara, 1974; (with J. Hajdu and B. Stringer) The Global System Levels: Space in Change, 1973, 1974; (with L. Bryant) Australia and New Zealand: A New Geography, 1974, 1980; China's Changing Landscapes, 1979; China, 1982; Using the Earth, 1982, 1983; Using the Earth's Resources, 1983; The Changing Earth, 1985; People and Environments, 1986; (with A. Reed) The World Now, 1986; (with L. Bryant) People in Australia: A Social Geography, 1986; Jacaranda Junior Geography Book 1 and 2, 1989.   Add: 41 Yarra St., Abbotsford 3067, Australia.

PASSOW, A. Harry.   American, b. 1920.   Education.   Jacob H. Schiff Prof. of Education, Teachers Coll., Columbia Univ., NYC, since 1952. *Publs:* (with R. Doll and S. Corey) Organizing for Curriculum, 1953; (with M. Goldberg, A. Tannenbaum and W. French) Planning for Talented Youth, 1955; (with M. Miles, S. Corey and D. Draper) Training Curriculum Leaders for Cooperative Research, 1955; (with F. Stratemeyer, M. McKim and H. Forkner) Developing a Curriculum for Modern Living, 1957; (with H. McNally) Improving the Quality of Public Schools Programs, 1960; Secondary Education for All: The English Approach, 1961; (ed. and contrib.) Curriculum Crossroads, 1962; (ed. and contrib.) Education in Depressed Areas, 1963; (ed.) Intellectual Development: Another Look, 1963; (ed.) Nurturing Individual Potential, 1964; (with M. Goldberg and J. Justman) The Effects of Ability Grouping, 1966; (with M. Goldberg, R. Neill and D. Camm) Comparison of Mathematics Programs for Bright Junior High School Students, 1966; (with J. Raph and M. Goldberg) Bright Underachievers, 1966; Toward Creating a Model Urban School System, 1967; (with M. Goldberg and A. Tannenbaum)

Education of the Disadvantaged Readings, 1967; (ed. and contrib.) Developing Programs for the Educationally Disadvantaged, 1968; (ed. and contrib) Reaching the Disadvantaged Learner, 1970; (ed. and contrib.) Reactions to Silberman's Crisis in the Classroom, 1971; (ed. and contrib.) Urban Education in the 1970's, 1971; (ed. and contrib.) Opening Opportunities for Disadvantaged Learners, 1972; (with H. Noah and M. Eckstein) The National Case Study: An Empirical Study of 20 Educational Systems, 1975; Secondary Education Reform: Retrospect and Prospect, 1976; American Secondary Education: The Conant Influence, 1977; (ed. and contrib.) The Gifted and the Talented: Their Education and Development, 1979; Education for Gifted Children and Youth: An Old Issue, A New Challenge, 1980; Reforming Schools in the 1980's, 1984. Add: 394 Eton St., Englewood, N.J. 07631, U.S.A.

PASTAN, Linda. American, b. 1932. Poetry. *Publs:* A Perfect Circle of Sun, 1971; On the Way to the Zoo, 1975; Aspects of Eve, 1975; The Five Stages of Grief, 1978; Selected Poems, 1979; Setting the Table, 1980; Waiting for My Life, 1981; PM/AM: New and Selected Poems, 1982; A Fraction of Darkness, 1985; The Imperfect Paradise, 1988. Add: 11710 Beall Mountain Rd., Potomac, Md. 20854, U.S.A.

PATAI, Raphael. American, b. 1910. Anthropology/Ethnology. Instr. of Hebrew Language, 1938-42, and Research Fellow in Ethnology, 1943-47, Hebrew Univ., Jerusalem; Prof. of Anthropology, Dropsie Coll., Philadelphia, Pa. 1948-57; Lectr. in Anthropology, New York Univ., NYC, 1951-53; Pres., American Friends of the Tel Aviv Univ., 1956-68; Dir. of Research, Herzl Inst., 1956-71; Prof. of Anthropology, Fairleigh Dickinson Univ., New Jersey, 1966-76. *Publs:* Shire R. Yisrael Berekhya Fontanella, 1933; HaMayim, 1936; HaSapanut ha'Ivrith, 1938; (ed. with Z. Wohlmuth) Mivhar haSippur ha Artzizraeli, 2 vols., 1938; Adam wa Adama, 2 vols., 1942-43; Masorot Historiyot, 1945; (ed. with J.J. Rivlin) Edoth, 3 vols., 1945-48; ed. (with J.J. Rivlin) Studies in Folklore and Ethology, 5 vols., 1946-48; (ed. with R. Bachi) Social Studies, 2 vols., 1946-48; Mada'ha Adam, 2 vols., 1947-48; Man and Temple in Ancient Jewish Myth and Ritual, 1947, 1967; Israel Between East and West: A Study in Human Relations, 1953, 1970; (ed.) The Hashemite Kingdom of Jordan, 1956; (ed.) The Republic of Lebanon, 2 vols., 1956; (ed.) The Republic of Syria, 2 vols., 1956; Annotated Bibliography of Syria, Lebanon and Jordan, 1957; The Kingdom of Jordan, 1958; Current Jewish Social Research, 1958, 1961; (ed.) Herzl Year Book, 7 vols., 1958-71; Sex and Family in the Bible and the Middle East (in U.K. as Family, Love and the Bible), 1959; (ed.) The Complete Diaries of Theodor Herzl, 5 vols., 1960; (ed. with F. Utley and D. Noy) Studies in Biblical and Jewish Folklore, 1960; Golden River to Golden Road: Society, Cultural and Change in the Middle East, 1963, 3rd ed. 1969; (with R. Graves) Hebrew Myths, 1964; The Hebrew Goddess, 1967, 1978; (ed.) Myth and Legend in Ancient Israel, by Angelo Rappaport, 3 vols., 1967; (ed.) Women in the Modern World, 1967; Tents of Jacob: The Diaspora Yesterday and Today, 1971; (ed.) Encyclopedia of Zionism and Israel, 2 vols., 1971; Myth and Modern Man, 1972; The Arab Mind, 1973, 1983; (with J.P Wing) The Myth of the Jewish Race, 1975; The Jewish Mind, 1978; The Messiah Texts, 1979; Gates to the Old City, 1980; The Vanished Worlds of Jewry, 1980; On Jewish Folklore, 1983; The Seed of Abraham, 1986; Nahum Goldmann: His Missions to the Gentiles, 1987; Ignaz Goldziher and His Oriental Diary, 1987; Apprentice in Budapest: Memories of a World That Is No More, 1988. Add: 39 Bow St., Forest Hills, N.Y. 11375, U.S.A.

PATCHETT, Mary Elwyn (Osborne). Has also written as David Bruce. Australian, b. 1897. Novels/Short stories, Children's fiction. *Publs:* novels for adults—Wild Brother, 1954; Cry of the Heart, 1956; The Saffron Woman, 1958; Brit, 1961; In a Wilderness, 1962, in U.S. as Dingo, 1963; The Last Warrior, 1965; Hunting Cat, 1976; fiction for children—Ajax, The Warrior (in U.S. as Ajax, Golden Dog of the Australian Bush), 1953; Kidnappers of Space (in U.S. as Space Captives of the Golden Men), 1953; The Lee Twins, 1953; Tam the Untamed, 1954; Lost on Venus (in U.S. as Flight to the Misty Planet), 1954; Evening Star, 1954; Adam Troy, Astroman, 1954; "Your Call, Miss Gaynor," 1955; Treasure of the Reef, 1955, in U.S. as The Great Barrier Reef, 1958; Undersea Treasure Hunters, 1955, in U.S. as the Chance of Treasure, 1957; Send for Johnny Danger, 1956; Return to the Reef, 1956; Sally's Zoo, 1957; Outback Adventure, 1957; Caribbean Adventures, 1957; The Mysterious Pool, 1958; The Brumby series, 5 vols., 1958-72; The Call of the Bush, 1959; Quest of Ati Manu, 1960; Warrimoo, 1961; The End of the Outlaws, 1961; Dangerous Assignment, 1962; The Golden Wolf, 1962; The Venus Project, 1963; Ajax and the Haunted Mountain, 1963; Tiger in the Dark, 1964; Ajax and the Drovers, 1964; Stranger in the Herd, 1964; The White Dingo, 1965; Summer on Wild Horse Island, 1965; The Terror of Manooka, 1966; Summer on Boomerang Beach, 1967; Festival of Jewels, 1968; Farm

Beneath the Sea, 1969; Quarter Horse Boy, 1970; The Long Ride, 1970; Roar of the Lion, 1973; other—The Proud Eagles, 1960; A Budgie Called Fred, 1964; (as David Bruce) Bird of Jove, 1971. Add: c/o Abelard Schuman, 7 Leicester Pl., London WC2H 7BP, England.

PATEMAN, Trevor John. British, b. 1947. Communications systems, Education, Language/Linguistics, Philosophy. Reader in Education, Univ. of Sussex, Brighton, since 1985 (Lectr., 1979-85). *Publs:* (ed.) Counter Course: A Handbook for Course Criticism, 1972; Language, Truth and Politics: Toward a Radical Theory for Communication, 1975, 1980; Television and the February 1974 General Election, 1975; Can Schools Educate, 1980; (ed.) Languages for Life, 1982; Language in Mind and Language in Society, 1987; What Is Philosophy?, 1987. Add: Education Area, University of Sussex, Brighton BN1 9RG, England.

PATER, Elias. *See* **FRIEDMAN**, Jacob Horace.

PATERSON, Alistair (Ian Hughes). New Zealander, b. 1929. Poetry. Continuing Education Officer, New Zealand Education Dept., since 1978. Instructor/Officer, rising to the rank of Lt. Comdr., Royal New Zealand Navy, 1954-74; Dean of Gen. Studies, New Zealand Police Dept., 1974-78. *Publs:* Caves in the Hills: Selected Poems, 1965; Birds Flying, 1973; Cities and Strangers, 1976; The Toledo Room: A Poem for Voices, 1978; (ed.) 15 Contemporary New Zealand Poets, 1890; Qu'appelle, 1982; The New Poetry, 1982; Incantation for Warriors, 1982; Oedipus Rex, 1987; (ed.) Short Stories from New Zealand, 1988. Add: P.O. Box 9612, Newmarket, Auckland, New Zealand.

PATERSON, Katherine (Womeldorf). American, b. 1932. Children's fiction, Children's non-fiction, Literature. Elementary sch. teacher, Lovettsville, Va., 1954-55; Presbyterian missionary, Japan, 1957-61; Master, Pennington Sch. for Boys, N.J., 1963-65; reviewer, Washington Post. *Publs:* Who Am I?, 1966; The Sign of the Chrysanthemum, 1973; Of Nightingales That Weep, 1974; The Master Puppeteer, 1976; Bridge to Terabithia, 1977; The Great Gilly Hopkins, 1978; Angels and Other Strangers, 1979; Jacob Have I Loved, 1980; The Crane Wife, 1981; Gates of Excellence: On the Reading and Writing of Books for Children, 1981; Rebels of the Heavenly Kingdom, 1983; Come Sing, Jimmy Jo, 1985; Park's Quest, 1989. Add: c/o E.P. Dutton, 2 Park Ave., New York, N.Y. 10016, U.S.A.

PATERSON, Neil. British, b. 1916. Novels/Short stories, Plays/Screenplays. Consultant, Films of Scotland. Gov., British Film Inst., 1958-60; Chmn., Literature Cttee., Scottish Arts Council, 1966-76; Gov., National Film Sch., 1970-80; Member, Arts Council of Great Britain, 1974-76. Dir., Grampian Television, Aberdeen, 1960-86. *Publs:* The China Run, 1948; Behold Thy Daughter, 1950; And Delilah, 1951; Man on the Tight-Rope, 1953; The Kidnappers, 1957; screenplays—The Little Kidnappers; High Tide at Noon; The Shiralee; The Spiral Road; Keeper of My Heart; Room at the Top. Add: St Ronans, Crieff, Perthshire, Scotland.

PATERSON, Ronald (William Keith). British, b. 1933. Education, b-Philosophy, Biography. Lectr., then Sr. Lectr. in Philosophy, Dept. of Adult Education, Univ. of Hull, since 1962. Staff Tutor, Holly Royde Coll., Dept. of Extra-Mural Studies, Univ. of Manchester, 1959-61. *Publs:* The Nihilistic Egoist: Max Stirner, 1971; Values, Education, and the Adult, 1979. Add: 215 Boroughbridge Rd., York, England.

PATON, (Rev. Canon) David Macdonald. British, b. 1913. Theology/Religion. Missionary in China, 1940-50; Vicar of Yardley Wood, Birmingham, 1952-56; Ed., S.C.M. Press, 1956-59; Secty., Missionary and Ecumenical Council of the Church Assembly, 1959-69; Hon. Canon, Canterbury Cathedral, 1966-80; Rector, St. Mary de Crypt and St. John the Baptist, Gloucester, 1970-81; Chaplain to H.M. the Queen, 1972-83. *Publs:* Blind Guides?, 1939; Christian Missions and the Judgment of God, 1953; (with J.T. Martin) Paragraphs for Sundays and Holy Days, 1957; (ed.) Church and Race in South Africa, 1958; (ed.) Essays in Anglican Self-Criticism, 1958; (ed. with C.C. West) The Missionary Church in East and West, 1959; (ed.) The Ministry of the Spirit: Selected Writings of Roland Allen, 1960, 1965; Anglicans and Unity, 1962, 1963; (ed.) The Parish Communion Today, 1962; (ed.) Mission and Communication, 1963; One Church Renewed for Mission, 1964; (ed.) New Forms of Ministry, 1965; (with R. Latham) Point of Decision, 1968; (ed.) Reform of the Ministry: A Study in the Work of Roland Allen, 1968; (ed.) Breaking Barriers, 1976; (ed. with C.W. Long) Compulsion of the Spirit, 1984; RO: The Life and Times of Bishop Ronald Hall of Hong Kong, 1985. Add: 37A Cromwell St., Gloucester GL1 1RE, England.

PATON WALSH, Jill. British, b. 1937. Children's fiction. *Publs:* Hengest's Tale, 1966; The Dolphin Crossing, 1967; Fireweed, 1969; (with Kevin Crossley-Holland) Wordhoard, 1969; Goldengrove, 1972; Farewell Great King (for adults), 1972; Toolmaker, 1973; The Dawnstone, 1973; The Emperor's Winding Sheet, 1974; The Huffler, 1975; The Island Sunrise: Prehistoric Culture in the British Isles, 1975; Unleaving, 1976; Children of the Fox: Crossing to Salamis, 1977; The Walls of Athens, 1978; Persian Gold, 1978; A Chance Child, 1978; The Green Book, 1981; Babylon, 1982; Parcell of Patterns, 1983; Lost and Found, 1984; Gaffer Samson's Luck, 1985; Lapsing, 1985. Add: 72 Water Lane, Histon, Cambridge CB4 4LR, England.

PATRICK, John. American, b. 1907. Plays/Screenplays. Radio Writer, NBC, San Francisco, Calif., 1933–36; freelance writer, Hollywood, 1936–38. *Publs:* The Willow and I, 1943; The Hasty Heart, 1945; The Story of Mary Surratt, 1947; The Curious Savage, 1950; Lo and Behold!, 1951; The Teahouse of the August Moon, 1953, as Lovely Ladies, Kind Gentlemen, 1970; Everybody Loves Opal, 1961; Everybody's Girl, 1967; Scandal Point, 1968; A Barrel Full of Pennies, 1968; Love Is a Time of Day, 1969; Opal Is a Diamond, 1971; Macbeth Did It, 1972; The Dancing Mice, 1972; The Savage Dilemma, 1972; Anybody Out There?, 1972; Roman Conquest, 1973; Sex on the Sixth Floor: Three One-Act Plays, 1974; The Enigma, 1974; Opal's Baby: A New Sequel in Two Acts, 1974; A Bad Year for Tomatoes, 1975; Opal's Husband, 1975; Noah's Animals, 1976; People! Three One Act Plays: Boredom, Christmas Spirit, Aptitude, 1980; That's Not My Father! Three One Act Plays: Raconteur, Fettucine, Masquerade, 1980; That's Not My Mother: Three One Act Plays: Seniority, Redemption, Optimism, 1980; Opal's Million Dollar Duck, 1980; The Girls of the Garden Club, 1980; The Magenta Moth, 1983; It's a Dog's Life, 1984. Add: Fortuna Mill Estate, Box 2386, St. Thomas, Virgin Islands 00801, U.S.A.

PATRICK, Maxine. *See* **MAXWELL,** Patricia Anne.

PATRICK, Robert. (Robert Patrick O'Connor). American, b. 1937. Plays/Screenplays. Doorman, Caffe Cino, NYC, 1966–68; Feature Ed., Astrology Mag., 1971–72. *Publs:* Robert Patrick's Cheap Theatricks!, 1972; Play-by-Play: A Spectacle of Ourselves, 1972; Kennedy's Children, 1973; My Cup Runneth Over, 1978; Mutual Benefit Life, 1978; One Man, One Woman: Six One Act Plays, 1978; Mercy Drop and Other Plays, 1980; Michelangelo's Models, 1983. Add: c/o La Mama, 74-A E. 4th St., New York, N.Y. 10003, U.S.A.

PATRICK, Susan. *See* **LORRIMER,** Claire.

PATRIDES, C(onstantinos) A(postolos). American, 1930. Literature. G.B. Harrison Prof. of English, Univ., of Michigan, Ann Arbor, since 1978. Lectr. to Assoc. Prof., Univ. of California at Berkeley, 1957–64; Lectr. to Prof., Univ. of York, 1964–78. *Publs:* (ed.) Milton's Lycidas: The Tradition and the Poem, 1961; Milton and the Christian Tradition, 1966; (ed.) Milton's Epic Poetry, 1967; (ed.) Approaches to Paradise Lost, 1968; (ed.) The Cambridge Platonists, 1969; (ed.) Sir Walter Raleigh's The History of the World, 1971; (gen. ed.) The Poetry of John Milton, 1972; The Grand Design of God: The Literary Form of the Christian View of History, 1972; (ed.) John Milton: Selected Prose, 1974, 1986; (ed.) The English Poems of George Herbert, 1974; (ed.) Aspects of Time, 1976; (ed.) Sir Thomas Browne: The Major Works, 1977; (ed.) Approaches to Marvell, 1978; (co-ed.) The Age of Milton, 1980; (ed.) Approaches to Sir Thomas Browne, 1982; Premises and Motifs in Renaissance Thought and Literature, 1982; (ed.) George Herbert: The Critical Heritage, 1983; (co-ed.) The Apocalypse in English Renaissance Thought and Literature, 1984; (ed.) The Complete English Poems of John Donne, 1985; An Annotated Critical Bibliography of Milton, 1987. Add: Dept. of English, Univ. of Michigan, Ann Arbor, Mich. 48109, U.S.A.

PATTEN, Brian. British, b. 1946. Novels/Short stories, Children's fiction, Plays/screenplays, Poetry. Former Ed., Underdog, an underground mag. of poetry. *Publs:* Little Johnny's Confession, 1967; (with Adrian Henri and Roger McGough) The Mersey Sound (Penguin Modern Poets), 1967; Note to the Hurrying Man, 1969; The Elephant and the Flower, 1970; The Irrelevant Song, 1971; (ed. with P. Krett) The House that Jack Built, 1973; Jumping Mouse, 1973; Mr. Moon's Last Case, 1975; The Pig and the Junkle (play), 1975; Vanishing Trick, 1976; Emma's Doll (juvenile), 1976; The Sly Cormorant and the Three Fishes (juvenile), 1977; Grave Gossip, 1979; (ed.) Gangsters, Ghosts, and Dragonflies, 1981; Grave: Gossip, 1981; (ed.) Clare's Countryside, 1981; Love Poems, 1981; Blind Love (play), 1982; (with Adrian Henri and Roger McGough) New Volume, 1983; Gargling with Jelly (comic verse), 1985; Jimmy Tagalong, 1988; Storm Damage, 1988; Gurgling with Jelly—The Play, 1988.

Add: c/o Unwin-Hyman, 15-17 Broadwick St., London W1V 1FP, England.

PATTEN, Thomas H. (Jr.). American, b. 1929. Personnel management. Prof. of Management and Human Resources, California State Polytechnic, Univ., Pomona, since 1984. Industrial Relations Exec., Ford Motor Co., Detroit, Mich., 1957–65; Prof., Univ. of Detroit, 1965–67; Prof. of Organizational Behavior and Personnel Management, Michigan State Univ., East Lansing, 1967–84. *Publs:* The Foreman: Forgotten Man of Management, 1968; Manpower Planning and the Development of Human Resources, 1971; (ed.) OD: Emerging Dimensions and Concepts, 1973; (compiler) Compensation Planning and Administration: A Bibliography, 1960-1975, 1975, 3rd ed. 1987; Pay: Employee Compensation and Incentive Plans, 1977; Classics of Personnel Management, 1979; Organizational Development Through Teambuilding, 1981; A Manager's Guide to Performance Appraisal: Pride, Prejudice, and the Law of Equal Opportunity, 1982; Fair Pay: The Managerial Challenge of Comparable Job Worth and Job Evaluation, 1988. Add: Claremont, Cal. 91711, U.S.A.

PATTERSON, Elizabeth Chambers. American. Sciences, Biography. Prof., Physical Sciences, Albertus Magnus Coll., New Haven, Conn., since 1970, now Emeritus (Lectr., 1948 and 1958–60; Instr., 1960–62; Asst. Prof., 1963–67; Assoc. Prof., 1967–69). Consulting Ed., American Scientist, since 1971; Consultant, Choice, since 1970. Asst. Prof. of Chemistry, Univ. of Texas at Arlington, 1941–42; Research Asst. in Chemistry, Univ. of North Carolina, Chapel Hill, 1942–44. *Publs:* John Dalton and the Atomic Theory: The Biography, 1970; Mary Somerville, 1979; Mary Somerville and the Cultivation of Science 1815-1840, 1983. Add: 175 East Rock Rd., New Haven, Conn. 06511, U.S.A.

PATTERSON, Harry. *See* **PATTERSON,** Henry.

PATTERSON, Henry. Also writes as Hugh Marlowe, Jack Higgins, Martin Fallon, James Graham, and Harry Patterson. British, b. 1939. Mystery/Crime/Suspense, Westerns/Adventure. Worked in various commercial and civil service posts, 1950–55; History teacher, Allerton Comprehensive Sch., Leeds, 1958–64; Lectr. in Liberal Studies, Leeds Coll. of Commerce and Leeds Polytechnic, 1964–68; Sr. Lectr. in Education, James Graham Coll., New Farnley, Yorks., 1968–70; Tutor, Univ. of Leeds, 1971–73. *Publs:* (as Harry Patterson) Sad Wind from the Sea, 1959; (as Harry Patterson) Cry of the Hunter, 1960; (as Harry Patterson) The Thousand Faces of Night, 1961; (as Harry Patterson) Comes the Dark Stranger, 1962; (as Harry Patterson) Hell Is Too Crowded, 1962; (as Martin Fallon) The Testament of Caspar Schultz, 1962; Seven Pillars to Hell, 1963; (as Harry Patterson) Pay the Devil, 1963; (as Harry Patterson) The Dark Side of the Island, 1963; (as Martin Fallon) Year of the Tiger, 1963; Passage by Night, 1964; (as Harry Patterson) A Phoenix in the Blood, 1964; (as Harry Patterson) Thunder at Noon, 1964; (as Harry Patterson) Wrath of the Lion, 1964; (as Harry Patterson) The Graveyard Shift, 1965; (as Martin Fallon) The Keys of Hell, 1965; A Candle for the Dead, 1966 (as The Violent Enemy, 1969); (as Harry Patterson) The Iron Tiger, 1966; (as Martin Fallon) Midnight Never Comes, 1966; (as Harry Patterson) Brought in Dead, 1967; (as Martin Fallon) Dark Side of the Street, 1967; (as Harry Patterson) Hell Is Always Today, 1968; (as Jack Higgins) End of Desolation, 1968; (as Martin Fallon) A Fine Night for Dying, 1969; (as Jack Higgins) In the Hour Before Midnight, 1969 (as U.S. as The Sicilian Heritage, 1970); (as Jack Higgins) Night Judgment at Sinos, 1970; (as James Graham) A Game for Heroes, 1970; (as Harry Patterson) Toll for the Brave, 1971; (as Jack Higgins) The Last Place God Made, 1971; (as James Graham) The Wrath of God, 1971; (as Jack Higgins) The Savage Day, 1972; (as James Graham) The Khufra Run, 1972; (as Jack Higgins) A Prayer for the Dying, 1973; (as James Graham) Bloody Passage (in U.S. a The Run to Morning), 1974; (as Jack Higgins) The Eagle Has Landed, 1975; (as Harry Patterson) The Valhalla Exchange, 1976; (as Jack Higgins) Storm Warning, 1976; (as Jack Higgins) Day of Judgement, 1978; (as Harry Patterson) To Catch a King, 1979; (as Jack Higgins) Solo, 1980; (as Jack Higgins) Luciano's Luck, 1981; (as Jack Higgins) Touch the Devil, 1982; (as Jack Higgins) Exocet, 1983; (as Harry Patterson) Dillinger, 1983; (as Jack Higgins) Confessional, 1985; Night of the Fox, 1986; (as Harry Patterson) Walking Wounded (play), 1987. Add: c/o David Higham Assocs., 5-8 Lower John St., London W1R 4HA, England.

PATTERSON, Michael. British, b. 1939. Theatre. Lectr. in Theatre Studies, Univ. of Ulster, Coleraine, since 1987. Lectr. in German, Queen's Univ. of Belfast, 1965–70; Lectr. in Drama, University Coll. of N. Wales, Bangor, 1970–74; Sr. Lectr. in Drama and Theatre Arts, Univ. of Leeds, 1974–87. *Publs:* German Theatre Today, 1976; The Revolution in German Theatre 1900-1933, 1981; Peter Stein, 1981; (ed.) Buchner:

The Complete Plays, 1987. Add: Dept. of English, Theatre, and Media Studies, Univ. of Ulster, Coleraine, N. Ireland.

PATTERSON, (Horace) Orlando. Jamaican, b. 1940. Novels/Short stories, Sociology. Prof. of Sociology and Allston Burr Sr. Tutor, Harvard Univ., Cambridge, since 1971 (Assoc. Prof. of Afro-American Studies, 1970–71). Asst. Lectr. in Sociology, London Sch. of Economics, 1965–67; Member, Editorial Bd., New Left Review, London, 1965–66; Consultant and Tutor in Sociology, Hawker Siddeley Dynamics, London, 1966–67; Lectr. in Sociology, Univ. of the West Indies, 1967–70. *Publs:* The Children of Sisyphus, 1964; The Sociology of Slavery: An Analysis of the Origins, Development, and Structure of Negro Slavery Society in Jamaica, 1967; An Absence of Ruins, 1967; Die the Long Day, 1972; Ethnic Chauvinism, 1977; Slavery and Social Death: A Comparative Study, 1982. Add: Dept. of Sociology, Harvard Univ., Cambridge, Mass. 02138, U.S.A.

PATTERSON, Raymond R(ichard). American, b. 1929. Poetry. Assoc. Prof. in English, City Coll. of the City Univ. of New York, since 1985 (Lectr., 1968–85). Children's Supvr., Youth House for Boys, NYC, 1956–58; Instr. in English, Benedict Coll., Columbia, S.C., 1958–59; English teacher in NYC public schs., 1959–68. *Publs:* Get Caught: A Photographic Essay, 1964; Twenty-Six Ways of Looking at a Black Man and Other Poems, 1969; Elemental Blues: Poems 1981-1982, 1982. Add: 2 Lee Ct., Merrick, N.Y. 11566, U.S.A.

PAUK, Walter. American, b. 1914. Education. Prof. of Education Emeritus and Dir. of the Reading-Study Center, Cornell Univ., Ithaca, N.Y., since 1955. *Publs:* (with J. Millman) How to Take Tests, 1969; How to Read Factual Literature, 1970; (with J. Wilson) How to Read Creative Literature, 1970; (with J. Wilson) Reading for Facts, 1974; (with J. Wilson) Reading for Ideas, 1974; Six-Way Paragraphs, 1974, Middle Level, 1983, Advanced Level, 1983; How to Study in College, 4th ed. 1989; A Skill at a Time Series, 1975; (with J. Wilson) Reading in English for Arab Students, 1975; Single Skills Series, 60 vols., 1985; Study Skills for College Athletes, 1987; Study Skills for Community and Junior Colleges, 1987; High School Study Skills, 1987; A User's Guide to College: Making Notes and Taking Tests, 1987. Add: Reading Research Center, 250 Olin Hall, Cornell Univ., Ithaca, N.Y. 14853, U.S.A.

PAUL, Barbara. *See* **LAKER,** Rosalind.

PAUL, Thomas Francis. New Zealander, b. 1924. Administration/Management, Business/Trade/Industry. Accountant, Anglican Church Office, Auckland. Ed., The Chartered Secretary, now The Professional Administrator, New Zealand, 1969–86. *Publs:* Advanced Accounting, 1962; Land and Income Tax Handbook, 1963, 5th ed. 1975; (ed.) Secretarial Law and Practice, 6th ed. 1969; Secretarial and Administrative Practice, 1974; Meetings: Procedure, Law, and Practice, 1979; (consulting ed.) New Zealand Company Law and Practice, 3 vols., 1979–89; Office and Company Administration, 1982; Law and Administration of Incorporated Societies, 2nd ed. 1986; Precedents for Incorporated Societies, 1987; How to Form and Run a Club, 1989; Administering an Estate, 1989. Add: 16 Glenmore Rd., Sunnyhills, Pakuranga, Auckland 1706, New Zealand.

PAULEY, Barbara Anne (Cotton). American, b. 1925. Historical/Romance/Gothic. Feelance writer. Former Editorial Asst., Ideal Publishing Corp. *Publs:* Blood Kin, 1972; Voices Long Hushed, 1976. Add: Great Oaks, Landrum, SC 29356, U.S.A.

PAULIN, Tom. British, b. 1949. Plays, Poetry, Literature. *Publs:* Thomas Hardy: The Poetry of Perception, 1975; Theoretical Locations, 1975; A State of Justice, 1977; Personal Column, 1978; The Strange Museum, 1980; The Book of Juniper, 1981; Liberty Tree, 1983; Ireland and the English Crisis, 1985; The Riot Act (play), 1985; (ed.) The Faber Book of Political Verse, 1986; (co-ed.) Hard Lines 3, 1987; Fivemiletown, 1987; The Hillsborough Script: A Dramatic Satire, 1987. Add: c/o Faber and Faber Ltd., 3 Queen Sq., London WC1N 3AU, England.

PAULING, Linus (Carl). American, b. 1901. Chemistry. Research Prof., Linus Pauling Inst. of Science and Medicine, Menlo Park, then Palo Alto, Calif. since 1974. Research Prof., Center for the Study of Democratic Instns., Santa Barbara, Calif. Asst. Prof., Assoc. Prof. and Prof., 1927–64, and Chmn., Div. of Chemistry and Chemical Engineering, and Dir. of the Gates and Crellin Labs., 1936–58, California Inst. of Technology, Pasadena: Prof. of Chemistry, Stanford Univ., California, 1969–74. *Publs:* (with Goudsmit) The Structure of the Line Spectra, 1930; (with Wilson) Introduction to Quantum Mechanics, 1935; The Nature of

the Chemical Bond, 1939, 3rd ed. 1960; General Chemistry, 1947, 1953; College Chemistry, 1950, 3rd ed. 1964; No More War, 1958, 1962; (with Hayward) The Architecture of Molecules, 1965; The Chemical Bond, 1967; Vitamin C and the Common Cold, 1970; Vitamin C, the Common Cold and the Flu, 1976; (with Ewan Cameron) Cancer and Vitamin C, 1979; How to Live Longer and Feel Better, 1985. Add: Linus Pauling Inst. of Science and Medicine, 440 Page Mill Rd., Palo Alto, Calif. 94306, U.S.A.

PAULSEN, Gary. American, b. 1939. Novels, Children's fiction, Children's non-fiction, Homes/Gardens, Social commentary. Has worked as a teacher, electronics field engineer, actor, director, farmer, rancher, truck driver, trapper, professional archer, singer and sailor. *Publs:* children's fiction—Mr. Tucket, 1969; The C.B. Radio Caper, 1977; The Curse of the Cobra. 1977; The Foxman, 1977; The Golden Stick, 1977; Tiltawhile John, 1977; Winterkill, 1977; (with Ray Peekner) The Green Recruit, 1978; Hope and a Hatchet, 1978; The Night the White Deer Died, 1978; The Spitball Gang, 1980; Dancing Carl, 1983; Popcorn Days and Buttermilk Nights, 1983; Tracker, 1984; Dogsong, 1985; Sentries, 1986; The Crossing, 1987; Hatchett, 1987, in U.K. as Hatchet, 1989; The Island, 1988; The Voyage of the Frog, 1989; The Winter Stories, 1989; children's non-fiction—Dribbling, Shooting and Scoring Sometimes, 1976; The Grass Eaters, 1976; (with Dan Theis) Martin Luther King, The Man Who Climbed the Mountain, 1976; The Small Ones, 1976; Careers in an Airport, 1977; Hitting, Pitching, and Running Maybe, 1977; Riding, Roping, and Bulldogging—Almost, 1977; Forehanding and—Backhanding If You're Lucky, 1978; (with John Morris) Hiking and Backpacking, 1978; Running, Jumping, and Throwing—If You Can, 1978; (with John Morris) Canoeing, Kayaking, and Rafting, 1979; Downhill, Hotdogging, and Cross-Country—If the Snow Isn't Sticky, 1979; Facing Off, Checking, and Goaltending—Perhaps, 1979; Going Very Fast in a Circle—If You Don't Run Out of Gas, 1979; Launching, Floating High, and Landing—If Your Pilot Light Doesn't Go Out, 1979; Pummeling, Falling, and Getting Up—Sometimes, 1979; Track, Enduro, and Motocross—Unless You Fall Over, 1979; (with Roger Barrett) Athletics, 1980; (with Roger Barrett) Ice Hockey, 1980; (with Roger Barrett) Motor-Cycling, 1980; (with Roger Barrett) Motor Racing, 1980; (with Roger Barrett) Skiing, 1980; (with Roger Barrett) Tennis, 1980; (with Art Browne, Jr.) TV and Movie Animals, 1980; Sailing, From Jibs to Jibing, 1981; novels for adults—The Death Specialists, 1976; The Implosion Effect, 1976; C.B. Jockey, 1977; The Sweeper, 1980; Meteorite-Track 291, 1981; Survival Guide, 1981; Compkill, 1981; Clutterkill, 1981; The Meatgrinder, 1984; Murphy, 1987; Murphy's Gold, 1988; Night Rituals, 1989; The Madonna Stories, 1989; other for adults—(with Raymond Friday Locke) The Special War, 1966; Some Birds Don't Fly, 1968; The Building a New, Buying an Old, Remodeling a Used, Comprehensive Home and Shelter How-to-Do-It Book, 1976; Farm: A History and Celebration of the American Farmer, 1977; Successful Home Repair, 1978; Money-Saving Home Repair Guide, 1981. Add: c/o Jonathan Lazear, 430 First Ave., North, Suite 516, Minneapolis, Minn. 55401, U.S.A.

PAULSON, Ronald (Howard). American, b. 1930. Art, Literature. Prof. of English, Johns Hopkins Univ., since 1984 (also 1967–75). Instr., 1958–59, Asst. Prof., 1959–62, and Assoc. Prof., 1962–63, Univ. of Illinois; Prof. of English, Rice Univ., Houston, 1963–67, and Yale Univ., New Haven, 1975–84. *Publs:* Theme and Structure in Swift's Tale of a Tub; (ed. with T. Lockward) Fielding: The Critical Heritage; (ed.) Fielding: 20th Century Views; Hogarth's Graphic Works; The Fictions of Satire; Satire and the Novel; Hogarth: His Life, Art and Times; Rowlandson: A New Interpretation; Emblem and Expression in English Art of the 18th Century; (ed.) Satire: Modern Essays in Criticism; The Age of Hogarth; Popular and Polite Art in the Age of Hogarth and Fielding; Literary Landscape: Turner and Constable; Representations of Revolution; Book and Painting: Shakespeare, Milton, and the Bible, 1982. Add: Johns Hopkins Univ., Baltimore, Md. 21218, U.S.A.

PAULSTON, Rolland G. American, b. 1929. Education, Social commentary/phenomena. Prof., Intnl. and Development Education Prog., Sch. of Education, Univ. of Pittsburgh, since 1972 (Asst. Prof., 1968–69; Assoc. Prof., 1969–72). Social Studies Teacher, Los Angeles Public Schs., 1956–59, and American High Sch. of Tangier, 1959–62; Research Asst., 1963–65, and Visiting Asst. Prof. and Research Assoc., Center for Education in Latin America, 1966–68, Teachers Coll., Columbia Univ., NYC. *Publs:* Educational Change in Sweden, 1968; Society, Schools, and Progress in Peru, 1971; Non-Formal Education, 1972; Folk Schools in Social and Cultural Change, 1974; Education in Social Movements, 1975; Other Dreams, Other Schools, 1980. Add: Sch. of Education, Univ. of Pittsburgh, Pittsburgh, Pa. 15260, U.S.A.

PAULU, Burton. American, b. 1910. Media. Dir. Emeritus of Univ. Media Resources, Univ. of Minnesota, Minneapolis. *Publs:* British Broadcasting; British Broadcasting in Transition; Radio and Television Broadcasting on the European Continent; Radio and Television Broadcasting in Eastern Europe; Television and Radio Broadcasting in the United Kingdom. Add: 5005 Wentworth Ave. S., Minneapolis, Minn. 55419, U.S.A.

PAUST, Marian. American, b. 1908. Poetry. Member, Bd. of Dirs., Richland County Bank, since 1964; also, farm mgr. since 1960. Regional Vice-Pres., 1951–54, State Vice-Pres., 1954, Muse Letter Ed., 1954, Member of the Bd. of Dirs., 1954–78, State Historian, 1956–83, State Secty., 1960, and Member of the Anthology Bd., Wisconsin Fellowship of Poets; National Contest Chmn., National Fedn. of State Poetry Socs., 1963. *Publs:* One Hundred Years, 1960; Honey to Be Savored, 1968; Everybody Beats a Drum, 1970; History of Wisconsin Fellowship of Poets, 1974; Personal Poems, 1977; North Country, 1978; New Poems Hung Up to Dry, 1980; The Green Web, 1983. Add: Route 4, Double M Ranch, Richland Center, Wisc. 53581, U.S.A.

PAVEY, Don. British, b. 1922. Art, Design (general), Recreation/Leisure/Hobbies. Sr. Lectr. in charge of the experimental art and design workshop, Sch. of Liberal Studies, Kingston Polytechnic, Surrey, 1969–82 (Lectr. in Design and History of Art in predecessor instn., Kingston Coll. of Art, 1950–69). Member of the Council, Soc. for Education Through Art, 1972–83 (Ed., Athene, journal of the soc., 1972–80); Founder and Chmn., Jr. Arts and Science Centres, 1970–80. *Publs:* (ed.) Methuen Handbook of Colour and Colour Dictionary, 1963, 1967, 1978; Art-Based Games, 1979; Genius, 1980; Colour, 1981; The Artist's Colourmen's Story, 1985. Add: 30 Wayside, London SW14 7LN, England.

PAVLOWITCH, Stevan K. British, b. 1933. History. Reader in the History of the Balkans, Univ. of Southampton (member of the faculty since 1965). Journalist and Public Relations Officer, Stockholm, Brussels, Milan and London, 1958–65. *Publs:* Anglo-Russian Rivalry in Serbia 1837-1839, 1961; Yugoslavia, 1971; Bijou d'Art (on Bojidar Karageorgevitch), 1978; Unconventional Perceptions of Yugoslavia 1940-1945, 1985; The Improbable Survivor: Yugoslavia and Its Problems 1918-1988, 1988. Add: Univ. of Southampton, Southampton SO9 5NH, England.

PAWEL, Ernst. American, b. 1920. Novels/Short stories, Biography, Translations. *Publs:* The Island in Time (novel), 1951; From the Dark Tower (novel), 1957; In the Absence of Magic (novel), 1961; (trans.) Five Operas and Richard Strauss, by L. Lehmann, 1964; (trans.) The Great Debate: Theories of Nuclear Strategy, by Raymond Aron, 1965; The Nightmare of Reason: A Life of Franz Kafka, 1984. Add: c/o Farrar, Straus and Giroux, 19 Union Sq. W., New York, N.Y. 10003, U.S.A.

PAWLEY, Martin (Edward). Also writes as Rupert Spade and Charles Noble. British, b. 1938. Architecture. Architectural Correspondent, The Guardian newspaper, London. News Ed., The Architect's Journal, London, 1967–69; Housing Consultant to the Govt. of Chile, 1972–73; consultant on low-cost construction to the U.N., 1975–77; Consultant to the State Govt. of Florida, 1977–79; with the City of Los Angeles Planning Dept., 1979–80; Ed., Building Design, London, 1981–83. *Publs:* Architecture Versus Housing, 1971; Frank Lloyd Wright: Public Buildings, 1971; Le Corbusier, 1971; Mies van der Rohe, 1971; (as Rupert Spade) Eero Saarinen, 1972; (as Rupert Spade) Paul Rudolph, 1972; (as Rupert Spade) Oscar Niemeyer, 1972; (as Rupert Spade) Richard Neutra, 1972; (as Charles Noble) Philip Johnson, 1972; The Private Future, 1974; Garbage Housing, 1974; Home Ownership, 1979; Building for Tomorrow, 1982; Theory and Design in the Second Machine Age, 1989. Add: 21 Bramham Gdns., London SW5, England.

PAWLIKOWSKI, John Thaddeus. American, b. 1940. Theology/Religion. Prof., Catholic Theological Union, Chicago, since 1968 (Dean of Students, 1969–72; Acting Pres., 1975–76). Member, American Bishops Cttee. for Catholic-Jewish Relations, since 1972; Member, United States Holocaust Memorial Council, since 1980. Chmn., Israel Study Group, National Council of Churches' Faith and Order Commn., 1972–74. *Publs:* Epistle Homilies, 1966; Proposals for Church Sponsored New Housing, 1971; Catechetics and Prejudice, 1973; Sinai and Calvary, 1976; The Challenge of the Holocaust for Christian Theology, 1978, 1982; What Are They Saying about Christian-Jewish Relations?, 1980; Christ in Light of the Christian-Jewish Dialogue, 1982; (co-ed. with Donald Senior) Biblical and Theological Reflections on the Challenge of Peace, 1984; (ed. with David Byers) Justice in the Marketplace, 1985; (with James

A. Wilde) When Catholics Speak About Jews, 1987; (ed. with Donald Senior) Economic Justice: CTU's Pastoral Commentary on the Bishop's Letter on the Economy, 1988. Add: Catholic Theological Union, 5401 S. Cornell Ave., Chicago, Ill. 60615, U.S.A.

PAXTON, John. British, b. 1923. Business/Trade/Industry, History, International relations/Current affairs, Politics/Government. Ed., The Statesman's Year-Book, 1969–90. Consultant Ed., The New Illustrated Everyman's Encyclopedia, 1981–84. *Publs:* (ed. and compiler) Everyman's Dictionary of Abbreviations, 1974, 1986; World Legislatures, 1974; (ed. with C. Cook) European Political Facts 3 vols., 1974–85; (with A.E. Walsh) Competition Policy, 1974; (ed.) The Statesman's Year-Book World Gazetteer, 1975, 3rd ed. 1986; The Developing Common Market, 1976; A Dictionary of the European Communities, 1977, 1982; (ed. with C. Cook) Commonwealth Political Facts, 1978; (ed. with S. Fairfield) A Calendar of Creative Man, 1980; Companion to Russian History, 1984; Companion to the French Revolution, 1986; Penguin Dictionary of Abbreviations, 1989. Add: c/o Coutts and Co., 188 Fleet St., London EC4A 2HT, England.

PAXTON, Lois. *See* **LOW,** Dorothy Mackie.

PAYNE, Alan. *See* **JAKES,** John.

PAYNE, Bruce. American, b. 1911. Administration/Management. Pres., Bruce Payne and Assocs. Inc., since 1946. *Publs:* Planning for Company Growth, 1963; (with D.D. Swett) Office Operation Improvement, 1967. Add: Bruce Payne and Assocs., 140 West End Ave., New York, N.Y. 10023, U.S.A.

PAYNE, Donald Gordon. Writes as Donald Gordon, James Vance Marshall, and Ian Cameron. British, b. 1924. Novels, Travel, Biography. *Publs:* as Ian Cameron—The Midnight Sea, 1958; Red Duster, White Ensign, 1959; The Lost Ones, 1961; Wings of the Morning, 1962; Lodestone and Evening Star, 1965; The Impossible Dream, 1971; Magellan and the First Circumnavigation of the World, 1974; Antarctica: The Last Continent, 1974; The White Ship, 1975; The Young Eagles, 1979; To the Farthest Ends of the Earth (History of the Royal Geographical Society), 1980; Mountains of the Gods: The Himalayas and the Mountains of Central Asia, 1984; Exploring Antarctica, 1984; Exploring Africa, 1984; Exploring Australia, 1985; Exploring the Himalayas, 1985; Lost Paradise: The Exploration of the Pacific, 1987; Kingdom of the Sun God: A History of the Andes, 1989. As James Vance Marshall—Walkabout, 1959; A River Ran Out of Eden, 1962; My Boy John That Went to Sea, 1966; A Walk to the Hills of the Dreamtime, 1970; The Wind at Morning, 1973; Still Waters, 1982; as Donald Gordon—Star-Raker, 1962; Flight of the Bat, 1963; The Golden Oyster, 1967; Leap in the Dark, 1970. Add: Pippacre, Westcott Heath, Dorking, Surrey, England.

PAYNE, J. Gregory. American, b. 1949. History, Biography. Assoc. Prof. of Communication Studies and Co-Dir. of the News Study Group, Emerson Coll., Boston, since 1983. Pres. and Advisory Bd. Member, Outspoken Young Physicians of America, since 1987; Consultant to the Bechtel Corp., U.S. Treasury Dept., and California Credit Union. Assoc. Prof. of Communications, California Lutheran Coll., Thousand Oaks, 1976–77; Asst. Prof. of Rhetoric and Dir. of Debate, Occidental Coll., Los Angeles, 1976–83; Head Speech Writer, Tom Bradley's Gubernatorial Campaign, California, 1982–83. *Publs:* Kent State: A Wake, 1978; Mayday: Kent State, 1981; (with Scott C. Ratzan) Tom Bradley: The Impossible Dream, 1986. Add: 31094 Montessa Dr., Laguna Beach, Calif. 92677, U.S.A.

PAYNE, Laurence. British, b. 1919. Mystery/Crime/Suspense. Actor: has had numerous roles in stage, film, television, and radio productions; drama teacher, Royal Coll. of Music, London, and St. Catherine's Sch., Guildford, Surrey. *Publs:* The Nose on My Face, 1962, in U.S. paperback as The First Body, 1964; Too Small For His Shoes, 1962; Deep and Crisp and Even, 1964; Birds in the Belfry, 1966; Spy for Sale, 1969; Even My Foot's Asleep, 1971; Take the Money and Run, 1982; Malice in Camera, 1983; Vienna Blood, 1984; Dead for a Ducat, 1985; Late Knight (in U.S. as Knight Fall), 1987. Add: c/o Hodder and Stoughton, 47 Bedford Sq., London WC1B 3DP, England.

PEABODY, Robert Lee. American, b. 1931. Politics/Government, Public/Social administration. Prof., Dept. of Political Science, Johns Hopkins Univ., Baltimore, since 1969 (Asst. Prof., 1961–64; Assoc. Prof., 1965–68). Advisory Ed., Congressional Quarterly Press, 1976–84. *Publs:* (ed. with N.W. Polsby) New Perspectives on the House of Representatives, 1963, 3rd ed. 1977; Organizational Authority, 1964; (with

R.K. Huitt) Congress: Two Decades of Analysis, 1969; (ed.) Education of a Congressman: The New Letters of Morris K. Udall, 1972; (with J.M. Berry, W.G. Frasure and J. Goldman) To Enact a Law: Congress and Campaign Financing, 1972; Leadership in Congress: Stability, Succession and Change, 1976. Add: Dept. of Political Science, Johns Hopkins Univ., Baltimore, Md. 21218, U.S.A.

PEACOCK, (Sir) Alan (Turner). British, b. 1922. Economics, Education, Music. Research Prof. in Public Finance, Heriot Watt Univ; Exec. Dir., David Hume Inst. Chmn., Scottish Arts Council, since 1986. Lectr. in Economics, 1948–51, and Reader in Public Finance, 1951–56, London Sch. of Economics; Prof. of Economic Science, Univ. of Edinburgh, 1956–62; Prof. of Economics, Univ. of York, 1962–78; Chief Economic Adviser, Depts. of Trade, Industry and Consumer Protection, 1973–76; Principal, later Vice-Chancellor, Univ. of Buckingham, 1980–84. Publs: Economics of National Insurance, 1952; (trans.) Theory of the Market Economy, by H. von Stackelberg, 1953; (ed.) Income Redistribution and Social Policy, 1954; (with H.C. Edey) National Income and Social Accounting, 1954; (with D.G.M. Dosser) National Income of Tanganyika, 1958; (with J. Wiseman) Growth of Public Expenditure in the United Kingdom 1890-1955, 1961; (ed. with D. Robertson) Public Expenditure: Appraisal and Control, 1963; (with J. Wiseman) Education for Democrats, 1964; (with H. Glennerster and R. Lavers) Educational Finance, 1966; (ed.) Quantitative Analysis in Public Finance, 1969; (with G.K. Shaw) Economic Theory of Fiscal Policy, 1971, 1976; (with R. Weir) The Composer in the Market Place, 1975; (with C.K. Rowley) Welfare Economics, 1975; Credibility of Liberal Economics, 1977; The Economic Analysis of Government, 1979; (ed. with F. Forte) Political Economy of Taxation, 1981; The Regulation Game, 1984; (co-ed.) Public Expenditure and Government Growth, 1985; Waltz Contrasts, 1988. Add: 8 Gilmour Rd., Edinburgh EH16 5NF, Scotland.

PEACOCK, Ronald. British, b. 1907. Literature. Prof. of German, Univ. of Leeds, 1939–45; Henry Simon Prof. of German, 1945–62, Dean of the Faculty of Arts, 1954–56, and Pro-Vice-Chancellor, 1958–62, Univ. of Manchester; Visiting Prof., Cornell Univ., 1949, Univ. of Heidelberg, 1960–61, Univ. of Freiburg, 1965, 1967–68; Prof. of German Studies and Head of the Dept., Bedford Coll., 1962–75, now Emeritus. Publs: Holderlin, 1938; The Poet in the Theatre, 1946, 1960; The Art of Drama, 1957, 1960; Goethe's Major Plays, 1959; Criticism and Personal Taste, 1972. Add: Greenshade, Woodhill Ave., Gerrards Cross, Bucks. SL9 8DR, England.

PEAKE, Lilian. British. Historical/Romance/Gothic. Has worked as secty., typist, and journalist: reporter in High Wycombe, fashion writer in London, and writer for Daily Herald newspaper and Woman mag., London. Publs: Man of Granite, 1971; This Moment in Time, 1971; The Library Tree, 1972; Man Out of Reach, 1972; The Real Thing, 1972; A Girl Alone, 1972; Mist Across the Moors, 1972; No Friend of Mine, 1972; Gone Before Morning, 1973; Man in Charge, 1973; Familiar Stranger, 1973; Till the End of Time, 1973; The Dream on the Hill, 1974; A Sense of Belonging, 1974; Master of the House, 1974; The Impossible Marriage, 1975; Moonrise over the Mountains, 1975; Heart in the Sunlight, 1975; The Tender Night, 1975; The Sun of Summer, 1975; A Bitter Loving, 1976; The Distant Dream, 1976; The Little Impostor, 1976; Somewhere to Lay My Head, 1977; Passionate Involvement, 1977; No Second Parting, 1977; This Man Her Enemy, 1977; Day of Possession, 1978; Rebel in Love, 1978; Run for Your Love, 1978; Dangerous Deception, 1979; Enemy from the Past, 1979; Stranger on the Beach, 1979; Promise at Midnight, 1980; A Ring for a Fortune, 1980; A Secret Affair, 1980; Strangers into Lovers, 1981; Gregg Barratt's Woman, 1981; Across a Crowded Room, 1981; Stay Till Morning, 1982; Bitter Revenge, 1982; Passionate Intruder, 1982; No Other Man, 1982; A Woman in Love, 1984; The Bitter Taste of Love, 1988. Add: c/o Mills and Boon Ltd., Eton House, 18-24 Paradise Rd., Richmond, Surrey TW9 1SR, England.

PEAKE, Pamela (Joyce). New Zealander, b. 1940. Crafts, Natural history. Freelance designer. Research biologist and univ. demonstrator, 1960–62; grammar sch. biology teacher, 1964–66. Publs: Animals with Shells, 1969; (co-author) 80 Toys to Make for Children, 1973; Creative Soft Toy Making, 1974; How to Make Dinosaurs and Dragons, 1977; The Complete Book of Soft Dolls, 1979; Catcraft, 1984; The Book of Toymaking, 1986; Learn to Make Soft Toys, 1987. Add: Spring Cottage, Ightham, Sevenoaks, Kent TN15 9HN, England.

PEALE, Norman Vincent. American, b. 1898. Theology/Religion. Pastor, Marble Collegiate Reformed Church, NYC, since 1932. Publs: A Guide fo Confident Living, 1948; The Power of Positive Thinking, 1952; The Coming of the King, 1956; Stay Alive All Your Life, 1957;

The Amazing Results of Positive Thinking, 1959; The Tough-Minded Optimist, 1962; Adventures in the Holy Land, 1963; Sin, Sex and Self-Control, 1965; Jesus of Nazareth, 1966; The Healing of Sorrow, 1966; Enthusiasm Makes the Difference, 1967; Bible Stories, 1973; (ed.) Treasury of Courage and Confidence, 1974; You Can If You Think You Can, 1974; The Positive Principle Today, 1976; (with Smiley Blanton) The Art of Real Happiness, 1976; The Positive Power of Jesus Christ, 1980; Dynamic Imaging, 1981; Have a Great Day, 1984; The True Joy of Positive Living, 1984; Why Some Positive Thinkers Get Powerful Results, 1986; Power of the Plus Factor, 1987; (with Kenneth Blanchard) The Power of Ethical Management, 1988; The American Character, 1988. Add: 1025 Fifth Ave., New York, N.Y. 10028, U.S.A.

PEARCE, Brian Louis. British, b. 1933. Novels/Short stories, Plays/Screenplays, Poetry, Education. Sr. Lectr. and College Librarian, Richmond upon Thames Coll., Twickenham, since 1977. Reference Librarian, Twickenham Public Library, 1958–61; Librarian, Acton Technical Coll., 1962–66; Ed., Expression, 1965–67; Tutor and Librarian, Twickenham Coll. of Technology, 1966–77. Publs: Poems, 1956; The Americas and Other Poems, 1962; Conchubar, 1963; A Sense of Wonder, 1963; Saga, 1963; The Blind Man at the Gate of Lethe, 1964; (ed.) Old Ascot: The Diaries of George and G.A. Longhurst 1833-1881, 1964; My Grandfather's Uncle: A Memoir of the Rev. Caleb Mark Longhurst, 1964; Paolo and Francesca, 1965; The Frozen Forest, 1965; The Eagle and the Swan (play), 1966; The Ascot of Gilbert Longhurst, 1967; Thames Music: A Poem, 1968; Holman, 1969; Combe Hill: A Poem, 1969; The Argonauts and Other Poems, 1970; The Art of Eric Ratcliffe: An Appreciation, 1970; Requiem for the Sixties, 1971; (ed.) Twickenham Eyot: An Anthology, 1973; Twickenham College of Technology: The First Thirty-Five Years 1937-1972, 1974; Selected Poems 1951-1973, 1978; The Vision of Piers Librarian, 1981; Leaves for Palinurus, 1982; Office Hours, 1983; Ave Acton Vale, 1983; Browne Study, 1984; Bond Street Snatches, 1984; Free for All: The Public Library Movement in Twickenham, 1985; (ed.) Palgrave: Selected Poems, 1985; Gwen John Talking, 1985; Dutch Comfort: Poetry, Prose, Translations, 1985; Victoria Hammersmith (novel), 1988; Thomas-Twining of Twickenham: His Work, His Museum, and the Perryn House Estate, 1988. Add: 72 Heathfield South, Twickenham, Middx. TW2 7SS, England.

PEARCE, Mary E. British, b. 1932. Novels/Short stories. Publs: Apple Tree Lean Down, 1973; Jack Mercybright, 1975; The Sorrowing Wind, 1975; Cast a Long Shadow, 1977; The Land Endures, 1978; Seedtime and Harvest, 1980; Polsinney Harbour, 1983; The Two Farms, 1985. Add: Owls End, Shuthonger, Tewkesbury, Glos., England.

PEARCE, (Ann) Philippa. British. Children's fiction. Scriptwriter and producer, BBC Radio Schs. Broadcasting, 1945–58; Children's Ed., André Deutsch Ltd., publrs., London, 1960–67. Publs: Minnow on the Say, 1955; Tom's Midnight Garden, 1958; Mrs. Cockle's Cat, 1962; A Dog So Small, 1962; (with Harold Scott) From Inside Scotland Yard, 1963; The Strange Sunflower, 1966; (with Brian Fairfax-Lucy) The Children of the House, 1968; The Elm Street Lot, 1969; The Squirrel Wife, 1971; Beauty and the Beast, 1972; What the Neighbours Did and Other Stories, 1972; The Shadow Cage and Other Tales of the Supernatural, 1977; The Battle of Bubble and Squeak, 1978; Wings of Courage, 1982; The Way to Sattin Shore, 1983; Lion at School and Other Stories, 1985; Who's Afraid and Other Strange Stories, 1986; Emily's Own Elephant, 1987; The Toothball, 1987. Add: 4 The King's Mill Lane, Great Shelford, Cambridge CB2 5EN, England.

PEARCE, Roy Harvey. American, b. 1919. Literature. Prof. of American Literature, Univ. of California at San Diego, since 1963. Ed., with others, Centenary Edition of the Works of Nathaniel Hawthorne, since 1962. Instr., 1945–46, Assoc. Prof., 1949–54, and Prof., 1954–63, Ohio State Univ., Columbus; Asst. Prof., Univ. of California at Berkeley, 1946–49. Former Member of Editorial Bd., English Literary History, from 1946. Publs: (ed. with William Matthews) An Annotated Bibliography of American Diaries Written Prior to the Year 1861, 1945; The Savages of America: A Study of the Indian and the Ideal of Civilization, 1953, as Savagism and Civilization: A Study of the Indian and the American Mind, 1965; (with E.H. Cady and Frederick J. Hoffman) The Growth of American Literature, 1956; (ed.) Colonial American Writing, 1960, 1968; The Continuity of American Poetry, 1961; (ed.) Whitman: A Collection of Critical Essays, 1962; (ed.) The American, by Henry James, 1962; (ed.) Hawthorne Centenary Essays, 1964; (ed. with J. Hillis Miller) The Act of the Mind: Essays on the Poetry of Wallace Stevens, 1965; (ed.) Experience in the Novel, 1968; Historicism Once More: Problems and Occasions for the American Scholar, 1969; (ed.) Nathaniel Hawthorne, Tales and Sketches, 1982; (ed. with Gabriel Almond and Marvin Chodorow) Progress and Its Discontents, 1982; Gesta Humanorum: Studies in the Historical Mode. Add: 7858 Esterel Dr., La Jolla, Calif. 92037, U.S.A.

PEARLMAN, Moshe. Israeli, b. 1911. Archaeology/Antiquities, History, Documentaries/Reportage. Dir.-Gen., Israel Broadcasting Service, 1952–56; Adviser to the Israeli Prime Minister, 1956–60; Ambassador on Special Mission to Congo (Leopoldville), 1960. *Publs:* Collective Adventure, 1938; Mufti of Jerusalem, 1947; Adventure in the Sun, 1948; The Capture and Trial of Adolf Eichmann, 1962; Ben Gurion Looks Back, 1965; Historical Sites in Israel, 1966; The Zealots of Masada, 1967; (with Teddy Kollek) Jerusalem: A History of Forty Centuries, 1969; (with Teddy Kollek) Pilgrims to the Holy Land, 1970; The First Days of Israel: In the Footsteps of Moses, 1973; The Maccabees, 1973; Moses, 1974; In the Footsteps of the Prophets 1975; Digging Up the Bible, 1980; (with Y. Yannai) Historical Sites in the Holy Land, 1985. Add: 16 David Marcus St., Jerusalem, Israel.

PEARSALL, Derek (Albert). British, b. 1931. Literature. Prof. of English, Harvard Univ., Cambridge, Mass., since 1985. Asst. Lectr., then Lectr., Dept. of English, King's Coll., London, 1959–65; Lectr., Sr. Lectr. and Reader, 1965–76, and Prof. of English, 1976–85, Univ. of York. *Publs:* (ed.) The Floure and the Leafe and The Assembly of Ladies, 1962; (ed. with Elizabeth Salter) Piers Plowman: Selections from the C-Text, 1967; John Lydgate, 1970; (with Elizabeth Salter) Landscapes and Seasons of the Medieval World, 1973; Old English and Middle English Poetry, 1977; (ed.) Piers Plowman: An Edition of the C-Text, 1978; (ed. with I.C. Cunningham) The Anchinleck Manuscript, 1979; (ed.) Manuscripts and Readers in 15th Century England, 1983; (ed.) Chaucer, The Nun's Priest's Tale: Variorum Edition, 1984; The Canterbury Tales, 1985; (ed.) Manuscripts and Texts: Editorial Problems in Later Middle English Literature, 1987. Add: Dept. of English, Harvard Univ., Cambridge, Mass. 02138, U.S.A.

PEARSALL, Ronald. British, b. 1927. Antiques/Furnishings, Cultural/Ethnic topics, Music. *Publs:* Worm in the Bud, 1969; The Table-Rappers, 1972; Victorian Sheet Music Covers, 1972; Victorian Popular Music, 1973; Collecting Mechanical Antiques, 1973; Edwardian Life and Leisure, 1973; Collecting and Restoring Scientific Instruments, 1974; (with G. Webb) Inside the Antique Trade, 1974; Night's Black Angels, 1975; Collapse of Stout Party, 1975; Edwardian Popular Music, 1975; Popular Music of the 1920's 1976; The Belvedere, 1976; The Alchemists, 1976; Public Purity, Private Shame, 1976; Conan Doyle, 1977; Tides of War, 1978; The Iron Sleep, 1979; Tell Me Pretty Maiden, 1981; Practical Painting, 1984; Joy of Antiques, 1988. Add: c/o David and Charles, Brunel House, Newton Abbot, Devon TQ12 4PU, England.

PEARSON, Bill. (William Harrison Pearson). New Zealander, b. 1922. Novels/Short stories, Essays. Assoc. Prof. of English, Univ. of Auckland, 1970 until Retirement, 1986 (Lectr., 1954–66). Teacher, Blackball Sch., 1942, and Oxford District High Sch., 1949, New Zealand, and in London County Council Schools, 1952–53; Sr. Research Fellow, Dept. of Pacific History, Australian National Univ., Canberra, 1967–69. *Publs:* Coal Flat, 1963, 4th ed. 1985; (ed.) Collected Stories 1935-63, by Frank Sargeson, 1964; Henry Lawson among Maoris, 1968; (ed.) Brown Man's Burden and Later Stories, by Roderick Finlayson, 1973; Fretful Sleepers and Other Essays, 1974; Rifled Sanctuaries: Some Views of the Pacific Islands in Western Literature to 1900, 1984. Add: Dept. of English, Univ. of Auckland, Private Bag, Auckland, New Zealand.

PEARSON, Diane (Margaret). British, b. 1931. Novels/Short stories. Consultant Ed., Transworld Publishers Ltd., London, since 1963. With Production Dept., Jonathan Cape Ltd., London, 1948–52; with local govt., County Hall, London, 1952–60; with Advertising Dept., Purnells Publishing, London, 1962–63. *Publs:* Bride of Tancred, 1967; The Marigold Field, 1969; Sarah Whitman, 1971; Csardas, 1975; The Summer of the Barshinskeys, 1984. Add: c/o Macmillan Ltd., 4 Little Essex St., London WC2, England.

PEARSON, Gayle. American, b. 1947. Children's fiction. Admin. Asst., Univ. of California at San Francisco, since 1982. Asst. News Ed., Vance Publications, Chicago, 1970–71; Social Worker, Elgin State Hosp., Chicago, 1971–73; Child Care Worker, Ming Quong Children's Center, Los Gatos, Calif., 1973–75; Area Dir., Santa Clara County Information and Referrsal, San Jose, Calif., 1977–81. *Publs:* Fish Friday, 1986; This Coming Home Cafe, 1988. Add: 533-A Diamond St., San Francisco, Calif. 94114, U.S.A.

PEARSON, John. British, b. 1930. Novels/Short stories, Biography,

Documentaries/Reportage. Freelance writer since 1965. Previously worked for The Times, The Sunday Times (as staff reporter, columnist, and feature writer), and for BBC Television (as scriptwriter). *Publs:* Gone to Timbuctoo (novel), 1961; (with Graham Turner) The Persuasion Industry, 1965; Bluebird and the Dead Lake, 1965; The Life of Ian Fleming, 1966; The Colosseum, 1968; The Life of James Bond, 1970; The Profession of Violence: The Rise and Fall of the Kray Twins, 1972, 3rd ed. 1984; Edward the Rake, 1974; The Life of Biggles, 1975; "Facades," 1979; The Kindness of Dr. Avicenna, 1982; Stags and Serpents: The Story of the House of Cavendish and the Dukes of Devonshire, 1983; The Ultimate Family: The Making of the Royal House of Windsor, 1986; The Selling of the Royal Family: The Mystique of the British Monarchy, 1986. Add: c/o Ed Victor, 162 Wardour St., London W1, England.

PEARSON, John. American, b. 1934. Novels/Short stories. Served as Methodist Minister in Windsor and Napa, Calif.; Extension Prog. Co-ordinator, Dept. of Arts and Humanities, Univ. of California at Berkeley, 1966–74. *Publs:* To Be Nobody Else, 1968; Kiss the Joy as It Flies, 1970; The Sun's Birthday, 1973; Begin Sweet World, 1976; Magic Doors, 1977; Love Is Most Mad and Moonly, 1978; The Calligraphy of Nature, 1984. Add: 1343 Sacramento St., Berkeley, Calif. 94702, U.S.A.

PEARSON, Keith David. Australian. Institutions/Organizations, Theology/Religion. Dr., Joint Bd. of Christian Education, Australia and New Zealand, 1960–80; Dir., Continuing Education for Ministry, since 1980. *Publs:* Why Do We Baptize Our Children?, 1961; The Meaning of Church Membership, 1962; A Programme for Church and Home, 1964; (ed.) The Elder Serving the Church, 1967; (compiler) Introduction to Group Dynamics, 1968; (compiler) Introduction to Organization Development, 1973; Introduction to Systems Thinking, 1980; Praying the Bible, 1982. Add: 73 Walpole St., Kew, Vic. 3101, Australia.

PEARSON, Lionel (Ignatius Cusack). British, b. 1908. Classics. Prof. of Classics Emeritus, Stanford Univ., California, since 1973 (Asst. Prof. to Assoc. Prof., 1940–54; Prof., 1954–73). Lectr. in Greek, Glasgow Univ., 1930–31; Lectr. and Asst. Prof., Dalhousie Univ., Halifax, N.S., 1932–38; Visiting Prof. of Classics, Univ. of Sydney, Aust., 1968, and Yale Univ., New Haven, Conn., 1974–75. *Publs:* Early Ionian Historians, 1939; The Local Historians of Attica, 1942; The Lost Histories of Alexander the Great, 1960; Popular Ethics in Ancient Greece, 1962; (trans. and ed. with F. Sandbach) Plutarch: Moralia, vol. XI, Loeb Classical Library series, 1965; (ed. with commentary) Demosthenes: Six Private Speeches, 1972; The Art of Demosthenes, 1976; (ed. with S.A. Stephens) Didymus, in Demosthenem Commenta, 1983; Selected Papers, 1983; The Greek Historians of the West: Timaeus and His Predecessors, 1988. Add: 12123 Foothill Lane, Los Altos Hills, Calif. 94022, U.S.A.

PEARSON, Roy. American, b. 1914. Theology/Religion. Minister, Southville Federated Church, Massachusetts, 1936–38, First Congregational Church, Swanzey, N.H., 1938–40, and Amherst, Mass., 1940–47, and Hancock Congregational Church, Lexington, Mass., 1947–54; Pres., Andover Theological Seminary, Newton Centre, Massachusetts, 1954–65; Bartlet Prof. of Sacred Rhetoric, 1954–79, and Pres., 1965–79, Andover Newton Theological Sch., Newton Centre, Mass., now retired. *Publs:* Here's a Faith for You, 1953; This Do—and Live, 1954; The Hard Commands of Jesus, 1957; Seeking and Finding God, 1958; The Ministry of Preaching, 1959; Hear Our Prayer, 1961; The Preacher: His Purpose and Practice, 1963; The Believer's Unbelief, 1963. Add: Stony Brook Rd., New London, N.H. 03257, U.S.A.

PEARSON, Scott Roberts. American, b. 1938. Economics. Prof., Food Research Inst., Stanford Univ., California, since 1980 (Asst. Prof., 1968–74; Assoc. Prof., 1974–80). *Publs:* Petroleum and the Nigerian Economy, 1970; (co-author) Commodity Exports and African Economic Development, 1974; (co-author) Rice in West Africa: Policy and Economics, 1981; (co-author) Food Policy Analysis, 1983; (co-author) The Cassava Economy of Java, 1984; (co-author) Portuguese Agriculture in Transition, 1987; (co-author) The Policy Analysis Matrix for Agricultural Development, 1989. Add: c/o Food Research Inst., Stanford Univ., Stanford, Calif. 94305, U.S.A.

PECHMAN, Joseph. American, b. 1918. Economics. Sr. Fellow, Brookings Instn., Washington, D.C., since 1962 (formerly Dir. of Economic Studies). Statistician, National Research Project, Philadelphia, 1937; Research Asst., Dept. of Economics, Univ. of Wisconsin, Madison, 1937–38; Asst. Dir., Wisconsin Income Tax Study, Wisconsin Tax Commn., 1938–39; Research Assoc., Univ. of Wisconsin, 1939–41; Economist, Office of Price Admin., Washington, 1941–42; Meteorologist, U.S. Army, 1942–45; Asst. Dir., Tax Advisory Staff, U.S. Treasury Dept.,

Washington, 1946–53; Assoc. Prof. of Finance, Sch. of Industrial Management, Massachusetts Inst. of Technology, Cambridge, 1953–54; Economist, Council of Economic Advisers, Washington, 1954–56, and Cttee. for Economic Development, Washington, 1956–60. Member, Bd. of Editors, American Economic Review, 1961–64; Chmn., President's Task Force on Intergovernmental Fiscal Relations, Washington, 1964; Irving Fisher Research Prof., Yale Univ., New Haven, Conn., 1966–67; Pres., American Finance Assn., 1971, Fellow, Center for Advanced Study of the Behavioural Sciences, Palo Alto, Calif., 1975–76; Pres. American Economic Assn., 1989. *Publs:* Federal Tax Policy, 1966, 5th ed., 1987; (with H. Aaron and M. Taussig) Social Security: Perspective for Reform, 1968; (with B. Okner) Who Bears the Tax Burden?, 1974; (ed. with P.M. Timpane) Work Incentives and Income Guarantees, 1975; Setting National Priorities, 1977–82; Who Paid the Taxes 1966-1985?, 1985; The Rich, The Poor, and the Tax They Pay, 1986; (ed.) The Role of the Economist in Government, 1989. Died 1989.

PECK, John (Frederick). American, b. 1941. Poetry. Lecturer, Univ. of Zurich, since 1985. Instr. in English, 1968–70, and Visiting Lectr., 1972–75, Princeton Unv., New Jersey; Asst. Prof., 1977–79, and Prof. of English, 1980–82, Mount Holyoke Coll., South Hadley, Mass. *Publs:* Shagbark, 1972; The Broken Blockhouse Wall, 1978. Add: c/o Englisches Seminar, Plattenstr. 47, 8032 Zurich, Switzerland.

PECK, M(organ) Scott. American, b. 1936. Psychology, Theology/Religion. Asst. Chief of Psychiatry and Neurology, Office of the Surgeon General, Washington, D.C., 1970–72; in private practice of psychiatry in New Preston, Conn. 1972–84. *Publs:* The Road Less Traveled: A New Psychology of Love, Traditional Values, and Spiritual Growth, 1978; People of the Lie; The Hope for Healing Human Evil, 1983; (with Marilyn von Waldener and Patricia Kay) What Return Can I Make?: The Dimensions of the Christian Experience, 1985. Add: c/o Simon and Schuster, 1230 Ave. of the Americas, New York, N.Y. 10020, U.S.A.

PECK, Merton Joseph. American, b. 1925. Economics. Prof. of Economics, Yale Univ., New Haven, since 1963. Asst. to Assoc. Prof. of Business Admin., Harvard Univ., Cambridge, Mass., 1956–61; Deputy Asst. Comptroller and Dir. of Systems Analysis, Office of the Secty. of Defense, Washington, D.C., 1961–62; Member, Council of Economic Advisers, Exec. Office of the President, 1968–69. *Publs:* (with W. Haber, J. Carroll and M. Kahn) The Maintenance of Way Employment on U.S. Railroads, 1957; (with J. Meyer, J. Stenason and C. Zwick) Economics of Competition in the Transportation Industries, 1959; Competition in the Aluminium Industry 1945-1958, 1961; (with F.M. Scherer) Weapons Acquisition: An Economic Analysis, 1962; (with R. Nelson and E. Kalachek) Technology, Economic Growth and Public Policy, 1967; (with R. Noll and J. McGowan) Economic Aspects of Television Regulation, 1973. Add: Dept. of Economics, Yale Univ., 37 Hillhouse Ave., New Haven, Conn. 06520, U.S.A.

PECK, Richard (Wayne). American, b. 1934. Children's fiction. *Publs:* (with Norman Strasma) Old Town: A Compleat Guide, 1965; (ed. with Ned E. Hoopes) Edge of Awareness: Twenty-Five Contemporary Essays, 1966; (ed.) Sounds and Silence, 1970; (ed.) Mindscapes: Poems for the Real World, 1971; (with Mortimer Smith and George Weber) A Consumer's Guide to Educational Innovations, 1972; Don't Look and It Won't Hurt, 1972; Dreamland Lake, 1973; Through a Brief Darkness, 1973; (with Stephen N. Judy) The Creative Word 2, 1973; (ed.) Urban Studies: A Research Paper Casebook, 1973; Representing Super Doll, 1974; (ed.) Transitions: A Literary Paper Casebook, 1974; The Ghost Belonged to Me, 1975; Are You in the House Alone?, 1976; (ed.) Pictures That Storm Inside My Head (poetry anthology), 1976; Monster Night at Grandma's House, 1977; Ghosts I Have Been, 1977; Father Figure, 1978; Secrets of the Shopping Mall, 1979; Close Enough to Touch, 1981; The Dreadful Future of Blossom Culp, 1983; Remembering the Good Times, 1985; Blossom Culp and the Sleep of Death, 1986; Princess Ashley, 1987; Those Summer Girls I Never Met, 1988; Voices After Midnight, 1989. Add: c/o Delacorte Press, 1 Dag Hammerskjold Plaza, New York, N.Y. 10017, U.S.A.

PECK, Robert Newton. American. Novels/Short stories, Children's fiction, Plays/Screenplays, Poetry. *Publs:* A Day No Pigs Would Die, 1972; Millie's Boy, 1973; Path of Hunters: Animal Struggle in a Meadow, 1973; Soup, 1974; Soup for Me, 1975; Wild Cat, 1975; Bee Tree and Other Stuff (verse), 1975; Fawn, 1975; I Am the King of Kazoo, 1976; Rabbits and Redcoats, 1976; Hamilton, 1976; Hang for Treason, 1976; (music and lyrics) King of Kazoo (play), 1976; Last Sunday, 1977; Trig, 1977; Patooie, 1977; The King's Iron, 1977; Soup for President, 1978;

Eagle Fur, 1978; Trig Sees Red, 1978; Basket Case, 1979; Hub, 1979; Mr. Little, 1979; Clunie, 1979; Soup's Drum, 1980; Secrets of Successful Fiction, 1980; Trig Goes Ape, 1980; Soup of Wheels, 1981; Justice Lion, 1981; Trig or Treat, 1982; Banjo, 1982; Soup in the Saddle, 1983; Soup's Goat, 1984; Spanish Hoof, 1985; Soup on Ice, 1985; Jo Silver, 1985; Soup on Fire, 1987; My Vermont, 1987; Hallapoosa, 1988; The Horse Hunters, 1988; Soup's Uncle, 1988; My Vermont II, 1988; Arly, 1989; Soup's Hoop, 1989. Add: 500 Sweetwater Club Circle, Longwood, Fla. 32779, U.S.A.

PECKHAM, Morse. American, b. 1914. Literature. Distinguished Prof. Emeritus of English and Comparative Literature, Univ. of South Carolina, Columbia, since 1980 (Distinguished Prof., 1967–80). Asst. Prof., The Citadel, Charleston, S.C., 1938–41; served in the U.S. Army Air Force, 1941–46; Instr., 1946–47, and Asst. Prof., 1948–49, Rutgers Univ., New Brunswick, N.J.; Asst. Prof., 1949–52, Assoc. Prof., 1952–61, Dir. of the Inst. for Humanistic Education for Business Executives, 1953–54, and of the Univ. Press, 1953–55, and Prof., 1961–67, Univ. of Pennsylvania, Philadelphia. *Publs:* (ed.) On the Origin of Species: A Variorum Text, by Charles Darwin, 1959; Humanistic Education for Business Executives: An Essay in General Education, 1960; (ed. with Seymour Chapman) Word, Meaning, Poem: An Anthology of Poetry, 1961; Beyond the Tragic Vision: The Quest for Identity in the Nineteenth Century, 1962; Man's Rage for Chaos: Biology, Behavior and the Arts, 1965; (ed.) Romanticism: The Culture of the Nineteenth Century, 1965; (ed.) Paracelsus, by Robert Browning, 1969; Art and Pornography: An Experiment in Explanation, 1969; The Triumph of Romanticism: Collected Essays, 1970; Victorian Revolutionaries: Speculation on Some Heroes of a Culture Crisis, 1970; (ed.) Pippa Passes, by Robert Browning, 1971; (ed.) Luria, by Robert Browning, 1973; Romanticism and Behavior: Collected Essays II, 1976; (ed.) Sordello, by Robert Browning, 1977; Explanation and Power: The Control of Human Behavior, 1979; Romanticism and Ideology, 1985; The Birth of Romanticism, 1986. Add: 6478 Bridgewood Rd., Columbia, S.C. 29206, U.S.A.

PEDEN, William (Harwood). American, b. 1913. Novels/Short stories, Literature. Prof. Emeritus of English, Univ. of Missouri, Columbia, since 1979 (Assoc. Prof., 1946–50; Prof. 1950–79; Dir. of the Univ. Press, 1958–62). Member, Editorial Cttee., Studies in Short Fiction, since 1963; Gen. Ed., Twayne Critical History of the Modern Short Story series, 9 vols., since 1979. Instr., 1938–42, Prof. of English, 1942–44, and Visiting Prof., 1971, Univ. of Maryland, College Park. Book Ed., Missourian, Columbia, 1955–63; Ed., Story mag., 1959–62. *Publs:* Some Aspects of Jefferson Bibliography, 1940; (ed. with Adrienne Koch) Life and Selected Writings of Thomas Jefferson, 1944; (ed. with Adrienne Koch) Selected Writings of John and John Quincy Adams, 1946; (ed.) Testimony Against Prophane Customs, 1953; (ed.) Notes on the State of Virginia, 1955; (ed.) 29 Stories, 1960, 1967; (ed.) The American Short Story: Front Lines in the National Defense of Literature, 1964, rev. ed. as The American Short Story: Continuity and Change 1940-1975, 1975; Night in Funland and Other Stories, 1968; (ed.) Collected Stories of Hubert Crackanthorpe, 1969; (ed. with George Garrett) New Writing from South Carolina, 1971; Short Fiction: Shape and Substance, 1971; Twilight at Monticello, 1973. Add: 408 Thilly, Columbia, Mo. 65201, U.S.A.

PEDLER, (Sir) Frederick (Johnson). British, b. 1908. Economics, Geography, History. Hon. Fellow, London Sch. of Oriental and African Studies. With U.K. Colonial Office, 1930–47; Managing Dir., United Africa Co. Ltd., London, 1955–68; Dir., Unilever, 1956–68. *Publs:* Post-War England, 1933, 4th ed. 1937; West Africa, 1951, 1959; Economic Geography of West Africa, 1955; The Lion and the Unicorn in Africa: The United Africa Company 1787-1931, 1974; Main Currents of West Africa History 1940-1978, 1979; A Pedler Family History, 1984; A Wider Pedler Family History, 1989. Add: 36 Russell Rd., Moor Park, Northwood, Middx. HA6 2LR, England.

PEDOE, Daniel. Anglo-American, b. 1910. Mathematics/Statistics. Prof. of Mathematics, Univ. of Minnesota, Minneapolis, 1964–81, now retired. Member of the faculty, Univ. of London, 1947–52, Univ. of Khartoum, 1952–59, Univ. of Singapore, 1959–62, and Purdue Univ., Lafayette, Ind., 1962–64. *Publs:* Methods of Algebraic Geometry, 3 vols., 1947–53; Circles, 1957, 1979; The Gentle Art of Mathematics, 1957–72; Geometric Introduction to Linear Algebra, 1963, 1976; Introduction to Projective Geometry, 1963; A Course of Geometry for Colleges and Universities, 1970; Geometry and the Liberal Arts, 1976, 1978. Add: 1956 E. River Terr., Minneapolis, Minn. 55414, U.S.A.

PEEKNER, Ray. *See* **PUECHNER,** Ray.

PEEL, Bruce Braden. Canadian, b. 1916. History. Chief Librarian, Univ. of Alberta, Edmonton, 1955–82, now retired. *Publs:* (with E. Knowles) The Saskatoon Story, 1952; (compiler) A Bibliography of the Prairie Provinces to 1953 with Biographical Index, 1956, 1973; (ed.) Librarianship in Canada 1946 to 1967, 1967; Steamboats on the Saskatchewan, 1972; Early Printing in the Red River Settlement, 1974; The Rossville Mission Press, 1974. Add: Cameron Library, Univ. of Alberta, Edmonton, Alta. T6G 2J8, Canada.

PEEL, Edwin (Arthur). British, b. 1911. Psychology. Reader in Psychology, 1946–48, and Prof. of Educational Psychology, 1948–50, Univ. of Durham; Prof. of Education, 1950–78, now Emeritus, and Chmn. of the Sch. of Education, 1964–70, Univ. of Birmingham. Pres. British Psychological Soc., 1960–61, and Assn. for Programmed Learning, 1966–68. *Publs:* The Psychological Basis of Education, 1956; The Pupil's Thinking, 1960; The Nature of Adolescent Judgment, 1971. Add: 47 Innage Rd., Northfield, Birmingham B31 2DY, England.

PEEL, H(azel) M(ary). British, b. 1930. Novels/Short stories, Children's fiction. *Publs:* Fury, Son of the Wilds, 1959; Pilot, the Hunter, 1962; Pilot, The Chaser, 1964; Easter, The Show Jumper, 1965; Jago, 1966; Nightstorm, the Flat Racer, 1966; Dido and Rogue, 1967; Gay Darius, 1968; Untamed, 1969; Land and Power, 1974; Law of the Wilds, 1974; Pocket Dictionary of the Horse, 1978. Add: c/o Soc. of Authors, 84 Drayton Gardens, London SW10, England.

PEEL, Malcolm L. American, b. 1936. Theology/Religion. Exec. Dir, Greater Cedar Rapids Community Foundn., Iowa, since 1989. Research Assoc., Inst. for Antiquity and Christianity, Claremont Univ. and Grad. Sch., California; Instr., Practical Theology, Yale Divinity School, 1960–62; Asst. Prof. of Religion and Foreign Languages, Lycoming Coll., Williamsport, Pa., 1965–69; Asst. Prof. of Religion, and Chmn. of Core Course, 1969–71, Assoc. Prof. 1971–78, and Prof. and Chmn., Dept. of Philosophy and Religion, 1978–81, 1983–86, Coe Coll., Cedar Rapids, Iowa; Dir., Herbert Hoover Endowment, Hoover Presidential Library Assn., West Branch, Iowa, 1981–83; Alston Prof. and Chmn. of the Dept. of Bible and Religion, Agnes Scott Coll., Decatur, Ga., 1986–89. Dir., Religion and Public Schs. of Iowa Project, 1977–78. *Publs:* (co-ed.) Yale Gnosticism Seminar, 1964; Epistle to Rheginos: A Valentinian Letter on the Resurrection—Translation from Coptic and Commentary, 1969; Gnosis und Auferstehung, 1974; (with J. Zandee) The Teachings of Silvanus, 1976; A Library of Faith (TV series), 1984; The Arrival of a New Age, 1986; (with others) Mercer Dictionary of the Bible, 1989. Add: Cedar Rapids Community Foundn., SGA Bldg., Cedar Rapids, Iowa 52401, U.S.A.

PEEPLES, Edwin (Augustus). American, b. 1915. Novels/Short stories, Children's fiction, Writing/Journalism, Essays. *Publs:* Fantasy on an Empty Stage (play), 1941; Swing Low (novel), 1945; A Professional Story Writer's Handbook, 1960; Blue Boy, 1964; A Hole in the Hill, 1969; Summary for a Sesqui (history), 1977; An Inquisitive Eye, 1989. Add: Vixen Hill, R.D.2, Phoenixville, Pa. 19460, U.S.A.

PEET, Bill. American, b. 1915. Children's fiction. Former artist and screenwriter for Walt Disney Productions. *Publs:* Hubert's Hair-Raising Adventure, 1959; Huge Harold, 1961; Smokey, 1962; The Pinkish Purplish Bluish Egg, 1963; Ella, 1964; Randy's Dandy Lions, 1964; Kermit the Hermit, 1965; Chester the Worldly Pig, 1965; Capyboppy, 1966; Farewell to Shady Glade, 1966; Jennifer and Josephine, 1967; Buford the Little Big-Horn, 1967; Fly Homer Fly, 1969; The Whingdingdilly, 1970; The Wump World, 1970; How Droofus the Dragon Lost His Head, 1971; The Caboose Who Got Loose, 1971; Countdown to Christmas, 1972; The Ant and the Elephant, 1972; The Spooky Tail of Preewit Peacock, 1973; Merle the High Flying Squirrel, 1974; The Gnats of Knotty Pine, 1975; Big Bad Bruce, 1976; Eli, 1978; Cowardly Clyde, 1979; Encore for Eleanor, 1981; The Luckiest One of All, 1982; No Such Things, 1983; Pamela Camel, 1984; The Kweeks of Kookatumdee, 1985; Jethro and Joel Were a Troll, 1987; Bill Peet: An Autobiography, 1989. Add: c/o Houghton Mifflin Co., 1 Beacon St., Boston, Mass. 02107, U.S.A.

PEHNT, Wolfgang. German, b. 1931. Architecture. Editor for Arts and Architecture, Deutschlandfunk. *Publs:* (ed.) Encyclopedia of Modern Architecture, 1964; New German Architecture 1960-70, 1970; Expressionist Architecture, 1973, 1979; (ed.) Die Stadt in der Bundesrepublik, 1974; Der Anfang der Bescheidenheit, Kritische Aufsatze zur Architektur des 20. Jahrhunderts, 1983; Das Ende der Zuversicht, 1983; Expressionist Architectural Drawings, 1985; Karljosef Schattner: Ein Architekt ans Eichstätt, 1988. Add: Danziger Strasse 2A, 5000 Cologne 40, West Germany.

PEIRCE, Neal R. American, b. 1932. Politics/Government, Social commentary/phenomena. Co-Founder and Contrib. Ed., The National Journal, Washington, D.C., since 1969; Syndicated Columnist, Washington Post Writers Group. Political Ed., Congressional Quarterly, 1960–69; Fellow, Woodrow Wilson Intnl. Center for Scholars, 1971–74. *Publs:* The People's President, 1968, 1981; The Megastates of America, 1972; The Pacific States of America, 1972; The Mountain States of America, 1972; The Great Plains States of America, 1973; The Deep South States of America, 1974; The Border South States, 1975; The New England States, 1976; The Mid-Atlantic States of America, 1977; The Great Lakes States of America, 1980; The Book of America, 1983; Corrective Capitalism, 1987. Add: 610 G St. S.W., Washington, D.C. 20024, U.S.A.

PELIKAN, Jaroslav. American, b. 1923. Theology/Religion. Titus Street Prof. of Ecclesiastical History since 1962, and Sterling Prof. of History since 1972, Yale Univ., New Haven, Conn. (Acting Dean, Grad. Sch., 1973–78, and Dean, 1975–78; Dir., Div. of Humanities, 1974–76). Member Editorial Bd., Collected Works of Erasmus, since 1978. Staff Member, Valparaiso Univ., Indiana, 1946–49, Concordia Theological Seminary, St. Louis, 1949–53, and Univ. of Chicago, 1953–62. Ed., Luther's Works, American Ed., 22 vols., 1955–70; Chmn., Council of Scholars, Library of Congress, 1980–83. *Publs:* From Luther to Kierkegaard, 1950; Fools for Christ, 1955; The Riddle of Roman Catholicism, 1959; (ed.) The Book of Concord, 1959; Luther the Expositor, 1959; The Shape of Death: Life, Death, and Immortality in the Early Fathers, 1961; The Light of the World: A Basic Image in Early Christian Thought, 1962; Obedient Rebels: Catholic Substance and Protestant Principle in Luther's Reformation, 1964; The Finality of Jesus Christ in an Age of Universal History: A Dilemma of the Third Century, 1965; The Christian Intellectual, 1966; (ed.) Makers of Modern Theology, 5 vols., 1966–68; (ed.) Interpreters of Luther, 1968; Spirit Versus Structure: Luther and the Institutions of the Church, 1968; Development of Christian Doctrine: Some Historical Prolegomena, 1969; Twentieth Century Theology in the Making, 3 vols., 1969–70; Historical Theology, 1971; The Christian Tradition, 4 vols., 1971–84; The Preaching of Augustine, 1973; The Growth of Medieval Theology, 1978; Scholarship and Its Survival, 1983; Reformation of Church and Dogma, 1984; The Vindication of Tradition, 1984; Jesus Through the Centuries, 1985; The Mystery of Continuity, 1986; Bach among the Theologians, 1986; The Excellent Empire, 1987; The Melody of Theology, 1988. Add: 156 Chestnut Lane, Hamden, Conn. 06518, U.S.A.

PELLING, Henry Mathison. British, b. 1920. History, Politics/Government, Biography. Fellow, St. John's Coll., Cambridge (Reader in Recent British History, Cambridge Univ., 1977–80). *Publs:* Origins of the Labour Party, 1954, 1965; (ed.) The Challenge of Socialism, 1954; America and the British Left, 1956; (with F. Bealey) Labour and Politics 1900-1906, 1958; American Labor, 1960; Modern Britain 1885-1955, 1960; A Short History of the Labour Party, 1961, 8th ed. 1985; A History of British Trade Unionism, 1963, 4th ed. 1987; Social Geography of British Elections, 1967; Popular Politics and Society in Late Victorian Britain, 1968, 1979; Britain and the Second World War, 1970; Winston Churchill, 1974, 1989; The Labour Governments 1945-51, 1984; Britain and the Marshall Plan, 1989. Add: St. John's Coll., Cambridge CB2 1TP, England.

PEMBERTON, Margaret. British, b. 1943. Novels/Short stories. *Publs:* Rendezvous with Danger, 1974; The Mystery of Saligo Bay, 1976; Tapestry of Fear, 1979; The Guilty Secret, 1979; Vengeance in the Sun, 1979; Harlot, 1980; Lion of Languedoc, 1981; Pioneer Girl, 1982; The Flower Garden, 1982; African Enchantment, 1982; Flight to Verechenko, 1983; Devil's Palace, 1983; Forever, 1983; Silver Shadows, Golden Dreams, 1985; Never Leave Me, 1986; A Multitude of Sins, 1988. Add: 13 Manor Lane, London SE13, England.

PEMBERTON, Nan. *See* PYKARE, Nina.

PEN, Jan. Dutch, b. 1921. Economics, Politics/Government. Prof. of Economics, Groningen Univ., since 1956. Dir., Gen. Economic Policy, Ministry of Economic Affairs, 1952–56. *Publs:* The Wage Rate under Trade Unions, 1959; Modern Economics, 1962; Harmony and Conflict in Modern Society, 1966; A Primer on International Trade, 1967; Income Distribution, 1971; Among Economists, 1985. Add: Dept. of Economics, State Univ., Groningen, The Netherlands.

PENDER, Lydia (Kathleen). Australian, b. 1907. Children's fiction, Poetry. Past Secty., Children's Book Council of Australia, New South Wales Branch. *Publs:* Marbles in My Pocket, 1957; Barnaby and the

Horses, 1961, 1980; Dan McDougall and the Bulldozer, 1963, 1987; Sharpur the Carpet Snake, 1967, 1982; (with M. Gilmore) Poems to Read to Young Australians, 1968; Brown Paper Leaves, 1971; Barnaby and the Rocket, 1972; The Useless Donkeys, 1979; Morning Magpie (poems), 1984; An Australian Alphabet, 1989. Add: 10 Blenheim Rd., Lindfield, N.S.W. 2070, Australia.

PENDLETON, Don(ald Eugene). Also writes as Dan Britain and Stephan Gregory. American, b. 1927. Novels/Short stories, Mystery/Crime/Suspense, Sex. Telegrapher, Southern Pacific Railroad, San Francisco, 1948–55; Air Traffic Control Specialist, Federal Aviation Admin., Western Region, 1957–61; Engineering Supervisor, Martin Co., Denver, 1961–64; Engineering Administrator, General Electric, 1964–66, and Lockheed Corp., Marietta, Ga. 1966–67; Sr. Ed. and Columnist, Orion mag., 1967–70. *Publs:* mystery novels—(as Stephan Gregory) Frame Up, 1960; (as Stephan Gregory) The Insatiables, 1967; (as Stephan Gregory) The Sex Goddess, 1967; (as Stephan Gregory) Madame Murder, 1967; (as Stephan Gregory) The Sexy Saints, 1967; (as Stephan Gregory) The Hot One, 1967; War Against the Mafia, 1969; Death Squad, 1969; Battle Mask, 1970; Miami Massacre, 1970; Continental Contract, 1971; Assault on Soho, 1971; Nightmare in New York, 1971; Chicago Wipe-Out, 1971; Vegas Vendetta, 1971; Caribbean Kill, 1972; California Hit, 1972; Boston Blitz, 1972; Washington IOU, 1972; San Diego Siege, 1972; Panic in Philly, 1973; Jersey Guns, 1974; Texas Storm, 1974; Detroit Deathwatch, 1974; New Orleans Knockout, 1974; Firebase Seattle, 1975; Hawaiian Hellground, 1975; Canadian Crisis, 1975; St. Louis Showdown, 1975; Colorado Kill-Zone, 1976; Acapulco Rampage, 1976; Dixie Convoy, 1976; Savage Fire, 1977; Command Strike, 1977; Cleveland Pipeline, 1977; Arizona Ambush, 1977; Tennessee Smash, 1978; Monday's Mob, 1978; Terrible Tuesday, 1979; Wednesday's Wrath, 1979; Thermal Thursday, 1979; Friday's Feast, 1979; Satan's Sabbath, 1980; Sicilian Slaughter, 1981; Bloodsport, 1982; Double Crossfire, 1982; The Iranian Hit, 1982; The Libyan Connection, 1982; The New War, 1982; Paramilitary Plot, 1982; Renegade Agent, 1982; Return to Vienna, 1982; Terrorist Summit, 1982; The Violent Streets, 1982; Ashes to Ashes, 1986; Copp for Hire, 1987; Fire in the Sky, 1988; Anvil of Hell, 1988; Moving Target, 1989; Blowoot, 1989; Copp in Deep, 1989; other—(as Stephan Gregory) All the Trimmings (novel), 1966; (as Stephan Gregory) The Huntress (novel), 1966; (as Stephan Gregory) Color Her Adultress (novel), 1967; The Search (verse), 1967; The Place (verse), 1967; (as Stephan Gregory) All Lovers Accepted (novel), 1968; Revolt (novel), 1968 (rev. ed. as Civil War II, 1971); All Heart (short stories), 1968; The Day God Appeared (short stories), 1968; (as Stephan Gregory) How to Achieve Sexual Ecstasy, 1968; (as Stephan Gregory) The Sexually Insatiable Female, 1968; (as Stephan Gregory) Hypnosis and the Sexual Life, 1968; (as Stephan Gregory) Religion and the Sexual Life, 1968; (as Stephan Gregory) Society and the Sexual Life, 1968; (as Stephan Gregory) Sex and the Supernatural, 1968; (as Stephan Gregory) ESP and the Sex Mystique, 1968; (as Stephan Gregory) Dialogues on Human Sexuality, 1968; (as Stephan Gregory) Secret Sex Desires, 1968; (as Stephan Gregory) The Sexuality Gap, 1968; The Olympians (novel), 1969; Cataclysm (novel), 1969; (as Stephan Gregory) Hypnosis and the Free Female, 1969; The Truth about Sex, 1969; The Guns of Terra 10 (novel), 1970; 1989: Population Doomsday (novel), 1970; (as Dan Britain) The Godmakers (novel), 1970; The Executioner's War Book, 1977. Add: c/o Scott Meredith Literary Agency, 845 Third Ave., New York, N.Y. 10022, U.S.A.

PENICK, James Lal, Jr. American, b. 1932. History. Prof. of History, Loyola Univ., Chicago, since 1972 (Asst. Prof., 1965–68; Assoc. Prof., 1968–72). Asst. Research Historian, Univ. of California, Berkeley, 1961–63; Intermediate Instr., California State Polytechnic, 1963–65. *Publs:* Progressive Politics and Conservation: The Ballinger-Pinchot Affair, 1968; Politics of American Science 1939 to the Present, 1965, 1972; The New Madrid Earthquakes, 1976, 1981; The Great Western Land Pirate: John A. Murrell in Legend and History, 1981. Add: 923 Wesley Ave., Evanston, Ill. 60202, U.S.A.

PENN, John. *See* **TROTMAN,** Jack.

PENNINGTON, Donald Henshaw. British, b. 1919. History. Emeritus Fellow, Balliol Coll., Oxford, since 1982 (Fellow and Tutor, 1965–82). Lectr., 1946–56, Sr. Lectr., 1956–60, and Reader, 1960–65, Univ. of Manchester. *Publs:* (with D. Brunton) Members of the Long Parliament, 1954; (with I.A. Roots) The Committee at Stafford, 1957; Seventeenth-Century Europe, 1970; (ed. with Keith Thomas) Puritans and Revolutionaries, 1978. Add: Rose Cottage, Linton Hill, near Ross- on-Wye, England.

PEPPE Rodney (Darrell). British, b. 1934. Children's fiction. Freelance graphic designer and illustrator, since 1965. Art Dir., S. H. Benson and J. Walter Thompson, London, 1960–65; Consultant Designer, Ross Foods Ltd., London 1965–72, and Syon Park, Brentford, Middx., 1972–73. *Publs:* The Alphabet Book, 1968; Circus Numbers, 1969; The House That Jack Built, 1970; Hey Riddle Diddle!, 1971; Simple Simon, 1972; Cat and Mouse, 1973; Odd One Out, 1974; Humpty Dumpty, 1974; Henry series, 7 vols., 1975–78; Picture Stories, 1976; Puzzle Book, 1977; Humphrey the Number Horse, 1978; Ten Little Bad Boys, 1978; Three Little Pigs, 1979; Moving Toys, 1980; Indoors, 1980; Outdoors, 1980; The Mice Who Lived in a Shoe, 1981; Run Rabbit, Run!, 1982; The Kettleship Pirates, 1983; Little Toy Board Books series, 5 vols., 1983; Make Your Own Paper Toys, 1984; Hello Henry, 1984; Hurrah for Henry, 1984; Block Books series, 4 vols., 1985; The Mice and the Flying Basket, 1985; Press Out Circus, 1986; Press Out Train, 1986; Tell the Time with Mortimer, 1986; The Mice and the Clockwork Bus, 1986; Open House, 1987; Thumbprint Circus, 1988; First Nursery Rhymes, 1988. Add: Barnwood House, Whiteway, Stroud, Glos. GL6 7ER, England.

PERCIVAL, Alicia C(onstance). British, b. 1903. History, Biography. Former Vice-Principal and Principal Lectr. in Education, Trent Park Coll. of Education, London, until retirement in 1967. *Publs:* The English Miss Today and Yesterday, 1938; (with M. Mare) Victorian Best Seller, 1947; Youth Will Be Led, 1951; The Origins of the Headmaster's Conference, 1969; Very Superior Men, 1973; Tho. James Pyne-Dixon Family Book, 1977; About Vincent Square, 1979. Add: Univ. Women's Club, 2 Audley Sq., South Audley St., London W1, England.

PERCIVAL, Robert C. British, b. 1908. Medicine/Health. Consulting Surgeon, Dept. of Obstetrics and Gynaecology, The London Hosp., since 1973 (Surgeon, 1947–73; Dir., Obstetrics and Gynaecology Unit, 1968–73). Surgeon Lt.-Comdr., R.N.V.R., Royal Navy, Surgical Specialist, 1941–46; Gynaecological Surgeon, King George Hosp., Ilford, Essex, 1946–68. Pres., Section of Obstetrics and Gynaecology, Royal Soc. of Medicine, London, 1973–74. *Publs:* (co-author) British Obstetric Practice, 3rd ed. 1963; (ed.) Holland and Brews Obstetrics, 14th ed. 1980. Add: Coker Wood Cottage, Pendomer, nr. Yeovil, Somerset BA22 9PD, England.

PERCY, Douglas C. Canadian, b. 1914. Novels/Short stories, Theology/Religion, Biography. Former Dir. of Public Relations, Ontario Bible Coll. *Publs:* Doctor to Africa, 1950; Hidden Valley, 1950; Gabartarwar Litafi Mai Tsarki, 2 vols., 1950; When the Bamboo Sings, 1957; Beyond the Tangled Mountain, 1960; Flight to Glory, 1965; (co-author) Encounter in Post Christian Era, 1970; (co-author) Rethinking Church Music, 1973; (co-author) Old Testament in Contemporary Preaching, 1974; (co-author) Emotional Problems and the Gospel, 1978; (co-author) The Old Testament in the New, 1980. Add: 73 Binswood Ave., Toronto, Ontario M4C 3N8, Canada.

PERCY, Walker. American, b. 1916. Novels/Short stories. *Publs:* The Moviegoer, 1961; The Last Gentleman, 1966; Love in the Ruins: The Adventures of a Bad Catholic at a Time Near the End of the World, 1971; The Message in the Bottle, 1975; Lancelot, 1977; The Second Coming, 1980; Lost in the Cosmos, 1984; The Thanatos Syndrome, 1987. Add: P.O. Box 510, Covington, La. 70433, U.S.A.

PERELMAN, Lewis J. American, b. 1946. Environmental science/Ecology. Policy Analyst, Policy Planning Section, Colorado Dept. of Highways. Pres., Colorado Assn. for the Future, since 1976. Project Dir., Growth and Education, Western Interstate Commn. for Higher Education, 1974. *Publs:* The Global Mind: Beyond the Limits to Growth, 1976; (co-ed.) Energy Transitions, 1981; The Learning Enterprise: Adult Learning, Human Capital and Economic Development, 1984. Add: Policy Planning Section, Colorado Dept. of Highways, 4201 E. Arkansas, Denver, Colo. 80222, U.S.A.

PERKINS, Dwight Heald. American, b. 1934. Economics, History, International relations/Current affairs. Prof. of Economics, since 1969, and Dir., Harvard Inst. for Intnl. Development, since 1980, Harvard Univ., Cambridge, Mass. (Instr. to Assoc. Prof., 1963–69; Assoc. Dir., East Asian Research Center, 1973–77; Chmn., Dept. of Economics, 1977–80). Research Assoc., Inst. of Economic Research, Hitotsubashi Univ., Tokyo, 1968–69. *Publs:* (with M.H. Halperin) Communist China and Arms Control, 1965; Market Control and Planning in Communist China, 1966; Agricultural Development in China 1368-1968, 1969; China's Modern Economy in Historical Perspective, 1975; (with others) Rural Small-Scale Industry in the People's Republic of China, 1977; (with S.H. Ban and P.Y. Moon) Rural Development in Korea, 1980; (with E.S. Mason and others) Economic and Social Modernization in Korea, 1980; (with S. Yusuf) Rural Development in China, 1984; China: Asia's Next Economic Giant?, 1986. Add: Harvard Inst. for Intnl. Development, 1 Eliot St., Harvard Univ., Cambridge, Mass. 02138, U.S.A.

PERKINS, George (Burton). American, b. 1930. Literature. Prof. of English since 1967, and Gen. Ed. of The Journal of Narrative Technique since 1971, Eastern Michigan Univ., Ypsilanti (Assoc. Prof., 1967–70; Dir. of Grad. Studies in English, 1969–73). Teaching Asst., Cornell Univ., Ithaca, N.Y., 1955–57; Instr., Washington Univ., St. Louis, 1957–60; Asst. Prof., Baldwin-Wallace Coll., Berea, Ohio, 1960–63, and Fairleigh Dickinson Univ., Rutherford, N.J., 1963–66; Lectr. in American Literature, Univ. of Edinburgh, 1966–67; Fellow, Inst. for Adv. Studies in the Humanities, Univ. of Edinburgh, 1981. *Publs:* Writing Clear Prose, 1964; (ed.) Varieties of Prose, 1966; (ed.) The Theory of the American Novel, 1970; (ed.) Realistic American Short Fiction, 1972; (ed.) American Poetic Theory, 1972; (ed. with Bradley, Beatty, and Long) The American Tradition in Literature, 4th ed., 1974, 7th ed. 1990; (ed. with Frye and Baker) The Practical Imagination, 1980, compact ed. 1987; (with Frye and Baker) The Practical Imagination: An Introduction to Poetry, 1983; (with Frye and Baker) The Harper Handbook to Literature, 1985; (with B. Perkins) Contemporary American Literature, 1988. Add: 1316 King George Blvd., Ann Arbor, Mich. 48108, U.S.A.

PERKINS, James (Alfred). American, b. 1911. Education. Chmn. and Chief Exec. Officer, Intnl. Council for Educational Development, NYC, since 1970. Dir., Center for Inter-American Relations; Trustee, Carnegie Foundn. for the Advancement of Teaching; Dir., Overseas Development Council, and Council on Foreign Relations; Member, Carnegie Council on Policy Studies in Higher Education; Chmn., Presidential Advisory Panel on the National Academy of Foreign Affairs; Member, Gen. Advisory Cttee., U.S. Arms Control and Disarmament Agency. Instr. in Political Science, 1937–39, and Asst. Prof. and Asst. Dir., Sch. of Public and Intnl. Affairs, 1939–41, Princeton Univ., New Jersey; Dir., Pulp and Paper Div., Office of Price Admin., Washington, D.C., 1941–43; Asst. to the Administrator, Foreign Economic Admin., Washington, 1943–45; Vice-Pres., Swarthmore Coll., Pennsylvania, 1945–50; Exec. Assoc., 1950–51, and Vice-Pres., 1955–63, Carnegie Foundn. for the Advancement of Teaching; Pres., Cornell Univ., Ithaca, N.Y., 1963–69; Chmn. and Exec. Dir., Center for Educational Enquiry, NYC, 1969–70. Trustee, Inst. for Defense Analysis, 1958–61; Dir., Rand Corp., 1960–70; Dir., American Council on Education, 1963–65; Trustee, 1964–68, and Chmn., 1967–68, Educational Testing Service; Chmn., United Negro Coll. Fund, 1965–69; Chmn., New York State Regents Advisory Cttee. on Educational Leadership, 1965–69; Chmn., Presidential Gen. Advisory Cttee. on Foreign Assistance Programs, 1965–69. *Publs:* The University in Transition, 1966; Higher Education: From Autonomy to Systems, 1972; The University as an Organization, 1973. Add: 94 North Rd., Princeton, N.J. 08540, U.S.A.

PERKINS, Michael. American, b. 1942. Novels/Short stories, Poetry, Literature. Case Worker, Dept. of Welfare, NYC, 1963–66; Ed., Croton Press Ltd., 1967–72; Chmn., Artists' Cooperative, Woodstock, N.Y., 1973–74; Ed., Ulster Arts mag., 1978–80; Dir., with Ed. Sanders, Woodstock Poetry Festival, 1978–82. *Publs:* The Blue Woman (poetry), 1966; Shorter Poems, 1968; Evil Companions, 1968; Renie Perkins, 1969; The Secret Record (literary criticism), 1976; The Persistence of Desire (poetry), 1977; Praise in the Ears of Clouds, 1982. Add: Ohayo Mt. Road, Glenford, N.Y. 12433, U.S.A.

PERL, Ruth June. American, b. 1929. Autobiography/Memoirs/Personal. Secty. and Treas., Hebrew Christian Witness, San Bernardino, Calif., since 1956. *Publs:* Thy People Shall Be My People, 1968, condensation as Let My People Know, 1969. Add: 4477 N. Genevieve Lane, San Bernardino, Calif. 92407, U.S.A.

PERLOFF, Marjorie (Gabrielle). American (born Austrian), b. 1931. Literature. Prof. of English and Comperative Literature, Stanford Univ., Calif., since 1986. Member, Academy of Literary Studies. Instr. to Assoc. Prof., Catholic Univ. of America, Washington, D.C., 1965–71; Assoc. Prof. to Prof., Univ. of Maryland, College Park, 1971–76; Florence R. Scott Prof., Univ. of Southern California, Los Angeles, 1976–86. Member of Exec. Council, Modern Language Assn., 1977–81. *Publs:* Rhyme and Meaning in the Poetry of Yeats, 1970; The Poetic Art of Robert Lowell, 1973; Frank O'Hara: Poet among Painters, 1977; The Poetics of Indeterminary: Rimbaud to Cage, 1981; The Dance of Intellect: Studies in the Poetry of the Pound Tradition, 1985; The Futurist Moment: Avant-Garde, Avant-Guerre, and the Language of Rupture, 1986; (assoc. ed.) Columbia Literary History of the U.S., 1988; (ed.) Postmodern Genres,

1988. Add: 1467 Amalfi Dr., Pacific Palisades, Calif. 90272, U.S.A.

PERRETT, Bryan. British, b. 1934. History, Military/Defence. Served in the Royal Armoured Corps, Regular and Territorial Army, 1952–70. *Publs:* Fighting Vehicles of the Red Army, 1969; NATO Armour, 1971, 1974; The Valentine in North Africa 1942–43, 1972; The Matilda, 1973; The Churchill, 1974; Through Mud and Blood, 1975; Tank Tracks to Rangoon, 1978; The Lee/Grant Tank in British Service, 1978; Allied Tank Destroyers, 1979; Wavell's Offensive, 1979; Sturmartillerie and Panzerjager, 1979; The Churchill Tank, 1980; The Stuart Light Tank Series, 1980; The Panzerkampfwagen III IV and V, 3 vols., 1980–81; British Tanks in North Africa 1940–42, 1981; (with A. Lord) Czar's British Squadron, 1981; The Tiger Tanks 1981; History of Biltzkrieg, 1982; German Armoured Cars, 1982; German Light Panzers, 1982; Weapons of the Falklands Conflict, 1982; Mechanized Infantry, 1984; The Hawks, 1984; (ed. and contrib.) Elite Fighting Units, 1984; Lightning War, 1985; Allied Tanks Italy, 1985; Allied Tanks North Africa, 1986; Knights of the Black Cross, 1986; A Hawk at War, 1986; Soviet Armour since 1945, 1987; Desert Warfare, 1988. Add: 7 Maple Ave., Burscough, nr. Ormskirk, Lancs., England.

PERRINE, Laurence. American, b. 1915. Literature. Emeritus Prof. of English, Southern Methodist Univ., Dallas, since 1981 (Instr., 1946–48; Asst. Prof., 1948–55; Assoc. Prof., 1955–60; Prof., 1960–81). *Publs:* Sound and Sense: An Introduction to Poetry, 1956, 7th ed. 1987; Story and Structure, 1959, 7th ed. 1988; (ed.) Poetry: Theory and Practice, 1962; (with J.M. Reid and J. Ciardi) Poetry: A Closer Look, 1963; (with J.M. Reid) 100 American Poems of the Twentieth Century, 1966; Literature: Structure, Sound and Sense, 1970, 5th ed. 1988; Dimensions of Drama, 1973; The Art of Total Relevance: Papers on Poetry, 1976. Add: 7616 Royal Pl., Dallas, Tex. 75230, U.S.A.

PERRY, George. British, b. 1935. Film, History, Transportation. Films Ed., The Sunday Times mag., London (staff member since 1963). Film Critic, Illustrated London News, 1982–88. *Publs:* The Films of Alfred Hitchcock, 1965; (with Terence Kelly and Graham Norton) A Competitive Cinema, 1966; (with Alan Aldridge) The Penguin Book of Comics, 1967, 1971; (ed.) The Book of the Great Western, 1970; (ed.) King Steam, 1971; (ed.) Wheels of London, 1972; (ed. with Nicholas Mason) Rule Britannia—The Victorian World (in U.S. as The Victorians—A World Built to Last), 1974; The Great British Picture Show, 1974, 1985; The Movie-Makers: Hitchcock, 1975; Movies from the Mansion, 1976, 1982; (ed.) The Great British (photographs by Arnold Newman), 1979; Forever Ealing, 1981, 1985; Diana: A Celebration, 1982; Life of Python, 1983; (ed.) Give My Regards to Broad Street, 1984; (with Derek Jewell) Frank Sinatra, 1985; Rupert, 1985; Bluebell, 1985; The Complete Phantom of the Opera, 1987; (ed.) The Golden Screen (reviews of Dilys Powell), 1989. Add: 7 Roehampton Lane, London SW15 5LS, England.

PERRY, Gordon Arthur. British, b. 1914. Agriculture/Forestry, Biology, Environmental science/Ecology, Natural history. Editorial and Educational Consultant since 1972. Gen. Ed., Blandford Press Ltd., London, since 1967. Deputy Headmaster, 1945–47; Area Organizer, Rural Studies, East Sussex Education Cttee., 1947–51; Lectr., Sr. Lectr. and Principal Lectr. of Rural Studies, Easthampstead Park Coll. of Education, 1951–69; Principal Lectr. and Head of Dept. of Rural Studies, Berkshire Coll. of Education, 1969–72. *Publs:* Soils, 1965; (with J.M. Hirons) Common Wild Flowers and Fruits, 1965; Plant Life, 1965; The Farmer's Crops, 1966; (with M.J. Hirons) Progressive Biology, 3 vols., 1967–70; (ed.) Studies in Social Biology and Hygiene, 1968; Farms and Farm Life, 1968; (ed. with E. Jones and A. Hammersley) Teacher's Handbook for Environmental Studies, 1968; (ed.) Teacher's Guidebook: Environmental Studies, 4 vols., 1968–70; (ed.) Studies in Human Biology, 1969; Villages and Village Life, 1970; Minerals, Mines, and Mining, 1970; Fire and the Fire Service, 1972; Police and the Police Service, 1974; Shops, Stores, and Markets, 1975; Councils and Local Government, 1975; (with R. Holme) Quality of Life, 1977. Add: 14 St. Andrew's Close, Holt, Norfolk NR25 6EL, England.

PERRY, Margaret. American, b. 1933. Literature. Dir. of Libraries, Valparaiso Univ., Indiana, since 1982. Reference and Young Adult Librarian, New York Public Library, 1954–55, 1957–58; Army Librarian, U.S. Army, France and Germany, 1959–67; Circulation Librarian, U.S. Military Academy, West Point, N.Y., 1967–70; Education Librarian, 1970–75, Asst. Prof., then Assoc. Prof., 1972–82, Asst. Dir. of Libraries for Reader Services, 1975–82, and Acting Dir. of Libraries, 1976–77, and 1980, University of Rochester, New York. Asst. Treas., 1977–78, and 2nd Vice-Pres., 1978–80, Urban League of Rochester. *Publs:* A Bio-Bibliography of Countee P. Cullen 1903-46, 1971; Silence to the Drums: A

Survey of the Literature of the Harlem Renaissance, 1976; The Harlem Renaissance: An Annotated Bibliography and Commentary, 1982; The Short Fiction of Rudolph Fisher, 1987. Add: 1200 Wood St., Valparaiso, Ind. 46383, U.S.A.

PERRY, Michael Charles. British, b. 1933. Theology/Religion. Archdeacon of Durham, Church of England, since 1970. Ed., The Christian Parapsychologist, since 1977. Chief Asst. for Home Publishing, Soc. for Promoting Christian Knowledge, 1963–70; Secty. to the Archbishops' Commn. on Christian Doctrine, 1967–71; Ed., The Church Quarterly, 1968–71. *Publs:* The Easter Enigma, 1959; The Pattern of Matins and Evensong, 1961; Meet the Prayer Book, 1963; (with D.W. Cleverley Ford, D.N. Sargent and R. Cant) The Churchman's Companion, 1964; (ed.) Crisis for Confirmation (in U.S. as Confirmation Crisis), 1967; (with D. Morgan) Declaring the Faith: The Printed Word, 1969; Sharing in One Bread, 1973; The Resurrection of Man, 1975; Handbook of Parish Worship, 1977; The Paradox of Worship, 1977; (with P. Carter) Handbook of Parish Finance, 1981; Psychic Studies, 1984; (ed.) Deliverance, 1987. Add: 7 The College, Durham DH1 3EQ, England.

PERRY, Peter John. British, b. 1937. Agriculture/Forestry, Geography, History. Reader in Geography, Univ. of Canterbury, Christchurch, since 1966. Review Ed., New Zealand Geographer, since 1974. *Publs:* (ed.) British Agriculture 1875-1914, 1973; British Farming in the Great Depression 1875-1914, 1974; The Geography of 19th Century Britain, 1975. Add: Dept. of Geography, Univ. of Canterbury, Christchurch, New Zealand.

PERRY, Thomas. American. Mystery/Crime/Suspense. University administrator. Formerly: weapons mechanic; fisherman; laborer; maintenance man; and teacher. *Publs:* The Butcher's Boy, 1982; Metzger's Dog, 1983; Big Fish, 1985; Islands, 1988. Add: c/o Putnam, 200 Madison Ave., New York, N.Y. 10016, U.S.A.

PERSICO, Joseph E. American, b. 1930. History. Member of the staff of N.Y. Gov. Averell Harriman, 1956–59; Foreign Service Officer, U.S. Information Agency, Brazil and Argentina, 1959–63; Speechwriter, New York State Dept. of Health, 1964–66; Chief Speechwriter for Nelson A. Rockefeller, 1967–77. *Publs:* My Enemy, My Brother: Men and Days of Gettysburg, 1977; Piercing the Reich, 1979; The Spiderweb, 1979; The Imperial Rockefeller: A Biography of Nelson A. Rockefeller, 1982; Murrow: An American Original, 1988. Add: P.O. Box 108, Albury, N.Y. 12260, U.S.A.

PERTWEE, Michael (Henry Roland). British, b. 1916. Plays/Screenplays, Autobiography/Memoirs/Personal. *Publs:* plays— (with Roland Pertwee) The Paragon, 1949; (with Roland Pertwee) Meet the Grove Family, 1955; She's Done It Again, 1970; Don't Just Lie There, Say Something, 1973; (with Brian Rix) A Bit Between the Teeth, 1976; Sextet, 1979; (with John Chapman) Look, No Hans!, 1986; (with John Chapman) Holiday Sway, 1987; (adaptor) King's Rhapsody, 1988; (with Brian Rix) You'll Do for Me, 1989; also many one-act plays; autobiography—Name Dropping, 1974. Add: 34 Aylestone Ave., London NW6, England.

PERUTZ, Kathrin. American, b. 1939. Novels/Short stories, Human relations. Exec. Dir., Contact Prog. Inc. *Publs:* The Garden, 1962; A House on the Sound, 1964; The Ghost, 1966; Mother Is a Country: A Popular Fantasy, 1968; Beyond the Looking Glass: America's Beauty Culture (in U.K. as Beyond the Looking Glass: Life in the Beauty Culture), 1970; Marriage Is Hell: The Marriage Fallacy, 1972; Reigning Passions, 1978. Add: 16 Avalon Rd., Great Neck, N.Y. 10021, U.S.A.

PERUTZ, Max (Ferdinand). British (born Austrian), b. 1914. Biology, Chemistry. Member of the Scientific Staff, Medical Research Council Lab. of Molecular Biology, Cambridge, since 1979 (Chmn., 1962–79). Dir., Unit for Molecular Biology, Medical Research Council, Cambridge, 1947–62; Reader, Davy-Faraday Laboratory, Cambridge, 1954–68; Chmn., European Molecular Biology Organization, 1963–69; Fullerian Prof. of Psychology, Royal Institution, London, 1973–79. Recipient, Nobel Prize for Chemistry, with Sir John Kendrew, 1962. *Publs:* Proteins and Nucleic Acids: Structure and Function, 1962; (with G. Fermi) Atlas of Molecular Structures in Biology 2: Haemoglobin and Myoglobin, 1981; Ging's ohne Forschung besser?, 1982; Is Science Necessary?, 1989. Add: Lab. of Molecular Biology, Hills Rd., Cambridge CB2 2QH, England.

PESEK, Boris Peter. American, b. 1926. Economics, Money/Finance. Prof. of Economics, Univ. of Wisconsin, Milwaukee, since 1967. Asst.

Prof., 1957–60, Assoc. Prof., 1960–62, and Prof., 1962–67, Michigan State Univ., East Lansing. *Publs:* (co-author) A Study of Contemporary Czechoslovakia, 1955; Gross National Product of Czechoslovakia, 1965; (co-author) Money, Wealth, and Economic Theory, 1967; (co-author) The Foundations of Money and Banking, 1968; Microeconomics of Money and Banking and Other Essays, 1988. Add: Dept. of Economics, Univ. of Wisconsin, Milwaukee, Wisc. 53201, U.S.A.

PESKETT, William. British, b. 1952. Poetry. Has worked as a journalist and biology teacher. *Publs:* Cleaning Stables, 1974; The Nightowl's Dissection, 1975; A Killing in the Grove, 1977; A More Suitable Terrain, 1978; Survivors, 1980. Add: c/o Secker and Warburg, 81 Fulham Rd., London SW3 6RB, England.

PESSEN, Edward. American, b. 1920. History, Sociology. Distinguished Prof. of History, City Univ. of New York, since 1972 (Lectr. in History, 1948–54; Prof., 1956–72). Assoc. Prof. of History, Fisk Univ., Nashville, Tenn., 1954–56. *Publs:* Most Uncommon Jacksonians, 1967; (ed. and co-author) New Perspectives on Jacksonian Parties and Politics, 1969; Jacksonian America: Society, Personality, and Politics, 1969, 1978; Riches, Class, and Power Before the Civil War, 1973; (ed. and co-author) Three Centuries of Social Mobility in America, 1974; (ed.) Jacksonian Panorama, 1975; (ed. and co-author) The Many-Faceted Jacksonian Era: New Interpretations, 1977; The Log Cabin Myth: The Social Backgrounds of the Presidents, 1984. Add: 853 E. 18th St., Brooklyn, N.Y. 11230, U.S.A.

PETAJA, Emil (Theodore). American, b. 1915. Science fiction/Fantasy, Poetry, Art. Full-time writer since 1963; Owner, SISU Publrs., San Francisco, since 1972. Chmn., Bokanalia Memorial Foundn. Formerly office worker, film technician, and photographer. *Publs:* Alpha Yes, Terra No!, 1965; The Caves of Mars, 1965; Saga of Lost Earths, 1965; The Star Mill, 1965; Tramontane, 1966; The Stolen Sun, 1967; Lord of the Green Planet, 1967; The Prism, 1968; Doom of the Green Planet, 1968; The Time Twister, 1968; And Flights of Angels (non-fiction), 1968; The Path Beyond the Stars, 1969; The Nets of Space, 1969; Seed of the Dreamers, 1970; Stardrift and Other Fantastic Flotsam (short stories), 1971; As Dream and Shadow (poetry), 1972; (ed.) The Hannes Bok Memorial Showcase of Fantasy Art, 1974; (ed.) Photoplay Edition, 1975; Lost Earths (omnibus of 4 novels), 1979. Add: P.O. Box 14126, San Francisco, Calif., 94114, U.S.A.

PETER, Laurence (Johnston). Canadian, b. 1919. Education, Social commentary/phenomena. Columnist, Human Behavior mag., since 1976. Member, Advisory Council, Big Brothers of Greater Los Angeles. Teacher in Surrey and Chilliwack, B.C., 1941–47; Instr., British Columbia Prison Dept., 1947–48; Teacher in Vancouver, 1948–50; Counselor, Vancouver Secondary Schs., 1950–55; Sch. Psychologist, Vancouver, 1956–64; Instr., 1963–64, and Asst. Prof. of Education, 1964–66, Univ. of British Columbia; Consultant, Canadian Mental Health Assn., 1963–66; Consultant, British Columbia Assn. for Retarded Children, 1965–66; Assoc. Prof. of Education, 1966–69, Dir. of Frieden Center for Prescriptive Teaching, 1967–70, and Prof. of Education, 1969–70, Univ. of Southern California, Los Angeles; Prof. in Residence, John Tracy Clinic, 1970–73; Adjunct Prof. of Education, Univ. of California, Stanislaus, 1975–76. Founding Member, Big Brothers Assn. of British Columbia; Vice-Pres., British Columbia Div., Canadian Mental Health Assn., 1959–62. *Publs:* Prescriptive Teaching, 1965; (with R. Hull) The Peter Principle; or, Why Things Always Go Wrong, 1969; The Peter Prescription: How to Make Things Go Right, 1972; Therapeutic Instruction, 1975; Classroom Instruction, 1975; Individual Instruction, 1975; Teacher Education, 1975; The Peter Plan: A Proposal for Survival, 1976; Peter's Quotations, 1977; Peter's People and Their Marvelous Ideas, 1979; Peter's Almanac, 1982; (with Bill Dana) The Laughter Prescription, 1982; Why Things Go Wrong: or the Peter Principle Revisited, 1984; Process of Teaching, 1985; The Peter Pyramid: Will We Ever Get the Point, 1986. Add: 2332 Via Ancapa, Palos Verdes Estates, Calif. 90274, U.S.A.

PETERKIEWICZ, Jerzy. British (b. Polish), b. 1916. Novels/Short stories, Plays/Screenplays, Poetry, Literature. Prof. of Polish Language and Literature, Sch. of Slavonic and East European Studies, Univ. of London, since 1964 (Lectr., 1950–64). *Publs:* Prowincja, 1936; Wiersze i poematy, 1938; Sami swoi, 1949; The Knotted Cord, 1953; Loot and Loyalty, 1955; (ed.) Polish Prose and Verse, 1956; Future to Let, 1958; (ed. and trans.) Antologia liryki angielskiej, 1958; Isolation: A Novel in 5 Acts, 1959; (ed and trans. with Burns Singer) Five Centuries of Polish Poetry 1450-1950, 1960, rev. ed. with Jon Stallworthy as Five Centuries of Polish Poetry 1450-1970, 1970; The Quick and the Dead, 1961; That Angel Burning at My Left Side, 1963; Poematy londynskie i wiersze przedwojenne, 1965; Inner Circle, 1966; Green Flows the Bile, 1969; The Other Side of Silence: The Poet at the Limits of Language, 1970; The Third Adam, 1975; (trans.) Easter Vigil, by Karol Wojtyla, 1979; Kula magiczna (Poems 1934-1952), 1980; (trans.) Collected Poems, by Karol Wojtyla, 1982; Poezje wybrane (Selected Poems), 1986; Literatura polska w perspektywie europejskiej (Polish Literature in Its European Context; essays translated from English), 1986. Add: 7 Lyndhurst Terr., London NW3, England.

PETERS, Elizabeth. *See* **MICHAELS,** Barbara.

PETERS, Ellis. *See* **PARGETER,** Edith.

PETERS, Geoffrey. *See* **PALMER,** Madelyn.

PETERS, Lenrie (Leopold). Gambian, b. 1932. Novels, Poetry. Surgeon in private practice, Banjul, since 1972. Chmn., National Library Bd., Gambia; Chmn., Bd. of Govs., Gambia Coll.; Chmn., West African Examinations Council. Surgical Registrar, Northampton Gen. Hosp., England, 1966–69; Surgeon, Victoria Hosp., Gambia, 1969–72. *Publs:* Poems, 1964; The Second Round (novel), 1965; Satellites, 1967; Katchikali, 1971; Selected Poetry, 1981. Add: Westfield Clinic, P.O. Box 142, Banjul, Gambia.

PETERS, Margot (McCullough). American, b. 1933. Literature, Theatre, Women, Biography. Prof. of English, Univ. of Wisconsin-Whitewater, since 1969. Asst. Prof. of English, Northland Coll., Ashland, Wisc., 1963–66. Kathe Tappe Vernon Prof. of Biography, Dartmouth Coll., Hanover, N.H., 1978. *Publs:* Charlotte Brontë: Style in the Novel, 1973; Unquiet Soul: A Biography of Charlotte Brontë, 1975; Bernard Shaw and the Actresses, 1980; Mrs. Pat: The Life of Mrs. Patrick Campbell, 1984; The House of Barrymore, 1990. Add: 511 College St., Lake Mills, Wisc. 53551, U.S.A.

PETERS, Maureen. Also writes as Veronica Black, Catherine Darby, Levanah Lloyd, Judith Rothman, and Sharon Whitby. British, b. 1935. Mystery/Crime/Suspense, Historical/Romance/Gothic, Biography. *Publs:* Elizabeth the Beloved, 1965; Katheryn, The Wanton Queen, 1967; Mary, The Infamous Queen, 1968; Bride for King James, 1968; Joan of the Lilies, 1969; The Rose of Hever, 1969, in U.S. as Anne, The Rose of Hever, 1971; Flower of the Greys, 1969; (as Veronica Black) Dangerous Inheritance, 1969; (as Veronica Black) Portrait of Sarah, 1969; Princess of Desire, 1970; Struggle for a Crown, 1970; (as Veronica Black) The Wayward Madonna, 1970; (as Veronica Black) A Footfall in the Mist, 1971; (as Veronica Black) Master of Malcarew, 1971; Shadow of a Tudor, 1971; Seven for St. Crispin's Day, 1971; The Cloistered Flame, 1971; Jewel of the Greys, 1972; The Woodville Wench, 1972; Henry VIII and His Six Wives (novelization of screenplay), 1972; The Peacock Queen, 1972; The Virgin Queen, 1972; The Queen Who Never Was, 1972; Royal Escape, 1972; (as Veronica Black) Enchanted Grotto, 1972; (as Veronica Black) Moonflete, 1972; (as Veronica Black) Fair Kilmeny, 1972; Jean Ingelow, Victorian Poetess (biography), 1972; Destiny's Lady, 1973; The Gallows Herd, 1973; The Maid of Judah, 1973; (as Veronica Black) Minstrel's Leap, 1973; Flawed Enchantress, 1974; So Fair and Foul a Queen, 1974; The Willow Maid, 1974; Curse of the Greys, 1974; (as Veronica Black) Spin Me a Shadow, 1974; (as Veronica Black) The House That Hated People, 1974; An Enigma of Brontës (biography), 1974; (as Judith Rothman) With Murder in Mind, 1975; The Queenmaker, 1975; Kate Alanna, 1975; (as Veronica Black) Tansy, 1975; (as Sharon Whitby) The Last of the Greenwood, 1975; (as Sharon Whitby) The Unforgotten Face, 1975; (as Catherine Darby) A Falcon for a Witch, 1975; (as Catherine Darby) The King's Falcon, 1975, in U.K. as A Game of Falcons, 1976; (as Catherine Darby) Fortune for a Falcon, 1975; A Child Called Freedom, 1976; (as Catherine Darby) Season of the Falcon, 1976; (as Catherine Darby) Falcon Royal, 1976, in U.K. as A Pride of Falcons, 1977; (as Catherine Darby) Falcon Tree, 1976; (as Catherine Darby) The Falcon and the Moon, 1976; (as Catherine Darby) Falcon Rising, 1976; (as Catherine Darby) Falcon Sunset, 1976; (as Catherine Darby) Whisper Down the Moon, 1977; (as Catherine Darby) Frost on the Moon, 1977; (as Catherine Darby) The Flaunting Moon, 1977; (as Catherine Darby) Sing Me a Moon, 1977; (as Veronica Black) Echo of Margaret, 1978; (as Catherine Darby) Seed of the Falcon, 1978; (as Catherine Darby) Falcon's Claw, 1978; (as Catherine Darby) Falcon to the Lure, 1978; (as Catherine Darby) Cobweb Across the Moon, 1978; (as Catherine Darby) Moon in Pisces, 1978; (as Belinda Grey) The Passionate Puritan, 1978; (as Catherine Darby) Dream of Fair Serpents, 1979; (as Veronica Black) Greengirl, 1979; (as Veronica Black) Pilgrim of Desire, 1979; (as Belinda Grey) Loom of Love, 1979; (as Belinda Grey) Sweet Wind of Morning, 1979; Beggar Maid, Queen, 1980; I, The Maid, 1980; The Snow Blossom, 1980; (as Veronica Black) Flame in the Snow, 1980; (as Sharon Whitby) Here Be Dragons, 1980; (as Sharon Whitby) The Silky, 1980; (as Belinda Grey) Moon of Laughing Flame, 1980; Night of the Willow, 1981; Ravenscar, 1981; (as Sharon Whitby) The Houseless One, 1981; (as Sharon Whitby) No Song at Morningside, 1981; (as Belinda Grey) Daughter of Isis, 1981; (as Belinda Grey) Glen of Frost, 1981; (as Levanah Lloyd) A Maid Called Wanton, 1981; (as Levanah Lloyd) Mail Order Bride, 1981; (as Levanah Lloyd) Cauldron of Desire, 1981; (as Levanah Lloyd) Dark Surrender, 1981; (as Veronica Black) The Dragon and the Rose, 1982; Red Queen, White Queen, 1982; Imperial Harlot, 1983; My Lady Troubadour, 1983; Alianor, 1983; Lackland's Bride, 1983; (as Veronica Black) Bond Wife, 1983; (as Sharon Whitby) Children of the Rainbow, 1983; (as Catherine Darby) A Circle of Rowan, 1983; A Song for Marguerite, 1984; My Philippa, 1984; (as Veronica Black) Hoodman Blind, 1984; (as Catherine Darby) The Rowan Maid, 1984; (as Catherine Darby) Song of the Rowan, 1984; (as Catherine Darby) Sangreal, 1984; Fair Maid of Kent, 1985; Isabella, The She Wolf, 1985; The Vinegar Seed, 1985; (as Catherine Darby) Sabre, 1985; (as Catherine Darby) Sabre's Child, 1985; (as Catherine Darby) Silken Sabre, 1985; (as Catherine Darby) House of Sabre, 1986; (as Catherine Darby) Heart of Flame, 1986; The Vinegar Blossom, 1986; (as Catherine Darby) A Breed of Sabres, 1987; (as Catherine Darby) Morning of a Sabre, 1987; The Luck Bride, 1987; The Vinegar Tree, 1987; Lady for a Chevalier, 1987; My Catalina, 1988; The Noonday Queen, 1988; Incredible, Fierce Desire, 1988; Wife in Waiting, 1989; Patchwork, 1989. Add: c/o Hale, 45-47 Clerkenwell Green, London EC1R 0HT, England.

PETERS, Natasha (pseud.) Historical/Romance/Gothic. *Publs:* Savage Surrender, 1977; Dangerous Obsession, 1978; The Masquers, 1979; The Enticers, 1981; The Immortals: A Novel of Shanghai, 1983; Darkness into Light, 1984; Wild Nights, 1986. Add: c/o Ballantine Books, 201 E. 50th St., New York, N.Y. 10022, U.S.A.

PETERS, Richard Stanley. British, b. 1919. Education, Philosophy, Psychology. Prof. Emeritus of Philosophy of Education, Inst. of Education, Univ. of London, since 1982 (Lectr. in Philosophy and Psychology, and Reader in Philosophy, Birkbeck Coll., 1949–62; Dean, Faculty of Education, 1971–74; Prof. of Philosophy of Education, 1962–82). Ed., Intnl. Library of Philosophy of Education, and Philosophy of Education section of Students' Library of Education, Routledge and Kegan Paul Ltd., publrs., London. *Publs:* Brett's History of Psychology, 1953, 1962; Hobbes, 1956, 1967; The Concept of Motivation, 1958, 1960; (co-author) Social Principles and the Democratic States, 1959; Authority, Responsibility and Education, 1960, 1973; Ethics and Education, 1966; (ed.) The Concept of Education, 1967; (ed.) Perspectives on Plowden, 1969; (co-author) The Logic of Education, 1970; (co-ed.) Hobbes and Rousseau: A Collection of Critical Essays, 1972; (co-ed.) Education and the Development of Reason, 1972; Reason, Morality and Religion, 1972; (ed.) Philosophy of Education, 1973; Reason and Compassion: Lindsay Memorial Lectures, 1973; Psychology and Ethical Development, 1974; (ed.) Nature and Conduct, 1975; (ed.) The Role of the Head, 1976; Essays on Education and the Education of Teachers, 1977; (ed.) John Dewey Reconsidered, 1978; Essays on Educators, 1981; Moral Development and Moral Education, 1981. Add: Dept. of Philosophy, Univ. of London Inst. of Education, Flat 3, 16 Shepherd's Hill, London N6 5AQ, England.

PETERS, Robert. American, b. 1924. Plays, Poetry, Literature. Prof. of English, Univ. of California at Irvine, since 1967. Asst. Prof. of Humanities, Boston Univ., 1952–54; Asst. Prof. of English, Ohio Wesleyan Univ., Delaware, 1954–57; Assoc. Prof. of English, Wayne State Univ., Detroit, 1957–63; Prof., Univ. of California at Riverside, 1963–67. *Publs:* Victorians on Literature and Art, 1961; The Crowns of Apollo: Swinburne's Principles of Literature and Art, 1965; (co-ed.) America: The Diary of a Visit by Edmund Gosse, 1966; (co-ed.) Pioneers of Modern Poetry, 1967; (co-ed.) The Letters of John Addington Symonds, 3 vols., 1967–69; Songs for a Son, 1967; The Sow's Head and Other Poems, 1969; Fuck Mother (play), 1970; Connection: In the English Lake District, 1973; Byron Exhumed, 1973; Red Midnight Moon, 1974; Holy Cow: Parable Poems, 1974; Cool Zebras of Light, 1974; Bronchial Tangle, Heart System, 1974; The Gift to Be Simple, 1975; Gauguin's Chair: Selected Poems, 1975; The Poet as Ice-Skater, 1976; Hawthorne, 1977; The Drowned Man to the Fish (poetry), 1978; The Great American Poetry Bake-Off (criticism), 3 vols., 1979–87; The Picnic in the Snow: Ludwig II of Bavaria (poetry), 1982; The Peters Black and Blue Guides to Literary Journals (criticism), 1984, 1985; What Dillinger Meant to Me (poetry), 1984; Hawker (poetry), 1985; Kane (poetry), 1985; The Blood Countess, 1987; Shaker Light (poetry), 1988; Letters to a Tutor, 1988. Add: Dept. of English, Univ. of California, Irvine, Calif. 92717, U.S.A

PETERS, William C(allier). American, b. 1920. Earth sciences. Prof. Emeritus of Mining and Geological Engineering, Univ. of Arizona, Tucson, since 1982 (Prof., 1964–82). Geologist, New Jersey Zinc Co., Gilman, Colo., 1948–50, and FMC Corp., Denver, 1950–59; Chief Geologist, Utah Copper Div., Kennecott Copper Corp., Salt Lake City, 1959–64. Chmn., Tucson Section, American Inst. of Mining and Metallurgical Engineers, 1968; Pres., Arizona Geological Soc., 1970–71, Southwest Minerals Exploration Assn , 1972, and Mining Club of the Southwest, 1987. *Publs:* (ed.) Mining and Ecology in the Arid Environment, 1970; Exploration and Mining Geology, 1978, 1987. Add: 5702 E. 7th St., Tucson, Ariz. 85711, U.S.A.

PETERSEN, Donald. American, b. 1928. Poetry. Prof. of English, State Univ. of New York, Oneonta (member of the English Dept. since 1956). Asst. Ed., Western Review, Iowa City, 1950–55; taught at the Univ. of Iowa, Iowa City, 1954–56. *Publs:* The Spectral Boy, 1964. Add: Dept. of English, State Univ. of New York, Oneonta, N.Y. 13820, U.S.A.

PETERSON, Bruce Henry. Australian, b. 1918. Psychiatry, Psychology, Sex, Theology/Religion. Consultant psychiatrist in private practice, 1955 until retirement, 1988. Hon. Federal Treas., 1963–70, and Pres., 1971–72, Australian and New Zealand Coll. of Psychiatrists; Hon. Psychiatrist, Sydney Hosp., 1964–73; Clinical Lectr. in Psychiatry, Sydney Univ., 1965–73. Pres., Family Life Movement of Australia, 1963–75; Ed., Australian Journal of Sex, Marriage, and Family, 1980–86. *Publs:* The Voices of Conscience, 1967; Understanding Psychosexual Development, 1970; Growing in Love and Sex, 1981. Add: 49/1 Lauderdale Ave., Fairlight, N.S.W. 2094, Australia.

PETERSON, Christmas. *See* **CHRISTMAS,** Joyce.

PETERSON, Edward N. American, b. 1925. History. Chmn., Dept. of History, Univ. of Wisconsin at River Falls, since 1954. *Publs:* Hjalmar Schacht: For and Against Hitler; The Limits of Hitler's Power; (asst. ed.) Pierce County Heritage, 8 vols., 1971–85; Retreat to Victory: The American Occupation of Germany, 1978. Add: 936 W. Maple St., River Falls, Wisc. 54022, U.S.A.

PETERSON, Edwin Loose. American, b. 1915. Cultural/Ethnic topics, Geography. Prof. of Geography, Utah State Univ., Logan, since 1937, now Emeritus. *Publs:* Cultural Geography of Europe, 1960; Cultural Geography of Asia, 1960; Cultural Geography of the Americas, 1960; Geography of World War II, 1970; World Cultural Geography, 1973. Add: 139 East 1st North, Logan, Utah 84321, U.S.A.

PETERSON, Elmer. American, b. 1930. Literature. Prof. of French, Colorado Coll., Colorado Springs, since 1960. Corresp., French XX Bibliography. *Publs:* Tristan Tzara, 1971; Z1 with Notes, 1972; (ed. with Michel Sanouillet) Marcel Duchamp, Salt Seller, 1973; (ed. with Ronald Sutherland) Dentelle Indented (poetry anthology), 1982. Add: Dept. of French, Colorado Coll., Colorado Springs, Colo. 80903, U.S.A.

PETERSON, Harold Bruce. American, b. 1939. Environmental science/ Ecology, Mythology/Folklore, Social commentary/phenomena. Dir. of Publications, Univ. of Wisconsin, Platteville. Ed. and Publisher, Almost Free mag., since 1975. Formerly, Staff Writer, Time Inc., NYC; Faculty Member, Utah State Univ., Logan, 1969–70. *Publs:* The Last of the Mountain Men, 1969, 1975; The Man Who Invented Baseball, 1973; Being Free, 1979. Add: c/o Backeddy Books, Box 301, Cambridge, Idaho 83610, U.S.A.

PETERSON, Helen Stone. American, b. 1910. Children's non-fiction. *Publs:* Henry Clay, 1964; Jane Addams, 1965; Abigail Adams, 1967; Roger Williams, 1968; Electing Our Presidents, 1970; Susan B. Anthony, 1971; Sojourner Truth, 1972; Give Us Liberty!: The Story of the Declaration of Independence, 1973; The Making of the Constitution, 1974; The Supreme Court in America's Story, 1976; Oliver Wendell Holmes, 1979. Add: 519 Caswell Rd., Chapel Hill, N.C. 27514, U.S.A.

PETERSON, John Eric. American, b. 1933. History. Prof. of History, Fourah Bay Coll., Univ. of Sierra Leone, since 1968 (Visiting Research Fellow, 1966–67). Acting Dir., Inst. of African Studies, Univ. of Sierra Leone; Ed., Sierra Leone Studies. Asst. Prof. of History, 1961–66, and Assoc. Prof., 1966–68, Kalamazoo Coll., Michigan. *Publs:* Province of Freedom: A History of Sierra Leone 1787-1870, 1969; Oman in the 20th Century, 1978; Yemen, 1982; Defending Arabia, 1986. Add: Dept. of History, Fourah Bay Coll., Univ. of Sierra Leone, Freetown, Sierra Leone.

PETERSON, Merrill D. American, b. 1921. History, Biography. Thomas Jefferson Foundn. Prof. of History, Univ. of Virginia, Charlottesville, since 1963, now Emeritus. Asst. Prof. to Prof. of History, Brandeis Univ., Waltham, Mass., 1949–55 and 1958–63; Asst. Prof. of History, Princeton Univ., New Jersey, 1955–58. *Publs:* The Jefferson Image in the American Mind, 1960; (ed.) Democracy, Liberty and Property: The State Constitutional Convention Debates of the 1820's, 1966; Thomas Jefferson and the New Nation: A Biography, 1970; James Madison: A Biography in His Own Words, 1974; (ed.) The Portable Thomas Jefferson, 1974; Adams, and Jefferson: A Revolutionary Dialogue, 1976; Olive Branch and Sword: The Compromise of 1833, 1982; (ed.) Thomas Jefferson, Writings, 1984; Thomas Jefferson: A Reference Biography, 1986; The Great Triumvirate: Webster, Clay, and Calhoun, 1987; (ed.) The Virginia Statute for Religious Freedom: Its Evolution and Consequences in American History, 1988; (ed.) Visitors to Monticello, 1989. Add: 901 Old Farm Road, Charlottesville, Va. 22903, U.S.A.

PETERSON, Randolph Lee. Canadian, b. 1920. Biology, Zoology. Curator, Dept. of Mammalogy, Royal Ontario Museum, Toronto, 1950–85, now Emeritus (Acting Curator, 1946–50); Prof. of Zoology, Univ. of Toronto, 1968–85, now Emeritus. *Publs:* North American Moose, 1955; The Mammals of Eastern Canada, 1966. Add: Dept. of Mammalogy, Royal Ontario Museum, Toronto, Ont. M5S 2C6, Canada.

PETERSON, Richard Austin. American, b. 1932. Cultural/Ethnic topics, Sociology. Prof. of Sociology, since 1967, and Chmn., Dept. of Soc. and Anthropology, 1982–87, Vanderbilt Univ., Nashville; Visiting Senior Lectr., Leeds Univ., England, 1985–86. Assoc. Ed., American Journal of Sociology, Journal of Popular Music, and Social Inquiry. Ed., American Sociological Assn. Sociology of Culture Section Newsletter. Asst. Prof., Univ. of Wisconsin, Madison, 1960–64. *Publs:* (with A.W. Gouldner) Notes on Technology and the Moral Order, 1962; (ed. with N.J. Demerath) System, Change and Conflict: A Reader in Sociological Theory, 1967; (ed.) With the Indian Army in the Great War 1916-1919, by Harold H. Peterson, 1970; (ed. with R.S. Denisoff) Sounds of Social Change, 1972; (ed.) The Peterson Nursery: A Victorian Episode, by Harold H. Peterson, 1972; The Industrial Order and Social Policy, 1973; The Dynamics of Industrial Society, 1973; The Production of Culture, 1976; Arts Audience Statistics and Culture Indicators, 1980; (ed. and contrib.) Patterns of Cultural Choice, 1984. Add: Box 1635B, Vanderbilt Univ., Nashville, Tenn. 37235, U.S.A.

PETERSON, Wallace C(arroll). American. Economics.George Holmes Prof. of Economics, Univ. of Nebraska, Lincoln, since 1952 (Chmn., 1965–75). *Publs:* The Welfare State in France, 1960; Income, Employment and Economic Growth, 1962, 6th ed. 1988; Elements of Economics, 1974; Our Overloaded Economy: Inflation, Unemployment, and the Crisis in American Capitalism, 1982; Market Power and the Economy, 1988. Add: 4549 South St., Lincoln, Nebr. 68506, U.S.A.

PETHYBRIDGE, Roger William. British, b. 1934. Area studies, History, Politics/Government. Prof., and Dir. of the Centre of Russian and East European Studies, University Coll. of Swansea, since 1962. *Publs:* A Key to Soviet Politics: The Crisis of the Anti-Party Group, 1962; (ed.) The Development of the Communist Bloc, 1965; (ed.) Witnesses to the Russian Revolution, 1965; A History of Postwar Russia, 1966; The Spread of the Russian Revolution: Essays on 1917, 1972; The Social Prelude to Stalinism, 1974. Add: Centre of Russian and East European Studies, University Coll., Swansea, Wales.

PETRAKIS, Harry Mark. American, b. 1923. Novels/Short stories, Plays/Screenplays, Autobiography/Memoirs/Personal, Biography. Writer-in-Residence, Chicago Public Library, 1976–78, and Chicago Bd. of Education, 1978–79. *Publs:* Lion at My Heart, 1959; The Odyssey of Kostas Volakis, 1963; Pericles on 31st Street, 1965; The Founder's Touch (biography), 1965; A Dream of Kings, 1966, screenplay 1969; The Waves of Night, 1969; Stelmark: A Family Recollection, 1970; In the Land of Morning, 1973, screenplay 1974; The Hour of the Bell, 1976; A Petrakis Reader, 1978; Nick the Greek, 1979; Days of Vengeance, 1983; Reflections: A Writer's Life—A Writer's Work, 1983; Collected Stories, 1987. Add: 80 East Rd., Dune Acres, Chesterton, Ind. 46304, U.S.A.

PETRAS, John W. American, b. 1940. Sociology. Prof. of Sociology, Central Michigan Univ., Mt. Pleasant, since 1966. Ed., Sociological Focus, 1971–74. *Publs:* G.H. Mead: Essays on His Social Philosophy, 1968; Sociology of Knowledge, 1970; Sexuality in Society, 1973; (with Bernard N. Meltzer and Larry T. Reynolds) Symbolic Interaction Theory: Genesis, Varieties, Criticisms, 1974; Sex: Male/Gender: Masculine, 1975; Social Meaning of Human Sexuality, 1978; (with Jennifer J. Aho) Learning about Sex, 1978; (with Jennifer J. Aho) Learning about Sexual Abuse, 1985. Add: Dept. of Sociology and Anthropology, Central Michigan Univ., Mt. Pleasant, Mich. 48859, U.S.A.

PETRIE, Catherine. American, b. 1947. Children's fiction. Owner and Dir., Professional Tour Consultants Inc., Lake Geneva, since 1981. Reading consultant, Pine Ridge, S.D., 1970–72, Edgewater, Colo., 1972–78, San Dimas, Calif., 1978–80, and Lake Geneva, 1980–81. *Publs:* Hot Rod Harry, 1982; Sandbox Betty, 1982; Joshua James Like Trucks, 1982; Seed, 1983; Night, 1983; Rain, 1983. Add: Route 2, Petrie Rd., Lake Geneva, Wisc. 53147, U.S.A.

PETRIE, Paul (James). American, b. 1928. Poetry. Prof. of English, Univ. of Rhode Island, Kingston, since 1969 (member of the English Dept., since 1959). *Publs:* Confessions of a Non-Conformist, 1963; The Race with Time and the Devil, 1965; The Leader: For Martin Luther King, Jr., 1968; From under the Hill of Night: Poems, 1969; The Idol, 1973; The Academy of Goodbye, 1974; Light from the Furnace Rising, 1978; Time Songs, 1979; Not Seeing Is Believing, 1983; Strange Gravity: Songs, Physical and Metaphysical, 1984; The Runners, 1988. Add: 200 Dendron Rd., Peace Dale, R.I. 02879, U.S.A.

PETRIE, Rhona. *See* BUCHANAN, Marie.

PETRY, Ann (Lane). American, b. 1908. Novels/Short stories, Children's fiction, Children's non-fiction. Pharmacist, Old Saybrook and Old Lyme, Conn., 1931–38; Writer and Reporter, Amsterdam News, NYC, 1938–41, and People's Voice, NYC, 1941–44; Visiting Prof. of English, Univ. of Hawaii, Honolulu, 1974–75. *Publs:* The Street, 1946; Country Place, 1947; The Drugstore Cat, 1949; The Narrows, 1953; Harriet Tubman: Conductor on the Underground Railroad (in U.K. as A Girl Called Moses: The Story of Harriet Tubman), 1955; Tituba of Salem Village, 1964; Legends of the Saints, 1970; Miss Muriel and Other Stories, 1971. Add: c/o Russell and Volkening Inc., 50 W. 29th St., New York, N.Y. 10001, U.S.A.

PETTIGREW, Thomas Fraser. American, b. 1931. Race relations. Prof. of Social Psychology, Univ. of California at Santa Cruz, since 1980, and Univ. of Amsterdam, since 1986. Asst. Prof. of Psychology, Univ. of North Carolina, Chapel Hill, 1956–57; Asst. Prof., 1957–62, Lectr., 1962–64, Assoc. Prof., 1964–68, and Prof. of Social Psychology and Sociology, 1968–80, Harvard Univ., Cambridge, Mass. *Publs:* (with E.Q. Campbell) Christians in Racial Crisis: A Study of the Little Rock Ministry, 1959; A Profile of the Negro American, 1964; Racially Separate or Together?, 1971; (ed.) Racial Discrimination in the United States, 1975; (ed.) The Sociology of Race Relations: Reflection and Reform, 1980; (with others) Prejudice, 1982; (with D.A. Alston) Tom Bradley's Campaigns for Governor: The Dilemma of Race and Political Strategies, 1988. Add: Psychology Bd., Stevenson Coll., Univ. of California, Santa Cruz, Calif. 95064, U.S.A.

PETTY, W(illiam) H(enry). British, b. 1921. Poetry, Administration/Management. County Education Officer, Kent County Council, 1973–84 (Deputy County Education Officer, 1963–73). Held various posts in admin. and teaching, 1946–63. Chmn., Assn. of Education Officers, 1979–80; Pres., Soc. of Education Officers, 1980–81; Chmn., County Education Officers Soc., 1982–83. *Publs:* No Bold Comfort, 1957; Conquest, 1967; (co-author) Educational Administration, 1980. Add: Willow Bank, Moat Rd., Headcorn, Kent TN29 9NT, England.

PETUCHOWSKI, Jakob Josef. American, b. 1925. Intellectual history, Theology/Religion. Sol and Arlene Bronstein Prof. of Judaeo-Christian Studies, Hebrew Union Coll., Jewish Inst. of Religion, Cincinnati, since 1981 (Asst. Prof. of Rabbinics, 1956–59; Assoc. Prof., 1959–63; Prof., 1963–65; Prof. of Rabbinics and Jewish Theology, 1965–74; Research Prof. of Jewish Theology and Liturgy, 1974–81). Member, Editorial Bd., Judaism—A Quarterly, since 1962. *Publs:* The Theology of Haham David Nieto, 1954, 1970; Ever since Sinai, 1964, 3rd ed. 1979; (ed. with Ezra Spicehandler) Peraqim Beyahaduth, 1963; Zion Reconsidered, 1966; Prayerbook Reform in Europe, 1968; Heirs of the Pharisees, 1970; (ed.) Contributions to the Scientific Study of Jewish Liturgy, 1970; Understanding Jewish Prayer, 1972; Beten im Judentum, 1976; Theology and Poetry, 1978; The Lord's Prayer and Jewish Liturgy, 1978; Melchisedech—Urgestalt der Okumene, 1979; Es Lehrten unsere Meister, 1979; Ferner Lehrten unsere Meister, 1980; Die Stimme vom Sinai, 1981; Gottesdienst des Herzens, 1981; Our Masters Taught, 1982; Wie unsere Meister die Schrift Erklaren, 1982; Feiertage des Herrn, 1984; Defining a Discipline, 1984; When Jews and Christians Meet, 1988. Add: 7836 Greenland Pl., Cincinnati, Ohio 45237, U.S.A.

PEYTON, K. M. Also writes as Kathleen Herald. British, b. 1929. Children's fiction. *Publs:* (as Kathleen Herald) Sabre the Horse from the Sea, 1948; (as Kathleen Herald) The Mandrake, 1949; (as Kathleen Herald) Crab the Roan, 1953; North to Adventure, 1958; Stormcock Meets Trouble, 1961; The Hard Way Home (in U.S. as Sing a Song of Ambush), 1962; Windfall (in U.S. as Sea Fever), 1962; Brownsea Silver, 1964; The Maplin Bird, 1964; The Plan for Birdsmarsh, 1965; Thunder in the Sky, 1966; Flambards, 1967; Fly by Night, 1968; The Edge of the Cloud, 1969; Flambards in Summer, 1969; Pennington's Seventeenth Summer, 1970; The Beethoven Medal, 1971; A Pattern of Roses, 1972; Pennington's Heir, 1973; The Team, 1975; The Right-Hand Man, 1977; Prove Yourself a Hero, 1977; A Midsummer Night's Death, 1978; Marion's Angels, 1979; Flambards Divided, 1981; Dear Fred, 1981; Going Home, 1982; The Last Ditch, 1983; Froggett's Revenge, 1985; The Sound of Distant Cheering, 1986; Downhill All the Way, 1988; Plain Jack, 1988; Darkling, 1989. Add: Rookery Cottage, N. Fambridge, Essex, England.

PFEFFER, Susan Beth. American, b. 1948. Children's fiction. *Publs:* Just Morgan, 1970; Better Than All Right, 1972; Rainbows and Fireworks, 1973; The Beauty Queen, 1974; Whatever Words You Want to Hear, 1974; Marly the Kid, 1975; Kid Power, 1977; Starring Peter and Leigh, 1979; Awful Evelina, 1979; Just Between Us, 1980; About David, 1980; What Do You Do When Your Mouth Won't Open?, 1981; A Matter of Principle, 1982; Courage, Dana, 1983; Fantasy Summer, 1984; Paperdolls, 1984; Kid Power Strikes Back, 1984; Truth or Dare, 1984; Starting with Melodie, 1985; Make Me a Star series, 6 vols., 1986; The Friendship Pact, 1986; Getting Even, 1986; Hard Times High, 1986; The Year Without Michael, 1987. Add: 14 S. Railroad Ave., Middletown, N.J. 10940, U.S.A.

PHELAN, Mary Kay. American, b. 1914. Children's non-fiction. *Publs:* The White House, 1962; The Circus, 1963; Mother's Day, 1965; Mr. Lincoln Speaks at Gettysburg, 1966; The Fourth of July, 1966; Election Day, 1967; Four Days in Philadelphia, 1967; Midnight Alarm: The Story of Paul Revere's Ride, 1968; Probing the Unknown: The Story of Dr. Florence Sabin, 1969; The Great Chicago Fire, 1971; Martha Berry, 1971; Mr. Lincoln's Inaugural Journey, 1972; The Story of the Boston Tea Party, 1973; The Burning of Washington 1814, 1975; The Story of the Boston Massacre, 1976; Waterway West: The Story of the Erie Canal, 1977; The Story of the Louisiana Purchase, 1979; The Story of the United States Constitution, 1987. Add: G 207 Vicar's Landing Way, Ponte Vedra Beach, FL 32082, U.S.A.

PHELPS, Gilbert (Henry, Jr.). British, b. 1915. Novels/Short stories, Plays/Screenplays, Poetry, Literature. Asst. Supvr. of English Studies, St. John's Coll., Cambridge, 1937–40; Lectr. and Tutor, Cambridge Univ. Bd. of Extra-Mural Studies, 1938–40; Lectr. in English, British Council Inst., Lisbon, 1940–42; Sr. English Master, Blundell's Sch., Tiverton, Devon, 1943–45; Talks Producer, BBC, Bristol, 1945–50; Supvr., Educational Talks, 1950–52, Producer, Third Prog., 1950–53, Gen. Instr., 1953–56, and Chief Instr., 1956–60, Staff Training Dept., BBC, London; Ed., Latin American Adventure and Makers of Empire Series. *Publs:* (ed.) Living Writers, 1947; The Dry Stone, 1953, rev. ed. as The Heart in the Desert, 1954; A Man in His Prime, 1955; The Russian Novel in English Fiction, 1956; The Winter People (radio play), 1958, 1964, abridged versions, 1963, 1973; The Centenarians: A Fable, 1958; The Winter People (novel and radio play), 1958; The Early Phases of British Interest in Russian Literature, vol. I, 1958, vol. II, 1960; The Tankerdown Skull (radio play), 1960; The Love Before the First, 1960; The Tide Comes In (radio play), 1960; The Spanish Cave (radio play), 1960; A Short History of English Literature, 1962, rev. ed. as A Survey of English Literature, 1965, 1979; The Last Horizon: Travels in Brazil (in U.S. as Green Horizons: Travels in Brazil), 1964; Latin America, 1965; (ed.) Vanity Fair, by Thackeray, 1967; Deliberate Adventure (radio play and serial), 1968; (ed.) Question and Response: A Critical Anthology of English and American Poetry, 1969; Latin America, 1970; Tenants of the House, 1971; (ed.) The Byronic Byron: A Selection from the Poems of Lord Byron, 1971; The Old Believer (in U.S. as Mortal Flesh), 1973; (ed.) Romeo and Juliet, by Shakespeare, 1973; (ed.) Villette, by Charlotte Brontë, 1973; (ed.) Wanderings in South America, by Charles Waterton, 1973; Arnold Bennett, The Old Wives' Tale, 1973; (ed.) Byron: An Autobiographical Anthology, 1974; (ed.) The Rare Adventures and Painful Peregrinations of William Lithgow, 1974; (ed.) Henry Esmond, by Thackeray, 1974; The Low Roads, 1975; Tragedy of Paraguay, 1975; Squire Waterton of Walton Hall, 1976; (ed.) Arlott and Truman on Cricket, 1977; Story of the British Monarchy, 1977; Fifty British Novels 1650-1900, 1979; (co-ed.) Animals Wild and Tame, 1979; From Myth to Modernism: A Short History of World Fiction, 1988; Post-War Literature and Drama, 1988. Add: The Cottage, School Rd., Finstock, Oxford OX7 3DJ, England.

PHENIX, Philip Henry. American, b. 1915. Education, Philosophy, Theology/Religion. Arthur I. Gates Prof. Emeritus of Philosophy and Education, Teachers Coll., Columbia Univ., NYC, since 1980 (Assoc. Prof., 1954–56; Prof. 1956–58 and since 1960). Assoc. Prof. of Religion and Coll. Chaplain, 1946–48 and 1950–53, and Dean of the Coll., 1958–60, Carleton Coll., Northfield, Minn.; Prog. Assoc., Edward W. Hazen Foundn., New Haven, Conn., 1953–54. *Publs:* Intelligible Religion, 1954; Philosophy of Education, 1958; Religious Concerns in Contemporary Education, 1959; (ed.) Philosophies of Education, 1961; Education and the Common Good, 1961; Realms of Meaning, 1964; Man and His Becoming, 1964; Education and the Worship of God, 1966. Add: 127 Rosewood Circle, Bridgewater, Va. 22812, U.S.A.

PHILIPP, Elliot Elias. Also writes as Philip Embey, Anthony Havil, and Victor Tempest. British, b. 1915. Medicine/Health, Sex, Biography. Consultant Gynaecologist and Obstetrician, Royal Northern Hosp. and City of London Maternity Hosp., 1964–80, now Hon. Consultant; Gynaecologist, French Dispensary, since 1952. Registrar and Sr. Registrar, University Coll. Hosp., St. Thomas's Hosp., Royal Free Hosp., and Middlesex Hosp., London, 1947–52; Consultant Gynaecologist, Oldchurch Hosp., Romford, Essex, 1952–64. *Publs:* (as Anthony Havil) The Technique of Sex, 1939, 7th ed. 1985; (as Anthony Havil) Talks on a Vital Subject, 1941; (as Victor Tempest) Near the Sun, 1946; (as Anthony Havil) The Aspect of Sex in Marriage, 1946 (vol. II of The Technique of Sex); (with E.W. Walls) Hilton's Rest and Pain, 1950; (as Anthony Havil) Birth Control and You, 1951; (as Philip Embey) Woman's Change of Life, 1955; (with I.C. Rubin) Childless Marriage, 1957; (co-author as Philip Embey) You and Your Baby, 1957, 1974; From Sterility to Fertility, 1957; (with E. Wright) Easy Childbirth, 1961; From Sterility and Impotency to Fertility and Virility, 1962; (with E. Crisp) Midwifery for Nurses, 1962, 1964; Obstetrics and Gynaecology for Students, 1962, 1970; (with K.L. Gearing) The Student Nurse in the Operating Theatre, 1964; (trans.) Sex Development and Maternity, by Dr. Pierre Vellay, 1968; (with R. Forbes) Easier Childbirth, 1969; (as Anthony Havil) The Making of a Woman, 1969; (ed. with J. Barnes and M. Newton) Scientific Foundations of Obstetrics and Gynaecology, 1970, 3rd ed. 1985; Having Your Baby, 1972; (ed.) From Conception to Birth, 1972; The Change of Life, 1977; Childlessness, 1978; Childbirth, 1978; (with G. Chamberlain) British Births 1970, vol. II, 1978; (with G. Barry Carruthers) Infertility, 1980; Hysterectomy, 1982; Overcoming Childlessness; (with Leila Hanna) Infertility and In Vitro Fertilisation, 1987; Safe Sex, 1987; Caesareans, 1988. Add: 78 Nottingham Terr., London NW1 4QE, England.

PHILIPS, (Sir) Cyril (Henry). British, b. 1912. History. Prof. of Oriental History, Univ. of London, 1946–80, now retired (Dir. of the Sch. of Oriental and African Studies, 1957–76, and Vice-Chancellor, 1969–70, 1972–76). With the Dept. of Training, The Treasury, 1943–46. *Publs:* The East Indian Company, 1940, 1961; India, 1949; Handbook of Oriental History, 1951, 1962; Correspondence of David Scott, 1951; Historians of India, Pakistan and Ceylon, 1961; The Evolution of India and Pakistan, 1962; Politics and Society in India, 1963; Fort William-India House Correspondence, 1964; History of the School of Oriental and African Studies 1917-67, 1967; The Partition of India, 1970; Young Wellington in India, 1973; (co-ed.) Indian Society and the Beginnings of Modernization, 1976; The Correspondence of Lord William Bentinck, 1977. Add: Sch. of Oriental and African Studies, Malet St., London WC1E 7HP, England.

PHILLIPS, Caryl. British, b. 1958. Novels, Plays/Screenplays, Travel. Writer-in-Residence, Factory Community Centre, London, 1981–82, Literary Criterion Centre, Mysore, India, 1987, and Stockholm Univ., Sweden, 1989. Member, Production Bd., British Film Inst., 1985–88. *Publs:* plays—Strange Fruit, 1981; Where There Is Darkness, 1982; The Shelter, 1984; The Wasted Years (in Best Radio Plays of 1984), 1985; Playing Away, 1987; novels—The Final Passage, 1985; A State of Independence, 1986; Higher Ground, 1989. Travel—The European Tribe, 1987. Add: c/o Judy Daish Assocs., 83 Eastbourne Mews, London W2 6LQ, England.

PHILLIPS, Derek L. American, b. 1934. Sociology. Prof. of Sociology, Univ. of Amsterdam, since 1971. Instr., Wellesley Coll., Massachusetts, 1962–63; Asst. Prof., Dartmouth Coll., Hanover, N.H., 1963–66; Assoc. Prof. and Prof., New York Univ., 1966–71. *Publs:* (ed.) Studies in American Society, 2 vols., 1965, 1967; Knowledge from What? Theories and Methods in Social Research, 1971; Abandoning Method, 1973; Wittgenstein and Scientific Knowledge, 1977; Equality, Justice and Rectification, 1979; Toward a Just Social Order, 1986. Add: Nieuwe Looiersstraat 124, 1017VG, Amsterdam, The Netherlands.

PHILLIPS, Dewi Zephaniah. Welsh, b. 1934. Education, Philosophy, Theology/Religion. Prof. of Philosophy, University Coll., Swansea, since 1971 (Lectr., 1965–67; Sr. Lectr., 1967–70). Ed., Philosophical Investigations. Lectr., Queen's Coll., Dundee, 1961–63, and Univ. Coll., Bangor, 1963–65. Gen. Ed., Studies in Ethics, and The Philosophy of Religion, Routledge and Kegan Paul, London, 1968–74. *Publs:* The Concept of Prayer, 1965; (ed.) Religion and Understanding, 1967; (ed.) Morality and Purpose, by J.L. Stocks, 1969; (with H.O. Mounce) Moral Practices, 1970; Death and Immortality, 1970; Faith and Philosophical Enquiry, 1970; (with I. Dilman) Sense and Delusion, 1971; Athronyddu Am Grefydd, 1974; Religion Without Explanation, 1976; Dramau Gwenlyn Parry, 1982; Through a Darkening Glass: Philosophy, Literature, and Social Change, 1982; Belief, Change and Forms of Life, 1986; R.S. Thomas: Poet of the Hidden God, 1986; Faith after Foundationalism, 1988. Add: Dept. of Philosophy, University Coll., Singleton Park, Swansea SA2 8PP, Wales.

PHILLIPS, Gerald M(arvin). American, b. 1928. Education, Human relations, Sociology, Speech/Rhetoric. Prof. of Speech Communication, Pennsylvania State Univ., University Park, since 1964. Series Ed., Southern Illinois Univ. Press. Former Asst. Prof. of Speech, Washington State Univ., Pullman, and Instr. in Speech, North Dakota Agricultural Coll. *Publs:* (with J. Wigley and S. Crandell) Speech: A Course in Fundamentals, 1963; Communication and the Small Group, 1966, 1973; (with D. Truby and E. Murray) Speech: Science-Art, 1969; (with R. Brubaker, R. Dunham and D. Butt) Development of Oral Communication in the Classroom, 1970; (with E. Erickson) Interpersonal Dynamics of the Small Group, 1970; (with D. Butt and N. Metzger) Communication in Education: Rhetoric of Schooling and Learning, 1974; (with N. Metzger) Intimate Communication, 1976; (with D. Pederson and J. Wood) Group Discussion, 1978, 1988; (with Julia T. Wood) Communication and Human Relations, 1983; (with J. Lloyd Goodall, Jr.) Loving and Living, 1983; Support Your Cause and Win, 1984; (with Julia T. Wood) Emergent Issues in Decision Making, 1984; (with H. Lloyd Goodall, Jr.) Making It in Any Organization, 1984; (with Kathleen Kougl and Lynne Kelly) Communicating in Public and Private, 1985; (with J. Jerome Zolten) Speaking to an Audience, 1985; (with Lawrence Eisenstein) Adult Problem Solving, 1986; (with Dr. J. Alfred Jones) Communicating with Your Doctor, 1988; (with Nancy J. Wyatt) Studying Organizations, 1988; A Theory of Rhetorical Incompetent, 1990. Add: 1212 S. Pugh St., State College, Pa. 16801, U.S.A.

PHILLIPS, James Atlee. Also writes as Philip Atlee. American, b. 1915. Novels/Short stories, Mystery/Crime/Suspense. *Publs:* mystery novels, as Philip Atlee—The Green Wound, 1963 (as The Green Wound Contract, 1967); The Silken Baroness, 1964 (as The Silken Baroness Contract, 1966); The Death Bird Contract, 1966; The Irish Beauty Contract, 1966; The Paper Pistol Contract, 1966; The Star Ruby Contract, 1967; The Skeleton Coast Contract, 1968; The Rockabye Contract, 1968; The Ill Wind Contract, 1969; The Fer-de-Lance Contract, 1970; The Canadian Bomber Contract, 1971; The White Wolverine Contract, 1971; The Judah Lion Contract, 1972; The Kiwi Contract, 1972; The Shankill Road Contract, 1973; The Spice Route Contract, 1973; The Kowloon Contract, 1974; The Underground Cities Contract, 1974; The Black Venus Contract, 1975; The Last Domino Contract, 1976; mystery novels, as James Atlee Phillips—The Case of the Shivering Chorus Girls, 1942; Suitable for Framing, 1949; Pagoda, 1951; The Deadly Mermaids, 1954; novels, as James Atlee Phillips—The Inheritors, 1940; The Naked Year, 1954. Add: c/o Fawcett Books, Random House, 201 E. 50th St., New York, N.Y. 10022, U.S.A.

PHILLIPS, Jayne Anne. American, b. 1952. Novels/Short stories. Has taught at Humboldt State Univ., Arcata, Calif.; Boston Univ.; and Williams College, Williamstown, Mass. *Publs:* Sweethearts (short stories), 1976; Counting (short stories), 1978; Black Tickets (short stories). 1979; How Mickey Made It (short stories), 1981; Fast Lanes (short stories), 1984; Machine Dreams (novel), 1984. Add: c/o ICM, 40 W. 57th St., New York, N.Y. 10019, U.S.A.

PHILLIPS, John Lawrence, Jr. American, b. 1923. Education, Psychology. Prof. and Chmn., Dept. of Psychology, Boise State Univ., Idaho, 1968 until retirement, 1988. (Chmn., Div. of Social Sciences, 1959–68). *Publs:* (ed.) Counselor's Guide to Idaho Colleges, 1965, 4th ed. 1971; (co-author) Counseling and Confidentiality, 1968; (co-author) Freedom and Determinism in Counseling Psychology, 1968; The Origins of Intellect: Piaget's Theory, 1969, 1975; Statistical Thinking: A Structural Approach, 1973, 1982; Piaget's Theory: A Primer, 1981. Add: 3233 Edson Dr., Boise, Idaho, U.S.A.

PHILLIPS, Louis Christopher. American, b. 1939. Novels/Short stories, Poetry. Assoc. Prof., and Dir. of Creative Writing, Central State Univ., Wilberforce, Ohio, since 1966. *Publs:* Dream Winners (novel), 1967; Love Ode: Plastic Surgical Pill Surreal, 1968; Sistine Cartoons, 1969; Bloodlines, 1971; Cheap Zoom Shots, 1974; Disco Candy and Other Stories, 1979; Twelve Muscle Tones, 1980. Add: 1812 Pueblo Dr., Xenia, Ohio 45385, U.S.A.

PHILLIPS, Mark. *See* **JANIFER**, Laurence.

PHILLIPS, Michael Joseph. American, b. 1937. Poetry, Literature. Visiting Fellow, Harvard Univ., Cambridge, Mass., 1976–77. *Publs:* Libretto for Twenty-Three Poems, 1967; Girls, Girls, Girls, 1967; Nine Concrete Poems, 1967; Seven Poems for Audrey Hepburn, 1968; Four Poster Poems, 1968; Four Poems for a Chocolate Princess, 1969; Four Gothic Twilight Poems, 1970; Eight Page Poems, 1970; Three Poems of the Cross, 1970; The Concrete Book, 1971; Kinetics and Concretes, 1971; Concrete Sonnets, 1973; Love, Love, Love, 1973; Concrete Haiku, 1975; Visual Poems, 1975; Visual Sequences, 1975; Haiku II, 1975; Concrete Sonnets, 1975; Abstract Poems, 1977; A Girl, 1978; More Women, 1978; Twenty-Two Concrete Poems Written While at Harvard, 1978; Beginnings of Samantha, 1979; Underworld Love Poems, 1979; 21 Erotic Haiku for Samantha, 1979; 31 Erotic Concrete Sonnets for Samantha, 1979; Edwin Muir, 1979; (ed.) 4 Major Visual Poets, 1980; Selected Love Poems, 1980; 35 Boogie Woogie Haiku, 1980; Betop Beauts, 1982; Indy Dolls, 1982; Superbeauts, 1983; Adornings, 1986; Imaginary Women, 1986; Selected Concrete Poems, 1986. Add: 101 S. Glenwood Ave., Bloomington, Ind. 47401, U.S.A.

PHILLIPS, R(obert) A(rthur) J(ohn). Canadian, b. 1922. Economics, Geography, History, Public/Social administration. Dir. of Northern Admin., 1963–65; Asst. Secty. to the Cabinet, 1965–69; Deputy Dir.-Gen., Information Canada, 1970–72; Exec. Dir., Heritage Canada, Ottawa, 1973–78. *Publs:* Canada, Giant of the North, 1965; The Yukon and Northwest Territories, 1966; Canada's North, 1967; The East Block of the Parliament Buildings, 1967; Canada's Railways, 1968; The Cottager's Handbook, 1987. Add: P.O. Box 319, Cantley, Que. J0X 1L0, Canada.

PHILLIPS, Robert (Schaeffer). American, b. 1938. Novels/Short stories, Poetry, Literature. Chmn., Cultural Events Cttee., Katonah Village Library, and Ed., Modern Poetry Studies, both since 1970; Assoc. Ed., The Paris Review, since 1977; Contrib. Ed., The Ontario Review, since 1977. Instr., The New Sch., NYC, 1969–71. *Publs:* Inner Weather, 1966; Land of Lost Content, 1970; (ed.) Aspects of Alice, 1971; The Confessional Poets, 1973; Denton Welch, 1974; (ed.) Moonstruck, 1974; The Pregnant Man, 1978; (ed.) Last Poems of Delmore Schwartz, 1979; William Goyen, 1979; Running on Empty, 1981; (ed.) Collected Stories of Noel Coward, 1983; (ed.) Letters of Delmore Schwartz, 1984; (ed.) Stories of Denton Welch, 1985; Personal Accounts: New and Selected Poems 1966-1986, 1986; (ed.); The Ego Is Always at the Wheel: Bagatelles, by Delmore Schwartz, 1986; The Wounded Angel, 1987; (ed.) The Triumph of Night: 20th Century Ghost Stories, 1989. Add: Cross River Rd., Box AF, Katonah, N.Y. 10536, U.S.A.

PHILLIPS, William. American, b. 1906. Literature, Politics. Founding Ed., with Philip Rahv, 1937–69, and sole ed., since 1969, Partisan Review. Prof., Boston Univ., since 1978. Prof. of English, Rutgers Univ., New Brunswick, N.J., 1963–78; has taught at New School for Social Research, NYC, Sarah Lawrence Coll., Bronxville, N.Y., and Univ. of Minnesota, Minneapolis. Add: A Sense of the Present, 1967; A Partisan View: Five Decades of the Literary Life, 1983. Add: c/o Partisan Review, 236 Bay State Rd., Boston, Mass. 02215, U.S.A.

PHILLIPSON, David W. British, b. 1942. Anthropology/Ethnology, Archaeology/Antiquities. Curator, Cambridge Univ. Museum of Archaeology and Anthropology, since 1981. Secty./Inspector, Zambia National Monuments Commn., 1964–72; Asst. Dir., British Inst. in Eastern Africa, Nairobi, 1973–79; Keeper of Archaeology, Ethnography, and History, Glasgow Museums and Art Galleries, 1979–81. *Publs:* (with B.M. Fagan and S.G.H. Daniels) Iron Age Cultures in Zambia, vol. II, 1969; National Monuments of Zambia, 1973; (ed. and contrib.) Mosi-oa-Tunya: A Handbook to the Victoria Falls Region, 1974; The Prehistory of Eastern Zambia, 1976; The Later Prehistory of Eastern and Southern Africa, 1977; (with L. Phillipson) East Africa's Prehistoric Past, 1978; African Archaeology, 1985. Add: Univ Museum of Archaeology and Anthropology, Downing St., Cambridge CB2 3DZ, England.

PHILLPOTTS, (Mary) Adelaide (Eden). Also writes as Mary Adelaide Eden Ross. British, b. 1896. Novels/Short stories, Plays/Screenplays, Poetry, Travel/Exploration/Adventure. *Publs:* Illyrion and Other Poems, 1916; Arachne, 1920; Man: A Fable, 1922; The Friend, 1923; Savitri the Faithful, 1923; Camillus and the Schoolmaster, 1923; (with Eden Phillpotts) Yellowsands (play), 1926, novel 1930; Lodgers in London, 1926; Akhnaton, 1926; Tomek the Sculptor, 1927; A Marriage, 1928; The Atoning Years, 1929; The Youth of Jacob Ackner, 1931; Founder of Shandon, 1932; The Growing World, 1934; Onward Journey, 1936; Broken Allegiance, 1937; What's Happened to Rankin, 1938; The Gallant Heart, 1939; The Round of Life, 1940; Laugh with Me, 1941; Our Little Town, 1942; From Jane to John, 1943; The Adventurers, 1944; The Lodestar, 1945; The Fosterling, 1946; Stubborn Earth, 1951; A Song of Man, 1969; Panorama of the World, 1969; (ed.) Letters from John Cooper Powys to Nicholas Ross, 1971; A Wild Flower Wreath, 1974; Reverie (autobiography), 1981; Village Love (novel), 1988. Add: Cobblestones, Kilkhampton, Bude, Cornwall EX23 9QW, England.

PHILMUS, Robert M(ichael). American, b. 1943. Literature. Prof. of English, Loyola Coll., Concordia Univ., Montreal, since 1976 (Asst. Prof., 1968–72; Assoc. Prof., 1972–76). Instr. of English, Carleton Coll., Northfield, Minn., 1967–68. Member, Bd. of Eds., 1973–78, and Ed., 1978–89, Science Fiction Studies. *Publs:* Into the Unknown: The Evolution of Science-Fiction from Francis Godwin to H.G. Wells, 1970, 1983; (ed. and contrib. with D.Y. Hughes) H.G. Wells: Early Writings in Science and Science Fiction, 1974; (ed. with D. Suvin) H.G. Wells and Modern Science Fiction, 1977; (ed. with P. Parrinder) H.G. Wells's Literary Criticism, 1980; H.G. Wells "The Island of Dr. Moreau": A Variorum Text, 1989. Add: Dept. of English, Concordia Univ., 7141 Sherbrooke St. W., Montreal, Que. H4B 1R6, Canada.

PHILP, (Dennis Alfred) Peter. British, b. 1920. Antiques/Furnishings, Literature. *Publs:* Beyond Tomorrow, 1946; The Castle of Deception, 1952; Love and Lunacy, 1954; Antiques Today, 1956; Antique Furniture for the Smaller Home, 1962; (with M. Holland and J. Salentoff) Antiques: A Popular Guide, 1972; Furniture of the World, 1974; (co-author) World Furniture, 1980; (co-author) Sotheby's Concise Encyclopedia of Furniture, 1989. Add: 77 Kimberley Rd., Cardiff CF2 5DP, Wales.

PHILPS, (Frank) Richard. British, b. 1914. Medicine/Health, Natural history. R.A.F. Medical Service, 1940–46; Medical Registrar, 1950–54, Research Asst., 1954–60, and Consultant in Cytology, 1960–73, University Coll. Hosp., London, now retired. *Publs:* A Short Manual of Respiratory Cytology, 1964; Watching Wild Life, 1968; Breve Manuale di Broncocitologia, 1974; Watching Wild Life, 1978. Add: Woodlands, Lewdown, Okehampton EX20 4PP, England.

PHIPPS, Grace May. New Zealander. Historical/Romance/Gothic. *Publs:* Marriage with Eve, 1955; The Women of the Family, 1956; The Life for Louise, 1957; Concerning Eve, 1959; The Young Wife, 1962; A Nurse Like Kate, 1963; Two Sisters in Love, 1966; Doctor on the Scene, 1967; The Tender-Hearted Nurse, 1968; No Wife for a Parson, 1969; Marriage While You Wait, 1970; The Bridal Boutique, 1971; And Be My Love, 1972; The Doctor's Three Daughters, 1973; We Love You, Nurse Peters, 1974; Maternity Hospital, 1976; A Doctor Like Ross, 1978; Doctor Gregory on Call, 1979; Nurse Penny's Patients, 1980; Tenants of Linden Lodge, 1982. Add: c/o Hale, 45-47 Clerkenwell Green, London EC1R 0HT, England.

PHIPPS, William Eugene. American, b. 1930. Theology/Religion. Prof. of Religion and Philosophy, Davis and Elkins Coll., since 1956. *Publs:* Was Jesus Married? The Distortion of Sexuality in the Christian Tradition, 1970; The Sexuality of Jesus: Theological and Literary Perspectives, 1973; Recovering Biblical Sensuousness, 1975; Influential Theologians on Wo/Man, 1980; Encounter Through Questioning Paul: A Fresh Approach to the Apostle's Life and Letters, 1982; Paul Against Supernaturalism, 1987; Death: Confronting the Reality, 1987; Cremation Concerns, 1989; Genesis and Gender, 1989. Add: Davis and Elkins Coll., Elkins, W. Va. 26241, U.S.A.

PHIPSON, Joan. Australian, b. 1912. Novels/Short stories, Children's fiction. Freelance writer and grazier. *Publs:* Good Luck to the Rider, 1953; Six and Silver, 1954; It Happened One Summer, 1957; The Boundary Riders, 1962; The Family Conspiracy, 1962; Threat to the Barkers, 1963; Birkin, 1965; The Crew of the Merlin (in U.S. as Cross Currents), 1966; A Lamb in the Family, 1966; Peter and Butch, 1969; The Haunted Night, 1970; Bass and Bill Martin, 1972; The Way Home, 1973; Polly's Tiger, 1973; Helping Horse (in U.S. as Horse with Eight Hands), 1974; The Cats, 1976; Fly into Danger, 1977 (in Australia as The Bird Smugglers, 1979); Hide till Daytime, 1977; Keep Calm (in U.S. as When the City Stopped), 1978; No Escape (in U.S. as Fly Free), 1979; Mr. Pringle and the Prince, 1979; A Tide Flowing, 1981; The Watcher in the Gardens, 1982; Beryl the Rainmaker, 1984; The Grannie Season, 1985; Dinko, 1985; Hit and Run, 1985; Bianca, 1988. Add: Wongalong, Mandurama, N.S.W. 2792, Australia.

PHOENICE, Jay. (Juliet Mary Fox Hutchinson). British, b. 1911. Poetry. *Publs:* The Harbour; The Third Day; A Rainbow of Paths; Peke Posy; From the Kyloe Hills; Remembering Vernon: A Personal Memoir of Lord Barnby (prose), 1984; Poems of Gratitude, 1988. Add: Kyloe Old Vicarage, Berwick-on-Tweed TD15 2PG, England.

PHYTHIAN, Brian A(rthur). British, b. 1932. Education, History, Language/Linguistics, Literature. Headmaster, Langley Park Boys' Sch., Beckenham, since 1970. Gen. Ed., New Sch. Series, English Univs. Press, since 1965. Sr. English Master, Manchester Grammar Sch., 1965–70. *Publs:* R.B. Sheridan, 1964; (ed. with J.A. Graham) Manchester Grammar School 1515-1965, 1965; (with G.P. Fox) Starting Points, 1967; (ed.) Considering Poetry, 1970; (with G. Summerfield and others) English in Practice, 1971; (compiler) Concise Dictionary of English Idioms, 1973; (compiler) Concise Dictionary of Slang, 1975; (ed.) Henry V, 1975; Correct English, 1979; Teach Yourself English Grammar, 1980; (compiler) Concise Dictionary of Foreign Expressions, 1981; Teach Yourself Good English, 1985; Concise Dictionary of Confusables, 1989. Add: Langley Park Boys' Sch., Beckenham, Kent, England.

PIANKA, Eric R. American, b. 1939. Biology, Environmental science/Ecology. Denton A. Cooley Centennial Prof., Univ. of Texas at Austin, since 1986 (Asst. Prof., 1968–72; Assoc. Prof., 1972–77; Prof. of Zoology, 1977–86). Managing Ed., The American Naturalist, 1971–74, Ed. Bd., 1975–77; Gov., American Assn. of Ichthyologists and Herpetologists, 1975–79; Member, Editorial Bd., Bioscience, 1975–79; Bd. of Editors, Natl. Geographic Research, 1985. *Publs:* Evolutionary Ecology, 1974, 4th ed. 1987; (co-ed.) Lizard Ecology: Studies of a Model Organism, 1983; Ecology and Natural History of Desert Lizards, 1986. Add: Dept. of Zoology, Univ. of Texas, Austin, Tex. 78712, U.S.A.

PICARD, Barbara Leonie. British, b. 1917. Children's fiction, Children's non-fiction, History, Mythology/Folklore. *Publs:* The Mermaid and the Simpleton, 1949; The Faun and the Woodcutter's Daughter, 1951; The Odyssey of Homer, 1952; Tales of Norse Gods and Heroes, 1953; The Lady of the Linden Tree, 1954; French Legends, Tales and Fairy Stories, 1955; Stories of King Arthur and His Knights, 1955; Ransom for a Knight, 1956; German Hero-Sagas and Folk-Tales, 1958; The Iliad of Homer, 1960; The Story of Rama and Sita, 1960; Tales of the British People, 1961; The Tower and the Traitors, 1961; Lost John, 1962; Hero Tales from the British Isles, 1963; The Goldfinch Garden, 1963; Celtic Tales, 1964; One Is One, 1965; The Young Pretenders, 1966; Twice Seven Tales, 1968; The Story of the Pandavas, 1968; Three Ancient Kings, 1972; Tales of Ancient Persia, 1972. Add: c/o Oxford Univ. Press, Walton St., Oxford, England.

PICK, John Barclay. British, b. 1921. History, Recreation/Leisure/Hobbies, Biography, Humour/Satire. Dir., J. Pick and Sons Ltd., 1957–81. *Publs:* Under the Crust, 1946; Out of the Pit, 1950; The Lonely Aren't Alone, 1952; Phoenix Dictionary of Games, 1952; 180 Games for One Player, 1954; Spectators' Handbook, 1956; (co-author) A Land Fit for Eros, 1957; The Fat Valley (in U.S. as The Last Valley), 1959; (co-author) The Strange Genius of David Lindsay, 1971; 100 Games for One Player, 1974; 100 More Games for One Player, 1976; Freedom Itself, 1979; (co-author) Neil M. Gunn: A Highland Life, 1981. Add: Hollins, Balmaclellan, Castle Douglas, Kirkcudbrightshire DG7 3QH, Scotland.

PICKARD, Tom. British, b. 1946. Poetry. Co-Founder and Mgr. of the Modern Tower Book Room, 1963–72, and the Ultima Thule Bookshop, 1969–73, Newcastle. *Publs:* High on the Walls, 1967; New Human Unisphere, 1969; An Armpit of Lice, 1970; The Order of Chance, 1971; Guttersnipe (novel), 1972; Dancing under Fire, 1973; Squire (television play), 1974; Jarrow March (radio documentary), 1976; Hero Dust: New and Selected Poems, 1979; The Jarrow March, 1982; Custom and Exile, 1985; Left Over People (TV play), 1986; We Make Ships (documentary film), 1987, as book 1989; Tell Them in Gdansk (documentary film), 1989. Add: c/o Judy Daish Assocs., 83 Eastbourne Mews, London W2 6LQ, England.

PICKER, Martin. American, b. 1929. Music. Prof. of Music, Rutgers Univ., since 1969 (Asst. Prof., 1961–65; Assoc. Prof., 1965–69). Ed.-in-Chief, Journal of the American Musicological Soc., 1969–71, and Chmn., Publications Comm., American Musicological Soc., 1976–81. *Publs:* The Chanson Albums of Marguerite of Austria, 1965; (with M.

Bernstein) An Introduction to Music, 4th ed. 1972; Fors Seulement, 1981; The Motet Books of Andrea Antico, 1987. Add: Dept. of Music, Rutgers Univ., New Brunswick, N.J. 08903, U.S.A.

PICKERING, Robert Easton. British, b. 1934. Novels/Short stories. *Publs:* Himself Again (in U.S. as The Uncommitted Man), 1966; In Transit, 1968; The Word Game, 1982. Add: 07150 Lagorce, France.

PICTON, Bernard. *See* **KNIGHT**, Bernard.

PIELMEIER, John. American, b. 1949. Plays/Screenplays. Actor, 1973–82. *Publs:* Agnes of God, 1983; Haunted Lives (A Witch's Brew, A Ghost Story, A Gothic Tale), 1984. Add: c/o Jeannine Edmunds, Artists Agency, 230 W. 55th St., New York, N.Y. 10019, U.S.A.

PIERARD, Richard V. American, b. 1934. Politics/Government, Theology/Religion. Prof. of History, Indiana State Univ., Terre Haute, since 1972 (Asst. Prof., 1964–67; Assoc. Prof., 1967–72). Member Editorial Council, Journal of Church and State, since 1989. Member, Indiana Gov.'s Advisory Commn. on Libraries and Information Services, 1980–81. *Publs:* (ed. with R.G. Clouse and R.D. Linder) Protest and Politics: Christianity and Contemporary Affairs, 1968; The Unequal Yoke: Evangelical Christianity and Political Conservatism, 1970; (ed. with R.G. Clouse and R.D. Linder) The Cross and the Flag, 1972; (with R.D. Linder) Politics: Case for Christian Action, 1973; (with R.D. Linder) Twilight of the Saints, 1978; (with R.G. Clouse) Streams of Civilization, vol. II, 1980; Bibliography on the Religious Right in America, 1986; (with R.D. Linder) Civil Religion and the Presidency, 1988. Add: Dept. of History, Indiana State Univ., Terre Haute, Ind. 47809, U.S.A.

PIERCE, Joe E. American, b. 1924. Novels/Short stories, Language/Linguistics. Prof. of Anthopology, Portland State Univ., Oregon. Exec. Ed., The HaPi Press, Portland, since 1971. Asst. Prof. of Linguistics and the English Language, Georgetown Univ., Washington, D.C., 1955–61; Prof. of English, Osaka Univ. of Education, Japan, 1967–68. *Publs:* Spoken English for Turks, 1955; Development of a Mass Literacy Program in Turkey, 1964; Life in a Turkish Village, 1964; A Linguistic Method of Teaching Second Languages, 1968; Red Runs the Earth, 1969; The Sapien Homo, 1972; A Theory of Language, Culture and Human Behavior, 1972; Shades of Minos, 1973; Languages and Linguistics, 1975; A Revolution in English Grammar, 1985. Add: 512 S.W. Maplecrest Dr., Portland, Ore. 97219, U.S.A.

PIERCE, John R(obinson). American, b. 1910. Engineering, Sciences. Visiting. Prof. of Music Emeritus, Stanford Univ., California, since 1983; Prof. of Engineering Emeritus, California Inst. of Technology, Pasadena, since 1979 (Prof. since 1971; Chief Technologist, Jet Propulsion Laboratory, 1979–82). Member of staff, Bell Telephone Lab., 1936–71: Exec. Dir., Research Communication Sciences Div., 1961–71. *Publs:* (with E.E. David) Man's World of Sound, 1958; The Beginning of Satellite Communication, 1968; Science, Art and Communication, 1968; Quantum Electronics and Waves and Messages, 1972; Almost All about Waves, 1974; Introduction to Communication Science and Systems, 1980; Signals, 1982; The Science of Musical Sound, 1983; (with Hiroshe Inose) Information Technology and civilization, 1984. Add: Dept. of Music, Stanford Univ., Calif. 94305, U.S.A.

PIERCE, Meredith Ann. American, b. 1958. Children's fiction. Library Asst., Alachua County Library District, Gainesville, Fla., since 1987. Bookseller, Bookland, 1981, and Waldenbooks, 1981–87, Gainesville. *Publs:* The Darkangel, 1983; A Gathering of Gargoyles, 1984; Birth of the Firebringer, 1985; The Woman Who Loved Reindeer, 1985; Where the Wild Geese Go, 1988; The Pearl of the Soul of the World, 1989. Add: 703 N.W. 19th St., Gainesville, Fla. 32603, U.S.A.

PIERCE, Richard Austin. American, b. 1918. History. Prof. of History, Queen's Univ., Kingston, 1959–84, now Emeritus; Prof. of History, Univ. of Alaska, Fairbanks, since 1988. Alaska History Series, Limestone Press, Kingston, since 1972. *Publs:* Russian Central Asia 1867-1917: A Study in Colonial Rule, 1960; (with A.S. Donnelly) Cities of Central Asia, 1961; (ed.) Mission to Turkestan: Being the Memoirs of Count K.K. Pahlen 1908-1909, 1964; (trans. and ed.) Russia's Hawaiian Adventure 1815-1817, 1965; (ed. with J.H. Winslow) H.M.S. Sulphur at California 1838 and 1839, 1969; (ed.) Rezanov Reconnoiters California 1806, 1972; (with G.V. Lantzeff) Eastward to Empire: Exploration and Conquest on the Russian Open Frontier to 1750, 1973; (trans. and ed. with A.S. Donnelly) A History of the Russian-American Company, by P.A. Tikhmenev, 1978; (ed.) Journals of Iakov Netsvetov: The Atkha Years 1828-1844, 1980; (ed.) Siberia and Northwestern American 1788-1792:

The Journal of Carl Heinrich Merck, 1980; (trans.) Russian-American Company Correspondence, 1984.　Add: Dept. of History; Univ. of Alaska, Fairbanks, Alaska 99775, U.S.A.

PIERCE, Roy. American, b. 1923. Politics/Government. Prof. of Political Science, Univ. of Michigan, Ann Arbor, since 1964 (Asst. Prof., 1956–59; Assoc. Prof., 1959–64). *Publs:* Contemporary French Political Thought, 1966; French Politics and Political Institutions, 1968, 1973; (with Philip E. Converse) Political Representation in France, 1986. Add: 211 McCotter Dr., Ann Arbor, Mich. 48103, U.S.A.

PIERCY, Marge. American, b. 1936. Novels/Short stories, Plays, Poetry, Essays. *Publs:* Breaking Camp (poetry), 1968; Hard Loving (poetry), 1969; (with B. Hershon, E. Jarrett and D. Lourie) 4-Telling (poetry), 1971; Going Down Fast, 1969; Dance the Eagle to Sleep, 1972; To Be of Use (poetry), 1973; Small Changes, 1973; Living in the Open (poetry), 1976; Woman on the Edge of Time, 1976; The High Cost of Living, 1978; The Twelve-Spoked Wheel Flashing (poetry), 1978; Vida, 1980; (with Ira Wood) The Last White Class (play), 1980. The Moon Is Always Female (poetry), 1980; Braided Lives, 1982; Circles on the Water (poetry), 1982; Parti-Colored Blocks for a Quilt (essays), 1982; Stone, Paper, Knife (poetry), 1983; Fly Away Home, 1984; My Mother's Body (poetry), 1985; Gone to Soldiers, 1987; Available Light (poetry), 1988. Early Ripening, 1988. Add: Box 1473, Wellfleet, Mass. 02667, U.S.A.

PIERRE, Clara. American, b. 1939. Fashion/Costume. Instr. of Journalism, New York Univ.; Member, Editorial Staff, Harper's Bazaar. Researcher, Intnl. Legal and Political Affairs, The World Law Fund, NYC, 1968–71; Member of the faculty, New Sch. for Social Research, NYC, 1977–78. *Publs:* Looking Good: The Liberation of Fashion, 1976; (coauthor) Clotheswise, 1982. Add: 697 West End Ave., New York, N.Y. 10025, U.S.A.

PIERSON, George Wilson. American, b. 1904. History, Humanities (general). Prof. Emeritus of History, Yale Univ., New Haven, since 1973 (joined faculty, 1926; Prof., 1944–46; Larned Prof. of History, 1946–73; Chmn., Dept. of History, 1956–62; Dir., Div. of the Humanities, 1964–70). *Publs:* Tocqueville and Beaumont in America, 1938; Yale College: An Educational History 1871–1921, 1952; Yale: The University College 1921–1937, 1955; Tocqueville in America, 1959; (ed.) Computers for the Humanities?: A Record of the Conference, 1965; The Education of American Leaders: Comparative Contributions of U.S. Colleges and Universities, 1969; (collaborator) Gustave de Beaumont: Lettres d'-Amerique, 1973; The Moving American, 1973; Yale: A Short History, 1976, 1979; A Yale Book of Numbers: Historical Statistics of the College and University 1701-1976, 1983; The Founding of Yale: The Legend of the Forty Folios, 1988. Add: 1691 Yale Station, New Haven, Conn. 06520, U.S.A.

PIERSON, Robert. American, b. 1911. Theology/Religion. Pres., Gen. Conference of Seventh-Day Adventists, 1966–79 (ordained minister, 1933). *Publs:* Your Bible Speaks, 1943; Wonderful Jesus, 1948; Paddles Over the Kamarang, 1953; Road to Happiness, 1948; Triumphs of the Cross, 1951; Secret of Happiness, 1958; Give Us This Day, 1959; Road to True Riches, 1965; 501 Illustrations, 1965; What Shall I Speak About?, 1966; So You Want to Be a Leader!, 1966; (co-author) Final Countdown, 1966; Faith on Tiptoe, 1967; Though the Winds Blow, 1968; Heart to Heart, 1970; (co-author) Bible Answers to Today's Questions, 1973; Faith Triumphant, 1974; We Still Believe, 1975; Angels over Elisabethville, 1975; Goodbye, Planet Earth, 1976; In Step with Jesus, 1977; Beloved Leaders, 1978; How to Be a Successful Christian Leader, 1978; What's Just Ahead, 1978; Miracles Happen Every Day, 1982; Here Comes Adventure, 1984; Love Come Home, 1987. Add: 127 Fulton Dr., Hendersonville, N.C. 28739, U.S.A.

PIET, John H. American, b. 1914. Theology/Religion. Prof. of Bible and Missions, Western Theological Seminary, Holland, Mich., 1960–84, now Emeritus; Pastor, Yokohama Union Church, since 1987. Vice-Principal, Voorhees Coll., Vellore, S. India, 1941–55; Prof. of Religion, Arcot Theological Seminary, Vellore, 1955–60. Pastor, Kathmandu, Nepal, 1984–87. *Publs:* Leaflet Evangelism, 1951; A Logical Presentation of the Saiva Siddhanta Philosophy, 1952; The Road Ahead: A Theology for the Church in Mission, 1970; The Key to the Good News, 1974; A Path Through the Bible, 1981. Add: 66 Yamate cho, Maga ku, Yokohama 231, Japan.

PIGGOTT, Alan (Derek). British, b. 1923. Recreation/Leisure/Hobbies, Autobiography/Memoirs/Personal. Chief Flying Instr., Lasham Gliding Centre, nr. Alton, Hants., since 1954. R.A.F. Pilot, 1942–53.

Publs: Gliding: A Handbook on Soaring Flight, 1958, 5th ed. 1986; Beginning Gliding, 1975; Understanding Gliding, 1977; Delta Papa: A Life of Flying (autobiography), 1977; Going Solo, 1978. Add: c/o Lasham Gliding Centre, nr. Alton, Hants., England.

PIKE, Charles R. *See* **GILMAN,** George G.

PIKE, Diane Kennedy. American, b. 1938. Supernatural/Occult topics, Theology/Religion, Autobiography/Memoirs/Personal. Writer, lectr. and group facilitator, since 1968. Co-Ed., Emerging mag. (formerly The Seeker), since 1972. Pres., Love Project, since 1972. Missionary-Teacher, United Methodist Church, Montevideo, Uruguay, 1959–62; Dir. of Youth and Children's Work, First United Methodist Church, Palo Alto, Calif., 1965–67; Pres., The Bishop Pike Foundn., 1969–72. *Publs:* (with James A. Pike) The Other Side (personal experience/parapsychology); Search (autobiography); (with R. Scott Kennedy) The Wilderness Revolt (history/religion); (with Arleen Lorrance) Channeling Love Energy: Life Is Victorious!; Cosmic Unfoldment; The Exodus Pattern; Journey into Self, Phase I, 1979; (with Arleen Lorrance) The Love Project Way; The Process of Awakening: An Overview. Add: P.O. Box 7601, San Diego, Calif. 92107, U.S.A.

PIKUNAS, Justin. American, b. 1920. Psychology. Prof. of Psychology, 1961–87, and Dir. of the Child and Family Center 1980–87, Univ. of Detroit, now Emeritus (Instr., 1951–52; Asst. Prof., 1952–56; Asst. Prof., 1956–61; Chmn., 1974–78). *Publs:* The Graphoscopic Scale: Manual, 1953, 3rd ed. 1982; Fundamental Child Psychology, 1957, 1965; Human Development: A Science of Growth, 1969, 3rd ed. 1976. Add: Dept. of Psychology, Univ. of Detroit, Detroit, Mich. 48221, U.S.A.

PILAPIL, Vicente R. Filipino-American, b. 1941. Biographer. Prof., California State Univ., Los Angeles, since 1970. Visiting Prof., Univ. of Calif., Los Angeles, 1968–69. Asst. Prof., Loyola Coll., Baltimore, 1961–64, and State Univ. of New York at Cortland, 1967–68. *Publs:* Alfonso XIII, 1969. Add: Dept. of History, California State Univ., Los Angeles, Calif. 90032, U.S.A.

PILARSKI, Laura P. American, b. 1926. Business/Trade/Industry, Children's non-fiction, Cultural/Ethnic topics. Chief Corresp., McGraw-Hill World News, Zurich, 1965–88 (freelance corresp., Poland, 1962–63); Special Corresp., McGraw-Hill Publication, since 1989. General News Reporter, Milwaukee Journal, 1949–60; Asst. to the Associated Press Corresp., Warsaw, 1962–63. *Publs:*(contrib. ed.) The Businessman's Guide to Europe, 1965; They Came from Poland (juvenile), 1969; Tibet: Heart of Asia, 1974; Pan Am's World Guide, 1976–78. Add: Kornelius-Strasse 3, 8008 Zurich, Switzerland.

PILCHER, Rosamunde. Also writes as Jane Fraser. British, b. 1924. Historical/Romance/Gothic, Plays/Screenplays. *Publs:* as Jane Fraser— Half-Way to the Moon, 1949; The Brown Fields, 1951; Dangerous Intruder, 1951; Young Bar, 1952; A Day Like Spring, 1953; Dear Tom, 1954; Bridge of Corvie, 1956; A Family Affair, 1958; A Long Way from Home, 1963; The Keeper's House, 1963; as Rosamunde Pilcher—A Secret to Tell, 1955; April, 1957; On My Own, 1965; Sleeping Tiger, 1967; Another View, 1969; The End of the Summer, 1971; Snow in April, 1972; The Empty House, 1973; The Day of the Storm, 1975; Under Gemini, 1977; Wild Mountain Thyme, 1978; The Carousel, 1981; Voices in Summer, 1984; The Blue Bedroom and Other Stories, 1985; The Shell Seekers, 1987; plays (with C.C. Gairdner)—The Piper of Orde; The Dashing White Sergeant, 1955; The Tulip Major, 1959. Add: Over Pilmore, Invergowrie, by Dundee, Scotland.

PILE, Stephen. British, b. 1949. Humour/Satire. Columnist, The Sunday Times, London, since 1980. Worked for local newspapers, 1972–75, the Times Higher Education Supplement, London, 1975–78, and the Sunday Telegraph, London, 1978–80. *Publs:* The Book of Heroic Failures, 1979. Add: c/o The Sunday Times, 1 Pennington St., London E1 9XW, England.

PILGRIM, Anne. *See* **ALLAN,** Mabel Esther.

PILGRIM, Derral. *See* **ZACHARY,** Hugh.

PILKINGTON, Francis Meredyth. British, b. 1907. Children's fiction, Mythology/Folklore. *Publs:* The Three Sorrowful Tales of Erin, 1965; Shamrock and Spear: Tales and Legends from Ireland, 1966. Add: Brookleaze, Nettlebridge, Oakhill, nr. Bath, Somerset, England.

PILKINGTON, Roger Windle. British, b. 1915. Children's non-fiction, Philosophy, Sex, Travel/Exploration/Adventure. Former research geneticist. *Publs:* Males and Females, 1948; Stringer's Folly, 1951; Biology; Man and God, 1951; Sons and Daughters, 1951; How Your Life Began, 1953; Revelation Through Science, 1954; Jan's Treasure, 1955; In the Beginning, 1955; Thames Waters, 1956; The Facts of Life, 1956; Small Boat Through Belgium, 1957; The Chesterfield Gold, 1957; The Great South Sea, 1957; The Ways of the Sea, 1957; The Missing Panel, 1958; Small Boat Through Holland, 1959; Robert Boyle: Father of Chemistry, 1959; How Boats Go Uphill, 1959; Small Boat to the Skager-rak, 1960; World Without End, 1960; The Dahlia's Cargo, 1960; Don John's Ducats, 1960; Small Boat to Sweden, 1961; Small Boat to Alsace, 1961; The Ways of the Air, 1961; Who's Who and Why, 1961; Small Boat to Bavaria, 1962; Nepomuk of the River, 1962; Boats Overland, 1962; How Boats Are Navigated, 1962; The River, 1963; (with Noel Streatfeild) Confirmation and After, 1963; Facts of Life for Parents, 1963; Small Boat to Germany, 1963; The Eisenbart Mystery, 1963; Heavens Alive, 1964; Small Boat Through France, 1964; Small Boat in Southern France, 1965; Glass, 1965; Small Boat on the Thames, 1966; The Boy from Stink Alley, 1966; Small Boat on the Meuse, 1967; Small Boat to Luxembourg, 1967; Small Boat on the Moselle, 1968; Small Boat to El-sinore, 1968; Small Boat in Northern Germany, 1969; Small Boat on the Lower Rhine, 1970; Small Boat on the Upper Rhine, 1971; Waterways in Europe, 1972; The Ormering Tide, 1974; The Face in the River, 1975; Small Boat Down the Years, 1988; Small Boat in the Midi, 1989. Add: La Maison du Coti, Mont Arthur, St. Aubin, Jersey, Channel Islands.

PILLING, Ann. Also writes as Ann Cheetham. British, b. 1944. Children's fiction. Has taught English in secondary schools. Publications officer, Federation of Children's Book Groups, 1978–81. *Publs:* (as Ann Cheetham) The Black Harvest, 1983; The Year of the Worm, 1984; (as Ann Cheetham) The Beggar's Curse, 1984; Henry's Leg, 1985; The Friday Parcel, 1986; No Guns, No Oranges, 1986; (as Ann Cheetham) The Witch of Lagg, 1986; (ed., with Anne Wood) Our Best Stories, 1986; The Big Pink, 1987; (as Ann Cheetham) The Pit, 1987; The Beast in the Basement, 1988; Dustbin Charlie, 1988; On the Lion's Side, 1988; Stan, 1988; The Big Biscuit, 1989; The Jungle Sale, 1989; Our Kid, 1989. Add: 57 St. John St., Oxford OX1 2LQ, England.

PILLING, Christopher (Robert). British, b. 1936. Poetry. Asst. in English, Ecole Normale, Moulins, France, 1957–58; French teacher, Wirral Grammar Sch., Cheshire, 1959–61, King Edward's Grammar Sch., Birmingham, 1961–62, and Ackworth Sch., Pontefract, Yorks., 1962–71, 1972–73; Head of the Dept. of Modern Languages, Knottingley High Sch., Yorkshire, 1973–78; Tutor in English, Univ. of Newcastle upon Tyne, 1978–80; Head of the French Dept., Keswick Sch., Cumbria, 1980–88. *Publs:* Snakes and Girls, 1970; Fifteen Poems, 1970; In All the Spaces on All the Lines, 1971; Wren and Owl, 1971; Andrée's Bloom and the Anemones, 1973; Light Leaves, 1975; War Photographer since the Age of 14, 1983. Add: 25 High Hill, Keswick, Cumbria CA12 5NY, England.

PIMENTEL, George C. American, b. 1922. Chemistry. Prof. of Chemistry, Univ. of California, Berkeley (joined faculty, 1949). Chmn., National Research Council Cttee. to Survey Opportunities in the Chemical Sciences, 1985. *Publs:* (with F.D. Rossini, K.S. Pitzer, R.L. Arnett and R.M. Braun) Selected Values of Physical and Thermodynamic Properties of Hydrocarbons and Related Compounds, 1953; (with A.R. Olson and C.W. Koch) Introductory Quantitative Chemistry, 1956; (with A.L. Mc-Clellan) The Hydrogen Bond, 1960; (ed.) Chemistry: An Experimental Science, 1960; (with R.D. Spratley) Understanding Chemical Ther-modynamics, 1969; (with Spratley) Chemical Bonding Clarified Through Quantum Mechanics, 1969; (with Spratley) Understanding Chemistry, 1971; (with Janice H. Coonrod) Opportunities in Chemistry, Today and Tommorrow, 1987. Add: Dept. of Chemistry, Univ. of California, Berkeley, Calif. 94720, U.S.A.

PINCHER, (Henry) Chapman. British, b. 1914. Novels/Short stories, Biology, Military/Defense, Sex, Writing/journalism. Columnist and Spe-cial Writer, Daily Express, Beaverbrook Newspapers, London, 1946–79; Fellow, King's Coll., London, 1979. *Publs:* a Breeding of Farm Animals, 1946; A Study of Fishes, 1947; Into the Atomic Age, 1947; Spotlight on Animals, 1950; Evolution, 1950; Sleep, and How to Get More of It, 1954; Not with a Bang, 1965; The Giantkiller, 1967; The Penthouse Con-spirators, 1970; Sex in Our Time, 1973; The Skeleton at the Villa Wolkonsky, 1975; The Eye of the Tornado, 1976; The Four Horses, 1978; Inside Story, 1978; Dirty Tricks (novel), 1980; Their Trade Is Treachery, 1981; The Private World of St. John Terrapin (novel), 1982; Too Secret Too Long, 1984; The Secret Offensive, 1985; Traitors, 1987; A Web of Deception, 1987. Add: Church House, Church St. Kintbury, Berks., England.

PINCHOT, Ann. American. Novels/Short stories, Medicine/Health, Biography. Sr. Ed., Trade Div., Prentice-Hall Inc., Englewood Cliffs, N.J., 1962–66. *Publs:* Hear This Woman, 1950; Hagar, 1952; 52 West, 1960; Jacqueline Kennedy, 1964; On Thin Ice, 1965; (with Lillian Gish) The Movies, Mr. Griffith and Me, 1967; The Man Chasers, 1970; Weep No More, My Lady, 1972; The Heart Doctor's Heart Book, 1974; An Independent Heart, 1976; Love Will Find Me, 1977; Vanessa, 1978; Cer-tain Rich Girls, 1979; Doctors and Wives, 1980; The Luck of the Lius-cotts, 1982; A Moment in the Sun, 1984. Add: 88 Maltbie Ave., Stamford, Conn. 06902, U.S.A.

PINE, William. *See* **GILMAN,** George G.

PINES, Maya. American. Medicine/Health, Psychology. Reporter, Life mag., NYC, 1952–60; behavior columnist, New York Times, 1982. *Publs:* (with C. Capa) Retarded Children Can Be Helped, 1957; (with R. Dubos) Health and Disease, 1965; Revolution in Learning: The Years from Birth to Six, 1967; The Brain Changers: Scientists and the New Mind Control, 1973; Inside the Cell; 1980. Add: 4701 Willard Ave., Chevy Chase, Md. 20815, U.S.A.

PINION, F(rancis) B(ertram). British, b. 1908. Literature. Formerly Reader in English Studies, Univ. of Sheffield (Lectr., 1961–68, and Sr. Lectr., 1968–73, Dept. of Education). Ed., The Thomas Hardy Society Review, 1975–84. Hon. Vice-Pres., Thomas Hardy Soc. *Publs:* (ed.) Men and Women, 1963; A Hardy Companion, 1968; (ed.) Dramatis Per-sonae, 1969; (ed.) One Rare Fair Woman, 1972; A Jane Austen Com-panion, 1973; (ed.) Thomas Hardy and the Modern World, 1974; (ed.) Two on a Tower, Short Stories, and The Famous Tragedy of the Queen of Cornwall, by Hardy, 4 vols., 1974–77; A Brontë Companion, 1975; (ed.) Budmouth Essays on Hardy, 1976; A Commentary on the Poems of Hardy, 1977; Thomas Hardy: Art and Thought, 1977; A D.H. Lawrence Companion, 1978; A George Eliot Companion, 1981; A George Eliot Mis-cellany, 1982; A Wordsworth Companion, 1984; A Tennyson Companion, 1984; A T.S. Eliot Companion, 1986; A Wordsworth Chronology, 1988; (ed. with M. Pinion) The Collected Sonnets of Charles (Tennyson) Turner, 1988; A Thomas Hardy Dictionary, 1989; Hardy the Writer, 1990. Add: 65 Ranmoor Cres., Sheffield, Yorks. S10 3GW, England.

PINKETT, Harold Thomas. American, b. 1914. History, Librarian-ship, Biography. Consultant archivist and historian, since 1979. Super-vising Archivist, 1959–71, and Chief Archivist, 1971–79, Legislative and Natural Resources Branch, National Archives, Washington, D.C.; Lectr., Dept. of History, Howard Univ., 1970–76, and American Univ., 1976–77, both Washington, D.C. Ed., Soc. of American Archivists Journal, 1968–71; Pres., Forest History Soc., 1976–78, and Agricultural Historical Soc., 1982–83. *Publs:* Gifford Pinchot, Private and Public Forester, 1970; Re-search in the Administration of Public Policy, 1975. Add: 5741 27th St. N.W., Washington, D.C. 20015, U.S.A.

PINKWATER, Daniel Manus. Also writes as Manus Pinkwater. American, b. 1941. Children's fiction, Animals/Pets. Regular commen-tator, "All Things Considered," National Public Radio. Art Instr., Children's Aid Soc., 1967–69, Lower West Side Visual Arts Center, 1969, and Henry Street Settlement, 1969, all NYC, and Bonnie Brae Farm for Boys, Millington, N.J., 1969; Asst. Project Dir., Inner City Summer Arts Prog., Hoboken, N.J., 1970. *Publs:* children's fiction—(as Manus Pinkwater) The Terrible Roar, 1970; (as Manus Pinkwater) Bear's Picture, 1972; Wizard Crystal, 1973; Magic Camera, 1974; (as Manus Pinkwater) Fat Elliot and the Gorilla, 1974; (as Manus Pinkwater) Blue Moose, 1975; (as Manus Pinkwater) Three Big Hogs, 1975; (as Manus Pinkwater) Wingman, 1975; (as Manus Pinkwater) Around Fred's Bed, 1976; Lizard Music, 1976; The Big Orange Splot, 1977; The Blue Thing, 1977; Fat Men from Space, 1977; The Hoboken Chicken Emergency, 1977; The Last Guru, 1978; Alan Mendelsohn: The Boy from Mars, 1979; Pickle Creature, 1979; Return of the Moose, 1979; Yobgorble, Mystery Monster of Lake Ontario, 1979; (with Luqman Keele) Java Jack, 1980; The Magic Moscow, 1980; The Wuggie Norple Story, 1980; Attila the Pun, 1981; Tooth-Gnasher Superflash, 1981; The Worms of Kukumlima, 1981; Roger's Umbrella, 1982; Slaves of Spiegel, 1982; The Snarkout Boys and the Avocado of Death, 1982; Young Adult Novel, 1982; I Was a Second Grade Werewolf, 1983; Devil in the Drain, 1984; Ducks!, 1984; The Snarkout Boys and the Baconburg Horror, 1984; The Frankenbagel Monster, 1986; The Moosepire, 1986; The Muffin Fiend, 1986; Aunt Lulu, 1988; Guys from Space, 1989; Uncle Melvin, 1989; other—(with Jill Pinkwater) Superpuppy: How to Choose, Raise, and Train the Best Pos-sible Dog for You, 1977. Add: c/o Susan Cohen, Writers House Inc., 21 W. 26th St., New York, N.Y. 10010, U.S.A.

PINKWATER, Manus, *See* **PINKWATER,** Daniel Manus.

PINNER, David. British, b. 1940. Novels/Short stories, Plays/Screenplays. Professional actor. *Publs:* Fanghorn (play), 1966; Ritual (novel), 1967; Dickon (play), 1967; With My Body (novel), 1968; The Drums of Snow (play), 1968; Shakebag (play), 1976; The Potsdam Quartet (play), 1980; There'll Always Be an England (novel), 1984. Add: 18 Leconfield Ave., London SW13, England.

PINSKER, Sanford S. American, b. 1941. Poetry, Literature. Prof. of English, Franklin and Marshall Coll., Lancaster, since 1967. *Publs:* The Schlemiel as Metaphor; Still Life (poetry); The Languages of Joseph Conrad; The Comedy That Hoits: An Essay on the Fiction of Philip Roth; Between Two Words: The American Novel in the 1960's; Memory Breaks Off (poetry); Conversations with Contemporary American Writers, 1985; Whales at Play (poetry), 1987. Add: 700 N. Pine St., Lancaster, Pa. 17604, U.S.A.

PINSKY, Robert. American, b. 1940. Poetry, Literature. Prof. of English, Univ. of California, Berkeley, since 1980. Poetry Ed., New Republic, Washington, D.C., since 1978. Asst. Prof. of Humanities, Univ. of Chicago, 1967–68; Prof. of English, Wellesley Coll., Massachusetts, 1968–80. *Publs:* Landor's Poetry, 1968; Sadness and Happiness (verse), 1975; The Situation of Poetry: Contemporary Poetry and Its Traditions, 1976; An Explanation of America (verse), 1979; (with others) Five American Poets, 1979; History of My Heart, 1984; Poetry and the World, 1988. Add: Dept. of English, Univ. of California, Berkeley, Calf. 94720, U.S.A.

PINSON, William M(eredith), Jr. American, b. 1934. Human relations, Social commentary/phenomena, Theology/Religion. Exec. Dir., Baptist Gen. Convention of Texas, since 1982. Prof. of Christian Ethics, Southwestern Baptist Theological Seminary, Ft. Worth, Tex., 1963–75; Pastor, First Baptist Church, Wichita Falls, Tex., 1975–77; Pres., Golden Gate Theological Seminary, Mill Valley, Calif., 1977–82. *Publs:* Ambassadors and Christian Citizenship, 1963; How to Deal with Controversial Issues, 1966; Resource Guide to Current Social Issues, 1968; No Greater Challenge, 1969; (with T.B. Maston) Right or Wrong, 1971; (with C.E. Fant) Twenty Centuries of Great Preaching, 13 vols., 1971; A Program of Application for the Local Church, 1972; (with B. Glass) Don't Blame the Game, 1972; (with C.E. Fant) Contemporary Christian Trends, 1972; The Local Church in Ministry, 1973; The Five Worlds of Youth, 1974; (co-author) Growing Disciples Through Preaching, 1976; Families with Purpose, 1978; Introduction to Christian Ethics, 1979; The Biblical View of the Family, 1981; World Topical Bible, 1981; Ready to Minister, 1984. Add: 333 N. Washington, Dallas, Tex. 75246, U.S.A.

PINTER, Harold. British, b. 1930. Plays/Screenplays, Poetry. Professional actor, 1949–60, also a director: Assoc. Dir., National Theatre, London, 1973–83. *Publs:* The Birthday Party, 1958, 1965; The Caretaker, 1960; The Birthday Party and Other Plays, 1960, in U.S. as The Birthday Party, and The Room (includes The Dumb Waiter), 1961; A Slight Ache and The Dumb Waiter, 1961; Three Plays: A Slight Ache, The Collection, The Dwarfs, 1962; The Collection, 1962; The Collection, and The Lover, 1963, The Lover published separately, 1965; Tea Party, 1965, 1968; The Homecoming, 1965, 1968; The Dwarfs and Eight Revue Sketches, 1965; Tea Party and Other Plays, 1967; The Lover, The Tea Party, The Basement, 1967; Mac, 1968; Landscape, 1968; Landscape and Silence (includes Night), 1969; Five Screenplays, 1971; Old Times, 1971; Monologue, 1973; No Man's Land, 1975; Plays, 3 vols., 1975–78; The Proust Screenplay: A La Recherche du Temps Perdu, 1977; Poems and Prose 1949-1977, 1978; Betrayal, 1978; I Know the Place (poetry), 1979; The Hothouse, 1980; Family Voices, 1981; The French Lieutenant's Woman and Other Screenplays, 1981; Other Places (Family Voices, Victoria Station, A Kind of Alaska), 1982; One for the Road, 1985; Collected Poems and Prose, 1986; Modern Language, 1988; The Heat of the Day, 1989; Reunion and Other Screenplays, 1990. Add: c/o Judy Daish Assocs., 83 Eastbourne Mews, London W2 6LQ, England.

PINTO, Jacqueline. Wrote as Jacqueline Blairman before 1957. British, b. 1927. Children's fiction, Children's non-fiction. Formerly, Sub-Ed., Homes and Gardens mag. *Publs:* (as Jacqueline Blairman) Headmistress in Disgrace; (as Jacqueline Blairman) Rebel at St. Agatha's; (as Jacqueline Blairman with M. Biggs) Triplets at Royders; Moses Mendelssohn, 1960; School Dinner Disaster, 1983; School Gala Disaster, 1985; School Library Disaster, 1986; School Outing Disaster, 1987; School Donkey Disaster, 1988. Add: 89 Uphill Rd., Mill Hill, London NW7 4QD, England.

PIPES, Richard. American, b. 1923. History, Intellectual history, International relations/Current affairs, Biography. Prof. of History since 1963, and currently Frank B. Baird Jr. Prof. of History, Harvard Univ., Cambridge, Mass. (joined faculty, 1950; Dir., Russian Research Center, 1968–73). Sr. Research Consultant, Stanford Research Inst., Washington, D.C., 1973–78; Dir., East European and Soviet Affairs, National Security Council, 1981–82. *Publs:* Formation of the Soviet Union, 1954, 1964; Karamzin's Memoir on Ancient and Modern Russia, 1959; (ed.) Russian Intelligentsia, 1961; Social Democracy and the St. Petersburg Labor Movement 1885-1897, 1963; (ed.) Revolutionary Russia, 1967; Europe since 1815, 1968; Struve: Liberal on the Left 1870-1905, 1970; (ed.) Collected Works of P.B. Struve, 15 vols., 1970; Russia under the Old Regime, 1974; Soviet Strategy in Europe, 1976; Struve: Liberal on the Right 1905-1944, 1980; U.S.-Soviet Relations in the Era of Detente, 1981; Survival Is Not Enough, 1984. Add: Dept. of History, Harvard Univ., Cambridge, Mass. 02138, U.S.A.

PIRIE, David (Tarbat). British, b. 1946. Novels/Short stories, Plays/Screenplays, Film. Film Critic, Options, since 1982. Film Critic, Time Out mag., London, 1974–81; Film Critic, BBC Radio 4, BBC World Service, and Capital Radio, 1976–81. *Publs:* Roger Corman: The Millennic Vision, 1970; A Heritage of Horror, 1973; The Vampire Cinema, 1977; Novels and Novelists, 1980; Mystery Story (novel), 1980; Anatomy of the Movies, 1981; filmscripts—Mystery Story, 1982; Rainy Day Women, 1983; Total Eclipse of the Heart, 1984; Love-Act, 1985; Wild Things (BBC film), 1986; Never Come Back (BBC serial), 1988. Add: c/o BBC Publications, 80 Wood Lane, London W12 0TT, England.

PISERCHIA, Doris (Elaine). Also writes as Curt Selby. American, b. 1928. Science fiction/Fantasy. *Publs:* Mister Justice, 1973; Star Rider, 1974; A Billion Days of Earth, 1976; Earthchild, 1977; Spaceling, 1978; The Spinner, 1980; The Fluger 1980; Earth in Twilight, 1981; Doomtime, 1981; (as Curt Selby) Blood County, 1981; (as Curt Selby) I, Zombie, 1982; The Dimensioneers, 1982; The Deadly Sky, 1983. Add: c/o DAW Books, New American Library, P.O. Box 120, Bergenfield, N.J. 07621, U.S.A.

PITCHER, George. American, b. 1925. Philosophy. Emeritus Prof. of Philosophy, Princeton Univ., New Jersey, since 1981 (Instr., 1956–60; Asst. Prof., 1960–63; Assoc. Prof., 1963–70; Prof., 1970–81). *Publs:* (ed.) Truth, 1964; The Philosophy of Wittgenstein, 1964; (ed.) Wittgenstein: A Collection of Critical Essays, 1966; (ed. with O.P. Wood) Ryle, 1970; A Theory of Perception, 1971; Berkeley, 1977; A Life of Grace, 1987. Add: 18 College Rd. West, Princeton, N.J. 08540, U.S.A.

PITCHER, Harvey John. British, b. 1936. Area studies, Literature. Asst. Lectr. in Russian, Glasgow Univ., 1961–63; Lectr. in Russian, Univ. of St. Andrews, 1963–71. *Publs:* Understanding the Russians, 1964; (ed.) Everyday Russian: A Reader, 1966; (ed.) N.V. Gogol: The Tale of How Ivan Ivanovich Quarrelled with Ivan Nikiforovich, 1970; The Chekhov Play: A New Interpretation, 1973; (trans. with James Forsyth) Chuckle with Chekhov, 1975; When Miss Emmie Was in Russia, 1977; Chekhov's Leading Lady, 1979; (trans. with Patrick Miles) Chekhov: The Early Stories (1883-88), 1982; The Smiths of Moscow, 1984; Lily: An Anglo-Russian Romance, 1987. Add: 37 Bernard Rd., Cromer, Norfolk, England.

PITCHFORD, Kenneth S(amuel). American, b. 1931. Poetry. Freelance editor, NYC. Member, Dept. of English, New York Univ., 1958–62; Assoc. Ed., The New Intnl. Yearbook, NYC, 1960–66. *Publs:* The Blizzard Ape: Poems, 1958; A Suite of Angels and Other Poems, 1967; Color Photos of the Atrocities: Poems, 1973; (trans.) The Sonnets to Orpheus, by Rilke, 1981. Add: c/o Purchase Press, P.O. Box 5, Harrison, N.Y. 10528, U.S.A.

PITRONE, Jean Maddern. American, b. 1920. Biography. Editorial Assoc., Writers' Digest Sch., Cincinnati, since 1967. *Publs:* Trailblazer: Negro Nurse in the American Red Cross; The Touch of His Hand; Chavez: Man of the Migrants; Myra: The Life and Times of Myra Wolfgang, Trade-Union Leader, 1980; The Dodges: The Auto Family, Fortune and Misfortune, 1981; Jean Hoxie: The Robin Hood of Tennis, 1985; Hudson's: Hub of America's Heartland, 1989; Tangled Web: Legacy of Auto Pioneer John F. Dodge, 1989. Add: 3878 Pare Lane, Trenton, Mich. 48183, U.S.A.

PITT, Barrie (William Edward). British, b. 1918. History. Military service, Europe and Middle East, 1939–46; Surveyor, England, 1946–60; Information Officer, U.K. Atomic Energy Authority, 1960–63; Historical Adviser, "The Great War," BBC-TV, 1963–64; Ed., Purnell's History of the Second World War, and Purnell's History of the First World War, 1964–70; Ed.-in-Chief, Ballantine's Illustrated History of the Violent Century, 1968–75. *Publs:* Zeebrugge: St. George's Day 1918, 1958; The Edge of Battle (novel), 1958; Coronel and Falkland, 1960; 1918: The Last Act, 1962; The Battle of the Atlantic, 1979; The Crucible of War: Western Desert 1941, 1980; Churchill and the Generals, 1981; The Crucible of War: 1942, Year of Alamein, 1982; Special Boat Squadron, 1983; (with Francis Pitt) The Chronological Atlas of World War II, 1989. Add: Fitzhead Ct., Fitzhead, Taunton, Somerset TA4 3JP, England.

PITT, David Charles. New Zealander, b. 1938. Anthropology/Ethnology, Sociology. Consultant, Intnl. Union for the Conservation of Nature, since 1976; Chargé de Recherches, Inst. Intnl. de recherches pour la paix, Geneva, since 1984. Asst. Prof. of Anthropology and Sociology, Univ. of Victoria, B.C., 1965–67; Prof. of Sociology, Univ. of Waikato, 1968–71, and Univ. of Auckland, 1971–79. Consultant, Intnl. Labour Org., 1968–70, Unesco, 1970–71, and World Health Org., 1979–83. *Publs:* Tradition and Economic Progress, 1970; Historical Documents in Anthropology and Sociology, 1972; (with C. MacPherson) Emerging Pluralism, 1974; Development from Below, 1976; Social Dynamics of Development, 1976; (with G. Sterky) Child Labour and Health, 1981; (with J. McNeely) Culture and Conservation, 1984; (with T. Weiss) The United Nations Bureaucracy, 1986; (with G. Thompson) Nuclear Free Zones, 1987; (with S. Bricens) New Ideas in Environmental Education, 1988; (with J. Ives) Deforestation, 1988; The Future of the Environment, 1988; (with P. Turner) The Anthropology of War and Peace, 1989; The Dying Mountains, 1989; AIDS and Society, 1989. Add: IUCN, 1196 Glard, Switzerland.

PITTENGER, (W.) Norman. American, b. 1905. History, Philosophy, Theology/Religion, Biography. Member of the Divinity Faculty, Cambridge Univ., since 1966, and Sr. Resident, King's Coll., Cambridge, since 1966. Prof., General Seminary, NYC, 1933–66. *Publs:* Approach to Christianity, 1939; Christ and Christian Faith, 1941; Christian Belief and Practice, 1942; (with B.I. Bell) Life of Jesus, 1943; Stewards of the Mystery of Christ, 1945; His Body the Church, 1946; The Divine Action, 1946; Living Faith, 1946; Sacraments, Signs, Symbols, 1949; (with T.S.K. Scott-Craig) The College Militant, 1949; Historic Faith and Changing World, 1950; The Christian Sacrifice, 1951; (with J.A. Pike) Faith of the Church, 1952; Christ in the Haunted Wood, 1953; (with J.V. Butler) What Is Priesthood?, 1954; Christian View of Sexual Behavior, 1954; Theology and Reality, 1954; Christian Affirmations, 1954; Principles and Practice, 1955; Rethinking the Christian Message, 1956; Tomorrow's Faith Today, 1956; Church, Ministry, Reunion, 1957; Episcopal Way of Life, 1957; The Word Incarnate, 1959; Pathway to Believing, 1960; Proclaiming Christ Today, 1962; Christian Understanding of Human Nature, 1964; Love Is the Clue, 1967; Time for Consent, 1967; God in Process, 1967; Life of Jesus Christ, 1968; Reconception in Christian Thinking, 1968; Life Light Love, 1968; Life of St. Paul, 1968; Process Thought and Christian Faith, 1968; Martin Luther, 1969; Whitehead, 1969; Thomas Aquinas, 1969; God's Way with Men, 1969; The Christian Situation, 1969; Henry VIII of England, 1970; Richard the Lion-Hearted, 1970; Goodness Distorted, 1970; Christology Reconsidered, 1970; Last Things in Christian Perspective, 1970; Making Sexuality Human, 1970; St. Peter, 1971; Plato, 1971; Early Britain, 1972; Christian Church as Social Process, 1972; Life in Christ, 1972; Trying to Be Christian, 1972; Life as Eucharist, 1973; Christian Faith and the Question of History, 1973; Love and Control in Human Sexuality, 1974; A Vision and a Way, 1974; Praying Today, 1974; The Holy Spirit, 1974; The Divine Trinity, 1977; Cosmic Love and Human Wrong, 1978; Loving Says It All, 1978; The Lure of Divine Love, 1979; After Death: Life in God, 1980; Abounding Love, 1981; Catholic Faith in a Process Perspective, 1981; The Meaning of Being Human, 1982; Picturing God, 1982; Ministry of All Christians, 1983; Preaching the Gospel, 1984; Passion and Perfection, 1985; Before the Ending of the Day, 1985; The Pilgrim Church, 1986; Freed to Love, 1987; Becoming and Belonging, 1989. Add: King's Coll., Cambridge, England.

PITTER, Ruth. British, b. 1897. Poetry. Painter for Walberswick Peasant Pottery Co., Suffolk, 1918–30; Partner, Deane and Forester, London, from 1930; now retired. *Publs:* First Poems, 1920; First and Second Poems 1912-1925, 1927; Persephone in Hades, 1931; A Mad Lady's Garland, 1934; A Trophy of Arms: Poems 1926-1935, 1936; The Spirit Watches, 1939; The Rude Potato, 1941; Poem, 1943; The Bridge: Poems 1939-1944, 1945; Pitter on Cats, 1947; Urania, 1950; The Ermine: Poems 1942-1952, 1953; Still by Choice, 1966; Poems 1926-1966 (in U.S. as Collected Poems), 1968; End of Drought, 1975. Add: The Hawthorns, Chilton Rd., Long Crendon, Aylesbury, Bucks., England.

PITTOCK, Joan (Hornby). British, b. 1930. Literature. Sr. Lectr. in English, Univ. of Aberdeen, since 1978 (Asst. Lectr., and Lectr., 1966–78): Member, Editorial Bd., British Journal for 18th Century Studies, since 1980 (Founder Ed., 1978–80). Pres., British Soc. for 18th Century Studies, 1980–82. *Publs:* The Ascendancy of Taste, 1973; (ed.) Joseph Warton: Odes on Various Subjects 1746, 1977; (ed.) George Hardinge: Rowley and Chatterton in the Shades 1782, 1979; (ed. with J.J. Carter) Aberdeen and the Enlightenment, 1987. Add: Dept. of English, Univ. of Aberdeen, Taylor Bldg., King's Coll., Old Aberdeen AB9 2UB, Scotland.

PIZER, Vernon. American, b. 1918. History, Sciences. Freelance writer. *Publs:* Rockets, Missiles and Space, 1962; (with W.R. Anderson) The Useful Atom, 1966; The World Ocean, 1967; The United States Army, 1967; Glorious Triumphs, 1968; Ink, Ark, and All That, 1976; You Don't Say, 1978; Short Changed by History, 1979; Take My Word for It, 1981; Eat the Grapes Downward, 1983; The Irrepressible Automobile, 1986. Add: 2206 Newbern Dr., Valdosta, Ga. 31602, U.S.A.

PLAGEMANN, Bentz. American, b. 1913. Novels/Short stories, Historical/Romance/Gothic, Children's non-fiction, Autobiography/Memoirs/Personal. Worked in bookstores in Cleveland, Chicago, Detroit, and New York, 1932–42; Instr. in Journalism, New York Univ., 1946–47. *Publs:* William Walter, 1941; All for the Best, 1946; Into the Labyrinth, 1948, in U.S. paperback as Downfall, 1952, 2nd U.S. paperback ed. as The Sin Underneath, 1956; My Place to Stand (autobiography), 1949; This Is Gogle; or, The Education of a Father (in U.K. as My Son Goggle), 1955; The Steel Cocoon, 1958; Half the Fun, 1961; Father to the Man, 1964; The Best Is Yet To Be, 1966; The Heart of Silence, 1967; A World of Difference, 1969; This Happy Place: Living the Good Life in America (reminiscences), 1970; How to Write a Story (juvenile), 1971; The Boxwood Maze (gothic novel), 1972; Wolfe's Cloister (gothic novel), 1974. Lives in Palisades, N.Y. Add: c/o Harold Matson Co., 276 Fifth Ave., New York, N.Y. 10001, U.S.A.

PLAIDY, Jean. *See* **HOLT,** Victoria.

PLAIN, Belva. American, b. 1918. Novels/Short stories. *Publs:* Evergreen, 1978; Random Winds, 1980; Eden Burning, 1982; Crescent City, 1984; The Golden Cup, 1986; Tapestry, 1988. Add: c/o Delacorte Press, 1 Dag Hammarskjold Plaza, 245 E. 47th St., New York, N.Y. 10017, U.S.A.

PLANO, Jack Charles. American, b. 1921. Institutions/Organizations, International relations/Current affairs. Prof. of Political Science since 1952, Chmn. of Dept. since 1979, and Ed. of New Issues Press, Western Michigan Univ., Kalamazoo. Visiting Fellow, Univ. of Sussex, Brighton, 1971–72. *Publs:* The United Nations and the India-Pakistan Dispute, 1966; (with M. Greenberg) The American Political Dictionary, 1962, 8th ed. 1989; (with R.E. Riggs) Forging World Order, 1967, 1971; (with R. Olton) The International Relations Dictionary, 1969, 4th ed. 1988; (with R.E. Riggs) Dictionary of Political Analysis, 1973, rev. ed., with R.E. Riggs and H.S. Robin, 1982; (with M. Greenberg, R. Olton and R.E. Riggs) Political Science Dictionary, 1973; International Approaches to the Problems of Marine Pollution; (with Ernest E. Rossi) The Latin American Political Dictionary, 1980; (with R. Chandler) The Public Administration Dictionary, 1982, 1988; (with R.E. Riggs) The United Nations, 1988. Add: Dept. of Political Science, Western Michigan Univ., Kalamazoo, Mich. 49001, U.S.A.

PLANTE, David (Robert). American, b. 1940. Novels/Short stories, Translations. Henfield Fellow, Univ. of East Anglia, Norwich, 1976; Writer-in-Residence, King's Coll., Cambridge, 1984–85. *Publs:* (trans. with N. Stangos) Argo; or, The Voyage of a Balloon, by A. Embiricos, 1967; The Ghost of Henry James, 1970; Slides, 1971; Relatives, 1972; The Darkness of the Body, 1974; Figures in Bright Air, 1976; The Family, 1978; The Country, 1980; The Woods, 1982; Difficult Women, 1983; The Foreigner, 1984; The Catholic, 1985; The Native, 1987. Add: c/o Deborah Rogers Agency, 20 Powis Mews, London W11 1JN, England.

PLANTINGA, Alvin (Carl). American. Philosophy, Theology/Religion. Prof. of Philosophy, Univ. of Notre Dame, Ind., since 1982. Prof. of Philosophy, Calvin Coll., Grand Rapids, 1963–82. *Publs:* (ed.) Faith and Philosophy, 1963; (ed.) The Ontological Argument, 1965; God and Other Minds, 1967; The Nature of Necessity, 1974; God, Freedom, and Evil, 1974; Does God Have a Nature?, 1980; (ed. with Nicholas Wolterstorff) Faith and Rationality, 1983. Add: Dept. of Philosophy, Univ. of Notre Dame, Notre Dame, Ind. 46556, U.S.A.

PLANZ, Allen. American, b. 1937. Poetry, Natural history. Formerly taught at Hunter Coll., NYC, Univ. of North Carolina, Chapel Hill, and Queens Coll., NYC; Poetry Ed., The Nation, NYC, 1969–70. *Publs:* Poor White and Other Poems, 1964; Heir to Anger, 1965; Studsong, 1968; A Night of Rioting, 1969; American Wilderness, 1970; Wild Craft, 1975. Add: Box 212, East Hampton, N.Y. 11937, U.S.A.

PLATER, Alan (Frederick). British, b. 1935. Novels, Children's fiction, Plays/Screenplays. Qualified as an architect, 1961; regular contributor to The Architects' Journal, London, and Yorkshire Post, Leeds, 1959–63. Founder-Member, Hull Arts Centre, 1970. *Publs:* (adaptor) Close the Coalhouse Door, 1969; You and Me: Four Plays, 1973; The Trouble with Abracadabra (juvenile), 1975; The Fosdyke Saga, 1976; The Beiderbecke Affair (novel), 1985; The Beiderbecke Tapes (novel), 1986; Misterioso, 1987. Add: c/o Margaret Ramsay Ltd., 14a Goodwin's Ct., London WC2N 4LL, England.

PLATT, Charles. British, b. 1944. Science fiction/Fantasy, Poetry. Freelance writer, mainly of science fiction short stories, photographer, and book jacket designer. Formerly worked for Clive Bingley publrs., London; Designer and Production Asst., New Worlds mag., London. *Publs:* The Garbage World, 1967; The City Dwellers, 1970, in U.S. as Twilight of the City, 1977; (with Thomas M. Disch and Marilyn Hacker) Highway Sandwiches (poetry), 1970; The Gas (poetry), 1970; Planet of the Voles, 1971; (ed. with Michael Moorcock) New Worlds 6, 1973, in U.S. as New Worlds 5, 1974; (ed. with Hilary Bailey) New Worlds 7, 1974, in U.S. as New Worlds 6, 1975; Sweet Evil, 1977; Dream Makers: The Uncommon People Who Write Science Fiction, 1980; Free Zone, 1989. Add: c/o Gollancz, 14 Henrietta St., London WC2E 8QJ, England.

PLATT, Colin. British, b. 1934. Archaeology/Antiquities, History. Prof. of History, Univ. of Southampton, since 1983 (Lectr., 1964–74; Sr. Lectr., 1974–79; Reader, 1979–83). Lectr. in Archaeology, Leeds Univ., 1962–64. *Publs:* The Monastic Grange in Medieval England, 1969; Medieval Southampton: The Port and Trading Community, 1973; (with R. Coleman-Smith) Excavations in Medieval Southampton, 2 vols., 1975; The English Medieval Town, 1976; Medieval England, 1978; The Atlas of Medieval Man, 1979; The Parish Churches of Medieval England, 1981; The Castle in Medieval England and Wales, 1982; The Abbeys and Priories of Medieval England, 1984; Medieval Britain from the Air, 1984; Traveller's Guide to Medieval England, 1985; National Trust Guide to Late Medieval and Renaissance Britain, 1986. Add: Dept. of History, Univ. of Southampton, Southampton SO9 5NH, England.

PLATT, Eugene (Robert). American, b. 1939. Poetry. Writer/Ed., U.S. Commission on Civil Rights, Washington, D.C., since 1979. Asst. to the Vice-Pres. for Student Affairs, Clarion State Coll., Pennsylvania, 1970–76; with the Bureau of Indian Affairs, Washington, D.C., 1976–78; Writer/Ed., New Orleans Continental Shelf Office, 1978–79. Poetry Ed., Sandlapper: The Mag. of South Carolina, 1974–78. *Publs:* Coffee and Solace, 1970; Six of One/Half Dozen of the Other, 1971; Allegheny Reveries, 1972; (ed.) A Patrick Kavanagh Anthology, 1973; An Original Sin, 1974; (ed.) Don't Ask Me Why I Write These Things, 1974; South Carolina Line, 1980; (ed.) An Outer Banks Anthology, 1981. Add: 6907 Kincaid Ave., Falls Church, Va. 22042, U.S.A.

PLAUT, W. Gunther. American/Canadian, b. 1912. Novels/Short stories, History, Theology/Religion, Autobiography/Memoirs/Personal. Sr. Scholar, Holy Blossom Temple, Toronto, since 1978 (Sr. Rabbi, 1961–77). Past Pres., Canadian Jewish Congress and Central Conference of American Rabbis. *Publs:* Die materielle Eheungultigkeit im deutschen und schweizerischen internationalen Privatrecht, 1935; Mount Zion: The First Hundred Years, 1956; The Jews in Minnesota, 1959; The Book of Proverbs: A Commentary, 1961; Judaism and the Scientific Spirit, 1962; The Rise of Reform Judaism, 1963; The Case for the Chosen People: The Role of the Jewish People Yesterday and Today, 1965; The Growth of Reform Judaism, 1965; Your Neighbor Is a Jew, 1967; Page Two: Ten Years of "News and Views", 1971; Genesis: A Modern Commentary, 1974; Time to Think, 1977; Hanging Threads, 1978, in U.S. as The Man in the Blue Vest and Other Stories, 1980; Numbers: A Commentary, 1979; Exodus: A Commentary, 1980; The Torah: A Modern Commentary, 1981; Unfinished Business (autobiography), 1981; The Letter, 1986; The Man Who Would Be Messiah 1988; The Magen David: How the Star of David Became the Jewish Symbol, 1989. Add: 1950 Bathurst St., Toronto, Ont. M5P 3K9, Canada.

PLEASANTS, Ben. American, b. 1940. Plays/Screenplays, Poetry. Teacher of special education, Los Angeles City Schs., since 1968. Writer, Los Angeles Free Press; Poetry Contrib., Los Angeles Times

(Reviewer, 1968–69). *Publs:* The Gluttons (play), 1968; 53 Stations, 1973; Transcontinental, 1974; Winter in Mongolia (play), 1975. Add: 321 S. Doheny, Beverly Hills, Calif. 90211, U.S.A.

PLEASANTS, Henry. American, b. 1910. Music. London Music Critic, International Herald Tribune, and London Ed., Stereo Review, NYC, since 1967. Music Critic, Philadelphia Evening Bulletin, 1930–42; Central European Music Corresp., New York Times, 1945–55. *Publs:* (trans. and ed.) Vienna's Golden Years of Music: A Selection from the Music Criticism of Eduard Hanslick, 1950; The Agony of Modern Music, 1955; Death of a Music?, 1961; (trans. and ed.) The Musical Journeys of Louis Spohr, 1961; (trans. and ed.) The Musical World of Robert Schumann, 1965; The Great Singers—From the Dawn of Opera to Our Own Time, 1966; Serious Music—And All That Jazz, 1969; The Great American Popular Singers, 1974; (trans. and ed.) The Music Criticism of Hugo Wolf, 1979. Add: 95 Roebuck House, London SW1E 5BE, England.

PLIMPTON, George (Ames). American, b. 1927. Children's fiction, History, Literature, Sports, Autobiography/Memoirs/Personal, Biography, Humor/Satire. Principal Ed., Paris Review, since 1953. Contrib. Ed., Sports Illustrated mag., NYC, since 1967. Instr., Barnard Coll., NYC, 1959–61; Advisor on John F. Kennedy Oral History Project. *Publs:* The Rabbit's Umbrella (juvenile), 1955; (ed.) Writers at Work: The Paris Review Interviews, 7 vols., 1957–86; Out of My League (baseball), 1961; Paper Lion (football), 1966; The Bogey man (golf), 1968; (co-ed.) The American Literary Anthology, 3 vols., 1968–70; (ed.) American Journey: The Life and Times of Robert Kennedy, by Jean Stein, 1970; (with Alex Karras and John Gordy) Mad Ducks and Bears, 1973; One for the Record: The Inside Story of Hank Aaron's Chase for the Home-Run Record, 1974; One More July (football), 1976; Shadow Box (boxing), 1976; (with Neil Leifer) Sports!, 1978; (with Jean Stein) Edie: An American Biography, 1982; (with Arnold Roth) A Sports Bestiary, 1982; (ed.) D.V.: The Memoirs of Diana Vreeland, 1984; Fireworks: A History and Celebration, 1984; Open Net (hockey), 1985; Curious Case of Sidd Finch, 1987. Add: 541 E. 72nd St., New York, N.Y. 10021, U.S.A.

PLISCHKE, Elmer. American, b. 1914. International relations/Current affairs, Politics/Government. Prof. of Govt. and Politics Emeritus, Univ. of Maryland, College Park, since 1979 (Asst. Prof., 1948–49; Assoc. Prof., 1949–52; Prof, since 1952; Head, Dept. of Govt. and Politics, 1954–68); Adjunct Scholar, American Enterprise Inst., since 1978. Asst. Prof., DePauw Univ., Greencastle, Ind., 1946–48; Adjunct Prof., Gettysburg Coll., Pennsylvania, 1979–85. *Publs:* Conduct of American Diplomacy, 1950, 3rd ed. 1967; (with R.G. Dixon) American Government: Basic Documents and Materials, 1950; Berlin: Development of Its Government and Administration, 1952; International Relations: Basic Documents, 1953, 1962; American Foreign Relations: A Bibliography of Official Sources, 1955; American Diplomacy: A Bibliography of Biographies, Autobiographies, and Commentaries, 1957; Summit Diplomacy: Personal Diplomacy of the President of the United States, 1958; Contemporary Governments of Germany, 1961, 1969; Government and Politics of Contemporary Berlin, 1963; (ed. and contrib.) Systems of Integrating the International Community, 1964; Foreign Relations Decision-Making: Options Analysis, 1973; United States Diplomats and Their Missions: A Profile of American Diplomatic Emissaries since 1778, 1975; Microstates in World Affairs: Policy Problems and Options, 1977; Modern Diplomacy: The Art and the Artisans, 1979; U.S. Foreign Relations: A Guide to Information Sources, 1980; Diplomat in Chief: The President at the Summit, 1986; Presidential Diplomacy: Summit Visits, Trips and Meetings, 1986; Foreign Relations: Analysis of Its Anatomy, 1988; Contemporary United States Foreign Policy: Documents and Commentary, 1989. Add: 227 Ewell Ave., Gettysburg, Pa. 17325, U.S.A.

PLOWDEN, Alison (Margaret Chichele). British, b. 1931. History, Documentaries/Reportage. Former member of Staff, Features Dept., then Drama Dept. (Radio), BBC, London. *Publs:* The Young Elizabeth, 1971; As They Saw Them: Elizabeth I, 1971; Mistress of Hardwick (from BBC TV series), 1972; Danger to Elizabeth, 1973; The Case of Eliza Armstrong (from BBC TV series), 1974; The House of Tudor, 1976; Marriage with My Kingdom, 1977; Tudor Women, 1979; Elizabeth Regina, 1980; The Young Victoria, 1981; Elizabethan England: Life in an Age of Adventure, 1982; Two Queens in One Isle, 1984; Lords of the Land, 1984; Lady Jane Grey and the House of Suffolk, 1985; Caroline and Charlotte: The Regent's Wife and Daughter, 1988. Add: c/o John Johnson, 45-47 Clerkenwell Green, London EC1R 0HT, England.

PLOWDEN, David. American, b. 1932. Photography. Writer and photographer since 1962; Lectr., Sch. of Journalism and Mass Communications, Univ. of Iowa, Iowa City, since 1984. Visiting Assoc. Prof., 1978–80, and Assoc. Prof., 1980–86, Inst. of Design, Illinois Inst. of Technology, Chicago. *Publs:* (all self-illustrated) Farewell to Steam, 1965; (ed.) Lincoln and His America 1809-1865, 1970; The Hand of Man on America, 1971; The Floor of the Sky: The Great Plains, 1972; Commonplace, 1974; Bridges: The Spans of North America, 1974; Tugboat, 1976; Steel, 1981; An American Chronology: Photographs of David Plowden, 1982; Industrial Landscape, 1985; A Time of Trains, 1987. Add: c/o W. W. Norton, 500 Fifth Ave., New York, N.Y. 10110, U.S.A.

PLOWMAN, Edward E. American, b. 1931. Theology/Religion. Sr. Ed., Christianity Today, since 1978 (News Ed., 1970–78). Former Youth Minister, First Baptist Church, National City, Calif.; Sr. Minister, Park Presidio Baptist Church, San Francisco. *Publs:* The Jesus Movement in America, 1971; Washington: Christians in the Corridors of Power, 1976. Add: 1014 Washington Bldg., Washington, D.C. 20005, U.S.A.

PLOWMAN, Stephanie. British, b. 1922. Children's fiction. Formerly, History Teacher, St. James's Sch., West Malvern, Worcs. *Publs:* Nelson, 1955; Sixteen Sail in Aboukir Bay, 1956; To Spare the Conquered, 1960; The Road to Sardis, 1965; Three Lives for the Czar, 1969; My Kingdom for a Grave, 1970; A Time to Be Born and a Time to Die, 1975; The Leaping Song, 1976. Add: c/o Bodley Head Ltd., 32 Bedford Sq., London WC1B 3SE, England.

PLUCKROSE, Henry (Arthur). Pseud: Richard Cobbett. British, b. 1931. Children's non-fiction, Education. Head teacher, Prior Weston Sch., London, 1968–84, now freelance educational consultant. Ed., Let's Go series. Teacher of elementary school-aged children in Inner London, 1954–68. *Publs:* Let's Make Pictures, 1965; Creative Arts and Crafts: A Handbook for Teachers in Primary Schools, 1966; Introducing Crayon Techniques, 1967; Lets Work Large: A Handbook of Art Techniques for Teachers in Primary Schools, 1967; Introducing Acrylic Painting, 1968; (compiler) The Art and Craft Book, 1969; (ed. with Frank Peacock) A Dickens Anthology, 1970; Creative Themes, 1970; (ed.) A Book of Crafts, 1971; Art and Craft Today, 1971; (ed.) Let's Use the Locality, 1971; (ed.) Let's Paint, 1971; (ed.) Let's Print, 1971; (ed.) Let's Make a Picture, 1971; (ed.) Let's Make a Puppet, 1971; Art, 1972; Churches, 1975; Castles, 1975; Open School, Open Society, 1975; Houses, 1976; Monasteries, 1976; Seen in Britain, 1978; (with Peter Wilby) The Condition of English Schooling, 1979; Saxon and Norman England, 1979; Mediaeval England, 1979; Children in Their Primary Schools, 1980; (with Peter Wilby) Education 2000, 1980; Victorian Britain, 1981; 20th Century Britain, 1981; Tudor Britain, 1981; Stuart Britain, 1981; Ancient Greeks, 1981; Arctic Lands, 1982; Hearing, 1985; Smelling, 1985; Tasting, 1985; Touching, 1985; Seeing, 1985; Growing, 1986; Shape, 1986; Floating and Sinking, 1986; Moving, 1987; Counting, 1987; Painting, 1987; What Is Happening in Our Primary Schools?, 1987; School, A Place for Children, 1988; Seen Locally, 1989. Add: 3 Butts Lane, Danbury, Essex, England.

PLUM, Jennifer. *See* **KURLAND,** Michael.

PLUMB, (Sir) John (Harold). British, b. 1911. History, Humanities, Biography. Univ. Lectr. in History, 1946–62, Reader in Modern English History, 1962–65, Prof. of Modern English History, 1965–74, and Chmn. of the History Faculty, 1966–68, Cambridge Univ.; Master of Christ's Coll., Cambridge, 1978–82. Ed., History of Human Society, since 1959, and Library of World Biography, since 1974, both Hutchinson; Historical Advisory Ed., Horizon mag., since 1959, and Penguin Books, since 1960. *Publs:* England in the Eighteenth Century, 1950; (with C. Howard) West African Explorers, 1951; Chatham, 1953; (ed.) Studies in Social History, 1955; Sir Robert Walpole: The Making of a Stateman, vol. I, 1956; The First Four Georges, 1956; The Renaissance, 1961; Men and Places, 1963; (ed.) Chrisis in the Humanities, 1964; The Growth of Political Stability in England 1675-1725, 1967; (co-author) Churchill Revised (Churchill the Historian), 1969; The Death of the Past, 1969; In the Light of History, 1972; The Commercialisation of Leisure, 1974; (with Huw Weldon) Royal Heritage, 1977; Georgian Delights, 1980; Royal Heritage: The Reign of Elizabeth II, 1980; (with Neil McKendrick and John Brewer) The Birth of a Consumer Society, 1982; Collected Esseys, Vol. I, 1988. Add: Christ's Coll., Cambridge CB2 3BU, England.

PLUMLY, Stanley. American, b. 1939. Poetry. Prof. of English, Univ. of Houston, since 1979. Visiting Poet, Louisiana State Univ., Baton Rouge, 1968–70, Ohio Univ., Athens, 1970–73, Univ. of Iowa, Iowa City, 1974–76, Princeton Univ., New Jersey, 1976–78, Columbia Univ., NYC, 1977–79, and Univ. of Houston, 1979–81. Poetry Ed., Ohio Review, Athens, 1970–75, and Iowa Review, Iowa City, 1976–78. *Publs:* In the Outer Dark, 1970; Giraffe, 1973; How the Plains Indians Got Hor-

ses, 1975; Out-of-the-Body Travel, 1977; Summer Celestial, 1983. Add: Dept. of English, Univ. of Houston, Houston, Tex. 77004, U.S.A.

PLUMMER, Ben. *See* **BINGLEY,** David Ernest.

PLUMMER, (Arthur) Desmond (Herne); Lord Plummer of St. Marylebone. British, b. 1914. Regional/Urban planning. Chmn., Portman Building Soc., London, since 1983 (Vice-Chmn., 1979–82); Chmn., National Employers Life Assurance, since 1983. Member, St. Marylebone Borough Council, London, 1952–65, and Mayor of St. Marylebone, 1958–59; Member, 1964–76, and Leader, 1967–73, Greater London Council; Chmn., Horserace Betting Levy Bd. (U.K.), 1974–82. *Publs:* Time for Change in Greater London, 1966; Report to London, 1970; Planning and Participation, 1973. Add: 4 The Lane, St. John's Wood, London NW8 0PN, England.

PLUNKETT, James. Irish, b. 1920. Novels/Short stories, Plays/Screenplays. Sr. Producer, Radio Telefis Eireann, since 1974 (Asst. Head of Drama, 1955–60; Head of Television Features, 1961–71). Branch Secty., Workers Union of Ireland, 1946–55. *Publs:* The Trusting and the Maimed, 1955; Big Jim, 1955; The Risen People, 1958; When Do You Die, Friend?, 1966; Strumpet City, 1969; The Gems She Wore, 1972; Farewell Companions, 1977; Collected Short Stories, 1977; The Boy on the Back Wall (essays), 1987. Add: Coolakeagh, Old Long Hill, Kilmacanogue, Co. Wicklow, Ireland.

POAGUE, Leland. American, b. 1948. Film. Prof., Dept. of English, Iowa State Univ., Ames, since 1986 (Asst. Prof., 1978–81; Assoc. Prof., 1981–86). Instr., 1973–74, and Asst. Prof. of English, 1974–78, State Univ. of New York Coll. at Geneseo. *Publs:* The Cinema of Frank Capra: An Approach to Film Comedy, 1975; The Cinema of Ernst Lubitsch: The Hollywood Films, 1978; The Hollywood Professionals, vol. 7: Wilder and McCarey, 1980; Howard Hawks, 1982; (with William Cadbury) Film Criticism: A Counter Theory, 1982; (co-ed.) A Hitchcock Reader, 1986. Add: English Dept., Iowa State Univ., Ames, Iowa 50011, U.S.A.

POCOCK, Hugh (Raymond Spilsbury). British, b. 1904. Poetry, History, Biography. Gen. Mgr., Shell Chile Ltd., 1948–49, and Shell Brazil Ltd., 1949–54; Secty., Royal Dutch Shell Group Coordination Cttee., London, 1957–59. Commnr., St. John Ambulance Brigade, Jersey, 1961–66. *Publs:* The Conquest of Chile, 1968; (with Lord Coutanche) The Memoirs of Lord Coutanche, 1975; Farmyard Comedian (poems), 1975. Add: Les Niemes, St. Peter, Jersey, Channel Islands.

POCOCK, Tom. (Thomas Allcot Guy Pocock). British. Art, Travel/Exploration/Adventure, Military/Defence, Biography. War Corresp., Leader Mag., 1945; Naval and Military Corresp., Daily Mail, London, 1948–52; Naval Corresp., The Times, London, 1952–55, Daily Express, 1956–57; Joint Ed., Elizabethan Mag., 1957–59; Defence Corresp., 1960–73, Travel Ed., 1973–82, and Special Writer, 1982–88, Evening Standard, London. *Publs:* Nelson and His World, 1968; Chelsea Reach, 1970; London Walks, 1973; Fighting General, 1973; Remember Nelson, 1977; The Young Nelson in the Americas, 1980; 1945: The Dawn Came Up Like Thunder, 1983; East and West of Suez, 1986; Horatio Nelson, 1987. Add: 22 Lawrence St., London SW3, England.

PODGORECKI, Adam. Polish, b. 1925. Novels/Short stories, Law, Sociology. Prof. of Sociology, Carleton Univ., Ottawa. Former Prof., Warsaw Univ. *Publs:* Principles of Legal Policy, 1957; Sociology of Law, 1962; Characteristics of Practical Social Sciences, 1962; Legal Phenomena in Public Opinion, 1964; Prestige of Law, 1966; Principles of Social Engineering, 1966; (ed.) Sociotechnics, 1968, 4th ed. 1974; Pathology of Social Life, 1969; (co-author) Attitudes of the Polish Population Toward Morality and Law, 1971; Elements of Sociology of Law, 1971; The Stories Parables, Tales, Fables, Fairy Tales, Short Stories, Anecdotes, Adages, Sayings, Stories and Parables, Aphorisms, Apothegms, Enigmas, Epigrams, Narratives, Conundrums, Cameos, Puzzles, Ellipses, Maxims, Riddles, Axioms, Theorems of Si-Tien, 23 vols., 1971–87; (co-ed.) Utilization of Social Sciences, 1973; (co-author) Knowledge and Opinion about Law, 1973; Law and Society, 1974; Sociology of Law, 1974; Practical Social Sciences, 1975; (with M.W. Los) Multidimensional Sociology, 1979; (co-ed.) Sociological Approaches to Law, 1981; Legal Systems and Social Systems, 1985. Add: Dept. of Sociology, Carleton Univ., Ottawa, Ont. K1S 5B6, Canada.

PODHORETZ, Norman. American, b. 1930. International relations/Current affairs, Literature, Social commentary/phenomena, Autobiography/Memoirs/Personal. Ed., Commentary mag., NYC, since 1960 (Asst. Ed., 1955; Assoc. Ed., 1956–58). *Publs:* Doings and Undoings:

The Fifties and After in American Writing, 1964; (ed.) The Commentary Reader: Two Decades of Articles and Stories, 1966; Making It (autobiography), 1967; Breaking Ranks: A Political Memoir, 1979; The Present Danger, 1980; Why We Were in Vietnam, 1982; The Bloody Crossroads: Where Literature and Politics Meet, 1986. Add: c/o Commentary, 165 E. 56th St., New York, N.Y. 10022, U.S.A.

POGANSKI, Donald John. American, b. 1928. Theology/Religion. Pastor, Lutheran Church-Missouri Synod, Zion Lutheran Church, San Luis Obispo, Calif., since 1970. Pastor, Christ Lutheran Church, Cincinnati, 1955–63, and Trinity Lutheran Church, Montclair, Calif., 1963–70. *Publs:* 50 Object Lessons, 1967; 40 Object Lessons, 1973. Add: 1010 Foothill Blvd., San Luis Obispo, Calif. 93401, U.S.A.

POGREBIN, Letty Cottin. American, b. 1939. Politics, Sociology, Women. Ed. and Writer, Ms. mag., NYC, since 1971. Vice-Pres., Bernard Geis Assocs., publrs., NYC, 1960–70; Columnist, "The Working Woman", Ladies Home Journal, NYC, 1971–81. *Publs:* How to Make It in a Man's World, 1970; Getting Yours, 1975; Growing Up Free, 1980; Family Politics, 1983; Among Friends, 1987. Add: c/o Ms. Mag., One Times Sq., New York, N.Y. 10036, U.S.A.

POGUE, Forrest Carlisle. American, b. 1912. History, Biography. Biographer, George C. Marshall Research Foundn., since 1956 (Dir., George C. Marshall Research Center, 1956–65; Exec. Dir., George M. Marshall Research Foundn., and Dir., George C. Marshall Research Library, 1965–74); Dir., Dwight D. Eisenhower Inst. for Historical Research, Museum of American History, Smithsonian Instn., Washington, D.C., 1974–84. *Publs:* The Supreme Command: Eisenhower's Command in North West Europe, 1954; George C. Marshall: Education of a General 1880-1939, 1964, Ordeal and Hope 1939-43, 1966, Organizer of Victory 1943-45, 1973, and Statesman 1945-59, 1987. Add: 1111 Army-Navy Dr., B-211, Arlington, Va. 22202, U.S.A.

POHL, Frederik. American, b. 1919. Novels/Short stories, Science fiction. Member of the Council, 1976–84, and Midwest Rep. to Council, since 1984, Author's Guild. Book Ed. and Assoc. Circulation Mgr., Popular Science Publ. Co., NYC, 1946–49; literary agent, NYC, 1949–53; Ed., Galaxy Publishing Co., NYC, 1960–69; Exec. Ed., Ace Books, NYC, 1971–72; Science Fiction Ed., Bantam Books, NYC, 1973–79. Pres., Science Fiction Writers of America, 1974–76; Pres., World SF, 1980–82. *Publs:* (ed.) Beyond the End of Time, 1952; (with C.M. Kornbluth) The Space Merchants, 1953; (ed.) Star Science Fiction Stories, 3 vols., 1953–54; (ed.) Assignment in Tomorrow, 1954; (ed.) Star Short Novels, 1954; (with C.M. Kornbluth) Search the Sky, 1954; (with Jack Williamson) Undersea Quest, 1954; (with C.M. Kornbluth) A Town Is Drowning, 1955; (with C.M. Kornbluth) Gladiator-at-Law, 1955; Alternating Currents (short stories), 1956; (with C.M. Kornbluth) Presidential Year, 1956; (with Jack Williamson) Undersea Fleet, 1956; Slave Ship, 1957; Edge of the City, 1957; The Case Against Tomorrow, 1957; (with Jack Williamson) Undersea City, 1958; Tomorrow Times Seven, 1959; (with C.M. Kornbluth) Wolfbane, 1959; (ed.) Star of Stars, 1960; Drunkard's Walk, 1960, expanded version 1961; The Man Who Ate the World, 1960; Turn Left at Thursday (short stories), 1961; (ed.) The Expert Dreamers, 1962; (ed.) Time Waits for Winthrop and Other Short Novels, 1962; (with C.M. Kornbluth) The Wonder Effect, 1962; A Plague of Pythons, 1963, rev. ed. as Demon in the Skull, 1984; The Abominable Earthman, 1963; (ed.) The Seventh Galaxy Reader, 1964; (with Jack Williamson) The Reefs of Space, 1964; (with Jack Williamson) Starchild, 1965; (ed.) Star Fourteen, 1966; (ed.) The If Reader of Science Fiction, 1966; The Frederik Pohl Omnibus, 1966; Digits and Dastards, 1968; The Age of Pussyfoot, 1969; (with Jack Williamson) Rogue Star, 1969; Day Million (short stories), 1970; (ed.) Nightmare Age, 1970; Practical Politics 1972, 1971; (ed. with C. Pohl) Science Fiction: The Great Years, 1974; Man Plus, 1977; Gateway, 1978; Jem, 1979; Beyond the Blue Event Horizon, 1980; The Cool War, 1981; Syzygy, 1982; Starburst, 1982; (with Jack Williamson) Wall Around a Star, 1983; Midas World, 1983; Heechee Rendezvous, 1984; The Years of the City, 1984; Black Star Rising, 1985; The Coming of the Quantum Cats, 1986; (ed. with Elizabeth Anne Hull) Tales from the Planet Earth, 1986; Chernobyl, 1987; The Annals of the Heechee, 1987; Narabedla Ltd., 1988; (with Jack Williamson) Land's End, 1988; The Day the Martians Came, 1988; Homegoing, 1989. Add: 855 S. Harvard Dr., Palatine, Ill. 60067, U.S.A.

POIRIER, Richard (William). American, b. 1925. Literature. Distinguished Prof. of English since 1963, Rutgers Univ., New Brunswick, N.J. (Chmn. of the Dept., 1963–72). Ed., Raritan Review, since 1981; Founder and Vice-Pres., Literary Classics of U.S. Inc. Served in the U.S. Army, 1943–45; Instr., Williams Coll., Williamstown, Mass., 1950–52;

Instr., 1958–60, and Asst. Prof., 1960–63, Harvard Univ., Cambridge, Mass. Ed., Partisan Review, New Brunswick, N.J., 1963–73. *Publs:* The Comic Sense of Henry James: A Study of the Early Novels, 1960; (ed.) Prize Stories: The O. Henry Awards, 4 vols., 1961–64; (ed. with Reuben A. Brower) In Defense of Reading, 1962; (ed. with William Abrahams) Prize Stories: The O. Henry Awards, 2 vols., 1965–66; A World Elsewhere: The Place of Style in American Literature, 1966; (ed. with W.L. Vance) American Literature, 1970; (ed. with Frank Kermode) The Oxford Reader, 1971; The Performing Self: Compositions and Decompositions in the Languages of Contemporary Life, 1971; Norman Mailer, 1972; The Aesthetics of Contemporary American Radicalism, 1972; Robert Frost: The Work of Knowing, 1977; The Renewal of Literature: Emersonian Reflections, 1987. Add: Raritan Quarterly, 165 College Ave., New Brunswick, N.J. 08903, U.S.A.

POLACH, Jaroslav G(eorge). American (b. Czechoslovakian), b. 1914. Economics, Management, International relations/Current affairs. Lectr. in Economics and Economics of Industrial Organizations, Univ. of Maryland, College Park, since 1970; with JP Intnl. Assocs., Oxon Hill, Md., since 1984. Exec. Bd. Member, American Sokol, Washington, since 1973. Law Clerk, Appellate Court Judges, Ostrava, Czechoslovakia, 1938–39; Secty. to the Head of Mission, Czechoslovak Special Mission, Budapest, 1939–41; Head of the Legal Dept. and Gen. Counsel for Intnl. Matters, Continental Steel Co., Prague; Head of the Legal Dept. and Gen. Counsel for Intnl. Matters, Czechoslovak Metallurgical Works at Ferromet, Prague, 1946–48; Intnl. Economist and Legal Analyst, Central Intelligence Agency, Washington, D.C., 1948–60; Staff Economist and Research Assoc., Resources for the Future Inc., Washingtòn, 1961–70; Dir., Intnl. Research Inst. Inc., Rockville, Md., 1968–69; Sr. Industry Economist, Economic Advisory Group, U.S. Internal Revenue Service, 1970–75; Sr. Adviser in Energy and Intnl. Economics, Office of the Secty., U.S. Dept. of the Treasury, 1975–84; Sr. Research Assoc., Center for Intnl. Studies, Univ. of Pittsburgh, 1986–87. Exec. Bd. Member, Czechoslovak Soc. of Arts and Sciences in America, 1960–68, 1974–78. *Publs:* (ed.) International Political Causes of the Czechoslovak Tragedies of 1938 and 1948, by A. Heidrich, 1962; Euratom: Its Background, Issues, and Economic Implications, 1964; Economic Development in the Countries of Eastern Europe, 1970; (with Joel Darmstadter and Perry Teitelbaum) Energy in the World Economy, 1972; The Structure of the International Petroleum Industry, 1976; (with Cathryn Goddard) The Implications of the Iranian Crisis for World Petroleum Situation, 1979. Add: 225 Panorama Dr., Oxon Hill, Md. 20745, U.S.A.

POLAKOFF, Keith (Ian). American, b. 1941. History. Prof. of History, since 1978, and Asst. Vice-Pres. for Academic Affairs and Dean of Grad. Studies, since 1986, California State Univ. at Long Beach (Asst. Prof., 1969–73; Assoc. Prof., 1973–78; Acting Dean, Sch. of Fine Arts, 1984–85). Lectr. in History, Herbert H. Lehman Coll., City Univ. of New York, 1967–69. Ed., 1972–77, and Production Mgr., 1977–80, The History Teacher mag. *Publs:* The Politics of Inertia: The Election of 1876 and the End of Reconstruction, 1973; (co-author) Generations of Americans: A History of the United States, 1976; Political Parties in American History, 1980. Add: 2971 Druid Lane, Rossmoor, Calif. 90720, U.S.A.

POLAND, Dorothy (Elizabeth Hayward). Writes as Alison Farely and Jane Hammond. British, b. 1937. Historical/Romance/Gothic. *Publs:* as Alison Farely—The Shadows of Evil, 1963; Plunder Island, 1964; High Treason, 1966; Throne of Wrath, 1967; Crown of Splendour, 1968; The Lion and the Wolf, 1969; Last Roar of the Lion, 1969; Leopard from Anjou, 1970; King Wolf, 1974; Kingdom under Tyranny, 1974; Last Howl of the Wolf, 1975; The Cardinal's Nieces, 1976; The Tempetuous Countess, 1976; Archduchess Arrogance, 1980; Scheming Spanish Queen, 1981; Spain for Mariana, 1982; as Jane Hammond—The Hell Raisers of Wycombe, 1970; Fire and the Sword, 1971; The Golden Courtesan, 1975; Shadow of the Headsman, 1975; The Doomtower, 1975; Witch of the White House, 1976; Gunpowder Treason, 1976; The Red Queen, 1976; The Queen's Assassin, 1977; The Silver Madonna, 1977; Conspirators' Moonlight, 1977; Woman of Vengeance, 1977; The Admiral's Lady, 1978; The Secret of Petherick, 1982; The Massingham Topaz, 1983; Beware the King's Enchantress, 1983; Moon in Aries, 1984; Eagle's Talon, 1984; Death in the New Forest, 1984. Add: Horizons, 95 Dock View Rd., Barry, Glam., Wales.

POLAND, Marguerite. S. African, b. 1950. Novels, Children's fiction. Asst., South African Museum, Cape Town, 1972; Research Asst., Inst. for Social Research, Natal Univ., 1973–75. *Publs:* children's fiction— The Mantis and the Moon: Stories for the Children of Africa, 1979; Nqalu, The Mouse with No Whiskers, 1979; Once at Kwa Fubesi, 1981; The

Bush Shrike, 1982; The Fiery-Necked Nightjar: A Christmas Story, 1983; The Wood-Ash Stars, 1983; Marcus and the Boxing Gloves (Go-Kart), 2 vols, 1984–88; Shadow of the Wild Hare, 1986; The Small Clay Bull, 1986; other for adults—Train to Doringbult (novel), 1987. Add: 54 Ronalds Rd., Kloof 3610, Durban, Natal, S. Africa.

POLE, Jack Richon. British, b. 1922. History, Intellectual history, Politics/Government. Asst. Lectr., then Lectr. in American History, University Coll., London, 1953–63; Visiting Assoc. Prof., Univ. of California, Berkeley, 1960–61; Fellow, Center for Advanced Study in the Behavioral Sciences, Stanford, Calif., 1969–70; Reader in American History and Govt., and Fellow, Churchill Coll., Cambridge, 1963–79; Rhodes Prof. of American History and Institutions, and Fellow of St. Catherine's Coll., Oxford Univ., 1979–89. *Publs:* Abraham Lincoln and the Working Classes of Britain, 1959; Abraham Lincoln, 1964; Abraham Lincoln and American Commitment, 1966; Political Representation in England and the Origins of the American Republic, 1966; (ed.) The Advance of Democracy, 1967; (ed.) The Revolution in America 1754-1788: Documents on the Internal Development of America During the Revolutionary Era, 1971; (ed. with M. Meyers) The Meanings of American History, 1971; Foundations of American Independence 1763-1815, 1972; (ed.) Slavery, Secession and Civil War, 1974; The Decision for American Independence, 1975; The Idea of Union, 1977; The Pursuit of Equality in American History, 1978; Paths of the American Past, 1979; The Gift of Government: From the English Restoration to the American Revolution, 1983; (co-ed.) Colonial British American, 1984; (ed.) The American Constitution: For and Against, 1987. Add: St. Catherine's Coll., Oxford, England.

POLENBERG, Richard. American, b. 1937. History. Smith Prof. of American History, Cornell Univ., Ithaca, since 1986 (Asst. Prof., 1966–67; Assoc. Prof., 1967–70; Prof., 1970–86). Lectr., Queens Coll., NYC, 1960–61; Lectr., 1961–64, Instr., 1964–65, and Asst. Prof., 1965–66, Brooklyn Coll., NYC. Pres., Temple Beth-El, Ithaca, 1980–81. *Publs:* Reorganizing Roosevelt's Government 1936-1939, 1966; (ed.) America at War: The Home Front 1941-1945, 1968; War and Society: The United States 1941-1945, 1972; (ed.) Radicalism and Reform in the New Deal, 1972; (with Walter LaFeber and Nancy Woloch) The American Century: A History of the United States since the 1890's, 1975, 3rd ed. 1985; One Nation Divisible: Class, Race, and Ethnicity in the United States since 1938, 1980; Fighting Faiths: The Abrams Case, The Supreme Court, and Free Speech, 1987. Add: Dept. of History, McGraw Hall, Cornell Univ., Ithaca, N.Y. 14853, U.S.A.

POLIAKOFF, Stephen. British, b. 1953. Plays/Screenplays. *Publs:* (with others) Lay-By, 1972; Hitting Town and City Sugar, 1976; Strawberry Fields, 1977; Shout Across the River, 1979; American Days, 1979; The Summer Party, 1980; Favourite Nights and Caught on a Train, 1982; Banners, and Soft Targets, 1984; Breaking the Silence, 1984; Coming In to Land, 1987. Add: c/o Margaret Ramsay Ltd., 14a Goodwin's Ct., London WC2N 4LL, England.

POLITELLA, Dario. Also writes as Tony Granite and David Stewart. American, b. 1921. Writing/Journalism, Humor/Satire. Prof. of Journalistic Studies, Univ. of Massachusetts, Amherst, since 1965. Bureau Mgr., Geneva Daily Times, New York, 1949–50; Asst. Prof., Sch. of Journalism, Kent State Univ., Ohio, 1950–55; Instr. Sch. of Journalism, Syracuse Univ., New York, 1955–57; Managing Ed., Henry Publishing Co., NYC, 1957; Assoc. Ed., Ziff-Davis Publishing Co., NYC, 1957–58; TV Writer, CBS-TV, NYC, 1958; Sr. Publicist, O.S. Tyson and Co., NYC, 1958–69; Public Relations Rep., Lockheed Corp., 1960–62; Asst. Prof. of Mass Communications, Ball State Univ., Muncie Ind., 1962–65; Instr., Chautauqua Instn., Summers 1968–86. *Publs:* When Hell Froze Over (poetry), 1953; Standard Operating Procedures for Student Publications, 1953; Operation Grasshopper, 1958; Directory of the Student College Press in America, biennially since 1967; Guidelines for the Student Press, 1969; The Illustrated Anatomy of Campus Humor, 1970; The Making of a Journalist, 1973. Add: N. Main St., Sunderland, Mass. 01375, U.S.A.

POLITI, Leo. American, b. 1908. Children's fiction. *Publs:* Little Pancho, 1938; Pedro, The Angel of Olvera Street, 1946; Young Giotto, 1947; Juanita, 1948; Song of the Swallows, 1949; Saint Francis and the Animals, 1959; A Boat for Peppe, 1950; Little Leo, 1951; The Mission Bell, 1953; The Butterflies Come, 1957; Moy Moy, 1961; Rosa, 1963; Lito and the Clown, 1964; Bunker Hill, Los Angeles Reminiscences of Bygone Days, 1964; Picolo's Park, 1965; Tales of the Los Angeles Parks, 1966; The Poinsettia, 1968; Mieko, 1969; Emmet, 1971; The Nicest Gift, 1973; Three Stalks of Corn, 1976; Mr. Fong's Toy Shop, 1978. Add: Macmillan Publishing Co., Inc., 866 Third Ave., New York, N.Y. 10022,

U.S.A.

POLKING, Kirk. American, b. 1925. Children's non-fiction, Writing/ Journalism. Dir., Writer's Digest Sch., F and W Publishing Corp., since 1976. Editorial Asst, 1948–52, and Ed., 1963–73, Writer's Digest; Editorial Asst. Modern Photography, 1948–52; Circulation Mgr., Farm Quarterly, 1952–57. *Publs:* Let's Go with Lewis and Clark, 1963; Let's Go with Henry Hudson, 1964; Let's Go See Congress at Work, 1966; Let's Go to an Atomic Energy Town, 1968; (ed. with Rose Adkins) The Beginning Writer's Answer Book 1971, 3rd ed 1987; (ed.) How to Make Money in Your Spare Time by Writing, 1971; The Private Pilot's Dictionary and Handbook, 1974, 1986; (ed.) Artist's Market, 1974; Law and the Writer, 1978, 1985; (ed.) Internships, 1981; Oceans of the World: Our Essential Resource, 1983; Freelance Jobs for Writers, 1984; (ed.) Writer's Encyclopedia, 1986; (ed.) The Beginner's Guide to Getting Published, 1987. Add: 1507 Dana Ave., Cincinnati, Ohio 45207, U.S.A.

POLLACK, Reginald. American, b. 1924. Children's fiction, art. Freelance writer, illustrator and painter. Visiting Critic in Art, Yale Univ. Grad. Sch. of Art, 1962–63; Instr., Cooper Union, NYC, 1963–64; Art Resource Staff Member, National Training Labs., Univ. of California, Arrowhead, 1966; art resource therapist and consultant to psychoanalysts, 1966–69; Staff member, Lighthouse Child Guidance Center, Presbyterian Hosp., Los Angeles, 1966–69, and Quaker Half-way House, Los Angeles, 1968. Trustee, Washington D.C. Project for the Arts, 1975–80; Visiting Artist, Materials Research Lab., Univ. of Pennsylvania, Philadelphia, 1977–78. *Publs:* The Magician and the Child, 1971; multi-media plays— The War of the Angels, 1974; The Twelve Gifts of Christmas, 1974; A Glory of Sights and Sounds, 1977. Add: Route 1, Box 955, Waterford, Va. 22190, U.S.A.

POLLAND, Madeleine A(ngela). Also writes as Frances Adrian. British, b. 1918. Novels/Short stories, Children's fiction. Asst. Librarian, Letchworth Public Library, Hertfordshire, 1939–42, 1945–46. *Publs:* Children of the Red King, 1960; The Town Across the Water, 1961; Beorn the Proud, 1961; Fingal's Quest, 1961; The White Twilight, 1962; Chuiraquimba and the Black Robes, 1962; City of the Golden House, 1963; The Queen's Blessing, 1963; Flame over Tara, 1964; Thicker Than Water, 1964; Mission to Cathay, 1965; Queen Without Crown, 1965; Deirdre, 1967; The Little Spot of Bother (in U.S. as Minutes of a Murder), 1967; To Tell My People, 1968; Stranger in the Hills, 1968; Random Army (in U.S. as Shattered Summer), 1969; To Kill a King, 1970; Alhambra, 1970; A Family Affair, 1971; Package to Spain, 1971; Daughter to Poseidon (in U.S. as Daughter of the Sea), 1972; Prince of the Double Axe, 1976; (as Frances Adrian) Double Shadow, 1977; Sabrina, 1979; All Their Kingdoms, 1981; The Heart Speaks Many Ways, 1982; No Price Too High, 1984; As It Was in the Beginning, 1987; Rich Man's Flowers, 1989. Add: Edificio Hercules 406, Avenida Gamonal, Arroyo de la Miel, Malaga, Spain.

POLLARD, Arthur. British, b. 1922. Literature. Consultant Prof. of English, Univ. of Buckingham, since 1984. Asst. Lectr., 1949–52, Lectr., 1952–64, and Sr. Lectr., 1964–67, Univ. of Manchester; Prof. of English, Univ. of Hull, 1967–84. *Publs:* (ed. with M.M. Hennell) Charles Simeon 1759-1836, 1959; (ed.) Let Wisdom Judge: University Addresses and Sermon Outlines by Charles Simeon, 1959; (ed.) New Poems of George Crabbe, 1960; English Hymns, 1960; English Sermons, 1963; (ed.) Sylvia's Lovers, by Mrs. Gaskell, 1964; Mrs. Gaskell, Novelist and Biographer, 1965; Richard Hooker, 1966; (ed. with J.A.V. Chapple) The Letters of Mrs. Gaskell, 1966; Charlotte Brontë, 1968; Trollope's Political Novels, 1968; (ed.) The Victorians, vol. 6 of the Sphere History of Literature in the English Language, 1970, 1987; Satire, 1970; (ed.) Crabbe: The Critical Heritage, 1972; (ed.) Webster's New World Companion to English and American Literature, 1973; (ed.) Silver Poets of the Eighteenth Century, 1976; Anthony Trollope, 1978; (ed.) Thackeray: Vanity Fair: A Casebook, 1978; (ed.) Marvell's Poems: A Casebook, 1980; The Victorian Period (excluding the novel), 1983; The Landscape of the Brontë's, 1988; (ed. with Norma Dalrymble-Champneys) The Complete Poetical Works of George Crabbe, 3 vols, 1988. Add: School of History, Politics and English, Univ. of Buckingham, Buckingham, England.

POLLARD, John (Richard Thornhill). British, b. 1914. History, Humanities (general), Travel/Exploration/Adventure, Biography. Sr. Lectr. in Classics, University Coll. of North Wales, Bangor, 1966 until retirement, 1988 (Lectr., 1949–66). Classics Master, Herne Bay Coll., 1938–39; Asst. in Classics, St. Andrews Univ., 1948–49. *Publs:* Journey to the Styx, 1955; Adventure Begins in Kenya, 1957; Africa for Adventure, 1961; African Zoo Man, 1963; Wolves and Werewolves, 1964; Helen of Troy, 1965; Seers, Shrines and Sirens, 1965; The Long Safari, 1967;

(with C. Day Lewis) Virgil: The Aeneid Appreciation, 1969; Birds in Greek Life and Myth, 1977; Divination and Oracles: Greece, Civilization of the Ancient Mediterranean, 1988. Add: The Yard, Red Wharf Bay, Anglesey LL75 8RX, Wales.

POLLARD, Sidney. British, b. 1925. Economics, History. Prof. of Economic History, Univ. of Bielefeld, since 1980. Fellow, Lectr., and Prof., Univ. of Sheffield, 1950–80. *Publs:* Three Centuries of Sheffield Steel, 1954; (with D.C. Coleman and K.G.T. McDonnell) A Survey of English Economic History, 1957, 3rd ed. 1967; A History of Labour in Sheffield, 1959; The Development of the British Economy 1914-1950, 1962, 3rd ed. 1914-80, 1983; The Genesis of Modern Management, 1965; The Idea of Progress, 1968; (with D.W. Crossley) The Wealth of Britain 1085-1966, 1968; (ed. with C. Holmes) Documents of European Economic History, 3 vols., 1968–73; (ed.) The Gold Standard and Employment Policies Between the Wars, 1970; (ed. with J.P.P. Higgins) Aspects of Capital Investment in Great Britain 1750-1850, 1971; (ed. with J. Salt) Robert Owen, Prophet of the Poor, 1971; (ed.) The Sheffield Outrages, 1971; European Economic Integration 1815-1970, 1974; (ed. with C. Holmes) Essays in the Economic and Social History of South Yorkshire, 1977; (with P.L. Robertson) The British Shipbuilding Industry 1870-1914, 1978; Peaceful Conquest, 1981; The Wasting of the British Economy, 1982; (with C.H. Feinstein) Studies in Capital Formation in the United Kingdom 1750-1920, 1988; Britain's Prime and Britain's Decline, 1988. Add: Loebellstrasse 14, 4800 Bielefeld I, W. Germany.

POLLARD, Thomas Evan. Australian, b. 1921. Theology/Religion. Prof. of New Testament Studies, Theological Hall, Knox Coll., Dunedin, 1963–82, now retired. Minister, Presbyterian Church of New South Wales, 1949–62; Teacher of New Testament, Univ. of Sydney, 1958–62; Hon. Lectr., Univ. of Otago, Dunedin, 1963–82. *Publs:* Johannine Christology and the Early Church, 1970; Fullness of Humanity: Christ's and Ours, 1982. Add: 22 Judith Ave., Mt. Riverview, N.S.W. 2774, Australia.

POLLEY, Judith Anne. Also writes as Judith Hagar, Helen Kent, Valentina Luellen, and Judith Stewart. British, b. 1938. Novels/Short stories, Historical/Romance/Gothic. *Publs:* The Countess, 1967; Maria Elena, 1968; Journey into Love, 1968; Master of Karatangi, 1968; A Pride of MacDonalds, 1968; Slightly Scarlet, 1969; Children of the Devil, 1970; The Flowering Desert, 1970; A Man for Melanie, 1970; Madelon, 1970; The King's Cavalier, 1971; Dangerous Deception, 1972; Castle of the Mist, 1972; The Secret of Val Verde, 1974; The King's Shadow, 1975; Francesca, 1977; Keeper of the Flame, 1977; Laird's French Bride, 1978; The Captive Heart, 1978; Place of Happiness, 1978; To Touch the Stars, 1979; Beloved Enemy, 1980; Don't Run from Love, 1981; Moonshadow, 1981; Prince of Deception, 1981; Shadow of the Eagle, 1982; Beloved Adversary, 1982; Silver Salamander, 1982; The Wind of Change, 1982; Wild Wind in the Heather, 1983; The Measure of Love, 1983; The Peaceful Homecoming, 1983; The Valley of Tears, 1984; Moonflower, 1984; Elusive Flame of Love, 1984; Mistress of Tanglewood, 1984; Black Ravenswood, 1985; The Lord of Darkness, 1985; Devil of Talland, 1985; The Passionate Pirate, 1986; Where the Heart Leads, 1986; Love the Avenger, 1986; The Devil's Touch, 1987; My Lady Melisande, 1987. Add: c/o Mills and Boon, 15-16 Brooks Mews, London W1A 1DR, England.

POLLOCK, (Rev.) John Charles. British. History, Theology/Religion, Travel/Exploration/Adventure, Biography. Capt., Coldstream Guards, 1943–45; Asst. Master., Wellington Coll., Berkshire, 1947–49; Rector of Horsington, Somerset, 1953–58. *Publs:* Candidate for Truth, 1950; A Cambridge Movement, 1953; The Cambridge Seven, 1955, 1985; Way to Glory: Life of Havelock of Lucknow, 1957; Shadows Fall Apart, 1958; The Good Seed, 1959; Earth's Remotest End, 1960; Hudson Taylor and Maria, 1962; Moody Without Sankey, 1963; The Christians from Siberia (in U.S. as The Faith of the Russian Evangelicals), 1964; The Keswick Story, 1964; Billy Graham, 1966; The Apostle: A Life of St. Paul, 1969; A Foreign Devil in China: The Life of Nelson Bell, 1971, 1989; George Whitefield and the Great Awakening, 1973; Wilberforce, 1977; Billy Graham: Evangelist to the World, 1979; The Siberian Seven, 1979; Amazing Grace: John Newton's Story, 1981; The Master: A Life of Jesus, 1984; Billy Graham: Highlights of the Story (in U.S. as To All the Nations), 1984; Shaftesbury, the Poor Man's Earl, 1985; A Fistful of Heroes, 1988; John Wesley, 1989. Add: Rose Ash House, South Molton, Devonshire, England.

POLLOCK, Sharon. Canadian, b. 1936. Plays/Screenplays. Member of the Drama Dept., Univ. of Alberta, Edmonton, 1976–77; Head of Playwright's Colony, Banff Centre of Fine Arts, 1977–80; Playwright-in-Residence, Alberta Theatre Projects, 1977–79; Artist-in-Residence, Na-

tional Arts Centre, Ottawa, 1981, 1982. Member, 1978–80, and Chmn., 1979–80, Advisory Arts Panel, Canada Council; Member of the Advisory Cttee., National Theatre Sch., 1979–80; Vice-Chmn., Playwrights Canada National Exec., 1981–83. *Publs:* A Compulsory Option; Walsh, 1973; The Komagata Maru Incident, 1978; Blood Relations and Other Plays, 1981. Add: 319 Manora Dr. N.E., Calgary, Alta. T2A 4R2, Canada.

POLONSKY, Antony (Barry). British, b. 1940. History, Politics/Government. Lectr. in Intnl. History, London Sch. of Economics, since 1970, and London Univ., since 1981. Secty., Assn. of Contemporary Historians, London, since 1975. Lectr. in East European History, Univ. of Glasgow, 1968–70. *Publs:* Politics in Independent Poland, 1972; The Little Dictator, 1975; The Great Powers and the Polish Question, 1976; (with B. Druckier) The Beginnings of Communist Rule in Poland, 1978; (co-author) The History of Poland since 1863, 1981; The Jews in Poland, 1986; (ed.) Polin, Vol. 1, 1987. Add: 27 Dartmouth Park Rd., London NW5, England.

POLUNIN, Nicholas. British, b. 1909. Environmental science/Ecology. Ed., Environmental Conservation, since 1974 (Biological Conservation, 1967–74); Pres., Foundn. for Environmental Conservation, since 1975; Pres., World Council for the Biosphere, since 1984; Convener and Gen. Ed., Environmental Monographs and Symposia; Chmn., Editorial Bd., Cambridge Studies in Environmental Policy. Fielding Curator and Keeper of the Univ. Herbaria, Fellow of New Coll., and Univ. Demonstrator and Lectr. in Botany, Oxford Univ., 1939–47; Visiting Prof., 1946–47, and Macdonald Prof. of Botany, 1947–52, McGill Univ., Montreal; Guggenheim Fellow and Research Fellow, Harvard Univ., Cambridge, Mass., 1950–53; Lectr. in Plant Science and Research Assoc., Yale Univ., New Haven, Conn., 1953–55; Ed., World Crops Books, 1954–76, and Plant Science Monographs, 1954–78; Prof. of Plant Ecology and Taxonomy, Head of the Dept. of Botany, and Dir. of the Univ. Herbarium, Univ. of Baghdad, 1956–58; Guest Prof., Univ. of Geneva, 1959–61; Prof. and Head of the Dept. of Botany, and Founding Dean, Faculty of Science, Univ. of Ife, Nigeria, 1962–66. Leader or member of numerous scientific expeditions, especially in arctic regions, 1930–38, 1946–65. *Publs:* Russian Waters, 1931; The Isle of Auks, 1932; Botany of the Canadian Eastern Arctic, vol. I, 1940, vol. II, 1947, vol. III, 1948; Arctic Unfolding, 1949; Circumpolar Arctic Flora, 1959; Introduction to Plant Geography, 1960; Elléments de Géographie botanique, 1967; (ed.) The Environmental Future, 1972; Growth Without Ecodisasters?, 1980; Ecosystem Theory and Application, 1986; (with Sir John Burnett) Maintenance of the Biosphere, 1989. Add: 7 Chemin Taverney, 1218 Grand-Saconnex, Geneva, Switzerland.

POLYA, John Bela. Australian, b. 1914. Chemistry, Medicine/Health. Assoc. Prof. of Chemistry, Univ. of Tasmania, Hobart, 1954–79, now retired. *Publs:* Absorptionsspektrographische und chemische Untersuchungen ueber chemische Kampstoffe, 1937; Are We Safe?: A Layman's Guide to Controversy in Public Health, 1964; 1, 2, 4—Triazoles, 1984. Add: 18 Carinya Rd., Greensborough, Vic. 3088, Australia.

POMERANCE, Bernard. American, b. 1940. Plays/Screenplays. Founder, Foco Novo theatre group, London. *Publs:* The Elephant Man, 1979; Quantrill in Lawrence, 1981; We Need to Dream All This Again (novel), 1987. Add: c/o Faber and Faber Ltd., 3 Queen Sq., London WC1N 3AU, England.

POMEROY, Ralph. American, b. 1926. Poetry. Art dealer, art critic, and freelance writer: Assoc. Dir., Forum Gallery, NYC, since 1979; Contrib. Ed., Arts mag., since 1981; Co-Ed., A Just God (literary mag.), since 1982; Visiting Lectr. on Painting, NY School of Interior Design, since 1983. Member, Editorial Staff, Artnews, NYC, 1963–68, and Art and Artists, London, 1966–73; Dir., Anna Leonowens Gallery, Coll. of Art and Design, Halifax, N.S., 1969–70; Visiting Lectr., Machaelis Coll. of Art, Univ. of Capetown, S. Africa, 1973; Visiting Lectr., Winchester Sch. of Art and Cardiff Coll. of Art, U.K., 1975–76; Contrib. Ed. on Art, House Beautiful, 1978; Assoc. Ed., "The Collector's Catalogue", 1979. *Publs:* verse—Book of Poems, 1948; Stills and Motives, 1961; The Canaries as They Are, 1965; In the Financial District, 1968; other—Stamos, 1974; The Ice Cream Connection: All You'd Love to Know about Ice Cream, 1975; First Things First: A Connoisseur's Companion to Breakfast, 1977. Add: 115 W. 71st St., New York, N.Y. 10023, U.S.A.

POMPIAN, Richard. American, b. 1935. Advertising/Public relations, Writing/Journalism. Pres., Pompian Advertising Inc., formerly ProSell Communications, since 1969; Partner, The Pompians, training consultants, since 1976; Asst. Prof. of Communication Arts, St. John's Univ., NYC, since 1980 (Adjunct Asst. Prof., 1979–80). Copywriter, Dancer-

Fitzgerald-Sample Inc., NYC, 1960–68. Ed., The Northeast Gazette, 1976–80; Adjunct Lectr. in Media Studies, Fordham Univ., NYC, 1979–80. *Publs:* Advertising, 1970; (ed.) The Rhythm Book, by Peter Phillips, 1971; Writing for Professionals, 1981. Add: 300 Riverside Dr., New York, N.Y. 10025, U.S.A.

POND, Grace (Isabelle). British, b. 1910. Animals/Pets. Ed., Cat Lovers Diary, Collins; Hon. Organiser, National Cat Club Show, Olympia, London; intnl. cat judge; Pres. of the Governing Council, The Cat Fancy. *Publs:* The Observer Book of Cats, 1959; Persian Cats, 1963; The Perfect Cat Owner, 1966; The Complete Cat Guide, 1968; The Long-Haired Cats, 1968; Batsford Book of Cats, 1969; Cats, 1970; (with E. Towe) Cats, 1970; (with A. Ashford), Rex, Abyssinian and Turkish Cats, 1972; The Complete Cat Encyclopaedia, 1972; (with C. Ing) Champion Cats of the World, 1972; (ed.) The Cat Lovers Bedside Book, 1974; (with M. Calder) The Long-Haired Cats, 1974; (with A. Sayer) The Intelligent Cat, 1977; (with I. Raleigh) The Standard Guide to Cat Breeds, 1979; Purnell's Pictorial Encyclopedia of Cats, 1980; (with J. Dineen) Cats, 1981; Longhaired Cats, 1983; (with M. Dunnill) Cat Shows and Showing, 1985; The New Observer's Book of Cats, 1987. Add: Greenhayes, 35 Blackwater Lane, Pound Hill, Crawley, Sussex, England.

PONDER, Patricia. *See* **MAXWELL,** Patricia Anne.

PONSONBY, D(oris) A(lmon). Also writes as Doris Rybot and Sarah Tempest. British, b. 1907. Historical/Romance/Gothic, Animals/Pets, Biography. *Publs:* The Gazebo, 1945, in U.S. as If My Arms Could Hold, 1947; Sophy Valentine, 1946; Merry Meeting, 1948; Strangers in My House, 1948; Bow Window in Green Street, 1949; Call a Dog Hervey, 1949; Family of Jaspard, 1950, as The General and The Fortunate Adventure, 2 vols., 1971; The Bristol Cousins, 1951; The Foolish Marriage, 1952; The Widow's Daughters, 1953; (as Doris Rybot, with Lydia Ingleton) The Popular Chow Chow, 1954; Royal Purple, 1954; Dogs in Clover, 1954; Conquesta's Caravan, 1955; Unhallowed House, 1956; The Lost Duchess, 1958; (as Doris Rybot) Romany Sister, 1960; So Bold a Choice, 1960; A Living to Earn, 1961; A Prisoner in Regent's Park, 1961; (as Doris Rybot) A Japanese Doll, 1961; The Orphans, 1962; (as Doris Rybot) My Kingdom for a Donkey, 1963, 1973; Bells Along the Neva, 1964; The Jade Horse of Merle, 1966; (as Doris Rybot) A Donkey and a Dandelion, 1966; An Unusual Tutor, 1967; (as Sarah Tempest) A Winter of Fear, 1967; The Forgotten Heir, 1969; The Heart in the Sand, 1970; Mr. Florian's Fortune, 1971; Flight from Hanover Square, 1972; (as Doris Rybot) It Began Before Noah (on zoos), 1972; The Gamester's Daughter, 1974; The Heir to Holtwood, 1975; The Unnamed Gentlewoman, 1976; Kaye's Walk, 1977; Sir William, 1978; Exhibition Summer, 1982; A Woman Despised, 1988. Add: c/o Curtis Brown Ltd., 162-168 Regent St., London W1R 5TB, England.

POOLE, Josephine. (Mrs. Jane Penelope Josephine Helyar). British, b. 1933. Novels/Short stories, Children's fiction. *Publs:* A Dream in the House, 1961; Moon Eyes, 1965; The Lilywhite Boys, 1968; Catch as Catch Can, 1969; Yokehem, 1970; Billy Buck (in U.S. as The Visitor), 1972; Touch and Go, 1976; When Fishes Flew, 1978; The Open Grave, 1979; The Forbidden Room, 1979; Hannah Chance, 1980; Diamond Jack, 1983; Country Companion, 1983; Three for Luck, 1985; Wildlife Tales, 1986; Puss in Boots, 1988; The Sleeping Beauty, 1988; The Loving Ghosts, 1988. Add: Poundsford Lodge, Poundisford, Taunton, Somerset, England.

POOVEY, William Arthur. American, b. 1913. Plays/Screenplays, Theology/Religion, Essays. Prof. of Preaching, Wartburg Seminary, Dubuque, Iowa, 1958–77. *Publs:* (with N.E. Marsh) Hymn Dramatizations, 1942; Questions That Trouble Christians, 1946; Problems That Plague the Saints, 1950; No Hands But Ours, 1954; Your Neighbor's Faith, 1961; And Pilate Asked, 1965; Cross Words, 1968; What Did Jesus Do?, 1969; Mustard Seeds and Wineskins, 1972; Let Us Adore Him, 1972; Signs of His Coming, 1973; Stand Still and Move Ahead, 1973; Six Faces of Lent, 1974; Banquets and Beggars, 1974; The Power of the Kingdom, 1974; Celebrate with Drama, 1975; That Wonderful Word Shalom, 1975; The Days Before Christmas, 1975; The Prayer He Taught, 1976, 1977; The Days Before Easter, 1976; Six Prophets for Today, 1977; Planning a Christian Funeral, 1978; Faith Is the Password, 1979; Prodigals and Publicans, 1979; We Sing Your Praise, O Lord, 1980; How to Talk to Christians about Money, 1982. Add: 10418 Applegate, San Antonio, Tex. 78230, U.S.A.

POPE, Dudley (Bernard Egerton). British, b. 1925. Historical/Romance/Gothic, History, Biography. Naval Corresp., 1944–57, and Deputy Foreign Ed., 1957–59, Evening News, London. *Publs:* Flag 4,

1954; The Battle of the River Plate, 1956; 73 North, 1958; England Expects, 1959; At 12 Mr. Byng Was Shot, 1962; The Black Ship, 1963; Guns, 1965; Ramage series, 18 vols., 1965–88; The Great Gamble, 1972; Harry Morgan's Way, 1977; Convoy, 1979; Life in Nelson's Navy, 1981; Buccaneer, 1981; Admiral, 1982; Decoy, 1983; Galleon, 1986. Add: c/o Campbell Thomson and McLaughlin Ltd., 31 Newington Green, London N16 9PU, England.

POPE, Ray. British, b. 1924. Children's fiction. Geography Teacher, Chippenham High Sch. for Girls, since 1966. *Publs:* Strosa Light, 1965; Nut Case, 1966; Salvage from Strosa, 1967; The Drum, 1969; Desperate Breakaway, 1969; One's Pool, 1969; The Model-Railway Men series, 3 vols., 1970–78; Is It Always Like This?, 1970; Telford series, 5 vols., 1970–79; Hayseed and Company, 1972. Add: The Vatican, 49 High St., Marshfield, Chippenham, Wilts., England.

POPE-HENNESSY, (Sir) John (Wyndham). British, b. 1913. Art. Prof. of Art, New York Univ., since 1977. Keeper, Dept. of Architecture and Sculpture, 1954–66, and Dir., 1967–73, Victoria and Albert Museum, London; Dir. of the British Museum, London, 1973–76; Consultative Chmn., Dept. of European Paintings, Metropolitan Museum of Art, New York, 1977–87. Slade Prof. of Fine Art, Oxford Univ., 1956–57, and Cambridge Univ., 1964–65. *Publs:* Giovanni di Paolo, 1937; Sassetta, 1939; Sienese Quattrocento Painting, 1947; A Sienese Codex of the Divine Comedy, 1947; The Drawings of Domenichino at Windsor Castle, 1948; A Lecture on Nicholas Hilliard, 1949; Donatello's Ascension, 1949; The Virgin with the Laughing Child, 1949; (ed.) Autobiography of Benvenuto Cellini, 1949; Paolo Uccello, 1950; Italian Gothic Sculpture in the Victoria and Albert Museum, 1952; Fra Angelico, 1952; Italian Gothic Sculpture, 1955; Italian Renaissance Sculpture, 1958; Italian High Renaissance and Baroque Sculpture, 1963; Catalogue of Italian Sculpture in the Victoria and Albert Museum, 1964; Renaissance Bronzes in the Kress Collection, 1965; The Portrait in the Renaissance, 1967; Essays on Italian Sculpture, 1968; Catalogue of Sculpture in the Frick Collection, 1970; Raphael, 1970; Luca della Robbia, 1980; The Study and Criticism of Italian Sculpture, 1980; Cellini, 1985; The Robert Lehman Collection I: Italian Paintings, 1987. Add: 28 via de' Bardi, 50125 Florence, Italy.

POPHAM, Hugh. British, b. 1920. Novels/Short stories, Poetry, History, Documentary/Reportage. *Publs:* Against the Lightning, 1944; The Journey and the Dream, 1945; To the Unborn—Greetings, 1946; Beyond the Eagle's Rage, 1951; Sea Flight, 1954; Cape of Storms, 1957; Monsters and Marlinspikes (in U.S. as The Fabulous Voyage of the Pegasus), 1958; The Sea Beggars, 1961; The Shores of Violence, 1963; The House at Cane Garden, 1965; The Somerset Light Infantry, 1968; Gentlemen Peasants, 1968; Into Wind, 1969; The Dorset Regiment, 1970; A Thirst for the Sea, 1979; F.A.N.Y: The Story of the Women's Transport Service, 1985. Add: 32 Tower Park, Fowey, Cornwall, PL23 1JD, England.

POPOVIC, Nenad D. American, b. 1909. Economics, Money/Finance, Politics/Government. Prof. Emeritus of Economics, Syracuse Univ., N.Y. (joined faculty, 1961). Exec. Dir., Intnl. Monetary Fund, Washington, D.C., 1950–52; Alternate Exec. Dir., World Bank, Washington, 1952–53; Vice-Gov., Yugoslav National Bank, 1953–55; Asst. State Secty. for Foreign Trade, 1955–60, and Plenipotentiary Minister, Ministry of Foreign Affairs, 1960–61, Yugoslavia. *Publs:* (co-author) Yugoslav Foreign Controls (economics), 1936; The Truth about Ethiopia (politics), 1937; Lectures on Statistics, 1947; Lectures in National Economic Planning, 1949; International Financial Organizations, 1965, 1967; Yugoslavia: The New Class in Crisis, 1968. Add: 319 Wedgewood Terr., Syracuse, N.Y. 13214, U.S.A.

POPPER, Frank James. American, b. 1944. Public administration, Regional/Urban planning. Self-employed Consultant, since 1975; Prof., since 1983, and Chmn., since 1986, Urban Studies Dept., Rutgers Univ., New Brunswick N.J. Research Assoc., 1968–69, and Dir., State Land Use Planning Project, 1975–81, Twentieth Century Fund, NYC; Staff Assoc., Public Admin. Service, Chicago, 1971–73; Sr. Research Assoc., American Soc. of Planning Officials, 1973–74; Sr Assoc., Environmental Law Inst., 1979–80; Gilbert White Fellow, Resources for the Future, 1982–83. *Publs:* The President's Commissions, 1970; Urban Nongrowth, 1976; The Politics of Land-Use Reform, 1981; Land Reform, American Style, 1984. Add: Urban Studies Dept. Rutgers Univ., New Brunswick, N.J. 08903, U.S.A.

POPPER, (Sir) Karl (Raimund). British, b. 1902. Philosophy, Autobiography/Memoirs/Personal. Prof. Emeritus, Univ. of London, (faculty member since 1945). William James Lectr., Harvard Univ., 1950. *Publs:* The Open Society and Its Enemies, 1945; The Poverty of

Historicism, 1957; The Logic of Scientific Discovery, 1959; Conjectures and Refutations: The Growth of Scientific Knowledge, 1963; Objective Knowledge: An Evolutionary Approach, 1972; Unended Quest: An Intellectual Autobiography, 1976; (with Sir John Eccles) The Self and Its Brain, 1977; The Open Universe, 1982; Quantum Theory and the Schism in Physics, 1982; Realism and the Aim of Science, 1983; The Pocket Popper, 1983. Add: c/o London Sch. of Economics, Houghton St., London WC2A 2AE, England.

POPPINO, Rollie E(dward). American, b. 1922. History. Prof. of History, Univ. of California at Davis, since 1961 (Chmn. of the Dept., 1978–87). Instr., Dept. of History, Stanford Univ., California, 1953–54; Intelligence Research Specialist, Dept. of State, Washington, D.C., 1954–61; Lectr., Sch. of Intnl. Service, American Univ., Washington, D.C., 1959–61. *Publs:* International Communism in Latin America: A History of the Movement 1917-1963, 1964; Feira de Santana, 1968; Brazil: The Land and People, 1968, 1973. Add: Dept. of History, Univ. of California, Davis, Calif. 95616, U.S.A.

POPPLE, James. British, b. 1927. Geography. Teacher, Nanaimo District Sr. Secondary Sch., British Columbia, since 1960. Teacher in the U.K., 1953–60. *Publs:* The Landscape of Europe, 1966, 1969; The Landscape of Japan, 1973. Add: 2490 Holyrood Dr., Nanaimo, B.C. V9S 4K8, Canada.

PORCH, Douglas. American, b. 1944. History. Sr. Lectr. in History, University Coll., Aberystwyth (Univ. Fellow, 1972–73). Research Student, Corpus Christi Coll., Cambridge, 1969–71; Research Fellow, Ecole Normale Superieure, Paris, 1971–72. *Publs:* Army and Revolution: France 1815-1848, 1974; The Making of a Military Revolutionary, 1974; The Portuguese Armed Forces and the Revolution, 1977; The March to the Marne: The French Army 1871-1914, 1981; The Conquest of Morocco, 1983; The Conquest of the Sahara, 1984. Add: History Dept., University Coll., Aberystwyth, Wales.

PORN, (Gustav) Ingmar. Finnish, b. 1935. Philosophy, Social sciences. Prof. of Philosophy, Univ. of Helsinki, since 1978. Lectr. in Philosophy, Univ. of Birmingham, 1964–78. *Publs:* The Logic of Power, 1970; Elements of Social Analysis, 1971; Action Theory and Social Science, 1977; (ed.) Essays in Philosophical Analysis, 1981. Add: Dept. of Philosophy, University of Helsinki, 00170 Helsinki 17, Finland.

PORTAL, Ellis. *See* POWE, Bruce.

PORTEN, Bezalel. American/Israeli, b. 1931. Archaeology/Antiquities, Theology/Religion. Assoc. Prof. in Jewish History, Hebrew Univ., Jerusalem, since 1969. Member of the faculty, Univ. of California, at Berkeley, 1964–65, and Davis, 1965–68; York Univ., Toronto, 1975–76. *Publs:* Archives from Elephantine: The Life of an Ancient Jewish Military Colony, 1968; (with J.C. Greenfield) Jews of Elephantine and Arameans of Syene: Fifty Aramaic Texts with Hebrew and English Translations, 1974; (with J.C. Greenfield) The Bisitun Inscription of Darius the Great: Aramaic Version, 1982; (ed. and trans. with A. Yardeni) Textbook of Aramaic Documents from Ancient Egypt, 2 vols., 1986–89. Add: 28 Efrata, Jerusalem 93384, Israel.

PORTEOUS, Leslie (Crichton). British, b. 1901. Novels/Short stories, Geography, Autobiography/Memoirs/Personal, Biography. *Publs:* Farmer's Creed, 1938; Teamsman, 1939; Land Truant, 1940; The Cottage, 1941; The Farm by the Lake, 1942; The Snow, 1943; The Earth Remains, 1944; Sons of the Farm, 1947; Changing Valley, 1948; Pioneers of Fertility, 1948; Wild Acres, 1949; Caves and Caverns of Peakland, 1949; The Beauty and Mystery of Well-Dressing, 1949; Derbyshire, 1951; Call of the Soil, 1953; Peakland, 1953; Man of the Moors, 1954; Chuckling Joe, 1954; The Battle Mound, 1955; Death in the Fields, 1956; Broken River, 1956; Great Men of Derbyshire, 1956; Pill-Boxes and Bandages, 1958; Lucky Columbell, 1959; The Well-Dressing Guide, 1959; Toad Hole, 1960; Derbyshire Customs, 1960; Strike, 1962; Portrait of Peakland, 1962; Man of the Fields: Richard Jefferies, 1964. Add: 18 the Parkway, Darley Dale, Matlock, Derbyshire, England.

PORTER, Andrew. British, b. 1928. Music. Music Critic, The New Yorker, NYC, since 1972. Music Critic, The Financial Times, London, 1952–72. *Publs:* A Musical Season, 1974; The Ring of the Nibelung, 1976; Music of Three Seasons, 1978; Music of Three More Seasons 1981; (ed.) Verdi's Macbeth: A Sourcebook, 1984; Musical Events 1980–1983, 1987. Add: c/o The New Yorker, 25 W. 43rd St., New York, N.Y. 10036, U.S.A.

PORTER, Bern. American, b. 1911. Poetry, Essays. Chmn. of the Bd., Bern Porter Books Inc., Belfast, Me., since 1929, and Inst. of Advanced Thinking, Belfast, since 1959. Founding Fellow, Intnl. Poetry Soc., London, 1978. *Publs:* Map of Houlton High School, 1929; Alpha Particles from Radium, 1933; Art Scrapbook, 1935; Art Reproductions, 1937; Books Book of Physics, 1938; Colloidal Graphite, 1939; Map of Physics, 1939; Map of Ricker, 1940; Map of Chemistry, 1941; Waterfight, 1941; Doldrums, 1941; Me, 1943; Cosmic Sight, 1943; All Over the Place, 1944; Miller Bibliography, 1946; Map of Joyceana, 1946; Art Techniques, 1947; Union of Science and Art, 1948; Elements of Typography, 1948; Schillerhaus, 1949; Drawings, 1954-1955, 1956; Rocket Data Book, 1956; Rocket Terminology, 1956; (with Richard Bowman) Science and Art, 1956; Mencken Bibliography, 1958; Drawings 1955-1956, 1959; Physics for Tomorrow, 1959; F. Scott Fitzgerald Publications, 1960; Aphasia, 1961; Scandinavian Summer, 1961; The Waste-Maker, 1961; Circle: Reproduction of Art Work 1944-47, 1963; Art Assorted, 1963; Reporting and Preventive Maintenance Forms for the 475L Program, 1963; Charcoal Drawings 1935-37, 1963; I've Left, 2nd ed. 1963, 3rd ed. 1971; Applicable 465L Publications, 1963; Day Notes for Mother, 1964; Native Alphabet, 1964; Scigraffiti, 1964; Aloiio, 1964; What Henry Miller Said and Why It's Important, 2nd ed. 1965, 3rd ed. 1978; Dynamic Test Vehicle Instrumentation and Data Sytem Criteria, 1965; Dynamic Test Vehicle Data Reduction and Correlation Requirements, 1965; Mathematics for Electronics, 1965; Art Productions 1928-1965, 1965; 468B, 1965; Captive Firing of Flight Stage Reliability Study, 1966; System Methodologies and Their Utilization, 1966; Moscow, 1966; Founds, 1966; Cut Leaves, 1966; The Box, 1968; The First Publications of F. Scott Fitzgerald, 1969; Knox County, Maine, 1969; The 14th of February, 1971; Found Poems, 1972; Hand Coated Chocolates, 1972; Contemporary Italian Painters, 1973; Trattoria Due Forni, 1973; The Manhattan Telephone Book, 1975; Run-On, 1975; Where to Go, What to Do, When in New York, Week of June 17, 1972, 1975; Selected Founds, 1975; Gee-Whizzles, 1976; Bern, 1976; The Last Acts of Saint Fu, 1976; Time, 1979; Il Recordi Di Firenze, 1980; Isle Vista, 1981; Me, 1982; The Book of Dos, 1982; Here Comes Everybody's Don't Book, 1983; Collected Poems, 1983; The Book of Death, 1983; Porter's Book, 1983; My Dear Me, 1985; Horizontal Hold, 1986; Devil's Wishbone, 1986; Never Ends, 1986; Left Leg, 1988; Sweet End, 1989. Add: 22 Salmond Rd., Belfast, Me. 04915, U.S.A.

PORTER, Bernard (John). British, b. 1941. History. Reader in History, Univ. of Hull, since 1988 (Lectr., 1968–78; Sr. Lectr., 1978–88). Fellow, Corpus Christi Coll., Cambridge, 1966–68. *Publs:* Critics of Empire: British Radical Attitudes to Colonialism in Africa 1896-1914, 1968; The Lion's Share: A Short History of British Imperialism 1850-1983, 1984; The Refugee Question in Mid-Victorian Politics, 1979; Britain, Europe and the World 1850-1982: Delusions of Grandeur, 1983, 1987; The Origins of the Vigilant State: The London Metropolitan Police Special Branch Before the First World War, 1987; Plots and Paranoia: A History of Political Policing in Britain, 1790 to the Present Day, 1989. Add: Dept. of History, Univ. of Hull, Hull HU6 7RX, England.

PORTER, Brian (Ernest). British, b. 1928. History, International relations/ Current affairs. Hon. Lectr. in Intnl. Relations, Univ. of Kent, Canterbury, since 1984. Lectr. in Political Science, Univ. of Khartoum, 1963–65; Sr. Lectr. in Intnl. Politics, Univ. Coll., Aberystwyth, 1971–85 (Lectr., 1965–71); Acting Vice-Consul, Muscat, 1967. *Publs:* Britain and the Rise of Communist China, 1967; (ed.) The Aberystwyth Papers: International Politics 1919-1969, 1972; (jt. author) The Reason of States, 1978; (jt. author) The Community of States, 1982; (jt. author) Home Fires and Foreign Fields: British Social and Military Experience in the First World War, 1985. Add: Rutherford Coll., Univ. of Kent, Canterbury, Kent, England.

PORTER, Burton F. American, b. 1936. Philosophy. Prof. and Head of the Dept. of Philosophy, Drexel Univ., Philadelphia, since 1987. Lectr. in Philosophy, European Div., Univ. of Maryland, London, 1968–71; Assoc. Prof. of Philosophy, King's Coll., Wilkes-Barre, Pa., 1969–71; Assoc. Prof., Russell Sage Coll., Troy, N.Y., 1971–87. *Publs:* Deity and Morality, with Regard to the Naturalistic Fallacy, 1968; (ed. and contrib.) Philosophy: A Literary and Conceptual Approach, 1974, 1980; (ed. and contrib.) Personal Philosophy, 1976; The Good Life: Alternatives in Ethics, 1980; Reasons for Living: A Basic Ethics, 1988. Add: Dept. of Humanities and Communications, Drexel Univ., Philadelphia, Pa. 19104, U.S.A.

PORTER, (Sir) George. British, b. 1920. Chemistry. Fullerian Prof. of Chemistry, Royal Instn. of Great Britain; Pres., Assn. for Science Education. Asst. Dir. of Research in Physical Chemistry, Cambridge Univ., 1952–54; Prof. of Physical Chemistry, 1955–63, and Firth Prof.

and Head of the Dept. of Chemistry, 1963–66, Univ. of Sheffield. *Publs:* Chemistry for the Modern World, 1962; Laws of Disorder (TV series), 1965; Time Machines (TV series), 1969; Controversy, 1971–75; (ed.) Progress in Reaction Kinetics, 5 vols; (co-ed.) Advice to Lecturers, 1974. Add: The Royal Instn., 21 Albemarle St., London W1X 4BS, England.

PORTER, Joshua Roy. British, b. 1921. Poetry, Theology/Religion, Essays. Fellow, Chaplain and Tutor, Oriel Coll., Oxford, and Univ. Lectr. in Theology, Oxford Univ., 1949–62; Dean, Faculty of the Arts, 1968–71, Dept. Head and Prof. of Theology, 1972–86, Univ. of Exeter; Canon and Prebendary of Wrightring, Chichester Cathedral, and Theological Lectr., 1965–88. *Publs:* (with J. Heath-Stubbs and S. Keyes) Eight Oxford Poets, 1941; (with F.F. Bruce) Promise and Fulfilment, 1963; Moses and Monarcy, 1963; The Extended Family in the Old Testament, 1967; (with R.C. Walton) A Source Book of the Bible for Teachers, 1970; (ed. with J.I. Durham) Proclamation and Presence, 1970; The Non-Juring Bishops, 1973; (with H.R.E. Davidson) The Journey to the Other World, 1975; The Book of Leviticus, 1976; (ed. with W.D.M. Russell) Animals in Folklore, 1978; The Monarchy, 1978; The Crown and the Church, 1978; (with G.W. Anderson) Tradition and Interpretation, 1979; (with R.C. Walton) A Basic Introduction to the Old Testament, 1980; (co-ed.) Folklore Studies in the Twentieth Century, 1980; (with M. Loewe and C. Blacker) Divination and Oracles, 1981; (with H.R.E. Davidson) The Folklore of Ghosts, 1981; (co-author) Israel's Prophetic Tradition, 1982; (co-author) Tracts for Our Times, 1983; (with C. Blacker) The Hero in Traditional Folklore, 1984; (with I. Netton) Arabia and the Gulf: From Traditional Society to Modern States, 1986; (with H.R.E. Davidson) The Seer in Folklore, 1989; (trans.) The Living Psalms, 1989. Add: 36 Theberton St., London N1, England.

PORTER, Joyce. British, b. 1924. Mystery/Crime/Suspense. WRAF Officer, 1949–63. *Publs:* Dover One, 1964; Dover Two, 1965; Dover Three, 1965; Sour Cream with Everything, 1966; Dover and the Unkindest Cut of All, 1967; The Chinks in the Curtain, 1967; Dover Goes to Pott, 1968; Neither a Candle nor a Pitchfork, 1969; Dover Strikes Again, 1970; Rather a Common Sort of Crime, 1970; Only with a Barge-Pole, 1971; A Medler and Her Murder, 1972; It's Murder with Dover, 1973; The Package Included Murder, 1975; Dover and the Claret Tappers, 1977; Who the Heck Is Sylvia, 1977; Dead Easy for Dover, 1978; The Cart Before the Crime, 1979; Dover Beats the Band, 1980. Add: 68 Sand St., Longbridge Deverill, nr. Warminster, Wilts., England.

PORTER, Peter (Neville Frederick). Australian, b. 1929. Poetry, Travel/Exploration/Adventure. Former journalist, bookseller and clerk; also worked in advertising. Compton Lectr. in Poetry, Univ. of Hull, 1970–71. *Publs:* Once Bitten, Twice Bitten: Poems, 1961; (with Kingsley Amis and Dom Moraes) Penguin Modern Poets 2, 1962; Poems Ancient and Modern, 1964; Words Without Music, 1968; Solemn Adultery at Breakfast Creek: An Australian Ballad, 1968; A Porter Folio: New Poems, 1969; The Last of England, 1970; Epigrams by Martial, 1971; After Martial, 1972; Preaching to the Converted, 1972; (ed.) New Poems 1971-72: A P.E.N. Anthology of Contemporary Poetry, 1972; (ed.) A Choice of Poe's Verse, 1972; Jonah, 1973; (with Anthony Thwaite) Roloff Beny in Italy, 1974; (ed. with Anthony Thwaite) The English Poets: From Chaucer to Edward Thomas, 1974; Living in a Calm Country, 1975; The Lady and the Unicorn, 1975; The Cost of Seriousness, 1978; English Subtitles, 1981; The Animal Programme, 1982; Collected Poems, 1983; Fast Forward, 1984; Narcissus, 1984; The Run of Your Father's Library, 1984; The Automatic Oracle, 1987; Mars, 1988. Add: 42 Cleveland Sq., London W2, England.

PORTER, Sheena. British, b. 1935. Children's fiction. Library Asst., Leicester City Library, 1954–57; Regional Children's Librarian, Nottingham County Library, 1957–60; Editorial Asst., Oxford Univ. Press, London, 1960–61; Regional Children's Librarian, Shropshire County Library, 1961–62. *Publs:* The Bronze Chrysanthemum, 1961; Hills and Hollows, 1962; Jacob's Ladder, 1963; Nordy Bank, 1964; The Knockers, 1965; Deerfold, 1966; The Scapegoat, 1968; The Valley of Carreg-Wen, 1971; The Hospital, 1973. Add: Dunning House, 57 Gravel Hill, Ludlow, Shropshire, England.

PORTER, Sylvia (Field). American, b. 1913. Economics, Money/Finance. Syndicated columnist: associated with the New York Post, 1935–77, and the New York Daily News, since 1978; Ed.-in-Chief, Sylvia Porter's Personal Finance Mag., since 1983, and Sylvia Porter's Active Retirement Newsletter, since 1988. *Publs:* How to Make Money in Government Bonds, 1939; If War Comes to the American Home, 1941; (co-author) How to Live Within Your Income, 1948; Managing Your Money, 1953, 1961; How to Get More for Your Money, 1961; Sylvia Porter's Income Tax Guide, 1961, and annually; Sylvia Porter's Money Book, 1975; Sylvia Porter's New Money Book for the 80's, 1980; Sylvia Porter's Your Own Money, 1983; Love and Money, 1985; Your Financial Security, 1988. Add: 2 Fifth Ave., New York, N.Y. 10011, U.S.A.

PORTIS, Charles (McColl). American, b. 1933. Westerns/Adventure. Freelance writer since 1964. Reporter, Commercial Appeal, Memphis, 1958, Arkansas Gazette, Little Rock, 1959–60, and New York Herald-Tribune, 1960–64. *Publs:* Norwood, 1966; True Grit, 1968; The Dog of the South, 1979; Masters of Atlantis, 1985. Add: 7417 Kingwood, Little Rock, Ark. 72207, U.S.A.

PORTOBELLO, Petronella. *See* **ANDERSON,** Flavia.

POSNER, Michael Vivian. British, b. 1931. Economics. Secty.-Gen., European Science Foundn., since 1986. Fellow, Pembroke Coll., Cambridge, 1960–83; Dir. of Economics, Ministry of Power, 1966–67; Economic Adviser to H.M. Treasury, 1967–71; Chmn., Social Science Research Council, 1979–83; Economic Dir., National Economic Development Office, 1984–86. *Publs:* (with S.J. Woolf) Italian Public Enterprise, 1966; Fuel Policy: A Study in Applied Economics, 1973; (ed.) Public Sector Resource Allocation, 1978; (ed.) Demand Management in the United Kingdom, 1978; (co-author) Energy Economics, 1981; (ed.) Problems of International Money 1972-1985, 1986. Add: Rushwood, Jack Straw's Lane, Oxford, England.

POSNER, Rebecca. British, b. 1929. Language/Linguistics. Prof. of the Romance Languages, and Fellow, St. Hugh's Coll., Oxford Univ., since 1978. Fellow, Girton Coll., Cambridge, 1960–63; Prof. of French Studies, Univ. of Ghana, 1963–65; Reader in Language, York Univ., 1965–78. *Publs:* Consonantal Dissimilation in the Romance Languages, 1961; The Romance Languages, 1966; (with J. Orr and I. Iordan) Introduction to Romance Linguistics, 1970; (co-ed.) Trends in Romance Linguistics and Philology, 4 vols., 1980–82. Add: St. Hugh's College, Oxford OX2 6LE, England.

POSNER, Richard. Also writes as Dayle Courtney, Jonathan Craig, Iris Foster, Beatrice Murray, Dick Wine, Alayna Richards, Erica Mitchell, and Paul Todd. American, b. 1944. Novels/short stories, Mystery/Crime/Suspense, Romance, Science fiction/Fantasy, Children's fiction. English Teacher, Sachem High Sch., Ronkonkoma, N.Y.; Instr. of Composition, Adelphi University, Garden City, N.Y.; Queensborough Community Coll., Bayside N.Y.; Suffolk Community College, Selden, N.Y. *Publs:* (as Beatrice Murray) The Dark Sonata, 1971; (with Jonathan Craig) The New York Crime Book, 1972; (as Iris Foster) The Moorwood Legacy, 1972; (as Iris Foster) Deadly Sea, Deadly Sand, 1972; (as Iris Foster) Nightshade, 1973; (as Iris Foster) The Sabath Quest, 1973; (as Iris Foster) The Crimson Moon, 1973; (as Dick Wine) Allegro With Passion, 1973; The Mafia Man, 1973; The Seven-Ups (1973); The Trigger Man (1974); Welcome, Sinner (1974); (as Paul Todd) Blood All Over, 1975; The Image and the Flesh, 1975; Lucas Tanner: A Question of Guilt, 1975; Lucas Tanner: A Matter of Love, 1975; Lucas Tanner: For Her to Decide, 1975; The Lovers, 1978; The Impassioned, 1980; Infidelities, 1982; (as Dayle Courtney) The Foxworth Hunt, 1982; (as Alayna Richards) Tycoon, 1983; (with Marie Castoire) The Gold Shield, 1984; (as Erica Mitchell) Jade Moon, 1984; (as Erica Mitchell) Bright Desire, 1985; Sweet Pain, 1987; Sparrow's Flight, 1988; Goodnight, Cinderella, 1989. Add: c/o Henry Morrison, Inc., P.O. 235, Bedford Hills, NY 10507, U.S.A.

POSPISIL, Leopold Jaroslav. American, b. 1923. Anthropology/Ethnology, Law. Prof. of Anthropology, Curator and Dir., Div. of Anthrpology, Peabody Museum, and Ed. of Univ. Publs. in Anthropology, Yale Univ., New Haven, since 1965 (Research Asst., Peabody Museum, 1953–56; Instr. in Anthropology, 1956–57; Asst. Curator, 1956–60; Asst. Prof. 1957–60; Assoc. Prof. and Assoc. Curator, 1960–65). *Publs:* Law among the Kapauku of Netherlands New Guinea, 1956; Kapauku Papuans and Their Law, 1958; Kapauku Papuan Economy, 1963; The Kapauku Papuans of Western New Guinea, 1964; Anthropology of Law, 1971; The Ethnology of Law, 1972, 1976; Anthropologie des Rechts, 1982. Add: Peabody Museum of Natural History, Yale Univ., New Haven, Conn. 06520, U.S.A.

POST, Mortimer. *See* **BLAIR,** Walter.

POST, Steve. American, b. 1944. Communications media/Broadcasting. Morning Host, WNYC-FM radio station, New York. Member, Bd. of Dirs., Pacifica Foundn. Inc. Producer, Host, and Gen. Mgr., WBAI-

FM radio station, NYC, 1965–80. *Publs:* Playing in the FM Band: A Personal Account of Free Radio, 1974. Add: 155 W. 71st St., New York, N.Y. 10023, U.S.A.

POSTER, Cyril Dennis. British, b. 1924. Education, Literature. Freelance consultant in education management, since 1986. Ed., Routledge Education Management series, since 1985. Headmaster, Lawrence Weston Sch., Bristol, 1959–69, and Sheppey Sch., Kent, 1970–76; Principal, Groby Community Coll., Leicester, 1977–83; Deputy Dir., National Development Centre for Sch. Mgmt. Training, Sch. of Education, Univ. of Bristol, 1984–86. *Publs:* Read Write Speak, 1964; (with Albert) Story of English Literature, 1965; Times and Seasons, 1966; The School and the Community, 1971; School Decision-Making, 1976; Community Education, 1982; (ed. with Day) Partnership in Education Management, 1988. Add: 83 Downs Park, E. Henleaze, Bristol BS6 7QG, England.

POSTER, Mark. American, b. 1941. Intellectual history. Prof. of History, Univ. of California at Irvine, since 1978. Member, Editorial Bd., The 18th Century: A Journal of Interpretation. *Publs:* The Utopian Thought of Restif de la Bretonne, 1971; (ed.) Harmonian Man: Selected Writings of Charles Fourier, 1971; Existential Marxism in Postwar France, 1976; Critical Theory of the Family, 1978; Sartre's Marxism, 1979; Foucault, Marxism and History, 1984; (ed.) Jean Baudrillard: Selected Writings, 1988. Add: History Dept., Univ. of California at Irvine, Irvine, Calif. 92717, U.S.A.

POTOK, Chaim. American, b. 1929. Novels/Short stories. Special Projects Ed., Jewish Publ. Soc. of America, Philadelphia, since 1974 (Ed., 1965–74). *Publs:* The Chosen, 1967; The Promise, 1969; My Name Is Asher Lev, 1972; In the Beginning, 1975; Wanderings: Chaim Potok's History of the Jews, 1978; The Book of Lights, 1981; Davita's Harp, 1985; Theo Tobiasse: Artist in Exile, 1987. Add: c/o Alfred Knopf Inc., 201 E. 50th St., New York, N.Y. 10022, U.S.A.

POTOKER, Edward Martin. American, b. 1931. Literature, Biography. Prof. of English since 1979, Bernard M. Baruch Coll., City Univ. of New York (Lectr., 1960–62; Asst. Prof., 1963–71; Chmn. of Dept., 1971–76; Assoc. Prof., 1972–79). Book Reviewer, New York Times Book Review, since 1962, and Saturday Review, since 1965. Member, Editorial Staff, New Yorker mag., 1957–58; Instr. in English, Univ. of Rochester, 1958–59; Lectr. in English, Hunter Coll., NYC, 1960. Former Contrib., Encyclopedia of World Literature in the 20th Century and Groliers Encyclopaedia International; Founding Member, The Journal of Critical Analysis, 1969. *Publs:* The Corn Grain, 1956; Ronald Firbank, 1969; John Braine, 1978; (ed.) A Tragedy in Green and When Widows Love: Two Stories by Ronald Firbank, 1978; (ed.) Ronald Firbank/Carl Van Vechten Correspondence, 1988. Add: 186 Riverside Dr., New York, N.Y. 10024, U.S.A.

POTTER, Dennis (Christopher George). British, b. 1935. Novels/Short stories, Plays/Screenplays. Book Reviewer, The Guardian, London, since 1973. Member of the Current Affairs Staff, BBC Television, London, 1959–61; Feature Writer, then Television Critic, Daily Herald, London, 1961–64; Leader Writer, The Sun, London, 1964; Television Critic, New Statesman, London, 1967, 1972; Book Reviewer, The Times, London, 1967–73. *Publs:* The Glittering Coffin, 1960; The Changing Forest: Life in the Forest of Dean Today, 1962; The Nigel Barton Plays, 1968; Son of Man, 1969; Hide and Seek (novel), 1973; Brimstone and Treacle, 1978; Pennies from Heaven (novelization of TV series), 1979; Sufficient Carbohydrate, 1983; Waiting for the Boat: Dennis Potter on Television, 1984; Ticket to Ride (novel), 1986; The Singing Detective, 1986; Blackeyes (novel), 1987. Add: Morecambe Lodge, Duxmere, Ross-on-Wye, Herefordshire, England.

POTTER, Jeremy. British, b. 1922. Mystery/Crime/Suspense, Historical/Romance/Gothic, History. *Publs:* Hazard Chase, 1964; Death in Office, 1965; Foul Play, 1967; The Dance of Death, 1968; A Trail of Blood, 1970; Going West, 1972; Disgrace and Favour, 1975; Death in the Forest, 1977; Good King Richard? (history), 1983; Pretenders (history), 1986; Independent Television in Britain, vol. 3: Politics and Control 1968-80, 1989. Add: c/o Constable and Co., 10 Orange St., London WC2H 7EG, England.

POTTER, Margaret (Newman). Also writes as Anne Betteridge, Anne Melville, and Margaret Newman. British, b. 1926. Mystery/Crime/Suspense, Historical/Romance/Gothic, Children's fiction. Teacher in England and Egypt, 1947–50; Ed., The King's Messenger children's mag., London, 1950–55; Adviser, Citizen's Advice Bureau, Twickenham, 1962–70. *Publs:* as Anne Betteridge unless otherwise

noted—(as Margaret Newman) Murder to Music (crime), 1959; The Foreign Girl, 1960; The Young Widow, 1961; Spring in Morocco, 1962; The Long Dance of Love, 1963; The Younger Sister, 1964; Return to Delphi, 1964; Single to New York, 1965; The Chains of Love, 1965; The Truth Game, 1966; A Portuguese Affair, 1966; A Little Bit of Luck, 1967; Shooting Star, 1968; (as Margaret Potter) The Touch-and-Go Year (juvenile), 1968; Love in a Rainy Country, 1969; (as Margaret Potter) The Blow-and-Grow Year, 1969; Sirocco, 1970; The Girl Outside, 1971; (as Margaret Potter) Sandy's Safari (juvenile), 1971; Journey from a Foreign Land, 1972; The Sacrifice, 1973; The Stranger on the Beach, 1974; (as Margaret Potter) The Story of the Stolen Necklace (juvenile), 1974; A Time of Their Lives (short stories), 1974; (as Margaret Potter), Trouble on Sunday (juvenile), 1974; The Temp, 1976; (as Margaret Potter), The Motorway Mob (juvenile), 1976; (as Margaret Potter) Tony's Special Place (juvenile), 1977; A Place for Everyone (short stories), 1977; (as Anne Melville) The Lorimer Line, 1977; The Tiger and the Goat, 1978; (as Anne Melville) The Lorimer Legacy (in U.S. as Alexa), 1979; as Anne Melville) Lorimers at War, 1980, in U.S. with Lorimers in Love, as Blaize, 1981; (as Anne Melville) Lorimers in Love (in U.S. with Lorimers at War, as Blaize), 1981; (as Anne Melville) The Last of the Lorimers (in U.S.A. as Family Fortunes), 1983; (as Anne Melville) Lorimer Loyalties, 1984; (as Margaret Potter) The Boys Who Disappeared (juvenile), 1985; (as Margaret Potter) . . . Unto the Fourth Generation, 1986; (as Anne Melville) The House of Hardie, 1987; (as Margaret Potter) Tilly and the Princess (juvenile), 1987; (as Anne Melville) The House of Hardie, 1987; (as Margaret Potter) Lochandar, 1988; (as Anne Melville) Grace Hardie, 1988; (as Anne Melville) The Dangerfield Diaries, 1989; (as Anne Melville) Snapshots, 1989. Add: c/o Peters Fraser and Dunlop, The Chambers, Chelsea Harbour, Lots Rd., London SW10 0XF, England.

POTTER, Vincent G. American, b. 1928. Philosophy, Theology/Religion, Translations. Prof. of Philosophy, Fordham Univ., Bronx, N.Y., since 1973 (Asst. Prof., 1965–69; Assoc. Prof., 1969–73). Ed., International Philosophical Quarterly, since 1985. *Publs:* Peirce's Ontological Pragmatism, 1966; C.S. Peirce on Norms and Ideals, 1968; Social Interaction: Arabia and USA Universities, 1982; Philosophy of Knowledge, 1985; Readings in Epistemology, 1986; (trans.) Pecham's On the Eternity of the World, 1987; (ed.) Doctrine and Experience, 1988. Add: Dept. of Philosophy, Fordham Univ., Bronx, N.Y. 10458, U.S.A.

POTTS, Jean. American, b. 1910. Mystery/Crime/Suspense. *Publs:* Someone to Remember (non-mystery novel), 1943; Go, Lovely Rose, 1954; Death of a Stray Cat, 1955; The Diehard, 1956; The Man with the Cane, 1957; Lightning Strikes Twice, 1958 (as Blood Will Tell, 1959); Home Is the Prisoner, 1960; The Evil Wish, 1962; THe Only Good Secretary, 1965; The Footsteps on the Stairs, 1966; The Trash Stealer, 1968; The Little Lie, 1968; An Affair of the Heart, 1970; The Troublemaker, 1972; My Brother's Killer, 1975. Add: 53 Irving Pl., Apt. 6-D, New York, N.Y. 10003, U.S.A.

POTTS, Richard. British, b. 1938. Children's fiction. Head Teacher, Great Ouseburn Primary Sch., York. *Publs:* An Owl for His Birthday, 1966; The Haunted Mine, 1968; A Boy and His Bike, 1976; Tod's Owl, 1980; Battleground, 1987. Add: 142 Main St., Fulford, York, England.

POULIN, A(lfred A.), Jr. American, b. 1938. Poetry, Translations. Prof. of English, State Univ. of New York at Brockport (joined faculty, 1971). Ed.-at-Large, American Poetry Review, Philadelphia, since 1972; Founding Ed., BOA Editions, Brockport, N.Y., since 1976. Asst. Prof. of English, 1962–64, 1968–71, Chmn., Div. of Humanities, 1968–71, and Asst. to Pres., Curr. and Dev., 1970–71, St. Francis Coll., Univ. of New England, Maine; Lectr., Univ. of Maryland European Div., Heidelberg, 1965, and Univ. of New Hampshire, Durham, 1965–66; Dir., Brockport Writers Forum, State Univ. of NY, Coll. of Brockport, 1972–75; Lit. Panel, The NY State Council on the Arts, 1977–80; Univ. Wide Committee on the Arts, State Univ. of NY, 1978; Exec. Dir., The NY State Literary Center, Inc., Brockport/Fairport, 1978–80; Task Force on the Individual Artist, The NY State Council on the Arts, 1980–81. *Publs:* (ed. with David A. DeTurk) The American Folk Scene, 1967; (ed.) Contemporary American Poetry, 1971; In Advent (verse), 1972; Catawba: Omens, Prayer, and Songs (verse), 1977; The Widow's Taboo: Poems after Catawba, 1977; (trans.) Duino Elegies and the Sonnets to Orpheus, by Rainer Maria Rilke, 1977; (trans.) Saltimbanques: Prose Poems, by Rainer Maria Rilke, 1978; The Nameless Garden (verse), 1978; (trans.) The Roses and The Windows, by Rainer Maria Rilke, 1979; (trans.) Poems by Anne Hebert, 1980; The Slaughter of Pigs: A Sequence of Poems, 1981; (trans.) The Astonishment of Origins: Poems by Rainer Maria Rilke, 1982; (trans.) Orchards: Poems by Rainer Maria Rilke, 1982; (ed.) A Ballet for the Ear: Interviews, Essays and Reviews, 1983; (trans.) The Migration of Powers:

Poems by Rainer Maria Rilke, 1985; A Nest of Sonnets, 1985; (trans.) The Complete French Poems of Rainer Maria Rilke, 1986; (trans.) Selected Poems, by Anne Hebert, 1987; A Momentary Order: Poems, 1987. Add: 92 Park Ave., Brockport, N.Y. 14420, U.S.A.

POURNELLE, Jerry (Eugene). Also writes as Wade Curtis. American, b. 1933. Novels/Short stories, Science fiction/Fantasy, Engineering/Technology. Freelance writer, lectr., and consultant, since 1970. Fellow, Operations Research Soc. of America and American Assn. for the Advancement of Science. Research Asst., Univ. of Washington Medical Sch., 1954–57; Aviation Psychologist and Systems Engineer, Boeing Corp., Seattle, 1957–64; Mgr. of Special Studies, Aerospace Corp., San Bernardino, Calif., 1964–65; Research Specialist and Proposal Mgr., American Rockwell Corp., 1965–66; Prof. of Political Science, Pepperdine Univ., Los Angeles, 1966–69; Exec. Asst. to the Major of Los Angeles, 1969–70.Contrib. of non-fiction articles to Galaxy mag., 1974–78; Pres., Science Fiction Writers of America, 1974. *Publs:* (as Wade Curtis) Red Heroin (novel), 1969; (with Stefan T. Possony) The Strategy of Technology: Winning the Decisive War, 1970; (as Wade Curtis) Red Dragon (novel), 1971; A Spaceship for the King, 1973; Escape from the Planet of the Apes (novelization of screenplay), 1973; (with Larry Niven) The Mote in God's Eye, 1974; (ed.) 20/20 Vision, 1974; Birth of Fire, 1976; (with Larry Niven) Inferno, 1976; West of Honor, 1976; High Justice (short stories) 1977; The Mercenary, 1977; (with Larry Niven) Lucifer's Hammer, 1977; Exiles to Glory, 1978; (ed.) Black Holes, 1979; A Step Further Out (non-fiction), 1980; Janissaries, 1980; (with Larry Niven) Oath of Fealty, 1981; (with Roland Green) Clan and Crown, 1982; (co-ed.) There Will Be War, 1983; (with Dean Ing) Mutual Assured Survival, 1984; (co-ed.) Men of War, 1984; (co-ed.) Blood and Iron, 1984; (co-ed.) Day of the Tyrant, 1985; (with Larry Niven) Footfall, 1985; (co-ed.) Warriors, 1986; (co-ed.) Imperial Stars: The Stars at War, Republic and Empire, 2 vols., 1986–87; (co-ed.) Guns of Darkness, 1987; (with Roland Green) Storms of Victory (novel), 1987; (with Larry Niven) Legacy of Heorot (novel), 1987; (ed. with John Carr) Call to Battle, 1988; Mercenary Prince (novel), 1989. Add: 3960 Laurel Canyon Blvd., Suite 372, Studio City, Calif. 91604, U.S.A.

POWE, Bruce Allen. Also writes as Ellis Portal. Canadian, b. 1925. Novels/Short stories, Science fiction/Fantasy, Humor/Satire. Vice-Pres. of Public Affairs, Canadian Life and Health Insurance Assn., Toronto, since 1966. Special Asst., Minister of Mines and Technical Surveys, 1951–57; Editorial Asst., Imperial Oil Ltd., 1957–60; Exec. Dir. Ontario Liberal Assn., 1960–63; Vice-Pres., Public Relations, Baker Advertising Ltd., 1964–66. *Publs:* Expresso '67, 1966; (as Ellis Portal) Killing Ground: The Canadian Civil War, 1968, under own name, 1972; The Last Days of the American Empire, 1974; The Aberhart Summer, 1983; The Ice Eaters, 1987. Add: 158 Ridley Blvd., Toronto, Ont. M5M 3M1, Canada.

POWELL, Anthony (Dymoke). British, b. 1905. Novels/Short stories, Plays/Screenplays, Literature, Autobiography/Memoirs/Personal. With Duckworth, publrs., London, 1926–35; Literary Ed., Punch, London, 1953–59. Trustee, National Portrait Gallery, London, 1962–76. *Publs:* Afternoon Men, 1931; Venusburg, 1932; From a View to a Death (in U.S. as Mr. Zouch: Superman: From a View to a Death), 1933; Agents and Patients, 1936; What's Become of Waring, 1939; (ed.) Novels of High Society from the Victorian Age, 1947; John Aubrey and His Friends, 1948, 3rd ed. 1988; (ed.) Brief Lives and Other Selected Writings of John Aubrey, 1949; A Question of Upbringing, 1951; A Buyer's Market, 1952; The Acceptance World, 1955; At Lady Molly's, 1957; Casanova's Chinese Restaurant, 1960; The Kindly Ones, 1962; The Valley of Bones, 1964; The Soldier's Art, 1966; The Military Philosophers, 1968; The Garden God and The Rest I'll Whistle: The Text of Two Plays, 1971; Books Do Furnish a Room, 1971; Temporary Kings, 1973; Hearing Secret Harmonies, 1975; Infants of the Spring, 1976; Messengers of Day, 1978; Faces in My Time, 1980; The Strangers All Are Gone, 1982; O, How the Wheel Becomes It!, 1983; The Fisher King, 1986. Add: The Chantry, nr. Frome, Somerset, England.

POWELL, Craig. Australian, b. 1940. Poetry. In private practice as psychoanalyst, Sydney, Aust., since 1982. Psychiatrist, Parramatta Psychiatric Centre, Sydney, 1968–72, Brandon Mental Health Center, Manitoba, 1972–75, and London Psychiatric Hosp., Ontario, 1976–82. *Publs:* A Different Kind of Breathing, 1966; I Learn by Going, 1968; A Country Without Exiles, 1972; Selected Poems 1963-1977, 1977; Rehearsal for Dancers, 1978; A Face in Your Hands, 1984. Add: 24 Minga St., Ryde, N.S.W. 2112, Australia.

POWELL, (John) Enoch. British, b. 1912. Poetry, Classics, History, Politics/Government, Translations. Ulster Unionist Member of Parliament (U.K.) for South Down, N. Ire., 1974–87 (Conservative M.P. for Wolverhampton South-West, 1950–74). *Publs:* The Rendel Harris Papyri, 1936; First Poems, 1937; A Lexicon to Herodotus, 1938; The History of Herodotus, 1939; Casting Off and Other Poems, 1939; Herodotus, Book VIII, 1939; Llyfr Blegywryd, 1942; Thucydidis Historia, 1942; (trans.) Herodotus, 1949; (with others) One Nation, 1950; Dancer's End and the Wedding Gift, 1951; The Social Services: Needs and Means, 1952; (with others) Change Is Our Ally, 1954; (with A. Maude) Biography of a Nation, 1955; Saving in a Free Society, 1960; Great Parliamentary Occasions, 1960; Nation Not Afraid, 1965; A New Look at Medicine and Politics, 1966; (with K. Wallis) The House of Lords in the Middle Ages, 1968; Freedom and Reality, 1969; Income Tax at 4/3 in the Pound, 1970; The Common Market: The Case Against, 1971; Still to Decide, 1972; No Easy Answers, 1973; Wrestling with the Angel, 1977; Joseph Chamberlain, 1977; A Nation or No Nation, 1978. Add: 33 South Eaton Pl., London SW1, England.

POWELL, Eric (Frederick William). Also writes as Peter Rusholm. British, b. 1899. Biology, Medicine/Health. *Publs:* Water Treatments, 1929; Cell Nutrition, 1934; Balance: Spiritual, Physical, Intellectual, 1934; Health Secrets of All Ages, 1935; Life Abundant, 1943; A Simple Way to Successful Living, 1951; Health from the Kitchen, 1959; The Group Remedy Prescriber, 1960; Lady, Be Beautiful, 1961; Building a Healthy Heart, 1961; The Natural Home Physician, 1962; The Biochemic Pocket Book, 1963; The Biochemic Prescriber, 1964; Biochemistry Up-to-Date, 1965; Tranquilisation with Harmless Herbs, 1965; Kelp the Health Giver, 1968; Health from Earth, 1970; (as Peter Rusholm) Air and Water Country Medicines, 1971; About Dandelions, 1972; A Home Course in Nutrition, 1978. Add: 51 Luton Rd., Markyate, Herts. AL3 8QD, England.

POWELL, Geoffrey (Stewart). Also writes as Tom Angus. British, b. 1914. History, Military/Defence, Autobiography. Served in the British Army, 1939–64, and in government service, 1964–76; Deputy Colonel, The Green Howards, 1982–84. *Publs:* The Green Howards, 1968, 1983; The Kandyan Wards, 1973; (as Tom Angus) Men at Arnhem, 1976; as Geoffrey Powell, 1986; (co-author) Suez: The Double War, 1979; The Book of Camden, 1982, 1984; The Devil's Birthday, 1984. Add: Army and Navy Club, Pall Mall, London SW1, England.

POWELL, Gordon George. Australian, b. 1911. History, Theology/Religion. Minister, Port Adelaide Presbyterian Church, South Australia, 1938–41; Asst. Minister, Scots Presbyterian Church, Melbourne, 1941–43; Chaplain, Royal Australian Air Force, 1943–45; Minister, Independent Church, Melbourne, 1946–52, and St. Stephen's Presbyterian (now Uniting) Church, Sydney, 1952–65; Minister, Scots Presbyterian Church, Melbourne, 1966–75; Minister, Christ Church on Quaker Hill, Pawling, N.Y., 1975–81, now retired. *Publs:* Two Steps to Tokyo, 1945; Personal Peace and Power, 1949; Happiness Is a Habit, 1954; The Blessing of Belief, 1956; The Secret of Serenity, 1957, rev. ed. as Power Through Acceptance, 1976; Freedom from Fear (in U.S. as Release from Guilt and Fear), 1960; The Innkeeper of Bethlehem, 1960; The Shepherd of Bethlehem, 1961; New Solutions to Difficult Sayings of Jesus, 1962; The Secret of Bethleham, 1963; Surprise Treasure, 1965; Famous Birthdays, 1988. Add: 26 Burgundy Dr., Doncaster, Vic. 3108, Australia.

POWELL, James. American, b. 1942. Westerns/Adventure.Conservationist for the Dept. of Agriculture, in Capitan, 1965–67, Deming, 1967–68, Silver City, 1968–72, and since 1972 in Las Cruces, all in New Mexico. *Publs:* A Man Made for Trouble, 1976; Deathwind, 1979; Stage to Seven Springs, 1979; Vendetta, 1980; The Malpais Rider, 1981; The Hunt, 1982; Apache Moon, 1983; A Summer with Outlaws, 1984; The Mule Thieves, 1986; The Last Stronghold, 1987. Add: c/o Doubleday, 666 Fifth Ave., New York, N.Y. 10103, U.S.A.

POWELL, Neil. British, b. 1948. Poetry, Literature. Teacher, Kimbolten Sch., Huntingdonshire, 1971–74, and St. Christopher Sch., Letchworth, Herts., 1974–88. *Publs:* A Commentary on Henry V, 1973; At Little Gidding, 1974; Afternoon Dawn, 1975: Suffolk Poems, 1975; At the Edge, 1977; Out of Time, 1979; Carpenters of Light: A Critical Study of Contemporary British Poetry, 1979; A Season of Calm Weather, 1982. Add: 3 Sun St., Baldock, Herts. SG7 6QA, England.

POWELL, Padgett. American, b. 1952. Novels/Short stories. Assoc. Prof. of English, Univ. of Florida, Gainesville. *Publs:* Edisto (novel), 1984, as screenplay, 1984; A Woman Named Drown (novel), 1987. Add: c/oLynn Nesbit, International Creative Management, 40 West 57th., New York, N.Y. 10019, U.S.A.

POWELL, Sumner Chilton. American, b. 1924. Historical/Romance/Gothic, History. Pres., Powell Assocs. *Publs:* Venture to Windward, 1957; From Mythical to Mediaeval Man, 1958; Puritan Village: The Formation of a New England Town, 1963; Venture to the Windward Isles, 1969; Pure Food: History of the William Underwood Food Company 1822-1972, 1972; Troubled Souls (fiction), 1972; 17th Century Constitutions, 1973; When I Was Five, 1974. Add: c/o Wesleyan University Press, 110 Mt. Vernon St., Middletown, Conn. 06457, U.S.A.

POWELL, Talmage. Also writes as Jack McCready, Ellery Queen, and Anne Talmage. American, b. 1920. Novels, Mystery/Crime/Suspense. *Publs:* novels—The Girl from Big Pine, 1961; The Cage, 1969; Mission: Impossible—The Priceless Particle, 1969; The Thing in B-3, 1969; Mission: Impossible—The Money Explosion, 1970; (as Anne Talmage) Dark over Arcadia, 1971; mystery novels—The Killer Is Mine, 1959; The Smasher, 1959; The Girl's Number Doesn't Answer, 1960; Man-Killer, 1960; The Girl Who Killed Things, 1960; What a Madman Behind Me, 1962; Start Screaming Murder, 1962; (as Jack McCready) The Raper, 1962; (as Ellery Queen) Murder with a Past, 1963; (as Ellery Queen) Beware the Young Stranger, 1965; Corpus Delectable, 1965; (as Ellery Queen) Where is Bianca?, 1966; (as Ellery Queen) Who Spies, Who Kills?, 1966; other—Cellar Team (juvenile), 1972; Written for Hitcock: Twenty-Five Twisted Tales, 1989. Add: 33 Caledonia Rd., Kenilworth, Asheville, N.C. 28803, U.S.A.

POWELL, Violet. British, b. 1912. Literature, Autobiography/Memoirs/Personal, Biography. *Publs:* Five Out of Six, 1960; A Substantial Ghost, 1967; The Irish Cousins, 1970; A Compton-Burnett Compendium, 1973; Within the Family Circle, 1976; Margaret, Countess of Jersey, 1978; Flora Annie Steel, Novelist of India, 1981; The Constant Novelist, 1983; (ed.) The Album of Anthony Powell's Dance to the Music of Time, 1987; The Life of a Provincial Lady: A Study of E.M. Delafield and Her Works, 1988. Add: The Chantry, nr. Frome, Somerset, England.

POWELL-SMITH, Vincent. British, b. 1939. Mystery/Crime/Suspense, Genealogy/Heraldry, Law, Supernatural/Occult topics. Lectr. in Law, Univ. of Aston, Birmingham, since 1968. Ed., Advisor and Reader, Butterworth and Co., London, since 1968; Consultant Legal Adviser, News of the World newspaper, London, since 1965 (Legal Adviser, 1964–65). *Publs:* Law of Boundaries and Fences, 1966, 1975; Law for Builders and Surveyors, 1967; (with W.S. Whyte) Building Regulations Explained and Illustrated, 1967, 5th ed. 1975; (ed.) Blackwell's Law of Meetings, 9th ed. 1968; Questions and Answers on "A" Level Law, 1968, 1971; Know Your Contract Cases, 1968; (with R.S. Sim) Casebook on Contract, 1968, 1972; (with R.S. Sim) Casebook on Industrial Law, 1969; (with R.S. Sim) Casebook on Land Law, 1969; (with P.V. Barber) British Constitution Notebook—Tort Notebook—Contract Notebook, 1969–71; (ed.) Topham's Law of Real Property, 11th ed. 1969; (ed.) The Transport Act of 1968, 1969; (ed.) The Law of Company Directors, 1970; (ed.) Law Students' Companion: Contract, 1970, 6th ed. 1982; (ed.) Law Students' Companion: Tort, 1970; (ed.) Questions and Answers Series, 1972; (ed.) Emden and Gill's Building Contracts, 1973; (ed.) The Law Students' Annual, 1973; The Health and Safety at Work Act, 1974; (ed.) C.L. Berry: The Young Pretender's Mistress, 1974; The Demolition Contracting Industry, 1974; (with G. Biggs) Episcopal Heraldry in England and Wales, 1975; (ed.) Summer's Treatise on Ghosts, 1975; Horse and Stable Management, 1984; (with D. Chappell) Building Contract Dictionary, 1985; (with J. Sims) Determination and Suspension of Construction Contracts, 1985; (with D. Chappell) Building Contracts Compared and Tabulated, 1987; The Systems of the Horse, 1987. Add: c/o Collins, 8 Grafton St., London W1X 3LA, England.

POWELSON, John Palen. American, b. 1920. Economics. Prof. of Economics since 1966, and Research Assoc., Inst. of Behavioural Science, since 1968, Univ. of Colorado, Boulder. Jr. Accountant, 1942–44, and Sr. Asst. Accountant, 1944, Haskins and Sells, NYC; Teaching Fellow in Economics, Harvard Univ., Cambridge, Mass., 1946–48; Sr. Accountant, Price Waterhouse and Co., Paris, 1949–50; Asst. Prof. of Accounting, Univ. of Buffalo, N.Y., 1949–50; Economist, Research Dept., 1950–54, and Asst. Chief of Training, 1954–58, Intnl. Monetary Fund, Washington, D.C.; Prof. of Economic Development, Sch. of Advanced Intnl. Studies of Johns Hopkins Univ., Washington, D.C., 1958–64, and Univ. of Pittsburgh, 1964–66. *Publs:* Economic Accounting, 1955, National Income and Flow of Funds Analysis, 1960; Latin America: Today's Economic and Social Revolution, 1964; Institutions of Economic Growth: A Theory of Conflict Management in Development Countries, 1972; (ed. with P. Ndegwa) Employment in Africa, 1973; (ed. with W. Loehr) Economic Development, Poverty, and Income Distribution, 1977; (with William Loehr) The Economics of Development and Distribution, 1981; (with Wil-

liam Loehr) Threat to Development: Pitfalls of the NIEO (New International Economic Order), 1982; (co-author) The Peasant Betrayed: Agriculture and Land Reform in the Third World, 1987; Facing Social Revolution: The Personal Journey of a Quaker Economist, 1987; Dialogue with Friends, 1988; The Story of Land: A World History of Land Tenure and Agrarian Reform, 1988. Add: 45 Bellevue Dr., Boulder, Colo. 80302, U.S.A.

POWERS, Anne. American, b. 1913. Novels/Short stories. *Publs:* The Gallant Years, 1946; Ride East, Ride West, 1947; No Wall So High, 1949; The Ironmaster, 1951; The Only Sin, 1954; The Thousand Fires, 1957; Ride with Danger, 1958; No King But Caesar, 1960; Rachel, 1973; The Four Queens, 1977; The Royal Consorts, 1978; The Young Empress, 1978; Eleanor, the Passionate Queen, 1981; The Secret Splendor, 1986; Queen's Ransom, 1986. Add: 3800 N. Newhall St., Milwaukee, Wisc. 53211, U.S.A.

POWERS, Bill. American, b. 1931. Children's fiction, Children's nonfiction. Freelance writer and photographer, NYC, since 1969. Commercial artist, NYC, 1956–65; Dir., Second Story Players, NYC, 1965–68. *Publs:* Break Him Down!, 1977; The Weekend, 1978, 1984; Flying High, 1978; Love Lost and Found, 1979; A Test of Love, 1979; Behind the Scenes of a Broadway Musical, 1982. Add: 72 Barrow St., New York, N.Y. 10014, U.S.A.

POWERS, J(ames) F(arl). American, b. 1917. Novels/Short stories. Member of the faculty, St. John's Univ., Collegeville, Minn., since 1976. Member of the faculty, Marquette Univ., Milwaukee, 1949–51, Univ. of Michigan, Ann Arbor, 1956–57, and Smith Coll., Northampton, Mass., 1965–66. *Publs:* Prince of Darkness and Other Stories, 1947; The Presence of Grace (short stories), 1956; Morte d'Urban (novel), 1962; Look How the Fish Live (short stories), 1975; Wheat That Springeth Green, 1988. Add: c/o Alfred Knopf Inc., 201 E. 50th St., New York, N.Y. 10022, U.S.A.

POWERS, M.L. *See* **TUBB** E.C.

POWERS, Nora. *See* **PYKARE,** Nina.

POWERS, Robert M. American, b. 1942. Air/Space topics, Astronomy. Taught at Pima Coll., Tucson, 1969–70, and Colorado Sch. of Mines Research Inst., 1975; formerly, Exec. Dir., Metropolitan Science Center, Denver, from 1979. *Publs:* (with others) Viking Mission to Mars, 1975; (consulting ed.) Colonies in Space, 1977; Planetary Encounters, 1978, 1980; Shuttle: World's First Space Ship, 1979; Coattails of God, 1981; Other Worlds Than Ours, 1983; Mars, 1986. Add: P.O. Box 12158, Denver, Colo. 80212, U.S.A.

POWERS, Tim. American. Science fiction. *Publs:* The Skies Discrowned, 1976; The Drawing of the Dark, 1979; The Anubis Gates, 1983; Dinner at Deviant's Palace, 1985; On Stranger Tides, 1987. Add: c/o Ace Books, 200 Madison Ave., New York, N.Y. 10016, U.S.A.

POWERS, William T. American, b. 1926. Psychology. With the Dept. of Technical Services, Chicago Sun-Times. Medical Physicist, V.A. Research Hosp., Chicago, 1954–60; Electronic Systems Engineer, Dept. of Astronomy, Northwestern Univ., Evanston, Ill., 1960–71. *Publs:* Behavior: The Control of Perception, 1973; (with W. Glasser) Stations of the Mind, 1981. Add: 1138 Whitfield Rd., Northbrook, Ill. 60062, U.S.A.

POWERSCOURT, Sheila. *See* **WINGFIELD,** Sheila.

POWLEDGE, Fred. American, b. 1935. Civil liberties/Human rights, Human relations, Race relations, Urban studies. Ed.-Writer, Associated Press, New Haven, Conn., 1958–60; Reporter, Atlanta Journal, 1960–63, and the New York Times, 1963–66. *Publs:* Black Power/White Resistance, 1967; To Change a Child, 1967; Model City, 1970; Mud Show: A Circus Season, 1975; Born in the Circus, 1976; The Backpacker's Budget Food Book, 1977; Journeys Through the South, 19779; So You're Adopted, 1982; Water, 1982; A Forgiving Wind, 1983; Fat of the Land, 1984; The New Adoption Maze, 1985; You'll Survive, 1986. Add: c/o Virginia Barber Agency, 353 W. 21st St., New York, N.Y. 10011, U.S.A.

POWLING, Chris. British, b. 1943. Children's fiction, Biography. Senior Lectr. in English, King Alfred's Coll., Winchester, since 1985. Occasional Contrib. and Presenter, B.B.C. Radio 4, since 1976. Primary sch. teacher, 1966–75, and head teacher, 1975–85, London. *Publs:* children's fiction—Daredevils or Scaredycats, 1979; Mog and the Rectifier, 1980; The Mustang Machine, 1981; Uncle Neptune, 1982; The Conker as Hard as a Diamond, 1984; Stuntkid, 1985; The Phantom Carwash, 1986; Fingers Crossed, 1987; Flyaway Frankie, 1987; Bella's Dragon, 1988; Hiccup Harry, 1988; Hoppity-Gap, 1988; Ziggy and the Ice Ogre, 1988; Harry's Party, 1989; other—Roald Dahl, 1983. Add: The Old Chapel, Easton, near Winchester, Hants. SO21 1EG, England.

POWNALL, David. British, b. 1938. Novels, Children's fiction, Plays/Screenplays, Poetry, Travel. Worked for Ford Motor Co., Dagenham, Essex, 1960–63, and Anglo-American, Zambia, 1963–69; resident writer, Century Theatre touring group, 1970–72, Duke's Theatre, Lancaster, 1972–75, and Paines Plough Theatre, London, 1975–80. *Publs:* verse—(with J. Hill) An Eagle Each, 1972; Another Country, 1978; fiction—The Raining Tree War, 1974; African Horse, 1975; My Organic Uncle and Other Stories 1976; God Perkins, 1977; Light on a Honeycomb, 1978; Beloved Latitudes, 1981; The White Cutter, 1988; plays—The Dream of Chief Crazy Horse, 1975; Music to Murder By, 1978; Motocar, and Richard III, Part Two, 1979; An Audience Called Edouard, 1979; Beef (in Best Radio Plays of 1981), 1982; Master Class, 1983; Ploughboy Monday (in Best Radio Plays of 1985), 1986; other—Between Ribble and Lune: Scenes from the North-West, 1980; The Bunch from Bananas (for children), 1980. Add: 136 Cranley Gardens, London N10 3AH, England.

POYER, Joe. American, b. 1939. Novels/Short stories. Proposal Writer and Ed., Beckman Instruments Inc., California, 1965–67; Mgr., Interdisciplinary Communications, Bioscience Planning Inc., California, 1967–68. Sr. Project Mgr., Allergan Pharmaceuticals Inc., Santa Ana, Calif., 1972–77; Instr. in Novel Writing, Golden West Coll., Huntington Beach, Calif., 1973–75. *Publs:* Operation Malacca, 1968; North Cape, 1969; The Balkan Assignment, 1971; The Chinese Agenda, 1972; The Shooting of the Green, 1973; Day of Reckoning, 1976; The Contract, 1978; Tunnel War, 1979; Vengeance 10, 1980. Add: c/o Wallace and Sheil Agency Inc., 1977 E. 70th St., New York, N.Y. 10021, U.S.A.

POYNTER, John Riddoch. Australian, b. 1929. History, Biography. Deputy Vice-Chancellor, Univ. of Melbourne, since 1975 (Dean of Trinity Coll., 1953–64; Prof. of History, 1966–75; Dean of Arts, 1971–73; Pro-Vice-Chancellor, 1972–75). Section Ed., Australian Dictionary of Biography, since 1972; Australian Secty., Rhodes Trust, since 1974. *Publs:* Russell Grimwade, 1967; Society and Pauperism: English Ideas on Poor Relief 1795-1830, 1969; Alfred Felton, 1974. Add: Univ. of Melbourne, Parkville, Vic. 3052, Australia.

POZZESSERE, Heather Graham. Also writes as Heather Graham and Shannon Drake. American. Historical/Romance. *Publs:* A Circumstantial Affair, 1985; Night Moves, 1985; Double Entendre, 1986; The DiMedici Bride, 1986; The Game of Love, 1986; A Matter of Circumstance, 1987; All In the Family, 1987; Bride of the Tiger, 1987; King of the Castle, 1987; Strangers in Paradise, 1988; Angel of Mercy, 1988; Dark Stranger, 1988; Lucia in Love, 1988; Rides a Hero, 1988; This Rough Magic, 1988; romance novels as Heather Graham—A Season for Love, 1983; Forbidden Fruit, 1983; Quiet Walks the Tiger, 1983; Tempestuous Eden, 1983; Tender Taming, 1983; When Next We Love, 1983; Night, Sea and Stars, 1983; Arabian Nights, 1984; Hours to Cherish, 1984; Red Midnight, 1984; Serena's Magic, 1984; Tender Deception, 1984; Golden Surrender, 1985; Hold Close the Memory, 1985; An Angel's Share, 1985; Sensuous Angel, 1985; Queen of Hearts, 1985; Dante's Daughter, 1986; Devil's Mistress, 1986; Eden's Spell, 1986; Handful of Dreams, 1986; The Maverick and the Lady, 1986; Every Time I Love You, 1987; Liar's Moon, 1987; Siren from the Sea, 1987; Sweet Savage Eden, 1989; Rides a Hero, 1989; romance novels as Shannon Drake—Tomorrow the Glory, 1985; Blue Heaven, Black Night, 1986; Lie Down in Roses, 1988; Ondine, 1988; Conquerors, 1989; Princess of Fire, 1989. Add: c/o Silhouette Books, 300 E. 42nd St., New York, N.Y. 10017, U.S.A.

PRALL, Stuart E. American, b. 1929. History. Prof. of History, Queens Coll., and Grad. Sch., City Univ. of New York, since 1972 and Exec. Officer of the Ph.D. Program in History at the Grad. Sch., since 1988. (Instr., 1960–63; Asst. Prof., 1964–66; Assoc. Prof., 1967–71). *Publs:* The Agitation for Law Reform During the Puritan Revolution 1640-1660, 1966; (ed.) The Puritan Revolution: A Documentary History, 1968; The Bloodless Revolution: England 1688, 1972; (with D.H. Willson) A History of England, 3rd ed. 1984. Add: 1479 Court Pl., Hewlett, N.Y. 11557, U.S.A.

PRANGER, Robert (J.). American, b. 1931. International relations/Current affairs, Military/Defence, Politics/Government. Dir., Intnl.

Programs, and Resident Scholar, American Enterprise Inst. for Public Policy Research, Washington, D.C., since 1971; Adjunct Prof., Georgetown Univ., and Johns Hopkins Univ. Sch. for Advanced Intnl. Studies, Washington. Assoc. Prof. of Political Science, Univ. of Washington, Seattle, 1968–71; Deputy Asst. Secty. of Defense for Near East and South Asian Affairs, Intnl. Security Affairs, 1969–70; Deputy Asst. Secty. of Defense for Policy Plans and National Security Council Affairs, Office of Intnl. Security Affairs, 1970–71. *Publs:* The Eclipse of Citizenship, 1968; Action, Symbolism and Order, 1968; American Policy for Peace in the Middle East, 1971; Defense Implications of International Indeterminacy, 1972; Nuclear Threat in the Middle East, 1975; Detente and Defense, 1976; Nuclear Strategy and National Security, 1977. Add: American Enterprise Inst., 1150 17th St. N.W., Washington, D.C. 20036, U.S.A.

PRATCHETT, Terry. British, b. 1948. Science fiction. *Publs:* Carpet People, 1971; The Dark Side of the Sun, 1976; The Colour of Magic, 1983; The Light Fantastic, 1986; Equal Rites, 1987; Mort, 1987; Sourcery, 1988; Wyrd Sisters, 1988. Add: c/o Colin Smythe, P.O. Box 6, Gerrards Cross, Bucks. SL9 8XA, England.

PRATHER, Richard Scott. Also writes as David Knight and Douglas Ring. American, b. 1921. Mystery/Crime/Suspense. Former Dir., Mystery Writers of America. Creator of the fictional detective Shell Scott. *Publs:* Case of the Vanishing Beauty, 1950; Bodies in Bedlam, 1951; Everybody Has a Gun, 1951; Find This Woman, 1951; Way of a Wanton, 1952; Darling It's Death, 1952; Lie Down, Killer, 1952; Dagger of Flesh, 1952; (as David Knight) Pattern for Murder, 1952; (as Douglas Ring) The Peddler, 1952; Too Many Crooks, 1953; Always Leave 'em Dying, 1954; Pattern for Panic, 1954; Strip for Murder, 1955; The Wailing Frail, 1956; (as David Knight) Dragnet: Case No. 561, 1956; Have Gat, Will Travel (collection), 1957; Three's a Shroud (collection), 1957; Slab Happy, 1958; Take a Murder, Darling, 1958; Over Her Dear Body, 1959; (with Stephen Marlowe) Double in Trouble, 1959; Dance with the Dead, 1960; (ed.) The Comfortable Coffin (anthology), 1960; Shell Scott's Seven Slaughters (collection), 1961; Dig That Crazy Grave, 1961; Kill the Clown, 1962; The Cockeyed Corpse, 1964; Dead Heat, 1964; The Trojan Hearse, 1964; Kill Him Twice, 1965; Dead Man's Walk, 1965; The Meandering Corpse, 1965; The Kubla Khan Caper, 1966; Gat Heat, 1967; The Cheim Manuscript, 1969; The Shell Scott Sampler, 1969; Kill Me Tomorrow, 1969; Shell Scott's Murder Mix, 1970; Dead-Bang, 1971; The Sweet Ride, 1972; The Sure Thing, 1975; The Amber Effect, 1986; Shellshock, 1987. Add: c/o Tor, St. Martin's Press, 175 Fifth Ave., New York, N.Y. 10010, U.S.A.

PRATT, John Clark. American, b. 1932. Novels/Short stories, Literature. Prof. of English, Colorado State Univ., Fort Collins, since 1974 (Chmn. of Dept., 1974–80). Gen. Ed., Writing from Scratch series. Prof. of English, U.S. Air Force Academy, Colorado Springs, 1960–74. *Publs:* The Meaning of Modern Poetry, 1962; John Steinbeck, 1970; (ed.) Ken Kesey's One Flew Over the Cuckoo's Nest, 1973; The Laotian Fragments, 1974, 1985; (with V.A. Neufeldt) George Eliot's "Middlemarch" Notebooks: An Edition, 1979; Vietnam Voices, 1984; (with T. Lomperis) Reading the Wind: The Literature of the Vietnam War, 1986; Writing from Scratch: The Essay, 1987. Add: Dept. of English, Colorado State Univ., Ft. Collins, Colo. 80523, U.S.A.

PRAWER, S(iegbert) S(alomon). British, b. 1925. Film, Literature, Language. Fellow and Dean of Degrees, Queen's Coll., Oxford, and Taylor Prof. of German Language and Literature, Oxford Univ., since 1969, now Emeritus Prof. Lectr., Birmingham Univ., 1948–63; Prof. of German, Westfield Coll., London Univ., 1964–69. Co-Ed., Oxford German Studies, 1971–75, and Anglica Germanica, 1973–79. *Publs:* German Lyric Poetry, 1952; Morike und seine Leser, 1960; Heine's Buch der Lieder: Critical Study, 1960; Heine, The Tragic Satirist, 1962; (ed.) The Penguin Book of Lieder, 1964; The Uncanny in Literature (lecture), 1965; (co-ed.) Essays in German Language, Culture, and Society, 1969; (ed.) The Romantic Period in Germany, 1970; Heine's Shakespeare (lecture), 1970; (ed.) Seventeen Modern German Poets, 1971; Comparative Literary Studies, 1973; Karl Marx and World Literature, 1976; Caligari's Children: The Film as Tale of Terror, 1980; Heine's Jewish Comedy, 1983; Frankenstein's Island: England and the English in the Writings of Heinrich Heine, 1986. Add: Queen's College, Oxford, England.

PREBBLE, John (Edward Curtis). British, b. 1915. Novels/Short stories, Plays/Screenplays, History, Biography. *Publs:* Where the Sea Breaks, 1944; The Edge of Darkness (in U.S. as The Edge of the Night), 1948; Age Without Pity, 1950; The Mather Story, 1954; The Brute Streets, 1954; The High Girders (in U.S. as Disaster at Dundee), 1956; My Great-

Aunt Appearing Day, 1958, reissued with additions as Spanish Stirrup, 1973; (with John A. Jordan) Mongaso (in U.S. as Elephants and Ivory), 1959; Spanish Stirrup, 1959; The Buffalo Soldiers, 1959; Culloden, 1961; The Highland Clearances, 1963; Glencoe, 1966; The Darien Disaster, 1968; The Lion in the North, 1971; Mutiny, 1975; John Prebble's Scotland, 1984; The King's Jaunt, 1988. Add: Hill View, The Glade, Kingswood, Surrey KT20 6LL, England.

PRELUTSKY, Jack. American, b. 1940. Children's fiction, Poetry, Translation. Full-time writer. Has worked as store assistant, cab driver, bus boy, photographer, furniture mover, potter, folksinger and actor. *Publs:* (trans.) The Bad Bear, 1967; A Gopher in the Gardens and Other Animal Poems, 1967; (trans.) No End of Nonsense, 1968; Lazy Blackbird and Other Verses, 1969; Three Saxon Nobles and Other Verses, 1969; The Terrible Tiger (verse), 1969; Toucans Two and Other Poems, 1971; Circus (verse), 1974; The Pack Rats's Day and Other Poems, 1974; Nightmares: Poems to Trouble Your Sleep, 1976; It's Halloween Christmas, Thanksgiving, Valentine's Day; verse, 4 vols., 1977–83; The Snopp on the Sidewalk and Other Poems, 1977; The Mean Old Mean Hyena (verse), 1978; The Queen of Eene (verse), 1978; The Headless Horseman Rides Tonight: More Poems to Trouble Your Sleep, 1980; Rainy Day Saturday (verse), 1980; Rolling Harvey Down the Hill (verse), 1980; The Sheriff of Rottenshot (verse), 1982; Kermit's Garden of Verses, 1982; The Baby Uggs Are Hatching (verse), 1982; The Random House Book of Poetry for Children, 1983; It's Snowing! It's Snowing!, 1984; What I Did Last Summer, 1984; New Kid on the Block, 1984; My Parents Think I'm Sleeping, 1985; Ride a Pink Pelican, 1986; Tyrannosaurus Was a Beast, 1988. Add: c/o Greenwillow Books, 105 Madison Ave., New York, N.Y. 10016, U.S.A.

PRESCOTT, Caleb. *See* **BINGLEY**, David Ernest

PRESCOTT, J(ohn) R(obert) V(ictor). Australian, b. 1931. Geography, Politics/Government. Prof. of Geography, Univ. of Melbourne (member of the faculty since 1961). Lectr. in Geography, University Coll., Ibadan, Nigeria, 1956–61. *Publs:* The Geography of Frontiers and Boundaries, 1965, rev. as Frontiers and Boundaries, 1978; The Geography of State Policies, 1968; The Evolution of Nigeria's International and Regional Boundaries 1861-1971, 1971; Political Geography, 1972; The Political Geography of the Oceans, 1975; The Map of Mainland Asia by Treaty, 1975; (with W.G. East) Our Fragmented World: An Introduction to Political Geography, 1975; (with H.J. Collier and D.F. Prescott) The Frontiers of Asia and Southeast Asia, 1976; (with P. Lovering) The Last of Lands: Antarctica, 1979; (with others) Australia's Continental Shelf, 1979; Maritime Jurisdiction in Southeast Asia, 1981; Australia's Maritime Boundaries, 1985; The Maritime Political Boundaries of the World, 1985; Political Frontiers and Boundaries, 1987. Add: Dept. of Geography, Univ. of Melbourne, Parkville, Vic. 3052, Australia.

PRESS, John (Bryant). British, b. 1920. Poetry, Literature. Served with the British Council in Greece, 1946–50, India and Ceylon, 1950–52, Birmingham, 1952–54, Cambridge, 1955–62, London, 1962–65, Paris, 1966–71, and Oxford, 1971–78; Literary Advisor, London, 1978–80. *Publs:* The Fire and the Fountain, 1955; Uncertainties, 1956; (ed.) Poetic Heritage, 1957; The Chequer'd Shade, 1958; Andrew Marvell, 1958; Guy Fawkes Night, 1959; Herrick, 1961; Rule and Energy, 1963; Louis MacNeice, 1964; (ed.) Palgrave's Golden Treasury, Book V, 1964; Map of Modern English Verse, 1969; The Lengthening Shadows, 1971; John Betjeman, 1974; Spring at St. Clair, 1974; Aspects of Paris, 1975; (with Edward Lowbury and Michael Riviere) Troika, 1977; Poets of World War I, 1983; Poets of World War II, 1984; A Girl with Beehive Hair, 1986. Add: 5 S. Parade, Frome, Somerset BA11 1EJ, England.

PRESS, O(tto) Charles. American, b. 1922. Politics/Government, Public/Social administration, Urban studies. Prof. of Political Science, Michigan State Univ., East Lansing, since 1965 (Asst. Prof., 1958–62; Assoc. Prof., 1962–65; Chmn. of Political Science Dept., 1966–73). Member of staff, Inst. of Community Development, Michigan State Univ. Faculty member, North Dakota Agricultural Coll., 1954–56; Dir., Grand Rapids Metropolitan Area Study, 1956–57; faculty member, Univ. of Wisconsin, 1957–58. *Publs:* When One Third of a City Moves to the Suburbs; A Report on the Grand Rapids Metropolitan Area, 1959; (with C. Adrian) Convention Report, 1962; Main Street Politics; (ed. with O.P. Williams) Democracy in Urban America, 1964; (with C.R. Adrian) The American Political Process, 1965; (ed. with A. Arian) Empathy and Ideology, 1966; (ed. with O.P. Williams) Democracy in the Fifty States, 1966, 1968; (with C.R. Adrian) Governing Urban American, 5th ed. 1977; (with C. Adrian) American Politics Reappraised, 1974; (with K. VerBerg) State and Community Governments in a Federal System, 1979, 1983; (with

K. VerBerg) American Policy Studies, 1981; The Political Cartoon, 1981. Add: Dept. of Political Science, Michigan State Univ., East Lansing, Mich. 48824, U.S.A.

PRESTON, Fayrene. Has also written as Jaelyn Conlee. American. Historical/Romance. *Publs:* (as Jaelyn Conlee) Satin and Steel, 1982; Silver Miracles, 1983; That Old Feeling, 1983; The Seduction of Jason, 1983; For the Loves of Sami, 1984; Rachel's Confession, 1985; Mississippi Blues, 1985; Fire in the Rain, 1986; Burke, the Kingpin, 1986; Mysterious, 1986; Allure, 1987; Sydney, The Temptress, 1987; Robin and Her Merry People, 1987; Copper Fire, 1988; Silken Thunder, 1988; Emerald Sunshine, 1988; Sapphire Lightning, 1988; Leah's Story, 1989; Alexander's Story, 1989; Raine's Story, 1989. Add: c/o Bantam Publishing, 666 Fifth Ave., New York, N.Y. 10103, U.S.A.

PRESTON, Ivy (Alice). New Zealander, b. 1913. Historical/Romance/Gothic, Autobiography/Memoirs/Personal. *Publs:* The Silver Stream (autobiography), 1959; Where Rats Twine, 1960; None So Blind, 1961; Magic in Maoriland, 1962; Rosemary for Remembrance, 1962; Island of Enchantment, 1963; Tamarisk in Bloom, 1963; Hearts Do Not Break, 1964; The Blue Remembered Hills, 1965; Secret Love of Nurse Wilson, 1965; Enchanted Evening, 1966; Hospital on the Hill, 1967; Nicolette, 1967; Red Roses for a Nurse, 1968; Ticket of Destiny, 1969; April in Westland, 1969; A Fleeting Breath, 1970; Interrupted Journey, 1970; (co-author) Springbrook, 1971; Portrait of Pierre, 1971; Petals in the Wind, 1972; Release the Past, 1973; Romance in Glenmore, 1974; Voyage of Destiny, 1974; Moonlight on the Lake, 1975; House above the Bay, 1976; Sunlit Seas, 1977; Where Stars May Lead, 1978; One Broken Dream, 1979; Mountain Magic, 1979; Summer at Willowbank, 1980; Interlude in Greece, 1982; Nurse in Cofusion, 1983; Enchantment at Hillcrest, 1984; Fair Accuser, 1985; To Dream Again, 1985; Flight from Heartbreak, 1986. Add: 95 Church St., Timaru, New Zealand.

PRESTON, Reginald Dawson. British, b. 1908. Biology, Botany. Emeritus Prof. of Plant Biophysics, Univ. of Leeds, since 1973 (1851 Exhibition Fellow, 1932–35; Prof., 1953–73; Joint Head of Botany Dept., 1953–62; Head of Astbury Dept. of Biophysics, 1962–73). Fellow, Inst. of Physics since 1942, Linnean Soc. since 1948, Royal Soc. since 1954, and Intnl. Academy of Wood Science since 1974; Hon. Fellow, Royal Microscopical Society, since 1967; Assoc. Ed., Journal of Experimental Botany, since 1950; member of Editorial Panel, Annals of Botany, Biorheology, Experimental Plant Pathology, and Journal of Bioenergetics. *Publs:* Molecular Architecture of Plant Cell Walls, 1952; (ed.) Advances in Botanical Research (3 vols.), 1963, 1965, 1970; The Physical Biology of Plant Cell Walls, 1974. Add: 117 St. Anne's Rd., Leeds LS6 3NZ, England.

PRESTON, Richard. *See* **LINDSAY**, Jack.

PRESTON, Richard (Arthur). Canadian, b. 1910. History. Formerly, W.K. Boyd Prof. of History, Duke Univ., Durham; Prof. of History, Royal Military Coll. of Canada. Past Pres., Canadian Historical Assn. and Assoc. for Canadian Studies in the United States. *Publs:* Gorges of Plymouth Fort, 1953; (co-author) Men in Arms: A Short History of Warfare, 1956; (co-ed.) Royal Fort Frontenac, 1958; (ed.) Kingston Before the War of 1812, 1959; Canada in World Affairs 1959-61, 1964; Canada and Imperial Defence, 1968; Canada's RMC, 1969; (ed.) Contemporary Australia, 1969; The Influence of the United States on Canadian Development, 1971; For Friends at Home: Letters of a Scottish Immigrant, 1974; The Defence of the Undefended Border, 1977; The Squat Pyramid: Canadian Studies in the United States, 1980. Add: Dept. of History, Duke Univ., Durham, N.C., U.S.A.

PREUSS, Paul. American, b. 1942. Science fiction. Freelance writer since 1978. Marketing Planning Projects Dir., Batten Barton Durstine and Osborn, NYC, 1966–67; Floor Dir., King-TV, 1967–68, and Unit Mgr., 1968–69, Production Mgr., 1969–70, and Creative Dir., 1970–72, King Screen Productions, Seattle; Staff Consultant, Biological Science Curriculum Study, Boulder, Colo., 1972–73; independent film producer, 1974–81, and Assoc. Producer, Ed., and Post-Production Supervisor, Lee Mendelson Film Productions, 1975–81. *Publs:* The Gates of Heaven, 1980; Re-Entry, 1981; Broken Symmetries, 1983; Human Error, 1985; (with Arthur C. Clarke) Breaking Strain, 1987; Stanfire, 1988; (with Arthur C. Clarke) Maelstrom, 1988; (with Arthur C. Clarke) Hide and Seek, 1989. Add: c/o Jean Naggar, The Jean V. Naggar Literary Agency, Inc., 216 E. 75th St., New York, N.Y. 10021, U.S.A.

PREVIN, André (George). American, b. 1929. Music. Conductor and composer: Principal Conductor, Royal Philharmonic Orchestra, London, since 1985, and Music Dir., Los Angeles Philharmonic Orchestra, since 1986. Composer of film scores (U.S.A.), 1950–62; Music Dir., Houston Symphony, 1967–69; Principal Conductor, London Symphony Orchestra, 1968–79 (now Conductor Emeritus); Music Dir., Pittsburgh Symphony Orchestra, 1976–84. *Publs:* Music Face to Face, 1971; (ed.) Orchestra, 1979; André Previn's Guide to Music, 1983. Add: c/o Harrison/ Parrott Ltd., 12 Penzance Pl., London W11 4PA, England.

PREWITT, Kenneth. American, b. 1936. Politics/Government. Vice-Pres., The Rockefeller Foundn., NYC. Formerly, Prof. of Political Science and Dir., National Opinion Research Center, Univ. of Chicago. *Publs:* (with Eliot, Chambers and Salisbury) American Government: Readings and Problems for Analysis, 1965; (with Knowles) Institutional Racism in America, 1969; (with Dawson) Political Socialization, 1969; Recruitment of Political Leaders, 1970; Education and Political Values: Essays on East Africa, 1971; (with H. Eulau) Labyrinths of Democracy: Adaptations, Linkages, Representation, and Policies in Urban Politics, 1973; (with A. Stone) Elites and American Democracy, 1973; (with S. Verba) Introduction to American Government, 1987. Add: 1133 Ave. of the Americas, New York, N.Y. 10036, U.S.A.

PRIBRAM, Karl H(arry). American. Psychiatry, Psychology. Prof., Depts. of Psychiatry and Psychology, and Head, The Neuropsychology Labs., Stanford Univ., Calif., since 1962 (Fellow, Center for Advanced Study in the Behavioral Sciences, 1958–59; Assoc. Prof., 1959–62). Research Asst. Prof., 1948–51, and Lectr., 1951–58, Yale Univ. Sch. of Medicine, New Haven, Conn.; Dir., Neurophysiological Research Labs., Inst. of Loving, Hartford, Conn., 1951–58. *Publs:* (with G.A. Miller and E. Galanter) Plans and the Structure of Behavior, 1960; (ed.) Brain and Behavior, 4 vols., 1969; (ed. with D. Broadbent) Biology of Memory, 1970; What Makes Man Human, 1971; Languages of the Brain: Experimental Paradoxes and Principles in Neuro-Psychology, 1971 5th ed. 1982; (with R. Isaacson) The Hippocampus, vols. I and II, 1976; (with M. Gill) Freud's "Project" Re-Assessed, 1976; (ed. with A.R. Luria) Psychophysiology of the Frontal Lobes, 1973; The Mind Machine, 1983. Add: 346 Costello Ct. W., Los Altos, Calif., U.S.A.

PRICE, Anthony. British, b. 1928. Mystery/Crime/Suspense. Ed., Oxford Times weekly group, 1972–88. *Publs:* The Labyrinth Makers, 1970; The Alamut Ambush, 1971; Colonel Butler's Wolf, 1972; October Men, 1973; Other Paths to Glory, 1974; Our Man in Camelot, 1975; War Game, 1976; The '44 Vintage, 1978; Tomorrow's Ghost, 1979; The Hour of the Donkey, 1980; Soldier No More, 1981; The Old Vengeful, 1982; Gunner Kelly, 1983; Sion Crossing, 1984; Here Be Monsters, 1985; For the Good of the State, 1986; A New Kind of War, 1987; A Prospect of Vengeance, 1988. Add: Wayside Cottage, Horton-cum-Studley, Oxford, England.

PRICE, Cecil (John Layton). British, b. 1915. Literature, Theatre. Biography. Lectr., 1949–59, and Sr. Lectr., 1959–61, Univ. Coll. of Wales, Aberystwyth; Prof. of English, 1961–80, and Dean of the Faculty of Arts, 1971–73, Univ. Coll. of Swansea. *Publs:* The English Theatre in Wales in the Eighteenth and Nineteenth Centuries, 1948; Cold Caleb, 1956; (ed.) The Letters of Richard Brinsley Sheridan, 1966; (ed.) The Dramatic Works of Richard Brinsley Sheridan, 1973; Theatre in the Age of Garrick, 1973; Gwyn Jones, 1975; The Professional Theatre in Wales, 1984. Add: 86 Glanbrydan Ave., Swansea SA2 0JH, Wales.

PRICE, Kingsley Blake. American, b. 1917. Education, Philosophy. Prof. of Philosophy, Johns Hopkins Univ., Baltimore, Md., since 1963 (Asst. Prof., 1953–57; Assoc. Prof., 1957–63). Teaching Fellowships, 1940–42, 1944–46, and Lectr. in Philosophy, 1946–47, Univ. of California, Berkeley; Prof., Dept. of Philosophy, Sarah Lawrence Coll., Bronxville, N.Y., 1948–51; Acting Asst. Prof., Dept. of Philosophy, Univ. of Washington, Seattle, 1951–53. *Publs:* Education and Philosophical Thought, 1962, 1967; (ed.) On Criticizing Music: Five Philosophical Perspectives, 1981. Add: 3945 Cloverhill Rd., Baltimore, Md. 21218, U.S.A.

PRICE, (Edward) Reynolds. American, b. 1933. Novels/Short stories, Poetry, Theology/Religion, Essays. James B. Duke Prof. of English, Duke Univ., Durham, N.C., since 1977 (joined faculty, 1958). Advisory Ed., Shenandoah, Lexington, Va., since 1964. Ed., The Archive, Durham, N.C., 1954–55. *Publs:* A Long and Happy Life, 1962; The Names and Faces of Heroes (short stories), 1963; A Generous Man, 1966; Love and Work, 1968; Late Warning: Four Poems, 1968; Permanent Errors (short stories), 1970; Things Themselves (essays), 1972; Presence and Absence: Version from the Bible, 1973; The Surface of Earth, 1975; Early Dark (play), 1977; A Palpable God, 1978; The Source of Light, 1981;

Vital Provisions, 1982; Mustian, 1983; Private Contentment, 1984; The Laws of Ice (poetry), 1986; Kate Vaiden, 1986; Good Hearts, 1988; The Common Room: Essays 1954-1987, 1988; Clear Pictures: First Loves, First Guides, 1989. Add: 4813 Duke Station, Durham, N.C. 27706, U.S.A.

PRICE, Roger (David). British, b. 1944. History. Reader in History, Univ. of East Anglia, Norwich. *Publs:* The French Second Republic: A Social History, 1972; The Economic Modernization of France, 1975; (ed. and contrib.) Revolution and Reaction: 1848 and the Second French Republic, 1975; 1848 in France, 1975; An Economic History of Modern France, 1981; The Modernization of Rural France: Communications Networks and Agricultural Market Structures in 19th Century France, 1983; A Social History of 19th-Century France, 1987; The Revolutions of 1848, 1988. Add: Sch. of Modern Languages and European History, Univ. of East Anglia, Norwich NR4 7TJ, England.

PRICE, Ronald Francis. British, b. 1926. Education. Sr. Lectr., Sch. of Education, La Trobe Univ., since 1970 (Lectr., 1967–70). Former teacher in England, Ghana, Bulgaria, and Peking, 1953–67. *Publs:* A Reference Book of English Words and Phrases for Foreign Science Students, 1966; Education in Communist China, 1970, 1975, as Education in Modern China, 1979; Marx and Education in Russia and China, 1977; Marx and Education in Late Capitalism, 1986. Add: Sch. of Education, La Trobe Univ., Bundoora, Vic. 3083, Australia.

PRICE, Stanley. British, b. 1931. Novels/Short stories, Plays/ Screenplays. *Publs:* novels—Crusading for Kronk, 1960; Just for the Record, 1961; A World of Difference, 1962; The Biggest Picture, 1964; screenplays—Arabesque, 1968; Gold, 1974; Shout at the Devil, 1975; television plays—All Things Being Equal, 1970; Exit Laughing, 1971; Minder, 1980; The Kindness of Mrs. Radcliffe, 1981; Moving, 1985; Star Quality (series), 1986; The Bretts, 1986–87; stage plays—Horizontal Hold, 1967; The Starving Rich, 1972; The Position Grotesque, 1973; The Two of Me, 1975; Moving, 1980; Why Me?, 1985. Add: c/o Douglas Rae, 28 Charing Cross Rd., London WC2, England.

PRICE, Susan. British, b. 1955. Children's fiction. Supermarket shelf-filler, Co-operative Soc., 1973–75. *Publs:* Devil's Piper, 1973; Twopence a Tub, 1975; Sticks and Stones, 1976; Home from Home, 1977; Christopher Uptake, 1981; The Carpenter (stories), 1981; In a Nutshell, 1983; From Where I Stand, 1984; Ghosts at Large, 1984; Odin's Monster, 1986; The Ghost Drum, 1987; Ghostly Tales, 1987; Here Lies Price, 1987; The Bone Dog, 1988; Master Thomas Katt, 1988; Miss Sanders, 1988; Crack-a-Story, 1989. Add: c/o Faber and Faber Ltd., 3 Queen Sq., London WC1N 3AU, England.

PRICE, Victor (Henry John). British, b. 1930. Novels, Poetry, Translations. Head of German Language Service, BBC External Services (Features Producer, Hong Kong, 1960–63; Greek Prog. Organizer, 1965–66; Head of Central Talks and Features, 1971–84). Held teaching appointments in Northern Ireland, 1952–54, and in W. Germany, 1954–55. *Publs:* The Death of Achilles, 1963; The Other Kingdom, 1964; Caliban's Wooing, 1966; (trans.) The Plays of Georg Buchner, 1971; Two Parts Water (verse), 1982. Add: 33 Pembridge Sq., London W2, England.

PRICKETT, Stephen. British, b. 1939. Mystery/Crime/Suspense, Architecture, Literature. Regius Prof. of English, Univ. of Glasgow, since 1990. Former Reader in English, Univ. of Sussex, Brighton, then member of the English Dept., Australian National Univ., Canberra. *Publs:* Do It Yourself Doom (crime), 1962; Coleridge and Wordsworth, 1970; (ed.) Cambridge New Architecture, 1970; Wordsworth and Coleridge: The Lyrical Ballads, 1975; Romanticism and Religion, 1976; Victorian Fantasy, 1979; (ed.) The Romantics, 1981; Words and the Word, 1986; England and the French Revolution, 1988. Add: c/o Dept. of English, Univ. of Glasgow, Glasgow, Scotland.

PRIDE, John Bernard. British, b. 1929. Language/Linguistics. Prof. of English Language, Victoria Univ. of Wellington, since 1969. Lectr. in English Language and Linguistics, Univ. of Leeds, 1965–69. *Publs:* The Social Meaning of Language, 1971; (ed. with J. Holmes) Sociolinguistics, 1972, 1986; Sociolinguistic Aspects of Language Learning and Teaching, 1980. Add: English Dept., Victoria Univ., Wellington, New Zealand.

PRIEST, Christopher (McKenzie). British, b. 1943. Novels/Short stories, Science fiction/Fantasy, Children's non-fiction, Film. Freelance writer. Lectr. in Science Fiction, Univ. of London, 1973–78. *Publs:* Indoctrinaire, 1970; Fugue for a Darkening Island (in U.S. as Darkening Island), 1972; Inverted World, 1974; Your Book of Film-Making, 1974;

Real-Time World, 1974; The Space Machine, 1976; A Dream of Wessex (in U.S. as The Perfect Lover), 1977; (ed.) Anticipations, 1978; An Infinite Summer, 1979; (co-ed.) Stars of Albion, 1979; The Affirmation, 1981; The Glamour, 1984. Add: c/o A.P. Watt, 30 John St., London WC1N 2DR, England.

PRIETO, Mariana Beeching. American, b. 1912. Children's fiction, Children's non-fiction. Teacher of Creative Writing, Dade County Schs. Adult Div., Miami, since 1956. Teacher of Creative Writing, Univ. of Miami, 1960–62. Writer of travel articles, Intnl. Travel News, 1982. Publs: Spanish and How, 1944; Pattern for Beauty, 1945; His Cuban Wife (novel), 1954; The Wise Rooster, 1962; El Gallo and Itzo, 1964; A Kite for Carlos, 1965; Tomato Boy, 1966; Johnny Lost, 1969; When the Monkeys Wore Sombreros, 1969; (ed.) Play It in Spanish, 1973; The Birdman of Papantla, 1973; Fun Jewelry, 1973; Hickless Cocktails and Harmless Highballs, 1980. Add: 2499 S.W. 34th Ave., Miami, Fla. 33145, U.S.A.

PRIME, Derek James. British, b. 1931. Children's fiction, Theology/Religion. Head of Religious Knowledge, Battersea Grammar Sch., London, 1954–57; Minister of Lansdowne Evangelical Free Church, 1957–69; Minister, Charlotte Baptist Chapel, Edinburgh, 1969–87. Pres., Fellowship of Independent Evangelical Churches, 1966–67. Ed., Christian Guide Series, Hodder and Stoughton, London. Publs: A Christian's Guide to Prayer, 1963; A Christian's Guide to Leadership, 1964; Tell Me the Answer Books, 6 vols., 1965–67; This Way to Life, 1968; Questions on the Christian Faith, 1967; Bible Guidelines, 1979; Created to Praise, 1981; From Trials to Triumphs, 1982; Practical Prayer, 1985; Directions for Christian Living, 1986; Pastors and Teachers, 1989. Add: 44 Spottiswoode St., Endinburgh EH9 1DG, Scotland.

PRIMMER, Phyllis (Griesbach). Also writes children's fiction as P.C. Fredricks. Canadian, b. 1926. Historical/Romance/Gothic, Children's fiction. Publs: Til Night Is Gone, 1953; At the River's Turning, 1960; Beyond the Bend, 1965; (as P.C. Fredricks) Battle at Blue Line; (as P.C. Fredricks) Rebound. Add: Shanty Bay, Ont. L0L 2L0, Canada.

PRINCE, Alison. British, b. 1931. Children's fiction, Children's non-fiction, Animals/Pets. Head of Art Dept., Elliott Comprehensive Sch., London, 1954–58; Fellow in Creative Writing, Jordanhill Coll. of Education, Glasgow, 1988. Publs: children's fiction—The House on the Common, 1969; The Red Alfa, 1971, in U.S. as The Red Jaguar, 1972; (with Chris Connor) Ben's Fish, 1972; The Doubting Kind, 1975; The Turkey's Nest, 1979, in U.S. as Willow Farm, 1980; The Night I Sold My Boots, 1979; Haunted Children (stories), 1982; Mill Green on Fire, 1982; Mill Green on Stage, 1982; The Sinister Airfield, 1983; Goodbye Summer, 1983; Night Landings, 1983; A Spy at Mill Green, 1983; The Ghost Within (stories), 1984; Hands Off Mill Green!, 1984; The Others, 1984; Scramble!, 1984; Rock On, Mill Green, 1985; A Job for Merv, 1986; Nick's October, 1986; The Type One Super Robot, 1987; How's Business, 1987; The Blue Moon Day, 1988; A Haunting Refrain (stories), 1988; children's non-fiction—(with Jane Hickson) Whosaurus? Dinosaurus!, 1975; Who Wants Pets?, 1988; other for adults—The Good Pets Guide, 1981. Add: Burnfoot House, Whiting Bay, Isle of Arran KA27 8QL, Scotland.

PRINCE, F(rank) T(empleton). British, b. 1912. Poetry, Literature, Translations. Prof. of English, Univ. of Southampton, 1957–74; Prof. of English, Univ. of the West Indies, Jamaica, 1975–78; Fannie Hurst Prof., Brandeis Univ., Waltham, Mass., 1978–80; Visiting Prof., Washington Univ., St. Louis, 1980–81, and Sana'a Univ., North Yemen, 1981–83. Publs: Poems, 1938; Soldiers Bathing and Other Poems, 1954; The Italian Element in Milton's Verse, 1954; The Stolen Heart, 1957; (ed.) Samson Agonistes, by Milton, 1957; In Defence of English: An Inaugural Lecture, 1959; (ed.) The Poems, by Shakespeare, 1960; (trans.) Sir Thomas Wyatt, by Sergio Baldi, 1961; (ed.) Paradise List, books I and II, by Milton, 1962; The Doors of Stone: Poems 1938-1962, 1963; William Shakespeare: The Poems, 1963; (ed.) Comus and Other Poems, by Milton, 1968; Memoirs in Oxford, 1970; (with John Heath-Stubbs and Stephen Spender) Penguin Modern Poets 20, 1971; Drypoints of the Hasidim, 1975; Afterword on Rupert Brooke, 1977; Collected Poems, 1979; The Yuan Chen Variations, 1981; Later On, 1983; Walks in Rome, 1988. Add: 32 Brookvale Rd., Southampton, Hants., England.

PRINCE, Peter. British, b. 1942. Novels/Short stories, Plays/Screenplays. Ed., BPC Publishing Ltd., London, 1969–71. Publs: Play Things, 1972; Dogcatcher, 1974; The Floater (TV play); Agents of a Foreign Power, 1977; Last Summer (TV play), 1977; Cold Harbour (TV play), 1978; Oppenheimer (TV series) 1980; The Good Father (novel),

1983; The Hit film), 1984; A Song for Europe (TV play), 1985. Add: 31 Meteor St., London SW11, England.

PRINGLE, John (Martin Douglas). British, b. 1912. Art, Politics/Government, Autobiography/Memoirs/Personal, Essays. Member, Editorial Staff, 1934–39, and Asst. Ed., 1944–48, Manchester Guardian; Special Writer, The Times, London, 1948–52; Ed., Sydney Morning Herald, 1953–57; Deputy Ed., The Observer, London, 1958–63; Managing Ed., Canberra Times, 1964–65; Ed., Sydney Morning Herald, 1965–70. Publs: (with M. Rajchmann) China Struggles for Unity, 1938; Australian Accent, 1958; Australian Painting Today, 1962; On Second Thoughts, 1971; Have Pen, Will Travel, 1973; (ed.) Parramatta Tales: The Best of Ethel Anderson, 1974; The Last Shenachie, 1976; The Shorebirds of Australia, 1987. Add: 8/105A Darling Point Rd., Darling Point, Sydney, N.S.W. 2027, Australia.

PRIOR, Allan. British, b. 1922. Novels/Short stories, Mystery/Crime/Suspense, Plays/Screenplays. Publs: A Flame in the Air, 1951; The Joy Ride, 1952; The One-Eyed Monster, 1958; One Away, 1961; The Interrogators, 1965; The Operators, 1966; The Loving Cup, 1968; The Contract, 1970; Paradiso, 1972; Affair, 1976; Never Been Kissed in the Same Place Twice, 1978; Theatre, 1981; A Cast of Stars, 1983; The Big March, 1983; Her Majesty's Hit Man, 1986. Add: Summerhill, Waverley Rd., St. Albans, Herts., England.

PRIOR, Kenneth Francis William. British, b. 1926. Theology/Religion. Minister, St. John's Downshine Hill, London, since 1987. Rector of Sevenoaks, Kent, since 1970; Hon. Canon, Rochester Cathedral, since 1982. Vicar, St. Paul's, Onslow Sq., London, 1953–65, and Bishop Hannington Memorial Church, Hove, Sussex, 1965–70; Rector of Sevenoaks, Kent, 1970–86. Publs: God and Mammon, 1965; The Way of Holiness, 1967, 1982; The Gospel in a Pagan Society, 1975. Add: 41 Osidge Lane, London N14 5JL, England.

PRITCHARD, R(obert) John. American, b. 1945. History, Politics/Government. Freelance writer and broadcaster since 1981; Dir./Secty., Integrated Dictionary Systems Ltd., since 1986. Teaching Asst. in History, Univ. of California at Riverside, 1968–70; Visiting Lectr. in History, Deep Springs Coll., California, 1973; Research Asst. in Intnl. History, London Sch. of Economics, 1974–81. Managing Ed., Millennium: Journal of International Studies, 1974–76; Course Tutor, The Open Univ., London, 1975, 1976, 1979. Publs: The Reichstag Fire: Ashes of Democracy, 1972; (contrib.) Cry Sabotage, 1972; (contrib.) Proceedings of the British Association for Japanese Studies, 1976, 1977, 1978; Far Eastern Influences upon British Strategy Towards the Great Powers 1937-39, 1979, 1987; (ed. and compiler) The Tokyo War Crimes Trial: The Complete Transcripts of the Proceedings of the International Military Tribunal for the Far East (vols. 1-20: Pre-Trial Documents; Indictment; Transcripts of the Court Proceedings; Judgement, with Annexes; vol. 21: Separate Opinions; vol. 22; Documents Relating to Review of the Judgement, by the Supreme Commander for the Allied Powers; Proceedings in Chambers), 1981; The Tokyo War Crimes Trial: Index and Guide, 5 vols., 1981–87; (with others) The Tokyo War Crimes Trial: An International Symposium, 1986; (with others) Unit 731: The Japanese Army's Secret of Secrets, 1989; Total War: Causes and Courses of the Second World War, 1989. Add: 28 Star Hill, Rochester, Kent ME1 1XB, England.

PRITCHARD, William H. American, b. 1932. Literature, Biography, Essays. Henry Clay Folger Prof. of English, Amherst Coll., Massachusetts. Publs: Wyndham Lewis, 1968; Wyndham Lewis: Profile in Literature, 1972; (ed.) W.B. Yeats (Penguin Critical Anthology), 1972; Seeing Through Everything: English Writers 1918-1940, 1977; (ed. with others) The Norton Anthology of American Literature, 1979, 3rd ed. 1989; Lives of the Modern Poets, 1980; Frost: A Literary Life Reconsidered, 1984; Randall Jarrell: A Literary Life, 1989. Add: Dept. of English, Amherst Coll., Amherst, Mass. 01002, U.S.A.

PRITCHETT, (Sir) V(ictor) S(awdon). British, b. 1900. Novels/Short stories, Literature, Autobiography/Memoirs/Personal. Critic, New Statesman, London, since 1926 (Dir., 1946–78). Pres., Soc. of Authors; Vice-Pres., Royal Soc. of Literature. Worked in the leather trade, London, 1916–20, and in the shellac, glue and photographic trades, Paris, 1920–23; Corresp., Christian Science Monitor, in Ireland and Spain, 1923–26. Pres., English P.E.N. Club, 1970. Publs: Marching Spain, 1928; Claire Drummer, 1929; The Spanish Virgin and Other Stories, 1930; Shirley Sanz (in U.S. as Elopement into Exile), 1932; Nothing Like Leather, 1935; Dead Man Leading, 1937; You Make Your Own Life, 1938; (ed.) This England, 1938; In My Good Books, 1942; It May Never Happen and Other Stories, 1945; (ed.) Novels and Stories, by Robert Lewis

Stevenson, 1945; The Living Novel, 1946, 1964; (ed.) Turnstile One: A Literary Miscellany from the New Statesman, 1948; Why Do I Write: An Exchange of Views Between Elizabeth Bowen, Graham Greene and V.S. Pritchett, 1948; Mr. Beluncle, 1951; Books in General, 1953; The Spanish Temper, 1955; Collected Stories, 1956; The Sailor, The Sense of Humour, and Other Stories, 1956; When My Girl Comes Home, 1961; London Perceived, 1962, 1974; The Key to My Heart, 1963; Foreign Faces (in U.S. as The Offensive Traveller), 1964; New York Proclaimed, 1965; The Working Novelist, 1965; Dublin: A Portrait, 1967; A Cab at the Door: Childhood and Youth 1900-1920 (in U.S. as A Cab at the Door: A Memoir), 1968; Blind Love and Other Stories, 1969; George Meredith and English Comedy, 1970; By My Own Hand, 1971; Midnight Oil, 1971; Balzac: A Biography, 1973; The Camberwell Beauty and Other Stories, 1974; The Gentle Barbarian: A Life of Turgenev, 1977; Selected Stories, 1978; On the Edge of the Cliff, 1979; The Myth Makers, 1979; The Tale Bearers, 1980; (ed.) The Oxford Book of Short Stories, 1981; Collected Stories, ·1982; More Collected Stories, 1983; A Man of Letters, 1985; Chekov: A Spirit Set Free, 1989. Add: 12 Regent's Park Terr., London NW1, England.

PROCHNOW, Herbert Victor. American, b. 1897. Business/Trade/Industry, Economics, International relations/Current affairs, Money/Finance, Speech/Rhetoric. Consultant and Hon. Member, Intnl. Monetary Conference (Pres., 1968); Secty., Federal Advisory Council, Federal Reserve System, since 1945. Former Asst. Prof. of Business Admin., Indiana Univ., and Lectr., Loyola Univ. and Northwestern Univ., Chicago; Dir., Summer Grad. Sch. of Banking, Univ. of Wisconsin, Madison, 1945–81; Asst. Cashier, 1933–36, Asst. Vice-Pres., 1936–47, Vice-Pres., 1947–55, Gen. Vice-Pres., 1956–59, Exec. Vice-Pres., 1960–62, Dir., 1960–68, Pres., 1962–68, and Hon. Dir., 1968–73, First National Bank of Chicago; Deputy Under-Secty. of State for Economic Affairs, and U.S. Alternate Gov., Intnl. Bank and Intnl. Monetary Fund, Washington, D.C., 1955–56; Financial Columnist, Chicago Tribune, 1968–70. Publs: (co-author) The Next Century Is America's, 1938; (co-author) Practical Bank Credit, 1939, 1963; (co-author) The Public Speaker's Treasure Chest, 1942, 4th ed. 1985; Great Stories from Great Lives, 1944; Meditations on the Ten Commandments, 1946; The Toastmaster's Handbook, 1949; Term Loans and Theories of Bank Liquidity, 1949; Successful Speakers Handbook, 1951; (ed.) American Financial Institutions, 1951; 1001 Ways to Improve Your Conversation and Speeches, 1952; Meditations on the Beatitudes, 1952; The Speaker's Treasury of Stories for All Occasions, 1953; (ed.) Determining the Business Outlook, 1954; The Speaker's Handbook of Epigrams and Witticisms, 1955; Speaker's Treasury for Sunday School Teachers, 1955; A Treasury of Stories, Illustrations, Epigrams and Quotations for Ministers and Teachers, 1956; A New Guide for Toastmasters, 1956; Meditations on the Lord's Prayer, 1957; The New Speaker's Treasury of Wit and Wisdom, 1958; A Family Treasury of Inspiration and Faith, 1958; (ed.) The Federal Reserve System, 1960; The Complete Toastmaster, 1960; Speaker's Book of Illustrations, 1960; (with H.V. Prochnow, Jr.) A Dictionary of Wit, Wisdom and Satire, 1962; 1000 Tips and Quips for Speakers and Toastmasters, 1962; 1400 Ideas for Speakers and Toastmasters, 1964; (ed.) World Economic Problems and Politics, 1965; (co-author) The Successful Toastmaster, 1966; (ed.) The Five-Year Outlook for Interest Rates, 1968; (co-author) A Treasury of Humorous Quotations, 1969; (ed.) The One-Bank Holding Company, 1969; (ed.) The Eurodollar, 1970; (with E.M. Dirksen) Quotation Finder, 1971; Tree of Life, 1972; Speaker's Source Book, 1972; (ed.) The Five-Year Outlook for Interest Rates in the United States and Abroad, 1972; Speaker's Treasury for Educators, Convocation Speakers, 1973; The Speaker's and Toastmaster's Handbook, 1973; (co-author) The Changing World of Banking, 1974; The Toastmaster's Treasure Chest, 1979, 1988; Dilemmas Facing the Nation, 1979; Bank Credit, 1981; Toastmaster's Quips and Stories and How to Use Them, 1982; A Treasure Chest of Quotations for All Occasions, 1983. Add: 2950 Harrison St., Evanston, Ill. 60201, U.S.A.

PROCKTER, Noel James. British, b. 1910. Homes/Gardens. Freelance horticultural consultant since 1972. Nursery Mgr., J. Cheal and Sons., Crawley, Sussex, 1940–45; Asst. Ed., Amateur Gardening mag., London, 1946–72. Publs: Simple Propagation, 1950, 8th ed. 1981; Garden Hedges, 1960; Climbing and Screening Plants, 1973, 1983; Perennials, 1983; Shrubs and Small Trees, 1984. Add: Shamrock Cottage, Bashley Rd., New Milton, Hants. BH25 5RX, England.

PROCTOR, George W. Also writes as Zach Wyatt. Novels/Short stories, Westerns, Science fiction. Add: novels—Enemies, 1983; (as Zach Wyatt) The Texians, comprising The Texians, 1984, The Horse Marines, 1984, War Devils, 1984, Blood Moon, 1985, Death's Shadow,

1985, and Comanche Ambush, 1985; (with Robert E. Vardeman) Death's Acolyte, 1985; (with Robert E. Vardeman) A Yoke of Magic, 1985; science fiction novels—The Esper Transfer, 1978; Shadowman, 1980; Fire at the Center, 1981; Starwings, 1984; V: The Chicago Conversion (novelization of TV series), 1984. Add: c/o Pinnacle Books, 1430 Broadway, New York, N.Y. 10018, U.S.A.

PROCTOR, Thelwall. American, b. 1912. Literature. Emeritus Prof. of Russian, Humboldt State Univ., Calfornia (joined faculty; 1959). Publs: Dostoevski and the Belinski School of Literary Criticism, 1969. Add: 2970 Greenbriar Lane, Arcata, Calif. 95521, U.S.A.

PROCTOR, William Gilbert, Jr. American, b. 1941. Business/Trade/Industry, Medicine/Health, Theology/Religion. Reporter, New York Daily News, 1969–73; formerly, Owner, Creative Christians, literary consulting service, from 1973. Publs: Survival on the Campus: A Handbook for Christian Students, 1972; Help Wanted: Faith Required, 1974; (with Moishe Rosen) Jews for Jesus, 1974; The Born Again Christian Catalog, 1979; (with Kenneth Bon) The Return of the Star of Bethlehem, 1980; (with Nick Pirovolus) Too Mean to Die, 1982; (with Larry Burkett) How to Prosper in the Underground Economy, 1982; (with Sally Langendoen) The Preconception Gender Diet, 1982; (with George Gallup, Nr.) Adventures in Immortality, 1982; (with William Dooner) How to Go from Rags to Riches in Real Estate, 1982; An Interview with Chiara Lubich, 1983. Add: P.O. Box 311, Grand Central Station, New York, N.Y. 10163, U.S.A.

PROKHOVNIK, Simon Jacques. Australian, (born French), b. 1920. Physics. Assoc. Prof. of Mathematics, Univ. of New South Wales, Sydney, 1956–81, now retired (former Lectr. and Sr. Lectr.). Biochemist and bacteriologist, 1939–45; Industrial chemist, 1947–53. Publs: The Logic of Special Relativity, 1967, 1978; The Origins of Modern Cosmology, 1978; Light in Einstein's Universe, 1985. Add: Sch. of Mathematics, Univ. of New South Wales, Kensington, N.S.W. 2033, Australia.

PRONZINI, Bill. Also writes as Jack Foxx, Alex Saxon, and William Jeffery. American, b. 1943. Mystery/Crime/Suspense. Full-time writer since 1969. Member, Bd. of Dirs., Mystery Writers of America. Publs: fiction—The Stalker, 1971; The Snatch, 1971; (as Jack Foxx) The Jade Figurine, 1972; Panic!, 1972; (as Alex Saxon) A Run in Diamonds, 1973; The Vanished, 1973; Undercurrent, 1973; Snowbound, 1974; (as Jack Foxx) Dead Run, 1975; Games, 1976; (with Barry N. Malzberg) The Running of Beasts, 1976; (as Jack Foxx) Freebooty, 1976; Blowback, 1977; (with Barry N. Malzberg) Acts of Mercy, 1977; (with Collin Wilcox) Twospot, 1978; (as Jack Foxx) Wildfire, 1978; (with Barry N. Malzberg) Night Screams, 1979; Labyrinth, 1980; (with Barry N. Malzberg) Prose Bowl, 1980; (with Jack Anderson) The Cambodia File, 1981; Hoodwink, 1981; Masques, 1982; Scattershot, 1982; Dragonfire, 1982; Bindlestiff, 1983; (as William Jeffery with Jeffery M. Wallmann) Day of the Moon, 1983; Quicksilver, 1984; (with John Lutz) The Eye, 1984; Nightshades, 1984; (with Marcia Muller) Double, 1984; Bones, 1985; Quincannon, 1985; Graveyard Plots (short stories), 1985; Deadfall, 1986; (with Marcia Muller) Beyond the Grave, 1986; (with Marcia Muller) The Lighthouse, 1987; The Last Days of Horse-Shy Halloran, 1987; Shackles, 1988; The Hangings, 1988; other—Gun in Cheek, 1982; (with Marcia Muller) 1001 Midnights, 1986; Son of Gun in Cheek, 1987; other (ed. or co-ed.)—Tricks and Treats, 1976, in U.K. as Mystery Writers Choice, 1977; Midnight Specials, 1977; Dark Sins, Dark Dreams, 1978; Werewolf, 1979; Shared Tomorrows, 1979; Bug-Eyed Monsters, 1980; The Edgar Winners, 1980; Voodoo!, 1980; Mummy!, 1980; Creature!, 1981; The Arbor House Treasury of Horror and the Supernatural, 1981; The Arbor House Necropolis, 1981; The Arbor House Treasury of Mystery and Suspense, 1981; Specter!, 1981; The Arbor House Treasury of Great Western Stories, 1982; The Arbor House Treasury of Detective and Mystery Stories, 1983; The Web She Weaves, 1983; The Mystery Hall of Fame, 1984; The Western Hall of Fame, 1984; Child's Play, 1984; The Lawmen, 1984; The Outlaws, 1984; Witches' Brew, 1984; The Reel West, 1984; The Cowboys, 1985; The Warriors, 1985; The Railroaders, 1985; The Ethnic Detectives, 1985; 13 Short Mystery Novels, 1985; Chapter and Hearse, 1985; The Second Reel West, 1985; She Won the West, 1985; A Treasury of Civil War Stories, 1985; A Treasury of World War II Stories, 1985; Dark Lessons, 1985; The Deadly Arts, 1985; 13 Short Espionage Novels, 1985; The Wickedest Show on Earth, 1985; Wild Westerns, 1986; Great Modern Police Stories, 1986; 101 Mystery Stories, 1986; Locked Room Puzzles, 1986; Mystery in the Mainstream, 1986; The Third Reel West, 1986; The Railroaders, 1986; The Steamboaters, 1986; The Cattlemen, 1987; The Horse Soldiers, 1987; Uncollected Crimes, 1987; Prime Suspects, 1987; Suspicious Characters, 1987; The Gunfighters, 1988; Women Sleuths, 1988. Add: c/o St. Martin's Press,

175 Fifth Ave., New York, N.Y. 10010, U.S.A.

PROOPS, Marjorie. British. Social commentary/phenomena. Asst. Ed. and Advice Columnist, Daily Mirror newspaper, London, 1939–45, and since 1954; Television broadcaster since 1976; Dir., Mirror Group Newspapers. Member of the Council, One Parent Families: Member, Royal Commn. on Gambling. Columnist, Daily Herald, London, 1945–54. *Publs:* Pride, Prejudice and Proops, 1975; Dear Marje, 1976. Add: 9 Sherwood Close, London SW13, England.

PROSCH, Harry. American, b. 1917. Humanities (general), Intellectual history, Philosophy, Theology/Religion. Prof. of Philosophy, Skidmore Coll., Saratoga Springs, 1962–87, now Emeritus (Chmn., 1962–76). Head of Humanities Staff, Shimer Coll., Mt. Carroll, Ill., 1955–56; Assoc. Prof. and Prof. of Philosophy, Southern Methodist Univ., Dallas, 1956–62. *Publs:* The Genesis of Twentieth Century Philosophy, 1964, 1971; (with M. Polanyi) Meaning, 1975; Michael Polanyi: A Critical Exposition, 1986. Add: 9 Loughberry Rd., Saratoga Springs, N.Y. 12866, U.S.A.

PROSE, Francine. American, b. 1947. Novels/Short stories. Member of the faculty, Master of Fine Arts Program, Warren Wilson Coll., Swannanoa, N.C., since 1984. Creative Writing Teacher, Harvard Univ., Cambridge, Mass., 1971–72; Visiting Lectr. in Fiction, Univ. of Arizona, Tucson, 1982–84; Instr., Breadloaf Writers Conference, Vermont, Summer 1984. *Publs:* Judah the Pious, 1973; The Glorious Ones, 1974; Stories from Our Living Past, 1974; Marie Laveau, 1977; Animal Magnetism, 1978; Household Saints, 1981; Hungry Hearts, 1983; Bigfoot Dreams, 1987; Women and Children First and Other Stories, 1988. Add: Warren Wilson Coll., Swannanoa, N.C. 28778, U.S.A.

PROSSER, Harold Lee. American, b. 1944. Novels/Short stories, Poetry, Literature. *Publs:* Dandelion Seeds: Eighteen Stories, 1974; The Capricorn and Other Fantasy Stories, 1974; The Cymric and Other Occult Poems, 1976; The Day of the Grunion and Other Stories, 1977; Spanish Tales, 1977; Goodbye, Lon Chaney, Jr., Goodbye (novelette), 1978; Christian Existentialism, 1978; Summer Wine (stories), 1979; The Alien and Other Fantasy Poems, 1980; Topoxte Island and Other Erotic Love Poems, 1980; Robert Bloch, 1987; Desert Woman Visions: 100 Poems, 1987; Jack Bimbo's Touring Circus Poems: 100 Poems, 1988. Add: 1313 S. Jefferson Ave., Springfield, Mo. 65808, U.S.A.

PRUITT, William O. Canadian, b. 1922. Zoology. Prof. of Zoology, Univ. of Manitoba, Winnipeg, since 1969. *Publs:* Animals of the North, 1967; Boreal Ecology, 1978; Wild Harmony, 1983. Add: Dept. of Zoology, Univ. of Manitoba, Winnipeg, Man. R3T 2N2, Canada.

PRUTTON, Martin. British, b. 1934. Physics. Chair in Physics, Univ. of York, since 1965. Research Physicist, ICL, Stevenage, Herts., 1957–65. *Publs:* Thin Ferromagnetic Films, 1964; (with J.C. Anderson) The Use of Thin Films in Physical Investigations, 1966; Surface Physics, 1976; (ed.) Electronic Properties of Surface, 1984. Add: Dept. of Physics, Univ. of York, Heslington, York YO1 5DD, England.

PRYBYLA, Jan S. American, b. 1927. Economics, International relations/Current affairs. Prof. of Economics, Pennsylvania State Univ.,University Park, since 1965 (Asst. Prof., 1958–62; Assoc. Prof., 1962–65). Asst. to the Pres., Coll. of Free Europe, Strasbourg-Paris, 1953–58. *Publs:* (with E. Atwater and K. Forster) World Tensions: Conflict and Accommodation, 1967, 1972; (ed. with H.G. Shaffer) From Underdevelopment to Affluence: Western, Soviet and Chinese Views, 1968; (ed.) Comparative Economic Systems, 1969; The Political Economy of Communist China, 1970; The Chinese Economy, 1978, 1980; Issues in Socialist Economic Modernization, 1980; Market and Plan under Socialism: The Bird in the Cage, 1987. Add: Dept. of Economics, Pennsylvania State Univ., 523 Kern Bldg., University Park, Pa. 16802, U.S.A.

PRYCE-JONES, David. British, b. 1936. Novels/Short Stories, Travel/Exploration/Adventure, Documentaries/Reportage, Essays. Literary Ed., Time and Time, 1960–61, and The Spectator, 1964. *Publs:* Owls and Satyrs, 1961; Graham Greene, 1962; The Sands of Summer, 1963; Next Generation, 1964; Quondam, 1965; The Stranger's View, 1967; The Hungarian Revolution, 1968; Running Away, 1969; The Face of Defeat, 1972; (ed.) Evelyn Waugh and His World, 1973; The England Commune, 1974; Unity Mitford: A Quest, 1976; Vienna, 1978; Shirley's Guild, 1979; Paris in the Third Reich, 1981; Cyril Connolly, Journal and Memoir, 1983; The Afternoon Sun, 1986; The Closed Circle, 1989. Add: Peters Fraser and Dunlop, The Chambers, Chelsea Harbour, Lots Rd., London SW10 0XF, England.

PRYNNE, J(eremy) H(alward). British, b. 1936. Poetry. Univ. Lectr. in English, and Librarian, Gonville and Caius Coll., Cambridge. *Publs:* Force of Circumstance and Other Poems, 1962; Kitchen Poems, 1968; Day Light Songs, 1968; Aristeas, 1968; The White Stones, 1969; Fire Lizard, 1970; Brass, 1971 Into the Day, 1972; A Night Square, 1973; Wound Response, 1974; High Pink on Chrome, 1975; News of Warring Clans, 1977; Down Where Changed, 1979; Poems, 1982; The Oval Window, 1983; Marzipan, 1986. Add: c/o Gonville and Caius Coll., Cambridge CB2 1TA, England.

PRYOR, Adel. (Adel Wasserfall). South African, b. 1918. Novels/Short stories. *Publs:* Tangled Paths, 1959; Clouded Glass, 1961; Hidden Fire, 1962; Out of the Night, 1963; Hearts in Conflict, 1964; Forgotten Dream, 1969; Her Secret Fear, 1971; A Norwegian Romance, 1976; All is Not Gold, 1979. Add: P.O. Box 3155, Cape Town 8000, South Africa.

PRYOR, Vanessa. *See* YARBRO, Chelsea Quinn.

PRYS-JONES, A(rthur) G(lyn). British, b. 1888. Poetry, History. Hon. Pres., English Section, Welsh Academy. Staff Inspector, Secondary Education, Wales, 1919–49, now retired. *Publs:* (ed.) Welsh Poets, 1917; Poems of Wales, 1923; Green Places: Poems of Wales, 1948; (ed.) The Fountain of Life: Prose and Verse from the Authorized Version of the Bible, 1949; A Little Nonsense, 1954; Gerald of Wales: His "Itinerary" Through Wales and His "Description" of the Country, 1955; (literary ed.) The National Songs of Wales, 1959; High Heritage: Poems of Wales, 1969; The Story of Carmarthenshire, 2 vols., 1959, 1972; Valedictory Verses, 1978. Add: 50 Coombe Lane West, Kingston-upon-Thames, Surrey KT2 7BY, England.

PUECHNER, Ray. Also writes as Charles B. Victor and Ray Peekner. American, b. 1935. Novels/Short stories. Literary Agent, Ray Peekner Literary Agency, since 1973. Exec. Dir., 1961–66, and Contrib. Ed., 1966–73, Literary Times, Chicago; Humor Ed., and Columnist, Chicagoland mag., 1965–69. *Publs:* The LSD and Sex and Censorship and Vietnam Cookbook, 1968; (as Charles B. Victor) The Whole Sky Burned, 1968; (as Charles B. Victor with Jack Tiger) Can't Help Being Beautiful, 1972; A Grand Slam, 1973; (as Ray Peekner, with Gary Paulsen) The Green Recruit, 1978. Add: c/o Ray Peekner Literary Agency, 3210 S. 7th St., Milwaukee, Wisc. 53215, U.S.A.

PUGH, John Charles. British, b. 1919. Geography. Prof. of Geography 1964–84, and Head of the Dept. 1966–84, King's Coll., Univ. of London, now Prof. Emeritus (Reader, 1956–64; Dean, Faculty of Natural Science, 1969–72). Co-Ed., with W.B. Morgan, Field of Geography series, Methuen Ltd., London, since 1971. Land Surveyor, Survey Dept., Nigeria, 1942–48; Lectr. in Geography, 1949–55, Dean, Faculty of Arts, 1950–52, and Sr. Lectr., 1955–56, University Coll., Ibadan, Nigeria. *Publs:* (with K.M. Buchanan) Land and People in Nigeria, 1955; (with A.E. Perry) A Short Geography of West Africa, 1960; (with W.B. Morgan) West Africa, 1969; Surveying for Field Scientists, 1974. Add: 4 Connaught Way, Tunbridge Wells, Kent TN4 9QJ, England.

PUGH, John Wilbur. American, b. 1912. Money/Finance. Banker, 1937–73: retired as Asst. Vice-Pres., Crocker National Bank, 1973; Instr., American River Coll., Sacramento, Calif., 1954–66, 1973–78; Faculty member, Anthony Sch. of Real Estate, 1973–78. *Publs:* Bankers Handbook, 1941; (with W. Hippaka) California Real Estate Finance, 1966, 5th ed. 1984. Add: 3820 San Juan Ave., Fair Oaks, Calif. 95628, U.S.A.

PUGH, Patterson David Gordon. British, b. 1920. Crafts, History, Medicine/Health. Surgeon Rear Admiral, 1975–78 (joined Naval Medicine Service, 1945); Medical Officer, Prison Medical Service, 1978–80. Ed., Practical Nursing, 1945–69. *Publs:* Nelson and His Surgeons, 1968; Staffordshire Portrait Figures and Allied Subjects of the Victorian Era, 1970, 1987; Naval Ceramics, 1971; Heraldic China Mementoes of the First World War, 1972; Pugh of Carshalton, 1973. Add: 3 Chilworth Rd., Camps Bay, Cape Town 8001, South Africa.

PULASKI, Mary Ann (Spencer). American, b. 1916. Education, Psychology. Clinical Prof. of Psychology, Grad. Inst. of Adelphi Univ., Garden City, N.Y., 1982–85. Member, Nassau County Mental Health Bd., N.Y. Member of the faculty, Buckley Country Day Sch., 1955–64, and Queens Coll., City Univ. of New York, 1964–67; Psychologist, Herricks Public Schs., New Hyde Park, N.Y., 1967–79; Pres., Nassau County Psychological Assn., 1973–74; former Bd., Member and Exec. Bd., N.Y. State Psychological Assn; Fellow, Am. Psychological Assn. *Publs:* Learning to Use Our Language: A Simplified Introduction to English

Grammar, 1965; Understanding Piaget: An Introduction to Children's Cognitive Development, 1971, 1980; (with J.L. Singer) The Child's World of Make-Believe: Experimental Studies in Imaginative Play, 1973; Step-by-Step Guide to Correct English, 1974, 1982; Your Baby's Mind and How It Grows: Piaget's Theory for Parents, 1978. Add: 19 Lynn Rd., Port Washington, N.Y. 10050, U.S.A.

PULLEIN-THOMPSON, Christine. British, b. 1930. Children's fiction. Dir., Grove Riding Schs. Ltd., Oxford, 1945–54. *Publs:* Riders from Afar, 1954; Phantom Horse, 1955; A Day to Go Hunting, 1955; The First Rosette, 1956; Stolen Ponies, 1957; Three to Ride, 1958; Ride by Night, 1960; The Horse Sale, 1960; Giles and the Elephant, 1960; The Empty Field, 1961; The Open Gate, 1962; Bandits in the Hills, 1962; The Gypsy Children, 1962; Homeless Kate, 1963; No One at Home, 1963; The Eastmans in Brittany, 1963; Granny Comes to Stay, 1964; The Boys from the Cafe, 1965; The Eastmans Move House, 1965; We Rode to the Sea, 1965; Stolen Ponies, 1965; Goodbye to Hounds, 1965; The Lost Cow, 1966; The Eastmans Find a Boy, 1966; A Day to Remember, 1966; Little Black Pony, 1967; Robbers in the Night, 1967; Room to Let, 1968; Dog in a Pram, 1969; Nigel Eats His Words, 1969; Three to Ride, 1973; Good Riding, 1974; (with Diana and Josephine Pullein-Thompson) Black Beauty's Clan, 1975; Riding for Fun, 1976; (with Diana and Josephine Pullein-Thompson) Black Beauty's Family, 1978, 1982; Pony Parade, 1978; Prince at Black Pony Inn, 1978; Black Velvet, 1979; Father Unknown, 1982; Ponies in the Park, 1982; Ponies in the Forest, 1983; Ponies in the Blizzard, 1984; Jessie, 1985; Stay at Home Ben, 1987; Please Save Jessie, 1987; Careless Ben, 1988; The Big Storm, 1988; Smoke in the HIlls, 1989; Candy Stops a Train, 1989; Candy Goes to a Gymkhana, 1989. Add: The Old Parsonage, Mellis, Eye, Suffolk 1PS 8EE, England.

PULLEIN-THOMPSON, Diana. Also writes as Diana Farr. British. Novels, Children's fiction, Literature, Biography. *Publs:* I Wanted a Pony, 1946; Three Ponies and Shannan, 1947; The Pennyfields, 1949; A Pony to School, 1950; A Pony for Sale, 1951; Janet Must Ride, 1953; Horses at Home, 1954; Riding with the Lyntons, 1956; Riding for Children, 1956; The Boy and the Donkey, 1958; The Secret Dog, 1959; The Hidden River, 1960; The Boy Who Came to Stay, 1960; The Battle of Clapham Common, 1962; Bindi Must Go, 1962; (with Christine and Josephine Pullein-Thompson) Black Beauty's Clan, 1975; The Hermits Horse, 1976; (with Christine and Josephine Pullein-Thompson) Black Beauty's Family, 1978, 1982; Ponies on the Trail, 1978; Ponies in Peril, 1979; Ponies in the Valley, 1979; (as Diana Farr) Gilbert Cannan: A Georgian Prodigy, 1978; Cassidy in Danger, 1979; Only a Pony, 1980; The Pony Seekers, 1981; Candy Has Her Foal, 1981; A Pony Found, 1983; (as Diana Farr) Five at Ten, 1985; (as Diana Farr) Choosing (adult novel), 1988; Dear Pup (humour), 1988. Add: 35 Esmond Rd., London W4 1JG, England.

PULLEIN-THOMPSON, Josephine (Mary Wedderburn). Also writes as Josephine Mann. British. Mystery/Crime/Suspense, Children's fiction. Gen. Secty., English Centre, P.E.N., since 1976. *Publs:* Six Ponies, 1946; I Had Two Ponies, 1947; Plenty of Ponies, 1949; Pony Club Team, 1950; The Radney Club, 1951; Prince Among Ponies, 1952; One Day Event, 1954; Show Jumping Secret, 1955; Patrick's Pony, 1956; Pony Club Camp, 1957; The Trick Jumpers, 1958; Gin and Murder, 1959; They Died in the Spring, 1960; All Change, 1961; How Horses Are Trained, 1961; Ponies in Colour, 1962; Murder Strikes Pink, 1963; Learn to Ride Well, 1966; (ed.) Horses and Their Owners, 1970; Race Horse Holiday, 1971; Poud Riders, 1973; Ride Better and Better, 1974; (with Chrisine and Diana Pullein-Thompson) Black Beauty's Clan, 1975; Star Riders of the Moor, 1976; Fear Treks the Moor, 1978; (with Christine and Diana Pullein-Thompson) Black Beauty's Family, 1978, 1982; Night Shade, 1978; Ride to the Rescue, 1979; Black Ebony, 1979; Ghost Horse on the Moor, 1980; The No Good Pony, 1981; Treasure on the Moor, 1982; The Prize Pony, 1982; The Hidden Horse, 1982; Black Raven, 1982; (as Josephine Mann) A Place with Two Faces, 1982. Pony Club Cup, 1983; Pony Club Challenge, 1984; Save the Ponies, 1984; Mystery on the Moor, 1984; Pony Club Trek, 1985; Suspicion Stalks the Moor, 1986. Add: 16 Knivet Rd., London SW6 1JH, England.

PULLEYBLANK, Edwin George. Canadian, b. 1922. Area studies, History, Language/Linguistics. Prof., Emeritus, Dept. of Asian Studies, Univ. of British Columbia, Vancouver, since 1988 (Prof. since 1966; Head of the Dept., 1968–75). Prof. of Chinese, Cambridge Univ., 1953–66. *Publs:* The Background of the Rebellion of An Lu-shan, 1955; (ed. with W.G. Beasley) Historians of China and Japan, 1961; Middle Chinese, 1984. Add: Dept. of Asian Studies, Univ. of British Columbia, Vancouver, B.C. V6T 1W5, Canada.

PULMAN, Michael Barraclough. American, b. 1933. History. Assoc. Prof., Univ. of Denver, since 1971. Teaching Asst., Univ. of California, Berkeley, 1961–62; member of the faculty, Florida State Univ., Tallahassee, 1964–71. *Publs:* The Elizabethan Privy Council in the 1570's, 1971. Add: History Dept., Univ. of Denver, Denver, Colo. 80208, U.S.A.

PULVERTAFT, (Isobel) Lalage. Also writes as Hilary March. British, b. 1925. Novels/Short stories. Editorial Asst., C.A. Doxiadis, Athens, 1971–73; Gulbenkian Research Scholar, Lucy Cavendish Coll., Cambridge, 1973–74. *Publs:* No Great Magic, 1955; The Thing Desired: Golden October; (as Hilary March) Either/Or (in U.S. as A Question of Love), 1966. Add: 96A Chalmers Rd., Cambridge, England.

PULZER, Peter George Julius. British, b. 1929. History, Politics/Government. Gladstone Prof. of Govt. and Public Admin. and Fellow, All Souls Coll., Oxford Univ. Official Student and Tutor in Politics, Christ Church, Oxford, 1962–84 (Lectr., 1957–62). *Publs:* The Rise of Political Anti-Semitism in Germany and Austria, 1964, 1988; Political Representation and Elections in Britain, 1967, 3rd ed. 1974. Add: All Souls Coll., Oxford OX1 4AL, England.

PUMPHREY, William Idwal. British, b. 1922. Engineering/Technology. Self-employed consultant, Newspaper Columnist and Short story writer. *Publs:* (with L. Aitchison) Engineering Steels, 1953; Researches into the Welding of Aluminium, 1955; (with L. Aitchison) Using Steel Wisely, 1958. Add: 28 Fitzwilliam Hse., The Little Green, Richmond, Surrey TW9 1QW, England.

PUNDEFF, Marin V. American, b. 1921. History, Politics/Government, Biography. Prof. of History, California State Univ. at Northridge, since 1958. Staff Member, Library of Congress, Washington, D.C., 1950–55; Lectr., Univ. of Southern California, Los Angeles, 1956–58. *Publs:* (co-author) Government, Law and Courts in the Soviet Union and Eastern Europe, 2 vols., 1959; (co-author) Eastern Europe in the Sixties, 1963; (co-author) Soviet Foreign Relations and World Communism, 1965; Bulgaria: Bibliographic Guide, 1965; History in the U.S.S.R., 1968; (co-author) Nationalism in Eastern Europe, 1969; (co-author) South-Eastern Europe: Guide to Basic Publications, 1969; (co-author) The Changing Face of Communism in Eastern Europe, 1970; (co-author) Leaders of the Communist World, 1971; (co-author) Yearbook on International Communist Affairs, 1972; (co-author) Religion and Atheism in the U.S.S.R. and Eastern Europe, 1975; (co-author) East Central and Southeast Europe: A Handbook of Literary and Archival Resources in North America, 1976; (co-author) Bulgaria Past and Present, 1982; (co-author) Encyclopedia of World Biography: 20th Century Supplement, 1988. Add: Dept. of History, California State Univ., Northridge, Calif. 91330, U.S.A.

PUNNETT, Robert Malcolm. British, b. 1936. Politics/Government, Public/Social administration. Reader in Politics, Univ. of Strathclyde, since 1983 (Lectr., 1964–74; Sr. Lectr., 1974–83). Asst. Lectr. in Politics, Univ. of Sheffield, 1963–64; Visiting Asst. Prof., Carleton Univ., Ottawa, 1967–68; Visiting Prof., McMaster Univ., Ont., 1976–77. *Publs:* British Government and Politics, 1968, 5th ed. 1987; Front-Bench Opposition, 1973; The Prime Minister in Canadian Government and Politics, 1977. Add: 78 Clober Rd., Milngavie, Glasgow G62 7SR, Scotland.

PURCELL, Sally (Anne Jane). British, b. 1944. Poetry, Translations. *Publs:* The Devil's Dancing Hour, 1968; (trans.) Provençal Poems, 1969; (ed. with L. Purves) The Happy Unicorns: The Poetry of the Under-25s, 1971; The Holly Queen, 1972; (ed.) George Peele, 1972; (ed. and trans.) Monarchs and the Muse: Poems by Monarchs and Princes of England, Scotland, and Wales, 1972; (trans.) The Exile of James Joyce, by Hélène Cixous, 1972; (ed.) Charles d'Orléans, 1973; Dark of Day, 1977; By the Clear Fountain, 1980; (ed.) The Early Italian Poets, 1981; (trans.) Gaspara Stampa, 1984; Guenever and the Looking Glass, 1984; Lake and Labyrinth, 1985; (trans.) Amorgos, by Nikos Gatsos, 1986. Add: c/o Anvil Press Poetry, 69 King George St., London SE10 8PX, England.

PURCELL, William. British, b. 1909. Theology/Religion, Biography. Literary Adviser, A.R. Mowbrays and Co. Ltd., Publrs., since 1955. Religious Broadcasting Dir., Midlands Region, BBC, 1953–66; Canon of Coventry Cathedral, 1960–66, and Worcester Cathedral, 1966–76. Ed., The Sign, 1970–86. *Publs:* Onward Christian Soldier: S. Baring Gould, 1957; Pilgrim's Programme; A Plain Man Looks at Himself, 1962; Woodbine Willie: G. Studdert Kennedy, 1962; A Plain Man Looks at the Commandments, 1966; Fisher of Lambeth, 1969; Him We Declare; Portrait of Soper, 1972; A Time to Die, 1979; Pilgrim's England, 1980; Modern Martyrs, 1983; Seekers and Finders, 1985. Add: 14 Conifer Close, Oxford OX2 9HP, England.

PURDOM, Tom. (Thomas Edward Purdom). American, b. 1936. Science fiction/Fantasy. Reservation Agent, United Airlines, 1957–58; Science Writer, Univ. of Pennsylvania, 1968–69; Visiting Prof. of English, Temple Univ., 1970–71; Adjunct Prof. of English, Drexel Univ., 1975; Instr. in Science Fiction, Inst. for Human Resources Development, 1976–77—all in Philadelphia. Vice-Pres., Science Fiction Writers of America, 1970–72. *Publs:* Want the Stars, 1964; The Tree Lord of Imeten, 1966; Five Against Arlane, 1967; (ed.) Adventures in Discovery, 1969; Reduction in Arms, 1971; The Barons of Behavior, 1972. Add: c/o Scott Meredith Literary Agency, 845 Third Ave., New York, N.Y. 10022, U.S.A.

PURDY, A(lfred) W(ellington). Canadian, b. 1918. Poetry. Poet-in-Residence, Univ. of Winnipeg, 1975–76, and Univ. of Western Ontario, London, 1977–78. *Publs:* The Enchanted Echo, 1944; Pressed on Sand, 1955; Emu, Remember!, 1956; The Crafte So Longe to Lerne, 1959; Poems for All the Annettes, 1962, 1968; The Blur in Between: Poems 1960-1961, 1962; The Cariboo Horses, 1965; North of Summer: Poems from Baffin Island, 1967; Wild Grape Vine, 1968; Spring Song, 1968; (ed.) The New Romans: Candid Canadian Opinions of the United States, 1968; (ed.) Fifteen Winds: A Selection of Modern Canadian Poems, 1969; (ed.) I've Tasted My Blood: Poems 1956-68, by Milton Acorn, 1969; Love in a Burning Building, 1970; The Quest for Ouzo, 1970; (ed.) Storm Warning: The New Canadian Poets, 1971; Selected Poems, 1972; Hiroshima Poems, 1972; On the Bearpaw Sea, 1973; Sex and Death, 1973; In Search of Owen Roblin, 1974; Sundance at Dusk, 1976; To Feed the Sun, 1976; The Poems of Al Purdy, 1976; At Marsport Drugstore, 1977; A Handful of Earth, 1977; No Other Country, 1977; Being Alive: Poems 1958-78, 1978; Moths in the Iron Curtain, 1979; The Stone Bird, 1981; (ed.) Into a Blue Morning: Poems Selected and New 1968-1981, by C.H. Gervais, 1982; Piling Blood, 1984. Add: R.R.1, Ameliasburgh, Ont. K0K 1A0, Canada.

PURDY, James. American, b. 1923. Novels/Short stories, Plays/Screenplays, Poetry. *Publs:* Don't Call Me by My Right Name and Other Stories, 1956; 63: Dream Palace (in U.K. as 63: Dream Palace: A Novella and Nine Stories), 1956, recorded 1968; Color of Darkness: Eleven Stories and a Novella, 1957, recorded as Eventide and Other Stories from Color of Darkness, 1969; Malcolm, 1959; The Nephew, 1960; Children Is All (stories and plays), 1962; Cracks (play), 1963; Cabot Wright Begins, 1964; Eustace Chisholm and the Works, 1967; An Oyster Is a Wealthy Beast (stories and poetry), 1967; Mr. Evening: A Story and Nine Poems, 1968; On the Rebound: A Story and Nine Poems, 1970; Jeremy's Version: Part One of Sleepers in Moon-Crowned Valleys, 1970; Part Two: The House of the Solitary Maggot, 1974; The Running Sun (poetry), 1971; I Am Elijah Thrust, 1972; Sunshine Is an Only Child (poetry), 1973; In a Shallow Grave, 1976; A Day After the Fair (anthology), 1977; Narrow Rooms, 1978; Lessons and Complaints (poems), 1978; Two Plays, 1979; Proud Flesh, 1980; Mourners Below, 1981; The Berry Picker, and Scrap of Paper (plays), 1981; On Glory's Course, 1984; The Candles of Your Eyes (story), 1985; Don't Let the Snow Fall (poem) and Dawn (story), 1985; In the Hollow of His Hand, 1986; The Candles of Your Eyes: 14 Collected Stories, 1987; Garments the Living Wear, 1989; Collected Poems, 1989. Add: 236 Henry St., Brooklyn, N.Y. 11201, U.S.A.

PURSER, John W(hitley). British, b. 1942. Plays/Screenplays, Poetry. Freelance writer and composer since 1965; freelance lectr., Glasgow Univ. Extramural Dept., since 1965. 'Cello Tutor, Lanarkshire County Council, 1964–67; Freelance Music Critic, The Scotsman, 1967–70; Dir., Scottish Intnl., 1968–70, and Occasional Words Ltd., 1969; Mgr., Scottish Music Information Centre, 1984–88. *Publs:* The Counting Stick (poetry), 1976; A Share of the Wind (poetry), 1980; Amoretti (poetry), 1985; Is the Red Light On?, 1987. Add: 27 Banavie Rd., Glasgow G11 5AW, Scotland.

PURSER, Philip (John). British, b. 1925. Novels/Short stories, Plays/Screenplays, Autobiography/Memoirs/Personal. Television Critic, The Sunday Telegraph, London, 1961–87. *Publs:* Peregrination 22, 1962; Four Days to the Fireworks, 1964; The Twentymen, 1967; Night of Glass, 1968; The Holy Father's Navy, 1971; The Last Great Tram Race, 1974; Where Is He Now?, 1978; The One and Only Phyllis Dixey, 1978; A Small Explosion, 1979; (with L. Halliwell) Television Companion, 1982, 1986. Add: Blakesley, Towcester, Northants., England.

PURTILL, Richard L. American, b. 1931. Mystery/Crime/Suspense, Science fiction/Fantasy, Philosophy. Prof. of Philosophy, Western Washington Univ., Bellingham, since 1970. Lectr. in Philosophy, San Francisco State Coll., 1969–70. *Publs:* Logic for Philosophers, 1971; Logical Thinking, 1972; Lord of the Elves and Eldils: Fantasy and Philosophy in C.S. Lewis and J.R.R. Tolkien, 1974; Reason to Believe, 1974; Philosophically Speaking, 1975; Thinking About Ethics, 1976; Thinking About Religion, 1978; Logic: Argument Refutation and Proof, 1979; The Golden Gryphon Feather, 1979; The Stolen Goddess, 1980; C.S. Lewis's Case for the Christian Faith, 1981; Murdercon, 1982; The Mirror of Helen, 1983; The Parallel Man, 1984; J.R.R. Tolkien: Myth, Morality and Religion, 1984; (ed.) Moral Dilemmas: Readings in Ethics and Social Philosophy, 1985; (with others) Philosophical Questions: An Introductory Anthology, 1985; Enchantment at Delphi, 1986. Add: Dept. of Philosophy, Western Washington Univ., Bellingham, Wash. 98225, U.S.A.

PUSHKAREV, Boris S. American, b. 1929. Regional/Urban planning, Transportation. Vice Pres., Research and Planning, Regional Plan Assn., NYC, since 1969 (Chief Planner, 1961–68; Planning Dir., 1968–69). Chmn., Russian Research Foundn. for the Study of Alternatives to Soviet Policy, since 1981; Member. Ed. Board, Possev, Russian Political monthly. Instr., Yale Univ., New Haven, Conn., 1958–61. Adjunct Prof., New York Univ., NYC, 1967–78. *Publs:* (with C. Tunnard) Man-Made America: Chaos or Control, 1963; Urban Space for Pedestrians: A Quantitative Approach, 1975; (with J. Zupan) Public Transportation and Land Use Policy, 1977; Urban Rail in America, 1982. Add: 300 Winston Dr., Apt. 921, Cliffside Park, N.J. 07010, U.S.A.

PUTNAM, Hilary. American, b. 1926. Philosophy. Walter Beverly Pearson Prof. of Modern Mathematics and Mathematical Logic, Harvard Univ., Cambridge, since 1965. Instr. in Philosophy, Northwestern Univ., Evanston, Ill., 1952–53; Asst. Prof. of Philosophy, 1953–60, and Assoc. Prof. of Philosophy, 1960–61, Princeton Univ., New Jersey; Prof. of the Philosophy of Science, Massachusetts Inst. of Technology, Cambridge, 1961–65. Pres., American Philosophical Assn., Eastern Div., 1976–77, Philosophy of Science Assn., 1977–78, Assn. for Symbolic Logic, 1977–80, and Charles S. Peirce Soc., 1988–89. *Publs:* (ed. with P. Benacerraf) Philosophy of Mathematics, 1964; Philosophy of Logic, 1971; Mathematics, Matter and Method (essays), 1975, 2nd ed. (including Philosophy of Logic), 1979; Mind, Language and Reality, 1975; Meaning and the Moral Sciences, 1978; Reason, Truth, and History, 1981; The Many Faces of Realism, 1987; Representation and Reality, 1988. Add: Dept. of Philosophy, Emerson Hall, Harvard Univ., Cambridge, Mass. 02138, U.S.A.

PUTNEY, Gail J. *See* **FULLERTON,** Gail.

PUTNEY, John. *See* **BECKWITH,** Burnham Putnam.

PUZO, Mario. American, b. 1920. Novels/Short stories, Children's fiction, Plays/Screenplays. Former Administrative Asst., U.S. Govt. *Publs:* The Dark Arena, 1955; The Fortunate Pilgrim, 1965; The Runaway Summer of Davie Shaw, 1966; The Godfather, 1969; The Godfather Papers and Other Confessions, 1972; (with Francis Ford Coppola) The Godfather (screenplay), 1972; Earthquake (screenplay), 1974; (with F.F. Coppola) The Godfather, Part Two (screenplay), 1975; Las Vegas, 1977; Fools Die, 1978; (with others) Superman (screenplay), 1978; The Sicilian, 1984. Add: c/o G.P. Putnam and Sons Inc., 200 Madison Ave., New York, N.Y. 10016, U.S.A.

PYBUS, Rodney. British, b. 1938. Poetry. Feature Writer and Literary Ed., The Journal, Newcastle, 1962–64; Writer/Producer, Tyne Tees Television, Newcastle, 1964–76; Lectr. in English, Macquarie Univ., Sydney, 1976–79; Literature Officer, Northern Arts, Cumbria, 1979–81; Tutor, Univ. of Liverpool, 1981–82. *Publs:* In Memoriam Milena, 1973; Bridging Loans, 1976; At the Stone Junction, 1978; (co-ed.) Adam's Dream: Poems from Cumbria and Lakeland, 1981; The Loveless Letters, 1981; (with others) Wall, 1981; (with David Constantine) Talitha Cumi, 1983; Cicadas in Their Summers: New and Selected Poems, 1987. Add: 21 Plough Lane, Sudbury, Suffolk CO10 6AU, England.

PYE, Michael (Kenneth). British, b. 1946. Novels, Film, History, Media. Staff Writer, The Scotsman, Edinburgh, 1967–71, and The Sunday Times, London, 1971–78. *Publs:* (with Lynda Myles) The Movie Brats: How the Film Generation Took Over Hollywood, 1979; Moguls: Inside the Business of Show Business, 1980; The King over the Water: The Windsors in the Bahamas, 1981, in paperback as The Windsors in Exile, 1982; Eldorado (novel), 1983, in U.S. as Kingdom Come, 1985; Reckoning (novel), 1987; The Pirelli Calendar Album, 1988. Add: c/o Curtis Brown Ltd., 162-168 Regent St., London W1R 5TA, England.

PYE, Virginia (Frances Kennedy). British, b. 1901. Novels/Short stories, Children's fiction. *Publs:* St. Martin's Summer, 1930; Red-Letter Holiday, 1940; Snow Bird, 1941; Primrose Polly, 1942; Half-Term

Holiday, 1943; The Prices Return, 1946; The Stolen Jewels, 1948; Johanna and the Prices, 1951; Holiday Exchange, 1953. Add: Cuttmill Cottage, Shackleford, Godalming, Surrey, GU8 6BJ, England.

PYKARE, Nina. Also writes as Ann Coombs, Nina Coombs, Nan Pemberton, Nora Powers and Regina Towers. American. Historical/Romance. *Publs:* (as Ann Coombs) The Fire Within, 1978; Love's Promise, 1979; The Scandalous Season, 1979; (as Nora Powers) Affairs of the Heart, 1980; (as Nora Powers) Design for Love, 1980; Lady Incognita, 1980; (as Nan Pemberton) Love's Delusion, 1980; (as Regina Towers) The Rake's Companion, 1980; Love's Folly, 1980; Love in Disguise, 1980; The Dazzled Heart, 1980; Man of Her Choosing, 1980; Love Plays a Part, 1981; The Innocent Heart, 1981; A Matter of Honor, 1982; Heritage of the Heart, 1982; (as Nora Powers) Promise Me Tomorrow, 1982; (as Nora Powers) Dream of the West, 1983; (as Nora Powers) In a Moment's Time, 1983; (as Nora Powers) Time Stands Still, 1983; (as Nina Coombs) Love So Fearful, 1983; (as Nina Coombs) Forbidden Joy, 1983; (as Nina Coombs) Passion's Domain, 1983; (as Nora Powers) In a Stranger's Arms, 1984; (as Nora Powers) This Brief Interlude, 1984; (as Nina Coombs) Sun Spark, 1984; (as Nora Powers) A Different Reality, 1985; (as Nora Powers) A Woman's Wiles, 1985; (as Nora Powers) No Man's Kisses, 1986; (as Nina Coombs) Before It's Too Late, 1986; (as Nora Powers) Woman of the West, 1989. Add: c/o Silhouette Books, 300 E. 42nd St., New York, N.Y. 10017, U.S.A.

PYKE, Magnus. British, b. 1908. Medicine/Health, Sciences, Social commentary/phenomena. Chief Chemist, Vitamins Ltd., London, 1934–40; Principal Scientific Officer, Ministry of Food, Scientific Adviser's Div., London, 1940–45 and 1946–48; Nutritional Adviser, Allied Commn. for Austria, British Element, Vienna, 1945–46; Mgr., Distillers Co. Ltd., Glenochil Research Station, Menstrie, Scotland, 1948–73; Secty., British Assn. for the Advancement of Science, London, 1973–77. *Publs:* Manual of Nutrition, 1945; Industrial Nutrition, 1950; Townsman's Food, 1950; Automation: Its Purpose and Future, 1956; Nothing Like Science, 1957; Slaves Unaware, 1959; About Chemistry, 1959; The Boundaries of Science, 1961; Teach Yourself Nutrition, 1962; The Science Myth, 1962; Food, Science and Technology, 1964; What Scientists Are Up To, 1966; The Science Century, 1967; The Human Predicament, 1967; Food and Society, 1968; Man and Food, 1970; Synthetic Food, 1970; Food Glorious Food, 1971; Technological Eating, or Where Does the Fish-Finger Point?, 1972; Catering Science and Technology, 1973; Success in Nutrition, 1975; Butter Side Up, 1977; There and Back, 1978; Our Future, 1980; The Six Lives of Pyke, 1981; (with P. Moore) Everyman's Scientific Facts and Feats, 1981; Curiouser and Curiouser, 1983; Red Rag to a Bull: Dr. Magnus Pyke's Dictionary of Fallacies, 1983; 101 Inventions, 1986. Add: 3 St. Peter's Villas, London W6 9BQ, England.

PYLE, A(lbert) M(offett). American, b. 1945. Mystery/Crime/Suspense. Fulltime writer since 1982. Drama Instr., Resident Arts and Humanities Consortium, Cincinnati, 1972–73; Planner and Planning Supervisor, Employment and Training Div., City of Cincinnati, 1974–80; Exec. Dir., Bluegrass Employment and Training Program, Lexington, Ky., 1980–82; Columnist, Cincinnati Post, 1982–85. *Publs:* Trouble Making Toys, 1985; Murder Moves In, 1987. Add: c/o Al Hart, Public Ledger Bldg., Philadelphia, Pa. 19106, U.S.A.

PYNCHON, Thomas. American, b. 1937. Novels/Short stories. Former Editorial Writer, Boeing Aircraft Corp., Seattle, Wash. *Publs:* V. 1963; The Crying of Lot 49, 1966; Gravity's Rainbow, 1973; Mortality and Mercy in Vienna, 1976; Low-Lands, 1978; The Secret Integration, 1980; The Small Rain, 1980; Slow Learner: Early Stories, 1984; In the Rocket's Red Glare, 1986. Add: c/o Little Brown, 34 Beacon St., Boston, Mass. 02106, U.S.A.

Q

QUALE, G(ladys) Robina. American, b. 1931. History. Prof. of History, Albion Coll., Michigan, since 1970 (Instr., 1957–60; Asst. Prof., 1960–65; Assoc. Prof., 1965–70). *Publs:* Eastern Civilizations, 1966, 1975; History of Marriage Systems, 1988. Add: Dept. of History, Albion Coll., Albion, Mich. 49224, U.S.A.

QUALTER, Terence H. Canadian, b. 1925. Politics/Government. Prof. of Political Science, Univ. of Waterloo, since 1967 (Lectr., 1960–61; Asst. Prof., 1961–64; Assoc. Prof., 1964–67; Chmn. of Dept. 1964–68, and 1970–73). *Publs:* Propaganda and Psychological Warfare, 1962; The Election Process in Canada, 1970; Graham Wallas and the Great Society, 1980; Opinion Control in the Democracies, 1985; Conflicting Political Ideas in Liberal Democracies, 1986. Add: Dept. of Political Science, Univ. of Waterloo, Waterloo, Ont. N2L 3G1, Canada.

QUANDT, Richard (Emeric). American, b. 1930. Economics. Hughes-Rogers Prof. of Economics, Princeton Univ., since 1976 (Member of the Faculty, since 1956). *Publs:* (with J. Henderson) Microeconomic Theory: Mathematical Approach, 1958, 3rd ed. 1980; (with W. Thorp), The New Inflation, 1959; (with B. Malkiel) Strategies and Rational Decisions in the Securities Options Market, 1969; (ed.) The Demand for Travel: Theory and Measurement, 1970; (with S.S. Goldfeld) Nonlinear Methods in Econometrics, 1972; (ed.) Studies in Nonlinear Estimation, 1976; (co-ed.) Prices, Competition, and Equilibrium, 1986; (with P. Asch) Racetrack Betting: The Professors' Guide to Strategies, 1986; (with H.S. Rosen) The Conflict Between Equilibrium and Disequilibrium Theories, 1988; The Econometrics of Disequilibrium, 1988. Add: Dept. of Economics, Princeton Univ., Princeton, N.J. 08544, U.S.A.

QUANDT, William Bauer. American, b. 1941. Politics/Government. Sr. Fellow, Brookings Instn., Washington D.C., since 1979, and Sr. Assoc., Cambridge Energy Research Assocs., Cambridge, Mass., since 1983. With Rand Corp., 1968–72, and National Security Council Staff, Washington, D.C., 1972–74; Prof. of Political Science, Univ. of Pennsylvania, Philadelphia, 1974–76. Office Dir. for Middle East Affairs, National Security Council Staff, Washington, D.C., 1977–79. *Publs:* Revolution and Political Leadership: Algeria 1954-58, 1969; The Comparative Study of Political Elites, 1970; (co-author) The Politics of Palestinian Nationalism, 1973; Decade of Decisions: American Policy Toward the Arab-Israeli Conflict 1967-1976, 1977; Camp David: Peacemaking and Politics, 1986. Add: 2318 44th St. N.W., Washington, D.C. 20007, U.S.A.

QUANTRILL, Malcolm. British, b. 1931. Novels, Architecture. Distinguished Prof. of Architecture, Texas A.M. Univ., College Station, since 1986. Asst. Prof., Louisiana State Univ., 1955–60; Lectr., Univ. of Wales, Cardiff, 1962–65, and University Coll., London, 1965–66; Asst. to the Dir., 1966–67, and Dir., 1967–69, Architectural Assn., London; Lectr., Univ. of Liverpool, 1970–73; Dean, Sch. of Environmental Design, Polytechnic of North London, 1973–80; Prof. of Architecture and Urban Design, Univ. of Jordan, Amman, 1980–83; Fellow, Graham Foundn., Chicago, 1984. *Publs:* The Gotobed Trilogy (novels), 1962–64; Ritual and Response in Architecture, 1974; Monuments of Another Age, 1975; On the Home Front (novel), 1977; The Art of Government and the Government of Art, 1978; Alvar Aalto: A Critical Study, 1982; Reima Pietilä: Architecture, Context, and Modernism, 1984; The Environmental Memory, 1987; Reima Pietilä: One Man's Odyssey in Search of Finnish Architecture, 1988. Add: 18 Causton Rd., London N6, England.

QUARRIE, Bruce. British, b. 1947. History, Recreation/Leisure/Hobbies. Managing Ed., Patrick Stephens Ltd., Cambridge, since 1978 (ed. 1972–78). Deputy News Ed., Medical News, 1968–70; Ed., Heating and Ventilating News, 1971–72. *Publs:* (ed.) Airfix Magazine Annual for Modellers, 7 vols., 1973–78; Napoleonic Wargaming, 1974; Tank Battles in Miniature, 2, 3 and 5, 1975–78; Afrika Korps, 1976; World War 2 Wargaming, 1976; Napoleon's Campaigns in Miniature, 1977; Panzer-Grenadier Division Grossdeutschland, 1977; Fallschirm-Panzer Division Hermann Goring, 1978; 2nd SS-Panzer Division Das Reich, 1978; Panzers in the Desert, 1978; Waffen-SS in Russia, 1978; Modelling Military Vehicles, 1978; Panzers in North-West Europe, 1979; German Paratroops in the Med, 1979; Panzers in Russia 1941-43, 1979; Panzers in Russia 1943-45, 1980; German Mountain Troops, 1980; PSL Guide to Wargaming, 1980; Panzers in the Balkans and Italy, 1981; Fallschirmjager, 1983; Hitler's Samurai, 1983, 1984; The World's Elite Forces, 1985; Hitler's Teutonic Knights, 1986; Secret Police Forces of the World, 1986; Beginner's Guide to War Gaming, 1987; Armored Wargaming: A Detailed Guide to Model Tank Warfare, 1988. Add: c/o Patrick Stephens Ltd., Dennington Estate, Wellingborough, Northants. NN8 2QD, England.

QUARRY, Nick. *See* **ALBERT,** Marvin H.

QUARTERMAIN, James. *See* **LYNNE,** James Broom.

QUAYLE, Eric. British, b. 1921. Literature. *Publs:* Ballantyne the Brave, 1967; The Ruin of Sir Walter Scott, 1968; R.M. Ballantyne—A Bibliography of First Editions, 1968; The Collector's Book of Books, 1971; The Collector's Book of Children's Books, 1971; The Collector's Book of Detective Fiction, 1972; The Collector's Book of Boys' Stories, 1973; Old Cook Books, 1978; The Magic Ointment and Other Cornish Legends, 1986; The Shining Princess and Other Japanese Legends, 1989. Add: Carn Cobba, Zennor, Cornwall TR26 3BZ, England.

QUEEN, Ellery. *See* **POWELL,** Talmage.

QUENNELL, Peter. British, b. 1905. Literature, Biography, Essays. Ed., The Cornhill Mag., London, 1944–51, and History Today mag., London, 1951–79. *Publs:* Poems, 1926; The Phoenix-Kind, 1929; Baudelaire and the Symbolists, 1929; Aspects of Seventeenth Century Verse, 1933; Sympathy and Other Stories, 1933; Byron: The Years of Fame, 1935; (with G. Paston) To Lord Byron, 1939; Caroline of England, 1939; Byron in Italy, 1941; Four Portraits, 1945; John Ruskin: The Portrait of a Prophet, 1949; The Singular Preference, 1952; Hogarth's Progress, 1955; The Sign of the Fish, 1960; Shakespeare: The Poet and His Background, 1963; Alexander Pope: The Education of Genius 1688-1728, 1968; Romantic England: Writing and Painting 1717-1851, 1970; Samuel Johnson: His Friends and Enemies, 1972; History of English Literature, 1973; Byron, 1974; (ed.) Memoirs of William Hickey, 1975; The Marble Foot, 1977; The Wanton Chase (autobiography), 1980; Customs and Characters, 1982. Add: 2 Chamberlain St., London NW1, England.

QUEST, Erica. *See* **SAWYER,** John and **SAWYER,** Nancy.

QUESTER, George (Herman). American, b. 1936. International relations/Current affairs. Chmn., Dept. of Govt. and Politics, Univ. of Maryland, College Park, since 1982. Instr. in Govt. and Asst. Prof. of Govt., 1967–70, Harvard Univ., Cambridge; Assoc. Prof., 1970–73, and Prof. of Govt., 1973–82, Cornell Univ., Ithaca, N.Y. *Publs:* Deterrence Before Hiroshima, 1966; Nuclear Diplomacy, 1970; The Politics of

Nuclear Proliferation, 1973; The Continuing Problem of International Politics, 1974; Offense and Defense in the International System, 1977; American Foreign Policy: The Lost Consensus, 1982; The Future of Nuclear Deterrence, 1986. Add: 5124 N. 37th St., Arlington, Va. 22207, U.S.A.

QUILLER, Andrew. *See* **BULMER**, Henry Kenneth.

QUIMBY, George (Irving). American, b. 1913. Anthropology/Ethnology. Archaeology/Antiquities. Curator of Ethnology and Prof. of Anthropology since 1965, and Dir. of the Burke Memorial Washington State Museum since 1968, Univ. of Washington, Seattle, Emeritus since 1983; Research Assoc. in North American Archaeology and Ethnology, Field Museum, Chicago, since 1965 (Curator of Exhibits, 1943–53; Asst. Curator, Anthropology Dept., and Curator, North American Archaeology and Ethnology, 1954–65). Pres., Central States Anthropological Soc., 1949, and Soc. for American Archaeology, 1958. *Publs:* Indian Life in the Upper Great Lakes 11,000 B.C. to A.D. 1800, 1960; Indian Culture and European Trade Goods: The Archaeology of the Historic Period in the Western Great Lakes Region, 1966; (co-author) Edward S. Curtis in the Land of the War Canoes: Pioneer Cinematographer in the Pacific Northwest, 1980. Add: Thomas Burke Memorial Washington State Museum, Univ. of Washington, Seattle, Wash. 98195, U.S.A.

QUINE, Willard V(an Orman). American, b. 1908. Mathematics, Philosophy. Edgar Pierce Prof., Emeritus of Philosophy, Harvard Univ., Cambridge (Inst. in Philosophy, 1936–41, Assoc. Prof., 1941–48; Prof. of Philosophy, 1948–78). Pres., Assn. for Symbolic Logic, 1951–55, American Philosophical Assn., 1957. *Publs:* A System of Logistic, 1934; Mathematical Logic, 1940; Elementary Logic, 1941; O Sentido da Nova Logica, 1944; Methods of Logic, 1950; From a Logical Point of View, 1953; Word and Object, 1960; Set Theory and Its Logic, 1963; The Ways of Paradox and Other Essays, 1966, 1976; Selected Logic Papers, 1966; Ontological Relativity and Other Essays, 1969; (with J. Ullian) The Web of Belief, 1970; Philosophy of Logic, 1970; The Roots of Reference, 1974; Theories and Things, 1981; The Time of My Life, 1985; Quiddities, 1987; La Scienza e i Dati di Senso, 1987; Pursuit of Truth, 1989. Add: Emerson Hall, Harvard Univ., Cambridge, Mass. 02138, U.S.A.

QUINN, David (Beers). British, b. 1909. History. Emeritus Andrew Geddes and John Rankin Prof. of Modern History, Univ. of Liverpool, since 1976 (Prof., 1957–76). Vice-Pres., The Hakluyt Soc., since 1988 (Member of the Council, 1950–54, 1956–60; Vice-Pres., 1960–82; Pres., 1983–87). Asst. Lectr., 1934–37, and Lectr., 1937–39, Univ. Coll., Southampton, Hants.; Lectr. in History, Queen's Univ., Belfast, 1939–44; Prof. of History, University Coll., Swansea, 1944–57. Secty., Ulster Soc. for Irish Historical Studies, 1939–44; Member of Council, 1951–55, 1956–60, Vice Pres., 1964–68, and Hon. Vice-Pres., 1983, Royal Historical Soc.; Hon. Fellow, British Academy, 1984. *Publs:* The Port Books or Petty Customs Accounts of Southampton for the Reign of Edward IV, 2 vols., 1937–38; The Voyages and Colonising Enterprises of Sir Humphrey Gilbert, 2 vols., 1940; Raleigh and the British Empire, 1947; The Roanoke Voyages 1584–90, 2 vols., 1955; (with H. Cronne and T. Moody) Essays in British and Irish History in Honour of J.E. Todd, 1949; (with P. Hulton) The American Drawings of John White 1577–1590, 2 vols., 1964; (with R. Skelton) Hakluyt's Principall Navigations, 1965; The Elizabethans and the Irish, 1966; (ed.) Richard Hakluyt, Editor, 2 vols., 1967; North American Discovery, 1971; (with W.P. Cumming and R.A. Skelton) The Discovery of North America, 1971; (with N.M. Cheshire) The New Found Land of Stephen Parmenius, 1972; (with A.M. Quinn) Virginia Voyages, 1973; (ed.) The Hakluyt Handbook, 2 vols., 1974; England and the Discovery of America, 1974; North America from Earliest Discovery to First Settlements, 1977; (ed.) New American World, 5 vols., 1979; (ed.) Early Maryland in a Wider World, 1982; (ed. with A.M. Quinn) The English New England Voyages 1602-8, 1983; Set Fair for Roanoke, 1985; (ed.) The Image of Ireland 1581, by John Derricke, 1986. Add: 9 Knowsley Rd., Liverpool L19 0PF, England.

QUINN, Derry. British, b. 1918. Novels/Short stories. Former film and television scriptwriter, and story ed. *Publs:* The Limbo Connection, 1976; The Solstice Man, 1977; The Fear of God, 1978. Add: 29 A, Ifield

Rd., London SW10 9A2, England.

QUINN, Kenneth (Fleming). New Zealander, b. 1920. Classics. Prof. of Classics, University Coll., Toronto. Lectr. in Classics, Victoria Univ. of Wellington, 1948–55; Sr. Lectr. and Reader in Classics, Univ. of Melbourne, 1955–65; Prof. of Classics, Univ. of Otago, Dunedin, 1965–69. Member, Australian Humanities Research Council, 1963–65. *Publs:* The Catullan Revolution, 1959; Latin Explorations, 1963; Virgil's Aeneid: A Critical Description, 1968; (ed.) Catullus: The Poems, 1970; (ed.) Approaches to Catullus, 1972; Catullus: An Interpretation, 1972; Texts and Contexts: The Roman Writers and Their Audience, 1979; How Literature Works, 1982. Add: 70 Rosetta Rd., Raumati South, New Zealand.

QUINN, Martin. *See* **SMITH**, Martin Cruz.

QUINN, Peter (John). Australian, b. 1941. Biology. Reader in Biophysical Chemistry, King's Coll., Univ. of London, since 1986 (Lectr., 1974–80, and Sr. Lect. in Biochemistry, 1980–86, Chelsea Coll.). Research Fellow, Univ. of Sydney, 1967, Agricultural Research Council Inst. of Animal Physiology, Cambridge, 1968–69, and Univ. of Oxford, 1972–74; Research Instr., Dept. of Psychiatry, Washington Univ. Medical Sch., St. Louis, 1970; Visiting Instr., Dept. of Endocrinology and Metabolism, Northwestern Univ. Medical Sch., Chicago, 1971. *Publs:* The Molecular Biology of Cell Membranes, 1976. Add: Biochemistry Dept., King's Coll., London, SW3 6LX, England.

QUINN, Simon. *See* **SMITH**, Martin Cruz.

QUINNEY, Richard. American, b. 1934. Criminology/Law enforcement/Prisons. Prof., Northern Illinois Univ., since 1983. Instr., St. Lawrence Univ., Canton, N.Y., 1960–62; Asst. Prof. Univ. of Kentucky, Lexington, 1962–65; Assoc. Prof., 1965–70, and Prof., 1970–72, New York Univ.; Prof., Boston College, 1978–83. *Publs:* (with Marshall B. Clinard) Criminal Behavior Systems, 1967, 1973; (ed.) Crime and Justice in Society, 1969; The Problem of Crime, 1970, 1977; The Social Reality of Crime, 1970; (ed.) Criminal Justice in America, 1974; Critique of Legal Order, 1974; Criminology, 1975; Class, State, and Crime, 1977, 1980; Providence, 1980; Social Existence, 1982. Add: Dept. of Sociology, Northern Illinois Univ., Dekalb, Ill. 60115, U.S.A.

QUINTON, Lord; Anthony Meredith Quinton. British, b. 1925. Intellectual history, Philosophy. Chmn. of the Bd., British Library, since 1985. Fellow, All Souls Coll., 1949–55, and New Coll., 1955–78, Oxford; Pres., Trinity Coll., Oxford, 1978–87; Member, Arts Council, 1979–81. *Publs:* (ed.) Political Philosophy, 1967; The Nature of Things, 1973; Utilitarian Ethics, 1973, 1989; (co-trans.) K. Ajdukiewicz: Problems and Theories of Philosophy, 1973; The Politics of Imperfection, 1978; Francis Bacon, 1980; Thoughts and Thinkers, 1982. Add: c/o British Library Bd., 2 Sheraton St., London W1V 4BH, England.

QUIRK, (Sir) Randolph. British, b. 1920. Language/Linguistics. Pres., British Academy. Former Prof.of English, Univ. of Durham, and Quain Prof. of English, Univ. Coll., London, and Vice-Chancellor, Univ. of London. *Publs:* The Concessive Relation in Old English Poetry, 1954, 1973; (with C.L. Wrenn) An Old English Grammar, 1955, 1958; (with P.G. Foote) The Saga of Gunnlaug Serpent-Tongue, 1957; (with A.H. Smith) The Teaching of English, 1958, 1964; The Use of English, 1962, 1968; (with D. Crystal) Systems of Prosodic and Paralinguistic Features in English, 1964; (with J. Svartvik) Investigating Linguistic Acceptability, 1966; Essays on the English Language, 1968; (with S. Greenbaum) Elicitation Experiments in English: Linguistic Studies in Use and Attitude, 1970; (with S. Greenbaum, G. Leech and J. Svartvik) A Grammar of Contemporary English, 1972; The English Language and Images of Matter, 1972; (with S. Greenbaum) A University Grammar of English, 1973; The Linguist and the English Language, 1974; (co-author) Old English Literature, 1975; (with J. Svartvik) A Corpus of English Conversation, 1980; Style and Communication, 1982; (with S. Greenbaum, G. Leech, and J. Svartvik) A Comprehensive Grammar of the English Language, 1985; Words at Work: Lectures on Textual Structure, 1986. Add: University Coll., Gower St., London WC1, England.

QUYTH, Gabriel. *See* **JENNINGS**, Gary.

R

RABAN, Jonathan. British, b. 1942. Literature. Asst. Lectr., University Coll. of Wales, Aberystwyth, 1965–67; Lectr., Univ. of East Anglia, Norwich, 1967–69. *Publs:* The Technique of Modern Fiction, 1968; Mark Twain: Huckleberry Finn, 1968; The Society of the Poem, 1971; Soft City, 1974; (ed.) Robert Lowell's Poems: A Selection, 1974; Old Glory, 1981; Foreign Land, 1985; Coasting, 1986; For Love and Money, 1987. Add: 29 Ennismore Gardens, London SW7 1AD, England.

RABB, Theodore K. American (b. British), b. 1937. History. Prof. of History, Princeton Univ., since 1977 (Assoc. Prof., 1967–77). Instr., Stanford Univ., California, 1961–62, and Northwestern Univ., Evanston, Ill., 1962–63; Asst. Prof., Harvard Univ., Cambridge, Mass., 1963–67; Visiting Assoc. Prof., Johns Hopkins Univ., Baltimore, 1970, and State Univ. of New York and Binghamton, 1973–74. *Publs:* (ed.) The Thirty Years' War, 1964, 1972; Enterprise and Empire, 1967; (co-ed.) Action and Conviction in Early Modern Europe, 1969; (co-ed.) The Family in History, 1973; The Struggle for Stability in Early Modern Europe, 1976; (co-ed.) Marriage and Fertility, 1980; Climate and History, 1981; (co-ed.) Industrialization and Urbanization, 1981; (co-ed.) The New History, 1982; (co-ed.) Hunger and History, 1983; (co-ed.) Population and Economy, 1986; (co-ed.) Art and History, 1986; (co-ed.) The Origin and Prevention of Major Wars, 1988. Add: Dept. of History, Princeton Univ., Princeton, N.J. 08544, U.S.A.

RABE, Berniece (Louise). American, b. 1928. Children's fiction. Instr. of Creative Writing, Columbia Coll., Chicago. Exec. Bd. Member, Fox Valley Writers, and Off Campus Writers, since 1973. Model, Patricia Stevens Agency, Chicago, 1945–46; Teacher and tutor in special education, Elgin, Ill., 1963–67; Teacher-Trainer, Church of Jesus Christ of Latter-Day Saints, Chicago, 1966–76. *Publs:* Rass, 1973; Naomi, 1975; The Girl Who Had No Name, 1977; The Orphans, 1978; Who's Afraid, 1980; The Balancing Girl, 1980; Margaret's Moves, 1987; A Smooth Move, 1987; Rehearsal for the Bigtime, 1988; Where's Chimpy?, 1988; Tall Enough to Own the World, 1989. Add: 860 Willow Lane, Sleepy Hollow, Ill. 60118, U.S.A.

RABE, David. American, b. 1940. Plays/Screenplays. Consultant, Villanova Univ., Pennsylvania, since 1972 (Asst. Prof., 1970–72). Feature Writer, New Haven Register, Connecticut, 1969–70. *Publs:* The Basic Training of Pavlo Hummel, and Sticks and Bones: Two Plays, 1973; The Orphan, 1973; In the Boom Boom Room, 1975; Streamers, 1977; I'm Dancing as Fast as I can (screenplay), 1982; Hurlyburly, 1985. Add: c/o Ellen Neuwald Inc., 902 N. Ronda Sevilla, Laguna Hills, Calif. 92653, U.S.A.

RABIN, Chaim. British/Israeli, b. 1915. Archaeology/Antiquities, Language/Linguistics. Cowley Lectr. in Post-Biblical Hebrew, Oxford Univ., 1941–56; Prof. of Hebrew Language, Hebrew Univ., Jerusalem, 1956–85; Pres., Israel Assn. of Applied Linguistics, 1974–82. *Publs:* (with H.M. Nahmad) Everyday Arabic, 1940; Everyday Hebrew, 1942; (with C. Singer) Prelude to Modern Science, 1946; Arabic, 1947; Hebrew, 1948; Ancient West-Arabian, 1951; (trans.) Maimonides, 1952; (ed.) The Zadokite Documents, 1954; Qumran Studies, 1957; (ed. with Y. Yadin) Aspects of the Dead Sea Scrolls, 1958; The Revival of Hebrew, 1958; (ed.) Studies in the Bible: Scripta Hierosolymitana VIII, 1961; Sociological Factors in the History of the Hebrew Language, 1967; A Short History of the Hebrew Language, 1974. Add: P.O. Box 7158, Jerusalem, Israel.

RABINOVITZ, Rubin. American, b. 1938. Literature. Prof. of

English, Univ. of Colorado, Boulder. Chmn., Bd. of Trustees, Colorado Associated Univs. Press. Instr. to Asst. Prof. of English, Columbia Univ., NYC, 1964–74. Vice-Chmn., Colorado Humanities Prog., 1979–80. *Publs:* The Reaction Against Experiment in the English Novel 1950–1960, 1967; Iris Murdoch, 1968; The Development of Samuel Beckett's Fiction, 1984. Add: 3938 Wonderland Hill Ave., Boulder, Colo. 80304, U.S.A.

RABINOWICZ, Mordka Harry. British, b. 1919. History, Theology/Religion, Biography. Rabbi, Willesden Synagogue, London, since 1978. Rabbi, Dollis Hill Synagogue, London, 1951–78. *Publs:* Guide to Hasidism, 1960; The Slave Who Saved the City, 1960; The Jewish Literary Treasures of England and America, 1962; The Legacy of Polish Jewry, 1965; A Guide to Life, 1968; The World of Hasidism, 1970; Treasures of Judaica, 1971; Hasidism and the State of Israel, 1982; Hasidic Story Book, 1984; Hasidism: The Movement and Its Leaders, 1988. Add: 31 Sherwood Rd., London NW4, England.

RABINOWITZ, Sandy. American, b. 1954. Animals/Pets, Children's fiction. Author and illustrator of children's books since 1975. *Publs:* (all self-illustrated) The Red Horse and the Bluebird, 1975; What's Happening to Daisy?, 1977; A Colt Named Mischief, 1979; How I Trained My Colt, 1981. Add: Carmel Rd., Bethany, Conn. 06525, U.S.A.

RABOW, Gerald. American, b. 1928. Engineering, Technology. Engineer, 1952–61, and Sr. Scientist, 1961–74, ITT, Nutley, N.J.; Prog. Dir., Otis Elevator Co. Corporate Research Center, 1974–77; member of the technical staff, Bell Labs, N.J., 1979–86. *Publs:* The Era of the System: How the Systems Approach Can Help Solve Society's Problems, 1969. Add: 21 Berkeley Terr., Livingston, N.J. 07039, U.S.A.

RABY, Derek (Graham). British, b. 1927. Plays/Screenplays. *Publs:* The Office, 1973; Tiger, 1974; A Cat Called Willie, 1975; Bandstand, 1975; We Need a Man, 1975; Put an Egg in Your Tank, 1977; Passing Through, 1977; Robinson, 1978; Night Shift, 1979; Letters to the Editor, 1979; Red Bottle, 1981; To Kill a Town, 1981; Tomantha, 1983. Add: The Little House, Elm Grove Rd., Cobham, Surrey, England.

RACHMAN, Stanley Jack. Also writes as Jack Durac. British, b. 1934. Medicine/Health, Sciences. Prof. of Psychology, Univ. of British Columbia, Vancouver, since 1983. Ed., Behaviour Research and Therapy, since 1963. Lectr., Univ. of the Witwatersrand, South Africa, 1954–59; Lectr., 1961–67, Sr. Lectr., 1967–73, Reader, 1973–78, and Prof. of Abnormal Psychology, 1978–83, Univ. of London. *Publs:* (ed.) Critical Essays on Psychoanalysis, 1961; (with H.J. Eysenck) Causes and Cures of Neurosis, 1965; Phobias: Their Nature and Control 1968; (with J. Teasdale) Aversion Therapy and the Behavior Disorders, 1969; (with J. Bergold) Verhaltenstherapie bei Phobien, 1969; The Effects of Psychotherapy, 1971; The Meanings of Fear, 1974; (with C. Philips) Psychology and Medicine, 1974; (as Jack Durac) A Matter of Taste, 1976; Fear and Courage, 1978; Wines and the Art of Tasting, 1978; (ed.) Contributions to Medical Psychology, 1979; (with G.T. Wilson) The Effects of Psychological Therapy, 1980; (with R. Hodgson) Obsessions and Compulsions, 1980; (with J. Maser) Panic: Psychological Perspectives, 1988. Add: Dept. of Psychology, Univ. of British Columbia, Vancouver, B.C. V6T 1W5, Canada.

RACTLIFFE, John Fuller. British, b. 1910. Information science/Computers, Mathematics/Statistics. Lectr., Lanchester Polytechnic, Coventry, since 1960. *Publs:* Elements of Mathematical Statistics, 1962,

1967; (with R. Wooldridge) Introduction to ALGOL Programming, 1963, 1968; ALGOL in Brief, 1971. Add: 20 Innis Rd., Coventry, England.

RADCLIFF-UMSTEAD, Douglas. American, b. 1944. Novels, Literature. Member, Editorial Bd., Pirandello Newsletter, and America Latina; Ed., Italian Culture. Asst. Prof. of Italian and French, Univ. of California at Santa Barbara, 1964–68; Former Dir., Centre for Medieval Studies, Univ. of Pittsburgh. *Publs:* The Birth of Modern Comedy in Renaissance Italy, 1969; Ugo Foscolo, 1970; (trans.) Last Letters of Jacopo Ortis, by Ugo Foscolo, 1970; (with Patrizio Rossi) Italiano Oggi, 1971; (ed.) Innovation in Medieval Literature, 1971; (ed.) The University World: A Synoptic View of Higher Education in the Middle Ages and Renaissance, 1973; The Mirror of Our Anguish: A Study of Pirandello, 1979; Carnival Comedy and Sacred Play, 1985; The Exile into Eternity: A Study of Bassani, 1987; Wait for Me, Little Girl (novel), 1989. Add: Romance Language Dept., Kent State Univ., Kent, Ohio 44242, U.S.A.

RADDALL, Thomas Head. Canadian, b. 1903. Novels/Short stories, History, Autobiography/Memoirs/Personal. *Publs:* The Pied Piper of Dipper Creek and Other Tales, 1939; His Majesty's Yankees, 1942; Roger Sudden, 1945; Tambour and Other Stories, 1945; Pride's Fancy, 1946; The Wedding Gift and Other Stories, 1947; West Novas: A History of the West Nova Scotia Regiment, 1948; Halifax, Warden of the North, 1948; The Nymph and the Lamp, 1950; Son of the Hawk, 1950; Tidefall, 1953; A Muster of Arms and Other Stories, 1954; The Wings of Night, 1956; The Path of Destiny: Canada from the British Conquest to Home Rule, 1957; The Rover: The Story of a Canadian Privateer, 1958; The Governor's Lady, 1960; Hangman's Beach, 1966; Footsteps on Old Floors, 1968; In My Time (autobiography), 1976; The Mersey Story, 1979. Add: 44 Park St., Liverpool, N.S. B0T 1KO, Canada.

RADIN, Ruth Yaffe. American, b. 1938. Children's fiction. Full-time writer. Has worked as a librarian, elementary sch. teacher, and a reading specialist. *Publs:* A Winter Place, 1982; Tac's Island, 1986; Tac's Turn, 1987; High in the Mountains, 1989. Add: c/o Macmillan Publishing Co., 866 Third Ave., New York, N.Y. 10022, U.S.A.

RADLEY, Eric John. British, b. 1917. Country life/Rural societies, Economics, History. Self-employed farmer; Chmn., Gloucestershire County Council, since 1985. Former Lectr. in English and Economic History, West Gloucestershire Coll. of Further Education, Cinderford. *Publs:* Notes on British Economic History, 1967; Country Diary, 1976; Objective Tests in Economic and Social History, 1979; A Country Diary from the Forest of Dean, 1986. Add: Elton Farm, Newnham on Severn, Glos., England.

RADLEY, Sheila. *See* **ROBINSON**, Sheila.

RADZINOWICZ, (Sir) Leon. British, b. 1906. Criminology/Law enforcement/Prisons, History. Fellow of Trinity Coll., Cambridge, since 1948 (Asst. Dir. of Research, 1946–49, Dir., Dept. of Criminal Science, 1949–59, Wolfson Prof. of Criminology, 1959–73, and Dir., Inst. of Criminology, 1960–72, Cambridge Univ.); Assoc. Fellow, Silliman Coll., Yale Univ., since 1966 (Walter E. Meyer Research Prof. of Law, 1962–63). Visiting Adjunct or Research Prof., Columbia Univ., NYC, 1964–67, Rutgers Univ., New Brunswick, N.J., 1968–72, 1979–81, Univ. of Virginia, Charlottesville, 1968–69, 1970–74, Univ. of Pennsylvannia, Philadelphia, 1970–74, John Jay Coll., City of New York Univ., 1978–79, Benjamin N. Cardozo Law Sch., Yeshiva Univ., NYC, 1978–79. Ed., Cambridge Studies in Criminology, 52 vols., 1940–84. *Publs:* History of English Criminal Law, vols. I-IV, 1948–68, vol. V (with R.G. Hood), 1986; Sir James Fitzjames Stephen, 1957; In Search of Criminology, 1961; The Need for Criminology, 1965; Ideology and Crime, 1966; (ed. with M.E. Wolfgang) Crime and Justice, 3 vols., 1971, 1977; (with R.G. Hood) Criminology and the Administration of Criminal Justice: A Bibliography, 1976; (with Joan King) The Growth of Crime, 1977; The Cambridge Institute of Criminology: The Background and Scope, 1988. Add: Trinity Coll., Cambridge, CB2 1TQ, England.

RAE, (Margaret) Doris. British, b. 1907. Novels/Short stories. Chief Clerk and Cashier, Newcastle upon Tyne Magistrates Courts, until 1972. *Publs:* Sings the Nightingale, 1956; The Whispering Wind, 1958; Flame on the Peaks, 1958; Journey into Paradise, 1959; Painted Waters, 1959; The Music and the Splendour, 1959; Golden Dawn, 1960; The Rowans Are Red, 1960; The Lying Jade, 1961; The Flowering Summer, 1961; Serenade to a Nurse, 1962; The Gossamer Web, 1962; Bright Particular Star, 1962; The Shadow and the Sun, 1963; Enchantment in the Snow, 1963; Highland Nurse, 1964; Blue is the Lake, 1964; Blaze of Gladness, 1965; Magic Spring, 1965; The Painted Fan, 1966; The Constant Star,

1967; Echo of Romance, 1967; The Golden Hours, 1968; Flame of the Forest, 1969; The Joyous Prelude, 1971; Honeysuckle in the Hedge, 1973; The Spirit and the Fire, 1974; Duet in Low Key, 1974; Awake to the Dawn, 1976; A Fair Wind Stirring, 1976; Summer Noon, 1976; Spring Song, 1977; Sing a Quiet Tune, 1977; Come Walk with Me, 1978; Mist on the Moors, 1979; The Spell of Solitude, 1981; Rich the Treasure, 1984. Add: Grange Lea Rest Home, North Rd., Ponteland, Northumberland, England.

RAE, Hugh C(rawford). Also writes as Robert Crawford, R.B. Houston, Stuart Stern, Jessica Stirling, and James Albany. British, b. 1935. Novels/Short stories, Mystery/Crime/Suspense, Romance/Historical, Plays/Screenplays. *Publs:* Skinner, 1964; Night Pillow, 1965; A Few Small Bones, 1966; The Interview, 1967; The Saturday Epic, 1968; The Marksman, 1969; The Dear Ones, 1969; (as Robert Crawford) The Shroud Society, 1970; (as Robert Crawford) Cockleburr, 1970; The Rock Harvest, 1971; (as Robert Crawford) Kiss the Boss Goodbye, 1971; The Revenue Men, 1971; The Shooting Gallery, 1972; (as Robert Crawford) The Badger's Daughter, 1972; (as Robert Crawford) Whip Hand, 1972; (as R.B. Houston) Two for the Grave, 1972; The Freezer, 1972; The Rookery, 1974; Harkfast, 1974; (as Jessica Stirling, with M. Coghlan) The Spoiled Earth, 1975; (as Jessica Stirling) The Dresden Finch, 1977; (as Jessica Stirling) The Dark Pasture, 1977; (as Stuart Stern, with S. Ungar) The Minotaur Factor, 1977; (as Stuart Stern) The Poison Tree, 1978; Sullivan, 1978; The Travelling Soul, 1978; (as Jessica Stirling) The Deep Wall at Noon, 1979; The Haunting at Waverley Falls, 1980; The Blue Evening Gone, 1980; The Gates of Midnight, 1982; Treasures on Earth, 1985; Creature Comforts, 1986; Hearts of Gold, 1987; The Good Provider, 1988; The Asking Price, 1989. Add: Drumore Farm Cottage, Gartness Rd., Balfron Station, Stirlingshire, Scotland.

RAE, John Bell. American, b. 1911. History, Transportation. Emeritus Prof. of the History of Technology, Harvey Mudd Coll., Claremont, Calif., since 1976 (Prof., 1959–76). Instr., Asst. Prof., and Assoc. Prof. of History, Massachusetts Inst. of Technology, Cambridge, 1939–59; Exchange Assoc. Prof., Case Inst. of Technology (now Case Western Reserve Univ.), Cleveland, Ohio, 1956–57; Visiting Prof. of History, Univ. of Manchester, Inst. of Science and Technology, U.K., 1965–66. *Publs:* (with T.H.D. Mahoney) The United States in World History, 1949, 3rd ed. 1964; (ed. with S.G. Morse and L. Foster) Readings on the American Way, 1953; American Automobile Manufacturers, 1959; The American Automobile, 1965; Climb to Greatness: The American Aircraft Industry, 1968; (ed.) Henry Ford, 1969; The Road and the Car in American Life, 1971; The Development of the Railway Land Subsidy Policy in the United States, 1979; Nissan/Datsun: A History of Nissan Motor Corporation in U.S.A. 1960–1980, 1982; The American Automobile Industry, 1984. Add: 437 W. 11th St., Claremont, Calif. 91711, U.S.A.

RAE, John Malcolm. British, b. 1931. Novels/Short stories, Children's fiction, Politics/Government. Dir., The Observer newspaper, London, and the Laura Ashley Foundn., since 1986. Head Master, Taunton Sch., Somerset, 1966–70, and Westminster Sch., London, 1970–86. *Publs:* The Custard Boys (novel), 1960; Conscience and Politics, 1970; The Golden Crucifix, 1974; The Treasure of Westminster Abbey, 1975; Christmas Is Coming, 1976; Return to the Winter Palace, 1979; The Third Twin, 1980; The Public School Revolution, 1981; Letters From School, 1987. Add: 101 Millbank Ct., 24 John Islip St., London SW1P 4LG, England.

RAEBURN, Antonia. British, b. 1934. History, Women. Art and Craft teacher, Hertfordshire primary schs., 1955–59, Holt Hall Sch., Norfolk, 1959–62; with Bath Academy of Art, 1962–67; worked on BBC TV documentary, Votes for Women, 1968, and has worked as picture researcher for TV and books. *Publs:* The Militant Suffragettes, 1971; The Suffragette View, 1975. Add: Deviock Farm House, Deviock, Torpoint, Cornwall PL11 3DL, England.

RAEFF, Marc. American, b. 1923. History. Bakhmeteff Prof. of Russian Studies, Columbia Univ., NYC, now Emeritus (joined faculty, 1961). Member of the faculty, Clark Univ., 1949–61. *Publs:* Siberia and the Reforms of 1822, 1956; M.M. Speransky, Statesman of Imperial Russia, 1957, 1969; (ed.) Peter the Great Changes Russia, 1963, 1972; Origins of the Intelligentsia: The 18th Century Nobility, 1966; (ed.) Russian Intellectual History: An Anthology, 1966; (ed.) The Decembrist Movement, 1966; (ed.) Plans for Political Reform in Imperial Russia, 1966; Imperial Russia: The Coming of Age of Modern Russia, 1970; (ed.) Catherine II: A Profile, 1971; Comprehendre l'ancien régime russe, 1982, as Understanding Imperial Russia, 1984; The Well-Ordered Police State: Social and Institutional Change Through Law in the Germanies and Russia 1600–

1800, 1984. Add: Dept. of History, Columbia Univ., New York, N.Y. 10027, U.S.A.

RAFFERTY, S.S. Pseud. for John J. Hurley. American, b. 1930. Mystery/Crime/Suspense. Reporter, Bridgeport Post Telegram, Connecticut, 1955–57; Sr. Vice-Pres., Rozene Advertising, Connecticut, 1957–61; Vice-Pres., Gaynor and Ducas Advertising, NYC, 1961–70. *Publs:* Fatal Flourishes (short stories), 1979; Die Laughing, 1984; Cork of the Colonies, 1984. Add: c/o Avon, 1790 Broadway, New York, N.Y. 10019, U.S.A.

RAINE, Craig. British, b. 1944. Poetry. Poetry Ed., Faber and Faber, publishers, London, since 1981. Lectr. in Oxford: Exeter Coll., 1971–72, Lincoln Coll., 1974–75, and Christ Church, 1976–79; Books Ed., New Review, London, 1977–78; Ed., Quarto, London, 1979–80; Poetry Ed., New Statesman, London, 1981. *Publs:* The Onion, Memory, 1978; A Martian Sends a Postcard Home, 1979; A Journey to Greece, 1979; A Free Translation, 1981; Rich, 1984; The Electrification of the Soviet Union, 1986; (ed.) A Choice of Kipling's Prose, 1987. Add: c/o Faber & Faber, 3 Queen Sq., London WC1N 3AU, England.

RAINE, Kathleen (Jessie). British, b. 1908. Poetry, Literature, Autobiography/Memoirs/Personal, Translations. Research Fellow, Girton Coll., Cambridge, 1955–61. *Publs:* Stone and Flower: Poems 1935–1943, 1943; (trans.) Talk of the Devil, by Dénis de Rougemont, 1945; Living in Time: Poems, 1946; (ed. with Max-Pol Fouchet) Aspects de Littérature Anglaise, 1918–1945, 1947; (trans.) Existentialism, by Paul Foulquié (trans.) Cousin Bette, by Honoré de Balzac, 1948; The Pythoness and Other Poems, 1949; (ed.) Letters of Samuel Taylor Coleridge, 1950; William Blake, 1951; Lost Illusion, by Honoré de Balzac, 1951; Selected Poems, 1952; The Year One: Poems, 1952; Coleridge, 1953; The Collected Poems of Kathleen Raine, 1956; (ed.) Selected Poems and Prose of Coleridge, 1957; Poetry in Relation to Traditional Wisdom, 1958; Christmas, 1960; Blake and England, 1960; The Hollow Hill and Other Poems, 1960–64, 1965; Defending Ancient Springs (essays), 1967; The Written Word, 1967; Six Dreams and Other Poems, 1968; Ninfa Revisited, 1968; Pergamon Poets 4: Kathleen Raine and Vernon Watkins, 1968; Blake and Tradition, 1968; (trans. with R.M. Nadal) Life's a Dream, by Calderon de la Barca, 1968; A Question of Poetry, 1969; (ed. with G.M. Harper) Thomas Taylor the Platonist: Selected Writings, 1969; (with David Gascoyne and W.S. Graham) Penguin Modern Poets 17, 1970; The Lost Country, 1971; William Blake, 1971; Faces of Day and Night (autobiography), 1972; Yeats, The Tarot and the Golden Dawn, 1972; Three Poems Written in Ireland, 1973; On a Deserted Shore, 1973; Farewell Happy Fields (autobiography), 1973; Death in Life, Life in Death (on Yeats), 1974; Blake and Antiquity, 1974; David Jones: Solitary Perfectionist, 1974; (ed.) A Choice of Blake's Verse, 1974; (ed.) Shelley, 1974; The Lake Unknown (autobiography), 1975; The Inner Journey of the Poet, 1976; The Oval Portrait and Other Poems, 1977; The Lion's Mouth (autobiography), 1977; Fifteen Short Poems, 1978; From Blake to "A Vision", 1978; David Jones and the Actually Loved and Known, 1978; The Oracle in the Heart: Poems 1974–1978, 1979; Blake and the New Age, 1979; Collected Poems, 1981; The Human Face of God, 1981; The Inner Journey of the Poet, 1982; Yeats to Initiate: Essays on Certain Themes in the Writings of W.B. Yeats, 1985; The Presence (poetry), 1987; Selected Poems, 1988; India Seen Afar, 1989. Add: 47 Paultons Sq., London SW3, England.

RAINEY, Gene Edward. American, b. 1934. International relations/Current affairs, Politics/Government. Prof. of Political Science, Univ. of North Carolina, Asheville, since 1969. Chmn., Buncombe Co. Bd. of Commissioners, since 1988. Asst. Dean, Sch. of Intnl. Service, 1963–64, and Assoc. Dean, Grad. Sch., 1964–66, American Univ., Washington, D.C.; Asst. Prof. of Political Science, Ohio State Univ., Columbus, 1966–69. *Publs:* (ed.) Contemporary American Foreign Policy: The Official Voice, 1969; Patterns of American Foreign Policy, 1975. Add: 19 Reynolds Pl., Asheville, N.C. 28804, U.S.A.

RAITT, Alan William. British, b. 1930. Literature. Fellow, Magdalen Coll., Oxford, since 1966 (Fellow by Examination, 1953–55), and Reader in French Literature, Oxford Univ., since 1979. Fellow, Exeter Coll., Oxford, 1955–56. *Publs:* (ed.) Balzac: Short Stories, 1964; (ed. with P.-G. Castex) Villiers de l'Isle-Adam: Le Prétendant, 1965; Villiers de l'Isle-Adam et le Mouvement Symboliste, 1965; French Life and Letters: The Nineteenth Century, 1965; Prosper Mérimée, 1970; (ed.) L'Education Sentimentale, by Flaubert, 1979; The Life of Villiers de l'Isle-Adam, 1981; (ed. with P.-G. Castex) Villiers de l'Isle-Adam: Oeuvres Complètes, 1986; Villiers de l'Isle-Adam exorciste du Réel, 1987. Add: Magdalen Coll., Oxford, England.

RAJAN, M(annarswamighala) S(reeranga). Indian, b. 1920. International relations/Current affairs. Prof. Emeritus since 1986 of Intnl. Org., Sch. of Intnl. Studies, Jawaharlal Nehru Univ., New Delhi (Prof., 1962–84). Research Secty., Indian Council of World Affairs, New Delhi, 1957–59; Ed., Intnl Studies, 1963–74; Dir., Indian Sch. of Intnl. Studies, New Delhi, 1965–71. Asian Fellow, Australian National Univ., Canberra, 1971–72; Ed., International Studies, 1963–74; Ed., India Quarterly and Foreign Affairs Reports, New Delhi, 1974–80. *Publs:* United Nations and Domestic Jurisdiction, 1958, 1962; The Post-War Transformation of the Commonwealth: Reflections on the Asian-African Contribution, 1963; India in World Affairs 1954–56, 1964; Non-alignment, India and the Future, 1970; (ed.) Studies in Politics: National and International, 1970; (ed.) India's Foreign Relations During the Nehru Era, 1976; Sovereignty over Natural Resources, 1978; (ed.) Great Power Relations, World Order, and the Third World, 1980; (ed.) India and the International System, 1980; The Expanding Jurisdiction of the United Nations, 1982; (with A. Appadorai) India's Foreign Policy and Relations, 1985, 1988; Studies on Nonalignment and the Nonaligned Movement, 1986; (ed.) The Nonaligned and the United Nations, 1987. Add: Sch. of Intnl. Studies, Jawaharlal Nehru Univ., New Delhi 110067, India.

RAJAN, Tilottama. Canadian, b. 1951. Poetry, Literature. Prof. of English, Univ. of Wisconsin, Madison, since 1985. Asst. Prof. of English, Huron Coll., Univ. of Western Ontario, 1977–80; Asst. and then Assoc. Prof. of English, Queen's Univ., Kingston, Ont. 1980–85. *Publs:* Myth in Metal Mirror, 1967; Dark Interpreter: The Discourse of Romanticism, 1980. Add: Dept. of English, Helen White Hall, 600 N. Park St., Univ. of Wisconsin, Madison, Wisc. 53704, U.S.A.

RAJU, Poolla Tirupati. Indian, b. 1904. Cultural/Ethnic topics, Philosophy, Theology/Religion. Prof. of Philosophy and Psychology, Univ. of Rajasthan, Jaipur, India, 1949–62; Professor of Philosophy and Indian Studies, The Coll. of Wooster, Ohio, 1962–73; Prof. of Philosophy, H.H. Lehman Coll., City Univ. of New York, 1973–75. *Publs:* Thought and Reality, 1937; (co-author) Comparative Studies in Philosophy, 1951; India's Culture and Her Problem, 1952; Idealistic Thought of India, 1953; Telugu Literature, 1954; (co-author) The Concept of Man, 1960, 1966: Indian Idealism and Modern Challenges, 1961; Introduction to Comparative Philosophy, 1970; (co-author) The Great Asian Religions, 1972; The Philosophical Traditions of India, 1972; Spirit, Being, and Self, 1982; Structural Depths of Indian Thought, 1985. Add: The Coll. of Wooster, Wooster, Ohio 44691, U.S.A.

RAKOFF, Alvin. Canadian, b. 1927. Plays/Screenplays. Freelance film and television dir., since 1952. Journalist in Toronto, 1949–53; Writer, Dir., and Producer, BBC television, London, 1953–57. *Publs:* A Flight of Fancy, 1953; (co-adaptor) The Troubled Air, 1953; Thunder in the Realm, 1955; (adaptor) Our Town, 1957; (adaptor) The Caine Mutiny Court Martial, 1957; Say Hello to Yesterday, 1967; (adaptor) Summer and Smoke, 1971; (adaptor) A Kiss Is Just a Kiss, 1971; (adaptor) A Man About a Dog, 1972; Rooms, 1974; O Canada, 1974; Mineshaft, 1975; (adaptor) Lulu Street, 1975; (adaptor) In Praise of Love, 1975; (adaptor) Romeo and Juliet, 1978; (co-author) City on Fire, 1979. Add: 1 The Orchard, London W4 1JZ, England.

RAKOSI, Carl. American, b. 1903. Poetry. Instr., Univ. of Texas, Austin, 1928–29; Social Worker, Chicago, New Orleans, Brooklyn, St. Louis, and Cleveland, 1929–45, Exec. Dir., Jewish Family and Children's Service, Minneapolis, Minn., 1945–68; in private practice of psychotherapy, Minneapolis, 1955–71; Writer-in-Residence, Univ. of Wisconsin, Madison, 1969–70, and Michigan State Univ., E. Lansing, 1972. *Publs:* Selected Poems, 1941; Two Poems, 1942; Amulet, 1967; Ere-VOICE, 1971; Ex Cranium, Night, 1975; My Experiences in Parnassus, 1977; Droles de Journal, 1981; History, 1981; Spiritus I, 1983; Collected Prose, 1984; Collected Poems, 1986. Add: 126 Irving St., San Francisco, Calif. 94122, U.S.A.

RALPHS, Sheila. British, b. 1923. Literature. Sr. Lectr., Univ. of Manchester, 1964–82 (Asst. Lectr., 1951–54; Lectr., 1954–64). *Publs:* Etterno Spiro: A Study in the Nature of Dante's Paradise, 1959; Dante's Journey to the Centre, 1972. Add: Univ. of Manchester, Manchester M13 9PL, England.

RAMANUJAN, A(ttipat) K(rishnaswami). Indian, b. 1929. Poetry, Translations. Member of the faculty since 1962, Prof. of Dravidian Studies and Linguistics since 1968, and Member, Commn. on Social Thought, since 1972, Univ. of Chicago. *Publs:* (trans.) Fifteen Poems from a Classical Tamil Anthology, 1965; The Striders, 1966; (trans.) The Yellow Fish, by Shouri, 1966; (trans.) The Interior Landscape: Love

Poems from a Classical Tamil Anthology, 1967; No Lotus in the Navel: Kannada Poems, 1969; Relations, 1972; (trans.) Speaking of Siva, 1973; (co-author) The Literatures of India, 1975; (trans.) Samskara, 1976; Selected Poems, 1976; Mattu Itara Padyagalu, 1977; Mattobbana Atmacaritre, 1979; (trans.) Hymns for the Drowning, 1981; (trans.) Poems of Love and War: From the Eight Anthologies and the Ten Songs of Classical Tamil, 1985; Second Sight (poems), 1986; (ed. with S. Blackburn) Another Harmony: New Essays on South Asian Folklore, 1986. Add: 5629 S. Dorchester Ave., Chicago, Ill. 60637, U.S.A.

RAMO, Simon. American, b. 1913. Sciences, Sports. Vice Chmn. of Bd., and Chmn. of Exec. Cttee., Thompson Ramo Wooldridge (TRW) Inc., Redondo Reach, Calif.; Research Assoc., California Inst. of Technology, Pasadena, since 1946; Dir., Times Mirror Co., and Union Bancorp Inc. Member, White House Energy Research and Development Advisory Council, U.S. State Dept. Advisory Cttee. on Science and Foreign Affairs, Conference Bd. Sr. Executives Council, and the Atlantic Council Energy Steering Cttee.; Dir., U.S. Chamber of Commerce; Trustee, California Inst. of Technology, Pasadena. With General Electric Co., Schenectady, N.Y., 1936–46; Lectr., Union Coll., Schenectady, 1941–46; Vice Pres., Hughes Aircraft Co., Culver City, Calif. 1946–53; Exec. Vice Pres., and Dir., Ramo Wooldridge Corp., Los Angeles, 1953–58; Scientific Dir., U.S. Air Force Ballistic Missiles Progs., Thor, Atlas and Titan, 1954–58. *Publs:* (with J.R. Whinnery) Fields and Waves in Modern Radio, 1944; 2nd ed. (with others) as Fields and Waves in Communication Electronics, 1984; Introduction to Microwaves, 1945; (ed., with others) Peacetime Uses of Outer Space, 1961; Cure for Chaos, 1969; Century of Mismatch, 1970; Extraordinary Tennis for the Ordinary Player, 1970, 1977; The Islands of E, Cono and My, 1973; The Management of Technological Corporations, 1980; America's Technology Slip, 1980; What's Wrong with Our Technological Society and How to Fix It, 1983; Tennis by Machiavelli, 1984; The Business of Science: Winning and Losing in the High-Tech Age, 1988. Add: TRW Inc., 1 Space Park, Redondo Beach, Calif. 90278, U.S.A.

RAMPLING, Anne. *See* **RICE,** Anne.

RAMSDEN, E. H. British. Art. Joint Ed., Eidos; Journal of Painting, Sculpture and Design, 1950–52. *Publs:* Introduction to Modern Art, 1940, 1949; Twentieth Century Sculpture, 1949; Sculpture: Theme and Variations, 1953; The Letters of Michaelangelo, 2 vols., 1963; Michaelangelo, 1966, 5th ed. 1978; 'Come, Take this Lute': A Quest for Identities in Italian Renaissance Portraiture, 1983. Add: 30 Mallord St., London SW3, England.

RAMSDEN, Herbert. British, b. 1927. Language/Linguistics, Literature. Prof. Emeritus of Spanish Language and Literature, Univ. of Manchester, since 1982 (Asst. Lectr. in Spanish, 1954–57; Lectr., 1957–61; Prof., 1961–82). *Publs:* An Essential Course in Modern Spanish, 1959; Weak-Pronoun Position in the Early Romance Languages, 1963; (ed.) Azorin's La ruta de Don Quijote, 1966; Angel Ganivet's Idearium Espanol: A Critical Study, 1967; The 1898 Movement in Spain, 1974; (ed.) Garcia Lorca's Bodas de sangre, 1980; Baroja's La busca, 1982; Po Baroja: La busca 1903 to La busca 1904, 1982; (ed.) Garcia Lorca's La casa de Bernarda Alba, 1983; Lorca's Romancero gitano: Eighteen Commentaries, 1988; (ed.) Garcia Lorca's Romancero gitano, 1988. Add: 7 Burford Ave., Bramhall, Cheshire, England.

RAMSDEN, John Andrew. British, b. 1947. History, Politics/Government. Reader in History, Queen Mary Coll., Univ. of London, since 1980. Research Student, Nuffield Coll., Oxford, 1969–72. *Publs:* (with others) By-Elections in British Politics, 1973; (with others) The Conservatives, 1977; (with others) Trends in British Politics since 1945, 1978; The Age of Balfour and Baldwin 1902–1940, 1978; The Shaping of Conservative Policy: The Conservative Research Department since 1929, 1980; Real Old Tory Politics, 1984. Add: Dept. of History, Queen Mary Coll., Mile End Rd., London E1, England.

RAMSEY, Gordon Clark. American, b. 1941. History, Biography. Organist, Second Church of Christ, Scientist, Hartford, since 1983. Secty. to Faculty Senate, and Adjunct Instr. in English, Univ. of Hartford, since 1986. Asst. to Headmaster, Alumni Dir., and Instr. in English, Worcester Academy, Mass., 1963–69; Secty. of the Bd., Yale Alumni Fund, 1969–71, Asst. and Exec. Dir., Assn. of Yale Alumni, 1972–77; Dir. of Financial Development, Avon Old Farms Sch., 1978–80; Development Consultant, Stoneleigh-Burnham Sch., Greenfield, Mass., 1980–82. *Publs:* Agatha Christie: Mistress of Mystery, 1967; (ed.) These Fields and Halls: A Book of Prayers and Meditations for Independent People, 1974; An Undertaking Sett Forward (history of Yale Alumni Fund), 1976;

Aspiration and Perseverance: The History of Avon Old Farms School, 1984. Add: 92 Cambridge St., W. Hartford, Conn. 06110-2305, U.S.A.

RAMSEY, Jarold. American, b. 1937. Plays, Poetry, Libretti. Assoc. Prof. to Prof. of English, Univ. of Rochester, N.Y., since 1971 (Asst. Prof., 1966–71). *Publs:* The Space Between Us, 1970; Love in an Earthquake, 1973; The Lodge of Shadows, (Libretto), 1974; (ed.) Coyote Was Going There (anthology of Indian myths), 1977; Coyote Goes Upriver (play), 1981; Dermographia, 1982; Reading the Fire: Essays in the Traditional Indian Literatures of the Far West, 1983. Add: 519 Wellington Ave., Rochester, N.Y. 14619, U.S.A.

RAMSEY, Norman F(oster). American, b. 1915. Physics. Higgins Prof. of Physics, Harvard Univ., Cambridge, Mass., since 1966 (Assoc. Prof., 1947–66); Sr. Fellow, Harvard Soc. of Fellows, since 1971. Assoc. Prof., Columbia Univ., NYC, 1943–47; Chmn., Physics Dept., Brookhaven National Lab., 1945–47; Eastman Prof., Oxford Univ., 1973–74. Pres., Universities Research Assn., 1966–81, American Physical Soc., 1978–79. *Publs:* (co-author) Experimental Nuclear Physics, 1951; Nuclear Moments, 1953; Molecular Beams, 1955, 1986; (co-author) Quick Calculus, 1965, 1986. Add: Lyman Physics Lab., Harvard Univ., Cambridge, Mass. 02138, U.S.A.

RAMSEY, Paul. American, b. 1924. Poetry, Literature. Poet-in-Residence since 1966, and Guerry Prof. of English since 1980, Univ. of Tennessee, Chattanooga (Prof. of English, 1966–70; Alumni Distinguished Service Prof., 1970–80); Pres., DuLeslin Agency and Dir., Tennessee Poetry Circuit. Teacher, Univ. of Alabama, Tuscaloosa, 1948–50 and 1953–57, Elmira Coll., N.Y., 1957–62, Raymond Coll., Stockton, Calif., 1962–64, and Univ. of South, Sewanee, Tenn., 1964–66; Research Fellow, Yale Univ., New Haven, Conn., 1980. *Publs:* The Lively and the Just, 1962; (with S. Kahn and J. Taylor) Triptych, 1964; In an Ordinary Place, 1965; A Window for New York, 1968; The Doors, 1968; The Art of John Dryden, 1968; The Naming of Adam, 1974; No Running on the Boardwalk, 1975; Antiphon, 1975; Eve, Singing, 1976; The Fickle Glass: A Study of Shakespeare's Sonnets, 1979; The Flight of the Heart, 1981; The Keepers, 1984; The Truth of Value: A Defence of Moral and Literary Judgement, 1985; (ed.) Contemporary Religious Poetry, 1987. Add: P.O. Box 4146, Chattanooga, Tenn. 37405, U.S.A.

RANA, J. *See* **BHATIA,** Jamunadevi.

RAND, J.H. *See* **HOLLAND,** James R.

RANDALL, Clay. *See* **ADAMS,** Clifton.

RANDALL, Dale B(ertrand) J(onas). American, b. 1929. Literature. Prof. of English, Duke Univ., Durham, since 1970 (Asst. Prof., 1960–65; Assoc. Prof., 1965–70; Asst. Dean of the Grad. Sch., then Assoc Dean., 1970–74). Member, Central Exec. Cttee., Folger Inst., since 1983; Advisory Council, Southeastern Renaissance Conference, since 1984; Ed., Renaissance Papers, since 1984. Co-Chmn., 1968–69, 1974–75, and Chmn., 1970–74, 1975–76, Southeastern Inst. of Medieval and Renaissance Studies. *Publs:* The Golden Tapestry: A Critical Survey of Non-Chivalric Spanish Fiction in English Translation 1543–1657, 1963; Joseph Conrad and Warrington Dawson: The Record of a Friendship, 1968; Jonson's Gypsies Unmasked: Background and Theme of "The Gypsies Metamorphos'd," 1975; (ed.) Medieval and Renaissance Studies, vol. VI, 1976, and vol. VIII, 1979; (ed. with George Walton Williams) Studies in the Continental Background of Renaissance English Literature: Essays Presented to John L. Lievsay, 1977; Gentle Flame: The Life and Verse of Dudley, Fourth Lord North (1602–1677), 1983; "Theatres of Greatness": A Revisionary View of Ford's "Perkin Warbeck", 1986. Add: Dept. of English, Duke Univ., 323 Allen Bldg., Durham, N.C. 27706, U.S.A.

RANDALL, Dudley. American, b. 1914. Poetry, Literature. Librarian since 1969, and Instr. since 1970, Univ. of Detroit (Poet-in-Residence, 1969–74); Founding Publisher, Broadside Press, Detroit. Member, Advisory Panel on Literature, Michigan Council for the Arts, and Cttee. for the Arts, New Detroit Inc., both since 1970. *Publs:* (with M. Danner) Poem Counterpoem, 1966; (ed. with M. Burroughs) For Malcolm, 1967; Cities Burning, 1968; (ed.) Black Poetry, 1969; Love You, 1970; More to Remember, 1971; (ed.) The Black Poets, 1971; After the Killing, 1973; A Litany of Friends: Poems Selected and New, 1981, 1983. Add: c/o Lotus Press Inc., P.O. Box 21607, Detroit, Mich. 48221, U.S.A.

RANDALL, Florence Engel. American, b. 1917. Historical/Romance/Gothic, Children's fiction. Freelance writer. *Publs:* Hedgerow, 1967;

The Place of Sapphires, 1969; The Almost Year (juvenile), 1971; Haldane Station, 1973; A Watcher in the Woods (juvenile), 1976; All the Sky Together (juvenile), 1983. Add: 88 Oxford Blvd., Great Neck, N.Y. 11023, U.S.A.

RANDALL, Francis Ballard. American, b. 1931. Cultural/Ethnic topics, History, International relations/Current affairs. Historian, Sarah Lawrence Coll., Bronxville, N.Y., since 1961. Member of faculty, Amherst Coll., Massachusetts, 1956–59, and Columbia Univ., NYC, 1959–61, 1967–68. *Publs:* (co-author) Essays in Russian and Soviet History, 1963; Stalin's Russia: An Historical Reconsideration, 1965; N.G. Chernyshevskii, 1967; Vissarion Belinskii, 1987. Add: 425 Riverside Dr., New York, N.Y.10025, U.S.A.

RANDALL, Janet. *See* **YOUNG, Janet Randall.**

RANDALL, John L(eslie). British, b. 1933. Psychology, Supernatural/Occult topics. Biology teacher, King Henry VIII Sch., Coventry, since 1979. Science Master, Oken High Sch., Warwick, 1958–62; Tutor in Biology, Leamington Coll., Leamington Spa, Warwicks., 1962–79. *Publs:* Parapsychology and the Nature of Life, 1975; Psychokinesis, 1982. Add: King Henry VIII Sch., Warwick Rd., Coventry, England.

RANDALL, Julia. American, b. 1923. Poetry. Former Assoc. Prof. of English, Hollins Coll., Virginia. *Publs:* The Solstice Tree: Poems, 1952; Mimic August: Poems, 1960; 4 Poems, 1964; The Puritan Carpenter, 1965; Adam's Dream, 1966; Adam's Dream: Poems, 1969; The Farewells, 1981; Moving in Memory, 1987. Add: Rt. 1, Box 64, N. Bennington, Vt. 05257, U.S.A.

RANDALL, Margaret. American, b. 1936. Poetry, Politics, Women, Translations. Ed., El Corno Emplumado, English-Spanish quarterly, Mexico City, 1962–69. *Publs:* Giant of Tears and Other Poems, 1959; Ecstasy Is a Number: Poem, 1961; Poems of the Glass, 1964; Small Sounds of the Bass Fiddle, 1964; October, 1965; 25 Stages of My Spine, 1967; Water I Slip Into at Night, 1967; So Many Rooms Has a House, But One Roof, 1968; Getting Rid of Blue Plastic: Poems Old and New, 1968; (ed.) Los Hippies: Expression de Una Crisis, 1968; (ed.) Las Mujeres, 1970; (trans.) Let's Go!, by Otto-René Castillo, 1970; (ed.) La Mujer Cubana Ahora, 1972; (ed.) Mujeres en la Revolucion, 1973; (ed.) Poems from Latin America, 1973; Part of the Solution: Portrait of a Revolutionary (miscellany), 1973; With Our Hands, 1974; Carlota: Poems and Prose from Havana, 1978; Doris Tijerino: Inside the Nicaraguan Revolution, 1978; (trans.) These Living Songs, 1978; We, 1978; Reflections from Cuba, 1978; Cuban Women: Twenty Years Later, 1979; (trans.) Breaking the Silences, 1981; Sandino's Daughters, 1982; Testimonios, 1983; Christians in the Nicaraguan Revolution, 1984; Risking a Somersault in the Air: Conversations with Nicaraguan Writers, 1984; (trans.) Carlos, The Dawn Is No Longer Beyond Our Reach, by Tomas Borge Martnez, 1984; The Coming Home Poems, 1986; Albuquerque: Coming Back to the USA, 1986; This Is about Incest, 1987; Memory Says Yes, 1988; (with Ruth Hubbard) The Shape of Red: Insider/Outsider Reflections, 1988. Add: 50 Cedar Hill Rd., N.E., Albuquerque, N. Mex. 87122, U.S.A.

RANDALL, Marta. American, b. 1948. Science fiction/Fantasy, Office Mgr., H. Zimmerman, Oakland, Calif., since 1968. Pres., Science Fiction Writers of America, 1982–84. *Publs:* A City in the North, 1976; Islands, 1976, 1980; Journey, 1978; Dangerous Games, 1980; (ed. with Robert Silverberg) New Dimensions 11, 1980; The Sword of Winter, 1983; Those Who Favor Fire, 1984. Add: P.O. Box 13243, Station E, Oakland, Calif. 94661, U.S.A.

RANDALL, Robert. *See* **SILVERBERG, Robert.**

RANDALL, Rona. British. Historical/Romance/Gothic. Fellow, Intnl. P.E.N.; Vice-Chmn., Women's Press Club of London, 1961–63. *Publs:* The Moon Returns, 1942; Doctor Havelock's Wife, 1943; Rebel Wife, 1944; The Late Mrs. Lane, 1945; The Howards of Saxondale, 1946; That Girl, Jennifer!, 1946; The Fleeting House, 1947; I Married a Doctor (in U.S. as The Doctor Takes a Wife), 1947; The Street of the Singing Fountain, 1948; Shadows on the Sand, 1949; Delayed Harvest, 1950; Young Doctor Kenway, 1950; The Island Doctor, 1951; Bright Morning, 1952; Girls in White, 1952; Young Sir Galahad, 1953; Journey to Love, 1953; Faith, Hope, and Charity, 1954; The Merry Andrews, 1954; Desert Flower, 1955; Journey to Arcady, 1955; Leap in the Dark, 1956; A Girl Called Ann, 1956; Runaway from Love, 1956; The Cedar Tree, 1957; The Doctor Falls in Love, 1958; Nurse Stacey Comes Aboard, 1958; Love and Dr. Maynard, 1959; Enchanted Eden, 1960; Sister at Sea, 1960; Hotel

De Luxe, 1961; Girl in Love, 1961; House Surgeon at Luke's, 1962; Walk into My Parlour, 1962, as Lyonhurst, 1977; Lab Nurse, 1962; The Silver Cord, 1963; The Willow Herb, 1965; Seven Days from Midnight, 1965; The Arrogant Duke, 1966; Leap in the Dark, 1966; Knight's Keep, 1967; Jordan and the Holy Land (non-fiction), 1968; Broken Tapestry, 1969; The Witching Hour, 1970; Silent Thunder, 1971; Mountain of Fear, 1972; Time Remembered, Time Lost, 1973; Glenrannoch (in U.S. as The Midnight Walker), 1973; Dragonmede, 1974; The Watchman's Stone, 1975; The Eagle at the Gate, 1977; The Mating Dance, 1979; The Ladies of Hanover Square, 1981; Curtain Call, 1983; The Drayton Legacy, 1985; The Potter's Niece, 1987; The Model Wife, 19th Century Style (non-fiction), 1989; Add: Conifers, Pembury Rd., Tunbridge Wells, Kent TN2 4ND, England.

RANDELL, Beverley. Pseud. for Beverley Price. New Zealander, b. 1931. Children's fiction. Ed., Price Milburn and Co. Ltd., New Zealand, 1962–84, Heinemann-New Zealand, 1984–86. *Publs:* PM Felt Books, 1965; Methuen Caption Books, 1966; Methuen Number-Story-Caption-Books, 1967; (co-author) PM Country Readers, 1967; (ed.) Mark and Meg Books, 1968; Wheaton's Tiny Readers, 1968; Guide to the Ready to Read Series, 1968, 1978; Bowmar Primary Reading Series, 1969; (ed.) PM Advanced Readers, 1969; John the Mouse Who Learned to Read, 1970; Listening Skillbuilders, 1971; The First Men on the Moon, 1971; (ed.) PM Town Readers 1971; (ed.) Methuen Concept Science, 1971; (ed.) PM Everyday Stories, 1971; Twelve Times Twelve, 1971; (ed.) Instant Readers, 1971; Methuen Story Readers, 1972; Cyfres Darllen Cyflym, 1973; Llyfar Pum Munud, 1973; (co-author) Methuen Country Books, 1973; (ed.) Red Car Stories, 1973; (ed.) Dinghy Books, 1973; PM Creative Workbooks, 1973; (with C. Harper) PM Animal Books, 1973; (ed.) PM Seagulls, 1974; (ed.) People at Work, 1974; (co-author) Methuen Country Books, 1974; First Phonics, 1974; The Cat with the Longest Whiskers, 1978; (ed. and co-author) PM Readalongs, 1978; 1982; Kisim Save Buk Helpim (in Pidgin), 1979; (ed.) Early Days, 1982; Nelson Joining-in Books: Rhyme and Rhythm, 1985; Look and Listen, 1985; Heinemann (New Zealand) Windmill Books, 1985; PM Readalong Rhythms, 1985; Ginn Rhythm and Rhyme books, 1986. Add: 24 Glasgow St., Kelburn, Wellington, New Zealand.

RANDI, James. Canadian, b. 1928. Paranormal, Social commentary. Professional magician (also known professionally as The Amazing Randi and Prince Ibis), since 1948. Founding Fellow and Exec. Bd. Member, Cttee. for Scientific Investigation of Claims of the Paranormal, and Member of the Editorial Bd. of its journal, since 1976. Regents Lectr., Univ. of California at Los Angeles, 1984. *Publs:* The Magic of Uri Geller, 1975, as The Truth about Uri Geller, 1982; (with Bert Randolph Sugar) Houdini: His Life and Art, 1976; Flim-Flam!: The Truth about Unicorns, Parapsychology, and Other Delusions, 1980; Test Your ESP Potential: A Complete Kit, 1982; The Faith Healers, 1987. Add: 1200 N.W. 8th St., Plantation, Fla. 33325, U.S.A.

RANDISI, Robert J(oseph). Also writes as Nick Carter, Tom Cutter, and J.R. Roberts. American, b. 1951. Mystery/Crime/Suspense, Westerns/Adventure. Full-time writer since 1982. Admin. aide, New York City Police Dept., 1973–81. *Publs:* mystery novels—The Disappearance of Penny, 1980; (with Warren Murphy) Midnight Man, 1981; Eye in the Ring, 1982; The Steinway Collection, 1983; Full Contact, 1984; mystery novels as Nick Carter—Pleasure Island, 1981; Chessmaster, 1982; The Mendoza Manuscript, 1982; The Greek Summit, 1983; The Decoy Hit, 1983; The Caribbean Coup, 1984; The Ham Reporter, 1986; No Exit from Brooklyn, 1987; western novels as J.R. Roberts—The Gunsmith series: Macklin's Woman, 1982; The Chinese Gunmen, 1982; The Woman Hunt, 1982; The Guns of Abilence, 1982; Three Guns for Glory, 1982; Leadtown, 1982; The Longhorn War, 1982; Quanah's Revenge, 1982; Heavyweight Gun, 1982; New Orleans Five, 1982; One-Handed Gun, 1982; The Canadian Payroll, 1983; Draw to an Inside Death, 1983; Dead Man's Hand, 1983; Bandit Gold, 1983; Buckskins and Six-guns, 1983; Silver War, 1983; High Noon at Lancaster, 1983; Bandido Blood, 1983; The Dodge City Gang, 1983; Sasquatch Hunt, 1983; Bulletts and Ballots, 1983; The Riverboat Gang, 1983; Killer Grizzly, 1984; North of the Border, 1984; Eagle's Gap, 1984; novels as Tom Cutter—The Blue Cut Job, 1983; Lincoln County, 1983; The Winning Hand, 1983; Chinatown Chance, 1983; other—(ed.) The Eyes Have It, 1984; (ed.) Mean Streets, 1986; (ed.) Eye for Justice, 1988. Add: c/o St. Martin's Press, 175 Fifth Ave., New York N.Y. 10010, U.S.A.

RANGLEY, Olivia. *See* **ZACHARY, Hugh.**

RANIS, Gustav. American, b. 1929. Economics. Trustee, Brandeis Univ., Waltham, Mass. Asst. Admin., U.S. Agency for Intnl. Development, 1965–67; Frank Altschul Prof. of Intnl. Economics, and Dir. of the Economic Growth Center, Yale Univ., New Haven, Conn., 1967–75. *Publs:* (with J. Fei) Development of the Labor Surplus Economy, 1964; (ed.) The U.S. and the Developing Economies, 1964; (ed.) The Government and Economic Development, 1971; The Gap Between Rich and Poor Nations, 1972; (ed. with W. Beranek) Science, Technology and Economic Development: A Historical and Comparative Study, 1979; (with J. Fei and S. Kuo) Growth with Equity: The Taiwan Case, 1979. Add: 7 Mulberry Rd., Woodbridge, Conn., U.S.A.

RANKIN, Herbert David. British, b. 1931. Classics, Philosophy. Prof. of Ancient Philosophy, Univ. of Southampton, since 1988 (Prof. of Classics, 1973–88). Foundn. Prof. of Classical Studies, Monash Univ., Clayton, Vic., 1965–73. *Publs:* Plato and the Individual, 1964; Petronius the Artist, 1971; Archilochus of Paros, 1977; Sophists, Socratics and Cynics, 1983; Antisthenes Sokratikos, 1986; Celts and the Classical World, 1987. Add: Dept. of Philosophy, Univ. of Southampton, Southampton SO9 5NH, England.

RANKINE, John. *See* **MASON,** Douglas Rankine.

RANSFORD, Oliver (Neil). British, b. 1914. History. Consultant Anaesthetist, Bulawayo Group of Hosps., Zimbabwe, since 1947. Medical Officer, H.M. Colonial Service, 1938–47. *Publs:* Livingstone's Lake, 1966; The Battle of Majuba Hill, 1967; The Rulers of Rhodesia, 1968; Bulawayo, 1968; The Battle of Spion Kop, 1969; The Slave Trade, 1971; Rhodesian Tapestry, 1971; The Greak Trek, 1972; (with T.W. Baxter) Livingstone in Africa, 1973; Livingstone: The Dark Interior, 1978; Bid the Sickness Cease, 1983. Add: 8 Heyman Rd., Suburbs, Bulawayo, Zimbabwe.

RANSLEY, Peter. British, b. 1931. Novels, Plays/Screenplays. Journalist and social worker, then free-lance writer. *Publs:* Disabled (in Plays and Players), 1971; Ellen (in Plays and Players), 1971; The Price (novel), 1984; The Hawk (novel), 1988. Add: c/o Peters Fraser Dunlop, The Chambers, Chelsea Harbour, Lots Rd., London SW10 0XF, England.

RANSOM, Candice F. Also writes as Kate Kenyon. American, b. 1952. Historical/Romance, Children's fiction. Full-time writer since 1980. Secty., Computer Sciences, Silver Springs, Md., 1973–77. *Publs:* The Silvery Past, 1982; Amanda, 1984; Susannah, 1984; Kathleen, 1985; Emily, 1985; Breaking the Rules, 1985; Blackbird Keep, 1986; Sabrina, 1986; Nicole, 1986; Cat's Cradle, 1986; Thirteen, 1986; (as Kate Kenyon) The Day the Eighth Grade Ran the School, 1987; Kaleidoscope, 1987; Fourteen and Holding, 1987; Fifteen at Last, 1987; Going on Twelve, 1988; My Sister the Meanie, 1988; My Sister the Traitor, 1989; My Sister the Creep, 1989. Add: 14400 Awbrey Patent Dr., Centreville, Va. 22020, U.S.A.

RANSOM, Harry Howe. American, b. 1922. International relations/Current affairs, Military/Defence, Politics/Governments. Prof. of Political Science, Vanderbilt Univ., Nashville, since 1961, Emeritus since 1987. Instr., Vassar Coll., Poughkeepsie, N.Y., 1948–52; Congressional Fellow, American Political Science Assn., 1953–54; Asst. Prof., Michigan State Univ., East Lansing, 1955; Research Assoc., Harvard Univ., Cambridge, Mass., 1955–61; Fellow, Woodrow Wilson Intnl. Center for Scholars, Washington, D.C., 1974–75. *Publs:* Central Intelligence and National Security, 1958; Can American Democracy Survive Cold War?, 1963; (ed.) An American Foreign Policy Reader, 1965; The Intelligence Establishment, 1970; Strategic Intelligence, 1974. Add: Dept. of Political Science, Vanderbilt Univ., Nashville, Tenn. 37235, U.S.A.

RANSOM, Jay Ellis. American, b. 1914. Anthropology/Ethnology, Chemistry, Earth sciences, Writing/Journalism. Exec. Dir., Western America Inst. for Exploration, since 1954. Science and mathematics teacher, 1936–49; Sr. Technical Writer, Northrop Aircraft Inc., Hawthorne, Calif., 1950–52; Farm Ed./Photojournalist, Enterprise-Courier, Oregon City, Ore., 1955–56; Sr. Technical Ed., Aerojet-Gen. Corp., Azusa, Calif., 1958–59; Ed. Dir. and Chief Proposals Writer, American Electronics Inc., El Monte, Calif., 1959–60; Sr. Technical Writer and Ed. Dir., Hercules Powder Co., Salt Lake City, 1962; City Ed., Siskiyou Daily News, Yreka, Calif., 1965; Reporter and Photographer, Press-Courier, Oxnard, Calif., 1965–67; Sr. Technical Ed. and Writer, Genge Industries Inc., Oxnard, 1967–69; Chief Technical Ed., Sass-Widders Corp., Oxnard, 1969–70. *Publs:* High Tension, 1953; Arizona Gem Trails and the Colorado Desert of California, 1955; Petrified Forest Trails, 1955; The Rock-Hunter's Range Guide, 1962; Fossils in America, 1964; Range Guide to Mines and Minerals, 1964; Gems and Minerals of America, 1975; The Gold Hunter's Field Book, 1975; A Complete Field Guide to North

American Wildlife, Western Ed., 1981; Writing for Publication, 1982; Anthropology and Native American Linguistics at the University of Washington 1934–1941, 1982; Archaeolinguistics and Paleoethnography of Ancient Rock Structures in Western North America, 1984. Add: 1821 E. 9th St., The Dalles, Ore. 97058, U.S.A.

RAO, Raja. Indian, b. 1909. Novels/Short stories. Prof. of Philosophy, Univ. of Texas at Austin, since 1965. *Publs:* Kanthapura, 1938; (ed. with Iqbal Singh) Changing India, 1939; The Cow of the Barricades and Other Stories, 1947; (with I. Singh) Whither India, 1948; The Serpent and the Rope, 1960; The Cat and Shakespeare: A Tale of India, 1965; Comrade Kirillov, 1976; The Policeman and the Rose, 1977; The Chess Master and His Moves, 1978. Add: Dept. of Philosophy, Univ. of Texas, Austin, Tex. 78712, U.S.A.

RAPHAEL, Chaim. Writes mystery novels as Jocelyn Davey. British, b. 1908. Mystery/Crime/Suspense, History, Theology/Religion. Univ. Lectr., Oxford, 1933–39. Engaged in government work, 1939–70: Liaison Officer for Internment Camps, 1939–42; Economics Adviser, 1942–45, and Economics Dir., 1945–57, British Information Services, New York; Deputy Head, 1957–1959, and Head of the Information Div., 1959–69, Dept. of the Treasury; Head of the Information Div., Civil Service Dept., 1969–70; Research Fellow in Jewish Social History, Univ. of Sussex, Brighton, 1970–76. *Publs:* mystery novels, as Jocelyn Davey— The Undoubted Deed (in U.S. as A Capitol Offense), 1956; The Naked Villainy, 1958; A Touch of Stagefright, 1960; A Killing in Hats, 1965; A Treasury Alarm, 1976; Murder in Paradise, 1982; A Dangerous Liaison, 1987; other, as Chaim Raphael—Memoirs of a Special Case, 1962; The Walls of Jerusalem: An Excursion into Jewish History, 1968; A Feast of History: Passover Through the Ages, 1972; A Coat of Many Colours: Memoirs of Jewish Experience (in U.S. as Encounters with the Jewish People) 1979; The Springs of Jewish Life, 1982; The Road from Babylon, 1985; A Jewish Book of Common Prayer, 1986. Add: The Priory, Kingsway, Hove, E. Sussex BN3 2RQ, England.

RAPHAEL, David Daiches. British, b. 1916. Philosophy. Sr. Research Fellow since 1983, and Hon. Fellow, since 1987, Imperial Coll., London. Asst. Principal, then Principal, Ministry of Labour and National Service, 1941–46; Prof. of Philosophy, Univ. of Otago, N.Z., 1946–49; Lectr., then Sr. Lectr., 1949–60, and Prof. of Political and Social Philosophy, 1960–70, Univ. of Glasgow; Prof. of Philosophy, Univ. of Reading, 1970–73, and Imperial Coll., Univ. of London, 1973–83. *Publs:* The Moral Sense, 1947; (ed.) Review of the Principal Questions in Morals, by Richard Price, 1948, 1974; Moral Judgement, 1955, 1978; The Paradox of Tragedy, 1960, 1961; (ed. and contrib.) Political Theory and the Rights of Man, 1967; (ed.) British Moralists 1650–1800, 1969; Problems of Political Philosophy, 1970, 1976; (ed. with A.L. Macfie) The Theory of Moral Sentiments, by Adam Smith, 1976, 1979; Hobbes: Morals and Politics, 1977; (co-ed.) Lectures on Jurisprudence, by Adam Smith, 1978; (co-ed.) Essays on Philosophical Subjects, by Adam Smith, 1980; Justice and Liberty, 1980; Moral Philosophy, 1981; (trans. with Sylvia Raphael) Richard Price as Moral Philosopher and Political Theorist, by Henri Laboucheix, 1982; Adam Smith, 1985. Add: Humanities Programme, Imperial Coll., London SW7 2BX, England.

RAPHAEL, Frederic (Michael). America, b. 1931. Novels/Short stories, Plays/Screenplays, Biography. Contrib., Sunday Times, London, since 1962 (Fiction Critic, 1962–65). *Publs:* Obbligato, 1956; The Earlsdon Way, 1958; The Limits of Love, 1960; A Wild Surmise, 1961; A Man on the Bridge (play), 1961; The Graduate Wife, 1962; The Trouble with England, 1962; Lindmann, 1963; Nothing But the Best (screenplay), 1964; Darling (novel), 1965, screenplay, 1965; Two for the Road (screenplay), 1967; Far from the Madding Crowd (screenplay), 1967; Orchestra and Beginners, 1967; Like Men Betrayed, 1970; A Severed Head (screenplay), 1971; Who Were You with Last Night?, 1971; April, June and November, 1972; Richard's Things, 1973; Bookmarks, 1974; Daisy Miller (screenplay), 1974; California Times (novel), 1975; The Glittering Prizes (television series), 1976; Rogue Male (screenplay), 1976; Somerset Maugham and His World, 1977; (co-trans.) The Poems of Catullus, 1978; (co-trans.) The Oresteia of Aeschylus, 1979; Sleeps Six (stories), 1979; Cracks in the Ice, 1979; A List of Books, 1980; Oxbridge Blues (stories), 1981; Richard's Things (screenplay), 1981; Byron, 1972; Oxbridge Blues (screenplay), 1984; Heaven and Earth, 1985; Think of England (stories), 1986; After the War, 1988. Add: The Wick, Langham, Colchester, Essex CO4 5PE, England.

RAPHAEL, Rick. American, b. 1919. Mystery/Crime/Suspense, Science fiction/Fantasy. Full-time writer since 1979. Newspaper reporter, writer, and ed., 1945–58; Copy Ed., Idaho Daily Statesman,

Boise, 1958–59; Asst. News Ed., and Political Ed., KBOI-TV and Radio, Boise, 1959–65; Press Secty. for Senator Frank Church, 1965–69; Exec. for J.C. Penney Co., 1969–79. *Publs:* The Thirstquenchers, 1964; Code Three, 1965; The Defector, 1980; The President Must Die, 1981. Add: 5320 Thotland Rd., Golden Valley, Minn. 55422, U.S.A.

RAPOPORT, Robert Norman. American, b. 1924. Anthropology/Ethnology, Medicine/Health, Psychology, Sociology. Dir., Inst. of Family and Environmental Research, London, since 1971. Former Lectr., Harvard Univ., Cambridge, Mass., and Prof., Northeastern Univ., Boston; Social Scientist, Tavistock Inst. of Human Relations, London, 1965–71. *Publs:* Changing Navaho Religious Values, 1954; Community as Doctor, 1960; Midcareer Development, 1970; (with R. Rapoport) Dual-Career Families, 1971; (with M. Fogarty and R. Rapoport) Sex, Career and Family, 1971; (with R. Rapoport and Z. Strelitz) Leisure and the Family Life Cycle, 1975; (co-author) Fathers, Mothers and Others, 1977; (with R. Rapoport and J. Bumstead) Working Couples, 1978; (co-ed.) Families in Britain, 1982; Children, Youth and Families, 1985; New Interventions for Children and Youth, 1987. Add: 7a Kidderpore Ave., London NW3 7SX, England.

RAPOPORT, Roger (Dale). American, b. 1946. Travel, Environmental science/Ecology, Medicine/Health, Sciences. *Publs:* (with L.J. Kirshbaum) Is the Library Burning?, 1969; The Great American Bomb Machine, 1971; The Superdoctors, 1977; (with Margot Lind) The California Catalogue, 1977; (with Ken Uston) The Big Player, 1977; California Dreaming, 1982, 22 Days in California, 1988; (with B. Willes) 22 Days in Asia, 1989. Add: 409 13th, Oakland, Calif, 94612, U.S.A.

RAPSON, Richard L. American, b. 1937. History, Humanities (general), Intellectual history, Social commentary/phenomena. Prof. of History, Univ. of Hawaii, Honolulu, since 1966 (Dir. of New Coll., 1970–73). *Publs:* (ed.) Individualism and Conformity in the American Character, 1967; Britons View Americans: Travel Commentary 1860–1935, 1971; (ed.) The Cult of Youth in Middle-Class America, 1971; (gen. ed. and contrib.) The Literature of History, 1971; The Pursuit of Meaning: America 1600-2000, 1977; Denials of Doubt: An Interpretation of American History, 1978; Fairly Lucky You Live Hawaii!: Cultural Pluralism in the Fiftieth State, 1980, American Yearnings: Love, Money, and Endless Possibility, 1988. Add: Dept. of History, Univ. of Hawaii, Honolulu, Hawaii 96822, U.S.A.

RATCLIFF, Carter. American, b. 1941. Art, Biography. Art critic and writer; Instr. in Art History and Criticism, School of Visual Arts, NYC, since 1971. Workshop Dir., Poetry Project, St. Mark's Church, NYC, 1969–70; Ed., Art News, 1969–72; Advisory Ed., Art International, 1970–75; Contr. Ed., Art in America, 1977; Contr., American Academy of Encyclopedias, 1979–80. *Publs:* Art Criticism: Other Minds, Other Eyes, 6 parts, 1974–75; Willem de Kooning, 1975; Alexander Liberman, 1978; Robert Smithson, 1979; Rafael Ferrer, 1980; (ed.) Lucas Samaras: Sittings, 1980; Fernando Botero, 1980; Jean Dubuffet, Partitions, 1980–81; Psycho-Sies, 1981, 1982; John Singer Sargent, 1982; (with Sarah McFadden) Art Materialized, Selections from the Fabric Workshop, 1982; Andy Warhol, 1983; Fever Coast: Give Me Tomorrow, 1983; (with Carol Squires) Aperture, No. 91, 1983; Red Grooms, 1984; Pressures of the Hand: Expressionist Impulses in Recent American Art, 1984; Jorge Castillo: Drawings, New York 1980-83, 1984; Pat Steir: Paintings, 1986; Gilbert and George: The Complete Pictures 1971-1985, 1987; Lynda Benglis and Keith Sonnier: A Ten Year Retrospective 1977-1987, 1987. Add: c/o Rizzoli International Publications Inc., 597 Fifth Ave., New York, N.Y. 10017. U.S.A.

RATCLIFFE, E. Jane. British, b. 1917. Natural history, Autobiography/Memoirs/Personal. *Publs:* Through the Badger Gate, 1974, 1983; Fly Fish, Run Free, 1979, 1984; Wildlife in My Garden, 1986. Add: Deer Close, Fellside, Tower Wood, Windermere, Cumbria LA23 3PW, England.

RATCLIFFE, Eric Hallam. British. Poetry, Essays. Founder and Ed., Ore Mag., since 1954. Experimental Officer, National Physical Lab., Teddington, 1945–66; Higher Scientific Officer, Water Research Centre, Stevenage, 1966–80; Asst. Ed., Inst. of Electrical Engineers, Stevenage, 1980–83. *Publs:* The Visitation, 1952; Little Pagan, 1955; The Ragnarok Rocket bomb, 1957; Transitions, 1957; The Chronicle of the Green Man, 1960; Mist on My Eyes, 1961; Gleanings for a Daughter of Aeolus, 1968; Out of the Thickets, 1969; Leo Poems, 1972; Warrior of the Icenian Queen, 1973; Romantic Acausalism, 1974; Commius the Atrebates: The Man and the Memory, 1975; Commius, 1975; A Sun-Red Mantle, 1976; Nightguard of the Quaternary, 1979; The Great Arthurian Timeslip,

1978; (with Vanessa Kembery) Sheila Ann Ratcliffe 1969-1983—A Biographical Memoir, 1984; Ballet Class, 1986; Intimations, 1989. Add: 7 The Towers, Southgate, Stevenage, Herts. SG1 1HE, England.

RATHBONE, Julian. British, b. 1935. Novels, Mystery/Crime/Suspense. Teacher of English, Ankara Koleji, Turkey, 1959–62; Teacher of English in U.K., 1962–70; Head of English, Bognor Regis Sch., Sussex, 1970–73; Literature Consultant to Royal Berkshire Libraries, 1983–84. *Publs:* Diamonds Bid, 1967; Hand Out, 1968; With My Knives I know I'm Good, 1969; Trip Trap, 1971; Kill Cure. 1973; Bloody Marvellous, 1974; King Fisher Lives, 1975; Carnival, 1975; (with Hugh Ross Williamson) The Princess, a Nun, 1978; A Raving Monarchist, 1978; The Euro-Killers, 1979; Joseph, 1979; A Last Resort, 1980; Base Case, 1981; A Spy of the Old School, 1982; Watching the Detectives, 1983; Wellington's War, 1984; Nasty Very, 1984; Lying in State, 1985; Zdt, 1986; The Crystal Contract, 1988. Add: c/o Margaret Hanbury, 27 Walcot Sq., London SE11 4UB, England..

RATHMELL, Neil. British, b. 1947. Novels/Short stories. Asst. Adviser for English and Drama, Shropshire Education Authority, since 1988. Teacher, Ellesmere Port, 1968–71, County Durham, 1971–75, and Shropshire, 1975–88 *Publs:* The Old School, 1976. Add: 3 Bridge Lane, Hanwood, Shrewsbury, Salop., England.

RATIU, Ion. Stateless, b. 1917. International relations/Current affairs. Dir., Free Romanian Press, since 1956, and the Free Romanian mag., since 1985. Chancellor, Romanian Legation, London, 1940; Prog. Asst., BBC, 1949–56. *Publs:* General Theory of Tort, 1936; Succession Ab Intestat, 1937; Policy for the West, 1957; (with Jane Cobb) Templeton, 1958; Contemporary Romania, 1975; Cartea Memorandului, 1979; Moscow Challenges the World, 1986. Add: Chalet Lani, Steinmatte, 3920-Zermatt, Switzerland.

RATNER, Lorman. American, b. 1932. History. Prof. of History and Dean, Coll. of Liberal Arts, Univ. of Tennessee, Knoxville, since 1986. Asst. Prof. of History, Ithaca Coll., New York, 1959–60; Prof. of History and Dean of Social Sciences, Lehman Coll., City Univ. of New York, 1961–77; Prof. of History and Vice-Chan./Dean of Faculty, Univ. of Wisc.-Parkside, 1977–82. *Publs:* Pre-Civil War Reform: The Variety of Principles and Programs, 1967; Northern Opposition to Anti-Slavery Movement, 1968; Antimasonry: The Crusade and the Party, 1969; (ed. with S. Coben and contrib.) The Development of an American Culture, 1970; Dialogue in American History, 1972; (gen. ed.) American Historical Sources Series, 8 vols. Add: Coll. of Liberal Arts, 226 Ayres Hall, Univ. of Tennessee, Knoxville, Tenn. 37996-1320, U.S.A.

RATNER, Rochelle. American, b. 1948. Novels/Short stories, Poetry, Essays, Translations. Columnist/Ed., Hand Book, since 1976, and American Book Review, since 1978. Book Review Ed., The East Village Other, NYC, 1970–72; Columnist/Ed., Soho Weekly News, NYC, 1975–82. *Publs:* A Birthday of Waters, 1971; False Trees, 1973; (trans.) Paul Colinet: Selected Poems, 1975; The Mysteries, 1976; The Tightrope Walker, 1977; Pirate's Song, 1978; Quarry, 1978; Combing the Waves, 1979; Hide and Seek, 1979; Sea Air in a Grave Ground Hog Turns Toward, 1980; Practicing to Be a Woman: New and Selected Poems, 1982; Trying to Understand What It Means to Be a Feminist (essays), 1984; Bobby's Girl (novel), 1986. Add: 609 Columbus Ave., New York, N.Y. 10024, U.S.A.

RATTRAY, Simon. *See* **TREVOR,** Elleston.

RAUCH, Irmengard. American, b. 1933. Anthropology/Ethnology, Language/Linguistics. Prof. of German. Univ. of California, Berkeley, since 1979. Instr., then Asst. Prof. of German and Linguistics, Univ. of Wisconsin, Madison, 1962–66; Assoc. Prof. of German and Linguistics, Univ. of Pittsburgh, 1966–68; Assoc. Prof., then Prof., Univ. of Illinois, Urbana, 1968–79. *Publs:* The Old High German Diphthongization, 1967; (co-ed.) Approaches in Linguistic Methodology, 1967; 1970 (co-ed.) Der Heliand, 1973; (co-ed.) Linguistic Method, 1978; (co-ed.) The Signifying Animal: The Grammar of Language and Experience, 1980; (co-ed.) Language Change, 1983; (co-ed.) The Semiotia Bridge, 1989. Add: Dept. of German, Univ. of California, Berkeley, Calif. 94720, U.S.A.

RAUCHER, Herman. American, b. 1928. Novels/Short stories, Plays/Screenplays. Advising dir., writer, and consultant. *Publs:* novels—Watermelon Man, 1970; Summer of '42, 1971; A Glimpse of Tiger, 1973; Ode to Billy Joe, 1975; There Should Have Been Castles, 1978; Maynard's House, 1980; screenplays—Sweet November, 1968; Can Hieronymus Merkin Ever Forget Mercy Humppe and Find True Happiness, 1969; Watermelon Man, 1970; Summer of '42, 1972; Ode to Billy Joe, 1976; The Other Side of Midnight, 1977. Add: c/o William Morris Agency, 105 Madison Ave., New York, N.Y. 10016, U.S.A.

RAUDKIVI, A(rved) J(aan). New Zealander, b. 1920. Engineering/Technology. Prof. of Civil Engineering, Univ. of Auckland, since 1970 (Lectr., Sr. Lectr. and Assoc Prof., 1956–69). With New Zealand Ministry of Works, 1950–55. *Publs:* Loose Boundary Hydraulics, 1967, 3rd ed. 1989; (with R.A. Callander) Introduction to Advanced Fluid Mechanics, 1975; (with R.A. Callander) Analysis of Groundwater Flow, 1976; Hydrology, 1979; Grundlagen des Sedimenttransports, 1982. Add: Univ. of Auckland, Sch. of Engineering, Auckland, New Zealand.

RAVEN, Ronald William. British, b. 1904. Medicine/Health. Consulting Surgeon, Westminster Hosp., and Royal Marsden Hosp., London, since 1969 (Consultant Surgeon, Westminster Hosp., 1948–69; Sr. Consultant Surgeon, Royal Marsden Hosp., 1962–69). Member of the Council, 1968–76, and of the Court of Patrons since 1976, Royal Coll. of Surgeons of England; Chmn., Marie Curie Memorial Foundn., since 1961; Chmn., Epsom Coll., since 1954. Pres., Assn. of Head and Neck Oncologists of Great Britain, 1967–70, and Oncology Section, Royal Soc. of Medicine, 1973–74; Pres., British Assn. of Surgical Oncology, 1973–78. *Publs:* (ed. with E. Fletcher) War Wounds and Injuries, 1940; Treatment of Shock, 1942; Surgical Care, 1942, 1952; (with P.E.T. Hancock) Cancer in General Practice, 1952; (with H. Burrows) Surgical Instruments and Appliances, 1952; Hand Book on Cancer for Nurses and Health Visitors, 1953; Cancer and Allied Diseases, 1955; (ed. and contrib.) Cancer, 7 vols., 1957–60; Cancer of Pharynx, and Oesophagus and Its Surgical Treatment, 1958; (ed.) Cancer Progress, 2 vols., 1960–63; (ed. with F.J.C. Roe) The Prevention of Cancer, 1967; (ed. and contrib.) Modern Trends in Oncology, 1973; (ed. and contrib.) The Dying Patient, 1975; (ed. and contrib.) Principles of Surgical Oncology, 1977; (ed. and contrib.) Outlook on Cancer, 1977; Foundations of Medicine, 1978; (with I.W.F. Hanham and R.F. Mould) Cancer Care: An International Survey, 1986; Rehabilitation and Continuing Care in Cancer, 1987; The Gospel According to St. John, 1987. Add: 29 Harley St., London W1N 1DA, England.

RAVEN, Simon (Arthur Noel). British, b. 1927. Novels/Short stories, Plays/Screenplays, Memoirs, Essays. *Publs:* The Feathers of Death, 1959; Brother Caine, 1959; Doctors Wear Scarlet, 1960; (ed.) The Best of Gerald Kersh, 1960; The English Gentlemen: An Essay in Attitudes (in U.S. as The Decline of the English Gentlemen), 1961; Close of Play, 1962; Boys Will Be Boys and Other Essays, 1963; The Sconcing Stoup (play), 1964; The Rich Pay Late, 1964; Friends in Low Places, 1965; Royal Foundation and Other Plays, 1966; The Sabre Squadron, 1966; Fielding Gray, 1967; The Judas Boy, 1968; Places Where They Sing, 1970; Sound the Retreat, 1971; Unman, Wittering, and Zigo (screenplay), 1971; Come Like the Shadows, 1972; The Pallisers (TV series based on novels by Anthony Trollope), 1974; Bring Forth the Body, 1974; The Survivors, 1976; The Fortunes of Fingel, 1976; Edward and Mrs Simpson (TV series), 1978; Roses of Picardie, 1980; Love in a Cold Climate (dramatization of novels by Nancy Mitford), 1980; An Inch of Fortune, 1980; Shadows on the Grass (memoir), 1982; September Castle, 1983; Morning Star, 1984; The Face of the Waters, 1985; Before the Cock Crow, 1986; The Old School (belles lettres), 1986; New Seed for Old, 1988; The Old Gang: A Memoir, 1988. Add: c/o Curtis Brown Ltd., 162–168 Regent St., London W1R 5TA, England.

RAVENSCROFT, Arthur. British, b. 1924. Literature. Jr. Lectr. in English, Univ. of Cape Town, 1946; Lectr. in English, 1947–56, and Sr. Lectr., 1957, Univ. of Stellenbosch, South Africa; Lectr. in English, University Coll. of Rhodesia and Nyasaland, Salisbury, 1958–63; Lectr. in English, 1963–66, and Sr. Lectr., 1966–83, Univ. of Leeds. Co-Ed., Film Review, Cape Town, 1949–55; Chmn., English Assn., Rhodesia, 1960–63; Ed., The Journal of Commonwealth Literature, 1965–79. *Publs:* (trans. with C.K. Johnman) Van Riebeeck's Journal 1659–1662, 1958; Chinua Achebe, 1969, 1977; Nigerian Writers and the African Past, 1978; (with H. Blamires and P. Quartermaine) A Guide to Twentieth Century Literature in English, 1983; "Teaching Words" in African Literature, 1986. Add: 24 The Avenue, Roundhay, Leeds LS8 1JG, England.

RAVETZ, Alison. British, b. 1930. Architecture, Regional/Urban planning, Urban studies. Lectr., Leeds Polytechnic, since 1981. Research Officer, Quarry Hill Flats Project, Univ. of Leeds, 1968–71; Lectr., Hull Sch. of Architecture, 1975–80. *Publs:* Model Estate: Planned Housing at Quarry Hill, Leeds, 1974; Remaking Cities: Contradictions of the Recent Urban Environment, 1980; The Government of Space: Town Planning in Modern Society, 1986. Add: 15 Hanover Sq., Leeds LS3 1AP, England.

RAVITCH, Norman, American, b. 1936. History. Prof. of History, Univ. of California at Riverside, since 1962 (Assoc. Dean of Humanities, 1970–75, and of Humanities and Social Sciences, 1979–86). *Publs:* Sword and Mitre, 1966; (ed.) Images of Western Man, 1973. Add: Dept. of History, Univ. of California, Riverside, Calif. 92521, U.S.A.

RAVITZ, Abe (Carl). American, b. 1927. Intellectual history, Literature, Biography. Prof. of English, California State Univ., Dominguez Hills, since 1966 (Chmn. of Dept., 1966–80). Asst. Prof. of English, Pennsylvania State Univ., University Park, 1953–58; Prof., Hiram Coll., Ohio, 1958–66. *Publs:* Clarence Darrow and the American Literary Tradition, 1962; The Haywood Case, 1963; David Graham Phillips, 1965; The American Disinherited: A Profile in Fiction, 1970; The Disinherited: Plays, 1974; Alfred Henry Lewis, 1979. Add: Dept. of English, California State Univ., 1000 E. Victoria, Carson, Calif. 90747, U.S.A.

RAWLEY, James A. American, b. 1916. History, Biography. Regents Prof. of History, Univ. of Nebraska, Lincoln, since 1986, Emeritus since 1987 (Prof., 1964–86; Chmn., 1966–67, 1973–82). Instr., Columbia Univ., NYC, 1946–47, New York Univ., 1946–51, and Hunter Coll., NYC, 1951–53; Assoc. Pr f., and subsequently Prof., 1953–64, and Dept. Chmn., 1953–57 and 1961–64, Div. of Social Studies, Sweet Briar Coll., Virginia. Pres., Nebraska State Historical Soc., 1973–74. *Publs:* Edwin D. Morgan 1811–1883: Merchant in Politics, 1955; (ed.) The American Civil War: An English View, 1965; Turning Points of the Civil War, 1966; Race and Politics: Bleeding Kansas and the Coming of Civil War, 1969; (ed.) Lincoln and Civil War Politics, 1969; The Politics of Union, 1974; The Trans-Atlantic Slave Trade: A History, 1981; Secession, 1989. Add: Dept. of History, Univ. of Nebraska, Lincoln, Nebr. 68588, U.S.A.

RAWLS, John. American, b. 1921. Philosophy. John Cowles Prof, Harvard Univ., Cambridge, Mass., since 1976 (Prof., 1962–76). Instr., Princeton Univ., 1950–52; Asst. Prof., Cornell Univ., Ithaca, New York, 1953–62. *Publs:* A Theory of Justice, 1971. Add: Dept. of Philosophy, Harvard Univ., Cambridge, Mass. 02138, U.S.A.

RAWORTH, Tom. (Thomas Moore Raworth). British, b. 1938. Novels/Short stories, Plays/Screenplays, Poetry. Owner and Publr., Matrix Press, and Ed., Outburst, London, 1959–64; Founding Ed., Goliard Press, London, 1965–67; Poet-in-Residence, Dept. of Literature, Univ. of Essex, Colchester, 1969–70; Fiction Instr., Bowling Green State Univ., Ohio, 1972–73; Poet-in-Residence, Northeastern Illinois Univ., Chicago, 1973–74; Visiting Lectr., Univ. of Texas at Austin, 1974–75; Poet-in-Residence, King's Coll., Cambridge, 1977–78. *Publs:* (with Anselm Hollo and Gregory Corso) The Minicab War (parodies), 1961; Weapon Man, 1965; Continuation, 1966; A Plague on Both Your Houses (screenplay), 1966; The Relation Ship: Poems, 1967; Betrayal (novel), 1967; (with J. Esam and A. Hollo) Haiku, 1968; The Big Green Day, 1968; A Serial Biography (novel), 1969; Lion, Lion, 1970; Moving, 1971; (with John Ashbery and Lee Harwood) Penguin Modern Poets 19, 1971; Pleasant Butter, 1972; Tracking, 1972; (with A. Benveniste and R. DiPalma) Time Being, 1972; Here, 1973; An Interesting Picture of Ohio, 1973; Back to Nature, 1973; (trans. with V. Raworth) From the Hungarian, 1973; Ace, 1974; Bolivia, 1974; Sic Him Oltorf! (novel), 1974; Cloister, 1976; Common Sense, 1976; The Mask, 1976; Log-book, 1977; Sky Tails, 1978; Four Door Guide, 1979; Cancer, 1979; Nicht Wahr, Rosie?, 1979; Waiting, 1982; Writing, 1983; Lèvre de Poche, 1983; Heavy Light, 1984; Tottering State: New and Selected Poems 1963–1983, 1984; Tractor Parts, 1984; Visible Shivers, 1988. Add: c/o T.A. Raworth, 8 Avondale Rd., Welling, Kent, England.

RAWSON, Claude Julien. British, b. 1935. Literature. Prof. of English, Yale Univ., New Haven, since 1986. Gen. Ed., Unwin Critical Library, since 1975. Lectr. in English, Univ. of Newcastle upon Tyne, 1959–65; Lectr., 1965–68, Sr. Lectr., 1968–71, and Prof. of English, 1971–85, Univ. of Warwick; George Sherburn Prof. of English, Univ. of Illinois, 1985–86. Pres., British Soc. for Eighteenth-Century Studies, 1974–75. *Publs:* Henry Fielding: Profiles in Literature, 1968; (author and ed.) Focus Swift, 1971; Henry Fielding and the Augustan Ideal under Stress, 1972; Gulliver and the Gentle Reader: Studies in Swift and Our Time, 1973; (ed.) Fielding: A Critical Anthology, 1973; (ed.) Yeats and Anglo-Irish Literature: Studies by Peter Ure, 1974; (ed.) The Character of Swift's Satire: A Revised Focus, 1982, 1983; (ed.) English Satire and the Satiric Tradition, 1984; Order from Confusion Sprung: Studies in 18th Century Literature, 1985; (ed. with F.P. Lock) Complete Poems of Thomas Parnell, 1988. Add: English Dept., Yale Univ., New Haven, Conn. 06520, U.S.A.

RAY, Cyril. British, b. 1908. Cookery/Gastronomy/Wine. History.

Founder and Past Pres., Circle of Wine Writers. British War Corresp., 1940–45; Foreign Corresp., The Sunday Times, London, and Unesco, 1945–56; Asst. Ed., The Spectator, London, 1958–62; Wine Corresp., The Director mag., London, 1958–76, The Observer, London, 1959–73, and Punch, London, 1978–85. *Publs:* (ed.) Scenes and Characters from Surtees, 1948; From Algiers to Austria: The History of the 78th Division, 1952; The Pageant of London, 1958; Merry England, 1960; Regiment of the Line: The Story of the Lancashire Fusiliers, 1963; (ed.) The Gourmet's Companion, 1963; (ed.) Morton Shand's Book of French Wines, 1964; (ed.) Best Murder Stories, 1965; The Wines of Italy, 1966; In a Glass Lightly, 1967; Lafite: The Story of Chateau Lafite Rothschild, 1968; Bollinger: The Story of a Champagne, 1971, 1982; Cognac, 1973, 1985; Mouton: The Story of Mouton-Rothschild, 1974; (with Elizabeth Ray) Wine with Food, 1975; The Wines of France, 1976; The Wines of Germany, 1977; The Complete Book of Spirits and Liqueurs, 1978; The St. Michael Guide to Wine, 1978; (with C. Mozley) Ruffino: The Story of a Chianti, 1979; Lickerish Limericks, 1979; Ray on Wine, 1979; The New Book of Italian Wines, 1982; Robert Mondavi of the Napa Valley, 1984; Vintage Tales, 1984; (ed.) The Compleat Imbiber, 1956–71, 1986. Add: Albany, Piccadilly, London W1, England.

RAY, David. American, b. 1932. Novels/Short stories, Poetry. Prof. of English, Univ. of Missouri, Kansas City, since 1971. Lectr., Cornell Univ., Ithaca, N.Y., 1960–64, Reed Coll., Portland, Ore., 1964–66, and Writer's Workshop, Univ. of Iowa, Iowa City, 1969–70; Ed., New Letters, 1971–85. *Publs:* (ed.) The Chicago Review Anthology, 1959; X-Rays, 1965; (ed.) From the Hungarian Revolution, 1966; (ed. with R. Bly) A Poetry Reading Against the Vietnam War, 1966; Dragging the Main, 1968; Hill in Oklahoma, 1972; (ed. with R. Farnsworth) Richard Wright: Impressions and Perspectives, 1973; Gathering Firewood, 1974; Enough of Flying, 1977; The Mulberries of Mingo and Other Stories, 1978; The Tramp's Cup, 1978; (ed. with Jack Salzman) The Jack Conroy Reader, 1979; (ed. with Judy Ray) New Asian Writing, 1979; (ed.) From A to Z: 200 Contemporary American Poets, 1980; (ed.) Collected Poem of E.L. Mayo, 1981; The Touched Life: Selected Poems, 1982; (ed. with Amritjit Singh) India, An Anthology of Contemporary Writing, 1983; Not Far From the River, Translations from the Gatha Saptasati, 1983; (ed.) New Letters Readers I and II, 1984; (co-author) The Deepest Hunger (play), 1984; On Wednesday I Cleaned Out My Wallet, 1985; Elysium in the Halls of Hell, 1986; Sam's Book, 1987; The Maharani's New Wall, 1989. Add: 5517 Crestwood Dr., Kansas City, Mo. 64110, U.S.A.

RAY, Dorothy Jean. American, b. 1919. Anthropology/Ethnology, Cultural/Ethnic topics. Freelance consulting anthropologist and writer. *Publs:* Artists of the Tundra and the Sea, 1961, 1980; (ed.) The Eskimo of St. Michael and Vicinity, as Related by H.M.W. Edmonds, 1966; Eskimo Masks: Art and Ceremony, 1967, 1975; Graphic Arts of the Alaskana Eskimo, 1969; (ed.) Contemporary Indian Artists: Montana/Wyoming/Idaho, 1972; The Eskimos of Bering Strait 1650-1898, 1975; Eskimo Art:Tradition and Innovation in North Alaska, 1977; (with Louis L. Renner) Pioneer Missionary to the Bering Strait Eskimos: Bellarmine Lafortune, S.J., 1979; Aleut and Eskimo Art: Tradition and Innovation in South Alaska, 1980; Ethnohistory in the Arctic: The Bering Strait Eskimo, 1983. Add: P.O. Box 586, Port Townsend, Wash. 98368, U.S.A.

RAY, Judy. British, b. 1939. Poetry. Independent poet and photographer. Assoc. Ed., New Letters mag., Kansas City, 1973–85; Co-Producer, New Letters on the Air, radio program, 1982–86. *Publs:* Pebble Rings, 1980; (ed. with David Ray) New Asian Writing, 1979. Add: 5517 Crestwood Dr., Kansas City, Mo. 64110, U.S.A.

RAY, Mary (Eva Pedder). British, b. 1932. Children's fiction, Songs, lyrics and libretti, Children's non-fiction, Librettist. Civil servant, 1962–78. *Publs:* The Voice of Apollo, 1963; The Eastern Beacon, 1964; Standing Lions, 1968; Spring Tide, 1969; Living in Earliest Greece, 1969; Shout Against the Wind, 1970; A Tent for the Sun, 1971; The Ides of April, 1974; Sword Sleep, 1976; Beyond the Desert Gate, 1977; Song of Thunder, 1978; Rain from the West, 1980; The Windows of Elissa, 1982; The Mary Rose (libretto), 1983; Dragons and Dinosaurs (libretto); The Golden Bees, 1984; The Dolphin Boy (libretto), 1985. Add: 2 Harcourt Dr., Canterbury, Kent, CT2 8DP, England.

RAY, Sheila G(raham). British, b. 1930. Librarianship, Literature. Assoc. Ed., Bookbird; Ed., School Librarian. Librarian, West Riding of Yorkshire, Lincolnshire, and Leicestershire 1952–68; Sr. Lectr. in Librarianship, City of Birmingham Polytechnic, 1968–83. *Publs:* Children's Fiction: A Handbook for Librarians, 1970, 1972; Library Services to Schools, 1968, 3rd ed., 1982; (with Melvyna Barnes) Youth Library Work, 1976; Children's Librarianship, 1979; The Blyton

Phenomenon, 1982. Add: Tan-y-Capel, Bont Dolgadfan, Llanbrynmair, Powys SY19 7BB, Wales.

RAY, Sib Narayan. Indian, b. 1921. Poetry, History, Literature, Politics/Government. Reader and Chmn., Dept. of Indian Studies, Univ. of Melbourne, since 1966 (Sr. Lectr. and Head of Indian Studies, 1963–66). Member, Bd. of Dirs., Indian Renaissance Inst., since 1960; Fellow, Inst. of Historical Studies, Calcutta, since 1970; Exec. Member, Australian Assn. of South-Asian Scholars, since 1972. Prof., City Coll., Calcutta Univ., 1945–56, 1958–60; Rockefeller Foundn. Fellow, Univs. of London and Chicago, 1956–58; Prof., Bombay Univ., 1960–63. *Publs:* Prekshita, 1945; Radicalism, 1946; Indian Constituent Assembly, 1947; (with Ellen Roy) In Man's Own Image, 1948; (trans.) Sartre: Les Mains Sales (Nongrahat), 1949; Sahitya-chinta, 1955; Explorations, 1956; (ed.) M.N. Roy: Philosopher-Revolutionary, 1958; Prabasher Journal, 1959; NayakerMritya (The Dying Hero), 1960; Moumachhitantra, 1961; Democracy inIndia, 1964; (ed.) Vietnam: Seen from East and West, 1966; Kathara TomarMon, 1968; (ed.) Gandhi, India and the World, 1970; Abhijnan, 1971; Autumnal Equinox, 1973; (ed. and trans. with Marian Maddern) I Have Seen Bengal's Face: Modern Bengali Poetry 1930-72, 1974; Kavir Nirvasan, 1974; (ed.) Vak, 1975; Apartheid in Shakespeare, 1977; (ed.) The World Her Village, 1979; Democracy, Culture and Decadence, 1980; The Role of the Intelligentsia in Contemporary Asian Societies, 1981; Srotera biruddhe, 1984; (ed) Selected Works of M.N. Roy 1917-1922, vol. I, 1988. Add: Dept. of Indian Studies, Univ. of Melbourne, Parkville, Vic. 3052, Australia.

RAYBURN, Robert G(ibson). American, b. 1915. Theology/Religion, Autobiography/Memoirs/Personal. Prof. of Practical Theology, Covenant Theological Seminary, St. Louis (Pres., 1956–77). Pastor, College Church of Christ, Wheaton, Ill., 1946–50; Pres., Highland Coll., Pasadena, Calif., 1952–55, and Covenant Coll., St. Louis, 1955–65. *Publs:* Fight the Good Fight, 1955; What about Baptism?, 1957; O Come Let Us Worship, 1980. Add: Covenant Theological Seminary, 12330 Conway Rd., St. Louis, Mo. 63141, U.S.A.

RAYFIELD, (Patrick) Donald. British, b. 1942. Literature, Biography, Translations. Reader in Russian, Queen Mary Coll., Univ. of London (joined faculty, 1967). Lectr. in Russian, Univ. of Queensland, 1964–66. *Publs:* Chekhov: Evolution of His Art, 1975; (trans.) Ati Leksi, by Galaktion Tabidze, 1975; The Dream of Lhasa, 1976; (trans.) Three Poems by Vazha Pshavela, 1981; Confessions of Victor X, 1984. Add: Dept. of Russian, Queen Mary Coll., Mile End Rd., London E1 4NS, England.

RAYMOND, Derek. *See* **COOK,** Robin.

RAYMOND, Diana Joan. British, b. 1916. Novels/Short stories. *Publs:* Joanna Linden, 1952; The Small Rain, 1954; Between the Stirrup and the Ground, 1956; Strangers' Gallery, 1958; The Five Days, 1959; Guest of Honour, 1960; The Climb, 1962; People in the House, 1964; The Noonday Sword, 1965; Front of the House, 1967; Are You Travelling Alone?, 1969; The Best of the Day, 1972; Incident on a Summer's Day, 1974; Horseman, Pass By, 1977; The Dark Journey, 1978; Emma Pride, 1982; The Dancers All Are Gone, 1983; House of the Dolphin, 1985; Lily's Daughter, 1988. Add: 22 The Pryors, East Heath Rd., London NW3, England.

RAYMOND, Ellsworth. American, b. 1912. Economics, Politics/Government. Prof. of Politics, New York Univ., NYC, since 1949. Research Analyst, U.S. Embassy, Moscow, 1938–43; Head, U.S.S.R. Economic Section, U.S. Military Intelligence, 1944–46; Sr. Slavic Fellow, Hoover Instn., Stanford, Calif., 1948. *Publs:* (trans.) Industrial Management in the U.S.S.R., 1950; (co-author) Soviet Power and Policy, 1954; Soviet Economic Progress, 1957, 1960; (ed.) Karl Marx, 1966; (ed.) The Russian Revolution, 1967; The Soviet State, 1968, 1978; (with John Stuart Martin) A Picture History of Eastern Europe, 1971. Add: c/o New York University Press, New York, N.Y. 10003, U.S.A.

RAYMOND, Mary. *See* **KEEGAN,** Mary.

RAYMOND, Patrick (Ernest). British, b. 1924. Novels/Short stories. Served in the Royal Air Force, rising to the rank of Group Capt., 1942–77. *Publs:* A City of Scarlet and Gold, 1963; The Lordly Ones, 1965; The Sea Garden, 1970; The Last Soldier, 1974; A Matter of Assassination, 1977; The White War, 1978; The Grand Admiral, 1980, Daniel and Esther, 1989. Add: Tara Cottage, Chalk Hill, Great Cressingham, Thetford, Norfolk IP25 6NP, England.

RAYNER, Claire. Also writes as Sheila Brandon. British, b. 1931.

Historical/Romance/Gothic, Medicine/Health. Columnist and Broadcaster, London. Formerly, Sister, Paediatric Dept., Whittington Hosp., London. *Publs:* Mothers and Midwives, 1962; (as Sheila Brandon) The Final Year, 1962; (as Sheila Brandon) Cottage Hospital, 1963; What Happens in Hospital, 1963; The Calendar of Childhood, 1964; (as Sheila Brandon) Children's Ward, 1964; Shilling a Pound Pears, 1964; Your Baby, 1965; (as Sheila Brandon) The Lonely One, 1965; Careers with Children, 1966; Essentials of Out-Patient Nursing, 1967; For Children: Equipping a Home for a Growing Family, 1967; The House of the Fen, 1967; Shall I Be a Nurse?, 1967; 101 Facts an Expectant Mother Should Know, 1967; 101 Key Facts of Practical Baby Care, 1967; Housework—The Easy Way, 1967; Home Nursing and Family Health, 1967; (as Ann Lynton) Mothercraft, 1967; Starch of Aprons, 1967, in paperback as The Hive, 1968; A Parent's Guide to Sex Education, 1968; (as Sheila Brandon) The Doctors of Downlands, 1968; Lady Mislaid, 1968; People in Love, 1968, in paperback as About Sex, 1972; (as Isobel Saxe) Desperate Remedies, 1968; Death on the Table, 1969; The Meddlers, 1970; Protecting Your Baby, 1971; Women's Medical Dictionary, 1971; (as Sheila Brandon) The Private Wing, 1971; When to Call the Doctor—What to Do Whilst Waiting, 1972; (as Sheila Brandon) Nurse in the Sun, 1972; A Time to Heal, 1972; The Burning Summer, 1972; The Shy Person's Book, 1973; Childcare Made Simple, 1973; Gower Street, 1973; The Haymarket, 1974; Where Do I Come From?, 1975; Paddington Green, 1975; Soho Square, 1976; (contrib. ed.) Atlas of the Body and Mind, 1976; (with Keith Fordyce) Kitchen Garden, 1976; (with Keith Fordyce) More Kitchen Gardens, 1977; Bedford Row, 1977; Family Feelings, 1977; Claire Rayner Answers Your 100 Questions on Pregnancy, 1977; (with Keith Fordyce) Clare and Keith's Kitchen Garden, 1978; The Body Book, 1978; Long Acre, 1978; Sisters, 1978; Related to Sex, 1979; Charing Cross, 1979; (with Keith Fordyce) Greenhouse Gardening, 1979; Everything Your Doctor Would Tell You If He Had the Time, 1980; The Strand, 1980; Reprise, 1980; Claire Rayner's Lifeguide, 1980; The Running Years, 1981; Handle with Care, 1981; Baby and Young Child Care, 1981; Chelsea Reach, 1982; Shaftesbury Avenue, 1983; Growing Pains, 1984; Claire Rayner's Marriage Guide, 1984; Family Chorus, 1984; Piccadilly, 1985; The Getting Better Book, 1985; The Virus Man, 1985; Seven Dials, 1986; Lunching at Laura's 1986; Woman, 1986; When I Grow Up, 1986; Jubilee, 1987; Safe Sex, 1987; Maddie, 1988: Flanders, 1988; Claire Rayner Talking, 1988; The Don't Spoil Your Body Book, 1989; Clinical Judgements, 1989. Add: Holly Wood House, Roxborough Ave., Harrow-on-the-Hill, Middx. HA1 3BU, England.

RAYNER, John Desmond. British, b. 1924. Theology/Religion. Sr. Minister, Liberal Jewish Synagogue, London, since 1961 (Assoc. Minister, 1957–61); Lectr. in Jewish Law, Leo Baeck Coll., London, since 1966, Chmn., Council of Reform and Liberal Rabbis, 1969–71 and 1982–84. *Publs:* Towards Mutual Understanding Between Jews and Christians, 1960; (ed. with C. Stern) Service of the Heart, 1967; (ed. with C. Stern) Gate of Repentance, 1973; Guide to Jewish Marriage, 1975; (with B. Hooker) Judaism for Today, 1978; (ed.) Passover Haggadah, 1981; (with D. Goldberg) The Jewish People: Their History and Their Religion, 1988. Add: The Liberal Jewish Synagogue, 28 St. John's Wood Rd., London NW8, England.

RAYNER, Mary (Yoma, née Grigson). British, b. 1933. Children's fiction. Freelance writer and illustrator. Copywriter, Longmans Green, publr., London, 1959–62. *Publs:* The Witch-Finder, 1975; Mr. and Mrs. Pig's Evening Out, 1976; Garth Pig and the Icecream Lady, 1977; The Rain Cloud, 1980; Mrs. Pig's Bulk Buy, 1981; Crocodarling, 1985; Mrs. Pig Gets Cross, 1986; Reilly, 1987; Oh Paul!, 1988; Rug, 1989. Add: c/o Macmillan Children's Books, 4 Little Essex St., London WC2R 3LF, England.

RAYNER, William. British, b. 1929. Novels/Short stories, Children's fiction. Formerly, teacher and lectr. *Publs:* The Reapers (novel), 1961; The Barebones (novel), 1962; The Tribe and Its Successors: An Account of African Traditional Life and European Settlement in Southern Rhodesia, 1962; The Last Days (novel), 1968; The Knife-Man: The Last Journal of Judas Iscariot (novel), 1969; The World Turned Upside Down (novel), 1970, retitled as Redcoat, 1971; The Bloody Affray at Riverside Drive (novel; in U.S. as Seth and Belle and Mr. Quarles and Me), 1972; Stag Boy (for children), 1972; Big Mister (for children), 1974; The Trail to Bear Paw Mountain (novel), 1974; A Weekend with Captain Jack (novel), 1975; The Day of Chaminuka (novel), 1976; Eating the Big Fish (novel; in U.S. as Interface Transfer), 1977; Chief Joseph, 1978; The Wheels of Fortune (novel), 1979; Knave of Swords (novel), 1980. Add: Spurriers Close, West Porlock, nr. Minehead, Somerset, England.

RAYNOR, Henry (Broughton). British, b. 1917. Music, Biography,

Schoolmaster, Whitchurch, Southport, Liverpool, London, and Guildford, now retired. Asst. Ed., Victoria Publs., 1955–56; freelance correspondent, The Times, 1958–71; also broadcaster and extramural lectr., Univs. of London and Surrey. *Publs:* Joseph Haydn, 1961; Radio and Television, 1971; A Social History of Music from the Middle Ages to Beethoven, 1979; Mahler, 1975; Music and Society since 1815, 1976; The Orchestra, 1978; Mozart, 1978; Music in England, 1980. Add: 1 Park Field Rd., Worthing, W. Sussex, England.

READ, Anthony. British, b. 1935. Plays/Screenplays, History, Military/Defence, Theatre, Biography. Full-time writer since 1973. Asst. Publicity Mgr., Birlec Ltd., 1956–58; Ed., Jonathan Cape Ltd., London, 1958–63; Producer and Story Ed., BBC, London, 1963–73. *Publs:* The True Book about the Theatre, 1964; (with Kenneth Bulmer) The Professionals: Where the Jungle Ends, 1978; (with Ken Blake) The Professionals: II: The Long Shot, 1978; (with David Fisher) Operation Lucy: The Most Secret Spy Ring of the Second World War, 1980, 1981; Colonel Z (biography), 1983; (with David Fisher) The Deadly Embrace: Hitler, Stalin, and the Nazi-Soviet Pact 1939-1941, 1988. Add: c/o W. W. Norton and Co. Inc., 500 Fifth Ave., New York, N.Y. 10110, U.S.A.

READ, Brian. British, b. 1927. Children's fiction, Children's non-fiction. Free-lance Writer, South Oxfordshire District Council, 1974–81. Public Health Inspector, 1951–74. *Publs:* The Long Chase, 1963; The Empty Cottage, 1964; A Friend for Anna, 1964; Lucy and the Chinese Eggs, 1969; Healthy Cities, 1969; The Water Wheel, 1970; The Water We Use, 1973; Men of Iron, 1974; Building a House, 1977; How Your House Works, 1979; Underground, 1985; General Conway and His Jersey Temple, 1986. Add: 50 St. Mark's Rd., Henley-on-Thames, Oxon RG9 1LW, England.

READ, David (Haxton Carswell). American, b. 1910. Theology/Religion. Minister, Madison Ave. Presbyterian Church, NYC, 1956–89. Minister, Greenbank Church of Scotland, Edinburgh, 1939–49; First Chaplain, Univ. of Edinburgh, 1949–55; Chaplain to H.M. the Queen in Scotland, 1952–55. *Publs:* The Spirit of Life, 1939; (trans.) The Church to Come, 1939; Prisoner's Quest: Lectures on Christian Doctrine in a POW Camp, 1944; Communication of the Gospel, 1952; The Christian Faith, 1955; I Am Persuaded, 1961; Sons of Anak, The Gospel and the Modern Giants, 1964; God's Mobile Family, 1966; Holy Common Sense, 1966, 1968; Whose God Is Dead?, 1966; The Pattern of Christ, 1967; The Presence of Christ, 1968; Virginia Woolf Meets Charlie Brown, 1968; Christian Ethics, 1968; Giants Cut Down to Size, 1970; Religion Without Wrappings, 1970; Overheard, 1971; Curious Christians, 1972; An Expanding Faith, 1973; Sent From God, 1974; Good News in Letters of Paul, 1975; Go and Make Disciples, 1978; Unfinished Easter, 1978; The Faith is Still There, 1980; This Grace Given, 1984; Grace Thus Far, 1986; Preaching about the Needs of Real People, 1988. Add: 1165 Fifth Ave., New York, N.Y., 10029, U.S.A.

READ, Donald. British, b. 1930. History, Biography. Prof. of Modern English History, Univ. of Kent, since 1974 (Sr. Lectr. in History, 1965–69; Reader in Modern English History, 1969–73). Knoop Research Fellow, Univ. of Sheffield, 1955–56; Lectr. in History, Univ. of Leeds, 1956–65. Pres., The Historical Assn., 1985–89. *Publs:* Peterloo, the Massacre and Its Background; Press and People, Opinion in Three English Cities; The English Provinces: Cobden and Bright; Edwardian England; England 1868-1914: The Age of Urban Democracy; Peel and the Victorians; (ed.) Documents from Edwardian England; (with E. Glasgow) Feargus O'Connor, Irishman and Chartist. Add: Darwin Coll., Univ. of Kent, Canterbury, Kent, England.

READ, Elfreida. Canadian, b. 1920. Children's fiction, Autobiography. *Publs:* The Dragon and the Jadestone, 1958; The Magic of Light, 1959; The Enchanted Egg (in U.S. as the Magical Egg), 1963; The Spell of Chu Chu Chan, 1966; Magic for Granny, 1967; Twin Rivers, 1968; No-one Need Ever Know, 1971; Brothers by Choice, 1974; The Message of the Mask, 1981; Kirstine and the Villains, 1982; Race Against the Dark, 1983; Growing Up in China (adult poetry), 1985; A Time of Cicadas (autobiography), 1989. Add: 2686 W. King Edward Ave., Vancouver 8,B.C., Canada.

READ, Gardner. American, b. 1913. Music. Prof. Emeritus of Composition, Boston Univ. Sch. for the Arts (Composer-in-Residence, 1948–78). Head, Composition Dept., St. Louis Inst. of Music, Mo., 1941–43; Kansas City Conservatory of Music, Mo., 1943–45, and Cleveland Inst. of Music, Ohio, 1945–48. *Publs:* Thesaurus of Orchestral Devices, 1953; Music Notation: A Manual of Modern Practice, 1964, 1969; Contemporary Instrumental Techniques, 1976; Modern Rhythmic Notation,

1978; Style and Orchestration, 1979; Genesis of an Opera, 1980; 20th Century Notation, 1986; Source Book of Proposed Music Notation, Reforms, 1987, 20th-Century Microtonal Notation, 1989. Add: 47 Forster Rd., Manchester, Mass. 01944, U.S.A.

READ, Jan. (John Hinton Read). British, b. 1917. Plays/Screenplays, Cookery/Gastronomy/Wine, History, Travel/Exploration/Adventure. Commonwealth Fund Fellow in Cinematography, 1946–47; Scenario Ed., Gainsborough Pictures, 1947–49; Asst. to Exec. Producer, Rank Org., 1950–52; Dir., Triangle Film Productions, London, 1952–73. *Publs:* (with Ted Willis) The Blue Lamp (play), 1952; (with Antonio Mingote) History for Beginners, 1960; The Wines of Spain and Portugal, 1973; The Moors in Spain and Portugal, 1974; (with Maite Manjon) Paradores of Spain, 1977; War in the Peninsula, 1977; Guide to the Wines of Spain and Portugal, 1977; (with Maite Manjon) Flavours of Spain, 1978; The Catalans, 1978; (with Maite Manjon) Visitors Scotland, 1979; The New Conquistadors, 1980; (with Maite Manjon) The Great British Breakfast, 1981; The Wines of Spain, 1982; The Wines of Portugal, 1982; Pocket Guide to Spanish Wines, 1983; Wines of the Rioja, 1984; (with Maite Manjon and Hugh Johnson) The Wine and Food of Spain, 1987, (with Hugh Johnson) Chilean Wines, 1988; Sherry and Sherry Bodegas, 1988; screenplays—The Blue Lamp (original story), 1950; White Corridors, 1951; Street Corner, 1953; Jason and the Argonauts, 1963; First Men in the Moon, 1964; television—Dr. Finlay'sa Casebook; Sherlock Holmes. Add: Donaldson Gardens, St. Andrews, Fife KY16 9DH, Scotland.

READ, Miss. Pseud. for Dora Jessie Saint. British, b. 1913. Novels/Short stories, Children's fiction. *Publs:* Village School, 1955; Village Diary, 1957; Storm in the Village 1958; Hobby Horse Cottage, 1958; Thrush Green, 1959; Fresh from the Country, 1960; Winter in Thrush Green, 1961; Miss Clare Remembers, 1962; The Market Square, 1966; The Howards of Caxley, 1967; Country Cooking, 1969; News from Thrush Green, 1970; Tyler's Row, 1972; Christmas Mouse, 1973; Battles at Thrush Green 1975; No Holly for Miss Quinn, 1976; Village Affairs, 1977; Return to Thrush Green, 1978; The White Robin, 1979; Village Centenary, 1980; Gossip from Thrush Green, 1981; A Fortunate Grandchild, 1982; Affairs at Thrush Green, 1983; Summer at Fairacre, 1984; At Home in Thrush Green, 1985; Time Rembered, 1986; The School at Thrush Green, 1987; The World of Thrush Green, 1988. Add: c/o Michael Joseph Ltd., 27 Wrights Lane, London W8 5TZ, England.

READ, Piers Paul. British, b. 1941. Novels/Short stories, Plays/Screenplays, Documentaries/Reportage. Sub-Ed., Times Literary Supplement, London, 1964–65. *Publs:* Game in Heaven with Tussy Marx, 1966; Coincidence (television play), 1968; The Junkers, 1968; Monk Dawson, 1970; The Family Firm (radio play), 1970; The Professor's Daughter, 1971; The House on Highbury Hill (television play), 1972; The Upstart, 1973; Alive: The Story of the Andes Survivors, 1974; Polanaise, 1976; The Train Robbers, 1978; A Married Man, 1979; The Villa Golitsyn, 1981; The Free Frenchman, 1986; A Season in the West, 1988. Add: 50 Portland Rd., London W11, England.

READ, Sylvia Joan. British. Novels/Short stories, Plays/Screenplays, Poetry. Leading Actress, and Scriptwriter, Theatre Roundabout Ltd., London, since 1964. Ed., Here and Now, 1940–49; former Lectr., Poets' Theatre Guild. *Publs:* The Poetical Ark, 1946; Harvest, 1951; Burden of Blessing, 1952; A Case of Arms, 1962; Travelling Actors, 1973; Singing Christmas, 1984; (with William Fry) Christian Theatre, 1986. Add: 859 Finchley Rd., London NW11 8LX, England.

READE, Brian Edmund. British, b. 1913. Poetry, Art, Literature. Asst. Keeper, 1936–58, and Deputy Keeper, 1958–73, now retired, Dept. of Prints and Drawings, Victoria and Albert Museum, London. Pres., Eighteen Nineties Soc., 1977. *Publs:* Edward Lear's Parrots, 1948, 1978; The Dominance of Spain, 1951; Regency Antiques, 1953; Art Nouveau and Alphonse Mucha, 1963; Aubrey Beardsley, 1966; Ballet Designs and Illustrations, 1967; Beardsley, 1967, 1987; (ed.) Sexual Heretics, 1970; Eye of a Needle (poetry), 1971; Louis Wain, 1972; B.E. Reade Collection, Torre Abbey, 1983; Beardsley Re-Mounted, 1989. Add: 42 Trumlands Rd., St. Marychurch, Torquay TQ1 4RN, England.

READE, Hamish. *See* **GRAY, Simon.**

READER, William Joseph. British, b. 1920. History, Biography. Held various positions in advertising, market research and public relations, Unilever Ltd., London, 1950–64; Visiting Prof., Univ. of Delaware, 1973, 1976; Texaco Fellow, London Sch. of Economics, 1979–80. *Publs:* (with C.H. Wilson) Men and Machines: A History of D. Napier & Son 1808-1958, 1958; Life in Victorian England, 1964; Professional Men: The Rise of the Professional Classes in 19th Century England, 1966; Architect of AirPower: A Life of the First Viscount Weir, 1968; Hard Roads and Highways: History of SPD Ltd., 1969; Imperial Chemical Industries: A History, 2 vols., 1970–1975; The Weir Group: A Centenary History, 1971; The Middle Classes, 1972; Victorian England, 1973; Metal Box: a History, 1976; A House in the City, 1979; Fifty Years of Unilever, 1980; Macadam, 1980; Bowater, A History, 1981; A History of the Institution of Electrical Engineers, 1987; At Duty's Call, 1988. Add: 46 Gough Way, Cambridge CB3 9LN, England.

READING, Peter. British, b. 1946. Poetry. Schoolteacher in Liverpool, 1967–68; Lectr., Dept. of Art History, Liverpool Coll. of Art, 1968–70. *Publs:* Water and Waste, 1970; For the Municipality's Elderly, 1974; The Prison Cell & Barrel Mystery, 1976; Nothing for Anyone, 1977; Fiction, 1979; Tom o' Bedlam's Beauties,·1981; Diplopic, 1983; $5 \times 5 \times 5 \times 5 \times 5$, 1983; C, 1984; Ukulele Music, 1985; Essential Reading (selected poems), 1986; Stet, 1986; Final Demands, 1988; Perduta Gente, 1989. Add: 1 Ragleth View, Little Stretton, Shropshire, England.

REANEY, James (Crerar). Canadian, b. 1926. Children's fiction, Plays/Screenplays, Poetry. Prof. of English, Middlesex Coll., Univ. of Western Ontario, London, since 1964 (Assoc. Prof., 1960–63). Member of faculty, 1949–57, and Asst. Prof. of English, 1957–60, Univ. of Manitoba, Winnipeg; Founding Ed., Alphabet mag., London, Ont., 1960–71. *Publs:* The Red Heart (poetry), 1949; A Suit of Nettles (poetry), 1958; Twelve Letters to a Small Town (poetry), 1962; The Killdeer and Other Plays, 1962; The Dance of Death at London, Ontario (poetry), 1963; Let's Make a Carol: A Play with Music for Children, 1965; Listen to the Wind, 1965; The Boy with an "R" in His Hand (children's fiction), 1965; Colours in the Dark, 1970; Masks of Childhood (plays), 1972; Poems, 1972; Names and Nicknames, 1972; Ignoramus, 1972; Geography Match, 1972; Apple Butter and Other Plays for Children, 1973; The Donnellys: A Trilogy, 1973–75; (with Ron Cameron) Masque, 1974; Selected Longer and Shorter Poems, 2 vols., 1976; All the Bees and All the Keys (children's play), 1976; (with Marty Gervais) Baldoon, 1976; Fourteen Barrels from Sea to Sea, 1977; The Dismissal, 1978; Wacousta, 1979; Gyroscope, 1980; King Whistle, 1980; The Canadian Brothers, 1984; Imprecations—The Art of Swearing, 1984; Take the Big Picture (children's fiction), 1986. Add: c/o Sybil Hutchinson, Apt. 409, Ramsden Pl., 50 Hillsboro Ave., Toronto, Ont. M5R 1S8, Canada.

REARDON, Bernard M(orris) G(arvin). British, b. 1913. Philosophy, Theology/Religion. Rector of Kelly, Devon, 1947–59; Rector of Parham, Sussex, 1959–63; Lectr. in Divinity, Bishop Otter Coll., Chichester, 1960–63; Lectr. in Divinity, 1960–63, Sr. Lectr. in Religious Studies, 1963–69, Reader, 1960–73, and Dept. Head, 1973–78. *Publs:* Henry Scott Holland, 1962; (trans.) Man and Metaphysics, by R. Jolivet, 1963; Religious Thought in the Nineteenth Century, 1966; Liberal Protestantism, 1968; Roman Catholic Modernism, 1970; From Coleridge to Gore, 1971; Liberalism and Tradition: Aspects of Catholic Thought in Nineteenth-Century France, 1975; Hegel's Philosophy of Religion, 1977; Religious Thought in the Reformation, 1981; Il pensiero religioso, della Riforma, 1984; Religion in the Age of Romanticism, 1985; Kant as Philosophical Theologian, 1987. Add: Dept. of Religious Studies, Univ. of Newcastle upon Tyne, England.

REARDON, Dennis J. American, b. 1944. Plays/Screenplays. Playwright-in-Residence, Univ. of Michigan, Ann Arbor, 1970–71, and Hartwick Coll., Oneonta, N.Y., 1980. *Publs:* The Happiness Cage, 1971; The Leaf People (in Plays from the New York Shakespeare Festival), 1986. Add: 106 MacDougal St., Apt. 9, New York, N.Y. 10012, U.S.A.

REAVER, J. Russell. American, b. 1915. Novels/Short stories, Literature. Univ. Service Prof. of English, Florida State Univ., Tallahassee, 1982–84, now Emeritus (Asst. and Assoc. Prof., 1947–63; Prof., 1963–82; Prof., Florida State Study Center, Florence, Italy, 1968–69). Asst. Prof. of English, The Citadel, Charleston, S.C., 1942–44; Instr. in English, Univ. of Illinois, 1944–47. *Publs:* Emerson as Mythmaker, 1954; (ed. with R.F. Davidson, Sarah Herndon and William Ruff) The Humanities in Contemporary Life, 1960; (with George Boswell) Fundamentals of Folk Literature, 1962; (ed. with R.F. Davidson, Sarah Herndon, William Ruff and Nathan Starr) The Humanistic Tradition, 1964; (compiler) An O'Neill Concordance, 3 vols., 1969; (with E.W. Carlson, Reginald L. Cook et al.) Emerson's Relevance Today, 1971; Somewhere Safe to Sea (novel), 1973; Moments of Transition: Processes of Structuring in Man, Society and Art, 1982; (co-author) Perspectives on Contemporary Legends, 1984; (co-author) First Citizens and Other Florida Folks, 1984; Florida Folktales, 1987. Add: 1228 Cherokee Dr., Tallahassee, Fl. 32301, U.S.A.

REAVES, J. Michael. American. Science fiction. *Publs:* (with Byron Preiss) Dragonworld, 1979, 1983; Darkworld Detective (short stories), 1982; The Shattered World, 1982; (with Steve Perry) Sword of the Samurai, 1984. Add: c/o Bantam Books, 666 Fifth Ave., New York, N.Y. 10019, U.S.A.

REBERT, M. Charles. American, b. 1920. Poetry. Teacher of Creative Writing and English, Littlestown High Sch., Pennsylvania, 1960–85. Poetry Consultant, teacher and lectr., St. David's Writers Conferences, 1958–74; Contrib. Ed., Time of Singing, Judson Coll., 1960–63. *Publs:* Shadow Prints, 1958; I Remember, 1964; Waiting for the Red Light, 1965; Like Sudden Roses, 1967; An Armistice of Flesh, 1967; The Glass Scene, 1973; American Majolica 1850-1900, 1982. Add: 140 Meade Ave., Hanover, Pa. 17331, U.S.A.

RECHY, John (Francisco). American, b. 1934. Novels/Short stories. *Publs:* City of Night, 1963; Numbers, 1967; This Day's Death, 1970; The Vampires, 1971; The Fourth Angel, 1972; The Sexual Outlaw: A Documentary. 1977; Momma as She Became—Not as She Was (play), 1978; Rushes, 1979; Bodies and Souls, 1983; Tigers Wild (play), 1986; Marilyn's Daughter, 1988. Add: c/o Georges Borchardt Inc., 136 E. 57th St., New York, N.Y. 10022, U.S.A.

RECK, Andrew Joseph. American, b. 1927. Philosophy. Prof. of Philosophy since 1958, Chmn., Dept. of Philosophy, since 1 69, and Dir., Master of Liberal Arts Prog., since 1984, Tulane Univ., New Orleans. Member, Editorial-Advisory Bd., Southern Journal of Philosophy, Tulane Studies in Philosophy, Intnl. Journal on World Peace, and Transactions of the Charles S. Peirce Soc.; Contributing Ed., The Reader's Adviser, since 1988. Instr. of Philosophy, Yale Univ., New Haven, Conn., 1955–58; Visiting Prof., Fordham Univ., 1979. *Publs:* Recent American Philosophy, 1964; (ed.) George Herbert Mead: Selected Writings, 1964, 1981; Introduction to William James, 1967; New American Philosophers, 1968; Speculative Philosophy, 1972; (ed.) Knowledge and Value: Essays in Honor of Harold N. Lee, 1972. Add: Dept. of Philosophy, Tulane Univ., New Orleans, La. 70118, U.S.A.

RECKORD, Barry. Jamaican. Plays/Screenplays. *Publs:* Skyvers (in New English Dramatists 9), 1966; Does Fidel East More Than Your Father: Cuban Opinion, 1971. Add: c/o ICM, 40 W. 57th St., New York, N.Y. 10019, U.S.A.

REDDAWAY, Peter (Brian). British, b. 1939. Politics/Government, International relations/Current affairs (Slavic studies), Biography. Sr. Lectr. in Political Science with special reference to Russia, London Sch. of Economics and Political Science, since 1972 (Lectr., 1965–72). Adviser, Amnesty Intnl. *Publs:* (ed. with Leonard Schapiro, and contrib.) Lenin: The Man, the Theorist, the Leader: A Reappraisal, 1967; (with others) Religion and the Search for New Ideals in the USSR, 1967; (ed.) Soviet Short Stories, Vol. II, 1968; (with others) USSR: Dibattito nella Communita Cristiana, 1968; (with others) Rights and Wrongs: Some Essays on Human Rights, 1969; (ed. and trans.) Uncensored Russia: Protest and Dissent in the Soviet Union, 1972; (with S. Bloch) Psychiatric Terror: The Abuse of Psychiatry in the Soviet Union, 1977; (ed. with T.H. Rigby and A.H. Brown) Authority, Power and Policy in the USSR, 1980; Schapiro, Leonard Bertram: 1908-1983, 1986. Add: London Sch. of Economics and Political Science, Houghton St., London WC2, England.

REDDAWAY, William Brian. British, b. 1913. Economics. Fellow Clare Coll., Cambridge, since 1938 (Lectr. in Economics, 1939–55, Dir., Dept. of Applied Economics, 1955–69, and Prof. of Political Economy, 1969–80, Cambridge Univ.). Member, National Bd. for Prices and Incomes, 1967–71; Ed., Economic Journal, 1971–76. *Publs:* The Russian Financial System, 1935; The Economics of a Declining Population, 1939; (with Carter and Stone) The Measurement of Production Movements, 1948; The Development of the Indian Economy, 1962; Effects of U.K. Direct Investment Overseas, 1967, 1968; The Effects of the Selective Employment Tax; First Report, 1970, Final Report, 1973; Some Key Issues for the Development of the Economy of Papua New Guinea, 1986. Add: 12 Manor Ct., Grange Rd., Cambridge CB3 9BE, England.

REDDING, David A(sbury). American, b. 1923. Theology/Religion, Minister, Liberty Presbyterian Church, Delaware, Ohio, since 1974. Teacher of English, Speech and History, and Asst. Basketball Coach, Doylestown High Sch., Ohio, 1947–49; Presbyterian Church, Plain City, Ohio, 1952–55; Instr. of English Bible, Univ. of Cincinnati, and Pastor, First Presbyterian Church, Glendale, Ohio, both 1955–63; Pastor and Head of Staff, First Presbyterian Church, East Cleveland, Ohio, 1963–66; Writer-in-Residence, Counselor and Preacher, Tarkio Coll., Missouri,

1966–67; Instr., Dept. of Philosophy, Flagler Coll., and Sr. Minister, Flagler Memorial Church, St. Augustine, Fla., 1968–74. *Publs:* The Parables He Told, 1962;The Psalms of David, 1963; The Miracles of Christ, 1964; If I Could Pray Again, 1965; The New Immorality, 1967; The Couch and the Altar, 1968; What Is the Man?, 1969; Songs in the Night, 1970; Flagler and His Church, 1970; The Faith of Our Fathers, 1971; The Miracles and the Parables, 1971; Until You Bless Me, 1972; God Is Up to Something, 1972; Jesus Makes Me Laugh, 1976; Lives He Touched, 1978; The Prayers I Love, 1978; Before You Call, I Will Answer, 1985; Amazed by Grace, 1987; The Golden String, 1988. Add: Liberty Presbyterian Church, 7080 Oleantangy River Rd., Delaware, Ohio, 43015, U.S.A.

REDGROVE, Peter. British, b. 1932. Novels/Short stories, Plays/Screenplays, Poetry, Anthropology/Ethnology. Resident Writer, Falmouth Sch. of Art, Cornwall, 1966–83. *Publs:* The Collector, 1960; The Nature of Cold Weather, 1961; At the White Monument, 1963; The Force, 1966; Dr. Faust's Sea-Spiral Spirit, 1972; Three Pieces for Voices, 1972; (with Penelope Shuttle) The Hermaphrodite Album, 1973; In the Country of the Skin, 1973; (with P. Shuttle) The Terrors of Dr. Treviles, 1974; Sons of My Skin: Selected Poems 1954-74, 1975; The Glass Cottage (novel), 1976; Miss Carstairs Dressed for Blooding and Other Plays, 1976; From Every Chink of the Ark: New Poems American and English, 1977; (with P. Shuttle) The Wise Wound: Every Woman and Eve's Curse, 1978; The Weddings at Nether Powers: Poems 1975-77, 1979; The God of Glass (novel), 1979; The Sleep of the Great Hypnotist (novel), 1979; (ed. with Jon Silkin) New Poetry 5, 1979; The Apple-Broadcast (verse), 1981; The Facilitators (novel), 1982; (ed.) Cornwall in Verse, 1982; The Working of Water (verse), 1984; A Man Named East and other New Poems, 1985; The Mudlark Poems, 1986; In the Hall of the Saurians (verse), 1987; The Moon Disposes (verse), 1987; The Black Goddess and the Sixth Sense, 1987; The One Who Set Out to Study Fear (stories), 1989; The First Earthquake (poetry), 1989. Add: c/o David Higham Assocs., 5-8 Lower John St., London W1R 4HA, England.

REDMAN, Lister Appleton. British, b. 1933. Children's non-fiction, Marketing, Physics. Sr. Science Master, Kirkham Grammar Sch, since 1972 (Sr. Physics Master, 1958–72). Dir., F.C. Curtis (Safety Training Aids) Ltd., since 1976; Producer of slide-tape programmes on safety, since 1977. *Publs:* Nuclear Energy, 1963; Physics in Action, 1966; (ed.) The Physics Teachers Handbook, 1966; Essential Elementary Physics, 1967; (ed.) The Physics Teachers Handbook Supplement One, 1967; (ed.) The Physics Teaching Handbook, 1971; The Young Student's Laboratory Guide, 1972; Sales Forum, 1972; (ed.) A-Level Physics Comprehension Book I, 1972; (with G.T. Brown) Getting to Know Physics, 5 vols., 1973–75; Essential GCSE Physics Students Worksheet [and Answers], 1988. Add: 6 Miletas Pl., Fairhaven, Lytham St. Annes, Lancs. FY8 1BQ, England.

REDMAYNE, Barbara. *See* **HOWE**, Muriel.

REDMOND, Eugene B. American, b. 1937. Poetry. Prof. of English, and Poet-in-Residence, California State Univ., Sacramento. Contrib. Ed., Confrontation: A Journal of Third World Literature; Editorial Dir., Black Anthology Project, a campus-prison-residential cooperative; Dir., Poetry-in-Schools Project, and Adviser, Community Poets Prog. and Writing Club, Sacramento. Dir. of Language Workshops and Poet-in-Residence, Southern Illinois Univ. Experiment in Higher Education, Carbondale, 1967–69; Writer-in-Residence, Oberlin Coll., Ohio, 1969–70. *Publs:* A Tale of Two Toms, 1968; A Tale of Time and Toilet Tissue, 1969; (ed.) Sides of the River (poetry/fiction), 1969; (ed. with Hale Chatfield) Poetry for My People, 1970; (with Chatfield) Ark of Bones and Other Stories, by Henry Dumas, 1970; Sentry of the Four Golden Pillars, 1970; River of Bones and Flesh and Blood, 1971; Songs from an Afro/Phone, 1972; In a Time of Rain and Desire, 1973; (ed.) Play Ebony Play Ivory, by Henry Dumas, 1973; (ed.) Ark of Bones and Other Stories, by Henry Dumas, 1973; Consider Loneliness as These Things, 1973; Bloodlinks and Sacred Places (record), 1973; Kwanza: A Ritual in 7 Parts, 1974; Into the Canaan of the Self (record), 1974; Handbook to Black Poetry, 1976; (ed.) Griefs of Joy, 1976. Add: c/o Black River, P.O. Box 15853, Sacramento, Calif. 95813, U.S.A.

REDMOND, Gerald. British, b. 1934. Sports/Physical education/Keeping fit. Prof., Univ. of Alberta, Edmonton. School teacher in London and Kent, England, 1957–64; Faculty member, Univ. of Otago, New Zealand, 1965–68, and Univ. of Massachusetts, Amherst, 1968 and 1973; with National Playing Fields Assn., 1970. *Publs:* The Caledonian Games in 19th Century America; (co-author) Sporting Heritage: A Guide to Halls of Fame, Sports Museums, and Special Collections in the United

States and Canada; Soccer Practice, 1978; Sports Canadiana, 1980; The Sporting Scots of 19th Century Canada, 1982. Add: Faculty of Physical Education, Univ. of Alberta, Edmonton, Alta. TG6 2H9, Canada.

REDWOOD, John (Alan). British, b. 1951. Economics, Money/Finance. Merchant banker and Industrialist; Fellow, All Souls Coll., Oxford, since 1972. Head of Prime Minister's Policy Unit, 1983–85. Member, Oxfordshire County Council, 1973–77; Gov., Oxford Polytechnic, 1974–77. *Publs:* Reason, Ridicule and Religion, 1976; European Science in the Seventeenth Century, 1977; Public Enterprise in Crisis, 1980; (with J.V. Hatch) Value for Money Audits, 1981; Controlling Public Enterprise, 1982; Going for Broke, 1983; Equity for Everyman, 1986; Popular Capitalism, 1988; Signals from a Railway Conference, 1988. Add: The Millbank Ct., John Islip St., London SW1, England.

REED, Eliot. *See* **AMBLER,** Eric.

REED, H(erbert) Owen. American, b. 1910. Music. Prof. Emeritus of Music Composition, Michigan State Univ., East Lansing (joined faculty, 1939; Chmn., Music Dept., 1957–58). *Publs:* A Workbook in the Fundamentals of Music, 947; Basic Music, 1954; Basic Music Workbook, 1954; Composition Analysis Chart, 1958; (with P. Harder) Basic Contrapuntal Technique, 1964; (with P. Harder) Basic Contrapuntal Technique Workbook, 1964; (with J.T. Leach) Scoring for Percussion, 1969; (with R.G. Sidnell) The Materials of Music Composition, book I, Fundamentals, 1979, and book II, Exploring the Parameters, 1980. Add: 4690 Ottawa Dr., Okemos, Mich. 48864, U.S.A.

REED, Ishmael. American, b. 1938. Novels/Short stories, Poetry. Vice-Pres. (Editorial), Yardbird Publishing Corp., Berkeley, Calif., since 1971. *Publs:* The Free-Lance Pallbearers, 1967; Yellow Back Radio Broke-Down, 1969; Catechism of D Neoamerican HooDoo Church (poetry), 1970; (ed.) 19 Necromancers from now, 1970; Mumbo-Jumbo, 1972; Conjure: Selected Poems 1963-1970, 1972; Chattanooga (poetry), 1973; The Last Days of Louisiana Red, 1974; Flight into Canada, 1976; Secretary to the Spirits (poetry), 1977; Shrovetide in Old New Orleans (essays), 1978; (ed.) Calafia: The California Poetry, 1979; God Made Alaska for the Indians (essays), 1982; The Terrible Twos (novel), 1982; (ed.) Quilt 2-3, 2 vols., 1981–82; Reckless Eyeballing, 1986; Writin' Is Fightin'; 37 Years of Boxing on Paper (non-fiction), 1988; The Terrible Threes (novel), 1989. Add: c/o Atheneum Publishers, 866 Third Ave., New York, N.Y. 10022. U.S.A.

REED, James. British, b. 1922. Literature, Mythology/Folklore. English teacher in various schs. in Newcastle upon Tyne and Yorkshire, 1951-64; Head of Humanities, Bingley Coll., Yorkshire, 1975-78. *Publs:* The Border Ballads, 1973; Sir Walter Scott: Landscape and Locality, 1980. Add: 83 Raikes Rd., Skipton-in-Craven, Yorks. BD13 1LS, England.

REED, Joseph W. American, b. 1932. Film, History, Literature, Biography. Prof. of English and American Studies, Wesleyan Univ., Middletown, Conn., since 1973 (Instr., 1960–61; Asst. Prof., 1961–67; Assoc. Prof., 1967–71; Chmn., 1971–73, 1975–76). Ed., Yale Boswell, since 1974. Ed., Yale Walpole, 1970–74. *Publs:* (ed. with G.R. Creeger) Selected Prose and Poetry of the Romantic Period, 1964; English Biography in the Early Nineteenth Century 1801-1838, 1966; (ed. with W.S. Lewis) The Castle of Otranto, by Horace Walpole, 1969; (ed.) American Diary 1857-1858, by Barbara Bodichon, 1972; (ed. with W.S. Lewis) Walpole's Family Correspondence, 1973; (ed. with J. Basinger and J. Frazer) Working with Kazan, 1973; Faulkner's Narrative, 1973; (ed. with F.A. Pottle) Boswell, Laird of Auchinleck 1778-1783, 1977; Three American Originals: John Ford, William Faulkner and Charles Ives, 1984. Add: Box 6075, Wesleyan Station, Middletown, Conn. 06457-6802, U.S.A.

REED, Kit (Lillian Craig). American, b. 1932. Novels/Short stories, Science fiction/Fantasy. Visiting Prof. of English, Wesleyan Univ., Middletown, Conn., since 1974. Reporter, St. Petersburg Times, 1954–55, and New Haven Register, Connecticut, 1956–59. *Publs:* Mother Isn't Dead She's Only Sleeping, 1961; At War as Children, 1964; When We Dream (juvenile), 1966; The Better Part, 1967; Mr. Da V. and Other Stories, 1967; Armed Camps (SF novel), 1969; Cry of the Daughter, 1971; Tiger Rag, 1973; (ed.) Fat, 1974; Captain Growup, 1976; The Killer Mice (SF short stories), 1976; The Ballad of T. Rantula, 1979; Magic Time (SF novel), 1980; Other Stories and: The Attack of the Giant Baby, 1981; Story First: The Writer as Insider, 1982; Fort Privilege, 1985; The Revenge of the Senior Citizens, 1986; Catholic Girls, 1987. Add: 45

Lawn Ave., Middletown, Conn. 06457, U.S.A.

REED, Rex. American, b. 1938. Novels, Cultural/Ethnic topics, Film, Social commentary/phenomena. Show business interviewer, and columnist. *Publs:* Do You Sleep in the Nude?, 1968; Big Screen, Little Screen, 1971; People Are Crazy Here, 1974; Valentines and Vitriol, 1977; Travolta to Keaton, 1979; Personal Effects (novel), 1985. Add: c/o Macmillan Inc., 866 Third Ave., New York, N.Y. 10022, U.S.A.

REED, Robert Rentoul, Jr. American, b. 1911. Poetry, Literature. Instr., New York Univ., NYC, 194719650; Asst. Prof. to Prof., Pennsylvania State Univ., 1950–77. *Publs:* Young April (poetry), 1937; Bedlam on the Jacobean Stage, 1952; The Occult on the Tudor and Stuart Stage, 1965; Richard II: From Mask to Prophet, 1968; East of Hatteras (poetry), 1969; Crime and God's Judgement in Shakespeare, 1984. Add: 621 E. McCormick Ave., State College, Pa. 16801, U.S.A.

REED, Stanley. British, b. 1911. Children's non-fiction, Film. Teacher and Visual Aids Officer, West Ham Education Cttee., London, 1932–50; Secty., 1950–64, and Dir., 1964–71, British Film Inst. *Publs:* The Cinema, 1952; (with John Huntley) How Films Are Made, 1955; A Guide to Good Viewing, 1961. Add: 54 Felstead Rd., Wanstead, London E11, England.

REED, T(erence) J(ames). British, b. 1937. Literature, Translations. Taylor Prof. of the German Language and Literature and Fellow of the Queen's Coll., Oxford Univ., since 1988 (Fellow and Tutor, St. John's Coll., and Lectr. in Modern Languages, 1963–88). Co-Ed., Oxford German Studies, since 1965; Ed., Oxford Magazine, since 1985. *Publs:* (ed.) Der Tod in Venedig, by Thomas Mann, 1971; Thomas Mann: The Uses of Tradition, 1974; The Classical Centre: Goethe and Weimar 1775-1832, 1980; Goethe, 1984; (trans.) Heine: Deutschland: A Not So Sentimental Journey, 1986. Add: The Queen's Coll., Oxford, England.

REED, Thomas Thornton. Australian, b. 1902. Poetry, History, Literature, Biography. Archdeacon of Adelaide, 1949–53, Dean of Adelaide, 1953–57, Bishop of Adelaide, 1957–73, and Archbishop of Adelaide, 1973–74, Church of England in Australia, now retired. *Publs:* Henry Kendall: A Critical Appreciation, 1960; Sonnets and Songs, 1962; (ed.) The Poetical Works of Henry Kendall, 1966; History of Saint Peter's Cathedral, Adelaide, 1969; Historic Churches of Australia, 1978; Anglican Clergymen in South Australia in the Nineteenth Century, 1986. Add: P.O. Box 130, North Adelaide, S.A. 5006, Australia.

REEDY, George E(dward). American, b. 1917. Military/Defence, Politics/Government, Biography. Nieman Prof. of Journalism, Marquette Univ., Milwaukee, since 1972 (Dean of the Coll. of Journalism, 1972–77). Congressional Correspondent, except for four years of military service, United Press, Washington, D.C., 1939–52; Exec. Dir., Senate Democratic Policy Cttee., Washington, 1952–60; Special Asst. to the Vice-Pres., Washington, 1961–64; Press Secty., White House, Washington, 1964–66; Pres., Struthers Research and Development Corp., Washington, 1966–68; Special Asst. to the President, Washington, D.C., 1968–69; Fellow, Woodrow Wilson Inst., Washington, 1970–72. *Publs:* Who Will Do Our Fighting for Us?, 1969; The Twilight of the Presidency, 1970; The Presidency in Flux, 1973; The Omniscient President: A Myth Collapses, 1975; (adv. ed.) The Presidency, 1975; Lyndon B. Johnson: A Memoir, 1982; The U.S. Senate: Paralysis or a Search for Consensus, 1986; The Twilight of the Presidency, Johnson to Reagan, 1987. Add: Coll. of Journalism, Marquette Univ., Milwaukee, Wisc. 53233, U.S.A.

REEMAN, Douglas (Edward). Also writes as Alexander Kent. British, b. 1924. Novels/Short stories. *Publs:* A Prayer for the Ship, 1958; High Water, 1959; Send a Gunboat, 1960; Dive in the Sun, 1961; The Hostile Shore, 1962; The Last Raider, 1963; With Blood and Iron, 1964; H.M.S. Saracen, 1965; Path of the Storm, 1966; The Deep Silence, 1967; The Pride and the Anguish, 1968; To Risks Unknown, 1969; The Greatest Enemy, 1970; Against the Sea, 1971; Rendezvous—South Atlantic, 1972; Go in and Sink!, 1973; The Destroyers, 1974; Winged Escort, 1975; Surface with Daring, 1976; Strike from the Sea, 1978; A Ship Must Die, 1979; Torpedo Run, 1981; Badge of Glory, 1982; The First to Land, 1984; D-Day—A Personal Reminiscence, 1984; The Volunteers, 1985; The Iron Pirate, 1986; In Danger's Hour, 1988; as Alexander Kent—To Glory We Steer, 1968; Form Line of Battle!, 1969; Enemy in Sight, 1970; The Flag Captain, 1971; Sloop of War, 1972; Command a King's Ship, 1973; Signal—Close Action, 1975; Richard Bolitho: Midshipman, 1975; Passage to Mutiny, 1976; In G llant Company, 1977; Midshipman Bolitho and the "Avenger," 1978; The Inshore Squadron, 1978; Stand into Danger, 1980; A Tradition of Victory, 1981; Success to the Brave, 1983; Colours

Aloft!, 1986; Honour This Day, 1987. Add: Blue Posts, Eaton Park Rd., Cobham, Surray KT11 2JH, England.

REES, Albert Lloyd George. Australian, b. 1916. Chemistry. Chief, CSIRO Div. of Chemical Physics, Victoria, 1958–78. Fellow, 1954, Member of the Council, 1963–68, 1969–73, Secty. of Physical Sciences, 1964–68, and Foreign Secty., 1969–73, Australian Academy of Science; Member of the Council, 1957–59, 1966–68, and Pres., 1967–68, Royal Australian Chemical Inst.; Member, Bureau and Exec. Cttee., 1963–73, Vice-Pres., 1967–69, and Pres., 1969–71, Intnl. Union of Pure and Applied Chemistry; Member, Exec. Cttee., Intnl. Council of Scientific Unions, 1969–72. *Publs:* Chemistry of the Defect Solid State, 1954; (co-ed.) The Australian Academy of Science: The First Twenty-Five Years 1954-79, 1980. Add: 9 Ajana St., North Balwyn, Vic. 3104, Australia.

REES, Barbara. British, b. 1934. Novels/Short stories. Arts Council Fellow in Creative Writing, Polytechnic of North London, 1976–78. *Publs:* Try Another Country, 1969; Diminishing Circles, 1970; Prophet of the Wind, 1973; George and Anna, 1976; The Victorian Lady, 1977; Harriet Dark, 1978. Add: 102 Savernake Rd., London NW3 2JR, England.

REES, David (Bartlett). British, b. 1936. Novels/Short stories, Children's fiction, Essays. Freelance writer, since 1984. Schoolmaster, Wilson's Grammar Sch., London, 1960–65, and Vyners Sch., Ickenham, Middx., 1965–68; Sr. Lectr. in English, St. Luke's Coll., Exeter, 1968–78; Lect. in Education, Univ. of Exeter, 1978–84. *Publs:* Storm Surge, 1975; Quintin's Man, 1976; The Missing German, 1976; Landslip, 1977; The Spectrum, 1977; The Ferryman, 1977; Risks, 1977; The Exeter Blitz, 1978; The House That Moved, 1978; In the Tent, 1979; Silence, 1979; The Green Bough of Liberty, 1980; The Lighthouse, 1980; Miss Duffy Is Still with Us, 1980; The Night Before Christmas Eve, 1980; The Marble in the Water, 1980; Holly, Mud and Whisky, 1981; A Beacon for the Romans, 1981; The Milkman's on His Way, 1982; The Mysterious Rattle, 1982; Waves, 1983; The Estuary, 1983; Painted Desert, Green Shade, 1984; Out of the Winter Gardens, 1984; Islands, 1985; A Better Class of Blond, 1985; The Hunger, 1986; Watershed, 1986; The Burglar, 1987; Friends and Neighbours, 1987; Twos and Threes, 1987; The Flying Island, 1988; Flux, 1988; The Wrong Apple, 1988; Quince, 1988; The Colour of His Hair, 1989. Add: 69 Regent St., Exeter, Devon, England.

REES, Henry. British, b. 1916. Geography, Regional/Urban planning, Transportation. Principal Lectr. in Geography, St. Paul's Coll. of Education, Newbold Revel, 1959–78. *Publs:* (ed.) A Geography of Commodities, 1957, 7th ed. 1974; British Ports and Shipping, 1958; Australasia: The New Certificate Geographies, Advanced Level, 1962, 4th ed. 1974; The British Isles: A Regional Geography, 1966, 1972; (with K.R. Sealy) Regional Studies of the United States and Canada, 1968; The Industries of Britain: A Geography of Manufacture and Power Together with Farming, Forestry and Fishing, 1970; (co-author and ed.) Urban Field Studies for Coventry Schools, 1970; Italy, Switzerland and Austria: A Geographical Study, 1974. Add: 68 Woodside Ave. N., Coventry CV3 6BD, England.

REES, Ioan Bowen. British, b. 1929. Politics/Government, Public/Social administration, Recreation/Leisure/Hobbies. Chief Exec., Gwynedd County Council, since 1980 (Secty., 1973–80). City Prosecutor, Cardiff, 1961–65; Deputy Clerk of the Council, 1967–73, and Deputy Clerk of the Peace, 1967–71, County of Pembroke. *Publs:* Galwady Mynydd (mountaineering), 1961; The Welsh Political Tradition, 1962; Dringo Mynyddoedd Cymru (mountaineering), 1965; (with Owen Dudley Edwards, Hugh MacDiarmid and others) Celtic Nationalism, 1967; Local Government in Switzerland, 1969; Government by Community, 1971; Mynyddoedd (mountaineering), 1974; Staffing Levels in Swiss Government, 1983; The Mountains of Wales, 1987. Add: County Offices, Caenarfon, Gwynedd, Wales.

REES, Joan. Also writes as Susan Strong. British, b. 1927. Historical/Romance/Gothic, Biography. Editorial Asst., British Kinematograph Soc., 1954–56, and Food and Agriculture Org., U.N., Rome, 1957–63. *Publs:* First Adventure, 1962; Voyage to Happiness, 1963; First Love, 1965; Bright Star, 1968; (as Susan Strong) This Thing Called Love, 1969; My Own True Love, 1970; Queen of Hearts, 1974; Jane Austen, Woman and Writer, 1976; The Bride in Blue, 1977; The Summer of 1560, 1977; (as Susan Strong) Error of Judgment, 1977; (as Susan Strong) Love Remembered, 1977; Lass from the Sea, 1979; (as Susan Strong) Emma's Dilemma, 1980; Drama of Love, 1981; Will to Love, 1982; By Love Cast Out, 1982; Far East Assignment, 1983; The Winter Queen, 1983; (as Susan Strong) Jo's Awakening, 1984; North to the Sun, 1985; Shelley's Jane

Williams, 1985; profligate Son: Branwell Brontë and His Sisters, 1986; (as Susan Strong) Swedish Rhapsody, 1987; Romantic Assignment, 1988. Add: 20 Harraby Green, 40 Wallace Rd., Broadstone, Dorset, England.

REES, (George) Leslie (Clarke). Australian, b. 1905. Children's fiction, Theatre, Travel/Exploration/Adventure, Autobiography/Memoirs/Personal. Drama Critic, Era, London, 1931–35; Co-Founder, 1937, and Hon. Chmn., Playwrights Advisory Bd., Sydney; Federal Drama Ed., and Deputy Dir. of Drama until 1966, ABC; Writer-in-Residence, Mt. Lawley Coll. of Advanced Education, Perth, 1975, and Curtin Univ., Perth, 1988. Pres., Sydney Centre of Intnl. P.E.N., 1967–75. *Publs:* Digit Dick on the Great Barrier Reef (and the Tasmanian Devil, in Black Swan Land and the Magic Jabiru, and the Zoo Plot, and the Lost Opals), 6 vols., 1942–57; The Story of Shy the Platypus (Karrawingi the Emu, Sarli the Barrier Reef Turtle, Shadow the Rock Wallaby, Aroora the Red Kangaroo, Wy-Lah the Cockatoo, Russ the Australian Tree Kangaroo), 7 vols., 1944–64; Gecko, The Lizard Who Lost His Tail, 1944; (ed.) Australian Radio Plays, 1946; Mates of the Kurlalong fiction), 1948; Bluecap and Bimbi, The Blue Wrens, 1948; The Story of Kurri Kurri the Kookaburra (Koonaworra the Black Swan), 2 vols., 1950, 1957; Quokka Island, 1951; (ed.) Modern Story Plays, 1951; Two Thumbs: The Story of a Koala, 1953; Towards an Australian Drama, 1953; (with Coralie Rees) Spinifex Walkabout: Hitch-Hiking in Remote North Australia, 1953; Danger Patrol, 1954; (with Coralie Rees) Westward from Cocos: Indian Ocean Travels, 1956; (with Coralie Rees) Coasts of Cape York: Travels Around Australia's Pearl-Tipped Peninsula, 1960; (ed.) Mask and Microphone: Plays, 1963; Boy Lost on Tropic Coast: Adventure with Dexter Hardy, 1968; (with Coralie Rees) People of the Big Sky Country, 1970; Mokee the White Possum, 1973; A History of Australian Drama, 2 vols., 1973–78; Panic in the Cattle Country, 1974; A Treasury of Australian Nature Stories, 1974; Hold Fast to Dreams: 50 Years in Theatre, Radio and Books (Memoirs), 1982. Add: 4/5 The Esplanade, Balmoral Beach, N.S.W. 2088, Australia.

REES, Paul Stromberg. American, b. 1900. Theology/Religion. Ed.-at-Large, World Vision, 1977–85 (Ed., 1971–77). Pastor, First Evangelical Covenant Church, Minneapolis, 1938–58; Vice-Pres. at Large, World Vision Intnl., Monrovia, Calif., 1958–77. Assoc. Ed., The Herald mag., 1955–578; Member, Bd. of Dirs., Christianity Today, 1956–80; Columnist, Covenant Companion mag., 1959–72. *Publs:* If God Be for Us, 1940; Things Unshakeable, 1947; The Radiant Cross, 1949; The Face of Our Lord, 1951; Stir Up the Gift, 1952; Prayer and Life's Highest, 1956; Christian: Commit Yourself, 1957; The Adequate Man, 1958; Stand Up in Praise to God, 1960; Triumphant in Trouble, 1962; Proclaiming the New Testament: Philippians, Colossians, Philemon, 1964; Men of Action in the Book of Acts, 1966; Pictures That Probe the Present, 1966; Free to Live, 1967; (ed.) Nairobi to Berkeley, 1967; Don't Sleep Through the Revolution, 1969, 3rd ed. 1972. Add: 2121 N. Ocean Blvd., Boca Raton, Fla. 33431, U.S.A.

REES, William Linford (Llewelyn). British, b. 1914. Medicine/Health, Psychiatry, Psychology. Consulting Physician, St. Bartholomews Hosp., since 1980; Prof. of Psychiatry, Univ. of London, 1966–80, now Emeritus, Treas., World Psychiatric Assn., since 1966. Asst. Medical Officer, Worcester City and County Mental Hosp., Powick, and Claybury Hosp., London, 1938–40; Psychiatrist, Specialist, and Deputy Physician Suprv., Mill Hill War Emergency Hosp., London, 1940–45; Specialist, Prisoner of War Neurosis Univ., 1945–46; Postgrad. Teacher and Asst. Physician, Maudsley Hosp., London, 1946–47; Consultant Psychiatrist and Deputy Physician Suprv., Whitchurch Hosp., Cardiff, 1947–48; Regional Adviser in Psychiatry for Wales, and Consultant Psychiatrist to Hosps. in Cardiff and South Wales, 1948–54; Consultant Physician, Maudsley Hosp. and Bethlem Royal Hosp., London, 1954–66. Pres., Royal Coll. of Psychiatrists, 1975–78; Pres., British Medical Assn., 1978–79. *Publs:* A Short Textbook of Psychiatry, 1967, 1976; (ed.) Anxiety in Comprehensive Medical Care, 1973; (co-ed.) Progress in the Pharmacotherapy of Depression—Mianserin HC1, 1979. Add: 62 Oakwood Ave., Purley, Surrey, England.

REEVE, F(ranklin) D(olier). American, b. 1928. Novels/Short stories, Poetry, Literature, Translations. Prof. of Letters, Wesleyan Univ., Middletown, Conn., since 1988 (Assoc. Prof. and Chmn. of the Russian Dept., 1962–64; Prof. of Russian 1964–66; Adjunct Prof., 1969–88); Visiting Prof., Yale Univ., New Haven, Conn., since 1973. Taught at Columbia Univ., NYC, 1952–61. Ed., The Poetry Review, 1982–84; Bd. of Dirs., Poets House. *Publs:* (ed. and trans.) Five Short Novels of Turgenev, 1961; (ed. and trans.) An Anthology of Russian Plays, 2 vols., 1961, 1963; Aleksandr Blok: Between Image and Idea, 1962; (ed. and trans.) Great Soviet Short Stories, 1963; The Stone Island (poetry), 1964; Six Poems,

1964; Robert Frost in Russia, 1964; On Some Scientific Concepts in Russian Poetry at the Turn of the Century, 1966; The Russian Novel, 1966; In the Silent Stones: Poems, 1968; The Red Machines (novel), 1968; (ed. and trans.) Contemporary Russian Drama, 1968; Just Over the Border (novel), 1969; The Brother (novel), 1971; The Blue Cat (poetry), 1972; The Three-Sided Cube (play), 1972; (ed. and trans) Nobel Lecture by Alexander Solzhenitsyn, 1972; White Colors (novel), 1973; Angling (poetry), 1984; (co-ed. and trans.) An Arrow in the Wall, by Andrei Voznesensky, 1987; Nightway (poetry), 1987; The White Monk: An Essay on Dostoevsky and Melville, 1989; Concrete Music and Other Poems, 1989; (ed. and trans.) Selected Poems, by Bella Akhmadulina, 1990. Add: Coll. of Letters, Wesleyan Univ., Middletown, Conn. 06457, U.S.A.

REEVE, Joel. *See* **COX,** William R.

REEVES, Elton T. American, b. 1912. Administration/Management, Psychology. Prof. of Mgmt., Univ. of Wisconsin Extension, Madison (joined faculty, 1969). Formerly in industry. *Publs:* Management Development, 1969; The Dynamics of Group Behavior, 1970; So You Want to Be a Supervisor!, 1972; So You Want to Be a Manager!, 1972; So You Want to Be an Executive!, 1972; How to Get Along with (Almost) Everybody, 1973; Practicing Effective Management, 1975. Add: c/o American Management Assoc., 135 W. 50th St., New York, N.Y. 10020, U.S.A.

REEVES, Marjorie E. British, b. 1905. Children's non-fiction, Education, History. Hon. Fellow, St. Anne's Coll., Oxford (Vice-Principal and Fellow, St. Anne's Coll., Oxford, and Univ. Lectr., Oxford Univ., until 1972; joined staff, 1939). *Publs:* Growing Up in a Modern Society, 1946; Then and There series (The Medieval Village; The Medieval Town; The Medieval Monastery; The Medieval Castle; Alfred and the Danes; The Norman Conquest; Elizabethan Court; A Medieval King Governs; Elizabethan Citizen; Explorers in the Elizabeth Age; Elizabeth Country House), 1956–78; (ed.) Eighteen Plus: Unity and Diversion in Higher Education, 1965; The Influence of Prophecy in the Later Middle Ages, 1969; (co-author) The Figurae of Joachim of Fiore, 1972; Joachim and the Prophetic Future, 1976; Sheepbell and Ploughshare, 1977; Why History?, 1980; (with Warwick Gould) Joachim of Fiore and the Myth of the Eternal Evangel in the Nineteenth Century, 1987; The Spanish Armada, 1988; The Crisis in Higher Education: Competence, Delight and the Common Good, 1988; (co-author) The Diaries of Jeffery Whitaker, 1989. Add: 38 Norham Rd., Oxford OX2 6SQ, England.

REEVES, Thomas C. American, b. 1936. History, Biography. Prof. of History, Univ. of Wisconsin-Parkside, Kenosha, since 1970. Asst. Prof., Univ. of Colorado, Boulder, 1966–70. *Publs:* Freedom and the Foundation: The Fund for the Republic in the Era of McCarthysim, 1969; (ed.) Foundations under Fire, 1970; (ed.) McCarthyism, 1973, 3rd ed. 1989; Gentleman Boss: The Life of Chester Alan Arthur, 1975; (ed.) James De Koven, Anglican Saint, 1978; The Life and Times of Joe McCarthy, 1982. Add: 5039 Cynthia Lane, Racine, Wisc. 53406, U.S.A.

REGENSTREIF, S(amuel) Peter. Canadian, b. 1936. Politics/ Government. Prof. of Political Science, Univ. of Rochester, since 1971 (Research Assoc., 1961–63; Asst. Prof., 1963–66; Assoc. Prof., 1966–71). Editorial Consultant, Chicago Sun-Times, since 1987; Pres., Policy Concepts, Inc., Toronto. *Publs:* The Diefenbaker Interlude: Parties and Voting in Canada, 1965. Add: Dept. of Political Science, Univ. of Rochester, Rochester, N.Y. 14627, U.S.A.

REGER, Roger. American, b. 1933. Psychology. Dir. of Special Education, Bd. of Coop. Educational Services, Buffalo, N.Y., since 1965. Part-time Instr., Grad. Sch., Syracuse Univ., New York, since 1975. *Publs:* School Psychology, 1965; (with W. Schroeder and K. Uschold) Special Education: Children with Learning Problems, 1968; (ed. and contrib.) Programming for Preschool Handicapped Children, 1970; Preschool Programming of Children with Disabilities, 1974. Add: c/o C.C. Thomas, 2600 S. First St., Springfield, Ill. 62717, U.S.A.

REGHABY, Heydar. Iranian, b. 1932. Poetry, Philosophy, Politics/Government. Chmn., Natural Science Dept., D.Q. Univ., Davis, Calif., since 1978. Teacher, Univ. of California Extension, Berkeley, Foothill and De Anza Colleges' Community Service Progs. Special Lectr., Dept. of Religion, Columbia Univ., NYC, 1964–66; Asst. Prof. of Philosophy and Political Science, Ball State Univ., Muncie, Ind., 1966–67; Asst. Prof. of Philosophy, Univ. of Oklahoma, Norman, 1967–68; Assoc. Prof. of Philosophy, California State Univ., San Jose, 1968–71. *Publs:* Philosophy and Freedom, 1970; (co-author and ed.) Philosophy of the Third World, 1974. Add: c/o Philosophical Library, 200 W. 57th St., New York, N.Y. 10019, U.S.A.

REICHART, Walter A. American, b. 1903. Literature. University Prof. of German, Univ. of Michigan, Ann Arbor, now retired (joined faculty, 1925). *Publs:* (ed.) Storm: Pole Poppenspaler, 1934; (ed.) Stehr: Der Geigenmacher, 1935; (ed.) Hauptmann: Der arme Heinrich, 1936; (with F.A. Voigt) Hauptmann and Shakespeare, 1938; (ed.) Hauptmann: Die Finsternisse, 1947; Washington Irving and Germany, 1957; (with H. Burgin and E. Neumann) Das Werk Thomas Mann, 1959; Gerhart-Hauptmann-Bibliographie, 1969; (ed.) Washington Irving: Journals and Notebooks 1819-1827, 1970; (ed. with Lillian Schlissel) Washington Irving: Journals and Notebooks 1807-1818, 1980. Add: 2106 Londonderry Rd., Ann Arbor, Mich. 48104, U.S.A.

REICHENBACH, Bruce. American, b. 1943. Philosophy. Prof. of Philosophy, Augsburg Coll., Minneapolis, since 1968. Visiting Prof., Morija Theological Seminary, Lesotho, 1976–77; Visiting Prof., Juniata College, 1985–86. *Publs:* The Cosmological Argument: A Reassessment, 1972; Is Man the Phoenix? A Study of Immortality, 1978, 1982; Evil and a Good God, 1982. Add: Augsburg Coll., 731 21st Ave. S., Minneapolis, Minn. 55454, U.S.A.

REID, Alastair. British, b. 1926. Children's fiction, Poetry, Translations. Staff Writer and Corresp., The New Yorker, since 1959. Taught at Sarah Lawrence Coll., Bronxville, N.Y., 1950–55; Visiting Prof. of Latin American Studies, Antioch Coll., Yellow Springs, Ohio, 1969–70; Seminar Instr. in Latin American Literature, Oxford Univ. and St. Andrews Univ., 1972–73. *Publs:* To Lighten My House: Poems, 1953; I Will Tell You of a Town, 1955; Fairwater, 1956; a Balloon for a Blunderbuss, 1957; Allth, 1958; Ounce Dice Trice, 1961; (with B. Gill) Millionaires, 1959; Supposing, 1960; Oddments Inklings Omens Moments: Poems, 1959; Passwords: Places, Poems, Preoccupations, 1963; To Be Alive, 1966; (with A. Kerrigan) Mother Goose in Spanish, 1967; Uncle Timothy's Traviata, 1967; (trans.) We Are Many, by Pablo Neruda, 1968; (trans. with A. Kerrigan) Jorge Luis Borges: A Personal Anthology, 1967; (trans. with B. Belitt) A New Decade: Poems 1958-1967, by Pablo Neruda, 1968; (trans.) Extravagaria, by Pablo Neruda, 1972; La Isla Azul, 1973; (trans.) Sunday Sunday, by Mario Vargas Llasa, 1973; (trans.) Fully Empowered, by Pablo Neruda, 1975; (trans.) Don't Ask Me How the Time Goes By, by J.E. Pachuco, 1978; Weathering: Poems and Translations, 1978; (trans.) Isla Negra, by Pablo Neruda, 1979; (ed. with Emir Rodriguez Monegal) Borges: A Reader, 1981; (trans. with Andrew Horley) Legacies: Selected Poems, by Herberto Padille, 1982; Whereabouts: Notes on Being a Foreigner, 1987. Add: c/o The New Yorker, 25 W. 43rd St., New York, N.Y. 10036, U.S.A.

REID, Andrew H. British, b. 1940. Psychiatry. Consultant Psychiatrist, Dundee Psychiatric Services, and Royal Dundee Liff Hospital, and Hon. Sr. Lectr. in Psychiatry, Univ. Dept. of Psychiatry, Ninewells Hospital and Medical School, Dundee, since 1972. Regional Adviser in Psychiatry, since 1981, and Member of the Council, since 1983, Royal Coll. of Psychiatrists. *Publs:* The Psychiatry of Mental Handicap, 1982; (co-author) Handbook of Studies on Psychiatry and Old Age, ed. by D.W.K. Kay and G.D. Burrows, 1984. Add: The Cottage, Main St., Longforgan, Dundee DD2 5ET, Scotland.

REID, Charles L. American, b. 1927. Philosophy. Prof. of Philosophy, Youngstown State Univ., Ohio, since 1976 (Assoc. Prof. 1968–76). *Publs:* Basic Philosophical Analysis, 1971; Choice and Action: An Introduction to Ethnics, 1981. Add: 465 Catalina Ave., Youngstown, Ohio 44504, U.S.A.

REID, Christopher. British, b. 1949. Poetry. *Publs:* Arcadia, 1979; Pea Soup, 1982; Caterina Brac, 1985. Add: 5/7 Camden Park Road, London NW1, England.

REID, Clyde Henderson, Jr. American, b. 1928. Psychology, Religion. Pastoral Counselor; Psychotherapist in private practice. Asst. Prof. of Practical Theology, Union Theological Seminary, NYC, 1960–64; Secty. for Evangelism, United Church of Christ, NYC, 1965–67; Assoc. Dir., Inst. for Advanced Pastoral Studies, Bloomfield Hills, Mich., 1967–70; Assoc. Prof. of Interpersonal Ministries, Iliff Sch. of Theology, Denver, 1971–74; Founder and Dir., Center for New Beginnings, 1974–79. *Publs:* I Belong, 1964; Why I Belong, 1964; The God-Evaders, 1966; The Empty Pulpit, 1967; Groups Alive—Church Alive, 1969; 21st Century Man Emerging, 1971; Help! I've Been Fired, 1971; Celebrate the Temporary, 1972; (with J. Kerns) Let It Happen: Creative Worship for the Emerging Church, 1973; The Return to Faith: Finding God in the Unconscious, 1974; You Can Choose Christmas, 1975; Dreams: Discovering

Your Inner Teacher, 1983. Add: 4 Benthaven Pl., Boulder, Colo. 80303, U.S.A.

REID, Frances P. American, b. 1910. Poetry. English Teacher: Diamond High Sch., Missouri, 1931–32, Castleford High Sch., Idaho, 1935–36, Filer High Sch., Idaho, 1936–39, Clinton Jr. High Sch., Tulsa, Okla, 1939–40, and Borah High Sch., Boise, 1958–76, now retired. *Publs:* None So Small, 1958; Thy Word in My Heart, 1962; Walk a Rainbow Trail, 1974; In the Lee of Mountains, 1976; Given to Time, 1978; No Leave-Taking, 1982. Add: 6117 Lubkin, Boise, Idaho 83704, U.S.A.

REID, Helen Evans. Canadian, b. 1911. History, Travel/Exploration/Adventure, Biography. Dir. of Medical Publs., Hosp. for Sick Children, Toronto, and Asst. Prof. of Paediatrics, Univ. of Toronto, 1967–74. *Publs:* A World Away: A Canadian Adventure on Easter Island, 1965; All Silent, All Damned: The Search for Isaac Barr, 1969. Add: R.R. 1, Loretto, Ont., LOG 1LO, Canada.

REID, Henrietta. Historical/Romance/Gothic. *Publs:* Island of Secrets, 1965; Return to Candelriggs, 1966; Daughter of Lir, 1966; Man of the Islands, 1966; My Dark Rapparee, 1966; Substitute for Love, 1967; Bridal Tapestry, 1967; Falcon's Keep, 1968; Beloved Sparrow, 1968; Laird of Storr, 1968; Reluctant Masqerade, 1969; The Thorn Tree, 1969; The Black Delaney, 1970; Hunter's Moon, 1970; Rival Sisters, 1970; The Made Marriage, 1971; Sister of the Bride, 1971; Garth of Tragillis, 1972; The Torrent, 1972; Bride of Ravenscourt, 1972; Dark Usurper, 1972; Bird of Prey, 1973; Intruder at Windgates, 1973; Dragon Island, 1974; The Man at the Helm, 1975; The Tartan Ribbon, 1976; Love's Puppet, 1976; Greek Bridal, 1976; Push the Past Behind, 1977; Tommorow Brings Enchantment, 1978; Paradise Plantation, 1979; Lord of the Isles, 1981; New Boss at Birchfields, 1982. Add: c/o Mills·and Boon Ltd., Eton House, 18-24 Paradise Rd., Richmond, Surrey TW9 1SR, England.

REID, John (Kelman Sutherland). British, b. 1910. Theology/Religion, Translations. Joint Ed., Scottish Journal of Theology, since 1948; Prof of Philosophy, Univ. of Calcutta, 1935–37; Minister, Craigmillar Park Parish Church, Edinburgh, 1939–52; Hon. Secty., Joint Cttee. on New English Bible, 1947–82; Chaplain to British Territorial Army, 1948–62; Prof. of Theology, Univ. of Leeds, 1962–61; Prof. of Systematic Theology, Univ. of Aberdeen, 1961–76. *Publs:* (ed. and trans.) Calvin's Theological Treatises, 1954; The Biblical Doctrine of the Ministry, 1955; The Authority of the Scripture, 1957, 3rd ed. 1981; (ed. and trans.) Calvin's Concerning the Eternal Predestination of God, 1961, 1982; Our Life in Christ, 1963; Presbyterians and Unity, 1966; Christian Apologetics, 1969. Add: 8 Abbotsford Ct., 18 Colinton Rd., Edinburgh EH10 5EH, Scotland.

REID, John P(hillip). American, b. 1930. History, Law, Biography. Prof. of Law, New York Univ. Sch. of Law, since 1966 (Instr., 1960–62; Asst. Prof., 1962–64; Assoc. Prof., 1964–66). *Publs:* Chief Justice: The Judicial World of Charles Doe, 1967; An American Judge: Marmaduke Dent of West Virginia, 1968; A Law of Blood: The Primitive Law of the Cherokee Nation, 1970; A Better Kind of Hatchet, 1976; In a Defiant Stance, 1977; In a Rebellious Spirit, 1979; Law for the Elephant, 1980; In Defiance of the Law, 1981; (ed.) The Briefs of the American Revolution, 1981; Constitutional History of the American Revolution, 1986; The Concept of Liberty in the Age of the American Revolution, 1988. Add: New York Univ. Sch. of Law, 40 Washington Sq. South, New York, N.Y. 10012, U.S.A.

REID, Loren. American, b. 1905. History, Speech/Rhetoric, Biography. Prof. of Speech, Univ. of Missouri, Columbia, since 1944 (Instr. in English, 1935–37; Asst. Prof., 1937–39; Visiting Prof., U.K. Div., Univ. of Maryland, 1952–53 and 1960–61). *Publs:* Teaching Speech, 1960, 4th ed. 1971; Speaking Well, 1962, 4th ed. 1982; Charles James Fox, 1969; Hurry Home Wednesday, 1978; Finally It's Friday, 1981. Add: 200 E. Brandon Rd., Columbia, Mo. 65203, U.S.A.

REID, Meta Mayne. British. Novels/Short stories, Children's fiction, Poetry. Hon. Secty., Belfast P.E.N. Centre, Northern Ireland. Pres., Irish P.E.N., 1970–72. *Publs:* The Land is Dear; Far Off Fields Are Green; Phelim and the Creatures, 1952; Carrigmore Castle, 1954; All Because of Dawks, 1955; Dawks Does It Again, 1956; Tiffany and the Swallow Rhyme, 1956; Cuckoo at Coolnean, 1956; Dawks on Robber's Mountain, 1957; Strangers in Carrigmore, 1958; Dawks and the Duchess, 1958; McNeills at Rathcapple, 1959; Storm on Kildoney, 1961; Sandy and the Hollow Book, 1961; Tobermillin Oracle, 1962; With Angus in the Forest, 1963; Tinkers' Summer, 1965; Silver Fighting Cocks, 1966; House at Spaniard's Bay, 1967; Glen Beyond the Door, 1968; The Two

Rebels, 1969; Beyond the Wide World's End, 1972; Plotters of Pollnashee, 1973; Snowbound at the White-water, 1974; No Ivory Tower (poetry), 1974; The Noguls and the Horse, 1976; A Dog Called Scampi, 1980. Add: c/o Abelard-Schuman, Blackie Children's Books, 7 Leicester Pl., London WC2H 7BP, England.

REID, Robert (William). British, b. 1933. History, Sciences, Biography. Chmn., VATV Ltd. Programme Dir., COPUS: Cttee. on the Public Understanding of Science. Ed., BBC Horizon series, 1967–70; Head of Science and Features, BBC Television, 1970–73. *Publs:* The Spectroscope, 1965; Tongues of Conscience, 1969; Marie Curie, 1974; Microbes and Men, 1974; My Children, My Children, 1977; Land of Lost Content: The Luddite Revolt 1812, 1986. Add: 50 Westcroft Sq., London W6 0TA, England.

REID, Vic(tor Stafford). Jamaican, b. 1913. Novels/Short stories, Children's fiction. Managing Dir. and Chmn. of a printing and publishing co. in Kingston. Formerly, newspaper reporter, ed., and foreign corresp.; also worked in advertising. *Publs:* New Day, 1949; The Leopard, 1958; Sixty-Five, 1960; The Young Warriors, 1967; Buildings in Jamaica, 1970; Mount Ephraim, 1972; The Sun and Juan de Bolas, 1974; The Jamaicans (short stories), 1978; Nanny-Town, 1983. Add: c/o Inst. of Jamaica Press, 2A Suthermere Rd., Kingston, Jamaica.

REID BANKS, Lynne. British, b. 1929. Novels/Short stories, Children's fiction, Plays/Screenplays. Actress in British repertory companies, 1949–53; Interviewer, Reporter and Scriptwriter, Independent Television News, London, 1955–62; Teacher, Kibbutz Yasur Sch. and Na'aman High Sch., Israel, 1963–71. *Publs:* Miss Pringle Plays Portia (play); It Never Rains (play), 1954; The Killer Dies Twice (play), 1956; All in a Row (play), 1956; The L-Shaped Room, 1960; An End to Running (in U.S. as House of Hope), 1962; The Unborn (play), 1962; Already It's Tomorrow (play), 1962; The Gift (play), 1965; Children at the Gate, 1968; The Backward Shadow, 1970; One More River, 1972; Two Is Lonely, 1974; The Adventures of King Midas, 1974; Sarah and After, 1975; Dark Quartet, 1976; The Farthest-Away Mountain, 1976; Path to the Silent Country, 1977; My Darling Villain, 1977; I, Houdini, 1978; Letters to My Israeli Sons, 1979; The Indian in the Cupboard, 1980; Defy the Wilderness, 1981; The Writing on the Wall, 1981; Maura's Angel, 1984; Defy the Wilderness (screenplay), 1983; The Warning Bell, 1984; The Rebel Fairy, 1985; Return of the Indian, 1986; Casualties, 1986; Melusine: A Mystery, 1988; The Secret of the Indian, 1989. Add: c/o Sheila Watson, Suite 8, 26 Charing Cross Road, WC2H 0DG, England.

REILE, Louis. American, b. 1925. Novels/Short stories, Film, Autobiography/Memoirs/Personal, Essays. Prof. of Literature and Cinema Arts, St. Mary's Univ., San Antonio (joined faculty, 1965). Columnist, Alamo Messenger, San Antonio, 1966–72, and Parent-Educator, 1970–72. *Publs:* Battle and Brother Louis (autobiography), 1959; Running Giant (novel), 1966; Films in Focus, 1970; Pater Wilhelm J. Chaminade (biography); Winding Flows the River, 1975; The Prism Cross, 1977; Take Me to the Cross, 1987; I Believe, 1988. Add: One Camino Santa-Maria, San Antonio, Tex. 78284, U.S.A.

REILLY, Robert Thomas. American, b. 1922. Novels/Short stories, Children's fiction, Biography, Documentaries/Reportage. Prof. of Journalism, Univ. of Nebraska, Omaha, since 1972, now Emeritus. Public Relations Consultant, Holland Dreves Reilly Inc., Omaha (Vice-Pres. and Partner, 1966–75). Production Mgr., Lawrence Advertising Agency, 1946–50; Dir. of Public Relations, Creighton Univ., Omaha, 1950–66. *Publs:* Red Hugh, Prince of Donegal, 1957; Christ's Exile, 1957; Massacre at Ash Hollow, 1960; Rebels in the Shadows, 1962; Irish Saints, 1964; Come Along to Ireland, 1969; Kibbutz on Tall Grass Mountain (TV script), 1975; The Lakota (TV script), 1976; Walking to Nalemba (TV script), 1977; The Creighton Story (TV script), 1978; Windows (TV script), 1979; Travel and Tourism Marketing Techniques, 1980; Public Relations in Action, 1980; Handbook of Tour Management, 1982. Add: 9110 N. 52nd Ave., Omaha, Nebr. 68152, U.S.A.

REILLY, (David) Robin. British, b. 1928. Antiques/Furnishings, Art, History, Biography. Sr. Mgmt., Josiah Wedgwood and Sons Ltd., 1952–64; Partner, Hogarth Galleries, New Orleans, 1971–78. *Publs:* The Rest to Fortune: The Life of Major-General James Wolfe, 1960; The Sixth Floor, 1969; Wedgwood Jasper, 1972; (with George Savage) Wedgwood: The Portrait Medallions, 1973; Wedgwood Portrait Medallions: An Introduction, 1973; The British at the Gates, 1974; British Watercolours, 1974; Pitt the Younger, 1978; (with George Savage) The Dictionary of Wedgwood, 1980; The Collector's Wedgwood, 1980. Add: c/o Curtis Brown Ltd., 162-168 Regent St., London W1R 5TA, England.

REIMANN, Arnold Luehrs. Australian, b. 1898. Physics. Research Physicist, Research Labs., Gen. Electric Co., Wembley, England, 1926–36; Leverhulme Research Fellow, Cavendish Lab., Cambridge, 1936–38; Lectr. in Physics, 1939–49, and Research Prof., 1950–68, Univ. of Queensland, Brisbane. *Publs:* Thermionic Emission, 1934; Vacuum Technique, 1952; Physics, 3 vols., 1971, 1973. Add: 52 Lucinda St., Taringa, Brisbane, Qld. 4068, Australia.

REINDORP, George Edmund. British, b. 1911. Theology/Religion. Curate, St. Mary Abbot, Kensington, 1937–39; Chaplain, R.N.V.R., 1939–46; Vicar, St. Stephen, 1946–57; Provost of Southwark and Rector of St. Saviour with All Hallows, Southwark, 1957–61; Bishop of Guildford, 1961–73, and of Salisbury, 1973–81. *Publs:* What about You?, 1956; No Common Task, 1957; Putting It Over: Ten Points for Preachers, 1961; Over to You, 1964; Preaching Through the Christian Year, 1973; Commentary on Holy Communion, series III, 1973. Add: Mole Coll., Bramley, nr. Guildford GU5 0AS, England.

REISCHAUER, Edwin O(ldfather). American, b. 1910. History, Prof. Emeritus, Harvard Univ., Cambridge, since 1981 (Instr., 1939–41; Assoc. Prof., 1946–50; Prof. of Japanese History, 1950–61, Univ. Prof., 1966–81). American Ambassador to Japan, 1961–66. *Publs:* Japan, Past and Present, 1946, 1963; The United States and Japan, 1957, 1965; Wanted: An Asian Policy, 1955; Ennin's Diary: The Record of a Pilgrimage to China in Search of the Law, 1955; Ennin's Travels in T'ang China, 1955; (with J.K. Fairbank) East Asia: The Great Tradition, 1960; (with others) East Asia: The Modern Transformation, 1965; Beyond Vietnam: The United States and Japan, 1967; Japan: The Story of a Nation, 1970, 3rd ed. 1988; (with Fairbank and Craig) East Asia: Tradition and Transformation, 1973; Toward the 21st Century: Education for a Changing World, 1973; The Japanese, 1977; My Life Between Japan and America, 1986; The Japanese Today: Change and Continuity, 1987. Add: 1737 Cambridge St., Cambridge, Mass. 02138, U.S.A.

REISS, Ira Leonard. American, b. 1925. Sex, Sociology. Prof. of Sociology, Univ. of Minnesota, Minneapolis, since 1969 (Dir., Family Study Center, 1969–74). Prof. of Sociology, Bowdoin Coll., Brunswick, Me., 1953–55, Coll. of William and Mary, Williamsburg, Va., 1955–59, Bard Col., Annandale-on-Hudson, N.Y., 1959–61, and Univ. of Iowa, Iowa City, 1961–69. *Publs:* Premarital Sexual Standards in America, 1960; The Social Context of Premarital Sexual Permissiveness, 1967; Family Systems in America, 1971, 4th ed. 1988; (ed.) Readings on the Family System, 1972; (ed.) Contemporary Theories about the Family, 2 vols., 1979; Journey Into Sexuality, 1986. Add: Dept. of Sociology, 1031 Social Science Bldg., Univ. of Minnesota, Minneapolis, Minn. 55455, U.S.A.

REJAI, Mostafa. Iranian, b. 1931. Politics/Government. Distinguished Prof., Miami Univ., Oxford, Ohio, since 1983 (Asst. Prof., 1964–67; Assoc. Prof., 1967–70; Prof., 1970–83). Assoc. Ed., Journal of Political and Military Sociology. *Publs:* (ed. and co-author) Democracy: The ontemporary Theories, 1967; (ed.) Mao Tse Tung on Revolution and War, 1970; (co-author) Ideologies and Modern Politics, 1971, 3rd ed. 1981; (ed. and co-author) Decline of Ideology, 1971; The Strategy of Political Revolution, 1973; The Comparative Study of Revolutionary Strategy, 1977; Leaders of Revolution, 1979; World Revolutionary Leaders, 1983; Comparative Political Ideologies, 1984; Loyalists and Revolutionaries: Political Leaders Compared, 1988. Add: Dept. of Political Science, Miami Univ., Oxford, Ohio 45056, U.S.A.

REMBAR, Charles. American, b. 1915. History, Law, Politics/Government. Partner, Rembar and Curtis, attorneys, NYC. *Publs:* The End of Obscenity, 1968; Perspective, 1975; The Law of the Land, 1980. Add: Lily Pond Lane, East Hampton, N.Y. 11937, U.S.A.

REMINGTON, Mark. *See* **BINGLEY,** David Ernest.

RENAN, Sheldon (Jackson). American, b. 1941. Plays/Screenplays, Film. Independent film and television producer/dir. Advertising copywriter in New York, San Francisco and Tokyo, 1964–68; Dir., Pacific Film Archive, Univ. Art Museum, Univ. of California, Berkeley, 1968–74. *Publs:* Introduction to American Underground Film (in U.K. as The Underground Film: An Introduction to its Development in America), 1967; Basic Film Terms (screenplay), 1970; (with Edwin O. Reischauer and D. Richie) The Japanese Film (television series), 1975; The International Animation Festival (television series), 1975; Basic Television Terms: A Video Dictionary (screenplay), 1976; The Electronic Rainbow: An Introduction to Television (screenplay), 1977; Burn Emergency (screenplay), 1977; Eye Emergency (screenplay), 1978; Treasure, 1984. Add: c/o Warner Books Inc., 666 Fifth Ave., New York, N.Y. 10103, U.S.A.

RENDELL, Joan. British. Crafts, History, Recreation/Leisure/Hobbies. Freelance writer, lectr., and broadcaster. Hon. Ed., British Matchbox Label and Booklet Soc., since 1952. *Publs:* Collecting Matchbox Labels, 1963; Flower Arrangement with a Marine Theme, 1967; Matchbox Labels, 1968; Collecting Natural Objects, 1972; Collecting Out of Doors, 1974; Country Crafts, 1975; Your Book of Corn Dollies, 1976; Your Book of Pressed and Dried Flowers, 1978; Along the Bude Canal, 1979; Lundy Island, 1979; Hawker Country, 1980; Gateway to Cornwall, 1981; Cornish Churches, 1982; The Match, The Box, and the Label, 1983; North Cornwall in the Old Days, 1983; Around Bude and Stratton, 1985; The Story of the Bude Canal, 1987; A Parish Album of Werrington, 1989. Add: Tremarsh, Launceston, Cornwall, England.

RENDELL, Ruth. Also writes as Barbara Vine. British, b. 1930. Mystery/Crime/Suspense. *Publs:* From Doon with Death, 1964; To Fear a Painted Devil, 1965; Vanity Dies Hard, 1965 (in U.S. as In Sickness and in Health, 1966); A New Lease of Death, 1967; (in U.S. paperback as Sins of the Fathers, 1970); Wolf to the Slaughter, 1967; The Secret House of Death, 1968; The Best Man to Die, 1969; A Guilty Thing Surprised, 1970; No More Dying Then, 1971; One Across, Two Down, 1971; Murder Being Done Once, 1972; Some Lie and Some Die, 1973; The Face of Trespass, 1974; Shake Hands for Ever, 1975; The Fallen Curtain and Other Stories, 1976; A Demon in My View, 1976; A Judgement in Stone, 1977; A Sleeping Life, 1978; Make Death Love Me, 1979; Means of Evil and Other Stories, 1979; The Lake of Darkness, 1980; Put On by Cunning (in U.S. as Death Notes), 1981; Master of the Moor, 1982; The Fever Tree and Other Stories, 1982; The Speaker of Mandarin, 1983; The Killing Doll, 1984; The Tree of Hands, 1984; An Unkindness of Ravens, 1985; The New Girl Friend and Other Stories, 1985; Live Flesh, 1986; Heartstones, 1986; Talking to Strange Men, 1987; A Warning to the Curious, 1987; The Veiled One, 1988; The House of Stairs, 1988; The Bridesmaid, 1989; Ruth Rendell's Suffolk (non-fiction), 1989. as Barbara Vine—The Dark-Adapted Eye, 1986; A Fatal Inversion, 1987. Add: Nussteads, Polstead, Colchester CO6 5DN, England.

RENDLE-SHORT, John. British, b. 1919. Medicine/Health, Biography. Emeritus Prof. of Child Health, Univ. of Queensland, Brisbane, since 1961. *Publs:* (with O.P. Gray) Synopsis of Children's Diseases, 6th ed. 1985; (co-author) The Father of Child Care: Life of William Cadogan 1711-1797; The Child: A Guide for the Paediatric Team, rev. ed. 1977. Add: Dept. of Child Health, Univ. of Queensland, Brisbane, Qld. 4067, Australia.

RENDON, Armando B. American, b. 1939. Civil liberties/Human rights, International relations/Current affairs. Public Information officer, U.S. Bureau of Census, since 1979; Pres., Ollin and Assoc., Inc., Public Relations, since 1983. Deputy Information Officer, U.S. Commn. on Civil Rights, 1967–69; Vice-Pres., ATM Corp., 1972–73; Assoc. Prof., American Univ., Washington, D.C., 1975–79. Pres., Los Cerezos TV Co., 1980–82, Member, Bd. of Trustees, Univ. of District of Columbia, 1976–79. *Publs:* Chicano Manifesto, 1971; We Mutually Pledge, 1978; Ethnicity and U.S. Foreign Policy, 1981; The Treaty of Guadelupe Hidalgo, 1983. Add: P.O. Box 5480, Washington, D.C. 20016, U.S.A.

RENFIELD, Richard Lee. American, b. 1932. Education, Translations. Translator, since 1974, and Asst. Division Chief, since 1986, Intnl. Monetary Fund, Washington, D.C. Project Secty. and Asst. Secty., Educational Policies Commn., Washington, D.C., 1958–67. *Publs:* (trans.) Winter Notes on Summer Impressions, by Fyodr Dostoevsky, 1955; If Teachers Were Free, 1969, 1972. Add: 2200 Leeland Dr., Falls Church, Va. 22043, U.S.A.

RENFREW, (Andrew) Colin. British, b. 1937. Archaeology. Master, Jesus Coll., Cambridge, and Disney Prof. of Archaeology, Cambridge Univ., since 1981. Member, Ancient Monuments Bd. for England, since 1974; Trustee, Antiquity Trust, since 1974. Lectr., 1965–70, Sr. Lectr., 1970–72, and Reader, 1972, Univ. of Sheffield; Prof. of Archaeology, Southampton Univ., 1972–81. Excavations at Saliagos, 1964–65, Sitagroi, 1968–70, Quanterness, 1972–74, Maes Howe, 1973–74, Liddle Farm, 1973–74, Ring of Brodgar, 1974, and Phylakopi, 1974–76. *Publs:* (with J.D. Evans) Excavations at Saliagos near Antiparos, 1968; The Emergence of Civilisation, 1972; (ed.) The Explanation of Culture Change, 1973; Before Civilisation, 1973; (ed.) British Prehistory, 1974; Investigations in Orkney, 1979; (ed.) Transformations: Mathematical Approaches to Culture Change, 1979; Problems in European Prehistory, 1979; (with J.M. Wagstaff) An Island Polity, 1982; (ed.) Theory and Explanation in Archaeology, 1982; Approaches to Social Archaeology, 1984; (ed.) The Prehistory of Orkney, 1985; The Archaeology of Cult, 1986; Archaeology And Language, 1987. Add: Master's Lodge, Jesus Coll.,

Cambridge CB5 8BL, England.

RENFROE, Earl W(iley). American, b. 1907. Medicine/Health. Prof. Emeritus of Orthodontics, Univ. of Illinois Coll. of Dentistry, Chicago, since 1973 (Instr. in Dentistry, 1933–46; Instr. in Orthodontics, 1946–47; Asst. Prof., 1947–53; Assoc. Prof., 1953–57; Prof., 1957–73; Head of the Dept., 1966–73). Pres., Chicago Assn. of Orthodontists, 1963–64; Vice-Pres., Chicago Council on Foreign Relations, 1968–69. *Publs:* Technique Training in Orthodontics, 1960; Edgewise, 1975. Add: c/o Lea and Febiger, 600 S. Washington Sq., Philadelphia, Pa. 19106, U.S.A.

RENIER, Elizabeth. Pseud. for Betty Doreen (Flook) Baker. British, b. 1916. Historical/Romance, Children's fiction. Former doctor's secty.; volunteer, Family Planning Assn., 1958–62. *Publs:* The Generous Vine, 1962; The House of Water, 1963; Blade of Justice, 1965; If This Be Treason, 1965, in U.S. as If This Be Love, 1971; Valley of Nightingales, 1966; A Singing in the Woods, 1966; Prelude to Freedom, 1967, in U.S. as Prelude to Love, 1972; The House of Granite, 1968; By Sun and Candelight, 1968; Tomorrow Comes the Sun, 1969; The Spanish Doll, 1970; Valley of Secrets, 1970; Woman from the Sea, 1971; The Renshawe Inheritance, 1972; A Time for Rejoicing, 1973; Ravenstor, 1974; Yesterday's Mischief, 1975; The Moving Dream, 1977; The Lightkeepers (juvenile), 1977; Landscape of the Heart, 1978; The Stone People (juvenile), 1978; The Dangerous Journey, 1979; The Post-Rider (juvenile), 1980; The Mail-Coach Driver (juvenile), 1985; Night of The Storm (juvenile), 1986; The Hiding-Place (juvenile), 1987; The Secret Valley (juvenile), 1988. Add: 4 Cranford Close, Exmouth, Devon EX8 2EY, England.

RENNIE, Basil Cameron. British, b. 1920. Mathematics. Ed., James Cook Mathematical Notes, since 1975, and The Mathematical Scientist, since 1985. Prof., R.A.A.F. Academy, Victoria, 1962–65; Prof. of Mathematics, James Cook Univ. of N. Queensland, Townsville, 1966–85. *Publs:* The Theory of Lattices, 1951. Add: 66 Hallett Rd., Burnside, S. Aust. 5066, Australia.

RENWICK, Charles (Cyril). Australian, b. 1920. Economics. Dir. of Research, Hunter Valley Research Foundn., Newcastle, N.S.W., since 1956. Chmn., New South Wales State Advisory Cttee., Australian Broadcasting Commn. Lectr. and Sr. Lectr. in Economics, Univ. of Sydney, 1944–53; Assoc. Prof. of Economics, New South Wales Univ. of Technology, Kensington, 1954; Head, Div. of Commerce, Newcastle University Coll., 1958–63; Hon. Prof., Univ. of Newcastle, 1963. Member, New South Wales Regional Boundaries Cttee., 1965; member, Australian Govt.'s Delegation, Water for Peace Conference, Washington, D.C., 1968; Member, Royal Commn. on F.M. Radio in Australia, 1973–74. *Publs:* Economists and Their Environment, 1947; (with G. Simpson-Lee) The Economic Pattern, 1951; The Hunter Valley Region, 1968; The Road to Decentralization, 1972; A Study of Wine in the Hunter Region of New South Wales, 1977. Add: Hunter Valley Research Centre, Newcastle, N.S.W. 2300, Australia.

RENWICK, Fred Blackwell. American, b. 1930. Economics, Money/Finance. Prof. of Finance. Leonard N. Stern Sch. Of Business-Graduate Div., New York Univ., NYC, since 1970 (Instr., 1966–67; Asst. Prof., 1967–68; Assoc. Prof., 1968–70). Member, Editorial Advisory Bd., American Journal of Economics and Sociology, since 1974. *Publs:* Introduction to Investments and Finance: Theory and Analysis, 1971. Add: 90 Trinity Pl., New York, N.Y. 10006, U.S.A.

REPS, John W(illiam). American, b. 1921. Regional/Urban planning. Prof. of City and Regional Planning, Cornell Univ., Ithaca, N.Y., 1960–87, now Emeritus (Lectr., 1948–50; Assoc. Prof., 1952–59). *Publs:* The Making of Urban America, 1965; Monumental Washington, 1967; Town Planning in Frontier America, 1969; Tidewater Towns, 1972; Cities on Stone, 1976; Cities of the American West, 1978; The Forgotten Frontier, 1981; Panoramas of Promise, 1984; Views and Viewmakers of Urban America, 1984. Add: 102 Needham Pl., Ithaca, N.Y. 14850, U.S.A.

RESNICK, Mike. (Michael Diamond Resnick). American, b. 1942. Science fiction, Hobbies, Sports. Freelance writer since 1964; Owner, Briarwood Pet Motel, Cincinnati, since 1976. Ed., National Tattler, 1965–66, and National Insider, 1966–69, for National Features Syndicate, Chicago; Ed. and Publisher, Oligarch Publishing, Chicago, 1969–70; Columnist, Collie Cues Mag., Hayward, 1969–80. *Publs:* science fiction—The Forgotten Sea of Mars (short stories), 1965; The Goddess of Ganymede, 1967; Pursuit on Ganymede, 1968; Redbeard, 1969; (with Glen A. Larson) Battlestar Galactica 5: Galactica Discovers Earth, 1980;

The Soul Eater, 1981; Birthright: The Book of Man, 1982; Walpurgis III, 1982; Tales of the Galactic Midway, comprising Sideshow, 1982, The Three-Legged Hootch Dancer, 1983, The Wild Alien Tamer, 1983, and The Best Rootin' Tootin' Shootin' Gunslinger in the Whole Damned Galaxy, 1983; The Branch, 1984; Tales of the Velvet Comet, comprising Eros Ascending, 1984, Eros at Zenith, and Eros Descending, 1985, and Eros at Nadir, 1986; Unauthorized Autobiographies (short stories), 1984; Adventures, 1985; The Inn of the Hairy Toad (short stories), 1985; Santiago, 1986; Stalking The Unicorn, 1987; The Dark Lady, 1987; Ivory, 1988; Paradise, 1989; Second Contact, 1990; other—Official Guide to the Fantastics, 1976; Official Guide to Comic Books and Big Little Books, 1977; Gymnastics and You: The Whole Story of the Sport, 1978; Official Guide to Comic and Science Fiction Books 1979. Add: 10547 Tanager Hills Dr., Cincinnati, Ohio 45249, U.S.A.

RESTAK, Richard M(artin). American, b. 1942. Medicine/Health. Physician: in private practice of neurology, Washington, D.C., since 1973. Member, Bd. of Dirs., Inst. for Psychiatry and Foreign Affairs, since 1984. *Publs:* Premeditated Man: Bioethics and the Control of Future Human Life, 1975; The Brain: The Last Frontier: Explorations of the Human Mind and Our Future, 1979; The Self Seekers, 1982; The Brain, 1984; The Infant Mind, 1986; The Mind, 1988. Add: 1800 R St. N.W., Suite C-3, Washington, D.C. 20009, U.S.A.

RESTON, James (Barrett). American (b. British), b. 1909. Media, Documentaries/Reportage. Columnist and Consultant, the New York Times, NYC, since 1974 (Reporter, 1939–42, 1944–55; Washington Bureau Chief, 1953–64; Assoc. Ed., 1964–68; Exec. Ed., 1968–69; Vice-Pres., 1969–74). *Publs:* Prelude to Victory, 1942; Sketches in the Sand, 1967; Artillery of the Press, 1967; The Innocence of Joan Little, 1977; Sherman's March and Vietnam, 1985; Reston's Washington, 1986. Add: c/o New York Times, 1000 Connecticut Ave., N.W., Washington, D.C. 20036, U.S.A.

REUBEN, David. American, b. 1933. Medicine/Health, Psychology, Sex. In private practice of psychiatry, Arizona and Illinois, Clinical Research Assoc., Harvard Univ. Sch. of Medicine, Cambridge, Mass., 1959–61. *Publs:* Everything You Always Wanted to Know about Sex (But Were Afraid to Ask), 1969; Any Woman Can!, 1971; The Save-Your-Life Diet, 1975; How to Get More Out of Sex, 1975; Everything You Alays Wanted to Know about Nutrition, 1978; Dr. David Reuben's Mental First-Aid Manual, 1982. Add: c/o Habib, 9950 Grosalia Way, La Mesa, Calif., U.S.A.

REUBER, Grant Louis. Canadian, b. 1927. Economics. Sr. Vice-Pres. and Chief Economist, Bank of Montreal, since 1978. Prof. of Economics, 1957–78, Dean of Social Sciences, 1968–74, and Vice-Pres. and Provost, 1974–78, Univ. of Western Ontario, London. *Publs:* Britain's Export Trade with Canada, 1960; Canada-United States Trade: Its Growth and Changing Composition, 1960; (with R.J. Wonnacott) The Cost of Capital in Canada, 1961; The Objectives of Monetary Policy, 1964; (with R.G. Bodkin, E.P. Bond and T.R. Robinson) Price Stability and High Employment: The Options for Canadian Economic Policy, 1967; (with F. Roseman) The Take-Over of Canadian Firms 1945-61; An Empirical Analysis, 1969; (with R.E. Caves) Canadian Economic Policy and the Impact of International Capital Flows, 1969; (with R.E. Caves) Capital Transfers and Economic Policy: Canada 1951-62, 1970; Wage Determination in Canadian Manufacturing 1953-66, 1971; Private Foreign Investment in Development, 1973; (ed. with T.N. Guinsburg) Perspectives on the Social Sciences in Canada, 1974; Canada's Political Economy, 1980. Add: 101 Wychwood Ct., London, Ont., Canada.

REVELEY, Edith. American, b. 1930. Novels/Short stories. *Publs:* The Etruscan Couple and Other Stories, 1976; A Pause for Breath, 1979; Skin Deep and Other Stories, 1980; In Good Faith, 1983. Add: c/o Mary Irvine, 4 Coombe Gardens, Wimbledon, London SW20 0QU, England.

REVELL, John Robert Stephen ("Jack"). British, b. 1920. Economics, Money/Finance. Dir., Instr. of European Finance, Bangor, 1973–85, now Consultant Dir. Research Officer and Sr. Research Officer, Dept. of Applied Economics, Cambridge Univ., 1957–68; Fellow, and Tutor and Sr. Tutor, Fitzwilliam Coll., Cambridge, 1965–68. Prof. of Economics, 1968–83, and Vice-Principal, 1978–83, Univ. Coll. of N. Wales, Bangor. *Publs:* (with John Moyle) The Owners of Quoted Ordinary Shares: A Study for 1963, 1966; The Wealth of the Nation, 1967; Changes in British Banking: The Growth of a Secondary Banking System, 1968; Financial Structure and Government Regulation in the United Kingdon 1952-1980, 1972; The British Financial System, 1973; Solvency and Regulation of Banks, 1975; Savings Flows in Europe 1976; (ed.) Competition and

Regulation of Banks, 1978; Inflation and Financial Institutions, 1979; Costs and Margins in Banking: An International Survey, 1980; A Study of the Spanish Banking System, 1980; Banking and Electronic Fund Transfers, 1983: Changes in Spanish Banking, 1984; Mergers and the Role of Large Banks, 1987. Add: 12 Rustat Rd., Cambridge CB1 3QT, England.

REWALD, John. American, b. 1912. Art. Assoc., Museum of Modern Art, since 1943; Prof. of Art History, Graduate Center, City Univ. of New York, since 1971. Prof., Univ. of Chicago, 1964–71. *Publs:* Cezanne et Zola, 1936, as Cezanne, 1939; (ed.) Cezanne: Correspondance, 1937, 5th ed. as Cezanne Letters, 1985; Gauguin, 1938; Maillol, 1939; (co-ed.) Pissarro: Letters to His Son Lucien, 1943; The Woodcuts of Maillol, 1943; Seurat, 1943; Degas: Works in Sculpture, 1944; Renoir Drawings, 1946; The History of Impressionism, 1946, 4th ed. 1973; Manet Pastels, 1947; Bonnard, 1948; The History of Post-Impressionism, 1956, 3rd ed., 1978; Manzu, 1966; Morandi, 1967; Studies in Impressionism, 1986; Studies in Post-Impressionism, 1986. Add: 535 E. 80th St., New York, N.Y. 10021, U.S.A.

REX, John Arderne. British, b. 1925. Race relations, Sociology. Dir., Social Science Research Council's Research Unit on Ethnic Relations, and Visiting Prof., Univ. of Birmingham, since 1979. Ed., Intnl. Library of Sociology, Routledge and Kegan Paul. Lectr., Leeds Univ., 1949–62, an Birmingham Univ., 1962–64; Prof., Univ. of Durham, 1964–70; Prof. of Sociology, Univ. of Warwick, 1970–79. *Publs:* Key Problems of Sociological Theory, 1961; (with R. Moore) Race Community and Conflict, 1967; Race Relations in Sociological Theory, 1970; Race Colonialism and the City, 1973; Discovering Sociology, 1973; Sociology and the Demystification of the Modern World, 1974; (ed.) Approaches to Sociology, 1974; (with S. Tomlinson) Colonial Immigrants in a British City, 1980; Social Conflict, 1981; Race and Ethnicity, 1986; (with D. Mason) Theories of Race and Ethnic Relations, 1986. Add: C.R.E.R., Univ. of Warwick, Coventry CV4 7AL, England.

REY, Margret. American, b. 1906. Children's fiction, Children's non-fiction. Writer and photographer. *Publs:* all with H.A. Rey—How the Flying Fishes Came into Being, 1938; Raffy and the Nine Monkeys, 1939; Anybody at Home?, 1939; How Do You Get There?, 1941; Curious George series (in U.K. as Zozo series), 7 vols., 1941–66; Elizabite, 1942; Tit for Tat, 1942; Where's My Baby?, 1943; Feed the Animals, 1944; Pretzel, 1944; Spotty, 1945; Pretzel and the Puppies, 1946; Billy's Picture, 1948; Mary Had a Little Lamb, 1951; See the Circus, 1956. Add: 14 Hilliard St., Cambridge, Mass. 02138, U.S.A.

REYBURN, Wallace (Macdonald). British, b. 1913. Novels/Short stories, Sports/Physical education/Keeping fit. Reporter, and Asst. Ed., 1931–34, and London Corresp., 1935–36, New Zealand newspapers; Asst. Ed., 1937–40, and Ed., 1946–50, various mags. in Toronto and Montreal; War Corresp., Montreal Standard, 1941–45; Asst. and Features Ed., various London mags., 1950–53; London Columnist, Toronto Telegram, 1954–67; Deputy Ed., Queen mag., London, 1965–66. *Publs:* Rehearsal for Invasion, 1943; Glorious Chapter, 1943; Some of It Was Fun, 1948; Follow a Shadow (novel), 1956; Port of Call (novel), 1957; The Street That Died (novel), 1958; Three Women (novel), 1959; Good and Evil (novel), 1960; Getting the Boy (novel), 1965; The World of Rugby, 1966; The Lions, 1967: The Unsmiling Giants, 1968; Frost: Anatomy of Success 1968; (ed.) Best Rugby Stories, 1969; The Rugby Companion, 1969; Flushed with Pride: The Story of Thomas Crapper, 1969; There Was Also Some Rugby, 1970; Bust Up: The Story of Otto Titzling, 1971; A History of Rugby, 1972; Bridge Across the Atlantic, 1973; The Inferior Sex, 1973; The Winter Men, 1973; Twickenham: The Story of a Rugby Ground, 1976; All about Rugby Football, 1976; Gilbert Harding, 1978; Mourie's Men, 1979; (with R. Bosenguet) Let's Get Through Wednesday, 1980. Add: c/o Michael Joseph, 27 Wright's Lane, London W8 5TZ, England.

REYNOLDS, Barrie. Australian, b. 1932. Anthropology/Ethnology, Cultural/Ethnic topics. Prof. of Material Culture, James Cook Univ. of North Queensland, Townsville. Keeper of Ethnography, 1955–64, and Dir., 1964–66, Rhodes-Livingstone Museum, Zambia; Chief Curator, Centennial Museum, Vancouver, 1968–69; Chief Ethnologist, Canadian Ethnology Service, National Museums of Canada, Ottawa, 1969–75. *Publs:* (ed.) The Fishing Devices of Central and Southern Africa, 1958; Magic, Divination and Witchcraft among the Barotse of Northern Rhodesia, 1963; (ed.) The Material Culture of the Ambo of Northern Rhodesia, 1964; Somalia Museum Development, 1966; The Material Culture of the Peoples of the Gwembe Valley, Northern Rhodesia, 1968; (ed. with M. Stott) Material Anthropology: Contemporary Approaches to Material Culture, 1987. Add: Material Culture Unit, James Cook Univ. of North Queensland, Townsville, Qld., Australia.

REYNOLDS, Ernest Randolph. British, b. 1910. Plays/Screenplays, Poetry, Antiques/Furnishings, Music, Theatre. British Council Lectr., Baghdad and Lisbon, 1940–44; Lectr. in English, Univ. of Birmingham, 1946–55. *Publs:* Tristram and Iseult, 1930; Early Victorian Drama 1830-1870, 1936; Mephistopheles and the Golden Apples: Fantastic Symphony in Verse, 1943; Five Portuguese Plays, 1943, 1944; Modern English Drama, 1949, 1951; The Plain Man's Guide to Antique Collecting, 1963; The Plain Man's Guide to Opera, 1964; Collecting Victorian Porcelain, 1966; Northamptonshire Treasures, 1972; Northampton Town Hall, 1974; Northampto Repertory Theate, 1976; Candlemas Night (radio play); The Three Musketeers (play); Queens of England (play). Add: 43 Wantage Rd., Abington Park, Northampton, England.

REYNOLDS, Graham. British, b. 1914. Art. Member of staff, 1937–74, and Keeper of the Dept. of Paintings, Prints and Drawings, 1959–74, Victoria and Albert Museum, London. *Publs:* Twentieth Century Drawings, 1946; Nicholas Hilliard and Isaac Oliver, 1947, 1971; Nineteenth Century Drawings 1850-1900, 1949; Thomas Bewick, 1949; An Introduction to English Water-Colour Painting, 1950, 1988; (ed.) Gastronomic Pleasures, 1950; Elizabethan and Jacobean Costume, 1951; English Portrait Miniatures, 1952, 1988; Painters of the Victorian Scene, 1953; Catalogue of the Constable Collection, Victoria and Albert Museum, 1960, 1973; Constable, the Natural Painter, 1965; Victorian Painting, 1966, 1987; The Engravings of S.W. Hayter, 1967; The Etchings of Anthony Gross, 1968; Turner, 1969; (ed.) Catalogue of Charles Dickens Centenary Exhibition, 1970; A Concise History of Water Colour Painting, 1972; (ed.) John Constable Sketchbooks of 1813 and 1814, 1973; Catalogue of Portrait Miniatures, Wallace Collection, 1980; (ed.) Constable with His Friends in 1806, 1981; Constable's England, 1983; The Later Paintings and Drawings of John Constable, 2 vols., 1984. Add: The Old Manse, Bradfield St. George, Bury St. Edmunds, Suffolk, England.

REYNOLDS, John. *See* **WHITLOCK,** Ralph.

REYNOLDS, Lloyd (George). American, b. 1910. Economics. Sterling Prof. of Economics, Yale Univ., New Haven, since 1952 (Assoc. Prof. of Economics, 1945–47, and Prof. of Economics, 1947–52; Chmn. of the Dept., 1951–59). Pres., Indu trial Relations Research Assn., 1955; Vice-Pres., American Economic Assn., 1959. *Publs:* The British Immigrant in Canada, 1935; Control of Competition in Canada, 1940; Labor and National Defense, 1941; An Index to Trade Union Publications, 1945; Labor Economics and Labor Relations, 1949; The Structure of Labor Markets, 1951; The Evolution of Wage Structure, 1956; Economics: A General Introduction, 1963; Wages Productivity and Industrialization in Puerto Rico, 1965; The Three Worlds of Economics, 1971; Agriculture in Development Theory, 1975; Image and Reality in Economic Development, 1977; Economic Growth in the Third World, 1850-1980, 1985. Add: Dept. of Economics, Yale Univ., New Haven, Conn. 06520, U.S.A.

REYNOLDS, Madge. *See* **WHITLOCK,** Ralph.

REYNOLDS, Philip Alan. British, b. 1920. International relations/Current affairs, Politics/Government. Wilson Prof. of Intnl. Politics, 1950–64, and Vice-Principal, 1961–63, University Coll., Aberystwyth; Prof. of Politics, 1964–80, and Vice-Chancellor, 1980–85, Univ. of Lancaster. *Publs:* War in the Twentieth Century, 1951; British Foreign Policy in the Inter-War Years, 1954; Introduction to International Relations, 1971, 1980; (with E.J. Hughes) The Historian as Diplomat: Sir Charles Kingsley Webster 1939-46, 1977. Add: Lattice Cottage, Borwick, Carnforth LA6 1JR, England.

REYNOLDS, William J. American, b. 1956. Novels/Short stories. Assoc. Ed., 1979–80, Sr. Ed., 1980–83, and Managing Ed., 1983–84, TWA Ambassador mag., St. Paul, Minn. *Publs:* The Nebraska Quotient, 1984; Moving Targets, 1986; Money Troubles: A Nebraska Mystery, 1988. Add: c/o Lescher and Lescher, 155 E. 71st St., New York, N.Y. 10021, U.S.A.

REZITS, Joseph. American, b. 1925. Music. Prof. of Music (Piano), Indiana Univ., Bloomington, since 1966. Asst. Prof. of Music, New Jersey State Coll., 1957–62. *Publs:* Source Materials for Piano Techniques, 1965; Source Materials for Keyboard Skills, 1975; The New Scribner Music Library Teachers Guide; (with Gerald Deatsman) Piano Music in Print and Literature on the Pianist Art, 2nd ed. 1978; The Guitarist's Resource Guide, 1982. Add: Sch. of Music, Indiana Univ., Bloomington, Ind. 47405, U.S.A.

REZLER, Julius. American, b. 1911. Economics, Industrial relations, Personnel management. Prof. Emeritus of Economics, Loyola Univ., Chicago, since 1976 (Prof., 1957–76; Dir., Inst. of Industrial Relations, 1965–69). Labor Arbitrator, American Arbitration Assn., since 1966, and National Academy of Arbitration, since 1980. Dir., Hungarian Inst. of Labor Studies, Budapest, 1943–45; Section Chief, Ministry of Reconstruction, Budapest, 1945–48; Fulbright Prof., India, 1961–62. *Publs:* (co-author) The Immigrant Scholar in America, 1968; Automation and Industrial Labor, 1969; (co-author) Western European Labor and the American Corporation, 1970; (co-author) Handbook of Modern Personnel Administration, 1972; (co-author) Ethnicity in Eastern Europe, 1980; (co-author) Arbitration in Health Care, 1982. Add: 22W 765 Tamarack Dr., Glen Ellyn, Ill. 60137, U.S.A.

RHINEHART, Susan Oneacre. American, b. 1938. Children's fiction. Attorney. Publications Dr., New Mexico Municipal League, 1973–83; Teacher, Intnl. Nursey Sch. and Kindergarten, Jamaica, N.Y., 1970–71, and NYC Public Schs., 1971–72. *Publs:* Something Old, Something New, 1961. Add: P.O. Box 9688, Santa Fe, N.M. 87504, U.S.A.

RHODES, Anthony. British, b. 1916. Novels/Short stories, Art, History, Travel/Exploration/Adventure. Officer, British Army, 1937 until invalided out with rank of Capt. in 1947. *Publs:* Sword of Bone (war memoirs), 1942; The Uniform (novel), 1949; A Sabine Journey (travel), 1952; A Ball in Venice (novel), 1953; The General's Summer House (novel), 1954; The Dalmatian Coast (travel), 1954; Where the Turk Trod (travel), 1955; The Poet as Superman (biography), 1959; The Prophet's Carpet (novel), 1960; The Rise and Fall of Louis Renault, 1965; Art Treasures of Eastern Europe, 1971; The Vatican in the Age of the Dictators, 1973; Princes of the Grape (travel), 1971; Propaganda: Art of Persuasion, 1976; The Power of Rome (1870-1922), 1982. Add: 40 Lower Belgrave St., London SW1, England.

RHODES, Philip. British, b. 1922. Medicine/Health. Prof. of Post-Grad. Medical Education, Univ. of Southampton, 1980 until retirement, 1987. Obstetric Physician, 1958–64, Prof. of Obstetrics and Gynaecology, 1964–74, and Dean, 1968–74, St. Thomas's Hosp. Medical Sch., London; Dean, Faculty of Medicine, Univ. of Adelaide, 1974–77; Postgrad. Dean of Medicine, Univ. of Newcastle upon Tyne, 1977–79. *Publs:* Fluid Balance in Obstetrics, 1960; Preparing for Your Baby, 1961; Expecting a Baby, 1967; Woman: A Biological Study, 1969; Reproductive Physiology, 1969; The Value of Medicine, 1977; Dr. John Leake's Hospital: The Birth, Life and Death of a Maternity Hospital, 1978; Letters to a Young Doctor, 1983; An Outline History of Medicine, 1985. Add: Fairford House, Lyndhurst Rd., Brockenhurst, Hants. SO42 7RH, England.

RHONE, Trevor D. Jamaican, b. 1940. Plays/Screenplays. Free-lance writer, since 1969. Writer, Jamaican Broadcasting Corp., 1958–60; teacher, 1963–64, 1965–69; actor in England, 1964–65; founder, Theatre '77 (Barn Theatre), Kingston, 1965. Add: Old Story Time and Other Plays, 1981; Two Can Play, 1986. Add: c/o Drumbeat Series, Longman Group, 5 Bentinck St., London W1M 5RN, England.

RHUE, Morton. *See* STRASSER, Todd.

RHYMES, Douglas Alfred. British, b. 1914. Theology/Religion. Hon. Canon, Southwark Cathedral. Vicar, All Saints, New Eltham, London, 1954–62; Dir. of Lay Training, Diocese of Southwark, London, 1962–68; Vicar of St. Giles, Camberwell, London, 1968–76; Parish priest of Woldingham, 1976–84. *Publs:* (co-ed.) Laymans Church, 1962; No New Morality, 1963; Prayer in the Secular City, 1968; Through Prayer to Reality, 1974; (co-ed.) Dropping the Bomb, 1984. Add: Chillington Cottage, 7 Duke's Rd., Fontwell, W. Sussex BH18 0SP, England.

RHYNE, Charles S. American, b. 1912. Law. Sr. Partner, Rhyne and Rhyne, Washington; Gen. Counsel, National Inst. of Municipal Law officers; Dir., National Savings and Trust Co., Washington. Trustee, Duke Univ., Durham, N.C. Pres., Bar Assn. of the District of Columbia, 1955–56; Vice-Pres., National Legal Aid Assn., 1957–58, and Inter-merican Bar Assn., 1957–58; Pres., 1957–58, and Chmn. of the Special Cttee. on World Peace Through Law, 1958–65, American Bar Assn.; Member, Commn. on Intnl. Rules of Judicial Procedure, 1958–62; Gen. Counsel, and Member, Bd. of Dirs., U.S. Cttee. for the Atlantic Congress, 1958–62; Pres., American Bar Foundn., 1959–60; Chmn. of the Bd. and Pres., World Peace Through Law Foundn., 1964–65; Chmn., Commn. on National Inst. of Justice, 1972–74. *Publs:* Civil Aeronautics Act Annotated, 1939; Airports and the Courts, 1944; Labor Unions and Municipal Employee Law, 1946; Aviation Accident Law, 1947; Airport Lease and Concession Agreements, 1948; The Law of Municipal Contracts, 1952; Municipal Law,

1957; International Law, 1972; Law of Local Government Operations, 1980. Add: 1404 Langley Pl., McLean, Va. 22101, U.S.A.

RHYS, Francis Stephen. British, b. 1926. Music. Prof. and Tutor, Royal Academy of Music, London, since 1963. Conductor of choirs and organist, London; Conductor, Richmond Orchestra, London. Formerly Music Dir., Convent of the Sacred Heart, Tunbridge Wells, Kent. *Publs:* Six Inventions for Two Oboes, 1950; (with C.K. Palmer) ABC of Church Music, 1967. Add: 7 Well Lane, East Sheen, London SW14, England.

RIASANOVSKY, Nicholas V(alentine). American, b. 1923. History. Sidney Hellman Ehrman Prof. of European History, Univ. of California, Berkeley, since 1969 (joined faculty, 1957). Co-Ed., California Slavic Studies, since 1960; Member of the Editorial Bd., The Russian Review. Asst. Prof. to Assoc. Prof., State Univ. of Iowa, Iowa City, 1949–57. *Publs:* Russia and the West in the Teaching of the Slavophiles: A Study of Romantic Ideology, 1952; Nicholas I and Official Nationality in Russia 1825–1855, 1959; A History of Russia, 1963, 4th ed. 1984; The Teaching of Charles Fourier, 1969; A Parting of Ways: Government and the Educated Public in Russia 1801–1855, 1976; The Image of Peter the Great in Russian History and Thought, 1985. Add: Dept. of History, Univ. of California, Berkeley, Calif. 94720, U.S.A.

RIBMAN, Ronald (Burt). American, b. 1932. Plays/Screenplays. Asst. Prof. of English, Otterbein Coll., Westerville, Ohio, 1962–63. *Publs:* The Journey of the Fifth Horse, and Harry, Noon and Night, 1967; Journey of the Fifth Horse published separately, 1974; The Ceremony of Innocence, 1968; Passing Through from Exotic Places, 1970; The Poison Tree, 1977; Cold Storage, 1978; Five Plays, 1978; Buck, 1983. Add: c/o Leo Bookman, William Morris Agency, 1350 Ave. of the Americas, New York, N.Y. 10019, U.S.A.

RICE, Anne. Has also written as Anne Rampling and A.N. Roquelaure. American, b. 1941. Novels/Short stories. *Publs:* Interview with the Vampire, 1976; The Feast of All Saints, 1980; Cry to Heaven, 1982; The Vampire Lestat, 1985; The Queen of the Damned, 1988; The Mummy, or Ramses the Great, 1989. Add: c/o Simon and Schuster, 1230 Ave. of the Americas, New York, N.Y. 10020, U.S.A.

RICE, Brian Keith. British, b. 1932. Sociology, Theology/Religion. Clerk in Holy Orders, since 1957; Social Responsibility Officer, County of Cleveland, and Chaplain to local govt. in N.E. Diocesan Dir. of Stewardship, Derby, 1960–66; Education Secty., United Soc. for the Propagation of the Gospel, 1966–72; Dir. of Education, Dioces of Birmingham, 1972–84. *Publs:* What Is Christian Giving?, 1958; Stewardship and Evangelism, 1963; Affluence and Christian Responsibility, 1964; (with R.H. Fuller) Christianity and the Affluent Society, 1966. Add: 39 Darlington Rd., Hartburn, Stockton on Tees, Cleveland TS18 5EJ, England.

RICE, C(harles) Duncan. British, b. 1942. History. Prof. of History, and Dean, Faculty of Arts and Sciences, New York Univ., since 1985. Henry Fellow, Harvard Univ., Cambridge, Mass., 1965–66; Lectr. in History, Univ. of Aberdeen, Scotland, 1966–70; Assoc. Prof. of History, 1975–79, and Dean of Saybrook Coll., 1972–79, Yale Univ., New Haven (Asst. Prof., 1969–75); Prof. of History and Dean, Hamilton Coll., Clinton, N.Y., 1979–85. *Publs:* The Rise and Fall of Black Slavery, 1975; The Scots Abolitionists 1833-1861, 1981. Add: N.Y.U. Faculty of Arts and Sciences, 5 Washington Sq. N., New York, N.Y. 10003, U.S.A.

RICE, Donald L. American, b. 1938. Novels/Short stories, Plays/Screenplays, Humor/Satire. Worked for various newspapers in Ohio, Wisconsin, Rhode Island, and Massachusetts, 1957–66; Technical Ed., Cooper-Bessemer, Mt. Vernon, Ohio, 1966–72; Ed., Schism, 1969–75. *Publs:* The President's Coming, 1970; (ed.) The Agitator, 1972; The Tryouts, 1973; The Situation on Earth, 1974; How to Publish Your Own Magazine, 1978; Mammals: A Clipbook, 1979; Birds: A Clipbook, 1980; Software, 1980; Fishes, Reptiles and Amphibians: A Clipbook, 1980; (co-ed.) The Friendly Stars, 1982; The New Testament: A Pictorial Archive from 19th Century Sources, 1985. Add: 1109 W. Vine St., Mt. Vernon, Ohio 43050, U.S.A.

RICE, Otis K(ermit). American, b. 1919. History. Prof. of History, West Virginia Inst. of Technology, Montgomery, since 1960, Emeritus since 1987. (Asst. Prof., 1957–59; Assoc. Prof., 1959–60; Chmn., Dept. of History and Social Sciences, 1962–72; Dir., Div. of Humanities and Sciences, 1968–72; Acting Dean, 1969; Dean Sch. of Human Studies, 1984–87). *Publs:* The Allegheny Frontier: West Virginia Beginnings 1730-1830, 1970; West Virginia: The State and Its People, 1972; Frontier

Kentucky, 1975; The Hatfields and the McCoys, 1978; Charleston and the Kanawha Valley, 1981; West Virginia: A History, 1985. Add: Box 147, Hugheston, W. Va. 25110, U.S.A.

RICH, Adrienne (Cecile). American, b. 1929. Poetry. Prof. of English and Feminist Studies, Stanford Univ., Calif., since 1986. Taught at the YM-YWHA Poetry Center Workshop, NYC, 1966–67; Visiting Poet, Swarthmore Coll., Pennsylvania, 1966–68; Adjunct Prof., Grad. Writing Div., Columbia Univ., NYC, 1967–69; Lectr., 1968–70, Instr., 1970–71, and Asst. Prof. of English, 1971–72; City Coll. of New York; Fannie Hurst Visiting Prof. of Creative Writing, Brandeis Univ., Waltham, Mass., 1972–73; Prof. of English, Douglass Coll., 1976–78; A.D. White Poet-at-Large, Cornell Univ., Ithaca, N.Y., 1982–85; Visiting Prof., San Jose State Univ., Calif., 1984–86. *Publs:* A Change of World, 1951; (Poems), 1952; The Diamond Cutters and Other Poems, 1955; Snapshots of a Daughter-in-Law: Poems 1954-1962, 1963; Necessities of Life: Poems 1962-1965, 1966; Selected Poems, 1967; Leaflets: Poems 1965-1968, 1969; The Will to Change: Poems 1969-1970, 1971; Diving into the Wreck: Poems 1971-1972, 1973; Poems Selected and New 1950-74, 1975; Of Woman Born: Motherhood as Experience and Institution, 1976; Women and Honor: Some Notes on Lying, 1977; The Dream of a Common Language: Poems 1974-1977, 1978; On Lies, Secrets, and Silence: Selected Prose 1966-1978, 1979; A Wild Patience Has Taken Me This Far: Poems 1978-1981, 1981; The Fact of a Doorframe: Poems 1950-84, 1984; Your Native Land, Your Life (poems), 1986; Blood, Bread, and Poetry (essays), 1986; Time's Power, 1989. Add: c/o W.W. Norton Co., 500 Fifth Ave., New York, N.Y. 10110, U.S.A.

RICH, Elaine Sommers. American, b. 1926. Children's fiction, Women. Columnist, Mennonite Weekly Review. *Publs:* (ed.) Breaking Bread Together, 1958; Hannah Elizabeth, 1964; Tomorrow, Tomorrow, Tomorrow, 1966; Am I This Countryside?, 1980; Mennonite Women, 1983; Spiritual Elegance: A Biography of Pauline Krehbiel Raid, 1987. Add: 112 S. Spring St., Bluffton, Ohio 45817, U.S.A.

RICHARD, Adrienne. American, b. 1921. Novels/Short stories. *Publs:* Pistol, 1969; The Accomplice, 1973; Wings, 1974; Into the Road, 1976; Managing Your Own Epilepsy, 1990. Add: 45 Chiltern Rd., Weston, Mass. 02193, U.S.A.

RICHARD, Cliff. British, b. 1940. Religion. Singer and actor: awarded 12 gold discs for records; films include: Serious Charge, 1959; Expresso Bongo, 1960; The Young Ones, 1962; Summer Holiday, 1963; Wonderful Life, 1964; Finders Keeps, 1966; Two a Penny, 1968; His Land, 1970; Take Me High, 1973. *Publs:* Questions, 1970; The Way I See It, 1972; The Way I See It Now, 1975; Which One's Cliff, 1977; Happy Christmas from Cliff, 1980; You, Me and Jesus, 1983; Mine to Share, 1984; Jesus, You, and Me, 1985; Single-Minded, 1988; Mine for Ever, 1989. Add: c/o Peter Gormley, P.O. Box 46C, Esher, Surrey KT10 9AA, England.

RICHARD, Susan. *See* **ELLIS,** Julie.

RICHARDS, Christine-Louise. American, b. 1910. Children's fiction, Songs, lyrics and libretti. Founder, Owner, and Pres., Blue Star Music Publishing Co., New Berlin and Morris, N.Y., since 1946; also independent artist. *Publs:* Blue Star Fairy Book of Stories for Children, 1950; Blue Star Fairy Book of More Stories for Children, 1969; The Blue Star Fairy Book of New Stories for Children, 1980; Branches, 1983. Add: Springslea, P.O. Box 185, Morris, N.Y. 13808, U.S.A.

RICHARDS, Clare. *See* **TITCHENER,** Louise.

RICHARDS, Denis George. British, b. 1910. History. Sr. Narrator and Official Historian, Air Ministry, Historial Branch, 1943–49; Principal, Morley Coll., London, 1950–65; Longman Fellow, Univ. of Sussex, Brighton, 1965–68. *Publs:* Modern Europe, 1939; (with H.St.G. Saunders) Royal Air Force 1939-1945, 3 vols., 1953–54 (C.P. Robertson Trophy); (with J.W. Hunt) Modern Britain, 1950; (with J.E. Cruikshank) The Modern Age, 1955; Britain under the Tudors and Stuarts, 1958; Offspring of the Vic: A History of Morley College, 1958; (with A. Quick) Britain 1714-1851, 1961; (with J. Bolton) Britain and the Ancient World, 1963; (with A. Quick) Britain 1851-1945, 1967; (with A. Quick) Twentieth Century Britain, 1968; (with A.E. Ellis) Medieval Britain, 1973; Portal of Hungerford, 1978. Add: 16 Broadlands Rd., London N6, England.

RICHARDS, (Sir) James Maude. British, b. 1907. Architecture, Travel. Vice-Pres., National Council on Inland Transport, since 1963.

Asst. Ed., The Architects' Journal, London, 1933; Asst. Ed., 1935–37, and Ed., 1937–71, The Architectural Review, London; Ed., Publications Div., 1942–43, and Dir. of Publications, Middle East, Cairo, 1943–46, U.K. Ministry of Information; Gen. Ed., The Architectural Press, London, 1946–71; Architectural Corresp., The Times newspaper, London, 1947–71; Hoffman Wood Prof. of Architecture, Univ. of Leeds, 1957–59; Ed., European Heritage, 1973–75. Member, Exec. Cttee., Modern Architectural Research Group, 1946–54; Member, Advisory Council, Inst. of Contemporary Arts, 1947–68; Member of the Council, Architectural Assn., London, 1948–51, 1958–61; Regular Member, BBC Critics Panel, 1948–68; Member, Architecture Council, Festival of Britain, 1949–51; Member, British Cttee., Intnl. Union of Architects, 1950–66, Royal Fine Art Commn., 1951–66, Fine Art Cttee. of the British Council, 1954–79, and the Council of Industrial Design, 1955–61; Member, Ministry of Transport Cttee. on Traffic Signs, 1962–63. *Publs:* Miniature History of the English House, 1938; (with E. Ravilious) High Street, 1938; Introduction to Modern Architecture, 1940; (with J. Summerson) The Bombed Buildings of Britain, 1942; Edward Bawden, 1946; The Castles on the Ground, 1946, 1973; The Functional Tradition in Early Industrial Buildings, 1958; An Architectural Journey in Japan, 1963; Guide to Finnish Architecture, 1966; A Critic's View, 1971; (ed. with Nikolaus Pevsner) The Anti-Rationalists, 1973; The Professions: Architecture, 1974; Provision for t e Arts, 1976; (ed.) Who's Who in Architecture from 1400 to the Present Day, 1977; Eight Hundred Years of Finnish Architecture, 1978; Memoirs of an Unjust Fella (autobiography), 1980; National Trust Book of English Architecture, 1981; Goa, 1982; National Trust Book of Bridges, 1984. Add: 29 Fawcett St., London SW10, England.

RICHARDS, Mark. British, b. 1922. Plays/Screenplays, Poetry. Teacher, Takapuna Grammar Sch., Auckland, since 1954. *Publs:* Solomon Grundy, 1958; Jericho Road, 1964; The Ballad of Dunken Bay, 1967; Long Weekend, 1972; Liberation Ode, 1976; Collected Poems 1952-83, 1984; A Burnt Child: Collected Plays 1960-85, 1986; Satan's Complaint: Poems 1984-88, 1988. Add: 41 Norwood Rd., Bayswater, Auckland, New Zealand.

RICHARDSON, Baron; John Samuel Richardson. British, b. 1910. Medicine/Health. Emeritus Consulting Physician, St. Thomas's Hosp., London. Pres., Intnl. Soc. of Internal Medicine, 1966–70, Royal Soc. of Medicine, 1969–71, and the British Medical Assn., 1970–71; Master, Soc. of Apothecaries, 1971–72; Chmn., Council for Postgrad. Medical Education in England and Wales, 1972–80; Pres., Gen. Medical Council, 1973–80. *Publs:* (ed.) The Practice of Medicine, 1956, 1960; Connective Tissue Disroders, 1963; (with G.I.C. Ingram) Anticoagulant Prophylaxis and Treatment, 1965; (ed.-in-chief) Medical Progress, 1969–73. Add: Windcutter, Lee, nr Ilfracombe, North Devon, England.

RICHARDSON, Alan. British, b. 1923. Social sciences. Prof. of Psychology, Univ. of Western Australia, since 1987 (Sr. Lectr., 1957–69; Reader, 1970–87). Asst. Lectr., Bedford Coll., Univ. of London, 1953–56. *Publs:* Mental Imagery, 1969; British Immigrants and Australia, 1974; Man in Society, 1974; The Experiential Dimension of Psychology, 1984. Add: Dept. of Psychology, Univ. of Western Australia, Nedlands, W.A. 6009, Australia.

RICHARDSON, Anne. *See* **ROIPHE,** Anne Richardson.

RICHARDSON, David (Horsfall Stuart). British, b. 1942. Botany, Environmental science/Ecology. Univ. Prof. of Botany, Trinity Coll., Dublin. *Publs:* The Vanishing Lichens, 1975; The Biology of Mosses, 1981; Biological Indicators of Pollution, 1987. Add: c/o Trinity Coll., Dublin 2, Ireland.

RICHARDSON, Frank McLean. British, b. 1904. History, Medicine/Health, Sex. British Army Officer, Army Medical Service, retired as Maj. Gen. (Dir., Medical Services, BAOR, 1957–61). Medical Adviser for Civil Defence, Scotland, 1963–69. *Publs:* Napoleon: Bisexual Emperor, 1972; Napoleon's Death: An Inquest, 1974; Fighting Spirit: Psychological Factors in War, 1978; The Public and the Bomb, 1981; Mars Without Venus: A Study of Some Homosexual Generals, 1981; (with Seumas MacNeill) Piobaireachd and Its Interpretation, 1987. Add: 4B Barnton Ave. W., Edinburgh EH4 6DE, Scotland.

RICHARDSON, Geoffrey Alan. British, b. 1936. Environmental science/Ecology, Geography. Principal, Queen's Coll., Glasgow, since 1976. Geography Master, Chislehurst and Sidcup Boys Grammar Sch., Kent, 1959–62, and Kings Sch., New South Wales, 1963–66; Geography Lectr. and Warden, Edge Hill Coll. of Education, 1966–73; the Sr. Tutor, Ilkley Coll. of Education, 1973–76. *Publs:* Case Studies in the

Australian Environment, 1970; The Southern Continents, 1975. Add: Queen's Coll., Park Dr., Glasgow G3 6LP, Scotland.

RICHARDSON, George Barclay. British, b. 1924. Economics. Warden of Keble Coll., Oxford, since 1989 (Tutorial Fellow, St. John's Coll., 1951–89; Secty. to the Delegates and Chief Exec., Oxford Univ. Press, 1974–88). *Publs:* Information and Investment, 1961; Economic Theory, 1964. Add: Oxford Univ. Press, Walton St., Oxford OX2 6DP, England.

RICHARDSON, Harry W(ard). British, b. 1938. Economics. Dir. of the Centre for Research in the Social Sciences, Univ. of Kent, Canterbury, since 1969. Asst. Lectr. in Economics, 1960–62, and Sr. Lectr., 1966–68, Univ. of Aberdeen; Lectr. in Economics, Univ. of Newcastle upon Tyne, 1962–64, and Univ. of Strathclyde, Glasgow, 1964–65. *Publs:* Economic Recovery in Britain 1932-1939, 1967; (with D.H. Aldcroft) Building in the British Economy Between the Wars, 1968; Regional Economics: Location Theory, Urban Structure and Regional Change, 1969; Elements of Regional Economics, 1969; (with D.H. Aldcroft) The British Economy 1870-1939, 1969; (ed.) Regional Economics: A Reader, 1970; Urban Economics, 1971; Regional Growth Theory, 1973; Regional Development Policy and Planning in Spain, 1975; New Urban Economics, 1977; Urban Economics, 1978; Regional and Urban Economics, 1979; (co-ed.) Economic Prospects for the Northeast, 1984. Add: Centre for Research in the Social Sciences, Univ. of Kent, Canterbury, Kent, England.

RICHARDSON, Henry V.M. American. b. 1923. Novels/Short stories. Prof. of Humanities, Walla Walla Valley Coll., Washington, since 1968. Lectr. to Asst. Prof. of Scandinavian Literature, Univ. of Washington, Seattle, 1959–64; Asst. Prof. of Literature and Languages, Eastern Washington Univ., Cheney, 1964–68. *Publs:* Not All Our Pride, 1965; Skarra, 1975; The Lady of Skarra, 1979. Add: 615 E. Washington St., Walla Walla, Wash. 99362, U.S.A.

RICHARDSON, Jack. American, b. 1935. Novels/Short stories, Plays/Screenplays, Autobiography/Memoirs/Personal. *Publs:* The Prodigal, 1960; The Prison Life of Harris Filmore (novel), 1961; Gallows Humor, 1961; Xmas in Las Vegas, 1966; Memoir of a Gambler (autobiography), 1979. Add: c/o Simon and Schuster, 1230 Ave. of the Americas, New York, N.Y. 10020, U.S.A.

RICHARDSON, Joanna. British. Literature, Biography. Member of Council, Royal Soc. of Literature, 1961–86. *Publs:* Fanny Brawne: A Biography, 1952; Rachel, 1956; Théophile Gauter: His Life and Times, 1958; Sarah Bernhardt, 1959; Edward FitzGerald, 1960; The Disastrous Marriage: A Study of George IV and Caroline of Brunswick, 1960; My Dearest Uncle: A Life of Leopold, First King of the Belgians, 1961; (ed.) FitzGerald: Selected Works, 1962; The Everlasting Spell: A Study of Keats and His Friends, 1963; (ed.) Essays by Divers Hands, 1963; Edward Lear, 1965; George IV: A Portrait, 1966; Creevey and Greville, 1967; Princess Mathilde, 1969; The Bohemians, 1969; Verlaine, 1971; La Vie Parisienne 1852-1870, 1971; Enid Starkie, 1973; (ed.) Verlaine: Poems in Translation, 1974; Stendhal: A Critical Biography, 1974; Baudelaire: Poems in Translation, 1975; Victor Hugo, 1976; Zola, 1978; Keats and His Circle, 1980; The Life and Letters of John Keats, 1981; Letters from Lambeth, 1981; Paris under Siege, 1982; Colette, 1983; Judith Gautier, 1987. Add: 55 Flask Walk, London NW3, England.

RICHARDSON, Midge Turk. Formerly wrote as Midge Turk. American, b. 1930. Children's non-fiction, Autobiography/Memoirs/Personal. Group Ed.-in-Chief, Seventeen mag. and Good Food mag., since 1988 (Exec. Ed., 1975–79, and Ed.-in-Chief. 1979–88, Seventeen mag.). Former Nun, Sisters of the Immaculate Heart of Mary; High Sch. Principal, Los Angeles, 1959–66; Asst. Dean, New York Univ., 1966–67; College Ed., Glamour mag., 1967–74; Ed.-in-Chief, and Editorial Dir., Co-Ed and Forecast mags., 1974–75. *Publs:* The Buried Life: A Nun's Journey, 1971; Gordon Parks: A Biography, 1971. Add: Seventeen Magazine, 850 Third Ave., New York, N.Y. 10022, U.S.A.

RICHARDSON, Miles. American, b. 1932. Anthropology/Ethnology. Prof. of Anthropology, Louisiana State Univ., Baton Rouge, since 1965. *Publs:* San Pedro, Colombia: Small Town in a Developing Society, 1970; (ed.) The Human Mirror: Material and Spatial Images of Man, 1974; (ed.) Place: Experience and Symbol, 1984; (ed. with Malcolm C. Webb) The Burden of Being Civilized, 1986. Add: Dept. of Geography and Anthropology, Louisiana State Univ., Baton Rouge, La. 70803, U.S.A.

RICHARDSON, Richard Judson. American, b. 1935. Politics/Government. Burton Craig Prof., Dept. of Political Science, Univ. of North Carolina, Chapel Hill, since 1977 (Assoc. Prof., 1969–73; Prof. since

1973; Dept. Chmn., 1975–80, and since 1985). Research Assoc., Inst. for Research in Social Science, since 1969. Grad. Teaching Asst., 1960–62, and Instr., Arts and Science Faculty, 1962–65, Tulane Univ., New Orleans; Asst. Prof., 1965–67, and Assoc. Prof., 1967–69, Western Michigan Univ., Kalamazoo. *Publs:* (with Kenneth N. Vines) The Politics of Federal Courts: Lower Courts in the United States, 1970, 1973; (co-author) The Politics of American Democracy, 1977, 1981. Add: Dept. of Political Science, Univ. of North Carolina, Chapel Hill, N.C. 27514, U.S.A.

RICHARDSON, Robert Galloway. British, b. 1926. History, Medicine/Health. Consultant medical ed. and freelance writer. Ed., Spectrum Intnl., since 1974; Consultant Ed., Intnl. Medicine, since 1979, and Cardiovascular Focus, since 1981. Medical Officer, Eaton Hall Officer Cadet Sch., Chester, 1952–54; Medical Ed., Butterworths Medical Publs., 1955–63; Asst. Ed., Medical News, 1963–67; Abbottempo, 1967–72; Consultant Ed., Intake, 1970–80, and Info, 1974–80. *Publs:* The Surgeon's Tale: The Story of Modern Surgery, 1958; Surgery: Old and New Frontiers, 1968; The Surgeon's Heart: A History of Cardiac Surgery, 1969; The Scapel and the Heart, 1970; (ed.) The Second World Conference on Smoking and Health, 1972; The Menopause: A Neglected Crisis, 1973; The Abominable Stoma: A Historical Survey of the Artificial Anus, 1973; The Hairs of Your Head Are Numbered, 1974; Larrey: Surgeon to Napoleon's Imperial Guard, 1974; Blood: A Very Special Juice, 1975; Nurse Sarah Anne: With Florence Nightingale at Scutari, 1977. Add: Apple Tree Cottage, French St., near Westerham, Kent TN16 1PW, England.

RICHETTI, John J. American, b. 1938. Literature. Sugarman Prof. of English Literature, Univ. of Pennsylvania, Philadelphia, since 1987. Asst. Prof. of English, Columbia Univ., NYC, 1967–70; Assoc. Prof., then Prof., Rutgers Univ., New Brunswick, N.J., 1970–87. *Publs:* Popular Fiction Before Richardson: Narrative Patterns 1700-1739, 1969; Defoe's Narratives: Situations and Structures, 1975; Philosophical Writing: Locke, Berkeley, Hume, 1983; Daniel Defoe, 1987. Add: Dept. of English, Univ. of Pennsylvania, Philadelphia, Pa. 19104, U.S.A.

RICHIE, Donald. American, b. 1924. Novels/Short stories, Anthropology/Ethnology, Film, Sex, Travel/Exploration/Adventure. Literary Ed., The Japan Times, Tokyo, since 1973; Adviser, Publishing and the Arts, Intnl. House of Japan, Tokyo, since 1981. Film Critic, Pacific Stars and Stripes, 1947–49, and The Japan Times, 1954–69; Curator of Film, Museum of Modern Art, New York, 1968–73. *Publs:* This Scorching Earth (novel), 1956; (with Joseph Anderson) The Japanese Film: Art and Industry, 1959; Land and People of Japan, 1960; The Japanese Movie, 1966; The Erotic Gods, 1966; Companions of the Holiday (novel), 1968; The Films of Akira Kuroswa, 1965; George Stevens: American Romantic, 1970; Japanese Cinema, 1971; Ozu, 1974; The Inland Sea (diary-novel) 1978; Introducing Japan, 1978; The Japanese Tattoo, 1980; Zan Inklings, 1982; Notes for a Study of Shohei Imamura, 1983; Some Aspects of Japanese Popular Culture, 1981; A Taste of Japan, 1985; Viewing Film, 1985; Introducing Tokyo, 1987; Different People (biography), 1987; Tokyo Nights (novel), 1988; Japanese Cinema, 1989; (ed.) Willard van Dyke: Memoirs, 1989. Add: 304 Shato Nezu, Yanaka 1, 1-18, Taito-ku, Tokyo 110, Japan.

RICHLER, Mordecai. Canadian, b. 1931. Novels/Short stories, Plays/Screenplays, Essays. Writer-in-Residence, Sir George Williams Univ., Montreal, 1968–69; Visiting Prof. of English, Carleton Univ., Ottawa, 1972–74. *Publs:* The Acrobats, 1954; Son of a Smaller Hero, 1955; A Choice of Enemies, 1957; No Love for Johnnie (screenplay), 1959; The Apprenticeship of Duddy Kravitz, 1959; The Incomparable Atuk (in U.S. as Stick Your Neck Out), 1963; Young and Willing (screenplay), 1964; Life at the Top (screenplay), 1965; Cocksure, 1968; The Street: Stories (in U.K. as The Street: A Memoir), 1969; Hunting Tigers under Glass: Essays and Reports, 1969; (ed.) Canadian Writing Now, 1970; St. Urbain's Horseman, 1971; Shoveling Trouble, 1973; Notes on an Endangered Species and Others, 1974; Jacob Two-Two Meets the Hooded Fang, 1975; The Street (memoirs), 1975; Images of Spain, 1977; Joshua Then and Now, 1980; Home Sweet Home; My Canadian Album, 1984. *Publs:* 1321 Sherbrooke St. W., Apt. 80C, Montreal, Que. H3G 1J4, Canada.

RICHMOND, Anthony Henry. Canadian, b. 1925. Sociology. Prof. of Sociology, York Univ., Toronto, since 1965 (Dir., Inst. for Behavioural Research, 1979–82). Lectr., Univ. of Edinburgh, 1952–63; Reader, Bristol Coll. of Science and Technology, now Bath Univ., 1963–65; Sr. Assoc. Member, St. Anthony's Coll., Oxford, 1984–85. *Publs:* Colour Prejudice in Britain, 1954, 1971; The Colour Problem, 1955, 1961; Post-War Immigrants in Canada, 1967; Readings in Race and Ethnic Relations, 1972; (with B. Neumann and R. Mezoff) Immigrant Integration and Urban Renewal in Toronto, 1972; Migration and Race Relations in an English City, 1973; (with D. Kubat) Internal Migration: The New World and the Third World, 1976; (with W.E. Kalabach) Factors in the Adjustment of Immigrants and Their Descendants, 1980; Immigration and Ethnic Conflict, 1988; Caribbean Immigrants, 1989. Add: Dept. of Sociology, York Univ., 4700 Keele St., Downsview, Ont. M3J 1P3, Canada.

RICHMOND, Hugh Macrae. British, b. 1932. Literature. Prof. of English, Univ. of California, Berkeley (joined faculty as Instr., 1957). *Publs:* The School of Love: The Evolution of the Stuart Love Lyric, 1964; Shakespeare's Political Plays, 1967, 1974; (ed.) Shakespeare's King Henry IV, part I, 1967; Shakespeare's Sexual Comedy, 1971; (ed.) Shakespeare's Henry VIII, 1971; Renaisance Landscapes: English Lyrics in a European Tradition, 1973; The Christian Revolutionary: John Milton, 1974; Puritans and Libertines: Anglo-French Literary Relations in the Reformation, 1981. Add: Dept. of English, Univ. of California, Berkeley, Calif. 94708, U.S.A.

RICHMOND, Leigh (Tucker). American. Science fiction/Fantasy. Reporter, photographer, newspaper ed., and research anthropologist; Pres., Centric Foundn. *Publs:* all with Walt Richmond (died, 1977)—Shock Waves, 1967; The Lost Millennium, 1967, as SIVA!, 1979; Phoenix Ship, 1969, expanded ed. as Phase Two, 1980; Positive Charge (short stories), 1970; Gallagher's Glacier, 1970, 1979; Challenge the Hellmaker, 1976; The Probability Corner, 1977. Add: P.O. Box 908, Maggie Valley, N.C. 28751, U.S.A.

RICHMOND, Robert P. American, b. 1914. Children's fiction, History, Biography. With Payroll Dept., Veterans Admin., White River Junction, Vt., 1960–73, now retired. *Publs:* Day the Indians Came, 1966; Powder for Bunker Hill, 1968; Powder Alarm—1775, 1971; John Stark, Freedom Fighter, 1976, 1988; Legacy of the Bloody Bride, 1979; Dick Whittington's Cat (musical play), 1988. Add: 51 Springdale Ave., Waterbury, Conn. 06708, U.S.A.

RICHMOND, Roe. (Roald Frederick Richmond). American, b. 1910. Novels/Short stories, Westerns/Adventure, Biography. Freelance writer since 1972. Sports Ed., Orleans County Monitor, Barton, Vt., 1933–36; State Ed. and Supvr., Federal Writers Project, Montpelier, Vt., 1936–42; Inspector, Jones and Lamson Machine Co., Springfield, Vt., 1942–47; freelance writer, Rutland, Vt., 1947–55, 1958–59; Proofreader, Alan S. Browne Co., Brattleboro, Vt., 1955–58; Ed. and Proofreader, S.N.H. Typesetting, Concord, N.H., 1959–72. *Publs:* Conestoga Cowboy, 1949, in paperback as The Utah Kid, 1953; Maverick Heritage, 1951; Riders of Red Butte, 1951, in paperback as The Hard Men, 1958; Mojave Guns, 1952; Island Fortress: The Story of Francis Marion, 1952; Death Rides the Dondrino, 1954; Montana Bad Man, 1957; Wyoming Way, 1958; Lash of Idaho, 1958; The Kansan, 1960; The Deputy (novelization of TV series), 1960; Forced Gigolos, 1960; The Wild Breed, 1961, as Legacy of a Gunfighter, 1980; The Blazing Star, 1963; War in the Panhandle, 1979; Showdown at Fire Hill, 1980; Rio Grande Riptide, 1980; Crusade on the Chisholm, 1980; Hell on a Holiday, 1980; Guns at Goliad, 1980; Nevada Queen High, 1980; An End to Summer, 1980; The Blaze of Autumn, 1980; Kelleway's Luck, 1981; Lifeline of Texas, 1981; Stakes Plains Rendezvous, 1981; El Paso del Norte, 1982; Carikee Crossfire, 1986; The Saga of Simon Fry, 1986. Add: 7 Fayette St., Concord, N.H. 03301, U.S.A.

RICHTER, Harvena. American, b. 1919. Novels/Short stories, Literature. Copywriter, Saks Fifth Ave., 1942–43, and R.H. Macy, 1943–46, both NYC; Copy Chief, Elizabeth Arden Co. Inc., NYC, 1946–47; Advertising Dir., I. Miller, 1947–48; Lectr., New York Univ., NYC, 1955–66, and Univ. of New Mexico, Albuquerque, 1969–89. *Publs:* The Human Shore (novel), 1959; Virginia Woolf: The Inward Voyage, 1970; (ed.) The Rawhide Knot and Other Stories, by Conrad Richter, 1978; Writing to Survive: The Private Notebooks of Conrad Richter, 1988. Add: c/o Ray Lincoln, Elkins Park House Apts., York Rd., Elkins Park, Pa. 19117, U.S.A.

RICKETTS, Ralph Robert. British, b. 1902. Novels/Short stories. Former Sub-Ed., London Mercury. *Publs:* A Lady Leaves Home, 1934; Camilla, 1937; The Manikin, 1956; Love in Four Flats, 1959; (ed.) We Are Happy, 1960; Henry's Wife, 1961; Bid the World Good Night, 1982. Add: Old Alresford Lodge, Alresford, Hants., England.

RICKMAN, Hans Peter. British, b. 1918. Intellectual history,

Philosophy. Visiting Prof., formerly Reader in Philosophy, The City Univ., London, since 1967 (Sr. Lectr., 1962–67). Staff Tutor in Philosophy and Psychology, Univ. of Hull, 1949–61. *Publs:* Meaning in History: Dilthey's Thought on History and Society (in U.S. as Pattern and Meaning in History), 1961; Preface to Philosophy, 1964; Living with Technology, 1967; Understanding and the Human Studies, 1967; (ed.) Selected Writings, by W. Dilthey, 1976; W. Dilthey, Pioneer of the Human Studies, 1979; The Adventure of Reason, 1983; Dilthey Today, 1988. Add: 12 Fitzroy Ct., 57 Shepherds Hill, London N6 5RD, England.

RICKS, Christopher. British, b. 1933. Literature. Prof. of English, Boston Univ., since 1986. Gen. Ed., Penguin English Poets; Co-Ed., Essays in Criticism. Fellow and Tutor, Worcester Coll., Oxford, and Lectr., Oxford Univ., 1958–68; Prof. of English, Univ. of Bristol, 1968–75, and Cambridge Univ., 1975–86. *Publs:* (ed.) Dissertation Upon English Typographical Founders and Foundries, 1962; Milton's Grand Style, 1963; (ed.) Poems and Critics: An Anthology of Poetry and Criticism from Shakespeare to Hardy, 1966; Tennyson's Methods of Composition, 1966; (ed.) A.E. Housman: A Collection of Critical Essays, 1968; (ed.) The Poems of Tennyson, 1969, 1987; (ed.) Milton's Paradise Lost, and Paradise Regained, 1968; (ed.) English Poetry and Prose 1540-1674, 1970; (ed.) English Drama to 1710, 1971; (ed.) Selected Criticism of Matthew Arnold, 1972; Tennyson: A Biographical and Critical Study, 1972; Keats and Embarrassment, 1974; (ed.) The State of the Language, 1980; The Force of Poetry, 1984; (ed.) The New Oxford Book of Victorian Verse, 1987; (ed.) A.E. Housman: Collected Poetry and Selected Prose, 1987; T.S. Eliot and Prejudice, 1988. Add: Dept. of English, Boston Univ., Boston, Mass. 02215, U.S.A.

RIDDEL, Joseph Neill. American, b. 1931. Literature. Prof. of English, Univ. of California at Los Angeles, since 1973. Asst. Prof. of English, Duke Univ., Durham, N.C., 1960–65; Assoc. Prof., 1965–68, and Prof. of English, 1968–72, State Univ. of New York at Buffalo. *Publs:* (with S.F. Morse and J. Bryer) Wallace Stevens Checklist and Bibliography of Stevens Criticism, 1963; The Clairvoyant Eye: The Poetry and Poetics of Wallace Stevens, 1965; C. Day Lewis, 1971; The Inverted Bell: Modernism and the Counterpoetics of William Carlos Williams, 1974. Add: 5044 Vanalden Ave., Tarzana, Calif. 91356, U.S.A.

RIDE, W(illiam) D(avid) L(indsay). Australian, b. 1926. Natural history, Zoology. Principal, Canberra Coll. of Advanced Education, since 1987 (Fellow in Life Sciences, 1980–82; Head, Sch. of Applied Science, 1982–87). Departmental Demonstrator in Vertebrate Zoology, Dept. of Zoology and Comparative Anatomy, Oxford, 1954–55; Hulme Lectr. in Zoology, Brasenose Coll., Oxford, 1955–57; Dir., Western Australian Museum, 1957–75; Dir., Australian Biological Resources Study, 1975–80. *Publs:* A Guide to the Native Mammals of Australia, 1970; Index to the Genera and Species of Fossil Mammalia Described from Australia, 1975; International Code of Zoological Nomenclature, 1985. Add: P.O. Box 1, Belconnen, A.C.T. 2616, Australia.

RIDGEWAY, Jason. *See* **MARLOWE,** Stephen.

RIDGWAY, John. British, b. 1938. Children's non-fiction, Recreation/ Leisure/Hobbies, Travel/Exploration/Adventure, Autobiography/ Memoirs/Personal. Proprietor, John Ridgway Sch. of Adventure, Sutherland, Scotland, since 1968. With Parachute Regiment, 1959–68. *Publs:* (co-author) A Fighting Chance, 1966; Journey to Ardmore, 1971; Amazon Journey, 1972; Cockleshell Journey, 1974; Gino Watkins, 1974; Round the World with Ridgway, 1978; (co-author) Round the World Non-Stop, 1985; Road to Elizabeth, 1986; Floodtide, 1988. Add: John Ridgway Sch. of Adventure, Ardmore, Rhiconich by Lairg, Sutherland, Scotland.

RIDGWAY, Matthew B(unker). American, b. 1895. History, Autobiography/Memoirs/Personal. Gen., U.S. Army, retired as Chief of Staff, 1955. *Publs:* (with Harold H. Martin) Soldier (memoirs), 1956; The Korean War, 1967. Add: 918 W. Waldheim Rd., Fox Chapel, Pittsburgh, Pa. 15215, U.S.A.

RIDING, Laura. (Mrs. Schuyler B. Jackson). Has also written as Laura Riding Gottschalk; now writes as Laura (Riding) Jackson. American, b. 1901. Novels/Short stories, Poetry, Language/Linguistics, Literature. *Publs:* (as Laura Riding Gottschalk) The Close Chaplet, 1926; Voltaire: A Biographical Fantasy, 1927; (with Robert Graves) A Survey of Modernist Poetry, 1927; Love as Love, Death as Death, 1928; (with Robert Graves) A Pamphlet Against Anthologies (in U.S. as Against Anthologies), 1928; Contemporaries and Snobs (criticism), 1928; Anarchism Is Not Enough (criticism and essays), 1928; Poems: A Joking Word, 1930; Twenty Poems Less, 1930; Though Gently, 1930; Experts Are Puzzled (short stories), 1930; Four Unposted Letters to Catherine (for children), 1930; Laura and Francisca: A Poem, 1931; The Life of the Dead, 1933; Poet: A Lying Word, 1933; (ed.) Everybody's Letters, 1933; Americans, 1934; (with G. Ellidge) 14A (story), 1934; Progress of Stories (collection), 1935, expanded ed. 1981; (contrib. ed.) Epilogue I, II and III, 1935, 1936, 1937; (trans. with Robert Graves) Almost Forgotten Germany, by Georg Schwarz, 1936; (as Madeleine Vara) Convalescent Conversations (prose), 1936; A Trojan Ending (novel), 1937, 1984; Collected Poems, 1938, expanded ed. 1980; The World and Ourselves (on world affairs), 1938; Lives of Wives (historical stories), 1939, 1988; Selected Poems: In Five Sets, 1970; The Telling (a personal evangel, with commentary), 1972; Description of Life (story), 1980; Communications of Broad Reference, 1983. Add: Box 35, Wabasso, Fla. 32970, U.S.A.

RIDLER, Anne (Barbara). British, b. 1912. Plays/Screenplays, Poetry, Libretti. Member of the Editorial Dept., Faber and Faber, publrs., London, 1935–40. *Publs:* (ed.) Shakespeare Criticism 1919-1935, 1936; Poems, 1939; A Dream Observed and Other Poems, 1941; (ed.) The Little Book of Modern Verse, 1941; The Nine Bright Shiners, 1943; Cain, 1943; The Shadow Factory, 1945; Henry Bly and Other Plays, 1950; The Golden Bird and Other Poems, 1951; (ed.) The Faber Book of Modern Verse, rev. ed. 1951; The Trial of Thomas Cranmer, 1956; (ed.) The Image of the City and Other Essays, by C. Williams, 1958; A Matter of Life and Death, 1959; Selected Poems, 1961; Who Is My Neighbour?, and How Bitter the Bread, 1963; (ed.) Shakespeare Criticism 1935-1960, 1963; (ed.) Poems and Some Letters, by J. Thomson, 1963; (ed.) Thomas Traherne: Poems, Centuries and Three Thanksgivings, 1966; (ed. with C. Bradby) Best Stories of Church and Clergy, 1966; Olive Willis and Downe House: An Adventure in Education, 1967; The Jesse Tree: A Masque in Verse, 1972; Some Time After and Other Poems, 1972; (trans.) L'Orfeo, by Monteverdi, 1975; (trans.) L'Eritrea, by Cavalli, 1976; Italian Prospect: Six Poems, 1976; (ed.) Selected Poems of George Darley, 1979; The Lambton Worm (libretto), 1979; Dies Natalis (verse), 1980; (ed.) The Poems of William Austin, 1984; A Victorian Family Postbag, 1988. Add: 14 Stanley Rd., Oxford, England.

RIDLEY, Anthony. British, b. 1933. History, Sciences (general), Transaportation. Principal Lectr., Middlesex Polytechnic, London. Asst. Master, Erith Grammar Sch., Kent, 1959–62. *Publs:* An Illustrated History of Transport, 1969; Living in Cities, 1971; (with D. Williams) Simple Experiments in Textile Science, 1974; At Home, 1976; Nuffield Home Economics: The Basic Course, Fibres and Fabrics Section, 1982. Add: 12 Hillfield Park, Winchmore Hill, London N21, England.

RIDLEY, Jasper (Godwin). British, b. 1920. History, Biography. *Publs:* Nicholas Ridley, 1957; Law of Carriage of Goods, 1957; Thomas Cranmer, 1962; John Knox, 1968; Lord Palmerston, 1970; Mary Tudor, 1973; Garibaldi, 1974; The Roundheads, 1976; Napoleon III and Eugenie, 1979; The History of England, 1981; The Statesman and the Fanatic: Cardinal Wolsey and Sir Thomas More, 1982; Henry VIII, 1984; Elizabeth I, 1987; The Tudor Age, 1988. Add: 6 Oakdale Rd., Tunbridge Wells, Kent, England.

RIDOUT, Ronald. British, b. 1916. Children's non-fiction, Language/Linguistics, Recreation/Leisure/Hobbies. Publisher's Rep., Ginn and Co. Ltd., London, 1946–50. *Publs:* English Today, 5 vols., 1948; English Workbooks, 10 vols., 1950; Self-Help English, 5 vols., 1952; Reading to Some Purpose, 7 vols., 1953; Wide Horizon Readers, 5 vols., 1953; English for Africans, 3 vols., 1954; Word Perfect, 10 vols., 1957; (with McGregor) English for Australian Schools, 5 vols., 1957; (with R. Ainsworth) Look Ahead Readers, 32 vols., 1958; Carnatic English Course, 7 vols., 1959; International English, 6 vols., 1960; Better English, 6 vols., 1961; (with N.K. Vaniasingham) English Today for South East Asia, 1962; Transition English, 2 vols., 1962; (with P. Townsend) This Is Life, 1963; (with L.H. Christie) The Facts of English, 1963, 1964; New English Workbooks, 10 vols., 1963; (with R. Ainsworth) Books for Me to Read, 24 vols., 1964; (with J. Gunn) Self-Help English for Australia, 5 vols., 1964; (with P. Sherlock) Self-Help English for the Caribbean, 5 vols., 1964; World-Wide English, 15 vols., 1965; English Now, 5 vols., 1966; (with E. Jones) Adjustments, 1966; English Workbooks for the Caribbean, 1966; (with P. Clements) Ahmed and Rehan Workbooks, 7 vols., 1966; Structural English Workbooks, 8 vols., 1967; (with C. Witting) English Proverbs Explained, 1967; (with S. Mason) Modern English Structures, 4 vols., 1968; English for Schools and Colleges in West Africa, 11 vols., 1968; Books for Me to Write In, 6 vols., 1968; (with M. Vodden) English for India, 10 vols., 1971; (with W. Clarke) Reference Book of English, 1971; Books for Me to Count In, 6 vols., 1971; (with M. Holt) Now I Can Read, 4 vols., 1971; (with V. Moll) In English, Please, 7 vols., 1971; (with T. Creed) Guided Conversations, 2 vols., 1971; (with M. Holt) The

Big Book of Puzzles, 2 vols., 1971; (with D. Faulds) Mastering English, 9 vols., 1972; Fun with Words, 3 vols., 1972; Books for Me to Begin In, 6 vols., 1972; The Facts of English, 1972; (with A. Hern) Word Puzzles, 1973; Dragon Puzzle Books, 6 vols., 1975; All Round English, 9 vols., 1975; Write Now, 1975; Puzzle It out, 5 vols., 1975; Evans Graded Readers, 2 vols., 1976; Evans Graded Verse, 5 vols., 1977; Just the Word, 6 vols., 1978; My Learning to Write Books, 6 vols., 1978; Say It in English, 11 vols., 1978; Macmillan Modern Primary English for Hong Kong, 30 vols., 1979; Nationwide English for Nigeria, 18 vols., 1979; The Pan Spelling Dictionary, 1980; The Nelson ELT Pocket Dictionary, 1980; Positive English Workbooks, 4 vols., 1980; My Dictionary, 6 vols., 1980; Basic Skills in English, 1981; Openings in English, 5 vols., 1981; Ann's Picture, 1982; Where Is Konky?, 1982; Stories in English, 1982; Superbook 1-6, 1983; Examining English, 1 & 2, 1983; Ronald Ridout's Children's Dictionary, 1983; Please Tick, 1983; Your English, 8 vols., 1984; Clever Crosswords, 4 vols., 1984; Now I Can Write, 10 vols., 1985; Now I Can Spell, 10 vols., 1985; Ronald Ridout's Puzzle Box, 4 vols., 1985; Sierra Leone Primary English 1-6, 1985; A-Z in English, 1986; Getting On with Spelling, 1986; Getting On with Writing, 1986; Methuen's Activity Dictionary, 1987; Match Them, 1988. Add: 6 Bryanston Sq., London W1, England.

RIEFE, Alan. Also writes historical romance novels as Barbara Riefe. American, b. 1925. Mystery/Crime/Suspense, Historical/Romance/Gothic, Westerns, Recreation/Leisure/Hobbies. Freelance writer. *Publs:* Tales of Horror (short stories), 1965; Vip's Illustrated Woman Driver's Manual, 1966; (with others) Am I Your President? (non-fiction), 1972; (ed. with Dick Harrington) Sanford and Son (non-fiction), 1973; suspense novels—The Lady Killers, 1975; The Conspirators, 1975; The Black Widower, 1975; The Silver Puma, 1975; The Bullet-Proof Man, 1975; The Killer with the Golden Touch, 1975; Tyger at Bay, 1976; Tyger by the Tail, 1976; The Smile on the Face of the Tyger, 1976; Tyger and the Lady, 1976; Hold that Tyger, 1976; Tyger, Tyger, Burning Out, 1976; historical romance novels (as Barbara Riefe)—Barringer House, 1976; Rowleston, 1976; Auldearn House, 1976; This Ravaged Heart, 1977, Far Beyond Desire, 1978; Fire and Flesh, 1978 (trilogy); Tempt Not This Flesh, 1979; Blackfire, 1980; So Wicked the Heart, 1980; Olivia, 1981; Wild Fire, 1981; Julia, 1981; Lucretia, 1981; Wicked Fire, 1983; This Proud Love, 1986; An Extraordinary Woman, 1986; westerns—Fortunes West series, Tucson, 1988, Cheyenne, 1988, San Francisco, 1989, and Salt Lake City, 1989. Add: c/o Knox Burger Assocs., 39 Washington Sq. S., New York, N.Y. 10012, U.S.A.

RIEFE, Barbara. *See* **RIEFE,** Alan.

RIEFF, Philip. American, b. 1922. Psychology, Sociology. Prof. of Sociology, Univ. of Pennsylvania, Philadelphia, since 1961. Contributing Ed., Harper and Row, NYC, since 1969. Teaching Fellow, 1946, and Instr., 1947–52, Univ. of Chicago; Asst. Prof., Brandeis Univ., Waltham, Mass., 1952–58; Chief Editorial Consultant, Beacon Press, Boston, 1952–58; Fellow, Center for Advanced Study in the Behavioral Sciences, Palo Alto, Calif., 1957–58; Assoc. Prof., Univ. of California, Berkeley, 1958–61. *Publs:* The Mind of the Moralist, 1959, 3rd ed. 1979; (ed.) The Collected Papers of Sigmund Freud, 1963; The Triumph of the Therapeutic: Uses of Faith after Freud, 1966; (compiler) On Intellectuals: Theoretical Studies, Case Studies, 1969; Fellow Teachers, 1973. Add: Dept. of Sociology, Univ. of Pennsylvania, Philadelphia, Pa. 19174, U.S.A.

RIEHL, Herbert. American, b. 1915. Meteorology/Atmospheric sciences. Sr. Scientist, National Center for Atmospheric Research, and Cooperative Inst. for Research in the Environmental Sciences, Univ. of Colorado, Boulder, since 1976. Teacher at the Univ. of Chicago, 1942–60, Colorado State Univ., 1960–72, and Freie Universitaet, Berlin, 1972–76. *Publs:* Tropical Meteorology, 1954; Introduction to the Atmosphere, 1965, 3rd ed. 1978; Climate and Weather in the Tropics, 1979. Add: 4390 Caddo Parkway, Boulder, Colo. 80303, U.S.A.

RIESMAN, David. American, b. 1909. Sociology. Henry Ford II Prof. of Social Sciences, Harvard Univ., Cambridge, since 1958. Law Clerk to Justice Brandeis, U.S. Supreme Court, Washington, 1935–36; member of the law firm of Lyne, Woodworth, and Evarts, Boston, 1936–37; Prof. of Law, Univ. of Buffalo, N.Y., 1937–41; Deputy Asst. District Attorney, New York County, 1942–43; Asst. Treas., Sperry Gyroscope Co., Lake Success, N.Y., 1943–46; Prof. of Social Sciences, Univ. of Chicago, 1946–58. *Publs:* The Lonely Crowd: A Study of the Changing American Character, 1950; Faces in the Crowd, 1952; Thorstein Veblen, 1953; Individualism Reconsidered and Other Essays, 1954; Constraint and Variety in American Education, 1956; Abundance for What and Other

Essays, 1963; Conversations in Japan: Modernization, Politics and Culture, 1967; The Academic Revolution, 1968; Academic Values and Mass Education, 1970; (ed.) Academic Transformation, 1973; (with S.M. Lipset) Education and Politics at Harvard, 1975; The Perpetual Dream, 1978; On Higher Education, 1980. Add: Harvard Univ., Cambridge, Mass. 02138, U.S.A.

RIFKIN, Jeremy. American, b. 1945. Economics, Environmental issues. Head, Foundn. on Economic Trends, since 1977. Founded People's Bicentennial Commn., Washington, D.C., 1971; Dir. with Randy Barber, People's Business Commn., 1976–77. *Publs:* How to Commit Revolution American Style, 1972; Own Your Own Job, 1977; (with Ted Howard) Who Should Play God?, 1977; (with Randy Barber) The North Will Rise Again: Pensions, Politics, and Power in the 1980s, 1978; (with Ted Howard) The Emerging Order: God in the Age of Scarcity, 1979; (with Ted Howard) Entropy, 1980; (with Nicanor Perlas) Algeny, 1983; Declaration of a Heretic, 1985; Time Wars: The Primary Conflict in Human History, 1987. Add: c/o Foundation on Economic Trends, Room 630, 1130 17th St. N.W., Washington, D.C. 20036, U.S.A.

RIFKIN, Shepard. Has also written as Jake Logan and Dale Michaels. American, b. 1918. Mystery/Crime/Suspense, Westerns/Adventure. *Publs:* Texas, Blood Red, 1956; Desire Island, 1960; What Ship? Where Bound?, 1961; Atlantic First, 1961; (as Dale Michaels) The Warring Breed, 1962; King Fisher's Road, 1963; (ed.) The Savage Years, 1967; Ladyfingers, 1969; The Murderer Vine, 1970; McQuaid, 1974; (as Jake Logan) Across the Rio Grande, 1975; (as Jake Logan) Slocum's Woman, 1976; The Snow Rattlers, 1977; McQuaid in August, 1979; 12 pseudonymous western novels, 1981–85. Add: 105 Charles St., New York, N.Y. 10014, U.S.A.

RIGGS, Robert E(dwon). American, b. 1927. International relations/Current affairs, Law, Politics/Government. Prof. of Law, Brigham Young Univ. Law School, since 1975. Instr. to Asst. Prof. of Political Science, Brigham Young Univ., Provo, Utah, 1955–60; Rockefeller Research Fellow i Intnl. Org., Columbia Univ., NYC, 1957–58; Research Specialist, Bureau of Business and Public Research, Univ. of Arizona, Tucson, 1960–63; private practice of law, 1963–64; Assoc. Prof., 1964–68, and Prof., 1968–75, Univ. of Minnesota, Minneapolis. *Publs:* Laws affecting Planning: Arizona, Pima County, 1952; Politics in the United Nations: A Study of United States Influence in the General Assembly, 1958; The Movement for Administrative Reorganization in Arizona, 1961; Arizona State Personnel Policies, 1962; Vox Populi: The Battle of 103, 1964; (with J.C. Plano) Forging World Order: The Politics of International Organization, 1967; US/UN: Foreign Policy and International Organization, 1971; (with J.C. Plano) Dictionary of Political Analysis, 1973, (with J.C. Plano and Helenan Robin), 1982; (with J.C. Plano and others) Political Science Dictionary, 1973; (with I.J. Mykletun) Beyond Functionalism, 1979; (with J.C. Plano) The United Nations, 1988. Add: 1158 S. 350 W., Orem, Utah 84057, U.S.A.

RIGONI, Orlando (Joseph). Also writes as Leslie Ames, James Wesley, and Carolyn Bell. American, b. 1917. Novels/Short stories, Historical/Romance/Gothic, Westerns/Adventure. *Publs:* Brand of the Bow; (as Leslie Ames) Bride of Donnebrook; Twisted Trails; Ambuscade; Pikabo Stage; House of Haddon; Headstone for a Trailboss; (as James Wesley) Texas Justice; (as Leslie Ames) Hill of Ashes; (as Leslie Ames) Castle on the Island; Sixgun Song; Showdown at Skeleton Flat; Massacre Ranch; A Nickle's Worth of Lead; (as Carolyn Bell) House of Clay; The Guns of Folly; A Close Shave at Pozo; Bullet Breed; Hunger Range; Drover Man; (as Leslie Ames) The Hungry Sea; (as Leslie Ames) The Hidden Chapel; (as James Wesley) Showdown at Mesa Bend; (as Leslie Ames) The Phantom Bride; (as Leslie Ames) Wind over the Citadel; The Big Brand; Muskeg Marshal; (as Leslie Ames) King's Castle; (as James Wesley) Maverick Marshal; Brand X; (as Leslie Ames) The Angry Wind; (as James Wesley) Four Graves to Jericho; (as James Wesley) Showdown at the MB Ranch; (as James Wesley) Diamond Range; (as James Wesley) Trail to Boothill; (as James Wesley) Bitterroot Showdown, 1985. Add: 2900 Dogwood Ave., Morro Bay, Calif. 93442, U.S.A.

RILEY, Carroll L. American, b. 1923. Anthropology/Ethnology, Archaeology/Antiquities, History. Research Assoc., Lab of Anthropology, Museum of New Mexico, since 1987; Distinguished Prof. of Anthropology, 1986–87, now Emeritus, and Curator of the Univ. Museum since 1978, Southern Illinois Univ., Carbondale (Curator of Physical Anthropology Museum, 1955–61; Asst. Prof., 1955–60; Assoc. Prof., 1960–67; Prof., 1967–86; Dir., 1972–74, Assoc. Dir., 1974–77, Univ. Museum; and Chmn. of Dept., 1979–82). Consultant, Lands Div., U.S. Dept. of Justice, 1952–70; Instr. in Anthropology, Univ. of Colorado, Boulder, 1953–54;

Asst. Prof. of Anthropology, Univ. of North Carolina, Chapel Hill, 1954–55. *Publs:* (co-ed.) Southwestern Journals of Adolph F. Bandelier 1880-1882, 1966, 1883-84, 1970, 1885-88, 1975 and 1889-92, 1984; (co-ed.) American Historical Anthropology, 1967; The Origins of Civilization, 1969, 1972; (co-ed.) Man Across the Sea, 1971; (co-ed.) The North Mexican Frontier, 1971; (co-author) Coras, Huicholes y Tepehuanes, 1972; Historical and Cultural Dictionary of Saudi Arabia, 1972; (co-ed.) The Classic Southwest, 1973; (co-ed.) The Mesoamerican Southwest, 1974; (co-ed.) Across the Chichimec Sea, 1978; (co-ed.) New Frontiers in the Archaeology and Ethno-history of the Greater Southwest, 1980; The Frontier People, 1982, 1987. Add: 1106 6th St., Las Vegas, N.M. 87701, U.S.A.

RILEY, Dick. (Richard Anthony Riley). American, b. 1946. Novels/Short stories. Former reporter for Associated Press, and the New York Post, NYC. *Publs:* (with T. Harris and S. Maull) Black Sunday, 1975; Rite of Expiation, 1976; (ed.) Critical Encounters: Writers and Themes in Science Fiction, 1978; (ed. with Pam McAllister) The Bedside Bathtub and Armchair Companion to Agatha Christie, 1979; Middleman Out (play), 1980; (ed. With Pam McAllister) The New Bedside, Bathtub and Armchair Guide to Agatha Christie, 1986. Add: c/o Ungar Publishing Co., 370 Lexington Ave., New York, N.Y. 10017, U.S.A.

RILEY, Edward Calverley. British, b. 1923. Literature. Prof. of Hispanic Studies, Univ. of Edinburgh, since 1970. Fellow, 1957–70, Reader in Spanish, 1957–65, and Prof., 1965–70, Trinity Coll., Dublin. *Publs:* Cervantes's Theory of the Novel, 1962; (ed. and contrib.) Suma Cervantina, 1973; Don Quixote, 1986. Add: Dept. of Hispanic Studies, Univ. of Edinburgh, David Hume Tower, George Sq., Edinburgh EH8 9JX, Scotland.

RILEY, Madeleine (Veronica). British, b. 1933. Novels/Short stories. *Publs:* A Spot Bigger Than God, 1966; Brought to Bed, 1968; Diary for Two, 1969; An Ideal Friend, 1977. Add: The Manor House, Wolston, Warwicks., England.

RIMLINGER, Gaston V. American, b. 1926. Economics. Hargrove Prof. of Economics, Rice Univ., Houston, since 1972 (Prof., 1960–69). Asst. Prof., Princeton Univ., New Jersey, 1955–60; Economic Prog. Adviser, Ford Foundn. in West Africa, 1969–72. *Publs:* Welfare Policy and Industrialization in Europe, America, and Russia, 1971; (with Carolyn Stremlau) Indigenisation and Management Development in Nigeria, 1974; Labor Markets, Wages and Unemployment, 1982. Add: Dept. of Economics, Rice Univ., Houston, Tex. 77001, U.S.A.

RIMMINGTON, Gerald Thorneycroft. British, b. 1930. Social sciences. Vicar of Cosby and Dir. of Continuing Ministerial Education, Diocese of Leicester, since 1986. District Education Officer, Ministry of Education, Nyasaland, 1961–63; Asst. Prof. of Education, 1963–65, and Assoc. Prof. 1965–67, Acadia Univ., Wolfville, N.S.; Prof. of Education and Dean, Faculty of Education, Brandon Univ., Manitoba 1967–73; Prof. of Education, Mt. Allison Univ., N.B., 1973–81; Rector of Paston, Diocese of Peterborough, 1981–86. *Publs:* (with Pike) Malawi: A Geographical Study, 1965; (with Logan) Social Studies: A Creative Direction, 1969; (with Traill and Logan) Teaching the Social Sciences, 1972; Education, Politics and Society in Leicester 1833-1903, 1978; The Comprehensive School Issue in Leicester 1945-74, 1984; Your Assembly in School 1984, 1988; The Education of Maladjusted Children in Leicester 1892-1974, 1985; Your 100 Prayers for School and Church, 1986; The Rise and Fall of Elected School Boards in England, 1986. Add: Cosby Vicarage, Leicester LE9 5UU, England.

RING, Douglas. *See* **PRATHER,** Richard Scott.

RINGENBERG, Lawrence Albert. American, b. 1915. Mathematics/Statistics. Prof. Emeritus of Mathematics since 1980, and Dean Emeritus of the Coll. of Arts and Sciences since 1980, Eastern Illinois Univ., Charleston (Head, Mathematics Dept., 1947–67; Prof., 1947–80; Dean of Coll. of Arts and Sciences, 1961–80). *Publs:* Portrait of 2, 1956; Informal Geometry, 1967; College Geometry, 1968; (with R. Presser) Geometry, 1971;. Add: Coll. of Arts and Sciences, Eastern Illinois Univ., Charleston, Ill. 61920, U.S.A.

RINGER, Barbara Alice. American, b. 1925. Law. Register of Copyrights, Copyright Office, Library of Congress, Washington, D.C., since 1973 (Asst. Register of Copyrights for Examining, 1963–65; Asst. Register of Copyrights, 1965–72). Adjunct Prof. of Law, Georgetown Univ., Washington, 1962–72; Dir., Copyright Div. of Unesco, Paris, 1972–73. *Publs:* Bibliography of Design Protection, 1955; Renewal of

Copyright, 1960; Unauthorized Duplication of Sound Recordings, 1960; Notice of Copyright, 1960; (with P. Gitlin) Copyrights, rev. ed. 1965; The Role of the U.S. in International Copyright, 1968; The Demonology of Copyright, 1974; Copyright and the Future Authorship, 1976; First Thoughts on the Copyright Act of 1976, 1977; The Unfinished Business of Copyright Revision, 1977; Copyright Law, 3 vols., 1983. Add: Copyright Office, Library of Congress, Washington, D.C. 20559, U.S.A.

RINGER, Robert J. American, b. 1938. Business/Trade/Industry, Social commentary/phenomena. *Publs:* Winning Through Intimidation, 1974; Looking Out for Number One, 1977; Restoring the American Dream, 1979. Add: c/o Harper and Row Inc., 10 E. 53rd St., New York, N.Y. 10022, U.S.A.

RINGOLD, Clay. *See* **HOGAN,** Ray.

RINHART, Floyd (Lincoln). American, b. 1915. Art, History, Photography. Consultant, American Pioneer Photography, Ohio State Univ., Columbia, since 1973. Lumber Sales Exec., South Florida, 1949–65. *Publs:* all with Marion Rinhart—American Daguerreian Art, 1967; American Miniature Case Art, 1969; America's Affluent Age, 1971; America's Centennial Celebration, 1976; Summertime, 1978; The American Daguerreotype, 1981; Victorian Florida, 1986. Add: c/o Peachtree Publications, Ltd., 494 Armour Circle, N.E., Atlanta, Ga. 30324, U.S.A.

RINHART, Marion (Hutchinson). American, b. 1916. Art, History, Photography. Consultant, American Pioneer Photography, Ohio State Univ., Columbus, since 1973. *Publs:* all with Floyd Rinhart—American Daguerreian Art, 1967; American Miniature Case Art, 1969; America's effluent Age, 1971; America's Centennial Celebration, 1976; Summertime, 1978; The America Daguerreotype, 1981; Victorian Florida, 1986. Add: c/o Peachtree Publications, Ltd., 494 Armour Circle, N.E., Atlanta, Ga. 30324, U.S.A.

RIORDAN, James (William). British, b. 1936. Children's fiction, Area Studies, Dance, International relations/Current affairs, Sports/Physical education/Keeping fit. Prof. of Russian Studies, Univ. of Surrey, Guildford. Vice-Pres. Intnl. Sports History Assn., and of the Soc. for Cultural Relations with the U.S.S.R. Sr. Translator, Progress Publishers, Moscow, 1962–65; Lectr. in Liberal Studies, Portsmouth Polytechnic, 1965–69. *Publs:* Mistress of the Copper Mountain (folk tales), 1975; Tales from Central Russia (folk tales), 1977; Sport in Soviet Society, 1977; Tales from Tartary (folk tales), 1978; (ed.) Sport under Communism, 1978; (with E. Colwell) Little Grey Neck, 1978; Sleeping Beauty, 1979; Beauty and the Beast, 1979; Soviet Sport: Background to the Olympics, 1980; A World of Folk Tales Fairy Tales 2 vols., 1981–82; Tales of King Arthur, 1982; Woman in the Moon, 1984; Tales From the Ballet, 1985; The Soviet Union: Land and Peoples, 1986; Folktales of the British Isles, 1987; Eastern Europe: Land and Peoples, 1987; Soviet Education: The Gifted and the Handicapped, 1988; Pinocchio, 1988; Soviet Youth Culture, 1989; Snowmaiden, 1989. Add: c/o Century Hutchinson, 62-65 Chandos Pl., London WC2N 4NW, England.

RIPLEY, Jack. *See* **WAINWRIGHT,** John.

RIPLEY, Randall Butler. American, b. 1938. Politics/Government, Public/Social administration. Prof. and Chmn. of Political Science Dept., Ohio State Univ., Columbus, since 1969 (Assoc. Prof., 1967–69). Member of the Governmental Studies Staff, Brookings Inst., Washington, D.C., 1963–67. *Publs:* (ed.) Public Policies and Their Politics, 1966; Party Leaders in the House of Representatives, 1967; Majority Party Leadership in Congress, 1969; Power in the Senate, 1969; The Politics of Economic and Human Resource Development, 1972; (ed. with T.J. Lowi) Legislative Politics U.S.A., 4th ed., 1978; American National Government and Public Policy, 1974; Congress, 1975, 4th ed. 1988; (ed. with G.A. Franklin) Policy-Making in the Federal Executive Branch, 1975; (with G.A. Franklin) Congress, The Bureaucracy, and Public Policy, 1976, 4th ed. 1987; (ed. with G.A. Franklin) National Government and Policy in the United States, 1977; (co-author) A More Perfect Union, 1979, 4th ed. 1989; (with G.A. Franklin) Policy Implementation and Bureaucracy, 1982, 1986; (with G.A. Franklin) CETA: Politics and Policy 1973-1982, 1984; Policy Analysis in Political Science, 1985; (with E.E. Slotnick) Readings in American Government and Politics, 1988. Add: Dept. of Political Science, Ohio State Univ., Columbus, Ohio 43210, U.S.A.

RIPPLEY, La Vern J. American, b. 1935. History, Language/Linguistics, Literature. Prof. of German, St. Olaf Coll., Northfield, Minn. Co-

Ed., Yearbook of German American Studies, Lawrence, Kans., since 1981. *Publs:* The Columbus, Ohio Germans, 1968; Of German Ways, 1970; Excursion Through America, 1973; Russian-German Settlements in the United States, 1974; The German-Americans, 1976; Research Possibilities in the German-American Field, 1980; Immigrant Wisconsin, 1985. Add: 909 Ivanhoe Dr., Northfield, Minn. 55057, U.S.A.

RISCHIN, Moses. American, b. 1925. History, Race relations, Biography. Prof. of History, San Francisco State Univ., since 1964. Ed., American Minority History series, Northern Illinois Univ. Press, since 1973; Member, Bd. of Eds., Journal of American Ethnic History, since 1980. Lectr. in History, Univ. of California at Los Angeles, 1962–64. Pres., Immigration History Soc., 1976–79. *Publs:* An Inventory of American Jewish History, 1954; Our Own Kind; Voting by Race, Creed or National Origin, 1960; The Promised City: New York's Jews 1870-1914, 1962, 3rd ed. 1977; (ed.) The American Gospel of Success: Individualism and Beyond, 1965, 1974; (ed.) The Spirit of the Ghetto, by Hutchins Hapgood, 1967; (ed. with S.J. Hurwitz) A Liberal Between Two Worlds: Essays of Solomon F. Bloom, 1968; (ed.) Concentration Camps, U.S.A., 1971; (ed.) Bonds of Loyalty, 1974; (ed.) The Abolitionists, 1974; (ed.) Modern Jewish Experience series, 59 vols., 1975; (ed.) First Majority, Last Minority, 1976; (ed.) Immigration and the American Tradition, 1976; The Jews of the West: The Metropolitan Years, 1979; The Jews and Pluralism: Toward an American Freedom Symphony, 1980; Grandma Never Lived in America: The New Journalism of Abraham Cahan, 1985; (ed.) Like All the Nations? The Life and Legacy of Judah L. Magnes, 1987; (ed.) The Jews of North America, 1987. Add: 350 Arballo Dr., San Francisco, Calif. 94132, U.S.A.

RISTE, Olav. Norwegian, b. 1933. History. Dir., Inst. for Defence Studies, National Defence Coll., since 1980 (with Defence Historical Office, 1964–80); Prof. of History, Univ. of Bergen, since 1980. *Publs:* The Neutral Ally: Norway's Relations with Belligerent Powers in the First World War, 1965; (ed. and author with J. Andenaes and M. Skodvin) Norway and the Second World War, 1966, 1974; (with B. Nokleby) Norway in World War II: The Resistance Movement, 1970, 1973; London-regjeringa: Norge i krigsalliansen, 1940–1945, 2 vols., 1973–79; (ed.) Western Security: The Formative Years, 1985; Utefront, 1987. Add: Husarveien 18, 1362 Billingstad, Norway.

RISTOW, Walter W. American, b. 1908. Librarianship. U.S. Editorial Advisor, The Map Collector intnl. quarterly. Chief Geography and Map Div., Library of Congress, Washington, D.C., 1968–78, now retired (Asst. Chief, and Assoc. Chief, 1946–67). Head, Map Room, and Chief Map Div., New York Public Library, NYC, 1937–46. *Publs:* Aviation Cartography, 1956, 1960; Marketing Maps of the United States, 1958; (with C.E. LeGear) Guide to Historical Cartography, 1960; (ed.) Survery of the Roads of the United States of America 1789, 1961; Three-Dimensional Maps, 1964; (compiler and co-author) A La Carte, 1972; Guide to the History of Cartography, 1973; Maps for an Emerging Nation: Commercial Cartography in Nineteenth Century America, 1977; (with R.A. Skelton) Nautical Charts on Velum in the Library of Congress, 1977; The Emergence of Maps in Libraries, 1980; American Maps and Mapmakers, 1985. Add: 10450 Lottsford Rd., No. 4115, Mitchellville, Md. 20716, U.S.A.

RIVENBURGH, Viola K. American, b. 1897. Poetry, History, Mythology /Folklore, Writing/Journalism, Biography. Teacher of literature and creative writing, City of Seattle Education Dept., since 1970; Prof. of English Emeritus, Univ. of Washington, Seattle, since 1967 (joined faculty, 1942). Prof. of English, Univ. of Hawaii, Honolulu, 1924–26. *Publs:* Princess Kaiulani, 1960; Words at Work, 1965; Hawaii: From Monarch to Annexation—50th State, 1975; Aeolus Sings (verse), 1978; Tales of the Menehune, The Little Pixie Folk of Hawaii 1980; Adventure in Early Alaska, 1985; Web World (verse), 1987. Add: 500 W. Olympic Pl., Seattle, Wash. 98119, U.S.A.

RIVERS, Joan. Pseud. for Joan Sandra Molinsky. American, b. 1933. Plays/Screenplays, Autobiography/Memoirs, Humor/Satire. Comedienne, writer, actress, and talk show hostess. National Chairperson, Cystic Fibrosis Foundn., since 1982. Member, Second City Improvisational Theatre Co., Chicago, 1961–62; syndicated columnist, Chicago Tribune, 1973–76; Hostess, syndicated talk shows: "That show," 1969–71, "The Tonight Show," 1983–86, and "The Late Show Starring Joan Rivers," 1986–87. *Publs:* (with Lester Colodny and Edgar Rosenberg) Fun City: A Comedy in Two Acts, 1970; The Girl Most Likely To (television screenplay), 1973; Having a Baby Can Be a Scream, 1974; (with Jay Redack) Rabbit Test (screenplay), 1978; The Life and Hard Times of Heidi Abromowitz: A Totally Unauthorized Biography, 1984; (with Richard

Meryman) Enter Talking (autobiography), 1986. Add. c/o Bill Sammeth Org., 9200 Sunset Blvd., Suite 1001, Los Angeles, Calif. 90069, U.S.A.

RIVET, Albert Lionel Frederick. British, b. 1915. Archaeology/Antiquities, Classics. Prof. of Roman Provincial Studies, Univ. of Keele, 1974–81, now Emeritus (Lectr. in Classics, 1964–67; Reader in Romano-British Studies, 1967–74). Asst. Archaeology Officer, Ordnance Survey, 1951–64. Pres., Soc. for the Promotion of Roman Studies, 1977–80; Member, Royal Commn. on Historical Monuments (England), 1979–85. Chmn., British Academy's Tabula Imperii Romani Cttee., 1981–86. *Publs:* Town and Country in Roman Britain, 1958, 1964; (ed.) The Iron Age in Northern Britain, 1966; (ed. and contrib.) The Roman Villa in Britain, 1969; (with C.C. Smith) The Place-Names of Roman Britain, 1979; (ed.) Consolidated Index of Britannica, I-X, 1983; (with S.S. and N.H.H. Sitwell) Tabula Imperii Romani, Sheet N30/030 (Britannia Septentrionalis), 1987; Gallia Narbonensis, 1988. Add: 7 Springpool, Univ. of Keele, Keele, Staffs. ST5 5BN, England.

RIVKIN, Ellis. American, b. 1918. History International relations/Current affairs, Theology/Religion. Adolph S. Ochs Prof. of Jewish History, Hebrew Union Coll./Jewish Inst. of Religion, Cincinnati, since 1965 (Asst. Prof., 1949–51; Assoc. Prof., 1951–53; Prof. of Jewish History, 1953–65). Pres., Globalist Research Foundn., since 1978. Instr. of Jewish History, Gratz Coll., Philadelphia, 1946–49. *Publs:* Leon da Modena and the Kol Sakhal, 1952; The Dynamics of Jewish History, 1970; The Shaping of Jewish History: A Radical New Interpretation, 1971; A Hidden Revolution: The Pharisee's Search for the Kingdom Within, 1978; What Crucified Jesus?: The Political Execution of a Charismatic, 1984. Add: c/o Hebrew Union Coll./Jewish Inst. of Religion, 3101 Clifton Ave., Cincinnati, Ohio 45220, U.S.A.

ROARK, Dallas M. American, b. 1931. Intellectual history, Philosophy, Theology/Religion. Prof. of Philosophy, Emporia State Univ., Kansas, since 1966. Pastor of Baptist churches in Bonaparte and West Branch, Iowa, 1955–60; Instr., 1960–63, Asst. Prof., 1963–65, and Assoc. Prof. of Religion, 1965–66, Wayland Baptist Coll., Plainview, Tex. *Publs:* (ed.) The Wayland Lectures, 1962; The Christian Faith, 1969; Dietrich Bonhoffer, 1972; Introduction to Philosophy, 1979. Add: c/o Baker Book House, P.O. Box 6287, 6030 E. Fulton, Grand Rapids, Mich. 49506, U.S.A.

ROAZEN, Paul. American, b. 1936. Politics/Government, Psychology. Prof. of Social and Political Science, York Univ., Toronto, since 1974 (Assoc. Prof., 1971–74). With Dept. of Govt., Harvard Univ., 1965–71. *Publs:* Freud: Political and Social Thought, 1968; Brother Animal: The Story of Freud and Tausk, 1969; (ed.) Sigmund Freud, 1973; Freud and His Followers, 1975; Erik H. Erikson: The Power and Limits of a Vision, 1976; Helene Deutsch: A Psychoanalyst's Life, 1985; (ed.) The Public Philosophy, by Walter Lippmann, 1989; Encountering Freud: The Politics and Histories of Psychoanalysis, 1989. Add: 31 Whitehall Rd.,Toronto, Ont. M4W 2C5, Canada.

ROBB, James Harding. New Zealander, b. 1920. Sociology. Prof. Emeritus of Sociology, Victoria Univ. of Wellington, since 1986 (Lectr. and Sr. Lectr., 1954–64; Assoc. Prof., 1965–66; Prof., 1966–86). Caseworker, Family Discussion Bureau, 1949–51; Research Worker., Tavistock Inst. of Human Relations, 1951–54. *Publs:* Working Class Anti-Semite, 1954; Family Discussion Bureau, 1949–51; Research Worker, Tavistock Inst. of (with Anthony Somerset) Report to Masterton, 1957; (with Margaret Carr) The City of Porirua, 1969; Life and Death of Official Social Research in New Zealand, 1987. Add: 9 Allen Terr., Tawa, New Zealand.

ROBBARDS, Karen. American, b. 1954. Novels/Short stories, Historical/ Romance. *Publs:* Island Flame, 1981; Sea Fire, 1982; Forbidden Love, 1983; Amanda Rose, 1984; To Love a Man, 1985; Dark Torment, 1985; Wild Orchids, 1986; Loving Julia, 1986; Some Kind of Hero, 1987; Night Magic, 1987. Add: c/o Shirley Burke, 370 E. 76th St., Suite B-704, New York, N.Y. 10021, U.S.A.

ROBBINS, Harold. American, b. 1912. Novels/Short stories. *Publs:* Never Love a Stranger, 1948; The Dream Merchants, 1949; A Stone for Danny Fisher, 1952; Never Leave Me, 1953; 79 Park Avenue, 1955; Stiletto, 1960; The Carpetbaggers, 1961; Where Love Has Gone, 1962; The Adventurers, 1966; The Inheritors, 1969; The Betsy, 1971; The Pirate, 1974; The Lonely Lady, 1976; Dreams Die First, 1977; Memories of Another Day, 1979; Goodbye Janette, 1981; Spellbinder, 1982; Descent from Xanadu, 1984; The Storyteller, 1985. Add: c/o Simon and Schuster, 1230 Ave. of the Americas, New York, N.Y. 10020, U.S.A.

ROBBINS, John Albert. American, b. 1914. Literature. Prof. Emeritus of English, Indiana Univ., Bloomington, since 1983 (Instr., 1946–50; Asst. Prof., 1950–55; Assoc. Prof., 1955–63; Prof., 1963–83). Ed., American Literary Scholarship, 1968–72, 1976, 1978, 1980, 1982, 1984–85, 1988, Duke Univ., Durham, N.C. *Publs:* (co-author) American Literary Manuscripts: A Checklist of Holdings in Academic, Historical and Public Libraries, Museums, and Authors' Homes in the United States, 1960, 1977; (ed.) EP to LU: Nine Letters Written to Louis Untermeyer by Ezra Pound, 1963; The Merrill Checklist of Edgar Allan Poe, 1969; An Interlude with Robert Frost, 1982. Add: Dept. of English, Indiana Univ., Bloomington, Ind. 47405, U.S.A.

ROBBINS, Kay. *See* **HOOPER,** Kay.

ROBBINS, Tom. American, b. 1936. Novels/Short stories. *Publs:* Guy Anderson, 1965; Another Roadside Attraction, 1971; Even Cowgirls Get the Blues, 1976; Still Life with Woodpecker, 1980; Jitterbug Perfume, 1984. Add: c/o Bantam, 666 Fifth Ave., New York, N.Y. 10019, U.S.A.

ROBENS OF WOLDINGHAM, Lord; Alfred Robens. British, b. 1910. Business/Trade/Industry, Engineering, Industrial relations, Autobiography/Memoirs/Personal. Chmn., Alfred Robens Assocs., since 1984. Labour Member of Parliament (U.K.) for Wansbeck Div. of Northumberland, 1945–50, and for Blyth, 1950–60: Parliamentary Private Secty. to the Minister of Transport, 1945–47; Parliamentary Secty. to the Minister of Fuel and Power, 1947–51; and Minister of Labour and National Service, 1951; Chmn., National Coal Bd., 1961–71; Chmn., Vickers Ltd., 1971–79. Chancellor, Univ. of Surrey, 1966–77. *Publs:* Engineering and Economic Progress, 1965; Industry and Government, 1970; Human Engineering, 1970; Ten Year Stint, 1972. Add: House of Lords, London SW1, England

ROBERT, Adrian. *See* **ST. JOHN,** Nicole.

ROBERT, Lionel. *See* **FANTHORPE,** R. Lionel.

ROBERTIELLO, Richard C. American, b. 1923. Psychiatry, Psychology, Sex. Practitioner of psychiatry and psychoanalysis, NYC, since 1947. Supervising Psychiatrist, Community Guidance Service, since 1956. Dir., Psychiatric Services, Long Island Consultation Center, 1953–78. *Publs:* Voyage from Lesbos, 1959; A Handbook of Emotional Illness and Treatment, 1961; (co-author) The Analyst's Role, 1963; Sexual Fulfillment and Self-Affirmation, 1964; Hold Them Very Tight, Then Let Them Go, 1974; (co-author) Big You—Little You, 1977; Your Own True Love, 1978; A Man in the Making, 1979; A Psychoanalyst's Quest, 1986; (co-author) 101 Common Therapeutic Blunders, 1987; (co-author) The WASP Mystique, 1987. Add: 49 E. 78th St., New York, N.Y. 10021, U.S.A.

ROBERTS, (Edward) Adam. British, b. 1940. International relations/Current affairs. Montague Burton Prof. of Intnl. Relations, Oxford Univ., since 1986, and Fellow of Balliol Coll. Asst. Ed., Peace News Ltd., 1962–65; Noel Buxton Fellow in Intnl. Relations, London Sch. of Economics, 1965–68; Lectr. in Intnl. Relations, London Sch. of Economics, 1968–81. *Publs:* (ed.) The Strategy of Civilian Defence: Non-Violent Resistance to Aggression, 1967; (with P. Windsor) Czechoslovakia 1968; Reform, Repression and Resistance, 1969; (trans. with A. Lieven) End of a War: Indochina 1954, by P. Devillers and J. Lacouture, 1969; Nations in Arms: The Theory and Practice of Territorial Defence, 1976, 1986; (with R. Guelff) Documents on the Laws of War, 1982, 1989; (with F. Newman and B. Joergensen) Academic Freedom Under Israeli Military Occupation, 1984; (with B. Kingsbury) United Nations, Divided World, 1988. Add: Balliol Coll., Oxford OX1 3BJ, England.

ROBERTS, Benjamin Charles. British, b. 1917. Industrial Relations, International relations/Current affairs. Prof. Emeritus, Univ. of London. Ed., British Journal of Industrial Relations, since 1963; Member, National Reference Tribunal of Coal Mining Industry, since 1970. Lectr., 1949–56, Reader, 1956–62, and Prof. of Industrial Relations, 1962–85, London Sch. of Economics. Pres., British Univs. Industrial Relations Assn., 1965–68, and Intnl. Industrial Relations Assn., 1967–73; Chmn., Economists' Bookshop, 1979–87. *Publs:* Trade Union Government and Administration in Great Britain, 1956; The Trades Union Congress 1868-1921, 1958; National Wages Policy in War and Peace, 1958; Unions in America, 1959; Trade Unions in a Free Society, 1959, 1962; (ed.) Industrial Relations, 1962, 3rd ed. 1968; Labour in the Tropical Territories of the Commonwealth, 1964; (with L. Greyfie de Bellecombe) Collective Bargaining in African Countries, 1967; (ed.) Industrial Relations: Contemporary Issues, 1968; (with J. Lovell) A Short History of the T.U.C.,

1968; (with R.D. Clarke and D.J. Fatchett) Workers Participation in Management in Britain, 1972; (with R. Loveridge and D. Gennard) Reluctant Militants: A Study of Industrial Technicians, 1972; (ed.) Towards Industrial Democracy, 1979; (with Hideaki Okomoto and George C. Lodge) Collective Bargaining and Employee Participation in Western Europe, North America and Japan, 1979; (ed.) Industrial Relations in Europe: Imperatives of Change, 1985. Add: London Sch. of Economics, Houghton St., Aldwych, London WC2A 2AE, England.

ROBERTS, Brian. British, b. 1930. History, Biography. Teacher of English and History, 1955–65. *Publs:* Ladies in the Veld, 1965; Cecil Rhodes and the Princess, 1969; Churchills in Africa, 1970; The Diamond Magnates, 1972; The Zulu Kings, 1974; Kimberley: Turbulent City, 1976; The Mad Bad Line: The Family of Lord Alfred Douglas, 1981; Randolph: A Study of Churchill's Son, 1984; Cecil Rhodes: Flawed Colossus, 1987. Add: North Knoll Cottage, 15 Bridge St., Frome BA11 1BB, England.

ROBERTS, Catherine. American, b. 1917. Philosophy, Sciences. Microbiologist, Carlsberg Lab., Copenhagen, 1946–61. *Publs:* The Scientific Conscience, 1967; Science, Animals, and Evolution, 1980. Add: 36 Tamalpais Rd., Berkeley, Calif. 94708, U.S.A.

ROBERTS, Chalmers (McGeagh). American, b. 1910. International relations/Current affairs. Columnist, Washington Post, since 1971 (Reporter, 1933–34; rejoined newspaper, 1949; Chief Diplomatic Reporter, 1959–71). Reporter, Pittsburgh Bureau, Associated Press, 1934–35, Toledo News-Bee, 1936–38, and Japan Times, Tokyo, 1938–39; Asst. Managing Ed., Washington Daily News, 1939–41; Sunday Ed., Washington Times-Herald, 1941; with the Office of War Information, London and Washington, 1941–43; with Life mag., 1946–47, and the Washington Star, 1947–49. *Publs:* Washington Past and Present, 1950; Can We Meet the Russians Half Way, 1958; The Nuclear Years: The Arms Race and Arms Control, 1945-70, 1970; First Rough Draft, 1973; The Washington Post: The First 100 Years, 1977. Add: 6699 MacArthur Blvd., Bethesda, Md. 20816, U.S.A.

ROBERTS, (Sir) Denys (Tudor Emil). British, b. 1923. Novels/Short stories, Humour/Satire. Chief Justice, Negara Brunei Darussalam, since 1979. Attorney-Gen., Gibraltar, 1960–62; Solicitor-Gen., 1962–66, Attorney-Gen., 1966–73, Chief Secty., 1973–78, and Chief Justice, 1979–88, Hongkong. *Publs:* Smuggler's Circuit, 1954; Beds and Roses, 1956; The Elwood Wager, 1958; The Bones of the Wajingas, 1960; How to Dispense with Lawyers, 1964; Doing Them Justice, 1987. Add: P.O. Box 338, Paphos, Cyprus.

ROBERTS, Derek Harry. British, b. 1931. Medicine/Health. Formerly, Hon. Lectr., Eastman Dental Hosp., Inst. of Dental Surgery, London. *Publs:* (with J. Sowray) Local Analgesia in Dentistry, 1970, 3rd ed. 1987; Fixed Bridge Prostheses, 1970, 1980; (ed. with F.J. Harty) Restorative Procedures for the Practicing Dentist, 1970; Precision Pendulum Clocks, 1986; British Skeleton Clocks, 1987. Add: 24 Shipbourne Rd.,Tonbr-idge, Kent TN10 3DN, England.

ROBERTS, Eric. British, b. 1914. Children's fiction, Plays/Screenplays, Natural history. Writer of syndicated daily column on the countryside since 1953. *Publs:* plays—Tremlett's Mole, 1949; Mrs. Griffin's Silver, 1950; Mr. Trotter's Animal Noises, 1955; The Magic Idol, 1955; Sky Adventure, 1956; The Mandarin's Cat, 1956; The Tunnel Escape, 1956; The Speaker in the House, 1957; Art and Sally Higgins, 1957; Whose Deal?, 1958; Ring for Higgins, 1959; Murder by Arrangement, 1962; Ring for Hartley, 1964; books—Adventure in the Sky, 1960; Oddities of Animal Life, 1962; Animal Ways and Means, 1963. Add: Gatesgarth, 53 Sywell Rd., Overstone, Northampton NN6 OAG, England.

ROBERTS, I.M. *See* ROBERTS, Irene.

ROBERTS, Iolo Francis. British, b. 1925. Chemistry, Education. Fellow, Univ. of Keele, since 1982 (Lectr., 1962–70; Sr. Lectr. in Education, 1970–82). *Publs:* (with L.M. Cantor) Further Education in England and Wales, 1969, 1972; Crystals and Their Structures, 1974; (with L.M. Cantor) Further Education Today: A Critical Review, 1979, 3rd ed. 1986. Add: Green Downs, 83 Whitmore Rd., Newcastle, Staffs., England.

ROBERTS, Irene. Also writes as Roberta Carr, Elizabeth Harle, I.M. Roberts, Ivor Roberts, Iris Rowland, and Irene Shaw. British, b. 1925. Mystery/Crime/Suspense, Historical/Romance/Gothic, Children's fiction. Tutor in Creative Writing, Kingsbridge Community Coll., since 1978. Woman's Page Ed., South Hams Review, 1977–79. *Publs:* Love Song of the Sea, 1960; (as Ivor Roberts) Jump into Hell!, 1960; (as Ivor Roberts) Trial by Water, 1961; (as Ivor Roberts) Green Hell, 1961; Squirrel Walk, 1961; Only to Part, 1961; Wind of Fate, 1961; Beloved Rascals, 1962; The Shrine of Marigolds, 1962; Come Back Beloved, 1962; The Dark Night, 1962; (as Iris Rowland) The Tangled Web, 1962; (as Iris Rowland) Island in the Mist, 1962; Sweet Sorrel, 1963; Tangle of Gold Lace, 1963; Cry of the Gulls, 1963; (as Iris Rowland) The Morning Star, 1963; (as Iris Rowland) With Fire and Flowers, 1963; (as Roberta Carr) Red Runs the Sunset, 1963; Laughing Is for Fun (juvenile), 1963; The Whisper of Sea-Bells, 1964; (as Iris Rowland) Golden Flower, 1964; (as Elizabeth Harle) Golden Rain, 1964; Holiday's for Hanbury (juvenile), 1964; Echo of Flutes, 1965; The Mountain Song, 1965; (as Roberta Carr) Sea Maiden, 1965; (as Elizabeth Harle) Gay Rowan, 1965; Where Flamingoes Fly, 1966; (as Iris Rowland) A Fountain of Roses, 1966; A Handful of Stars, 1967; (as Iris Rowland) Valley of Bells, 1967; (as Iris Rowland) Blue Feathers, 1967; (as Iris Rowland) A Veil of Rushes, 1967; (as Roberta Carr) Fire Dragon, 1967; (as Elizabeth Harle) Sandy, 1967; (as Irene Shaw) The House of Lydia, 1967; Shadows on the Moon, 1968; Jungle Nurse, 1968; Love Comes to Larkswood, 1968; Alpine Nurse, 1968; (as Iris Rowland) To Be Beloved, 1968; (as Irene Shaw) Moonstone Manor, 1968; in U.S. as Murder's Mansion, 1976; (as Irene Shaw) The Olive Branch, 1968; Nurse in the Hills, 1969; The Lion and the Sun, 1969; Thunder Heights, 1969; (as Iris Rowland) Rose Island, 1969; (as Iris Rowland) Cherries and Candlelight, 1969; (as Iris Rowland) Nurse at Kama Hall, 1969; (as Iris Rowland) Moon over Moncrieff, 1969; Surgeon in Tibet, 1970; Birds Without Bars, 1970; The Shrine of Fire, 1970; (as Iris Rowland) The Knave of Hearts, 1970; (as Iris Rowland) Star-Drift, 1970; (as Iris Rowland) Rainbow River, 1970; (as Iris Rowland) The Wild Summer, 1970; (as Roberta Carr) Golden Interlude, 1970; Gull Haven, 1971; Sister at Sea, 1971; (as Iris Rowland) Orange Blossom for Tara, 1971; (as Iris Rowland) Blossoms in the Snow, 1971; (as Elizabeth Harle) Spray of Red Roses, 1971; (as Elizabeth Harle) The Silver Summer, 1971; Moon over the Temple, 1972; The Golden Pagoda, 1972; (as Iris Rowland) Sister Julia, 1972; (as Elizabeth Harle) Buy Me a Dream, 1972; (as I.M. Roberts) The Throne of Pharaohs, 1974 (as Iris Rowland) To Lisa with Love, 1975; (as Iris Rowland) Golden Bubbles, 1976; (as I.M. Roberts) Hatshepsut, Queen of the Nile, 1976; Desert Nurse, 1976; Nurse in Nepal, 1976; Stars above Raffael, 1977; (as Iris Rowland) Hunter's Dawn, 1977; (as Iris Rowland) Forgotten Dreams, 1978; (as Iris Rowland) Golden Triangle, 1978; Hawks Barton, 1979; (as Elizabeth Harle) The Burning Flame, 1979; Symphony of Bells, 1980; Nurse Moonlight, 1980; (as Iris Rowland) Dance Ballerina Dance, 1980; Weave Me a Moonbeam, 1982; Jasmine for a Nurse, 1982; Sister on Leave, 1982; Nurse in the Wilderness, 1983; (as Iris Rowland) Temptation, 1983; (as Elizabeth Harle) Come To Me Darling, 1983; (as Iris Rowland) Theresa, 1985; (as I.M. Roberts) Hour of the Tiger, 1985; Moonpearl, 1986; Kingdom of the Sun, 1987; Sea Jade, 1987; Song of the Nile, 1987. Add: Alpha House, Higher Town, Marlborough, Kingsbridge, S. Devon TQ7 3RL, England.

ROBERTS, Ivor. *See* ROBERTS, Irene.

ROBERTS, J.R. *See* RANDISI, Robert J.

ROBERTS, James D(eotis, Sr.). American, b. 1927. Philosophy, Race relations, Theology/Religion. Dean, Sch. of Theology, Virginia Union Univ., Richmond, since 1973. Prof. of Systematic Theology, Sch. of Religion, Howard Univ., Washington, D.C. 1958–73. *Publs:* Faith and Reason in Pascal, Bergson and James, 1962; From Puritanism to Platonism in Seventeenth Century England, 1968; Liberation and Reconciliation: A Black Theology, 1971; (ed. with James Gardner) Quest for a Black Theology, 1971; Extending Redemption and Reconciliation, 1973; Black Theology Today, 1984. Add: c/o Christopher Publishing House, 1405 Hanover St., Box 1014, W. Hanover, Mass. 02339, U.S.A.

ROBERTS, James Hall. *See* DUNCAN, Robert L.

ROBERTS, Joan Ila. American, b. 1935. Education. Prof., Dept. of Child and Family Studies, Syracuse Univ., New York, since 1985. (Chmn. of Dept., 1978–80 and Assoc. Prof., 1978–84). Member, Research Staff, Makerere Coll., Kampala, Univ. of London, Teachers Coll., of Columbia Univ., NYC, 1961–63; Research Assoc., Hunter Coll., NYC, 1964–67; Asst. Prof., Dept. of Educational Policy Studies, Univ. of Wisconsin, Madison, 1968–75; Assoc. Prof., Upstate Medical Center, State Univ. of New York, 1976–83. *Publs:* (ed.) School Children in the Urban Slum: Readings in Social Science Research, 1967, 1968; Scene of the Battle: Group Behavior in Urban Classrooms, 1970; (ed.) Beyond Intellectual Sexism, 1976; Educational Patterns and Cultural Configurations, 1976; Schooling in the Cultural Context, 1976. Add: Coll. for Human Development, 202 Slocum Hall, Syracuse Univ., Syracuse, N.Y 13210, U.S.A.

ROBERTS, John. *See* **BINGLEY,** David Ernest.

ROBERTS, John Morris. British, b. 1928. History. Warden, Merton Coll., Oxford, since 1984. Fellow, Magdalen Coll., Oxford, 1951–53, and Fellow, Merton Coll., Oxford, 1953–79; Member, Inst. for Advanced Study, Princeton, N.J., 1960; Vice-Chancellor, Univ. of Southampton, 1979–85. *Publs:* (ed.) French Revolution Documents, vol. I, 1966; Europe 1880-1945, 1967; The Mythology of the Secret Societies, 1972; The Paris Commune from the Right, 1973; Revolution and Improvement, 1776-1847, 1974; The History of the World, 1976; The French Revolution, 1978; Illustrated History of the World, 1980; The Triumph of the West, 1985. Add: Merton Coll., Oxford, England.

ROBERTS, Keith (John Kingston). British, b. 1935. Historical/Romance/Gothic, Science fiction/Fantasy. Freelance graphic designer and advertising copywriter. Asst. Ed., Science Fantasy and Science Fiction Impulse, 1965–66 (Managing Ed., Science Fiction Impulse, 1966). *Publs:* The Furies, 1966; Pavane, 1968; The Inner Wheel, 1970; Anita, 1970; The Boat of Fate, 1971; Machines and Men, 1973; The Chalk Giants, 1974; The Grain Kings, 1975; Ladies from Hell, 1979; Molly Zero, 1980; Kiteworld, 1985; Kaeti and Company, 1986; The Lordly Ones, 1986; Tears in a Glass Eye, 1989. Add: 23 New St., Henley-on-Thames, Oxon. RG9 2BP, England.

ROBERTS, Kevin. Canadian, b. 1940. Novels/Short stories, Plays, Poetry. *Publs:* Cariboo Fishing Notes (poetry), 1973; Five poems, 1974; West Country (poetry), 1975; Deepline (poetry), 1978; S'Ney'mos (poetry), 1980; Heritage (poetry), 1981; Stonefish (poetry), 1982; Flash Harry and the Daughters of Divine Light (fiction), 1982; Black Apples (play), 1983; Nanoose Bay Suite (poetry), 1984; Picking the Morning Colour (fiction), 1985. Add: Box 55, Lantzville, B.C. V0R 2H0, Canada.

ROBERTS, Michael. British, b. 1908. History. Lectr., Merton Coll., Oxford, 1932–34; Asst. Lectr., Univ. of Liverpool, 1934–35; Prof. of History, Rhodes Univ., Grahamstown, 1935–53; Prof. of Modern History, Queen's Univ., Belfast, 1954–73; Dir., Inst. for Social and Economic Research, Rhodes Univ., 1974–76. British Council Representative, Stockholm, 1944–46. *Publs:* The Whig Party 1807-1812, 1939; (with A.E.G. Trollip) The South African Opposition 1939-1945, 1947; Gustavus Adolphus: A History of Sweden 1611-1632, 2 vols., 1953–58; (ed.) Historical Studies, 1959; Essays in Swedish History, 1967; The Early Vasas: A History of Sweden 1523-1611, 1968; (ed.) Sweden as a Great Power, 1611-1697, 1968; Sverige och Europa, 969; Gustav Vasa, 1970; Gustavus Adolphus and the Rise of Sweden, 1973; (ed.) Sweden's Age of Greatness, 1973; The Swedish Imperial Experience, 1979; Sverige som stormakt 1560-1718, 1980; British Diplomacy and Swedish Politics 1758-1773, 1980; The Age of Liberty: Sweden 1719-1772, 1986; (ed. and trans.) Swedish Diplomats at Cromwell's Court 1655-56, 1989. Add: 1 Allen St., Grahamstown 6140, South Africa.

ROBERTS, Nancy Correll. American, b. 1924. Children's fiction, Local history/Rural topics, Medicine/Health, Paranormal. Freelance writer. Town Commissioner, Maxton, N.C., 1952–56; Ed. and Publisher, Scottish Chief, Maxton, 1953–57; Pres., Maxton Development Corp., 1954–55. *Publs:* An Illustrated Guide to Ghosts and Mysterious Occurrences in the Old North State, 1959; Ghosts of the Carolinas, 1962; David, 1968; Sense of Discovery: The Mountain, 1969; A Week in Robert's World: The South, 1969; (with Bruce Roberts) Where Time Stood Still: A Portrait of Appalachia, 1970; (with Bruce Roberts) This Haunted Land, 1970; The Governor, 1972; The Goodliest Land: North Carolina, 1973; (with Bruce Roberts) Ghosts and Specters: Ten Supernatural Stories from the Deep South, 1974; The Faces of South Carolina, 1976 (with Bruce Roberts) Ghosts of the Wild West, 1976; (with Bruce Roberts) America's Most Haunted Places, 1976; (with Bruce Roberts) You and Your Retarded Child, 1977; Appalachian Ghosts, 1978; Southern Ghosts, 1979; Help for the Parents of a Handicapped Child, 1981; South Carolina Ghosts: From the Mountains to the Coast, 1983; Ghosts and Specters of the Old South, 1984; Haunted Houses: Tales from 32 American Homes, 1988; This Haunted Southland: Where Ghosts Still Roam, 1988. Add: 3600 Chevington Rd., Charlotte, N.C. 28226, U.S.A.

ROBERTS, Nora. American, b. 1950. Novels/Short stories, Historical/Romance. Full-time writer since 1979. Legal Secty., Wheeler and Korpeck, Silver Spring, Md., 1968–70; Clerk, The Hecht Co., Silver Spring, 1970–72; Secty., R and R Lighting, Silver Spring, 1972–75. *Publs:* Irish Thoroughbred, 1981; Blithe Images, 1982; Song of the West, 1982; Search for Love, 1982; Island of Flowers, 1982; The Heart's Victory, 1982; From This Day, 1983; Her Mother's Keeper, 1983; Reflections, 1983; Once More with Feeling, 1983; Untamed, 1983; Dance of Dreams, 1983; Tonight and Always, 1983; This Magic Moment, 1983; Endings and Beginnings, 1984; Storm Warning, 1984; Sullivan's Woman, 1984; Rules of the Game, 1984; Less of a Stranger, 1984; A Matter of Choice, 1984; The Law Is a Lady, 1984; First Impressions, 1984; Opposites Attract, 1984; Promise Me Tomorrow, 1984; Playing the Odds, 1985; Partners, 1985; The Right Path, 1985; Tempting Fate, 1985; Boundary Lines, 1985; All the Possibilities, 1985; One Man's Art, 1985; Summer Desserts, 1985; Dual Image, 1985; Night Moves, 1985; The Art of Deception, 1986; Affaire Royale, 1986; One Summer, 1986; Treasures Lost, Treasures Found, 1986; Risky Business, 1986; Lessons Learned, 1986; Second Nature, 1986; A Will and a Way, 1986; Home for Christmas, 1986; For Now, Forever, 1987; Mind over Matter, 1987; Command Performance, 1987; Brazen Virtue, 1988; The Last Honest Woman, 1988. Add: c/o Amy Berkower, Writers House, 21 W. 26th St., New York, N.Y. 10010, U.S.A.

ROBERTS, Paula. *See* **LORIN,** Amii.

ROBERTS, Philip Davies. Canadian, b. 1938. Poetry, Language. Full-time writer since 1980. English teacher, Madrid, 1963; Sub-Ed., Reuters, London, 1964–66; Public Relations Consultant, Peters Bishop and Partners, London, 1966–67; Lectr., 1967–74, and Sr. Lectr. in English, 1974–80, Univ. of Sydney. Poetry Ed., Sydney Morning Herald, 1970–74; Founding Ed., Island Press. Sydney, 1970–79. *Publs:* (ed.) The Inside Eye: A Study in Pictures of Oxford College Life, 1961; Just Passing Through, 1969; (with Geoff Page) Two Poets, 1971; (ed. with J.C. and P.M. Bright) Models of English Style (textbook), 1971; Crux, 1973; Will's Dream, 1975; Selected Poems, 1978; How Poetry Works, 1986; Plain English: A User's Guide, 1987; Letters Home, 1989. Add: P.O. Box 557, Annapolis Royal, N.S. B0S 1A0, Canada.

ROBERTS, Sally. *See* **JONES,** Sally Roberts.

ROBERTS, Wagner. *See* **OVERHOLSER,** Wayne.

ROBERTS, Willo Davis. American, b. 1928. Mystery/Crime/Suspense, Historical/Romance/Gothic, Science fiction/Fantasy. *Publs:* Murder at Grand Bay, 1955; Girl Who Wasn't There, 1957; Murder Is So Easy, 1961; Suspected Four, 1962; Nurse Kay's Conquest, 1966; Once a Nurse, 1966; Nurse at Mystery Villa, 1967; Return to Darkness, 1969; Waiting Darkness, 1970; Shroud of Fog, 1970; Devil Boy, 1970; Shadow of a Past Love, 1970; House at Fern Canyon, 1970; The Tarot Spell, 1970; Invitation to Evil, 1970; Terror Trap, 1971; King's Pawn, 1971; Gates of Montrain, 1971; The Watchers, 1971; Ghosts of Harrel, 1971; Inherit the Darkness, 1972; Nurse in Danger, 1972; Becca's Child, 1972; Sing a Dark Song, 1972; The Nurses, 1972; Face of Danger, 1972; Dangerous Legacy, 1972; Sinister Gardens, 1972; The M.D., 1972; The Evil Children, 1973; The Gods in Green, 1973; Nurse Robin, 1973; Didn't Anybody Know My Wife, 1974; White Jade, 1975; Key Witness, 1975; The View from the Cherry Tree, 1975; Expendable, 1976; The Jaubert Ring, 1976; Act of Fear, 1977; Cape of Black Sands, 1977; Don't Hurt Laurie, 1977; House of Imposters, 1977; Dark Dowry, 1978; The Minden Curse, 1978; The Cade Curse, 1978; The Stuart Stain, 1979; Devil's Double, 1979; Radkin Revenge, 1979; The Hellfire Heritage, 1979; The Macomber Menace, 1979; The Gresham Ghost, 1980; The Search for Willie, 1980; Destiny's Women, 1980; More Minden Curses, 1980; Girl with the Silver Eyes, 1980; The Face at the Window, 1981; A Long Time to Hate, 1982; The Gallant Spirit, 1982; Days of Valor, 1983; House of Fear, 1983; No Monsters in the Closet, 1983; The Pet Sitting Peril, 1983; Sniper, 1984; Keating's Landing, 1984; Eddie and the Fairy Godpuppy, 1984; Elizabeth, 1984; Babysitting Is a Dangerous Job, 1985; Caroline, 1985; Victoria, 1985; The Magic Book, 1985; The Annalise Experiment, 1985; My Rebel, My Love, 1986; To Share a Dream, 1986; Sugar Isn't Everything, 1987; Madawaska, 1988; Megan's Island, 1988; What Could Go Wrong?, 1989; Nightmare, 1989; To Grandmother's House We Go, 1990. Add: 12020 Engebretson Rd., Granite Falls, Wash. 98252, U.S.A.

ROBERTSON, Barbara Anne. Canadian, b. 1931. Biography. *Publs:* (compiler with M.A. Downie) The Wind Has Wings, 1968, enlarged ed. as The New Wind Has Wings, 1984; Wilfrid Laurier: The Great Conciliator, 1971; (with M.A. Downie) The Well-Filled Cupboard, 1987. Add: 52 Florence St., Kingston, Ont. K7M 1Y6, Canada.

ROBERTSON, Elspeth. *See* **ELLISON,** Joan Audrey.

ROBERTSON, James I., Jr. American, b. 1930. History. C.P. Miles Prof. of History, Virginia Polytechnic Inst. and State Univ., Blacksburg. Ed., Civil War History, 1959–61; Exec. Dir., U.S. Civil War Centennial Commn., 1961–65; Assoc. Prof., Univ. of Montana, Missoula, 1965–67.

Publs: (ed.) A Confederate Girl's Diary, 1960; (ed.) From Manassas to Appomattox, 1960; Virginia 1861-1865, 1961; (ed.) Four Years with General Lee, 1962; (ed.) The Diary of Dolly Lunt Burge, 1962; The Stonewall Brigade, 1963; The Civil War, 1963; (ed.) One of Jackson's Foot Cavalry, 1964; (ed.) The Civil War Letters of General Robert Mc-Allister, 1965; (ed.) Civil War Books: A Critical Bibliography, 2 vols., 1967–69; (ed.) Four Years in the Stonewall Brigade, 1971; The Concise Illustrated Hist-ory of the Civil War, 1971; The 4th Virginia Infantry, C.S.A., 1982; Civil War Sites in Virginia, 1982; The 18th Virginia Infantry, C.S.A., 1984; General A.P. Hill, 1987; Soldiers Blue and Gray, 1988. Add: Dept. of History, Virginia Polytechnic Inst. and State Univ., Blacksburg, Va. 24061, U.S.A.

ROBERTSON, John Monteath. British, b. 1900. Chemistry. Prof. Emeritus, Univ. of Glasgow, since 1970 (Gardiner Prof. of Chemistry, 1942–70; Dir., Chemical Labs, 1955–70). Ed., MTP Intnl. Review of Science, Butterworth and Co., publrs., London, since 1972. Co-Ed., Structure Reports, Intnl. Union of Crystallography, Oosthock publrs., Utrecht, 1940–61. *Publs:* Organic Crystals and Molecules: Theory of X-Ray Structure Analysis with Applications to Organic Chemistry, 1953. Add: 11 Eriskay Rd., Inverness IV2 3LX, Scotland.

ROBERTSON, Keith (Carlton). Also writes as Carlton Keith. American, b. 1914. Novels/Short stories, Children's fiction. Freelance writer since 1947. Refrigeration engineer, 1937–41; worked for a publisher, 1945–47. *Publs:* Ticktock and Jim (in U.K. as Watch for a Pony), 1948; Ticktock and Jim, Deputy Sheriffs, 1949; The Dog Next Door, 1950; The Missing Brother, 1950; The Lonesome Sorrel, 1952; The Mystery of Burnt Hill, 1952; Mascot of the Melroy, 1953; Outlaws of the Sourland, 1953; Three Stuffed Owls, 1954; The Wreck of the Saginaw, 1954; Ice to India, 1955; The Phantom Rider, 1955; The Pilgrim Goose, 1956; The Pinto Deer, 1956; The Crow and the Castle, 1957; Henry Reed Inc., 1958; If Wishes Were Horses, 1958; The Navy: From Civilian to Sailor, 1958; (as Carlton Keith) The Diamond-Studded Typewriter (novel), 1958; retitled as Gem of Murder, 1959; (as Carlton Keith) Missing, Presumed Dead, 1961; (as Carlton Keith) Rich Uncle, 1963; Henry Reed's Journey Baby-Sitting Service, Big Show, Think Tank, 4 vols., 1963–86; (as Carlton Keith) The Hiding-Place, 1965; (as Carlton Keith) The Crayfish Dinner (in U.K. as The Elusive Epicure), 1966; (as Carlton Keith) A Taste of Sangria (novel; in U.K. as The Missing Bookkeeper), 1968; The Year of the Jeep, 1968; The Money Machine, 1969; In Search of a Sandhill Crane, 1973; Tales of Myrtle the Turtle, 1974. Add: c/o Viking Press, 40 W. 23rd St., New York, N.Y. 10010, U.S.A.

ROBERTSON, Marian. South African, b. 1921. History. Freelance writer. *Publs:* Show Me the Mountain, 1970; Diamond Fever: South African Diamond History from Primary Sources 1866-1869, 1974; (with Mendel and Solomon Kaplan) From Shtetl to Steelmaking, 1979; Building for Permanence: The Story of a Building Society in the Life of South Africans 1883-1983, 1983; Living with the 1820 Settlers, 1985; (with Mendel Kaplan) Jewish Roots in the South African Economy, 1986; (with Rudy Frankel) Tiger Tapestry, 1988; (with Mendel Kaplan) Dear Son, 1988. Add: Waterford, Massinger Rd., off de Waal Rd., Diep River, Cape 7945, South Africa.

ROBESON, Kenneth. *See* **GOULART,** Ron.

ROBIN, Arthur de Quetteville. Australian, b. 1929. Theology/Religion, Biography. Vicar of Kallista, Vic., 1956–59, and Croydon, Vic., 1961–64; Sub-Warden, St. George's Coll., Perth, 1964–68; Visiting Tutor in History, Univ. of Western Australia, Nedlands, 1964–68; Vicar of St. Paul's Church, Geelong, Vic., 1969–78, and Rural Dean of Geelong, 1971–78; Vicar of Holy Trinity, Kew, Vic., 1978–84. *Publs:* Charles Perry, Bishop of Melbourne: The Challenges of a Colonial Episcopate 1847-1876, 1967; Mathew Blagden Hale: The Life of an Australian Pioneer Bishop, 1976; Making Many Rich: A Memoir of Joseph John Booth, 1978; (ed.) Australian Sketches: The Journals and Letters of Frances Perry, 1984. Add: 8 Poley Ct., Grovedale, Vic. 3216, Australia.

ROBINETT, Stephen. American, b. 1941. Science fiction/Fantasy. Lawyer. *Publs:* Stargate, 1976; The Man Responsible, 1978; Projections (short stories), 1979. Add: 718 Fernleaf Ave., Corona del Mar, Calif. 92625, U.S.A.

ROBINS, Patricia. *See* **LORRIMER,** Claire.

ROBINS, Robert Henry. British, b. 1921. Language/Linguistics. Prof. of Gen. Linguistics, Univ. of London, since 1966, now Emeritus (Lectr., Sch. of Oriental and African Studies, 1948–54; Reader, 1954–65). Hon.

Secty. 1961–88, and Pres. since 1988, Philological Soc.; Pres., Intnl. Cttee. of Linguists, since 1977; Hon. Member Linguistic Soc. of America, since 1980. *Publs:* Ancient and Mediaeval Grammatical Theory in Europe, 1951; The Yurok Language, 1958; General Linguistics: An Introductory Survey, 1964; A Short History of Linguistics, 1967; Diversions of Bloomsbury: Selected Writings on Linguistics, 1970; Ideen-und Problem-geschichte der Sprachwissenschaft, 1973. Add: Sch. of Oriental and African Studies, Univ. of London, London WC1H 0XG, England.

ROBINSON, A(ntony) M(eredith) Lewin. South African, b. 1916. History. Lectr. in Bibliography, Univ. of Cape Town Sch. of Librarianship, since 1962. Asst. Dir., 1945–61, and Dir., 1961–81, South African Library, Cape Town. *Publs:* None Daring to Make Us Afraid: A Study of English Periodical Literature in the Cape Colony 1824-1835, 1962; Systematic Bibliography: A Practical Guide to the Work of Compilation, 1966, 3rd ed. 1979; (ed.) Thomas Pringle's Narrative of a Residence in South Africa, 1966; (ed.) The Letters of Lady Anne Barnard to Henry Dundas: From the Cape and Elsewhere 1793-1803, 1973; (ed. with J.C. Quinton) François Le Vaillant: Traveller in South Africa and His Collection of 165 Water Colour Paintings, 1781-1784, 2 vols., 1973; (ed.) Notes on a Visit to South Africa 1889, by Stanley Leighton, 1975; Short-Title Catalogue of Early Printed Books in South African Libraries 1470-1550, 1977; (ed.) Selected Articles from the Cape Monthly Magazine 1870-75, 1978; From Monolith to Microfilm, 1979; (ed.-in-chief) A South African Bibliography to the Year 1925, 4 vols., 1979. Add: 136 Camp Ground Rd., Newlands, Cape Town, South Africa.

ROBINSON, Basil William. British, b. 1912. Art. Keeper Emeritus, Victoria and Albert Museum, London, 1972–76, now retired (Asst. Keeper, 1939–54; Deputy Keeper, 1954–66; Keeper, Dept. of Metalwork, 1966–72). Founder, 1954, and Chmn., Aldrich Catch Club; Hon. Vice-Pres., Arms and Armour Soc., since 1965; Hon. Pres., To-Ken Soc. of Great Britain, since 1970. Pres., Royal Asiatic Soc., 1970–73. *Publs:* Arms and Armour of Old Japan, 1951; Catalogue of a Loan Exhibition of Persian Miniatures, 1951; Persian Paintings, 1952; The Kevorkian Collection: Islamic . . . Paintings and Drawings, 1953; Persian Painting, 1953; Summary Catalogue of Drawings by Kuniyoshi, 1953; A Primer of Japanese Sword-Blades, 1955; Persian Miniatures, 1957; Japanese Landscape Prints of the 19th Century, 1957; (trans. with R. Eldon) Trafalgar, by Rene Maine, 1957; Catalogue of the Persian Paintings in the Bodleian Library, 1958; Bottle-Tickets, 1958; (co-author) The Chester Beatty Library: Catalogue of the Persian Manuscripts and Miniatures, vol. II, 1960, vol. III, 1962; Kuniyoshi, 1961; The Arts of the Japanese Sword, 1961; Hiroshige: Persian Drawings, 1965; Persian Miniature Painting from Collections in the British Isles, 1967; (with B. Gray) The Persian Art of the Book, 1972; Chinese Cloisonné Enamels, 1972; Miniatures Persanes: Donation Pozzi, 1974; Persian Paintings in the India Office Library, 1976; (ed. and co-author) Islamic Painting in the Keir Collection, 1976; Japanese Sword-Fittings in the Baur Collection, 1980; Persian Paintings in the John Rylands Library, 1980; Kuniyoshi, the Warrior Prints, 1982; The Aldrich Book of Catches, 1989. Add: 41 Redcliffe Gardens, London SW10 9JH, England.

ROBINSON, Derek. British, b. 1932. Economics. Sr. Research Officer, Inst. of Economics and Statistics, since 1961, and Fellow, Magdalen Coll., Oxford, since 1969. Member, Civil Service, 1948–55; Economic Adviser, National Bd. for Prices and Incomes, 1965–67; Visiting Prof., Univ. of Calfornia, Berkeley, 1968; Sr. Economic Adviser, Dept. of Employment and Productivity, London, 1968–70; Deputy Chmn., The Pay Bd., London, 1973–74; Chmn., Social Science Research Council (U.K.), 1975–78. *Publs:* Non-Wage Incomes and Prices Policy, 1966; Wage Drift, Fringe Ben-efits and Manpower Distribution, 1968; Workers' Negotiated Savings Plans for Capital Formation, 1970; (ed.) Local Labour Markets and Wage Structures, 1970; (with H. Suppanz) Prices and Incomes Policy: The Austrian Experience, 1972; Incomes Policy and Capital Sharing in Europe, 1973; (with J. Vincens) Research into Labour Market Behaviour, 1974; Solidaristic Wage Policy in Sweden, 1974; (ed. with Ken Mayhew) Pay Policies for the Future, 1983; Monetarism and the Labour Market, 1986; Introduction to Economics, 1986. Add: 56 Lonsdale Rd., Oxford, England.

ROBINSON, Derek. Also writes as Dirk Robson. British, b. 1932. Novels, Sport, Humour. *Publs:* novels—Goshawk Squadron, 1971; Rotten with Honour, 1973; Kramer's War, 1977; The Eldorado Network, 1979; Piece of Cake 1983; War Story, 1987; sports—Rugby: Success Starts Here, 1969; Get Squash Straight, 1978; Run with the Ball!, 1984; humour—Krek Waiter's Peak Bristle (guide to West Country dialect), 1970; Son of Bristle, 1971; Bristle Rides Again, 1972; other—A Shocking History of Bristol, 1973; Just Testing, 1985. Add: c/o Macmillan London

Ltd., 4 Little Essex St., London WC2R 3LF, England.

ROBINSON, Frank M(alcolm). American, b. 1926. Science fiction/ Fantasy. Freelance writer since 1973. Office boy, Ziff-Davis Publishing Co., Asst. Ed., Family Weekly, 1955–56, and Science Digest, 1956–59; Ed., Rogue mag., 1959–65; Managing Ed., Cavalier, 1965–66; Ed., Censorship Today, 1967; Staff Writer, Playboy Mag., 1969–73. *Publs:* The Power, 1956; (ed. with Earl Kemp) The Truth about Vietnam, 1966; (ed. with Nat Lehrman) Sex, American Style, 1971; (with Thomas N. Scortia) The Glass Inferno, 1974; (with Thomas N. Scortia) The Prometheus Crisis, 1975; (with Thomas N. Scortia) The Nightmare Factor, 1978; (with Thomas N. Scortia) The Gold Crew, 1980; A Life in the Day of, and Other Stories, 1980; (with John Levin) The Great Divide, 1982; (with Thomas N. Scortia) Blow-Out!, 1987. Add: 4100 Twentieth St., San Francisco, Calif. 94114, U.S.A.

ROBINSON, Gilbert de Beauregard. Canadian, b. 1906. Mathematics/ Statistics, Biography. Prof. of Mathematics, Univ. of Toronto, since 1931 (Vice-Pres., Research, 1965–71; with Inst. of the Environment, 1971–72, and Faculty of Education, 1972–74). Production Ed., C.R. Math Reports R.S.C., since 1979. Managing Ed., Canadian Journal of Mathematics, 1949–77; Pres., Canadian Mathematics Congress, 1953–57; Pres., Canadian Soc. of History and Philosophical Science, 1979–81. *Publs:* Foundations of Geometry, 1940, 4th ed. 1959; Representation Theory of the Symmetric Group, 1961; Vector Geometry, 1962; Collected Papers of Alfred Young, 1978; History of Mathematics Dept. at University of Toronto, 1979, Percy James Robinson 1873-1953, 1981; Sermons at Go Home Bay, 1983. Add: 877 Yonge St., Apt. 305, Toronto, Ont. M4W 3M2, Canada.

ROBINSON, J(ohn). Lewis. Canadian, b. 1918. Geographer. Emeritus Prof. of Geography, Univ. of British Columbia, Vancouver. Pres., Assn. of Pacific Coast Geographers, 1950, Canadian Assn.of Geographers, 1955, and British Columbia Geographers Assn., 1958. *Publs:* The Canadian Arctic, 1952; Resources of the Canadian Shield, 1969; British Columbia: 100 Years of Geographical Change, 1973; Concepts and Themes in the Regional Geography of Canada, 1983, 1989. Add: Dept. of Geography, Univ. of British Columbia, Vancouver, B.C. V6T 1W5, Canada.

ROBINSON, Kim Stanley. American, b. 1952. Science fiction, Literature. Visiting Lectr., Univ. of California at Davis, 1982–84, 1985, and at San Diego, 1982, 1985. *Publs:* The Novels of Philip K. Dick, 1984; The Wild Shore, 1984; Icehenge, 1985; The Memory of Whiteness, 1985; The Planet on the Table, 1986, The Gold Coast, 1988. Add: 17811 Romelle Ave., Santa Ana, Calif. 92705, U.S.A.

ROBINSON, Marguerite S. American, b. 1935. Anthropology/Ethnology, Politics/Government. Inst. Fellow, Harvard Inst. for Intnl. Development, Cambridge, since 1985 (Fellow, 1980–85). (Lectr., 1964–65; Asst. Prof., 1965–72; Assoc. Prof., 1972–78; Prof. of Anthropology, 1978–85, and Dean of the Coll., 1973–75). Brandeis Univ., Waltham, Mass. Undertook field work in Ceylon, 1963 and 1967; National Science Foundn. Fellow, Newnham Coll., Cambridge, England, 1966–67; field work in Andhra Pradesh, India, 1969 and 1980; Research Fellow, Peabody Museum, Harvard Univ., 1969–76; Project Officer, National Inst. of Health, 1971–72. *Publs:* (contrib.) Cambridge Papers in Social Anthropology, vol. III, 1962, vol. V, 1968; (contrib.) Structuralism: A Reader, 1970; Political Structure in a Changing Sinhalese Village, 1974. Add: Harvard Inst. for Intnl. Development, Eliot St., Cambridge, Mass. 02138, U.S.A.

ROBINSON, Marilynn. American, b. 1943. Novels, Social commentary. *Publs:* House-Keeping, 1980; Mother Country (non-fiction), 1989. Add: c/o Farrar Straus, 19 Union Sq. W., New York, N.Y. 10003, U.S.A

ROBINSON, Philip (Bedford). British, b. 1926. Novels/Short stories, Information science/Computers, Language/Linguistics. Produce Exporter in India, 1950–58; Principal Technical Officer, Intnl. Computers Ltd., 1962–78. *Publs:* The Pakistani Agent, 1965; Masques of a Savage Mandarin, 1969; (ed. with G. Cuttle) Executive Programs and Operating Systems, 1970; (with E. Humby) Computers, 1971; Computer Programming, 1972; Advanced COBOL:ANS74, 1976; Import/Export, 1977; (with A. Beesley) English for Your Business Career, vols. III-IV, 1977–78; Insurance, 1978; Trading Round the World, 1978; It Pays to Be Insured, 1978; Computers Do Better, 1979. Add: 154 Hersham Rd., Walton-on-Thames, Surrey, England.

ROBINSON, Robert. British, b. 1927. Novels, Humour/Satire. Television Broadcaster, BBC, London, since 1956. *Publs:* Landscape with Dead Dons, 1956; Inside Robert Robinson, 1965; The Conspiracy, 1968; The Dog Chairman, 1982; (ed.) The Everyman Book of Light Verse, 1984; Bad Dreams, 1989. Add: c/o BBC, Broadcasting House, Portland Pl., London W1, England.

ROBINSON, Roland (Edward). British, b. 1912. Poetry, Anthropology/ Ethnology, Mythology/Folklore, Autobiography/Memoirs/Personal. Book Reviewer, Sydney Morning Herald (Ballet Critic, 1956–66); Ed., Poetry Mag., Sydney; Pres., Poetry Soc. of Australia. Member, Kirsova Ballet, 1944–47. *Publs:* Beyond the Grass-Tree Spears: Verse, 1944; Language of the Sand, 1948; Legend and Dreaming: Legends of the Dream-Time of the Australian Aborigines, 1952; Tumult of the Swans, 1953; The Feathered Serpent: The Mythological Genesis and Recreative Ritual of the Aboriginal Tribes of the Northern Territory of Australia, 1956; Black-Feller, White-Feller, 1958; Deep Well, 1962; The Man Who Sold His Dreaming, 1965; Aborigine Myths and Legends, 1966; Grendel, 1967; The Australian Aborigine in Colour, 1968; (ed.) Wandjina: Children of the Dreamtime: Aboriginal Myths and Legends, 1968; Selected Poems, 1971; The Drift of Things, 1914-1952 (autobiography), 1973; The Shift of Sands 1952-1962 (autobiography), 1976; A Letter to Joan (autobiography), 1978; Selected Poems, 1984. Add: 42 Old Belmont Rd., Belmont North, N.S.W. 2280, Australia.

ROBINSON, Sheila (Mary). Also writes as Sheila Radley and Hester Rowan. British, b. 1928. Mystery/Crime/Suspense, Historical/Romance/Gothic. *Publs:* (as Hester Rowan) Overture in Venice, 1976; (with others) Writers of East Anglia (anthology), 1977; (as Hester Rowan) The Linden Tree, 1977; (as Hester Rowan) Snowfall, 1978; (as Sheila Radley) Death and the Maiden, 1978; (as Sheila Radley) The Chief Inspector's Daughter, 1981; (as Sheila Radley) A Talent for Destruction, 1982; (as Sheila Radley) Blood on the Happy Highway, 1983; (as Sheila Radley) Fate Worse Than Death, 1985; (as Sheila Radley) Who Saw Him Die?, 1987; (as Sheila Radley) This Way out, 1989. Add: c/o Curtis Brown Ltd., 162–168 Regent St., London W1R 5TA, England.

ROBINSON, Spider. American, b. 1948. Science fiction/Fantasy. Freelance writer since 1973. Realty Ed., Long Island Commercial Review, Syosset, N.Y., 1972–73. Book Reviewer, Galaxy mag., 1975–77. *Publs:* Telempath, 1976; Callahan's Crosstime Saloon (short stories), 1977; (with Jeanne Robinson) Stardance, 1979; Antinomy (short stories), 1980; Time Travelers Strictly Cash (short stories), 1981; Mindkiller, 1982; Melancholy Elephants (short stories), 1984; Night of Power, 1985; Callahan's Secret (short stories), 1986; Time Pressure, 1987; Callahan and Company (short stories), 1988; Callahan's Lady, 1989; (with Jeanne Robinson) Starseed; 1990. Add: c/o Eleanor Wood, Spectrum Agency, 432 Park Ave. S., New York, N.Y. 10016, U.S.A.

ROBINSON, W(illiam) R(onald). American, b. 1927. Film, Literature. Prof. of English, Univ. of Florida, Gainesville, since 1971 (Assoc. Prof., 1967–71). Asst. Prof., Univ. of Virginia, Charlottesville, 1962–67. *Publs:* Edwin Arlington Robinson: A Poetry of the Act, 1967; (ed.) Man and the Movies, 1967. Add: English Dept., Univ. of Florida, Gainesville, Fla. 32601, U.S.A.

ROBISON, Mary. American, b. 1949. Novels/Short stories. Member of the English Dept., Harvard Univ., Cambridge, Mass. *Publs:* Days (short stories), 1979; Oh! (novel), 1981; An Amateur's Guide to the Night (short stories), 1983; Believe Them (short stories), 1988. Add: Dept. of English, Harvard Univ., Cambridge, Mass. 02138, U.S.A.

ROBOTTOM, John (Carlisle). British. Children's non-fiction, History. Freelance writer since 1987. Sch. teacher, 1956–65; Lectr. in History, Bingley Coll. of Education, Yorkshire, 1966–68; Sr. and Principal Lectr., Crewe Coll. of Education, Cheshire, 1968–74; Education Officer, BBC, 1974–86. *Publs:* Modern China, 1967; China in Revolution, 1970; Modern Russia, 1970; (ed. and contrib.) Making the Modern World: The 20th Century, 1970, 1972; Twentieth-Century China, 1973; (ed. and contrib.) Making the Modern World: The 19th Century, 1975; (with W. Claypole) Caribbean Story, 2 vols., 1980–81; Russia in Change, 1984; A Social and Economic History of Industrial Britain, 1986; (with A. Leake) Tutorial Topics, 1988. Add: 4 Hampton Lane, Solihull B91 2PS, England.

ROBSON, Brian Turnbull. British, b. 1939. Geography, Urban studies. Prof. of Geography, Manchester Univ., since 1977. Gen. Ed., Cambridge Human Geography Series, since 1983. Lectr. University Coll. of Wales, Aberystwyth, 1964–67; Lectr., Cambridge Univ., 1967–77; Hon. Ed.,

AREA, Inst. of British Geographers, 1971–74. *Publs:* Urban Analysis: A Study of City Structure, 1969; Urban Growth: An Approach, 1973; Urban Social Areas, 1975; (ed.) Houses and People in the City, 1976; (ed.) Man's Impact on Past Environments, 1976; (ed.) Geographical Agenda for a Changing World, 1982; Where is the North?, 1985; Managing the City, 1987; Those Inner Cities, 1988. Add: Dept. of Geography, Manchester Univ., Manchester 13, England.

ROBSON, Derek Ian. British, b. 1935. Education, History. Principal, Education Dept. of Victoria, since 1983 (Asst. Teacher, 1959–60; Sr. Teacher, 1970–77; Deputy Principal, 1978–82). Ed., Staff Development Journal, since 1974. Member, Education Dept. Secondary History Cttee., since 1965. Correspondence Lectr. in British History, Royal Melbourne Inst. of Technology, 1967–71. *Publs:* A Student's British History, 1964; A Student's Asian History, 1968; Indonesia: A Brief Survey, 1968; (co-author) The Use of Sources, 1969; (co-author) Evaluation, 1974; (ed.) Studies in Administration, 17 vols., 1977–88. Add: 2 Apple Ct., Burwood E., Melbourne, Vic. 3151, Australia.

ROBSON, Dirk. *See* **ROBINSON,** Derek.

ROBSON, Jeremy. British, b. 1939. Poetry. Managing Dir., Robson Books, London, since 1974. Poetry Critic, Tribune, London, 1962–77; Ed., Aldus Books, London, 1963–69; Chief Ed., Vallentine Mitchell, publrs., London, 1969–72; Ed., Woburn Press, London, 1972–73. *Publs:* Pamphlet, 1961; Poems for Jazz, 1963; Thirty-Three Poems, 1964; (ed.) Letters to Israel: Summer 1967, 1968; (ed.) Poems from Poetry and Jazz in Concert: An Anthology, 1969; In Focus, 1970; Poems Out of Israel, 1970; (ed.) The Young British Poets, 1971; (ed. Corgi Modern Poets in Focus 2 and 4, 2 vols., 1971; Travelling, 1972; (ed.) Poetry Dimension I: A Living Record of the Poetry Year, 1973. Add: Robson Books, Bolsover House, 5-6 Clipstone St., London W1P 7EB, England.

ROBY, Mary Linn. Also writes as Pamela D'Arcy; Georgina Grey, Elizabeth Welles, and Mary Wilson. American, b. 1930. Historical/Romance/ Gothic. English Teacher, Concord/Carlisle High School, Mass., since 1972. Former History Teacher, State College High Sch., Pa. *Publs:* Still as the Grave, 1964; Afraid of the Dark, 1965; Before I Die, 1966; Cat and Mouse, 1967; In the Dead of the Night, 1969; Pennies on Her Eyes, 1969; All Your Lovely Words are Spoken, 1970; Some Die in Their Beds, 1970; If She Should Die, 1970; Lie Quiet in Your Grave, 1970; That Fatal Touch, 1970; Dig a Narrow Grave, 1971; This Land Turns Evil Slowly, 1971; Reap the Whirlwind, 1972; And Die Remembering, 1972; When the Witch Is Dead, 1972; The White Peacock, 1972, in U.K. as The Cry of the Peacock, 1974; Shadow over Grove house, 1973; Speak No Evil of the Dead, 1973; The House at Kilgallen, 1973; The Broken Key, 1973; Marsh House, 1974; The Tower Room, 1974; The Silent Walls, 1974; (as Mary Wilson) The Changeling, 1975; (as Mary Wilson) Wind of Death, 1976; Christobel, 1976; The Treasure Hunt, 1976; (as Elizabeth Welles) Seagull Crag, 1977; The Hidden Book, 1977; Trapped, 1977; A Heritage of Strangers, 1978; (as Georgina Grey) The Hesitant Heir, 1978; Fortune's Smile, 1979; My Lady's Mask, 1979; (as Georgina Grey) Turn of the Cards, 1979; Passing Fancy, 1980; (as Georgina Grey) Both Sides of the Coin, 1980; (as Georgina Grey) Fashion's Frown, 1980; (as Georgina Grey) Franklin's Folly, 1980; (as Georgina Grey) The Last Cotillion, 1980; (as Pamela D'Arcy) Angel in the House, 1980; (as Pamela D'Arcy) Heritage of the Heart, 1980; (as Pamela D'Arcy) Magic Moment, 1980; Love's Wilful Call, 1981; (as Georgina Grey) The Bartered Bridegroom, 1981; (as Georgina Grey) The Queen's Quadrille, 1981; (as Georgina Grey) The Reluctant Rivals, 1981; (as Georgina Grey) Lingering Laughter, 1982. Add: c/o New American Library, 1633 Broadway, New York, N.Y. 10019, U.S.A.

ROBY, Pamela Ann. American, b. 1942. Sociology. Prof. of Sociology, Univ. of California at Santa Cruz, since 1973. Asst. Prof. of Sociology, Brandeis Univ., Waltham, Mass., 1971–73. *Publs:* (with S.M. Miller) The Future of Inequality, 1970; (ed.) Child Care—Who Cares?: Foreign and Domestic Infant and Early Childhood Development Policies, 1973; (ed.) The Poverty Establishment, 1974; Women in the Workplace, 1981. Add: Merrill Coll., Univ. of California, Santa Cruz, Calif. 95064, U.S.A.

ROCHARD, Henri. *See* **CHARLIER,** Roger Henri.

ROCHE, John P. American, b. 1923. Politics/Government. John M. Olin Distinguished Prof. Civilization and Foreign Affairs, and Academic Dean, Fletcher Sch. of Law and Diplomacy, Tufts Univ., Medford. Founding Trustee, Woodrow Wilson Intnl. Center for Scholars, Smithsonian Instn., Washington; Member, Council on Foreign Relations; Mem-

ber, President's Gen. Advisory Council on Arms Control and Disarmament, since 1982; Member, Sub-Commission on Prevention of Discrimination and Protection of Minorities, UN Human Rights Comm., since 1984. Asst. Prof. to Assoc. Prof. of Political Science, Haverford Coll., Pennsylvania, 1949–56; Prof. of Politics and History, Brandeis Univ., Waltham, Mass., 1956–73. Special Consultant to the U.S. President, 1966–68; Member, National Council on the Humanities, 1967–70; Member, Presidential Commn. on Intnl. Broadcasting, 1972–73; Member, U.S. Bd. for Intnl. Broadcasting, Washington, 1974–77; syndicated columnist, 1968 –82. *Publs:* (with M. Stedman) The Dynamics of Democratic Govern-ment, 1954; Courts and Rights, 1961, 1967; The Quest for the Dream: Civil Liberties in Modern America, 1963; Shadow and Substance: Studies in the Theory and Structure of Politics, 1964; (ed.) American Political Thought, vol. I, 1965, vol. II, 1967; John Marshall, 1966; Sentenced to Life: Reflections on Politics, Education and Law, 1974; (with Uri Ra'anan) Ethnic Resurgence in Modern Democracies, 1980; History and Impact of Marxist-Leninist Organizational Theory, 1984; (contr.) National Security Policy: The Decision-making Process, 1984. Add: 15 Bay State Rd., Weston, Mass. 02193, U.S.A.

ROCHE, Paul. British, b. 1928. Novels/Short stories, Plays/Screenplays, Poetry, Translations. Instr., Smith Coll., Northampton, Mass., 1957–59; Poet-in-Residence, California Inst. of the Arts, Valencia, 1972–74. *Publs:* The Rat and the Convent Dove and Other Tales and Fables, 1952; O Pale Galilean (novel), 1954; (trans.) The Oedipus Plays of Sophocles, 1958; The Rank Obstinacy of Things: A Selection of Poems, 1962; Vessel of Dishonour (novel), 1962; (trans.) The Orestes Plays of Aeschylus, 1963; (trans.) Prometheus Bound, by Aeschylus, 1964; 22 November 1963 (The Catherisis of Anguish), 1965; Ode to the Dissolution of Morality, 1966; All Things Considered: Poems (in U.S. as All Things Considered and Other Poems), 1966; (trans.) The Love-Songs of Sappho, 1966; To Tell the Truth: Poems, 1967; Te Deum for J. Alfred Prufrock, 1967; Oedipus the King (screenplay), 1967; (trans.) 3 Plays of Plautus, 1968; (trans.) Philoctetes, lines 676-729, by Sophocles, 1971; Lament for Erica: A Poem, 1971; (trans.) Three Plays of Euripides: Alcestis, Medea, The Bacchae, 1974; Enigma Variations and . . ., 1974; The Kiss, 1974; New Tales from Aesop for Reading Aloud, 1982; With Duncan Grant in Southern Turkey, 1982. Add: c/o New American Library, 1633 Broadway, New York, N.Y. 10019, U.S.A.

ROCKLAND, Michael Aaron. American, b. 1935. History. Prof. and Chmn., Dept. of American Studies, Douglass Coll., Rutgers Univ., New Brunswick, N.J., since 1969 (Asst. Dean of Douglass Coll., 1969–72). Contrib. Ed., New Jersey Monthly; Reporter, New Jersey News, PBS-TV. Asst. Cultural Attache, U.S. Embassies in Argentina and Spain, 1961–68; Exec. Asst. to the Chancellor of Higher Education, State of New Jersey, 1968–69. *Publs:* Sarmiento's Travels in the United States in 1847, 1970; (ed.) America in the Fifties and Sixties: Julian Marias on the United States, 1972; (co-author) Three Days on Big City Waters (TV screenplay), 1974; The American Jewish Experience in Literature, 1975; Homes on Wheels, 1980; (co-author) Looking for America on the New Jersey Turnpike, 1989; Anudaba, 1989. Add: 11 Farragut Pl., Morristown, N.J. 07960, U.S.A.

ROCKLEY, L(awrence) E(dwin). British, b. 1916. Business/Trade/ Industry, Money/Finance. Principal, Rockley-Evans Assocs., business mgmt. and educational consultants, since 1966; Managing Dir., Cailvale Ltd., mgmt. and environmental consultants, since 1973; Fellow Emeritus, Coventry Polytechnic, since 1986. Deputy Chief Internal Auditor, City of Leicester Corp., 1947–57; Area Chief Auditor, National Coal Bd., 1957–60; Lectr. to Reader in Finance, Lanchester Polytechnic, Coventry, 1965–80. *Publs:* Capital Investment Decisions, 1968; Finance for the Non-Accountant, 1970, 4th ed. 1984; The Non-Accountants Guide to Finance, 1972; Investment for Profitability, 1973; The Non-Accountants Guide to the Balance Sheet, 1973; Public and Local Authority Accounts, 1974, 1978; The Meaning of Balance Sheets and Company Reports, 1975, 1983; Finance for the Purchasing Executive, 1978; Policy for Disclosure, 1979; (with O.A. Hill) Security: Its Management and Control, 1981; Business Accounting, 1987. Add: Charnwood, 121 Windy Arbor, Kenilworth, Warwicks. CV8 2BJ, England.

ROCKWELL, Anne (née Foote). American, b. 1934. Children's fiction, Children's non-fiction. *Publs:* Children's fiction—(ed.) Savez-Vous Planter les Choux? and Other French Songs, 1962; Paul and Arthur Search for an Egg, 1964; Gypsy Girl's Best Shoes, 1966; Sally's Caterpillar, 1966; Molly's Woodland Garden 1971; Paul and Arthur and the Little Explorer, 1972; (with Harlow Rockwell) Thruway, 1972; The Awful Mess, 1973; Gift for a Gift, 1974; The Gollywhopper Egg, 1974; The Story Snail, 1974; (ed.) The Three Bears and 15 Other Stories, 1975;

Big Boss, 1975; No More Work, 1976; Albert B. Cub and Zebra: An Alphabet Storybook, 1977; A Bear, A Bobcat, and Three Ghosts, 1977; Buster and the Bogeyman, 1978; Gogo's Car Breaks Down, 1978; Gogo's Pay Day, 1978; Timothy Todd's Good Things Are Gone, 1978; Willy Runs Away, 1978; (with Harlow Rockwell) Blackout, 1979; The Bump in the Night, 1979; Henry the Cat and the Big Sneeze, 1980; Honk Honk!, 1980; (with Harlow Rockwell) Out to Sea, 1980; Walking Shoes, 1980; (with Harlow Rockwell) Happy Birthday to Me, 1981; (with Harlow Rockwell) My Barber, 1981; (with Harlow Rockwell) I Play in My Room, 1981; Thump! Thump! Thump!, 1981; Big Bad Goat, 1982; (with Harlow Rockwell) Can I Help?, 1982; (with Harlow Rockwell) How My Garden Grew, 1982; (with Harlow Rockwell) I Love My Pets, 1982; (with Harlow Rockwell) Sick in Bed, 1982; (with Harlow Rockwell) The Night We Slept Outside, 1983; (with Harlow Rockwell) My Backyard, 1984; (with Harlow Rockwell) Our Garage Sale, 1984; (with Harlow Rockwell) When I Go Visiting, 1984; First Comes Spring, 1985; In Our House, 1985; My Babysitter, 1985; At Night, 1986; At the Playground, 1986; In the Morning, 1986; In the Rain, 1986; Come to Town, 1987; Handy Hank Will Fix It, 1988; Hugo at the Window, 1988; Things to Play with, 1988; My Spring Robin, 1989; On Our Vacation, 1989; children's non-fiction— Filippo's Dome, 1967; Glass, Stones and Crown: The Abbe Suger and the Building of St. Denis, 1968; The Good Llama, 1968; The Stolen Necklace: A Picture Story from India, 1968; Temple on a Hill: The Building of the Parthenon, 1968; The Wonderful Eggs of Furicchia (retelling), 1969; (with Harlow Rockwell) Olly's Polliwogs, 1970; When the Drum Sang: An African Folktale, 1970; The Monkey's Whiskers: A Brazilian Folktale, 1971; Paintbrush and Peacepipe: The Story of George Catlin, 1971; (with Harlow Rockwell) The Toolbox, 1971; Tuhurahura and the Whale: A Maori Legend, 1971; What Bobolino Knew (retelling), 1971; The Dancing Stars: An Iroquois Legend, 1972; Machines, 1972; (with Harlow Rockwell) Toad, 1972; The Boy Who Drew Sheep, 1973; Games (and How to Play Them), 1973; (with Harlow Rockwell) Head to Toe, 1973; The Wolf Who Had a Wonderful Dream: A French Folktale, 1973; Befana: A Christmas Story (retelling), 1974; Poor Goose: A French Folktale, 1976; I Like the Library, 1977; The Girl with a Donkey Tail, 1979; The Old Woman and Her Pig, and 10 other stories (retelling), 1979; (with Harlow Rockwell) The Supermarket, 1979; Up a Tall Tree, 1981; When We Grow Up, 1981; Boats, 1982; Cars, 1984; (with Harlow Rockwell) Nice and Clean, 1984; Trucks, 1984; (with Harlow Rockwell) The Emergency Room, 1985, in UK as Going to Casualty, 1987; Planes, 1985; Big Wheels, 1986; Fire Engines, 1986; Things That Go, 1986; (with Harlow Rockwell) At the Beach, 1987; Bear Child's Book of Hours, 1987; Bikes, 1987; (with Harlow Rockwell) The First Snowfall, 1987; Puss in Boots and Other Stories, 1988; Trains, 1988. Add: P.O. Box 379, Old Greenwich, Conn. 06870. U.S.A.

ROCKWELL, Thomas. American, b. 1933. Children's Fiction. *Publs:* Rackety-Bang and Other Verses; Humpf!; The Neon Motorcycle; How to Eat Fried Worms and Other Plays; Hiding Out; Tin Cans; Squawwwk!; The Portmanteau Book; The Thief; Hey, Lover Boy; Oatmeal Is Not for Mustaches; How to Fight a Girl. Add: R.D. 3, Poughkeepsie, N.Y. 12603, U.S.A.

RODAHL, Kaare. American, b. 1917. Medicine/Health, Travel/Exploration/Adventure. Chief, Dept. of Physiology, 1950–52, and Dir. of Research, 1954–57, Arctic Aeromedical Lab., Fairbanks, Alaska; Asst. Prof. of Physiology, Univ. of Oslo, 1952–54; Dir. of Research, Lankenau Hosp., Philadelphia, 1957–65; Dir., Inst. of Work Physiology, 1965–87, and Prof., Norweigian Coll. of Physical Education, 1966–87. *Publs:* The Ice Capped Island, 1946; North, 1953; (ed.) Bone as a Tissue, 1960; (ed.) Muscle as a Tissue, 1962; The Last of the Few, 1963; (ed.) Fat as a Tissue, 1964; Be Fit for Life, 1966; (ed.) Nerve as a Tissue, 1966; (co-author) Textbook of Work Physiology, 1970, 3rd ed. 1986; Stress, 1972; Akiviak, 1974. Add: Maltrostveien 40, Oslo 3, Norway.

RODD, John. Canadian, b. 1905. Antiques/Furnishings, Recreation/Leisure/Hobbies. Cabinetmaker and restorer of antiques, Sydney, B.C., since 1927. *Publs:* The Repair and Restoration of Furniture, 1954, as Repairing and Restoring Antique Furniture, 1976. Add: 1830 McMicken Rd., R.R. 3, Sydney, B.C. V8L 3X9, Canada.

RODDICK, Alan. New Zealander, b. 1937. Poetry. Public servant. Ed., Radio Poetry Prog., New Zealand Broadcasting Corp., 1968–69, 1973–74. *Publs:* The Eye Corrects: Poems 1955-1965, 1967; (ed.) Home Ground: Poems, by Charles Brasch, 1974; Allen Curnow, 1981; (ed.) Collected Poems, by Charles Brasch, 1984. Add: 18 Wilfrid St., Christchurch 4, New Zealand.

RODDY, Lee. American, b. 1921. Novels/Short Stories, children's fic-

tion, Children's non-fiction, History, Theology/Religion, Biography. Owner, Roddy Publications, Ceres, Calif., since 1969, Founding Dir. and Vice-Pres., Orcom Inc. and Adam II Productions Inc., since 1982. Writer and mgr. in radio broadcasting and advertising, Los Angeles, 1947–65; Ed., Publisher, then Corp. Vice-Pres., Regional Times Publishers, Ceres, 1966–73; Staff Writer and Researcher, Shick Sunn Classic Pictures, 1976–79; Founding Dir and Vice-Pres., Codemakers Inc., 1982–85. *Publs:* (with Paul F. Peppin) The Family Necessary Book, 1975; (with Charles E. Sellier Jr. and David Balsiger) The Lincoln Conspiracy, 1977; (with Charles E. Sellier Jr.) The Life and Time of Grizzly Adams, 1977; Robert E. Lee, 1977; Gentleman, 1977; (with George B. Derkatch) Word of Fire, 1977; (with Charles E. Sellier Jr.) In Search of Historic Jesus, 1979; The Taming of the Cheetah, 1979; Intimate Portraits of Women in the Bible, 1980; Search for the Avenger, 1980; The Mystery of Aloha House, 1981; Love's Far Horizon, 1981; On Wings of Love, 1981; (with Steve Douglass) Making the Most of Your Mind, Here's Life, 1983; (with Rachel Banner) The Impatient Blossom, 1985; D. J. Dillion and the Hair-Pulling Bear Dog, 1985; D. J. Dillon and the City Bear's Adventures, 1985; D. J. Dillon and Dooger, the Grasshopper Hound, 1985; D. J. Dillon and the Ghost Dog of Stoney Ridge, 1985; D. J. Dillon and the Mad Dog of Lobo Mountain, 1986; D. J. Dillon and the Legend of the White Raccoon, 1986; D. J. Dillon and the Mystery of the Black Hole Mine, 1987; D. J. Dillon and the Ghost of the Moaning Mansion, 1987. Add: c/o Roddy Publications, P.O. Box 700, Penn Valley, Calif. 95946, U.S.A.

RODEFER, Stephen. American, b. 1940. Poetry, Translations. Curator, Archive for New Poetry, and Lectr., Dept. of Literature Univ. of California, San Diego, since 1985. Research Asst., 1965–66, and Instr. in English, 1966–67, State Univ. of New York at Buffalo; Asst. Prof. of English and Co-Dir. of the Creative Writing Prog., Univ. of New Mexico, Albuquerquo, 1967–71; Ed., Fervent Valley, Placitas, N.M., 1972–75; Poetry Specialist, Berkeley, Calif. Unified Sch. District, 1976–80; Lectr. in English, San Francisco State Univ., 1981–85. *Publs:* The Knife, 1965; After Lucretius, 1973; (trans.) Villon, 1976; One or Two Love Poems from the White World, 1976; Safety, 1977; The Bell Clerk's Tears Keep Flowing, 1978; (trans.) Orpheus, 1981; Plane Debris, 1981; Four Lectures, 1982; (with Benjamin Friedlander) Oriflamme Day, 1985; Emergency Measures, 1987. Add: Dept. of Literature, Univ. of Calif. San Diego, La Jolla, Calif. 92093, U.S.A.

RODERUS, Frank. American, b. 1942. Westerns. Freelance writer since 1980. Formerly, Journalist: Reporter, Tampa Times, 1965–66, Lakeland Ledger, 1966–68, and Tampa Tribune, 1968–72, all Florida, Waterloo Courier, Iowa, 1972–75, and Colorado Springs Gazette Telegraph, 1979–80. *Publs:* Journey to Utah, 1977; The 33 Brand, 1977; The Keystone Kid, 1978; Easy Money, 1978; Home to Texas, 1978; The Name Is Hart, 1979; Hell Creek Cabin, 1979; Sheepherding Man, 1980; Jason Evers, His Own Story, 1980; Old Kyle's Boy, 1981; Cowboy, 1981; The Ordeal of Hogue Bynell, 1982; Leaving Kansas, 1983; Reaching Colorado, 1984; Finding Nevada, 1985; Stillwater Smith, 1986; Billy Ray and the Good News, 1987; The Ballad of Bryan Drayne, 1987. Add: 92 High Park Rd., Florissant, Colo., U.S.A.

RODES, John Edward. American, b. 1923. History. Prof., Occidental Coll., Los Angeles (joined faculty, 1950). Member of the faculty, Univ. of Southern California, Los Angeles, 1947–48, 1955, and Simmons Coll., Boston, 1948–50; Fulbright Lectr., Univ. of the Saarland, W. Germany, 1974–75; Member of the faculty, Univ. of Puget Sound, Tacoma, Wash., 1977–78. *Publs:* Germany: A History, 1964; A Short History of the Western World, 1970; Quest for Unity, 1971. Add: 416 E. Mendocino, Altadena, Calif. 91001, U.S.A.

RODGERS, Carolyn M. American. Novels, Poetry. Former Midwest Ed., Black Dialogue, NYC. *Publs:* Paper Soul, 1968; Two Love Raps, 1969; Songs of a Blackbird, 1969; Now Ain't That Love, 1969; For H.W. Fuller, 1970; Long Rap/Commonly Known as a Poetic Essay, 1971; How I Got Ovah: New and Selected Poems, 1975; The Heart as Ever Green, 1978; Translation, 1980; Eden and Other Poems, 1983; A Little Lower Than the Angels (novel), 1984. Add: 12750 S. Sangamon, Chicago, Ill. 60643, U.S.A.

RODGERS, (Sir) John (Charles, Bt.). British, b. 1906. Economics, Geography, History, Politics/Government. Deputy Chmn., J. Walter Thompson Co. Ltd., London, 1931–70; Conservative Member of Parliament (U.K.) for Sevenoaks, Kent, 1950–79; Undersecty. of State, Bd. of Trade, 1958–61. Chmn., Radio Luxembourg, London, 1979. Vice-Chmn., Exec. Cttee., Political and Economic Planning (PEP), 1960–68; Pres., Inst. of Practitioners in Advertising, 1967–69; Pres., Inst. of Statisticians, 1971–78. Founder, History Today. *Publs:* Mary Ward Settlement, 1930; The Old Public Schools of England, 1939; The English Woodland, 1941; English Rivers, 1948; (with others) One Nation, 1950; York: A History, 1951; (ed.) Thomas Gray's Poems, 1953; (with others) Change Is Our Ally, 1954; One Nation at Work, 1976. Add: 72 Berkeley House, Hay Hill, London W1; or, The Dower House, Groombridge, Kent, England.

RODGERS, Mary. American, b. 1931. Novels/Short stories, Children's fiction, Plays/Screenplays, Songs, lyrics and libretti. Script Ed. and Asst. to the Producer, New York Philharmonic Young People's Concerts, CBS-TV, 1957–71; Script Writer, Hunter Coll. Little Orch. Soc., NYC, 1958–59; Columnist ("Of Two Minds"), with Dorothy Rodgers, McCalls mag, NYC. *Publs:* (music and lyrics only) Davy Jones' Locker, by Arthur Birnkrant and Waldo Salt, 1959; (lyrics only) Three to Make Music, 1959; The Rotten Book (children's fiction), 1969; (with Dorothy Rodgers) A Word to the Wives, 1970; Freaky Friday (children's fiction), 1972; screenplay 1977; Pinocchio (for marionettes), 1973; A Billion for Boris (children's fiction), 1974; The Devil and Max Devlin (film), 1980; Summer Switch (children's fiction), 1983. Add: 91 Central Park W., New York, N.Y. 10023, U.S.A.

RODITI, Edouard (Herbert). American, b. 1910. Poetry, Art, Biography. Art Critic, L'Arche; Contrib. Ed., Antaeus and Conjunctions, NYC, European Judaism, Amsterdam, and Third Rail, Los Angeles. *Publs:* Poems for F, 1935; Prison Within Prison: Three Elegies on Hebrew Themes, 1941; (with P. Goodman and M. Liben) Pieces of Three, 1942; (trans.) Young Cherry Trees Secured Against Hares, by André Breton, 1946; Oscar Wilde, 1947, 1986; Poems 1928-1948, 1949; (trans.) The Pillar of Salt, by Albert Memmi, 1956; (trans.) The Essence of Jewish Art, by Ernest Namenyi, 1960; Dialogues on Art, 1960; Joachim Karsch, 1960; (trans.) Memed, My Hawk, by Yashar Kemal, 1961; (trans.) Toros y Toreros, by Pablo Picasso, 1961; De l'Homosexualité, 1962; (trans.) Art Nouveau, by Robert Schmutzler, 1964; New Hieroglyphic Tales: Prose Poems, 1968; Magellan of the Pacific, 1973; Emperor of Midnight, 1974; The Delights of Turkey (short stories), 1974; The Disorderly Poet and Other Essays, 1975; Meetings wih Conrad, 1977; In a Lost World, 1978; Thrice Chosen, 1981; New Old and New Testaments, 1983; Etre un Autre: Poems in French, 1983; More Dialogues on Art, 1983; (trans.) Contes Hieroglyphiques, by Horace Walpole, 1986; (trans.) The Wandering Fool, by Yunus Emre, 1987; Propos sur l'Art, 1987; (trans) Mon Piaffeur Noir, by Ronald Firbank, 1987; L'Art de Jef Van Hoof, 1989; Dialogues, 1989. Add: 142 Blvd. Massena, no. 1070, Paris 13, France.

RODNEY, William. Canadian, b. 1923. History, Politics/Government, Biography. Prof. of European and Canadian History, Royal Roads Militaory Coll., Victoria, B.C, since 1969, Emeritus since 1989. (Asst. Prof., 1962–65; Assoc. Prof., 1965–68). *Publs:* Soldiers of the International: A History of the communist Party of Canada 1919-1929, 1968; Kootenai Brown His Life and Times, 1969; Joe Boyle: King of the Klondike, 1974. Add: Faculty of Arts, Royal Roads Military Coll., FMO, Victoria, B.C. V0S 1B0, Canada.

RODRIGUEZ, Judith (Green). Has also written as Judith Green. Australian, b. 1936. Poetry. Lectr., Foundations of Professional Writing, Royal Melbourne Inst. of Technology, since 1988; Poetry Consultant, Penguin Books–Australia, since 1989. Lectr., Dept. of External Studies, Univ. of Queensland, Brisbane, 1959–60; Lectr. in English, Univ. of the West Indies, Kingston, 1963–65; Lectr., St. Mary's Coll. of Education, Twickenham, Middx., England, 1966–68; Lectr. and Sr. Lectr. in English La Trobe Univ., Melbourne, 1969–85; Lectr. in English, Macarthur Inst. of Higher Education, Sydney, 1987. Poetry Ed., Meanjin, Melbourne, 1979–82; Writer, Poetry Column, Sydney Morning Herald, 1984–86. *Publs:* (as Judith Green; with others) Four Poets, 1962; Nu-Plastik Fanfare Red and Other Poems, 1973; Broadsheet Number Twenty-Three, 1976; Water Life, 1976; Shadow on Glass, 1978; 3 Poems, 1979; Angels, 1979; Arapede, 1979; Mudcrab at Gambaro's, 1980; Witch Heart, 1982; (with others) Mrs. Noah and the Minoan Queen, 1983; Floridian Poems, 1986; The House by Water: New and Selected Poems, 1988. Add: 62 Cremorne Rd., Cremorne, N.S.W. 2090, Australia.

RODWAY, Allan Edwin. British, b. 1919. Poetry, Literature. Reader in English, Univ. of Nottingham, since 1952, now retired. Prof., Univ. of Oregon, 1960–61. *Publs:* Godwin and the Age of Transition, 1952; (with V. de S. Pinto) the Common Muse, 1957; The Romantic Conflict, 1963; Science and Modern Writing, 1964; (with Malcolm Bradbury) Two Poets, 1967; (ed.) Poetry of the 1930's, 1967; (ed.) Midsummer Night's Dream, 1969; The Truths of Fiction, 1970; English Comedy, Its Role and Nature from Chaucer to the Present Day, 1975; The Craft of Criticism, 1982; Preface to Auden, 1983. Add: The White House, 63 Radford

Bridge Rd., Nottingham, England.

RODWIN, Lloyd. American, b. 1919. Urban studies. Ford Intnl. Prof. and Dir., Special Prog. for Urban and Regional Studies of Developing Areas, Massachusetts Inst. of Technology, Cambridge, since 1967, Emeritus since 1987 (Research Assoc., 1946–47; Asst. Prof., 1947–51; Assoc. Prof., 1951–59; Head, Dept. of Urban Studies and Planning, 1969–73). Head, Faculty Policy Committee, 1959–69; Jt. Centre for Urban Studies of Massachusetts Inst. of Technology and Harvard Univ., Ed., Cities and Development series; Member Editorial Bd., International Regional Science Review; Pres., Regional Science Assoc., 1986–87. *Publs:* The British New Towns Policy, 1956; (ed.) Planning Urban Growth and Regional Development, 1960; Housing and Economic Progress, 1961; (ed.) The Future Metropolis, 1961; Nations and Cities: A Comparison of Strategies for Urban Growth, 1970; Cities and City Planning, 1981; (ed. with R. Hollister) Cities of the Mind; (ed.) Shelter, Settlement, and Development, 1987; (ed.with Hidihiko Sazanami) De-industrialization and Regional Economics Transformation: The Experience of the United States, 1989. Add: 15 Arlington St., Cambridge, Mass., U.S.A.

ROE, Derek Arthur. British, b. 1937. Archaeology/Antiquities. Univ. Lectr., since 1965, and Fellow of St. Cross Coll., since 1971, Univ. of Oxford. Archaeological Corresp., The Times, London, 1961–65. *Publs:* A Gazetteer of British Lower and Middle Palaeolithic Sites, 1968; Prehistory: An Introduction, 1970; The Lower and Middle Palaeolithic Periods in Britain, 1981; (ed.) Adlun in the Stone Age, 3 vols., 1983; (ed.) Studies in the Upper Paleolithic of British and Northwest Europe, 1986. Add: Dept. of Ethnology and Prehistory, Oxford Univ., 60 Banbury Rd., Oxford OX2 6PN, England.

ROE, Ernest. Australian, b. 1920. Education, Librarianship. Prof. and Dir., Tertiary Education Inst., Univ. of Queensland, St. Lucia, since 1973, now Emeritus. Foundn. Prof. and Dean of Eduction, Univ. of Papua and New Guinea, 1967–72. *Publs:* (with F.J. Schonell) Promise and Performance, 1962; (with J.A. Passmore, S.W. Cohen and L. Short) Teaching Methods in Australian Universities, 1965; Teachers, Librarians and Children, 1965; Some Dilemmas of Teaching, 1971; Using and Misusing the Materials of Teaching and Learning, 1975; Academics, Librarians, Resource Management, and Resource Use, 1981; (with R. McDonald) Informed Professional Judgment: A Guide to Evaluation in Post-Secondary Education, 1984; (with R. McDonald and I. Moses) Reviewing Academic Performance: Approaches to the Evaluation of Departments and Individuals, 1986; (with I. Moses) Running a Department, 1990. Add: Tertiary Education Inst., Univ. of Queensland, St. Lucia, Qld. 4067, Australia.

ROEBUCK, Derek. British, b. 1935. Prof. and Head of Law, City Polytechnic of Hong Kong, since 1987. Prof. of Law, Univ. of Tasmania, Hobart, 1969–78; Head of Research, Amnesty Intnl., London, 1979–82; Prof. of Law, Univ. of Papua New Guinea, 1982–87. *Publs:* The Law of Contract: Text and Materials for Students of Business, 2 vols., 1966–68; Law in the Study of usiness, 1967; (with P.C. Duncan and A. Szakats) Law of Commerce, 1968; (with D.E. Allan and M.E. Hiscock) Asian Contract Law: A Survey of Current Problems, 1969; (with K.K. Lian, D.E. Allan and M.E. Hiscock) Credit and Security in Singapore: The Legal Problems of Development Finance, 1973; (with S. Gautama, D.E. Allan and M.E. Hiscock) Credit and Security in Indonesia: The Legal Problems of Development Finance, 1973; (with H. Tanikawa, D.E. Allan and M.E. Hiscock) Credit and Security in Japan: The Legal Problems of Development Finance, 1973; (with W. Weerasooria, D.E. Allan M.E. Hiscock) Credit and Security in Ceylon: The Legal Problems of Development finance, 1973; (with S.T.J. de Guzman, D.E. Allan and M.E. Hiscock) Credit and Security in the Philippines: The Legal Problems of Development Finance, 1973; (with K.Y. Chick, D.E. Allan and M.E. Hiscock) Credit and Security in Korea: The Legal Problems of Development Finance, 1973; (with C. Tingsabadh, D.E. Allan and M.E. Hiscock) Credit and Security in Thailand: The Legal Problems of Development Finance, 1973; (with L. Jen-kong, D.E. Allan and M.E. Hiscock) Credit and Security in the Republic of China in Taiwan: The Legal Problems of Development Finance, 1973; Law of Contract: Text and Materials, 1974; (with D.E. Allan and M.E. Hiscock) Credit and Security: The Legal Problems of Development Financing, 1974; (with R.J.K. Chapman) The Court as the Public Conscience: Conservation, Pollution and the Law, 1976; (with Mr. Justice Beattie and P.A. Cornford) Admiralty: Australian and New Zealand Commentary of the Laws of England, 1976; (with L. Masel, D.E. Allan and M.E. Hiscock) Credit and Security in Australia: The Legal Problems of Development Finance, 1977; (with Wilfred Burchett) The Whores of War, 1977; Custom and Usage: Australia and New Zealand Commentary of the Laws of England, 1979; (with J. Singh, D.E.

Allan and M.E. Hiscock) Credit and Security in West Malaysia: The Legal Problems of Development Finance, 1980; The Background of the Common Law, 1983, 1988; (with D.K. Srivastava and J. Nonggorr) The Context of Contract in Papua New Guinea, 1984; (with D.K. Srivastava and J. Nonggorr) Pacific Contract Law, 1987; Cheques, 1989; (with C.P.Chui) Hong Kong Contracts, 1989. Add: Dept. of Law, CPHK, 700 Nathan Rd., Mong Kok, Kowloon, Hong Kong.

ROFES, Eric Edward. American, b. 1954. Children's non-fiction, Sex, Social commentary. Teacher, and Co-Dir., Fayerweather Street Sch., Cambridge, Mass., since 1978. Member of the Massachusetts Cttee. for Children and Youth; Member, Bd. of Dirs., Gay Community News. *Publs:* (ed.) The Kids' Book of Divorce: By, for and about Kids, 1981; "I Thought People Like That Killed Themselves": Lesbians, Gay Men, and Suicide, 1982; (ed.) The Kids' Book about Parents, 1984; (ed.) The Kids' Book about Death and Dying: By and for Kids, 1985; Socrates, Plato and Guys Like Me: Confessions of a Gay Schoolteacher, 1985; Gay Life: Leisure, Love and Living for the Contemporary Gay Male, 1986; The Kids' Book of Sex, 1987. Add: c/o Helen Rees Literary Agency, 308 Commonwealth Ave., Boston, Mass. 02116, U.S.A.

ROGALY, (Henry) Joseph. British, b. 1935. Social commentary/ phenomena. Writer, Financial Times, London, 1965–80 and since 1987. With Rand Daily Mail, Johannesburg until 1959, and The Economist, London, 1960–65. *Publs:* Parliament for the People, 1976; Grunwick, 1977. Add: c/o Deborah Rogers Ltd., 49 Blenheim Cres., London W11 2EF, England.

ROGERS, Floyd. *See* **SPENCE,** William John Duncan.

ROGERS, Franklin Robert. American, b. 1921. Literary critic. Prof. of English, San José State Univ., Calif., 1964–87, now Emeritus. Prof. of English, Univ. of Wisconsin-Milwaukee, 1958–63. *Publs:* Mark Twain's Burlesque Patterns . . ., 1960; The Pattern for Mark Twain's Roughing It. . ., 1961; (ed.) Simon Wheeler, Detective, by Mark Twain, 1963; (ed.) Mark Twain's Satires and Burlesques, 1967; (ed.) Roughing It, by Mark Twain, 1972; Painting and Poetry: Form, Metaphor, and the Language of Literature, 1985. Add: Dept. of English, San José State Univ., San José Calif. 95192, U.S.A.

ROGERS, George William. American, b. 1917. Economics, Politics/ Government. Research Prof., Univ. of Alaska, Juneau, 1960–83, now Emeritus. Member, Cttee. on Polar Research, National Academy of Sciences, Washington, D.C., since 1972 (member, Cttees. on Alaska Earthquake, 1964–73, Arctic Science and Technology, 1971–72, and Environmental Impact of Oil and Gas Production on the Outer Continental Shelf, 1973–74). Economist, Office of Price Admin., 1943–46, and Dept. of the Interior, 1946–47 and 1949–56; Staff Social Scientist, Arctic Inst. of North America, 1956–60. Chmn., Bd. of Trustees, Alaska Permanent Fund, 1981–82. *Publs:* Alaska in Transition: The Southeast Region, 1960: The Future of Alaska: The Economic Consequences of Statehood, 1962; (ed.) Change in Alaska: People, Petroleum and Politics, 1971; (with A. Tussing and V. Fischer) Alaska Pipeline Report, 1971; (co-author) The Circumpolar North: A Political and Economic Geography, 1978; (co-author) Issues in Alaska Development, 1978. Add: 1790 Evergreen Ave., Juneau, Alaska 99801, U.S.A.

ROGERS, Katharine M. American, b. 1932. Literature. Prof. of English, Brooklyn Coll., and Doctoral Faculty, City Univ. of New York, since 1974 (Instr., Asst. Prof. and Assoc. Prof., 1958–73); Research Prof., American Univ., since 1989. *Publs:* The Troublesome Helpmate: A History of Misogyny in Literature, 1966; William Wycherley, 1972; (ed.) The Signet Classic Book of Eighteenth and Nineteenth Century British Drama, 1979; Selected Writings of Samuel Johnson, 1981; Feminism in Eighteenth Century England, 1982; (co-ed.) The Meridian Anthology of Early Women Writers, 1987. Add: 6202 Perthshire Ct. Bethesda, Md. 20817, U.S.A.

ROGERS, Keith. *See* **HARRIS,** Marion Rose.

ROGERS, Pamela. British, b. 1927. Children's fiction. Formerly a teacher and riding sch. owner. *Publs:* The Runaway Pony, 1961; The Rag and Bone Pony, 1962; Dan and His Donkey, 1964; Secret in the Forest, 1964; Thomasina, 1966; The Lucky Bag, 1969; Fish and Chips, 1970; The Magic Egg, 1971; The Big Show, 1971; The Tractor, 1971; The Rainy Picnic, 1972; Sports Day, 1972; The Weekend, 1972; The Visitor, 1973; The Rare One, 1973; The Jinx, 1973; All Change, 1974; To Market, 1974; Anne and Her Mother, 1974; The Magnolia Tree 1974; Outing for Three, 1974; Sometimes Stump, 1975; The Stone Angel, 1976;

The Playing Field Horses, 1976; Little Stick and Big Who, 1976; Martin's Christmas, 1977. Add: Beaumans Cottage, Wards Lane, Wadhurst, Sussex, England.

ROGERS, Pat. British, b. 1938. Literature, Biography. DeBartolo Prof. in the Liberal Arts, Univ. of South Florida, Tampa, since 1986. Fellow, Sidney Sussex Coll., Cambridge, 1964–69; Lectr., King's Coll., Univ. of London, 1969–73; Prof. of English, University Coll. of N. Wales, Bangor, 1973–76, and Univ. of Bristol, 1977–86. *Publs:* (ed.) A Tour Through Great Britain, by Daniel Defoe, 1971, 1989; Grub Street: Studies in a Subculture, 1972, rev. ed. as Hacks and Dunces, 1980; (ed.) Defoe: The Critical Heritage, 1972; The Augustan Vision, 1974; An Introduction to Pope, 1976; (ed.) The Eighteenth Century, 1978; Henry Fielding: A Biography, 1979; Robinson Crusoe, 1979; (ed.) Swift: Complete Poems, 1983; Literature and Popular Culture in the Eighteenth Century, 1983; Eighteenth-Century Encounters, 1985; (ed.) The Oxford Illustrated History of English Literature, 1987. Add: Dept. of English, Univ. of South Florida, Tampa, Fla. 33620, U.S.A.

ROGERS, Rosemary. American, b. 1932. Historical/Romance/Gothic. Secty., Solano County Parks Dept., California, 1969–74. *Publs:* Sweet Savage Love, 1974; The Wildest Heart, 1974; Dark Fires, 1975; The Crowd Pleasers, 1978; The Insiders, 1979; Last Love, Last Love, 1980; Love Play, 1981; Surrender to Love, 1982; The Wanton, 1985. Add: Darien, Conn., U.S.A.

ROGERS, Thomas (Hunton). American, b. 1927. Novels/Short stories. Member of faculty, Dept. of English, Pennsylvania State Univ., University Park. *Publs:* The Pursuit of Happiness, 1968; The Confession of a Child of the Century, 1972; At the Shores, 1980. Add: Dept. of English, Pennsylvania State Univ., University Park, Pa. 16802, U.S.A.

ROGERS, William (Cecil). American, b. 1919. Education, International relations/Current affairs, Politics/Government. Consultant, Minnesota Intnl. Center, since 1984; Assoc. Ed., Livable Writer Newsletter. Dir., World Affairs Center, Univ. of Minnesota, Minneapolis, 1949–84. *Publs:* Community Education in World Affairs, 1956; A Guide to Understanding World Affairs, 1966; Global Dimensions in U.S. Education: The Community, 1972; The Winter City Book: A Survival Guide for the Frost Belt, 1980. Add: 3510 McKinley St. N.E., Minneapolis, Minn. 55418, U.S.A.

ROGERSON, Alan Thomas. British, b. 1943. Mathematics/Statistics, Theology/Religion. Lectr. in Mathematics, Queens Coll., Oxford; Research Dir., The Sch. of Mathematics Project, since 1973. Schoolmaster, Charterhouse, Godalming, Surrey, 1966–69; Jr. Research Fellow, Wolfson Coll., Oxford, 1971–73. *Publs:* Millions Now Living Will Never Die—A Study of Jehovah's Witnesses, 1969; (co-author) Vectors and Mechanics, 1971; (co-author) Differential Equations and Circuits, 1971; (co-ed.) Revised Advanced Mathematics, 2 vols., 1973; Numbers and Infinity, 1981. Add: Wolfson Coll., Oxford, England.

ROGLER, Lloyd Henry. American, b. 1930. Anthropology/Ethnology, Psychiatry, Sociology. Albert Schweitzer Univ. Prof., since 1974, and Dir., Hispanic Research Center, since 1977, Fordham Univ., Bronx, N.Y. Member, National Advisory Mental Health Council, National Inst. of Mental Health, U.S. Dept. of Health, Education and Welfare. Assoc. Prof., Yale Univ., New Haven, Conn., 1960–68; Prof. of Sociology, Case Western Reserve Univ., Cleveland, Ohio, 1968–74. *Publs:* (with A.B. Hollingshead) Trapped: Families and Schizophrenia, 1965; Migrant in the City: The Life of a Puerto Rican Action Group, 1972; Puerto Rican Familites in NYC: Intergenerational Processes. Add: Hispanic Research Center, Fordham Univ., Bronx, N.Y. 10458, U.S.A.

ROGO, D. Scott. American, b. 1950. Paranormal, Psychology.Consulting Ed., Fate mag., since 1978. Lectr., John F. Kennedy Univ., Orinda, Calif. *Publs:* NAD: A Study of Some Unusual Other-World Experiences, 1970; NAD Volume 2: A Psychic Study of "The Music of the Spheres", 1972; Methods and Models for Education in Parapsychology, 1973; The Welcoming Silence, 1973; An Experience of Phantoms, 1974; Parapsychology: A Century of Enquiries, 1975; In Search of the Unknown, 1976; Exploring Psychic Phenomena, 1976; The Haunted Universe, 1977; Mind Beyond the Body, 1978; Minds and Motion, 1978; The Haunted House Handbook, 1978; The Poltergeist Experience, 1979; (with R. Bayless) Phone Calls from the Dead, 1979; (with J. Clark) Earth's Secret Inhabitants, 1979; (with A. Druffel) The Tujunga Canyon Contacts, 1980; UFO Abduction, 1980; Miracles, 1982; ESP and Your Pet, 1982; Leaving the Body, 1983; Our Psychic Potentials, 1984; The Search for Yesterday, 1985; On the Track of the Poltergeist, 1985; Mind over Matter,

1986; Life after Death, 1986; Psychic Breakthroughs Today, 1987; The Infinite Boundary: A Psychic Look at Spirit, Possession, Madness, and Multiple Personality, 1987. Add: 18132 Schoenborn St., Northridge, Calif. 91324, U.S.A.

ROGOW, Arnold A(ustin). American, b. 1924. Intellectual history, Politics/Government, Psychiatry, Biography. Member of faculty, Univ. of Iowa, Iowa City, 1952–58, and Stanford Univ., California, 1959–66; Prof. of Political Science, City Univ. of New York, 1966–85. *Publs:* The Labour Government and British Industry, 1945-51, 1955; (with H.D. Lasswell) Power, Corruption, and Rectitude, 1963; James Forrestal: A Study of Politics, Personality and Policy, 1964; The Psychiatrists, 1970; The Dying of the Light: A Searching Look at America Today, 1975; Thomas Hobbes: Radical in the Service of Reaction, 1986. Add: 1100 Madison Ave., New York, N.Y. 10028, U.S.A.

ROHMER, Richard. Canadian, b. 1924. Science fiction/Fantasy, Environmental science/Ecology, Biography. Law Partner, Rohmer and Swayze, then Counsel, Frost and Redway, Toronto, since 1951. Chmn., Bd. of Governors, Univ. of Canada North. Chmn., Royal Commn. on Publishing, 1970–72; Counsel, Royal Commn. on Metropolitan Toronto, 1975–77. *Publs:* The Green North (non-fiction), 1970; The Arctic Imperative: An Overview of the Energy Crisis, 1973; Ultimatum, 1973; Exxoneration, 1974; Exodus/UK, 1975; Separation, 1976; E.P. Taylor (biography), 1978; Balls!, 1979; Periscope Red, 1980; Separation II, 1981; Triad, 1981; Patton's Gap (non-fiction), 1981; Retaliation, 1982; How to Write a Best-Seller, 1984; Massacre 747 (non-fiction), 1984; Starmageddon, 1986; Hour of the Fox, 1981. Add: c/o New American Library, 1633 Broadway, New York, N.Y. 10019, U.S.A.

ROHNER, Ronald P. American, b. 1935. Anthropology/Ethnology, Psychology. Prof. of Anthropology and Family Studies, Univ. of Connecticut, Storrs, since 1975 (Asst. Prof. of Anthropology, 1964–67; Assoc. Prof., 1967–75). *Publs:* The People of Gilford: A Contemporary Kwakiutl Village, 1967; The Ethnography of Franz Boas: Letters and Diaries of Franz Boas Written on the Northwest Coast from 1886 to 1931, 1969; (with E.C. Rohner) The Kwakiutl Indians of British Columbia, 1970; They Love Me, They Love Me Not: A Worldwide Study of the Effects of Parental Acceptance and Rejection, 1975; (with C.C. Nielson) Parental Acceptance and Rejection: A Review and Annotated Bibliography of Research and Theory, 2 vols., 1978; (with E.C. Rohner) Worldwide Tests of Parental Acceptance-Rejection Theory, 1980; Handbook for the Study of Parental Acceptance and Rejection, 1980, 1984; The Warmth Dimension: Foundations of Parental Acceptance-Rejection Theory, 1986; (with M. Chaki-Sircar) Woman and Children in a Bengali Village, 1988. Add: Dept. of Anthropology, Univ. of Connecticut, Storrs, Conn. 06269-2158, U.S.A.

ROHRBACH, Peter Thomas. Also writes as James R. Cody. American, b. 1926. Novels/Short stories. Ed., Spiritual Life mag., 1966–70. *Publs:* A Girl and Her Teens, 1959, 7th ed. 1965; The Disillusioned, 1959; A Gentle Fury, 1959; Bold Encounter, 1960; Search for St. Therese, 1961; Conversation with Christ, 1965, 10th ed. 1982; Journey to Carith, 1966; (as James R. Cody) The D.C. Man; (as James R. Cody) Search and Destroy; Stagecoach East, 1983; American Issue, 1985. Add: 9609 Barkston Ct., Potomac, Md. 20854, U.S.A.

ROHRBOUGH, Malcolm Justin. American, b. 1932. History. Prof. of History, Univ. of Iowa, Iowa City, since 1971 (Asst. Prof. and Assoc. Prof., 1964–71). Dept. of History, Princeton Univ., N.J., 1962–64. *Publs:* The Land Office Business: The Settlement and Administration of American Public Lands, 1789-1837, 1968; The Trans-Appalachian Frontier: People, Societies, and Institutions, 1775-1850, 1978; Aspen: The History of a Silver Mining Town 1879-1893, 1986. Add: Dept. of History, Univ. of Iowa, Iowa City, Iowa 52242, U.S.A.

ROIPHE, Anne Richardson. Has also written as Anne Richardson. American, b. 1935. Novels, Psychology. *Publs:* (as Anne Richardson) Digging Out, 1967; Up the Sandbox!, 1970; Long Division, 1972; (as Anne Richardson) Torch Song, 1977; (with Herman Roiphe) Your Child's Mind: The Complete Guide to Infant and Child Emotional Well-Being, 1986; Lovingkindness, 1987; A Season for Healing: Reflections on the Holocaust, 1988. Add: c/o Summit Books, 1230 Ave. of the Americas, New York, N.Y. 10020, U.S.A.

ROLAND SMITH, Gordon. British, b. 1931. Children's non-fiction, Crafts, Theology/Religion. Public Relations Officer, Gen. Conference of the New Church, since 1984; freelance design consultant. Pres., Missionary Soc. of the New Church, 1970–77, and since 1979. Teacher,

1951–55, 1958–64, and Head of Art and Jr. Dept., 1968–83, Cannock Sch., Kent; Graphic Designer, Marley Group, 1955–57. *Publs:* First Models in Cardboard, 1963, 1969; Creative Crayon Craft, 1964; My Side of the Grave, 1970; Making a Model Village, 1970; The Zebra Book of Papercraft, 1972; Make It from Paper, 1974; Paper for Play, 1975; Thinks, 1979; I Suppose I Shall Survive, 1982; 100 Plus Calligraphy Projects, 1989. Add: Melilot, Well Hill Lane, Chelsfield, Orpington, Kent BR6 7QJ, England.

ROLFE, Sheila Constance. Canadian, b. 1935. Children's fiction. *Publs:* Amulets and Arrowheads, 1967; Sasquatch Adventure, 1975. Add: 4267 Yuculta Cres., Vancouver, B.C. V6N 4A9, Canada.

ROLL OF IPSDEN, Baron; Eric Roll. British, b. 1907. Economics, History, Money/Finance. Banker and Joint Chmn., S.G. Warburg and Co. Ltd., London, since 1974 (Deputy Chmn., 1967–74). Prof. of Economics and Commerce, University Coll. of Hull, 1935–46; formerly with the U.K. Civil Service: Permanent Under-Secty. of State, Dept. of Economic Affairs, 1964–66. *Publs:* An Early Experiment in Industrial Organisation, 1930; Spotlight on Germany, 1933; About Money, 1934; Elements of Economic Theory, 1935; A History of Economic Thought, 1938, 4th ed. 1973; The Combined Food Board, 1957; The World After Keynes, 1968; The Uses and Abuses of Economics, 1978; (ed.) The Mixed Economy, 1982; Crowded Hours (autobiography), 1985. Add: D2 Albany, Piccadilly, London W1, Engand.

ROLLE, Andrew. American, b. 1922. History, Biography. Cleland Prof. of History, Occidental Coll., Los Angeles (joined faculty, 1952). American Vice-Consul, Genoa, 1945–48. *Publs:* Riviera Path, 1948; An American in California, 1956; The Road to Virginia City, 1960; (with A. Nevins and I. Stone) Lincoln: A Contemporary Portrait, 1962; Occidental College: The First Seventy-Five Years, 1962; California: A History, 1963, 4th ed. 1987; (ed.) A Century of Dishonor: The Early Crusade for Indian Reform, 1965; The Lost Cause: Confederate Exiles in Mexico, 1965; California: A Students' Guide to Localized History, 1965; The Golden State, 1965, 1978; Los Angeles: A Students' Guide to Localized History, 1966; The Immigrant Upraised: Italian Adventures and Colonists in an Expanding America, 1968; (ed.) Life in California, 1970; The American Italians: Their History and Culture, 1973; (co-author) Essays and Assays: California History Reconsidered, 1973; The Italian-Americans: Troubled Roots, 1981; Los Angeles: From Pueblo to City of the Future, 1982; Occidental College: A Centennial History, 1987. Add: Dept. of History, Occidental Coll., Los Angeles, Calif. 90041, U.S.A.

ROLLIN, Roger B. American, b. 1930. Literature. William James Lemon Prof. of Literature, Clemson Univ., South Carolina, since 1975. Prof. of English, Franklin and Marshall Coll., Lancaster Pa., 1959–75. *Publs:* Robert Herrick, 1966; (ed.) Hero/Anti-Hero, 1973; (ed. with J. Max Patrick) Trust to Good Verses: Herrick Tercentenary Essays, 1978; (ed.) The Americanization of the Global Village: Essays in Comparative Popular Culture, 1989. Add: Rt. 5, Box 233, Seneca, S.C. 29678, U.S.A.

ROLLINS, Wayne Gilbert. American, b. 1929. Theology/Religion. Prof. of Religious Studies, and Dir. of the Ecumenical Inst., Assumption Coll., Worcester, Mass., since 1974. Instr. in Religion, Princeton Univ., New Jersey, 1958–59; Asst. Prof. of Biblical Studies, Wellesley Coll., Massachusetts, 1959–66; Prof. of Biblical Studies, Hartford Seminary Foundn., Connecticut, 1966–74. *Publs:* The Gospels: Portraits of Christ, 1964; Jung and the Bible, 1983. Add: 75 Craigmoor Rd., West Hartford, Conn. 06107, U.S.A.

ROLLO, Vera Foster. American, b. 1924. Air/Space topics, Geography, History. Publr., Maryland Historical Press. Former Lightplane Ed., American Aviation Publs., Washington, D.C. *Publs:* Maryland's Constitution and Government, 1968, 1985; Maryland Personality Parade, 1970; Your Maryland, 2nd ed. 1971, 4th ed. 1985; Henry Harford: Last Proprietor of Maryland, 1976; Aviation Law: An Introduction, 1979, 1985; Ask Me! (About Maryland): A Geography, 1980; The Black Experience in Maryland, 1980, 1984; A Geography of Maryland, 1981; Maryland's Government, 1986; Aviation Insurance, 1987; The Proprietorship of Maryland, 1988. Add: c/o Maryland Historical Press, 9205 Tuckerman St., Lanham, Md. 20706, U.S.A.

ROLLS, Eric Charles. Australian, b. 1923. Poetry, Children's non-fiction, History, Natural history. Self-employed farmer and grazier. *Publs:* Sheaf Tosser, 1967; They All Ran Wild, 1969; Running Wild, 1973; The River, 1974; The Green Mosaic, 1977; Miss Strawberry Verses, 1978; A Million Wild Acres, 1981; Celebration of the Senses, 1984; Doorways: A Year of the Cumberdeen Diary, 1989; Selected Poetry, 1990. Add:

Cumberdeen, Baradine, N.S.W. 2396, Australia.

ROLO, Paul Jacques Victor. British, b. 1917. History, Biography. Prof. of History, Univ. of Keele, since 1972 (Lectr. in History and Politics, 1951–61; Sr. Lectr., 1961–72). Lectr., Balliol Coll., Oxford, 1946–49. *Publs:* George Canning, 1965; Entente Cordiale, 1969; Britain and the Briand Plan, 1973. Add: Dept. of History, Univ. of Keele, Keele, Staffs., England.

ROLPH, C.H. (Cecil Rolph Hewitt). British, b. 1901. Criminology/Law enforcement/prisons,Law, Autobiography/Memoirs/Personal. Dir., Statesman Publishing Co., London, since 1965. Former Chief Inspector, City of London Police. Member, Parole Bd., 1967–69. *Publs:* A Licensing Handbook, 1947; Crime and Punishment, 1950; Towards My Neighbour, 1950; On Gambling, 1951; Personal Identity, 1956; (ed.) The Human Sum, 1957; Mental Disorder, 1958; Commonsense about Crime and Punishment, 1961; The Trial of Lady Chatterley, 1961; (with Arthur Koestler) Hanged by the Neck, 1961; All Those in Favour? (the ETU Trial), 1962; The Police and the Public, 1962; Law and the Common Man, 1967; Books in the Dock, 1969; Kingsley, 1973; Believe What You Like, 1973; Living Twice (autobiography), 1974; Mr. Prone, 1977; The Queen's Pardon, 1978; London Particulars (autobiography), 1980; The Police (history for children), 1980; As I Was Saying (collected essays), 1985; Further Particulars (autobiography), 1987. Add: Rushett Edge, Bramley, Surrey, England.

ROMANO, Louis. American, b. 1921. Children's fiction, Children's non-fiction, Education. Prof. of Education, Michigan State Univ., East Lansing, since 1966. Exec. Dir., Michigan Assn. of Middle Sch. Educators, since 1975. Teacher and Asst. Supt. of Schs., Shorewood Public Schs., Wisconsin, 1944–64; Supt. of Schs., Wilmette, Ill., 1965–66. *Publs:* (with N.P. Georgiady) Exploring Wisconsin, 1957; (with N.P. Georgiady) Gertie the Duck, 1959; (with N.P. Georgiady) Anden Agda, 1959; (with N.P. Georgiady) Anden Gertrud, 1959; (with N.P. Georgiady) Trudi La Cane, 1960; (with N.P. Georgiady) Tulita La Patita, 1960; (with N.P. Georgiady) This is a Department Store, 1962; (with N.P. Georgiady) Our Country's Flag, 1963; (with N.P. Georgiady) Our National Anthem, 1963; (co-author) A Guide to Successful Parent-Teacher Conferences, 1964; Challenge to the Fives, 1965; (with N.P. Georgiady) Quack, die Ente, 1965; (with N.P. Georgiady) Wisconsin Indians, Wisconsin Women, Wisconsin Men, Wisconsin Historical Sights, all 1966; (with N.P. Georgiady) Know about Money, Know about Banks, The Ironclad, The Boston Tea Party, Thomas Jefferson, all 1966; (with N.P. Georgiady) Illinois Indians, Illinois Women, Illinois Men, Illinois Historical Sights, all 1967; (with N.P. Georgiady) Michigan Indians, Michigan Women, Michigan Men, Michigan Historical Sights, all 1967; (with N.P. Georgiady) Indiana Indians, Indiana Women, Indiana Men, Indiana Historical Sights, all 1968; (with N.P. Georgiady) The History of the Nation's Capitol, Monuments and Memorials in Our Nation's Capitol, Famous People in the Early History of Our Capitol, Important Buildings in Our Nation's Capitol, all 1968; (with N.P. Georgiady and R.L. Green) Daniel Hale Williams, Benjamin Banneker, Jan Matzeliger, Percy Lavon Julian, Charles Richard Drew, Mary McLeod Bethune, W.E.B. DuBois, Carter G. Woodson, Mordecai Johnson, John Hope Franklin, Thurgood Marshall, Ralph Bunche, William H. Heard, Oscar DePriest, Carl B. Stokes, John Merrick, John H. Johnson, Maggie Lena Walker, Charles Spaulding, Robert S. Abbott, Estebanico, Jean Baptiste Pointe DuSable, James Beckwourth, Matthew Henson, Maj. Robert H. Lawrence, Garrett Morgan, Granville T. Woods, Ernest Just, George W. Carver, Paul Williams, Richard Wright, James Baldwin, Paul Laurence Dunbar, Langston Hughes, Charles W. Chestnutt, Sojourner Truth, Frederick Douglas, Martin Luther King Jr., Crispus Attucks, Harriet Tubman, Sidney Poitier, Burt Williams, Ethel Waters, Paul Robeson, Ida Aldridge, Jackie Robinson, Jack Johnson, Joe Louis, Althea Gibson, Jimmy Brown, Meta Warrick Fuller, Henry O. Tanner, Archibald J. Motley Jr., Jacob Lawrence, Horace Pippin, Marian Anderson, William C. Handy, Louis Armstrong, Duke Ellington, Harry Belafonte, all 1968; (with J. Heald and N.P. Georgiady) Selected Readings on General Supervision, 1972; (with N.P. Georgiady) Introduction to the Defenders, Pope, Tecumseh, King Philip, all 1973; (with N.P. Georgiady), A. Kloster and R. Featherstone) The Management of Educational Personnel, 1973, 1977; (with N.P. Georgiady and J. Heald) The Middle School, 1973; (with N.P. Georgiady) Know about Airports, Know about Shopping Centers, Know about Computers, Know about Skyscrapers, Know about Assembly Lines, Know about Highways, Know about Banks, Know about Money, Know about Stamp Collecting, all 1975; A Guide to an Effective Middle School, 1984. Add: Erickson Hall 419, Michigan State Univ., East Lansing, Mich. 48824, U.S.A.

ROME, Anthony. *See* **ALBERT,** Marvin H.

ROME, Margaret. British. Historical/Romance/Gothic. *Publs:* The Lottery for Matthew Devlin, 1968; The Marriage of Caroline Lindsay, 1968; (A Chance to Win, 1969; Flower of the Marsh, 1969; Man of Fire, 1970; Bird of Paradise, 1970; Chateau of Flowers, 1971; The Girl at Eagles' Mount, 1971; Bride of the Rif, 1972; Island of Pearls, 1973; The Bartered Bride, 19 3; Palace of the Hawk, 1974; Valley of Paradise, 1975; Cove of Promises, 1975; The Girl at Dane's Dyke, 1975; Adam's Rib, 1976; Bride of Zarco, 1976; Lion of Venice, 1977; The Thistle and the Rose, 1977; Son of Adam, 1978; Castle of the Fountains, 1979; Champagne Spring, 1979; Isle of Calypso, 1979; Marriage by Capture, 1980; Miss High and Mighty, 1980; The Wild Man, 1980; Second-Best Bride, 1981; King of Kielder, 1981; Castle in Spain, 1981; Rapture of the Deep, 1982; Valley of Gentians, 1982; Bay of Angels, 1983; Castle of the Lion, 1983; Lord of the Land, 1983. Add: c/o Mills and Boon Ltd., Eton House, 18-24 Paradise Rd., Richmond, Surrey TW9 1SR, England.

ROMER, (Louis) John. British, b. 1941. Archaeology, History. Pres., Theban Foundn., Berkeley, since 1979. Lectr. in the history of art, 1968–72; artist, Oriental Inst. Epigraphic Survey, Luxor, Egypt, 1973–77; archaeologist for the Brooklyn Museum excavation in Luxor, 1977–79. *Publs:* Valley of the Kings, 1981; Romer's Egypt (in U.S. as People of the Nile), 1982; Ancient Lives: Story of the Pharaoh's Tombmakers, 1984; Testament: Bible and History, 1988. Add: Theban Foundn., 2134 Allston Way, Berkeley, Calif. 94704, U.S.A.

ROMERIL, John. Australian, b. 1945. Plays/Screenplays, Literature. Dir. and actor; resident writer, Australian Performing Group, Melbourne, 1974, W.A. Inst. of Technology, Bentley, 1977, Univ. of Newcastle, N.S.W., 1978, Jigsaw Theatre Co., Canberra, 1980, Troupe, Adelaide, 1981, Flinders Univ., Bedford Park, S.A., 1984, Magpie, Adelaide, 1985, and Vict. Arts Centre, Melbourne, 1985. *Publs:* plays—Chicago Chicago (in Plays), 1970; Two Plays, 1971; I Don't Know Who to Feel Sorry For, 1973; The Floating World, 1975, 1982; Bastardy, 1982; Mrs. Thrally F (in Seven One-Act Plays), 1983; Waltzing Matilda, 1984; The Accidental Poke (in Popular Short Plays for the Australian Stage), 1985; The Kelly Dance, 1986; (co-author) Legends, 1986; other—6 of the Best, 1984. Add: c/o Almost Managing, P.O. Box 34, Carlton, Vic. 3053, Australia.

ROMNEY, Steve. *See* **BINGLEY,** David Ernest.

RONAN, Colin Alistair. British, b. 1920. Astronomy, Children's non-fiction, History, Sciences, Biography. Secty., East Asian History of Science Trust; U.K. and Project Coordinator, Needham Research Inst., Cambridge. Sr. Staff Member, Secretariat of the Royal Soc., London, 1949–60. *Publs:* Changing Views of the Universe, 1961; Earth from Pole to Pole, 1961; The Meaning of Light, 1962; Man Probes the Universe, 1964; Clocks and Watches, 1964; Radio Astronomy, 1964; The Astronomers, 1964; Optical Astronomy, 1964; The Stars, 1965; The Easy Way to Understand Photography, 1966; Exploring Space, 1966; The Universe, 1966; Their Majesties' Astronomers (in U.S. as Astronomers Royal), 1967; The Meaning of Sound, 1967; Isaac Newton, 1969; Edmond Halley, 1969; Invisible Astronomy, 1969; A Book of Science, 1970; Discovering the Universe, 1971; Astronomy, 1973; Lost Discoveries, 1973; Galileo, 1974; The Shorter Science and Civilisation in China, 3 vols., 1978–85; The Practical Astronomer, 1980; Deep Space, 1982; An Illustrated History of World's Science, 1982; The Cambridge Illustrated History of the World's Science, 1988. Add: 13 Acorn Ave., Bar Hill, Cambridge CB3 8DT, England.

RONSLEY, Joseph. Canadian, b. 1931. Literature. Prof. of English, McGill Univ., Montreal, since 1983 (Asst. Prof., 1969–73, Assoc. Prof., 1973–83). Asst. Prof. of English, Univ. of Wisconsin, Madison, 1967–69. *Publs:* Yeats's Autobiography: Life as Symbolic Pattern, 1968; (ed.) Myth and Reality in Irish Literature, 1977; (ed.) Denis Johnston: A Retrospective, 1981; (ed.) Selected Plays of Denis Johnston, 1983; (ed.) Omnium Gatherum: Essays for Richard Ellmann, 1989. Add: Dept. of English, McGill Univ., Montreal, Que. H3A 2T6, Canada.

ROOK, (William) Alan. British, b. 1909. Poetry, Cookery/Gastronomy/Wine, Literature. Managing Dir., Skinner, Rook and Chambers Ltd., wine merchants, since 1947. *Publs:* (ed. with A.W. Sandford) Oxford Poetry, 1936, 1936; Songs from a Cherry Tree, 1938; Soldiers, This Solitude, 1942; These Are My Comrades: Poems, 1943; We Who Are Fortunate, 1945; Not as a Refuge (literary criticism), 1948; Diary of an English Vineyard, 1972. Add: Stragglethorpe Hall, Lincoln, England.

ROOK, Tony. British, b. 1932. Mystery/Crime/Suspense, Archaeology/Antiquities. Ed., Hertfordshire Archaeological Review; Dir., Welwyn Archaeological Soc.; Education Officer, Lockleys Archaeological Trust; Extra-Mural Lectr., Univ. of London. Bldg. Technologist, G. Wimpey Ltd., and CLAIRA, 1957–63; Sr. Science Teacher, Sherrardswood Sch., 1963–73. *Publs:* Roman Villa, 1973; Roman Legionary, 1974; Strange Mansion, 1974; Pompeiian House, 1978; Roman Bath House, 1978; The Labrador Trust, 1983; A History of Hertfordshire, 1984. Add: Old Rectory, 23 Mill Lane, Welwyn, Herts. AL6 9EU, England.

ROOKE, Daphne (Marie). British/South African, b. 1914. Novels/Short stories, Children's fiction. *Publs:* The Sea Hath Bounds (in U.S. asGrove of Fever Trees), 1946; Mittee, 1951; Ratoons, 1953; The South African Twins (in U.S. as Twins in South Africa), 1953; The Australian Twins (in U.S. as Twins in Australia), 1954; New Zealand Twins, 1957; Wizards' Country, 1957; Beti, 1959; A Lover for Estelle, 1961; The Greyling, 1962; Diamond Jo, 1965; Boy on the Mountain, 1969; Double Ex!, 1971; Margaretha de la Porte, 1974; A Horse of His Own, 1976. Add: 34 Bent St., Fingal Bay, N.S.W. 2315, Australia.

ROONEY, Andrew A(itken). (Andy Rooney). American, b. 1919. Humor, Essays. Writer-Producer, CBS-TV, since 1959; Newspaper Columnist, Tribune Co. Syndicate, since 1979. *Publs:* (with O.C. Hutton) Air Gunner, 1944; The Story of Stars and Stripes, 1946; Conquerors' Peace, 1947; The Fortunes of War, 1962; A Few Minutes with Andy Rooney, 1981; And More by Andy Rooney. 1982; Pieces of My Mind, 1984; The Most of Andrew Rooney, 1986; Word for Word, 1986; Not That You Asked, 1989. Add: c/o CBS News, 524 W. 57th St., New York, N.Y. 10019, U.S.A.

ROOP, Connie. (Constance Betzer Roop). American, b. 1951. Children's fiction, Children's non-fiction. *Publs:* (all with Peter Roop)—Space Out!, 1984; Go Hog Wild!, 1984; Out to Lunch!, 1984; Keep the Lights Burning, Abbie, 1985; Buttons for General Washington, 1986; Stick Out Your Tongue!, 1986; Going Buggy!, 1986; Let's Celebrate!, 1986; The Extinction of the Dinosaurs, 1987; Mysteries of the Solar System, 1987; Poltergeists, 1987. Add: 2601 N. Union St. Appleton, Wisc. 54911, U.S.A.

ROOP, Peter. American, b. 1951. Children's fiction, Children's non-fiction. Teacher, Appleton Area Sch. District, Wisconsin, since 1973; Instr., Univ. of Wisconsin Sch. of the Arts, Rhinelander, since 1986. Fulbright Exchange teacher, Kingston, England, 1976–77; Instr., Univ. of Wisconsin, Fox Valley, 1983–84. *Publs:* The Cry of the Conch, 1984; Little Blaze and the Buffalo Jump, 1984; Siskimi,984; Natosi, 1984; (with Connie Roop) Space Out!, 1984; (with Connie Roop) Go Hog Wild, 1984; (with Connie Roop) Out to Lunch!, 1984; (with Connie Roop) Keep the lights Burning, Abbie, 1985; (with Connie Roop) Buttons for General Washington, 1986; (with Connie Roop) Stick Out Your Tongue!, 1986; (with Connie Roop) Going Buggy!, 1986; (with Connie Roop) Let's Celebrate!, 1986; (with Connie Roop) The Extinction of the Dinosaurs, 1987; (with Connie Roop) Mysteries of the Solar System, 1987; (with Connie Roop) Poltergeists, 1987. Add: 2601 N. Union St., Appleton, Wisc. 54911, U.S.A.

ROOS, Kelley. *See* **ROOS**, William.

ROOS, Noralou P. Canadian, b. 1942. Administration/Management, Medicine/Health, Politics/Government, Public/Social administration. Prof., Faculty of Admin. Studies, and Prof., Faculty of Medicine, Univ. of Manitoba, Winnipeg, since 1973. Asst. Prof. of Political Science, 1968–69, Massachusetts, Inst. of Technology, Cambridge; Asst. Prof. of Org. Behavior, Grad. Sch. of Mgmt., Northwestern Univ., Evanston, Ill., 1969–72; Research Assoc., Hosp. Research and Educational Trust, 1971–72; National Health Scientist, Health and Welfare, Canada, 1973. *Publs:* (with L.L. Roos) Managers of Modernization, 1971. Add: Faculty of Medicine, Univ. of Manitoba, Winnipeg, Man., Canada.

ROOS, William. Wrote mysteries, with Audrey Roos (now deceased), as Kelley Roos. American, b. 1911. Mystery/Crime/Suspense, Plays/Screenplays. *Publs:* mystery novels, with Audrey Roos, as Kelley Roos—Made Up to Kill, 1940, in U.K. as Made Up for Murder, 1941; If the Shroud Fits, 1941, as Dangerous Blondes, 1951; The Frightened Stiff, 1942; Sailor, Take Warning!, 1944; There Was a Crooked Man, 1945; Ghost of a Chance, 1947; Murder in Any Language, 1948; Triple Threat, 1949; Beauty Marks the Spot, 1951; The Blonde Died Dancing, 1956, in U.K. as She Died Dancing, 1957; Speaking of Murder (play), 1957; Requiem for a Blonde, 1958, in U.K. as Murder Noon and Night, 1959; Scent of Mystery (novelization of screenplay), 1959; Grave Danger, 1965; Necessary Evil, 1965; A Few Days in Madrid, 1965; Cry in the

Night, 1966; One False Move, 1966; Who Saw Maggie Brown?, 1967; To Save His Life, 1968; Suddenly One Night, 1970; What Did Hattie See?, 1970; Bad Trip, 1971; Murder on Martha's Vineyard, 1981; other, as William Roos—The Hornet's Longboat (novel), 1940; January Thaw (play), 1946; Boy Wanted (play), 1947; As he Girls Go (musical), 1948; (as William Rand) Ellery Queen's The Four of Hearts Mystery (play), 1948; Courtin' Time (musical), 1951; Belles on Their Toes (play), 1952. Add: c/o Dodd Mead, 79 Madison Ave., New York, N.Y. 10016, U.S.A.

ROOSE-EVANS, James. British, b. 1927. Children's fiction, Plays/Screenplays, Theatre. Freelance theatre dir., author and actor; Columnist ("Something Extra"), Woman mag., since 1986. Founder and Chmn., Bleddfa Trust-Centre for Caring and the Arts in Mid-Wales, since 1974. Founder Hampstead Theatre Club, London, 1959 (Artistic Dir., 1959–73), and Stage Two, London, 1969. Member of the faculty, Juilliard Sch. of Music, NYC, 1955–56; Staff Member and Judge, Royal Academy of Dramatic Art, London, 1957–62. *Publs:* Directing a Play, 1968; Experimental Theatre, 1970, 4th ed. 1989; The Adventures of Odd and Elsewhere, 1971; The Secret of the Seven Bright Shiners, 1972; Odd and the Great Bear, 1973; Elsewhere and the Gathering of the Clowns, 1974; The Return of the Great Bear, 1 75; The Secret of Tippity-Witchit, 1975; The Female Messiah (radio documentary), 1975; Actor Training 2, 1976; The Lost Treasure of Wales, 1977; London Theatre, 1977; Topsy and Ted, (radio play), 1977; Acrobats of God (BBC documentary), 1977; Pride of Players (dramatic anthology), 1978; The Third Adam (radio documentary), 1978; A Well-Conducted Theatre (radio documentary), 1979; Lady Managers (BBC documentary), 1980; 84 Charing Cross Road (play), 1981; Odd to the Rescue, 1983; Inner Journey, Outer Journey, 1987; (ed.) Darling Ma: Letters of Joyce Grenfell, 1988; Re Joyce! (play), 1988; (ed.) The Time of My Life: The Wartime Journals of Joyce Grenfell, 1989. Add: c/o David Higham Assocs., 5-8 Lower John St., London W1R 4HA, England.

ROOSEVELT, Elliott. American, b. 1910. Mystery/Crime/Suspense, History, Biography. Pres. and Dir., Dalco Uranium, Inc., since 1957. Worked in advertising, editing, and broadcasting, 1920–41; Vice-Pres., Aeronautical Chamber of Commerce of America, 1934–35; mayor of Miami Beach, Fla., 1965–69. *Publs:* As He Saw It, 1946; (ed.) F.D.R.: His Personal Letters, 3 vols., 1947–50; (with James Brough) An Untold Story: The Roosevelts of Hyde Park, 1973; (with James Brough) A Rendezvous with Destiny: The Roosevelts of the White House, 1975; (with James Brough) Mother R.: Eleanor Roosevelt's Untold Story, 1977; Eleanor Roosevelt, with Love: A Centenary Remembrance, 1984; The Hyde Park Murder, 1985; Murder and the First Lady, 1985; Murder at Hobcaw Barony, 1986; The White House Pantry Murder, 1987; Murder at the Palace, 1988. Add: c/o St. Martin's Press, Inc., 175 Fifth Ave., New York, N.Y. 10010, U.S.A.

ROOT, Phyllis. American, b. 1949. Children's fiction. Full-time writer. Formerly worked as an admin. asst., bicycle repair person, costume seamstress, and architectural draftsperson. *Publs:* Hidden Places, 1983; (with Carol A. Marron) Gretchen's Grandma, 1983 (with Carol A. Marron) Just One of the Family 1984; (with Carol A. Marron) No Place for a Pig, 1984; My Cousin Charlie, 1984; Moon Tiger, 1985; Joshua Holly's Big Family Blues, 1985; Soup for Supper, 1986. Add: 3842 Bloomington Ave. S., Minneapolis, Minn. 55407, U.S.A.

ROOT, William Pitt. American, b. 1941. Novels/Short stories, Poetry, Translation. Assoc. Prof., Hunter Coll., NYC, since 1986. Asst. Prof., Michigan State Univ., East Lansing, 1967–68; Visiting writer, Univ. of Montana, Missoula, 1978, 1980–81, 1983–86. *Publs:* The Storm and Other Poems, 1969; Striking the Dark Air for Music, 1973; The Port of Galveston, 1974; (ed.) What A World, What a World!: Poetry by Young People in Galveston Schools, 1974; Coot and Other Characters, 1977; (ed.) Timesoup (poetry), 1980; Fireclock, 1981; Reasons for Going It on Foot, 1981; In the World's Common Grasses, 1981; Faultdancing, 1986. Add: Add: English Dept., Hunter Coll., New York, N.Y. 10021, U.S.A.

ROOTHAM, Jasper St. John. British, b. 1910. Poetry. Private Secty. to the Prime Minister, 1938–39; Asst. to the Gov. of the Bank of England, 1966–67; Managing Dir., Lazard Bros. and Co. Ltd., London, 1967–75. *Publs:* Miss-Fire, 1946; Demi-Paradise (prose), 1960; Verses 1928-1972, 1973; The Celestial City, 1975; Reflections from a Crag, 1978; Selected Poems 1980; Stand Fixed in Steadfast Gaze, 1981; Affirmation, 1982; Lament for a Dead Sculptor and Other Poems, 1985. Add: 30 West St., Wimborne Minster, Dorset BH21 1JS, England.

ROPER, Laura Wood. Also writes as Laura Newbold Wood. American, b. 1911. Biography. *Publs:* as L.N. Wood—Walter Reed,

Doctor in Uniform, 1943; Raymond Ditmars: His Exciting Career, 1944; Louis Pasteur (children), 1948; as Laura Wood Roper—F.L.O.: A Biography of Frederick Law Olmsted, 1973. Add: 3405 O St. N.W., Washington, D.C. 20007, U.S.A.

ROQUELAURE, A.N. *See* **RICE**, Anne.

ROSAND, David. American, b. 1938. Art. Prof. of Art History, Columbia Univ., NYC, since 1964. *Publs:* Art History and Criticism, 1974; Titian, 1978; Painting in Cinquecento Venice: Titian, Veronese, Tintoretto, 1982; The Portrait, The Courtier, and Death in Castiglione, 1938. Add: Dept. of Art History, Columbia Univ., New York, N.Y. 10028, U.S.A.

ROSBERG, Rose. American, b. 1916. Poetry. Librarian, NYC Bd. of Education. *Publs:* Trips: Without LSD, 1969. Add: 880 W. 181st St., New York, N.Y. 10033, U.S.A.

ROSE, Al. American, b. 1916. Songs, lyrics and libretti, Music. Self-employed artist, writer, recording dir., film actor and radio commentator. Writer and commentator, Journeys into Jazz, radio series, Southern Illinois Univ. Radio Network, Carbondale. *Publs:* (with Souchon) New Orleans Jazz; A Family Album, 1967; (co-author) Storyville Portraits, 1970; Storyville, New Orleans, 1974; Eubie Blake, 1979; Born in New Orleans, 1983; I Remember Jazz, 1987. Add: 728 Tyler St., Hollywood, Fla. 33022, U.S.A.

ROSE, Elinor K. American, b. 1920. Poetry. Syndicated Feature Writer, The Detroit News, since 1955. Lectr., Michigan Council for the Arts Sch. Progs. *Publs:* Relax, Chum; Sugar and Spice; Rhyme and Reason; (co-ed.) Echoes from the Moon, 1976; Born in New Orleans, 1984. Add: 350 E. Ocean Ave., Hypoluxo Island, Flor. 33462, U.S.A.

ROSE, Eliot Joseph Benn. British, b. 1909. Race relations. Co-Founder and Chmn., The Runnymede Trust, since 1968. Literary Ed., The Observer newspaper, London, 1948–51; Dir., Intnl. Press Inst., Zurich, 1951–62; Dir., Survey of Race Relations in Britain, 1963–69; Editorial Dir., Westminster Press, London, 1970–74; Chmn., Penguin Books Ltd., London, 1973–80. Chmn., Inter-Action Trust, 1968–84. *Publs:* (with Nicholas Deakin) Colour and Citizenship, 1969. Add: 37 Pembroke Sq., London W8, England.

ROSE, Ernst. American, b. 1899. Literature, Translations. Prof. Emeritus, New York Univ., Washington Sq., Coll., NYC, since 1966 (Instr., 1925–29; Asst. Prof., 1929–38; Assoc. Prof., 1938–49; Prof., 1949–66; Chmn., Dept. of German, 1948–65; Head, Dept. of German, 1958–65). *Publs:* (with C.M. Purin) Deutsche Kulturkunde, 1926; Contemporary German Literature from Sensuous to Spiritual Poetry 1880-1930, 1930; (ed. with H. Rose) Neue deutsche Maerchen und Erzaehlungen, 1934; Geschichte der deutschen Dichtung, 1936; Fliessend Deutsch, 1951; A History of German Literature, 1960; Faith from the Abyss: Hermann Hesse's Way from Romanticism to Modernity, 1965; (ed. with F. Semmler) Grosse Vergangenheit, 1968; (trans. with Sheila Wilson) Walter Hinz: The Corner Stone, 1977; Blick nach Osten, 1981. Add: 256 Clifton, Mt. Holly, N.J. 08060, U.S.A.

ROSE, Evelyn (Gita). Pseud.: Gita Davis. British, b. 1925. Cookery/Gastronomy/Wine. Consultant home economist, writer and broadcaster; Cookery Ed., Jewish Chronicle and Cheshire Life; Columnist, Decanter mag. nChmn. of Home Economics Advisory Cttee., Salford Coll. of Technology, since 1968; Member, Consumers' Cttee. of Great Britain, since 1985; Member, Meat and Livestock Commn. and Chmn. of its Statutory Consumers' Cttee. since 1986. National Chmn., Assn. of Home Economics, 1971–73. *Publs:* More Fun with Your Food, 1958; Cooking and Eating for Health, 1959; The Jewish Home, 1969; The Complete International Jewish Cookbook, 1976; The Entertaining Cookbook, 1980; (with J. Rose) The First Time Cookbook, 1982; The New Jewish Cuisine, 1985; (with S. Leon) Master Class for Creative Cooks, 1987; Evelyn Rose Goes Microwave in the Jewish Kitchen, 1989. Add: 27 Gibwood Rd. Northenden, Manchester M22 4BR, England.

ROSE, Jennifer. *See* **WEBER**, Nancy.

ROSE, Kenneth (Vivian). British, b. 1924. History, Biography. Asst. Master, Eton Coll., 1984; Member, Editorial Staff, 1952, and Columnist, 1961, Daily Telegraph newspaper, London. *Publs:* Georgiana: Seven Portraits, 1948; Superior Person: A Portrait of Curzon and His Circle in Late Victorian England, 1969; The Later Cecils, 1975; King George V, 1983; Curzon: A Most Superior Person, 1985; Kings, Queens, and Courtiers: Intimate Portraits of the Royal House of Windsor from Its Foun-

dation to the Present Day, 1985. Add: 38 Brunswick Gardens, London W8 4AL, England.

ROSE, Marilyn Gaddis. American, b. 1930. Biography, Translations. Prof. of Comparative Literature, and Dir., Translation Research and Instruction Prog., State Univ. of New York at Binghamton, since 1968. Ed., Translation Perspectives, since 1983. *Publs:* (trans.) Axel, by Villiers de l'Isle-Adam, 1971; Julian Green, 1971; Jack B. Yeats, 1972; Katharine Tynan, 1973; (ed.) Translation in the Humanities, 1977; Transcriptions/Inscriptions, 1979; Doubles/Dialogs, 1980; Translation Spectrum, 1980; (trans.) Eve of the Future Eden, by Villiers de l'Isle-Adam, 1981; Shared Experiences, 1982; (trans.) Lui: A View of Him, by Louise Colet, 1986. Add: 4 Johnson Ave., Binghamton, N.Y. 13905, U.S.A.

ROSE, Norman Anthony. British, b. 1934. History, International relations/Current affairs, Biography. Chaim Weizmann Prof. of Intnl. Relations, Hebrew Univ., Jerusalem, since 1982 (Sr. Lectr., 1974–78; Assoc. Prof. 1978–82). Sr. Research Ed., The Weizmann Letters, 1968–70. *Publs:* The Gentile Zionists: A Study in Anglo-Zionist Diplomacy 1929-39, 1973; (ed.) Baffy: The Diaries of Blanche Dugdale 1936-1947, 1973; Vansittart: Study of a Diplomat, 1978; Lewis Namier and Zionism, 1980; (ed.) The Letters of Chaim Weizmann Jan. 1939-June 1940, 1980; Chaim Weizmann: A Biography, 1986. Add: Dept. of Intnl Relations, Hebrew Univ., Jerusalem, Israel.

ROSE, Paul (Bernard). British, b. 1935. History, Law, Politics. Barrister since 1957; H. M. Coroner (South London); Part-Time Immigration Adjudicator, since 1987. Legal Adviser, Cooperative Union Ltd., 1957–60; Lectr., Salford Univ., 1960–62; Labour Member of Parliament (U.K.) for Blackley, Manchester, 1964–79; Deputy Circuit Judge, 1975–88. *Publs:* Law Relating to Industrial and Provident Societies, 1962; Weights and Measures Law, 1964; The Manchester Martyrs, 1970; Backbencher's Dilemma, 1981; The Moonies Unmasked, 1981; History of the Fenian Movement in England, 1982. Add: Coroner's Office, The Law Courts, Barclay Rd., Croydon CR9 3NE, Surrey.

ROSE, Peter I(saac). American, b. 1933. Education, Race Relations, Sociology. Sophia Smith Prof. of Sociology and Anthropology, Smith Coll., Northampton, Mass., since 1973 (Asst. Prof., 1960–63; Assoc. Prof., 1963–67; Prof. 1967–73). Member of Graduate Faculty, Univ. of Massachusetts, since 1965. Assoc. Ed., Journal of Refugee Studies, since 1987. Teaching Asst., 1954–57, and Acting Project Dir., 1957–58, Cornell Univ., Ithaca, N.Y.; Instr., Goucher Coll., Maryland, 1958–60. Ed., Research Bulletin on Intergroup Relations, Soc. for the Study of Social Problems and Soc. for the Psychological Study of Social Issues, 1959–63; Assoc. Ed., Social Problems, 1967–70; Consulting Ed., Time-Life Books, 1972–77. *Publs:* They and We, 1964, 4th ed. 1989; The Study of Society, 1967, 4th ed. 1977; The Subject Is Race:Traditional Ideologies and the Teaching of Race Relations, 1968; (ed. and contrib.) The Ghetto and Beyond: Essays on Jewish Life in America, 1969; (ed. and contrib.) Americans from Africa, vol. I, Slavery and Its Aftermath, 1970, vol. II, Old Memories, New Moods, 1970; (ed.) Nation of Nations, 1971; (ed. and contrib.) Seeing Ourselves, 1972, 1975; Many Peoples, Many Nations, 1973; (ed. with S. Rothman and W.J. Wilson) Through Different Eyes, 1973; (with M. Glazer and P.M. Glazer) Sociology: Inquiring into Society, 1977; Strangers in Their Midst, 1978; (ed.) Views from Abroad, 1978; (ed.) Socialization and the Life Cycle, 1979; Mainstream and Margins, 1983; (ed.) Working with Refugees, 1986. Add: 66 Paradise Rd., Northampton, Mass. 01060, U.S.A.

ROSE, Richard. American, b. 1933. International relations/Current affairs, Politics/Government. Prof. of Public Policy since 1982, and Dir. of the Centre for the Study of Public Policy since 1976, Univ. of Strathclyde, Glasgow (Prof. of Politics, 1966–82). Hon. Secty., Cttee. on Political Sociology, Intnl. Political Science Assn. and Intnl. Sociology Assn. Reporter, St. Louis Post-Dispatch, 1955–57; Lectr. in Govt., Univ. of Manchester, 1961–66; Fellow, Stanford Univ., California, 1967, Woodrow Wilson Center, Washington, D.C., 1974, Brookings Instn., 1976, American Enterprise Inst., 1980, and Intnl. Monetary Fund, 1984. *Publs:* (with D.E. Butler) The British General Election of 1959, 1960; (with M. Abrams) Must Labour Lose?, 1960; Politics in England, 1964, 2nd ed. as Politics in England Today, 1974, 3rd ed. as Politics in England, 1980, 5th ed. 1989; (ed.) Studies in British Politics, 1966, 1969, 1976; Influencing Voters, 1967; (ed.) Policymaking in Britain, 1969; People in Politics, 1970; Governing Without Consensus: An Irish Perspective, 1971; (ed. with M. Dogan) European Politics, 1971; (ed.) Lessons from America, 1974; (with T.T. Mackie) International Almanac of Electoral History, 1974, 3rd ed. 1990; (ed.) Electoral Behavior, 1974; (ed.) The Management of Urban Change in Britain and Germany, 1974; The Problem of Party

Government, 1974; Northern Ireland: Time of Choice, 1976; (ed.) The Dynamics of Public Policy, 1976; Managing Presidential Objectives, 1976; (ed. with J. Wiatr) Comparing Public Policies, 1977; (ed. with D. Kavanagh) New Trends in British Politics, 1977; What Is Governing? Purpose and Policy in Washington, 1978; (with Guy Peters) Can Government Go Bankrupt?, 1978; (co-ed.) Elections Without Choice, 1978; Do Parties Make a Difference?, 1980, 1984; (ed.) Challenge to Governance: Studies in Overloaded Polities, 1980; (co-ed.) Britain: Progress and Decline, 1980; (co-ed.) Presidents and Prime Ministers, 1980; (ed.) Electoral Participation, 1980; (co-ed.) United Kingdom Facts, 1982; Understanding the United Kingdom, 1982; (co-ed.) The Territorial Dimension in United Kingdom Politics, 1982; (co-ed.) Fiscal Stress in Cities, 1982; (with Ian McAllister) The Nationwide Competition for Votes, 1984; Understanding Big Government, 1984; Public Employment in Western Nations, 1985; (with Ian McAllister) Voters Begin to Choose, 1986; (with Rei Shiratoni) Welfare State East and West, 1986; (with Denis Van Mecehelen) Patterns of Parliamentary Legislation, 1986; Ministers and Ministries, 1987; (with Terence Karran) Taxation by Political Inertia, 1987; The Postmodern Presidency, 1988; Ordinary People in Public Policy, 1989. Add: Bennochy, 1 East Abercromby St., Helensburgh, Dunbartonshire G84 7SP, Scotland.

ROSEMAN, Kenneth David. American, b. 1939. Children's fiction, Children's non-fiction, Theology/Religion. Rabbi, Temple Beth-El, Madison, Wisc., since 1976. Dean and Instr. in Jewish American History, Hebrew Union Coll.—Jewish Inst. of Religion, Cincinnati, Ohio, 1972–74; Dir., Inst. for Jewish Life, NYC., 1974–76. *Publs:* The Cardinal's Snuffbox, 1982; The Melting Pot: An Adventure in New York, 1984; Escape from the Holocaust, 1985; The Tenth of Av, 1988. Add: 117 Shiloh Dr., Madison, Wisc. 53705, U.S.A.

ROSEN, Gerald. American, b. 1938. Novels/Short stories, Literature. Assoc. Prof. of Creative Writing to Univ. Writer-in-Residence, California State Univ., Sonoma, since 1971. *Publs:* Blues for a Dying Nation, 1972; Zen in the Art of J.D. Salinger, 1977; The Carmen Miranda Memorial Flagpole, 1977; Dr. Ebenezer's Book and Liquor Store, 1980; Growing Up Bronx, 1984. Add: English Dept., California State Univ., Sonoma, Rohnert Park, Calif. 94928, U.S.A.

ROSEN, Michael (Wayne). British, b. 1946. Children's fiction, Plays/Screenplays, Poetry. Freelance writer and broadcaster: created "Everybody Here" series, Channel 4 Television, London, 1982–83. *Publs:* Backbone (play), 1968; Stewed Figs (play), 1968; Regis Debray (radio play), 1971; Mind Your Own Business (children's verse), 1974; Once There Was a King Who Promised He Would Never Chop Anybody's Head Off (children's fiction), 1976; Wouldn't You Like to Know (children's verse), 1977; The Bakerloo Flea (children's fiction), 1979; (with Roger McGough) You Tell Me (children's verse), 1979; You Can't Catch Me! (children's verse), 1981; I See a Voice (on poetry), 1981; (with Susanna Steele) Inky Pinky Ponky: Collected Playgound Rhymes (children's verse), 1982; Nasty (children's fiction), 1982; A Cat and Mouse Story (children's fiction), 1982; (ed.) Everybody Here (TV series), 1982; Quick, Let's Get Out of Here (children's verse), 1983; Bloody Liars (adult verse), 1984; Hairy Tales and Nursery Crimes, 1984; Speaking to You (Anthology for children), 1984; Don't Put Mustard in the Custard (children's verse), 1985; (ed.) Kingfisher Book of Children's Poetry, 1985; Under the Bed (miscellany for children), 1986; Smelly Jelly Smelly Fish (miscellany for children), 1986; When Did You Last Wash Your Feet (verse), 1986; (ed.) That'd Be Telling (story anthology), 1986; Hard Boiled Legs (miscellany), 1987; You're Thinking About Doughnuts (children's fiction), 1987; The Hypnotiser (children's verse), 1987; (ed.) A Spider Bought a Bicycle (anthology for children), 1987; Did I Hear You Write?, 1987; Norma and the Washing Machine, 1988; Down at the Doctor's, 1988; The Class Two Monster, 1989. Add: 49 Parkholme Rd., London E8 3AQ, England.

ROSEN, Sam. American, b. 1920. Economics. Prof. of Economics, Univ. of New Hampshire, Durham, 1957–85, now Emeritus. Faculty member, Univ. of Wyoming, Laramie, 1949–51, and Univ. of Delaware, Newark, 1952–57. *Publs:* National Income, 1963; National Income and Other Social Accounts, 1972. Add: Whittemore Sch., Univ. of New Hampshire, Durham, N.H. 03824, U.S.A.

ROSEN, Sidney. American, b. 1916. Children's fiction, Sciences (general), Biography. Prof. Emeritus of Physical Science, Univ. of Illinois, Urbana (Visiting Assoc. Prof., 1958–60; Assoc. Prof., 1960–64; Prof. from 1964). Asst. Prof. of Physical Science, Brandeis Univ., Waltham, Mass., 1955–58; Science Specialist, Ford Foundn., Colombia, 1963–64. *Publs:* Galileo and the Magic Numbers, 1958; Doctor Paracel-

sus, 1959; The Harmonious World of Johann Kepler, 1961; (with R. Siegfried and J. Dennison) Concepts in Physical Science, 1965; Wizard of the Dome, 1969; (with D. Rosen) Death and Blintzes, 1985. Add: 341 Astronomy, Univ. of Illinois, Urbana, Ill. 61801, U.S.A.

ROSEN, Stanley Howard. American, b. 1929. Poetry, Philosophy. Prof. of Philosophy, Pennsylvania State Univ., since 1966 (Instr., 1956–58; Asst. Prof., 1958–63; Assoc. Profs., 1963–66). *Publs:* Death in Egypt (poetry), 1950; Plato's Symposium, 1968, 1987; Nihilism, 1969; G.W.F. Hegel, 1974; The Limits of Analysis, 1980; Plato's Sophist: The Drama of Original and Image, 1983; Hermeneutics as Politics, 1987; The Quarrel Between Philosophy and Poetry, 1988; The Ancients and the Moderns, 1989. Add: 1256 S. Garner St., State College, Pa. 16801, U.S.A.

ROSENBERG, Bruce Alan. American, b. 1934. Mythology/Folklore. Prof., Brown Univ., Providence, since 1977. Faculty member, Univ. of California, Santa Barbara, 1965–67, and Univ. of Virginia, Charlottesville, 1967–69; Prof., Pennsylvania State Univ., University Park, 1969–77. *Publs:* The Folksongs of Virginia, 1969; (with Jerome Mandel) Medieval Literature and Folklore Studies, 1970; The Art of the American Folk Preacher, 1970; Custer and the Epic of Defeat, 1974; The Code of the West, 1981; The Spy Story, 1987; Can These Bones Live?, 1988. Add: American Civilization Prog., 82 Waterman St., Providence, R.I. 02912, U.S.A.

ROSENBERG, Claude N., Jr. American, b. 1928. Money/Finance. Sr. Partner, Rosenberg Capital Mgmt., San Francisco, since 1970. Partner, J. Barth and Co., San Francisco, 1955–70. *Publs:* Stock Market Primer, 1962; The Common Sense Way to Stock Market Profits, 1968, 1978; Psycho-Cybernetics and the Stock Market, 1970; Investing with the Best, 1986. Add: Four Embarcadero Center, San Francisco, Calif. 94111, U.S.A.

ROSENBERG, George Stanley. American, b. 1930. Social sciences. Prof. of Sociology, Case Western Reserve Univ., Cleveland, since 1973 (Assoc. Prof., 1967–72). Research Assoc., Bureau of Social Science Research, Washington, D.C., 1961–67. *Publs:* The Worker Grows Old, 1970; Working Class Kinship, 1973. Add: Dept. of Sociology, Case Western Reserve Univ., Cleveland, Ohio 44106, U.S.A.

ROSENBERG, J. Mitchell. American, b. 1906. History, Law. Lectr., Political Science, Brooklyn College Institute for Retired Professionals and Executives, since 1983; Special Referee Disciplinary Proceedings, Appellate Division, 2nd Dept., since 1981; Administrative Law Judge, since 1986. Asst. District Attorney, Kings County, N.Y., 1940–76; Sr. Attorney, N.Y. State Dept., Justice Services, 1976–78. Asst. Prof., Univ. of Rhode Island, Kingston, 1966–67; Lectr. in Political Science, Brooklyn Coll., N.Y., 1967–69; Lectr. in Social Science, Kingsborough Community Coll., 1969–70; Lectr. in Political Science, New Sch. for Social Research, NYC, 1970–76; Adjunct Asst. Prof., Criminal Justice, Long Island Univ., 1973; Lectr., Dept. of Political Science, Jersey City State Coll., N.J. 1980. *Publs:* Story of Zionism, 1946; Jerome Frank: Jurist and Philosopher, 1970; Our Crime-Riddled Society, 1978. Add: 901 Ave. H, Brooklyn, N.Y. 11230, U.S.A.

ROSENBERG, John D(avid). American, b. 1929. Literature. Prof. of English, Columbia Univ., NYC (joined faculty, 1962). *Publs:* The Darkening Glass: A Portrait of Ruskin's Genius, 1961; (ed.) The Genius of John Ruskin: Selections, 1963; (ed.) Swinburne: Selected Poetry and Prose, 1968; The Fall of Camelot: A Study of Tennyson's Idylls of the King, 1973; (ed.) The Poems of Alfred, Lord Tennyson, 1975; Carlyle and the Burden of History, 1985. Add: Dept. of English, Columbia Univ., New York, N.Y. 10027, U.S.A.

ROSENBERG, Marvin. American. Literature. Prof. of Dramatic Art, Univ. of California, Berkeley, since 1948. Former Dir., Thai Section, Intnl. Broadcasting Div., U.S. State Dept. *Publs:* The Masks of Othello; The Masks of King Lear, 1972; The Masks of Macbeth, 1978. Add: Dept. of Dramatic Art, Univ. of California, Berkeley, Calif. 94720, U.S.A.

ROSENBERG, Morris. American, b. 1922. Sociology. Prof. of Sociology, Univ. of Maryland, College Park, since 1975. Lectr., Columbia Univ., NYC, 1949–51; Asst. Prof., Cornell Univ., Ithaca, N.Y., 1951–56; Chief, Section on Social Structure, National Inst. of Mental Health, 1957–74; Prof. of Sociology, State Univ. of New York, Buffalo, 1974–75. *Publs:* (ed. with P.F. Lazarsfeld) The Language of Social Research, 1955; Occupations and Values, 1957; (with R.K. Goldsen, R.M. Williams and E.A. Suchman) What College Students Think, 1960; Society and the Adolescent Self-Image, 1965; The Logic of Survey Analysis, 1968; (ed.

with P.F. Lazarsfeld and A.K. Pasanella) Continuities in the Language of Social Research, 1972; (co-author) Black and White Self-Esteem, 1972; Conceiving the Self, 1979; (ed. with R.H. Turner) Social Psychology: Sociological Perspectives, 1981; (ed. with H.B. Kaplan) Social Psychology of the Self-Concept, 1982. Add: Dept. of Sociology, Univ. of Maryland, College Park, Md. 20742, U.S.A.

ROSENBERG, Wolfgang. New Zealander, b. 1915. Economics, Money/ Finance, Politics/Government. Barrister and solicitor. Formerly, Reader in Economics, Univ. of Canterbury (faculty member, 1946–80). *Publs:* Full Employment in New Zealand, 1960; The Effect of Import Controls and Industrialization in New Zealand, 1965; A Guidebook to New Zealand's Future, 1968; Import Controls and Full Employment, 1972; Money in New Zealand, 1973; What Every New Zealander Should Know about the Coming Depression and How to Overcome It, 1978; CER (Closer Economic Relations with Australia): Sanity or Sell-Out, 1982; The Magic Square: What Every New Zealander Should Know about Rogernomics, 1986. Add: 14 Sherwood Lane, Christchurch, New Zealand.

ROSENBLATT, Joseph. Canadian, b. 1933. Poetry. Ed., Jewish Dialog mag., Toronto, since 1969. Former labourer, factory worker, plumber's mate, grave digger, and civil servant. *Publs:* Voyage of the Mood, 1963; The LSD Leacock: Poems, 1966; Winter of the Luna Moth, 1968; Greenbaum, 1971; The Bumble-bee Dithyramb, 1972; The Blind Photographer, 1973; Dream Craters, 1974; Vampires and Virgins, 1975; Top Soil, 1976; Loosely Tied Hands, 1978; Snake Oil, 1978; The Sleeping Lady, 1979; Tommy Fry and the Ant Colony, 1979; Brides of the Stream, 1983. Add: c/o Oolichan Books, Box 10, Lantzville, B.C. V0R 2H0, Canada.

ROSENBLOOM, Joseph R. American, b. 1928. History, Theology/ Religion. Adjunct Prof. of Classics, Washington Univ., St. Louis, since 1961. Rabbi, Temple Emanuel, St. Louis, since 1961. *Publs:* Biographical Dictionary of Early American Jewry, 1960; Literary Analysis of the Dead Sea Isaiah Scroll, 1970; A Living Faith, 1970; Conversion to Judaism, 1978. Add: Washington Univ., Box 1050, St. Louis, Mo. 63130, U.S.A.

ROSENBLOOM, Noah H. American, b. 1915. Philosophy, Theology/ Religion. Prof., Stern Coll., Yeshiva Univ., NYC, since 1954. Member, Editorial Bd., Tradition. *Publs:* Luzzatto's Ethico-Psychological Interpretation of Judaism, 1965; (trans.) The Foundation of the Torah, by Luzzatto, 1965; Tradition in a Reform Age, 1976; The Threnody and the Threnodist of the Holocaust, 1980; (trans.) Song of the Murdered Jewish People, by Katzenelson, 1980; The Exodus Epic of the Enlightenment and Traditional Exegesis, 1983; Malbim, 1988. Add: 1066 E. 85th St., Brooklyn, N.Y. 11236, U.S.A.

ROSENBLUM, Robert. American, b. 1927. Art. Prof. of Fine Arts, New York Univ., NYC, since 1966. Prof. of Art and Archaeology, Princeton Univ., New Jersey, 1956–66; Slade Prof. of Fine Art, Oxford Univ., 1971–72. *Publs:* Cubism and Twentieth-Century Art, 1960; Transformations in Late Eighteenth Century Art, 1967; Jean-Auguste-Dominique Ingres, 1967; Frank Stella, 1971; Modern Painting and the Northern Romantic Tradition: Friedrich to Rothko, 1975; French Painting 1774-1830 (exhibition catalogue), 1975; Andy Warhol: Portraits of the Seventies, 1979; (with H.W. Janson) Nineteenth Century Art, 1984; The Dog in Art from Rococo to Post-Modernism, 1988; The Romantic Child from Runge to Sendak, 1988. Add: Dept. of Fine Arts, New York Univ., New York, N.Y. 10003, U.S.A.

ROSENSAFT, Menachem Z. American, b. 1948. Poetry, International relations/Current affairs, Literature, Essays. Attorney: Assoc., Kaye Scholer Fierman Hays and Handler, since 1982. Pres., Labor Zionist Alliance, since 1988. Founding Chmn., Intnl. Network of Children of Jewish Holocaust Survivors. Ed., Bergen-Belsen Youth Mag., Bergen-Belsen Memorial Press, 1965; Adjunct Lectr. in Jewish Studies, City Coll. of New York, 1972–75; Book Review, Ed., Columbia Journal of Transnational Law, NYC, 1978–79; Law Clerk to U.S. District Court Judge Whitmann Knapp, Southern District of New York, 1979–81; Assoc., Proskauer Rose Goetz and Mendelsohn, 1981–82. *Publs:* Moshe Sharett: Statesman of Israel, 1966; Fragments, Past and Future (poetry), 1968; Not Backward to Belligerency: Israel and the Arab States, 1969. Add: 179 E. 70th St., New York, N.Y. 10021, U.S.A.

ROSENTHAL, Bernard G. American, b 1922. Cultural/Ethnic topics, Psychology. Prof. of Social Psychology, Illinois Inst. of Technology, Chicago, since 1964; Prof. of Psychology, Forest Inst. of Professional

Psychology, 1979–86, now Emeritus. Exec. Ed., American Editorial Bd., The Human Context, since 1968; Consultant, Drug Treatment Prog., Evanston, Ill., since 1976. Asst. Prof., Univ. of Chicago, 1948–55; Lectr. and Research Assoc., Harvard Univ., Cambridge, Mass. 1957–60; Prof., Mundelein Coll., Chicago, 1975–79. *Publs:* The Images of Man, 1971; (co-author) The Nature and Development of the Encounter Movement in Confrontations, Encounters in Self and Interpersonal Awareness, 1971; The Development of Self-Identification in Relation to Attitudes Toward the Self in the Chippewa Indians, 1974; (co-author) In Search for Community: Encounter Groups and Social Change, 1978; Crowding Behavior and the Future, 1982; Von der Armut der Psychologie—und wie ihr Abzuhefen Ware, 1974. Add: 212 S. Orange Dr., Los Angeles, Calif. 90036, U.S.A.

ROSENTHAL, Donald B. American, b. 1937. Politics/Government. Prof. of Political Science, State Univ. of New York at Buffalo, since 1964. *Publs:* (with R.L. Crain and Elihu Katz) The Politics of Community Conflict, 1969; The Limited Elite, 1970; (ed.) The City in Indian Politics, 1976; The Expansive Elite, 1977; Sticking-Points and Ploys in Federal-Local Relations, 1979; (ed.) Urban Revitalization, 1980; Urban Housing and Neighborhood Revitalization, 1988. Add: SUNY/Buffalo, Amherst Campus, Buffalo, N.Y. 14260, U.S.A.

ROSENTHAL, Erwin (Isak Jacob). British, b. 1904. Area Studies, History, Theology/Religion. Emeritus Reader in Oriental Studies, Univ. of Cambridge, since 1971 (Lectr. in Hebrew, 1948–59; Reader, 1959–71); Emeritus Fellow, Pembroke Coll., Cambridge, since 1971 (Fellow, 1962–71). Goldsmid Lectr. in Hebrew, and Head, Dept. of Hebrew, Univ. Coll., Univ. of London, 1933–36; Lectr. in Semitic Languages and Literatures, Univ. of Manchester, 1936–44. Pres., Soc. for Near Eastern Studies, Cambridge, 1957–79, 1972–74, 1979; Pres., British Assn. for Jewish Studies, 1977. *Publs:* Ibn Khalduns Gedanken uber den Staat, 1932; (ed. and co-author) Law and Religion, 1938; (ed. and co-author) Saadya Studies, 1942; (ed. and trans.) Averroes' Commentary on Plato's Republic, 1956, 3rd ed. 1969; Political Thought in Medieval Islam, 1958, 4th ed. 1985; Griechisches Erbe in der judischen Religionsphilosophie des Mittelalters, 1960; Judaism and Islam, 1961; Islam in the Modern National State, 1965; Studia Semitica, 2 vols., 1971. Add: 199 Chesterton Rd., Cambridge CB4 1AH, England.

ROSENTHAL, M(acha) L(ouis). American, b. 1917. Poetry, Literature. Prof. of English, New York Univ., since 1961 (joined faculty, 1945). Poetry Ed., Present Tense, NYC, since 1973. *Publs:* (with W. Hummel and E. Leichty) Effective Reading: Methods and Models, 1944; (ed. with T. Jameson) A Selection of Verse, 1952; (with A.J.M. Smith) Exploring Poetry, 1955, 1973; A Primer of Ezra Pound, 1960; The Modern Poets: A Critical Introduction, 1960; (ed. with G. Sanders and J. Nelson) Chief Modern Poets of Britain and America, 1962, 1970; (ed.) Selected Poems and Two Plays of W.B. Yeats, 1962, 3rd ed. (with three plays), 1986; Blue Boy on Skates: Poems, 1964; (ed.) The William Carlos Williams Reader, 1966; The New Poets: American and British Poetry since World War II, 1967; (ed.) The New Modern Poetry: An Anthology of British and American Poetry since World War II, 1967, 1969; (ed.) 100 Postwar Poems: British and American, 1968; Beyond Power: New Poems, 1969; The View from the Peacock's Tail: Poems, 1972; Randall Jarrell, 1972; Poetry and the Common Life, 1974; She: A Sequence of Poems, 1977; Sailing into the Unknown: Yeats, Pound, and Eliot, 1978; Poems 1964-1980, 1981; (with Sally M. Gall) The Modern Poetic Sequence: The Genius of Modern Poetry, 1983; (trans.) The Adventures of Pinocchio, by Collodi, 1983; (gen. ed.) Poetry in English: An Anthology, 1987; The Poet's Art, 1987; As for Love: Poems and Translations, 1987. Add: Dept. of English, New York Univ., 19 University Pl., New York, N.Y. 10003, U.S.A.

ROSHWALD, Mordecai. American, b. 1921. Science fiction/Fantasy, Philosophy, Politics/Government. Prof. of Humanities, Univ. of Minnesota, Minneapolis, 1972–84 (joined faculty, 1957). Lectr. in Political Theory, Hebrew Univ., Jerusalem, 1951–55. *Publs:* The Education of Man, 1954; Humanism in Practice, 1955; Level 7 (novel), 1959; A Small Armageddon (novel), 1962; (with Miriam Roshwald) Moses: Leader, Prophet, Man, 1969. Add: G-2 Glacier Dr., Nashua, N.H. 03062, U.S.A.

ROSKAMP, Karl Wilhelm. American, b. 1923. Economics. Prof. of Economics, Wayne State Univ., Detroit, Mich., since 1960. Vice-Pres., since 1978, and Pres., 1984–87, Intnl. Inst. of Public Finance. Assoc. Prof., Univ. of Paris II, 1977–83, 1986–87. *Publs:* (with W.F. Stolper) The Structure of the East German Economy, 1960; Capital Formati n in West Germany, 1965; Die Amerikanische Wirtschaft: Eine Einfuehrung, 1975; The American Economy 1929-1970, 1977; (ed.) Public Choice and

Public Finance, 1978; (co-ed.) Reforms of Tax Systems, 1979; (co-ed.) Public Finance and Economic Growth, 1981; (co-ed.) Public Sector and Political Economy Today, 1985; (ed.) International Institute of Public Finance: Semicentennial 1937-1987, 1987. Add: Dept. of Economics, Wayne State Univ., Detroit, Mich. 48202, U.S.A.

ROSKILL, Mark Wentworth. British, b. 1933. Art. Prof. of History of Modern Art, Univ. of Massachusetts, Amherst, since 1972 (Assoc. Prof., 1968–72). Instr., 1959–60, and Asst. in Teaching, 1960–61, Dept. of Art and Archaeology, Princeton Univ., N.J.; Instr., 1961–63, and Asst. Prof., 1963–68, Dept. of Fine Arts, Harvard Univ., Cambridge, Mass. *Publs:* English Painting from 1500-1865, 1959; (ed.) The Letters of Vincent Van Gogh, 1963; Dolce's Aretino and Venetian Art Theory of the Cinquecento, 1968; Van Gogh, Gauguin and the Impressionist Circle, 1970; What Is Art History?, 1975; (with David Carrier) Truth and Falsehood in Visual Images, 1984; The Interpretation of Cubism, 1985; The Interpretation of Pictures, 1989. Add: Dept. of Art, Univ. of Massachusetts, Amherst, Mass. 01003, U.S.A.

ROSS, Alan. British, b. 1922. Poetry, Sports. Travel/ Exploration/Adventure, Biography, Memoirs. Managing Dir., London Mag. Eds., formerly Alan Ross Publrs., London, since 1965; Ed., London Mag., since 1961. Staff member, British Council, 1947–50; staff member, The Observer, London, 1950–71. *Publs:* Summer Thunder, 1941; The Derelict Day: Poems in Germany, 1947; Time Was Away: A Notebook in Corsica, 1948; The Forties: A Period Piece, 1950; (ed.) Selected Poems of John Gay, 1950; The Gulf of Pleasure (travel), 1951; Poetry 1945-50, 1951; (ed. with J. Ross) Borrowed Time, by F. Scott Fitzgerald, 1951; Something of the Sea: Poems 1942-52, 1954; The Bandit on the Billiard Table: A Journey Through Sardinia, 1954; rev. ed. as South to Sardinia, 1960; Australia 55: A Journal of the MCC Tour (cricket), 1955; Cape Summer, and The Australians in England, 1957; (ed.) Abroad: Travel Stories, 1957; To Whom It May Concern: Poems 1952-57, 1958; The Onion Man, 1959; Danger on Grass Island, 1960; Through the Caribbean: The MCC Tour of the West Indies, 1959-60 (cricket), 1960; (ed.) The Cricketers Companion, 1960; African Negatives, 1962; Australia 63 (cricket), 1963; The West Indies at Lord's (cricket), 1963; (ed.) Poetry Supplement, 1963; (ed.) London Magazine Stories 1-9, 1964–74; North from Sicily: Poems in Italy 1961-64, 1965; The Wreck of Moni, 1965; A Castle in Sicily, 1966; (ed.) Leaving School, 1966; Poems 1942-67, 1967; A Calcutta Grandmother, 1971; Tropical Ice, 1972; The Taj Express: Poems 1967-73, 1973; (ed.) Living in London, 1974; Open Sea, 1975; Death Valley, 1980; (ed.) The Turf, 1982; Colours of War: War Art 1939-45, 1983; Ranji, Prince of Cricketers, 1984; Blindfold Games, 1986; The Emissary, 1986; Coastwise Lights, 1988. Add: 4 Elm Park Lane, London SW3, England.

ROSS, Angus. New Zealander, b. 1911. History. Emeritus Prof. of History, Univ. of Otago, since 1976 (Lectr., 1937–56; Reader, 1956–64; Prof., 1965–76). *Publs:* 23rd New Zealand Battalion, 1959; New Zealand: Aspirations in the Pacific in the 19th Century, 1964; New Zealand in the Pacific World, 1966; (ed. and contrib.) New Zealand's Record in the Pacific Islands in the 20th Century, 1969: They Built in Faith, 1976; (with others) The First British Commonwealth, 1980. Add: 134 Cannington Rd., Maori Hill, Dunedin, New Zealand.

ROSS, Angus. Pseudonym for Kenneth Giggal. British, b. 1927. Mystery/Crime/Suspense, Biography. Served in the Fleet Air Arm, Royal Navy, 1944–52; Sales Mgr., D.C. Thomson, publishers, Dundee and London, 1952–71. *Publs:* The Manchester Thing, 1970; The Huddersfield Job, 1971; The London Assignment, 1972; The Dunfermline Affair, 1973; The Bradford Business, 1974; The Amsterdam Diversion, 1974; The Leeds Fiasco, 1975; The Edinburgh Exercise, 1975; The Ampurias Exchange, 1976; The Aberdeen Conundrum, 1977; The Hamburg Switch, 1980; The Menwith Tangle, 1982; The Darlington Jaunt, 1983; The Greenham Plot, 1984; The Luxembourg Run, 1985; (with Anthony Dicks) Famous Fighting Planes (non-fiction), 1985; The Tyneside Ultimatum, 1988; Classic Sailing Ships (non-fiction), 1988; The Leipzig Manuscript, 1990. Add: The Old Granary, Bishop Monkton, near Harrogate, North Yorkshire, England.

ROSS, Catherine. *See* **BEATY,** Betty.

ROSS, Clarissa. *See* **ROSS,** William.

ROSS, Dana. *See* **ROSS,** William.

ROSS, Diana. British, b. 1910. Children's fiction. Art teacher, 1930–34. *Publs:* The World at Work (Getting You Things, Making You

Things), 2 vols., 1939; The Story of the Beetle Who Lived Alone, 1941; (with Antony Denney) Uncle Anty's Album, 1942; The Golden Hen and Other Stories, 1942; The Little Red Engine Gets a Name, 1942; The Wild Cherry, 1943; Nursery Tales, 1944; The Story of the Little Red Engine, 1945; The Story of Louisa, 1945; The Little Red Engine Goes to Market (Goes to Town, Goes Travelling, and the Rocket, Goes Home, Goes to Be Mended, and the Taddlecombe Outing, Goes Carolling), 8 vols., 1946–71; Whoo, Whoo, the Wind Blew, 1946; The Tooter and Other Nursery Tales, 1951; The Enormous Apple Pie and Other Miss Pussy Tales, 1951; Ebenezer the Big Balloon, 1952; The Bridal Gown and Other Stories, 1952; The Bran Tub, 1954; William and the Lorry, 1956; Child of Air, 1957; The Dreadful Boy, 1959; The Merry-Go-Round, 1963; Old Perisher, 1965; Nothing to do, 1966; I Love My Love with an A: Where Is He?, 1972. Add: Minster House, Shaw, Melksham, Wilts., England.

ROSS, Helaine. *See* **DANIELS,** Dorothy.

ROSS, Jonathan. *See* **ROSSITER,** John.

ROSS, Laurence. *See* **HYLAND,** Ann.

ROSS, Leonard Q. *See* **ROSTEN,** Leo.

ROSS, Malcolm. *See* **ROSS-MACDONALD,** Malcolm.

ROSS, Marilyn. *See* **ROSS,** William.

ROSS, Murray George. Canadian, b. 1910. Education, Public/Social administration. Pres. Emeritus, York Univ., Toronto, Ont., since 1972 (Pres., 1960–70; Univ. Prof. of Social Science, 1970–72). Prof., 1950–55, and Vice-Pres., 1955–60, Univ. of Toronto. *Publs:* (ed.) Towards Professional Maturity, 1948; Religious Beliefs of Youth, 1950; The Y.M.C.A. in Canada, 1951; Community Organization: Theory and Principles, 1955, 1965; (with C.E. Hendry) New Understandings of Leadership: A Survey and Application of Research, 1957; Case Histories in Community Organization, 1958; The New University, 1961; New Universities in the Modern World, 1965; The University: The Anatomy of Academe, 1976; Canadian Corporate Directors on the Firing Line, 1980. Add: York Univ., Glendon Coll., 2275 Bayview Ave., Toronto, Ont. M4N 3M6, Canada.

ROSS, Ralph Gilbert. American, b. 1911. Education, Philosophy, Social sciences (general). Emeritus Alexander Prof. of Humanities, and Prof. of Philosophy, Scripps Coll., Claremont, Calif. (Prof. since 1966). Instr. in Philosophy, Univ. of Newark, N.J., 1935–40, and Queens Coll., NYC, 1940–45; Asst. Prof., 1945–47, and Assoc. Prof. of Philosophy, 1947–51, New York Univ.; Prof. of Philosophy and Humanities, and Chmn. of The Humanities Prog., Univ. of Minnesota, Minneapolis, 1951–66. *Publs:* Scepticism and Dogma, 1940; (ed.) Ethical Studies, by F.H. Bradley, 1951; (with E. van den Haag) The Fabric of Society, 1957; (with J. Berryman and A. Tate) The Arts of Reading, 1960; (co-ed.) The Philosophy of Edmund Burke, 1961; (ed.) Three Lectures on Aesthetic, by Bernard Bosanquet, 1963; (with E. van den Haag) Passion and Social Constraint, 1963; Symbols and Civilization, 1963; The Nature of Communism, 1963; Obligation: A Social Theory, 1970; (co-ed.) Literature and the Arts, 1974; (co-ed.) Thomas Hobbes in His Time, 1974; (ed.) Makers of American Thought, 1974. Add: 429 Baughman Ave., Claremont, Calif. 91711, U.S.A.

ROSS, Sam. American, b. 1912. Novels/Short stories, Plays/Screenplays. *Publs:* He Ran All the Way, 1947, screenplay, 1951; Someday, Boy, 1948; The Sidewalks Are Free, 1950, as Melov's Legacy, 1984; Port Unknown, 1951; This, Too, Is Love, 1953; You Belong to Me, 1955; The Tight Corner, 1956; The Hustlers, 1956; Ready for the Tiger, 1964; Day of the Shark, 1967; Hang-Up, 1968; The Fortune Machine, 1970; The Golden Box, 1971; Solomon's Palace, 1973; Windy City, 1979. Add: c/o Academy Chicago Publications, Ltd., 213 W. Institute Pl., Chicago, Ill. 60610, U.S.A.

ROSS, Sinclair. Canadian, b. 1908. Novels/Short stories. With Royal Bank of Canada, in Winnipeg, 1931–42, and in Montreal, 1946 until retirement in 1968. *Publs:* As for Me and My Home, 1941; The Well, 1958; The Lamp at Noon and Other Stories, 1968; Whir of Gold, 1970; Sawbones Memorial, 1974; The Race (short stories), 1982. Add: c/o McClelland and Stewart, 481 University Ave., Toronto M5G 2E9, Canada.

ROSS, Tony. British, b. 1938. Children's fiction. Graphic Designer, Littlewoods, Liverpool, 1961–62, and Smith Kline and French Pharmaceuticals, Welwyn Garden City, Herts., 1962–64; Art Dir., Brunnings

Advertising, Manchester, 1964–65; Lectr. in Illustration, Manchester Polytechnic, 1965–86. *Publs:* (all self-illustrated)—Tales from Mr. Toffy's Circus: Big Ethel, Blodwen, Bop, Mr. Toffy, Samuel, Tiger Hary, 6 vols., 1973; Hugo and the Man Who Stole Colours, 1977; Hugo and the Wicked Winter, 1977; Norman and Flop Meet the Toy Bandit, 1977; Hugo and Oddsock, 1978; The Greedy Little Cobber, 1979; The True Story of Mother Goose and Her Son Jack, 1979; Hugo and the Ministry of Holidays, 1980, in U.S. as Hugo and the Bureau of Holidays, 1982; Naughty Nigel, 1982, in U.S. as Naughty Nicky, 1983; Jack the Giantkiller, 1983; I'm Coming to Get You, 1984; Towser series, 6 vols., 1984–85; Lazy Jack, 1985; I Want My Potty, 1986; Oscar Got the Blame, 1987; Super Dooper Jezebel, 1988; I Want a Cat, 1988; retellings—Goldilocks and the Three Bears, 1976; The Pied Piper of Hamelin, 1977; Little Red Ridding Hood, 1978; Jack and the Beanstalk, 1980; Puss in Boots, 1981; The Three Pigs, 1983; The Boy Who Cried Wolf, 1985; Foxy Fables, 1986; Playschool Book of Songs, 1987; Stone Soup, 1987. Add: Rivendell House, Kerswell, Cullompton, Devon EX15 2EF, England.

ROSS, William (Edward Daniel). Also writes as Marilyn Carter, Clarissa Ross, Dana Ross, and Marilyn Ross. Canadian, b. 1912. Writer of romance, mystery, western and gothic mystery novels. Past Pres., New Brunswick Branch of Canadian Author's Assn. *Publs:* author of more than 320 novels, latest are: Dark Shadows, 1967; China Shadow, 1974; Moscow Mists, 1977; Jade Princess, 1977; Eternal Desire, 1979; Pleasure's Daughter; Casablancea Intrigue, 1979; Fan the Wanton Flame, 1980; Only Make Believe, 1980; Forbidden Flame, 1982; Denvers' Lady, 1985; Smiles of Summer, 1985; Portrait of Love, 1985; Shadows over Briarcliff, 1986; Castle Malice, 1986; The Reluctant Debutante, 1987; Summer Playhouse, 1987. Add: 80 Horto Rd., E. Riverside, St. John, N.B. E2H 1P8, Canada.

ROSS, Zola (Helen Girdey). Also writes mystery novels as Helen Arre, Bert Iles, and Z.H. Ross. American, b. 1912. Mystery/Crime/Suspense, Westerns/Adventure, Children's fiction. Adult education teacher, Lake Washington Schs., Kirkland, Wash., since 1956. Assoc. Prof. of Creative Writing, Univ. of Washington, 1948–55. *Publs:* (as Z.H. Ross) Three Down Vulnerable, 1946; (as Z.H. Ross) Overdue for Death, 1947; (as Z.H. Ross) One Corpse Missing, 1948; Bonanza Queen: A Novel of the Comstock Lode, 1949; Tonapah Lady, 1950; Reno Crescent, 1951; The Green Land, 1952; (as Helen Arre) The Corpse by the River, 1953; Cassy Scandal, 1954); (as Helen Arre) No Tears at the Funeral, 1954; The Golden Witch, 1955; A Land to Tame, 1956; (as Helen Arre) Write It Murder, 1956; (as Bert Iles) Murder in Mink, 1956; Spokane Saga, 1957; (as Helen Arre) The Golden Shroud, 1958; (as Helen Arre) Murder by the Book, 1960; juvenile novels, with Lucile McDonald—The Mystery of Catesby Island, 1950; Stormy Year, 1952; Friday's Child, 1954; Mystery of the Long House, 1956; Pigtail Pioneer, 1956; Wing Harbor, 1957; The Courting of Ann Maria, 1958; Assignment in Ankara, 1959, as Stolen Letters, 1959; Winter's Answer, 1961; The Sunken Forest, 1968; For Glory and the King, 1969. Add: 16907 72nd Ave. N.E., Bothell, Washington 98011, U.S.A.

ROSSABI, Morris. American, b. 1941. History, International Relations, Politics. Prof. of History, City Univ. of New York and Columbia Univ., NYC, since 1987. Smithsonian Fellowship, 1968–69; Fellow, Fulbright-Hays Prog., 1969–70; Prof. of History, Case Western Reserve Univ., Cleveland, 1970–87. Fellowship, American Council of Learned Socs., 1972–73, 1978–79; Fellow, National Endowment for the Humanities, and Research Fellow, Harvard Univ., East Asian Research Center, both 1974–75. *Publs:* China and Inner Asia, 1400–1970, 1975; (co-author) Cambridge History of Inner Asia, 1975; (co-author) From Ming to Ch'ing, 1979; (co-author) China under Mongol Rule, 1981; China Among Equals, 1982; Khubilai Khan, 1988. Add: 175 Riverside Dr., New York, N.Y. 10024, U.S.A.

ROSSE, Ian. *See* **STRAKER**, J.R.

ROSSEL, Seymour (H.). American, b. 1945. Children's fiction, Children's non-fiction. Chief Exec. of Rossel Books, since 1981; Pres., Rossel Computer Consulting Inc., since 1988. Former Exec. Vice-Pres., Behrman House Publrs. Inc., from 1972–81. *Publs:* (co-author and co-ed.) Lessons from Our Living Past, 1972; When a Jew Prays, 1973; (co-ed.) Stories from Our Living Past, 1974; When a Jew Seeks Wisdom: The Sayings of the Fathers, 1975; Judaism, 1976; Family, 1980; The Holocaust, 1981; Introduction to Jewish History, 1981; Mitzvah: The Teacher's Guide, 1982; Journey Through Jewish History, 1983; Israel: Covenant People, Covenant Land, 1985; Managing the Jewish Classroom: How to Transform Yourself into a Master Teacher, 1987; A Child's Bible:

Lessons from the Torah, 1987; The Holocaust: The Fire That Raged, 1988; A Child's Bible: Lessons from the Prophets and Writings, 1989. Add: 15512 Golden Creek, Dallas, Tex. 75248, U.S.A.

ROSSITER, John. Also writes as Jonathan Ross. British, b. 1916. Mystery/Crime/Suspense. Detective Chief Supt., Wiltshire Constabulary, 1939–69. Columnist, Wiltshire Courier, Swindon, 1963–64. *Publs:* (as Jonathan Ross) The Blood Running Cold, 1968; (as Jonathan Ross) Diminished by Death, 1968; (as Jonathan Ross) Dead at First Hand, 1969; (as Jonathan Ross) The Deadest Thing You Ever Saw, 1969; The Murder Makers, 1970; The Deadly Green, 1970; The Victims, 1971; A Rope for General Dietz, 1972; (as Jonathan Ross) Here Lies Nancy Frail, 1972; The Manipulators, 1973; (as Jonathan Ross) The Burning of Billy Toober, 1974; The Villains, 1974; The Golden Virgin (in U.S. as The Deadly Gold), 1975; (as Jonathan Ross) I Know What It's Like to Die, 1976; The Man Who Came Back (non-mystery novel), 1978; (as Jonathan Ross) A Rattling of Old Bones, 1979; Dark Flight (non-mystery novel), 1981; (as Jonathan Ross) Dark Blue and Dangerous, 1981; (as Jonathan Ross) Death's Head, 1982; (as Jonathan Ross) Dead Eye, 1983; (as Jonathan Ross) Dropped Dead, 1984; (as Jonathan Ross) Burial Deferred, 1985; (as Jonathan Ross) Fate Accomplished, 1987; (as Jonathan Ross) Sudden Departure, 1988; A Time for Dying, 1989. Add: 2 Church Close, Orcheston, nr. Salisbury, Wilts. SP3 4RP, England.

ROSS-MACDONALD, Malcolm (John). Also writes as Malcolm Ross and Malcolm Macdonald. British, b. 1932. Novels/Short stories, Plays/Screenplays, Sciences (general). Exec. Ed., Aldus Books, 1964–66. *Publs:* The Big Waves, 1962; (with D. Longmore) Spare Part Surgery, 1968; (with D. Longmore) Machines in Medicine, 1969; (with D. Longmore) The Heart, 1971; (compiler) World Wildlife Guide, 1971; Beyond the Horizon, 1971; Kristina's Winter, 1972; Conditional People, 1973; Every Living Thing, 1973; Life in the Future, 1974; World from Rough Stones, 1974; The Origin of Johnny, 1975; The Rich Are with You Always, 1976; Sons of Fortune, 1978; Abigail, 1979; The Dukes, 1980; Goldeneye, 1981; Tessa d'Arblay, 1983; In Love and War (In U.S. as For They Shall Inherit), 1984; Mistress of Pallas (in U.S. as On a Far Wild Shore), 1986; The Silver Highways, 1987; The Sky with Diamonds (in U.S. as Honor and Obey), 1988; A Notorious Woman, 1988; His Father's Son, 1989; In Her Innocence, 1989. Add: c/o David Higham Ltd., 5/8 Lower John St., London W1R 4HA, England.

ROSSNER, Judith. American, b. 1935. Novels/Short stories. *Publs:* To the Precipice, 1966; Nine Months in the Life of an Old Maid, 1969; Any Minute I Can Split, 1972; Looking for Mr. Goodbar, 1975; Attachments, 1977; Emmeline, 1980; August, 1983. Add: c/o Julian Bach Agency, 747 Third Ave., New York, N.Y. 10017, U.S.A.

ROSTEN, Leo. Has also written as Leonard Q. Ross. American, b. 1908. Novels/Short stories, Plays/Screenplays, Politics/Government, Social sciences, Essays, Humor/Satire. Lectr., Columbia Univ., NYC, since 1955. Editorial Advisor, Look mag., NYC, 1949–71. *Publs:* The Washington Correspondents, 1937; (as Leonard Q. Ross) The Education of Hyman Kaplan, 1937; (as Leonard Q. Ross) The Strangest Places, 1939; (as Leonard Q. Ross) Dateline: Europe (in U.K. as Balkan Express), 1939; (as Leonard Q. Ross) Adventure in Washington, 1940; Hollywood: The Movie Colony, The Movie Makers, 1941; 112 Gripes about the French, 1944; The Dark Corner, 1945, screenplay, 1946; Sleep My Love, 1946, screenplay, 1948; The Velvet Touch (screenplay), 1948; Where Danger Lies (screenplay), 1950; Double Dynamite (screenplay), 1951; Walk East on Beacon (screenplay), 1952; (ed.) A Guide to the Religions of America (in U.K. as Religions of America), 1957, rev. ed. as Religions in America, 1963; The Return of Hyman Kaplan, 1959; Captain Newman, M.D., 1961; The Story Behind the Painting, 1962; It's Only Money (screenplay), 1962; The Many Worlds of Leo Rosten (in U.K. as The Leo Rosten Bedside Book), 1964; A Most Private Intrigue, 1967; The Joys of Yiddish, 1968; A Trumpet for Reason, 1970; People I Have Loved, Known or Admired, 1970; Rome Wasn't Burned in a Day: The Mischief of Language, 1972; (ed.) The Look Book, 1975; The 3:10 to Anywhere, 1976; The Power of Positive Nonsense, 1977; Passions and Prejudices, 1978; (ed.) Infinite Riches, 1979; Silky, 1979; King Silky, 1980; Hooray for Yiddish: A Book About English, 1982; Giant Book of Laughter, 1985. Add: 36 Sutton Pl. S., New York, N.Y. 10022, U.S.A.

ROSTON, Murray. British/Israeli, b. 1928. Art history, Intellectual history, Literature, Theatre. Prof. of English Literature, Bar-Ilan Univ., Ramat Gan, Israel (joined faculty 1956). *Publs:* Prophet and Poet: The Bible and the Growth of Romanticism, 1965; Biblical Drama in England from the Middle Ages to the Present Day, 1968; The Soul of Wit: A Study of John Donne, 1974; Milton and the Baroque, 1980; Sixteenth-Century

English Literature, 1982; Renaissance Perspectives in Literature and the Visual Arts, 1987. Add: 51 Katznelson St., Kiryat Ono, Israel.

ROSTOW, Eugene V. American, b. 1913. Business/Trade/Industry, Law, Politics/Government. Sterling Prof. of Law and Public Affairs, Yale Univ., New Haven, 1965–84, now Emeritus (Dean of the Law Sch., 1955–65). Distinguished Visiting Research Prof. of Law and Diplomacy, Natl. Defense Univ., Washington, D.C., since 1984. Pitt Prof. of American History, and Fellow of King's Coll., Cambridge Univ., England, 1959–60; U.S. Under Secty. of State for Political Affairs, 1966–69; Eastman Prof., Oxford Univ., England, 1970–71; Dir., U.S. Arms Control and Disarmament Agency, 1981–83. *Publs:* A National Policy for the Oil Industry, 1949; Planning for Freedom, 1959; The Sovereign Prerogative, 1962; Law, Power and the Pursuit of Peace, 1968; (ed.) Is Law Dead?, 1971; Peace in the Balance, 1972; (ed.) The Middle East, 1977; The Ideal in Law, 1978. Add: 1315 4th St. S.W., Washington, D.C. 20024, U.S.A.

ROSTOW, Walt W. American, b. 1916. Economics, History, International relations/Current affairs, Politics/Government. Prof. of Economics and History, Univ. of Texas, since 1969. Instr. in Economics, Columbia Univ., NYC, 1940–41; served in Office of Strategic Services, 1941–45; Asst. Chief, German-Austrian Div., Dept. of State, 1945–46; Harmsworth Prof. of American History, Oxford Univ., 1946–47; Special Asst. to the Exec. Secty., U.N. Economic Commn. for Europe, Geneva, 1947–49; Pitt Prof. of American History, Cambridge Univ., 1949–50; Prof. of Economic History, Massachusetts Inst. of Technology, Cambridge, 1950–61, and staff member, Center for Intnl. Studies, MIT, 1951–61; Counsellor and Chmn., Policy Planning Council, Dept. of State, 1961–66; Special Asst. to the Pres., The White House, Washington, D.C., 1966–69 (Deputy Spec. Asst. to Pres., 1961). *Publs:* The American Diplomatic Revolution, 1946; British Economy of the Nineteenth Century, 1948; The Process of Economic Growth, 1952, 1960; (with A. Levin and others) The Dynamics of Soviet Society, 1952; (with A.D. Gayer and A.J. Schwartz) The Growth and Fluctuation of the British Economy, 1790-1850, 2 vols., 1953, 1975; (co-author) The Prospects for Communist China, 1954; (with R.W. Hatch) An American Policy in Asia, 1955; (with M.F. Millikan) A Proposal: Key to an Effective Foreign Policy, 1957; The Stages of Economic Growth, a Non-Communist Manifesto, 1960, 1972; The United States in the World Arena, 1960; (ed.) The Economics of Take-off into Sustained Growth, 1963; View From the Seventh Floor, 1964; A Design for Asian Development, 1965; (with W.E. Griffith) East-West Relations: Is Detente Possible?, 1969; Politics and the Stages of Growth, 1971; The Diffusion of Power, 1972; How It All Began, 1975; The World Economy: History and Prospect, 1978; Getting from Here to There, 1978; Why the Poor Get Richer and the Rich Slow Down, 1980; British Trade Fluctuations 1868-1896: A Chronicle and a Commentary, 1981; Pre-Invasion Bombing Strategy: General Eisenhower's Decision of March 25, 1944, 1981; The Division of Europe after World War II: 1946, 1981; Europe after Stalin: Eisenhower's Three Decisions of March II, 1953, 1982; Open Skies: Eisenhower's Proposal of July 21, 1955, 1982; The Barbaric Counter-Revolution! Cause and Cure, 1983; Eisenhower, Kennedy and Foreign Aid, 1985; The U.S. and the Regional Organ. of Asia and the Pacific 1965-1984, 1985; Rich Countries and Poor Countries: Reflections on the Past, Lessons for the Future, 1987; Essays on a Half Century: Ideas, Policies, and Action, 1988; Theorists of Economic Growth from David Hume to the Present, 1989. Add: One Wildwind Pt., Austin, Tex. 78746, U.S.A.

ROTBLAT, Joseph. British, b. 1908. International relations/Current affairs, Medicine/Health, Physics, Sciences. Prof., Medical Coll. of St. Bartholomew's Hosp., Univ. of London, 1950–76, now Emeritus. Member, Pugwash Continuing Cttee., since 1957; Pres., Pugwash Conferences on Science and World Affairs, since 1988. Ed., Physics in Medicine and Biology, 1960–73. *Publs:* (co-author) Progress in Nuclear Physics, 1950;(ed.) Atomic Energy: A Survey, 1954; (with G.O. Jones and G.J. Whitrow)Atoms and the Universe, 1959, 1973; (with Sir James Chadwick) Radioactivity and Radioactive Substances, 1961; Science and World Affairs, 1962;(co-author) The Uses and Effects of Nuclear Energy, 1964; (ed.) Aspects of Medical Physics, 1966; Pugwash: The First Ten Years, 1967; Scientists in the Quest for Peace: A History of the Pugwash Conferences, 1972; Nuclear Reactors: To Breed or Not to Breed, 1977; Nuclear Energy and Nuclear Weapon Proliferation, 1979; Nuclear Radiation in Warfare, 1981; Scientists, the Arms Race and Disarmament, 1982; The Arms Race at a Time of Decision, 1984; Nuclear Strategy and World Security, 1985; World Peace and the Developing Countries, 1986; Strategic Defence and the Future of the Arms Race, 1987; Coexistence, Cooperation and Common Security, 1988. Add: 8 Asmara Rd., London NW2 3ST, England.

ROTH, Andrew. British (born American), b. 1919. International relations/Current affairs, Politics/Government, Biography. Research Dir., Parliamentary Profiles, London, since 1955. London Ed., Singapore Standard, 1950–59, France Observateur, 1950–60, and Sekai, Tokoyo, 1950–70; Political Corresp., Manchester Evening News, 1972–84. *Publs:* Japan Strikes South, 1941; (co-author) French Interests and Policies in the Pacific, 1943; Dilemma in Japan, 1945; Business Background of MP's, 8 eds., 1955–81; MPs' Chart, 1967, 5th ed. 1979; Enoch Powell: Tory Tribune, 1970; Can Parliament Decide?, 1971; Heath and the Heathmen, 1972; Sir Harold Wilson: Yorkshire Walter Mitty, 1977; Parliamentary Profiles, 4 vols., 1984–85, 1988–90. Add: 2 Queen Anne's Gate Bldgs., Dartmouth St., London SW1H 9BP, England.

ROTH, Henry. American, b. 1906. Novels/Short stories. Teacher, Roosevelt High Sch., NYC, 1939–41; precision metal grinder, 1941–46; teacher, Montville, Me., 1947–48; Attendant, Maine State Hosp., 1949–53; waterfowl farmer, 1953–62; tutor, 1956–65. *Publs:* Call It Sleep, 1934; Shifting Landscape, 1987. Add: c/o 2600 New York Ave. N.W., Albuquerque, N.M. 87104, U.S.A.

ROTH, June. American, b. 1926. Cookery/Gastronomy/Wine, Medicine/Health. Nationally syndicated newspaper columnist ("Special Diets/Nutrition Hotline"). Vice-Pres., 1980–81, 1985–86, and Pres., 1982–83, American Soc. of Journalists and Authors. *Publs:* Freeze and Please Home Freezer Cookbook, 1963; Rich and Delicious Figure Slimming Cookbook, 1964; Thousand Calorie Cookbook, 1967; Fast and Fancy Cookbook, 1969; How to Cook Like a Jewish Mother, 1969; Take Good Care of My Son Cookbook for Brides, 1969; How to Use Sugar to Lose Weight, 1969; The Indoor/Outdoor Barbecue Book, 1970; The Pick of the Pantry Cookbook, 1970; Let's Have a Brunch Cookbook, 1971; The On-Your-Own Cookbook, 1972; (with E. Boe) Edith Bunker's All in the Family Cookbook, 1972; Healthier Jewish Cookery: The Unsaturated Fat Way, 1972; Elegant Desserts, 1973; Old-Fashioned Candymaking, 1974; Salt-Free Cooking with Herbs and Spices, 1975; The Troubled Tummy Cookbook, 1976; The Galley Cookbook, 1977; Cooking for Your Hyperactive Child, 1977; The Food/Depression Connection, 1978; The Bagel Book, 1978; The Pritikin Program of Diet and Exercise (recipes), 1979; (with Don Mannerberg, M.D.) Aerobic Nutrition, 1981; The Allergic Gourmet, 1983; Living Better with a Special Diet, 1983; The Pasta-Lovers Diet Book, 1984; (with H.M. Ross, M.D.) The Executive Success Diet, 1986; (with Dr. Julian Whitaker) Reversing Health Risks, 1988. Add: 1057 Oakland Court, Teaneck, N.J. 07666, U.S.A.

ROTH, Philip. American, b. 1933. Novels/Short stories, Essays. *Publs:* Goodbye, Columbus, 1959; Letting Go, 1962; When She Was Good, 1967; Portnoy's Complaint, 1969; Our Gang, 1971; The Breast, 1972; The Great American Novel, 1973; My Life as a Man, 1974; Reading Myself and Others, 1975; The Professor of Desire, 1977; The Ghost Writer, 1979; A Philip Roth Reader, 1980; Zuckerman Unbound, 1981; The Anatomy Lesson, 1983; Zuckerman Bound, 1985; The Prague Orgy, 1985; The Counterlife, 1987; The Facts, 1988. Add: c/o Farrar Straus and Giroux, 19 Union Sq. W., New York, N.Y. 10003, U.S.A.

ROTH, Robert Joseph. American, b. 1920. Philosophy, Theology/Religion. Prof. of Philosophy, Fordham Univ., Bronx, N.Y., since 1970 (Instr., 1953–57; Asst. Prof., 1957–64; Assoc. Prof. 1964–70; Chmn. of the Dept., 1970–73; Pres., Faculty Senate, 1972–74; Dean, Fordham Coll., 1974–79). *Publs:* John Dewey and Self-Realization, 1963; American Religious Philosophy, 1967; (ed.) God Knowable and Unknowable, 1973; (ed.) Person and Community: A Philosophical Exploration, 1975. Add: Dept. of Philosophy, Fordham Univ., Bronx, N.Y. 10458, U.S.A.

ROTHENBERG, Jerome. American, b. 1931. Poetry, Translations. Prof. of English and Creative Writing, State Univ. of New York, Binghamton, since 1986. Prof., Visual Arts and Literature, Univ. of California at San Diego, 1977–86. Ed., New Wilderness Letter, NYC; Founder and Publr., Hawk's Well Press, NYC; Ed., Floating World, NYC; Ed., with David Antin, Some/Thing, NYC; Ethnopoetics Ed., Stony Brook, NYC; Ed., with Dennis Tedlock, Alcheringa: A First Mag. of Ethnopoetics; Ed., New Wilderness Letter, NYC. *Publs:* (trans.) New Young German Poets, 1959; White Sun Black Sun, 1960; The Seven Hells of the Jigoku Zoshi, 1962; Sightings I-IX, 1964; (trans.) The Deputy, by Rolf Hochhuth, 1965; The Gorky Poems, 1966; (ed.) Ritual: A Book of Primitive Rites and Events, 1966; Between: Poems 1960-1963, 1967; (trans.) The Flight of Quetzalcoatl, 1967; Conversations, 1968; Sightings and Red Easy Color, 1968; Poems 1964-1967, 1968; (trans. with M. Hamburger) Poems for People Who Don't Read Poems, by Hans Magnus Enzensberger, 1968; (trans.) The Book of Hours and Constellations, by Eugen Gomringer, 1968; (ed.) Technicians of the Sacred: A Range of

Poetries from Africa, America, Asia and Oceania, 1968, 1985; Poland/1931, 1969; (trans.) The 17 Horse-Songs of Frank Mitchell: X-XIII, 1970; A Book of Testimony, 1971; Poems for the Game of Silence, 1971; (ed.) Shaking the Pumpkin: Traditional Poetry of the Indian North Americas, 1972, 1986; Esther K. Comes to America, 1973; Seneca Journal I: A Poem of Beavers, 1973; (ed. with G. Quasha) America a Prophecy: A New Reading of American Poetry from Pre-Columbian Times to Present, 1973; Poland/1931, 1974; The Cards, 1974; (ed.) Revolution of the World: A New Gathering of American Avant Garde Poetry 1914-1945, 1974; The Pirke and the Pearl, 1975; Seneca Journal: Midwinter, and The Serpent, 2 vols., 1975–77; (co-trans.) Gematria 27, 1977; Narratives and Realtheatre Pieces, 1978; Poèmes pour le jeu du silence, 1978; (ed.) A Big Jewish Book, 1978; Numbers and Letters, 1979; Vienna Blood, 1980; Pre-Faces, 1981; (ed. with D. Rothenberg) Symposium of the Whole, 1982; Poems for the Society of Mystic Animals, 1982; Altar Pieces, 1982; That Dada Strain, 1983; 15 Flower World Variations, 1984; The Riverside Interviews, 1984; A Merz Sonata, 1986; New Selected Poems, 1986. Add: c/o New Directions Publrs., 80 Eighth Ave., New York, N.Y. 10011, U.S.A.

ROTHENBERG, Robert Edward. American, b. 1908. Medicine/Health. Attending Surgeon, French and Polyclinic Medical Sch. and Health Center, NYC; Dir. of Surgical Research, Cabrini Medical Center; Prof. of Surgery, New York Medical Coll. *Publs:* Group Medicine and Health Insurance in Action, 1949; (ed. and author) Understanding Surgery, 1955; (ed.) The New Illustrated Medical Encyclopedia, 4 vols., 1959; The New American Medical Dictionary and Health Manual, 1962; Health in the Later Years, 1964; (ed. and author) Reoperative Surgery, 1964; (ed. and author) The New Illustrated Child Care Encyclopedia, 12 vols., 1966; The Doctors' Premarital Medical Advisor, 1969; The Fast Diet Book, 1971; (ed. and author) The Complete Surgical Guide, 1974; (ed. and author) The Complete Home Medical Encyclopedia, 20 vols., 1974; What Every Patient Wants to Know, 1975; The Complete Book of Breast Care, 1975; First Aid, 1976; Disney's Growing Up Healthy, 4 vols., 1977; (ed.) The Plain Language Law Dictionary, 1981. Add: 35 Sutton Pl., New York, N.Y. 10022, U.S.A.

ROTHENSTEIN, (Sir) John (Knewstub Maurice). British, b. 1901. Novels/Short stories, Art, Autobiography/Memoirs/Personal, Biography. Hon. Fellow, Worcester Coll., Oxford, since 1963; Fellow, University Coll., London, since 1978. Dir., Tate Gallery, London, 1938–64; Rector, Univ. of St. Andrews, Scotland, 1964–67; Ed., The Masters, 1965–67. *Publs:* The Artist of the 1890's, 1928; Morning Sorrow (novel), 1930; British Artists and the War, 1931; An Introduction to English Painting, 1933; The Life and Death of Conder, 1938; Augustus John, 1944; Edward Burra, 1945; Modern English Painters, 3 vols., 1952, 1956, 1974, rev. ed. 1984; The Tate Gallery, 1958; (with Martin Butlin) Turner, 1962; British Art since 1900, 1962; Francis Bacon, 1964; (with Ronald Alley) Summer's Lease, 1965; Brave Day, Hideous Night, 1966; Time's Thievish Progress, 1970; (with others) Edward Burra, 1973; Victor Hammer: Artist and Craftsman, 1978; Stanley Spencer the Man: Correspondence and Reminiscences, 1979; John Nash, 1983. Add: Beauforest House, Newington, Dorchester-on-Thames, Oxford, England.

ROTHMAN, David J. American. Civil liberties/Human rights, Criminology/Law enforcement/Prisons, History. Prof. of History, Columbia Univ., NYC, since 1971 (Asst. Prof., 1964–67; Assoc. Prof., 1967–71). Co-ed., Women and Children First series. *Publs:* Politics and Power: The United States Senate 1869-1901, 1966; The Discovery of the Asylum: Social Order and Disorder in the New Republic, 1971; (ed. with Sheila M. Rothman) On Their Own: The Poor in Modern America, 1972; (ed. with Sheila M. Rothman) The Sources of the American Social Tradition, 1975; (ed.) The World of the Adams Chronicles, 1976; (co-author) Doing Good: The Limits of Benevolence, 1978; (ed. with Stanton Wheeler) Social History and Social Policy, 1980; Reforming the Asylum: Conscience and Convenience in Progressive America, 1980. Add: 522 Fayerweather Hall, Columbia Univ., New York, N.Y. 10027, U.S.A.

ROTHMAN, Joel. American, b. 1938. Children's fiction, Children's non-fiction. *Publs:* Secrets with Ciphers and Codes, 1969; At Last to the Ocean, 1971; Night Lights, 1972; A Moment in Time, 1973; I Can Be Anything You Can Be, 1973; Once There Was a Stream, 1973; The Antcyclopedia, 1974; Compleat Drum Technique, 1974; The Compleat Show Drummer, 1975; Which One Is Different, 1975; Around the Drums Compleatly, 1976; (with Gar Whaley) Compleat Drum Reader, 1976; This Can Lick a Lollypop, 1979. Add: c/o Doubleday, 245 Park Ave., New York, N.Y. 10167, U.S.A.

ROTHMAN, Judith. *See* **PETERS,** Maureen.

ROTHSCHILD, Joseph. American, b. 1931. History, Politics/Government. Prof. of Government since 1968, and Class of 1919 Prof. of Political Science since 1978, Columbia Univ., NYC (Instr., 1955–58; Asst. Prof., 1958–62; Assoc. Prof., 1962–68; Chmn., Prog. on Contemporary Civilization, 1968–71, and Dept. of Political Science, 1971–75). *Publs:* The Communist Party of Bulgaria, 1959; Introduction to Contemporary Civilization in the West, 2 vols., 1960; (ed. with B. Wishy) Chapters in Western Civilization, 2 vols., 1961; Communist Eastern Europe, 1964; Pilsudski's Coup d'Etat, 1966; East Central Europe Between the Two World Wars, 1974; Ethnopolitics, 1981; Return to Diversity, 1989. Add: 445 Riverside Dr., New York, N.Y. 10027, U.S.A.

ROTHSCHILD, Kurt William. Austrian, b. 1914. Economics. Prof. of Economics, Univ. of Linz, since 1966, now Emeritus. Lectr., Glasgow Univ., 1940–47; Sr. Research Worker, Austrian Inst. for Economic Research, Vienna, 1947–66. *Publs:* Austria's Economic Development Between the Two Wars, 1947; The Austrian Economy since 1945, 1950; The Theory of Wages, 1954; Wage-Theory, 1963; Market Forms, Wages and Foreign Trade, 1966; Economic Forecasting, 1969; Development of Income Distribution in Western Europe, 1971; (ed.) Power in Economics, 1971; (with E. Nowotny) Determinants of Money Wage Movements, 1972; (with H. Schmahl) The Decline in the Value of Money, 1973; (co-author) The Utilisation of Social Sciences in Policy Making, 1977; Unemployment in Austria 1955-1975, 1977; Introduction to Disequilibrium Theory, 1981; (co-ed.) Roads to Full Employment, 1986; Theories of Unemployment, 1988. Add: Doblinger Hauptstrasse 77a, A-1190 Vienna, Austria.

ROTHSTEIN, Samuel. Canadian, b. 1921. Librarianship. Prof., Sch. of Librarianship, Univ. of British Columbia, Vancouver, 1961–86, now Emeritus (Jr. Librarian, 1947–48; Head of Acquisitions, 1948–51; Asst. Univ. Librarian, 1954–59; Assoc. Univ. Librarian, 1959–61; Acting Univ. Librarian, 1961–62; Dir., Sch. of Librarianship, 1961–70). *Publs:* The Development of Reference Services, 1955; (co-ed.) As We Remember It, 1970; (co-author) The Library—The University, 1972. Add: 1416 W. 40th Ave., Vancouver, B.C. V6M 1V6, Canada.

ROTHWEILER, Paul R. Also writes as Jonathan Scofield. American, b. 1931. Novels/Short stories. *Publs:* The Sensuous Southpaw, 1976; The Sophomore Jinx, 1979; Blood Sports, 1980; (as Jonathan Scofield) The King's Cannon, 1981; Railroad King, 1981; Fortune's Mistress, 1982; Empire Builder, 1982; Troubled Empire, 1982; Cry of the Condor, 1983; Track of the Assassin, 1987. Add: c/o Avon Books, 105 Madison Ave., New York, N.Y. 10016, U.S.A.

ROTHWELL, Kenneth Sprague. American, b. 1921. Literature. Prof. of English, Univ. of Vermont, Burlington, since 1970. Co-Ed., Shakespeare on Film newsletter. Asst. Prof., 1957–62, Assoc. Prof., 1962–66, and Prof. of English, 1966–70, Univ. of Kansas, Lawrence. *Publs:* Questions of Rhetoric and Usage, 1971, 1974; (ed.) A Goodly Heritage: The Episcopal Church in Vermont, 1973; A Mirror for Shakespeare, 1980, 1982; (ed.) Shakespeare on Film Newsletter, 1981. Add: Dept. of English, Univ. of Vermont, Burlington, Vt. 05405, U.S.A.

ROTHWELL, Victor Howard. British, b. 1945. History. Lectr. in History, Univ. of Edinburgh, since 1970. *Publs:* British War Aims and Peace Diplomacy 1914-1918, 1971; Britain and the Cold War 1941-1947, 1982. Add: History Dept., William Robertson Bldg., George Sq., Edinburgh 8, Scotland.

ROTIMI, Ola. Nigerian, b. 1938. Plays/Screenplays. Head of Dept. of Creative Arts, since 1982, and dir. of univ. theatre, since 1977, Univ. of Port Harcourt. Artistic dir., Univ. of Ife Theatre, 1973–77. *Publs:* The Gods Are Not to Blame, 1971; Kurunmi, 1971; Ovonramwen Nogbaisi, 1974; Our Husband Has Gone Mad Again, 1977; Holding Talks, 1979; If: A Tragedy of the Ruled, 1983; Hopes of the Living Dead, 1988. Add: Dept. of Creative Arts, Univ. of Port Harcourt, P.M.B. 5323, Port Harcourt, Nigeria.

ROTSLER, William. Has also written as Victor Appleton, William Arrow and John Ryder Hall. American, b. 1926. Science fiction/Fantasy, Film. Photographer and filmmaker since 1959; writer, producer, and dir. of commercials, documentaries, and industrial feature films; also actor and dir., and writer of screenplays. Rancher in Camarillo, Calif., 1942–44, 1946; sculptor, 1950–59. *Publs:* Contemporary Erotic Cinema, 1973; Patron of the Arts, 1974; (as John Ryder Hall) Futureworld (novelization of screenplay), 1976; (as William Arrow) Man: The Hunted

Animal (novelization of screenplay), 1976; To the Land of the Electric Angel, 1976; (as William Arrow) Visions of Nowhere (novelization of screenplay), 1976; (as John Ryder Hall) Sinbad and the Eye of the Tiger (novelization of screenplay), 1977; Zandra, 1978; Iron Man: Call My Killer . . . Modok, 1979; Dr. Strange, 1979; The Far Frontier, 1980; (with Gregory Benford) Shiva Descending, 1980; (as Victor Appleton, with Sharman DiVono) Tom Swift, 1–6, 1981; Mr. Merlin, 1981; Blackhawk, 1982; Vice Squad, 1982; Star Trek II Biographies, 1982; Star Trek: Distress Call, 1982; Star Trek II Short Stories, 1982; The Hidden Worlds of Zandra, 1983; Magnum, P.I.: Maui Mystery, 1983; The A-Team, No. 1. Defense Against Terror, 1983; Star Trek: The Vulcan Treasure, 1984; Star Trek III Short Stories, 1984; The A-Team, No. 2. The Danger Maze, 1984; Plot-It-Yourself Adventure: Goonies Cavern of Horror, 1985   Add: c/o Richard Curtis Assocs., 164 E. 64th St., New York, N.Y. 10021, U.S.A.

ROUECHE, Berton. American, b. 1911. Novels, Medicine/Health (medical journalism), Travel. Staff writer, and originator and sole proprietor of "Annals of Medicine" Dept., The New Yorker, NYC., since 1944. Reporter, Kansas City Star, 1934–41, St. Louis Globe Democrat, 1941–42, and St. Louis Post-Dispatch, Dispatch, 1942–44; Faculty Member, Bread Loaf Writers' Conference, Middlebury, Vt., 1958, and Indiana Univ. Writers' Conference, Bloomington, 1962. *Publs:* Black Weather (novel), 1945; Greener Grass and Some People Who Found It, 1948; Eleven Blue Men, 1953; The Last Enemy (novel), 1959; The Incurable Wound, 1958; The Delectable Mountains, 1959; The Neutral Spirit, 1960; (ed.) Curiosities of Medicine, 1963; A Man Named Hoffman, 1955; Annals of Epidemiology, 1967; Field Guide to Disease, 1967; What's Left: Reports on a Diminishing America, 1969; The Orange Man and Other Narratives of Medical Detection, 1971; Feral (novel), 1974; Fago (novel), 1977; The River World and Other Explorations, 1978; The Medical Detectives, 1980; Sea to Shining Sea: People, Travel, Places, 1987. Add: c/o Harper and Row, 10 E. 53rd St., New York, N.Y. 10022, U.S.A.

ROUNDS, Glen (Harold). American, b. 1906. Novels/Short stories, Children's fiction, Plays/Screenplays. *Publs:* also illustrator—Ol' Paul, The Mighty Logger, 1936, 3rd ed. 1976; Lumber Camp, 1937, The Whistle Punk of Camp 15, 1959; Pay Dirt, 1938; School of the Air (radio plays), 1938–39; The Blind Colt, 1941; Whitey series, II vols., 1942–63; Stolen Pony, 1948, 1969; Rodeo: Bulls, Broncos, and Buckaroos, 1949; Hunted Horses, 1951; Buffalo Harvest, 1952; Lone Muskrat, 1953; Swamp Life: An Almanac, 1957; Wildlife at Your Doorstep: An Illustrated Almanac, 1958; Beaver Business: An Almanac, 1960; Wild Orphans, 1961; Rain in the Woods and Other Small Matters, 1964; (ed.) Trail Drive, from Log of a Cowboy, by Andy Adams, 1965; The Snake Tree, 1966; (ed.) Mountain Men, by George F. Ruxton, 1966; (ed.) The Boll Weevil, 1967; The Treeless Plains, 1967; The Prairie Schooners, 1968; (ed.) Casey Jones, 1968; Wild Horses of the Red Desert, 1969; (ed.) The Strawberry Roan, 1970; Once We Had a Horse, 1971; The Cowboy Trade, 1972; The Day the Circus Came to Lonetree, 1973; (ed.) Sweet Betsy from Pike, 1973; Mr. Yowder series, 6 vols., 1976–83; The Beaver: How He Works, 1976; Blind Outlaw, 1980; Wild Appaloosa, 1983; The Morning the Sun Refused to Shine, 1984; Washday on Noah's Ark, 1985; Old MacDonald Had a Farm, 1989. Add: Box 763, Southern Pines, N.C. 28387, U.S.A.

ROUNTREE, Thomas J. American, b. 1927. Literature. Prof. of English, Univ. of South Alabama, Mobile, since 1971 (Chmn., Dept. of English, 1971–74). Faculty member, Southeastern Louisiana Coll., Hammond, 1958–60, and East Texas State Univ., Commerce, 1960–61; Prof. of English, 1961–71, and Dir. of the Creative Writing Prog., 1962–71, Univ. of Alabama, Tuscaloosa. Member, Literary Arts Cttee., Allied Arts Council, Mobile, 1974–75. *Publs:* This Mighty Sum of Things, 1965; The Last of the Mohicans: Notes, 1965; Emma: Notes, 1967; (ed.) Critics on Hawthorne, 1972; (ed.) Critics on Melville, 1972; (ed.) Critics on Emerson, 1973. Add: Route 16, Box 351, Mobile, Ala. 36619, U.S.A.

ROUSE, Irving. American, b. 1913. Anthropology/Ethnology, Archaeology/ Antiquities. Charles J. MacCurdy Prof. of Anthropology, Yale Univ., New Haven, 1970–84, now Emeritus (Instr. in Anthropology, 1939–43; Asst. Prof., 1943–48; Assoc. Prof., 1948–54; Prof., 1954–70). *Publs:* Prehistory in Haiti: A Study in Method, 1939; Culture of the Fort Liberte Region, Haiti, 1941; Archaeology of the Maniabon Hills, Cuba, 1942; A Survey of Indian River Archaeology, Florida, 1951; Puerto Rican Prehistory, 1952; (with J.M. Cruxent) An Archaeological Chronology of Venezuela, 2 vols., 1958–59; (with J.M. Cruxent) Venezuelan Archaeology, 1963; Introduction to Prehistory, 1972; Migrations in Prehistory, 1986. Add: Dept. of Anthropology, Yale Univ., New Haven, Conn. 06520, U.S.A.

ROUSE, Parke Shepherd, Jr. American, b. 1915. Art, History, Biog-

raphy. Columnist Editorialist, Newport News Daily Press, Va. Dir. of Publs., Colonial Williamsburg, Va., 1951–55; Sunday Ed., Richmond Times-Dispatch, 1952–54; Dir. of Public Relations, Virginia Chamber of Commerce, 1954–55; Dir., Jamestown-Yorktown Foundn., Virginia, until retirement in 1980. *Publs:* Virginia: The English Heritage in America, 1966; Planters and Pioneers, 1967; Tidewater Virginia in Color, 1968; Below the James Lies Dixie, 1968; Endless Harbor, 1969; James Blair of Virginia, 1971; Roll, Chesapeake, Roll, 1972; The Great Wagon Road, 1973; Cows on Campus, 1974; Virginia: A Pictorial History, 1975; Richmond in Color, 1979; A House for a President, 1983; The Good Old Days, 1985. Add: 14 Bayberry Lane, Williamsburg, Va. 23185, U.S.A.

ROUSSEAU, George S. American, b. 1941. Intellectual history, Literature. Prof. of Eighteenth-Century Studies, Univ. of California at Los Angeles (joined faculty, 1968). Osgood Fellow in English Literature, Princeton Univ., New Jersey, 1965–66; Instr. in English Literature, Harvard Univ., Cambridge, Mass., 1966–68. *Publs:* (with Marjorie Hope Nicolson) This Long Disease My Life: Alexander Pope and the Sciences, 1968; (ed.) John Hill's Hypochondriasis, 1969; (ed. with Eric Rothstein) The Augustan Milieu: Essays Presented to Louis A. Landa, 1970; (co-ed.) Tobias Smollett: Bicentennial Essays Presented to Lewis M. Knapp, 1971; (ed.) Organic Form: The Life of an Idea, 1972; (ed. with Neil Rudenstine) English Poetic Satire: Wyatt to Byron, 1972; Goldsmith: The Critical Heritage, 1974; The Renaissance Man in the 18th Century, 1978; (ed. with Roy Porter) The Ferment of Knowledge: Studies in the Historiography of Eighteenth-Century Science, 1980; The Letters and Papers of Sir John Hill, 1982; Tobias Smollett: Essays of Two Decades, 1982; (ed.) Literature and Science, 1985; (co-ed.) Sexual Underworlds of the Enlightenment, 1987; (co-ed.) Exoticism and the Enlightenment, 1988; (with Roy Porter) Hysteria in Western Civilization, 1990. Add: 2424 Castillian Dr., Outpost Estates, Los Angeles, Calif. 90068, U.S.A.

ROUTH, Francis John. British, b. 1927. Music. Freelance writer and composer. Ed., Composer. *Publs:* Playing the Organ, 1958; Contemporary Music, 1968; (ed.) The Patronage and Presentation of Contemporary Music, 1970; Contemporary British Music, 1972; Early English Organ Music, 1973; Stravinsky, 1974; (with I. Bruce, D. Castillejo, C. Cornford and C. Gosford) Patronage of the Creative Artist, 1974. Add: 68 Barrowgate Rd., Chiswick, London W4 4QU, England.

ROVER, Constance Mary. British, b. 1910. History, Women. Former Deputy Head, Dept. of Sociology and Law, Polytechnic of North London, retired 1972 (joined faculty, 1957). *Publs:* The Punch Book of Women's Rights, 1967; Women's Suffrage and Party Politics 1866-1914, 1967; Love, Morals and the Feminists, 1970. Add: Flat 3, 42 Shorncliffe Rd., Folkestone, Kent CT20 2NB, England.

ROVIT, Earl. American, b. 1927. Novels/Short stories, Literature. Prof. of English, City Coll. of New York, since 1965. *Publs:* Herald to Chaos, 1960; Ernest Hemingway, 1963, rev. ed. (with G. Brenner), 1986; The Player King (novel), 1965; A Far Cry (novel), 1967; Saul Bellow, 1967; Crossings (novel), 1973. Add: c/o English Dept., City Coll. of New York, New York, N.Y. 10031, U.S.A.

ROWAN, Deirdre. *See* **WILLIAMS**, Jeanne.

ROWAN, Hester. *See* **ROBINSON**, Sheila.

ROWAT, Donald C(ameron). Canadian, b. 1921. Politics/Government, Public/Social administration. Prof. of Political Science, Carleton Univ., Ottawa, since 1958 (Asst. Prof., 1950–53; Assoc. Prof., 1953–58; Acting Dir., Sch. of Public Admin., 1957–58; Chmn., Dept. of Political Science, 1962–65; Supvr., Grad. Studies in Political Science, 1965–66). Research Asst., Dept. of Finance, Ottawa, 1943–44; Administrative Officer, Dept. of National Health and Welfare, Ottawa, 1944–45; Dir. of Research, Inst. of Public Affairs, and Lectr. in Political Science, Dalhousie Univ., Halifax, 1947–49; Lectr. in Political Science, Univ. of British Columbia, Vancouver, 1949–50. *Publs:* The Reorganization of Provincial-Municipal Relations in Nova Scotia, 1949; The Public Service of Canada, 1953; Your Local Government, 1955, 1975; (ed.) Basic Issues in Public Administration, 1961; (ed.) The Ombudsman: Citizen's Defender, 1965, 1968; The Canadian Municipal System: Essays on the Improvement of Local Government, 1969; (with R. Hurtubise) The University, Society and Government, 1970; (ed. with R. Hurtubise) Studies on the University, Society and Government, 1970; (ed.) Provincial Government and Politics: Comparative Essays, 1972, 1973; (ed.) The Government of Federal Capitals, 1972; The Ombudsman Plan: The Worldwide Spread of an Idea, 1973, 1985; (ed.) The Finnish Parliamentary Ombudsman, by Mikael Hiden, 1973; (ed.) Urban Politics in Ottawa-Carleton, 1974; (co-ed.) The

Provincial Political Systems, 1976; (co-ed.) Political Corruption in Canada, 1976; (ed.) The Referendum and Separation Elsewhere: Implications for Quebec, 1978; (ed.) Administrative Secrecy in Developed Countries, 1979; (ed.) The Right to Know: Essay on Governmental Publicity and Public Access to Information, 1980, 1981; (ed.) International Handbook on Local Government Reorganization, 1980; (ed.) Provincial Policy-Making, 1981; (ed.) Global Comparisons in Public-Administration, 1981; (ed.) Recent Urban Politics in Ottawa-Carleton, 1985; (ed.) The Making of the Federal Access Act, 1985; (ed.) Bureaucracy in Developed Democracies, 1986; (ed.) Cases on Canadian Policy-Making, 1987; (ed.) Issues in Provincial Politics, 1988; (ed.) Public Administration in Developed Democracies, 1988; (ed.) Canada and the Crisis of Environmental Destruction, 1989. Add: Dept. of Political Science, Carleton Univ., Colonel by Dr., Ottawa K1S 5B6, Canada.

ROWBOTHAM, David (Harold). Australian, b. 1924. Novels/Short stories, Poetry. Literary Ed., The Courier-Mail, Brisbane, since 1980 (Literary and Theatre Critic, 1955–64; Chief Book Reviewer, 1964–69; Arts Ed., 1969–80). Advisory Ed., Poetry Mag., Sydney; Council Member, Australian Soc. of Authors, since 1964. Editorial Staff Member, The Australian Encyclopedia, 1950–51; Columnist, Toowoomba Chronicle, 1952–55; Broadcaster, ABC National Book Review Panel, 1957–63; Sr. Tutor in English, Univ. of Queensland, Brisbane, 1965–69. *Publs:* Ploughman and Poet, 1954; Town and City: Tales and Sketches, 1956; (ed.) Queensland Writing, 1957; Inland: Poems, 1958; All the Room, 1964; The Man in the Jungle (novel), 1964; Brisbane, 1964; Bungalow and Hurricane: New Poems, 1967; The Makers of the Ark, 1970; The Pen of Feathers, 1971; Selected Poems, 1975; Maydays, 1980. Add: 28 Percival Terr., Holland Park, Brisbane, Qld. 4121, Australia.

ROWBOTHAM, Sheila. British, b. 1943. Women. Teacher, Workers Educational Assn. Formerly, Member of Staff, Black Dwarf newspaper, London. *Publs:* Women, Resistance and Revolution, 1973; Woman's Consciousness, Man's World, 1973; Hidden from History: 300 Years of Women's Oppression and the Fight Against It, 1973, 3rd ed. 1977; A New World for Women, 1977; (with Jeff Weeks) Socialism and the New Life, 1977; (with Jean McCrindle) Dutiful Daughters, 1977; (with Lynne Segal and Hilary Wainwright) Beyond the Fragments, 1979; Dreams and Dilemmas: Collected Writings, 1983; Friends of Alice Wheeldon, 1986; The Past Is Before Us: Feminism in Action from the Late 1960's, 1989. Add: c/o Virago Press, 20-23 Mandela St., London NW1 0HQ, England.

ROWE, D(enis) Trevor. British, b. 1929. History, Transportation. Mgr., Foreign Touring Service, Camping and Caravanning Club, since 1982. Shipping Officer, British Council, 1958–62; Cargo Supvr., British Caledonian Airways, 1966–80. *Publs:* Railway Holiday in Spain, 1966; Continental Railway Handbook: Spain and Portugal, 1970; Railways of South America, 1975; European Narrow Gauge Steam, 2 vols., 1975–76. Add: 70 Hevers Ave., Horley, Surrey, England.

ROWELL, Douglas Geoffrey. British, b. 1943. History, Theology/Religion. Chaplain-Fellow, Keble Coll., Oxford, since 1972; Canon of Chichester Cathedral, since 1981. Asst. Chaplain and Hastings Rashdall Student, New Coll., Oxford, 1968–72. *Publs:* Hell and the Victorians: A Study of the 19th Century Theological Controversies Concerning Eternal Punishment and the Future Life, 1974; (co-ed.) Rock-Hewn Churches of Ea tern Tigray, 1974; The Liturgy of Christian Burial, 1977; The Vision Glorious: Themes and Personalities of the Catholic Revival in Anglicanism, 1983; (ed.) Tradition Renewed: The Oxford Movement Conference Papers, 1986; (ed.) To the Church of England: Essays and Papers and the Preface to Crockford's Clerical Directory 1987-88, by Gareth Bennett, 1988. Add: Keble Coll., Oxford, England.

ROWELL, George. British, b. 1923. Plays/Screenplays, Songs, lyrics and libretti, Theatre. Chmn., Soc. for Theatre Research, since 1989. Reader in Theatre History, Univ. of Bristol, 1979–87 (Jr. Fellow, 1951; Asst. Lectr., 1951–54; Lectr., 1954–62; Sr. Lectr., 1962–69; Special Lectr., 1969–79). *Publs:* (ed.) Nineteenth Century Plays, 1953; The Victorian Theatre, 1956, 1978; (adaptor with K. Mobbs) Engaged!, 1963; (librettist and lyricist with J. Slade) Sixty Thousand Nights, 1967; (ed.) Late Victorian Plays 1890-1914, 1968; (adaptor) The Lyons Mail, 1969; (ed.) Victorian Dramatic Criticism, 1971; (adaptor with A. Woods and J. Slade) Trelawny, 1974; Queen Victoria Goes to the Theatre, 1978; Theatre in the Age of Irving, 1981; (ed.) Plays by W.S. Gilbert, 1982; (with Anthony Jackson) The Repertory Movement, 1984; (ed.) Plays by A.W. Pinero, 1985; William Terriss and Richard Prince, 1987. Add: 11 Stoke Paddock Rd., Bristol BS9 2DJ, England.

ROWEN, Herbert H(arvey). American, b. 1916. History, Translations.

Prof. of History, Rutgers Univ., New Brunswick, N.J., since 1964, now Emeritus. Instr., Brandeis Univ., Waltham, Mass., 1950–53; Asst. Prof. of History, Univ. of Iowa, Iowa City, 1953–57; Assoc. Prof., Elmira Coll., New York, 1957–60; Prof., Univ. of Wisconsin, Milwaukee, 1960–64. *Publs:* (trans.) German History: Some New German Views, 1954; (ed.) La Relation de mon ambassade en Hollande, by S.N. Arnauld de Pomponne, 1955; The Ambassador Prepares for War: The Dutch Embassy of Arnauld de Pomponne 1669-1671, 1957; A History of Early Modern Europe, 1960; (ed.) From Absolutism to Revolution 1648-1848, 1963; (trans.) France and the Atlantic Revolution of the 18th Century 1770-1799, by Jacques Godechot, 1965; (with B. Lyon and T. Hamerow) A History of the Western World, 1969; (ed. and trans.) The Low Countries in Early Modern Times, 1972; (ed. and trans.) America: A Dutch Historian's Vision from Afar and Near, by Johan Huizinga, 1972; John de Witt, Grand Pensionary of Holland 1625-1672, 1978; The King's State: Proprietary Dynasticism in Early Modern France, 1980; (trans.) The Dutch Republic and American Independence, by J.W. Schulte Nordholt, 1982; John de Witt: Statesman of the "True Freedom", 1986; The Princes of Orange: The Stockholders in the Dutch Republic, 1988. Add: 3 Lemore Circle, Rocky Hill, N.J. 08553, U.S.A.

ROWETT, Helen (Graham Quiller). British, b. 1915. Biology, Zoology. Principal Lectr. in Educational Technology, Plymouth Polytechnic, 1973–76, now retired (Lectr. in Zoology, 1944–67; Sr. Lectr., 1968–73). *Publs:* Dissection Guides: I Frog, 1950, II Dogfish, III Rat, 1951, IV Rabbit, 1952, and V Invertebrates, 1953; Histology and Embryology, 1953; Histology, 1957; The Rat as a Small Mammal, 1957, 1974; Basic Anatomy and Physiology, 1959, 3rd ed. 1987; Guide to Dissection, 1962; Two MoorsWay, 1975, 3rd ed. 1987. Add: 3 Manor Park, Dousland, Yelverton, Devon PL20 6LX, England.

ROWLAND, Arthur Ray. American, b. 1930. History, Librarianship. Librarian, since 1961, Prof., since 1976, Augusta Coll., Georgia. Circulation Librarian, George State Coll., Atlanta, 1952–54; Librarian, Armstrong Coll., Savannah, Ga., 1954–56; Head, Circulation Dept., Auburn Univ. Library, Alabama, 1956–58; Librarian, Jacksonville Univ., Alabama, 1958–61. Vice-Pres., 1973–75, and Pres., 1975–77, Georgia Library Assn. *Publs:* (ed.) Reference Services, 1964; (ed.) Historical Markers of Richmond County, Georgia, 1966, 1971; A Bibliography of the Writings on Georgia History, 1966, 1978; A Guide to the Study of Augusta and Richmond County, Georgia, 1967; (ed.) The Catalog and Cataloguing, 1969; (with Helen Calla an) Yesterday's Augusta, 1976; (ed.) The Librarian and Reference Service, 1977; (ed.) Reminiscence of Augusta Marines, 1985. Add: 1339 Winter St., Augusta, Ga. 30904, U.S.A.

ROWLAND, Iris. *See* **ROBERTS,** Irene.

ROWLAND, J(ohn) R(ussell). Australian, b. 1925. Poetry. Member of the Australian Dept. of Foreign Affairs: served Canberra, 1944, 1949–52, 1959–65, Moscow, 1946–48, London, 1948–49, 1957–59, Saigon, 1952–55, Washington, D.C., 1955–57; Ambassador to the U.S.S.R., 1965–68; High Commnr. in Malaysia, 1969–72; Ambassador to Austria, Czechoslovakia, and Hungary, 1973–74; Deputy Secty., Dept. of Foreign Affairs, 1975–78; Ambassador to France, 1978–82. *Publs:* The Feast of Ancestors: Poems, 1965; Snow, 1971; Times and Places, 1975; The Clock Inside, 1979; The Sculptor of Candles, 1985; Sixty, 1989. Add: 15 Grey St., Deakin, A.C.T. 2600, Australia.

ROWLAND, Peter Kenneth. British, b. 1938. History, Biography. Admin. Officer, London Waste Regulation Authority. *Publs:* The Last Liberal Governments: The Promised Land 1905-1910, 1968; The Last Liberal Governments: Unfinished Business 1911-1914, 1971; Lloyd George, 1975; (ed.) Macaulay's History of England in the 18th Century, 1980; (ed.) Macaulay's History of England from 1485 to 1685, 1985; (ed.) Autobiography of Charles Dickens, 1988. Add: 65 Essex Rd., London E10 6EG, England.

ROWNTREE, Derek (G.F.). British, b. 1936. Education, Information science/Computers, Mathematics/Statistics. Prof. of Educational Development, Open Univ. (U.K.). Ed.-in-Chief, Educational Materials, U.S. Industries (G.B.) Ltd., 1961–66; Sr. Lectr. in Programmed Learning, Brighton Coll. of Education, 1967–70. *Publs:* Basic Statistics, 16 vols., 1964–72; Basically Branching: A Handbook for Programmers, 1966; Learn How to Study, 1970, 3rd ed. as Learn How to Study: A Programmed Guide to Better Study Techniques, 1983; Educational Technology in Curriculum Development, 1974, 1982; Assessing Students: How Shall We Know Them?, 1977, 1987; A Dictionary of Education, 1981; Statistics Without Tears, 1981; Developing Courses for Students, 1981; Probability Without Tears, 1984; Who Needs a Home Computer?, 1985; Teaching

Through Self-Instruction, 1986. Add: Oak Cottage, Farthinghoe, Northants, NN13 5NY, England.

ROWSE, A(lfred) L(eslie). British, b. 1903. Poetry, History, Literature. Fellow, All Souls Coll., Oxford, 1925–74, now Emeritus. Pres. of the English Assn., 1952; Research Assoc., Huntington Library, San Marino, California, 1962–69. *Publs:* On History: A Study of Present Tendencies (in U.S. as Science and History: A New View of History), 1927; Politics and the Younger Generation, 1931; The Question of the House of Lords, 1934; (with G.B. Harrison) Queen Elizabeth and Her Subjects, 1935; Mr. Keynes and the Labour Movement, 1935; (ed. with M. Henderson) Studies in Cornish History, by Charles Henderson, 1935; Sir Richard Grenville of the Revenge: An Elizabethan Hero, 1937; Tudor Cornwall: Portrait of a Society, 1941, 1969; A Cornish Childhood: Autobiography of a Cornishman, 1942; Poems of a Decade 1931-1941, 1942; The Spirit of English History, 1943; The English Spirit: Essays in History and Literature, 1944, 1966; Poems Chiefly Cornish, 1944; The Use of History, 1946, 1963; Poems of Deliverance, 1946; The End of an Epoch: Reflections on Contemporary History, 1947; (ed.) The West in English History, 1949; The England of Elizabeth: The Structure of Society, 1950; The English Past: Evocations of Places and Persons, 1951, rev. ed. as Times, Persons, Places: Essays in Literature, 1965; A New Elizabethan Age?, 1952; (trans.) History of France, by Lucien Romier, 1953; An Elizabethan Garland, 1953; The Expansion of Elizabethan England, 1955; The Early Churchills: An English Family, 1956; The Later Churchills (in U.S. as The Churchills: From the Death of Marlborough to the Present), 1958, in 2 vols. as The Churchills: The Story of a Family, 1966; The Elizabethans and America, 1959; Poems Party American, 1959; St. Austell: Church, Town, Parish, 1960; All Souls and Appeasement: A Contribution to Contem-porary History (in U.S. as Appeasement: A Study in Political Decline 1933-1939), 1961; Ralegh and the Throckmortons (in U.S. as Sir Walter Ralegh, His Family and Private Life), 1962; William Shakespeare: A Biography, 1962; Christopher Marlowe: A Biography (in U.S. as Christopher Marl-owe: His Life and Works), 1964; (ed.) Shakespeare's Sonnets, 1964, rev. ed. as Shakespeare's Sonnets: The Problems Solved, 1973; A Cornishman at Oxford: The Education of a Cornishman, 1965; Shakespeare's Southampton: Patron of Virginia, 1965; Bosworth Field and the Wars of the Roses (in U.S. as Bosworth Field: From Medieval to Tudor England), 1966; Poems of Cornwall and America, 1967; (ed.) A Cornish Anthology, 1968; The Contribution of Cornwall and Cornishmen to Britain, 1969; The Cornish in America (in U.S. as The Cousin Jacks: The Cornish in America), 1969; (ed.) The Two Chiefs of Dunboy: A Story of 18th Century Ireland, by J.A. Froude, 1969; The Elizabethan Renaissance, vol. I, The Life of the Society, 1971, vol. II, The Cultural Achievement, 1972; The Tower of London in the History of the Nation, 1972; Strange Encounter, 1972; Shakespeare the Man, 1973; Windsor Castle in the History of the Nation, 1974; Simon Forman: Sex and Society in Shakespeare's Age, 1974; Peter, The White Cat of Trenarren, 1974; (ed. with John Betjeman) Victorian and Edwardian Cornwall from Old Photographs, 1974; Oxford in the History of England, 1975; Jonathan Swift: Major Prophet, 1975; Discoveries and Reviews, 1975; A Cornishman Abroad, 1976; Brown Buck: A Californian Fantasy, 1976; Matthew Arnold: Poet and Prophet, 1976; Homosexuals in History, 1977; Milton the Puritan: Portrait of a Mind, 1977; The Road to Oxford: Poems, 1978; The Byrons and Trevanions, 1978; (ed.) Illustrated, Annotated Shakespeare, 1978; Three Cornish Cats, 1979; (ed.) Roper's Life of Sir Thomas More, with Letters, 1979; Portraits and Views, Literary and Historical, 1979; A Man of the Thirties, 1979; Story of Britain, 1979; Memories of Men and Women, 1980; Shakespeare's Globe (in U.S. as What Shakespeare Read and Thought), 1981; A Life: Collected Poems, 1981; Eminent Elizabethans, 1983; Shakespeare's Characters: A Complete Guide, 1984; Night at the Carn (short stories), 1984; Prefaces to Shakespeare's Plays, 1984; Shakespeare's Self-Portrait, 1984; Glimpses of the Great, 1985; A Quartet of Cornish Cats, 1986; Stories from Trenarren, 1986; The Little Land of Cornwall, 1986; (ed.) The First Colonists: Hakluyt's Voyages to North American, 1986; Reflections on the Puritan Revolution, 1986; In Shakespeare's Land, 1986; The Poet Auden: A Personal Memoir, 1987; Court and Country: Studies in Tudor Social History, 1987; The Victorian Froude: Historian and Man of Letters, 1987; (ed.) Froude's Spanish Story of the Armada, 1988; A.L. Rowse's Cornwall, 1988; Transatlantic, Later Poems, 1989; Friends and Contemporaries, 1989; Discovering Shakespeare: A Chapter in Literary History, 1989. Add: Trenarren, St. Austell, Cornwall, England.

ROY, Archie E. (Archibald Edmiston Roy). British, b. 1924. Novels/Short stories, Astronomy. Prof. of Astronomy, Univ. of Glasgow, since 1977 (Lectr., 1958–66; Sr. Lectr., 1966–73; Reader, 1973–77). Co-ed., Vistas in Astromony, since 1983. Science Teacher, Shawlands Academy, Glasgow, 1954–58. *Publs:* Great Moments in Astronomy, 1963; The Foundations of Astrodynamics, 1965; Deadlight, 1968; (trans.) Concise Encyclopedia of Astronautics, 1968; The Curtained Sleep, 1969; All Evil Shed Away, 1970; Sable Night, 1973; The Dark Host, 1976; (with D. Clarke) Astronomy: Principles and Practice, 1977; (with D. Clarke) Astronomy: Structure of the Universe, 1977; Orbital Motion, 1978; Devil in the Darkness, 1978; (ed.) Long-Term Behaviour of Natural and Artificial N-Body Systems, 1988. Add: Dept. of Physics and Astronomy, Univ. of Glasgow, Glasgow G12 8QQ, Scotland.

ROY, James (Henry Barstow). British, b. 1922. Agriculture/Forestry, Medicine/Health. Agricultural Research Worker, National Inst. for Research in Dairying, Shinfield, Reading, 1949–85. *Publs:* The Calf, 1955, 4th ed. 1980; Inte national Encyclopaedia of Food and Nutrition, 1969. Add: Bruncketts, The Street, Mortimer, Reading, Berks., England.

ROYAL, Rosamund. *See* **SHERWOOD**, Valerie.

ROYCE, James E. American, b. 1914. Philosophy, Psychology. Prof. of Psychology, Seattle Univ., since 1948 (Dean, Coll. of Arts and Sciences, 1965–73). Member, Bd. of Dirs., National Council on Alcoholism, since 1976. Pres., Div. of Philosophical Psychology, American Psychological Assn., 1964–65, and American Assn. of State Psychology Bds., 1966–67. *Publs:* Personality and Mental Health, 1954; Man and His Nature, 1961; Man and Meaning, 1969; Alcohol Problems and Alcoholism, 1981, 1989; Ethics for Addiction Professionals, 1987. Add: Seattle Univ., Seattle, Wash. 98122, U.S.A.

ROYCE, Joseph Russell. American. Psychology. Research Prof., Center for Advanced Study in Theoretical Psychology, Univ. of Alberta, Edmonton, since 1984 (Prof. and Head, Dept. of Psychology, 1960–67; Dir., Center for Advanced Studies in Theoretical Psychology, 1967–84). *Publs:* The Encapsulated Man: An Interdisciplinary Essay on the Search for Meaning, 1964; (ed. and co-author) Psychology and the Symbol: An Interdisciplinary Symposium, 1965; (ed.) Toward Unification in Psychology, 1970; (ed. with W.W. Rozeboom) The Psychology of Knowing, 1972; (ed.) Multivariate Analysis and Psychological Theory, 1973; (ed. with L.P. Mos) Theoretical Advances in Behavior Genetics: The Fourth Banff Conference on Theoretical Psychology, 1979; (ed. with L.P. Mos) Humanistic Psychology: Concepts and Criticisms, 1981; (with A. Powell) Theory of Personality and Individual Differences: Factors, Systems, Processes, 1983; (ed. with L.P. Mos) Annals of Theoretical Psychology, 2 vols., 1984. Add: Center for Advanced Study in Theoretical Psychology, Univ. of Alberta, Edmonton, Alta. T6G 2E9, Canada.

ROYCE, Kenneth. Pseud. for Kenneth Royce Gandley; also writes as Oliver Jacks. British, b. 1920. Mystery/Crime/Suspense. *Publs:* My Turn to Die, 1958; The Soft Footed Moor, 1959; The Long Corridor, 1960; No Paradise, 1961; The Night Seekers, 1962; The Angry Island, 1963; The Day the Wind Dropped, 1964; Bones in the Sand, 1967; A Peck of Salt, 1968; A Single to Hong Kong, 1969; The XYY Man, 1970; The Concrete Boot, 1971; The Miniatures Frame, 1972; Spider Underground (in U.S. as The Masterpiece Affair), 1973; Trap Spider, 1974; (as Oliver Jacks) Man on a Short Leash, 1974; The Woodcutter Operation, 1975; Bustillo, 1976; (as Oliver Jacks) Assassination Day, 1976; (as Oliver Jacks) Autumn Heroes, 1977; The Satan Touch, 1978; The Third Arm, 1980; (as Oliver Jacks) Implant, 1980; 10,000 Days, 1981; Channel Assault, 1982; The Stalin Account, 1983; The Crypto Man, 1984; The Mosley Receipt, 1985; Hashimi's Revenge, 1986; No Way Back, 1986; The President Is Dead, 1988; Fall-Out, 1989. Add: 3 Abbotts Close, Abbotts Ann, Andover, Hants., England.

ROYKO, Mike. American, b. 1922. Social commentary/phenomena. Reporter and Columnist, Chicago Tribune (formerly with the Chicago Daily News and Chicago Sun Times), since 1959. Reporter, Chicago North Side Newspapers, 1956; Reporter and Asst. City Ed., Chicago City News Bureau, 1956–59. *Publs:* Up Against It, 1967; I May be Wrong But I Doubt It, 1968; Boss: Richard J. Daley of Chicago, 1971; Slats Grobnik and Some Other Friends, 1976; Sez Who? Sez Me, 1982; Like I Was Sayin', 1984. Add: Chicago Tribune, 435 N. Michigan Ave., Chicago, Ill. 60611, U.S.A.

ROYSTER, Vermont. American, b. 1914. International relations/Current affairs, Politics/Government, Essays. Prof. of Public Affairs, Univ. of North Carolina, Chapel Hill, since 1971. Contrib. Ed., The Wall Street Journal, NYC, since 1971 (Writer and Columnist, 1936–71; Ed., 1958–71). *Publs:* Journey Through the Soviet Union, 1962; A Pride of Prejudices (essays), 1967; The American Press and the Revolutionary Tradition, 1974; My Own, My Country's Time (memoirs), 1983; The Essential Royster (essays), 1985. Recipient: Pulitzer Prize for Commentary, 1953 and 1984.   Add: 903 Arrowhead Rd., Chapel Hill, N.C. 27514, U.S.A.

RUBENS, Bernice.   British, b. 1928.   Novels/Short stories.   Documentary film writer and dir., for the U.N. and other organizations, since 1950. Teacher of English, Handsworth Grammar Sch. for Boys, Birmingham, 1948–49.   *Publs:* Set on Edge, 1960; Madame Sousatzka, 1962; Mate in Three, 1965; The Elected Member (in U.S. as Chosen People), 1969; Sunday Best, 1971; Go Tell the Lemming, 973; I Sent a Letter to My Love, 1975; The Ponsonby Post, 1977; A Five Year Sentence (in U.S. as Favors), 1978; Spring Sonata, 1979; Birds of Passage, 1981; Brothers, 1984; Mr. Wakefield's Crusade, 1985; Our Father, 1987; Kingdom Come, 1989.   Add: 16A Belsize Gardens, London NW3 4LD, England.

RUBENSTEIN, Richard E.   American, b. 1938.   Law, Politics/Government.   Assoc. Prof. of Political Science, Roosevelt Univ., Chicago, since 1969.   Asst. Dir., Adlai Stevenson Inst., Chicago, 1967–70.   *Publs:* (ed. with Robert Fogelson) Mass Violence in America, 44 vols. of reprints, 1969; Rebels in Eden: Mass Political Violence in the United States, 1970; Left Turn: Origins of the Next American Revolution, 1973; (ed.) Great Courtroom Battles, 1973; The Cunning of History, 1978; Reflections on Religion and Public Policy, 1984; Alchemists of Revolution: Terrorism in the Modern World, 1987.   Add: Dept. of Political Science, Roosevelt University, Chicago, Ill. 60605, U.S.A.

RUBENSTEIN, Richard Lowell.   American, b. 1924.   History, Politics/ Government, Psychology, Theology/Religion, Autobiography/ Memoirs/Personal, Essays.   Distinguished Prof. of Religion since 1977, and Dir. of the Center for Study of Southern Religion, Florida State Univ., Tallahassee (Prof., 1970–77).   Pres., Washington Inst. for Values in Public Policy, Washington, D.C., since 1982.   Adjunct Prof. of Humanities, Univ. of Pittsburgh, 1964–70.   *Publs:* After Auschwitz, 1966; The Religious Imagination, 1968; Morality and Eros, 1970; My Brother Paul, 1972; Power Stuggle (autobiography), 1974; The Cunning of History, 1975; (ed.) Modernization: The Humanist Response to Its Promise and Problems, 1982; The Age of Triage, 1984; (with John K. Roth) Approaches to Auschwitz, 1987; (ed.) The Dissolving Alliance: The United States and the NATO Alliance, 1987; (ed.) Spirit Matters: The Worldwide Impact of Religion on Public Policy, 1987; (ed. with John K. Roth) The Political Significance of Latin-American Liberation Theology, 1988.   Add: 751 Shore Dr., Tallahassee, Fla. 32312, U.S.A.

RUBIN, Larry (Jerome).   American, b. 1930.   Novels/Short stories, Poetry, Literature.   Prof. of English, Georgia Inst. of Technology, Atlanta, since 1973 (Instr., 1956–58; Asst. Prof., 1958–65; Assoc. Prof., 1965–73).   *Publs:* The World's Old Way, 1963; Lanced in Light, 1967; All My Mirrors Lie, 1975.   Add: Box 15014, Druid Hills Branch, Atlanta, Ga. 30333, U.S.A.

RUBIN, Stanley.   British, b. 1928.   History, Medicine/Health. Palaeopathologist to Liverpool Univ. Rescue Archaeology Unit. Supt. Physio-therapist, Alderhey Children's Hosp., Liverpool, 1964–82. Supt. Physio-therapist, City of Liverpool Sch. Health Service, 1959–64. Justice of the Peace, since 1960.   *Publs:* Medieval English Medicine AD 500-1300: A Survey of the Sources, 1974; A Beginner's Guide to Biomedical Instrumentation, 1987.   Add: c/o Year Book Medical Publishers, c/o Wolfe Medical Publs., 3 Conway St., London W1P 6HE, England.

RUBIN, Theodore I.   American, b. 1923.   Psychiatry.   Psychiatrist in private practice, NYC, since 1956.   Former Pres., Bd. of Trustees, American Inst. of Psychoanalysis; Training and Supervising Psychoanalyst, New Sch. of Social Research, NYC.   Former Contrib. Columnist, Ladies Home Journal.   *Publs:* Jordi, 1960; Lisa and David, 1961; In the Life, 1961; Sweet Daddy, 1963; Platzo and the Mexican Pony Rider, 1965; The Thin Book by a Formerly Fat Psychiatrist, 1966; The 29th Summer, 1966; Cat, 1966; Coming Out, 1967; The Winner's Notebook, 1967; The Angry Book, 1969; Forever Thin, 1970; Emergency Room Diary, 1972; Doctor Rubin Please Make Me Happy, 1974; Shrink, 1974; Compassion and Self-Hate, 1976; Love Me, Love My Fool, 1976; Reflections in a Goldfish Tank, 1977; (with David C. Berliner) Understanding Your Man, 1971; Alive and Fat and Thinning in America, 1978; Reconciliations, 1980; Through My Own Eyes, 1980; One to One, 1981; Not to Worry, 1983; Overcoming Indecisiveness, 1985; Lisa and David Story, 1986; Miracle at Bellvue, 1986; Real Love, 1989.   Add: 219 E. 62nd St., New York, N.Y. 10021, U.S.A.

RUBINOFF, Lionel.   Canadian, b. 1930.   Social commentary, Social sciences, Theology/Religion.   Prof. of Philosophy since 1971, and Vice-Dean, Arts and Sciences, 1980–85, Trent Univ., Peterborough, Ont. Lectr.,

1960–63, Asst. Prof., 1968–70, and Prof. of Social Science and Philosophy, 1970–71, York Univ., Toronto.   Trustee, North York Bd. of Education, 1970–73.   *Publs:* The Pornography of Power, 1968; (ed.) The Presuppositions of Critical History, by F.H. Bradley, 1968; (ed.) Faith and Reason: Essays in the Philosophy of Religion, by R.G. Collingwood, 1968; Collingwood and the Reform of Metaphysics, 1970; (ed.) Tradition and Revolution, 1971; The Dialectic of Work and Labour in the Ontology of Man, 1971; Violence and the Retreat from Reason, 1974; Auschwitz and the Theology of Holocaust, 1974; Nationalism and Celebration, 1975; Vico and the Verification of Historical Interpretation, 1976; Auschwitz and the Pathology of Jew-Hatred, 1976; Technology and the Crisis of Rationality, 1977; The Metaphysics of Technology and the Crisis of Rationality, 1978; In Nomine Diaboli: The Voices of Evil, 1978; On Theorizing Human Conduct, 1979; Hymn to Apollo: Philosophy, Justice, and the Condition of Pluralism, 1981; Utopianism and the Eschatology of Violence, 1981; Multiculturalism and the Metaphysics of Pluralism, 1982; Beyond the Domination of Nature: Moral Foundations of a Conserver Society, 1985; Obligations to Future Generations, 1988.   Add: R.R.7, Peterborough, Ont. K9J 6X8, Canada.

RUBINSTEIN, Gillian (née Hanson).   British, b. 1942.   Children's fiction.   Ed., Tom Stacey Publishers, London, 1969–72.   *Publs:* Space Demons, 1986; Answers to Brut, 1988; Beyond the Labyrinth, 1988; Melanie and the Night Animal, 1988.   Add: 29 Seaview Rd., Lynton, S.A. 5062, Australia.

RUBINSTEIN, Hilary (Harold).   British, b. 1926.   Travel.   Dir., A.P. Watt Ltd., literary agents, London, since 1965, Chmn. and Managing Dir. since 1982.   Dir., Victor Gollancz Ltd., London, 1953–63; Special Features Ed., The Observer newspaper, London, 1963; Deputy Ed., The Observer Mag., 1964–65.   *Publs:* The Complete Insomniac (in U.S. as Insomniacs of the World, Goodnight), 1974; (ed.) The Good Hotel Guide (in U.S. as Europe's Wonderful Little Hotels and Inns), 1978 (and annually); Hotels and Inns: An Anthology, 1984.   Add: 61 Clarendon Rd., London W11, England.

RUBY, Robert H.   American.   History, Transportation, Biography. Physician in private practice since 1955.   *Publs:* The Oglala Sioux, 1955; (with J.A. Brown) Half-Sun on the Columbia: A Biography of Chief Moses, 1965; (with J.A. Brown) The Spokane Indians, 1970; (with J.A. Brown) The Cayuse Indians, 1972; (with J.A. Brown) Ferryboats on the Columbia River, 1974; (with J.A. Brown) The Chinook Indians, 1976; (with J.A. Brown) Myron Eells and the Puget Sound Indians, 1976; (with J.A. Brown) Indians of the Pacific Northwest, 1981; (with J.A. Brown) A Guide to the Indian Tribes of the Pacific Northwest, 1986; (with J.A. Brown) Dreamer-Prophets of the Columbia Plateau, 1989.   Add: 1022 Ivy, Moses Lake, Wash. 98837, U.S.A.

RUCHELMAN, Leonard I.   American, b. 1933.   Criminology/Law enforcement/Prisons, Politics/Government.   Assoc. Prof. of Govt. since 1969, and Dir. of Urban Studies, Lehigh Univ., Pennsylvania.   *Publs:* (ed.) Big City Mayors, 1969; Political Careers: Recruitment Through the Legislature, 1970; (ed.) Who Rules the Police?, 1973; Police Politics: A Comparative Study of Three Cities, 1974; A Workbook in Program Design for Public Managers, 1985; A Workbook in Redesigning Public Services, 1989.   Add: 3019 Oakland Rd., Bethlehem, Pa., U.S.A.

RUCKER, Rudy.   American, b. 1946.   Science fiction, Poetry, Sciences.   Free-lance writer since 1982.   Taught at State Univ. of New York, Geneseo, 1972–78, and Randolph-Macon Woman's Coll., Lynchburg, Va., 1980–82.   Add: science fiction—White Light, 1980; Spacetime Donuts, 1981; Software, 1982; The Sex Sphere, 1983; The Fifty-Seventh Franz Kafka (stories), 1983; Master of Space and Time, 1984; The Secret of Life, 1985; Mind Tools, 1987; other—Geometry, Relativity, and the Fourth Dimension, 1977; (ed.) Speculations on the Fourth Dimension: Selected Writings of Charles H. Hinton, 1980; Infinity and the Mind, 1982; Light Fuse and Get Away (poetry), 1983; The Fourth Dimension, 1985.   Add: c/o Houghton Mifflin Co., 1 Beacon St., Boston, Mass. 02108, U.S.A.

RUDD, Margaret.   *See* **NEWLIN**, Margaret Rudd.

RUDKIN, (James) David.   British, b. 1936.   Plays/Screenplays, Translations.   Playwright.   Asst. Master of Latin, Greek, and Music, County High Sch., Bromsgrove, Worcs., 1961–64.   *Publs:* (trans.) Moses and Aaron, by Schoenberg, 1965; Afore Night Come, 1966; The Grace of Todd, 1970; Cries from Casement as His Bones Are Brought to Dublin, 1974; Penda's Fen, 1974; Ashes, 1977; (trans.) Hippolytus, by Euripides, 1980; The Sons of Light, 1981; The Triumph of Death, 1981; (trans.)

Peer Gynt, by Ibsen, 1983; The Saxon Shore, 1986. Add: c/o Margaret Ramsay Ltd., 14a Goodwin's Ct., London WC2, England.

RUDLOE, Jack. American, b. 1943. Marine Science/Oceanography. Pres., Gulf Specimen Co., Inc., Panacea, Fla., since 1964. *Publs:* The Sea Brings Forth, 1968; The Erotic Ocean, 1971; The Living Dock at Panacea, 1977; Time of the Turtle, 1978; Wilderness Coast, 1988. Add: c/o Dutton, 2 Park Ave., New York, N.Y. 10016, U.S.A.

RUDOLF, Anthony. British, b. 1942. Poetry, Translations. Co-Founder and Ed., Menard Press, London, since 1969. Jr. Exec., British Travel Assn., London and Chicago, 1964–66; English and French teacher, 1967–68; worked in bookshops, London, 1969–71; London Ed., Stand mag., Newcastle upon Tyne, 1969–72; Literary Ed., 1970–72, and Managing Ed., 1972–75, European Judaism, London; Advisory Ed., Heimler Foundn. Publications, London, 1974–76, and Jewish Quarterly, London, 1975–80. *Publs:* (trans.) Selected Poems, by Yves Bonnefoy, 1968, 1986; The Manifold Circle (verse), 1971; (ed. with Richard Burns) An Octave for Octavio Paz, 1972; The Soup Complex (adaptation of a play by Ana Novac), 1972; (trans.) Two Poems from Veines, by Jean-Paul Guibbert, 1972; (trans.) Tyorkin, and The Stovemakers: Poetry and Prose of Alexander Tvardovsky, 1974; (trans.) Relative Creatures: Victorian Women in Society and the Novel 1837-1867, by Francoise Basch, 1974; (trans. with Peter Jay and Petru Popescu) Boxes, Stairs and Whistle Time: Poems, by Popescu, 1975; The Same River Twice (verse), 1976; (ed.) Poems from Shakespeare IV, 1976; (trans. with Daniel Weissbort) The War Is Over: Selected Poems, by Evgeny Vinokurov, 1976; (trans.) A Share of Ink, by Edmond Jabes, 1979; (ed. with Howard Schwartz) Voices i the Ark: The Modern Jewish Poets, 1980; After the Dream: Poems 1964-1979, 1980; Byron's Darkness: Lost Summer and Nuclear Winter, 1986. Add: 8 The Oaks, Woodside Ave., London N12 8AR, England.

RUDOMIN, Esther. *See* **HAUTZIG**, Esther.

RUDRUM, Alan (William). British, b. 1932. Literature. Prof. of English, Simon Fraser Univ., Burnaby, B.C., since 1969. Lectr. in English, Adelaide Univ., South Australia, 1958–64, and Queen's Univ., Belfast, 1964–66; Asst. Prof. of English, Univ. of California, 1966–68; Prof., Kent State Univ., Ohio, 1968–69. *Publs:* (ed.) Poems of Johnson, 1965; Milton's Paradise Lost: A Critical Commentary, 1966; A Critical Commentary on Milton's Comus and Shorter Poems, 1967; (ed.) Modern Judgements on Milton, 1968; A Critical Commentary on Milton's Samson Agonistes, 1969; (ed.) Complete Poems of Henry Vaughan, 1976; Writers of Wales: Henry Vaughan, 1981; (ed.) The Works of Thomas Vaughan, 1984. Add: Dept. of English, Simon Fraser Univ., Burnaby, B.C. V5A 1S6, Canada.

RUDY, Willis. American, b. 1920. History. Prof. Emeritus of History, Fairleigh Dickinson Univ., Rutherford, N.J., since 1982 (Prof., 1963–82). Instr. and Lectr., Harvard Univ., Cambridge, Mass., 1949–52, 1953, 1957. *Publs:* The College of the City of New York: A History 1847-1947, 1949, 1976; (with John S. Brubacher) Higher Education in Transition, 1958, 3rd ed. 1976; The Liberal Arts College Curriculum: A Historical Review of Basic Themes, 1960; Schools in an Age of Mass Culture, 1965; The Universities of Europe, a History, 1984. Add: 161 W. Clinton Ave., Tenafly, N.J. 07670, U.S.A.

RUE, Leonard Lee III. American, b. 1926. Natural history. *Publs:* Animals in Motion, 1956; Tracks and Tracking, 1956; (with Dorothy Knight) American Animals, 1961; World of the White-Tailed Deer, 1962; World of the Beaver, 1963; New Jersey Out-of-Doors, 1964; World of the Raccoon, 1964; Cottontail, 1965; (with John Bailey) Our Wild Animals, 1965; Pictorial Guide to the Mammals of North America, 1967; Sportsman's Guide to Game Animals, 1968, 1979; The World of the Red Fox, 1969; Pictorial Guide to Birds of North America, 1970; The World of the Ruffed Grouse, 1973; Game Birds of North America, 1973; The Deer of North America, 1978, 1989; Furbearing Animals of North America, 1981; When Your Deer Is Down, 1981; How I Photograph Wildlife and Nature, 1984; (with William Owen) Meet the Opossum [Moose, Beaver], 3 vols., 1984–86; (with others) The Outdoor Life Deer Hunters Encyclopedia, 1985; Add: 138 Millbrook Rd., Blairstown, N.J. 07825, U.S.A.

RUEF, John Samuel. American, b. 1927. Theology/Religion. Chaplain, Dean of Instruction, and Head of the Dept. Religious Studies, Chatham Hall, Virginia, since 1985. Prof. of New Testament, Berkeley Divinity Sch., New Haven, Conn., 1960–71; Dir., Inst. of Religious Studies, Buffalo, N.Y., 1972–74; Dean, Nashotah House, 1974–85. *Publs:* Understanding the Gospels, 1963; The Gospels and the Teachings

of Jesus, 1967; The First Letter of Paul to Corinth, 1971; The New Testament and the Sacraments of the Church, 1973. Add: Box 1143, Chatham, Va 24531 U.S.A.

RUELL, Patrick. *See* **HILL**, Reginald.

RUETHER, Rosemary Radford. American, b. 1936. Theology/Religion, Women, Biography. Harkness Prof., Garrett Seminary, Evanston, Ill., since 1976. With Immaculate Heart Coll., Los Angeles, 1965–66; Lectr., George Washington Univ., Washington, D.C., 1966–67; Lectr. in Roman Catholic Studies, Harvard Divinity Sch., Cambridge, Mass., 1972–73; Lectr. in Theology and Women's Studies, Yale Divinity Sch., New Haven, Conn., 1973–74; Asst. Prof., 1967–72, and Assoc. Prof., 1974–76, Howard Univ. Sch. of Religion, Washington, D.C. *Publs:* The Church Against Itself, 1967; Communion Is Life Together, 1968; Gregory Nazianzus: Rhetor and Philosopher, 1969; The Radical Kingdom: The Western Experience of Messianic Hope, 1970; Liberation Theology: Human Hope Confronts Christian History and American Power, 1972; (ed. and contrib.) Religion and Sexism: The Image of Women in the Judeo-Christian Tradition, 1974; Faith and Fratricide: The Image of the Jews in Early Christianity, 1974; (with E. Bianchi) From Machismo to Mutuality: Essays on Sexism and Woman-Man Liberation, 1975; The New Woman and the New Earth: Essays on Sexist Ideologies and Human Liberation, 1975; Mary: The Feminine Face of the Church, 1977; (with Eleanor McLaughlin) Women of Spirit, 1978; (with Rosemary Keller) Women and Religion in America, 1981; To Change the World, 1981; Disputed Questions: On Being a Christian, 1982; Women and Religion in America: The Colonial Period, 1983; Sexism and God-Talk, 1984; Womanguides, 1986; Women and Religion in America: 1900-1968, 1986; Women-Church: Theology and Practice of Feminist Liturgical Communities, 1986; Catholicism Today: Crises and Challenges, 1987; Contemporary Catholicism, 1987. Add: 1426 Hinman, Evanston, Ill. 60201, U.S.A.

RUHEN, Olaf. New Zealander, b. 1911. Novels/Short stories, Geography, History, Autobiography/Memoirs/Personal. *Publs:* Land of Dahori, 1957; Naked under Capricorn, 1958; White Man's Shoes, 1960; Tangaroa's Godchild, 1962; The Flockmaster, 1963; Minerva Reef, 1963; Mountains in the Clouds, 1963; Lively Ghosts, 1964; Harpoon in My Hand, 1966; The Broken Wing, 1965; Corcoran's the Name, 1967; The Rocks, Sydney, 1966; (with Maurice Shadbolt) Isles of the South Pacific, 1968; (ed.) South Pacific Adventure, 1966; Scan the Dark Coast, 1969; Australia 2000, 1970; Parramatta Sketch Book, 1971; Port Macquarie, 1971; (with Cedric Emanuel) Australia This Changing Land, 1972; Historic Buildings of Sydney, 1972; The Day of the Diprotodon, 1976; Port of Melbourne 1835-1976, 1976; (with W. Hudson Shaw) Lawrence Hargrave, 1977; (with Lawrence Collings) On and Around Sydney Harbour, 1978; Bullock Teams: The Building of a State, 1980; (with R.M. Williams) Beneath Whose Hand, 1984. Add: Cross St., Mosman, N.S.W. 2088, Australia.

RULE, Jane. Canadian, b. 1931. Novels/Short stories, Literature, Social commentary/phenomena. Teacher of English, Concord Academy, Massachusetts, 1954–56; Asst. Dir. of Intnl. House, 1958–59, Intermittent Lectr. in English, 1959–70, and Visiting Lectr. in Creative Writing, 1972–73, Univ. of British Columbia, Vancouver. *Publs:* The Desert of the Heart, 1964; This Is Not for You, 1970; Against the Season, 1971; Lesbian Images, 1975; Themes for Diverse Instruments, 1975; The Young in One Another's Arms, 1977; Contract with the World, 1980; Outlander, 1981; Inland Passage, 1985; A Hot-Eyed Moderate, 1985; Memory Board, 1987; After the Fire, 1989. Add: The Fork, R.R.1, Galiano, B.C. VON 1PO, Canada.

RULON, Philip Reed. American, b. 1934. History. Prof. of History, Northern Arizona Univ., Flagstaff, snce 1980 (Assoc. Prof., 1971–80). Member, National Bd. of Advisors, American Biographical Inst., Raleigh, N.C. Faculty member, Oklahoma State Univ., Stillwater, 1964–67. Member, Editorial Bd., Historian, 1974–79. *Publs:* Oklahoma State University, 1975; Compassionate Samaritan: The Life of Lyndon Baines Johnson, 1981; Letters from Hill Country: The Correspondence of Rebekah and Lyndon Baines Johnson, 1981; (with William H. Lyon) Speaking Out: An Oral History of the American Past, 2 vols., 1981; (ed.) Navajo Trader, by Gladwell Richardson, 1986; Add: Box 5725, Northern Arizona Univ., Flagstaff, Ariz. 86001, U.S.A.

RUMAKER, Michael. American, b. 1932. Novels/Short stories, Plays/Screenplays. Teacher of Writing Workshops, Rockland Center for the Arts, West Nyack, N.Y., since 1978. Lectr. in Writing, New Sch. for Social Research, NYC, 1967–71; Writer-in-Residence and Lectr., City

Coll. of New York, 1969–71, 1985. *Publs:* The Butterfly, 1962; Exit 3 and Other Stories, 1966; Gringos and Other Stories, 1967; Queers (play), 1970; A Day and a Night at the Baths, 1979; My First Satyrnalia, 1981. Add: 139 S. Broadway, South Nyack, N.Y. 10960, U.S.A.

RUMENS, Carol. British, b. 1944. Novels, Poetry, Literature. Poetry Ed., Literary Review, London; book reviewer, The Observer, London. Publicity asst., 1974–77, and advertising copywriter, 1977–81, in London; Poetry Ed., Quarto, London, 1981–82; Creative Writing Fellow, Univ. of Kent, Canterbury, 1983–85. *Publs:* Strange Girl in Bright Colours, 1973; A Necklace of Mirrors, 1978; Unplayed Music, 1981; Scenes from the Gingerbread House, 1982; Star Whisper, 1983; Direct Dialing, 1985; (ed.) Making for the Open: The Chatto Book of Post-Feminist Poetry 1964-1984, 1985; Icons, Waves, 1986; Selected Poems, 1987; Plato Park (novel), 1987; The Greening of the Snow Beach, 1988. Add: c/o Chatto and Windus, 40 William IV St., London WC2N 4DF, England.

RUNCIMAN, (Sir) Steven (James Cochran Stevenson). British, b. 1903. History. Fellow of Trinity Coll., 1927–38, and Lectr., Cambridge Univ., 1932–38; Prof. of Byzantine Art and History, Univ. of Istanbul, 1942–45; Rep., British Council, Greece, 1945–47. Chmn., Anglo-Hellenic League, 1951–67; Member, Advisory Council, Victoria and Albert Museum, London, 1957–73; Trustee, British Museum, London, 1960–68; Pres., British Inst. of Archaeology at Ankara, 1960–75. *Publs:* The Emperor Romanus Lecapenus, 1929; The First Bulgarian Empire, 1930; Byzantine Civilization, 1933; The Mediaeval Manichee, 1947; A History of the Crusades, vol. I, 1951, vol. II, 1952, vol. III, 1954; The Eastern Schism, 1955; The Sicilian Vespers, 1958; The White Rajahs, 1960; The Fall of Constantinople 1453, 1965; The Great Church in Captivity, 1968; The Last Byzantine Renaissance, 1970; The Orthodox Church and the Secular State, 1971; Byzantine Styles and Civilization, 1975; The Byzantine Theocracy, 1977; Mistra, 1980. Add: Elshieshields Tower, Lockerbie, Dumfriesshire, Scotland.

RUNDLE, Anne. Also writes as Marianne Lamont, Alexandra Manners, Joanne Marshall, and Jeanne Sanders. British. Historical/Romance/Gothic, Children's fiction. *Publs:* The Moon Marriage, 1967; Swordlight, 1968; (as Joanne Marshall) Cuckoo at Candelmas, 1968; (as Joanne Marshall) Cat on a Broomstick, 1969; (as Joanne Marshall) The Dreaming Tower, 1969; Forest of Fear, 1969; Dragonscale (juvenile), 1969; Rakehell, 1970; Tamlane (juvenile), 1970; (as Marianne Lamont) Darkchangeling, 1970; (as Marianne Lamont) Green Glass Moon, 1970; (as Joanne Marshall) Flower of Silence, 1970; (as Joanne Marshall) Babylon Was Dust, 1971; (as Marianne Lamont) Bitter Bride Bed, 1971; Lost Lotus, 1972; Amberwood, 1972; (as Joanne Marshall) Wildboar Wood, 1973; The Trelised Walk, 1973; Sea-Song, 1973; (as Alexandra Manners) The Stone Maiden, 1973; (as Alexandra Manners) Candles in the Wood, 1974; Heron Brook, 1974; (as Jeanne Sanders) Spindrift, 1974; (as Joanne Marshall) Follow a Shadow, 1974; (as Joanne Marshall) Valley of Tall Chimneys, 1974; (as Alexandra Manners) The Singing Swans, 1975; Judith Lammeter, 1976; (as Alexandra Manners) Sable Hunter (in U.S. paperback as Cardigan Square), 1977; (as Marianne Lamont) Nine Moons Wasted, 1977; Grey Ghyll, 1978; (as Joanne Marshall) The Peacock Bed, 1978; (as Alexandra Manners) Wildford's Daughter, 1978, in U.K. as The White Moths, 1979; (as Marianne Lamont) Horns of the Moon, 1979; (as Alexandra Manners) Echoing Yesterday, 1981; (as Marianne Lamont) Horns of the Moon, 1981; (as Alexandra Manners) Karran Kinrade, 1982; (as Marianne Lamont) A Serpent's Tooth, 1983; (as Alexandra Manners) The Red Bird, 1984; (as Alexandra Manners) The Gaming House, 1984; Moonbranches (juvenile), 1986. Add: Cloy Cottage, Knowe Rd., Brodick, Arran, Scotland.

RUPP, Richard H. American, b. 1934. Literature, Education. Assoc. Prof. to Prof., Appalachian State Univ., Boone, N.C., since 1975 (Dean of the Grad. Sch., 1975–79). Asst. Prof., Georgetown Univ., Washington, D.C., 1961–68; Asst. Prof., Univ. of Miami, 1968–72; Assoc. Prof., Brooklyn Coll., City Univ. of New York, 1972–74. *Publs:* Celebration in Postwar American Fiction 1945-67, 1970; (ed.) The Marble Faun; or, The Romance of Mente Beni, by Nathaniel Hawthorne, 1971; (ed.) Critics on Whitman, 1972; (ed.) Critics on Emily Dickinson, 1972; Getting Through College, 1984. Add: 634 Poplar Summit, Boone, N.C. 28607, U.S.A.

RUPPENTHAL, Karl M(axwell). American, b. 1917. Business/Trade/Industry, Industrial relations, Politics/Government, Transportations. UPS Foundn. Prof., and Dir. of the Centre for Transportation Studies, Univ. of British Columbia, Vancouver, 1971–84, now Emeritus. Founder, Farwest Press; Consultant to the Canadian Ministry of Transport, Transport Canada, and the National Harbours Bd. Pilot, Trans-World

Airlines, 1942–68; Dir., Transportation Mgmt. Prog., Stanford Univ., California, 1959–70; Ryder Foundn. Prof. of Transportation, Univ. of Miami, 1970. *Publs:* Revolution in Transportation, 1960; Challenge to Transportation, 1961; Transportation Frontiers, 1962; The Air Line Dispatcher in North America, 1962; New Dimensions in Business Logistics, 1963; Perspectives in Transportation, 1963; Transportation Progress, 1964; Developments in Business Logistics, 1964; Issues in Transportation Economics, 1965; Transportation and Tomorrow, 1966; Business Logistics in American Industry, 1968; Air Transportation: A Forward Look, 1970; Transportation Subsidies: Nature and Extent, 1974; Regulation, Competition, and the Public Interest, 1976; Case Problems in Air Transportation, 1978, 3rd ed. 1982; The British Columbia Railway: A Railway Derailed, 1979; Canada's Ports and Waterborne Trade, 1982. Add: 3755 W. 2nd Ave., Vancouver, B.C. V6R 1J8, Canada.

RUSH, Christopher. British, b. 1944. Novels/Short stories, Poetry. Asst. Principal and English Teacher, George Watson's Coll., Edinburgh, since 1972. Secondary Sch. English teacher, Edinburgh, 1970–72. *Publs:* Peace Comes Dropping Slow, 1983; A Resurrection of a Kind, 1984; A Twelvemonth and a Day, 1985. Add: 2 Peel Terr., Edinburgh EH9 2AY, Scotland.

RUSH, Philip. British, b. 1908. Historical/Romance/Gothic, Children's fiction, Children's non-fiction, Biography. *Publs:* Rogue's Lute, 1944; Mary Read, Buccaneer, 1945; Freedom Is the Man, 1946; Crispin's Apprentice, 1948; He Sailed with Dampier, 1948; A Cage of Falcons, 1954; Queen's Treason, 1954; Red Man's Country, 1955; King of the Castle, 1956; Great Men of Sussex, 1956; My Brother Lambert, 1957; The Minstrel Knight, 1957; Strange People, 1957; London's Wonderful Bridge, 1957; He Went with Dampier, 1957; More Strange People, 1958; Strange Stuarts, 1959; He Went with Franklin, 1960; How Roads Have Grown, 1960; Apprentice-at-Arms, 1960; The Young Shelley, 1961; (with J. O'Keefe) Weights and Measures, 1962; The Castle and the Harp, 1963; The Book of Duels, 1964; Frost Fair, 1965; That Fool of a Priest, 1970; A Face of Stone, 1973; Guns for the Armada, 1975; Death to the Strangers, 1977; Pierce Allard, 1981; Quayle, 1982. Add: 45 Castle St., Canterbury, Kent CT1 2PY, England.

RUSHDIE, Salman. British, b. 1947. Novels/Short stories. *Publs:* Grimus, 1975; Midnight's Children, 1981; Shame, 1983; The Jaguar Smile, 1987; The Satanic Verses, 1988. Add: c/o Aitken and Stone, 29 Fernshaw Rd.,London SW10 0TE, England.

RUSHER, William Allen. American, b. 1923. Politics/Government, Documentaries/Reportage. Publr., National Review, NYC, 1957–88. Attorney-at-Law, NYC, 1948–56; Assoc. Counsel, Internal Security Subcttee., U.S. Senate, Washington, D.C., 1956–57. *Publs:* Special Counsel, 1968; (with A Schardt and Mark Hatfield) Amnesty?, 1973; The Making of the New Majority Party, 1975; How to Win Arguments, 1981; The Rise of the Right, 1983; The Coming Battle for the Media, 1988. Add: 150 E. 35th St., New York, N.Y. 10016, U.S.A.

RUSHING, Jane Gilmore. American, b. 1925. Novels/Short stories, Westerns/Adventure, History. Reporter, Abilene Reporter-News, Tex., 1946–47; English Teacher, Ira High Sch., 1947–48, Snyder High Sch., 1948–52, and Levelland High Sch., 1953–56, all Tex.; Instr., Univ. of Tennessee, Knoxville, 1957–59; Part-time teacher, Texas Tech. Univ., 1959–79. *Publs:* Walnut Grove, 1964; Against the Moon, 1968; Tamzen, 1972; Mary Dove, 1974; (with Kline A. Nall) Evolution of a University: Texas Tech's First Fifty Years, 1975; The Raincrow, 1977; Covenant of Grace, 1982; Winds of Blame, 1983. Add: 3809 39th St., Lubbock, Tex. 79413, U.S.A.

RUSHOLM, Peter. *See* **POWELL,** Eric.

RUSHTON, William (George). British, b. 1937. Humour/Satire. Actor, author and cartoonist. Founder Ed., 1961, and Contributor, Private Eye mag., London; numerous appearances on the stage, in film, and as broadcaster. *Publs:* William Rushton's Dirty Book, 1964; How to Play Football: The Art of Dirty Play, 1968; The Day of the Grocer, 1971; The Geranium of Flut, 1975; Superpig, 1976; Pigsticking: A Joy for Life, 1977; The Reluctant Euro, 1980; The Filth Amendment, 1981; W.G. Grace's Last Case, 1984; Adam and Eve, 1985; Willie Rushton's Great Moments of History, 1985; Don't Open That Trapdoor, 1986; The Alternative Gardener, 1986; Vile Pile, 1986; Yecch!, 1986; The Flyin' Wotsit Fingy, 1986; Marylebone Versus the Rest of the World, 1987; (ed.) Spy Thatcher, 1987. Add: c/o Andre Deutsch Ltd., 105 Great Russell St., London WC1B 3LJ, England.

RUSS, Joanna. American, b. 1937. Science fiction/Fantasy. Prof. of English, Univ. of Washington, Seattle, since 1984 (Assoc. Prof., 1977–84). Asst. Prof., Cornell Univ., Ithaca, N.Y., 1967–68 and 1971–72, State Univ. of New York, Binghamton, 1972–73 and 1974–75, and Univ. of Colorado, Boulder, 1975–77. *Publs:* Picnic on Paradise, 1968; And Chaos Died, 1970; The Female Man, 1975; We Who Are about to, 1977; The Two of Them, 1978; Kittatinny: A Tale of Magic, 1978; On Strike Against God, 1980; The Adventures of Alyx (short stories), 1983; The Zanzibar Cat (short stories), 1983; How to Suppress Women's Writing, 1983; Extra (Ordinary People), 1984; The Other Side of the Moon (short stories), 1987. Add: Dept. of English, Univ. of Washington, Seattle, Wash. 98195, U.S.A.

RUSSELL, Brian Fitzgerald. British, b. 1904. History, Medicine/Health. Asst, Physician, Dept. of Dermatology, St. Bartholomew's Hosp., London, 1948–52; Physician, Dept. of Dermatology, The London Hosp., and St. John's Hosp. for Diseases of the Skin, 1952–69; Dean, Inst. of Dermatology, London, 1959–64. *Publs:* (with Eric Wittkower) Emotional Factors in Skin Diseases, 1953; St. John's Hospital for Diseases of the Skin 1863-1963, 1963. Add: "Arches," Hilltop Lane, Saffron Walden, Essex CB11 4AS, England.

RUSSELL, Conrad (Sebastian Robert). British, b. 1937. History. Prof. of History, Yale Univ., New Haven. Lectr./Reader in Modern History, Bedford Coll., Univ. of London, 1960–79. *Publs:* The Crisis of Parliaments: English History 1509-1660 (Shorter Oxford History of the Modern World), 1971; (ed. and co-author) The Origins of the English Civil War, 1973; Parliaments and English Politics 1621-1629, 1979. Add: Dept. of History, Yale Univ., New Haven, Conn. 06520, U.S.A.

RUSSELL, David Syme. British, b. 1916. Theology/Religion. Principal, Rawdon Coll., Leeds, 1953–64; Joint Principal, Northern Baptist Coll., Manchester, 1964–67; Moderator, Free Church Federal Council, 1974–75; Gen. Secty., Baptist Union of Great Britain and Ireland, 1967–82. *Publs:* Between the Testaments, 1960; (with M.R. Bielby) Two Refugees: Ezekiel and Second Isaiah, 1962; The Method and Message of Jewish Apocalyptic, 1964; The Jews from Alexander to Herod, 1967; The Background to Biblical Interpretation in the New Testament, 1971; Apocalyptic, Ancient and Modern, 1978; The Daily Study Bible: Daniel, 1981; In Journeyings Often, 1982; From Early Judaism to Early Church, 1987; The Old Testament Pseudepigrapha: Patriarchs and Prophets in Early Judaism, 1987; David: An Active Volcano, 1989. Add: 40 Northumbria Dr., Henleaze, Bristol BS9 4HP, England.

RUSSELL, Francis. American, b. 1910. History, Literature, Biography. *Publs:* Three Studies in 20th Century Obscurity, 1953; The Pioneer Spirit, 1959; Tragedy in Dedham, 1962; The French and Indian Wars, 1963; The Great Interlude, 1964; Lexington, Concord and Bunker Hill, 1964; The Shadow of Blooming Grove, 1968; President Harding, 1969; The Age of Duerer, 1969; The Making of the Nation, 1969; The Confident Years, 1970; Forty Years On, 1971; Concise History of Germany, 1972; A City in Terror, 1975; Adams: An American Dynasty, 1976; The President Makers, 1976; The Secret War, 1982; Sacco-Vanzetti: The Case Resolved, 1986; The Knave of Boston, 1987. Add: The Lindens, Sandwich, Mass., 02563, U.S.A.

RUSSELL, Franklin (Alexander). Canadian, b. 1926. Children's fiction, Natural history. *Publs:* Watchers at the Pond, 1961; Argen the Gull, 1963; The Frightened Hare, 1965; Hawk in the Sky, 1965; The Honeybees, The Secret Islands, 1966; Searchers at the Gulf, 1970; The Atlantic Shore, 1971; The Okefenokee Swamp, 1973; The Sea Has Wings, 1973; Season on the Plain, 1974; Wild Creatures, 1975; The Audubon Society Book of Wild Birds, 1976; Wings on the Southwinds, 1984; Hunting Animals, 1985. Add: 27 Spring Close Highway, East Hampton, N.Y. 11937, U.S.A.

RUSSELL, Helen Ross. American, b. 1915. Children's non-fiction, Education. Freelance writer and consultant since 1966. Ed., Nature Study, since 1981. Teacher in public schs., 1934–46; Prof., 1946–56, and Academic Dean, 1956–66, Fitchburg State Coll. Pres., American Nature Study Soc., 1974. *Publs:* City Critters, 1969, 1975; True Book of Buds, 1970; Clarion the Killdeer, 1970; Winter Search Party, 1971; Winter: A Field Trip Guide, 1972; Small Worlds: A Field Trip Guide, 1972; Soil: A Field Trip Guide, 1972; The True Book of Springtime Tree Seeds, 1972; Ten Minute Field Trips, Using the School Grounds for Environmental Studies (teachers book), 1973; Water: A Field Trip Guide, 1973; Earth the Great Recycler, 1973; Foraging for Dinner, 1975; Wave Hill Trail Guide, 1978. Add: 44 College Dr., Jersey City, N.J. 07305, U.S.A.

RUSSELL, James. *See* **GILMAN**, George G.

RUSSELL, Jeffrey Burton. American, b. 1934. History, Theology/Religion. Prof. of Medieval and Church History, Univ. of California at Santa Barbara, since 1979. Asst. Prof. of History, Univ. of New Mexico, Albuquerque, 1960–61; Jr. Fellow, Soc. of Fellows, Harvard Univ., Cambridge, Mass., 1961–62; Asst. Prof., 1962–65, Assoc. Prof., 1965–69, and Prof., 1969–75, Univ. of California at Riverside, 1962–65; Michael P. Grace Prof. of Medieval Studies and Dir. of Medieval Inst., Univ. of Notre Dame, Indiana, 1975–79. *Publs:* Dissent and Reform in the Early Middle Ages, 1965; (with others) The Transformation of the Roman World, 1966; Medieval Civilization, 1968; A History of Medieval Christianity: Prophecy and Order, 1968; (ed.) Religious Dissent in the Middle ages, 1971; Witchcraft in the Middle Ages, 1972; The Devil: Perceptions of Evil from Antiquity to Primitive Christianity, 1977; A History of Witchcraft: Sorcerers, Heretics and Pagans, 1980; (with Carl T. Berkhout) Medieval Heresies: A Bibliography 1969-1979, 1981; Satan: The Early Christian Tradition, 1981; The Devil in the Middle Ages, 1984; Mephistopheles: The Devil in the Modern World, 1986; The Prince of Darkness: Radical, Evil and the Power of Good in History, 1988. Add: Dept. of History, University of California, Santa Barbara, Calif. 93106, U.S.A.

RUSSELL, Jeremy (Longmore). British, b. 1935. International relations/Current affairs. Industry Adviser to the Nature Conservancy Council. Formerly, Mgr., Business Environment and Planning, Shell U.K. Ltd. *Publs:* Energy as a Factor in Soviet Foreign Policy, 1976; Geopolitics of Natural Gas, 1983. Add: 97 Queen's Rd., Richmond, Surrey, England.

RUSSELL, Joan Mercedes. British, b. 1921. Dance/Ballet. Sr. Tutor and Head of Dance Dept., Worcester Coll. of Higher Education, 1948–82. Chmn. of Dance Section, Assn. of Teachers in Colls. and Depts. of Education, 1958–68. *Publs:* Modern Dance in Education, 1958; Creative Dance in the Primary School, 1965, 3rd ed. 1988; Creative Dance in the Secondary School, 1969, 1979. Add: Hawkhurst House, Cradley, Malvern, Worcs., England.

RUSSELL, John. British, b. 1919. Art. Art Critic since 1974, and Chief Art Critic since 1982, The New York Times. Hon. Attaché, Tate Gallery, 1940–41; served in the Ministry of Information, 1941–43, and the Naval Intelligence Div., Admiralty, London, 1943–46; Regular Contributor, 1945–49, and Art Critic, 1949–74, The Sunday Times, London. *Publs:* Shakespeare's Country, 1942; British Portrait Painters, 1945; Switzerland, 1950; Logan Pearsall Smith, 1950; Erich Kleiber, 1956; Paris, 1960, 1983; Seurat, 1965; (with Bryan Robertson and Lord Snowdon) Private View, 1965; Max Ernst, 1967; Henry Moore, 1968; Ben Nicholson, 1969; (with Suzi Gablik) Pop Art Redefined, 1969; The World of Matisse, 1970; Francis Bacon, 1971; Edouard Vuillard, 1971; The Meanings of Modern Art, 1981. Add: 166 E. 61st St., New York, N.Y. 10021, U.S.A.

RUSSELL, John Leonard. British, b. 1906. Philosophy, Theology/Religion. Lectr. in Philosophy, Heythrop Coll., Univ. of London, since 1947, now retired. Roman Catholic priest, ordained 1945. *Publs:* Science and Metaphysics, 1958; (with E. Nemesszeghy) Theology of Evolution, 1972. Add: Heythrop Coll., 11 Cavendish Sq., London W1M 0AN, England.

RUSSELL, Kenneth Victor. British, b. 1929. Criminology/Law enforcement/Prisons, Sociology, Theology/Religion. Principal Lectr., School of Law, Leicester Polytechnic (formerly Coll. of Education), since 1963. *Publs:* (with J.D. Tooke) Learning to Give, 1967; (with Tooke) Crime Is Our Business, 1973; (with Tooke) Projects in Religious Studies, 1974; Complaints Against the Police, 1976, 3rd ed., 1985; Police Acts 1964 and 1976: Complaints Against the Police Which Are Withdrawn, 1986; (with R. MacKay) Psychiatry and the Criminal Process, 1986. Add: 6 St. Peters Close, Glenfield, Leicester LE3 8QB, England.

RUSSELL, Martin (James). British, b. 1934. Mystery/Crime/Suspense. Reporter, 1951–62, and Sub-ed., 1961–73, Croydon Advertiser, Surrey. *Publs:* No Through Road, 1965; No Return Ticket, 1966; Danger Money, 1968; Hunt to a Kill, 1969; Deadline, 1971; Advisory Service, 1971; Concrete Evidence, 1972; Double Hit, 1973; Crime Wave, 1974; Phantom Holiday, 1974; The Client, 1975; Murder by the Mile, 1975; Double Deal, 1976; Mr. T., 1977; Dial Death, 1977; Daylight Robbery, 1978; A Dangerous Place to Dwell, 1978; Touchdown, 1979; Death Fuse, 1980; Catspaw, 1980; Backlash, 1981; Rainblast, 1982; All Part of the Service, 1982; The Search for Sara, 1983; A Domestic Affair, 1984; Censor, 1984; The Darker Side of Death, 1985; Prime Target, 1985; Dead Heat, 1986; The Second Time Is Easy, 1987; House Arrest, 1988. Add: 15 Breckonmead, Wanstead Rd., Bromley, Kent, England.

RUSSELL, Norman H. American, b. 1921. Poetry, Botany. Prof. of Biology and Creative Studies, Central State Univ., Edmond, Okla., since 1979 (Prof. of Biology, 1951–72; Dean Sch. of Math and Science, 1972–79). *Publs:* An Introduction to the Plant Kingdom, 1958; Violets of Central and Eastern United States, 1965; Night Dog and Other Poems, 1971; Open the Flower, 1974; An Introduction to Plant Science, 1975; Russell, the Man, the Teacher, the Indian, 1975; Indian Thoughts: I Am Old, 1976; Indian Thoughts: The Children of God, 1976; Indian Thoughts: My Journey, 1980; The Longest March, 1980. Add: Central State Univ., Edmond, Okla. 73034, U.S.A.

RUSSELL, (Irwin) Peter. British, b. 1921. Poetry, Translations. Owner of bookshop and poetry press, 1950–63. *Publs:* Picnic to the Moon, 1944; (ed.) Ezra Pound: A Collection of Essays . . . to Be Presented to Ezra Pound on His Sixty-Fifth Birthday, 1950, 1974; Descent: A Poem Sequence, 1952; (ed. with K. Sing) A Note . . . on G.V. Desani's "All about H. Hatterr" and "Hali", 1952; (ed.) ABC of Economics, by Ezra Pound, 1953; (trans.) Three Elegies of Quintilius 1954; The Spirit and the Body: An Orphic Poem, 1956; Images of Desire: Discrete Sonnets, 1962; Dreamland and Drunkenness, 1963; Complaints of Circe, 1963; Visions and Ruins: An Existentialist Poem, 1964; (trans.) Landscapes by Camillo Pennati, 1964; Agamemnon in Hades, 1965; The Golden Chain: Lyrical Poems 1964-1969, 1970; Paysages Legendaires, 1971; (trans.) The Elegies of Quintilius, 1973; Acts of Recognition: Four Visionary Poems, 1978; Theories, 1978; Epigrammata: Malice Aforethought; or, The Tumour in the Brain, 1981; Elemental Disorders, 1982; The Vitalist Reader: A Selection of the Poetry of Anthony L. Johnson, William Oxley, and Peter Russell, 1982; All for the Wolves: Selected Poems 1947-1975, 1984. Add: c/o Anvil Press Poetry, 69 King George St., London SE10 8PX, England.

RUSSELL, Ray. American, b. 1924. Novels/Short stories, Mystery/Crime/Suspense, Screenplays, Poetry. Assoc. Ed., 1954–55, Exec. Ed., 1955–60, and Contrib. Ed., 1968–75; Playboy mag. *Publs:* Sardonicus (stories), 1961; The Case Against Satan, 1962; The Little Lexicon of Love, 1966; Unholy Trinity (stories), 1967; The Colony, 1969; Sagittarius, 1971; Prince of Darkness (stories), 1971; Holy Horatio, 1976; Incubus, 1976; Princess Pamela, 1979; The Devil's Mirror, 1980; The Book of Hell, 1980; The Bishop's Daughter, 1981; Haunted Castles, 1985; The Night Sound (poetry), 1987; Dirty Money, 1988. Add: c/o H.N. Swanson Inc., 8523 Sunset Blvd., Los Angeles, Calif. 90069, U.S.A.

RUSSELL, Ronald. British, b. 1924. Archaeology/Antiquities, Art, Country Life/Rural societies, Health, Travel/Exploration/Adventure. Moderator and Examiner, Univ. of Cambridge Local Examinations Syndicate, since 1969. Head of English, Monmouth Sch., 1956–70, and Soham Grammar Sch., 1971; Head of English, 1972–85, and Sr. Teacher, 1973–85, City of Ely Coll. *Publs:* Lost Canals of England and Wales, 1971; Waterside Pubs, 1974; Discovering Lost Canals, 1975; (with John Boyes) Canals of Eastern England, 1977; Rivers, 1978; Guide to British Topographical Prints, 1979; Lost Canals and Waterways of Britain, 1982; Discovering Antique Prints, 1982; (ed.) Walking Canals, 1984; Cambridgeshire and Cambridge, 1988; Swimming for Life, 1989. Add: 4 Maners Way, Cambridge CB1 4SL, England.

RUSSELL, Roy. British, b. 1918. Novels/Short stories, Plays/Screenplays, Documentaries/Reportage. *Publs:* plays—Return to Bedlam; Rope Enough; Thanksgiving Day; The Eleventh Commandment; television—The Troubleshooters; A Man of Our Times; Crime of Passion; A Family at War; Intimate Strangers; A House in Regent Place; The Onedin Line; Tales of the Unexpected; The Irish R.M.; Last Video and Testament; The Woodcutter Operation; Documentaries—The Lonely Sea and the Sky; Prince Charles, Pilot Royal; other—A Family at War Towards Victory (novel). Add: c/o Harvey Unna and Stephen Durbridge Ltd., 24 Pottery Lane, London W11 4LZ, England.

RUSSELL, W(illiam) M(oy) S(tratten). British, b. 1925. Science fiction/Fantasy, Animals/Pets, Psychology. Reader in Sociology, Univ. of Reading, Berks., since 1971 (Lectr. in Sociology, 1966–71). Hon. Librarian, Folklore Soc., since 1977. *Publs:* (with Claire Russell) Human Behaviour: A New Approach, 1961; Man, Nature and History, 1967; (with C. Russell) Violence, Monkeys and Man, 1968; (ed. with J.R. Porter) Animals in Folklore, 1978. Add: c/o David Higham Assocs. Ltd., 5-8 Lower John St., Goldent Sq., London W1R 4HA, England.

RUSSELL, Willy. (William Martin Russell). British, b. 1947. Plays. Fellow of Creative Writing, Manchester Polytechnic, 1977–78; assoc. dir., Liverpool Playhouse, 1981–83. *Publs:* Breezeblock Park, 1978; One for the Road, 1980, 1985; Educating Rita, 1981; Stags and Hens, 1984; Blood Brothers, 1984; Shirley Valentine, 1986. Add: c/o Margaret Ramsay Ltd., 14A Goodwin's Ct., London WC2N 4LL, England.

RUSSELL TAYLOR, Elisabeth. British, b. 1930. Novels, Children's fiction, Homes/Gardens, Travel/Exploration/Adventure. Freelance Broadcaster and Journalist for B.B.C., The Times, The Observer, New Library World, Medical News, Amateur Gardening, Living, and Queen, Library Assn. Record, etc. *Publs:* Wish You Were Here (travel), 1976; London Lifelines, 1977; The Gifts of the Tarns (children's fiction), 1977; Tales from Barleymill (children's fiction), 1978; The Loadstone (children's fiction), 1978; The Potted Garden, 1980; The Diabetic Cookbook, 1981; Marcel Proust and His Contexts, 1981; Turkey in the Middle (Children's fiction), 1983; Swann Song (adult fiction), 1988; Divide and Rule, 1989. Add: 21 Steeles Rd., London NW3 4SH, England.

RUSSETT, Bruce Martin. American, b. 1935. International relations, Military/Defence, Politics/Government. Dean Acheson Prof. of Intnl. Relations and Political Science, Yale Univ., New Haven, Conn., since 1985 (Asst. Prof., 1962–66; Assoc. Prof., 1966–68; Prof., 1968–85). Ed., Journal of Conflict Resolution, since 1972. Instr., Massachusetts Inst. of Technology, Cambridge, 1961–62. *Publs:* Community and Contention: Britain and America in the Twentieth Century, 1963; World Handbook of Political and Social Indicators, 1964; (with H. Alker) World Politics and the General Assembly, 1965; Trends in World Politics, 1965; International Regions and the International System, 1967; (ed.) Economic Theories of International Politics, 1968; What Price Vigilance? The Burdens of National Defense, 1970; No Clear and Present Danger: A Skeptical View of the United States Entry into World War II, 1972; (ed.) Peace, War, and Numbers, 1972; (ed. with A. Stepan) Military Force and American Society, 1973; Power and Community in World Politics, 1974; (with E.C. Hanson) Interest and Ideology: The Foreign Policy Beliefs of American Businessmen, 1975; (ed. with B. Blair) Progress in Arms Control?, 1979; (ed. with R. Merritt) From National Development to Global Community, 1981; (with H. Starr) World Politics: The Menu for Choice, 1981, 1985; The Prisoners of Insecurity, 1983; (ed. with Fred Chernoff) Arms Control and the Arms Race, 1985. Add: Box 3532 Yale Station, Yale Univ., New Haven, Conn. 06520, U.S.A.

RUTHERFORD, Douglas. *See* **McCONNELL,** J.D.R.

RUTHERFORD, Phillip R. American, b. 1939. Language/Linguistics. Prof. of English, Univ. of Maine at Portlant-Gorham, since 1966. *Publs:* Dissertations in Linguistics 1900-1964, 1967; The Dictionary of Maine Place Names, 1971, 1982; Fifty Years in Texas, 1985. Add: c/o Cumberland Press, P.O. Box 1082, Portland, Me. 04104, U.S.A.

RUTMAN, Darrett Bruce. American, b. 1929. History. Grad. Research Prof., Univ. of Florida, Gainesville, since 1984. Instr. to Assoc. Prof. Univ. of Minnesota, Minneapolis, 1959–68; Prof. of History, Univ. of New Hampshire, Durham, 1968–84. *Publs:* (ed.) The Old Dominion: Essays for Thomas Perkins Abernethy, 1964; (co-author) Law and Authority in Colonial America, 1965; Winthrop's Boston: Portrait of a Puritan Town 1630-1649, 1965; Husbandmen of Plymouth: Farms and Villages in the Old Colony 1620-1692, 1966; American Puritanism: Faith and Practice, 1970; (ed.) The Great Awakening: Event and Exegesis, 1971; The Morning of America 1603-1789, 1971; (co-author) Insights and Parallels: Problems and Issues of American Social History, 1973; John Winthrop's Decision for America 1629, 1975; A Militant New World 1607-1640, 1979; (co-author) The Chesapeake in the Seventeenth Century, 1980; (co-auther) A Place in Time: Middlesex County, Virginia 1650-1750, 2 vols., 1984; (co-auther) Generations and Change: Genealogical Perspectives in Social History, 1986. Add: Dept. of History, 4131 Turlington Hall, Univ. of Florida, Gainesville, Fla. 32611, U.S.A.

RUTSALA, Vern A. American, b. 1934. Poetry. Prof. of English, Lewis and Clark Coll., Portland, since 1961. Ed. December mag., Western Springs, Ill., 1959–62. *Publs:* The Window: Poems, 1964; Small Songs: A Sequence of Poems, 1969; The Harmful State, 1971; (ed.) British Poetry 1972, 1972; Laments, 1975; The Journey Begins, 1976; Paragraphs, 1978; The New Life, 1978; Walking Home from the Icehouse, 1981; Backtracking, 1985; Ruined Cities, 1987. Add: Dept. of English, Lewis and Clark Coll., Portland, Ore. 97219, U.S.A.

RUTTER, Michael (Llewellyn). British, b. 1933. Psychiatry, Psychology. Prof. of Child Psychiatry, Univ. of London, Inst. of Psychiatry, since 1973 (Sr. Lectr., then Reader, 1965–73). Hon. Consultant Child Psychiatrist, Bethlem Royal and Maudsley Hosps., London, since 1966 (Registrar and Sr. Registrar, 1958–61; Member of the Scientific Staff, Medical Research Council Social Psychiatry Research Unit, 1962–65);

Hon. Dir., Medical Research Council Child Psychiatry Unit, since 1984 (Member of Scientific Staff, Psychiatry Research Unit, 1962–65); European Ed., Journal of Autism and Development Disorders. *Publs:* Children of Sick Parents, 1966; (with J. Tizard and K. Whitmore) Education, Health and Behaviour, 1970; (with P. Graham and W. Yule) A Neuropsychiatric Study in Childhood, 1970; (ed.) Infantile Autism: Concepts, Characteristics and Treatment, 1971; Maternal Deprivation Reassessed, 1972, 1981; (ed. with J.A.M. Martin) The Child with Delayed Speech, 1972; Helping Troubled Children, 1975; (with D. Shaffer and M. Shepherd) A Multi-Axial Classification of Child Psychiatric Disorders, 1975; (with N. Madge) Cycles of Disadvantage, 1976; (ed. with L. Hersov) Child Psychiatry: Modern Approaches, 1977; (ed. with E. Schopler) Autism: A Reappraisal of Concepts and Treatments, 1978; (with others) Fifteen Thousand Hours, 1979; Changing Youth in a Changing Society, 1979; (ed.) Scientific Foundations of Developmental Psychiatry, 1980; (ed. with R. Russell Jones) Lead Versus Health: Sources and Effects of Low Level Lead Exposure, 1983; (ed. with N. Garmezy) Stress, Coping and Development, 1983; (ed.) Developmental Neuropsychiatry, 1983; A Measure of Our Values: Goals and Dilemmas in the Upbringing of Children, 1983; (with H. Giller) Juvenile Delinquency: Trends and perspectives, 1983; (ed. with L. Hersov) Child and Adolescent Psychiatry: Modern Approaches, 2nd ed., 1985; (ed. with C. Izard and P. Read) Depression in Young People: Developmental and Clinical Perspectives, 1986; (with others) Treatment of Autistic Children, 1987; (ed. with W. Yule) Language Development and Disorders, 1987; (co-ed.) Assessment and Diagnosis in Child Psychopathology, 1988; (ed.) Studies of Psychosocial Risk: The Power of Longitudinal Data, 1988. Add: Dept. of Child and Adolescent Psychiatry, Inst. of Psychiatry, De Crespigny Park, London SE5 8AF, England.

RYALLS, Alan. British, b. 1919. Recreation/Leisure/Hobbies, Travel/Exploration/Adventure. Overseas Corresp., Motor Caravan and Motorhome, London, since 1975. Ed., Camping and Caravanning mag., London, 1956–75. *Publs:* Enjoy Camping Holidays, 1963; Your Guide to Hungary, 1967; Your Guide to Cyprus, 1969; Camping with B.P., 1969; Bulgaria for Tourists, 1971; (with R. Marchant) Better Camping, 1973; Modern Camping, 1975. Add: Acres End, Field Way, Helmdon, Brackley, Northants. HN13 5QN, England.

RYAN, Alan. British, b. 1940. Philosophy. Fellow since 1969, and Reader in Politics since 1978, New Coll., Oxford. Lectr. in Philosophy, Univ. of Keele, 1963–66; Lectr. in Politics, Univ. of Essex, Colchester 1966–69; Visiting Prof. of Political Science, City Univ. of New York, 1967–68. *Publs:* The Philosophy of John Stuart Mill (in U.S. as John Stuart Mill), 1970, 1987; Philosophy of the Social Sciences, 1970; (ed.) Social Explanation, 1973; J.S. Mill, 1975; (ed.) The Idea of Freedom, 1979; Property and Political Theory, 1984; (ed.) Utilitarianism and Other Essays, 1987. Add: Savile House, Mansfield Rd., Oxford, England.

RYAN, John. Irish, b. 1925. Literature, Autobiography/Memoirs/Personal. Ed., The Dublin Mag.; Dir., Anna Livia Books; Writer and Reader, Sunday Morning Miscellany, Irish Radio, since 1969. Secty., The James Joyce Inst. of Ireland., 1970–74, and The Irish Academy of Letters, 1974–76. *Publs:* (ed.) A Bash in the Tunnel: James Joyce Through Irish Eyes, 1970; Remembering How We Stood, 1975; A Wave of the Sea, 1981. Add: Elstow, Knapton Rd., Dun Laoghaire, Co. Dublin, Ireland.

RYAN, John (Gerald Christopher). British, b. 1921. Children's fiction, Humour/Satire. Cartoonist, Catholic Herald, since 1965. Asst. Art Master, Harrow Sch., Middx., 1947–54. *Publs:* Pugwash series, 14 vols.; The John Ryan Ecclesiastical Fun Book; The Noah's Ark series, 1977–82; Dodo's Delight, 1978; Doodle's Homework, 1979; One Dark and Stormy Night, 1986; A Bad Year for Dragons, 1986. Add: Gungarden Lodge, The Gungardens, Rye, E. Sussex TN31 7HH, England.

RYAN, Peter Allen. Australian, b. 1923. Writing/Journalism, Autobiography/Memoirs/Personal, Biography. Secty. To The Bd. of Examiners for Barristers and Solicitors, Victoria, Australia, since 1988. Dir., Melbourne Univ. Press and Asst. to the Vice Chancellor, Univ. of Melbourne, both since 1962. Gen. Ed., Encyclopaedia of Papua and New Guinea; Pres., Assn. of Australian Univ. Presses. *Publs:* Fear Drive My Feet, 1959; The Preparation of Manuscripts, 1966; Redmond Barry, 1972; Encyclopaedia of Papua New Guinea, 1982. Add: Box 319, Flemington, Vic. 3031, Australia.

RYAN, Rachel. *See* **BROWN**, Sandra.

RYAN, William (Michael). American, b. 1948. Novels/Short stories, Poetry. Report Writer, Audience Studies Inc., Hollywood, Calif., 1969;

Announcer, producer, scriptwriter and host of weekly educational radio progs., 1980–81; Instr. in English, Colorado State Univ., Fort Collins, 1982, Western New England Coll., Springfield, Mass., 1985–86, and Univ. of Massachusetts, Amherst, 1986–87. *Publs:* Blaming the Victim, 1972; Tales of Moon and Beast, 1972; Equality, 1981; Eating the Heart of the Enemy, 1985; Dr. Excitement's Elixir of Longevity, 1985. Add: c/o Wieser and Wieser, 118 E. 25th St., New York, N.Y. 10010, U.S.A.

RYAN, William M(artin). American, b. 1918. Language/Linguistics, Literature, Mythology/Folklore. Prof. of English, Univ. of Missouri, Kansas City, since 1955. Taught at St. Ambrose Coll., Davenport, Iowa, 1946–52. *Publs:* William Langland, 1968; (with others) Studies in Language, Literature, and Culture in the Middle Ages and Later, 1969; (ed.) The Linguists and the Literature, 1971. Add: Dept. of English, Univ. of Missouri, Kansas City, Mo. 64110, U.S.A.

RYBCZYNSKI, Witold. Canadian, b. 1943. Architecture, Technology. Prof. of Architecture, McGill Univ., Montreal (joined faculty, 1975). Consultant, Banco de Mexico, 1974–80, U.N. Environment Program, 1976, Intnl. Development Research Centre, 1977, and World Bank, 1978. *Publs:* Paper Heroes: A Review of Appropriate Technology, 1980; Taming the Tiger: The Struggle to Control Technology, 1983, 1985; Home: A Short History of An Idea, 1986, 1987; The Most Beautiful House in the World, 1989. Add: The Boathouse, 206 Covey Hill, Hemmingford, Que. J0L 1HO, Canada.

RYBOT, Doris. *See* **PONSONBY**, D.A.

RYCHLAK, Joseph F(rank). American, b. 1928. Philosophy, Psychology, Social sciences. Maude C. Clarke Prof. of Humanistic Psychology, Loyola Univ. of Chicago, since 1983. Asst. Prof. of Psychology, Florida State Univ., Tallahassee, 1957–58; Asst. Prof. of Psychology, Washington State Univ., Pullman, 1958–61; Assoc. Prof. of Psychology, 1961–65, and Prof., 1965–69, St. Louis Univ., Mo; Prof. of Psychology, Purdue Univ., West Lafayette, Ind., 1969–83. *Publs:* A Philosophy of Science for Personality Theory, 1968, 1981; Introduction to Personality and Psychotherapy: A Theory-Construction Approach, 1973, 1981; The Psychology of Rigorous Humanism, 1977, 1987; Discovering Free Will and Personal Responsibility, 1979; Personality and Life-Style of Young Male Managers: A Logical Learning Theory Analysis, 1982; (with Norman Cameron) Personality and Development: A Dynamic Approach, 1985. Add: Dept. of Psychology, Loyola Univ. of Chicago, 6525 N. Sheridan Rd., Chicago, Ill. 60626, U.S.A.

RYCROFT, Charles. British, b. 1914. Psychiatry. Psychoanalyst in private practice. Consultant in Psychotherapy, Tavistock Clinic, London, 1956–68. *Publs:* (contrib. ed.) Psychoanalysis Observed, 1966; Imagination and Reality, 1968; Anxiety and Neurosis, 1968; Critical Dictionary of Psychoanalysis, 1968; Reich, 1971; The Innocence of Dreams, 1979; Psychoanalysis and Beyond, 1985. Add: 18 Wimpole St., London W1, England.

RYDBERG, Ernie. American, b. 1901. Children's fiction. *Publs:* Bright Summer, 1953; Sixteen Is Special, 1954; The Silver Fleet, 1955; The Golden Window, 1956; Conquer the Winds, 1957; Mystery in the Jeep, 1959; The Day the Indians Came, 1964; The Dark of the Cave, 1965; The Yellow Line, 1969; Footsy, 1973; (with Lou Rydberg) The Shadow Army, 1976. Add: 3742 Tennyson, San Diego, Calif. 92107, U.S.A.

RYDELL, Forbes. *See* **FORBES**, Stanton.

RYDELL, Wendell. *See* **RYDELL**, Wendy.

RYDELL, Wendy. Also writes as Wendell Rydell. American, b. 1927. Children's non-fiction, Sports/Physical education/Keeping fit. *Publs:* (as Wendell Rydell) Football, 1971; (as Wendell Rydell) Basketball, 1971; (as Wendell Rydell) Baseball, 1972; (with Steven Schepp) Pot, Pills, Powers: The Truth about Drugs, 1972; Instant Sewing Handbook, 1972; (with Bob Heit) Sports Greats Past and Present, 1973; The Name of the Game: Football, 1973; The Name of the Game: Basketball, 1973; The Name of the Game: Baseball, 1973; (with George Gilbert) The Great Book of Magic, 1976; Fossils, 1977; Landslides and Avalanches, 1977; Islands, 1978; Deserts, 1978; The A to Z Handbook of Recreational Drugs, 1980; The Complete Home Decorator, 1981. Add: 51 Wintercress Lane, East Northport, N.Y. 11731, U.S.A.

RYDER, Arthur John. British, b. 1913. History, Politics/Government. Education Officer, Control Commn. in Germany, 1946–56; Member, Conservative Party Research Dept., London, 1958–62; Asst. Lectr., 1962–64, Lectr. in History, 1964–69, Sr. Lectr., 1969–76, and Reader in History, 1976–80, St. David's Univ. Coll., Lampeter, Wales. *Publs:* The German Revolution of 1918, 1967; Twentieth Century Germany: From Bismarck to Brandt, 1973. Add: 74 Clifton Hill, London NW8, England.

RYDER, G(eoffrey) H(arwood). British, b. 1920. Engineering. Principal Lectr., Royal Military Coll. of Science, Swindon, since 1952. *Publs:* Strength of Materials, 1973; (with P. Gates) Jigs, Fixtures, Tools, and Gauges, 1973; (with M.D. Bennett) Mechanics of Machines, 1975. Add: Royal Military Coll. of Science, Shrivenham, Swindon, Wilts., England.

RYDER, Jonathan. *See* **LUDLUM,** Robert.

RYDER, M(ichael) L(awson). Also writes as Michael Lawson. British, b. 1927. Agriculture, Archaeology, Biology, History. With the Wool Industries Research Assn., Leeds, 1950–59; Sr. Lectr., Sch. of Rural Science, Univ. of New England, Australia, 1960–62; Principal Scientific Officer, Press Officer and Ed., Agricultural Research Council, Animal Breeding Research Org., Edinburgh, 1962–84; Principal Scientific Officer, Hill Farming Research Org., Edinburgh, 1984–87. *Publs:* (with S.K. Stephenson) Wool Growth, 1968; Animal Bones in Archaeology, 1969; Hair, 1973; Sheep and Wool for Handicraft Workers, 1978; Sheep and Man, 1983; Cashmere and Mohair for Breeders and Spinners, 1987. Add: 4 Osprey Close, Southampton SO1 8EX, England.

RYDER, Thom. *See* **HARVEY,** John B.

RYKEN, Leland. American, b. 1942. Literature. Teacher, Wheaton Coll., Illinois, since 1968. *Publs:* The Apocalyptic Vision in Paradise Lost, 1970; The Literature of the Bible, 1974; Triumphs of the Imagination: Literature in Christian Perspective, 1979; The Christian Imagination: Essays on Literature and the Arts, 1981; Milton and Scriptural Tradition: The Bible into Poetry, 1984; The New Testament in Literary Criticism, 1984; How to Read the Bible as Literature, 1984; Windows to the World, 1985; Culture in Christian Perspective, 1986; Worldly Saints: The Puritans as They Really Were, 1986; Words of Delight: A Literary Introduction to the Bible, 1987; Words of Life: A Literary Introduction to the New Testament, 1987; Work and Leisure in Christian Perspective, 1987; Effective Bible Teaching, 1988. Add: Dept. of English, Wheaton Coll., Wheaton, Ill. 60187, U.S.A.

RYKWERT, Joseph. British, b. 1926. Architecture, Art. Prof. of Architecture, Univ. of Pensylvania, Philadelphia, since 1988. Visiting Lectr., Hochschule für Gestaltung, Ulm, 1959–60; Librarian, Royal Coll. of Art, London, 1961–67; Prof. of Art, Univ. of Essex, Colchester, 1967–80; Lectr., 1980–85, and Reader in Architecture, 1985–85, Cambridge Univ. Member of the Commn., Venice Biennale, 1974–77. *Publs:* The Golden House, 1947; (ed.) Ten Books on Architecture of L.B. Alberti, 1955; The Idea of a Town, 1963, 1976; Church Building, 1966; On Adam's House in Paradise, 1972; (ed.) Parole nel Vuoto (essays by A. Loos), 1972; G.B. Nolli's Plan of Rome, 1977; The First Moderns: Architects of the Eighteenth Century, 1980; The Necessity of Artifice (collected essays on art and architecture), 1982; (with Anne Rykwert) The Brothers Adam, 1985; (trans.) On the Art of Building, by Alberti, 1988. Add: Ph. D. Program in Architecture, Univ. of Pennsylvania, Philadelphia, PA. 19104, U.S.A.

RYLANT, Cynthia. American, b. 1954. Children's fiction. *Publs:* When I was Young in the Mountains, 1982; Miss Maggie, 1983: This Year's Garden, 1984; Waiting to Waltz: A Childhood (verse), 1984; A Blue-Eyed Daisy, 1985; The Relatives Came, 1985; Every Living Thing (stories), 1985; A Fine White Dust, 1986; Night in the Country, 1986; Birthday Presents, 1987; Children of Christmas (in U.K. as Silver Packages and Other Stories), 1987; All I See, 1988; A Kindness, 1989; Mr. Grigg's Work, 1989. Add: P.O. Box 5031, Kent, Ohio 44240, U.S.A.

RYLE, Anthony. British, b. 1927. Psychiatry, Psychology. Consultant Psychotherapist, St. Thomas' Hospital, London. Gen. Practitioner, Caversham Centre Group Practice, London, 1952–64; Dir., Univ. of Sussex Health Service, 1964–79. *Publs:* Neurosis in the Ordinary Family, 1967; Student Casualties, 1969; Frames and Cages, 1975; Psychotherapy: A Cognitive Integration of Theory and Practice, 1982. Add: Psychotherapy Unit, St. Thomas' Hosp., London SE1 7EH, England.

S

SAAL, Jocelyn. *See* **SACHS**, Judith.

SABERHAGEN, Fred(erick Thomas). American, b. 1930. Science fiction/Fantasy. Freelance writer, 1962–67, and since 1973. Electronics Technician, Motorola Inc., Chicago, 1956–62; Asst. Ed., Encyclopaedia Britannica, Chicago, 1967–73. *Publs:* The Golden People, 1964; The Water of Thought, 1965, 1981; Berserker (short stories), 1967; Brother Assassin (in U.K. as Brother Berserker), 1969; Berserker's Planet, 1975; The Dracula Tape, 1975; The Book of Saberhagen (short stories), 1975; Specimens, 1976; The Holmes-Dracula File, 1978; The Veils of Azlaroc, 1978; The Empire of the East (novel trilogy; published separately as The Broken Lands, 1968; The Black Mountains, 1971; Changeling Earth, 1973), 1979; Love Conquers All, 1979; Mask of the Sun, 1979; Berserker Man, 1979; An Old Friend of the Family, 1979; The Ultimate Enemy (short stories), 1979; A Matter of Taste, 1980; Thorn, 1980; (with Roger Zelazny) Coils, 1980; The Berserker Wars, 1981; Octagon, 1981; (ed.) A Spadeful of Spacetime, 1981; (co-ed.) Pawn to Infinity, 1982; Earth Descended, 1982; Dominions, 1982; The First Second, Third Book of Swords, 3 vols., 1983–84; A Century of Progress, 1983; The Berserker Throne, 1985; Berserker: Blue Death, 1985; The Frankenstein Papers, 1986; The First Book of Lost Swords: Woundhealer's Story, 1986; Pyramids, 1987. Add: c/o Virginia Kidd, Box 278, Milford, Pa. 18337, U.S.A.

SABINE, Ellen S. American, b. 1908. Antiques/Furnishings, Art. Member, Esther Stevens Brazer Guild, Hospital Soc. of Early American Decoration Inc. Instr. in American Antique Decoration, Young Women's Christian Assn., NYC, 1948–73. *Publs:* American Antique Decoration, 1956; American Folk Art, 1958; Early American Decorative Patterns, 1962; Treasury of American Folk Patterns, 1982. Add: 9-D Sterling St. Lakehurst, N.J. 08733, U.S.A.

SABINE, William Henry Waldo. British, b. 1903. Poetry, History, Psychology. Partner, Colburn and Tegg, book and print dealers, Hollis, N.Y., since 1954. *Publs:* The Fairy King, 1929; (ed.) Diary of a Public School Girl, 1930, 4th ed., 1932; Guido and the Girls, 1933, 4th ed. 1934; Second Sight in Daily Life, 1949; Suppressed History of General Nathaniel Woodhull, 1954; (ed.) New-York Diary of Lt. Jabez Fitch, 1776-1777, 1954; Woodhull and Washington, 1955; (ed.) Historical Memoirs of Chief Justice William Smith, 1763-1778, 2 vols., 1956, 1958; Katrina van Buskirk (stage play), 1957; Echoes from the Crag, 1957; (ed.) A Prophecy Concerning the Swedish Monarchy, 1968; (ed.) Verse by Charles and M.E. Sabine, 2 vols., 1968; (ed.) Historical Memoirs of Chief Justice William Smith, 1778-1783, 1971; Murder, 1776, and Washington's Policy of Silence, 1973. Add: 19709 Hollis Ave., Hollis, N.Y. 11412, U.S.A.

SABLE, Martin Howard. American, b. 1924. Area studies, Librarianship. Prof., Sch. of Library Science, Univ. Wisconsin, Milwaukee, since 1972 (Assoc. Prof., 1968–72). Advisory ed. on Latin America, Encyclopedia Americana, since 1967; Editorial Bd. Member, Intnl. Library Review, since 1982, and The Reference Librarian, since 1987. Research Assoc., Latin American Center, Univ. of California-Los Angeles, 1965–68; Visiting Prof., Grad. Library Sch., Hebrew Univ., Jerusalem, 1972–73. *Publs:* A Selective Bibliography in Science and Engineering, 1964; Master Directory of Latin America, 1965; Periodicals for Latin American Economic Development, Trade and Finance: An Annotated Bibliography, 1965; A Guide to Latin American Studies, 1967; UFO Guide 1947-1967, 1967; Communism in Latin America, an International Bibliography: 1900-

1945, 1960-67, 1968; A Bio-Bibliography of the Kennedy Family, 1969; Latin American Agriculture: a Bibliography, 1970; Latin American Studies in the Non-Western World and Eastern Europe, 1970; Latin American Urbanization: A Guide to the Literature, Organizations and Personnel, 1971; International and Area Studies Librarianship: Case Studies, 1973; The Guerrilla Movement in Latin America, an International Bibliography, 1977; Latin American Jewry: A Research Guide, 1978; Exobiology: A Research Guide, 1978; A Guide to Nonprint Materials for Latin American Studies, 1979; The Latin American Studies Directory, 1981; A Bibliography of the Future, 1981; The Protection of the Library: An International Bibliography, 1984; Industrial Espionage and Trade Secrets: An International Bibliography, 1985; Mexican and Mexican-American Agricultural Labor in the United States: A Research Guide, 1986; Holocaust Studies: A Directory and Bibliography of Bibliographies, 1987; A Guide to the Writings of Pioneer Latin Americanists of the U.S.A., 1989. Add: 4518 Larkin St., Milwaukee, Wisc. 53211, U.S.A.

SABRE, Dirk. *See* **LAFFIN**, John.

SACHS, Judith. American, b. 1947. Also writes as Petra Diamond, Rebecca Diamond, Jocelyn Saal, Jennifer Sarasin; with Anthony Bruno under joint pseudonym Antonia Saxon; under house pseudonym as Emily Chase. Novels/Short stories, Historical/Romance. Full-time writer since 1979. Editorial Asst., The Magazine, NYC, 1969–70; Asst., then Assoc. Ed., Saturday Review Press, NYC, 1970–73; Managing Ed., Arbor House Publishing, NYC, 1973; Sr. Ed., Delacorte Press, NYC, 1973–77, and Hawthorn Books, NYC, 1977–79. *Publs:* (as Rebecca Diamond) Summer Romance 1982; (as Jocelyn Saal) Dance of Love, 1982; (as Jocelyn Saal) Trusting Hears, 1982; (as Jocelyn Saal) Running Mates, 1983; (as Jocelyn Saal) On Thin Ice, 1983; (as Antonia Saxon) Paradiso, 1983; (as Jennifer Sarasin) Spring Love, 1983; (with Anthony Bruno) Smoky Joe's High Ride, 1983; (as Antonia Saxon) Above the Moon, 1984; (as Jennifer Sarasin) The Hidden Room, 1984; (as Emily Chase) The Big Crush, 1984; (as Petra Diamond) Confidentially Yours, 1984; (with Anthony Bruno) Just Another Friday Night, 1984; (as Petra Diamond) Night of a Thousand Stars, 1985; (as Emily Chase) With Friends Like That, 1985; (as Jennifer Sarasin) Splitting, 1985; (as Jennifer Sarasin) Cheating, 1985; (as Jennifer Sarasin) Living It Up, 1986; (as Petra Diamond) Play It Again, Sam, 1986; (as Jennifer Sarasin) Taking Over, 1987; (as Jennifer Sarasin) Together Again; 1987; Rites of Spring, 1987. Add: 404 Burd St., Pennington, N.J. 08534, U.S.A.

SACHS, Marilyn (Stickle). American, b. 1927. Children's fiction. Children's Librarian, Brooklyn Public Library, N.Y., 1949–59; Part-time Children's Librarian, San Francisco Public Library, Calif., 1960–65. *Publs:* Amy Moves In, 1964; Laura's Luck, 1965; Amy and Laura, 1966; Veronica Ganz, 1968; Peter and Veronica, 1969; Marv, 1970; The Bears' House, 1971, The Truth About Mary Rose, 1973; A Pocket Full of Seeds, 1973; Matt's Mitt, 1975; Dorrie's Book, 1975; A December Tale, 1976; A Secret Friend, 1978; A Summer's Lease, 1979; Bus Ride, 1980; Class Pictures, 1980; Fleet Footed Florence, 1981; Hello . . . Wrong Number, 1981; Call Me Ruth, 1982; Beach Towels, 1982; Fourteen, 1983; The Fat Girl, 1984; Thunderbird, 1985; Underdog, 1985; Baby Sister, 1986; Almost Fifteen, 1987; Fran Ellen's House, 1987; Just Like a Friend, 1989. Add: 733 31st Ave., San Francisco, Calif. 94121, U.S.A.

SACHS, Mendel. American, b. 1927. Sciences. Prof. of Physics, State Univ. of New York at Buffalo, since 1966. Theoretical Physicist, Univ. of California Radiation Lab., Livermore, 1954–56; Asst. Prof. of

Physics, San Jose State Coll., Calif., 1957–61; Assoc. Prof. of Physics, Boston Univ., 1962–66. Member, Bd. of Eds., Intnl. Journal of Theoretical Physics, 1967–76. *Publs:* Solid State Theory, 1963; The Search for Theory of Matter, 1971; The Field Concept in Contemporary Science, 1973; Ideas of the Theory of Relativity, 1974; Ideas of Matter, 1981; General Relativity and Matter, 1982; Quantum Mechanics from General Relativity, 1986; Einstein Versus Bohr, 1988. Add: 95 Carriage Circle, Williamsville, N.Y. 14221, U.S.A.

SACHS, Murray. American (b. Canadian), b. 1924. Literature. Prof. of French and Comparative Literature, Dept. of Romance and Comparative Literature, Brandeis Univ., Waltham, Mass., since 1966 (Asst. Prof., 1960–61 Assoc. Prof., 1961–66; Chmn., 1981–84). Member, Editorial Advisory Bd., Nineteenth-Century French Studies, State Univ. Coll., Fredonia, N.Y.; Member, Editorial Advisory Bd., Purdue University Monographs in Romance Languages. Asst. Prof., Williams Coll., Williamstown, Mass., 1954–60. Pres., Assn. of Depts. of Foreign Languages, 1985. *Publs:* (ed. with E.M. and R.B. Grant) French Stories, Plays and Poetry, 1959; The Career of Alphonse Daudet, 1965; (ed.) The French Short Story in the Nineteenth Century, 1969, Anatole France: The Short Stories, 1974. Add: Dept. of Romance and Comparative Literature, Brandeis Univ., Waltham, Mass. 02254, U.S.A.

SACKS, Oliver (Wolf). British, b. 1933. Medicine/Health. Prof. in Neurology, Albert Einstein Coll. of Medicine. Add: Migraine, 1970, 1986; Awakenings, 1973, 1982; A Leg to Stand On, 1984; The Man Who Mistook His Wife For a Hat, 1985; Seeing Voices: A Journey into the World of the Deaf, 1989. Add: c/o Summit Books, 1230 Ave. of the Americas, New York, N.Y. 10020, U.S.A.

SADDLEMYER, (Eleanor) Ann. Canadian, b. 1932. Literature. Prof., of English, Victoria Coll., Univ., of Toronto, since 1971, and Master of Massey Coll. since 1988. (Dir., Grad. Drama Centre, 1972–77; Acting Dir., 1985–86). Prof. of English, Univ. of Victoria, B.C., 1968–71; Co-ed., Theatre History in Canada, 1978–86. *Publs:* (with R. Skelton) The World of W.B. Yeats, 1965; In Defence of Lady Gregory, Playwright, 1966; (ed.) the Plays of J.M. Synge: Books One and Two, 1968; Synge and Modern Comedy, 1968, (ed.) J.M. Synge: Plays, 1969; (ed.) The Plays of Lady Gregory, Books I-IV 1970; (ed.) A Selection of Letters from J.M. Synge to W.B. Yeats and Lady Gregory, 1971; (ed.) Letters to Molly: J.M. Synge to Maire O'Neill, 1971; Theatre Business: The Correspondence of the First Abbey Theatre Directors, 1982; The collected Letters of John M. Synge, vol. 1, 1983, vol. 2, 1984; (co-ed.) Lady Gregory Fifty Years After, 1987. Add: 100 Lakeshore Rd. East, Oakville, Ont. L6J 6M9, Canada.

SADDLER, Allen. Pseud. for Ronald Charles Richards. British, b. 1923. Novels/Short stories, Plays/Screenplays, Children's non-fiction, Humor/Satire. Theatre Critic, The Guardian newspaper, London, Plays and Players, and Plays International. *Publs:* The Great Brain Robbery, 1965; Gilt Edge, 1966; Talking Turkey, 1968; Betty, 1974; (ed. and contrib.) The Western Front (radio series), 1974; All Basic Comforts (play), 1977; Them (play), 1977; NAF (play), 1980; Kindly Leave the Stage (play), 1980; radio plays—The Penstone Commune; Willie Banks and the Technological Revolution; Who Needs Money?; The Road; Penstone Revisited; Willie Banks and the Administrative Machine; Ahead of the Game; Archie's Watergate; Revolution at the Palace; The Giveaway; Daddy Good; Old and Blue; The Price Strike; Undesirable Alien; Arson in Berlin; Working the System; The Day War Breaks Out; Man of the People; Up Against the Wall; I Should Say So; Spring; for children—The King and Queen series, 1982; Smudger's Seaside Spectacular; Smudger's Saturday Special; Jerry and the Monsters; Jerry and the Inventions; The Relay Race. Add: 5 St. John's Hall, Station Rd., Totnes, Devon TQ9 5HW, England.

SADIE, Stanley (John). British, b. 1930. Music. Ed., The New Grove Dictionary of Music and Musicians, since 1970. Music Critic, The Times, 1964–81; Ed., The Musical Times, London, 1967–87. Prof., Trinity Coll. of Music, London, 1957–65. *Publs:* Handel, 1962; (with A. Jacobs) The Pan Book of Opera (in U.S. as The Opera Guide), 1964, 3rd ed. 1984; Mozart, 1965; Beethoven, 1967; Handel, 1968; Handel Concertos, 1973; (ed.) New Grove Dictionary of Music and Musicians, 20 vols., 1980; Mozart, 1982; (ed.) New Grove Dictionary of Musical Instruments, 3 vols., 1984; The Cambridge Music Guide (in U.S. as Stanley Sadie's Music Guide), 1986; Mozart Symphonies, 1986; (ed. with H. Wiley Hitchcock) The New Grove Dictionary of American Music, 4 vols., 1986; The Brief Music Guide, 1987; (ed.) The Grove Concise Dictionary of Music (in U.S. as The Norton/Grove Encyclopedia of Music), 1988; (ed.) History of Opera, 1989; (ed. with H. M. Brown) Performance Prac-

tice, 1989; (series ed.) Man and Music, 8 vols., 1989–. Add: 12 Lyndhurst Rd., London NW3 5NL, England.

SADLER, Mark. *See* **LYNDS**, Dennis.

SAFDIE, Moshe. Canadian (b. Israeli), b. 1938. Architecture. Principal, Moshe Safdie Assocs., Montreal, since 1964, Jerusalem, since 1971, and Boston, since 1978. Prof. of Architecture, Harvard Univ., Cambridge, Mass., since 1978. With Van Ginkle and Assocs., architects/planners, Montreal, 1961–62; with Louis I. Kahn, architect, Philadelphia, 1962–63; Section Head, and Architect/Planner with the Canadian Corp. for 1967 World Exhibition, Montreal, 1963–64; Visiting Prof. of Architecture, McGill Univ., Montreal, 1970; Charlotte Shepherd Davenport Prof. of Architecture, Yale Univ., New Haven, Conn., 1971. *Publs:* Habitat, 1967; Beyond Habitat, 1970; For Everyone a Garden, 1974; Form and Purpose, 1980; Harvard Jerusalem Studio, 1986; Jerusalem: The Future of the Past, 1989. Add: 100 Properzi Way, Somerville, Mass. 02174, U.S.A.

SAFIRE, William. American, b. 1929. Politics/Government, Language/Linguistics. Columnist, New York Times, Washington, since 1973. Reporter, New York Herald-Tribune Syndicate, 1949–51; Correspondent, WNBC-WNBT, Europe and the Middle East, 1951; Radio-TV Producer, WNBC, NYC, 1954–55; Vice-Pres., Tex McCrary Inc., 1955–60; Pres., Safire Public Relations, 1960–68; Special Asst. to President Nixon, 1969–73. *Publs:* The Relations Explosion, 1963; Plunging into Politics, 1964; Safire's Political Dictionary, 1968, 3rd ed. 1978; Before the Fall, 1975; Full Disclosure, 1977; Safire's Washington, 1980; On Language, 1980; What's the Good Word?, 1982; (with Leonard Safir) Good Advice, 1982; I Stand Corrected, 1984; Take My Word for It, 1986; Freedom, 1987; You Could Look It Up, 1988. Add: New York Times, 1627 Eye St. N.W., Washington, D.C. 20006, U.S.A.

SAGAN, Carl. American, b. 1934. Novels/Short stories, Astronomy, Sciences. David Duncan Prof. of Astronomy and Space Sciences, and Dir., Lab for Planetary Studies, Cornell Univ., Ithaca, N.Y. (joined faculty, 1968); Pres., Carl Sagan Productions, since 1977. Ed.-in-Chief, Icarus: Intnl. Journal of Solar System Studies, NYC, since 1968. Member, NASA, and National Academy of Science, since 1959; Council Member, Smithsonian Instn., since 1975. *Publs:* (with W.W. Kellogg) The Atmospheres of Mars and Venus, 1961; (with I.S. Shklovskii) Intelligent Life in the Universe, 1966; (with J. Leonard) Planets, 1966; Planetary Exploration, 1970; (ed. with K.Y. Kondratyev and M. Rycroft) Space Research XI, 2 vols., 1971; (ed. with T. Owen and H.J. Smith) Planetary Atmospheres, 1971; (ed. with T. Page) UFOs: A Scientific Debate, 1972; The Cosmic Connection: An Extraterrestrial Perspective, 1973; (ed.) Communication with Extraterrestrial Intelligence, 1973; (with R. Bradbury, A.C. Clarke, B. Murray and W. Sullivan) Mars and the Mind of Man, 1973; Other Worlds, 1975; The Dragons of Eden, 1977; Murmurs of Earth: Voyager Interstellar Record, 1978; Broca's Brain (novel), 1979; Cosmos, 1980; Contact, 1985; Comet, 1985. Add: Space Science Bldg., Cornell Univ., Ithaca, N.Y. 14853, U.S.A.

SAGE, Lorna. British, b. 1943. Literature. Sr. Lectr. in English Literature, since 1975, and Dean of the Sch. of English and American Studies since 1985, Univ. of East Anglia, Norwich (Asst. Lectr., 1965; Lectr., 1968); also journalist and critic. Tucker Visiting Prof., Wellesley Coll., Massachusetts, 1981. *Publs:* (ed.) Peacock: Satirical Novels, 1976; Doris Lessing, 1983. Add: Sch. of English and American Studies, Univ. of East Anglia, Norwich NR4 7TJ, England.

SAGGS, Henry (William Frederick). British, b. 1920. Archaeology/Antiquities, History. Prof. of Semitic Languages, Univ. Coll., Cardiff, since 1966. Lectr., then Reader in Akkadian, Sch. of Oriental and African Studies, Univ. of London, 1953–66. *Publs:* The Greatness That Was Babylon: A Sketch of the Ancient Civilization of the Tigris-Euphrates Valley, 1962, 1987; Everyday Life in Babylonia and Assyria, 1965, 1987; (ed.) H.A. Layard: Nineveh and Its Remains, 1970; The Encounter with the Divine in Mesopotamia and Israel, 1978; The Might That Was Assyria, 1984; Civilization Before Greece and Rome, 1989. Add: Eastwood, Bull Lane, Long Melford, Suffolk, England.

SAHAKIAN, William S(ahak). American, b. 1921. Education, Philosophy, Psychiatry, Psychology. Prof. of Philosophy and Psychology, Suffolk Univ., Boston, Mass., since 1946. Book Reviewer, Boston Globe; Advisory Ed., Rand McNally Publishing Co.; Abstractor, Psychological Abstracts. Former Professorial Lectr. in Psychology, Massachusetts Coll. of Pharmacy; Psychological Consultant, Mendota Research Group; Lectr. in Psychology, Sociology, and Philosophy,

Northeastern Univ.; Advisor to the Pres., Curry Coll., 1954–56. *Publs:* Systems of Ethics and Value Theory, 1963, 1968, as Philosophies of Life, 1979; Psychology of Personality, 1965, 3rd ed. 1977; (with Mabel Lewis Sahakian) Realms of Philosophy, 1965, 3rd ed. 1981; Philosophies of Religion, 1965; (with Mabel Lewis Sahakian) Ideas of the Great Philosophers, 1966, 1981; Philosophy, 1968; History of Psychology, 1968, 1980; History of Philosophy, 1968; Psychotherapy and Counseling, 1969, 1976; Psychopathology Today, 1970, 3rd ed. 1985; Psychology of Learning, 1970, 1976; Social Psychology: Experimentation, Theory and Research, 1972; Systematic Social Psychology, 1974, as History and Systems of Social Psychology, 1982; Ethics: Theories and Problems, 1974; (with Mabel Lewis Sahakian) Rousseau as Educator, 1974; History and Systems of Psychology, 1975; (with Mabel Lewis Sahakian) John Locke, 1975; (with Mabel Lewis Sahakian) Plato, 1975; Introduction to Psychology of Learning, 1976; (with J. Fabry and R. Bulka) Logotherapy in Action, 1979. Add: P.O. Box 12, 49 Eisenhower Circle, Wellesley, Mass. 02181, U.S.A.

SAHGAL, Nayantara (Pandit). Indian, b. 1927. Novels/Short stories, History, Autobiography/Memoirs/Personal. *Publs:* Prison and Chocolate Cake, 1954; A Time to Be Happy, 1958; From Fear Set Free, 1962; This Time of Morning, 1965; Storm in Chandigarh, 1969; History of the Freedom Movement, 1970; The Day in Shadow, 1971; A Situation in New Delhi, 1977; Rich Like Us, 1985; Plans for Departure, 1985; Mistaken Identity, 1988. Add: 181-B Rajpur Rd., Dehra Dun 248009, U.P., India.

SAHLINS, Marshall (David). American, b. 1930. Anthropology. Prof. of Anthropology, Univ. of Chicago. Lectr. in Anthropology, Columbia Univ., 1955–57; Asst. Prof., 1957–61, Assoc. Prof., 1961–64, and Prof. from 1964, Univ. of Michigan, Ann Arbor. *Publs:* Social Stratification in Polynesia, 1958; (ed. with Elman R. Service) Evolution and Culture, 1960; Maola: Culture and Nature on a Fijian Island, 1962; Tribesmen, 1968; Stone Age Economics, 1972; The Use and Abuse of Biology: An Anthropological Critique of Sociobiology, 1976; Culture and Practical Reason, 1977; Historical Metaphors and Mythical Realities: Structure in the Early History of the Sandwich Islands Kingdom, 1981; Islands of History, 1985. Add: Dept. of Anthropology, Univ. of Chicago, Chicago, Ill. 60637, U.S.A.

SAID, Edward W. American, b. 1935. Literary criticism, International relations/Current Affairs. Prof. of English and Comparative Literature, Columbia Univ., NYC, since 1970 (Instr., 1963–65; Asst. Prof., 1965–68; Assoc. Prof., 1968–70). Fellow, Center for Advanced Study, Univ. of Illinois, Urbana, 1967–68; Fellow, Center for Advanced Study in the Behavioral Sciences, Stanford Univ., California, 1975–76. *Publs:* Joseph Conrad and the Fiction of Autobiography, 1966; Beginnings: Intention and Method, 1975; Orientalism, 1979; The Question of Palestine, 1980; Covering Islam: How the Media and the Experts Determine How We See the Rest of the World, 1981; The World, the Text, and the Critic, 1983; After the Last Sky: Palestinian Lives, 1986; (ed.) Literature and Society, 1986; (with Christopher Hitchens) Blaming the Victims: Spurious Scholarship and the Palestinian Question, 1987. Add: Dept. of English, Columbia Univ., New York, N.Y. 10027, U.S.A.

SAIL, Lawrence (Richard). British, b. 1942. Poetry. Teacher, Exeter Sch., Devon, since 1982. Admin. Officer, Greater London Council, 1965–66; Head of Modern Languages, Lenana Sch., Nairobi, 1966–70; Part-time Teacher, Millfield Sch., Somerset, 1973–74; Teacher, 1976–80, and Visiting Writer, 1980–81, Blundells Sch., Devon. Ed., South West Review, Exeter, 1980–85. *Publs:* Opposite Views, 1974; (with Teresa Sail) Children in Hospital (non-fiction), 1976; The Drowned River, 1978; The Kingdom of Atlas, 1980; Devotions, 1987; Aquamarine, 1989; (ed.) First and Always, 1989. Add: Richmond Villa, 7 Wonford Rd., Exeter, Devon, England.

SAINER, Arthur. American, b. 1924. Plays/Screenplays, Theatre. Book Critic since 1961, and Drama Critic since 1969, Village Voice, NYC (Book Ed., 1962; Drama Critic, 1961–65); Theatre and Film Ed., American Book Review, since 1986. Member, Academic Council, and Prog. Advisor, Campus-Free Coll., Boston, since 1971; Playwriting Instr., New Sch. for Social Research, NYC, since 1985. New York Ed., TV Guide mag., NYC, 1956–61; Film Critic, Show Business Illustrated mag., Chicago, 1961; Member of English Dept., C.W. Post Coll., Brookville, N.Y., 1963–67, and 1975; Co-Producer, The Bridge Theatre, NYC, 1965–66; Founding Ed., Ikon Mag., NYC, 1967; Member of Drama Dept., Bennington Coll., Vt., 1967–69; Member of English Dept., Adelphi Univ., Garden City, N.Y., 1975; Member of Theatre Dept., Wesleyan Univ., Middletown, Conn., 1977–80, and Hunter Coll., NYC, 1980–81. *Publs:* The Sleepwalker and the Assassin: A Study of the Contemporary Theatre,

1964; The Thing Itself (in Playwrights for Tomorrow 6), 1969; I Piece Smash (in The Scene 2), 1974; The Radical Theatre Notebook, 1973. Add: 565 West End Ave., New York, N.Y. 10024, U.S.A.

SAINI, B(alwant) S(ingh). Australian, b. 1930. Architecture. Prof. of Architecture, Univ. of Queensland, Brisbane, since 1972. Sr. Lectr. in Architecture, Delhi Sch. of Planning and Architecture, 1956–59; Sr. Lectr., then Reader in Architecture, Univ. of Melbourne, 1959–72. Member, Australian National Commn. for Unesco, 1977–84. *Publs:* Architecture in Tropical Australia, 1970; Building in Hot Dry Climates, 1980; The Australian House, 1982. Add: 11 Montrose Rd., Taringa, Qld. 4068, Australia.

SAINSBURY, Maurice Joseph. Australian, b. 1927. Psychiatry. Sr. Specialist, Mental Health Services, New South Wales Dept. of Health, since 1983. Consultant Psychiatrist (Col.), Army Office, since 1976. Gen. Practitioner, 1953–57, and in England, 1957–62; Psychiatrist and Deputy Medical Supt., North Ryde Psychiatric Centre, N.S.W., 1962–68; Dir., New South Wales Inst. of Psychiatry, 1968–83; Chief Examiner in Psychiatric Medicine, New South Wales Nurse Registration Bd., 1969–71; Pres., Royal Australian and N.Z. Coll. of Psychiatrists, 1976. *Publs:* Key to Psychiatry, 1974, 3rd ed. 1980. Add: 3 Bimbil Pl., West Killara, N.S.W., Australia 2071.

SAINT, Andrew (John). British, b. 1946. Architecture, Biography. Historian, Historic Buildings and Monuments Commn's London Div., since 1986. Lectr., Univ. of Essex, 1971–74; Architectural Ed., Survey of London, Greater London Council, 1974–86. *Publs:* Richard Norman Shaw, 1976; The Image of the Architect, 1983; Towards a Social Architecture, 1987. Add: 14 Burghley Rd., London NW5, England.

ST. AUBYN, Giles (Rowan). British, b. 1925. Philosophy, Biography. Master, Eton Coll., 1947–85. *Publs:* Macaulay, 1952; The Art of Argument, 1957; A Victorian Eminence, 1958; The Royal George, 1963; A World to Win, 1968; Infamous Victorians, 1971; Edward VII, Prince and King, 1979; The Year of Three Kings: 1483, 1983. Add: Cornwall Lodge, Cambridge Park, St. Peter Port, Guernsey, Channel Islands.

ST. CLAIR, Elizabeth. *See* **COHEN,** Susan.

ST. CLAIR, Margaret (Neeley). American, b. 1911. Science fiction/Fantasy. Full-time writer since 1945. Horticulturist, St. Clair Rare Bulb Gardens, El Sobrante, Calif., 1938–41. *Publs:* Agent of the Unknown, 1956; The Green Queen, 1956; The Games of Neith, 1960; Sign of the Labrys, 1963; Message from the Eocene, 1964; Three Worlds of Futurity (short stories), 1964; The Dolphins of Altair, 1967; The Shadow People, 1969; The Dancers of Noyo, 1973; Change the Sky and Other Stories, 1974; The Best of Margaret St. Clair, 1985; The Lack of Teddy Bears (autobiography), 1989. Add: Star Rt., Manchester, Calif. 95459, U.S.A.

ST. CLAIRE, Erin. *See* **BROWN,** Sandra.

ST. GEORGE, Judith. American, b. 1931. Children's fiction and non-fiction. Member, Rutgers Univ. Advisory Council on Children's Literature, since 1977. Chmn., Brooklyn Bridge Centennial Commn. Educational Cttee., 1981–83. *Publs:* Turncoat Winter, Rebel Spring, 1970; The Girl with Spunk, 1975; By George, Bloomers!, 1976; The Chinese Puzzle of Shag Island, 1976; The Shad Are Running, 1977; The Shadow of the Shaman, 1977; The Halo Wind, 1978; The Halloween Pumpkin Smasher, 1978; Mystery at St. Martin's 1979; The Amazing Voyage of the New Orleans, 1980; Haunted, 1980; Call Me Margo, 1981; The Mysterious Girl in the Garden, 1981; The Brooklyn Bridge: They Said It Couldn't Be Built, 1982; Do You See What I See?, 1982; In the Shadow of the Bear, 1983; (adapter) Grand Constructions, 1983; (adapter) Great Painters, 1984; (author from screenscript) Tales of the Gold Monkey, 1983; (author from filmscript) A View to a Kill, 1985; The Mount Rushmore Story, 1985; What's Happening to My Junior Year?, 1986; Who's Scared? Not Me!, 1987; Panama Canal: Gateway to the World, 1989. Add: 290 Roseland Ave., Essex Fells, N.J. 07021, U.S.A.

SAINT JAMES, Andrew. *See* **STERN,** James.

ST. JOHN OF FAWSEY Baron; Norman (Anthony Francis) St. John-Stevas. British, b. 1929. Law, Biography. Conservative M.P. (U.K.) for Chelmsford, Essex, 1964–87 (Chancellor of the Duchy of Lancaster, Leader of the House of Commons, and Minister for the Arts, 1979–81). Called to the Bar, Middle Temple, London, 1952; Lectr., Southampton Univ., 1952–53, King's Coll., Univ. of London, 1953–56; Tutor in

Jurisprudence, Christ Church, Oxford, 1953–55, and Merton Coll., Oxford, 1955–57; Fellow, Yale Univ., New Haven, Conn., 1957; Legal and Political Corresp., The Economist, London, 1959–64. *Publs:* Obscenity and the Law, 1956; Walter Bagehot, 1959; Life, Death and the Law, 1961; The Right to Life, 1963; Law and Morals, 1964; (ed.) Walter Bagehot: The Works, 11 vols., 1966–78; The Agonising Choice, 1971; John Paul II: His Travels and Mission, 1982; The Two Cities, 1984. Add: 21 Charles St., London WIX 7HD, England.

ST. JOHN, Bruce (Carlisle). Barbadian, b. 1923. Poetry. Sr. Lectr. in Spanish, Univ. of the West Indies, Bridgetown, since 1976 (Lectr., 1964–75). Member, National Council for Arts and Culture, Barbados. Asst. Master, St. Giles' Boys' Sch., Barbados, 1942–44, and Combermere Sch., Barbados, 1944–64. Ed., Ascent series of poetry chap-books, 1982. *Publs:* The Foetus Pains (verse), 1972; The Foetus Pleasures (verse), 1972; Bruce St. John at Kairi House (verse), 1974, 1975; Joyce and Eros and Varia (verse), 1976; The Vests (verse play), 1977; (ed.) Aftermath: An Anthology, 1977; Por el Mar de las Antillas: A Spanish Course for Caribbean Secondary Schools, 4 vols., 1979; (ed.) Caribanthology, 1981; Bumbatuk 1 (verse), 1982. Add: P.O. Box 64, Bridgetown, Barbados.

ST. JOHN, David. *See* **HUNT,** E. Howard.

ST. JOHN, Nicole. Also writes as Elizabeth Bolton, Catherine E. Chambers, Kate Chambers, Pamela Dryden, Lavinia Harris, Norma Johnston, and Adrian Robert. American. Novels/Short stories, Mystery/Crime/Suspense, Historical/Romance/Gothic, Children's fiction, Children's non-fiction, Mythology/Folklore. Pres., St. John Inst. of Arts and Letters. Has worked as retailer, producer/director, actress, teacher and businesswoman. *Publs:* as Norma Johnston—The Wishing Star, 1963; The Wider Heart, 1964; Ready or Not, 1965; The Bridge Between, 1966; The Keeping Days, 1973; Glory in the Flower, 1974; Of Time and Of Seasons, 1975; Strangers Dark and Gold, 1975; A Striving After Wind, 1976; The Sanctuary Tree, 1977; A Mustard Seed of Magic, 1977; The Swallow's Song, 1978; If You Love Me, Let Me Go, 1978; The Crucible Year, 1979; Pride of Lions, 1979; A Nice Girl Like You, 1980; Myself and I, 1981; The Days of the Dragon's Seed, 1982; Timewarp Summer, 1982; Gabriel's Girl, 1983; The Carlisle Chronicles, 3 vol. series, 1986; Shadow on Unicorn Farms, 1986; Watcher in the Mist, 1986; Shadow of a Unicorn, 1987; Whisper of the Cat, 1988; The Potter's Wheel, 1988; The Tangiers Truth, 1988; as Nicole St. John—The Medici Ring, 1975; Wychwood, 1976; Guinever's Gift, 1977; as Pamela Dryden—Mask for My Heart, 1982; Riding Home, 1988; as Lavinia Harris—Dreams and Memories, 1982; The Great Rip-Off, 1984; A Touch of Madness, 1985; Soaps in the Afternoon, 1985; Cover-Up!, 1986; The Packaging of Hank and Celia, 1986; as Kate Chambers—The Secret of the Singing Strings, 1983; Danger in the Old Fort, 1983; The Case of the Dog-Lover's Legacy, 1983; Secrets on Beacon Hill, 1984; The Legacy of Lucian Van Zandt, 1984; The Threat of the Pirate Ship, 1984; as Catherine Chambers—California Gold Rush: Search for Treasure, 1984; Daniel Boone and the Wilderness Road, 1984; Flatboats on the Ohio: Westward Bound, 1984; Frontier Dream: Life on the Great Plains, 1984; Frontier Farmer: Kansas Adventures, 1984; Frontier Village: A Town Is Born, 1984; Indian Days: Life in a Frontier Town, 1984; Log-Cabin Home: Pioneers in the Wilderness, 1984; Texas Roundup: Life on the Range, 1984; Wagons West: Off to Oregon, 1984; as Elizabeth Bolton—Ghost in the House, 1985; The Case of the Wacky Cat, 1985; The Secret of the Ghost Piano, 1985; The Secret of the Magic Potion, 1985; The Tree House Detective Club, 1985; as Adrian Robert—The Awful Mess Mystery, 1985; Ellen Ross, Private Detective, 1985; My Grandma, the Witch, 1985; The Secret of the Haunted Chimney, 1985; The Secret of the Old Barn, 1985. Add: Box 299, 103 Godwin Ave., Midland Park, N.J. 07432, U.S.A.

ST. JOHN, Patricia Mary. British, b. 1919. Children's fiction, Theology/Religion, Biography. Missionary nurse in Morocco, 1949–76. *Publs:* Tanglewood Secret, 1948; Treasures of the Snow, 1950; Star of Light, 1953; Four Candles, 1956; Poems, 1956; Harold St. John, 1960; A Missionary Muses on the Creed, 1961; Hudson Pope, 1962; Rainbow Garden, 1963; Missing the Way, 1966; Twice Freed, 1968; Breath of Life, 1970; Man of Two Worlds, 1972; The Mystery of Pheasant Cottage, 1978; Where the River Begins, 1981; Nothing Else Matters (in U.S. as If You Love Me), 1982; Would You Believe It?, 1983; The Victor (in U.S. as The Runaway), 1983; The Other Kitten (for children), 1984; Friska My Friend (for children), 1985; Courageous Journey: The Story of a Family's Will to Survive, 1988. Add: 10 Preston Close, Canley, Coventry, England.

ST. JOHN, Philip. *See* **del REY,** Lester.

ST. JOHN, Robert. American, b. 1902. Novels/Short stories, History, Media, Race relations, Travel/Exploration/Adventure, Autobiography/Memoirs/Personal, Biography. Former Assoc. Press and National Broadcasting Co., Foreign Corresp. *Publs:* From the Land of Silent People, 1942; It's Always Tomorrow, 1944; The Silent People Speak, 1948; Shalom Means Peace, 1949; Tongue of the Prophets, 1952; This Was My World, 1953; Through Malan's Africa, 1954; Foreign Correspondent, 1957; Ben-Gurion, 1959; The Boss, 1960; Builder of Israel, 1961; Israel, 1961; They Came from Everywhere, 1962; The Man Who Played God, 1962; Roll Jordan Roll, 1965; Encyclopedia of Radio and Television Broadcasting, 1967; Jews, Justice and Judaism, 1969; Once Around Lightly, 1970; South America More or Less, 1971; Eban by St. John, 1972; Ben-Gurion (for children), 1986; Builder of Israel, 1988. Add: 16605 Bealle Hill, Waldorf, Md. 20601, U.S.A.

ST. OMER, Garth. West Indian. Novel/Short stories. *Publs:* A Room on the Hill, 1968; Shades of Grey, 1968; Nor Any Country, 1969; J. Black Bam and the Masqueraders, 1972; The Lights on the Hill, 1985. Add: c/o Faber & Faber Ltd., 3 Queen Sq., London WC1N 3AU, England.

SAKOL, Jeannie. American, b. 1928. Novels/Short stories, Social commentary/phenomena. *Publs:* What about Teen-Age Marriage?, 1961; The Inept Seducer, 1967; Gumdrop, 1972; I Was Never the Princess, 1974; New Year's Eve, 1975; Flora Sweet, 1977; All Day, All Night, All Woman, 1978; The Wonderful World of Country Music, 1979; Promise Me Romance, 1979; Hot 30, 1980; Mothers and Lovers, 1980; (with Caroline Latham) The Royals: An Intimate Look at the Lives and Lifestyles of Britain's Royal Family, 1988. Add: 230 East 48th St., New York, N.Y. 10017, U.S.A.

SALAMAN, Raphael A. British, b. 1906. History. Engineer, Marks and Spencer Ltd., 1938–63, now retired. *Publs:* Dictionary of Tools Used in the Woodworking and Allied Trades, 1700-1970, 1975; Dictionary of Leather-Working Tools, c.1700-1950, and the Tools of Allied Trades, 1985. Add: 21 Kirkdale Rd., Harpenden, Herts. AL5 2PT, England.

SALAZAR, Rachel. American, b. 1954. Novels/Short stories. Full-time writer since 1983. Asst. to the Vice-Pres., Council on Foreign Relations, NYC, 1979–80; Instr. in English, Brooklyn Coll., 1981–83; Managing Ed., Fiction, Collective Inc., 1982–84; Ed., Grove Press Inc., NYC., 1984–86. *Publs:* Spectator, 1986. Add: P.O. Box 1812, Canal St. Station, New York, N.Y. 10013-0871, U.S.A.

SALE, Kirkpatrick. American, b. 1937. Social commentary. Bd. Member, PEN American Center, since 1976, Exploratory Project for Conditions of Peace, since 1984, and Learning Alliance, since 1985; Co-Dir., E.F. Schumacher Soc., U.S.A., since 1986 (Secty., 1980–86); Contributing Ed., Nation, NYC, since 1986. *Publs:* S.D.S., 1973; Power Shift, 1975; Human Scale, 1980; Dwellers In the Land: The Bioregional Vision, 1985. Add: 113 W. 11th St., New York, N.Y. 10011, U.S.A.

SALE, Richard (Bernard). American, b. 1911. Novels/Short stories, Screenplays, Mystery/Crime/Suspense. Screenwriter for Paramount, 1944, Republic, 1945–48, Twentieth Century Fox, 1948–52, British Lion, 1953–54, United Artists, 1954, and Columbia, 1956; television writer, dir. and producer, CBS, 1958–59. *Publs:* novels—Not Too Narrow, Not Too Deep, 1936; Is Ship Burning?, 1937; The Oscar, 1963; The White Buffalo, 1975; mystery novels—Cardinal Rock, 1940; Lazarus No. 7, 1942, in U.K. as Death Looks In, 1943; Sailor, Take Warning, 1942; Passing Strange, 1942; Destination Unknown, 1943 (in U.S. as Death at Sea, 1948); Benefit Performance, 1946; Home Is the Hangman, 1949; Murder at Midnight, 1950; For the President's Eyes Only (in U.K. as The Man Who Raised Hell), 1971. Add: 138 S. Camden Dr., Beverly Hills, Calif. 90212, U.S.A.

SALINGER, Herman. American, b. 1905. Poetry, Literature, Translations. Prof. of Germanic Languages and Comparative Literature, Duke Univ., Durham, N.C., from 1955. Prof. of German, Grinnell Coll., Iowa, 1947–55. *Publs:* (ed. and compiler) Index to the Poems of Rainer Maria Rilke, 1942; (trans.) Germany: A Winter's Tale, 1844, by Heinrich Heine, 1944; Angel of Our Thirst: Poems, 1950; (trans. and ed.) Twentieth-Century German Verse: A Selection, 1952; (ed. and rans. with H.M. Block) The Creative Vision: European Writers on Their Art, 1960; (trans.) Ballad of the Buried Life, by Rudolf Hagelstange, 1962; A Sigh is the Sword (poetry), 1962; (ed. with H. Reichert) Studies in Arthur Schnitzler, 1963; (trans.) Poems Against Death, by Karl Krolow, 1969; (ed. with A. Arnoldner) Prinzipien der Literaturwissenschaft, by Ernst Elster, 1972; (trans.) Hamlet, Fables and Other Poems, by Peter Henisch, 1980. Add:

German Dept., Duke Univ., Durham, N.C. 27707, U.S.A.

SALINGER, J(erome) D(avid). American, b. 1919. Novels/Short stories. *Publs:* The Catcher in the Rye (novel), 1951; Nine Stories (in U.K. as For Esmé—With Love and Squalor and Other Stories), 1953; Franny and Zooey (short stories), 1961; Raise High the Roof Beam, Carpenters, and Seymour: An Introduction, 1963. Add: c/o Harold Ober Assocs., 40 East 49th St., New York, N.Y. 10017, U.S.A.

SALINGER, Pierre (Emil George). American, b. 1925. Novels/Short stories, Biography. Chief Foreign Correspondent and Sr. Ed., Europe, ABC News, London, since 1988 (Bureau Chief, Paris, 1979–88). Trustee, Robert F. Kennedy Memorial Foundn., Washington; Honorary Chmn., Bd. of Trustees, American Coll. in Paris. Reporter and Night City Ed., San Francisco Chronicle, 1942–55; West Coast and Contrib. Ed., Collier's Mag., NYC, 1955–56; Investigator, U.S. Senate Select Cttee. on Improper Activities in the Labor-Management Field, 1957–59; Press Secty. to Senator, then President John F. Kennedy, 1959–63; Senator from California (Democrat), U.S. Senate, Washington, 1964–65; Vice Pres., Continental Airlines, and Continental Air Services, 1965–68; Sr. Vice Pres., MPROP Inc., 1969; Roving Ed., L'Express, Paris, 1973–79. Guest Lectr., in Journalism, Mills Coll., Oakland, Calif., 1950–55; Press Officer, Stevenson for President Campaign, Calif., 1952, and Richard Graves for Gov. of California Campaign, 1954. *Publs:* (ed.) A Tribute to John F. Kennedy, 1964; With Kennedy, 1966; A Tribute to Robert F. Kennedy, 1968; On Instructions of My Government (novel), 1971; Je Suis un Americain, 1975; La France et Le Nouveau Monde, 1976; America Held Hostage, 1981; The Dossier (novel), 1984; Mortal Games (novel), 1988. Add: 39 Lennox Gardens, Flat 4, London SW1, England.

SALISBURY, Frank B(oyer). American, b. 1926. Biology, Botany, Theology/Religion. Prof. of Plant Physiology since 1966, and Prof. of Botany since 1968, Utah State Univ., Logan (Head of Plant Science, 1966–70). Chief Ed., for North America and Pacific Rim, Journal of Plant Physiology since 1989. Asst. Prof. of Botany, Pomona Coll., Claremont, Calif., 1954–55; Asst. Prof. of Plant Physiology, 1955–61, and Prof., 1961–66, Colorado State Univ., Fort Collins; National Science Foundn. Postdoctoral Fellow, Tubingen, W. Germany, and Innsbruck, Austria, 1962–63; Technical Rep. in Plant Physiology, U.S. Atomic Energy Commn., 1973–74. *Publs:* The Flowering Process, 1963; (with R.V. Parke) Vascular Plants: Form and Function, 1964, 1970; Truth by Reason and by Revelation, 1965; (with C. Ross) Plant Physiology, 1969, 3rd ed. 1985; The Biology of Flowering, 1971; (with W.A. Jensen) Botany, 1972, 1984; The Utah UFO Display: A Biologist's Report, 1974; The Creation, 1976; (co-author) Biology, 1977. Add: 2020 North 1250 East, North Logan, Utah 84321, U.S.A.

SALISBURY, Harrison E. American, b. 1908. History, International relations/Current affairs. Assoc. Ed., The New York Times 1972–74 (joined staff, 1949). Pres., American Academy and Inst. of Arts and Letters, 1975–77, Authors League (U.S.), 1980–85. *Publs:* Russia on the Way, 1946; American in Russia, 1955; The Shook Up Generation, 1958; To Moscow and Beyond, 1960; Moscow Journal, 1961; The Northern Palmyra Affair, 1962; A New Russia, 1965; (ed.) The Soviet Union: The First Fifty Years, 1967; Behind the Lines, 1967; Orbit of China, 1967; The Nine Hundred Days: The Siege of Leningrad, 1969; The Coming War Between Russia and China, 1969; The Many Americas Shall Be One, 1971; To Peking and Beyond, 1973; The Gates of Hell, 1975; Travels Around America, 1976; The Unknown War, 1978; Black Night, White Snow, 1978; Russia in Revolution, 1978; Without Fear or Favor: The New York Times and *Its* Times, 1980; A Journey for Our Times, 1983; China: 100 Years of Revolution, 1983; The Long March: The Untold Story, 1985; A Time of Change, 1988. Add: c/o Harper and Row, 10 E. 53rd St., New York, N.Y. 10022, U.S.A.

SALISBURY, John. *See* **CAUTE,** David.

SALISBURY, Robert H(olt). American, b. 1930. Politics/Government. Prof., Washington Univ., St. Louis (joined faculty, 1955; Chmn., Dept. of Political Science, 1966–73, and since 1986 Chmn., Center for the Study of Public Affairs, 1974–76). *Publs:* (co-author) Functions and Policies of American Government, 1958, 3rd ed. 1967; (with Eliot, Chambers and Prewitt) American Government: Readings and Problems, 1959, 1965; (ed. with Chambers) Democracy in the Mid-Twentieth Century, 1960, as Democracy Today, 1962; (with Master and Eliot) State Politics and the Public Schools, 1964; Interest Group Politics in America, 1970; Governing America: Public Choice and Political Action, 1973; Citizen Participation in the Public Schools, 1980; (with Prewitt and Verba) An Introduction to American Government, 1987. Add: 337 Westgate, St. Louis, Mo. 63130, U.S.A.

SALKEY, (Felix) Andrew (Alexander). Jamaican, b. 1928. Novels/Short stories, Children's fiction, Poetry. Prof. of Writing, Hampshire Coll., Amherst, Mass., since 1976. Regular outside contrib., interviewer, and scriptwriter, BBC External Services (Radio), London, 1952–76; English teacher in a London comprehensive sch., 1957–59. *Publs:* A Quality of Violence, 1959; Escape to an Autumn Pavement, 1960; (ed.) West Indian Stories, 1960; Hurricane, 1964; Earthquake, 1965; (ed.) Stories from the Caribbean (in U.S. as Island Voices), 1965; (ed.) Young Commonwealth Poets '65, 1964; Drought, 1966; The Shark Hunters, 1966; Riot, 1967; (ed.) Caribbean Prose, 1967; The Late Emancipation of Jerry Stover, 1968; The Adventures of Catullus Kelly, 1969; Jonah Simpson, 1969; Havana Journal, 1971; (ed.) Breaklight: Caribbean Poetry, 1971; Georgetown Journal, 1972; (ed.) Caribbean Essays, 1972; (ed.) Breaklight: An Anthology of Caribbean Poetry (in U.S. as Breaklight: The Poetry of the Caribbean), 1972; Anancy's Score (stories), 1973; (ed.) Caribbean Essays, 1973; Jamaica (verse), 1973; (ed.) Caribbean Folk Tales and Legends, 1975; Come Home, Malcolm Heartland, 1976; (ed.) Writing in Cuba since the Revolution, 1977; In the Hills Where Her Dreams Live, 1979; The River that Disappeared, 1980; Danny Jones, 1980; Away (verse), 19 0. Add: Flat 8, Windsor Ct., Moscow Rd., Queensway, London W2, England.

SALLIS, James. American, b. 1944. Science fiction/Fantasy, Music. Full-time writer. Formerly, college instr., editor, and publisher's reader. *Publs:* Few Last Words (SF short stories), 1969; (ed.) The War Book, 1969; (ed.) The Shores Beneath, 1970; The Guitar Player (non-fiction), 1971; (ed.) Jazz Guitars: An Anthology, 1984; Difficult Lives (non-fiction), 1990. Add: c/o Meredith Bernstein, 470 West End Ave., New York, N.Y. 10023, U.S.A.

SALLIS, John C(leveland). American, b. 1938. Philosophy. Prof. of Philosophy, Duquesne Univ., Pittsburgh, since 1970 (Assoc. Prof., 1960–70). *Publs:* Introduction to the Techniques of Symbolic Logic, 1966; Heidegger and the Path of Thinking, 1970; Phenomenology and the Return to Beginnings, 1973; Being and Logos: The Way of Platonic Dialogue, 1975; The Gathering of Reason, 1978; Delimitations: Phenomenology and the End of Metaphysics, 1986; Spacings—of Reason and Imagination in Texts of Kant, Fichte, Hegel, 1987. Add: c/o Univ. of Chicago Press, 5801 Ellis Ave., Chicago, Ill. 60637, U.S.A.

SALMON, Edward Togo. Canadian, b. 1905. History. Instr., Cambridge Univ., 1926–27; Asst. Prof., Acadia Univ., 1929–30; Prof., McMaster Univ., Hamilton, 1930–73; Corresponding Ed., Phoenix mag., 1959–69; Member, Monograph Cttee., American Philological Assn., 1963–66. *Publs:* A History of the Roman World from 30 B.C. to A.D. 138, 1944, 6th ed. 1968; Samnium and the Samnites, 1967; Roman Colonization under the Republic, 1969; The Nemesis of Empire, 1974; The Making of Roman Italy, 1982. Add: 36 Auchmar Rd., Hamilton, Ont. L9C 1C5, Canada.

SALMON, John (Hearsey McMillan). New Zealand, b. 1925. History, Biography. Marjorie Walter Goodhart Prof. of History, Bryn Mawr Coll., Pa., since 1969. Prof. of History, Univ. of New South Wales, Australia, 1960–65; Dean of Humanities and Prof. of History, Univ. of Waikato, NZ, 1965–69. *Publs:* The French Religious Wars in English Political Thought, 1959; A History of Goldmining in New Zealand, 1963; (ed.) the French Wars of Religion, 1967; Cardinal de Retz: The Anatomy of Conspirator, 1969; (ed. with R.E. Giesey and trans.) Francogallia, by Francois Hotman, 1972; Society in Crisis: France in the 16th Century, 1975, 1979; Renaissance and Revolt: Essays in the Intellectual and Social History of Early Modern France, 1987. Add: Bryn Mawr Coll., Bryn Mawr, Pa. 19010, U.S.A.

SALMOND, John. Australian, b. 1937. History. Prof. of History, La Trobe Univ., Bundoora, Vic., since 1969 (Dept. Chmn., 1971–73, 1979–80, 1982–83; Dean, Sch. of Humanities, 1974–75). *Publs:* The Civilian Conservation Corps, 1967; The New Deal, 1970; (with W.J. Breen) An Ideal of Freedom, 1978; A Southern Rebel, 1983. Add: 45 Ramsay Ave., East Kew, Vic. 3102, Australia.

SALSBURY, Stephen. American, b. 1931. Economics, History. Prof. of Economic History, and Dept. Chmn. since 1977, and Dean of the Faculty of Economics since 1980, University of Sydney.Asst. Prof., 1963–67, Assoc., Prof., 1968–70, and Prof. of History, 1970–77, Univ. of Delaware, Newark. *Publs:* The State, The Investor, and the Railroad: The Boston and Albany, 1825-1869, 1967; (with A.D. Chandler) Pierre S. du Pont and the Making of the Modern Corporation, 1971; (ed.) Essays on the History of the American West, 1975; No Way to Run a Railroad: The Untold Story of the Penn Central, 1982; (with Kay Sweeney) The Bull, the Bear and the Kangaroo: The History of the Sydney Stock Exchange, 1988. Add: Dept. of Economic History, Univ. of Sydney, Sydney, N.S.W. 2006, Australia.

SALTER, Cedric. *See* **KNIGHT**, Frank.

SALTER, Lionel. British, b. 1914. Music, Translations. Critic, Gramophone, since 1948. Head of Television Music, 1956–63, Head of Opera, 1963–67, and Asst. Controller of Music, 1967–74, BBC, London; General Ed., BBC Music Guides, 1971–75. Record Critic, The Music Teacher, 1952–79. *Publs:* Going to a Concert, 1950; Going to the Opera, 1955; The Musician and His World, 1963; (trans.) Opera Guides—Mozart, 3 vols., 1971; (with J. Bornoff) Music and the Twentieth Century Media, 1972; Gramophone Guide to Classical Composers, 1978.Add: c/o Salamander Books, 52 Bedford Row, London WCIR 4LR, England.

SALTER, Mary D. *See* **AINSWORTH**, Mary D. Salter.

SALVADORI, Max William. (Massimo Salvadori-Paleotti). British/Italian, b. 1908. Economics, History, Politics/Government. Prof. Emeritus of History, Smith Coll., Northampton, Mass.With Inst. of Foreign Trade, Rome, 1931–32; Farm Mgr., Njoro, Kenya, 1934–37; Lectr., Univ. of Geneva, 1937–39; Prof., St. Lawrence Univ., Canton, N.Y., 1939–41, Bennington Coll., Vt., 1945–62, and Smith Coll., Northampton, Mass., 1947–75; with Unesco, 1948–49, NATO Secretariat, 1952–53, and ENI, Rome, 1956–57. *Publs:* L'Unita del Mediterraneo, 1931; La Penetrazione Europea in Africa, 1932; La Colonisation Européenne au Kenya, 1938; Problemi di Liberta, 1949; Resistenza ed Azione, 1951; (ed.) Lettere di Giacinta Salvadori, 1953; The Rise of Modern Communism, 1953, rev. ed. 1975; Storia della Resistenza Italiana, 1955; Capitalismo Demoncratico, 1956; NATO, 1957; Liberal Democracy, 1957; (ed.) Locke and Liberty, 1959; The Economics of Freedom, 1959; Prospettive Americane, 1960; Western Roots in Europe, 1961; Cavour and the Unification of Italy, 1961; La Resistenza nell' Anconetano e nel Piceno, 1962; (ed.) The American Economic System, 1963; Da Roosevelt a Kennedy, 1964; Italy, 1965; (ed.) Modern Socialism, 1968; (ed.) European Liberalism, 1972; A Pictorial History of the Italian People, 1972; Breve Storia della Resistenza Italiana, 1974; Free Market Economics, 1977; The Liberal Heresy, 1977; L'Eresia Liberale 2 vols., 1984.Add: 36 Ward Ave., Northampton, Mass. 01060, U.S.A.

SALVAN, Jacques Léon. merican, b. 1898. Literature, Philosophy. Prof. Emeritus, Univ. of Arizona, Tucson, since 1971 (Visiting Prof., Dept. of Romance Languages, 1964–71).Member of faculty, Univ. of Kansas, Lawrence, 1920–23.Member of faculty, Washington Univ., St. Louis, Mo., 1923–29; Member of faculty, 1929–64, and Prof. and Chmn., Dept. of French, 1959–61, Wayne State Univ., Detroit, Mich. *Publs:* Le Romantisme français et l'Angleterre victorienne, 1949; To Be and Not to Be: An Analysis of Jean-Paul Sartre's Ontology, 1952; The Scandalous Ghost: Sartre's Existentialism as Related to Vitalism, Humanism, Mysticism, Marxism, 1967.Add: Four Mile Village, Santa Rose Beach, Fla. 32459, U.S.A.

SAMBROOK, A(rthur) J(ames). British, b. 1931.Literature, Biography.Prof. of English, Univ. of Southampton, since 1981 (Lectr. in English, 1964–71; Sr. Lectr., 1971–75; Reader, 1975–81).Lectr. in English, St. David's Coll., Lampeter, 1957–64. *Publs:* A Poet Hidden: The Life of R.W. Dixon, 1833–1900, 1962; (ed.) The Scriberiad, 1967; (ed.) James Thomson's The Seasons and the Castle of Indolence, 1972; William Cobbett: An Author Guide, 1973; (ed.) Pre-Raphaelitism: Patterns of Literary Criticism, 1974; (ed.) James Thomson's The Seasons, 1981; English Pastoral Poetry, 1983; (ed.) James Thomson's Liberty, the Castle of Indolence, and Other Poems, 1986; The Intellectual and Cultural Context of English Literature 1700-1789, 1986.Add: Dept. of English, Univ. of Southampton, Southampton, England.

SAMBROT, William Anthony. American, b. 1920. Novels/Short stories. *Publs:* Island of Fear, 1962. Add: c/o Curtis Brown Ltd., 10 Astor Pl., New York, N.Y. 10003, U.S.A.

SAMELSON, William. American, b. 1928. Novels/Short stories, Language/Linguistics, Literature. Chmn., Dept. of Foreign Languages, San Antonio Coll., Tex., since 1960. *Publs:* Gerhart Herrmann Mostar: A Critical Profile, 1965; (ed.) Der Sinn des Lesens, 1968; All Lie in Wait (novel), 1969; English as a Second Language: Phase One: Let's Converse, 1973, Phase Two: Let's Read, 1974, Phase Three: Let's Write, 1975, Phase

Four: Let's Continue, 1979, and Phase Zero Plus: Let's Begin, 1980. Add: Dept. of Foreign Languages, San Antonio Coll., 1300 San Pedro Ave., San Antonio, Tex. 78284, U.S.A.

SAMPSON, Anthony (Terrell Seward). British, b. 1926. International relations/Current affairs, Politics/Government. Ed., Drum mag., Johannesburg, 1951–55; Staff member, 1955–66, and Chief American Corresp., 1973–74, The Observer, London; former Ed., Observer mag. *Publs:* Drum: A Venture into the New Africa, 1956; The Treason Cage, 1958; Commonsense about Africa, 1960; (with S. Pienaar) South Africa: Two Views of Separate Development, 1960; Anatomy of Britain, 1962; Anatomy of Britain Today, 1965; Macmillan: A Study in Ambiguity, 1967; The New Europeans, 1968; The New Anatomy of Britain, 1971; The Sovereign State: The Secret History of ITT, 1973; The Seven Sisters: The Great Oil Companies and the World They Made, 1975; The Arms Bazaar, 1977; The Money Lenders, 1981; The Changing Anatomy of Britain, 1982; Empires of the Sky, 1984; Black and Gold: Tycoons, Revolutionaries, and Apartheid, 1987. Add: 27 Ladbroke Grove, London W11, England.

SAMPSON, Edward E. American, b. 1934. Psychology, Sociology. Dean, Sch. of Social and Behavioral Science, California State Univ., Northridge, since 1986. Prof. of Psychology, Univ. of Calif., Berkeley, 1960–70; Prof. of Sociology and Psychology, Clark Univ., Worcester, Mass., 1971–82; Dean, Wright Inst., Berkeley, Calif., 1982–86. *Publs:* Approaches, Contexts, and Problems of Social Psychology, 1964; Student Activism and Protest, 1970; Social Psychology and Contemporary Society, 1971, 1976; Ego at the Threshold, 1975; Group Process for the Health Professions, 1978, 1981; Introducing Social Psychology, 1980; Justice and the Critique of Pure Psychology, 1983. Add: 55BS, California State Univ., Northridge, Calif. 91330, U.S.A.

SAMPSON, Geoffrey (Richard). British, b. 1944. Language/Linguistics, Philosophy, Politics/Government, Information technology. Prof. of Linguistics, Univ. of Leeds, since 1985. Fellow, Queen's Coll., Oxford, 1969–72; Lectr.,London School of Economics, 1972–74; Lectr., 1974–76, and Reader, 1976–84, Univ. of Lancaster. *Publs:* The Form of Language, 1975; Liberty and Language, 1979; Making Sense, 1980; Schools of Linguistics, 1980; An End to Allegiance, 1984; Writing Systems, 1985; (with Garside and Leech) The Computational Analysis of English, 1987. Add: Dept. of Linguistics, Univ. of Leeds, Leeds LS2 9JT, England.

SAMPSON, Ronald Victor. British, b. 1918. Human relations, Intellectual history, Politics/Government, Sociology. Lectr. in Politics, Univ. of Bristol, 1953–81. *Publs:* Progress in the Age of Reason, 1957; Equality and Power (in U.S. as The Psychology of Power), 1965; Tolstoy: The Discovery of Peace, 1973. Add: Beechcroft, Hinton Charterhouse, Bath, Avon, England.

SAMS, Eric. British, b. 1926. Literature, Music. Principal Officer, Dept. of Employment, London, 1950–78. *Publs:* Brahms Songs, 1972; The Songs of Robert Schumann, 1975; The Songs of Hugo Wolf, 1983; Shakespeare's Lost Play "Edmund Ironside," 1986. Add: 32 Arundel Ave., Sanderstead, Surrey, England.

SAMUELS, Warren J(oseph). American, b. 1933. Economics, Law, Politics/Government. Prof. of Economics, Michigan State Univ., East Lansing, since 1968 (Dir. of Grad. Progs., and Placement Officer, Dept. of Economics, 1969–73). Asst. Prof. of Economics, Univ. of Missouri, 1957–58, and Georgia State Coll., Atlanta, 1958–59; Asst. Prof. of Economics, 1959–62, and Assoc. Prof., 1962–68, Univ. of Miami, Fla. Member, Editorial Bd., History of Political Economy, 1969–88; Pres., Economics Soc. of Michigan, 1972–73; Member, Public Utilities Taxation Cttee., National Tax Assn., 1971–73; Ed., Journal of Economic Issues, 1971–81; Member of Exec. Cttee., 1972–73, and Pres., 1981–82, History of Economics Soc.; Pres., Assn. for Social Economics, 1988. *Publs:* The Classical Theory of Economic Policy, 1966; (ed. with H.M. Trebing) A Critique of Administrative Regulation of Public Utilities, 1972; Pareto on Policy, 1974; (ed.) The Economy as a System of Power, 2 vols., 1979; (co-ed.) Taxing and Spending Policy, 1980; (ed.) The Methodology of Economic Thought, 1980; (ed.) Research in the History of Economic Thought and Methodology, vol. 1, 1983. Add: 4397 Cherrywood Dr., Okemos, Mich. 48864, U.S.A.

SAMUELSON, Paul Anthony. American, b. 1915. Economics. Inst. Prof., Massachusetts Inst. of Technology, since 1966, Emeritus since 1986 (Asst. Prof. of Economics, 1940–44; Assoc. Prof. and staff member, Radiation Lab., 1944–45; Prof., 1947–66). Consultant, National Resources Planning Bd., 1941–43; Prof., Intnl. Economic Relations, Fletcher

Sch. of Law and Diplomacy, Medford, Mass., 1945–47; Consultant, U.S. Treasury, 1945–52; Member, Advisory Bd., National Commn. on Money and Credit, 1958–60; Consultant, Council of Economic Advisors, 1960–68. *Publs:* Foundations of Economic Analysis, 1947, 1983; Economics, 1948, 13th ed. (with W. Nordhaus) 1989; (ed.) Readings in Economics, 1955; (with R. Dorfman and R.M. Solow) Linear Programming and Economic Analysis, 1958; The Collected Scientific Papers of Paul A. Samuelson, vols. I and II, 1966, vol. III, 1972, vol. IV, 1978, vol.V, 1986. Recipient: Nobel Prize, 1970. Add: 75 Clairemont Rd., Belmont, Mass. 02178, U.S.A.

SANBORN, Margaret. American, b. 1915. History, Natural history, Biography. *Publs:* Robert E. Lee, a Portrait: 1807-1861, 1966; Robert E. Lee, the Complete Man: 1861-1870, 1967; The American: River of El Dorado, 1974; The Grand Tetons, 1978; Yosemite: Its Discovery, Its Wonders, and Its People, 1981; Mark Twain, The Bachelor Years: A Biography, 1989. Add: 527 Northern Ave., Mill Valley, Calif. 94941, U.S.A.

SANCHEZ, Sonia. American, b. 1934. Children's fiction, Plays/Screenplays, Poetry. Assoc. Prof. of English, Temple Univ., Philadelphia, since 1977. Staff member, Downtown Community Sch., 1965–67, and Mission Rebels in Action, 1968–69, San Francisco, Calif.; Instr., San Francisco State Coll., 1967–69; Lectr. in Black Literature, Univ. of Pittsburgh, Pa., 1969–70, Rutgers Univ., New Brunswick, N.J., 1970–71, Manhattan Community Coll., NYC, 1971–73, and Amherst Coll., Mass., 1972–75. *Publs:* Homecoming, 1969; WE a BaddDDD People, 1970; Broadside No. 34, 1970; The Bronx Is Next, 1970; It's a New Day; Poems for Young Brothas and Sistuhs, 1971; Sister Son/ji, 1971; Dirty Hearts '72, 1971; (ed.) Three Hundred Sixty Degrees of Blackness Comin' at You, 1972; Love Poems, 1973; A Blues Book for Blue Black Magical Women, 1973; The Adventures of Fat Head, Smallhead, and Squarehead (juvenile), 1973; Sound Investment (short stories), 1979; I've Been a Woman: New and Selected Poems, 1979; Homegirls and Handgrenades, 1984; Under a Soprano Sky, 1987. Add: Dept. of English, Temple Univ., Philadelphia, Pa. 19041, U.S.A.

SANCTUARY, Brenda. Also writes as Bridget Campbell. British, b. 1934. Cookery/Gastronomy/Wine. Columnist on cookery as Bridget Campbell, Woman's Mirror, 1959–60, Reveille, 1959 and 1967–72, and Value Today, 1974. *Publs:* Eat Cheaply and Well, 1975; (with Roger Grounds and Robin Howe) Fresh from the Garden, 1979. Add: Priory Mead, The Green, Datchet, Slough SL3 9JL, England.

SANDBURG, Helga. American, b. 1918. Novels/Short stories, Children's fiction, Poetry. Independent lectr. on reminiscence, folk song, and the art of writing, since 1959. Secty. to her father, Carl Sandburg, 1944–51. *Publs:* The Wheel of Earth, 1958; Measure My Love, 1959; The Owl's Roost, 1962; Blueberry, 1963; Sweet Music: A Book of Family Reminiscence and Song, 1963; Joel and the Wild Goose, 1963; Gingerbread, 1964; Bo and the Old Donkey, 1965; The Unicorns (poems), 1965; The Wizard's Child, 1967; (with G. Crile) Above and Below (non-fiction), 1969; Anna and the Baby Buzzard, 1970; To a New Husband (poems), 1970; Children and Lovers: 15 Stories by Helga Sandburg, 1976; A Great and Glorious Romance: The Story of Carl Sandburg and Lilian Steichen, 1978; . . .Where Love Begins, 1989. Add: 2060 Kent Rd., Cleveland, Ohio 44106, U.S.A.

SANDERLIN, George. American, b. 1915. History, Biography. Emeritus Prof. of English, San Diego State Univ., California (joined faculty, 1955). Assoc. Prof. of English, Univ. of Maine, Orono, 1938–55. *Publs:* (ed.) College Reading, 1953, 1958; St. Jerome and the Bible, 1961; (co-author) Effective Writing and Reading, 1962; First Around the World, 1964; St. Gregory the Great, 1964; Eastward to India, 1965; Effective Writing, 1966; Across the Ocean Sea, 1966; 1776: Journals of American Independence, 1968; The Sea-Dragon, 1969; Benjamin Franklin, 1971; (trans. and ed.) Bartolome de Las Casas: A Selection of His Writings, 1971; The Settlement of California, 1972; A Hoop to the Barrel, 1974; Washington Irving, 1975; Mark Twain, 1978. Add: 997 Vista Grande, El Cajon, Calif., U.S.A.

SANDERLIN, Owenita. American, b. 1916. Children's fiction, Children's non-fiction, Education, Autobiography/Memoirs/Personal. Consultant and resource teacher in gifted education, San Diego City Schs. Gifted Progs., 1971–73 and since 1981. *Publs:* Jeanie O'Brien, 1965; Johnny, 1968; Creative Teaching, 1971, Teaching Gifted Children, 1973; Tennis Rebel, 1978; Match Point, 1979. Add: 997 Vista Grande Rd., El Cajon, Calif. 92019, U.S.A.

SANDERS, David. American, b. 1926. Literature. Miller Prof. of

Humanities, Harvey Mudd Coll., Claremont, since 1985 (joined faculty, 1959; member, Dept. of Humanities and Social Sciences, 1959–70; Chmn. of the Dept., 1973–77; Prof. of English, 1977–85). Chmn., Dept. of Humanities, Clarkson Coll., Potsdam, N.Y., 1970–73. *Publs:* John Hersey, 1967; (ed.) Studies in "U.S.A." (essays), 1972; John Dos Passos: A Comprehensive Bibliography, 1987. Add: 1630 Rutgers Ct., Claremont, Calif. 91711, U.S.A.

SANDERS, Ed(ward). American, b. 1939. Novels/Short stories, Poetry, Social commentary/phenomena. Ed. and Publr., Fuck You: A Mag. of the Arts, NYC, 1962–65; Organizer and Lead Singer of The Fugs, a literary-political rock group, 1964–69; Owner, Peace Eye Bookstore, NYC, 1965–69. *Publs:* Poem from Jail, 1963; King Lord—Queen Freak, 1964; The Toe-Queen: Poems, 1964; (ed.) Bugger: An Anthology, 1964; Peace Eye, 1965, rev. ed. 1967; Shards of God, 1971; The Family: The Story of Charles Manson's Dune Buggy Attack Battalion, 1971; Egyptian Hieroglyphics, 1973; Tales of Beatnik Glory, 1975; 20,000 A.D., 1976; Fame and Love in New York (novel), 1980; The Z-D Generation, 1982; Thirsting for Peace in a Raging Century: Selected Poems 1961-1985, 1986. Add: Box 729, Woodstock, N.Y. 12498, U.S.A.

SANDERS, James Edward. New Zealander, b. 1911. Novels/Short stories, History, Autobiography/Memoirs/Personal. Journalist, since 1936; Columnist, Feature and Financial Writer, Wilson & Horton Ltd., since 1971. Journalist, New Zealand Observer and Northland Times, 1936–39; Proprietor, James Sanders Advertising Ltd., 1954–69. *Publs:* The Time of My Life, 1967; The Green Paradise, 1971; The Shores of Wrath, 1972; Kindred of the Winds, 1973; High Hills of Gold, 1973; Our Explorers, 1974; New Zealand Victoria Cross Winners, 1974; Fire in the Forest, 1975; The Lamps of Maine, 1975; Where Lies the Land?, 1976; Desert Patrols, 1976; Chase the Dragon, 1978; Dateline—NZPA, 1979; Frontiers of Fear, 1980; Venturer Courageous, 1983; The Colourful Colony, 1983; A Long Patrol, 1986; Of Wind and Water, 1989. Add: 508A East Coast Rd., Mairangi Bay, Auckland 10, New Zealand.

SANDERS, Jeanne. See **RUNDLE**, Anne.

SANDERS, Lawrence. American, b. 1920. Novels/short stories, Mystery/Crime/Suspense. *Publs:* (ed.) Thus Be Loved: A Book for Lovers, 1966; (with Richard Carol) Handbook of Creative Crafts, 1968; The Anderson Tapes, 1970; The Pleasures o Helen, 1971; Love Songs, 1972; The First Deadly Sin, 1973; The Tomorrow File, 1975; The Tangent Objective, 1976; The Second Deadly Sin, 1977; The Marlow Chronicles, 1977; The Tangent Factor, 1978; The Sixth Commandment, 1979; The Tenth Commandment, 1980; The Third Deadly Sin, 1981; The Case of Lucy Bending, 1982; The Seductions of Peter S, 1983; The Passion of Molly T, 1984; The Fourth Deadly Sin, 1985; The Loves of Harry Dancer, 1986; The Eighth Commandment, 1986; Tales of the Wolf, 1986; The Dream Lover, 1987; The Timothy Files, 1987; Timothy's Game, 1988; Love Songs, 1989; Capital Crimes, 1989. Add: c/o Putnam, 200 Madison Ave., New York, N.Y. 10016, U.S.A.

SANDERS, Peter (Basil). British, b. 1938. History, Translations. Chief Exec., Commn. for Racial Equality, London, since 1988 (Dir., 1977–88). Administrative Officer, Lesotho (formerly Basutoland), 1961–66; Principal Conciliation Officer, 1973–74, and Deputy Chief Officer, Race Relations Bd., London 1974–77. *Publs:* Moshweshwe of Lesotho, 1971; (ed. and trans. with M. Damane) Lithoko: Sotho Praise Poems, 1974; Moshoeshoe, Chief of the Sotho, 1975; The Simple Annals: The History of an Essex and East End Family, 1989. Add: 5 Bentfield End Causeway, Stansted Mountfitchet, Essex, England.

SANDERS, Ronald. American, b. 1932. History, Race relations, Autobiography/Memoirs/Personal, Biography. Rudolph Prof. of Jewish Studies, Syracuse Univ., New York, since 1989. Instr. in History, Queens Coll., NYC, 1958–65; Assoc. Ed., 1966–73, and Ed., 1973–75, Midstream Monthly Jewish Review. *Publs:* (ed. with A. Fried) Socialist Thought: A Documentary History, 1964; Israel: the View From Masada, 1966; The Downtown Jews, 1969; Reflections on a Teapot, 1972; Lost Tribes and Promised Lands, 1978; The Days Grow Short: The life and Music of Kurt Weill, 1980; The High Walls of Jerusalem, 1984; Shores of Refuge, 1988. Add: 49 W. 12th St., New York, N.Y. 10011, U.S.A.

SANDERSON, Stewart F(orson). British, b. 1924. Literature, Mythology/Folklore. Dir. of the Inst. of Dialect and Folk Life Studies, Univ. of Leeds, since 1964 (Lectr. in Folk Life Studies and Dir. of the Folk Life Survey, 1960–64; Chmn., Sch. of English, 1980–83). Member of the British Library Advisory Cttee. on the National Sound Archive, since 1983. Secretary-Archivist, 1952–58, and Sr. Research Fellow, and Ed.

of Scottish Studies, 1957–60, Univ. of Edinburgh. Joint Secty., Section H, British Assn. for the Advancement of Science, 1957–63; Pres., Folklore Soc., 1971–73; member of the Council, Soc. for Folk Life Studies, 1974–79, 1981–83; Gov., British Inst. of Recorded Sound, 1979–83; Chmn., Literature Cttee., Scottish Arts Council, 1983–88. *Publs:* Hemingway, 1961, 1970; (with others) The City of Edinburgh, 1963; (with others) Studies in Folk Life, 1969; (ed.) The Secret Common-Wealth and A Short Treatise of Charms and Spels, 1976; (with others) To Illustrate the Monuments, 1976; (ed. with H. Orton and J. Widdowson) The Linguistic Atlas of England, 1978; Ernest Hemingway: For Whom the Bell Tolls (criticism), 1980; (ed. with J. Kirk and J. Widdowson) Studies in Linguistic Geography, 1985; (with C. Upton and J. Widdowson) Word Maps: A Dialect Atlas of England, 1987; (ed.) The Silver Bough, vol.1, 1989. Add: Primside Mill Farmhouse, Kelso, Roxburghshire TD5 8PR, Scotland.

SANDFORD, Jeremy. British, b. 1934. Novels/short stories, Civil liberties/Human rights, Sociology, Travel/Exploration/Adventure. *Publs:* Cathy Come Home (novel), 1966; Synthetic Fun (sociology), 1967; Down and Out in Britain, 1970; Edna the Inebriate Woman (novel), 1971; In Search of the Magic Mushroom (travel), 1972; Gypsies (sociology), 1973; Tomorrow's People (sociology), 1974; Prostitutes (sociology), 1975; Virgin of the Clearways (novel), 1978. Add: 7 Earls Court Sq., London SW5, England.

SANDLER, Irving (Harry). American, b. 1925. Art. Prof. of Art History, State Univ. of New York at Purchase, since 1971. Instr. in Art History, New York Univ., NYC, 1960–71; Art critic, New York Post, 1960–65. *Publs:* The Triumph of American Painting: A History of Abstract Expressionism, 1970; The New York School: Painters and Sculptors of the Fifties, 1978; Alex Katz, 1979; Twenty Artists: Yale School of Art 1950–1970, 1981; Concepts in Construction 1910–1980, 1982; (ed.) Mark Rothko: Paintings 1948–1969, 1983; Al Held, 1984; (co-ed.) Defining Modern Art: Selected Writings of Alfred H. Barr, 1986; American Art of the 1960's, 1987. Add: 100 Bleecker St., New York, N.Y. 10012, U.S.A.

SANDLER, Merton. British b. 1926. Medicine/Health. Physician: Consultant Chemical Pathologist, Queen Charlotte's Maternity Hosp., London, since 1958; Prof. of Chemical Pathology, Inst. of Obstetrics and Gynaecology, Univ. of London, since 1973. *Publs:* Mental Illness in Pregnancy and the Puerperium, 1978; The Psychopharmacology of Aggression, 1979; Enzyme Inhibitors as Drugs, 1980; Amniotic Fluid and Its Clinical Significance, 1980; The Psychopharmacology of Alcohol, 1980; The Psychopathology of Anticonvulsants, 1981; Leeds Castle Migraine Workshop, 1989. Add: 27 St. Peter's Rd., Twickenham, Middx. TW1 1QY, England.

SANDMAN, Peter (Mark). American, b. 1945. Education, Environmental science/Ecology, Media, Writing/Journalism. Prof. of Journalism, since 1983, and Dir., Environmental Communication Research Prog., Rutgers Univ., New Brunswick, N.J. (Assoc. Prof., 1977–83). Member, Editorial Bd., Environment and Bahavior, and Public Relations Research and Education. Asst. Prof., Dept. of Journalism, Ohio State Univ., Columbus, 1971–72; Asst. Prof., 1972–75, and Assoc. Prof., 1975–77, Univ. of Michigan, Ann Arbor. *Publs:* Where the Girls Are, 1967; (with D.R. Goldenson) How to Succeed in Business Before Graduating, 1968; The Unabashed Career Guide, 1969; (ed.) Five Hundred Back-to-Work Ideas for Housewives, 1970; (ed.) From Campus Coed to Working Woman, 1970; (ed. with Frank Philpot) Three Months to Earn, 1970; (ed.) The Independent Teenager, 1970; (ed.) Not Quite Ready to Retire, 1970; (ed.) Careers After High School, 1970; Students and the Law, 1971; (with D.M. Rubin and D.B. Sachsman) Media: An Introductory Analysis of American Mass Communications, 1972, 1982; (ed. with D.M. Rubin and D.B. Sachsman), Media Casebook: An Introductory Reader in American Mass Communications, 1972, 1977; (co-author) Emerging Issues in Environmental Education, 1974; (with J. Myer and J.B. Garry) Writing about Wildlife, 1974; (ed. with B.G. Yarrison) Source Book of Educational and Training Resources in Agriculture, Home Economics, and Natural Resources of Institutions on the Title XII Registry, 1979; (with others) Report on the Accident at Three Mile Island, 1980; Green Acres in the 1980s: Meeting New Jersey's Needs for Open Space and Recreation, 1983; (with C.S. Klompus and B.G. Yarrison) Scientific and Technical Writing, 1985; (with N.D. Weinstein and M.L. Klotz) Public Response to the Risk from Radon, 1987; (with D.B. Sachsman and M.R. Greenberg) The Environmental News Source, 1987; (with others) Environmental Risk and the Press, 1987; (with Billie J. Hance and Caron Chess) Improving Dialogue with Communities, 1988; (ed. with David B. Sachsman and Michael R. Greenberg) Environmental Reporter's Handbook, 1988. Add: Environmental Communication Research Prog., Rutgers Univ., New Brunswick,

N.J. 08903, U.S.A.

SANDON, J.D. *See* **HARVEY,** John B.

SANDOZ, G(eorge) Ellis. American, b. 1931. Philosophy, Politics/Government. Prof. of Political Science, Louisiana State Univ., Baton Rouge, since 1978. Instr. to Prof., Louisiana Technological Univ., Ruston, 1959–68; Prof. and Head of Political Science Dept., East Texas State Univ., Commerce, 1968–78. *Publs:* Political Apocalypse; A Study of Dostoevsky's Grand Inquisitor, 1971; Conceived in Liberty, 1978; (co-ed.) A Tide of Discontent: The 1980 Elections and Their Meaning, 1981; The Voegelinian Revolution: A Biographical Introduction, 1981; (ed.) Eric Voegelin's Thought: A Critical Appraisal, 1982; (co-ed.) Election '84; Landslide Without a Mandate?, 1985. Add: Dept. of Political Science, Louisiana State Univ., Baton Rouge, La. 70803, U.S.A.

SANDS, Martin. *See* **BURKE,** John.

SANDY, Stephen. American, b. 1934. Poetry. Prof. of English, Bennington Coll., Vermont, since 1975 (joined faculty, 1969). Instr., 1963–67, and Councillor for English, Grad. Soc., 1967–74, Harvard Univ. *Publs:* Caroms, 1960; Mary Baldwin, 1962; Destruction of Bullfinch's House, 1964; Stresses in the Peaceable Kingdom, 1967; Home Again, Looking Around, 1968; (trans.) Catullus LVIII, 1969; Japanese Room, 1969; Jerome, 1970; Roofs, 1971; The Difficulty, 1975; The Austin Tower, 1975; Freestone: Sections 25 and 26, 1977; End of the Picaro, 1977; Arch, 1977; The Hawthorne Effect, 1980; The Raveling of the Novel: Studies in Romantic Fiction from Walpole to Scott, 1980; After the Hunt, 1982; Flight of Steps, 1982; Riding to Greylock, 1983; To a Mantis, 1987; Man in the Open Air, 1988. Add: Box 524, North Bennington, Vt. 05257, U.S.A.

SANECKI, Kay Naylor. British. Homes/Gardens, Horticulture, Biography. *Publs:* Wild and Garden Herbs, 1956; (co-author) Practical Herb Gardening, 1968; Discovering English Gardens, 1969; Discovering Herbs, 1970, 4th ed. 1985; (ed.) Discovering Period Gardens, 1970; (ed.) Gardening for the Disabled, 1971; (ed.) Discovering Flower Arrangement, 1971; (ed. and contrib.) What Is That Flower, 1974; Humphrey Repton, 1974; The Complete Book of Herbs, 1974; Gardens in Britain, 1979, 3rd ed. 1987; Old Garden Tools, 1979, 1987; The Fragrant Garden, 1981; Fragrant and Aromatic Plants, 1985. Add: c/o David and Charles, Brunel House, Newton Abbot, Devon TQ12 4PU, England.

SANER, Reg(inald Anthony). American, b. 1931. Poetry. Prof. of English, Univ. of Colorado, Boulder, since 1972 (Asst. Prof., 1962–67; Assoc. Prof., 1967–72). Freelance photographer in Illinois, 1953–54; photographer and writer, Montgomery Publishing Co., Los Angeles and San Francisco, 1956; Asst. Inst., 1956–60, Instr., 1961–62, Univ. of Illinois. *Publs:* Climbing into the Roots, 1965; So This is the Map, 1981; Essay on Air, 1984. Add: 1925 Vassar, Boulder, Colo. 80303, U.S.A.

SANGER, Marjory Bartlett. American, b. 1920. Children's fiction, Biology, Children's non-fiction, Biography. Chmn. and Public Relations Ed., Bulletin, Massachusetts Audubon Soc., Boston, 1954–57; Advisory Bd., Roll ns Coll. Writers Conference, Winter Park, Fla., 1968–76. *Publs:* The Bird Watchers, 1957; Greenwood Summer, 1958; Mangrove Island, 1963; Cypress Country, 1965; World of the Great White Heron, 1967; Checkerback's Journey, 1969; Billy Bartram and His Green World, 1972; Escoffier, 1976; Forest in the Sand, 1983. Add: Box 957, Winter Park, Fla. 32790, U.S.A.

SANJIAN, Avedis K. American, b. 1921. History, Literature. Prof. of Armenian, Univ. of California, Los Angeles, since 1968 (Assoc. Prof., 1965–68). Post-Doctoral Research Fellow in Armenian Studies, 1957–61, Asst. Prof. of Armenian, 1961–65, Harvard Univ., Cambridge, Mass. *Publs:* The Armenian Communities in Syria Under Ottoman Dominion, 1965; Colophons of Armenian Manuscripts, 1301-1480: A Source For Middle Eastern History, 1969; A Catalogue of Medieval Armenian Manuscripts in the United States, 1976; (trans. and ed. with A. Tietze) Eremia Chelebi Komurjian's Armeno-Turkish Poem, The Jewish Bride, 1981; The Private Letters of the Poet Vahan Tekeyan, 1983; David Anhaght': The "Invincible" Philosopher, 1986. Add: 545 Muskingum Pl., Pacific Palisades, Calif. 90272, U.S.A.

SARASIN, Jennifer. *See* **SACHS,** Judith.

SARBAN, Pseud. for John W. Wall. British. Science fiction/Fantasy. *Publs:* Ringstones and Other Curious Tales, 1951; The Doll Maker and Other Tales of the Uncanny, 1953; The Sound of His Horn (SF novel),

1960. Add: c/o Ballantine Books Inc., 201 E. 50th St., New York, N.Y. 10022, U.S.A.

SARGENT, Lyman T(ower). American, b. 1940. Politics/Government. Prof. of Political Science, Univ. of Missouri-St. Louis, since 1975 (Asst. Prof. 1965–70; Dir., Political Science Lab., 1968–69; Chmn., Dept. of Political Science, 1969–71, 1975–78; Assoc. Prof., 1970–75). Instr., Univ. of Wyoming, Laramie, 1964–65; Visiting Prof., Univ. of Exeter, 1978–79, 1983–84, and London Sch. of Economics, 1985–86. Member, Inst. for Advanced Study, Princeton Univ., N.J., 1981–82. *Publs:* Contemporary Political Ideologies: A Comparative Analysis, 1969, 7th ed., 1987; (with Thomas A. Zant) Techniques of Political Analysis: An Introduction, 1970; New Left Thought: An Introduction, 1972; (ed.) Consent, 1979; British and American Utopian Literature, 1988. Add: Dept. of Political Science, Univ. of Missouri-St. Louis, Mo. 63121, U.S.A.

SARGENT, Pamela. American, b. 1948. Science fiction/Fantasy. Freelance writer and editor since 1971. *Publs:* (ed.) Women of Wonder: Science Fiction Stories by Women about Women, 1975; (ed.) More Women of Wonder: Science-Fiction Novelettes by Women about Women, 1976; (ed.) Bio-Futures: Science Fiction Stories about Biological Metamorphosis, 1976; Cloned Lives, 1976; Starshadows (short stories), 1977; (ed.) The New Women of Wonder: Recent Science-Fiction by Women about Women, 1978; The Sudden Star, 1979, in U.K. as The White Death, 1980; Watchstar, 1980; The Golden Space, 1982; The Alien Upstairs, 1983; Earthseed, 1983; Eye of the Comet, 1984; Homesmind, 1984; Venus of Dreams, 1986; The Shore of Women, 1986; (co-ed.) Afterlives, 1986; The Best of Pamela Sargent (short stories), 1987; Alien Child, 1988; Venus of Shadows, 1988. Add: c/o Joseph Elder Agency, 150 W. 87th St., New York, N.Y. 10024, U.S.A.

SARICKS, Ambrose. American, b. 1915. History, Biography. Prof. Emeritus of History, Univ. of Kansas, Lawrence, since 1984 (Asst. Prof., 1950–56; Assoc. Prof., 1956–62; Prof., 1962–82; Assoc. Dean, Grad. Sch., 1966–70; Vice Chancellor, Academic Affairs, 1972–75). Dean, Grad. Sch., Wichita State Univ., Kans., 1970–72. *Publs:* (ed.) A Bibliography of the Frank E. Melvin Collection of Pamphlets of the French Revolution in the University of Kansas Libraries, 2 vols., 1960; Pierre Samuel du Pont de Nemours, 1965. Add: 2552 Arkansas, Lawrence, Kans. 66046, U.S.A.

SARKAR, Anil Kumar. Indian, b. 1912. Philosophy, Psychology, Theology/Religion. Prof. Emeritus, California State Univ., Hayward, and California Inst. of Asian Studies, San Francisco, since 1980 (Prof. of Philosophy, California State Univ., 1965–80; Dir., South-Asian Studies, California Inst. of Asian Studies, 1968–80). Prof. of Philosophy, Rajendra Coll., Chapra, India, 1940–44; Sr. Lectr., Univ. of Ceylon, Colombo and Peradeniya, 1944–64; Visiting Prof., Univ. of New Mexico, Albuquerque, 1954–65. *Publs:* An Outline of Whitehead's Philosophy, 1940; Changing Phases of Buddhist Thought, 1968; Whitehead's Four Principles: From West-East Perspectives, 1974; Dynamic Facets of Indian Thought, Vol. I, 1980. Add: 818 Webster St., Hayward, Calif. 94544, U.S.A.

SARNA, Jonathan D(aniel). American, b. 1955. History, Theology/Religion, Biography. Prof. of American Jewish History, Hebrew Union Coll.-Jewish Inst. of Religion, Cincinnati, since 1988 (Visiting Lectr., 1979–80; Asst. Prof., 1980–84; Assoc. Prof., 1984–88) Dir., Center for the Study of the American Jewish Experience, since 1984 (Academic Adviser, 1981–84). Dir., Cincinnati Chapter, American Jewish Cttee., since 1981; Member of the Academic Council, American Jewish Historical Soc., since 1982; Member, Bd. of Dirs., Assn. for Jewish Studies, since 1984. *Publs:* (ed.) Jews in New Haven, 1978; Jacksonian Jew: The Two Worlds of Mordecai Noah, 1981; (ed. and trans.) People Walk on Their Heads: Moses Weinberger's Jews and Judaism in New York, 1982; The American Jewish Experience, 1986; (with Alexandra S. Korros) American Synagogue History: A Bibliography and State-of-the-Field Survey, 1988. Add: 3101 Clifton Ave., Cincinnati, Ohio 45220, U.S.A.

SARNA, Nahum M. American, b. 1923. Theology/Religion. Emeritus Golding Prof. of Biblical Studies, Brandeis Univ., Waltham, Mass. (Chmn., Dept. of Near Eastern and Jewish Studies, 1969–75). Gen. Ed., Jewish Publ. Soc. Bible Commentary, since 1974. Librarian, 1957–63, and Assoc. Prof. of Bible, 1963–65, Jewish Theological Seminary, NYC. *Publs:* Understanding Genesis, 1966, 1970; (trans. and ed. with M. Greenberg and J. Greenfield) The Book of Psalms, 1973; The Book of Job, 1980; The Writings (Kethubim), 1982; Exploring Exodus, 1986; Commentary to Genesis, 1989. Add: 39 Green Park, Newton, Mass. 02158, U.S.A.

SARNAT, Marshall. Israeli, b. 1929. Administration/Management, Business/Trade/Industry, Economics, Money/Finance. Prof. of Finance, since 1976, and Dir., Inst. of Business Research, since 1972, Hebrew Univ. (Instr., 1959–65; Lectr., 1965–67; Sr. Lectr., 1967–72; Assoc. Prof., 1972–76). *Publs:* The Development of the Securities Market in Israel, 1966; Savings and Investment through Retirement Funds, 1966; (with H. Levy) Investment and Portfolio Analysis, 1972; (with H. Levy) Financial Decision-Making under Uncertainty, 1977; (with H. Levy) Capital Investment and Financial Decisions, 1978; Inflation and Capital Markets, 1978; (with G. Szego) International Finance and Trade, 1980; (with G. Szego Saving, Investment and Capital Markets in an Inflationary Economy, 1982; (with H. Levy) Portfolio and Investment Selection, 1984; (with H. Levy) Principles of Financial Management, 1988. Add: Nayot 34, Jerusalem, Israel.

SARNO, Ronald Anthony. American, b. 1941. History, Media, Sex, Theology/Religion. Consultant on grantswriting for hosps., educational instns., and charities; Consultant on medical practice mgmt. since 1978; Mgr., Belair Klein and Evans, NYC, since 1988. Teacher, Xavier High Sch., NYC, 1966–69; Scriptwriter, Sacred Heart Radio Prog., 1969–75, and Sacred Heart TV Prog., 1974–75; Grantswriter, St. Joseph's Hosp. and Medical Center, Paterson, N.J., 1976–79; Admin., Mountainview Medical Assocs., Nyack, N.Y., 1980–82; Chief Development Officer, Caldwell Coll., New Jersey, 1982–83; Chief Fiscal Officer, Family Dynamics Inc., 1983–86; Admin. Mgr., Memorial Sloan-Kettering Cancer Centre, NYC., 1986–88. Asst. Ed., Sacred Heart Mag., 1967–68; Contributing Ed., National Jesuit News, 1972–74; Ed., Inisfada Report, 1973. *Publs:* Achieving Sexual Maturity, 1969; Let Us Proclaim the Mystery of Faith, 1970; The Story of Hope: The Nation, The Man, The Kingdom, 1972; Prayers for Modern, Urban, Uptight Man, 1974; (co-ed.) Liturgical Handbook for CLCs, 1974; The Cruel Caesars: Their Impact on the Early Church, 1976; David and Bathsheba (libretto), 1977; (with Len Badia) Morality: How We Live It Today, 1979; Using Media in Religious Education, 1987. Add: 145 N. Walnut St., Ridgewood, N.J. 07450, U.S.A.

SARNOFF, Dorothy. American. Human relations, Speech/Rhetoric. Chmn., Speech Dynamics Inc., NYC, since 1964. Lectr., Conductor of Seminars, and Consultant to business corp. *Publs:* Speech Can Change Your Life, 1975; Make the Most of Your Best, 1981; Never Be Nervous Again, 1988. Add: 111 West 57th St., New York, N.Y. 10019, U.S.A.

SARNOFF, Irving. American, b. 1922. Psychology, Sex, Social commentary/phenomena. Prof. of Psychology, New York Univ., NYC, since 1962. *Publs:* Personality Dynamics and Development, 1962; Society with Tears, 1966; Testing Freudian Concepts: An Experimental Social Approach, 1971; (with Suzanne Sarnoff) Sexual Excitement/Sexual Peace: The Place of Masturbation in Adult Relationships, 1979; (with Suzanne Sarnoff) Love-Centered Marriage in a Self-Centered World, 1989. Add: 100 Bleecker St., New York, N.Y. 10012, U.S.A.

SAROYAN, Aram. American, b. 1943. Novels, Poetry, Plays, Biography. Publr., Lines Books, NYC (Founding Ed., Lines, 1964–65). *Publs:* (with J. Caldwell and R. Kolmar) Poems, 1963; In, 1964; Top, 1965; Works, 1966; Sled Hill Voices, 1966; Coffee Coffee, 1967; Aram Saroyan, 1968; (Poems), 1968; Pages, 1969; Words and Photographs, 1970; The Beatles, 1970; 5 Mini-Books, 1971; Cloth: An Electric Novel, 1971; The Rest, 1971; Poems, 1972; (with V. Bockris) By Airmail, 1972; The Street (novel), 1974; The Bolinas Book, 1974; Marijuana and Me, 1974; The Street: An Autobiographical Novel, 1975; O My Generation and Other Poems, 1976; Genesis Angels: The Saga of Lew Welch and the Beat Generation, 1979; Last Rites: The Death of William Saroyan, 1982; William Saroyan, 1983; Trio: Gloria Vanderbilt, Carol Matthau, Oona Chaplin, 1985; The Romantic: A Novel, 1988; Pasternak and Mandelstam (play), 1988. Add: 229, Poplar Crest Ave., Thousand Oaks, Calif. 91320, U.S.A.

SARTON, May. American, b. 1912. Novels/Short stories, Plays/Screenplays, Poetry, Animals/Pets, Autobiography/Memoirs/Personal. Apprentice, then member, and Dir. of Apprentice Group, Eva Le Gallienne's Civic Repertory Theatre, NYC, 1930–33; Founder and Dir., Apprentice Theatre, NYC, and Associated Actors Inc., Hartford, Conn., 1933–36; Teacher of Creative Writing and Choral Speech, Stuart Sch., Boston, Mass., 1937–40; Documentary Scriptwriter, Office of War Information, 1944–45; Briggs-Copeland Instr. in Composition, Harvard Univ., Cambridge, Mass., 1950–53; Lectr. Breadloaf Writer's Conference, Middlebury, Vt., 1951–52, and Boulder Writers' Conference, Colo., 1953–54; Phi Beta Kappa Visiting Scholar, 1959–60; Danforth Lectr., 1960–61; Lectr. in Creative Writing, Wellesley Coll., Mass., 1960–63. *Publs:* Encounter in April (poetry), 1937; The Single Hound, 1938; Inner Landscape (poetry), 1939; The Bridge of Years, 1946; Underground River (play), 1947; The Lion and the Rose (poetry), 1948; The Leaves of the Tree (poetry), 1950; Shadow of a Man, 1950; A Shower of Summer Days, 1952; The Land of Silence and Other Poems, 1953; Faithful are the Wounds, 1955; The Birth of a Grandfather, 1957; In Time Like Air (poetry), 1957; The Fur Person: The Story of a Cat, 1957; I Knew a Phoenix: Sketches for an Autobiography, 1959; Cloud, Stone, Sun, Vine: Poems, Selected and New, 1961; The Small Room, 1961; Joanna and Ulysses, 1963; Mrs. Stevens Hears the Mermaids Singing, 1965; Miss Pickthorn and Mr. Hare: A Fable, 1966; A Private Mythology: New Poems, 1966; As Does New Hampshire and Other Poems, 1967; Plant Dreaming Deep (autobiography), 1968; The Poet and the Donkey, 1969; Kinds of Love, 1970; A Grain of Mustard Seed (poetry), 1971; A Durable Fire: New Poems, 1972, As We Are Now, 1973; Journal of Solitude, 1973; Collected Poems, 1974; Crucial Conversations, 1975; A World of Light, 1976; The House by the Sea, 1977; A Reckoning, 1978; Selected Poems, 1978; Halfway to Silence (poetry), 1980; Recovering: A Journal, 1980; Writings on Writing, 1980; Anger, 1982; Letters from Maine (poetry), 1984; The Magnificent Spinster, 1985; The Silence Now: New and Uncollected Earlier Poems, 1988; A Self-Portrait, 1988; After a Stroke: A Journal, 1988; The Education of Harriet Hatfield (novel), 1989. Add: P.O. Box 99, York, Maine 03909, U.S.A.

SASSER, Charles W(anye). American, b. 1942. Novels/Short stories, Mystery/ Crime/Suspense. Freelance writer since 1979; Pres., Cedar Press Publishing Co., since 1981. Officer, Miami Police Dept., 1965–68; homicide detective, Tulsa Police Dept., 1969–79; also, Instr. in Sociology, Tulsa Jr. Coll., 1974; Dir., Criminal Justice Dept., American Christian Coll., Tulsa, 1975–78. *Publs:* No Gentle Streets, 1984; (with others) The Soldier of Fortune, 1986; I Have Come to Step Over Your Soul, 1987. Add: c/o Ethan Ellenberg, 548 Broadway, Suite 5-C, New York, N.Y. 10012, U.S.A.

SAUER, Gordon C. American, b. 1921. Art, Medicine/Health. In private practice as dermatologist, Kansas City, Mo., since 1954. Clinical Prof. of Medicine, Univ. of Kansas Sch. of Medicine (Head, Dermatology Section, 1958–70). *Publs:* Manual of Skin Diseases, 5th ed. 1985; Teen Skin, 1973; Gould Bird Print Reproductions, 1977; John Gould, The Bird Man, 1982. Add: 6400 Prospect Ave., Kansas City, Mo. 64132, U.S.A.

SAUL, Leon Joseph. American, b. 1901. Psychiatry. In private practice of psychiatry and psychoanalysis. Emeritus Prof. of Psychiatry, Sch. of Medicine, Univ. of Pennsylvania, since 1969 (Prof. of Clinical Psychiatry, 1948–60; Prof. of Psychiatry, 1960–69); Emeritus Training and Supvr. Analyst, Philadelphia Psychoanalytic Inst., since 1970; Emeritus Chief Psychiatric Consultant, Swarthmore Coll., Pa., since 1971; Hon. Consultant, Inst. of the Pennsylvania Hosp., Philadelphia, since 1970. *Publs:* Emotional Maturity, 1947, 3rd ed. 1971; Bases of Human Behavior, 1951, 1972; The Hostile Mind, 1956; Technic and Practice of Psychoanalysis, 1958; Fidelity and Infidelity, 1967; (with Henri Parens) Dependence in Man, 1971; Psychodynamically Based Psychotherapy, 1972; Psychodynamics of Hostility, 1976; The Childhood Emotional Pattern, 1977; The Childhood Emotional Pattern and Corey Jones, 1977; The Childhood Emotional Pattern in Marriage, 1979; The Childhood Emotional Pattern and Maturity, 1979; The Childhood Emotional Pattern and Psychodynamic Therapy, 1980; The Childhood Emotional Pattern and Human Hostility, 1980; (with Silas Warner) The Psychotic Personality, 1982. Add: 275 Highland Ave., Media, Pa. 19063, U.S.A.

SAUNDERS, Ann Loreille. Has also written as Ann Cox-Johnson. British, b. 1930. Archaeology/Antiquities, Architecture, History. Ed., Costume, since 1967; Ed., London Topographical Record, since 1975. Deputy Librarian, Lambeth Palace, London, 1952–55; Asst. Keeper, British Museum, London, 1955–56; Archivist, St. Marylebone Public Library, London, 1956–63; Sub-ed., Journal of the British Archaeological Assn., 1964–75. *Publs:* (ed. as Ann Cox-Johnson) Handlist to the Ashbridge Collection on the History and Topography of St. Marylebone, 1959; (as Ann Cox-Johnson) John Bacon, R.A. 1740-1799, 1961; (ed. as Ann Cox-Johnson) Handlist of Painters, Sculptors, and Architects Associated with St. Marylebone, 1760-1900, 1963; Regent's Park, 1969, 1981; Arthur Mee's King's England: London North of the Thames, except the City and Westminster, 1972; London: The City and Westminster, 1975; The Regent's Park Villas, 1981; The Art and Architecture of London: An Illustrated Guide, 1984, 1988. Add: 3 Meadway Gate, London NW11 7LA, England.

SAUNDERS, (Dame) C(icely) M. British, b. 1918. Medicine/Health. Chmn., St. Christopher's Hospice, London (Medical Dir., 1967–85). Medical Social Worker, 1947–51, and Houseman, 1957–58, St. Thomas'

Hospital, London; Research Fellow, St. Joseph's Hospice, London, 1958–65. Member, Medical Research Council, 1976–79. *Publs:* The Management of Terminal Disease, 1978, 1984; Living with Dying, 1982. Add: St. Christopher's Hospice, 51-59 Lawrie Park Rd., London SE26, England.

SAUNDERS, James A. British, b. 1925. Plays/Screenplays. Formerly taught in London. *Publs:* Alas, Poor Fred: A Duologue in the Style of Ionesco, 1960; Double, Double, 1962; Next Time I'll Sing to You, 1963; A Scent of Flowers, 1964; Barnstable, 1965; (adaptor with I. Murdoch) The Italian Girl, 1967; Neighbors and Other Plays, 1968; Haven, later as A Man's Best Friend, 1969; (adaptor) The Travails of Sancho Panza, 1969; The Borage Pigeon Affair, 1969; Games, 1973; After Liverpool, 1973; Bodies, 1979; Savoury Meringue and Other Plays, 1980; Bye Bye Blues and Other Plays, 1980; Fall, 1985; Scandella, 1985; Emperor Waltz, 1986. Add: c/o Margaret Ramsey, 14a Goodwin's Court, London WC2, England.

SAUNDERS, Jean. Also writes as Sally Blake, Jean Innes, and Rowena Summers. British, b. 1932. Novels/Short stories, Historical/Romance/Gothic, Children's fiction, Writing. *Publs:* The Fugitives, 1974; (as Jean Innes) Ashton's Folly, 1975; (as Jean Innes) Sands of Lamanna, 1975; (as Jean Innes) The Golden God, 1975; Only Yesterday, 1975; (as Jean Innes) The Whispering Dark, 1975; (as Jean Innes) White Blooms of Yarrow; (as Jean Innes) Boskelly's Bride, 1976; (as Jean Innes) The Wishing Stone, 1976; Nightmares, 1977; The Tender Trap, 1977; Roses All the Way, 1978; (as Jean Innes) The Dark Stranger, 1979; The Tally-Man, 1979; Lady of the Manor, 1979; Cobden's Cottage, 1979; Rainbow's End, 1979; (as Rowena Summers) Blackmaddie, 1980; Anchor Man, 1980; Dangerous Enchantment, 1980; (as Jean Innes) Silver Lady, 1981; (as Sally Blake) The Devil's Kiss, 1981; The Kissing Time, 1982; (as Rowena Summers) The Savage Moon, 1982; Love's Sweet Music, 1982; (as Sally Blake) Moonlight Mirage, 1982; The Spider's Web, 1982; The Language of Love, 1982; (as Jean Innes) Scent of Jasmine, 1982; (as Jean Innes) Enchanted Island, 1982; (as Jean Innes) Legacy of Love, 1982; (as Jean Innes) Seeker of Dreams, 1983; Taste the Wine, 1983; (as Rowena Summers) The Sweet Red Earth, 1983; Partners in Love, 1984; (as Rowena Summers) Willow Harvest, 1984; Scarlet Rebel, 1985; Golden Destiny, 1986; The Craft of Writing Romance (non-fiction), 1986; (as Rowena Summers) Killigrew Clay, 1986; (as Rowena Summers) Clay Country, 1987; (as Rowena Summers) Family Ties, 1988; Writing Step by Step (non-fiction), 1988; All in the April Morning, 1989; (as Jean Innes) Buccanneer's Bride, 1989; (as Sally Blake) Outback Woman, 1990; The Bannister Girls, 1990. Add: 2 Kingfisher Rd., Worle, Weston-super-Mare, Avon, England.

SAUNDERS, (Sir) Owen (Alfred). British, b. 1904. Sciences (general). Prof. of Mechanical Engineering Emeritus, Imperial Coll. of Science and Technology, Univ. of London, since 1965 (Prof., 1946–65; Vice-Chancellor, Univ. of London, 1965–69). *Publs:* The Calculation of Heat Transfer, 1932; An Introduction to Heat Transfer, 1952. Add: Oakbank, Sea Lane, Middleton-on-Sea, Sussex, England.

SAUNDERS, Wes. *See* **BOUNDS,** Sydney.

SAUVAIN, Philip Arthur. British, b. 1933. Children's non-fiction, Environmental science/Ecology, Geography, History, Humanities (general). Freelance writer. Head of Geography Dept., Steyning Grammar Sch., Sussex, 1957–61, and Penistone Grammar Sch., nr. Sheffield, 1961–63; Sr. Lectr. in Geography, James Graham Coll., Leeds, 1963–68; Head of Environmental Studies Dept., Charlotte Mason Coll. of Education, Ambleside, 1968–74. *Publs:* A Map Reading Companion, 1961; A Geographical Field Study Companion, 1964; Exploring at Home, 1966; Exploring Britain, 1966; Exploring the World, 1967; Hulton's Practical Geography (4 books), 1969–72; Discovery series (6 books), 1970; Lively History series (4 books), 1970–72; The Great Wall of China, 1972; The First Men on the Moon, 1972; A First Look at Maps, 1973; Exploring the World of Man series (10 books), 1973–77; Breakaway series (8 books), 1973–76; Environment Books: First Series (4 books), 1974, Second Series (4 books), 1978; Looking Around Town and Country, 1975; A First Look at Winds (Dinosaurs, Discoveries, Rain, Ice and Snow), 5 vols., 1975–78; Imagining the Past: First Series (6 books), 1976, Second Series (6 books), 1979; Looking Back, 1977; Macmillan Local Studies Kit, 1979; Looking Around Cards, 1979; Certificate Mapwork, 1980; The British Isles, 1980; Story of Britain series (4 books), 1980; Science Discussion Pictures, 1981, 1983; Britain's Living Heritage, 1982; History of Britain (4 books), 1982; Theatre, 1983; Macmillan Junior Geography (4 books), 1983; Hulton New Geographies (5 books), 1983; History Map Books (2 books), 1983, 1985; Hulton New Histories (5 books), 1984, 1985; France and the French, 1985;

European and World History 1815-1919, 1985; Modern World History 1919 Onwards, 1985; How History Began, 1985; Castles and Crusaders, 1986; What to Look For (series; 4 books), 1986; British Economic and Social History, 2 vols., 1987; Wind and Water Power, 1987; Wood and Coal, 1987; Carrying Energy, 1987; Oil and Natural Gas, 1987; GCSE History Companions (3 books), 1988; Mine, 1989. Add: 70 Finborough Rd., Stowmarket, Suffolk 1P14 1PU, England.

SAVA, George. British (born Russian), b. 1903. Novels/Short stories, History, Medicine/Health, Politics/Government, Autobiography/Memoirs/Personal. Consulting surgeon. *Publs:* The Hunting Knife, 1937; Beauty from the Surgeon's Knife, 1938; A Surgeon's Destiny, 1939; Donkey's Serenade, 1940; Twice the Clock Round, 1941; A Ring at the Door, 1941; Surgeon's Symphony, 1944; Russia Triumphant, 1943; A Tale of Ten Cities 1943; They Stayed in London, 1943; Valley of Forgotten People, 1943; The Chetniks; Rasputin Speaks; School for War, 1943; War Without Guns, 1944; Land Fit for Heroes, 1945; Link of Two Hearts, 1945; Gissy, 1946; Call it Life, 1946; The Knife Heals Again, 1948; The Way of a Surgeon, 1949; Strange Cases, 1950; A Doctor's Odyssey, 1951; Patients' Progress, 1952; A Surgeon Remembers, 1953; Surgeon Under Capricorn, 1954; The Lure of Surgery, 1955; A Surgeon at Large, 1957; All This and Surgery Too, 1958; Appointments in Rome, 1963; A Surgeon in New Zealand, 1964; A Surgeon in Cyprus, 1966; The Gates of Heaven are Narrow, 1968; A Surgeon in Australia; Alias Doctor Holtzman, 1968; A Skeleton for My Mate, 1971; The Beloved Nemesis, 1971; The Imperfect Surgeon; The Sins of Andrea, 1972; On the Wings of Angeles, 1972; Tell Your Grief Softly, 1972; Return from the Valley, 1973; Pretty Polly, 1976; Of Men and Medicine, 1976; Mary Mary Quite Contrary, 1977; Cruasader's Clinic, 1977; No Man is Perfect, 1978; A Surgeon and His Knife, 1978; A Stranger in His Skull, 1979; Secret Surgeon, 1979; Crimson Eclipse, 1980; Betrayal in Style, 1984; Double Identity, 1984; A Smile Through Tears, 1985; Bill of Indictment, 1986. Add: c/o A.P. Watt Ltd., 26-28 Bedford Row, London WC1R 4HL, England.

SAVAGE, Ernest. American, b. 1918. Mystery/Crime/Suspense. *Publs:* Two If by Sea, 1982. Add: 6104 Oliver Rd., Paradise, Calif. 95969, U.S.A.

SAVERY, Constance Winifred. British, b. 1897. Novels/Short stories, Children's fiction, Biography. *Publs:* Forbidden Doors (in U.S. as Tenthragon), 1929; Nicolas Chooses White May, 1930; There Was a Key (in U.S. as Pippin's House), 1930; Peter of Yellow Gates, 1935; Moonshine in Candle Street, 1937; Danny and the Alabaster Box, 1937; Green Emeralds for the King (in U.S. as Emeralds for the King), 1938; Enemy Brothers, 1943; The Good Ship Red Lily (in U.K. as Flight to Freedom), 1944; Blue Fields, 1947; Dark House on the Moss, 1948; Up a Winding Stair, 1949; Three Houses in Beverley Road, 1950; Redhead at School, 1951; Scarlet Plume, 1953; Meg Plays Fair, 1953; Young Elizabeth Green, 1954; Five Wonders for Wyn, 1955; Tabby Kitten, 1956; Welcome, Santza, 1956; Four Lost Lambs, 1957; Thistledown Tony, 1957; The Boy from Brittany, 1957; To the City of Gold, 1958; In Apple Alley, 1958; Magic in My Shoes, 1959; The Sea Urchins, 1959; Rebel Jacqueline, 1960; The [Reb] and the Redcoats, 1961; All Because of Sixpence, 1961; The White Kitling, 1962; The Royal Caravan, 1963; Joric and the Dragon, 1964; The Sea Queen, 1965; Please Buy My Pearls, 1965; The Golden Cap, 1966; The Strawberry Feast, 1967; The Silver Angel, 1968; Lavender's Tree, 1969; The Sapphire Ring, 1969; Gilly's Tower, 1969; The City of Flowers, 1969; God's Arctic Adventurer (biography), 1970; Drifting Sands, 1971; No King But Christ, 1976. Add: Cherry Trees, 5 Garden Close, Dumbleton, Nr. Evesham, Worcs. W11 6TT, England.

SAVITT, Sam. American. Children's fiction, Animals/Pets, Sports/Physical education/Keeping fit, Documentaries/Reportage. Freelance writer and artist. *Publs:* Step-A-Bit, 1956; Midnight, 1957; There was a Horse, 1961; Around the World with Horses, 1962; Rodeo: Cowboys, Bulls, and Broncos, 1963; Sam Savitt Guide to Horses, 1963; Vicki and the Black Horse, 1964; Day at the L.B.J. Ranch, 1965; America's Horses, 1966; Horse of the West, 1966; Equestrian Olympic Sketchbook, 1968; Sam Savitt's True Horse Stories, 1970; Sam Savitt Horse Information Chart, 1970; Sam Savitt World of Ponies, 1972; Wild Horse Running, 1973; (with Suzanne Wilding) Ups and Downs, 1973; Sam Savitt Horse Through Time, 1974; (with Herb Marlin) What to Do for Your Horse Before the Vet Comes, 1975; Vicki and the Brown Mare, 1976; (with William Steinkraus) Great Horses of the U.S. Equestrian Team, 1977; The Dingle Ridge Fox and Other Stories, 1978; Springfellow, 1978; (with Robert Kraus) Springfellow: Foal's First Day, 1979; Draw Horses with Sam Savitt, 1980; One Horse, One Hundred Miles, One Day, 1980; Sam Savitt Draft Horse, 1981; A Horse to Remember, 1984; Sam Savitt Guide to Polo, 1987. Add: Box 302, North Salem, N.Y. 10560,

U.S.A.

SAVORY, Teo. American. Novels/Short stories, Poetry, Translations. Ed.-in-Chief, Unicorn Press and Unicorn Journal, Santa Barbara, Calif., later Greensboro, N.C., since 1966. *Publs:* The Landscape of Dreams, 1960; The Single Secret, 1961; A Penny for the Guy (in U.S. as A Penny for His Pocket), 1963; Traveler's Palm: A Poetry Sequence, 1967; The House Wrecker, 1967; A Christmas Message Received During a Car Ride, 1967; (trans.) Corbière, Supervielle, Prévert, Jammes, Michaux, Guillevic, Queneau, Eich, 8 vols., 1967–71; Snow Vole: A Poetry Sequence, 1968; To a High Place (novel), 1971; (trans.) The Cell, by Horst Bienek, 1972; Transitions, 1973; Dragons of Mist and Torrent, 1974; (trans.) Selected Guillevic, 1974; (trans.) Zen Poems, by Nhat Hanh, 1974; A Clutch of Fables, 1975; (trans.) Euclidians, by Guillevic, 1975; Stonecrop (novel), 1977; A Childhood (novella), 1978; (trans.) Words for All Weather, by Prévert, 1979; To Raise Rainbow (novel), 1980; West to East (short stories), 1989. Add: Unicorn Press Inc., P.O. Box 3307, Greensboro, NC. 27402, U.S.A.

SAWYER, John. Writes with Nancy (Buckingham) Sawyer under joint pseuds, Nancy Buckingham, Nancy John, and Erica Quest. British, b. 1919. Historical/Romance/Gothic. Full-time writer. Former dir. of a London advertising agency. *Publs:* all with Nancy Sawyer—(as Nancy Buckingham) Victim of Love (in U.S. as The Hour Before Moonrise), 1967; (as Nancy Buckingham) Cloud over Malverton, 1967; (as Nancy Buckingham) Heart of Marble (in U.S. as Storm in the Mountains), 1967; (as Nancy Buckingham) Romantic Journey (in U.S. as The Legend of Baverstock Manor), 1968; (as Nancy Buckingham) The Dark Summer, 1968; (as Nancy Buckingham) Call of Glengarron, 1968; (as Nancy Buckingham) Kiss of Hot Sun, 1969; (as Nancy Buckingham) Shroud of Silence (in U.S. as The Secret of the Ghostly Shroud), 1970; (as Nancy Buckingham) The House Called Edenhythe, 1970; (as Nancy Buckingham) Return to Vienna, 1971; (as Nancy Buckingham) Quest for Alexis, 1973; (as Nancy Buckingham) Valley of the Ravens, 1973; (as Nancy Buckingham) The Jade Dragon, 1974; (as Nancy Buckingham) The Other Cathy, 1978; (as Erica Quest) The Silver Castle, 1978; (as Nancy Buckingham) Vienna Summer, 1979; (as Erica Quest) The October Cabaret, 1979; (as Nancy Buckingham) Marianna, 1981; (as Erica Quest) Design for Murder, 1981; (as Nancy John) The Spanish House, 1981; (as Nancy John) Tormenting Flame, 1981; (as Nancy John) To Trust Tomorrow, 1981; (as Nancy John) A Man for Always, 1981; (as Nancy John) So Many Tomorrows, 1982; (as Nancy John) Web of Passion, 1982; (as Nancy John) Outback Summer, 1982; (as Nancy John) Summer Rhapsody, 1983; (as Nancy John) Never Too Late, 1983; (as Nancy John) Make-Believe Bride, 1983; (as Nancy John) Dream of Yesterday, 1984; (as Nancy John) Window to Happiness, 1984; (as Nancy John) Night with a Stranger, 1984; (as Nancy John) Champagne Nights, 1985; (as Nancy John) Rendezvous, 1985; (as Nancy John) The Moongate Wish, 1985; (as Nancy John) Lookalike Love, 1986; (as Nancy John) Secret Love, 1986. Add: c/o A.M. Heath, 40-42 William IV St., London WC2N 4DD, England.

SAWYER, Nancy (Buckingham). Writes with John Sawyer under joint pseuds. Nancy Buckingham, Nancy John, and Erica Quest. British, b. c1924. Historical/Romance/Gothic.Full-time writer.Vice-Pres., Romantic Novelists Assn. Formerly medical social worker. *Publs:* all with John Sawyer—(as Nancy Buckingham) Victim of Love (in U.S. as The Hour Before Moonrise), 1967; (as Nancy Buckingham) Cloud over Malverton, 1967; (as Nancy Buckingham) Heart of Marble (in U.S. as Storm in the Mountains), 1967; (as Nancy Buckingham) Romantic Journey (in U.S. as The Legend of Baverstock Manor), 1968; (as Nancy Buckingham) The Dark Summer, 1968; (as Nancy Buckingham) Call of Glengarron, 1968; (as Nancy Buckingham) Kiss of Hot Sun, 1969; (as Nancy Buckingham) Shroud of Silence (in U.S. as Secret of the Ghostly Shroud), 1970; (as Nancy Buckingham) The House Called Edenhythe, 1970; (as Nancy Buckingham) Return to Vienna, 1971; (as Nancy Buckingham) Quest for Alexis, 1973; (as Nancy Buckingham) Valley of the Ravens, 1973; (as Nancy Buckingham) The Jade Dragon, 1974; (as Nancy Buckingham) The Other Cathy, 1978; (as Erica Quest) The Silver Castle, 1978; (as Nancy Buckingham) Vienna Summer, 1979; (as Erica Quest) The October Cabaret, 1979; (as Nancy Buckingham) Marianna, 1981; (as Erica Quest) Design for Murder, 1981; (as Nancy John) The Spanish House, 1981; (as Nancy John) Tormenting Flame, 1981; (as Nancy John) To Trust Tomorrow, 1981; (as Nancy John) A Man for Always, 1981; (as Nancy John) So Many Tomorrows, 1982; (as Nancy John) Outback Summer, 1982; (as Nancy John) Web of Passion, 1982; (as Nancy John) Summer Rhapsody, 1983; (as Nancy John) Never Too Late, 1983; (as Nancy John) Make-Believe Bride, 1983; (as Nancy John) Dream of Yesterday, 1984; (as Nancy John) Window to Happiness, 1984; (as Nancy John) Night with a Stranger, 1984; (as Nancy John) Champagne Nights, 1985; (as Nancy John) Rendezvous, 1985; (as Nancy John) The Moongate Wish, 1985; (as Nancy John) Lookalike Love, 1986; (as Nancy John) Secret Love, 1986. Add: c/o A.M. Heath, 40-42 William IV St., London WC2N 4DD, England.

SAWYER, Roger. British, b. 1931. Civil liberties/Human rights, History, Race relations. Examiner in English, Univ. of London, since 1965. Asst. Master, Forton House Preparatory Sch., Chard, Somerset, 1950–52; Housemaster, Blue Coat Sch., Edgbaston, Birmingham, 1958–60; Deputy Head, 1960–77, and Headmaster, 1977–83, Bembridge Preparatory Sch., Isle of Wight. *Publs:* Casement: The Flawed Hero, 1984; Slavery in the Twentieth Century, 1985; Children Enslaved, 1988. Add: Dover Cottage, Dennet Rd., Bembridge, Isle of Wight PO35 5XD, England.

SAX, Joseph L. American, b. 1936. Environmental science/Ecology, Law. Prof. of Law, Univ. of California, Berkeley, since 1987. Attorney, Washington, D.C., 1959–62; Prof. of Law, Univ. of Colorado, Boulder, 1962–65; Prof. of Law, Univ. of Michigan, Ann Arbor, 1966–86. *Publs:* (with R.E. Clark) Waters and Water Rights, 1967; Water Law, Planning and Policy, 1968; The Environmental Crisis: Man's Struggle to Live with Himself, 1970; Defending The Environment, 1971; Mountains Without Handrails, 1980; Legal Control of Water Resources, 1985.Add: Boalt Hall, Univ. of California, Berkeley, Calif. 94720, U.S.A.

SAXON, Alex. *See* PRONZINI, Bill.

SAXON, Antonia. *See* SACHS, Judith.

SAXTON, Josephine (Howard). British, b. 1935. Science fiction/Fantasy. *Publs:* The Hieros Gamos of Sam and An Smith, 1969; Vector for Seven; or, The Weltanshauung of Mrs. Amelia Mortimer and Friends, 1971; Group Feast, 1971; The Travails of Jane Saint, 1981; The Power of Time and Other Stories, 1985; Little Tours of Hell: Tales of Food and Holidays, 1986; The Queen of the States (novel), 1986. Add: 4 Albany Terrace, Flat 3, Leamington Spa, Warwicks. CV32 5LP, England.

SAXTON, Judith. *See* TURNER, Judy.

SAYLES, John. American, b. 1950. Novels/Short stories, Plays/screenplays. *Publs:* Pride of the Bimbos (novel), 1975; Union Dues (novel), 1977; Anarchists' Convention (short stories), 1979; screenplays—Piranah, 1978; The Lady in Red, 1979; Alligator, 1980; A Perfect Match, 1980; Battle Beyond the Stars, 1980; The Return of the Secaucus Seven (also dir.), 1980; The Howling, 1981; The Challenge, 1982; Lianna (also dir.), 1983; Baby, It's You (also dir.), 1983; The Brother from Another Planet (also dir.), 1984; Enormous Changes at the Right Moment, 1985; other—Thinking in Pictures: The Making of the Movie Matewan, 1987. Add: c/o Scribner's, 866 Third Ave., New York, N.Y. 10022, U.S.A.

SAYLOR, J(ohn) Galen. American, b. 1902. Education, Genealogy/Heraldry. Prof. Emeritus of Secondary Education, Univ. of Nebraska, Lincoln, since 1971 (Prof., 1940–71).Dir. of Research, Nebraska State Education, 1936–38; Research Assoc., Teachers Coll., Columbia Univ., NYC, 1938–40; Fulbright Lectr. in Education, Univ. of Jyvaskyla, Finland, 1962–63. *Publs:* Factors Associated with Participation in Cooperative Programs of Curriculum Planning, 1941; (with W.M. Alexander) Secondary Education: Basic Principles and Practices, 1950; (with W.M. Alexander) Curriculum Planning for Better Teaching and Learning, 1954; (with W.M. Alexander) Modern Secondary Education: Basic Principles and Practices, 1959; (with W.M. Alexander) Curriculum Planning for Modern Schools, 1966; (with W.M. Alexander) The High School: Today and Tomorrow, 1971; (with W.M. Alexander) Planning Curriculum for Schools, 1974, 2nd ed. (with W.M. Alexander and Arthur J. Lewis) 1981; Antecedent Developments in the Movement to Competency-Based Programs of Teachers Education, 1976; Who Planned the Curriculum: A Curriculum Plans Reservoir Model, with Historical Examples, 1982; A History of the Department of Secondary Education, University of Nebraska, Lincoln, 1871-1980, 1982; A Saylor Lineage, 1983; A Smith Lineage, 1985; The Gilchrist Lineage, 1987.Add: 3001 S. 51st St., No. 377, Lincoln, Nebr. 68506, U.S.A.

SCAGLIONE, Aldo. American, b. 1925. Language/Linguistics, Literature. Prof. of Italian Studies, New York Univ., since 1987 Prof., Univ. of Toulouse, 1949–51, Univ. of Chicago, 1951–52, Univ. of California, Berkeley, 1952–68, Yale Univ., 1954–65, and City Univ. of N.Y., 1971–72; W.R. Kenan Prof. of Romance Languages and Comparative Literature, Univ. of North Carolina, Chapel Hill, 1968–87. *Publs:* (ed.) Orlando Innamorato, Amorum Libri, by Matteo Maria Boiardo, 1951,

1963; Nature and Love in the Late Middle Ages: An Essay on the Cultural Context of the Decameron, 1963; Ars Grammatica: A Bibliographic Survey, Two Essays on the Grammar of the Latin and Italian Subjunctive, and A Note on the Ablative Absolute, 1970; The Classical Theory of Composition from Its Origins to the Present, 1972; (ed.) Francis Petrarch, Six Centuries Later: A Symposium, 1975; (ed.) Ariosto 1974 in America, 1976; The Theory of German Word Order, 1981; Komponierte Prosa von der Antike bis zur Gegenwart, 2 vols., 1981; (ed.) The Emergence of National Languages, 1983; The Liberal Arts and the Jesuit College System, 1986. Add: Room 600, 19 University Place, New York Univ., New York, N.Y. 10003, U.S.A.

SCALAPINO, Robert Anthony. American, b. 1919. International relations/Current affairs, Politics/Government. Robson Research Prof. of Government, since 1977, and Dir., Inst. of East Asian Studies, Univ. of California, Berkeley (Asst. Prof., 1949–51; Assoc. Prof., 1951–56; Prof. of Political Science, 1956–77). Ed., Asian Survey journal, since 1962. Instr., Harvard Univ., Cambridge, Mass., 1948–49. *Publs:* Democracy and the Party Movement in Pre-War Japan, 1953; (with J. Masumi) Parties and Politics in Contemporary Japan, 1962; (ed.) North Korea Today, 1964; The Japanese Communist Movement 1920-1966, 1968; (with Chong-Sik Lee) Communism in Korea, 2 vols., 1972; (ed. and contrib.) Elites in the People's Republic of China, 1972; American-Japanese Relations in a Changing Era, 1972; Asia and the Major Powers, 1972; Asia and the Road Ahead, 1975; (ed.) The Foreign Policy of Modern Japan, 1977; The Early Japanese Labor Movement, 1984; (with G.T. Yu) Modern China and Its Revolutionary Process, vol. I, 1985; Major Power Relations in Northeast Asia, 1987. Add: Inst. of East Asian Studies, Univ. of California, Berkeley, Calif. 94720, U.S.A.

SCAMMON, Richard M. American, b. 1915. Politics/Government. Dir., Elections Research Center, Washington, D.C., 1955–61, and since 1965. Trustee, National Council on Public Polls (Pres., 1969–70). Chief, Div. of Research for Western Europe, U.S. Dept. of State, 1948–55; Dir. of the Census (U.S.), 1961–65; Chmn., President's Commn. on Registration and Voting Participation, 1963, and Select Commn. on Western Hemisphere Immigration, 1966–68; Member, U.S. Delegation to the 1973 U.N. General Assembly; Member, U.S. Delegation to observe Salvadoran Elections, 1982; Member, Kissinger Commn. on Central America, 1983–84. *Publs:* (ed.) America Votes, vols. I-XVIII, 1956–89; (ed.) America at the Polls, 1965; (co-author) This U.S.A., 1965; The Real Majority, 1970; America at the Polls 2, 1988. Add: 5508 Greystone St., Chevy Chase, Md. 20815, U.S.A.

SCANLAN, Arthur Brian. New Zealander, b. 1907. History. Ed., Taranaki Herald, 1937–64. *Publs:* Mountain of Maoriland, 1949; Pukekura Park and Brooklands, 1950; Egmont: The Story of a Mountain, 1961; (ed. and co-author) Mt. Egmont Handbook, 1964, 1970; 100 Years of Firefighting, 1966; Hospital on the Hill, 1967; Historic New Plymouth, 1968; Harbour at the Sugar Loaves, 1975; Taranaki's First Railway, 1977; Pukekura, 1978; Taranaki People and Places, 1985. Add: 30 Holsworthy Rd., New Plymouth, New Zealand.

SCANNELL, Vernon. British, b. 1922. Novels/Short stories, Poetry, Literature, Autobiography/Memoirs/Personal. Former amateur and professional boxer; Teacher of English, Hazlewood Sch., Limpsfield, Surrey, 1955–62. *Publs:* Graves and Resurrections, 1948; The Fight, 1953; The Wound and the Scar, 1954; A Mortal Pitch, 1957; The Masks of Love, 1960; The Face of the Enemy, 1961; The Dividing Night, 1962; A Sense of Danger, 1962; Edward Thomas, 1962; (ed. with P. Beer and T. Hughes) New Poems, 1962; The Big Time, 1965; Walking Wounded, 1965; Epithets of War, 1969; Mastering the Craft, 1970; The Dangerous Ones, 1970; Selected Poems, 1971; The Tiger and the Rose: An Autobiography, 1971; The Loving Game, 1974; Not Without Glory: Poetry of World War II, 1976; A Proper Gentleman, 1977; A Lonely Game (juvenile), 1979; New and Collected Poems, 1980; Winterlude, 1982; Ring of Truth (novel), 1983; Funeral Games (poems), 1987; (ed.) Sporting Literature, 1987; Argument at Kings (autobiography), 1987. Add: 51 North St., Otley, W. Yorks, LS21 1AH, England.

SCARBOROUGH, William Kauffman. American, b. 1933. History. Prof. of History since 1976, and Chmn. of the Dept. since 1980, Univ. of Southern Mississippi, Hattiesburg (Assoc. Prof., 1964–76). Asst. Prof. of History, Millsaps Coll., Jackson, Miss., 1961–63, and Northeast Louisiana Univ., Monroe, 1963–64, and Pres., Mississippi Historical Soc., 1979–80. *Publs:* The Overseer: Plantation Management in the Old South, 1966; (ed.) The Diary of Edmund Ruffin, vol. I, Toward Independence, 1972, vol. II, The Years of Hope, 1976, vol. III, A Dream Shattered, 1989. Add: Southern Station, Box 8371, Hattiesburg, Miss. 39406, U.S.A.

SCARF, Maggie. American, b. 1932. Psychiatry, Psychology. Assoc. Fellow, Jonathan Edwards Coll., Yale Univ., New Haven, Conn. Contributing Ed., The New Republic mag. *Publs:* Meet Benjamin Franklin, 1968; Antarctica: Bottom of the World, 1970; Body, Mind, Behavior, 1976; Unfinished Business: Pressure Points in the Lives of Women, 1980; Intimate Partners: Patterns in Love and Marriage, 1987. Add: 88 Blake Road, Hamden, Conn. 06517, U.S.A.

SCARFE, Wendy (Elizabeth). Australian, b. 1933. Novels/Short stories, Poetry, Race relations, Third World problems, Biography. Secondary sch. teacher, Warrnambool High Sch., since 1976. Taught at St. Annes Coll., 1972–76. *Publs:* Shadow and Flowers (poetry), 1974; The Lotus Throne (novel), 1976; Neither Here Nor There (novel), 1984; all the following with Allan John Scarfe—A Mouthful of Petals, 1967; Tiger on a Rein, 1969; People of India, 1972; The Black Australians, 1974; Victims or Bludgers? Case Studies in Poverty in Australia, 1974; J.P., His Biography, 1975; Victims or Bludgers? A Poverty Inquiry for Schools, 1981; Labor's Titan: The Story of Percy Brookfield 1878-1921, 1983. Add: 8 Bostock St., Warrnambool, Vic. 3280, Australia.

SCARGILL, David Ian. British, b. 1935. Geography, Travel/Exploration/Adventure. Univ. Lectr., Oxford Univ., and Coll. Fellow, St. Edmund Hall, Oxford, since 1962. *Publs:* Economic Geography of France, 1968; (ed.) The Massif Central, 1973; (ed.) North East England, 1973; (ed.) The Mezzogiorno, 1973; (ed.) The Paris Basin, 1973; (ed.) Randstad Holland, 1973; The Dordogne Region of France, 1974; (ed.) Scotland's Highlands and Islands, 1974; (ed.) Northern Ireland, 1974; (ed.) The Scandinavian Northlands, 1974; (ed.) North Rhine Westphalia, 1974; (ed.) The Eastern Alps, 1975; (ed.) The Franco-Belgian Border Region, 1975; (ed.) Andalusia, 1975; (ed.) The Lower Rhone and Marseille, 1975; (ed.) Poland's Western and Northern Territories, 1975; (ed.) The Moscow city Region, 1976; (ed.) Saar-Lorraine, 1976; (ed.) London: Metropolis and Region, 1976; The Form of Cities, 1979; (with A.G. Crosby) Oxford and Its Countryside, 1982; Urban France, 1983. Add: St. Edmund Hall, Oxford, England.

SCARROTT, Michael. *See* **FISHER**, A. Stanley T.

SCARRY, Richard. American, b. 1919. Children's fiction. *Publs:* Tinker and Tanker series, 7 vols., 1960–78; Best Ever series, 7 vols., 1963–79; Busy, Busy World, 1965; Storybook Dictionary, 1966; What Do People Do All Day, 1968; Look and Learn Library, 1971; Great Big Air Book, 1971; ABC Workbook, 1971; Funniest Storybook Ever, 1972; Great Big Mystery Book, 1972; Please and Thank You Book, 1973; Find Your ABC's, 1973; Cars and Trucks and Things That Go, 1974; Animal Nursery Tales, 1975; Look-Look Books, 1976; Color Books, 1976; Early Words, 1976; Busiest People Ever, 1976; Best Make-It Book Ever, 1977; Postman Pig, 1978; Toy Book, 1978; Lowly Worm series, 1979; Easy to Read Books, 1981. Add: Schwyzerhus, 3780 Gstaad, Switzerland.

SCHACHT, Richard. American, b. 1941. Philosophy. Prof. of Philosophy, Univ. of Illinois at Urbana-Champaign. *Publs:* Alienation, 1970; Hegel and After, 1975; Nietzsche, 1983; Classical Modern Philosophers, 1984. Add: Dept. of Philosophy, 105 Gregory Hall, 810 S. Wright St., Univ. of Illinois, Urbana, Ill. 61801, U.S.A.

SCHAEFFER, Susan Fromberg. American, b. 1941. Novels/Short stories, Children's fiction, Poetry. Prof., Brooklyn Coll., N.Y., since 1974 (Asst. Prof., 1966–72; Assoc. Prof., 1973–74). Asst. Prof., Illinois Inst. of Technology, Chicago, 1964–66. *Publs:* The Witch and the Weather Report (poetry), 1972; Falling, 1973; Anya, 1974; Granite Lady (poetry), 1974; Rhymes and Runes of the Toad (poetry), 1975; Alphabet for the Lost Years (poetry), 1976; Time in Its Flight, 1978; The Bible of the Beasts of the Little Field (poetry), 1980; The Queen of Egypt (short fiction), 1980; Love (novel), 1981; The Madness of a Seduced Woman (novel), 1983; Mainland (novel), 1985; The Injured Party (novel), 1986; The Dragons of North Chittendon (for children), 1986; The Four Hoods and Great Dog (for children), 1988; Buffalo Afternoon (novel), 1989. Add: c/o Russell and Volkening Inc., 50 W. 29th St., New York, N.Y. 10001, U.S.A.

SCHALK, Adolph F(rancis). American, b. 1923. Social commentary/phenomena, Documentaries/Reportage. Ed., Today mag., Chicago, 1951–55; Ed., The Bridge, Hamburg, W. Germany, 1957–62. *Publs:* Eyes On Modern World, 1964; The Germans, 1971, 1972; Germans in

America, 1973. Add: CH 6579 Indemini, Ticino, Switzerland.

SCHALLER, George B(eals). American, b. 1933. Zoology. Dir. for Science, Wildlife Conservation International, N.Y. Zoological Soc., since 1979 (assoc. with the Soc. since 1966). Research Assoc., Johns Hopkins Univ., Baltimore, 1963–66. *Publs:* The Mountain Gorilla: Ecology and Behavior, 1963; The Year of the Gorilla, 1964; The Deer and the Tiger: A Study of Wildlife in India, 1967; (with Millicent E. Selsam) The Tiger: Its Life in the Wild (juvenile), 1969; The Serengeti Lion: A Study of Predator-Prey Relations, 1972; Golden Shadows, Flying Hooves, 1973; Mountain Monarchs: Wild Sheep and Goats of the Himalaya, 1977; Stones of Silence: Journeys in the Himalaya, 1980; (with others) The Giant Pandas of Wolong, 1985. Add: Wildlife Conservation Intnl., New York Zoological Soc., Bronx Park, N.Y. 10460, U.S.A.

SCHAMA, Simon (Michael). American (born British), b. 1945. History. Prof. of History, Harvard Univ., Cambridge, Mass., since 1980. Fellow and Dir. of Studies in History, Christ's Coll., Cambridge, 1966–76; Fellow of Brasenose Coll., Oxford, 1976–80. *Publs:* (ed. with Eric Homberger and William Janeway) The Cambridge Mind, 1970; Patriots and Liberators: Revolution in the Netherlands 1780-1813, 1977; Two Rothschilds and the Land of Israel, 1979; Affluence and Anxiety: A Social Interpretation of Dutch Culture in Its Golden Age, 1983; The Embarrassment of Riches: An Interpretation of Dutch Culture in the Golden Age, 1987; Citizens: A Chronicle of the French Revolution, 1989. Add: c/o Knopf Inc., 201 E. 50th St., New York, N.Y. 10022, U.S.A.

SCHAPIRO, Meyer. American (b. Russian), b. 1904. Art. Prof. Emeritus of Fine Arts, Columbia Univ., since 1973 (Lectr., 1928–36; Asst. Prof., 1936–46; Assoc. Prof., 1946–52; Prof. of Art History and Archaeology, 1952–65; Univ. Prof., 1965–73). *Publs:* The Romanesque Sculpture of Moissac, 1931; Van Gogh, 1950; Paul Cézanne, 1952; The Parma Ildefonsus: A Romanesque Illuminated Manuscript from Cluny and Related Work, 1964; Words and Pictures, 1973; Selected Papers: vol. I, Romanesque Art, 1976, vol. II, Modern Art, 1978, and vol. III, Late Antique, Early Christian and Medieval Art, 1980; Style, Artiste et Société 1983. Add: 279 W. 4th St., New York, N.Y. 10014, U.S.A.

SCHAPSMEIER, Edward Lewis. American, b. 1927. History, Biography. Distinguished Prof. of History, Illinois State Univ., Normal, since 1967. Instr. in History, Ohio State Univ., Columbus, 1965–66. *Publs:* with Frederick Schapsmeier—Henry A. Wallace of Iowa: The Agrarian Years 1910-1940, 1968; Walter Lippmann: Philosopher-Journalist, 1969; Henry A. Wallace and the War Years 1940-1965, 1970: Abundant Harvests: The Story of American Agriculture, 1973; Encyclopedia of American Agricultural History, 1975; Agriculture in the West, 1979; Dictionary of Political Parties and Civic Action Groups, 1980; Dirkson of Illinois, 1985; Date with Destiny: A Political Biography of Gerald R. Ford, 1987. Add: 3103 Winchester Dr., Bloomington, Ill. 61704, U.S.A.

SCHAPSMEIER, Frederick H(erman). American, b. 1927. History, Biography. Rosebush Prof. of History, Univ. of Wisconsin-Oshkosh, since 1980 (Assoc. Prof., 1965–70; Prof. since 1970). Lectr., 1963–64, and Asst. Prof. of American History, 1964–65, Univ. of Southern California, Los Angeles. *Publs:* with Edward L. Schapsmeier—Henry A. Wallace of Iowa: The Agrarian years 1910-1940, 1968; Walter Lippmann: Philosopher-Journalist 1969; Henry A. Wallace and the War Years 1940-1965, 1970; Abundant Harvests: The Story of American Agriculture, 1973; Dictionary of American Agricultural History, 1975; Agriculture in the West, 1979; Dictionary of Political Parties and Civic Action Groups, 1980; Dirkson of Illinois, 1985; Date with Destiny: The Political Career of Gerald R. Ford, 1987. Add: Dept. of History, Univ. of Wisconsin, Oshkosh, Wisc. 54901, U.S.A.

SCHARF, Aaron. American, b. 1922. Art, Photography. Head of the Dept. of Art History and Complementary Studies, St. Martin's Sch of Art, London, 1961–69; Prof. of the History of Art, The Open Univ., Milton Keynes, England, 1969–82. Member, Photography Sub-Cttee., Arts Council of Great Britain, 1972–78. *Publs:* Creative Photography, 1965; Art and Photography, 1968; (ed. with Christopher Harvie and Graham Martin) Industrialisation and Culture, 1830-1914, 1971, 1983; (with Jiri Mucha and Marina Henderson) Alphonse Mucha, 1971; Introduction to Art, 1971, 1978; Art and Industry, 1971; Art and Politics in France: From David to Daumier, 1972; The Roots of Modern Art, 1975; Pioneers of Photography, 1975; A New Beginning: Primitivism and Science in Post-Impressionist Art, 1976; The Emerging of Modern Art in the Early Twentieth Century, 1976; Art in the French Revolution 1848-1851, 1976; William Hogarth, 1979. Add: Tithe Barn Lane, Briston, Melton Constable, Norfolk, England.

SCHARFF, Edward E. American, b. 1946. Business/Trade/Industry, History. Asst. Managing Ed., Institutional Investor, NYC, since 1983. Reporter, Washington Star, 1970–78, Staff Writer, 1978–80, and Economy and Business Writer, 1980–82, Money, NYC. *Publs:* World Power: The Making of the Wall Street Journal, 1986. Add: 41 Hillcrest Park Rd., Old Greenwich, Conn. 06870, U.S.A.

SCHECHTER, Ruth Lisa. American. Poetry. Founder and Ed., Croton Review. Consultant Poetry Therapist, Odyssey House, NYC, 1971–78. *Publs:* Near the Wall of Lion Shadows, 1969, 1970; Movable Parts, 1971; Suddenly Thunder, 1972; offshore, 1974; Double Exposure, 1978; Clockworks, 1979; Speedway, 1983; Chords and Other Poems, 1986; Many Rooms in a Winter Night, 1989. Add: 9 Van Cortland Pl., Croton-on-Hudson, N.Y. 10520, U.S.A.

SCHEDVIN, Carl Boris. Australian, b. 1936. Economics, History. Prof. of Economic History, Univ. of Melbourne, since 1979. Lectr., then Sr. Lectr. in Economic History, Univ. of Sydney, 1966–73; Official War Historian, 1968–73; Reader in Economic History, Monash Univ., 1973–79. *Publs:* Australia and the Great Depression, 1970; (co-ed.) Urbanization in Australia: The Nineteenth Century, 1974; (co-author) War Economy 1942-45, 1977; (co-ed.) Australian Capital Cities: Historical Essays, 1978; Shaping Science and Industry, 1987; (co-ed.) Australian Financiers: Biographical Essays, 1988. Add: Faculty of Economics, Univ. of Melbourne, Parkville, Vict., Australia 3052.

SCHEELE, Roy. American, b. 1942. Poetry. Poet for the Poet-in-the-Schools Program, Nebraska Arts Council, since 1976; Instr. of English as a Second Language, Midwest Inst. for Intl. Studies, Doane Coll., Crete, Nebr., since 1982. Instr. in English, Univ. of Tennessee at Martin, 1966–68; Research Librarian, City Library, Lincoln, Nebr., 1969–70; Instr. in English, Theodor Heuss Gymnasium, Waltrop, Germany, 1974–75; Lectr. in Classics, Creighton Univ., Omaha, 1977–79; Visiting Instr. in Classics, Univ. of Nebraska, 1980–81. *Publs:* Grams and Epigrams, 1973; Accompanied, 1974; Noticing, 1979; The Sea-Ocean, 1981; Pointing out the Sky, 1985; The Voice We Call Human, 1989. Add: 2020 S. 25th St., Lincoln, Nebr. 68502, U.S.A.

SCHEER, Wilbert E. American, b. 1909. Administration/Management, Language/Linguistics, Personnel management. Faculty member, Northwestern Univ., Evanston, Ill., since 1967. Office Mgr. and Asst. Operations Mgr., McKesson & Robbins, Chicago, 1928–46; Personnel Dir., Illinois Agricultural Assn., Illinois Farm Bureau, 1946–51; Dir. of Personnel, 1951–69, and Editorial and Research Asst., 1969–74, Blue Cross/Blue Shield, Chicago; Teacher, Adult Evening Prog., Central YMCA, 1956–66. *Publs:* You Can Improve Your Communication, 1962; The Art of Successful Self-Expression and Communication, 1965; Personnel Director's Handbook, 1969; Corporate Growth Through Internal Management Development, 1972; How to Develop an Effective Company Growth Plan, 1975; Personnel Administration Handbook, 1979; Outside Influences on Personnel Management, 1981; People Policies: Successful Personnel Management, 1984. Add: 804 Austin Ave., Park Ridge, Ill. 60068, U.S.A.

SCHEFFER, Victor B(lanchard). American, b. 1906. Animals/Pets, Environmental science/Ecology. Biologist, U.S Fish and Wildlife Service, 1937–69; Antarctic Observer, U.S. Arms Control and Disarmament Agency, 1964; Lectr. in Zoology and Forest Resources, Univ. of Washington, Seattle, 1966–72; Chmn., U.S. Marine Mammal Commn., 1973–76. *Publs:* The Year of the Whale, 1969; The Year of the Seal, 1970; The Seeing Eye, 1971; A Voice for Wildlife, 1974; A Natural History of Marine Mammals, 1976; Adventures of a Zoologist, 1980; The Amazing Sea Otter, 1981; Spires of Form, 1983. Add: 14806 S.E. 54th St., Bellevue, Wash. 98006, U.S.A.

SCHEIBER, Harry N. American, b. 1935. History, Politics/Government. Prof. of Law and History, Univ. of California, Berkeley, since 1980. Co-Ed., History of American Economy Series, Johnson Reprint; Member of Editorial Bds., Publius: Journal of Federalism and Reviews in American History. Faculty Member, Dartmouth Coll., Hanover, N.H. 1960–71; Prof. of History, Univ. of California at San Diego, 1971–80. *Publs:* The Wilson Administration and Civil Liberties, 1960; (ed.) United States Economic History, 1964; (co-author) America: Purpose and Power, 1965; The Condition of American Federalism, 1966; (co-author and assoc. ed.) The Frontier in American Development, 1969; (ed.) The Old Northwest, 1969; Ohio Canal Era, 1820-1861, 1969, 1987; (with J. Scheiber) Black Labor in America, 1970; (co-author) Law in American History, 1972; (with J. Shideler) Agriculture in the Development of the Far West, 1975; (co-author) American Economic History, 1976; (co-ed.)

American Law and the Constitutional Order, 1978, 1987; (co-author) Technology, the Economy, and Society: The American Experience, 1987; (ed.) Federalism in Perspective, 1987. Add: Sch. of Law, Univ. of California, Berkaley, Calif. 94720, U.S.A.

SCHELL, Jonathan (Edward). American, b. 1943. Social commentary/phenomena, Documentaries/Reportage. Staff Writer, The New Yorker mag. *Publs:* The Village of Ben Suc (reportage), 1967; The Military Half (reportage), 1968; The Time of Illusion 1975; The Fate of the Earth, 1982; The Abolition, 1984; History in Shermanark: An American Family During the Reagan-Mondale Election, 1987; The Real War: The Classic Reporting on the Vietnam War, 1987. Add: c/o Alfred Knopf, 201 E. 50th St., New York, N.Y. 10022, U.S.A.

SCHELL, Orville (Hickok). American, b. 1940. Environmental science/ Ecology, International relations/Current affairs, Social commentary/phenomena. Member, National Committee on U.S.-China Relations. *Publs:* (ed. with Herbert Franz Schurmann) The China Reader, 1966; (with Frederick Crews) Starting Over, 1970; (with Joseph Esherick) Modern China, 1972; The Town That Fought to Save Itself, 1974; In the People's Republic, 1976; Brown, 1978; Watch Out for the Foreign Guests: China Encounters the West, 1981; Modern Meat, 1984; To Get Rich Is Glorious: China in the 1980's, 1986; Discos and Democracy: China in the Throes of Reform, 1988. Add: Niman-Schell Ranch, Box 56 Overlook Rd., Bolinas, Calif. 94924, U.S.A.

SCHELLENBERG, James A. American, b. 1932. Psychology, Sociology. Prof. of Sociology, Indiana State Univ., Terre Haute, since 1976. Prof. of Sociology, Western Michigan Univ., Kalamazoo, 1969–76. *Publs:* An Introduction to Social Psychology, 1970, 1974; Selected Readings and Projects in Social Psychology, 1971; (ed. with Richard MacDonald) Masters of Social Psychology, 1978; The Science of Conflict 1982; Conflict Between Communities, 1987. Add: 87 Heritage Dr., Terre Haute, Ind 47803, U.S.A.

SCHELLING, Thomas C. American, b. 1921. Economics, International relations/Current affairs, Social sciences. Prof. of Economics since 1958, and Lucius N. Littauer Prof. of Political Economy since 1978, John F. Kennedy Sch. of Govt., Harvard Univ., Cambridge. Assoc. Prof. of Economics, Yale Univ., New Haven, Conn., 1953–58. *Publs:* National Income Behavior, 1951; International Economics, 1958; The Strategy of Conflict, 1960; (with Morton Halperin) Strategy and Arms Control, 1961; Arms and Influence, 1966; Micromotives and Macrobehavior, 1978; (ed.) Incentives for Environmental Protection, 1983; Choice and Consequence, 1984. Add: 79 Kennedy St., Cambridge, Mass. 02138, U.S.A.

SCHENCK, Hilbert. American, b. 1926. Science fiction, Engineering, Sports. Test Engineer, Pratt and Whitney Aircraft, East Hartford, Conn., 1952–56; Asst. Prof. to Prof., Clarkson Coll., Potsdam, N.Y., 1956–66; Prof., 1966–83, and Dir. of the Scuba Safety Project, 1968–80, Univ. of Rhode Island, Kingston. *Publs:* science fiction—Wave Rider (short stories), 1980; At the Eye of the Ocean (novel), 1980; A Rose for Armageddon (novel), 1982; other—(with Henry Kendall) Shallow Water Diving for Pleasure and Profit, 1950; (with Henry Kendall) Underwater Photography, 1954; (with Henry Kendall) Shallow Water Diving and Spearfishing, 1954; Skin Diver's and Spearfisherman's Guide to American Waters, 1955; Heat Transfer, 1959; (with R. Kenyon) Thermodynamics, 1961; An Introduction to the Engineering Research Project, 1962; Fortran Methods in Heat Flow, 1963; Theories of Engineering Experimentation, 1963, 3rd ed. 1978; (ed.) Introduction to Ocean Engineering, 1975. Add: c/o St. Martin's Press, 175 Fifth Ave., New York, N.Y. 10010, U.S.A.

SCHERMERHORN, Richard A. American, b.1903. Cultural/Ethnic topics, Race relations. Prof. Case Western Reserve Univ., Cleveland, Ohio, 1948–72; Visiting Prof., Univ. of Lucknow, India, 1959–60; Visiting Prof., Indian Inst. of Technology, Kanpur, 1968–70. *Publs:* These Our People: Minorities in American Culture, 1949; Society and Power, 1961; Psychiatric Index for Interdisciplinary Research, 1964; Comparative Ethnic Relations, 1970; Ethnic Plurality in India, 1978. Add: 650 W. Harrison, Claremont, Calif. 91711, U.S.A.

SCHEVILL, James (Erwin). American, b. 1920. Novels/Short stories, Plays/Screenplays, Poetry, Theatre. Prof. of English, Brown Univ., Providence, R.I., since 1969. Member of Faculty, Calforina Coll. of Arts and Crafts, Oakland, 1950–59; Member of Faculty, 1959–68, and Dir. of Poetry Center, 1961–68, San Francisco State Coll., Calif. *Publs:* Tensions (poetry), 1947; The American Fantasies (poetry), 1951; Sherwood Anderson: His Life and Work, 1951; High Sinners, Low Angels, 1953; The Right to Greet (poetry), 1956; The Roaring Market and the Silent

Tomb (biography), 1956; (ed.) Six Historians, by Ferdinand Schevill, 1956; Selected Poems, 1945-1959, 1959; Voices of Mass and Capital A, 1962; Private Dooms and Public Destinations: Poems, 1945-1962, 1962; The Master, 1963; The Stalingrad Elegies (poetry), 1964; The Black President and Other Plays, 1965; Release (poetry), 1968; Violence and Glory: Poems, 1962-1968, 1969; Lovecraft's Follies (play), 1971; Breakout! In Search of New Theatrical Environments, 1972; The Buddhist Car and Other Characters (poetry), 1973; Pursuing Elegy, 1974; Cathedral of Ice, 1975; The Arena of Ants (novel), 1977; The Mayan Poems, 1978; Fire of Eyes: A Guatemalan Sequence, 1979; Edison's Dream, 1982; The American Fantasies: Collected Poems 1945-1982, 1983; The Invisible Volcano (poem), 1985; Oppenheimer's Chair (play), 1985; Collected Short Plays, 1986; Ambiguous Dancers of Fame: Collected Poems 1945-1986, 1987. Add: Dept. of English, Brown Univ., Providence, R.I. 02912, U.S.A.

SCHICKEL, Richard (Warren). American, b. 1933. Film. Television writer, dir. and producer. Film Critic, Time mag., since 1973. Sr. Ed., Look mag., 1956–60; Sr. Ed., Show mag., 1960–63; Film Critic, Life mag., 1965–73. *Publs:* The World of Carnegie Hall, 1960; The Stars, 1962; Movies: The History of an Art and an Institution, 1964; The Gentle Knight, 1964; The Disney Version, 1968; The World of Goya, 1968; Second Sight: Notes on Some Movies, 1972; His Picture in the Papers, 1974; The Men Who Made the Movies, 1974; The Platinum Years, 1974; The Fairbanks Album, 1975; The World of Tennis, 1975; Another I, Another You, 1978; Singled Out, 1981; Cary Grant: A Celebration, 1983; D.W. Griffith: An American Life, 1984; Intimate Strangers: The Culture of Celebrity, 1985; James Cagney: A Celebration, 1985; The Disney Version, 1985; (with Michael Walsh) Carnegie Hall: The First Hundred Years, 1987; Striking Poses: Photographs from the Kobal Collection, 1988. Add: 33 Harrison St., New York, N.Y. 10013, U.S.A.

SCHILPP, Paul A(rthur). American, (born German), b. 1897. Education, Philosophy, Theology/Religion. Emeritus Prof. of Philosophy, North-western Univ., Evanston, Ill., since 1965 (Lectr., Assoc. Prof. and Prof. of Philosophy 1936–65); Prof. Emeritus, Southern Illinois Univ., Carbondale, since 1980 (Visiting Distinguished Research Prof., 1965–82). Adjunct Prof. of Philosophy, Univ. of California at Santa Barbara, since 1982. Prof. of Psychology, Bible and Religious Education, Univ. of Puget Sound, Wash., 1922–23; Assoc. Prof. of Philosophy, Univ. of the Pacific, San Jose, Calif., 1923–24; Prof. of Philosophy, 1924–34, and Assoc. Prof. of German, 1935–36, Univ. of the Pacific, Stockton, Calif. Founder, Pres., and Ed., Library of Living Philosophers, 1938–81. *Publs:* Do We Need a New Religion?, 1929; (ed.) Higher Education Faces the Future, 1930; (ed.) College of the Pacific Publications in Philosophy, 3 vols., 1932–34; Kant's Pre-Critical Ethics, 1938; The Quest for Religious Realism: Some Paradoxes of Religion, 1938; (ed.) Philosophy of John Dewey, 1939; (ed.) Philosophy of George Santayana, 1940; (ed.) Theology and Modern Life, 1940; (ed.) Philosophy of Alfred North Whitehead, 1941; (ed.) Philosophy of G.E. Moore, 1942; (ed.) Philosophy of Bertrand Russell, 1944; (ed.) Philosophy of Ernst Cassirer, 1949; (ed.) Albert Einstein: Philosopher-Scientist, 1949; (ed.) Philosophy of Sarvepalli Radhakrishnan, 1952; Human Nature and Progress, 1954; (ed.) Philosophy of Karl Jaspers, 1957; (ed.) Philosophy of C.D. Broad, 1959; (ed.) Philosophy of Rudolf Carnap, 1963; The Crisis in Science and Education, 1963; (ed.) Philosophy of Martin Buber, 1967; (ed.) Philosophy of C.I. Lewis, 1968; Philosophy of Karl Popper, 1974; Philosophy of Brand Blanshard, 1980; The Philosophy of Jean-Paul Sartre, 1981; (ed. with Lewis E. Hahn) The Philosophy of Gabriel Marcel, 1984; The Philosophy of W.V. Quine, 1986; The Philosophy of Georg Henrik von Wright, 1988. Add: 9 Hillcrest Dr., Carbondale, Ill. 62901, U.S.A.

SCHISGAL, Murray. American, b. 1926. Plays/Screenplays. Musician, 1947–50; practiced law, 1953–55; teacher, 1955–59. *Publs:* The Typist and the Tiger, 1960; Ducks and Lovers, 1961; Luv, 1964; Fragments, Windows and Other Plays, 1965; Jimmy Shine, 1969; The Chinese and Doctor Fish, 1970; An American Millionaire, 1974; All Over Town, 1974; The Pushcart Peddlers, The Flatulist, and Other Plays, 1980; Luv and Other Plays, 1983; Closet Madness and Other Plays, 1984; Popkins, 1984; Jealousy, and There Are No Sacher Tortes in Our Society!, 1985; Old Wine in a New Bottle, 1987; Road Show, 1987; Man Dangling, 1988. Add: c/o Bridget Aschenberg, ICM, 40 W. 57th St., New York, N.Y. 10019, U.S.A.

SCHLEE, Ann. British, b. 1934. Novels/Short stories, Children's fiction. *Publs:* children's fiction—The Strangers, 1971; The Consul's Daughter, 1972; The Guns of Darkness, 1973; Ask Me No Questions, 1976; Lost, 1977; The Vandal, 1979; adult fiction—Rhine Journey, 1981;

The Proprietor, 1983; Laing, 1987. Add: David Higham Assocs., 5-8 Lower John St., London WIR 4HA, England.

SCHLEIN, Miriam. American. Children's fiction. Children's non-fiction. Past Pres., Forum of Writers for Young People. *Publs:* A Day at the Playground, 1951; Tony s Pony, 1952; Shapes, 1952; Go with the Sun, 1952; Fast Is Not a Ladybug: A Book about Fast and Slow Things, 1953; The Four Little Foxes, 1953; When Will the World Be Mine?, 1953; Heavy Is a Hippopotamus, 1954; The Sun Looks Down, 1954; How Do You Travel?, 1954; Elephant Herd, 1954; It's About Time, 1955; City Boy, Country Boy, 1955; Oomi, The New Hunter, 1955; Little Red Nose, 1955; Puppy's House, 1955; Big Talk, 1955; Lazy Day, 1955; Henry's Ride, 1956; Deer in the Snow, 1956; Something for Now, Something for Later, 1956; Little Rabbit, The High Jumper, 1957; Amazing Mr. Pelgrew, 1957; The Big Cheese, 1958; The Bumblebee's Secret, 1958; Home, The Tale of a Mouse, 1958; Herman McGregor's World, 1958; Kittens, Cubs and Babies, 1959; The Fisherman's Day, 1959; My Family, 1960; The Sun, The Wind, The Sea, and the Rain, 1960; Laurie's New Brother, 1961; Amuny, Boy of Old Egypt, 1961; The Pile of Junk, 1962; Snow Time, 1962; The Snake in the Carpool, 1963; The Way Mothers Are, 1963; Who? . . . 1963; The Big Green Thing, 1963; Big Lion, Little Lion, 1964; Billy, The Littlest One, 1966; The Best Place, 1968; My House, 1971; Moon-Months and Sun-Days, 1972; Juju-Sheep and the Python's Moonstone, and Other Moon Stories from Different Times and Different Places, 1973; The Rabbit's World, 1973; What's Wrong with Being a Skunk?, 1974; The Girl Who Would Rather Climb Trees, 1975; Metric: The Modern Way to Measure, 1975; Bobo the Troublemaker, 1976; Giraffe, The Silent Giant, 1976; I, Tut, 1978; On the Track of the Mystery Animal, 1978; Snake Fights, Rabbit Fights and More, 1979; Lucky Porcupine, 1980; Antarctica, the Great White Continent, 1980; Billions of Bats, 1982; Project Panda Watch, 1984; The Dangerous Life of the Sea Horse, 1986; What the Elephant Was, 1986; Big Talk, 1988. Add: 19 E. 95th St., New York, N.Y. 10028, U.S.A.

SCHLESINGER, Arthur (Meier), Jr. American, b. 1917. History, Politics/Government. Albert Schweitzer Prof. of the Humanities, City Univ. of New York, since 1966. With Office of War Information, 1942–43, and Office of Strategic Services, 1943–45; Assoc. Prof. of History, 1946–54 and Prof. of History, 1954–61, Harvard Univ.; Consultant, Economic Cooperation Admin., 1948, and Mutual Security Admin., 1951–52; Special Asst. to Presidents Kennedy and Johnson, 1961–64. *Publs:* Orestes A. Brownson: A Pilgrim's Progress, 1939; The Age of Jackson, 1945; The Vital Center, 1949; (with R.H. Rovere) The General and the President, 1951; The Age of Roosevelt, 3 vols., 1957–60; Kennedy or Nixon, 1960; The Politics of Hope, 1963; (ed. with M. White) Paths of American Thought, 1963; A Thousand Days: John F. Kennedy in the White House, 1965; The Bitter Heritage: Vietnam and American Democracy 1941-1966, 1967; The Crisis of Confidence: Ideas, Power and Violence in America, 1969; (ed. with F.L. Israel) History of American Presidential Elections, 1971; (ed.) History of U.S. Political Parties, 1972; The Imperial Presidency, 1973; (ed.) The Dynamics of World Power, 5 vols., 1973; (ed.) Foreign Travelers in America, 39 vols., 1974; (ed. with Roger Bruns) Congress Investigates, 5 vols., 1975; Robert Kennedy and His Times, 1978; (ed.) The Almanac of American History, 1983; The Cycles of American History, 1986. Add: City Univ. of New York, 33 W. 42nd St., New York, N.Y. 10036, U.S.A.

SCHLESINGER, Benjamin. Canadian, b. 1928. Family planning, Sociology. Prof., Faculty of Social Work, Univ. of Toronto, since 1960. *Publs:* (ed.) The Multi-Problem Family, 1967; (ed.) Poverty in Canada and the United States, 1968; (ed.) The One-Parent Family, 1969, 5th ed. 1985; (ed.) The Jewish Family, 1971; Families: A Canadian Perspective, 1972; (ed.) Family Planning in Canada, 1974; (ed.) Sexual Behavior in Canada, 1977; Families: Canada, 1979; One in Ten: The One-Parent Family in Canada, 1979; Sexual Abuse of Children: A Resource Guide and Annotated Bibliography, 1982; Remarriage: A Review and Annotated Bibliography, 1983; The One-Parent Family in the 1980's, 1985; Sexual Abuse of Children in the 1980's, 1986; Jewish Family Issues, 1987; (with Rachel Schlesinger) Abuse of the Elderly: Issues and Annotated Bibliography, 1988. Add: Faculty of Social Work, Univ. of Toronto, 246 Bloor St. W., Toronto, Ont., Canada M5S 1A1.

SCHLOSSSTEIN, Steven. American, b. 1941. Novels/Short stories, Business/Trade/Industry. Pres., SBS Assocs. Inc., Princeton, N.J., NYC and Tokyo, since 1982. Vice-Pres. in Hong Kong, NYC, Tokyo, Dusseldorf, and Sydney, Morgan Guaranty Trust Co., 1969–82. *Publs:* Kensei, 1983; Trade War: Greed, Power, and Industrial Policy on Opposite Sides of the Pacific, 1984; Yakuza: The Japanese Godfather, 1987. Add: P.O. Box 1507, Princeton, N.J. 08540, U.S.A.

SCHMANDT, Henry J. American, b. 1918. Politics/Government, Urban studies. Prof. of Urban Affairs and Political Science, Univ. of Wisconsin, Milwaukee, since 1960. Asst. Prof. of Political Science, Univ. of Detroit, 1952–54; Assoc. Prof. of Political Science, St. Louis Univ., 1955–59. *Publs:* History of Political Philosophy, 1960; (with J. Bollens) Exploring the Metropolitan Community, 1961; (with P. Stenibicker and G. Wendel) Metropolitan Reform in St. Louis, 1961; Milwaukee Metropolitan Study Commission, 1965; Courts in the American Political System, 1968; (ed. with W. Bloomberg) Power, Poverty and Urban Life, 1968; (ed. with W. Bloomberg) The Quality of Urban Life, 1969; (with D. Vogel and J. Goldbach) Milwaukee: A Contemporary Urban Profile, 1971; (with J. Bollens) The Metropolis: Its People, Politics and Economic Life, 3rd ed. 1975; (with G.D. Wendel) Federal Aid to St. Louis, 1983. Add: Dept. of Urban Affairs, Univ. of Wisconsin, Milwaukee, Wisc. 53201, U.S.A.

SCHMEISER, Douglas A. Canadian, b. 1934. Civil liberties/Human rights, Criminology/Law enforcement/Prisons, Law. Prof. of Law, Univ. of Saskatchewan, since 1961 (Dir. of Grad. Legal Studies, 1969–74; Dean of Law, 1974–77). Me ber of the National Council, Canadian Human Rights Foundn. Member, Advisory Academic Panel, Canada Council, 1971–74; Pres., Canadian Assn. of Law Teachers, 1973–74; Chmn., Law Reform Commn. of Saskatchewan, 1982–87. *Publs:* Civil Liberties in Canada, 1964; Cases and Comments on Criminal Law, 1966; Criminal Law: Cases and Comments, 2nd ed. 1973, 4th ed. 1981, 5th ed. 1985; The Native Offender and the Law, 1974. Add: Coll. of Law, Univ. of Saskatchewan, Saskatoon, Sask., S7N OWO, Canada.

SCHMIDT, Michael (Norton). Mexican, b. 1947. Poetry, Literature, Translations. Ed. Dir., Carcanet Press Ltd., Manchester, since 1969. Ed., PN Review; Special Lectr. in Poetry, Manchester Univ. *Publs:* Black Buildings, 1969; One Eye Mirror Cold, 1970; Bedlam and the Oakwood, 1970; Desert of Lions, 1972; (ed. with G. Lindop) British Poetry since 1960; It Was My Tree, 1972; (tr. with E. Kissam) Flower and Song, 1975; My Brother Gloucester, 1976; (ed.) Ten British Poets, 1976; A Change of Affairs, 1978; (ed.) A Reader's Guide to Fifty Poets, 2 vols., 1979; The Colonist, 1980; in U.S. as Green Island, 1982; (ed.) Eleven British Poets, 1980; Choosing a Guest: New and Selected Poems, 1983; (ed.) Some Contemporary Poets of Britain and Ireland, 1983; The Dresden Gate, 1986; (trans.) Octavio Paz: On Poets and Others, 1986. Add: 208 Corn Exchange Bldgs., Manchester M4 3BQ, England.

SCHMIDT, Stanley (Albert). American, b. 1944. Science fiction/Fantasy. Ed., Analog mag., NYC, since 1978. Asst. Prof. of Physics, Heidelberg Coll., Tiffin, Ohio, 1969–78. *Publs:* Newton and the Quasi-Apple, 1975; The Sins of the Fathers, 1976; Lifeboat Earth, 1978; (ed.) Analog's Golden Anniversary Anthology Children of the Future, Lighter Side, War and Peace, Reader's Choice, Writer's Choice, 6 vols., 1980–82; (ed.) Aliens from Analog, 1983; (ed.) From Mind to Mind, 1984; Tweedlioop, 1986. Add: c/o Analog, 380 Lexington Ave., New York, N.Y. 10017, U.S.A.

SCHMIDT-NIELSEN, Knut. American, b. 1915. Zoology. James B. Duke Prof. of Physiology, Dept. of Zoology, Duke Univ., Durham, N.C., since 1963 (Prof., 1952–63). Member, Bd. of Consultant Eds., Annals of Arid Zone, since 1962; Member of Editorial Bd., American Journal of Physiology. Member, Editorial Bds., Comparative Physiology, 1963–64, Physiological Zoology, 1959–70, and Journal of Cellular and Comparative Physiology, 1961–66; Chief Ed., News in Physiological Sciences, 1985–88. *Publs:* Animal Physiology, 1960, 3rd ed. 1970; Desert Animals: Physiological Problems of Heat and Water, 1964; How Animals Work, 1972; (ed. with L. Bolis and S.H.P. Maddrell) Comparative Physiology, 3 vols., 1973–78; Animal Physiology: Adaptation and Environment, 1975, 3rd ed. 1983; Scaling: Why Is Animal Size So Important?, 1984. Add: Dept. of Zoology, Duke Univ., Durham, N.C. 27706, U.S.A.

SCHMITTHOFF, Clive Macmillan. British, b. 1903. Business/Trade/Industry, Law. Prof. Emeritus, City of London Polytechnic; Hon. Prof. of Law, Univ. of Kent, Canterbury; Hon. Prof. of Law, Ruhr-Universitat, Bochum; Barrister. Founder, 1957, and Ed., Journal of Business Law. *Publs:* The English Conflict of Laws, 3rd ed. 1954; (ed.) The Sources of the Law of International Trade, 1964; The Sale of Goods, 2nd ed. 1966; (co-author) Palmer's Company Law, 21st ed. 1968, 24th ed. 1987; The Export Trade, 5th ed. 1969, 8th ed. 1986, (co-author) Mercantile Law, 12th ed. 1972, 14th ed. 1984; The Harmonisation of European Company Law, 1973; (ed.) European Company Law Texts, 1974; Commercial Law in a Changing Economic Climate, 1977, 1981. Add: 29 Blenheim Rd., London W4 1ET, England.

SCHMITZ, Dennis. American, b. 1937. Poetry. Prof. of English, California State Univ., Sacramento, since 1974 (joined faculty, 1966). Instr. in English Literature, Illinois Inst. of Technology, Chicago, 1961–62, and Univ. of Wisconsin, Milwaukee, 1962–66. *Publs:* We Weep for Our Strangeness, 1969; Double Exposures, 1971; Goodwill, Inc., 1976; String, 1980; Singing, 1985; Eden, 1989. Add: Dept. of English, California State Univ., Sacramento, Calif. 95819, U.S.A.

SCHMOKEL, Wolfe W(illiam). American, b. 1933. History. Prof. of History, Univ. of Vermont, Burlington, since 1971 (Instr., 1962–63; Asst. Prof., 1963–67; Assoc. Prof., 1967–71). Visiting Prof., Boston Univ., Mass., 1965–66, and Middlebury Coll., Vt., 1968–69 and 1973–74. *Publs:* Dream of Empire: German Colonialism, 1919-1945, 1964; (with A.J. Andrea) The Living Past: Western Historiographical Traditions, 1975. Add: Dept. of History, Univ. of Vermont, Burlington, Vt. 05405, U.S.A.

SCHNEEBAUM, Tobias. American, b. 1921. Autobiography/Memoirs/ Personal. Dir. of Research and Documentation, Asmat Museum of Culture and Progress, Agats, Irian Jaya, Indonesia. *Publs:* Keep the River on Your Right, 1969; Wild Man, 1979; (with Gunter and Ursula Konrad) Asmat: Life with the Ancestors, 1981; Asmat Images, 1985; Where the Spirits Dwell, 1988. Add: 463 West St., New York, N.Y. 10014, U.S.A.

SCHNEIDER, Ben Ross, Jr. American, b. 1920. Literature, Autobiography/Memoirs/Personal. Prof. of English, Lawrence Univ. (joined faculty, 1955). *Publs:* Wordsworth's Cambridge Education, 1957; (co-author) Themes and Research Papers, 1961; Ethos of Restoration Comedy, 1971; Travels in Computerland, 1974; My Personal Computer and Other Family Crises, 1984. Add: Dept. of English, Lawrence Univ., Appleton, Wisc., 54911, U.S.A.

SCHNEIDER, B(etty) V(ance) H(umphreys). Also writes as B.V. Humphreys. American, b. 1927. Business/Trade/Industry, Industrial relations, Personnel management. Research Economist since 1954, and Dir. of California Public Employee Relations Research and Publ. Prog. since 1969, Inst. of Industrial Relations, Univ. of California, Berkeley. Ed., California Public Employee Relations, since 1969. Ed., Inst. of Industrial Relations Bulletin, 1957–68 and Industrial Relations, 1961–68; Lectr., Mills Coll., Oakland, Calif., 1968–74, and Central Michigan Univ., 1984. *Publs:* (ed.) Statistics of Labor-Management Relations, 1956; Industrial Relations in the Pacific Coast Longshore Industry, 1956; Industrial Relations in the California Aircraft Industry, 1956; Industrial Relations in the West Coast Maritime Industry, 1958; (as B.V. Humphreys) Clerical Unions in the Civil Service, 1958; The Older Worker, 1962; (ed.) Labor and Management in Industrial Society, by Clark Kerr, 1964; Canadian Trailblazer: The New Collective Bargaining Law, 1968; (with M. Ross) California's Meet and Confer Laws, 1968; (ed.) Affirmative Action Versus Seniority: Is Conflict Inevitable? by Bonnie G. Cebulski, 1977; (ed.) Local Option in the Administration of Public Sector Employment Relations: California Experience and Prospects, by Philip Tamoush, 1977; (ed.) A Symposium on California's High Education Employer-Employee Relations Act of 1978, 1978; Approaching the State Unit Problem, 1978; (ed.) A Statistical Analysis of Agreements in California Local Government, 1979; Layoffs and Attrition: A Summary of Recent Reports, 1979; A Post-13 Update on Public Employment Trends, 1979; (ed.) Public-Sector Labor Legislation, 1979, 1988; (ed.) Pocket Guide to the Public Safety Officers Procedural Bill of Rights Act Meyers-Milias-Brown Act, Educational Employment Relations Act, 3 vols., 1986–89; Conferring Strike Rights by Statute: Experience Outside California, 1987. Add: 2114 Marin Ave., Berkeley, Calif. 94707, U.S.A.

SCHNEIDER, Robert W. American, b. 1933. Literature, Biography. Prof., Northern Illinois Univ., since 1973 (Asst. Prof., 1961–65; Assoc. Prof., 1965–73). Instr., Univ. of Minnesota, Minneapolis, 1958–59; Instr., Coll. of Wooster, Ohio, 1959–61. *Publs:* Five Novelists of the Progressive Era, 1965; Novelist to a Generation: The Life and Thought of Winston Churchill, 1976. Add: Dept. of History, Northern Illinois Univ., DeKalb, Ill. 60115, U.S.A.

SCHOEN, Barbara. American, b. 1924. Novels/Short stories. Assoc. Prof., State Univ. of New York, Purchase, since 1978 (Asst. Prof., 1973–78). *Publs:* A Place and a Time, 1965; A Spark of Joy, 1967. Add: 101 Park Ave., Bronxville, N.Y. 10708, U.S.A.

SCHOENBRUN, David (Franz). American, b. 1915. International relations/Current affairs. News Commentator and Chief Corresp., Metromedia, NYC, 1964, and since 1965. Sr. Lectr., New Sch. for Social Research, since 1970. High Sch. Language Teacher, NYC, 1934–36;

Labor Relations Adjuster, 1936–40, and Ed., Trade newspaper, 1937–40, Dress Manufacturers Assn., NYC; Freelance writer for mags. and newspapers, 1940–41; Bureau Chief, European Propaganda Desk, U.S. Office of War Information, 1942–43; with U.S. Army Intelligence, 1943–45; Chief of Allied Forces Newsroom and Commentator for U.N. Radio, Algiers, 1943; U.S. Intelligence Liaison Officer with French Army, 1944–45; Combat Corresp., U.S. Seventh Army, 1945; Bureau Chief, Overseas News Agency, Paris, 1945–47; Bureau Chief, Paris Bureau, 1945–50, Chief Corresp. and Chief of Washington, D.C. Bureau, 1960–63, CBS Inc.; Guest Commentator, ABC News, 1967–70; Sr. Lectr., Columbia Univ., NYC, 1968–70. *Publs:* As France Goes, 1957; The Three Lives of Charles de Gaulle, 1965; Viet Nam: How We Got In, How We Get Out, 1968; The New Israelis, 1973; Triumph in Paris, 1976; Soldiers of the Night: The Story of the French Resistance, 1980; America Inside Out: At Home and Abroad from Roosevelt to Reagan, 1984. Add: c/o N.S. Bienstock Inc., 10 Columbus Circle, New York, N.Y. 10019, U.S.A.

SCHOENFELD, Maxwell Philip. American, b. 1936. History, Autobiography/Memoirs/Personal. Prof. of History, Univ. of Wisconsin-Eau Claire, since 1964. *Publs:* The Restored House of Lords, 1967; The War Ministry of Winston Churchill, 1972; Sir Winston Churchill: His Life and Times, 1973, 1986; Fort de la Presqu'ile, 1979; Charles Vernon Gridley: A Naval Career, 1983. Add: Dept. of History, Univ. of Wisconsin, Eau Claire, Wisc. 54701, U.S.A.

SCHOENHERR, Richard Anthony. American, b. 1935. Institutions/Organizations, Sociology. Prof. of Sociology since 1982, Project Dir., Comparative Religious Org. Studies, and Co-Investigator, Dane County Health and Social Agency Study, since 1973, Univ. of Wisconsin (Asst. Prof., 1971–76). Ordained Roman Catholic Priest, 1961 (Assoc. Pastor, St. Benedict's Church, Pontiac, Mich., 1961–64; Part–time Asst. Pastor, St. Sabina Church, Chicago, 1964–70). Assoc. Study Dir., 1969–70, and Sr. Study Dir., 1970–71, National Opinion Research Center, and Research Assoc. and Asst. Prof. of Sociology, 1971, Univ. of Chicago. *Publs:* (with Peter M. Blau) The Structure of Organizations, 1971; (co-author) The Catholic Priest in the United States: Sociological Investigations, 1972; (co-author) The Political Economy of Diocesan Advisory Councils, 1980; (with A. Sorensen) From the Second Vatican to the Second Millennium: Decline and Change in the U.S. Catholic Church, 1981. Add: Dept. of Sociology, 3454 Social Science Bldg., Univ. of Wisconsin, Madison, Wisc. 53706, U.S.A.

SCHOFIELD, Michael. British, b. 1919. Civil liberties/Human rights, Sex, Social commentary/phenomena, Social sciences (general). Social research consultant. Research Dir., Central Council for Health Education, London, 1961–65, Govt. Advisory Cttee. on Drug Dependence, 1967, Wootton Cttee. on Cannabis, 1969, and Police Powers of Arrest and Search, 1970. *Publs:* The Sexual Behaviour of Young People, 1965; The Sociological Aspects of Homosex ality, 1965; Society and the Young School Leaver, 1967; Drugs and Civil Liberties, 1968; Social Research, 1969; (co-author) Behind the Drug Scene, 1970; The Strange Case of Pot, 1971; (co-author) The Rights of Children, 1972; The Sexual Behaviour of Young Adults, 1973; Promiscuity, 1976; The Sexual Containment Act, 1978. Add: 28 Lyndhurst Gardens, London NW3 5NW, England.

SCHOFIELD, Paul. See TUBB, E.C.

SCHOFIELD, Sylvia Anne. Also writes as Sylvia A. Matheson and Max Mundy. British. Mystery/Crime/Suspense, Archaeology/Antiquities, Travel/Exploration/Adventure. Creative Copywriter, J. Walter Thompson, London, 1951–56; Public Relations Officer, British Horse Soc., London, 1965–66. *Publs:* (as Max Mundy) Death is a Tiger, 1960; (as Sylvia A. Matheson) Time Off to Dig, 1961; (as Max Mundy) Dig for a Corpse, 1962; (as Max Mundy) Pagan Pagoda, 1964; (as Max Mundy) Death Cries Olé, 1966; (as Sylvia A. Matheson) The Tigers of Baluchistan, 1967; (as Sylvia A. Matheson) Persia: An Archaeological Guide, 1972, 1979; (as Sylvia A. Matheson) Leathercraft in the Lands of Ancient Persia, 1978; (as Sylvia A. Matheson) Rajasthan, Land of Kings, 1984 (photos by Roloff Beny). Add: Casa Carob, VA.CA.33, Javea (Alicante), Spain.

SCHOLEFIELD, Alan. Also writes as Lee Jordan. South African, b. 1931. Novels/Short stories, Plays/Screenplays, History. Former member of Foreign Staff, Sydney Morning Herald, and Defence Corresp., The Scotsman. *Publs:* A View of Vultures, 1966; Great Elephant, 1967; The Eagles of Malice, 1968; Wild Dog Running, 1970; The Young Masters; The Hammer of God; Lion in the Evening; The Alpha Raid, Venom; Point of Honour; Berlin Blind; The Stone Flower; The Sea Cave; Fire in the Ice; King of the Golden Valley; The Last Safari; The Lost Giants; (as Lee Jordan) Cat's Eyes; Criss Cross; The Deadly Side of the Square; The Toy Cupboard; Chain Reaction; The Dark Kingdoms (history); Chaka (screenplay); Treasure Island (stage adaptation). Add: c/o Elaine Greene Ltd., 31 Newington Green, London N16 9PU, England.

SCHOLEY, Arthur (Edward). British, b. 1932. Children's fiction, Plays/Screenplays. *Publs:* (with Donald Swann) The Song of Caedmon, 1971; Christmas Plays and Ideas for Worship, 1973; The Discontented Dervishes, 1977; Sallinka and the Golden Bird, 1978; Twelve Tales for a Christmas Night, 1978; (with Donald Swann) Wacky and His Fuddlejig, 1978; (with Donald Swann) Singalive, 1978; (with Ronald Chamberlain) Herod and the Rooster, 1979; The Dickens Christmas Carol Show, 1979; (with Donald Swann) Baboushka, 1979; (with Donald Swann) Candletree, 1981; Five Plays for Christmas, 1981; Four Plays about People, 1983; Martin the Cobbler, 1983; The Hosanna Kids, 1985; Make a Model Crib, 1988; (with Donald Swann) Brendan A-hoy!, 1989. Add: 1 Cranbourne Rd., London N10 2BT, England.

SCHONBERG, Harold C(harles). American, b. 1915. Music, Biography. Assoc. Ed., American Music Lover, 1946–48; Music Critic, New York Sun, 1946–50; Contrib. Ed. and Record Columnist, Musical Courier, 1948–52; Columnist, The Gramophone, London, 1948–60; Music and Record Critic, 1950–60, Music Critic, 1960–80, and Cultural Corresp., 1980–85, New York Times. *Publs:* The Guide to Long-Playing Records: Chamber and Solo Instrument Music, 1955; The Collector's Chopin and Schumann, 1959; The Great Pianists, 1963; The Great Conductors, 1967; Lives of the Great Composers, 1970, 1981; Grandmasters of Chess, 1973; Facing the Music, 1981; The Glorious Ones: Classical Music's Legendary Performers, 1985; The Virtuosi: Classical Music's Great Performers from Paganini to Pavarotti, 1988. Add: c/o New York Times, 229 W. 43rd St., New York, N.Y. 10036, U.S.A.

SCHORR, Mark. American, b. 1953. Also writes as Scott Ellis. Mystery/Crime/ Suspense. Instr. in Journalism, Univ. of California at Los Angeles, since 1983. Reporter, Los Angeles Herald Examiner, 1980–82; producer in the Investigations Unit, KNXT-TV, Los Angeles, 1983. *Publs:* Red Diamond, Private Eye, 1983; Ace of Diamonds, 1984; Diamond Rock, 1985; Bully!, 1985; (as Scott Ellis) The Borzoi Control, 1986; The Microbe Solution, 1988. Add: c/o Michael Carlisle, William Morris Agency, 1350 Ave. of the Americas, New York, N.Y. 10019, U.S.A.

SCHOTT, Penelope Scambly. American, b. 1942. Novels, Poetry. Asst. Prof., Rutgers Univ., New Brunswick, N.J., 1971–78; Asst. Prof., and Coordinator of Accelerated Progs., Somerset County Coll., North Branch, N.J., 1978–83; Assoc. Research Scientist, Educational Testing Service, Princeton, N.J., 1983–87. *Publs:* My Grandparents Were Married for Sixty-five Years (poetry), 1977; A Little Ignorance (novel), 1986; These Are My Same Hands (poetry), 1989. Add: Box 215, Rocky Hill, N.J. 08553, U.S.A.

SCHRAG, Peter. American, b. 1931. Education, Politics/Government, Sociology. Editorial Page Ed., Sacramento Bee, since 1978. Reporter, El Paso Herald Post, Texas, 1953–55; Asst. Secty., Amherst Coll., Massachusetts, 1955–66; Assoc. Education Ed., 1966–68, Exec. Ed., 1968–73, Saturday Review, NYC: Ed., Change, NYC, 1969–70; Lectr., Univ. of Massachusetts, 1970–71, and Univ. of California, Berkeley, 1974–78. *Publs:* Voices in the Classroom, 1965; Village School Downtown, 1967; Out of Place in America, 1970; The Decline of the WASP (in U.K. as The Vanishing American), 1972; The End of the American Future, 1973; Test of Loyalty, 1974; (with Diane Divoky) The Myth of the Hyperactive Child, 1975; Mind Control, 1978. Add: Sacramento Bee, 21st and Q Sts., Sacramento, Calif. 95813, U.S.A.

SCHRANK, Jeffrey. American, b. 1944. Communications media, Education, Psychology. Ed., Media Mix Newsletter, since 1968. *Publs:* Interpersonal Communication (audio tape series), 1971; Teaching Human Beings: 101 Subversive Activities for the Classroom, 1972; Freedom: Now and When?, 1972; Feelings: Exploring Inner Space, 1973; The Seed Catalog: Teaching/Learning Resource Guide, 1974; Deception Detection: An Educator's Guide to the Art of Insight, 1975; Understanding Mass Media, 1975; Guide to the Short Film, 1978; Snap, Crackle, and Popular Taste, 1978; Snap, Crackle and Write, 1979; Guide to Checking and Savings Accounts, 1979. Add: c/o Diamandis Communications, 1515 Broadway, New York, N.Y. 10036, U.S.A.

SCHREINER, Samuel (Agnew, Jr.). American, b. 1921. Novels/Short stories. Reporter, Pittsburgh Sun-Telegraph, Pa., 1946–51; Asst. Managing Ed., Parade Magazine, 1951–55; Sr. Ed., The Reader's Digest, 1955–

74. *Publs:* Thine Is The Glory, 1975; Pleasant Places, 1977; The Condensed World of the Reader's Digest, 1977; Angelica, 1978; The Possessors and the Possessed, 1980; The Van Alens, 1981; A Place Called Princeton, 1984; The Trials of Mrs. Lincoln, 1987. Add: 111 Old King Highway, S. Darien, Conn. 06820, U.S.A.

SCHROEDER, Andreas (Peter). Canadian, b. 1946. Novels/short stories, Plays/Screenplays, Poetry, Translations. Editorial Bd. Member, The Canadian Fiction Mag., Toronto, since 1971. Chmn., Public Lending Right Commn., since 1986. Assoc. Prof., Univ. of Victoria, B.C., 1974–75; Assoc. Prof., Univ. of British Columbia Creative Writing Dept., 1984–87. Co-Founding Ed., Contemporary Literature in Translation, Vancouver, 1969–83; Chmn., Writers Union of Canada, 1975–76. *Publs:* The Ozone Minotaur, 1969; (trans. with M. Bullock) The Stage and Creative Arts, 1969; (ed. with J. Yates) Contemporary Poetry of British Columbia, 2 vols., 1970, 1972; File of Uncertainties, 1971; (with D. Frith) uniVERSE, 1971; The Late Man (short stories), 1971; The Late Man (screenplay), 1972; (ed. with R. Wiebe) Stories from Pacific and Arctic Canada, 1974; (trans.) Collected Stories of Ilse Aichinger, 1974; Shaking It Rough: A Prison Memoir, 1976; The Illegal Smile (fiction), 1978; Words Inside Out (verse), 1984; Toccata in D (novella), 1985; Dust-Ship Glory (novel), 1986. Add: Box 3127, Mission City, B.C. V2V 4J3, Canada.

SCHROETER, Louis C. American, b. 1929. Administration/Management, Chemistry. Corp. Sr. Vice-Pres. for Worldwide Distribution, Mfg. and Engineering, The Upjohn Co., Kalamazoo, Mich. since 1977 (Research Assoc., 1959–63; Head, Pharmacy Research, 1963–65; Head, Sterile Products Development, 1965–66; Head, Tablet and Capsule Development, 1966–68; Asst. Mgr., Product Research, 1968–70; Mgr., Pharmacy Research, 1970–73; Vice-Pres. for Manufacturing, 1974–77; Vice-Pres. and Gen. Mgr., Domestic Pharmaceutical Div., 1978–85). Exec. Dir., Merck Sharp & Dohme Research Lab., Rahway, N.J. *Publs:* Sulfur Dioxide, 1966; Ingredient X, 1969; Organizational Elan, 1970; Self-Discipline, 1978. Add: 5371 Colony Woods Dr., Portage, Mich. 49009, U.S.A.

SCHUETTINGER, Robert (Lindsay). American, b. 1936. History, Philosophy, Politics/Government. Dir. of Studies, The Heritage Foundn., Washington, D.C., since 1977; Ed., Policy Review, since 1977. Asst. Prof. of Political Science, Catholic Univ. of America, Washington, D.C., 1965–67; Visiting Lectr., St. Andrews Univ., Scotland, 1968–70; Asst. Prof. of Political Science, Lynchburg Coll., Virginia, 1970–73; Sr. Research Assoc., Republican Study Cttee., Washington, D.C., 1973–77; Visiting Lectr., Yale Univ., New Haven, Conn., 1974–75. *Publs:* The Conservative Tradition in European Thought, 1970; Toward Liberty: Essays in Honor of Ludwig Von Mises, 1971; (ed.) South Africa, 1976; (co-author) China: The Turning Point, 1976; (co-author) Korea in the World Today, 1976; (co-author) The Illusion of Wage and Price Control, 1976; Saving Social Security, 1977; Lord Acton, 1977; (with E.F. Butler) Forty Centuries of Wage and Price Control, 1978. Add: c/o Heritage Foundation, 214 Massachusetts Ave. N.E., Washington, D.C. 20002, U.S.A.

SCHUH, G(eorge) Edward. American, b. 1930. Agriculture/Forestry. Dean, Humphrey Inst. of Public Affairs, Univ. of Minnesota, Minneapolis, since 1987. Prof. of Agricultural Economics, Purdue Univ., Indiana, 1959–79; Prof. and Head, Dept. of Agricultural and Applied Economics, Univ. of Minnesota, St. Paul, 1978–84; Dir., Agriculture and Rural Development, The World Bank, Washington, D.C., 1984–87. Prof. Advisor to the Ford Foundn., 1966–72; Sr. Staff Economist, President's Council of Economic Advisors, 1974–75; Dir., Center for Public Policy and Public Admin., 1976–77; Deputy Under Secty. for Intnl. Affairs and Commodity Programs, U.S. Dept. of Agriculture, 1978–79. *Publs:* The Agricultural Development of Brazil, 1971; Research on Agricultural Development in Brazil, 1972; (co-author) The Development of Sao Paulo Agriculture, 1973; (with H. Tollini) Costs and Benefits of Agricultural Research, 1979; (with J. McCoy) Food and Development in the Pacific Basin, 1985; The United States and the Developing Countries: An Economic Perspective, 1986. Add: Humphrey Center, 301 19th Ave., S., Minneapolis, Minn. 55455, U.S.A.

SCHULBERG, Budd (Wilson). American, b. 1914. Novels/Short stories, Plays/Screenplays, Biography. Pres., Schulberg Enterprises, NYC, since 1958, and Douglass House Foundn., NYC; Founder, Watts Writers Workshop, Los Angeles, Calif., since 1965. Screenwriter in Hollywood, 1936–39; Member, New York Council, Authors' Guild, 1958–60. *Publs:* (with F. Scott Fitzgerald) Winter Carnival (screenplay), 1939; What Makes Sammy Run? (novel), 1941, play with S. Schulberg, 1964; (with M. Berkeley) City Without Men (screenplay), 1943; The Harder

They Fall, 1947; The Disenchanted, 1950, play with H. Breit, 1958; Some Faces in the Crowd (short stories), 1953; On the Waterfront (screenplay), 1954; Waterfront (novel), 1955; A Face in the Crowd: A Play for the Screen, 1957; Across the Everglades: A Play for the Screen (screenplay as Wind Across the Everglades), 1958; (ed.) From the Ashes: The Voices of Watts, 1967; Sanctuary V, 1970; Loser and Still Champion: Muhammad Ali, 1972; The Four Seasons of Success, 1972; Swan Watch, 1975; Everything That Moves, 1980; Moving Pictures, 1983. Add: c/o Alyss Dorese Agency, 1400 Ambassador St., Los Angeles, Calif. 90035, U.S.A.

SCHULLER, Gunther. American, b. 1925. Music. Composer and Conductor; Publr. and Ed., Margun Music Inc., Newton Centre, Mass; Dir., Festival at Sandpoint, Idaho, since 1985. First Chair, French Horn, Cincinnati Symphony, 1943–45; Solo French Horn, Metropolitan Opera Orchestra, NYC, 1949–59; Assoc. Prof. of Music, Yale Univ., New Haven, Conn., 1964–67; Head, Composition Dept., 1965–84 and Artistic Dir., 1974–84, Berkshire Music Centre, Tanglewood, Mass.; Pres., New England Conservatory of Music, Boston, 1967–77. *Publs:* Horn Technique, 1962; Early Jazz: Its Roots and Musical Development, 1968; Musings, 1985; The Swing Era, 1988. Add: 167 Dudley Rd., Newton Centre, Mass. 02159, U.S.A.

SCHULLER, Robert H(arold). American, b. 1926. Administration/Management, Human relations, Psychology, Theology/Religion. Founder and Sr. Pastor, Crystal Cathedral of the Reformed Church in America, formerly Garden Grove Community Church, Calif., since 1955. Pres., Bd. of Dirs., Christian Counseling Service Inc., since 1969; Founder and featured Pastor, Hour of Power national television prog., since 1970; Founder and Pres., Robert Schuller Inst. for Successful Church Leadership, since 1970; Member, Bd. of Dirs., Religion in American Life, since 1975. Pastor, Ivanhoe Church, Ill., 1950–55. *Publs:* God's Way to the Good Life, 1963; Your Future Is Your Friend, 1964; Move Ahead with Possibility Thinking, 1967; Self-Love; The Dynamic Force of Success, 1969; Power Ideas for a Happy Family, 1972; You Can Become the Person You Want to Be, 1973; The Greatest Possibility Thinker That Ever Lived, 1973; Your Church Has Real Possibilities, 1974; Love or Loneliness: You Decide, 1974; Reach Out for New Life, 1977; Peace of Mind Through Possibility Thinking, 1977; It's Possible, 1978; The Courage of Carol, 1978;Turn Your Stress into Strength, 1978; Bloom, Where Are You Planted, 1978; Positive Prayers, 1978; The Peak to Peek Principle, 1980; Self-Esteem: The New Reformation, 1982; Tough Times Never Last, But Tough People Do!, 1983; Tough Minded Faith for Tender Hearted People, 1984; The Be-Happy Attitudes, 1985; The Power of Being Debt Free, 1985; Be Happy You Are Loved, 1986; Success Is Never Ending, Failure Is Never Final, 1988. Add: 12141 Lewis St., Garden Grove, Calif. 92640, U.S.A.

SCHULTZ, Samuel J. American, b. 1914. Theology/Religion. Emeritus Prof. of Bible and Theology, Wheaton Coll., Illinois, since 1980 (Prof., 1949–80; Chmn., Div. of Biblical Studies, Wheaton Coll., and Wheaton Graduate Sch.); Prof. of Old Testament and Bible Exposition, Tampa Bay Theological Seminary, Florida, since 1987. Member, Bd. of Trustees, Gordon Conwell Theological Seminary, South Hamilton, Mass., since 1980. *Publs:* The Old Testament Speaks, 1960, 3rd ed. 1980; Old Testament Survey: Law and History, 1964; The Prophets Speak, 1968; Deuteronomy: Gospel of Love, 1971; The Gospel of Moses, 1974; Interpreting the Word of God, 1976; Leviticus: God among His People, 1983; Message of the Old Testament, 1986. Add: 143 East St., Lexington, Mass. 02173, U.S.A.

SCHULTZ, Theodore W. American, b. 1902. Economics. Charles L. Hutchinson Distinguished Service Prof. of Economics, Univ. of Chicago, since 1952 (joined faculty as Prof. of Economics, 1943). Recipient, Nobel Prize in Economics, 1979. *Publs:* Redirecting Farm Policy, 1943; Agriculture in an Unstable Economy, 1945; The Economic Organization of Agriculture, 1953; The Economic Value of Education, 1963; Transforming Traditional Agriculture, 1964; Economic Growth and Agriculture, 1968; Investment in Human Capital: The Role of Education and Research, 1971; Human Resources: Policy Issues and Research Opportunities, 1972; (ed.) Distortions of Agricultural Incentives, 1978; Investing in People: The Economics of Population Quality, 1981. Add: 5620 S. Kimbark Ave., Chicago, Ill. 60637, U.S.A.

SCHULZ, Charles (Monroe). American, b. 1922. Humor/Satire. Created syndicated strip cartoon, Peanuts, 1950: since 1952, more than 110 titles based on strip reprints, TV progs., feature films, etc. *Publs:* Peanuts, 1952; More Peanuts, 1954; Good Grief, More Peanuts, 1956; Good Ol' Charlie Brown, 1962; Snoopy, 1962; You're Out of Your Mind, Charlie Brown, 1962; But We Love You Charlie Brown, 1962; Peanuts

Revisited, 1962; Go Fly a Kite, Charlie Brown, 1962; Peanuts Every Sunday, 1962; You Can Do It, Charlie Brown, 1962; Happiness Is a Warm Puppy, 1962; Love Is Walking Hand in Hand, 1965; A Charlie Brown Christmas, 1965; You Need Help, Charlie Brown, 1966; Charlie Brown's All-Stars, 1966; You've Had It, Charlie Brown, 1969; Peanuts Jubilee: the Art of Charles Schulz, 1975; Speak Softly and Carry a Beagle, 1975; Charlie Brown's Super Book of Things to Do and Collect, 1975; Be My Valentine, Charlie Brown, 1976; It's a Mystery, Charlie Brown, 1976; He's Your Dog, Charlie Brown, 1977; Hooray for You, Charlie Brown, 1977; Play Ball, Snoopy, 1978; Race for Your Life, Charlie Brown, 1978; And a Woodstock in a Birch Tree, 1979; And the Beagles and the Bunnies Shall Lie Down Together: The Theology in Peanuts, 1984; Big League Peanuts, 1985; By Supper Possessed, 1988; Talk Is Cheap, Charlie Brown, 1988. Add: Snoopy Place, Santa Rosa, Calif. 95401, U.S.A.

SCHULZ, Max Frederick. American, b. 1923. Literature. Prof. of English, Univ. of Southern California, Los Angeles, since 1963 (Chmn., 1968–80). Assoc. Ed., Critique mag., 1971–85. *Publs:* The Poetic Voices of Coleridge, 1963, rev. ed., 1965; (ed.) Essays in American and English Literature, Presented to Bruce Robert McElderry, Jr., 1967; Radical Sophistication: Studies in Contemporary Jewish-American Novelists, 1969; Bruce Jay Friedman, 1973; Black Humor Fiction of the Sixties: A Pluralistic Definition of Man and His World, 1973; Paradise Preserved: Recreations of Eden in 18th and 19th Century England, 1985. Add: Dept. of English, Univ. of Southern California, Los Angeles, Calif. 90089, U.S.A.

SCHULZE, Franz. American, b. 1927. Architecture, Art. Hollender Prof. of Art, Lake Forest Coll., Illinois, since 1974. Contributing Ed., Art News, and Inland Architect; Corresponding Ed., Art in America; Member, Advisory Bd., Koffler Foundn., Chicago, since 1971. Instr. of Art, Purdue Univ., Indiana, 1950–52; Lectr. in Humanities, Univ. of Chicago, 1952–53; Art Critic, Chicago Sun-Times, 1978–85. *Publs:* Art, Architecture and Civilization, 1968; Fantastic Images: Chicago Art since 1945, 1971; (with Oswald W. Grube and Peter C. Pran) 100 Years of Architecture in Chicago: Continuity of Structure and Form, 1976; Mies van der Rohe: A Critical Biography, 1985; The University Club of Chicago, 1987. Add: Dept. of Art, Lake Forest Coll., Lake Forest, Ill. 60045, U.S.A.

SCHULZE, Hertha. Also writes as Kate Wellington. American, b. 1935. Novels/Short stories, Romance. Member of Staff, Dept. of Independent Study, Univ. of Minnesota, Minneapolis, since 1986. Instr. in Theatre, Michigan State Univ., East Lansing, 1963–66; Asst. Prof. of Theatre, Univ. of Minnesota, 1967–68; Assoc. Prof. of Art, Rochester Inst. of Technology, New York, 1970–80; Assoc. Prof. of Theatre, Colorado Col., Colorado Springs, 1980-81; freelance writer, 1981–86. *Publs:* (ed.) Ecclesia, 1980; (as Kate Wellington) A Delicate Balance, 1984; Solid Gold Prospect, 1987. Add: c/o Steven J. Axelrod, Axelrod Agency, 125 Fifth Ave., New York, N.Y. 10011, U.S.A.

SCHUSKY, Ernest L. American, b. 1931. Anthropology/Ethnology. Race relations. Prof. of Anthropology, Southern Illinois Univ., Edwardsville, since 1960. Member of faculty, South Dakota State Univ., Brookings, 1958–60; Fulbright Prof., Seoul National Univ., 1982. *Publs:* A Manual for the Analysis of Kingship, 1964, 1972; (with T.P. Culbert) Introducing Culture, 1967, 3rd ed. 1978; The Right to Be Indian, 1970; Variation in Kinship, 1973; The Study of Cultural Anthropology, 1975; The Forgotten Sioux, 1975; (ed.) the Political Organization of Native North Americans, 1980; Introduction to Social Science, 1981; Culture and Agriculture, 1989. Add: 412 Willowbrook, Collinsville, Ill. 62234, U.S.A.

SCHUTZ, Will(iam C.). American, b. 1925. Human relations, Psychology. Dir., Center for Holistic Studies, Antioch Univ., West, San Francisco, since 1978. Member of faculty Univ. of Chicago, 1950–51, Tufts Univ., Medford, Mass., 1953–54, and Harvard Univ. Cambridge, Mass., 1954–58, Univ. of California, Berkeley, 1958–63, and Albert Einstein Coll. of Medicine, Bronx, N.Y., 1963–67; Assoc.-in-Residence, Esalen Inst., Big Sur, Calif., 1967–75. *Publs:* Firo: A Three Dimensional Theory of Interpersonal Behavior, 1958 (reissued as The Interpersonal Underworld), 1966; Joy, 1967; Here Comes Everybody, 1971; Elements of Encounter, 1973; Body Fantasy, 1977; Leaders of Schools, 1977; Profound Simplicity, 1979; The Truth Option, 1984. Add: c/o Irvington Publishers, 740 Broadway, New York, N.Y. 10003, U.S.A.

SCHUYLER, James (Marcus). American, b. 1923. Novels/Short stories, Plays/Screenplays, Poetry. *Publs:* Alfred and Guinevere, 1958; Salute, 1960; (with Kenward Elmslie) Unpacking the Black Trunk, 1965;

May 24th or So, 1966; (with John Ashbery) A Nest of Ninnies, 1969; Freely Espousing: Poems, 1969; The Crystal Lithium, 1972; (with Kenneth Koch and K. Elmslie) Penguin Modern Poets 24, 1973; Hymn to Life: Poems, 1974; The Fireproof Floors of Witley Court, 1976; The Home Book: Prose and Poems, 1977; What's for Dinner?, 1978; The Morning of the Poem (poetry), 1980; A Few Days, 1985; Selected Poems. 1988. Add: c/o Maxine Groffsky, 2 Fifth Ave., New York, N.Y. 10011, U.S.A.

SCHWAMM, Ellen. American, b. 1934. Novels/Short stories. *Publs:* Adjacent Lives, 1978; How He Saved Her, 1983. Add: 255 W. 88th St., New York, N.Y. 10024, U.S.A.

SCHWARTZ, Barry. American, b. 1942. Novels/Short stories, Poetry, Art, Social commentary/phenomena. Planner in Arts and Humanities, Univ. of California, Los Angeles, since 1973. Advisory and Contrib. Ed., Arts-in-Society, since 1972; Ed., The New Writer, and Columnist, Video Views in Today's Filmaker, since 1972. Former Co-Ed., The Human Futures Series, Prentice-Hall, Inc., Englewood Cliffs, N.J., and Ed., Etcetera Mag. *Publs:* (with R.E.L. Masters, Jean Houston and Stanley Krippner) Psychedelic Art, 1968; (ed. with Robert Disch) White Racism: History, Pathology and Practice, 1970; (ed. with Disch) Hard Rains: Conflict and Conscience in American Society, 1970; (ed. with Disch) Killing Time, 1972; (ed.) Affirmative Education, 1972; (ed.) Human Connection Prisoners of Their Passions (poetry), 1973; The Voyeur of Our Times (poetry), 1974; The New Humanism: Art in a Time of Change, 1974; Queuing and Waiting, 1975; (ed.) The Changing Face of the Suburbs, 1976; (ed.) The Psychology of Learning and Behavior, 1978, 1984; Vertical Classification, 1981; (with H. Lacey) Behaviorism, Science, and Human Nature, 1983; The Battle for Human Nature, 1986; George Washington: The Making of a Modern Symbol, 1987. Add: c/o Norton, 500 Fifth Ave., New York, N.Y. 10110, U.S.A.

SCHWARTZ, Eli. American, b. 1921. Economics, Money/Finance. Prof. of Economics and Finance, Coll. of Business and Economics, Lehigh Univ., Bethlehem, Pa., since 1962 (joined faculty, 1954). *Publs:* (coauthor) Study of the Probable Effects of a Move Toward Land Value Taxation in the City of Bethlehem, 1958; Corporation Finance, 1962; (ed. and co-author with J.R. Aronson) Management Policies in Local Government Finance, 1975, 1981; Trouble in Eden: A Comparison of the British and Swedish Economies, 1980. Add: Drown Hall No. 35, Lehigh Univ., Bethlehem, Pa. 18015, U.S.A.

SCHWARTZ, Elliott S. American, b. 1936. Music. Prof. of Music, Bowdoin Coll., Brunswick, Me., since 1975 (Asst. Prof., 1965–70; Assoc. Prof., 1970–75). *Publs:* The Symphonies of Ralph Vaughan Williams; (ed. with B. Childs) Contemporary Composers on Contemporary Music; Electronic Music: A Listener's Guide; Music: Ways of Listening. Add: 5 Atwood Lane, Brunswick, Me. 04011, U.S.A.

SCHWARTZ, Joseph. American, b. 1925. Language/Linguistics, Literature, Writing/Journalism. Prof. of English, Marquette Univ., Milwaukee, Wisc., since 1950. Ed., Renascence mag., since 1978. *Publs:* (with J.W. Archer) A Reader for Writers, 1962; (with J.A. Rycenga) Perspectives on Language, 1963; (with J.A. Rycenga) Province of Rhetoric, 1965; (with J.W. Archer) Exposition, 1966; (with R.C. Roby) Poetry: Meaning and Form, 1969; Hart Crane: An Annotated Critical Bibliography, 1970; (with R.C. Schweik) Hart Crane: A Descriptive Bibliography, 1972; Hart Crane: A Reference Guide, 1983. Add: Dept. of English, Marquette Univ., Milwaukee, Wis. 53233, U.S.A.

SCHWARTZ, Kessel. American, b. 1920. Literature. Prof. since 1962, and Chmn., 1962–64, 1973–83, Dept. of Foreign Languages, Univ. of Miami, Coral Gables, Fla. (Dir. of Grad. Studies, 1964–65). Member, Editorial Advisory Bd., Anales de la Narrativa Espanola Contemporanea, since 1977, and Folio, since 1979. Asst. Instr., Univ. of Missouri, Columbia, 1940–42; Dir. of cultural centers in Nicaragua, Ecuador, and Observer in Costa Rica, State Dept., 1946–48; Asst. Prof., Hamilton Coll., Clinton, N.Y., 1950–51, Colby Coll., Waterville, Me., 1951–53, and Univ. of Vermont, Burlington, 1953–57; Prof. and Chmn., Univ. of Arkansas, Fayetteville, 1957–62. *Publs:* The Contemporary Novel of Ecuador, 1953; (with R. Chandler) A New History of Spanish Literature, 1961; (ed.) Fiestas, by Juan Goytisolo, 1964; (with R. Chandler) A New Anthology of Spanish Literature, 2 vols., 1967; Introduction to Modern Spanish Literature, 1968; Vicente Aleixandre, 1969; The Meaning of Existence in Contemporary Hispanic Literature, 1970; Juan Goytisolo, 1970; A New History of Spanish American Fiction, 2 vols., 1972; Studies on Twentieth-Century Spanish and Spanish-American Literature, 1983. Add: 6400 Maynada, Coral Gables, Fla. 33146, U.S.A.

SCHWARTZ, Louis Brown. American, b. 1913. Criminology/Law enforcement/Prisons, Law. Prof. of Law, Hastings Coll. of Law, Univ. of California at San Francisco, since 1983. Prof. of Law, Univ. of Pennsylvania, Philadelphia, 1946–83. Chief, Decree Section, Antitrust Div., U.S. Dept. of Justice, 1945–46; Reporter, Model Penal Code of the American Law Inst., 1957–62; Dir., National Commn. on Reform of Federal Criminal Laws, 1968–71. *Publs:* (reporter with H. Wechsler) Model Penal Code, 1962; (with S.A. Goldstein) Law Enforcement Handbook, 1970, 1980; Proposed Federal Criminal Code and Commentaries, 1971; (with J.J. Flynn) Antitrust and Regulatory Alternatives, 5th ed. 1977, 6th ed., with J.J. Flynn and H. First, 1983; Studying Law for Fun and Profit, 1980. Add: Hastings Coll. of Law, Univ. of California, 200 McAllister St.,San Francisco, Calif. 94102, U.S.A.

SCHWARTZ, Lynne Sharon. American, b. 1939. Novels/Short stories. Full-time writer. Visiting Lectr., Univ. of Iowa Writers' Workshop, Iowa City, 1982–83; Lectr., Columbia Univ. Gen. Studies Writing Program, NYC, 1983–84; Visiting Asst. Prof., Boston Univ. Creative Writing Program, 1984, 1987. *Publs:* Rough Strife (novel), 1980; Balancing Acts (novel), 1981; Disturbances in the Field (novel), 1983; Acquainted with the Night (stories), 1984; We Are Talking about Homes (stories), 1985; The Melting Pot and Other Subversive Stories, 1987; Leaving Brooklyn (novel), 1989. Add: Amanda Urban, ICM, 40 W. 57th St., New York, N.Y. 10019, U.S.A.

SCHWARTZ, Mildred Anne. Canadian, b. 1932. Politics/Government, Race relations, Sociology. Prof. of Sociology, Univ. of Illinois at Chicago, since 1969 (Assoc. Prof., 1966–69). Asst. Prof., Univ., of Calgary, Alta., Canada, 1962–64; Study Dir., National Opinion Research Center, 1964–66. *Publs:* Trends in White Attitudes Toward Negroes, 1966; Public Opinion and Canadian Identity, 1967; (co-author) Political Parties and the Canadian Social Structure, 1967; Politics and Territory, 1974; (co-author) Canadian Political Parties: Origin, Character, Impact, 1975; The Environment for Policy-Making in Canada and the United States, 1981; A Sociological Perspective on Politics, 1990; The Party Network: The Robust Organisation of the Illinois Republicans, 1990. Add: Box 4348, Univ. of Illinois, Chicago, Ill. 60680, U.S.A.

SCHWARTZ, Sheila R. American. Novels/Short stories, Education, Literature. Prof., State Univ. Coll., New Paltz, N.Y., since 1963. Lectr., Hofstra Univ. Hempstead, N.Y., 1958–60; Instr., City Coll. of New York, 1962–63. *Publs:* all with G. Ruben—How People Lived in Ancient Greece and Rome, 1967; (with Nancy Lynn Schwartz) How People Live in Mexico, 1969; Teaching the Humanities: Selected Readings, 1970; Earth in Transit, 1977; Like Mother, Like Me, 1978; Growing Up Guilty, 1978; Teaching Adolescent Literature, 1978; The Solid Gold Circle, 1980; The Hollywood Writers' Wars (completed for Nancy Lynn Schwartz), 1981; One Day You'll Go, 1982; Jealousy, 1983; Sorority, 1987; Bigger Is Better, 1987; The Most Popular Girl, 1988. Add: English Education, State University Coll., New Paltz, N.Y. 12561, U.S.A.

SCHWARZ, Henry G. American, b. 1928. History, Politics/Government. Prof., Center for East Asian Studies since 1969 and Ed., Studies on East Asia, Western Washington Univ., Bellingham, since 1971. Fulbright Prof., Univ. of the Philippines, Diliman, Quezon City, 1964–65; Asst. Prof., Far Eastern Inst., Univ. of Washington, Seattle, 1965–69. *Publs:* Leadership Patterns in China's Frontier Regions, 1964; China: Three Facets of a Giant, 1966; Liu Shao-ch'i and "People's War," 1969; Chinese Policies Toward Minorities, 1971; Mongolian Short Stories, 1974; Bibliotheca Mongolica, Part 1, 1978; Studies in Mangolia, 1979; The Minorities of Northern China, 1984. Add: Center for East Asian Studies, Western Washington Univ., Bellingham, Wash. 98225, U.S.A.

SCHWARZENBERGER, Georg. British, b. 1908. Law, Politics/Government. Vice-Pres., London Inst. of World Affairs, since 1984 (Dir., 1943–84), and Emeritus Prof. of Intnl. Law, Univ. of London, since 1975 (Lectr., 1938–45, Reader, 1945–62, Dean, Faculty of Laws, University Coll., 1965–67, Prof., 1962–75). Barrister, Gray's Inn, London. Co-Ed. (with Keeton), The Library of World Affairs, and The Year Book of World affairs, 1947–84, and of Current Legal Problems, 1948–72. *Publs:* Power Politics: A Study of World Society, 1941, 3rd ed. 1964; International Law as Applied by International Courts and Tribunals, vol. I, 1945, 3rd ed. 1957, vol. II, 1968, vol. III, 1976, vol. IV, 1986; A Manual of International Law, 1947, 7th ed. 1976; The Legality of Nuclear Weapons, 1958; The Frontiers of International Law, 1962; The Inductive Approach to International Law, 1965; International Law and Order, 1971; The Dynamics of International Law, 1976. Add: 4 Bowers Way, Harpenden, Herts., England.

SCHWEITZER, Arthur. American, b. 1905. Economics. Prof. of Economics, Indiana Univ., Bloomington, since 1951 (Assoc. Prof. of Economics, 1947–51). Instr. and Assoc. Prof., Univ. of Wyoming, Laramie, 1939–47. *Publs:* Spiethoffs Konjunkturlehre, 1938; Big Business in the Third Reich, 1964; Nazifizierung des Mittelstandes, 1970; The Age of Charisma, 1984. Add: Dept. of Economics, Indiana Univ., Bloomington, Ind. 47401, U.S.A.

SCHWERNER, Armand. American, b. 1927. Poetry. Prof. of English, Coll. of Staten Island, City Univ. of New York, since 1973 (joined faculty, 1964). *Publs:* The Lightfall, 1963; (with D. Kaplan) The Domesday Dictionary, 1965; (if personal), 1968; The Tablets I-VIII, 1968; Seaweed, 1969; The Tablets I-XV, 1971; The Bacchae Sonnets, 1974; (author and adaptor) Redspell, 1975; The Tablets XVI-XVIII, 1975; This Practice, 1976; The Work, The Joy, and the Triumph of the Will, 1978;Sounds of the River Naranjana, 1982. Add: 30 Catlin Ave., Staten Island, N.Y. 10304, U.S.A.

SCHWINGER, Julian. American, b. 1918. Physics. Prof. of Physics, Univ. of California at Los Angeles, since 1972. Instr. and Asst. Prof., Purdue Univ., Lafayette, Ind., 1941–43; Staff Member, Radiation Lab., Massachusetts Inst. of Technology, Boston, 1942–45; Staff Member, Metallurgy Lab., Univ. of Chicago, 1943; Assoc. Prof., 1945–47, Prof., 1947–66, and Higgens Prof. of Physics, 1966–72, Harvard Univ., Cambridge, Mass. Recipient (jointly), Nobel Prize in Physics, 1965. *Publs:* Differential Equations of Quantum Field Theory, 1956; The Theory of Fundamental Interactions, 1957; (ed.) Quantum Electrodynamics, 1958; Lectures on Quantum Field Theory, 1967; (with David Saxon) Discontinuities in Waveguides, 1968; Particles and Sources, 1969; Particles, Sources, and Fields, 2 vols., 1970–73; Quantum Kinematics and Dynamics, 1970; Selected Papers, 1979; Einstein's Legacy, 1986. Add: Dept. of Physics, Univ. of California, Los Angeles, Calif. 90024, U.S.A.

SCIAMA, Dennis (William). British, b. 1926. Physics. Extraordinary Reseach Fellow, Churchill Coll., Cambridge, since 1986; Prof. of Astrophysics, Intnl. Sch. of Advanced Studies, Trieste, since 1983. Fellow, Trinity Coll., Cambridge, 1952–56; Member, Inst. for Advanced Study, Princeton, N.J., 1954–55; Agassiz Fellow, Harvard Univ., Cambridge, Mass., 1955–56; Research Assoc., King's Coll., London, 1958–60; Visiting Prof., Cornell Univ., Ithaca, N.Y., 1960–61; Lectr. in Maths, 1961–70, andFellow of Peterhouse, 1963–70, Cambridge Univ.; Sr. Research Fellow, All Souls Coll., Oxford 1970–85. *Publs:* The Unity of the Universe, 1959; The Physical Foundations of General Relativity, 1969; Modern Cosmology, 1971, 1975. Add: 7 Park Town, Oxford, England.

SCOFIELD, Jonathan. *See* ROTHWEILER, Paul R.

SCOTLAND, Jay. *See* JAKES, John.

SCOTT, Alexander. British, b. 1920. Plays/Screenplays, Poetry, Literature, Biography. Head of Dept. of Scottish Literature, Glasgow Univ., since 1971 (Lectr., 1948–63, Sr. Lectr., 1963–67). Secty., Univs. Cttee. on Scottish Literature, since 1968. Ed., Northeast Review, 1945–46, Scots Review, 1950–51, Satire Review, Edinburgh, 1954–57; Asst. Lectr., Edinburgh Univ., 1947–68; Gen. Ed., The Scottish Library, Calder & Boyars, publrs., London, 1968–71. *Publs:* Prometheus 48, 1948; The Latest in Elegies, 1949; Selected Poems, 1950; (ed.) Selected Poems of William Jeffrey, 1951; (ed.) The Poems of Alexander Scott, 1530-1584, 1952; Untrue Thomas, 1952; Mouth Music: Poems and Diversions, 1954; Right Royal, 1954; Shetland Yarn, 1954; Tam O'Shanter's Tryst, 1955; (ed.) Diaries of a Dying Man, by William Soutar; The Last Time I Saw Paris, 1957; Truth to Tell, 1958; Still Life: William Soutar 1898-1943, 1958; Cantrips, 1968; (ed. with N. MacCaig) Contemporary Scottish Verse, 1970; Greek Fire, 1971; Double Agent, 1972; The MacDiarmid Makars, 1923-1972 (criticism), 1972; (ed. with M. Grieve) The Hugh MacDiarmid Anthology: Poems in Scots and English, 1972; (ed. with D. Gifford) Neil M. Gunn: The Man and the Writer, 1973; Selected Poems 1943-1974, 1975; (ed.) Modern Scots Verse, 1978; Poems in Scots, 1978; (ed.) Scotch Passion, 1982; (ed. with James Aitchison) New Writing Scotland 2, 1984; (ed.) Voices of Our Kind: Scottish Poetry 1920-1985, 1985; (ed.) Diaries of a Dying Man, 1988. Add: 5 Doune Gardens, Glasgow G20 6DJ, Scotland.

SCOTT, Amoret (Tanner). British, b. 1930. Antiques/Furnishings, Cookery/Gastronomy/Wine, Recreation/Leisure/Hobbies, Biography. *Publs:* Hedgerow Harvest, 1979; A Murmur of Bees, 1980; Parrots, 1982; with Christopher Scott—A-Z of Antique Collecting, 1963; Collecting Bygones, 1964; Dummy Board Figures, 1966; Tobacco and the Collector,

1966; Collecting, 1967; Antiques as an Investment, 1967; Discovering Staffordshire Figures, 1969; Discovering Smoking Antiques, 1970; Treasures in Your Attic, 1971; Discovering Stately Homes, 1973, 1989; Wellington, 1973; Smoking Antiques, 1981; Staffordshire Figures, 1984. Add: The Footprint, Padworth Common, Reading, Berks. RG7 4QG, England.

SCOTT, Arthur Finley. British, b. 1907. History, Literature. Member, Inst. of Education, since 1952, and Univ. Teacher since 1968, Univ. of London (Examiner in English, 1955–69). Sr. English Master, Oakham Sch., 1930–33, and Taunton Sch., 1933–43, and Headmaster, Kettering Grammar Sch., 1943–51; Sr. Lectr., Borough Rd. Coll., of Education, 1952–73, now retired. *Publs:* Meaning and Style, 1938; Poetry and Appreciation, 1939; English Composition (4 books), 1951–53; Illustrated English (4 books), 1954–55; Poems for Pleasure (3 books), 1955; New Reading (10 books), 1956–60; The Poet's Craft, 1957; A Bridge to English (2 books), 1958; Parrish Poetry Books (4 books), 1958–59; (with D. Mukerjee) English Composition and Translation, 1962; The Craft of Prose, 1963; Current Literary Terms: Dictionary of Their Origin and Use, 1965; Plain English (5 books), 1966; (with N.K. Aggarwala) New Horizons (10 books), 1968–71; Close Readings, 1968; Every One a Witness series: The Georgian Age, 1970, The Stuart Age, 1974, The Plantagenet Age, 1974; Witch, Spirit, Devil, 1974; Who's Who in Chaucer, 1974; The Tudor Age, 1975; The Norman Age, 1976; The Roman Age, 1977; The Saxon Age, 1979; The EarlyHanoverian Age, 1980; America Grows, 1982; What Fires Kindle Genius?, 1982; What Makes a Prose Genius?, 1983. Add: 59 Syon Park Gardens, Osterley, Isleworth, Middx., England.

SCOTT, Bill. (William Neville Scott). Australian, b. 1923. Novels/Short stories, Children's fiction, Poetry, Songs/Lyrics and Libretti, Cultural/Ethnic topics, Music, Mythology/Folklore, Autobiography/Memoirs/Personal. Full-time writer. Served in the Royal Australian Navy, 1942–46; Bookseller, publisher and editor in the 1950's and 1960's. *Publs:* Focus on Judith Wright, 1967; Some People (short stories), 1968; Brother and Brother (verse), 1972; (ed.) The Continual Singing: An Anthology of World Poetry, 1973; Portrait of Brisbane, 1976; (ed.) The Complete Book of Australian Folklore, 1976; (ed.) Bushranger Ballads, 1976; My Uncle Arch and Other People (short stories), 1977; Boori (children's fiction), 1978; Tough in the Old Days (autobiography), 1979; (with John Meredith) Ned Kelly After a Century of Acrimony, 1980; (ed.) The Second Penguin Australian Songbook, 1980; Darkness Under the Hills (children's fiction), 1980; (ed.) Reading 360 series (The Blooming Queensland Side, On the Shores of Botany Bay, The Golden West, Bound for South Australia, Upon Van Diemen's Land, The Victorian Bunyip), 6 vols., 1981; Australian Bushrangers, 1983; (ed.) Reading 360 Series, 6 vols., 1983; (ed.) Penguin Book of Australian Humorous Verse, 1984; Shadows Among the Leaves (children's fiction), 1984; The Long and the Short and the Tall (folklore), 1985; Following the Gold (children's poems), 1989; Many Kinds of Magic (children's fiction), 1989. Add:157 Pratten St., Warwick, Qld. 4370, Australia.

SCOTT, Christopher. British, b. 1930. Antiques/Furnishings, Recreation/Leisure/Hobbies, Biography. *Publs:* all with Amoret Scott—A-Z of Antique Collecting, 1963; Collecting Bygones, 1964; Dummy Board Figures, 1966; Tobacco and the Collector, 1966; Collecting, 1967; Antiques as an Investment, 1967; Discovering Staffordshire Figures, 1969; Discovering Smoking Antiques, 1970; Treasures in Your Attic, 1971; Discovering Stately Homes, 1973; Wellington, 1973; Smoking Antiques, 1981; Staffordshire Figures, 1986. Add: c/o Shire Publs., Cromwell House, Church St., Princes Risborough, Aylesbury HP17 9AJ, England.

SCOTT, David L. British, b. 1920. Medicine/Health. Retired Consultant Anaesthetist. Head, Dept. of Anaesthesia, County Hosp., Sundsvall, Sweden, 1950–60. *Publs:* Modern Hospital Hypnosis—Especially for Anaesthetists. Add: Ravelstone, Manley, Cheshire WA6 9ED, England.

SCOTT, Donald Fletcher. British, b. 1930. Medicine/Health, Psychology. Consultant Electroencephalographer, London Hosp., since 1967. Former Research Fellow, Mayo Clinic, Rochester, Minn. *Publs:* (co-author) Neurological and Neurosurgical Nursing, 1967; About Epilepsy, 1969, 3rd ed. 1982; The Psychology of Work, 1970; Fire and Fire Raisers, 1974; Understanding EEG, 1976. Add: EEG Dept., London Hosp., Whitechapel, London E1 1BB, England.

SCOTT, Franklin D. American, b. 1901. History, International relations/Current affairs, Social sciences, Biography. Curator, Nordic Collections, Honnold Library, Claremont Colls., Calif., since 1970. Prof.

Emeritus of History, Northwestern Univ., Evanston, Ill., since 1969 (Prof., 1935–69); Dir., Westergaard Prog., Pomona Coll., Claremont, Calif., since 1970 (Visiting Prof., 1969–70). *Publs:* Bernadotte and the Fall of Napoleon, 1935; (compiler) The Twentieth Century World, 1938, 12th ed. 1963; (with E. Teigler) Guide to the American Historical Review, 1946; The United States and Scandinavia, 1950, 1975; (ed.) Pictorial History of Northwestern University, 1951; Scandinavia Today, 1951; (ed. and trans.) Baron Klinkowstrom's America, 1818-1820, 1952; The American Experience of Swedish Students, 1956; (co-author) Contemporary Civilization, 1958; (with R. Beringer) Emigration and Immigration, 1963; (trans.) Wertmuller: Artist and Immigrant Farmer, 1963; (ed.) World Migration in Modern Times, 1968; The Peopling of America, 1972; Sweden: The Nation's History, 1977, 1988; Transatlantica: Essays on Scandinavian Migration and Culture, 1979. Add: Honnold Library, Claremont, Calif. 91711, U.S.A.

SCOTT, Gavin (Duncan). British, b. 1950. Novels/Short stories. Reporter/Presenter with BBC Radio and TV, London, on World at One, Newsnight, etc. Reporter, New Zealand Broadcasting Corp., 1971–73, and with the Times Educational Supplement, London, 1973–75. *Publs:* Hot Pursuit, 1977; Flight of Lies, 1980; How to Get Rid of the Bomb, 1982. Add: 10 Vanbrugh Rd., London W4, England.

SCOTT, Jane. *See* **McELFRESH, Adeline.**

SCOTT, Janey. *See* **LINDSAY, Rachel.**

SCOTT, John Anthony. American, b. 1916. Education, History, Politics/Government, Biography. Lectr. in Legal History, Rutgers Univ., Sch. of Law, Newark, N.J., since 1967. Ed., Living History Library, Alfred A. Knopf Inc., NYC, since 1966, and Makers of America series, Facts on File, NYC, since 1985. *Publs:* Republican Ideas and the Liberal Tradition in France, 1951; (ed. and author) Frances A. Kemble: Journal of a Residence on a Georgian Plantation in 1838-39, 1961, 1984; (ed. and contrib.) Living Documents in American History, vol. I, 1964, vol. II, 1968; (ed. and trans.) The Defense of Gracchus Babeuf before the High Court of Vendome, 1964; The Ballad of America: The History of the United States in Song and Story, 1965, 1983; (ed. and contrib.) Frank Moore: The Diary of the American Revolution, 1967; Settlers on the Eastern Shore, 1607-1750, 1967; Trumpet of a Prophecy: Revolutionary America 1763-1783, 1969; Teaching for a Change, 1972; Fanny Kemble's America, 1973; Hard Trials on My Way: Slavery and the Struggle Against It, 1800-1860, 1974; Woman Against Slavery: The Life of Harriet Beecher Stowe, 1978; The Story of America, 1984; John Brown of Harper's Ferry, 1987. Add: Rutgers Univ., Sch. of Law, 15 Washington St., Newark, N.J. 07102, U.S.A.

SCOTT, Nathan A., Jr. American, b. 1925. Literature, Philosophy, Theology/Religion. William R. Kenan, Jr., Prof. of Religious Studies and Prof. of English, Univ. of Virginia, Charlottesville, since 1976. Advisory Ed., Modernist Studies, Religion and Literature, and The Virginia Quarterly Review. Assoc. Prof. of Humanities, Howard Univ., Washington, D.C. 1948–55; Shailer Mathews Prof. of Theology and Literature, and Co-Ed., The Journal of Religion, Univ. of Chicago, 1955–76. Fellow, Sch. of Letters, Indiana Univ., Bloomington, 1965–72. *Publs:* Rehearsals of Discomposure: Alienation and Reconciliation in Modern Literature, 1952; (ed.) The Tragic Vision and the Christian Faith, 1957; Modern Literature and the Religious Frontier, 1958; Albert Camus, 1962; Reinhold Niebuhr, 1963; (ed.) The New Orpheus: Essays Toward a Christian Poetic, 1964; (ed.) The Climate of Faith in Modern Literature, 1964; Samuel Beckett, 1965; (ed.) Four Ways of Modern Poetry, 1965; (ed.) Man in the Modern Theatre, 1965; The Broken Center: Studies in the Theological Horizon of Modern Literature, 1966; Ernest Hemingway, 1966; (ed.) The Modern Vision of Death, 1967; (ed.) Adversity and Grace: Studies in Recent American Literature, 1968; Craters of the Spirit: Studies in the Modern Novel, 1968; Negative Capability: Studies in the New Literature and the Religious Situation, 1969; The Unquiet Vision: Mirrors of Man in Existentialism, 1969; Nathanael West, 1971; The Wild Prayer of Longing: Poetry and the Sacred, 1971; Three American Moralists: Mailer, Bellow, Trilling, 1973; (ed.) The Legacy of Reinhold Niebuhr, 1975; The Poetry of Civic Virtue: Eliot, Malraux, Auden, 1976; Mirrors of Man in Existentialism, 1978; The Poetics of Belief: Studies in Coleridge, Arnold, Pater, Santayana, Stevens, and Heidegger, 1985. Add: Dept. of Religious Studies, Univ. of Virginia, Charlottesville, Va. 22903, U.S.A.

SCOTT, Roy Vernon. American, b. 1927. Agriculture/Forestry, History. Prof. of History since 1964, and Distinguished Prof. since 1978, Mississippi State Univ. (Asst. Prof., 1960–62; Assoc. Prof., 1962–64).

Research Assoc., Business History Foundn., 1958–59 and 1963–64; Visiting Asst. Prof., Univ. of Missouri, Columbia, 1959–60. *Publs:* The Agrarian Movement in Illinois, 1880-1896, 1962; The Reluctant Farmer: The Rise of Agricultural Extension to 1914, 1970; (with J.G. Shoalmire) The Public Career of Cully A. Cobb: A Study in Agricultural Leadership, 1973; (ed. with George L. Robson, Jr.) Southern Agriculture Since the Civil War, 1979; Railroad Development Programs in the Twentieth Century, 1985; (with Ralph W. Hidy and others) The Great Northern Railway: A History, 1988. Add: Dept. of History, Mississippi State Univ., Mississippi State, Miss. 39762, U.S.A.

SCOTT, Tom. Scottish b. 1918. Poetry, Children's non-fiction, Literature. Former Ed., Scottish Literature Series, Pergamon Press, Oxford. *Publs:* Seven Poems of Maister Francis Villon, 1953; An Ode til New Jerusalem, 1956; The Ship and Ither Poems, 1963; A Possible Solution to the Scotch Question, 1963; Dunbar: A Critical Exposition of the Poems, 1966; (ed. with J. MacQueen) The Oxford Book of Scottish Verse, 1966; (ed.) Late Medieval Scots Poetry: A Selection from the Makars and Their Heirs down to 1610, 1967; At the Shrine o the Unkent Sodger: A Poem for Recitation, 1968; Tales of King Robert the Bruce, 1969; (ed.) The Penguin Book of Scottish Verse, 1970; Brand the Builder, 1975; The Tree, 1977; Tales of Sir William Wallace, 1981; The Dirty Business, 1986. Add: Duddingston Park, Edinburgh 15, Scotland.

SCOTT, Warwick. *See* **TREVOR, Elleston.**

SCOTTI, R.A. American, b. 1946. Mystery/Crime/Suspense. Formerly: Publicist, Holt Publishing Co., NYC; Copywriter, Book-of-the-Month Club, NYC; Ed., Star-Ledger, Newark, N.J., 1967–68. *Publs:* The Kiss of Judas, 1958; The Devil's Own, 1985; The Hammer's Eye, 1987. Add: 224 E. 18th St., New York, N.Y. 10003, U.S.A.

SCOUTEN, Arthur H(awley). American, b. 1910. Literature, Biography. Instr., Texas A. and M. Coll., 1942–43, and the Univ. of Texas, 1943–46; Prof. of English, Univ. of Pennsylvania, Philadelphia, 1947–80; Prof. of English, Univ. of Delaware, Wilmington, 1981. *Publs:* (ed. with Leo Hughes) Ten English Farces, 1948; (ed.) The London Stage: 1660-1800, part 3, 2 vols., 1961; (ed.) A Bibliography of the Writings of Jonathan Swift, 1963; (ed. with E.L. Avery) The London Stage 1660-1800, part 1, 1965; (ed. with R.D. Hume) The Country Gentleman, by Sir Robert Howard and George Villiers, 2nd Duke of Buckingham, 1976; (with J. Loftis, R. Southern, and M. Jones) The Revels History of Drama in English, vol. V: 1660-1750, 1976; Jonathan Swift's Progress from Prose to Poetry, 1981. Add: 8419 Shawnee St., Chestnut Hill, Philadelphia, Pa. 19118, U.S.A.

SCOVELL, E(dith) J(oy). British, b. 1907. Poetry. *Publs:* Shadows of Chrysanthemums and Other Poems, 1944; The Midsummer Meadow and Other Poems, 1946; The River Steamer and Other Poems, 1956; The Space Between, 1982; Listening to Collared Doves, 1986; Collected Poems, 1988. Add: 61 Park Town, Oxford OX2 6SL, England.

SCOVILLE, James Griffin. American, b. 1940. Economics, Industrial relations. Prof. of Industrial Relations, Univ. of Minnesota, Minneapolis, since 1979 (Dir., Industrial Relations Center, 1979–82). Instr., 1964–65, and Asst. Prof. of Economics, 1966–69, Harvard Univ., Cambridge, Mass.; Economist, Intnl. Labour Office, Geneva, Switzerland, 1965–66; Assoc. Prof., 1969–75, and Prof. of Economics and Labor and Industrial Relations, 1975–79, Univ. of Illinois, Urbana, Ill. *Publs:* The Job Content of the U.S. Economy, 1940-70, 1970; (ed.) Perspectives on Poverty and Income Distribution, 1971; Manpower and Occupational Analysis: Concepts and Measurements, 1972; (ed. with Adolf Sturmthal and contrib.) The International Labor Movement in Transition, 1973. Add: 4849 Girard Ave. S., Minneapolis, Minn. 55409, U.S.A.

SCREECH, M(ichael) A(ndrew). British, b. 1926. Intellectual history, Literature. Sr. Research Fellow, All Souls Coll., Oxford, since 1984. Asst., French Dept., University Coll., 1950–51; Asst. Lectr., Lectr., and Sr. Lectr., Univ. of Birmingham, 1951–61; Reader, then Prof. of French, 1961–71, and Fielden Prof. of French Language and Literature, 1971–84, University Coll., Univ. of London. *Publs:* The Rabelaisian Marriage: Aspects of Rabelais's Religion, Ethics, and Comic Philosophy, 1958; L'Evangelisme de Rabelais: Aspects de la satire religieuse au xvie siècle, 1959; (ed.) Le Tiers Livre de Pantagruel, 1964, 1975; (ed.) Le fèvre d'Etaples: Cinquante-deux semaines de l'an, 1964; (ed.) Joachim du Bellay: Les regrets et autres oeuvres poetiques, 1966, 3rd ed. 1979; (ed.) Gargantua (text by Ruth Calder), 1970; (ed.) La Pantagrueline Prognostication, 1975; Rabelais, 1980; Ecstasy and the Praise of Folly, 1981, 1988;

Montaigne and Melancholy, 1983; (with Anne Reeve) Erasmus' Annotations on the New Testament: The Gospels, 1986; (with Stephen Rawles) A New Rabelais Bibliography: Editions Before 1626, 1987; (ed. and trans.) Montaigne: An Apology for Raymond Sebond, 1987. Add: All Souls Coll., Oxford OX1 4AL, England.

SCROGGIE, Marcus Graham. British, b. 1901. Engineering/Technology. Independent consultant, since 1932. Chief Engineer, Burndept Wireless Ltd., 1928–1931; Squadron Leader, R.A.F., Technical Branch, 1943–45. *Publs:* Television, 1935; Radio and Electronic Laboratory Handbook, 1938, 9th ed. 1980; Foundations of Wireless and Electronics, 1943, 10th ed. 1984; Second Thoughts on Radio Theory, 1955; Fundamentals of Semiconductors, 1960; Principles of Semiconductors, 1961; The Electron in Electronics, 1965; Phasor Diagrams, 1966; Essays in Electronics, 1963. Add: 12 Pinewoods, Bexhill-on-Sea, East Sussex TN39 3UD, England.

SCRUTON, Roger. British, b. 1944. Architecture, Philosophy, Politics/Government. Prof. of Aesthetics, Birkbeck Coll., Univ. of London, since 1985 (Lectr., subsequently Reader in Philosophy, 1971-85). Fellow, Peterhouse, Cambridge, 1969–71. *Publs:* (co-author) Morality and Moral Reasoning 1971; Art and Imagination, 1974; The Aesthetics of Architecture, 1979; The Meaning of Conservatism, 1980; A Short History of Modern Philosophy, 1981; Fortnight's Anger, 1981; The Politics of Culture, 1981; Kant, 1982; A Dictionary of Political Thought, 1982; The Aesthetic Understanding, 1983; Thinkers of the New Left, 1985; Sexual Desire, 1986; Spinoza, 1986; A Land Held Hostage, 1987; Untimely Tracts, 1987. Add: 6 Linden Gardens, London W2, England.

SCULLY, James (Joseph). American, b. 1937. Poetry, Literary criticism, Translations. Assoc. Prof. to Prof. of English, Univ. of Connecticut, Storrs, since 1964. Instr., Rutgers Univ., New Brunswick, N.J., 1963–64; taught at Hartford Street Academy, Conn., 1968–69. *Publs:* (ed.) Modern Poetics (in U.K. as Modern Poets on Modern Poetry), 1965; The Marches: A Book of Poems, 1967; Communications, 1970; Avenue of the Americas, 1971; Santiago Poems, 1975; (trans. with C. Herington) Prometheus Bound, by Aeschylus, 1975; Scrap Book, 1977; (trans with Maria Proser) Quechua Peoples Poetry, 1977; (trans. with Maria Proser and Arlene Scully) De Repente/All of a Sudden, by Teresa de Jesus, 1979; May Day, 1980; Apollo Helmet, 1983; Line Break: Poetry as Social Practice, 1988. Add: 250 Lewiston Ave., Willimantic, Conn. 06226, U.S.A.

SCUPHAM, (John) Peter. British, b. 1933. Poetry. Chmn. of the English Dept., St. Christopher Sch., Letchworth, Herts., since 1961; Ed., Cellar Press, and Owner, Mandeville Press, both in Hitchin, Herts. English Teacher, Skegness Grammar Sch., Lincs., 1957–61. *Publs:* The Small Containers, 1972; The Snowing Globe, 1972; Children Dancing, 1972; The Nondescript, 1973; The Gift, 1973; Prehistories, 1975; The Hinterland, 1977; Natura, 1978; Summer Palaces, 1980; (with John Mole) Christmas Past, 1981; Transformation Scenes: A Sequence of Five Poems, 1982; Winter Quarters, 1983; (with John Mole) Christmas Games, 1983; (with John Mole) Christmas Visits, 1985; Out Late, 1986; (with John Mole) Christmas Emblems, 1986; The Air Show, 1988; (with John Mole) Christmas Gifts, 1988. Add: 2 Taylor's Hill, Hitchin, Herts. SG4 9AD, England.

SEABORG, Glenn (Theodore). American, b. 1912. Chemistry. University Prof. of Chemistry, Univ. of California, Berkeley, since 1971; also, Assoc. Dir. of the Lawrence Berkeley Lab., since 1972, and Dir. of the Lawrence Hall of Science, Berkeley, since 1982 (joined faculty, 1937; Instr., 1939–41; Asst. Prof., 1941–45; Prof., 1945–71; Chancellor, 1958–61). Pres., American Assn. for the Advancement of Science, 1972, and American Chemical Soc., 1976. Co-discoverer of: nuclear energy source isotopes Pu-239 and U-233; and of the elements: 94, plutonium; 95, americium; 96, curium; 97, berkelium; 98, californium; 99, einsteinium; 100, fermium; 101, mendelevium; 102, nobelium. Recipient, Nobel Prize for Chemistry, 1951. *Publs:* The Chemistry of the Actinide Elements, 1958; The Transuranium Elements, 1958; Elements of the Universe, 1958; Man-Made Transuranium Elements, 1963; Education and the Atom, 1964; The Nuclear Properties of the Heavy Elements, 1964; Oppenheimer, 1969; Man and Atom, 1971; Nuclear Milestones, 1972; (ed.) Transuranium Elements: Products of Modern Alchemy, 1978; Kennedy, Khrushchev and the Test Ban, 1981; (co-ed.) Nuclear Chemistry, 1982; Stemming the Tide: Arms Control in the Johnson Years, 1987. Add: Lawrence Berkeley Lab., Univ. of California, Berkeley, Calif. 94720, U.S.A.

SEABROOK, Jeremy. British, b. 1939. Sociology, Autobiography/Memoirs/Personal. Dramatist, mainly in collaboration with Michael

O'Neill. Taught in secondary-modern sch. for two years; Social Worker for Inner London Education Authority, 1967–69, and with Elfrida Rathbone Assn., 1973–76. *Publs:* The Unprivileged: A Hundred Years of Family Life and Tradition in a Working-Class Street, 1967; City Close-Up, 1971; The Everlasting Feast, 1974; A Lasting Relationship: Homosexuals and Society, 1976; What Went Wrong? Working People and the Ideals of the Labour Movement, 1978; Mother and Son: An Autobiography, 1980; Working Class Childhood, 1982; A World Still to Win: The Reconstruction of the Post-War Working Class, 1985; Landscapes of Poverty, 1985; Life and Labour in a Bombay Slum, 1987; (with Trevor Blackwell) The Politics of Hope, 1988; The Leisure Society, 1988; The Race for Riches, 1988. Add: c/o Curtis Brown, 162-168 Regent St., London W1R 5TB, England.

SEABURY, Paul. American, b.1923. Politics/Government. Prof. of Political Science, Univ. of California, Berkeley, 1963–65 and since 1967 (joined faculty, 1953; Asst. Dean, Coll. of Letters and Science, 1963–64; Vice Chmn., Dept. of Political Science, 1964–65; Chmn. Coll. of Letters and Science, 1967–69). Vice Chmn., Bd. of Foreign Scholarships, U.S. Dept. of State; Vice Chmn., Univ. Centers for Rational Alternatives, NYC.; Dir., Pumpkin Papers Irregulars, since 1979; Chmn., Intnl. Council on the Future of the Univ.; Member, President's Foreign Intelligence Advisory Bd., since 1982. Lectr. then Instr., Columbia Univ., NYC, 1947–53; Prof. of Govt. and Provost, Univ. of California at Santa Cruz, 1966–67. Consultant, U.S. Dept. of State, 1965–69. *Publs:* The Wilhelmstrasse, 1954; Power, Freedom and Diplomacy, 1963; The Balance of Power, 1965; The Rise and Decline of the Cold War, 1966; The Game of Croquet, 1968; (with A. Wildavsky) U.S.vForeign Policy: Perspectives and Proposals, 1969; The Foreign Policy of the United States of America, 1972; Universities in the Western World, 1976; (ed. and contrib.) Bureaucrats and Brainpower, 1980; America's Stake in the Pacific, 1981; (co-ed.) The Grenada Papers, 1984. Add: Dept. of Political Science, Univ. of California, Berkeley, Calif. 94705, U.S.A.

SEAGER, Ralph William. American, b. 1911. Poetry. Emeritus Prof. of English, Keuka Coll., Keuka Park, N.Y. (joined faculty, 1960). *Publs:* Songs from a Willow Whistle, 1956; Beyond the Green Gate, 1958; Christmas Chimes in Rhyme, 1962; The Sound of an Echo, 1963; Cup, Flagon, and Fountain, 1965; A Choice of Dreams, 1970; Wheatfields and Vineyards, 1975; Little Yates and the United States, 1976; The Manger Mouse and Other Christmas Poems, 1977; Hiding in Plain Sight, 1982; The Love Tree, 1985; (with others) The First Quartet, 1988. Add: 311 Keuka St., Penn Yan, N.Y. 14527, U.S.A.

SEAGRAVE, Barbara Ann Garvey. *See* **JACKSON,** Barbara Ann Garvey Seagrave.

SEALE, Sara. Pseud. for A.D.L. MacPherson. Historical/Romance/Gothic. *Publs:* Beggars May Sing, 1932; Chase the Moon, 1933; Summer Spell, 1937; Grace Before Meat, 1938; This Merry Bond, 1938; Spread Your Wings, 1939; Green Grass Growing, 1940; Stormy Petrel, 1941; Barn Dance, 1941; The Silver Sty, 1941; House of Glass, 1944, in Can. as Maggy, 1959; Folly to Be Wise, 1946; The Reluctant Orphan, 1947, in Can. as Orphan Bride, 1962; The English Tutor, 1948; The Gentle Prisoner, 1949; These Delights, 1949; Then She Fled Me, 1950; The Young Amanda, 1950; The Dark Stranger, 1951; Wintersbride, 1951; The Lordly One, 1952; The Forbidden Island, 1953; Turn to the West, 1953; The Truant Spirit, 1954; Time of Grace, 1956; Child Friday, 1956; Sister to Cinderella, 1956; I Know My Love, 1957; Trevallion, 1957; Lucy Lamb, 1958; Charity Child, 1959; Dear Dragon, 1959; Cloud Castle, 1960; The Only Charity, 1961; Valentine's Day, 1962; The Reluctant Landlord, 1962; Doctor's Ward, 1962; By Candlelight, 1963; The Youngest Bridesmaid, 1963; The Third Uncle, 1964; To Catch a Unicorn, 1964; Green Girl, 1965; The Truant Bride, 1966; Penny Plain, 1967; That Young Person, 1969; The Queen of Hearts, 1969; Dear Professor, 1970; Mr. Brown, 1971, in Can. as The Unknown Mr. Brown, 1972; My Heart's Desire, 1976. Add: c/o Mills and Boon Ltd., Eton House, 18-24 Paradise Rd., Richmond, Surrey TW9 1SR, England

SEALE, William. American, b. 1939. Architecture, History, Biography. Specialist in the restoration of historic buildings; consultant on various restorations. *Publs:* Texas Riverman, 1966; Sam Houston's Wife, 1970; Texas in Our Time, 1971; The Tasteful Interlude: American Interiors 1860–1917, 1975; (with H.R. Hitchcock) Temples of Democracy: The State Capitols of the USA, 1976; Courthouse, 1978; Recreating the Historic House Interior, 1979; The President's House, 1986. Add: 805 Prince St., Alexandria, Va. 22314, U.S.A.

SEALEY, Leonard (George William). British, b. 1923. Children's non-fiction, Education, Mathematics/Statistics. Self-employed educational writer and consultant, since 1968. Adviser to Primary Schs., Leics., 1956–65; Principal, North Bucks. Coll. of Education, 1965–67; Dir., Regional Educational Lab. Prog., Newton, Mass., 1967–68. *Publs:* The Creative Use of Mathematics, 1961; (co-author) Communication and Learning, 1962; Finding Out About the World of Numbers, 1963; (co-author) Beginning Mathematics, 1963; About Numbers, 1964; The Teaching of Elementary School Mathematics, 1964; The Shapes of Things, 1965; Introducing Mathematics, 1968; Exploring Language, 1968; Basic Skills in Learning, 1970; First School Mathematics, 1971; Let's Find Out About Mathematics, 1971; The Post Office Books, 1971; Introducing Computation, 1971; Practice and Processes, 1972; Lively Reading, 1973; Macmillan Children's Encyclopedia, 2 vols., 1974; Open Education, 1977; (co-author) Children's Writing, 1979. Add: 11 Chilton St., Plymouth, Mass. 02360, U.S.A.

SEALTS, Merton M., Jr. American, b. 1915. Literature, Biography. Emeritus Henry A. Pochmann Prof. of English, Univ. of Wisconsin, Madison, since 1982 (Prof., 1965–75; Henry A. Pochmann Prof., 1975–82). Instr. in English, Univ. of Missouri, 1941–42; Instr. in English, Wellesley Coll., 1946–48; Asst. Prof., 1948–51, Assoc. Prof., 1951–58, and Prof. of English, 1958–65, Lawrence Univ. *Publs:* Melville as Lecturer, 1957; (ed. with H. Hayford) Billy Budd, Sailor, by Herman Melville, 1962; (ed.) The Journals and Miscellaneous Notebooks of Ralph Waldo Emerson 1835-1838, vol. V, 1965; Melville's Reading: A Check-List of Books Owned and Borrowed, 1966, 1988; (ed. with A.R. Ferguson) Emerson's Nature: Origin, Growth, Meaning, 1969, 1979; (ed.) The Journals and Miscellaneous Notebooks of Ralph Waldo Emerson 1847-1848, vol. X, 1973; The Early Lives of Melville: Nineteenth Century Biographical Sketches and Their Authors, 1974; Pursuing Melville, 1940-1980: Chapters and Essays, 1982. Add: 4006 Mandan Cres., Madison, Wisc. 53711, U.S.A.

SEAMAN, Gerald Roberts. British, b. 1934. Music. Assoc. Prof. of Musicology, Univ. of Auckland, since 1970 (Sr. Lectr., 1965–69; Acting Head of Dept., 1978). Lectr. in Music, Nottingham Training Coll., 1962–64; Sr. Assoc. Member, St. Antony's Coll. Oxford, 1980. *Publs:* History of Russian Music, vol. I, 1968; The Rimksy-Korsakov Research Manual: A Bibliography and Research Guide, 1989. Add: Dept. of Music, Univ. of Auckland, Private Bag, Auckland, New Zealand.

SEAMAN, Sylvia Sybil. Also writes with F. Schwartz under joint pseud. Francis Sylvin. American, b. 1910. Novels/Short stories, Medicine/Health, Humor/ Satire. *Publs:* (as Francis Sylvin) Rusty Carrousel, 1943; (as Francis Sylvin) Miracle Father, 1952; (as Francis Sylvin) Test-Tube Father; Always a Woman, 1965; How to Be a Jewish Grandmother, 1979. Add: 244 W. 74th St., New York, N.Y. 10023, U.S.A.

SEARE, Nicholas. *See* **TREVANIAN.**

SEARLE, Graham William. British, b. 1937. History, Theology/Religion. Dir., Independent Schools Careers Organization, since 1988. Asst. Master, Strathallan Sch., Perthshire, 1962–66; Head of History, Stamford Sch., 1966–75; Headmaster, Colston's Sch., Bristol, 1975–88. *Publs:* The Counter Reformation, 1974. Add: 35 Buttermere Dr., Camberley, Surrey, England.

SEARLE, John R(ogers). American, b. 1932. Philosophy. Prof. of Philosophy, Univ. of California, Berkeley, since 1966 (Asst. Prof., 1959–64; Assoc. Prof., 1964–66; Special Asst. to the Chancellor, 1965–67). *Publs:* Speech Acts: An Essay in the Philosophy of Language, 1969; The Campus War, 1971; (ed.) The Philosophy of Language, 1971; Expression and Meaning: Studies in the Theory of Speech Acts, 1979; (ed. with others) Speech Act Theory and Pragmatics, 1980; Intentionality: An Essay in the Philosophy of Mind, 1983; Minds, Brains, and Science, 1984; (with D. Vanderveken) Foundations of Illocutionary Logic, 1985. Add: Dept. of Philosophy, Univ. of California, Berkeley, Calif. 94720, U.S.A.

SEARLE, Ronald (William Fordham). British, b. 1920. Humour/Satire. Graphic artist and cartoonist: creator of St. Trinian's series. *Publs:* Forty Drawings, 1946; Le Nouveau Ballet Anglais, 1947; Hurrah for St. Trinian's!, 1948; The Female Approach, 1949; Back to the Slaughterhouse, 1951; Souls in Torment, 1953; Rake's Progress, 1955; Merry England, 1956; Which Way Did He Go, 1961; Searle in the Sixties, 1965; From Frozen North to Filthy Lucre, 1964; Pardong M'sieur, 1965; Searle's Cats, 1967; The Square Egg, 1968; Hello—Where Did All the People Go?, 1969; Hommage à Toulouse Lautrec, 1969; Secret Sketchbook, 1970; The Addict, 1971; More Cats, 1975; Drawings from

Gilbert and Sullivan, 1975; The Zoodiac, 1977; Ronald Searle, 1978; The King of Beasts, 1980; The Big Fat Cat Book, 1982; Winespeak, 1983; Ronald Searle in Perspective, 1984; Ronald Searle's Golden Oldies, 1985; To the Kwai—and Back, 1986; Something in the Cellar, 1986; Ah, Yes, I Remember It Well: Paris 1961-1975, 1987; Ronald Searle's Non-Sexist Dictionary, 1988. Add: c/o Tessa Sayle, 11 Jubilee Pl., London SW3 3TE, England.

SEARLES, (William) Baird. American, b. 1934. Literature (science fiction). Columnist, "On Books," in Isaac Asimov's Magazine of Science Fiction, since 1981; Consulting Ed., Popular Library/Questar Books, since 1985. Professional dancer, 1954–69; Assoc. Ed., Science Fiction Review Monthly, 1965–68; Dir. of Drama and Literature Programming, WBAI-FM Radio, NYC, 1969–73; Columnist, "Films and Television," Magazine of Fantasy and Science Fiction, 1970–84; Owner, Science Fiction Shop, NYC, 1974–86. *Publs:* Stranger in a Strange Land and Other Works, 1975; (with Martin Last) The Science Fiction Quizbook, 1976; (with others) A Reader's Guide to Science Fiction, 1979; (with Ben Meacham and Michael Franklin) A Reader's Guide to Fantasy, 1982; Films of Science Fiction and Fantasy, 1988. Add: 135 Charles St. New York, N.Y. 10014, U.S.A.

SEARLS, Hank. (Henry Hunt Searls, Jr.). American, b. 1922. Novels/Short stories, Science fiction/Fantasy, Biography. Freelance writer since 1959. Writer for Hughes Aircraft, Culver City, Calif., 1955–56, Douglas Aircraft, Santa Monica, Calif., 1956–57, and Warner Brothers, Burbank, Calif., 1959. *Publs:* The Big X, 1959; The Crowded Sky, 1960; The Astronaut, 1960; The Pilgrim Project, 1964; The Hero Ship, 1969; The Lost Prince: Young Joe, The Forgotten Kennedy, 1969; Pentagon (novel), 1971; Never Kill a Cop (novel), 1977; Overboard, 1977; Jaws 2 (novelization of screenplay), 1978; Firewind (novel), 1981; Sounding, 1982; Blood Song, 1984; Jaws: The Revenge, 1987; Kataki, 1987. Add: c/o Scott Meredith Literary Agency, 845 Third Ave., New York, N.Y. 10022, U.S.A.

SEARS, David O('Keefe). American, b. 1935. Politics/Government, Psychology. Prof. of Psychology and Political Science, since 1971, and Dean of Social Sciences, since 1983, Univ. of California at Los Angeles, (Asst. Prof., 1961–67; Assoc. Prof. of Psychology, 1967–69; Assoc. Prof. of Psychology and Political Science, 1969–71). *Publs:* (with R.E. Lane) Public Opinion, 1964; (with J.L. Freedman and J.M. Carlsmith) Social Psychology, 1970; (with Freedman and Carlsmith) Readings in Social Psychology, 1971; (with J.B. McConahay) The Politics of Violence, 1973; (with J. Citrin) Tax Revolt, 1982; (with R. Lan) Political Cognition, 1986. Add: Dept. of Psychology, Univ. of California, Los Angeles, Calif. 90024, U.S.A.

SEBASTIAN, Lee. *See* **SILVERBERG,** Robert.

SEBASTIAN, Margaret. *See* **GLADSTONE,** Arthur M.

SEBEOK, Thomas A(lbert). American (b. Hungarian), b. 1920. Anthropology/Ethnology, Language/Linguistics, Mythology/Folklore. Distinguished Prof. of Linguistics since 1967, and of Semiotics since 1978, Prof. of Anthropology, and of Uralic and Altaic Studies, Indiana Univ., Bloomington (—joined faculty, 1943; Dir. of Human Relations Area Files, 1965–69). Pres., Semiotic Soc. of America since 1984 (Exec. Dir., 1976–80; Chmn., Editorial Bd., 1976–80; Vice-Pres., 1983). Asst. Dir., 1952, 1953, Assoc. Dir., 1958, 1975, and Dir., 1964, Linguistic Inst. of Linguistic Soc. of America; Pres., Linguistic Soc. of America, 1975. *Publs:* Guide's Manual for Spoken Hungarian, 1945; Spoken Hungarian, 1945; Spoken Finnish, 1947; Studies in Cheremis Folklore, vol. 1, with others, 1952, vol. 2 The Supernatural, with F.J. Ingemann, 1955, vol. 3 The First Cheremis Grammar (1775), with A. Raun, 1956, vol. 5, The Cheremis, 1956, vol. 6, Games, with P.G. Brewster, 1958, vol. 8, Concordance and Thesaurus of Poetic Language, with V.J. Zeps, 1961, vol. 9, An Eastern Cheremis Manual: Phonology, Grammar, Texts, and Glossary, with F.J. Ingemann, 1961; (ed. and co-author with C.E. Osgood) Psycholinguistics: Survey of Theory and Research Problems, 1954; (ed.) Myth: A Symposium, 1958; The Mari Region, USSR, 1959; (co-ed.) American Studies in Uralic Linguistics, 1960; (ed.) Style in Language, 1960; (ed.) Current Trends in Linguistics, 14 vols., 1963–76; (ed. with A.S. Hayes and M.C. Bateson) Approaches to Semiotics: Cultural Anthropology, Education, Linguistics, Psychiatry, Psychology, 1964; Portraits of Linguists: A Biographical Source Book for the History of Western Linguistics, 1746-1963, 2 vols., 1966; (ed.) Selected Writings of Gyula Laziczius, 1966; (co-author) Communication Systems and Resources in the Behavioral Sciences, 1967; (ed.) Animal Communication: Techniques of Study and Results of Research, 1968; (ed. with A.

Ramsay) Approaches to Animal Communication, 1969; Perspectives in Zoosemiotics, 1972; Structure and Texture: Selected Essays in Cheremis Verbal Art, 1974; (ed.) The Tell-Tale Sign, 1975; Contributions to the Doctrine of Signs, 1975; From the Life of the Cheremis, 1975; (co-ed) Speech Surrogates: Drum and Whistle System, 1976; (ed.) Native Languages of the Americas, 2 vols., 1976–77; (ed.) How Animals Communicate, 1977; (ed.) A Perfusion of Signs, 1977; (ed.) Aboriginal Sign Languages of the Americas and Australia, 2 vols., 1978; (ed.) Cheremis Literary Reader, 1978; Semiosis in Nature and Culture, 1978; (ed.) Sight, Sound, and Sense, 1978; (ed. with Jean Umiker-Sebeok) Speaking of Apes: A Critical Anthology of Two-Way Communication with Man, 1980; (with Jean Umiker-Sebeok) You Know My Method: A Juxtaposition of Charles S. Peirce and Sherlock Holmes, 1980; (ed. with Robert Rosenthal) The Clever Hans Phenomenon: Communication with Horses, Whales, Apes, and People, 1981; The Play of Musement, 1981; (ed. with Umberto Eco) The Sign of Three, 1983; (co-author and co-ed.) Classics of Modern Semiotics, 1985; (ed.-in-chief) Encyclopedic Dictionary of Semiotics, 1985; (ed. with Jean Umiker-Sebeok) The Semiotic Sphere, 1985; Shizen to Bunka no kigo, 1985. Add: 1104 Covenanter Dr., Bloomington, 47401, U.S.A.

SEBESTYEN, Ouida. American, b. 1924. Children's fiction. *Publs:* Words by Heart, 1979; Far from Home, 1980; IOU's, 1982; On Fire, 1985; The Girl in the Box, 1988. Add: 115 S. 36th St., Boulder, Colo. 80303, U.S.A.

SEDERBERG, Arelo (Charles). American, b. 1931. Novels/Short stories, Money/Finance. Asst. Managing Ed., Economic News, Los Angeles Herald Examiner, since 1978. Reporter, Los Angeles Mirror, 1954–63; Financial Writer, Los Angeles Times, 1963–70; Public Relations Exec., Carl Byoir and Assocs. Inc., Los Angeles and Las Vegas, 1970–78. *Publs:* The Stock Market Investment Club Handbook, 1971; A Collection for J.L., 1973, in paperback as How to Kidnap a Millionaire, 1974; Sixty Hours of Darkness, 1974; Casino, 1977; Breedlove, 1979; The Power Players, 1980. Add: 447 W. Duarte Rd., no. 6, Arcadia, Calif., U.S.A.

SEDWICK, Frank. American, b. 1924. Language/Linguistics, Literature. Prof. of Spanish, Univ. of Maryland, College Park, 1947–49, U.S. Naval Academy, Annapolis, Md., 1951–53, Univ. of Wisconsin, Milwaukee, 1953–58, Ohio Wesleyan Univ., 1958–63, and Rollins Coll., Winter Park, Fla., 1963–80. *Publs:* (ed.) Dos comedias de Unamuno, 1960; (ed.) La forja de los suenos, 1960; The Tragedy of Manuel Azana and the Fate of the Spanish Republic, 1963; A History of the Useless Precaution Plot in Spanish and French Literature, 1964; (co-ed.) La gloria de Don Ramiro, 1966; (co-ed) Selecciones de Madariaga, 1969; Conversation in Spanish, 1969, 5th ed. 1989; (co-author) Conversaciones con madrilenos, 1974; Spanish for Careers, 1980; The Practical Book of Cobs, 1987. Add: 2033 Cove Trail, Maitland, Fla. 32751, U.S.A.

SEE, Carolyn. Also writes as Monica Highland. American, b. 1934. Novelist and journalist. Adjunct Prof., then Prof. of Literature, Univ. of California at Los Angeles. *Publs:* The Rest Is Done with Mirrors, 1970; Blue Money, 1974; Mothers, Daughters, 1977; Rhine Maidens, 1981; Golden Days, 1987; Making History, 1989; as Monica Highland—Lotus Land, 1983; 1-10 Shanghai Road, 1985; Greetings from Southern California, 1988. Add: P.O. Box 107, Topanga, Calif., U.S.A.

SEED, Jenny (Cecile Eugenie Seed). South African, b. 1930. Children's fiction. *Publs:* Peter the Gardener, 1966; To the Rescue, 1966; Tombi's Song, 1966; Timothy and Tinker, 1967; The River Man, 1968; Canvas City, 1968; The Voice of the Great Elephant, 1968; Kulumi the Brave, 1970; The Prince of the Bay (in U.S. as The Vengeance of the Zulu King), 1970; The Great Thirst, 1971; The Broken Spear, 1972; The Red Dust Soldiers, 1972; The Sky Green Lizard, 1973; The Bushman's Dream, 1974; The Unknown Land, 1976; Strangers in the Land, 1976; The Year One, 1981; The Policeman's Button, 1981; Gold Dust, 1982; The New Fire, 1983; The Spy Hill, 1984; Place among the Stones, 1987; Hurry, Hurry, Sibusiso, 1988. Add: 10 Pioneer Cres., Northdene, Queensburgh, Natal, South Africa.

SEELEY, Ivor Hugh. British, b. 1924. Engineering/Technology. Head, Dept. of Surveying, and Dean of Environmental Studies, Trent Polytechnic, Nottingham, 1970–82, now Emeritus Prof.; Visiting Prof., Essex Inst. of Higher Education. Series Ed., Macmillan Bldg.and Surveying Series. Engineer and Surveyor, Haverhill Urban District Council, Suffolk, 1956–60; Engineer and Surveyor, Newport-Pagnell Rural District Council, 1960–61. *Publs:* Building Quantities Explained; Civil Engineering Quantities; Municipal Engineering Practice: Civil Engineering

Specification; Outdoor Recreation and the Urban Environment; Building Economics; Building Technology; Planned Expansion of Country Towns; Building Maintenance; Local Government Explained; Advanced Building Measurement; Quantity Surveying Practice; Building Surveys, Reports and Dilapidations; Civil Engineering Contract Administration and Control. Add: 36A Mapperley Hall Dr., Nottingham NG3 5EW, England.

SEELYE, John (Douglas). American, b. 1931. Novels/Short stories, Film, Literature. Grad. Research Prof., Univ. of Florida, Gainesville, since 1984. Consulting Ed., Penguin Books, NYC, since 1979. Assoc. Prof. of English, Univ. of California at Berkeley, 1960–65; Assoc. Prof, 1966–71, and Prof., 1971–74, Univ. of Connecticut, Storrs; Prof. of English, Univ. of North Carolina, Chapel Hill, 1974–84. Contrib. Ed., New Republic, Washington, D.C., 1971–79; Member of Editorial Bd., American Literature, Durham, N.C., 1974–78. *Publs:* (ed.) Arthur Gordon Pym, Benito Cereno, and Related Writings, 1967; (ed.) Etchings of a Whaling Cruise, by J. Ross Browne, 1968; The True Adventures of Huckleberry Finn, as told by John Seelye, 1970; Melville: The Ironic Diagram, 1970; The Kid, 1972; Dirty Tricks, or, Nick Noxin's Natural Nobility, 1974; Prophetic Waters: The River in Early American Life and Literature, 1977; Mark Twain in the Movies: A Meditation with Pictures, 1977; (Ed.) The Adventures of Huckleberry Finn, by Twain, 1985; (ed.) The Adventures of Tom Sawyer, by Twain, 1986; (ed.) The Virginian, by Owen Wister, 1988; (ed.) Yankee Drover: Being the Unpretending Life of Asa Sheldon, 1988. Add: 439 N.E. 9th Ave., Gainesville, Fla. 32601, U.S.A.

SEFTON, Catherine. Pseudonym for Martin Waddell. Irish, b. 1941. Novels/Short stories, Children's fiction. Full-time writer. *Publs:* children's fiction—In a Blue Velvet Dress, 1972; The Sleepers on the Hill, 1973; The Back House Ghosts, 1974, in USA as The Haunting of Ellen, 1975; The Ghost and Bertie Boggin, 1980; Emer's Ghost, 1981; The Finn Gang, 1981; A Puff of Smoke, 1982; The Emma Dilemma, 1982; Island of the Strangers, 1983; My Gang, 1984; The Blue Misty Monsters, 1985; The Ghost Girl, 1985; The Ghost Ship, 1985; Flying Sam, 1986; Starry Night, 1986; Shadows on the Lake, 1987; Bertie Boggin and the Ghost Again, 1988; The Day Smells Went Wrong, 1988; Frankie's Story, 1988; The Haunted Schoolbag, 1989; The Beat of The Drum, 1989. children's fiction as Martin Waddell—Ernie's Chemistry Set Flying Trousers, 2 vols., 1978; Napper Goes for Goal Strikes Again, 2 vols., 1981; The Great Green Mouse Disaster, 1981; Harriet and the Crocodiles Haunted School, Robot, Flying Teachers, 4 vols., 1982–87; The House under the Stairs, 1983; Solve-It-Yourself Mysteries: The Mystery Squad and the Dead Man's Message the Artful Dodger, the Whistling Thief, Mr. Midnight, the Creeping Castle, the Camera, the Robot's Revenge, the Cannonball Kid, 8 vols., 1983–86; Going West, 1983; Big Bad Bertie, 1984; Napper's Golden Goals, 1984; The Budgie Said GRRR, 1985; The School Reporter's Notebook, 1985; Owl and Billy, 1986; The Day It Rained Elephants, 1986; Our Wild Weekend, 1986; Little Dracula's First Bite Christmas, at the Seaside, Goes to School, 4 vols., 1986–87; The Tough Princess, 1986; Owl and Billy and the Space Days, 1987; The Tall Story of Wilbur Small, 1987; Can't You Sleep, Little Bear?, 1988; Great Gran Gorilla to the Rescue, 1988; Great Gran Gorilla and the Robbers, 1988; Alice the Artist, 1988; Class Three and the Beanstalk, 1988; novels as Martin Waddell—Otley, 1966; Otley Pursued Forever, Victorious, 3 vols., 1967–69; Come Back When I'm Sober, 1969; A Little Bit British, Being the Diary of an Ulsterman, 1970; other—(ed.) A Tale to Tell, 1982. Add: 139 Central Promenade, Newcastle, Co. Down, Northern Ireland.

SEGAL, Erich. American, b. 1937. Novels/Short stories, Plays/Screenplays, Classics. Adjunct Prof. of Classics, Yale Univ., New Haven, Conn, since 1981; Research Fellow, University Coll. London, since 1982; Supernumerary Fellow, Wolfson Coll., Oxford, since 1985. Teaching Fellow, Harvard Univ., Cambridge, Mass., 1959–64; Lectr. in Classics 1964, Asst. Prof., 1965–68, and Assoc. Prof., 1968–73, Yale Univ., Visiting Prof. of Classics, Princeton Univ., New Jersey, 1974–75; Tel Aviv, 1976; Visiting Prof. in Comparative Literature, Dartmouth Coll., Hanover, N.H., 1976–78; Visiting Fellow, Wolfson Coll., Oxford, 1979–80. *Publs:* (ed.) Euripides: A Collection of Critical Essays, 1968; Roman Laughter: The Comedy of Plautus, 1968; (ed. and trans.) Plautus: Three Comedies, 1969; Love Story (novel) 1970; Fairy Tale, 1973; Odyssey (play), 1975; Oliver's Story (novel), 1977; Man, Woman and Child (novel), 1980; Problems in Plautus, 1981; (ed.) The Oxford Readings in Greek Tragedy, 1983; (co-ed.) Caesar Augustus: Seven Essays, 1984; The Birth of Comedy, 1984; The Class (novel), 1984; (ed.) Plato's Dialogues, 1985; Doctors (novel), 1988. Add: Wolfson Coll., Oxford OX2 6UD, England.

SEGAL, Harriet. American, b. 1931. Novels/Short stories. Full-time writer since 1980. Member, Exec. Bd. of Assocs., Marine Biological Lab., Woods Hole, Mass., since 1982. Asst. Account Exec., 1954–55, and Art Buyer, 1955–57, McCann-Erickson Inc.; Asst. Account Exec. and Copywriter, Albert Frank-Guenther Law Inc., San Francisco, 1958–60; Asst. to the Air Dir., SHOW, NYC, 1960–61; Writer and Ed., U.S. Information Service, New Delhi, 1962–63; freelance writer and ed., 1963–80; Reporter, Greenburgh Independent, 1969–72. *Publs:* Susquehanna, 1984, in U.K. as On Flows the River, 1985; Catch the Wind, 1987. Add: c/o Rollene W. Saal, 200 E. 82nd st., New York, N.Y. 10028, U.S.A.

SEGAL, Lore. American (born Austrian), b. 1928. Novels/Short stories. Prof., Univ. of Illinois, Chicago, since 1978. Prof. of Creative Writing and Literature, Columbia Univ., NYC, 1969–78, Princeton Univ., New Jersey, 1973–77, Sarah Lawrence Coll., Bronxville, N.Y., 1975–76. *Publs:* Other People's Houses, 1964; (trans. with W.D. Snodgrass) Gallows Songs by Christian Morgenstern, 1968; Tell Me a Mitzi, 1970; All the Way Home, (trans.) The Juniper Tree and Other Tales from Grimm, 1973; Tell Me: A Trudy, 1977; Lucinella (novel), 1978; The Story of Old Mrs. Brubeck and How She Looked for Trouble and Where She Found Him, 1978; Her First American, 1985; The Story of Mrs. Lovewright and Purrless Her Cat, 1985; (trans) The Book of Adam to Moses, 1987. Add: 280 Riverside Dr., New York, N.Y. 10025, U.S.A.

SEGAL, Ronald (Michael). British, b. 1932. International relations/Current affairs, Politics/Government, Race relations, Autobiography/Memoirs/Personal. Publisher and Ed., Africa South, subsequently Africa South in Exile, 1956–61; Founder and Gen. Ed., Penguin African Library, London, 1961–84. Convenor Intl. Conference on Ecnomic Sanctions Against South Africa, 1964; and Intl. conference on South West Africa 1966, *Publs:* The Tokolosh, 1961; Political Africa: A Who's Who of Personalitie and Parties, 1961; African Profiles, 1962; Into Exile, 1963; (ed.) Sanctions Against South Africa, 1964; The Crisis of India (in U.S. as The Anguish of India), 1965; The Race War, 1966; (ed. with R. First) South West Africa: Travesty of Trust, 1967; America's Receding Future (in U.S. as The Americans: A Conflict of Creed and Reality), 1968; The Struggle Against History, 1971; Whose Jerusalem?, 1973; The Decline and Fall of the American Dollar, 1974; The Tragedy of Leon Trotsky, 1979; (with M. Kidron) The State of the World Atlas, 1981; The New State of the World Atlas, 1984; The Book of Business, Money and Power, 1987. Add: The Old Manor House, Walton-on-Thames, Surrey, England.

SEGAL, S(tanley) S(olomon). British, b. 1919. Education. Educational Consultant since 1968, and Principal, 1970–86, Ravenswood Village for the Care of the Mentally Handicapped; Prof. of Special Education, Bulmershe Coll. of Higher Education, since 1981. Honorary Ed., British Journal of Special Education, formerly Special Education: Forward Trends, since 1973 (Ed., 1956–73). Headmaster, Special Sch. for the Educationally Subnormal, 1956–65, and Special Sch. for Physically Handicapped Pupils, 1966–69, I.L.E.A. *Publs:* Eleven-Plus Rejects, 1961; Teaching Backward Pupils, 1963; Space Age Readers, 1964; (ed.) Backward Pupils in the U.S.S.R., 1965; No Child Is Ineducable, 1967, 1974; Number the Home, 1967; (ed.) The Working World, 1967; From Care to Education, 1972; Mental Handicap: A Select Annotated Bibliography, 1972; Society and Mental Handicap: Are We Ineducable?, 1984. Add: 11 Ravensdale Ave., Finchley, London N12, England.

SEGRÈ, Emilio. American (b. Italian), b. 1905. Physics, Biography. Prof. of Physics Emeritus, Univ. of California, Berkeley, since 1972 (Prof., 1946–72). Recipient, Nobel Prize in Physics, 1959. *Publs:* (ed. and contrib.) Experimental Nuclear Physics, 1953, 1959; Nuclei and Particles, 1963, 1977; Enrico Fermi Physicist, 1970; From X-Rays to Quarks: Modern Physicists and Their Discoveries, 1980; From Falling Bodies to Radio Waves: Classical Physicists and Their Discoveries, 1984. Add: 3802 Quail Ridge Rd., Lafayette, Calif. 94549, U.S.A.

SEGUN, Mabel D(orothy), née Aig-Imoukhuede). Nigerian, b. 1930. Children's fiction, Poetry, Essays, Autobiography. Sr. Research Fellow, Inst. of African Studies, Univ. of Ibadan, since 1982. Teacher, Nigeria, 1953–59; Ed., Hansard, Western Nigeria Legislature, Ibadan, 1959–61; Information Office, Western Nigeria Ministry of Information, Ibadan, 1961–63; Copywriter, Lintas Ltd., Lagos, 1964; Trainee Ed., Silver Burdett, publishers, Morristown, N.J., 1965, and Harper and Row, NYC, 1966; Ed., Modern Woman, Lagos, 1966–67, and Franklin Book Programmes, Lagos, 1967; Education Officer, 1967–68, and Head, 1969–70, Federal Ministry of Education Broadcasting Unit, Lagos; Head, Dept. of English and Social Studies, 1971–73, 1974–79, and Acting Vice-Principal, 1978–79, National Technical Teachers Coll., Lagos; Deputy Permanent

Delegate of Nigeria to Unesco, Paris, 1979–81; Chief Federal Inspector of Education, Federal Ministry of Education, Lagos, 1981–82. *Publs:* My Father's Daughter (autobiography), 1965; Friends, Nigerians, Countrymen (essays), 1977, in Nigeria as Sorry No Vacancy, 1985; (ed. with Neville Grant) Under the Mango Tree (poetry), 2 vols., 1980; Youth Day Parade (children's fiction), 1983; Olu and the Broken Statue (children's fiction), 1985; Conflict and Other poems, 1986; My Mother's Daughter (autobiography), 1987; (ed.) Illustrating for Children, 1988; Ping Pong: Twenty-Five Years of Table Tennis, 1989. Add: Inst. of African Studies, Univ. of Ibadan, Ibadan Nigeria.

SEIDEL, Frederick (Lewis). American, b. 1936. Poetry. Advisory Ed., Paris Review, Paris and NYC, since 1961 (Paris Ed., 1960–61). *Publs:* Final Solutions: Poems, 1963; Sunrise, 1980; Men and Women: New and Selected Poems, 1984. Add: 251 W. 92nd St., New York, N.Y. 10025, U.S.A.

SEIDEL, George Joseph. American, b. 1932. Philosophy. Chmn., Dept. of Philosophy, St. Martin's Coll., Olympia, Wash., since 1962. Fulbright Fellow, Univ. of Freiburg, Germany, 1961–62; Org. of American States Fellow, Univ. del Salvador, Buenos Aires, 1965. Pres., Northwest Conference on Philosophy, 1971. *Publs:* Martin Heidegger and the Pre-Socratics: An Introduction to His Thought, 1964; Crisis of Creativity, 1966; A Contemporary Approach to Classical Metaphysics, 1969; Being, Nothing, and God: A Philosophy of Appearance, 1970; Activity and Ground: Fichte, Schelling and Hegel, 1976. Add: St. Martin's Coll., Lacey, Wash. 98503, U.S.A.

SEIDEL, Kathleen Gilles. American. Romance. *Publs:* The Same Last Name, 1983; A Risk Worth Taking, 1983; Mirrors and Mistakes, 1984; After All These Years, 1984; When Love Isn't Enough, 1984; Don't Forget to Smile, 1984. Add: c/o Adele Leone Agency, 26 Nantucket Pl., Scarsdale, N.Y. 10583, U.S.A.

SEIDLER, Ann. American, b. 1925. Children's fiction, Speech/ Rhetoric. Assoc. Prof. of Speech, Montclair State Coll., Upper Montclair, since 1967. Teacher of Speech and Drama, Punahau Sch., Honolulu, Hawaii, 1946–47; Speech Consultant to National Hosp. for Speech Disorders, NYC, 1949–51, Mountainside Hosp., Montclair, N.J., 1953–54, and Cedar Grove Bd. of Education, N.J., 1954–62. *Publs:* all with J. Slepian unless otherwise noted—Magic Arthur and the Giant, 1964; The Cock that Couldn't Crow, 1964; Roaring Dragon of Red Rose, 1964; Alfie and the Dream Machine, 1964; Mr. Sipple and the Naughty Princes, 1964; Lester and the Sea Master, 1964; The Best Invention of All, 1967; The Silly Listening Book, 1967; Ding Dong Bing Bong, 1964; The Hungry Thing, 1967; An Ear Is to Hear, 1967; Bendemolena, 1967 (co-author) Make Yourself Clear, 1974; The Cat Who Wore a Pot on Her Head, 1981; (with Doris Bianchi) Voice And Diction Fitness: A Comprehensive Approach, 1988. Add: 15 Undercliff Rd., Montclair, N.J. 08042, U.S.A.

SEIDLER, Harry. Australian, b. 1923. Architecture. Architect, Harry Seidler & Assocs. Sydney, since 1948. *Publs:* Houses, Interiors and Projects, 1954; (contrib.) Harry Seidler 1955-1963, 1963; (contrib.) Architecture for the New World—The Work of Harry Seidler, 1973. Add: 2 Glen St., Milsons Point, N.S.W. 2061, Australia.

SEIDLER, Tor. American, b. 1952. Children's fiction. *Publs:* The Dulcimer Boy, 1979; Terpin, 1982; A Rat's Tale, 1986; The Tar Pit, 1987; Add: 121 W. 78th St., New York, N.Y. 10024, U.S.A.

SEIDMAN, Hugh. American, b. 1940. Poetry. Faculty Member, New School for Social Research, since 1976. Poet/Writer-in-Residence, Yale Univ., 1971, 1973, City Coll. of City Univ. of New York, 1972–75, Wilkes Coll., 1975, Wichita State Univ., 1978, Aspen Writers Conference, 1979, Washington Coll., 1979, Univ. of Wisconsin-Madison, 1981, Coll. of William and Mary, 1982, N.Y. State Poets in the Schools, 1978–81, and Columbia Univ., NYC, 1985. *Publs:* Collecting Evidence, 1970; (ed. with Richard Zarro) Westbeth Poets, 1971; (ed. with Frances Whyatt) Equal Time, 1972; Blood Lord, 1974; Throne/Falcon/Eye, 1982. Add: 463 West St., New York, N.Y. 10014, U.S.A.

SEIFMAN, Eli. American, b. 1936. Education, History. Prof. of Social Science, The State Univ. of New York, Stony Brook, since 1964 (Dir. of Teacher Preparation, 1964–68; Dir. of Teacher Preparation and Chmn. Dept. of Education, 1965–70). General Ed., Stony Brook American Historical Assn. History Education Project Occasional Paper Series. Social Studies Teacher, Harold G. Campbell Jr. High Sch., NYC, 1957–63; Lectr.

in Education, Queens Coll., Univ. City of New York, 1961–64. *Publs:* A History of the New York State Colonization Society, 1966; (ed. with M. Feldman) The Social Studies: Structure, Models, and Strategies, 1969; (ed. with D. Allen) The Teacher's Handbook, 1971; (co-ed.) Toward a New World Outlook, 1976; (co-ed.) Education and Socialist Modernization, 1987. Add: Social Science Interdisciplinary Program, State Univ. of New York, Stony Brook, N.Y. 11794, U.S.A.

SEKLER, Eduard F(ranz). Austrian, b. 1920. Architecture, Urban studies. Architect in Vienna, since 1946; Prof. of Architecture since 1960, and Osgood Hooker Prof. of Visual Arts since 1970, Harvard Univ., Cambridge (Dir., Carpenter Center for the Visual Arts, 1966–76; Chmn., 1972–73, and Acting Chmn., 1975, Dept. of Visual and Environmental Studies). Teaching and Research Asst., 1945–53, Lectr., 1953, and Prof. Extraordinarius, 1960, Vienna Technical Univ. Expert Member, Unesco Intnl. Cttee. on Monuments, Artistic, Historical and Archaeological Sites, Paris, 1951–56; Member, Bd. of Dirs., Soc. of Architectural Historians, Philadelphia, 1963–66, 1970–73, and of the Boston Architectural Center, 1966–68; Consultant to the Historic Monuments Office, Vienna, 1971; Head, Unesco Intnl. Team for a Master Plan for the Preservation of the Cultural Heritage of the Kathmandu Valley, 1975. *Publs:* Das Punkthaus im europaischen Wohnungsbau, 1952; Wren and His Place in European Architecture, 1956; (ed.) Historic Urban Spaces I-IV, 1962–71; Proportion: Measure of Order, 1965; (with others) Kathmandu Valley: The Preservation of Physical Environment and Cultural Heritage: Protective Inventory, vols., 1975; (ed.) Master Plan for the Conservation of the Cultural Heritage in the Kathmandu Valley, 1977, 1979; (with others) Le Corbusier at Work: The Genesis of the Carpenter Center for the Visual Arts, 1978; Josef Hoffmann, 1982. Add: Carpenter Center for the Visual Arts, Harvard Univ., Cambridge, Mass. 02138, U.S.A.

SELBOURNE, David. British, b. 1937. Plays, Politics. *Publs:* The Play of William Cooper and Edmund Dew-Nevett, 1968; The Two-Backed Beast, 1969; Dorabella, 1970; Samson, and Alison Mary Fagan, 1971; The Damned, 1971; Class Play, 1973; Brook's Dream: The Politics of Theatre, 1974; What's Acting, and Think of a Story, Quickly!, 1977; An Eye to India, 1977; An Eye to China, 1978; Through the Indian Looking-Glass, 1982; The Making of a Midsummer Night's Dream, 1983; Against Socialist Illusion: A Radical Argument, 1985; (ed.) In Theory and In Practice: Essays on the Politics of Jayaprakash Narayan, 1986; Left Behind: Journeys into British Politics, 1987; A Doctor's Life (non-fiction), 1989. Add: c/o Curtis Brown, 162-168 Regent St., London W1R 5TB, England.

SELBY, Elliott. *See* **NICHOLSON,** Hubert.

SELBY, Hubert, Jr. American, b. 1928. Novels/Short stories, Plays/ Screenplays. *Publs:* Last Exit to Brooklyn, 1964; The Room, 1971; Third Commandment (screenplay); The Demon, 1976; Requiem for a Dream, 1978; Song of the Silent Snow (stories), 1986. Add: c/o Grove Press, 841 Broadway, New York, N.Y. 10003, U.S.A.

SELDEN, George. Pseud. for George Selden Thompson. American, b. 1929. Children's fiction, Plays/Screenplays, Biography. *Publs:* The Dog that Could Swim Under Water (fiction), 1956; The Garden Under the Seafiction), 1957, as Oscar Lobster's Fair Exchange, 1966; The Cricket in Times Square (fiction), 1960; I See What I See! (fiction), 1962; The Mice, The Monks, and the Christmas Tree (fiction), 1963; Heinrich Schliemann: Discoverer of Buried Treasure, 1964; Sir Arthur Evans: Discoverer of Knossos, 1964; Sparrow Socks (fiction), 1965; The Children's Story (play, adaptation of the work by James Clavell), 1966; The Genie of Sutton Place (television play); The Dunkard (fiction), 1968; Tucker's Countrysidefiction), 1969; The Genie of Sutton Place (fiction), 1973; Harry Cat's Pet Puppy (fiction), 1974; Chester Cricket's Pigeon Ride (fiction), 1981; Irma and Jerry (fiction), 1982; Chester Cricket's New Home, 1983; Harry Kitten and Tucker Mouse, 1987; The Old Meadow, 1987. Add: c/o Farrar Straus & Giroux Inc., 19 Union Sq. W., New York, N.Y. 10003, U.S.A.

SELDES, George. American, b. 1890. History, Writing/Journalism, Biography. Reporter, Pittsburgh Leader, Pa., 1909–10; Night Ed., Pittsburgh Post, Pa., 1910–16; Managing Ed., Pulitzer's Weekly, NYC, 1916; War Corresp., American Expeditionary Force, 1918–19; Head, Berlin Bureau, 1920–27, and Rome Branch, 1925, Chicago Tribune; Ed., In Fact (weekly newsletter), 1940–50. *Publs:* You Can't Print That (in U.K. as The Truth Behind the News), 1929; Can These Things Be?, 1931; World Panorama, 1933; The Vatican: Yesterday, Today, Tomorrow, 1934; Iron, Blood and Profits, 1934; Sawdust Caesar, 1935; Lords of the Press, 1938; You Can't Do That, 1938; The Catholic Crisis, 1940; Witch Hunt, 1940;

The Facts Are..., 1942; Facts and Fascism, 1943; 1000 Americans, 1947; The People Don't Know, 1949; Tell the Truth and Run, 1953; (compiler and ed.) The Great Quotations, 1961; Never Tire of Protesting, 1968; Even the Gods Cannot Change History, 1976; (ed.) The Great Thoughts, 1985; Witness to a Century, 1987. Add: R.D. 1, Box 412, Windsor, Vt. 05089, U.S.A.

SELF, Margaret Cabell. American, b. 1902. Novels/Short stories, Children's fiction, Recreation/Leisure/Hobbies. Founding Ed., photographer, and reporter, Block Island Times, R.I., since 1970. Founder and Commandant, New Canaan Mounted Troop, Jr. Cavalry of America, 1938–63. *Publs:* Teaching the Young to Ride, 1935; Red Clay Country, 1936; Horses: Their Selection, Care and Handling, 1943; Those Smith Kids, 1945; The Horseman's Encyclopedia, 1945; Ponies on Parade, 1945; Fun on Horseback, 1945, rev. ed. 1967; Chitter Chat Stories, 1946; (ed.) A Treasury of Horse Stories, 1946; Riding Simplified, 1948; Come Away, 1948; Horseman's Companion, 1949; Horsemastership, 1953; Irish Adventure, 1954; The American Horse Show, 1958; Jumping Simplified, 1959; Riding with Mariles, 1960; The How and Why of Horses, 1961; Complete Book of Horses and Ponies, 1965; Riding Step by Step, 1965; The Happy Year, 1965; Horses of Today, 1965; The Shaggy Little Burro of San Miguel, 1965; The Horseman's Almanac, 1966; Henrietta, 1966; At the Horse Show with Margaret Cabell Self, 1966; The Morgan Horse in Pictures, 1967; The Quarter Horse in Pictures, 1969; The Young Rider and His First Pony, 1969; Sky Rocket: The Story of a Little Bay Horse, 1970; How to Buy the Right Horse, 1971; The Hunter in Pictures, 1972; The Nature of the Horse, 1971; The Problem Horse and the Problem Horseman, 1976. Add: Block Island, R.I. 02807, U.S.A.

SELLERS, Alexandra. British. Romance. *Publs:* The Indifferent Heart, 1980; Captive of Desire, 1981; Fire in the Wind, 1982; Season of Storm, 1983; The Forever Kind, 1984; The Real Man, 1984; The Male Chauvinist, 1985; The Old Flame, 1986. Add: c/o P. Tornetta, Box 423, Croton-on-Hudson, N.Y. 10521, U.S.A.

SELLIN, Eric. American, b. 1933. Poetry, Literature. Prof. of French and Franco-African Literatures, Temple Univ., Philadelphia, Pa., since 1970 (Instr., 1962–65; Asst. Prof., 1965–67; Assoc. Prof., 1967–70). Founder and Ed., CELFAN Review. Lectr. de Littérature Américaine, Univ. of Bordeaux, France, 1956–57; Instr. of French, Clark Univ., Worcester, Mass., 1958–59. Founder, Center for the Study of the Francophone Literature of North Africa, 1981. *Publs:* Night Voyage, 1964; The Dramatic Concepts of Antonin Artaud, 1968; Trees at First Light, 1973; Tanker Poems, 1973; Borne kilométrique, 1973; As-Shamsu, 1973; The Inner Game of Soccer, 1976; Soccer Basics, 1977; Marginalia: Poems, 1979; Crépuscule prolongé à El Biar, 1982; Nightfall over Lubumbashi, 1982; Night Foundering, 1985. Add: 312 Kent Rd., Bala-Cynwyd, Pa. 19004, U.S.A.

SELLMAN, Hunton D. American, b. 1900. Theatre. Prof. Emeritus of Drama, San Diego State Univ. (joined faculty, 1946). Theatre bldg. and lighting consultant, since 1932. Assoc. Prof. of Dramatic Art, State Univ. of Iowa, 1930–46. *Publs:* (co-author) Stage Scenery and Lighting; (co-author) Modern Theatre Practice; (with Merrill Lessley) Essentials of Stage Lighting, 2nd ed. 1982. Add: 5015 Campanile Dr., San Diego, Calif. 92115, U.S.A.

SELLMAN, Roger Raymond. British, b. 1915. History. County Inspector of Schs., Devon, 1960–69. *Publs:* Modern British Economic and Social History, 1947, 1973; Modern European History, 1949, 1974; Survey of British History, 2 vols., 1949, 1950; Student's Atlas of Modern History, 1952, 1973; Atlas of Eastern History, 1954; Castles and Fortresses, 1954; Roman Britain, 1956; English Churches, 1956; The Elizabethan Seamen, 1957; The Vikings, 1957; Prehistoric Britain, 1958; Civil War and Commonwealth, 1958; The Anglo-Saxons, 1959; Norman England, 1960; Ancient Egypt, 1960; Mediaeval English Warfare, 1960; Illustrations of Dorset History, 1961; The First World War, 1961; Illustrations of Devon History, 1962; Historical Atlas From 1789, 1963, 1973; The Second World War, 1964; Devon Village Schools in the Nineteenth Century, 1968; Outline Atlas of World History, 1970; Modern World History, 1972; Garibaldi and the Unification of Italy, 1973; Bismarck and the Unification of Germany, 1973; The Prairies, 1974; Modern British History, 1976; Aspects of Devon History, 1985. Add: Pound Down Corner, Whitestone, Devon EX4 2HP, England.

SELTZER, Leon F(rancis). American, b. 1940. Literature. Psychotherapist in private practice. Asst. Prof., Queens Coll., City Univ. of New York, 1967–70; Assoc. Prof. of English, Cleveland State Univ., 1970–78. *Publs:* The Vision of Melville and Conrad: A Comparative

Study, 1970; Paradoxical Strategies in Psychotherapy, 1986. Add: 14195 Mango Dr., San Diego, Calif. 92014, U.S.A.

SELVON, Samuel (Dickson). Trinidadian, b. 1923. Novels/Short stories. Journalist, Trinidad Guardian, 1946–50; Civil Servant with Indian High Commnr., London, 1950–53. *Publs:* A Brighter Sun, 1952; An Island is a World, 1955; The Lonely Londoners, 1956; Ways of Sunlight, 1958; Turn Again, Tiger, 1958; I Hear Thunder, 1963; The Housing Lark, 1965; The Plains of Caroni, 1969; Those Who Eat the Cascadura, 1972; Moses Ascending, 1975; Moses Migrating, 1983.

SELWYN, Francis. British, b. 1935. Mystery/Crime/Suspense. Freelance translator and regular contributor to Penthoog use, London, since 1971. Adult Education Organizer, 1961–65; Research Asst., BBC, London, 1966–71. *Publs:* Sergeant Verity series, 5 vols., 1975–80; Gangland: The Case of Bentley and Craig (non-fiction), 1988; Rotten to the Core: The Life and Death of Neville Heath (non-fiction), 1988. Add: c/o Andre Deutsch Ltd., 105 Great Russell St., London WC1B 3LJ, England.

SELZ, Peter. American, b. 1919. Art. Prof., Dept. of Art History, Univ. of California, Berkeley (Dir., Univ. Art Museum, 1965–73). Ed., Art in America. Prof. of Art History, Inst. of Design, Chicago, 1949–55; Chmn., Art Dept., Pomona Coll., Claremont, Calif., 1955–58; Curator of Painting and Sculpture Exhibitions, Museum of Modern Art, NYC, 1958–65. Dir., College Art Assn. of America, 1958–62, and 1964–68. *Publs:* German Expressionist Painting, 1957; New Images of Man, 1959; Art Nouveau, 1960; The Work of Jean Dubuffet, 1962; Emil Nolde, 1963; Max Beckmann, 1964; Mark Rothko, 1961; Alberto Giacometti, 1965; Seven Decades of Modern Art, 1966; Directions in Kinetic Sculpture, 1966; Funk, 1967; Harold Paris: The California Years, 1972; Ferdinand Hodler, 1972; Sam Francis, 1975, 1982; Art in Our Times, 1981; Chillida, 1986. Add: Dept. of Art History, Univ. of California, Berkeley, Calif. 94720, U.S.A.

SEMAAN, Khalil I.H. American, b. 1920. Language/Linguistics. Asst. Prof. since 1965, and Prof. of Arabic since 1970, State Univ. of New York, Binghamton (Assoc. Prof., 1966–70). Lectr. in Semitic Languages, New York Univ., NYC, 1955–56; Lectr., in Arabic, Columbia Univ., NYC, 1957; Asst. Prof. of Oriental Languages, Univ. of California, Los Angeles, 1957–59; Reference Librarian, Library of Congress, Washington, D.C., 1960–62; Dir., Afro-Asian Research Inst., Stockholm, Sweden, 1962–64; Visiting Scholar, Columbia Univ. Teachers Coll., NYC, 1964–65. *Publs:* Ash-Shafi'i's Risalah, 1962; Ibn Sina's Risalah On The Points Of Articulation Of The Speech-Sounds, 1963; Linguistics in the Middle Ages: Phonetic Studies In Early Islam, 1968; Murder In Baghdad (trans. of Salah Abd al-Sabur's verse play, Ma'sat al-Hallaj), 1972; (ed.) Islam and the Medieval West, 1980; Arabic Phonetics. Add: 713 Country Club Rd., Binghamton, N.Y. 13903, U.S.A.

SEMMLER, Clement William. Australian, b. 1914. Literary critic and biographer. Deputy Gen. Mgr., A.B.C., Sydney, 1965–77, now retired (Supvr., Youth Education, S.A., 1942–46; Asst. Dir. of Variety, 1947–48; Asst. Controller of Progs., 1948–60; Asst. Gen. Mgr. of Progs., 1960–64). Consulting Ed., Poetry Australia; Book Reviewer, The Australian, Brisbane Courier Mail, The Bulletin, and Quadrant; Member, National Library of Australia's Advisory Cttee. on Humanities; Deputy Pres. of the Council, State Library of New South Wales; Chmn. of the Council, Alexander Mackie Coll. of Advanced Education; Chmn., Commonwealth Immigration Publicity Council. *Publs:* For the Uncanny Man: Essays on James Joyce and Others, 1963; (ed. with Derek Whitelock) Literary Australia, 1965; Barcroft Boake: Poet of the Stockwhip, 1965; A.B. Banjo Paterson, 1965; (ed.) Stories of the Riverina, 1965; Kenneth Slessor, 1966; (ed.) Coast to Coast 1965-66: Collection of Australian Short Stories, 1966; The Banjo of the Bush, 1966; (ed.) The World of Banjo Paterson, 1967; (ed.) Twentieth Century Australian Literary Criticism, 1967; A.B. Paterson: Great Australian, 1967; The Art of Brian James and Other Essays on Australian Literature, 1972; Douglas Stewart, 1974; The ABC: Aunt Sally and Sacred Cow, 1980; (ed.) A Frank Hardy Swag, 1982; (ed.) The War Diaries War Despatches of Kenneth Slessor, 2 vols., 1985–87. Add: The Croft, St. Clair St., Bowral 2576, Australia.

SEN, Amartya K(umar). Indian, b. 1933. Economics. Lamont Univ. Prof., And Prof Economics and Philosophy, Harvard Univ., Cambridge, Mass., since 1988. Prof. of Economics, Jadavpur Univ., Calcutta, 1956–58; Prize Fellow, 1957–61, and Staff Fellow, 1961–63, Trinity Coll., Cambridge; Prof. of Economics, Delhi Univ., 1963–71; Prof. of Economics, London School of Economics, 1971–77; at Oxford Univ.: Fellow, Nuffield Coll., 1977–80; Prof. of Economics, 1977–80; Fellow, All

Souls Coll., and Drummond Prof. of Political Economy, 1980–88. Pres., Econometric Soc., 1984, and Intnl. Economic Assn., 1986–89. *Publs:* Choice of Techniques: An Aspect of Planned Economic Development, 1960, 3rd ed., 1968; Growth Economics, 1970; Collected Choice and Social Welfare, 1970; On Economic Inequality, 1973; Employment, Technology and Development, 1975; Poverty and Famines, 1981; (co-ed.) Utilitarianism and Beyond, 1982; Choice, Welfare, and Measurement, 1982; Resources, Values, and Development, 1984; Commodities and Capabilities, 1985; The Standard of Living, 1987; On Ethics and Economics, 1987. Add: Littauer Center, Harvard Univ., Cambridge, Mass. 02138, U.S.A.

SENDAK, Maurice. American, b. 1928. Children's fiction. *Publs:* Kenny's Window, 1956; Very Far Away, 1957; The Sign on Rosie's Door, 1960; The Nutshell Library, 1962; Where the Wild Things Are, 1963; Hector Protector, and As I Went Over the Water, 1965; Higglety Pigglety Pop, or There Must Be More to Life, 1967; In the Night Kitchen, 1970; The Juniper Tree, and Other Stories from Grimm, 1973; King Grisly-Beard, 1974; Really Rosie, 1975; Some Swell Pup, 1976; Seven Little Monsters, 1977; Outside Over There, 1981; Hector Protector, 1984; Posters, 1986; On Books and Pictures, 1986. Add: 200 Chestnut Hill Rd., Ridgefield, Conn. 06877, U.S.A.

SENIOR, Michael. British, b. 1940. Plays/Screenplays, Geography, Travel/Exploration/Adventure, Biography. *Publs:* The Coffee Table (radio play), 1964; Portrait of North Wales, 1973; Portrait of South Wales, 1974; Greece and Its Myths, 1978; Myths of Britain, 1979; (with others) Heroes and Heroines, 1980; (ed.) Sir Thomas Malory's Tales of King Arthur, 1980; Life and Times of Richard II, 1981. Add: c/o Robert Hale & Co., Clerkenwell House, Clerkenwell Green, London EC1R 0HT, England.

SENNETT, Richard. American, b. 1943. Sociology. Prof. of Sociology, New York Univ., since 1969. Founder, New York Inst. for the Humanities. Member, Editorial Bd., Theory and Society, since 1974, Psychoanalysis and Contemporary Thought, since 1976, and Literature and Society, since 1978; Member of the Bd., P.E.N., since 1977. *Publs:* (ed.) Classic Essays on the Culture of Cities, 1969; (ed., with Stephen Thernstrom, and contrib.) Nineteenth Century Cities, 1969; Families Against the City: Middle Class Homes of Industrial Chicago 1872-1890, 1970; The Uses of Disorder, 1970; (with Jonathan Cobb) The Hidden Injuries of Class, 1972; (ed.) The Psychology of Society, 1977; The Fall of Public Man, 1977; (with others) Beyond the Crisis Society, 1977; Authority, 1980; The Frog Who Dared to Croak, 1982; An Evening of Brahms, 1984; Palais Royale, 1987. Add: Inst. for the Humanities, 26 University Pl., New York, N.Y. 10003, U.S.A.

SERJEANT, Richard. *See* VAN ESSEN, W.

SERLE, (Alan) Geoffrey. Australian, b. 1922. History. General Ed., Australian Dictionary of Biography, since 1975. *Publs:* (ed. with J. Grant) The Melbourne Scene, 1803-1956, 1957; The Golden Age: A History of the Colony of Victoria, 1851-1861, 1963; The Rush to be Rich: A History of the Colony of Victoria, 1883-1889, 1971; From Deserts the Prophets Come: The Creative Spirit in Australia, 1788-1972, 1973; John Monash: A Biography, 1982. Add: Australian Dictionary of Biography, Australian Natl. Univ., Canberra, A.C.T. 2600, Australia.

SERLING, Robert J(erome). American, b. 1918. Novels/Short stories, Air/Space topics. Air safety lectr., and consultant, since 1966. *Publs:* The Probable Cause, 1960; The Electra Story, 1962; The Left Seat, 1964; The President's Plane Is Missing, 1967; The Newsman and Air Accidents, 1967; Loud and Clear, 1969; She'll Never Get Off the Ground, 1971; Ceiling Unlimited, 1973; The Only Way to Fly: The Story of Western Airlines, 1976; McDermott's Sky, 1977; Wings, 1978; From the Captain to the Colonel, 1980; The Jet Age, 1982; Eagle: The History of American Airlines, 1985; Air Force 1 Is Haunted, 1985. Add: c/o Doubleday & Co. Inc., 666 Fifth Ave., New York, N.Y. 10103, U.S.A.

SERRAILLIER, Ian (Lucien). British, b. 1912. Children's fiction, Poetry, Children's non-fiction. *Publs:* (co-author) Three New Poets, 1942; The Weaver Birds, 1944; Thomas and the Sparrow, 1946, 1951; They Raced for Treasure, 1946, as Treasure Ahead, 1954; Flight to Adventure, 1947, as Mountain Rescue, 1955; Captain Bounsaboard and the Pirates, 1949; The Monster Horse, 1950; There's No Escape, 1950, 1963; The Ballad of Kon-Tiki, 1952; Belinda and the Swans, 1952; Jungle Adventure, 1953, 1956; The Adventures of Dick Varley, 1954, 1956; Beowulf the Warrior, 1954; Making Good, 1955, 1956; Everest Climbed, 1955; Guns in the Wild, 1956; The Silver Sword, 1956, reissued in U.S. as

Escape from Warsaw, 1963; Katy at Home, 1957; Poems and Pictures, 1958; (co-author) A Puffin Quartet of Poets, 1958, rev. ed. 1964; Katy at School, 1959; The Ivory Horn, 1960, 1962; The Gorgon's Head, 1961; The Windmill Book of Ballads, 1962; The Way of Danger, 1962, 1965; Happily Ever After, 1963; The Clashing Rocks, 1963, 1971; The Midnight Thief, 1963; The Enchanted Island (in U.S. as Murder at Dunsinane), 1964; The Cave of Death, 1965; Fight for Freedom, 1965; Ahmet the Woodseller, 1965; A Fall From the Sky, 1966; The Challenge of the Green Knight, 1966; Robin in the Greenwood, 1967; Chaucer and his World, 1967; The Turtle Drum, 1967, 1968; Havelok the Dane, 1967, in U.K. as Havelok the Warrior, 1968; Robin and His Merry Men, 1969; The Tale of Three Landlubbers, 1970; Heracles the Strong, 1970; The Ballad of St. Simeon, 1970; A Pride of Lions, 1971; The Bishop and the Devil, 1971; Have You Got Your Ticket?, 1972; Marko's Wedding, 1972; I'll Tell You a Tale, 1973, 1976; Pop Festival, 1973; Suppose You Met a Witch, 1973; The Robin and the Wren, 1974; How Happily She Laughs, 1976; The Sun Goes Free, 1977; The Road to Canterbury, 1979; All Change at Singleton, 1979; (with Richard Pailthorpe) Goodwood Country in Old Photographs, 1987. Add: Singleton, Chichester, Sussex, England.

SERVADIO, Gaia (Cecilia Gemmalina). British, b. 1938. Novels/ Short stories, Criminology/Law enforcement/Prisons, Travel/Exploration/Adventure. *Publs:* Melinda: tanto gentile e tanto onesta, 1967; Don Juan-Salome: Don Giovanni-L'azione Consiste, 1968; Il Metodo, 1970; A Siberian Encounter, 1971; Angelo La Barbera: Profile of a Mafia Boss, 1974; Mafioso, 1976; Insider Outsider, 1978; To a Different World, 1979; Luchino Visconti, 1981; La donna nel Rinascimento, 1986; Il Lamento di Arianna (novel), 1988; Una Infanzia Diversa (autobiography), 1988. Add: 31 Bloomfield Terr., London SW1, England.

SERVENTY, Vincent Noel. Australian. Children's fiction, Animals, Natural history. Pres., Wildlife Preservation Soc. of Australia; Trustee, World Wildlife Fund (Australia); Co-Producer, Australian Ark television series, Nature Walkabout series. *Publs:* Australia's Great Barrier Reef, 1955; A Continent in Danger, 1965; Landforms of Australia, 1966; Nature Walkabout, 1966; Wildlife of Australia, 1968; Southern Walkabout, 1969; Dryandra, 1969; Turtle Bay Adventure, 1970; Australia's National Parks, 1970; Australian Wildlife Conservation, 1970; The Singing Land, 1972; The Great Barrier Reef, 1972; (with D.L. Serventy and J. Warham) The Handbook of Australian Seabirds, 1973; Desert Walkabout, 1974; Australia's Wildlife Heritage, 5 vols., 1975; Zoo Walkabout, 1979; Glovebox Guide to Australian Nature, 1980; Plantlife of Australia, 1981; Australian Landfor s (Birds, Wildlife, Mother and Baby Animals), 4 vols., 1981; (with others) Land Beyond Time, 1984; Australian Trees, 1984; The Desert Sea, 1985; Australia's World Heritage, 1986; Saving Australia, 1988. Add: 8 Reiby Rd., Hunters Hill, N.S.W. 2110, Australia.

SETH, Vikram. Indian, b. 1952. Novels, Poetry, Travel. Sr. Ed., Stanford Univ. Press, Calif. 1985–86. *Publs:* Mappings (poems), 1980; From Heaven Lake: Travels Through Sinkiang and Tibet, 1983; The Humble Administrator's Garden (poems), 1985; The Golden Gate: A Novel in Verse, 1986, From Heaven Lake, 1987. Add: c/o Irene Skolnick, Curtis Brown Inc., 10 Astor Pl., New York, N.Y.

SETHI, Narendra Kumar. Indian, b. 1935. Poetry, Administration/ Management. Prof. of Mgmt., St. John's Univ., Jamaica, N.Y., since 1966. Instr., Henry George Sch., NYC, 1961–70; Prof. of Mgmt., Long Island Univ., N.Y., 1962–63, 1965–66; Instr., New Sch. for Social Research, N.Y., 1963. *Publs:* Shabda Ki Chalna, 1962; The World Is Split, 1962; Hindu Proverbs, 1963; Song Lines of a Day, 1968; Bibliography of Indian Management, 1969; Management Perspectives, 1972; Social Sciences in Management, 1972; Managerial Mirage, 1974; Managerial Dynamics, 1978; Antar Bodh, 1982; Operations Management, 1984. Add: Dept. of Management, St. John's Univ., Jamaica, N.Y. 11439, U.S.A.

SETHNA, M(inocher) J(ehangirji). Indian, b. 1911. Novels/Short stories, Law, Philosophy, Photography. Prof. of Law, Univ. of Bombay, since 1960. Lectr. in Mercantile and Co. Laws, Batliboi's Accountancy Inst., Bombay, 1936–52; Prof. of Law, Govt. Law Coll., Bombay, 1952–60. *Publs:* Indian Company Law, 1956, 10th ed. 1987; Photography, 1970; Art of Living, 1972; Jurisprudence, 1973; Health and Happiness, 1974; Society and the Criminal, 1980, 1989; The Beauty That Is Kashmir, 1982. Add: Sethna House, 251 Tardeo Rd., Bombay 7, India.

SETON, Anya. American. Historical/Romance/Gothic, Children's fiction. *Publs:* My Theodosia, 1941; Dragonwyck, 1944; Turquoise, 1946; The Hearth and the Eagle, 1948; Foxfire, 1951; Katherine, 1954; Mistletoe and Sword (juvenile), 1955; The Winthrop Woman, 1958; Washington Irving (juvenile), 1960; Devil Water, 1962; Avalon, 1965;

Green Darkness, 1972; Smouldering Fires (juvenile), 1975. Add: Binney Lane, Old Greenwich, Conn. 06870, U.S.A.

SEUSS, Dr. (Theodor Seuss Geisel). Also writes as Theo Le Sieg. American, b. 1904. Children's fiction. Pres., Beginner Books, Random House, publrs., NYC. Former advertising illustrator, and illustrator for Life, Judge, Vanity Fair, Redbook and Saturday Evening Post mags. *Publs:* And to Think That I Saw It on Mulberry Street, 1937; The 500 Hats of Bartholomew Cubbins, 1938; The King's Stilts, 1939; Horton Hatches the Egg, 1940; McElligot's Pool, 1947; Thidwick, The Big-Hearted Moose, 1948; Bartholomew and the Oobleck, 1949; If I Ran the Zoo, 1950; Scrambled Eggs Super, 1953; Horton Hears a Who, 1954; On Beyond Zebra, 1955; If I Ran the Circus, 1956; How the Grinch Stole Christmas, 1957; The Cat in the Hat 1957; The Cat in the Hat Comes Back, 1958; Yertle the Turtle, 1958; Happy Birthday to You, 1959; One Fish Two Fish Red Fish Blue Fish, 1960; Green Eggs and Ham, 1960; The Sneetches and Other Stories, 1961; Dr. Seuss's Sleep Book, 1962; Hop on Pop, 1963; Dr. Seuss's ABC Book, 1963; Fox in Socks, 1965; I Had Trouble in Getting to Solla Sellew, 1965; The Cat in the Hat Songbook, 1967; The Foot Book, 1968; I Can Lick 30 Tigers Today, and Other Stories, 1969; My Book about Me, 1969; I Can Draw It Myself, 1970; Mr. Brown Can Moo, Can You?, 1970; Did I Even Tell You How Lucky You Are?, 1973; Great Day for Up, 1974; The Shape of Me, and Other Stuff, 1974; There's a Wocket in My Pocket, 1974; Oh the Thinks You Can Think, 1975; The Cat's Quizzer, 1976; I Can Read with My Eyes Shut, 1978; Oh, Say Can You Say?, 1979; Hunches in Bunches, 1982; The Butter Battle Book, 1984; You're Only Old Once, 1986; I Am Not Going to Get Up Today, 1987; as Theo LeSieg—Ten Apples up on Top, 1961; I Wish That I Had Duck Feet, 1965; Come Over to My House, 1966; The Eye Book, 1968; I Can Write (By Me, Myself), 1971; In a People House, 1972; The Many Mice of Mr. Brice, 1973; Wacky Wednesday, 1974; Would You Rather Be a Bullfrog, 1975; Hooper Humperdink, 1976; Please Try to Remember The First of Octember, 1977; Maybe You Should Fly a Jet! Maybe You Should Be a Vet!, 1980; The Tooth Book, 1981. Add: c/o Random House, 201 E. 50th St., New York, N.Y. 10022, U.S.A.

SEVERIN, Timothy. British, b. 1940. History. *Publs:* Tracking Marco Polo, 1964; Explorers of the Mississippi, 1967; The Golden Antilles, 1970; The African Adventure, 1973; Vanishing Primitive Man, 1973; The Oriental Adventure, 1976; The Brendan Voyage, 1978; The Sindbad Voyage, 1982; The Jason Voyage, 1985; The Ulysses Voyage, 1987. Add: Courtmacsherry, Co. Cork, Ireland.

SEVERN, David. *See* **UNWIN,** David.

SEWELL, Brocard. Also writes as Joseph Jerome. British, b. 1912. Literature, Autobiography/Memoirs/Personal. Biography. Roman Catholic priest: Carmelite friar. Ed. of The Aylesford Review (literary quarterly), and Dir. of St. Albert's Press, Aylesford, Kent, 1955–68; Lectr. in Pre-Raphaelite and 1890's Studies, Dept. of English, St. Francis Xavier Univ., Antigonish, Nova Scotia, 1969–72. *Publs:* (ed.) Arthur Machen, 1960; (with Cecil Woolf) The Clerk Without a Benefice: A Study of Fr. Rolfe, Baron Corvo, 1961; (ed., with Cecil Woolf) Corvo 1860-1960, 1961; (ed.) Two Friends: John Gray and Andre Raffalovich, 1963; (as Joseph Jerome) Montague Summers: A Memoir, 1965: My Dear Time's Waste (autobiography), 1966; Footnote to the Nineties: A Memoir of John Gray and Andre Raffalovich, 1968; The Vatican Oracle, 1970; Olive Custance: Her Life and Work, 1975; Cecil Chesterton, 1978; (ed.) Henry Williamson: The Man, The Writings, 1980; St. Dominic's Press, 1916-1936, 1979; Like Black Swans: Some People and Themes, 1982; In the Dorian Mode: A Life of John Gray, 1983; Frances Horovitz, Poet: A Memoir, 1987; Cancel All Our Vows, 1988. Add: Whitefriars, Tanners St., Faversham, Kent, England.

SEWELL, Stephen. Australian, b. 1953. Plays/Screenplays. Resident writer, Nimrod Theatre, Sydney, 1981–82. *Publs:* The Father We Loved on a Beach by the Sea, 1976; Traitors, 1983; The Blind Giant Is Dancing, 1983; Welcome to the Bright World, 1983; Dreams in an Empty City, 1986. Add: c/o Currency Press, 87 Jersey Rd., Woollahra, N.S.W. 2025, Australia.

SEWELL, William (Hamilton). American, b. 1909. Sociology. Vilas Research Prof. of Sociology, Univ. of Wisconsin, Madison, since 1965 (Prof. of Sociology since 1946; Chmn. of the Dept., 1958–63; Chancellor, 1968–69). Pres., American Sociological Assn.; Member of Exec. Cttee., Behavioral Science Div., National Research Council. Asst. Prof. of Sociology, 1937–38, Assoc. Prof., 1938–40, and Prof. 1940–44, Oklahoma State Univ., Stillwater. Assoc. Ed., American Sociological Review,

1954–57, and Sociometry, 1955–58. *Publs:* Scandinavian Students on an American Campus, 1962; (co-ed.) Uses of Sociology, 1967; Education, Occupation and Earnings, 1975; (ed.) Schooling and Achievement in American Society, 1976. Add: 1005 Merrill Springs Rd., Madison, Wisc. 53705, U.S.A.

SEXTON, Linda Gray. American, b. 1953. Psychology, Women. Member, Editorial Bd., Radcliffe Quarterly, Cambridge, Mass., since 1976. *Publs:* (ed.) 45 Mercy Street, by Anne Sexton, 1976; (ed.) Anne Sexton: A Self-Portrait in Letters, 1977; (ed.) Words for Dr. Y, by Anne Sexton, 1978; Between Two Worlds: Young Women in Crisis, 1979; Rituals, 1982; Mirror Images, 1985; Points of Light, 1988. Add: c/o Houghton Mifflin, 2 Park St., Boston, Mass. 02107, U.S.A.

SEXTON, Virginia Staudt. American, b. 1916. Psychology. Prof. Emeritus of Psychology, Herbert H. Lehman Coll., City Univ. of New York, since 1979 (Prof., 1968–79); Prof., St. John's Univ., since 1979. Elementary Teacher, St. Peter and St. Paul's Sch., Bronx, N.Y., 1936–39; Clerk, Dept. of Welfare, NYC, 1939–44; Guidance Dir., and Lectr., and subsequently Assoc. Prof. and Chmn., Dept. of Psychology, Notre Dame Coll. of Staten Island, N.Y., 1944–52; Lectr., Seton Hall Univ., South Orange, N.J., 1947–52 and 1954–55; Lectr., Adult Education Prog., Fordham Univ., Bronx, N.Y., 1952–54; Instr., 1953–56, Asst. Prof. 1957–60, Assoc. Prof. 1961–66, and Prof. 1967–68, Hunter Coll., City Univ. of New York. *Publs:* all with H. Misiak—Catholics in Psychology: A Historical Survey, 1954; History of Psychology: An Overview, 1966; Historical Perspectives in Psychology: Readings, 1971; Phenomenological, Existential, and Humanistic Psychologies: A Historical Survey, 1973; Psychology Around the World, 1976. Add: 188 Ascan Ave., Forest Hills, N.Y. 11375, U.S.A.

SEYERSTED, Per. Norwegian. Literature, Biography. Prof. of American Literature, Univ. of Oslo, since 1973 (Dir., American Inst., 1973–79). Vice-Chmn., Nordic Assn. for Canadian Studies, since 1984. Chmn., Nordic Assn. for American Studies, 1973–79. *Publs:* (ed.) Gilgamesj, 1967; Kate Chopin, 1969; (ed.) The Complete Works of Kate Chopin, 2 vols., 1969; Leslie Marmon Silko, 1980; From Norwegian Romantic to American Realist, 1984. Add: c/o American Inst., Postboks 1002 Blindern, Oslo 3, Norway.

SEYMOUR, A(rthur) J(ames). Guyanese, b. 1914. Poetry, Literature. Cultural Relations Adviser, Ministry of Information, Culture and Youth, and Deputy Chmn., Dept. of Culture, Guyana. Ed., Kyk-over-Al literary mag., Georgetown, 1945–61; Chief Information Officer, Govt. Information Service, British Guiana, 1954–62; Development Officer, Caribbean Org., Puerto Rico, 1962–64; Public Relations Officer, Demerara Bauxite Co. Ltd./Guyana Bauxite Co. Ltd., Guyana, 1965–73. *Publs:* Verse, 1937; More Poems, 1940; Over Guiana, Clouds, 1945; Sun's in My Blood, 1945; The Guiana Book, 1948; A Survey of West Indian Literature, 1950; Leaves from the Trees, 1951; Caribbean Literature (radio talks), 1951; Water and Blood: A Quincunx, 1952; Window on the Caribbean, 1952; (ed.) Anthology of West Indian Poetry, 1952, 1957; (ed.) Anthology of Guyanese Poetry, 1954; (ed.) Themes of Song, 1959; Selected Poems, 1965; Monologue, 1968; Edgar Mittelholzer: The Man and His Work, 1969; Patterns, 1970; I, Anancy, 1971; Introduction to Guyanese Writing, 1971; (ed. with E. Seymour) My Lovely Native Land, 1971; Black Song, 1972; Passport, 1972; (ed.) New Writing in the Caribbean, 1972; Song to Man, 1973; Italic, 1974; Looking at Poetry, 1974; Live in Georgetown, 1974; Growing Up in Guyana, 1976; Cultural Policy in Guyana, 1977; Nine Caribbean Essays, 1977; (ed.) Independence Ten: Guyanese Writing 1966-1976, 1977; Family Impromptu, 1977; Pilgrim Memories, 1977; Images of Majority: Collected Poems 1968-1978, 1978; The Making of Guyanese Literature, 1979; (ed.) A Treasury of Guyanese Poetry, 1980; Religious Poems, 1980; Studies in West Indian Poetry, 1981; Lord of My Life (verse), 1981; Poems for Export Only, 1982; The Poetry of Frank A. Collymore, 1982; The Poetry of Phyllis Shand Allfrey, 1982; Thirty Years A Civil Servant, 1982; Studies of Ten Guyanese Poems, 1982; The Years in Puerto Rico and Mackenzie, 1983; 70th Birthday Poems, 1984; (ed.) Dictionary of Guyanese Biography, 1984. Add: 23 North Rd., Bourda, Georgetown, Guyana.

SEYMOUR, Alan. Australian, b. 1927. Novels, Plays/Screenplays. TV Critic and writer in Australia, 1940's and 1950's; theatre critic, London Mag., 1963–65; producer, BBC TV, London, 1974–77. *Publs:* The One Day of the Year (play), 1962, novel version, 1967; The Coming Self-Destruction of the United States of America (novel), 1969. Add: 74 Upland Rd., London SE22 0DB, England.

SEYMOUR, Gerald (William Herschel Kean). British, b. 1941. Mystery/Crime/Suspense. Reporter, ITV News, 1963–78. *Publs:* Harry's Game, 1975; The Glory Boys, 1976; Kingfisher, 1977; Red Fox, 1979; The Contract, 1980; Archangel, 1982; In Honour Bound, 1984; Field of Blood, 1985; Supergrass, 1985; A Song in the Morning, 1986; At Close Quarters, 1987; The Contract, 1987; An Eye for an Eye, 1988; Home Run, 1989. Add: c/o A.D. Peters & Co. Ltd., The Chambers, Lots Rd., Chelsea Harbour, London SW10 0XF, England

SEYMOUR, Miranda (Jane). British, b. 1948. Novels/Short stories. Ed., Lorrimer Publishing, London, since 1974. Member of staff, Kasmin Gallery, 1966, Brods Gallery, 1966, Christies, 1966–67, Spinks Gallery, 1967–68, Plumbers Gallery, 1969–70, National Trust, 1970–72, and Daily Express, 1972–74. *Publs:* The Stones of Maggiare (in U.S. as The Bride of Sforza), 1974; Count Manfred, 1976; Daughter of Darkness (in U.S. as Daughter of Shadows), 1977; The Goddess, 1979; Madonna of the Island, 1980; Medea, 1981; Casper and the Secret Kingdom, 1986; Vampire of Verdonia, 1988. Add: 15 Hanover Terr., London NW1, England.

SEYMOUR-SMITH, Martin. British, b. 1928. Poetry, Literature, Sex, Biography. Member, Editorial Bd., Preview, since 1989. Sch. master, 1954–60; Editorial Asst., The London Mag., 1955–56; Poetry Ed., Truth mag., London, 1955–57, and The Scotsman, Edinburgh, 1964–67; Literary Adviser, Hodder & Stoughton, publrs., London, 1963–65; General Ed., Gollancz Classics series, Victor Gollancz Ltd., publrs., London, 1967–69. *Publs:* (with R. Taylor and T. Hards) Poems, 1952; (Poems), 1953; (ed.) Poetry from Oxford, 1953; All Devils Fading, 1954; Robert Graves, 1956, 1970; (ed.) Shakespeare's Sonnets, 1963; Tea with Miss Stockport: 24 Poems, 1963; (ed.) A Cupful of Tears: Sixteen Victorian Novelettes, 1965; Bluff Your Way in Literature, 1966, 1972; (ed.) Every Man in His Humour, by Ben Jonson, 1966, 1983; (ed. with J. Reeves) A New Canon of English Poetry, 1967; Fallen Women: A Sceptical Inquiry into the Treatment of Prostitutes, Their Clients, and Their Pimps in Literature, 1969; Poets Through Their Letters, 1969; (ed. with J. Reeves) The Poems of Andrew Marvell, 1969; (ed.) Longer Elizabethan Poems, 1970; (with J. Reeves) Inside Poetry, 1970; Reminiscences of Norma: Poems 1963-1970, 1971; Guide to Modern World Literature (in U.S. as Funk and Wagnalls' Guide to World Literature), 1973, 3rd ed. as Macmillan Guide to Modern World Literature (in U.S. as New Guide to Modern World Literature) 1986; Sex and Society, 1975; Who's Who in Twentieth-Century Literature, 1976; (ed.) The English Sermon 1550-1650, 1976; (ed.) Selected Poems, by Walt Whitman, 1976; (ed.) The Mayor of Casterbridge, by Thomas Hardy, 1979; Fifty European Novels, 1979; Novels and Novelists, 1980; The New Astrologer, 1981; Robert Graves: His Life and Work, 1982; (ed.) Nostromo, by Conrad, 1983; (ed.) The Secret Agent, by Conrad, 1984; Rudyard Kipling, 1989; (compiler) Everyman Dictionary of Fictional Characters, 1989. Add: 36 Holliers Hill, Bexhill-on-Sea, Sussex TN40 2DD, England.

SHACKLE, George Lennox Sharman. British, b. 1903. Economics, Mathematics/Statistics. Emeritus Prof., Univ. of Liverpool, since 1969 (Brunner Prof. of Economic Science, 1951–69). Member, Statistical Branch, Admiralty and Cabinet Office, London, 1939–45; Reader in Economic Theory, Univ. of Leeds, Yorks., 1950; Member, Council, Royal Economic Soc., 1955–69; Pres., Section F. British Assn. for the Advancement of Science, 1966. *Publs:* Expectations, Investment and Income, 1938, 1968; Expectation in Economics, 1949, 1952; Mathematics at the Fireside, 1952; (ed. with C.F. Carter and G.P. Meredith) Uncertainty and Business Decisions, 1954, 1957; Uncertainty in Economics, 1955; Time in Economics, 1958; (ed.) A New Prospect of Economics, 1958; Economics for Pleasure, 1959, 1968; Decision, Order and Time in Human Affairs, 1961, 1969; A Scheme of Economic Theory, 1965; The Nature of Economic Thought, 1966; The Years of High Theory, 1967; Expectation, Enterprise and Profit, 1970; Epistemics and Economics, 1972; An Economic Querist, 1973; Keynesian Kaleidics, 1974; Imagination and the Nature of Choice, 1979. Add: Rudloe, Alde House Drive, Aldeburgh, Suffolk IP15 5EE, England.

SHACKLETON, Lord, of Burley; Edward Arthur Alexander Shackleton. British, b. 1911. Geography, Travel/Exploration/Adventure, Biography. Labour Peer, House of Lords (Minister of Defence for the R.A.F., 1964–67; Minister without Portfolio and Deputy Leader, House of Lords, 1967–68; Lord Privy Seal, 1968; Paymaster-Gen., 1968; Lord Privy Seal and Leader of the House of Lords, 1968–70; Chmn., House of Lords Select Cttee. on Science and Technology, 1988). ; an Adviser to the RTZ Corp., London, since 1982 (Dir., 1973–82, Deputy Chmn., 1975–82, Chmn., RTZ Development Enterprises, 1973–83). Labour Member of (UK) Parliament for Preston, 1946–50, and for Preston South, Lancs., 1950–55; Chmn., Anglesey Aluminium Ltd., 1981–85. Pres., Assn. of Special

Libraries and Information Bureaux (ASLIB), 1963–65; Chmn., British Standards Instn., 1977–80, East European Trade Council, 1977–86, and British-Australia Soc., 1984–88. *Publs:* Arctic Journeys, 1937; (co-author) Borneo Jungle, 1938; Nansen, The Explorer, 1956; Economic Survey of the Falkland Islands, 1976, 1982; U.K. Anti-Terrorist Legislation, 1978. Add: 19 St. James's Sq., London SW1, England.

SHADBOLT, Maurice (Francis Richard). New Zealander, b. 1932. Novels/Short stories, Travel/Exploration/Adventure. Journalist for various New Zealand publs., 1953–54; Documentary Scriptwriter and Dir., New Zealand National Film Unit, 1954–57. *Publs:* The New Zealanders:Sequence of Stories, 1959; Summer Fires and Winter Country, 1963; (with B. Brake) New Zealand: Gift of the Sea, 1963; Among the Cinders, 1965: The Presence of Music: 3 Novellas, 1967; The Shell Guide to New Zealand, 1968; (with O. Ruhen) Isles of the South Pacific, 1968; The Summer's Dolphin, 1969; Strangers and Journeys, 1972; A Touch of Clay, 1974; Danger Zone, 1976; Figures in Light, 1979; The Lovelock Version, 1980; Once on Chanuk Bair, 1982; Season of the Jew, 1986. Add: Box 60028, Titirangi, Auckland 7, New Zealand.

SHAFER, Neil. American, b. 1933. Economics, Money/Finance. Joined Western Publishing Co. Inc., Racine, 1962: Sr. Numismatic Ed., 1974–81; Ed.-in-Chief, New England Journal of Numismatics, 1985–87. Asst. Dir., Racine Symphony Orchestra, 1963–72; Dir., Kiwanis Youth Symphony, Racine, 1966–79. *Publs:* United States Territorial Coinage for the Philippine Islands, 1961; A Guide Book of Philippine Paper Money, 1964; A Guide Book of Modern United States Currency, 1965, 8th ed. 1979; Philippine Emergency and Guerrilla Currency of World War II, 1974; Let's Collect Paper Money, 1976; (co-ed.) Standard Catalogue of World Paper Money, 2 vols, 1982–86; (co-author) Standard Catalogue of Depression Scrip of the United States, 1985. Add: P.O. Box 17138, Milwaukee, Wisc. 53217, U.S.A.

SHAFER, Robert (Eugene). American, b. 1925. Education. Prof. of English, Arizona State Univ., Tempe. *Publs:* Success in Reading, 8 vols., 1968–73; Developing Reading Efficiency, 1975; (with John S. Simmons and Gail West) Decisions about the Teaching of English, 1976; Applied Linguistics and Reading, 1979; (with Karen Smith and Clare Staab) Language Functions and School Success, 1983; (ed. with James Britton and Ken Watson) Teaching English Worldwide, 1989. Add: Dept. of English, Arizona State Univ., Tempe, Ariz. 85287, U.S.A.

SHAFFER, Anthony (Joshua). Has also written novels with Peter Shaffer as Peter Anthony. British, b. 1926. Novels/Plays. *Publs:* (with Peter Shaffer as Peter Anthony) How Doth the Crocodile?, 1951; (with Peter Shaffer as Peter Anthony) Woman in the Wardrobe, 1952; (with Peter Shaffer) Withered Murder, 1955; Sleuth (play), 1970; (with Robin Hardy) The Wicker Man (novelization of screenplay), 1978; (with Peter Shaffer as Peter Anthony) Absolution (novelization of screenplay), 1979; Murderer (play), 1979; Evil under the Sun (screenplay), 1982; Whodunnit (play), 1983. Add: Fraser & Dunlop Scripts Ltd., The Chambers, Lots Rd., Chelsea Harbour, London SW10, England.

SHAFFER, Dale Eugene. American, b. 1929. Librarianship. Library Consultant, since 1971. Prof. of Economics, Bethany Coll., W. Va., 1958–59; Business and Technical Librarian, South Bend Public Library, Ind., 1960–61; Chief Librarian and Head, Library Science Dept., Glenville State Coll., W. Va., 1963–65; Head Librarian, Ocean County Coll., Toms River, N.J., 1965–67; Dir. of Library, Capital Univ., Columbus, Ohio, 1968–71; Dir. of Library and Assoc. Prof., Univ. of Pittsburgh, Johnstown, Pa., 1972–73. *Publs:* The Maturity of Librarianship as a Profession, 1968; The Library Picture File: A Complete System of How to Process and Organize, 1970; The Pamphlet Library: Use of the Sha-Frame System, 1972; the Filmstrip Collection: Complete Instructions on How to Process and Organize, 1972; The Audio-Tape Collection: A Library Manual on Sources, Processing, and Organization, 1973; A Basic Audio-Tape Collection: Lecture Programs for the Academic Library, 1973; Library Job Descriptions: Examples Covering Major Work Areas, 1973; Library Resources for Nurses: A Basic Collection for Supporting the Nursing Curriculum, 1973; Creativity for Librarians: A Management Guide to Encourage Creative Thinking, 1973; A Library of 1,500 Free Pamphlets: Titles and Sources for Every Librarian and Teacher, 1974; Sources of Free Teaching Material, 1975; Career Education Pamphlets, 1976; A Handbook of Library Ideas, 1977; Posters for Teachers and Librarians, 1978; Management Concepts for Improving Libraries: A Guide for the Professional Librarian, 1979; Criteria for Improving the Professional Status of Librarianship, 1980; Educator's Sourcebook of Posters, 1981; A Guide to Writing Library Job Descriptions, 1981; Marbles—A Forgotten Part of Salem History, 1983; Some Remembrances of Salem's Past, 1983;

Sourcebook of Teaching Aids—Mostly Free: Posters and Handbooks for Educators, 1984; Reflections of Salem's Past, 1984; Views of Salem History, 1985; Yesterday in Salem: A Collection of Nostalgic Articles, 1986; Historical Firsts in Salem, 1987; Flashbacks of Salem History, 1988. Add: 437 Jennings Ave., Salem, Ohio 44460, U.S.A.

SHAFFER, Harry G. American, b. 1919. Economics. Prof. of Economics, Soviet and East European Studies, Univ. of Kansas, Lawrence, since 1969 (Instr., 1956–59; Asst. Prof., 1959–64; Assoc. Prof., 1964–69). Instr. of Economics and Business, Concord Coll., Athens, W. Va., 1948–49; Instr. of Economics, Univ. of Alabama, 1950–56. *Publs:* (ed.) The Soviet Economy: A Collection of Western and Soviet Views, 1963, 1969; (ed.) The Soviet System in Theory and Practice: Selected Western and Soviet Views, 1965, 1984; (ed.) The Communist World: Marxist and Non-Marxist Views, 1967; (ed. with J.S. Prybyla) From Under-Development to Affluence: Western, Soviet and Chinese Views, 1968; The Soviet Treatment of the Jews, 1974; The U.S. Conquers the West, 1974; Periodicals on the Socialist Countries and on Marxism: A New Annotated Index, 1977; Soviet Agriculture, 1977; Women in the Two Germanies, 1981. Add: 2510 Jasu Dr., Lawrence, Kans. 66046, U.S.A.

SHAFFER, Jerome Arthur. American, b. 1929. Philosophy. Prof. of Philosophy, and Chmn., Univ. of Connecticut, Storrs, since 1967. Assoc. Prof., Swarthmore Coll., Pa., 1955–67. *Publs:* Philosophy of Mind, 1968; Reality, Knowledge and Value, 1971; Violence, 1971. Add: Dept. of Philosophy, Univ. of Connecticut, Storrs, Conn. 06268, U.S.A.

SHAFFER, Peter (Levin). Has also written novels with Anthony Shaffer as Peter Anthony. British, b. 1926. Novels/Short stories, Plays/Screenplays. With Acquisition Dept., New York Public Library, 1951–54; with Boosey & Hawkes, music publrs., 1954–55; Literary Critic, Truth, 1956–57; Music Critic, Time and Tide, 1961–62. *Publs:* (with A. Shaffer as Peter Anthony) How Doth the Little Crocodile?, 1951; (Peter Anthony) Woman in the Wardrobe, 1952; (with A. Shaffer) Withered Murder, 1955; Five Finger Exercise, 1958; The Private Ear and The Public Eye, 1962; The Royal Hunt of the Sun: A Play Concerning the Conquest of Peru, 1965; Black Comedy, Including White Lies: Two Plays, 1967; Equus, 1973; Shrivings, 1974; Amadeus, 1980; The Collected Plays of Peter Shaffer, 1982; Yonadab, 1985; Lettice and Lovage, 1987. Add: c/o Macnaughton-Lowe, 200 Fulham Rd., London SW10, England.

SHAGAN, Steve. American, b. 1927. Novels/Short stories, Plays/Screenplays. Screenwriter/Producer. Member, Bd. of Dirs., Writers Guild of America, West. Publicist, Paramount Studios, Hollywood, 1962–63; Producer, Tarzan series, NBC-TV, 1965–66; Producer, TV movies, Universal Studios, Hollywood, 1968–70; Producer/Writer, "Save the Tiger," Paramount Pictures, 1972; Exec. Producer, "W.W. and the Dixie Dance Kings," 20th Century Fox, 1974; Producer, "The Formula," MGM, 1980. *Publs:* Save the Tiger (novel), 1973, as a screenplay, 1973; City of Angels (novel), 1975 (as screenplay entitled Hustle); (with David Butler) Voyage of the Damned (screenplay), 1976; The Formula (novel), 1980, as screenplay 1980; The Circle, 1982; The Discovery, 1984; Vendetta, 1986. Add: c/o Morrow, 105 Madison Ave., New York, N.Y. 10016, U.S.A.

SHAH, (Sayed) Idries. British, b. 1924. Cultural/Ethnic topics, Philosophy, Psychology. Dir. of Studies, Inst. for Cultural Research, London, since 1966. Proprietor, Intnl. Press Agency, London, 1958–64. *Publs:* Oriental Magic, 1956; Destination Mecca, 1957; (compiler and trans.) The Secret Lore of Magic, 1957; Special Problems in the Study of Sufi Ideas, 1966; (trans. and compiler) The Exploits of the Incomparable Mulla Nasrudin, 1966; (compiler and trans.) Tales of the Dervishes, 1967; Reflections 1968; (compiler) Caravan of Dreams, 1968; (compiler and trans.) The Way of the Sufi, 1968; (compiler and trans.) Wisdom of the Idiots, 1969; (trans.) The Book of the Book, 1969; The Sufis, 1969; (compiler and ed.) Textos Sufis, 1969; (compiler) The Dermis Probe, 1970; Thinkers of the East, 1971; The Magic Monastery, 1972; Lo que un pajaro deberia Parecer 1972; (compiler and trans.) The Subtleties of Nasrudin, 1973; (compiler and trans.) The Pleasantries of the Incredible Mulla Nasrudin, 1973; The Elephant in the Dark, 1974; A Veiled Gazelle, 1977; Special Illumination, 1977; Neglected Aspects of Sufi Study, 1977; A Perfumed Scorpion, 1978; The Hundred Tales of Wisdom, 1978; (trans.) Learning How to Learn, 1978; (ed. and trans.) World Tales, 1979; Seeker after Truth, 1982; Kara Kush, 1986; Darkest England, 1987; The Natives Are Restless, 1988; The Commanding Self, 1989. Add: c/o A.P. Watt Ltd., 20 John St., London WC1N 2DL, England.

SHAHANE, Vasant A(nant). Indian, b. 1923. Novels/Short stories, Poetry, Literature. Sr. Prof. of English, 1947–83, and Prof. Emeritus since 1984, Osmania Univ., Hyderabad, India (Principal, Univ. Coll. of Arts and Commerce, 1973–74). *Publs:* E.M. Forster: A Reassessment, 1962; Perspectives on Forster's A Passage to India, 1968; Khushwant Singh, 1972; Notes on Whitman's Leaves of Grass, 1972; Rudyard Kipling: Activist and Artist, 1973; (ed.) Indian Essays on A Passage to India, 1974; E.M. Forster:A Study in Double Vision, 1975; Ruth Prawer Jhabvala, 1976; (ed.) Indian Poetry in English: A Critical Assessment, 1980; The Flute and the Drum, 1980; (ed.) Modern Indian Fiction, 1981; (ed.) Approaches to E.M. Forster, 1981; A Passage to India, by Forster (York Notes), 1982; The Waste Land:A Study, 1982; Prajapati: God of the People (novel), 1984; Doctor Fauste (novel), 1987. Add: 3-4-1013/22, Barkatpura, Hyderabad 500027 (A.P.), India.

SHALLCRASS, John James. New Zealander, b. 1922. Education. Reader, Victoria Univ. of Wellington, since 1968. Sr. Lectr., 1959–63, and Vice-Principal, 1963–67, Wellington Teachers Coll.; Ed., Liberal Studies Briefs, Price-Milburn & Co. Ltd., publrs., Wellington, 1968–74. *Publs:* Educating New Zealanders, 1967; (ed. with J.L. Ewing) An Introduction to Maori Education, 1973; (ed. and contrib.) Secondary Schools in Change, 1974; (ed. and contrib.) The Spirit of an Age; Forward to Basics; (ed.) Recreation Reconsidered; (with J. Wilson) No Stone Unturned; (ed.) Civil Liberties in a Changing World. Add: 24 Newcombe Cres., Wellington 5, New Zealand.

SHALLOW, Robert. *See* ATKINSON, Frank.

SHANE, John. *See* DURST, Paul.

SHANGE, Ntozake. American. Novels/Short stories, Plays/Screenplays, Poetry. Former teacher, Mills Coll., Oakland, Calif., Sonoma State Univ., Rohnert Park, Calif., Medgar Evers Coll., Brooklyn, N.Y., and the Univ. of California at Berkeley. *Publs:* For Colored Girls Who Have Considered Suicide When the Rainbow is Enuf, 1976, 1977; Sassafrass: A Novella, 1976; Nappy Edges (poetry), 1978; Three Pieces: Spell No. 7, A Photograph: Lovers in Motion, Boogie Woogie Landscapes, 1981; Sassafrass, Cypress and Indigo, 1982; A Daughter's Geography, 1983; From Okra to Greens: Poems, 1984; Betsey Brown, 1985; Ridin' the Moon in Texas (poetry), 1988. Add: c/o St. Martin's Press, 175 Fifth Ave., New York, N.Y. 10010, U.S.A.

SHANK, Margarethe Erdahl. American, b. 1910. Novels/Short stories, Autobiography/Memoirs/Personal, Humor/Satire. Formerly Prof. of English, Glendale Community Coll., Arizona. *Publs:* The Coffee Train, 1953; Call Back the Years, 1966. Add: 1645 W. State Ave., Phoenix, Ariz. 85021, U.S.A.

SHANK, Theodore. American, b. 1929. Plays/Screenplays, Theatre. Prof., Dept. of Dramatic Art, Univ. of California at Davis, since 1956; Dir., Magic Theatre, San Francisco; Actors Theatre of Louisville; Los Angeles Theatre Center; and Minnesota Opera New Music-Theatre Ensemble. Member, Advisory Bd., West Coast Plays, since 1977; Advising Ed., Praxis, since 1979; Member, Bd. of Dirs., Snake Theatre, since 1979; Soon 3 Theatre, since 1981; and San Francisco Intnl. Theatre Festival, since 1981; Advisory Ed., New Theatre Quarterly, since 1986. Contributing Ed., The Drama Review, NYC, 1976–86. *Publs:* The Bowery Theatre 1826-1836, 1956; (ed.) 500 Plays: Outlines and Production Notes, 1963; The Art of Dramatic Art, 1969; (with others) Them Inc. (stage play with music), 1969; (with others) The Crimes and Trials of the Chicago 8 – 1 + 2 (play), 1971; (with others) Undead (play), 1972; (with others) The Moving Bed Show (play), 1976; (with others) Sheet Dreams (play), 1977; Theatre in Real Time, 1980; American Alternative Theatre, 1982; Wild Indian (play), 1985; Codex (play), 1987; Fly Away All (opera libretto), 1987. Add: Dept. of Dramatic Art, Univ. of California, Davis, Calif. 95616, U.S.A.

SHANKLAND, Peter Macfarlane. British, b. 1901. History, Biography. *Publs:* (co-author) Malta Convoy, 1961; (co-author) Dardanelles Patrol, 1964; The Phantom Flotilla, 1968; Byron of the Wager, 1975; Beware of Heroes, 1975; (co-author) The Royal Baccarat Scandal, 1977; (co-author) Murder with a Double Tongue, 1978; (co-author) Tragedy in Three Voices, 1980; Death of an Editor: The Caillaux Drama, 1981. Add: Bowden House, 9 Market St., Poole, Dorset, England.

SHANNON, Doris. Canadian, b. 1924. Novels/Short stories. Bank Teller in Napanee, Ont., 1942–47, and Vancouver, 1948–49, for the Royal Bank of Canada. *Publs:* The Whispering Runes, 1972; Twenty-two Hallowfield, 1974; The Seekers, 1975; Hawthorn Hill, 1976; Lodestar Legacy, 1976; Cain's Daughters, 1978; Beyond the Shining Mountains, 1979; Little Girls Lost, 1981; The Punishment, 1981; Family Money,

1984. Add: 10580 154A St., Surrey, B.C., Canada.

SHANNON, Steve. *See* **BOUMA,** J. L.

SHAPCOTT, Thomas W(illiam). Australian, b. 1935. Novels, Plays/Screenplays, Poetry, Songs, lyrics and libretti, Art, Literature. Dir., Literature Bd. of Australia Council, since 1983. Clerk, H.S. Shapcott, Public Accountant, Ipswich, Qld., 1951–63; Partner, Shapcott & Shapcott, Accountants, Ipswich, 1963–72; Public Accountant, Sole Trader, Ipswich, 1972–78. *Publs:* Time on Fire: Poems, 1961; Twelve Bagetelles, 1962; The Mankind Thing, 1964; Sonnets 1960-1963, 1964; A Taste of Salt Water: Poems, 1967; Focus on Charles Blackman (art monograph), 1967; (ed. with R. Hall) New Impulses in Australian Poetry, 1968; Inwards in the Sun: Poems, 1969; Fingers at Air: Experimental Poems, 1969; (ed.) Australian Poetry Now, 1969; the Seven Deadly Sins, 1970; (ed.) Poets on Record, 1970–73; Begin with Walking, 1972; Interim Report, 1972; Shabbytown Calendar: Poems, 1975; (ed.) Contemporary American and Australian Poetry, 1976; Seventh Avenue Poems, 1976; Selected Poems, 1978; Travelling Full Circle: Prose Poems, 1978; Those Who Are Compelled, 1980; Stump and Grape and Bopple-nut, 1981; (ed.) Consolidation, 1982; The Birthday Gift (novel), 1982; Welcome! (poetry), 1983; White Stag of Exile (novel), 1984; Holiday of the Ikon (novel), 1985; Hotel Belleview (novel), 1986; Travel Dice (poetry), 1987; Limestone and Lemon Wine (stories), 1988; Selected Poems 1956-88, 1989; The Search for Galina (novel), 1989; Charles Blackman (Art monograph), 1989. Add: 62 Cremorne Rd., Cremorne, N.S.W. 2060, Australia.

SHAPIRO, David (Joel). American, b. 1947. Poetry, Art. Ed. Asst., Art News, NYC, since 1970. Instr., Columbia Univ., 1972–81. *Publs:* Poems, 1960; A Second Winter, 1961; When Will the Bluebird, 1962; January: A Book of Poems, 1965; (ed. with Kenneth Koch) Learn Something, America, 1968; Poems from Deal, 1969; (ed. with Ron Padgett) An Anthology of New York Poets, 1970; A Man Holding an Acoustic Panel, 1971; The Dance of Things, 1971; The Page-Turner, 1973; (trans.) Writings of Sonia Delaunay, 1974; (co-trans.) The New Art of Color: The Writings of Robert and Sonia Delaunay, 1978; Lateness, 1978; John Ashbery: An Introduction to His Poetry, 1979; Jime Dine: Painting What One Is, 1981; To an Idea (verse), 1983; Jasper Johns: Drawings 1954-1984, 1984; House Blow Apart, 1988. Add: c/o Overlook Press, 12 W. 21st., New York, N.Y. 10010, U.S.A.

SHAPIRO, Eli. American, b. 1916. Economics. Sloane Prof. of Management, Massachusetts Inst. of Technology, Cambridge, since 1976 (Prof., 1952–61). Instr., Brooklyn Coll., N.Y., 1936–41; Research Assoc., 1938–39, Consultant, 1939–42, and Member of Research Staff, 1955–62, National Bureau of Economic Research; Asst. Prof. of Finance, 1946–47, Assoc. Prof., 1948–52, and Prof., 1952, Univ. of Chicago; Prof. of Finance, 1962–70, and Sylvan C. Coleman Prof. of Financial Management, 1968–70, Harvard Business Sch., Boston. *Publs:* (with others) Personal Finance Industry and Its Credit Standards, 1939; Money and Banking, (with Steiner) 1941, (with Steiner and Solomon) 1958; Development of the Wisconsin Credit Union Movement, 1947; (with D. Meiselman) Measurement of Corporate Sources and Uses of Funds, 1964; (with Solomon and W.L. White) Money and Banking, 1968; (with Wolf) The Role of Private Placement in Corporate Finance, 1972; (co-ed.) Capital for Productivity and Growth, 1977. Add: 180 Beacon St., Boston, Mass. 02116, U.S.A.

SHAPIRO, Harry L. American, b. 1902. Anthropology. Prof. Emeritus of Anthropology, Columbia Univ., NYC, since 1974 (Prof., 1939–73); Curator Emeritus, Dept. of Anthropology, American Museum of Natural History, NYC, since 1970 (Asst. Curator, 1926–31, Assoc. Curator, 1931–42, Curator, and Chmn., Dept. of Anthropology, 1942–70). Member of Bd., Louise Wise Services, since 1985. Vice Pres., American Assn. of Physical Anthropology, 1941–42; Pres., American Ethnological Soc., 1942–43, and American Anthropological Assn., 1948. *Publs:* Heritage of the Bounty, 1936; Migration and Environment, 1939; Aspects of Culture, 1956; The Jewish People, 1960; Peking Man, 1975. Add: c/o American Museum of Natural History, Central Park W. at 79th St., New York, N.Y. 11572, U.S.A.

SHAPIRO, Harvey. American, b. 1924. Poetry. Deputy Ed., New York Times mag., since 1983 (Staff Member, New York Times mag., 1957–75; Ed., New York Times Book Review, 1975–83). Instr. in English, Cornell Univ., Ithaca, N.Y., 1949–52; Creative Writing Fellow, Bard Coll., NYC, 1950–51; Staff member, Commentary mag., 1953–54, and New Yorker mag., 1954–55. *Publs:* The Eye, 1953; The Book and Other Poems, 1955; Mountain, Fire, Thornbush, 1961; Battle Report, 1966; This World, 1971; Lauds, 1975; Lauds and Nightsounds, 1978; The

Light Holds, 1984; National Cold Storage Company, 1988. Add: c/o New York Times, 229 W. 43rd St., New York, N.Y. 10036, U.S.A.

SHAPIRO, Herman. American, b. 1922. Intellectual history, Philosophy. Prof. of Philosophy, San Jose State Univ., California, since 1965 (Asst. Prof., 1960–62; Assoc. Prof., 1962–65). Member of faculty, Hunter Coll., 1956–57, and Queens Coll., 1957–58, City Coll. of New York, and Univ. of Connecticut, Storrs, 1958–60. *Publs:* Motion, Space and Time, According to William Ockham, 1957; Medieval Philosophy, 1964; (ed.) Hellenistic Philosophy, 1966; (co-ed.) The Italian Philosophers, 1972; (co-ed.) The Transalpine Thinkers, 1973; Renaissance Philosophy, 1977. Add: c/o Random House Inc., 201 E. 50th St., New York, N.Y. 10022, U.S.A.

SHAPIRO, Karl (Jay). American, b. 1913. Novels/Short stories, Poetry, Literature, Essays, Autobiography. Prof. of English, Univ. of California, Davis, since 1968. Consultant in Poetry, Library of Congress, Washington, D.C., 1946–47; Assoc. Prof., Johns Hopkins Univ., Baltimore, Md., 1947–50; Ed., Poetry, Chicago, 1950–56, Newbery Library Bulletin, Chicago, 1953–55, and Prairie Schooner, Lincoln, Nebr. 1956–66; Visiting Prof., Loyola Univ., Chicago, 1951–52; Visiting Prof., Univ. of California, Berkeley and Davis, 1955–56, and Univ. of Indiana, Bloomington, 1956–57; Prof. of English, Univ. of Nebraska, Lincoln, 1956–66, and Univ. of Illinois, Chicago Circle, 1966–68. *Publs:* Poems, 1935; Person, Place and Thing, 1942; The Place of Love, 1942; V-Letter and Other Poems, 1944; Essay on Rime, 1947; Trial of a Poet and Other Poems, 1947; English Prosody and Modern Poetry, 1947; A Bibliography of Modern Prosody, 1948; Beyond Criticism, 1953, as A Primer for Poets, 1965; Poems 1940-1953, 1953; (ed. with L. Untermeyer and R. Wilbur) Modern American and Modern British Poetry, rev. shortened ed., 1955; The Tenor (play), 1956; The House, 1957; Poems of a Jew, 1958; In Defense of Ignorance (essays), 1960; (with J.E. Miller and B. Slote) Start with the Sun: Studies in Cosmic Poetry, 1960; (ed.) American Poetry, 1960; (ed.) Prose Keys to Modern Poetry, 1962; The Bourgeois Poet, 1964; (with Ralph Ellison) The Writer's Experience, 1964; (with R. Beum) A Prosody Handbook, 1965; Randall Jarrell, 1967; To Abolish Children and Other Essays, 1968; Selected Poems, 1968; White-Haired Lover, 1968; Edsel (novel), 1971; The Poetry Wreck: Selected Essays, 1975; Adult Bookstore, 1976; Collected Poems, 1978; Love and War, Art and God (poetry), 1984; New and Selected Poems 1940-1986, 1987; The Younger Son (autobiography), 1988. Add: 904 Radcliffe Dr., Davis, Calif. 95616, U.S.A.

SHAPIRO, Stanley. American, b. 1925. Novels, Plays/Screenplays. Pres., Stanley Shapiro Prods., since 1985. Formerly Pres. of Nob Hill Prods., Lankershim Prods., and Samesta Prods. *Publs:* The Engagement Baby (play), 1973; Simon's Soul (novel), 1977; A Time to Remember (novel), 1986; screenplays include Pillow Talk, Operation Petticoat, Lover Come Back, Touch of Mink, The Seniors, Carbon Copy, etc. Add: 9938 Robbins, Beverly Hills, Calif. 90212, U.S.A.

SHARAT CHANDRA, G. S. American, b. 1938. Poetry, Translations. Instr., Iowa State Univ., 1968–79; Asst. Prof., Iowa Wesleyan Coll., 1969–72; Asst. Prof. and Poet-in-Residence, Dept. of English, Washington State Univ., Pullman, 1972–78; Fulbright Sr. Prof. in Creative Writing and American Literature, Malaysia, 1978–79. *Publs:* (trans.) On the Death of a Day Old Child, 1968; (trans.) How to Go, 1968; Will This Forest, 1969; Reasons for Staying, 1970; April in Nanjangud, 1971; Once or Twice, 1974; (trans.) Offsprings of Servagna, 1978; The Ghost of Meaning, 1978; Heirloom, 1982. Add: 2505 Debden Ct., Tallahassee, Fla. 32308, U.S.A.

SHARKANSKY, Ira. American/Israeli, b. 1938. Economics, Politics/Government. Prof. of Political Science, Hebrew Univ. of Jerusalem, since 1975. Asst. Prof. of Political Science, Ball State Univ., Muncie, Ind., 1964–65; Asst. Prof., Florida State Univ., Tallahassee, 1965–66; Assoc. Prof., 1968–71, and Prof. of Political Science, 1971–75, Univ. of Wisconsin, Madison. *Publs:* Spending in the American States, 1968; Politics of Taxing and Spending, 1969; Regionalism in American Politics, 1970; The Routines of Politics, 1970; Public Administration: Policy-Making in Government Agencies, 1970, 1972; The Maligned States, 1972; (with Robert L. Lineberry) Urban Politics and Public Policy, 1974; The United States, 1975; Wither the State?, 1979; What Makes Israel Tick?, 1985; The Political Enemy of Israel, 1987. Add: Dept. of Political Science, Hebrew Univ., Jerusalem, Israel.

SHARKEY, Jack. (John Michael Sharkey). Also writes as Mike Johnson, Rick Abbot and Monk Ferris. American, b. 1931. Mystery/Crime/Suspense, Science fiction/Fantasy, Plays/Screenplays.

Professional writer since 1952; Asst. Ed., Playboy mag., Chicago, 1963–64; Ed., Aim, later Good Hands, for Allstate Insurance Co., Northbrook, Ill., 1964–75. *Publs:* Murder, Maestro, Please (mystery novel), 1960; The Secret Martians (SF novel), 1960; Death for Auld Lang Syne (mystery novel), 1962; The Addams Family (mystery novel), 1965; Ultimatum in 2050 A.D. (SF novel), 1965; plays—Here Lies Jeremy Troy, 1969; M Is for Million, 1971; How Green Was My Brownie, 1972; Kiss or Make Up, 1972; Meanwhile, Back on the Couch..., 1973; A Gentleman and a Scoundrel, 1973; Roomies, 1974; Spinoff, 1974; Who's on First, 1975; (with Dave Reiser) What a Spot!, 1975; Saving Grace, 1976; Take a Number, Darling, 1976; The Creature Creeps!, 1977; Dream Lover, 1977; (with Dave Reiser) Hope for the Best, 1977; Rich Is Better, 1977; The Murder Room, 1977; (with Ken Easton) Pushover, 1977; Once Is Enough, 1977; (as Mike Johnson) The Clone People, 1978; Double Exposure, 1978; Missing Link, 1978; (with Ken Easton) Turnabout, 1978; (with Dave Reiser) Not the Count of Monte Cristo?, 1978; Turkey in the Straw, 1979; (with Dave Reiser) Operetta!, 1979; My Son the Astronaut, 1980; Par for the Corpse, 1980; (as Rick Abbot) June Groom, 1980; (as Rick Abbot) Play On!, 1980; (as Rick Abbot) A Turn for the Nurse, 1980; (as Rick Abbot) But Why Bump Off Barnaby?, 1981; Honestly Now!, 1981; (as Mike Johnson) The Return of the Maniac, 1981; (with Dave Reiser) Slow Down, Sweet Chariot, 1982; (with Dave Reiser) Woman Overboard, 1982; Your Flake or Mine?, 1982; (with Dave Reiser) The Picture of Dorian Gray, 1982; (with Dave Reiser) The Saloonkeeper's Daughter, 1982; The Second Lady, 1983; (with Dave Reiser) And on the Sixth Day, 1984; (with Mel Buttorff) And Then I Wrote..., 1984; (with Dave Reiser) Jekyll Hydes Again!, 1984; (with Dave Reiser and Ira and Brady Rubin) My Husband the Wife, 1984; (as Monk Ferris) Don't Tell Mother, 1984; (as Monk Ferris) This Must be the Place!, 1984; (as Monk Ferris) Let's Murder Marsha!, 1984; (with Tim Kelly) The Great All-American Disaster Musical, 1985; (with Tim Kelly) Money, Power, Murder, Lust, Revenge and Marvelous Clothes, 1985; (as Monk Ferris) A Fine Monster *You* are!, 1985; (as Monk Ferris) Bone-Chiller, 1985; One Toe in the Grave, 1986; (with Dave Reiser) Zingo!, 1986; (as Rock Abbot) Class Musical!, 1986; (with Dave Reiser) Love With a Twist, 1987; (with Tim Kelly) The Woman in White, 19877; (with Tim Kelly) Cinderella Meets the Wolfman!, 1987; (with Tim Kelly) Sherlock Holmes and the Gaint Rat Of Sumatra, 1987; (with Tim Kelly) The Three-and-a-Half Musketeers, 1987; (with Tim Kelly) Tim and Time Again, 1987; (as Rick Abbot) The Bride Of Brackenloch!, 1987; (as Monk Ferris) Hamlet, Cha-Cha-Cha!, 1987; Nell of the Ozarks, 1988; While the Lights Were Out, 1988; (with Dave Reiser) Coping, 1988; (With Dave Reiser) The Pinchpenny Phantom of the Opera, 1988; Allocating Annie, 1989; Oh, Fudge!, 1989; (with Leo Sears) 100 Lunches, 1989. Add: 24276 Ponchartrain Lane, Lake Forest, Calif. 92630, U.S.A.

SHARMAT, Marjorie Weinman. Also writes as Wendy Andrews. American, b. 1928. Children's fiction. *Publs:* Rex, 1967; Goodnight Andrew, Goodnight Craig, 1969; Gladys Told Me to Meet Her Here, 1970;Hot Thirsty Day, 1971; 51 Sycamore Lane, 1971; Getting Something on Maggie Marmelstein, 1971; A Visit with Rosalind, 1972; Nate the Great series, 11 vols., 1972–89; Sophie and Gussie, 1973; Morris Brookside, A Dog, 1973; Morris Brookside is Missing, 1974; I Want Mama, 1974; I'm Not Oscar's Friend Anymore, 1975; Walter the Wolf, 1975; Maggie Marmelstein for President, 1975; Burton and Dudley, 1975; The Lancelot Closes at Five, 1976; The Trip and Other Sophie and Gussie Stories, 1976; Mooch the Messy, 1976; Edgemont, 1977; I'm Terrific, 1977; I Don't Care, 1977; (with others) Just for Fun, 1977; A Big Fat Enormous Lie, 1978; Thornton the Worrier, 1978; Mitchell Is Moving, 1978; Mooch the Messy Meets Prudence the Neat, 1979; Scarlet Monster Lives Here, 1979; Mr. Jameson and Mr. Philips, 1979; Uncle Boris and Maude, 1979; The 329th Friend, 1979; (with Mitchell Sharmat) I Am Not a Pest, 1979; Octavia Told Me a Secret, 1979; Say Hello, Vanessa, 1979; Griselda's New Year, 1979; Little Devil Gets Sick, 1980; The Trolls of 12th Street, 1979; What Are We Going to Do about Andrew?, 1980; Sometimes Mama and Papa Fight, 1980; Taking Care of Melvin, 1980; Gila Monsters Meet You at the Airport, 1980; Grumley the Grouch, 1980; (with Mitchell Sharmat) The Day I Was Born, 1980; Twitchell the Wishful, 1981; Chasing After Annie, 1981; Rollo and Juliet, Forever! 1981; The Sign, 1981; Lucretia the Unbearable, 1981; The Best Valentine in the World!, 1982; Two Ghosts on a Bench, 1982; Mysteriously Yours, Maggie Marmelstein, 1982; Square Pegs (adaptation of CBS-TV sit-com), 1982; Frizzy the Fearful, 1983; I Saw Him First, 1983; How to Meet a Gorgeous Guy, 1983; Rich Mitch, 1983; The Story of Bently Beaver, 1984; Bartholomew the Bossy, 1984; How to Meet a Gorgeous Girl, 1984; Sasha the Silly, 1984; He Noticed I'm Alive . . . and Other Hopeful Signs, 1984; (as Wendy Andrews) Vacation Fever!, 1984; (as Wendy Andrews) Supergirl, 1984; My Mother Never Listens to Me, 1984; Two Guys Noticed Me . . . and Other Miracles, 1985; Attila the Angry, 1985; (as

Wendy Andrews) Are We There Yet?, 1985; How to Have a Gorgeous Wedding, 1985; Get Rich Mitch!, 1985; The Son of the Slime Who Ate Cleveland, 1985; One Terrific Thanksgiving, 1985; Helga High-Up, 1986; Hurray for Mother's Day!, 1986; Who's Afraid of Ernestine?, 1986; Marjorie Sharmat's Sorority Sisters, 8 vols., 1986–87; Helga High Up, 1987; Hooray for Father's Day!, 1987; Go to Sleep, Nicholas Joe, 1987; (with Mitchell Sharmat) Surprises, Treasures, Kingdoms, 3 Vols., 1989; (with Mitchell Sharmat) Olivia Sharp, Agent for Secrets, 2 vols., 1989. Add: c/o Dell Publishing Co., 666 Fifth Ave., New York, N.Y. 10103, U.S.A.

SHAROT, Stephen. British, b. 1943. Sociology. Assoc. Prof., Dept. of Behavioural Sciences, Ben-Gurion Univ. of the Negev, Israel, since 1980. Lectr., Dept. of Sociology, Leicester Univ., U.K., 1970–74; Lectr., 1974–76, and Sr. Lectr., 1976–79, Dept. of Sociology, Hebrew Univ. of Jerusalem. *Publs:* Modern Judaism: A Sociology, 1976; Messianism, Mysticism, and Magic: A Sociological Analysis of Jewish Religious Movements, 1982. Add: Dept. of Behavioural Sciences, Ben-Gurion Univ. of the Negev, Beer Sheva, Israel.

SHARP, Clifford Henry. British, b. 1922. Transportation. Reader in Transport Economics, Univ. of Leicester, since 1973 (Lectr., 1965–68; Sr. Lectr., 1968–73). Dir., Pearce Sharp and Assocs., since 1975. Specialist Adviser, House of Commons Estimates Cttee., 1968–69, and Select Cttee. on Nationalised Industries, 1972–73. *Publs:* The Problem of Transport, 1965; Problems of Urban Passenger Transport, 1967; Transport Economics, 1973; Living with the Lorry, 1973; Transport and the Environment, 1976; The Economics of Time, 1981. Add: 18 Guilford Rd., Leicester, England.

SHARP, Dennis. British, b. 1933. Architecture. Principal of Dennis Sharp Architects, London, since 1964. Regular contributor on architecture, building, building design, A+U (Tokyo), etc., since 1979; Prof., Intnl. Academy of Architecture, since 1987. Dir., CICA, Intnl. Cttee. of Architectural Critics. Asst. Architect, British Rail, London, 1957, Bedfordshire County Architects Dept., 1958–59, William Holford and Partners, Liverpool, Arnold Weisner, Liverpool, Graeme Shankland and Partners, and Gerald Beech and Assocs., all Liverpool, 1961–63; Architect and Technical Officer, Civic Trust, Manchester, 1963–64; Lectr., Manchester Univ. Sch. of Architecture, 1964–68; Sr. Lectr. in charge of History Course, Architectural Assn. Sch., London, and Gen. Ed., Architectural Assn., 1968–82. *Publs:* Area Rejuvenation: Rochdale, 1965; Modern Architecture and Expressionism, 1966; Sources of Modern Architecture, 1967; (ed.) Planning and Architecture, 1968; (ed.) Glass in Modern Architecture, 1968; The Picture Palace and Other Buildings for the Movies, 1969; (ed.) Manchester, 1969; The Bauhaus, 1970; (ed.) Glass Architecture by P. Scheerbart, 1972; A Visual History of Twentieth Century Architecture, 1974; (ed.) Henri van de Velde: Theatres 1904-14, 1974; (co-ed.) Form and Function, 1975; (ed.) The Rationalists, 1978; (ed.) The English House by H. Muthesius, 1979; Sources of Modern Architecture: A Critical Bibliography, 1981; Alfred C. Bossoms' American Architecture 1903-1926, 1984. Add: 1 Woodcock Lodge, Epping Green, Hertford SG13 8ND, England.

SHARP, Doreen Maud. British, b. 1920. Business/Trade/Industry. Lectr., 1952–70, and Sr. Lectr., 1970–78, Bromley Coll. of Technology. Member, Secretarial Studies Cttee., Business Education Council, 1977–82; Co-Chmn., European Assn. of Professional Secretaries, 1979–81. *Publs:* Typing Mailable Copy, 1973; Through Practice to Production, 1974; The Secretary in Europe, 1976; Beginners, Please! with Pitman 2000, 1977; The Theory of Typewriting, 1978; Typewriting in Three Languages, 1981; Office Typewriting, 1984; Mailable Copy and How to Produce It, 1984; Electronic Keyboarding, 1985; Realistic Business Dictation, 1985; The PA's Handbook, 3rd ed. 1986; (consultant ed.) Chambers Office Oracle, 1987. Add: 41 Reservoir Rd., Pymble, N.S.W. 2073, Australia.

SHARP, Margery. British, b. 1905. Novels/Short stories, Children's fiction, Plays/Screenplays. *Publs:* Rhododendron Pie, 1930; Fanfare for Tin Trumpets, 1932; The Nymph and the Nobleman, 1932; The Flowering Thorn, 1933; Meeting at Night (play), 1934; Sophy Cassmajor, 1934; Four Gardens, 1935; The Nutmeg Tree, 1937; Harlequin House, 1939; The Stone of Chastity, 1940; Lady in Waiting (play), 1940; Three Companion Pieces: Sophy Cassmajor, The Tigress on the Hearth, and The Nymph and the Nobleman, 1955; Cluny Brown, 1944; Britannia Mews, 1946; The Foolish Gentlewoman, 1948, play, 1950; Lise Lillywhite, 1951; The Gypsy in the Parlour, 1954; The Eye of Love, 1957; The Rescuers, 1959; Melisande, 1960; Something Light, 1960; Miss Bianca series, 5 vols., 1962–72; Martha in Paris, 1962; The Turret, 1963; Martha, Eric and George, 1964; The Sun in Scorpio, 1965; Lost at the Fair, 1965; In Pious

Memory, 1967; Rosa, 1969; The Innocents, 1971; the Lost Chapel Picnic and Other Stories, 1973; Children Next Door, 1974; The Magical Cockatoo, 1974; The Faithful Servants, 1975; Bernard the Brave, 1976; Summer Visits, 1977; Bernard Into Battle, 1979. Add: c/o William Heinemann Ltd., 81 Fulham Rd., London SW3 6RB, England.

SHARPE, Tom. (Thomas Ridley Sharpe). British, b. 1928. Novels. Full-time novelist since 1971. Social worker, 1952, teacher, 1952–56, and photographer, 1956–61, in South Africa; Lectr. in History, Cambridge Coll. of Arts and Technology, 1963–71. *Publs:* Riotous Assembly, 1971; Indecent Exposure, 1973; Porterhouse Blue, 1974; Blot on the Landscape, 1975; Wilt, 1976; The Great Pursuit, 1977; The Throwback, 1978; The Wilt Alternative, 1979; Ancestral Vices, 1980; Vintage Stuff, 1982; Wilt on High, 1984. Add: c/o Richard Scott Simon Ltd., 43 Doughty St., London WC1N 2LF England.

SHARR, Francis Aubie. British, b. 1914. Botany, Librarianship. State Librarian of Western Australia, 1953–76; Adviser to Govt. of Northern Nigeria, 1962–63; Pres., Library Assn. of Australia, 1969–70. *Publs:* (with Edgar Osborne) County Library Practice, 1950; County Library Transport, 1951; The Library Needs of Northern Nigeria, 1963; Western Australian Plant Names and Their Meanings: A Glossary, 1978. Add: 58 The Avenue, Nedlands, W.A. 6009, Australia.

SHATTUCK, Roger. American, b. 1923. Poetry, Literature, Translations. University Prof. and Prof. of Modern Language, Boston Univ, since 1985. Asst. Prof., and Prof. of French and English, Univ. of Texas, Austin, 1956–71; Chmn., Advisory Bd., National Trans. Center, 1965–69; Commonwealth Prof. of French, Univ. of Virginia, Charlottesville, 1974–88. *Publs:* (ed. and trans.) Selected Writings of Guillaume Apollinaire, 1950; The Banquet Years, 1958; (ed. and trans.) Mount Analogue, by René Daumal, 1959; (ed. with W. Arrowsmith) The Craft and Context of Translation, 1961; Proust's Binoculars, 1963; (ed. with S.W. Taylor) Selected Works of Alfred Jarry, 1964; Half Tame, 1964; (trans. with F. Brown) Occasions, by Paul Valéry, 1971; Marcel Proust, 1974 (National Book Award); The Forbidden Experiment, 1980; The Innocent Eye, 1984. Add: Univ. Profs. Program, Boston Univ., 745 Commonwealth Ave., Boston, Mass. 02215, U.S.A.

SHAW, Bob. British, b. 1931. Science fiction/Fantasy. Press Officer, Short Bros. and Harland, Belfast, 1971–73; Publicity Officer, Vickers Shipbldg. Group, 1973–75. *Publs:* Night Walk, 1967; The Two-Timers, 1968; The Shadow of Heaven, 1969; The Palace of Eternity, 1969; One Million Tomorrows, 1970; The Ground Zero Man, 1971, rev. ed. as The Peace Machine, 1985; Other Days, Other Eyes, 1972; Tomorrow Lies in Ambush, 1973; Orbitsville, 1974; A Wreath of Stars, 1976; Cosmic Kaleidoscope, 1976; Medusa's Children, 1977; Who Goes Here?, 1977; Ship of Strangers, 1978; Vertigo, 1978; Dagger of the mind, 1979; The Ceres Solution, 1981; Galactic Tours, 1981; A Better Mantrap (short stories), 1982; Orbitsville Departure, 1983; Fire Pattern, 1984; The Ragged Astronauts, 1986; The Wooden Spaceships, 1988; Dark Night in Toyland (short stories), 1989; Killer Planet, 1989. Add: 66 Knutsford Rd., Grappenhall, Warrington, Cheshire WA4 2PB, England.

SHAW, Brian. *See* **TUBB**, E. C.

SHAW, Bynum G(illette). Also writes articles as Bob Gillette. American, b. 1923. Novels/Short stories, Plays/Screenplays. Lectr. to Prof. of Journalism, Wake Forest Univ., Winston-Salem, N.C., since 1965. *Publs:* The Sound of Small Hammers, 1962; The Nazi Hunter, 1968; (with E. Hunter) Reprisal (screenplay), 1970; Divided We Stand: The Baptists in American Life, 1974; Days of Power, Nights of Fear, 1980; (with E. Folk) W.W. Holden: A Political Biography, 1982; History of Wake Forest College, vol. IV, 1988. Add: 2700 Speas Rd., Winston-Salem, N.C. 27106, U.S.A.

SHAW, David T. American (born Chinese), b. 1938. Engineering/Technology, Environmental science/Ecology. Prof., Dept. of Electrical Engineering, since 1977, and Dir. of the Lab. for Power and Environmental Studies since 1978, State Univ. of New York at Buffalo (Asst. Prof., Div. of Interdisciplinary Studies and Research, 1964–67; Assoc. Prof., Faculty of Engineering and Applied Sciences, 1967–74; Prof., Electrical Engineering and Nuclear, Aerospace and Engineering Science Depts., 1974–77). Ed. with P. Powers, Energy, Power and Environment series, since 1977. *Publs:* (ed.) Assessment of Airborne Radioactivity, 1978; (ed.) Recent Developments in Aerosol Science, 1978; Fundamentals of Aerosol Science, 1978; (with J. Bricard) The Physics of Aerosols, 1983. Add: Lab. for Power and Environmental Studies, State Univ. of New York at Buffalo, 330 Bonner Hall, Amherst, N.Y. 14260, U.S.A.

SHAW, Felicity. Writes mystery novels as Anne Morice. British, b. 1918. Novels/Short stories, Mystery/Crime/Suspense. *Publs:* novels, as Felicity Shaw—The Happy Exiles, 1956; Sun Trap, 1958; mystery novels, as Anne Morice—Death in the Grand Manor, 1970; Murder in Married Life, 1971; Death of a Gay Dog, 1971; Murder on French Leave, 1972; Death and the Dutiful Daughter, 1973; Death of a Heavenly Twin, 1974; Killing with Kindness, 1974; Nursery Tea and Poison, 1975; Death of a Wedding Guest, 1976; Murder in Mimicry, 1977; Scared to Death, 1977; Murder by Proxy, 1978; Murder in Outline, 1979; The Hen in Her Death, 1980; Hollow Vengeance, 1982; Sleep of Death, 1982; Murder Post-Dated, 1983; Getting Away with Murder?, 1984; Dead on Cue, 1985; Publish and Be Killed, 1986; Treble Exposure, 1987; Fatal Charm, 1988. Add: 41 Hambleden Village, Henley-on-Thames, Oxon, England.

SHAW, Henry I., Jr. American, b. 1926. History, Military/Defence. Chief Historian since 1962, and Asst. Head, Historical Branch, since 1967, History and Museums Div., Headquarters, U.S. Marine Corps., Washington, D.C. (Historian, 1951–62). Managing Ed., Military Collector and Historian, 1954–58; Ed.-in-Chief, 1958–71, and Consulting Ed., 1971–86, Company of Military Historians. *Publs:* (with C.S. Nichols) Okinawa: Victory in the Pacific, 1955; (with F.O. Hough and V.E. Ludwig) Pearl Harbor to Guadalcanal, 1958; (with D.T. Kane) Isolation of Rabaul, 1963; (with B.A. Nalty and E.T. Turnbladh) Central Pacific Drive, 1966; (with B.M. Frank) Victory and Occupation, 1968; Tarawa: A Legend Is Born, 1969; (with J. Ringler) USMC Operations in the Dominican Republic 1965, 1970; (with R.M. Donnelly) Blacks in the Marine Corps, 1975. Add: History and Museums Div., Headquarters, U.S. Marine Corps, Washington, D.C. 20380, U.S.A.

SHAW, Irene. *See* **ROBERTS**, Irene.

SHAW, Russell B(urnham). American, b. 1935. Philosophy, Theology/Religion. Secty. for Public Affairs, National Conference of Catholic Bishops, United States Catholic Conference, since 1975 (Dir., National Catholic Office for Information, 1969–73; Assoc. Secty. for Communication, 1973–74). Staff Writer, The Catholic Standard, 1957, and National Catholic News Service, 1957–66; Dir. of Publs. and Information, National Catholic Educational Assn., 1966–69. *Publs:* The Dark Disciple, 1961; Abortion on Trial, 1968; (ed. with M.P. Sheridan) Catholic Education Today and Tomorrow, 1968; (ed. with R.J. Hurley) Trends and Issues in Catholic Education, 1969; (with C.A. Koob) S.O.S. for Catholic Schools, 1970; (with G.G. Grisez) Beyond the New Morality, 1974, 1980; Church and State, 1979; Choosing Well, 1982; Why We Need Confession, 1986; Renewal, 1986; Signs of the Times, 1986; Does Suffering Make Sense, 1987. Add: 2928 44th Pl. N.W., Washington, D.C. 20016, U.S.A.

SHAW, Stanford Jay. American, b. 1930. History. Prof. of History, Univ. of California at Los Angeles, since 1968. Ed. in Chief, Intnl. Journal of Middle East Studies, Cambridge Univ. Press, since 1968. Assoc. Prof. of History, Harvard Univ., Cambridge, Mass., 1958–68. *Publs:* The Financial Administrative Organization and Development of Ottoman Egypt, 1517-1798, 1962; Ottoman Egypt in the Eighteenth Century: The Nizammame-i Misir of Ahmed Cezzar Pasha, 1962; Ottoman Egypt in the Age of the French Revolution, 1964; The Budget of Ottoman Egypt, 1968; Between Old and New: The Ottoman Empire under Sultan Selim III, 1789-1807, 1971; History of the Ottoman Empire and Modern Turkey, 2 vols., 1977–78. Add: History Dept., Univ. of California, Los Angeles, Calif. 90024, U.S.A.

SHAW, Thurstan. British, b. 1914. Archaeology/Antiquities. Curator, Museum of Anthropology, Achimota Coll., Ghana, 1937–45; with Cambridgeshire Education Cttee., 1945–51; Tutor, Cambridge Inst. of Eduction, 1951–63; Prof. of Archaeology, Univ. of Ibadan, Nigeria, 1963–74; Ed., West African Archaeological Newsletter, Nos. 1-12, 1964–70, and West African Journal of Archaeology, Vols. 1-5, 1971–75; Dir. of Studies in Archaeology and Anthropology, Magdalene Coll., Cambridge, 1976–79. *Publs:* Excavation at Dawu, 1961; Archaeology and Nigeria, 1964; (ed. and co-author) Nigerian Prehistory and Archaeology, 1969; Igbo-Ukwu: An Account of Archaeological Discoveries in Eastern Nigeria, 2 vols., 1970; Africa and the Origins of Man, 1973; Why "Darkest" Africa?, 1975; (ed. and co-author) Discovering Nigeria's Past, 1975; Unearthing Igbo-Ukwu, 1977; Nigeria: Its Archaeology and Early History, 1978; Filling Gaps in Afric Maps: Fifty Years of Archaeology in Africa, 1984; (with S. E. H. Daniels) Excavations At Iwo Eleru, Ondo State, Nigeria, 1987. Add: 37 Hawthorne Rd., Stapleford, Cambridge CB2 5DU, England.

SHAWCROSS, John T. American, b. 1924. Literature. Prof. of English, Staten Island Community Coll., NYC, and Grad. Center of the

City Univ. of New York, since 1970. Member of the faculty, rising to Prof. of English, Rutgers Univ., New Brunswick, N.J., 1963–67, and Univ. of Wisconsin, Madison, 1967–70. *Publs:* (ed.) The Complete English Poetry of John Milton, 1963, 1971; (ed. with Ronald D. Emma) Language and Style in Milton, 1967; (ed.) The Complete Poetry of John Donne, 1967; Seventeenth-Century Poetry, 1969; Poetry and Its Conventions, 1972; (ed.) Milton: The Critical Heritage, 2 vols., 1970–72; Myths and Motifs in Literature, 1973; (ed. with Michael J. Lieb) Achievements of the Left Hand: Essays on Milton's Prose, 1974; With Mortal Voice: The Creation of Paradise Lost, 1982; Milton: A Bibliography for the Years 1624-1700 1984; Paradise Regain'd: Worthy t' Have Not Remain'd So Long Unsung, 1988. Add: c/o Duquesne Univ. Press., 600 Forbes Ave., Pittsburgh, Pa. 15282, U.S.A.

SHAWCROSS, William. British, b. 1946. International relations/Current affairs. Freelance journalist in Czechoslovakia, 1968–69; Corresp. for The Sunday Times, London, 1969–72. *Publs:* Dubcek, 1970; Crime and Compromise: Janos Kadar and the Politics of Hungary since Revolution, 1974; Sideshow: Kissinger, Nixon, and the Destruction of Cambodia, 1979; Quality of Mercy: Cambodia, The Holocaust, and the Modern Conscience, 1985; The Shah's Last Ride, 1989. Add: c/o Chatto and Windus, 30 Bedford Sq., London WC1B 3RP, England.

SHAWN, Frank S. *See* **GOULART,** Ron.

SHAWN, Wallace. American, b. 1943. Plays/Screenplays. Taught English, Indore Christian Coll., India, 1965–66; taught English, Latin, and Drama, Day Sch., NYC, 1968–70; Shipping clerk, Laurie Love Ltd., NYC, 1974–75; Xerox Machine Operator, Hamilton Copy Center, NYC, 1975–76. *Publs:* Marie and Bruce, 1980; (with André Gregory) My Dinner with André (screenplay), and Marie and Bruce, 1983; Aunt Dan and Lemon, 1985. Add: c/o Margaret Ramsay Ltd., 14a Goodwin's Court, London WC2N 4LL, England.

SHEAFFER, Louis. Pseud. for Louis Sheaffer Slung. American, b. 1912. Literature, Biography. Theatre Critic, Brooklyn Eagle, 1949–55. *Publs:* O'Neill, Son And Playwright, 1968; O'Neill, Son And Artist (Pulitzer Prize for Biography), 1973. Add: c/o Little, Brown & Co., 34 Beacon St., Boston, Mass. 02106, U.S.A.

SHEAHAN, John. American, b. 1923. Economics. Prof. of Economics, Williams Coll., Williamstown, Mass., since 1954. Member, Colombia Advisory Group, Harvard Univ. Development Advisory Service, Bogota, 1963–65. Visiting Prof., El Colegio de Mexico, 1970–71; Fulbright Research Prof., Université de Grenoble, 1974–75; Visiting Fellow, University of Sussex, Brighton, 1981–82. *Publs:* Promotion and Control of Industry in Postwar France, 1963; The Wage-Price Guideposts, 1967; An Introduction to the French Economy, 1969; Patterns of Development in Latin America, 1987. Add: Dept. of Economics, Williams Coll., Williamstown, Mass. 01267, U.S.A.

SHEARMAN, John (Kinder Gowran). British, b. 1931. Art. Prof. of Fine Arts, Harvard Univ., since 1987. Lectr., 1957–67, Reader, 1967–74, Prof. of the History of Art, 1974–79, and Deputy Dir., 1974–78, Courtauld Inst., London; Prof., 1979–87, and Chmn., 1979–85, Dept. of Art and Archaeology, Princeton Univ., New Jersey. *Publs:* Andrea del Sarto, 1965; Drawings of Nicolas Poussin IV; Landscape Drawings, 1963; (ed.) Studies in Renaissance and Baroque Art Presented to Anthony Blunt, 1967; Mannerism, 1967, 7th ed. 1986; Raphael's Cartoons, 1972; Catalogue of the Early Italian Paintings in the Collection of H.M. the Queen, 1983; Funzione e Illusione, 1983. Add: 3 Clement Circle, Cambridge, Mass. 02138, U.S.A.

SHECKLEY, Robert. American, b. 1928. Mystery/Crime/Suspense, Science fiction/Fantasy. TV and radio writer; fiction ed., Omni, 1980–82. *Publs:* Untouched by Human Hands (short stories), 1954; Citizen in Space (short stories), 1955; Pilgrimage to Earth (short stories), 1957; Immortality Delivered, 1958; as Immortality Inc., 1959; Store of Infinity (short stories), 1960; The Status Civilization, 1960; Notions: Unlimited (short stories), 1960; Calibre .50 (suspense), 1961; Dead Run (suspense), 1961; Live Gold (suspense), 1962; The Man in the Water (suspense), 1962; Journey Beyond Tomorrow, 1962, in U.K. as Journey of Joenes, 1978; Shards of Space (short stories), 1962; White Death (suspense), 1963; The Game of X (suspense), 1965; The Tenth Victim, 1965; Mindswap, 1966; Time Limit (suspense), 1967; Dimension of Miracles, 1968; The People Trap (short stories), 1968; Can You Feel Anything When I Do This? (short stories), 1971; The Robert Sheckley Omnibus, ed. by Robert Conquest, 1973; In a Land of Clear Colors, 1974; Options, 1975; Crompton Divided (in U.K. as The Alchemical Marriage of Alistair Crompton), 1978; Futuropolis, 1978; The Robot Who Looked Like Me (short stories), 1978; The Wonderful World of Robert Sheckley (short stories), 1979; Dramocles, 1983; Is That What People Do? (short stories), 1984; Victim Prime, 1987; Hunter/Victim, 1988; The Draconian Alternative, 1988. Add: c/o Marty Shapiro, Shapiro-Lichtman Talent, 8827 Beverly Blvd., Los Angeles, Calif. 90048, U.S.A.

SHECTER, Ben. American. Novels/Short stories, Children's fiction. *Publs:* Emily, Girl Witch of New York, 1963; Partouche Plants a Seed, 1966; Conrad's Castle, 1967; Someplace Else, 1971; If I Had a Ship, 1971; Game for Demons, 1972; Across the Meadow, 1973; Stone House Stories, 1973; Night Whispers, 1974; The Whistling Whirligig, 1974; Molly Patch and Her Animal Friends, 1975; The Stocking Child, 1976; The Hiding Game, 1977; Hester the Jester, 1977; A Summer Secret, 1977; The River Witches, 1979; The Discontented Mother, 1980; Sparrow Song, 1981. Add: c/o Harper and Row, 105 E. 53rd St., New York, N.Y. 10022, U.S.A.

SHEED, Wilfrid (John Joseph). American (born British), b. 1930. Novels/Short stories, Social commentary/phenomena, Biography, Essays. Columnist, New York Times Book Review, NYC, since 1971. Film Critic, 1957–61, and Assoc. Ed., 1959–66, Jubilee mag., NYC: Drama Critic, Esquire mag., NYC, 1967–69; Visiting Lectr. in Creative Arts, Princeton Univ., N.J., 1970–71. *Publs:* Joseph, 1958; (ed.) G.K. Chesterton's Essays and Poems, 1958; A Middle Class Education, 1960; The Hack, 1963; Square's Progress, 1965; Office Politics, 1966; The Blacking Factory, and Pennsylvania Gothic: A Short Novel and a Long Story, 1969; Max Jamison (in U.K. as The Critic), 1970; The Morning After (essays), 1971; People Will Always Be Kind, 1973; Vanishing Species of America, 1974; Muhammad Ali, 1975; Three Mobs: Labor, Church and Mafia, 1975; The Good Word and Other Words (essays), 1978; Transatlantic Blues, 1978; Clare Booth Luce, 1982; Frank and Maisie: A Memoir with Parents, 1985; (ed.) 16 Short Novels, 1986; The Boys of Winter, 1987. Add: Donadio Assocs., 231 W. 22nd St., New York, N.Y. 10011, U.S.A.

SHEEHAN, Neil. American, b. 1936. International affairs. Reporter, New York Times, based in NYC, Djakarta, Saigon, and now Washington, D.C., since 1964. Served with the U.S. Army, 1959–62; Vietnam Bureau Chief, United Press Intnl., 1962–64. *Publs:* The Arnheiter Affair, 1972; A Bright Shining Lie: John Paul Vann and America in Vietnam, 1988, (National Book Award). Add: 4505 Klingle St. N.W., Washington, D.C. 20016, U.S.A.

SHEEHAN, Susan. American, b. 1937. Social sciences. Staff Writer, New Yorker mag., since 1962. Editorial Asst., Esquire-Coronet mags., 1959–60. *Publs:* Ten Vietnamese, 1967; A Welfare Mother, 1976; A Prison and a Prisoner, 1978; Is There No Place on Earth for Me?, 1982; Kate Quinton's Days, 1984; A Missing Plane, 1986. Add: c/o New Yorker, 25 W. 43rd St., New York, N.Y. 10036, U.S.A.

SHEEHY, Gail. American. Social commentary/phenomena. Contributing Ed., Vanity Fair mag., NYC, since 1986. Fashion Ed., Democrat and Chronicle, Rochester, N.Y., 1961–63; Feature Writer, New York Herald Tribune, 1963–66; Contrib. Ed., New York mag., 1968–79. *Publs:* Lovesounds, 1970; Panthermania: The Clash of Black Against Black in One American City, 1971; Speed Is of the Essence, 1971; Hustling: Prostitution in Our Wide Open Society, 1973; Passages: The Predictable Crises of Adult Life, 1976; Pathfinders, 1981; Spirit of Survival, 1986; Character: America's Search for Leadership, 1988. Add: c/o Morrow, 105 Madison Ave., New York, N.Y. 10014, U.S.A.

SHEFFIELD, Charles. British. Novels, Science fiction, Sciences. Chief Scientist, Earth Satellite Corp. Formerly Pres., American Astronautical Soc., and Science Fiction Writers of America. *Publs:* Sight of Proteus, 1978; The Web Between the Worlds, 1979; Vectors, 1980; Hidden Variables, 1981; Earthwatch: A Survey of the World from Space, 1981; (ed. with John L. McLucas) Commercial Operations in Space 1980-2000, 1981; (with David F. Bischoff) The Selkie (novel), 1982; My Brother's Keeper, 1982; Erasmus Magister, 1982; Man on Earth (non-fiction), 1983; The McAndrew Chronicles, 1983; (with Carol Rosin) Space Careers, 1984; Between the Strokes of Night, 1985; The Nimrod Hunt, 1986; Trader's World, 1988; Proteus Unbound, 1989. Add: 6812 Wilson Lane, Bethesda, Md. 20817, U.S.A.

SHELBOURNE, Cecily. *See* **EBEL,** Suzanne.

SHELBY, Graham. British, b. 1940. Historical novels. Former advertising copywriter, film extra, and book reviewer. *Publs:* The Knights of Dark Renown, 1969; The Kings of Vain Intent, 1970; The Villains of the Piece, 1972; The Devil Is Loose, 1973; The Wolf at the Door, 1975; The Cannaways, 1978; The Cannaway Concern, 1980; The Edge of the Blade, 1986. Add: c/o Rogers Coleridge and White Ltd., 20 Powis Mews, London W11 1JN, England.

SHELDON, Lee. *See* **LEE**, Wayne C.

SHELDON, Roy. *See* **TUBB**, E. C.

SHELDON, Sidney. American, b. 1917. Novels/Short stories, Plays/Screenplays. Television show creator, producer, and writer, since 1963. *Publs:* (adaptor, with Ben Roberts) The Merry Widow (operetta), 1943; Jackpot, 1944; Dream with Music, 1944; Alice in Arms, 1945; The Bachelor and the Bobby-Soxer (screenplay), 1947; (with Albert Hackett and Frances Goodrich) Easter Parade (screenplay), 1948; Annie Get Your Gun (screenplay), 1950; Rich, Young, and Pretty (screenplay), 1951; Dream Wife, 1953; Anything Goes (screenplay), 1956; Never Too Young, 1956; The Buster Keaton Story (screenplay), 1957; Redhead, 1959; Roman Candle, 1960; Billy Rose's Jumbo (screenplay), 1962; The Naked Face (novel), 1970; The Other Side of Midnight, 1974; Bloodline, 1977; Rage of Angels, 1980; The Master of the Game, 1982; If Tomorrow Comes, 1985; Windmills of the Gods, 1986; The Sands of Time, 1988. Add: c/o Press Relations, William Morrow, 105 Madison Ave., New York, N.Y. 10016, U.S.A.

SHELTON, Richard. American, b. 1933. Poetry. Prof. of English, Univ. of Arizona, Tucson, since 1979 (joined faculty, 1960). *Publs:* Journal of Return, 1969; The Tattooed Desert, 1971; The Heroes of Our Time, 1972; Of All the Dirty Words, 1972; Among the Stones, 1973; Chosen Place, 1974; You Can't Have Everything, 1975; The Bus to Veracruz, 1978; Selected Poems: 1969-1981, 1982; A Kind of Glory, 1982; Hohokam, 1986; The Other Side of the Story, 1987. Add: Dept. of English, Univ. of Arizona, Tucson, Ariz. 85721, U.S.A.

SHENKER, Israel. American, b. 1925. Language/Linguistics, Writing/Journalism, Essays, Humor/Satire. Reporter, New York Times, NYC, since 1968. Corresp., Time Mag., NYC, 1949–68. *Publs:* (ed. with M. Shenker) As Good as Golda, 1970; Words and Their Masters, 1974; (with Zero Mostel) Zero Mostel's Book of Villains, 1977; Nothing Is Sacred, 1979; In the Footsteps of Johnson and Boswell, 1984; Coat of Many Colors, 1985. Add: c/o New York Times, 229 W. 43rd St., New York, N.Y. 10036, U.S.A.

SHENNAN, Joseph Hugh. British, b. 1933. History. Prof. of European History since 1979, and Pro-Vice-Chancellor since 1984, Univ. of Lancaster (Reader in History, 1971–74; Prof. of European Studies, 1974–79). Asst. Lectr., and Lectr. in History, Univ. of Liverpool, 1960–65. *Publs:* The Parlement of Paris, 1968; Government and Society in France, 1461-1661, 1969; (exec. ed.) Dictionary of World History, 1973; The Origins of the Modern European State, 1450-1725, 1974; Philippe, Duke of Orléans: Regent of France 1715-23, 1979; Liberty and Order in Early Modern Europe: The Subject and the State 1650-1800, 1986. Add: Furness Coll., Univ. of Lancaster, Bailrigg, Lancaster, England.

SHENTON, James (Patrick). American, b. 1925. History. Prof. of American History, Columbia Univ., NYC, since 1967 (joined faculty, 1951). *Publs:* Robert John Walker, 1959; Reconstruction: The South after the War, 1963; (co-author) An Historian's History of the United States, 1967; The Melting Pot, 1971; (co-ed.) Ethnic Groups in American Life, 1978. Add: 80 Passaic Ave., Passaic, N.J. 07055, U.S.A.

SHEPARD, Leslie Alan. British, b. 1917. Mythology/Folklore, Paranormal. European Ed. and Researcher, Gale Research Co., Detroit, Mich., since 1966. London Ed., Univ. Books Inc., NYC, since 1965. Organiser, Dir., Scriptwriter, Ed., and Producer, Paul Rotha Productions Ltd., and Data Film Productions Ltd., both London, 1942–57; Production Controlling Officer, Central Office of Information, London, 1960–62. *Publs:* The Broadside Ballad: A Study in Origins and Meaning, 1962, 1978; John Pitts, Ballad Printer of Seven Dials, London 1765-1844: With a Short Account of his Predecessors in the Ballad and Chapbook Trade, 1969; The History of Street Literature, 1973; (ed.) Dracula Book of Great Vampire Stories, 1977; (ed.) Encyclopedia of Occultism and Parapsychology, 1978, rev. ed., 3 vols., 1984–85; How to Protect Yourself Against Black Magic and Witchcraft, 1978; (ed.) Dracula Book of Great Horror Stories, 1981; (with others) Oxford English, 1986; Occultism Update, 2 vols., 1987–88. Add: 1 Lakelands Close, Stillorgan, Blackrock, Co. Dublin, Ireland.

SHEPARD, Lucius. American. Science fiction. *Publs:* Green Eyes, 1984; Life During Wartime, 1987; The Jaguar Hunter, 1988. Add: c/o Ace Books, 200 Madison Ave., New York, N.Y. 10016, U.S.A.

SHEPARD, Martin. American, b. 1934. Psychiatry, Psychology, Autobiography/Memoirs/Personal. *Publs:* (with Marjorie Lee) Games Analysts Play, 1970; (with Marjorie Lee) Marathon 16, 1970; The Love Treatment, 1971; (with Marjorie Lee) Sexual Marathon, 1972; A Psychiatrist's Head (autobiography), 1972; The Do-It-Yourself Psychotherapy Book, 1973; Beyond Sex therapy, 1975; Fritz, 1975; A Question of Values, 1976; Someone You Love Is Dying, 1976; The Seducers, 1981; The Reluctant Exhibitionist, 1985. Add: R.D.2, Noyac Rd., Sag Harbor, N.Y. 11963, U.S.A.

SHEPARD, Richmond. American, b. 1929. Sports/Physical education/Keeping fit, Theatre. Dir., Richmond Shepard Mime theatre, since 1952. Prof., Drama Dept., California State Univ., Los Angeles, 1967–76. *Publs:* (with Mick Schulster) Karate: The Deadly Defense, 1964; Reality, Mr. Kaufman (screenplay), 1968; The Fast Draw (screenplay), 1971; Mime: The Technique of Silence, 1971; Creating Comedy Through Theatre Games and Improvisation, 1981; Mime: Advanced Technique and Style, 1983; (with John Sinclair) Lord Buckley's Finest Hour (play), 1983; Designer Genes (play), 1987; I Could Be Short (play), 1987. Add: 6468 Santa Monica Blvd., Hollywood, Calif. 90038, U.S.A.

SHEPARD, Sam. Pseud. for Samuel Shepard Rogers. American, b. 1943. Novels/Short stories, Plays/Screenplays. Actor. *Publs:* La Turista, 1968; Five Plays: Chicago, Icarus's Mother, Red Cross, Fourteen Hundred Thousand, Melodrama Play, 1967; Operation Sidewinder, 1970; The Unseen Hand and Other Plays, 1971; Mad Dog Blues and Other Plays, 1971; Hawk Moon (short stories), 1973; The Tooth of Crime, and Geography of a Horse Dreamer, 1974; Action, and The Unseen Hand, 1975; Angel City and Other Plays, 1976; Rolling Thunder Logbook, 1977; Buried Child and Other Plays, 1979, in U.K. as Buried Child, and Seduced, and Suicide in B Flat, 1980; Four One-Act Plays, 1980; True West, 1981; Seven Plays, 1981; Motel Chronicles, 1982; Fool for Love and Other Plays, 1984; Paris, Texas (screenplay), 1984; A Lie of the Mind, 1985. Add: c/o Loris Berman, Little Theatre Bldg., 240 W. 44th St., New York, N.Y. 10036, U.S.A.

SHEPHARD, Roy Jesse. Canadian, b. 1929. Medicine/Health, Sports/Physical education/Keeping fit. Dir. of the Sch. of Physical and Health Education, and Prof. of Applied Physiology, Faculty of Medicine, Univ. of Toronto, since 1964. Consultant, Toronto Rehabilitation Centre, Gage Research Inst., and Defence and Civil Inst. of Environmental Medicine, since 1968; Ed.-in-Chief, Year Book of Sports Medicine, since 1979. Cardiac Research Fellow, Guy's Hosp., London, 1952–54; Medical Officer, RAF Inst. of Aviation Medicine, Farnborough, 1953–56; Asst. Prof. of Preventive Medicine, Univ. of Cincinnati, Ohio, 1956–58; Principal Scientific Officer, Ministry of Defence, Chemical Defence Establishment, 1958–64. *Publs:* (ed.) Proceedings, International Symposium on Physical Activity and Cardiovascular Health, 1967; Endurance Fitness, 1969, 1977; (with K.L. Andersen, H. Denolin, E. Varnauskas and R. Masironi) Fundamentals of Exercise Testing, 1971; (ed. and co-author) Frontiers of Fitness, 1971; Alive, Man: The Physiology of Physical Activity, 1972; Men at Work: Applications of Ergonomics to Performance and Design, 1974; The Fit Athlete, 1978; (with Hugues Lavallée) Physical Fitness Assessment, 1978; Human Physiological Work Capacity, 1978; Physical Activity and Aging, 1978, 1987; Ischaemic Heart Disease and Physical Activity, 1981; Textbook of Exercise Physiology and Biochemistry, 1982; Physical Activity and Growth, 1982; The Risks of Passive Smoking, 1982; Carbon Monoxide, The Silent Killer, 1983; Exercise Biochemistry, 1983; (with P. Welsh) Current Therapy in Sports Medicine, 1985, 1989; Fitness and Health in Industry, 1986; Economic Benefits of Enhanced Fitness, 1986; (with J. Taunton) Foot and Ankle in Sports Medicine, 1986; Fitness of a Nation, 1986; Fundamentals of Exercise Physiology, 1987. Add: 29 Poplar Plains Rd., Toronto, Ont. M4V 2M7, Canada.

SHEPHERD, George W. American, b. 1926. Politics/Government, Race relations. Prof. and Dir., Intnl. Race Relations Center, Univ. of Denver, since 1968 (Asst. Prof., 1961–1968). *Publs:* They Wait in Darkness, 1955; Politics of African Nationalism, 1962; Nonaligned Black Africa, 1970; Racial Influences on U.S. Foreign Policy, 1970; Anti-Apartheid, 1977; The Trampled Grass: Tributary States and Self-Reliance in the Indian Ocean Zone of Peace, 1987. Add: 6053 S. Platte Canyon Rd., Littleton, Colo. 80120, U.S.A.

SHEPHERD, Michael. *See* **LUDLUM**, Robert.

SHEPPARD, David Stuart. British, b. 1929. Urban studies, Autobiography/Memoirs/Personal. Anglican clergyman; Bishop of Liverpool since 1975 (Curate, St. Mary's, Islington, 1955–57; Warden, Mayflower Family Centre, Canning Town, 1957–69; Bishop of Woolwich, 1969–75). Played cricket 22 times for England, 1950–63. *Publs:* Parson's Pitch (autobiography), 1964; Built as a City, 1974; Bias to the Poor, 1983; The Other Britain, 1984; (With Archbishop Derek Worlock) Better Together, 1988. Add: Bishop's Lodge, Woolton Park, Liverpool L25 6DT, England.

SHEPPARD-JONES, Elisabeth (Maia). British, b. 1920. Children's fiction, Autobiography/Memoirs/Personal. *Publs:* I Walk on Wheels, 1958; Welsh Legendary Tales, 1959; The Search for Mary, 1960; Scottish Legendary Tales, 1962; The Empty House, 1965; The Reluctant Nurse, 1965; The Byrds' Nest, 1968; Emma and the Awful Eight, 1968; Cousin Charlie, 1973; Stories of Wales: Told for Children, 1978.. Add: Draenen Wen, Meadow Lane, Penarth, Glamorgan, Wales.

SHEPPERSON, Wilbur (Stanley). American, b. 1919. History, Biography. Prof. and Chmn., Dept. of History, Univ. of Nevada, Reno, since 1966. Ed., Halcyon, since 1979. Asst. Ed., Univ. of Nevada Press, 1968–75; Ed., Nevada Historical Quarterly, 1970–73. *Publs:* British Emigration to North America, 1957; Samuel Roberts of Wales, 1961; Emigration and Disenchantment, 1965; Retreat to Nevada, 1966; Restless Strangers, 1970; Questions from the Past, 1973; Hardscrabble: A Narrative of the California Hill Country, 1975. Add: 2490 Pioneer Dr., Reno, Nev. 89502, U.S.A.

SHERATON, Neil. *See* **SMITH,** Norman Edward Mace.

SHERATSKY, Rodney E(arl). American, b. 1933. Film. Teacher of Humanities and Film Production, Northern Valley Regional High Sch., Demarest, N.J., since 1961. Contributing Ed., Sightlines mag., NYC, 1971–72. *Publs:* (ed. with J.L. Reilly) The Lively Arts: Four Representative Types, 1964; (ed. with M.E. Keisman) The Creative Arts: Four Representative Types, 1968; Film: The Reality of Being, 1969; (with Anthony W. Hodgkinson) Humphrey Jennings: More Than a Maker of Films, 1982. Add: Northern Valley Regional High Sch., Demarest, N.J. 07627, U.S.A.

SHERBURNE, Donald W. American, b. 1929. Philosophy. Prof. of Philosophy, Vanderbilt Univ., Nashville, Tenn. (Asst. Prof. of Philosophy, 1960–64; Assoc. Prof. of Philosophy, 1964–68). Instr. in Philosophy, Yale Univ., New Haven, Conn., 1959–60. Ed., Soundings: An Interdisciplinary Journal, 1980–85. *Publs:* A Whiteheadian Aesthetic, 1961; A Key to Whitehead's Process and Reality, 1966; (co-ed.) Corrected Edition of Whitehead's Process and Reality, 1978. Add: 227 Leonard Ave., Nashville, Tenn. 37205, U.S.A.

SHERIDAN, Jane. *See* **WINSLOW,** Pauline Glen.

SHERIDAN, Lee. *See* **LEE,** Elsie.

SHERIDAN, Lionel Astor. British, b. 1927. Law. Prof. of Law, Univ. of Malaya, Singapore, 1956–63; Prof. of Comparative Law, Queen's Univ., Belfast, 1963–71; Prof. of Law, University Coll., Cardiff, 1971–88 (Acting Principal, 1988). *Publs:* Fraud in Equity, 1957; (with V.T.H. Delany) The Cy-Pres Doctrine, 1959; (ed.) Malaya, Singapore, The Borneo Territories: The Development of Their Laws and Constitutions, 1961; (with H.E. Groves) The Constitution of Malaysia, 1967, 4th ed. 1987; (with G.W. Keeton) The Modern Law of Charities, 3rd ed. 1983; (ed.) Survey of the Land Law of Northern Ireland, 1971; (ed. with G.W. Keeton) A Case-Book on Equity and Trusts, 2nd ed. 1974; Rights in Security, 1974; (with G.W. Keeton) The Law of Trusts, 11th ed. 1983; (with G.W. Keeton) Equity, 3rd ed. 1987; (with G.W. Keeton) The Comparative Law of Trusts in the Commonwealth and the Republic of Ireland, 1976, supplement, 1981; (with G.W. Keeton) Digest of the English Law of Trusts, 1979. Add: Cherry Trees, St. Nicholas, S. Glamorgan, Wales.

SHERIDAN, Thomas. Australian, b. 1938. Industrial relations. Sr. Lectr., Dept. of Economics, Univ. of Adelaide, since 1968. *Publs:* Mindful Militants: The Amalgamated Engineering Union in Australia 1920–1972, 1975; Division of Labour: Industrial Relations in the Chifley Years 1945-48, 1989. Add: Dept. of Economics, Univ. of Adelaide, S.A. 5001, Australia.

SHERLAW-JOHNSON, Robert. British, b. 1932. Music. Univ. Lectr. in Music, Oxford Univ., and Fellow of Worcester Coll., Oxford, since 1970. Composer and pianist. Lectr., York Univ., 1965–70.

Publs: Messiaen, 1975. Add: Malton Croft, Woodlands Rise, Stonesfield, Oxon OX7 2PL, England.

SHERLOCK, (Sir) Philip (Manderson). Jamaican, b. 1902. Area studies, History, Biography. Vice-Pres., Caribbean Resources Development Foundn. Inc., since 1983. Headmaster, Wolmer's Boys Sch., Jamaica, 1933–38; Secty., Inst. of Jamaica, 1939–44; Education Officer, Jamaica Welfare, 1944–47; Dir., Extra-Mural Dept., 1947–60, Vice Principal, 1952–62, University Coll. of the West Indies; Vice Chancellor, Univ. of the West Indies, 1963–69; Secty.-Gen., Assn. of Caribbean Universities and Research Insts. Foundn. Inc., 1969–79; Secty., Assn. of Caribbean Univs. Foundn., 1979–83. *Publs:* Anansi the Spider Man, 1956; (with J. Parry) Short History of the West Indies, 1956; Caribbean Citizen, 1957; West Indian Story, 1960; Three Finger Jack, 1961; Jamaica: A Junior History, 1966; West Indian Folk Tales, 1966; The West Indies, 1966; The Land and the People of the West Indies, 1967; The Iguana's Tail, 1969; West Indian Nations, 1973; Ears and Tails and Common Sense, 1974; Shout for Freedom, 1976; Norman Manley, 1980; Keeping Company with Jamaica, 1984. Add: 7855 N.W. 12th St., Suite 217, Miami, Fla. 33126, U.S.A.

SHERMAN, Arnold. Israeli, b. 1932. Poetry, Air/Space topics, Military/Defence, Humor/Satire. Public Relations Dir., EL AL Israel Airlines, since 1965. Exec. Vice-Chmn., Technion Univ. News Ed., Aviation Week, 1958–63. *Publs:* A Thought in the Night (poetry), 1950; Impaled on a Cactus Bush (humour), 1970; In the Bunkers of Sinai (military), 1971; To the Skies (aviation), 1972; Lightning in the Skies (aviation), 1973; When God Judged and Men Died (military), 1973; The EL AL Story, 1973; Impaled on a Rhino's Horn (humour), 1974; The Druse, 1975; Pomeranz Connection, 1976; Israel on $10 a Day, 1976; In Search of Rahamim (autobiography), 1977; Blue Sky, Red Sea, 1977; The Ship (novel), 1978; Challenging the Skies (aviation), 1979; Wings of Icarus (novel), 1980; Splintered Cedar (Lebanon), 1981; Israel High Technology, 1984. Add: Moshav, Michmoret, Israel.

SHERMAN, Ingrid. American, b. 1919. Poetry, Medicine/Health, Psychology. Founder, Dir. and Counselor, Peace of Mind Studio, since 1958. Teacher of Metaphysics and poetry therapy study courses, Yonkers, N.Y., since 1963. *Publs:* Thoughts for You, 1966; Ripples of Wisdom, 1966; Poems that Speak of Love, 1966; For Your Reading Pleasure, 1966; Gems from Above, 1967; Prayer Poems that Heal, 1967; Radiations for Self Help, 1967; Philosophical Tidbits, 1967; Strange Patterns, 1967; Let Thy Heart Sing, 1967; Health, Natural Remedies for Better Health, 1970; Significant Roses, 1975; The Simple Life, 1977; In Praise of God, 1978; On Healing, 1978. Add: 108 121st Ave., Treasure Island, Fla. 33706, U.S.A.

SHERMAN, Martin. American, b. 1938. Plays/Screenplays. Resident writer, Playwrights Horizons, NYC, 1976–77. *Publs:* Things Went Badly in Westphalia (in The Best Short Plays of 1970), 1970; Bent, 1979; Messiah, 1982; Passing By (in Gay Plays 1), 1984; Cracks (in Gay Plays 2), 1986. Add: c/o Margaret Ramsay Ltd., 14-A Goodwin's Ct., London WC2N 4LL, England.

SHERMAN, Richard B. American, b. 1929. History, Race relations. Prof. of History, Coll. of William and Mary, Williamsburg, Va., since 1970 (Asst. Prof., 1960–65; Assoc. Prof., 1965–70). Instr. in History, Pennsylvania State Univ., University Park, 1957–60; Fulbright Prof., Univ. of Stockholm, Sweden, 1966–67. *Publs:* (ed.) The Negro and the City, 1970; The Republican Party and Black America, 1973. Add: Dept. of History, Coll. of William and Mary, Williamsburg, Va. 23185, U.S.A.

SHERMAN, Roger. American. Economics. Brown-Forman Prof. of Economics, and Chmn., Univ. of Virginia, Charlottesville (Asst. Prof., 1965–68; Assoc. Prof., 1969–71; Prof. since 1971). *Publs:* Oligopoly: An Empirical Approach, 1972; The Economics of Industry, 1974; Antitrust Policies and Issues, 1978; Perspectives on Postal Service Issues, 1980; The Regulation of Monopoly, 1989. Add: 408 E. Market St., No. 304, Charlottesville, Va. 22901, U.S.A.

SHERMAN, Steve (Barry). American, b. 1938. Novels, Travel, Exploration. Freelance writer since 1971. High school English teacher in Glendale, Calif., 1961– 63; elementary sch. teacher in Ruby, Alaska, 1963–64; Research Librarian, Univ. of Alaska, Fairbanks, 1967–69; Reporter, Anchorage Daily News, Alaska, 1971. *Publs:* ABC's of Library Promotion, 1971; Bike Hiking, 1974; The Wood Stove and Fireplace Book, 1976; Appalachian Odyssey: Walking the Trail from Georgia to Maine, 1977; Christmas Wreaths, 1987; The Maple Sugar Murders, 1987, Wreathes for All Seasons, 1988. Add: c/o Walker and Co.,

720 Fifth Ave., New York, N.Y. 10019, U.S.A.

SHERRIN, Ned. (Edward George Sherrin). British, b. 1931. Novels/Short stories, Plays/Screenplays, Songs, lyrics and libretti, Autobiography, Biography. Film, theatre and TV producer. Producer, ATV, 1956–58, and BBC, 1958–65: produced and directed TV satire prog., That Was the Week That Was. *Publs:* (with C. Brahms) Cindy-Ella (novel), 1962; (ed. with David Frost) That Was the Week That Was, 1963; (with C. Brahms) Rappel 1910 (novel), 1964; (with C. Brahms) Benbow Was His Name (novel), 1967; (with C. Brahms) Ooh La La! (short stories), 1973; (with C. Brahms) After You Mr. Feydeau (short stories), 1975; A Small Thing Like An Earthquake (memoirs), 1983; (with C. Brahms) Song by Song, 1984; Cutting Edge, 1984; (with N. Shand) 1956 and All That, 1984; (with Alistair Beaton) The Metropolitan Mikado (libretto), 1985; (with C. Brahms) Too Dirty for the Windmill (memoir), 1986. Add: c/o Margaret Ramsay Ltd., 14a Goodwin's Court, London WC2, England.

SHERRY, Norman. British, b. 1925. Literature. Prof. of Literature, Trinity Univ. San Antonio, Texas. Formerly: Lectr. in English, Univ. of Singapore, 1960–66; Lectr., 1966–68, and Sr. Lectr. in English, 1968–70, Univ. of Liverpool; Prof. of English, Univ. of Lancaster, from 1970. *Publs:* Conrad's Eastern World, 1966; Jane Austen, 1966; Charlotte and Emily Brontë, 1969; Conrad's Western World, 1971; Conrad and His World, 1973; The Life of Graham Greene, vol. 1: 1904-1939, 1989. Add: c/o Viking Press, 40 W. 23rd St., New York, N.Y. 10010, U.S.A.

SHERRY, Sylvia. British. Novel/Short stories, Children's fiction. Primary sch. teacher, 1949–51; Teacher, Church High Sch., 1951–53; Lectr., Kenton Lodge Coll. of Ed cation, Newcastle upon Tyne, 1953–61. *Publs:* Street of the Small Night Market, 1966; Frog in a Coconut Shell, 1967; A Pair of Jesus Boots, 1969; The Loss of the Night Wind, 1970; Snake in the Old Hut, 1972; Dark River, Dark Mountain, 1974; Mat, The Little Monkey, 1977; Girl in a Blue Shawl (for adults), 1978; South of Red River (for adults), 1981; A Pair of Desert-Wellies (for children), 1985; Rocky and the Ratman, 1988. Add: 6 Gillison Close, Melling, nr. Carnforth, Lancs, LA6 2RD, England.

SHERWIN, Judith Johnson. American, b. 1936. Novels/Short stories, Poetry. Asst. Prof. of English, State Univ. of New York at Albany, since 1981 (Poet-in-Residence, 1980–81). Pres., Poetry Soc. of America, 1975–78. *Publs:* Uranium Poems, 1969; The Life of Riot (short stories), 1970; Impossible Buildings (poetry) 1973; Waste, 3 vols., 1977–79; How the Dead Count: New Poems, 1978. Add: Dept. of English, State Univ. of New York, Albany, N.Y. 12203, U.S.A.

SHERWOOD, Hugh C. American, b. 1928. Money/Finance, Writing/Journalism. Editorial Services Officer, Irving Trust Co., NYC, since 1977. Assoc. Ed., Medical Economics, 1955–59; Assoc. Ed., 1963; Sr. Ed., 1963–66, and Managing Ed., 1966–69; Business Mgmt., Greenwich, Conn; Contributing Ed. and Investment Columnist, Industry Week, 1971–78; Contributing Ed., Physician's Mgmt., 1972–76. *Publs:* The Journalistic Interview, 1969, 1972; How To Invest in Bonds, 1974, 1983; How Corporate and Municipal Debt Is Rated, 1976. Add: L6, 109 N. Broadway, White Plains, N.Y. 10603, U.S.A.

SHERWOOD, John H(erman Mulso). British, b. 1913. Mystery/Crime/Suspense, Biography. Freelance writer. Former Head of the French Language Service, BBC, London. *Publs:* The Disappearance of Dr. Bruderstein; Mr. Blessington's Imperialist Plot; Ambush for Anatol; Two Died in Singapore; Vote Against Poison; Undiplomatic Exit; The Half Hunter; No Golden Journey: A Biography of James Elroy Flecker; Honesty Will Get You Nowhere; The Limericks of Lachasse; The Hour of the Hyenas; A Shot in the Arm, 1982; Green Trigger Fingers, 1984; A Botanist at Bay, 1985; The Mantrap Garden, 1986; Flowers of Evil, 1987; Menacing Groves, 1988. Add: 36 High St., Charing, Ashford, Kent, England.

SHERWOOD, Morgan Bronson. American, b. 1929. History. Prof., Dept. of History, Univ. of California, Davis, since 1974 (Asst. Prof., 1965–69; Assoc. Prof., 1969–74). Editorial Adviser, Agricultural History, since 1965, and Alaska History, since 1985. Asst. Prof. of History, Univ. of Cincinnati, Ohio, 1964–65. *Publs:* Exploration of Alaska, 1965, 1969; (ed. with J.L. Penick, C.W. Pursell and D.C. Swain) The Politics of American Science, 1939-Present, 1965, 1972; (ed.) Alaska and Its History, 1967; (ed.) The Cook Inlet Collection, 1974; Big Game in Alaska, 1981. Add: Dept. of History, Univ. of California, Davis, Calif. 95616, U.S.A.

SHERWOOD, Valerie. Also writes as Rosamund Royal. American. Romance. *Publs:* This Loving Torment, 1977; These Golden Pleasures, 1977; This Towering Passion, 1978; (as Rosamund Royal) Rapture, 1979; Her Shining Splendor, 1980; Bold Breathless Love, 1981; Rash Reckless Love, 1981; Wild Wilful Love, 1982; Lovely Lying Lips, 1983; Rich Radiant Love, 1983; Born to Love, 1984; Lovesong, 1985; Windsong, 1986; Nightsong, 1986; To Love a Rogue, 1987; Lisbon, 1988. Add: c/o New American Library, 1633 Broadway, New York, N.Y. 10019, U.S.A.

SHIBLES, Warren. American, b. 1933. Children's non-fiction, Philosophy. Asst. Prof. of Philosophy, Univ. of Wisconsin, Whitewater, since 1967. *Publs:* Philosophical Pictures, 1969, 1971; Models of Ancient Greek Philosophy, 1971; An Analysis of Metaphor, 1971; Essays on Metaphor, 1971; Metaphor: An Annotated Bibliography, 1971; Emotions, 1974; Wittgenstein: Language and Philosophy, 1974; Death: An Interdisciplinary Analysis, 1974; Rational Love, 1978; Ethics for Children, 1978; Emotion (Humor, Time): A Critical Analysis for Children, 3 vols., 1978; Good and Bad Are Funny Things: A Rhyming Book of Ethics for Children, 1978; Lying: A Critical Analysis, 1985. Add: Box 342, Whitewater, Wisc. 53190, U.S.A.

SHIBUTANI, Tamotsu. American, b. 1920. Psychology, Sociology. Prof. of Sociology, Univ. of California, Santa Barbara, since 1966 (Assoc. Prof. 1962–66). Instr. in Sociology, Univ. of Chicago, 1948–51; Asst. Prof. of Sociology, Univ. of California, Berkeley, 1951–57. *Publs:* Society and Personality, 1961; (with K.M. Kwan) Ethnic Stratification, 1965; Improvised News: A Sociological Study of Rumor, 1966; (ed.) Human Nature and Collective Behavior: Papers in Honor of Herbert Blumer, 1970; The Derelicts of Company K, 1978; Social Processes, 1986. Add: 2088 Cliff Dr., Santa Barbara, Calif. 93109, U.S.A.

SHIDELER, Mary M(cDermott). American, b. 1917. Psychology, Theology/Religion. Freelance writer, since 1955. Pres., American Theological Soc., Midwest Div., 1976–77; Ed., The Descriptive Psychology Bulletin, 1978–79; Pres., Soc. for Descriptive Psychology, 1981–82. *Publs:* The Theology of Romantic Love: A Study in the Writings of Charles Williams, 1962; Charles Williams, 1966; A Creed for a Christian Skeptic, 1968; Consciousness of Battle: An Interim Report on a Theological Journey, 1969; Mother and the Flying Saucer, and Other Fables, 1976; In Search of the Spirit, 1985; Persons, Behavior, and Worlds: The Descriptive Psychology Approach, 1988. Add: 501 Sky Trail Rd., Jamestown Star Route, Boulder, Colo. 80302, U.S.A.

SHIEH, Francis. American, b. 1926. Economics, Language/Linguistics. Researcher, Inst. of American Studies, Chinese Academy of Social Sciences, Beijing; Visiting Prof., Shenyang Polytechnic Univ., China. Formerly Prof. of Economics, Prince George Community Coll., Largo, Md., from 1966 (Coordinator, 1967–69; Chmn., Dept of Economics, 1971–73). *Publs:* A Glimpse of the Chinese Language; Keys for Economic Understanding, 1971; Keys to Economic Understanding, 1976; Work and Study Cycle Theory, 1978. Add: 11201 Woodlawn Blvd., Upper Marlboro, Md. 20772, U.S.A.

SHIKES, Ralph Edmund. American, b. 1912. Art, Biography. Publisher and Member, Editorial Bd., Washington Spectator, since 1976. Pres., 1960–73, and Sr. Consultant, 1973–76, Science and Medicine Publishing Co., Inc., NYC. *Publs:* (ed. with Louis Untermeyer) The Best Humor Annual, 1951, 1952 and 1953; (ed.) Slightly Out of Order (caricature collection), 1958; The Indignant Eye: The Artist as Social Critic in Prints and Drawings from the Fifteenth Century to Picasso, 1969; (with Paula Harper) Pissarro: His Life and Work, 1980; The Art of Satire: Painters as Caricaturists from Delacroix to Picasso, 1984. Add: 16 West 77th St., New York, N.Y. 10024, U.S.A.

SHILLINGLAW, Gordon. American, b. 1925. Business/Trade/Industry. Prof. of Accounting, Graduate Sch. of Business, Columbia Univ. NYC, since 1966 (Assoc. Prof., 1961–66). Asst. Prof., Hamilton Coll., Clinton, 1951–52; Consulting Assoc., Joel Dean Assocs., 1952–55; Asst. Prof., Massachusetts Inst. of Technology, Cambridge, 1955–61; Visiting Prof., IMEDE Mgmt. Development Inst., Lausanne, Switzerland, 1964–65 and 1967–69. *Publs:* Cost Accounting: Analysis and Control, 1961, 5th ed. as Managerial Cost Accounting, 1982; (with M.J. Gordon) Accounting: A Management Approach, 1964, 8th ed. with P. Meyer, 1986; Financial Accounting: Concepts and Applications, 1989. Add: 196 Villard Ave., Hastings-on-Hudson, N.Y. 10706, U.S.A.

SHILOH, Ailon. American, b. 1924. Anthropology/Ethnology, Medicine/Health, Sociology. Prof. and Dir., Grad. Studies, Dept. of Anthropology, Univ. of South Florida, Tampa, since 1973. Research

Assoc. Hadassah Medical Org., 1954–65; Prof of Anthropology, Grad. Sch. of Public Health, Univ. of Pittsburgh, Pa., 1965–73. *Publs:* The Total Institution: Profiles of Mental Patient Perception and Adaptation, 1966; Peoples and Cultures of the Middle East, 1969; Studies in Human Sexual Behavior: The American Scene, 1970; Alternatives to Doomsday: Considerations of the Population/Pollution Syndrome, 1971; By Myself I'm a Book: An Oral History of the Early Jewish Experience in Pittsburgh, 1972; (ed. with I.C. Selavan) Ethnic Groups of America: Their Morbidity, Mortality, and Behavior Disorders, 2 vols., 1973; Christianity Against Jesus, 1977; Faith Healing: The Religious Experience as Therapeutic Process, 1981; Travellers Across Time: Peoples and Cultures of the Middle East (TV univ. course), 1987. Add: Dept. of Anthropology, Coll. of Social and Behavioral Sciences, Univ. of South Florida, Tampa, Fla. 33620, U.S.A.

SHINAGEL, Michael. American, b. 1934. Literature. Dean of Continuing Education and Univ. Extension, and Sr. Lectr. in English, Harvard Univ., Cambridge, Mass., since 1975. Former Prof. of English, Union Coll., Schenectady, N.Y., (joined faculty, 1967). *Publs:* Daniel Defoe and Middle-Class Gentility, 1968; (ed.) Concordance to the Poems of Jonathan Swift, 1972; (ed.) Robinson Crusoe, by Daniel Defoe, 1975. Add: Harvard Univ., 20 Garden St., Cambridge, Mass. 02138, U.S.A.

SHINE, Frances L(ouise). American, b. 1927. Novels/Short stories. Former Elementary sch. teacher, Juniper Hill Sch., Framingham Public Schs., Mass. (joined faculty, 1953); now retired. *Publs:* The Life-Adjustment of Harry Blake, 1968; Johnny Noon, 1973; Conjuror's Journal, 1978. Add: 17 Clark St., Framingham, Mass. 01701, U.S.A.

SHIPLER, David K(arr). American, b. 1942. International relations/Current affairs. Journalist, New York Times: News Clerk, 1966–68; Reporter, Metropolitan Staff, 1968–73; Correspondent, Saigon, 1973–75; Correspondent, 1975–79, and Bureau Chief, 1977–79, Moscow Bureau; Bureau Chief, Jerusalem, 1979–84; Visiting Scholar (on leave from New York Times), Brookings Instn., Washington, D.C., 1984–85; Corresp., Washington Bureau, 1985–87; Chief Diplomatic Corresp., since 1987. *Publs:* Russia: Broken Idols, Solemn Dream, 1983; Arab and Jew: Wounded Spirits in a Promised Land, 1986 (Pulitzer Prize). Add: 4005 Thornapple St., Chevy Chase, Md. 20815, U.S.A.

SHIPMAN, David. British, b. 1932. Film. European Rep., Curtis Publishing Co., 1961–63; Freelance rep., 1964–66. *Publs:* The Great Movie Stars: The Golden Years, 1970, 3rd ed. 1989; The Great Movie Stars: The International Years, 1972, 3rd ed. 1989; Brando, 1974; The Story of Cinema: From the Beginnings to Gone With the Wind, 1982; The Good Film and Video Guide, 1984, 1986; The Story of Cinema: From Citizen Kane to the Present Day, 1984; A Pictorial History of Science Fiction Films, 1985; Caught in the Act: Sex and Eroticism in the Cinema, 1985; Movie Talk: Who Said What about Whom in the Movies, 1988; Marlon Brando, 1989. Add: c/o Frances Kelly Agency, 111 Clifton Rd., Kingston-upon-Thames, Surrey KT2 6PL, England.

SHIPMAN, Henry Longfellow. American, b. 1948. Astronomy. Prof. of Physics, Univ. of Delaware, Newark, since 1981 (Asst. Prof., 1974–77; Assoc. Prof., 1977–81). Teaching Asst., California Inst. of Technology, Pasadena, 1969–71; J.W. Gibbs Instr., Yale Univ., New Haven, Conn., 1971–73; Asst. Prof., Univ. of Missouri, St. Louis, 1973–74. *Publs:* Black Holes, Quasars, and the Universe, 1976, 1980; The Restless Universe: An Introduction to Astronomy, 1978; Space 2000: Meeting the Challenge ofa New Era, 1987. Add: Physics and Astronomy Dept., Univ. of Delaware, Newark, Del. 19716, U.S.A.

SHIPPEN, Zoë American, b. 1902. Cookery/Gastronomy/Wine. *Publs:* Cooking With a Light Touch, 1966; Four for Lunch, Dinner for Eight, 1975; Cooking Can Be Fun, 1988. Add: 220 Fairview Rd., Palm Beach, Fla. 33480, U.S.A.

SHIPPEY, T(homas) A(lan). British, b. 1943. Literature. Prof. of English Language and Medieval Literature, Sch. of English, Univ. of Leeds, since 1979. Lectr. in English, Univ. of Birmingham, 1965; Fellow, St. John's Coll., Oxford, 1972. *Publs:* Old English Verse, 1972; (ed. and trans.) Poems of Wisdom and Learning in Old English, 1976; Beowulf, 1978; The Road to Middle-Earth, 1982. Add: 22 Falkland Ct., Leeds LS17 6JE, England.

SHIRAS, Wilmar H(ouse). Also writes as Jane Howes. American, b. 1908. Science fiction/Fantasy. *Publs:* (as Jane Howes) Slow Dawning, 1946; Children of the Atom, 1953. Add: 3720 Rhoda Ave., Oakland, Calif. 94602, U.S.A.

SHIRER, William L(awrence). American, b. 1904. History. Foreign Corresp. for U.S. Newspapers, in Europe, India, and Near East, 1925–45; Columnist, New York Herald Tribune, 1942–48; Pres., Authors' Guild, 1956–57. *Publs:* Berlin Diary, 1941; End of a Berlin Diary, 1947; Midcentury Journey, 1952; The Challenge of Scandinavia, 1955; The Consul's Wife, 1956; The Rise and Fall of the Third Reich, 1960; The Rise and Fall of Adolf Hitler, 1961; The Sinking of the Bismarck, 1962; The Collapse of the Third Republic: An Enquiry into the Fall of France in 1940, 1969; 20th Century Journey: A Memoir of a Life and the Times, vol. I, The Start, 1976, vol. II, The Nightmare Years, 1984; Gandhi: A Memoir, 1980. Add: P.O. Box, 487, Lenox, Mass. 01240, U.S.A.

SHIRLEY, Frances Ann. American, b. 1931. Literature. Prof. of English, Wheaton Coll., Norton, Mass., since 1973 (Instr., 1960–63; Asst. Prof., 1963–67; Assoc. Prof., 1967–73; Asst. Dean, 1963; Chmn. of Dept., 1972–81; Dir., Prog. for Writing Competence, 1977–79; A. Howard Meneely Research Prof., 1980–81; Assoc. Provost, 1984–88). *Publs:* Shakespeare's Use of Off-Stage Sound, 1963; (ed.) Devil's Law-Case, by John Webster, 1972; Swearing and Perjury in Shakespeare's Plays, 1979; (ed.) King John and Henry VIII: Critical Essays, 1988. Add: Dept. of English, Wheaton Coll., Norton, Mass. 02766, U.S.A.

SHIRLEY, John (Patrick). American, b. 1953. Novels, Science fiction. Fruit picker, dancer, and office worker; regularly performs as lead singer with rock bands. *Publs:* Transmaniacon, 1979; Dracula in Love, 1979; Three-Ring Psychus, 1980; City Come A'Walkin', 1981; The Brigade (novel), 1982; Cellars, 1983; Eclipse, 1985; A Splendid Chaos, 1988. Add: c/o Bluejay Books, St. Martin's Press, 175 Fifth Ave., New York, N.Y. 10010, U.S.A.

SHIRREFFS, Gordon Donald. Has also written as Gordon Donalds, Jackson Flynn, Stewart Gordon and Art MacLean. American, b. 1914. Novels/Short stories, Westerns, Children's fiction, Children's non-fiction. *Publs:* Rio Bravo, 1956; Code of the Gun, 1956; (as Gordon Donalds) Arizona Justice, 1956; Range Rebel, 1956; Fort Vengeance, 1957; (as Stewart Gordon) Gunswift, 1957; Bugles on the Prairie, 1957; Massacre Creek, 1957; Son of the Thunder People, 1957; (as Gordon Donalds) Top Gun, 1957; Shadow Valley, 1958; Ambush on the Mesa, 1958; Swiftwagon, 1958; Last Train from Gun Hill, 1958; The Brave Rifles, 1959; The Lonely Gun, 1959; Roanoke Raiders, 1959; Fort Suicide, 1959; Trail's End, 1959; Shadow of a Gunman, 1959; Renegade Lawman, 1959; Apache Butte, 1960; They Met Danger, 1960; The Mosquito Fleet, 1961; The Rebel Trumpet, 1961; The Proud Gun, 1961; Hangin' Pards, 1961; Ride a Lone Trail, 1961; The Gray Sea Raiders, 1961; Powder Boy of the Monitor, 1961; The Valiant Bugles, 1962; Tumbleweed Trigger, 1962; The Haunted Treasure of the Espectros, 1962; Voice of the Gun, 1962; Rio Desperado, 1962; Action Front!, 1962; The Border Guidon, 1962; Mystery of Lost Canyon, 1963; Slaughter at Broken Bow, 1963; The Cold Seas Beyond, 1963; The Secret of the Spanish Desert, 1964; Quicktrigger, 1964; Too Tough to Die, 1964; The Nevada Gun, 1964; The Hostile Beaches, 1964; The Hidden Rider of Dark Mountain, 1964; Blood Justice, 1964; Gunslingers Three, 1964; Judas Gun, 1964; Last Man Alive, 1964; Now He Is Legend, 1965; The Lone Rifle, 1965; The Enemy Seas, 1965; Barranca, 1965; The Bolo Battalion, 1966; Southwest Drifter, 1967; Torpedoes Away!, 1969; The Godless Breed, 1968; Five Graves to Boothill, 1968; The Killer Sea, 1968; The Mystery of the Lost Cliffdwelling, 1968; Showdown in Sonora, 1969; Jack of Spades, 1970; The Manhunter, 1970; Brasada, 1972; Bowman's Kid, 1973; Renegade's Trail, 1974; (as Jackson Flynn) Shootout, 1974; Apache Hunter, 1975; The Marauders, 1977; Rio Diablo, 1977; Legend of the Damned, 1977; Captain Cutlass, 1978; Calgaich, The Swordsman, 1980; The Untamed Breed, 1981; Showdown in Sonora, 1981; Bold Legend, 1982; Glorieta Pass, 1984; The Ghost Dancers, 1986; Hell's Forty Acres, 1987; Maximilian's Gold, 1988; The Walking Sands, 1989. Add: 17427 San Jose St., Granada Hills, Calif. 91344, U.S.A.

SHIVERS, Jay Sanford. American, b. 1930. Public/Social administration. Prof. and Supvr., Recreational Service Education, Univ. of Connecticut, Storrs, since 1970. *Publs:* Public Administration of Park and Recreational Services, 1962; Leadership in Recreational Service, 1963; Principles and Practices of Recreational Service, 1967; Camping: Administration, Counseling, Programming, 1971; (with G. Hjelte) Planning Recreational Places, 1971; (with G. Hjelte) Public Administration of Recreational Services, 1972, 1978; (with C.R. Calder) Recreational Crafts: Instructional Techniques and Programming, 1974; (with H.F. Fait) Therapeutic and Adapted Recreational Service, 1974; Essentials of Recreational Services, 1978; Leisure: Emergence and Expansion, 1979; Recreational Leadership: Group Dynamics and Human Relations, 1980; Urban Recreational Problems, 1980; (with Hollis F. Fait) Recreational

Services for the Aging, 1980; Leisure and Recreation Concepts: A Critical Analysis, 1981; (with C.A. Bucher) Recreation for Today's Society, 2nd ed., 1984; (with H.F. Fait) Special Recreational Services Therapeutic and Adapted, 1985; Recreational Leadership, 1986; Recreational Safety, 1986; Introduction to Recreational Service Administration, 1987; Camping: Organization and Operation, 1989. Add: U-34, Univ. of Connnecticut, Storrs, Conn. 06269-2034, U.S.A.

SHNEIDMAN, J. Lee. American, b. 1929. History. Prof. of History, Adelphi Univ., Garden City, N.Y., since 1970 (Assoc. Prof., 1965–70); Chmn., Columbia Univ. Seminar on History of Legal and Political Thought and Institutions, since 1985. Ed., Bulletin of the Intnl. Psychohistorical Assn. *Publs:* Rise of the Aragonese-Catalan Empire, 1200-1350, (2 vols.) 1970; Spain and Franco, 1949-1959, 1973; (with Peter Schwab) John F. Kennedy, 1974. Add: History Dept., Adelphi Univ., Garden City, N.Y. 11530, U.S.A.

SHNEOUR, Elie Alexis. American, b. 1926. Biology, Social sciences. Chmn., Science Advisors Prog., American Soc. of Biological Chemists, since 1973; Member, Advisory Council, The Cousteau Soc., since 1977; Dir. of Research, Biosystems Research Inst., and Pres. Biosystems Assocs. Ltd., La Jolla, since 1974 (founder, 1964). Prof. of Biology, Univ. of Utah, Salt Lake City, 1965–69; Research Neurochemist, City of Hope Medical Center, Duarte, Calif., 1969–71; Dir. of Research, Calbiochem Inc., La Jolla, Calif., 1971–74. Member, Exec. Cttee., National Academy of Science Study Group on Biology and the Exploration of Mars, 1964; Chmn., Western Regional Council Research on Basic Biosciences for Manned Orbiting Missions, American Inst. of Biological Sciences, NASA, 1966–69; Council Member, American Soc. of Neurochemistry, 1971–73. *Publs:* (with Samuel Moffat) Life Beyond the Earth, 1965, 1967; The Search for Extraterrestrial Life, 1966; The Malnourished Mind, 1974. Add: Biosystems Research Inst., P.O. Box 1414, La Jolla, Calif. 92038, U.S.A.

SHOBIN, David. American, b. 1945. Novels/Short stories. Attending Physician, St. John's Smithtown Hosp., and Smithtown Gen. Hosp., Smithtown, N.Y., since 1975; Asst. Prof. of Clinical Obstetrics and Gynecology, State Univ. of New York at Stony Brook, since 1978; Pres., David Shobin, professional service corp., Smithtown, since 1980. *Publs:* The Unborn, 1980. Add: c/o The Linden Press, Simon and Schuster, 1230 Ave. of the Americas, New York, N.Y. 10020, U.S.A.

SHOCK, Nathan W(etherill). American, b. 1906. Biology, Medicine/Health, Psychology. Scientist Emeritus, Gerontology Research Center, National Inst. of Aging, since 1977 (Chief, 1941–76). Research Assoc., Dept. of Pediatrics, Univ. of Chicago, 1930–32; Asst. Prof. of Physiology, Univ. of California, Berkeley, 1933–41; Pres., Gerontological Soc., USA, 1960, and Intnl. Assn. of Gerontology, 1969–72. *Publs:* (ed.) Problems of Aging, 1950; A Classified Bibliography of Gerontology and Geriatrics, 1951, supplement 1957; Trends in Gerontology, 1951, 1957; (ed.) Aging: Some Social and Biological Aspects, 1960; (ed.) Biological Aspects of Aging, 1962; (ed.) Perspectives in Experimental Gerontology, 1966; The International Association of Gerontology: A Chronicle 1950-1987, 1988. Add: Gerontology Research Center, Francis Scott Key Medical Center, Baltimore, Md. 21224, U.S.A.

SHOCKLEY, Ann Allen. American, b. 1927. Novels/Short stories. Assoc. Librarian for Special Collections and University Archivist, Fisk Univ., Nashville (formerly Assoc. Librarian for Public Services and Assoc. Prof. of Library Science). Ed., American Library Assn.'s Black Caucus Newsletter, since 1972. Asst. Librarian, Delaware State Coll., 1959–60; Asst. Librarian, and subsequently Assoc. Librarian, and Curator of the Negro Collection, Univ. of Maryland, Eastern Shore, 1960–69. *Publs:* (ed. with Sue P. Chandler) Living Black American Authors: A Biographical Directory, 1973; Loving Her (novel), 1974; (with E.J. Josey) Handbook of Black Librarianship, 1977; The Black and White of It (short stories), 1980; Say Jesus and Come to Me (novel), 1982; Afro-American Women Writers: An Anthology and Critical Guide, 1988. Add: 1809 Morena St., Apt. G-4, Nashville, Tenn. 37208, U.S.A.

SHOESMITH, Kathleen A. British, b. 1938. Historical/Romance/Gothic, Children's non-fiction. Teacher, West Riding County Council, since 1958. *Publs:* Three Poems for Children, 1965; Playtime Stories (6 titles), 1966; Judy Stories (4 titles), 1967; Easy to Read (6 titles), 1967; How Do They Grow? (4 titles), 1967; Jack O'Lantern, 1969; Cloud Over Calderwood, 1969; Do You Know About? (4 titles), 1970; The Tides of Tremanion, 1970; Mallory's Luck, 1971; Return of the Royalist, 1971; Reluctant Puritan, 1972; Do You Know About (16 titles), 1972–73; Use Your Senses (5 titles), 1973; The Highwayman's Daughter,

1973; Belltower, 1973; The Black Domino, 1975; Elusive Legacy, 1976; The Miser's Ward, 1977; Smuggler's Haunt, 1978; Guardian at the Gate, 1979; Brackenthorpe, 1980; Autumn Escapade, 1981; Rustic Vineyard, 1982; A Minor Bequest, 1984. Add: 351 Fell Lane, Keighley, West Yorks, England.

SHONE, Ronald. British, b. 1946. Business/Trade/Industry, Economics, Psychology. Sr. Lectr. in Economics, Univ. of Stirling, since 1982 (Lectr., 1976–82). Lectr., 1971–73, and Esmeé Fairbairn Research Fellow, 1974–76, Univ. of Sheffield. *Publs:* The Pure Theory of International Trade, 1972; Microeconomics: A Modern Treatment, 1975; (with F. Neal) Economic Model Building, 1976; Applications in Intermediate Microeconomics, 1981; Autohypnosis, 1982; Issues in Macroeconomics, 1984; Creative Visualization, 1984; Advanced Autohypnosis, 1985; Microeconomics, 1987; (with D.N. King) Microeconomics: An Introduction to Theory and Applications, 1987; Open Economy Macroeconomics, 1989. Add: Dept. of Economics, Univ. of Stirling, Stirling FK9 4LA, Scotland.

SHONTZ, Franklin C(urtis). American, b. 1926. Psychology. Prof., Dept. of Psychology, Univ. of Kansas, Lawrence, since 1960. *Publs:* Research Methods in Personality; Perceptual and Cognitive Aspects of Body Experience; (with W. Epstein) Psychology in Progress; Psychological Aspects of Physical Illness and Disability; (with J. Spotts) Cocaine Users; Fundamentals of Research in the Behavioral Sciences: Principles and Practice. Add: Dept. of Psychology, Univ. of Kansas, Lawrence, Kans. 66045, U.S.A.

SHORE, Norman. *See* **SMITH,** Norman Edward Mace.

SHORT, Philip. British, b. 1945. Politics/Government, Biography, Documentaries/Reportage. Chief of BBC Paris Bureau, since 1981 (Moscow Corresp., 1974–76; Peking Corresp., 1977–81). Freelance corresp., Malawi, 1967–70; and Uganda, 1971–73. *Publs:* Banda, 1974; The Dragon and the Bear, 1982. Add: c/o Lloyds Bank, 20 Badminton Rd., Downend, Bristol, England.

SHORT, Robert Stuart. British, b. 1938. Art, Literature. Sr. Lectr., Sch. of Modern Languages and European History, Univ. of East Anglia, Norwich, since 1967. Asst. Lectr., Hull Univ., 1965–67. *Publs:* (with Roger Cardinal) Surrealism: Permanent Revelation, 1971; Paul Klee, 1979; Dada and Surrealism, 1980; (with Peter Webb) Hans Bellmer, 1985. Add: Sch. of Modern Languages and European History, Univ. of East Anglia, Norwich NR4 7TJ, England.

SHORTER, Edward. American, b. 1941. History, Medicine/Health. Prof. of History, Univ. of Toronto, since 1967. *Publs:* The Historian and the Computer, 1971; (with Charles Tilly) Strikes in France, 1974; The Making of the Modern Family, 1975; A History of Women's Bodies, 1983; Beside Manners: The Troubled History of Doctors and Patients, 1985; The Health Century, 1987. Add: Dept. of History, Univ. of Toronto, Toronto, Ont. M5S 1A1, Canada.

SHOTWELL, Louisa R(ossiter). American, b. 1902. Children's fiction, Children's non-fiction, Sociology. *Publs:* The Harvesters: Story of the Migrant People, 1961; Roosevelt Grady, 1963; Beyond the Sugarcane Field, 1964; Adam Bookout, 1967; Magdalena, 1971. Add: 1570 East Ave., Apt. 619, Rochester, N.Y. 14610, U.S.A.

SHRAKE, Edwin. American, b. 1931. Westerns/Adventure. Reporter, Fort Worth Press, and Dallas Times Herald; columnist, Dallas Morning News; Assoc. Ed., Sports Illustrated, NYC. *Publs:* Blood Reckoning, 1962; But Not for Love, 1964; Blessed McGill, 1968; Strange Peaches, 1972; Peter Arbiter, 1973; (with Dan Jenkins) Limo, 1976. Add: 1505 Wildcat Hollow, Austin, Tex. 78746, U.S.A.

SHRAND, David. South African, b. 1913. Children's fiction, Law, Money/Finance. Chartered accountant since 1940; Tax consultant and financial adviser, since 1971. Former Lectr. on Income Tax and Executorship, Univ. of Cape Town, and Examiner on Trustee Diploma, Inst. of Bankers in South Africa. *Publs:* What Every Attorney (Real Estate Agent/Property Owner, Professional Person, Salaried Person, Taxpayer) Should Know About Income Tax, 5 vols.; The 1971/1972 Income Tax Statutory Amendments; The Administration of Insolvent Estates in South Africa; Real Estate in South Africa; The Financial and Statistical Digest of South Africa; Studies in Income Tax; The Taxation of Companies in South Africa; (co-author) The Registration, Management and Winding-up of Companies in South Africa; (co-author) The Farmer's Legal and Financial Handbook; Today and Yesterday; The Administration of Deceased Estates in South Africa; Trusts in South Africa; A Guide to General Sales Tax; The Taxation of Co-Operative Societies in South Africa; Shrand on the Sectional Titles Act; The Law and Practice of Insolvency, Winding-up of Companies, and Judicial Management; Law and Finance for the Farmer; The Making of a Will; The Taxation of Fringe Benefits; Every Man His Own Income Tax Consultant; The Law and Practice of Close Corporations; The Vicarious Society; In Search of God, 1988.. Add: P.O. Box 3461, Cape Town, 8000, South Africa.

SHRAPNEL, Norman. British, b. 1912. Politics/Government, Social commentary/phenomena. Parliamentary correspondent and columnist, The Guardian, 1958–75. *Publs:* (with W. Papas) Parliament, 1966; A Bluffer's Guide to Politics, 1974; A View of the Thames, 1977; The Performers: Politics as Theatre, 1978; The Seventies: Britain's Inward March, 1980. Add: 27A Shooters Hill Rd., London SE3, England.

SHREVE, Susan R(ichards). American, b. 1939. Novels/Short stories, Children's fiction. Former secondary sch. English teacher. *Publs:* A Fortunate Madness, 1974; The Nightmares of Geranium Street, 1977; A Woman Like That, 1977; Loveletters, 1978; Children of Power, 1979; Family Secrets, 1979; The Masquerade, 1980; Miracle Play, 1981; The Bad Dreams of a Good Girl, 1982; The Revolution of Mary Leary, 1982; Dreaming of Heroes, 1984; The Flunking of Joshua T. Bates, 1984; How I Saved the World on Purpose, 1985; Queen of Hearts, 1987; Lily and the Runaway Baby, 1987; A Country of Strangers, 1989. Add: c/o Russell and Volkening, 50 W. 29th St., New York, N.Y. 10001, U.S.A.

SHRIMSLEY, Bernard. British, b. 1931. Novels. Assoc. Ed., Daily Express, London, since 1983. Asst. Ed., Daily Mirror, London, 1964–68; Ed., Liverpool Daily Post, 1968–69; Deputy Ed., 1969–72, and Ed., 1972–75, The Sun, London; Ed., News of the World, London, 1975–80; Ed, The Mail on Sunday, London, 1982. *Publs:* The Candidates, 1968; Lion Rampant, 1984. Add: c/o John Farquharson Ltd., 162 Regent St., London W1R 5TB, England.

SHUBIN, Seymour. American. Novels/Short stories, Medicine/Health, Psychiatry, Documentaries/Reportage. Former Managing Ed., Official Detective Stories Mag., and The Psychiatric Reporter, and Ed., J.B. Lippincott Publishing Co., Philadelphia, Pa. *Publs:* Anyone's My Name, 1953; Stranger to Myself, 1954; Manta, 1958; Wellville, U.S.A., 1961; The Captain, 1982; Holy Secrets, 1984; Voices, 1985; Never Quite Dead, 1989. Add: 122 Harrogate Rd., Overbrook Hills, Pa. 19151, U.S.A.

SHUGRUE, Michael Francis. American, b. 1934. Literature. Prof. of English, Staten Island Coll., City Univ. of New York, since 1979 (Dir. of Academic Development, City Coll., 1972–74; Dean of Faculties, Richmond Coll. 1974–79). Dir. of English Progs., Modern Language Assn. of America, NYC, 1965–73; Gen. Ed., Foundns. of the Novel, Garland Press, NYC, 1972–75. *Publs:* (ed. with W. McBurney) The Virtuous Orphan, by Marivaux, 1965; (ed.) The Recruiting Officer, by Farquhar, 1966; How the New English Will Help Your Child, 1966; (ed.) Selected Poetry and Prose of Daniel Defoe, 1968; English in a Decade of Change, 1968; (ed. with H. Finestone) Prospects for the 70s, 1973; (ed. with H. Finestone and C. Shrodes) The Conscious Reader, 1974, 4th ed., 1985; The Essay, 1981. Add: 1205 Evergreen Ave., Plainfield, N.J. 07060, U.S.A.

SHUKMAN, Harold. British, b. 1931. History, Translations. Fellow since 1961, and Lectr. in Modern Russian History since 1969, St. Antony's Coll., Oxford. Gen. Ed., Longman's History of Russia. *Publs:* (trans. with M. Hayward) E. Shvarts: The Dragon, 1965; (trans. with M. Glenny) I. Babel: Marya, 1965; Lenin and the Russian Revolution, 1966; (trans. with M. Hayward) V. Kataev: The Holy Well, 1967; (with G. Katkov) Lenin's Path to Power, 1971; (with F.W. Deakin and H.T. Willetts) A History of World Communism, 1975; (trans.) Heavy Sand, by A. Rybakov, 1981; (trans.) All Stalin's Men by Roy Medvedev, 1983; (trans.) China and the superpowers, by Roy Medvedev, 1986; (ed.) The Blackwell Encyclopedia of the Russian Revolution, 1988; (trans.) Children of the Arbat, by Anatoli Rybakov, 1988; (trans.) Memories, by Andrei Gromyko, 1989. Add: St. Antony's Coll., Oxford, England.

SHULMAN, Irving. American, b. 1913. Novels/Short stories, Social commentary/phenomena, Biography. Teaching Asst., Univ. of California, Los Angeles, 1962–64; Prof., California State Coll., Los Angeles, 1964–65. *Publs:* The Amboy Dukes, 1947; Cry Tough, 1949; The Big Brokers, 1953; The Square Trap, 1953; Children of the Dark, 1956; Good Deeds Must be Punished, 1956; Calibre, 1957; The Velvet Knife, 1961; The Short End of the Stick and Other Stories, 1959; (with P. Bristol) The Roots of Fury (biography), 1961; Harlow, 1964; Valentino, 1967;

"Jackie!" The Exploitation of a First Lady, 1970; The Devil's Knee, 1973; Saturn's Child, 1976. Add: c/o Doris Halsey, Reece Halsey Agency, 8733 Sunset Blvd., Los Angeles, Calif. 90069, U.S.A.

SHULMAN, Marshall D(arrow). American, b. 1916. International relations/Current affairs, Politics/Government. Adlai E. Stevenson Prof. of Intnl. Relations since 1974, and Dir. of the Harriman Inst. for Advanced Study of the Soviet Union, since 1982, Columbia Univ., NYC (Prof. of Govt., and Dir., Russian Inst., 1967–74). Assoc. Dir., 1954–62, and Research Assoc., 1962–67, Russian Research Center, and Lectr. in Govt., 1956–60, Harvard Univ., Cambridge, Mass.; Prof. of Intnl. Politics, Fletcher Sch. of Law and Diplomacy, Tufts Univ., Medford, Mass., 1961–68. *Publs:* Stalin's Foreign Policy Reappraised, 1963; Beyond the Cold War, 1966; (co-ed.) East-West Tensions in the Third World, 1986. Add: 420 West 118th St., New York, N.Y. 10027, U.S.A.

SHULMAN, Milton. Canadian, b. 1913. Novels/Short stories, Children's fiction, History, Media, Essays. Theatre Critic since 1953, and Columnist, Evening Standard, London (Film Critic, 1948–58; Television Critic, 1964–72). Broadcaster ("Stop the Week"), BBC Radio. Book Critic, Sunday Express, London, 1957–58; Exec. Producer, Granada Television, London, 1958–62; Asst. Controller of Progs., Rediffusion Television, London, 1962–64; Current Affairs Columnist, Daily Express, London, 1973–74; Film Critic, Vogue Mag., 1975–88. *Publs:* Defeat in the West, 1948; How to Be a Celebrity, 1950; Preep, 1964; Kill 3, 1967; Preep in Paris, 1967; Preep and the Queen, 1970; (with H. Kretzmer) Every Home Should Have One, 1970; The Least Worst Television in the World, 1973; The Ravenous Eye, 1973. Add: 51 Eaton Sq., London SW1, England.

SHULTZ, George P(ratt). American, b. 1920. Business/Trade/Industry, Economics, Industrial relations. Member of faculty, Mass. Inst. of Technology, Cambridge, 1948–57; Prof. of Industrial Relations, 1957–68, and Dean, Grad. Sch. of Business, 1962–68, Univ. of Chicago; U.S. Secty. of Labor, Washington, 1969–70; Dir., Office of Mgmt. and Budget, Washington, 1970–72; Secty. of the Treasury, and Chmn. of the Cost of Living Council, Washington, 1972–74; Prof. of Mgmt. and Public Policy, Stanford Univ., 1974; Exec. Vice-Pres., 1974–75, Pres., 1975–79, Vice-Chmn., 1980, and Pres., 1980–82, Bechtel Corp; U.S. Secty. of State, 1982–88. Sr. Staff Economist, President's Council of Economic Advisers, 1955–56; Consultant to Office of U.S. Secty. of Labor, 1959–60; Member, Illinois Gov.'s Cttee. on Unemployment, 1961–62; Consultant to Pres., Advisory Commn. on Labor-Management Policy, 1961–62; Chmn., U.S. Dept. of Labor Task Force on U.S. Employment Service, 1965–68; Member, U.S. Dept. of Labor National Manpower Policy Task Force, 1966–68; Pres., Industrial Relations Research Assn., 1968; Chmn., President's Economic Advisory Bd., 1981–82. *Publs:* Pressures on Wage Decisions, 1951; (with C. Myers) The Dynamics of a Labor Market, 1951; (with T. Whisler) Management Organization and The Computer, 1960; (with A. Weber) Strategies for the Displaced Woqsrker, 1966; (with R. Aliber) Guidelines, Informal Controls, and the Marketplace, 1966; (with A. Rees) Workers and Wages in the Urban Labor Market, 1970; (with Kenneth W. Dam) Economic Policy Beyond the Headlines, 1979. Add: c/o Office of Secty. of State, 2201C St. N.W., Washington, D.C. 20520, U.S.A.

SHUMAKER, (Charles) Wayne. American, b. 1910. History, Literature. Prof. of English, Univ. of California, Berkeley, 1946–77. *Publs:* Elements of Critical Theory, 1952; English Autobiography, 1954; Literature and the Irrational, 1960; (ed. and contrib.) An Approach to Poetry, 1965; Unpremeditated Verse, 1967; The Occult Sciences in the Renaissance, 1972; (with John Heilbron) John Dee on Astronomy, 1978; Renaissance Curiosa, 1982; Natural Magic: Four Treatises 1590-1667, 1989. Add: Dept. of English, 322 Wheeler Hall, Univ. of California, Berkeley, Calif. 94720, U.S.A.

SHUMAN, Samuel I. American, b. 1925. Law, Politics/Government. Lawyer: Called to Michigan Bar, 1954, and to Texas Bar, 1979. Law Teacher, Wayne State Univ., Detroit, 1954–80. *Publs:* Legal Positivism: Its Scope and Limitations, 1963; (with N.D. West) Austrian Penal Code, 1966; (ed.) The Future of Federalism, 1968; (ed. and contrib. with G.L. Dorsey) Validation of New Forms of Social Organization, 1968; (ed. and contrib.) Law and Disorder, 1971; (with N.D. West) Introduction to American Law: Cases and Materials, 1971; Psychosurgery and the Medical Control of Violence, 1978. Add: 730 N. Post Oak, Suite 400, Houston, Tex. 77024, U.S.A.

SHUMSKY, Zena. *See* COLLIER, Zena.

SHURA, Mary Francis. *See* **CRAIG,** Mary.

SHUTTLE, Penelope (Diane). British, b. 1947. Novels/Short stories, Plays/Screenplays, Poetry. *Publs:* An Excusable Vengeance (novel), 1967; All the Us]ual Hours of Sleeping (novel), 1969; Nostalgia Neurosis, 1968; Jesusa (novel), 1972; (with Peter Redgrove) The Hermaphrodite Album, 1973; Midwinter Mandala, 1973; Wailing Monkey Embracing a Tree (novel), 1974; Photographs of Persephone, 1974; Autumn Piano, 1974; Songbook of the Snow, 1974; (with Peter Redgrove) The Terrors of Doctor Treviles (novel), 1974; The Girl Who Lost Her Glove (radio play), 1974; The Dream (verse), 1975; Webs of Fire (verse), 1975; Period (verse), 1976; Four American Sketches (verse), 1976; Rainsplitter in the Zodiac Garden (novel), 1976; The Dauntless Girl (radio play), 1978; (with Peter Redgrove) The Wise Wound (non-fiction), 1978; The Mirror of the Giant (novel), 1980; The Orchard Upstairs, 1981; The Child-Stealer, 1983; The Lion from Rio (poetry), 1986; Adventures with My Horse (verse), 1988. Add: c/o David Higham Assocs., 5-8 Lower John St., London W1R 4HA, England.

SICHEL, Werner. American, b. 1934. Economics. Prof. of Economics, and Dept. Chmn., Western Michigan Univ., Kalamazoo, since 1960. Pres., Economics Soc. of Michigan, 1975–76; and Midwest Business Ecnmics Assn., 1989–90. *Publs:* (ed.) Industrial Organization and Public Policy: Selected Readings, 1967; (ed.) Antitrust Policy and Economic Welfare, 1970; (with Peter Eckstein) Basic Economic Concepts, 1974, 1977; (ed.) Public Utility Regulation, 1975; (ed.) The Economic Effects of Multinational Corporations, 1975; (ed.) Salvaging Public Utility Regulation, 1976; (ed.) Economic Advice and Executive Policy: Recommendations from Past Members of the Council of Economic Advisers, 1978; (ed.) Public Utility Rate Making in an Energy Conscious Environment, 1979; (ed. with Thomas G. Gies) Applications of Economic Principles in Public Utility Industries, 1981; (ed. with Thomas G. Gies) Deregulation: Appraisal Before the Fact, 1982; (with Martin Bronfenbrenner and Wayland Gardner) Economics, 1984, 3rd ed. 1990; (with Beatrice Sichel) Economics Journals and Serials: An Analytical Guide, 1986; (ed.) The State of Economic Science: The Views of Six Nobel Laureates, 1989. Add: Dept. of Economics, Western Michigan Univ., Kalamazoo, Mich. 49008, U.S.A.

SIDNEY, Neilma. Pseud. for Neilma Gantner. Australian, b. 1922. Novels/Short stories. Member, Australian Exec. Intnl. Social Service, 1955–69, and Intnl. Exec. of Intnl. Social Service, 1965–69. *Publs:* Saturday Afternoon, 1959; Beyond the Bay, 1966; The Eye of the Needle, 1970; The Return, 1976; Journey to Mourilyan, 1986; Sunday Evening (short stories), 1988. Add: P.O. Box 497, South Yarra, Vic. 3141, Australia.

SIEGEL, Benjamin. Also writes as Matthew Benn. American, b. 1914. Novels/Short stories. *Publs:* The Sword and the Promise, 1959; A Kind of Justice, 1960; The Principal, 1963; Doctors and Wives, 1970; Case History, 1971; The Jurors, 1973; Four Doctors, 1975; (as Matthew Benn) Private Practice, 1975; This Healing Passion, 1978; The Adventures of Richard O'Boy, 1980. Add: 203 Forest Dr., Ithaca, N.Y. 14850, U.S.A.

SIEGEL, Bernie S(hepard). American, b. 1932. Medicine/Health. Surgeon, practising in New Haven, Conn., since 1961; Founder and Dir., Exceptional Cancer Patients (therapy and healing program). *Publs:* Love, Medicine, and Miracles, 1986. Add: c/o Harper and Row, 10 E 53rd St., New York, N.Y. 10022, U.S.A.

SIEGEL, Irving H(erbert). American, b. 1914. Business/Trade/Industry, Economics, Mathematics/Statistics. Consulting economist, since 1979. Asst. Chief, Productivity Div., Bureau of Labor Statistics, U.S. Dept. of Labor, Washington, D.C., 1941–43; Chief Economist, Veterans Admin., Washington, D.C., 1945–49; Operations Analyst, Johns Hopkins Operations Research Office, 1949–51, and 1961–63; Project Co-Dir., Twentieth Century Fund, 1951–55; Sr. Economist, Council of Economic Advisers, 1953–60; Consultant, Patent Research Inst., George Washington Univ., Washington, D.C., 1955–72; Member of Research Council, Research Analysis Corp., 1963–65; Economist, Upjohn Inst. for Employment Research, 1965–72; Economic Adviser, Bureau of Domestic Business Development, U.S. Dept. of Commerce, Washington, D.C., 1972–79. *Publs:* (with H. Magdoff and M. Davis) Production, Employment and Productivity in 59 Manufacturing Industries: 1919-36, 1939; Soviet Labor Productivity, 1952; (ed. with S. Levitan and contrib.) Dimensions of Manpower Policy: Programs and Research, 1966; (ed. and contrib.) Manpower Tomorrow: Prospects and Priorities, 1967; (co-author) Chemistry in the Economy, 1973; Company Productivity: Measurement for Improvement, 1980; Fuller Employment with Less Inflation, 1981; (with Edgar Wein-

berg) Labor-Management Cooperation: The American Experience, 1982; Productivity Measurement in Organizations: Private Firms and Public Agencies, 1986. Add: 8312 Bryant Dr., Bethesda, Md. 20034, U.S.A.

SIEGEL, Paul N. American, b. 1916. Literature. Prof. Emeritus of English, Long Island Univ., Brooklyn, N.Y., since 1978 (Chmn., English Dept., 1956–71; Prof., 1956–78). Instr. in English, City Coll., City Univ., NYC, 1946–49; Assoc. Prof., 1949–52, and Prof. of English, 1952–56, Ripon Coll., Wisc.; Prof., Grad. Sch., New York Univ., NYC, 1968; Prof., Shakespeare Inst., Stratford, Conn., 1969; Prof., World Centre for Shakespeare Studies, London, 1972. *Publs:* Shakespearean Tragedy and the Elizabethan Compromise, 1957; (ed.) His Infinite Variety: Major Shakespearean Criticism since Johnson, 1964; Shakespeare in His Time and Ours, 1968; (ed.) Leon Trotsky on Literature and Art, 1970; (ed.) Macbeth, 1970; Revolution and the Twentieth-Century Novel, 1979; Shakespeare's English and Roman History Plays: A Marxist Approach, 1986; The Meek and the Militant: Religion and Power Across the World, 1986. Add: 101 W. 85th St., New York, N.Y. 10024, U.S.A.

SIGAL, Clancy. American, b. 1926. Novels. Asst. to the Wage Coordinator, United Auto Workers, Detroit, Mich., 1946–47; Story Analyst, Columbia Pictures, Hollywood, Calif., 1952–54; Agent, Jaffe Agency, Los Angeles, Calif., 1953–56. *Publs:* Weekend in Dinlock, 1960; Going Away:Report, A Memoir, 1963; Zone of the Interior, 1976. Add: c/o Journalism Sch., Univ. of Southern California, Los Angeles, Calif. 90089-1695, U.S.A.

SIGBAND, Norman Bruce. American, b. 1920. Business/Trade/Industry, Writing/Journalism. Prof. of Business Communication, Univ. of Southern California, Los Angeles, since 1965. Prof., De Paul Univ., Chicago, 1946–65. *Publs:* Practical English for Everyday Use, 1954; Effective Report Writing for Business, Industry, and Government, 1960; Communication for Management, 1969; Management Communications for Decision Making, 1973; Communications for Management and Business, 1976, 5th ed. 1989; Communicating in Business, 1981, 3rd ed. 1989. Add: 3109 Dona Susana Dr., Studio City, Calif. 91604, U.S.A.

SIGWORTH, Oliver F(rederic). American, b. 1921. Intellectual history, Literature, Biography, Essays. Prof. of English, Univ. of Arizona, Tucson, since 1953. *Publs:* Four Styles of a Decade, 1961; Nature's Sternest Painter: Five Essays on the Poetry of George Crabbe, 1965; William Collins, 1965; (ed. and contrib.) Criticism and Aesthetics 1660-1800, 1971. Add: Dept. of English, Univ. of Arizona, Tucson, Ariz. 85721, U.S.A.

SIIRALA, Aarne Johannes. Canadian, b. 1919. Psychiatry, Psychology, Theology/Religion. Prof. of Religion and of Systematic Theology, Wilfrid Laurier Univ., Waterloo Lutheran Seminary, Ontario, since 1963. Principal, Adult Educational Centre of the Church of Finland, since 1952 (Teacher, 1946–52). Visiting Scholar, Union Theological Seminary, NYC, 1960–63. *Publs:* (trans.) Luther's Lära om Kallelsen, by Gustaf Wingren, 1946; Gottes Gebot bei Martin Luther, 1956; (with Martti Siirala) Elaman Ykseys, 1960; The Voice of Illness: A Study of Therapy and Prophecy, 1963, 1982; Divine Humanness, 1970; (ed.) Gotthard Booth, The Cancer Epidemic: Shadow of the Conquest of Nature, 1980. Add: 310 Bridgeport Rd., Waterloo, Ont., Canada.

SILBER, Sherman J(ay). American, b. 1941. Medicine/Health. In private practice, St. Louis; consulting Urologist, St. Luke's Hosp.-West, and St. John's Mercy Medical Center. Asst. Surgeon, Dept. of Surgery, Univ. of Melbourne, 1973–74; Asst. Prof. of Urology, and Vice-Chmn., Div. of Urology, Univ. of Calfornia Medical Center, San Francisco, and Chief of Urology, Veterans Admin. Hosp., San Francisco, 1974–76. *Publs:* Transurethral Resection, 1977; Microsurgery, 1979; How to Get Pregnant, 1980; The Male, 1981; How Not to Get Pregnant: Your Guide to Simple, Reliable Contraception, 1987. Add: 224 S. Woods Mill, Suite 730, St. Louis, Mo. 63017, U.S.A.

SILBER, William L. American, b. 1942. Economics, Money/Finance. Prof. of Economics and Dir. of Doctoral Prog., Grad. Sch. of Bus. Admin., New York Univ. Assoc. Ed., Review of Economics and Statistics, and Journal of Finance. *Publs:* Portfolio Behavior of Financial Institutions, 1970; (with L.S. Ritter) Money, 1970, 5th ed. 1985; (with L.S. Ritter) Principles of Money, Banking and Financial Markets, 1974, 5th ed. 1986; (ed.) Financial Innovation, 1975. Add: c/o Basic Books, 10 E. 53rd St., New York, N.Y. 10022, U.S.A.

SILBERMAN, Charles Eliot. American, b. 1925. Criminology/Law enforcement/Prisons, Education, Social commentary/phenomena, Social sciences. Dir., The Study of Jewish Life, since 1979. Lectr. in Economics, Columbia Univ., NYC, 1948–66; Assoc. Ed., 1953–61, and Member, Bd. of Eds., 1961–71, Fortune mag. *Publs:* (co-author) Markets of the Sixties, 1960; Crisis in Black and White, 1964; The Myths of Automations, 1966; Crisis in the Classroom, 1970; (ed.) The Open Classroom Reader, 1973; Criminal Violence, Criminal Justice, 1978; A Certain People, 1985. Add: 535 E. 86th St., New York, N.Y. 10028, U.S.A.

SILK, Dennis (Peter). Israeli/British, b. 1928. Poetry. Ed., The Jerusalem Post. *Publs:* A Face of Stone, 1964; (with Harold Schimmel and Robert Friend) Now, 1964; (ed.) Retrievements: A Jerusalem Anthology, 1968, 1977; (ed. with Harold Schimmel) 14 Israeli Poets: A Selection of Modern Hebrew Poetry, 1976; The Punished Land, 1980; Hold Fast, 1984; Catwalk and Overpass, 1988. Add: P.O. Box 8103, German Colony, Jerusalem, Israel.

SILK, Joseph (Ivor). British, b. 1942. Astronomy. Prof. of Astronomy, Univ. of California, Berkeley, since 1970. *Publs:* The Big Bang, 1980, 1988; (with I. Appenzeller and J. Lequeux) Star Formation, 1980; (with J. Barrow) The Left Hand of Creation, 1983. Add: 3074 Buena Vista Way, Berkeley, Calif. 94720, U.S.A.

SILK, Leonard S. American, b. 1918. Plays/Screenplays, Business/Trade/Industry, Economics, Politics/Government. Columnist, The New York Times, since 1970 (member, Editorial Bd., 1970–76). Former Chmn. of Editorial Bd., and Editorial Page Ed., Business Week mag., NYC; Poynter Fellow, Yale Univ., New Haven, Conn. 1974–75. *Publs:* Sweden Plans for Better Housing, 1948; Forecasting Business Trends, 1959; The Research Revolution, 1960; Veblen (play), 1966; (with P. Saunders) The World of Economics, 1969; Contemporary Economics, 1970; Nixonomics, 1972; (ed. and contrib.) Capitalism: The Moving Target, 1973; The Economists, 1976; Economics in Plain English, 1978, 1986; (with Mark Silk) The American Establishment, 1980; Economics in the Real World, 1985. Add: c/o The New York Times, 229 West 43rd St., New York, N.Y. 10036, U.S.A.

SILKIN, Jon. British, b. 1930. Poetry, Literature. Founding Co-Ed. since 1952, and Ed. since 1968, Stand, Newcastle upon Tyne; Co-Founding Ed., Northern House, publrs., Newcastle upon Tyne, since 1964. *Publs:* The Portrait and Other Poems, 1950; The Peaceable Kingdom, 1954; The Two Freedoms, 1958; (with M. de Sausmarez) Isaac Rosenberg, 1890-1918: Catalogue of the Exhibition Held at Leeds University, May-June 1959; Together with the Text of Unpublished Material, 1959; (ed.) Living Voices: An Anthology of Contemporary Verse, 1960; The Re-ordering of the Stones, 1961; Flower Poems, 1964; (with Richard Murphy and Nathaniel Tarn) Penguin Modern Poets 7, 1965; Nature with Man, 1965; Poems New and Selected, 1966; (trans.) Against Parting, by Nathan Zach, 1968; Three Poems, 1969; Killhope Wheel, 1971; Amana Grass, 1971; Out of the Battle: Poetry of the Great War (criticism), 1972; Air That Pricks Earth, 1973; (ed.) Poetry of the Committed Individual: A "Stand" Anthology of Poetry, 1973; The Principle of Water, 1974; The Little Time-Keeper, 1976; (ed.) The Penguin Book of First World War Poetry, 1978; Into Praising, 1978; The Lapidary Poems, 1979; The Psalms with Their Spoils, 1980; Selected Poems, 1980, 1988; Autobiographical Stanzas, 1984; (ed. with Michael Blackburn and Lorna Tracy) Stand One: An Anthology of Stand Magazine Short Stories, 1984; Footsteps on a Downcast Path, 1984; Gurney: A Play in Verse, 1985; The Ship's Pasture, 1986. Add: 19 Haldane Terr., Newcastle upon Tyne NE2 3AN, England.

SILKO, Leslie (Marmon). American, b. 1948. Novels/Short stories, Westerns/Adventure, Poetry. *Publs:* Laguna Woman: Poems, 1974; Ceremony (novel), 1977; Storyteller (includes short stories), 1981; (with James A. Wright) With the Delicacy and Strength of Lace: Letters, 1986. Add: c/o Seaver Books, 333 Central Park W., New York, N.Y. 10025, U.S.A.

SILLITOE, Alan. British, b. 1928. Novels/Short stories, Children's fiction, Plays/Screenplays, Poetry. *Publs:* Without Beer or Bread, 1957; Saturday Night and Sunday Morning, 1958, screenplay 1960; The Loneliness of the Long Distance Runner, 1959, screenplay 1961; The Rats and Other Poems, 1960; The General, 1960; Key to the Door, 1961; The Ragman's Daughter, 1963, screenplay 1970; A Falling Out of Love and Other Poems, 1964; The Road to Volgograd (travel), 1964; The Death of William Posters, 1965; A Tree on Fire, 1967; (with Ruth Fainlight) All Citizens Are Soldiers (adaptation), 1967; The City Adventures of Marmalade Jim, 1967; Guzman Go Home, 1968; Shaman and Other Poems, 1968; Love in the Environs of Voronezh and Other Poems, 1968; This Foreign Field, 1970; A Start in Life, 1971; Travels in Nihilon, 1971; (with T. Hughes and R. Fainlight) Poems, 1971; Raw Material, 1972; Men,

Women, and Children, 1973; The Flame of Life, 1974; Mountains and Caverns, 1975; The Widower's Son, 1976; Three Plays, 1978; Snow on the North Side of Lucifer (verse), 1979; The Storyteller (novel), 1979; More Lucifer, 1980; The Second Chance (stories), 1981; Her Victory, 1982; The Saxon Shore Way (travel), 1982; The Lost Flying Boat (novel), 1983; Down from the Hill (novel), 1984; Sun Before Departure: Poems 1974-1982, 1984; Malmalade Jim and the Fox (for children), 1985; Life Goes On (novel), 1986; (with David Sillitoe) Nottinghamshire (travel), 1987; Out of the Whirlpool (novel), 1987. Add: 21 The Street, Wittersham, Kent, England.

SILMAN, Roberta. American, b. 1934. Novels/Short stories, Children's fiction. Full-time writer. *Publs:* Somebody Else's Child, 1976; Blood Relations, 1977; Boundaries, 1979; The Dream Dredger, 1986. Add: 18 Larchmont St., Ardsley, N.Y. 10502, U.S.A.

SILVER, Daniel J. American, b. 1928. Philosophy, Theology/Religion. Rabbi, The Temple, Cleveland, Ohio, since 1956. Adjunct Prof. of Religion, Case Western Reserve Univ., Cleveland, since 1974; Adjunct Prof. of Religion, Cleveland State Univ., since 1974. Sr. Ed., CCAR Journal, 1964–73. *Publs:* (ed.) In the Time of Harvest, 1963; Maimonidean Criticism and Maimonidean Controversy 1180-1240, 1965; (ed. and contrib.) Judaism and Ethics, 1970; History of Judaism, vol. I, 1974; Images of Moses, 1982; History of Scripture, 1988. Add: The Temple, University Circle at Silver Park, Cleveland, Ohio 44106, U.S.A.

SILVER, Eric. British, b. 1935. Biography. Israel Corresp., The Observer newspaper, London, since 1987. Joined The Guardian, London, 1960; Jerusalem Correspondent, The Guardian and The Observer newspaper, 1972–83; South Asia Corresp, The Guardian, 1984–87). Chmn., Foreign Press Assn. in Israel, 1975. *Publs:* Victor Feather, T.U.C., 1973; Begin: A Biography (in U.S. as Begin: The Haunted Prophet), 1984. Add: 64 Street of the Prophets, Jerusalem 95141, Israel.

SILVER, Harold. British, b. 1928. Education, History, Sociology. Researcher and consultant. Lectr., Hull Coll. of Commerce, 1956–58, and Huddersfield Coll. of Technology, 1958–60; Lectr. and Prof. of Education, Chelsea Coll., Univ. of London, 1961–78; Principal, Bulmershe Coll. of Higher Education, Reading, 1978–86. *Publs:* (trans.) V.I. Chuikov: The Beginning of the Road (in U.S. as The Battle for Stalingrad), 1963; The Concept of Popular Education, 1965; (ed.) Robert Owen on Education, 1969; (with Judith Ryder) Modern English Society, 1970; (with S.J. Teague) The History of British Universities 1800-1969; (ed.) Equal Opportunity in Education, 1973; (with John Lawson) A Social History of Education in England, 1973; (with Pamela Silver) The Education of the Poor, 1974; English Education and the Radicals 1780-1850, 1975; Education and the Social Condition, 1980; Education as History, 1983; (with John Brennan) A Liberal Vocationalism, 1988. Add: 2 William Orchard Close, Headington, Oxford, England.

SILVER, Richard. *See* **BULMER,** Henry Kenneth.

SILVERBERG, Robert. Also writes as Walter Chapman, Ivar Jorgensen, Calvin M. Knox, David Osborne, Lee Sebastian, and with Randall Garrett (now deceased) under joint pseud. Robert Randall. American, b. 1935. Science fiction/Fantasy, Children's fiction, Children's non-fiction, History, Sciences, Biography. Full-time writer. *Publs:* science fiction—Revolt on Alpha (juvenile), 1955; The Thirteenth Immortal, 1957; Master of Life and Death, 1957; (as Robert Randall) The Shrouded Planet, 1957; Invaders from Earth, 1958; Starman's Quest (juvenile), 1958; (as David Osborne) Invincible Barriers, 1958; Stepsons of Terra, 1958; (as David Osborne) Aliens from Space, 1958; (as Ivar Jorgensen) Starhaven, 1958; (as Calvin M. Knox) Lest We Forget Thee, Earth, 1958; (as Calvin M. Knox) The Plot Against Earth, 1959; (as Robert Randall) The Dawning Light, 1959; The Planet Killers, 1959; Lost Race of Mars (juvenile), 1960; Collision Course, 1961; The Seed of Earth, 1962; Recalled to Life, 1962; Next Stop the Stars (short stories), 1962; The Silent Invaders, 1963; Regan's Planet, 1964; (as Calvin M. Knox) One of Our Asteroids Is Missing, 1964; Godling, Go Home! (short stories), 1964; Time of the Great Freeze (juvenile), 1965; Conquerors from the Darkness (juvenile), 1965; Needle in a Timestack (short stories), 1966; The Gate of Worlds (juvenile), 1967; To Open the Sky, 1967; Thorns, 1967; Those Who Watch, 1967; The Time-Hoppers, 1967; Planet of Death, 1967; Hawksbill Station, 1968; in U.K. as The Anvil of Time, 1969; The Masks of Time, 1968, in U.K. as Vornan-19, 1970; (as Ivar Jorgensen) Whom the Gods Would Slay, 1968; The Calibrated Alligator (juvenile short stories), 1969; Dimension Thirteen (short stories), 1969; Up the Line, 1969; Nightwings, 1969; Across a Billion Years (juvenile), 1969; The Man in the Maze (juvenile), 1969;

Three Survived (juvenile), 1969; To Live Again, 1969;World's Fair, 1992 (juvenile), 1970; Downward to the Earth, 1970; Tower of Glass, 1970; Parsecs and Parables (short stories), 1970; The Cube Root of Uncertainty (short stories), 1970; Moonferns and Starsongs (short stories), 1971; The World Inside, 1971; A Time of Changes, 1971; Son of Man, 1971; (as Ivar Jorgensen) The Deadly Sky, 1971; The Reality Trip and Other Implausibilites (short stories), 1972; The Book of Skulls, 1972; Dying Inside, 1972; The Second Trip, 1972; Valley Beyond Time (short stories), 1973; Unfamiliar Territory (short stories), 1973; Earth's Other Shadow (short stories), 1973; Born with the Dead (short stories), 1974; Sundance (short stories), 1974; Sunrise on Mercury (juvenile short stories), 1975; The Feast of St. Dionysus (short stories), 1975; The Stochastic Man, 1975; Shadrach in the Furnace, 1976; The Shores of Tomorrow (short stories), 1976; The Best of Robert Silverberg (short stories), 1976; Capricorn Games (short stories), 1976; The Songs of Summer (short stories), 1979; Lord Valentine's Castle, 1980; Majipoor Chronicles, 1982; World of a Thousand Colors (short stories), 1982; Valentine Pontifex, 1983; Land of Darkness, 1983; The Conglomeroid Cocktail Party, 1984; Tom O'Bedlam, 1985; Sailing to Byzantium, 1985; Star of the Gypsies, 1986; Beyond the Safe Zone (stories), 1986; At Winter's End, 1988; other—Treasures Beneath the Sea (juvenile), 1960; First American into Space, 1961; Lost Cities and Vanished Civilizations (juvenile), 1962; The Fabulous Rockefellers, 1963; Sunken History: The Story of Underwater Archaeology (juvenile), 1963; 15 Battles That Changed the World, 1963; Home of the Red Man: Indian North America Before Columbus (juvenile), 1963; Empires in the Dust, 1963; The Great Doctors (juvenile), 1964; Akhnaten, The Rebel Pharaoh, 1964; The Man Who Found Nineveh: The Story of Austen Henry Layard (juvenile), 1964; Man Before Adam, 1964; (ed.) Great Adventures in Archaeology, 1964; (as Walker Chapman) The Loneliest Continent, 1965; Scientists and Scoundrels: A Book of Hoaxes, 1965; The World of Coral (juvenile), 1965; The Mask of Akhnaten (juvenile), 1965; Socrates (juvenile), 1965; The Old Ones: Indians of the American Southwest, 1965; Men Who Mastered the Atom, 1965; The Great Wall of China, 1965; Niels Bohr, The Man Who Mapped the Atom (juvenile), 1965; Forgotten by Time: A Book of Living Fossils (juvenile), 1966; Frontiers of Archaeology, 1966; (as Walker Chapman) Kublai Khan, Lord of Xanadu (juvenile), 1966;The Long Rampart: The Story of the Great Wall of China, 1966; (as Lee Sebastian) Rivers (juvenile), 1966; Bridges, 1966; To the Rock of Darius: The Story of Henry Rawlinson (juvenile), 1966; (ed.) Earthmen and Strangers, 1966; (ed. as Walker Chapman) Antarctic Conquest, 1966; (ed.) The Voyagers in Time, 1967; The Dawn of Medicine, 1967; The Adventures of Nat Palmer, Arctic Explorer, 1967; The Auk, The Dodo, and the Oryx, 1967; The Golden Dream: Seekers of El Dorado, 1967; Men Against Time; Salvage Archaeology in the United States, 1967; The Morning of Mankind, 1967; The World of the Rain Forest, 1967; Light for the World: Edison and the Power Industry, 1967; Four Men Who Changed the Universe (juvenile), 1968; Ghost Towns of the American West, 1968; Mound Builders of Ancient America, 1968; (as Lee Sebastian) The South Pole (juvenile), 1968; Stormy Voyager: The Story of Charles Wilkes, 1968; The World of the Ocean Depths, 1968; (ed.) Men and Machines, 1968; (ed.) Mind to Mind, 1968; Bruce of the Blue Nile (juvenile), 1969; The Challenge of Climate: Man and His Environment, 1969; Vanishing Giants: The Story of the Sequoias, 1969; Wonders of Ancient Chinese Science, 1969; The World of Space, 1969; (ed.) Tomorrow's Worlds, 1969; (ed.) Dark Stars, 1969; (ed.) Three for Tomorrow, 1969; If I Forget Thee, O Jerusalem: American Jews and the State of Israel, 1970; Mammoths, Mastodons, and Man, 1970; The Pueblo Revolt, 1970; The Seven Wonders of the Ancient World (juvenile), 1970; (ed.) The Mirror of Infinity: A Critics' Anthology of Science Fiction, 1970; (ed.) Science Fiction Hall of Fame I, 1970; (ed.) The Ends of Time, 1970; (ed.) Great Short Novels of Science Fiction, 1970; (ed.) Worlds of Maybe, 1970; (ed.) Alpha 1-9, 9 vols., 1970–78; Before the Sphinx, 1971; Clocks for the Ages: How Scientists Date the Past, 1971; To the Western Shore: Growth of the United States 1776-1853, 1971; (with Arthur C. Clarke) Into Space, 1971; (ed.) Four Futures, 1971; (ed.) The Science Fiction Bestiary, 1971; (ed.) New Dimensions 1-11 (vol. 11 ed. with Marta Randall), 11 vols., 1971–80; John Muir: Prophet among the Glaciers, 1972; The Longest Voyage: Circumnavigation in the Age of Discovery, 1972; The Realm of Prester John, 1972; The World Within the Ocean Wave, 1972; The World Within the Tide Pool, 1972; (ed.) The Day the Sun Stood Still, 1972; (ed.) Invaders from Space, 1972; (ed.) Beyond Control, 1972; (ed.) Deep Space, 1973; (ed.) Chains of the Sea, 1973; (ed.) No Mind of Man, 1973; (ed.) Other Dimensions, 1973; (ed.) Three Trips in Time and Space, 1973; Drug Themes in Science Fiction, 1974; (ed.) Mutants, 1974; (ed.) Threads of Time, 1974; (ed.) Infinite Jest, 1974; (ed.) Windows into Tomorrow, 1974; (ed. with Roger Elwood) Epoch, 1975; (ed.) Explorers of Space, 1975; (ed.) The New Atlantis,

1975; (ed.) Strange Gifts, 1975; (ed.) The Aliens, 1976; (ed.) The Crystal Ship, 1976; (ed.) Triax, 1977; (ed.) Trips in Time, 1977; (ed.) Earth Is the Strangest Planet, 1977; (ed.) Galactic Dreamers, 1977; (ed.) The Infinite Web, 1977; (ed.) The Androids Are Coming, 1979; (ed) Lost Worlds, Unknown Horizons, 1979; (ed.) Edge of Space, 1979; (ed. with Martin H. Greenberg and Joseph D. Olander) Car Sinister, 1979; (ed with Martin H. Greenberg and Joseph D. Olander) Dawn of Time: Prehistory Through Science Fiction, 1979; (ed.) The Best of New Dimensions, 1979; (ed. with Martin H. Greenberg) The Arbor House Treasury of Modern Science Fiction, 1980; (ed. with Martin Greenberg) The Arbor House Treasury of Great Science Fiction Short Novels, 1980; (ed. with Martin H. Greenberg) The Arbor House Treasury of Science Fiction Masterpieces, 1983; (ed. with Martin H. Greenberg) The Time Travelers: A Science Fiction Quartet, 1985; Project Pendulum (juvenile), 1987; (ed.) Robert Silverberg's Worlds of Wonder, 1987. Add: c/o Arbor House, 105 Madison Ave., New York, N.Y. 10016, U.S.A.

SILVERLOCK, Anne. *See* **TITCHENER,** Louise.

SILVERMAN, Hillel E. American, b. 1924. Theology/Religion, Rabbi, Sinai Temple, Los Angeles, Calif., 1964–81, and Temple Sholom, Greenwich, Conn., since, 1981. *Publs:* (with M. Silverman) Prayer Book for Summer Camp, 1954; (with M. Silverman) Selihot Service, 1955; (with M. Silverman) Tishav B'av Service, 1955; Judaism Looks at Life, 1968; Judaism Meets the Challenge, 1972; From Week to Week, 1974; From Heart to Heatrt, 1979. Add: c/o Prayer Book Press, 1363 Fairfield Ave., Bridgeport, Conn. 06605, U.S.A.

SILVERMAN, Jerry. American, b. 1931. Music, Mythology/Folklore, Translations. *Publs:* Folk Blues, 1958; Folksinger's Guitar Guide, 1962; Art of the Folk Blues Guitar, 1964; Beginning the Folk Guitar, 1964; Folksinger's Guitar Guide, vol. 2, 1966; (trans.) Russian Songs, 1966; Flat Picker's Guitar Guide, 1966; Sixty-Two Outrageous Songs, 1966; A Folksinger's Guide to Note Reading and Music Theory, 1966; The Chord Player's Encyclopedia, 1967; How to Play the Guitar, 1968; Graded Guitar, 10 vols., 1970; That Good Old Razza Ma Tazz, 1970; Folksongs for Schools and Camps, 1971; The Liberated Woman's Songbook, 1971; How to Play Better Guitar, 1972; Beginning the Five-String Banjo, 1974; Jerry Silverman Folk Guitar Method Book, 1974; Jerry Silverman Folk Harmonica, 1974; Jerry Silverman Blues Harmonica, 1974; The Folksong Encyclopedia, 1975; Ragtime Guitar, 1975; How to Play Country Fiddle, 1975; Favorite Folk Songs, 1976; Children's Songs, 1976; Blues, 1976; Love Songs, 1976; Bluegrass, 1976; Folksongs for Flute, 1977; Folk Guitar—Folk Songs, 1977; How Can I Keep from Singing, 1977; Folksongs for Voice and Classical Guitar, 1977; The Back Packer's Song Book, 1977; Favorite Christmas Songs and Carols, 1977; Ragtime Solos and Duets, 1978; No More Booze, 1978; Look, Listen, and Learn Guitar, 1979; Guitar Folk Styles, 1979; The Young Guitarist, 2 vols., 1980; Sing and Play Blues, 1980; Sing and Play Ragtime, 1980; Easy Folk Fiddle, 2 vols., 1980; Play Guitar in 15 Lessons, 1982; Bass Runs and Arpeggios for Guitar, 1982; How to Play Blues Guitar, 1982; How to Play Ragtime Guitar, 1982; How to Play Bluegrass Guitar, 1982; How to Sing Higher and Lower, 1982; Scales into Chords, 1982; Pop Guitar Hits—Fingerstyle, 1983; Country and Western Guitar Hits—Fingerstyle, 1983. Add: 160 High St., Hastings-on-Hudson, N.Y. 10706, U.S.A.

SILVERN, Leonard C(harles). American, b. 1919. Education, Engineering/ Technology, Physics. Pres., Education and Training Consultants Co., Sedona, Ariz., since 1968 (Principal Scientist, 1964–66; Vice-Pres., 1967–68); Pres., Systems Engineering Labs. Reviewer, Computing Reviews, Assn. for Computing Machinery, since 1962; Registered professional consulting engineer, State of California, since 1969. Adjunct Prof., Univ. of Southern California, 1957–65; Visiting Prof., Univ. of California Extension, 1963–72; Contrib. Ed., Educational Technology, 1968–73. *Publs:* Fundamentals of Teaching Machine and Programmed Learning Systems, 3 vols., 1964; Administrative Factors Guide for Fundamentals Course, 1964; (with D. Perrin) Systems Engineering of Learning: The Training System, 1964; Systems Engineering of Education series, 19 vols., 1965–79; Basic Analysis, 1965; Administrative Factors Guide to Basic Analysis, 1965; (with G.M. Silvern) Elements of EYBOL, 1966; Analysis asProcess, 1966; Model Concepts and Simulation, 1966; Systems Using Feedback, 1966; Examination of System Conceptualizations, 1914-1964; 1966; Synthesis as a Process, 1966; Basic Synthesis, 1970; Systems Engineering Applied to Training, 1972; Simulating a Real-life Problem on the General System Model, 1972; Roles of Feedback and Feedforward During Simulation, 1974; Application of Systems Thinking to the Administration of Instruction, 1976; Preparing Occupational Instruction, 1977; Systems Engineering Applied to Radio Communications

(SEARCH), 1980; (ed.) Proceedings of the National Solid Waste Management Symposium, 1989. Add: Box 2085, Sedona, Ariz. 86336, U.S.A.

SILVERSTEIN, Shel(by). Also writes as Uncle Shelby. American, b. 1932. Children's fiction, Poetry, Humor/Satire. Free-lance writer and cartoonist for Playboy, Chicago, and other magazines; also composer and song writer. *Publs:* Now Here's My Plan: A Book of Futilities (drawings), 1960; Uncle Shelby's ABZ Book: A Primer for Tender Young Minds (children's fiction), 1961; Playboy's Teevee Jeebies (drawings), 1963; Uncle Shelby's Story of Lafcadio, The Lion Who Shot Back (children's fiction), 1963; Who Wants a Cheap Rhinoceros? (children's fiction), 1964; The Giving Tree (children's fiction), 1964; Uncle Shelby's A Giraffe and A Half (children's verse), 1964; Uncle Shelby's Zoo: Don't Bump the Glump! (children's verse), 1964; More Playboy Teevee Jeebies (drawings), 1965; Where the Sidewalk Ends: The Poems and Drawings of Shel Silverstein (children's verse), 1974; The Missing Piece (children's fiction), 1976; Different Dances (drawings), 1979; The Missing Piece Meets the Big O (children's fiction), 1981; A Light in the Attic: Poems and Drawings (children's verse), 1982; (with David Mamet) Things Change (screenplay), 1988. Add: c/o Harper and Row, 10 E. 53rd Street, New York, N.Y. 10022, U.S.A.

SILVERSTEIN, Theodore. American, b. 1904. Literature, Philosophy, Theology/Religion. Prof. of English Emeritus, Univ. of Chicago (former Prof. of English, and Chmn., Cttee. for the Analysis of Ideas and the Study of Methods). *Publs:* Visio Sancti Pauli: A Study of the Apocalypse in Latin Together with Nine Texts, 1935; Medieval Latin Scientific Writings in the Barberini Collection: A Provisional Catalogue, 1957; (ed.) Medieval English Lyrics (in U.S. as English Lyrics Before 1500), 1971; Sir Gawain and the Green Knight, 1974; (trans.) Poeti e Filosofi Medievali, 1975; Salerno and the Development of Theory, 1978; Sir Gawain and the Green Knight: A New Critical Edition, 1984. Add: 5807 South Dorchester Ave., Chicago, Ill. 60637, U.S.A.

SILVERWOOD, Jane. *See* **TITCHENER,** Louise.

SILVESTER, Frank. *See* **BINGLEY,** David Ernest.

SIM, Katharine Phyllis. British, b. 1913. Novels/Short stories, Travel/Exploration/Adventure, Biography. *Publs:* Malayan Landscape, 1946; These I Have Loved, 1947; Malacca Boy, 1957; The Moon at My Feet, 1959; Flowers of the Sun: An Appreciation of the Malay Pantun, 1959; Costumes of Malaya, 1960; Black Rice, 1960; The Jungle Ends Here, 1961; Journey Out of Asia, 1962; Desert Traveller: The Life of Jean Louis Burckhardt, 1969; David Roberts, R.A., 1983. Add: Maescanol, Pencarreg, Llanybydder, SA40 9QJ, Wales.

SIME, Mary. British, b. 1911. Education, Psychology. Freelance lectr., and external examiner. Principal Lectr. in Education, Chorley Coll. of Education, Lancs., 1963–76, now retired. *Publs:* A Child's Eye View: Piaget for Young Parents and Teachers, 1973; Read Your Child's Thought: Preschool Learning Piaget's Way, 1980. Add: 105 Mell Rd., Tollesbury, Essex, England.

SIMIC, Charles. American, b. 1938. Poetry, Translations. Assoc. Prof. of English, Univ. of New Hampshire, Durham, since 1974. Editorial Asst., Aperture mag., NYC, 1966–69. *Publs:* What the Grass Says, 1967; Somewhere Among Us a Stone Is Taking Notes, 1969; (ed. and trans.) Five Gardens, by Luan Lauc, 1970; (ed. and trans.) Selected Poems, by Ivan V. Lalic, 1970; (ed. and trans.) Four Yugoslav Poets: Ivan V. Lalic, Brank Miljkovic, Milorad Pavic, Ljubomir Simovic, 1970; (ed. and trans.) The Little Box: Poems, by Vaco Popa, 1970; Dismantling the Silence, 1971; White, 1972; Return to a Place Lit by a Glass of Milk, 1974; (co-ed.) Another Republic, 1976; Charon's Cosmology, 1977; (trans.) Key to Dreams According to Djordje, 1978; Brooms: Selected Poems, 1978; School for Dark Thoughts, 1978; Classic Ballroom Dances, 1980; Shaving at Night, 1982; Austerities, 1982; Weather Forecast for Utopia and Vicinity: Poems 1967-1982, 1983; Selected Poems 1963-83, 1985; The Uncertain Certainty, 1985; Unending Blues, 1986; The World Doesn't End, 1989. Add: Dept. of English, Univ. of New Hampshire, Durham, N.H. 03824, U.S.A.

SIMMIE, James (Martin). British, b. 1941. Public/Social administration, Regional/Urban planning, Sociology. Lectr. in Urban Sociology, University Coll., London, since 1970. Ed., Sociology, Politics, and Cities, since 1976. Sr. Lectr., Oxford Polytechnic, 1965–70. *Publs:* The Sociology of Internal Migration, 1972; Citizens in Conflict, 1974; Power, Property, and Corporatism, 1981; (with S. French) Corporatism, Participation, and Planning: The Case of Contemporary London, 1989. Add:

University Coll., Gower St., London WC1, England.

SIMMONS, D(avid) R(oy). New Zealander, b. 1930. Anthropology/Ethnology. Ethnologist, Auckland Inst. and Museum, since 1968 (Asst. Dir., 1978–85). Asst. Keeper in Anthropology, 1962–64, and Keeper, 1965–67, Otago Museum, Dunedin. *Publs:* (ed.) C. Servant: Habits and Customs of the New Zealanders 1838-42, 1972; (ed.) J.D.H. Buchanan: Maori History and Place Names of Hawkes Bay, 1973; The Great New Zealand Myth: A Study of the Origin and Migration Traditions of the Maori, 1975; (with Brian Brake and James McNeish) Art of the Pacific, 1979; A Catalogue of Maori Artefacts in the Museums of Canada and the U.S.A., 1982; Whakairo: Maori Tribal Art, 1985; Ta Moko: The Art of Maori Tattooing, 1986. Add: 12 Minto Rd., Remuera, New Zealand.

SIMMONS, Jack. British. History, Literature, Transportation. Lectr., Oxford Univ., 1943–47; Prof. of History, 1947–75, Pro-Vice-Chancellor, 1960–63, and Public Orator, 1965–68, Univ. of Leicester. Pres., Leicestershire Archaeological and Historical Soc., 1966–77; Chmn., Leicester Broadcasting Council, 1967–70; Member, Advisory Council, Science Museum, London. 1969–84; Chmn. of the Cttee., National Railway Museum, York, 1981–84. *Publs:* (with Margery Perham) African Discovery: An Anthology of Exploration, 1942; Southey, 1945; (ed.) Letters from England, by Southey, 1951; (ed.) Journeys in England: An Anthology, 1951; Parish and Empire: Studies and Sketches, 1952; Livingstone and Africa, 1955; New University, 1958; The Railways of Britain: An Historical Introduction, 1961, 3rd ed. 1986; Transport, 1962; Britain and the World, 1965; St. Pancras Station, 1968; Transport Museums in Britain and Western Europe, 1970; (ed.) A Devon Anthology, 1971; Leicester Past and Present, 2 vols., 1974; (ed.) Rail 150: The Stockton and Darlington Railway and What Followed, 1975; The Railway in England and Wales 1830-1914, 1978; A Selective Guide to England, 1978; Dandy Cart to Diesel: The National Railway Museum, 1981; (ed.) The Men Who Built Railways, 1983; The Railway in Town and Country 1830-1914, 1986. Add: Flat 6, 36 Victoria Park Rd., Leicester LE2 1XB, England.

SIMMONS, James (Stewart Alexander). British, b. 1933. Poetry. Member of English Dept., New Univ. of Ulster, Coleraine, 1968 until retirement, 1984; Writer-in-Residence, Queen's Univ. of Belfast, since 1989. Ed., Poetry and Audience, Leeds, 1957–58; Founder, The Honest Ulsterman, Portrush, N. Ire., 1963. *Publs:* (ed.) Out on the Edge, 1958; Ballad ofMarriage, 1966; (with T.W. Harrison) Aikin Mata: The Lysistrata of Aristophanes, 1966; In the Wilderness and Other Poems, 1969; Songs for Derry, 1969; No Ties, 1970; Energy to Burn: Poems, 1971; No Land is Waste, Dr. Eliot, 1972; The Long Summer Still to Come, 1971; West Strand Visions, 1974; (ed.) Ten Irish Poets: An Anthology, 1974; Judy Garland and the Cold War, 1976; The Selected James Simmons, 1978; Constantly Singing, 1980; Sean O'Casey, 1983; From the Irish, 1985; Poems 1956-1986, 1986. Add: 134 My Lady's Rd., Belfast, Northern Ireland.

SIMMONS, Marc (Steven). American, b. 1937. History. Visiting Asst. Prof. of History, Univ. of New Mexico, 1965–66 and 1967–68. *Publs:* (trans. and ed.) Border Comanches, 1967; Spanish Government in New Mexico, 1968; Yesterday in Santa Fe, 1969; The Little Lion of the Southwest: A Life of Manuel Antonio Chaves, 1973; Witchcraft in the Southwest, 1974; Turquoise and Six-Guns, 1974; New Mexico, 1977; People of the Sun, 1979; Southwestern Colonial Ironwork, 1980; Albuquerque: A Narrative History, 1982;Ranchers, Ramblers, and Renegades, 1984; Following the Santa Fe Trail, 1984; (ed.) On the Santa Fe Trail, 1986; Taos to Tome, 1986. Add: Box 51, Cerrillos, N.M. 87010, U.S.A.

SIMMS, Eric (Arthur). British, b. 1921. Natural history. Member, Advisory Cttee. on Bird Sanctuaries in the Royal Parks, London, since 1972; Vice-Pres., Friends of the Brent Gomis Symphony Orch., since 1975; Member, Advisory Panel, World Wildlife Fund, since 1976. Schoolmaster, 1946–50; Resident Naturalist to BBC, 1951–57; Producer, BBC television, 1958–67; Justice of the Peace, 1965–68. Council Member, Royal Soc. for the Protection of Birds, 1953–63. *Publs:* Bird Migrants, 1952; Voices of the Wild, 1957; (co-author) Witherby's Sound-Guide to British Birds, 1958; Woodland Birds, 1971; Wild Life in the Royal Parks, 1974; Birds of Town and Suburb, 1975; Live and Let Live, 1975; Birds of the Air (autobiography), 1976; British Thrushes, 1978; Public Life of the Street Pigeon, 1979; Natural History of Britain and Ireland, 1979; Wild Life Sounds and Their Recordings, 1979; Natural History of Birds, 1982. Add: Meon, 85 Brook Rd., Dollis Hill, London NW2 7DR, England.

SIMON, Arthur. American, b. 1930. Social commentary phenomena. Exec. Dir., Bread for the World. Pastor, Trinity Lutheran Church, NYC, 1961–74. *Publs:* Faces of Poverty, 1966; Stuyvesant Town U.S.A.:Pattern for Two Americas, 1970; Breaking Bread with the Hungry, 1971; Bread for the World, 1976, 1985; Christian Faith and Public Policy, 1987. Add: 602 E. 9th St., New York, N.Y. 10009, U.S.A.

SIMON, Edith. British, b. 1917. Novels/Short stories, Children's fiction, History, Translations. Painter and sculptor. *Publs:* Somersaults and Strange Company (children's fiction), 1937; (trans.) Arthur Koestler: The Gladiators, 1938; The Chosen, 1940; Biting the Blue Finger, 1942; Wings Deceive, 1943; The Other Passion, 1947; The Golden Hand, 1952; The Past Masters (in U.S. as The House of Strangers), 1953; The Twelve Pictures, 1955; The Sable Coat, 1956; The Piebald Standard (in U.S. as Knights Templars), 1957; The Great Forgery, 1960; The Making of Frederick the Great, 1962; The Reformation, 1968; The Saints, 1969; Luther Alive: The Making of the Reformation, 1970; The Anglo-Saxon Manner, 1972. Add: 11 Grosvenor Cres., Edinburgh EH12 5EL, Scotland.

SIMON, Herbert A(lexander). American, b. 1916. Administration/ Management, Psychology. Richard King Mellon Univ. Prof. of Computer Sciences and Psychology, Carnegie-Mellon Univ., Pittsburgh, since 1965 (Prof. of Admin. and Psychology, 1949–65). Assoc. Prof. and Prof., Illinois Inst. of Technology, 1945–49. Chmn., Div. of Behavioral Sciences, National Research Council, 1968–70; Member, President's Science Advisory Cttee., 1968–71. *Publs:* (with C.E. Ridley) Measuring Municipal Activities, 1938; (with others) Determining Work Loads for Professional Staff in a Public Welfare Agency, 1941; Fiscal Aspects of Metropolitan Administration, 1943; (with others) Fire Losses and Fire Risks, 1943; Administrative Behavior: A Study of Decision-Making Processes in Administrative Organization, 1947; Techniques of Municipal Administration, 1947; (with others) Public Administration, 1950; (with others) Centralization vs. Decentralization in Organizing the Controller's Department, 1954; Models of Man, Social and Rational: Mathematical Essays on Rational Human Behavior in a Social Setting, 1957; (with John G. March) Organizations, 1958; The New Science of Management Decision, 1960, as The Shape of Automation for Men and Management, 1965; The Sciences of the Artificial, 1969; (with A. Newell) Human Problem Solving, 1972; Models of Discovery and Other Topics in the Methods of Science, 1977; Models of Thought, 2 vols., 1979, 1989; Models of Bounded Rationality, 2 vols., 1982; Reason in Human Affairs, 1983; (with K.A. Ericsson) Protocol Analysis, 1984; (with others) Scientific Discovery, 1987. Add: Dept. of Psychology, Carnegie-Mellon Univ., Pittsburgh, Pa. 15213, U.S.A.

SIMON, Julian L(incoln). American, b. 1932. Advertising/Public relations, Demography, Economics, Marketing. Prof. of Marketing, Univ. of Illinois, Urbana, since 1969. First Lipson Prof. of Intnl. Marketing, Hebrew Univ., Jerusalem, 1970–71. *Publs:* How to Start and Operate a Mail-Order Business, 1965, 4th ed. 1987; Basic Research Methods in Social Science, 1969, 3rd ed. 1985; (with H.H. Fussler) Patterns of Use of Books in Large Research Libraries, 1969; Issues in the Economics of Advertising, 1970; The Management of Advertising, 1971; The Effects of Income on Fertility, 1973; Applied Managerial Economics, 1974; The Economics of Population Growth, 1975; (ed.) Research in Population Economics, 4 vols., 1978–82; The Ultimate Shortage, 1980; The Ultimate Resource, 1982; (co-ed.) The Resourceful Earth: Population and Economic Growth Theory, 1985; Effort, Opportunity and Wealth, 1987. Add: Dept. of Marketing, Univ. of Illinois, Urbana, Ill. 61801, U.S.A.

SIMON, Michael A. American, b. 1936. Philosophy, Sciences (general). Prof. of Philosophy, State Univ. of New York, Stony Brook, since 1985 (Assoc. Prof., 1978–85). Instr. of Philosophy, Hamilton Coll., Clinton, N.Y., 1964–66; Asst. Prof., 1966–71, and Assoc. Prof., 1971–78, Univ. of Connecticut, Storrs. *Publs:* The Matter Of Life: Philosophical Problems of Biology, 1971; Understanding Human Action: Social Explanation and the Vision of Social Science, 1982. Add: 320 N. Village Ave., Rockville Centre, N.Y. 11570, U.S.A.

SIMON, (Marvin) Neil. American, b. 1927. Plays/Screenplays. Writer for television, 1951–60, for the stage and screen, since 1961. *Publs:* Plays—(with W. Friedberg) Adventures of Marco Polo: A Musical Fantasy, 1959; (adaptor with W. Friedberg) Heidi, 1959; (with D. Simon) Come Blow Your Horn, 1961; Little Me, 1962; Barefoot in the Park, 1964; The Odd Couple, 1966 (Tony Award); Sweet Charity, 1966; The Star-Spangled Girl, 1967; Plaza Suite, 1969; Promises, Promises, 1969; Last of the Red Hot Lovers, 1970; The Gingerbread Lady, 1971; The Prisoner of Second Avenue, 1972; The Comedy of Neil Simon, 1972; The Sunshine Boys, 1973; The Good Doctor, 1974; God's Favorite, 1975; California Suite, 1977; Chapter Two, 1979; Collected Plays 2, 1979; They're Playing Our Song, 1980; I Ought to Be in Pictures, 1981; Fools, 1982; Brighton Beach Memoirs, 1984; Actors and Actresses, 1984; Biloxi Blues, 1985 (Tony Award); The Odd Couple (female version), 1985; Broadway Bound, 1986; Rumours, 1988. Add: c/o Da Silva and Da Silva, 502 Park Ave., Suite 10G, New York, N.Y. 10022, U.S.A.

SIMON, Rita J(ames). American, b. 1931. Law, Sociology. Dir., Law and Society Program, and Prof. of Sociology, Law and Communications Research, Univ. of Illinois, Urbana, since 1975 (Assoc. Prof. and Prof. in the Sociology Dept. and Inst. of Communications Research, 1963–67; Prof. and Head of the Sociology Dept., 1968–70; Prof. of Sociology, Research; Prof. of Communications, and Prof. in the Coll., of Law, 1971–74). Member of the Council, American Sociological Assn., 1971–73; Ed., American Sociological Review 1977–80. *Publs:* The Jury and the Defense of Insanity, 1967; (ed.) As We Saw the Thirties, 1967; (ed.) Readings in the Sociology of Law, 1968; (with Jeffrey O' Connell) Payment for Pain and Suffering, 1972; American Public Opinion: 1937-1970, 1974; Women and Crime, 1975; (ed.) The Jury System, 1975; (with Howard Altstein) Transracial Adoption, 1977; Continuity and Change: A Study of Two Ethnic Communities in Israel, 1978; (ed.) Research in Law and Sociology, 1978; (ed. with Freda Adler) The Criminology of Deviant Women, 1979; The American Jury, 1980; New Lives: The Adjustment of Soviet Jewish Immigrants in the United States and Israel, 1985; (co-ed.) International Migration: The Female Experience, 1986. Add: Dept. of Sociology, Univ. of Illinois, Urbana, Ill, 61801, U.S.A.

SIMON, Robert. *See* **MUSTO, Barry.**

SIMON, Roger L(ichtenberg). American, b. 1943. Novels/Short stories, Mystery/Crime/Suspense. *Publs:* Heir, 1968; The Mama Tass Manifesto, 1970; The Big Fix, 1973; Wild Turkey, 1975; Peking Duck, 1979; California Roll, 1985; The Straight Man, 1986; Dead Meet, 1988; Raising the Dead, 1988. Add: c/o Warner Books, 666 Fifth Ave., New York, N.Y. 10103, U.S.A.

SIMON, Seymour. American, b. 1931. Children's non-fiction. Former science teacher. *Publs:* Animals in Field and Laboratory: Science Projects in Animal Behaviour, 1968; Look-It-Up Book of the Earth, 1968; Motion, 1969; Discovering What Earthworms Do, 1969; Discovering What Frogs Do, 1969; Exploring with a Microscope, 1969; Let's Try It Out; Wet and Dry, 1969; Weather and Climate, 1969; Discovering What Goldfish Do, 1970; Handful of Soil, 1970; Light and Dark, 1970; Science in a Vacant Lot, 1970; Chemistry in the Kitchen, 1971; Discovering What Gerbils Do, 1971; Finding Out with Your Senses, 1971; Paper Airplane Book, 1971; Science at Work: Easy Models You Can Make, 1971; Science at Work: Projects in Space Science, 1971; Hot and Cold, 1972; Science at Work: Projects in Oceanography, 1972; Science Projects in Ecology, 1972; Science Projects in Pollution, 1972; A Building on Your Street, 1973; Discovering What Crickets Do, 1973; From Shore to Ocean Floor: How Life Survives in the Sea, 1973; The Paper Airplane Book, 1973; Projects with Plants: A Science at Work Book, 1973; The Rock-Hound's Book, 1973; A Tree on Your Street, 1973; Birds on Your Street, 1974; Life in the Dark: How Animals Survive at Night, 1974; Water on Your Street, 1974; Pets in a Jar, 1975; Projects with Air, 1975; Discovering What Garter Snakes Do, 1975; Ghosts, 1976; Life on Ice, 1976; Everything Moves, 1976; The Optical Illusion Book, 1976; Tropical Saltwater Aquariums, 1976; Life and Death, 1976; Animals in Your Neighborhood, 1976; Discovering What Puppies Do, 1977; Beneath Your Feet, 1977; Space Monsters, 1977; What Do You Want to Know about Guppies, 1977; Look to the Night Sky, 1977; Exploring Fields and Lots, 1978; Killer Whales, 1978; About Your Lungs, 1978; Animal Fact/Animal Fable, 1979; Danger from Below, 1979; The Secret Clocks, 1979; Meet the Giant Snakes, 1979; Creatures from Lost Worlds, 1979; The Long View into Space, 1979; Deadly Ants, 1979; About the Foods You Eat, 1979; Strange Mysteries, 1980; Mirror Magic, 1980; Silly Animal Jokes and Riddles, 1980; Einstein Anderson series, 6 vols., 1980–82; Science Sleuth, 1980; Poisonous Snakes, 1981; Mad Scientists, 1981; About Your Brain, 1981; Strange Creatures, 19 1; Body Sense/Body Nonsense, 1981; The Smallest Dinosaurs, 1982; How to Be a Space Scientist in Your Own Home, 1982; The Long Journey from Space, 1982; How to Talk to Your Computer, 1985; Saturn, 1985; Shadow Magic, 1985; Jupiter, 1985; The Largest Dinosaurs, 1985; Stars, 1986; The Sun, 1986; Mars, 1987; Uranus, 1987; Icebergs and Glaciers, 1987; Galaxies, 1988; Volcanoes, 1988; How to be an Ocean Scientist in Your Own Home, 1988; Storms, 1989; The New Question and Answer Book about Dinosaurs, 1989; Whales, 1989. Add: 4 Sheffield Rd., Great Neck, N.Y. 11021, U.S.A.

SIMON, Sheldon Weiss. American, b. 1937. Politics/Government, Third World problems. Prof. of Political Science, Arizona State Univ., Tempe, since 1975. Asst. Prof., 1966–69, Assoc. Prof., 1969–74, and Prof., 1974–75, Univ. of Kentucky, Lexington. *Publs:* The Broken Triangle: Peking, Djakarta and the PKI, 1969; War and Politics in Cambodia: A Communications Analysis, 1974; Asian Neutralism and U.S. Policy, 1975; The Military and Security in the Third World, 1978; The Asean States and Regional Security, 1982; The Future of Asian-Pacific Security Collaboration, 1988. Add: Dept. of Political Science, Arizona State Univ., Tempe, Ariz. 85281, U.S.A.

SIMONS, Beverley. Canadian, b. 1938. Novels/Short stories, Plays/Screenplays. *Publs:* The Beauty (short story), 1965; The Elephant and the Jewish Question, 1968; Green Lawn Rest Home, 1969; Crabdance, 1969, 1972; Preparing (includes Prologue, Triangle, Crusader, and Green Lawn Rest Home), 1975. Add: 5202 Marine Dr., W. Vancouver, B.C. V7W 2P8, Canada.

SIMONSON, Harold P. American, b. 1926. Literature, Theology/Religion, Biography. Prof. of English, Univ. of Washington, Seattle, since 1968. *Publs:* (ed.) Cross Currents, 1959; Zona Gale, 1962; (with P. Hager) Salinger's Catcher in the Rye, 1963; (ed.) Trio: Stories, Plays, Poems, 1963; Writing Essays, 1966; Francis Grierson, 1966; (ed.) American Perspectives, 1968; (ed.) Quartet: Stories, Plays, Poems, Critical Essays, 1970; (ed.) Significance of the Frontier in American History, by F.J. Turner, 1970; (ed.) The Valley of Shadows, by F. Grierson (memoirs), 1970; The Closed Frontier, 1970; Strategies in Criticism, 1971; (with J. Magee) Dimensions of Man, 1973; Jonathan Edwards: Theologian of the Heart, 1974; Radical Discontinuities: Romantic Imagination and Christian Consciousness, 1983; Prairies Within: The Tragic Trilogy o f Ole Rolvaag, 1987; Beyond the Frontier: Writers, Western Regionalism, and a Sense of Place, 1989. Add: P.O. Box 7487, Tacoma, Wash. 98407, U.S.A.

SIMPSON, A(lfred) W(illiam) Brian. British, b. 1931. History, Law. Prof. of Law, Univ. of Michigan, Ann Arbor, since 1987. Fellow and Tutor in Jurisprudence, Lincoln Coll., Oxford, 1955–73; Prof. of Law, Univ. of Kent at Canterbury, 1973–84, and Univ. of Chicago, 1984–87. *Publs:* Introduction to the History of the Land Law, 1961; (ed. and contrib.) Oxford Essays in Jurisprudence: Second Series, 1973; A History of the Common Law of Contract, 1975; Pornography and Politics, 1983; (ed. and contr.) A Biographical Dict. of the Common Laws, 1984; Cannibalism and the Common Law, 1984; Invitation to Law, 1987; Legal Theory and Legal History, 1987. Add: Univ. of Michigan Law Sch., Ann Arbor, Mich. 48109-1215, U.S.A.

SIMPSON, Colin. Australian, b. 1908. Travel/Exploration/Adventure. Journalist, 1928–47; Radio Documentary Writer, A.B.C., 1947–50. *Publs:* Adam in Ochre, 1951; Come Away Pearler, 1952; Adam with Arrows, 1953; Adam in Plumes, 1954; Islands of Men, 1955; The Country Upstairs (in U.K. as Picture of Japan; in U.S. as Japan, An Intimate View), 1956, rev. ed. 1969; Australian Image, 1956; Wake Up Europe (in U.S. as Europe, An Intimate View) 1959; Show Me a Mountain, 1961; Asia's Bright Balconies, 1962; Take Me to Spain, 1963; Take Me to Russia (in U.S. as This is Russia), 1964; The Viking Circle, 1966; Katmandu, 1967; Greece, The Unclouded Eye, 1968; The New Australia, 1971; Bali and Beyond, 1971; Off to Asia, 1972; This is Japan, 1975; Wake Up to New Zealand, 1976; Pleasure Islands of the South Pacific, 1979; Blue Africa, 1981. Add: 4/13 Moruben Rd., Mosman, N.S.W. 2088, Australia.

SIMPSON, David Penistan. British, b. 1917. Classics. Asst. Master, Eton Coll, 1946–81: Head of Classical Dept., 1954–61; House Master, 1956–72. *Publs:* Cassell's New Latin Dictionary, 1959; Cassell's New Compact Latin Dictionary, 1963; First Principles of Latin Prose, 1965; (with P.H. Vellacott) Writing in Latin, 1970. Add: Ailanthi, Shepton Beauchamp, Ilminster, Somerset, England.

SIMPSON, Dick. American, b. 1940. Politics/Government. Assoc. Prof. of Political Science, Univ. of Illinois at Chicago, since 1972 (Instr., 1967–68; Asst. Prof., 1968–72). Exec. Dir., Metro-Chicago Clergy and Laity Concerned, since 1987. Alderman, 44th Ward, City of Chicago, 1971–79. *Publs:* Who Rules? Introduction to the Study of Politics, 1970, 1972; (with others) The Politics of Cultural Subnationalism, 1972; Winning Elections: A Handbook in Participatory Politics, 1972, 3rd ed. 1980; (with George Beam) Strategies for Change, 1976; (ed.) Chicago's Future, in a Time of Change, 1976, 3rd ed. 1988; Neighborhood Government in Chicago's 44th Ward, 1979; (with others) Illinois: Political Processes and Government Performance, 1980; (with others) Volunteerism in the

Eighties, 1982; (ed. with Charles Williams) Blueprint of Chicago Government, 1983; (with George Beam) Political Action, 1984; (ed. with Clinton Stockwell) Justice Ministries: Fighting Against Hunger, Homelessness and Joblessness, 1984, 1987; (ed. with Clinton Stockwell) Justice Ministries: The Struggle for Peace, Justice and Sanctuary, 1985; The Politics of Compassion and Transformation, 1989. Add: Dept. of Political Science, Univ. of Illinois at Chicago Circle, Box 4348, Chicago, Ill. 60680, U.S.A.

SIMPSON, Dorothy (née Preece). British, b. 1933. Mystery/Crime/Suspense. Teacher of English and French, Dartford Grammar Sch. for Girls, Kent, 1955–59, and Erith Grammar Sch., Kent, 1959–61; Teacher of English, Senacre Sch., Maidstone, Kent, 1961–62; marriage guidance counsellor, 1969–82. *Publs:* Harbingers of Fear, 1977; The Night She Died, 1981; Six Feet Under, 1982; Puppet for a Corpse, 1983; Close Her Eyes, 1984; Last Seen Alive, 1985; Dead on Arrival, 1986; Element of Doubt, 1987; Suspicious Death, 1988; Dead by Morning, 1989. Add: c/o Anne McDermid, Curtis Brown, 162-168 Regent St., London W1R 5TA, England.

SIMPSON, E(rvin) P(eter) Y(oung). American (b. New Zealander), b. 1911. History, Theology/Religion. Holder of C. Shirley Donnelly Chair of History, and Prof. of History, Alderson-Broaddus Coll., Philippi, W. Va., 1969–77, now retired. Engaged in pastoral ministry, Baptist Union of New Zealand, 1936–49; Assoc. Prof. of Biblical Studies, 1950–55, and Prof. of Church History, 1955–67, Berkeley Baptist Divinity Sch., Calif.; Prof. of Church History, Grad. Theological Union, Berkeley, Calif., 1963–67; Sr. Lectr. in History, Massey Univ., Palmerston North, NZ, 1967–69. *Publs:* The History of the New Zealand Baptist Missionary Society, 1949; A History of the Baptists in New Zealand, 1953; Ordination and Christian Unity, 1966; A Plan for the Development of an Indian University at Bacone College, 1980; History of Alderson-Broaddus College 1812-1951, 1983. Add: 13 Greystone Dr., Philippi, W. Va 26416, U.S.A.

SIMPSON, Jacqueline (Mary). British, b. 1930. History, Language/Linguistics, Mythology/Folklore, Translations. *Publs:* (ed.) Heimskringla: The Olaf Sagas, 2 vols., 1964; (trans. and ed.) The Northmen Talk, 1965; (with G.N. Garmonsway) The Penguin English Dictionary, 1965, 3rd ed. 1979; Everyday Life in the Viking Age, 1967, 1969; (trans. with G.N. Garmonsway) Beowulf and Its Analogues, 1968; (trans. and ed.) Icelandic Folktales and Legends, 1972; The Folklore of Sussex, 1973; (trans. and ed.) Legends of Icelandic Magicians, 1975; The Folklore of the Welsh Border, 1976; The Viking World, 1980; British Dragons, 1980; European Folklore, 1987; Scandinavian Folktales, 1988. Add: 9 Christchurch Rd., Worthing, Sussex BN11 1JH, England.

SIMPSON, Lewis P(earson). American, b. 1916. Intellectual history, Literature. Boyd Prof. of English, and Co-Ed., The Southern Review, Louisiana State Univ., Baton Rouge, now Emeritus (joined faculty, 1948). Ed., Library of Southern Civilization, Louisiana State Univ. Press, since 1970.Member, Editorial Bd., American Literature, 1969–72; Selection Bd. Member, Library of America, since 1979. *Publs:* (ed.) The Federalist Literary Mind, 1962; (ed.) Profile of Robert Frost, 1971; The Man of Letters in New England and the South, 1973; The Dispossessed Garden: Pastoral and History in Southern Literature, 1975; (ed.) The Possibilities of Order: The Work of Cleanth Brooks, 1976; The Brazen Face of History: Studies in the Literary Consciousness in America, 1980; (sr. ed.) The History of Southern Literature, 1985; (ed. with others) Stories from the Southern Review, 1988; (ed. with others) The Southern Review and Modern Literature, 1935-1985, 1989; Mind and the American Civil War: A Meditation on Lost Causes, 1989. Add: Southern Review, Louisiana State Univ., Baton Rouge, La 70803, U.S.A.

SIMPSON, Louis (Aston Marantz). American, b. 1923. Poetry, Literature, Biography. Prof. of English, State Univ. of New York, Stony Brook, since 1967. Ed., Bobbs-Merrill Publishing Co., NYC, 1950–55; Instr., Columbia Univ., NYC, 1955–59; Prof. of English, Univ. of California, Berkeley, 1959–67. *Publs:* The Arrivistes: Poems 1940-49, 1949; Good News of Death and Other Poems, 1955; (ed. with D. Hall and R. Pack) New Poets of England and America, 1957; A Dream of Governors: Poems, 1959; Riverside Drive, 1962; James Hogg: A Critical Study, 1962; At the End of the Open Road: Poems, 1963; Selected Poems, 1965; (ed.) An Introduction to Poetry, 1967; Adventures of the Letter I, 1971; Air with Armed Men (in U.S. as North of Jamaica), 1972; Three on the Tower (on Pound, Eliot, and Williams), 1975; Searching for the Ox: Poems, 1977; A Revolution in Taste: Studies of Dylan Thomas, Allen Ginsberg, Sylvia Plath, and Robert Lowell, 1978; Caviare at the Funeral: Poems, 1980; A Company of Poets, 1981; The Best Hour of the Night, 1983; People Live Here: Selected Poems 1949-1983, 1983; The Character of the Poet, 1986; Collected Poems, 1988; Selected Prose, 1989. Add: 1 Highview Ave., Setauket, N.Y. 11733, U.S.A.

SIMPSON, Michael Andrew. South African, b. 1944. Medicine/-Health. Physician: Dir. of Programme Development, Clinic Holdings, Pretoria, since 1987. Psychiatrist, Guy's Hosp., London, 1970; Asst. Prof. of Psychiatry, McMaster Univ., Hamilton, Ont., Canada, 1973; Sr. Lectr. in Psychiatry and Medicine, Royal Free Hosp. Sch. of Medicine, Univ. of London, 1976; Prof. of Psychiatry, Family Practice and Community Health, Temple Univ., Philadelphia, 1979; Prof. of Medical Education, and Deputy Dean, Univ. of Natal, South Africa, 1984–87. *Publs:* Publs: Medical Education: A Critical Approach, 1972; Continuing Education in the Health Sciences, 1978; The Facts of Death, 1979; Dying, Death and Grief: A Critical Annotated Bibliography, 1979; (co-ed.) Primary Care and Medical Education, 1979; Psycholinguistics in Clinical Practice: Languages of Illness and Healing, 1982: Dying and Grief II, 1987; (with others) AIDS: Principles, Practices and Politics, 1988. Add: P.O. Box 51, Pretoria 0001, South Africa.

SIMPSON, Mona. American, b. 1957. Novels. *Publs:* Anywhere But Here, 1987. Add: c/o Alfred Knopf Inc., 201 E. 50th St., New York, N.Y. 10022, U.S.A.

SIMPSON, Myrtle Lillias. British, b. 1931. Children's fiction, Travel/Exploration/Adventure, Autobiography/Memoirs/Personal, Biography. *Publs:* Far and Near Readers (5 books); Home is a Tent, 1964; White Horizons, 1966; Due North, 1970; Simpson the Obstetrician, 1972; Greenland Summer, 1973; Armadillo Stew, 1974; Vikings, Scots and Scraelings, 1978; Skisters: The Story of Scottish Skiing, 1982. Add: Farletter, Insh, Kingussie, Inverness-shire, Scotland.

SIMPSON, N(orman) F(rederick). British, b. 1919. Novels/Short stories, Plays/Screenplays. Teacher, City of Westminster Coll., London, and extramural lectr., 1946–62; Literary Mgr., Royal Court Theatre, London, 1976–78. *Publs:* A Resounding Tinkle, 1958; The Hole, 1958; One Way Pendulum, 1960; The Form, 1961; The Hole and Other Plays and Sketches, 1964; The Cresta Run, 1966; Some Tall Tinkles: Television Plays, 1968; Was He Anyone?, 1973; Harry Bleachbaker (novel), 1974, in U.S. as Man Overboard, 1976; (trans.) Inner Voices, 1983. Add: c/o Deborah Rogers Ltd., 49 Blenheim Cres., London W11 2EF, England.

SIMPSON, Robert. British, b. 1921. Music. Composer. Music Producer, BBC, London, 1951–80. *Publs:* Carl Nielsen: Symphonist, 1952, 1979; Bruckner and the Symphony, 1963; The Essence of Bruckner, 1966, 1978; Sibelius and Nielsen, 1965; (ed.) The Symphony, 1966; The Beethoven Symphonies, 1970; The Proms and Natural Justice, 1980. Add: Siochain, Killelton, near Camp, Tralee, Co. Kerry, Ireland.

SIMPSON, R(obert) Smith. American, b. 1906. International relations/ Current affairs. Foreign Service Officer, U.S. Dept. of State, 1944–62. *Publs:* El Movimento Obrero en los Estados Unidos de Norteamerica, 1951; Anatomy of the State Department, 1967; (ed. and contrib.) Resources and Needs of American Diplomacy, 1968; (ed. and contrib.) Instruction in Diplomacy: The Liberal Arts Approach, 1972; The

ant Ed., Encyclopaedia of Forms and Precedents. Sr. Legal Asst., Bd. of Inland Revenue, 1947–53; Chief Legal Officer, Industrial and Commercial Finance Corp. Ltd., 1953–61. *Publs:* Control of Company Finance, 1958; Sergeant and Sims on Stamp Duties, 9th ed. 1988. Add: 89 Dovehouse St., London SW3 6JZ, England.

SIMS, George. British, b. 1923. Mystery/Crime/Suspense. Dealer in rare books and manuscripts, G.F. Sims (Rare Books), Hurst, since 1948. *Publs:* The Terrible Door, 1964, Sleep No More, 1966; The Last Best Friend, 1967; The Sand Dollar, 1969; Deadhand, 1971; Hunters Point, 1973; The End of the Web, 1976; Rex Mundi, 1978; Who Is Cato?, 1981; The Keys of Death, 1982; Coat of Arms, 1984. Add: Peacocks, Hurst, Reading, Berks, RG10 0DR, England.

SIMS, Patsy. American, b. 1938. Social commentary. Reporter: Feature Writer for the Philadelphia Inquirer, since 1973. Reporter, then Women's Ed. and Special Assignment Writer, New Orleans States-Item, 1958–72; worked for the San Francisco Chronicle, 1973. *Publs:* The Klan, 1978; New Orleans: The Passing Parade, 1980; Cleveland Benjamin's Dead!: A Struggle for Dignity in Louisiana's Cane Country, 1981; Can Somebody Shout Amen? Inside the Tents and Tabernacles of American Revivalists, 1988. Add: c/o St. Martin's Press, 175 Fifth Ave., New York, N.Y. 10010, U.S.A.

SIMSOVA, Sylvia. British, b. 1931. Librarianship. Information systems consultant, DataHelp, since 1986. Asst. Lectr., 1964–66, Lectr., 1966–76, and Principal Lectr., 1976–86, Sch. of Librarianship, Polytechnic of North London. *Publs:* (ed.) Lenin, Krupskaia and Libraries, 1968; (ed.) Nicholas Rubakin and Bibliopsychology, 1968; (with M. Mackee) A Handbook of Comparative Librarianship, 1970, 1974; (with A.D. Burnett and R.K. Gupta) Studies in Comparative Librarianship: Three Essays Presented for the Sevensma Prize, 1973; Tibetan and Related Dog Breeds: A Guide to Their History, 1979; A Primer of Comparative Librarianship, 1982; Library Needs of Chinese in London (Vietnamese in Britain), 2 vols., 1982. Add: DataHelp, 18 Muswell Ave., London N10 2EG, England.

SINCLAIR, Alasdair. *See* **CLYNE,** Douglas.

SINCLAIR, Andrew (Annandale). British, b. 1935. Novels/Short stories, Plays/Screenplays, History, Translations. Managing Dir., Lorrimer Publishing Ltd., since 1967, and Film Dir., and Screenwriter, Timon Films, since 1969, both London. Fellow and Dir. of Historical Studies, Churchill Coll., Cambridge, 1961–63; Fellow, American Council of Learned Socs., 1963–64; Lectr. in American History, Univ. Coll., London, 1965–67. *Publs:* The Breaking of Bumbo, 1959, screenplay 1970; My Friend Judas (novel and play), 1959; The Project, 1960; Prohibition: The Era of Excess, 1962; The Hallelujah Bum (in U.S. as The Paradise Bum), 1963; The Raker, 1964; The Available Man: The Life Behind the Masks of Warren Gamaliel Harding, 1965; The Better Half: The Emancipation of the American Woman, 1965; Adventures in the Skin Trade (adaptation), 1966;Concise History of the United States, 1967; Gog, 1967; (trans.) Selections from the Greek Anthology, 1967; (trans.) Bolivian Diary: Ernesto "Che" Guevara, 1968; (trans. with M. Alexandre) La Grande Il-

tion: A Study of New Zealand Policy and Opinion 1880-1914, 1955; The Origin of the Maori Wars, 1957, 1961; A History of New Zealand, 1959, 4th ed. 1980; (ed.) The Maori King, by John Eldon Gorst, 1959; (with W. Mandle) Open Account: A History of the Bank of New South Wales in New Zealand 1861-1961, 1961; (ed.) Distance Looks Our Way: The Effects of Remoteness on New Zealand, 1961; (ed. with R. Chapman) Studies in a Small Democracy: Essays in Honour of Willis Airey, 1963; A Time to Embrace, 1963; William Pember Reeves: New Zealand Fabian, 1965; The Liberal Government, 1891-1912: First Steps Towards a Welfare State, 1967; The Firewheel Tree, 1973; Walter Nash, 1976; The Reefs of Fire (children's story), 1977; (with Wendy Harrex) Looking Back: Photographic History of New Zealand, 1978; (ed.) A Soldier's View of Empire: The Reminiscences of James Bodell 1831-1892, 1982; History of the University of Auckland 1883-1983, 1983; (with Judith Bassett and Marcia Stenson) The Story of New Zealand (for children), 1985; A Destiny Apart: New Zealand's Search for National Identity, 1986. Add: Dept. of History, Univ. of Auckland, Private Bag, Auckland 1, New Zealand.

SINCLAIR, Keith Val. Australian, b. 1926. Art, Literature. Prof. of Medieval French, Univ. of Connecticut, Storrs, since 1972. Assoc. Prof. of French, Univ. of Sydney, 1968–71. *Publs:* The Melbourne Livy: A Study of Bersuire's Translation, 1961; Bibliographical Essay on Medieval Studies in Australia, 1966; Catalogue of the Exhibition of Medieval Manuscripts, 1967; Medieval and Renaissance Treasures of the Ballarat Art Gallery, 1969; Descriptive Catalogue of Medieval and Renaissance Manuscripts in Australia, 1969; Tristan de Nanteuil: Chanson de geste inédite, 1971; Prières en ancien français, 1978; French Devotional Texts of the Middle Ages, 1979, supplements, 1982, 1988. Add: Dept. of Romance Languages, Univ. of Connecticut, Storrs, Conn. 06268, U.S.A.

SINCLAIR, Olga (Ellen). Also writes as Ellen Clare and Olga Daniels. British, b. 1923. Novels/Short stories, Children's fiction, Children's non-fiction. *Publs:* Gypsies (juvenile), 1967; Man at the Manor, 1967; Man of the River, 1968; Hearts by the Tower (in U.S. paperback as Night of the Black Tower), 1968; Dancing in Britain (juvenile), 1970; Bitter Sweet Summer, 1970; Children's Games (juvenile), 1972; Wild Dream, 1973; Tenant of Binningham Hall, 1975; Toys and Toymaking (juvenile), 1975; My Dear Fugitive, 1976; Where the Cigale Sings, 1976; Never Fall in Love, 1977; Master of Melthorpe, 1979; Gypsy Julie, 1979; Gypsy Girl (juvenile), 1981; (as Ellen Clare) Ripening Vine, 1981; (as Olga Daniels) Lord of Leet Castle, 1984; (as Olga Daniels) The Gretna Bride, 1985; Orchids from the Orient, 1986; (as Olga Daniels) The Bride from Faraway, 1987; When Wherries Sailed By (non-fiction), 1987; (as Olga Daniels) The Untamed Bride, 1988; Gretna Green (non-fiction), 1989. Add: Dove House Farm, Potter Heigham, Norfolk NR29 5LJ, England.

SINGER, Adam. *See* **KARP,** David.

SINGER, Benjamin D. Canadian, b. 1931. Communications, Media, Sociology. Prof. of Sociology, Univ. of Western Ontario, London, since 1972 (Assoc. Prof., 1966–72). Ed., Grosse Pointe Press, Mich., 1952; Advertising Mgr., Palmer-Pann Corp., Detroit, 1953–55; Pres., Singer-Kingswood Advertising Co., Detroit, 1957–61. *Publs:* (with R. Osborn and J. Geschwender) Black Rioters, 1970; (ed.) Communications in Canadian Society, 1972; Social Functions of Radio in a Community Emergency, 1972; Feedback and Society, 1973; Racial Factors in Psychiatric Intervention, 1977; Social Functions of the Telephone, 1981.Add: c/o R and E Research Assocs., 936 Industrial Ave., Palo Alto, Calif. 94303, U.S.A.

SINGER, Isaac Bashevis. American, b. 1904. Novels/Short stories, Children's fiction, Autobiography/Memoirs/Personal, Translations. Journalist, Jewish Daily Forward, NYC, since 1935. Proofreader and trans. Literariske Bleter, Warsaw, 1923–33. *Publs:* Pan, by Knut Hamsen, 1928; (trans.) All Quiet on the Western Front, Erich Maria Remarque, 1930; (trans.) The Magic Mountain, by Thomas Mann, 4 vols., 1930; (trans.) The Road Back, by Erich Maria Remarque, 1930; (trans.) From Moscow to Jerusalem, by Leon S. Glaser, 1938; The Family Moskat, 1950; Satan in Goray, 1955; Gimpel the Fool and Other Stories, 1957; The Magician of Lublin, 1960; The Spinoza of Market Street and Other Stories, 1961; The Slave, 1962; Short Friday and Other Stories, 1964; (ed. with E. Gottlieb) Prism 2, 1965; Selected Short Stories, 1966; In My Father's Court, 1966; Zlateh the Goat and Other Stories, 1966; Mazel and Schlimazel: or The Milk of a Lioness, 1966; The Fearsome Inn, 1967; The Manor, 1967; The Séance and Other Stories, 1968; When Schlemiel Went to Warsaw and Other Stories, 1968; A Day of Pleasure: Stories of a Boy Growing Up in Warsaw, 1969; Elijah the Slave, 1970; Joseph and Koza; or The Sacrifice to the Votuda, 1970; The Estate, 1970; A Friend

of Kafka and Other Stories, 1970; Alone in the Wild Forest, 1971; The Topsey-Turvey Emperor of China, 1971; Enemies: A Love Story, 1972; The Wicked City, 1972; The Hasidim: Paintings, Drawings and Etchings, 1973; The Fools of Chelm and Their History, 1973; A Crown of Feathers and Other Stories, 1973; Schlemiel the First (play), 1974; Yentl, the Yeshiva Boy (play), 1974; Why Noah Chose the Dove, 1974; Passions and Other Stories, 1975; A Tale of Three Wishes, 1976; A Little Boy in Search of God, 1976; A Young Man in Search of Love, 1978; Shosha, 1978; Old Love, 1979; A Day of Pleasure, 1980; The Golem, 1982; The Penitent, 1983; Stories for Children, 1984; The Image and Other Stories, 1985; Love and Exile (memoirs), 1985; Stories for Children, 1987. Add: 209 West 86th St., New York, N.Y. 10024, U.S.A.

SINGER, J. David. American, b. 1925. International relations/Current affairs. Military/Defence, Politics/Government, Social sciences. Prof. of Political Science since 1965, and Co-ordinator of World Politics Prog., since 1969, Univ. of Michigan, Ann Arbor (Visiting Prof., 1958–60; Sr. Scientist, Mental Health Research Inst., 1960–83; Assoc. Prof., 1963–65). Instr. Vassar Coll., Poughkeepsie, N.Y., 1955–57. *Publs:* (ed. with George Kish) The Geography of Conflict, 1960; Financing International Organization: The United Nations Budget Process, 1961; Deterrence, Arms Control and Disarmament: Toward a Synthesis in National Security Policy, 1962, 1984; (ed.) Weapons Management in World Politics, 1963; (ed.) Human Behavior and International Politics: Contributions from the Social-Psychological Sciences, 1965; (ed.) Quantitative International Politics: Insights and Evidence, 1968; A General Systems Taxonomy for Political Science, 1971; Individual Values, National Interests, and Political Development in the International System, 1971; On the Scientific Study of Politics: An Approach to Foreign Policy Analysis, 1972; (with M. Small) The Wages of War, 1816-1965; A Statistical Handbook, 1972; (with S. Jones) Beyond Conjecture in International Politics: Abstracts of Data-Based Research, 1972; (with Dorothy LaBarr) The Study of International Politics, (source guide), 1976; (ed.) The Correlates of War I: Research Origins and Rationale, 1979; (ed. with Michael Wallace) To Augur Well: Early Warning Indicators in World Politics, 1979; Explaining War, 1979; (ed.) The Correlates of War II: Testing Realpolitik Models, 1980;. Resort to Arms: International and Civil War 1816-1980, 1982; Quantitative Indicators in World Politics, 1984. Add: Dept. of Political Science, Univ. of Michigan, Ann Arbor, Mich. 48109, U.S.A.

SINGER, Marcus George. American, b. 1926. Philosophy. Prof. of Philosophy, Univ. of Wisconsin, Madison, since 1963 (Instr., 1952–55; Asst. Prof., 1955–59; Assoc. Prof., 1959–63; Chmn., Dept. of Philosophy, 1963–68). Instr. in Philosophy, Cornell Univ., Ithaca, N.Y., 1951–52. *Publs:* Generalization in Ethics, 1961, 1971; (ed. with R. Ammerman) Introductory Readings in Philosophy, 1960; (ed. with W.H. Hay) Reason and the Common Good: Selected Essays of Arthur E. Murphy, 1963; (ed. with R. Ammerman) Belief, Knowledge, and Truth, 1970; (ed.) Morals and Values, 1977; (ed.) American Philosophy, 1986. Add: 5021 Regent St., Madison, Wisc. 53705, U.S.A.

SINGER, Peter. Australian, b. 1946. Animals, Philosophy. Prof. of Philosophy, Monash Univ., Clayton, Vic., since 1977; Dir., Centre for Human Bioethics, since 1983. Co-Ed., Bioethics journal, since 1986. *Publs:* Democracy and Disobedience, 1973; Animal Liberation: A New Ethics for Our Treatment of Animals, 1975, 1989; (ed. with Thomas Regan) Animal Rights and Human Obligations: An Anthology, 1976, 1989; Practical Ethics, 1979; Marx, 1980; (with James Mason) Animal Factories, 1980; The Expanding Circle: Ethics and Sociobiology, 1981; Hegel, 1983; (with Deane Wells) The Reproduction Revolution, 1984; (ed.) In Defence of Animals, 1985; (with Helga Kuhse) Should the Baby Live?, 1985; (ed.) Applied Ethics, 1986. Add: Centre for Human Bioethics, Monash Univ., Wellington Rd., Clayton, Vic. 3168, Australia.

SINGER, Sarah Beth. American, b. 1915. Teacher, Hillside Hosp., Glen Oaks, N.Y., 1965–76; Teacher of Creative Writing, Samuel Field YM-YWCA, Long Island, Queens, N.Y., 1979–83. Consultant Ed., Poet Lore, 1975–81. Vice-Pres., Poetry Soc. of America, 1974–78; Exec. Dir., Poetry Soc. of America, 1979–83. *Publs:* After the Beginning, 1975; Of Love and Shoes, 1987. Add: 2360 43rd Ave. E, Unit 415, Seattle, Wash. 98112, U.S.A.

SINGH, Amritjit. Indian, b. 1945. Literature, Biography, Translations. Prof. of English, Rhode Island Coll., Providence, since 1986. Lectr. in English, Univ. of Delhi, 1965–68; Lectr. in English, Herbert Lehman Coll., City Univ. of New York, 1970–71; Instr. in English, New York Univ., 1971–72; Asst. Prof., Lehman Coll., 1973–73; Academic Assoc., American Studies Research Centre, 1974–77; Reader in English, Univ. of Hyderabad, 1977–78; Prof. of English, Univ. of Rajasthan, 1978–83;

ACLS Visiting Fellow, Yale Univ., 1983–84; Prof. of English, Hofstra Univ., Hempstead, N.Y., 1984–86. *Publs:* The Novels of the Harlem Renaissance: Twelve Black Writers, 1923-1933, 1976; (co-ed.) Afro-American Poetry and Drama 1760-1975 (annotated bibliography), 1979; (co-ed.) Indian Literature in English 1827-1979 (annotated bibliography), 1981; (co-ed.) India: An Anthology of Contemporary Writing, 1983; (co-ed.) The Harlem Renaissance: Revaluations, 1989; (co-ed.) The Magic Circle of Henry James, 1989. Add: 27 Briarwood Rd., Lincoln, R.I. 02865, U.S.A.

SINGH, Khushwant. Indian, b. 1915. Novels/Short stories, History, Biography, Translations. Practising Lawyer, High Court, Lahore, 1939–47; Press Attaché, Indian Foreign Service, London and Ottawa, 1947–51; Member of the Communications Staff, Unesco, Paris, 1954–56; Ed., Yejna, Indian Govt. publ., New Delhi, 1956–58; Ed., Illustrated Weekly of India, Bombay, 1969–78, and National Herald, 1978–80; Ed., Hindustan Times, New Delhi, 1980–83. *Publs:* The Mark of Vishnu and Other Stories, 1950; The Voice of God and Other Stories: A Bride for the Sahib and Other Stories; The Sikhs, 1952; (with P. Russell) A Note on G.V. Desani's All About Hatterr and Hali, 1952; Train to Pakistan (in U.S. as Mano Majra), 1955; I Shall Not Hear the Nightingale, 1959; Jupji: The Sikh Morning Prayer, 1959; The Sikhs Today: Their Religion, History, Culture, Customs, and Way of Life, 1959; rev. ed. 1964; (trans. with M.A. Husain) Umrao Jan Ada: Courtesan of Lucknow, by M. Ruswa, 1961; Fall of the Kingdom of the Punjab, 1962; A History of the Sikhs, 1469-1964 (2 vols.), 1963, 1966; Ranjit Singh: Maharajah of the Punjab, 1780-1839, 1963; (ed.) Sunset of the Sikh Empire, by Dr. Sita Ram Kohli, 1967; (ed.) Sacred Writings of the Sikhs; (with A. Joshi) Shri Ram: A Biography, 1963; (trans.) The Skeleton, by Amrita Pritam, 1964; (trans.) Land of the Five Rivers, by Java Thadani, 1965; (trans.) I Take this Woman, by Rajinder Singh Bedi; (with S. Singh) Ghadar, 1919; India's First Armed Revolution, 1966; (with S.V. Singh) Homage to Guru Gobind Singh, 1966; Hymns of Hanak the Guru, 1969; Black Jasmine, 1971; On War and Peace, 1976; Good People, Bad People, 1977; India Without Humbug, 1977; Indira Gandhi Returns, 1979; Delhi: A Profile, 1982; The Sikhs, 1984; Punjab Tragedy, 1984; The Sikhs Today, 1987. Add: 49E Sujan Singh Park, New Delhi 110 003, India.

SINKANKAS, John. American. b. 1915. Earth sciences. Officer, U.S. Navy, 1936–61, retired; Research Assoc., Univ. of California at San Diego, 1962–72; Former Visiting Assoc. Prof. of Geology, San Diego State Univ.; now retired. *Publs:* Gem Cutting, 1955, 3rd ed. 1984; Gemstones of North America. 2 vols., 1959–76; Gemstones and Minerals, 1961, as Prospecting for Gemstones and Minerals, 1970; Mineralogy for Amateurs, 1964; Mineralogy: A First Course, 1966; Standard Catalogue of Gems, 1968; (ed.) Earth Science Studio Handbook of Minerals, by Helmuth Boegel (in U.K. as A Collector's Guide to Minerals and Gemstones), 1971; Gemstone and Mineral Data Book, 1972; Emeralds and Other Beryls, 1981; (with Peter G. Read) Beryl, 1986. Add: 5372 Van Nuys Ct., San Diego, Calif. 92109, U.S.A.

SINOR, Denis. French, b. 1916. History. Distinguished Prof. Emeritus of Uralic and Altaic Studies, Indiana Univ., Bloomington, since 1986 (Prof., 1962–86; Dir., Inner Asian and Uralic National Resource Center, 1964–88). Ed., Journal of Asian History, since 1967. Univ. Lectr. Cambridge Univ., 1948–62. *Publs:* (ed.) Orientalism and History, 1954, 1970; A Modern Hungarian-English Dictionary, 1957; History of Hungary, 1959; Introduction àl'étude de l'Eurasie Centrale, 1963; (trans. with M. McKellar) Conqueror of the World, by René Grousset, 1966; (ed.) Studies in South, East and Central Asia, 1968; Inner Asia: History, Civilization, Languages: A Syllabus, 1969, 1971; Inner Asia and Its Contacts with Medieval Europe, 1977; (ed.) Modern Hungary: A Reader, 1977; Tanulmányok, 1982; (ed.) Handbook of Uralic Studies, 1988; (ed.) Cambridge History of Inner Asia, 1988. Add: Dept. of Uralic and Altaic Studies, Goodbody Hall, Indiana Univ., Bloomington, Ind. 47405, U.S.A.

SIODMAK, Curt. (Kurt Siodmak). American (b. German), b. 1902. Mystery/Crime/Suspense, Science fiction/Fantasy. Screenwriter and dir., for Gaumont British, 1931–37, and in the U.S., since 1937. Formerly, railroad engineer and factory worker. *Publs:* Schluss in Tonfilmatelier, 1930; Stadt Hinter Nebeln, 1931; F.P. 1 Antwortet Nicht (science fiction), 1931, trans. by H.W. Farrell as F.P. 1 Does Not Reply (in U.K. as F.P. 1 Fails to Reply), 1933; Die Madonna aus der Markusstrasse, 1932; Bis ans Ende der Welt, 1932; Rache im Ather, 1932; Die Macht im Dunkeln, 1937; Donovan's Brain (science fiction), 1943; Whomsoever I Shall Kiss, 1952; Skyport (science fiction), 1959; For Kings Only, 1961; Hauser's Memory (science fiction), 1968; The Third Ear (science fiction), 1971; City in the Sky (science fiction), 1974.

SIRC, Ljubo. British, b. 1920. Economics, Autobiography. Dir., Centre for Research into Communist Economies, London, since 1983. Member of faculty, Univ. of Dacca, Bangladesh, 1960–61, and Univ. of St. Andrews, Dundee, 1962–65; Lectr., 1965–68, and Sr. Lectr., 1968–83, Univ. of Glasgow. *Publs:* (with M. Miller, T.M. Piotrowicz and H. Smith) Communist Economy under Change, 1963; Economic Devolution in Eastern Europe, 1969; Outline of International Trade, 1973; Outline of International Finance, 1974; (co-author) Can Workers Manage?, 1977; The Yugoslav Economy under Selfmanagement, 1979; Between Hitler and Tito (autobiography), 1989. Add: Univ. of Glasgow, Glasgow G12, Scotland.

SISLER, Harry Hall. American, b. 1917. Poetry, Chemistry. Distingushed Service Prof. of Chemistry, Univ. of Florida, Gainesville, since 1979 (Chmn., Dept. of Chemistry, 1957–68; Dean, Coll. of Arts and Sciences, 1968–70; Exec. Vice Pres., 1970–73; Dean of the Grad. Sch., 1973–79). Consulting Ed., Van Nostrand Reinhold Publishing Corp., NYC, 1963–71, and Dowden Hutchinson & Ross, 1971–78. *Publs:* (with C.A. VanderWerf and A.W. Davidson) General Chemistry: A Systematic Approach, 1949, 1959; (with W.T. Lippincott and J.J. Stewart) A Systematic Laboratory Course in General Chemistry, 1950, 1961; (with A.B. Garrett and J.F. Haskins) Essentials of Chemistry, 1951, 1959; (with A.B. Garrett, J.F. Haskins and M. Kurbatov) Essentials of Experimental Chemistry, 1951, 1959; (with W.L. Evans and A.B. Garrett) Semi-Micro Qualitative Analysis, 1951, 1967; (with C.A. VanderWerf and A.W. Davidson) College Chemistry: A Systematic Approach, 1953, 1961; Chemistry in Non-Aqueous Solvents, 1961; Electron Structure, Properties, and the Periodic Law, 1961; (with C.A. VanderWerf, A.W. Davidson and R.D. Dresdner) College Chemistry, 3rd ed. 1967; (ed. with W.L. Jolly) Metal-Ammonia Solutions, 1972; (ed. with R.G. Pearson) Hard and Soft Acids and Bases, 1973; Starlight (poetry), 1976; (ed.w with L.K. Krannich) Compounds Containing As-N Bonds, 1976; (ed. with S.E. Frazier) Chloramination Reactions, 1977; (with R.D. Dresdner and W. Mooney) College Chemistry, 1980; Of Outer and Inner Space (poetry), 1981. Add: 6014 N.W. 54th Way, Gainesville, Fla. 32606, U.S.A.

SISSON, C(harles) H(ubert). British, b. 1914. Novels/Short stories, Poetry, Literature, Essays, Translations, Autobiography. Asst. Principal, 1936–42, Principal, 1945–53, Asst. Secty., 1953–62, and Under Secty., 1962–68, Ministry of Labour, London; Asst. Under Secty. of State, 1968–71 and Dir. of Occupational Safety and Health, 1971–73, Dept. of Employment, London. *Publs:* An Asiatic Romance (novel), 1953; Versions and Perversions of Heine, 1955; Poems, 1959; The Spirit of British Administration and Some European Comparisons, 1959; Twenty-One Poems, 1960; The London Zoo: Poems, 1961; Numbers, 1965; Art and Action (essays), 1965; Christopher Homm (novel), 1965; Catullus, 1966; The Discarnation: or, How the Flesh Became Word and Dwelt Among Us, 1967; Essays, 1967; Metamorphoses: Poems, 1968; Roman Poems, 1968; English Poetry 1900-1950: An Assessment, 1971; The Case of Walter Bagehot, 1972; In the Trojan Ditch: Collected Poems and Selected Translations, 1974; The Corridor, 1975; (trans.) The Poetic Art, by Horace, 1975; (trans.) Lucretius, 1976; Anchises, 1976; (ed.) Selected Poems of Swift, 1977; (ed.) Hardy's Jude the Obscure, 1978; The Avoidance of Literature (essays), 1978; (trans.) Selected Contes, by La Fontaine, 1979; (trans.) The Divine Comedy of Dante, 1980; Exactions, 1980; (ed.) Philip Mairet's Autobiographical and Other Papers, 1981; Selected Poems, 1981; Anglican Essays, 1983; Collected Poems 1943-1983, 1984; (trans.) The Aeneid of Virgil, 1986; (trans.) Racine's Britannicus, Phaedra, Athaliah, 1987; God Bless Karl Marx (poems), 1987; On the Look-out (autobiography), 1989. Add: Moorfield Cottage, The Hill, Langport, Somerset, England.

SISSON, Rosemary Anne. British, b. 1923. Novels/Short stories, Children's fiction, Plays/Screenplays, Biography. *Publs:* The Adventures of Ambrose, 1951; The Impractical Chimney Sweep, 1956; Mr. Nobody, 1956; The Queen and the Welshman (play), 1958; Fear Came to Supper (play), 1959; The Splendid Outcasts (play), 1959; The Young Shakespeare, 1959; The Isle of Dogs, 1959; The Young Jane Austen, 1962; The Young Shaftesbury, 1964; Bitter Sanctuary (play), 1964; The Man in the Case (play), 1965; The Exciseman, 1972; Catherine of Aragon: Six Wives of Henry VIII (television play), 1972; The Marriage Game: Elizabeth R (television play), 1972; The Killer of Horseman's Flats, 1973; (with R. Morley) A Ghost on Tiptoe (play), 1975; The Stratford Story, 1974; Horse in the House (television play), 1976; Escape from the Dark, 1976; Duchess of Duke Street (television series), 1977; The Dark Horse (play), 1978; Talking Parcel (television play), 1978; The Queen and the Welshman, 1979; (with A. Nixon) The Manions of America, 1982; Bury Love Deep, 1985; Beneath the Visiting Moon, 1986; The Bretts, 1987.

Add: 167 New King's Rd., London SW6, England.

SIZER, John. British, b. 1938. Administration/Management, Business/Trade/Industry. Prof. of Financial Mgmt., Loughborough Univ. of Technology, since 1970. Lectr., Univ. of Edinburgh, 1965–68; Sr. Lectr., London Grad. Sch. of Business Studies, 1968–70. Member, University Grants Cttee., 1984–89. *Publs:* An Insight into Management Accounting, 1969, 1979; Case Studies in Management Accounting, 1974, 1979; (ed.) Readings in Management Accounting, 1980; Perspectives in Management Accounting, 1980; (jt. ed.) Casebook of British Management Accounting, 2 vols., 1984–85; Institutional Response to Financial Reductions in the University Sector, 1987. Add: Dept. of Mgmt. Studies, Loughborough Univ. of Technology, Loughborough, Leics., England.

SIZER, Theodore Ryland. American, b. 1932. Education, History. Prof., Brown Univ., Providence, R.I. Teacher, Roxbury Latin Sch., West Roxbury, Mass., 1955–56, and Melbourne Grammar Sch. Australia, 1958; Asst. Prof. of Education, 1961–64, and Dean of Faculty of Education, 1964–72, Harvard Univ., Cambridge, Mass.; Headmaster, Phillips Academy, Andover, Mass., 1972–81. *Publs:* The Age of Academies, 1964; Secondary Schools at the Turn of the Century, 1964; (ed.) Religion and Public Education, 1967; (ed.) Moral Education: Five Lectures, 1970; Places for Learning, Places for Joy, 1973; Horace's Compromise, 1984. Add: 47 Nisbet St., Providence, R.I. 02906, U.S.A.

SKALDASPILLIR, Sigfriour. *See* **BROXON,** Mildred Downey.

SKARSTEN, Malvin Olai. American, b. 1892. Autobiography/Memoirs/Personal, Biography. Dir., Student Teaching, Black Hills State Coll., S.D., 1926–44; Head, Dept. of Education, and Dir., Grad. Sch., Pacific Univ., Forest Grove, Ore., 1944–65. *Publs:* George Drouillard, Hunter and Interpreter for Lewis and Clark, 1964; The Least of These, 1975; Those Remarkable People, The Dakotas. Add: 430 Oriole St., Apt. G-17, Spearfish, S.D. 57783, U.S.A.

SKELTON, Geoffrey (David). British, b. 1916. Music, Theatre, Biography, Translations. With BBC External Services News, 1956–59, and Producer and Prog. Organiser, German Service, 1956–67; Theatre Critic, BBC Radio, Brighton, 1968–83. *Publs:* Flowers for the Leader, 1939; Summer Night, 1939; Have You Seen My Lady?, 1948; Memories for Sale, 1955; (trans.) The White Horseman, 1962; Wagner at Bayreuth: Experiment and Tradition, 1965, 1976; (trans. and adaptor with A. Mitchell) The Persecution and Assassination of Marat as Performed by the Inmates of the Asylum of Charenton under the Direction of the Marquis de Sade, by Peter Weiss, 1965; (trans.) Arden Must Die, 1967; (trans.) A Monotonous Landscape, 1968; (trans.) Discourse on . . . Vietnam, 1970; (trans.) God's First Love, 1970; Wieland Wagner: The Positive Sceptic, 1971; (trans.) Trotsky in Exile, 1971; (trans.) Frieda Lawrence, 1973; (ed. and trans. with R.L. Jacobs) Wagner Writes from Paris, 1973; (trans.) Friedrich Heer: Challenge of Youth, 1974; (trans.) Max Frisch: Sketchbook 1966-1971, 1974, and 1946-49, 1977; Paul Hindemith: The Man Behind the Music, 1975; (trans.) Max Frisch: Montauk, 1976; (trans.) Cosima Wagner's Diaries, vol. 1, 1978, vol. 2, 1980; (trans.) Max Frisch: Man in the Holocene, 1980; (trans.) Max Frisch: Triptych, 1981; Richard and Cosima Wagner: Biography of a Marriage, 1982; (trans.) Le Grand Macabre, 1982; (trans.) Max Frisch: Bluebeard, 1983; (trans.) Ruth Breslav: Living For Brecht, 1987. Add: 49 Downside, Shoreham, Sussex BN43 6HF, England.

SKELTON, Peter. British, b. 1929. Novels/Short stories, Animals/Pets, Travel/Exploration/Adventure. Ed., Cherry Tree Books; writer of features, News of the World, London, since 1967; Feature Writer, Holland Herald, since 1969; Book Reviewer, Daily Telegraph. Gen. Production Ed., Sunday Times Newspaper Group, London, 1950–53; Founder, Pins and Needles mag., Sunday Times mag., and Fantasy Books, 1952; Ed., GO Travel Mag., 1953. *Publs:* The Charm of Hours, 1954; Animals All, 1957; All About Paris, 1959; The Promise of Days, 1962; The Blossom of Months, 1973; The Flowering of Seasons, 1975; (with E. Bishop) The London Ritz, 1980; Tiger Kub and the Royal Jewel, 1984. Add: St. Anthony, Nr. Woodfield, Torquay, Devon, England.

SKELTON, Robin. Canadian, b. 1925. Poetry, Literature. Prof. of English since 1963, and Ed., Malahat Review, Since 1966, Univ. of Victoria. Ed., Sono Nis Press, since 1976. *Publs:* poetry—Patmos and Other Poems, 1955; Third Day Lucky, 1958 Begging the Dialect, 1960; The Dark Window, 1962; An Irish Gathering, 1964; Inscriptions, 1967; Selected Poems 1947-1967, 1968; An Irish Album, 1969; Georges Zuk; Selected Verse, 1969; Answers, 1969; The Hunting Dark, 1971; Two Hundred Poems from the Greek Anthology, 1971; A Private Speech, 1971;

Three for Herself, 1972; Musebook, 1972; Timelight, 1974; Georges Zuk; The Underwear of the Unicorn, 1975; Callsigns, 1976; Because of Love, 1977; Three Poems, 1977; Landmarks, 1979; The Collected Shorter Poems 1947-1977, 1981; Limits, 1981; De Nihilo, 1982; Zuk, 1982; Wordsong, 1983; Collected Longer Poems 1947-1977, 1985; Openings, 1988; fiction—The Man who Sang in His Sleep, 1984; The Parrot who Could, 1987; Telling the Tale, 1987; The Fires of the Kindred, 1987; literary criticism—The Poetic Pattern, 1956; Poetry, 1963; The Writings of J.M. Synge, 1971; The Practice of Poetry, 1971; J.M. Synge, 1972; The Poet's Calling, 1975; Poetic Truth, 1978; Spellcraft, 1978; They Call It the Cariboo, 1979; House of Dreams, 1983; Talismanic Magic, 1985; Memoirs of a Literary Blockhead (autobiography), 1988; biographies—J.M. Synge and His World, 1971; ed. of following—J.M. Synge: Translations, 1961; J.M. Synge: Four Plays and the Aran Islands, 1962; J.M. Synge: Collected Poems, 1962; Edward Thomas: Selected Poems, 1962; Selected Poems of Byron, 1965; David Gascoyne: Collected Poems, 1965; J.M. Synge: Riders to the Sea, 1969; (with A. Clodd) David Gascoyne: Collected Verse Translations, 1970; Synge/Petrach, 1971; The Collected Plays of Jack B. Yeats, 1971; Two Hundred Poems from the Greek Anthology, 1971; Thirteen Irish Writers on Irish Writers on Ireland, 1973; symposia—(with A. Sadlemyer) The World of W.B. Yeats, 1965; (with D.R. Clark) Irish Renaissance, 1965; Herbert Read; A Memorial Symposium, 1970. Add: Dept. of English, Univ. of Victoria, Victoria, B.C. V8W 2Y2, Canada.

SKEMP, Joseph Bright. British, b. 1910. Classics, Philosophy. Emeritus Prof. of Greek, Univ. of Durham (Reader, 1949–50; Ed. Durham Univ. Journal, 1953–57). Former Fellow of Gonville and Caius Coll., Cambridge, and Lectr. in Classics, Univ. of Manchester; Co-Ed., Phronesis periodical, Van Gorcum Assen, Holland, 1955–64. *Publs:* Plato's Theory of Motion, 1942, enlarged ed. 1967; (trans.) Plato's Statesman, 1962, 1987; The Greeks and the Gospel, 1963; Plato, 1976. Add: 6A Westfield Park, Bristol BS6 6LT, England.

SKEMP, Richard Rowland. British, b. 1919. Mathematics, Psychology. Prof. of Education, Univ. of Warwick, 1973–86, now Emeritus. Lectr., 1955–66, and Sr. Lectr., 1966–73, Dept. of Psychology, Univ. of Manchester. *Publs:* Understanding Mathematics (5 books), 1964–70; The Psychology of Learning Mathematics, 1971; Intelligence, Learning, and Action, 1979; Mathematics in the Primary School, Structured Activities for Primary Mathematics, 1989. Add: Mathematics Inst., Univ. of Warwick, Coventry, CV4 7AL, England.

SKENDI, Stavro. Albanian, b. 1906. Cultural/Ethnic topics, History, International relations/Current affairs, Mythology/Folklore. Prof. Emeritus of Balkan Languages and Cultures, Columbia Univ., NYC, since 1972 (joined faculty, 1954). Co-Ed., Zeitschrift für Balkanalogie, W. Germany, since 1964; Member, Ed. Bd., Südost-Forschungen, Munich, since 1971; Hon. Pres., Soc. of Albanian Studies, since 1979. Special Lectr., Toronto Univ., 1952–53; Member, Inst. for Advanced Study, Princeton, N.J., 1972–73. *Publs:* Albanian and South Slavic Oral Epic Poetry, 1954; The Political Evolution of Albania, 1912-1944, 1954; (ed. and contrib.) Albania, 1956; The Albanian National Awakening, 1878-1912, 1967; Balkan Cultural Studies, 1980. Add: 50 E. 72nd St., Apt. 8-C, New York, N.Y. 10021, U.S.A.

SKENE, Anthony. British. Plays/Screenplays. *Publs:* File on Harry Jordan; In the Night; Chicane; The Waiting Game; Love Thy Neighbor; The Fleapit; Day of Heroes; West of Eden; The Lovemakers; Square on the Hypotenuse; What's In It For Me?; A Walk Through the Forest; Wicked Women; Seasons of the Year; Rose and Fern; Last Land; Who Killed Lamb?; Blunt Instrument; Thought they Died Years Ago; A Gift of Tongues; The Prisoner; Special Branch; Rivals of Sherlock Holmes; Name of the Game; Upstairs, Downstairs; Wilde Alliance; Thomas and Sarah; Thundercloud; The Adventures of Sherlock Holmes; And No One Could Save Her (screenplay); The Lodger (play). Add: 5A Furlong Rd., London N7 8LS, England.

SKIDMORE, Max J(oseph, Sr.). American, b. 1933. Language/Linguistics, Politics/Government. Dean, Coll. of Arts and Sciences and Prof. of Political Science, Univ. of Missouri, Kansas City, since 1985. Member of Editorial Bd., American Studies journal, since 1972. Teacher, Missouri Public schs., 1954–55; Supt. of Schs., Climax Springs, Mo., 1956–57; Mgmt. Analyst, Social Security Admin., Dept. of Health, Education and Welfare, Washington, D.C., 1959–62; Admin. Asst., Office of Commnr. of Social Security, 1962–64; Assoc. Prof. and Dir. of American Studies, Univ. of Alabama, Tuscaloosa, 1965–68; Prof. and Head, Dept. of Political Science, Southwest Missouri State Univ., 1968–82; Pres., Missouri Political Science Assn., 1971–72; Member, Editorial Bd., American

Studies Journal, 1972–76, 1977–85; Pres., Mid-Continent American Studies Assn., 1975–76; Dir., American Studies Research Center, Hyderabad, India, 1978–79; Dean of Arts and Sciences, Eastern New Mexico Univ., 1982–84. *Publs:* Medicare and the American Rhetoric of Reconciliation, 1970; (ed.) Word Politics: Essays on Languages and Politics, 1972; (with Marshall Carter Wanke) American Government, 1974, 5th ed. 1989; American Political Thought, 1978; (with James Barnes and Marshall Carter) The World of Politics, 1981, 1984; Ideologies: Politics in Action, 1989. Add: Coll. of Arts and Sciences, Univ. of Missouri, Kansas City, Mo. 64110, U.S.A.

SKINNER, Ainslie. *See* **GOSLING,** Paula.

SKINNER, B(urrhus) F(rederic). American, b. 1904. Novels/Short stories, Psychology, Autobiography/Memoirs/Personal. Prof. of Psychology Emeritus, Harvard Univ., Cambridge, Mass., since 1975 (Prof. 1948–75). Jr. Fellow, Harvard Soc. of Fellows, 1933–36; Instr. in Psychology, 1936–37, Asst. Prof., 1937–39, and Assoc. Prof., 1939–45, Univ. of Minnesota, Minneapolis; Prof. of Psychology and Chmn. of Dept., Indiana Univ., Bloomington, 1945–48. *Publs:* Behavior of Organisms, 1938; Walden Two (novel), 1948; Science and Human Behavior, 1953; Verbal Behavior, 1957; (with C.B. Ferster) Schedules of Reinforcement, 1957; Cumulative Record, 1959, rev. ed. 1961; (with J.G Holland) The Analysis of Behavior, 1961; The Technology of Teaching, 1968; Contingencies of Reinforcement, 1969; Freedom and Dignity, 1971; About Behaviorism, 1974; Particulars of My Life (autobiography), 1976; Reflections on Behaviorism and Society, 1978; The Shaping of a Behaviorist (autobiography), 1979; Notebooks, 1980; Skinner for the Classroom, 1982; (with Margaret E. Vaughan) Enjoy Old Age, 1983; A Matter of Consequences (autobiography), 1983; Upon Further Reflection, (autobiography) 1987; The Selection of Behavior, 1988. Add: 11 Old Dee Rd., Cambridge, Mass. 02138, U.S.A.

SKINNER, Knute (Rumsey). American, b. 1929. Poetry. Prof. of English, Western Washington Univ., since 1962. Member of faculty, Univ. of Iowa, 1960–61 and Oklahoma Coll. for Women, 1961–62. *Publs:* Stranger with a Watch, 1965; A Close Sky Over Killaspuglonane, 1968; In Dinosaur Country, 1969; The Sorcerers: A Laotian Tale, 1972; Hearing of the Hard Times, 1981; The Flame Room, 1982; Selected Poems, 1985; Learning to Spell "Zucchini", 1988. Add: P.O. Box 4065, Bellingham, Wash. 98227, U.S.A.

SKINNER, Martyn. British, b. 1906. Poetry. *Publs:* Sir Elfadore and Mabyna, 1935; Letters to Malaya, 3 vols., 1941–47; Two Colloquies, 1949; The Return of Arthur, 1966; Old Rectory: Prologue, 1970; Old Rectory: The Session, 1973; Old Rectory: The Epilogue, 1977; (with R.C. Hutchinson) Two Men of Letters, 1979; Alms for Oblivion, 1983; Old Rectory (omnibus), 1984. Add: Fitzhead, Taunton, Somerset, England.

SKINNER, Quentin (Robert Duthie). British, b. 1940. History, Intellectual history. Fellow of Christ's Coll., Cambridge, since 1962, and Prof. of Political Science, Cambridge Univ., since 1978 (Lectr. in History, 1967–78). Member, Sch. of Social Science, Inst. for Advanced Study, Princeton, N.J., 1976–79. *Publs:* (ed., with P. Laslett and W.G. Runciman) Philosophy, Politics and Society, 1972; The Foundations of Modern Political Thought, vol. I, The Renaissance, 1978, vol. II, The Age of Reformation, 1978; Machiavelli, 1981; (co-ed. and contrib.) Philosophy in History, 1984; (ed. and contrib.) The Return of the Grand Theory in the Human Sciences, 1985; (co-ed. and contributor) The Cambridge History of Renaissance Philosophy, 1988; Meaning and Context, 1988; (co-ed.) The Prince, by Machiavilli, 1988. Add: Christ's Coll., Cambridge CB2 3BU, England.

SKIPP, Victor (Henry Thomas). British, b. 1925. History, Philosophy, Head of History, Sheldon Heath Comprehensive Sch., Birmingham, 1955–59; Principal Lectr. in History, and Head, Dept. of Environmental Studies, Bordesley Coll. of Education, Birmingham, 1964–78. *Publs:* Discovering Sheldon, 1960; (with R.P. Hastings) Discovering Bickenhill, 1963; An Eighteenth Century Farm Labourer's Family, 1963; Out of the Ancient World, 1967; (with H.P.R. Finberg) Local History: Objective and Pursuit, 1967; Honest to Man, 1967; Medieval Yardley, 1970; The Origins of Solihull, 1977; Crisis and Development: An Ecological Case Study of the Forest of Arden, 1570-1674, 1978; The Centre of England, 1979; A History of Greater Birmingham—Down to 1830, 1980; The Making of Victorian Birmingham, 1983. Add: 5 Clay Lane, Birmingham B26 1DU, England.

SKLAR, Kathryn Kish. American, b. 1939. History, Women. Assoc. Prof. to Prof., Dept. of History, Univ. of California, Los Angeles, since

1974. Member of faculty, Dept. of History, Univ. of Michigan, Ann Arbor, 1969–74, and Radcliffe Inst., Harvard Univ., Cambridge, Mass., 1973–74. *Publs:* Catharine Beecher: A Study in American Domesticity 1973; (ed.) The Writings of Harriet Beecher Stowe, 1982; (ed.) Notes of Sixty Years: The Autobiography of Florence Kelley 1849-1926, 1984. Add: Dept. of History, Univ. of California, Los Angeles, Calif. 90024, U.S.A.

SKLAR, Robert (Anthony). American, b. 1936. Cultural/Ethnic topics, Film, Literature. Prof., Dept. of Cinema Studies, New York Univ., since 1977 (Chmn., 1977–81). Asst. Prof. of History, 1965–69, Assoc. Prof., 1969–75, and Prof. of History, 1975–76, Univ. of Michigan, Ann Arbor. *Publs:* F. Scott Fitzgerald: The Last Laocoon, 1967; (ed.) The Plastic Age: 1917-1930, 1970; Movie-Made America: A Cultural History of the American Movies, 1975; Prime-Time America: Life On and Beyond the Television Screen, 1980. Add: 284 Lafayette St., New York, N.Y. 10012, U.S.A.

SKLARE, Marshall. American, b. 1921. Cultural/Ethnic topics, Sociology, Theology/Religion. Klutznick Family Prof. of Contemporary Jewish Studies and Sociology since 1979, and Dir. Center for Modern Jewish Studies since 1980, Brandeis Univ., Waltham, Mass. (Prof., 1970–79). Prof. of Sociology, Yeshiva Univ., NYC, 1966–70; former Dir., Div. of Scientific Research, American Jewish Cttee. *Publs:* (ed.) The Jews: Social Patterns of an American Group, 1958; (co-author) Jewish Identity on the Suburban Frontier, 1967, 1979; America's Jews, 1971; Conservative Judaism: An American Religious Movement, rev. ed. 1972; (ed.) The Jew in American Society, 1974; (ed.) The Jewish Community in America, 1974; Understanding American Jewry, 1982; American Jews: A Reader, 1983. Add: Lown Bldg., Brandeis Univ., Waltham, Mass. 02254, U.S.A.

SKOGLUND, John E. American, b. 1912. Theology/Religion. Cornelius Woelfkin Prof. of Preaching, Emeritus, Colgate-Rochester/Bexley Hall/Crozer, N.Y. (joined faculty, 1958). Prof. of Theology, American Baptist Seminary of the West, 1940–47; Foreign Secty., American Baptist Foreign Mission Soc., Valley Forge, Pa., 1947–54; Pastor, First Baptist Church, Seattle, Wash., 1954–58; Visiting Prof., United Theological Coll., Bangalore, India, 1974–77, Chinese Univ., Hong Kong, 1981–82, and Betelseminariet, Stockholm, 1983; Adjunct Prof., American Baptist Seminary of the West, 1984–87. *Publs:* The Spirit Tree, 1951; They Reach for Life, 1955; Come and See, 1956; To the Whole Creation, 1958; (with J.R. Nelson) Fifty Years of Faith and Order, 1964; The Baptists, 1965; Worship in the Free Churches, 1965; (ed.) Worship and Renewal, 1965; (ed.) Worship in a Secular Age, 1967; A Manual for Worship, 1968. Add: 1909 San Antonio Ave., Berkeley, Calif. 94707, U.S.A.

SKOLNIKOFF, Eugene B. American, b. 1928. Politics/Government, Sciences (general). Prof. of Political Science, Massachusetts Inst. of Technology, Cambridge, since 1963 (Research Asst., 1948–50; Member, Administrative Staff, 1952–55; Chmn., Political Science Dept., 1970–74; Dir. of Center for Intnl. Studies, 1972–87). Research Assoc., Center for European Studies, Harvard Univ., Cambridge, Mass., since 1973. Systems Analyst, Inst. for Defense Analysis, 1957–58; staff member, 1958–63, and Sr. Consultant, 1977–81, Office of Science and Technology Policy, Exec. Office of the Pres. *Publs:* Science, Technology and American Foreign Policy, 1967; (with D.A. Kay) World Eco-Crisis, 1972; The International Imperatives of Technology, 1972. Add: MIT E38-648, Cambridge Mass. 02139, U.S.A.

SKORNIA, Harry Jay. American, b. 1910. Media, Sociology. Prof. Emeritus of Radio and Television, Dept. of Speech and Theatre, Univ. of Illinois, Urbana, since 1975 (Prof., 1953–75). Adjunct Prof. of Mass Communication, Univ. of South Florida. Head, Dept. of Radio and Television, Indiana Univ., Bloomington, 1940–53. Pres., National Assn. of Educational Broadcasters, 1953–61; Chancellor, United Community Church Coll., Sun City, Fla., 1981–82. *Publs:* Handbuch uber die Grundlagen des freien deutschen Rundfunks, 1948; (with R.H. Lee and F. Brewer) Creative Broadcasting, 1950; Television and Society, 1965; Television and the News, 1968; (ed. with J.W. Kitson) Problems and Controversies in Television and Radio, 1968. Add: Westwood Retirement Center, #534-535, 1001 Mar Walt Dr., Fort Walton Beach, Fla. 32548, U.S.A.

SKUPSKY, Donald S. American, b. 1948. Business/Trade/Industry, Information science/Computers, Law. Pres. and Gen. Counsel, Information Requirements Clearinghouse, Denver, since 1984. Sr. Staff Attorney and Project Office Mgr., National Center for State Courts, Williamsburg, Va. and Denver, 1974–84. *Publs:* (with others) Microfilm and the Courts: Guide for Court Managers and Reference Manual, 1976; (with others) Business Equipment and the Courts: Guide for Court Managers and Reference Manual, 1977; (with others) Date Processing and the Courts: Guide for Court Managers, 1977; (with others) Comparative Records Management Systems and the Courts, 1980; Legal Requirements for Business Records: Federal Requirements, 1984; Legal Requirements for Business Records: State Requirements, 1985; Recordkeeping Requirements, 1988. Add: c/o Information Requirements Clearinghouse, 3801 E. Florida Ave., Suite 400, Denver, Colo. 80210, U.S.A.

SKUTCH, Alexander F. Costa Rican (born American), b. 1904. Natural history, Philosophy. Prof. of Ornithology, Univ. de Costa Rica, 1964, 1979. *Publs:* Life Histories of Central American Birds, 3 vols., 1954–69; The Quest of the Divine, 1956; Life Histories of Central American Highland Birds, 1967; The Golden Core of Religion, 1970; A Naturalist in Cost Rica, 1971; Studies of Tropical American Birds, 1972, and New Studies, 1981; The Life of the Hummingbird, 1973; Parent Birds and Their Young, 1976; A Bird Watcher's Adventures in Tropical America, 1977; Aves de Costa Rica, 1977; The Imperative Call, 1979; A Naturalist on a Tropical Farm, 1980; Birds of Tropical America, 1983; Nature Through Tropical Windows, 1983; Life Ascending, 1985; The Life of the Woodpecker, 1985; Helpers at Birds' Nests, 1987; A Naturalist amid Tropical Splendor, 1987; Life of the Tanager, 1989; Birds Asleep, 1989. Add: Quizarrá, 8000 San Isidro de. El General, Costa Rica.

SKVORECKY, Josef. Canadian, b. 1924. Novels/Short stories, Film. Prof. of English and Prof. of Film, Univ. of Toronto, Ont., since 1975 (Special Lectr., 1969–70; Writer-in-Residence 1970–71; Assoc. Prof. 1971–75). Member, Central Cttee. of the Czechoslovak Writers Union, 1967–68. *Publs:* The Cowards, 1970; All the Bright Young Men and Women film history), 1972; The Mournful Demeanour of Lieutenant Boruvka, 1974; Miss Silver's Past, 1974; The Bass Saxophone, 1977; The Swell Season, 1982; Jiri Menzel and the History of the Closely Watched Trains, 1983; The Engineer of Human Souls, 1984; Dvorak in Love, 1986. Add: 487 Sackville St., Toronto, Ont. M4X 1T6, Canada.

SKY, Kathleen. Pseud. for Kathleen Mckinney Goldin. American, b. 1943. Science fiction/Fantasy. Freelance writer since 1968. Children's barber, Bullock's Dept. Store, Pasadena, Calif., 1964–71; also former volunteer worker for the Humane Soc., Pasadena, and film extra. *Publs:* Birthright, 1975; Ice Prison, 1976; Vulcan!, 1978; Death's Angel, 1980; Witchdame, 1985. Add: c/o Berkley, 200 Madison Ave., New York, N.Y. 10016, U.S.A.

SLACK, Edwin Brian. New Zealander, b. 1923. Environmental science/Ecology. Research Officer, Lister Inst. of Preventive Medicine, London, 1943–47; Lectr. in Bio-Chemistry, King's Coll., Newcastle upon Tyne, 1947–50; Managing Dir., Plasticisers Ltd., Bradford, 1950–59; Reader in Applied Fisheries, 1962–88, and Dir. of Environmental Studies, 1974–84, Victoria Univ. of Wellinhton. *Publs:* Coarse Fibres, 1957; The Sea Fisheries, 1969; Fisheries in New Zealand, 1969; Environment New Zealand, 1979. Add: 19 Milton Terr., Picton, New Zealand.

SLADE, Bernard. (Bernard Slade Newbound). Canadian, b. 1930. Plays/Screenplays. Actor, 1949–57; co-founder, Garden Centre Theatre, Vineland, Ont., 1954; television writer, 1957–74. *Publs:* Same Time, Next Year, 1975; Tribute, 1978; Fling!, 1979; Romantic Comedy, 1980; Special Occasions, 1982; Fatal Attraction, 1986; An Act of the Imagination, 1987; Return Engagements, 1989. Add: 1262 Lago Vista Pl., Beverly Hills, Calif. 90210, U.S.A.

SLADE, Peter. British, b. 1912. Education, Psychology, Theatre. Pres., Educational Drama Assn., since 1978; Vice-Pres., National Assn. of Dramatherapists, since 1978. Dir., First Children's Theatre Co., 1932, BBC Children's Hour, 1936, and Worcestershire Arts Centre, 1938; Drama Adviser, Staffordshire County, 1943–47; Dir. Pear Tree Players, 1945–47; Drama Adviser, Birmingham Education Authority, 1947–77. *Publs:* The Value of Drama in Religion, Education, and Therapy, 1939; Child Drama, 1954; Introduction to Child Drama, 1958; Dramatherapy as an Aid to Becoming a Person, 1959; (with J. Hudson) A Chance for Everyone, Book I, 1966, Book II, 1969; Experience of Spontaneity, 1968; Natural Dance, 1977. Add: Swingletrees, Park Crescent, Stow-on-the-Wold, Glos. GL54 1DT, England.

SLADEK, John (Thomas). Also writes with Thomas M. Disch under joint pseuds. Thom Demijohn and Cassandra Knye. American, b. 1937. Mystery/Crime/Suspense, Science fiction/Fantasy, Supernatural/Occult topics. Engineering Asst., Univ. of Minnesota, 1959–61; Technical Writer, Technical Publs. Inc., St. Louis Park, Minn., 1961–62; Switchman,

Great Northern Railway, Minneapolis, 1962–63; draftsman, NYC, 1964–65; Ed. with Pamela A. Zoline, Ronald Reagan: The Magazine of Poetry, London, 1968. *Publs:* (as Cassandra Knye) The House That Fear Built, 1966; (as Cassandra Knye but without Thomas M. Disch) The Castle and the Key, 1967; (as Thom Demijohn) Black Alice, 1968; The Reproductive System (SF novel), 1968; The Müller-Fokker Effect (SF novel), 1971; The Steam-Driver Boy and Other Strangers (SF short stories), 1973; The New Apocrypha: Guide to Strange Science and Occult Beliefs, 1973; Black Aura, 1974; Keep the Giraffe Burning (SF short stories), 1977; Invisible Green, 1977; Roderick; or, The Education of a Young Machine (SF novel), 1980; The Best of John Sladek (SF short stories), 1981; Alien Accounts (SF short stories), 1982; Roderick at Random (SF novel), 1982; Tik-Tok, 1983; Lunatics of Terra, 1984; Bugs (SF novel), 1989. Add: c/o A.P. Watt Ltd., 26-28 Bedford Row, London WC1R 4HL, England.

SLATER, Mary. British, b. 1909. Cookery/Gastronomy/Wine, Recreation/Leisure/Hobbies, Travel/Exploration. *Publs:* Simple Clothes for Children; More Clothes for Children; Clothes for Teens to Twenties; The Caribbean Islands; Cooking the Caribbean Way; Caribbean Cooking for Pleasure, Caribbean Cooking, 1984. Add: 105 Hallam St., London W1N 5LU, England.

SLATZER, Robert (Franklin). American, b. 1927. Westerns/Adventure, Biography. Exec. Producer, Jaguar Pictures Co., Hollywood, Calif., since 1959. Producer, Columbia Pictures Corp., Hollywood, 1948, 1969–74; Screenwriter, RKO Radio Pictures, 1949; Screenwriter and Dir., Monogram Studios, 1949–50; Screenwriter and Dir., Paramount Pictures Corp., Hollywood, 1951–53; Exec. Producer, Television Series, Republic Studios, 1953–54; Pres., Slatzer Oil and Gas Co., 1960–63; Member, Bd. of Dirs., United Mining and Milling Corp., 1967–69. Dir., National Academy of TV Arts and Sciences, 1972; Bd. Dir., Millionaire's Club, 1977. *Publs:* The Hellcats, 1968; Cowboy and the Heiress, 1970; The Young Wildcats, 1971; Campaign Girl, 1972; The Punishment Pawn, 1973; The Life and Curious Death of Marilyn Monroe, 1974; Duke of Thieves, 1976; Daphne, 1978; Bing Crosby: The Hollow Man, 1981; Duke: The Life and Times of John Wayne, 1986. Add: P.O. Box 1075, Hollywood, Calif. 90078, U.S.A.

SLAUGHTER, Carolyn. British, b. 1946. Novels. Advertising Copywriter in London agencies, 1969–76. *Publs:* The Story of the Weasel, 1976; Columba, 1977; Magdalene, 1979; Dreams of the Kalahari, 1981; Heart of the River, 1982; The Banquet, 1983; A Perfect Woman, 1984; The Innocents, 1986; The Widow, 1989. Add: 2805 Main St., Lawrenceville, N.J. 08648, U.S.A.

SLAUGHTER, Eugene Edward. American, b. 1909. Education. Prof. Emeritus of English Language and Literature, Southeastern Oklahoma State Univ., Durant, since 1974 (Assoc. Prof., 1932–45; Dir. of Publicity, 1935–42 and 1946–49; Acting Librarian, 1952–53 and 1954–55; Prof., 1946–74). Chief, Modern Language Insts. Branch, Div. of Educational Personnel Training, U.S. Office of Education, Washington, D.C., 1965–67. *Publs:* Virtue According to Love—In Chaucer, 1957, 1970; (co-author) The National Interest and the Teaching of English, 1961; A Generous University Education, 1985. Add: Southeastern Oklahoma State Univ., Durant, Okla. 74701, U.S.A.

SLAUGHTER, Frank G(ill). Also writes as C.V. Terry. American, b. 1908. Historical/Romance/Gothic, Medicine/Health. Medical practitioner, since 1930. Formerly practised surgery, Riverside Hosp., Fla. *Publs:* The Warrior, 1941; That Non Should Die, 1941; Spencer Brade, M.D., 1942; Air Surgeon, 1943; Battle Surgeon, 1944; A Touch of Glory, 1945; In a Dark Garden, 1945; The New Science of Surgery, 1946; The Golden Isle, 1947; Medicine for Moderns, 1947; Sangaree, 1948; Divine Mistress, 1949; Immortal Magyar, 1949; The Stubborn Heart, 1950; The Road to Bithynia, 1950; Fort Everglades, 1951; East Side General, 1952; The Galileans, 1953; Storm Haven, 1954; The Song of Ruth, 1955; Apalachee Gold, 1955; (as C.V. Terry) Buccaneer Surgeon, 1955; (as C.V. Terry) Darien Venture, 1955; (as C.V. Terry) The Deadly Lady of Madagascar, 1956; (as C.V. Terry) The Golden Ones, 1956; The Healer, 1956; Flight from Natchez, 1957; The Scarlet Cord, 1958; Sword and Scalpel, 1959; The Mapmaker, 1960; Daybreak, 1961; The Thorn of Arimathea, 1962; The Crown and the Cross, 1962; Lorena, 1963; The Land and the Promise, 1963; Pilgrims in Paradise, 1964; Epidemic!, 1964; The Curse of Jezebel, 1965; David: Warrior and King, 1965; Tomorrow's Miracle, 1966; Upon This Rock, 1966; A Savage Place, 1966; The Purple Quest, 1967; Constantine, 1967; Surgeon, U.S.A., 1968; God's Warrior, 1968; Doctor's Wives, 1968; The Sins of Herod, 1969; Surgeon's Choice, 1970; Countdown, 1971; Code Five, 1972; Convention, M.D., 1973; Women in White, 1974; Stonewall Brigade, 1975; Deep Is the Shadow,

1975; Devil's Gamble, 1976; The Passionate Rebel, 1979; Gospel Fever, 1980; Doctor's Daughters, 1981; Doctor at Risk, 1982; No Greater Love, 1984; Transplant, 1987. Add: Box 14, Ortega Station, Jacksonville, Fla. 32210, U.S.A.

SLAVITT, David (Rytman). Also writes as Henry Sutton. American, b. 1935. Novels/Short stories, Poetry, Translations. Lectr. in English Columbia Univ., NYC, since 1985. Assoc. Ed., Newsweek Mag., 1958–65; Assoc. Prof. of English, Temple Univ., Philadelphia, 1978–80. *Publs:* Suits for the Dead, 1961; The Carnivore, 1965; Rochelle, or Virtue Rewarded, 1966; (as Henry Sutton) The Exhibitionist, 1967; Feel Free, 1968; (as Henry Sutton) The Voyeur, 1969; Day Sailing, 1969; Anagrams, 1970; (as Henry Sutton) Vector, 1970; (trans.) The Eclogues of Virgil, 1971; Child's Play, 1972; ABCD, 1972; (trans.) The Eclogues and the Georgics of Virgil, 1972; (as Henry Sutton) The Liberated, 1973; The Outer Mongolian, 1973; The Killing of the King, 1974; Vital Signs, 1975; (with P. Secord and C. Backman) Essentials of Social Psychology, 1976; King of Hearts, 1976; Jo Stern, 1978; The Sacrifice, 1978; Rounding the Horn, 1978; The Idol, 1979; Dozens, 1981; Ringer, 1982; Big Nose, 1983; Alice at 80, 1984; The Elegies to Delia of Albius Tibullus, 1985; (with Bill Adler) Secrets, 1985; The Walls of Thebes, 1985; (with Bill Adler) The Agent, 1986; (ed.) Adrien Stoutenberg: New and Selected Poems, 1986; Physicians Observed (non-fiction), 1987; The Hussar (novel), 1987. Add: c/o William Morris Agency, 1350 Ave. of the Americas, New York, N.Y. 10019, U.S.A.

SLAVUTYCH, Yar. American, b. 1918. Poetry, Language/Linguistics, Literature, Translations. Prof. of Slavic Languages, Univ. of Alberta, Edmonton, since 1979 (Asst. Prof., 1960–65). Instr. in Ukrainian, U.S. Army Language Sch., Monterey, Calif., 1955–60; Poet Laureate from Ukrainian Mohylo-Mazepian Academy of Science, Ottawa, 1982. *Publs:* Spivaje kolos (poetry), 1945; Homin vikiv (poetry), 1946; Pravdonostsi (poetry), 1948; Spiegel und Erneuerung (poetry), 1949; Spraha (poetry), 1950; Moderna ukrajins'ka poezija, 1900-1950, 1950; Don'ka bez imeny (poetry), 1952; Rozstriliana muza, 1955; The Muse in Prison (poetry), 1956; Mistsiamy zaporoz'kymy, 1957, 3rd ed. 1985; (trans.) Vybrani poeziji: Selected Poems by John Keats in Ukrainian, 1958; Oasis, Selected Poems, 1959; Ivan Franko i Rosija, 1959; Conversational Ukrainian, 1959, 5th ed. 1987; Oaza (poetry), 1960; Velych Shevchenka, 1961; Majestat (poetry), 1962; Trofeji, 1938-1963 (poetry), 1963; (ed.) Pivnichne siajvo, vols. I-V, 1964–71; Shevchenkova poetyka, 1964; Ukrainian Literature in Canada, 1966; (co-ed.) Slavs in Canada, I, 1966; Zavojovnyky prerij, 1968; Mudroschchi mandriv (poetry), 1972; (ed.) Zakhidnokanads'kyj zbirnyk, 2 vols., 1973–75; Kozak i Amazonka, 1973; The Conquerors of the Prairies, 1974, 1984; (ed.) An Anthology of Ukrainian Poetry in Canada, 1898-1973, 1975; Ukrajins'ka poezija v Kanadi, 1976; L'Oiseau de feu (selected poems), 1976; Zibrani tvory, 1938-1978, 1978; The Poetry of Yar Slavutych: A Symposium, 1978; Zhyvi smoloskypy, 1983; (trans.) Valogatott versek, 1983; Izbrannoe (poetry), 1986; (ed.) Ukrainian Shakespeariana in the West, 1987; Standard Ukrainian Grammar, 1987; U vyri bahatokul'turnosty (memoirs), 1988; Oaza" tesknoty, 1989; Vybranae, 1989. Add: 72 Westbrook Dr., Edmonton, Alta. T6J 2E1, Canada.

SLEATOR, William (Warner, III). American, b. 1945. Children's fiction. Accompanist for ballet classes, Royal Ballet Sch., London, 1967–68; rehearsal pianist, Boston Ballet Co., 1974–83. *Publs:* The Angry Moon (retelling), 1970; Blackbriar, 1972; Run, 1973; House of Stairs, 1974; Among the Dolls, 1975; (with William H. Redd) Take Charge: A Personal Guide to Behavior Modification (non-fiction), 1976; Into the Dream, 1979; Once, Said Darlene, 1979; The Green Futures of Tycho, 1981; That's Silly, 1981; Fingers, 1983; Interstellar Pig, 1984; Singularity, 1985; The Boy Who Reversed Himself, 1986; The Duplicate, 1988; Strange Attractors, 1989. Add: 77 Worcester St., Boston, Mass. 02118, U.S.A.

SLEMON, Gordon Richard. Canadian, b. 1924. Engineering/ Technology. Prof. of Electrical Engineering, Univ. of Toronto, since 1955 (Dean, 1979–86). Chmn., Innovation Foundn., since 1980, and Microelectronics Development Centre, since 1982. Pres., Electrical Engineering Consociates, 1976–79. *Publs:* (with J.M. Ham) Scientific Basis of Electrical Engineering, 1960; Magnetoelectric Devices, 1965; (with A. Straughen) Electric Machines, 1980; (with S.B. Dewan and A. Straughen) Power Semiconductor Drives, 1984. Add: 40 Chatfield Dr., Don Mills, Ont., Canada.

SLESAR, Henry. American, b. 1927. Novels/Short stories, Mystery/ Crime/Suspense, Plays/Screenplays. Headwriter, Somerset, NBC, 1971–73, The Edge of Night, 1968–83, and Capitol, TV series, 1984–86.

Publs: The Grey Flannel Shroud, 1959; Enter Murderers, 1960; Clean Crimes and Neat Murders (stories), 1960; A Crime for Mothers and Others (stories), 1961; The Bridge of Lions, 1963; Two on a Guillotine (screenplay), 1968; The Seventh Mask, 1969; The Thing at the Door, 1974; Murders Most Macabre (stories), 1987. Add: 125 East 72nd St., New York, N.Y. 10021, U.S.A.

SLESINGER, Warren. American, b. 1933. Poetry, Literature. Ed., Univ. of South Carolina Press, since 1986. Resident, Poets-In-The-School Prog., Indiana, Delaware, Ohio, and Pennsylvania. Member of Sales Staff, Macmillan Co., NYC, 1961–64; Mgr., Holt, Rinehart & Winston, NYC, 1961–68; Ed., D.C. Heath & Co., Lexington, Mass., 1969; Asst. Prof. of English, Coll. of Wooster, Ohio, 1969–75; Ed. and Market Mgr., Univ. of Pennsylvania Press, Philadelphia, 1976–81; East Coast Rep., Univ. of Chicago Press, 1981–86. *Publs:* Field with Figurations, 1970; Heartland II (anthology), 1975; With Some Justification, 1985. Add: c/o Univ. of South Carolina Press, 508 Assembly St., Columbia, S.C. 29208, U.S.A.

SLIDE, Anthony (Clifford). British, b. 1944. Communications media, Film, Theatre. Freelance writer, researcher and film scholar, Los Angeles; Ed., Filmmakers series, Scarecrow Press. Asst. Ed., Intnl. Film Guide, London, 1968–71; Louis B. Mayer Research Assoc., American Film Inst., Los Angeles, 1971–72; Assoc. Archivist, American Film Inst., Washington, D.C., 1972–75; Resident Film Historian, Academy of Motion Picture Arts and Sciences, Los Angeles, 1975–80. *Publs:* Early American Cinema, 1970; The Griffith Actresses, 1973; (with Edward Wagenknecht) The Films of D.W. Griffith, 1975; The Idols of Silence, 1976; The Big V: A History of the Vitagraph Company, 1976; 1988; Early Women Directors, 1977, 1984; Aspects of American Film History Prior to 1920, 1978; Films on Film History, 1979; The Kindergarten of the Movies: A History of the Fine Arts Company, 1980; (with Edward Wagenknecht) Fifty Great American Silent Films 1912-1920, 1980; The Vaudevillians, 1981; Great Radio Personalities in Historic Photographs, 1982, 1988; (ed.) Selected Film Criticism, 5 vols., 1982; A Collector's Guide to Movie Memorabilia, 1983; (ed.) Selected Film Criticism: Foreign Films 1930-1950, 1984; (ed.) International Film, Radio and Television Journals, 1985; (ed.) Selected Film Criticism 1951-1960, 1985; Fifty Classic British Films 1932-1982, 1985; (ed.) The Best of Rob Wagner's Script, 1985; (ed.) Selected Theatre Criticism, 3 vols., 1985; A Collector's Guide to TV Memorabilia, 1986; (ed.) Filmfront, 1986; The American Film Industry: A Historical Dictionary, 1986; Great Pretenders, 1986; Fifty French Films, 1912-1982, 1987; (ed.) Selected Radio and Television Criticism 1987; (with Patricia and Stephen Hanson) Sourcebook for the Performing Arts, 1988; The Cinema and Ireland, 1988; (ed.) Picture Dancing on a Screen, 1988; The International Film Industry: A Historical Dictionary, 1989; Silent Portraits, 1989. Add: 4118 Rhodes Ave., Studio City, Calif. 91604, U.S.A.

SLIVE, Seymour. American, b. 1920. Art. Gleason Prof. of Fine Arts since 1973, and Dir. of the Fogg Art Museum, 1975–82, now Emeritus, Harvard Univ., Cambridge, Mass. (joined faculty, 1954). Taught at Oberlin Coll., Ohio, 1950–51, and Pomona Coll., California, 1952–54. *Publs:* Rembrandt and His Critics 1630-1730, 1953; Drawings of Rembrandt, 2 vols., 1965; (co-author) Dutch Art and Architecture 1600-1800, 1966; Frans Hals, 3 vols., 1970–74; Jacob van Ruisdael, 1981. Add: Fogg Art, Museum Harvard Univ., Cambridge, Mass. 02138, U.S.A.

SLOANE, Peter J(ames). British, b. 1942. Economics, Industrial relations. Prof. and Head, Dept. of Economics, Univ. of Aberdeen, since 1984. Member of the Council, Scottish Economic Soc., since 1983. Asst. Lectr., 1966–67, and Lectr. 1967–69, Dept. of Political Economy, Univ. of Aberdeen; Lectr. in Industrial Economics, Univ. of Nottingham, 1969–75; Economic Adviser (on Secondment), Dept. of Employment Unit for Manpower Studies, London, 1973–74; Prof. of Economics and Management, Paisley Coll., 1975–84. Member, Nottingham and District Local Employment Cttee., 1967–74. *Publs:* Changing Patterns of Working Hours, 1975; (with Brian Chiplin) Sex Discrimination in the Labour Market, 1976; Sport in the Market, 1980; (ed.) Women and Low Pay, 1980; The Earnings Gap Between Men and Women in Britain, 1981; (with H.C. Jain) Equal Employment Issues, 1981; (with B. Chiplin) Tackling Discrimination, 1982; (with others) Labour Economics, 1985. Add: The Eaves, Kincardine Rd., Torphins, Aberdeenshire AB3 4HH, Scotland.

SLOBODKINA, Esphyr. American (born Russian), b. 1908. Writer and illustrator of children's fiction. Pres., Urquhart-Slobodkina Inc., Great Neck, N.Y. and Hallandale, Fl., since 1968. Painter, sculptor and designer represented in Metropolitan Museum, and Whitney Museum, NYC, Corcoran Gall. and Smithsonian, Washington, D.C., Philadelphia

Museum of Art, New York State Museum, Albany, etc. Pres., Art Development Co., NYC, 1945–68; Asst. Export Mgr., CBS/Hytron, Danvers, Mass., and NYC, 1948–57. *Publs:* Caps for Sale, 1940; The Wonderful Feast, 1955; Little Dog Lost, Little Dog Found, 1956; The Clock, 1956; The Little Dinghy, 1958; Behind the Dark Window Shade, 1958; Billie, 1959; Pinky and the Petunias, 1959; Moving Day for the Middlemans, 1960; Jack and Jim, 1961; The Long Island Ducklings, 1961; Boris and His Balalaika, 1964; Pezzo The Peddlar and the Circus Elephant, 1970; The Thirteen Silly Thieves, 1970; The Flame, The Breeze, and the Shadow, 1969; Notes for a Biographer, 4 vols., 1977–83; Billy, the Condominium Cat, 1980. Add: 309 S.W. 8th St., Hallandale, Fla. 33009, U.S.A.

SLOMAN, Albert Edward. British, b. 1921. Education, Literature. Vice-Chancellor, Univ. of Essex, 1962–87. Lectr. in Spanish, Univ. of California, Berkeley, 1946–47; Reader in Spanish, Univ. of Dublin, 1947–53; Prof. of Spanish, Univ. of Liverpool, 1953–62. *Publs:* The Sources of Calderon's El Principe Constante, 1950; The Dramatic Craftsmanship of Calderon, 1958; (ed.) Calderon: La Vida es Sueno, 1961; A University in the Making, 1964; British Universities and Their Students, 1970. Add: 19 Inglis Rd., Colchester, Essex, CO3 3HU, England.

SLONIM, Reuben. Canadian, b. 1914. History, Theology/Religion, Travel/Exploration/Adventure. Founding Pres., Assn. For the Living Jewish Spirit, Toronto, since 1983. Rabbi, McCaul St. Synagogue, Toronto, 1937–54; Assoc. Ed., Toronto Telegram, 1955–71; Rabbi, Habonim Congregation, Toronto, 1960–83. *Publs:* In the Steps of Pope Paul, 1965; Both Sides Now, A 25-Year Encounter with Arabs and Israelis, 1971; Family Quarrel: The United Church and the Jews, 1977; Grand To Be An Orphan, 1983; To Kill a Rabbi, 1987. Add: 625 Roselawn Ave., Apt. 1105, Toronto, Ont., Canada.

SLOSBERG, Mike. American, b. 1934. Novels/Short stories, Humor/Satire. Exec. Creative Dir., EA Exclusives Inc., Boston, since 1987. Pres., Wunderman, Ricotta and Kline, advertising agency, NYC, 1978–83 (subsidiary of Young and Rubicam Inc.—with Young and Rubicam: Copywriter, San Francisco Office, 1960–62; Creative Supvr., San Francisco Office, 1962–65; Vice Pres. and Creative Dir., NYC Office, 1965–69; Vice Pres. and Creative Dir., West Coast Office, 1969–71; Sr. Vice-Pres. and Assoc. Creative Dir., NYC, 1972–78); Exec. Vice-Pres., Marsteller Inc., NYC, 1983–84; Exce. Vice-Pres., 1984–86, and Pres., Direct Marketing Div., 1986–88, Bozell Jacobs, Kenyon and Eckhardt, NYC. *Publs:* (author and illustrator) Klan-Destined (cartoon book), 1965; The August Strangers (novel), 1977. Add: c/o Ea Exclusives Inc., 530 Atlantic Ave., Boston, Mass. 02210, U.S.A.

SLOTE, Alfred. Also writes as A. H. Garnet. American. Novels, Children's fiction. Has worked as an educational television producer, journalist, and teacher. *Publs:* children's fiction—The Princess Who Wouldn't Talk, 1964; The Moon in Fact and Fancy (non-fiction), 1967, 1971; Air in Fact and Fancy, 1968; Stranger on the Ball Club, 1970; Jake, 1971; The Biggest Victory, 1972; My Father, The Coach, 1972; Hang Tough, Paul Mather, 1973; Tony and Me, 1974; Matt Gargan's Boy, 1975; My Robot Buddy, 1975; The Hot Shot, 1977; My Trip to Alpha I, 1978; Love and Tennis, 1979; The Devil Rides with Me and Other Fantastic Stories, 1980; C.O.L.A.R.: A Tale of Outer Space, 1981; Clone Catcher, 1982; Rabbit Ears, 1982; Omega Station, 1983; The Trouble on Janus, 1985; Moving In, 1988; A Friend Like That, 1988; Make-Believe Ballplayer, 1989; adult fiction—Denham Proper, 1953; Lazarus in Vienna, 1956; Strangers and Comrades, 1965; (with Woodrow W. Hunter) Preparation for Retirement (short stories), 1968; Termination: The Closing at Baker Plant (non-fiction), 1969; (as A. H. Garnet; with Garnet Garrison) The Santa Claus Killer, 1981; (as A. H. Garnet; with Garnet Garrison) Maze, 1982. Add: c/o Lippincott, 10 E. 53rd St., New York, N.Y. 10022, U.S.A.

SLOVENKO, Ralph. American, b. 1927. Law, Psychiatry, Psychology, Criminology. Prof. of Law and Psychiatry, Wayne State Univ., Detroit, Mich., since 1969. Member, Bd. of Dirs., American Orthopsychiatric Assn., and American Law-Psychology Assn.; Ed., American Series in Behavioral Science and Law. Law Clerk, Louisiana Supreme Ct., 1953; U.S. District Ct. Commnr., 1960; Sr. Asst. District Attorney, New Orleans, La., 1964–65. *Publs:* (ed.) Sexual Behavior and the Law, 1965; (ed.) Crime, Law and Corrections, 1966; Psychotherapy, Confidentiality and Privileged Communications, 1966; (co-ed.) Motivations in Play, Games and Sports, 1967; Handbook of Criminal Procedure, 1967; Creditors' and Debtors' Rights in Louisiana Civil Law, 1968; Psychiatry and Law, 1973; Tragicomedy in Court Opinions, 1974. Add: Wayne State Univ. Law Sch., Detroit, Mich, 48202, U.S.A.

SMALL, Beatrice. American, b. 1937. Romance. Secty., Young and Rubicam Advertising, NYC, 1959–60; Sales Asst., Weed Radio and TV Representatives, NYC, 1960–61, and Edward J. Petrie and Co., NYC, 1961–63; Owner, The Fat Cat gift shop, Southold, New York, 1976–81. *Publs:* The Kadin, 1978; Love Wild and Fair, 1978; Adora, 1980; Skye O'Malley, 1980: Unconquered, 1982; Beloved, 1983; All the Sweet Tomorrows, 1984; This Heart of Mine, 1985; A Love for All Time, 1968; Enchantress Mine, 1987; Blaze Wyndham, 1988; Lost Love Found, 1989. Add: P. O. Box 765, Southold, N.Y. 11971, U.S.A.

SMALL, Ernest. *See* **LENT**, Blair.

SMALLEY, Stephen S(tewart). British, b. 1931. Architecture, Theology/Religion. Dean of Chester, since 1987. Dean and Chaplain, Peterhouse, Cambridge, 1960–63; Lectr. then Sr. Lectr., Dept. of Religious Studies, Univ. of Ibadan, Nigeria, 1963–69; Lectr., 1970–77, and Sr. Lectr., 1977, Univ. of Manchester; Canon Residentiary and Precentor, Coventry Cathedral, 1977–86. *Publs:* Building for Worship: Biblical Principles in Church Design, 1967; Heaven and Hell: A Study of Last Things, 1968; The Spirit's Power: The Teaching of the Bible about the Holy Spirit, 1972; (ed. with B. Lindars) Christ and Spirit in the New Testament: Essays in Honour of Professor C.F.D. Moule, 1973; John: Evangelist and Interpreter, 1978; 1, 2, 3 John, 1984. Add: The Deanery, 7 Abbey St., Chester CH1 2JF, England.

SMART, Alastair. British, b. 1922. Art, Biography. Emeritus Prof. of Fine Art, Univ. of Nottingham. Tutor in Art History, Univ. of Hull, 1949–56; Member, Inst. for Advanced Study, Princeton, N.J., 1966–67. Former Member, Art Panel, Arts Council of Great Britain, and of the Council, Walpole Soc. *Publs:* The Life and Art of Allan Ramsay, 1952; (with John Woodward) Victorian Painting, 1959; Paintings and Drawings by Allan Ramsay, 1713-1784, 1964; The Assisi Problem and the Art of Giotto, 1971; Introducing Francis Cotes, R.A. (1726-1770), 1971; The Renaissance and Mannerism in Italy, 1972; The Renaissance and Mannerism Outside Italy, 1972; Thomas Shotter Boys, 1974; (with A. Brooks) Constable and His Country, 1976; The Dawn of Italian Painting, 1978; (with R. Simon) The Art of Cricket, 1983. Add: Rosings, 5 North Street West, Uppingham, Rutland, Leics., England.

SMART, John Jamieson Carswell. British and Australian, b. 1920. Philosophy. Emeritus Prof., Univ. of Adelaide, since 1972 (Hughes Prof. of Philosophy, 1950–72); Emeritus Prof., since 1986, Australian National Univ. (Prof. of Philosophy, Inst. of Advanced Studies, 1976–85). Fellow, Australian Academy of the Humanities, since 1969. Jr. Research Fellow, Corpus Christi Coll., Oxford, 1948–50; Reader in Philosophy, La Trobe Univ., 1972–76. *Publs:* An Outline of a System of Utilitarian Ethics, 1961; Philosophy and Scientific Realism, 1963; (ed.) Problems of Space and Time, 1964; Between Science and Philosophy, 1968; (with Bernard Williams) Utilitarianism: For and Against, 1973; Ethics, Persuasion and Truth, 1984; Essays Metaphysical and Moral, 1987. Add: 74 Mackenzie St., Hackett, A.C.T., Australia 2602.

SMART, (Roderick) Ninian. British, b. 1927. Classics, Education, Philosophy, Religion. Prof. of Religious Studies, Univ. of Lancaster, since 1967 (former Pro-Vice-Chancellor); Prof. of Comparative Religions, Univ. of California, Santa Barbara. Lectr. in Philosophy, Univ. of Wales, 1952–56; Lectr. in History and Philosophy of Religion, Univ. of London, 1956–61; H.G. Wood Prof. of Theology, Univ. of Birmingham, 1961–67. *Publs:* Reasons and Faiths, 1958; World Religions: A Dialogue, 1960; Historical Selections in the Philosophy of Religion, 1962; Doctrine and Argument in Indian Philosophy, 1964; Philosophers and Religious Truth, 1964; The Teacher and Christian Belief, 1966; Secular Education and the Logic of Religion, 1968; The Yogi and the Devotee, 1968; The Religious Experience of Mankind, 1969; the Philosophy of Religion, 1970; The Concept of Worship, 1972; The Phenomenon of Religion, 1973; The Science of Religion and the Sociology of Knowledge, 1974; Mao, 1974; A Companion for the Long Search, 1977; Background to the Long Search, 1977; The Phenomenon of Christianity, 1979; In Search of Christianity, 1979; Beyond Ideology, 1981; (with Richard Hecht) Sacred Texts of the World, 1982; Worldviews, 1983; (with Peter Merkl) Religion and Politics in the Modern World, 1983; (with Swami Purnananda) Prophet of a New Hindu Age, 1983; Concept and Empathy, 1986; Religion and the Western World, 1987; The World's Religions, 1989. Add: Religious Studies, UCSB, Santa Barbara, Calif. 93106, U.S.A.

SMELSER, Neil Joseph. American, b. 1930. Sociology. Univ. Prof. of Sociology, Univ. of California, Berkeley, since 1972 (Asst. Prof., 1958–60; Assoc. Prof., 1920–62; Prof., 1962–72; Asst. Chancellor for Educational Development, 1966–68). *Publs:* (with T. Parsons) Economy and Society, 1956; Social Change in the Industrial Revolution, 1959; Theory of Collective Behaviour, 1962; The Sociology of Economic Life, 1963; (ed. with W.T. Smelser) Personality and Social Systems, 1963; 1971; (co-ed.) Social Structure and Mobility in Economic Development, 1967; (ed.) Sociology, 1967, 1973; Essays in Sociological Explanation, 1968; Sociological Theory: A Contemporary View, 1971; (ed.) Karl on Society and Social Change, 1972; (with G. Almond) Public Higher Education in California, 1973; (with Stephen Warner) Sociological Theory: Historical and Formal, 1976; Comparative Methods in Social Science, 1976; (with Robin Content) The Changing Academic Market, 1980; (ed. with Erik H. Erikson) Themes of Work and Love in Adulthood, 1980; Sociology, 1981, 1984; (ed.) Handbook of Sociology, 1988. Add: 109 Hillcrest Rd., Berkeley,Calif. 94705, U.S.A.

SMERK, George M. American, b. 1933. Transportation, Urban studies. Prof. of Transportation, Sch. of Business, since 1969, and Dir. of Inst. for Urban Transportation, Indiana Univ., Bloomington, since 1969 (Teaching Assoc., 1960–63; Assoc. Profs., 1966–69). Writer, Newsline newsletter, Transportation Research Bd., since 1976; Columnist, Bus Ride mag., and Railfan and Railroad Mag., since 1982. Exec. Dir., Indiana Transportation Assn., since 1987. Asst. Prof. of Transportation, Univ. of Maryland, College Park, 1963–66. *Publs:* Urban Transportation: The Federal Role, 1965; (ed.) Readings in Urban Transportation, 1968; (ed.) Transportation Horizons, 1970; (ed.) Essays on Transportation Problems of the 1970s, 1970; (co-author) Mass Transit Management: A Handbook for Small Cities, 1971, 3rd ed. 1988; (with W.R. Black) Mass Transit Technical Study for Bloomington, Indiana, 1971; Urban Mass Transportation: A Dozen Years of Federal Policy, 1974. Add: Sch. of Business, Indiana Univ., Bloomington, Ind. 47405, U.S.A.

SMITH, Alfred G. American, b. 1921. Communications Media, Cultural/Ethnic topics. Prof. of Anthropology, Coll. of Communication, Univ. of Texas, Austin, since 1973. Member, Bd. of Dirs., Journal of Communication, since 1973. With Research and Analysis, Far East, Office of Strategic Services, 1942–45; Acting Instr., Univ. of Wisconsin, 1946–50; Supvr. of Linguistics, Office of the High Commnr., Trust Territory of the Pacific Islands, 1950–53; Asst. Prof. of Anthropology, Antioch Coll., Ohio, 1953–56; Assoc. Prof. of Anthropology, Emory Univ, Atlanta, Ga., 1956–62; Prof. of Anthropology, of Community Service, and Public Affairs, Univ. of Oregon, Eugene, 1962–73; Dir., 1971–72, and Pres., 1973–74, Intnl. Communication Assn. *Publs:* (ed.) Communication and Culture, 1966; Communication and Status, 1966; Cognitive Styles in Law Schools, 1979. Add: 1801 Lavaca, Austin, Texas 78701, U.S.A.

SMITH, Anna Hester. South African, b. 1912. History. City Librarian and Dir. of Africana Museum, Johannesburg, 1960–75, now retired (with Library since 1938, and Museum since 1959). Contrib. since 1943, and Ed. 1960–75, Africana Notes and News quarterly mag. Library Asst., Univ. of Stellenbosch, Cape Province, 1934–38. *Publs:* (with J. Ploeger) Pictorial Atlas of the History of the Union of South Africa, 1949; Pictorial History of Johannesburg, 1956; The Spread of Printing: Eastern Hemisphere—South Africa, 1971; Johannesburg Street Names, 1971; (ed.) Africana Curiosities, 1973; (ed.) Africana Byways, 1976; Treasures of the Africana Museum, 1977; Cape Views and Customs, 1978. Add: 103 Montevideo, 9th St., Killarney, Johannesburg, South Africa.

SMITH, Anthony. British, b. 1926. Environmental science/Ecology, Sciences, Travel/Exploration/Adventure. Science Corresp., Manchester Guardian, 1953, 1956–57, and Daily Telegraph, London, 1957–63. *Publs:* Blind White Fish in Persia, 1953; Sea Never Dry, 1958; High Street Africa, 1961; Throw out Two Hands, 1963; The Body, 1968, 1985; The Seasons, 1970; The Dangerous Sort, 1970; Mato Grosso, 1971; Beside the Seaside, 1972; (with Jill Southam) Good Beach Guide, 1973; The Human Pedigree, 1975; Animals on View, 1977; Wilderness, 1978; A Persian Quarter Century, 1979; A Sideways Look, 1983; The Mind, 1984; Smith and Son, 1984; The Great Rift, 1988; Explorers of the Amazon, 1989. Add: 10 Aldbourne Rd., London W12, England.

SMITH, Arthur L. *See* ASANTE, Molefi K.

SMITH, Arthur L. Jr. American, b. 1927. History, International relations/Current affairs. Prof. of History, California State Univ., Los Angeles, since 1956. *Publs:* The Deutschtum of Nazi Germany and the United States, 1965; Churchill's German Army, 1977; World War II: Policy and Strategy, 1979; Die Hexe von Buchenwald, 1983; Heimkehr aus dem Zweiten Weltkrieg, 1985; Hitler's Gold, 1989. Add: 5151 State Univ. Dr., Los Angeles, Calif. 90032, U.S.A.

SMITH, Barbara Herrnstein. Has also edited as Barbara Herrnstein. American, b. 1932. Literature. Prof. of Comparative Literature and English, Duke Univ., Durham, N.C., since 1987. Assoc. Ed., Poetics Today. Instr., Dept. of English and American Literature, Brandeis Univ., Waltham, Mass., 1960–61; Member of faculty, Literature Div., Bennington Coll., Vt., 1961–74; Prof., Univ. of Pennsylvania, Philadelphia, 1974–87. Member, Editorial Bd., Critical Inquiry and PMLA, 1978–80. *Publs:* (ed. as Barbara Herrnstein) Discussions of Shakespeare's Sonnets, 1964; Poetic Closure: A Study of How Poems End, 1968; (ed.) William Shakespeare: Sonnets, 1969; On the Margins of Discourse, 1978; Contingencies of Value: Alternative Perspectives for Critical Theory, 1988. Add: 325 Allen Bldg., Duke Univ., Durham, N.C. 27706, U.S.A.

SMITH, Bernard (William). Australian, b. 1916. Art. Lectr., 1955, Sr. Lectr., 1956–63, and Reader 1964–66, Univ. of Melbourne; Prof. of Contemporary Art, and Dir. of the Power Inst. of Fine Arts, Univ. of Sydney, 1967–77; Pres., Australian Academy of the Humanities, 1977–80. Secty., Australian Humanities Research Council, 1962–65; Member, Australian Unesco Cttee. for Letters, 1965; Chmn., Intnl. Art Critics Assn., 1966–69. *Publs:* Place, Taste and Tradition: A Study of Australian Art Since 1788, 1945, 1979; Education Through Art in Australia, 1958; European Vision and the South Pacific, 1960, 1980; Australian Painting, 1962, 1972; The Architectural Character of Glebe, Sydney, 1973; Concerning Contemporary Art, 1975; Documents on Art and Taste in Australia, 1975; Antipodean Manifesto: Essays in Art and History, 1977; The Spectre of Truganini (Boyer Lectures), 1980; The Boy Adeodatus, 1984; (with R. Joppien) The Art of Captain Cook's Voyages, 3 vols., 1985–87; The Death of the Artist as Hero, 1988; (with A. Wheeler) The Art of the First Fleet, 1988; The Critic as Advocate, 1989;. Add: c/o Yale Univ. Press, 302 Temple St., New Haven, Conn. 06520, U.S.A.

SMITH, Bert(ha) Kruger. American, b. 1915. Novels/Short stories, Education, Psychology. Exec. Assoc., Hogg Foundn. for Mental Health, Austin, Tex., since 1952. *Publs:* (with R.L. Sutherland, W.H. Holtzman and E.A. Koile) Personality Factors on the College Campus, 1962; No Language But a Cry, 1964; (with R.L. Sutherland) Understanding Mental Health, 1965; Your Non-Learning Child: His World of Upside Down, 1968; A Teaspoon of Honey (novel), 1970; Insights for Uptights, 1973; Aging in America, 1973; Pursuit of Dignity: New Living Alternatives for the Elderly, 1977; Looking Forward, 1983. Add: 5818 Westslope Dr., Austin, Tex. 78731, U.S.A.

SMITH, Bradley F. American, b. 1931. Education, Biography. Instr., Cabrillo Coll., Aptos, Calif., since 1960. Member of Program Cttee., American Historical Assn. Instr., Miles Coll., Birmingham, Ala., 1967–69. *Publs:* Adolf Hitler: His Family, Childhood and Youth, 1967, 1975; Heinrich Himmler: A Nazi in the Making, 1971, 1974; (ed. with Agnes F. Peterson) Himmler Geheimreden, 1974; Reaching Judgement at Nuremberg, 1977; (with Elena Agarossi) Operation Sunrise, 1979; The Road to Nuremberg, 1981; The American Road to Nuremberg: The Documentary Record, 1981; The Shadow Warriors, 1984; The War's Long Shadow, 1986. Add: Box 1225, Soquel, Calif. 95073, U.S.A.

SMITH, Brian (Clive). British, b. 1938. Political science, Public/ Social administration. Prof. of Political Science and Social Policy, Univ. of Dundee, since 1989. Ed., Public Administration and Development, since 1984. Asst. Lectr. in Politics, Univ. of Exeter, 1963–65; Lectr. in Public Admin., Inst. of Admin., Ahmadu Bello Univ., Nigeria, 1965–66; Lectr. in Politics, Univ. of Exeter, 1966–70; Lectr. in Public Admin., Civil Service Coll., London, 1970–72; Sr. Lectr., 1972–80, and Reader in Public Admin., 1980–89, Univ. of Bath. Ed., Public Administration Bulletin, 1970–76. *Publs:* Regionalism in England, 1965; Field Administration, 1967; Advising Ministers, 1969; (with J. Stanyer) Administering Britain, 1976; Policy Making in British Government, 1976; (with D.C. Pitt) Government Departments, 1981; (with D.C. Pitt) The Computer Revolution in Public Administration, 1984; Decentralization, 1985; Bureaucracy and Political Power, 1988. Add: Political Science Dept., Univ. of Dandee, Dundee, Scotland.

SMITH, C. Busby. *See* SMITH, John.

SMITH, Caesar. *See* TREVOR, Elleston.

SMITH, C(alvin) Ray. American, b. 1929. Architecture, Design, Theatre. Freelance writer and editor; Teacher, Parsons Sch. of Design, NYC, since 1977, and Fashion Inst. of Technology, NYC, since 1985. Sr. Ed., Progressive Architecture, Stamford, Conn., 1961–70; Ed., Theatre Crafts, NYC, 1969–74, and Interiors, NYC, 1974–76. Pres., U.S. Inst. for Theatre Technology Inc., 1968–71; Managing Dir., The Aston Magna

Foundn. for Music, 1973–75. *Publs:* (ed.) The Shapes of Our Theatre, 1970; The American Endless Weekend, 1972; (ed.) The Theatre Crafts Book of Costume, 1973; (ed.) The Theatre Crafts Book of Makeup, Masks, and Wigs, 1974; Supermannerism: New Attitudes in Post-Modern Architecture, 1977; Graphic Design USA: 1, 1980; Interior Design in Twentieth Century America: A History, 1987. Add: P.O. Box 32, Lenhartsville, Pa. 19534, U.S.A.

SMITH, C(hristopher) U(pham) M(urray). British, b. 1930. Biology. Sr. Lectr. in Biology, Univ. of Aston, Birmingham, since 1959. *Publs:* The Architecture of the Body, 1964; Molecular Biology: A Structural Approach, 1968; The Brain: Towards an Understanding, 1970; The Problem of Life: An Essay on the Origins of Biological Thought, 1974. Add: c/o Faber & Faber, 3 Queen Sq., London WC1N 3AU, England.

SMITH, Clifford Thorpe. British, b. 1924. Geography. Emeritus Prof., Univ. of Liverpool (Prof. of Latin American Geography from 1970; Dir., Center for Latin American Studies, 1970–82). Lectr. in Geography, Univ. of Cambridge, 1951–70; Fellow, St. John's Coll., Cambridge, 1960–70. Co-Ed., Journal of Latin-American Studies, 1970–81. *Publs:* (co-author) The Making of the Broads: A Reconsideration of Their Origin in the Light of New Evidence, 1960; An Historical Geography of Western Europe Before 1800, 1967; (co-ed.) Latin America: Geographical Perspectives, 1971; (co-author) Geography of the Third World, 1983; Population and Development in Peru, 1987. Add: 91 Ennisdale Dr., West Kirby, Wirral, Merseyside L48 9UF, England.

SMITH, Dave. (David Jeddie Smith). American, b. 1942. Poetry. Prof. of English, Virginia Commonwealth Univ., Richmond, since 1982. Teacher of English and French, and football coach, Poquoson High Sch., Virginia, 1965–67; Part-time instr., Christopher Newport Coll., Newport News, Va., 1970–72, Thomas Nelson Community Coll., Hampton, Va., 1970–72, and Coll. of William and Mary, Williamsburg, Va., 1971; Instr., Western Michigan Univ., Kalamazoo, 1974–75; Asst. Prof., Cottey Coll., Nevada, Mo., 1975–76; Asst. Prof., 1976–79, Assoc. Prof. of English, 1979–81, and Dir. of the Creative Writing Program, 1976–80, Univ. of Utah, Salt Lake City; Visiting Prof. of English, State Univ. of New York, Binghamton, 1980–81; Assoc. Prof. of English, and Dir. of Creative Writing, Univ. of Florida, Gainsville, 1981–82. *Publs:* Bull Island, 1970; Mean Rufus Thrown Down, 1973; The Fisherman's Whore, 1974; Drunks, 1975; Cumberland Station, 1976; In Dark, Sudden with Light, 1977; Goshawk, Antelope, 1979; Blue Spruce, 1981; Homage to Edgar Allan Poe, 1981; Onliness (novel), 1981; Dream Flights, 1981; (ed.) The Pure Clear Word: Essays on the Poetry of James Wright, 1982; Gray Soldiers, 1983; Southern Delights (short stories), 1984; Local Assays: On Contemporary American Poetry, 1985; The Roundhouse Voices: Selected and New Poems, 1985; (ed. with David Bottoms) The Morrow Anthology of Younger American Poets, 1985; Cuba Night (poems), 1990; (ed.) The Essential Poe, 1990. Add: 2821 E. Brigstock Rd., Midlothian, Va. 23113, U.S.A.

SMITH, David E. American, b. 1939. Medicine/Health, Sociology. Founder and Medical Dir., Haight-Ashbury Free Clinic, and Pres., Youth Projects, Inc., San Francisco, since 1967; Research Dir., Merritt Perralta Chemical Dependence Recovery Hosp., and Assoc. Clinical Prof. of Toxicology, Univ. of California Medical Center, San Francisco, since 1967. Founder and Ed., Journal of Psychoactive Drugs (formerly Journal of Psychedelic Drugs); Founder and Bd. Chmn., National Free Clinic Council (former Pres.); consultant and lectr. Formerly: Physician, Presbyterian Alcoholic Clinic and Contra Costa Alcoholic Clinic: Dir., Alcohol and Drug Abuse Screening Unit, and Consultant on Drug Abuse, Dept. of Psychiatry, San Francisco Gen. Hosp. *Publs:* Drug Abuse Papers, 1969; The New Social Drug: Medical, Legal and Cultural Perspectives on Marijuana, 1970; (co-author) Love Needs Care: A History of San Francisco's Haight-Ashbury Free Clinic, 1971; (co-author) The Free Clinic: Community Approaches to Health Care and Drug Abuse, 1972; (co-author) It's So Good, Don't Even Try It Once: Heroin in Perspective, 1972; (co-author) Drugs in the Classroom, 1973; (co-author) Uppers and Downers, 1973; (co-author) Barbiturate Use, Misuse, and Abuse, 1977; A Multicultural View of Drug Abuse, 1978; Amphetamine Use, Misuse and Abuse, 1979; PCP: Problems and Prevention, 1982; Substance Abuse and Industry, 1983; The Benzodiazepines: Current Standard Medical Practice, 1984; Treating the Cocaine Abuse, 1985; Drug Free, 1986; A Physician's Guide to Psycho Active Drugs, 1987; The Haight Asbury Free Clinic: Still Free After All These Years, 1988; Treating Opiate Dependency, 1989. Add: c/o Youth Projects Inc., Haight-Ashbury Free Medical Clinic, 409 Clayton St., San Francisco, Calif. 94117, U.S.A.

SMITH, David Marshall. British, b. 1936. Geography, Urban studies.

Prof. of Geography, Queen Mary Coll., Univ. of London, since 1973. Lectr., Univ. of Manchester, 1963–66; Assoc. Prof., Southern Illinois Univ., Carbondale, 1966–70; Assoc. Prof. of Geography and Urban Studies, Univ. of Florida, Gainesville, 1970–72. *Publs:* The Industrial Archaeology of the East Midlands, 1965; Industrial Britain: The North West, 1969; Industrial Location, 1971, 1981; The Geography of Social Wellbeing in the USA, 1973; (with M.R. Smith) The United States: How They Live and Work, 1973; Patterns in Human Geography, 1975; Human Geography: A Welfare Approach, 1977; Where the Grass Is Greener: Living in an Unequal World, 1979; Living under Apartheid: Aspects of Urbanisation and Social Change in South Africa, 1982; Apartheid in South Africa, 1987; Geography, Inequality and Society, 1988. Add: Geography Dept., Queen Mary Coll., Mile End Rd., London E1 4NS, England.

SMITH, Delia. British. Food and wine. Writer, columnist, and broadcaster: Cookery Writer, Evening Standard newspaper, later The Standard, London, 1972–85; Columnist, Radio Times; presenter of several BBC-TV series. *Publs:* How to Cheat at Cooking, 1973; Country Fare, 1973; Recipes from Country Inns and Restaurants, 1973; Family Fare, books 1 and 2, 1973–74; Evening Standard Cook Book, 1974; Country Recipes from "Look East," 1975; More Country Recipes from "Look East", 1976; Frugal Food, 1976; Book of Cakes, 1977; Recipes from "Look East," 1977; Food for Our Times, 1978; Cookery Course, 2 parts, 1978–81; The Complete Cookery Course, 1982; A Feast for Lent, 1983; A Feast for Advent, 1983; One Is Fun, 1985; (ed.) Food Aid Cookery Book, 1986; A Journey into God, 1988. Add: c/o BBC Publications, 35 Marylebone High St., London WIM 4AA, England.

SMITH, Dodie. (Dorothy Gladys Smith). Has also written as C.L. Anthony. British. Novels/Short stories, Children's fiction, Plays/Screenplays, Biography. *Publs:* plays—(as C.L. Anthony) Autumn Crocus, 1931; (as C.L. Anthony) Service, 1932; (as C.L. Anthony) Touch Wood, 1934; Call It a Day, 1935; Bonnet Over the Windmill, 1937; Dear Octopus, 1938; Lovers and Friends, 1943; Letter From Paris, 1952; I the Castle, 1954; Amateur Means Lover, 1962; novels and children's books—I Capture the Castle, 1948; The Hundred and One Dalmatians, 1956; The New Moon with the Old, 1963; The Town in Bloom, 1965; It Ends with Revelations, 1967; The Starlight Barking, 1967; A Tale of Two Families, 1970; The Girl from the Candlelit Bath, 1978; The Midnight Kittens, 1978; autobiographies—Look Back with Love, 1974; Look Back with Mixed Feelings, 1978; Look Back with Astonishment, 1979; Look Back with Gratitude, 1985. Add: The Barretts, Finchingfield, Essex, England.

SMITH, Doris Buchanan. American, b. 1934. Children's fiction. *Publs:* A Taste of Blackberries, 1973; Kick a Stone Home, 1974; Tough Chauncey, 1974; Kelly's Creek, 1975; Up and Over, 1976; Dreams and Drummers, 1978; Salted Lemons, 1980; Last Was Lloyd, 1981; Moonshadow of Cherry Mountain, 1982; The First Hard Times, 1983; Laura Upside-Down, 1984; Return to Bitter Creek, 1986; Karate Dancer, 1987; Voyages, 1989. Add: c/o Viking Penguin Inc., 40 W. 23rd St., New York, N.Y. 10010, U.S.A.

SMITH, Doris E(dna Elliott). Irish, b. 1919. Historical/Romance/Gothic. Has worked for an insurance group, Dublin, since 1938. *Publs:* Star to My Barque, 1964; The Thornwood, 1966; Song from a Lemon Tree, 1966; The Deep Are Dumb, 1967; Comfort and Keep, 1968; Fire Is for Sharing, 1968; To Sing Me Home, 1969; Seven of Magpies, 1970; Cup of Kindness, 1971; The Young Green Corn, 1971; Dear Deceiver, 1972; The One and Only, 1973; The Marrying Kind, 1974; Green Apple Love, 1974; Haste to the Wedding, 1974; Cotswold Honey, 1975; Smuggled Love, 1976; Wild Heart, 1977; My Love Came Back, 1978; Mix Me a Man, 1978; Back o' the Moon, 1981; Noah's Daughter, 1982; Marmalade Witch, 1982. Lives in Dublin. Add: c/o Robert Hale Ltd., 45–47 Clerkenwell Green, London EC1R 0HT, England.

SMITH, Duane Allan. American, b. 1937. History. Prof. of History, Fort Lewis Coll., Durango, Colo., since 1964. *Publs:* Rocky Mountain Mining Camps: The Urban Frontier, 1967; (with Ubbelohde and Benson) A Colorado History, 1972, 6th ed. 1988; Horace Tabor: His Life and the Legend, 1973; Silver Saga: The Story of Caribou, Colorado, 1974; Colorado Mining, 1977; (with Weber) Fortunes Are for the Few: Letters of Forty-Niner, 1977; Rocky Mountain Boom Town: A History of Durango, 1980, 1986; Secure the Shadow: Lachlan McLean, Colorado Mining Photographer, 1980; (with Vandenbusche) A Land Alone: Colorado's Western Slope, 1981; (with Ubbelohde and Benson) A Colorado Reader, 1982; Song of the Hammer and Drill, 1982; When Coal Was King: A History of Crested Butte, Colorado 1880-1952, 1984; (with Lamm) Pioneers and Politicans: Ten Colorado Governors in Profile, 1984; (with Metcalf and Noel) Colorado: Heritage of the Highest State, 1984; Mining

America: The Industry and the Environment 1800-1980, 1987; Mesa Verde National Park, 1988. Add: 2911 Cedar Ave., Durango, Colo. 81301, U.S.A.

SMITH, (Sir) Dudley. British, b. 1926. Politics/Government, Biography. Conservative M.P. (U.K.) for Warwick and Leamington Spa, since 1968 (M.P. for Brentford and Chiswick, 1959–66; Opposition Whip, 1965–66; Opposition Spokesman on Employment and Productivity, 1969–70; Under Secty of State, Dept. of Employment, 1970–74; Under-Secty. for Defence, 1984). A Deputy Lt. of Warwickshire. Journalist and Newspaper Exec., 1943–66 (Asst. News Ed., Sunday Express, 1953–59); Divisional Dir. and Sr. Exec., The Beecham Group Ltd., 1966–70. *Publs:* They Also Served, 1945; Harold Wilson: A Critical Biography, 1963. Add: Church Farm, Weston-under-Wetherley, nr. Leamington Spa, Warwicks., England.

SMITH, Dwight L. American, b. 1918. History, Travel/ Exploration/Adventure. Prof., American Western and Canadian History, Miami Univ., Oxford, Ohio, since 1953–84, now Emeritus. Ed., The Old Northwest. Instr., Ohio State Univ., Columbus, 1949–53. Research Historian, Ohio Historical Soc., 1950–51; Ed. and Consultant, American Biographical Centre, 1966–81. *Publs:* From Greene Ville to Fallen Timbers, 1952; The Western Journals of John May: Ohio Company Agent and Business Adventurer, 1961; (with C.G. Crampton) The Hoskaninni Papers: Mining in Glen Canyon, 1961; Down the Colorado, 1965; Western Life in the Stirrups, 1965; The Photographer and the River, 1967; John D. Young and the Colorado Gold Rush, 1969; (with L.W. Garrison) The American Political Process, 1972; (ed.) Afro-American History, 2 vols., 1974–81; (ed.) Indians of the United States and Canada, 1974, vol. 2, 1983; (ed.) Era of the American Revolution, 1975; The American and Canadian West, 1979; (ed.) The History of Canada, 1983; (ed.) The War of 1812, 1985; (with C.G. Crampton) The Colorado River Survey, 1987; A Frustrated Westward Trek, 1988. Add: 409 Emerald Woods Dr., Oxford, Ohio 45056, U.S.A.

SMITH, Edwin H. American, b. 1919. Education. Prof. of Education, Florida State Univ., Tallahassee, since 1971 (joined faculty, 1962). *Publs:* (with C. and R. Geeslin) Reading Development Kits A, B, and C, 1968, 1969; Literacy Education for Adolescents and Adults, 1969; (with C.G. Rowell) The Sound Spelling Program, 1971; (with M. Martin) Guide to Curricula for Disadvantaged Adult Programs, 1972; (with C.G. Rowell and L. Hafner) The Sound Reading Program, 1972; (wIth B. Guice and N. Frederick) Learning and Teaching the Decoding Skills, 1974; (with B. Guice and N. Frederick) Informal Reading Diagnosis and Correction, 1975; Teaching Reading to Adults, 1975; (with B. Palmer and W. McCall) Test Lessons in Figurative Language, 1980; (with W. McCall) Test Lessons in Reading/Reasoning, 1980. Add: Coll. of Education, Florida State Univ., Tallahassee, Fla. 32306, U.S.A.

SMITH, Ella. American, b. 1933. Novels, Film, Biography. Freelance dir. and writer in theater, television and film, Los Angeles; Acting coach, Tracy Roberts Actors Studio. Asst. Prof. of Theater and Film, Rhode Island Coll., Providence, 1964–71; Asst. Prof. of Dramatic Arts, Univ. of Connecticut, Storrs, 1971–72. *Publs:* Starring Miss Barbara Stanwyck, 1974, 1985; Introduction to A World of Movies 1974; The Transference, 1982. Add: Box 366, Beverly Hills, Calif. 90213, U.S.A.

SMITH, Elsdon Coles. American, b. 1903. Language/Linguistics. Lawyer, Chicago, since 1930; Book Review Ed., Names, Journal of the American Name Soc., since 1953. *Publs:* Naming Your Baby, 1943; Story of Our Names, 1950; (compiler) Personal Names, 1952; Dictionary of American Family Names, 1956; Treasury of Name Lore, 1967; American Surnames, 1969; New Dictionary of American Family Names, 1973; The Book of Smith, 1978. Add: 8001 Lockwood Ave., Skokie, Ill. 60077. U.S.A.

SMITH, Elton Edward. American, b. 1915. Literature. Prof. of Victorian Literature, Univ. of South Florida, Tampa, since 1961. Visiting Prof., Univ. of Algiers, 1968–70, Mohammed V Univ., Rabat, Morocco, 1974–75, Univ. of London, 1982, Univ. of Paris, 1983. *Publs:* The Two Voices: A Tennyson Study, 1964; (with E.M.G. Smith) William Godwin, 1965; Louis MacNeice, 1970; The Angry Young Men of the Thirties: Day Lewis, Spender, MacNeice, Auden, 1975; Charles Reade, 1977. Add: c/o Twayne, 70 Lincoln St., Boston, Mass. 02111, U.S.A.

SMITH, Emma. British, b. 1923. Novels/Short stories, Children's Fiction. *Publs:* Maidens' Trip, 1948; The Far Cry, 1949; Emily: The Story of a Traveller (in U.S. as Emily: The Travelling Guinea Pig), 1959; Out

of Hand, 1963; Emily's Voyage, 1966; No Way of Telling, 1972; The Opportunity of a Lifetime, 1978. Add: c/o Curtis Brown, 162-168 Regent St., London W1R 5TA, England.

SMITH, Evelyn E(lizabeth). American, b. 1937. Mysteries. Contributor to numerous women's mags. *Publs:* The Perfect Planet, 1962; (as Delphine C. Lyons) Valley of Shadows, 1968; (as Delphine C. Lyons) The Armchair Shoppers Guide; Depths of Yesterday; Flower of Evil; House of Four Widows; Unpopular Planet, 1975; The Copy Shop, 1985; Miss Melville Regrets, 1986; Miss Melville Returns, 1987; Miss Melville's Revenge, 1988. Add: P.O. Box 226, Ansonia Station, New York, N.Y. 10023, U.S.A.

SMITH, Frederick E(screet). Also writes as David Farrell. British, b. 1922. Novels/short stories, Plays/Screenplays. *Publs:* Of Masks and Minds, 1954; Laws Be Their Enemy, 1955; 633 Squadron, 1956; Lydia Trendennis, 1957; The Sin and the Sinners, 1958; The Grotto of Tiberius, 1961; (as David Farrell) Temptation Isle, 1962; (as David Farrell) the Other Cousin, 1962; The Devil Behind Me, 1962; (as David Farrell) Two Loves, 1963; The Storm Knight, 1966; A Killing for the Hawks, 1966; (as David Farrell) Valley of Conflict, 1967; (as David Farrell) Strange Enemy, 1967; (as David Farrell) Mullion Rock, 1968; The Wider Sea of Love, 1969; Waterloo, 1970; The Tormented, 1974; 633 Squadron: Operation Rhine Maiden, 1975; Saffron's War, 1975; Saffron's Army, 1976; 633 Squadron: Operation Crucible, 1977; 633 Squadron: Operation Valkyrie, 1978; The War God, 1980; 633 Squadron: Operation Cobra, 1981; 633 Squadron: Operation Titan, 1982; The Obsession. 1984; Rage of the Innocent, 1986; A Meeting of Stars, 1987; A Clash of Stars, 1987; In the Presence of My Foes, 1988; Years of the Fury, 1989. Add: 3 Hathaway Rd., Southbourne, Bournemouth, Dorset BH6 3HH, England.

SMITH, George H(enry). Also writes as Jan Hudson, Jerry Jason, Diana Summers and with M. Jane Deer Smith under joint pseud. M.J. Deer. American, b. 1922. Historical/Romance/Gothic, Science fiction/Fantasy, Biography. Freelance writer since 1950. *Publs:* Satan's Daughter, 1961; 1976: Year of Terror, 1961; Scourge of the Blood Cult, 1961; The Coming of the Rats, 1961; Doomsday Wing, 1963; (as M.J. Deer) A Place Called Hell (romance), 1963; (as M.J. Deer) Flames of Desire, 1963; The Unending Night, 1964; The Forgotten Planet, 1965; (as Jerry Jason) The Psycho Makers, 1965; The Four Day Weekend, 1966; Druid's World, 1967; (as Jan Hudson) The Hell's Angels (non-fiction), 1967, in U.K. as The New Barbarians, 1973; (as Jan Hudson) The People in the Saucers (non-fiction) 1967; Who Is Ronald Reagan? (biography), 1968; Kar Kaballa, 1969; Witch Queen of Lochlann, 1969; Martin Luther King, Jr. (biography), 1971; Bikers at War (non-fiction), 1976; The Second War of the Worlds, 1978; The Island Snatchers, 1978; (as Diana Summers) Wild Is the Heart (romance) 1978; (as Diana Summers) Love's Wicked Ways (romance), 1979; The Devil's Breed, 1979; The Rogues, 1980; The Firebrands, 1980; (as Diana Summers) Fallen Angel, 1981; (as Diana Summers) Louisana, 1984; (as Diana Summers) The Emperor's Lady, 1984. Add: 4113 W. 180th St., Torrance, Calif. 90504, U.S.A.

SMITH, Gregory Blake. American, b. 1951. Novels. Asst. Prof. of English, Carleton Coll., Northfield, Minn., since 1987. *Publs:* The Devil in the Dooryard, 1986. Add: Dept. of English, Carleton Coll., Northfield, Minn. 55057, U.S.A.

SMITH, Grover Cleveland. American, b. 1923. Intellectual history, Literature. Prof. of English, Duke Univ., Durham, N.C., since 1966 (Instr., 1952–55; Asst. Prof., 1955–61; Assoc. Prof., 1961–66). Pres., T.S. Eliot Soc., since 1989. Instr., Rutgers Univ., N.J., 1946–48, and Yale Univ., New Haven, Conn., 1948–52. *Publs:* T.S. Eliot's Poetry and Plays: A Study in Sources and Meaning, 1956, 1974; (ed.) Josiah Royce's Seminar, 1913-1914: As Recorded in the Notebooks of Harry T. Costello, 1963; (ed.) Letters of Aldous Huxley, 1969; Archibald MacLeish, 1971; Ford Madox Ford, 1972; The Waste Land, 1983. Add: Box 6043, College Station, Durham, N.C. 27708, U.S.A.

SMITH, Hedrick (Laurence). American, b. 1933. International relations/Current affairs. Washington Corresp., New York Times Mag., since 1987 (Foreign Affairs Writer, New York Times, Washington, 1962–63; Saigon Corresp., 1963–64; Cairo Corresp., 1964–66; Diplomatic Corresp., 1966–69 and 1970–71; Moscow Bureau Chief, 1971–74; Deputy National Ed., 1975–76; Bureau Chief, Washington, 1976–79; Chief Washington Corresp., 1979–85). Reporter in Atlanta, Nashville, and Memphis, United Press, 1959–62; Visiting Journalist, American Enterprise Inst., 1985–86. Recipient: Pulitzer Prize for public service, 1972, and international reporting, 1974. *Publs:* (with N. Sheehan, E.W. Kenworthy, and F. Butterfiel) The Pentagon Papers, 1971; The Russians, 1976; (with A.

Clymer, R. Bart and L. Silk) Reagan: The Man, The President, 1980; Beyond Reagan: The Politics of Upheaval, 1986; (with others) The Power Game, 1988. Add: New York Times, 1717 K St. N.W., Washington, D.C. 20036, U.S.A.

SMITH, Hobart Muir. American, b. 1912. Biology, Zoology. Prof. of EPO Biology, Univ. of Colorado, since 1968. Instr. of Biology, Univ. of Rochester, N.Y., 1941–45; Assoc. Prof. of Wildlife Mgmt., Texas A & M Univ., College Station, 1946; Instr. to Prof. of Zoology, Univ. of Illinois, Urbana, 1947–68. Publs: Handbook of Amphibians and Reptiles of Kansas, 1950, 1956; (with E.H. Taylor) An Annotated Checklist and Key to the Reptiles of Mexico Exclusive of the Snakes, 1950; (with H.S. Zim) Reptiles and Amphibians, 1953, 1956; Snakes as Pets 1953, 4th ed., 1977; Lectures in Comparative Anatomy, 1954; (with J.L. Bronson) Pet Turtles, 1954; Pet Turtles, 1955; Evolution of Chordate Structure, 1957, 1960; Laboratory Studies of Chordate Structure, 1957, 7th ed. 1973; A Golden Stamp Book: Snakes, Turtles and Lizards, 1958; (with F.G. Boys) Poisonous Amphibians and Reptiles: Recognition and Bite Treatment, 1959; Glossary of Terms for Comparative Anatomy, 1961; (with T.P. Maslin and R.L. Brown) Summary of the Distribution of the Herpetofauna of Colorado, 1965; (with E.H. Taylor) Herpetology of Mexico, 1966; Turtles, 1967; Early Foundations of Mexican Herpetology: An Annotated and Indexed Bibliography of the Herpetological Publications of Alfredo Duges 1826-1910, 1969; (with J.C. Oldham and S.A. Miller) A Laboratory Perspectus of Snake Anatomy, 1970; (with R.B. Smith) Synopsis of the Herpetofauna of Mexico, 6 vols., 1971–80; (with J.C. Oldham) Laboratory Anatomy of the Iguana, 1974; Amphibians of North America, 1978; Reptiles of North America, 1982. Add: Dept. of EPO Biology, Univ. of Colorado, Boulder, Colo. 80309, U.S.A.

SMITH, Howard E., Jr. American, b. 1927. Children's non-fiction. Ed., Gen. Book Div., McGraw-Hill Book Co., NYC, 1967–75. Publs: From Under the Earth: America's Metals, Fuels and Minerals, 1967; Play with the Wind, 1972; (with L. Norris) The Newsmakers: The Press and the Presidents, 1974; Play with the Sun, 1975; Dreams in Your Life, 1975; The Unexplored World, 1976; The Sensual Explorer, 1977; Giant Animals, 1977; The Complete Beginner's Guide to Mountain Climbing, 1977; (with L. Norris) An Oak Tree Dies and a Journey Begins, 1979; Animal Olympics, 1979; Animal Marvels, 1981; Living Fossils, 1982; Killed Weather, 1982; Larousse: The World We Live In, 1982; A Naturalist's Guide to the Year, 1985; Disarmament: The Road to Peace, 1986; Small Worlds: Communities of Living Things, 1987; Daring the Unknown: A History of NASA, 1987. Add: 128 Willow St., Brooklyn, N.Y. 11201, U.S.A.

SMITH, Howard K(ingsbury). American, b. 1914. International relations/Current affairs, Politics/Government, Children's non fiction. Freelance news commentator, author and lectr., since 1979. Foreign Corresp., United Press, London, 1939; Berlin Corresp., 1941, Chief European Corresp. and Dir., London, 1946–57, Washington Corresp., 1957–61, and Chief Corresp. and Gen. Mgr., 1961–62, all CBS; Radio and Television News Commentator, ABC, Washington, D.C., 1962–79. Publs: Last Train from Berlin, 1942; The State of Europe, 1949; Washington, D.C., 1967. Add: 6450 Brooks Lane, Bethesda, Md. 20816, U.S.A.

SMITH, Howard Ross. American, b. 1917. Administration/Management, Business/Trade/Industry, Economics. Prof. of Mgmt., Univ. of Georgia, Athens, since 1963 (Assoc. Prof. of Economics, 1946–49; Prof. of Economics, 1949–61). Publs: (ed.) Statistical Abstract of Georgia, 1953; Economic History of the United States, 1955; Government and Business, 1958; Democracy and Public Interest, 1960; The Capitalistic Imperative, 1976; (with others) Management: Making Organizations Perform, 1980, and A Book of Readings, 1980. Add: Dept. of Mgmt., Coll. of Business Admin., Univ. of Georgia, Athens, Ga. 30602, U.S.A.

SMITH, Iain Crichton. British, b. 1928. Novels/Short stories, Poetry. Secondary Sch. Teacher, Clydebank, 1953–55; English teacher, Oban High Sch., Argyllshire, 1955–77. Publs: (in English): The Long River, 1955; (co-author) New Poets 1959, 1959; Deer on the High Hills, 1960; Thistles and Roses, 1961; The Law and the Grace, 1965; At Helensburgh, 1968; Consider the Lilies (in U.S. as The Alien Light), 1969; The Last Summer, 1969; (trans.) Ben Dorain, by D.B. Macintyre, 1969; Survival Without Error and Other Stories, 1970; From Bourgeois Land, 1970; Selected Poems, 1970; (trans.) Poems to Eimhir, by Sorley MacLean, 1971; My Last Duchess, 1971; (co-author) Penguin Modern Poets 22, 1972; Love Poems and Elegies, 1972; Hamlet in Autumn, 1972; The Black and the Red, 1973; Goodbye, Mr Dixon, 1974; The Notebooks of Robinson Crusoe and Other Poems, 1974; In the Middle, 1977; The Hermit and Other Stories, 1977; River, River: Poems for Children, 1978; An End

to Autumn (novel), 1978; Murdo and Other Stories, 1981; A Field Full of Folk (novel), 1982; Selected Poems 1955-80, 1982; The Search (novel), 1983; The Exiles (poetry), 1984; Mr. Trill in Hades and Other Stories, 1984; The Tenement (novel), 1985; Selected Poems, 1985; A Life (poetry), 1986; Towards the Human (criticism), 1987; In the Middle of the Wood (novel), 1987. Add: Tigh Na Fuaran, Taynuilt, Argyll PA35 1JW, Scotland.

SMITH, James L(eslie Clarke). British, b. 1936. Literature. Sr. Lectr., Dept. of English, Univ. of Southampton, since 1980 (Lectr. 1965–80). Henry Fellowship, Yale Univ., 1962–63; Lectr., Dept. of English, Univ. of British Columbia, Vancouver, 1963–64. Publs: Melodrama, 1973; (ed.) Sir John Vanbrugh's The Provoked Wife, 1974; (ed.) Victorian Melodramas, 1976; (ed.) William Wycherley's The Plain Dealer, 1979; (ed.) Dion Boucicault's London Assurance, 1984. Add: Sansomes Farmhouse, Whiteparish, nr. Salisbury, Wilts, England.

SMITH, Joan. Canadian, b. 1938. Historical/Romance/Gothic, children's fiction. Publs: An Affair of the Heart, 1977; Escapade, 1977; La Comtesse, 1978; Imprudent Lady, 1978; Dame Durden's Daughter, 1978; Aunt Sophie's Diamonds, 1979; Flowers of Eden, 1979; Sweet and Twenty, 1979; Talk of the Town, 1979; Aurora, 1980; Babe, 1980; Endure My Heart, 1980; Lace for Milady, 1980; Delsie, 1981; Lover's Vows, 1981; Love's Way, 1982; Reluctant Bride, 1982; Reprise, 1982; Wiles of a Stranger, 1982; Prelude to Love, 1983; Grandmother's Donkey, 1983; Grandmother's Secret, 1983; Royal Rebels, 1985; Midnight Masquerade, 1985; The Devious Duchess, 1985; True Lady, 1986; Bath Belles, 1986; A Country Wooing, 1987; Love's Harbinger, 1987; Country Flirt, 1987; Larcenous Lady, 1988. Add: c/o Fawcett, 201 E. 50th St., New York, N.Y. 10022, U.S.A.

SMITH, John. Has also written as C. Busby Smith. British, b. 1924. Children's fiction, Plays/Screenplays, Poetry, Literature. Dir., 1946–58, and Managing Dir., 1959–71, Christy and Moore Ltd., literary agents, London. Ed., Poetry Review, London, 1962–65. Publs: (as C. Busby Smith) Gates of Beauty and Death: Poems, 1948; The Dark Side of Love, 1952; The Birth of Venus: Poems, 1954; The Mask of Glory, 1956; Mr. Smith's Apocalypse: A Jazz Cantata, 1957; Excursus in Autumn., 1958; (ed. with W. Seymour) The Pattern of Poetry, 1963; A Discreet Immorality, 1965; (ed.) My Kind of Verse, 1965; (ed.) Modern Love Poems, 1966; Five Songs of Resurrection, 1967; Four Ritual Dances, 1968; (ed. with W. Seymour) Happy Christmas, 1968; (with H. Read and J. Cassou) Jan Le Witt: An Appreciation of His Work, 1971; The Broken Fiddlestick, 1971; The Early Bird and the Worm, 1972; Entering Rooms, 1973; (ed.) My Kind of Rhymes, 1973; The Arts Betrayed, 1978; A Landscape of My Own: Selected Poems 1948-1982, 1982; Songs for Simpletons, 1984. Add: 3 Adelaide Ct., Hove, Sussex, England.

SMITH, Kathleen J(oan). British, b. 1929. Novels, Plays/Screenplays, Poetry, Criminology/Law enforcement/Prisons. Asst. Gov., Holloway Prison, London, 1957–60. Publs: Twelve Months, Mrs. Brown, 1965; A Cure for Crime, 1965; The Young and the Pity, 1966; Devil's Delight, 1968; The Company of God, 1975; Help for the Bereaved, 1978; The Stages of Sorrow, 1979; Old Welsh Country Life, 1984; Meditations for Eagles, 1987. Add: Felin Faesog, Clynnog, Caernarvon, Gwynedd, North Wales.

SMITH, Kay Nolte. American, b. 1932. Mystery/Crime/Suspense, Translations. Writing and Speech Consultant, AT & T Bell Laboratories, New Jersey, since 1978. Advertising copy-writer, Stern Brothers, NYC, 1957–59, and Fletcher Richards Calkins and Holden, NYC, 1959–62; professional actress, as Kay Gillian, 1962–75; Instr., Trenton State Coll., N.J., 1975–80; and Brookdale Coll., Lincroft, N.J., 1975–82. Publs: The Watcher, 1980; Catching Fire, 1982; Mindspell, 1983; Elegy for a Soprano, 1985; (transl.) Chantecler, by Edmond Rostand, 1986; Country of the Heart, 1988. Add: 73 Hope Rd., Tinton Falls, N.J. 07724, U.S.A.

SMITH, Ken(neth John). British, b. 1938. Poetry. Ed., Stand, Newcastle upon Tyne, 1963–69; taught in an elementary sch., Dewsbury, Yorks., 1963–64, and in a technical coll., Batley, Yorks., 1964–65; Tutor, Exeter Coll. of Art, Devon, 1965–69; Instr. in Creative Writing, Slippery Rock State Coll., Pa., 1969–72; Visiting Poet, Clark Univ., Worcester, Mass., 1972–73; Yorkshire Arts Fellow, Leeds Univ., 1976–78; Ed., South West Review, Exeter, 1976–79; Writer-in-Residence, Kingston Polytechnic, Surrey, 1979–81, and H.M. Prison Wormwood Scrub, 1985–87. Publs: Eleven Poems, 1964; The Pity, 1967; Academic Board Poems, 1968; A Selection of Poems, 1969; Work, Distances: Poems, 1972; The Wild Rose, 1973; Hawk Wolf, 1974; Frontwards in a Backwards Movie, 1975; Anus Mundi, 1975; Wasichi, 1975; Henry the Navigator, 1976; Tristam Crazy, 1978; Burned Books, 1981; Fox Running, 1981; Abel Baker Charlie Delta Epic Sonnets, 1982; The Poet Reclining, 1982; Terra, 1986; A Book of Chinese Whispers, 1987; Wormwood, 1987; Inside Time, 1989. Add: 78 Friars Rd., London E6 1LL, England.

SMITH, L. Neil. American. Science fiction. *Publs:* Their Majesties' Buccaneers, 1981; The Venus Belt, 1981; The Nagasaki Vector, 1983; Lando Calrissian and the Flamewind of Oseon, 1983; Lando Calrissian and the Mindharp of Sharu, 1983; Lando Calrissian and the Starcave of ThonBoka, 1983; Tom Paine Maru, 1984; The Crystal Empire, 1986. Add: c/o Ballantine Books, 201 E. 50th St., New York, N.Y. 10020, U.S.A.

SMITH, Lacey Baldwin. American, b. 1922. History, Biography. Prof. of English History, Northwestern Univ., Evanston, Ill., since 1955. Instr., Princeton Univ., N.J., 1951–53; Asst. Prof., Massachusetts Inst. of Technology, Cambridge, 1953–55. *Publs:* Tudor Prelates and Politics, 1953; A Tudor Tragedy: The Life and Times of Catherine Howard, 1961; This Realm of England 1399-1689, 1966, 3rd ed. 1975; The Elizabethan Epic (in U.S. as The Elizabethan World), 1966; (with Jay Williams) The Spanish Armada, 1966; Henry VIII: The Mask of Royalty, 1971; Elizabeth Tudor: Portrait of a Queen, 1975; (with Jean R. Smith) Essentials of World History, 1979; (with Jean R. Smith) The Past Speaks to 1688, 1981; Treason in Tudor England: Politics and Paranoia, 1986. Add: Dept. of History, Northwestern Univ., Evanston, Ill. 60201, U.S.A.

SMITH, Lew. *See* FLOREN, Lee.

SMITH, Mark (Richard). American, b. 1935. Novels/Short stories. Prof. of English, Univ. of New Hampshire, Durham, since 1975 (Instr., 1966–68; Asst. Prof., 1968–71; Assoc. Prof., 1971–75). Adviser to the Rockefeller Foundn., 1967–69. *Publs:* Toyland, 1965; The Middleman, 1967; The Death of the Detective, 1974; The Moon Lamp, 1976; The Delphinium Girl, 1980; Doctor Blues, 1983; Smoke Street, 1984; A Book of Lilies, 1985. Add: Dept. of English, Hamilton-Smith, Univ. of New Hampshire, Durham, N.H. 03824, U.S.A.

SMITH, Martin Cruz. Also writes as Nick Carter, Jake Logan, Martin Quinn, and Simon Quinn. American, b. 1942. Novels/Short stories, Mystery/Crime/Suspense. Reporter, Philadelphia Daily News, 1965, and Magazine Management, 1966–69. *Publs:* novels—(as Martin Smith) The Indians Won, 1970; (as Martin Quinn) The Adventures of the Wilderness Family (novelization of screenplay), 1976; (as Jake Logan) North to Dakota, 1976; (as Jake Logan) Ride for Revenge, 1977; mystery novels—Gypsy in Amber, 1971; The Analog Bullet, 1972; Canto for a Gypsy, 1972; Nightwing, 1977; Gorky Park, 1981; Stallion Gate, 1986; Polar Star, 1989; mystery novels as Nick Carter—The Inca Death Squad, 1972; Code Name: Werewolf, 1973; The Devil's Dozen, 1973; mystery novels as Simon Quinn—His Eminence, Death, 1974; Nuplex Red, 1974; The Devil in Kansas, 1974; The Midas Coffin, 1975; Last Rites for the Vulture, 1975; The Human Factor (novelization of screenplay), 1975. Add: c/o Knox Burger Assocs., 391 Washington Sq. S., New York, N.Y. 10012, U.S.A.

SMITH, Michael. American, b. 1935. Plays, Poetry, Theatre. Asst. Press Secty. and Speechwriter for Mayor Koch, NYC, since 1986. Dramatist and dir.; Theatre Critic, 1959–74, and Assoc. Ed., 1962–65, Village Voice, NYC (Obie Award judge, 1962–68, 1972–74); Instr., New Sch. for Social Research, NYC, 1964–65; Mgr., Sundance Festival Theatre, Upper Black Eddy, Pa., 1966–68; Producer, Caffe Cino, NYC, 1968; Dir., Theatre Genesis, NYC, 1971–75; Instr., Project Radius, Dalton, Ga., 1972, and Hunter Coll., NYC, 1972; Arts Ed., Taos News, N.M., 1977–78; Arts Critic, New London Day, Connecticut, 1982–86. *Publs:* (ed.) Eight Plays from Off-Off-Broadway, 1966; Theatre Journal, Winter 1967, 1968; Theatre Trip, 1969; The Next Thing (in The Best of Off-Off-Broadway), 1969; Captain Jack's Revenge (in New American Plays 4), 1971; Country Music (in More Plays from Off-Off-Broadway), 1972; American Baby (poetry), 1983; A Sojourn in Paris (poetry), 1985. Add: 463 West St., Apt. D-604, New York, N.Y. 10014, U.S.A.

SMITH, Michael. Irish, b. 1942. Poetry. Teacher of Latin and English, St. Paul's Coll., Raheny, Dublin. Ed., New Irish Poets series of the New Writers Press, Dublin, and of The Lace Curtain, Dublin. *Publs:* With the Woodnymphs, 1968; Dedications, 1968; Homage to James Thompson (B.V.) at Portobello, 1969; Poems, 1971; Times and Locations, 1972; (ed.) Selected Poems of James Clarence Mangan, 1974; (trans.) Del Camino, by Antonio Machado, 1974. Add: 19 Warrenmount Pl., SCR, Dublin 8, Ireland.

SMITH, Morton. American, b. 1915. Classics, Ancient history, Theol-

ogy/Religion. Prof. Emeritus of History, since 1985, and Adjunct Prof. of Religion since 1988, Columbia Univ., NYC, (Asst. Prof., 1957–60; Assoc. Prof., 1960–62; Prof., 1962–85; Special Lectr. in Religion 1986–88). Asst. Prof. of Biblical Literature, Brown Univ., Providence, R.I., 1950–56. *Publs:* Tannatic Parallels to the Gospels, 1951; The Ancient Greeks, 1960; (with M. Hadas) Heroes and Gods, 1965; Palestinian Parties and Politics that Shaped the Old Testament, 1971; The Secret Gospel, 1973; Clement of Alexandria and a Secret Gospel of Mark, 1973; (with E. Bickerman) The Ancient History of Western Civilization, 1976; Jesus the Magician, 1978; Hope and History, 1980. Add: 165 W. 66 St., Apt. 20j, New York, N.Y. 10023, U.S.A.

SMITH, Norman Edward Mace. Writes as Neil Sheraton and Norman Shore. British, b. 1914. Mystery/Crime/Suspense. Pilot, R.A.F., 1940–45, and British Overseas Airways Corp., 1946–71. *Publs:* (as Neil Sheraton) African Terror, 1957; (as Neil Sheraton) Cairo Ring, 1958; (as Neil Sheraton) Clear Sky Above, 1959; (as Neil Sheraton) They Found a Way Back, 1960; (as Neil Sheraton) The Princess and the Pilot, 1961; (as Norman Shore) The Lonely Russian, 1972; (as Norman Shore) Hong Kong Nightstop, 1973; (as Norman Shore) Russian Hi-Jack, 1975. Add: 67 St. Alban's Ave., Bournemouth BH8 9EG, England.

SMITH, Page. American, b. 1917. History, Biography. Prof. Emeritus of Historical Studies, Cowell Coll., Univ. of California at Santa Cruz, since 1973 (Provost, 1964–70; Prof. 1970–73). Fellow, Inst. of Early American History and Culture, 1951–53; Asst. to Prof., Univ. of California at Los Angeles, 1953–64. *Publs:* James Wilson, Founding Father, 1956; John Adams, 1962; The Historian and History, 1964, as a City Upon a Hill: The Town in American History, 1966; Daughters of the Promised Land: Women in American History, 1970; Jefferson, 1976; A New Age Now Begins: A People's History of the American Revolution, 1976; (co-author) The Chicken Book, 1976; A Letter from My Father, 1976; (ed.) The Religious Origins of the American Revolution, 1976; The Constitution: A Documentary and Narrative History, 1978; The Shaping of America, 1980, The Nation Comes of Age, 1981, Trial by Fire: The Civil War and Reconstruction, 1982, and American Enters the World, 1985 (vols III, IV, VI and VIII of A People's History of the United States); Dissenting Opinion: The Selected Essays of Page Smith, 1984. Add: 235 Pine Flat Rd., Santa Cruz, Calif. 95060, U.S.A.

SMITH, Peter Charles Horstead. British, b. 1940. Novels/Short stories, History. Ed., Photo Precision Ltd., printers and publrs., 1972–75. *Publs:* Destroyer Leader, 1968; Task Force 57, 1969; Pedestal, 1970; Stuka at War 1970, 1980; Hard Lying, 1971; British Battle Cruisers, 1972; (with Edwin Walker) War in the Aegean, 1974; Heritage of the Sea, 1974; Royal Navy Ships' Badges, 1974; (ed.) The Haunted Sea, 1974; (with Edwin Walker) Battles of the Malta Striking Forces, 1974; Destroyer Action, 1974; R.A.F. Squadron Badges, 1974; The Story of the Torpedo Bomber, 1974; Per Mare Per Terram: A History of the Royal Marines, 1974; Arctic Victory, 1975; Fighting Flotilla, 1976; (ed. and contrib.) Undesirable Properties, 1977; The Great Ships Pass, 1977; Hit First, Hit Hard, 1979; (ed. and contrib.) The Phantom Coach, 1979; Action Imminent, 1980; (ed. and contrib.) Haunted Shores, 1980; Impact! The Dive Bomber Pilots Speak, 1981; (with J.R. Dominy) Cruisers in Action, 1981; Dive Bomber!, 1982; Rendezvous Skerki Bank (fiction), 1982; Hold the Narrow Sea, 1984; Uninvited Guests, 1984; H.M.S. Wild Swan, 1985; Into the Assault, 1985; Vengeance, 1986; The Jungle Dive Bombers, 1987; Victoria's Victories, 1987; (with D.A. Oakley) The Royal Marines: A Pictorial History, 1988; Battleship Royal Sovereign, 1988; Massacre at Tobruk, 1988; Eagle's War, 1989; Strike from the Sky, 1989. Add: "Foxden," 12 Brocklands Rd., Riseley, Bedford MK44 1EE, England.

SMITH, Peter J. Canadian, b. 1931. Geography. Prof. of Geography, Univ. of Alberta, Edmonton, since 1969 (Asst. Prof., and Assoc. Prof., 1959–69). Research Planner, City Planning Dept., Calgary, Alta., 1956–59. *Publs:* Population and Production: An Introduction to Some Problems in Economic Geography, 1967, rev. ed. 1971; (ed.) Studies in Canadian Geography: The Prairie Provinces, 1972; (ed.) Edmonton: The Emerging Metropolitan Pattern, 1978; The Edmonton-Calgary Corridor, 1978 (ed.) Environment and Economy: Essays on the Human Geography of Alberta, 1984. Add: Dept. of Geography, Univ. of Alberta, Edmonton, Alta. T6G 2H4, Canada.

SMITH, Ralph Bernard. British, b. 1939. Area Studies, History. Reader in International History of Asia, Sch of Oriental and African Studies., Univ. of London, since 1988 (Lectr., 1962–71; Reader since 1971). *Publs:* Viet-Nam and the West, 1968, 1971; Land and Politics in the England of Henry VIII: The West Riding of Yorkshire 1530-46,

1970; (ed. with W. Watson) Early South East Asia, 1979; An International History of the Vietnam War, I, 1955-61, 1983, II, 1961-65, 1985　Add: Sch. of Oriental and African Studies, London WC1, England.

SMITH, Ralph Lee. American, b. 1927. Communications media/ Broadcasting, Medicine/Health, Money/Finance, Politics/Government. Dir., Corp. Relations, Smart House Project, NAHB Research Foundn., since 1986. Performing musician on Appalachian dulcimer, banjo, and harmonica. Ed., National Better Business Bureau, NYC, 1954–57; freelance writer, 1958–70; Sr. Research Assoc., Sloan Commn. on Cable Communications, NYC, 1970–71; with Telecommunications Dept., MITRE Corp., McLean, Va., 1971–72; Assoc. Prof., Sch. of Communications, Howard Univ., Washington, D.C., 1973–76; Exec., Bertman Group, 1980–83. *Publs:* The Health Hucksters, 1960; The Bargain Hucksters, 1962; The Grim Truth about Mutual Funds, 1963; (with B. Watenberg) The New Nations of Africa, 1963; Getting to Know the World Health Organization, 1963; The Tarnished Badge, 1965; At Your Own Risk, 1969; The Wired Nation, 1972; Songs and Tunes of the Blue Ridge and Great Smoky Mountains, 1983; The Story of the Dulcimer, 1986; Smart House: The Coming Revolution in Housing, 1987. Add: 400 Prince Georges Blvd., Upper Marlboro, Md. 20772-8731, U.S.A.

SMITH, Robert Ellis. American, b. 1940. Civil liberties/Human rights, Law. Publisher, Privacy Journal, Washington, D.C., and Providence, R.I., since 1974. Reporter, Detroit Free Press, 1962–63, 1966; Ed., The Southern Courier, Montgomery, Ala., 1965–66; Reporter and Ed., Newsday, Long Island, N.Y., 1967–70; Asst. Dir., Office for Civil Rights, U.S. Dept. of Health, Education and Welfare, Washington, D.C., 1973–74. *Publs:* Compilation of State and Federal Privacy Laws, 1976, 6th ed. 1988; Privacy: How to Protect What's Left of It, 1979; Workrights, 1983; The Big Brother Book of Lists, 1984. Add: P.O. Box 15300, Washington, D.C. 20003, U.S.A.

SMITH, Rowland (James). Canadian, b. 1938. Literature. Mc-Culloch Prof. in English and Acting, Dean, Faculty of Arts and Social Sciences, Dalhousie Univ., Halifax, since 1988 (Asst. Prof., 1967–70; Assoc. Prof., 1970–77; Prof, from 1977; Dir., Centre for African Studies, 1976–77). Lectr. in English, Univ. of the Witwatersrand, Johannesburg, 1963–67. Asst. Ed., English Studies in Africa, Johannesburg, 1964–67; Secty.-Treas., Assn. of Canadian Univ. Teachers of English, 1968–70; Pres., Canadian Assn. of Chmn. of English, 1982–83; Vice-Pres., 1981–82, Exec. Member, 1985–86, and Chmn. of Div. 33, 1984, Modern Language Assn.; Member, Aid to Publs. Cttee., Canadian Fedn. for the Humanities, 1979–85. *Publs:* Lyric and Polemic: The Literary Personality of Roy Campbell, 1972; (ed.) Exile and Tradition: Studies in African and Caribbean Literature, 1976. Add: Dept. of English, Dalhousie Univ., Halifax, N.S. B3H 3J5, Canada.

SMITH, Shelley. Pseud. for Nancy Hermione Bodington. British, b. 1912. Mystery/Crime/Suspense. *Publs:* Background for Murder, 1942; Death Stalks a Lady, 1945; This Is the House, 1945; Come and Be Killed!, 1946; He Died of Murder!, 1947; The Woman in the Sea, 1948; Man with a Calico Face, 1950; (as Nancy Bodington) How Many Miles to Babylon? (stories), 1950; Man Alone (in U.S. as The Crooked Man), 1952; An Afternoon to Kill, 1953; The Party at No. 5 (in U.S. as The Cellar at No. 5), 1954; Rachel Weeping: A Triptych, 1957; The Lord Have Mercy, 1956; The Ballad of the Running Man, 1961; A Grave Affair, 1971; A Game of Consequences, 1978. Add: Chequers Orchard, Steyning, Sussex BN4 3GE, England.

SMITH, Vivian (Brian). Australian, b. 1933. Poetry, Children's non-fiction, Literature, Biography. Reader in English, Univ. of Sydney. Literary Ed., Quadrant. Former Lectr. in French, Univ. of Tasmania. *Publs:* The Other Meaning: Poems, 1956; James McAuley, 1965, 1970; An Island South, 1967; Les Vigé en Australie, 1967; (ed.) Australian Poetry, 1969; Vance Palmer, 1971; Robert Lowell, 1974; Familiar Places (poems), 1978; (ed.) Letters of Vance and Nettie Palmer, 1978; (ed.) Young St. Poets Anthology, 1981; (ed. with Peter Coleman and Lee Shrubb) Quadrant: Twenty-Five Years, 1982; Tide Country, 1982; Tasmania and Australian Poetry, 1984; (ed. with Margaret Scott) Effects of Light: The Poetry of Tasmania, 1985; Selected Poems, 1985; Australian Poetry 1986, 1986; Nettie Palmer, 1988; Australian Poetry 1988, 1988. Add: 19 McLeod St., Mosman, N.S.W., Australia 2088.

SMITH, Wilbur (Addison). British, b. 1933. Novels/Short stories. *Publs:* When the Lion Feeds, 1964; The Dark of the Sun, 1965; The Sound of Thunder, 1966; Shout at the Devil, 1968; Goldmine, 1970, screenplay as Gold, 1974; Diamond Hunters, 1971; The Sunbird, 1972; Eagle in the Sky, 1974; Eye of the Tiger, 1975; Cry Wolf, 1976; A Sparrow Falls,

1977; Hungry Is the Sea, 1978; Wild Justice, 1979; A Falcon Flies, 1980; Men of Men, 1981; The Angels Weep, 1982; The Leopard Hunts in Darkness, 1984; The Burning Shore, 1985; Power of the Sword, 1986; Rage, 1987; Time to Die, 1989. Add: c/o Charles Pick Consultancy, 3 Bryanston Pl., Flat 3, London W1H 7FN, England.

SMITH, Wilfred Cantwell. Canadian, b. 1916. History, Theology/Religion. Prof. of Comparative Religion, and Dir., Inst. of Islamic Studies, McGill Univ., Montreal, 1949–63; McCullough Prof. of Religion, Dalhousie Univ., Halifax, N.S., 1973–78; Prof., of World Religions, 1964–73 and Prof. of Comparative History of Religion, 1978–84, Harvard Univ., Cambridge, Mass.; Sr. Killam Fellow, Univ. of Toronto, 1985–87. *Publs:* Modern Islam in India, 1943; Islam in Modern History, 1957; The Faith of Other Men, 1962; The Meaning and End of Religion, 1963; Modernization of a Traditional Society, 1965; Questions of Religious Truth, 1967; Belief and History, 1977; Faith and Belief, 1979; Towards a World Theology, 1981; On Understanding Islam, 1981. Add: 476 Brunswick Ave., Toronto, Ont. M5R 2Z5, Canada.

SMITH, William Jay. American, b. 1918. Children's verse, Poetry, Literature, Translations. Writer-in-Residence, 1965–66, and Prof. of English, 1967–68, 1970–80, now Emeritus, Hollins Coll., Virginia. Asst. in French, Washington Univ., St. Louis, Mo. 1939–41; Instr. in English and French, 1946–47, and Visiting Prof. of Writing, and Acting Chmn., Writing Div., Sch. of the Arts, 1973, 1974–75, Columbia Univ., NYC; Instr. in English, 1951, Poet-in-Residence and Lectr. in English, 1959–64, 1966–67, Williams Coll., Williamstown, Mass.; Democratic Member, Vermont House of Reps., 1960–62; Poetry Reviewer, Harper's Mag., NYC, 1961–64; Editorial Consultant, Grove Press, NYC, 1968–70; Consultant in Poetry, 1968–70, and Hon. Consultant, 1970–74, Library of Congress, Washington, D.C., Poet-in-Residence, Cathedral of St. John the Divine, NYC, 1985–88. *Publs:* Poems, 1947; Celebration at Dark: Poems, 1950; (trans.) Scirroco, by Romualdo Romano, 1951; Typewriter Birds, 1954; Laughing Time, 1955; (trans.) Poems of a Multimillionaire, by Valery Larabaud, 1955; (ed. and trans.) Selected Writings of Jules Laforgue, 1956; The Bead Curtain: Calligrams, 1957; Poems 1947-1957, 1957; Boy Blue's Book of Beasts, 1957; Puptents and Pebbles: A Nonsense ABC, 1959; Typewriter Town, 1960; The Spectra Hoax (criticism), 1961; What Did I See?, 1962; (ed.) Herrick, 1962; My Little Book of Big and Little: Little Dimity, Big Gumbo, Big and Little, 3 vols., 1963; Prince Souvanna Phouma: An Exchange Between Richard Wilbur and William Jay Smith, 1963; Ho for a Hat!, 1964; The Straw Market, 1965; (ed. with L. Bogan) The Golden Journey: Poems for Young People, 1965; The Tin Can and Other Poems, 1966; If I Had a Boat, 1966; (ed.) Poems from France, 1967; Mr. Smith and Other Nonsense, 1968; Around My Room and Other Poems, 1969; Grandmother Ostrich and Other Poems, 1969; (with V. Haviland) Children and Poetry; A Selective Annotated Bibliography, 1969; New and Selected Poems, 1970; A Rose for Katherine Anne Porter, 1970; (trans.) Two Plays by Charles Bertin: Christopher Columbus and Don Juan, 1970; (trans.) Children of the Forest, by Else Baskow, 1970; (trans.) The Pirate Book, by Lennar Hellsing, 1970; Louise Bogan: A Woman's Words, 1971; The Streaks of the Tulip: Selected Criticism, 1972; (ed.) Poems from Italy, 1972; At Delphi: For Allen Tate on His Seventy-Fifth Birthday, 19 November 1974, 1974; Venice in the Fog, 1975; (ed.) Light Verse and Satires, by Witter Bynner, 1978; (with Richard Wilbur) Verses on the Times, 1978; Journey to the Dead Sea, 1979; (trans.) Agadir by Artur Lundkvist, 1979; The Tall Poets, 1979; The Traveler's Tree: New and Selected Poems, 1980; Army Brat: A Memoir, 1980; (ed.) A Green Place: Modern Poems (for children), 1982; (ed. with Emanuel Brasil) Brazilian Poetry 1950-1980, 1983; (with James S. Holmes) Dutch Interior: Post-war Poetry of the Netherlands and Flanders, 1984; (trans.) Moral Tales, by Jules Laforgue, 1985; Collected Translations: Italian, French, Spanish, Portuguese, 1985; (with Dana Gioia) Poems from Italy, 1985; (trans. with Leif Sjöberg) Wild Bouquet: Nature Poems by Harry Martinson, 1985; (ed. with F.D. Reeve) An Arrow in the Wall: Selected Poetry and Prose, by Andrei Voznesensky, 1987; The Tin Can, 1988; Journey to the Interior, 1988; Plain Talk, 1988; (trans, with Edwin Morgan and others) Eternal Moment by Sándor Weöres, 1989; (trans. with Sonja Haussmann Smith) The Madmen and the Medusa, by Tchicaga U Tam'Si, 1989. Add: 1675 York Ave., Apt. 20K, New York, N.Y. 10128, U.S.A.

SMITHER, Elizabeth. New Zealander, b. 1941. Novels, Children's fiction, Poetry, Literature. Librarian, New Plymouth Public Library, 1959–63, and since 1979. *Publs:* Here Come the Clouds, 1975; You're Very Seductive William Carlos Williams, 1978; The Sarah Train (juvenile), 1978; The Legend of Marcello Mastroianni's Wife, 1981; Casanova's Ankle, 1981; Shakespeare's Virgins, 1983; First Blood (novel), 1983; Tug Brothers (for children), 1983; Professor Musgrove's Canary, 1986; Brother-love Sister-love (novel), 1986; Gorilla/Guerilla,

1986; Animaux, 1988.   Add: 19-A Mount View Pl., New Plymouth, New Zealand.

SMITHERS, (Sir) Peter. British, b. 1913. Biography. Conservative Member of Parliament (U.K.) for Winchester, 1950–64; U.K. Delegate, U.N. Gen. Assembly, 1960–64; Under-Secty. of State, Foreign Office, 1962–64; Secty. Gen., Council of Europe, 1964–69. *Publs:* The Life of Joseph Addison, 1954, 1968. Add: 6911 Vico Morcote, Switzerland.

SMITHSON, Alison (Margaret). British, b. 1928. Novels/Short stories, Architecture, Urban studies. Partner, A & P Smithson, Architects, London, since 1949. *Publs:* (co-author) Without Rhetoric: An Architectural Aesthetic, 1955, 1972; Portrait of a Female Mind as Young Girl, 1966; (co-author) Urban Structuring, 1967; (ed.) Team 10 Primer, 1968; The Euston Arch, 1968; (co-author) Ordinariness and Light: Urban Theories 1952–60 and Their Application in a Building Project, 1970; The Christmas Tree, 1977; Calendar of Christmas, 1977; Place Worth Inheriting, 1978; Anthology of British (and Scottish) Christmas, 2 vols., 1979–80; (co-author) The Shift in Our Aesthetic: Ephemera: 1950–1978, 1982; AS in DS: An Eye on the Road, 1983; Upper Lawn, 1986. Add: 24 Gilston Rd., London SW10 9SR, England.

SMITHSON, Peter (Denham). British, b. 1923. Architecture, Urban studies. Partner, A & P Smithson, Architects, London, since 1949. *Publs:* (co-author) Urban Structuring, 1967; (co-author) Ordinariness and Light: Urban Theories 1952-60 and Their Applications in a Building Project, 1970; Bath: Walks Within the Walls, 1971, 1980; (co-author) Without Rhetoric: An Architectural Aesthetic, 1955-1972, 1973; (co-author) The Shift in Our Aesthetic: Ephemera: 1950-1978, 1982. Add: 24 Gilston Rd., London SW10 9SR, England.

SMITHYMAN, (William) Kendrick. New Zealander, b. 1922. Poetry, Literature. Primary sch. teacher 1946–63; Sr. Tutor, Dept. of English, Univ. of Auckland, 1963–87. *Publs:* Seven Sonnets, 1946; The Blind Mountain and Other Poems, 1950; The Gay Trapeze, 1955; Inheritance: Poems, 1962; A Way of Saying: A Study of New Zealand Poetry, 1965; Flying to Palmerston: Poems, 1968; (ed.) The Land of the Lost, by William Satchell, 1971; Earthquake Weather, 1972; The Seal in the Dolphin Pool, 1974; Dwarf with a Billiard Cue, 1978; Stories about Wooden Keyboards, 1985; (ed.) The Toll of the Bush, by William Satchell, 1985; Are You Going to the Pictures?, 1987. Add: 66 Alton Ave., Northcote, Auckland, New Zealand.

SMUCKER, Barbara Claassen. American: Canadian Landed Immigrant, b. 1915. Children's fiction. Teacher of journalism and English, Harper High School, Kansas, 1937–38; reporter, Newton Evening Kansan, 1939–41; teacher, Ferry Hall School, Lake Forest, Ill., 1960–63; Children's Librarian, Kitchener Public Library, Ontario, 1969–77; Head Librarian, Renison Coll., Univ. of Waterloo, Ontario, 1977–82. *Publs:* Henry's Red Sea, 1955; Cherokee Run, 1957; Wigwam in the City, 1966, published as Susan, 1972; Underground to Canada (in U.S. as Runaway to Freedom), 1977; Days of Terror, 1979; Amish Adventure, 1983; White Mist, 1985; Jacob's Little Giant, 1987. Add: 57 McDougall Rd., Waterloo, Ont. N2L 2W4, Canada.

SMYTH, Harriet Rucker. American, b. 1926. Biology, Natural history. Teacher of English, Torrington High Sch., Conn., since 1970. *Publs:* Amphibians and Their Ways, 1962. Add: Valley Rd., New Preston, Conn. 06777, U.S.A.

SMYTH, James Desmond. British, b. 1917. Zoology. Emeritus Prof. of Parasitology, Imperial Coll. of Science and Technology, Univ. of London, since 1982 (Prof., 1971–82). Prof. of Experimental Biology, Trinity Coll., Dublin, 1955–59; Prof. of Zoology, Australian National Univ., Canberra, 1959–70. *Publs:* An Introduction to Animal Parasitology, 1962, 1976; The Physiology of Trematodes, 1966, (with D.W. Halton) 1984; The Physiology of Cestodes, 1969; (with M.M. Smyth) Frogs as Host Parasite Systems, 1980. Add: London Sch. of Hygiene and Tropical Medicine, Keppel St., London WC1E 7HT, England.

SMYTHIES, John R(aymond). British, b. 1922. Medicine/ Health, Philosophy, Psychiatry, Psychology. C.B. Ireland Prof. of Psychiatry, Univ. of Alabama, Birmingham, since 1973, Emeritus since 1989. Reader in Psychiatry, Univ. of Edinburgh, 1961–73; Consultant, W.H.O., 1963–68. *Publs:* Analysis of Perception, 1956; (ed. and contrib.) Brain and Mind, 1965; The Neurological Foundations of Psychiatry, 1966; (ed. and co-author, with H.E. Himwich and S. Kety) Amines and Schizophrenia, 1967; Biological Psychiatry, 1968; (ed. and co-author with Arthur Koestler) Beyond Reductionism, 1969; Brain Mechanism and Be-

havior, 1970; (with L. Corbett) Psychiatry for Students of Medicine, 1976; (co-ed.) International Review of Neurobiology, vols. 29-30, 1988. Add: Cedarstone, Hill Brow, Liss, Hants. GU33 7PB, England.

SNAVELY, Tipton Ray. American, b. 1890. Economics. Prof. of Economics Emeritus, Univ. of Virginia, Charlottesville, since 1961 (joined faculty, 1918). *Publs:* The Taxation of Negroes in Virginia, 1917; Public Utilities, 1933; (co-author) State Grants-in-Aid in Virginia, 1933; The Fiscal System of Tennessee, 1936; George Tucker as Political Economist, 1954; The Department of Economics at the University of Virginia, 1825-1956, 1967. Add: 1421 Gentry Lane, Charlottesville, Va. 22903, U.S.A.

SNEDDON, Ian Naismith. British, b. 1919. Mathematics, Physics. Simson Prof. of Mathematics, Univ. of Glasgow, since 1957, Emeritus since 1985 (Lectr. in Natural Philosophy, 1946–50). Prof. of Mathematics, Univ. Coll. of North Staffordshire (now Keele Univ.), 1950–56. *Publs:* (with N.F. Mott) Wave Mechanics and Its Applications, 1948; Fourier Transforms, 1951; The Special Functions of Mathematical Physics and Chemistry, 1956, 3rd ed. 1980; Elements of Partial Differential Equations, 1957; (with J. G. Defares) An Introduction to the Mathematics of Biology and Medicine, 1960, 1973; Fourier Series, 1961; Zagadnienie Szczelin w Matematycznej Teorii Sprezystosci, 1962; Mixed Boundary Value Problems, 1966; (with M. Lowengrub) Crack Problems in the Mathematical Theory of Elasticity, 1969; The Linear Theory of Thermoelasticity, 1974; Metoda Transformacji Calkowych w Mieszanych Zagadnieniach Bizegowych Klasycznej Teorii Sprezystosci, 1974; The Use of Integral Transforms, 1982; (with E.L. Ince) Solution of Ordinary Differential Equations, 1987. Add: 19 Crown Terrace, Glasgow G12 9ES, Scotland.

SNELLGROVE, Laurence Ernest. British, b. 1928. History, Language/Linguistics. *Publs:* From Kitty Hawk to Outer Space, 1960; From Steamcarts to Minicars, 1961; From Coracles to Cunarders, 1962; From Rocket to Railcar, 1963; Suffragettes and Votes for Women, 1964; Franco and Spanish Civil War, 1965; Modern World since 1870, 1968, 1981; (with R.J. Cootes) The Ancient World, 1970; Hitler, 1971; Second World War, 1971; Early Modern Age, 1972; (with J.R.C. Yglesias) Mainstream English, vols., 1974; Picture the Past, 5 vols., 1978; Wide Range Histories, 1978; (with David Thornton) History Around You, 4 vols., 1982–83; Modern World, 1984; Britain since 1700, 1985; Storyline Histories, 4 vols., 1986; Modern World History, 1989. Add: 13 Captains Walk, Saundersfoot, Dyfed, Wales.

SNODGRASS, Anthony McElrea. British, b. 1934. Archaeology/ Antiquities. Laurence Prof. of Classical Archaeology, Cambridge Univ., since 1976. Chmn., Antiquity Publications Ltd., since 1987. Lectr., 1961–69, Reader, 1969–75, and Prof., 1975–76, Univ. of Edinburgh. Member, Editorial Bd., Soc. for the Promotion of Hellenic Studies, 1972–87. *Publs:* Early Greek Armour and Weapons, 1964; Arms and Armour of the Greeks, 1967; The Dark Age of Greece, 1971; Archaeology and the Rise of the Greek State, 1977; Archaic Greece, 1980; An Archaeology of Greece, 1987. Add: Museum of Classical Archaeology, Sidgwick Ave., Cambridge CB3 9DA, England.

SNODGRASS, W(illiam) D(eWitt). Also writes as S.S. Gardons. American, b. 1926. Poetry, Literature, Translations. Prof., Univ. of Delaware, Newark. Instr. in English, Cornell Univ., Ithaca, N.Y., 1955–57, Univ. of Rochester, N.Y., 1957–58, and Wayne State Univ., Detroit, Mich., 1959–67; Prof. of English, Syracuse Univ., N.Y., 1968–77. *Publs:* Heart's Needle, 1959; (trans. with Lore Segal) Gallows Songs, by Christian Morgenstern, 1967; After Experience: Poems and Translations, 1968; (ed.) Syracuse Poems 1969, 1969; (as S.S. Gardons) Remains: Poems, 1970; In Radical Pursuit: Critical Essays and Lectures, 1975; The Führer Bunker, 1977; (trans.) Six Troubadour Songs, 1977; (trans.) Traditional Hungarian Songs, 1978; If Birds Built with Your Hair, 1979; The Boy Made of Meat, 1983; Magda Goebbels, 1983; (trans.) Six Minnesinger Songs, 1983; (trans.) The Four Seasons, 1984; D.D. Byrde Calling Jennie Wrenn, 1984; Selected Poems 1957-1987, 1987; (with paintings by De-Loss McGraw) Midnight Carnival (poems), 1988. Add: R.D.1, Erieville, N.Y. 13061, U.S.A.

SNOW, Helen Foster. Also writes as Nym Wales. American, b. 1907. Novels/Short stories, Poetry, Genealogy/Heraldry, History, Autobiography/ Memoirs/Personal. *Publs:* The Left-Wing Painters and Modern Art in China, 1933–35; The Chinese Student Movement, 1935–36; The Sian Incident, 1936; The Beginnings of the Industrial Cooperatives in China, 1938; Inside Red China, 1939; China Builds for Democrary, 1941; Song of Ariran: The Life Story of an Asian Revolutionary, 1941; The

Chinese Labor Movement, 1941; Red Dust, 1952, as The Chinese Communists: Sketches and Autobiographies of the Old Guard, 2 vols., 1972; Fables and Parables, 1952; (as Nym Wales) Historical Notes on China, 6 vols., 1961; An American Experience in Yenan, retitled My Yenan Notebooks, 1960; Women in Modern China, 1967; Korea and the Life of Kim San, 1972; The Land Beyond the Kuttawoo, 1974; The Guilford Story, 1974; The History of Damariscove Island in Maine, 1976; The Saybrook Story, 1978; Totemism, The T'ao-T'ieh, and the Chinese Ritual Bronzes, 1978; The China Years (autobiography), 1983; My China Years (autobiography), 1984. Add: 148 Mungertown Rd., Madison, Conn. 06443, U.S.A.

SNOW, Keith Ronald. British, b. 1943. Biology, Children's non-fiction, Medicine/Health, Zoology. Principal Lectr., Polytechnic of East London, since 1988 (Lectr., North East London Polytechnic, 1970–88). Reviewer, Times Educational Supplement, since 1969; Major Contrib., Book of the British Countryside, Drive Publs., since 1973. *Publs:* The Arachnids: An Introduction, 1970; Insects and Disease, 1974; Flies, 1978; I Am a Fox (Squirrel, Badger, Hedgehog, Rabbit, Frog), 6 vols., 1978–82; A Garden of Birds, 1981; Birds in Your Garden, 1984; British Mosquitoes (Culicidae), 1987. Add: Sch. of Science, Polytechnic of East London, Romford Rd., London E15 4LZ, England.

SNOW, Lyndon. *See* **ELSNA,** Hebe.

SNOW, Philip (Albert). British, b. 1915. Administration, Anthropology, Archaeology, History, Sports, Travel/Exploration/Adventure, Biography. Justice of the Peace, Warwicks, 1952–75, and West Sussex, since 1976. Examiner on Pacific Subjects, Oxford and Cambridge Univs., since 1955; Permanent Rep. of Fiji, Intnl. Cricket Conference, since 1965; First Chmn., Associate Member Countries, Intnl. Cricket Conterence, since 1982. Administrator and Magistrate, Fiji and Western Pacific, 1938–52; Bursar, Rugby Sch., Warwickshire, 1952–76. Ed., Civil Service Journal, Fiji, 1944; Chmn., Public Schools Bursars Assn., Great Britain and Commonwealth, 1962–65. *Publs:* Civil Defence Services, Fiji, 1942; (ed. with G.K. Roth) Fijian Customs, 1944; Cricket in the Fiji Islands, 1949; Rock Carvings in Fiji, 1950; Bula, 1959; (with D.M. Sherwood and F.J. Walesby) Visit of Three Bursars to Schools and Universities in U.S.A. and Canada, 1964; (ed.) Best Stories of the South Seas, 1967; (with J.S. Woodhouse) Visit of Her Majesty the Queen and H.R.H. Prince Philip to Rugby School on the Occasion of the Quatercentenary Year 1567-1967, 1967; Bibliography of Fiji, Tonga and Rotuma, vol. I, 1969; (with Stefanie Waine) The People from the Horizon: An Illustrated History of the Europeans among the South Sea Islanders, 1979; Stranger and Brother: A Portrait of C.P. Snow, 1982. Add: Gables, Station Rd., Angmering, Sussex, England.

SNOW, Richard F(olger). American, b. 1947. Novels/Short stories, poetry, History. Managing Ed., American Heritage mag., NYC, since 1979 (joined staff, 1970; Assoc. Ed., 1972–77; Sr. Ed., Book Div., 1977–78). *Publs:* The Funny Place (poetry), 1975; Freelon Starbird: Being a Narrative of the Extraordinary Hardships Suffered by an Accidental Soldier in a Beaten Army During the Autumn and Winter of 1776, 1976; The Iron Road: A Portrait of American Railroading, 1978; The Burning, 1981; Coney Island: A Postcard Journey to the City of Fire, 1984. Add: 490 West End Ave., New York, N.Y. 10024, U.S.A.

SNOWMAN, Daniel. British, b. 1938. History, Music, Politics/Government. Producer, BBC, London, since 1967. Lectr. in Politics and American Studies, Univ. of Sussex, 1963–67. *Publs:* USA: The Twenties to Vietnam, 1968; Eleanor Roosevelt, 1969; Kissing Cousins (in U.S. as Britain and America), 1977; (ed.) If I Had Been . . ., 1979; The Amadeus Quartet, 1981; The World of Placido Domingo, 1985. Add: 47 Wood Lane, London N6, England.

SNYDER, Anne. American, b. 1922. Children's fiction. Teacher of Creative Writing for Gifted Children's Assn. of San Fernando Valley, 1970, 1971; Teacher of Juvenile Fiction Writing, California State Univ., 1979, 1980. *Publs:* 50,000 Names For Jeff, 1969; Nobody's Family, 1975; First Step, 1975; Kids and Drinking, 1977; My Name Is Davy — I'm an Alcoholic, 1977; The Old Man and the Mule, 1978; Goodbye, Paper Doll (novel), 1980; Counter Play (novel), 1981; Two Point Zero (novel), 1982; Nobody's Brother (novel), 1982; The Best That Money Can Buy (novel), 1983; You Want to Be What? (novel), 1984; The Truth About Alex (novel), 1987. Add: 20713 Exhibit Ct., Woodland Hills, Calif. 91367, U.S.A.

SNYDER, Cecil. American, b. 1927. Novels/Short stories. Instr. in English, Santa Ana Coll., Calif., 1961–62; Assoc. in English, Univ. of

California, Los Angeles and Riverside, 1963–67; Lectr. in English, California State Univ., Pomona, 1967–71. *Publs:* Big with Vengeance, 1969. Add: 20345 Stanford Ave., Riverside, Calif. 92507, U.S.A.

SNYDER, Francis Gregory. American, b. 1942. Law, Politics/Government. Reader in European Community Law, University Coll., London, since 1987. Book Review Ed., Journal of Legal Pluralism, since 1975; Ed., Review of African Political Economy, since 1983; European Law Ed., Modern Law Review, since 1988. Asst. Prof., 1971–74, and Assoc. Prof., 1974–78, Osgoode Hall Law Sch., and Div. of Social Science, York Univ., Downsview, Ont; Sr. Lectr., 1979–81, and Reader, 1981–87, Sch. of Law, Warwick Univ., England. *Publs:* One Party Government in Mali, 1965; (with M.A. Savané) Law and Population in Senegal, 1977; Capitalism and Legal Change, 1981; Law of the Common Agricultural Policy, 1985; (co-ed.) The Political Economy of Law, 1987; (co-ed.) Labour, Law and Crime, 1987. Add: Bentham House, 4-8 Endsleigh Gardens, London WC1H 0EG, England.

SNYDER, Gary (Sherman). American, b. 1930. Poetry, Philosophy. Prof. of English, Univ. of California, Davis, since 1986. Lectr. in English, Univ. of California, Berkeley, 1964–65. *Publs:* Riprap, 1959; Myths and Texts, 1960; Hop, Skip, and Jump, 1964; Nanao Knows, 1975; Riprap and Cold Mountain Poems, 1965; Six Sections from Mountains and Rivers Without End, 1965; Three Worlds, Three Realms, Six Roads, 1966; A Range of Poems, 1966; The Back Country, 1967; The Blue Sky, 1969; Four Changes, 1969; Sours of the Hills, 1969; Earth House Hold: Technical Notes and Queries to Fellow Dharma Revolutionaries, 1969; Regarding Wave, 1970; Anasazi, 1971; The Fudo Trilogy, 1973; Turtle Island, 1974; All in the Family, 1975; The Old Ways (essays), 1977; He Who Hunted Birds in His Father's Village, 1978; The Real Work, 1980; True Night, 1980; Axe Handles, 1983; Passage Through India, 1984; Left Out in the Rain, 1986. Add: c/o North Point Press, 850 Talbot, Berkeley, Calif. 94706, U.S.A.

SNYDER, Graydon. American, b. 1930. Theology/Religion. Prof. of New Testament and Academic Dean, Chicago Theological Seminary, since 1987. Prof. of Biblical Studies, 1959–86, and Dean, 1975–86, Bethany Theological Seminary, Oak Brook, Ill. *Publs:* (ed. with W. Klassen) Current Issues in New Testament Interpretation, 1962; In His Hands, 1965; The Shepherd of Hermas, 1967; (with R. Ruether) Power and Violence, 1971; (with Neff and Miller) Using Biblical Simulations, 2 vols., 1973–75; Ante Pacem, 1985. Add: Chicago Theological Seminary, 5757 S. University Ave., Chicago, Ill. 60637, U.S.A.

SNYDER, Louis L. American, b. 1907. History, Documentaries/Reportage. Prof. Emeritus of History, City Coll. and City Univ. of New York, since 1977 (Instr., 1933–41; Asst. Prof., 1941–49; Assoc. Prof., 1949–53; Prof., 1953–77). Gen. Ed., Anvil series of original paperbacks in story. Paris Ed., New York Herald, 1928–31. *Publs:* Hitlerism: The Iron Fist in Germany, 1932; From Bismarck to Hitler: The Background of German Nationalism, 1935; Mastery Units in Modern History, 1936; Race: History of Modern Ethnic Theories, 1939; A Survey of European Civilization: vol. I: To the End of the Middle Ages, 1941, 8th ed. 1962, vol. II: From 1500 to the Present, 1942, 7th ed. 1962, (ed. with R.B. Morris and J.E. Wisan) A Handbook of Civilian Protection, 1942; (ed. with R.B. Morris) A Treasury of Great Reporting, 1949, 1962; (with J.A. Fenton) Vitalized Modern History, 1949; (ed.) A Treasury of Intimate Biographies, 1950; (ed. with R.B. Morris) They Saw It Happen, 1952; German Nationalism: The Tragedy of a People, 1952, 1962; The Meaning of Nationalism, 1954; The Age of Reason, 1955; The World in the 20th Century; (ed.) Fifty Major Documents of the 20th Century, 1955, 1962; (ed.) Fifty Major Documents of the 19th Century, 1955; A Basic History of Modern Germany, 1957; (ed.) Documents of German History, 1958; The First Book of World War I, 1958, 1980; The First Book of World War II, 1959; The First Book of the Soviet Union, 1959, 3rd ed. 1972; Hitler and Nazism, 1961; The War: A Concise History 1939-1945, 1960; (ed.) The Imperialism Reader: Documents and Readings in Modern Expansionism, 1962; The Idea of Racialism, 1962; (ed.) Masterpieces of War Reporting, 1964; The First Book of the Long Armistice, 1964; (ed.) The Dynamics of Nationalism: Readings in Its Meaning and Development, 1964; The Military History of the Lusitania, 1965; (ed. with M. Perry and B. Mazen) Panorama of the Past, 2 vols., 1966; The Weimar Repblic, 1966; Western Europe: A Scholastic Multi-Text on World Affairs, 1966; The Making of Modern Man: Western Civilization since 1500, 1967, 1972; The Blood-and-Iron Chancellor: A Documentary Biography, 1967; (with I.M. Brown) Frederick the Great: Prussian Warrior and Statesman, 1968; The New Nationalism, 1968; (ed.) Frederick The Great, 1971; (with I.M. Brown) The Dreyfus Affair, 1971; Great Turning Points in History, 1971; The Dreyfus Case: A Documentary History, 1973; Varieties of

Nationalism, 1975; Encyclopedia of the Third Reich, 1976; Roots of German Nationalism, 1977; Hitler's Third Reich: A Documentary History, 1980; Louis L. Snyder's Historical Guide to World War II, 1982; Global Mini-Nationalisms: Autonomy or Independence, 1982; Macro-Nationalisms: A History of the Pan-Movements, 1984; National Socialist Germany, 1984; Diplomacy in Iron: The Life of Herbert von Bismarck, 1985; The Third Reich, 1933-1945: A Bibliographical Guide to German National Socialism, 1987. Add: Carnegie Lake Estates, 21 Dogwood Lane, Princeton, N.J. 08540, U.S.A.

SNYDER, Zilpha Keatley. American, b. 1927. Novels/Short stories, Children's fiction, Poetry. Elementary sch. teacher, California, New York, Washington, D.C., and Alaska, 1948–62. *Publs:* Season of Ponies, 1964; The Velvet Room, 1965; Black and Blue Magic, 1966; The Egypt Game, 1967; Eves in the Fishbowl, 1968; Today Is Saturday (verse), 1969; The Changeling, 1970; The Headless Cupid, 1971; The Witches of Worm, 1972; The Princess and the Giants, 1973; The Truth about Stone Hollow, 1974; Below the Root, 1975; And All Between, 1976; Until the Celebration, 1977; Heirs of Darkness, 1978; The Famous Kidnapping Case, 1979; Heirs of Darkness (for adults), 1980; A Fabulous Creature, 1981; Come on Patsy, 1982; The Birds of Summer, 1983; Blair's Nightmare, 1984; The Changing Maze, 1985; And Condors Danced, 1987; Squeak Saves the Day, 1988; Janie's Private Eyes, 1989. Add: 52 Miller Ave., Mill Valley, Calif. 94941, U.S.A.

SOBIN, Gustaf. American, b. 1935. Children's fiction, Poetry, Translations. *Publs:* The Tale of the Yellow Triangle (for children), 1973; Wind Chrysalid's Rattle, 1980; Celebration of the Sound Through, 1982; The Earth as Air, 1984; (trans.) Ideograms in China, by Henri Michaux, 1984; Voyaging Portraits, 1988. Add: c/o New Directions, 80 Eighth Ave, New York, N.Y. 1001, U.S.A.

SOBOL, Donald J. American, b. 1924. Children's fiction, Children's non-fiction. Reporter, New York Sun, 1946–47, and Long Island Daily Press, 1947–52; buyer, Macy's, New York, 1953–55; columnist, 1959–68. *Publs:* The Double Quest, 1958; The Lost Dispatch, 1958; The First Book of Medieval Man, 1959; Two Flags Flying, 1960; The Wright Brothers at Kitty Hawk, 1961; (ed.) A Civil War Sampler, 1961; The First Book of the Barbarian Invaders (Stocks and Bonds), 2 vols., 1962–63; Encyclopedia Brown, Boy Detective series, 24 vols., 1963–85; (ed.) An American Revolutionary War Reader, 1964; Lock, Stock, and Barrel, 1965; (ed.) The Strongest Man in the World, 1967; Secret Agents Four, 1967; Greta the Strong, 1970; Milton, The Model A, 1971; The Amazons of Greek Mythology, 1972; True Sea Adventures, 1975; Disasters, 1979; Angie's First Case, 1981; Encyclopedia Brown (omnibus), 1983; The Amazing Power of Ashur Fine, 1986. Add: c/o McIntosh and Otis, 475 Fifth Ave., New York, N.Y. 10017, U.S.A.

SOBOL, Ken. American, b. 1938. Children's non-fiction, Sports/Physicial education/Keeping fit, Biography. *Publs:* The Clock Museum, 1968; Babe Ruth and the American Dream, 1974; A Cosmic Christmas, 1979; The Devil and Daniel Mouse, 1979. Add: c/o Philip Spitzer Literary Agency, 788 Ninth Ave., New York, N.Y. 10019, U.S.A.

SOCOLOFSKY, Homer Edward. American, b. 1922. History, Biography. Prof. of History, Kansas State Univ., Manhattan (joined faculty, 1947). *Publs:* Kansas History in Graduate Study, 1959, rev. ed. 1970; Arthur Capper: Publisher, Politician, Philanthropist, 1962; The Cimarron Valley, 1969; (with H. Self—) Historical Atlas of Kansas, 1972, 1988; The Socolofsky Family, 1973; Landlord William Scully, 1979; (with A. Spetter) The Presidency of Benjamin Harrison, 1987. Add: 801 Willard Place, Manhattan, Kans. 66502, U.S.A.

SOFTLY, Barbara (Charmian). British, b. 1924. Children's fiction, Children's non-fiction. Former sch. teacher. *Publs:* Plain Jane, 1961; Place Mill, 1962; A Stone in a Pool, 1965; Ponder and William, 1966; Magic People, 1966; Ponder and William on Holiday, 1968; More Magic People, 1969; Hippo, Potta and Muss, 1969; A Lemon Yellow Elephant Called Trunk, 1970; Geranium, 1972; Ponder and William at Home, 1972; Ponder and William at the Weekend, 1974; Queens of England, 1977. Add: Bundels, Ridgway Lane, Sidbury, Devon, England.

SOHL, Jerry. (Gerald Allen Sohl). Also writes as Nathan Butler, Roberta Jean Mountjoy, and Sean Mei Sullivan. American, b. 1913. Mystery/Crime/ Suspense, Science fiction/Fantasy, Recreation/Leisure/Hobbies. Freelance writer since 1958: Staff Writer, Star Trek, Aldred Hitchcock Presents, and The New Breed; also concert pianist. Reporter, Telegraph Ed., Photographer, and Feature Writer, Bloomington Daily Pantagraph, Ill., 1945–58. *Publs:* The Haploids,

1952; Costigan's Needle, 1953; The Transcendent Man, 1953; The Altered Ego, 1954; Point Ultimate, 1955; The Mars Monopoly, 1956; The Time Dissolver, 1957; Prelude to Peril (suspense), 1957; The Odious Ones, 1959; One Against Herculum, 1959; Night Slaves, 1965; The Lemon Eaters (suspense), 1967; The Anomaly, 1971; The Spun Sugar Hole (suspense), 1971; The Resurrection of Frank Borchard (suspense), 1973; (as Nathan Butler) Dr. Josh (suspense), 1973; Underhanded Chess, 1973; (as Nathan Butler) Mamelle (suspense), 1974; (as Sean Mei Sullivan) Supermanchu, Master of Kung Fu (suspense), 1974; Underhanded Bridge, 1975; I, Aleppo, 1976; (as Nathan Butler) Blow-Dry (suspense), 1976; (as Nathan Butler) Mamelle, The Goddess (suspense), 1977; (as Roberta Jean Mountjoy) Night Wind, 1981; (as Roberta Jean Mountjoy) Black Thunder, 1983; Death Sleep (science fiction), 1983; (as Nathan Butler) Kaheesh (suspense), 1983. Add: P.O. Box 1336, Thousand Oaks, Calif. 91360, U.S.A.

SOHN, Louis B(runo). American, b. 1914. Law. Woodruff Prof. of Intnl. Law, Univ. of Georgia Law Sch., Athens, since 1981. Vice-Pres., American Branch of Intnl. Law Assn. since 1959; Chmn., Commn. to Study the Org. of Peace, since 1968. Research Fellow, 1946–47, Lectr. on Law, 1947–51, Asst. Prof., 1951–53, John Harvey Gregory Lectr. on World Org., 1951–81, Prof. of Law, 1953–61, and Bemis Prof. of Intnl. Law, 1961–81, Harvard Law Sch., Cambridge, Mass. Counselor on Intnl. Law, Dept. of State, Washington, D.C., 1970–71. *Publs:* (ed.) Cases on World Law, 1950; (ed.) Cases on United Nations Law, 1956, 1967; (with Grenville Clark) World Peace through World Law, 1958, 3rd ed. 1966; (ed.) Basic Documents of African Regional Organizations, 4 vols., 1971–72; (ed. with Thomas Buergenthal) International Protection of Human Rights, 1973; (with K. Gustafson) The Law of the Sea, 1984; (ed.) International Organization and Integration, 1986. Add: Univ. of Georgia Law Sch., Room 309, Athens, Ga. 30602, U.S.A.

SOLBERG, Richard William. American, b. 1917. History, Theology/Religion. Inst. in History, St. Olaf Coll., Northfield, Minn., 1940–41; Pastor, Trinity Lutheran Church, Ingleside, Ill., 1943–45; Prof. of History, Augustana Coll., Sioux Falls, S.D., 1945–49, 1950–53, and 1956–64; Religious Affairs Advisor, U.S. High Commn. for Germany, 1949–50; Sr. Rep. in Germany, Lutheran World Fedn., 1953–56; Vice-Pres. for Academic Affairs, Thiel Coll., Greenville, Pa., 1964–73; Dir., Dept. for Higher Education, Lutheran Church in America, 1973–82; Dir., History Project, Lutheran Educational Conference of North America, 1982–85. *Publs:* As Between Brothers, 1957; God and Caesar in East Germany, 1961; How Church-Related Are Church-Related Colleges?, 1980; Lutheran Higher Education in North America, 1985. Add: 3678 Corte de los Reyes, Thousand Oaks, Calif. 91360, U.S.A.

SOLBRIG, Otto Thomas. American, b. 1930. Biology, Botany, Ecology. Paul C. Mangelsdorf Prof. of Natural Sciences, Harvard Univ., Cambridge, since 1984 (Prof. of Biology, 1969–84; Supervisor of the Bussey Inst. and Dir. of the Gray Herbarium, 1978–84). Prof. of Botany, Univ. of Michigan, Ann Arbor, 1966–69. *Publs:* Evolution and Systematics, 1966; Principles and Methods of Plant Biosystematics, 1969; (with T. Gadella) Biosystematic Literature; (with G. Orians) Convergent Evolution in Warm Deserts; (with D.J. Solbrig) Introduction to Population, Biology and Evolution; Topics in Plant Population Biology, 1979. Demography and Evolution in Plant Populations, 1980. Add: 22 Divinity Ave., Cambridge, Mass. 02138, U.S.A.

SOLERI, Paolo. American (b. Italian), b. 1919. Architecture, Environmental science/Ecology. Pres., the Cosanti Foundn., Scottsdale, Ariz., since 1956; engaged in the construction of Arcosanti (community for 5,000 people), near Cordes Junction, Ariz., since 1970. In private practice, Turin and Southern Italy, 1950–55. *Publs:* Arcology: The City in the Image of Man, 1970; The Sketchbooks of Paolo Soleri, 1971; The Bridge Between Matter and Spirit Is Matter Becoming Spirit, 1973; The Omega Seed; Fragments; (with Scott M. Davis) Paolo Soleri's Earth Casting, 1984; Arcosanti: An Urban Laboratory, 1984; Space for Peace, 1984; Technology and Cosmogenesis, 1986. Add: Cosanti Foundn., 6433 Doubletree Rd., Scottsdale, Ariz. 85253, U.S.A.

SOLOMON, Ezra. American, b. 1920. Economics. Dean Witter Prof. of Finance, Stanford Univ., since 1961. Member of Faculty, Univ.of Chicago, 1948–60. Ed., Journal of Business, 1953–57; Member, Council of Economic Advisers, Exec. Office of the President, Washington, 1971–73. *Publs:* The Management of Corporate Capital, 1959; Metropolitan Chicago: An Economic Analysis, 1960; The Theory of Financial Management, 1963; Money and Banking, 1968; The Anxious Economy, 1975; (with J.J. Pringle) Introduction to Financial Management, 1977; Beyond the Turning Point, 1981; (ed.) International Patterns of Inflation: A Study in Contrasts, 1984. Add: Grad. Sch. of Business, Stanford Univ., Stanford, Calif. 94305, U.S.A.

SOLOMON, Richard H(arvey). American, b. 1937. International relations/ Current affairs, Politics/Government. Member, Exec. Panel, Office of the Chief of Naval Operations, Washington, D.C., since 1983; Dir., Policy Planning Staff, Dept. of State, Washington, since 1986. With Polaroid Corp., Cambridge, Mass., 1959–62, Brookings Inst., Washington, D.C., 1962, Simulmatics Corp., NYC, 1967, Bendix Aerospace Corp., 1967–68, Univ. of Michigan, Ann Arbor, 1966–71, and Johns Hopkins Univ., Baltimore, Md., 1972–75; Member of National Security Council, Washington, D.C., 1971–76; Head, Political Science Dept., Rand Corp., Santa Monica, Calif., 1976–86. Member of Boston World Affairs Council, 1963. *Publs:* Mao's Revolution and the Chinese Political Culture, 1971; A Revolution Is Not a Dinner Party: A Feast of Images of the Maoist Transformation of China, 1975; Asian Security in the 1980's, 1979; The China Factor: Sino-American Relations and the Global Scene, 1981. Add: Policy Planning Staff, Dept. of State, Washington, D.C. 20520, U.S.A.

SOLOMON, Robert C. American, b. 1942. Philosophy. Prof. of Philosophy, Univ. of Texas, Austin, since 1972. Faculty Member, Princeton Univ., 1966–68, Univ. of California at Los Angeles, 1968–69, Univ. of Pittsburgh, 1969–71, and City Univ. of New York, 1971. *Publs:* From Rationalism to Existentialism, 1972; (ed.) Phenomenology and Existentialism, 1972; (ed.) Nietzsche, 1973; (ed.) Existentialism, 1974; The Passions, 1976; Introducing Philosophy, 1977; History and Human Nature, 1979; Introducing the Existentialists, 1980; Love: Emotion, Myth and Metaphor, 1981; In the Spirit of Hegel, 1983; It's Good Business, 1985; From Hegel to Existentialism, 1987; Continental Philosophy since 1750, 1988; About Love, 1988; A Passion for Justice, 1989. Add: Dept. of Philosophy, Univ. of Texas, Austin, Tex. 78712, U.S.A.

SOLOMONS, David. American (b. British), b. 1912. Administration/Management, Business/Trade/Industry, Economics. Arthur Young Prof. of Accounting Emeritus, Wharton Sch., Univ. of Pennsylvania, Philadelphia. Pres., American Accounting Assn., 1977–78. *Publs:* Divisional Performance: Measurement and Control, 1965; (ed.) Studies in Cost Analysis, 1968; (with R.C. Jones and R.A. Zelten) The Cost of Physicians' and Certain Paramedical Services in New York Municipal Hospitals, 1973; Prospectus for a Profession, 1974; (ed.) The Conceptual Frameworth of Accounting, 1977; (ed.) Improving the Financial Discipline of States and Cities, 1980; Collected Papers, 2 vols., 1984; Making Accounting Policy, 1986; (ed.) Standard Setting for Financial Reporting, 1987; Guidelines for Financial Reporting Standards, 1989. Add: 205 Elm Ave., Swarthmore, Pa. 19081, U.S.A.

SOLOW, Robert (Merton). American, b. 1924. Economics. Prof. of Economics, Mass. Inst. of Technology, Cambridge (Asst. Prof. of Statistics, 1950–54, Assoc. Prof. of Economics, 1954–58). Vice Pres. for Social and Economic Science, American Assn. for the Advancement of Science; Member, Exec. Cttee. Econometric Soc. (Pres., 1964). Sr. Economist, U.S. Council of Economic Advisers, 1961–62; Member, National Commn. on Technology, Automation and Economic Progress, 1963–64; Vice Pres., 1968, and Pres., 1979, American Economic Assn.; Member, President's Commn. on Income Maintenance Programs, 1968–69; Eastman Visiting Prof., Oxford Univ., 1968–69; Dir., 1975–80, and Chmn., 1979–80, Federal Reserve Bank of Boston. *Publs:* (with Dorfman and Samuelson) Linear Programming and Economic Analysis, 1958; Capital Theory and the Rate of Return, 1963; The Nature and Sources of Unemployment in the US., 1964; Price Expectations and the Behavior of the Price Level, 1970; Growth Theory: An Exposition, 1970. Add: 528 Lewis Wharf, Boston, Mass. 02110, U.S.A.

SOLT, Mary Ellen. American, b. 1920. Poetry. Prof. of the Comparative Literature Dept., Indiana Univ., since 1980 (Asst. Prof., 1970–73; Assoc. Prof., 1973–80). English Teacher, Dinsdale High ch., Iowa, 1941–42, Hubbard High Sch., Iowa, 1942–44, Estherville High Sch., Iowa, 1944–46, Univ. High Sch., Iowa City, 1946–48, Bentley Sch., NYC, 1949–52. *Publs:* Flowers in Concrete, 1960; (ed. with W. Barnstone) Concrete Poetry: World View, 1968; A Triology of Rain, 1970; Eyewords, 1972; The Peoplemover, 1978; (ed.) Dear Ez: Letters from William Carlos Williams to Ezra Pound, 1985. Add: Dept. of Comparative Literature, Indiana Univ., Bloomington, Ind. 47401, U.S.A.

SOLTIS, Jonas F. American, b. 1931. Education, Philosophy. William Heard Kilpatrick Prof. of Philosophy and Education, Teachers Coll., Columbia Univ., NYC, since 1964. Ed., Teachers Coll. Record. Instr. in History and Philosophy, Univ. of Connecticut, Waterbury, 1958–60;

Instr. in Education, Wesleyan Univ., Middletown, Conn., 1962–64; Consultant, Addison-Wesley Publishing Co., Reading, Mass., 1965–68. *Publs:* Seeing, Knowing, and Believing: A Study in the Language of Visual Perception, 1966; An Introduction to the Analysis of Educational Concepts, 1968, 1978; (ed. with B. Chazan) Moral Education, 1973; (ed.) Philosophy of Education since Mid-Century, 1981; (ed.) Philosophy and Education: Eightieth Yearbook of the National Society for the Study of Education, 1981; (with K. Strike) The Ethics of Teaching, 1985; (with D.C. Phillips) Perspectives on Learning, 1985; (with W. Feinberg) School and Society, 1985; (with D. Walker) Curriculum and Aims, 1986; (with G. Fenstermacher) Approaches to Teaching, 1986. Add: Teachers Coll., Columbia Univ., New York, N.Y. 10027, U.S.A.

SOMERS, Jane. *See* **LESSING,** Doris.

SOMERS, Paul. *See* **GARVE,** Andrew.

SOMERS, Suzanne. *See* **DANIELS,** Dorothy.

SOMERSET FRY, Plantagenet. British, b. 1931. Children's non-fiction, History, Biography. Gen. Ed., Macmillan History in Pictures (series of books for children); Sr. Member, Wolfson Coll., Cambridge, since 1984 (Visiting Senior Member, 1980–84). Member, Technical Journal Staff, 1957–58, Mag. Staff, 1958, Public Relations Officer, and Account Exec., 1960–63, Dir., 1963–64, and Information Officer, 1965–67, Incorporated Assn. of Architects and Surveyors (IAAS); Information Officer, Ministry of Public Building and Works, 1967–70; Head of Information Services, Council for Small Industries in Rural Areas, 1970–74; Ed., H.M. Stationery Office, 1975–80. *Publs:* Mysteries of History, 1957; The Cankered Rose, 1959; Rulers of Britain, 1967; They Made History, 1970; The World of Antiques, 1970; Constantinople, 1970; The Wonderful Story of the Jews, 1970; Antique Furniture, 1971; Children's History of the World, 1972; Answer Book of History, 1972; Zebra Book of Famous Men, 1972; Zebra Book of Famous Women, 1972; Collecting Inexpensive Antiques, 1973; Zebra Book of Castles, 1974; Great Caesar, 1974; British Mediaeval Castles, 1974; 1000 Great Lives, 1975; Questions, 1976; 2000 Years of British Life, 1976; Chequers: The Country Home of Britain's Prime Ministers, An Official History, 1977; 3000 Questions and Answers Book, 1977; Boudicca, 1978; The Roman World, 1980; David and Charles Book of Castles, 1980; Fountains Abbey, 1981; Beautiful Britain, 1981; Great Cathedrals, 1982; History of Scotland, 1982; Rebellion Against Rome, 1983; Roman Britain: History and Sites, 1984; Battle Abbey and the Battle of Hastings (souvenir guide), 1984; 3,000 More Questions and Answers, 1984; Antiques, 1984; Rievaulx Abbey, 1986; Children's Illustrated Dictionary, 1987; (with Fiona Somerset Fry) History of Ireland, 1988. Add: Wood Cottage, Wattisfield, Bury St. Edmunds, Suffolk, England.

SOMERVILLE, James Hugh Miller. British, b. 1922. Recreation. Assoc. Ed., 1950–58, and Ed., 1958–65, Yachtsman. Yachting Corresp., The Sunday Times, London, 1952–82; British Corresp., Yachting (USA), 1958–79. *Publs:* Yacht Racing Rules Simplified, 1955; Yacht and Dinghy Racing, 1957; (ed.) Dinghy Year Book, 1957; Sceptre, 1958; Leisureguide: Sailing, 1975; Short History of the Royal Northern Yacht Club, 1974; History of Nautical Inn Signs, 1974. Add: Hollenden House, Buckhurst Rd., Bexhill-on-Sea, E. Sussex, England.

SOMERVILLE-LARGE, Peter. Irish, b. 1928. Mystery/Crime/Suspense, History, Travel/Exploration/Adventure. *Publs:* Tribes and Tribulations, 1966; Caviar Coast, 1968; The Coast of West Cork, 1972; From Bantry Bay to Leitrim, 1974; Couch of Earth, 1975; Irish Eccentrics, 1975; Eagles Near the Carcase, 1977; Dublin, 1979; A Living Dog, 1981; The Grand Irish Tour, 1983; Hang Glider, 1985; Cappaghglass, 1985; To the Navel of the World, 1987; Skying, 1989. Add: c/o Hamish Hamilton, 27 Wrights Lane, London W8 5TZ, England.

SOMTOW, S. P. *See* **SUCHARITKUL,** Somtow.

SONDHEIM, Stephen (Joshua). American, b. 1930. Songs, lyrics and libretti. Also a composer. Pres., Dramatists Guild (USA), 1973–81. *Publs:* lyrics—West Side Story, 1957; Gypsy, 1959; A Funny Thing Happened on the Way to the Forum, 1963; Anyone Can Whistle, 1965; Do I Hear a Waltz?, 1966; Company, 1971; Follies, 1972; A Little Night Music, 1973; The Frogs, 1974; Pacific Overtures, 1977; Sweeney Todd, 1979; Merrily We Roll Along, 1981; Sunday in the Park with George, 1984; Into the Woods, 1986. Add: c/o Flora Roberts Inc., 157 W. 57th St., New York, N.Y. 10019, U.S.A.

SONNICHSEN, C(harles) L(eland). American, b. 1901. History,

Literature, Mythology/Folklore, Biography. Emeritus Prof. of English, Univ. of Texas at El Paso, since 1972 (H.Y. Benedict Prof., 1968–72). Sr. Ed., Journal of Arizona History, Tucson, since 1978 (Chief of Publs. and Ed., 1972–78). Asst. Master, St. James Sch., Faribault, Minn., 1924–26; Instr. of English, Carnegie Inst. of Technology, 1927–29; Assoc. Prof. of English, Texas Coll. of Mines, El Paso, 1931–33; Prof. of English and Chmn. of Dept., Texas Coll. of Mines and Texas Western Coll. (now Univ. of Texas at El Paso), 1933–60; Dean, Grad. Sch., Texas Western Coll., 1960–67. Pres.: Texas Folklore Soc., 1935; Western Literature Assoc., 1966; Assn. of Texas Grad. Schs., 1966–67; Western Writers of America, 1977; Western History Assn., 1984. *Publs:* Billy King's Tombstone, 1942; Roy Bean: Law West of the Pecos, 1943; Cowboys and Cattle Kings, 1950; I'll Die Before I'll Run, 1951; (with W.V. Morrison) Alias Billy the Kid, 1957; Ten Texas Feuds, 1957; The Mescalero Apaches, 1958; Tularosa: Last of the Frontier West, 1960, 1980; The El Paso Salt War, 1961; The Southwest in Life and Literature (anthology), 1962; Outlaw: Bill Mitchell, Alias Baldy Russell, 1964; Pass of the North, 1968, as 2 vols., 1980; (with M.G. McKinney) The State National Bank of El Paso, 1971; White Oaks, New Mexico, 1971; Colonel Greene and the Copper Skyrocket, 1974; (with George W. Chambers) San Agustn: First Cathedral Church in Arizona, 1974; The Grave of John Wesley Hardin (folklore biography), 1979; From Hopalong to Hud: The American Western Novel (essays), 1978; The Ambidextrous Historian (essays), 1981; Tucson: The Life and Times of an American City, 1982; Pioneer Heritage, 1984; The Laughing West, 1988. Add: c/o Texas Western Press, E1 Paso Texas 79968-0633, U.S.A.

SONTAG, Susan. American, b. 1933. Novels/Short stories, Plays/Screenplays, Essays. Instr. in English, Univ. of Connecticut, Storrs, 1953–54; Teaching Fellow in Philosophy, Harvard Univ., Cambridge, Mass., 1955–57; Ed., Commentary, NYC, 1959; Lectr. in Philosophy, City Coll. of New York, and Sarah Lawrence Coll., Bronxville, N.Y., 1959–60; Instr., Dept. of Religion, Columbia Univ., NYC, 1960–64; Writer-in-Residence, Rutgers Univ., New Brunswick, N.J. 1964–65. Pres., PEN American Center, 1987–89. *Publs:* The Benefactor, 1963; Against Interpretation (essays), 1966; Death Kit, 1967; Duet for Cannibals (screenplay), 1969; Trip to Hanoi, 1969; Styles of Radical Will (essays), 1969; Brother Carl (screenplay), 1971; On Photography, 1976; Illness as Metaphor, 1978; I, etcetera, 1978; Under the Sign of Saturn (essays), 1980; A Susan Sontag Reader, 1982. Add: c/o Farrar, Straus & Giroux, Inc., 19 Union Sq. West, New York, N.Y. 10003, U.S.A.

SOOTHILL, Keith (Leonard). British, b. 1941. Criminology/Law enforcement/Prisons, Sociology. Sr. Lectr. in Sociology, Cartmel Coll., Univ. of Lancaster, since 1978 (Lectr., 1972–78). Research Asst., Queen Elizabeth Coll., London, 1965–66; Research Officer, Apex Charitable Trust, 1966–69; Research Worker, Inst. of Psychiatry, Univ. of London, 1970–72. *Publs:* The Prisoner's Release, 1974; (with P.J. Pope) Medical Remands in Magistrates' Courts, 1974; (with T.C.N. Gibbens and P.J. Pope) Medical Remands in the Criminal Court, 1977; (co-author) Contemporary British Society, 1988. Add: Dept. of Sociology, Univ. of Lancaster, Bailrigg, Lancaster, England.

SOPER, Lord; Donald Oliver Soper. British, b. 1903. Theology/Religion. Methodist Clergyman. Supt. Minister of West London Mission, 1936–78. Past Chmn. of Shelter. *Publs:* Christianity and Its Critics; Popular Fallacies about the Christian Faith; Will Christianity Work; Practical Christianity Today; Questions and Answers in Ceylon; It is Hard to Work for God; The Advocacy of the Gospel; Tower Hill 12.30; Aflame with Faith; Christian Politics, 1977; Calling for Action, 1984. Add: 19 Thayer St., London W1M 5LJ, England.

SOPER, Eileen Louise. New Zealander, b. 1900. Children's fiction, History, Autobiography/Memoirs/Personal. Assoc. Ed., Otago Witness, 1924–32; Ed., Notes for Women, Otago Daily Times, 1932–38; Pres., Otago Business and Professional Women's Club, 1932–38; Provincial Commnr., Otago Girl Guides Assn., 1941–54; Pres., Victoria League of Otago, 1964–66. *Publs:* The Otago of Our Mothers, 1948; Young Jane, 1955; The Green Years (autobiography), 1969; The Month of the Brittle Star, 1971; The Leaves Turn (autobiography), 1973. Add: 6 Howard St., Macandrew Bay, Dunedin, New Zealand.

SOPER, Tony. British. Natural history. Freelance film maker, and contributor to BBC Natural History Unit programmes. *Publs:* The Bird Table Book, 1965; (with C. Gill and F. Booker) The Wreck of the Torrey Canyon, 1967; (with J. Sparks) Penguins, 1967; (with J. Sparks) Owls, 1970; The Shell Book of Beachcombing, 1972; The New Bird Table Book, 1973; Wildlife Begins at Home, 1975; Everyday Birds, 1976; Beside the Sea, 1978; Birdwatch, 1982; Discovering Birds, 1983; The National Trust

Guide to the Coast, 1984; Discovering Animals, 1985; Go Birding, 1988; A Passion for Birds, 1988; Birds in Your Garden, 1989. Add: Gerston Point, Kingsbridge, Devon TQ7 3BA, England.

SOREL, Julia. *See* **DREXLER,** Rosalyn.

SOREL, Nancy Caldwell. American, b. 1934. Biography. Columnist, "First Encounters", Atlantic mag. News Writer, Massachusetts Inst. of Technology, 1958–60; Staff Ed., Columbia Encyclopedia, 1962–63; English Language Teacher, New Sch. For Social Research, and U.N., NYC, 1963–65; English Teacher, Brooklyn Friends Sch., N.Y. 1965–66. *Publs:* Word People, 1970; (contrib.) The People's Almanac II, 1978; (with Merle Miller) Lyndon, 1980; Ever Since Eve, 1984. Add: 156 Franklin St., New York, N.Y. 10013, U.S.A.

SORENSEN, Theodore (Chaikin). American, b. 1928. Politics/Government, Social commentary/phenomena. Lawyer with Paul Weiss, Rifkind Wharton, and Garrison, NYC, since 1966. Dir., The Twentieth Century Fund, since 1984. Asst. to Sen. John Kennedy, 1953–61; Special Counsel to the Pres. of the United States, 1961–64; Visiting Lectr. in Public and Intnl. Affairs, Princeton Univ., N.J., 1966–68. *Publs:* Decision Making in the White House, 1963; Kennedy, 1965; The Kennedy Legacy, 1969; Watchman in the Night: Presidential Accountability after Watergate, 1975; A Different Kind of Presidency, 1984; (with Ralf Dahrendorf) A Widening Atlantic? Domestic Change and Foreign Policy, 1986; (ed) Let the Word Go Forth: The Speeches, Statements and Writings of John F. Kennedy, 1988. Add: 1285 Ave. of the Americas, New York, N.Y. 10019, U.S.A.

SORENSEN, Thomas Chaikin. American, b. 1926. International relations/Current affairs, Politics/Government. Vice-Pres., Capital International, since 1980. Deputy Dir., U.S. Information Agency, 1961–65; Vice-Pres., Univ. of California, 1966–68; Pres., Advest Intnl. and Sr. Vice-Pres., and Dir., Advest Group, 1974–80. *Publs:* The Word War: The Story of American Propaganda, 1968. Add: The Pines, Matfield, Kent, England.

SORENSEN, Virginia. (Mrs. Alec Waugh). American, b. 1912. Novels/Short stories, Children's fiction. *Publs:* A Little Lower Than the Angels, 1942; On This Star, 1946; The Neighbors, 1947; The Evening and the Morning, 1949; The Proper Gods, 1951; Curious Missie, 1953; Many Heavens, 1954; The House Next Door, 1954; Plain Girl, 1955; Miracles on Maple Hill, 1956; Kingdom Come, 1960; Lotte's Locket, 1964; Where Nothing Is Long Ago, 1964; Around the Corner, 1971; The Man with the Key, 1974; Friends of the Road, 1978. Add: c/o Curtis Brown Ltd., 10 Astor Pl., New York, N.Y. 10003, U.S.A.

SORLEY WALKER, Kathrine. British. Poetry, Dance/Ballet, Biography. Ballet, Dance and Mime Critic, The Daily Telegraph, London, since 1968. Freelance writer and ed., The Dancing Times, Vandance, Dance Chronicle, and other specialist periodicals. *Publs:* Brief for Ballet, 1948; Beauty Is Built Anew, 1949; Robert Helpmann, 1957; The Heart's Variety, 1959; (trans.) Haydn, 1959; (co-ed.) Raymond Chandler Speaking, 1962; Eyes on the Ballet, 1963, rev. ed. 1965; Joan of Arc, 1964; Eyes on Mime, 1969; Saladin: Sultan of the Holy Sword, 1971; Dance and Its Creators, 1972; Emotion and Atmosphere, 1975; (co-ed.) Writings on Dance 1938-68 by A.V. Coton, 1975; Ballet for Boys and Girls, 1980; The Royal Ballet: A Picture History, 1981, 1986; De Basil's Ballets Russes, 1982; Ninette de Valois: Idealist Without Illusions, 1987. Add: 60 Eaton Mews West, London SW1W 9ET, England.

SORRENSON, Maurice Peter Keith. New Zealander, b. 1932. History, Race relations. Prof. of History, Univ. of Auckland, since 1968 (Lectr., 1964–65; Sr. Lectr., 1965–66; Assoc. Prof., 1966–67; Head of the History Dept., 1974–76, 1978–80, 1984-87). Research Fellow, East African Inst. of Social Research, Makerere Univ., Kampala, 1963–64. *Publs:* Land Reform in Kikuyu Country, 1967; Maori and European since 1870: A Study in Adaptation and Adjustment, 1967; The Origins of European Settlement in Kenya, 1968; Europe and Southern Africa, 1972; Integration or Identity: Cultural Integration in New Zealand since 1911, 1977; Separate and Unequal: Cultural Integration in South Africa 1919-1961, 1977; Maori Origins and Migrations, 1979; Na To Hoa Aroha: From Your Dear Friend: The Correspondence Between Sir Apirana Ngata and Sir Peter Buck, 1925-50, 3 vols., 1986–88 Add: History Dept., Univ. of Auckland, Private Bag, Auckland, New Zealand.

SORRENTINO, Gilbert. American, b. 1929. Novels/Short stories, Poetry, Literature. Prof. of English, Stanford Univ., Calif. Ed. and Publr., Neon mag., NYC, 1956–60; Ed., Grove Press, NYC, 1965–70.

Publs: The Darkness Surrounds Us, 1960; Black and White, 1964; The Sky Changes (novel), 1966; The Perfect Fiction, 1969; Steelwork (novel), 1970; Corrosive Sublimate, 1971; Imaginative Qualities of Actual Things (novel), 1971; Splendide-Hotel, 1973; Flawless Play Restored: The Masque of Fungo, 1974; Elegiacs of Sulpicia, 1977; The Orangery, 1978; Mulligan Stew (novel), 1979; Aberration of Starlight (novel), 1980; Crystal Vision (novel), 1981; Selected Poems 1958-80, 1981; Blue Pastoral (novel), 1983; Something Said (critical essays), 1984; Odd Number (novel), 1985; Rose Theatre (novel), 1987. Add: Dept. of English, Stanford Univ., Stanford, Calif. 94305, U.S.A.

SOSKIN, V. H. *See* **ELLISON**, Virginia Howell.

SOTO, Gary. American, b. 1952. Poetry. Assoc. Prof. of English, Univ. of California, Berkeley. Former Member of the Dept. of English, San Diego State Univ., Calif. *Publs:* (with others) Entrance: Four Chicano Poets, 1976; The Elements of San Joaquin, 1977; The Tale of Sunlight, 1978; Father Is a Pillow Tied to a Broom, 1980; Where Sparrows Work Hard, 1981; Living up the Street, 1985; Small Faces, 1986; California Childhood, 1988; Lesser Evils, 1988; Who Will Know Us?, 1990; Baseball in April, 1990. Add: c/o Univ. of Pittsburgh Press, 127 N. Bellefield Ave., Pittsburgh, Pa. 15260, U.S.A.

SOULSBY, E(rnest) J(ackson) L(awson). British, b. 1926. Veterinary medicine. Fellow, Wolfson Coll., Cambridge, and Prof. of Animal Pathology, Cambridge Univ., since 1978 (Lectr., 1954–63). Veterinary Officer, Edinburgh, 1949–52; Lectr. in Clinical Parasitology, Univ. of Bristol, 1952–54; Prof. of Parasitology, Univ. of Pennsylvania, Philadelphia, 1964–78. *Publs:* Textbook of Veterinary Clinical Parasitology, 1965; Biology of Parasites, 1966; Reaction of the Host to Parasitism, 1968; Helminths, Arthropods, and Protozoa of Domesticated Animals, 6th ed. 1968, 7th ed. 1982; Immunity to Animal Parasites, 1972; Parasitic Zoonoses, 1974; Pathophysiology of Parasitic Infections, 1976; Epidemiology and Control of Nematodiasis in Cattle, 1981; Immune Responses in Parasitic Infections, vols., 1987. Add: Old Barn House, Swaffham Prior, Cambridge CB5 0LD, England.

SOUPER, Patrick C(harles). British, b. 1928. Education. Lectr. in Education, Univ. of Southampton, from 1970. Freelance Flautist, 1942–52; Chaplain to Derby Cathedral and Derby City Hosp., 1957–63, Central Colleges, Univ. of London, 1963–65 and St. Paul's Sch., 1965–70. Pres., Southampton Local Assn. of Univ. Teachers, 1974–75. *Publs:* About to Teach: An Introduction to Method in Teaching, 1976; (with W.K. Kay) The School Assembly Debate 1942-1982, 1982; (with Kay) The School Assembly in Hampshire, 1982; (with Kay) Worship in the Independent Day School, 1983; (ed.) The Spiritual Dimension of Education, 1985. Add: 3 Kolokotroni St., 741.000 Rethymnon, Crete, Greece.

SOUSTER, Raymond. Also writes as Raymond Holmes and as John Holmes. Canadian, b. 1921. Novels/Short stories, Poetry. Staff member, Canadian Imperial Bank of Commerce, Toronto, Ont., from 1939, now retired. *Publs:* When We are Young, 1946; Go to Sleep World, 1947; (as Raymond Holmes) The Winter of Time, 1949; Selected Poems, 1956; A Local Pride, 1962; Place of Meeting, 1962; The Colour of the Times, 1964; Ten Elephants on Yonge Street, 1965; As Is, 1967; (ed.) New Wave Canada, 1966; Lost and Found, 1968; So Far So Good, 1969; (ed. with R. Woollatt) Generation Now, 1970; (ed. with D. Lochhead) Made in Canada, 1970; The Years, 1971; Selected Poems, 1972; (as John Holmes) On Target, 1972; (ed. with D. Lochhead) 100 Poems of 19th Century Canada, 1974; Change Up, 1974; (ed. with R. Wollatt) Sights and Sounds, 1974; (ed. with R. Woollatt) These Loved, These Hated Lands, 1974; Double Header, 1975; Rain Check, 1975; Extra Innings, 1977; (ed.) Vapour and Blue: The Poetry of W.W. Campbell, 1978; Hanging In: New Poems, 1979; (ed.) Comfort of the Fields: The Best Known Poems of Archibald Lampman, 1979; Collected Poems, 5 vols., 1980–84; Going the Distance: New Poems 1979-82, 1983; (ed. with Douglas Lochhead) Powassan's Drum: Selected Poems of Duncan Campbell Scott, 1983; (with Bill Brooks) Queen City, Toronto in Poems and Pictures, 1984; Jubilee of Death: The Raid on Dieppe, 1984; (ed. with Douglas Lochhead) Windflower: The Selected Poems of Bliss Carman, 1986; It Takes All Kinds: New Poems, 1986; The Eyes of Love, 1987; Asking for More, 1988. Add: 39 Baby Point Rd., Toronto, Ont. M6S 2G2, Canada.

SOUTHALL, Ivan (Francis). Australian, b. 1921. Children's fiction, Children's non-fiction. *Publs:* The Weaver from Meltham, 1950; Simon Black series, 9 vols., 1950–62; They Shall Not Pass Unseen, 1956; The Story of the Hermitage, 1956; Bluey Truscott, 1958; Softly Tread the Brave, 1960; Journey into Mystery, 1961; Hill's End, 1962; Woomera, 1962; Parson on the Track, 1963; Rockets in the Desert, 1965; Indonesia

Face to Face, 1965; Lawrence Hargrave, 1965; Ash Road, 1965; Indonesian Journey, 1965; The Fox Hole, 1967; The Sword of Esau, 1968; To the Wild Sky, 1968; Let the Balloon Go, 1968; Curse of Cain, 1968; Finn's Folly, 1969; Walk a Mile and Get Nowhere, 1970; Bread and Honey, 1970; Chinaman's Reef is Ours, 1970; Josh, 1971; Over the Top, 1972; Head in Clouds, 1973; Matt and Jo, 1973; Benson Boy, 1973; Seventeen Seconds, 1974; Fly West, 1974; A Journey of Discovery: On Writing for Children, 1975; What about Tomorrow, 1977; King of the Sticks, 1979; The Golden Goose, 1981; The Long Night Watch, 1983; A City Out of Sight, 1984; Christmas in the Tree, 1985; Rachel, 1986; Blackbird, 1988. Add: Box 25, Healesville, Vic. 3777, Australia.

SOUTHAM, B(rian) C(harles). British, b. 1931. Literature. Publisher, The Athlone Press, London. Lectr. in English Literature, Univ. of London, 1961–63. *Publs:* (ed.) Volume the Second, 1963; Jane Austen's Literary Manuscripts, 1964; Tennyson, 1971; (ed.) Selected Poems of Lord Tennyson, 1974; (ed.) Jane Austen: The Critical Heritage 2 vols., 1966–88; (ed.) Critical Essays on Jane Austen, 1968; (ed. with R.W. Chapman) Minor Works of Jane Austen, 1969; A Student's Guide to the Selected Works of T.S. Eliot, 1969, 4th ed. 1981; Jane Austen, 1975; (ed.) Jane Austen: Northanger Abbey and Persuasion, 1976; (ed.) Jane Austen: Sense and Sensibility, Pride and Prejudice, and Mansfield Park (casebooks), 3 vols., 1976; (ed.) T.S. Eliot (casebook), 1978; (ed.) Sir Charles Grandison, 1981. Add: 3 W. Heath Dr., London NW11, England.

SOUTHERN, Terry. Also writes as Maxwell Kenton. American, b. 1924. Novels/Short stories, Plays/Screenplays, Film. *Publs:* (with D. Burnett) Candy Kisses (screenplay), 1955; Flash and Filigree, 1958; (with Mason Hoffenberg as Maxwell Kenton) Candy, 1958, under real names, 1964; The Magic Christian, 1959, screenplay, 1971; (co-ed.) Writers in Revolt, 1963; (with S. Kubrick) Dr. Strangelove (screenplay), 1964; (with Christopher Isherwood) The Loved One (screenplay), 1965; The Journal of "The Loved Ones": The Production Log of a Motion Picture, 1965; (with Ring Lardner, Jr.) The Cincinnati Kid (screenplay), 1966; Barbarella (screenplay), 1967; Red-Dirt Marijuana and Other Tastes (short stories), 1967; Easy Rider (screenplay), 1968; End of the Road (screenplay), 1969; Blue Movie, 1970; The Rolling Stones on Tour, 1978. Add: R.F.D., East Canaan, Conn. 06024, U.S.A.

SOUTHGATE, Vera. British. Children's fiction, Education. Lectr. in Curriculum Development, 1960–72, and Sr. Lectr. in Education, 1972–79, Univ. of Manchester. Dir., Extending Beginning Reading Project, Schs. Council, 1973–77. *Publs:* (with J. Havenhand) Sounds and Words, 10 books, 1959–67; Southgate Group Reading Tests, 2 vols., 1962; (with J. Havenhand) Ladybird Easy Reading Books: People at Work Series, 4 books, 1962–65; Game Series, 2 books, 1964; Well-loved Tales, 28 books, 1964–75; Swallow Books, 3 books, 1964; Penny the Poodle, 5 books, 1964; First Words, 12 books, 1968; (with F.W. Warburton) i.t.a.: An Independent Evaluation, 1969; (with G.R. Roberts) Reading: Which Approach?, 1970; i.t.a.: What is the Evidence?, 1970; Beginning Reading, 1972; (ed.) Literacy at all Levels, 1972; (co-author) Extending Beginning Reading, 1981; (ed.) Star Series, 15 vols., 1982; Children Who Do Read, 1983. Add: 3 Mere Ct., Chester Rd., Mere, Knutsford, Cheshire WA16 6LQ, England.

SOUTHWOOD, Sir (Thomas) Richard (Edmund). British, b. 1931. Environmental science/Ecology, Zoology. Linacre Prof. of Zoology, since 1979, and Vice-Chancellor since 1989, Oxford Univ., Delegate, Oxford Univ. Press, since 1980. Ed., Entomologists Monthly mag., since 1962; Chmn., National Radiological Protection Bd., since 1986. Dean, Royal Coll. of Science, 1971–72; Prof. of Zoology, Univ. of London, 1967–79. Pres., British Ecological Soc., 1976–78; Gen. Ed., Arnold's Resources and Environmental Science Series, 1977–86; Chmn., Royal Commn. on Environmental Pollution, 1981–86; Pres., Royal Entomological Soc., 1983. *Publs:* (with D. Leston) Land and Water Bugs of the British Isles, 1959; Life of the Wayside and Woodland, 1963; Ecological Methods, 1966, 1978; (ed.) Insect Abundance, 1968; (with D. Strong and J.L. Lawton) Insect Communities on Plants, 1982; (ed. with B. Juniper) Insects and the Plant Surface, 1986, (ed. with R.R. Jones) Radiation and Health 1987. Add: Merton Coll., Oxford, England.

SOUTHWORTH, Warren H. American, b. 1912. Education, Medicine/Health. Prof. Emeritus of Health Education, Sch. of Education, and Prof. of Preventive Medicine, Medical Sch., Univ. of Wisconsin, Madison, since 1981 (Prof., 1944–81). Consultant, Unesco and WHO, since 1971; Consultant, Coronet Instructional Media, since 1970. Prof., Health Education and Science, Panzer Coll., East Orange, N.J., 1942–44; Coordinator of Sch. Health Prog., Wisconsin Dept. of Public Instruction, 1944–48. *Publs:* Manual for Emergency Medical Teams, 1952; (with

A.F. Davis) Hygiene, 1954; (with A.F. Davis) Science of Health, 1957; (with B.R. Moss) Health Education, 1961; Some Filtered Facts about Smoking and Health, 1971; Curriculum Planning and Some Current Health Problems, 1974; Basic Concepts in Patient Education for Health Care Facilities, 1982; Educational Therapy for Spinal Cord Injury Persons, 1985; Staff Handbook on Educational Therapy for Spinal Cord Injury Persons, 1985. Add: 3207 Stevens St., Madison, Wisc. 53705, U.S.A.

SOYINKA, Wole. (Akinwande Oluwole Soyinka). Nigerian, b. 1934. Novels/Short stories, Plays/Screenplays, Poetry, Translations. Goldwin Smith Prof. of African Studies and Theatre Arts, Cornell Univ., Ithaca, N.Y., since 1988. Play Reader, Royal Court Theatre, London, 1958–59; Research Fellow in Drama, Univ. of Ibadan, 1960–61; Lectr. in English, Univ. of Ife, 1962–64; Sr. Lectr. in English, Univ. of Lagos, 1964–67; Dir., Sch. of Drama, Univ. of Ibadan, 1969–72; Research Prof. of Drama, 1972–75, and Prof. of Comparative Literature, 1975–85, Univ. of Ife. Founding Dir. of the Orisun Theatre, and the 1960 Masks Theatre, Lagos and Ibadan. *Publs:* The Lion and the Jewel, 1959; Dance of the Forests, 1960; Camwood on the Leaves, 1960; Three Plays: The Trials of Brother Jero, the Swamp Dwellers, The Strong Breed, 1963; Kongi's Harvest, 1964; Five Plays: A Dance of the Forests, The Lion and the Jewel, The Swamp Dwellers, The Trials of Brother Jero, The Strong Breed, 1964; Before the Blackout, 1964; The interpreters (novel), 1965; The Road, 1965; Idanre, and Other Poems, 1967; (trans.) Forest of a Thousand Daemons: A Hunter's Saga, by D.A. Fagunwa, 1968; Madmen and Specialists, 1970; The Jero Plays, 1972; A Shuttle in the Crypt (poems), 1972; The Man Died: Prison Memoirs, 1972; (adaptor) The Bacchae, 1973; (ed.) Poems of Black Africa (in U.S. as Anthology of Black Verse), 1973; Colected Plays, 2 vols., 1973–74; Camwood on the Leaves, and Before the Blackout: Two Short Plays, 1974; Season of Anomy (novel), 1974; Myth, Literature, and the African World, 1976; Death and the King's Horseman, 1976; Ogun Abibiman (verse), 1976; (adaptor) Opera Wonyosi, 1981; Ake The Years of Childhood (autobiography), 1981; A Play of Giants, 1984; Six Plays, 1984; Mandela's Earth and Other Poems, 1988; Art, Dialogue and Outrage (essays), 1988; Isara: A Voyage Round Essay, 1989. Add: African Studies Dept., Cornell Univ., Ithaca, N.Y. 14850, U.S.A.

SPACHE, George D. American, b. 1909. Education. Prof. Emeritus, Univ. of Florida, Gainesville, since 1969 (joined faculty 1949). Pres., Spache Educational Consultants Inc. *Publs:* (with O. Spache and R. Tetart) Parlons Francais-Premier, Parlons Francais-Deuxieme, 1940, rev. ed. 1941; Good Books for Poor Readers, 1954; Resources in Teaching Reading, 1955; (with P.C. Berg) The Art of Efficient Reading, 1955, 4th ed. 1984; Binocular Reading Test, 1955; (with P.C. Berg) Faster Reading for Business, 1958; Good Reading for Poor Readers, 1958, 10th ed. 1978; (with L.P. Boone) Writing Elements, 1958; (with H. Roxwell and W. Schramm) Steps to Better Reading: Books I and II, 1963–64; Toward Better Reading, 1963; Diagnostic Reading Scales, 1963, 3rd ed. 1981; (with E.B. Spache) Reading in the Elementary School, 1964, 5th ed. 1985; Good Reading for The Disadvantaged Reader, 1970, 1975; The Teaching of Reading, 1972; Investigating the Issues of Reading Disabilities, 1976; Diagnosing and Correcting Reading Disabilities, 1976, 1981; (with Ken McIlroy and P.C. Berg) Case Studies in Reading Disability, 1981; (with E.B. Spache) Project Achievement: Reading, Books A-G, 1982–86. Add: 4042 Wilshire Circle East, Lakeshore Village, Sarasota, Fla. 34242, U.S.A.

SPACKS, Barry. American, b. 1931. Novels/Short stories, Poetry. Visiting Prof., Univ. of California, Santa Barbara, since 1980. Asst. Prof., Univ. of Florida, Gainesville, 1957–59; Prof. of English, Massachusetts Int. of Technology, Cambridge, 1960–83. *Publs:* Twenty Poems, 1967; The Company of Children (verse), 1968; The Sophomore (novel), 1969; Something Human (verse), 1972; Orphans (novel), 1972; Teaching the Penguins to Fly (verse), 1975; Imagining a Unicorn (verse), 1978; Spacks Street: New and Selected Poems, 1982; Brief Sparrow (verse), 1988. Add: 1111 Bath St., Santa Barbara, Calif. 93101, U.S.A.

SPACKS, Patricia Meyer. American, b. 1929. Literature. Prof. of English, Univ. of Virginia, Charlottesville, since 1989. Instr. in English, Indiana Univ., Bloomington, 1954–56; Instr. in Humanities, Univ. of Florida, 1958–59; Instr., 1959–61, Asst. Prof., 1961–65, Assoc. Prof., 1965–68, and Prof. of English, 1968–79, Wellesley Coll., Massachusetts; Prof. of English, 1979–89, and Chmn. of the Dept., 1985–88, Yale Univ., New Haven, Conn. *Publs:* The Varied God, 1969; The Insistence of Horror, 1962; (ed.) 18th Century Poetry, 1964; John Gay, 1965; Poetry of Vision, 1967; (ed.) Late Augustan Prose, 1971; An Argument of Images, 1971; (ed.) Late Augustan Poetry, 1973; The Female Imagination, 1975;

Imagining a Self, 1976; (ed.) Contemporary Women Novelists, 1977; The Adolescent Idea, 1981; Gossip, 1985. Add: Dept. of English, Univ. of Virginia, Charlottesville, Va. 22903, U.S.A.

SPADE, Rupert. *See* **PAWLEY, Martin.**

SPALDING, Keith. Formerly wrote as Karl Heinz G. Spalt. British, b. 1913. Language/Linguistics, Literature. Prof. and Head, Dept. of German, Univ. Coll. of North Wales, Bangor, 1950–80, now Emeritus. Ed., Historical Dictionary of German Figurative Usage, Basil Blackwell, Oxford, since 1952. Assoc. Ed., Muret-Sanders Encyclopaedic Dictionary, 1952–74. *Publs:* Kultur oder Vernichtung, 1932; Introduction to the German Language through Lyric Poetry, 1940; Der weite Weg, 1946; (ed.) Ackermann aus Bohmen, 1950; (ed.) Selections from Adalbert Stifter, 1952; (ed.) German Advanced Unseens, 1958; (ed.) German Word Patterns, 1962; (ed.) German Simple Unseens, 1963; (ed.) Grillparzer's Sappho, 1965; (ed.) Stifter's Abdias, 1966; (ed.) Goethe's Hermann und Dorothea, 1968. Add: Gower House, Llanfairpwll, Anglesey, Gwynedd LL61 5NX, Wales.

SPALDING, Ruth. Has also written as Marion Jay. British. Plays, Biography, Documentaries/Reportage. Formerly, Gen. Directing and Acting Mgr., The Rock Theatre Co. Ltd.; a National Adviser and Lectr., National Union of Townswomen's Guilds; Gen. Secty., Assn. of Head Mistresses, 1960–74. *Publs:* (as Marion Jay, with Alison Graham-Campbell) With This Sword (play), 1954; (as Marion Jay) The Word (Christmas mime), 1957; (as Marion Jay) Pleasure or Pain in Education (play), 1958; (as Marion Jay, with Alison Graham-Campbell) Mistress Bottom's Dream (play), 1958; (as Marion Jay and Lucile Spalding, with Alison Graham-Campbell and Helen Anderson) Why Not Write a Documentary Play?, 1960; The Improbable Puritan: A Life of Bulstrode Whitelocke, 1605-1675, 1975. Add: 34 Reynards Rd., Welwyn, Herts, AL6 9TP, England.

SPANN, Weldon Oma. American, b. 1924. Novels/Short stories. Electronics technician since 1964. *Publs:* Outlaw Town, 1965; Return to Violence, 1969; Discharge to Danger, 1969; The Stink of Murder, 1969; Hunter for Hire, 1970; Wall of Jeopardy, 1970; Plunge into Peril, 1970. Add: 1712 Pike Ave., North Little Rock, Ark. 72114, U.S.A.

SPANNER, Valerie. *See* **GRAYLAND, Valerie.**

SPARK, Muriel (Sarah). British. Novels/Short stories, Children's fiction, Plays/Screenplays, Poetry, Literature. Worked in the Political Intelligence Dept. of the British Foreign Office during World War II; Gen. Secty., Poetry Soc., and Ed., Poetry Review, London, 1947–49. *Publs:* (ed. with D. Stanford) Tribute to Wordsworth, 1950; Child of Light: A Reassessment of Mary Shelley, 1951; The Fanfarlo, 1952; (ed.) A Selection of Poems by Emily Brontë, 1952; (with D. Stanford) Emily Brontë; Her Life and Works, 1953; John Masefield, 1953; (ed. with D. Stanford) My Best Mary: The Letters of Mary Shelley, 1953; (ed.) The Brontë Letters, 1954; (ed. with D. Stanford) Letters of John Henry Newman, 1957; The Comforters, 1957; Robinson, 1958; The Go-Away Bird and Other Stories, 1958; Memento Mori, 1959; The Ballad of Peckham Rye, 1960; The Bachelors, 1960; The Prime of Miss Jean Brodie, 1961; Voices at Play, 1961; Doctors of Philosophy (play), 1963; The Girls of Slender Means, 1963; The Mandelbaum Gate, 1965; Collected Poems I, 1967; Collected Stories I, 1967; The Public Image, 1968; The Very Fine Clock, 1969; The Driver's Seat, 1970; Not to Disturb, 1971; The Hothouse by the East River, 1973; The Abbess of Crewe, 1974; The Takeover, 1976; Territorial Rights, 1979; Loitering with Intent, 1981; Bang-Bang You're Dead and Other Stories, 1982; Going Up to Sotheby's and Other Poems, 1982; The Only Problem, 1984; The Stories of Muriel Spark, 1986; Mary Shelley, 1988; A Far Cry from Kensington, 1988. Add: c/o David Higham Assocs., 5-8 Lower John St., London W1R 4HA, England.

SPARNON, Norman. Australian, b. 1913. Crafts, Translations. Freelance teacher and artist, since 1958. *Publs:* Japanese Flower Arrangement: Classical and Modern, 1960; Beauty of Wildflowers, 1967; Magic of Camellias, 1968; A Guide to Japanese Flower Arrangement, 1969; Ikebana with Roses, 1969; Poetry of Leaves, 1970; (trans.) Rikka: The Soul of Japanese Flower Arrangement, 1974; Creative Japanese Flower Arrangement, 1982. Add: 41 Darling Point Rd., Darling Point, N.S.W. 2027, Australia.

SPARSHOTT, Francis (Edward). Canadian, b. 1926. Poetry, Philosophy. Prof. of Philosophy, Victoria Coll., Univ. of Toronto, since 1964 (Lectr. in Philosophy, 1950–55; Lectr. in Classics, 1955–70; Asst.

Prof. of Philosophy, 1955–62; Assoc. Prof., 1962–64; Chmn., Dept. of Philosophy, 1966–70). Pres., Canadian Philosophical Assn., 1975–76, and League of Canadian Poets, 1977–79; Pres., American Soc. for Aesthetics, 1981–82. *Publs:* An Enquiry into Goodness and Related Concepts, 1958; The Structure of Aesthetics, 1963; A Divided Voice (verse), 1965; The Concept of Criticism, 1967; A Cardboard Garage, 1969; A Book by Cromwell Kent (humour), 1970; Looking for Philosophy, 1972; The Naming of the Beasts (verse), 1979; The Rainy Hills (verse), 1979; The Theory of the Arts, 1982; The Cave of Trophonius (verse), 1983; The Hanging Gardens of Etobicoke (verse), 1983; Storms and Screens (verse), 1985; Off the Ground: First Steps in the Philosophy of the Art of Dance, 1988. Add: 50 Crescentwood Rd., Scarborough, Ont. M1N 1E4, Canada.

SPATZ, Kenneth Christopher, Jr. American, b. 1940. Psychology. Prof. of Psychology, Hendrix Coll., Conway, Ark., since 1973. Instr. in Psychology, Univ. of the South, Sewanee, Tenn., 1966–69; Assoc. Prof. of Psychology, Univ. of Arkansas, Monticello, 1971–73. *Publs:* A Laboratory Manual for Experimental Psychology, 1970; (with J.O. Johnston) Basic Statistics: Tales of Distributions, 1976, 4th ed. 1989. Add: Dept. of Psychology, Hendrix Coll., Conway, Ark. 72032, U.S.A.

SPEAIGHT, George. British, b. 1914. History, Theatre, Travel. Gen. Ed. of Publs., Soc. for Theatre Research, London, since 1970. Ed., Rainbird Publishing Group, London, 1960–73; Co-ed., Theatre Notebook, London, 1969–76. *Publs:* Juvenile Drama: The History of the English Toy Theatre, 1947; The History of the English Puppet Theatre, 1955; Professional and Literary Memoirs of Charles Dibdin the Younger, 1956; The History of the English Toy Theatre, 1969; Punch and Judy: A History, 1970; Bawdy Songs of the Early Music Hall, 1975; The Book of Clowns, 1980; A History of the Circus, 1981; The Life and Travels of Richard Barnard, Marionette Proprietor, 1981; Memories of Circus, Variety, etc. by Henry Whiteley, 1981; The New Shell Guide to Britain, 1985; Collecting Theatre Memorabilia, 1988. Add: 6 Maze Rd., Kew Gardens, Richmond, Surrey, England.

SPEAR, Allan Henry. American, b. 1937. History, Race relations. Assoc. Prof. of History, Univ. of Minnesota, Minneapolis, since 1967 (Lectr., 1964–65; Asst. Prof., 1965–67). State Senator, Minn., since 1973. *Publs:* Black Chicago: The Making of a Negro Ghetto, 1890-1920, 1967. Add: 2429 Colfax Ave. S., Minneapolis, Minn., U.S.A.

SPEAR, Hilda D. British, b. 1926. Literature. Sr. Lectr. in English since 1987, and Sr. Adviser of Studies, 1979–83, Univ. of Dundee (Lectr., 1969–87). Held various teaching and lecturing posts, London and Leicester, 1946–57; Lectr., Purdue Univ., West Lafayette, Ind., 1957–58; Lectr. in English and Education in Leicester, 1958–60, 1965–68. *Publs:* (ed.) The English Poems of Charles Stuart Calverley, 1974; (ed.) The Poems and Selected Letters of C.H. Sorley, 1978; Remembering, We Forget, 1979; Hardy's The Mayor of Casterbridge, 1980; Lawrence's The Rainbow, 1980; Conrad: Youth and Typhoon, 1980; William Golding: The Inheritors, 1983; Emily Brontë Wuthering Heights, 1985; William Golding: The Spire, 1986; E.M. Forster: A Passage to India, 1986; Forster in Egypt: A Graeco-Alexandrian Encounter, 1987. Add: Dept. of English, The University, Dundee DD1 4HN, Scotland.

SPEARE, Elizabeth George. American, b. 1908. Children's fiction, Children's non-fiction. *Publs:* Calico Captive, 1957; The Witch of Blackbird Pond, 1958; The Bronze Bow, 1961; Life in Colonial America, 1963; The Prospering, 1966; The Sign of the Beaver, 1983. Add: 48 Bibbins Rd., Easton, Conn. 06612, U.S.A.

SPEARS, (Marion) Heather. Canadian, b. 1934. Poetry. Freelance writer and graphic artist. *Publs:* Asylum Poems, 1958; The Danish Portraits, 1966; From the Inside, 1972; Drawings from the Newborn, 1986; How to Read Faces, 1986. Add: Oslo Plads 1611, 2100 Copenhagen O, Denmark.

SPEARS, Monroe K(irk). American, b. 1916. Literature. Moody Prof. of English, Rice Univ., Houston, 1964–86, now Emeritus. Instr. in English, Univ. of Wisconsin, Madison, 1940–42; Asst. Prof. of English, 1946–49, and Assoc. Prof., 1949–52, Vanderbilt Univ., Nashville; Prof., Univ. of the South, Sewanee, 1952–64. Ed., The Sewanee Review, 1952–61. *Publs:* (ed. with H. Bunker Wright) The Literary Works of Matthew Prior, 2 vols., 1959; The Poetry of W.H. Auden, 1963; (ed.) Auden: A Collection of Critical Essays, 1964; Hart Crane, 1965; Dionysus and the City: Modernism in Twentieth Century Poetry, 1970; Space Against Time in Modern American Poetry, 1972; The Levitator and other Poems, 1975; American Ambitions (essays), 1987. Add: Carruthers Rd., Sewanee, Tenn. 37375, U.S.A.

SPECTOR, Jack Jerome. American, b. 1925. Art, Psychology. Prof. of Art History, Rutgers Univ., New Brunswick, N.J., since 1972 (Instr., 1962–64; Asst. Prof., 1964–67: Assoc. Prof., 1967–72; Chmn., Dept. of Art, and Dir., Grad. Prog. in Art History, 1969–71; Dir., Rutgers Jr. Year in France, Paris and Tours, 1971–73). Sr. Fellow, Center for Advanced Study in the Visual Arts, 1985–86. *Publs:* The Murals of Eugene Delacroix at Saint-Sulpice, 1967; The Aesthetics of Freud, 1973; Delacroix's "Death of Sardanapalus", 1974. Add: Dept. of Art, Rutgers Univ., New Brunswick, N.J. 08903, U.S.A.

SPECTOR, Leonard S. American, b. 1945. Military/Defence, Technology. Affiliated with the Carnegie Endowment for International Peace, Washington, D.C., since 1984. Assoc., Wald, Harkrader and Ross, Washington, D.C., 1973–75; Special Counsel to the Commissioner, U.S. Nuclear Regulatory Commn., Washington, D.C., 1975–77; Chief Counsel, Senate Energy and Non-Proliferation Subcttee., Washington, 1978–82; Dir. of the Non-Proliferation Project, Roosevelt Center for American Policy Studies, Washington, 1982–83 *Publs:* The Spread of Nuclear Weapons, 1984; Nuclear Proliferation Today, 1984; The New Nuclear Nations, 1985; Going Nuclear, 1987 Add: c/o Ballinger Publishing Co., 54 Church St., Cambridge, Mass. 02138, U.S.A.

SPECTOR, Robert D(onald). American, b. 1922. Literature. Dir. of Humanities and Prof. of English, Long Island Univ., Brooklyn, N.Y. (joined faculty, 1948). *Publs:* (ed.) Seven Masterpieces of Gothic Horror, 1963; (ed.) Vicar of Wakefield, 1964; (ed.) Hard Times, 1964; (ed.) Scarlet Letter, 1965; (ed.) Essays on the 18th Century Novel, 1965; (ed.) Tom Sawyer, 1966; English Literary Periodicals, 1966; (ed.) Frankenstein, 1967; (ed.) Emma, 1969; Tobias George Smollett, 1969, 1989; (ed.) Great Short British Novels, 1970; Pär Lagerkvist, 1973; (ed.) Candle and the Tower, 1974; Arthur Murphy, 1979; Tobias Smollett: A Reference Guide, 1980; The English Gothic, 1984; Backgrounds to Restoration and Eighteenth-Century English Literature, 1989. Add: 1761 E. 26th St., Brooklyn, N.Y. 11229, U.S.A.

SPECTOR, Sherman David. American, b. 1927. History, Politics/Government. Prof. of History and Govt., Russell Sage Coll., Troy, N.Y., since 1960. Asst. Prof., State Univ. of New York, Albany, 1957–60. *Publs:* Rumania at the Paris Peace Conference, 1962; (with R. Ristelhueber) History of the Balkan Peoples, 1972; (ed.) The History of the Romanian Peoples, 1974. Add: 6 Comely Lane, Latham, N.Y. 12110, U.S.A.

SPEED, Frank Warren. Australian, b. 1911. Military/Defence, Politics/Government, Travel/Exploration/Adventure, Documentaries/Reportage. Australian Corresp., Army Quarterly and Defence Journal. Officer in Australian Regular Army, retired as Brigadier, 1939–66. *Publs:* South East Asian Peninsula Today, 1970; Indonesia Today, 1971; Your Journey into the South East Asian Peninsula, 1973; Your Journey into Indonesia, 1973; Malaysia and Singapore, 1973; Indonesia Today, 1975; Comd. Structure of Australian Defence Policy, 1987. Add: Vanwall Rd., Moggill, Qld. 4070, Australia.

SPEED, F(rederick) Maurice. British, b. 1912. Mystery/Crime/Suspense, Film. Ed. and Compiler, Film Review Annual, London, since 1945; Film Critic, What's On in London (Managing Ed., 1935–76). Ed. and Compiler, The Western Film Annual, Macdonald Publs. Ed., The Film Diary, 1987–89. *Publs:* They Rubbed Him Out; Movie Cavalcade; Star Parade; The Moviegoers' Quiz Book. Add: 4 The Farm, 10 Princes Way, London SW19 6QF, England.

SPEICHER, Helen Ross. Writes with Kathryn Borland under joint pseuds. Alice Abbott, Jane Land, and Jane and Ross Land. American, b. 1915. Novels/Short stories, Historical/Romance/Gothic, Children's fiction, Children's non-fiction. Ed., Intnl. Typographical Union, Indianapolis, 1937–41; Plant mag., Intnl. Harvester, Indianapolis, 1942–44. *Publs:* all with Kathryn Borland—(as Alice Abbott) Southern Yankees, 1960; (as Alice Abbott) Allan Pinkerton, Young Detective, 1962; (as Jane and Ross Land) Miles and the Big Hat, 1963; (as Alice Abbott) Everybody Laughed and Laughed, 1964; (as Alice Abbott) Eugene Field, Young Poet, 1964; (as Alice Abbott) Phillis Wheatley, Young Colonial Poet, 1968; (as Alice Abbott) Harry Houdini, Young Magician, 1969; (as Alice Abbott) Clocks, From Shadow to Atom, 1969; (as Alice Abbott) Good-by to Stony Crick, 1974; (as Alice Abbott) The Third Tower (romance novel), 1974; (as Jane Land) Stranger in the Land (novel), 1974; (as Alice Abbott) Good-bye, Julie Scott (romance novel), 1975.

SPEIGHT, Johnny. British, b. 1921. Plays. Radio and television scriptwriter for the BBC, London, since 1955; Creator of BBC series,

Till Death Us Do Part. *Publs:* If There Weren't Any Blacks You'd Have to Invent Them, 1965; Till Death Us Do Part, play and screenplay, 1973; It Stands to Reason: A Kind of Autobiography, 1973; The Thoughts of Chairman Alf, 1973; Pieces of Speight, 1974; The Garnett Chronicles, 1986. Add: Fouracres, Heronsgate, Chorleywood, Herts., England.

SPELLMAN, Cathy Cash. American. Romance. *Publs:* Notes to My Daughter (non-fiction), 1981; So Many Partings, 1983; An Excess of Love, 1985; Fancy, 1989. Add: c/o Collins, 8 Grafton St., London W1X 3LA, England.

SPELLMAN, Roger G. *See* **COX,** William R.

SPENCE, Duncan. *See* **SPENCE,** William John Duncan.

SPENCE, Eleanor. Australian, b. 1928. Children's fiction, Autobiography. Teaching Asst., Autistic Children's Assn. of New South Wales, since 1974. Children's Librarian, Coventry City Libraries, Warwicks., 1952–54. *Publs:* Patterson's Track: Summer In-Between; Lillipilly Hill; The Green Laurel, 1964; Year of the Currawong, 1965; The Switherby Pilgrims, 1967; Jamberoo Road, 1969; The Nothing Place; Time to Go Home; The Travels of Hermann, 1973; The October Child (in U.K. as The Devil Hole), 1976; A Candle for St. Antony, 1977; The Seventh Pebble, 1980; The Leftovers, 1983; Me and Jeshua, 1984; Miranda Going Home, 1985; Mary and Frances, 1986; Deezle Boy, 1987; Another October Child (autobiography), 1988. Add: 85 Rickard Rd., Empire Bay, N.S.W. 2256, Australia.

SPENCE, William John Duncan. Also writes as Jim Bowden, Hannah Cooper, Kirk Ford, Floyd Rogers, and Duncan Spence. British, b. 1923. Novels/Short stories, Westerns/Adventure, History. Sch. teacher, 1940–43; Store Mgr., 1946–77. *Publs:* as Duncan Spence—Dark Hell, 1959; (with Joan Spence) Romantic Ryedale, 1977, 1987; (with Joan Spence) The Medieval Monasteries of Yorkshire, 1981; (with Joan Spence) Handy Facts: North Yorkshire, 1984; as Jim Bowden—The Return of the Sheriff, 1960; Waymans Ford, 1960; Two Gun Justice, 1961; Roaring Valley, 1962; Revenge in Red Springs, 1962; Black Water Canyon, 1963; Arizona Gold, 1963; Trail of Revenge, 1964; Brazos Freud, 1965; Guns along the Brazos, 1967; Gun Loose, 1969; Valley of Revenge, 1971; Trail to Texas, 1973; Thunder in Montana, 1973; Showdown in Salt Fork, 1975; Hired Gun, 1976; Incident at Bison Creek, 1977; Cap, 1978; Dollars of Death, 1979; Renegade Riders, 1980; Gunfight at Elm Creek, 1980; Shadow of Eagle Rock, 1982; Pecos Trail, 1983; Incident at Elm Creek, 1984; Hangman's Trail, 1986; Return of the Gunmen, 1988; as Floyd Rogers—The Man from Cheyenne Wells, 1964; Revenge Rider, 1964; The Stage Riders, 1967; Montana Justice, 1973; Hangman's Gulch, 1974; Incident at Elk River, 1979; as Kirk Ford—Trail to Sedalia, 1967; Feud Riders, 1974; as Bill Spence—Harpooned: The Story of Whaling, 1980; Bomber's Moon, 1981; Secret Squadron, 1986; as Hannah Cooper—Time Will Not Wait, 1983. Add: Post Office, Ampleforth Coll., York, England.

SPENCER, Charles. British, b. 1920. Art. Lectr. in Art and Theatre, Croydon Coll., Surrey. Consultant, Grosvenor Gallery, London, 1962–65; Ed., Art and Artists, 1965–68, and Eds. Alecto, 1968–70. *Publs:* Erté, 1970; (ed.) Decade of Printmaking, 1973; (ed. and contrib.) The Aesthetic Movement, 1973; Léon Bakst, 1973; (with P. Dyer) The World of Serge Diaghilev, 1974; (ed. with C. Bernard) The World of Flo Ziegfeld, 1974; Cecil Beaton: Stage and Film Designs, 1975. Add: 24A Ashworth Rd., London W9 1JY, England.

SPENCER, Christopher. American, b. 1930. Literature, Biography. Prof. of English, Univ. of North Carolina at Greensboro, since 1970. Chmn., Div. of Humanities, and Head, Dept. of English, Little Rock Univ., Ark., 1958–62; Assoc. Prof. of English, 1962–65, and Prof., 1965–70, Illinois State Univ., Normal. *Publs:* (ed. and author) Davenant's Macbeth from the Yale Manuscript, 1961; (ed. and author) Five Restoration Adaptations of Shakespeare, 1965; Nahum Tate, 1972; The Genesis of Shakespeare's Merchant of Venice, 1988. Add: Dept. of English, Univ. of North Carolina at Greensboro, Greensboro, N.C. 27412, U.S.A.

SPENCER, Colin. British, b. 1933. Novels/Short stories, Cookery/Gastronomy/Wine. Freelance writer, dramatist, and painter. *Publs:* An Absurd Affair, 1961; Anarchists in Love (in U.S. as The Anarchy of Love), 1963; Asylum, 1966; Poppy, Mandragora, and the New Sex, 1966; The Tyranny of Love, 1967; Spitting Image, 1968; Lovers in War, 1970; Panic, 1972; Summer at Camber-39, 1973; How the Greeks Captured Mrs. Nixon, 1974; The Victims of Love, 1978; Gourmet Cooking for Vegetarians, 1978; Good and Healthy, 1983; Colin Spencer's Cordon Vert, 1985; Mediterranean Vegetarian Cooking, 1986; (with Tom Sanders) The

Vegetarians' Healthy Diet Book, 1986; The New Vegetarian, 1986; Colin Spencer's Fish Cookbook, 1986; One Course Feasts, 1986; Feast for Health, 1987; Al Fresco, 1987; The Romantic Vegetarian, 1988; The Worldly Vegetarian, 1989. Add: Two Heath Cottages, Tunstall, Woodbridge, Suffolk IP12 2HQ, England.

SPENCER, Dora (Margaret). Australian, b. 1916. Autobiography/Memoirs/Personal. MacLeay Fellow, Univ. of Sydney, 1939–40; Lectr. in Zoology, Univ. of New England, Armidale, N.S.W., 1940–45; Tutor in Zoology, Commonwealth Reconstruction Training Scheme, Univ. of Sydney, 1946–48; Entomologist, Dept. of Public Health, Papua New Guinea, 1954–61, 1971, 1975–78. *Publs:* Doctor's Wife in New Guinea, 1959; Doctor's Wife in Papua, 1964; Doctor's Wife in Rabaul, 1967; John Howard Lidgett Cumpston 1880-1954: A Biography, 1987. Add: 1 George St., Tenterfield, N.S.W. 2372, Australia.

SPENCER, Elizabeth. American, b. 1921. Novels/Short stories. Adjunct Prof., Concordia Univ., Montreal, since 1981 (Visiting Prof., 1976–81). Instr., Northwest Mississippi Jr. Coll., Senatobia, 1943–44, and Ward-Belmont Coll., Nashville, Tenn., 1944–45; Reporter, The Nashville Tennessean, 1945–46; Instr., 1948–49, and Instr. in Creative Writing, 1949–51 and 1952–53, Univ. of Mississippi, Oxford. *Publs:* Fire in the Morning, 1948; This Crooked Way, 1952; The Voice at the Back Door, 1956; The Light in the Piazza, 1960; Knights and Dragons, 1965; No Place for an Angel, 1967; Ship Island and Other Stories, 1968; The Snare, 1972; The Stories of Elizabeth Spencer, 1981; Marilee, 1981; The Salt Line, 1984; Jack of Diamonds and Other Stories, 1988. Add: c/o Viking Press, 40 W. 23rd St., New York, N.Y. 10010, U.S.A.

SPENCER, John (Walter). British, b. 1922. Language/Linguistics. Prof. of English Language, Univ. of Bayreuth. Member of faculty, Univ. of Lund, Sweden, 1949–52, Univ. of Edinburgh, 1955–56, Univ. of Allahabad, India, 1956–58, Univ. of Lahore, Pakistan, 1958–59, Univ. of Ibadan, Nigeria, 1959–62, Univ. of Leeds, 1962–82; Prof. of English, Hong Kong Univ., 1982–84. Ed., West African Language Monograph Series, CUP, 1963–74; Ed., Journal of West African Languages, 1964–71. *Publs:* Workers for Humanity, 1963; (ed.) Language in Africa, 1963; (with N.E. Enkvist and M. Gregory) Linguistics and Style, 1964; (ed. with M. Wollmann) Modern Poems for the Commonwealth, 1966; (ed. and co-author) The English Language in West Africa, 1971. Add: Univ. of Bayreuth, Postfach H-101251, 8580 Bayreuth, Germany.

SPENCER, LaVyrle. American. Romance. *Publs:* The Fulfillment, 1979; The Endearment, 1982; A Promise to Cherish, 1983; Humingbird, 1983; Sweet Memories, 1984; Twice Loved, 1984; Separate Beds, 1985; The Hellion, 1985; Forsaking All Others, 1985; Spring Fancy, 1985; A Heart Speaks, 1986; Years, 1986; The Gamble, 1987; Vows, 1988; Morning Glory, 1989. Add: c/o Putnam, 200 Madison Ave., New York, N.Y. 10016, U.S.A.

SPENCER, Paul. British, b. 1932. Anthropology/Ethnology, Demography, Medicine/Health, Sociology. Reader in African Anthropology, Sch. of Oriental and African Studies, Univ. of London, since 1971. Staff member, Inst. for Operational Research, Tavistock Inst., London, 1962–71. *Publs:* The Samburu: A Study of Gerontocracy in a Nomadic Tribe, 1965; General Practice and Models of the Referral Process, 1971; Nomads in Alliance: Symbiosis and Growth among the Rendille and Samburu of Kenya, 1973; (ed.) Society and the Dance: The Social Anthropology of Process and Performance, 1985; The Maasai of Matapato: A Study of Rituals of Rebellion, 1988. Add: Sch. of Oriental and African Studies, Thornaugh St., London WC1, England.

SPENCER, Ross H. American, b. 1921. Crime/Mystery. *Publs:* The Data Caper, 1978; The Reggis Arms Caper, 1979; The Stranger City Caper, 1980; The Abu Wahab Caper, 1980; The Radish River Caper, 1981; Echoes of Zero, 1981; The Missing Bishop, 1985; Monastery Nightmare, 1986; Kirby's Last Circus, 1987; Death Wore Gloves, 1987. Add: 551 N. Dunlap Ave., Youngstown, Ohio 44509, U.S.A.

SPENCER, Scott. American. Novels/Short stories. *Publs:* Last Night at the Brain Thieves Ball, 1973; Preservation Hall, 1976; Endless Love, 1979; Waking the Dead, 1986. Add: c/o ICM, 40 W. 57th St., New York, N.Y. 10019, U.S.A.

SPENCER, William. American, b. 1922. History, Travel/Exploration/Adventure. Chief of Publs., Education Dept., 1962–64, and Field Expert in Public Admin., Morocco, 1964, both Unesco; Dir., Inst. of Non-Western Studies, American Univ., Washington, D.C., 1965–68; Prof. of Middle East History, Florida State Univ., Tallahassee, 1968–80; Visiting Prof.,

Rollins Coll., Florida, 1982–85. *Publs:* Land and People of Turkey, 1958, 1971; Land and People of Morocco, 1965, 1972; Land and People of Tunisia, 1967, 1972; Land and People of Algeria, 1969; Story of North Africa, 1975; Algiers in the Age of the Corsairs, 1976; Historical Dictionary of Morocco, 1980; The Islamic States in Conflict, 1983; Global Cultures: The Middle East, 1986; Portrait of Turkey: The Land and People, 1989; World Hunger and Food Resources, 1989. Add: P.O. Box 1702, Suite 52, Gainesville, Fla., U.S.A.

SPENDER, (Sir) Stephen (Harold). British, b. 1909. Poetry, Novels, Plays, Literature, Travel/Exploration/Adventure, Autobiography/Memoirs/ Personal. Prof. of English Literature, Univ. Coll., London, 1970–77, now Emeritus. Ed., Horizon mag., London, 1939–41; Co-Ed., 1953–66, and Corresponding Ed., 1966–67, Encounter mag., London; Consultant in Poetry in English, Library of Congress, Washington, D.C., 1965–66. Pres., English Centre, P.E.N., 1975. *Publs:* Nine Experiments by S.H.S.: Being Poems Written at the Age of Eighteen, 1928; 20 Poems, 1930; Poems, 1933, 1934; Vienna, 1935; At Night, 1935; The Destructive Element: A Study of Modern Writers and Beliefs, 1935; The Burning Cactus (short stories), 1936; Forward from Liberalism, 1937; Trial of a Judge, 1938; The Still Centre, 1939; (with G. Rees) Danton's Death, adaptation of a play by Georg Buchner, 1939; The New Realism: A Discussion, 1939; Selected Poems, 1940; I Sit by the Window, 1940; The Backward Son (novel), 1940; Ruins and Visions, 1942; Life and the Poet, 1942; Spiritual Exercises (To Cecil Day Lewis), 1943; (with W. Sansom and J. Gordon) Jim Braidy: The Story of Britain's Firemen, 1943; Citizens in War—and After, 1945; Botticelli, 1945; Poems of Dedication, 1946; European Witness (on Germany), 1946; Poetry since 1929, 1946; Returning to Vienna, 1947; Nine Sketches, 1947; The Edge of Being, 1949; To the Island, 1951; World Within World: The Autobiography of Stephen Spender, 1951; Europe in Photographs, 1951; Shelley, 1952; Learning Laughter (on Israel), 1952; The Creative Element: A Study of Vision, Despair, and Orthodoxy among Some Modern Writers, 1953; Sirmione Peninsula, 1954; Collected Poems 1928-1953, 1955, 1928-1985, 1986; The Making of a Poem (essays), 1955; Mary Stuart, adaptation of the play by Schiller, 1957; Inscriptions, 1958; Lulu, adaptation of the play by Frank Wedekind, 1958; Engaged in Writing, and The Fool and the Princess (short stories), 1958; The Imagination in the Modern World: Three Lectures, 1962; Rasputin's End, 1963; The Struggle of the Modern, 1963; Selected Poems, 1964; (with P. Fermor) Ghika: Paintings, Drawings, Sculpture, 1964; The Magic Flute: Retold, 1966; Chaos and Control in Poetry, 1966; The Year of the Young Rebels, 1969; The Generous Days: Ten Poems, 1969, augmented ed. as The Generous Days, 1971; Descartes, 1970; Art Student, 1970; (with John Heath-Stubbs and F.T. Prince) Penguin Modern Poets, 20, 1971; Love-Hate Relations: A Study of Anglo-American Sensibilities, 1974; W.H. Auden: A Tribute, 1975; Eliot, 1975; The Thirties and After, 1978; Recent Poems, 1978; (with Fulvio Roiter) Venice, 1979; (with Paul Hogarth) America Observed, 1979; Letters to Christopher: Stephen Spender's Letters to Christopher Isherwood 1929-1939, 1980; (with David Hockney) China Diary, 1982; Rasputin's End (libretto), 1983; Oedipus Trilogy, 1985; Journals 1939-1983, 1985; In Irina's Garden, 1986; The Temple (novel), 1988. Add: 15 Loudoun Rd., London NW8, England.

SPERLICH, Peter W(erner). American, b. 1934. Civil liberties/Human rights, Human relations, Psychology. Prof. of Law, since 1963, and of Political Science, since 1980, Univ. of California, Berkeley. *Publs:* Conflict and Harmony in Human Affairs, 1971; Single Family Defaults and Foreclosures, 1975; Trade Rules and Industry Practice, 1976; Over-the-Counter Drug Advertisements, 1977; Residing in a Mobile Home, 1977; An Evaluation of the Emerging School Act Nonprofit Organization, 1978. Add: 210 Barrows Hall, Univ. of California, Berkeley, Calif. 94720, U.S.A.

SPICER, Bart. With Bette Coe Spicer also writes as Jay Barbette. American, b. 1918. Novels/Short stories, Mystery/Crime/Suspense. *Publs:* mystery novels—The Dark Light, 1949; Blues for the Prince, 1950; (as Jay Barbette) Final Copy, 1950; The Golden Door, 1951; Black Sheep, Run, 1951; The Long Green, 1952 (in U.K. as Shadow of Fear, 1953); (as Jay Barbette) Dear Dead Days, 1953 (in U.S. paperback, Death's Long Shadow, 1955); The Taming of Carney Wilde, 1954; The Day of the Dead, 1955; (as Jay Barbette) The Deadly Doll, 1958; Exit, Running, 1959; (as Jay Barbette) Look Behind You, 1960; Act of Anger, 1962; The Burned Man, 1966; Kellogg Junction, 1969; The Adversary, 1974; novels—The Wild Ohio, 1954; The Tall Captains, 1957; Brother to the Enemy, 1958; The Day Before Thunder, 1960; Festival, 1970. Add: c/o Putnam, 200 Madison Ave., New York, N.Y. 10016, U.S.A.

SPIEGEL, Henry William. American, b. 1911. Economics. Prof. Emeritus of Economics, Catholic Univ. of America, Washington, D.C., since 1977 (Lectr., 1943–46; Assoc. Prof., 1946–50; Prof., 1950–77). Member, Bd. of Eds., Social Science mag., since 1953, and History of Political Economy mag., since 1973. *Publs:* Der Pachtvertrag der Kleingartenvereine, 1933; Land Tenure Policies At Home and Abroad, 1941; The Economics of Total War, 1942; The Brazilian Economy, 1949; Current Economic Problems, 1949, 3rd ed. 1961; Introduction to Economics, 1951; (ed. and trans.) Development of Economic Thought, 1952; (ed. and trans.) DuPont on Economic Curves, 1955; (ed.) The Rise of American Economic Thought, 1960; The Growth of Economic Thought, 1971, 1983; (ed. with Warren Samuels) Contemporary Economists in Perspective, 1983. Add: Dept. of Economics, Catholic Univ. of America, Washington, D.C. 20064, U.S.A.

SPIELBERG, Peter. American, b. 1929. Novels/Short stories, Literature. Prof. of English, Brooklyn Coll., N.Y., since 1961. *Publs:* James Joyce's Letters and Manuscripts at the University of Buffalo, 1962; (with S. Galin) Reference Books: How to Select and Use Them, 1969; Bedrock, 1973; Twiddledum Twaddledum, 1974; (co-ed.) Statements 2, 1976; The Hermetic Whore, 1977; Crash-Landing, 1985. Add: Dept. of English, Brooklyn Coll., Brooklyn, N.Y. 11210, U.S.A.

SPILHAUS, Athelstan. American (born South African), b. 1911. Meteorology/Atmospheric sciences, Sciences. Pres., Pan Geo Inc., since 1984. Consultant, National Oceanic and Atmospheric Admin., Dept. of Commerce, Washington, D.C., since 1974. Prof. of Physics, Univ. of Minnesota Inst. of Technology, Minneapolis, since 1966 (Dean, 1949–66). Research Asst., Massachusetts Inst. of Technology, Cambridge, Mass., 1933–35; Asst. Dir. of Technical Services, Union of South Africa Defense Forces, 1935–36; Research Asst. in Oceanography, 1936–37, Investigator, 1938–60, and Assoc. in Physical Oceanography, 1960, Woods Hole Oceanographic Instn., Mass.; Asst. Prof. of Meteorology, 1937–39, Founder and Chmn., Dept. of Meteorology and Oceanography, 1938–47, Assoc. Prof., 1939–42, Prof., 1942–48, and Dir. of Research, 1946–48, New York Univ., NYC; Reorganizer of Meteorological Services, and Meterological Adviser to Union of South Africa Govt., 1947. *Publs:* (with James E. Miller) Workon on Meteorology, 1942; Weathercraft, 1951; (with W.E.K. Middleton) Meteorological Instruments, 1953; Satellite of the Sun, 1958, 1964; Turn to the Sea, 1959; The Ocean Laboratory, 1966; Experimental Cities, 1966; Waste Management, The Next Industrial Revolution, 1966; Oceanography 1966—Achievements and Opportunities, 1967; (with Kathlean Spilhaus) Mechanical Toys: How Old Toys Work, 1989. Add: Box 1063, Middleburg, Va. 22117, U.S.A.

SPILLANE, Mickey. (Frank Morrison Spillane). American, b. 1918. Mystery/Crime/Suspense. *Publs:* I, the Jury, 1947; Vengeance is Mine!, 1950; My Gun is Quick, 1950; The Big Kill, 1951; One Lonely Night, 1951; The Long Wait, 1951; Kiss Me, Deadly, 1952; The Deep, 1961; The Girl Hunters, 1962; Me, Hood!, 1963; Day of the Guns, 1964; The Snake, 1964; Killer Mine, 1965; Bloody Sunrise, 1965; The Death Dealers, 1965; The Twisted Thing, 1966; The By-Pass Control, 1967; The Body Lovers, 1967; The Delta Factor, 1967; Survival: Zero, 1970; Tough Guys, 1970; The Erection Set, 1972; The Last Cop Out, 1973; The Day the Sea Rolled Back (juvenile), 1979; The Ship That Never Was (juvenile), 1982; Tomorrow I Die (short stories), 1984; The Killing Man, 1989. Add: c/o Mysterious Press, 129 W. 56th St., New York, N.Y. 10019, U.S.A.

SPINDLER, George Dearborn. American, b. 1920. Anthropology/Ethnology, Education, Psychology. Emeritus Prof. of Anthropology and Education, Stanford Univ., Calif., since 1978 (Asst. Prof., 1950–53; Assoc. Prof., 1954–60; Prof., 1960–78); Visiting Prof., Univ. of Wisconsin since 1979. Series Ed. since 1960, and Consulting Ed. since 1965, Holt, Rinehart, and Winston, NYC. Ed., American Anthropologist, 1962–67; Pres., Council for Anthropology and Education, 1982. *Publs:* Menomini Acculturation, 1955; (ed.) Education and Anthropology, 1955; Transmission of American Culture, 1959; (ed. and contrib.) Education and Culture, 1963; (with A. Beals and L. Spindler) Culture in Process, 1967, rev. ed. 1973; (ed. and contrib.) Being an Anthropologist, 1970; (with L. Spindler) Dreamers Without Power: The Menomini Indians, 1971; Burgbach: Urbanization and Identity in a German Village, 1973; (ed. and contrib.) Education and Cultural Process: Toward an Anthropology of Education, 1974; The Making of Psychological Anthropology, 1978; Doing the Ethnography of Schooling, 1982; Interpretive Ethnography at Home and Abroad, 1987; Education and Cultural Process: Anthropological Approaches, 1987; The American Cultural Dialogue, 1989. Add: Ethnographics, P.O. Box 38, Calistoga, Calif. 94515, U.S.A.

SPINGARN, Lawrence (Perreira). American, b. 1917. Novels/Short stories, Poetry. Dir., Perivale Press, Van Nuys, Calif., since 1968. Special Asst., Hispanic Desk, Library of Congress, Washington, D.C., 1941–43; Instr. in English, Pomona Coll., 1948–49. *Publs:* Rococo Summer and Other Poems, 1947; The Lost River, 1951; Letters from Exile, 1961; Madame Bidet and Other Fixtures, 1968; Freeway Problems—and Others, 1970; (ed.) Poets West, 1975; The Blue Door, 1977; The Dark Playground: Poems, 1979; The Belvedere: A Tale, 1982; Moral Tales, 1983; Going Like Seventy: Poems, 1988. Add: c/o Perivale Press, 13830 Erwin St., Van Nuys, Calif. 91401, U.S.A.

SPINK, Ian. British, b. 1932. Music. Prof. of Music, Royal Holloway and Bedford New Coll., Univ. of London, since 1974 (Sr. Lectr., 1969–71; Reader, 1971–74). Sr. Lectr., Music Dept., Univ. of Sydney, Australia, 1962–68. *Publs:* (ed.) Ayres, Songs and Dialogues, by Robert Johnson, 1961; (ed.) Songs (1604) and Ayres (1618)), by Greaves, Mason, Earsden, 1962; (ed.) Manuscript Songs, by Alfonso Ferrabosco II, 1966; An Historical Approach to Musical Form, 1967; (ed.) English Songs 1625-1660, 1971; English Song: Dowland to Purcell, 1974; (ed.) The Judgment of Paris, by T.A. Arne, 1978. Add: Royal Holloway and Bedford New Coll., Egham, Surrey, England.

SPINK, Reginald. British, b. 1905. Area studies, History, Mythology/Folklore, Translations. Member, Exec. Cttee., Translators Assn., 1965–68, 1972–75. *Publs:* (with J.O. Krag) England bygger op, 1947; (trans.) My Childhood, by Carl Nielsen, 1953; (trans.) Living Music, by Carl Nielsen, 1953; (trans.) The Roman, by Palle Lauring, 1956; (trans.) The Galathea Deep Sea Expedition, 1956; The Land and People of Denmark, 1956; (adapter) Three Comedies, by Ludvig Holberg, 1957; (trans.) The Land of the Tollund Man, by Palle Lauring, 1957; (trans.) Hans Andersen's Fairy Tales, 1958; (trans.) The Buzzard, by Frank Wenzel, 1959; (trans.) Terry in the South Seas, by Bengt Danielsson, 1959; (trans. and ed.) Fairy Tales and Stories, by Hans Christian Andersen, 1960; (trans.) Daughters of Allah, by Henny Harald Hansen, 1960; (trans.) Chavante, by Rolf Blomberg, 1960; Fairy Tales of Denmark, 1961; (trans.) Ulu: The World's End, by Jorgen Bisch, 1961; The Young Hans Andersen, 1962; (trans.) Behind the Veil of Arabia, by Jorgen Bisch, 1962; (trans.) And It Was Morning, by Poul Borchsenius, 1962; (trans.) Gauguin in the South Seas, by Bengt Danielsson, 1962; (trans.) Mongolia: Unknown Land, by Jorgen Bisch, 1963; (trans.) Vasari's Life and Lives, by Einar Rud, 1963; (trans.) A Christmas Greeting to My English Friends, by Hans Christian Andersen, 1965; Hans Christian Andersen and His World, 1972; Hans Christian Andersen: The Man and His Work, 1972; (trans.) New Tales, by Hans Christian Andersen, 1973; (trans.) Denmark: An Official Handbook, 14th ed. 1974; (trans.) Danish Akvavit, by Henning Kirkeby, 1975; (trans.) Hans Christian Andersen as an Artist, 1977; DBC: The Story of the Danish Bacon Company 1902-1977, 1977; (trans.) Symbols Around Us, by Sven Tito Achen, 1978; (trans.) Copenhagen University: 500 Years of Science and Scholarship, by Svend E. Stybe, 1979; (trans.) On the Threshold of a Golden Age, by Leif L. Ludvigsen, 1979; (trans.) The Danish Foreign Service, 1980; (trans.) Denmark, by Bent Rying, 2 vols., 1981, 1988; (trans.) Hans Christian Andersen, by Erling Nielsen, 1983; (trans.) Soren Kierkegaard, by P.P. Rohde, 1983; (trans.) N.F.S. Grundtvig, by Poul Dam, 1983; 40 År efter (memoirs), 1983. Add: 6 Deane Way, Eastcote, Ruislip, Middx. HA4 8SU, England.

SPINRAD, Norman. American, b. 1940. Novels/Short stories, Science fiction/Fantasy, Writing. *Publs:* The Solarians, 1966; Agent of Chaos, 1967; The Men in the Jungle, 1967; Bug Jack Barron, 1969; Fragments of America, 1970; The Last Hurrah of the Golden Horde, 1970; (ed.) The New Tomorrows, 1971; The Iron Dream, 1972; (ed.) Modern Science Fiction, 1974; Passing Through the Flame, 1975; No Direction Home, 1975; A World Between, 1979; Songs from the Stars, 1980; The Mind Game, 1980; The Void Captain's Tale, 1983; Staying Alive: A Writer's Guide, 1983; Child of Fortune, 1985; Little Heroes, 1987; Agent of Chaos, 1988; Other Americas (novellas), 1988. Add: c/o Jane Rotrosen, 318 E. 51st St., New York, N.Y. 10022, U.S.A.

SPIRO, Herbert (John). American, b. 1924. Politics/Government. Prof. of Political Science, Free Univ., Berlin, since 1980; Visiting Scholar, Univ.of Texas, since 1984. Teaching Fellow in Govt., 1950–53, Instr. in Govt., 1954–57, and Asst. Prof. of Govt., 1957–61, Harvard Univ., Cambridge, Mass.; Assoc. Prof. of Political Science, Amherst Coll., Massachusetts, 1961–65; Chmn., Asian and African Studies Prog., Univ. of Massachusetts, Amherst Coll., Mount Holyoke Coll., and Smith Coll., 1964–65; Prof. of Political Science, Univ. of Pennsylvania, Philadelphia, 1965–70; with the U.S. Dept. of State: Member, Policy Planning Staff, 1970–75; Ambassador to Equatorial Guinea, 1975–76; Ambassador to the United Republic of Cameroon, 1975–77; Fellow, Woodrow Wilson Intnl. Center for Scholars, Smithsonian Instn., 1977–79; Visiting Prof., Defense

Intelligence Sch., 1979–80. Member, Editorial Bd., Journal of Politics, 1967–71; Council Member, American Political Science Assn., 1968–70. *Publs:* (co-author) Governing Post-War Germany, 1953; The Politics of German Codetermination, 1958; (co-author) Patterns of Government: The Political Systems of Europe, 1958, 1962; Government by Constitution: The Political Systems of Democracy, 1959; Politics in Africa: Prospects South of the Sahara, 1961; (co-author) Five African States 1963; World Politics: The Global System, 1966; Africa: The Primacy of Politics, 1967; (ed.) Patterns of African Development, 1968; (co-author) Why Federations Fail, 1968; The Dialectic of Representation 1619-1969, 1969; Responsibility in Government: Theory and Practice, 1969; Politics as the Master Science: From Plato to Mao, 1970; A New Foreign Policy Consensus?, 1979; (co-author) The Legacy of the Constitution, 1987. Add: Towers of Town Lake, 401 H-35 North, Ste. 4B3, Austin, Tex. 78701, U.S.A.

SPITZ, Lewis William. American, b. 1922. History, Biography. Prof. of History, Stanford Univ., Calif., since 1960. Instr. to Assoc. Prof., Univ. of Missouri, Columbia, 1953–60. *Publs:* Conrad Celtis: The German Arch-Humanist, 1957; (ed.) Career of the Reformer IV: Luther's Works XXXIV, 1960; (ed.) The Reformation: Material or Spiritual?, 1962, as The Reformation: Basic Interpretations, 1972; The Religious Renaissance of the German Humanists, 1963; (ed. with Richard W. Lyman) Major Crises in Western Civilization, 1965; (ed.) The Protestant Reformation, 1966; Life in Two Worlds: A Biography of William Sihler, 1967; The Renaissance and Reformation Movements, 1971, 1987; (ed.) The Northern Renaissance, 1972; (ed. with Wenzel Lohff) Discord, Dialogue, and Concord: The Lutheran Reformation's Formula of Concord, 1977; (ed.) Humanismus und Reformation in der deutschen Geschichte, 1981; The Protestant Reformation 1517-1559, 1985. Add: 827 Lathrop Dr., Stanford, Calif. 94305, U.S.A.

SPITZER, Lyman (Jr.). American, b. 1914. Astronomy, Physics. Charles A. Young Prof. Emeritus of Astronomy, Princeton Univ., N.J., since 1982 (Prof. of Astronomy, 1947–52; Chmn., Dept. of Astrophysical Sciences, and Dir. of the Univ. Observatory, 1947–79; Charles A. Young Prof., 1952–82; Dir., Project Matterhorn, 1953–61; Chmn., Exec. Cttee., Princeton Plasma Physics Lab., 1961–66; Chmn., Univ. Research Bd., 1967–72). Instr. in Physics and Astronomy, 1939–42, and Assoc. Prof. of Astrophysics, 1946–47, Yale Univ., New Haven, Conn.; Scientist, Special Studies Group, Columbia Univ. Div. of War Research, N.Y., 1942–44; Dir., Sonar Analysis Group, 1944–46. *Publs:* (ed.) Physics of Sound in the Sea, 1946; Physics of Fully Ionized Gases, 1956, 1962; Diffuse Matter in Space, 1968; Physical Processes in the Interstellar Medium, 1978; Searching Between the Stars, 1982; Dynamical Evolution of Globular Clusters, 1987. Add: Princeton Univ. Observatory, Peyton Hall, Princeton, N.J. 08544, U.S.A.

SPIVACK, Charlotte. American, b. 1926. Literature, Biography. Prof. of English, Univ. of Massachusetts, Amherst, since 1971 (Visiting Lectr., 1964–66; Assoc. Prof., 1967–70). Asst. Prof., 1958–60, and Assoc. Prof., 1961–64, Fisk Univ., Nashville, Tenn. *Publs:* (with W. Bracy) Early English Drama, 1966; George Chapman, 1967; The Comedy of Evil on Shakespeare's Stage, 1978; Ursula K. Le Guin, 1984; Merlin's Daughters: Contemporary Women Writers of Fantasy, 1987. Add: English Dept., Univ. of Massachusetts, Amherst, Mass. 01003, U.S.A.

SPIVACK, Kathleen (Romola Drucker). American, b. 1938. Poetry. Fellow, Radcliffe Inst. for Independent Study, 1969–72. *Publs:* Flying Inland, 1973; The Jane Poems, 1974; Swimmer in the Spreading Dawn, 1981; The Breakup Variations, 1984; The Beds We Lie In: Selected and New Poems, 1986. Add: 53 Spruce St., Watertown, Mass. 02172, U.S.A.

SPOCK, Benjamin (McLane). American, b. 1903. Child development, Human relations, Medicine/Health, Disarmament. Instr. in Pediatrics, Cornell Medical Coll., NYC, 1933–47; Consultant in Psychiatry, Mayo Clinic, Rochester, Minn., and Assoc. Prof. of Psychiatry, Mayo Found., Univ. of Minnesota, Rochester, 1947–51; Prof. of Child Development, Univ. of Pittsburgh, 1951–55, and Western Reserve Univ., Cleveland, 1955–67. *Publs:* Baby and Child Care, 1946, rev. ed. 1976; (with J. Reinhart and W. Miller) A Baby's First Year, 1955; (with M.E. Lowenberg) Feeding Your Baby and Child, 1955; Dr. Spock Talks with Mothers, 1961; Problems of Parents, 1962; (with M. Lerrigo) Caring for Your Disabled Child, 1964; (with M. Zimmermann) Dr. Spock on Vietnam, 1968; Decent and Indecent, 1970; A Young Person's Guide to Life and Love, 1971; Raising Children in a Difficult Time, 1974. Add: P.O. Box 1890, St. Thomas, Virgin Islands 00803, U.S.A.

SPRACKLING, Michael Thomas. British, b. 1934. Physics. Sr.

Lectr. in Physics, King's Coll., London, since 1985. Asst. Master, King Edward VI Sch., Stourbridge, 1958–60; Asst. Lectr., 1960–62, Lectr., 1962–83, and Sr. Lectr. in Physics, 1983–85, Queen Elizabeth Coll., London. *Publs:* The Mechanical Properties of Matter, 1970; Plastic Deformation of Simple Ionic Crystals, 1977; Liquids and Solids, 1985. Add: 35 Princes Gardens, London W3 0LX, England.

SPREIREGEN, Paul (David). American, b. 1931. Architecture, Urban studies. Architect and planner in private practice, Washington, D.C., since 1970. Urban designer, Adams Howard & Greeley, Boston Govt. Center, 1958–59, and "Downtown Progress", Washington, D.C., 1960–62; Dir. of Urban Design Progs., American Inst. of Architects, 1962–66; Dir. for Architecture and Design, National Endowment for the Arts, 1966–70; Emons Distinguished Prof. of Architecture, Ball State Univ., Muncie, Ind., 1973–74. *Publs:* Urban Design: The Architecture of Towns and Cities, 1965; The Modern Metropolis: Its Origins, Form, Characteristics, and Planning: Selected Essays of Hans Blumenfeld, 1967; (ed.) On the Art of Designing Cities: Selected Essays of Elbert Peets, 1968; (with H. Von Hertzen) Building a New Town: The Story of Finland's New Garden City, Tapiola, 1971, 1973; (ed.) Metropolis and Beyond: Selected Essays of Hans Blumenfeld, 1978; Design Competitions, 1979; The Architecture of William Morgan, 1987. Add: 2215 Observatory Pl. N.W., Washington, D.C. 20007, U.S.A.

SPRIGGE, Timothy (Lauro Squire). British, b. 1932. Intellectual history, Philosophy. Prof. of Logic and Metaphysics, Univ. of Edinburgh, since 1979. Lectr. in Philosophy, Univ. Coll., London, 1961–63; Lectr., 1963–70, and Reader in Philosophy, 1970–79, Univ. of Sussex, Brighton. *Publs:* (ed.) The Correspondence of Jeremy Bentham, vols. 1 and 2, 1968; Facts, Words, and Beliefs, 1970; Santayana: An Examination of His Philosophy, 1974; The Vindication of Absolute Idealism, 1983; Theories of Existence, 1984; The Rational Foundations of Ethics, 1988. Add: David Hume Tower, George Sq., Edinburgh, Scotland.

SPRINKEL, Beryl (Wayne). American, b. 1923. Economics, Money/Finance. Chmn., Council of Economic Advisers, The White House, Washington, D.C., 1985–89 (Under-Secty. for Monetary Affairs, U.S. Treasury, 1981–85). Member, Bd. of Economists, Time Mag., NYC, since 1969. With Harris Trust and Savings Bank, Chicago, 1952–81: Exec. Vice-Pres., 1974–81. Dir., U.S. Chamber of Commerce, 1969–75, and Intnl. Monetary Market of Chicago Mercantile Exchange, 1972–75. *Publs:* Money and Stock Prices, 1964; Money and Markets: A Monetarist View, 1971; (with Robert Genetski) Winning with Money, 1977. Add: c/o Council of Economic Advisers, The White House, Washington, D.C. 20500, U.S.A.

SPRUILL, Steven. American, b. 1946. Science fiction. Full-time writer since 1981. Biological technician, Hazleton Labs., Falls Church, Va., 1969–73; psychology intern, Veterans Admin. Hosp., Washington, D.C., 1978–79, and Mt. Vernon Community Health Center, Alexandria, Va., 1979–80. *Publs:* Keepers of the Gate, 1977; The Psychopath Plague, 1978; Hellstone, 1980; The Imperator Plot, 1983; The Genesis Shield, 1985; Paradox Planet, 1988. Add: 123 N. Park Dr., Arlington, Va. 22203, U.S.A.

SPURLING, Hilary. British, b. 1940. Literature, Biography. Reviewer, The Daily Telegraph, London. Theatre Critic, 1964–70, and Literary Ed., 1967–70, Spectator mag., London. *Publs:* Ivy when Young: The Early Life of Ivy Compton Burnett, 1974; (ed.) Mervyn Peake: Drawings, 1974; Handbook to Anthony Powell's Music of Time, 1977; Secrets of a Woman's Heart: The Later Life of Ivy Compton Burnett, 1984; Elinor Fettiplace's Receipt Book, 1986. Add: c/o David Higham Assocs., 5-8 Lower John St., London W1R 4HA, England.

SPURLING, John. British, b. 1936. Novels, Plays/Screenplays, Literature. Announcer, BBC Radio, London, 1963–66; Henfield Writing Fellow, Univ. of East Anglia, 1973; Art Critic, New Statesman, London, 1976–88. *Publs:* MacRune's Guevara, 1969; In the Heart of the British Museum, 1972; Samuel Beckett: A Study of His Plays, 1972; Shades of Heathcliff, and Death of Captain Doughty, 1975; The British Empire, part I, 1982; Graham Greene, 1983, The Ragged End (novel), 1989. Add: c/o MLR Ltd., 200 Fulham Rd., London SW10, England.

SQUIRES, (James) Radcliffe. American, b. 1917. Poetry, Literature, Biography. Ed., Chicago Review, 1945–46; Instr., Dartmouth Coll., Hanover, N.H., 1946–48; Fulbright Prof. of American Culture, Salonika, Greece, 1959–60; Prof. of English, Univ. of Michigan, Ann Arbor, 1963–81. *Publs:* Cornar, 1940; Where the Compass Spins, 1951; The Loyalties of Robinson Jeffers, 1956; The Major Themes of Robert Frost, 1963;

Frederic Prokosch, 1964; Fingers of Hermes: Poems, 1965; The Light under Islands: Poems, 1967; Daedalus, 1968; Allen Tate: A Literary Biography, 1971; (ed.) Allen Tate and His Work: Critical Evaluations, 1972; Waiting in the Bone, 1973; Gardens of the World, 1980; Journeys, 1981; The Envoy (broadside), 1983; The Garden of Prometheus (broadside), 1985. Add: Dept. of English, Univ. of Michigan, Ann Arbor, Mich. 48109, U.S.A.

STAAR, Richard F. American, b. 1923. Politics/Government. Coordinator, Intnl. Studies Program, formerly Sr. Fellow, Hoover Inst. on War, Revolution, and Peace, Stanford Univ., Calif., since 1969; Ed., Yearbook on Intnl. Communist Affairs, since 1969. Prof. of Political Science, Emory Univ., Atlanta, 1959–69; U.S. Ambassador to MBFR, Vienna, 1981–83. *Publs:* Poland 1944-1962, 1962; Aspects of Modern Communism, 1968; Communist Regimes in Eastern Europe, 1971, 5th ed., 1988; (ed.) Arms Control: Myth Versus Reality, 1984; USSR Foreign Policies after Detente, 1985, 3rd ed. 1989; (co-author) Soviet Military Policies Since World War II, 1986; (ed.) Public Diplomacy: USA Versus USSR, 1986; (ed.) The U.S. and Eastern Europe in the 1990's, 1989; (ed.) The USSR in the 1990's, 1990. Add: 36 Peter Coutts Circle, Stanford, Calif. 94305, U.S.A.

STABLEFORD, Brian M(ichael). British, b. 1948. Science fiction/Fantasy. Lectr. in Sociology, Univ. of Reading, 1977–88. *Publs:* Cradle of the Sun, 1969; The Blind Worm, 1969; The Days of Glory, 1970; In the Kingdom of the Beasts, 1970; Day of Wrath, 1970; To Challenge Chaos, 1971; The Halcyon Drift, 1972; Rhapsody in Black, 1973, 1975; Promised Land, 1974; The Paradise Game, 1974; The Fenris Device, 1974; The Face of Heaven, 1974; Mind Riders, 1975; Mysteries of Modern Science, 1977; Critical Threshold, 1977; The Realms of Tartarus, 1977; Wildeblood's Empire, 1977; The City of the Sun, 1978; The Last Days of the Edge of the World (juvenile), 1978; Balance of Power, 1979; The Walking Shadow, 1979; The Paradox of the Sets, 1979; A Clash of Symbols: The Triumph of James Blish, 1979; Optiman, 1980, in U.K. as War Games, 1981; The Castaways of Tanagar, 1981; Journey to the Center, 1982; The Gates of Eden, 1983; Future Man, 1984; (with David Langford) The Third Millennium, 1985; Scientific Romance in Britain, 1985; The Sociology of Science Fiction, 1987; The Empire of Fear, 1989; The Way to Write Science Fiction, 1989. Add: 113 St. Peter's Rd., Reading, Berks. RG6 1PG, England.

STACEY, Margaret. British, b. 1922. Sociology. Prof. of Sociology, Univ. of Warwick, since 1974. Lectr., 1963–70, and Sr. Lectr., 1970–74, Univ. Coll. of Swansea, Wales. Pres., British Sociological Assn., 1981–83. *Publs:* Tradition and Change: A Study of Banbury, 1960; Methods of Social Research, 1969; (ed.) Comparability in Social Research, 1969; (ed.) Hospitals, Children and Their Families, 1970; (ed.) Power, Persistence, and Change: A Second Study of Banbury, 1974; (ed.) Sociology of the National Health Service, 1976; (co-ed.) Health and the Division of Labour, 1977; (co-ed.) Health Care and Health Knowledge, 1977; (co-ed.) Beyond Separation: Further Studies of Children in Hospital, 1979; (with Marion Price) Women Power and Politics, 1981; (co-ed.) Concepts of Health, Illness, and Healing, 1986; The Sociology of Health and Healing: A Text Book, 1988. Add: Dept. of Sociology, Univ. of Warwick, Coventry CV4 7AL, England.

STACEY, Nicholas (Anthony Howard). British. Business/Trade/Industry, History, Intellectual history. Chmn., Nicholas Stacey Assocs., since 1962. Member of Editorial Staff, Financial Times, London, 1944–46; Asst. Secty., Assn. of Certified and Corporate Accountants, 1946–51; Visiting Scholar, Grad. Sch. of Business, Columbia Univ., NYC, 1951–53; Economic and Marketing Advisor, General Electric Co. Ltd., 1954–62; Chmn., Chesham Amalgamations and Investments Ltd., 1962–83. *Publs:* English Accountancy, 1800-1954, A Study in Social and Economic History, 1954; (with A. Wilson) The Changing Pattern of Distribution, 1958, 1965; Problems of Export Marketing, 1962; (with A. Wilson) Industrial Marketing Research: Management and Technique, 1962; Mergers in Modern Business, 1966, 1970; Psychological Attributes of Mergers, 1980; Living in an Alibi Society, 1988. Add: c/o Scottish Academic Press, 33 Montgomery St., Edinburgh EH7 5JX, Scotland.

STACEY, Tom. British, b. 1930. Novels, Short stories, Travel/Exploration. Chmn., Stacey Intnl., since 1974 (Tom Stacey Ltd. until 1974). Staff Writer, Picture Post, London and the Far East, 1952–54; African Corresp., Daily Express, London, 1954–55; Canada and Latin America Reporter, Montreal Star, 1955–56; Foreign Corresp., in the Middle East, 1956–57; American Columnist, 1957, and Diplomatic and Roving Corresp., 1957–60, Daily Express; Chief Roving Corresp., Sunday Times, London, 1960–65; Columnist, Evening Standard, London, 1965–

67; Ed.-in-Chief, Correspondents World Wide, 1967–73, and Chambers' Encyclopaedia Yearbook, 1969–72. *Publs:* The Hostile Sun: A Malayan Journey, 1953; The Brothers M (novel), 1960; Summons to Ruwenzori, 1963; (ed.) Today's World, 1969; (ed.) Here Come the Tories, 1970; Immigration and Enoch Powell, 1970; The Living and the Dying (novel), 1975; The Pandemonium (novel), 1980; The Worm in the Rose (novel), 1985; Deadline (screenplay and novel), 1988; Bodies and Souls (short stories), 1989. Add: 128 Kensington Church St., London W8, England.

STACK, Edward MacGregor. American, b. 1919. Language/Linguistics. Prof. of Foreign Languages and Literatures, North Carolina State Univ., Raleigh, since 1963. Visiting Asst. Prof. of Romance Languages, Louisiana State Univ., Baton Rouge, 1950–51; Instr. in Romance Languages, Univ. of Virginia, Charlottesville, 1951–52; Asst. Prof. of Romance Languages, Univ. of Texas, Austin, 1952–58; Prof. and Chmn., Whittier Coll., Calif., 1958–60; Prof., Villanova Univ., Pa., 1960–61; Dir., Consultant and Lectr., Electronic Teaching Labs., Professorial Lectr., George Washington Univ., and American Univ., and U.S. Specialist Lectr. in Krakow and Warsaw, Poland, Vienna, and Stockholm, all 1963. *Publs:* Reading Scientific French, 1954, 3rd ed. 1979; (trans.) Selected Maxims of La Rochefoucauld, 1956; Reading French in the Arts and Sciences, 1957, 4th ed. 1987; (with E. Haden and E.T. Book) Oral French, 1957; Elementary Oral and Written French, 1959; French Handbook and Guide, 1960; The Language Laboratory and Modern Language Teaching, 1960, 3rd ed. 1978; Le Pont Neuf: A Structural Review Grammar, 1966, 3rd ed. 1978. Add: 3925 Arrow Dr., Raleigh, N.C. 27612, U.S.A.

STACK, George. American, b. 1932. Philosophy. Prof. of Philosophy, State Univ. of New York at Brockport, since 1970 (Asst. Prof., 1967–68; Assoc. Prof., 1968–70). Instr., 1963–64, and Asst. Prof., 1964–67, Post Coll., Long Island Univ., N.Y. *Publs:* Berkeley's Analysis of Perception, 1970; On Kierkegaard, 1976; Kierkegaard's Existential Ethics, 1977; Sartre's Philosophy of Social Existence, 1977; Lange and Nietzsche, 1983. Add: Dept. of Philosophy, State Univ. of New York at Brockport, Brockport, N.Y. 14420, U.S.A.

STADE, George. American, b. 1933. Literature. Prof. of English and Comparative Literature, Columbia Univ., NYC, since 1971 (Asst. Prof., 1965–68; Assoc. Prof., 1968–71). Ed.-in-Chief, European Writers, Scribners, since 1979. Instr., Rutgers Univ., Newark, N.J., 1961–65. *Publs:* Robert Graves, 1969; (ed. with F.W. Dupee) Selected Letters of E.E. Cummings, 1968; (ed.) Six Modern British Novelists, 1974; (ed.) Six Contemporary British Novelists, 1976; (ed.) Columbia Essays on Modern Writers, 1976; Confessions of a Lady-Killer, 1979. Add: Dept. of English, Columbia Univ., New York, N.Y. 10027, U.S.A.

STADTMAN, Verne August. American, b. 1926. Education, History. Vice-Pres., The Carnegie Foundn. for the Advancement of Teaching, since 1980. Managing Ed., California Monthly, California Alumni Assn., Berkeley, 1950–64; Centennial Ed., Univ. of California, Berkeley, 1964–69; Ed., 1969–73, Staff Assoc., 1972, Asst. Dir., 1973–73, and Assoc. Dir., 1973, Carnegia Commn. on Higher Education, Berkeley; Assoc. Dir. and Ed., Carnegie Council on Policy Studies in Higher Education, Berkeley, 1974–80. *Publs:* California Campus, 1960; (compiler and ed.) Centennial Record of the University of California, 1967; University of California 1868-1968, 1970; (ed. with David Riesman) Academic Transformation—Seventeen Institutions Under Pressure, 1973; Academic Adaptations: Higher Education Prepares for the 1980's and 1990's, 1980. Add: 66 Shady Brook Lane, Princeton, N.J. 08540, U.S.A.

STAFF, Frank William. British, b. 1908. History, Recreation/Leisure/ Hobbies. Tour Mgr., Thomas Cook & Son Ltd., London, 1936–72. *Publs:* The Transatlantic Mail, 1956; The Penny Post: 1680–1918, 1964; The Picture Postcard and Its Origins, 1966, 1979; The Valentine and Its Origins, 1969; Picture Postcards and Travel, 1979. Add: Stonehaven, West Bay, Bridport, Dorset, Stonehaven, DT6 4HR England.

STAFFORD, David (Christopher). British, b. 1943. Economics, Money/ Finance. Head of the Dept. of Economics, Univ. of Exeter, since 1987 (Tutor, 1971–72; Lectr., 1972–79; Sr. Lectr., 1979–87). With Swiss Bank Corp., London and Switzerland, 1962–68. *Publs:* China Clay Sand: Liability or Asset?, 1972; Open-ended Funds: Bank Experience in France and Britain, 1975; Mutual Funds in the European Economic Community and Switzerland, 1976; Economics of Housing Policy, 1977; Bank Competition and Advertising, 1982; Key Developments in Personal Finance, 1985; Directory of Unit Trust Management, 1987, 1988; Risk Ratio, 1987; Rent Control, 1987; Housing Policy and Finance, 1988. Add: The Old Vicarage, Holman Way, Topsham, Exeter, Devon, England.

STAFFORD, William (Edgar). American, b. 1914. Poetry, Literature, Autobiography/Memoirs/Personal. Member, Oregon Bd., Fellowship of Reconciliation, since 1959. Prof. of English, Lewis and Clark Coll., Portland, Ore., 1960–80, now retired (member of the English Dept., 1948–54, 1957–60). Asst. Prof. of English, Manchester Coll., Ind., 1955–56; Prof. of English, San Jose State Coll., Calif., 1956–57; Consultant in Poetry, Library of Congress, Washington, D.C., 1970–71. *Publs:* Down in My Heart (experience as a conscientious objector during World War II), 1947; West of Your City: Poems, 1960; Traveling Through the Dark, 1962; The Rescued Year, 1966; (ed. with F. Candelaria) The Voices of Prose, 1966; Friends to This Ground: A Statement for Readers, Teachers, and Writers of Literature, 1967; (ed.) The Achievement of Brother Antoninus: A Comprehensive Selection of His Poems with a Critical Introduction, 1967; Eleven Untitled Poems, 1968; Weather: Poems, 1969; Allegiances, 1970; Temporary Facts, 1970; (with R. Bly and W. Matthews) Poems for Tennessee, 1971; (ed. with R. Ross) Poems and Perspectives, 1971; Someday, Maybe, 1973; That Other Alone: Poems, 1973; Leftovers, A Care Package: Two Lectures, 1973; Stories That Could Be True (poetry), 1977; The Design in the Oriole, 1977; Two about Music, 1978; Writing the Australian Crawl: Views on the Writer's Vocation, 1978; Things That Happen Where There Aren't Any People, 1980; Sometimes Like a Legend, 1981; A Glass Face in the Rain: New Poems, 1982; Roving Across Fields, 1983; (with Marvin Bell) Segues: A Correspondence in Poetry, 1983; Smoke's Way: Poems from Limited Editions 1968-1981, 1983; A Glass Face in the Rain (poetry), 1983; Listening Deep, 1984; Stories, Storms and Strangers, 1984; You Must Revise Your Life, 1987; An Oregon Message (poetry), 1987. Add: 1050 Sunningdale, Lake Oswego, Ore. 97034, U.S.A.

STAGG, Frank. American, b. 1911. Theology/Religion. Emeritus Prof. of New Testament Interpretation, Southern Baptist Theological Seminary, since 1982 (James Buchanan Harrison Prof., 1964–77; Sr. Prof., 1977–82). Pastor, First Baptist Church, DeRidder, La., 1941–44; Prof. of New Testament and Greek, New Orleans Baptist Seminary, La., 1945–64. *Publs:* The Book of Acts: The Early Struggle for an Unhindered Gospel, 1955; Exploring the New Testament, 1961; New Testament Theology, 1962; Studies in Luke's Gospel, 1967; (co-author) Glossolalia: Tongue Speaking in Biblical, Historical and Psychological Perspective, 1967; Polarities of Man's Existence in Biblical Perspective, 1973; The Holy Spirit Today, 1973; (with Evelyn Stagg) Woman in the World of Jesus, 1978; Knox Preaching Guides: Galations/Romans, 1980; The Bible Speaks on Aging, 1981; The Doctrine of Christ, 1985. Add: 5610 Ahuawa Pl., Bay St. Louis, Miss. 39520, U.S.A.

STALLWORTHY, (Sir) John. New Zealander, b. 1906. Medicine/ Health. Emeritus Nuffield Prof. of Obstetrics and Gynaecology, Oxford Univ., since 1973 (Nuffield Prof., 1967–73). Dir., Area Dept. of Obstetrics and Gynaecology, United Oxford Hosps., 1939–67. Pres., Royal Soc. of Medicine, 1974–75. *Publs:* (with others) Problems of Fertility in General Practice, 1948; (with Gordon Bourne) Recent Advances in Obstetrics and Gynaecology, 1966, 12th ed., 1977; (with John Howkins) Bonney's Gynaecological Surgery, 1974; (co-ed.) The Medical Effects of Nuclear War, 1983; (with others) Cancer of the Uterine Cervix, 1984. Add: 8A College Green, Gloucester GL1 2LX, England.

STALLWORTHY, Jon (Howie). British, b. 1935. Poetry, Literature, Biography, Translations. Fellow of Wolfson Coll., Oxford, and Reader in English Literature, Oxford Univ., since 1986. Ed., Oxford Univ. Press, London, 1959–71; and Clarendon Press, Oxford, 1972–77; Visiting Fellow, All Souls Coll., Oxford, 1971–72; John Wendell Anderson Prof. of English Literature, Cornell Univ., Ithaca, N.Y., 1977–86. *Publs:* The Earthly Paradise, 1958; The Astronomy of Love, 1961; Out of Bounds, 1963; Between the Lines: Yeats's Poetry in the Making, 1963; The Almond Tree, 1967; A Day in the City, 1967; (ed.) Yeats: Last Poems: A Casebook, 1968; Root and Branch, 1969; Positives, 1969; Vision and Revision in Yeats's "Last Poems", 1969; (trans. with J. Peterkiewicz) Five Centuries of Polish Poetry, rev. ed. 1970; (trans. with P. France) The Twelve and Other Poems, by Alexander Blok, 1970, in paperback as Alexander Blok, 1974; A Dinner of Herbs, 1970; (ed. with Seamus Heaney and Alan Brownjohn) New Poems 1970–1971; (ed.) The Penguin Book of Love Poetry (in U.S. as A Book of Love Poetry), 1973; Hand in Hand, 1974; The Apple Barrel: Selected Poems 1956-1963, 1974; Wilfred Owen, 1974; A Familiar Tree, 1978; (trans. with P. France) Selected Poems, by Boris Pasternak, 1982; (ed.) The Complete Poems and Fragments, by Wilfred Owen, 2 vols., 1983; (ed.) The Oxford Book of War Poetry, 1984; (ed.) The Poems of Willfred Owen, 1985; The Anzac Sonata: New and Selected Poems, 1986. Add: Long Farm, Elsfield Rd., Old Marston, Oxford, England.

STAMBLER, Irwin. American, b. 1924. Air/Space topics, Children's non-fiction, History, Music, Recreation/Leisure/Hobbies, Sports/Physical education/Keeping fit, Travel/Exploration/Adventure. Co-Publr. and Editorial Dir., Technology Forecasts and Technology Surveys newsletter, since 1969; syndicated newspaper columnist ("Pop, Rock and Soul"), since 1977; Publr. and Ed., Alternative Energy newsletter, since 1980. Western Ed., Research and Development mag., since 1966; Ed., Tape Cartridge/ Cassette Industry, since 1970. Sr. Engineer, Chase Aircraft, NYC, 1950–53; Structure Engineer, Republic Aviation, Farmingdale, N.Y., 1953–54; Engineering Ed., Space Aeronautics mag., 1954–66; Corresp., Airline Mgmt. and Marketing mag., 1967–69. *Publs:* Space Ship: Story of the X-15, 1961; The Battle for Inner Space: Undersea Warfare and Weapons, 1962; Wonders of Underwater Exploration, 1962; Breath of Life: Story of Our Atmosphere, 1963; Build the Unknown, 1963; Project Gemini, 1964; Encyclopedia of Popular Music, 1965; Supersonic Transport, 1965; Orbiting Space Stations, 1965; Automobiles of the Future, 1966; Great Moments in Auto Racing, 1967; Guide to Model Car Racing, 1967; Weather Instruments, 1968; Worlds of Sound, 1968; Ocean Liners of the Air, 1969; (with G. Landon) Encyclopedia of Folk, Country and Western Music, 1969, 1981; World of Microelectronics, 1969; Project Viking, 1970; Guitar Years: Popular Music from Country and Western to Hard Rock, 1970; (with G. Landon) Golden Guitars: The Story of Country Music, 1971; Great Moments in Stock Car Racing, 1971; Unusual Automobiles of Today and Tomorrow, 1972; Shorelines of America, 1972; Automobile Engines of Today and Tomorrow, 1973; Revolution in Light, 1973; The Supercars and the Men Who Drive Them, 1974; Speed Kings: The World's Fastest Humans, 1974; Women in Sports, 1975; Encyclopedia of Pop, Rock and Soul, 1975, 1989; The Supercars and the Men Who Race Them, 1975; Bill Walton, Super Center, 1976; Catfish Hunter, 1976; Here Come the Funny Cars, 1976; Minibikes and Small Cycles, 1977; New Automobiles of the Future, 1978; Top Fuelers, 1978; Racing the Sprint Cars, 1979; Dream Machines: Vans and Pickups, 1980; (with G. Landon) New Encyclopedia of Folk, Country and Western Music, 1983; Off-Roading, 1984. Add: Suite 208, 205 S. Beverly Dr., Beverly Hills, Calif. 90212, U.S.A.

STAMM, Martin L. American, b. 1917. Education, Human relations. Prof. of Education and Chmn. and Supvr., Div. of Student Personnel Services, Trenton State Coll., N.J., since 1966. Administrative Asst. to Supt. of Curriculum, 1956–57 and Dir., 1957–62, Guidance and Pupil Personnel Services, South Bend, Ind.; District Dir. of Guidance, Scotch Plains, N.J., 1964–66; Member of Editorial Staff, ASCA Yearbook, American Sch. Counselors Assn. Publs., 1967. *Publs:* all with Blossom Nissman—Alphabet Land, 1970; Ask Counselor, 1970; New Dimensions in Elementary Guidance, 1971; Your Child and Drugs: A Preventitive Approach, 1973; What You Always Wanted to Know About Tests But Were Afraid to Ask!, 1973; Implications and Applications of Assessment Instruments, 1978. Add: Student Personnel Services, Trenton State Coll., Trenton, N.J. 08625, U.S.A.

STAMPER, Alex. *See* **KENT,** Arthur.

STAMPP, Kenneth M(ilton). American, b. 1912. History. Morrison Prof. of American History, Univ. of California, Berkeley, since 1957, now Emeritus (Asst. Prof., 1946–49; Assoc. Prof., 1949–51; Prof., 1951–57). *Publs:* Indiana Politics during the Civil War, 1949; And the War Came, 1959; The Peculiar Institution, 1956; (ed.) The Causes of the Civil War, 1959; (co-author) The National Experience, 1963; The Era of Reconstruction 1865-1877, 1965; (co-ed.) Reconstruction: An Anthology of Revisionist Writings, 1969; The Imperiled Union: Essays on the Background of the Civil War, 1980. Add: 682 San Luis Rd., Berkeley, Calif. 94707, U.S.A.

STANDEN, John Derek. British, b. 1937. History. Principal Lectr. in History, Gipsy Hill Centre, Kingston Polytechnic, since 1974 (Lectr., 1964–67; Sr. Lectr., 1967–74). Asst. Master, Kingsdale Sch., 1960–64. Founder and Ed., Teaching History, 1968–75. *Publs:* The Victorian Age., 1967; The End of an Era, 1968; The Edwardians, 1968; After the Deluge, 1969; The Great Exhibition, 1973. Add: Flat 1, 30 New Compton St., London WC2H 8DN, England.

STANDER, Siegfried. South African, b. 1935. Novels/Short stories. *Publs:* This Desert Place, 1961; The Emptiness of the Plains, 1963; Strangers, 1965; The Journeys of Josephine, 1966; The Horse, 1968; The Fortress, 1972; Leopard in the Sun, 1973; (with Christiaan Barnard) The Unwanted, 1974; Flight from the Hunter, 1977; (with Christiaan Barnard) In the Night Season, 1977; Into the Winter, 1983. Add: Cliff Cottage, P.O. Box 23, Plettenberg Bay, South Africa.

STANFIELD, Anne. *See* **COFFMAN,** Virginia.

STANFORD, Barbara. American, b. 1943. Education, Literature, Mythology/Folklore, Women. Teacher, Vashon High Sch., St. Louis, Mo., 1964–70; Teacher, Fairview High Sch., Boulder, Colo., 1970–72; taught in Education Prog., Utica Coll. of Syracuse Univ., Utica, N.Y., 1973–79. *Publs:* Negro Literature for High School Students, 1968; (with G. Stanford) Learning Discussion Skills Through Games, 1969; (with D. Turner) Theory and Practice in the Teaching of Literature by Afro-Americans; (ed.) I, Too, Sing America, 1971; (ed. with G. Stanford) Changes, 1971; (ed. with G. Stanford) Mix, 1971; (ed. with G. Stanford) Strangers to Themselves: Myths and Modern Man; (ed.) On Being Female; (ed. with G. Stanford) Love has Many Faces; Peacemaking, 1976; (co-author) Designs for English, 1977; (with K. Amin) Black Literature for High School Students, 1978. Add: 12406 Colleen Dr., Little Rock, Ark. 72212, U.S.A.

STANFORD, Derek. British, b. 1918. Poetry, Literature. Literary Reviewer, Birmingham Post; Literary Corresp., The Statesman, Karachi. Lectr. on creative writing and the history of literature, City Literary Inst., London, 1957–69; Fiction Reviewer, The Scotsman, Edinburgh, 1968–84; Poetry Reviewer, Books and Bookmen, London, 1970–84. *Publs:* (with John Bayliss) A Romantic Miscellany (verse), 1946; The Freedom of Poetry: Studies in Contemporary Verse, 1947; Music for Statues (verse), 1948; (with Muriel Spark) Tribute to Wordsworth, 1950; Christopher Fry: An Appreciation, 1951; Christopher Fry Album, 1952; (with Muriel Spark) Emily Brontë: Her Life and Work, 1953; (ed., with Muriel Spark) My Best Mary: The Selected Letters of Mary Shelley, 1953; (ed., with Muriel Spark) Letters of John Henry Newman, 1957; Movements in English Poetry 1900-1958, 1959; (with Ada Harrison) Ann Brontë: Her Life and Work, 1959; John Betjeman: A Study, 1961; Muriel Spark: A Biography and Critical Study, 1963; Dylan Thomas: A Literary Study, 1964; (ed.) Poets of the Nineties, 1965; (ed.) Prose of This Century, 1966; (ed.) Aubrey Beardsley's Erotic Universe, 1967; (ed.) The Arts of Sport and Recreation, 1967; (ed.) Short Stories of the Nineties, 1969; (ed.) Landmarks in Post-War British Drama, 1969; (ed.) Critics of the Nineties, 1970; (ed.) Writing of the Nineties, 1971; (ed.) The Witticisms of Oscar Wilde, 1971; Pre-Raphaelite Writing, 1973; Inside the Forties: Literary Memoirs 1937-57, 1977; The Traveller Hears the Strange Machine: Selected Poems 1946-1979, 1980; The Vision and Death of Aubrey Beardsley (poem sequence), 1985; Introduction to the Nineties, 1987. Add: c/o Sidgwick and Jackson Ltd., 1 Tavistock Chambers, Bloomsbury Way, London WC1A 2SG, England.

STANFORD, Don(ald Elwin). American, b. 1913. Poetry, Literature, Essays. Alumni Prof. Emeritus, Louisiana State Univ., Baton Rouge, since 1983 (Prof. of English, 1953–83, Alumni Prof., 1979–83; Ed., Southern Review, 1963–83); Ed. Emeritus, The Southern Review, since 1983. Visiting Assoc. Prof., Duke Univ., Durham, N.C., 1961–62; Ed., Humanities Series, Louisiana State Univ. Press, 1962–67. *Publs:* New England Earth, 1941; The Traveler, 1955; (ed.) The Poems of Edward Taylor, 1960; (ed.) Nine Essays in Modern Literature, 1965; (ed.) Selected Poems of Robert Bridges, 1974; (ed.) Selected Poems of S. Foster Damon, 1974; In the Classic Mode: The Achievement of Robert Bridges, 1978; (ed.) Selected Letters of Robert Bridges, 1983; Revolution and Convention in Modern Poetry, 1983; (ed.) John Masefield: Letters to Margaret Bridges, 1984; (ed.) Selected Poems of John Masefield, 1984; The Cartesian Lawnmower, 1984. Add: 776 Delgado Dr., Baton Rouge, La. 70808, U.S.A.

STANFORD, Sondra. American. Romance. *Publs:* A Stranger's Kiss, 1978; Bellfleur, 1980; Golden Tide, 1980; Shadow of Love, 1980; No Trespassing, 1980; Storm's End, 1980; Long Winter's Night, 1981; And Then Came Dawn, 1981; Whisper Wind, 1981; Yesterday's Shadow, 1981; Tarnished Vows, 1982; Silver Mist, 1982; Magnolia Moon, 1982; Sun Lover, 1982; Love's Gentle Chains, 1983; The Heart Knows Best, 1984; For All Time, 1984; A Corner of Heaven, 1984; Cupid's Task, 1985; Bird in Flight, 1986; Equal Shares, 1986; Stolen Trust, 1987; Heart of Gold, 1988; Through All Eternity, 1988; Proud Beloved, 1989. Add: 4117 Birchwood Dr., Corpus Christi, Tex. 78412, U.S.A.

STANIER, Maida. British, b. 1909. Novels/Short stories, Plays/Screenplays, Poetry. Freelance broadcaster and journalist. *Publs:* Light and Shade (poetry), 1953; Culex's Guide to Oxford (poetry), 1955; Free and Easy (poetry), 1957; The New Oxford Spy (poetry), 1969; The Ruins of Time (plays), 1969; The Singing Time (novel), 1975; Talking about Oxford; More Talking about Oxford; The Adventure of Captain Jason and His Little Mate (for children), 1980; Portrait of a Schoolmaster (biography), 1984. Add: Flat 20, Wyndham House, Plantation, Rd., Oxford,

England.

STANKIEWICZ, Wladyslaw Jozef. British/Canadian, b. 1922. Philosophy, Politics/Government. Prof. of Political Science, Univ. of British Columbia, Vancouver, since 1965 (Asst. Prof., 1957–61; Assoc. Prof., 1961–65). Lectr. in Political Science, Polish University Coll., London, 1947–52; Research Assoc., Mid-European Studies Center, NYC, 1952–54; Visiting Fellow, Center of Intnl. Studies, Princeton Univ., New Jersey, 1954–55; Economist, Govt. of Ontario, 1956–57. *Publs:* (with J.M. Montias) Institutional Changes in the Postwar Economy of Poland, 1955; Politics and Religion in Seventeenth Century France: A Study of Political Ideas from the Monarchomachs to Bayle, as Reflected in the Toleration Controversy, 1960; (ed.) Political Thought Since World War II: Critical and Interpretive Essays, 1964; (ed.) The Living Name: A Tribute to Stefan Stykolt from Some of His Friends, 1964; (ed.) Crisis in British Government: The Need for Reform, 1967; (ed.) In Defense of Sovereignty (critical anthology), 1969; What Is Behavioralism? (essay), 1971; Relativism: Thoughts and Aphorisms, 1972; Canada-U.S. Relations and Canadian Foreign Policy, 1973; (ed.) British Government in an Era of Reform, 1976; Aspects of Political Theory: Classical Concepts in an Age of Relativism, 1976; A Guide to Democratic Jargon (aphorisms), 1976; Approaches to Democracy: Philosophy of Government at the Close of the Twentieth Century, 1980; (ed.) The Tradition of Polish Ideals, 1981. Add: Dept. of Political Science, Univ. of British Columbia, Vancouver, B.C. V6T 1W5, Canada.

STANLEY, Bennett. *See* **HOUGH,** S. B.

STANLEY, Diane. American, b. 1943. Children's fiction. Freelance medical illustrator, 1970–74; Art Dir. of Children's Books, Putnam's, Publishers, NYC, 1978–79 *Publs:* The Conversation Club, 1983; Birdsong Lullaby, 1985; A Country Tale, 1985; The Good Luck Pencil, 1986; Peter the Great, 1986; Captain Whiz-Bang, 1987 Add: c/o Macmillan, 866 Third Ave., New York, N.Y. 10022, U.S.A.

STANLEY, Julian C(ecil), Jr. American, b. 1918. Education, Psychology. Prof. of Psychology, and Dir., Study of Mathematically Precocious Youth, Johns Hopkins Univ., Baltimore, Md., since 1971 (Prof. of Education and Psychology, 1967–71). Assoc. Prof. of Educational Psychology, George Peabody Coll. for Teachers, 1949–53; Assoc. Prof. of Education, 1953–57, Prof., 1957–62, Prof. of Educational Psychology, 1962–67, Chmn., Dept. of Educational Psychology, 1962–63, and Dir., Lab. of Experimental Design, 1961–67, Univ. of Wisconsin, Madison. *Publs:* Measurement in Today's Schools, 4th ed. 1964; (with D.T. Campbell) Experimental and Quasi-experimental Designs for Research, 1966; (ed.) Improving Experimental Design and Statistical Research, 1967; (with G.V. Glass) Statistical Methods in Education and Psychology, 1970; (with G.H. Bracht and K.D. Hopkins) Perspectives in Educational and Psychological Measurement, 1972; (with K.D. Hopkins) Educational and Psychological Measurement and Evaluation, 1972, 3rd ed. 1989; (ed.) Preschool Programs for the Disadvantaged, 1972; (ed.) Compensatory Education Ages Two to Eight, 1973; (ed. with D.P. Keating and L.H. Fox) Mathematical Talent: Discovery, Description, and Development, 1974; (ed. with W.C. George and C.H. Solano) The Gifted and the Creative: A Fifty-Year Perspective, 1977; Educational Programs and Intellectual Prodigies, 1978; (ed. with W.C. George and S.J. Cohn) Educating the Gifted: Acceleration and Enrichment, 1979; (ed. with Camilla P. Benbow) Academic Precocity: Aspects of Its Development, 1983. Add: 430 Gilman Hall, Johns Hopkins Univ., Baltimore, Md. 21218, U.S.A.

STANLEY, Oliver. British, b. 1925. Law, Money/Finance. Chmn., Rathbone Bros. PLC, London, Liverpool, Amsterdam, and Geneva, since 1971. H.M. Inspector of Taxes, 1953–65; Dir., Gray DawesCo. Ltd., London, 1966–71. *Publs:* Guide to Taxation, 1967; (with David Ross) Tax and Insurance, 1969; (co-author) Simon's Taxes, 1970; Taxology, 1972; (ed.) The Creation and Protection of Capital, 1974; Taxation of Farmers and Landowners, 1981, 3rd ed. 1987; Offshore Tax Planning, 2nd ed. 1989. Add: 5 The Park, London NW11 7SR, England.

STANSKY, Peter (David Lyman). American, b. 1932. History, Literature, Biography. Frances and Charles Field Prof. of History, Stanford Univ., Calif., since 1974 (Assoc. Prof., 1968–74). Ed., Conference on British Studies Biographical Series, Cambridge Univ. Press., 1970–74. *Publs:* Ambitions and Strategies, 1964; (co-author) Journey to the Frontier, 1966; (ed.) The Left and the War, 1969; (ed.) John Morley: 19th Century Essays, 1970; (co-author) The Unknown Orwell, 1972; England Since 1867, 1973; (ed.) Churchill, 1973; (ed.) The Victorian Revolution, 1974; Gladstone, 1979; (co-author) Orwell: The Transformation, 1979; William Morris, 1983; (ed.) On Nineteen Eighty-Four, 1983; Redesigning the World, 1985. Add: Dept. of History, Stanford Univ., Stanford, Calif. 94305, U.S.A.

STANTON, Paul. *See* **BEATY,** David.

STANTON, Vance. *See* **AVALLONE,** Michael.

STAPLES, M.J. *See* **STAPLES,** Reginald.

STAPLES, Reginald (Thomas). Also Writes as M.J. Staples, Robert Tyler Stevens and James Sinclair. British, b. 1911. Novels/ Short stories. Managing Dir., Fullerton and Lloyd (Publishers) Ltd., since 1954; Dir., Town and Country Studios Ltd., since 1968; Chmn., Vista Sports Ltd., since 1971, all in Croydon. Managing Dir., Staples and Hancock Ltd., Croydon, 1953–66; Dir., H.D. Vincent (Printers) Ltd., Worthing, 1958–66. *Publs:* (as Robert Tyler Stevens) The Summer Day Is Done, 1976; (as Robert Tyler Stevens) Flight from Bucharest, 1977; (as James Sinclair) Warrior Queen, 1977; (as Robert Tyler Stevens) Appointment in Sarajevo, 1978; (as Robert Tyler Stevens) Woman of Cordova, 1979; (as James Sinclair) Canis the Warrior, 1979; (as Robert Tyler Stevens) The Fields of Yesterday, 1982; Shadows in the Afternoon, 1983; The Hostage, 1985; The Woman in Berlin, 1986; A Professional Gentleman, 1988; (as M. J. Staples) Down Lambeth Way, 1988. Add: Wenvoe, Dome Hill, Caterham, Surrey, England.

STAPLES, Robert Eugene. American, b. 1942. Human relations, Humanities, Race relations, Sociology. Prof. of Sociology, Univ. of California, San Francisco, since 1984 (Assoc. Prof., 1973–84). Asst. Prof., California State Univ., Hayward, 1968–69; Asst. Prof. of Sociology, Fisk Univ., Nashville, Tenn., 1969–70; Member of faculty, Univ. of California, Irvine, 1970–71; Assoc. Prof. of Sociology, Howard Univ., Washington, D.C., 1971–73. *Publs:* The Lower-Income Negro Family in Saint Paul, 1967; The Black Family: Essays and Studies, 1971; The Black Woman in America, 1973; Introduction to Black Sociology, 1976; The World of Black Singles, 1981; Black Masculinity, 1982; The Urban Plantation, 1987. Add: Grad. Prog. in Sociology, Univ. of California, San Francisco, Calif. 94143, U.S.A.

STAPLETON, (Katharine) Laurence. American, b. 1911. Poetry, Literature, Politics/Government. Prof. Emeritus of English, Bryn Mawr Coll., Pa. (joined faculty, 1934; Prof. of English, and of Political Theory, 1948–64; Mary E. Garrett Prof. of English, 1964–80; Chmn., Dept. of English, 1954–65). Registrar, Massachusetts Public Employment Service, 1933–34. *Publs:* Justice and World Society, 1944; The Design of Democracy, 1949; (ed.) H.D. Thoreau: A Writer's Journal, 1959; Yushin's Log and Other Poems, 1969; The Elected Circle: Studies in the Art of Prose, 1973; Marianne Moore, 1978. Add: 229 N. Roberts Rd., Bryn Mawr, Pa. 19010, U.S.A.

STARBUCK, George (Edwin). American, b. 1931. Poetry. Prof. of English, Boston Univ., since 1971. Fiction Ed., Houghton Mifflin Co., Boston, Mass., 1958–61; Member of English Dept., State Univ. of New York, Buffalo, 1963–64; Assoc. Prof., 1964–67, and Dir., Writers Workshop, 1967–70, Univ. of Iowa, Iowa City. *Publs:* Bone Thoughts, 1960; White Paper: Poems, 1966; Three Sonnets; Elegy in a Country Church Yard, 1975; Desperate Measures, 1978; Talking B.A. Blues, 1980; The Argot Merchant Disaster: Poems New and Selected, 1982; Space-Saver Sonnets, 1986; Richard the Third in a Fourth of a Second, 1986. Add: Dept. of English, Boston Univ., Boston, Mass. 02215, U.S.A.

STARK, (Dame) Freya. British, b. 1893. History, Travel/ Exploration/Adventure, Autobiography/Memoirs/Personal, Essays. With Ministry of Information, 1939–41; Attaché, British Foreign Service, 1941–44. *Publs:* Baghdad Sketches, 1932, 1937; The Valley of Assassins, 1934; The Southern Gates of Arabia, 1936; Seen in the Hadhramaut, 1938; A Winter in Arabia, 1940; Letters from Syria, 1942; East Is West, 1945; Perseus in the Wind, 1948; Traveller's Prelude, 1950; Beyond Euphrates, 1951; The Coast of Incense, 1953; Ionia: A Quest, 1954; The Lycian Shore, 1956; Alexander's Path, 1958; Riding to the Tigris, 1959; Dust in the Lion's Paw, 1961; The Journey's Echo, 1963; Rome on the Euphrates, 1966; The Zodiac Arch, 1968; Time, Space and Movement in Landscape, 1969; The Minaret of Djam, 1970; Turkey, 1970; Letters, 6 vols., 1974–81; A Peak in Darien, 1976; Rivers of Time, 1982. Add: c/o John Murray, 50 Albemarle St., London W1X 4BD, England.

STARK, Joshua. *See* **OLSEN,** T. V.

STARK, Richard. *See* **WESTLAKE,** Donald E.

STARK, Werner. American, b. 1909. History, Sociology, Theology/ Religion. Prof. of Sociology, Fordham Univ., NYC, since 1963. Hon. Prof. of Sociology, Univ. of Salzburg, since 1974. Lectr. in Social Studies, Univ. of Edinburgh, 1945–51; Reader in History of Economic Thought, Univ. of Manchester, 1951–63. *Publs:* Ursprung and Aufsteig des landwirtschaftlichen Grossbetriebs in den bomischen Landern, 1934; Sozialpolitik, 1936; The Ideal Foundations of Economic Thought, 1943; The History of Economics in Its Relations to Social Development, 1944; America: Ideal and Reality: The United States of 1776 in Contemporary European Philosophy, 1947; (ed.) Rare Masterpieces of Philosophy and Science, 17 vols., 1950–66; (ed.) Jeremy Bentham's Economic Writings, 3 vols., 1952–54; The Sociology of Knowledge, 1958; Social Theory and Christian Thought, 1959; Montesquieu: Pioneer of the Sociology of Knowledge, 1960; The Fundamental Forms of Social Thought, 1962; The Sociology of Religion, 5 vols., 1966–72; Grundriss der Religionssoziologie, 1974; The Social Bond, 4 vols., 1976–82. Add: Dept. of Sociology, Fordham University, Bronx, N.Y. 10458, U.S.A.

STARKE, Joseph Gabriel. Australian, b. 1911. History, International relations/Current affairs, Law, Psychiatry. Queen's Counsel, since 1961 (Barrister since 1939). Prof. of Humanitarian Law, Intnl. Inst. of Humanitarian Law, San Remo, Italy, since 1975; Member, Panel of Arbitrators, Intnl. Court of Justice, since 1969; Gen. Ed., Australian Law Journal, since 1974; Consultant, Inter-State Commn., since 1985. Member, League of Nations Secretariat, Geneva, 1935–40. *Publs:* Introduction to International Law, 1947, 10th ed. 1989; The ANZUS Treaty Alliance, 1965; Studies in International Law, 1965; The Law of Town and Country Planning in New South Wales, 1966; (ed.) The Protection and Encouragement of Private Foreign Investment, 1966; (ed.) Australian Year Book of International Law 1965, 1966; (with P.F.P. Higgins) Cheshire and Fifoot on Contracts, Australian Ed., 1966, 4th ed. 1981; Introduction to the Science of Peace, 1968; Assignments of Choses in Action in Australia, 1972; The Validity of Psycho-Analysis, 1973; Contributions to Irenology in the Writings of Leonard Nelson, 1974; (co-author) Casebook on the Law of Contract, 1975; The Changing Legal Scene in New South Wales: An Overview, 1986; The Science of Peace, 1986. Add: 2 Kemp Close, Swinger Hill, Phillip, A.C.T. 2606, Australia.

STARR, Chester G. American, b. 1914. Archaeology/Antiquities, History. Bently Prof. of History, Univ. of Michigan, Ann Arbor, since 1970. Prof. of History, Univ. of Illinois, 1940–70. *Publs:* Roman Imperial Navy, 1940, 1960; From Salerno to the Alps, 1948; Emergence of Rome, 1950; Civilization and the Caesars, 1954; (co-author) History of the World, 1960; Origins of Greek Civilization, 1961; History of the Ancient World, 1965; Rise and Fall of the Ancient World, 1965; Awakening of Greek Historical Spirit, 1968; Athenian Coinage, 1970; Ancient Greeks, 1971; Ancient Romans, 1971; Early Man, 1973; Political Intelligence in Classical Greece, 1974; Economic and Social Growth of Early Greece, 1977; Essays on Ancient History, 1979; The Beginnings of Imperial Rome, 1980; The Roman Empire: A Study in Survival, 1973, 1982; Individual and the Community: The Rise of the Polis, 1986; Past and Future in Ancient History, 1987. Add: Dept. of History, Univ. of Michigan, Ann Arbor, Mich. 48109, U.S.A.

STARR, Henry. *See* **BINGLEY,** David Ernest.

STARR, Kate. *See* **DINGWELL,** Joyce.

STASHEFF, Christopher. American, b. 1944. Science fiction. Asst. Prof. of Speech and Theatre, Montclair State Coll., New Jersey, since 1977 (Instr., 1972–77). *Publs:* The Warlock in Spite of Himself, 1969; King Kobold, 1971; A Wizard in Bedlam, 1979; The Warlock Unclocked, 1982; Escape Velocity, 1983; King Kobold Revived, 1984; The Warlock Enraged, 1985; Her Majesty's Wizard, 1986; The Warlock Is Missing, 1986; The Warlock Wandering, 1986; The Warlock Insane, 1989. Add: Dept. of Speech and Theatre, Montclair State Coll., Upper Montclair, N.J. 07043, U.S.A.

STASSINOPOULOS, Arianna. Greek, b. 1950. Social commentary/ phenomena, Women, Biography. *Publs:* The Female Woman, 1973; The Other Revolution, 1978; Maria: Beyond the Callas Legend, 1980; The Gods of Greece, 1983; Picasso, Creator and Destroyer, 1988. Add: c/o Watkins Loomis, 150 E. 35th St., New York, N.Y. 10016, U.S.A.

STATLER, Oliver. American, b. 1915. Art, History, Travel/ Exploration/Adventure. Adjunct Prof., Univ. of Hawaii at Manoa. *Publs:* Modern Japanese Prints: An Art Reborn, 1956; Shiko Munakata, 1958; Japanese Inn, 1961; The Black Ship Scroll, 1964; Shimoda Story, 1961; Americans in the Opening of Japan, 1971; Japanese Pilgrimage, 1983.

Add: 1619 Kamamalu Ave., Honolulu, Hawaii, 96813, U.S.A.

STAVE, Bruce M. American, b. 1937. Politics/Government, Urban studies. Prof. of History since 1975, Dir. of the Center for Oral History, since 1979, and Chmn. of History Dept., since 1985, Univ. of Connecticut, Storrs (Asst. Prof., 1970–72; Assoc. Prof., 1971–75). Assoc. Ed., Journal of Urban History, since 1976. Instr., 1965–66, and Asst. Prof. of History, 1966–70, Univ. of Bridgeport, Conn.; Fulbright Prof. of American History, Marathwada and Bhagalpur Univs., India, 1968–69, in Australasia, 1977, and Peking Univ., China, 1984–85. *Publs:* The New Deal and the Last Hurrah: Pittsburgh Machine Politics, 1970; (ed.) Urban Bosses, Machines, and Progressive Reformers, 1972, 1984; (ed. with LeRoy Ashby) The Discontented Society: Interpretations of 20th Century American Protest, 1972; (ed.) Socialism and the Cities, 1975; The Making of Urban History, 1977; Modern Industrial Cities: History, Policy and Survival, 1984; Talking about Connecticut: Oral History in the Nutmeg State, 1985. Add: 200 Broad Way, Coventry, Conn. 06238, U.S.A.

STAVIS, Barrie. American, b. 1906. Novels/Short stories, Plays/ Screenplays, Songs, lyrics and libretti, History. Foreign Corresp. in Europe, 1937–38; Co-Founder, and Member, Bd. of Dirs., New Stage theatre group, 1947; Member, Bd. of Dirs., U.S. Inst. for Theatre Technology, 1961–64, 1969–72. *Publs:* plays—Refuge: A One-Act Play of the Spanish War, 1939; Lamp at Midnight: A Play about Galileo, 1947, 3rd ed. 1974, oratorio version, as Galileo Galilei, 1975; The Man Who Never Died: A Play about Joe Hill, 1955, 3rd ed. 1972, opera version, as Joe Hill, 1970; Banners of Steel: A Play about John Brown, 1967, as Harpers Ferry, 1967; Coat of Many Colors: A Play about Joseph in Egypt, 1968; novels—The Chain of Command, 1945; Home, Sweet Home!, 1949; others—(ed. with F. Harmon) The Songs of Joe Hill, 1955; Notes on Joe Hill and His Times, 1964; Joe Hill: Poet/Organizer, 2 vols., 1964; John Brown: The Sword and the Word, 1970.

STAVRIANOS, Leften S. American, b. 1913. History, International relations/Current affairs, Third World problems. Adjunct Prof. of History, Univ. of California, San Diego, since 1975. Lectr., Queens Univ., Canada, 1937–38; Instr., and Asst. Prof., Smith Coll., Northampton, Mass., 1939–46; Assoc. Prof. of History, 1946–56, and Prof., 1956–73, Northwestern Univ., Evanston, Ill. *Publs:* Balkan Federation, 1944; Greece: American Dilemma and Opportunity, 1952; The Balkans since 1453, 1958; (co-author) Global History of Man, 1962; World since 1500, 1966; World to 1500, 1970; Man the Toolmaker, 1973; The Promise of the Coming Dark Age, 1976; Global Rift: The Third World Comes of Age, 1981; Lifelines from Our Past, 1989. Add: Univ. of California-San Diego, La Jolla, Calif. 92093, U.S.A.

STEAD, C(hristian) K(arlson). New Zealander, b. 1932. Novels/Short stories, Poetry, Literature. Lectr. in English, Univ. of New England, N.S.W., 1956–57; faculty member, 1960–86, and Prof. of English, 1969–86, Auckland Univ. Chmn., N.Z. Literary Fund, 1973–75. *Publs:* Whether the Will Is Free: Poems 1954-62, 1964; The New Poetic: Yeats to Eliot, 1964; (ed.) New Zealand Short Stories: Second Series, 1966; Smith's Dream (novel), 1971; (ed.) Measure for Measure: A Casebook, 1971; Crossing the Bar, 1972; (ed.) Selected Letters and Journals of Katherine Mansfield, 1973; Quesada: Poems 1972-74, 1975; Walking Westward, 1978; Five for the Symbol (short stories), 1981; In the Glass Case: Essays on New Zealand Literature, 1981; (ed.) Collected Stories of Maurice Duggan, 1981; Geographies, 1982; Poems of a Decade, 1983; Paris, 1984; All Visitors Ashore (novel), 1984; Pound, Yeats, Eliot, and the Modernist Movement, 1986; The Death of the Body (novel), 1986; Between (poems), 1988; Sister Hollywood (novel), 1989; Answering to the Language (essays), 1989. Add: 37 Tohunga Cres., Parnell, Auckland 1, New Zealand.

STEAD, Philip John. British, b. 1916. Novels/Short stories, Criminology/Law enforcement/Prisons, Biography. Prof. of Comparative Police Science, John Jay Coll. of Criminal Justice, City Univ. of New York, since 1974 (Dean of Grad. Studies, 1979–82). Ed., Police Studies, since 1978. Dean of Academic Studies, The Police Staff Coll., Bramshill, England, 1953–74. *Publs:* In the Street of the Angel, 1947; (ed.) Songs of the Restoration Theatre, 1948; The Charlatan, 1948; Fausta, 1950; Mr. Punch, 1950; (ed. and trans.) The Memoirs of Lacenaire, 1952; Vidocq: A Biography, 1953; The Police of Paris, 1957; Second Bureau, 1959; (ed. with J.C. Alderson) The Police We Deserve, 1973; Police: A Description of the Regular Police Service of England and Wales, 1974; (ed.) Pioneers in Policing, 1977; The Police of France, 1983. Add: John Jay Coll. of Criminal Justice, 444 West 56th St., New York, N.Y. 10019, U.S.A.

STEANE, J(ohn) B(arry). British, b. 1928. Literature, Music. Teacher, Merchant Taylors Sch. Northwood, since 1952. Member of Reviewing Staff, The Gramophone, since 1973. *Publs:* Marlowe: A Critical Study, 1964; (ed.) Dekker: The Shoemaker's Holiday, 1965; Tennyson, 1966; (ed.) Jonson: The Alchemist, 1967; (ed.) Marlowe: The Complete Plays, 1969; (ed.) Nashe: The Unfortunate Traveller and Other Works, 1972; The Grand Tradition: Seventy Years of Singing on Record, 1974; (with others) Opera on Record, 3 vols., 1979–85. Add: Merchant Taylors Sch., Northwood, Middx., England.

STEARN, Jess. American. Paranormal, Biography. *Publs:* The Sixth Man, 1961; The Door of the Future, 1964; The Grapevine, 1965; Yoga, Youth, and Reincarnation, 1965; Edgar Cayce: The Sleeping Prophet, 1968; The Second Life of Susan Ganier, 1969; Seekers, 1969; Adventures into the Psychis, 1971; A Time for Astrology, 1971; Dr. Thompson's New Way to Cure Your Aching Back, 1973; The Search for the Soul, 1973; A Prophet in His Own Country: The Young Edgar Cayce, 1974; (with Taylor Caldwell) The Romance of Atlantis, 1975; Miracle of the Mind: The Power of Alpha-Thinking, 1976; A Matter of Immortality, 1976; (with Taylor Caldwell) I, Judas, 1978; The Truth about Elvis, 1980; In Search of Taylor Caldwell, 1981; Elvis: His Spiritual Journey, 1982; Soulmates, 1985. Add: c/o Bantam, 666 Fifth Ave., New York, N.Y. 10103, U.S.A.

STEARN, William Thomas. British, b. 1911. Botany, Horticulture, Sciences, Biography. Librarian, Royal Horticultural Soc., 1933–41, 1946–52; Botanist, then Sr. Principal Scientific Officer, British Museum of Natural History, 1952–76, London; Visiting Prof., Dept. of Botany, Univ. of Reading, 1977–83; now retired. Pres., Ray Soc., 1974–77; Pres., Garden History Soc., 1977–82; Pres., Linnean Soc. of London, 1979–82. *Publs:* (with H.B.D. Woodcock) Lilies of the World, 1950; (with E. Blatter and W.S. Millard) Some Beautiful Indian Trees, 1955; Introduction to the Species Plantarum of Carl Linnaeus, 1957; Early Leyden Botany, 1961; Botanical Latin, 1966, 1983; (ed.) Humboldt, Bonpland, Kunth, and Tropical American Botany, 1968; (with C.N. Goulimis) Wild Flowers of Greece, 1968; (with A.W. Smith) Gardener's Dictionary of Plant Names, 1972; (with W. Blunt) Captain Cook's Florilegium, 1973; (with W. Blunt) Australian Flower Paintings of Ferdinand Bauer, 1976; The Wondrous Transformation of Caterpillars: M.S. Merian, 1978; The Natural History Museum at South Kensington, 1981; (with E. Rucker) Maria Sibylla Merian in Surinam, 1982; Plant Portraits from the Flora Danica, 1983; (with P.H. Davis) Peonies of Greece, 1984; (with M. Page) Culinary Herbs, 2nd ed. 1985; (with M. Rix) Redoute's Fairest Flowers, 1987; (With C. Brickell) An English Florilegium, 1987; (with A.T. Gage) A Bicentenary History of the Linnean Society of London, 1988. Add: 17 High Park Rd., Kew Gardens, Richmond, Surrey TW9 4BL, England.

STEBBINS, Robert A. Canadian, b. 1938. Criminology/Law enforacement/ Prisons, Education, Leisure, Sociology. Prof. of Sociology, Univ. of Calgary, since 1976. Asst. Prof., 1965–68, Assoc. Prof. and Head of Dept., 1968–71, and Prof., 1972–73, Dept. of Sociology and Anthropology, Memorial Univ. of Newfoundland; Prof. of Sociology, Univ. of Texas at Arlington, 1973–76. *Publs:* Commitment to Deviance: The Non-professional Criminal in the Community, 1971; The Disorderly Classroom: Its Physical and Temporal Conditions, 1974; Teachers and Meaning: Definitions of Classroom Situations, 1975; Amateurs: On the Margin Between Work and Leisure, 1979; Fieldwork Experience: Qualitative Approaches to Social Research, 1980; The Sociology of Deviance, 1982; The Magician: Career, Culture and Social Psychology in a Variety Art, 1984; Sociology: The Study of Society, 1987, 1990; Canadian Football: The View from the Helmet, 1987; Deviance: Tolerable Differences, 1988; The Laugh Makers: Stand-Up Comedy as Art, Business, and Life-Style, 1989. Add: Dept. of Sociology, Univ. of Calgary, Calgary, Alta. T2N 1N4, Canada.

STEBBINS, Robert C(yril). American, b. 1915. Natural history. Prof. Emeritus of Zoology, and Curator of Herpetology, Univ. of California, Berkeley. *Publs:* (with C.A. Stebbins) What Bird Is That?, 1951; (with C.A. Stebbins) Birds of Lassen Volcanic National Park, 1942; (with L. Miller) Birds of the Campus, 1947; Amphibians of Western North America, 1951; Amphibians and Reptiles of Western North America, 1954; Reptiles and Amphibians of San Francisco Bay Region, 1959; Nature Next Door, 1962; (with A.H. Miller) Lives of Desert Animals in Joshua Tree National Monument, 1964; (with D.C. Ibsen and G. Gillfillan) Animal Coloration, 1966; A Field Guide to Western Reptiles and Amphibians, 1966, 1985; (with T.I. Storer, R.L. Usinger and J.W. Nybakken) General Zoology, 5th ed., 1972, 6th ed. 1979; Amphibians and Reptiles of California, 1972. Add: Museum of Vertebrate Zoology, 2593 Life Sciences Bldg., Univ. of California, Berkeley, Calif. 94720, U.S.A.

STEEGMULLER, Francis. Also writes as David Keith and Byron Steel. American, b. 1906. Novels/Short stories, Literature, Biography. *Publs:* (as Byron Steel) O Rare Ben Jonson, 1927; (as Byron Steel) Java-Java, 1928; The Musicale, 1930; (as Byron Steel), Sir Francis Bacon: The First Modern Mind, 1930; (with M.D. Lane) America on Relief, 1938; Flaubert and Madame Bovary: A Double Portrait, 1939, 3rd ed. 1966; (as David Keith) A Matter of Iodine, 1940; (as David Keith) A Matter of Accent, 1943; States of Grace, 1946; French Follies and Other Follies, 1946; (as David Keith) Blue Harpsichord, 1949; Maupassant: A Lion in the Path (in U.K. as Maupassant), 1949; (trans.) Impressionists and Symbolists, by Lionello Venturi, 1950; The Two Lives of James Jackson Jarves, 1951; (trans.) The Selected Letters of Gustave Flaubert, 1953; The Grand Mademoiselle, 1956; (trans.) Madame Bovary, by Gustave Flaubert, 1957; The Christening Party, 1960; (trans.) Le Hibou et la Poussiquette, by Edward Lear, 1961; Apollinaire: Poet among the Painters, 1963; (ed. and co-trans. with N. Guterman) Selected Essays, by Sainte-Beuve, 1963; (trans. with N. Guterman) Papillot, Clignot, et Dodo, by Eugene Field, 1964; (ed.) November, by Gustave Flaubert, 1966; (trans.) Intimate Journal 1840-1841, by Gustave Flaubert, 1967; Cocteau: A Biography, 1970; Stories and True Stories, 1972; (ed. and trans.) Flaubert in Egypt, 1973; (ed.) Your Isadora: The Love Story of Isadora Duncan and Gordon Craig (in U.K. as Your Isadora: The Love Story of Isadora Duncan and Gordon Craig Told Through Letters and Diaries Never Before Published), 1974; Silence at Salerno, 1978; (ed. and trans.) The Letters of Gustave Flaubert 1830-1857, 1980; (ed. and trans.) The Letters of Gustave Flaubert 1857-1880, 1983. Add: 200 East 66th St., New York, N.Y. 10021, U.S.A.

STEEL, Byron. *See* **STEEGMULLER,** Francis.

STEEL, Danielle. American, b. 1947. Historical/Romance/Gothic. *Publs:* Going Home, 1973; Passion's Promise, 1977, in U.K. as Golden Moments, 1980; Now and Forever, 1978; The Promise (novelization of screenplay), 1978; Season of Passion, 1979; The Ring, 1980; Loving, 1980; To Love Again, 1980; Remembrance, 1981; Palomino, 1981; Love Poems, 1981; Summer's End, 1981; A Perfect Stranger, 1982; Once in a Lifetime, 1982; Crossings, 1982; Thurston House, 1983; Changes, 1983; Full Circle, 1984; Having a Baby (non-fiction), 1984; Secrets, 1985; Family Album, 1985; Wanderlust, 1986; Fine Things, 1987; Kaleidoscope, 1987; Zoya, 1988; Star, 1989; Martha series (juvenile), 3 vols., 1989; Max series (juvenile), 3 vols., 1989. Add: c/o Dell Publishing Co., One Dag Dammarskjold Plaza, New York, N.Y. 10017, U.S.A.

STEEL, David (Martin Scott). British, b. 1938. Politics/Government. Social and Liberal Democrat Member of Parliament (U.K.) for Tweeddale, Ettrick and Lauderdale, since 1983 (for Roxburgh, Selkirk and Peebles, 1965–83), and Leader of the Liberal Party 1976–88. *Publs:* Boost for the Borders, 1964; Out of Control, 1968; No Entry, 1969; The Liberal Way Forward, 1975; A New Political Agenda, 1976; Militant for the Reasonable Man, 1977; New Majority for a New Parliament, 1978; High Ground of Politics, 1979; A House Divided, 1980; (with Judy Steel) David Steel's Border Country, 1985; Partners in One Nation, 1985; (with David Owen) The Time Has Come, 1987; (with Judy Steel) Mary Stuart's Scotland, 1987. Add: c/o House of Commons, London SW1A 0AA, England.

STEEL, D(avid) R(obert). British, b. 1948. Administration/Management, Politics/Government. Secty., Scottish Health Bd. Chmn.'s Funeral Mgrs. Group, since 1986. Lectr. in Politics, Univ. of Exeter, 1972–84; Asst. Dir., National Assn. of Health Authorities, 1984–86. *Publs:* (with R.G.S. Brown) The Administrative Process in Britain, 2nd ed. 1979; (with D.A. Heald) Privatising Public Enterprises, 1984. Add: 29 Park Rd., Edinburgh EH6 4LA, Scotland.

STEEL, Ronald. American, b. 1931. History, Politics/Government, Biography. Member, Council of Foreign Relations, NYC. *Publs:* The End of Alliance: America and the Future of Europe, 1964; Pax Americana, 1967; (with J.J. Servan Schreiber) The American Challenge, 1968; Imperialists and Other Heroes, 1971; Walter Lippmann and the American Century, 1980. Add: c/o Janklow Assocs., 598 Madison Ave., New York, N.Y. 10022, U.S.A.

STEELE, Harwood E(lmes Robert). Also writes as Howard Steele. Canadian, b. 1897. Westerns/Adventure, Poetry, Children's non-fiction, International relations/Current affairs. Asst. Press Rep., Canadian Pacific Railway, 1923–25; Historian, Canadian Govt. Arctic Expedition, 1925; Military Adviser, CBC, 1937–39. *Publs:* (as Howard Steele) Cleared for Action (poetry), 1914; The Canadians in France 1915-1918, 1920; Spirit-of-Iron (Manitou-Pewabic) (novel), 1923; I Shall Arise (novel), 1926; The Ninth Circle (novel), 1927, The Long Rise: A Short History of the 17th Duke of York's Royal Canadian Hussars, 1934; Policing the Arctic: The Story of the Conquest of the Arctic by the Royal Canadian, Formerly North-West, Mounted Police, 1936; India: Friend or Foe?, 1947; To Effect an Arrest: Adventures of the Royal Canadian Mounted Police (short stories), 1947; Ghosts Returning (novel), 1950; The Marching Call (juvenile), 1955; The Red Serge: Stories of the Royal Canadian Mounted Police, 1961; The R.C.M.P.: Royal Canadian Mounted Police, 1969. Add: 20 Brant St., Orillia, Ont., Canada.

STEELE, Howard. *See* **STEELE,** Harwood E.

STEELE, Mary Q(uintard). Also writes as Wilson Gage. American, b. 1922. Children's fiction, Natural history. *Publs:* (as Wilson Gage) Secret of Fiery Gorge, 1960; (as Wilson Gage) A Wild Goose Tale, 1961; (as Wilson Gage) Dan and the Miranda, 1962; (as Wilson Gage) Big Blue Island, 1964; (as Wilson Gage) Miss Osborne—the Mop, 1965; (as Wilson Gage) Ghost of Fire Owl Farm, 1966; Journey Outside, 1969; (as Wilson Gage) Mike's Toads, 1970; The Living Year, 1972; The First of the Penguins, 1973; (with W.O. Steele) The Eye in the Forest, 1975; Because of the Sand Witches There, 1975; The True Men, 1976; (as Wilson Gage) Squash Pie, 1976; (as Wilson Gage) Down in the Boondocks, 1977; (ed.) The Fifth Day, 1978; The Owl's Kiss, 1978; Wish, Come True, 1979; (as Wilson Gage) Mrs. Gaddy and the Ghost, 1979; The Life (and Death) of Sarah Elizabeth Harwood, 1980; (as Wilson Gage) Cully Cully and the Bear, 1982; (as Wilson Gage) The Crow and Mrs. Gaddy, 1984; (as Wilson Gage) Mrs. Gaddy and the Fast Growing Vine, 1985; The First of the Penguins, 1985; Anna's Summer Songs, 1988; Anna's Garden Songs, 1989. Add: c/o Greenwillow, Morrow, 105 Madison Ave., New York, N.Y. 10016, U.S.A.

STEELE, (Henry) Max(well). American, b. 1922. Novels/Short stories, Children's fiction, Literature. Prof. of English, Univ. of North Carolina, Chapel Hill, since 1972 (Lectr., 1955–58 and 1967–68; Writer-in-Residence, 1966–67; Assoc. Prof., 1968–72). Advisory Ed., Paris Review, Paris and NYC, since 1952. *Publs:* Debby, 1950; Goblins Must Go Barefoot, 1965; Where She Brushed Her Hair (short stories), 1968; The Cat and the Coffee Drinkers (for children), 1969; The Hat of My Mother: Stories, 1988. Add: Dept. of English, Univ. of North Carolina, Chapel Hill, N.C. 27514, U.S.A.

STEELE, Peter. British, b. 1935. Medicine/Health, Travel/Exploration/Adventure. General Medical Practitioner, Whitehorse, Yukon. *Publs:* Two and Two Halves to Bhutan, 1970; Doctor on Everest, 1972; Medical Care for Mountain Climbers, 1976; Medical Handbook for Mountaineers, 1988. Add: 11 Sunset Dr. N., Whitehorse, Yukon Y1A 4M7, Canada.

STEELMAN, Robert J(ames). American, b. 1914. Westerns/Adventure. Civilian electronics engineer, for U.S. Army Signal Corps, 1939–46, and for U.S. Navy, 1949–69. *Publs:* Stages South, 1956; Apache Wells, 1959; Winter of the Sioux, 1959; Call of the Arctic, 1960; Ambush at Three Rivers, 1964; Cheyenne Vengeance, 1974; Dakota Territory, 1974; The Fox Dancer, 1975; Sun Boy, 1975; Portrait of a Sioux, 1976; Lord Apache, 1977; The Galvanized Reb, 1977; White Medicine Man, 1979; Surgeon to the Sioux, 1979; The Great Yellowstone Steamboat Race, 1980; The Man They Hanged, 1980; The Prairie Baroness, 1981; Border Riders, 1983; Blood and Dust, 1987. Add: 875 Amiford Dr., San Diego, Calif. 92107, U.S.A.

STEFFANSON, Con. *See* **GOULART,** Ron.

STEGENGA, James A. American, b. 1937. International relations/Current affairs. Prof. of Intnl. Relations, Purdue Univ., West Lafayette, Ind., since 1968. Book Review Ed., Armed Forces and Society Mag., since 1977. *Publs:* The United Nations Force in Cyprus, 1968; (ed.) Issues before the 25th General Assembly, 1970; (with A.W. Axline) The Global Community, 1972, 1982; (ed.) Toward a Wiser Colossus, 1972. Add: Dept. of Political Science, Purdue Univ., West Lafayette, Ind. 47907, U.S.A.

STEGNER, Wallace (Earle). American, b. 1909. Novels/Short stories, History, Biography. Instr., Augustana Coll., Rock Island, Ill., 1934; Univ. of Utah, Salt Lake City, 1934–37, and Univ. of Wisconsin, Madison, 1937–39; Faculty Instr., Harvard Univ., Cambridge, Mass., 1939–45; Prof. of English, 1945–69, and Jackson Eli Reynolds Prof. of the Humanities, 1969–71, Stanford Univ., Calif.; Hon. Consultant, Library of Congress, 1973–77. *Publs:* Remembering Laughter, 1937; The Potter's House, 1938; On a Darkling Plain, 1940; Fire and Ice, 1941; Mormon Country, 1942; The Big Rock Candy Mountain, 1943; (co-author) One Nation, 1945; Second Growth, 1947; The Women on the Wall, 1950; The Preacher

and the Slave, 1950, reissued as Joe Hill: A Biographical Novel, 1969; Beyond the Hundredth Meridian, 1954; The City of the Living, 1956; A Shooting Star, 1961; Wolf Willow, 1962; The Gathering of Zion, 1964; All the Little Live Things, 1967; The Sound of Mountain Water, 1969; Angle of Repose, 1971; The Uneasy Chair, 1974; The Spectator Bird, 1976; Recapitulation, 1979; (with Page Stegner) American Places, 1981; One Way to Spell Man, 1982; Crossing to Safety, 1987. Add: 13456 S. Fork Lane, Los Altos Hills, Calif. 94022, U.S.A.

STEIG, William. American, b. 1907. Children's fiction, Poetry, Humor/Satire. Free-lance humorous artist, since 1930. *Publs:* Man about Town (drawings), 1932; About People: A Book of Symbolical Drawings, 1939; The Lonely Ones (drawings), 1942; All Embarrassed (drawings), 1944; Small Fry (New Yorker cartoons), 1944; Persistent Faces (drawings), 1945; Till Death Do Us Part: Some Ballet Notes on Marriage (drawings), 1947; The Agony in the Kindergarten (drawings), 1950; The Rejected Lovers (drawings), 1951; Dreams of Glory and Other Drawings, 1953; The Steig Album (drawings), 1953; Continuous Performance (cartoons), 1963; Roland, the Minstrel Pig, 1968; CDB!, 1968; Sylvester and the Magic Pebble, 1969; The Bad Island, 1969; An Eye for Elephants (verse), 1970; The Bad Speller (reader), 1970; Male/Female (drawings), 1971; Amos and Boris, 1971; Dominic, 1972; The Real Thief, 1973; Farmer Palmer's Wagon Ride, 1974; Abel's Island, 1976; The Amazing Bone, 1976; Caleb and Kate, 1977; Tiffky Doofky, 1978; Gorky Rises, 1980; Doctor De Soto, 1982; Yellow and Pink, 1984; Rotten Island, 1984; Solomon the Rusty Nail, 1985. Add: Box 416, Kent, Conn. 06757, U.S.A.

STEIN, Benjamin. American, b. 1944. Novels, Social Commentary. Full-time writer since 1977. Trial Lawyer with the Federal Trade Commn., Washington, D.C., 1970–73; speechwriter for President Nixon, 1973–74, and President Ford, 1974; Member, Editorial Page Staff, Wall Street Journal, NYC, 1976–76; creative consultant and scriptwriter for Norman Lear, Los Angeles, 1976–77. *Publs:* (with Herbert Stein) On the Brink (novel), 1977; (with William J. McGuiness) Building Technology: Mechanical and Electrical Systems, 1977; Fernwood U.S.A.: An Illustrated Guide from the Folks Who Brought You Mary Hartman, Marty Hartman, 1977; The Croesus Conspiracy (novel), 1978; Dreemz (nonfiction), 1978; (as Ben Stein) The View from Sunset Boulevard: America as Brought to You by the People Who Make Television, 1979; (as Ben Stein; with Herbert Stein) Moneypower: How to Make Inflation Make You Rich, 1980; Bunkhouse Logic: How to Bet on Yourself and Win, 1981; 'Ludes: A Ballad of the Drug and the Dreamer, 1982; Her Only Sin: A Novel of Hollywood, 1986; Hollywood Days, Hollywood Nights: The Diary of a Mad Screenwriter, 1988. Add: St. Martin's Press, 175 Fifth Ave., New York, N.Y. 10010, U.S.A.

STEIN, Bruno. American, b. 1930. Economics, Industrial Relations, Public/Social administration. Prof. of Economics, since 1968 (Asst. Prof., 1959–63; Assoc. Prof., 1963–68), and Dir., Inst. of Labor Relations, since 1974, New York Univ., NYC. *Publs:* (with C.K. Leung) Local Manpower Data Programs: An Analysis, 1968; (ed.) The Economics of Poverty and Public Welfare, 1971; (ed. with S.M. Miller) Incentives and Planning in Social Policy, 1973; Work and Welfare in Britain and the U.S.A., 1976; Social Security and Pensions in Transition: Understanding the American Retirement System, 1980. Add: Dept. of Economics, New York Univ., New York, N.Y. 10003, U.S.A.

STEIN, Herbert. American, b. 1916. Economics. Member, Bd. of Contributors, Wall St. Journal, since 1974; Ed., AEI Economist, since 1977; also, Dir., Reynolds Metals Co. Consultant, Congressional Budget Office, since 1976; Sr. Fellow, American Enterprise Inst., since 1977 (Adjunct Scholar, 1975–77); Member, President's Council of Economic Advisers, Washington, since 1969 (Chmn., 1972–74); Member, President's Blue Ribbon Commn. on Defense Mgmt., since 1985. Economist, National Defense Advisory Commn., 1940–41, War Production Bd., 1941–44, and Office of War Mobilization and Reconversion, 1945; Economist, Commn. for Economic Development, from 1945: Assoc. Dir., Research, 1948–56; Dir. of Research, 1955–56; Vice-Pres. and Chief Economist, 1966–67; Sr. Fellow, Brookings Instn., 1967–69; A Willis Robertson Prof. of Economics, Univ. of Virginia, Charlottesville, 1974–84. Weekly Columnist, "The Economy Today," Scripps-Howard newspapers, 1974–80. *Publs:* U.S. Government Price Policy During the World War, 1938; (with others) Jobs and Markets, 1946; (ed.) Policies to Combat Depression, 1956; The Fiscal Revolution in America, 1969; Economic Planning and the Improvement of Public Policy, 1975; (with W. Leontief) The Economic System in an Age of Discontinuity, 1976; (with Benjamin Stein) On the Brink, 1977; Money Power, 1980; Presidential Economics, 1984, 1988; Washington Bedtime Stories: The Politics of Money and Jobs, 1986.

Add: c/o Free Press, Macmillan, 866 Third Ave., New York, N.Y. 10022, U.S.A.

STEIN, Michael B. Canadian, b. 1940. Politics/Government. Prof. of Political Science, McMaster Univ., Hamilton, since 1977 (Chmn. of Dept., 1980–83). Asst. Prof. of Political Science, Carleton Univ., Ottawa, 1965–68; Assoc. Prof. of Political Science, McGill Univ., Montreal, 1968–77. *Publs:* (ed. with Robert J. Jackson) Issues in Comparative Politics, 1971; The Dynamics of Right-Wing Protest: A Political Analysis of Social Credit in Quebec, 1973. Add: Dept. of Political Science, McMaster Univ., Hamilton, Ont. L8S 4M4, Canada.

STEIN, Peter (Gonville). British, b. 1926. History, Law. Regius Prof. of Civil Law and Fellow, Queens' Coll., Cambridge, since 1968. Fellow, British Academy, since 1974. Prof. of Jurisprudence, Univ. of Aberdeen, 1956–68. *Publs:* Fault in the Formation of Contract in Roman Law and Scots Law, 1958; (ed.) W.W. Buckland's Textbook of Roman Law, 3rd ed. 1963; Regulae Iuris: From Juristic Rules to Legal Maxims, 1966; Roman Law and English Jurisprudence, 1969; (with J. Shand) Legal Values in Western Society, 1974; (co-ed.) Adam Smith's Lectures on Jurisprudence, 1978; Legal Evolution, 1980; (co-ed.) Studies in Justinian's Institutes, 1983; Legal Institutions, 1984; The Character and Influence of the Roman Civil Law: Essays, 1988. Add: Queens' Coll., Cambridge, CB3 9ET, England.

STEIN, Sol. American, b. 1926. Novels/Short stories, Plays/Screenplays. Associated with The Colophon Corp., Scarborough, N.Y. Lectr., Social Studies, City Coll., NYC, 1948–51; Ed., Voice of America, U.S. State Dept., 1951–53; Consultant, Harcourt Brace Jovanovich, NYC, 1958–59; Lectr., Columbia Univ., NYC, 1958–60; Exec. Vice-Pres., Mid-Century Book Soc., 1959–62; Pres., Stein and Day, publishers, New York, 1962–89. *Publs:* The Illegitimist (play), 1953; A Shadow of My Enemy (play), 1957; The Husband, 1969; The Magician, 1971; Living Room, 1974; The Childkeeper, 1975; Other People, 1979; The Resort, 1980; The Touch of Treason, 1985; A Deniable Man, 1989; A Feast for Lawyers (non-fiction), 1989. Add: c/o The Colophon Corp., 43 Linden Circle, Scarborough, N.Y. 10510, U.S.A.

STEINBERG, Erwin R. American, b. 1920. Language, Literature. Thomas S. Baker Prof. of English and Interdisciplinary Studies, Carnegie-Mellon Univ., Pittsburgh, since 1981 (Instr., 1946–49; Asst. Prof., 1949–55; Assoc. Profs., 1955–61; Dean, Margaret Morrison Carnegie Coll., 1960–73; Prof. of English, 1961–80; Dean, Coll. of Humanities and Social Studies, 1965–75; Dir. of Communications Design Center, 1979–81). Coordinator, Project English, U.S. Office of Education, Washington, D.C., 1963–64; Visiting Scholar, Center for Advanced Study in the Behavioral Sciences, Stanford, Calif., 1970–71. *Publs:* (with William M. Schutte) Communication in Business and Industry, 1960, 1983; (ed. with William M. Schutte) Personal Integrity, 1961; (with William M. Schutte) Communication Problems in Business and Industry, 1961, 1983; (ed.) The Rule of Force, 1962; (gen. ed.) Insight, 14 vols., 1968–74; (ed. with Alan Markman) English Then and Now, 1970; (ed. with Lois Josephs) English Education Today, 1970; The Stream of Consciousness and Beyond in Ulysses, 1973; (ed.) The Stream of Consciousness Technique in the Modern Novel, 1979; (ed. with Lee W. Gregg) Cognitive Processes in Writing, 1980; (ed.) La Tecnica del Fluir de la Consciencia en la Novela Moderna, 1982; (ed. with Alan Markman) Exercises in the History of English, 1983; (ed.) Plain Language: Principles and Practice, 1989. Add: Carnegie Mellon Univ., Pittsburgh, Pa. 15213, U.S.A.

STEINBERG, Jonathan. American, b. 1934. History, Translations. Univ. Lectr. in History and Tutor, Trinity Hall, Cambridge, since 1966. *Publs:* (trans.) M. Boveri's Treason in the Twentieth Century, 1961; Yesterday's Deterrent: Tirpitz and the Birth of the German Battle Fleet, 1965; (trans.) F. Heer's Intellectual History of Europe, 1966; Why Switzerland?, 1976; (trans.) P. Arlacchi' Mafia, Peasants and Great Estates: Society in Traditional Calabria, 1983; Silent Mutiny: How the Italians Saved Jews from Their German Allies 1941-43, 1990. Add: Trinity Hall, Cambridge CB2 1TJ, England.

STEINBERG, Leo. American (b. Russian), b. 1920. Art. Prof. of Art History, Univ. of Pennsylvania, Philadelphia, since 1975. Prof. of Art History, Hunter Coll. and Graduate Center, City Univ., NYC, 1961–75; American Academy of Arts and Sciences Fellow, 1978; Fellow, University Coll., London, 1979. *Publs:* Other Criteria: Confrontations with 20th-Century Art, 1972; Michelangelo's Last Paintings, 1975; Borromini's San Carlo alle Quattro Fontane, 1977; The Sexuality of Christ in Renaissance Art and in Modern Oblivion, 1984. Add: c/o Dept. of Art History, Univ. of Pennsylvania, Philadelphia, Pa. 19174, U.S.A.

STEINER, George. American, b. 1929. Novels/Short stories, Literature. Extraordinary Fellow, Churchill Coll., Cambridge, since 1969 (Fellow and Dir. of English Studies, 1961–69); Prof. of English and Comparative Literature, Univ. of Geneva, since 1974. Member, Editorial Staff of The Economist, London, 1952–56; Fellow, Inst. for Advanced Study, Princeton, N.J., 1959–60. *Publs:* Tolstoy or Dostoevsky, 1958; The Death of Tragedy, 1960; Anno Domini, 1964; Language and Silence, 1967; (ed.) Penguin Book of Modern Verse Translation, 1967; Extraterritorial, 1971; In Bluebeard's Castle, 1971; The Sporting Scene (in U.S as Fields of Force: Fischer and Spassky at Reykjavik), 1973; After Babel, 1975; Heidegger, 1978; On Difficulty and Other Essays, 1978; The Portage to San Cristobal of A.H., 1981; Antigones, 1984; George Steiner: A Reader, 1984. Add: Churchill Coll., Cambridge, England.

STEINER, George A. American. Administration/Management, Business/Trade/Industry, Public/Social administration. Harry and Elsa Kunin Prof. of Business and Society, and Prof. of Mgmt. and Public Policy Emeritus, Grad. Sch. of Mgmt., Univ. of California, Los Angeles, since 1956 (Dir., Div. of Research, 1956–71). Asst. in Economics, 1934–37 and Prof. of Economics, 1947–56, Univ. of Illinois, Urbana; Instr. and Asst. Prof. of Finance, Indiana Univ., Bloomington, 1937–42; Asst. Dir., Bureau of Business Research, and Ed., Indiana Business Review, both 1937–39; Dir., Reports and Analysis, Controller Div., War Production Bd., 1942–43; Dir., Requirements Cttee. Staff, and later Dir. of Policy, Defense Production Admin., and Dir. of Policy, Office of Defense Mobilization, Exec. Office of the Pres., all 1951–53; Sr. Economic Advisor, Development Planning, Lockheed Aircraft Corp., Burbank, Calif. 1954–56. Dir., Center for Research and Dialogue on Business in Soc., 1971–80; Pres., National Academy of Mgmt., 1972. *Publs:* The Tax System and Industrial Development, 1938; Indiana State Disbursements, 1938; (with G.W. Starr) Retail Trade Turnover, 1940; (ed. and contrib.) Economics of National Defense, 1941; (ed. and contrib.) Economic Problems of War, 1942; (with D. Novick) Wartime Industrial Statistics, 1950; Government's Role in Economic Life, 1953; National Defense and Southern California 1961-1970, 1961; (ed. and contrib.) Managerial Long-Range Planning, 1963; (with W. Cannon) Multinational Corporate Planning, 1966; (with W.G. Ryan) Industrial Project Management, 1968; Strategic Factors in Business Success, 1969; Top Management Planning, 1969; Business and Society, 1971, 1974; Instructor's Manual for Business and Society, 1971, 1974; Issues in Business and Society, 1972, 1977; Comprehensive Managerial Planning, 1972; Pitfalls in Comprehensive Corporate Planning, 1972; Cases in Business and Society, 1973; Business and Society: Cases and Questions, 1974; (with J. Corson) Measuring Business's Social Performance: The Corporate Social Audit, 1974; (with J.B. Miner) Management Policy and Strategy, 1977, 3rd ed. 1986; Strategic Managerial Planning, 1977; Strategic Planning: What Every Manager Must Know, 1979; (with John F. Steiner) Business, Government, and Society, 1980, 3rd ed. 1988; The New CED, 1983. Add: Grad. Sch. of Business Admin., Univ. of California, Los Angeles, Calif. 90024, U.S.A.

STEINER, Kurt. American, b. 1912. Law, Politics/Government. Prof. of Political Science, Stanford Univ., California, 1962–77, now Emeritus (Assoc. Prof., 1955–62; Assoc. Chmn., Dept. of Political Science, 1959–63; Dir., Stanford in Germany, 1961; Dir., Center for Japanese Studies, Tokyo, 1961–62). Attorney, Vienna, Austria, 1935–38; Dir., Berlitz Schs., Cleveland and Pittsburgh, 1939–43; Prosecuting Attorney, Intnl. Prosecution Section, 1947–48, and Chief, Civil Affairs and Civil Liberties Branch, Legal Section, 1949–51, Supreme Commander for Allied Powers, Tokyo. *Publs:* (ed. and contrib. with T. Smith) City and Village in Japan, 1960; Local Government in Japan, 1965; Politics in Austria, 1972; (ed. and contrib. with S. Flanagan and E. Krauss) Political Opposition and Local Politics in Japan, 1980; (ed.) Modern Austria, 1981; Tradition and Innovation in Contemporary Austria, 1982. Add: 832 Sonoma Terr., Stanford, Calif. 94305, U.S.A.

STEINKRAUS, Warren Edward. American, b. 1922. Philosophy. Prof. of Philosophy, State Univ. Coll. of New York, Oswego, since 1964, Emeritus since 1987; Exchange scholar, State Univ. of New York, since 1976. Literature Ed., Idealistic Studies Journal, since 1974. Prof. of Philosophy and Chmn. of Dept., Union Coll., Barbourville, Ky., 1959–64. *Publs:* (ed. and contrib.) New Studies in Berkeley's Philosophy, 1966; (with G.R. Malkani) A Discussion on the Law of Karma, 1966; (ed. and contrib.) New Studies in Hegel's Philosophy, 1971; Philosophy of Art, 1974, 1984; (ed. with K. Schmitz) Art and Logic in Hegel's Philosophy, 1979; (ed.) Representative Essays of Borden P. Bowne, 1980; (ed. with R.N. Beck) E.S. Brightman: Studies in Personalism, 1988. Add: 89 Sheldon Ave., Oswego, N.Y. 13126, U.S.A.

STEINMETZ, Lawrence Leo. American, b. 1938. Administration/ Management, Business/Trade/Industry, Human relations, Personnel management. Pres., High Yield Mgmt. Inc., since 1969 (Vice Pres., 1968–69). Prof. of Mgmt., Univ. of Colorado, Boulder, 1964–77. *Publs:* Interviewing Skills for Supervisors; Managing the Marginal and Unsatisfactory Performer; (with J.B. Kline and D.P. Stegall) Managing the Small Business; (with R. Johnson and A.D. Allen) Labor Law: Grass Roots Approach to Industrial Peace; (with H.R. Todd, Jr.) First Line Management; The Art and Skill of Delegation; Human Relations; People and Work; Nice Guys Finish Last. Add: 245 Fair Pl., Boulder, Colo. 80302, U.S.A.

STENHOUSE, David. British/New Zealander, b. 1932. Education, Environmental Science/Ecology, Psychology, Zoology. Sr. Lectr. in Psychology, Massey Univ., since 1966. Lectr. in Zoology, Lincoln Coll., Univ. of New Zealand, 1958–59; Lectr. in Zoology and Psychology, Univ. of Queensland, 1960–65. *Publs:* Crisis in Abundance, 1966; (ed. and author) Unstated Assumptions in Education, 1972; The Evolution of Intelligence: A General Theory and Some of Its Implications, 1974; Active Philosophy in Education and Science, 1985. Add: Massey Univ., Palmerston North, New Zealand.

STENT, Gunther S(iegmund). American, b. 1924. Biology, Philosophy. Prof. of Molecular Biology since 1959, Chmn. of Molecular Biology since 1980, and Dir. of the Virus Lab., since 1980, Univ. of California, Berkeley (Asst. Research Biochemist, 1952–56; Assoc. Prof. of Bacteriology, 1956–59). Member, Editorial Bds.: Molecular and General Genetics, 1962–68, Genetics, 1963–68, Journal of Molecular Biology, 1965–68, and Annual Review of Genetics, 1965–69. *Publs:* (ed.) Papers in Bacterial Viruses, 1960, 1966; Molecular Biology of Bacterial Viruses, 1963; (ed. with J. Cairns and J.D. Watson) Phage and the Origin of Molecular Biology, 1967; The Coming of the Golden Age: A View of the End of Progress, 1969; Molecular Genetics, 1971, (with R. Calendar) rev. ed., 1978; (ed.) Function and Formation of Neural Systems, 1977; (ed.) Morality as a Biological Phenomenon, 1978; Paradoxes of Progress, 1979; (ed.) Critical Edition of the Double Helix, by J.D. Watson, 1980; (ed. with K.J. Muller and J.G. Nicholls) Neurobiology of the Leech, 1981; (ed.) Mind from Matter?, by M. Delbrick, 1985. Add: 145 Purdue Ave., Berkeley, Calif. 94708, U.S.A.

STEPANCHEV, Stephen. American, b. 1915. Poetry, Literature. Prof. of English, Queens Coll, City Univ. of New York, Flushing, 1949–85. *Publs:* Three Priests in April, 1956; American Poetry Since 1945: A Critical Survey, 1965; Spring in the Harbor, 1967; A Man Running in the Rain, 1969; The Mad Bomber, 1972; Mining the Darkness, 1975; Medusa and Others, 1975; The Dove in the Acacia, 1977; What I Own, 1978; Descent, 1988. Add: 140-60 Beech Ave., Flushing, N.Y. 11355, U.S.A.

STEPHENS, Alan (Archer). American, b. 1925. Poetry. Member of the English Dept., Univ. of California, Santa Barbara, since 1959: Prof. of English, since 1967. Asst. Prof. of English, Arizona State Univ., Tempe, 1954–58. *Publs:* The Sum: Poems, 1958; (ed.) Selected Poems, by Barnaby Googe, 1961; Between Matter and Principle, 1963; The Heat Lightning, 1967; Tree Meditation and Others, 1970; White River Poems, 1975; In Plain Air: Poems 1958-1980, 1982; Stubble Burning, 1988. Add: 326 Canon Dr., Santa Barbara, Calif. 93105, U.S.A.

STEPHENS, Casey. *See* **WAGNER**, Sharon Blythe.

STEPHENS, Frances. Pseud. for Margaret Bentley; also writes as Kathy Ellis and Faith Alexander. British, b. 1926. Novels/Short stories. *Publs:* Dolly Don't Cry, 1967; Cage a Skylark, 1970; A Tree Full of Birds, 1971; Clover for Tea, 1972; The Way to Paradise, 1974; Wings of the Morning, 1980; River Girl, 1981; (as Kathy Ellis) Where the Wilderness Ends, 1982; (as Faith Alexander) The Shifting Sands, 1985; (as Faith Alexander) Where Wild Winds Blow, 1987; Rainbow Through the Rain, 1988. Add: Green Hedges, 111 Westfield Lane, Wyke, nr. Bradford, W. Yorks., England.

STEPHENS, F(rank) Douglas. Australian, b. 1913. Medicine/Health. Prof. of Surgery and Urology, Northwestern Univ., 1975-84, now Emeritus. Medical Officer, Royal Melbourne and Children's Hosps., 1937–39; Nuffield Research Fellow, Hosp. for Sick Children, Great Ormond St., London, 1947–50; Clinical Surgical Teacher, Univ. of Melbourne, 1950–75; Hon. Consultant Paediatric Surgeon, Royal Women's Hosp., Melbourne, 1953–75; Dir., Surgical Research Unit, Royal Children's Hosp. Research Foundn., Melbourne, 1957–75; Attending Urologist, 1975–80, and Dir. of Surgical Education and Research, 1982-

86, Children's Memorial Hosp., Chicago. *Publs:* Congenital Malformations of Rectum, Anus and Genito-urinary Tracts, 1963; (with E. Durham Smith) Anorectal Malformations in Children, 1971; Congenital Malformations of the Urinary Tract, 1983. Add: Dept. of Urology, Children's Memorial Hosp., 2300 Children's Plaza, Chicago, Ill. 60614, U.S.A.

STEPHENS, Meic. Welsh, b. 1938. Poetry, Literature. Literature Dir., Welsh Arts Council, since 1967. Ed., with R.B. Jones, Writers of Wales series, since 1969. French Master, Ebbw Vale Grammar Sch., 1962–66; Journalist, Western Mail, Cardiff, 1966–67; Ed., Poetry Wales magazine, 1965–73. *Publs:* Triad, 1962; (ed. with J.S. Williams) The Lilting House, 1969; (ed.) Artists in Wales I-III, 1971–77; Exiles All, 1973; (ed.) The Welsh Language Today, 1973; (ed.) A Reader's Guide to Wales, 1973; Linguistic Minorities in Western Europe, 1976; (ed.) Green Horse, 1978; (ed.) The Arts in Wales 1950-75, 1979; (ed.) The Curate of Clyro: Extracts from the Diary of Francis Kilvert, 1983; (ed.) The Oxford Companion to the Literature of Wales, 1986; (ed.) A Book of Wales, 1987; (trans.) The White Stone, 1987; (ed.) A Cardiff Anthology, 1987; (ed.) A Dictionary of Literary Quotations, 1989. Add: 9 Museum Pl., Cardiff CF1 3NX, Wales.

STEPHENS, Robert Oren. American, b. 1928. Literature. Prof. of English, since 1968, and Chmn., 1981–88, Univ. of North Carolina at Greensboro (Asst. Prof., 1961–66; Assoc. Prof., 1966–68). Instr. in English, Univ. of Texas, Austin, 1958–61. *Publs:* Hemingway's Nonfiction: The Public Voice, 1968; Hemingway: The Critical Reception, 1977. Add: Dept. of English, Univ. of North Carolina, Greensboro, N.C. 27412, U.S.A.

STEPHENS, Thomas M. American, b. 1931. Education. Prof., and Assoc. Dean, Coll. of Education, Ohio State Univ., Columbus, since 1970. Owner and Publr., Cedars Press; Ed. and Publr., The Directive Teacher mag.; Assoc. Ed., Behavioral Disorders, Teacher Education in Special Education and Exceptional Child Quarterly; Consulting Ed., Charles E. Merrill, publisher. Admin., Ohio Dept. of Education, 1965–66; Assoc. Prof., Sch. of Education, Univ. of Pittsburgh, 1966–70. Developer, Criterion Referenced Curriculum Series, Charles E. Merrill Inc., 1982. *Publs:* Ohio's Academically Gifted 1960-61, 1961; (with W.B. Barbe) Educating Tomorrow's Leaders, 1961; Ohio's Academically Gifted 1961-62, 1962; A Look at Ohio's Gifted-Status Study, 1962; (ed. with Barbe) Attention to the Gifted a Decade Later, 1962; (ed.) Acceleration and the Gifted, 1963; (ed.) Pathways to Progress, 1964; Orthopedically Handicapped in Ohio Schools, 1964; Using Behavioral Approaches with Delinquent Youth, 1970; Directive Teaching of Children with Learning and Behaviorial Handicaps, 1970; Implementing Behavioral Approaches in Elementary and Secondary Schools, 1974; Teaching Skills to Learning Disabled Children, 1977; Teaching Children Basic Skills, 1978; Social Skills in the Classroom, 1978. Add: 1753 Blue Ash Pl., Columbus, Ohio 43229, U.S.A.

STEPHENS, William Peter. British, b. 1934. History, Theology/ Religion, Translations. Prof. of Church History, Univ. of Aberdeen, since 1986. Asst. Tutor in New Testament, 1958–61, and Holder of Ranmoor Chair of Church History, 1971–73, Hartley Victoria Coll., Manchester; Methodist Chaplain, Univ. of Nottingham, 1961–65; Minister, Methodist Church, Shirley, Croydon, 1967–71; Holder of Randles Chair of Theology, Wesley Coll., Bristol, 1973–80; Fellow, 1980–81, and Tutor in Church History, 1981–86, The Queen's Coll., Birmingham. Bristol City Councillor, 1976–83. *Publs:* (trans.) Luther's Works vol. 41; Church and Ministry, 1966; The Holy Spirit in the Theology of Martin Bucer, 1970; Faith and Love (sermons), 1971; The Holy Spirit, 1974; Christians Conferring, 1978; (with John Todd) Our Churches, 1978; Methodism in Europe, 1981; The Theology of Huldrych Zwingli, 1986. Add: King's Coll., Old Aberdeen AB9 2UB, Scotland.

STEPHENS-HODGE, Lionel (Edmund Howard). British, b. 1914. Poetry, Theology/Religion. Lectr., London Coll. of Divinity, 1956–64; Rector, St. James's, Church of England, Brindle, 1964–74; Member, Church of England Liturgical Commn., 1969–75. *Publs:* A Sense of Direction, 1943; The Collects: An Introduction and Exposition, 1961; New Testament People: Champions of Faith (verse), 1984. Add: 1 Manor Park, Clyst St. Mary, Exeter EX5 3BW, England.

STEPHENSON, Andrew M(ichael). British, b. 1946. Science fiction/ Fantasy. Design Engineer, Plessey Telecommunications Research, Taplow, Bucks., 1969–76. European Rep., Science Fiction Writers of America, 1976–78. *Publs:* Nightwatch, 1977; The Wall of Years, 1979. Lives in High Wycombe, Bucks. Add: c/o A.P. Watt Ltd., 26-28 Bedford Row, London WC1R 4HL, England.

STEPTOE, John (Lewis). American, b. 1950. Children's fiction. *Publs:* Stevie, 1969; Uptown, 1970; Train Ride, 1971; Birthday, 1972; My Special Best Words, 1974; Marcia, 1976; Daddy Is a Monster . . . Sometimes, 1980; Jeffrey Bear Cleans Up His Act, 1983; The Story of Jumping Mouse, 1984; Mufaro's Beautiful Daughters, 1987; Baby Says, 1988. Add: 840 Monroe St., Brooklyn, N.Y. 11221, U.S.A.

STERLING, Bruce. American, b. 1954. Science fiction. *Publs:* Involution Ocean, 1977; The Artificial Kid, 1980; Schismatrix, 1985; (ed.) Mirrorshades, 1986; Islands in the Net, 1988. Add: c/o William Morrow, 105 Madison Ave., New York, N.Y. 10016, U.S.A.

STERLING, Claire. American, b. 1919. International relations/Current affairs. Freelance journalist and author since 1968. Labour Ed., 1949–51, and Foreign Correspondent, 1951–68, The Reporter, NYC. *Publs:* The Masaryk Case, 1969; The Terror Network: The Secret War of International Terrorism, 1981; The Time of the Assasians, 1984 Add: c/o Atlas World Press Review, 230 Park Ave., New York, N.Y. 10017, U.S.A.

STERLING, Maria Sandra. *See* **FLOREN,** Lee.

STERN, Axel. British, b. 1912. Philosophy. Tutor, Smith Coll. (U.S.A.), Geneva, 1946–47; Science and Language Teacher, Frensham, Surrey, 1948, and Villars, Switzerland, 1949; Asst., Moral Philosophy, Univ. of Edinburgh, 1950–54; Asst. Lectr., 1954–55, Lectr., 1955–67, and Sr. Lectr. in Philosophy, 1967–79, Univ. of Hull; Visiting Prof., Tubingen Univ., Germany, 1974–75. *Publs:* Un Poème Méta-Physique en Prose, 1941; Morale de La Liberté, 1944; L'existentialisme contre l'existence, 1944; Le Vrai en Art et en Science, 1946; (ed.) I. Benrubi: Conaissance et Morale, 1947; Metaphysical Reverie, 1956; The Science of Freedom, 1969. Add: The Old Vicarage, 16 Egerton Rd., Monton, Manchester M30 9LR, England.

STERN, Clarence A. American, b. 1913. History, Politics/Government. Assoc. Prof. of History, Univ. of Wisconsin, Oshkosh, since 1965, and Univ. of Wisconsin, Fond du Lac, since 1975. Teacher, Michigan Public Schs., 1934–42 and 1954–55; Asst. Prof., Lawrence Inst. of Technology, Coll. of Engineering, Detroit, Mich., 1946–50; Assoc. Prof. of History and Political Science, Wayne State Coll., Nebr., 1958–65. *Publs:* Republican Heyday: Republicanism through the McKinley Years, 1962, 1969; Resurgent Republicanism: The Handiwork of Hanna, 1963, 1968; Golden Republicanism: The Crusade for Hard Money, 1964, 1970; Protectionist Republicanism: Republican Tariff Policy in the McKinley Period, 1971. Add: 1625 Elmwood Ave., Oshkosh, Wisc. 54901, U.S.A.

STERN, Daniel. American, b. 1928. Novels/Short stories. Vice-Pres. and Creative Dir., Lubard-Southard Inc., NYC, since 1973; Vice-Pres. of Promotion, East Coast, CBS Entertainment, NYC, since 1979. Fellow, Center for the Humanities, Wesleyan Univ., Middletown, Conn., since 1969 (Visiting Prof. of English and Letters, 1976–79). Cellist, Indianapolis Symphony Orchestra, Ind., 1948–49; freelance mag. writer, NYC, 1955–58; former Copywriter, Doner & Peck Advertising Agency, NYC; Sr. Vice-Pres., and Managing Dir., McCann-Erickson Advertising Inc., NYC, 1964–69; Vice-Pres. of Advertising and Publicity Worldwide, Warner Bros., 1969–72; Vice-Pres., and Dir. of Marketing, Longchamps Inc., NYC, 1972–73. *Publs:* The Girl with the Glass Heart, 1953; The Guests of Fame, 1955; Miss America, 1959; Who Shall Live, Who Shall Die, 1963; After the War, 1967; The Suicide Academy, 1968; The Rose Rabbi, 1971; Final Cut, 1975; An Urban Affair, 1980; Twice Told Tales: Stories, 1989. Add: CBS Entertainment Div., CBS, Inc., 51 W. 52nd St., New York, N.Y. 10019, U.S.A.

STERN, Ellen Norman. American, b. 1927. Children's non-fiction, Biography. *Publs:* Embattled Justice: The Story of Louis Dembitz Brandeis, 1971; Dreamer in the Desert: A Portrait of Nelson Glueck, 1980; Elie Wiesel: Witness for Life, 1982. Add: 135 Anbury Lane, Willow Grove, Pa. 19090, U.S.A.

STERN, Fritz. American, b. 1926. History, Politics/Government. Seth Low Prof. of History, Columbia Univ., NYC, since 1967 (Instr. 1946–51; Member of faculty, 1953–63; Prof., 1963–67). Permanent Visiting Prof., Univ. of Konstanz, Germany, since 1967; Member, Bd. of Eds., Foreign Affairs, since 1978. *Publs:* (ed.) The Varieties of History, 1956; The Politics of Cultural Despair, 1961, 1974; (ed.) Geschichte und Geschichtschreibung, 1963; (ed. with L. Krieger) The Responsibility of Power: Historical Essays in Honor of Hajo Holborn, 1967; Bethman Hollweg und der Krieg: die Grenzen der Verantwortung, 1968; The Failure of Illiberalism: Essays on the Political Culture of Modern Germany, 1972;

Gold and Iron: Bismarck, Bleichroeder, and the Building of the German Empire, 1977; Dreams and Delusions: The Drama of German History, 1987. Add: Dept. of History, Columbia Univ., New York, N.Y. 10027, U.S.A.

STERN, Gerald. American, b. 1925. Poetry. Prof. of English, Univ. of Iowa City, since 1982. Consultant in Poetry, Pennsylvania Arts Council, since 1973. Instr., Temple Univ., Philadelphia, 1957–63; Prof., Indiana Univ. of Pennsylvania, 1963–67; Prof., Somerset County Coll., New Jersey, from 1968. *Publs:* The Naming of Beasts and Other Poems, 1973; Rejoicings, 1973; Lucky Life, 1977; The Red Coat, 1981; Paradise Poems, 1984; Rejoicings, 1984; Lovesick, 1987. Add: Creative Writing Prog., Dept. of English, Univ. of Iowa, Iowa City, Iowa 52242, U.S.A.

STERN, James (Andrew). Also translates as Andrew St. James. British, b. 1904. Novels/Short stories, Autobiography/Memoirs/Personal, Translations. Farmer in Rhodesia, 1925–26; Bank Clerk in London and Germany, 1927–29; Asst. Ed., London Mercury, 1929–30. *Publs:* The Heartless Land, 1932; Something Wrong, 1938; (trans. as Andrew St. James) Brazil: Land of the Future, by S. Zweig, 1941; (trans. at Andrew St. James) Amerigo Vespucci, by S. Zweig, 1942; (trans.) The Rise and Fall of the House of Ullstein, by H. Ullstein, 1943; (ed.) Grimm's Fairy Tales, 1944; (trans. as Andrew St. James with E.B. Ashton) The Twins of Nuremberg, by H. Kesten, 1946; The Hidden Damage, 1947; The Man Who Was Loved, 1951; (trans.) Spark of Life, by E.M. Remarque, 1952; (trans. with T. Stern) Selected Prose, by Hugo von Hofmannsthal, 1952; (trans. with T. Stern) Letters to Milena, by F. Kafka, 1953; (trans.) A Woman in Berlin, 1954; (trans. with R. Pick) Casanova's Memoirs, 1955; (trans.) The Foreign Minister, by L. Lania, 1956; (trans. with T. Stern and W.H. Auden) The Caucasian Chalk Circle, by B. Brecht, 1960; (trans. with T. Stern) Description of a Struggle and Other Stories, by F. Kafka, 1960; The Stories of James Stern, 1968; (trans. with E. Duckworth) Letters to Felice Bauer, by F. Kafka, 1972. Add: Hatch Manor, Tisbury, Wilts., England.

STERN, Jay B. American, b. 1929. Education, Social commentary/phenomena, Theology/Religion. Dir., Jewish Education Mgmt. Assocs., since 1982. Educational Dir., Temple Beth El, Rochester, N.Y., 1954–74; Instr. in Hebrew, Colgate-Rochester Divinity Sch., 1967–69, and Univ. of Rochester, N.Y., 1970–74; Pres., Midrasha Coll. of Jewish Studies, Southfield, Mich., 1975–79; Headmaster, Jewish Day Sch. of Greater Washington, 1979–82. *Publs:* Know Your School, 1961; Shalom Yisrael, 1961; Heroes of Modern Jewish Thought, 1966; Pathways Through Jewish History, 1967; Siddur Meforash, 1967; Principal's Principles, 1968; On Teaching History, 1968; (ed.) The Parent and Jewish Education, 1968; Integrated History Instruction, 1969; To Live as a Jew, 1971; (ed.) Three Western Scriptures, 1975; (ed.) A Curriculum for the Afternoon Jewish School, 1977; What's A Nice God Like You Doing in a Place Like This!, 1987; Case Studies in Ten Jewish Schools, 1987. Add: 10802 Cavalier Dr., Silver Spring, Md. 20901, U.S.A.

STERN, Madeleine B. American, b. 1912. History, Biography. Partner, Leona Rostenberg Rare Books, NYC, since 1945. *Publs:* The Life of Margaret Fuller, 1942; Louisa May Alcott, 1950; Purple Passage: The Life of Mrs. Frank Leslie, 1953; Imprints on History: Book Publishers and American Frontiers, 1956; We the Women: Career Firsts of 19th Century America, 1963; So Much in a Lifetime: The Story of Dr. Isabel Barrows, 1964; Queen of Publishers' Row: Mrs. Frank Leslie, 1965; The Pantarch: A Biography of Stephen Pearl Andrews, 1968; Heads and Headlines: The Phrenological Fowlers, 1971; (ed.) Women on the Move, 4 vols., 1972; (ed.) The Victoria Woodhull Reader, 1974; (with L. Rostenberg) Old and Rare: Thirty Years in the Book Business, 1974; (ed.) Louisa's Wonder Book: An Unknown Alcott Juvenile, 1975; (ed.) Behind a Mask: The Unknown Thrillers of Louisa May Alcott, 1975; (ed.) Plots and Counterplots: More Thrillers of Alcott, 1976; (with L. Rostenberg) Between Boards: New Thoughts on Old Books, 1978; Books and Book People in 19th-Century America, 1978; (with L. Rostenberg) Bookman's Quintet: Five Catalogues about Books, 1980; (ed.) Publishers for Mass Entertainment in 19th-Century America, 1980; A Phrenological Dictionary of Nineteenth-Century Americans, 1982; (ed.) Critical Essays on Louisa May Alcott, 1984; Antiquarian Bookselling in the United States: A History from the Origins to the 1940s, 1985; (ed.) A Modern Mephistopheles and Taming a Tartar, by Louisa May Alcott, 1987; (co-ed.) The Selected Letters of Louisa May Alcott, 1987; (ed.) A Double Life: Newly Discovered Thrillers of Louisa May Alcott, 1988; (co-ed.) The Journals of Louisa May Alcott, 1989. Add: 40 E. 88th St., New York, N.Y. 10128, U.S.A.

STERN, Richard G(ustave). American, b. 1928. Novels/Short stories,

Essays. Prof. of English, Univ. of Chicago, since 1965 (joined faculty, 1955). Lektor, Univ. of Heidelberg, 1950–51; Instr., Connecticut Coll., New London, 1951–52; Visiting Lectr., Univ. of Venice, 1962–63. *Publs:* Golk, 1960; Europe; or, Up and Down with Schreiber and Baggish (in U.K. as Europe; or, Up and Down with Baggish and Schreiber), 1961; In Any Case, 1963; Teeth, Dying, and Other Matters, and The Gamesman's Island: A Play, 1964; Stitch, 1965; (ed.) Honey and Wax: Pleasures and Powers of Narrative: An Anthology, 1966, 1968; A Short Novel, An Urban Idyll, Five Stories and Two Trade Notes, 1970; The Books in Fred Hampton's Apartment (essays), 1973; Other Men's Daughters, 1973; Natural Shocks, 1978; Packages, 1980; The Invention of the Real, 1982; A Father's Words, 1986; The Position of the Body, 1987; Noble Rot: Stories 1949-1988, 1989. Add: Dept. of English, Univ. of Chicago, 1050 East 59th St., Chicago, Ill. 60637, U.S.A.

STERN, Richard Martin. American, b. 1915. Novels/Short stories, Mystery/Crime/Suspense. Pres., Mystery Writers of America, 1971. *Publs:* The Bright Road to Fear, 1958; Suspense, 1959; The Search for Tabatha Carr, 1960; These Unlucky Deeds, 1961; High Hazard, 1962; Cry Havoc, 1963; Right Hand, Opposite, 1964; I Hide, We Seek, 1965; The Kessler Legacy, 1967; Merry Go Round, 1969; Brood of Eagles, 1969; Manuscript for Murder, 1970; Murder in the Walls, 1971; You Don't Need an Enemy, 1972; Stanfield Harvest, 1972; Death in the Snow, 1972; The Tower, 1973; Power, 1974; The Will, 1976; Snowbound Six, 1977; Flood, 1979; The Big Bridge, 1982; Wildfire, 1985; Tsunami, 1988; Tangled Murders, 1989; Missing Man, 1990. Add: Rt. 9, Box 55, Santa Fe, N.M. 87501, U.S.A.

STERN, Robert A.M. American, b. 1939. Architecture. Principal, Robert Stern Architects, since 1976; Prof. of Architecture, Columbia Univ., NYC, since 1982 (Lectr., 1970–73; Asst. Prof., 1973–77; Assoc. Prof., 1977–82; Dir., Temple Hoyne Buell Center for American Architecture, 1984–88). Ed., Perspecta, the Yale Architectural Journal, 1965; Partner, Robert Stern and John Hagmann, Architects, 1969–76. *Publs:* New Directions in American Architecture, 1969, 1977; George Howe: Towards a Modern American Architecture, 1975; (with Deborah Nevins) The Architect's Eye, 1979; (co-author) East Hampton's Heritage, 1982; Raymond Hood, 1982; (co-author) New York 1900, 1983; Pride of Place, 1986; (co-author) New York 1930, 1987; Modern Classicism, 1988. Add: 211 W. 61st St., New York, N.Y. 10023, U.S.A.

STERN, Stuart. *See* **RAE,** Hugh C.

STERNBERG, Robert J(effrey). American, b. 1949. Psychology (cognitive science). Prof. of Psychology and Dir. of Graduate Studies in Psychology, Yale Univ., New Haven. *Publs:* Intelligence, Information Processing, and Analogical Reasoning: The Componential Analysis of Human Abilities, 1977; (ed.) Handbook of Human Intelligence, 1982; (ed.) Advances in the Psychology of Human Intelligence, 3 vols., 1982–86; Beyond IQ: A Triarchic Theory of Human Intelligence, 1985. Add: Dept. of Psychology, Yale Univ., Box 11A Yale Station, New Haven, Conn. 06520, U.S.A.

STERNE, Richard S(tephen). American, b. 1921. Sociology. Assoc. Prof. of Urban Studies and Sociology, Univ. of Akron, Ohio, since 1973. Budget Dir., Rhode Island Community Chests Inc., Providence, 1951–55; Research and Budget Dir., Delaware Valley United Fund, Trenton, N.J., 1955–60; Research Dir., Social Service Council of Greater Trenton, N.J., 1960–62; Assoc. Prof. of Sociology, Univ. of Miami, Coral Gables, Fla., and Research Dir., Welfare Planning Council of Dade Co., Miami, Fla., both 1962–68; Dir. of Social Research, Council Social Agencies, Rochester, N.Y., 1968–73. *Publs:* Delinquent Conduct and Broken Homes, 1966; (with J. Phillips and A. Rabushka) The Urban Elderly Poor: Social and Bureaucratic Conflict, 1974; (co-ed.) Public Rule or Ruling Classes, 1978. Add: 4062 Greenwich Rd., Norton, Ohio 44203, U.S.A.

STERNLICHT, Sanford. American, b. 1931. Poetry, History, Literature, Biography. Prof. of Theatre, State Univ. of New York at Oswego, 1972–86, now Emeritus (Instr. of English, 1959–60; Asst. Prof., 1960–62; Prof., 1962–72). Adjunct Prof. of English, Syracuse Univ., N.Y., since 1982. *Publs:* Gull's Way, 1961; Uriah Phillips Levy, 1961; Love in Pompeii, 1967; (with E.M. Jamison) The Black Devil of the Bayous, 1970; John Webster's Imagery and the Webster Canon, 1972; John Masefield, 1978; McKinley's Bulldog: The Battleship Oregon, 1978; C.S. Forester, 1981; (with E.M. Jameson) U.S.F. Constellation: Yankee Racehorse, 1981; (ed.) Selected Short Stories of Padraic Colum, 1985; Padraic Colum, 1985; (ed.) Selected Plays of Padraic Colum, 1986; John Galsworthy, 1987; R.F. Delderfield, 1988; (ed.) Selected Poems of Padraic Colum, 1988. Add: 100 Buckingham Ave., Syracuse, N.Y. 13210, U.S.A.

STEVENS, (John) Austin. British. Novels/Short stories, History. Ed., Mercier Press, Cork, 1968–71. *Publs:* Time and Money, 1959; On the Market, 1960; The Moon Turns Green, 1961; The Antagonists, 1963; The Dispossessed: The German Jewish Refugees in Britain, 1975. Add: c/o Richard Scott Simon Ltd., 32 College Cross, London N1 1PR, England.

STEVENS, Christopher. British, b. 1948. Economics, Politics/Government, Third World problems. Research Fellow, Université Libre de Bruxelles; Research Officer, Overseas Development Inst., London. Tutor, Univ. of Ghana, Accra, 1971–72; Lectr., Lanchester Polytechnic, Coventry, 1973; Economist and Planning Officer, Govt. of Botswana, Gaborone, 1973–75. *Publs:* The Soviet Union and Black Africa, 1976; Food Aid and the Developing World, 1979; (ed.) EEC and the Third World: A Survey 1-6, 6 vols., 1981–87; Nigeria: Economic Prospects to 1985, 1982; The Political Economy of Nigeria, 1984. Add: Overseas Development Inst., Regent's Coll., Inner Circle – Regent's Park, London NW1 4NS, England.

STEVENS, Dan J. *See* **OVERHOLSER,** Wayne D.

STEVENS, James R(ichard). Canadian, b. 1940. Fantasy, History, Mythology/Folklore. *Publs:* Sacred Legends of the Sandy Lake Cree, 1971; (ed.) Recollections of an Assinaboine Chief, 1973; (ed.) Great Leader of the Ojibway, 1973; Paddy Wilson's Gold Fever, 1976; (ed.) Phillip Neault: Pioneer, 1977; (ed.) Legends from the Forest, 1985; Killing the Shamen, 1985. Add: R.R. 13, Thunder Bay, Ont. P7B 5E4, Canada.

STEVENS, Joan. New Zealander, b. 1908. Literature. Sr. Lectr.-Prof., Victoria Univ. of Wellington, 1947–73, now retired. *Publs:* The New Zealand Novel 1860-1960, 1961, rev. ed., 1860-1965, 1966; (ed.) New Zealand Short Stories, 1968; (ed.) Mary Taylor, Friend of Charlotte Brontë Letters from New Zealand and Elsewhere, 1972; (ed.) The London Journal of Edward Jerningham Wakefield, 1972. Add: 27 Raukawa St., Otaki, New Zealand.

STEVENS, John. *See* **TUBB,** E.C.

STEVENS, John (Edgar). British, b. 1921. Literature, Music. Fellow, since 1950, and President, since 1983, Magdalene Coll., Cambridge, and Prof. of Medieval and Renaissance English, Cambridge Univ., since 1978, Emeritus since 1988 (Lectr. in English, 1954–74, and Reader in English and Musical History, 1974–78). *Publs:* Medieval Carols, 1952; Music and Poetry in the Early Tudor Court, 1961; Music at the Court of Henry VIII, 1962; (with Richard Axton) Medieval French Plays, 1971; Medieval Romance, 1973; Early Tudor Songs and Carols, 1975; Words and Music in the Middle Ages, 1986. Add: 4-5 Bell's Court, Cambridge, England.

STEVENS, Mark. American, b. 1951. Novels/Short stories, Art. Freelance writer since 1975; Art Critic, Newsweek, NYC, since 1977, and the New Republic, Washington, D.C., since 1986. *Publs:* Richard Diebenkorn: Etchings and Dryprints 1949-1980, 1981; Summer in the City, 1984. Add: c/o Kathy P. Robbins, The Robbins Office, 2 Dag Hammarskjold Plaza, 866 Second Ave., New York, N.Y. 10017, U.S.A.

STEVENS, Peter (Stanley). Canadian, b. 1927. Poetry. Assoc. Prof. to Prof. of English, Univ. of Windsor, Ont., since 1969. Chmn. of The English Dept., Hillfield Coll., Hamilton, Ont., 1957–64; Lectr., Extension Div., McMaster Univ., 1961–64; Asst. Prof. of English, Univ. of Saskatchewan, Saskatoon, 1964–69. *Publs:* Plain Geometry, 1968; Nothing But Spoons, 1969; (ed.) The McGill Movement: A.J.M. Smith, F.R. Scott, and Leo Kennedy, 1969; A Few Myths, 1970; (ed.) Forum: Canadian Life and Letters 1920-1970: Selections from "The Canadian Forum", 1972; Breadcrusts and Glass, 1972; Family Feelings and Other Poems, 1974; Momentary Stay, 1974; And the Dying Sky Like Blood, 1974; The Bogman Pavese Tactics, 1977; Modern Canadian Poetry, 1978; Coming Back, 1981; Revenge of the Mistresses, 1981; Out of the Willow Trees, 1986. Add: 2055 Richmond St., Windsor, Ont. N8Y 1L3, Canada.

STEVENS, Richard P. American, b. 1931. History, International relations/Current affairs, Politics/Government. Asst. Dir., Kuwait Univ. Office, Washington, D.C., since 1979 (Visiting Prof. and Academic Adviser, Univ. of Kuwait, 1977–79); Adjunct Prof., Georgetown Univ., Washington, D.C., since 1981. Prof. of History and Govt., King's Coll., Wilkes-Barre, Pa., 1959–61; Chmn., Dept. of Political Science, Pius XII Univ. Coll., Lesotho, Basutoland, 1962–63; Prof. of Political Science, Lincoln Univ., Pa., 1964–74, and Univ. of Khartoum, Sudan, 1974–76

Publs: American Zionism and U.S. Foreign Policy 1942-1947, 1962; Lesotho, Botswana, and Swaziland: The Former High Commission Territories in Southern Africa, 1967; Zionism and Palestine Before the Mandate: A Phase of Western Imperialism, 1972; Smuts and Weizmann: A Study in South African-Zionist Cooperation, 1974; Historical Dictionary of Botswana, 1975; Israel and South Africa, 1977. Add: 7739 Rocton Ct., Chevy Chase, Md. 20015, U.S.A.

STEVENS, Robert Tyler. *See* **STAPLES,** Reginald.

STEVENS, William Christopher. *See* **ALLEN,** Steve.

STEVENSON, Anne. American/British, b. 1933. Poetry, Literature, Biography. Sch. teacher, Lillesden Sch., Kent, 1955–56, Westminster Sch., Ga., 1959–60, and Cambridge Sch., Mass., 1961–62; Advertising Mgr., A. & C. Black, publrs., London, 1956–57; Tutor, Dept. of Extra-Mural Studies, Univ. of Glasgow, 1970–73; Counsellor, Open Univ., Paisley, Renfrew, 1972–73; Writer in Residence, Univ. of Dundee, 1973–75; Fellow, Lady Margaret Hall, Oxford, 1975–77; Writing Fellow, Bulmershe Coll., Reading, 1978; Co-Proprietor, Poetry Bookshop, Hay-on-Wye, 1978–81; Co-ed., Other Poetry mag., Oxford, 1978–84; Writer-in-Residence, Univ. of Edinburgh, 1987–89. *Publs:* Living in America, 1965; Elizabeth Bishop, 1966; Reversals, 1969; Correspondence: A Family History in Letters, 1974; Travelling Behind Glass: Selected Poems, 1963-1973, 1975; Enough of Green, 1977; Minute by Glass Minute, 1982; Making Poetry, 1983; A Legacy, 1983; Black Grate Poems, 1984; The Fiction-Makers, 1985; Selected Poems, 1987; Bitter Fame: A Life of Sylvia Plath, 1989; The Other House: New Poems, 1990. Add: 30 Logan St., Langley Park, Durham DH7 9YN, England.

STEVENSON, Anne. American. Mystery/Crime/Suspense, Historical/Romance/Gothic. *Publs:* Ralph Dacre, 1967; Flash of Splendour, 1968; A Relative Stranger, 1970; A Game of Statues, 1972; The French Inheritance, 1974; Coil of Serpents, 1977; Mask of Treason, 1979; Turkish Rondo, 1981. Add: c/o William Morrow Inc., 105 Madison Ave., New York, N.Y. 10016, U.S.A.

STEVENSON, David. British, b. 1942. History. Reader, Dept. of History, and Dir. of the Centre for Scottish Studies, Univ. of Aberdeen. *Publs:* The Scottish Revolution, 1637-44: The Triumph of the Covenanters, 1973; Revolution and Counter-Revolution in Scotland 1644-51, 1977; Alasdair Mac Colla and the Highland Problem in the Seventeenth Century, 1980; Scottish Covenanters and Irish Confederates, 1981; The Government of Scotland under the Covenanters 1638-51, 1982; (with Wendy B. Stevenson) Scottish Texts and Calendars: An Analytical Guide to Serial Publications, 1987; The Origins of Freemasonry, 1988; The First Freemasons: The Early Scottish Lodges and Their Members, 1988. Add: Dept. of History, Univ. of Aberdeen, Aberdeen AB9 2UB, Scotland.

STEVENSON, Dwight Eshelman. American, b. 1906. Archaeology/Antiquities, History, Theology/Religion. Prof. of Religion and Philosophy, Bethany Coll., W. Va., 1933–47; Prof. of Homiletics, 1947–74, and Dean, 1969–74, Lexington Theological Seminary, Ky.; Coordinator, Theological Education Assn. of Mid-America (TEAM-A), 1974–81. *Publs:* Faiths that Compete for My Loyalty, 1946; Voice of the Golden Oracle, 1946; (co-author) Home to Bethphage, 1948; Strong Son of God, 1949; Beginning at Jerusalem, 1950, 1960; The Church After Paul, 1951, 1955; Faith Takes a Name, 1954; The Fourth Witness, 1954, 1961; Preaching on the Books of the New Testament, 1956; (co-author) Reaching People from the Pulpit, 1958; Your Face in This Mirror, 1959; Preaching on the Books of the Old Testament, 1961; The Church: What and Why, 1962; On Holy Ground, 1963; Lexington Theological Seminary 1865-1965, 1964; The False Prophet, 1965; In the Biblical Preacher's Workshop, 1967; A Way in the Wilderness, 1968; Disciple Preaching in the First Generation, 1969; Monday's God, 1976. Add: 1600 Texas St. #407, Fort Worth, Tex. 76102, U.S.A.

STEVENSON, Elizabeth. American, b. 1919. History, Literature, Biography. Candler Prof. Emeritus, Graduate Inst. of the Liberal Arts, Emory Univ., Atlanta (Asst. to Dean of Emory Coll., 1960–74; Research Assoc., Asst. Prof., to Prof., from 1974). Library Asst. Atlanta Public Library, Ga., 1948–56. *Publs:* The Crooked Corridor: A Study of Henry James, 1949; Henry Adams, 1955 (Bancroft Prize); (ed.) A Henry Adams Reader, 1958; Lafcadio Hearn, 1961; Babbitts and Bohemians: The American 1920s, 1967; Park Maker: A Life of Frederick Law Olmsted, 1977. Add: 532 Daniel Ave., Decatur, Ga. 30032, U.S.A.

STEVENSON, Florence. Also writes as Zandra Colt, Lucia Curzon, Zabrina Faire, Ellen Fitzgerald, and Pamela Frazier. American. His-

torical/Romance/Gothic, Children's fiction. Drama Columnist, Mirror newspaper, Los Angeles, 1949–50; Editorial Asst., Mademoiselle mag., NYC, 1956–57; Press Asst., James D. Proctor, 1957–58; Asst. Ed., 1959–60, and Contrib. Ed., 1960–70, Opera News, NYC; Columnist, "Opera Boutique", Metropolitan Opera Program, NYC; Columnist, "Things of Beauty", Lincoln Center Program, NYC; Assoc. Ed., FM Guide, NYC, 1964–65; Contrib. Ed., Weight Watchers, 1968–75, and New Ingenue, 1974–75, both NYC. *Publs:* The Story of Aida, Based on the Opera by Guiseppe Verdi (juvenile), 1965; Ophelia, 1968; Feast of Eggshells, 1970; The Curse of the Concullens, 1970; The Witching Hour, 1971; Where Satan Dwells, 1971; (with Patricia Hagan Murray) Bianca, 1973; Kilmeny in the Dark Wood, 1973; Altar of Evil, 1973; The Mistress of Devil's Manor, 1973; The Sorcerer of the Castle, 1974; Dark Odyssey, 1974; The Ides of November, 1975; A Shadow on the House, 1975; Witch's Crossing, 1975; The Silent Watcher, 1975; A Darkness on the Stairs, 1976; The House at Luxor, 1976; Dark Encounter, 1977; The Horror from the Tombs, 1977; (with Sara Halbert) Call Me Counselor (non-fiction), 1977; Julie, 1978; The Golden Galatea, 1979; The Moonlight Variations, 1981; The Household, 1988; as Zabrina Faire—Lady Blue, 1979; The Midnight Match, 1979; The Romany Rebel, 1979; Enchanting Jenny, 1979; Wicked Cousin, 1980; Athena's Airs, 1980; Bold Pursuit, 1980; Pretender to Love, 1981; Pretty Kitty, 1981; Tiffany's True Love, 1981; as Lucia Curzon—The Chadbourne Luck, 1981; Adverse Alliance, 1981; The Mourning Bride, 1982; Queen of Hearts, 1982; The Dashing Guardian, 1983; as Zandra Colt—The Cactus Rose, 1982; The Splendid Savage, 1983; as Ellen Fitzgerald—A Novel Alliance, 1984; Lord Caliban, 1985; The Irish Heiress, 1985; Rogue's Bride, 1985; The Dangerous Dr. Langhorne, 1985; The Forgotten Marriage, 1986; Lessons in Love, 1986; The Heirs of Bellair, 1986; Venetian Masquerade, 1987; A Streak of Luck, 1987; Romany Summer, 1988; as Pamela Frazier—The Virtuous Mistress, 1988. Add: 227 E. 57th St., New York, N.Y. 10022, U.S.A.

STEVENSON, Ian (Pretyman). American, b. 1918. Psychiatry, Paranormal phenomena. Carlson Prof. of Psychiatry, Univ. of Virginia, Charlottesville (joined faculty, 1957; former Chmn., Dept. of Psychiatry, Sch. of Medicine). *Publs:* The Diagnostic Interview, 1960, 1970; Twenty Cases Suggestive of Reincarnation, 1966, 1974; The Psychiatric Examination, 1969; Telepathic Impressions, 1970; Xenoglossy, 1974; Cases of Reincarnation Type: vol. I, Ten Cases in India, 1975, vol. II, Ten Cases in Sri Lanka, 1977, vol. III, Twelve Cases in Lebanon and Turkey, 1980, and vol. IV, Twelve Cases in Thailand and Burma, 1983; Unlearned Language: New Studies in Xenoglossy, 1984; Children Who Remember Previous Lives, 1987. Add: Box 152, Div. of Personality Studies, Univ. of Virginia Health Sciences Center, Charlottesville, Va. 22908, U.S.A.

STEVENSON, James. American, b. 1929. Novels, Children's fiction. Artist and writer for The New Yorker mag. since 1956. *Publs:* children's fiction—Walker, The Witch, and the Striped Flying Saucer, 1969; The Bear Who Had No Place to Go, 1972; Here Comes Herb's Hurricane!, 1973; Could be Worse!, 1977; Wilfred the Rat, 1977; (with Edwina Stevenson) Help! Yelled Maxwell, 1978; The Sea View Hotel, 1978; Winston, Newton, Elton, and Ed, 1978; The Worst Person in the World, 1978; Fast Friends: Two Stories, 1979; Monty, 1979; Clams Can't Sing, 1980; Howard, 1980; That Terrible Halloween Night, 1980; The Night after Christmas, 1981; The Wish Card Ran Out!, 1981; Oliver, Clarence, and Violet, 1982; We Can't Sleep, 1982; Barbara's Birthday, 1983; Grandpa's Great City Tour, 1983; The Great Big Especially Beautiful Easter Egg, 1983; What's under My Bed!, 1983; Worse Than Willy!, 1984; Yuck!, 1984; Are We Almost There?, 1985; Emma, 1985; That Dreadful Day, 1985; Fried Feathers for Thanksgiving, 1986; No Friends, 1986; There's Nothing to Do!, 1986; When I Was Nine, 1986; Higher on the Door, 1987; Happy Valentine's Day, Emma!, 1987; No Need for Monty, 1987; Will you Please Feed Our Cat?, 1987; The Supreme Souvenir Factory, 1988; We Hate Rain!, 1988; The Worst Person in the World at Crab Beach, 1988; Oh No, It's Waylon's Birthday!, 1989; for adults—Do Yourself a Favor, Kid (novel), 1962; The Summer Houses (novel), 1963; Sorry, Lady—This Beach Is Private! (cartoons), 1963; Sometimes, But Not Always (novel), 1967; Something Marvelous Is About to Happen, 1971; Cool Jack and the Beanstalk (comic strip novel), 1976; Let's Boogie! (cartoons), 1978; Uptown Loca, Downtown Express, 1983. Add: c/o Liz Darhansoff, 1220 Park Ave., New York, N.Y. 10128, U.S.A.

STEVENSON, John P. *See* **GRIERSON,** Edward.

STEVENSON, William (Henri). Canadian, b. 1924. Novels/Short stories, Children's fiction, Politics/Government, Travel/Exploration/Adventure. *Publs:* The Yellow Wind: An Excursion in and Around Red China, 1959; After Nehru, What?, 1961; Canada and the World, 1962; Birds' Nests in Their Beards (travel in Malaysia), 1964; The Bushbabies (fiction), 1965; Strike Zion!, 1967 (in U.K. as Israeli Victory); Zanek! A Chronicle of the Israeli Air Force, 1971; The Borman Brotherhood, 1973; A Man Called Intrepid: The Secret War, 1976; The Ghosts of Africa (novel), 1980; Intrepid's Last Case, 1984; Eclipse, 1986; Booby Trap, 1987. Add: c/o Phil Gitlin, 7 W. 51st St., New York, N.Y. 10019, U.S.A.

STEWART OF FULHAM, Lord; Michael Stewart. British, b. 1906. Politics/Government, Autobiography/Memoirs/Personal. Labour Member of Parliament (U.K.) for East Fulham, 1945–55, and for Fulham, 1955–79; Under-Secty. of State for War, 1947–51; Secty. of State for Education and Science, 1964–65, for Foreign Affairs, 1965–66, and for Foreign and Commonwealth Affairs, 1968–70; First Secty. of State, 1966–68. *Publs:* The British Approach to Politics, 1938, 1965; Modern Forms of Government, 1959, 1961; Life and Labour (autobiography), 1980. Add: 11 Felden St., London SW6, England.

STEWART, A(gnes) C(harlotte). British. Novels/Short stories, Children's fiction. *Publs:* The Boat in the Reeds, 1960; Falcon's Crag, 1969; The Quarry Line Mystery, 1971; Elizabeth's Tower, 1972; Dark Dove, 1974; Ossian House, 1974; Beyond the Boundary, 1976; Silas and Con, 1977; Brother Raimon Returns, 1978; Biddy Grant of Craigengill, 1979; Wandering Star (for adults), 1981. Add: Knowetop, Corsock, Castle Douglas, Kirdcudbrightshire DG7 3EB, Scotland.

STEWART, Ann Harleman. American. Linguistics, Literature. Visiting Scholar, Program in American Civilization, Brown Univ., Providence, since 1986. Asst. Prof. of English, Rutgers Univ., New Brunswick, N.J., 1973–74; Asst. Prof. of English, 1974–79, and Assoc. Prof. of English, 1979–84, Univ. of Washington, Seattle; Visiting Assoc. Prof. and Research Affiliate, Writing Program, Massachusetts Inst. of Technology, Cambridge, 1984–86. Chmn., Exec. Cttee. on General Linguistics, Modern Language Assn., 1983–87. *Publs:* Graphic Representation of Models in Linguistic Theory, 1976; (with Bruce A. Rosenberg) Ian Fleming: A Critical Biography, 1989. Add: 55 Summit Ave., Providence, R.I. 02906, U.S.A.

STEWART, Daniel Kenneth. American, b. 1925. Advertising/Public relations, Writing, Communications. Prof. of Communication Studies, Northern Illinois Univ., DeKalb, since 1970. Dir., Basic Science Unit, Campbell-Ewald Co., Detroit, Mich., 1967–69; Ed.-in-Chief, Journal of Advertising, 1971–75. *Publs:* The Psychology of Communication, 1969; Advertising and Consumer Behavior, 1981. Add: Dept. of Communication Studies, Northern Illinois Univ., DeKalb, Ill. 60115, U.S.A.

STEWART, David. *See* POLITELLA, Dario.

STEWART, Donald Charles. American, b. 1930. Writing/Journalism. Prof. of English, Kansas State Univ., since 1981 (Asst. Prof., 1968–75; Assoc. Prof., 1975–81). Ed., Kansas English, 1971–79; Asst. Chmn., 1981, Assoc. Chmn., 1982, and Chmn., 1983, Conference on Coll., Composition and Communication. *Publs:* The Authentic Voice, 1972; The Versatile Writer, 1986; (with Paul Bryant and Patricia Stewart) The Eclectic Reader, 1988; My Yellowstone Years, 1989. Add: Dept. of English, Kansas State Univ., Manhattan, Kans. 66506, U.S.A.

STEWART, Donald H(enderson). American, b. 1911. History, Biography. Distinguished Teaching Prof. Emeritus of American History, State Univ. of New York at Cortland, since 1980 (Assoc. Prof., 1956–57; Prof., 1957–75; Distinguished Teaching Prof., 1975–80). Assoc. Prof. of History, Union Coll., Barbourville, Ky., 1940–46; with U.S. Army, 1942–46, and U.S. Army Reserve, 1948 until retirement with rank of Lt. Col. in 1966; Asst. Prof., 1947–51, and Assoc. Prof., 1951–56, Drake Univ., Des Moines, Iowa. *Publs:* (with Ralph A. Brown) A Student Guide to the American Story, 1956; (with others) Concise Dictionary of American Biography, 1964; The Opposition Press of the Federalist Period, 1969; (with others) McGraw-Hill Encyclopedia of World Biography, 1973. Add: 13 Warren St., Cortland, N.Y. 13045, U.S.A.

STEWART, Fred M(ustard). American, b. 1936. Novels/Short stories. *Publs:* The Mephisto Waltz, 1969; The Methuselah Enzyme, 1970; Lady Darlington, 1971; The Mannings, 1973; Star Child, 1974; Six Weeks, 1976; Rage Against Heaven, 1978; Century, 1981; Ellis Island, 1983; The Titan, 1985; Lady Darlington, 1985. Add: c/o William Morris Agency, 1350 Ave. of the Americas, New York, N.Y. 10019, U.S.A.

STEWART, Harold (Frederick). Australian, b. 1916. Poetry, Theology/Religion, Essays, Translations. *Publs:* Phoenix Wings, 1948; Orpheus and Other Poems, 1956; (trans.) A Net of Fireflies, 1960; (trans.) A Chime of Windbells, 1969; The Exiled Immortal, 1980; (co-trans.) Tan-

nisho, 1980; By the Old Walls of Kyoto, 1981. Add: 501 Keifuku Daini Manshon, Shugakuin, Sakyo-ku, Kyoto 606, Japan.

STEWART, James Stuart. British, b. 1896. Theology/Religion. Prof. Emeritus of New Testament Language, Literature and Theology, Univ. of Edinburgh, since 1966 (faculty member since 1947). Minister of Religion, since 1924; Extra Chaplain to Her Majesty the Queen in Scotland, since 1966 (Chaplain, 1952–66). Minister, Auchterarder, Perthshire, 1924–28, Beechgrove, Aberdeen, 1928–35, and North Morningside, Edinburgh, 1935–46. *Publs:* (ed. with H.R. Mackintosh) Schleiermacher's The Christian Faith, 1928; The Life and Teaching of Jesus Christ, 1932; A Man in Christ: Theology of St. Paul, 1935; The Gates of New Life, 1937; The Strong Name, 1941; Heralds of God, 1945; A Faith to Proclaim, 1953; Thine is the Kingdom, 1956; The Wind of the Spirit, 1968; River of Life, 1972; King for Ever, 1974. Add: St. Raphael's Home, 6 Blackford Ave, Edinburgh EH9 2LB, Scotland.

STEWART, J(ohn) I(nnes) M(ackintosh). Also writes as Michael Innes. British, b. 1906. Novels/Short stories, Mystery/Crime/Suspense, Literature. Lectr. in English, Univ. of Leeds, 1930–35; Jury Prof. of English, Univ. of Adelaide, 1935–45; Lectr., Queen's Univ. of Belfast, 1946–48; Student of Christ Church, 1949–73, and Reader in English Literature, 1969–73, Oxford Univ. *Publs:* as J.I.M. Stewart—(ed.) Montaigne's Essays: John Florio's Translation, 1931; Educating the Emotions, 1944; Character and Motive in Shakespeare, 1949; Mark Lambert's Supper, 1954; A Use of Riches, 1957; The Man Who Wrote Detective Stories, and Other Stories, 1959; The Man Who Won the Pools, 1961; The Last Tresilians, 1963; Eight Modern Writers, 1963; An Acre of Grass, 1965; Rudyard Kipling, 1966; The Aylwins, 1966; Vanderlyn's Kingdom, 1967; Joseph Conrad, 1968; Cucumber Sandwiches, 1969; Avery's Mission, 1971; Thomas Hardy, 1971; Palace of Art, 1972; The Gaudy, 1974; Young Pattullo, 1975; A Memorial Service, 1976; The Madonna of the Astrolabe, 1977; Full Term, 1978; Our England Is a Garden, 1979; Andrew and Tobias, 1980; The Bridge at Arta, 1981; A Villa in France, 1982; My Aunt Christina and Other Stories, 1983; An Open Prison, 1984; The Naylors, 1985; Parlour 4 and Other Stories, 1986; as Michael Innes—Death at the President's Lodging (in U.S. as Seven Suspects), 1937; Hamlet, Revenge!, 1937; Lament for a Maker, 1938; Stop Press (in U.S. as The Spider Strikes), 1939; The Secret Vanguard, 1940; There Came Both Mist and Snow (in U.S. as A Comedy of Terrors), 1940; Appleby on Ararat, 1941; The Daffodil Affair, 1942; The Weight of the Evidence, 1944; Appleby's End, 1945; From London Far (in U.S. as Unsuspected Chasm), 1946; What Happened at Hazelwood, 1946; Night of Errors, 1947; The Journeying Boy (in U.S. as The Case of the Journeying Boy), 1949; (with Rayner Heppenstall) Three Tales of Hamlet, 1950; Operation Pax (in U.S. as Paper Thunderbolt), 1951; Private View (in U.S. as One Man Show), 1952; Christmas at Candleshoe, 1953; Appleby Talking (in U.S. as Dead Man's Shoes), 1954; The Man from the Sea, 1955; Old Hall, New Hall (in U.S. as A Question of Queens), 1956; Appleby Talks Again, 1956; Appleby Plays Chicken (in U.S. as Death on a Quiet Day), 1957; The Long Farewell, 1958; Hare Sitting Up, 1959; The New Sonia Wayward (in U.S. as The Case of Sonia Wayward), 1960; A Connoisseur's Case (in U.S. as The Crabtree Affair), 1962; Money from Home, 1966; The Bloody Wood, 1966; A Change of Heir, 1966; Death by Water, 1968; Appleby at Allington, 1968; A Family Affair (in U.S. as A Picture of Guilt), 1969; Death at the Chase, 1970; An Awkward Lie, 1971; The Open House, 1972; Appleby's Other Story, 1973; The Mysterious Commission, 1974; The Appleby File, 1975; The Gay Phoenix, 1976; Honeybath's Haven, 1977; The Ampersand Papers, 1978; Going It Alone, 1979; Lord Mullion's Secret, 1981; Sheiks and Adders, 1982; Appleby and Honeybath, 1983; Carson's Conspiracy, 1984; Appleby and the Ospreys, 1986. Add: Lower Park House, Occupation Rd., Lindley, Huddersfield HD3 3EE, England.

STEWART, Judith. *See* POLLEY, Judith Anne.

STEWART, (Lady) Mary (Florence Elinor). British, b. 1916. Mystery/Crime/Suspense, Historical/Romance/Gothic, Children's fiction. Lectr. in English, Durham Univ., 1941-45. *Publs:* Madam, Will You Talk?, 1955; Wildfire at Midnight, 1956; Thunder on the Right, 1957; Nine Coaches Waiting, 1958; My Brother Michael, 1959; The Ivy Tree, 1961; The Moon-Spinners, 1962; This Rough Magic, 1964; Airs above the Ground, 1965; The Gabriel Hounds, 1967; The Wind off the Small Isles, 1968; The Crystal Cave, 1970; The Little Broomstick (for children), 1971; The Hollow Hills, 1973; Ludo and the Star Horse (for children), 1975; Touch Not the Cat, 1976; The Last Enchantment, 1979; A Walk in Wolf Wood (for children), 1980; The Wicked Day, 1983; Thornyhold, 1988. Add: c/o Hodder & Stoughton Ltd., Mill Rd., Dunton Green, Sevenoaks, Kent TN13 2YA, England.

STEWART, Michael. *See* **STEWART OF FULHAM,** Lord.

STEWART, Michael (James). British, b. 1933. Economics. Reader in Political Economy, University Coll., London, since 1969. Sr. Economic Advisor, Cabinet Office, London, 1967; Economic Advisor to Kenya Treasury, 1967-69; Special Economic Advisor to Foreign and Commonwealth Secty., 1977-78. *Publs:* Keynes and After, 1967; The Jekyll and Hyde Years: Politics and Economic Policy since 1964, 1977; The Age of Interdependence: Economic Policy in a Shrinking World, 1983; (with Peter Jay) Apocalypse 2000: Economic Breakdown and the Suicide of Democracy 1989-2000, 1987. Add: 79 South Hill Park, London NW3 2SS, England.

STEWART, Rosemary. British. Administration/Management. Fellow in Organizational Behaviour, Templeton Coll.: Oxford Centre for Mgmt. Studies, since 1966. Fellow in Mgmt. Studies, London Sch. of Economics, 1964-66; Dir., Acton Soc. Trust, 1956-61. *Publs:* (co-author) Management Succession, 1956; (with R. Lewis) The Boss: The Life and Times of the British Businessman, 1958; The Reality of Management, 1963, 1986; Managers and Their Jobs, 1967, 1987; The Reality of Organizations, 1970, 1986; How Computers Affect Management, 1971; Contrasts in Management, 1976; (with others) The District Administrator in the National Health Service, 1980; Choices for the Manager, 1982; Leading in the NHD: A Practical Guide, 1989. Add: Templeton Coll., Oxford Centre for Mgmt. Studies, Kennington Rd., Kennington, Oxford OX1 5NY, England.

STEWART, William Alexander Campbell. British, b. 1915. Education. Sr. English Master, Friends Sch., Saffron Walden, Essex, 1938-43, and Abbotsholme Sch., Rocester, 1943-44; Asst. Lectr., and Lectr. in Education, Univ. Coll. of Nottingham, 1944-47; Lectr. in Education, Univ. of Wales, 1947-50; Prof. of Education, 1950-67, and Vice-Chancellor, 1967-79, Univ. of Keele; Visiting Professorial Fellow, Univ. of Sussex, Brighton, 1979-85. *Publs:* Quakers Education, 1953; (ed. with J. Eros) Systematic Sociology by K. Mannheim, 1957; (with K. Mannheim) An Introduction to the Sociology of Education, 1962; (with P. McCann) The Educational Innovators vol. I, 1750-1880, 1967, (sole author) vol. II, 1881-1967, 1968; Progressives and Radicals in English Education 1750-1970, 1972; Higher Education in Postwar Britain, 1989. Add: Flat 4, 74 Westgate, Chichester, West Sussex P019 3HH, England.

STIERLIN, Helm. American/German, b. 1926. Psychiatry. Acting Chief, Family Studies Section, Adult Psychiatry Branch, National Inst. of Mental Health, Bethesda, Md., since 1969 (Visiting Scientist, 1965; Head of Psychotherapy Unit, Family Studies Section, 1966-71). Asst. Prof. of Psychiatry, Johns Hopkins Univ., Baltimore, since 1969; Faculty member, 1957-62, and since 1971, Washington Sch. of Psychiatry, and Washington Psychoanalytic Inst., since 1972. Staff member, Chestnut Lodge, Rockville, Md., 1957-62; Sr. Supervising Analyst, Sanatorium Bellevue, Kreuzlingen, Switzerland, 1963-64. *Publs:* Der gewalttaetige Patient: Eine Untersuchung ueber die von Geisteskranken an Aertzter und Pflegepersonen veruebten Angriffe, 1956; Conflict and Reconciliation: A Study in Human Relations and Schizophrenia, 1969; Das Tun der Einen ist das Tun des Anderen, 1917, 1972; Separating Parents and Adolescents: A Perspective on Running Away, Schizophrenia, and Waywardness, 1974; Hitler: A Family Perspective, 1977; Psychoanalysis in Family Therapy, 1977; (with I. Rucker-Embden) First Interview with the Family, 1980; (co-ed.) Familiar Realities, 1987. Add: c/o Aronson Inc., 230 Livingston St. Northvale, N.J. 07647, U.S.A.

STIGLER, George J(oseph). American, b. 1911. Economics, Intellectual history. Charles R. Walgreen Distinguished Service Prof. of American Instns., Univ. of Chicago, since 1958. Asst. Prof. of Economics, Iowa State Coll., 1936-38; Asst. Prof., 1938-41, Assoc. Prof., 1941-44, and Prof., 1944-46, Univ. of Minnesota, Minneapolis; Prof., Brown Univ., Providence, R.I., 1946-47, and Columbia Univ., NYC, 1947-58. Research Staff Member, National Bureau of Economic Research, 1941-76; Vice-Chmn., Securities Investors Protective Commn., 1971-74. Recipient: Nobel Prize in economic science. *Publs:* Production and Distribution Theories, 1940; The Theory of Competitive Price, 1942; The Theory of Price, 1946, 4th ed. 1987; (with Friedman) Roofs or Ceilings, 1946; Domestic Servants in the United States, 1947; Trends in Output and Employment, 1947; Five Lectures on Economic Problems, 1949; Employment and Compensation in Education, 1950; (with K. Boulding) Readings in Price Theory, 1952; Trends in Employment in the Service Industries, 1956; (with D. Blank) Supply and Demand for Scientific Personnel, 1957; Capital and Rates of Return in Manufacturing, 1963; The Intellectual and the Market Place and Other Essays, 1963, 1984; Essays in the History of Economics, 1965; The Organization of Industry,

1968; (with J.K. Kindahl) The Behavior of Industrial Prices, 1970; (with Manuel Cohen) Can Regulatory Agencies Protect the Consumer?, 1971; The Citizen and the State, 1975; The Economist as Preacher, 1982; Memoirs of an Unregulated Economist, 1988. Add: Univ. of Chicago, 1101 E. 58th St., Chicago, Ill. 60637, U.S.A.

STILES, Lindley J(oseph). American, b. 1913. Poetry, Education. Prof. of Education for Interdisciplinary Studies, Sociology and Political Science, Northwestern Univ., Evanston, Ill., since 1966. Dean, Sch. of Education, Univ. of Virginia, Charlottesville, 1949–55, and Univ. of Wisconsin, Madison, 1955–66. *Publs:* (with I.O Helseth) Supervision as Guidance, 1946; (with M.F. Dorsey) Democratic Teaching in Secondary Schools, 1950; Moods and Moments (poetry), 1955; (ed.) The Teacher's Role in American Society, 1957; (ed. and contrib.) Teacher Education in the United States, 1960; (ed. and contrib.) Secondary Education in the United States, 1962; (co-ed. and contrib.) Education in Urban Society, 1962; Ideas and Images for Life with Young People (poetry), 1964; The Scholar Teacher: The Present State of Neglect, 1967; Introduction to College Education, 1969; (co-author) Criticism, Conflict and Change: Readings in American Education, 1970; (co-author) Profiles in College Teaching: Models at Northwestern, 1972; (co-author) Teaching and Technology, 1972; (co-author) Controversy in Education, 1972, 1974; (co-author) Perspectives on Social Change, 1972; Policy and Perspective at the Growing Edge of Education, 1973; (co-author) Processes and Phenomena of Social Change, 1973; (co-author) New Prospectives on Teacher Education, 1973; Theories in Teaching, 1974; (ed. with Bruce D. Johnson) Morality Examined, 1977. Add: c/o Princeton Book Co., Box 57, Pennington, N.J. 08534, U.S.A.

STILL, Richard (Ralph). American, b. 1921. Marketing. Prof. of Marketing and Intnl. Business Studies, Coll. of Business Admin., Univ. of Georgia, Athens, since 1968. Asst. Prof. of Business, Univ. of Rochester, N.Y., 1953-55; Prof. of Marketing, Syracuse Univ., N.Y., 1955-68. External Examiner, and Visiting Prof., Univ. of West Indies, Jamaica, 1966-76. *Publs:* Sales Management, 1958, 5th ed. 1988; Basic Marketing, 1964, 1971; Essentials of Marketing, 1966, 1972; Cases in Marketing, 1972, 1985; Fundamentals of Modern Marketing, 1973, 4th ed., 1985. Add: 3010 Emathla St., Miami, Fla. 33133, U.S.A.

STILL, William N. American, b. 1932. History. Prof. of History, and Dir., Prog. in Maritime History and Underwater Research, East Carolina Univ., Greenville, N.C. since 1974 (Assoc. Prof., 1968-74). *Publs:* Confederate Shipbuilding, 1969; Iron Afloat: The Story of the Confederate Armorclads, 1971; North Carolina's Revolutionary War Navy, 1976; American Sea Power in the Old World: The United States Navy in European and Near Eastern Waters 1865-1917, 1980. Add: 124 Oxford Rd., Greenville, N.C. 27834, U.S.A.

STILLINGER, Jack. American, b. 1931. Literature. Prof. of English, Univ. of Illinois at Urbana-Champaign, since 1964 (Asst. Prof., 1958–61; Assoc. Prof., 1961–64). *Publs:* (ed.) The Early Draft of John Stuart Mill's Autobiography, 1961; (ed.) Anthony Munday's Zelauto, 1963; (ed.) William Wordsworth: Selected Poems and Prefaces, 1965; (ed.) The Letters of Charles Armitage Brown, 1966; (ed.) Twentieth Century Interpretations of Keats's Odes, 1968; (ed.) John Stuart Mill: Autobiography, 1969; (ed.) John Stuart Mill: Autobiography and Other Writings, 1969; The Hoodwinking of Madeline and Other Essays on Keats's Poems, 1971; The Texts of Keats's Poems, 1974; (ed.) The Poems of John Keats, 1978; (ed.) Mill's Autobiography, and Literary Essays, 1981; (ed.) Keats's Complete Poems, 1982. Add: Dept. of English, 608 S. Wright St., Univ. of Illinois, Urbana, Ill. 61801, U.S.A.

STILLMAN, Richard J(oseph). American, b. 1917. Administration/ Management, Military/Defense, Money/Finance. Prof. Emeritus of Mgmt., Univ. of New Orleans, La., since 1982 (Prof., 1967–82), Pres., Richard J. Stillman Co., since 1984. Commissioned in the Regular Army: 2nd Lt. through Colonel, 1942–65, retired 1965; Prof. of Business Admin., Dir. of Mgmt. Development Progs., Dir. of Center for Economic Opportunity, Ohio Univ., Athens, 1965–67. *Publs:* U.S. Infantry: Queen of Battle, 1965; (with F. Henri) Bitter Victory: A History of Black Soldiers in World War I, 1970; Guide to Personal Finance: Lifetime Program of Money Management, 1972, 5th ed. 1988; Do It Yourself Contracting to Build Your Own Home: A Managerial Approach, 1974, 1981; Personal Finance Guide and Workbook: A Managerial Approach to Successful Household Record Keeping, 1977, 1979; Moneywise, 1978; More for Your Money: Personal Finance Techniques to Cope with Inflation and the Energy Shortage, 1980; Your Personal Financial Planner: Sourcebook of Tools to Help Beat Inflation and the Energy Shortage, 1980; Small Business Management: How to Start and Stay in Business, 1983; Six Steps to Your Financial Success: A Managerial Approach to Family Budgeting, 1986; Dow Jones Industrial Average: History and Role in an Investment Strategy, 1986; (with John Page) How to Use Your Personal Computer to Manage Your Personal Finances, 1987; How to Establish Your Own Successful Business at Home, 1990. Add: 2311 Oriole St., New Orleans, La. 70122, U.S.A.

STINE, G(eorge) Harry. Also writes science fiction as Lee Correy. American, b. 1928. Science fiction/Fantasy, Children's fiction, Air/Space topics, Children's non-fiction. Freelance consultant and writer, since 1976. Founder, and past Pres., National Assn. of Rocketry: Assoc. Fellow, American Inst. of Aeronautics. Chief of the Propulsion Branch, Controls and Instruments Section, 1952–55, and Chief of Range Operations Div. and Navy Flight Safety Engineer, 1955–57, White Sands Proving Ground, N.M.; Design Specialist, Martin Co., Denver, Colo., 1957; Pres. and Chief Engineer, Model Missiles, Denver, 1957–59; Vice-Pres. and Chief Engineer, Micro-Dynamics, Broomfield, Colo., 1959; Design Engineer, Stanley Aviation, Denver, 1959–60; Asst. Dir. of Research, Huyck Corp., Stamford, Conn., 1960–65; freelance consultant, 1965–73; Marketing Mgr., Flow Technology, Phoenix, 1973–76. Ed., Missile Away!, 1953–57; Columnist, Mechanix Illustrated, 1956–57; Ed., The Model Rocketeer, 1957–64, 1976–79. Publs: (as Lee Correy) Starship Through Space (juvenile), 1954; (as Lee Correy) Contraband Rocket, 1955; (as Lee Correy) Rocket Man (juvenile), 1955; Rocket Power and Space Flight, 1957; Earth Satellites and the Race for Superiority, 1957; Man and the Space Frontier, 1962; Handbook of Model Rocketry, 1965, 5th ed. 1983; The Model Rocket Manual, 1975, 1977; The Third Industrial Revolution, 1975; Shuttle into Space: A Ride in America's Space Transportation System (juvenile), 1978; (as Lee Correy) Star Driver, 1980; (as Lee Correy) Space Doctor, 1981; (as Lee Correy) Shuttle Down, 1981; (as Lee Correy) The Abode of Life, 1982; (as Lee Correy) Manna, 1983; The Hopeful Future, 1983; The Silicon Gods, 1984; On the Frontiers of Science: Strange Machines You Can Build, 1985; Handbook for Space Colonists, 1985; (as Lee Correy) A Matter of Metalaw, 1986; The Corporate Survivors, 1986; Warbots, 7 vols., 1988–89. Add: 616 W. Frier Dr., Phoenix, Ariz. W. Frier Dr., Phoenix, Ariz. 85021, U.S.A.

STINE, Hank. (Henry Eugene Stine). American, b. 1945. Science fiction/ Fantasy. Ed., Starblaze Books. Formerly, film dir., Ed., Galaxy mag., 1978–79. Publs: Season of the Witch, 1968; Thrill City, 1969; The Prisoner: A Day in the Life (novelization of TV series), 1970; Light Years: The Science Fiction Round Robin, 1982; (with J.R. Frank) The New Eves: Heroines of Science Fiction, 1989. Add: c/o Jeremy P. Tarcher Inc., 9110 Sunset Blvd., Suite 250, Los Angeles, Calif. 90069, U.S.A.

STINSON, Jim. (James Emerson Stinson, Jr.) American, b. 1937. Novels. Publs: Double Exposure, 1985; Low Angles, 1986; Truck Shot, 1989. Add: 252 Annandale Rd., Pasadena, Calif. 91105, U.S.A.

STIRLING, Jessica. See **RAE,** Hugh C.

STIRLING, Nora B(romley). American, b. 1900. Plays/Screenplays, Children's non-fiction, History, Biography. Publs: No Strings Attached, 1947; The Ins and Outs, 1949, 1968; Scattered Showers, 1949; Fresh Variable Winds, 1949; High Pressure Area, 1949 . . . and You Never Know, 1951; The Case of the Missing Handshake, 1952; The Room Upstairs, 1953; (with N. Ridenour) My Name Is Legion, 1953; Return to Thine Own House, 1954; Random Target, 1954; Tomorrow Is a Day, 1955; Point of Beginning, 1955; What Did I Do?, 1957; Treasure Under the Sea, 1957; Broken Circle, 1957; The Daily Special, 1958; The Second Look, 1958; According to Size, 1958; Eye of the Hurricane, 1959; The Green Blackboard, 1959; Present Pleasure, 1959; Ticket to Tomorrow, 1960; Exploring for Lost Treasure, 1960; Ever Since April, 1960; Apples for Teacher, 1960; Boys at Large, 1960; The Pink Telephone, 1961; Family Life Plays, 1961; The Picnic Basket, 1961; Three Maple Street, 1962; You Never Told Me, 1962; The Long View, 1962; Our Kind, 1962; The Day the Sky Went to School, 1962; A Choice to Make, 1963; Up from the Sea, 1963; Night of Reckoning, 1964; Heart of the House, 1964; The Picnic Basket, 1964; Who Wrote the Classics?, 3 vols., 1965–70; Breakthrough, 1965; Wonders of Engineering, 1966; Let's Get Basic, 1967; You Would If You Loved Me, 1969; Stop, Look and Listen . . . Children Ahead, 1970; All the Caterpillars You Want, 1970; Your Money or Your Life, 1974; Pearl Buck, Woman in Conflict, 1983. Add: c/o Harold Ober Assocs., 40 E. 49th St., New York, N.Y., U.S.A.

STIVENS, Dal(las George). Australian, b. 1911. Novels/Short stories. Served in the Australian Dept. of Information, 1944–50; Press Officer, Australia House, London, 1949–50; Foundn. Pres., 1963–64, Vice Pres., 1964–66, and Pres., 1967–73, Australian Soc. of Authors; Member,

N.S.W. Advisory Cttee., A.B.C., 1971–73; Chmn., Literary Cttee., Capt. Cook Bicentenary Celebrations, 1969–70. Publs: The Tramp and Other Stories, 1936; The Courtship of Uncle Henry: Short Stories, 1946; Jimmy Brockett: Portrait of a Notable Australian, 1951; The Gambling Ghost and Other Stories, 1946; Ironbark Bill, 1955; The Wide Arch, 1958; (ed.) Coast to Coast: Australian Stories, 1957-58, 1959; (with B. Jefferis) A Guide to Book Contracts, 1967; Three Persons Make a Tiger, 1968; A Horse of Air, 1970; The Incredible Egg: A Billion Year Journey, 1974; The Unicorn and Other Tales, 1976; The Bushranger, 1979; The Demon Bowler and Other Cricket Stories, 1979; The Portable Dal Stivens, 1982. Add: 5 Middle Harbour Rd., Lindfield, N.S.W., Australia 2070.

STOCKMAN, David A(llen). American, b. 1946. Politics/Government. Managing Dir., Salomon Brothers, NYC, since 1985. Special Asst. to Congressman John Anderson, 1970–72; Exec. Dir., House Republic Conference, U.S. House of Representatives, Washington, D.C., 1972–75; U.S. Congressman from the 4th district of Michigan, 1971–81; Chmn., Republican Economic Policy Task Force, Washington, D.C., 1977–81; Dir., U.S. Office of Management and Budget, Washington, 1981–85. Publs: The Triumph of Politics: Why the Reagan Revolution Failed (in U.K. as The Triumph of Politics: The Crisis in American Government and How It Affects the World), 1986. Add: c/o Salomon Brothers, 1 New York Plaza, New York, N.Y. 10004, U.S.A.

STOCKWIN, (James) Arthur (Ainscow). Australian and British, b. 1935. Politics/Government. Nissan Prof. of Modern Japanese Studies, and Dir. of Nissan Inst. of Japanese Studies, Univ.of Oxford, since 1982. Lectr., 1964–66, Sr. Lectr., 1966–72, and Reader in Political Science, 1972–81, Australian Natl. Univ. Publs: The Japanese Socialist Party and Neutralism: A Study of a Political Party and Its Foreign Policy, 1968; (ed.) Japan and Australia in the Seventies, 1972; Japan: Divided Politics in a Growth Economy, 1982;(ed.) Dynamic and Immobilist Politics in Japan, 1988. Add: Nissan Inst. of Japanese Studies, 1 Church-Walk, Oxford OX2 6LY, England.

STOCKWOOD, (Arthur) Mervyn. British, b. 1913. Theology/Religion, Travel/ Exploration/Adventure, Biography. Anglican clergyman: Vicar, St. Matthew, Moorfields, Bristol, 1941–55; Vicar, University Church, Cambridge, 1955–59; Bishop of Southwark, 1959–80. Publs: There Is a Tide, 1946; Whom They Pierced, 1948; I Went to Moscow, 1955; The Faith Today, 1959; Cambridge Sermons, 1959; Bishop's Journal, 1965; The Cross and the Sickle, 1978; From Strength to Strength, 1980; Chanctonbury Ring (autobiography), 1982. Add: 15 Sydney Bldgs., Bath, Avon BA2 6BZ, England.

STODDARD, Alan. British, b. 1915. Medicine/Health. Private practice in medicine, Chichester, Sussex. Consultant in Physical Medicine, Brook Hosp., London, 1948–73. Publs: Manual of Osteopathic Technique, 1959; Manual of Osteopathic Practice, 1969; The Back: Relief from Pain, 1979. Add: The Anchorage, Spinney Lane, Itchenor, Chichester, Sussex PO20 7DJ, England.

STOESSINGER, John G. American, b. 1927. Intellectual history, International relations/Current affairs. Prof. of Political Science, City Univ. of New York, since 1967. Acting Dir., Political Affairs Div., U.N., NYC, since 1967. Various teaching posts at Harvard Univ., Massachusetts Inst. of Technology, Cambridge, Mass. and Columbia Univ., NYC, 1954–67. Publs: The Refugee and the World Community, 1956; The Might of Nations: World Politics in Our Time, 1962, 8th ed. 1986; Financing the United Nations System, 1964; The United Nations and the Superpowers, 1965, 4th ed. 1977; (co-ed.) Power and Order, 1968; Nations in Darkness: China, Russia, and America, 1973, 4th ed. 1986; (co-ed.) Divided Nations in a Divided World, 1974; Why Nations Go To War, 1974; 4th ed. 1986; Henry Kissinger, 1976; Night Journey, 1978; Crusaders and Pragmatists, 1979. Add: 275 Central Park West, New York, N.Y. 10024, U.S.A.

STOLLER, Alan. Australian, b. 1911. Psychiatry. Member of Faculty of Medicine, Melbourne Univ., and Monash Univ., Clayton, Vic. Ed. Emeritus, Australian and New Zealand Journal of Psychiatry; Member, Expert Advisory Panel on Mental Health, World Health Org. Research Asst., Maudsley Hosp., Univ. of London Inst. of Psychiatry, 1946–47; Headquarters Consultant Psychiatrist, Commonwealth Repatriation Dept., Australia, 1947–53; Chief Clinical Officer, Victorian Mental Health Authority, and Dir., Mental Health Research Inst., 1953–69, and Chmn., Victorian Health Authority, Melbourne, 1969–76. Member of Exec. Bd., 1949–53, and Pres., 1954, World Fedn. for Mental Health; WHO Consultant in Thailand, 1958–59, in Indonesia, 1963, 1969; Consultant to the Australian Govt., 1953; Pres., Victorian Council of Mental Hygiene,

1967–68; Pres., Australian and New Zealand Coll. of Psychiatrists, 1970–71. *Publs:* Mental Health Facilities and Needs of Australia, 1955; (ed.) Growing Up: Problems of Old Age in the Australian Community, 1960; (ed.) The Family Today: Its Role in Personal and Social Adjustment, 1961; (ed.) New Faces: Immigration and Family Life in Australia, 1962; The Health of a Metropolis, 1972; Family in Australia, 1974. Add: 71 Glen Shian Lane, Mt. Eliza, Vic. 3930, Australia.

STOLTZFUS, Ben Frank(lin). American, b. 1927. Novels/Short stories, Literature. Prof. of French and Comparative Literature, and Creative Writing, Univ. of Calfornia, Riverside, since 1960. Instr. in French, Smith Coll., Northampton, Mass., 1958–60. *Publs:* Alain Robbe-Grillet and the New French Novel, 1964; Georges Chennevière et L'Unanimisme, 1965; The Eye of the Needle, 1967; Gide's Eagles, 1969; Black Lazarus, 1972; Gide and Hemingway: Rebels Against God, 1978; Alain Robbe-Grillet: The Body of the Text, 1985; Postmodern Poetics: Nouveau Roman and Innovative Fiction, 1987; Alain Robbe-Grillet: Life, Work, and Criticism, 1987; Red White and Blue, 1989. Add: Dept. of Literatures and Languages, Univ. of California, Riverside, Calif. 92521, U.S.A.

STOLZ, Mary (Slattery). American, b. 1920. Novels/Short stories, Children's fiction. *Publs:* To Tell Your Love, 1950; The Organdy Cupcakes, 1951; The Sea Gulls Woke Me, 1951; The Leftover Elf, 1952; In a Mirror, 1953; Ready or Not, 1953; Truth and Consequence, 1953; Pray Love, Remember, 1954; Two by Two, 1954, as A Love or a Season, 1964; Rosemary, 1955; Hospital Zone, 1956; The Day and the Way We Met, 1956; Good-bye My Shadow, 1957; Because of Madeline, 1957; And Love Replied, 1958; Second Nature, 1958; Emmett's Pig, 1959; Some Merry-Go-Round Music, 1959; The Beautiful Friend and Other Stories, 1960; A Dog on Barkham Street, 1960; Belling the Tiger, 1961; Wait for Me, Michael, 1961; The Great Rebellion, 1961; Frédou, 1962; Pigeon Flight, 1962; Siri, The Conquistador, 1963; The Bully of Barkham Street, 1963; Who Wants Music on Monday?, 1963; The Mystery of the Woods, 1964; The Noonday Friends, 1965; Maximilian's World, 1966; A Wonderful, Terrible Time, 1967; Say Something, 1968; The Dragons of the Queen, 1969; The Story of a Singular Hen and Her Peculiar Children, 1969; Juan, 1970; By the Highway Home, 1971; Leap Before You Look, 1972; Lands End, 1973; The Edge of Next Year, 1974; Cat in the Mirror, 1975; Ferris Wheel, 1977; Cider Days, 1978; Go and Catch a Flying Fish, 1979; What Time of Night Is It?, 1981; Cat Walk, 1983; Quentin Corn, 1985; Explorer of Barkham Street, 1985; Night of Ghosts and Hermits, 1985; The Cuckoo Clock, 1986; Ivy Larkin, 1986; The Scarecrows and Their Child, 1987; Zekmet the Stone Carver, 1988; Storm in the Night, 1988; Pangur Ban, 1988. Add: P.O. Box 82, Longboat Key, Fla. 34228, U.S.A.

STONE, Alan A. American, b. 1929. Law, Psychiatry. Prof. of Law and Psychiatry, Faculty of Law and Medicine, Harvard Univ., Cambridge, Mass., since 1972 (Instr. 1961–65, Assoc., 1954–66, Asst. Prof., 1966–69, and Assoc. Prof., 1969–72, Medical Sch.; Visiting Lectr., Psychiatry and Psychoanalysis, 1968–69, and Lectr. in Law, 1969–72, Law Sch.). Dir., Resident Education, McLean Hosp., Belmont, Mass., 1962–63. Past Pres., American Psychiatric Assn. *Publs:* (with G. Onque) Longitudinal Studies of Child Personality, 1959; (with S. Stone) The Abnormal Personality Through Literature, 1966; Mental Health and the Law, 1976; Law, Psychiatry and Morality: Essays and Analysis, 1984. Add: Harvard Law Sch., Cambridge, Mass. 02138, U.S.A.

STONE, Brian (Ernest). British, b. 1919. Autobiography/Memoirs/Personal, Literature, Translations. Reader in Literature, The Open Univ., Milton Keynes, 1969–85. Head of English, Brighton Coll. of Education, 1963–69. *Publs:* Prisoner from Alamein, 1944; (trans.) Sir Gawain and the Green Knight, 1959, 1974; Medieval English Verse, 1963; The Owl and the Nightingale, 1971; (with Pat Scorer) Sophocles to Fugard, 1977; Chaucer: Love Visions, 1983; Chaucer, 1987; (trans.) King Arthur's Death), 1988. Add: c/o Penguin, 27 Wrights Lane, London W8 5TZ, England.

STONE, Gerald (Charles). British, b. 1932. History, Language/Linguistics. Univ. Lectr., Oxford Univ., and Fellow and Tutor, Hertford Coll., Oxford, both since 1972. Lectr., Univ. of Nottingham, 1966–71; Asst. Dir. of Research, Cambridge Univ., 1971–72. *Publs:* The Smallest Slavonic Nation: The Sorbs of Lusatia, 1972; (with B. Comrie) The Russian Language since the Revolution, 1978; An Introduction to Polish, 1980; (ed. with D. Worth) The Formation of the Slavonic Literary Languages, 1985. Add: Hertford Coll., Oxford OX1 3BW, England.

STONE, Irving. American, b. 1903. Novels/Short stories, History, Biography. Founder and Pres., Eugene V. Debs Foundn., Terre Haute,

Ind., and Member, Advisory Bd., Univ. of California Inst. for the Creative Arts, since 1963; Pres., Affiliates of the Dept. of English, Univ. of California, Los Angeles, since 1969; Regents Prof., Univ of California, Los Angeles, since 1984. Teaching Fellow in Economics, Univ. of Southern California, Los Angeles, 1923–24, and Univ, of California, Berkeley, 1924–26; Art Critic, Los Angeles Mirror-News, 1956–60; Pres., California Writers Guild, 1960–61; Founder, Academy of American Poets, 1962, and California State Colls. Cttee. for the Arts, 1967; Trustee, Douglas House Foundn., Watts, Los Angeles, Calif., 1967–68. *Publs:* Pageant of Youth, 1933; Lust for Life, 1934; (ed. with J. Stone) Dear Theo: Autobiography of Vincent van Gogh, 1937; Sailor on Horseback, 1938; False Witness, 1940; Clarence Darrow for the Defense (in U.K. as Darrow for the Defense), 1941; They Also Ran: The Story of the Men who were Defeated for the Presidency, 1943; Immortal Wife, 1944; Adversary in the House, 1947; Earl Warren, 1948; The Passionate Journey, 1949; (with R. Kennedy) We Speak for Ourselves: Self Portrait of America, 1950; The President's Lady, 1951; Love Is Eternal, 1954; Men to Match My Mountains: The Opening of the Far West 1840-1900, 1956; The Biographical Novel: Three Views of the Novel, 1957; The Agony and the Ecstasy, 1961; (ed. with A. Nevens) Lincoln: A Contemporary Portrait, 1962; (ed. with J. Stone) I, Michelangelo: An Autobiography through Letters, 1962; The Irving Stone Reader, 1963; The Story of Michelangelo's Pieta, 1964; The Great Adventure of Michelangelo, 1965; Those Who Love, 1965; There Was Light: Autobiography of a University, Berkeley, 1867-1968, 1970; Passions of the Mind, 1971; The Greek Treasure: A Biographical Novel of Henry and Sophia Schliemann, 1975; (ed.) Jack London, 1977; The Origin, 1980; Depths of Glory, 1985. Died, 1989.

STONE, Lawrence. American, b. 1919. History. Dodge Prof. of History, Princeton Univ., N.J., since 1963; Dir., Shelby Collum David Center for History Studies, since 1968. *Publs:* Sculpture in Britain: The Middle Ages, 1955; An Elizabethan: Sir Horatio Palavicino, 1956; The Crisis of the Aristocracy 1558-1641, 1965; The Causes of the English Revoution 1629-1642, 1972; Family and Fortune: Finance in the Sixteenth and Seventeenth Centuries, 1973; (ed.) Schooling and Society, 1976; Family, Sex and Marriage: England 1500-1800, 1977; The Past and the Present, 1984; (with J.C. Fawtier Stone) An Open Elite? England 1540-1880, 1984; The Past and the Present Revisited, 1988. Add: 266 Moore St., Princeton, N.J. 08540, U.S.A.

STONE, Lesley. *See* **TREVOR,** Elleston.

STONE, Merlin (David). British, b. 1948. Marketing. Dir., Granbate Ltd., and Taba Midas Ltd. Esmée Fairbairn Research Scholar, Univ. of Sussex, 1970–72; Lectr., Dept. of Management Sciences, Inst. of Science and Technology, Univ. of Manchester, 1972–75; Sr. Lectr., Sch. of Economics and Politics, Kingston Polytechnic, 1975–77; Product Mgr. and Market Analyst, Iscar Ltd., Israel, 1977–78; Course Coordinator, Jerusalem Inst. of Management, 1978–79; Sr. Lectr., Sch. of Management Education, Kingston Polytechnic, 1979–80; Business Planning Mgr., Rank Xerox, 1980–83; Lectr. in Marketing, Henley Management Coll., 1983–86. *Publs:* Product Planning, 1976; Marketing and Economics, 1980; (with H. MacArthur) How to Market Computers and Office Systems, 1984; (with A. Wilde) Field Service Management, 1985; (with R. Shaw) Database Marketing, 1988. Add: 31 Guilford Ave., Surbiton, Surrey KT5 8DG, England.

STONE, (Sir) (John) Richard (Nicholas). British, b. 1913. Economics. Fellow of King's Coll., since 1945, and Leake Prof. of Finance and Accounting, Cambridge Univ., 1955–80 (Dir., Dept. of Applied Economics, 1945–55). With C.E. Heath and Co., 1936–39; served in the Ministry of Economic Warfare, 1939–40, and Office of the War Cabinet, Central Statistical Office, 1940–45. Pres., Econometric Soc., 1955. Recipient, Nobel Prize in Economics, 1984. *Publs:* The Role of Measurement in Economics, 1951; (with others) The Measurement of Consumers' Expenditure and Behaviour in the United Kingdom 1920-1938, vol. I, 1954, vol. II, 1966; Quantity and Price Indexes in National Accounts, 1956; Input-Output and National Accounts, 1961; (with G. Stone) National Income and Expenditure, 9th ed. 1972; Mathematics in the Social Sciences and Other Essays, 1966; Mathematical Models of the Economy and Other Essays, 1970; Demographic Accounting and Model Building, 1971; Aspects of Economic and Social Modelling, 1980. Add: 13 Millington Rd., Cambridge, England.

STONE, Robert (Anthony). American, b. 1937. Novels, Screenplays. Editorial Asst., New York Daily News, 1958–60; Writer-in-Residence, Princeton Univ., New Jersey, 1971–72, 1985; taught at Amherst Coll.,

Massachusetts, 1972–75, 1977–78, Stanford Univ., California, 1979, Univ. of Hawaii, Manoa, 1979–80, Harvard Univ., Cambridge, Mass., 1981, Univ. of California at Irvine, 1982, New York Univ., 1983–84, and Univ. of California at San Diego, 1985. *Publs:* A Hall of Mirrors, 1967; Dog Soldiers, 1974; (with Judith Rascoe) Who'll Stop the Rain (screenplay), 1978; A Flag for Sunrise, 1981; Children of Light, 1986. Add: c/o Candida Donadio and Assocs., 231 W. 22nd St., New York, N.Y. 10011, U.S.A.

STONE, Thomas H. *See* **GILMAN,** George G.

STONE, William S(idney). American, b. 1928. Recreation/Leisure/ Hobbies. Advertising Writer, then Assoc. Creative Dir., Doremus & Co., NYC, since 1983. Ed., Zeiss Historica Journal. Advertising Writer, Batten Barton Durstine & Osborne Inc., NYC, 1954–1983. *Publs:* Guide to American Sports Car Racing, 1960, 4th ed. 1971; MG Guide, 1964; Mustang Guide, 1965; VW 1600 Guide, 1966; Buying a Used Sports Car, 1967; Guide to Racing Driving Schools, 1972. Add: 222 East 80th St. (6E), New York, N.Y. 10021, U.S.A.

STONE, Zachary. *See* **FOLLETT,** Ken.

STONEHOUSE, Bernard. British, b. 1926. Natural history, Travel/ Exploration/Adventure, Zoology. Ed., Polar Record. Reader in Zoology, Univ. of Canterbury, NZ, 1964–68; Sr. Lectr. in Ecology, Univ. of Bradford, 1972–82. *Publs:* Het Bevroren Continent: The Frozen Continent: A History of Antarctic Exploration, 1958; Wideawake Island: The Story of BOU Centenary Expedition to Ascension Island, 1960; Whales, 1963; Gulls and Terns, 1964; Penguins, 1968; Birds of the New Zealand Shore, 1968; Animals of the Arctic (Antarctic), 2 vols., 1971–72; Young Animals, 1973; (ed.) The Way Your Body Works, 1974; (ed.) The Biology of Penguins, 1974; Mountain Life, 1975; Penguins, 1975; (ed.) Biology of Marsupials, 1977; (ed.) Evolutionary Ecology, 1977; (ed.) Animal Marking: Recognition Marking of Animals in Research, 1978; A Closer Look at Reptiles, 1978; Whales and Dolphins, 1978; Kangaroos, 1978; Penguins, 1978; (consultant co-ed.) Atlas of Earth Resources, 1979; The Living World of the Sea, 1979; (with M. Borner) Orang-Utan, 1979; (ed.) Philips Illustrated Atlas of the World, 1980; Bears, 1980; Saving the Animals, 1981; (ed.) Biological Husbandry, 1981; Charles Darwin and Evolution, 1981; Venomous Snakes, 1981; Parrots, 1981; Buffaloes, 1981; (co-ed.) Arctic Ocean, 1982; Britain from the Air, 1982; Pocket Guide to the World, 1985; Sea Mammals of the World, 1985; (ed.) Arctic Air Pollution, 1986; Polar Ecology, 1988. Add: Scott Polar Research Institute, Lensfield Rd., Cambridge, England.

STONEMAN, Paul. British, b. 1947. Economics. Reader in Economics, Univ. of Warwick, Coventry, since 1973. *Publs:* Technological Diffusion and the Computer Revolution, 1976; (with others) Mergers and Economic Performance, 1979; The Economic Analysis of Technological Change, 1983; The Economic Analysis of Technology Policy, 1987; (ed. with P. Dasgupta) Economic Policy and Technological Performance, 1987. Add: Dept. of Economics, Univ. of Warwick, Coventry CV4 7AL, England.

STOPPARD, Miriam. British, b. 1937. Medicine/Health. Physician: Resident Fellow, Dept. of Chemical Pathology, 1963–65, Registrar in Dermatology, 1965–66, and Sr. Registrar in Dermatology, 1966–68, Univ. of Bristol; Assoc. Medical Dir., 1968–71, Deputy Medical Dir., 1971–74, Medical Dir., 1974–76, Deputy Managing Dir., 1976–77, and Managing Dir., 1977–81, Syntext Pharmaceuticals Ltd. *Publs:* Miriam Stoppard's Book of Baby Care, 1977; (with others) My Medical School, 1978; Miriam Stoppard's Book of Health Care, 1979; The Face and Body Book, 1980; Everywoman's Lifeguide, 1982; Your Baby, 1982; Fifty Plus Lifeguide, 1982; Your Growing Child, 1983; Baby Care, 1983; Baby and Child Medical Handbook, 1986. Add: Iver Grove, Iver, Bucks., England.

STOPPARD, Tom. British, (born Czechoslovakian), b. 1937. Novels/ Short stories, Plays/Screenplays. Journalist, Western Daily Press, Bristol, 1954–58, and Bristol Evening World, 1958–60; freelance journalist, 1960–63. *Publs:* Enter a Free Man, 1968; (with others) Introduction 2 (short stories), 1964; Lord Malquist and Mr. Moon (novel), 1966; (adaptor) Tango, 1966; A Separate Peace, 1966; Rosencrantz and Guildenstern Are Dead, 1967; The Real Inspector Hound, 1968; Albert's Bridge and If You're Glad I'll Be Frank: Two Plays for Radio, 1969; After Magritte, 1971; Jumpers, 1972; Travesties, 1974; Dirty Linen and New-Found-Land, 1976; The Fifteen Minute Hamlet, 1976; Albert's Bridge and Other Plays, 1977; Every Good Boy Deserves Favour, and Professional Foul, 1978; Night and Day, 1978; (adaptor) Undiscovered Country, by Schnitzler, 1980; Dog's Hamlet, Cahoot's Macbeth, 1980; (adaptor) On

the Razzle, by Johann Nestroy, 1981; The Dog It Was That Died and Other Plays, 1983; The Real Thing, 1984; Four Plays for Radio, 1984; Rough Crossing, from play by Molnar, 1985; Dalliance, 1986; Hapgood, 1987. Add: Iver Grove, Iver, Bucks., England.

STORER, James Donald. British, b. 1928. Air/Space topics, Engineering/Technology, Transportation. With Design Office, British Aircraft Corp., Weybridge, Surrey, 1948–66; Asst. Keeper, 1966–78, and Keeper, 1978–85, Dept. of Technology, Royal Scottish Museum, Edinburgh; Keeper, Dept. of Science, Technology, and Working Life, National Museums of Scotland, 1985 until retirement, 1988. *Publs:* Steel and Engineering, 1959; Behind the Scenes in an Aircraft Factory, 1965; It's Made Like This: Cars, 1967; The World We Are Making: Aviation, 1968; A Simple History of the Steam Engine, 1969; How to Run an Airport, 1971; How We Find Out About Flight, 1973; Flying Feats, 1977; Book of the Air, 1979; Great Inventions, 1980; (with others) Encyclopaedia of Transport, 1983; (jt. author) East Fortune: Museum of Flight and History of the Airfield, 1983; Ship Models in the Royal Scottish Museum, 1986. Add: 2 Dale Rd., Coalbrookdale, Telford TF8 7DT, England.

STOREY, Anthony. British, b. 1928. Novels, Plays/Screenplays, Biography. Psychology Tutor, Cambridge Univ., since 1966. Professional rugby player, 1947–60; Schoolmaster, Wakefield, 1950–53; Psychologist, Newton-le-Willows, 1957–60, and Armagh, N. Ire. and Suffolk, 1960–66. *Publs:* Jesus Iscariot, 1967; Graceless Go I (novel), 1969, screenplay, 1973, television play with L. Hughes, 1974; The Rector, 1970; The Plumed Serpent (screenplay), 1971; Platinum Jag: A Psycho-Thriller, 1972; The Centre Holds, 1973; Zulu Dawn (screenplay), 1974; Platinum Ass, 1975; Brothers Keepers, 1975; Stanley Baker (biography), 1978; The Saviour, 1979; On Becoming a Virgin, 1985. Add: Beyton Cottage, Beyton, Bury St. Edmunds, Suffolk, England.

STOREY, David (Malcolm). British, b. 1933. Novels/Short stories, Plays/Screenplays. *Publs:* This Sporting Life, 1960; Flight into Camden, 1961; Radcliffe, 1963; The Restoration of Arnold Middleton, 1967; In Celebration, 1969; The Contractor, 1970; Home, 1970; The Changing Room, 1971; Pasmore, 1972; The Farm, 1973; Cromwell, 1973; A Temporary Life, 1973; Life Class, 1974; Mother's Day, 1976; Saville, 1976; Early Days, Sisters, Life Class, 1980; A Prodigal Child, 1982; Present Times, 1984. Add: c/o Jonathan Cape, 32 Bedford Sq., London WC1B 3EL, England.

STOREY, Edward. British, b. 1930. Poetry, Songs, lyrics and libretti, Travel/Exploration/Adventure, Autobiography/Memoirs/Personal, Biography. Member, Literature Panel, Eastern Arts Assn., since 1970. Former Lectr., Adult Education Centre, Peterborough. *Publs:* North Bank Night, 1969; Portrait of the Fen Country, 1970, 1982; A Man in Winter, 1972; Four Seasons in Three Countries, 1974; Katharine of Aragon (libretto); The Solitary Landscape, 1975; Call It a Summer Country, 1978; The Dark Music, 1979; Old Scarlett (libretto), 1981; A Right to Song: The Life of John Clare, 1982; Spirit of the Fens, 1985; Fen, Fire and Flood, 1986; Summer Journeys Through the Fens, 1988. Add: Westwood House, Thorpe Rd., Peterborough PE3 6JF, Canada.

STOREY, Graham. British, b. 1920. Literature. Fellow of Trinity Hall, Cambridge, since 1949, and Reader in English, Cambridge Univ., since 1981, now Emeritus (Sr. Tutor, 1958–68, and Vice-Master, 1970–74, Trinity Hall; Lectr. in English, Cambridge Univ., 1965–81; Chmn., Faculty Bd. of English, 1972–74). *Publs:* Reuters' Century, 1951; (ed. with Humphry House) Journals and Papers of G.M. Hopkins, 1959; (ed.) A.P. Rossiter, Angel with Horns, 1961; (ed.) Selected Verse and Prose of G.M. Hopkins, 1966; (co-ed.) Letters of Charles Dickens, vol. I, 1965, vol. II, 1969, vol. III, 1974, vol. V, 1981, vol. VI, 1988; A Preface to Hopkins, 1981; (ed. with Howard Erskine-Hill) Revolutionary Prose of the English Civil War, 1983; Bleak House: A Critical Study, 1987. Add: Trinity Hall, Cambridge, England.

STOREY, Margaret. British, b. 1926. Children's fiction, Mystery. Private tutor, 1956–59; English Teacher, Miss Ironside's Sch., London, 1959–69; Sr. Teacher, Vale Sch., London, 1969–72; Sr. English Teacher, The Study, Wimbledon, 1972–77, and Putney Park Sch., London, 1977. *Publs:* Kate and the Family Tree, 1965 (in U.S. as The Family Tree, 1973); Pauline, 1976; The Smallest Doll, 1966; The Smallest Bridesmaid, 1966; Timothy and Two Witches, 1966; The Stone Sorcerer, 1967; The Dragon's Sister, and Timothy Travels, 1967; A Quarrel of Witches, 1970; The Mollyday Holiday, 1971; The Sleeping Witch, 1971; Wrong Gear, 1973; Keep Running, 1974, in U.S. as Ask Me No Questions, 1975; A War of Wizards, 1976; The Double Wizard, 1979; (with Jill Staynes) Goodbye, Nanny Gray, 1987; A Knife at the Opera, 1988; Body of Opinion, 1988. Add:

c/o Curtis Brown, 162 Regent St., London W1R 5TB, England.

STOREY, R(obin) L(indsay). British, b. 1927. History. Prof. of Medieval History, Nottingham Univ., since 1983 (Lectr., 1962–64; Sr. Lectr., 1964–66; Reader in History, 1966–73; Prof. of English History, 1973–83). Asst. Keeper, Public Record Office, 1953–62. *Publs:* (ed.) Register of Thomas Langley, Bishop of Durham 1406-1437, 6 vols., 1956–70; Thomas Langley and the Bishopric of Durham, 1961; The End of the House of Lancaster, 1966; The Reign of Henry VII, 1968; (co-ed. and contrib.) The Study of Medieval Records, 1971; Chronology of the Medieval World 800-1491, 1973. Add: Dept. of History, Univ. of Nottingham, Nottingham NG7 2RD, England.

STORM, Christopher. *See* **OLSEN**, T.V.

STORM, Virginia. *See* **CHARLES**, Theresa.

STORR, (Charles) Anthony. British, b. 1920. Psychiatry. Fellow, Royal College of Physicians, London: qualified as physician, 1944; served various internships, 1944–58; Consultant Psychiatrist, Chase Farm Hosp., 1956–61; Consultant Psychotherapist and Clinical Lectr. in Psychiatry, Oxford Univ., 1974–84. Member of the Council, Section of Psychiatry, Royal Soc. of Medicine, 1955–57; Chmn., Medical Section, British Psychological Soc., 1968; Fellow, Adlai Stevenson Inst. for Intnl. Affairs, Chicago, 1971–74. *Publs:* The Integrity of the Personality, 1960; Sexual Deviation, 1964; Human Aggression, 1968; Human Destructiveness, 1972; The Dynamics of Creation, 1972; Jung, 1973; The Art of Psychotherapy, 1979; (ed.) The Essential Jung, 1983; Solitude: A Return to the Self, 1988; Churchill's Black Dog, Kafka's Mice, and Other Phenomena of the Human Mind, 1989; Freud, 1989. Add: 45 Chalfont Rd., Oxford OX2 6TJ, England.

STORR, Catherine. (Lady Balogh). British, b. 1913. Novels/Short stories, Children's fiction. Physician: Asst. Psychiatrist, West London Hosp., 1948–50; Sr. Hosp. Medical Officer, Dept. of Psychological Medicine, Middlesex Hosp., London, 1950–62; Asst. Ed., Penguin Books, London, 1966–70. *Publs:* Clever Polly series, 3 vols., 1952–80; Stories for Jane, 1952; Marianne Dreams, 1958; Marianne and Mark, 1950; Robin, 1962; Flax into Gold (libretto), 1964; Lucy, 1964; The Catchpole Story, 1965; Rufus, 1969; Puss and Cat, 1969; Thursday, 1971; Kate and the Island, 1972; Black God, White God, 1972; (ed.) Children's Literature, 1973; The Chinese Egg, 1975; The Painter and the Fish, 1975; Unnatural Fathers, 1976; The Story of the Terrible Scar, 1976; Tales from the Psychiatrist's Couch (short stories), 1977; Winter's End, 1978; Vicky, 1981; The Bugbear, 1981; February Yowler, 1982; The Castle Boy, 1983; Two's Company, 1984; Cold Marble, 1986; The Boy and the Swan, 1987; The Underground Conspiracy, 1987. Add: Flat 5, 12 Frognal Gardens, London NW3, England.

STORY, Jack Trevor. British, b. 1917. Novels/Short stories. *Publs:* The Trouble with Harry, 1949; Protection for a Lady, 1950; Green to Pagan Street, 1952; The Money Goes Round and Round, 1958; Mix Me a Person, 1959; Man Pinches Bottom, 1962; Live Now, Pay Later, 1963; Something for Nothing, 1963; The Urban District Lover, 1964; Company of Bandits, 1965; I Sit in Hanger Lane, 1968; Dishonourable Member, 1969; Hitler Needs You, 1970; The Season of the Skylark, 1970; The Blonde and the Boodle, 1970; One Last Mad Embrace, 1970; Little Dog's Day, 1971; Whistle While I'm Dead: The Wind in the Snottygobble Tree, 1971; Letters to an Intimate Stranger: A Year in the Life of Jack Trevor Story, 1972; Crying Makes Your Nose Run, 1974; Story on Crime, 1975; Morag's Flying Fortress, 1976; Up River, 1979; Jack on the Box, 1979. Add: c/o Leveret Press, Stacy Hill Farm, Wolverton, Milton Keynes, England.

STOTLAND, Ezra. American, b. 1924. Criminology/Law enforcement/ Psychology. Prof. of Psychology since 1965, and Dir. of Prog. in Soc. and Justice since 1971, Univ. of Washington, Seattle. Grad. Asst., 1949, Research Asst., Bureau of Psychological Services, 1949–50, Research Asst., Navy Conference Research, 1950, Research Asst., Research Center for Group Dynamics, 1950–53, Research Assoc., Research Center for Group Dynamics, 1953–56, Lectr. in Extension Service, 1953–57, and Lectr. and Research Assoc., Dept. of Psychology, 1957, Univ. of Michigan, Ann Arbor; Consultant, Veterans Admin., 1959–71. Formerly, Consulting Ed., Behavior and Criminal Justice, and Journal of Research in Crime and Delinquency. *Publs:* (with A. Zander and A.R. Cohen) Role Relations in the Mental Health Profession, 1957; (with A.L. Kobler) The End of Hope: A Social-Clinical Study of Suicide, 1964; (with A.L. Kobler) Life and Death of a Mental Hospital, 1965; (co-ed.) Comparative Administrative Theory, 1968; Psychology of Hope: An Integration of Ex-

perimental, Social, and Clinical Approaches, 1969; (with S. Sherman and K.G. Shaver) Empathy and Birth Order: Some Experimental Explorations, 1971; (with L.K. Canon) Social Psychology: A Cognitive Approach, 1972; (co-author) Investigation of White Collar Crime, 1977; (with others) Empathy, Fantasy and Helping, 1978; (co-ed.) White Collar Crime: Theory and Research, 1983. Add: Society and Justice Prog., Univ. of Washington, Seattle, Wash. 98195, U.S.A.

STOTT, John Robert Walmsley. British, b. 1921. Theology/Religion. Rector Emeritus, All Souls Church, London, since 1975 (Curate, 1945–50, Rector, 1950–75); Pres., London Inst. for Contemporary Christianity, since 1986 (Dir., 1982–86). Ordained Minister since 1945; conducted missions in the univs. of Cambridge, Oxford, and in Canada, U.S.A., Australia, South, East and West Africa, and South-East Asia, since 1952; Hon. Chaplain to H.M. the Queen, since 1959. *Publs:* Men With a Message (in U.S. as Basic Introduction to the New Testament), 1954; Basic Christianity, 1958; 1971; Your Confirmation, 1958; What Christ Thinks of the Church, 1958; The Preacher's Portrait, 1961; The Epistles of John, 1964; The Canticles and Selected Psalms, 1966; Men Made New, 1966; The Message of Galatians, 1968; One People, 1969; Christ the Controversialist, 1970; Understanding the Bible, 1972; Guard the Gospel, 1973; Balanced Christianity, 1975; Christian Mission in the Modern World, 1975; Baptism and Fullness, 1975; The Lausanne Covenant, 1975; Christian Counter-Culture, 1978; Focus on Christ, 1979; God's New Society, 1979; I Believe in Preaching (in U.S as Between Two worlds), 1982; The Bible Book for Today, 1982; Issues Facing Christians Today, 1984, in U.S. as Involvement, 2 vols., 1985; The Authentic Jesus, 1985; The Cross of Christ, 1986; (co-author) Essentials, 1988. Add: 13 Bridford Mews, London W1N 1LQ, England.

STOTT, (Charlotte) Mary. British b. 1907. Autobiography/Memoirs/ Personal. Women's Ed., The Guardian newspaper, London, 1957–72. *Publs:* Forgetting's No Excuse, 1973; Organization Woman, 1978; (ed. with J. King) Is This Your Life?, 1977; Ageing for Beginners, 1981; Before I Go . . . , 1985; (ed.) Women Talking, 1987. Add: 4/11 Morden Rd., London SE3 0AA, England.

STOTT, Mike. British, b. 1944. Plays/Screenplays. Stage Mgr. at the Scarborough Library Theatre, and Play-reader for the Royal Shakespeare Theatre, for three years; Script Ed., BBC Radio, London, 1970–72; Resident Writer, Hampstead Theatre Club, London, 1975. *Publs:* Soldiers Talking, Cleanly, 1978; Funny Peculiar, 1978; Lenz, adaptation of the story by Georg Buchner, 1979. Add: c/o Michael Imison Playwrights Ltd., 28 Almeida St., London N1 1TD, England.

STOUT, Joseph A., Jr. American, b. 1939. History. Prof. of History, Oklahoma State Univ., Stillwater, since 1983 (Asst. Prof., 1972–74; Assoc. Prof., 1974–83). Asst. Prof. of History, Missouri Southern Coll., Joplin, 1971–72. *Publs:* (with Odie B. Faulk) The Mexican War: Changing Interpretations, 1973; The Liberators: The Filibustering Expeditions into Mexico, 1848, and the Last Gasp of Manifest Destiny, 1973; (ed.) Ether and Me or Just Relax, by Will Rogers, 1973; Apache Lightning: The Last Great Battles of the Ojo Calientes, 1974; (ed.) There's Not a Bathing Suit in Russia and Other Bare Facts, by Will Rogers, 1974; (ed.) The Cowboy Philosopher on the Peace Conference, 1974; (with Odie B. Faulk) A Short History of the American West, 1974; Cattle Country: A History of the Oklahoma Cattleman's Association, 1981. Add: Oklahoma State Univ., Dept. of History, Stillwater, Okla. 74074, U.S.A.

STOVER, John Ford. American, b. 1912. History, Transportation. Emeritus Prof. of American History, Purdue Univ., Lafayette, Ind. since 1978 (Instr., 1947–52; Asst. Prof., 1952–55; Assoc. Prof., 1955–59; Prof. 1959–78). *Publs:* The Railroads of the South: 1865-1900, 1955; American Railroads, 1961; A History of American Railroads, 1967; Turnpikes, Canals and Steamboats, 1969; Transportation in American History, 1970; Life and Decline of the American Railroad, 1970; History of the Illinois Central Railroad, 1975; Iron Road to the West, 1978; Sixty-five Years of Kiwanis in Indiana, 1981; History of the Baltimore and Ohio Railroad, 1987. Add: 615 Carrolton Blvd., West Lafayette, Ind. 47906, U.S.A.

STOVER, Leon (Eugene). American, b. 1929. Science fiction/Fantasy, Anthropology/Ethnology, History, Literature. Prof. of Anthropology, Illinois Inst. of Technology, Chicago, since 1974 (Assoc. Prof., 1965–74). Instr., American Museum of Natural History, NYC, 1955–57; Asst. Prof. of Anthropology, Hobart Coll. and William Smith Coll., Geneva, N.Y., 1957–63; Visiting Prof., Tokyo Univ., 1963–65. Formerly, Script Writer, Encyclopaedia Britannica Films, Chicago; Science Ed., Amazing and Fantastic mags., 1968–69. *Publs:* (ed. with Harry Harrison) Apeman,

Spaceman: Anthropological Science Fiction, 1968; (ed. with Willis E. McNelly) Above the Human Landscape: Anthology of Sociological Science Fiction, 1972; (with Harry Harrison) Stonehenge (SF novel), 1972, rev. as Stonehenge: Where Atlantis Died, 1983; La Science-Fiction Américaine: Essai d'Anthropologie Culturelle, 1972; The Cultural Ecology of Chinese Civilization, 1973; (with Takeko Stover) China: An Anthropological Perspective, 1975; (with Bruce Kraig) Stonehenge: The Indo-European Heritage (in U.K. as Stonehenge and the Origins of Western Culture), 1978; The Shaving of Karl Marx: An Instant Novel of Ideas, 1982; The Prophetic Soul: A Reading of H.G. Wells's "Things to Come", 1987; Robert A. Heinlein, 1987, Harry Harrison, 1990. Add: Dept. of Social Sciences, Illinois Inst. of Technology, Chicago, Ill. 60616, U.S.A.

STOW, (Julian) Randolph. Australian, b. 1935. Novels/Short stories, Poetry. Former Anthropological Asst., Northwest Australia and Papua New Guinea; Lect. in English and Commonwealth Literature, Univ. of Leeds, 1962, 1968–69, Univ. of Western Australia, 1963–64. *Publs:* A Haunted Land, 1956; The Bystander, 1957; Act One: Poems, 1957; To the Islands, 1958; Outrider: Poems 1956-1962, 1962; Tourmaline, 1963; (ed.) Australian Poetry 1964, 1964; The Merry-Go-Round in the Sea, 1965; Midnite: The Story of a Wild Colonial Boy, 1967; A Counterfeit Silence: Selected Poems, 1969; Eight Songs for a Mad King, 1969; Miss Donnithorne's Maggot, 1974; Visitants, 1979; The Girl Green as Elderflower, 1980; The Suburbs of Hell, 1984. Add: c/o Richard Scott Simon Ltd., 43 Doughty St., London WCIN 2LF, England.

STOWE, David Metz. American, b. 1919. Theology/Religion. Consultant. Exec. Vice Pres., United Church Bd. for World Ministries 1970–85, now retired (Missionary, China, 1947–50; Educational Secty., 1956–61; Gen. Secty., Interpretation and Personnel, 1961–62; Prof., Near East Sch. of Theology, 1962–63). Assoc. Minister, First Congregational Church, Berkeley, Calif., 1943–45, and 1951–53; Chaplain and Chmn., Dept. of Religion, Carleton Coll., Northfield, Minn. 1953–56; Exec. Secty., Div. of Foreign Missions, National Council of Churches, NYC, 1963–70. *Publs:* The Church's Witness in the World, 1963; When Faith Meets Faith, 1963, 4th ed., 1972; Partners with the Almighty, 1966; Ecumenicity and Evangelism, 1970. Add: 54 Magnolia Ave., Tenafly, N.J. 07670, U.S.A.

STRACHAN, J(ohn) George. Canadian, b. 1910. Medicine/Health, Psychology. Dir., Milwaukee Information and Referral Center, 1947–53; Exec. Dir., Alcoholism Foundn. of Alberta, Edmonton, 1953–65; Consultant, Govt. of the Province of Alberta, 1965–72; Dir. and Founder, Alberta Drivers Prog., Edmonton, 1970–73; Pres., Gillain Foundn., Victoria, B.C., 1973–79. Secty., Canadian Council, and the Canadian Foundn. on Alcoholism, 1954–64; Vice Pres. and Dir., North American Assn. Alcoholism Prog., Washington, D.C., 1955–64; Special Projects Consultant, Christopher D. Smithers Foundn., NYC, 1965–68. *Publs:* A History and Minute Book of the Canadian Council on Alcoholism, 1959; A History and Minute Book of the North American Association of Alcoholism Programs, 1959; Alcoholism: Treatable Illness, 1968, 1982; Practical Alcoholism Programming, 1971; (ed. with J.A.L. Gilbert) Evaluation in Medical Education, 1971; The Alberta Impaired Drivers Program: A Manual, 1973; Recovery from Alcoholism, 1975. Add: 2035 Summergate Blvd., Sidney, B.C. V8L 4K6, Canada.

STRADLING, Leslie Edward. British, b. 1908. Theology/Religion. Curate of St. Paul, Newington, London, 1933–38; Vicar of St. Luke, Camberwell, London, 1938–43, and St. Anne, Wandsworth, London, 1943–45; Bishop of Masasi, 1945–52, South West Tanganyika, 1952–61, and Johannesburg, 1961–74. *Publs:* A Bishop on Safari, 1958; The Acts through Modern Eyes, 1963; An Open Door, 1966; A Bishop at Prayer, 1971; Prayers of Love, 1973; Prayers of Faith, 1974; Praying Now, 1976; Praying the Psalms, 1978. Add: Braehead House, Auburn Rd., Kenilworth 7700, South Africa.

STRAIGHT, Michael (Whitney). American, b. 1916. Novels/Short stories, History, Biography, Autobiography. Economist, Dept. of State, Washington, D.C., 1937–38; Ghost Writer, Washington, D.C., 1938–41; Contrib. Ed., 1941–43, Publr., 1946–48, and Ed., 1948–56, New Republic, Washington, D.C.; Deputy Chmn., National Endowment for the Arts, Washington, D.C., 1969–78. National Chmn., American Veterans Cttee., 1950–52. *Publs:* Make This the Last War, 1943; Trial by Television, 1954; Carrington, 1960; A Very Small Remnant, 1963; (with others) Three West, 1970; In Great Decades, 1979; After Long Silence (autobiography), 1983; Nancy Hanks: An Intimate Portrait, 1988. Add: 5910 Bradley Blud., Bethesda, Md., U.S.A.

STRAKER, J(ohn) F(oster). Also writes as Ian Rosse. British, b. 1904. Mystery/Crime/Suspense, Travel/Exploration/Adventure. Sr. Mathematics Master, Kingsland Grange Sch., Shrewsbury, Salop., 1927–35; Headmaster, Blackheath Preparatory Sch., London, 1936–39; Sr. Mathematics Master, Cumnor House Sch., Danehill, Sussex, 1945–78. *Publs:* Postman's Knock, 1954; Pick Up the Pieces, 1955; The Ginger Horse, 1956; Gun to Play With, 1956; Goodbye, Aunt Charlotte!, 1958; Hell Is Empty, 1958; Death of a Good Woman, 1961; Murder for Missemily, 1961; A Coil of Rope, 1962; Final Witness, 1963; The Shape of Murder, 1964; Rocochet, 1965; Miscarriage of Murder, 1967; Sin and Johnny Inch, 1968; A Man Who Cannot Kill, 1969; Tight Circle, 1970; A Letter for Obi, 1971; The Goat, 1972; (as Ian Rosse) The Droop (non-mystery novel), 1972; Arthur's Night, 1976; Swallow Them Up, 1977; Death on a Sunday Morning, 1978; Pity It Wasn't George, 1979; Countersnatch, 1980; Southeast England, 1981; Another Man's Poison, 1983; A Choice of Victims, 1984. Add: Lincoln Cottage, Horsted Keynes, Sussex RH17 7AW, England.

STRAND, Kenneth A(lbert). American, b. 1927. Art, History, Theology/Religion. Univ. Prof., Andrews Univ., Berrien Springs, Mich., since 1959. Ed., Andrews Univ. Seminary Studies, since 1974 (Book Review Ed., 1966–67; Assoc. Ed., 1967–74). Engaged in pastoral service, Mich., 1952–59. *Publs:* A Reformation Paradox, 1960; Reformation Bibles in the Crossfire, 1961; (ed.) Dawn of Modern Civilization: Studies in Renaissance, Reformation and Other Topics Presented to Honor Albert Hyma, 1962, 1964; (author and compiler) Reformation Bible Pictures: Woodcuts from Early Lutheran and Emserian New Testaments, 1963; German Bibles Before Luther: The Story of 14 High-German Editions, 1966; Early Low-German Bibles, 1967; Three Essays on Early Church History, with Emphasis on the Roman Province of Asia, 1967; (author and compiler) Woodcuts to the Apocalypse in Dürer's Time, 1968; (ed.) Essays on the Nothern Renaissance, 1968; (ed.) Essays on Luther, 1969; (author and compiler) Woodcuts to the Apocalypse from the Early 16th Century, 1969; The Open Gates of Heaven: Brief Introduction to Literary Analysis of the Book of Revelation, 1970, 1972; (author and compiler) Reform Essentials of Luther and Calvin: A Source Collection, 1971; Essays on the Sabbath in Early Christianity, 1972; (author and compiler) Luther's "September Bible" in Facsimile, 1972; Perspectives in the Book of Revelation: Essays on Apocalyptic Interpretation, 1975; Interpreting the Book of Revelation, 1976, 1979; The Early Christian Sabbath, 1979; (ed.) The Sabbath in Scripture and History, 1982; Catholic German Bibles of the Reformation Era, 1982. Add: Seminary Hall, Andrews Univ., Berrien Springs, Mich. 49104, U.S.A.

STRAND, Mark. American, b. 1934. Poetry, Translations. Distinguished Prof. of English Univ. of Utah, Salt Lake City. Instr., Univ. of Iowa, Iowa City, 1962–65; Fulbright Lectr., Univ. of Brazil, Rio de Janeiro, 1965–66; Assoc. Prof., Brooklyn Coll., N.Y., 1970–72. *Publs:* Sleeping with One Eye Open, 1964; Reasons for Moving: Poems, 1968; (ed.) The Contemporary American Poets: American Poetry since 1940, 1969; (ed.) New Poetry of Mexico, 1970; Darker: Poems, 1970; (trans.) 18 Poems from the Quechua, 1971; The Story of Our Lives, 1973; The Sergeantville Notebook, 1973; Elegy for My Father, 1973; (ed. and trans.) The Owl's Insomnia: Selected Poems of Rafael Alberti, 1973; (co-ed.) Another Republic, 1976; The Late Hour, 1978; The Monument, 1978; Selected Poems, 1980; The Planet of Lost Things (for children), 1982; (ed.) Art of the Real: Nine American Figurative Painters, 1983; The Night Book (for children), 1985; Mr. and Mrs. Baby and Other Stories, 1985; Rembrandt Takes a Walk, 1986; William Bailey, 1987; New Poems, 1990. Add: 716 4th Ave., Salt Lake City, Utah 84103, U.S.A.

STRANGER, Joyce. Pseud. for Joyce Muriel Wilson. British. Novels/Short stories, Children's fiction, Poetry, Animals/Pets. *Publs:* Wild Cat Island, 1961; Circus All Alone, 1965; The Running Foxes, 1965; Breed of Giants, 1966; Rex, 1967; Casey (in U.S. as Born to Trouble), 1968; Rusty (in U.S. as The Wind on the Dragon), 1969; One for Sorrow, 1969; Zara, 1970; Jason—Nobody's Dog, 1970; Chia, The Wildcat, 1971; Lakeland Vet, 1972; The Honeywell Badger, 1972; Paddy Joe, 1973; The Hare at Dark Hollow, 1973; Trouble for Paddy Joe, 1973; Walk a Lonely Road, 1973; A Dog Called Gelert and Other Stories, 1974; The Secret Herds: Animal Stories, 1974; Never Count Apples, 1974; Never Tell a Secret, 1975; Paddy Joe at Deep Hollow Farm, 1975; The Fox at Drummer's Darkness, 1976; The Wild Ponies, 1976; Joyce Stranger's Book of Hanak Animals (verse), 1976; Flash, 1976; Kym: The True Story of a Siamese Cat, 1976; Khazan, 1977; Two's Company (autobiography), 1977; A Walk in the Dark, 1978; The Curse of Seal Valley, 1978; The January Queen, 1979; How to Get a Sensible Dog, 1979; Vet on Call, 1980; Double Trouble, 1980; All about Your Pet Puppy, 1980; The Stallion, 1981; Vet Riding High, 1981; No More Horses, 1981; Dial V.E.T.,

1981; Marooned!, 1982; Two for Joy, 1983; Jasse, 1983; Stranger than Fiction, 1984; A Dog in a Million, 1984; Shadows in the Dark, 1984; The Family at Fool's Farm, 1985; The Hounds of Hades, 1985; Dog Days, 1986; Double or Quit, 1987; Paddy Joe and Tomkin's Folly, 1976; How to Own A Sensible Dog, 1988; Spy—The No Good Pup, 1989. Add: c/o Aitken and Stone, 29 Fernshaw Rd., London SW10 0TG, England.

STRASSER, Todd. Also writes as Morton Rhue. American, b. 1950. Novels/Short stories, Children's fiction. Freelance writer since 1975; Founding Pres., Toggle Inc., NYC, since 1978. Reporter, Times Herald Record, Middletown, N.Y., 1974–76; Copywriter, Compton Advertising, NYC, 1976–77; Researcher, Esquire mag., NYC, 1977–78. *Publs:* Angel Dust Blues, 1979; Friends Till the End, 1981; (as Morton Rhue) The Wave, 1981; Rock 'n' Roll Nights, 1982; Workin' for Peanuts, 1983; Turn It Up!, 1984; The Complete Computer Popularity Program, 1984; A Very Touchy Subject, 1985; Ferris Bueller's Day Off, 1986; Wildlife, 1987; The Mall from Outer Space 1987; The Family Man, 1988; The Accident, 1988. Add: 310 W. 79th St., New York, N.Y. 10024, U.S.A.

STRATTON, Rebecca. Also writes as Lucy Gillen. British. Historical Romance/Gothic. Full-time writer since 1967. Civil servant for the Coventry County Ct., 1957–67. *Publs:* (as Lucy Gillen) The Ross Inheritance, 1969; (as Lucy Gillen) Good Morning, Doctor Houston, 1969; (as Lucy Gillen) The Silver Fishes, 1969; (as Lucy Gillen) A Wife for Andrew, 1969; (as Lucy Gillen) Heir to Glen Ghyll, 1970; (as Lucy Gillen) Nurse Helen, 1970; (as Lucy Gillen) Doctor Toby, 1970; (as Lucy Gillen) The Girl at Smuggler's Rest, 1970; (as Lucy Gillen) My Beautiful Heathen, 1970; (as Lucy Gillen) The Whispering Sea, 1971; (as Lucy Gillen) Winter at Cray, 1971; (as Lucy Gillen) Dance of Fire, 1971; (as Lucy Gillen) Marriage by Request, 1971; (as Lucy Gillen) Summer Season, 1971; (as Lucy Gillen) The Enchanted Ring, 1971; (as Lucy Gillen) Sweet Kate, 1971; (as Lucy Gillen) That Man Next Door, 1971; (as Lucy Gillen) A Time Remembered, 1971; (as Lucy Gillen) The Pretty Witch, 1971; (as Lucy Gillen) Dangerous Stranger, 1972; (as Lucy Gillen) Glen of Sighs, 1972; (as Lucy Gillen) Means to an End, 1972; (as Lucy Gillen) The Changing Years, 1972; (as Lucy Gillen) Painted Wings, 1972; (as Lucy Gillen) The Pengelly Jade, 1972; (as Lucy Gillen) The Runaway Bridge, 1972; (as Lucy Gillen) An Echo of Spring, 1973; (as Lucy Gillen) Moment of Truth, 1973; (as Lucy Gillen) A Touch of Honey, 1973; (as Lucy Gillen) Gentle Tyrant, 1973; (as Lucy Gillen) A Handful of Stars, 1973; (as Lucy Gillen) The Stairway to Enchantment, 1973; The Golden Madonna, 1973; The Bride of Romano, 1973; (as Lucy Gillen) Come, Walk with Me, 1974; (as Lucy Gillen) Web of Silver, 1974; Castles in Spain, 1974; The Yellow Moon, 1974; Island of Darkness, 1974; Autumn Concerto, 1974; The Flight of the Hawk, 1974; Run from the Wind, 1974; Fairwinds, 1974; (as Lucy Gillen) All the Summer Long, 1975; (as Lucy Gillen) Return to Deepwater, 1975; The Warm Wind of Farik, 1975; Firebird, 1975; The Fire and the Fury, 1975; The Goddess of Mavisu, 1975; Isle of the Golden Drum, 1975; Moon Tide, 1975; (as Lucy Gillen) The Hungry Tide, 1976; (as Lucy Gillen) The House of Kingdom, 1976; The White Dolphin, 1976; Proud Stranger, 1976; The Road to Gafsa, 1976; Gemini Child, 1976; Chateau d'Armor, 1976; (as Lucy Gillen) Master of Ben Ross, 1977; Dream of Winter, 1977; Girl in a White Hat, 1977; More Than a Dream, 1977; Sprindrift, 1977; (as Lucy Gillen) Back of Beyond, 1978; (as Lucy Gillen) Heron's Point, 1978; Lost Heritage, 1978; Image of Love, 1978; Bargain for Paradise, 1978; The Corsican Bandit, 1978; The Eagle of the Vincella, 1978; Inherit the Sun, 1978; The Sign of the Ram, 1978; The Velvet Glove, 1978; (as Lucy Gillen) Hepburn's Quay, 1979; Close to the Heart, 1979; Lark in an Alien Sky, 1979; The Tears of Venus, 1979; (as Lucy Gillen) The Storm Eagle, 1980; Trader's Cay, 1980; The Leo Man, 1980; The Inherited Bride, 1980; Apollo's Daughter, 1980; The Black Invader, 1981; Dark Enigma, 1981; The Silken Cage, 1981; Charade, 1982; The Golden Spaniard, 1982, The Man from Nowhere, 1982. Add:c/o Mills and Boon, Eton House, 18-24 Paradise Rd., Richmond, Surrey TW9 1SR, England.

STRATTON, Thomas. *See* **COULSON,** Robert and **DeWEESE,** Gene.

STRAUB, Peter (Francis). American, b. 1943. Novels/Short stories, Poetry. Teacher of English, Milwaukee Univ. Sch., 1966–69. *Publs:* Ishmael (poems), 1972; Open Air (poems), 1972; Marriages (novel), 1973; Julia (novel), 1975; If You Could See Me Now (novel), 1977; Ghost Story (novel), 1979; Shadowland (novel), 1980; Floating Dragon (novel), 1983; Leeson Park and Belsize Park (poems), 1983; (with Stephen King) The Talisman (novel), 1984; Blue Rose (novella), 1984; Koko (novel), 1988. Add: 1 Beachside Common, Westport, Conn., U.S.A.

STRAUMANN, Heinrich (Enrico). Swiss, b. 1902. Literature, Essays. Hon. Prof.of English Philology, Univ. of Zurich, Switzerland, since 1971

(Lectr., 1933–38; Prof., 1939–71). Pres., P.E.N., Zurich Chapter, 1942–46; Pres., Swiss British Soc., 1946–52; Rector, Univ. of Zurich, 1960–62. *Publs:* Justinus Kerner, 1928; Newspaper Headlines, 1935; Byron and Switzerland, 1949; American Literature in the Twentieth Century, 1951; Phoenix und Taube, 1954; William Faulkner, 1968; (with M. Bircher) Shakespeare und die Deutsche Schweiz, 1971; Contexts of Literature: An Anglo-Swiss Approach, 1973. Add: 76 Drusbergstrasse, 8053 Zurich, Switzerland.

STRAUS, Dorothea. American, b. 1916. Novels/Short stories, Memoirs. *Publs:* Thresholds, 1971; Showcases (memoirs), 1974; Palaces and Prisons, 1976; Under the Canopy, 1982; The Birthmark, 1987. Add: 160 E. 65th St., New York, N.Y. 10021, U.S.A.

STRAUS, Murray A. American, b. 1926. Psychology, Sociology. Prof. of Sociology and Dir. of the Family Research Lab., Univ. of New Hampshire, Durham, since 1968. Consultant, U.S. National Inst. of Mental Health, and National Science Foundn. Assoc. Prof., Cornell Univ., Ithaca, N.Y., 1959–61; Prof. of Sociology, Univ. of Minnesota, Minneapolis, 1961–68. *Publs:* (with J.I. Nelson) Sociological Analysis: An Empirical Approach Through Replication, 1968; Family Analysis: Readings and Replications, 1969; Family Measurement Techniques, 1969, (with Bruce Brown) rev. ed. 1978; (co-ed.) Family Problem Solving, 1971; (with Gerald Hotaling) The Social Causes of Husband-Wife Violence, 1980; (co-author) Behind Closed Doors: Violence in the American Family, 1980; (with others) The Dark Side of Families: Current Family Violence Research, 1983; (with Alan Lincoln) Crime and the Family, 1985; (with Arnold S. Linsky) Social Stress in the United States: Links to Regional Patterns of Crime and Illness, 1986; Intimate Violence, 1988; Physical Violence in American Families, 1989; The Social Origins of Rape in the United States, 1989. Add: Dept. of Sociology, Univ. of New Hampshire, Durham, N.H. 03824, U.S.A.

STRAUSS, Walter L(eopold). American (born German), b. 1932. Art. Gen. Ed., The Illustrated Bartsch, 66 vols. Taught at the State Univ. of New York, Binghamton, 1979–83, and Cooper Union, NYC, 1984–85. *Publs:* Albrecht Dürer's Complete Engravings, Woodcuts, and Dry-Points, 1972; The German Single-Life Woodcut 1500-1550, 4 vols., 1974; Complete Drawings of Albrecht Dürer, 6 vols., 1975; (ed.) Tribute to Wolfgang Stechow, 1976; (with D. Alexander) The German Single-Life Woodcut of the 17th Century, 1978; (with M. van der Meulen) The Rembrandt Documents, 1979. Add: Box 325, Scarborough, N.Y. 10510, U.S.A.

STRAWSON, (Sir) Peter (Frederick). British, b. 1919. Philosophy. Fellow, Magdalen Coll., Oxford, since 1968 (Fellow, Univ. Coll., 1948–68), and Waynflete Prof. of Metaphysics, Oxford Univ., 1968–87 (Lectr., 1949–66; Reader, 1966–68). *Publs:* Introduction to Logical Theory, 1952; Individuals, 1959; The Bounds of Sense, 1966; (ed.) Philosophical Logic, 1967; (ed.) Essays in the Philosophy of Thought and Action, 1968; Logico-Linguistic Papers, 1971; Freedom and Resentment, 1974; Subject and Predicate in Logic and Grammar, 1974; Skepticism and Naturalism: Some Varieties, 1985; Analyse et Métaphysique, 1985. Add: Magdalen Coll., Oxford, England.

STREET, Julia Montgomery. American, b. 1898. Children's fiction, Poetry. Field Worker, N.C. Children's Home, Greensboro, 1921–23; Primary teacher, Winston-Salem schs., N.C., 1923–24; Script writer and script-writing teacher, WSJS Radio Council, Winston-Salem, N.C. *Publs:* Street Lights, 1939; Salem Christmas Eve, 1940; Fiddler's Fancy, 1956; Moccasin Tracks, 1958; Candle Love Feast, 1959; Drover's Gold, 1961; Dolcie's Whale, 1963; (with R. Walser) North Carolina Parade, 1966; Judaculla's Handprint and Other Mysterious Tales from North Carolina, 1976. Add: 545 Oaklawn Ave., Winston-Salem, N.C. 27104, U.S.A.

STREETEN, Paul Patrick. British, b. 1917. Economics, Public/Social administration. Dir., World Development Inst., and Prof., Boston Univ. Chmn., Editorial Bd., World Development. Fellow, Balliol Coll., 1948–66, 1968–78, and Dir., Inst. of Commonwealth Studies, 1968–78, Oxford, Univ. Deputy Dir., Gen. Economic Planning, Ministry of Overseas Development, 1964–66; Fellow and Acting Dir., Inst. of Development Studies, 1966–68; Dir., Commonwealth Development Corp., 1967–73. *Publs:* (ed.) Value in Social Theory, 1958; Economic Integration, 1964; (ed. with M. Lipton) The Crisis of Indian Planning, 1968; (ed.) Unfashionable Economics, 1970; (ed. with H. Corbet) Commonwealth Policy in a Global Context, 1971; (with D. Elson) Diversification and Development, 1971; The Frontiers of Development Studies, 1972; Aid to Africa, 1972; Trade Strategies for Development; (with S. Lall) Foreign Investment, Transnationals, and Developing Countries, 1977; Development

Perspectives, 1981; First Things First, 1981; (ed.) Recent Issues in World Development, 1981; What Price Food?, 1987; (ed.) Beyond Structural Adjustment, 1988. Add: World Development Inst., Boston Univ., 270 Bay State Rd., Boston, Mass. 02215, U.S.A.

STREITWIESER, Andrew, Jr. American, b. 1927. Chemistry. Prof. of Chemistry, Univ. of California, Berkeley, since 1963 (Instr., 1952–54; Asst. Prof., 1954–59; Assoc. Prof., 1959–63). Co-Ed., Progress in Physical Organic Chemistry, vols. I-XI, Wiley Interscience, NYC, 1963–74. *Publs:* Molecular Orbital Theory for Organic Chemists, 1961; Solvolytic Displacement Reactions, 1962; (with J.I. Brauman) Supplemental Tables of Molecular Orbital Calculations, 1965; (with C.A. Coulson) Dictionary of Electron Calculations, 1965; (with P. Owens) Orbital and Electron Density Diagrams: An Application of Computer Graphics, 1973; (with C.J. Heathcock) Organic Chemistry: An Introductory Text, 1976, 3rd ed., 1985. Add: Dept. of Chemistry, Univ. of California, Berkeley, Calif. 94720, U.S.A.

STRENG, Frederick John. American, b. 1933, Theology/Religion. Prof. of History of Religions, Southern Methodist Univ., Dallas, Tex., since 1974 (Assoc. Prof., 1966–74). Gen. Ed., Religious Life of Man series, Wadsworth Publ. Co. Asst. Prof. of History of Religions, Univ. of Southern California, 1963–66. *Publs:* Emptiness: A Study in Religious Meaning, 1967; Understanding Religious Life, 1969, 1985; (co-ed.) Ways of Being Religious, 1973; (co-ed.) Buddhist-Christian Dialogue, 1986; (co-ed.) Spoken and Unspoken Thanks, 1989. Add: Dept. of Religous Studies, Southern Methodist Univ., Dallas, Tex. 75275, U.S.A.

STRETE, Craig. Pseud. for a Cherokee Indian writer. American, b. 1950. Science fiction/Fantasy, Children's fiction. Ed., Red Planet Earth mag. *Publs:* If All Else Fails, We Can Whip the Horse's Eyes and Make Him Cry and Sleep, 1976; The Bleeding Man and Other Science Fiction Stories (juvenile), 1977; Paint Your Face on a Drowning in the River, 1978; When Grandfather Journeys into Winter (juvenile fiction), 1979; Dark Journey (verse), 1979; Burn Down the Night, 1982; To Make Death Love Us, 1985; Death in the Spirit House, 1986; Death Chants, 1986; Night Walker, 1986. Add: Kirby McCauley Ltd., 432 Park Ave. S., Suite 1509, New York, N.Y. 10016, U.S.A.

STRETTON, Hugh. Australian, b. 1924. Politics/Government, Urban studies. Reader in History, Univ. of Adelaide, 1969–89 (Prof. of History, 1954–68). Member, S. Australian Housing Trust, since 1971. *Publs:* The Political Sciences, 1969; Ideas for Australian Cities, 1970; Housing and Government, 1974; Capitalism, Socialism and the Environment, 1976; Urban Planning in Rich and Poor Countries, 1978; Political Essays, 1987. Add: 61 Tynte St., North Adelaide, S.A. 5006, Australia.

STRICKLAND, Margot. British, b. 1937. Short stories, Biography. *Publs:* The Byron Women, 1974; Angela Thirkell: Portrait of a Lady Novelist, 1977. Add: c/o Duckworth, 43 Gloucester Cres., London NW1 7DY, England.

STROM, Robert. American, b. 1935. Education, Psychology. Prof. of Education since 1973, and Dir., Office of Parent Development Intnl., Arizona State Univ., Tempe (Chmn., Dept.of Elementary Education, 1969–73). *Publs:* Teaching in the Slum School, 1965; (ed. with P. Torrance) Mental Health and Achievement, 1965; Psychology for the Classroom, 1969; (ed.) Teacher and the Learning Process, 1971; The Urban Teacher, 1971; (ed.) Values and Human Development, 1973; (ed. with P. Torrance) Education for Affective Achievement, 1973; (ed.) Teaching and Its Preconditions, 1974; Parent and Child in Fiction, 1977; Growing Together: Parent and Child Development, 1978; Growing Through Play, 1980; Educational Psychology, 1982; Human Development and Learning, 1987. Add: 6017 E. Cambridge Ave., Scottsdale, Ariz. 85257, U.S.A.

STRONG, Eithne. Irish, b. 1923. Novels/Short stories, Poetry. *Publs:* Songs of Living, 1962; Sarah, in Passing, 1974; Degrees of Kindred, 1979; Flesh—The Greatest Sin, 1980; Cirt Oibre, 1980; Patterns, 1981; Fuil Agus Fallai, 1983; My Darling Neighbour, 1985. Add: 17 Eaton Sq., Monkstown, Co. Dublin, Ireland.

STRONG, Pat. *See* **HOUGH,** Richard.

STRONG, (Sir) Roy (Colin). British, b. 1935. Art, History. Asst. Keeper, 1959–67, and Dir., Keeper, and Secty., 1967–74, National Portrait Gallery, London; Museum Dir., Victoria and Albert Museum, 1974–87. *Publs:* Portraits of Queen Elizabeth I, 1963; (with J.A. Van Dorsten)

Leicester's Triumph, 1964; Holbein and Henry VIII, 1967; Tudor and Jacobean Portraits, 1969; The English Icon, 1969; (with J.T. Oman) Elizabeth R, 1971; Van Dyck, Charles I on Horseback, 1972; (with J.T. Oman) Mary Queen of Scots, 1972; (with S. Orgel) Inigo Jones: The Theatre of the Stuart Court, 1973; Splendour at Court, 1973; (with C. Ford) An Early Victorian Album: The Hill/Adamson Collection, 1974; Nicholas Hilliard, 1975; The Cult of Elizabeth: Elizabeth Portraiture and Pageantry, 1977; When Did You Last See Your Father? The Victorian Painter and British History, 1978; The Renaissance Garden in England, 1979; Britannia Triumphant: Inigo Jones, Rubens, and Whitehall Palace, 1980; (co-author) The English Miniature, 1981; (co-author) Designing for the Dancer, 1981; (with J.T. Oman) The English Year, 1982; (co-author) The New Pelican Guide to English Literature, 1982; The English Renaissance Miniature, 1983; (with J. Murrell) Artists of the Tudor Court Catalogue, 1983; Art and Power, 1984; (co-author) Glyndebourne: A Celebration, 1984; Strong Points, 1985; Henry, Prince of Wales and England's Lost Renaissance, 1986; Creating Small Gardens, 1986; Gloriana: Portraits of Queen Elizabeth I, 1987; The Small Garden Designer's Handbook, 1987; Cecil Beaton: The Royal Portraits, 1988. Add: Curtis Brown Ltd., 162-168 Regent St., London W1R 5TB, England.

STRONG, Susan. *See* **REES,** Joan.

STROUP, Herbert. American, b. 1916. Education, Philosophy, Sociology, Theology/Religion. Prof. of Sociology, Brooklyn Coll., City Univ. of New York, since 1954 (Tutor, to Assoc. Prof., 1942–54; Dean of Students, 1954–69). *Publs:* (ed.) A Symphony of Prayer, 1945; The Jehovah's Witnesses, 1945; Social Work: An Introduction to the Field, 1948; Community Welfare Organization, 1952; Bureaucracy in Higher Education, 1966; Organized Student Activities, 1967; Church and State in Confrontation, 1967; Four Religions of Asia, 1968; (with R. Farson and P. Hauser) The Future of the Family, 1969; Like a Great River: An Introduction to Hinduism, 1972; Founders of Living Religions, 1974; Social Welfare Pioneers, 1983. Add: 171 Fairlawn Ave., West Hempstead, N.Y. 11552, U.S.A.

STRUTTON, Bill. (William Harold Strutton). Australian, b. 1918. Novels/Short stories, Science fiction/Fantasy, Plays/Screenplays, Military/ Defence.Feature Writer, Australian Consolidated Press, 1945–58. *Publs:* A Jury of Angels, 1957; (with M. Pearson) The Secret Invaders, 1958; Island of Terrible Friends, 1961; Doctor Who and the Zarbi, 1965; The Carpaccio Caper (in U.K. as A Glut of Virgins), 1973; (with V. Guest and M. Foster) Department K (screenplay). Add: Federico Marti Carreras 2,6,4, 17200 Pala frugell, Gerona, Spain.

STRYK, Lucien. American, b. 1924. Poetry, Translations. Member of English Dept. since 1958, and currently Prof. of English, Northern Illinois Univ., DeKalb. Visiting Lectr., Niigata Univ., Japan, 1956–58, and Yamaguchi Univ., Japan, 1962–63; Fulbright Lectr., Iran, 1961–62. *Publs:* Taproot: A Selection of Poems, 1953; The Trespasser: Poems, 1956; Notes for a Guidebook, 1965; (ed. and trans. with T. Ikemoto) Zen: Poems, Prayers, Sermons, Anecdotes, Interviews, 1965; (ed.) Heartland: Poets of the Midwest, 2 vols., 1967–75; (ed.) World of the Buddha: A Reader, 1968; The Pit and Other Poems, 1969; (ed. and trans. with T. Ikemoto) Afterimages: Zen Poems of Shinkichi Takahashi, 1970; Awakening, 1973; (trans. with T. Ikemoto) Zen Poems of China and Japan: The Crane's Bill, 1973; (trans. with T. Ikemoto) Twelve Death Poems of the Chinese Zen Masters, 1973; Selected Poems, 1976; (co-trans.) The Penguin Book of Zen Poetry, 1977; The Duckpond, 1978; (ed.) Prairie Voices: A Collection of Illinois Poets, 1980; Encounter with Zen: Writings on Poetry and Zen, 1981; Collected Poems 1953-1983, 1984; On Love and Barley: Haiku of Basho, 1985; Triumph of the Sparrow: Zen Poems of Shinkichi Takahashi, 1986; Bells of Lombardy, 1986. Add: Dept. of English, Northern Illinois Univ. DeKalb, Ill. 60115, U.S.A.

STUART, Alex R. *See* **GORDON,** Stuart.

STUART, Dabney. American, b. 1937. Novels/Short stories, Poetry, Literature. Prof. of English, Washington and Lee Univ., Lexington, Va. (joined faculty, 1965); Ed., Shenandoah, since 1988. Instr. in English, Coll. of William and Mary, Williamsburg, Va., 1961–65; Poet-in-Residence, Univ. of Virginia, Charlottesville, 1981–82. Poetry Ed., Shenandoah, 1966–76. *Publs:* The Diving Bell, 1966; A Particular Place, 1969; The Other Hand, 1974; Friends of Yours, Friends of Mine, 1974; Round and Round, 1977; Nabokov: The Dimensions of Parody, 1978; Rockbridge Poems, 1981; Common Ground, 1982; Don't Look Back, 1987. Add: Dept. of English, Washington and Lee Univ., Lexington, Va. 24450, U.S.A.

STUART, Forbes. British, b. 1924. Children's fiction, Children's non-fiction, History. Documentary film producer, 1951–62; in public relations 1962–69. *Publs:* South African Towns Tell Tales, 1954; Horned Animals Only, 1966; A Medley of Folk Songs, 1971; The Boy on the Ox's Back, 1971; Stories of Britain in Song, 1972; The Magic Bridle, 1974; The Magic Horns, 1975; The Dancer of Burton Fair, 1976; The Mermaid's Revenge, 1979. Add: 6 Somerton Rd., London NW2, England.

STUART, (Henry) Francis (Montgomery). Irish, b. 1902. Novels/Short stories, Plays/Screenplays, Poetry, Translations. Founder Member, Irish Academy of Letters. *Publs:* Nationalism and Culture, 1924; Mystics and Mysticism, 1929; Women and God, 1931; We Have Kept the Faith (poetry), 1932; Pigeon Irish, 1932; The Coloured Dome, 1932; Men Crowd Me Round (play), 1933; Try the Sky, 1933; Glory, 1933, play, 1936; Things to Love For: Notes for an Autobiography, 1934; In Search of Love, 1935; The Angel of Pity, 1935; The White Hare, 1936; The Bridge, 1937; Julie, 1938; The Great Square, 1939; Strange Guest (play), 1940; The Pillar of Cloud, 1948; Redemption, 1949; The Flowering Cross, 1950; Good Friday's Daughter, 1952; The Chariot, 1953; The Pilgrimage, 1955; Victors and Vanquished, 1958; Angels of Providence, 1959; Flynn's Last Dive (play), 1962; Who Fears to Speak (play), 1970; Black List, Section H, 1971; Memorial, 1973; (trans.) The Captive Dreamer, by Christian de la Maziere, 1974; A Hole in the Head, 1976; The High Consistery, 1980; The Abandoned Snail-Shell, 1987. Add: 2 Highfield Park, Dublin 14, Ireland.

STUART, Ian. Also writes as Malcolm Gray. British, b. 1927. Mystery/Crime/Suspense. Fulltime writer since 1984. Formerly, Mgr., Barclays Bank. *Publs:* The Snow on the Ben, 1961; Golf in Hertfordshire (non-fiction), 1972; Death from Disclosure, 1976; Flood Tide, 1977; Sand Trap, 1977; Fatal Switch, 1978; A Weekend to Kill, 1978; Pictures in the Dark, 1979; The Renshaw Strike, 1980; End on the Rocks, 1981; The Garb of Truth, 1982; Thrilling-Sweet and Rotten, 1983; A Growing Concern, 1985; (as Malcolm Gray) Look Back on Murder, 1985; (as Malcolm Gray) Stab in the Back, 1986; Sandscreen, 1987; (as Malcolm Gray) A Matter of Record, 1987; The Margin, 1988; (as Malcolm Gray) An Unwelcome Presence, 1989. Add: 218 Watford Rd., Chiswell Green, St. Albans, Herts. AL2 3EA, England.

STUART, Sidney. *See* AVALLONE, Michael.

STUART, Simon. British, b. 1930. Education. English teacher, King's Sch., Canterbury, 1954–57, Stowe Sch., Bucks., 1958–61, and Haberdashers' Aske's Sch., Elstree, 1961–78. *Publs:* (with John Wilson and M.C. Hinton) Moral Education in Schools, 1969; New Measure 10, 1969; Say: An Experiment in Learning, 1969, 1973; New Phoenix Wings (literary criticism), 1979. Add: 16 Neville Dr., London N2, England.

STUBBS, Harry Clement. *See* CLEMENT, Hal.

STUBBS, Jean (Yvonne). British, b. 1926. Mystery/Crime/Suspense, Historical/Romance/Gothic. Regular Reviewer, Books and Bookmen, London, 1966–80. *Publs:* The Rose Grower, 1962; The Travellers, 1963; Hanrahan's Colony, 1964; The Straw Crown, 1966; My Grand Enemy, 1967; The Passing Star (in U.S. as Eleanor Duse), 1970; The Case of Kitty Ogilvie, 1970; An Unknown Welshman, 1972; Dear Laura, 1973; The Painted Face, 1974; The Golden Crucible, 1976; Kit's Hill, 1978, in U.S. as By Our Beginnings, 1979; The Ironmaster (in U.S. as An Imperfect Joy), 1981; The Vivian Inheritance, 1982; The Northern Correspondent, 1984; 100 Years Around the Lizard, 1985; A Lasting Spring, 1987; Great Houses of Cornwell, 1988; Like We Used to Be, 1989. Add: Trewin, Nancegollan, nr. Helston, Cornwall TR13 0AJ, England.

STUBBS, Peter Charles. British, b. 1937. Economics, History. Reader in Economics, Univ. of Manchester, since 1980 (Lectr., 1969–72; Sr. Lectr., 1972–80; Dean of Faculty, 1985–87). Staff member, The Economist mag., London, 1960–62; Research Fellow, Inst. of Applied Economic Research, Univ. of Melbourne, 1963–68. *Publs:* Innovation and Research, 1968; The Australian Motor Industry, 1972; (with N. Lee) The History of Dorman Smith, 1972; (co-author) Transport Economics, 1980, 1984; Technology and Australia's Future, 1980; Australia and the Maritime Industries, 1983. Add: c/o Dept. of Economics, Univ. of Manchester, Manchester M13 9PL, England.

STUHLMUELLER, Carroll. American, b. 1923. Theology/Religion. Ordained Roman Catholic priest, 1950; Prof. of Scripture, Catholic Theological Union, Chicago, since 1968. Asst. Prof. of Scripture, Passionist Theologate, Louisville, Ky., 1954–65; Assoc. Prof. of Scripture, St. Mary's Grad. Sch. of Theology, Notre Dame, Ind., 1957–64; Assoc.

Prof. of Scripture, St. Meinrad Seminary, Ind., 1965–68; Prof. of Scripture, St. John's Univ., NYC, 1970–75; Assoc. Ed., Catholic Biblical Quarterly, 1973–77; Ed., The Bible Today, 1980–85; Assoc. Ed., Journal of Biblical Literature, 1987–90. *Publs:* The Gospel of St. Luke, 1960, 1964; The Book of Leviticus, 1960; The Books of Aggai, Zacharia, Malachia, Jona, Joel, Abdia, 1961; (ed.) Hew Horizons, by Barnabas M. Ahern, 1961; The Prophets and the Word of God, 1964, 1966; The Book of Isaiah, chapters 40-66, 1965; Creative Redemption in Deutero-Isaiah, 1970; (ed. with E.H. Maly and W. Heidt) The Bible Today Reader, 1973; Thirsting for the Lord, 1977; Biblical Meditations for Lent, 1978; (ed.) Women and Priesthood, 1978; Biblical Meditations for the Easter Season, 1980; Biblical Meditations for Advent and Christmas Season, 1980; Biblical Meditations for Ordinary Time, 3 vols., 1985; Psalms, 2 vols., 1983; (with Donald Senior) The Biblical Foundations for Mission, 1983; Rebuilding with Hope, 1988. Add: Catholic Theological Union, 5401 S. Cornell Ave., Chicago, Ill. 60615, U.S.A.

STUMPF, Samuel (Enoch). American, b. 1918. Law, Philosophy. Prof. of Jurisprudence, Sch. of Law, and Prof. of Medical Philosophy, Sch. of Medicine, Vanderbilt Univ., Nashville, since 1974 (Chmn., and Prof., Philosophy Dept., 1948–67; Lectr. in Jurisprudence, Law Sch., 1950–58; Consultant, Medical Sch., 1963–67). Pres., Cornell Coll., Mt. Vernon, Iowa, 1967–74. *Publs:* A Democratic Manifesto, 1954; Socrates to Sartre: A History of Philosophy, 1966, 4th ed. 1988; Morality and Law, 1966; (ed.) Philosophical Problems, 1971, 3rd ed. 1989; Philosophy: History and Problems, 1971, 4th ed. 1989; Elements of Philosophy, 1979, 1983. Add: 424 Page Rd., Nashville, Tenn. 37205, U.S.A.

STUPAK, Ronald J(oseph). American, b. 1934. International relations/Current affairs, Politics/Government, Public/Social administration. Sr. Faculty Member, Prof. of Political Science and Contemporary Affairs, and Asst. Dean for Progs., Federal Executive Inst., Charlottesville, Va., since 1975. Instr., 1966–67, Asst. Prof., 1967–70, Assoc. Prof., 1970–74, and Prof., 1974–75, Miami Univ., Oxford, Ohio; Consultant, Public Affairs Center, Univ. of Southern California, Los Angeles, 1973–82. *Publs:* (ed. with Richard U. Sherman) Readings in National Security Policy, 1963; The Shaping of Foreign Policy: The Role of the Secretary of State as Seen by Dean Acheson, 1969; American Foreign Policy, 1976; (co-author) Understanding Political Science, 1977; (co-author) Inside the Bureaucracy, 1978. Add: Federal Executive Inst., Route 29 N., Charlottesville, Va. 22903, U.S.A.

STURROCK, Jeremy. *See* HEALEY, Ben.

STYAN, J(ohn) L(ouis). British, b. 1923. Literature, Theatre. Franklyn Bliss Snyder Prof. of English Literature since 1977, and Prof. of Theatre, Now Emeritus, Northwestern Univ., Evanston. Staff Tutor, then Sr. Staff Tutor in Literature and Drama, Dept. of Adult Education, Univ. of Hull, England, 1950–65; Prof. and Chmn., Dept. of English, Univ. of Michigan, Ann Arbor, 1965–74; Andrew Mellon Prof. of English, Univ. of Pittsburgh, 1974–77. *Publs:* The Elements of Drama, 1960; The Dark Comedy, 1962, 1968; The Dramatic Experience, 1965; Shakespeare's Stagecraft, 1967; Chekhov in Performance, 1971; The Challenge of the Theatre, 1972; Drama, State and Audience, 1975; The Shakespeare Revolution, 1977; Modern Drama in Theory and Practice, 3 vols., 1981; Max Reinhardt, 1982; Shakespeare in Performance: All's Well That Ends Well, 1984; The State of Drama Study, 1984; Restoration Comedy in Performance, 1986. Add: Oak Apple Cottage, Barnes Lane, Milford on Sea, Hants. SO41 0RP, England.

STYLES, Frank Showell. *See* CARR, Glyn.

STYRON, William. American, b. 1925. Novels/Short stories, Plays/Screenplays. Fellow, Silliman Coll., Yale Univ., New Haven, Conn., since 1964. Advisory Ed., Paris Review, Paris and NYC, since 1952; Member, Editorial Bd., The American Scholar, Washington, D.C., since 1970. *Publs:* Lie Down in Darkness, 1951; The Long March, 1956; (ed.) Best Short Stories from The Paris Review, 1959; Set This House on Fire, 1960; The Confessions of Nat Turner, 1967; In the Clap Shack (play), 1973; Sophie's Choice, 1979; This Quiet Dust and Other Writings, 1982. Add: R.F.D., Roxbury, Conn. 06783, U.S.A.

SUBOND, Valerie. *See* GRAYLAND, Valerie.

SUCHARITKUL, Somtow. Also writes as S.P. Somtow. Born in Bangkok, Thailand, 1952. Novels, Science fiction. Conductor and composer: Dir., Bangkok Opera Soc., 1977–78, and Asian Composers Conference/Festival, Bangkok, 1978. *Publs:* science fiction—Mallworld, 1981; Inquestor, comprising Light on the Sound, 1982, The

Throne of Madness, 1983, and Utopia Hunters, 1984; Fire from the Wine-Dark Sea, 1983; The Aquiliad, 1983; Starship and Haiku, 1984; The Darkling Wind, 1985; Symphony of Tenor, 1988. novels—(as S.P. Somtow) Vampire Junction, 1984; (as S.P. Somotow) The Shattered Horse, 1986. Add: c/o Tor Books, St. Martin's Press, 175 Fifth Ave., New York, N.Y. 10010, U.S.A.

SUDA, Zdenek Ludvik. American, b. 1920. Economics, History, Politics/Government, Sociology. Assoc. Prof. of Sociology, Univ. of Pittsburgh, since 1968. Asst. Head of Dept., Intnl. Secretariate of the European Movement, Paris, 1951–54; Supervising Prog. Ed., Free Europe Cttee. Inc., 1954–68. *Publs:* La division internationale socialiste dutravail, 1967; The Czechoslovak Socialist Republic, 1969; Zealots and Rebels, 1980; (ed.) Directions of Change, 1981. Add: Dept. of Sociology, Univ. of Pittsburgh, Pittsburgh, Pa. 15260, U.S.A.

SUDBERY, Rodie. British, b. 1943. Children's fiction. *Publs:* The House in the Wood, 1968; Cowls, 1969; Rich and Famous and Bad, 1970; The Pigsleg, 1971; Warts and All, 1972; A Curious Place, 1973; Inside the Walls, 1973; Ducks and Drakes, 1975; Lightning Cliff, 1975; The Silk and the Skin, 1977; Long Way Round, 1977; Somewhere Else, 1978; A Tunnel with Problems, 1979; The Village Secret, 1980; Night Music, 1983; Grandmother's Footsteps, 1984. Add: 5 Heslington Croft, Fulford, York YO1 4NB, England.

SUELFLOW, August R(obert). American, b. 1922. Librarianship, Theology/Religion. Dir., Dept. of Archives and History, Concordia Historical Inst., St. Louis, Mo., since 1948, and Assoc. Ed., the inst.'s quarterly, since 1950; Archivist, Missouri District, Lutheran Church-Missouri Synod, St. Louis, since 1966 (Asst. Curator, 1946–66; Archivist, Western District, 1948–66). Instr., Washington Univ., St. Louis, Mo., 1967–83; (guest lectr., 1952–69, 1974). Asst. Pastor of churches in Richmond Heights, Mo., 1948–56, and St. Louis, 1958–75. *Publs:* Heart of Missouri, 1954; (ed.) Directory of Religious Historical Depositories in America, 1963; (ed.) Microfilm Index and Bibliography, 1966; (ed.) A Preliminary Guide to Church Records Repositories, 1969; Religious Archives: An Introduction, 1980. Add: 801 DeMun Ave., St. Louis, Mo. 63105, U.S.A.

SUGGS, M(arion) Jack. American, b. 1924. Theology/Religion. Prof. of New Testament, 1956–89, and Dean 1977–89, Brite Divinity Sch., Texas Christian Univ., Fort Worth (Asst. Prof., 1952–54; Assoc. Prof., 1954–56). *Publs:* The Layman Reads His Bible, 1957; The Gospel Story, 1960; (ed. with B.L. Daniels) Studies in the History and Text of the New Testament, 1967; Wisdom, Christology and Law in Matthew's Gospel, 1970; (co-ed.) Oxford Study Edition of the New English Bible, 1976. Add: 5605 Winifred Dr., Fort Worth, Tex. 76122, U.S.A.

SUINN, Richard M. American, b. 1933. Psychology, Sports. Prof and Head Dept. of Pysycdhology, Colorado State Univ., Sports State Univ., Fort Collins, since 1972. Counselor, Counseling Center, Stanford Univ., Calif., 1958–59; Asst. Prof. of Psychology, Whitman Coll., Walla Walla, Wash., 1959–64; Research Assoc., Stanford Medical Sch., 1964–66; Assoc. Prof., Psychology Dept., Univ. of Hawaii, Honolulu, 1966–68. Consultant Psychologist, U.S. Biathlon and U.S. Nordic Ski Teams, 1976, and U.S. Women's Track and Field Teams, 1980, Olympic Games. *Publs:* The Predictive Validity of Projective Measures, 1969; The Fundamentals of Behavior Pathology, 1970; (with R. Weigel) The Innovative Psychological Therapies, 1975; (with R. Weigel) The Innovative Medical-Psychiatric Therapies, 1978; Psychology in Sports: Methods and Applications, 1980; Fundamentals of Abnormal Psychology, 1984; Seven Steps to Peak Performance, 1986. Add: Dept. of Psychology, C-71 Social Science Bldg., Colorado State Univ., Fort Collins, Colo. 80523, U.S.A.

SUKENICK, Ronald. American, b. 1932. Novels/Short stories, Literature. Prof. of English, Univ. of Colorado, Boulder, since 1974 (Dir., Creative Writing Prog., 1975–77). Publisher, American Book Review. Lectr., Brandeis Univ., Waltham, Mass., 1956–57, and Hofstra Univ., Hempstead, N.Y., 1961–62; part-time teacher, 1963–66; Asst. Prof. of English, City Coll. of New York, 1966–67, and Sarah Lawrence Coll., Bronxville, N.Y., 1968–69; Writer-in-Residence, Cornell Univ., Ithaca, N.Y., 1969–70, and Univ. of California at Irvine, 1970–72. Founding Member, Fiction Collective; Chmn., Coordinating Council of Literary Mags., 1975–77. *Publs:* Wallace Stevens: Musing the Obscure, 1967; Up, 1968; The Death of the Novel and Other Stories, 1969; Out, 1973; 98.6, 1975; Long Talking Bad Conditions Blues, 1979; In Form: Digressions on the Act of Fiction, 1985; Blown Away, 1985; The Endless Short Story, 1986; Down and In, 1987. Add: Dept. of English, Univ. of

Colorado, Boulder, Colo. 80309, U.S.A.

SUKNASKI, Andrew, Jr. Canadian, b. 1942. Poetry. Ed., Three Legged Coyote mag. and Press, Wood Mountain, Sask. Formerly, Ed., Anak Press, Deodar Shadow Press, and "Elfin Plot" and "Sundog", all Wood Mountain. Writer-in-Residence, St. John's Coll., Univ. of Manitoba, Winnipeg, 1977–78. *Publs:* The Shadow of Eden Once, 1970; Circles, 1970; In Mind ov Xrossroads ov Mythologies, 1971; Rose Way in the East, 1972; Old Mill, 1972; The Nightwatchman, 1972; The Zen Pilgrimage, 1972; Y th Evolution into Ruenz, 1972; (with others) Four Parts Sand: Concrete Poems, 1972; Wood Mountain Poems, 1973, expanded ed. 1976; Suicide Notes, Book One, 1973; Phillip Well, 1973; These Fragments I've Gathered for Ezra, 1973; Leaving, 1974; On First Looking Down from Lion's Gate Bridge, 1974, rev. ed. 1976; Blind Man's House, 1974; Leaving Wood Mountain, 1975; (trans.) The Shadow of Sound, by Andrei Voznesensky, 1975; Writing on Stone: Poemdrawings 1966-1976, 1976; Octomi, 1976; Almighty Voice, 1977; Moses Beauchamp, 1978; The Ghosts Call You Poor, 1978; (with George Morrissette) Two for Father, 1978; East of Myloona, 1979; The Ghost Gun, 1981; The Land They Gave Away: Selected and New Poems 1971-1982, 1982; Montage for an Interstellar Cry, 1982; Silk Trail, 1984. Add: Wood Mountain, Sask. S0H 4L0, Canada.

SULEIMAN, Michael Wadie. American, b. 1934. International relations/Current affairs, Politics/Government. Prof. of Political Science, Kansas State Univ., Manhattan, since 1972 (Asst. Prof., 1965–68; Assoc. Prof., 1968–72; Dept. Head, 1975–82). *Publs:* Political Parties in Lebanon: The Challenge of a Fragmented Political Culture, 1967; American Images of Middle East Peoples: Impact of the High School, 1977; The Arabs in the Mind of American, 1987; (co-ed.) Arab-Americans: Continuity and Change in Adaptive Experience, 1989. Add: 427 Wickham Rd., Manhattan, Kans. 66502, U.S.A.

SULLIVAN, Alvin D. American, b. 1942. Literature. Prof. of English, Southern Illinois Univ. (joined faculty as Instr. 1968). Ed., Papers on Language and Literature, since 1973 (Asst. Ed., 1970–73). *Publs:* (with Nicholas Joost) D.H. Lawrence and The Dial, 1970; (with Joost) The Dial: Two Author Indexes, 1971; (compiler) An Annotated Checklist of D.H. Lawrence Criticism; (ed.) British Literary Magazines, 4 vols., 1982–86. Add: Dept. of English, Southern Illinois Univ., Edwardsville, Ill. 62026, U.S.A.

SULLIVAN, Clara K. American, b. 1915. Economics, Money/Finance. Free-lance Consultant on tax policy, since 1981. Member, Tax Policy Advisory Bd. of Tax Analysts, Washington, D.C. Economist, Harvard Law Sch. Intnl. Prog. in Taxation, Cambridge, Mass., 1958–63; Sr. Economist, Intnl. Economic Integration Prog., Columbia Univ., NYC, 1963–64; Economics Ed., Houghton Mifflin Co., Boston, Mass., 1967–69. *Publs:* The Search for Tax Principles in the Economic Community, 1963; The Tax on Value Added, 1965. Add: 336 Pensacola Rd., Venice, Fla. 34285, U.S.A.

SULLIVAN, George E(dward). American, b. 1927. Children's non-fiction, Sciences, Sports/Physical education/Keeping fit. Adjunct Prof., Fordham Coll., Fordham Univ., NYC, since 1969. Public Relations Dir., Popular Library, 1952–55; Publicity Dir., American Machine and Foundry Co., NYC, 1955–62. *Publs:* (with F. Clause) How to Win at Bowling, 1961; (with D. Weber) The Champion's Guide to Bowling, 1963; (with F. Clause and P. McBride) Junior Guide to Bowling, 1963; The Story of the Peace Corps., 1964; (with I. Crane) The Young Sportsman's Guide to Pocket Billiards, 1964; The Story of Cassius Clay, 1964; Harness Racing, 1964; (with L. Lassiter) The Modern Guide to Pocket Billiards, 1964; The Champion's Guide to Golf, 1965; Better Ice Hockey for Boys, 1965; (with F. Larsen) Skiing for Boys and Girls, 1965; How Do They Make It?, 1965; (with L. Scott) Teenage Guide to Skin and Scuba Diving, 1965; The Modern Guide to Softball, 1965; Seven Modern Wonders of the World, 1966; Football's Unforgettable Games, 1966; The Complete Book of Autograph Collecting, 1971; Understanding Architecture, 1971; Inflation-Proof Your Future, 1971; Tom Seaver of the Mets, 1971; The Rise of the Robots, 1971; How Do They Run It?, 1971; The Gamemakers, 1972; Pro Football Plays in Pictures, 1972; How Do They Build It?, 1972; Pitchers and Pitching, 1972; Understanding Photography, 1972; By Chance a Winner: The History of Lotteries, 1972; The Backpacker's Handbook, 1973; Sports for Your Child, 1973; Baseball's Art of Hitting, 1973; Hank Aaron, 1974; Roger Staubach: A Special Kind of Quarterback, 1974; Queens of the Court, 1974; How Does It Get There?, 1974; Pro Football A to Z, 1975; Understanding Hydrophonics, 1975; Supertanker!, 1976; Dave Cowens, 1976; Home Run!, 1976; Wind Power for Your Home, 1977; Better Gymnastics for Girls, 1977; Nada Comanici, 1977;

This Is Pro Soccer, 1978; The Sports Dictionary, 1978; Modern Olympic Superstars, 1979; The Supercarriers, 1979; Gary Player's Book for Young Golfers, 1980; Discover Archaeology, 1980; Marathon Madness, 1980; Track for Girls, 1981; Anwar el-Sadat: The Man Who Changed Mid-East History, 1982; Inside Nuclear Submarines, 1982; Mr. President, 1983; Mary Lou Retton, 1984; The Thunderbirds, 1985; The Story of Ronald Reagan, 1985; Famous Blimps and Airships, 1988; Great Escapes of World War II, 1988; How the White House Really Works, 1989. Add: 330 E. 33rd St., New York, N.Y. 10016, U.S.A.

SULLIVAN, John Patrick. British, b. 1930. Classics, Literature, Translations. Prof. of Classics, Univ. of California, Santa Barbara, since 1978. Assoc. Ed., Petronian Soc. Newsletter, since 1984. Fellow and Tutor in Classics, 1955–63, and Dean, 1960–61, Lincoln Coll., Oxford, England; Assoc. Prof., and Acting Chmn., Dept. of Classical Languages, 1962, Prof., 1963–69, and Chmn., Dept. of Classics, 1963–65, Univ. of Texas, Austin; Faculty Prof., 1969–78, and Provost, 1972–75, State Univ. of New York, Buffalo. Co-Ed., Arion Journal of Classical Culture, 1961–69; Contributing Ed., The Texas Observer, 1969–76; Ed., Arethusa, 1971–75. *Publs:* (ed.) Critical Essays on Roman Literature: Elegy and Lyric, 1962; (ed.) Critical Essays on Roman Literature: Satire, 1963; Ezra Pound and Sextus Propertius: A Study in Creative Translation, 1964; (trans.) Petronius: The Satyricon and the Fragments, 1965; The Satyricon of Petronius: A Literary Study, 1968; (ed.) The Penguin Critical Anthologies: Ezra Pound, 1970; (ed.) The Date and Author of the Satyricon, 1971; Propertius: A Critical Introduction, 1975; The Jaundiced Eye (poetry), 1976; (trans.) Petronius: Satyricon, and Seneca: Apocolocyntosis, 1977; (ed.) Women in Antiquity: The Arethusa Papers, 1983; Literature and Politics in the Age of Nero, 1985; (ed.) Epigrams of Martial Englished by Divers Hands, 1987; Martial: The Unexpected Classic, 1989. Add: 1020 Palermo Dr., Santa Barbara, Calif. 93105, U.S.A.

SULLIVAN, Marion F. Also writes as James M. Brooks. American, b. 1899. Biography. *Publs:* Westward the Bells, 1971, 1987; Save That Tree, 1974; (as James M. Brooks) Finding the Right Job, 1978; Cooking the All American Way, 1981. Add: 7327 Garden Highway, Yuba City, Calif. 95991, U.S.A.

SULLIVAN, (Donovan) Michael. American, b. 1916. Art. Prof. of Oriental Art, 1966–75, and Christensen Prof. 1975–85, Stanford Univ., California; Fellow, St. Catherine's Coll., Oxford, since 1979. Lectr. in Asian Art, Univ. of London, 1960–66; Slade Prof. of Fine Art, Oxford Univ., 1973–74; Slade Prof. of Fine Art, Cambridge Univ., 1983–84. *Publs:* Chinese Art in the XX Century, 1959; An Introduction to Chinese Art, 1961; The Birth of Landscape Painting in China, 1962; Chinese Ceramics, Bronzes, and Jades in the Collection of Alan and Lady Barlow, 1963; Chinese and Japanese Art, 1966; A Short History of Chinese Art, 1967; The Cave Temples of Maichishan, 1969; Chinese Art: Recent Discoveries, 1973; The Arts of China, 1973, 3rd ed. 1984; The Meeting of Eastern and Western Art, 1973, 1989; The Three Perfections, 1974; Chinese Landscape Painting in the Sui and T'ang Dynasties, 1979; Symbols of Eternity: The Art of Landscape Painting in China, 1979. Add: St. Catherine's Coll., Oxford OX1 3UJ, England.

SULLIVAN, Sean Mei. *See* SOHL, Jerry.

SULLIVAN, Walter (Seager). American, b. 1918. Sciences, Travel/Exploration/Adventure. Science Ed., New York Times, 1964–87 (joined newspaper, 1940; Foreign Corresp., 1948–56; Science News Ed., 1962–63). *Publs:* Quest for a Continent, 1957; White Land of Adventure, 1957; Assault on the Unknown: The International Geophysical Year, 1961; Polar Regions, 1962; (ed. and contrib.) America's Race for the Moon, 1962; We Are Not Alone: The Search for Intelligent Extra-Terrestrial Life, 1964, rev. ed. 1966; (co-author) The Soviet-Union: The Fifty Years, 1967; (co-author) The Gentle Art of Walking, 1971; (co-author) UFO's: A Scientific Debate, 1972; Continents in Motion: The New Earth Debate, 1974; Black Holes: The Edge of Space, the Edge of Time, 1979; Landprints: On the Magnificent American Landscape, 1984. Add: c/o New York Times, 229 West 43rd St., New York, N.Y. 10036, U.S.A.

SULTAN, Stanley. American, b. 1928. Novels/Short stories, Literature. Prof. of English, Clark Univ., Worcester, Mass., since 1968 (Asst. Prof., 1959–62; Assoc. Prof., 1962–68). Asst. Ed., National Lexicographic Bd. Ltd., NYC, 1951–55; Instr. in English, Smith Coll., Northampton, Mass., 1955–59. *Publs:* The Argument of Ulysses, 1965; (ed.) The Playboy of the Western World, by J.M. Synge, 1971; Yeats at His Last, 1975; Ulysses, The Wasteland, and Modernism, 1977; Rabbi, 1978; (co-author) Galley Bliss, 1980; Eliot, Joyce, and Company, 1987. Add: 25 Hardwick St., Boston, Mass. 02135, U.S.A.

SULTANA, Donald Edward. Maltese, b. 1924. Literature, Biography. Hon. Fellow, Univ. of Edinburgh, since 1982 (Lectr., 1965–72; Sr. Lectr., 1973–78; Reader in English Literature, 1979–81). Lectr. in English Literature, Royal Univ. of Malta, 1951–64. *Publs:* Samuel Taylor Coleridge in Malta and Italy 1804-1806, 1969; Benjamin Disraeli in Spain, Malta, and Albania 1830-32, 1976; "The Siege of Malta" Rediscovered: An Account of Sir Walter Scott's Mediterranean Journey and His Last Novel, 1977; (ed.) New Approaches to Coleridge: Biographical and Critical Essays, 1981; The Journey of Sir Walter Scott to Malta, 1987; The Journey of William Frere to Malta in 1832, 1988. Add: 5 Howe St., Edinburgh EH3 6TE, Scotland.

SULZBERGER, C(yrus) L(eo, II). American, b. 1912. Novels/Short stories, History, International relations/Current affairs, Politics/Government, Autobiography/Memoirs/Personal. Foreign Affairs Columnist, New York Times, 1954–78, now retired (Corresp. in London Office, covering the Balkans, Russia and the Middle East, 1940–44; Chief of the Foreign Service, Paris, 1944–54). Reporter and Rewrite Man, Pittsburgh Press, 1934–35; Reporter, United Press, Washington D.C., 1935–38; Foreign Corresp., Evening Standard, London, 1938–39; with United Press, North American Newspaper Alliance, and BBC, 1939–40. *Publs:* Sit-Down with John L. Lewis, 1938; The Big Thaw: A Personal Exploration of the "New" Russia and the Orbit Countries, 1956; What's Wrong with United States Foreign Policy, 1959; My Brother Death, 1961; The Resistentialist, 1962, as Unconquered Souls: The Resistentialists, 1973; The Test: De Gaulle and Algeria, 1962; Unfinished Revolution: America and the Third World, 1965; (co-author) The American Heritage Picture History of World War II, 1966, 1970; A Long Row of Candles: Memoirs and Diaries 1934-1954, 1969; The Last of the Giants (memoirs), 1970; The Tooth Merchant, 1973; An Age of Mediocrity, 1973; The Conflict War: Russia's Game in China, 1974; Fall of Eagles, 1976; Go Gentle into the Night, 1976; Seven Continents and Forty Years, 1977; The Tallest Liar, 1977; Marina, 1978; How I Committed Suicide, 1982; Such a Peace: Yalta Revisited, 1982; The World and Richard Nixon, 1987; Fathers and Children, 1987. Add: 25 Blvd. du Montparnasse, 75006 Paris, France.

SUMMERS, Anthony (Bruce). British, b. 1942. History, Documentaries/Reportage. Researcher, World in Action prog., Granada-TV, 1963; Newsreader and writer, Swiss Broadcasting Corp., 1964–65; Scriptwriter, BBC-TV News, 1965; Sr. Film Producer, BBC-TV Current Affairs Progs., 1965–73. *Publs:* (with Tom Mangold) The File on the Tsar, 1976; Conspiracy (Who Killed President Kennedy?), 1980; Goddess: The Secret Lives of Marilyn Monroe, 1985; (with Stephen Dorril) Honeytrap: The Secret Worlds of Stephen Ward, 1987. Add: c/o Sterling Lord Literistic Inc., One Madison Ave., New York, N.Y. 10010, U.S.A.

SUMMERS, Diana. *See* SMITH, George H.

SUMMERS, Essie. New Zealander, b. 1912. Romance, Autobiography. Formerly worked for Londontown Drapers, Christchurch; also worked as a costing clerk, and as a columnist. *Publs:* New Zealander Inheritance, 1957, in Can. as Heatherleigh, 1963; The Time and the Place, 1958; Bachelors Galore, 1958; The Lark in the Meadow, 1959, in Canada as Nurse Abroad, 1961; The Master of Tawhai, 1959, in Moon over the Alps, 1960; Come Blossom-Time, My Love, 1961; No Roses in June, 1961; The House of the Shining Tide, 1962; South to Forget, in Canada as Nurse Mary's Engagement, 1963; Where No Roads Go, 1963; Bride in Flight, 1964; The Smoke and the Fire, 1964; No Legacy for Lindsay, 1965; No Orchids by Request, 1965; Sweet Are the Ways, 1965; Heir to Windrush Hill, 1966; His Serene Miss Smith, 1966; Postscript to Yesterday, 1966; A Place Called Paradise, 1967; Rosalind Comes Home, 1968; Meet on My Ground, 1968; The Kindled Fire,, 1969; Revolt—and Virginia, 1969; The Bay of Nightingales, 1970; Summer in December, 1970; Return to Dragonshill, 1971; The House on Gregor's Brae, 1971; South Island Stowaway, 1972; The Forbidden Valley, 1973; A Touch of Magic, 1973; Through All the Years, 1974; The Gold of Noon, 1974; The Essie Summers Story (autobiography), 1974; Anne of Strathallan, 1975; Beyond the Foothills, 1976; Not by Appointment, 1976; Adair of Starlight Peaks, 1977; Goblin Hill, 1977; The Lake of the Kingfisher, 1978; Spring in September, 1978; My Lady of the Fuchsias, 1979; One More River to Cross, 1979; The Tender Leaves, 1980; Autumn in April, 1981; Daughter of the Misty Gorges, 1981; A Lamp for Jonathan, 1982; A Mountain for Luenda, 1983; Season of Forgetfulness, 1983; MacBride of Tordarroch, 1984; Winter in July, 1984; To Bring You Joy, 1985; High Country Governess, 1987. Add: Eton House, 18-24 Paradise Rd., Richmond, Surrey TW9 1SR, England.

SUMMERS, Gene F. American, b. 1936. Psychology, Sociology. Prof., Dept of Rural Sociology, Univ. of Wisconsin, Madison, since 1975

(Assoc. Prof., 1970–75). *Publs:* (with Richard L. Hough, John T. Scott and Clinton Folse) Before Industrialization: A Rural Social System Base Study, 1969; Attitude Measurement, 1970; Industrial Invasion of Nonmetropolitan America, 1976; Nonmetropolitan Economic Growth and Community Change, 1979; Energy Resource Communities, 1982; Technology and Social Change in Rural Areas, 1983; Deindustrialization: Restructuring the Economy, 1984; Needs Assessment: Theory and Methods, 1988. Add: Dept of Rural Sociology, Univ. of Wisconsin-Madison, 340C Agric. Hall, Madison, Wisc. 53706, U.S.A.

SUMMERS, Hal. (Henry Forbes Summers). British, b. 1911. Poetry. Former Under-Secty., Dept. of the Environment. *Publs:* Smoke After the Flame, 1944; Hinterland, 1947; Poems in Pamphlet, 1951; Tomorrow Is My Love, 1978; The Burning Book, 1982. Add: Folly Fields, Linden Gardens, Tunbridge Wells, Kent TN2 5QU, England.

SUMMERS, Hollis (Spurgeon, Jr.) Also writes as Jim Hollis. American, b. 1916. Novels/Short stories, Poetry. Distinguished Prof. of English, Ohio Univ., Athens, since 1959. Teacher, Homes High Sch., Covington Ky., 1937–44; Prof. of English, Georgetown Coll., 1945–49, and Univ. of Kentucky, Lexington, 1949–59; Lectr., Arts Prog., Assn. of American Colls., 1958–63; Danforth Lectr., 1963–66. *Publs:* City Limit (novel), 1948; Brighten the Corner (novel), 1952; (ed.) Kentucky Story: A Collection of Short Stories, 1954; (with James Rourke as Jim Hollis) Teach You a Lesson (novel), 1955; The Weather of February (novel), 1957; The Walks Near Athens, 1959; (ed. with E. Whan) Literature: An Introduction, 1960; (ed.) Discussions of the Short Story, 1963; Someone Else: Sixteen Poems about Other Children, 1962; Seven Occasions, 1965; The Peddler and Other Domestic Matters, 1967; The Day After Sunday (novel), 1968; Sit Opposite Each Other, 1970; Start from Home, 1972; The Garden (novel), 1972; Dinosaurs, 1978; Standing Room (short stories), 1984; After the Twelve Days, 1987; Other Concerns and Brother Clark, 1988. Add: 181 N. Congress St., Athens, Ohio 45701, U.S.A.

SUMMERS, Joseph Holmes. American, b. 1920. Literature. Prof. of English, Univ. of Rochester, N.Y., 1969–85, now Emeritus. Assoc. Prof., Univ. of Connecticut, Storrs, 1955–59; Prof. of English, Washington Univ., St. Louis, 1959–66; Fulbright Prof. and Visiting Fellow, All Souls Coll., Oxford, 1966–67; Prof. of English, Michigan State Univ., East Lansing 1966–69. *Publs:* George Herbert: religion and Art, 1954; (ed.) Andrew Marvell: Selected Poems, 1961; The Muse's Method: An Introduction to Paradise Lost, 1962; (ed.) The Lyric and Dramatic Milton: Selected Papers for the English Institute, 1965; (ed.) George Herbert: Selected Poetry, 1967; The Heirs of Donne and Jonson, 1970; Dreams of Love and Power in Shakespeare's Plays, 1984. Add: 179 Crosman Terr., Rochester, N.Y. 14620, U.S.A.

SUMMERS, Judith (Anne). British, b. 1953. Novels, History. Full-time writer since 1985. Freelance London tourist guide/lectr., 1976–85; Asst. Film Ed., BBC Television, London, 1978–81. *Publs:* Dear Sister, 1985; I, Gloria Gold, 1988; Soho: A History, 1989. Add: c/o Bloomsbury Publishing, 2 Soho Sq., London W1V 5DE, England.

SUMMERS, Rowena. *See* SAUNDERS, Jean.

SUMMERSON, Sir John (Newenham). British, b. 1904. Architecture, Art. Inst. in Architecture, Edinburgh Coll. of Art 1923–30; Asst. Ed., Architect and Building News, 1933–41; Deputy Dir., National Buildings Record, 1941–45; Lectr. in the History of Architecture, Architectural Assn., London 1949–62, and Birbeck Coll., Univ. of London, 1950–67; Slade Prof. of Fine Art, Oxford Univ., 1958–59; Ferens Prof. of Fine Art, Univ. of Hull, 1960–61, 1970–71; Slade Prof. of Fine Art, Cambridge Univ., 1966–67. Member of the Council, Architectural Assn., 1940–45; Member, 1944–66, and Chmn., 1960–62, Listed Buildings Cttee., Ministry of Housing and Local Govt.; Member, Royal Fine Art Commn., 1947–54, Arts Council Art Panel, 1953–56, Royal Commn. on Historical Monuments (England), 1953–74, and Historic Buildings Council, 1953–78; Chmn., National Council for Diplomas in Art and Design, 1961–70; Trustee, National Portrait Gallery, 1966–73; Member, Advisory Council on Public Records, 1968–74. *Publs:* (with C. Williams-Ellis) Architecture Here and Now, 1945; John Nash, Architect to George IV, 1935; (with J.M. Richards) The Bombed Buildings of Britain 1942, 1945; Georgian London 1946, 3rd ed. 1988; The Architectural Association (centenary history), 1947; Ben Nicholson (Penguin Modern Painters), 1948; Heavenly Mansions (essays), 1949; Sir John Soane, 1952; Sir Christopher Wren, 1953; Architecture in Britain 1530-1830 (Pelican History of Art) 1953, 7th ed. 1983; New Description of Sir J. Soane's Museum, 1955; The Classical Language of Architecture, 1964; The Book of John Thorpe, 1966;

Inigo Jones, 1966; Victorian Architecture, 1969; (ed.) Concerning Architecture, 1969; The London Building World of the Eighteen-Sixties, 1974; (with H.M. Colvin and others) The History of the King's Works, vol. III 1976, vol. IV 1982; The Architecture of the 18th Century, 1986; The Unromantic Castle (essays), 1989. Add: 1 Eton Villas, London NW3, England.

SUMNER, (Edith) Aurea. British, b. 1913. Novels/Short stories, Children's non-fiction. Music Mistress, Scotholme Central Girls Sch., 1934–38; Divinity Mistress, Hill Secondary Modern Sch., 1948–53. *Publs:* Listen and Do, 1958; More Listen and Do, 1959; The Hand, 1982. Add: Galatea, 535 Main Rd., Dovercourt Bay, Harwich, Essex CO12 4NH, England.

SUNDERLAND, Eric. British, b. 1930. Anthropology/Ethnology, Biology, Demography. Principal, University Coll. of North Wales, Bangor, since 1984. Book Review Ed., Annals of Human Biology, since 1973. Prof. of Anthropology, 1971–84, and Pro-Vice-Chancellor, 1979–84, Univ. of Durham. *Publs:* (ed. with D.F. Roberts) Genetic Variation in Britain, 1973; Some Bio-Social Aspects of Anthropology, 1973; Elements of Human and Social Geography: Some Anthropological Perspectives, 1973; The Exercise of Intelligence: The Bio-Social Preconditions for the Operation of Intelligence, 1980; (ed. with P.S. Harper) Population Studies in Wales, 1986. Add: University Coll. of North Wales, Bangor LL57 2DG, Wales.

SUNDERLAND, (Sir) Sydney. Australian, b. 1910. Medicine/Health. Emeritus Prof. of Experimental Neurology, Univ. of Melbourne (Prof. of Anatomy, 1939–61; Dean, Faculty of Medicine, 1953–71; Prof. of Experimental Neurology, 1961–75). Chmn., Safety Review Cttee., Australian Atomic Energy Commn., and Protective Chemistry Research Advisory Cttee.; Member, Australian Univs. Commn., Defence Research and Development Policy Cttee., Defence Medical Services Cttee., and Cttee. of Mgmt., Royal Melbourne Hosp.; Trustee, National Museum of Victoria. Member, National Health and Medical Research Council, 1953–69; Member, 1953–69, and Chmn., 1964–69, Medical Research Cttee. of the National Health and Medical Research Council; Member of the Council, and Secty., Div. of Biological Sciences, Australian Academy of Science, 1955–58; Australian Rep., Pacific Science Council, 1957–69; Chmn., National Radiation Advisory Cttee., 1959–64. *Publs:* Nerves and Nerve Injuries, 1968, 1978. Add: Dept. of Experimental Neurology, Univ. of Melbourne, Parkville, Vic., Australia 3052.

SUNDQUIST, James (Lloyd). American, b. 1915. Politics/Government. Sr. Fellow Emeritus, Brookings Instn., Washington. *Publs:* Politics and Policy: The Eisenhower, Kennedy and Johnson Years, 1968; Making Federalism Work, 1969; Dynamics of the Party System, 1973, 1983; Dispersing Population, 1975; The Decline and Resurgence of Congress, 1981; Constitutional Reform and Effective Government, 1986. Add: 3016 N. Florida St., Arlington, Va. 22207, U.S.A.

SUPER, Robert Henry. American, b. 1914. Literature, Biography. Prof. Emeritus of English, Univ. of Michigan, Ann Arbor (joined faculty, 1947). *Publs:* The Publication of Landor's Works, 1954; Walter Savage Landor: A Biography, 1954; (ed.) The Complete Prose Works of Matthew Arnold, 11 vols., 1960–77; The Time-Spirit of Matthew Arnold, 1970; Trollope in the Post Office, 1981; (ed.) Trollope's Marion Fay, 1982; (ed. with M. Allott) The Oxford Arnold, 1986; The Chronicler of Barsetshire: A Life of Anthony Trollope, 1988. Add: 1221 Baldwin Ave., Ann Arbor, Mich. 48104, U.S.A.

SUPPLE, Barry E(manuel). British, b. 1930. Economics, History. Master, St. Catharine's Coll., Cambridge, and Prof. of Economic History, Cambridge Univ., since 1981. Asst. Prof. of Business History, Harvard Univ. Graduate School of Business Admin., Boston, 1955–60; Assoc. Prof. of Economic History, McGill Univ., Montreal, 1960–62; Lectr., Reader, then Prof. of Economic and Social History, 1962–78, Dean, School of Social Sciences, 1965–68, and Pro-Vice-Chancellor, 1968–72, Univ. of Sussex, Brighton; Professorial Fellow, Nuffield Coll., Oxford, and Reader in Recent Social and Economic History, Oxford Univ., 1978–81. Member of the Council, Social Science Research Council, 1972–77; Co-Ed., Economic History Review, 1973–82. *Publs:* Commercial Crisis and Change in England 1600-42, 1959; (ed.) The Experience of Economic Growth, 1963; Boston Capitalists and Western Railroads, 1967; The Royal Exchange Assurance: A History of British Insurance 1720-1970, 1970; (ed.) Essays in Business History, 1977; History of British Coal Industry, 1987. Add: St. Catharine's Coll., Cambridge, England.

SURTEES, Virginia. British. Art, Biography. *Publs:* Dante Gabriel

Rossetti: Drawings and Paintings, 2 vols., 1971; (ed.) Sublime and Instructive, 1972; Charlotte Canning, 1975; A Beckford Inheritance, 1977; (ed.) Reflections of a Friendship, 1979; (ed.) The Diaries of G.P. Boyce, 1981; (ed.) The Diary of Ford Madox Brown, 1981; The Ludovisi Goddess, 1984; Jane Welsh Carlyle, 1986; The Artist and The Autocrat, 1988. Add: Royal Bank of Scotland, 43 Curzon St., London W1, England.

SUSSMAN, Barry. American, b. 1934. Politics/Government. Survey Ed., Washington Post, Washington, D.C., since 1980 (joined staff, 1965). *Publs:* The Great Coverup: Nixon and the Scandal of Watergate, 1974; What Americans Really Think, 1988. Add: Washington Post, 1150 15th St., Washington, D.C. 20071, U.S.A.

SUTCLIFF, Rosemary. British, b. 1920. Novels/Short stories, Children's fiction, History, Autobiography/Memoirs/Personal. *Publs:* The Chronicles of Robin Hood, 1950; The Queen Elizabeth Story, 1950; The Armourer's House, 1951; Brother Dusty-Feet, 1952; Simon, 1953; The Eagle of the Ninth, 1954; Outcast, 1955; The Shield-Ring, 1956; Lady in Waiting, 1956; The Silver Branch, 1957; Warrior Scarlet, 1958; The Lantern Bearers, 1959; Knight's Fee, 1960; The Rider of the White Horse, 1960; Houses and History, 1960; Dawn Wind, 1961; Beowulf, 1962; Rudyard Kipling, 1962; Sword at Sunset, 1963; The Hound of Ulster, 1963; Heroes and History, 1965; The Mark of the Horse Lord, 1965; The High Deeds of Finn MacCool, 1967; The Chief's Daughter, 1967; Tristan and Iseult; The Changeling; A Circlet of Oak Leaves; The Truce of the Games; Capricorn Bracelet, 1973; Blood Feud, 1976; Sun Horse, Moon Horse, 1977; Song for a Dark Queen, 1978; The Light Beyond the Forest, 1979; Frontier Wolf, 1980; Eagle's Egg, 1981; The Road to Camlann, 1981; Blue Remembered Hills: A Recollection, 1982; Bonnie Dundee, 1983; Flame Coloured Taffeta, 1985; The Roundabout Horse, 1986; Blood and Sand 1987; Little Hound Found, 1989. Add: Swallowshaw, Walberton, Arundel, W. Sussex BN18 0PQ, England.

SUTCLIFFE, Reginald Cockcroft. British, b. 1904. Meteorology/Atmospheric sciences. Emeritus Prof. of Meterology, Univ. of Reading, Berks., since 1970 (Prof., 1965–70). With U.K. Meteorological Office, 1927–39; Sr. Meteorological Officer, Allied Expeditionary Air Force, later British Air Force of Occupation, Germany, 1944–46; returned to Meteorological Office, U.K., 1946: Dir. of Research, 1957–65. *Publs:* Meteorology for Aviators, 1938; Weather and Climate, 1966. Add: Pound Farm, Cadmore End, High Wycombe, Bucks. HP14 3PF, England.

SUTHERLAND, Efua (Theodora). Ghanian, b. 1924. Plays/Screenplays, Children's non-fiction. Founding Dir., Experimental Theatre Players, now Ghana Drama Studio, Accra, since 1958. Founder, Ghana Soc. of Writers, now Univ. of Ghana Writers Workshop; Cofounder, Okyeame mag., Accra. Schoolteacher in Ghana, 1951-54. *Publs:* Playtime in Africa (juvenile), 1960; The Roadmakers, 1961; Edufa (based on Alcestis by Euripedes), 1967; Foriwa, 1967; Vulture! Vulture! and Tahinta: Two Rhythm Plays, 1968; The Marriage of Anansewa, 1975. Add: c/o Longman Group, 5 Bentinck St., London W1M 5RN, England.

SUTHERLAND, Elizabeth. *See* **MARSHALL,** Elizabeth Margaret.

SUTHERLAND, James (Runcieman). British, b. 1900. Poetry, Literature. Emeritus Prof., University Coll., London, since 1967 (Sr. Lectr., 1930–36; Prof. of English Literature, Birkbeck Coll., 1936–44; Prof. of English Language and Literature, Queen Mary Coll., 1944–51; Lord Northcliffe Prof., 1951–67; Public Orator, 1957–62). Lectr., University Coll., Southampton, 1925; Lectr., Univ. of Glasgow, 1925–30. Ed., Review of English Studies, 1940–47. *Publs:* Leucocholy (poems), 1926; Jasper Weeple, 1930; The Medium of Poetry, 1934; Defoe, 1937; Background for Queen Anne, 1939; The Dunciad, 1943; English in the Universities, 1945; A Preface to Eighteenth Century Poetry, 1948; The English Critic, 1952; (ed.) The Oxford Book of English Talk, 1953; On English Prose, 1957; English Satire, 1958; English Literature in the Late Seventeenth Century, 1969; Daniel Defoe: A Critical Study, 1971; (ed.) The Oxford Book of Literary Anecdotes, 1975; The Restoration Newspaper and Its Development, 1986. Add: 16 Murray Ct., 80 Banbury Rd., Oxford OX2 6LQ, England.

SUTHERLAND, Margaret. New Zealander, b. 1941. Novels/Short stories, Children's fiction. *Publs:* The Fledgling, 1974; Hello I'm Karen (for children), 1974; The Love Contract, 1976; Getting Through, 1977; Dark Places, Deep Regions, 1980; The Fringe of Heaven, 1984. Add: c/o Migrant Health Unit, 90 Scott St., Sydney, N.S.W. 2297, Australia.

SUTHERLAND, Norman Stuart. British, b. 1927. Psychology. Prof. of Experimental Psychology, and Dir. of the Centre for Research on Perception and Cognition, Univ. of Sussex, since 1965. Fellow, Magdalen Coll., Oxford, 1953–57; Lectr., Univ. of Oxford, 1957–64; Fellow, Merton Coll., Oxford, 1962–64. Ed., Quarterly Journal of Experimental Psychology, 1970–72. *Publs:* (ed., with R.M. Gilbert) Animal Discrimination Learning, 1969; (with N.J. Mackintosh) Mechanisms of Animal Discrimination Learning, 1971; Breakdown: A Personal Crisis and a Medical Dilemma, 1976, 1987; (ed.) Tutorial Essays in Psychology, vol. I, 1977, vol. II, 1979; Discovering the Human Mind, 1982; Men Change Too, 1987; Macmillan Dictionary of Psychology, 1989. Add: Lab. of Experimental Psychology, Univ. of Sussex, Brighton, Sussex BN1 9QG, England.

SUTTON, Clive (Julian). British, b. 1937. Economics. Asst. Principal, Sheffield City Polytechnic, since 1978. With Esso Petroleum Co., London, 1960–62; Lectr., Polytechnic of Central London, 1962–66, and Univ. of Bristol, 1966–69; Sr. Lectr., Univ. of Stirling, 1969–78. *Publs:* (with R.W. Shaw) Industry and Competition, 1976; Economics and Corporate Strategy, 1980. Add: Sheffield City Polytechnic, Sheffield S1 1WB, England.

SUTTON, David. British, b. 1917. Medicine/Health. Consultant Radiologist, The National Hospitals for Nervous Diseases, London, 1951–83; Consultant Radiologist, St. Mary's Hosp. and Medical Sch., London, 1953–83, and Dir. of the Radiology Dept., 1963–83. Ed., Clinical Radiology, 1959–64; Pres., Radiology Section, Royal Soc. of Medicine, 1969. *Publs:* Arteriography, 1962; Radiology and Imaging for Medical Students, 1965, 4th ed. 1982; (ed.) A Textbook of Radiology and Imaging, 1969, 4th ed. 1987. Add: 21 Meadowbank, Primrose Hill Rd., London NW3 3AY, England.

SUTTON, David John. British, b. 1944. Poetry. Computer Programmer, ICL Ltd., since 1966. *Publs:* Out on a Limb, 1969; Absences and Celebrations, 1982; Flints, 1986. Add: 46 West Chiltern, Reading, Berks., England.

SUTTON, Denys. British, b. 1917. Art, Biography. Ed., Apollo mag., London, 1962–87. *Publs:* French Drawing of the 18th Century, 1949; American Painting, 1949; Bonnard, 1957; Christie's, 1959; Derain, 1959; Stael, 1960; (ed.) Vlaminck, 1961; (ed.) Stevenson's Velasquez, 1962; Lautrec, 1962; Whistler, 1964; Triumphant Satyr: Rodin, 1966; (ed.) Letters of Roger Fry, 1972; Walter Sickert, 1976; Robert Langton Douglas, 1979; Fads and Fancies, 1979; Delights of a Dilettante, 1980; Sacheverell Sitwell, 1981; Degas: Man and Work, 1986. Add: 22 Chelsea Park Gardens, London SW3, England.

SUTTON, Eve(lyn Mary). New Zealander (b. British), b. 1906. Children's fiction. *Publs:* My Cat Likes to Hide in Boxes, 1973; Green Gold, 1976; Tuppenny Brown, 1977; Johnny Sweep, 1977; Moa Hunter, 1978; Skip for the Huntaway, 1983; Surgeon's Boy, 1983; Kidnapped by Blackbirders, 1984; Valley of Heavenly Gold, 1987. Add: 84 Kohimarama Rd., Flat 1, Auckland 5, New Zealand.

SUTTON, Jane. American, b. 1950. Children's fiction. Full-time writer since 1979. Mental health worker, Harlem Valley State Hosp., Wingdale, N.Y., 1972–74; staff writer, Mid-Hudson Leisure, Poughkeepsie, N.Y., 1974–75; in public relations, Instrumentation Lab. Inc., Lexington, Mass., 1975–80. *Publs:* What Should a Hippo Wear?, 1979; Me and the Weirdos, 1981; Confessions of an Orange Octopus, 1983; Not Even Mrs. Mazursky, 1984; Definitely Not Sexy, 1988. Add: 11 Mason St., Lexington, Mass. 02173, U.S.A.

SUTTON, Henry. *See* **SLAVITT,** David.

SUTTON, Jean. (Eugenia Geneva Hansen Sutton). American, b. 1916. Children's fiction. Consultant asst. since 1971. Personnel Worker, U.S. Steel, Los Angeles, 1940–41; construction co. timekeeper, San Diego, 1942–45; Lathe Operator, Douglas Aircraft Co., Santa Monica, Calf., and social worker, Los Angeles; Exec. Secty., San Diego City Council, 1949–52; Administrative Asst., San Diego State Coll., 1953–55; and Social Studies Teacher, San Diego County High Schs., 1958–71. *Publs:* (with Jeff Sutton, died 1979)—The River, 1966; The Beyond, 1968; The Programmed Man, 1968; Lord of the Stars, 1969; Alien from the Stars, 1970; The Boy Who Had the Power, 1971. Add: 4318 Date Ave., La Mesa, Calif. 92041, U.S.A.

SUTTON, S. B. American, b. 1940. Urban studies, Biography. Research Fellow, Arnold Arboretum, Harvard Univ., Cambridge, 1971–74. *Publs:* Charles Sprague Sargent and the Arnold Arboretum, 1970; (ed.) Civilizing American Cities, 1971; Cambridge Reconsidered, 1976;

Crossroads in Psychiatry: A History of the McLean Hospital, 1986. Add: c/o Massachusetts Institute of Technology Press, Cambridge, Mass. 02142, U.S.A.

SVARTVIK, Jan. Swedish, b. 1931. Language/Linguistics. Prof. of English, Univ. of Lund, Sweden, since 1970. Research Asst., and Asst. Dir., Survey of English Usage, Univ. Coll., London, 1961–65; Lectr., 1965–66 and Reader, 1966–70, Univ. of Gothenburg. Co-ed., Lund Studies in English, 1970, and Studia Linguistica, 1975. *Publs:* On Voice in the English Verb, 1966; (co-author) Investigating Linguistic Acceptability, 1966; The Evans Statements: A Case for Forensic Linguistics, 1968; (ed.) Errata: Papers in Error Analysis, 1973; (co-ed.) A Corpus of English Conversation, 1980; (co-ed.) Studies in English Literature for Randolph Quirk, 1980; (co-author) A Comprehensive Grammar of the English Language, 1985. Add: Dept. of English, Helgonabacken 14, Univ. of Lund, 223 62 Lund, Sweden.

SWAIM, Alice Mackenzie. American, b. 1911. Poetry. Critic, National Writers' Club, and Columnist, Cornucopia, 1953–55; Poetry Columnist, Evening Sentinel, Carlisle, Pa., 1956–70; Member, Intnl. Exec. Cttee., Studie Scambi, Italy, 1961–71; Vice-Pres., 1964–47 and 1967–70, and Book Reviewer, 1967–74, American Poetry League; Columnist, Tejas mag., 1968–70; Rep. and Consultant, Assn. for Poetry Therapy, 1970–74. *Publs:* Let the Deep Song Rise, 1952; Up to the Stars, 1954; Sunshine in a Thimble, 1958; Crickets Are Crying Autumn, 1960; The Gentle Dragon, 1962; Pennsylvania Profile, 1966; Scented Honey Suckle Days, 1966; Here on the Threshold, 1966; Beneath a Dancing Star, 1968; Beyond My Catnip Garden, 1970; Celebration of Seasons, 1978; And Miles to Go, 1982; Unicorn and Thistle, 1982; Children in Summer, 1983. Add: 322 N. 2nd St., Apt. 1606, Harrisburg, Pa. 17101, U.S.A.

SWALLOW, Norman. Also writes as George Leather. British, b. 1921. Media, Biography. Freelance Writer and Producer, since 1985. Writer and Producer, BBC Radio, 1946–50; Writer and Producer, 1950–57, Asst. Head of Film, 1957–60, Exec. Producer of Omnibus series, 1968–71, and Head of Arts Features, 1971–74, BBC Television; Dir., 1963–68, and Exec. Producer, 1974, Granada Television. *Publs:* Factual Television, 1966; Eisenstein: A Documentary Portrait, 1976. Add: 36 Crooms Hill, London SE10, England.

SWANBERG, W(illiam) A(ndrew). American, b. 1907. History, Biography. Ed., Dell Publishing Co., NYC, 1935–44; Writer-Ed., Office of War Information, 1944-45; then free-lance writer. *Publs:* Sickles the Incredible, 1956; Jim Fisk, 1959; First Blood, 1957; Citizen Hearst, 1961; Dreiser, 1965; Pulitzer, 1968; The Rector and the Rogue, 1971; Luce and His Empire, 1972; Norman Thomas, 1976; Whitney Father, Whitney Heiress, 1980. Add: 823-A Heritage Village, Southbury, Conn. 06488, U.S.A.

SWANN, Donald (Ibrahim). British, b. 1923. Songs, Music, Autobiography/Memoirs/Personal. Freelance writer, performer, and composer. *Publs:* Sing Round the Year, 1965; (with J.R.R. Tolkien) The Road Goes Ever On, 1968, 1978; The Space Between the Bars, 1968; The Rope of Love, 1973; Swann's Way Out: A Posthumous Adventure, 1975; (with Arthur Scholey) Sing Alive, 1978; Round the Piano with Donald Swann: Songs for Children and Others, 1979; Baboushka: Children's Opera, 1980; The Visitors (based on Tolstoy), 1985; Brendan A-hoy!, 1985; (with Evelyn Kirkhart and Mary Morgan) Mamahuhu (musical play), 1986; (with Richard Crane) Envy (musical play), 1986. Add: 13 Albert Bridge Rd., London SW11 4PX, England.

SWARD, Robert S. American Canadian, b. 1933. Novels/Short stories, Poetry. Member, Writing Prog., Cornell Univ., Ithaca, N.Y., 1962–64; Writer-in-Residence, Univ. of Victoria, B.C., 1969–73; Founding Ed., Soft Press, Victoria, 1970–77, and Hancock House Publishers, Victoria, 1976–79. *Publs:* Uncle Dog and Other Poems, 1962; Kissing the Dancer, 1964; Thousand-Year-Old Fiancée, 1965; In Mexico and Other Poems, 1966; Horgbortom Stringbottom, I Am Yours, You Are History, 1970; Quorum/Noah, 1970; (ed.) Vancouver Island Poems, 1973; (ed.) Cheers for Muktananda, 1974; Letter to a Straw Hat, 1974; The Jurassic Shales (novel), 1975; Lasqueti Island, B.C., 1978; Six Poems, 1980; Twelve Poems, 1982; Half-a-Life's History: Poems New and Selected, 1983; Movies: Left to Right, 1983; The Toronto Islands: An Illustrated History, 1983; (with Robert Priest and Robert Zend) The Three Roberts, 1984. Add: P.O. Box 7062, Santa Cruz, Calif. 95061-7062, U.S.A.

SWARTHOUT, Glendon. American, b. 1918. Novels/Short stories, Children's fiction. Assoc. Prof. of English, Michigan State Univ., East Lansing, 1951–59; Lectr., Arizona State Univ., Tempe, 1959–62. *Publs:*

Willow Run, 1943; They Came to Cordura, 1958; Where the Boys Are, 1960; Welcome to Thebes, 1962; (with K. Swarthout) The Ghost and the Magic Saber, 1963; The Cadillac Cowboys, 1964; (with K. Swarthout) Whichaway, 1966; The Eagle and the Iron Cross, 1966; Loveland, 1968; (with K. Swarthout) The Button Boat, 1969; Bless the Beasts and Children, 1970; (with K. Swarthout) TV Thompson, 1972; The Tin Lizzie Troop, 1972; Luck and Pluck, 1973; The Shootist, 1975; (with K. Swarthout) Whales to See the, 1975; The Melodeon, 1977; Skeletons, 1979; (with K. Swarthout) Cadbury's Coffin, 1982; The Old Colts, 1985; The Homesman, 1988. Add: 5045 Tamanar Way, Scottsdale, Ariz. 85253, U.S.A.

SWARTZ, Jon David. American, b. 1934. Psychology. Prof. of Education and Psychology, since 1978, and Assoc. Dean for Libraries and Learning Resources, since 1981, Southwestern Univ., Georgetown, Tex. Editorial Assoc., Current Anthropology, since 1971; Consulting Ed., Journal of Personality Assessment, since 1981; Book Review Ed., Journal of Biological Psychology, since 1982, and (for English language publs.) Revista Interamericana de Psicologia, since 1983; Series Ed., Southwestern Univ. Bibliographic series, since 1985. Taught at Univ. of Texas, Austin and Odessa, 1962–78. *Publs:* (with others) Inkblot Perception and Personality: Holtzman Inkblot Technique, 1961; (with C.C. Cleland) Mental Retardation: Approaches to Institutional Change, 1969; (with Cleland) Administrative Issues in Institutions for the Mentally Retarded, 1972; Multihandicapped Mentally Retarded: Training and Enrichment Strategies, 1973; Holtzman Inkblot Technique Annotated Bibliography, 1973; (with R. Diaz-Guerrero and W.H. Holtzman) Personality Development in Two Cultures: A Longitudinal Study of School Children in Mexico and the United States, 1975; (with R.K. Eyman and C.C. Cleland) Research with the Profoundly Retarded, 1978; (with C.C. Cleland) Exceptionalities Through the Lifespan: An Introduction, 1982; (with W.H. Holtzman and R.C. Reinehr) Holtzman Inkblot Technique, 1956-1982: An Annotated Bibliography, 1983. Add: A. Frank Smith Jr. Library Centre, Southwestern Univ., Georgetown, Tex. 78626, U.S.A.

SWEARER, Donald K(eeney). American, b. 1934. Theology/Religion. Prof., Swarthmore Coll., Pennsylvania, since 1976 (Assoc. Prof. 1970–75). Member, Editorial Bd., Journal of Religious Ethics, since 1978. Instr., of English, Bangkok Christian Coll., 1957–60; Admin Asst., Edward W. Hazen Foundn., 1961–63; Instr. and Asst. Prof., Oberlin Coll. Ohio, 1965–70; Acting Assoc. Prof., Univ. of Pennsylvania, 1970–72. Asst. Ed., Journal of Asian Studies, 1978–80. *Publs:* Buddhism in Transition, 1970; (ed.) Toward the Truth, 1971; (with Sobhana Dhammasudhi and Eshin Nishimura) Secrets of the Lotus: Studies in Buddhist Mediation, 1971; Southeast Asia, 1973; Theology of Dialogue, 1973; War Haripunjaya: The Royal Temple of the Buddha's Relic, 1976; (ed.) Buddhism, 1977; Dialogue: The Key to Understanding Other Religions, 1977; Buddhism and Society in SE Asia, 1981; (co-author) Focus on Buddhism: Audio-Visual Resources for Teaching Religion, 1981. Add: Dept. of Religion, Swarthmore Coll., Swarthmore, Pa. 19081, U.S.A.

SWEENEY, Leo. American, b. 1918. Intellectual history, Philosophy, Theology/Religion. Research Prof., Dept. of Philosophy, Loyola Univ. of Chicago, Ill., since 1974 (Visiting Prof., 1972–74). Corresponding Ed., The Modern Schoolman, St. Louis Univ., since 1967. Pres., U.S.A. Section, Intnl. Soc. for Neoplatonic Studies, since 1986 Prof., Dept of Philosophy, St. Louis Univ., 1954–68; Research Prof., Dept. of Philosophy, Creighton Univ., Omaha, Nebr. 1968–70; Visiting Prof., Sch., of Philosophy, Catholic Univ. of America, Washington, D.C., 1970–72. Pres., Jesuit Philosophical Assn., 1965–66; Pres., American Catholic Philosophical Assn., 1980–81. *Publs:* (ed.) Proceedings of the Annual Convention of the Jesuit Philosophical Assn., 1960, 1961, 1962; A Metaphysics of Authentic Existentialism, 1965; Wisdom in Depth: Essays in Honor of Henry Renard, 1966; Infinity in the Presocratics: A Bibliographical and Philosophical Study, 1972; Authentic Metaphysics in an Age of Unreality, 1988; Studies in Christian Philosophy, 2 vols., 1990. Add: Loyola Univ., 6525 North Sheridan, Chicago, Ill. 60626, U.S.A.

SWEETING, George. American, b. 1924. Social commentary/phenomena, Theology/Religion. Pres., Moody Bible Inst., Chicago, 1971–87 (Pastor, the Moody Church, 1966–71). Evangelist traveled world-wide, 1951–61; Pastor, Madison Ave. Baptist Church, Paterson, N.J. 1961–66. *Publs:* And the Greatest of These, 1968; Living Stones, 1970; The City: A Matter of Conscience, 1972; How to Solve Conflicts, 1973; Love is the Greatest, 1974; How to Begin the Christian Life, 1975; Special Sermons for Special Days (on Special Issues, on the Family), 3 vols., 1977–81; How to Witness Successfully, 1978; Talking It Over, 1979; Faith That Works, 1983; Your Future, 1984; You Can Climb Higher, 1985; Great Quotes and Illustrations, 1986 Add: 1209 Spruce Ct., Libertyville, Ill. 60048, U.S.A.

SWEETLAND, Nancy Rose. Pseud. for Nancy A. Rose. American, b. 1934. Children's fiction. Dir., Scripters Manuscript Group, since 1972. Ed., The Artist's Notebook, 1970–71; Dir., Institutional Writing Progr., Wisconsin Penal Inst., 1970–79; Member, Bd. of Dirs., Wisconsin Regional Writers Assn., 1971–79, and Wisconsin Fellowship of Poets, 1973–78. *Publs:* Funny Talk Freddy, 1970; The Dragon of Cobblestone Castle, 1970; Yelly Kelly, 1970; The Motherless Bug, 1971. Add: 215 Oak Hill Dr., Green Bay, Wisc. 54301, U.S.A.

SWEETMAN, David. British, b. 1943. Poetry, Children's non-fiction. Arts Producer, BBC Television, London. Formerly worked for the British Council for 8 years, mainly in Africa. *Publs:* for children— Queen Nzinga, 1971; Picasso, 1973; Captain Scott, 1974; The Borgias, 1976; Patrice Lamumba, 1978; Spies and Spying, 1981; The Amulet, 1980; The Moyo Kids, 1980; Skyjack over Africa, 1980; Bishop Crowther, 1981 Women Leaders in African History, 1984; poetry—Looking into the Deep End, 1981. Add: c/o Faber & Faber Ltd., 3 Queen Sq., London WC1N 3AU, England.

SWEETSER, Wesley. American, b. 1919. Literature, Biography. Emeritus Prof. of English, State Univ. of New York at Oswego, since 1982 (Assoc. Prof. of English, 1967–69; Prof., 1969–82). Instr., Univ. of Colorado, Boulder, 1945–48; Asst. Prof., Peru State Teachers Coll., Nebr., 1948–50; Assoc. Prof., U.S. Air Force Academy, 1957–63; Visiting Prof., Nebraska Wesleyan Coll., Lincoln, 1966–67. *Publs:* Arthur Machen, 1964; (with A. Goldstone) A Bibliography of Arthur Machen, 1965; Ralph Hodgson: A Bibliography, 1974, 1980. Add: R.R. 5, Box 76, Oswego, N.Y. 13126, U.S.A.

SWENSON, May. American, b. 1919. Plays, Poetry, Literature, Translations. Ed., New Directions Press, NYC, 1959–66; Poet-in-Residence, Purdue Univ., Lafayette, Ind., 1966–67; Poetry Seminar Instr., Univ. of North Carolina, Greensboro, 1968–69. *Publs:* Another Animal, 1954; A Cage of Spines, 1958; To Mix with Time: New and Selected Poems, 1963; The Contemporary Poet as Artist and Critic, 1964; Poems to Solve, 1966; Half Sun, Half Sleep: New Poems, 1967; Iconographs: Poems, 1970; More Poems to Solve, 1971; (trans.) Windows and Stones: Selected Poems, by Thomas Transtromer, 1972; The Guess and Spell Coloring Book (juvenile), 1976; New and Selected Things Taking Place, 1978; In Other Words (poems), 1987. Add: 73 The Boulevard, Sea Cliff, New York, N.Y. 11579, U.S.A.

SWETMAN, Glenn R(obert). American, b. 1936. Poetry. Prof. of English, Nicholls State Univ., Thibodaux, La., since 1971 (Head, Dept. of English, 1968–71). Consulting Ed., Paon Press, Dallas, Tex., since 1974; Book Reviewer and Literary Consultant, Mississippi State Times, since 1961. Instr., Univ. Coll. of Tulane Univ., New Orleans, La., 1961–64; Asst. Prof., Univ. of Southern Mississippi, Hattiesburg, 1964–66; Assoc. Prof., Louisiana Technical Univ., Ruston, 1966–67. *Publs:* (with C. Whittington and W. Sullivan) Poems from the McNeese Review, 1961; (with W. Read and J.R. Swetman) The Pagan Christmas, 1962; Tunel de Amor, 1973; Deka No. 1, 1973; Shards, 1979; Deka No. 2, 1979; Concerning Carpenters, 1980; Son of Igor, 1980; Poems of the Fantastic, 1986. Add: Dept. of English, Nicholls State Univ., Thibodaux, La. 70301, U.S.A.

SWIERENGA, Robert P. American, b. 1935. History. Prof. of History, Kent State Univ., Ohio, since 1968. Managing Ed., Social Science History. *Publs:* Pioneers and Profits: Land Speculation on the Iowa Frontier, 1968; (ed.) Quantification in American History: Theory and Research, 1970; (ed.) Beyond the Civil War Synthesis, 1975; Acres for Cents: Delinquent Tax Auctions in Frontier Iowa, 1976; (ed.) Bilateral Bicentennial: A History of Dutch-American Relations 1782-1982, 1982; (ed.) History and Ecology: James C. Malin's Studies of the Grassland, 1984; (ed.) Netherlanders in America: A Study of Emigration and Settlement in the 19th and 20th Centuries in the U.S.A., 1985; (ed.) The Dutch in America: Immigration, Settlement, and Cultural Change, 1985. Add: Dept. of History, Kent State Univ., Kent, Ohio 44242, U.S.A.

SWIFT, Bryan. *See* KNOTT, William C.

SWIFT, Graham (Colin). British, b. 1949. Novels/Short stories. *Publs:* The Sweet Shop Owner, 1980; Shuttlecock, 1981; Learning to Swim and Other Stories, 1982; Waterland, 1983; Out of This World, 1988. Add: c/o A.P. Watt Ltd., 20 John St., London WC1N 2DR, England.

SWIFT, (Sister) Mary Grace. American, b. 1927. Dance/Ballet, Biography. Member, Ursuline Order of Nuns. Prof. of History, Loyola Univ. (joined faculty, 1966). Elementary Sch. teacher in Kansas, 1947–56; Secondary sch. teacher in Kansas and Oklahoma, 1957–61. *Publs:* The Art of the Dance in the U.S.S.R., 1968; A Loftier Flight (biography), 1974; (ed.) With Bright Wings, 1976; Belles and Beaux on Their Toes, 1980. Add: c/o Dept. of History, Loyola Univ., New Orleans, La. 70118, U.S.A.

SWIFT, Richard Newton. American, b. 1924. International relations/Current affairs. Prof. of Politics, New York Univ., 1942–83, now Emeritus (joined faculty, 1949; Head, Dept. of Govt. and Intnl. Relations, 1963–69). Foreign Assoc., Royal Inst. of Intnl. Affairs, since 1975. Ed., Annual Review of U.N. Affairs (yearbooks), 15 vols., 1950–69; Vice-Chmn., Commn. to Study the Org. of Peace, 1971–82; Exec. Cttee. Member, Intnl. Law Assn., 1973–85. *Publs:* World Affairs and the College Curriculum, 1949; International Law: Current and Classic, 1969. Add: 72 Barrow St., Apt. 3-N, New York, N.Y. 10014, U.S.A.

SWIFT, W. Porter. American, b. 1914. Human relations, Psychology. Prof. of Psychology, Broome Community Coll., N.Y., since 1964. Consultant in private practice; Prof., Grad. Sch., Ithaca Coll., N.Y., 1954–59, and since 1965 (Chmn., Psychology Dept., 1954–59); Clinical Psychologist, Broome County Medical Health Clinic, since 1965. Chmn., Psychology Dept., State Univ. of New York at Binghamton, 1946–51; Consultant, The Hay Assocs., Philadelphia, 1959–64. Dir., Psychological Services, Villanova Univ., Pa., 1962–64. *Publs:* General Psychology, 1969; (with Donald Laird and R.T. Fruehline) Psychology: Human Relations and Motivation, 1974. Add: 3 Murray St., Binghamton, N.Y. 13905, U.S.A.

SWIHART, Thomas L. American, b. 1929. Astronomy, Physics. Prof. of Astronomy, and Astronomer at the Stewart Observatory, Univ. of Arizona, Tucson, since 1963. Assoc. Prof. of Physics and Astronomy, Univ. of Mississippi, Oxford, 1955–57; Staff Member, Los Alamos Scientific Lab., New Mexico, 1957–62; Asst. Prof. of Astronomy, Univ. of Illinois, Urbana, 1962–63. *Publs:* Astrophysics and Stellar Astronomy, 1968; Basic Physics of Stellar Atmospheres, 1971; Physics of Stellar Interiors, 1972; (with others) Introductory Theoretical Astrophysics, 1976; Journey Through the Universe, 1978; Radiation Tansfer and Stellar Atmospheres, 1981. Add: Steward Observatory, Univ. of Arizona, Tucson, Ariz. 85721, U.S.A.

SWINBURNE, Richard (Granville). British, b. 1934. Philosophy, Theology/Religion. Nolloth Prof. of the Philosophy of the Christian Religion, Oxford Univ., since 1985. Fereday Fellow, St. John's Coll., Univ. of Oxford, 1958–61; Leverhulme Research Fellow in the History and Philosophy of Science, Univ. of Leeds, Yorks., 1961–63; Lectr. in Philosophy, 1963–69, and Sr. Lectr., 1969–72, Univ. of Hull, Yorks.; Prof. of Philosophy, Univ. of Keele, 1972–84. *Publs:* Space and Time, 1968, 1980; The Concept of Miracle, 1971; An Introduction to Confirmation Theory, 1973; (ed.) The Justification of Induction, 1974; The Coherence of Theism, 1977; The Existence of God, 1979; Faith and Raison, 1981; (ed.) Space, Time and Causality, 1983; (with S. Shoemaker) Personal Identity, 1984; The Evolution of the Soul, 1986; (ed.) Miracles, 1989; Responsibility and Atonement, 1989. Add: Oriel Coll., Oxford OX1 4EW, England.

SWINDELLS, Madge. British. Romance. *Publs:* Summer Harvest, 1983; Song of the Wind, 1985; Shadows on the Snow, 1987; The Corsican Woman, 1988. Add: c/o Macdonald and Co. Ltd., Greater London House, Hampstead Rd., London NW1 7QX, England.

SWINDELLS, Robert (Edward). British, b. 1939. Children's fiction. Served in the Royal Air Force, 1957–60; Advertising Clerk, Bradford Telegraph and Argus, 1960–67; Engineer, Hepworth and Grandage, Bradford, 1967–69; elementary sch. teacher, Bradford, 1972–77; part-time teacher, 1977–80. *Publs:* When Darkness Comes, 1973; A Candle in the Night, 1974; as A Candle in the Dark, 1983; Voyage to Valhalla, 1976; The Ice-Palace, 1977; The Very Special Baby, 1977; Dragons Live Forever, 1978; The Moonpath and Other Stories, 1979; Norah's Ark, 1979; Norah's Shark, 1979; The Weather-Clerk, 1979; Ghost Ship to Ganymede, 1980; Norah and the Whale, 1981; Norah to the Rescue, 1981; World Eater, 1981; Brother in the Land, 1984; The Thousand Eyes of Night, 1985; The Ghost Messengers, 1986; Staying Up, 1986; Mavis Davis, 1988; The Postbox Mystery, 1988; A Serpent's Tooth, 1988. Add: 3 Upwood Park, Black Moor Rd., Oxenhope, Keithley, West Yorks. BD22 9SS, England.

SWORD, Wiley. American, b. 1937. History. Pres., Techni-Cast Inc., since 1960. *Publs:* Shiloh: Bloody April, 1974; President Washington's Indian War, 1985; Firepower from Abroad, 1986; Sharpshooter: Hiram Berdan, His Famous Sharpshooters, and Their Sharps Rifles, 1988. Add: 5640 Kolly Rd., Birmingham, Mich. 48010, U.S.A.

SYDENHAM, Michael John. British, b. 1923. History. Prof. of History, Carleton Univ., Ottawa, Ont., since 1968, Emeritus since 1988. Head, History Dept., City of Portsmouth Coll. of Education, 1957–68. *Publs:* The Girondins, 1961; The French Revolution, 1965; The First French Republic 1792-1804, 1974. Add: Dept. of History, Carleton Univ., Ottawa, Ont. K1S 5B6, Canada.

SYDNEY, Cynthia. *See* **TRALINS,** S. Robert.

SYERS, (William) Ed(ward). American, b. 1914. Novels/Short stories, History. Syndicated feature columnist. *Publs:* Seven-Navy Subchaser, 1960; Texas: Off The Beaten Trail, 3 vols., 1964–72; (co-ed.) The Will Rogers Book, 1973; The Devil Gun, 1976; Texas: The Beginning, 1978; Backroads of Texas, 1979; Ghost Stories of Texas, 1981; The Luckenbach Showdown, 1986; Handpressed, 1987; Backroads of Texas, 1988. Add: c/o Gulf Publishing, Box 2608, Houston, Tex. 77252, U.S.A.

SYKES, Alrene (Maud). Australian. Theatre. Sr. Lectr. in English, Univ. of Queensland, Brisbane, since 1969 (Lectr., 1962–68). Member of the Council, La Boite Theatre, Brisbane, since 1979. Play Ed., Australian Broadcasting Commn., Sydney, 1952–62. *Publs:* Harold Pinter, 1970; (ed.) Nightmares of the Old Obscenity Master (radio plays), 1975; (ed.) Five Plays for Stage, Radio and Television, 1977; (ed.) 2D and Other Plays (stage plays), 1978; (ed.) Can't You Hear Me Talking to You?, (stage plays), 1978; (ed.) Three Political Plays (stage plays), 1980. Add: Dept. of English, Univ. of Queensland, St. Lucia, Qld. 4067, Australia.

SYLVESTER, Philip. *See* **WORNER,** Philip.

SYLVIN, Francis. *See* **SEAMAN,** Sylvia Sybil.

SYME, (Sir) Ronald. New Zealander, b. 1903. History, Classics. Fellow and Tutor, Trinity Coll., Oxford, 1929–49; Camden Prof. of Ancient History, Univ. of Oxford, 1949–70. Pres., Intl. Fedn. of Classical Studies, 1951–54; Secty.-Gen., 1952,19671, and Pres., 1971–75, Intl. Council for Philosophy and Humanistic Studies. *Publs:* The Roman Revolution, 1939; Tacitus, 1958; Colonial Elites, 1958; Sallust, 1964; Ammianus and the Historia Augusta, 1968; Ten Studies in Tacitus, 1970; Emperors and Biography, 1971; Danubian Papers, 1971; The Historia Augusta: A Call for Clarity, 1971; History in Ovid, 1978; Roman Papers, 2 vols., 1979, vol. 3, 1984; Some Arval Brethren, 1980; Historia Augusta Papers, 1983; The Augustan Aristocracy, 1986. Add: Wolfson Coll., Oxford, England.

SYME, (Neville) Ronald. Irish, b. 1910. Children's fiction, Children's non-fiction, History, Travel/Exploration/Adventure. Cadet and Officer, 1930–34, and Gunner, 1939–40, British Merchant Service; Reporter and Foreign Corresp., 1934–39; Asst. Ed., John Westhouse & Peter Lunn Ltd., publishers, London, 1946–48; Public Relations Officer, British Rd. Federation, London, 1948–50. *Publs:* Full Fathom Five, 1946; That Must Be Julian, 1947; Hakluyt's Sea Stories, 1948; Julian's River War, 1949; Ben of the Barrier, 1949; Bay of the North: The Story of Pierre Radisson, 1950; The Story of British Roads, 1951; Cortes of Mexico, 1951 (in U.K. as Cortez: Conqueror of Mexico, 1952); I, Mungo Park (Captain Anson, Gordon of Khartoum), 3 vols., 1951–53; Champlain of the St. Lawrence, 1952; Columbus, Finder of the New World, 1952; The Story of Britain's Highways, 1952; La Salle of the Mississippi, 1953; Magellan, First Around the World, 1953; The Windward Islands: Frontiers of the Caribbean, Islands of the Sun, A Schooner Voyage in the West Indies, 3 vols., 1953; The Settlers of Carriacou, 1953; Gipsy Michael, 1954; John Smith of Virginia, 1954; The Story of New Zealand: We Dip into the Past, Life in New Zealand Today, A Tour of New Zealand, 3 vols., 1954; The Cook Islands, 1955; Henry Hudson (in U.K. as Hudson of the Bay), 1955; They Came to an Island, 1955; Isle of Revolt, 1956; Ice Fighter, 1956; Balboa, Finder of the Pacific,1956; De Soto, Finder of the Mississippi, 1957; The Amateur Company, 1957; The Great Canoe, 1957; The Forest Fighters, 1958; River of No Return, 1958; The Man Who Discovered the Amazon, 1958; Cartier, Finder of the St. Lawrence, 1958; On Foot to the Arctic: The Story of Samuel Hearne (in U.K. as Trail to the North), 1959; Vasco Da Gama, Sailor Towards the Sunrise,

1959; The Spaniards Came at Dawn, 1959; Thunder Knoll, 1960; The Buccaneer Explorer, 1960; Captain Cook, Pacific Explorer, 1960; Francis Drake, Sailor of the Unknown Seas, 1961; First Man to Cross America: The Story of Cabeza de Vaca, 1961; The Mountainy Men, 1961; Coast of Danger, 1961; Nose-Cap Astray, 1962; Walter Raleigh, 1962; The Young Nelson, 1962; African Traveler: The Story of Mary Kingslye, 1962; Two Passengers for Spanish Fork, 1963; Francisco Pizarro, Finder of Peru, 1963; Switch Points at Kamlin, 1964; The Dunes and the Diamonds, 1964; Invaders and Invasions, 1964; Nigerian Pioneer: The Story of Mary Slessor, 1964; Alexander Mackenzie, Canadian Explorer, 1964; Sir Henry Morgan, Buccaneer, 1965; Francisco Coronado and the Seven Cities of Gold, 1965; The Missing Witness, 1965; Quesada of Columbia,1966; William Penn, Founder of Pennsylvania, 1966; Garibaldi, The Man Who Made a Nation, 1967; The Saving of the Fair East Wind, 1967; Bolivar, The Liberator, 1968; Captain John Paul Jones, America's Fighting Seaman, 1968; Amerigo Vespucci, Scientist and Sailor, 1969; Frontenac of New France, 1969; Benedict Arnold, Traitor of the Revolution, 1970; Vancouver, Explorer of the Pacific Coast, 1970; Toussaint, The Black Liberator, 1971; Zapata, Mexican Rebel, 1971; The Travels of Captain Cook, 1971; John Cabot and His Son Sebastian, 1972; Juarez, The Founder of Modern Mexico, 1972; Verrazano, Explorer of the Atlantic Coast, 1973; Fur Trader of the North: The Story of Pierre de la Verendrye, 1973; John Charles Fremont, The Last American Explorer, 1974; Marquette and Joliet, Voyagers on the Mississippi, 1974; Geronimo, The Fighting Apache, 1975; Isle of the Frigate Bird (on the Cook Islands), 1975; Osceola, Seminole Leader, 1976; The Lagoon Is Lonely Now (autobiography), 1979. Add: c/o William Morrow Inc., 105 Madison Ave., New York, N.Y. 10016, U.S.A.

SYMMONS-SYMONOLEWICZ, Konstantin. American, b. 1909. Anthropology/Ethnology, Politics/Government, Sociology. Prof. Emeritus of Sociology and Anthropology, Allegheny Coll., Meadville, Pa., since 1976 (Prof., 1969–76). Prof. of Sociology and Anthropology, Wilkes Coll., Wilkes-Barre, Pa., 1945–62; Prof. of Sociology and Anthropology, MacMurry Coll., Jacksonville, Ill., 1962–69. *Publs:* Modern Nationalism: Toward a Consensus in Theory, 1968; Nationalist Movements: A Comparative View, 1970; (ed. and trans.) The Non-Slavic Peoples of the Soviet Union, 1972; National Consciousness in Poland: Origin and Evolution, 1983. Add: 540 Deissler Ct., Meadville, Pa. 16335, U.S.A.

SYMONDS, John. British. Novels/Short stories, Children's fiction, Plays/Screenplays, Supernatural/Occult topics, Biography. *Publs:* ua-William Waste, 1947; The Lady in the Tower, 1951; The Great Beast: The Life of Aleister Crowley, 1951, 1971; The Magic Currant Bun, 1952; Travellers Three, 1953; Sheila (play), 1953; The Isle of Cats, 1955; Away to the Moon, 1956; The Bright Blue Sky, 1956; Lottie, 1957; A Girl among Poets, 1957; The Magic of Aleister Crowley, 1958; Madame Blavatsky: Medium and Magician, 1959 (in U.S. as The Lady with the Magic Eyes, 1960, retitled in U.K. as In Astral Light, 1965); Elfrida and the Pig, 1959; The Only Thing That Matters, 1960; I, Having Dreamt, Awake (play), 1961; Thomas Brown and the Angels: A Study in Enthusiasm, 1961; Dapple Grey: The Story of a Rocking-Horse, 1962; Bezill, 1962; Light over Walter, 1963; The Story George Told Me, 1963; The Other House (play), 1963; Tom and Tabby, 1964; Grodge-Cat and the Window Cleaner, 1965; With a View on the Palace, 1966; The Stuffed Dog, 1967; The Hurt Runner, 1968; (ed. with Kenneth Grant) The Confessions of Aleister Crowley: An Autobiography, 1969; (ed., with Kenneth Grant) The Magical Record of Beast 666: The Diaries of Aleister Crowley 1914-1920, 1972; (ed., with Kenneth Grant) Magick, by Aleister Crowley, 1973; (ed. with Kenneth Grant) White Stains, by Aleister Crowley, 1973; Prophecy and Parasites, 1973; Harold: The Story of a Friendship, 1973; The Shaven Head, 1974; Conversations with Gerald, 1974; (ed., with Kenneth Grant) The Complete Astrological Writings of Aleister Crowley, 1974; (ed., with Kenneth Grant) Moonchild, by Aleister Crowley, 1974; Letters from England, 1975; The Child: Prologue to an Earthquake, 1976; The Bicycle Plays, and the Winter Forest (play), 1976; The Guardian of the Threshold, 1980; Collected Dramatic Works, 5 vols., 1981–87; Zélide (novel), 1984. Add: c/o Gerald Duckworth Ltd., The Old Piano Factory, 43 Gloucester Cres., London NW1 7DY, England.

SYMONDS, Pamela (Maureen Southey). British, b. 1916. Language/ Linguistics. Teacher, 1939–65. *Publs:* Let's Speak French, vol. I, 1962, vol. II, 1963; (with G. Lester) Gérard Vernier, 1965; (with G. Lester) Voyage en Scooter, 1966; French Through Action, vol. I, 1967, vol. II, 1969; (with R. Pérès) Un Mois dans le Midi, 1968; (with G. Chevallier) Les Skis de Virginie, 1970; (with R. Pérès) L'Idole, 1973; French from France, 5 vols., 1975–79; A l'Ecoute, 1982; French Talk, 1987. Add: 10 Bisham Gardens, London N6 6DD, England.

SYMONDS, (John) Richard. British, b. 1918. History, Institutions/ Organizations, International relations/Current affairs. Sr. Assoc. Member, St. Antony's Coll., Oxford Univ., since 1979. Served in the U.N. Development Programme, 1950–79; Resident Rep. in Ceylon, Yugoslavia, Europe, East Africa, and Southern Africa, 1950–65, Greece, 1972–75, and Tunisia, 1975–78. Sr. Research Officer, Inst. of Commonwealth Studies, Oxford Univ., 1963–65; Professorial Fellow, Inst. of Development Studies, Univ. of Sussex, Brighton, 1966–69; Rep. in Europe, U.N. Inst. for Training and Research, 1969–71. *Publs:* The Making of Pakistan, 1950; The British and Their Successors, 1966; (ed. and co-author) International Targets for Development, 1970; (with M. Carder) The United Nations and the Population Question, 1973; Oxford and Empire—The Last Lost Cause?, 1986; Alternative Saints, 1988. Add: 43 Davenant Rd., Oxford, England.

SYMONS, Geraldine. Also writes as Georgina Groves. British, b. 1909. Novels/Short stories, Children's fiction, Biography. *Publs:* All Souls, 1950; French Windows, 1952; Children in the Close, 1959; The Rose Window, 1964; The Quarantine Child, 1966; (as Georgina Groves) Morning Glory, 1966; The Workhouse Child, 1969; The Suckling, 1969; Miss Rivers and Miss Bridges, 1971; Mademoiselle, 1973; Now and Then, 1977; Second Cousins Once Removed, 1978. Add: 4 de Vaux Pl., Salisbury, Wilts., England.

SYMONS, Julian (Gustave). British, b. 1912. Mystery/Crime/ Suspense, Poetry, History, Biography. Reviewer, Sunday Times, London, since 1958. Ed., Twentieth Century Verse, London, 1937–39; Reviewer, Manchester Evening News, 1947–56; Chmn., Crime Writers Assn., 1958–59, and Cttee. of Mgmt., Soc. of Authors, 1969–71; Pres., Detection Club, 1976–85; Ed., Penguin Mystery Series, 1974–79. *Publs:* Confusions about X, 1938; (ed.) Anthology of War Poetry, 1942; The Second Man, 1944; The Immaterial Murder Case, 1945; A Man Called Jones, 1947; Bland Beginning, 1949; (ed.) Selected Writings of Samuel Johnson, 1949; The 31st of February, 1950; A.J.A. Symons: His Life and Speculations, 1950; Charles Dickens, 1951; Thomas Carlyle: The Life and Ideas of a Prophet, 1952; The Broken Penny, 1952; The Narrowing Circle, 1954; Horatio Bottomley, 1955; The Paper Chase (in U.S. as Bogues's Fortune), 1956; (ed.) Selected Works, Reminiscences and Letters, by Thomas Carlyle, 1956; The Colour of Murder, 1957; The General Strike: A Historical Portrait, 1957; The Gigantic Shadow (in U.S. as Pipe Dream), 1958; The Progress of Crime, 1960; The Thirties: A Dream Revolved, 1960; A Reasonable Doubt: Some Criminal Cases Re-examined, 1960; Murder, Murder, 1961; The Killing of Francie Lake (in U.S. as The Plain Man), 1962; The Detective Story in Britain, 1962; Buller's Campaign, 1963; The End of Solomon Grundy, 1964; The Belting Inheritance, 1965; Francis Quarles Investigates, 1965; England's Pride: The Story of the Gordon Relief Expedition, 1965; Crime and Detection: An Illustrated History from 1840 (in U.S. as A Pictorial History of Crime), 1966; Critical Occasions, 1966; The Man Who Killed Himself, 1967; The Man Whose Dreams Came True, 1969; (ed.) Essays and Biographies, by A.J.A. Symons, 1969; The Man Who Lost His Wife, 1971; The Players and the Game, 1972; Bloody Murder: From the Detective Story to the Crime Novel: A History (in U.S. as Mortal Consequences: A History from the Detective Story to the Crime Novel), 1972, 1985; Between the Wars: Britain in Photographs, 1972; Notes from Another Country, 1972; The Plot Against Roger Rider, 1973; The Object of an Affair and Other Poems, 1974; A Three Pipe Problem, 1975; (ed.) The Angry Thirties, 1976; The Tell-Tale Heart: Life and Works of Edgar Allan Poe, 1978; The Blackheath Poisonings, 1978; Seven Poems for Sarah, 1979; (ed.) Verdict of Thirteen: A Detection Club Anthology, 1979; Conan Doyle, 1979; Sweet Adelaide, 1979; The Great Detectives, 1981; Critical Observations, 1981; The Detling Murders, 1982; The Tigers of Subtopia, 1982; The Name of Annabel Lee, 1983; Crime and Detection Quiz, 1983; (ed.) New Poetry 9, 1983; (ed.) Classic Crime Omnibus, 1984; Dashiell Hammett, 1985; The Criminal Comedy of the Contented Couple (in U.S. as A Criminal Comedy), 1985; (ed.) Tchekov's The Shooting Party, 1986; The Kentish Manor Murders, 1988. Add: 330 Dover Rd., Walmer, Deal, Kent, England.

SYMONS, Leslie John. British, b. 1926. Geography. Prof. of Geography, Univ. Coll. of Swansea, since 1980 (Sr. Lectr., 1970–73; Reader, 1973–80). Lectr. in Geography, Queens Univ., Belfast, N. Ire., 1953–63; Simon Sr. Research Fellow, Univ. of Manchester, 1967–68; Sr. Lectr. in Geography, Univ. of Canterbury, N.Z., 1963–70. Ed., Textbook Series, Geography of the USSR, Hicks-Smith & Son, N.Z., 1968–70. *Publs:* (ed.) Land Use in Northern Ireland, 1963; Agricultural Geography, 1967, 1978; (with L. Hanna) Northern Ireland: A Geographical Introduction, 1967; Russian Agriculture: A Geographical Survey, 1972; (ed. with C. White) Russian Transport: An Historical and Geographical Survey, 1975; (ed.) The Soviet Union: A Systematic Geography, 1982; (ed. with J.

Ambler and D. Shaw) Soviet and East European Transport Problems, 1985; (co-ed.) Transport and Economic Development: Soviet Union and Eastern Europe, 1987. Add: Squirrels Jump, 17 Wychwood Close, Llangland, Swansea SA3 4PH, Wales.

SYMONS, (H.B.) Scott. Canadian, b. 1933. Novels/Short stories, Antiques/Furnishings. Curator, Sigmund Samuel Canadiana Collection and Canadian Gallery, Royal Ontario Museum, Toronto, Asst. Prof. of Fine Art, Univ. of Toronto, and Consultant, Smithsonian Instn., Washington, D.C., all since 1962. *Publs:* Place D'Armes, 1967; Civil Square, 1969; Heritage: A Romantic Look at Early Canadian Furniture, 1971; Helmet of Flesh, 1988. Add: c/o McClelland & Stewart Ltd., 481 University Ave., Toronto, Ont., M5G 2E9, Canada.

SYNAN, Edward A. American, b. 1918. Intellectual history. Prof., and Sr. Fellow, Pontifical Inst. of Mediaeval Studies, Toronto, since 1959 (Pres., 1973–79; Acting Pres., since 1989). Assoc. Ed., The Bridge mag., 1958–62. *Publs:* The Popes and the Jews in the Middle Ages, 1965; The Works of Richard Campsall, vol. I, 1968, vol. II, 1982; (trans.) The Fountain of Philosophy: A Translation of 12th Century Fons philosophiae of Godfrey of Saint Victor, 1972. Add: 59 Queen's Park Cres. East, Toronto, Ont. M5S 2C4, Canada.

SYNAN, (Harold) Vinson. American, b. 1934. History, Social commentary/ phenomena, Theology/Religion. Asst. Gen. Supt., officially commissioned Historian, Pentecostal Holiness Church (Pastor, 1956–74). Pres., Soc. for Pentecostal Studies, 1973–74. *Publs:* Emmanuel College: The First Fifty Years, 1969; Holiness-Pentecostal Movement in U.S., 1971; The Old Time Power, 1973; Charismatic Bridges, 1974; (ed.) Aspects of Pentecostal-Charismatic Origins, 1975; (ed.) Azusa Street, 1976; In the Latter Days, 12984; The Twentieth Century Pentecostal Explosion, 1987. Add: 7412 N. Ann Arbor, Oklahoma City, Okla. 73132, U.S.A.

SYNGE, Ursula. British, b. 1930. Children's fiction, Mythology/ Folklore. Bookseller, Pied Piper Bookshop, Bristol, 1957–85. *Publs:* Weland, Smith of the Gods, 1972; The People and the Promise, 1974; Andun and the Bear, 1975; Kalavala, 1977; The Giant at the Ford and Other Legends of the Saints, 1980; Swan's Wing, 1982. Add: 10 Highbury Villas, St. Michael's Hill, Bristol 2, England.

SYPHER, Lucy Johnston. American, b. 1907. Children's fiction, Autobiography/Memoirs/Personal. Teacher, Lassell Jr. Coll., Auburndale, Mass., 1929–69. *Publs:* The Edge of Nowhere, 1972; Cousins and Circuses, 1974; The Spell of the Northern Lights, 1975; The Turnabout Year, 1976. Add: Schooley Mt. Rd., Heath Village, Hackettstown, N.J. 07840, U.S.A.

SYROP, Konrad. British, b. 1914. History, Documentaries/Reportage, Translations. Chmn., Copyright Licensing Agency Ltd., since 1983. War Corresp., 1944, Head, European Production Dept., 1955–60, and External Services Production, 1960–69, Prog. Ed., 1969–71, Head, Central European Service, 1971–73, and Chmn., External Services' Working Party, 1973–78, BBC, London (joined staff, 1939). *Publs:* Spring in October: The Polish Revolution of 1956, 1957; (trans.) The Inquisitors, by G. Andrzejewski, 1960; (trans.) The Elephant, by S. Mrozek, 1962; (trans.) The Ugupu Bird, by S. Mrozek, 1968; Poland Between the Hammer and the Anvil, 1968; Poland in Perspective, 1982; radio documentaries—The White Divorce, 1970; The Search for Utopia, 1976; Marxism and the Marxists, 1977. Add: Flat 5, 15 St. German's Pl., London SE3 0NN, England.

SZASZ, Thomas Stephen. American, b. 1920. Law, Philosophy, Psychiatry, Psychology. Private practice of psychiatry and psychoanalysis and Prof., Dept. of Psychiatry, State Univ. of New York, Upstate Medical Centre, Syracuse, since 1956. Sr. and Visiting Scholar, Faculty Improvement Prog., Eli Lilly Foundn., since 1966; Member, Bd. of Govs., Intnl. Academy of Forensic Psychology, since 1968. Research Asst., 1949–50, and Staff member, 1950–56, Chicago Inst. for Psychoanalysis; Co-founder and Bd. of Dirs. Chmn., American Assn. for the Abolition of Involuntary Mental Hospitalization Inc., 1970. *Publs:* Pain and Pleasure: Study of Bodily Feelings, 1957; The Myth of Mental Illness: Foundations of a Theory of Personal Conduct, 1961, rev. ed. 1974; Law, Liberty, and Psychiatry: An Inquiry into the Social Uses of Mental Health Practices, 1963; Psychiatric Justice, 1965; The Ethics of Psychoanalysis: The Theory and Method of Autonomous Psychotherapy, 1965; Ideology and Insanity: Essays on the Psychiatric Dehumanization of Man, 1970; The Manufacture of Madness: A Comparative Study of the Inquisition and the Mental Health Movement, 1970; The Age of Madness, 1973.; The Second Sin, 1973; Ceremonial Chemistry: The Ritual Persecution of Drugs, Addicts and Pushers, 1974; Heresies, 1976; Schizophrenia: The Sacred Symbol of Psychiatry, 1976; Karl Kraus and the Soul-Doctors, 1976; Psychiatric Slavery, 1977; The Theology of Medicine, 1977; The Myth of Psychotherapy, 1978; Sex by Prescription, 1980; The Therapeutic State, 1984; Insanity: The Idea and Its Consequences, 1987. Add: State Univ. of New York, Upstate Medical Centre, 750 E. Adams St., Syracuse, N.Y. 13210, U.S.A.

SZEKELY, Endre. Australian, b. 1922. Psychology. Dir. of Clinical Studies, Cumberland Coll. of Health Sciences, Sydney, since 1974. Principal Clinical Psychologist, Bureau of Maternal and Child Health, New South Wales Dept. of Health, Sydney, 1960-69; Sr. Lectr. in Psychology, Univ. of Newcastle, N.S.W., 1969-74. *Publs:* Basic Analysis of Inner Psychological Functions, 1965; Functional Laws of Psychodynamics, 1979. Add: 67 Ronald Ave., Lane Cove, Sydney, N.S.W. 2066, Australia.

SZIRTES, George. British, b. 1948. Poetry. Head of Art, St. Christopher Sch., Letchworth, Herts., since 1981. Proprietor, Starwheel Press, Hitchin, Herts. Part-time teacher in colleges and schs., 1973-75; Head of Art, Hitchin Girls Sch., 1975-81. *Publs:* Poems, 1972; The Iron Clouds, 1975; Visitors, 1976; An Illustrated Alphabet, 1977; (with Neil Powell and Peter Scupham) A Mandeville Troika, 1977; At the Sink, 1978; Silver Age, 1978; The Slant Door, 1979; Sermon on a Ship, 1980; Homage to Cheval, 1980; November and May, 1981; The Kissing Place, 1982; Short Wave, 1983; The Photographer in Winter, 1986; Metro, 1988. Add: 20 Old Park Rd., Hitchin, Herts. SG5 2JR, England.

SZULC, Tad. American, b. 1926. History, International relations/Current affairs, Politics/Government, Sociology. Foreign and Diplomatic Corresp., New York Times, NYC, 1953–73. *Publs:* Twilight of the Tyrants, 1959; (withK.E. Meyer) The Cuban Invasion, 1962; Winds of Revolution, 1963; Dominican Diary, 1965; Latin America, 1966; Bombs of Palomares, 1967; Czechoslovakia since World War II, 1971; (ed.) The United States and the Caribbean, 1971; Portrait of Spain, 1972; Invasion of Czechoslovakia, 1974; Compulsive Spy, 1974; Innocents at Home, 1974; The Energy Crisis, 1974; Illusion of Peace, 1978; Diplomatic Immunity (novel), 1981; Fidel: A Critical Portrait, 1986. Add: 4515 29th St. N.W., Washington, D.C. 20008, U.S.A.

T

TABORI, George. British, b. 1914. Novels/Short stories, Plays/Screenplays. Resident Dir., Kammerspiele, Munich. Artistic Dir., Berkshire Theatre Festival. Dir., Bremen Theaterlab, Germany, 1976–78. *Publs:* Beneath the Stone the Scorpion (novel), 1945; Companions of the Left Hand (novel), 1946; Original Sin (novel), 1947; The Caravan Passes (novel), 1951; Flight into Egypt, 1953; The Emperor's Clothes, 1953; The Journey: Confession (novel), 1958; The Good One (novel), 1960; Brecht on Brecht, 1962; The Cannibals, 1968; The Guns of Carrar, adaptation of a play by Brecht, 1970; Son of a Bitch (short stories), 1980. Add: c/o Bertha Case, 42 West 53rd St., New York, N.Y. 10019, U.S.A.

TABORSKY, Edward J(oseph). American, b. 1910. International relation/Current affairs, Politics/Government. Prof. of Govt., Univ. of Texas at Austin, since 1949. Personal Secty. to Pres. E. Benes of Czechoslovakia, 1939–45; Minister Plenipotentiary and Envoy Extraordinary of Czechoslovakia to Sweden, 1945–48. *Publs:* The Czechoslovak Cause, 1944; Czechoslovak Democracy at Work, 1945; O novou demokracii, 1945; Nase vec, 1946; Pan President se nam vratil, 1946; Pravda zvitezila, 1947; Nase nova ustava, 1948; Conformity under Communism, 1958; Communism in Czechoslovakia 1948-1960, 1961; Communist Penetration of the Third World, 1973; President Edward Benes Between the East and the West 1938-1948, 1981. Add: 4503 Parkwood, Austin, Tex. 78722, U.S.A.

TAFEL, Edgar. American, b. 1912. Architecture. Architect in private practice, NYC. *Publs:* Apprentice to Genius: Years with Frank Lloyd Wright, 1979, in paperback as Years with Frank Lloyd Wright, 1985. Add: 14 E. 11th St., New York, N.Y. 10003, U.S.A.

TAGLIABUE, John. American, b. 1923. Poetry. Prof. of English, Bates Coll., Lewiston, since 1971 (joined faculty, 1953). Lectr. in American Literature, American Univ., Beirut, 1945–46; Fulbright Prof., Univ. of Pisa, 1950–52, Tokyo Univ., 1958–60, and Fudan Univ., Shanghai, 1984. Poet-in-Residence, Anatolia Coll., Thessalonika, Greece, 1979. *Publs:* Poems, 1959; A Japanese Journal, 1966; The Buddha Uproar, 1967; The Doorless Door, 1970; Every Minute a Ritual 1973; The Great Day: Poems 1962-1983, 1984. Add: 12 Abbott St., Lewiston, Me. 04240, U.S.A.

TAIT, George Edward. Canadian, b. 1910. Children's fiction, Children's non-fiction, History. Prof. Emeritus, Faculty of Education, Univ. of Toronto, since 1973 (former Prof. of Education, and Dir. of Elementary Education). Elementary sch. teacher, London, Ont., 1931–41; Dir., Anglo-American Sch., Bogota, Colombia, 1941–44; Public Sch. Inspector, Huntsville and Welland, Ont., 1944–50; Member of Franklin Probe, Arctic Expedition, with Commnr. of North West Territories, 1974. *Publs:* The Saddle of Carlos Perez, 1949; The Silent Gulls, 1950; Wake of the West Wind, 1952; (ed.) Famous Canadian Stories, 1953; Breastplate and Buckskin, 1953; The World Was Wide, 1954; The Upward Trail, 1956; Proud Ages, 1958; Fair Domain, 1960; (ed.) Aldine World Atlas, 1961; One Dominion, 1962, expanded ed., 1973; The Eagle and the Snake, 1966; (with others) Mathematics Enrichment; The Unknown People: Indians of North America, 1974. Add: 105 Golfdale Rd., Toronto, Ont. M4N 2B8, Canada.

TALARZYK, W. Wayne. American, b. 1940. Marketing. Prof. of Marketing, Ohio State Univ., Columbus, since 1978 (Asst. Prof., 1969–72; Assoc. Prof., 1972–78; Chmn. of Dept., 1980–89). *Publs:* (with J.F. Engel and C.M. Larson) Cases in Promotional Strategy, 1971, 1984; (with T.N. Beckman and W.R. Davidson) Marketing, 9th ed. 1973; Contemporary Cases in Marketing, 1974, 3rd ed. 1983; (with R.D. Blackwell and James F. Engel) Contemporary Cases in Consumer Behavior, 1977, 1984, 1990; Cases for Analysis in Marketing, 1977, 3rd ed. 1985; (with R.D. Blackwell and W.T. Johnston) Management Cases in marketing, 1983; Cases and Exercises in Marketing, 1987. Add: 1775 South College, Columbus, Ohio 43210, U.S.A.

TALBOT, Charlene Joy. American, b. 1924. Children's fiction. *Publs:* Tomas Takes Charge, 1966, as Children in Hiding, 1968; A Home with Aunt Florry, 1974; The Great Rat Island Adventure, 1977; An Orphan for Nebraska, 1977. Add: 568 Van Duzer St., Staten Island, New York 10304, U.S.A.

TALBOT, Godfrey Walker. British, b. 1908. History, Autobiography/Memoirs/Personal, Biography. Staff Corresp., 1937–69, Chief Reporter and War Corresp., 1941–E, and Corresp. accredited to Buckingham Palace, 1948–69, BBC, London. *Publs:* Speaking from the Desert, 1944; (ed.) Royalty Annual, 1952-56; Ten Seconds from Now, 1973; Queen Elizabeth the Queen Mother, 1973; Permission to Speak, 1976; Royal Heritage, 1977; Country Life Book of the Queen Mother, 1978; Country Life Book of the Royal Family, 1980. Add: Holmwell, Hook Hill, Sanderstead, South Croydon, Surrey, England.

TALBOT, Michael. American, b. 1953. Novels, Paranormal. Full-time writer since 1983. Media dir. for the Public Interest Research Group, Lansing, Mich., 1974–75; fiction agent, with John Brockman Assocs., literary agency, NYC, 1980–83. *Publs:* Mysticism and the New Physics, 1981; The Delicate Dependency: A Novel of the Vampire Life, 1982; The Bog (novel), 1986; Beyond the Quantum: Sciences Probes Deeper into Questions about God, the Riddle of Consciousness, and the Ultimate Relationship Between Mind and Reality, 1986; (with Danny Sugerman) Wonderland Avenue: Tales of Glamour and Excess, 1986; Come as You Were: A Handbook of Techniques for Opening Up Your Memories of Past Lives, 1986; To the Ends of the Earth, 1986; Night Things: A Novel of Supernatural Terror, 1988; A Wilful Woman, 1989. Add: c/o Knopf Inc., 201 E. 50th St., New York, N.Y. 10022, U.S.A.

TALBOT, Norman Clare. British, b. 1936. Poetry, Literature. Prof. of English, Univ. of Newcastle, N.S.W., since 1963. *Publs:* The Seafolding of Harri Jones, 1965; (ed.) XI Hunter Valley Poets + VII, 1966; The Major Poems of John Keats, 1968; Poems for a Female Universe, 1968; Son of a Female Universe, 1971; The Fishing Boy, 1973; (ed.) Hunter Valley Poets 1973, 1973; (ed.) IV Hunter Valley Poets, 1975; Find the Lady: A Female Universe Rides Again, 1977; (ed.) V Hunter Valley Poets, 1978; (co-ed.) The Terrible Echidna?, 1978, (ed.) I Is Invulnerable Green, 1979; Where Two Rivers Meet, 1980; (ed.) The Companion to This Place, 1980; (ed. with Ross Bennett) The Oak In an Egg, 1980; A Glossary of Poetic Terms, 1980, 1987; (ed.) Book Without Barriers, 1981; (ed.) Under Construction, 1981; (ed.) The Hawkesbury Vowels, 1981; (ed. with Zeny Giles) Contrast and Relief: Short Stories of Hunter Valley, 1981; (ed.) with Michael Orange) Australasian Victorian Studies Proceedings 1980, 1982; (ed. with T.H. Naisby) Mobile As They Come, 1983; (co-ed.) Listening to the Stars, 1984; The Kelly Haiku, 1985; (co-ed.) Contrary Modes: Proceedings of the World Science Fiction Conference, Melbourne 1985, 1985; (ed. with T.H. Naisby) The Young Hunter, 1986; (ed.) Another Site to Be Mined, 1987; (ed.) The Tiona Park Poems, 1988; (ed.) Wearing the Heterozosm, 1989. Add: 54 Addison Rd., New Lambton, N.S.W.

2305, Australia.

TALESE, Gay. American, b. 1932. Novels/Short stories, Autobiography/Memoirs/Personal. *Publs:* New York: A Serendipiter's Journey, 1961; The Overreachers, 1965; The Bridge, 1964; Fame and Obscurity, 1970, 1984; The Kingdom and the Power, 1970; Honor Thy Father, 1972; Thy Neighbor's Wife, 1980. Add: c/o Dell Publishing Co., 666 Fifth Ave., New York, N.Y. 10103, U.S.A.

TALLENT, Norman. American, b. 1921. Psychology. Private practice, psychology, Northampton, Mass. *Publs:* Clinical Psychological Consultation, 1963; Psychological Perspectives on the Person, 1967; (with Spungin) Psychology: Understanding Ourselves and Others, 1972, 3rd ed. 1983; Psychological Report Writing, 1976, 3rd ed., 1988; Psychology of Adjustment, 1978; Report Writing in Special Education, 1980. Add: 41 Hillside Rd., Northampton, Mass. 01060, U.S.A.

TALLY, Ted. American, b. 1952. Plays/Screenplays. *Publs:* Hooters, 1978; Terra Nova, 1981; Coming Attractions, 1982; Silver Linings, 1983; Little Footsteps, 1986. Add: c/o Helen Merrill, 337 W. 22nd St., New York, N.Y. 10011, U.S.A.

TALMAGE, Anne. *See* **POWELL,** Talmage.

TAMES, Richard Lawrence. British, b. 1946. History, Area studies. Head of External Services, Sch. of Oriental & African Studies, Univ. of London, since 1984 (joined faculty 1975). Sixth Form Master, Haberdashers' Aske's Sch., Elstree, Herts., 1967–70; Lectr., Chiswick Polytechnic, London, 1970–71; Secty. to the Council, Hansard Soc., 1973–74. *Publs:* Economy and Society in 19th Century Britain, 1972; William Morris, 1972; Isambard Kingdom Brunel, 1972; The Conquest of South America, 1974; Modern France: State and Society, 1976; Japan Today, 1976; The World of Islam: A Teacher's Handbook, 1977; China Today, 1978; People, Power, and Politics, 1978; The Japan Handbook: A Guide for Teachers, 1978; The Arab World Today, 1980; India in the 20th Century, 1981; Japan in the Twentieth Century, 1981; Emergent Nations, 1981; Journey into Japan, 1981; Servant of the Shogun, 1981; Approaches to Islam, 1982; The Muslim World, 1982; Case Studies in Development, 1982; The Japanese, 1982; Makers of Modern Britain, 1983; Growing Up in the 1960s, 1983; The Great War, 1984; Victorian London, 1984; Britain and the World in the 20th Century, 1984; Nazi Germany, 1985; Dictionaries of Religion: Islam, 1985; Radicals, Railways, and Reform: Britain 1815-51, 1986; Exploring Other Civilizations, 1987; Planters, Pilgrims, and Puritans, 1987; The American West, 1988; Passport to Japan, 1988; Japan since 1945, 1989; The First Day on the Somme, 1989; Journey Through Japan, 1989; Journey Through Canada, 1989; Anne Frank, 1989; Helen Keller, 1989. Add: 76 Regent Sq., London E3 3HW, England.

TANCOCK, John (Leon). British, b. 1942. Art. Head, Dept. of Impressionist and Modern Paintings, Sotheby Parke Bernet, NYC, since 1972. Assoc. Curator, Nineteenth and Twentieth Century Sculpture, Philadelphia Museum of Art, 1967–72. *Publs:* Multiples: The First Decade, 1971; The Sculpture of Auguste Rodin, 1976. Add: Sotheby, 1334 York Ave., New York, N.Y. 10021, U.S.A.

TANHAM, George Kilpatrick. American, b. 1922. Military/Defence. Assoc. Prof. of History, Calif. Inst. of Technology, 1947–55; Assoc. Dir., USOM (now U.S. AID), Vietnam, 1964–65; Special Asst. for Counterinsurgency, U.S. Embassy, Bangkok, Thailand, 1968–70; Vice-Pres., and Trustee, Rand Corp., 1970–82 (Research Staff member, 1955–58; Deputy to Vice-Pres., 1959–60). *Publs:* Communist Revolutionary Warfare: The Vietminh in Indochina, 1961, rev. ed. as Communist Revolutionary Warfare: From the Vietminh to the Viet Cong, 1967; War Without Guns: American Civilians in Rural Vietnam, 1966; Contribution a l'Histoire de la Resistance Belge, 1971; Trial in Thailand, 1974; Soviet Strategy and Islam, 1989. Add: Tumbling Run Farm, P.O. Box 373, Strasburg, Va. 22657, U.S.A.

TANN, Jennifer. Also writes as Geoffrey Booth. British, b. 1939. Business/Trade/Industry, History. Dir. of Continuing Education, Univ. of Newcastle upon Tyne, since 1986. Lectr., 1969–73, and Reader in Economic History, 1973–86, Univ. of Aston in Birmingham. *Publs:* Gloucestershire Woollen Mills, 1967; (co-author) Historic Towns, 1967; The Development of the Factory, 1971; (co-author) Archaeology of the Industrial Revolution, 1973; (as Geoffrey Booth) Industrial Archaeology, 1974; (ed.) Selected Papers of Boulton and Watt, vol. 1, 1982; A History of the Stock Exchange Birmingham, 1985. Add: 28A Church St., Durham DH1 3DG, England.

TANNAHILL, Reay. British, b. 1929. Historical/Romance/Gothic, Social commentary/phenomena. *Publs:* Food in History, 1973, 1988; Flesh and Blood: A History of the Cannibal Complex, 1975; Sex in History, 1980; A Dark and Distant Shore (historical novel), 1983; The World, The Flesh, and the Devil, 1985; Passing Glory, 1989. Add: c/o Rogers, Coleridge and White Ltd., 20 Powis Mews, London W11 1JN, England.

TANNER, John (Ian). British, b. 1927. Air/Space topics, Genealogy/Heraldry, History. Founding Dir., R.A.F. Museum, London, since 1963, Battle of Britain and Cosford Aerospace Museum, since 1978, and Bomber Command Museum, since 1980. Hon. Archivist, since 1980, and Sr. Research Fellow, since 1982, Pembroke Coll., Oxford; Visiting Fellow, Wolfson Coll., Cambridge, since 1985. Archivist-Librarian, Kensington Library, London, 1950–51, Leighton House Art Gallery and Museum, 1951–53; Curator, Librarian and Tutor, R.A.F. Coll., Cranwell, 1953–63; Extra-Mural Lectr. in the History of Art, Nottingham Univ., 1959–63. *Publs:* (co-author) An Encyclopaedic Dictionary of Heraldry, 1968; How to Trace Your Ancestors, 1971; Badges of the Fighting Services, 1973; History of Man in Flight, 1973; The Royal Air Force Museum: One Hundred Years of Aviation History, 1973; Man in Flight, 1973; (with W.E. May and W.Y. Carman) Badges and Insignia of the British Armed Services, Who's Famous in Your Family?, 1975, 1979; Wings of the Eagle (exhibition catalogue), 1976; (ed.) They Fell in the Battle, 1980; Royal Air Force Museum: The Official Guide, 1987. Add: 57 Drayton Gardens, London SW10, England.

TANNER, Stephen L. American, b. 1938. Literary criticism, Biography. Prof. of English, Brigham Young Univ., Provo, Utah, since 1981 (Assoc. Prof., 1978–81). Asst. Prof., Univ. of Idaho, Moscow, 1969–73; Sr. Fulbright Lectr., Univ. Federale de Minas Gerais, 1974–76, 1983, and at the Univ. of Coimbra, 1979. *Publs:* Ken Kesey, 1983; Paul Elmer More: Literary Criticism as the History of Ideas, 1987; Lionel Trilling, 1988. Add: 1756 South 290 East, Orem, Utah 84058, U.S.A.

TANNER, Tony. British, b. 1935. Literature. Fellow, King's Coll., Cambridge, since 1964, and Reader in the Faculty of English, Cambridge Univ., since 1981. *Publs:* Conrad: Lord Jim, 1963; The Reign of Wonder: Naivety and Reality in American Literature, 1965; Saul Bellow, 1965; (ed.) Mansfield Park, by Jane Austen, 1966; (ed.) Henry James: Modern Judgements, 1968; (ed.) Hawthorne, by Henry James, 1968; City of Words: American Fiction 1950-1970, 1971; Adultery in the Novel: Contact and Transgression, 1980; Jane Austen, 1986. Add: King's Coll., Cambridge, England.

TANSELLE, G(eorge) Thomas. American, b. 1934. Art, Literature. Vice-Pres., John Simon Guggenheim Memorial Foundn., NYC., since 1978; Adjunct Prof. of English and Comparative Literature, Columbia Univ., NYC, since 1980. Co-Ed., The Writings of Herman Melville, Northwestern Univ. Press and Newberry Library, since 1968. Instr., 1960–61, Asst. Prof., 1961–63, Assoc. Prof., 1963–68, and Prof. of English, 1968–78, Univ. of Wisconsin, Madison. *Publs:* Royall Tyler, 1967; Guide to the Study of United States Imprints, 1971; A Checklist of Editions of Moby Dick, 1976; Selected Studies in Bibliography, 1979; The History of Books as a Field of Study, 1981; Textual Criticism since Greg: A Cronicle, 1950-1985, 1988. Add: c/o Univ. Press of Virginia, P.O. Box 3608, Univ. Station, Charlottesville, Va. 22903, U.S.A.

TARGET, George William. British, b. 1924. Novels/Short stories, Politics/Government, Theology/Religion, Biography. With Book Production Dept., Cassell & Co. Ltd., London, 1959–64; Writer-in-Residence, Colorado State Univ., Ft. Collins, 1964. *Publs:* The Evangelists, 1958; The Teachers, 1960; The Missionaries, 1961; Watch With Me, 1961; The Shop Stewards, 1962; The Americans, 1964; We, the Crucifiers, The Scientists, 1966; Evangelism Inc., 1968; Under the Christian Carpet, 1969; Unholy Smoke, 1969; The Young Lovers, 1970; Tell it the Way it Is, 1970; Confound Their Politicks, 1970; The Patriots, 1974; Bernadette Devlin, 1974; Dear Dirty Dublin, 1974; The Nun in the Concentration Camp, 1974; The Triumph of Vice, 1976; Out of this World, 1985; How to Stop Smoking, 1985; Words That Shook the World, 1987; Your Hip and You, 1987. Add: Sea House, Coast Rd., Trimingham, Norfolk, England.

TARLING, (Peter) Nicholas. British, b. 1931. History. Prof. of History, Univ. of Auckland, since 1968 (Assoc. Prof., 1965–68). Lectr., 1957–61, and Sr. Lectr. in History, 1961–65, Univ. of Queensland. *Publs:* Anglo-Dutch Rivalry in the Malay World, 1780-1824, 1962; Piracy and Politics in the Malay World, 1963; A Concise History of Southeast Asia, 1966; (ed.) China and its Place in the World, 1967; British Policy in the Malay Peninsula and Archipelago, 1824-1871, 1969; (ed. with J.

Ch'en) Studies in the Social History of China and Southeast Asia, 1970; Britain, the Brookes and Brunei, 1971; Imperial Britain in Southeast Asia, 1975; Sulu and Sabah, 1978; The Burthen, The Risk, and the Glory, 1982; The Sun Never Sets, 1986; The Fourth Anglo-Burmese War, 1987. Add: Univ. of Auckland, Private Bag, Auckland, New Zealand.

TARN, Nathaniel. American (b. British), b. 1928. Poetry, Translations. Prof. of Comparative Literature, Rutgers Univ., New Brunswick, N.J., 1970–85, now Emeritus. Has worked as an anthropologist in Guatemala and Burma; former Member of the faculty, Univ. of Chicago, and Univ. of London; Gen. Ed., Cape Eds., and Dir., Cape Goliard Ltd., publrs., London, 1967–69. *Publs:* Old Savage/Young City, 1964; (with Richard Murphy and Jon Silkin) Penguin Modern Poets 7, 1965; (trans.) The Heights of Macchu Picchu, by Pablo Neruda, 1966; Where Babylon Ends, 1968; (trans.) Stelae, by Victor Segalen, 1969; The Beautiful Contradictions, 1969; October: A Sequence of Ten Poems Followed by Requiem Pro Duabus Filiis Israel, 1969; The Silence, 1970; A Nowhere for Vallejo: Choices, October, 1971; Lyrics for the Bride of God: Section: The Artemision, 1973; The Persephones, 1975; Lyrics for the Bride of God, 1975; The House of Leaves, 1976; The Microcosm, 1977; Bird Scapes, with Seaside, 1978; (with Janet Rodney) Atitlan/Alashka: New and Selected 1979; The Land Songs, 1981; Weekends in Mexico, 1982; The Desert Mothers, 1984; At the Western Gates, 1985; Seeing America First, 1989. Add: P.O. Box 566, Tesuque, N.M. 87574, U.S.A.

TÁRNOKY, András Laszlo. British, b. 1920. Chemistry. Hon. Research Fellow, Univ. of Reading, since 1985. Research Asst., Postgrad. Medical Sch., London, 1945; Research Chemist Chemotherapeutic Research Div., May & Baker Ltd., Dagenham, 1946–47; Biochemist, Mile End Hosp. Group, London, 1948–50, and United Reading Hosp., 1950, 19685. *Publs:* Clinical Biochemical Methods, 1958; (co-author) Chromatographic and Electrophoretic Techniques, 1968, 4th ed. 1976; (co-author) A Symposium on Carbenoxolone Sodium 1968; (co-author) Carbenoxolone Sodium, 1970; (co-author) Advances in Clinical Chemistry, vol. 21, 1980. Add: Dept. of Physiology and Biochemistry, Box 228, Whiteknights, Reading RG6 2AJ, England.

TARR, Joel Arthur. American, b. 1934. History, Urban studies. Prof. of History and Public Policy, Carnegie-Mellon Univ., Pittsburgh, since 1973, and Assoc. Dean, Coll. of Humanities and Social Science, since 1988 (Asst. Prof., 1967–70; Assoc. Prof., 1971–73; Acting Dean, Sch. of Urban and Public Affairs, 1986). Asst. Prof., California State Univ., Long Beach, 1961–66; Visiting Asst. Prof., Univ. of California, Santa Barbara, 1966–67. *Publs:* A Study in Boss Politics: William Lorimer of Chicago, 1971; (ed. with Anthony Penna and Edwin Fenton) Living in Urban America, 1974; (ed.) Patterns of City Growth, 1974; (ed.) Retrospective Technology Assessment, 1977; Pittsburgh-Sheffield: Sister Cities, 1986; (ed.) Rise of the Networked City in Europe and America, 1988. Add: Dept. of History, Carnegie-Mellon Univ., Pittsburgh, Pa. 15213, U.S.A.

TARRANT, John. *See* **EGLETON,** Clive.

TARRANT, John Rex. British, b. 1941. Agriculture/Forestry, Geography. Reader in Environmental Sciences, Univ. of East Anglia (joined faculty, 1968). Asst. Lectr. in Geography, University Coll., Dublin, 1966–68. *Publs:* (ed.) Computers in Geography, 1970; Agricultural Geography, 1974; Food Policies, 1980. Add: Sch. of Environmental Sciences, Univ. of East Anglia, Norwich NR4 7TJ, England.

TART, Charles T. American, b. 1937. Psychology. Prof. of Psychology, Univ. of California, Davis, since 1966. Lectr., Stanford Univ., Calif., 1964; Instr., Univ. of Virginia Sch. of Medicine, Charlottesville, 1965–66. *Publs:* (ed.) Altered States of Consciousness, 1969, 1972; On Being Stoned: A Psychological Study of Marijuana Intoxication, 1971; (ed.) Transpersonal Psychologies, 1975; States of Consciousness, 1975; Learning to Use Extrasensory Perception, 1976; Psi: Scientific Studies of the Psychic Realm, 1977; (ed.) Mind at Large, 1979; Waking Up, 1986; Open Mind, Discriminating Mind, 1989. Add: Dept. of Psychology, Univ. of California, Davis, Calif. 95616, U.S.A.

TATE, Ellalice. *See* **HOLT,** Victoria.

TATE, James (Vincent). American, b. 1943. Poetry. Poetry Ed., The Dickinson Review, N.D., since 1967; Visiting Prof., Univ. of Massachusetts, Amherst, since 1971; Assoc. Ed., Pym Randall Press, Cambridge, Mass., and Barn Dream Press: Consultant, Coordinating Council of Literary Mags. Visiting Lectr., Univ. of Iowa, Iowa City, 1965–67, and Univ. of California, Berkeley, 1967–68; Asst. Prof., Colum-

bia Univ., NYC, 1969–71, and Emerson Coll., Boston, Mass., 1970–71. *Publs:* Cages, 1966; The Destination, 1967; The Lost Pilot, 1967; The Torches, 1968, rev. ed. 1971; Notes of Woe: Poems, 1968; Mystics in Chicago, 1968; Camping in the Valley, 1968; Row with Your Hair, 1969; Is There Anything, 1969; Shepherds of the Mist, 1969; The Oblivion Ha-Ha, 1970; Amnesia People, 1970; Deaf Girl Playing, 1970; (with Bill Knott) Are You Ready Mary Baker Eddy?, 1970; Wrong Songs, 1970; Hints to Pilgrims, 1971; Apology for Eating Geoffrey Movius's Hyacinth, 1971; Nobody Goes to Visit the Insane Anymore, 1971; Absences: New Poems, 1971; Viper Jazz, 1976; Riven Doggeries, 1979; The Land of Little Sticks, 1982; Constant Defender, Reckoner, 1986. Add: Dept. of English, Univ. of Massachusetts, Amherst, Mass. 01003, U.S.A.

TATE, Joan. British, b. 1922. Children's fiction, Children's non-fiction, Translations. Freelance writer, trans., and publrs. reader. *Publs:* Jenny, 1964; The Crane, 1964; The Rabbit Boy, 1964; Coal Hoppy, 1964; Next Doors, 1964; Silver Grill, 1965; Picture Charlies, 1965; Lucy, 1965; The Tree (in U.S. as Tina and David), 1966; The Holiday, 1966; Tad, 1966; Bill, 1966; Mrs. Jenny, 1966; Bits and Pieces, 1966; The New House, 1967; The Soap Box Car, 1967; The Old Car, 1967; The Great Birds, 1967; The Circus, 1967; Letters to Chris, 1967; Wild Martin, 1967; Luke's Garden, 1967, augmented version 1976; Sam and Me, 1968; Out of the Sun, 1969; Whizz Kid (in U.S. as An Unusual Kind of Girl), 1969; The Train, 1969; The Letter, 1969; Puddle's Tiger, 1969; The Caravan, 1969; Edward and the Uncles, 1969; The Secret, 1969; Lucy, 1969; The Nest, 1969; The Cheapjack Man, 1969; The Gobbleydock, 1969; The Tree House, 1969; The Ball, 1969; Going Up, vol. I, 1969, vol. II, 1971, vol. III, 1974; Clipper, 1969; Ring on My Finger, 1971; The Long Road Home, 1971; Gramp, 1971; Wild Boy, 1972; Wump Day, 1972; Dad's Camel, 1972; Your Town, 1972; Jock and the Rock Cakes, 1973; Grandpa and My Little Sister, 1973; Taxi!, 1973; Night Out, 1973; The Match, 1973; Dinah, 1973; The Man Who Rang the Bell, 1973; Journal for One, 1973; Ben and Annie, 1973; Ginger Mick, 1974; The Runners, 1974; The Living River, 1974; Dirty Dan, 1974; Sandy's Trumpet, 1974; Your Dog, 1975; Disco Books, 8 vols, 1975; The House That Jack Built, 1976; The New House, 1976; Crow and the Brown Boy, 1976; Polly and the Barrow Boy, 1976; Billoggs, 1976; You Can't Explain Everything, 1976; See You and Other Stories, 1977; On Your Own, 1977; Cat Country, 1979; Helter Skelter (poems), 1979; Turn Again Whittington, 1980; Safari, 1980; Panda Car, 1980. Add: 7 College Hill, Shrewsbury SY1 1LZ, England.

TATE, Peter. British. Science fiction/Fantasy. Journalist. *Publs:* The Thinking Seat, 1969; Gardens One to Five (in U.K. as Gardens, 1, 2, 3, 4, 5), 1971; Country Love and Poison Rain, 1973; Moon on an Iron Meadow, 1974; Seagulls under Glass (short stories), 1975; Faces in the Flames, 1976; Greencomber, 1979. Add: 3 Seaway Ave., Friars Cliff, Christchurch, Hants., England.

TATTERSALL, (Honor) Jill. British, b. 1931. Historical/Romance/Gothic. *Publs:* A Summer's Cloud, 1965; Enchanter's Castle, 1966; The Midnight Oak, 1967; Lyonesse Abbey, 1968; A Time at Tarragon, 1969; Lady Ingram's Retreat, 1970, in U.S. as Lady Ingram's Room, 1981; Midsummer Masque, 1972; The Wild Hunt, 1974; The Witches of All Saints, 1975; The Shadows of Castle Fosse, 1976; Chanters Chase, 1978; Dark at Noon, 1978; Damnation Reef, 1979. Add: Nanny Cay, Tortola, British Virgin Islands.

TAVEL, Ronald. American, b. 1941. Novels/Short stories, Plays/Screenplays. Reader and Lectr., New York State Council on the Arts, since 1969; Founder Member, New York Theatre Strategy; Adviser and Contrib., Subplot Theatre. Screenwriter, Andy Warhol Films Inc., NYC, 1964–66; Founder, 1965, and Resident Playwright, 1965–67, Playhouse of the Ridiculous, NYC; Literary Adviser, Scripts mag., NYC, 1971–72; Resident Playwright, Theatre of the Lost Continent, NYC, 1971–73; Playwright, The Actors Studio, NYC, 1972; Resident Playwright, Yale Univ. Divinity Sch., New Haven, Conn., 1975, 1977; Resident Playwright, Williamstown Theatre Summer Festival, Mass., 1977; Resident Playwright, New Playwrights' Theatre of Washington, D.C., 1978–79; Resident Playwright, Cornell Univ., Ithaca, N.Y., 1980–81; Lectr., Mahidol Univ., Thailand, 1981–82. Teacher of Play and Screenwriting, 12th Annual Summer Writer's Conf., Hofstva Univ., 1984; Distinguished Visiting Assoc. Prof. in Creative Writing, Univ. of Colorado, Boulder, 1986–87, and Resident Playwright, The Actors Ensemble, Boulder, 1987. *Publs:* Street of Stairs (novel), 1968; Bigfoot and Other Plays, 1973. Add: 528 Gov. Nicholls, New Orleans, La. 70116, U.S.A.

TAVERNE, Dick. British, b. 1928. Politics/Government. Dir. PRIMA Europe, since 1987. Labour M.P. (U.K.) for Lincoln, 1962–74;

Independent M.P. for Lincoln 1974; Founder Dir., 1970, Dir.-Gen., 1979–81, and Chmn., 1981–82, Inst. for Fiscal Studies; Chmn., Public Policy Centre (U.K.), 1984–87. *Publs:* The Future of the Left: Lincoln and After, 1974. Add: 60 Cambridge St., London SW1, England.

TAYLOR, A(lan) J(ohn) P(ercivale). British, b. 1906. History. Hon. Fellow, Magdalen Coll., Oxford (Tutor in Modern History, 1938–63; Lectr. in Intnl. History, Oxford Univ., 1953–63). *Publs:* The Italian Problem in Diplomacy 1847-49, 1934; Germany's First Bid for Colonies 1884-85, 1938; The Habsburg Monarchy 1815-1918, 1941; The Course of German History, 1945; From Napoleon to Stalin, 1950; Rumours of Wars, 1952; The Struggle for Mastery of Europe 1848-1918, 1954; Bismarck, 1955; Englishmen and Others, 1956; The Troublemakers: Dissent over Foreign Policy 1792-1939, 1957; The Russian Revolution of 1917, 1958; The Origins of the Second World War, 1961; The First World War: An Illustrated History, 1963; Politics in Wartime and Other Essays, 1964; English History, 1914-45, 1965; From Sarajevo to Potsdam, 1966; Europe: Grandeur and Decline, 1967; War by Time-Table, 1969; (ed.) Lloyd George: Twelve Essays, 1970; (ed.) Lloyd George: A Diary by Frances Stevenson, 1971; Beaverbrook, 1972; (ed.) Off the Record: Political Interviews by W.P. Crozier 1933-1943, 1973; The Second World War: An Illustrated History, 1974; (ed.) My Darling Pussy: The Letters of Lloyd George and Frances Stevenson 1913-41, 1975; Essays in English History, 1976; The Last of the Old Europe, 1977; The War Lords, 1977; The Russian War 1941-45, 1978; How Wars Begin, 1979; Revolutions and Revolutionaries, 1980; Politicians, Socialism, and Historians, 1980; A Personal History (autobiography), 1983; An Old Man's Diary, 1984; How Wars End, 1985. Add: 32 Twisden Rd., London NW5 1DN, England.

TAYLOR, Andrew (McDonald). Australian, b. 1940. Poetry, Translations. Sr. Lectr. in English, Univ. of Adelaide, since 1975 (Lectr., 1971–74). Tutor, 1962–63, and Lockie Fellow, 1966–68, Univ. of Melbourne; Teacher, British Inst., Rome, 1964–65. *Publs:* (ed.) Byron: Selected Poems, 1971; The Cool Change, 1971; Ice Fishing, 1973; The Invention of Fire, 1976; The Cat's Chin and Ears: A Bestiary, 1976; Parabolas: Prose Poems, 1976; The Crystal Absences, The Trout, 1978; (ed., with Ian Reid) Number Two Friendly Street, 1978; Selected Poems, 1982; Bernie the Midnight Owl (for children), 1984; (trans. with Beate Josephi) Miracles of Disbelief, 1985; (ed. with Judith Rodriguez) Poems Selected from The Australian's Twentieth Anniversary Poetry Competition, 1985; Traveling, (ed.) Unsettled Areas, 1986; Reading Australian Poetry, 1987; Selected Poems 1960-1985, 1988. Add: Dept. of English, Univ. of Adelaide, Adelaide, S.A. 5001, Australia.

TAYLOR, Charles (Alfred). British, b. 1922. Education, Physics. Prof. Emeritus, University Coll. (formerly Prof. and Head, Physics Dept.); Prof. of Experimental Physics, Royal Instn. of Great Britain. Temporary Experimental Officer, Admiralty Signals Establishment, 1942, 19645; Research Physicist, Metropolitan Vickers Electrical Co., 1945–48; Lectr., and later Reader, Inst. of Science and Technology, Univ. of Manchester, 1948–65. Vice-pres. for Education, Inst. of Physics, London, 1970–75. *Publs:* (with H. Lipson) Fourier Transforms and X-ray Diffraction (textbook), 1958; (with H. Lipson) Optical Transforms, 1964; The Physics of Musical Sounds, 1965; (ed.) Penguin Physics Reference Books, 1973; Sounds of Music, 1976; Images, 1978; Diffraction, 1987; Art and Science of Lecture Demonstration, 1988. Add: 9 Hill Deverill, Warminister, Wilts. BA12 7EF, England.

TAYLOR, Constance Lindsay. *See* **CULLINGFORD,** Guy.

TAYLOR, David (Conrad). British, b. 1934. Animals/Pets, Zoology. Zoo Veterinary Consultant; Partner, Taylor & Greenwood, Zoo Veterinary Consultants. *Publs:* Zoovet, 1976; Doctor in the Zoo, 1978; Going Wild, 1980; The Dog, 1980; The Cat, 1980; Next Panda Please, 1982; The Wandering Whale, 1984; Dragon Doctor, 1985; You and Your Cat, 1986; You and Your Dog, 1986; The Zoo in You, 1987; The Zoo in the House, 1987; The Zoo in the Garden, 1987; The Zoo in the Town, 1987; The Complete "One by One," 1987; Animal Monsters, 1987; Animal Assassins, 1987; Animal Olympics, 1988; Animal Magicians, 1988. Add: 2 Withy Close, Lightwater, Surrey, England.

TAYLOR, Domini. *See* **LONGRIGG,** Roger.

TAYLOR, Dorothy A. British, b. 1938. Education, Music. Lectr. in Music Education, Univ. of London Inst. of Education, since 1979. *Publs:* Learning with Traditional Rhyme and Song, 6 vols., 1976; The Ladybird Book of Rhymes, 1977; Singing Rhymes, 1979; Skipping Rhymes, 1979; Music Now: A Guide to Recent Developments and Current Opportunities

in Music Education, 1979; (ed.) ISME Yearbook 8, 1981; (with K. Swanwick) Discovering Music, 1982. Add: Dept. of Music, Univ. of London Inst. of Education, 20 Bedford Way, London WC1H 0AL, England.

TAYLOR, Edward C(urtis). American, b. 1923. Chemistry. Prof., Princeton Univ., N.J., since 1964 (Asst. Prof. and Assoc. Prof., 1954, 19664). *Publs:* (co-ed.) Advances in Organic Chemistry: Methods and Results, 9 vols, 1960–76; (co-ed.) Pteridine Chemistry, 1964; (co-ed.) The Heterocyclic Derivatives of Phosphorus, Arsenic, Antimony and Bismuth, 1970; (co-ed.) The Pyrimidines, Supplement I, 1970, (co-author) Chemistry of Enaminonitrites and O-Aminonitriles, 1970; (co-ed.) Purines, 1971; (co-ed.) Mass Spectrometry of Heterocyclic Compounds, 1971, 1985; (co-ed.) 7-Membered Heterocyclic Compounds containing Oxygen and Sulphur, 1972; (co-ed.) Indoles, Parts 1-2, 1972, part 3, 1979; (co-ed.) Condensed Pyridazines Including Cinnolines and Phthalazines, 1973; (co-ed.) Pyridazines, 1973; (co-ed. NMR Spectra of Simple Heterocycles, 1973; (co-ed.) Benzofurans, 1974; (co-ed.) Heterocycles in Organic Synthesis, 1974; (co-ed.) Pyridine and Its Derivatives, Parts 1-4, 1974, part 5, 1984; Principles of Heterocyclic Chemistry: An ACS Audio Course, and ACS Film Course, 1974; (co-ed.) Photochemistry of Heterocyclic Compounds, 1976; (co-ed.) Special Topics in Heterocyclic Chemistry, 1977; (co-ed.) Chromenes, Chromanones and Chromones, 1977; (co-ed.) Stereochemistry of Heterocyclic Compounds, parts 1-2, 1977; (co-ed.) Quinolines, Part 1, (co-ed.) Chemistry of 1,2,3-Triazines and 1,2,4-Triazines, Tetrazines and Pentazines, 1978; (co-ed.) Thiazole and Its Derivatives, parts 1-3, 1979; (co-ed.) Condensed Pyrazines, 1979; (co-ed.) 1,2,3-Triazoles, 1980; (co-ed.) 1,2,4-Triazines, 1981; (co-ed.) Isoquinolines, part 1, 1981; (co-ed.) Chromans and Tocopherols, 1981; (co-ed.) Benzimidazoles and Congeneric Tricyclic Compounds, parts 1-2, 1981; (co-ed.) Small Ring Heterocycles, parts 1-2, 1983, part 3, 1985; (co-ed.) Azepines, parts 1-2, 1984; (co-ed.) 1,3-Dipolar Cycloaddition Chemistry, vols 1-2, 1984; (co-ed.) Physical Methods in Heterocyclic Chemistry, 1984; (co-ed.) Thiophene and Its Derivatives, part 1, 1985; parts 2 & 3, 1986; (co-ed.) Pyridine-Metal Complexes, parts 6A, B, C, 1985; (co-ed.) Oxazoles, 1986; (ed.) Fused Pyrimidines, part III, 1988; (ed.) Synthesis of Fused Heterocycles, 1988. Add: Dept. of Chemistry, Princeton Univ., Princeton, N.J. 08540, U.S.A.

TAYLOR, Fred J(ames). British, b. 1919. Food/Wine, Recreation (Fishing and Field Sports), Autobiography/Memoirs. Angling Corresp. and Columnist, Evening Standard, London, since 1966, Shooting Times, since 1973, and Sunday Telegraph (became Mail on Sunday, 1986) since 1979. *Publs:* Angling in Earnest, 1959; Favourite Swims, 1961; Fishing Here and There; Fish of Rivers, Lakes and Ponds, 1961; Tench Fishing, 1962; Tench; Game and Fish Cook Book, 3rd ed.; Guide to Ferreting; My Fishing Years, 1981; Fred J. Taylor's Guide to Terreting, 1988. Add: 42 Barkham Close, Cheddington, Leighton Buzzard, Beds. LU7 0RT,

TAYLOR, H. Baldwin. *See* **WAUGH,** Hillary.

TAYLOR, Henry. American, b. 1942. Poetry, Translations. Prof. of Literature since 1976, and Co-Dir. of the MFA Program in Creative Writing since 1982, American Univ., Washington, D.C. (Assoc. Prof., 1971–76; Dir. of American Studies Prog., 1983–85). Editorial Consultant, Magill's Literary Annual, since 1971; Instr. in English, Roanoke Coll., Va. 1966–68; Asst. Prof. of English, Univ. of Utah, Salt Lake City, 1968–71; Dir., Univ. of Utah Writers' Conference, 1969–72; Writer-in-Residence, Hollins Coll., Virginia, 1978. *Publs:* The Horse Show at Midnight, 1966; Breakings, 1971; An Afternoon of Pocket Billiards, 1974; (author and ed.) Poetry: Points of Departure, 1974; (ed.) The Water of Light: A Miscellany in Honor of Brewster Ghiselin, 1976; Desperado, 1979; (trans. with Robert A. Brooks) The Children of Herakles, translated from Euripides' Heraklaidai, 1981; The Flying Change (poetry), 1985 (Pulitzer Prize). Add: Box 85, Lincoln, Va. 22078, U.S.A.

TAYLOR, Janelle (Diane Williams). American, b. 1944. Historical/Romance. Orthodontic Nurse, Athens, Ga., 1962–65, and Augusta, Ga., 1967–68, 1973–74; Research Technologist, Medical Coll. of Georgia, Augusta, 1975–77; Lectr. on Writing, Georgia, 1982–88. *Publs:* Savage Ecstasy, 1981; Defiant Ecstasy, 1982; Forbidden Ecstasy, 1982; Brazen Ecstasy, 1983; Love Me with Fury, 1983; Tender Ecstasy, 1983; First Love, Wild Love, 1984; Golden Torment, 1984; Valley of Fire, 1984; Savage Conquest, 1985; Stolen Ecstasy, 1985; Destiny's Temptress, 1986; Moondust and Madness, 1986; Sweet, Savage Heart, 1986; Bittersweet Ecstasy, 1987; Wild Is My Love, 1987; Fortune's Flames, 1988; Passions Wild and Free, 1988; Wild Sweet Promise, 1989; Kiss of the Night Wind, 1989. Add: 4366 Deerwood Lane, Evans, Ga. 30809, U.S.A.

TAYLOR, Jayne. *See* **KRENTZ,** Jayne.

TAYLOR, Jennifer (Evelyn). Australian, b. 1935. Architecture. Assoc. Prof. of Architecture, Univ. of Sydney, since 1983 (Lectr. and Sr. Lectr. 1970–82). *Publs:* An Australian Identity: Houses for Sydney 1953-63, 1972, 1984; (with John Andrews) John Andrews: Architecture a Performing Art, 1982; Australian Architecture Since 1960, 1986. Add: Dept. of Architecture, Univ. of Sydney, Sydney, N.S.W. 2006, Australia.

TAYLOR, John (Gerald). British, b. 1931. Astronomy, Mathematics/Statistics, Physics. Prof. of Mathematics, King's Coll., Univ. of London, since 1971. Fellow, Christ's Coll., 1958–60, Asst. Maths lectr., Cambridge Univ., 1959–60, and Sr. Research Fellow, Churchill Coll., 1963–64, all Cambridge; Staff Member, Inst. for Advanced Study, Princeton, N.J., 1956–58 and 1961–63; Prof. of Physics, Rutgers Univ., New Brunswick, 1964–B; Lectr., Maths Inst., and Fellow, Hertford Coll., Oxford, 1966–67; Reader in Particles and Fields, Queen Mary Coll., Univ. of London, 1967–69; Prof. of Physics, Univ. of Southampton, 1969–71. *Publs:* Quantum Mechanics: An Introduction, 1969; The Shape of Minds to Come, 1970; The New Physics, 1972; Black Holes: The End of the Universe?, 1973; Superminds, 1975; Special Relativity, 1975; Science and the Supernatural, 1980; The Frontiers of Knowledge, 1982; (ed.) Supergravity '81, 1982; (ed.) Supersymmetry and Supergravity '82, 1983; (ed.) Tributes to Paul Dirac, 1987. Add: Dept. of Mathematics, King's Coll., London WC2R 2LS, England.

TAYLOR, John (Laverack). British, b. 1937. Education, Regional/Urban planning. Principal, and Bramley Prof. of Educational Development, Bretton Hall, since 1981; Dir., Sheffield Centre for Environmental Research; Sr. Lectr., Univ. of Sheffield. Head of the Trent Dept. of Town and Country Planning, Nottingham, 1975–79; Asst. Dir. and Dean of Environmental Studies, North East London Polytechnic, 1979–81. *Publs:* (with Robert Armstrong) Instructional Simulation Systems in Higher Education, 1970; Instructional Planning Systems, 1971; (ed. with Robert Armstrong) Feedback on Instructional Simulation, 1971; (with Rex Walford) Simulation in the Classroom, 1973; (ed.) Planning for Urban Growth, 1972; Learning and the Simulation Game, 1978; Unesco Guide on Simulation and Gaming for Environmental Education, 1984; (co-ed.) La Simulazione giocata, 1987. Add: Bretton Hall, W. Bretton, Wakefield WF4 4LG, England.

TAYLOR, John Russell. British, b. 1935. Film, Media, Theatre. Art Critic, The Times, London, since 1978 (Film Critic, 1962–72). Prof., Cinema Div., Univ. of Southern California, Los Angeles, 1972–78. *Publs:* Joseph L. Mankiewicz: An Index, 1960; Anger and After: A Guide to the New British Drama (in U.S. as The Angry Theatre), 1962, 1969; Anatomy of a Television Play, 1962; Cinema Eye, Cinema Ear: Some Key Film-Makers of the 60s, 1964; (ed.) Three Plays of John Arden, 1964; (ed.) New English Dramatists 8, 1965; Penguin Dictionary of the Theatre, 1966; The Art Nouveau Book in Britain, 1966; Art in London: A Guide, 1966; The Rise and Fall of the Well-Made Play, 1967; The Publications of T.N. Foulis, 1967; Look Back in Anger: A Casebook, 1968; The Art Dealers, 1969; Harold Pinter, 1969; (ed.) The Playwrights Speak, 1969; The Hollywood Musical, 1971; The Second Wave: British Dramatists for the Seventies, 1971; (ed.) The Pleasure Dome: Collected Film Criticism of Graham Greene, 1972; David Storey, 1974; Fifty Superstars, 1974; (ed.) Masterworks of British Cinema, 1974; Peter Shaffer, 1975; Directors and Directions: Cinema for the Seventies, 1978; Hitch: The Life and Times of Alfred Hitchcock, 1978; Impressionism, 1981; Strangers in Paradise: The Hollywood Emigrés 1933-1950, 1982; Ingrid Bergman, 1983; Alec Guinness: A Celebration, 1984; Vivien Leigh, 1984; Hollywood 1940s, 1985; Portraits of the British Cinema, 1985; Orson Welles, 1986; Edward Wolfe, 1986; Great Movie Moments, 1987. Add: P.O. Box 481, Virginia St., London E1 9BD, England.

TAYLOR, John Stephen. British, b. 1916. Novels/Short stories, History. Medical Practitioner, with own practice, since 1941. *Publs:* Essay on History of Thorne and Parish Affairs in Thorne in Reigns of George II III, 1953; Two Humber Keels and their Captains 100 Years Ago, 1955; Works and Days, 1835-72, 1956; Thorne 1723-1785, 1957; Two Essays on Old Thorne: A Chemist and Master Mason, 1958; Herod's Steward, 1964; Hatfield Chace, 1965. Add: Crust Mill House, Brooke St., Thorne, Doncaster, S. Yorks. DN8 4BB, England.

TAYLOR, John Vernon. British, b. 1914. Anthropology/Ethnology, Politics/Government, Theology/Religion. Warden, Bishop Tucker Theological Coll., Uganda, 1945–54; Research Worker, Intnl. Missionary Council, 1955–59; Africa Secty., 1959–63, and Gen. Secty., 1963–74, Church Missionary Soc.; Bishop of Winchester, 1975–85. *Publs:* Were You There?, 1950; Man in the Midst, 1955; Christianity and Politics in Africa, 1957; The Growth of the Church in Buganda, 1958; African Passion, 1958; Christians of the Copperbelt, 1961; The Primal Vision, 1963; For All the World, 1966; Change of Address, 1968; See for Yourself, 1968; The Go-Between God, 1972; Enough Is Enough, 1975; Weep Not for Me, 1986; A Matter of Life and Death, 1986. Add: Camleigh, 65 Aston St., Oxford, England.

TAYLOR, John William Ransom. British, b. 1922. Air/Space topics, History. Ed.-in-Chief and Compiler, Jane's All the World's Aircraft, London, since 1959 (Asst. Compiler, 1955–59). Contrib. Ed., Air Force Magazine, since 1971. Vice-Pres., Guild of Aviation Artists. Air Corresp., Meccano Mag., 1943–72; Ed., Aircraft Annual, 1949–74, and Aviation Book Adviser, 1967–74, Ian Allan Group, publrs., London; Ed., Air BP Mag., 1956–72. *Publs:* (with M. Allward) Spitfire, 1946; Civil Aircraft Markings, annually 1949-78; (with M. Allward) Wings for Tomorrow, 1951; Military Aircraft Recognition, 1952; Civil Airliner Recognition, 1953; Picture History of Flight, 1955; (ed.) Science in the Atomic Age, 1956; (with M. Allward) Rockets and Space Travel, 1956; (ed.) Best Flying Stories, 1956; (with B. Arkell) Helicopters Work Like This, 1956, 3rd ed. 1972; Royal Air Force, 1957; Fleet Air Arm, 1957; Jet Planes Like This, 1957, 6th ed. 1971; Russian Aircraft, 1957; Rockets and Missiles, 1958; CFS: Birthplace of Air Power, 1958, 1987; Rockets and Spacecraft Work Like This, 1959, 5th ed. 1970; British Airports, 1959; U.S. Military Aircraft, 1959; (with G. Swanborough) Warplanes of the World, 1959, rev. ed. as Military Aircraft of the World; (with M. Allward) Westland 50, 1965; Aircraft Aircraft, 1967, 4th ed. 1974; (with P.J.R. Moyes) Pictorial History of the Royal Air Force, 3 vols., 1968-71, 1980; (ed.) Combat Aircraft of the World, 1969; Light Plane Recognition, 1970; (with G. Swanborough) Civil Aircraft of the World, 1970, 4th ed. 1978; (ed.) The Lore of Flight, 1971; (with G. Swanborough) British Civil Aircraft Register, 1971; (with M.J.H. Taylor) Missiles of the World, 1972, 1975; (with D. Mondey) Spies in the Sky, 1972; (ed.) Jane's Aircraft Pocket Books, 10 vols., 1973-82; (ed. with M.J.H. Taylor and D. Mondey) Guinness Book of Air Facts and Feats, 1974, 1977; History of Aerial Warfare, 1974; (ed. with K. Munson) History of Aviation, 1974, 1978; (with S.H.H. Young) Airlines and Airliners of the World, 1975; Jets, 1976; (with R.A. Mason) Aircraft, Strategy, and Operations of the Soviet Air Forces, 1986. Add: 36 Alexandra Dr., Surbiton, Surrey KT5 9AF, England.

TAYLOR, Lester D. American, b. 1938. Economics. Prof., Univ. of Arizona, Tucson, since 1974 (Visiting Prof., 1972–73). Asst. Prof., Harvard Univ., Cambridge, Mass., 1964–68; Staff Economist, Council of Economic Advisors, 1964–65; Advisor, Harvard Advisory Development Services, Bogota, Colombia, 196719668; Assoc. Prof., Univ. of Michigan, Ann Arbor, 1969–74. *Publs:* (with H.S. Houthakker) Consumer Demand in the United States 1929-1970, 1966, 1970; (with M.L. Ingbar) Hospital Costs in Massachusetts: An Econometric Study, 1968; (with S.J. Turnovsky and T.A. Wilson) Inflationary Process in North American Manufacturing, 1973; Probability and Mathematical Statistics, 1974; Telecommunications Demand, 1980. Add: Dept. of Economics, Univ. of Arizona, Tucson, Ariz. 85721, U.S.A.

TAYLOR, Michael J(oseph). American, b. 1924. Theology/Religion. Prof. of Theology, Seattle Univ., Wash., since 1973 (Asst. Prof., 1961–66; Assoc. Prof., 1967–73). *Publs:* The Protestant Liturgical Renewal, 1963; (with R.P. Marshall) Liturgy and Christian Unity, 1965; (ed.) Liturgical Renewal in the Christian Churches, 1967; (ed.) The Sacred and the Secular, 1968; (ed.) The Mystery of Sin and Forgiveness, 1971; (ed.) Sex: Thoughts for Contemporary Christians, 1972; (ed.) The Mystery of Suffering and Death, 1973; (ed.) A Companion to Paul: Topical Readings in Pauline Theology, 1975; A Companion to John: Readings in Johannine Theology, 1977; (ed.) The Sacraments: Readings in Contemporary Sacramental Theology, 1980; John: The Different Gospel, 1983; The Sacraments as "Encasement", 1986. Add: Seattle Univ., Seattle, Wash. 98122, U.S.A.

TAYLOR, Mildred D. American. Children's fiction. Full-time English and History teacher with the Peace Corps in Ethiopia, two years, then Peace Corps recruiter in the U.S.; study skills co-ordinator, Univ. of Colorado Black Ed. Program, two years; worked in an office, Los Angeles. *Publs:* Song of the Trees, 1975; Roll of Thunder, Hear My Cry, 1976; Let the Circle Be Unbroken, 1981; The Gold Cadillac, 1987; The Friendship and Other Stories, 1987. Add: c/o Dial Press, Two Park Ave., New York, N.Y. 10016, U.S.A.

TAYLOR, Peter (Hillsman). American, b. 1919. Novels/Short stories, Plays/Screenplays. Prof. of English, Univ. of Virginia, Charlottesville, since 1967. Member of faculty, Univ. of North Carolina, Chapel Hill, 1946–67; Visiting Lectr., Kenyon Coll., Gambier, Ohio, 1952–57, and

Ohio State Univ., Columbus, 1957–63. *Publs:* A Long Fourth and Other Stories, 1958; A Woman of Means (novel), 1950; The Windows of Thornton (short stories), 1954; Tennessee Day in St. Louis (play), 1957; Happy Families Are All Alike: A Collection of Short Stories, 1959; Miss Leonora When Last Seen and 15 Other Stories, 1963; A Stand in the Mountains (play), 1965; (ed. with Robert Penn Warren and Robert Lowell) Randall Jarrell, 1914-1965, 1967; The Collected Stories of Peter Taylor, 1969; Presences: Seven Dramatic Pieces, 1973; In the Miro District and Other Stories, 1977; The Old Forest and Other Stories, 1985; A Summons to Memphis, 1986; Conversations with Peter Taylor, ed. by Hubert H. McAlexander, 1987. Add: Dept. of English, Wilson Hall, Univ. of Virginia, Charlottesville, Va. 22901, U.S.A.

TAYLOR, Robert Lewis. American, b. 1912. Novels/Short stories, Biography. Reporter, St. Louis Post-Dispatch, Mo., 1936-39; Profile Writer, The New Yorker, 1939-48. *Publs:* Adrift in a Boneyard, 1947; Doctor, Lawyer, Merchant, Chief, 1948; W.C. Fields: His Follies and Fortunes, 1949; The Running Pianist, 1950; Professor Fodorski: A Politico-Sporting Romance, 1950; Winston Churchill: An Informal Study in Greatness, 1952; The Bright Sands, 1954; Center Ring: The People of the Circus, 1956; The Travels of Jamie McPheeters, 1958; A Journey to Matecumbe, 1961; Two Roads to Guadalupe, 1964; Vessel of Wrath: The Life and Times of Carry Nation, 1966; Niagara, 1980. Add: Bulb Bridge Rd., Kent, Conn. 06757, U.S.A.

TAYLOR, Samuel. American, b. 1912. Plays/Screenplays. Chmn., Dramatists Play Service Inc., NYC. *Publs:* The Happy Time, 1950; Sabrina Fair, 1954; The Pleasure of His Company, 1959; First Love, 1961; (co-author) No Strings, 1962; Beekman Place, 1964; Avanti!, 1969; A Touch of Spring, 1975; Legend, 1976; Perfect Pitch, 1977. Add: East Blue Hill, Me. 04629, U.S.A.

TAYLOR, Telford. American, b. 1908. History, Law. Nash Prof. of Law Emeritus, Columbia Univ., NYC (joined faculty, 1958); Prof. of Law, Benjamin Cardozo Law Sch., NYC. Gen. Counsel, Federal Communications Commn., Washington, D.C., 1940–42; Chief Counsel, U.S. Office for the Prosecution of Axis Criminality, Nuremberg, 1946–49; Administrator, Small Defense Plants Admin., Washington, D.C., 1951–52; Chmn., New York City Advisory Bd. on Public Welfare, 1960–63. Special Master, U.S. District Court for the Southern District of New York, 1977–1983. *Publs:* Sword and Swastika: Generals and Nazis in the Third Reich, 1952; Grand Inquest: The Story of Congressional Investigations, 1954; The March of Conquest: The German Victories in Western Europe, 1959; The Breaking Wave: the Second World War in the Summer of 1940, 1967; Two Studies in Constitutional Interpretation, 1969; Nuremberg and Vietnam: An American Tragedy, 1970; Courts of Terror: Soviet Justice and Jewish Emigration, 1976; Munich: The Price of Peace, 1979. Add: 54 Morningside Dr., New York, N.Y. 10025, U.S.A.

TAYLOR, Theodore. American, b. 1921. Novels/Short stories, Children's fiction, Plays/Screenplays, Children's non-fiction. Writer, Perlberg-Seaton Productions, Paramount Pictures, Calif., 1956–61, and 20th Century-Fox Studios, 1965–68. *Publs:* The Magnificent Mitsher, 1954; Fire on the Beaches, 1958; The Body Trade, 1968; People Who Make Movies, 1967; The Cay, 1969; (with R. Houghton) Special Unit Senator, 1970; Air Raid: Pearl Harbor, 1971; The Children's War, 1971; The Maldonado Miracle, 1973; Rebellion Town, 1973; Showdown (screenplay), 1973; (with Kreskin) The Amazing World of Kreskin, 1973; Teetoncey, 1974; Battle in the Arctic Seas, 1976; The Odyssey of Ben O'Neal, 1977; A Shepherd Watches, A Shepherd Sings, 1977; Jule: The Story of Composer Jule Styne, 1979; The Girl Who Whistled the River Kwai (teleplay), 1980; The Trouble with Tuck, 1981; H.M.S. Hood vs. Bismarck, 1982; Battle in the English Channel, 1983; Sweet Friday Island, 1984; The Cats of Shambala, 1985; Rocket Island, 1985; Walking Up a Rainbow, 1986; The Stalker, 1987; The Hostage, 1988; Sniper, 1989. Add: 1856 Catalina St., Laguna Beach, Calif., U.S.A.

TAYLOR, Walter Harold. Australia, b. 1905. Engineering, Technology. Concrete Technologist in private practice, since 1976. Part-time Lectr. on Concrete Technology and Practice, Royal Melbourne Inst. of Technology, since 1945. Research Engineer, Div. of Bldg. Research, Commonwealth Scientific and Industrial Research Org., Highett, Vic., 1945–70; Technical Services Engineer, John Connell Group of Consulting Engineers, 1971–76. *Publs:* Concrete Technology and Practice, 1965, 4th ed. 1977. Add: 19 Lawson St., Hawthorn East, Vic., Australia 3123.

TAYLOR, Welford Dunaway. American, b. 1938. History, Literature, Biography, Humor/Satire. Prof. of English since 1964, and Chmn. of the Dept., 1978–86, Univ. of Richmond, Va. Member of faculty, Ran-

dolph-Macon Academy, Va., 1959, 19660, and St. Christopher's Sch., 1960–63. *Publs:* (ed.) The Buck Fever Papers, 1971; (ed.) Virginia Authors Past and Present, 1972; Amelie Rives (Princess Troubetzkoy), 1973; Sherwood Anderson, 1977. Add: 5 Calycanthus Rd., Richmond, Va. 23221, U.S.A.

TAYLOR, William. New Zealander, b. 1938. Children's fiction. Principal, Ohakune School, 1978–84. Mayor of Ohakune, 1980–88. *Publs:* Burnt Carrots Don't Have Legs, 1976; Pack Up Pick Up and Off, 1981; My Summer of the Lions, 1986; Shooting Through, 1986; Break a Leg!, 1987; Possum Perkins (in U.K. as Paradise Lane), 1987; The Worst Soccer Team Ever!, 1987; Making Big Bucks, 1987; The Kidnap of Jessie Parker, 1989; I Hate My Brother Maxwell Potter, 1989; Agnes the Sheep, 1989. Add: 96 Clyde St., Ohakune, New Zealand.

TEAL, G. Donn. American, b. 1932. Civil liberties/Human rights. Ed., High Fidelity mag., NYC, since 1988. Former Ed., Alfred A. Knopf, Inc., Harry N. Abrams, Inc., and Oration Magazine, NYC. *Publs:* The Gay Militants, 1971. Add: 304 W. 75th St., New York, N.Y. 10023, U.S.A.

TEDDER, John M(ichael). (Baron Tedder of Glenguin). British, b. 1926. Chemistry. Purdie Prof. of Chemistry, Univ. of St. Andrews, since 1969. Roscoe Prof. of Chemistry, Univ. of Dundee, 1964–69. *Publs:* (co-author) Basic Organic Chemistry, 5 vols.; (co-author) Valence Theory, 1964; The Chemical Bond, 1970; (co-author) Radicals; (co-author) Pictorial Orbital Theory. Add: Dept. of Chemistry, Univ. of St. Andrews, Purdie Bldg., St. Andrews KY169ST, Fife, Scotland.

TELLER, Neville. British, b. 1931. Mystery/Crime/Suspense, Plays/Screenplays, Architecture, Marketing, Politics/Government (Israeli affairs). Civil Servant Dept. of Health and Social Security, since 1970. Freelance radio writer, since 1956. Marketing Mgr., Butterworth Publs. Ltd., 1966–68; Marketing Dir., Granada Publs., 1968–69; Marketing Co-ordinator, The Times, London, 1969–70. *Publs:* Bluff Your Way in Marketing, 1966, 1969; (ed.) Whodunit: Ten Tales of Crime and Detection, 1970; (ed.) Hospice: The Living Idea, 1981; (ed.) British Architectural Design Awards, 1983 and annually; (ed.) British Construction Profile, 1984; Radio Plays—Party Going, 1981; Dizzy and the Faery Queen, 1981; The Sword in the Stone, 1981; The Daughter of Time, 1982; The Poisoned Chocolates Case, 1984; The Serpent's Smile, 1985; Shadows of Doubt, 1986; Regency Buck, 1986; The King's Commissar, 1988; We Two Together, 1988; The Skull Beneath the Skin, 1989. Add: 15 Ewhurst Close, Cheam, Surrey SM2 7LN, England.

TELLER, Walter Magnes. American, b. 1910. Agriculture/Forestry, Autobiography/Memoirs/Personal, Biography. *Publs:* The Farm Primer, 1941; (with P. Alston Waring) Roots in the Earth: The Small Farmer Looks 1943; An Island Summer, 1951; The Search for Captain Slocum, 1956; (ed.) The Voyages of Joshua Slocum, 1958; (ed.) Five Sea Captains, 1960; Area Code 215: A Private Line in Bucks County, 1963; Cape Cod and the Offshore Islands, 1970; Joshua Slocum, 1971; (ed.) Twelve Works of Naive Genius, 1972; (ed.) Walt Whitman's Camden Conversations, 1973; (ed.) On the River, 1976; Consider Poor I: The Life and Works of Nancy Luce, 1984. Add: 200 Prospect Ave., Princeton, N.J. 08540, U.S.A.

TELSER, Lester G(reenspan). American, b. 1931. Economics. Prof. of Economics, Univ. of Chicago, since 1965 (Research Asst., Cowles Commn. for Research in Economics, 1952–54; Cooperative Agent, U.S. Dept. of Agriculture, 1954–55; Asst. Prof., 1958–60; Assoc. Prof., 1960!9663). Asst. Prof. of Economics, Iowa State Univ., Ames, 1955–56. Assoc. Ed., Journal of American Statistical Assn., 1966, 19669. *Publs:* Competition, Collusion and Game Theory, 1972; (with R.L. Graves) Functional Analysis in Mathematical Economics, 1972; Economic Theory and the Core, 1978; A Theory of Efficient Co-operation and Competition, 1987; Theories of Competition, 1988. Add: Dept. of Economics, Univ. of Chicago, Chicago, Ill. 60637, U.S.A.

TEMIN, Peter. American, b. 1937. Economics. Prof. of Economics, Massachusetts Inst. of Technology, Cambridge, since 1970 (Teaching Asst., 1961, 19662; Asst. Prof. of Industrial History, 1965–67; Assoc. Prof. of Economic History, 1967–70). *Publs:* Iron and Steel in Nineteenth Century America: An Economic Enquiry, 1964; The Jacksonian Economy, 1969; (ed.) New Economic History, 1972; Causal Factors in American Economic Growth in the Nineteenth Century, 1975; Did Monetary Forces Cause the Great Depression?, 1975; Taking Your Medicine: Drug Regulation in the United States, 1980; The Fall of the Bell System, 1987. Add: Room E52-274, Dept. of Economics, Massachusetts Inst. of Technology, Cambridge, Mass. 02139, U.S.A.

TEMPERLEY, (Harold) Neville (Vazeille). British, b. 1915. Sciences Theology/Religion. Prof. of Applied Mathematics, Univ. Coll., Swansea, 1965–82, now retired. Fellow, King's Coll., Cambridge, 1941–54 (Lectr. in Physics, 1948–53); Visiting Prof. Physics, Univ. of Nebraska, 1953–54; Consultant, National Bureau of Standards, Washington, D.C., 1954–55; Sr. Principal Scientist, Atomic Energy Authority, Aldermaston, 1955–65. *Publs:* Properties of Matter, 1953; Changes of State, 1956; A Scientist Who Believes in God, 1961; The Physics of Simple Liquids, 1968; (with D.H. Trevena) Liquids and Their Properties, 1978; Graph Theory and Applications, 1981. Add: Thorney House, Thorney, Langport, Somerset, England.

TEMPERLEY, Nicholas. British/American, b. 1932. Music. Prof. of Musicology, Univ. of Illinois, Urbana, since 1972 (Assoc. Prof., 1967–72; Chmn., Musicology Div., 1972–75). Member, Editorial Bd., Nineteenth Music, since 1978. Asst. Lectr. in Music, Cambridge Univ., and Fellow and Dir. of Studies in Music, Clare Coll., Cambridge, 1961–66; Asst. Prof. of Music, Yale Univ., New Haven, Conn., 1966–67. Ed., Journal of the American Musicological Soc., 1978–80; Pres., Midwest Victorian Studies Assn., 1981–83. *Publs:* The Music of the English Parish Church, 1979; (ed.) The Athlone History of Music in Britain, vol. V, The Romantic Age 1800-1914, 1981; (with Charles G. Manns) Fuging Tunes in the Eighteenth Century, 1983; (ed.) The Lost Chord: Essays on Victorian Music, 1989. Add: 805 W. Indiana St., Urbana, Ill. 61801, U.S.A.

TEMPEST, Ian. *See* CHARLES, Theresa.

TEMPEST, Sara. *See* PONSONBY, D.A.

TEMPEST, Victor. *See* PHILIPP, Elliot Elias.

TEMPLE, Dan. *See* NEWTON, D.B.

TEMPLE, Nigel (Hal Longdale). British, b. 1926. Architecture, Children's non-fiction, Homes/Gardens (garden history). Painter and Photographer. With RAF, Meteorology, 1944–48; Member of faculty, Sheffield Coll. of Art, Yorks., 1953–55 and Wakefield Coll. of Art, 1955–58; Head of Visual Studies, Glos. Coll. of Education, 1958–78. *Publs:* Farnham Inheritance, 1956, 1965; Farnham Buildings and People, 1963, 1973; Looking at Things (filmstrips and handbooks), 1968; Seen and Not Heard, 1970; Blaise Hamlet, 1975, 1978; John Nash and the Village Picturesque, 1979. Add: Wendover Gardens, Cheltenham, Glos. GL50 2PA, England.

TEMPLE, Philip. New Zealander, b. 1939. Novels, Children's non-fiction, Communications Media (television), Film. Features Ed., New Zealand Listener, 1968–72; Assoc. Ed., Landfall, 1972–74. *Publs:* Nawok!, 1962; The Sea and the Snow, 1966; The World at Their Feet, 1969; Mantle of the Skies, (ed.) Castles in the Air, 1973; Christchurch: A City and Its People, 1973; Patterns of Water, 1974; South Island, 1975; The Explorer (novel), 1975; Guides to New Zealand Walking Tracks, 11 vols., 1976-; Ways to the Wilderness, 1977; Stations (novel), 1979; Beak of the Moon (novel), 1981; Sam (novel), 1984; Moa (for children), 1985; New Zealand Explorers, 1985; New Zealand From the Air, 1986; Legend of the Kea (for children), 1986; Kakapo (for children), 1988. Add: Eastbourne, Wellington, New Zealand.

TEMPLE, Robert (Kyle Grenville). American, b. 1945. Area Studies (Chinese civilization and Psychology), History, Sciences. Sr. Ed., Second Look mag., 1978–80; Sr. Research Fellow in History of Science, New Horizons Research Foundation, Canada, 1985; Co-Producer, BBC TV Documentary: "Byline: Richard Gregory," 1989. *Publs:* The Sirius Mystery, 1976; Gotter, Orakel, und Visionen, 1982; Strange Things, 1983; Conversations with Eternity, 1984; China: Land of Discovery and Invention (in U.S. as The Genius of China), 1986; Open to Suggestion: The Uses and Abuses of Hypnosis, 1989. Add: c/o David Higham Assocs. Ltd. (Agents), 5-8 Lower John St., Golden Sq., London W1R 4HA, England.

TEMPLE, Wayne C(alhoun). American, b. 1924. History. Archivist since 1964, and Chief Deputy Dir., Illinois State Archives, Springfield; Assoc. Ed., Lincoln Herald quarterly, since 1974 (Ed.-in-Chief, 1958–74). Gen., Illinois State Militia, Retired. Curator, Ethnohistory, Illinois State Museum, 1954–58; John Wingate Weeks Prof. of History, Lincoln Memorial Univ., Harrogate, Tenn., 1958–64. *Publs:* Historic Tribes, 1958, 4th ed., 1987; Lincoln the Railsplitter, 1961; (ed.) Campaigning with Grant, 1961; The Civil War Letters of Henry C. Bear, 1961; Abraham

Lincoln and Others at the St. Nicholas, 1969; Alexander Williamson, Tutor to the Lincoln Boys, 1971; Indian Villages of the Illinois Country: Atlas, 1975; Lincoln as a Lecturer on Discoveries, Inventions, and Improvements, 1982; Stephen A. Douglas: Freemason, 1982; By Square and Compasses: The Building of Lincoln's Home and Its Sage, 1984; Lincoln's Connections with the Illinois and Michigan, His Return from Congress in '48, and His Invention, 1986; Illinois' Fifth Capitol, 1988. Add: 1121 S. Fourth St. Ct., Springfield, Ill. 62703,

TEMPLETON, Edith. Also writes as Louise Walbrook. British, b. 1916. Novels/Short stories, Travel/Exploration/Adventure, Translations. Conference and Law Court Interpreter, British Forces in Germany, rank of Capt., 1945–46. *Publs:* Summer in the Country, 1950; Living on Yesterday, 1951; The Proper Bohemians, 1952; The Island of Desire, 1952; The Surprise of Cremona, 1954; Italienisches Capriccio, 1955; This Charming Pastime, 1955; (co-author) Stories of the New Yorker, 1960; (co-author) The Gourmet's Companion, 1963; (trans., as Louise Walbrook) Gordon, 1966; (co-author) Abroad, 1968; Three: A Coffee House Acquaintance, 1971; (co-author) The New Compleat Imbiber, 1986. Add: 76 Corso Europa, 18012 Bordighera, Italy.

TENN, William. Pseud. for Philip Klass. American, b. 1919. Science fiction/Fantasy. Member of the English Dept., Pennsylvania State Univ., State College, since 1966. Consulting Ed., Fantasy and Science Fiction mag., 1958. *Publs:* (ed.) Children of Wonder, 1953, as Outsiders, 1954; short stories—Of All Possible Worlds, 1955, 1956; The Human Angle, 1956; Time in Advance, 1958; The Seven Sexes, 1968; The Square Root of Man, 1968; novels—A Lamp for Medusa, 1968; Of Men and Monsters, 1968; (ed. with Donald E. Westlake) Once Against the Law, 1968. Add: W. Fairmont Ave., State College, Pa. 16802, U.S.A.

TENNANT, Emma (Christina). Also writes as Catherine Aydy. British, b. 1937. Mystery/Crime/Suspense, Science fiction/Fantasy, Children's fiction. Travel Corresp., Queen mag., 1963; Features Ed., Vogue mag., 1966; Ed., Bananas mag., 1975–78—all in London. *Publs:* (as Catherine Aydy) The Colour of Rain, 1964; The Time of the Crack (science fiction), 1973, as The Crack, 1978; The Last of the Country House Murders (science fiction), 1974; Hotel de Dream (science fiction), 1976; (ed.) Bananas, 1977; The Bad Sister, 1978; (ed.) Saturday Night Reader, 1979; Wild Nights, 1979; Alice Fell, 1980; The Boggart (juvenile), 1980; The Search for Treasure Island, 1981; Queen of Stones, 1982; Woman Beware Woman, 1983, in U.S. as The Half-Mother, 1985; The Ghost Child (juvenile), 1984; Black Marina, 1985; The Adventures of Robina, 1986; The House of Hospitalities, 1987; A Wedding of Cousins, 1988. Add: c/o Faber and Faber, 3 Queen Sq., London WC1, England.

TENNANT, (Sir) Peter (Frank Dalrymple). British, b. 1910. Cultural/Ethnic topics, Literature. Former Dir., Prudential Corp., C. Tennant and Sons Ltd., Northern Engineering Industries Intnl. Fellow, Queen's Coll., Cambridge, 1934–47; Member, U.K. Diplomatic Service, 1939–52; Overseas Dir. and Deputy Dir.-Gen., Fedn. of British Industries, 1952–64; Dir.-Gen., British National Export Council, 1965–72. Chmn. and Pres., London Chamber of Commerce, 1975–79. *Publs:* Ibsen's Dramatic Technique, 1947; The Scandinavian Book, 1951; Touchlines of War, 1989. Add: Blue Anchor House, Linchmere Rd., Haslemere, Surrey GU27 3QF, England.

TENNYSON, G(eorg) B(ernhard). American, b. 1930. Literature. Prof. of English, Univ. of California, Los Angeles, since 1970 (Asst. Prof., 1964–67; Assoc. Prof., 1967–70). Ed., Nineteenth-Century Fiction mag., 1971–74, and since 1983 (re-named Nineteenth Century Literature, 1986). Instr. in English, Univ. of North Carolina, Chapel Hill, 1962—64. *Publs:* Sartor called Resartus, 1964; An Introduction to Drama, 1967; (ed.) A Carlyle Reader, 1969, 1984; (ed. with E.E. Ericson) Religion and Modern Literature, 1974; (ed. with D.J. Gray) Victorian Literature: Prose and Poetry, 2 vols., 1975; (ed. with U.C. Knoepflmacher) Nature and the Victorian Imagination, 1977; (with E.J. Tennyson) An Index to "Nineteenth-Century Fiction", 1977; Victorian Devotional Poetry, 1981. Add: Dept. of English, Univ. of California, Los Angeles, Calif. 90024, U.S.A.

TENSEN, Ruth Marjorie. American. Children's fiction. Teacher of primary grades, Rochester, N.Y., 1926–61. *Publs:* Come to the Zoo, 1948; to the Farm, 1949; Come to the City, 1951; Come to the Pet Shop, 1954; Come to See the Clowns, 1963. Add: 1570 East Ave., Apt. 208, Rochester, N.Y. 14610, U.S.A.

TERKEL, Studs (Louis). American. Music, Social commentary/-phenomena. Compere, Wax Museum radio prog., since 1945, and Studs Terkel Almanac, both Chicago, since 1952. *Publs:* Giants of Jazz, 1956;

Division Street America, 1966; Amazing Grace (play), 1959; Hard Times, 1970; Working, 1974; Talking to Myself, 1977; American Dreams, Lost and Found, 1980; The Good War: An Oral History of World War II, 1984 (Pulitzer Prize); The Great Divide, 1988. Add: Pantheon, 201 E. 50th St., New York, N.Y. 10022, U.S.A.

TERPSTRA, Vern. American, b. 1927. Business/Trade/Industry, Marketing. Prof. of Intnl. Business, Univ. of Michigan, Ann Arbor, since 1966. Consulting Ed., Intnl. Business, Holt Rinehart & Winston, publrs., since 1971; Member, Editorial Bd., Journal of Intnl. Business Studies, since 1972. Asst. Prof., Univ. of Pennsylvania, Philadelphia, 1964, 19666; Pres., Academy of Intnl. Business, 1971, 1972. *Publs:* (co-ed.) Patents and Progress, 1965; (co-author) Comparative Analysis for International Marketing in the Common Market, 1967; (ed.) University Education for International Business, 1969; International Marketing, 1972, 4th ed. 1987; The Cultural Environment of International Business, 1978; International Dimensions of Marketing, 1982, 1988. Add: 750 Lans Way, Ann Arbor, Mich., U.S.A.

TERRACE, Herbert S. American, b. 1936. Psychology. Prof. of Psychology, Columbia Univ., NYC, since 1968 (joined faculty, 1961). Assoc. Ed., Behaviorism, since 1974, and Behavioral and Brain Sciences, since 1977, and Journal of Experimental Psychology: Animal Behavior Processes, since 1987. Member, Bd. of Dirs., Eastern Psychological Assn., since 1987. Pres., Soc. of Experimental Analysis of Behavior, 1973–75. *Publs:* (with S. Parker) Psychological Statistics, 1970; (with T.G. Bever) Psychology in Human Society, 1973; Nim, 1979; (with C. Locurto, and J. Autoshaping, 1980; (with P. Marler) Biology of Learning, 1983; (with H. Roitblat and T.G. Bever) Animal Cognition, 1984. Add: Dept. of Psychology, 418 Schermerhorn, Columbia Univ., New York, N.Y. 10027, U.S.A.

TERRAINE, John Alfred. British, b. 1921. History, Biography. Hon. Fellow, Keble Coll., Oxford. BBC Producer and Prog. Organiser, London, 1944–63. *Publs:* Mons, 1960; Douglas Haig: The Educated Soldier, 1963; The Western Front, 1964; The Great War: An Illustrated History, 1964; (ed.) General Jack's Diary, 1964; The Life and Times of Lord Mountbatten, 1968; (ed.) The Men Who Marched Away, 1968; Impacts of War, 1914 and 1918, 1970; (ed.) The Decisive Battles of the Western World, 1970; The Mighty Continent, 1974, TV series, 1974; TV series— (co-author) The Great War; (co-author) The Lost Peace; Trafalgar, 1976; The Road to Passchendaele, 1977; To Win a War: 1918, The Year of Victory, 1978; The Smoke and the Fire: Myths and Anti-Myths of War 1861-1945, 1981; White Heat: The New Warfare 1914-18, 1982; The Right of the Line: The Royal Air Force in the European War 1939-1945, 1985. Add: 74 Kensington Park Rd., London W11 2PL, England.

TERRIS, Susan. American, b. 1937. Children's fiction. *Publs:* The Upstairs Witch and the Downstairs Witch, 1970; The Backwards Boots, 1971; On Fire, 1972; The Drowning Boy, 1972; Plague of Frogs, 1973; Pickle, 1973; Whirling Rainbows, 1974; Amanda, the Panda, and the Red-head, 1975; The Pencil Families, 1975; No Boys Allowed, 1976; The Chicken Pox Papers, 1976; Two P's in a Pod, 1977; Tucker and the Horse Thief, 1979; Stage Brat, 1980; No Scarlet Ribbons, 1981; Wings and Roots, 1982; Octopus Pie, 1983; The Latchkey Kids, 1985; Baby-Snatcher, 1985; Nell's Quilt, 1987. Add: 11 Jordan Ave., San Francisco, Calif. 94118, U.S.A.

TERRY, C.V. *See* **SLAUGHTER,** Frank G.

TERRY, Megan. American, b. 1932. Plays/Screenplays. Stage and television director. Teacher of drama, Cornish Sch. of Allied Arts, Seattle, 1954–56; Writer-in-Residence, Yale Univ. Drama Sch., New Haven, Conn., 1966–67; Founding Member, 1963, and Dir., Playwrights Workshop, 1963–68, Open Theatre, NYC; Founding Member and Treas., New York Theatre Strategy, 1971; Founding Member, Women's Theatre Council, NYC, 1971. *Publs:* Calm Down Mother, 1966; Four Plays: Viet Rock, Comings and Goings, Keep Tightly Closed in a Cool Dry Place, and The Gloaming, Oh My Darling, 1967; The People vs. Ranchman, 1967; Home, 1968; Approaching Simone, 1970; Three One-Act Plays, 1972; Couplings and Groupings, 1972; The Pioneer, and Pro-Game, 1974; Hothouse, 1974; Hospital Play, 1974; Henna for Endurance, 1974; Fifteen Million Fifteen Year Olds, 1974; Sleazing Towards Athens, 1977; Willie-Walla-Bill's Dope Garden, 1977; Brazil Fado, 1977; American King's English for Queens, 1978; Attempted Rescue on Avenue B, 1979; Babes in the Big House, 1979; (with others) 100,001 Horror Stories of the Plains, 1979; Scenes from Maps, 1980; Objective Love, 1980; Running Gags (lyrics only), 1980; The Trees Blew Down, 1981; Mollie Bailey's Traveling Family Circus, 1983; Goona Goona, 1984; (with J.A. Schmidman)

Sea of Forms, 1986; (with Jo Ann Schmidman) Walking Through Walls, 1987; Amtrak, 1988; Headlights: Breakfast Serial, 1989; Censor, 1990. Add: c/o Omaha Magic Theatre, 1417 Farnam St., Omaha, Nebr. 68102, U.S.A.

TERRY, William. *See* **GILMAN,** George G.

TERSON, Peter. Pseud. for Peter Patterson. British, b. 1932. Children's Fiction, Plays/Screenplays. Playwright: Associated with the Victoria Theatre, Stoke on Trent, and the National Youth Theatre, London. *Publs:* The Apprentices, 1968; The of Gervase Beckett; or, The Man Who Changed Places, 1969; Zigger Zagger, and Mooney and His Caravans, 1970; Rattling the Railings, 1979; Prisoners of the War, 1983; Strippers, 1985; Hotel Dorado, 1986; One Act Plays for School, 2 vols., 1988; (ed.) Title.... Short Plays, 1988; Offents (children's novel), 1988; The Voyage (children's novel), 1988. Add: c/o Alan Williams, S and M House, Beacon St., Lichfield, Staff. WS13 7AA, England.

TESELLE, Eugene. American, b. 1931. Theology/Religion. Prof. of Church History and Theology, Divinity Sch., Vanderbilt Univ., Nashville, Tenn., since 1974 (Assoc. Prof., 1969–74). Asst. Minister, First Presbyterian Church, East Orange, N.J., 1955–58; Instr., Dept. of Religious Studies, 1962–65, and Asst. Prof., Dept. of Religious Studies, 1965–69, Yale Univ., New Haven, Conn. *Publs:* Augustine the Theologian, 1970; Augustine's Strategy as an Apologist, 1973; Christ in Context: Divine Purpose and Human Possibility, 1975. Add: 2007 Linden Ave., Nashville, Tenn. 37212, U.S.A.

TESICH, Steve. American (born Yugoslavian), b. 1942. Plays/Screenplays. *Publs:* Nourish the Beast, 1974; Gorky (musical), 1976; The Carpenters, 1976; Passing Game, 1978; Touching Bottom (trilogy: The Road, A Life, Baptismal), 1980; Division Street, 1982; Summer Crossing (novel), 1982; American Flyers, Eleni, 1985. Add: c/o Random House, 201 E, 50th St., New York, N.Y. 10022, U.S.A.

THACKRAY, Derek Vincent. British, b. 1926. Children's fiction, Education, Biography. Lectr. in Education, Leicester Univ., since 1978. Lectr., 1960–62, Sr. Lectr., 1962–66 and Head of Education Dept., 1966–78, St. Paul's Coll. of Education. Varied teaching appointments, 1945–60. *Publs:* Stories the Rhymes Tell, 1968; Tarzan Tortoise Series, 1969; Other Children Series, 1970; Readiness to Read, 1971; (with J. Downing) Reading Readiness, 1971; This is How We Live, 1971; This Is How We Work, 1971; This Is My Colour, 1973; This Is My Shape, 1973; Steps to Reading, 1973; This Is My Sound, 1975; Reading Readiness Inventory, 1975; Reading Readiness Profiles, 1974; Growth in Reading, Reading Readiness Workbooks, 1980; St. Peter and His Successors, 1982; Pope John Paul II, 1982. Add: University Centre, Barrack Rd., Northampton, England.

THADEN, Edward Carl. American, b. 1922. History. Prof. of History, Univ. of Illinois, Chicago, since 1968 (Dir. of Grad. Studies and Chmn., Dept. of History, 1970–73). Vice-Pres., Commn. Intnl. des Etudes Historiques Slaves, since 1985. Prof. of History, Pennsylvania State Univ., University Park, 1952–68. *Publs:* Conservative Nationalism in 19th-Century Russia, 1964; Russia and the Balkan Alliance of 1912, 1965; Russia since 1801: The Making of a New Society, 1971; (ed. and co-author) Russification in the Baltic Provinces and Finland 1855-1914, 1981; Russia's Western Borderlands 1710-1870, 1984. Add: Dept. of History, Univ. of Illinois, Chicago, Ill. 60680, U.S.A.

THALER, M.N. *See* **KERNER,** Fred.

THAMES, C.H. *See* **MARLOWE,** Stephan.

THANET, Neil. *See* **FANTHORPE,** R. Lionel.

THATCHER, Alice Dora. British, b. 1912. Children's fiction. *Publs:* Henry the Helicopter series, 12 vols., 1956–75; Tommy the Tugboat series, 12 vols., 1956–77; The Coracle Builders, 1964; Island Pony, 1966; Lezzie the Lifeboat, 1985. Add: Craig-y-Mor, Parrog, Newport, Pembrokeshire SA42 0RU, Wales.

THAYER, Geraldine. *See* **DANIELS,** Dorothy.

THEIL, Henri. Dutch, b. 1924. Economics. McKethan-Matherly Prof., Univ. of Florida, Gainesville, since 1981. Prof., and Dir., Center for Mathematical Studies in Business and Economics, Univ. of Chicago, 1965–81 (Visiting Prof., Dept. of Economics, 1955–56; Ford Foundn. Visiting Grad. Sch. of Business, 1964). Dir., Econometric Inst. of the

Netherlands Sch. of Economics, Rotterdam, 1956–66. *Publs:* Linear Aggregation of Economic Relations, 1954; Economic Forecasts and Policy, 1958, 1961; Optimal Decision Rules for Government and Industry, 1964; (with J.C.G. Boot and T. Kloek) Operations Research and Quantitative Economics: An Elementary Introduction, 1965; Applied Economic Forecasting, 1966; Economics and Information Theory, 1967; Principles of Econometrics, 1971; Statistical Decomposition Analysis with Applications in the Social and Administrative Sciences, 1972; Theory and Measurement of Consumer Demand, vol. I, 1975, vol. II, 1976; Introduction to Econometrics, 1978; The System-Wide Approach to Microeconomics, 1980; System-Wide Explorations in International Economics, Input-Output Analysis, and Marketing Research, 1980; (with F.E. Suhm and J.F. Meisner) International Consumption Comparisons, 1981; (with D.G. Fiebig) Exploiting Continuity, 1984; (with K.W. Clements) Applied Demand Analysis, 1987; (with C.-F. Chung and J.L. Seale, Jr.) International Evidence on Consumption Patterns, 1989. Add: 5918 NW 95th Way, Gainesville, Fla. 32606, U.S.A.

THEOBALD, Robert. British, b. 1929. Science fiction/Fantasy, Economics, Environmental science/Ecology, Politics/Government. Pres., Participation Publrs., since 1973. With the Org. for European Cooperation, Paris, 1953–57. *Publs:* The Rich and the Poor, 1959; The Challenge of Abundance, 1960; Free Men and Free Markets, 1963; (ed.) The Guaranteed Income, 1966; (ed.) Social Policies for America in the Seventies, 1968; Economizing Abundance, 1970; (with J.M. Scott) Teg's 1994, 1970; An Alternative Future for America II, 1970; Habit and Habitat, 1970; (ed.) Futures Conditional, 1971; (ed.) The Failure of Success, 1972; Beyond Despair, 1976; An Alternative Future for America's Third Century, 1976; We're Not Ready for That, Yet!, 1979; Avoiding 1984, 1982; The Rapids of Change, 1987; Victory 1992!, 1989. Add: Box 2240, Wickenburg, Ariz. 85358, U.S.A.

THEROUX, Alexander (Louis). American, b. 1939. Novels/Short stories, Children's fiction. Taught at Longwood Coll., Farmville, Va., Harvard Univ., Cambridge, Mass., and Phillips Academy, Andover, Mass. *Publs:* Three Wogs (short stories), 1972; Theroux Metaphrastes: An Essay on Literature, 1975; The Great Wheadle Tragedy (for children), 1975; The Schinocephalic Waif (for children), 1975; Master Snickup's Cloak (for children), 1979; Darconville's Cat (novel), 1981; An Adultery (novel), 1987. Add: c/o Doubleday, 245 Park Ave., New York, N.Y. 10167, U.S.A.

THEROUX, Paul. American, b. 1941. Novels/Short stories, Children's fiction, Literature, Travel. Lectr. in English, Soche Hill Coll., Limbe, Malawi, 1963–65, Makerere Univ., Kampala, Uganda, 1965–68, and Univ. of Singapore, 1968–71. *Publs:* Waldo, 1967; Fong and the Indians, 1968; Girls at Play, 1969; Murder in Mount Holly, 1969; Jungle Lovers, 1971; Sinning with Annie and Other Stories, 1972; V.S. Naipaul: An Introduction to His Work, 1972; Saint Jack, 1973; The Black House, 1974; The Great Railway Bazaar: By Train Through Asia, 1975; The Family Arsenal, 1976; The Consul's File, 1977; Picture Place, 1978; A Christmas Card (children's fiction), 1978; The Old Patagonian Express: By Train Through the Americas, 1979; World's End, 1980; London Snow (children's fiction), The Mosquito Coast, 1981; The London Embassy, 1982; The Kingdom by the Sea, 1983; Sailing Through China, 1983; Doctor Slaughter, 1984; Sunrise with Sea-Monsters, 1985; Imperial Way: Making Tracks from Peshawar to Chittagong, 1985; (with Bruce Chatwin) Patagonia Revisited, 1985; O-Zone, 1986; The White Man's Burden, 1987; Riding the Inn Rooster, 1988; My Secret History, 1989. Add: c/o Hamish Hamilton Ltd., 47 Wrights Lane, London W8 5TZ, England.

THESEN, Hjalmar Peter. South Africa, b. 1925. Novels/Short stories. Dir., Thesen and Co. (Pty.) Ltd., since 1950. *Publs:* The Echoing Cliffs; The Castle of Giants; Master of None; Country Days (personal experiences); A Deadly Presence, 1982. Add: Seaford, Thesen Hill, Knysna, South Africa.

THESIGER, Wilfred (Patrick). British, b. 1910. Travel/Exploration/Adventure. Served in the Sudan Political Service, 1935–40, Sudan Defence Force and Special Air Service, 1940–43; Explored the Danakil Desert, 1933–34, and the empty quarter of Arabia, 1945–50; Studied the Marsh Arabs of Iraq, 1950–58. *Publs:* Arabian Sands, 1959; The Marsh Arabs, 1964; Desert, Marsh and Mountain: The World of a Nomad, 1979; Life of My Choice, 1987; Vision of a Nomad, 1987. Add: 15 Shelley Court, Tite St., London SW3, England.

THIELE, Colin (Milton). Australian, b. 1920. Novels/Short stories, Children's fiction, Poetry, History, Biography. Dir., Wattle Park Teachers Coll., Adelaide (Lectr., 1957–62; Sr. Lectr. in English, 1962–63;

Principal, 1965–72; Dir., Teachers Centre, 1987–89). Council Member, Australian Soc. of Authors, since 1967 (Pres., 1987); Fellow, Australian Coll. of Education, since 1969 (member, 1964–68). *Publs:* Progress to Denial, 1945; Splinters and Shards, 1945; Burke and Wills (play), 1949; The Golden Lighning: Poems, 1951; The State of Our State, 1952; (ed.) Jindyworobak Anthology, 1953; Man in a Landscape, 1960; (ed.) Looking at Poetry, 1960; (ed. with I. Mudie) Australian Poets Speak, 1961; The Sun on the Stubble, 1962; Gloop, The Gloomy Bunyip, 1962, as Gloop the Bunyip, 1970; (ed. with G. Branson) One-Act Plays for Secondary Schools, 3 vols., 1962, 1964, rev. eds. as Setting the Stage, and The Living Stage, 1969, 1970; Storm Boy, 1963; (ed.) Favourite Australian Stories, 1963; (ed.) Handbook to Favourite Australian Stories, 1964; (ed. with G. Branson) Beginners, 1964; February Dragon, 1965; In Charcoal and Conté, 1966; The Rim of the Morning (short stories), 1966; Mrs. Munch and Puffing Billy, 1967; Barossa Valley Sketchbook, 1968; Heysen of Hahndorf (biography), 1968; Blue Fin, 1969; Yellow Jacket Jock, 1969; Selected Verse (1940-1970), 1970; Labourers in the Vineyard (novel, 1970; Flash Flood, 1970; Flip Flop and Tiger Snake, 1970; (ed. with G. Branson) Plays for Young Players, 1970; Coorong, 1972; The Fire in the Stone, 1973; Range Without Man, 1974; Albatross Two, 1974; Magpie Island, 1974; Uncle Gustav's Ghosts, 1974; The Little Desert, 1975; Grains of Mustard Seed, 1975; Heysen's Early Hahndorf, 1976; The Bight, 1976; The Hammerhead Light, 1976; The Shadow on the Hills, 1977; The Sknuks, 1977; Lincoln's Place, 1978; Maneater Man, 1979; River Murray Mary, 1979; Ballander Boy, 1979; Chadwick's Chimney, 1980; The Best of Colin Thiele, 1980; The Valley Between, 1981; The Undercover Secret, 1982; Pinquo, 1983; Coorong Captive, 1985; Seashores and Shadows, 1985; The Seed's Inheritance, 1986; Farmer Schulz's Ducks, 1986; South Australia Revisited, 1986; Shatterbelt, 1987; Ranger's Territory, 1987; Klontarf, 1988; The Ab Diver, 1988; Jodie's Journey, 1988; Stories Short and Tall, 1989. Add: 24 Woodhouse Cres., Wattle Park, S.A., Australia.

THIERAUF, Robert James. American, b. 1933. Administration/Management, Business/Trade/Industry, Information science/Computers. Chmn., Dept. of Mgmt. and Information Systems, Xavier Univ., Cincinnati, Ohio, 1968–80. *Publs:* Decision Making Through Operation Research, 1970, 1975; Data Processing for Business and Management, 1973; Systems Analysis and Design of Real-Time Management Information Systems, 1975; Management Principles and Practices, 1977; An Introductory Approach to Operations Research, 1978; Distributed Processing Systems, 1978; Management Auditing: A Questionnaire Approach, 1980; An Introduction to Data Processing for Business, 1980; Systems Analysis and Design: A Case Study Approach, 1980, 1986; Effective Information Systems Management, 1982; Decision Support Systems for Effective Planning and Control: A Case Study Approach, 1982; A Manager's Complete Guide to Effective Information Systems: A Questionnaire Approach, 1983; Effective Management Systems, 1984, 1987; Management Science: A Model Formulation Approach with Computer Application, 1985; A Problem-Finding Approach to Effective Corporate Planning, 1987; User-Oriented Decision Support Systems: A Problem-Finding Approach, 1988; Effective Information Centers: Guidelines for MIS and IC Managers, 1988; New Directions in MIS Management: Guidelines for the 1990's, 1988; Group Decision Support Systems for Effective Decision Making, 1989. Add: Xavier Univ., Victory Parkway, Cincinnati, Ohio 45207, U.S.A.

THIMANN, Kenneth Vivian. American, b. 1904. Biology. Prof. of Biology, Univ. of California, Santa Cruz, since 1965 (Dean of Sciences, 1965–67; Provost of Crown Coll., 1965–72). Prof. of Biology, 1935–62, and Higgins Prof. of Biology, 1962–65, Harvard Univ., Cambridge, Mass. *Publs:* (with F.W. Went) Phytohormones, 1937; (co-author and ed. with F. Brown and B. Scharrer) Action of Hormones in Plants and Invertebrates, 1948; (ed. and contrib.) The Physiology of Forest Trees, 1958; The Life of Bacteria, 1955, 1963; (with F. Skoog and C. West) The Natural Plant Hormones, 1972; Hormone Action in the Whole Life of Plants, 1977; (ed. and contrib.) Senescence in Plants, 1980; (with J. Langenheim) Botany: Plant Biology in Relation to Human Affairs, 1982. Add: 36 Pasatiempo Dr., Santa Cruz, Calif. 95060, U.S.A.

THIRSK, (Irene) Joan. British, b. 1922. History. Sr. Research Fellow in Agrarian History, Univ. of Leicester, 1951–65; Reader in Economic History, and Fellow of St. Hilda's Coll., Univ. of Oxford, 1965–83. Ed., Agricultural History Review, 1963–72. *Publs:* English Peasant Farming, 1957; Tudor Enclosures, 1958; (ed.) The Agrarian History of England and Wales, IV, 1500-1640, 1967, V, 1640-1750, 1985; Seventeenth Century Economic Documents, 1972; The Restoration, 1976; Economic Policy and Projects, 1978; The Rural Economy of England, 1984; England's Agricultural Regions and Agrarian History, 1500-1750, 1987.

Add: 1 Hadlow Castle, Hadlow, Tonbridge, Kent, England.

THODY, Philip (Malcoln Waller). British, b. 1928. Novels/Short stories, Literature, Biography. Prof. of French Literature, Univ. of Leeds, since 1965 (Chmn., French Dept., 1968–72, 1975–79; Chmn. of the Bd., Faculties of Arts, Economics, Social Studies and Law, 1972–74). *Publs:* Albert Camus: A Study of His Work, 1957; Jean-Paul Sartre: A Literary and Political Study, 1960; Albert Camus 1913-1960, 1961; Jean Genet: A Study of His Novels and Plays, 1968; Jean Anouilh, 1968; Choderlos de Laclos, 1970; Jean-Paul Sartre: A Biographical Introduction, 1971; Aldous Huxley: A Biographical Introduction, 1973; Roland Barthes, 1977; Dog Days in Babel (novel), 1979; Faux Amis and Key Words, 1985; Marcel Proust, Novelist, 1987; Albert Camus, Novelist, 1989; French Caesarism from Napoleon 1e to Charles de Gaulle, 1989. Add: French Dept., The University, Leeds LS2 9JT, England.

THOMAE, Betty Kennedy. American, b. 1920. Poetry, Songs, lyrics and libretti, Law. Secty., Delligatti, Hollenbaugh, Briscoe and Milless, Attorneys at Law, Columbus, Ohio, since 1958. With American Heritage Research Assn. Inc., since 1975. *Publs:* My Honey (song); Roses and Thorns (poetry), 1969; The Legal Secretary's Handbook with Forms, 1973; (ed. and co-author) Legal Secretary's Encyclopedic Dictionary, 1976; Stand Still Summer (poetry), 1987. Add: 1008 Hardesty Pl. West, Columbus, Ohio 43204, U.S.A.

THOMAS, Alan Gradon. British, b. 1911. Literature, Biography. Self-employed antiquarian bookseller (entered booktrade, 1927). *Publs:* Fine Books, 1967; (ed.) Spirit of Place: Letters and Essays on Travel by Lawrence Durrell, 1969; Great Books and Book Collectors, 1975. Add: c/o National Westminster Bank, 300 King's Rd., London SW3 5UJ, England.

THOMAS, Alfred Strickland. Australian, b. 1900. Horticulture. Self-employed gynaecologist. Hon. Asst. Gynaecologist, Prince Henry's Hosp., Melbourne, 1928–48. Pres., National Rose Soc. of Victoria, 1938–48, 1950–52, 1954–68; Foundn. Pres., National Rose Soc. of Australia, 1972. *Publs:* Better Roses, 1950; Roses—Growing, Knowing and Showing Them, 1975; Growing Roses, 1983. Add: 52 Kenny St., Balwyn N., Vic. 3104, Australia.

THOMAS, Audrey (Grace). Canadian, b. 1935. Novels/Short stories, Plays/Screenplays. *Publs:* Mrs. Blood, 1967, radio play, 1975; Ten Green Bottles (short stories), 1967; Munchmeyer, and Prospero on the Island (two short novels), 1972; Songs My Mother Taught Me, 1973; Once Your Submarine Cable is Gone (radio play), 1973; Blown Figures, 1974; Ladies and Escorts (short stories), 1977; Latakia, 1979; Real Mothers, 1981; Intertidal Life, 1984. Add: 3305 W. 11th Ave., Vancouver, B.C. V6R 2J7, Canada.

THOMAS, (Antony) Charles. Also writes as Percy Trevelyan. British, b. 1928. Archaeology/Antiquities, History, Military/Defence. Prof. of Cornish Studies, Univ. of Exeter, since 1972 and Dir., Inst. of Cornish Studies, Redruth, since 1972. Ed., Cornish Studies, since 1973. Lectr. in Archaeology, Univ. of Edinburgh, 1958–67; Prof. of Archaeology, Univ. of Leicester, 1967–72. Ed., Cornish Archaeology, 1961–78. *Publs:* (ed.) Rural Settlement in Roman Britain, 1966; Christian Antiquities in Camborne, 1967; Britain and Ireland in Early Christian Times, 1971; The Early Christian Archaeology of North Britain, 1971; (ed.) The Iron Age in the Irish Sea Province, 1972; (with A. Small and D.M. Wilson) St. Ninian's Isle and Its Treasure, 2 vols., 1973; (with D.E. Ivall) Military Insignia of Cornwall, 1974; (as Percy Trevelyan) Mr. Holmes in Cornwall, 1980; Christianity in Roman Britain to A.D. 500, 1981; Exploration of a Drowned Landscape, 1985; Celtic Britain, 1986; Views and Likenesses: Early Photographers in Cornwall and Scilly, 1988. Add: Inst. of Cornish Studies, Trevithick House, Pool, Redruth, Cornwall.

THOMAS, Clara McCandless. Canadian, b. 1919. Literature, Biography. Prof. of English, York Univ., Toronto, from 1969, now Emeritus (joined faculty as Instr., 1961); Canadian Studies Research Fellow, York Univ., Toronto, since 1984. Member of Editorial Bds.: Journal of Canadian Fiction, Journal of Canadian Studies, University of Ottawa Short Stories Series, and Literary History of Canada. Faculty member, Univ. of Western Ontario, 1947–61, and Univ. of Toronto, 1958–61. *Publs:* Canadian Novelists, 1946; The Clear Spirit, 1966; Love and Work Enough: The Life of Anna Jameson, 1967; Ryerson of Upper Canada, 1969; Margaret Laurence (literary criticism), 1969; Our Nature: Our Voices, 1972; (co-author) Read Canadian, 1972; The Manawaka World of Margaret Laurence, 1975; William Arthur Deacon: A Canadian Literary Life, 1982. *Publs:* 305 Scott Library, York Univ., 4700 Keele St.,

Downsview, Toronto, Ont., Canada.

THOMAS, Craig. Also writes as David Grant. British, b. 1942. Novels, Mystery/Crime/Suspense. School teacher in Stafford, 1966–68, Lichfield, 1968–73, and Walsall, 1973–77. *Publs:* Rat Trap, 1976; Firefox, 1977; Wolfsbane, 1978; Snow Falcon, 1979; (as David Grant) Moscow 5000, 1979; (as David Grant) Emerald Decision, 1980; Sea Leopard, 1981; Jade Tiger, 1982; Firefox Down, 1983; The Bear's Tears, 1985; Winter Hawk, 1987; All the Grey Cats, 1988. Add: c/o Curtis Brown Ltd., 162-168 Regent St., London W1R 5TA, England.

THOMAS, David. British, b. 1931. Agriculture, Geography. Prof. of Geography, Univ. of Birmingham, since 1978. Lectr. and Reader, Univ. Coll., Univ. of London, 1957–70; Prof. of Geography, Univ. of Wales 1970–78. *Publs:* Agriculture in Wales During the Napoleonic Wars, 1963; London's Green Belt, 1970; (ed. and contrib.) Geography of the British Isles, 1974; Wales: A New Study, 1978; Wales: The Shaping of a Nation, 1984. Add: Sch. of Geography, Univ. of Birmingham, Birmingham, B15 2TT, England.

THOMAS, David Arthur. British, b. 1925. History. *Publs:* With Ensigns Flying, 1958; Submarine Victory, 1962; What Do You Know?, 1964; Battle of the Java Sea, 1968; Crete 1941; The Battle at Sea, 1972; Nazi Victory: Crete 1941, 1973; Japan's War at Sea, 1978; Royal Admirals, 1982; The Canning Story 1785-1985, 1985; Compton Mackenzie: A Bibliography, 1986; Companion to the Royal Navy, 1987; The Illustrated Armada Handbook, 1988; The Atlantic Star 1939-45, 1989. Add: Cedar Lodge, Sheering, Bishop's Stortford, Herts., England.

THOMAS, David H(urst). American, b. 1945. Anthropology/Ethnology, Archaeology/Antiquities. Curator, Dept. of Anthropology, American Museum of Natural History, NYC, since 1982 (Asst. Curator, 1972–76 Assoc. Curator, 1976–82); Adjunct, Curator, Dept. of Anthropology, Florida Museum of Natural History, Guinesville, since 1987. Member, Advisory Bd., Cambridge Univ. Press, Academic Press, and Journal of Quantitative Archaeology, also, Member, National Science Foundn. Panel for Archaeology. Prof., City Coll. of the City Univ. of New York, 1971–72. *Publs:* Predicting the Past: An Introduction to Anthropological Archaeology, 1974; Figuring Anthropology: First Principles of Probability and Archaeology, 1976; Archaeology, 1979, 1989; Refiguring Anthropology, 1986; St. Catherines: An Island in Time, 1988. Add: Dept. of Anthropology, American Museum of Natural History, Central Park W. at 79th St., New York, N.Y. 10024, U.S.A.

THOMAS, David St. John. British, b. 1929. Transportation, Writing/Journalism. Chmn., David & Charles PLC., since 1960. *Publs:* Trains Work Like This, 1959; Great Moments with Trains, 1960; A Regional History of the Railways of Great Britain: vol. I: The West Country, 1960, 6th ed., 1987, in paperback as West Country Railway History, 1974, 1989; The Motor Revolution, 1961; (with G. Thomas) Double Two Generations of Railway Enthusiasm, 1963; (with S. Rocksborough Smith) Summer Saturdays in the West, 1973; A Guide to Writing and Publishing (with H. Bermont, in U.S. as Getting Published), 1974; The Great Way West, 1975; The Country Railway, 1976; The Breakfast Book, 1980; (with Patrick Whitehouse) The Great Western Railway: 150 Glorious Years, 1984; (with Patrick Whitehouse) The Great Days of the Country Railway, 1986; (with Patrick Whitehouse) LMS: A Century and a Half of Progress, 1987; (with Patrick Whitehouse) LMS 150, 1988; (with Patrick Whitehouse) SR 150, 1988. Add: c/o David & Charles, Brunel House, Forde Rd., Newton Abbot, Devon TQ12 4PU, England.

THOMAS, Denis. British, b. 1922. Art, Cultural affairs, Economics. Ed., Europe, London, since 1981. Critic and Leader Writer, Associated Newspapers, 1957–61; Deputy Ed., Independent Television News, 1961–64; Ed., Economic Age, 1968–70, all London. *Publs:* Challenge in Fleet Street, 1957; (ed.) Personal Opinion, 1963; The Story of Newspapers, 1965; Thomas Churchyard of Woodbridge, 1966; The Visible Persuaders, 1967; Copyright and the Creative Artist, 1967; (ed.) Concise Encyclopedia of Antiques, 1969; (ed.) The Mind of Economic Man, 1970; Guide to English Watercolours, 1961; The Impressionists, 1974; Picasso and His Art, 1975; Abstract Painting, 1976; Battle Art, 1977; The Face of Christ, 1979; Dictionary of Fine Arts, 1981; Rowland Hilder's England, 1986; The Age of the Impressionists, 1987. Add: Coach House, Oakwood Close, Chislehurst, Kent, England.

THOMAS, D(onald) M(ichael). British, b. 1935. Novels/Short stories, Poetry. Sr. Lectr. in English, Hereford Coll. of Education, since 1964. *Publs:* (with Peter Redgrove and D.M. Black) Penguin Modern Poets II,

1968; Two Voices, 1968; (ed.) The Granite Kingdom: Poems of Cornwall, 1970; Logan Stone, 1971; The Shaft, 1973; Poetry in Crosslight, 1975; Love and Other Deaths, 1975; (trans.) Poems of Akhmatova: Requiem and Poem Without a Hero, 1975; The Honeymoon Voyage, 1978; The Flute Player (novel), 1979; Birthstone (novel), 1980; The White Hotel (novel), 1981; Dreaming in Bronze, 1981; Ararat (novel), 1983; Selected 1983; (with Sylvia Kantaris) News from the Front (poetry), 1983; Swallow (novel), 1984; Sphinx (novel), 1986; Summit, 1987; Memories and Hallucinations (memoirs), 1988. Add: The Coach House, Rashleigh Vale, Truro, Cornwall TR1 1JJ, England.

THOMAS, Edmund Barrington. Australian, b. 1929. Education. Ed. and Publisher, The Professional Reading Guide for Educational Administrators; Dir., Educational and Staff Development Services. Principal, Charlton High Sch., Victoria, 1966–67, and Heywood High Sch., Victoria, 1968–70; Lectr. in Education, 1971–72, Sr. Lectr., 1973–76, and Sub-Dean and Dean of Education, 1971–74, Univ. of Papua New Guinea; Master, Earle Page Coll., Univ. of New England, New South Wales, 1976–79; Sr. Lectr. in Educational Admin., Univ. of New England, 1976–84, and Deakin Univ., Vic., 1984–86. Publs: Lets Talk of Many Things, 1966, 4th ed., 1986–87; Papua New Guinea Education, 1977; (with W.S. Simpkins and A.R. Thomas) Principal and Task: An Australian Perspective, 1982; (with W.S. Simpkins and A.R.Thomas) Principal and Change: The Australian Experience, 1987. Add: P.O. Box 104, Point Lonsdale, Vic. 3225, Australia.

THOMAS, Gordon. British, b. 1933. History. Foreign Corresp. for the London Daily Express in Middle East, Algeria, Cyprus, Kenya, and Uganda, 1955–60; Writer, Dir., and Producer with BBC, in London, Germany, South Africa, and North Africa, 1961–69. Publs: Descent into Danger, 1954; Physician Extraordinary, 1955; Bed of Nails, 1956; Heroes of the Royal Air Force, 1956; Miracle of Surgery, 1957; The National Health Service and You, 1958; (with R.C. Hutchinson) Turn by the Window, 1959; (with Ian Hudson) The Parents Home Doctor, 1959, 4th ed. 1971; (with Max Morgan Witts) The Day the World Ended, 1965; (with M.M. Witts) Earthquake, 1966; (with M.M. Witts) Shipwreck: The Strange Fate of the Morro Castle, 1968; (with M.M. Witts) Voyage of the Damned, 1970; (with M.M. Witts) Guernica: The Crucible of World War Two, 1973; Issels: The Biography of a Doctor, 1975; (with M.M. Witts) Ruin from the Air, 1977; (with M.M. Witts) Enola Gay, 1977; (with M.M. Witts) The Day the Bubble Burst, 1979; (with M.M. Witts) Trauma, 1981; (with M.M. Witts) Pontiff, 1983; (with M.M. Witts) The Year of Armageddon, 1984; The 1985; Desire and Denial, 1986; The Trial, 1987. Add: c/o Jonathan Clowes Ltd., 22 Prince Albert Rd., London NW1 7ST, England.

THOMAS, Graham Stuart. British, b. 1909. Horticulture. Garden Consultant, National Trust, London, since 1974 (Gardens Adviser, 1955–74). Mgr. T. Hilling & Co. Ltd. Chobham, Surrey, 1931–56; Mgr. and Assoc. Dir., Sunningdale Nurseries, Surrey, 1956–71. Publs: The Old Shrub Roses, 1955; The Manual of Shrub Roses, 1957; Colour in the Winter Garden, 1957; The Modern Florilegium, 1958; Shrub Roses of Today, 1962; Climbing Roses, Old and New, 1965; Plants for Ground Cover, 1970; Perennial Garden Plants, 1976; Gardens of the National Trust, 1979; Three Gardens, 1983; Trees in the Landscape, 1983; The Art of Planting, 1984; (ed.) Recreating the Period Garden, 1984; (with others) A Garden of Roses, 1987; The Complete Flower Paintings and Drawings of Graham Stuart Thomas, 1987; The Rock Garden and Its Plants, 1989. Add: 21 Kettlewell Close, Horsell, Woking, Surrey, England.

THOMAS, Hugh. (Lord Thomas of Swynnerton). British, b. 1931. Novels, History, Biography. Chmn., Centre for Policy Studies, since 1979. Prof. of History, Univ. of Reading, 1965–75. Publs: The World's Game (novel), 1957; The Oxygen Age (novel), 1958; (ed.) The Establishment (essays), 1959; Assault at Arms (political text), 1960; The Spanish Civil War, 1961, 1977; The Story of Sandhurst, 1961; The Suez Affair, 1967; (ed.) Crisis in the Civil Service, 1968; Cuba; or, The Pursuit of Freedom, 1971; (ed.) The Selected Writings of José Antonio Primo de Rivera, 1972; Goya and the Third of May 1808 (art history), 1972; John Strachey, 1973; An Unfinished History of the World, 1979, 1982; The Case for the Round Reading Room, 1983; Havannah (novel), 1984; Armed Truce, 1986; Klara (novel), 1988; Madrid: A Traveller's Companion, 1988. Add: 29 Ladbroke Grove, London W11 3BB, England.

THOMAS, Ivor. See **BULMER-THOMAS**, Ivor.

THOMAS, (Sir) Keith (Vivian). British, b. 1933. History, Religion. Pres. of Corpus Christi Coll., Oxford, since 1986 (Fellow, All Souls Coll.,

Oxford, 1955–57; Fellow, St. John's Coll., Oxford, 1957–86; Reader, 1978–85, and Prof. of Modern History, Oxford Univ., 1986). Ed., Past Masters series, since 1979; Delegate, Oxford Univ. Press, since 1980. Joint Literary Dir., 1970–74, Member of Council, 1975–78, and Vice Pres., 1980–84, Royal Historical Soc. Publs: Religion and the Decline of Magic, 1971; Rule and Misrule in the Schools of Early Modern England, 1976; Age and Authority in Early Modern England, 1977; (co-ed.) Puritans and Revolutionaries, 1978; Man and the Natural World, 1983. Add: Corpus Christi, Oxford, England.

THOMAS, Lee. See **FLOREN**, Lee.

THOMAS, Leslie (John). British, b. 1931. Novels/Short stories, Plays/Screenplays, Travel/Exploration/Adventure, Autobiography/Memoirs/Personal. Feature writer, London Evening News, 1956–66. Publs: This Next Week, 1964; The Virgin Soldiers, 1966; Orange Wednesday, 1967; The Love Beach, 1968; Some Lovely Islands, 1968; Come to the War, 1969; His Lordship, 1970; Onward Virgin Soldiers, 1971; Arthur McCann and All His Women, 1972; The Man with The Power, 1973; Tropic of Ruislip, 1974; Stand Up Virgin Soldiers, 1975; Dangerous Davies, 1976; Ormerod's Landing, 1977; That Old Gang of Mine, 1978; The Magic Army, 1982; The Hidden Places of Britain, 1982; A World of Islands, 1983; The Dearest and the Best, 1984; In My Wildest Dreams (autobiog.), 1985; The Adventures of Goodnight and Loving, 1986; Dangerous in Love, 1987. Add: Greatbridge House, Greatbridge, Romsey, Hants., England.

THOMAS, Lewis. American, b. 1913. Biology, Sciences, Essays. Prof. of Pathology and Medicine, Cornell Univ. Medical Sch., NYC, since 1973; Adjunct Prof., Rockefeller Univ., and Consultant, Rockefeller Univ. Hosp., NYC, since 1973. Member, Bd. of Overseers, Harvard Univ., Cambridge, Mass., 1976; Member, Governing Bd., National Academy of Sciences, since 1979; Member, President's Commn. on National Agenda for the '80's, since 1980; Member, Bd. of Dirs., Foundation for the Advancement of Intnl. Research in Microbiology, since 1980. Prof. and Chmn., Dept. of Pathology, 1954–58, and Dept. of Medicine, 1958–66, New York Univ. Bellevue Medical Center; Dean, New York Univ. Sch. of Medicine, 1966–69; Prof. and Chmn., Dept. of Pathology, Yale-New Haven Medical Centre, 1969–73, and Dean, Yale Univ. Medical Sch., New Haven, Conn., 1972–73. Pres. and Chief Exec. Officer, Memorial Sloan-Kettering Cancer Center, and Attending Physician, Memorial Hosp., NYC, 1973–80. Member, Bd. of Health of the City of New York, 1955–69; Member, President's Science Advisory Cttee., 1967–70; Member, Scientific Advisory Cttee., Massachusetts Gen. Hosp., Boston, 1969–72; Chmn., Cttee. to Review the National Cancer Plan, National Academy of Sciences, 1972; Chmn., Overview Cluster, President's Biomedical Research Panel, 1976–76. Publs: Notes of a Biology Watcher: The Lives of a Cell, 1974; More Notes of a Biology-Watcher: The Medusa and the Snail, 1979; Late Thoughts on Listening to Mahler's Ninth Symphony, 1983; The Youngest Science, 1983; The Lasker Awards: Four Decades of Scientific Medical Progress, 1986. Add: 333 E. 68th St., New York, N.Y. 10021, U.S.A.

THOMAS, Paul. Indian, b. 1908. Art, Cultural/Ethnic topics, Sociology, Theology/Religion. Dir., Horizon Publrs. Ltd., Trichur, since 1969. Officer, Indian Railways, 1928–40, and Bombay Port Trust, 1941–56. Publs: Women and Marriage in India, 1939; Epics, Myths and Legends of India, 1941; Hindu Religion, Customs and Manners, 1947; Christians and Christianity in India and Pakistan, 1954; Kama Kalpa: Hindu Ritual of Love, 1956; Story of the Cultural Empire of India, 1958; Colonists and Foreign Missionaries of Ancient India, 1963; Indian Women through the Ages, 1964; Churches in India, 1964; Incredible India, 1966; March of Free India, 1968; Kama Katha: Love Tales from Indian Classics, 1969; Humour, Wit and Satire from Indian Classics, 1969; Festivals and Holidays of India, 1971; American Holiday, 1976; Secrets of Sorcery Spells and Pleasure Cults of India, 1983; The Death of a Harijan, 1984; A Syncretic History of Religion, 1988. Add: V1/359 East Fort, Trichur 680 005, Kerala, India.

THOMAS, R(onald) S(tuart). Welsh, b. 1913. Children's fiction, Poetry, Literature. Ordained Deacon, 1936, Priest, 1937; Curate of Chirk, 1936–40, and of Hanmer, 1940–42; Rector of Manafon, 1942–54; Vicar of St. Michael's Eglwysfach, 1954–67, and of St. Hywyn, Aberdaron, with St. Mary, Bodferin, 1967–78. Publs: The Stones of the Field, 1946; An Acre of Land, 1952; The Minister, 1953; Song at the Year's Turning: Poems 1942-1954, 1955; Poetry for Supper, 1958; Judgment Day, 1960; Tares, 1961; (ed.) The Batsford Book of Country Verse, 1961; (with Lawrence Durrell and Elizabeth Jennings) Penguin Modern Poets 1, 1962; The Bread of Truth, 1963; (ed.) The Penguin Book of Religious

Verse, 1963; (ed.) Selected Poems, by Edward Thomas, 1964; Words and the Poet, 1964; Pieta, 1966; (ed.) A Choice of George Herbert's Verse, 1967; Not that He Brought Flowers, 1968; (with Roy Fuller) Pergamon Poets I, 1968; Postcard: Song, The Mountains, 1968; (ed.) A Choice of Wordsworth's Verse, 1971; Young and Old, 1972; H'm: Poems, 1972; Selected Poems 1946–1968, 1973; What is a Welshman?, 1974; Laboratories of the Spirit, 1975; Frequencies, 1978; Between Here and Now, 1981; Poet's Meeting, 1983; Later Poems: A Selection, 1983; Selected Prose, 1983; The Poems of R.S. Thomas, 1985; Experimenting with an Amen, 1986; The Echoes Return Slow, 1988. Add: Sarn-y-Plas Rhiw, Pwllheli, Gwynedd, Wales.

THOMAS, Rosie. American. Historical/Romance. *Publs:* Love's Choice, 1982; Celebration, 1982; Follies, 1983; Sunrise, 1984; The White Dove, 1986; Strangers, 1987; Bad Girls, Good Women, 1989. Add: c/o Bantam Publishing, 666 Fifth Ave., New York, N.Y. 10103, U.S.A.

THOMAS, Ross. Also writes as Oliver Bleeck. American, b. 1926. Novels/Short stories, Mystery/Crime/Suspense. *Publs:* The Cold War Swap, 1966; The Seersucker Whipsaw, 1967; Cast a Yellow Shadow, 1967; The Singapore Wink, 1968; The Fools in Town Are on Our Side, 1970; (as Oliver Bleeck) The Brass Go-Between, 1969; (as Oliver Bleeck) Protocol fora Kidnapping, 1971; The Backup Men, 1971; (as Oliver Bleeck) The Procane Chronicle (in U.K. as The Thief Who Painted Sunlight), 1972; The Porkchoppers, 1972; If You Can't be Good, 1973; (as Oliver Bleeck) The Highbinders, 1974; The Money Harvest, 1975; (as Oliver Bleeck) No Questions Asked, 1976; Yellow-Dog Contract, 1977; Chinaman's Chance, 1978; The Eighth Dwarf, 1979; The Mordida Man, 1981; Missionary Stew, 1983; Briarpatch, 1984; Out on the Rim, 1987. Add: 3947 Rambla Orienta, Malibu, Calif. 90265, U.S.A.

THOMAS, Ted. (Theodore L. Thomas). American, b. 1920. Science fiction. Patent lawyer, with Armstrong Cork Co., Lancaster, Pa., since 1955 (formerly practiced in Washington, D.C.). Columnist, Advocate, Stamford, Conn., 1949–79, and Fantasy and Science Fiction, NYV, 1964–67. *Publs:* (with Kate Wilhelm) The Clone, 1965; (with Kate Wilhelm) Year of the Cloud, 1970. Add: 1284 Wheatland Ave., Lancaster, Pa. 17603, U.S.A.

THOMAS, Vaughan. British, b. 1934. Sports/Fitness. Head, Dept. of Sport and Recreation Studies, Liverpool since 1971. Secty., Soc. of Sports Sciences. Lectr., Loughborough Technical Coll., 1966–68, and St. Mary's Coll., Inst. of Education, London Univ., 1968–71. England Basketball National Team Coach, 1962–63, and 1968–70, and Welsh Basketball National Team Coach, 1964–68; Hon. Adviser in Fitness Training, Badminton Assn. of England, 1970. *Publs:* Science and Sport, 1970; Basketball: Techniques and Tactics, 1972; Physiology of Exercise, 1975; Better Physical Fitness, 1979; Book of Fitness and Exercise, 1981. Add: Dept. of Sport and Recreation Studies, Liverpool Polytechnic, Byrom St., Liverpool, England.

THOMAS, Victoria. *See* DeWEESE, Gene.

THOMEY, Tedd. American, b. 1920. Mystery/Crime/Suspense, Cultural/Ethnic topics, Biography. Entertainment Columnist, Press-Telegram, Long Beach, Calif., since 1950. *Publs:* And Dream of Evil, 1954; Jet Pilot, 1954; Killer in White, 1956; Jet Ace, 1958; I Want Out, 1959; (with F. Aadland) The Big Love (biography), 1961; Flight to Takla-Ma, 1961; The Loves of Errol Flynn, 1961; The Sadist, 1961; Doris Day, 1962; All the Way, 1964; (with P. Hirsch) Hollywood Uncensored, 1965; (with P. Hirsch) Hollywood Confidential, 1967; (with Ed McBain) Crime Squad, 1968; (with N. Wilner) The Comedians, 1970; The Glorious Decade, 1971; The Prodigy Pilot, 1987; The Big Love (play), 1988. Add: 7228 Rosebay St., Long Beach, Calif. 90808, U.S.A.

THOMPSON, Brenda. British, b. 1935. Children's non-fiction, Education. Clinical Biochemist, 1957–60; Teacher, Flora Gardens Primary, 1964; Thornhill Primary, 1964–66, and Pooles Park Primary, 1966–71; Head Teacher, Northwold Sch., 1971–78, and Stamford Hill Primary Sch., 1978–81. Member, Press Council, 1973–74. *Publs:* Learning to Read, 1970; Learning to Teach, 1973; Volcanos, 1974; Under the Sea, 1974; Pirates, 1974; (ed.) Where Am I, 1974; The Pre-School Book, 1976; Reading Success, 1979. Add: Nantddu, Rhandirmwyn, Dyfed SA20 0NG, Wales.

THOMPSON, Donald Neil. Canadian, b. 1939.Economics, Marketing. Prof. of Admin. Studies, York Univ., Toronto, since 1971.Principal, Donald N. Thompson & Assoc., Economic Consultants, Toronto.Sr. Fellow, Harvard Law Sch., Cambridge, Mass., 1970–71; Visiting Prof., Lon-

don Sch. of Economics, 1977–78. *bPubls:* b Franchise Operations and Antitrust, 1971; (ed.) Contractual Marketing Systems, 1971; The Economics of Environmental Protection, 1973; Canadian Marketing: Problems and Prospects, 1973; Problems in Canadian Marketing, 1976; Conglomerate Mergers, 1978; (ed.) Macromarketing, 1979.Add: Faculty of Administrative Studies, York Univ., Toronto M3J 1P3, Canada.

THOMPSON, E(rnest) V(ictor). British, b. 1931. Historical/Romance, Travel/Exploration. *Publs:* historical/romance novels—Chase the Wind, 1977; Harvest of the Sun, 1978; The Music Makers, 1979; Ben Retallick, 1980; The Dream Traders, 1981; Singing Spears, 1982; The Restless Sea, 1983; Cry Once Alone, 1984, in U.S. as Republic, 1985; Polrudden, 1985; The Stricken Land, 1986; Becky, 1988; God's Highlander, 1989; other—Discovering Bodmin Moor, 1980; Discovering Corwall's South Coast, 1982; Sea Stories of Devon, 1984; E.V. Thompson's West Country, 1986. Add: c/o Macmillan Publishers Ltd., 4 Little Essex St., London WC2R 3IF, England.

THOMPSON, Francis George. Scottish, b. 1931. Engineering/Technology, Geography, Paranormal. Lectr., Lews Castle Coll., Scotland. Co-ed., Sruth Newspaper, Inverness, 1966–70. *Publs:* Electrical Installation and Workshop Technology, 3 vols., 1968–69, 1987; Harris Tweed, 1969; St. Kilda and Other Hebridean Outliers, 1970; The Ghosts, Spirits and Spectres of Scotland, 1973; (ed.) Highland Ways, and Byways, 1973; The Uists and Barra, 1974; The Highlands and Islands of Scotland, 1974; Victorian and Edwardian Highlands and Islands, 1976; Murder-Mystery in the Highlands, 1978; A Scottish Bestiary, 1978; Portrait of the River Spey, 1979; The National Mod, 1979; Crofting Years, 1984; Shell Guide to Northern Scotland and the Islands, 1987; Harris and Lewis, 1987; The Western Isles, 1988. Add: Rathad na Muilne, Stornoway, Isle of Lewis PA87 2TZ, Scotland.

THOMPSON, Gene. *See* LUTZ, Giles A.

THOMPSON, Ian Bently. British, b. 1936. Economics, Geography. Prof. in Geography, Glasgow Univ., since 1976. Asst. Lectr., Leeds Univ., 1959–62; Sr. Lectr. in Geography, Southampton Univ., 1962–76. *Publs:* The St. Malo Region, Brittany, 1968; Modern France: A Social and Economic Geography, 1970; Corsica, 1971; The Paris Basin, 1973, 1982; La France: Population Economie et Regions, 1973; (ed. and trans.) France: A Geographical Study, by Pierre George, 1973; The Lower Rhone and Marseille, 1974. Add: Dept. of Geography, Univ. of Glasgow, Glasgow G12 8QQ, Scotland.

THOMPSON, James. British, b. 1932. Librarianship. Librarian, Univ. of Birmingham, since 1987. Deputy Librarian, Univ. of Glasgow, 1965–67; Univ. Librarian, Univ. of Reading, 1967–87. *Publs:* The Librarian and English literature, 1968; Books: An Anthology, 1968; An Introduction to University Library Administration, 1970, 4th ed. (with R.P. Carr) 1987; English Studies: A Guide for Librarians to the Sources and Their Organisation, 1971; Library Power: A New Philosophy of Librarianship, 1974; A History of the Principles of Librarianship, 1977; (ed.) University Library History, 1980; The End of Libraries, 1982. Add: The Library, Univ. of Birmingham, Birmingham B15 2TT, England.

THOMPSON, Kenneth W(infred). American, b. 1921. International relations/Current affairs, Philosophy. Commonwealth Prof. of Govt. and Foreign Affairs, Univ. of Virginia, Charlottesville, since 1975. Vice-Pres., The Rockefeller Foundn., NYC, 1961–73. *Publs:* Christian Ethics and the Dilemmas of Foreign Policy, 1959; Political Realism and the Crisis of World Politics, 1960; American Diplomacy and Emergent Patterns, 1962; Moral Issue in Statecraft, 1966; Foreign Assistance: A View from the Private Sector, 1972; Understanding World Politics, 1975; Higher Education and Social Change, 2 vols., 1976–77; Interpreters and Critics of the Cold War, 1978; Foreign Policy and the Democratic Process, 1978; Ethics, Functionalism and Power, 1979; Masters of International Thought, 1980; Morality and Foreign Policy, 1980; Portraits of American Presidents: F.D.R. Through Carter, vols. I-VII, 1982–89; The Presidency and the Public Philosophy; Cold War Theories, 1943-53, vol. I; Winston Churchill's World View: Statesmanship and Power; Toynbee's Philosophy of World History and Politics, 1985; Moralism and Morality in Politics and Diplomacy, 1985; (ed.) Arms Control and National Security, vols. I-XV, 1986–89;Theory and Practice in International Relations, 1987. Add: Woodrow Wilson Dept. of Govt. and Foreign Affairs, Univ. of Virginia, Charlottesville, Va. 22901, U.S.A.

THOMPSON, Laurence Graham. American, b. 1920. Anthropology/Ethnology, History, Philosophy, Theology/Religion. Prof. of East Asian Languages and Cultures, Univ. of Southern California, Los Angeles,

1965–86, now Emeritus. U.S. Foreign Service Staff Officer, various Asian assignments, 1951–56; Rep., Asia Foundn., Korea and Taiwan, 1956–59; Prof. of Music, Taiwan Normal Univ., 1959–62; Asst. Prof. of Chinese Language and Literature, Pomona Coll., Calif., 1962–65. *Publs:* (trans.) Fifty Years of Chinese Philosophy, 1898-1950, 1956, 1965; (trans.) Ta T'ung Shu: The One-World Philosophy of K'ang Yu-Wei, 1958; Chinese Religion: An Introduction, 1969, 3rd ed. 1979; (ed.) The Chinese Way in Religion, 1973; (ed.) Studia Asiatica: Essays in Felicitation of the Seventy-Fifth Anniversary of Professor Ch'en Shou-Yi, 1974; (compiler) Studies of Chinese Religion: A Comprehensive and Classified Bibliography of Publications in English, French, and German Through 1970, 1975; Chinese Religions in Western Languages, 1976. Add: 5515 Medea Valley Dr., Agoura, Calif. 91301, U.S.A.

THOMPSON, Mervyn (Garfield). New Zealander, b. 1936. Plays, Autobiography. Lectr., Univ. of Canterbury, Christchurch, 1966–71; Co-Dir., Court Theatre, Christchurch, 1971–74; Artistic Dir., Downstage Theatre, Wellington, 1975–76; Sr. lectr. in Drama, Univ. of Auckland, 1977–86. *Publs:* plays—O! Temperance!, 1974; First Return, 1974; (with Y.B. Edwards) A Night at the Races, 1981; Songs to Uncle Scrim, 1983; Songs to the Judges, 1983; Coaltown Blues, 1986; autobiography—All My Lives, 1980. Add: c/o Playmarket, P.O. Box 9767, Wellington, New Zealand.

THOMPSON, Neil. Australian, b. 1929. Novels/Short stories, Cookery/ Gastronomy/Wine, Travel/Exploration/Adventure. Lectr. in English, Sturt Coll. of Advanced Education, since 1968 (joined staff in 1957). *Publs:* Shadow on the Sea, 1965; Ride the Hurricane In, 1966; The Elliston Incident, 1967; Storm North, 1968; Southern Backwash, 1969; Ask the Wind—Ask the Sea, 1970; Cocas Deadline, 1971; Written Communication, 1971; Hiri, 1975; Colour and Chaos, 1976; Write Now, 1981; Cruising Gulfs Log (travel guide), 1984; (with Val Thompson) Meg Merrilees Seafoods, 1984. Add: 44 Marlborough St., Brighton 5048, S. Australia.

THOMPSON, (Sir) Robert (Grainger Ker). British, b. 1916. Military/ Defence, Politics/Government. With Malayan Civil Service, 1938–61; served in the R.A.F., 1939–46; Head, British Advisory Mission, Vietnam, 1961–65. *Publs:* Defeating Communist Insurgency, 1966; The Royal Flying Corps, 1968; No Exit from Vietnam, 1969; Revolutionary War in World Strategy, 1970; Peace is Not at Hand, 1974; Make for the Hills, 1989. Add: Pitcott House, Winsford, Minehead, Somerset, England.

THOMPSON, Robert Bruce. New Zealander, b. 1920. Poetry. Retired Industrial Chemist. Sch. Master, 1952–62; Ed., Image mag., Press, Auckland, 1958–61. *Publs:* Cast on the Doting Sea, 1955; (co-ed.) Poems by Several Hands, 1976; Northern Aspects, 1976. Add: Taumarere, Bay of Islands, Northland, New Zealand.

THOMPSON, Robert Norman. Canadian, b. 1914. Economics, Politics/Government. Prof. of Political Science, Trinity Western Univ., Langley, B.C., since 1972 (Chmn., Bd. of Govs., 1968–72). Freelance writer and columnist since 1970. Ed., Freeman Report, Vanguard Inst., since 1978. Prof. of Political Science, Wilfred Laurier Univ., Waterloo, Ont., 1967–72. Fellow. Canadian Guild of Arthors. *Publs:* Canadians, It's Time You Knew, 1962; Commonsense for Canadians, 1967; (with Terrance Norr) Social Economics, 1979; A Voice from the Market Place, 1979; (with Cleon Skousen) A Model Constitution for Canada, 1982; Liberation: The First to Be Freed, 1987. Add: Box 430, Fort Langley, B.C. V0X 1J0, Canada.

THOMPSON, Roger Francis. British, b. 1933. History, Social commentary/phenomena. Reader in American History, Univ. of East Anglia, Norwich, since 1976 (Sr. Lectr., 1969–76). History Master, Eton Coll., Berks., 1957–67. *Publs:* The Golden Door: A History of the U.S.A., 1969; Women in Stuart England and America, 1974; (co-ed.) Contrast and Connection: Bicentennial Essays in Anglo-American History, 1976; (ed.) Samuel Pepys' Penny Merriments, 1976; Unfit for Modest Ears, 1979; The Witches of Salem, 1982; Sex in Middlesex, 1986. Add: 32 Cambridge St., Norwich NR2, 3BB, England.

THOMPSON, Thomas. American, b. 1913. Western/Adventure. Freelance writer since 1940. Former sailor, nightclub entertainer, secty., and furniture salesman, Co-Founder and Pres., 1957, 166, Western Writers of America. *Publs:* Range Drifter, 1949; Broken Valley, 1949; Sundown Riders, 1959; Gunman Brand, 1951; Shadow of the Butte, 1952; The Steel Web, 1953; King of Abilene, 1953; Trouble Rider, 1954; They Brought Their Guns (short stories), 1954; Forbidden Valley, 1955; Born to 1956; Rawhide Rider, 1957, in U.K. as Gun of the Stranger, 1960; Brand of

a Man, 1958; Bitter Water, 1960; Moment of Glory, 1961; Bonanza: One Man with Courage (novelization of TV series), 1966; Outlaw Valley, 1987. Add: 207 Third St., Newbury Park, Calif. 91320, U.S.A.

THOMPSON, Vivian L. American, b. 1911. Children's fiction. *Publs:* Camp-in-the-Yard, 1961; The Horse That Liked Sandwiches, 1962; Sad Day, Glad Day, 1962; Kimo Makes Music, 1962; Ah See and The Spooky House, 1963; Faraway Friends, 1963; George Washington, 1964; Hawaiian Myths of Earth, Sea, and Sky, 1966; Keola's Hawaiian Donkey, 1966, as play 1982; Meet the Hawaiian Menehunes, 1967; Hawaiian Legends of Tricksters and Riddlers, 1969; Maui-Full-of-Tricks, 1970; Hawaiian Tales of Heroes and Champions, 1971; Aukele the Fearless, 1972; The Protected One, 1981; Neat! Said Jeremy (play), 1982; The Scary Thing-Snatcher (play), 1982; Keola's Hawaiian Donkey (play), 1982; Hawaiian Tales of Heroes and Champions, 1987; Hawaiian Myths of Earth, Sea, and Sky, 1988. Add: 936 Kumukoa St., Hilo, Hawaii 96720, U.S.A.

THOMPSON, William B(ernard). British, b. 1914. Classics, Education. Hon. Fellow in Education about Europe, Univ. of Durham, since 1980. Head of Classics, King Edward VI Sch., Southampton, 1949–56; Sr. Lectr. in Education, Univ. of Leeds, 1956–79. *Publs:* Greece and Rome on Postage Stamps, 1947; Classical Novels, 1966, addenda 1975; (with J.D. Ridge) Catalogue of the National Collection of Greek and Latin School Text Books, 2 parts, 1970–74; European Studies 1983; (ed.) The Cultural Dimension in Education about Europe, 1984; (with D.A. McMurtrie) Eurotrails in the North East of England, 1985. Add: Sch. of Education, The Univ., Leeds LS2 9JT, England.

THOMPSON, William David. American, b. 1929. Theology/Religion. Prof. of Preaching, Eastern Baptist Theological Seminary, Philadelphia, since 1962, now retired; Minister, First Baptist Church of Philadelphia. Pres., American Academy of Homiletics. Former Assoc. Prof. of Homiletics, Northern Baptist Seminary, Chicago, Ill. *Publs:* A Listener's Guide to Preaching, 1966; (ed. with W. Toohey) Recent Homiletical Thought: A Bibliography, 1935-64, 1967; (co-author) Dialogue Preaching, 1969; (ed.) Abingdon Preacher's Library, 12 vols., 1980–81; Preaching Biblically, 1981; Listening on Sunday, 1983; Philadelphia's First Baptists, 1989. Add: 765 Ormond Ave., Drexel Hill, Pa. 19026, U.S.A.

THOMPSON, William Irwin. American, b. 1938. History, Essays. Chmn. of Bd. of Dirs., Lindisfarne Assn., NYC, since 1972 (Founder and Dir., 1972–81). Member, Editorial Bd., Main Currents in Modern Thought, New Rochelle, N.Y., since 1972. Instr. of Humanities, 1965–66, and Assoc. Prof. of Humanities, 1966–68, Massachusetts Inst. of Technology, Cambridge; Assoc. Prof. of Humanities, 1968–72, and Prof. of Humanities, 1972–79, York Univ., Toronto. *Publs:* The Imagination of an Insurrection: Dublin, Easter 1916, 1967; At the Edge of History, 1971; Passages about Earth: An Exploration of the New Planetary Culture, 1974; Evil and World Order, 1976; Darkness and Scattered Light, 1978; The Time Falling Bodies Take to Light, 1981; From Nation to Emanation, 1981; Islands Out of Time, 1985; Pacific Shift, 1986. Add: c/o Sierra Books, P.O. Box 5853, Pasadena, Calif. 91107, U.S.A.

THOMSON, D(aisy) H(icks). Also writes short stories for magazines and radio as Jonathan H. Thomson. British, b. 1918. Novels/Short stories. Asst. Welfare Officer, Bute County Council, and Asst. Registrar of Births, Rothesay, 1939–45. *Publs:* Prelude to Love, 1963; To Love and Honour, 1964; Jealous Love, 1964; Portrait of My Love, 196; Love for a Stranger, 1966; A Truce for Love, 1967; Be Love Betrayed, 1967; Journey to Love, 1967; Be My Love, 1968; My Only Love, 1969; The Italian for Love, 1970; Summons to Love, 1971; Woman in Love, 1973; Hello My Love, 1974; The Beginning of Love, 1975; The Summer of Love, 1976; My One and Only Love, 1976; From Solitude with Love, 1976; The Voice of Love, 1977; Myrtle for My Love, 1977; A Time for Love, 1977; In Love, in Vienna, 1978; Suddenly It Was Love, 1978; A Nightingale for Love, 1978; Love at Leisure, 1979; The Face of Love, 1979; The Web of Love, 1979; The Island of Love, 1980; I Love Your Julie, 1980; To Love and Be Wise, 1980; The Eve of Love, 1981; The Talisman of Love, 1982; Kiss Your Love Again, 1983; Inheritance of Love, 1983; The Colour of Love, 1983; Champagne for My Love, 1984; Quicksands of Love, 1984; Never Doubt My Love, 1985. Add: 28 Clover Ct., Church Rd., Haywards Health RH16 3UP, England.

THOMSON, Derick S(mith). Also writes in Gaelic as Ruaraidh MacThomais. British, b. 1921. Poetry, Literature. Prof. of Celtic, Univ. of Glasgow, since 1963 (Lectr. in Welsh, 1949–56). Ed., Gairm Quarterly since 1952; Pres., Scottish Gaelic Texts Soc., since 1964; Chmn., Gaelic Books Council, since 1969. Reader in Celtic, Univ. of Aberdeen, 1957–

63; Ed., Scottish Gaelic Studies, 1961–75. Member, Scottish Arts Council, 1975–77. *Publs:* (as Ruaraidh MacThomais) An Dealbh Briste, 1951; The Gaelic Sources of MacPherson's Ossian, 1952; Branwen Uerch Lyr, 1961; (with J.L. Campbell) Edward Lhuyd in the Scottish Highlands, 1699-1700, 1963; (as Ruaraidh MacThomais) Eadar Samhradh is Foghar, 1967; (with I. Grimble) The Future of the Highlands, 1968; (as Ruaraidh MacThomais) An Rathad Cian, 1970; The Far Road and Other Poems, 1971; An Introduction to Gaelic Poetry, 1974; The New Verse in Gaelic: A Structural Analysis, 1974; Ossian Prize, 1974; (as Ruaraidh MacThomais) Saorsa Agus an Iolaire, 1977; The New English-Gaelic Dictionary, 1980; Creachadh ma Clarsaich, 1982; Companion to Gaelic Scotland, 1983; Why Gaelic Matters, 1986. Add: c/o Blackwell, 108 Cowley Rd., Oxford OX2 0EL, England.

THOMSON, Edward. *See* **TUBB**, E.C.

THOMSON, Francis Paul. Scottish, b. 1914. Art, Finance, Biography. Consultant on Post office and Bank Giro Systems, since 1968. Initiator and Organiser, British Giro Banking Reform, 1946–65. *Publs:* Postal Cheques are Your Business, 1946; Giro—Europe's Wonder Bank, 1951; Giro Credit Transfer Systems, 1964; Money in the Computer Age, 1968; Banking Automation, 1971; (ed. with E.S. Thomson) History of Tapestry, by W.G. Thomson, 1973; Tapestry: Mirror of History, 1979; Home and Family Databook, 1979; The Sussex Tapestry, 1986; The Making of a Genius, 1987. Add: The Town House, Church Rd., Watford WD1 3PY, England.

THOMSON, George Henry. Canadian, b. 1924. Literature. Prof. of English Literature, Univ. of Ottawa, since 1969, retired 1990. Lectr., Asst. Prof., and Assoc. Prof., Mount Allison Univ., Sackville, N.B., 1953–66. *Publs:* The Fiction of E.M. Forster, 1967; (ed.) Albergo Empedocle and Other by E.M. Forster: Uncollected Writings, 1900-1915, 1971. Add: 655 Echo Dr., Ottawa, Ont., Canada.

THOMSON, George Malcolm. British, b. 1899. Novels/Short stories, History. Former Leader writer, Beaverbrook Press, London. *Publs:* Caledonia, or The Future of the Scots, 1927; A Short History of Scotland, 1930; Crisis in Zanat, 1942; The Twelve Days, 1964; The Crime of Mary Stuart, 1967; Vote of Censure, 1968; The Robbers Passing By, 1968; A Kind of Justice, 1970; Sir Francis Drake, 1972; The North-West Passage, 1975; Warrior Prince, 1976; The First Churchill, John, Duke of Marlborough, 1979; The Ball at Glenkerran, 1982; Kronstadt '21. Add: 5 The Mount Sq., London NW3 6SY, England.

THOMSON, James Miln. Australian, b. 1921. Marine science/Oceanography, Zoology. Prof. of Zoology, Univ. of Queensland, St. Lucia, since 1968 (Sr. Lectr., 1965–66; Reader, 1967–68; Pro-Vice-Chancellor, 1983–85). Deputy Vice-Chancellor, Northern Territory Univ., since 1989. Research Officer, 1945–53, Sr. Research Officer, 1953–57, and Principal Research Officer, 1957–63, Commonwealth Scientific and Industrial Research Org. Warden. Univ. Coll. of the Northern Territory, 1986–88. *Publs:* The Great Barrier Reef, 1966; (co-author) Zoology for Senior Forms, 1967; Fish of Ocean and Shore, 1974; A Field to the Common Sea and Estuarine Fishes of Non-Tropical Australia, 1977. Add: 28 Raffles Plaza, 1 Buffalo Ct., Darwin, N.T. 5790, Australia.

THOMSON, Jonathan H. *See* **THOMSON**, D.H.

THOMSON, June. British, b. 1930. Mystery/Crime/Suspense. *Publs:* Not One of Us, 1971; Death Cap, 1973; The Long Revenge, 1974; Case Closed, 1977; A Question of Identity, 1977; Deadly Relations (in U.S. as The Habit of Loving), 1979; Alibi in Time, 1980; Shadow of a Doubt, 1981; To Make a Killing, 1982, in U.S. as Portrait of Lilith, 1983; Sound Evidence, 1984; A Dying Fall, 1985; The Dark Stream, 1986; No Flowers by Request, 1987; Rosemary for Remembrance, 1988; The Spoils of Time, 1989. Add: c/o Constable, 10 Orange St., London WC2H 7EG, England.

THOMSON, Peter (William). British, b. 1938. Literature, Theatre. Prof. of Drama, Univ. of Exeter, since 1974. Trustee, Open Cast Theatre Co., since 1974; Chmn., Medium Fair Charitable Trust, since 1975; Colway Theatre Trust, since 1980, and Combined Arts Panel of South West Arts, since 1980. Lectr. in Drama, Univ. of Manchester, 1964–71, and Univ. of Wales, 1971–74. Member, Arts Council Community Arts Cttee., 1978–80. *Publs:* (ed.) Julius Caesar, 1968; (ed. with Kenneth Richards) Nineteenth Century British Theatre, 1970; (ed. with Kenneth Richards) The Eighteenth Century English Stage, 1971; (with Clive Goodhead) Ideas in Action, 1973; (with Jan Needle) Bertolt Brecht, 1980; Shakespeare's Theatre, 1983; (with Gamini Salgado) The Everyman Com-

panion to the Theatre, 1985; (ed.) Plays, by Dion Boucicault, 1985. Add: Dept. of Drama, Univ. of Exeter, Exeter, Devon, England.

THOMSON, Robert. British, b. 1921. Intellectual history, Psychology. Sr. Lectr. in Psychology, Univ. of Leicester, since 1964. Censor, Sr. Tutor, and Lectr. in Psychology, Univ. of Durham, 1949–64. *Publs:* The Psychology of Thinking, 1959; The Pelican History of Psychology, 1968; (with W. Sluckin) Fear in Animals and Man, 1979; (with others) Introducing Psychology, 1982. Add: Dept. of Psychology, Univ. of Leicester, Leicester, England.

THORELLI, Hans B. American, b. 1921. Administration/Management, Business/Trade/Industry. E.W. Kelley Prof. of Business Admin., Indiana Univ., Bloomington, since 1972 (Prof. 1964–72; Chmn., Marketing Dept., 1966–69). Member Advisory Bd., Industrial Marketing Mgmt., Journal of International Business, and Journal of Consumer Policy. Staff member, Corporate Marketing Services, Gen. Electric, NYC, 1956–59; Prof., Grad. Sch. of Business, Univ. of Chicago, 1959–64; Prof., Intnl. Mgmt. Development Inst., Lausanne Univ., Switzerland, 1964–65; Visiting Prof., London Grad. Sch. of Business, 1969–70. *Publs:* The Federal Antitrust Policy: Origination of an American Tradition, 1954; (co-author) The International Operations Simulation: With Comments on Design and Use of Management Games, 1964; (ed. and co-author) International Marketing Strategy, 1973, 1980; (co-author) Consumer Information Handbook: Europe and North America, 1974; (co-author) The Information Seekers: An International Study of Consumer Information and Advertising Image, 1975; (co-author) Consumer Information Systems and Consumer Policy, 1977; (ed. and co-author) Strategy Q Structure R Performance, 1977; (co-author) Consumer Emancipation and Economic Development: The Case of Thailand, 1982. Add: Sch. of Business, Indiana Univ., Bloomington, Ind. 47405, U.S.A.

THORNDIKE, John. American, b. 1942. Novels. *Publs:* Anna Delaney's Child, 1986; The Potato Baron, 1989. Add: 437 University Ave., Boulder, Colo. 80302, U.S.A.

THORNDIKE, Joseph J(acobs, Jr.). American, b. 1913. Social commentary/phenomena. Pres., Thorndike, Jensen and Partin Inc.; Ed.-in-Chief, American Heritage Publishing Co.; Vice Pres., Unitarian Publishing Co. Asst. Ed., Time Mag., 1934–36; Assoc. Ed., 1936–46, and Managing Ed., 1946–49, Life Mag. *Publs:* The Very Rich, 1976; The Magnificent Builders, 1978; (ed.) Three Centuries of American Architects, 1981. Add: c/o Crown Publishers, 225 Park Ave., New York, N.Y. 10003, U.S.A.

THORNE, Christopher (Guy). British, b. 1934. History, International relations/Current affairs. Prof. of Intnl. Relations, Univ. of Sussex, Brighton, since 1976 (Reader, 1968–76). Head of Further Education, BBC Radio, London, 1966–68. *Publs:* Ideology and Power, 1965; Chartism, 1966; The Approach of War 1938-39, 1967; The Limits of Foreign Policy: The West, the League and the Far Eastern Crisis of 1931-1933, 1972; Allies of a Kind: The United States, Britain, and the War Against Japan 1941-1945, 1978; The Issue of War: States, Societies and the Far Eastern Conflict of 1941-1945, 1985, in Paperbook as The Far Eastern War, 1987; American Political Culture and the Asian Frontier 1941-1973, 1988; Border Crossings: Studies in International History, 1988. Add: Sch. of European Studies, Univ. of Sussex, Brighton, Sussex BN1 9QN, England.

THORNE, Nicola. *See* **ELLERBECK**, Rosemary.

THORNTON, John Leonard. British, b. 1913. Librarianship, Medicine/Health, Biography. Library Asst., Univ. Coll., London, 1929–34, and Wellcome Historical Medical Library, 1934–37; Librarian, St. Bartholomew's Hosp. Medical Coll., 1938–78; Consultant Librarian, Royal Coll. of Obstetricians and Gynaecologists, 1961–80. *Publs:* Cataloguing in Special Libraries, 1938; Special Library Methods, 1940; Chronology of Librarianship, 1941; Mirror for Librarians, 1948; Medical Books, Libraries and Collectors, 1949, 1966; John Abernethy, 1953; (with R.I.J. Tully) Scientific Books, Libraries and Collectors, 1954, 3rd ed. 1971, Supplement 1969-75, 1978; Classics of Librarianship, 1957; (with A. Monk and E. Brooke) Select Bibliography of Medical Biography, 1961, 1970; Medical Librarianship, 1963; Selected Readings in the History of Librarianship, 1966; (ed. with V.C. Medvei) The Royal Hospital of Saint Bartholomew 1974; Jan Van Rymsdyk, 1982; (with C. Reeves) Medical Book Illustration, 1983. Add: 120 Grasmere Ave., Wembley, Middx. HA9 8TQ, England.

THORNTON, Michael. British, b. 1941. Biography. Special Features Writer, Sunday Express, London, 1969–76 (Film and Drama Critic, 1964–67). Show Business Ed., What's On in London, 1976–77. Special Features Writer, Daily Express, London, 1982, and Evening Standard, London, 1989. Contrib., The Times, London, The Stage, etc. *Publs:* (contrib.) Gilbert Harding by His Friends, 1961; Jessie Matthews, 1974; Forget Not, 1975; (with Margaret, Duchess of Argyll) Royal Feud: The Queen Mother and the Duchess of Windsor, 1985; Argyll Verses Argylle, 1989. Add: Dinah Wiener Ltd., 27 Arlington Rd., London NW1 7ER, England.

THORP, Roderick. American, b. 1936. Novels/Short stories, Sociology. Assoc. Prof. of Literature, Ramapo Coll., N.J., 1971–76. *Publs:* Into the Forest, 1961; The Detective, 1966; Dionysus, 1969; (with Robert Blake) The Music of Their Laughter, 1970; (with Robert Blake) Wives, 1971; Slaves, 1972; The Circle of Love, 1974; Westfield, 1977; Nothing Lasts Forever, 1979; Jenny and Barnum, 1982; Rainbow Drive, 1986. Add: c/o Raines & Raines, 71 Park Ave., New York, N.Y. 10016, U.S.A.

THORPE, James. American, b. 1915. Literature. Sr. Research Assoc., Huntington Library, San Marino, since 1966 (Dir., Huntington Library, Art Gallery and Botanical Gardens, 1966–83). Member, American Philosophical Soc., since 1982. Prof. of English, Princeton Univ., N.J., 1946–66. Member, Cttee. on Research Activities, Modern Language Assn., 1950–73; Trustee, Kent Sch., 1952–59; Member, Fulbright Selection Advisory Cttee., 1964–66, and Henry Francis DuPont Winterthur Advisory Cttee., 1967–71. *Publs:* Bibliography of the Writings of George Lyman Kittredge, 1948; (ed.) Rochester's Poems, 1950; (ed.) Milton Criticism, 1950; (ed.) Poems of Sir George Etherege, 1963; Literary Scholarship, 1964; (ed.) Aims and Methods of Scholarship, 1963, 3rd ed. 1971; (ed.) Relations of Literary Study, 1967; (ed.) Bunyan's Pilgrim's Progress, 1969; Principles of Textual Criticism, 1972, 1979; Use of Manuscripts in Literary Research, 1974, 1979; Gifts of Genius, 1980; the Scenes, 1980; A Word to the Wise, 1982; John Milton: The Inner Life, 1983; The Sense of Style: Reading English Prose, 1987. Add: Huntington Library, San Marino, Calif. 91108, U.S.A.

THORPE, Kay. Historical/Romance/Gothic. *Publs:* Devon Interlude, 1968; The Last of the Mallorys, 1968; Opportune Marriage, 1968; Rising Star, 1969; Curtain Call, 1971; Not Wanted on Voyage, 1972; Olive Island, 1972; Sawdust Season, 1972; Man in a Box, 1972; An Apple in Eden, 1973; The Man at Kambala, 1973; Remember This Stranger, 1974; The Iron Man, 1974; The Shifting Sands, 1975; Sugar Cane Harvest, 1975; The Royal Affair, 1976; Safari South, 1976; The River Lord, 1977; Storm Passage, 1977; Lord of La Pampa, 1977; Bitter Alliance, 1978; Full Circle, 1978; Timber Boss, 1978; The Wilderness Trail, 1978; Caribbean Encounter, 1978; The Dividing Line, 1979; The Man from Tripoli, 1979; This Side of Paradise, 1979; Chance Meeting, 1980; No Passing Fancy, 1980; Copper Lake, 1981; Floodtide, 1981; The New Owner, 1982; A Man of Means, 1982; The Land of the Incas, 1983; Never Trust a Stranger, 1983; Master of Morley, 1983; The Inheritance, 1984; Temporary Marriage, 1984; South Seas Affair, 1985; Dangerous Moonlight, 1985; Double Deception, 1985; Jungle Island, 1986; Win or Lose, 1986; Jungle Island, 1986; Time Out of Mind, 1987; Land of Illusion, 1988; Tokyo Tryst, 1988. Add: c/o Mills and Boon Ltd., 15–16 Brooks Mews, London W1A 1DR, England.

THORPE, Sylvia. Pseud. for June Sylvia Thimblethorpe. British, b. 1926. Historical/Romance/Gothic. Former secty., and teacher. *Publs:* The Scandalous Lady Robin, 1950; The Sword and the Shadow, 1951; Beggar on Horseback, 1953; Smugglers' Moon, 1955, in U.S. as Strangers on the Moor, 1966; The Golden Panther, 1956; Sword of Vengeance, 1957; Covenant, 1957; Captain Gallant, 1958; Beloved Rebel, 1959; Romantic Lady, 1960; The Devel's Bondsman, 1961; The Highwayman, 1962; The House at Bell Orchard, 1962; The Reluctant Adventuress, 1963; Fair Shines the Day, 1964; Spring Will Come Again, 1965; The Changing Tide, 1967; Dark Heritage, 1968, as Tarrington Chase, 1977; No More A-Roving, 1070; The Scarlet Domino, 1970; The Scapegrace, 1971; Dark Enchantress, 1973; The Silver Nightingale, 1974; The Witches of Conygton, 1976; A Flash of Scarlet, 1978; The Varleigh Medallion, 1979; The Avenhurst Inheritance, 1981; Mistress of Astington, 1983. Add: c/o Century Hutchinson, 62–65 Chandos Place, London WC2N 4NW, England.

THORPE, Trebor. *See* **FANTHORPE,** R. Lionel.

THRASHER, Peter Adam. British, b. 1923. Urban studies, Biography. Chartered Civil Engineer, Dept. of Planning and Transportation, G.L.C., since 1966. Member of Staff: Admiralty, 1937–57; L.C.C., 1957–64; Dept. of Environment, 1964–66. *Publs:* Pasquale Paoli: An Enlightened

Hero 1725-1807, 1970; (with K. Crawford) Standard Statistical Sectors for Greater London. Add: 1b Denbridge Rd., Bickley, Bromley, Kent BR1 2AG, England.

THRIBB, E.J. *See* **FANTONI,** Barry.

THUBRON, Colin Gerald Dryden. British, b. 1939. Novels/Short stories, History, Travel/Exploration/Adventure. Member of Editorial Staff, Hutchinson & Co., 1959–62, and Macmillan Co., 1964–65; Freelance documentary filmmaker, BBC, in Turkey, Morocco, and Japan, 1963, 1965. *Publs:* Mirror to Damascus, 1967; The Hills of Adonis: A Quest in Lebanon, 1968; Jerusalem, 1969; Journey into Cyprus, 1975; God in the Mountain, 1977; Emperor, 1978; The Royal Opera House, Covent Garden, 1982; Among the Russians, 1983; A Cruel Madness, 1984; Behind the Wall, 1987. Add: 27 St. Ann's Villas, London W11, England.

THUM, Marcella. American. Historical/Romance/Gothic, Children's fiction, Travel/Exploration/Adventure. Chief Librarian, AOS, Scott Air Force Base, Illinois, 1979–85. Pres., St. Louis Writers Guild, 1967; Member, Bd. of Dirs., Missouri Writers Guild, 1974–75. *Publs:* Mystery at Crane's Landing, 1964; Treasure of Crazy Quilt Farm, 1966; Anne of the Sandwich Islands, 1967; Librarian with Wings, 1967; Secret of the Sunken Treasure, 1969; (with G. Thum) The Persuaders: Propaganda in War and Peace (paperback as Propaganda), 1972; Fernwood (in U.K. as The Haunting Cavalier), 1973; Exploring Black America, 1975; Abbey Court, 1976; Exploring Literary America, 1979; The White Rose, 1980; Exploring Military America, 1982; (with G. Thum) Blazing Star, 1983; Jasmine, 1984; Wild Laurel, 1985; (with G. Thum) Airlift!, 1986; Margarite, 1987; Mistress of Paradise, 1988. Add: 6507 Gramond Dr., St. Louis, Mo. 63123, U.S.A.

THURSTON, Robert (Donald). American, b. 1936. Science fiction/Fantasy. Reporter, Union-Sun Journel, Lockport, N.Y., 1959–60; Asst. Prof., Alliance Coll., Cambridge Springs, Pa., 1967–68; Mgr., Glen Art Book Store, Williamsville, N.Y., 1968–71. *Publs:* Alicia II, 1978; (with Glen A. Larson) Battlestar Galactica, 1978; (with Glen A. Larson) Battlestar Galactica 2: The Cyclon Death Machine, 1979; (with Glen A. Larson) Battlestar Galactica 3: The Tombs of Kobol, 1979; (with Glen A. Larson) Battlestar Galactica 4: The Young Warriors, 1980; A Set of Wheels, 1983; Q Colony, 1985; For the Silverfish, 1985; (with Glen A. Larson) Battlestar Galactica 11: The Nightmare Machine, 1985; (with Glen A. Larson) Battlestar Galactica 12: Die, Chameleon!, 1986; (with Glen A. Larson) Battlestar Galactica 13: Apollo's War, 1987, (with Glen A. Larson) Battlestar Galachica 14: Surrender the Galactica, 1988; Robot Jox, 1989; Robot City No. 9: Intruder, 1990. Add: 86 Cedar St., Ridgefield Park, N.J. 07660, U.S.A.

THWAITE, Ann (Barbara). British, b. 1932. Children's fiction, Biography. Member, Editorial Bd., Cricket mag., since 1979. Contrib. Ed., Cricket and Company mag., 1974–78; Visiting Prof., Tokyo Women's Christian Univ., 1985–86. *Publs:* The House in Turner Square, 1960; Home and Away, 1967; (ed.) All Sorts 1–7, 1968–75; The Travelling Tooth, 1968; The Day with the Duke, 1969; The Camelthorn Papers, 1969; The Only Treasure, 1970; Waiting for the Party: The Life of Frances Hodgson Burnett, 1974; The Chatterbox, 1978; Tracks 1978; (ed.) Allsorts of Poems, 1978; A Piece of Parkin, 1980; Edmund Gosse: A Literary Landscape, 1984; Pennies For the Dog, 1985; Gilbert and the Birthday Cake, 1986; Amy and the Night-Time Visit, 1987. Add: The Mill House, Low Tharston, Norfolk NR15 2YN, England.

THWAITE, Anthony (Simon). British, b. 1930. Poetry, Literature, Travel. Visiting Lectr. in English Literature, Tokyo Univ., Japan, 1955–57; Radio Producer, BBC, London, 1957–62; Literary Ed., The Listener, London, 1962–65; Asst. Prof. of English, Univ. of Libya, Benghazi, 1965–67; Literary Ed., New Statesman, London, 1968–72; Co-Ed., Encounter, London, 1973–85. *Publs:* (Poems), 1953; Home Truths, 1957; Essays on Contemporary English Poetry: Hopkins to the Present Day, 1957, rev. ed. as Contemporary English Poetry: An Introduction, 1959; (ed. with Hilary Corke and W. Plomer) New Poems 1961, 1961; The Owl in the Tree: Poems, 1963; (ed. and trans. with G. Bownas) The Penguin Book of Japanese Verse, 1964; The Stones of Emptiness: Poems 1963-66, 1967; (with R. Beny) Japan in Colour, 1967; The Deserts of Hesperides: An Experience of Libya, 1969; A. Alvarez and Roy Fuller) Penguin Modern Poets 18, 1970; Points, 1972; Inscriptions, 1973; Poetry Today 1960-1973, 1973; New Confessions, 1974; (ed. with Peter Porter) The English Poets: From Chaucer to Edward Thomas, 1974; (with R. Beny and P. Porter) Roloff Beny in Italy, 1974; Beyond the Inhabited World, 1976; A Portion for Foxes, 1977; (ed. with Fleur Adock) New Poetry 4, 1978; Twentieth Century English Poetry, 1978; Victorian Voices, 1980; (with R. Beny)

Odyssey: Mirror of the Mediterranean, 1981; (ed.) Larkin at Sixty, 1982; Poems 1953-1983; Six Centuries of Verse, 1984; Letter from Tokyo, 1987 (ed.) Collected Poems of Philip Larkin, 1988. Add: The Mill House, Low Tharston, Norfolk NR15 2YN, England.

TIBBER, Robert. *See* **FRIEDMAN,** Rosemary.

TIBBER, Rosemary. *See* **FRIEDMAN,** Rosemary.

TIBBETTS, Orlando L. American, b. 1919. Co. Pastor, First Baptist Church in America, Providence, R.I., 1983–86. Exec. Minister, American Baptist Churches of Connecticut, Hartford, 1970–81. *Publs:* The Reconciling Community, 1969; Sidewalk Prayers, 1971; More Sidewalk Prayers, 1973; The Work of the Church Trustee, 1979; How to Keep Useful Church Records, 1983; The Minister's Handbook, 1986. Add: 199 S. Tara Dr., Tavares, Fla. 32778, U.S.A.

TICHENOR, Tom. American, b. 1923. Children's fiction, Recreation/Leisure/Hobbies. Puppeteer and Designer, Nashville Public Library, Tenn., since 1947. *Publs:* Folk Plays for Puppets, 1959; Smart Bear, 1970; Tom Tichenor's Puppets, 1971; Sir Patches and the Dragon, 1971; Tom Tichenor Christmas Tree Crafts, 1975; Neat-O The Supermarket Mouse, 1981. Add: 310 Thompson Lane, Nashville, Tenn. 37211, U.S.A.

TIERNEY, Kevin. British, b. 1942. Law. Barrister-at-Law, Lincoln's Inn, London; Prof., Hastings Coll. of the Law, San Francisco, since 1980 (Visiting Prof., 1979–80). Assoc. Lawyer, NYC, 1969–71; Assoc. Prof., 1971–75, and Prof., 1975–79, Wayne State Univ. Law Sch., Detroit. *Publs:* Courtroom Testimony: A Policeman's Guide, 1970; How to Be a Witness, 1971; Darrow, 1979. Add: c/o Crowell, 10 E. 53rd St., New York, N.Y. 10022, U.S.A.

TIGER, Lionel. Canadian, b. 1937. Anthropology/Ethnology. Prof. of Anthropology, Rutgers Univ., New Brunswick, N.J. Asst. Prof. of Sociology, Univ. of British Columbia, Vancouver, 1963–68; Research Dir., Guggenheim Foundn., 1972–84. *Publs:* (with C.W. Eliot, K. Naegele, M. Prang and M. Steinberg) Discipline and Discovery, 1966; Men in Groups, 1969; (with Robin Fox) The Imperial Animal, 1971; Women in the Kibbutz, 1975; (ed.) Female Hierarchies, 1978; Optimism, 1979; Men in Groups, 1984, 1985; (with Reinhart Wolf) China's Food, 1985; The Manufacture of Evil: Ethics, Evolution, and the Industrial System, 1987; (ed. with Michael J. Robinson) Man and Beast and Revisited, 1989; America Worked: The Photographs of Dan Weiner, 1989. Add: Dept. of Anthropology, Rutgers Univ., New Brunswick, N.J. 08903, U.S.A.

TIGERMAN, Stanley. American, b. 1930. Architecture. Principal, Stanley Tigerman and Assocs., architects, Chicago, since 1964. Prof. of Architecture, Univ. of Illinois, Chicago, 1967–71; Chmn., Design Cttee., American Inst. of Architects, 1976–77. *Publs:* Versus: An American Architect's Alternatives, 1982; (with S. G. Lewin) The California Condition: A Pregnant Architecture, 1982; The Architecture of Exile, 1988. Add: 920 N. Michigan Ave., Chicago, Ill. 60611, U.S.A.

TILL, Barry Dorn. British, b. 1923. History, Theology/Religion. Fellow, 1953–60, Chaplain, 1953–56, Dean, 1956–60, and Tutor, 1957–60, Jesus Coll., Cambridge; Dean of Hong Kong, 1960–64; Principal, Morley Coll., London, 1965–86. Member, Advisory Council, Victoria and Albert Museum, London, 1976–83. *Publs:* Change and Exchange, 1964; Changing Frontiers in the Mission of the Church, 1965; The Churches Search for Unity, 1972. Add: 44 Canonbury Sq., London N1 2AW, England.

TILLEY, Patrick. British, b. 1928. Novels, Science fiction, Film, Communications media (television scripts). Graphic designer and illustrator, 1954–68. *Publs:* Whatever Happened to the Likely Lads? (novelization of TV series), 1973; Fade-Out (science fiction novel), 1975; Mission (novel), 1981; The Amtrak Wars (science fiction novels), comprising Cloud Warrior, 1983, First Family, 1985, Iron Master, 1987, Blood River, 1988, Death-Bringer, 1989, Star-Child, 1990; Illustrated Guide to The Amtrah Wars, 1989. Add: Pen-yr-Allt, Llanrhychwyn, above Trefriw, Gwynedd LL27 0YX, North Wales.

TILLINGHAST, Richard. American, b. 1940. Poetry. Assoc. Prof. of English, Univ. of Michigan, Ann Arbor, since 1983. Asst. Prof. of English, Univ. of California, Berkeley, 1968–73; Instr., San Quentin Prison Coll. Program, California, 1975–78; Visiting Asst. Prof., Univ. of the South, 1979–80; Briggs-Copeland Lectr., Harvard Univ., Cambridge, Mass., 1980–83. *Publs:* The Keeper, 1968; Sleep Watch, 1969, 1983; The Knife and Other Poems, 1980, 1983; Sewanee in Ruins, 1981; Our

Flag Was Still There, 1984. Add: 1317 Granger Ave., Ann Arbor, Mich. 48104, U.S.A.

TIMBERLAKE, Richard Henry, Jr. American, b. 1922. Money/Finance. Prof. of Banking and Finance, Univ. of Georgia, Athens, since 1964. Assoc. Prof. of Economics, Florida State Univ., 1958–63; Research Consultant, Federal Reserve Bank of Richmond, Va. 1970–71. *Publs:* Money, Banking and Central Banking, 1965; (with E.B. Selby) Money and Banking, 1972; The Origins of Central Banking in the United States, 1978. Add: c/o Harvard Univ. Press, 79 Garden St., Cambridge, Mass. 02138, U.S.A.

TIMMS, Kathleen. Canadian, b. 1943. Mystery/Crime/Suspense. Administrator and accountant with a Toronto law firm since 1973. Officer mgr., Calgary, 1961–66; high sch. business teacher, Toronto, 1968–72. *Publs:* One-Eyed Merchants, 1986; Society's Child, 1987. Add: c/o Arnold P. Goodman, Goodman Assocs., 500 West End Ave., New York, N.Y. 10024, U.S.A.

TIMPERLEY, Rosemary Kenyon. British, b. 1920. Novels/Short stories. Ed., Ghost Books, Barrie & Jenkins Ltd., London, 1969–73. *Publs:* The Listening Child, 1955; A Dread of Burning, 1955; Web of Scandal, 1955; The Fairy Doll, 1955; Shadow of a Woman, 1955; Dreamers in the Dark, 1962; The Velvet Smile, 1962; Yesterday's Voices, 1962; Across a Crowded Room, 1962; Twilight Bar, 1962; The Bitter Friendship, 1962; Let Me Go, 1962; Broken Circle, 1963; The Veiled Heart, 1964; Devil's Paradise, 1964; The Suffering Tree, 1965; They Met in Moscow, 1965; Forgive Me, 1966; Blind Alley, 1966; My Room in Rome, 1967; Lights on the Hill, 1967; The Washers-up, 1968; The Catwalk, 1968; The Tragedy Business, 1969; Rome with Mrs. Evening, 1969; (ed.) Fifth, Sixth, Seventh, Eighth, and Ninth Ghost Books, 1969–73; Doctor Z, 1970; The Mask-shop, 1970; House of Secrets, 1971; Walk to San Michele, 1971; The Summer Visitors, 1971; The Passionate Marriage, 1972; The Long Black Dress, 1972; Shadows in the Park, 1973; Journey with Doctor Godley, 1973; The Echo-game, 1973; Juliet, 1974; The White Zig-Zag Path, 1974; The Egyptian Woman, 1975; The Private Prisoners, 1975; The Devil of the Lake, 1976; The Phantom Husband, 1976; The Stranger, 1977; The Man with the Beard, 1977; The Nameless One, 1978; Syrilla Black, 1978; Suspicion, 1978; Chidori's Room, 1983; The Office Party and After, 1984; Love and Death, 1985; Tunnel of Shadows, 1986; The Wife's Tale, 1986. Add: 21 Ellerker Gardens, Richmond, Surrey TW10 6AA, England.

TINDALL, Gillian (Elizabeth). British, b. 1938. Novels/Short stories, Literature, Urban studies, Biography. *Publs:* No Name in the Street (in U.S. as When We Had Other Names), 1959; The Water and the Sound, 1961; The Edge of the Paper, 1963; The Israeli Twins, 1963; A Handbook on Witchcraft, 1965; The Youngest, 1966; Someone Else, 1969; Fly Away Home, 1971; Dances of Death: Short Stories on a Theme, 1973; The Born Exile: George Gissing, 1974; The Traveller and the Child, 1976; The Fields Beneath, 1977; The Intruder, 1979; The China Egg and Other Stories, 1981; City of Gold: The Biography of Bombay, 1982; Looking Forward, 1983; Rosamond Lehmann: An Appreciation, 1985; To the City, 1987; Give Them All My Love, 1989. Add: c/o Curtis Brown Ltd., 162-168 Regent St., London W1R 5TA, England.

TINKER, Hugh (Russell). British, b. 1921. History, International relations/Current affairs, Politics/Government, Race relations. Emeritus Prof., Univ. of Lancaster. (Prof. of Politics, 1977–82). Dir., Inst. of Race Relations, London, 1970–72; Prof., 1963–69, and Research Fellow, 1972–77, Inst. of Commonwealth Studies, Univ. of London. *Publs:* The Foundations of Local Self-Government in India, Pakistan and Burma, 1954; The Union of Burma: A Study of the First Years of Independence, 1957; (co-author) Democratic Institutions in the World Today, 1958; India and Pakistan: A Political Analysis, 1962; Ballot Box and Bayonet: People and Government in Emergent Countries, 1961; Reorientations: Studies Asia in Transition, 1965; (co-author) The Glass Curtain Between Asia and Europe, 1965; South Asia: A Short History, 1966; (co-author) Asia Bureaucratic Systems Emergent from the British Imperial Tradition, 1966; Experiment with Freedom: India and Pakistan 1947, 1967; (ed.) Henry Yule's Narrative of the Mission to the Court of Ava in 1855, 1968; (co-author) The Study of International Affairs: Essays in Honour of Kenneth Younger, 1972; A New System of Slavery: The Export of Indian Labour Overseas, 1830-1920, 1974; Separate and Unequal: India and the Indians in the British Commonwealth 1920-1950, 1975; The Banyan Tree: Overseas Emigrants from India, Pakistan and Bangladesh, 1977; Race, Conflict, and the International Order, 1977; The Ordeal of Love: C.F. Andrews and India, 1979; Burma: The Struggle for Independence, 2 vols., 1983–84; Men Who Overturned Empires: Fighters, Dreamers, and Schemers, 1987.

Add: Montbegon, Hornby, Lancaster England.

TINNISWOOD, Peter. British, b. 1936. Novels/Short stories, Plays/Screenplays. Former journalist with Sheffield Star, Sheffield Telegraph, Liverpool Daily Post, and Western Mail. *Publs:* A Touch of Daniel, 1969; Mog, 1970; I Didn't Know You Cared, 1973; Except You're A Bird, 1974; The Stirk of Stirk, 1974; Tales (and More Tales) from a Long Room, 2 vols., 1981–82; Shemerelda, 1981; The Home Front, 1982; The Brigadier Down Under, 1983; The Brigadier in Season, 1984; Call It a Canary, 1985; Uncle Mort's North Country, 1986; The Brigadier's Collection, 1986; Tales from Witney Scrotum, 1987; Hayballs, 1989. Add: c/o Anthony Sheil Assocs., 43 Doughty St., London WC1N 2LF, England.

TINSLEY, Ernest John. British, b. 1919. Theology/Religion. Head of the Dept. of Theology, Univ. of Hull, 1954–61; Prof. of Theology, Univ. of Leeds, 1962–76; Bishop of Bristol, 1976–85. *Publs:* The Imitation of God in Christ, 1960; (ed.) The Gospel of Luke, 1965; (ed.) Modern Theology, 1973; Tragedy, Irony and Faith, 1984. Add: 100 Acre End St., Eynsham, OX8 1PD, England.

TIPPETTE, Giles. American, b. 1936. Novels/Short stories, Westerns/Adventure, Recreation/Leisure/Hobbies, Sports/Physical education/Keeping fit. Freelance writer. *Publs:* The Bank Robber, 1970, in paperback as The Spikes Gang, 1971; The Trojan Cow, 1971; The Brave Men (on auto racing and rodeo), 1972; Satuday's Children (on college football), 1973; Austin Davis, 1974; The Sunshine Killers, 1974; The Survivalist, 1975; The Mercenaries, 1976; Wilson's Gold (Luck, Choice, Revenge, Woman), 5 vols., 1980–82; The Texas Bank Robbing Company, 1982; Hard Luck Money, 1982. Add: c/o Doubleday 666 Fifth Ave., New York, N.Y. 10103, U.S.A.

TIPTON, David. British, b. 1934. Poetry, Biography, Translations. English teacher, Argentina and Peru, 1960–70. *Publs:* Poems in Transit, 1960; City of Kings, 1967; (ed. and trans. with M. Ahern) Peru the New Poetry: Twelve Peruvian Poems, 1970; (ed. and trans. with M. Ahern and W. Rowe) The Spider Hangs Too Far from the Ground, 1970; Millstone Grit, 1972; (trans.) Common Grave, 1973; Pachacamac, 1974; Atahualda, 1975; Graph of Love, 1976; Moving House, 1982; Sexual Disturbances, 1983; Wars of the Roses. Add: c/o Rivelin Grapherne Press, The Annexe, Kennet House, 19 High St., Hungerford, Berks RG17 0NL, England.

TIPTON, Ian Charles. British, b. 1937. Philosophy. Reader, Univ. Coll. of Swansea, Wales, since 1988. Lectr., Univ. of Keele, Staffs., 1964–67; Lectr., 1967–74, Sr. Lectr., 1974–87, and Reader, 1987–88, University Coll. of Wales, Aberystwyth. *Publs:* Berkeley: The Philosophy of Immaterialism, 1974; (ed.) Locke on Human Understanding: Essays, 1977. Add: Dept. of Philosophy, Univ. Coll. of Swansea, Singleton Pk., Swansea, Wales.

TISCHLER, Hans. American, b. 1915. Music. Prof. of Musicology, Indiana Univ., Bloomington, 1965–85, now Emeritus. Prof. of Music, West Virginia Wesleyan Coll., Buckhannon, 1945–47; Assoc. Prof. of Music History and Theory, Roosevelt Univ. of Chicago, 1947–65. Pres., Medieval Assn. of the Midwest, 1980–82. Member, Medieral Academy of America, and American and Antnl. Music Soc. *Publs:* The Perceptive Music Listener, 1955; Practical Harmony, 1964; A Structural Analysis of Mozart's Piano Concertos, 1966; (ed.) Essays in Musicology for Willi Apel, 1968; (trans. and ed.) History of Keyboard Music to 1700, 1973; A Medieval Motet Book, 1973; (ed.) The Montpelier Codex, 3 vols., 1978; Chanter m'estuet: Songs of the Trouvères, 1981; The Earliest Motets (to c. 1270): Complete Comparative Edition, 3 vols., 1982; The Style and Evolution of the Earliest Motets, 4 vols., 1985. The Parisian Two-Part Organa: Complete Comparative Edition, 2 vols., 1988. Add: Sch. of Music, Indiana Univ., Bloomington, Ind. 47405, U.S.A.

TISDELL, Clement Allan. Australian, b. 1939. Economics. Prof. of Economics, Univ. of Queensland, since 1989. Postdoctoral Travelling Scholar, 1965; Lectr. in Economics, 1966, Sr. Lectr. in Economics, 1967, and Reader in Economics, 1967–72, Australian National Univ., Canberra; Prof. of Economics, Univ. of Newcastle, N.S.W., 1972–89. *Publs:* The Theory of Price Uncertainty, Production and Profit, 1968; Microeconomics: Theory of Economic Allocation, 1972; Economics of Markets: An Introduction to Economic Analysis, 1974; Workbook to Accompany Economics of Markets, 1975; Microeconomia, 1978; Economics of Fibre Markets, 1979; Economics in Our Society, 1979, 1981; (co-ed.) The Economics of Structural Change and Adjustment, 1979; Science and Technology Policy, 1981; Micronomic Policy, 1981; Microeconomics of Markets, 1982; Wild Pigs, 1982; (co-author) Economics in Canadian Society, 1986; (co-author) Weed Control Economics, 1987; (co-ed.)

Techonological Change, Development and the Environment, 1988; (co-ed.) Economics of Tourism, 1988. Add: Dept. of Economics, Univ. of Queensland, St. Lucia, Qld. 4067, Australia.

TITCHENER, Louise. Writes as Josie March, Anne Silverlock, and Jane Silverwood; writes with Carolyn Males, Ellen Buckholtz, and Ruth Glick, under joint pseud. Alyssa Howard; with Ruth Glick as Alexis Hill Jordan; with Carolyn Males as Clare Richards. American, b. 1941. Historical/romance. Full-time writer since 1978. Instr. of English Composition, Howard Community Coll., Columbia, Md., and Univ. of Maryland, Catonsville, 1964–78. *Publs:* (as Alyssa Howard) Love Is Elected, 1981; (as Alyssa Howard) Southern Persuasion, 1983; (as Alexis Hill Jordan) The Arms of Love, 1983; (as Alexis Hill Jordan) Brian's Captive, 1983; (as Alexis Hill Jordan) Reluctant Merger, 1984; (as Alexis Hill Jordan) Summer Wine, 1984; (as Alexis Hill Jordan) Beginner's Luck, 1984; (as Anne Silverlock) Casanova's Master, 1984; (as Anne Silverlock) With Each Caress, 1985; (as Anne Silverlock) Aphrodite's Promise, 1985; (as Anne Silverlock) An Invincible Love, 1985; (as Jane Silverwood) Voyage of the Heart, 1985; (as Alexis Hill Jordan) Mistaken Image, 1985; (as Alexis Hill Jordan) Hopelessly Devoted, 1985; (as Alexis Hill Jordan) Summer Stars, 1985; (as Clare Richards) Renaissance Summer, 1985; (as Anne Silverlock) Fantasy Lover, 1986; (as Anne Silverlock) In the Heart of the Sun, 1986; (as Jane Silverwood) Slow Melt, 1986. Add: 5162 Phantom Court, Columbia, Md. 21044, U.S.A.

TITLEY, David Paul. British, b. 1929. History. Headmaster, Charlton Kings Secondary Sch., Cheltenham, from 1977, now retired. Sch. Master, Stoke-on-Trent, 1954–67; Deputy Headmaster, Dyson Perrins High Sch., Malvern, 1967–77. *Publs:* Machines, Money and Men, 1969, 1974; Look and Remember Histories, Books 1-5, 1969–71; Britain in History, Books 1-2, 1974–75; Look and Remember People and Events, Books 1a and 1b, 1975, 2a and 2b, 1976; Let's Make History, 4 vols., 1979. Add: 7 Leahill Close Malvern, Worcs., England.

TITTERTON, (Sir) Ernest (William). Australian, b. 1916. Physics. Prof. of Nuclear Physics, Australian National Univ., Canberra, since 1950 (Dean, 1966–68 and Dir., 1968–73, Research Sch. of Physical Sciences), Research Officer, British Admiralty, 1939–43; Member, British Scientific Mission to U.S.A. on Atomic Bomb Development, 1943–47; Sr. Member, Timing Group At First Atomic Bomb Test, Alamogordo, 1945; Adviser on Instrumentation, Bikini Atomic Weapon Test, 1946; Head of Electronics Div., Los Alamos Lab. U.S.A. 1946–47; Group Leader in Charge of Research Team, Harwell, 1947–50. Pres., Australian Inst. of Nuclear Science and Engineering, 1973–75. *Publs:* Facing the Atomic Future, 1954; (co-author) Inside the Atom, 1966; Uranium: Energy Source of the Future?, 1979. Add: P.O. Box 331, Jamison, A.C.T. 2614, Australia.

TITUS, Eve. Has also written as Nancy Lord. American, b. 1922. Children's fiction. *Publs:* Anatole series, 10 vols., 1956–79; Basil series, 5 vols., 1958–81; (as Nancy Lord) My Dog and I, 1958; The Mouse and the Lion, 1962; The Two Stonecutters, 1967; Mr. Shaw's Shipshape Shoeshop, 1970; Why the Wind God Wept, 1972. Add: McIntosh and Otis Inc., 475 Fifth Ave., New York, N.Y. 10017, U.S.A.

TOBIAS, Andrew P. American, b. 1947. Business/Trade/Industry, Marketing, Money/Finance. Columnist, Playboy mag., Chicago, since 1983. Pres., Harvard Student Agencies, Inc., Cambridge, Mass., 1967–68; Vice-Pres., National Student Marketing Corp., NYC, 1968–70; Contrib. Ed., New York mag., 1972–77, Esquire mag., NYC, 1977–83. *Publs:* (with A. Bortz and C. Weinberger) The Ivy League Guidebook, 1968; (ed.) How to Earn Money in College, 1968; Honor Grades on Fifteen Hours a Week, 1969; The Funny Money Game, 1971; Fire and Ice, 1976; The Only Investment Guide You'll Ever Need, 1978; Getting By on $100,000 a Year and Other Such Tales, 1980; The Invisible Bankers: Everything the Insurance Industry Never Wanted You to Know, 1982; Money Angles, 1984; Managing Your Money (computer software), 1984; The Only Other Investment Guide You'll Ever Need, 1987. Add: c/o MECA, 355 Riverside Ave., Westport, Conn. 06880, U.S.A.

TOBIAS, John Jacob. British, b. 1925. Criminology/Law enforcement/Prisons, History. Civil Servant, since 1974; Seconded as Chief Personnel Officer, States of Jersey, since 1983. Tutor, 1959–64, and Dir. of Academic Studies, 1964–74, The Police Coll., Bramshill. *Publs:* Crime and Industrial Society in the Nineteenth Century, 1967; Against the Peace, 1970; (ed.) Nineteenth Century Crime: Prevention and Punishment, 1972; In the Local Interest, 1972; Prince of Fences, 1974; Crime and Police in England 1700-1900, 1979. Add: Athenaeum, Pall Mall, London SW1, England.

TOBIAS, Richard C. American, b. 1925. Literature. Prof. of English, Univ. of Pittsburgh, since 1969 (Instr., 1957–59; Asst. Prof., 1959–64; Assoc. Prof., 1964–69). Ed., Guide to the Year's Work in Victorian Poetry, in Victorian Poetry, since 1962. Ed., Victorian Bibliography in Victorian Studies, 1975–84. *Publs:* Art of James Thurber, 1970; T.E. Brown (1830-1897), The Manx Poet, 1974, 1978; (ed. with Paul Zolbrod) Shakespeare's Last Plays, 1974. Add: Dept. of English, 526 CL, Univ. of Pittsburgh, Pittsburgh, Pa. 15260, U.S.A.

TOBIN, James. American, b. 1918. Economics. Sterling Prof. of Economics, Yale Univ., New Haven, Conn., since 1957 (Dir., Cowles Foundn. for Research in Economics, 1955–61; Acting Dir., 1964–65; Chmn., Dept. of Economics, 1968–69, 1974–78). Pres., Econometric Soc., 1958; Member, Council of Economic Advisers, 1961–62; Pres., American Economic Assn., 1971; Visiting Prof., Univ. of Nairobi, Kenya, 1972–73. *Publs:* (with S.E. Harris, C. Kaysen, and F.X. Sutton) The American Business Creed, 1956; National Economic Policy, 1966; (ed. with D. Hester) Risk Aversion and Portfolio Choice, 1967; (ed. with D. Hester) Studies of Behavior, 1967; (ed. with D. Hester) Financial Markets and Economic Activity, 1967; Essays in Economic, vol. I, Macroeconomics, 1971, vol. II, Consumption and Econometrics, 1975, vol. III, Theory and Policy, 1982; The New Economics One Decade Older, 1974; Asset Accumulation and Economic Activity: Reflections on Contemporary Macroeconomic Theory, 1980; Policies for Prosperity: Essays in a Keynsian Mode, 1987, (ed. with M. Weidengaum) Two Revolutions in Economic Policy: The First Economic Reports of Presidents Kennedy and Reagan, 1988. Add: Yale Univ., Box 2125, Yale Station, New Haven, Conn. 06520, U.S.A.

TOCH, Henry. British. Money/Finance, Public/Social administration. Sr. Lectr., City of London Polytechnic, since 1957; now retired. Taxation and financial consultant. H.M. Inspector of Taxes, 1949–56. *Publs:* How to Pay Less Income Tax, 1958; Tax Saving for the Business Man, 1959, 3rd ed. 1974; British Social and Political Institutions, 1960; Income Tax, 1966, 13th ed. 1983; Economics for Professional Studies, 1974, 1977; How to Survive Inflation, 1977; How to Pass Examinations in Taxation, 1979; Cases in Income Tax Law, 1981; Essentials of British Constitution and Government, 1982; Taxation 1984/85, 1984; Income Tax Made Simple, 1985; Taxation Made Simple, 1986; How to Pay Less Income Tax, 1986. Add: 49 Hawkshead Lane, North Mymms, Herts. AL9 7TD, England.

TOCZEK, Nick. British, b. 1950. Poetry. Founding Ed. and Publr., The Little Word Machine, L.W.M. Publs., since 1972, and of the Wool City Rocker, since 1979. Co-Ed., Black Columbus, mag., Birmingham Univ. Student's Union, 1969–71. *Publs:* Because the Evenings..., 1972; The Book of Number, 1973; (co-ed.) Midland Read, 1973; Evensong, 1974; Malignant Humour, 1975; Antrography of a Friend (novel), 1976; God Shave the Queen (humour), 1976; (co-ed.) Melanthika: An Anthology of Pan-Caribbean Writing, 1977; Acts of Violence (prose), 1979; Complete Strangers Tell You Nothing, 1979; Lies, 1979; The Credible Adventures of Nick Toczek (prose), 1979; Rock 'n' Roll Terrorism (prose/poems/lyrics), Add: 5 Beech Terrace, Undercliffe, Bradford BD3 0PY, England.

TODD, James Maclean. British, b. 1907. Archaeology/Antiquities, Classics, Translations. Asst. Master of Mathematics, Stowe Sch., Buckingham, 1934–48; Headmaster, The High Sch., Newcastle, Staffs. 1948–63; Examinations Secty., Oxford and Cambridge Schs. Examination Bd., Oxford, 1964–74. *Publs:* The Ancient World, 1938; (ed.) Hymns, Prayers and Psalms for Use in Newcastle High School, 1951; (compiler with Janet G. Todd) Voices from the Past: A Classical Anthology in Translation, 1955; (with Janet G. Todd) Peoples of the Past, 1963. Add: Foxton Lodge, Foxton Close, Oxford OX2 8LB, England.

TODD, John M(urray). British, b. 1918. Philosophy, Theology/Religion, Biography. Dir., Search Press, since 1970, and Tablet Publishing Co., since 1988. Publr., Longmans Green, 1956–59, London; Dir., and publr., Darton Longman & Todd Ltd., 1959–83. *Publs:* We Are Men, 1955; Catholicism and the Ecumenical Movement, 1955; (ed.) The Springs of Morality, 1956; John Wesley and the Catholic Church, 1958; (ed.) The Arts, Artists and Thinkers, 1958; (ed.) Work, 1960; African Mission, 1960; (ed.) Problems of Authority, 1962; Martin Luther, 1964; Reformation, 1971; Luther, 1982. Add: Doulting Manor, Shepton Mallet, Somerset BA4 4QE, England.

TODD, Paul. *See* **POSNER,** Richard.

TOFFLER, Alvin. American, b. 1928. Social commentary/phenomena. Washington corresp., 1957–59; Assoc. Ed., Fortune Mag., 1959–61; Visiting Scholar, Russell Sage Foundn., 1969–70. *Publs:* The Culture Consumers, 1964; (ed.) The Schoolhouse in the City, 1968; Future Shock, 1970; (ed.) The Futurists, 1972; (ed.) Learning for Tomorrow, 1973; The Eco-Spasm Report, 1975; The Third Wave, 1980; Previews and Premises, 1983; The Adaptive Corporation, 1984. Add: c/o McGraw-Hill, 1221 Ave. of the Americas, New York, N.Y. 10020, U.S.A.

TOFT, (Eric) John. British, b. 1933. Novels/Short stories. Lectr., Brighton Polytechnic, since 1965. Lectr., Malayan Teachers Coll., 1961–64. *Publs:* The Bargees, 1969; The Wedge, 1971; The House of the Arousing, 1973; The Underground Tree, 1978; The Dew, 1981. Add: 1 Clarendon Terr., Brighton, Sussex, England.

TOLAND, John (Willard). American, b. 1912. History, Politics/Government. *Publs:* Ships in the Sky, 1957; Battle: The Story of the Bulge, 1959; But Not in Shame 1961; The Dillinger Days, 1963; The Flying Tigers, 1963; The Last 100 Days, 1966; The Story of the Bulge, 1967; The Rising Sun: History of Japan 1936-1945, 1970; Adolf Hitler, 1976; Hitler: The Pictorial Documentary of His Life, 1977; No Man's Land, 1980; Infamy, 1982; Gods of War (novel), 1985; Occupation, 1987. Add: 1 Long Ridge Rd., Danbury, Conn. 06810, U.S.A.

TOLEDANO, Ralph de. American, b. 1916. Novels/Short stories, Poetry, Music, Politics/Government. Syndicated columnist, Copley News Service, Washington, D.C., since 1974. National Reports Ed., Newsweek mag., NYC, 1948–60; Syndicated columnist, King Features Syndicate, NYC, 1960–71, and National News-Research Syndicate, 1971–74. *Publs:* (ed. and contrib.) Frontiers of Jazz, 1947; Seeds of Treason, 1950; Spies, and Diplomats, 1952; Day of Reckoning (novel), 1954; Nixon, 1956; Lament for a Generation, 1960; The Greatest Plot in History, 1963; The Winning Side, 1963; (with P. Brennan) The Goldwater Story, 1964; RFK: The Man Who Would Be President, 1967; One Man Alone: Richard Nixon, 1969; (with P. Brennan) Claude Kirk, 1970; Little Cesar, 1971; J. Edgar Hoover: The Man in His Times, 1973; Let Our Cities Burn, 1975; The Municipal Doomsday Machine, 1976; Poems: You and I, 1978; Devil Take Him, 1979. Add: 825 New Hampshire Ave. N.W., Washington, D.C. 20037, U.S.A.

TOLIVER, Raymond Frederick. American, b. 1914. History. Former Officer, U.S. Air Force; Sales Rep. Lockheed Aircraft Corp., Burbank, Calf., 1965–74. *Publs:* (with T.J. Constable) Fighter Aces, 1965; (with T.J. Constable) Horrido!, 1968; (with T.J. Constable) The Blond Knight of Germany, 1971; (with T.J. Constable) Fighter Aces of the Luftwaffe, 1977; The Interrogator, 1978; (with T.J. Constable) Fighter Aces of the U.S.A., 1979. Add: 4116 Rhodes Way, Oceanside, Calif. 92056 U.S.A.

TOLL, Robert Charles. American, b. 1938. Theatre. Research Assoc., Inst. for the Study of Community and Race Relations, Berkeley, Calif., 1971–72; Lectr., St. Mary's Coll., Moraga, Calif., 1974; Lectr. in History, Univ. of California, Berkeley, 1975–76. *Publs:* Blacking Up: The Minstrel Show in Nineteenth Century America, 1974; (ed.) Old Slack's Reminiscences and Pocket History of the Colored Profession, 1974; On with the Show: The First Century of Show Business in America, 1976; The Entertainment Machine: American Show Business in the Twentieth Century, 1982. Add: c/o Oxford Univ. Press, 200 Madison Ave., New York, N.Y. 10016, U.S.A.

TOMALIN, Claire. British, b. 1933. Literature, Social commentary/phenomena. Literary Ed., The Sunday Times, London, 1980–86. *Publs:* The Life and Death of Mary Wollstonecraft, 1974; Shelley and His World, 1980; Parents and Children, 1981; Katherine Mansfield: A Secret Life, Add: 57 Gloucester Cres., London NW1 7EG, England.

TOMALIN, Ruth. Has also written as Ruth Leaver. British. Novels/Short stories, Natural history, Biography. Freelance press reporter, London law courts, since 1966. Staff reporter on various newspapers, 1942–65. *Publs:* Threnody for Dormice, 1946; The Day of the Rose, 1947; (as Ruth Leaver) Green Ink, 1951; Deer's Cry, 1952; All Souls, 1952; W.H. Hudson, 1954; (as Ruth Leaver) The Sound of Pens, 1955; The Daffodil Bird, 1959; The Sea Mice, 1962; The Garden House, 1964; The Spring House, 1968; (ed.) Best Country Stories, 1969; Away to the West, 1972; A Green Wishbone, 1975; A Stranger Thing, 1975; The Snake Crook, 1976; Gone Away, 1979; W.H. Hudson, 1982; Little Nasty, 1985; A Summer Ghost, 1986; Another Day, 1988; Long Since, 1989. Add: c/o Barclays Bank, 15 Langham Pl., London W1, England.

TOMESKI, Edward A. American, b. 1930. Human relations, Information science/Computers. Prof., Fordham Univ., Bronx. N.Y., since 1971

(Asst. Prof., 1966–71); Prof., Barry Coll., Miami, since 1977. Former Assoc. Ed., Journal of Systems Mgmt. *Publs:* Executive Use of Computers, 1969; Computer Revolution, 1970; (with Harold Lazarus) People-Oriented Computer Systems, 1974; Fundamentals of Computers in Business, 1979. Add: 501 Chicago Blvd., Sea Girt, N.J. 08750, U.S.A.

TOMKINS, Calvin. American, b. 1925. novels/Short stories, Art, Biography. Staff Writer, New Yorker mag., NYC, since 1961. Assoc. Ed., 1953–56, and Gen. Ed., 1956–60, Newsweek mag., NYC. *Publs:* Intermission, 1951; The Bride and the Bachelors, 1965, in U.K. paperback as Ahead of the Game: The Lewis and Clark Trail, 1965; The World of Marcel Duchamp, 1966; Eric Hoffer: An American odyssey, 1968; Merchants and masterpieces: The Story of the Metropolitan Museum of Art, 1970; Living Well is the Best Revenge, 1971; The Other Hampton, 1974; The Scene: Reports on Post-Modern Art, 1976; Off the Wall: Robert Rauschenberg and the Art World of Our Time, 1980; Post-to-Neo: The Art World of the 1980s, 1988. Add: c/o The New Yorker, 25 W. 43rd St., New York, N.Y. 10036, U.S.A.

TOMKINS, Jasper. Pseud. for Tom Batey. American, b. 1946. Children's fiction. Free-lance writer and artist, since 1978. Staff Artist, Bantam Books Inc., NYC, 1971–74; Art Dir., Great Northwest Publications, Bellevue, Wash., 1974–78. Publs: (all self-illustrated) The Catalog, 1981; Nimby: A Remarkable Cloud, 1982; The Hole in the Ocean!: A Daring Journey, 1984; The Sky Jumps into Your Shoes at Night, 1986; When a Bear Bakes a Cake, 1987; The Mountains Crack Up!, 1987; The Balancing City, 1988. Add: Rte. 1, Box 914, Eastsound, Wash. 98245, U.S.A.

TOMKINS, Oliver Stratford. British, b. 1908. Theology/Religion, Biography. Anglican Bishop of Bristol, 1959–75, now retired. Asst. Gen. Secty., Student Christian Movement, 1933–40; Ed., Student Movement Mag., 1937–40; Deacon, 1935; priest, 1936; Vicar of Holy Trinity, Millhouses, Sheffield, 1940–45; Assoc. Gen. Secty., World Council of Churches, and Secty., Commn. on Faith and Order, 1945–52; Warden, Lincoln Theological Coll., and Canon and Prebend, Lincoln Cathedral, 1953–59; Bishop of Bristol, 1959–75; Member, Central Cttee., World Council of Churches, 1968–75. *Publs:* (ed. and contrib.) The Universal Church in God's Design, 1948; The Wholeness of the Church, 1949; The Church in the Purpose of God, 1950; Intercommunion, 1951; (ed.) Faith and Order, 1953; Life of E.S. Woods, Bishop of Lichfield, 1957; A Time for Unity, 1964; Guarded by Faith, 1971; Lambeth Preparatory Essays, 1978; (with others) Imagination and the Future, 1980; A Fully Human Priesthood, 1986; Prayer for Unity, 1987. Add: 14 St. George's Sq., Worcester WR1 1HX, England.

TOMLINSON, (Alfred) Charles. British, b. 1927. Poetry, Literature. Member of faculty, currently Prof. of English Poetry, Univ. of Bristol, since 1956. Hon. Fellow, Queens' Coll., Cambridge. *Publs:* Relations and Contraries, 1951; The Necklace, 1955, rev. ed. 1966; Seeing is Believing, 1958; (trans. with H. Gifford) Versions from Fyodor Tyutchev 1803-1873, 1960; A Peopled Landscape: Poems, 1963; (trans. with H. Gifford) Castilian Ilexes: Versions from Antonio Machado, 1963, 1974; (with T. Connor and A. Clarke) Poems: A Selection, 1964; American Scenes and Other Poems, 1966; The Poems as Initiation, 1967; The Matachines, 1968; To Be Engraved on the Skull of a Cormorant, 1968; (with A. Brownjohn and M. Hamburger) Penguin Modern Poets 14, 1969; The Way of a World, 1969; America West Southwest, 1969; (trans. with H. Gifford) Ten Versions from Trilce, by César Vallejo, 1970; (ed.) Marianne Moore: A Collection of Critical Essays, 1970; Renga, 1971, 4th ed., 1983; (ed.) William Carlos Williams: A Collection of Critical Essays, 1972; Words and Images, 1972; Written on Water, 1972; The Way In, 1974; In Black and White: Graphics, 1975; (ed.) William Carlos Williams: Selected Poems, 1976, 1985; The Shaft, 1978; Selected Poems, 1978; (ed. and trans.) Selected Poems by Octavio Paz, 1979; The Flood, 1981; (ed.) The Oxford Book of Verse in English Translation, 1981; Some Americans, 1981; Airborn, 1981; Isaac Rosenberg of Bristol, 1982; Poetry and Metamorphosis (lectures), 1983; The Sense of the Past: Three Twentieth-Century Poets, 1983; Translations, 1983; Notes from New York and Other Poems, 1984; Collected Poems, 1985; Eden, 1985; The Return, 1987. Add: Brook Cottage, Ozleworth Bottom, Glos. GL12 7QB, England.

TOMPKINS, Edwin Berkeley. American, b. 1935. History. Exec. Dir., National Historical Publications Commn., Washington, since 1973. Dir., Philadelphia Maritime Museum, 1961; Member of History Faculty, 1963–71, Dean of Summer Session, 1965–68, and Sr. Fellow, Hoover Instn., 1968–71, Stanford Univ., California; Dir., Historical and Cultural Affairs, State of Delaware, 1971–73. *Publs:* Anti-Imperialism in the United States: The Great Debate 1890-1920, 1970; (ed.) Peaceful Change

in Modern Society, 1971; The United Nations in Perspective, 1972. Add: c/o Hoover Institution Press, Stanford Univ., Stanford, Calif. 94305, U.S.A.

TONG, Raymond. British, b. 1922. Poetry, Travel. Freelance writer. Served in Nigeria and Uganda for Overseas Education Service, 1949–61; British Council Officer in Argentina, Iraq, India, Kuwait and England, 1961–82. *Publs:* Today the Sun, 1947; Angry Decade, 1950; (ed.) African Helicon, 1954, 1975; Figures in Ebony (travel), 1958; Fabled City, 1960; A Matter of History, 1976; Crossing the Border, 1978; Add: 1B Beaufort Rd., Clifton, Bristol BS8 2JT, England.

TONOGBANUA, Francisco G. Filipino, b. 1900. Poetry, Literature, Travel/Exploration/Adventure, Essays. Ed.-in-Chief, PBGA Bulletin, of Columbus in the Philippines; Ed., Cross, since 1980. Principal, Binal-bagan Elementary Sch., 1919–21; Managing Ed., Philippine Collegian, 1923–26; Reporter and Chief Proofreader, Philippine Herald, 1925–26; Teacher of English, Manila West High Sch., 1926–28; Reporter and Literary Ed., Tribune, 1926–28; Teacher of English, Div. of City Schs., Manila, 1930–34; High Sch. Principal, 1934–39, and Gen. Supvr., 1939–41, Bureau of Education; Prof. of English, Head of Dept., Chmn. of Grad. Dept., and Secty. of Inst. of Arts and Sciences, Far Eastern Univ., 1946–66; Dean of Grad. Sch., Golden Gate Coll., Bantangas, 1966–73; Dean of Liberal Arts and Education, Central Colleges of the Philippines, Quezon City, 1973–75; Educational Consultant and Dean of Grad. Sch., Harvardian Coll., San Fernando, Pampanga, 1973–81. *Publs:* (ed. and compiler) Birthday Calendar, 1946; An Outline of English Literature, 1948; A Survey of American Literature, 1948; A Survey of English Literature, 1949; Fallen Leaves (poetry), 1951; Green leaves (poetry), 1954; A Survey of Filipino Literature, 1965, 1977; (ed. and compiler) Filipino Folk Songs, 1956; Forty-One Christmases (poetry), 1959; A Stone, a Leaf, a Door (poetry), 1962; Sonnets (125), 1964; Brown Leaves (poetry), 1965; Across the Pacific (travelogue), 1965; Cupid to Psyche (essays), 1966; My God, My Mercy (poetry), 1967; A History of the Knights of Columbus in the Philippines, 1981; Philippine Literature in English, 1984; My Early Poems, 1984; Christmas (poetry), 1984; The Philconsa Essays, 1986; Poems of Choice, 1986. Add: 32 Ragang, Manresa, Quezon City, Philippines.

TORDAY, Ursula. *See* **BLACKSTOCK,** Charity.

TORRANCE, Lee. Pseud. for Sidney Henry Sadgrove. British, b. 1920. Novels/Short stories, Plays/Screenplays. Artist, teacher and writer, since 1949. *Publs:* radio plays—You've Got to Do Something, 1967; A Touch of the Rabbits, 1968; The Suitability Factor, 1968; Stanislaus and the Princess, 1969; A Few Crumbs, 1971; Stanislaus and the Frog, 1972; Paradise Enow, 1972; Stanislaus and the Witch, 1973; The 1975; The Bag, 1977; Half Sick of Shadows, 1977; Bleep, 1977; Icary Dicary Doc, 1978; Filling, 1979; stage plays—All in the Mind, 1977; Angel, 1978; First Night, 1980; Hoodunnit, 1984; Pawn en Prise, 1985; Just for Comfort, 1986; Tiger, 1987; novels—Only on Friday, 1980; State of Play, 1986. Add: Pimp Barn, Withyham, Hartfield, Sussex TN7 4BB, England.

TORRANCE, Thomas Forsyth. British, b. 1913. History, Philosophy, Sciences, Theology/Religion. Ed. with J.K.S. Reid, Scottish Journal of Theology, since 1949. Prof. of Systematic Theology, Auburn, N.Y., 1938–39; Minister, Alyth Barony, Perthshire, 1940–47, and Beechgrove Parish, Aberdeen, 1947–50; Prof. of Church History, 1950–52, and Prof. of Christian Dogmatics, 1952–79, Univ. of Edinburgh. Pres., Académie Intl. des Sciences Religieuses, 1972–81. *Publs:* The Doctrine of Grace in the Apostolic Fathers, 1949; Calvin's Doctrine of Man, 1949; Royal Priesthood, 1955; Kingdom and Church, 1956; (ed. with G.W. Bromiley) Karl Barth: Church Dogmatics, 13 vols., 1956–75; When Christ Comes and Comes Again, 1957; (ed. and trans.) The Mystery of the Lord's Supper, by Robert Bruce, 1958; (ed.) Calvin's Tracts and Treatises, 3 vols., 1959; (co-author and compiler) The School of Faith, 1959; The Apocalypse Today, 1959; Conflict and Agreement in the Church, 2 vols., 1959, 1960; (ed. with D.W. Torrance) Calvin's News Testament Commentaries, 12 vols., 1959–73; Karl Barth: An Introduction to His Early Theology, 1962; Theology in Reconstruction, 1965; Theological Science, 1969; Space, Time and Incarnation, 1969; God and Rationality, 1971; Theology in Reconciliation, 1975; Space, Time, and Resurrection, 1976; The Ground and Grammar of Theology, 1980; Christian Theology and Scientific Culture, 1980; Divine and Contingent Order, 1981; Reality and Evangelical Theology, 1982; Juridical and Physical Law, 1982; James Clerk Maxwell, 1982; Transformation and Convergence in the Frame of Knowledge, 1984; The Christian Frame of Mind, 1985; Reality and Scientific Theology, 1985; The Hermeneutics of John Calvin, 1988; The

Trinitarian Faith, 1988. Add: 37 Braid Farm Rd., Edinburgh EH10 6LE, Scotland.

TORRO, Pel. *See* FANTHORPE, R. Lionel.

TOTTLE, Charles Ronald. British, b. 1920. Engineering, Technology, Sciences. Prof. Emeritus, Bath Inst. of Medical Engineering, since 1978. Deputy Dir., Dounreay Experimental Reactor Establishment, UKAEA 1958–59; Prof. and Head, Dept. of Metallurgy, 1959–67, and Dean, Faculty of Science, 1966–67, Univ. of Manchester; Prof., Univ. of Bath, 1967–77; Managing Dir., South Western Industrial Research Ltd., 1970–75. *Publs:* The Science of Engineering Materials, 1966; Encyclopedia of Metallurgy and Materials, 1984. Add: Thirdacre, Hilperton, Trowbridge, Wilts., England.

TOULMIN, Stephen E(delston). British, b. 1922. Philosophy, Intellectual history. Prof. of Philosophy, Northwestern Univ., Evanston, Ill. Prof., Cttee. on Social Thought, Univ. of Chicago, since 1973. Lectr. in the Philosophy of Science, Oxford Univ., 1949–55; Prof. of Philosophy, Univ. of Leeds, 1955–59; Dir., Unit for the History of Ideas, Nuffield Foundn., London, 1960–64; Prof. of History of Ideas and Philosophy, Brandeis Univ., Waltham, Mass., 1965–69; Prof. of Philosophy, Michigan State Univ., East Lansing, 1969–72; Provost of Crown Coll. and Prof. of Philosophy, Univ. of California at Santa Cruz, 1972–73. Member of the Council, Smithsonian Instn., Washington, D.C., 1967–76. *Publs:* An Examination of the Place of Reason in Ethics, 1950; The Philosophy of Science: An Introduction, 1953; (with others) Metaphysical Beliefs: Three Essays, 1957; The Uses of Argument, 1958; Foresight and Understanding: An Enquiry into the Aims of Science, 1961; (with others) Science and the Arts, 1961; (with June Goodfield) The Ancestry of Science, 3 vols., 1961–65; Night Sky at Rhodes, 1963; Human Understanding, vol. 1: The Collective Use and Development of Concepts, 1972; (with Allan Janik) Wittgenstein's Vienna, 1973; Knowing and Acting: An Introduction to Philosophy, 1976; (with Allan Janik and R. Rieke) An Introduction to Reasoning, 1979; The Inwardness of Mental Life, 1979; The Uses and Abuses of Casuistry, 1987. Add: Dept. of Philosophy, Northwestern Univ., Evanston, Ill. 60208, U.S.A.

TOULSON, Shirley. British, b. 1924. Poetry, Geography (topography), Mythology/Folklore. Features Ed., The Teacher (journal of the National Union of Teachers), London, since 1967. Former freelance journalist. *Publs:* Shadows in an Orchard, 1960; Circumcision's Not Such a Bad Thing After All and Other Poems, 1970; All Right Auden, I Know You're There: A Quick Thought, 1970; For a Double Time, 1970; The Fault, Dear Brutus: A Zodiac of Sonnets, 1972; (ed.) The Remind-Me-Hat and Other Stories, 1973; Education in Britain, 1974; Four Ways with a Ruin, 1976; The Drover's Roads of Wales, 1977; (with John Loveday) Bones and Angels, 1978; East Anglia, 1979; Derbyshire, 1980; Winter Solstice, 1981; The Moors of the Southwest, 2 vols., 1983–84; The Mendip Hills: A Threatened Landscape, 1984; Celtic Journeys: Scotland and the North of England, 1985; The Celtic Alternative: Reminder of the Christianity We Lost, 1987; Walking Round Wales: The Givaldus Journey, 1988. Add: 16 Priest Row, Wells, Somerset BA5 2PY, England.

TOURS, Hugh Berthold. British, b. 1910. History, Biography. Staff member, Archive Section, Bank of England, London, 1962–69 (joined staff in 1928). *Publs:* Parry Thomas, 1959; The Life and Letters of Emma Hamilton, 1963; The Leyland Eight, 1966; The Dart Valley Railway Story, 1972. Add: 15 Cresswell Place, London SW10 9RD, England.

TOWERS, Regina. *See* PYKARE, Nina.

TOWLE, Tony. American, b. 1939. Poetry. Asst. to the Dir., Universal Ltd. Art Eds., since 1964. *Publs:* After Dinner We Take a Drive into the Night, 1968; North, 1970; Autobiography, and Other Poems, 1977; Works on Paper, 1978. Add: 100 Sullivan St., New York, N.Y. 10012, U.S.A.

TOWNE, Peter. *See* NABOKOV, Peter.

TOWNES, Charles H(ard). American, b. 1915. Physics. Univ. Prof., Univ. of California, Berkeley, since 1967, now Emeritus. Assoc. Prof., 1948–50, Prof. of Physics, 1950–61, Exec. Dir. of the Radiation Lab., 1950–52, and Chmn. of the Physics Dept., 1952–55, Columbia Univ., New York; Provost and Prof. of Physics, 1961–66, and Inst. Prof., 1966–67, Massachusetts Inst. of Technology, Cambridge. Chmn., Science and Technology Advisory Cttee. for Manned Space Flight, NASA, 1964–69; Member, 1966–69, and Vice-Chmn., 1967–69, President's Science Advisory Commn; Pres., American Physical Soc., 1967; Member, President's Commn. on Science and Technology, 1976. Recipient, Nobel Prize in Physics, 1964. *Publs:* (with Paul Kisliuk) Molecular Microwave Spectra Tables, 1952; (with A.L. Schawlow) Microwave Spectroscopy, 1955; (ed.) International Conference on Quantum Electronics, 1960; Masers, Lasers, and Instrumentation, 1964. Add: Dept. of Physics, Univ. of California, Berkeley, Calif. 94720, U.S.A.

TOWNLEY, Ralph. British, b. 1923. Plays/Screenplays, International relations/Current affairs. Sr. Dir., U.N. Secretariat, NYC; now retired. *Publs:* The United Nations: A View from Within, 1968; (with Dr. B.B. Waddy) A Word or Two Before You Go, 1981; The Brides of Enderby, 1988; Madam, I'm Adam (play), 1989. Add: Box 654, 51 Main St., Marion, Mass. 02738, U.S.A.

TOWNSEND, John Rowe. British, b. 1922. Children's fiction, Literature. Sub-Ed., 1949–54, Art Ed., 1954–55, Ed., Manchester Guardian Weekly, 1955–69, and Children's Book Ed., 1968–78, The Guardian, London. *Publs:* Gumble's Yard, 1961; Hell's Edge, 1963; Widdershins Crescent, 1965; The Hallersage Sound, 1966; Pirate's Island, 1968; The Intruder, 1969; Goodnight, Prof., Love, 1970; A Sense of Story, 1971; (ed.) Poetry, 1971; The Summer People, 1972; Forest of the Night, 1974; Written for Children, 1974, 1987; Noah's Castle, 1975; Top of the World, 1976; The Xanadu Manuscript, 1977; A Sounding of Storytellers, 1979; King Creature Come, 1980; The Islanders, 1981; Clever Dick, 1982; A Foreign Affair, 1982; Dan Alone, 1983; Gone to the Dogs, 1984; Cloudy-Bright, 1984; Tom Tiddler's Ground, 1985; The Persuading Stick, 1986; Downstream, 1987; Rob's Place, 1987; The Golden Journey, 1989. Add: 72 Water Lane, Histon, Cambridge CB4 4LR, England.

TOWNSEND, Peter (Brereton). British, b. 1914. Sociology. Prof. of Social Policy, Univ. of Bristol, since 1982. Chmn., Child Poverty Action Group, since 1969, and of Disability Alliance, since 1974. Research Secty., Political and Economic Planning, 1952–54; Research Officer, Inst. of Community Studies, 1954–57; Research Fellow and Lectr., London Sch. of Economics, 1957–63; Prof. of Sociology, Univ. of Essex, Colchester, 1963–81. *Publs:* Family Life of Old People, 1957; (with R. Titmuss and B. Abel-Smith) National Superannuation, 1957; (with C. Woodroffe) Nursing Homes in England and Wales, 1961; The Last Refuge: A Survey of Residential Institutions and Homes for the Aged in England and Wales, 1962; (with D. Wedderburn) The Aged in the Welfare State, 1965; (with B. Abel-Smith) The Poor and the Poorest, 1965; (with R. Titmuss, B. Abel-Smith and R.H.S. Crossman) Socialism and Affluence, 1967; (co-author) Old People in Three Industrial Societies, 1968; (ed.) The Concept of Poverty, 1970; (ed. with N. Bosanquet) Labour and Inequality, 1972; The Social Minority, 1973; Sociology and Social Policy, 1975; Poverty in the United Kingdom, 1979; (ed. with N. Bosanquet) Labour and Equality, 1980; (co-author) Inequalities, in Health, 1980; (co-author) Manifesto, 1981; (ed. with A. Walker) Disability in Britain, 1981; The Family and Later Life, 1981; (co-ed.) Responses to Poverty: Lessons from Europe, 1984; (with P. Phillimore and A. Beattie) Inequalities in Health in the Northern Region, 1986; (with P. Corrigan and U. Kowarzik) Poverty and the London Labour Market, 1987; (with P. Phillimore and A. Beattie) Health and Deprivation: and the North, 1987; (co-authors) Inequalities in Health: The Black Report and the Health Divide, 1988; Inner City Deprivation and Premature Death in Greater Manchester, 1988; (co-auther) Service Provision and Living Standards in Islington, 1988. Add: Dept. of Philosophy, Northwestern Univ., Evanston, Ill. 60208, U.S.A.

TOWNSEND, Peter (Wooldridge). British, b. 1914. History, Third World Problems, Travel/Exploration/Adventure, Autobiography. Full-time writer. Group Capt., Royal Air Force; served War of 1939–45, Wing Comdr., 1941; Equerry to King George VI, 1944–52; Deputy Master of H.M. Household, 1950; Equerry to the Queen, 1952–53; Air Attache, Brussels, 1953–56. *Publs:* Earth, My Friend, 1959; Duel of Eagles, 1970; The Last Emperor, 1975; Time and Chance (autobiography), 1978; The Smallest Pawns in the Game, 1979; The Girl in the White Ship, 1981; The Postman of Nagasaki, 1984; Duel in the Dark, 1986. Add: La Mare aux Oiseaux, 78610 Saint-Leger-en-Yvelines, France.

TOWNSEND, Sue (Susan Townsend). British, b. 1946. Novels, Plays/Screenplays. *Publs:* plays—Bazaar and Rummage, Groping for Words, and Womberang, 1984; The Great Celestial Cow, 1984; The Secret Diary of Adrian Mole Aged 13, 1985 (novel version, 1984); other novels—The Growing Pains of Adrian Mole, 1984; The Adrian Mole Diaries (collection), 1985; Rebuilding Coventry (novel), 1988. Add: c/o Anthony Sheil Assocs., 43 Doughty St., London WC1N 2LF, England.

TOYNBEE, Polly. British, b. 1946. Novelss, Documentaries/ Reportage. News Reporter, since 1969. Social Affairs Ed., BBC TV and Radio, since 1988. Feature Writer, The Observer, London, 1973–77, and Columnist, The Guardian, London, 1977–88. *Publs:* Leftovers, 1966; A Working Life, 1970; Hospital (in U.S. as Patients), 1977; The Way We Live Now, 1982; Lost Children, 1985. Add: 1 Crescent Grove, London SW4, England.

TRACY, Clarence. Canadian, b. 1908. Literature, Biography. Prof. of English, Univ. of Saskatchewan, Saskatoon, 1950–66, Univ. of British Columbia, Vancouver, 1966–68, and Acadia Univ., Wolfville, N.S., 1968–73; Visiting Prof., Univ. of Toronto, 1973–75. *Publs:* Artificial Bastard: Life of Richard Savage, 1953; (ed.) Poetical Works of Richard Savage, 1962; The Spiritual Quixote, by Richard Graves, 1967; Browning's Mind and Art, 1968; Johnson's Life of Savage, 1971; The Rape Observed, 1974; A Portrait of Richard Graves, 1987. Add: Port Maitland, N.S. B0W 2V0, Canada.

TRACY, Leland. *See* **TRALINS,** S. Robert.

TRACY, Michael Alec. British, b. 1932. Agriculture (agricultural economics), History. Head, Agricultural Policies Div., Org. for Economic Cooperationa and Development, Paris, 1966–73; Dir., Council Secretariat of the European Communities, 1973–83; Visiting Prof., Wye Coll., Univ. of London, 1983–88. *Publs:* Agriculture in Western Europe 1964, 3rd ed., 1989; Japanese Agriculture at the Crossroads, 1972; (ed.) for Agriculture in the EEC, 1979. Add: "La Bergerie," 20 Rue Emile Francois, La Hutte, 1474-Ways, Belgium.

TRAILRIDER, *See* **HYLAND,** Ann.

TRAINOR, Francis. American, b. 1929. Biology. Prof. of Biology, Univ. of Connecticut, Storrs, since 1967 (Instr., 1957; Asst. Prof., 1960; Assoc. Prof., 1964). Pres., Phycological Soc. of America, 1969. *Publs:* Introductory Phycology, 1978. Add: Dept. of Ecology and Evolutionary Biology, Univ. of Connecticut, Storrs, Conn. 06269, U.S.A.

TRAINOR, Richard. *See* **TRALINS,** S. Robert.

TRALINS, S(andor) Robert. Also writes as Ray Z. Bixby, Norman A. King, Keith Miles, Sean O'Shea, Rex O'Toole, Leland Tracy, Richard Trainor, Ruy Traube, Cynthia Sydney, and Dorothy Verdon. American, b. 1926. Novels/Short stories, Plays/Screenplays, Psychology, Supernatural/ Occult topics. *Publs:* Dynamic Selling, 1960; How to be a Power Closer in Selling, 1961; Primitive Orgy, 1961; Five Wild Dames, 1961; Congo Lust, 1961; The Rapist, 1962; Hired Nymph, 1962; Four Nude Queens, 1962; The One and Only Jean, 1962; Naked Hills, 1962; Caesar's Bench, 1962; Law of Lust, 1962; Death Before Dishonor, 1962; Freak Lover, 1962; Torrid Island, 1962; Captain O'Six, 1962; They Make Her Beg, 1963; The Love Worshipers, 1963; Donna is Different, 1963; Artist Swinger, The Hillbilly, 1963; Pleasure Was My Business, 1963; (ghostwriter for Frank Russell) Billion Dollars at Your Fingertips, 1963; Devil's Hook, 1963; Smuggler's Mistress, 1963; Colossal Carnality, 1964; Jazzman in Nudetown, 1964; The Smugglers, 1964; The Pirates, 1964; Gunrunner, 1964; (as Norman A. King) French Leave, 1965; (as Cynthia Sydney) Trick or Treat, 1965; Slave King, 1965; (as Sean O'Shea) Whisper, 1965; Squaresville Jag, 1965; (as Sean O'Shea) Variations in Voyeurism, 1965; (as Sean O'Shea) Variations in Exhibitionism, 1965; The Cosmozoids, 1965; (as Sean O'Shea) The Nymphet Syndrome, 1965; (with Michael Gilbert) Psychological Study of 21 Abnormal Sex Offenders, 1965; Supernatural Happenings, 1965; Beyond Human Understanding, 1965; The Miss from S.I.S., 1966; The Chic Chick Spy, 1966; (as Norman A. King) So Cold, So Cruel, 1966; (as Dorothy Verdon) First Try, 1966; (as Cynthia Sydney) Stay until Morning, 1966; (as Cynthia Sydney) The Higher the Price, 1966; (as Cynthia Sydney) The Love Business, 1966; (as Rex O'Toole) Soft Sell, 1966; (as Cynthia Sydney) Take Me Out in Trade, 1966; (as Cynthia Sydney) Lost and Found, 1966; (as Norman A. King) Hide and Seek, 1966; (as Cynthia Sydney) Sin Point, 1966; (as Cynthia Sydney) Ripe and Ready, 1966; (as Cynthia Sydney) Office Swinger, 1966; Sexual Fetish, 1966; Gomer Pyle USMC, 1966; Dragnet '67, 1966; Psychokick, 1966; Remember to Die, 1966; (ghostwriter for William Hersey) How to Cash in on Your Hidden Memory Power; (as Sean O'Shea) What a Way to Go, 1966; (as Sean O'Shea) Operation Boudoir, 1967; (as Sean O'Shea) Win with Sin, 1967; (as Sean O'Shea) Nymph Island Affair, 1967; (as Sean O'Shea) Invasion of the Nymphs, 1967; Cairo Madam, 1967; (as Cynthia Sydney) Executive Wife, 1967; (as Norman A. King) The Flyers, 1967; (as Cynthia Sydney) Give and Take, 1967; (as Rex O'Toole) Soft Sell, 1967; The Ring-a-Ding UFOs, 1967; (as Ruy Traube) The Seduction Art, 1967; (as Ruy Traube) Memoirs

of a Beach Boy Lover, 1967; (as Ray Z. Bixby) Rites of Lust, 1967; (as Ruy Traube) Uninhibited, 1968; (as Rex O'Toole) Cheating and Infidelity, 1968; (as Richard Trainor) Yum-Yum Girl, 1968; (as Rex O'Toole) Confessions of an Exhibitionist, 1968; (as Sean O'Shea) The Topless Kitties, 1968; Strangers, 1968; Runaway Slave, 1968; (as Ruy Traube) Sex Cultists, 1969; (as Rex O'Toole) Gigolos, 1969; The Mind Code, 1969; Black Brute, 1969; Slave's Revenge, 1969; Clairvoyance in Women, 1969; ESP Forewarnings, 1969; Weird People of the Unknown, 1969; Children of the Supernatural, 1969; Panther John, 1970; Black Pirate, 1970; The Hidden Spectre, 1970; Ghoul Lover, 1971; (as Alfred D. Laurance) Homer Pickle the Greatest, 1971; Clairvoyant Women, 1972; Supernatural Strangers, 1972; Supernatural Warnings, 1973; (as Keith Miles) Dragon's Teeth, 1973; Android Armageddon, 1974; Illegal Tender (screenplay), 1975; Buried Alive, 1977. Add: c/o Fiesta Publishing Corp., 6360 NE Fourth Ct., Miami, Fla. 33138, U.S.A.

TRANTER, Clement John. British, b. 1909. Mathematics/Statistics. Bashforth Prof. of Mathematical Physics, Royal Military Coll. of Science, Shrivenham, 1953–74, now Emeritus (Sr. Lectr. in Mathematics, 1935–47; Assoc. Prof. of Mathematics, 1947–53). *Publs:* Integral Transforms in Mathematical Physics, 1951; Advanced Level Pure Mathematics, 1953; Techniques of Mathematical Analysis, 1957; (with C.G. Lambe) Differential Equations for Engineers and Scientists, 1961; Mathematics for Sixth Form Scientists, 1964; (with C.G. Lambe) Advanced Level Mathematics: Pure and Applied, 1966; Bessel Functions with Some Physical Applications, 1968. Add: Flagstones, 25 Trenchard Rd., Stanton Fitzwarren, nr. Swindon, Wilts, SN6 7RZ, England.

TRANTER, John (Ernest). Australian, b. 1943. Poetry. Asian Ed., Angus and Robertson, publishers, Singapore, 1971–73; Radio Producer, Australian Broadcasting Commn., Sydney and Brisbane, 1974–77. *Publs:* Parallax and Other Poems, 1970; Red Movie and Other Poems, 1972; The Blast Area, 1974; The Alphabet Murders: Notes from a Work in Progress, 1976; Crying in Early Infancy: One Hundred Sonnets, 1977; (ed.) The New Australian Poetry, 1979; Selected Poems, 1982; Under Berlin: New Poems 1988, 1988. Add: 59 View St., Annandale, N.S.W. 2038, Australia.

TRANTER, Nigel (Godwin). Also wrote western novels as Nye Tredgold. British, b. 1909. Historical/Romance/Gothic, Westerns/Adventure, Children's fiction, Architecture, Country life/Rural societies, History. Full-time writer, lecturer and broadcaster, since 1946. Accountant and inspector, family insurance co., Edinburgh, 1929–39. Chmn., Scottish Convention, 1948–51; Scottish Pres., P.E.N., 1962–66 (now Hon. Pres.); Scottish Chmn., Soc. of Authors, 1966–74, and National Book League, 1973–78. *Publs:* The Fortalices and Early Mansions of Southern Scotland 1400–1650, 1935; Trespass, 1937; Mammon's Daughter, 1939; Harsh Heritage, 1939; Eagles Feathers, 1941; Watershed, 1941; The Gilded Fleece, 1942; Delayed Action, 1944; Tinker's Pride, 1945; Man's Estate, 1946; Flight of Dutchmen, 1947; Island Twilight, 1947; Root and Branch, 1948; Colours Flying 1948; The Chosen Course, 1949; (as Nye Tredgold) Thirsty Range, 1949; (as Nye Tredgold) Heartbreak Valley, 1950; Fair Game, 1950; High Spirits, 1950; The Freebooters, 1950; Tidewrack, 1951; Fast and Loose, 1951; Bridal Path, 1952; Cheviot Chase, 1952; (as Nye Tredgold) The Big Corral, 1952; (as Nye Tredgold) Trail Herd, 1952; Ducks and Drakes, 1953; The Queen's Grace, 1953; (as Nye Tredgold) Desert Doublecross, 1953; Rum Week, 1954; The Night Riders, 1954; (as Nye Tredgold) Cloven Hooves, 1954; There Are Worse Jungles, 1955; Rio d'Oro, 1955; (as Nye Tredgold) Dynamite Trail, 1955; The Long Coffin, 1956; (as Nye Tredgold) Rancher Renegade, 1956; MacGregor's Gathering, 1957; The Enduring Flame, 1957; (as Nye Tredgold) Trailing Trouble, 1957; (as Nye Tredgold) Death Reckoning, 1957; Balefire, 1958; The Stone, 1958; (as Nye Tredgold) Bloodstone Trail, 1958; Spaniards' Isle (juvenile), 1958; Border Rising (juvenile), 1959; Nestor the Monster (juvenile), 1960; Birds of a Feather (juvenile), 1961; The Deer Poachers (juvenile), 1961; Kettle of Fish, 1961; The Master of Gray, 1961; Something Very Fishy (juvenile), 1962; The Fortified House in Scotland (non-fiction), 5 vols., 1962–66, as 1 vol., 1970; Drug on the Market, 1962; Gold for Prince Charlie, 1962; The Courtesan, 1963; Give a Dog a Bad Name (juvenile), 1963; Chain of Destiny, 1964; Silver Island (juvenile), 1964; Smoke Across the Highlands (juvenile), 1964; The Pegasus Book of Scotland (juvenile), 1964; Past Master, 1965; Pursuit (juvenile), 1965; Outlaw of the Highlands: Rob Roy (non-fiction), 1965; A Stake in the Kingdom, 1966; Lion Let Loose, 1967; Fire and High Water (juvenile), 1967; Tinker Tess (juvenile), 1967; Cable from Kabul, 1968; Black Douglas, 1968; To the Rescue (juvenile), 1968; (ed.) No Tigers in the Hindu Kush, by Philip Tranter, 1968; Land of the Scots (non-fiction), 1968; Robert the Bruce (trilogy): The Steps to the Empty Throne, 1969; The Path of the Hero King, 1970; The Price of the King's

Peace, 1971; The Queen's Scotland (non-fiction), 4 vol., 1971–77; The Young Montrose, 1972; Portrait of the Border Country (non-fiction), 1972; Montrose, The Captain-General, 1973; The Wisest Fool, 1974; The Wallace, 1975; Stewart Trilogy: Lords of Misrule, 1976; A Folly of Princes, 1977; The Captive Crown, 1977; Macbeth the King, 1978; Margaret the Queen, 1979; Portrait of the Lothians (non-fiction), 1979; David the Prince, 1980; True Thomas, 1981; Nigel Tranter's Scotland: A Very Personal View, 1981; The Patriot, 1982; Lord of the Isles, 1983; Unicorn Rampant, 1984; The Riven Realm, 1984; Traditions of Scottish Castles (non-fiction), 1985; James, By the Grace of God, 1985; Rough Wooing, 1986; Columba: The Story of Scotland (non-fiction), 1987; Cache Down, 1987; Flowers of Chiralry, 1988; Mail Royal, 1989. Add: Quarry House, Aberlady, East Lothian EH32 0QB, Scotland.

TRAPIDO, Barbara. South African, b. 1941. Novels/Short stories. Full-time writer since 1970. Secondary sch. English teacher, in London, 1964–70. *Publs:* Brother of the More Famous Jack, 1982; Noah's Ark, 1984. Add: 5 Southmoor Rd., Oxford OX2 6RS, England.

TRASLER, Gordon Blair. British, b. 1929. Psychology. Prof. of Psychology, Univ. of Southampton, since 1964 (Lectr., 1957–64; Dean of Social Sciences, 1970–73). Ed.-in-Chief, British Journal of Criminology, since 1980. Psychologist, H.M. Prisons at Wandsworth and Winchester, England, 1955–57. *Publs:* In Place of Parents, 1960; The Explanation of Criminality, 1962; The Shaping of Social Behaviour, 1967; (with J. Bowlby, B. Bernstein, D.M. Downes, P. Leach and C. Hindley) The Formative Years, 1968; (with M. Davies) Research and Penal Practice, 1975; (with D.P. Farrington) Behaviour Modification with Offenders, 1980. Add: Fox Croft, Old Kennels Lane, Oliver's Battery, Winchester SO22 4JT, England.

TRATTNER, Walter I. American, b. 1936. History, Social commentary/phenomena. Prof. of History, Univ. of Wisconsin—Milwaukee, since 1972 (Asst. Prof., 1965–67; Assoc. Prof., 1967–71). Asst. Prof. of History, Northern Illinois Univ., DeKalb, 1963–65. *Publs:* Homer Folks: Pioneer in Social Welfare, 1968; Crusade for the Children: A History of the National Child Labor Committee and Child Labor Reform in America, 1970; From Poor Law to Welfare State: A History of Social Welfare in America, 1974, 4th ed., 1989; Social Welfare or Social Control?, 1983; Social Welfare: An Annotated Bibliography, 1983; Biographical Dictionary of Social Welfare in America, 1986. Add: 4719 N. Elkhart Ave., Milwaukee, Wisc. 53211, U.S.A.

TRAUBE, Ruy. *See* **TRALINS**, S. Robert.

TRAVELL, Janet (Graeme). American, b. 1901. Autobiography/Memoirs/Personal. Physician in private practice, since 1933. Assoc. Physician, Dept. of Medicine (Cardiovascular Diseases), Beth Israel Hosp., NYC, since 1941; Clinical Prof. of Medicine Emerita, George Washington Sch. of Medicine, Washington, D.C., since 1970 (Assoc. Clinical Prof., 1961–70). Instr. in Pharmacology, 1933–47, Asst. Prof., 1947–51, and Assoc. Prof. in Clinical Pharmacology, 1951–63, Cornell Univ. Medical Coll., NYC; Physician, Outpatients, New York Hosp., NYC, 1941–66, and to the U.S. Pres., Washington, D.C. 1961–65; Special Consultant to the U.S. Air Force, Office of the Surgeon Gen., Washington, D.C., 1962–64. *Publs:* Office Hours: Day and Night, 1969; (with David G. Simons) Myofascial Pain and Dysfunction: The Trigger Point Manual, 1983. Add: 4525 Cathedral Ave. N.W., Washington, D.C. 20016, U.S.A.

TRAVER, Robert. Pseud. for John Donaldson Voelker. American, b. 1903. Novels/Short stories, Recreation/Leisure/Hobbies, Autobiography/Memoirs/Personal. Prosecuting Attorney, Marquette County, Michigan, 1935–50; Justice of the Michigan Supreme Court, 1957–60; Weekly Columnist, Detroit News, 1967–69. *Publs:* Troubleshooter: The Story of a Northwoods Prosecutor, 1943; Danny and the Boys: Being Some Legends of Hungry Hollow, 1951; Small Town D.A., 1954; Anatomy of a Murder (novel), 1958; Trout Madness, 1960; Hornstein's Boy (novel), 1962; Anatomy of a Fisherman, 1964; Laughing Whitefish (novel), 1965; The Jealous Mistress, 1968; Trout Magic, 1974; People Versus Kirk, 1981. Add: Deer Lake Road, Ishpeming, Mich. 49849, U.S.A.

TRAVERS, Basil Holmes. Australian, b. 1919. Sports/Physical education/Keeping fit, Biography. Headmaster, Launceston Church Grammar Sch., 1953–58, and Sydney Church of England Grammar Sch., 1959–84. *Publs:* Let's Talk Rugger, 1950; The Captain General, 1953. Add: 19 Edward St., Gordon, N.S.W. 2072, Australia.

TRAVERS, Kenneth. *See* **HUTCHIN**, Kenneth Charles.

TRAVERS, P(amela) L(yndon). British, b. 1906. Children's fiction, Essays. Journalist, actress, and dancer, in the 1920's; Regular contrib. to the Irish Statesman, Dublin, in 1920's and 1920's; worked for the British Ministry of Information in the U.S. during World War II; Writer-in-Residence, Radcliffe Coll., Cambridge, Mass., 1965–66, Smith Coll., Northampton, Mass., 1966–67, and Scripps Coll., Claremont, Calif., 1970. *Publs:* Mary Poppins series, 6 vols., 1934–88; Moscow Excursion, 1935; Happy Ever After, 1940; I Go by Sea, I Go by Land, 1941; The Fox at the Manger, 1962; Friend Monkey, 1971; About Sleeping Beauty, 1975; Two Pairs of Shoes, 1980; What The Bees Know (essays), 1989. Add: c/o William Collins Sons Ltd., 8 Grafton St., London W1, England.

TRAVERSI, Derek A(ntona). British, b. 1912. Literature. Emeritus Prof. of English, Swarthmore Coll., Pennsylvania. Dir. of the British Inst., Barcelona, 1945–48; Rep. of the British Council, Montevideo, 1948–50, Santiago, Chile, 1950–55, Teheran, 1955–59, Madrid, 1959–65, and Rome, 1965–70. *Publs:* An Approach to Shakespeare, 1938, 3rd ed. 1968; Shakespeare: The Last Phase, 1954; Shakespeare: From Richard II to Henry V, 1957; Shakespeare: The Roman Plays, 1963; T.S. Eliot: The Longer Poems, 1976; The Literary Imagination, 1981; The Canterbury Tales: A Reading, 1983; Chaucer: The Earlier Poetry, 1987. Add: 12 Richmond Mansions, Denton Rd., Twickenham, Middx. TW1 2HH, England.

TRAVIS, Dempsey J. American, b. 1920. Cultural/Ethnic topics, Autobiography, Biography. Press., Travis Realty Co., Chicago, since 1949; Pres., Urban Research Inst., Chicago, since 1969. Has served as: Dir., Sears Bank and Trust Co.; Chmn., Mayor of Chicago's Real Estate Review Cttee.; Member, Bd. of Dirs., Chicago World's Fair Cttee.; Member, Bd. of Trustees, Garrett-Evangelical Seminary Evanston, Ill., and Northwestern Memorial Hosp., Chicago. *Publs:* Don't Stop Me Now (autobiography), 1970; An Autobiography of Black Chicago, 1981; An Autobiography of Black Jazz, 1983; An Autobiography of Black Politics, 1987; Harold Washington, The People's Mayor, 1988. Add: 8001 S. Champlain, Chicago, Ill. 60619, U.S.A.

TRAWICK, Buckner Beasley. American, b. 1914. Literature, Autobiography/Memoirs/Personal. Prof. Emeritus of English, Univ. of Alabama, Tuscaloosa, since 1978 (Asst. Prof., 1946–51; Assoc. Prof., 1951 –62; Prof., 1962–78). Instr., Clemson Agricultural Coll., S.C., 1937–38, Univ. of Mississippi, University, 1938–40, and Temple Univ., Philadelphia, Pa., 1946. *Publs:* World Literature, vol. I, 1953, vol. II, 1955; (ed.) Selected Prose Works of Arthur Hugh Clough, 1964; The Bible as Literature, vol. I, 1968, vol. II, 1970; Shakespeare's Othello: Analysis and Criticism, 1969; Shakespeare and Alcohol, 1978; The Trawick Tree: Its Nuts and Fruits, 1982. Add: 7 Sycamore Lane, Tuscaloosa, Ala. 35405, U.S.A.

TREADGOLD, Donald Warren. American, b. 1922. History. Prof. of Russian History, Jackson Sch. of Intnl. Studies, Univ. of Washington, Seattle, since 1959 (Asst. Prof., 1949–55; Assoc. Prof., 1955–59; Chmn., Dept. of History, 1972–82; Chmn., Russian and East European Studies, 1983–86). Ed., Slavic Review, 1961–65, and 1968–75; Pres., American Assn. for the Advancement of Slavic Studies, 1977–78, and Pacific Coast Branch of the American Historical Assn., 1978–79. *Publs:* Lenin and His Rivals, 1955; The Great Siberian Migration, 1957; Twentieth Century Russia, 1959, 6th ed. 1987; (ed.) The Development of the USSR: An Exchange of Views, 1964; (ed.) Soviet and Chinese Communism: Similarities and Differences, 1967; The West in Russia and China: Religious and Secular Thought in Modern Times, 2 vols., 1973; (ed. with P.F. Sugar) The Lands of Partitioned Poland 1795-1918, by P.S. Wandycz, 1974; (ed. with P.F. Sugar) East Central Europe Between the Two World Wars, by J. Rothschild, 1974; (ed. with P.F. Sugar) Southeastern Europe under Ottoman Rule 1354-1804, 1977; (ed. with P.F. Sugar) The Establishment of the Balkan National States 1804-1920, by C. and B. Jelavich, 1977; A History of Christianity, 1979; (ed. with P.F. Sugar) The Peoples of the Eastern Habsburg Lands, 1526-1918, by Robert A. Kann and Zdenek V. David, 1984. Add: 900 University St., Seattle, Wash. 98101, U.S.A.

TREADGOLD, Mary. British, b. 1910. Novels, Children's fiction. Former BBC Producer and Literary Ed., Overseas Services. *Publs:* We Couldn't Leave Dinah, 1941; No Ponies, 1946; The Polly Harris, 1949; The Running Child (novel), 1951; The Heron Ride, 1961; The Winter Princess, 1962; Return to the Heron, 1963; The Weather Boy, 1964; Maid's Ribbons, 1965; Elegant Patty, 1967; Poor Patty, 1968; This Summer, Last Summer, 1968; The Humbugs, 1968; The Rum Day of the

Vanishing Pony, 1970; Journey from the Heron, 1981. Add: c/o Jonathan Cape, 32 Bedford Sq., London WC1, England.

TREASE, (Robert) Geoffrey. British, b. 1909. Novels/Short stories, Children's fiction, Plays, History, Autobiography/Memoirs/Personal. Member of the Council, Soc. of Authors, London, since 1974 (Chmn., Management Cttee., 1972–73). *Publs:* Bows Against the Barons, 1934; Comrades for the Charter, 1934; Call to Arms, 1935; Walking in England, 1935; Missing from Home, 1937; Red Comet, 1937; Mystery on the Moors, 1937; Christmas Holiday Mystery, 1937; Detectives of the Dales, 1938; In the Land of the Mogul, 1938; The Dragon Who Was Different (plays), 1938; Such Divinity, 1939; Colony (play), 1939; Only Natural, 1940; Cue for Treason, 1940; Running Deer, 1941; The Grey Adventurer, 1942; Black Night, Red Morning, 1944; Trumpets in the West, 1947; The Hills of Varna (in U.S. as Shadow of the Hawk), 1948; Silver Guard, 1948; Fortune My Foe (in U.S. as Sir Walter Raleigh, Captain and Adventurer), 1949; Young Traveller in India and Pakistan, 1949; No Boats on Bannermere, 1949; Mystery of Moorside Farm, 1949; Tales Out of School, 1949; The Secret Fiord, 1949; Under Black Banner, 1950; Enjoying Books, 1951; Black Banner Players, 1952; The Crown of Violet (in U.S. as Web of Traitors), 1952; The Barons' Hostage, 1952; Young Traveller in England and Wales, 1953; The Shadow of Spain (plays), 1953; The Silken Secret, 1953; The Seven Queens of England, 1953; Black Banner Abroad, 1954; The Fair Flower of Danger, 1955; Seven Kings of England, 1955; The Gates of Bannerdale, 1956; Word to Caesar (in U.S. as Message to Hadrian), 1956; The Young Traveller in Greece, 1956; Snared Nightingale, 1957; Mist Over Athelney (in U.S. as Escape to King Alfred), 1958; So Wild the Heart, 1959; Edward Elgar: Maker of Music, 1959; The Maythorn Story, 1960; Thunder of Valmy (in U.S. as Victory at Valmy), 1960; Wolfgang Mozart, 1961; The Young Writer, 1961; Change at Maythorn, 1962; The Italian Story, 1963; Follow My Black Plume, 1963; A Thousand for Sicily, 1964; Seven Stages, 1964; The Dutch are Coming, 1965; Bent is the Bow, 1965; This is Your Century, 1965; The Red Towers of Granada, 1966; The Grand Tour, 1967; The White Nights of St. Petersburg, 1967; (ed.) Matthew Todd's Journal, 1968; The Runaway Serf, 1968; Seven Sovereign Queens, 1968; Byron, A Poet Dangerous to Know, 1969; Nottingham, A Biography, 1970; The Condottieri, 1970; A Masque for the Queen, 1970; A Whiff of Burnt Boats: An Early Autobiography, 1971; Horsemen on the Hills, 1971; Samuel Pepys and His World, 1972; A Ship to Rome, 1972; Popinjay Stairs, 1973; D.H. Lawrence, the Phoenix and the Flame (in U.S. as The Phoenix and the Flame: D.H. Lawrence), 1973; Days to Remember, A Garland of Historic Anniversaries, 1973; A Voice in the Night, 1973; Laughter at the Door: A Continued Autobiography, 1974; The Chocolate Boy, 1975; London: A Concise History, 1975; The Iron Tsar, 1975; When the Drums Beat, 1976; Violet for Bonaparte, 1976; The Seas of Morning, 1976; The Spy Catchers, 1976; The Field of the Forty Footsteps, 1977; The Claws of the Eagle, 1977; Portrait of a Cavalier: William Cavendish, 1st Duke of Newcastle, 1979; Mandeville, 1980; A Wood by Moonlight, 1981; Saraband for Shadows, 1982; The Cormorant Venture, 1984; Timechanges, 1985; The Edwardian Era, 1986; Tomorrow Is a Stranger, 1987; The Arpino Assignment, 1988; A Slight of Angels, 1988; Hidden Treasure, 1989. Add: 1 Yomede Park, Newbridge Rd., Bath BA1 3LS, England.

TREAT, Lawrence. American, b. 1903. Mystery/Crime/Suspense. Founder and Past Pres., Mystery Writers of America. *Publs:* Bringing Sherlock Home (puzzle book), 1930; Run Far, Run Fast, 1937; B as in Banshee, 1940; (as Wail for the Corpses, 1943); D as in Dead, 1941; H as in Hangman, 1942; O as in Omen, 1943; The Leather Man, 1944; V as in Victim, 1945; H as in Hunted, 1946; Q as in Quicksand, 1947 (in U.K. as Step into Quicksand, 1959); T as in Trapped, 1947; F as in Flight, 1948; Over the Edge, 1948; Trial and Terror, 1949; Big Shot, 1951; Weep for a Wanton, 1956; Lady, Drop Dead, 1960; Venus Unarmed, 1961; (ed.) Murder in Mind, 1967; P as in Police (short stories), 1970; (ed.) The Mystery Writer's Handbook, 1976; Crime and Puzzlement (puzzles), 1981; (ed.) A Special Kind of Crime, 1982; Crime and Puzzlement, 2 (puzzles), 1982; You're the Detective (juvenile), 1983; The Armchair Detective, 1983; Crime and Puzzlement, 3 (puzzles), 1988. Add: RFD Box 475A, Edgartown, Mass. 02539, U.S.A.

TREDGOLD, Nye. *See* **TRANTER,** Nigel.

TREFIL, James. American, b. 1938. Physics. Prof. of Physics, Univ. of Virginia, Charlottesville, since 1975 (Assoc. Prof., 1970–75). *Publs:* Physics as a Liberal Art, 1978; From Atoms to Quarks, 1980; (with Robert T. Rood) Are We Alone?, 1981; Colonies in Space, 1981; The Moment of Creation: Big Bang Physics from Before the First Millisecond to the Present Universe, 1984; The Unexpected Vista: A Physicist's View of Nature, 1985; Meditations at Ten Thousand Feet: A Scientist in the Moun-

tains, 1986; Meditations at Sunset: A Scientist Looks at the Sky, 1987; Scientist at the Seashore, 1987; The Dark Side of the Universe: Searching for the Outer Limits of the Cosmos, 1988. Add: c/o Macmillan, 866 Third Ave., New York, N.Y. 10022, U.S.A.

TREFOUSSE, Hans Louis. American, b. 1921. History, Autobiography/ Memoirs/Personal, Biography. Distinguished Prof. of History, Brooklyn Coll., City Univ. of New York, since 1986 (Instr., 1950–57; Asst. Prof., 1958–61; Assoc. Prof., 1962–65; Prof. since 1966). Instr., Adelphi Coll., Garden City, N.Y., 1949–50. Ed., Twayne Series Rulers and Statesmen of the World, 1966–76. *Publs:* Germany and American Neutrality, 1939-41, 1951; Ben Butler: The South Called Him Beast, 1957; (ed.) What Happened at Pearl Habor?, 1958; Benjamin Franklin Wade: Radical Republican from Ohio, 1964; (ed.) The Cold War, 1965; The Radical Republicans: Lincoln's Vanguard for Racial Justice, 1969; (ed.) Background for Radical Reconstruction, 1970; Reconstruction: America's First Effort at Radical Democracy, 1971; (ed.) The Causes of the Civil War, 1971; Lincoln's Decision for Emancipation, 1975; Impeachment of a President: Andrew Johnson, the Blacks and Reconstruction, 1975; (ed.) Towards a New Viewpoint of America: Essays in Honor of Arthur C. Cole, 1977; (ed.) Germany and America: Essays on Problems of International Relations and Immigration, 1980; Carl Schurz: A Biography, 1982; Pearl Habor: The Continuing Controversy, 1982; Andrew Johnson: A Biography, 1989. Add: 22 Shore Acres Rd., Staten Island, N.Y. 10305, U.S.A.

TREGEAR, Thomas R. British, b. 1897. Economics, Geography. Lectr., 1923–27, and Prof. of Geography, 1946–51, Central China Univ., Wuchang: Geography Teacher, Sidcot Sch., Winscombe, Somerset, 1929–46; Lectr., Univ. of Hong Kong, 1952–59; Warden, Woodbrooke Coll., Birmingham, 1959–63. *Publs:* Land Use in Hong Kong and the New Territories, 1958; (with L. Berry) The Development of Hong Kong and Kowloon as told in Maps, 1959; A Geography of China, 1965; Economic Geography of China, 1970; The Chinese: How They Live and Work, 1973; China: A Geographical Survey, 1980. Add: 24 Portland Rd., Oxford, England.

TREGIDGO, Philip Sillince. British, b. 1926. Education, Language/Linguistics. Occasional Lectr. in English for British Council, London. Teacher in the U.K., 1951–54; Sr. Education Officer and English Teaching Organiser, Ghana, 1954–63. *Publs:* Practical English Usage for Overseas Students, 1959; A Background to English, 1961; (with P.A. Ogundipe) Practical English, Books 1-5, 1965–66; English for Tanzanian Schools, Standards 6 and 7, 1966–68; The Story of the Aeroplane, 1969; The Magic Rocks, 1969; (with I.K. Hoh) Longman New Ghana English Course, Books 1-3, 1970–78; The Story of the Motor Car, 1971; The Story of Trains, 1974; English Grammar in Practice, 1979; (with A.L. Mawasha) Advance with English Standard 6, 7, and 8, 1979–81; (with P.A. Ogundipe) New Practical English, Junior Books 1-3, 1985–86, Senior Books 1-3, 1986–88. Add: Winneba, 11 The Avenue, Petersfield, Hants., England.

TREHEARNE, Elizabeth. *See* **MAXWELL,** Patricia Anne.

TREITEL, G(ünter) H(einz). British, b. 1928. Law. Fellow, All Souls Coll., Oxford, and Vinerian Prof. of English Law, Oxford Univ., since 1979 (Lectr., University Coll., Oxford, 1953–54; Fellow, Magdalen Coll., Oxford, 1954–79; All Souls Reader in English Law, Oxford Univ., 1964–79). Trustee, British Museum, London, since 1983. Asst. Lectr., London Sch. of Economics, 1951–53. *Publs:* (co-ed.) Dicey's Conflict of Laws, 7th ed. 1958, and Dicey and Morris: Conflict of Laws, 8th ed. 1967; The Law of Contract, 1962, 7th ed. 1987; (co-ed.) Chitty on Contracts, 23rd ed. 1968; 25th ed. 1983; (co-ed.) Benjamin's Sale of Goods, 1974, 3rd ed., 1987; An Outline of the Law of Contract, 1975, 4th ed., 1989; Remedies for Breach of Contract: A Comparative Account, 1988. Add: All Souls Coll., Oxford OX1 4AL, England.

TREMAIN, Rose. British, b. 1943. Novels/Short stories, Children's fiction, Women, Biography. *Publs:* Freedom for Women, 1971; Stalin: An Illustrated Biography, 1974; Sadler's Birthday, 1976; Letter to Sister Benedicta, 1979; The Cupboard, 1981; The Colonel's Daughter and Other Stories, 1984; The Swimming Pool Season, 1985; Journey to the Volcano (for children), 1985; The Garden of the Villa Mollini, 1987. Add: 2 High House, Thorpe St. Andrew, Norwich NR7 0EZ, England.

TRENCH, John (Chenevix). British, b. 1920. Mystery/Crime/Suspense, Archaeology/Antiquities, History. Copy consultant. Creative Group Head, S.H. Benson Ltd., 1964–70; Creative Dir., 1970–74, and Account Dir., 1974–80, Foster Turner & Benson Ltd. *Publs:* Docken

Dead, 1953; Dishonoured Bones, 1954; What Rough Beast, 1957; Archaeology Without a Spade, 1960; History for Postmen, 1961; The Bones of Britain, 1962; (ed.) The Harp Book of Graces, 1962; Beyond the Atlas, 1963. Add: Windmill Farm, Coleshill, Amersham, Bucks., England.

TRENDALL, Arthur Dale. Australian, b. 1909. Archaeology/Antiquities. Resident Fellow, La Trobe Univ., since 1969. Librarian, British Sch. at Rome, 1936–38; Fellow, Trinity Coll., Cambridge, 1936–40; Prof. of Greek and Archaeology, 1939–54, and Dean, Faculty of Arts, 1947–50, Univ. of Sydney; Master of Univ. House, Australian National Univ., Canberra, 1954–69; Geddes-Harrower Prof. of Greek Art and Archaeology, Univ. of Aberdeen, 1966–67. *Publs:* Paestan Pottery, 1936; (with J.R. Stewart) Handbook to the Nicholson Museum, 2nd ed. 1948; Vasi antichi dipinti del Vaticano—Vasi italioti ed etruschi a fiture rosse, 2 vols., 1953, 1955, and Collezione Astarita: Vasi italioti ed estruschi, 1976; (with A. Cambitoglou) Apulian Red-figured Vase-Painters of the Plain Style, 1961; South Italian Vase Painting, 1966; The Red-figured Vases of Lucania, Campania and Sicily, 2 vols., 1967, supplements I, II, and III, 1970, 1973, 1984; Greek Vases in the Logie Collection, 1971; (with T.B.L. Webster) Illustrations of Greek Drama, 1971; Early South Italian Vase-painting, 1974; Greek Vases in the National Gallery of Victoria, 1978; (with A. Cambitoglou) The Red-figured Vases of Apulia, 2 vols., 1978–82, supplement I, 1984; (with Ian McPhee) Greek Red-figured Fish Plates, 1987; The Red-figured Vases of Paestum, 1987; Red-Figure Vases of South Italy and Sicily, 1988. Add: Menzies Coll., La Trobe Univ., Bundoora, Vic. 3083, Australia.

TRENGOVE, Alan Thomas. Australian, b. 1929. History, Medicine/Health, Sports/Physical education/Keeping fit, Biography. Feature Writer and Columnist, Herald & Weekly Times Ltd., Melbourne, Vic., 1955–75. *Publs:* (co-author) The Golden Mile, 1961; (co-author and ed.) The Art of Tennis (in U.S. as Tennis the Professional Way), 1964; (co-author) The Unforgiving Minute, 1966; (co-author) Living with Arthritis, 1969; John Grey Gorton: An Informal Biography, 1969; (ed.) Geoff Hunt on Squash, 1974; (co-author and co-ed.) The Australasian Book of Thoroughbred Racing, 1974; (co-author) Not Just for Openers, 1974; The BHP Story, 1975; Adventure in Iron, 1976; Menzies: A Pictorial Biography, 1978; Discovery: Stories of Modern Mineral Exploration, 1979; The Story of the Davis Cup, 1985. Add: 31 Trafalgar St., Mont Albert, Vic., Australia 3127.

TRENHAILE, John Stevens. British, b. 1949. Novels, Mystery/Crime/Suspense. *Publs:* Kyril, 1981; A View from the Square, 1983; Nocturne for the General, 1985; The Mahjong Spies, 1986; The Gates of Exquisite View, 1987; The Scroll of Benevolence, 1988; Krysalis, 1989. Add: c/o Blake Friedmann, literary agents, 37-41 Gower St., London WC1E 6HH, England.

TRENT, Olaf. *See* **FANTHORPE**, R. Lionel.

TRENTON, Gail. *See* **GRANT**, Neil.

TREPP, Leo. American, b. 1913. Philosophy, Theology/Religion. Prof. Emeritus of Philosophy and Humanities, Napa Coll., Calif. (Rabbi since 1936). Visiting Prof. of Religion, Univ. of Oldenburg, and Hamburg, W. Germany, 1972, 1979, Univ. of Mainz, W. Germany, 1983–87; Univ. Prof., since 1988. *Publs:* Taine, Montaigne, Richeome: ein Beitrag zur französichen Wesenkunde, 1935; Eternal Faith, Eternal People: A Journey into Judaism, 1962, rev. ed. as History of the Jewish Experince: Eternal Faith, Eternal People, 1973; Die Landesgemeinde der Juden in Oldenburg, 1965; Judaism, Development and Life, 1966, 3rd ed. 1981; Das Judentum, Geschichte und lebendige Gegenwart, 1970, 3rd ed. 1979; Die Oldenburger Judenschaft, 1973; The Complete Book of Jewish Observance, 1980; Una Historia de la Experiencia Judia, 1980; Die Juden, 1987. Add: 295 Montecito Blvd., Napa, Calif., 94558, U.S.A.

TRESIDDER, Argus John. American, b. 1907. Language/Linguistics, Mythology (classical). Foreign Service Officer, 1949–70, now retired. Former Prof. of English in American and foreign Univs. *Publs:* Reading to Others, 1940; (with L. Schubert and C. Jones) Writing and Speaking, 1943; Myths of Turkey, 1956; Ceylon: An Introduction to the Resplendent Land, 1960; The Basic Principles of Oral and Written Composition; Six Tickets to Effective Communication, 1977; Watch-Word!: A Glossary of Gobbledygook, Clichés, and Solecisms, 1981. Add: 4206 Cordell St., Annandale, Va. 22003, U.S.A.

TRESSELT, Alvin. American, b. 1916. Children's fiction, Mythology/Folklore. Instr. and Dean of Faculty, Inst. of Children's Literature, Redding Ridge, Conn., since 1974. Worked in a defense plant, 1943–46;

Display Designer and Advertising Copywriter, B. Altman Co., NYC, 1946–52; Ed., Humpty Dumpty's Mag., NYC, 1952–65; Ed., 1965–67, and Exec. Ed. and Vice Pres., 1967–74, Parents' Mag. Pres, NYC. *Publs:* Rain Drop Splash, 1946; White Snow Bright Snow, 1947; Johnny Maple-Leaf, 1948; The Wind and Peter, 1948; Bonnie Bess: The Weathervane Horse, 1949; Sun Up, 1949; Little Lost Sqirrel, 1950; Follow the Wind, 1950; Hi, Mr. Robin!, 1950; Autumn Harvest, 1951; A Day with Daddy, 1953; Follow the Road, 1953; I Saw the Sea Come In, 1954; Wake Up Farm!, 1955; Wake Up City!, 1957; The Rabbit Story, 1957; The Frog in the Well, 1958; The Smallest Elephant in the World, 1959; Timothy Robins Climbs the Mountain, 1960; An Elephant Is not a Cat 1962; Under the Trees and Through the Grass (ecology), 1962; The Mitten: An Old Ukrainian Folktale, 1964; How Far Is Far? (science), 1964; Hide and Seek Fog, 1965; The Old Man and the Tiger, 1965; A Thousand Lights and Fireflies, 1965; The World in the Candy Egg, 1967; The Tears of the Dragon, 1967; (with Nancy Cleaver) Legend of the Willow Plate, 1968; The Crane Maiden, 1968; Helpful Mr. Bear, 1968; Ma Lien and the Magie Brush, 1968; The Fox Who Travelled, 1968; It's Time Now!, 1969; How Rabbit Tricked His Friends, 1969; The Rolling Rice Ball, 1969; The Fisherman under the Sea, 1969; The Land of Lost Buttons, 1970; Eleven Hungry Cats, 1970; Gengoroh and the Thunder God, 1970; The Beaver Pond (ecology), 1970; A Sparrow's Magic, 1970; The Hare and the Bear and Other Stories, 1971; Stories from the Bible, 1971; Ogre and His Bride, 1971; Lum Fu and the Golden Mountain, 1971; The Little Mouse Who Tarried, 1971; Wonder Fish from the Sea, 1971; The Dead Tree (ecology), 1972; The Little Green Man, 1972; The Nutcracker, 1974; What Did You Leave Behind?, 1978. Add: 53 Dorethy Rd., W. Redding, Conn. 06896, U.S.A.

TRESSILLIAN, Richard. Also writes as Raynard Devine. British. Historical/Romance. *Publs:* The Bondmaster, 1977; Blood of the Bondmaster, 1977; The Bondmaster Breed, 1979; Fleur, 1979; Bondmaster Fury, 1982; Bondmaster's Revenge, 1983; Bondmaster Buck, 1984; (as Raynard Devine) Masters of the Black River, 1984; (as Raynard Devine) The Flesh Traders, 1985; (as Raynard Devine) Black River Affair, 1985; (as Raynard Devine) Black River Breed, 1985; (as Raynard Devine) Revenge at Black River, 1985; Bloodheart, 1985; Bloodheart Royal, 1986. Add: c/o Century Hutchinson Ltd., Brookmount House, 62-65 Chandos Pl., Covent Garden, London WC2N 4NW, England.

TRETHOWAN, William (Kenneth Illtyd). British, b. 1907. Philosophy, Theology/Religion. Benedictine Monk, Downside Abbey, Bath, since 1936. Ed., The Downside Review, 1946–52, 1960–64. *Publs:* Certainty: Philosophical and Theological, 1948; Christ in the Liturgy, 1950; (with M. Pontifex) The Meaning of Existence, 1954; An Essay in Christian Philosophy, 1954; The Basis of Belief, 1961; (with A. Dru) Maurice Blondel, 1966; Absolute Value, 1970; The Absolute and the Atonement, 1971; Mysticism and Theology, 1975; (trans.) The Christian Sacrifice, by E. Masure; (trans. with F. Sheed) The Philosophy of St. Bonaventure, by E. Gilson; (trans.) What is Faith?, E. by Joly; (trans.) Is There a Christian Philosophy?, by M. Nédoncelle; Process Theology and the Christian Tradition, 1985; (co-trans.) Christian Faith, by H. de Lubac, 1986. Add: Downside Abbey, Stratton on the Fosse, Bath, Somerset, England.

TREVANIAN. Pseud. for Rod Whitaker; also writes as Nicholas Seare. American, b. 1925. Novels, Mystery/Crime/Suspense, Film. Former Prof., Univ. of Texas, Austin. *Publs:* (as Rod Whitaker) The Language of Film, 1970; The Eiger Sanction, 1972; The Loo Sanction, 1973; (as Nicholas Seare) Thirteen Thirty Nine or So, 1975; The Main, 1976; Shibumi, 1979; The Summer of Katya, 1983. Add: c/o Crown, 225 Park Ave. S., New York, N.Y. 10003, U.S.A.

TREVELYAN, Humphrey. (Lord Trevelyan). British, b. 1905. History, Autobiography/Memoirs/Personal. Former Dir., British Petroleum Co. Ltd., Gen. Electric Co. Ltd., and British Bank of the Middle East; Former Chmn., Royal Inst. of Intnl. Affairs; Chmn. of the Trustees, British Museum; Pres., Council of Foreign Bondholders; entered Indian Civil Service, 1929, and U.K. Foreign Service, 1947; Economic and Financial Adviser, U.K. High Commn. for Germany, 1951–53; Charge d'Affaires, Peking, 1953–55; Ambassador to Egypt, 1955–56; Under Secty. at the U.N., 1958; Ambassador to Iraq, 1958–61; Deputy Under Secty. of State, Foreign office, London, 1962; Ambassador to the U.S.S.R., 1962 until retirement in 1965; High Commnr. in S. Arabia, 1967. *Publs:* The Middle East in Revolution, 1970; Worlds Apart, 1971; The India We Left, 1972; Diplomatic Channels, 1973; Public and Private, 1980. Add: 24 Duchess of Bedford House, London W8 7QN, England.

TREVELYAN, Percy. *See* **THOMAS**, Charles.

TREVELYAN, Raleigh. British, b. 1923. Novels/Short stories, History, Autobiography/Memoirs/Personal, Biography, Translations. Editorial Dir., Michael Joseph Ltd., London, 1962–73; Dir., Hamish Hamilton Ltd., London, 1974–80; Literary Adviser, Jonathan Cape, publishers, London, 1980–86. *Publs:* The Fortress, 1956; A Hermit Disclosed, 1960; (ed.) Italian Short Stories: Penguin Parallel Texts, 1965; The Big Tomato, 1966; (trans.) The Outlaws, by Luigi Meneghello, 1966; (ed.) Italian Writing Today, 1967; Princes Under the Volcano, 1972; The Shadow of Vesuvius, 1976; A Pre-Raphaelite Circle, 1978; Rome '44: The Battle for the Eternal City, 1981; Shades of the Alhambra, 1984; The Golden Oriole: Childhood Family and Friends in India, 1987. Add: St. Cadix, St. Veep, Lostwithiel, Cornwall, England.

TREVER, John Cecil. American, b. 1915. Archaeology/Antiquities, Theology/Religion. Voluntary dir., Dead Sea Scrolls Project, Sch. of Theology at Claremont, Calif., since 1980 (Dir., DSS Project, and Co-ordinator of Lay Education, 1975–80). Assoc. Prof. of Old Testament, Drake Univ., Des Moines, Iowa, 1944–47; Dir., Dept. of English Bible, National Council of Churches, 1948–53; A.J. Humphrey Prof. of Religion, Morris-Harvey Coll., 1953–59; Prof. of Religion, Baldwin-Wallace Coll., Berea, Ohio, 1959–75. *Publs:* (with M. Burrows and W. Brownlee) The Dead Sea Scrolls of St. Mark's Monastery, vol. I-II, 1950–51; The Cradle of Our Faith: The Holy Land, 1954; The Untold Story of Qumran, 1965; Scrolls from Qumran Cave I, 1972; The Dead Sea Scrolls: A Personal Account, 1978, 1988; The Bible and the Palestinian-Israeli Conflict, 1989. Add: 369 W. Radcliffe Dr., Claremont, Calif. 91711, U.S.A.

TREVES, Ralph. American, b. 1906. Crafts, Homes/Gardens. Former Reporter and Ed., New York Daily Mirror and New York Journal-American, and Assoc. Ed., Science Illustrated, McGraw-Hill Publishing Co., NYC; Medical and Science Writer, Physician Publs., NYC, 1967–73. Pres., National Assn. of Home Workshop Writers, 1974–78. *Publs:* Complete Book of Basement Finishing, 1954; Reproducing Early American Furniture, 1964; Recreation Rooms; Family Handyman Home Improvement Book; Home Protection; Homeowner's Complete Guide; The Book of Cleaning. Add: 311 Lake Evelyn Dr., W. Palm Beach, Fla. 33411, U.S.A.

TREVOR, Elleston. Also writes as Mansell Black, Roger Fitzalan, Adam Hall, Simon Rattray, Warwick Scott, Caesar Smith, and Lesley Stone. British. Mystery/Crime/Suspense, Children's fiction, Plays/Screenplays. *Publs:* Badger's Beech, 1948; The Wizard of the Wood, 1950; Chorus of Echoes, 1950; (as Warwick Scott) Image in the Dust, 1951; (as Simon Rattray) Knight Sinister, 1951; (as Mansell Black) Dead on Course, 1951; Redfern's Miracle, 1951; Tiger Street, 1951; (as Warwick Scott) the Domesday Story, 1952; (as Warwick Scott) Naked Canvas, 1952; (as Mansell Black) Sinister Cargo, 1952; A Blaze of Roses, 1952; The Passion and the Pity, 1953; The Big Pick-Up, 1955; Squadron Airborne, 1955; The Killing-Ground, 1956; Gale Force, 1956; The Pillars of Midnight, 1957; (as Caesar-Smith) Heatwave, 1958; The V.I.P., 1959; The Billboard Madonna, 1960; The Burning Shore, 1961; Flight of the Phoenix, 1964; (as Adam Hall) The Quiller Memorandum, 1964; (as Adam Hall) The Volcanoes of San Domingo, 1964; The Shoot, 1966; (as Adam Hall) The Ninth Directive, 1966; The Freebooters, 1967; (as Roger Fitzalan) A Blaze of Arms, 1967; A Place for the Wicked, 1968; (as Adam Hall) The Striker Portfolio, 1969; Bury Him Among Kings, 1970; Badger's Moon, 1970; Sweethallow Valley, 1970; Badger's Wood, 1970; (as Simon Rattray) Queen in Danger, 1971; (as Adam Hall) The Warsaw Document, 1971; (as Simon Rattray) Bishop in Check, 1972; (as Simon Rattray) Pawn in Jeopardy (originally as Dead Silence), 1973; (as Adam Hall) The Tango Briefing, 1973; (as Simon Rattray) Rook's Gambit (originally as Dead Circuit), 1974; (as Adam Hall) The Mandarin Cypher, 1975; The Paragon, 1975; (as Adam Hall) The Kobra Manifesto, 1976; The Theta Syndrome, 1977; Blue Jay Summer, 1977; Seven Witnesses, 1977; (as Adam Hall) The Sinkiang Executive, 1978; The Sibling, 1979; (as Adam Hall) The Scorpion Signal, 1979; (as Adam Hall) The Peking Target, 1982; (as Lesley Stone) Siren Song, 1985; (as Adam Hall) Quiller, in U.K. as Northlight, 1985; Deathwatch, 1985; (as Adam Hall) Quiller's Run, 1987; (as Adam Hall) Quiller KGB, 1989. Add: 6902 E. Dynamite, Cane Creek, Ariz. 85331, U.S.A.

TREVOR, (Lucy) Meriol. British, b. 1919. Novels/Short stories, Children's fiction, Biography. *Publs:* The Forest and the Kingdom, 1949; Hunt the King, Hide the Fox, 1950; The Fires and the Stars, 1951; Sun Slower, Sun Faster, 1955; The Other Side of the Moon, 1956; The Last of Britain, 1956; The New People, 1957; Merlin's Ring, 1957; The Treasure Hunt, 1957; The Caravan War, 1958; A Narrow Place, 1958; Four Odd Ones, 1958; The Sparrow Child, 1958; Newman, 2 vols., 1962; The Rose Round, 1963; William's Wild Day Out, 1963; The Midsummer

Maze, 1964; The King of the Castle, 1966; Lights in a Dark Town, 1966; Apostle of Rome, 1966; Pope John, 1967; Prophets and Guardians, 1969; The City and the World, 1970; The Holy Images, 1971; The Two Kingdoms, 1973; The Fugitives, 1973; The Marked Man, 1974; Enemy at Home, 1974; The Arnolds, 1974; Newman's Journey, 1974; The Forgotten Country, 1975; The Treacherous Paths, 1976; The Fortunate Marriage, 1976; The Civil Prisoners, 1977; The Fortunes of Peace, 1978; The Wanton Fires, 1979; The Sun with a Face, 1984; The Golden Palaces, 1986; The Shadow of a Crown (James II), 1988. Add: 70 Pulteney St., Bath BA2 4DL, England.

TREVOR, William. Pseud. for William Trevor Cox. Irish, b. 1928. Novels/Short stories, Plays/Screenplays. History Teacher, Armagh, Northern Ireland, 1951–53; Art Teacher, Rugby, England, 1953–55; sculptor in Somerset, 1955–60; advertising copywriter, London, 1960–64. *Publs:* A Standard of Behaviour, 1958; The Old Boys, 1964; The Boarding House, 1965; The Love Department, 1966; The Day We Got Drunk on Cake and Other Stories, 1967; The Girl (play), 1968; Mrs. Eckdorf in O'Neill's Hotel, 1969; Miss Gomez and the Brethren, 1971; The Old Boys (play), 1971; The Ballroom of Romance and Other Stories, 1972; Going Home (play), 1972; A Night with Mrs. Da Tanka (play), 1972; The Last Lunch of the Season, 1973; Elizabeth Alone, 1974; Marriages (play), 1974; Angels at the Ritz and Other Stories, 1975; The Children of Dynmouth, 1976; Lovers of Their Time and Other Stories, 1978; The Distant Past, 1979; Other People's Worlds, 1980; Beyond the Pale, 1981; Scenes from an Album (play), 1981; Fools of Fortune, 1983; The Stories of William Trevor, 1983; A Writer's Ireland: Landscape in Literature, 1984; The News from Ireland and Other Stories, 1986; Nights at the Alexandra, 1987; The Silence in the Garden, 1988. Add: c/o A.D. Peters, The Chambers, Chelsea Harbour, Lots Rd., London SW10 0XF, England.

TREVOR-ROPER, Hugh (Redwald). (Baron Dacre of Glanton). British, b. 1914. History. Regius Prof. of Modern History, Univ. of Oxford, 1957–80; Master of Peterhouse, Cambridge, 1980–87. *Publs:* Archbishop Laud, 1940; The Last Days of Hitler, 1947; The Gentry 1540-1640, 1953; (ed.) Hitler's Table Talk, 1953; (ed. with Bennett) The Poems of Richard Corbett, 1955; Historical Essays, 1957; (ed.) Hitler's War Directives 1939-45, 1964; (ed.) Essays in British History Presented to Sir Keith Feiling, 1964; The Rise of Christian Europe, 1965; Religion, the Reformation and Social Change, 1967; (ed.) The Age of Expansion, 1968; The Philby Affair, 1968; The European Witch-Craze of the 16th and 17th Centuries, 1970; The Plunder of the Arts in the Seventeenth Century, 1970; Hermit of Peking, 1976; Princes and Artists, 1976; Renaissance Essays, 1985; Catholic Anglicans and Puritans, 1988. Add: c/o A.D. Peters and Co., The Chambers, Chelsea Harbour, Lots Rd., London SW10 OXF, England.

TREVOR-ROPER, Patrick (Dacre). British, b. 1916. Medicine/Health, Music. Eye Surgeon, Westminster Hosp., 1947–82, and Moorfields Eye Hosp., London, 1961–81. Ed., Transactions of the Ophthalmological Soc., London, since 1949. *Publs:* Music at Court, by A. Yorke-Long, 1954; Ophthalmology: A Textbook for Diploma Students, 1955, 1962; Lecture Notes in Ophthalmology, 1959, 7th ed. 1986; (ed.) International Ophthalmology Clinics—The Cornea, 1962; The World Through Blunted Sight, 1970, 1988; The Eye and Its Disorders, 1974, 1984; (ed.) Recent Advances in Ophthalmology, 1974; (ed.) The Bowman Lectures, 1978; Ophthalmology: Pocket Consultant, 1981, 1985. Add: 3 Park Sq. West, London NW1, England.

TREW, Antony (Francis). South African, b. 1906. Novels/Short stories. Divisional Secty., Transvaal, 1932–36, Joint General Mgr., 1936–39, and Dir.-Gen., 1946–66, Automobile Assn. of South Africa. *Publs:* Two Hours to Darkness, 1963; Smoke Island, 1964; The Sea Break, 1966; The White Schooner, 1969; Towards the Tamarind Trees, 1970; The Moonraker Mutiny, 1972; Kleber's Convoy, 1974; The Zhukov Briefing, 1975; Ultimatum, 1976; Death of a Supertanker, 1978; The Antonov Project, 1979; Sea Fever, 1980; Running Wild, 1982; Bannister's Chart, 1984; Yashimoto's Last Dive, 1986; The Chalk Circle, 1989. Add: 1 Templemere, Oatlands Dr., Weybridge, Surrey, England.

TREWIN, John Courtenay. British, b. 1908. Poetry, Literature. Drama Critic, The Lady, since 1949, and The Birmingham Post, since 1955; Contrib. to the Observer, London, since 1937 (Editorial Staff Member, 1942–53; Literary Ed., 1943–48; Second Drama Critic, 1943–53; Ed., Plays of the Year series, 50 vols., since 1948. Editorial Staff Member, 1932–37, and Second Drama Critic, 1934–37, Morning Post, London; Drama Critic, Punch mag., 1944–45, John o'London's, 1945–54, and The Sketch, 1947–59; Ed., West Country Mag., 1946–52, and The Year's Work in the Theatre, British Council, 1949–51; Radio Drama Critic, The Listener, 1951–57; Drama Critic, The Illustrated London News, 1946–88. Pres., Critics' Circle, 1964–65; Chmn., West Country Writers' Assn., 1964–73. *Publs:* Shakespeare Memorial Theatre, 1932; The English Theatre, 1948; Up from the Lizard, 1948; We'll Hear a Play, 1949; (with H.J. Wilmott) London-Bodmin, 1950; Stratford-upon-Avon, 1950; The Theatre Since 1900, 1951; Th Story of Bath, 1951; Drama 1945-1950, 1951; Down to the Lion, 1952; (with E.M. King) Printer to the House, 1952; A Play To-night, 1952 (with T.C. Kemp) The Stratford Festival, 1953; Dramatists of Today, 1953; Edith Evans, 1954; (ed.) Theatre Programme, 1954; Mr. Macready, 1955; Sybil Thorndike, 1955; Verse Drama Since 1800, 1956; Paul Scofield, 1956; The Night Has Been Unruly, 1957; Alec Clunes, 1958; The Gay Twenties: A Decade of the Theatre, 1958; Benson and the Bensonians, 1960; The Turbulent Thirties, 1960; A Sword for a Prince, 1960; John Neville, 1961; The Birmingham Repertory Theatre, 1963; Shakespeare on the English Stage 1900-1964, 1964; Completion of Lamb's Tales, 1964; Drama in Britain 1951-1964, 1965; (with H.F. Rubinstein) The Drama Bedside Book, 1966; (ed.) Macready's Journals, 1967; Robert Donat, 1968; The Pomping Folk, 1968; Shakespeare's Country, 1970; (with Arthur Colby Sprague) Shakespeare's Plays Today, 1970; Peter Brook, 1971; (ed.) Sean, by Mrs. Eileen O'-Casey, 1971; I Call My Name (poems), 1971; Down South (poems), 1972; Portrait of Plymouth, 1973; Long Ago (poems), 1973; Theatre Bedside Book, 1974; Tutor to the Tsarevich, 1975; (ed.) Eileen, 1976; The Edwardian Theatre, 1976; Going to Shakespeare, 1977; (ed.) Nicoll, British Drama, 1978; Companion to Shakespeare, 1981; (with Lord Miles), Curtain Calls, 1981; (ed.) The West Country Book, 1981; (with Wendy Trewin) The Arts Theatre, London, 1986; Five-and-Eighty Hamlets, 1987. Add: 15 Eldon Grove, London NW3 5PT, England.

TRIBUS, Myron. American, b. 1921. Engineering/Technology, Environmental science/Ecology, Sciences (general). Dir., AKT Systems, Hayward, Calif., since 1986. Instr., and subsequently Asst. Prof., 1946–50, and Assoc. Prof. and subsequently Prof., 1953–61, Engineering Dept., Univ. of California at Los Angeles; Engineer, General Electric Co., Jet Engine Div., West Lynn, Mass. and Evendale, Ohio, 1950–51; Dir., Aircraft Icing Research Project, Univ. of Michigan, Ann Arbor, 1951–53; Dean, Thayer Sch. of Engineering, Dartmouth Coll., Hanover, N.H., 1961–69; Asst. Secty. of Commerce for Science and Technology, U.S. Dept. of Commerce, 1969–70; Sr. Vice-Pres., Xerox Corp., 1970–74; Dir., Centre for Advanced Engineering Study, MIT, Cambridge, Mass., 1974–86. *Publs:* Introductory Heat Transfer, 1950; Thermostatics and Thermodynamics, An Introduction to Energy, Information and States of Matter, 1961; Rational Descriptions, Decisions and Designs, 1969. Add: 350 Britto Terrace, Fremont, Calif. 94539, U.S.A.

TRICKETT, Joyce. Australian, b. 1915. Short stories, Plays, Poetry. Songwriter and artist. Retired singer-entertainer and speech-drama teacher. Formerly, radio announcer and TV featurist; presenter and creator of weekly radio prog. "The Poetry of the People". *Publs:* The Light Shines, 1962, 1977; Pool of Quiet, 1963, 1977; Bless This House, 1970, 4th ed. 1977; An Australian Vision, 1972; Christmas Is Forever, 1975; Seven to Ten and Back Again (children's poetry), 1979; Up to Six and Over (children's poetry), 1982; (self-illustrated) The Cattitudes of Chairman Miaow, 1986. Add: 23 Lavender Cres., Lavender Bay, North Sydney, N.S.W. 2060, Australia.

TRICKETT, (Mabel) Rachel. British, b. 1923. Novels/Short stories, Plays/Screenplays, Literature. Principal, St. Hugh's Coll., Oxford, since 1973. Asst. to the Curator, Manchester City Art Galleries, 1945–46; Lectr. in English, Univ. Coll. of Hull, York., 1946–54; Fellow and Tutor, St. Hugh's Coll., and Lectr., Oxford Univ., 1954–73. *Publs:* The Return Home, 1952; The Course of Love, 1954; Antigone (play), 1954; Point of Honour, 1958; Silas Marner (play), 1960; A Changing Place, 1962; The Elders, 1966; The Honest Muse: A Study in Augustan Verse, 1967; A Visit to Timon, 1969. Add: St. Hugh's Coll., Oxford, England.

TRIFFIN, Robert. Belgian, b. 1911. Economics. Frederick William Beinecke Prof. of Economics, and Master, Berkeley Coll., Yale Univ., New Haven, since 1951; Visiting Prof., Louvain La Neuve Univ., since 1977. Participated in creation of the European Payments Union, 1959; Originator of the Triffin Plan for Intnl. Monetary Reform. *Publs:* Gold and the Dollar Crisis, 1960; The World Money Maze, 1966; Our International Monetary System: Yesterday, Today and Tomorrow, 1968; (with Rainer S. Masera) Europe's Money: Problems of European Monetary Coordination and Integration, 1984. Add: IRES, Place Montesquieu, 1348 Louvain La Neuve, Belgium.

TRIGGER, Bruce Graham. Canadian, b. 1937. Anthropology/Ethnology, Archaeology/Antiquities. Prof. of Anthropology, McGill Univ., Montreal, since 1969 (Asst. Prof., 1964–67; Assoc. Prof., 1967–69). *Publs:* History and Settlement in Lower Nubia, 1965; The Late Nubian Settlement at Arminna West, 1967; Beyond History: The Methods of Prehistory, 1968; The Huron: Farmers of the North, 1969; The Impact of Europeans on Huronia, 1969; The Meroitic Funerary Inscriptions from Arminna West, 1970; (with J.F. Pendergast) Cartier's Hochelaga and the Dawson Site, 1972; The Children of Aataentsic, 1976; Nubia under the Pharaohs, 1976; Time and Traditions, 1978; Handbook of North American Indians, Northeast Volume, 1978; Gordon Childe: Revolutions in Archaeology, 1980; Natives and Newcomers: Canada's "Heroic Age" Reconsidered, 1985; A History of Archaeological Thought, 1989. Add: Dept. of Anthropology, McGill Univ., 855 Sherbrooke St. W., Montreal, Que. H3A 2T7, Canada.

TRILLIN, Calvin (Marshall). American, b. 1935. Social commentary. Staff writer, The New Yorker, since 1963; syndicated columnist, King Features, since 1986. Columnist, Nation mag., 1978–85. *Publs:* An Education in Georgia, 1964; Barnett Frummer Is an Unbloomed Flower, 1969; U.S. Journal, 1971; American Fried, 1974; Runestruck, 1977; Alice, Let's Eat, 1978; Floater, 1980; Uncivil Liberties, 1982; Third Helpings, 1983; Killings, 1984; With All Disrespect, 1985; If You Can't Say Something Nice, 1987. Add: c/o The New Yorker, 25 W. 43rd St., New York, N.Y. 10036, U.S.A.

TRILLING, Diana. American, b. 1905. Literature, Women, Essays, Biography. Freelance writer since 1949. Fiction Critic, The Nation, NYC, 1941–49; Guggenheim Fellow, 1950–51; Rockefeller Fellow, 1977–79. Member, American Academy of Arts and Sciences. *Publs:* (ed.) The Portable D.H. Lawrence, 1947; (ed.) Selected Letters of D.H. Lawrence, 1958; Claremont Essays, 1964; (ed.) Last Decade: Essays and Reviews 1965-75, 1975; We Must March, My Darlings, 1977; Reviewing the Forties, 1978; (ed.) Uniform Edition of the Works of Lionel Trilling 1978-80, 1980; (ed.) Speaking of Literature and Society, 1980; Mrs. Harris: The Death of the Scarsdale Diet Doctor, 1981. Add: 35 Claremont Ave., New York, N.Y. 10027, U.S.A.

TRIMBLE, Barbara Margaret. Writes as Margaret Blake and B.M. Gill. British, b. 1921. Novels/Short stories, Mystery/Crime/Suspense. Full-time writer. Has worked as clerk/typist, school teacher, and chiropodist. *Publs:* novels as Margaret Blake—Stranger at the Door, 1967; Bright Sun, Dark Shadow, 1968; The Rare and the Lovely, 1969; The Elusive Exile, 1971; Flight from Fear, 1973; Courier to Danger, 1973; Apple of Discord, 1975; Walk Softly and Beware, 1977; mystery novels as B.M. Gill—Target Westminster, 1977; Death Drop, 1979; Victims (in U.S. as Suspect), 1981; The Twelfth Juror, 1984; Seminar for Murder, 1985; Nursery Crimes, 1986. Add: c/o Patricia Robertson, 87 Caledonian Rd., London N1 9BT, England.

TRIMMER, Ellen (McKay). Canadian, b. 1915. Children's fiction, Education, Human relations. Staff Development Consultant, Ontario Ministry of Correctional Services; now retired. Probation Officer and Area Mgr., Ontario Probation and Parole Service, 1962–81, and Staff Training Consultant, 1981–83. *Publs:* The Cup; Tiny Tales'n Tunes; You and Yours; The Characters of Christmas Meet Christ; The Three Gifts of Christmas; The Gates of Christmas; Christmas Pathways; Home for Christmas; Christmas Wonders; The "Fear Nots" of Christmas. Add: 25 Widdicombe Hill, Apt. 809, Weston, Ont. M9R 1B1, Canada.

TRIMMER, Eric J(ames). Also writes as Eric Jameson. British, b. 1923. Medicine/Health. Ed., British Journal of Clinical Practice; Consultant Ed., British Journal of Sexual Medicine; Consultant, Medical Tribune Group. Former Medical Adviser, I.P.C. Mags. and Readers Digest. *Publs:* (as Eric Jameson) The National History of Quackery, 1961; A Young Man's Guide to Medicine, 1962; Look at the Body, 1962; Look at Doctors, 1963; Teach Your Child First Aid, 1964; Before Birth, 1965; Femina, 1966; I Swear and Vow, 1966; Live Long, Stay Young, 1965; Rejuvenation, 1967; Understanding Anxiety in Everyday Life, 1970; (as Dr. Philip Lawson) Ex-Smoker's Diet Book, 1973; Having a Baby, 1974; Basic Sexual Medicine, 1978; Visual Dictionary of Sex, 1978; The First Seven Years, 1978; Complete Book of Slimming and Diets, 1981; You're a Father, 1982; Ten Day Relaxation Plan, 1983; Good Housekeeping Guide to Medicine, 1984; The Magic of Magnesium, 1987; Selenium the Trace Element for Health and Life Extension. Add: Yew Tree Lodge, Lone Lane, Bembridge, I.W. PO35 5RY, England.

TRINKAUS, Charles. American, b. 1911. History, Philosophy, Theology/Religion. Prof. Emeritus of History, Univ. of Michigan, Ann Arbor (joined faculty, 1970). Member of faculty, Sarah Lawrence Coll.,

Bronxville, N.Y., 1936–70. *Publs:* Adversity's Noblemen, The Italian Humanists on Happiness, 1940, 1965; (ed.) Graduate Study in an Undergraduate College, 1956; In Our Image and Likeness: Humanity and Divinity in Italian Humanist Thought, 2 vols., 1970; (ed. and contrib.) The Pursuit of Holiness in Late Medieval and Renaissance Religion, 1974; The Poet as Philosopher: Petrarch and the Formation of Renaissance Consciousness, 1979; The Scope of Renaissance Humanism, 1983. Add: 59 Langdon Terrace, Bronxville, N.Y. 10708, U.S.A.

TRIPODI, Tony. American, b. 1932. Psychology, Sociology. Assoc. Dean and Prof. of Social Work, Univ. of Pittsburgh Sch. of Social Work, since 1987. Research Technician, California Dept. of Mental Hygiene, 1958–60; Research Analyst, California Youth Authority, 1959–60; Research Asst., 1962–63, and Asst. Prof., 1963–65, Columbia Univ., NYC; Research Assoc., Brooklyn Coll., N.Y., 1963–65; Asst. Prof., Univ. of California, Berkeley, 1965–66; Assoc. Prof., 1966–69, and Prof. of Social Work, 1969–87, Univ. of Michigan, Ann Arbor. *Publs:* (co-author) Clinical and Social Judgment, 1966; (co-ed.) Exemplars of Social Research, 1969; (with Phillip Fellin and Henry Meyer) The Assessment of Social Research, 1969 (co-author) Thought and Personality, 1970; (with Irwin Epstein and Philip Fellin) Social Program Evaluation, 1971; (co-ed.) Social Workers at Work, 1972; (co-author) Advances in Behavioral Theory, vol. 4, 1973; (co-author) Uses and Abuses of Social Research in Social Work, 1974; (co-author) Research Techniques for Program Planning, Monitoring and Evaluation, 1977; (co-author) Differential Social Program Evaluation, 1978; (co-author) Research Techniques for Clinical Social Workers, 1980; Evaluative Research for Social Workers, 1983. Add: 330 Hazelwood, Ann Arbor, Mich. 48103, U.S.A.

TRIPP, Miles (Barton). Also writes as Michael Brett. British, b. 1923. Novels/Short stories, Mystery/Crime/Suspense, Autobiography/Memoirs/Personal. Deputy Charity Commnr., Charity Commn., 1972–83. Chmn., Crime Writers Assn., 1968–69. *Publs:* Faith is a Windsock, 1952; The Image of Man, 1955; A Glass of Red Wine, 1960; Kilo Forty, 1963; (as Michael Brett) Diecast, 1963; The Skin Dealer, 1964; A Quarter of Three, 1965; (as Michael Brett) A Plague of Dragons, 1965; The Chicken, 1966; The Fifth Point of the Compass, 1967; One is One, 1968; Malice and the Maternal Instinct, 1969; The Eighth Passenger (autobiography), 1969; Man Without Friends, 1970; Five Minutes with a Stranger, 1971; The Claws of God, 1972; Obsession, 1973; Woman at Risk, 1974; A Woman in Bed, 1976; The Once a Year Man, 1977; The Wife-Smuggler, 1978; Cruel Victim, 1979; High Heels, 1980; Going Solo, 1981; One Lover Too Many, 1983; A Charmed Death, 1984; Some Predators Are Male, 1985; Death of A Man-Tamer, 1987; The Frightened Wife, 1987. Add: c/o Peters Fraser and Dunlop, The Chambers, Chelsea Harbour, Lots Rd., London SW10 0XF, England.

TRIVELPIECE, Laurel. Also writes as Hannah K. Marks. American, b. 1926. Novels/Short stories, Children's fiction, Plays/Screenplays, Poetry. Secty. and copywriter, Abbott Kimball, San Francisco, 1945–50; Copywriter, City of Paris, San Francisco, 1950–53, Berdorf Goodman, NYC, 1953 and Roy S. Durstine, San Francisco, 1954–55; freelance writer, mainly for Macy's Union Sq., San Francisco, 1955–57, 1963–77. *Publs:* Legless in Flight, 1978; During Water Peaches, 1979; (as Hannah K. Marks) Triad, 1980; In Love and Trouble, 1981; The New Job (play), 1984; Trying Not to Love You, 1985; Blue Hores, 1987; Just a Little Bit Lost, 1988. Add: 23 Rocklyn Ct., Corte Madera, Calif. 94925, U.S.A.

TROLLOPE, Joanna. Pseud for Joanna Curteis; also writes as Caroline Harvey. British, b. 1943. Novels, Historical fiction and non-fiction. Teacher in preparatory schs. and of adult and foreign student classes, since 1968. Feature writer, Harpers and Queen mag., London. *Publs:* Eliza Stanhope, 1978; Parson Harding's Daughter, 1979, in U.S. as Mistaken Virtues, 1980; Leaves from the Valley, 1980; (as Caroline Harvey) Charlotte, Alexandra, 1980; The City of Gems, 1981; The Steps of the Sun, 1983; Britannia's Daughters, 1983; The Taverners' Place, 1986; The Choir, 1988; A Village Affair, 1989. Add: Bloomsbury Publishing, 2 Soho Sq., London W1V 5DE, England.

TROTMAN, Jack. Also writes as John Penn. Canadian. British Army Intelligence Corps Officer, 1940–46; served in the Foreign Office, London, 1946–48; Joint Intelligence Bureau, Ottawa, 1949–65; Canadian Dept. of National Defence, 1965–73; NATO Intnl. Staff, Paris, 1973–77. Pres., Jersey Branch, Royal Commonwealth Soc., 1981–84, and Pres., The National Trust for Jersey, 1984–87. *Publs:* Notice of Death, in the U.S as An Ad for Murder, 1982; Deceitful Death, in U.S. as Stag-Dinner Death, 1983; A Will to Kill, 1983; Mortal Term, 1983; A Deadly Sickness, 1985; Unto the Grave, 1986; Barren Revenge, 1986; Accident Prone,

1987; Outrageous Exposures, 1988; A Feast of Death, 1989. Add: c/o Murray Pollinger, 4 Garrick Street, London WC2E 9BH, England.

TROTMAN-DICKENSON, Aubrey Fiennes. British, b. 1926. Chemistry. Principal, Univ. of Wales Coll. of Cardiff, since 1988 (Principal, Univ. Coll., Cardiff (UCC), 1977–88). Prof of Chemistry Univ. Coll. of Wales, Aberystwyth, 1960–68; Principal, Univ. of Wales Inst. of Science and Technology, Cardiff, 1968–88. *Publs:* Gas Kinetics, 1955; Free Radicals, 1959; (ed.) Comprehensive Inorganic Chemistry, 1973. Add: UWIST, P.O. Box 68, Cardiff CF1 3XA, Wales.

TROUT, Kilgore. *See* **FARMER,** Philip José

TROY, Katherine. *See* **MAYBURY,** Anne.

TROY, Una. Irish. Novels/Short stories, Plays/Screenplays. *Publs:* We Are Seven; Maggie; The Workhouse Graces; The Other End of the Bridge; Esmond; The Brimstone Halo; The Benefactors; Tiger Puss; The Castle that Nobody Wanted; Stop Press; Doctor Go Home; Out of the Everywhere; Caught-in-the-Furze; A Sack of Gold, 1979; So True a Fool, 1981; plays—Mount Prospect; Swans and Geese; The Old Road; An Apple Day; film script—(with T. Morrison) She Didn't Say No. Add: 6 Osborne Terr., Bonmahon, Co. Waterford, Ireland.

TRUDEAU, Garry (B). American, b. 1948. Humor/Satire. Creator of Doonesbury cartoons, syndicated in 400 newspapers in U.S.A. *Publs:* Still a Few Bugs in the System, 1972; The President Is a Lot Smarter Than You Think 1973; Doonesbury, 1973; But This War Had Such Promise, 1973; Call Me When You Find America, 1973; Don't Ever Change, Boopsie, 1974; Guilty, Guilty, Guilty, 1974; Even Revolutionaries Like Chocolate Chip Cookies, 1974; Joanie, 1974; Dare to be Great, Ms. Caucus, 1975; I Have No Son, 1975; What Do We Have for the Witnesses, Johnnie, 1975; Wouldn't a Gremlin Have Been More Sensible?, 1975; (with N. von Hoffman) We'll Take it from Here, Sarge, 1975; The Doonesbury Chronicles, 1975; (with David Leventhal) Hitler Moves East, 1977; As the Kid Goes for Broke, 1977; Any Grooming Hints for Your Fans, Rollie?, 1978; Doonesbury Greatest Hits, 1978; You're Never Too Old for Nuts and Berries, 1978; But the Pension Fund was Just Sitting There, 1979; We're Not Out of the Woods Yet, 1979; And That's My Final Offer, 1980; A Tad Overweight, But Violet Eyes to Die For, 1980; He's Never Heard of You, Either, 1981; In Search of Reagan's Brain, 1981; The People's Doonesbury, 1981; Adjectives Will Cost You Extra, 1982; Ask for May, Settle for June, 1982; Gotta Run, My Government is Collapsing, 1982; Unfortunately She was Also Wired for Sound, 1982; The Wreck of the Rusty Nail, 1983; You Give Great Meeting, Sid, 1983; Dressed for Failure, I See, 1984; Sir, I'm Worried about Your Mood Swings, 1984; Doonesbury: A Musical Comedy, 1984; Check Your Egos at the Door, 1985; Rap Master Ronnie, 1986; Doonesbury Deluxe, 1987; Downtown Doonesbury, 1987; Talkin' about my G-G-Generation, 1988; We're Eating More Beets!, 1988. Add: c/o Universal Press Syndicate, 4400 Johnson Drive, Fairway, Kans. 66205, U.S.A.

TRUEBLOOD, Paul G(raham). American, b. 1905. Literature, Biography. Prof. Emeritus of English, Willamette Univ., Salem, Ore. (Prof. of English and Chmn. of Dept., 1955–70). Instr., Univ. of Idaho' Moscow, 1937–40; Assoc. Profs., Stockton Coll., 1940–46; Asst. Prof., Univ. of Washington, 1947–52; Visiting Prof., Univ. of Oregon, Eugene, 1954–55. *Publs:* The Flowing of Byron's Genius, 1945, 1962; Lord Byron, 1969, 1977; (ed.) Byron's Political and Cultural Influence in Nineteenth Century Europe, 1981. Add: Capital Manor, P.O. Box 5000, Salem, Ore. 97304, U.S.A.

TRUITT, Anne. American, b. 1921. Art, Autobiography, Translations. Prof. of Art, Univ. of Maryland, College Park, since 1980. Dir., Corp. of Yaddo, Saratoga Springs, N.Y. *Publs:* (transl. with C.J. Hill) Marcel Proust and Deliverence from Time, 1956; Day Book: The Journal of an Artist, 1982; Turn: The Journal of an Artist, 1986. Add: 3506 35th St. N.W., Washington, D.C. 20016, U.S.A.

TRUMAN, Margaret. American, b. 1924. Mystery/Crime/Suspense, Autobiography/Memoirs/Personal, Biography. Dir., Riggs National Bank, Washington; Trustee, Harry S. Truman Inst., and George Washington Univ. Secty., Harry S., Truman Scholarship Fund. Concert Singer, 1947–54. *Publs:* Souvenir, 1956; White House Pets, 1969; Harry S. Truman, 1973; Women of Courage, 1976; Murder in the White House, 1980; Murder on Capitol Hill, 1981; Letters from Father, 1981; Murder in the Supreme Court, 1982; Murder in the Smithsonian, 1983; Murder on Embassy Row, 1984; Murder at the FBI, 1985; Murder in Georgetown, 1986. Add: c/o Scott Meredith, 845 Third Ave., New York, N.Y. 10022,

U.S.A.

TRUMAN, Ruth. American, b. 1931. Theology/Religion, Women, Autobiography/Memoirs/Personal, Humor/Satire. Dir., Extended Education for Prog. Servies, California State Univ., Fullerton, since 1986. Counselor and Instr., Citrus Coll., Azusa, Calif., 1967–70; Dir. of Counseling, California Lutheran Coll., Thousand Oaks, 1971–74; Special Asst., Bureau of Higher and Continuing Education, Washington, D.C., 1978; Consultant, 1978–82; Dir., Cancer Information Service of California, 1983–86. *Publs:* Underground Manual for Minister's Wives, 1974; The Mission of the Church College, 1978; How to Be a Liberated Christian, 1981; Spaghetti from the Chandelier, 1984. Add: 2814 E. Roberta Dr., Orange, Calif. 92669, U.S.A.

TRUSCOTT, Lucian K., IV. American, b. 1947. Novels/Short stories. Fellow, Alicia Patterson Foundation, New York, 1976. *Publs:* The Complete Van Book (non-fiction), 1976; Dress Gray (novel), 1979. Add: c/o Doubleday, 666 Fifth Ave., New York, N.Y. 1013, U.S.A

TUBB, E(dwin) C(harles). Also writes as Chuck Adams, Jud Cary, J.F. Clarkson, James S. Farrow, James R. Fenner, Charles S. Graham, Charles Grey, Volsted Gridban, Gill Hunt, E.F. Jackson, Gregory Kern, King Lang, Mike Lantry, P. Lawrence, Chet Lawson, Arthur Maclean, Carl Maddox, M.L. Powers, Paul Schofield, Brian Shaw, Roy Sheldon, John Stevens, and Edward Thomson. British, b. 1919. Mystery/Crime/Suspense, Westerns/Adventure, Science fiction/Fantasy. Has worked as a welfare officer, catering mgr., and printing machine salesman. Ed., Authentic Science Fiction mag., London, 1956–57. *Publs:* science fiction—(as King Lang) Saturn Patrol, 1951; (as Gill Hunt) Planetfall, 1951; (as Brian Shaw) Argentis, 1952; Alien Impact, 1952; Atom War on Mars, 1952; (as Volsted Gridban) Alien Universe, 1952; (as Volsted Gridban) Reverse Universe, 1952; (as Volsted Gridban) Planetoid Disposals Ltd., 1953; (as Volsted Gridban) DeBracy's Drug, 1953; (as Volsted Gridban) Fugitive of Time, 1953; (as Charles Grey) The Wall, 1953; (as Charles Grey) Dynasty of Doom, 1953; (as Charles Grey) The Tormented City, 1953; (as Charles Grey) Space Hunger, 1953; (as Charles Grey) I Fight for Mars, 1953; The Mutants Rebel, 1953; Venusian Adventure, 1953; Alien Life, 1954; (as Carl Maddox) The Living World, 1954; World at Bay, 1954; (as Roy Sheldon) The Metal Eater, 1954; Journey to Mars, 1954; (as Carl Maddox) Menace from the Past, 1954; City of No Return, 1954; The Stellar Legion, 1954; The Hell Planet, 1954; The Resurrected Man, 1954; (as Charles Grey) The Extra Man, 1954; (as Charles Grey) The Hand of Havoc, 1954; (as Charles Grey) Enterprise 2115, 1954, in U.S. as The Mechanical Monarch, 1958; Alien Dust, 1955; The Space-Born, 1956; (as Arthur Maclean) Touch of Evil, 1959; Moon Base, 1964; Ten from Tomorrow (short stories), 1966; Death Is a Dream, 1967; The Winds of Gath, 1967, in U.K. as Gath, 1968; C.O.D. Mars, 1968; Derai, 1968; S.T.A.R. Flight, 1969; Toyman, 1969; Escape into Space, 1969; Kalin, 1969; The Jester at Scar, 1970; Lallia, 1971; Technos, 1972; Century of the Manikin, 1972; A Scatter of Stardust (short stories), 1972; Mayenne, 1973; Veruchia, 1973; Jondelle, 1973; (as Gregory Kern) Galaxy of the Lost, 1973; (as Gregory Kern) Slave Ship from Sergan, 1973; (as Gregory Kern) Monster of Metelaze, 1973; Zenya, 1974; (as Gregory Kern) Enemy Within the Skull, 1974; (as Gregory Kern) Jewel of Jarhan, 1974; (as Gregory Kern) Seetee Alert!, 1974; (as Gregory Kern) The Gholan Gate, 1974; (as Gregory Kern) The Eater of Worlds, 1974; (as Gregory Kern) Earth Enslaved, 1974; (as Gregory Kern) Planet of Dread, 1974; (as Gregory Kern) Spawn of Laban, 1974; (as Gregory Kern) The Genetic Buccaneer, 1974; (as Gregory Kern) A World Aflame, 1974; (as Edward Thomson) Atilus the Slave, 1975; (as Edward Thomson) Atilus the Gladiator, 1975; Breakaway (novelization of Space 1999 TV series), 1975; Eloise, 1975; Eye of the Zodiac, 1975; Collision Course (novelization of Space 1999 TV series), 1975; (as Gregory Kern) The Ghosts of Epidoris, 1975; (as Gregory Kern) Mimics of Dephene, 1975; (as Gregory Kern) Beyond the Galactic Lens, 1975; Jack of Swords, 1976; Alien Seed (novelization of Space 1999 TV series), 1976; Spectrum of a Forgotten Sun, 1976; Rogue Planet (novelization of Space 1999 TV series), 1976; (as Gregory Kern) Das Kosmische Duelle, 1976; Earthfall (novelization of Space 1999 TV series), 1977; Haven of Darkness, 1977; Prison of Night, 1977; The Primitive, 1977; (as Edward Thomson) Gladiator, 1978; Incident on Ath, 1978; The Quillian Sector, 1978; Stellar Assignment, 1979; Web of Sand, 1979; Death Wears a White Face, 1979; Iduna's Universe, 1979; The Luck Machine, 1980; The Terra Data, 1980; Pawn of the Omphalos, 1980; Earth Is Heaven, 1982; The Coming Event, 1982; Stardeath, 1983; Melome, 1983; (as Gregory Kern) The Galactiad, 1983; Angado, 1984; Symbol of Terra, 1984; The Temple of Truth, 1985; suspense and western novels—(as Paul Schofield) The Fighting Fury, 1955; (as Mike Lantry) Assignment New York, 1955; (as E.F. Jackson) Commanche Capture, 1955; (as Jud Cary) Sands of Destiny, 1955; (as

J.F. Clarkson) Men of the Long Rifle, 1955; (as M.L. Powers) Scourge of the South, 1956; (as James S. Farrow) Vengeance Trail, 1956; (as John Stevens) Quest for Quantrell, 1956; (as Chuck Adams) Trail Blazers, 1956; (as P. Lawrence) Drums of the Prairie, 1956; (as Chet Lawson) Men of the West, 1956; (as Charles S. Graham) Wagon Trail, 1957; (as James R. Fenner) Colt Vengeance, 1957; Target Death, 1961; Lucky Strike, 1961; Calculated Risk, 1961; Too Tough to Handle, 1962; The Dead Keep Faith, 1962; The Spark of Anger, 1962; Full Impact, 1962; I Vow Vengeance, 1962; Gunflash, 1962; Hit Back, 1962; One Must Die, 1962; Suicide Squad, 1962; Airborne Commando, 1963; No Higher Stakes, 1963; Penalty of Fear, 1963. Add: 67 Houston Rd., London SE23 2RL, England.

TUCCI, Niccolo. American (b. Italian), b. 1908. Novels/Short stories, Plays/Screenplays, Essays. Writer for the New Yorker, NYC, since 1946, and contrib. to other mags. Polemicist and Corresp., Politics Mag., NYC, 1943–46; Co-Founder, 1954, and Columnist, The Press of Freedom, Village Voice, NYC; Writer-in-Residence, Columbia Univ., NYC, 1965–66; Co-Founder, The Wide Embrace theatre co., NYC, 1973. *Publs:* Posterity for Sale (play), 1939; Il Segreto, 1956; Those of the Lost Continent: Before My Time, 1962; Unfinished Funeral, 1964; Gli Atlantidi (autobiography), 1968; Love and Death, 1973; How to Get Away Without Murder (essays), 1973; Confessioni Involontaire (autobiography), 1977; The Sun and the Moon, 1977. Add: 25 E. 67th St., New York, N.Y. 10021, U.S.A.

TUCCILLE, Jerome. American, b. 1937. Money/Finance, Politics/ Government, Social commentary/phenomena. Investment broker, NYC. *Publs:* Radical Libertarianism, 1970; It Usually Begins with Ayn Rand, 1971; (ed. with M. Rothbard) The Right Wing Individualist Tradition in America, 1972; Here Comes Immortality, 1973; Who's Afraid of 1984?, 1975; Everything the Beginner Needs to Know to Invest Shrewdly, 1978; The Optimist's Guide to Making Money in the 1980's, 1979; Mind over Money, 1980; Dynamic Investing, 1981; Inside the Underground Economy, 1982; How to Profit from the Wall Street Mergers, 1983; Kingdom: The Story of the Hunt Family of Texas, 1984; Trump (biography), 1985; Wall Street Blues, 1988. Add: c/o Lyle Stuart Inc., 120 Enterprise Ave., Secaucus, N.J. 07094, U.S.A.

TUCKER, Anne W(ilkes). American, b. 1945. Photography. Curator of Photography, Museum of Fine Arts, Houston, since 1976. *Publs:* (with William Burback) Walker Evans: Photographs, 1971; (with Lee Witkin) Rare Books and Photographs (catalogue), 1973; (ed.) The Woman's Eye, 1973; (with William C. Agee) The Target Collection of American Photography (catalogue), 1977; (compiler) Photo Notes and Filmfront, 1977; (ed.) The Antony G. Cronin Memorial Collection, 1979; (ed.) Suzanne Bloom and Ed Hill, 1980; (ed.) 5 American Photographers, 1981; The Museum of Fine Arts, Houston: A Guide to the Collection, 1981; (ed.) In Sequence, 1982; Unknown Territory: Photography by Ray K. Metzer 1957-1983, 1984; (co-ed.) Robert Frank, 1986. Add: 4118 Bellefontaine St., Houston, Tex. 77025, U.S.A.

TUCKER, Anthony. British, b. 1924. Environmental Science/Ecology. Science Editor, The Guardian, London, 1964–88 (former Northern Features Ed., Art Critic). *Publs:* Climate for Living, 1967; The Toxic Metals, 1972; (with J.A. Lauwerys and Keith Reid) Man, Nature, and Ecololgy, 1974; (With J. Gleisner) Crusable of Despair: The Effects of Nuclear War, 1981. Add: 5 Spicer St., St. Albans AL3 4PH, England.

TUCKER, Helen. American, b. 1926. Novel/Short stories. Reporter, Times-News, Burlington, N.C., 1946–47, Times-News, Twin Falls, Idaho, 1948–49, Stateman, Boise, Idaho, 1950–51, and Raleigh Times, N.C., 1955–57; Continuity Writer, Radio KDYL, Salt Lake City, Utah, 1952–53; Continuity Supvr., Radio WPTF, Raleigh, N.C., 1953–55; Editorial Asst., Columbia Univ. Press, NYC, 1959–60; Dir. of Publicity and Publs., North Carolina Museum of Arts, Raleigh, 1967–70. *Publs:* The Sound of Summer Voices, 1969; The Guilt of Agust Feilding, 1971; No Need of Glory, 1972; The Virgin of Lontano, 1973; A Strange and Ill-Starred Marrige, 1979; A Mistress to the Regent, 1980; An Infamus Attachment, 1980; The Double Dealers, 1982; Season of Dishonor, 1982; Ardent Vows, 1983; Bounded by Honor, 1984. Add: 2930 Hosteler St., Raleigh, N.C. 27609, U.S.A.

TUCKER, (Allan) James. Also Write as David Craig and Bill James. British, b. 1929. Novel/Short stories, Literature. *Publs:* Equal Partner, 1960; The Righthand Man, 1961; The Lands of Chimney Hill (radio Play), 1962; Bruster, 1966; Honourable Estates, 1966; The Novels og Anthony Powell, 1976; Blage of Riot, 1978; The King's Friend, 1982; as Davis Craig—The Alias man, 1968; Message Ends, 1969; Contect Lost, 1970;

Young Men May Die, 1970; A Walk at Night, 1971; Up from the Grave, 1971; Double Take, 1972; Bolthole, 1973; Knifeman, 1973; Whose Little Girl Are You? 1974; A dead Liberty, 1974; The Albion Case, 1975; Faith, Hope, and Death, 1976; as Bill James—You'd Better Believe it, 1985; The Lolita Man, 1986; Halo Parade, 1987; Protection, 1988. Add: c/o Constable, 10 Orange St., London WC2H 7EG, England.

TUCKER, Link. *See* **BINGLEY,** David Ernest.

TUCKER, Martin. American, b. 1928. Poetry, Literature, Essays. Prof. of English, C.W. Post Coll. of Long Island Univ., N.Y. since 1968 (Asst. Prof., 1963–66; Assoc. Prof., 1966–68). Ed., Confrontation mag., Brookville, Long Island, since 1970. *Publs:* (ed. with R.Z. Temple) A Library of Literary Criticism: Modern British Literature, 3 vols., 1966; Africa in Modern Literature, 1967; (ed.) Moulton's Library of Literary Criticism, 4 vols., 1968; (ed.) The Criticial Temper, 4 vols., 1979, vol. V, 1989; (ed.) Undine, by Olive Schreiner, 1972; (ed. with R. Stein) A Library of Literary Criticism: Modern British Literature, vol. 4, 1974; Joseph Conrad, 1976; (ed. with J. Ferres) Modern Commonwealth Literature, 1977; Homes of Locks and Mysteries (poetry), 1982. Add: 90-A Dosoris Lane, Glen Cove, N.Y. 11542, U.S.A.

TUCKER, Robert C. American, b. 1918. Politics/Government. Prof. of Politics Emeritus, Princeton Univ., N.J., since 1984 (Prof. 1962–84). Attaché U.S. Embassy, Moscow, 1944–53; Assoc. Prof., and subsequently Prof. of Govt., Indiana Univ., Bloomington, 1958–62. *Publs:* Philosophy and Myth in Karl Marx, 1961, 1972; The Soviet Political Mind: Stalinism and After, 1963, 1971; (ed. with S.F. Cohen) The Great Purge Trial, 1965; The Marxian Revolutionary Idea, 1969; (ed.) The Marx-Engels Reader, 1972, 1978; Stalin as Revolutionary 1879-1929: A Study in History and Personality, 1973; (ed.) The Lenin Anthology, 1975; (ed.) Stalinism: Essays in Historical Interpretation, 1977; Politics as Leadership, 1981; Political Culture and Leadership in Soviet Russia: From Lenin to Gorbachev, 1987. Add: c/o Norton Inc., 500 Fifth Ave., New York, N.Y. 10110, U.S.A.

TUCKER, William Edward. American, b. 1932. Theology/Religion, Biography. Chancellor, Texas Christian Univ., Fort Worth, since 1979 (Asst. Dean, 1966–69, Assoc. Dean, 1969–71, and Dean and Prof. of Church History, 1971–76, Brite Divinity Sch. of Texas Christian Univ.). Prof., 1959–66, and Chmn., 1961–66; Dept. of Religion and Philosophy, Atlantic Christian Coll., Wilson, N.C.; Pres., Bethany Coll., West Virginia, 1976–79. *Publs:* J.H. Garrison and Disciples of Christ, 1964; Journey in Faith: History of the Christian Church (Disciples of Christ), 1975. Add: 2900 Simondale Dr., Fort Worth, Tex. 76109, U.S.A.

TUCKER, (Arthur) Wilson ("Bob"). American, b. 1914. Mystery/Crime/Suspense, Science fiction/Fantasy. Motion picture projectionist, 1933–72; and electrician for 20th Century Fox, and the Univ. of Illinois at Urbana and at Normal. Pubr. of many fan mags.: The Planetoid, 1932, Science Fiction News Letter, D'Journal, Le Zombie, 1938–75, Fantasy and Weird Fiction, 1938–39, Yearbook of Science, Fanewscard Weekly, Fanzine Yearbook, 1941–45, Fapa Variety, etc. Pres., National Fantasy Fan Fedn., 1942–43. *Publs:* The Chinese Doll, 1946; To Keep or Kill, 1947; The Dove, 1948; The Stalking Man, 1949; Red Herring, 1951; The City in the Sea (science fiction), 1951; The Long Loud Silence (science fiction), 1952; The Time Masters (science fiction), 1953, 1971; Wild Talent (science fiction), 1954, as Man from Tomorrow, 1955; The Science-Fiction Subtreasury (short stories), 1954, as Time: X, 1955; The Neo-Fan's Guide to Science Fiction Fandom (non-fiction), 1955; Time Bomb (science fiction), 1955, as Tomorrow Plus X, 1957; The Man in My Grave, 1956; The Hired Target, 1957; The Lincoln Hunters (science fiction), 1958; To the Tombaugh Station (science fiction), 1960; Last Stop, 1963; A Processional of the Damned, 1966; The Warlock, 1967; The Year of the Quiet Sun (science fiction), 1970; This Witch, 1971; Ice and Iron (science fiction), 1975; Resurrection Days (science fiction), 1981. Add: c/o Curtis Brown, 10 Astor Pl., New York, N.Y. 10003, U.S.A.

TUCKMAN, Bruce Wayne. American, b. 1938. Education. Prof. of Education, Florida State Univ., Tallahassee. Research Psychologist, Naval Medical Research Inst., 1963–65; Asoc. Prof. 1965–70, then Prof. of Education, Rutgers Univ., New Brunswick, N.J. *Publs:* (ed. with J.L.O'Brien) Preparing to Teach the Disadvantaged, 1969; Conducting Educational Research, 1972, 3rd ed. 1988; Measuring Educational Outcomes, 1975; Analyzing the Designing Educational Research, 1979; (with F.C. Johnson) Effective College Management, 1987; Testing for Teachers, 1988. Add: Coll. of Education, Florida State Univ., Tallahassee, Fla. 32306, U.S.A.

TUDOR, Andrew Frank. British, b. 1942. Film, Sociology. Sr. Lectr. in Sociology, Univ. of York, since 1975 (Lectr., 1970–75). Research Officer, and Lectr., Dept. of Sociology, Univ. of Essex, Colchester, 1966–70. Assoc. Ed., Screen, 1972–76. *Publs:* Theories of Film, 1974; Image and Influence: Studies in the Sociology of Film, 1974; Beyond Empiricism, 1982; Monsters and Mad Scientists, 1989. Add: Dept. of Sociology, Univ. of York, Heslington, York WO1 5DD, England.

TUDOR, Tasha. American, b. 1915. Children's fiction, Poetry. *Publs:* Pumpkin Moonshine, 1938; Alexander the Gander, 1939; The Country Fair, 1940; A Tale for Easter, 1941; Snow Before Christmas, 1941; Dorcas Porcus, 1942; The White Goose, 1943; Linsey Woolsey, 1946; Thistly B., 1949; The Dolls' Christmas, 1950; Amanda and the Bear, 1951; Edgar Allan Crow, 1953; A Is for Annabelle (verse), 1954; I Is One (verse), 1956; Around the Year (verse), 1957; Becky's Birthday, 1960; Becky's Christmas, 1961; (ed.) Book of Fairy Tales, 1961; (ed.) Wings from the Winds, 1964; (ed.) Favorite Stories, 1965; (ed.) Take Joy!, 1966; First Delights, 1966; Corgiville Fair, 1971; A Time to Keep: The Tasha Tudor Book of Holidays, 1977; Five Senses, 1978; The Springs of Joy, 1979; Tasha Tudor's Treasure, 3 vols., 1981; (ed.) All for Love, 1984; Seasons of Delight, 1986; Give Us This Day: The Lord's Prayer, 1987. Add: Putnam Publishing, 200 Madison Ave., New York, N.Y. 10016, U.S.A.

TUFTY, Barbara. American, b. 1923. Earth sciences, Environmental Science (conservation), Meteorology/Atmospheric sciences. Ed., Audubon Naturalist Soc., since 1985. Staff Writer and Corresp., Science News, 1948–70; Science Writer, National Academy of Sciences, 1970–72; Ed., National Science Foundn. Bulletin, Washington, D.C., 1972–84. *Publs:* (trans.) Crafts and Culture in the Ivory Coast, 1967; 1001 Questions Answered about Natural Land Disasters Storms 2 vols., 1970–72; Cells—Units of Life, 1973. Add: 3812 Livingston St., N.W., Washington, D.C. 20015, U.S.A.

TUGENDHAT, Christopher (Samuel). British, b. 1937. Business/-Trade/Industry, Politics/Government. Chmn., Civil Aviation Authority, since 1986; Dir., National Westminster Bank, and BOC Group, since 1985, and Commercial Union Assurance Co., since 1988. Chmn., Royal Inst. of Intnl. Affairs (Chatham House), since 1986. Feature and Leader Writer, Financial Times, London, 1960–70; Conservative Member of Parliament (U.K.) for Cities of London and Westminster, 1970–74, and for City of London and Westminster South, 1974–76; Shadow Spokesman for Employment, 1974–75, and Foreign and Commonwealth Affairs, 1975–76; Dir., Sunningdale Oils Ltd., 1971–76, and Phillips Petroleum Intnl. (U.K.) Ltd., 1972–76; Vice-Pres., Commn. of the European Communities, 1981–85. *Publs:* Oil: The Biggest Business, 1968; The Multinationals, 1971; Britain, Europe, and the Third World, 1976; Making Sense of Europe, 1986; (with William Wallace) Options for British Foreign Policy in the 1990s, 1988. Add: 35 Westbourne Park Rd., London W2 5QD, England.

TUGENDHAT, Julia. Writes as Julia Dobson. British, b. 1941. Children's fiction, Children's non-fiction. *Publs:* The Children of Charles I (history), 1975; The Smallest Man in England (historical novel), 1977; Children of the Tower (history), 1978; They Were at Waterloo (history), 1979; The Ivory Poachers: A Crisp Twins Adventure (novel), 1981; The Tomb Robbers (novel), 1981; Mountbatten, Sailor Hero (history), 1982; The Wreck Finders (novel), 1982; The Animal Rescuers (novel), 1982; Danger In the Magic Kingdom (novel), 1983; The Chinese Puzzle (novel), 1984. Add: 35 Westbourne Park Rd., London W2, England.

TUGWELL, Maurice A. J. Canadian, b. 1925. International relations/Current affairs, Military/Defence. Dir., Centre for Conflict Studies, Univ. of New Brunswick, Fredericton, since 1980. Retired Officer, British Army: joined as private, 1943; retired as brigadier, 1978. *Publs:* (ed. and co-author) The Unquiet Peace, 1957; By Air to Battle, 1971; Arnhem: A Case Study, 1975; Skiing for Beginners, 1977. Add: 15 Spruce Terrace, Fredericton, N.B. E3B 2S6, Canada.

TULCHIN, Joseph S. American, b. 1939. Area Studies, History, International relations/Current affairs, Politics/Government. Prof. of History since 1971, and Dir., Office of Intnl. Progs., since 1982, Univ. of North Carolina, Chapel Hill. Asst. Prof. of History, Yale Univ., New Haven, Conn., 1964–71. *Publs:* The Aftermath of War, 1971; (ed. with David J. Danielski) The Autobiographical Notes of Charles Evans Hughes, 1973; (ed.) Problems in Latin American History, 1973; (ed.) Hemispheric Perspectives on the United States, 1978; (ed. with Heraldo Munoz) Latin American Nations in World Politics, 1984; (ed.) Habitat, Health, and

Development, 1986; Argentina and the United States: A Conflicted Relationship, 1989. Add: Dept. of History, Univ. of North Carolina, Chapel Hill, N.C. 27514, U.S.A.

TULLETT, James Stuart. British, b. 1912. Novels/Short stories, History, Travel/Exploration/Adventure, Biography. Feature writer, Taranaki Newspaper Ltd., New Plymouth, 1962–82. *Publs:* Tar White, 1962; Yellow Streak, 1963; Red Abbott, 1964; White Pine, 1965; Hunting Black, 1966; (with Graham Alexander) The Super Men, 1967; Nairn Bus to Baghdad, 1969; Town of Fear, 1971; The Industrious Heart, A History of New Plymouth, 1980. Add: 191 Tukapa St., New Plymouth, New Zealand.

TUMIN, Melvin M. American, b. 1919. Sociology. Prof. of Sociology and Anthropology, Princeton Univ., N.J., 1947–89. Consultant, Curriculum Panel and Regional Advisory Panel, Office of Education, U.S. Dept. of Health, Education and Welfare; Consultant, Research and Development Section, U.S. AID; Consultant, Educational Testing Service; Member, Editorial Bd., Public Opinion Quarterly, Social Education, American Sociologist, and Social Problems. Asst. Prof. of Sociology and Anthropology, Wayne State Univ., Detroit, 1944–47. Pres., Soc. for the Study of Social Problems, 1966–67; Pres., Eastern Sociological Soc., 1967–68; Dir., Task Force on Individual Violence, National Commn. on Causes and Prevention of Violence, 1968–69. *Publs:* (with J.W. Bennett) Social Life: Structure and Function, 1948; Caste in a Peasant Society, 1952; Segregation and Desegregation: A Summary of Research 1951-56, 1957; Desegregation: Resistance and Readiness, 1958; An Inventory and Evaluation of Research and Theory in Anti-Semitism, 1960; Social Class and Social Change in Puerto Rico, 1961; (ed.) Race and Intelligence, 1963; Education, Social Class, and Intergroup Attitudes in England, France and Germany, 1964; Quality and Equality in American Education, 1966; Social Stratification, 1967, 1985; Education and National Goals: A Model for the Measurement of the Effectiveness of Educational Systems, 1969; Reader in Social Stratification, 1969; Comparative Perspective on Race Relations, 1969; Crimes of Violence: Preventions, 1969; Patterns of Society, 1973; (co-ed.) Pluralism in a Democratic Society, 1977. Add: 119 Fitz Randolph, Princeton, N.J., U.S.A.

TUNSTALL, C. Jeremy. British, b. 1934. Communications Media/Broadcasting, Sociology. Prof. of Sociology, City Univ., London, since 1974. Research Officer, London Sch. of Economics, 1962–65; Research Fellow, Univ. of Essex, 1965–69; Sr. Lectr. in Sociology, Open Univ., 1969–74. Consultant, Royal Commn. on the Press, 1975–76. *Publs:* The Fishermen, 1962; The Advertising Man, 1964; Old and Alone, 1966; The Westminster Lobby Correspondents, 1970; (ed.) Media Sociology, 1970; (ed. with Kenneth Thompson) Sociological Perspectives, 1971; Journalists at Work, 1971; (ed.) The Open University Opens, 1974; The Media Are American, 1977; (with D. Walker) Media Made in California, 1981; The Media in Britain, 1983; Communications Deregulation, 1986. Add: 19 S. Villas, Camden Sq., London NW1 9BS, England.

TUOHY, Frank (John Francis Tuohy). British, b. 1925. Novels/Short stories, Biography. Lectr., Turku Univ., Finland, 1947–48; Prof. of English Language and Literature, Univ. of Sao Paulo, Brazil, 1950–56; Contract Prof., Jagiellonian Univ., Krakow, Poland, 1958–60. *Publs:* The Animal Game, 1957; The Warm Nights of January, 1960; The Admiral and the Nuns and Other Stories, 1962; The Ice Saints, 1964; Fingers in the Door, 1970; Portugal, 1970; W.B. Yeats (biography), 1976; Live Bait, 1978; The Collected Stories, 1984. Add: Shatwell Cottage, Yarlington, Nr. Wincanton, Somerset BA9 8DL, England.

TURBOTT, Evan Graham. New Zealander, b. 1914. Natural history, Zoology. Dir. Emeritus, Auckland Inst. and Museum, since 1979 (Dir., 1964–79). Asst. Dir., Canterbury Museum, Christchurch, 1957–64. *Publs:* New Zealand Bird Life, 1947; (with R.A. Falla and R.B. Sibson) A Field Guide to New Zealand Birds, 1966, 1970, as The New Guide to the Birds of the New Zealand, 1979; (ed. and contrib.) Buller's Birds of New Zealand: A New Edition of Sir Walter Buller's A History of the Birds of New Zealand, 1967. Add: Auckland Inst. and Museum, Private Bag, Auckland 1, New Zealand.

TURCO, Lewis (Putnam). Also Writes as Wesli Court. American, b. 1934. Novels/Short stories, Poetry, Literary Criticism, Education (textbooks), Essays. Member of the faculty since 1965, Dir. of the Prog. in Writing Arts since 1969, and Prof. of English since 1971, State Univ. of New York at Oswego; Faculty Exchange Scholar, State Univ. of New York, since 1975. Member of the faculty, Univ. of Connecticut, 1959, Fenn Coll., Cleveland State Univ., 1960–64, and Hillsdale Coll., Michigan, 1964–65. Founding Dir., Cleveland State Univ. Poetry Center, 1961–64; Visiting Prof., State Univ. of New York at Potsdam, 1968–69;

Bingham Poet-in-Residence, Univ. of Louisville, 1982. *Publs:* First Poems, 1960; The Sketches and Livevil: A Mask, 1962; Awaken, Bells Falling: Poems 1959-1967, 1968; The Book of Forms: A Handbook of Poetics, 1968; (compiler) The Literature of New York: A Bibliography of Colonial and Native New York State Authors, 1970; Creative Writing in Poetry, 1970; The Inhabitant, 1970; Pocoangelini: A Fantography and Other Poems, 1971; Poetry: An Introduction Through Writing, 1973; The Weed Garden, 1973; Freshman Composition and Literature, 1974; (as Wesli Court) Courses in Lambents, 1977; (as Wesli Court) Curses and Lambents, 1978; A Cage of Creatures: Poems, 1978; (as Wesli Court) Murgatroyd and Mabel, 1978; Seasons of the Blood, 1980; American Still Lifes, 1981; (as Wesli Court) The Airs of Wales, 1981; The Compleat Melancholick, 1985; Visions and Revisions: of American Poetry, 1986; A Maze of Monsters, 1986; The New Book of Forms: A Handbook of Poetics, 1986; Dialogue, 1989; The Shifting Web: New and Selected Poems, 1989. Add: Box 362, 54 W. 8th St., Oswego, N.Y. 13126, U.S.A.

TURECK, Rosalyn. American, b. 1914. Music. Concert pianist: extensive U.S. tours since 1937, and European tours since 1947. Dir., Intnl. Bach Soc., NYC, since 1966; Hon. Life Fellow, St. Hilda's Coll., Oxford, since 1974. Member of faculty, Philadelphia Conservatory of Music, Pa., 1935–42, Mannes Sch. of Music, 1940–44, Juilliard Sch. of Music, 1943–55, and Columbia Univ., NYC, 1953–55; Prof. of Music, Univ. of California, San Diego, 1966–72; Prof. of Music, Univ. of Maryland, College Park, 1982. Founder-Dir., Composers of Today (Soc. for the Performance of Contemporary Music), NYC, 1951–55, Tureck Bach Players, London, 1957, Intnl. Bach Soc., 1966, Inst. for Bach Studies, 1968; Tureck Bach Players, NYC, 1981, and Tureck Bach Inst., 1981. *Publs:* An Introduction to the Performance of Bach, 3 vols., 1959–60; (transcriber) A. Scarlatti: Air and Gavotte; (transcriber) Paganini: Perpetuum Mobile; (transcriber) J.S. Bach: Sarabande, C minor, 1960; Italian Concerto (Tureck Bach Urtext series), 1981; Lute Suite in G minor, Set for Classical Guitar (Tureck Bach Urtext series), 1982; Lute Suite, C minor, Set for Classical Guitar, 1985. Add: c/o Ibbs and Tillett Ltd., 18B Pindock Mews, London W9 2PY, England.

TURK, Frances (Mary). British, b. 1915. Novels/Short stories, Poetry. Lectr., critic, and literary judge. Mag. Columnist, Cambridgeshire Life Mag. Member, Huntingdon and Peterborough Co. Library Cttee., 1950–73; Cttee. Member, Romantic Novelists' Assn., 1965–67. *Publs:* Paddy O'Shea, 1937; Doctor Periwinkle, 1937; The Song of the Nightingale, 1938; The Precious Hours, 1938; The Rector, Bless Him, 1939; Paradise Street, 1939; Green Garnet, 1940; Lovable Clown, 1941; Dear Professor, 1941; Angel Hill, 1942; Candle Corner, 1943; Wideawake, 1944; The Five Grey Geese, 1944; The House of Heron, 1946; Ancestors, 1947; Jerninghams, 1948; Three Bags Full, 1949; Salutation, 1949; Time and Tranquillity, 1950; The Small House at Ickley, 1951; The Gentle Flowers, 1952; The Lovely Things, 1952; The Laughing Fox, 1953; The Heart of a Rose, 1954; The Dark Wood, 1954; The Glory and the Dream, 1955; The Fruit of the Vine, 1955; Dinny Lightfoot, 1956; The Jagged Edge, 1956; No Through Road, 1957; A Vain Shadow, 1957; The House in Orange Street, 1958; The White Swan, 1958; The Land of Beulah, 1959; The Temple of Fancy, 1959; Journey to Eternity, 1960; A Time to Know, 1960; A Man Called Jeremy, 1961; The Golden Leaves, 1961; The Secret Places, 1962; The Living Fountains, 1962; A Lamp from Murano, 1963; The Mistress of Medlam, 1963; A Flush of Scarlet, 1963; A Visit to Marchmont, 1964; The Guarded Heart, 1964; The Summer Term, 1965; The Sour-Sweet Days, 1965; Goddess of Threads, 1966; The Rectory at Hay, 1966; Lionel's Story, 1966; Legacy of Love, 1967; The Flowering Field, 1967; The Martin Window, 1968; The Lesley Affair, 1968; Fair Recompense, 1969; For Pity, For Anger, 1970; The Absent Young Man, 1971; Whispers, 1972. Add: Hillrise, Buckden, Huntingdon PE18 9UH, England.

TURKLE, Brinton. American, b. 1915. Children's fiction. *Publs:* Obadiah the Bold, 1965; The Magic of Millicent Musgrave, 1967; The Fiddler of High Lonesome, 1968; Thy Friend, Obadiah, 1969; The Sky Dog, 1969; Mooncoin Castle; or, Skulduggery Rewarded, 1970; The Adventures of Obadiah, 1972; It's Only Arnold, 1973; Deep in the Forest, 1976; Rachel and Obadiah, 1978; Do Not Open, 1981. Add: c/o Dutton, 2 Park Ave., New York, N.Y. 10016, U.S.A.

TURNBULL, Colin M(acmillan). American (born British), b. 1924. Anthropology/Ethnology, Sociology. Anthropological field researcher in Ituri Forest, Congo, 1951, 1954–55, 1957–59; Asst. Curator, 1959–65, and 1965–69, American Museum of Natural History, NYC; Prof. of Anthropology, Virginia Commonwealth Univ., Richmond, 1973–75. Former consultant to U.S. State Dept., American Univ., and Agency for International Development. *Publs:* The Forest People, 1961; The Lonely

African, 1962; The Peoples of Africa, 1962; The Mbuti Pygmies: An Ethnographic Survey, 1965; Wayward Servants: The Two Worlds of the African Pygmies, 1965; Tradition and Change in African Tribal Life, 1966; (with Thubten Jigme Norbu) Tibet, 1968; The Mountain People, 1972; Man in Africa, 1976; The Human Cycle, 1983. Add: c/o Simon and Schuster, 1230 Ave. of the Americas, New York, N.Y. 10020, U.S.A.

TURNBULL, Gael (Lundin). British, b. 1928. Poetry. Full-time writer. Formerly, Gen. medical practitioner and anaesthetist. *Publs:* A Trampoline, 1968; Scantlings, 1970; Finger Cymbals, 1971; A Random Sapling, 1974; Thronging the Heart, 1976; Residues, 1976; If a Glance Could Be Enough, 1978; The Small Change, 1980; Rain in Wales, 1981; A Gathering of Poems 1950-1980, 1983; From the Language of the Heart, 1983; Traces, 1983; Circus, 1984; A Year and a Day, 1985; Spaces, 1986; A Winter Journey, 1987. Add: c/o Mariscat Press, 3 Mariscat Rd., Glasgow G41 4ND, Scotland.

TURNBULL, Stephen (Richard). British, b. 1948. History. District Health Education Officer, Dewsbury, since 1984. Secty., To-Ken Soc. of Great Britain, Northern Branch, since 1971. Health Education Officer, Leeds, 1971–84. *Publs:* The Samurai: A Military History, 1977; Samurai Armies 1550-1615, 1979; Warlords of Japan, 1979; The Mongols, 1980; The Book of the Samurai, 1982; The Book of the Medieval Knight, 1985; Samurai Warriors, 1987; Battles of the Manurai, 1987; Samurai Warlords: The Book of The Daimyo, 1989. Add: 9 Victoria Dr., Horsforth, Leeds LS18 4PN, England.

TURNER, (Sir) Alexander (Kingcome). New Zealander, b. 1901. Law. Pres. of the Court of Appeal of New Zealand, Wellington, 1972–73, now retired (became Judge of the Court, 1962). Called to the New Zealand Bar, 1923; Gen. Practice, Auckland, 1926–51; Queen's Counsel, 1952; Judge of the Supreme Court of New Zealand, 1953–62. Vice Pres., Univ. of Auckland, 1950–52. *Publs:* all with Spencer Bower—The Law Relating to Estoppel by Representation, 1966, 2nd ed. (by Turner only), 1979; Spencer Bower and Turner on the Doctrine of Res Judicata, 1969; Spencer Bower and Turner on the Law of Actionable Misrepresentation, 1974. Add: 14 St., Michael's Cres., Kelburn, Wellington 1, New Zealand.

TURNER, Amédée (Edward). British, b. 1929. Law. Patent Barrister, London, since 1954; Member of the European Parliament for Suffolk and South East Cambridgeshire, since 1984 (Member for Suffolk and Harwich, 1979–84). Advisor, Kenyon & Kenyon, New York Patent Attorneys, NYC, 1957–60; Queens Counsel (Q.C.), 1976. *Publs:* The Law of Trade Secrets, 1962, Supplement 1968; The Law of the New European Patent, 1979. Add: 1 Essex Ct., Temple, London EC4, England.

TURNER, Bryan S. British, b. 1945. Sociology, Theology/Religion, Third World. Prof. of Social Sciences, Univ. of Utrecht, Netherlands, since 1988. Member of Ed. Bd., Theory, Culture, and Society. Lectr. and Reader in Sociology, Univ. of Aberdeen, 1969–74, 1978–82, and Univ. of Lancaster, 1974–78; Prof. of Sociology, Flinders Univ. Bedford Pk., S.A., 1982–88. Alexander von Humboldt Fellow, Univ. of Bielefeld, W. Germany, 1987–88. *Publs:* Weber and Islam, 1974; Marx and the End of Orientalism, 1978; (with N. Abercrombie and S. Hill), The Dominant Ideology Thesis, 1980; For Weber: Essays on the Sociology of Fate, 1981; (with M. Hepworth), Confession: Studies in Deviance and Religion, 1982; Religion and Social Theory, 1983; (with N. Abercrombie and S. Hill) The Penguin Dictionary of Sociology, 1984; The Body and Society, 1984; Equality, 1986; Citizenship and Capitalism: The Debate over Reformism, 1986; (with R.J. Holton) Talcott Parsons on Economy and Society, 1986; (with N. Abercrombie and S. Hill) Sovereign Individuals of Capitalism, 1986; Medical Power and Social Knowledge, 1987; (with G. Stranth) Nietzsche's Dance, 1988; Status, 1988. Add: Faculty of Social Sciences, Univ. of Utrecht, Postbus 80140, 3508 TC Utrecht, The Netherlands.

TURNER, Darwin T. American, b. 1931. Poetry, Literature, Theatre. Univ. of Iowa Foundn. Distinguished Prof. of English, and Chmn., African American/World Studies, Univ. of Iowa City, since 1972 (Visiting Prof. of English, 1971–72). *Publs:* (ed.) A Guide to Composition, 1960; (ed.) Standards for Freshman Composition, 1961; Katharsis, 1964; (ed. with Turtu Rnernery. Bright) Images of the Negro in America, 1964; Nathaniel Hawthorne's The Scarlet Letter, 1967; (ed.) Black American Literature, 4 vols., 1969–70; Afro-American Writers, 1970; (ed.) Black Drama in America: An Anthology, 1971; In a Minor Chord: Three Afro-American Writers and Their Search for Identity, 1971; (ed. with J. Bright and R. Wright) Voices from the Black Experience, 1972; (with B. Stanford) Theory and Practice in the Teaching of Literature by Afro-Americans, 1972; Afro-American Writers, 1972; (ed. with P. Thompson) Responding Five, 1973; (ed.) The Wayward and the Seeking: Selected Writings of

Jean Toomer, 1980 (ed. with J. Sekora) The Art of Slave Narrative, 1983; (ed.) Cane, by J. Toomer, 1988. Add: 303 English/Philosophy Bldg., Univ. of Iowa, Iowa City, Iowa 52242, U.S.A.

TURNER, David. British, b. 1927. Plays/Screenplays, Communications media (television scripts). *Publs:* Semi-Detached, 1962; (adaptor) The Servant of Two Masters, 1968; The Prodigal Daughter, 1973; The Beggar's Opera, 1982. Add: c/o Balliol Coll., Oxford OX1 3BJ, England.

TURNER, E(rnest) S(ackville). British, b. 1909. History, Humor/Satire. Member, Punch Table, London. Ed., Soldier, British Army mag., 1946–57. *Publs:* Boys Will Be Boys, 1948, 1974; Roads to Ruin, 1950; Shocking History of Advertising, 1952; The Third Pip, 1952; A History of Courting, 1954; Maiden Voyage, 1954; Gallant Gentlemen, 1956; Call the Doctor, 1958; Court of St. James's, 1959; The Phoney War, 1961; What the Butler Saw, 1962; All Heaven in a Rage, 1964; How to Measure a Women, 1965; Taking the Cure, 1965; Hemlock Lane, 1968; May It Please Your Lordship, 1971; Amazing Grace, 1975; Dear Old Blighty, 1980; An ABC of Nostalgia, 1984. Add: 21 Woburn Ct., Stanmore Rd., Richmond, Surrey, England.

TURNER, Frederick C. American, b. 1938. International Relations/Current affairs, Politics/Government. Prof. of Political Science, Univ. of Connecticut, Storrs, since 1970 (Asst. Prof., 1965–68; Assoc. Prof., 1968–70). Latin American Rep., Roper Public Opinion Research Center, since 1972. Visiting Lectr., Dept. of Political Science, Yale Univ., New Haven, Conn., 1967–69. Pres., World Assn. for Public Opinion Research, 1988–90. *Publs:* The Dynamic of Mexican Nationalism, 1968; Catholicism and Political Development in Latin America, 1971; Responsible Parenthood: The Politics of Mexico's New Population Policies, 1974; Juan Peron and the Reshaping of Argentina, 1983; Racionalidad del peronismo, 1988. Add: 30 Timber Dr., Storrs., Conn. 06268, U.S.A.

TURNER, George (Reginald). Australian, b. 1916. Novels/Short stories, Science fiction. Employment Officer, Commonwealth Employment Service, Melbourne, 1945–49, and Wangaratta, Vic., 1949–50; Textile Technician, Buck Mills, Wangaratta, 1951–64; Sr. Employment Officer, Volkswagen Ltd., Melbourne, 1964–67. *Publs:* Young Man of Talent, 1959; A Stranger and Afraid, 1961; The Cupboard under the Stairs, 1962; A Waste of Shame, 1965; The Lame Dog Man, 1967; (ed.) The View from the Edge, 1977; Beloved Son, 1978; Transit of Cassidy, 1978; Vaneglory, 1982; Yesterday's Men, 1983; In the Heart or In the Head (memoir), 1984; The Sea and Summer, 1987. Add: 4/296 Inkerman St., E. St. Kilda, Vic. 3183, Australia.

TURNER, George William. Australian, b. 1921. Language/Linguistics. Member of Faculty, Univ. of Canterbury, N.Z., 1955–64; Reader in English, Univ. of Adelaide, 1965–86. *Publs:* The English Language in Australian and New Zealand, 1966, 1972; Stylistics, 1973; (ed.) Good Australian English, 1973; (ed.) The Australian Pocket Oxford Dictionary, 2nd ed. 1984; (ed.) Australian Concise Oxford Dictionary, 1986. Add: 3 Marola Ave., Rostrevor, S.A. 5073, Australia.

TURNER, Harold Walter. British, b. 1911. Theology/Religion. Hall Warden, 1941–51, and Ecumenical Chaplain, 1941–47, Otago Univ., N.Z.; Parish Minister, Dunedin, N.Z., 1951–54; Lectr. in Theology, Univ. Coll. of Sierra Leone, 1955–62; Sr. Lectr. in Religion, Univ. of Nigeria, 1963–66; Lectr. in Phenomenology and History of Religions, Leicester Univ., 1966–70; Prof. of World Religions, Emory Univ., Atlanta, Ga., 1970–72; Lectr., Sr. Lectr. and Hon. Research Fellow in Religious Studies, Univ. of Aberdeen, 1973–81; Founding Dir., Centre for New Religious Movements, Selly Oak Colleges, Birmingham, and Hon. Fellow, Dept. of Theology, Univ. of Birmingham, 1981–89. *Publs:* Halls of Residence, 1953; Profile through Preaching, 1965; (with R.C. Mitchell) Comprehensive Bibliography of Modern African Religious Movements, 1966, 1972; African Independent Church, 2 vols., 1967; Living Tribal Religions, 1971, 1973; Rudolf Otto, The Idea of the Holy: A Guide for Students, 1974; Bibliography of New Religious Movements in Primal Societies: Black Africa, 1977; North America, 1978; Religious Innovation in Africa, 1979; From Temple to Meeting House, 1979. Add: c/o St. John's Coll., Auckland 5, New Zealand.

TURNER, Henry A(ndrew, Jr.). American, b. 1919. Politics/Government. Academic Vice Chancellor, and Prof. of Political Science, Univ. of California, Santa Barbara. *Publs:* American Democracy: State and Local Government, 1968; (co-author) American Democracy in World Perspective, 4th ed. 1974; (co-author) The Government and Politics of

California, 4th ed. 1971; Reappraisals of Fascism, 1976; Hitler: Memoirs of a Confidant, 1985; German Big Business and the Rise of Hitler, 1985; The Two Germanies since 1945: East and West, 1987. Add: 703 Foxen Drive, Santa Barbara, Calif. 93105, U.S.A.

TURNER, Herbert Arthur (Frederick). British, b. 1919. Economics, Industrial Relations. Leverhulme Foundn. Sr. Research Fellow, Cambridge, since 1985; Fellow, Churchill Coll., Cambridge, and Emeritus Prof. of Industrial Relations, Cambridge Univ., since 1963. Member, Research and Economic Dept., 1944–47, and Asst. Education Secty., 1947–50, Trades Union Congress; Lectr., 1950–59, and Sr. Lectr., 1959–61, Manchester Univ.; Montague Burton Prof. of Industrial Relations, Univ. of Leeds., 1961–63. Member, Natl. Bd. for Prices and Incomes, 1967–71. *Publs:* Arbitration, 1951; Wage Policy Abroad, 1956; Trade Union Growth, Structure, and Policy, 1962; Wages: The Problems for Undeveloped Countries, 1965; Prices, Wages, and Incomes Policies, 1966; Labour Relations in the Motor Industry, 1967; Is Britain Really Strike-Prone?, 1969; Do Trade Unions Cause Inflation?, 1972, 3rd ed. 1978; Management Characteristics and Labour Conflicts, 1978; The Last Colony: Labour in Hong Kong, 1980. Add: Churchill College, Cambridge, England.

TURNER, John Christopher. British, b. 1928. Mathematics/ Statistics. Assoc. Prof. of Mathematics, and Dean, Sch. of Computing and Mathematical Sciences, Univ. of Waikato (joined faculty, 1970). Former Lectr. in Applied Mathematics, Univ. of Sierra Leone, Freetown; Sr. Lectr. in Statistics, Huddersfield Polytechnic, Yorks., 1965–67; Principal Lectr. in Statistics, Leeds Polytechnic, 1967–70. *Publs:* Modern Applied Mathematics, 1970; (with R. Hosking and D. Joyce) First Steps in Numerical Analysis, 1978; (with A. Schaake and D. Sedgwick) Braiding—Regular Knots, 1988. Add: Univ. of Waikato, Hamilton, New Zealand.

TURNER, John Frayn. British, b. 1923. History, Biography. Ed., R.A.F. Publicity, Ministry of Defence, 1963–73; Ed., Central Office of Information, London, 1973–84; Managing Ed, Brevet Publishing, 1984–86. *Publs:* Service Most Silent, 1955; VCs of the Royal Navy, 1956; Prisoner at Large, 1957; Hovering Angels, 1957; Periscope Patrol, 1957; Invasion '44, 1959; VCs of the Air, 1960; Battle Stations, 1960; Highly Explosive, 1961; The Blinding Flash, 1962; VCs of the Army, 1962; A Girl Called Johnnie, 1963; Famous Air Battles, 1963; British Aircraft of World War II, 1974; Destination Berchtesgaden, 1974; Famous Flights, 1978; American Aircraft of World War II, 1979; The Bader Wing, 1981; The Yanks Are Coming, 1983; Frank Sinatra, 1983; The Bader Tapes, 1986; The Good Spy Gride, 1988; Rupert Brooke: The Splendour and the Pain, 1989; Deanua Durbin, 1989. Add: The Metropole, Apt. 302, Folkestone, Kent, England.

TURNER, Judy. Also writes as Judith Saxton. British, b. 1936. Historical/Romance/Gothic. *Publs:* Ralegh's Fair Bess, 1972; Cousin to the Queen, 1972; Feather Light, Diamond Bright, 1974; (as Judith Saxton) The Bright Day Is Done, 1974; (as Judith Saxton) Princess in Writing, 1976; (as Judith Saxton) Winter Queen, 1976; Child of Passion, 1978; Merry Jade, 1978; (as Judith Saxton) The Pride, 1981; (as Judith Saxton) Family Feeling, 1987; (as Judith Saxton) All My Fortunes, 1988. Add: 110 Park Ave., Wrexham, Denbs., Wales.

TURNER, Katharine Charlotte. American, b. 1910. History, Writing/Journalism. Emeritus Prof. of English, Arizona State Univ., Tempe, since 1977 (Asst. Prof., 1946–49; Assoc. Prof., 1949–55; Prof., 1955–77). Asst. Prof. of English, Central Michigan Coll. Mount Pleasant, 1939–43; Cryptanalytic Aide, U.S. War Dept., 1943–46; Lectr. in American Literature, Formosa, 1955–56. *Publs:* Red Men Calling on the Great White Father, 1951; Writing: The Shapes of Experience, 1966. Add: 1216 Maple, Tempe, Ariz. 85281, U.S.A.

TURNER, Len. *See* **FLOREN,** Lee.

TURNER, Louis Mark. British, b. 1942. Business/Trade/Industry, International relations/Current affairs, Third World problems. Dir., Intnl. Business and Technology Prog., Royal Inst. of Intnl. Affairs, London. Researcher on Multinational Corps., Univ. of Salford, 1964–73. *Publs:* Politics and the Multinational Company, 1969; The Growth and Spread of Multinational Companies, 1969; Invisible Empires: Multinational Companies and the Modern World, 1970; Multinational Companies and The Third World, 1973; (with John Ash) The Golden Hordes: International Tourism and the Rise of the Pleasure Periphery, 1975; Oil Companies and the International System, 1978; (with James Bedore) Middle Eastern

Industrialization: The Saudi and Iranian Cases, 1979; (with others) Living with the Newly Industrializing Countries: Trade and Adjustment, 1982; (with John Stopford) Britain and the Multinationals, 1985; (with Valerie Yorke) European Interests in Gulf Oil, 1986; Industrial Collaboration with Japan, 1987. Add: 10 St. James's Sq., London SW1Y 4LE, England.

TURNER, Merfyn. British, b. 1915. Criminology/Law enforcement/Prisons. Social worker and freelance writer. *Publs:* Ship without Sails, 1953; Forgotten Men, 1960; Safe Lodging, 1961; A Pretty Sort of Prison, 1965; O Ryfedd Ryw, 1970; (with Whiteley and Briggs) Dealing with Deviants, 1971; Trwy'r Drws ac Allan, 1987. Add: 24 Harberton Rd., London N19, England.

TURNER, Paul (Digby Lowry). British, b. 1917. Literature, Biography, Translations. Emeritus Fellow, Linacre Coll., Oxford, since 1984 (Univ. Lectr. in English Literature, and Fellow, Linacre Coll., both 1964–84). Asst. Lectr. in English, King's Coll., London, 1946–48; Asst. Lectr. in English, Cambridge Univ., 1948–53; Lectr. in English, University Coll., London, 1955–61, and 1962–63; Prof. of English, Ankara Univ., 1961–62, and 1963–64. *Publs:* (trans.) Euphormio's Satyricon, 1954; (trans.) Daphnis and Chloe, 1956; (trans.) Apollonius of Tyre, 1956; (trans.) The Ephesian Story, 1957; (trans.) The King's Bride, 1959; (trans.) Undine, 1960; (trans.) Satirical Sketches, 1961; (ed.) Selection From Philemon Holland's Translation of Pliny's Natural History, 1962; (ed.) Selection from North's Plutarch, 1963; (ed.) Swift's Gulliver's Travels, 1971; (ed.) Browning's Men and Women, 1972; Tennyson, 1976; English Literature 1832-1890, Excluding the Novel, 1989. Add: c/o Linacre Coll., Oxford, England.

TURNER, Philip (William). Also writes as Stephen Chance. British, b. 1925. Children's fiction, Plays/Screenplays. Part-time Teacher, Malvern Coll., since 1975; now retired. Ordained Priest, Church of England, 1951; Anglican Parish Priest, St. Bartholomew's, Armley, Leeds, 1951–55, St. Peter's, Crawley, Sussex, 1955–60, and St. Matthew's, Northampton, 1960–65; Head of Religious Broadcasting, BBC Midland Region, 1965–70; Teacher, Droitwich High Sch., 1970–73; Chaplain, Eton Coll., Bucks., 1973–75. *Publs:* Christ in the Concrete City (play), 1953, 1960; Mann's End (play), 1953; Passion in Paradise Street (play), 1954; Cry Dawn in Dark Babylon: A Dramatic Mediation, 1959; (with Jack Windross) Tell It with Trumpets: Three Experiments in Drama and Evangelism (includes Mann's End, Passion in Paradise Street, Six-Fifteen to Eternity), 1959; Casey: A Dramatic Mediation on the Passion, 1961; This Is the Word, and Word Made Flesh (play), 1962; Colonel Sheperton's Clock (fiction), 1964; The Christmas Story: A Carol Service for Children, 1964; The Grange at High Force (fiction), 1965; Peter Was His Nickname, 1965; Sea Peril (fiction), 1966; So Long at the Fair (play), 1966; Men in Stone (play), 1966; Cantata for Derelicts (play), 1967; Steam on the Line (fiction), 1968; The Bible Story (in U.S. as Illustrated Bible Stories), 1968; War on the Darnel (fiction), 1969; Wig-wig and Homer (fiction), 1969; Devil's Nob (fiction), 1970; Powder Quay (fiction), 1971; (as Stephen Chance) Septimus series, 4 vols., 1971–79; Madonna in Concrete (play), 1971; Dunkirk Summer (fiction), 1973; Skull Island (fiction), 1977; Rookoo and Bree (fiction), 1978; Decision in the Dark: Tales of Mystery, 1978; Watch at the World's End (play), 1979; The Good Shepherd, 1986; How Many Miles to Bethlehem? (play), 1989; The Candlemass Treasure (fiction), 1988. Add: St. Francis, 181 W. Malvern Rd., Malvern, Worcs., England.

TURNER, Ralph. British, b. 1936. Crafts. Head of Exhibitions, Crafts Council, London, since 1974. Asst. Mgr., Ewan Phillips Gallery, London, 1963–67; Dir., Pace Gallery, London, 1967–69, and Co-Founder/Dir., Electrum Gallery, London, 1970–74. Adviser to Scottish Arts Council, 1975–76, and Stedelijk Museum, Amsterdam; Crafts Adviser, Penguin Books, London, 1978–85. *Publs:* Contemporary Jewellery, 1975; On Tour, 1975; Jewellery in Europe, 1975; Jewellery by Helga Zahn, 1976; The New Jewellery, 1985. Add: Crafts Council, 12 Waterloo Pl., London SW1Y 4AO, England.

TURNER, Ralph (Herbert). American, b. 1919. Sociology. Prof. of Sociology and Anthropology, Univ. of California, Los Angeles, since 1959 (Member of faculty since 1948, Chmn., Sociology Dept., 1963–68; Vice-Chmn., 1982–83, and Chmn., 1983–84, Statewide Academic Senate). Research Assoc., American Council on Race Relations, 1947–48. Pres., Pacific Sociological Assn., 1957; Member of Council, 1959–64, Chmn. of Social Psychology Section, 1960–61, Pres., 1968–69, Chmn. of Section on Theoretical Sociology, 1973–74, and Chmn., Collective Behavior Section, 1983–84, American Sociological Assn.; Member, 1961–66, and Chmn., 1963–64, Behavioral Sciences Study Section, National Insts. of Health; Dir.-at-Large, Social Science Research Council, 1965–66; Member, Bd. of Dirs., Foundations Fund for Research in Psychiatry, 1970–73; Chmn., Panel on Public Policy Implications of Earthquake Prediction, National Academy of Sciences, 1974–75; Member of the Council, 1974–78, and Vice-Pres., 1978–82, Intnl. Sociological Assn.; Ed., Annual Review of Sociology, 1980–86. Member, Cttee. on Earthquake Engineering Research, National Research Council, 1981–82; Pres., Soc. for the Study of Symbolic Interactions, 1982–83. Member, Editorial Staff, American Sociological Review, 1955–56; Assoc. Ed., Social Problems, 1959–62, 1967–69; Editorial Consultant, 1959–62, and Ed., 1962–64, Sociometry. *Publs:* (with L. Killian) Collective Behavior, 1957, 3rd ed., 1987; The Social Context of Ambition, 1964; Robert Park on Social Control and Collective Behavior, 1967; Family Interaction, 1970; Earthquake Prediction and Public Policy, 1975; (with J. Nigg and B. Shaw) Earthquake Threat: The Human Response in Southern California, 1979; (with J. Nigg and D. Paz) Waiting for Disaster: Earthquake Watch in California, 1986. Add: Dept. of Sociology, UCLA, 405 Hilgard Ave., Los Angeles, Calif. 90024, U.S.A.

TURNER, Thomas Coleman. American, b. 1927. Novels/Short stories. *Publs:* Buttermilk Road, 1963. Add: P.O. Box, 1586, Anniston, Ala. 36202, U.S.A.

TURNER, William Weyand. American, b. 1927. Criminology/Law enforcement/Prisons, International relations/Current affairs, Law. Ed., Police Evidence Library, National Lawyers Cooperative Publishing Co., and Bancroft-Whitney Co. *Publs:* The Police Establishment, 1968; Invisible Witness: The Use and Abuse of the New Technology of Crime Investigation, 1968; Hoover's FBI: The Men and the Myth, 1970; Power of the Right, 1971; (with E. Asinof and W. Hinckle) The Ten Second Jailbreak, 1973; (with John G. Christian) The Assassination of Robert F. Kennedy, 1978; (with Warren Hinckle) The Fish Is Red: The Story of the Secret War Against Castro, 1980. Add: 163 Mark Twain Ave., San Rafael, Calif. 94903, U.S.A.

TURNILL, Reginald. British, b. 1915. Air/Space topics. Reporter specialising in industry, Press Assn., London, 1930–56; Industrial corresp., 1956–58, and Air/Defense Corresp., 1958–76, BBC, London. *Publs:* Moonslaught: The Story of Man's Race to the Moon, 1969; The Language of Space: A Dictionary of Astronautics, 1971; Manned Spaceflight, 1972, 3rd ed. 1978; Unmanned Spaceflight, 1974; Spaceflight Directory, 1978; Space Age, 1980; Farnborough: The Story of RAE, 1980; Jane's Spaceflight Directory, 1984, 4th ed., 1988, Space Technology Technology International, 1989. Add: Somerville Lodge, Hillside, Sandgate, Kent CT20 3DB, England.

TURNOCK, David. British, b. 1938. Geography. Reader in Geography, Univ. of Leicester, since 1977 (Lectr., 1969–77). Asst. Lectr. and Lectr. in Geography, Univ. of Aberdeen, 1964–69. *Publs:* Patterns of Highland Development; Scotland's Highlands and Islands; An Economic Geography of Romania; Industrial Geography of Eastern Europe; The New Scotland; Human Geography of the Romanian Carpathians; Railways in the British Isles; Historical Geography of Scotland since 1707; The Romanion Economy; Historical Geography of Eastern Europe; Contemporary Human Geography of Eastern Europe; Regional Railway History: North Scotland. Add: 21 Ingarsby Dr., Leicester LE5 6HB, England.

TUROW, L. Scott. American, b. 1949. Novels/Short stories, Law. Lawyer: Assoc., Sonnenscheim, Carlin, Nath and Rosenthal, Chicago, since 1986. Jones Lectr. in Creative Writing, Stanford Univ., California, 1972–75; Assoc. Suffolk County District Attorney, Boston, 1977–78; Asst. U.S. Attorney, U.S. District Court, Chicago, 1978–86. *Publs:* One L: An inside account of Life in the First Year at Harvard Law School, 1977; Presumed Innocent (novel), 1987. Add: c/o Sonnenscheim, Carlin, Nath and Rosenthal, Sears Tower, Suite 8000, Chicago, Ill. 60606, U.S.A.

TURVEY, Ralph. British, b. 1927. Economics. Lectr., then Reader in Economics, London Sch. of Economics 1948–64 (Visiting Prof., 1973–75); Chief Economist, The Electricity Council, 1964–67; Joint Deputy Chmn., National Bd. for Prices and Incomes, 1967–71; Economic Adviser, Scientific Control Systems Ltd., London, 1971–75. Member, National Water Council. *Publs:* The Economics in Electric Supply, 1968; Economic Analysis and Public Enterprises, 1971; Demand and Supply, 1971, 1980; (with D. Anderson) Electricity Economics, 1977; Consumer Price Indices, 1989. Add: c/o OECD, 2001 L St. N.W., Suite 700, Washington, D.C. 20036, U.S.A.

TUSHINGHAM, A(rlotte) Douglas. Canadian, b. 1914. Archaeology/Antiquities, Art, Geography, History. Prof. Emeritus, Dept. of Near Eastern Studies, Univ. of Toronto, since 1979 (Prof., 1955–79). Head, Div.

of Art and Archaeology, 1955–64, and Chief Archaeologist, 1964–79, Royal Ontario Museum, Toronto. *Publs:* The Beardmore Relics: Hoax or History?, 1966; (with V.B. Meen) The Crown Jewels of Iran, 1968, rev. ed. 1974; (with D. Baly) Atlas of the Biblical World, 1971; Excavations at Dibon (Dhiban) in Moab, 1972; Studies in Ancient Peruvian Metalworking, 1979; Excavations in Jerusalem 1961-1967, vol. I, 1986. Add: 66 Collier St., Toronto, Ont. M4W 1L9, Canada.

TUSSING, Aubrey Dale. American, b. 1935. Economcs, Education. Prof. of Economics, Syracuse Univ., N.Y., since 1974 (Asst. Prof., 1966–69; Assoc. Prof., 1969–74); Dir., Maxwell Sch. Health and Society Prog., since 1984. Asst. Prof. of Economics, Washington State Univ., Pullman, Wash., 1964–66; Sr. Research Fellow, Educational Policy Research Center, Syracuse, N.Y., 1968–74; Research Prof. of Economics, Economic and Social Research Inst., Dublin, 1975–76, 1979–81. *Publs:* (with M.A. Eggers) Economic Processes: The Level of Economic Activity, 1965; (with M.A. Eggers) Economic Processes: The Composition of Economic Activity, 1965; (with J.C. Byrnes) The Financial Crisis in Higher Education: Past, Present and Future, 1971; (with L.D. DeWitt) The Supply and Demand for Graduates of Higher Education: 1970 to 1980, 1971; Poverty in a Dual Economy, 1974; Irish Educational Expenditures: Past, Present, and Future, 1978; Irish Medical Care Resources: An Economic Analysis, 1985; (with D. Rottman and M. Wiley) The Population Structure and Living Circumstances of Irish Travellers: Results from the 1981 Census of Traveller Families, 1986. Add: Dept. of Economics, Syracuse Univ., Syracuse, N.Y. 13244, U.S.A.

TUTE, Warren (Stanley). Also writes as Andrew Warren. British, b. 1914. Novels/Short stories, Plays/Screenplays, History, Biography. Head of the Script Unit, London Weekend Television, 1968–69. *Publs:* The Felthams, 1950; Chico, 1950; Lady in Thin Armour, 1951; Gentlemen in Pink Uniform, 1952; The Life of a Circus Bear, 1952; The Younger Felthams, 1953; Cockney Cats, 1953; Girl in the Limelight, 1954; The Cruiser, 1955; The Rock, 1957; Leviathan, 1959; The Golden Creek, 1960; The Grey Top Hat: The Story of Moss Bross, 1961; Atlantic Conquest: The Story of the North Atlantic Passenger Trade, 1962; The Admiral, 1963; Cochrane: The Story of the 10th Earl of Dundonald, 1964; (trans.) Le Petomane, 1967; A Matter of Diplomacy, 1969; The Powder Train, 1970; The Tarnham Connection, 1971; Escape Route Green: Flight from Stalag XXA, 1971; (as Andrew Warren) This Time Next October, 1971; The Deadly Stroke, 1973; The Resident, 1973; (with J. Costello and T. Hughes) D. Day, 1974; Next Saturday in Milan, 1975; Honours of War and Peace, 1976; The North African War, 1976; The Cairo Sleeper, 1977; (with Clare Francis) The Commanding Sea, 1981; The True Glory: The Story of the Royal Navy, 1983. Add: 83240 Auvillar, Rrance.

TUTTLE, Lisa. American, b. 1952. Mystery/Crime/Suspense, Science fiction/Fantasy, Children's fiction, Women's studies. Ed., Mathom fan mag., 1968–70; Television Columnist, Austin American Statesman, Tex., 1976–79. *Publs:* (with George R.R. Martin) Windhaven (science fiction), 1980; Catwitch (juvenile), 1983; Angela's Rainbow (fantasy), 1983; Familiar Spirit (suspense), 1983; (with Rosalind Ashe) Children's Literary Houses (juvenile), 1984; A Nest of Nightmares (short stories), 1986; Encyclopedia of Feminism, 1986; Gabriel (suspense), 1987; A Spaceship Built of Stone (short stories), 1987; Heroines: Women Inspired by Women, 1988. Add: c/o Howard Morhaim, 175 Fifth Ave., New York, N.Y. 10010, U.S.A.

TUTTLE, William McCullough, Jr. American, b. 1937. History, Biography. Prof. of United States History, Univ. of Kansas (joined faculty, 1967). *Publs:* Race Riot: Chicago in the Red Summer of 1919, 1970; W.E.B. Du Bois, 1973; (co-author) Plain Folk: The Life Stories of Undistinguished Americans, 1982; (co-author) A People and a Nation: A History of the United States, 1982, 1986. Add: Dept. of History, Univ. of Kansas, Lawrence, Kans. 66045, U.S.A.

TUTTON, Barbara. British, b. 1914. Novels/Short stories, Children's fiction. *Publs:* Mystery at Bracken Dale; Take Me Alive, Rich to Die; Black Widow; The Riddle of the Allabones; Plague Spot. Add: Wall Nooks, Belper, Derby DE5 2DN, England.

TUTUOLA, Amos. Nigerian, b. 1920. Novels/Short stories. Stores officer, Nigerian Broadcasting Co., Ibadan, since 1956. *Publs:* The Palm-Wine Drinkard and His Dead Palm-Wine Tapster in the Dead's Town, 1952; My Life in the Bush of Ghosts, 1954; Simbi and the Satyr of the Dark Jungle, 1955; The Brave African Huntress, 1958; The Feather Woman of the Jungle, 1962; Ajaiyi and His Inherited Poverty, 1967; The Witch-Herbalist of the Remote Town, 1981; The Wild Hunter in the Bush of Ghosts, 1982; Pauper, Brawler, and Slanderer, 1987. Add: c/o Federal

Radio Corp., Broadcasting House, New Court Rd., Ibadan, Nigeria.

TUWHARE, Hone. New Zealander Maori, b. 1922. Poetry. Member Auckland Boilermakers Union, since 1964. Pres., Te Mahoe Local, New Zealand Workers Union, 1962–64; Pres., Birkdale Maori Cultural Cttee., Auckland, 1966–68; Councillor, Borough of Birkenhead, Auckland, 1968–70. *Publs:* No Ordinary Sun: Poems, 1964; Come Rain Hail, 1970; Sapwood and Milk, 1972; Something Nothing, 1973; Making a Fist of It, 1978; Selected Poems, 1980; Year of the Dog, 1982. Add: c/o John McIndoe Ltd., 51 Crawford St., Dunedin, New Zealand.

TWIST, Ananias. *See* **NUNN,** William Curtis.

TY-CASPER, Linda. Philippine, b. 1931. Novels/Short stories. Lectr. in Creative Writing, Ateneo de Manila Univ., Summer 1978, 1980; Writer-in-Residence, Univ. of the Philippines Creative Writing Center, 1980, 1982. *Publs:* The Transparent Sun (short stories), 1963; The Peninsulars (novel), 1964; The Secret-Runner (short stories), 1974; The Three-Cornered Sun (novel), 1979; Dread Empire (novel), 1980; Hazards of Distance (novel), 1981; Fortress in the Plaza (novel), 1985; Awaiting Trespass (novel), 1985; Wings of Stone (novel), 1986; Ten Thousand Seeds (novel), 1987, A Small Party in a Garden (novel), 1988. Add: 54 Simpson Dr., Saxonville, Mass. 01701, U.S.A.

TYDEMAN, William (Marcus). British, b. 1935. Literature, Theatre. Prof. of English, University Coll. of North Wales, Bangor, since 1986 (Asst. Lectr., 1961–64; Lectr., 1964–70; Sr. Lectr., 1970–73; Reader, 1983–86). *Publs:* (ed.) English Poetry 1400-1580, 1970; (ed. with M.J. Heath) Six Christmas Plays, 1971; (ed. with A.R. Jones) Wordsworth: Lyrical Ballads (casebook), 1972; (ed. with A.R. Jones) Coleridge: The Ancient Mariner and Other Poems (casebook), 1973; The Theatre in the Middle Ages: Western European Stage Conditions c.800-1576, 1978; (ed. with A.R. Jones) Joseph Hucks: A Pedestrian Tour Through Wales, 1979; (ed.) Plays, by Tom Robertson, 1982; (ed.) Wilde: Comedies (casebook), 1982; (ed.) Four Tudor Comedies, 1984; Dr. Faustus: Text and Performance, 1984; English Medieval Theatre 1400-1500, 1986; Henry V, 1987; Marder in the Cathedral, The Cocktail Party: Text and Performance, 1988. Add: c/o Dept. of English, University Coll. of North Wales, Bangor, Gwynedd LL57 2DG, Wales.

TYLER, Anne. American, b. 1941. Novels/Short stories. *Publs:* If Morning Ever Comes, 1964; The Tin Can Tree, 1965; A Slipping Down Life, 1970; The Clock Winder, 1972; Celestial Navigation, 1974; Searching for Caleb, 1976; Earthly Possessions, 1977; Morgan's Passing, 1980; Dinner at the Homesick Restaurant, 1982; (ed. with Shannon Ravenel) The Best American Short Stories 1983, 1983; The Accidental Tourist, 1985; Breathing Lessons, 1988. Add: 222 Tunbridge Rd., Baltimore, Md. 21212, U.S.A.

TYLER, Cyril. British, b. 1911. Animals/Pets, Chemistry. Emeritus Prof. of Physiology and Biochemistry, Univ. of Reading (Lectr. in Agricultural Chemistry, 1939–47; Prof., 1947–58; Prof. of Physiology and Biochemistry, 1958–76; Deputy Vice-Chancellor, 1967–76). Lectr. in Agricultural Chemistry, Royal Agricultural Coll., Cirencester, 1935–39. *Publs:* Organic Chemistry for Students of Agriculture, 1946; Animal Nutrition, 2nd ed. 1964; Wilhelm von Nathusius 1821-1899 on Avian Eggshells, 1964. Add: Dept. of Physiology and Biochemistry, Univ. of Reading, Whiteknights, Reading RG6 2AJ, England.

TYLER, Stephen Albert. American, b. 1932. Anthropology/Ethnology, Language/Linguistics. Prof. of Anthropology and Linguistics since 1970, and Chmn., Dept. of Anthropology, since 1971, Rice Univ., Hous-

ton, Tex. Assoc. Ed., American Ethnologist, and Annual Review Inc; Assoc. Ed., Cultural Anthropology, Journal of Anthropological Research. Asst. Prof. of Anthropology, Univ. of California, Davis, 1964–67; Assoc. Prof., Tulane Univ., New Orleans, La., 1967–70. *Publs:* Koya: An Outline of Grammar, 1969; (ed.) Cognitive Anthropology, 1969; India: An Anthropological Perspective, 1973; The Said and the Unsaid: Mind, Meaning and Culture, 1978; The Unspeakable: Discourse, Dialogue and Rhetoric in the Post-Modern World, 1988. Add: 3106 Blue Bonnet, Houston, Tex. 77025, U.S.A.

TYLER-WHITTLE, Michael. Writes as Tyler Whittle and Mark Oliver. British, b. 1927. Novels/Short stories, Children's fiction, Children's non-fiction, Biography. *Publs:* all as Tyler Whittle unless otherwise noted—Spades and Feathers, 1954; The Runners of Orford, 1955; Castle Lizard, 1956; The Bullhead, 1957; (as Mark Oliver) As Though They Had Never Been (in U.S. as The Wanton Boys), 1958; (co-author) Heroes of Our Time, 1959; (as Mark Oliver) A Roll of Thunder, 1960; (co-author) Tales of Many Lands, 1960; (as Mark Oliver) Luke Benedict, 1961; (as Mark Oliver) Feet of Bronze, 1962; Young Plants and Polished Corners, 1963; (as Mark Oliver) Five Spinning Tops of Naples, 1964; Some Ancient Gentlemen, 1968; Common or Garden, 1970; The Last Plantagenet, 1970; The Plant Hunters, 1971; The Young Victoria, 1971; The Birth of Greece, 1972; Albert's Victoria, 1972; The World of Classical Greece, 1973; Royal and Republican Rome, 1974; Imperial Rome, 1974; The Widow of Windsor, 1974; Bertie, 1974; Edward, 1975; The Last Kaiser, 1977; Curtis' Wunderwelt der Blumen, 1979; Victoria and Albert at Home, 1980; Curtis's Flower Garden Displayed, 1981; The House of Flavell, 1981; Solid Joys and Lasting Treasure, 1985. Add: c/o Curtis Brown Ltd., 162-168 Regent St., London W1R 5TB, England.

TYRE, Nedra. American. Mystery/Crime/Suspense. *Publs:* Red Wine First (short stories), 1947; Mouse in Eternity, 1952 (as Death Is a Lover, 1953); Death of an Intruder, 1953; Journey to Nowhere, 1954; Hall of Death, 1960 (in U.S. in paperback, Reformatory Girls, 1962); Everyone Suspect, 1964; Twice So Fair, 1971. Add: 2900 Palmwood Cirde, Mechanicsville, Va. 2311, U.S.A.

TYRRELL, David Arthur John. British, b. 1925. Medicine/Health. Deputy Dir. and Head of Div. of Communicable Diseases, Clinical Research Centre, Harrow, Middx., 1970–84. Dir., Common Cold Unit, Salisbury, since 1982 (Member of the Scientific Staff, 1957–69). *Publs:* The Common Cold and Related Diseases, 1965; Interferon and Its Clinical Potential, 1976; Technologies for Rural Health, 1977; Microbial Disease: Diagnosis, Therapy, and Control, 1979; The Abolition of Infection—Hope or Illusion?, 1982. Add: Harvard Hospital, Common Cold Unit, Coombe Rd., Salisbury, Wilts. SP2 8BW, England.

TYSDAHL, Björn Johan. Norwegian, b. 1933. Literature. Prof. of English Literature, Univ. of Oslo, since 1985 (Univ. Lectr., 1965–72; Reader, 1972–84). *Publs:* Joyce and Ibsen, 1968; William Godwin as Novelist, 1981; Maurits Hansens fortellerkunst, 1988. Add: English Dept., Univ. of Oslo, Blindern, Oslo 3, Norway.

TYSON, Joseph B. American, b. 1928. History, Theology/Religion. Prof. of Religious Studies, Southern Methodist Univ., Dallas, Tex., since 1974 (Instr., 1958–60; Asst. Prof., 1960–65; Assoc. Prof., 1965–74). *Publs:* Study of Early Christianity, 1973; (with T.R.W. Longstaff) Synoptic Abstract, 1978; The New Testament and Early Christianity, 1984; The Death of Jesus in Luke – Acts, 1986; (ed.) Luke – Acts and the Jewish People, 1988. Add: Dept. of Religious Studies, Southern Methodist Univ., Dallas, Tex. 75275, U.S.A.

U

UCHIDA, Yoshiko. American, b. 1921. Novels, Children's fiction, Children's non-fiction, Mythology/Folklore. Teacher, Frankford Friends Sch., Philadelphia, 1944–45; Secty., Inst. of Pacific Relations, NYC, 1946–47, United Student Christian Council, NYC, 1947–52, and Lawrence Radiation Lab., Univ. of California, Berkeley, 1957–62; Ford Fndn. Foreign Study and Research Fellowship, 1952–53; Wrote series of articles on folk arts and crafts for Nippon Times, Tokyo, 1953–54, and Craft Horizons, NYC, 1955–64. *Publs:* The Dancing Kettle and Other Japanese Folk Tales, 1949; New Friends for Susan, 1951; We Do Not Work Alone: Kanjiro Kawai, 1953; The Magic Listening Cap: More Folk Tales from Japan, 1955; The Full Circle, 1957; Takao and the Grandfather's Sword, 1958; The Promised Year, 1959; Milk and the Prowler, 1960; Rokubei and the Thousand Rice Bowls, 1962; The Forever Christmas Tree, 1963; Sumi's Prize, 1964; The Sea of Gold and Other Tales from Japan, 1965; Sumi's Special Happening, 1966; In-Between Miya, 1967; Sumi and the Goat and the Tokyo Express, 1969; Hisako's Mysteries, 1969; Makoto, The Smallest Boy, 1970; Journey to Topaz, 1971; Samurai of Gold Hill, 1972; The Birthday Visitor, 1975; The Rooster Who Understood Japanese, 1976; Journey Home, 1978; A Jar of Dreams, 1981; Desert Exile: The Uprooting of a Japanese American Family (for adults), 1982; The Best Bad Thing, 1983; The Happiest Ending, 1985; The Two Foolish Cats, 1987; Picture Bride (novel for adults), 1987. Add: 1685 Solano Ave., Apt. 102, Berkeley, Calif. 94707, U.S.A.

UDE, Wayne. American, b. 1946. Western/Adventure. Community Development Specialist, Bear Paw Development Corp., Havre, Mont., 1969–70; Exec. Dir., Community Action Prog., Fort Bellknap Indian Reservation, Mont., 1970–71; Instr., Springfield Technical Community Coll., Mass., 1974; Exec. Dir., Council on Aging, Amherst, 1974–76; Asst. Prof., 1976–82, and Assoc. Prof. of English, 1982–84, Colorado State Univ., Fort Collins; Writer-in-Residence, Mankato State Univ., Minnesota, 1984–86. *Publs:* Buffalo and Other Stories, 1975; Becoming Coyote, 1981. Add: Box 53, Mankato State Univ., Mankato, Minn. 56001, U.S.A.

UDRY, J. Richard. American, b. 1928. Demography, Sociology. Prof. of Sociology since 1969, and Dir., Carolina Population Center since 1977, Univ. of North Carolina, Chapel Hill (Assoc. Prof., 1965–69, and Prof. of Maternal of Child Health, 1969). *Publs:* The Social Context of Marriage, 1966, 3rd ed. 1974; The Media and Family Planning, 1974; The Demographic Impact of Domestic Family Planning Programs, 1975. Add: Carolina Population Center, Univ. of North Carolina, Chapel Hill, N.C. 27514, U.S.A.

UDRY, Janice (May). American, b. 1928. Children's fiction. *Publs:* Little Bear and the Beautiful Kite, 1955; A Tree Is Nice, 1956; Theodore's Parents, 1958; The Moon Jumpers, 1959; Danny's Pig, 1960; Alfred, 1960; Let's Be Enemies, 1961; Is Susan Here?, 1962; The Mean Mouse and Other Mean Stories, 1962; End of the Line, 1962; Betsy-Back-in-Bed, 1963; Next Door to Laura Linda, 1965; What Mary Jo Shared, 1966; If You're a Bear, 1967; Mary Ann's Mud Day, 1967; What Mary Jo Wanted, 1968; Glenda, 1969; Emily's Autumn, 1969; The Sunflower Garden, 1969; Mary Jo's Grandmother, 1970; Angie, 1971; How I Faded Away; or, The Invisible Boy, 1976; Oh No, Cat!, 1976; Thump and Plunk, 1981. Add: 412 Elliott Rd., Chapel Hill, N.C. 27514, U.S.A.

UEDA, Makoto. Canadian, b. 1931. Literature, Biography, Translations. Prof. of Japanese and Comparative Literature, Stanford Univ., Calif., since 1971. Lectr., 1961–62, Asst. Prof., 1962–65, Assoc. Prof.,

1965–68, and Prof., 1968–71, Univ. of Toronto, Ont. *Publs:* (trans.) The Old Pine Tree and Other Noh Plays, 1962; Zeami, Basho, Yeats, Pound: A Study in Japanese and English Poetics, 1965; Literary and Art Theories in Japan, 1967; Matsuo Basho, 1970; Modern Japanese Haiku: An Anthology, 1976; Modern Japanese Writers and the Nature of Literature, 1976; Modern Japanese Poets and the Nature of Literature, 1983; (ed.) The Mother of Dreams and Other Short Stories, 1986. Add: Dept. of Asian Languages, Stanford Univ., Stanford, Calif. 94305, U.S.A.

UHNAK, Dorothy. American, b. 1933. Mystery/Crime/Suspense. Detective in NYC Transit Police Dept., 1953–67. *Publs:* Policewoman, 1964; The Bait, 1968; The Witness, 1969; The Ledger, 1970; Law and Order, 1973; The Investigation, 1977; False Witness, 1981; Victims, 1985. Add: c/o Simon & Schuster Inc., 1230 Sixth Ave., New York, N.Y. 10020, U.S.A.

ULAM, Adam Bruno. American, b. 1922. History, Politics/Government. Member of faculty since 1947, Research Assoc., Russian Research Center, since 1948, Prof. of Govt. since 1959, and Dir., Russian Research Center, 1973–76, and since 1980, Harvard Univ., Cambridge, Mass. (Gurney Prof. of History and Political Science, 1979). Research Assoc., Center for Intnl. Studies, Massachusetts Inst. of Technology, 1953–55. *Publs:* The Philosophical Foundations of English Socialism, 1951; Titoism and the Cominform, 1952; The Unfinished Revolution, 1960, 1979; The New Face of Soviet Totalitarianism, 1963; The Bolsheviks, 1965; Expansion and Coexistence, 1968; The Rivals, 1971; The Fall of the American University, 1972; Stalin: The Man and His Era, 1973; History of Soviet Russia, 1976; Ideologies and Illusions, 1976; In the Name of the People, 1976; Russia's Failed Revolutions, 1981; Dangerous Relations: The Soviet Union in World Politics, 1970–1982, 1982; The Kirov Affair, 1988. Add: 1737 Cambridge St., Cambridge, Mass. 02138, U.S.A.

ULLENDORFF, Edward. British, b. 1920. Area studies, Language/Linguistics, History, Religion. Emeritus Prof. of Ethiopian Studies and Semitic Languages, Sch. of Oriental and African Studies, Univ. of London, since 1982 (Prof. 1964–82). Fellow, British Academy, since 1965; (Vice-Pres., 1980–82). Research Officer, Oxford Univ., Inst. of Colonial Studies, 1948–49; Lectr. then Reader in Semitic Languages, St. Andrews Univ., 1950–59; Prof. of Semitic Languages, Univ. of Manchester, 1959–64; Joint Ed., Journal of Semitic Studies, 1961–64, and Ethiopian Studies, 1964; Manchester Univ. Press; Chmn., Editorial Bd., Bulletin of School of Oriental and African Studies, 1968–78. *Publs:* The Definite Article in the Semitic Languages, 1941; Exploration and Study of Abyssinia, 1945; Catalogue of Ethiopian Manuscripts in the Bodleian Library, Oxford, 1951; The Ethiopian Manuscripts in the Royal Library, Windsor Castle, 1953; The Semitic Languages of Ethiopia, 1955; The Ethiopians, 1959, 1973; (with S. Wright) Catalogue of Ethiopian Manuscripts in the Cambridge University Library, 1961; Comparative Semitics, 1961; (joint ed.) Studies in Honour of G.R. Driver, 1962; (with S. Moscati and others) Introduction to Comparative Grammar of the Semitic Languages, 1964; An Amharic Chrestomathy, 1965, 1978; The Challenge of Amharic, 1965; Ethiopia and the Bible, 1968, 1982; (co-author) Solomon and Sheba, 1974; The Autobiography of Emperor Haile Sellassie, 1976; Studies in Semitic Languages and Civilizations, 1977; (with M.A. Knibb) A New Edition of the Book of Enoch, 1978; The Bawdy Bible, 1979; (co-author) The Emperor Theodore's Amharic Letters to Queen Victoria and Her Special Envoy, 1979; (with C.F. Beckingham) The Hebrew Letters of Prester John, 1982; Tigrinya Chrestomathy, 1985; Studia Aethiopica et Semitica,

1987, The Two Zions, 1988.   Add: 4 Bladon Close, Oxford OX2 8AD, England.

ULLMANN, John E(manuel).   American, b. 1923.   Business/Industry, Economics.   Prof. of Mgmt., Hofstra Univ., Hempstead, N.Y., since 1961 (Chmn., Dept. of Mgmt., Marketing and Quantitative Methods, 1961–73); Consulting Engineer.   *Publs:* Waste Disposal Problems in Selected Industries, 1969; (with S. Gluck) Manufacturing Management, 1969, 1981; Potential Civilian Markets for the Military Electronics Industry, 1970; Business and Technical Determinants of Innovation, 1973; Quantitative Methods in Management, 1976; The Suburban Economic Network, 1977; The Improvement of Productivity, 1980; Social Costs in Modern Society, 1983; The Prospects of American Industrial Recovery, 1985; (ed.) A Handbook of Engineering Management, 1986, The Anatomy of Industrial Decline, 1988.   Add: 2518 Norwood Ave., North Bellmore, N.Y. 11710, U.S.A.

UNADA.   *See* **GLIEWE,** Unada G.

UNDERHILL, Charles.   *See* **HILL,** Reginald.

UNDERWOOD, Michael.   Pseudonym for John Michael Evelyn. British, b. 1916.   Mystery/Crime/Suspense.   Called to the Bar, Grays Inn, London, 1939; with the Dept. of Public Prosecutions, London, 1946–76: Asst. Dir., 1969–76.   *Publs:* Murder on Trial, 1954; Murder Made Absolute, 1955; Death on Remand, 1956; False Witness, 1957; Lawful Pursuit, 1958; Arm of the Law, 1959; Cause of Death, 1960; Death by Misadventure, 1960; Adam's Case, 1961; The Case Against Phillip Quest, 1962; Girl Found Dead, 1963; The Crime of Colin Wise, 1964; The Unprofessional Spy, 1964; The Anxious Conspirator, 1965; A Crime Apart, 1966; The Man Who Died on Friday, 1967; The Man Who Killed Too Soon, 1968; The Shadow Game, 1969; The Silent Liars, 1970; Shem's Demise, 1970; A Trout in the Milk, 1971; Reward for a Defector, 1973; A Pinch of Snuff, 1974; The Juror, 1975; Menaces, Menaces, 1976; Murder with Malice, 1977; The Fatal Trip, 1977; Crooked Wood, 1978; Anything but the Truth, 1978; Smooth Justice, 1979; Victim of Circumstance, 1979; A Clear Case of Suicide, 1980; Crime upon Crime, 1980; Double Jeopardy, 1981; Hand of Fate, 1981; Goddess of Death, 1982; A Party to Murder, 1983; Death in Camera, 1984; The Hidden Man, 1985; Death at Deepwood Grange, 1986; The Uninvited Corpse, 1987; The Injudicious Judge, 1987; Dual Enigma, 1988; A Compelling Case, 1989.   Add: c/o Macmillan, 4 Little Essex St., London WC2R 3LF, England.

UNDERWOOD, Peter.   British, b. 1923.   Film, Paranormal, Biography. *Publs:* A Gazetteer of British Ghosts, 1971; Into the Occult, 1972; Horror Man: The Life of Boris Karloff (in U.S. as Karloff), 1972; A Gazetteer of Scottish and Irish Ghosts, 1973, paperback as Gazetteer of Scottish Ghosts, 1974; A Host of Hauntings, 1973; (with Paul Tabori) The Ghosts of Borley, 1973; Haunted London, 1973; Life's A Drag: A Biography of Danny La Rue, 1974; The Vampire's Bedside Companion, 1975; (with Leonard Wilder) Lives to Remember: A Case-Book on Reincarnation, 1975; Deeper into the Occult, 1975; Hauntings, 1977; (ed.) Thirteen Famous Ghost Stories, 1977; Ghosts of North West England, 1978; Dictionary of the Supernatural, 1978, in paperback as Dictionary of the Occult and Supernatural, 1979; Ghosts of Wales, 1978; The Complete Book of Dowsing and Diving, 1980; A Ghost Hunter's Handbook, 1980; Ghosts of Hampshire and the Isle of Wight, 1982; Ghosts of Devon, 1982; Ghosts of Cornwall, 1983; No Common Task-The Autobiography of a Ghost Hunter, 1983; This Haunted Isle: The Ghosts and Legends of Britain's Historic Building, 1984; Ghosts of Kent, 1984; The Ghost Hunters, 1985; Ghosts of Somerset, 1985; West Country Hauntings, 1986; The Ghost Hunter's Guide, 1986; Queen Victoria's Other World, 1986; Jack the Ripper: 100 Years of Mystery, 1987; Ghosts of Dorset, 1988; Ghosts of Wiltshire, 1989.   Add: c/o The Savage Club, 9 Fitzmaurice Pl., London W1X 6JD, England.

UNGAR, Sanford J.   American, b. 1945.   Civil liberties/Human rights, Law, Politics/Government;   Member, National News Staff, the Washington Post, Washington, D.C., since 1972 (Member, Editorial Staff, 1969–70 and Metropoloitan Staff, 1970–71)   Dean, Sch. of Communication, The American Univ., Washington, since 1986, Instr., Metropolitan Inst., Univ. of Chicago, since 1974.   Corresp., United Press Intnl., Paris, 1967–69.   The Papers and the Papers: An Account of the Legal and Political Battle Over the Pentagon Papers: 1972; FBI, 1976; Africa: The People and Politics of an Emerging Continent, 1985; (ed.) Estrangement: America and the World, 1985.   Add: c/o The American Univ. Sch. of Communication 4400 Massachusetts Ave. N.W., Washington, D.C. 20016, U.S.A.

UNGERER, Miriam.   American, b. 1929.   Food and Wine.   Freelance writer since 1968; associated with the East Hampton Star, East Hampton, N.Y., since 1980; also, restaurant consultant.   Reporter, U.S. Information Services, Wiesbaden, West Germany, 1953–57; Sportswear Ed., Women's Wear Daily, NYC, 1958–60; Fashion and Features Reporter, New York Journal-American, 1960–62; Contributing Ed., Women's Features, New York Herald Tribune, 1962–64; engaged in design research and publicity, 1965–68.   *Publs:* (with Tomi Ungerer) Come Into My Parlour (juvenile), 1964; The Too Hot to Cookbook, 1966; Good Cheap Food, 1973, 1985; Country Food: A Seasonal Journal, 1983; Food for Friends, 1985; Summer Time Food, 1989.   Add: c/o Random House, 201E. 50th St., New York, N.Y. 10022, U.S.A.

UNSWORTH, Barry (Forster).   British, b. 1930.   Novels/Short stories, Plays/Screenplays.   Lectr. in English.   *Publs:* The Partnership, 1966; The Greeks Have a Word for It, 1967; The Hide, 1970; Mooncranker's Gift, 1973; The Stick Insect (television play), 1975; The Big Day, 1976; Pascali's Island, in U.S. as Idol Hunter, 1980; The Rage of the Vulture, 1982; Stone Virgin, 1985; Sugar and Rum, 1988.   Add: Hamish Hamilton, 22 Wright's Lane, London W8 5TZ, England.

UNTERBERGER, Betty Miller.   American.   History.   Prof. of History, Texas A & M Univ., College Station, since 1968.   Prof. and Chmn. of Grad. Studies, California State Univ., Fullerton, 1965–68.   Pres., Soc. of Historians of American Foreign Relations, 1985.   *Publs:* America's Siberian Expedition 1918-1920: A Study of National Policy, 1956, 1969, American Intervention in the Russian Civil War, 1969; American Views of Mohammed Ali Jinnah and the Pakistan Liberation Movement, 1981; Woodrow Wilson and the Russian Revolution, 1982; The United States, Revolutionary Russia and the Rise of Czeckoslavakia, 1989.   Add: Dept. of History, Texas A & M Univ., College Station, Tex. 77843, U.S.A.

UNWIN, David (Storr).   Also writes children's fiction as David Severn. British, b. 1918.   Novels/Short stories, Children's fiction.   *Publs:* all as David Severn unless otherwise noted—Rick Afire!, 1942; A Cabin for Crusoe, 1943; Waggon for Five, 1944; Hermit in the Hills, 1945; Forest Holiday, 1946; Ponies and Poachers, 1947; The Cruise of the Maiden Castle, 1948; Treasure for Three, 1949; Dream Gold, 1949; Bill Badger Omnibus, 1950; Crazy Castle, 1951; Drumbeats!, 1953; (as David Unwin) The Governor's Wife, 1954; (as David Unwin) A View of the Heath, 1956; The Future Took Us, 1957; The Green-Eyed Gryphon, 1958; Foxy-Boy, 1959 (in U.S. as The Wild Valley, 1963); Three at the Sea, 1959; Jeff Dickson, Cowhand, 963; Clouds Over the Alberhorn, 1963; A Dog for a Day, 1965; The Girl in the Grove, 1974; The Wishing Bone, 1977; (as David Unwin) Fifty Years with Father, 1982.   Add: Garden Flat 31, Belsize Pk., London NW3, England.

UNWIN, Rayner (Stephens).   British, b. 1925.   Literature.   Deputy Chmn., Unwin Hyman Publishers.   Formerly, Chmn., George Allan & Unwin Ltd., publrs., London (Dir., since 1951).   *Publs:* The Gulf of Years: Letters from John Ruskin to Kathleen Olander, 1953; The Rural Muse, 1954; The Defeat of John Hawkins, 1960.   Add: Limes Cottage, Little Missenden, nr. Amersham, Bucks., England.

UPDIKE, John (Hoyer).   American, b. 1932.   Novels/Short stories, Poetry, Literary Criticism.   Staff Reporter, The New Yorker, NYC, 1955–57.   *Publs:* The Carpentered Hen and Other Tame Creatures (in U.K. as Hoping for a Hooper) (poetry), 1959; The Poorhouse Fair, 1959; The Same Door (short stories), 1959; Rabbit, Run, 1960; Pigeon Feathers and Other Stories, 1962; The Magic Flute, 1962; The Centaur, 1963; Telephone Poles (poetry), 1963; Seventy Poems, 1963; The Ring, 1964: Of the Farm, 1965; Assorted Prose, 1965; The Music School (short stories), 1966; A Child's Calendar, 1966; Couples, 1968: Three Texts from Early Ipswich: A Pageant, 1968; (with others) Penguin Modern Stories 2, 1969; Midpoint and Other Poems, 1969; The Dance of the Solids (poetry), 1969; Bottom's Dream: Adapted from William Shakespeare's A Midsummer Night's Dream, 1969; Bech: A Book, 1970; (ed.) Pens and Needles, by David Levine, 1970; Rabbit Redux, 1971; Museums and Women and Other Stories, 1972; Warm Wine: An Idyll, 1973; Buchanan Dying (play), 1974; A Month of Sundays, 1975; Picked-Up Pieces, 1975; Marry Me, 1976; Tossing and Turning (poetry), 1977; The Coup, 1978; Problems and Other Stories, 1979; Talk from the Fifties, 1979; Sixteen Sonnets, 1978; Three Illuminations in the Life of an American Author (short stories), 1979; The Chaste Planet (short story), 1980; People One Knows: Interviews with Insufficiently Famous Americans, 1980; Hawthorne's Creed, 1981; Rabbit Is Rich (novel), 1981; The Beloved (short story), 1982; Bech Is Back (short stories), 1982; Hugging the Shore: Essays and Criticism, 1983; (ed. with Shannon Ravenel) The Best American Short Stories 1984, 1984; The Witches of Eastwick (novel), 1984; Facing Nature (poetry), 1985; Trust Me (short stories), 1986; S., a Novel, 1988; Self-Consciousness (memoirs), 1989. Add: Beverly Farms, Mass. 01915, U.S.A.

UPTON, Martin. British, b. 1933. Agriculture/Forestry, Economics. Prof., Univ. of Reading, since 1988 (Research Agriculturist, 1957–60; Lectr., 1967–78; Reader, 1978–88). Lectr. in Agricultural Economics, Univ. of Ibadan, Nigeria, 1960–66; Economist, Ministry of Agriculture, and Lectr., Queen's Univ., Belfast, 1966–67. *Publs:* (with Q.B.O. Anthonio) Farming as a Business (textbook), 1965, 1970; Farm Management in Africa, 1973; Agricultural Production Economics and Resource-Use, 1976; Success in Farming, 1984; African Farm Management, 1987. Add: Dept. of Agricultural Economics, Univ. of Reading, Reading, Berks. RG6 2AR, England.

UPWARD, Edward (Falaise). British, b. 1903. Novels/Short stories. Schoolmaster, 1928–62. *Publs:* Buddha, 1924; Journey to the Border, 1938; In the Thirties, 1962; The Rotten Elements, 1969; The Railway Accident and Other Stories, 1969; The Spiral Ascent, 1977; No Home But the Struggle, 1979; The Night Walk and Other Stories, 1987. Add: c/o William Heinemann Ltd., 81 Fulham Rd., London SW3 6RB, England.

URCH, Elizabeth. Also writes as Elise Brogan. British, b. 1921. Autobiography/Memoirs/Personal. Head Teacher, Logierait Sch., Tayside Education Authority, 1972–86 (Head Teacher, Newbigging Sch., 1969–72). Asst. Teacher, Moyal Sch., Larne, 1959–66, and Larne Grammar Sch., Northern Ireland, 1966–69. *Publs:* (as Elise Brogan) Queen of the Manse: The Musing of a Parson's Wife, 1957; Be Still My Soul, 1964; For God's Sake Watch Your Language, 1978; Ladders Up to Heaven, 4 vol., 1980–83. Add: Lochalsh, Tom-na-Moan Rd., Pitlochry, Scotland.

URDANG, Constance (Henriette). American, b. 1922. Novels/Short stories, Poetry. Copy Ed., Bellas Hess Inc., publrs., NYC, 1947–51; Ed., P.F. Collier and Son, publrs., NYC, 1952–54; Coordinator of the Writers' Program Washington Univ., St., Louis, 1977–84; Visiting Lectr., Princeton Univ., 1985. *Publs:* (ed. with P. Engle) Prize Stories '57, 1957; (ed. with P. Engle and C. Harnack) Prize Stories '59, 1959; (ed.) The Randam House Vest Pocket Dictionary of Famous People. 1962. Charades and Celebrations: Poems, 1965; Natural History (novel), 1969; The Picnic in the Cemetery, 1975, The Lone Woman and Others, 1980; Only the World, 1983; Lucha (novella), 1986; American Earthquakes (novella), 1988; The Woman Who Read Novels (novella), 1990. Add 6943 Columbia Pl., St. Louis, Mo. 63130, U.S.A.

URE, Jean. Also writes as Sarah McCulloch. Historical/Romance, Children's fiction, Translations. British, b. 1943. *Publs:* Dance for Two (in U.S. as Ballet Dance for Two), 1960; (trans.) City of a Thousand Drums, by Henri Vernes, 1966; (trans.) The Dinosaur Hunters, by Henri Vernes, 1966; (trans.) The Yellow Shadow, by Henri Vernes, 1966; (trans.) Cold Spell, by Jean Bruce, 1967; (trans.) Top Secret, by Jean Bruce, 1967; (trans.) White Gorilla, by Henri Vernes, 1967; (trans.) Operation Parrot, by Henri Vernes, 1968; (trans.) Strip Tease, by Jean Bruce, 1968; (trans.) The Snare, by Noel Calef, 1969; (trans.) March Battalion, by Sven Hassel, 1970; (trans.) Assignment Gestapo, by Sven Hassel, 1971; (trans.) Hitler's Plot to Kill the Big Three, by Laszlo Havas, 1971; (trans.) SS General, by Sven Hassel, 1972; (trans.) Reign of Hell, by Sven Hassel, 1973; All Thy Love, 1975; Marriage of True Minds, 1975; Hear No Evil, 1976; No Precious Time, 1976; All in a Summer Season, 1977; Early Stages, 1977; Bid Time Return, 1978; Curtain Fall, 1978; Dress Rehearsal, 1978; A Girl Like That, 1979; Masquerade, 1979; See You Thursday, 1981; If It Weren't for Sebastian, 1982; A Proper Little Nooryeff (in U.S. as What If They Saw Me Now?), 1982; Hi There, Supermouse!, 1983, in U.S. as Supermouse, 1984; The You-Two, 1984; You Win Some, You Lose Some, 1984; After Thursday, 1985; Megastar, 1985; Nicola Mimosa, 1985, in U.S. as The Most Important Thing, 1986; A Bottled Cherry Angel, 1986; Brenda the Bold, 1986; The Other Side of the Fence, 1986; Swings and Roundabouts, 1986; The Fright, 1987; One Green Leaf, 1987; Tea-Leaf on the Roof, 1987; War with Old Mouldy!, 1987; Who's Talking?, 1987; Frankie's Dad, 1988; Soppy Birthday, 1988; Trouble with Vanessa, 1988; A Muddy Kind of Magic, 1988; There's Always Danny, 1988; Two Men in a Boat, 1988; Plague, 1990, 1989; novels as Sarah McCulloch— Not Quite a Lady, 1980; A Lady for Ludovic, 1981; A Most Insistant Lady, 1981; Merely a Gentleman, 1982; A Perfect Gentleman, 1982. Add: 88 Southbridge Rd., Croydon, Surrey CR0 1AF, England.

URIS, Leon (Marcus). American, b. 1924. Novels/Short stories, Plays/Screenplays. *Publs:* Battle Cry, 1953, screenplay, 1955; The Angry Hills, 1955, Gunfight at the OK Corral (screenplays), 1957; Exodus, 1957, musical play as Ari, 1971; Exodus Revised (in U.K. as In

the Steps of Exodus), 1959; Mila 18, 1961, Armageddon: A Novel of Berlin, 1964; Topaz, 1967, The Third Temple, 1967, Q.B. VH, 1970, Ireland: A Terrible Beauty, 1975; Trinity, 1976; (with Jull Uris) Jerusalem, Song of Songs, 1981; The Haj, 1984, Mitla Pass 1988. Add: c/o Doubleday & Co. Inc., 666 Fifth Ave., New York, N.Y. 10103, U.S.A.

URQUHART, Brian Edward. British, b. 1919. Biography. Scholar-in-Residence, The Food Foundn., NYC, since 1986. Under-Secty.-Gen. for Special Political Affairs, U.N., 1974–86 (joined org., 1945). *Publs:* Hammarskjold, 1972; A Life in Peace and War, 1987; Decolonization and World Order, 1989. Add: 131 East 66th St., New York, N.Y. 10021, U.S.A.

URQUHART, Fred(erick Burrows). British, b. 1912. Novels/Short stories. Reader for a London literary agency, 1947–51, and for MGM, 1951–54; London Scout for Walt Disney Productions, 1959–60; former Reader for Cassell Co., & J.M. Dent & Sons, publrs., London. *Publs:* Time Will Knit, 1938; I Fell for a Sailor and Other Stories, 1940; The Clouds Are Big with Mercy, 1946; Selected Stories, 1946; (ed. with J. Maurice Lindsay) No Scottish Twilight: New Scottish Stories, 1947; The Last G.I. Bride Wore Tartan: A Novella and Some Short Stories, 1948; The Year of the Short Corn and Other Stories, 1949; The Ferret Was Abraham's Daughter, 1949; The Last Sister and Other Stories, 1950; Jezebel's Dust, 1951; The Laundry Girl and the Pole: Selected Stories, 1955; (ed.) W.S.C.: A Cartoon Biography, 1955; (ed.) Great True War Adventures, 1956; (ed.) Scottish Short Stories, 1957; (ed.) Men at War: The Best War Stories of All Time, 1957; (ed.) Great True Escape Stories, 1958; (ed.) The Cassell Miscellany, 1848-1958, 1958; Scotland in Colour, 1961; The Dying Stallion and Other Stories, 1967; The Ploughing Match and Other Stories, 1968; (co-ed.) Modern Scottish Short Stories, 1978; Palace of Green Days, 1979; Proud Lady in a Cage, 1980; A Diver in China Seas and Other Stories, 1980; (ed.) The Book of Horses, 1981; Seven Ghosts in Search, 1983; Full Score (short stories), 1989. Add: Spring Garden Cottage, Fairwarp, Uckfield, Sussex, England.

USBORNE, Richard A(lexander). British, b. 1910. Literature. Asst. Ed., Strand Mag., 1947–50; Dir., Graham & Gillies Advertising Agency, London, 1962–70. *Publs:* Clubland Heroes, 1953, 1974; Wodehouse at Work, 1961; (ed.) A Century of Summer Fields, 1964; Wodehouse at Work to the End, 1976; (ed.) Sunset at Blandings, 1977; (ed.) Vintage Wodehouse, 1977; A Wodehouse Companion, 1981; The Penguin Wodehouse Companion, 1988. Add: The Charter House, London EC1M 6NN, England.

USHER, George. British, b. 1930. Agriculture/Forestry, Biology, Botany. Rector of Credenhill, Hereford, since 1984. Scientific Officer, H.M. Colonial Overseas Civil Service, 1953–57; Sr. Biology Master, 1957–80. *Publs:* Biology Model Answers, 1963; Test Papers in O Level Biology, 1964; Dictionary of Botany, 1966; Introduction to Viruses, 1970; Textbook of Practical Biology, 1970; Dictionary of Plants Useful to Man, 1974; Human and Social Biology, 1977; A Level Biology Model Answers, 1978; Chemistry for O Level, 1980. Add: St. Mary's Rectory, Credenhill, Hereford HR4 7OL, England.

USHERWOOD, Stephen. British, b. 1907. History, Literature. Member, Editorial and Production Staff, BBC Radio, London, 1946–68. *Publs:* Reign by Reign, 1960; The Bible, Book by Book, 1962; Shakespeare, Play by Play, 1967; Place Names, Street Names, Festivals and Holidays, Coins, Inns, 1968–71; Britain, Century by Century, 1972; Europe, Century by Century, 1972; Food, Drink and History, 1972; The Great Enterprise, 1978; (with E. Usherwood) Visit Some London Catholic Churches, 1982. (with E. Usherwood) The Counter-Armada, 1596: The Journal of the Mary Rose, 1983; (with E. Usherwood) We Die for the Old Religion, 1987. Add: 24 St. Mary's Grove, Canonbury, London N1, England.

USTINOV, Peter (Alexander). British, b. 1921. Novels/Short stories, Plays/Screenplays, Autobiography/Memoirs/Personal. Actor and dir. Goodwill Ambassador, Unicef, since 1969. Rector, Univ. of Dundee, 1968–74. *Publs:* House of Regrets, 1942; The New Lot (documentary screenplay), 1943; Blow Your Own Trumpet, 1943; Beyond, 1943; The Banbury Nose, 1944; Plays About People, 1950; The Love of Four Colonels, 1951; The Moment of Truth, 1951; Romanoff and Juliet, 1956; And a Dash of Pity: Short Stories, 1959; The Loser (novel), 1961; Ustinov's Diplomats: A Book of Photographs, 1960; We Were Only Human (caricatures), 1961; Photo Finish, 1962; Five Plays, 1965; The Frontiers of the Sea, 1966; The Unknown Soldier and His Wife: Two Acts of War Separated by a Truce for Refreshment, 1967; Halfway up the Tree, 1967; The Wit of Peter Ustinov, 1969; Kumnagel (novel), 1971;

R Love J, 1973; Dear Me (memoirs), 1977; My Russia (memoirs/travel), 1983; Ustinov in Russia, 1987.   Add: 11 Rue de Silly, 92100 Boulogne, France.

UTLEY, Robert M(arshall).   American, b. 1929.   History.   Regional Historian, Southwest Region, 1957–64; Chief Historian 1964–72; Dir., Office of Archeology and Historic Preservation, 1972–77, and Asst. Dir., 1973–77, U.S. National Park Service; Deputy Dir., Advisory Council on Historic Preservation, 1977–80.   *Publs:* Custer and the Great Controversy: Origin and Development of a Legend, 1962; The Last Days of the Sioux Nation, 1963; (ed.) Battlefield and Classroom: Four Decades with the American Indian, 1867-1904, by Richard Henry Pratt, 1963; Frontiersmen in Blue: The U.S Army and the Indian, 1848-65, 1967; Frontier Regulars: The U.S. Army and the Indian, 1866-91 (in U.K. as Bluecoats and Redskins), 1973; (ed.) Life in Custer's Cavalry: Diaries and Letters of Albert and Jennie Barnitz 1867-68, 1977; (co-author) American Heritage History of the Indian Wars, 1977; The Indian Frontier of the American West 1846-1891, 1984; High Noon in Lincoln: Violence on the Western Frontier, 1987; Cavalier in Buckskin: George Armstrong Custer and the Western Military Frontier, 1988; Billy the Kid: A Short and Violent Life, 1989.   Add: 5 Vista Grande Ct., Eldorado, Sante Fe, M. Mex. 87505, U.S.A.

V

VACHSS, Andrew H(enry). American, b. 1942. Novels, Law. Lawyer in private practice, NYC, since 1976. Formerly social worker: caseworker, then unit supervisor of multi-problem ghetto casework team, Dept. of Social Services, NYC, 1966–69; Urban Coordinator, Community Development Foundn., Norwalk, Conn., 1969–70; Organizer and Coordinator, Calumet Community Congress, Lake County, Ind., 1970; Dir., Uptown Community Org., Chicago, 1970–71; Dir., Libra Inc., Cambridge, Mass., 1971; Deputy Dir., Medfield–Norfolk Prison Project, Medfield, Mass., 1971–72; Project Dir. and Dir. of Intensive Treatment Unit, Dept. of Youth Services, Boston, 1972–73; Planner and Analyst, Crime Control Coordinator's Office, Yonkers, N.Y., 1974–75. *Publs:* The Life-Style Violent Juvenile: The Secure Treatment Approach, 1979; Flood (novel), 1985; Strega (novel), 1987; Blue Bell (novel), 1988. Add: c/o Knopf Inc., 201 E. 5oth St., New York, N.Y. 10022, U.S.A.

VAHANIAN, Gabriel. French, b. 1927. Theology/Religion, Translations. Jeannette K. Watson Prof. of Religion, Syracuse Univ., N.Y., since 1975 (Asst. Prof., 1958–62; Assoc. Prof., 1962–67; Eliphalet Remington Prof., 1967–73); Prof. de théologe ethique, Univ. de Sciences Humaines, Strasbourg, since 1984. Instr., Princeton Univ., N.J., 1955–58; Visiting Prof., Univ. des Sciences Humaines, Strasbourg, 1972–75, 1975–76, 1979–80; Visting Prof., Univ of Toronto, Ontario, 1978. *Publs:* (trans.) La Confession de foi d'eglise (The Faith of the Church), by Karl Barth, 1960; The Death of God: The Culture of our Post-Christian Era, 1961; Wait Without Idols, 1964; No Other God, 1966; La Condition de Dieu, 1970; Dieu et l'Utopie, 1977; L'Etre et Dieu (collection), 1986. Add: 136 Palais Universitaire, 67084 Strasbourg, Cedax. France.

VAIZEY, Marina (Alandra; Lady Vaizey). British, b. 1938. Art. Art Critic of The Sunday Times newspaper, London, since 1974. Member, Exec. Cttee., Contemporary Art Society, since 1974; Member, Advisory Cttee., Royal Photographic Soc. Collection, since 1980; Member, Fine Arts Advisory Cttee., British Council, since 1987. Art Critic of the Financial Times newspaper, London, 1970–74; Dance Critic and Feature Writer, Now magazine, London, 1979–81. Member of the Council, Arts Council of Great Britain, 1975–78 (Deputy Chmn. of the Art Panel); Member, Advisory Cttee., Government Art Collection, Dept. of the Environment, 1975–82; Exec. Dir., Mitchell Prize for the History of Art, 1976–87. *Publs:* Keith Grant: A Journey to the Far North (catalogue), 1970; Critics' Choice (catalogue), 1974; Gilbert Spencer (catalogue), 1974; L.S. Lowry (catalogue), 1976; Alex Colville (catalogue), 1977; St. Michael Guide to Famous Paintings, 1979; Andrew Wyeth (catalogue), 1980; 100 Masterpieces of Painting, 1980; The Artist as Photographer, 1982; Printer as Photographer (catalogue), 1982; Personal Choice (catalogue), 1983; (with others) Andre Kertesz, 1984; Peter Blake, 1985. Add: 24 Heathfield Terr., London W4 4JE, England.

VALDES, Mario J. Canadian, b. 1934. Literature, Philosophy. Prof. of Hispanic Studies and Comparative Literature, Univ. of Toronto, since 1971 (Asst. Prof., 1963–66; Assoc. Prof., 1967–71). Ed., Canadian Review of Hispanic Studies, since 1976. *Publs:* Death in the Literature of Unamuno, 1964; (ed.) Miguel de Unamuno's Niebla, 1969; An Unamuno Source Book, 1973; (ed.) Critical Edition of Unamuno's San Manuel Bueno, 1974; (ed.) Interpretation of Narrative, 1978; Shadows in the Cave: Phenomenological Theory of Literary Criticism, 1982; Identity of the Literary Text, 1985; Inter-American Literary Relations, 1985; Phenomenological Hermeneutics and the Study of Literature, 1987. Add: Comparative Literature, Univ. of Toronto, 14045 Robarts Library,

Toronto, Ont., Canada.

VALDEZ, Luis (Miguel). American, b. 1940. Plays/Screenplays, Theatre. Founding Dir., El Teatro Campesino, Delano, 1965–69, Fresno, 1969–71, and since 1971, in San Juan Bautista, Calif. Union Organizer, United Farmworkers, Delano, Calif., to 1967. *Publs:* Actos (collection, including La quinta temporado, Las dos garas del patroncito, Los vendidos, La conquista de Mexico, No saco nada de la escuela, The Militants, Vietnam campesino, Huelguistas, Soldado razo), 1971; (ed. with Stan Steiner) Aztlan: An Anthology of Mexican American Literature, 1972; Pensamiento Serpentino: A Chicano Approach to the Theatre of Reality, 1973. Add: 705 Fourth St., San Juan Bautista, Calif. 95045, U.S.A.

VALE, Malcolm Graham Allan. British, b. 1942. History, Biography. Fellow and Tutor, St. John's College, Oxford, since 1978. Jr. Research Fellow, Queen's Coll., Oxford, 1966–69; Lectr. in History, Univ. of Warwick, Coventry, 1969–70; Lectr., Univ. of York, 1970–78. *Publs:* English Gascony, 1399-1453, 1970; Charles VII, 1974; War and Chivalry, 1981; The Angevin Legacy and the Hundred Years War, 1989. Add: St. John's Coll., Oxford, England.

VALENCY, Maurice. American, b. 1903. Plays/Screenplays, Songs, lyrics and libretti, Literature. Advisory Ed., Humanities Encyclopedia Americana. Former Brander Matthews Prof. of Dramatic Literature (now Prof. Emeritus), and Prof. of Comparative Literature, Columbia Univ., NYC. Dir. of Academic Studies, Juilliard Sch., NYC, 1971–85. *Publs:* The Tragedies of Herod, 1940; (adaptor) The Madwoman of Chaillot, 1948; (adaptor) The Enchanted, 1950; (adaptor) The Apollo of Bellac, 1954; (adaptor) Ondine, 1954; (adaptor) The Queen's Gambit, 1956; (adaptor) The Virtuous Island, 1956; La Perichole (libretto), 1958; (ed. and adaptor) Four Plays by Giraudoux, 1958; (adaptor) The Visit, 1958; In Praise of Love, 1958; The Gypsy Baron (libretto), 1959; Feathertop, 1959; (co-ed.) The Palace of Pleasure: An Anthology of the Novella, 1960; Battleship Bismarck, 1963; The Thracian Horses, 1963; The Flower and the Castle: An Introduction to the Drama, 1964; The Breaking String: The Plays of Chekhov, 1966; The Cart and the Trumpet: The Plays of Bernard Shaw, 1973; Regarding Electra, 1978; Conversation with a Sphinx, 1979; The End of the World, 1980; Ashby, 1984; Julie, 1989. Add: 404 Riverside Drive, New York, N.Y. 10025, U.S.A.

VALENTINE, Alec. *See* **ISAACS**, Alan.

VALENTINE, Jean. American, b. 1934. Poetry. Member, Dept. of Writing, Columbia Univ., NYC. Poetry Workshop Teacher, Swarthmore Coll., Pa., 1968–70, and Yale Univ., New Haven, Conn., 1970, 1974. *Publs:* Dream Barker and Other Poems, 1965; Pilgrims, 1969; Ordinary Things, 1974; The Messenger, 1979. Add: Dept. of Writing, Columbia Univ., New York, N.Y. 10027, U.S.A.

VALIN, Jonathan (Louis). American, b. 1947. Mystery/Crime/Suspense. Freelance writer since 1979. Lectr. in English, Univ. of Cincinnati, 1974–76, and Washington Univ., 1976–79. *Publs:* The Lime Pit, 1980; Final Notice, 1980; Dead Letter, 1981; Day of Wrath, 1982; Natural Causes, 1983; Life's Work, 1986; Fire Lake, 1987; Extenuating Circumstances, 1989. Add: c/o Dominick Abel Literary Agency, 498 West End Ave., New York, N.Y. 10024, U.S.A.

VALLIS, Val(entine Thomas). Australian, b. 1916. Poetry. Opera

Critic for The Australian, Opera and A.B.C. radio. Lectr. and Sr. Lectr. in Philosophy, 1950–65, Sr. Lectr. in English, 1965–73, then Reader, 1974–81, Univ. of Queensland, St. Lucia. *Publs:* Songs of the East Coast, 1947; (ed. with R.S. Byrnes) The Queensland Centenary Anthology, 1959; Dark Wind Blowing, 1961; (ed. with J. Wright and Ruth Harrison) Witnesses of Spring: Previously Unpublished Poems of John Shaw Neilson, 1970. Add: Dept. of English, Univ. of Queensland, St. Lucia, Brisbane, Australia 4067.

VAMPLEW, Wray. British, b. 1943. History, Sports/Physical education/Keeping fit. Sr. Reader in Economic History, Flinders Univ. of South Australia, since 1981 (Lectr., 1975–80). Lectr. in Economic History, Univ. of Edinburgh, Scotland, 1967–75. *Publs:* Salvesen of Leith, 1975; The Turf: A Social and Economic History of Horse-Racing, 1976; South Australian Historical Statistics, 1984; Australian: Historical Statistics 1987; Pay Up and Play the Game: Professional Sport in Britain 1875-1914. Add: 32 Shamrock Rd., Hallett Cove, S.A. 5158, Australia.

VAN ALLBURG, Chris. American, b. 1949. Children's fiction. Artist. *Publs:* (all illustrated by the author) The Garden of Abdul Gasazai, 1979; Jumanji, 1981; Benn's Dream, 1982; The Wreck of the Zephyr, 1983; The Mysteries of Harris Burdick, 1984; The Polar Express, 1985; The Stranger, 1986; The Alphabet Theater Proudly Presents How The Z Was Zapped, 1987; Two Bad Ants, 1988. Add: c/o Houghton Mifflin, 2 Park St., Boston, Mass. 02108, U.S.A.

VANCE, Jack. Also writes as John Holbrook Vance, Alan Wade, and Peter Held. American, b. 1916. Mystery/Crime/Suspense, Science fiction/Fantasy. Writer of scripts for Captain Video prog. *Publs:* The Dying Earth, 1950; The Space Pirate, 1953 (as The Five Gold Bands, 1963); Vandals of the Void, 1953; To Live Forever, 1956; (as Alan Wade) Isle of Peril, 1957; Big Planet, 1959; Slaves of the Klau, 1959; (as Peter Held) Take My Face, 1959; The Man in the Cage, 1960; The Dragon Masters, 1963; Demon Prince Series: The Star King, The Killing Machine, The Palace of Love, The Face, The Book of Dreams, 1963–81; The Houses of Iszm, 1964; Son of the Tree, 1964; Future Tense, 1964; Monsters in Orbit, 1965; The World Between, and Other Stories, 1965; Space Opera, 1965; The Blue World, 1966; The Brains of Earth, 1966; The Languages of Pao, 1966; Many Worlds of Magnus Ridolph, 1966; Eyes of the Overworld, 1966; The Fox Valley Murders, 1966; The Pleasant Grove Murders, 1967; The Last Castle, 1967; Planet of Adventure No. 1: City of the Chasch, 1968; The Deadly Isles, 1969; Planet of Adventure No. 2: The Servants of the Wankh, 1969; Eight Fantasms and Magics: A Science Fiction Adventure, 1969; Planet of Adventure No. 3: The Dirdir, 1969; Emphyrio, 1969; Planet of Adventure No. 4: The Pnume, 1970; The Durdane Trilogy: The Anome, The Brave Free Men, The Asutra, 1973–74; The Alastor Series: Trullion 2262, Marune 933, Wyst 1716, 1973–78; Bad Ronald, 1973; The Worlds of Jack Vance, 1976; Green Magic, 1979; The House on Lily Street, 1979; The View from Chickweed's Window, 1979; Lyonesse I, 1983; Cugel's Saga, 1983; Rhialto the Marvellous, 1984; Lyonesse II: The Green Pearl, 1985; The Cadwal Chronicles I: Araminta Station, 1987; Wankh, 1986; The Augmented Agent, 1986; The Dark Side of the Moon (stories), 1986. Add: 6383 Valley View Rd., Oakland, Calif. 94611, U.S.A.

VANCE, John Holbrook. *See* VANCE, Jack.

van de KAMP, Peter. American (born Dutch), b. 1901. Astronomy. Research Astronomer and Dir. Emeritus of Sproul Observatory, Swarthmore Coll., since 1972 (Assoc. Prof. of Astronomy, 1937–40; Dir. of Sproul Observatory, 1937–72; Prof., 1940–72). Asst., Kapteyn Astronomical Lab., Groningen, Netherlands, 1922–23; Research Assoc., McCormick Observatory, 1923–24, Instr., 1925–28, and Asst. Prof., 1928–37, Univ. of Virginia, Charlottesville; Martin Kellog Fellow, Lick Observatory, Univ. of California, Berkeley, 1924–25; Conductor, Swarthmore Coll. Orchestra, Pa. 1945–54; Dir.-at-Large, Assn. of Univs. for Research in Astronomy, and Pres., IAU Commn. No. 26 (Double Stars), Intnl. Astronomical Union, 1958–62; Member, U.S.A. National Cttee., IAU, 1964–68. *Publs:* Basic Astronomy, 1952; (with G. Honegger) Space, The Architecture of the Universe, 1961; Elements of Astromechanics, 1964; Principles of Astrometry, 1967; Stellar Paths, 1981; Dark Companions of Stars, 1986. Add: Amstel 244, AK 1017 Amsterdam, Netherlands.

van der POST, (Sir) Laurens (Jan). South African, b. 1906. Novels/Short stories, Travel/Exploration/Adventure. Military Attaché to the British Minister, Batavia, 1945–47; Explorer—has made several missions to Africa for the British Govt. and the Colonial Development Corp., including mission to Kalahari, 1952; Farmer, Orange Free State, South Africa, 1948–65. *Publs:* In a Province, 1934; Venture to the Interior, 1951; The Face Beside the Fire, 1953; Flamingo Feather, 1955; The Dark Eye in Africa, 1955; A Bar of Shadow, 1956; The Lost World of the Kalahari, 1958; The Heart of the Hunter, 1961; The Seed and the Sower, 1963; Journey into Russia (in U.S. as A View of All the Russias), 1964; The Hunter and the Whale: A Tale of Africa, 1967; A Portrait of All the Russias, 1967; A Portrait of Japan, 1968; The Night of the New Moon: August 6, 1945 . . . Hiroshima, 1970; A Story Like the Wind, 1972; A Far-Off Place, 1974; Jung: The Story of Our Time, 1975; First Catch Your Eland: A Taste of Africa, 1977; Yet Being Someone Other, 1982; (with Jane Taylor) Testament to the Bushmen, 1984; (with Jean-Marc Pottiez) A Walk with a White Bushman: Conversation, 1986. Add: c/o Hogarth Press, 30 Bedford Sq., London WC1B 3RP, England.

VAN DER SPUY, Una. South African, b. 1912. Homes/Gardens. *Publs:* Gardening in Southern Africa, 1942; Ornamental Shrubs and Trees, 1943; Garden Planning and Construction, 1943; Indigenous Trees and Shrubs for the Garden, 1971; South African Wild Flowers for the Garden, 1971; Gardening with Shrubs, 1973; Gardening with Ground Covers, 1975; Gardening with Climbers, 1976; Gardening with Trees, 1977. Add: Old Nectar, Box 127, Stellenbosch, South Africa.

van der ZEE, Karen. Pseud for Mona van Wieren. Dutch, b. 1947. Historical/Romance. *Publs:* Sweet Not Always, 1979; Love Beyond Reason, 1980; A Secret Sorrow, 1981; Going Underground, 1982; Waiting, 1982; One More Time, 1983; Soul Ties, 1984; Staying Close, 1984; Pelangi Haven, 1985; Fancy Free, 1986; Time For Another Dream, 1986; Shadows on Bali, 1988; Hot Pursuit, 1988; (as Mona van Wieren) Rhapsody in Bloom, 1989; Brazillian Fire, 1989. Add: c/o Mills and Boon Ltd., Eton House, 18-24 Paradise Rd., Richmond, Surrey TW9 1SR, England.

van de VALL, Mark. Dutch, b. 1923. Industrial relations, Institutions/Organizations, Sociology (social policy research, sociological practice). Adjunct Prof. of Sociology, State Univ. of New York at Buffalo, since 1963, and Prof. of Sociology and Social Research, Erasmus Univ., Rotterdam, since 1988. Special Research Fellow, Dept. of Health, Education and Welfare, Washington, D.C., 1969–70; Prof. of Sociology, Univ. of Leyden, Netherlands, 1977–88. *Publs:* Labor Organizations, a Macro and Micro-Sociological Analysis on a Comparative Basis, 1970; (with Charles D. King) Models of Industrial Democracy: Consultation, Co-Determination and Workers Management, 1978, Sociaal Beleidsonderzoek: Een Professioneel Paradigma, 1980, (with Frans L. Leeuw) Social Beleidsonderzoek: Differentiatie en Outwikkeling, 1987. Add: Sociological Inst., Erasmus Univ., Post Box 1738, 3000 DR Rotterdam, The Netherlands.

VAN DE WETERING, Janwillem. Dutch, b. 1931. Novels/Short stories, Mystery/Crime/Suspense, Children's fiction, Social commentary, Theology/Religion. Sergeant, Amsterdam Reserve Police, since 1965. Salesman for Dutch companies in South Africa, 1952–58; lived in a Buddhist monastery, Kyoto, Japan, 1958–59; company dir., Bogota, Colombia, 1959–62, and Lima, Peru, 1963; land salesman, Brisbane, Australia, 1964–65; textile co. dir., Amsterdam, 1965–67; member of the Buddhist group in Maine, U.S.A., 1975–80. *Publs:* De Legel Spiegal, 1971, in U.S. as the Empty Mirror: Experiences in a Japanese Zen Monastery, 1974; A Glimpse of Nothingness: Experiences in an American Zen Community, 1975; Outsider in Amsterdam, 1975; Tumbleweel, 1976; The Corpse on the Dike, 1976; Death of a Hawker, 1977; The Japanese Corpse, 1977; The Blond Baboon, 1978; Little Owl, 1978; The Maine Massacre, 1979; Hugh Pine, 1980; The Mind Murders, 1981; The Streetbird, 1983; The Rattle-Rat, 1985; Inspector Saito's Small Satori, 1985; Murder by Remote Control, 1986; The Sergeant's Cat, 1987; Hard Rain, 1988; Seesaw Millions, 1988. Add: c/o Ballantine Books, 201 E. 50th St., New York, N.Y. 10022, U.S.A.

VANDIVER, Frank Everson. American, b. 1925. History, Biography. Dir., Mosher Inst. for Defense Studies, Texas A and M Univ., since 1988 Pres., Jefferson Davis Assn., and Chief Advisory Ed., The Papers of Jefferson Davis, since 1963. Asst. Prof., 1955–56, Assoc. Prof., 1956–58, Prof., 1958–65, Harris Masterson, Jr. Prof. of History, 1965–79, Acting Pres., 1969–70, Provost, 1970–75, and Vice-Pres., 1975–79, Rice Univ., Houston, Tex.; Pres., North Texas State Univ., Denton, 1979–81. (Pres., Texas A and M Univ., 1981–88). *Publs:* (ed.) The Civil War Diary of General Josiah Gorgas, 1947; (ed.) Confederate Blockade-Running Through Bermuda 1861-1865, 1947; Ploughshares into Swords: Josiah Gorgas and Confederate Ordnance, 1952; (ed.) Proceedings of the Congress of the Confederate States of America, 3 vols., 1953; Rebel Brass: The Confederate Command System, 1956; Mighty Stonewall, 1957; (ed.) Narrative of Military Operations, by Joseph E. Johnston, 1959; (ed.) War

Memoirs, by Jubal A. Early, 1960; Jubal's Raid: General Early's Famous Attack on Washington in 1864, 1960; Fields of Glory: A Pictorial Narrative of American Wars, 1960; Basic History of the Confederacy, 1962; Jefferson Davis and the Confederate State, 1964; (ed.) The Idea of the South, 1964; John J. Pershing, 1967; Their Tattered Flags: The Epic of the Confederacy, 1970; The Southwest: South or West, 1975; Black Jack, 2 vols., 1977. Add: Texas A & M Univ., College Station, Tex. 77843, U.S.A.

VAN DUSEN, Albert. American, b. 1916. History. Ed., The Papers of Jonathan Trumbull Sr., since 1967. Instr., Dept. of History, Duke Univ., Durham, N.C., 1941–46; Instr., Dept. of History, Wesleyan Univ., Middletown, Conn., 1946–48; Historian, U.S. Dept. of the Army, 1948–49; Asst. Prof., 1949–55, Assoc. Prof., 1955–62, and Prof. of History, 1962–83, Univ. of Connecticut, Storrs. State Historian of Connecticut, 1952–85. *Publs:* Middletown and the American Revolution, 1953; The Public Records of the State of Connecticut, vol. IX, 1797-1799, 1953, vol. X, 1800-1801, 1965; Connecticut, 1961; (with F. Humphreville) This Is Connecticut, 1963; Puritans Against the Wilderness, 1975; Adventures for Another World: Jonathan Trumble's Commonplace Book, 1983. Add: 85 Ball Hill Rd., Storrs, Conn. 06268, U.S.A.

VAN DUSEN, C(larence) Raymond. American, b. 1907. Language/ Linguistics, Psychology, Speech/Rhetoric, Biography. Coordinator of Grad. Studies, and Prof. of Speech Pathology, Mississippi Univ. for Women, Columbus since 1967, now retired (Dir., Speech and Hearing Clinic, 1965–67). Consultant, Speech Pathologist, Regional Rehabilitation Center, Rupelo, Miss., since 1965. Instr., to Asst. Prof. in Speech, Michigan State Univ., East Lansing, 1937–40; Assoc. Prof. in Speech, Michigan State Univ., East Lansing, 1937–40; Assoc. Prof., to Prof. of Speech, Univ. of Miami, 1947–61; Dean, Brevard Community Coll., Cocoa Beach, Fla., 1961–64; Pres., Golden Hills Academy, 1964–65. *Publs:* Training the Voice for Speech, 1943, 1953; While You Were Away: A Guide to Veterans, 1945; (with H. van Smith) The New Speech-O-Gram Technique for Persuasive Public Speaking, 1962; (with H. Cromwell) Oral Approach to Phonetics, 1969; (with L. Eggert) Don't Muff the Punch Line, 1972; Stroke Prediction and Prevention, 1981; Speech Program for Stroke Patients, 1982. Add: c/o Royal Court Reports, 902 Cheryl Drive, P.O. Box 927, Aberdeen, Miss. 39730, U.S.A.

VAN DUYN, Mona. American, b. 1921. Poetry. Faculty member, Washington Univ., St. Louis (Lectr. in English, 1950–67). Instr. in English, Univ. of Iowa, Iowa City, 1944–46, and Univ. of Louisville, Ky., 1946–50. Ed., Perspective: A Quarterly of Literature, St. Louis, 1947–67. *Publs:* Valentines to the Wide World: Poems, 1959; A Time of Bees, 1964; To See, To Take: Poems, 1970; Bedtime Stories, 1972; Merciful Disguises: Published and Unpublished Poems, 1973; Letters from a Father and Other Poems, 1982. Add: 7505 Teasdale Ave., St. Louis, Mo. 63130, U.S.A.

VANDYKE, Henry. America, b. 1928. Novels/Short stories. Writer-in-Residence, Kent State Univ., since 1969. Assoc. Ed., Univ. Engineering, Research Inst., Ann Arbor, Mich., 1956–58; Corresp., Crowell-Collier-Macmillan Publ. Co., NYC, 1959–67. *Publs:* Ladies of the Rachmaninoff Eyes, 1965; Blood of Strawberries, 1969; Dead Piano, 1971; Lunacy and Caprice, 1987. Add: 40 Waterside Plaza, New York, N.Y. 10010, U.S.A.

VAN DYKE, Vernon B. American, b. 1912. International relations/Current affairs, Politics/Government. Prof. Emeritus of Political Science, Univ. of Iowa, Iowa City. Former Vice Pres., American Political Science Assn.; Sr. Fellow, National Endowment for the Humanities, and Fellow, Woodrow Wilson Intnl. Center for Scholars, Washington, 1972–73. *Publs:* Political Science: A Philosophical Analysis, 1960; Pride and Power: The Rationale of the Space Program, 1964; Human Rights, The United States, and World Community, 1970; International Politics, 3rd ed. 1972; Human Rights, Ethnicity, and Discrimination, 1985; Introduction to Politics, 1988. Add: Dept. of Political Science, Univ. of Iowa, Iowa City, Iowa 52242, U.S.A.

VANE, Bert. *See* **KENT,** Arthur.

VAN ESSEN, W(illiam). Also writes as Richard Serjeant. British, b. 1910. Medicine/Health, Photography, Recreation/Leisure/Hobbies. Hon. Consultant Surgeon, Woolwich Group of Hosps., London. *Publs:* (as Richard Sergeant) Private Flying for Leisure and Business, 1962; (with G. Catling) Miniature Photography for the Young Cameraman, 1962; (as Richard Serjeant) A Man May Drink, 1964; (with G. Catling) Movie Making for the Young Cameraman, 1964; (ed. with Alex Watson) The

Gliding Book, 1965, 1970; (as Richard Serjeant) The Spectrum of Pain, 1969; (as Richard Serjeant) Louis Pasteur and the Fight Against Disease, 1971. Add: 6 Hatlex Hill, Hest Bank, Lancaster LA2 6ET, England.

van FRAASSEN, Bas C. Canadian, b. 1941. Philosophy, Sciences. Prof. of Philosophy, Princeton Univ., since 1982. Asst. Prof., 1966–68, and Assoc. Prof. of Philosphy, 1968–69, Yale Univ., New Haven, Conn.; Prof. of Philosophy, Univ. of Toronto, 1969–81; Prof. of Philosophy, Univ. of Southern California, Los Angeles, 1976–81. Ed.-in-Chief, Journal of Philosophical Logic, 1971–77. *Publs:* An Introduction to the Philosophy of Time and Space, 1970; Formal Semantics and Logic, 1971; (with Karel Lambert) Derivation and Counterexample: An Introduction to Ghilosophical Logic, 1972; The Scientific Image, 1980; (ed. with E. Beltrametti) Current Issues in Quantum Logic, 1982. Add: Dept. of Philosophy, Princeton Univ., Princeton, N.J. 08544, U.S.A.

van HELLER, Marcus. *See* **ZACHARY,** Hugh.

van ITALLIE, Jean-Claude. American, b. 1936. Plays/Screenplays, Translations. Ed., Translatlantic Review, NYC, 1960-63; Playwright-in-Residence, Open Theatre, NYC, 1963–68; freelance writer on public affairs for NBC and CBS television, NYC, 1963–67; Teacher of playwriting, New Sch. for Social Research, NYC, 1967–68 and 1972; Lectr. in Playwriting, Naropa Inst., 1973–89, Princeton, N.J., 1974–83, Yale Sch. of Drama, 1986, New York Univ., 1986–88, Univ., of Colorado, Boulder, 1987–89. *Publs:* American Hurrah: Five Short Plays, 1967; War and Four Other Plays, 1967; (with S. Thie) Thoughts on the Instant of Greeting a Friend on the Street, 1968; (with Open Theatre) The Serpent: A Ceremony, 1968; (Obie award, 1969), The King of the United States, 1972; Mystery Play, 1973; (trans.) The Seagull, 1973; The Fable, 1975; (trans.) The Cherry Orchard, 1977; America Hurrah and Other Plays, 1978; (trans.) Three Sisters, 1979; Bag Lady, 1979; (trans.) Uncle Vanya, 1980; Picasso: A Writer's Diary (teleplay for BBC), 1980; The Tibetan Book of the Dead, 1982; (trans.) The Bakery, by Genet, 1985; The Traveller, 1986. Add: Box L, Charlemont, Mass. 01339, U.S.A.

VAN LAWICK, Hugo. Dutch, b. 1937. Natural history, Zoology. Film producer and photographer. *Publs:* (with Jane Goodall) Innocent Killers, 1970; Solo: The Story of an African Wild Dog, 1973; Savage Paradise, 1977; (with P. Matthiessen) Sand Rivers, 1981; (with Elspeth Huxley) Last Days in Eden, 1984; Among Predators and Prey, 1986. Add: c/o William Collins Sons & Co., 8 Grafton St., London W1X 3LA, England.

VAN LINH, Erik. *See* **del REY,** Lester.

VAN LUSTBADER, Eric. American, b. 1946. Novels, Science fiction. *Publs:* The Sunset Warrior, 1976; Shallows at Night, 1977; Dai-San, 1978; Beneath an Opal Moon, 1978; The Ninja, 1980; Sirens, 1982; Black Heat, 1983; The Miko, 1984, Jian, 1985; Shan, 1986; Zero, 1988. Add: c/o Henry Morrison Inc., Box 235, Bedford Hills, N.Y. 10507, U.S.A.

van PEURSEN, Cornelis A(nthonie). Dutch, b. 1920. Cultural/Ethnic topics, Philosophy. Extraordinary Prof. of Epistemology, Free Univ., Amsterdam, 1963–85. Member, Netherlands, Unesco Commn., since 1974 (Secty., Netherlands, Unesco, 1948–50). Reader in Philosphy, Univ. of Utrecht, 1950–53; Prof. of Philosophy, Univ. of Groningen, 1953–60; Prof. of Philosophy, Univ. of Leiden, 1960–83. *Publs:* Body, Soul, Spirit, 1965; L. Wittgenstein, 1969; Leibniz, 1969; Wirklichkeit als Ereignis, 1969; Wetenschappen en Werkelijkheid, 1970; Phenomenology and Analytical Philosophy, 1972; Phenomenology and Reality, 1972; The Strategy of Culture, 1974. Add: A Gogelweg, 39, 2517 JE. Den Haag, Holland.

VAN RIPER, Guernsey, Jr. American, b. 1909. Children's fiction, Children's non-fiction. Copywriter, Sidener & Van Riper, 1933–40; Ed., Bobbs-Merrill Co., publrs., 1941–48. *Publs:* Lou Gehrig, Boy of the Sand Lots, 1949; Will Rogers, Young Cowboy, 1951; Knute Rockne, Young Athlete, 1952; Babe Ruth, Baseball Boy, 1954; Jim Thorpe, Indian Athlete, 1956; Richard Byrd, Boy Who Braved the Unknown, 1958 (reissued as Richard Byrd, Boy of the South Pole); Yea Coach! Three Great Football Coaches, 1966; The Game of Basketball, 1967; World Series Highlights, 1970; The Mighty Macs: Three Famous Baseball Managers, 1972; Behind the Plate: Three Great Catchers, 1973; (with J. Newcombe and G. Sullivan) Football Replay, 1973; (with S. & B. Epstein and R. Reeder) Big League Pitchers and Catchers, 1973; Golfing Greats, 1975. Add: 4745 Kessler N. Dr., Indianapolis, Ind, 46208, U.S.A.

van RJNDT, Philippe. Canadian, b. 1950. Novels/Short stories. *Publs:* The Tetramachus Collection, 1976; Blueprint, 1977; The Trial of Adolf Hitler, 1978; Samaritan, 1983; Last Message to Berlin, 1984; Eclipse, 1986; Tides, 1988. Add: 50 Hillsboro Ave., No. 2303, Toronto, Ont. M5R 1S8, Canada.

VAN SCYOC, Sydney (Joyce). American, b. 1939. Science fiction/ Fantasy. Freelance writer, since 1962. Secty., 1975–77, and Pres., 1977–79, Starr King Unitarian Church, Hayward, Calif. *Publs:* Saltflower, 1971; Assignment: Nor'Dyren, 1973; Starmother, 1976; Cloudcry, 1977; Sunwaifs, 1981; Darkchild, 1982; Bluesong, 1983; Starsilk, 1984; Drowntide, 1987; Featherstroke, 1989. Add: 2636 East Ave., Hayward, Calif. 94541, U.S.A.

VANSITTART, Peter. British, b. 1920. Novels/Short stories, Children's non-fiction, History. *Publs:* I Am the World, 1942; Enemies, 1947; The Overseer, 1949; Broken Canes, 1950; A Verdict of Treason, 1952; A Little Madness, 1953; The Game and the Ground, 1956; Orders of Chivalry, 1958; The Tournament, 1959; A Sort of Forgetting, 1960; Carolina, 1961; Sources of Unrest, 1962; The Friends of God, 1963; The Siege, 1964; The Lost Lands, 1964; The Dark Tower, 1965; The Shadow Land, 1967; The Story Teller, 1968; Green Knights, Black Angels, 1969; Pastimes of a Red Summer, 1969; Landlord, 1970; Vladivostok: Figures in Laughter, 1972; Marlborough House School, 1974; Dictators, 1974; Worlds and Underworlds, 1974; Quintet, 1976; Lancelot, 1978; Flakes of History, 1978; Harry, 1980; The Death of Robin Hood, 1980; Voices from the Great War, 1981; Three Six Seven, 1982; Voices, 1870-1914, 1984; (ed.) John Masefield's Letters from the Front, 1984; Aspects of Feeling, 1985; Paths from a White Horse, 1985; The Ancient Mariner and the Old Sailor, 1985; Happy and Glorious!, 1988; Parsifal, 1988; Voices from the Revolution, 1989. Add: 9 Upper Park Rd., Hampstead, London NW3, England.

VAN STOCKUM, Hilda. American (born Dutch), b. 1908. Children's fiction, Translations. Art teacher in Ireland, Illustrator, and painter (honorary RHA). Montessori Instr., Child Education Foundn., N.Y., 1934; Instr. in Art and Creative Writing, Inst. of Lifetime Learning, Washington, D.C., 1965–74. Pres., Children's Book Guild, Washington, D.C., 1972–74. *Publs:* A Day on Skates, 1934; (trans.) Tilio, A Boy of Papua, by Rudolk Voorhoeve, 1937; The Cottage at Bantry Bay, 1938; Francie on the Run, 1939; Kersti and Saint Nicholas, 1940; Pegeen, 1941; Andries, 1942; Gerrit and the Organ, 1943; The Mitchells, 1945; Canadian Summer, 1948; Angels' Alphabet, 1948; (trans.) Marian and Marion, by J.M. Selleger-Elout, 1949; Patsy and the Pup, 1950; King Oberon's Forest, 1957; Friendly Gables, 1960; Little Old Bear, 1962; The Winged Watchman, 1962; (trans.) Corso, The Donkey, by Christina Pothast-Gimberg, 1962; Jeremy Bear, 1963; Bennie and the New Baby, 1964; New Baby Is Lost, 1964; Mogo's Flute, 1966; Penengro, 1972; Rufus Round and Round, 1973; (trans.) The Curse of Laguna Grande, by Siny R. van Interson, 1973; (trans.) The Smugglers of Buenaventura, by Siny R. van Interson, 1974; (trans.) In the Spell of the Past, by Siny R. van Interson, 1975; (trans.) Bruno, by Achim Broger, 1975; The Borrowed House, 1975; (trns.) Kasimir, by Achim Broger, 1976. Add: 8 Castle Hill, Berkhamsted, Herts., England.

VAN TASSEL, Dennie L. American. Information science/Computers. Member of staff and Lectr. in Computer Science, Univ. of California, Santa Cruz. *Publs:* Computer Security Management, 1972; Program Style, Design, Efficiency, Debugging, Testing, 1974, 1978; (ed.) The Compleat Computer, 1976, 1983; Computer, Computer, Computer, 1977; Introductory Cobol Programming, 1978; RPGII and RPGIII Programming, 1986. Add: Computer Center, Univ. of California, Santa Cruz, Calif. 95064, U.S.A.

VAN TIL, William. American, b. 1911. Education, Social commentary/phenomena, Travel/Exploration/Adventure. Coffman Distinguished Prof. Emeritus in Education, Indiana State Univ., Terre Haute, since 1977 (Coffman Distinguished Prof., 1967–77); Dir., Univ. Workshops in Writing for Professional Publs. since 1977. Instr., to Asst. Prof., Ohio State Univ., Columbus, 1934–45; Ed., Intercultural Education News, 1944–47; Prof., Univ. of Illinois, Urbana, 1947–51; Prof. and Div. Chmn., George Peabody Coll., Nashville, Tenn., 1951–57; Prof. and Dept. Chmn., New York Univ., 1957–67. Ed., Insights mag., John Dewey Soc., 1964–72; Columnist, One Way of Looking at It, in Contemporary Education, 1968–71, and Kappan, 1971–78. *Publs:* The Danube Flows Through Fascism, 1938; Time On Your Hands, 1945; Economic Roads for American Democracy, 1947; The Making of a Modern Educator, 1961; (with G.F. Vars and J.H. Lounsbury) Modern Education for the Junior High School Years, 1961, 1967; (ed. and contrib.) Curriculum: Quest for Relevance,

1971, 1974; Education: A Beginning, 1971, 1974; (with W.R. Stephens) Education in American Life, 1972; (ed. and contrib.) Issues in Secondary Education, 1976; Van Til on Education, 1977; Secondary Education: School and Community, 1978; Writing for Professional Publication, 1981, 1986; My Way of Looking At It, 1983; ASCD in Retrospect, 1986. Add: Sch. of Education, Indiana State Univ., Terre Haute, Ind. 47809, U.S.A.

van VOGT, A(fred) E(lton). American (b. Canadian), b. 1912. Mystery/Crime/Suspense, Science fiction/Fantasy, Medicine/Health, Money Finance, Autobiography/Memoirs/Personal. Census Clerk, Ottawa, 1931–32; Western Rep., Maclean Trade Papers, Winnipeg, 1936–39; Managing Dir., Hubbard Dianetic Research Foundn. of Calif., Los Angeles, 1950–52; and Owner, with his wife, Hubbard Dianetic Center, Los Angeles, 1953–61. Pres., California Assn. of Dianetic Auditors, 1958–81. *Publs:* Slan, 1946, 1951; The Weapon Makers, 1947, 3rd ed. as One Against Eternity, 1955; The Book of Ptath, 1947, as Two Hundred Million A.D., 1964; The World of A., 1948, in U.K. as The World of Null-A, 1969; (with E. Mayne Hull) Out of the Unknown (short stories), 1948, 1969, 2nd U.K. ed. as The Sea Thing and Other Stories, 1970; The Voyage of the Space Beagle, 1950, as Mission: Interplanetary, 1952; Masters of Time, 1950, as Earth's Last Fortress, 1960, in U.K. in Two Science Fiction Novels, 1973; The House That Stood Still, 1950, as The Mating Cry, 1960, 2nd U.K. ed. as The Undercover Aliens, 1976; The Weapon Shops of Isher, 1951; The Mixed Men, 1952, as Mission to the Stars, 1955; Away and Beyond (short stories), 1952; Destination: Universe!, 1952; The Universe Maker, 1953, in U.K. in The Universe Maker, and The Proxy Intelligence, 1967; (with E. Mayne Hull) Planets for Sale, 1954, in U.K. in A van Vogt Omnibus, 1967; The Pawns of Null-A, 1956, as The Players of Null-A, 1966; (with Charles Edward Cooke) The Hypnotism Handbook (non-fiction), 1956; Empire of the Atom, 1957; The Mind Cage, 1957; Triad (omnibus), 1959; The War Against the Rull, 1959; Siege of the Unseen, 1959, in U.K. in Two Science Fiction Novels, 1973; The Wizard of Linn, 1962; The Violent Man (suspense novel), 1962; The Beast, 1963, in U.K. as Moonbeast, 1969; The Twisted Men (short stories), 1964; Monsters (short stories), 1965, as The Blal, 1976; Rogue Ship, 1965; (with E. Mayne Hull) The Winged Man, 1966; The Far-Out Worlds of A.E. van Vogt (short stories), 1968, as the Worlds of A.E. van Vogt, 1974; The Silkie, 1969; Quest for the Future, 1970; Children of Tomorrow, 1970; The Battle of Forever, 1971; More Than Superhuman (short stories), 1971; The Proxy Intelligence and Other Mind Benders, 1971; M-33 in Andromeda (short stories), 1971; The Darkness on Diamondia, 1972; The Book of van Vogt (Short stories), 1972, as Lost: Fifty Suns, 1979; The Money Personality (non-fiction), 1972; Future Glitter, 1972, 2nd. U.K. ed. as Tyranopolis, 1977; The Secret Galactics, 1974, as Earth Factor X, 1976; The Man with a Thousand Names, 1974; The Best of A.E. van Vogt, 1974; Reflections of A.E. van Vogt (non-fiction), 1975; The Gyrb (short stories), 1976; The Anarchistic Colossus, 1977; Supermind, 1977; Pendulum (short stories), 1978; Renaissance, 1979; Cosmic Encounter, 1980; Computer World, 1983; Null-A Three, 1985. Add: c/o DAW Books Inc., 1633 Broadway, New York, N.Y. 10019, U.S.A.

van WIEREN, Mona. *See* **van der ZEE,** Karen.

VARDAMAN, Patricia Black. American, b. 1931. Institutions/ Organizations, Writings/Journalism. Vice-Pres., and Systems Analyst, Mgmt. Assocs., since 1967; Wine Importer, Vardaman Wine Imports, since 1981. With Finance Office, 1949–51, and Coll. of Law, 1951–67, Asst. to Dean, Systems Development, 1967–70, and Systems Analyst, 1970, Univ. of Denver. *Publs:* (with George T. Vardaman and Carroll C. Halterman) Cutting Communications Costs and Increasing Impacts, 1970; Forms for Better Communication, 1971; (with George T. Vardaman) Communication in Modern Organizations, 1973; (with George T. Vardaman) Successful Writing, 1977. Add: P.O. Box 691, Indian Hills, Colo. 80454, U.S.A.

VARDRE, Leslie. *See* **DAVIES,** L.P.

VARLEY, John. American, b. 1947. Science fiction/Fantasy. Freelance writer since 1973. *Publs:* The Ophiuchi Hotline, 1977; Titan, 1978; The Persistance of Vision (short stories; in U.K. as In the Hall of the Martian Kings), 1978; Wizard, 1980; The Barbie Murders and Other Stories, 1980; Millennium, 1983; Demon, 1984. Add: 2030 W. 28th, Eugene, Ore. 97405, U.S.A.

VARMA, Monika. Indian, b. 1916. Stories, Poetry, Translations. *Publs:* Dragonflies Draw Flame, 1962; Gita Govinda and Other Poems, 1966; (trans.) A Bunch of Poems, by Rabindranath Tagore, 1966; Green Leaves and Gold, 1970; Quartered Questions and Queries, 1971; Past Imperative, 1972; Across the Vast Spaces, 1975; Alakananda, 1976; Lord

Krishna, Love Incarnate, 1978; Blue Champagne (stories), 1986. Add: c/o Mr. Sanjaya Varma, B88 Sarvodaya Enclave, New Delhi 100 017, India.

VAS DIAS, Robert. American, b. 1931. Poetry. Lectr., Univ. of Maryland European Div., since 1981; Co-Ed., Ninth Decade, since 1983. Poet-in-Residence, Thomas Jefferson Coll., Grand Valley State Colls., Allendale, Mich., 1971–74; Gen. Secty., The Poetry Soc., London, 1975–78. *Publs:* The Counted, 1967; (ed.) Inside Outer Space: New Poems of the Space Age, 1970; The Life of Parts, 1972; Speech Acts and Happenings, 1972; Making Faces, 1976; Ode, 1977; Poems Begining: "The World," 1979. Add: 108 Hemingford Rd., London N1 1DE.

VASIL, Raj Kumar. Indian, b. 1931. History, Politics/Government, Race relations. Reader in Political Science, Victoria Univ., Wellington, since 1976 (Sr. Lectr., 1967–76). Ed., Asia Publishing House, Bombay, 1959–60; Lectr. in Intnl. Relations, Jadavpur Univ., Calcutta, 1960–67. *Publs:* Politics in a Plural Society: A Study of Non-Communal Political Parties in West Malaysia, 1971; The Malaysian General Election of 1969, 1972; Ethnic Politics in Malaysia, 1980; Public Service Unionism, 1980; Politics in Bi-Racial Societies: Third World Experience, 1984; Governing Singapore, 1984; Biculturalism: Reconciling Aotearoa with New Zealand, 1988. Add: Dept. of Political Science, Victoria Univ., P.O. Box 60, Wellington, New Zealand.

VASTA, Edward. American. b, 1928. Literature. Prof. of English, Univ. of Notre Dame, since 1969 (Instr., 1958–61; Asst. Prof., 1961–66; Assoc. Prof., 1966–69). *Publs:* The Spiritual Basis of Piers Plowman, 1965; (ed.) Middle English Survey: Critical Essays, 1965; (ed.) Interpretations of Piers Plowman, 1968; (ed.) Chaucerian Problems and Perspectives, 1979. Add: Dept. of English, Univ. of Notre Dame, Notre Dame, Ind. 46556, U.S.A.

VASUDEVA, Vishnudayal. *See* **BISSOONDOYAL,** Basdeo.

VATIKIOTIS, P(anayiotis) J. American, b. 1928. History, International relations/Current affairs, Politics/Government. Prof. of Politics with reference to the Near and Middle East, Univ. of London, since 1965 (Chmn., Centre for Middle Eastern Studies, Sch. of Oriental and African Studies, 1966–69). Prof. of Govt., Indiana Univ., Bloomington, 1963–65. *Publs:* The Fatimid Theory of the State, 1957, 1981; The Egyptian Army in Politics, 1961, 1975; Politics and the Military in Jordan, 1921-1957, 1967; (ed.) Egypt Since the Revolution, 1968; The Modern History of Egypt, 1969, 1980, 1985; Conflict in the Middle East, 1971; (ed.) Revolution in the Middle East and Other Case Studies, 1972; Greece: A Political Essay, 1975; Nasser and His Generation, 1978; Arab and Regional Politics in the Middle East, 1984; Islam and the Nation-State, 1987. Add: Sch. of Oriental and African Studies, Univ. of London, Malet St., London WC1E 7HP, England.

VAUGHAN, Alden T(rue). American, b. 1929. History. Prof. of History, Columbia Univ., NYC, since 1969 (Instr., 1961–64; Asst. Prof., 1964–66; Assoc. Prof., 1966–69). *Publs:* New England Frontier, 1965; (ed.) Chronicles of the American Revolution, 1965; (ed.) America Before the Revolution, 1967; (ed.) The American Colonies in the 17th Century, 1971; (co-ed.) The Structure of American History, 1971; (ed.) The Puritan Tradition in America, 1972; (co-author and co-ed.) Perspectives on Early American History, 1973; American Genesis, 1975; (co-ed.) Puritan New England, 1977; (ed.) New England's Prospect, by William Wood, 1977; (ed.) Early American Indian Documents: Treaties and Laws, 20 vols., 1979-; (co-author) Crossing the Cultural Divide, 1980; (co-ed.) Puritans Among the Indians, 1981. Add: 560 Riverside Dr., New York, N.Y. 10027, U.S.A.

VAUGHAN, Richard Patrick. American, b. 1919. Psychology, Theology/Religion. Roman Catholic Priest (Jesuit): in private practice as psychologist, Los Angeles, since 1977. Clinical Psychologist, St. Mary's Hosp., San Francisco, 1956–57; Prof. of Psychology, 1958–67, and Dean of the Coll. of Liberal Arts and Science, 1967–69, Univ. of San Francisco; Provincial Superior of Calfornia Jesuits, 1969–76. Instr., Loyola Marymount Univ., 1977–87. *Publs:* Mental Illness and the Religious Life, 1962; Introduction to Religious Counseling: A Christian Humanistic Approach, 1969; Basic Skills for Christian Counselors, 1987. Add: Jesuit Community, Loyola Marymount Univ., P.O. Box 45041, Los Angeles, Calif. 90045, U.S.A.

VAUGHAN-THOMAS, Wynford. British, b. 1908. Country life/Rural societies, History, Travel/Exploration/Adventure, Autobiography/Memoirs/Persona. Radio and television commentator with the BBC, 1936–66, and Harlech Television (also Dir.), 1967–80, now retired. Pres., The Kilvert Soc.; Pres., Welsh Council for Voluntary Action, since 1969; Gov., British Film Inst., since 1978. Add: Anzio (military history), 1961; Madly in All Directions (autobiography/travel), 1967; (with Alun Llewellyn) The Shell Guide to Wales, 1969; The Splendour Falls, 1973; Gower, 1975; The Countryside Companion, 1980; Trust to Talk, 1980; Wynford Vaughan-Thomas' Wales, 1981; The Prince of Wales, 1982; Wales: A History, 1985; How I Liberated Burgundy, 1985; South and Mid-Wales, 1987. Add: "Pentower", Tower Hill, Fishguard, Dyfed SA65 91A, Wales.

VAUGHAN WILLIAMS, Ursula. Also writes as Ursula Wood. British, b. 1911. Novels, Poetry, Songs, lyrics and libretti, Biography. *Publs:* No Other Choice, 1941; Fall of Leaf, 1944; Need for Speech, 1948; The Sons of Light (libretto), 1951; Wandering Pilgrimage, 1952; Silence and Music, 1959; Break to Be Built (libretto), 1961; Heirs and Rebels, 1963; Ralph Vaughan Williams, 1964; The Sofa (libretto), 1965; Metamorphoses, 1966; Set to Partners, 1968; Melita (libretto), 1968; The Brilliant and the Dark (libretto), 1969; David and Bathsheba (libretto), 1969; (co-author) Pictorial Biography of Ralph Vaughan Williams, 1971; The Icy Mirror (libretto), 1972; Serenade (libretto), 1973; Aspects (libretto), 1978; Ode to Compassion (libretto), 1978; King of Macedon (libretto), 1979; Aspects (verse), 1983; The Yellow Dress (novel), 1984; Echoes (libretto), 1986; Insect Play (libretto), 1986. Add: 66 Gloucester Cres., London NW1 7EG, England.

VAYDA, Andrew P. American, b. 1931. Anthropology/Ethnology, Environmental science/Ecology. Prof. of Anthropology and Ecology, Rutgers Univ., New Brunswick, N.J., since 1972. Prof., Colmmbia Univ., 1968–72. Ed., Human Ecology: An Interdisciplinary Journal, 1971–77. *Publs:* Maori Warfare, 1960, 1970; (ed. with A. Leeds) Man, Culture, and Animals, 1965; (ed.) Peoples and Cultures of the Pacific, 1968; (ed.) Environment and Cultural Behavior, 1969; War in Ecological Perspective, 1976. Add: Dept. of Human Ecology, Cook Coll., P.O. Box 231, Rutgers Univ., New Brunswick, N.J. 08903, U.S.A.

VELARDO, Joseph Thomas. American, b. 1923. Biology, Medicine/Health. Prof. of Anatomy, Strich Sch. of Medicine, Loyola Univ., Chicago, since 1967. Consultant, Intnl. Basic and Biomedical Curricula, since 1973. Research Fellow in Biology, 1952–53, Assoc. in Pathology, 1953–54, and Assoc. in Surgery, 1954–55, Harvard Univ. Grad. Sch. and Harvard Medical Sch., Cambridge and Boston, Mass.; Asst. in Surgery, Peter Bent Brigham Hosp., Boston, 1954–55; Asst. Prof. of Anatomy Endocrinology, Yale Univ. Sch. of Medicine, New Haven, Conn., 1955–61; Dir., Inst. for the Study of Human Reproduction, 1962–67. Co-Ed., CME (Journal of Continuing Medical Education), 1964–67. *Publs:* (ed. and contrib.) The Endocrinology of Reproduction, 1958; The Essentials of Human Reproduction, 1958; The Uterus, 1959; (contrib.) Trophoblast and Its Tumors, 1959; (contrib.) The Vagina, 1961; The Ovary, 1963; Human Steroids, 1964; Enzymes in the Female Genital System, 1963; (co-ed.) Biology of Reproduction: Basic and Clinical Studies, 1972; Human Reproduction, 1973; The Ureter, 1980, 1981. Add: 607 E. Wilson Ave., Old Grove East, Lombard, Ill. 60148, U.S.A.

VENABLES, Terry. *See* **WILLIAMS,** Gordon.

VENDLER, Helen (Hennessy). American, b. 1933. Literature. Kenan Prof. of English, Harvard Univ., Cambridge, Mass., since 1985. Instr., Cornell Univ., Ithaca, N.Y., 1960–63; Lectr., Swarthmore Co., Pennsylvania, and Haverford Coll., Pennsylvania, 1963–64; Asst. Prof., Smith Coll., Northampton, Mass., 1964–66; Asst. Prof., 1966–68, and Prof., 1968–85, Boston Univ. *Publs:* Yeats's Vision and the Later Plays, 1963; On Extended Wings: Wallace Stevens' Longer Poems, 1969; The Poetry of George Herbert, 1975; Part of Nature, Part of Us: Modern American Poets, 1981; The Odes of John Keats, 1983; Wallace Stevens: Words Chosen Ou of Desire, 1986; (ed.) The Harvard Book of Contemporary American Poetry, 1986; (ed.) Voices and Visions, 1987. Add: Dept. of English, Harvard Univ., Cambridge, Mass. 02138, U.S.A.

VENTURI, Robert. American, b. 1925. Architecture. Partner, Venturi, Rauch and Scott Brown, Architects and Planners, since 1964. Inst. to Assoc. Prof., Univ. of Pennsylvania, Philadelphia, 1957–65; Charlotte Shepherd Davenport Prof. of Architecture, Yale Univ., New Haven, Conn., 1966–70; Architect-in-Residence, American Academy in Rome, 1966. *Publs:* Complexity and Contradiction in Architecture, 1966, 1977; (with Denise Scott Brown and Steven Izenour) Learning from Las Vegas, 1972, 1977; (with Denise Scott Brown) A View from the Campidoglio: Selected Essays 1953-1984, 1984. Add: 4236 Main St., Philadelphia, Pa. 19127, U.S.A.

VERDON, Dorothy. *See* **TRALINS**, S. Robert.

VERDUIN, John Richard, Jr. American, b. 1931. Education. Prof. of Education, Southern Illinois Univ., Carbondale, since 1967. Assoc. Prof. of Education, State Univ. of New York, Geneseo, 1962–67. *Publs:* Cooperative Curriculum Improvement, 1967; Conceptual Models in Teacher Education: An Approach to Teaching and Learning, 1967; (co-author) Pre-Student Teaching Laboratory Experiences, 1970; (co-author) Project Follow Through, 1971; (co-author) Adults Teaching Adults: Principles and Strategies, 1977; (co-author) The Adult Educator: A Handbook for Staff Development, 1979; Curriculum Building for Adult Learning, 1980; (co-author) Adults and Their Leisure: The Need for Lifelong Learning, 1984; (co-author) Handbook for Differential Education of the Gifted, 1986. Add: 107 N. Lark Lane, Carbondale, Ill. 62901, U.S.A.

VERMES, Geza. British, b. 1924. History, Theology/Religion. Reader in Jewish Studies and Professorial Fellow, Wolfson Coll., Oxford, since 1965. Ed., Journal of Jewish Studies, since 1971. Lectr., 1957–64, and Sr. Lectr., 1964–65, Newcastle Univ. *Publs:* Les Manuscrits du Desert de Juda, 1953, 1954; Discovery in the Judean Desert, 1956; Scripture and Tradition in Judaism, 1961, 1973; The Dead Sea Scrolls in English, 1962, 1975, 1987; Jesus the Jew, 1973, 3rd ed. 1981; (co-ed.) E. Schurer, The History of the Jewish People in the Age of Jesus Christ, 3 vols., 1973–87; (co-ed.) P. Winter, On the Trial of Jesus, 1974; Post-Biblical Jewish Studies, 1975; The Dead Sea Scrolls: Qumran in Perspective, 1977, 1981; The Gospel of Jesus the Jew, 1981; Jesus and the World of Judaism, 1983; The Dead Sea Scrolls after Forty Years, 1987; (co-author) The Essenes According to the Classical Sources, 1989. Add: West Wood Cottage, Foxcombe Lane, Boars Hill, Oxford OX1 5DH, England.

VERMEULE, Emily Dickinson Townsend. American, b. 1928. Archaeology, Art, Classics, History. Zemurray-Stone-Radcliffe Prof., Harvard Univ., Cambridge, Mass., since 1970; also, Fellow for Research, Museum of Fine Arts, Boston, since 1963. Asst. Prof. of Classics, 1958–61, and Assoc. Prof., 1961–64, Boston Univ.; Prof. of Greek and Fine Arts, Wellesley Coll., Massachusetts, 1965–70. *Publs:* Euripides' Electra, 1959; Greece in the Bronze Age, 1964, 7th ed. 1980; The Trojan War in Greek Art, 1964; Gotterkult, Archaeologia Homerica V, 1974; The Art of the Shaft Graves, 1975; Death in Early Greek Art and Poetry, 1979; (with V. Karageorghis) Mycenaean Pictorial Vase-Painting, 1982. Add: Dept. of the Classics, Harvard Univ., Cambridge, Mass. 02138, U.S.A.

VERNEY, Douglas (Vernon). Canadian, b. 1924. Politics/Government. Prof. of Political Science, York Univ., Toronto, since 1962 (Assoc. Prof., 1961–62). Lectr. in Political Science, Univ. of Liverpool, England, 1949–61; Dir., Social Science Research Council of Canada, 1972–74; Member, Inst. for Advanced Study, Princeton, N.J., 1977–78. Past Pres., Canadian Political Science Assn.; Ed., Canadian Public Administration, 1970–74. *Publs:* Parliamentary Reform in Sweden 1866-1921, 1957; Public Enterprise in Sweden, 1959; The Analysis of Political Systems, 1959; (with Sir Denis Brogan) Political Patterns in Today's World, 1963, 1968; British Government and Politics, 1966, 3rd ed. 1976; Three Civilizations, Two Cultures, One State: Canada's Political Traditions, 1986. Add: Ross 657 South York Univ., N. York, Ontario M3J 1PJ, Canada.

VERNEY, (Sir) John. British, b. 1913. Novels/Short stories, Children's fiction. Painter and illustrator. *Publs:* Verney Abroad, 1954; Going to the Wars: A Journey in Various Directions, 1955; Friday's Tunnel, 1959, 1962; Look at Houses, 1959, 1970; February's Road, 1961; Every Advantage, 1961; The Mad King of Chichiboo, 1963; ismo, 1964; (ed. with Patricia Campbell) Under the Sun: Stories, Poems, Articles from Elizabethan Sources, 1964; A Dinner of Herbs (autobiographical), 1966; Seven Sunflower Seeds, 1968; Fine Day for a Picnic, 1968; Samson's Hoard, 1973. Add: The White House, Clare, Suffolk, England.

VERNEY, Michael Palmer. British, b. 1923. Recreation/Leisure/Hobbies. Marine craft consultant and chartered civil engineer, since 1951. Deputy Engineer, River Arun Catchment Bd., 1949–52; Area Engineer, West Sussex River Bd., 1952–65; Divisional Engineer, Sussex River Authority, 1965–74; District Engineer, Southern Water Authority, 1974–81. *Publs:* Amateur Boat Building, 1948; Practical Conversions and Yacht Repairs, 1951; Complete Amateur Boat Building, 1959; Yacht Repairs and Conversions, 1961; Umbau von Booten, 1951; Boat Maintenance, 1970; Boat Repairs and Conversions, 1972; The Care and Repair of Hulls, 1979; The Complete Book of Yacht Care, 1986; Building Chine Boats, 1987. Add: Hillsborough, The Parkway, Rustington, Sussex,

England.

VERNEY, Peter (Vivian Lloyd). British, b. 1930. History, Biography. Regular British Army Officer, 1954–70. *Publs:* The Standard Bearer, 1962; The Micks—The Story of the Irish Guards, 1971; The Battle of Blenheim, 1976; The Gardens of Scotland, 1976; Here Comes the Circus, 1978; Anzio 1944: An Unexpected Fury, 1978; The Earthquake Handbook, 1979; Homo Tyrannicus, 1979; Book of Sports Fitness, 1980; (ed.) Book of Sporting Verse, 1980; The Genius of the Garden, 1989. Add: Skiveralls House, Chalford Hill, Glos. GL6 8QJ, England.

VERNEY, Stephen Edmund. British, b. 1919. Human relations, Social commentary/phenomena, Theology/Religion. Retired Bishop, Church of England. Vicar of St. Francis, Clifton, 1952–58; Diocesan Missioner, Coventry Diocese, and Vicar of Leamington Hastings, 1958–64; Canon of Coventry Cathedral, 1964–70; Canon of Windsor, 1970–77; Bishop of Repton, 1977–85. *Publs:* Fire in Coventry, 1964; (co-author) People and Cities, 1969; Into the New Age, 1976; Water into Wine, 1985; The Dance of Love, 1989. Add: Charity School House, Church Rd., Blewbury, Oxon. OX11 9PY, England.

VERNON, Magdalen Dorothea. British, b. 1901. Psychology. Prof. of Psychology, Univ. of Reading, 1956–67. *Publs:* Experimental Study in Reading, 1931; Visual Perception, 1937; A Further Study of Visual Perception, 1952; The Psychology of Perception, 1962; (ed.) Experiments in Visual Perception, 1966; Human Motivation, 1969; Perception Through Experience, 1970; Reading and its Difficulties, 1971. Add: 13 Sunridge Ave., Bromley, Kent, England.

VERNON, Raymond. American, b. 1913. Economics, Politics/Government. Prof., Govt. Dept., Harvard Univ., Cambridge, Mass., 1978–84, now Emeritus (Prof., Business Sch., 1959–80). With the U.S. Dept. of State, 1946–54. *Publs:* (with Edgar M. Hoover) Anatomy of a Metropolis, 1959; The Changing Economic Function of the Central City, 1959; Metropolis 1985, 1960; The Dilemma of Mexico's Development, 1963; (ed.) Public Policy and Private Enterprise in Mexico, 1964; The Myth and Reality of Our Urban Problems, 1966; (ed.) How Latin America Views the United States Investor, 1966; Manager in the International Economy, 1968, 5th ed. 1986; (ed.) The Technology Factor in International Trade, 1970; Sovereignty at Bay; 1971; The Economic Environment of International Business, 1972, 4th ed. 1986; The Economic and Political Consequences of Multinational Enterprise: An Anthology, 1972; (ed.) Big Business and the State: Changing Relations in Western Europe, 1974; (ed.) The Oil Crisis, 1975; Storm over the Multinationals: The Real Issues, 1977; (ed.) State Owned Enterprises in the Western Economies, 1980; Two Hungry Giants: America and Japan in a Quest for Oil and Ores, 1983; Exploring the Global Environment, 1985; (ed.) The Promise of Privatization, 1988; (with Debora L. Spar) Beyond Globalism: Remaking American Foreign Economic Policy, 1989. Add: 1 Dunstable Rd., Cambridge, Mass. 02138, U.S.A.

VERRAL, Charles Spain. Has also written as George L. Eaton. Canadian, b. 1904. Children's fiction, Children's non-fiction, Sports/Fitness, Biography. Sport Columnist, Youngperson news journal, since 1983. Commercial artist, NYC, 1927–30; Ed. and Art Dir., Clayton Publs., 1930–35; Co-Author of Smith and Smith Publs. air adventure magazine series Bill Barnes, 1934–43; Script Writer, Mandrake the Magician, national radio prog., 1940–41; Continuity Writer of Hap Hopper, United Features syndicated adventure newspaper strip, 1941–47; Writer and ed., Western Publishing Co., 1960–62, and Reader's Digest, NYC, 1962–74. *Publs:* Captain of the Ice, 1953; Champion of the Court, 1954; Men of Flight, 1954; King of the Diamond, 1955; Mighty Men of Baseball, 1955; High Danger, 1955; The Wonderful World Series, 1956; Walt Disney's Great Locomotive Chase, 1956; Annie Oakley, 1957; Lassie and the Daring Rescue, 1957; Brave Eagle, 1957; Broken Arrow, 1957; The Lone Ranger and Tonto, 1957; Rin-Tin-Tin and the Outlaw, 1957; Lassie and Her Day in the Sun, 1958; Cheyenne, 1958; Andy Burnett, 1958; Play Ball, 1958; Zorro, 1958; Smokey the Bear, 1958; Rin-Tin-Tin and the Hidden Treasure, 1959; Zorro and the Secret Plan, 1959; Walt Disney's The Shaggy Dog, 1959; The Winning Quarterback, 1960; The Case of the Missing Message, 1960; Smokey the Bear and His Animal Friends, 1960; The Flying Car, 1961; Jets, 1962; Go! The Story of Outer Space, 1962; Robert Goddard, Father of the Space Age, 1963; Babe Ruth, Sultan of Swat, 1976; Casey Stengel: Baseball's Greatest Manager, 1978. Add: 79 Jane St., New York, N.Y. 10014, U.S.A.

VERVAL, Alain. *See* **LANDE**, Lawrence Montague.

VERYAN, Patricia. Pseud. for Patricia V. Bannister. British and

American (b. British), b. 1923. Historical/Romance/Gothic. Secty. since 1938: currently Secty. for Grad. Affairs, Univ. of California at Riverside, since 1971. *Publs:* The Lord and the Gypsy, 1978, in U.K. as Debt of Honour, 1980; Love's Duet, 1979, in U.K. as A Perfect Match, 1981; Mistress of Willovale, 1980; Nanette, 1981; Some Brief Folly, 1981; Feather Castles, 1982; Married Past Redemption, 1983; The Noblest Frailty, 1983; The Wagered Widow, 1984; Sanguinet's Crown, 1985; Practice to Deceive, 1985; Journey to Enchantment, 1986; Give All to Love, 1987; The Tyrant, 1987; Love Alters Not, 1987, Cherished Enemy, 1988; The Dedicated Villain, 1989. Add: 10129 Main St., Bellevue, Wash. 98004, U.S.A.

VESEY, Godfrey (Norman Agmondisham). British, b. 1923. Philosophy. Prof. of Philosophy, Open Univ., Milton Keynes, since 1969; retired, 1988 (Pro-Vice-Chancellor, 1975–77; Acting Vice-Chancellor, 1980). Lectr., then Reader in Philosophy, King's Coll., London, 1952–69; Visiting Prof., Carleton Coll., Minn. and Univ. of Oregon, 1966. Hon. Dir., Royal Inst. of Philosophy, 1965–79. *Publs:* (ed.) Body and Mind, 1964; The Embodied Mind, 1965; (ed.) The Human Agent, 1968; (ed.) Talk of God, 1969; (ed.) Knowledge and Necessity, 1970; Perception, 1970; (ed.) The Proper Study, 1971; (ed.) Reason and Reality, 1972; (ed.) Philosophy and the Arts, 1973; Personal Identity, 1974; (ed.) Understanding Wittgenstein, 1974; (ed.) Philosophy in the Open, 1974; (ed.) Impressions of Empiricism, 1976; (ed.) Communication and Understanding, 1977; (ed.) Human Values, 1978; (ed.) Idealism: Past and Present, 1982; (ed.) Philosophers Ancient and Modern, 1986; (with Antony Flew) Agency and Necessity, 1987; (ed.) The Philosophy of Christianity, 1990. Add: 73 Bushmead Ave., Bedford MK40 3QW, England.

VESEY, Paul. Pseud. for Samuel Washington Allen. American, b. 1917. Poetry. Prof. Emeritus of English, Boston Univ., since 1981 (Prof., 1971–81). Avalon Prof. of Humanities, Tuskegee Inst., Alabama, 1968–70; Visiting Prof. of English, Wesleyan Univ., Middletown, Conn., 1970–71. *Publs:* Ivory Tusks, 1956; Ivory Tusks and Other Poems, 1968; (co-ed.) Pan-Africanism Reconsidered, 1962 (ed.) Poems From Africa, 1973; Paul Vesey's Leger, 1975; Every Round, 1987. Add: 145 Cliff Ave., Winthrop, Mass. 02152, U.S.A.

VESPER, Karl H(amptom). American, b. 1932. Business/Trade/Industry, Engineering Technology. Prof. of Business Admin. and Prof. of Mechanical Engineering, Univ. of Washington, Seattle, since 1969. Dir. of Engineering Case Development, Stanford Univ., California, 1963–69. Ed., Mechanical Engineering Series, McGraw-Hill Book Co., New York, 1966–74. *Publs:* Engineers at Work, 1974; (with LaRue T. Hosmer and Arnold C. Cooper) The Entrepreneurial Function, 1977; New Venture Strategies, 1979. Add: Dept. of Business Admin., Univ. of Washington, Seattle, Wash. 98195, U.S.A.

VICTOR, Charles B. *See* PUECHNER, Ray.

VICTOR, Edward. American, b. 1914. Sciences. Prof. Emeritus of Science Education, Northwestern Univ. Sch. of Education, Evanston, Ill., since 1979 (Prof., 1958–78). Adjunct Prof. of Science Education, Arizona State Univ., Sch. of Education, Tempe, since 1979. Science Ed., Follett Publishing, since 1962, and Benefic Press, since 1965; Science Consultant, Cenco Films, since 1965; and McGraw-Hill Films, since 1970. Chemistry instr., Boston Univ., Mass., 1942–44; Head of Science Dept., Westbrook Jr. Coll., Portland, Me., 1944–51; Science Supvr., Newport, Rhode Island schs., 1951–57; Asst. Prof., Univ. of Virginia, Charlottesville, 1957–58. *Publs:* Friction, 1961; Machines, 1962; Magnets, 1962; Molecules and Atoms, 1963; Planes and Rockets, 1965; Heat, 1967; Electricity, 1967; Magnets and Electromagnets, 1967; Machines, 1969; Sound, 1969; Living Things, 1971; The Physical World, 1971; (co-author) A Sourcebook for Elementary Science, 2nd ed. 1971; (co-author) Investigation Science (Grades 1-6), 1972; (co-author) Readings in Science Education for the Elementary School, 3rd ed. 1975; Science for the Elementary School, 6th ed. 1989. Add: 9819 Calico Dr., Sun City, Ariz. 85373, U.S.A.

VIDAL, Gore. Has also written mysteries as Edgar Box. American, b. 1925. Novels/Short stories, Plays/screenplays. Member, President's Advisory Council on the Arts, 1961–63; Member, Advisory Bd., Partisan Review, 1960–71; Co-Chmn., The New Party, 1968–71. *Publs:* Williwaw, 1946; In a Yellow Wood, 1947; The City and the Pillar, 1948, rev. ed. 1965; The Season of Comfort, 1949; A Search for the King; A Twelfth Century Legend, 1950; Dark Green Bright Red, 1950; The Judgement of Paris, 1952; (as Edgar Box) Death in the Fifth Position, 1952; (as Edgar Box) Death Before Bedtime, 1953; (as Edgar Box) Death Likes It Hot, 955; Messiah, 1954, 1965; A Thirsty Evil: Seven Short Stories,

1956; Visit to a Small Planet and Other Television Plays, 1957; The Best Man: A Play of Politics, 1960; Romulus: A New Comedy (play), 1962; Three: Williwaw, A Thirsty Evil, Julian the Apostate, 1962; Three Plays (includes Visit to a Small Planet, The Best Man, Love Love Love), 1962; Rocking the Boat (essays), 1962; Julian, 1964; Romulus: The Broadway Adaptation, and the Original Romulus the Great by Friedrich Durrenmatt, translated by Gerhard Nelhaus, 1966; Washington D.C., 1967; Myra Breckinridge, 1968; Weekend, 1968; Reflections upon a Sinking Ship (essays), 1969; Two Sisters: A Novel in the Form of a Memoir, 1970; An Evening with Richard Nixon, 1972; Homage to Daniel Shays: Collected Essays, 1952–71 (in U.K. as Collected Essays: 1952–71), 1972; Burr, 1973; Myron, 1974; 1876; 1976; Matters of Fact and Fiction: Essays 1973–76, 1977; (with others) Great American Families, 1977; Kalki, 1978; (with Robert J. Stantion) Views from a Window: Conversations, 1980; Creation, 1981; The Second American Revolution and Other Essays, 1982 (in U.K. as Pink Triangle and Yellow Star and Other Essays); Duluth, 1983; Lincoln, 1984; Gore Vidal's Venice, 1985; Empire, 1987; Armageddon?, 1987; Hollywood: A Novel of America in the 1920's, 1990. Add: c/o Random House, 201 E. 50th St., New York, N.Y. 10022, U.S.A.

VIDGER, Leonard Perry. American, b. 1920. Business/Trade/Industry, Money/Finance. Prof. of Finance and Real Estate, Sch. of Business, San Francisco State Univ., Calif., since 1965 (Asst. Prof., 1955–60; Assoc. Prof., 1960–65; Dir., Real Estate Research Prog., 1965–70); Visiting Prof. of Finance, Univ. of Nebraska, Lincoln, 1970–72. *Publs:* Selected Cases and Problems in Real Estate, 1963; Suggested Solutions to Selected Cases and Problems in Real Estate, 1963; Borrowing and Lending on Residential Property, 1981. Add: 126 Highland Dr., Edmonds, Wash. 98020, U.S.A.

VIDLER, Alexander Roper. British, b. 1899. Theology/Religion. Hon. Fellow, King's Coll., Cambridge, since 1972 (Fellow and Dean, 1956–67). Warden, St. Deiniol's Library, Hawarden, 1939–48; Ed., Theology, 1939–64; Canon of Windsor, 1948–56; Mayor of Rye, 1972–74. *Publs:* Magic and Religion, 1930; Sex, Marriage and Religion, 1932; (with W.L. Knox) The Development of Modern Catholicism, 1933; The Modernist Movement in the Roman Church, 1934; A Plan Man's Guide to Christianity, 1936; (with W.L. Knox) The Gospel of God and the Authority of the Church, 1937; God's Demand and Man's Response, 1939; God's Judgement on Europe, 1940; Secular Despair and Christian Faith, 1941; Christ's Strange Work, 1944; The Orb and the Cross, 1945; (with W.A. Whitehouse) Natural Law, 1946; Christian Belief, 1950; Christian Belief and This World, 1956; Essays in Liberality, 1957; Windor Sermons, 1958 The Church in an Age of Revolution, 1961; (ed. and contrib.) Sounding, 1962; (ed. and contrib.) Objections to Christian Belief, 1963; A Century of Social Catholicism, 1964; Twentieth Century Defenders of the Faith, 1965; F.D. Maurice and Company, 1966; A variety of Catholic Modernists, 1970; (with M. Muggeridge) Paul: Envoy Extraordinary, 1972; Scenes from a Clerical Life, 1977; Read, Mark, Learn, 1980. Add: Saltcote Pl., Mill Rd., Rye, Sussex TN31 7NN, England.

VIERECK, Peter (Robert Edwin). American, b. 1916. Plays/Screenplays, Poetry, Philosophy, Politics/Government. Holder of Alumnae Found. Chair of Interpretive Studies, 1965–79, and William R. Kenan Jr. Chair of History, since 1979, Mt. Holyoke Coll., South Hadley, Mass. (Assoc. Prof., 1948–55; Prof. of History, 1955–65). Teaching Asst., 1941–42, Instr. in German, and Tutor in History and Literature, 1946–47, Harvard Univ. Cambridge, Mass.; Asst. Prof. of History, 1947–48, and Visiting Prof. of Russian History, 1948–49, Smith Coll., Northampton, Mass. *Publs:* Metapolitics: From the Romantics to Hitler, 1941, rev. ed. as Metapolitics: The Roots of the Nazi Mind, 1961; Terror and Decorum: Poems 1940-1948, 1948; Conservatism Revisited: The Revolt Against Revolt, 1815-1949, 1949; Strike Through the Mask! New Lyrical Poems, 1950; The First Morning: Lyrical Poems, 1952; Shame and Glory of the Intellectuals: Babbit Jr. vs. the Rediscovery of Values, 1953, rev. ed. 1965; Dream and Respnsibility: Four Test Cases of the Tension Between Poetry and Society, 1953; The Persimmon Tree: New Pastoral and Lyric Poems, 1956; The Unadjusted Man: A New Hero for Americans: Reflections on the Distinction Between Confirming and Conserving, 1956, rev. ed. 1962; Conservatism: From John Adams to Churchill, 1956; Inner Liberty: The Stubborn Grit in the Machine (lecture), 1957; The Tree Witch, 1961, published as The Tree Witch: A Poem and a Play (First of All a Poem), 1961; Conservatism Revisited, and the New Conservatism: What Went Wrong?, 1962, 1980; New and Selected Poems: 1932-1967, 1967; Archer in the Marrow: The Applewood Cycles 1967-1987, 1987. Add: 12 Silver St., South Hadley, Mass. 01075, U.S..

VIERTEL, Joseph. American, b. 1915. Novels/Short stories, Plays/Screenplays. Pres., Presidential Realty Corp. *Publs:* So Proudly We Hail (play), 1936; The Last Temptation, 1955; To Love and Corrupt,

for Edith Sitwell, 1948; Volume Two, 1949; Selected Poems and New, 1958; Poems in Praise of Love, 1952; Poems 55, 1962; Selected Stories, 1962; (ed.) The Doveglion Book of Philippine Poetry, 1962; The Portable Villa, 1963; The Essential Villa, 1965; (ed.) The New Doveglion Book of Philippine Poetry, 1975; Appassionate, 1978. Add: 780 Greenwich St., New York, N.Y. 10014, U.S.A.

VILLA-GILBERT, Mariana (Soledad Magdelena). British, b. 1937. Novels/Short stories. Gramophone Records Sales Asst., W.H. Smith & Son Ltd., London and Canterbury, since 1958. *Publs:* Mrs. Galbraith's Air, 1963; My Love All Dressed in White, 1964; Mrs. Cantello, 1966; A Jingle Jangle Song, 1968; The Others, 1970; Manuela (fantasy), 1973; The Sun in Horus, 1986. Add: 28 St. Martin's Rd., Canterbury, Kent CT1 1QW, England.

VINCENT, Claire. *See* **ALLEN,** Charlotte Vale.

VINCENT, John James. British, b. 1929. International relations/Current affairs, Race relations, Theology/Religion. Dir., Urban Theology Unit, London and Sheffield, since 1970. Leader, Ashram Community, since 1967; Methodist Supt., Sheffield Inner City Ecumenical Mission, since 1971; Ed., New City Journal, since 1972. Minister, Machester and Salford Mission, 1956–62; Supt. Minister, Rochdale Mission, 1962–69; Member, British Council of Churches Commn. on Defence and Disarmament, 1963–65, 1969–73; Founding Member, and Chmn., Alliance of Radical Methodists, 1971–74. *Publs:* Christ in a Nuclear World, 1962, 1963; (trans.) W.G. Kummel: Man in the New Testament, 1963; Christ and Our Stewardship: Six Bible Studies, 1963; Christian Nuclear Perspective, 1964; Christ and Methodism: Towards a New Christanity for a New Age, 1965, 1966; Here I Stand: The Faith of a Radical, 1967; Secular Christ: A Contemporary Interpretation of Jesus, 1968; The Working Christ: Christ's Ministries through His Church in the New Testament and in the Modern City, 1968; The Race Race, 1970; The Jesus Thing, 1973; The Jesus Thing Workbook, 1973; Disiple and Lord: Discipleship in Mark's Gospel, 1975; Alternative Church, 1976; Stirrings: Essays Christian and Radical, 1977; Alternative Journeys, 1979; Inner City Issues, 1980; Starting All Over Again, 1981; Into the City, 1982; OK Let's Be Methodists, 1984; Radical Jesus, 1985; (with J.D. Davies) Mark at Work, 1986; T.S.B.: The People's Bank, 1987; Ministry in the City, 1989; A British Liberation Theology, 1989. Add: 239 Abbeyfield Rd., Sheffield S4 7AW, England.

VINE, Barbara. *See* **RENDELL,** Ruth.

VINGE, Joan (Carol) D(ennison). American, b. 1948. Science fiction/Fantasy. Salvage archaeologist, San Diego Co., 1971. *Publs:* The Outcases of Heaven Belt, 1978; Fireship (short stories), 1978; Eyes of Amber and Other Stories, 1979; The Snow Queen, 1980; (ed. with Steven G. Spruill) Binary Star 4, 1980; Psion, 1982; World's End, 1984; Phoenix in the Ashes (short stories), 1985; Ladyhawke (novelization of screenplay), 1985; Catspaw, 1988. Add: 26 Douglas Rd., Chappaqua N.Y. 10514, U.S.A.

VINGE, Vernor (Steffen). American, b. 1944. Science fiction/Fantasy. Assoc. Prof. of Mathematics, San Diego State Univ., since 1972. *Publs:* Grimm's World, 1969; The witling, 1976; True Names, Peace War, 1984; Marooned in Realtime, 1986. Add: Dept. of Math., San Diego State Univ., San Diego, Calif. 92182, U.S.A.

VINING, Elizabeth Gray. Also writes as Elizabeth Janet Gray. American, b. 1902. Novels/Short stories, Children's fiction, Biography. Tutor to Crown Prince of Japan, 1946–50; Vice Pres., Bd. of Trustees, 1952–71, and Vice Chmn., Bd. of Dirs., 1952–71, Bryn Mawr Coll. *Publs:* as Elizabeth Janet Gray—Merediths' Ann, 1927; Tangle Garden, 1928; Tilly-Tod, 1929; Meggy Maclntosh, 1930; Jane Hope, 1933; Young Walter Scott, 1935; Beepy Marlowe of Charles Town, 1936; Penn, 1938; The Contributions of the Quakers, 1939; The Fair Adventure, 1940; Adam of the Road (Newbery Award), 1942; Sandy, 1945; The Cheerful Heart, 1959; I Will Adventure, 1962; as Elizabeth Gray Vining—Windows for the Crown Prince (autobiographical), 1952; The World in Tune, 1952; The Virginia Exiles, 1955; Friend of Life: The Biography of Rufus M. Jones, 1958; Return to Japan, 1960; I Will Adventure, 1962; Take Heed of Loving Me, 1964; Flora: A Biography (in U.K. as Flora MacDonald: Her Life in the Highlands and in America), 1966; I, Roberta, 1967; The Taken Girl, 1972; Mr. Whittier, 1974; Being Seventy: The Measure of a Year, 1978. Add: Kendal at Longwood, Box 194, Kennett Sq., Pa. 19348, U.S.A.

VINSON, Kathryn. (Kathryn Vinson Williams). American, b. 1911.

Children's fiction. Instr. in English, 1966–70, and Asst. Prof., 1970–71, Coll. of Orlando; Adjunct Instr. in English, Florida Technological Univ., now Univ. of Central Florida, 1969–71; Adjunct Instr. in Humanities, Valencia Community Coll., Orlando, 1971–72. *Publs:* The Luck of the Golden Cross, 1960; Run with the Ring, 1965. Add: 844 Kenilworth Terr., Orlando, Fla. 32803, U.S.A.

VIORST, Judith. American. Children's fiction, Poetry, Sciences. Contrib. Ed., and Columnist, Redbook mag., since 1968. Columnist, Washington Star Syndicate, 1970–72. *Publs:* (ed. with Shirley Moore) Wonderful World of Science, 1961; Projects: Space, 1962; One Hundred and Fifty Science Experiments, Step-by-Step, 13; Natural World, 1965; The Village Square (p), 1965; The Changing Earth, 1967; Sunday Morning, 1968; It's Hard to be Hip Over Thirty, and Other Tragedies of Married Life (p), 1968; I'll Fix Anthony, 1969; Try It Again, Sam: Safety When You Walk, 1970; (with Milton Viorst) The Washington D.C. Underground Gourmet, 1970; People and Other Aggravations (p), 1971; The Tenth Good Thing About Barney, 1971; Alexander and the Terrible, Horrible, No Good, Very Bad Day, 1972; Yes, Married: A Saga of Love and Complaint (prose pieces), 1973; My Mama Says There Aren't Any Zombies, Ghosts, Vampires, Creatures, Demons, Monsters, Fiends, Goblins, or Things, 1973; Rosie and Michael, 1974; How Did I Get to be Forty and Other Atrocities (p), 1976; A Visit from St. Nicholas to a Liberated Household, 1977; Alexander Who Used to be Rich Last Sunday, 1978; Love and Guilt and the Meaning of Life, Etc., 1979; If I Were in Charge of the World and Other Worries (p), 1981; Necessary Losses, 1986; When Did I Stop Being Twenty and Other Injustices (p), 1987; The Good-bye Book, 1988; Over Fifty and Other Negotiations (verse), 1989. Add: 3432 Ashley Terr., N.W., Washington, D.C. 20008, U.S.A.

VIORST, Milton. American, b. 1930. International relations/Current affairs, Politics/Government. Reporter, Washington Post, 1957–61; Washington Correspondent, New York Post, 1961–64; Syndicated Political Columnist, Washington Star, 1970–75. *Publs:* Hostile Allies: FDR and de Gaulle, 1964; (ed.) The Great Documents of Western Civilization, 1965; Fall From Grace: The Republican Party and the Puritan Ethic, 1968; Hustlers and Heroes: An American Political Panorama, 1970; Fire in the Streets: America in the, 1960;'s, 1980; (ed.) Making a Difference: The Peace Corps at Twenty-five, 1986; Lands of Sorrow: Israel's Journey from Independence, 1987. Add: 3432 Ashley Terr., N.W., Washington, D.C. 20008, U.S.A.

VIPONT, Charles. *See* **FOULDS,** Elfrida Vipont.

VIPONT, Charles. *See* **FOULDS,** Elfrida Vipont.

VISCOTT, David S(teven). American, b. 1938. Novels/Short stories. Psychiatry, Autobiography/Memoirs/Personal. Psychiatrist: Instr. in Psychiatry, Univ. Hosp., Boston, 1964–67. *Publs:* Labyrinth of Silence (novel), 1970; Feel Free (psychiatry), 1971; Winning (psychiatry), 1972; The Making of a Psychiatrist (autobiography), 1973; Dorchester Boy (autobiography), 1973; How to Live with Another Person, 1974; (with Jonah Kalb) What Every Kid Should Know, 1976; The Language of Feelings, 1976; Risking, 1978; The Viscott Method, 1984; Taking Care of Business, 1985; I Love You, Let's Work It Out, 1987. Add: c/o Pocket Books, 1230 Ave. of the Americas, New York, N.Y. 10020, U.S.A.

VITA-FINZI, Claudio. British, b. 1936. Earth sciences. Lectr., Univ. Coll., London, since 1964. Research Fellow, St. John's Coll., Cambridge, 1961–64. *Publs:* (with J.J.E. Aarons) The Useless Land, 1960; The Mediterranean Valleys, 1969; Recent Earth History, 1973; Archaeological Sites in Their Setting, 1978; Recent Earth Movements, 1986. Add: Univ. Coll., Gower St., London WC1E 6BT, England.

VITAL, David. Israeli, b. 1927. History (poltical and international), Politics/Government. Prof. of Political Science, since 1977, and Nahum Goldman Prof. of Diplomacy, since 1983, Tel Aviv Univ; Prof. of History and Khitznick Prof. of Jewish Civilization, Northwestern Univ., Evanston, since 1988. In govt. service, Israel, 1954–66; Lectr. in Intnl. Relations, Univ. of Sussex, Brighton, 1966–68; Assoc. Prof., and subsequently Prof. of Political Science, Bar-Ilan Univ., Ramat-Gan, Israel, 1968–72; Prof., Haifa Univ., 1972–77. *Publs:* The Inequality of States: A Study of the Small Power in International Relations, 1967; The Making of British Foreign Policy, 1968; The Survival of Small States: Studies in Small Power/Great Power Conflict, 1971; Medinot Ketanot Be-Mivham Ha-Kiyum, 1972; The Origins of Zionism, 1975; Zionism: The Formative Years, 1982; Zionism: The Crucial Phase 1987. Add: Dept. of History, Northwestern Univ., Evanston, Ill. 60208, U.S.A.

VITEK, Donna. Has also written as Donna Alexander. American. Historical/Romance. *Publs:* (as Donna Alexander) Red Roses, White Lilies, 1979; (as Donna Alexander) No Turning Back, 1979; (as Donna Alexander) In from the Storm, 1979; A Different Dream, 1980; Promises from the Past, 1981; Showers of Sunlight, 1981; Veil of Gold, 1981; Where the Heart Is, 1981; Valaquez Bride, 1982; A Game of Chance, 1982; Garden of the Moongate, 1982; Sweet Surrender, 1982; Morning Always Comes, 1982; Passion's Price, 1983; Blue Mist of Morning, 1983; Dangerous Embrace, 1983; No Promise Given, 1983; Warmed By the Fire, 1983; Never Look Back, 1983; An Unforgettable Caress, 1984; Breaking the Rules, 1984; Asking for Trouble, 1984; Thrill of the Chase, 1985; Deep in the Heart, 1985; Players in the Shadows, 1985; One Step Ahead, 1985; Best-Kept Secret, 1985; Dream Maker, 1986; Playing with Fire, 1986; Morning Glory, 1986; Laying Down the Law, 1986; First-Class Male, 1987; Adventure with a Stranger, 1987. Add: c/o Dell Publishing, 666 Fifth Ave., New York, N.Y. 10103, U.S.A.

VITERZOVIC, T. *See* **KUEHNELT-LEDDIHN,** Erik.

VIVANTE, Arturo. American (b. Italian), b. 1923. Novels/Short stories. Practised medicine in Rome until 1958; thereafter a full-time writer. Writer-in-Residence, Bennington Coll., Vermont, since 1980. Writer-in-Residence: Univ. of North Carolina, Greensboro, 1968–69, Boston Univ., 1969–70, Purdue Univ., 1972–74, Brandeis Univ., Waltham, Mass., 1976, Univ. of Michigan, Ann Arbor, 1977, Univ. of Iowa, Iowa City, 1977, Univ. of Texas at El Paso, 1977–78, and Univ. of Idaho, 1979–80. *Publs:* Poesie (verse), 1951; A Goodly Babe (novel), 1966; The French Girls of Killini (short stories), 1967; Doctor Giovanni (novel), 1969; Imagining Stories, 1975; Run to the Waterfall (short stories), 1979; (trans.) Essays on Art and Ontology, by Leone Vivante, 1980; Writing Fiction, 1980, (trans.) Poems: Giacomo Leopardi, 1988. Add: P.O. Box 3005, Wellfleet, Mass. 02667, U.S.A.

VOCKLER, John Charles. Australian, b. 1924. Theology/Religion. Ordained Anglican priest, 1948; Vice-Warden of St. John's Coll., Univ. of Queensland, 1950–53; Asst. Priest, Cathedral of St. John the Divine, NYC, 1954; Fellow and Tutor, Gen. Theological Seminary, NYC, 1954–56; Priest-in-Charge, St. Stephen's, NYC, 1956; Asst. Priest, Parish of Singleton, N.S.W., Australia, 1956–59; Lectr. in Theology, St. John's Theological Coll., Morpeth, N.S.W., 1956–59; Titular Bishop of Mt. Gambier and Asst. Bishop of Adelaide, 1959–62; Bishop of Polynesia, 1962–68; entered Soc. of St. Francis, 1969; Chaplain, to Third Order, Soc. of St. Francis, European Province, 1972–74; Guardian, Friary of St. Francis, Brisbane, 1975–77, and Islington, N.S.W., 1978–79; Warden, Community of St. Clare, Newcastle, N.S.W., 1975–80, and Soc. of Sacred Advent, 1976–80; Minister Provincial, Pacific Province, Soc. of St. Francis, 1976–81; Acting Warden, 1981–82, and Warden, 1982–83, Poor Clares of Reparation, Mt. Sinai, N.Y. *Publs:* Can Anglicans Believe Anything: The Nature and Spirit of Anglicanism, 1961; Forward Day by Day, 1962; (ed.) Believing in God, by M.L. Yates, 1962, 1983; One Man's Journey, 1972; St. Francis: Franciscanism and the Society of St. Francis, 1980. Add: St. Elizabeth's Friary, 1474 Boshwick Ave., Brooklyn, N.Y. 11207, U.S.A.

VOIGT, Cynthia. American, b. 1942. Children's Fiction. *Publs:* Homecoming, 1981; Tell Me If the Lovers Are Losers, 1982; Dicey's Song, 1982 (Newbery Medal); The Callender Papers, 1983; A Solitary Blue, 1983; Building Blocks, 1984; The Runner, 1985; Jackaroo, 1985; Izzy, Willy-Nilly, 1986; Come a Stranger, 1986; Stories about Rosie, 1986; Sons from Afar, 1987; Tree by Leaf, 1988; Seventeen Against the Dealer, 1989. Add: c/o Atheneum, 866 Third Ave., New York, N.Y. 10022, U.S.A.

VOIGT, Milton. American, b. 1924. Literature. Prof. of English Univ. of Utah, Salt Lake City, since 1960 (Dean, Coll. of Letters and Science, 1967–70; Dept. Chmn., 1971–75). Instr., Univ. of Idaho, Moscow, 1952–55, and Univ. of Kentucky, Lexington, 1956–60. *Publs:* Swift and the Twentieth Century. Add: Dept. of English, Univ. of Utah, Salt Lake City, Utah 84112, U.S.A.

VOITLE, Robert (Brown). American, b. 1919. Literature, Biography. Prof. Emeritus, Univ. of North Carolina, Chapel Hill (appointed Prof. of English, 1964). *Publs:* Samuel Johnson, the Moralist, 1961; The Third Earl of Shaftesbury, 1984. Add: 307 Country Club Rd., Chapel Hill, N.C. 27514, U.S.A.

VONDRA, Josef Gert. Australian, b. 1941. Novels/Short stories, Cookery/Gastronomy/Wine, Travel/Exploration/Adventure. Sub-Ed., Radio Australia, ABC, 1966–67. *Publs:* Timor Journey, 1968; The Other China, 1969; Hong Kong: City Without a Country, 1969; A Guide to

Australian Cheese, 1970; Paul Zwilling, 1974. Add: P.O. Box 5, South Yarra, Vic., Australia 3141.

von GLAHN, Gerhard Ernst. American, b. 1911. International relations/Current affairs. Emeritus Prof. of Political Science, Univ. of Minnesota, Duluth, since 1979; (Assoc. Prof., 1947–50; Prof. and Dept. Head, 1950–79). Instr., Political Science, Western Reserve Univ., Cleveland, Ohio, 1939–41; Instr. in Political Science, Duluth State Teachers Coll., 1941–47. *Publs:* The Occupation of Enemy Territory, 1957; Law Among Nations, 1965, 5th ed. 1986. Add: 2105 Vermilion Rd., Duluth, Minn. 55803, U.S.A.

von HOFFMAN, Nicholas. American, b. 1929. Social commentary, Biography. Journalist: staff member and columnist for the Washington Post, since 1966. Assoc. Dir., Industrial Area Foundn., Chicago, 1954–63; staff member, Chicago Daily News, 1963–66. *Publs:* Mississippi Notebook, 1964; The Multiversity: A Personal Report of What Happens to Today's Students at American Universities, 1966; We Are the People Our Parents Warned Us Against, 1968; Two, Three, Many More: A Novel, 1969; Left at the Post, 1970; (with Garry Trudeau) The Fireside Watergate, 1973; (with Garry Trudeau) Tales from the Margaret Mead Taproom: The Compleat Gonzo Governship of Doonesbury's Uncle Duke, 1976; Make-Believe Presidents: Illusions of Power from McKinley to Carter, 1978; Organized Crimes, 1987; Citizen Cohn: The Life and Times of Roy Cohn, 1988. Add: c/o Doubleday, 666 Fifth Ave., New York, N.Y. 10103, U.S.A.

VON LAUE, Theodore H. American, b. 1916. History. Emeritus Jacob and Frances Hiatt Prof. of European History, Clark Univ., Worcester, Mass., since 1983 (Jacob and Frances Hiatt Prof. 1970–83). Prof. of History, Univ. of California, Riverside, 1955–64, and Washington Univ. St. Louis, Mo., 1964–70. *Publs:* Leopold Ranke—The Formative Years, 1950; Sergie Witte and the Industrilization of Russia, 1963; Why Lenin?, Why Stalin? 1964; The Golbal City, 1969; The World Revolution of Westernization: The Twentieth Century in Global Persepective, 1987. Add: Clark Univ. Worcester, Mass. 01610, U.S.A.

von LEYDEN, Wolfgang (Marius). British, b. 1911. Philosophy, Politics/Government. Reader in Philosophy, Univ, Univ. of Durham, since 1962 (Lectr., 1946–56; Sr. Lectr., 1956–62). Visiting Prof., New York State Univ., Binghamton, 1966–67; Distinguished Visiting Scholar, London Sch. of Economics, 1978–81. *Publs:* (ed. and trans.) John Locke: Essays on the Law of Nature, 1954, 3rd ed., 1988; Remembering, 1961; Seventeenth Century Metaphysics, 1968; Hobbes and Locke: The Politics of Freedom and Obligation, 1981; Aristotle on Equality and Justice, 1985. Add: 5 Pimlico, Durham DH1 4QW, England.

von MEHREN, Arthur Taylor. American, b. 1922. Law. Story Prof. of Law, Harvard Univ. Cambridge Mass., since 1976 (joined faculty, 1946). *Publs:* (with J. Gordley) The Civil Law System: An Introduction to the Comparative Study of Law, 1951, 1977; (ed. with K. H. Nadelmann and J. N. Hazard) XXth Century Comparative and Conflicts Law, 1961; (ed.) Law in Japan: The Legal Order in a Changing Society, 1963; (with D. Trautman) The Law of Multistate Problems: Cases and Materials on Conflicts of Laws, 1965; Law in the United States: A General and Comparative View, 1988. Add: Harvard Law Sch., Langdell Hall, Cambridge, Mass. 02138, U.S.A.

VONNEGUT, Kurt, Jr. American, b. 1922. Novels/Short stories, Plays/ Screenplays, Essays. Teacher, Hopefield Sch., Sandwich, Mass., since 1965; Vice-Pres., P.E.N. American Center, since 1974. Visiting Lectr., Writers Workshop, Univ. of Iowa, Iowa City, 1965–67, and Harvard Univ., Cambridge, Mass., 1970–71. *Publs:* Player Piano, 1952; The Sirens of Titan, 1959; Canary in a Cathouse (short stories), 1961; Mother Night, 1961; Cat's Cradle, 1963; God Bless You, Mr. Rosewater: or, Pearls Before Swine, 1965; Welcome to the Monkey House: A Collection of Short Works, 1968, Slaughterhouse Five: or, The Children's Crusade: A Duty-Dance with Death, by Kurt Vonnegut, Jr. A Fourth-Generation German-American Now Living in Easy Circumstances on Cape Code (and Smoking Too Much) Who, as an American Infantry Scout Hors de Combat, as Prisoner of War, Witnessed the Fire-Bombing of Dresden, Germany, the Florence of the Elbe, a Long Time Ago, and Survived to Tell the Tale: This is a Novel Somewhat in the Telegraphic Schizophrenic Manner of Tales of the Planet Trakfanadire, Where the Flying Saucers Come From, 1969; Happy Birthday, Wanda June (play), 1970; Between Time and Timbuktu: or, Prometheus 5: A Space Fantasy (play), 1972; The Vonnegut Statement, 1973; Breakfast of Champions: or Goobye, Blue Monday, 21973; Wampeters, Foma, and Granfallons: Opinions, 1974;

Slapstic, 1976; Jailbird, 1979; Deadeye Dick, 1982; Galapagos, 1985, Bluebird, 1988. Add: Scudder's Lane, West Barnstable, Mass. 02668, U.S.A.

VOORHEES, Richard J. American, b. 1916. Literature, Essays. Prof. Emeritus of English, Purdue Univ., West Lafayette, Ind., since 1982 (instr., 1946–54; Asst. Prof., 1954–60; Assoc. Prof., 1960–64; Prof., 1964–82. *Publs:* The Paradox of George Orwell, 1961; P. G. Wodehouse, 1966. Add: 1700 Sheridan, West Lafayette, Ind. 47906, U.S.A.

VOTAW, Dow. American, b. 1920. Administration/Management, Business/Trade/Industry, Social commentary/phenomena. Prof. of Business Admin. Emeritus, Univ. of California, Berkeley, since 1948. Ed., with S.P. Sethi, Economic Institutions and Social Systems series for Prentice-Hall Inc. *Publs:* Modern Corporations, 1965; The Six-Legged Dog: Mattei and Eni, A Study in Power, 1965; Legal Aspects of Business Administration, 3rd ed. 1969; (with S.P. Sethi) The Corporate Dilemma, 1973; (with E.M. Epstein) Rationality, Legitimacy, Responsibility: The Search for New Directions in Business and Society, 1978. Add: 321

Camino al Mar, La Selva Beach, Calif. 95076, U.S.A.

VROOM, Victor H. American, b. 1932. Administration/Management, Psychology. Prof. of Psychology, and John G. Searle Prof., of Organisation and Management, Yale Univ. Sch. of Org. and Mgmt., New Haven, Conn., since 1972. Asst. Study Dir., Inst. for Social Research, Univ. of Michigan, Ann Arbor, 1955–58; Asst. Prof. of Psychology, Univ. of Pennsylvania, Philadelphia, 1960–63; Assoc. Prof. Carnegie Inst. of Technology, Pittsburgh, 1963–66; Prof. of Psychology and Industrial Admin., Carnegie-Mellon Univ., Pittsburgh, 1966–72 (formerly Carnegie Inst.). *Publs:* Some Personality Determinants of the Effects of Participation, 1960; (co-author) The Productivity of Work Groups, 1963; Work and Motivation, 1964; Motivation in Management, 1965; (ed.) Methods of Organization Research, 1967; (co-ed.) The Management of Motivation, 1970; (co-author) Leadership and Decision-Making, 1973; The New Leadership, 1988. Add: Sch. of Org. and Mgmt. Yale Univ., 56 Hilhouse Ave., New Haven, Conn. 06520, U.S.A.

W

WAAGENAAR, Sam. American, b. 1908. History, Travel/Exploration/Adventure, Biography. Freelance writer and photographer. European Dir. of Public Relations, Metro-Goldwyn-Meyer, 1930–35; Corresp., Netherlands News Agency, 1935–40; and Intnl. News Service, 1944–46. *Publs:* Asia, 1957; Countries of the Red Sea, 1957; Children of the World, 1958; Women of Rome, 1959; Women of Israel, 1960; The Little Five, 1960; Children of Israel, 1961; The Murder of Mata Hari (in U.S. as Mata Hari), 1964; The Pope's Jews, 1974. Add: 85 Via Luigi Bodio, 00191 Rome, Italy.

WABER, Bernard. American, b. 1924. Children's fiction. Graphic Designer, People mag., NYC, since 1974. Commercial Artist, Conde Nast Publications, and Seventeen mag., NYC, 1952–54; Graphic Designer, Life mag., NYC, 1955–72. *Publs:* Lorenzo, 1961; The House on East 88th Street (in U.K. as Welcome, Lyle), 1962; Rich Cat, Poor Cat, 1963; How to Go About Laying an Egg, 1963; Just Like Abraham Lincoln, 1965; Lyle, Lyle, Crocodile, 1965; Lyle and the Birthday Party, 1966; "You Look Ridiculous", Said the Rhinoceros to the Hippopotamus, 1966; An Anteater Named Arthur, 1967; Cheese, 1967; A Rose for Mr. Bloom, 1968; Loveable Lyle, 1969; A Firely Named Torchy, 1970; Nobody Is Perfick, 1971; Ira Sleeps Over, 1972; Lyle Finds His Mother 1974; I Was All Thumbs, 1975; But Names Will Never Hurt Me, 1976; Goodbye, Funny Dumpy-Lumpy, 1977; Mice on My Mind, 1977; The Snake, 1978; You're a Little Kid with a Big Heart, 1980; Dear Hildegarde, 1980; Bernard, 1982; Funny, Funny Lyle, 1987; Ira Says Goodbye, 1988. Add: c/o Houghton Mifflin Co., 2 Park St., Boston, Mass. 02107, U.S.A.

WACHTER, Oralee (Roberts). American, b. 1935. Children's non-fiction, Education, Medicine/Health, Sex. Film Dir.: Pres. and Dir., O.D.N. Productions, Inc., NYC, since 1974. Gen. Education Dir. at a day sch., San Francisco, 1965–67; Extension Instr., Univ. of California, Berkeley, 1969–72; Communications specialist for public school system, Berkeley, 1969–75; Instr., California Inst. for Women, Frontera, 1975. *Publs:* Acquaintance Rape Prevention, 1978; Spouse Abuse Handbook, 1981; The Abusive Partner, 1982; Talking Helps, 1983; No More Secrets for Me, 1983; Close to Home, 1986; Sex, Drugs, and AIDS, 1987. Add: 74 Varick St., New York, N.Y. 10013, U.S.A.

WADDELL, Evelyn (Lyn) Margaret. Writes as Lyn Cook. Canadian, b. 1918. Children's fiction. Librarian, Scarborough Public Libraries, since 1962. *Publs:* The Bells on Finland Stret, 1950; The Little Magic Fiddler, 1951; Rebel on the Trail, 1953; Jady and the General, 1955; Pegeen and the Pilgrim, 1957; The Road to Kip's Cove, 1961; Samantha's Secret Room, 1963; The Brownie Handbook for Canada, 1965; The Secret of Willow Castle, 1966; The Magical Miss Mittens, 1970; Toys from the Sky (picture story book), 1972; Jolly Jean-Pierre (picture story book), 1973, If I Were All These (picture story book), 1974; A Treasury for Tony, 1981; The Magic Pony (picture story book), 1981; Sea Dreams (picture story book), 1981. Add: 72 Cedarbrae Blvd., Scarborough, Ont. M1J 2K5, Canada.

WADDINGTON, Miriam. Canadian, b. 1917. Poetry, Literature, Biography, Essays. Member of English Dept. since 1964, and currently Prof. of Literature, York Univ., Toronto. Advisory Ed., Otto Rank Assn. Journal. Caseworker, Jewish Family Service, Toronto, 1942–44, 1957–60, and Philadelphia Child Guidance Clinic, 1944–46; Lectr. and Supvr. McGill Sch. of Social Work, Montreal, 1946–49; Caseworker, Montreal Children's Hosp. Speech Clinic, 1950–52, and John Howard Soc., 1955–57; Supvr., North York Family Service, 1960–62. *Publs:* Green World,

1945; The Second Silence, 1955; The Season's Lovers, 1958; The Glass Trumpet, 1966; Call Them Canadians, 1968; Say Yes, 1969; A.M. Klein, 1970; Dream Telescope, 1972; Driving Home: Poems New and Selected, 1972; (ed.) John Sutherland, 1973; (ed.) The Collected Poems of A.M. Klein, 1974; The Price of Gold, 1976; Mister Never, 1978; The Visitants (poems), 1981; Summer at Lonely Beach: Selected Short Stories, 1982; Collected Poems, 1986; Apartment Seven: Essays New and Selected, 1989. Add: 32 Yewfield Cres., Don Mills, Ont. M3B 2Y6, Canada.

WADDINGTON, Raymond B(ruce). American, b. 1935. Literature. Literary critic, particularly of 16th and 17th century English poetry. Prof. of English, Univ. of California at Davis, since 1982. Member, Editorial Bd., The Sixteenth Century Journal, since 1974. Instr. in English, Univ. of Houston, 1961–62; Asst. Prof. of English, Univ. of Kansas, Lawrence, 1962–65; Asst. Prof., Assoc. Prof., and Prof. of English, Univ. of Wisconsin, Madison, 1966–82. *Publs:* (ed. with T.O. Sloan) The Rhetoric of Renaissance Poetry, 1974; The Mind's Empire: Myth and Form in George Chapman's Narrative Poems, 1974; (ed. with C.A. Patrides) The Age of Milton: Backgrounds to Seventeenth Century Literature, 1980. Add: 39 Pershing Ave., Woodland, Calif. 95695, U.S.A.

WADDINGTON-FEATHER, John Joseph. British, b. 1933. Children's fiction, Plays, Poetry, History, Literature. Chaplain, Prestfeld Sch., since 1985. Ordained into Anglican Holy Orders, 1977; Auxiliary Chaplain, Shrewsbury Prison. Co-Ed., Poetry and Audience mag., 1953–54; Ed., Summer Bulletin (Yorkshire Dialect Soc.), 1963–74; Member, Editorial Bd., Platform mag., 1967–69. *Publs:* A Collection of Poems, 1963; (ed.) Northern Aspect, 1964; Of Mills, Moors and Men, 1966; Leeds, the Heart of Yorkshire, 1967, 3rd ed. 1985; Century of Model-Village Schooling, 1958; Yorkshire Dialect, 1970, 3rd ed. 1980; (co-ed.) Swing Back, 1971; Garlic Lane, 1970; Easy Street, 1973; (co-ed.) Ipso Facto, 1975; One Man's Road, 1977; Six More Characters in Seaqrch of an Author (play), 1978; Quill's Adventures in the Great Beyond [Wasteland; Grozzieland] (for children), 3 vols., 1980–88; Tall Tales from Yukon, 1984; Khartoum Trilogy and Other Poems, 1985. Add: Fair View, Old Coppice, Lyth Bank, Shrewsbury SY3 0BW, England.

WADDY, Charis. British, b. 1909. Area studies, History, Theology/Religion, Women. *Publs:* Baalbek Caravans, 1967; The Muslim Mind, 1976, 1982; Women in Muslim History, 1980. Add: 12 Norham Rd., Oxford OX2 6SF, England.

WADDY, Lawrence Heber. American, b. 1914. Plays/Screenplays, History. Asst., Saint James-by-the-Sea Episcopal Church, La Jolla, Calif. Chaplain, Winchester Coll., Hants., 1938–42, 1946–49, and Royal Navy, 1942–46; Headmaster, Tonbridge Sch., Kent, 1949–62; Hon. Canon, Diocese of Rochester, 1961–62; Lectr. in Classics, Univ. of Calif., San Diego, 1969–80. *Publs:* Pax Romana and World Peace, 1950; The Prodigan Son, 1963; The Bible as Drama, 1974; Faith of Our Fathers, 1976; Symphony, 1977; Drama in Worship, 1978; Mayor's Race, 1980; A Parish by the Sea, 1988. Add: 5910 Camino de la Costa, La Jolla, Calif. 92037, U.S.A.

WADE, Alan. *See* VANCE, Jack.

WADE, David. British b. 1929. Plays/Screenplays. Radio Critic, The Times, London, since 1967. Radio Critic, The Listener, London, 1965–67. *Publs:* Trying to Connect You; The Cooker; The Guthrie Process; The Gold Spinners; Three Blows in Anger; The Ogden File; The

Magician's Heart; The Carpet Maker of Samarkand; The Nightingale; Summer of '39; The Facts of Life; A Rather Nasty Crack; On Detachment; David Wade Collection, 1986. Add: c/o Eakin Press, P.O. Box 23069, Austin, Tex. 78735, U.S.A.

WADE, Jennifer. *See* **WEHEN**, Joy De Weese.

WADE, Mason. American, b. 1913. History, Biography/Public Affairs Officer, U.S. Embassy, Ottawa, 1951–53; Dir., Canadian Studies Prog., Univ. of Rochester, N.Y., 1955–65; Sr. Historian, Univ. of Western Ontario, London, 1965–72. Pres. Canadian Historical Assn., 1965. *Publs:* Margaret Fuller, 1940; (ed.) Selected Writings of Margaret Fuller, 1942; Francis Parkman, 1943; (ed.) Francis Parkman's Oregon Trail, 1943; French-Canadian Outlook, 1946; (ed.) Journal of Francis Parkman, 1947; (co-author) Essays on Contemporary Quebec, 1953; French Canadians, 1760-1945, 1955; (co-author) Our Living Traditions, 1957, vols. I and V, 1965; (co-author) Culture of Contemporary Canada, 1957; (ed.) Canadian Dualism, 1960; (co-author) United States and World Today, 1961; (co-author) Tradition, Values, and Socio-Economic Development, 1961; (co-author) United States and Canada, 1964; French Canadian, 1760-1967, 1968; (ed.) Regionalism in the Canadian Community, 1969; (ed.) International Megalopolis, 1969; (co-author) Attitudes of Colonial Powers Towards American Indian, 1970; (co-author) Quebec-Boston, 1980. Add: R.R.P2, Cornish, N.H. 03745, U.S.A.

WADE, Robert. Also writes as Wade Miller, Will Daemer, Whit Masterson, and Dale Wilmer; wrote with Bill Miller, under those pseudonyms, until Miller's death in 1961. American, b. 1920. Mystery/Crime/Suspense. *Publs:* (as Wade Miller) Deadly Weapon, 1946; (as Wade Miller) Guilty Bystander, 1947; (as Bob Wade and Bill Miller) Pop Goes the Queen, 1947 (in U.K. as Murder—Queen High, 1958); (as Wade Miller) Uneasy Street, 1948; (as Wade Miller) Devil on Two Sticks, 1949 (in U.S. paperback, Killer's Choice, 1950; (as Wade Miller) Calamity Fair, 1950; (as Wade Miller) Devil May Care, 1950; (as Will Daemer) The Case of the Lonely Lovers, 1951; (as Wade Miller) The Killer, 1951; (as Wade Miller) Shoot to Kill, 1951; (as Wade Miller) The Tiger's Wife, 1951; (as Dale Wilmer) Memo for Murder, 1951; (as Wade Miller) Branded Woman, 1952; (as Wade Miller) The Big Guy, 1953; (as Wade Miller) South of the Sun, 1953; (as Dale Wilmer) Deal Fall, 1954; (as Dale Wilmer) Jungle Heat, 1954; (as Wade Miller) Mad Baxter, 1955; (as Whit Masterson) All Through the Night, 1955 (in U.S. paperback, A Cry in the Night, 1956); (as Whit Masterson) Dead, She Was Beautiful, 1955; (as Wade Miller) Kiss Her Goodbye, 1956; (as Whit Masterson) Badge of Evil, 1956 (in U.S. paperback, Touch of Evil, 1958); (as Whit Masterson) A Shadow in the Wild, 1957; (as Wade Miller) Kitten with a Whip, 1959; (as Wade Miller) Sinner Take All, 1960; (as Whit Masterson) A Hammer in His Hand, 1960; (as Wade Miller) Nightmare Cruise (in U.K. as The Sargasso People), 1961; (as Whit Masterson) Evil Come, Evil Go, 1961; (as Wade Miller) The Girl from Midnight, 1962; (as Whit Masterson) 711—Officer Needs Help, 1965 (in U.K. as A Killer with a Badge, 1966; in U.S. paperback, Warning Shot, 1967); (as Robert Wade) The Stroke of Seven, 1965; (as Whit Masterson) Play Like You're Dead, 1967; (as Whit Masterson) The Last One Kills, 1969; (as Robert Wade) Knave of Eagles, 1969; (as Whit Masterson) The Death of Me Yet, 1970; (as Whit Masterson) The Gravy Train, 1971 (in U.S. paperback, The Great Train HiJack, 1976); (as Whit Masterson) Why She Cries, I Do Not Know, 1972; (as Whit Masterson) The Undertaker Wind, 1973; (as Whit Mastersons) The Man with Two Clocks, 1974; (as Whit Masterson) Hunter of the Blood, 1977; (as Whit Masterson) The Slow Gallows, 1979. Add: c/o Dodd Mead, 71 Fifth Ave., New York, N.Y. 10003, U.S.A.

WADE, Sir (Henry) William (Rawson). British, b. 1918. Law. Called to the Bar, Lincoln's Inn, London, 1946; Hon. Bencher, 1964. Fellow of Trinity Coll., 1946–61, Lectr., 1947, and Reader, 1959, Cambridge Univ.; Prof. of English Law, Oxford Univ., 1961–76. Master of Gonville and Caius Coll., Cambridge 1976–88; Rouse Ball Prof. of English Law, Cambridge Univ., 1978–82. *Publs:* (with Megarry) The Law of Real Property, 1957, 5th ed. 1984; Administrative Law, 1961, 6th ed., 1988; Towards Administrative Justice, 1963; (with Schwartz) Legal Control of Govern-ment 1972; Constitutional Fundamentals, 1980. Add: Master's Lodge, Caius Coll., Cambridge, England.

WADIA, Maneck S. Indian, b. 1931. Administration/Management Anthropology. Pres., Wadia Assocs., Management and Personal Consultants, since 1971. Asst. Prof. of Mgmt., Indiana Univ., 1958–60; Ford Foundn. Fellow, Administrative Science Center, Univ. of Pittsburgh, Pa., 1960–61; Member of the faculty, Grad. Sch. of Business, 1961–65, Research Assoc., Intnl. Center for the Advancement of Mgmt. Education,

1961–64, and Faculty Resident, 1964–65, Stanford Univ., Calif. *Publs:* The Nature and Scope of Management, 1966; (with H.W. Boyd) Marketing Management: Cases from Emerging Countries, 1966; Management and the Behavioral Sciences, 1968; Cases in International Business, 1970; Reflections of Culture. Add: 1660 Luneta Dr., Del Mar, Calif. 92014, U.S.A.

WAGENKNECHT, Edward. American, b. 1900. History, Literature, Biography. Prof. of English Emeritus, Boston Univ., Mass., since 1965 (Prof., 1947–65; Ed., Boston Univ., Studies in English, 1954–57). *Publs:* more than 60 books including—Cavalcade of the English Novel, 1943; (ed.) The Fireside Book of Christmas Stories, 1945; Cavalcade of the American Novel, 1952; The Movies in the Age of Innocence, 1962; Edgar Allan Poe: The Man Behind the Legend, 1963; Seven Daughters of the Theater, 1964; The Man Charles Dickens, rev. ed. 1966; Henry Wadsworth Longfellow: Portrait of an American Humanist, 1966; Mark Twain, the Man and His Work, rev. ed. 1967; As Far as Yesterday, 1968; Ralph Waldo Emerson: Portrait of a Balanced Soul, 1974; (ed.) The Letters of James Branch Cabell, 1975; Eve and Henry James: Portraits of Women and Girls in His Fiction, 1978; Henry David Thoreau: What Manner of Man, 1981; American Profile 1900-1909, 1982; Gamaliel Bradford, 1982; The Novels of Henry James, 1983; Daughters of the Covenant, 1983; The Tales of Henry James, 1984; Henry Wadsworth Longfellow: His Poetry and Prose, 1986; Stars of the Silents, 1987; Nathaniel Hawthorne: The Man, His Tales, and Romances, 1989. Add: 233 Otis St., West Newton, Mass. 02165, U.S.A.

WAGNER, (Sir) Anthony (Richard). British, b. 1908. Genealogy/Heraldry. Joint Registrar of the Court of Chivalry, since 1954; Clarenceaux King of Arms since 1978; Ed., Soc. of Antiquaries Dictionary of British Arms, since 1940. Portcullis Pursuivant, 1931–43, and Ministry of Town and Country Planning, 1943–46; Private Secty. to Minister, 1944–45; Secty., Order of the Garter, 1952–61; Registrar of Coll. of Arms, 1953–60; Genealogist of the Order of the Bath, 1961–72, and of the Order of St. John, 1961–75; Knight Principal, Imperial Soc. of Knights Bachelor, 1962–82; Pres., Chelsea Soc., London, 1967–73; Master of the Vintners Co., 1973; Dir., Heralds' Museum, Tower of London, 1978–82. *Publs:* (compiler) Catalogue of the Heralds' Commemorative Exhibition 1934, 1936; Historic Heraldry of Britain, 1939, 3rd ed. 1972; Heralds and Heraldry in the Middle Ages, 1939; Heraldry in England, 1946; Catalogue of English Mediaeval Rolls of Arms, 1950; The Records and Collections of the College of Arms, 1952; English Genealogy, 1960, 3rd ed. 1984; English Ancestry, 1961; Heralds of England, 1967; Pedigree and Progress, 1975; Heralds and Ancestors, 1978; Wagners of Brighton, 1983; How Lord Birkenhead Saved the Heralds, 1986; A Herald's World, 1988. Add: 68A Chelsea Sq., London SW3 6LD, England.

WAGNER, Diane. American, b. 1959. Criminology. Development writer, Filmation Assocs., Los Angeles. Member, Bd. of Dirs., Independent Writers of Southern California, 1984–87. *Publs:* Corpus Delicti, 1986. Add: c/o Peter Ginsberg, Curtis Brown Assocs., 10 Astor Place, New York, N.Y. 10003, U.S.A.

WAGNER, Jenny. Australian. Children's fiction. *Publs:* The Werewolf Knight, 1972; The Bunyip of Berkeley's Creek, 1973; Peter and the Zauberleaf, 1973; Aranea: A Story about a Spider, 1975; Hannibal, 1976; John Brown, Rose, and the Midnight Cat, 1977; The Nimbin, 1978; Jo-Jo and Mike, 1982; The Machine at the Heart of the World, 1983; (with Noela Hills) Goanna, 1987; The Windmill in the Paddock, 1988. Add: c/o Viking Publishers, P.O. Box 257, 487 Maroondah Highway, Ringwood, Victoria 3134, Australia.

WAGNER, Linda C. (Linda Wagner-Martin). American, b. 1936. Poetry, Literature. Prof. of English, Michigan State Univ., East Lansing, since 1968. Ed., The Centennial Review. Former teacher, Wayne State Univ., Detroit, and Bowling Green State Univ., Ohio. *Publs:* The Poems of William Carlos Williams, 1964; Denise Levertov, 1967; Intaglios, 1967; Phyllis McGinley, 1971; The Prose of William Carlos Williams, 1970; (ed.) William Faulkner: Four Decades of Criticism, 1973; (ed.) T.S. Eliot, 1974; (ed.) Ernest Hemingway: Five Decades of Criticism, 1974; Hemingway and Faulkner: Inventors/Masters, 1975; (with C. David Mead) Introducing Poems, 1976; Ernest Hemingway: A Reference Guide, 1977; Robert Frost: The Critical Heritage, 1977; Speaking Straight Ahead: Interviews with William Carlos Williams, 1977; William Carlos Williams: A Reference Guide, 1978; Des Passos: Artist as American, 1979; American Modern (essays), 1980; (ed.) Joyce Carol Oates: Critical Essays, 1979; Songs for Isadora, 1981; Ellen Glasgow: Beyond Convention, 1982; (ed.) Sylvia Plath: Critical Essays, 1984; Sylvia Plath: A Biography, 1987; (ed.) New Essays on The Sun Also Rises, 1987; (ed.) Ernest

Hemingway: Six Decades of Criticism, 1987. Add: Dept. of English, Michigan State Univ., East Lansing, Mich. 48823, U.S.A.

WAGNER, Rudolph Fred. American, b. 1921 Education, Psychology. Prof. of Psychology, Valdosta State Coll., Georgia, since 1983 (Assoc. Prof., 1977–83). Chief Psychologist, Richmond Public Schs., Virginia, 1959–77. *Publs:* Teaching Phonics with Success, 1969; Dyslexia and Your Child, 1971; Helping the Wordblind, 1976; Teaching Study Habits Today, 1977; Study Skills for Better Grades, rev. ed. 1978. Add: 2007 Pinecliff Dr., Valdosta, Ga. 31601, U.S.A.

WAGNER, Sharon Blythe. Also writes as Casey Stephens, M.E. Cooper, Carolyn Keene, and Ann Sheldon. American, b. 1936. Historical/Romance/Gothic, Westerns/Adventure, Children's fiction. *Publs:* Prairie Wind, 1967; Dude Ranch Mystery, 1968; Curse of Still Valley, 1969; Country of the Wolf, 1970; Maridu, 1970; Circle of Evil, 1971; Gypsy from Nowhere, 1971; Winter Evil, 1971; Moonwind, 1971; House of Shadows, 1972; (with B. Casey) Shadow on the Sun, 1972; Legacy of Loneliness, 1972; (with B. Casey) Cove in Darkness, 1972; Cry of the Cat, 1973; (with B. Casey) Haitian Legacy, 1973; (with B. Casey) Wind of Bitterness, 1973; Gypsy and Nimblefoot, 1973; Satan's Acres, 1974; Shades of Evil, 1974; Colors of Death, 1974; Havenhurst, 1974; Roses from Yesterday, 1974; Dark Waters of Death, 1974; Dark Side of Paradise, 1974; The Turquoise Talisman, 1974 (with B. Casey) Dark Sun at Midnight, 1974; (with B. Casey) Echoes of an Ancient, 1976; (with B. Casey) Bride of the Dullahan, 1976; Shadow of Her Eyes, 1979; Haunted Honeymoon, 1979; (with B. Casey) Love's Broken Promises, 1979; Gypsy and the Moonstone Stallion, 1980; House of Doom, House of Desire, 1980; Secrets, 1980; Embraces, 1980; (as Casey Stephens) Porterfield Legacy, 1980; (as Casey Stephens) The Shadows of Fieldcrest Manor, 1980; The Chadwicks of Arizona, 1981; Charade of Love, 1981; New Dreams for Kendra, 1982; Jacquelle's Shadow, 1982; Journey to Paradise, 1982; Tour of Love, 1983; Stranger's Who Love, 1983; Change partners, 1983; (as M.E. Cooper) Picture Perfect, 1986; House on the Hill, 1988; Rainbow Days, 1989; as Carloyn Keene—Kachina Doll Mystery, 1981; Elusive Heiress, 1982; Broken Anchor, 1983; Emerald-Eyed Cat, 1984; Campfire Stroies, 1984; Eskimo's Secret, 1985; as Ann Sheldon—Haunted Valley, 1982; Of the Old Sleigh, 1983; Emperor's Pony, 1983; Phantom of Dark Oaks, 1983. Add: 2137 East Bramble Ave., Mesa, Ariz. 85204, U.S.A.

WAGNER, Wenceslas J. American, b. 1917. Air/Space topics, Law, Politics/Government. Prof. of Law, Univ. of Detroit, since 1971. Visiting Prof. of Literature, Fordham Univ., Bronx, N.Y., 1948–49; Teaching Fellow in Comparative Law, Northwestern Univ., Sch. of Law, Chicago, 1950–53; Instr., 1953–54, Asst. Prof., 1954–57, Assoc. Prof., 1957–61, and Prof. of Law, 1961–62, Univ. of Notre Dame, Ind.; Prof. of Law, Univ. of Indiana, Bloomington, 1962–71. *Publs:* Les libertés de l'air, 1948; The Federal States and Their Judiciary, 1959; (ed. with J.N. Hazard) Legal Thought in the U.S. Under Contemporary Pressures, 1970; International Air Transportation as Affected by State Sovereignty, 1970; (ed. and contrib.) Polish Law Throughout the Ages; 1970. The Polish Law of Obligations, 1974; (ed. with J.N. Hazard) The Law of the U.S. in Social and Technological Change, 1974; (ed. with J.N. Hazard) The Law in the U.S. in the Bicentennial Era, 1978; (ed. with J.N. Hazard) Law in the U.S.A. for the 1980's, 1982; (ed. with J.N. Hazard) Law in the U.S.A. Faces Social and Scientific Change, 1986. Add: 651 E. Jefferson Ave., Detroit, Mich. 48226, U.S.A.

WAGONER, David (Russell). American, b. 1926. Novels/Short stories, Poetry. Prof. of English, Univ. of Washington, Seattle, since 1966 (Assoc. Prof., 1954–66). Ed., Poetry Northwest, Seattle, since 1966; Member, Bd. of Chancellors, Academy of American Poets, since 1978. Instr., De Pauw Univ., Greencastle, Ind., 1949–50, and Pennsylvania State Univ., University Park, 1950–54. Ed., Contemporary Poetry Series, Princeton Univ. Press, 1978–81. *Publs:* Dry Sun, Dry Wind (poetry), 1943; The Man in the Middle, 1954; Money, Money, Money, 1955; Rock, 1958; A Place to Stand (poetry), 1958; The Nesting Ground (poetry), 1963; The Escape Artist, 1965; Staying Alive (poetry), 1966; Baby, Come On Inside, 1968; New and Selected Poems, 1969; Working Against Time (poetry), 1970; Where Is My Wandering Boy Tonight?, 1970; Riverbed (poetry), 1972; (ed.) Straw for the Fire: From the Notebooks of Theodore Roethke, 1943-63, 1972; The Road to Many a Wonder, 1974; Sleeping in the Woods (poetry), 1974; Tracker, 1975; Travelling Light (poetry), 1976; Whole Hog, 1976; Collected Poems 1956-1976, 1976; Who Shall Be the Sun? (poetry), 1978; In Broken Country (poetry), 1979; The Hanging Garden (novel), 1980; Landfall (poetry), 1981; First Light (poetry), 1984; Through the Forest (poetry), 1987. Add: 1918 144th S.E., Mill Creek, Wash. 98012, U.S.A.

WAHL, Jan. American, b. 1933. Children's fiction, Plays/Screenplays, Poetry. Secty. to Isak Dinesen, Denmark, 1957–58. *Publs:* Paradise! Paradiseo! (play), 1954; Pleasant Fieldmouse, 1964; The Howards Go Sledding, 1964; Hello Elephant, 1964; The Beast Book (verse), 1964; Cabbage Moon, 1965; The Muffetumps: The Story of Four Dolls, 1966; Christmas in the Forest, 1967; Pocahontas in London, 1967; The Furious Flycycle, 1968; Push Kitty, 1968; Cobweb Castle, 1968; Rickety Rackety Rooster, 1968; Runaway Jonah and Other Tales, 1968; A Wolf of My Own, 1969; How the Children Stopped the Wars, 1969; The Fishermen, 1969; May Horses, 1969; The Norman Rockwell Storybook, 1969; The Prince Who Was a Fish, 1970; The Mulberry Tree, 1970; The Wonderful Kite, 1970; Doctor Rabbit, 1970; The Animals' Peace Day, 1970; Abe Lincoln's Beard, 1971; Anna Help Ginger, 1971; Crabapple Night, 1971; Margaret's Birthday, 1971; The Six Voyages of Pleasant Fieldmouse, 1971; Lorenzo Bear & Company, 1971; The Very Peculiar Tunnel, 1972; Magic Heart, 1972; Grandmother Told Me, 1972; Cristobal and the Witch, 1972; Juan Diego and the Lady, 1972; S.O.S. Bobomobile!, 1973; Crazy Brobobalou, 1973; The Five in the Forest, 1974; Pleasant Fieldmouse's Halloween Party, 1974; Mooga Mega Mekki, 1974; Jeremiah Knucklebones, 1974; The Muffletump Storybook, 1975; The Clumpets Go Sailing, 1975; The Bear, The Wolf, and the Mouse, 1975; The Screeching Door; or, What Happened at the Elephant Hotel, 1975; The Muffletumps' Christmas party, 1975; The Woman with the Eggs, 1975; Follow Me, Cried Bee, 1976; Great-Grandmother Cat Tales, 1976; Grandpa's Indian Summer, 1976; The Pleasant Fieldmouse Storybook, 1977; Doctor Rabbit's Foundling, 1977; Frankenstein's Dog, 1977; The Muffletumps' Halloween Scare, 1977; Pleasant Fieldmouse's Valentine Trick, 1977; Carrot Nose, 1978; Dracula's Cat, 1978; Jamie's Tiger, 1978; Youth's Magic Horn, 1978; Drakestail, 1978; Who Will Believe Tim Kitten?, 1978; The Teeny Tiny Witches, 1979; Sylvester Bear Overslept, 1979; Needle Noodle, 1979; Doctor Rabbit's Lost Scout, 1979; Old Hippo's Easter Egg, 1980; Button Eye's Orange, 1980; The Cucumber Princess, 1981; The Little Blind Goat, 1981; Grandpa Gus's Birthday Cake, 1981; Tiger Watch, 1982; The Pipkins Go Camping, 1982; Small One, 1983; Peter and the Troll Baby, 1983; More Room for the Pipkins, 1983; Humphrey's Bear, 1983; So Many Raccoons, 1985; The Toy Circus, 1986; Cheltenham's Party, 1985; Rabbits on Rollerskates, 1986; Let's Go Fishing, 1987; The Golden Christmas Tree, 1988; Tales of Fuzzy Mouse, 1988. Add: Aptdo. Postal 33, San Miguel Allende, Mexico.

WAIDSON, Herbert Morgan. British, b. 1916. Literature, Translations. Prof. of German, Univ. Coll. of Swansea, Univ. of Wales, 1960–83, now Emeritus. Lectr. to Sr.Lectr., Univ. of Hull, 1946–60. *Publs:* Jeremias Gotthelf: An Introduction to the Swiss Novelist, 1953; (ed.) Die schwarze Spinne, by J. Gotthelf, 1956; (trans.) The Black Spider, by J. Gotthelf, 1956; (ed.) German Short Stories 1945-1955, 1957; The Modern German Novel, 1959, as The Modern German Novel 1945-1965, 1971; (ed.) German Short Stories, 1900-1945, 1959; (ed.) German Short Stories 1955-1965, 1969; (ed.) Egmont, by Goethe, 1960; (trans.) Kindred by Choice, by Goethe, 1960; (ed.) Modern German Stories, 1961; (ed.) A History of the German Novelle, by E.K. Bennett, 1961; (ed. with G. Seidmann) Doktor Murkes gesammeltes Schweigen, by Böll, 1963; (ed. and trans.) Writings on Theatre and Drama, by F. Dürrenmatt, 1976; (trans.) Wilhelm Meister by Goethe, 1977-82; (trans.) Prophecies, by Paquet, 1983; (ed.) Anthology of Modern Swiss Literature, 1984. Add: 29 Myrtle Grove, Sketty, Swansea SA2 0SJ, Wales.

WAIN, John (Barrington). British, b. 1925. Novels/Short stories, Poetry, Literature. Lectr.in English, Univ. of Reading, Berks., 1947–55; First Holder, Fellowship in Creative Arts, Brasenose Coll., Oxford, 1971–72; Prof. of Poetry, Oxford Univ., 1973–78. *Publs:* Mixed Feelings, 1951; Hurry on Down (in U.S. as Born in Captivity), 1954; Living in the Present, 1955; (ed.) Interpretations: Essays on Twelve English Poems, 1955; A Word Carved on a Sill, 1956; Preliminary Essays, 1957; The Contenders, 1958; Gerard Manley Hopkins: An Idiom of Desperation, 1959; (ed.) International Literary Annual, 2 vols., 1959, 1960; A Travelling Woman, 1959; Nuncle and Other Stories, 1960; (ed.) Fanny Burney's Diary, 1960; Weep Before God: Poems, 1961; Strike the Father Dead, 1962; Sprightly Running: Part of an Autobiography, 1962; Essays on Literature and Ideas, 1963; (ed.) Anthology of Modern Poetry, 1963; The Living World of Shakespeare: A Playgoer's Guide, 1964; Wildtrack: A Poem, 1965; Death of the Hind Legs and Other Stories, 1966; (ed.) Selected Shorter Poems of Thomas Hardy, 1966; (ed.) The Dynasts, by Thomas Hardy, 1966; (ed.) Selected Shorter Stories of Thomas Hardy, 1966; The Smaller Sky, 1967; Arnold Bennett, 1967; (ed.) Shakespeare: Macbeth: A Casebook, 1968; Letters to Five Artists, 1969; A Winter in the Hills, 1970; The Life Guard, 1971; (ed.) Shakespeare: Othello: A Casebook, 1971; The Shape of Feng, 1972; A House for the Truth (critical essays), 1972; Samuel Johnson (in U.S. as Samuel Johnson: A Biography),

1974; Feng, 1975; Professing Poetry, 1977; (ed.) An Edmund Wilson Celebration, 1978; (ed.) Personal Choice (verse anthology), 1978; The Pardoner's Tale, 1978; King Caliban and Other stories, 1978; Poems 1949-1979, 1981; (ed.) Everyman's Book of English Verse, 1981; Lizzie's Floating Shop, 1981; Young Shoulders, 1982; (with K.K. Yung) Samuel Johnson 1709-84, 1984; Dear Shadows: Portraits from Memory, 1986; (ed) The Oxford Library of English Poetry, 3 vols., 1986; Open Spaces (poems), 1987; Where the Rivers Meet (novel), 1988. Add: c/o Century Hutchinson, 62-65 Chandos Pl., London WC2N 4NW, England.

WAINER, Cord. *See* **DEWEY,** Thomas B.

WAINWRIGHT, Geoffrey. British, b. 1939. Theology/Religion. Ordained Methodist Minister, since 1967; Prof. of Systematic Theology, Duke Univ., since 1983. Prof. of Systematic Theology, Protestant Faculty of Theology, Yaoundé, Cameroon, W. Africa, 1967–73; Lectr. in Systematic Theology, Queen's Coll., Birmingham, 1973–79; Roosevelt Prof. of Systematic Theology, Union Theological Seminary, NYC, 1979–83 Ed., Studio Liturgica, 1974–87. *Publs:* Christian Initiation, 1969; Eucharist and Eschatology, 1971, 1981; (co-ed.) The Study of Liturgy, 1978; Doxology, 1980; The Ecumenical Moment, 1983; (co-ed.) The Study of Spirituality, 1986; Geoffrey Wainright on Wesley and Calvin, 1987; (ed) Keeping the Faith: Essays to Mark the Centenary of Lux Mundi, 1988. add: The Divinity School, Duke Univ., Durham, N.C. 27706, U.S.A.

WAINWRIGHT, Gordon Ray. Also writes as Ray Gordon. British, b. 1938. Education Freelance Writer and Lectr., since 1987. Teacher of English, Manvers Sch., Nottingham, 1959–61; Asst. Lectr. in Liberal Studies, Coll. of Technology, Hull, 1961–65; Lectr. in Gen. Studies, Hebburn Technical Coll., Co. Durham, 1965–68; Head, Dept. of Liberal Studies, 1968–83, and Head of Communication and Industrial Development, 1983–85, Wearside Coll.; Mgr., Sunderland Open Learning, 1985–87. *Publs:* Efficiency in Reading, 1965; Towards Efficiency in Reading, 1968; Rapid Reading Made Simple, 1972; People and Communication, 1979; Report Writing, 1984; People and Communication: A Workbook, 1984; Teach Yourself Body Language, 1985; Teach Yourself Meetings and Committee Procedure, 1987. Add: 22 Hawes Ct., Seaburn Dene, Sunderland SR6 8NU, England.

WAINWRIGHT, Jeffrey. British, b. 1944. Poetry, Translations. Lectr., then Sr. Lectr. in English, Manchester Polytechnic, since 1973. Lectr. in American Literature, Univ. Coll. of Wales, Aberystwyth, 1967–72; Visiting Instr., Long Island Univ., New York, 1970–71. *Publs:* The Important Man, 1970; Heart's Desire, 1978; Selected Poems, 1985; (trans.) The Mystery of the Charity of Joan of Arc, by Charles Peguy, 1986; (trans) The Satin Slipper (play), by Paul Claudel, 1988. Add: 11 Hesketh Ave., Didsbury, Manchester M20 8QN, England.

WAINWRIGHT, John. Also writes as Jack Ripley. British, b. 1921. Mystery/Crime/Suspense, Autobiography/Memoirs/Personal. Police service, West Yorks., 1948–68. *Publs:* Death in a Sleeping City, 1965; Ten Steps to the Gallows, 1965; Evil Intent, 1966; The Crystalised Carbon Pig, 1966; Talent for Murder, 1967; The Worms Must Wait, 1967; Shall I Be a Policeman, 1967; Web of Silence, 1968; Edge of Extinction, 1968; The D rkening Glass, 1968; The Take-Over Men, 1969; The Big Tickle, 1969; Prynters Devil, 1970; Freeze Thy Blood Less Coldly, 1970; The Hard Hit, 1974; Kill the Girls and Make Them Cry, 1974; Landscape with Violence, 1975; Coppers Don't Cry, 1975; Acquital, 1976; Walther P. 38, 1976; Who Goes Next?, 1976; The Bastard, 1976; Pool of Tears, 1977; A Nest of Rats, 1977; Do Nothing till You Hear from Me, 1977; The Day of the Peppercorn Kill, 1977; The Jury People, 1978; Thief of Time, 1978; Death Certificate, 1978; Tail-End Charlie (memoirs), 1978; A Ripple of Murders, 1978; Braiwnash, 1979; Duty Elsewhere, 1979; Tension, 1979; The Reluctant Sleeper, 1979; Home Is the Hunter, and The Big Kayo, 1979; Take Murder..., 1979; The Eye of the Beholder, 1980; The Venus Fly Trap, 1980; Dominoes, 1980; Man of Law, 1980; A Kill of Small Consequence, 1980; The Tainted Man, 1981; All on a Summer's Day, 1981; An Urge for Justice, 1981; Blayde R.I.P., 1982; Anatomy of a Riot, 1982; The Distaff Factor, 1982; Their Evil Ways, 1983; Spiral Staircase, 1983; Heroes No More, 1983; Cul-de-Sac, 1984; The Forest, 1984; The Ride, 1984; Clouds of Guilt, 1985; All Through the Night, 1985; Portrait in Shadows, 1986; The Tenth Interview, 1986; Wainwright's Beat (memoirs), 1987; The Forgotten Murders, 1987; as Jack Ripley—Davis Doesn't Live Here Any More, 1971; The Pig Got Up and Slowly Walked Away, 1972; My Word You Should Have Seen Us, 1972; My God How the Money Rolls In, 1972. Add: c/o Macmillan & Co. Ltd., Little Essex St., London WC2R 3LF, England.

WAITE, Peter (Busby). Canadian, b. 1922. History. Prof. of History, Dalhousie Univ., Halifax, since 1961 (Lectr., 1951, Asst. Prof., 1955, Assoc. Prof., 1960, and Head of Dept., 1960–68). Pres., Canadian Historical Assn., 1968–69; Chmn., Humanities Research Council of Canada, 1968–70. *Publs:* The Life and Times of Confederation 1864-1867, 1962; (ed.) Debates on Confederations in the Province of Canada, 1963; (ed.) PreConfederation: Documents of Canadian History, 1965; (ed.) House of Commons Debates 1867-1868, 1968; Canada 1874-1896; Arduous Destiny, 1971; Confederation 1854-1867, 1972; John A. Macdonald: His Life and World, 1975; The Man from Halifax: Sir John Thompson, Prime Minister, 1985; Lord of Point Grey: N.A.M. MacKenzie 1894-1986, 1988. Add: 960 Ritchie Dr., Halifax, N.S., Canada.

WAKEFIELD, Dan. American, b. 1932. American, b. 1932. Social commentary/phenomena. Staff Writer, Nation mag., NYC, 1956–59; Visiting Lectr., Univ. of Massachusetts, Amherst, 1965–67; Visiting Lectr. in Journalism, Univ. of Illinois, 1968; Staff Member, Bread Loaf Writers Conference, 1966, 1968, 1970; Visiting Lectr. in English, Iowa Writers Workshop, Univ. of Iowa, 1972; Visiting Lectr. in English, Univ. of Mass. at Boston, 1981 (and 1965–67); Visiting Lectr. in Creative Writing, Emerson Coll., 1982–83. *Publs:* Island in the City, 1959; Revolt in the South, 1961; The Addict: An Anthology, 1963; Between the Lines, 1966; Supernation at Peace and War, 1968; Going All the Way, 1970; Starting Over, 1973; Home Free, 1977; James at 15 (TV series), 1977–78; The Seduction of Miss Leona (screenplay), 1980; Under the Apple Tree (novel), 1982; The Innocents Abroad, by Mark Twain (screenplay), 1983; Selling Out (novel), 1985; Returning: A Spiritual Journey, 1988. Add: c/o Doubleday, 666 Fifth Ave., New York, N.Y. 10103, U.S.A.

WAKEMAN, Evans. *See* **WAKEMAN,** Frederic Evans, Jr.

WAKEMAN, Frederic Evans, Jr. Also writes as Evans Wakeman. American, b. 1937. Novels/Short stories, History, International relations/ Current affairs, Politics/Government. Prof. of Chinese History, Univ. of California, Berkeley, since 1965 (Chmn., Center for Chinese Studies, 1972–79). Pres., Social Science Research Council, since 1986. Dir., Inter-Univ. Prog. in Chinese Language Studies, Taipei, Taiwan, 1967–68. *Publs:* (as Evans Wakeman) Seventeen Royal Palms Drive (novel), 1961; Strangers atthe Gate: Social Disorder in South China, 1966; (ed.) Nothing Concealed: Essays in Honor of Liu Yu-Yun, 1969; History and Will: Philosophical Perspectives of Mao Tse-Tung's Thought: The Fall of Imperial China; Ming and Qing Historical Studies in the People's Republic of China, 1981; The Coreat Enterprise, 1988. Add: c/o Univ of California Press, 2120 Berkeley Way, Berkeley, Calif. 94720, U.S.A.

WAKOSKI, Diane. American, b. 1937. Poetry, Literature. Member of the faculty, Michigan State Univ., East Lansing, since 1976. Clerk, British Book Centre, NYC, 1960–63; English Teacher, Jr. High Sch. 22, NYC, 1963–66. *Publs:* Coins and Coffins, 1962; (with others) Four Young Lady Poets, 1962; Discrepancies and Apparitions: Poems, 1966; The George Washington Poems, 1967; Greed, Parts One and Two, 1968; The Diamond Merchant, 1968; Inside the Blood Factory, 1968; (with R. Kelly and R. Loewinsohn) A Play and Two Poems, 1968; Thanking My Mother for Piano Lessons, 1969; Greed, Parts 3 and 4, 1969; The Moon Has a Complicated Geography, 1969; The Magellanic Clouds, 1970; Greed, Parts 5-7, 1970; The Lament of the Lady Bank Dick, 1970; Love, You Big Fat Snail, 1970; Black Dream Ditty for Billy "The Kid" Seen in Dr. Generosity's Bar Recruiting for Hell's Angels and Black Mafia, 1970; Exorcism, 1971; On Barbara's Shore, 1971; The Motorcycle Betrayal Poems, 1971; The Pumpkin Pie, or Reassurances Are Always False, Though We Love Them, Only Physics Counts, 1972; The Purple Finch Song, 1972; Sometimes a Poet Will Hijack the Moon, 1972; Smudging, 1972; Form is an Extension of Content, 1972; The Owl and the Snake: A Fable, 1973; Greed, Parts 8, 9, 11, 1973; Dancing on the Grave of a Son of a Bitch, 1973; Winter Sequences, 1973; Trilogy: Coins and Coffins, Discrepancies and Apparitions, The George Washington Poems, 1974; Virtuoso Literature for Two and Four Hands, 1975; Waiting for the King of Spain, 1976; The Man Who Shook Hands, 1978; Towards a New Poetry, 1980; Cap of Darkness, 1980; The Magician's Feast Letters, 1982; Saturn's Rings, 1982; The Lady Who Drove Me to the Airport, 1982; Divers, 1982; The Collected Greed, 1984; Why My Mother Likes Liberace, 1986; The Rings of Saturn, 1986; Emerald Ice: Selected Poems 1962-87, 1988. Add: 607 Division, East Lansing, Mich. 48823, U.S.A.

WALBANK, Frank William. British, b. 1909. Classics, Biography. Lectr., 1934–46, Prof. of Latin, 1946–51, and Prof. of Ancient History and Classical Archaeology, 1951–77, Univ. of Liverpool. Pres., Roman Soc., 1961–65, and The Classical Assn., 1969–70. *Publs:* Aratos of Sicyon, 1934; Philip V of Macedon, 1940; The Decline of the Roman

Empire in the West, 1946; Historical Commentary on Polybius, vol. I, 1957, vol. II, 1967, vol. III, 1979; The Awful Revolution, 1969; Polybius, 1972; The Hellenistic World, 1981; Selected Papers, 1985; (With N.G.L. Hammod) History of Macedonia, vol. III, 1988. Add: 64 Grantchester Meadows, Cambridge CB3 9JL, England.

WALBROOK, Louise. *See* **TEMPLETON**, Edith.

WALCOTT, Derek (Alton). British, b. 1930. Plays/Screenplays, Poetry. Founding Dir., Trinidad Theatre Workshop, since 1959. Former Feature Writer, Public Opinion, Kingston, and Trinidad Guardian, Port-of-Spain. *Publs:* Twenty-Five Poems, 1948; Epitaph for the Young, 1949; Henri Christophe: A Chronicle, 1950; Henri Dernier: A Play for Radio Production, 1951; Poems, 1953; Sea at Dauphin, 1954; Ione: A Play with Music, 1957; In a Green Night: Poems 1948-60, 1962; Selected Poems, 1964; The Castaways and Other Poems, 1965; The Gulf and Other Poems (in U.S. as The Gulf), 1969; Dream on Monkey Mountain and Other Plays, 1971; Another Life, 1973; Sea Grapes, 1976; Selected Poems, 1977; The Star-Apple Kingdom, 1978; The Joker of Seville, and O Babylon!, 1978; Remembrance, and Pantomime, 1980; The Fortunate Traveller, 1982; Midsummer, 1983; Three Plays, 1986; Collected Poems 1948-1984, 1986; The Arkansas Testament, 1987; Omeros (Verse), 1989. Add: 165 Duke of Edinburgh Ave., Diego Martin, Trinidad.

WALCUTT, Charles Child. American, b. 1908. Novels/Short stories, Education, Literature. Prof. of English, Queens Coll. and Grad. Center, City Univ. of New York, since 1951. Writer and Ed., J.B. Lippincott Co.—Harper and Row, Philadelphia, Pa., since 1961. Prof., Univ. of Oklahoma, Norman, 1938–44, Eastern Michigan Univ., Ypsilanti, 1944–47, and Washington Jefferson Coll., Washington, Pa., 1947–51. *Publs:* (ed. with L.F. Dean) The Mind in the Making, 1939; The Romantic Compromise in the Novels of Winston Churchill, 1951; American Literary Naturalism: A Divided Stream, 1956; (with S. Terman) Reading: Chaos and Cure, 1958; (ed. and co-author) Tomorrow's Illiterates: The State of Reading Instruction Today, 1961; An Anatomy of Prose, 1962; (with G. McCracken) Basic Reading, 1962, 1966–68, rev. ed. as Lippincott's Basic Reading, 13 vols., 1969–71, 4th ed. 1980–81; (with J.C. Daniels and H. Diack) Your Child's Reading: A Guide for Parents Who Want to Help, 1964; Phonics Guide to Basic Reading, 1965; (with G. McCracken) Reading Goals: The Red Book, 1966; (with G. McCracken) Reading Goals: The Blue Book, 1966; Jack London, 1966; Man's Changing Mask: Modes and Methods of Characterization in Fiction, 1966; (with J.E. Whitesell) The Explicator Cyclopedia: vol. I—Modern Poetry, 1966; (with G. McCracken) Reading Goals: The Orange Book, 1968; (with J.E. Whitesell) The Explicator Cyclopedia: vol. II—Poetry to 1860, 1969; (with G. McCracken) Reading Goals: The Purple Book, 1969; (with J.E. Whitesell) The Explicator Cyclopedia, vol. III—Prose, 1969; (ed.) Moby Dick, by Hermann Melville, 1969; Jude the Obscure, by Thomas Hardy, 1969; John O'Hara, 1969; (with G. McCracken) Codebooks to Lippincott's Basic Reading, 1969–71; (with G. McCracken) Reading Goals: The Gold Book, 1970; (with J. Reinach) My Book Book, 1971; (co-author) Teaching Reading: A Phonic/Linguistic Approach to Developmental Reading, 1974; (ed.) Seven Novelists in the American Naturalist Tradition, 1974. Add: 18 Knightsbridge Rd., Great Neck, N.Y. 11021, U.S.A.

WALDMAN, Anne. American, b. 1945. Poetry. Dir., M.F.A. in Poetics and Writing, The Summer Writing Program, Naropa Inst., Boulder, since 1974. Dir. of the Poetry Project, St. Mark's Church-in-the-Bowery, NYC, 1968–78; Ed., The World mag., NYC; Ed., Angel Hair and Angel Hair Books, NYC; Founding Ed., Full Court Press, NYC, 1973. *Publs:* On the Wing, 1967; Giant Night, 1968; O My Life!, 1969; "The World" Anthology: Poems from the St. Mark's Poetry Project, and Another World, 1969, 1971; Baby Breakdown, 1970; Giant Night: Selected Poems, 1970; Icy Rose, 1971; No Hassles, 1971; (with Ted Berrigan) Memorial Day, 1971; Holy City, 1971; Goodies from Anne Waldman, 1971; Light and Shadow, 1972; The West Indies Poems, 1972; Spin Off, 1972; (with J. Brainard) Self Portrait, 1973; Life Notes: Selected Poems, 1973; Fast Speaking Woman, 1975; Journals and Dreams: Poems, 1975; Joseph Cornell, 1976; Shaman, 1977; (with Reed Bye) 4 Travels, 1978; Mark Rothko, 1978; (ed. with Marilyn Webb) Talking Poetics from Naropa Institute, 2 vols., 1978–79; To a Young Poet, 1979; Countries, 1980; Cabin, 1982; First Baby Poems, 1982; Make-Up on Empty Space, 1984; Invention, 1985; Skin Meat Bones, 1985; The Romance Thing, 1987; Blue Mosque, 1988; Helping the Dreamer: New and Selected Poems, 1989. Add: Naropa Institute, 2130 Arapahoe Ave., Boulder, Colo. 80302, U.S.A.

WALDROP, Howard. American, b. 1946. Science fiction. Linotype operator, Daily News, Arlington, Tex., 1965–68; advertising copywriter,

Lindell-Keyes, Dallas, 1972; auditory research subject, Dynastat Inc., Austin, Tex., 1975–80. *Publs:* The Texas-Israeli War: 1999, with Jake Saunders, 1974; Them Bones, 1984; Howard Who?, 1986. Add: P.O. Box 49335, Austin, Tex. 78765, U.S.A.

WALES, Nym. *See* **SNOW**, Helen Foster.

WALES, Robert. British, b. 1923. Novels/Short stories, Plays/Screenplays. Freelance writer and TV producer. Chmn., Soc. of Authors Broadcasting Cttee., 1978–80. *Publs:* The Cell, 1971; Harry (novel), 1985. Add: 2 Thorn St., Barnes, London SW13 0PR, England.

WALFORD, A(lbert) J(ohn). British, b. 1906. Language/Linguistics, Librarianship. Library service at Stoke Newington, 1924–30, Lambeth, 1930–43, for Commercial Union Assurance Co., London, 1973–78, and attached to Library Assoc., 1978–80. Ed., Library Assoc. Record, 1953–59; Member Editorial Bd., The Reference Librarian, 1981–86. *Publs:* Guide to Reference Material, 1959, supplement, 1963, 4th ed. as Walford's Guide to Reference Material, 3 vols., 1980–87, and Concise Guide, 1981; A Guide to Foreign Language Grammars and Dictionaries, 1961, 3rd ed. 1977; Walford's Guide to Current British Periodicals in the Humanities and Social Sciences, 1986; Reviews and Reviewing, 1986. Add: 45 Parkside Drive, Watford, Herts. WD1 3AU, England.

WALKER, Alan. Australian, b. 1911. History, Race relations, Sociology, Theology/Religion. Principal, Pacific Coll. for Evangelism, since 1989. Supt., Central Methodist Mission, Sydney, 1958–78; Dir. of World Evangelism, World Methodist Council, 1978–88. Pres., Methodist Church, N.S.W., 1970–71. *Publs:* Concerning Teaching, 1936; There is Always God, 1938; Everybody's Calvary, 1943; Coal Town: A Sociological Survey of Cessnock, N.S.W., 1944; World Encounter, 1949; Christianity of the Offensive, 1949; Heritage Without End, 1953; Australia Finding God, 1954; Start Where You Are, 1955; My Faith is Enough, 1955; Plan for a Christian Australia, 1955; The Whole Gospel for the Whole World, 1957; A New Mind for a New Age, 1959; God is Where You Are, 1962; The Many Sided Cross, 1962; Christ is Enough, 1963; How Jesus Helped People, 1964; A Ringing Call to Mission, 1966; The Life Line Story, 1967; Breakthrough: Rediscovery of the Holy Spirit, 1969; Now for Newness, 1970; Jesus, The Liberator, 1973; God, The Disturber, 1973; The New Evangelism, 1975; Love in Action, 1977; Life Begins at Christ, 1979; The Promise and the Power, 1980; Life Grows with Christ, 1981; Standing Up to Preach, 1983; Life Ends in Christ, 1983; Your Life Can be Changed, 1985; Life in the Holy Spirit, 1986; Whither Australia, 1987. Add: 14 Owen Stanley Ave., Beacon Hill, N.S.W. 2100, Australia.

WALKER, Alexander. British, b. 1930. Film, Biography. Film Critic, The Standard newspaper, London, since 1959. Critic of the Year, Press Awards, 1970. Former lectr. in political philosophy, U.S.A., and feature writer, Birmingham Post. *Publs:* The Celluloid Sacrifice: Aspects of Sex in the Movies, 1966; Stardom: The Hollywood Phenomenon, 1970; Stanley Kubrick Directs, 1971; Hollywood, England: The British Film Industry in the Sixties, 1975; Rudolph Valentino, 1976; Double Takes: Notes and After-thoughts on the Movies 1956-76, 1977; Superstars, 1978; The Shattered Silents: How the Talkies Came to Stay, 1978; Garbo, 1980; Peter Sellers, 1981; Joan Crawford, 1983; Dietrich, 1984; (ed.) No Bells on Sunday: The Journals of Rachel Roberts, 1984; National Heroes: British Cinema Industry in the 1970s and 1980s, 1985; Bette Davis, 1986; (trans.) Woody Allen: Beyond Words, by Benayoun, 1986; Vivian: The Life of Vivian Leigh, 1987; It's Only a Movie, Ingrid: Encounters on and Off Screen, 1988. Add: 1 Marlborough, 38-40 Maida Vale, London W9 1RW, England.

WALKER, Alice. American, b. 1944. Novels/Short stories, Children's fictions, Poetry. Fulltime writer. *Publs:* In Love and Trouble (short stories); You Can't Keep a Good Woman Down (short stories); Once (poetry); Revolutionary Petunias (poetry); Goodnight, Willie Lee, I'll See You in the Morning (poetry); The Third Life of Grange Copeland (novel); Meridian (novel); The Color Purple (novel), 1983 (American Book Award; Pulitzer Prize); In Search of Our Mother's Gardens: Womanist Prose, 1983; Horses Make a Landscape Look More Beautiful (poetry), 1984; Living by the Word: Selected Writings 1973-87, 1986; To Hell with Dying (juvenile), 1988; The Temple of My Face, 1989. Add: P.O. Box 378, Navarro, Calif. 95463, U.S.A.

WALKER, Benjamin. Indian, b. 1923. History, Paranormal, Theology/Religion. Joint Ed., Asia, Saigon. *Publs:* Persian Pageant, 1950; Angkor Empire, 1955; Hindu World, 2 vols., 1968; Sex and the Supernatural, 1970; (co-author) Encyclopedia of the Unexplained, 1974; The

Human Double, 1974; Encyclopedia of Esoteric Man, 1977; Encyclopedia of Metaphysical Medicine, 1978; Masks of the Soul, 1981; Tantrism, 1982; Gnosticism Past and Present, 1983; Companion to the Kabala, 1989. Add: 84 Church Rd., Teddington, Middx., England.

WALKER, David (Harry). Canadian, b. 1911. Novels/Short stories, Children's fiction. Canadian Commnr., Roosevelt Campobello Intnl. Park Commn., since 1965. Served in British Army in Black Watch, 1931–47: in India, 1932–36, in Sudan, 1936–38, Aide-de-Camp to Gov. Gen. of Canada, 1938–39, Prisoner-of-War in Germany, 1940–45, Instr., Staff Coll., Camberley, Surrey, 1945–46, Comptroller to Viceroy of India, 1946–47, retired as Maj., 1947. *Publs:* The Storm and the Silence, 1949; Geordie, 1950; The Pillar, 1952; Digby, 1953; Harry Black, 1954; Sandy Was a Soldier's Boy, 1957; Where the High Winds Blow, 1960; Storms of Our Journey and Other Stories, 1962; Dragon Hill, 1962; Winter of Madness, 1964; Mallabec, 1965; Come Back, Geordie, 1966; Devil's Plunge (in U.S. as CAB—Intersec), 1968; Pirate Rock, 1969; Big Ben, 1970; The Lord's Pink Ocean, 1972; Black Dougal, 1973; Ash, 1976; Pot of Gold, 1977; Lean, Wind, Lean: A Few Times Remembered (memoirs), 1984. Add: Strathcroix, St. Andrews, N.B. E0G 2X0, Canada.

WALKER, David (Maxwell). British, b. 1920. Law. Regius Prof. of Law, Univ. of Glasgow, since 1958 (Prof. of Jurisprudence, 1954–58). Dir., Scottish Univs. Law Inst., 1974–80. *Publs:* (ed.) Faculty Digest of Decisions 1940–50, 1953; Law of Damages in Scotland, 1955; (ed.) Topham and Ivamy's Company Law, Scottish Part, 12th-16th eds. 1955–78; The Scottish Legal System, 1959, 5th ed. 1981; Law of Delict in Scotland, 1966, 1981; Scottish Courts and Tribunals, 1969, 5th ed. 1985; Principles of Scottish Private Law, 1970, 4th ed., 4 vols., 1988–89; Law of Prescription in Scotland, 1973, 3rd ed. 1981; Law of Civil Remedies in Scotland, 1974; Law of Contracts in Scotland, 1979, 1985; The Oxford Companion to Law, 1980; (ed.) Stair's Institutions, 6th ed., 1981; (ed.) Stair Tercentenary Studies, 1981; The Scottish Jurists, 1985; Legal History of Scotland, 2 vols. 1988–90. Add: Dept. of Private Law, Univ. of Glasgow, Glasgow, Scotland.

WALKER, George F. Canadian, b. 1947. Plays/Screenplays. Dramaturge, 1972–73, and Resident Playwright, 1972–76, Factory Theatre Lab, Toronto. *Publs:* The Prince of Naples, 1972; Ambush at Tether's End, 1972; Sacktown Rag, 1972; Bagdad Saloon, 1973; Beyond Mozambique, 1975; Ramona and the White Slaves, 1976; Zastrozzi, 1977; Three Plays, 1978; Filthy Rich, 1981; Theatre of the Film Noir, 1981; Science and Madness, 1982; The Art of War, 1983; The Power Plays, 1984; Criminals in Love, 1985; Nothing Sacred, 1988; The East End Plays, 1988. Add: c/o Great North Artists, 350 Dupont St., Toronto, Ont., Canada

WALKER, Harry. *See* WAUGH, Hillary.

WALKER, J. *See* CRAWFORD, John Richard.

WALKER, John. American, b. 1906. Art. Dir. Emeritus, The National Gallery of Art, Washington, since 1969 (Chief Curator, 1939–56, and Dir., 1956–59). Member, Intnl. Council of Museums, Commn. of Fine Arts, and the Catholic Commn. on Intellectual and Cultural Affairs; Trustee, American Fedn. of Arts, Los Angeles County Museum, National Opera Inst., A.W. Mellon Educational and Charitable Trust, and the Wallace Foundn.; Member, Art Advisory Panel, British National Trust. Formerly, Member, Federal Council on the Arts and Humanities, the Special Fine Arts Cttee. of the U.S. Dept. of State, and Chmn., Fine Arts Panel, U.S. Air Force Academy. *Publs:* (with A. Aldrich) A Guide to Villas and Gardens in Italy, 1938; (with H. Cairns) Masterpieces of Painting from the National Gallery of Art, 1944; Paintings from America, 1951; (with H. Cairns) Great Paintings from the National Gallery of Art, 1952; Bellini and Titian at Ferrara, 1957; (with H. Cairns) Treasures from the National Gallery of Art, 1963; (with H. Cairns) A Pageant of Painting from the National Gallery of Art, 1966; Self-Portrait with Donors, 1974; (ed.) National Gallery of Art, Washington: 1000 Masterpieces, 1976; Turner, 1976; Constable, 1978; The Scottish Sketches of R.B. Cunningham Graham, 1981; Portraits: 5000 Years, 1983. Add: 1729 H St. N.W., Washington, D.C. 20006, U.S.A.

WALKER, Joseph A. American, b. 1935. Plays/Screenplays. *Publs:* The River Niger, 1972. Add: c/o Hill & Wang, 19 Union Sq. W., New York, N.Y. 10003, U.S.A.

WALKER, Kenneth Richard. British, b. 1931. Economics. Prof. of Economics, Univ. of London, Sch. of Oriental and African Studies, since

1972 (Fellow, 1959–61; Lectr., 1961–64; Reader, 1964–72; Head of Dept. of Economic and Political Studies, 1972–86). Asst. Lectr. in Political Economy, Aberdeen Univ., 1956–59. *Publs:* Planning in Chinese Agriculture: Socialisation and the Private Sector 1956-62, 1965; Food Grain Consumption and Procurement in China, 1984. Add: Dept. of Economic and Political Studies, Sch. of Oriental and African Studies, Univ. of London, WC1, England.

WALKER, Kenneth Roland. American, b. 1928. Education, History. Prof. of History since 1966, and Head of Social Sciences and Philosophy Dept. since 1972, Arkansas Tech Univ., Russelville (Assoc. Prof., 1958–66; Dean of Sch. of Arts and Sciences, 1970–72). U.S. Air Force Officer, 1952–58. *Publs:* Days the Presidents Died, 1966; A History of the Middle West, 1972; History of First United Methodist Church of Russelville, Arkansas 1973-1984, 1984. Add: Arkansas Tech Univ., Russelville, Ark. 72801, U.S.A.

WALKER, Lucy. Pseud. for Dorothy Lucie (McClemans) Sanders; also awrites as Shelley Dean. Australian, b. 1907. Historical/Romance/Gothic. Teacher, in W.A., 1928–36, and in London, 1936–38. Former Member, State Advisory Bd. to the Australian Broadcasting Commn., and Member, State Library Bd., W.A. *Publs:* (as Dorothy Lucie Sanders) Fairies on the Doorstep, 1948, in U.S. as Lucy Walker) as Pool of Dreams, 1973; (as Dorothy Lucie Sanders) The Randy, 1948; (as Dorothy Lucie Sanders), Six for Heaven, 1952; (as Dorothy Lucie Sanders) Shining River, 1954; The One Who Kisses, 1954; Sweet and Faraway, 1955; Come Home, Dear!, 1956; (as Dorothy Lucie Sanders) Waterfall, 1956, in U.S. (as Lucy Walker) as The Bell Branch, 1971; Heaven Is Here, 1957; (as Dorothy Lucie Sanders) Ribbons in Her Hair, 1957; Master of Ransome, 1958; Orchard Hill, 1958; The Stranger from the North, 1959; Kingdom of the Heart, 1959; (as Dorothy Lucie Sanders) Pepper Tree Bay, 1959; Love in a Cloud, 1960; The Loving Heart, 1960; The Moonshiner, 1961, in U.S. as Cupboard Love, 1963; Wife to Order, 1961; (as Dorothy Lucie Sanders) Monday in Summer, 1961; The Distant Hills, 1962; Down in the Forest, 1962; The Call of the Pines, 1963; Follow Your Star, 1963; The Man from Outback, 1964; A Man Called Masters, 1965; The Other Girl, 1965; Reaching for the Stars, 1966; The Ranger in the Hills, 1966; (as Shelley Dean) South Sea Island, 1966; (as Shelley Dean) Island in the South, 1967; The River Is Down, 1967; Home at Sundown, 1968; The Gone-Away Man, 1969; Joyday for Jodi, 1971; The Mountain That Went to the Sea, 1971; Girl Alone, 1973; The Runaway Girl, 1975; Gamma's Girl, 1977; So Much Love, 1977. Add: 20 Jukes Way, Wembley Gardens, W.A. 6016, Australia.

WALKER, Margaret (Abigail). American, b. 1915. Novels/Short stories, Poetry. Prof. of English since 1949, and Dir. of Inst. for the Study of History, Life and Culture of Black Peoples since 1968, Jackson State Coll., Miss. Prof. of English, West Virginia State Coll. Institute, 1942–43, and Livingston Coll., Salisbury, N.C. 1945–46. *Publs:* For My People (poetry), 1942; Come Down from Yonder Mountain, 1962; Jubilee, 1965; Ballad for the Free (poetry), 1966; Prophets of a New Day, 1970; How I Wrote Jubilee, 1972; October Journey (poetry), 1973; A Poetic Equation: Convers tions Between Nikki Giovanni and Margaret Walker, 1974; The Daemonic Genius of Richard Wright, 1982. Add: 2205 Guynes St., Jackson, Miss. 39213, U.S.A.

WALKER, Max. *See* AVALLONE, Michael.

WALKER, Nigel (David). British, b. 1917. Criminology, Psychology. Staff member, Scottish Office, 1946–61; Fellow, Nuffield Coll., Oxford, and Reader in Criminology, Oxford Univ., 1961–73; Wolfson Prof. of Criminology. Cambridge Univ., 1973–88 (Dir., Inst. of Criminology, 1973–80). Member, Cttee. on Mentally Abnormal Offenders, 1972–75; Member, Advisory Council on the Penal System, 1970–79; Pres., National Assn. of Probation Officers, 1980–85. *Publs:* Delphi, 1936; A Short History of Psychotherapy, 1957; Morale in the Civil Service, 1961; Crime and Punishment in Britain, 1965; Crime and Insanity in England, 2 vols., 1968–72; Sentencing in a Rational Society, 1969; Crimes, Courts, and Figures, 1971; Explaining Misbehaviour (lecture), 1974; Treatment and Justice (lecture), 1976; Behaviour and Misbehaviour, 1977; Punishment, Danger, and Stigma, 1980; Sentencing Theory, Law, and Practice, 1986; Crime and Criminology, 1987; (co-author) Public Attitudes to Sentencing, 1988. Add: Inst. of Criminology, 7 West Rd., Cambridge, England.

WALKER, Samuel E. American, b. 1942. Criminology, History. Assoc. Prof., Dept. of Criminal Justice, Univ. of Nebraska at Omaha since 1974. *Publs:* A Critical History of Police Reform: The Emergence of Professionalism, 1977; Popular Justice: A History of American Criminal Justice, 1980; The Police in America: An Introduction, 1983; Sense and

Nonsense about Crime, 1984. Add: Dept. of Criminal Justice, Univ. of Nebraska at Omaha, Omaha, Neb. 68182, U.S.A.

WALKER, Stella Archer. British. Animals/Pets, Art, Sports. Art Corresp., Horse & Hound, since 1960–88. *Publs:* (compiler) In Praise of Kent, 1952; (compiler) In Praise of Horses, 1953; (compiler) In Praise of Spring, 1954; Horses of Renown, 1954; (compiler) Long Live the Horse, 1955; (with R.S. Summerhays) The Controversial Horse: Sporting Art: England 1700-1900, 1972; (ed.) Summerhay's Horseman's Encyclopedia, 1975; Enamoured of an Ass, 1977; British Sporting Art in the Twentieth Century, 1989. Add: Watermill Farm, Rushlake Green, Heathfield, E. Sussex TN21 9PX, England.

WALKER, Ted. British, b. 1934. Short stories, Poetry. Prof. of Creating Writing, New England Coll., Arundel, Sussex, since 1971. *Publs:* Those Other Growths, 1964; Fox on a Barn Door, 1965; The Solitaries, 1967; The Night Bathers, 1970; Gloves to the Hangman, 1973; Burning the Ivy, 1978; The Lion's Cavalcade, 1980; Big Jim and the Figaro Club, 1981; The High Path, 1982; A Family Man, 1983; You've Never Heard Me Sing, 1985; In Spain, 1987; Selected Poems, 1987. Add: Argyll House, Eastergate, Chichester, Sussex, England.

WALKER, William George. Australian, b. 1928. Administration/Management, Education. Chief Exec. and Principal, Australian Management Coll., Mt. Eliza, Vic., since 1980. Founding Ed., Journal of Educational Admin., and The Practising Manager. Teacher, N.S.W. Dept. of Education, 1948–51; Lectr. in Education, Wagga Teachers' Coll., N.S.W., 1952–56; Asst. to Dir., Bureau of Educational Research, Univ. of Illinois, 1956–58; Lectr. in Education, Armidale Teachers' Coll., 1959–61; Sr. Lectr., 1962–65, Assoc. Prof., 1966–68, and Prof. of Education, 1968–79, Univ. of New England, Armidale, N.S.W. Former Pres., Commonwealth Council for Educational Admin. *Publs:* (with A.R. Crane) Peter Board: His Contribution to the Development of Education in New South Wales, 1957; (with A.R. Crane and G.W. Bassett) Headmasters for Better Schools, 1963; The Principal at Work: Case Studies in School Administration, 1965; (ed. with G. Baron and D.H. Cooper) Educational Administration: International Perspectives, 1969; Theory and Practice in Educational Administration, 1970; (with C. Steel and J. Mumford) A Glossary of Educational Terms: age in Five English Speaking Countries, 1973; (ed. with A.R. Crane and A.R. Thomas) Explorations in Educational Administration, 1973; (with M. Kirby and S. Houston) A Touch of Healing, 1985. Add: "Kiah", A.M.C., Kunyung Rd., Mt. Eliza, Vic. 3930, Australia.

WALL, Joseph Frazier. American, b. 1920. History, Biography. Dir., Rosenfield Prog. in Public Affairs, Grinnell Coll., Iowa, since 1980 (Instr., 1947–51; Asst. Prof., 1951–55; Chmn. of Dept., 1954–57 and 1963–64; Assoc. Prof., 1955–57; Chmn., Div. of Social Studies, 1956–57 and 1959–60; Prof., 1957–61; Parker Prof. of History, 1961–80; Dean of Coll., 1969–73). *Publs:* Henry Watterson: Reconstructed Rebel, 1956; (with Robert Parks) Freedom, 1956; Andrew Carnegie, 1972; (ed. with Richard Lowitt) Interpreting the 20th Century, 1973; Iowa, 1978; Policies and People, 1979; Skibo, 1984. Add: 2000 Country Club Dr., Grinnell, Iowa 50012, U.S.A.

WALL, (Sir) Patrick (Henry Bligh). British, b. 1916. Politics/Government. Conservative Member of Parliament (U.K.) for the Haltemprice div. of Hull, 1954–55, for the Haltemprice div. of the East Riding of Yorkshire, 1955–83, and for Beverley, 1983–87: Parliamentary Private Secty. to the Minister of Agriculture, Fisheries and Food, 1950–57, and to the Chancellor of the Exchequer, 1958–59; Member, British Delegation to the U.N., 1962; Chmn., Conservative Parliamentary Fisheries Subcttee., 1962–83. Chmn., Military Cttee., North Atlantic Assembly, 1977–81 and Pres., 1983–85. *Publs:* Royal Marine Pocket Book, 1944; Student Power, 1968; Defence Policy, 1969; Overseas Aid, 1969; Europe's Back Door, 1972; The Indian Ocean and the Threat to the West, 1975; Prelude to Détente, 1975; The Southern Oceans and the Security of the Free World, 1977. Add: 8 Westminster Gdns., Marsham St., London SW1, England.

WALLACE, Barbara Brooks. American. Children's fiction. *Publs:* Claudia; Andrew the Big Deal; The Trouble with Miss Switch; Victoria; Can Do, Missy Charlie; The Secret Summer of L.E.B., 1974; Julia and the Third Bad Thing, 1975; Palmer Patch, 1976; Hawkins, 1977; The Contest Kid Strikes Again, 1980; Peppermints in the Parlor, 1980; Hawkins and the Soccer Solution, 1981; Miss Switch to the Rescue, 1981; Claudia and Duffy, 1982; Hello, Claudia!, 1982; The Barrel in the Basement, 1985; Argyle, 1987; Perfect Acres, Inc., 1988. Add: 2708 George Mason Pl., Alexandria, Va. 22305, U.S.A.

WALLACE, Bruce. American, b. 1920. Biology. Prof. of Biology, Virginia Polytechnic Inst. and State Univ., Blacksburg, Va., since 1981 (Univ. Distinguished Prof., 1983). With the Dept. of Genetics, Carnegie Instn. of Washington, 1947–49, and with The Biological Lab, 1949–58, both Cold Spring Harbor, N.Y.; Prof. of Genetics, Cornell Univ., Ithaca, N.Y., 1958–81. Secty., 1956–58, and Pres., 1972, American Soc. of Naturalists; Secty., 1968–70, and Pres., 1974, Genetics Soc. of America; Pres., Soc. for the Study of Evolution, 1974. *Publs:* (with T. Dobzhansky) Radiation, Genes and Man, 1959; (with A. Srb) Adaptation, 1961; Chromosomes, Giant Molecules and Evolution, 1966; Topics in Population Genetics, 1968; Genetic Load: Its Biological and Conceptual Aspects, 1970; Essays in Social Biology, 3 vols., 1972; Basic Population Genetics, 1981; (ed. with R. Lewontin, J. Moore, and W. Provine) Dobzhansky's Genetics of Natural Populations, 1981; (ed. and co-author) Human Culture: A Moment in Evolution, 1983; (with G. Simmons, Jr.) Biology for Living, 1987. Add: 940 McBryde Dr., Blacksburg, Va. 24060, U.S.A.

WALLACE, Doreen. British, b. 1897. Novels/Short stories. *Publs:* A Little Learning; The Gentle Heart; The Portion of the Levites; Creatures of an Hour; Even Such Is Time; Barnham Rectory, 1934; Latter Howe, 1935; So Long to Learn, 1936; Going to the Sea, 1936; Old Father Antic, 1937; The Faithful Compass, 1937; The Time of Wild Roses, 1938; A Handful of Silver, 1939; East Anglia, 1939; The Spring Returns, 1940; English Lakeland, 1941; Green Acres, 1941; Land from the Waters, 1944; Carlotta Green, 1944; The Noble Savage, 1945; Billy Potter, 1946; Willow Farm, 1948; How Little We Know, 1949; Only One Life, 1950; In a Green Shade, 1950; (with R. Bagnall-Oakeley) Norfolk, 1951; Root of Evil, 1952; Sons of Gentlemen, 1953; The Younger Son, 1954; Daughters, 1955; The Interloper, 1956; The Money Field, 1957; Forty Years On, 1958; Richard and Lucy, 1959; Mayland Hall, 1960; Lindsay Langton and Wives, 1961; Woman with a Mirror, 1963; The Mill Pond, 1966; Ashbury People, 1968; The Turtle, 1969; Elegy, 1970; An Earthly Paradise, 1971; A Thinking Reed, 1973; Changes and Chances, 1975; Landscape with Figures, 1976. Add: 2 Manor Gardens, Diss, Norfolk, England.

WALLACE, F(loyd) L. American. Mystery/Crime/Suspense, Science fiction/Fantasy. Freelance writer, mainly of science fiction short stories. *Publs:* Address: Centauri (science fiction), 1955; Three Times a Victim, 1957; Wired for Scandal, 1959. Add: c/o Ace Books, 51 Madison Ave., New York, N.Y. 10010, U.S.A.

WALLACE, Ian. Canadian, b. 1950. Children's fiction. Staff writer and illustrator, Kids Can Press, Toronto, 1974–76; Information Officer, Art Gallery of Ontario, Toronto, 1976–80. *Publs:* (all illustrated by the author) Julie News, 1974; The Sandwich, 1974; The Christmas Tree House, 1976; Chin Chiang and the Dragon's Dance, 1984; The Sparrow's Song, 1986; Morgan the Magnificant, 1987. Add: 370 Palmerston Blvd., Toronto, Ont. M6G 2N6, Canada.

WALLACE, Ian. Pseud. for John Wallace Pritchard. American, b. 1912. Novels/Short stories, Science fiction/Fantasy, Biography. Psychology Technician, Clinical Psychologist, Dept. Head, Administrative Asst., Dir., and Divisional Dir., Bd. of Education, Detroit, 1934–74; now retired. Part-time Lectr. in Education, Wayne State Univ., Detroit, 1955–74. *Publs:* (as John Wallace Pritchard, with others) Frank Cody, A Realist in Education, 1943; (as John Wallace Pritchard) Every Crazy Wind (novel), 1952; (as John Wallace Pritchard, with Paul H. Voelker) Off to Work (non-fiction), 1962; science fiction novels—Croyd, 1967; Dr. Orpheus, 1968; Deathstar Voyage, 1969; The Purloined Prince, 1971; Pan Sagittarius, 1973; Voyage to Dari, 1974; The World Asunder, 1976; The Sign of the Mute Medusa, 1977; Z-Sting, 1978; Heller's Leap, 1979; The Lucifer Comet, 1980; The Rape of the Sun, 1982; Megalomania, 1989. Add: c/o DAW Books, 1301 Ave. of the Americas, New York, N.Y. 10019, U.S.A.

WALLACE, Irving. American, b. 1916. Novels/Short stories, Cultural/ Ethnic topics. *Publs:* The Fabulous Originals, 1955; The Square Pegs, 1957; The Fabulous Showman, 1959; The Sins of Philip Fleming, 1959; The Chapman Report, 1960; The Twenty-Seventh Wife, 1961; The Prize, 1962; The Three Sirens, 1963; The Man, 1964; The Sunday Gentleman, 1965; The Plot, 1967; The Writing of One Novel, 1968; The Seven Minutes, 1969; The Nympho and Other Maniacs, 1971; The Word, 1972; The Fan Club, 1974; The People's Almanac 1, 1975, 2, 1978, 3, 1981; The R Document, 1976; The Book of Lists 1, 1977, 2, 1980, 3, 1983; The Two, 1978; The Pigeon Project, 1979; The Second Lady, 1980; The Book of Predictions, 1981; The Intimate Sex Lives of Famous People, 1981; The Almighty, 1982; The Miracle, 1984; The Seventh Secret, 1986;

The Celestial Bed, 1987. Add: P.O. Box 49328, Los Angeles, Calif. 90049, U.S.A.

WALLACE, John Malcolm. American, b. 1928. Literature. Prof. of English Literature, Univ. of Chicago, since 1967. Instr. in English, Cornell Univ., Ithaca, N.Y., 1960–63; Asst. Prof., 1963–66, and Assoc. Prof., 1966–67, Johns Hopkins Univ., Baltimore, Md. *Publs:* Destiny His Choice: The Loyalism of Andrew Marvell (literary criticism), 1968; (co-ed. with J. Max Patrick) Style, Rhetoric and Rhythm: Essays by Morris Croll, 1966; (ed.) The Golden and the Brazen World, 1985. Add: English Dept., Univ. of Chicago, Chicago, Ill. 60637, U.S.A.

WALLACE, Robert. *See* **DANIELS**, Norman A.

WALLACE, Sylvia. American. Novels/Short stories. West Coast Ed., Dell Publishing Co., 1944–48, and MacFadden Publishing Co., 1952–57. *Publs:* The Fountains, 1976; (with Irving Wallace, David Wallechinsky, and Amy Wallace) The Book of Lists 2, 1980; Empress, 1980; (with Irving Wallace, David Wallechinsky, and Amy Wallace) The Intimate Sex Lives of Famous People, 1981. Add: P.O. Box 429328, Los Angeles, Calif. 90049, U.S.A.

WALLACE-CRABBE, Christopher (Keith). Australian, b. 1934. Poetry, Literature, Essays. Prof., Univ. of Melbourne, since 1987 (Lockie Fellow, 1961–63; Sr. Lectr., 1963–76; Reader, 1976–87). *Publs:* The Music of Division, 1959; In Light and Darkness, 1963; Eight Metropolitan Poems, 1963; (ed.) Six Voices, 1963; The Rebel General, 1967; (ed.) Australian Poetry 1971, 1971; (ed.) The Australian Nationalists, 1971; Where the Wind Came, 1971; Selected Poems, 1974; Melbourne or the Bush, 1974; Act in the Noon, 1974; The Emotions Are Not Skilled Workers, 1979; Toil and Spin: Two Directions in Modern Poetry, 1979; (ed.) The Golden Apples of the Sun, 1980; Splinters (novel), 1981; Three Absences in Australian Writing, 1983; The Amorous Cannibal and Other Poems, 1985; I'm Deadly Serious, 1988. Add: 910 Drummond St., North Carlton, Vic. 3054, Australia.

WALLACH, Erica. American, b. 1922. Autobiography/Memoirs/Personal. *Publs:* Light at Midnight, 1967. Add: P.O. Box 669; Hopefield, Warrenton, Va. 22186, U.S.A.

WALLACH, Ira. American, b. 1913. Novels/Short stories, Plays/Screenplays. *Publs:* The Horn and the Roses, 1947; How to be Deliriously Happy, 1950; Hopalong-Freud, 1951; Hopalong-Freud Rides Again, 1952; Gutenberg's Folly, 1954; Sticks and Stones, 1954; Phoenix 55, 1955; How to Pick a Wedlock, 1956; Dig We Must, 1956; (with A.S. Ginnes) Drink to Me Only, 1959; Muscle Beach, 1959; The Absence of a Cello, 1960; Play, 1964; Smiling the Boy Fell Dead, 1961; Kaboom!, 1974; 5,000 Years of Foreplay, 1976. Add: 345 W. 58th St., New York, N.Y. 10019, U.S.A.

WALLER, George Macgregor. American. History, Biography. Prof. of History, Butler Univ., Indianapolis, Ind., since 1954. Member, Indiana American Revolution Bicentennial Commn., 1971–83; Pres., Ohio-Indiana American Studies Assn., 1980–81. *Publs:* (ed.) Puritanism in Early America, 1950, 1973; (ed.) Pearl Harbor, 1953, rev. ed. 1965; Samuel Vetch, Colonial Enterpriser, 1960; The American Revolution in the West, 1975. Add: Butler Univ., Indianapolis, Ind. 46208, U.S.A.

WALLER, Irene Ellen. British, b. 1928. Art, Crafts, Design. Textile Designer, Sculptor and British corresp. for Fiber Arts mag. Textile Designer, Simpson Godlee, Manchester, 1948–50; Interior Designer, Restall's, Birmingham, 1950–53; Head, Sch. of Woven Textiles, Birmingham Art Coll., 1953–70. *Publs:* Thread: An Art Form (in U.S. as Designing With Thread), 1973; Tatting, A Contemporary Art Form, 1974; Knots and Netting, 1976; The Craft of Weaving, 1976; Textile Sculptures, 1977; Fine Art Weaving, 1979; Design Sources for the Fiber Artist, 1979. Add: 13 Portland Rd., Edgbaston, Birmingham, England.

WALLER, Leslie. American, b. 1923. Novels/Short stories, Children's non-fiction, Money/Finance. *Publs:* Three Day Pass, 1944; Show Me the Way, 1946; The Bed She Made, 1950; Books to Begin On (non-fiction children's series), 1950–65; Phoenix Island, 1954; The Banker, 1963; K (in U.K. as The K Assignment), 1964; Will the Real Toulouse-Lautrec Please Stand Up?, 1964; Overdrive, 1965; The Family, 1966; New Sound, 1966; The American, 1967; A Change in the Wind, 1968; The Mob: The Story of Organized Crime (secondary sch. textbook), 1969; Number One, 1969; The Swiss Bank Connection (non-fiction), 1970; The Coast of Fear, 1971; The Swiss Account, 1973; Hide in Plain Sight (non-fiction), 1974; Trocadero, 1976; The Brave and the Free, 1978; Blood and Dreams, 1980;

Embassy, 1987; Amazing Faith, 1988. Add: c/o McGraw-Hill Books, 1221 Ave. of the Americas, New York, N.Y. 10020, U.S.A.

WALLOWER, Lucille. American, b. 1910. Children's fiction, Children's non-fiction. Sch. Librarian, Harrisburg Public Library, Pa., 1943–; Asst. Children's Librarian, 1944–46; Dir., Harrisburg Art Assn. Studio, 1943–48; Fashion Artist, Pomeroy's 1946–49, and Bowman's Inc., 1949–52, Harrisburg; Children's Librarian, 1959–70, and Librarian, 1970–75, Abington Library Soc., Pa. *Publs:* A Conch Shell for Molly, 1940; Chooky, 1942; The Roll of Drums, 1945; Your Pennsylvania, 1953; Old Satan, 1955; Indians of Pennsylvania, 1956, 1985; The Hippity Hopper, 1957; The Morning Star, 1957; All About Pennsylvania, 1958, 1984; They Came to Pennsylvania, 1960, 1985; The Lost Prince, 1963; Your State, 1963; Pennsylvania ABC, 1964; My Book About Abraham Lincoln, 1967; The Pennsylvania Primer, 1954, 1985; William Penn, 1968; Colonial Pennsylvania, 1969; The Pennsylvania Dutch, 1971; Introduction to Pennsylvania, 1974; Pennsylvania Bicentennial Workshop, 1975; African American Workshop, 1977; Pennsylvania, The Keystrone State, 1987. Add: 60 E. Main St., Cambridge, N.Y. 12816, U.S.A.

WALLS, Ian G. British, b. 1922. Horticulture. Horticultural Adviser, West of Scotland Agricultural Coll., 1940–78. *Publs:* Creating Your Garden, 1967; Greenhouse Gardening, 1970; Tomato Growing Today, 1972; Complete Book of the Greenhouse, 1973, 1988; (with A.S. Horsburgh) Making the Most of Your Greenhouse, 1973; (with A. Berrie and D. Harris) Hydroponics, 1975; Garden Problems A-Z, 1979; Care and Maintenance of Bowling Greens, 1979; Modern Greenhouse Methods: Flowers and Plants, Vegetables, 2 vols., 1982; Growing Vegetables, Fruit, and Flowers for Profit, 1986; Simple Tomato Growing, 1987. Add: 17 Dougalston Ave., Milngavie, Glasgow, Scotland.

WALSH, Chad. American, b. 1914. Children's fiction, Poetry, Literature, Theology/Religion. Prof. of English, 1952–77, and Writer-in-Residence, 1969–77, Beloit Coll., Wisc. (Member of English Dept., from 1945; Dept. Chmn., 1959–69); Asst. at St. Paul's Church, Beloit, Wisc., since 1948. Ordained Priest, Episcopal Church, 1949. *Publs:* Stop Looking and Listen: An Invitation to the Christian Life, 1947; The Factual Dark, 1949; C.S. Lewis: Apostle to the Skeptics, 1949; Early Christians of the 21st Century, 1950; Campus Gods on Trial, 1953, rev. ed. 1962; Knock and Enter (novel), 1953; Eden Two-Way, 1954; (with E. Montizambert) Faith and Behavior: Christian Answers to Moral Problems, 1954; Nellie and Her Flying Crocodile, 1956; Behold the Glory (meditations), 1956; The Rough Years (novel), 1960; God at Large, 1960; The Personality of Jesus, 1961; (with E. Walsh) Why Go to Church?, 1962; Doors into Poetry, 1962; From Utopia to Nightmare, 1962; The Psalm of Christ: Forty Poems on the Twenty-Second Psalm, 1963; The Story of Job, 1963; The Unknowing Dance, 1964; (ed.) Today's Poets: American and British Poetry since the 1930s, 1965; (ed.) Garlands for Christmas, 1965; (ed.) The Honey and the Gall: Poems of Married Life, 1967; The End of Nature: Poems, 1969; God at Large, 1971; (ed. with Eva T. Walsh) Twice Ten, 1976; The Literary Legacy of C.S. Lewis, 1979; Hang Me Up My Begging Bowl, 1979; A Rich Fest, 1981; (ed.) The Visionary Christian, 1981; Doors into Poetry (text book), 1982. Add: C-1 Meadowbrook, Joy Dr., South Burlington, Vt. 05401, U.S.A.

WALSH, (Sir) John (Patrick). New Zealander. Medicine/Health, Psychiatry, Theology/Religion. Former Dean and Dir., Prof. of Oral Surgery and Oral Medicine, Univ. of Otago Dental Sch., and Lectr. in Stomatology, Otago Univ., Dunedin. *Publs:* Stomatology, 1957; Living with Uncertainty, 1968; Psychiatry and Dentistry, 1977. Add: Unit 29, Hillsborough Heights Village, Auckland 4, New Zealand.

WALSH, P(atrick) G(erard). British, b. 1923. Classics, Literature, Theology/Religion, Translations. Prof. of Humanity, Univ. of Glasgow, since 1972. Lectr. in Classics, Univ. Coll., Dublin, 1952–59; Lectr., 1959–67, Reader in Humanity, 1967–71, and Prof. of Medieval Latin, 1971–72, Univ. of Edinburgh. *Publs:* Livy: His Historical Aims and Methods, 1961; (ed. with A. Ross) Aquinas, Courage, 1965; (trans.) Letters of Paulinus of Nola, 2 vols., 1966–67; The Roman Novel, 1970; Courtly Love in the Carmina Burana, 1972; (ed.) Livy Book XXI, 1973; Poems of Paulinus of Nola, 1974; Livy, 1974; (ed.) Thirty Poems from the Carmina Burana, 1976; (ed.) Andreas Capellanus on Love, 1982; (ed.) Teubner Livy Books XXVI-VII, 1982; (co-ed.) George Buchanan: Tragedies, 1982; (ed.) Divine Providence and Human Suffering, 1985; (ed.) Teubner Livy Books XXVIIIXXX, 1986; (co-ed.) William of Newburgh: History of English Affairs, 1988. Add: 17 Broom Rd., Glasgow G43 2TP, Scotland.

WALSH, Sheila. Also writes as Sophie Leyton. British, b. 1928. Historical/Romance. Secty., Romantic Novelists Assn. (Chmn. 1985–87). *Publs:* The Golden Songbird, 1975; Madalena, 1976; The Sergeant Major's Daughter, 1977; A Fine Silk Purse, 1978, in U.S. as Lord Gilmore's Bride, 1979; The Incomparable Miss Brady, 1980; (as Sophie Leyton) Lady Cecily's Dilemma, 1980, in U.S. as The Pink Parasol, 1985; The Rose Domino, 1981; A Highly Respectable Marriage, 1983; The Runaway Bride, 1984; Cousins of a Kind (in U.S. as The Diamond Waterfall), 1985; The Incorrigible Rake, 1985; Improper Acquaintances, 1986; An Insubstantial Pageant, in U.S. as The Wary Widow, 1986; Bath Intrigue, 1986; Lady Aurelia's Bequest, 1987; Minerva, Marquis, 1988; The Nabob, 1989. Add: 35 Coudray Rd., Southport, Merseyside PR9 9NL, England.

WALSH, Stephen. British, b. 1942. Music. Freelance music critic; Sr. Lectr. in Music, University Coll., Cardiff, since 1976. Producer, Gramophone Dept., BBC, London, 1964–65; Music Critic, Listener, London, 1965; Deputy Music Critic, Observer, London, 1966–85. *Publs:* The Lieder of Schumann, 1971; Bartok Chamber Music, 1982; The Music of Stravinsky, 1988. Add: The Cwm, Welsh Newton, Monmouth, Gwent NP5 3RW, Wales.

WALSH, William. British, b. 1916. Education, Literature. Prof. of Commonwealth Literature, Univ. of Leeds, since 1972, now Emeritus (Prof. of Education, and Head, Dept. of Education, 1957–72; Chmn., Combined Faculties of Arts, Economic and Social Studies and Law, 1964–66; Chmn., Bd. of Faculty of Education, 1968–70; Pro-Vice-Chancellor, 1965–67; Chmn., Bd. of Extramural Studies, 1969–76, and Sch. of English, 1973–78). Member, Univ. Grants Cttee., Education Sub-Cttee., 1965–70. *Publs:* The Use of Imagination: Educational Thought and the Literary Mind, 1959; A Human Idiom: Literature and Humanity, 1964; Coleridge: The Work and the Relevance, 1967; A Manifold Voice: Studies in Commonwealth Literature, 1970; R.K. Narayan, 1972; Commonwealth Literature, 1973; V.S. Naipaul, 1973; (ed.) Readings in Commonwealth Literature, 1973; D.J. Enright: Poet of Humanism, 1974; Patrick White: Voss, 1976; Patrick White's Fiction, 1977; F.R. Leavis, 1980; Introduction to Keats, 1981; R.K. Narayan, 1982. Add: 27 Moor Dr., Headingley, Leeds LS6 4BY, England.

WALSHE, R(obert) D(aniel). Australian, b. 1923. Education, History, Language/Linguistics, Writing/Journalism. Teacher of Creative Writing, Sutherland Shire Evening Coll. Former Managing Dir., Martindale Press Ltd.; Secondary sch. teacher, 1952–63; Editorial Dir., A.H. and A.W. Reed Publrs. (Aust.) Pty. Ltd., 1970–75. *Publs:* (with P.M. Wheeler) Mastering Words, 1961; Guide to World History since 1789, 1962; (with P. O'Heara and D. Shirley) How to Study Better, 1963; (with P.M. Wheeler) Mastering English, 1969; (ed.) Teaching the Process of Composition Writing, 1971; (ed. with N.A. Little) Ways We Teach History, 1971; (ed.) Exploring the New English, 1973; (with J.J. Cosgrove and E.B. McKillop) Power and Persuasion: Twenty Modern Biographies of Great Men, 1974; (ed.) The New English in Action, 1974; Better Writing, Clearer Thinking, 1979; Every Child Can Write, 1981; (with B. Dwyer) Learning to Read the Media, 1984; (ed. with P. March) Writing and Learning in Australia, 1986; Teaching Writing: K-12, 1988. Add: Unit 5, 74 Linden St., Sutherland, N.S.W. 2232, Australia.

WALTER, Elizabeth. British. Novels/Short stories, Translations. Freelance ed. and translator, and Ed. of Collins Crime Club. *Publs:* The More Deceived; The Nearest and Dearest; Snowfall; The Sin-Eater; Davy Jones's Tale; Come and Get Me; Dead Woman; A Christmas Scrapbook; Season's Greetings; A Wedding Bouquet; A Season of Goodwill; (trans.) A Scent of Lilies, by Claire Gallois; (trans.) Lord of the River, by Bernard Clavel; (trans.) A Matter of Feeling, by Janine Bloissard. Add: c/o Collins, 8 Grafton St., London W1X 3LA, England.

WALTER Mildred Pitts. American. Children's fiction. *Publs:* Lillie of Watts, 1969; Lillie of Watts Takes a Giant Step, 1971; Ty's One-Man Band, 1980; The Girl on the Outside, 1982; Because We Are, 1983; My Mama Needs Me, 1983; Brother to the Wind, 1985; Trouble's Child, 1985; Justin and the Best Biscuits in the World, 1986; Maria Loves Rock, 1988. Add: c/o Bradbury Press, 866 Third Ave., New York, N.Y. 10022, U.S.A.

WALTERS, Alan Arthur. British, b. 1926. Economics, Money/Finance. Prof. of Political Economy, Johns Hopkins Univ., Baltimore, since 1977. Lectr. and subsequently Sr. Lectr., 1952–61, and Prof. and Head, Dept. of Econometrics and Social Statistics, 1961–68, Univ. of Birmingham; Cassel Prof. of Economics, London Sch. of Economics, 1968–77. Adviser to the Prime Minister, 1981–83. *Publs:* (with R.W. Clower, G. Dalton and M. Harwitz) Growth Without Development, 1966; Integration in Freight Transport, 1968; The Economics of Road User Chargers,

1968; An Introduction to Econometrics, 1968, 1970; (with E. Bennathan) Economics of Ocean Freight Rates, 1969; Money in Boom and Slump, 1969, 3rd ed. 1971; Money and Banking, 1970; (with Anthony Churchill et al) Road Use Charges in Central America, 1972; (ed.) Money and Banking: Noise and Prices, 1975; (with P.R.G. Layard) Microeconomic Theory, 1977; (with Esra Bennathan) Port Pricing and Investment Policy for Developing Countries, 1979; Britain's Economic Renaissance, 1986. Add: 2820 P St. N.W., Washington, D.C., U.S.A.

WALTERS, Hugh. Pseud. for Walter Llewellyn Hughes. British, b. 1910. Children's fiction. Former Managing Dir., Bradsteds Ltd., engineers, and Chmn., Walter Hughes Ltd., furnishings. Justice of the Peace, 1947–74. *Publs:* Blast Off at Woomera, 1957, in U.S. as Blast-Off at 0300, 1958; The Domes of Pico, 1958, in U.S. as Menace from the Moon, 1959; Operation Columbus, 1960, in U.S. as First on the Moon, 1961; Moon Base One, 1961, in U.S. as Outpost on the Moon, 1962; Expedition Venus, 1962; Destination Mars, 1963; Terror by Satellite, 1964; Mission to Mercury, 1965; Journey to Jupiter, 1965; Spaceship to Saturn, 1967; The Mohole Mystery, 1968, in U.S. as The Mohole Menace, 1969; Nearly Neptune (in U.S. as Neptune One Is Missing), 1969; First Contact?, 1971; Passage to Pluto, 1973; Tony Hale, Space Detective, 1973; Murder on Mars, 1975; Boy Astronaut, 1977; The Caves of Drach, 1977; The Last Disaster, 1978; The Blue Aura, 1979; First Family on the Moon, 1979; The Dark Triangle, 1981; School on the Moon, 1981; "P.K.," 1986. Add: 16 Elm Ave., Bilston, W. Midlands WV14 6AS, England.

WALTERS, John Beauchamp. British, b. 1906. History, Philosophy, Biography. *Publs:* Will America Fight?, 1942; Light in the Window, 1942; Mind Unshaken, 1961; Essence of Buddhism, 1961; Splendour and Scandal, 1968; Aldershot Review, 1970; The Royal Griffin, 1972; (with Joan Walters) Chris, 1983. Add: Edificio Alca, Apt. A-5, El Botanico, Puerto de la Cruz, Tenerife, Canary Islands.

WALTHAM, Tony (A.C.) British, b. 1942. Earth sciences, Recreation/Leisure/Hobbies. Lectr. in Geology, Trent Polytechnic, Nottingham, since 1968. *Publs:* (ed.) Limestones and Caves of Northwest England, 1974; Caves, 1974; World of Caves, 1976; Catastrophe: The Violent Earth, 1978; Caves, Crags and Gorges, 1984; (with John Middleton) The Underground Atlas, 1986; Yorkshire Dales—Limestone Country, 1987; Yorkshire Dales National Park, 1987; Ground Subsidence, 1989. Add: Civil Engineering Dept.,Trent Polytechnic, Nottingham NG1 4BU, England.

WALTON, Henry John. British, b. 1924. Education, Psychiatry, Psychology. Prof. of Intnl. Medical Education, formerly Prof. of Psychiatry, Univ. of Edinburgh. Pres., World Federation for Medical Education; Foundn. Member and past Pres., Soc. for Research into Higher Education; Pres., Assn. for Medical Education in Europe. Past Chmn., Assn. for the Study of Medical Education, and Assn. of Univ. Teachers of Psychiatry. *Publs:* Small Group Methods in Medical Teaching, 1973; (co-author) Alcoholism, 1974, 1989; (ed.) Small Group Psychotherapy, 1974; (co-author) Examinations in Medicine, 1976; (co-ed.) Innovations in Medical Education, 1978; (ed.) Dictionary of Psychiatry, 1985; (ed.) Education and Training in Psychiatry, 1986; (co-ed.) Newer Developments in Assessing Clinical Competence, 1986. Add: 38 Blacket Pl., Edinburgh EH9 1RL, Scotland.

WALTON, James. British, b. 1911. Archaeology/Antiquities, Architecture. Publr., Longman Group, South Africa, since 1960 (Managing Dir., 1964–72). Deputy Dir. of Education, Lesotho, 1947–60. *Publs:* Homesteads of the Yorkshire Dales, 1947; Craftwork for African Schools, 1949; Homesteads and Villages of South Africa, 1952, 1965; Vroee Plase en Nedersettings in kie Orange Vrystaat, 1955; Timbered Buildings of the Huddersfield District, 1955; Father of Horses and Father of Kindness, 1958; Old Maseru, 1958; (ed.) The Mountain Bushmen of Basutoland, 1957; Early Ghoya Settlement in the Orange Free State, 1965; (ed. with J.R. Wahl) Thomas Pringle in South Africa, 1970; Water-Mills, Windmills, and Horse-Mills of South Africa, 1974; The Josephine Mill and Its Owners, 1978; Cape Dovecots and Fowl-runs, 1985. Add: 4 Mountain Rd., Claremont, Cape, South Africa.

WALTON, (Sir) John (Nicholas). British, b. 1922. Medicine. Physician: Warden, Green Coll., Oxford, since 1983. Research Asst., Univ. of Durham, 1951–56; First Asst. in Neurology, Newcastle upon Tyne, 1956–58; Consultant Neurologist, Newcastle Univ. Hospitals, 1958–63; Prof. of Neurology, 1968–83, and Dean of Medicine, 1971–81, Univ. of Newcastle upon Tyne. Pres., British Medical Assn., 1981–82; and Royal Soc. of Medicine, 1984–86; Pres., Gen. Medical Council

(U.K.), 1982–89. *Publs:* Subarachnoid Haemorrhage, 1956; (with R.D. Adams) Polymyositis, 1958; Essentials of Neurology, 1961, 6th ed. 1989; Disorders of Voluntary Muscle, 1964, 5th ed. 1988; Brain's Diseases of the Nervous System, 7th ed. 1969, 9th ed. 1985; (with F.L. Mastaglia) Skeletal Muscle Pathology, 1982; Introduction to Clinical Neuroscience, 1983, 1987; (with P.B. Beeson and R. Bodley Scott) Oxford Companion to Medicine, 1986. Add: Green Coll., Oxford OX2 6HG, England.

WALTON, Ortiz (Montaigne). American, b. 1933. Sociology. Freelance writer and musician. With Buffalo Philharmonic, N.Y., 1954–57, and Boston Symphony Orchestra, 1957–62; Member, Ethnic Studies Dept., Univ. of California, Berkeley, 1969–70, 1974–76. *Publs:* Coronation of the King: Contributions by Duke Ellington to Black Culture, 1969; A Comparative Analysis of the African and Western Aesthetic, 1970; Music: Black, White and Blue, 1972. Add: 1129 Bancroft Way, Berkeley, Calif. 94702, U.S.A.

WALTON, Richard J(ohn). American, b. 1928. Children's non-fiction, History, International relations/Current affairs, Politics/Government. Reporter, New York World Telegram and The Sun, NYC, 1955–59; Producer and Broadcaster of Report to Africa, Voice of America, Washington, D.C., 1959–62; U.N. Corresp., Voice of America, 1962–67. *Publs:* The Remnants of Power: The Tragic Last Years of Adlai Stevenson, 1968; America and the Cold War, 1969; Beyond Diplomacy, 1970; Cold War and Counter Revolution: The Foreign Policy of John F. Kennedy, 1972; The United States and Latin America, 1972; Canada and the U.S.A., 1972; Congress and American Foreign Policy, 1972; The United States and the Far East, 1973; Henry Wallace, Harry Truman, and the Cold War, 1976; The Power of Oil, 1977; Swarthmore College: An Informal History, 1986; John Brown's Tract: Lost Adirondack Empire, 1988. Add: 5 Grenore St., Warwick, R.I. 02888, U.S.A.

WALTZ, Kenneth N. American, b. 1924. International relations/Current affairs, Military/Defence, Politics/Government. Ford Prof. of Political Science and Comparative Studies, Univ. of California, Berkeley, since 1971. Lectr., 1953–56, and Asst. Prof., 1956–57, Columbia Univ., NYC; Assoc. Prof., 1957–64, and Prof., 1964–66, Swarthmore Coll., Pa.; Prof., Brandeis Univ., Waltham, Mass., 1966–71; Adlai Stevenson Prof. of Intnl. Politics, 1967–71. *Publs:* Man, The State, and War: A Theoretical Analysis, 1959; Foreign Policy and Democratic Politics: The American and British Experience, 1967; (with S. Speigel) Conflict in World Politics, 1971; (with R.J. Art) The Use of Force, 1971, 3rd ed. 1988; Theory of International Politics, 1979. Add: Dept. of Political Science, Univ. of California, Berkeley, Calif. 94720, U.S.A.

WALVIN, James. British, b. 1942. History, Race Relations, Sport. Reader in History, Univ. of York. *Publs:* (with M. Craton), A Jamaica Plantation: Worthy Park 1670-1870, 1970; The Black Presence: A Documentary of the Negro in Britain, 1971; Black and White: The Negro and English Society 1555-1945, 1973; The People's Game: A Social History of British Football, 1975; (co-ed.) Slavery, Abolition, and Emancipation, 1976; Beside the Seaside: A Social History of the Popular Seaside Holiday, 1978; Leisure and Society 1830-1950, 1978; (co-ed.) Abolition of the Atlantic Slave Trade, 1981; A Child's World: A Social History of English Childhood 1800-1914, 1982; (ed.) Slavery and British Society 1776-1848, 1982; (with E. Royle) English Radicals and Reformers 1776-1848, 1982; Slavery and the Slave Trade, 1983; Black Personalities: Africans in Britain in the Era of Slavery, 1983; (co-ed.) Leisure in Britain since 1800, 1983; Urban England 1776-1851, 1984; (co-ed.) Manliness and Morality, 1985; Football and the Decline of Britain, 1986; England, Slaves, and Freedom 1776-1838, 1986; Victorian Values, 1987. Add: Dept. of History, Univ of York, York YO1 5DD, England.

WALWORTH, Arthur. American, b. 1903. History, Travel/Exploration/Adventure, Biography. Instr., Yale-in-China, Changsha, 1925–26; Staff, Educational Dept., Houghton Mifflin Co., Boston, 1927–43. *Publs:* School Histories at War, 1938; Black Ships Off Japan, 1946; Cape Breton: Isle of Romance, 1948; Woodrow Wilson, 2 vols, (vol. I, Pulitzer Prize for Biography), 1958; America's Moment: 1918, American Diplomacy at the End of World War I, 1977; Wilson and His Peacemakers: American Diplomacy at the Paris Peace Conference 1919, 1986. Add: 865 Central Ave., E-206, Needham, Mass. 02192, U.S.A.

WALZER, Michael. American, b. 1935. Philosophy, Politics/Government. Prof. of Social Science, Inst. of Advanced Study, Princeton, N.J., since 1980. Member, Bd. of Govs., The Hebrew Univ., Jerusalem, since 1974; Ed., Dissent, New York, since 1976; Contrib. Ed., The New Republic, Washington, D.C., since 1977. Asst. Prof. of Politics, Princeton Univ., New Jersey, 1962–66; Prof. of Govt., Harvard Univ.,

Cambridge, Mass., 1966–80. *Publs:* The Revolution of the Saints, 1965; (ed., with Philip Green) The Political Imagination in Literature, 1969; Obligations: Essays on Disobedience, War, and Citizenship, 1970; Political Action, 1971; Regicide and Revolution, 1974; Just and Unjust Wars, 1977; Radical Principles, 1980; Spheres of Justice, 1983; Exodus and Revolution, 1985; Interpretation and Social Criticism, 1987; The Company of Critics, 1988. Add: Sch. of Social Science, Inst. of Advanced Study, Princeton, N.J. 08540, U.S.A.

WAMBAUGH, Joseph. American, b. 1937. Novels/Short stories, Criminology. Detective Sergeant, Los Angeles Police Force, 1960–74. *Publs:* The New Centurions, 1971; The Blue Knight, 1972; The Onion Field, 1973; The Choirboys, 1975; The Black Marble, 1978; The Glitter Dome, 1981; The Delta Star, 1983; Lines and Shadows, 1984; The Secrets of Harry Bright, 1985; Echoes in the Darkness, 1987; The Blooding, 1989. Add: 30 Linda Isle, Newport Beach, Calif. 92260, U.S.A.

WANDOR, Michelene. British, b. 1940. Novels/Short Stories, Plays/Screenplays, Poetry, Sex, Theatre, Women. Poetry ed., Time Out, London, 1971–82; resident writer, Univ. of Kent, Canterbury, 1982–83. *Publs: plays*—(with Dinah Brooke) Sink Songs, 1975; Care and Control (in Strike While the Iron Is Hot), 1980; Spilt Milk, and Mal de Mère (in Play Nine), 1981; Aurora Leigh (in Plays by Women 1), 1982; Five Plays, 1984; The Wandering Jew, 1987; *fiction*—(co-author) Tales and More Tales I Tell My Mother, 2 vols., 1978–87; Guests in the Body, 1986; (with Sara Maitland) Arky Types, 1987; *poetry*—Upbeat, 1982; (co-author) Touch Papers, 1982; Gardens of Eden, 1984; Collected Poems, 1990. *other*—(ed.) The Body Politic, 1972; (co-author) The Great Divide, 1976; (co-ed.) Cutlasses and Earrings, 1977; (ed.) Strike While the Iron Is Hot, 1980; Understudies: Theatre and Sexual Politics, 1981, rev. ed. as Carry On, Understudies, 1986; (ed.) Plays by Women 1-4, 4 vols., 1982–85; (ed.) On Gender and Writing, 1983; Look Back in Gender: Sexuality and the Family in Post-1956 British Drama, 1987; Wandor on Women Writers, 1989; Once a Feminist, 1990. Add: 71 Belsize Lane, London NW3 5AU, England.

WANG, Hui-Ming. Chinese, b. 1922. Poetry, Art, Mythology/Folklore, Recreation/Leisure/Hobbies, Translations. Prof. of Art, Univ. of Massachusetts, Amherst, Mass., since 1964; also independent painter and woodcutter. Member of Faculty, Yale Univ., New Haven, Conn., 1951–61. *Publs:* Epoh Studio Woodcuts, 1968; The Birds and the Animals, 1969; (trans.) The Boat Untied, 1971; (ed.) The Land on the Tip of a Hair, 1972; (with Robert Bly) Jumping Out of Bed, 1972; (trans.) Ten Poems and Lyrics by Mao Tse-tung, 1975; (with Anna Wang) The Chinese Book of Table Tennis, 1981; Folk Tales of the West Lakes, 1982; Small Is Not Little, 1986. Add: Greenfield Rd., Montague, Mass. 01351, U.S.A.

WARD, Alan J. American, b. 1937. History, Politics/Government. Prof. of Govt., Coll. of William and Mary, Williamsburg, Va., since 1967. Former Lectr. in Politics, Univ. of Adelaide, S.A. *Publs:* Ireland and Anglo-American Relations 1899-1921, 1969; The Easter Rising: Revolution and Irish Nationalism, 1980; Northern Ireland: Living with the Crisis, 1987. Add: Dept. of Govt., Coll. of William and Mary, Williamsburg, Va. 23185, U.S.A.

WARD, Christopher. British. Social commentary/phenomena. Former Columnist, Daily Mirror newspaper, London; Ed., Daily Express, London. *Publs:* How to Complain: The Indispensable Manual to Consumer Guerilla Warfare, 1974; Our Cheque Is in the Post, 1980. Add: c/o Redwood Publishing, 20-26 Brunswick Pl., London N1 6DJ, England.

WARD, David. British, b. 1938. Geography, History, Social sciences. Prof. of Geography, Univ. of Wisconsin, Madison, since 1966. Ed., Journal of Historical Geography. Ed., Assn. of American Geographers Monograph Series, 1972–75; Ed., Journal of Historical Geography, 1976–81. *Publs:* Cities and Immigrants: A Geography of Change in Nineteenth Century America, 1971; Geographic Perspectives on America's Past, 1979; Poverty, Ethnicity and the American City 1840-1925, 1989. Add: Dept. of Geography, Science Hall, Univ. of Wisconsin, Madison, Wisc. 53706, U.S.A.

WARD, Donald. British, b. 1909. Poetry. Former higher grade postman. *Publs:* The Dead Snake, 1971; A Few Rooks Circling Trees, 1975; Border Country, 1981; By the Luminous Water, 1984. Add: 50 Daleside, Orpington, Kent BR6 6EQ, England.

WARD, Douglas Turner. American, b. 1930. Plays/Screenplays. Actor and stage dir. Co-Founder, and Artistic Dir., since 1967, Negro

Ensemble Co., NYC. Journalist, 1948–51; with Paul Manns Actors Workshop, NYC, 1955–58. *Publs:* Happy Ending, and Day of Absence, 1966; The Reckoning, 1970; Brotherhood, 1970. Add: Negro Ensemble Co., 424 W. 55th St., New York, N.Y. 10019, U.S.A.

WARD, Elizabeth Honor. Also writes as Ward S. Leslie. British, b. 1926. Children's non-fiction, Physics, Theology/Religion. *Publs:* (as Ward S. Leslie) Touchdown to Adventure, 1958; Senior Physics (Books 1 and 2), 1965–66; (with G. Osae-Addo) Newtown Families, 1966; The Story of Creation, 1973; (with A.H. Ward) Essential Senior Physics, 1974; (with K.Baker) AIDS, Sex, and Family Planning: A Christian View, 1989. Add: Coaster's Cottage, Hermitage, Dorchester DT2 7BB, England.

WARD, Harry Merrill. American, b. 1929. History. Prof., Univ. of Richmond, Va., since 1978 (Assoc. Prof., 1965–78). Consultant to Bicentennial radio series produced by U.S. Bicentennial Media Group Inc. Formerly with: Georgetown Coll., Ky., 1959–61; Morehead State Univ., Ky., 1961–65; Visiting Assoc. Prof., Southern Illinois Univ., Carbondale, 1967–68. *Publs:* United Colonies of New England 1643-90, 1961; Department of War 1781-95, 1962, 1981; Unite or Die: Intercolony Relations 1690-1763, 1971; Statism in Plymouth Colony, 1973; (co-author) Richmond During the Revolution 1775-83, 1978; Duty, Honor, or Country: General George Weedon and the American Revolution, 1979; Richmond: An Illustrated History, 1985; Charles Scott and the "Spirit of '76", 1988; Major General Adam Stephen and the Cause of American Liberty, 1989; Colonial America 1607-1763, 1990. Add: Dept. of History, Univ. of Richmond, Richmond, Va. 23173, U.S.A.

WARD, John Manning. Australian, b. 1919. History. Vice-Chancellor and Principal, since 1981, and Prof. of History, since 1982, Univ. of Sydney (Challis Prof. of History, 1949–79; Deputy Vice Chancellor, 1979–81). Barrister, non-practising, Supreme Court of New South Wales. Chmn., Archives Authority of N.S.W., 1979–82. *Publs:* British Policy in the South Pacific 1786-1893, 1948, 3rd ed. 1976; (co-author) Trusteeship in the Pacific, 1949; Australia's First Governor-General: Sir Charles Fitzroy 1851-1855, 1953; Earl Grey and the Australian Colonies 1846-1857, 1958; (co-author) The Pattern of Australian Culture, 1963; Empire in the Antipodes: The British in Australia 1840-1860, 1966; (co-author) Historiography of the British Empire-Commonwealth, 1966; Changes in Britain 1919-1957, 1968; (co-author) Historians at Work, 1973; Colonial Self-Government, 1976; James Macarthur, Colonial Conservative 1798-1867, 1981. Add: Univ. of Sydney, Sydney, N.S.W. 2006, Australia.

WARD, (John Stephen) Keith. British, b. 1938. Philosophy, Theology/Religion. Prof. of the History and Philosophy of Religion, Univ. of London, since 1985 (F.D. Maurice Prof. of Moral and Social Theology, 1982–85). Lectr. in Logic, 1964–66, and Lectr. in Moral Philosophy, 1966–68, Univ. of Glasgow; Lectr. in Moral Philosophy, Univ. of St. Andrews, Scotland, 1969–71; Lectr. in Philosophy, King's Coll., Univ. of London, 1971–74; Dean of Trinity Hall, Cambridge, 1975–82. *Publs:* 50 Key Words in Philosophy, 1968; Ethics and Christianity, 1970; The Development of Kant's View of Ethics, 1972; The Concept of God, 1974; The Divine Image, 1976; The Promise, 1981; Rational Theology and the Creativity of God, 1982; Holding Fast to God, 1982; Battle for the Soul, 1985; The Turn of the Tide, 1986; Images of Eternity, 1987; The Rule of Love, 1988; Divine Action, 1990. Add: Old Brewery Cottage, Lower Froyle, Alton GU34 4LX, England.

WARD, Jonas. *See* **COX,** William R.

WARD, Jonas. *See* **GARFIELD,** Brian.

WARD, Norman. Canadian, b. 1918. Politics/Government, Autobiography/Memoirs/Personal, Essays, Humor/Satire. Prof. of Political Science, Univ. of Saskatchewan, Saskatoon, 1956–85, now Emeritus (Instr., 1945–48; Asst. Prof., 1948–51; Assoc. Prof., 1951–55). Chmn., Saskatchewan Public Admin. Foundn., 1963–65; Member, Advisory Cttee. on Election Expenses, 1964–65; Vice-Chmn., 1964–65, 1972–73, 1974–75, and Member, 1982–83, Saskatchewan Electoral Boundaries Commn.; Dir., Inst. for Research on Public Policy, 1972–76; Chmn., Saskatchewan Archives Bd., 1982. *Publs:* The Canadian House of Commons: Representation, 1950, 1963; Mice in the Beer, 1960; Government in Canada, 1961, 1964; The Public Purse: A Study in Canadian Democracy, 1962; The Fully Processed Cheese, 1964; (ed.) The Government of Canada, 1963, 6th ed. 1987; (ed.) A Party Politician: The Memoirs of Chubby Power, 1966; (ed. with D. Spafford) Politics in Saskatchewan, 1968; (with D. Hoffmann) Bilingualism and Biculturalism in the Canadian House of Commons, 1970; (ed.) Democratic Government in Canada, 1971, 5th ed.

1989; (ed.) The Politician, 1976; Her Majesty's Mice, 1977. Add: 412 Albert Ave., Saskatoon, Sask. S7N 1G3, Canada.

WARD, Philip. British, b. 1938. Plays/Screenplays, Poetry, Librarianship, Travel/Exploration/Adventure, Translations. Co-ordinator, Library Services, and Dir., Libyan Research Library, Oasis Oil Co. of Libya Inc., Tripoli, 1963–71; Dir., Indonesia library project, 1973–74. *Publs:* Collected Poems, 1960; The Quell-Finger Dialogues, 1965; Seldom Rains, 1967; A Survey of Libyan Bibliographical Resources, 2nd ed. 1967; Ambigamus, 1967; Touring Libya: The Western Provinces, 1967; Apuleius on Trial at Sabratha, 1967; Poems for Participants, 1968; At the Best of Times, 1968; A Musical Breakfast, 1968; Touring Libya: The Southern Provinces, 1968; The Poet and the Microscope, 1968; The Okefani Song of Nij Zitru, 1969; Touring Libya: The Eastern Provinces, 1969; A Lizard and Other Distractions, 1969; Tripoli, 1969; Maps on the Ceiling, 1969; Motoring to Nalut, 1970; Spanish Literary Appreciation, 1970; Garrity: Nine Plays, 1970; Sabratha, 1970; Touring Lebanon, 1971; The Way to Wadi al-Khail, 1971; Touring Cyprus, 1971; Touring Iran, 1971; Come with Me to Ireland, 1972; Pincers, 1973; The Aeolian Islands, 1974; A House on Fire, 1974; Bangkok, 1975; Indonesia: The Development of a National Library Service, 1975; A Maltese Boyhood, 1975; Indonesian Traditional Poetry, 1975; Indonesia: The Development of a Provincial Library Service, 1975; Television Plays, 1976; Impostors and Their Imitators, 1978; The Keymakers and Other Poems, 1978; The Oxford Companion to Spanish Literature, 1978; A Dictionary of Common Fallacies, 1978, 2nd ed. 2 vols., 1980; Cambridge Street Literature, 1978; (ed.) The Gold-Mines of Midian, by Richard F. Burton, 1979; (with Audrey J. Ward) The Small Publisher, 1979; Lost Songs, 1981; A Lifetime's Reading, 1982; (trans.) Greguerías, by R. Gomez de la Serna, 1982; Albania: A Travel Guide, 1983; (trans.) The Pure-Bred Arabian Horse, by Carlo Guarmani, 1984; Forgotten Games: A Novel of Cortés and Montezuma, 1984; Japanese Capitals, 1985; Travels in Oman, 1987; Finnish Cities, 1987; Polish Cities, 1988; Rajasthan, Agra, Delhi, 1989; Bulgaria: A Travel Guide, 1989. Add: c/o Oxford University Press, Walton St., Oxford, England.

WARD, Ralph Gerard. Australian, b. 1933. Geography, Social sciences. Dir., Research Sch. of Pacific Studies, Australian National Univ., Canberra, since 1980 (Prof. of Human Geography, 1971–80). Jr. Lectr., then Lectr., Univ. of Auckland, 1956–61; Lectr. in Geography, Univ. Coll., London, 1961–67; Prof. of Geography, Univ. of Papua New Guinea, 1967–71. *Publs:* (ed. with M.W. Ward) New Zealand's Industrial Potential, 1961; Islands of the South Pacific, 1961; Land Use and Population in Fiji, 1965; (ed.) American Activities in the Central Pacific 1790-1870, 1966–69; (ed. with D.A.M. Lea) An Atlas of Papua New Guinea, 1970; (ed.) Man in the Pacific Islands, 1972; (with M. Levison and J.W. Webb) The Settlement of Polynesia: A Computer Simulation, 1973; (ed. with A. Proctor) South Pacific Agriculture: Choices and Constraints, 1980; (with H.B.C. Brookfield and F. Ellis) Land, Cane, and Coconuts: Rural Economy in Fiji, 1985; (co-ed.) New Directions in the South Pacific, 1988. Add: 8 Booth Cres., Cook, A.C.T. 2614, Australia.

WARD, Russel (Braddock). Australian, b. 1914. History, Literature, Politics/Government, Autobiography. Member, Univ. Council, since 1960, and Deputy Chancellor, since 1983, Univ. of New England, Armidale (Lectr., 1957–60; Sr. Lectr., 1960–63; Assoc. Prof., 1963–67; Prof. of History, 1967–79). Pres., Canberra Branch, Fellowship of Australian Writers, 1956, Univ. of New England Teachers' Assn., 1959, and Univ. of New England Union, 1965, 1966. *Publs:* Three Street Ballads, 1957; The Australian Legend, 1958; (ed.) The Penguin Book of Australian Ballads, 1964; Australia, 1965; (with P. O'Shaughnessy and G. Inson) The Restless Years, 1968; (with J. Robertson) Such Was Life: Documents in Australian Social History 1788-1850, vol. 1, 1969, vol.2, 1984, vol. 3, 1986; (with G. Inson) The Glorious Years, 1971; (ed. and trans.) The New Australia, by E. Marin La Meslee, 1973; (ed. and trans.) Socialism Without Doctrine, by Albert Métin; A Nation for a Continent, The History of Australia: The Twentieth Century, 1977; Australia since the Coming of Man, 1982; Finding Australia, 1987; A Radical Life: The Autobiography of Russel Ward, 1988. Add: History Dept., Univ. of New England, Armidale, N.S.W. 2350, Australia.

WARDELL Phyl(lis, née Robinson). New Zealander, b. 1909. Children's fiction. *Publs:* Gold at Kapai, 1960; The Secret of the Lost Tribe of Te Anau, 1961; Passage to Dusky, 1967; Hazard Island, 1976; The Nelson Treasure, 1983; Beyond the Narrows, 1985. Add: 192 Salisbury St., Christchurch, New Zealand.

WARDEN, Lewis Christopher. American, b. 1913. Novels/Short stories, Law, Biography. Practice of Law, Ohio, 1938–45; Instr., Commercial Law, Ohio, 1939–41; Judge of the Court of Common Pleas, Ohio, 1944–50; Ed., 1950–78, Supervising Ed., 1961–62, and Project Ed., 1968–78, Lawyers Co-op. Publishing Co., Rochester, N.Y. Book Reviewer, Harvard Law Sch. Bulletin, 1971–74. *Publs:* The New Crusade, 1934; The Life of Blackstone, 1938; (contrib. ed.) American Law Reports, 1950–53; (contrib. ed.) Ohio Jurisprudence, 2nd ed., 1953–56; Torrent of the Willows, 1954; (contrib. ed.) Florida Jurisprudence, 1956–58; (contrib. ed.) New York Jurisprudence, 1958–62; (contrib. ed.) American Jurisprudence, 1962–78; Murder on Wheels, 1964; Running Against the Wind, 1981. Add: 8787 E. Mountain View, Scottsdale, Ariz. 85258, U.S.A.

WARDHAUGH, Ronald. Canadian, b. 1932. Language/Linguistics. Prof. Dept. of Linguistics, Univ. of Toronto, since 1975 (Chmn., 1975–86). Prof. of Lingusitics, Univ. of Michigan, Ann Arbor, 1972–75 (Asst. Prof., 1966–68, Assoc. Prof., 1968–72). Dir., Center for Research on Language and Language Behavior, 1969–71. *Publs:* Reading: A Linguistic Perspective, 1969; Introduction to Linguistics, 1972; Topics in Applied Linguistics, 1974; The Contexts of Language, 1976; (co-ed.) A Survey of Applied Linguistics, 1976; Language and Nationhood: The Canadian Experience, 1983; How Conversation Works, 1985; An Introduction ot Sociolinguistics, 1986; Languages in Competition, 1987. Add: 31 Walmer Rd, Apt.6, Toronto, Ont. M5R 2W7, Canada.

WARDLE, David. British, b. 1930. Education. Head, Dept. of Education, Padgate Coll. of Education, Stoke-on-Trent, since 1971. Principal Lectr. in Education, Alsager Coll. of Education, 1967–71. *Publs:* English Popular Education 1780-1970, 1970; Education and Society in Nineteenth Century Nottingham, 1971; The Rise of the Schooled Society, 1974; English Popular Education 1780-1975, 1976. Add: 151 Hassall Rd., Alsager, Stoke-on-Trent, England.

WARDLE, (John) Irving. British, b. 1929. Plays/Screenplays, Theatre, Biography. Drama Critic, The Times newspaper, London, since 1963. Deputy Theatre Critic, The Observer, London, 1960; Ed., Gambit, 1973–75. *Publs:* The Houseboy (play), 1974; The Theatres of George Devine, 1978. Add: 51 Richmond Rd., New Barnet, Herts., England.

WARDROPER, John Edmund. Canadian, b. 1923. History, Literature, Humor/Satire. Author and freelance journalist. Previously on staffs of British national newspapers, 1951–84 (The Sunday Times, 1972–84). *Publs:* (ed. and compiler) Love and Drollery, 1969; (ed. and compiler) Jest Upon Jest, 1970; (ed.) Demaundes Joyous, 1971; Kings, Lords and Wicked Libellers, 1973; The Caricatures of George Cruikshank, 1977; Juggernaut, 1981. Add: 60 St. Paul's Rd., London N1, England.

WARE, Jean. (Mrs. Hugh Hunt). British, b. 1914. Children's fiction, Biography. Weekly contrib. and script and feature writer, BBC Radio, 1949–66; Feature Writer, Liverpool Daily Post, 1951–66. *Publs:* Campau Dic, 1956; Rowdy House, 1961; (with Hugh Hunt) The Several Lives of a Victorian Vet, 1979. Add: 12 Vine Lane, Wrecclesham, Farnham, Surrey, England.

WARE, Kallistos (Timothy Richard). British, b. 1934. Theology/ Religion. Fellow of Pembroke Coll., and Lectr. in Eastern Orthodox Studies, Univ. of Oxford, since 1966. Member of the Monastic Brotherhood of St. John, Patmos, Greece; Asst. Bishop in the Orthdox Archdiocese of Thyateira and Great Britain. *Publs:* The Orthodox Church, 1963; Eustratios Argenti: A Study of the Greek Church Under Turkish Rule, 1964; (ed.) The Art of Prayer: An Orthodox Anthology, 1966; (trans. with Mother Mary) The Festal Menaion, 1969; The Lenten Triodion, 1978; (trans. with G.E.H. Palmer and P.S. Sherrard) The Philokalia, vol. I, 1979, vol. II, 1981, vol. III, 1984; The Orthodox Way, 1979; (with Georges Barrois) Women and the Priesthood, 1982; (ed.) The Jesus Prayer, 1987. Add: 15 Staverton Rd., Oxford OX2 6XH, England.

WARE, Wallace. *See* **KARP**, David.

WARHAM, John. British, b. 1919. Photography, Zoology. Reader in Zoology, Univ. of Canterbury, since 1966. *Publs:* The Technique of Bird Photography, 1956, 4th ed. 1983; The Technique of Wildlife Cinematography, 1966; (with D.L. and V.N. Serventy) The Handbook of Australian Seabirds, 1971. Add: Zoology Dept., Univ. of Canterbury, Christchurch, New Zealand.

WARMINGTON, William Allan. British, b. 1922. Administration/ Management, History, Industrial relations. Freelance writer and lectr. Research Fellow, West Africa Inst. of Social and Economic Research, Ibadan, Nigeria, 1953–56; Sr. Research Fellow., Inst. of Science and Tech-

nology, Manchester; Lectr., Manchester Sch. of Business, Univ. of Manchester, 1969–83. *Publs:* A West African Trade Union, 1960; (with E. and S. Ardener) Plantation and Village in the Cameroons, 1962; (with F.A. Wells) Studies in Industrialisation: Nigeria and the Cameroons, 1962; (co-author) Organisational Behaviour and Performance, 1977. Add: Westington Corner, Chipping Camden, Glos. GL55 6DW, England.

WARNER, Alan (John). British, b. 1912. Literature. Emeritus Prof. of English, New Univ. of Ulster, Coleraine, since 1978 (Prof., 1968–78). Lectr. in English, Rhodes University Coll., Grahamstown, South Africa, 1939–46; Lectr., then Sr. Lectr., Univ. of the Witwatersrand, Johannesburg, 1946–50; Prof., Makerere University Coll., Kampala, 1951–60, and Magee University Coll., Londonderry, 1961–68. *Publs:* (ed.) English Poems and Ballads, 1957; (ed.) Days of Youth, 1960; A Short Guide to English Style, 1961; Clay Is the Word: Patrick Kavanagh 1904-1967, 1973; William Allingham, 1975; (ed.) The Selected John Hewitt, 1981; A Guide to Anglo-Irish Literature, 1981; On Foot in Ulster, 1983. Add: 33 Lodge Rd., Coleraine, Co. Londonderry, Northern Ireland.

WARNER, Francis. British, b. 1937. Plays/Screenplays, Poetry. Vice-Master, Fellow and Tutor in English Literature, St. Peter's Coll., Oxford, and Univ. Lectr., Oxford Univ., since 1965. Member of faculty, St. Catharine's Coll., Cambridge, 1959–65. *Publs:* poetry—Perennia, 1962; Early Poems, 1964; Experimental Sonnets, 1965; Madrigals, 1967; The Poetry of Francis Warner, 1970; Lucca Quartet, 1975; Morning Vespers, 1980; Spring Harvest, 1981; Epithalamium, 1986; Collected Poems 1960-1984, 1985; plays—Maquettes, 1972; Requiem (Lying Figures, Killing Time, Meeting Ends), 1972–73; A Conception of Love, 1978; Light Shadows, 1980; Moving Reflections, 1983; Living Creation, 1985; Healing Nature: The Athens of Pericles, 1987. Add: St. Peter's Coll., Oxford OX1 2DL, England.

WARNER, Marina. British, b. 1946. Novels/Short stories, Children's fiction, History, Literature, Biography. Reviewer, The Independent newspaper, London; BBC radio; Times Literacy Supplement; New York Times Book Review. *Publs:* The Dragon Empress, 1972; Alone of All Her Sex: The Myth and the Cult of the Virgin Mary, 1976; In a Dark Wood (novel), 1977; The Crack in the Teacup (children's history), 1979; Queen Victoria's Sketchbook, 1979; Joan of Arc: The Image of Female Heroism, 1981; The Impossible Day (Night, Bath, Rocket) (children's stories), 1981–82; The Skating Party (novel), 1982; The Wobbly Tooth (children's story), 1984; Monuments and Maidens: The Allegory of the Female Form, 1985; Fawcett Puze, 1986; The Lost Father (novel), 1988. Add: Peters, Fraser and Dunlop 5th Floor, The Chambers, Chelsea Harbour, Lots Rd., London SW6 0XF, England.

WARNER, Matt. *See* **FICHTER**, George S.

WARNER, Philip. British, b. 1914. History. Formerly Sr. Lectr., Royal Military Academy, Sandhurst. *Publs:* Sieges of the Middle Ages, 1967; The Medieval Castle, 1971; The Special Air Service Regiment, 1971; The Crimean War, A Reappraisal, 1972; British Battlefields: The South, 1972; British Battlefields: The North, 1972; British Battlefields: The Midlands, 1973: British Battlefields: Scotland and the Borders, 1974; Distant Battle: A Retrospect of Empire, 1974; Dervish: The Rise and Fall of an African Empire, 1975; Stories of Famous Regiments, 1975; The Japanese Army of World War II, 1975; Army Life in the 90's, 1975; Guide to Castles in Britain, 1976; The Best of British Pluck: BOP, 1976; The Battle of Loos, 1976; The Soldier: His Daily Life Through the Ages, 1976; Making Model Forts and Castles, 1977; The Fields of War, 1977; Panzer, 1977; The Zeebrugge Raid, 1978; Famous Welsh Battles, 1978; Alamein, 1979; The D Day Landings, 1980; Invasion Road, 1980; Auchinleck: The Lonely Soldier, 1981; The SBS, 1983; Horrocks: The General Who Led from the Front, 1984; The British Cavalry, 1984; Kitchener: The Man Behind the Legend, 1985; The Secret Forces of World War II, 1985; Passchendaele, 1987; Firepower, 1988; World War II: The Untold Story, 1988. Add: c/o Jim Reynolds Assocs., Westbury Mill, Westbury, near Brackley, Northants NN13 5JC, England.

WARNER, Val. British, b. 1946. Poetry, Translations. Freelance Writer. Teacher, I.L.E.A., 1969–72; Writer-in-Residence, Univ. Coll. of Swansea, 1977–78, and Univ. of Dundee, 1979–81. *Publs:* These Yellow Photos, 1971; Under the Penthouse, 1973; (trans.) The Centenary Corbière, 1974; (ed.) Charlotte Mew: Collected Poems and Prose, 1982; Before Lunch, 1986. Add: c/o Carcanet, 208-12 Corn Exchange Buildings, Manchester M4 3BQ, England.

WARNER William W(hitesides). American, b. 1920. Environment/Ecology. Served with the U.S. Information Agency, 1951–62;

Latin American Program Coordinator, U.S. Peace Corps; Dir., Smithsonian Institution's Office of International Activities. *Publs:* Beautiful Swimmers: Watermen, Crabs, and the Chesapeake Bay, 1976 (Pulitzer Prize); Distant Water: The Fate of the North Atlantic Fisherman, 1983. Add: c/o Little Brown, 34 Beacon St., Boston, Mass. 02108, U.S.A.

WARNOCK, Baroness; (Helen) Mary Warnock. British, b. 1924. Philosophy. Mistress of Girton Coll., Cambridge, since 1985. Headmistress, Oxford High Sch., 1966–72; Research Fellow, Lady Margaret Hall, Oxford, 1972–76; Sr. Research Fellow, St. Hugh's Coll., Oxford, 1976–84. Member of Independent Broadcasting Authority, 1974–81. *Publs:* Ethics since 1900, 1960; The Philosophy of Jean-Paul Sartre, 1963; (ed.) Utilitarianism, 1964; Existentialist Ethics, 1966; Existentialism, 1970; Imagination, 1975; Schools of Thought, 1977; Education: A Way Forward, 1979; Memory, 1987; A Common Policy for Education, 1988. Add: c/o Girton Coll., Cambridge, England.

WARNOCK, (Sir) Geoffrey (James). British, b. 1923. Philosophy. Principal, Hertford Coll., Oxford, 1971–88. (Fellow and Tutor in Philosophy, Magdalen Coll., Oxford, 1953–71; Vice-Chancellor, Oxford Univ., 1981–85). *Publs:* Berkeley, 1953; English Philosophy since 1900, 1958, rev. ed. 1969; (ed. with J.O. Urmson) J.L. Austin's Philosophical Papers, 1961, rev. ed. 1970; (ed.) J.L. Austin's Sense and Sensibilia, 1962; Contemporary Moral Philosophy, 1967; The Object of Morality, 1971; J.L. Austen, 1989. Add: Brick House, Axford, Marlborough, Wilts SN8 2EX, England.

WARRACK, John (Hamilton). British, b. 1928. Music. Lectr. in Music, Oxford Univ., since 1984. Asst. Music Critic, Daily Telegraph, London, 1954–61; Chief Music Critic, Sunday Telegraph, 1961–72; Artistic Dir., Leeds Music Festival, 1977–83. *Publs:* Six Great Composers, 1958; (with H. Rosenthal) Concise Oxford Dictionary of Opera, 1964, 1979; Carl Maria von Weber, 1968, 1976; Tchaikovsky Symphonies and Concertos, 1969; Tchaikovsky, 1973, 1989; Tchaikovsky Ballet Music, 1979; (ed.) Writings on Music, by Weber, 1981. Add: Beck House, Rievaulx, Helmsley, York, England.

WARREN, Andrew. *See* **TUTE**, Warren.

WARREN, Charles Marquis. American, b. 1917. Novels/Short stories, Westerns/Adventure. Freelance writer, and film producer, director, and writer: Pres., Commander Films, since 1951, CMW Productions, since 1960, Emirau Productions, since 1962, and MW Productions, since 1987. Created the TV series Gunsmoke, 1955, Rawhide, 1958, and The Virginian, 1962. *Publs:* Only the Valiant, 1943; Valley of the Shadow, 1948; Deadhead, 1949. Add: 3250 Cornell Rd., Agoura Hills, Calif. 91301, U.S.A.

WARREN, Harris Gaylord. American, b. 1906. History, Politics/Government. Prof. of History Emeritus, Miami Univ., Oxford, Ohio, since 1971 (Prof. and Chmn. of Dept., 1957–71). Instr., Joliet Jr. Coll., 1930–36, Northwestern Univ., Evanston, Ill., 1937–38, and Michigan State Univ., East Lansing, 1938–39; Assoc. Prof., MacMurray Coll., 1939–40; Asst. Prof., Louisiana State Univ., Baton Rouge, 1940–46; Officer, U.S. Army, 1942–46; Prof., Univ. of Mississippi, University, 1946–57. *Publs:* (co-author) A Guidebook in Civics for High Schools, 1934; (ed. with F.J. Meine) Great Leaders, 1938; (ed.) A History of the World, 3 vols., 1937–38; The Sword Was Their Passport: A History of American Filibustering During the Mexican Revolution, 1943; Paraguay: An Informal History, 1949; (ed. with Faye Cooper-Cole) An Illustrated Outline History of Mankind, 1951; Herbert Hoover and the Great Depression, 1959; (with H.D. Leinenweber and Ruth O.M. Andersen) Our Democracy at Work, 1963, 1967; History Manual, 1965; Paraguay and the Triple Alliance: The Post-War Decade 1869-1878, 1978; The Rebirth of the Paraguayan Republic, 1985. Add: c/o Univ. of Pittsburgh Press, 127 N. Bellefield Ave., Pittsburgh. Penn. 19104, U.S.A.

WARREN, James E(dward), Jr. American, b. 1908. Poetry, Education. Sch. Historian and English Teacher, 1959–74, Chmn., Dept. of English, 1960–73, and Poet-in-Residence, 1974–75, The Lovett Sch., Atlanta, Ga. *Publs:* This Side of Babylon, 1938; Against the Furious Men, 1946; The Teacher of English, 1956; Earnest Family in Switzerland and America, 1961; Altars and Destinations, 1964; Trembling Still for Troy, 1965; Greener Year, Whiter Bough, 1966; Selected Poems, 1967; The Winding of Clocks, 1968; Listen, My Land, 1971; Mostly of Emily Dickinson, 1972; How to Write a Research Paper, 1972; Walking with Candles, 1973; A Kind of Fighting, 1974; A History of the Lovett School, 1975; Bequest/Request, 1976; Prie-Dieu and Jubilee, 1978; Collected Poems, 1979; The Elegance of God, 1980; Poems of Lovett, 1986. Add: 544 Deering

Rd. N.W., Atlanta, Ga. 30309, U.S.A.

WARREN, Kenneth. British, b. 1931. Geography, Regional/Urban planning. Univ. Lectr. in Geography, Univ. of Oxford, since 1970; Fellow and Tutor, Jesus Coll., Oxford, since 1970. Lectr. in Geography, Univ. of Leicester, until 1966, and Univ. of Newcastle upon Tyne, 1966–70. *Publs:* The British Iron and Steel Sheet Industry since 1840, 1970; (with G. Manners, D. Keeble, and B. Rogers) Regional Development in Britain, 1972, 1980; North East England, 1973; Mineral Resources, 1973; The American Steel Industry 1850-1970: A Geographical Interpretation, 1973; World Steel, 1975; The Geography of British Heavy Industry since 1800, 1976; Chemical Foundations: The Alkali Industry in Britain, 1980. Add: 12 New Yatt Rd., Witney, Oxon., England.

WARREN, Robert Penn. American, b. 1905. Novels/Short stories, Plays/Screenplays, Poetry, History, Literature. Prof. Emeritus of English, Yale Univ., New Haven, Conn., since 1973 (Prof. of Playwriting, 1950–56; Prof. of English, 1962–73). Member, Fugitive Group of Poets: Co-Founding Ed., The Fugitive, Nashville, Tenn., 1922–25; Asst. Prof., Southwestern Coll., Memphis, Tenn., 1930–31, and Vanderbilt Univ., Nashville, Tenn., 1931–34; Asst. and Assoc. Prof., Louisiana State Univ., Baton Rouge, 1934–42; Founding Ed., Southern Review, Baton Rouge, La., 1935–42; Prof. of English, Univ. of Minnesota, Minneapolis, 1942–50; Consultant in Poetry, Library of Congress, Washington, D.C. 1944–45. *Publs:* John Brown: The Making of a Martyr, 1929; (with others) I'll Take My Stand: The South and the Agrarian Tradition, 1930; Thirty-Six Poems, 1935; (ed. with C. Brooks and J.T. Purser) An Approach to Literature: A Collection of Prose and Verse with Analyses and Discussions, 1936, rev. ed. 1952; (ed.) A Southern Harvest: Short Stories by Southern Writers, 1937; (with C. Brooks) Understanding Poetry: An Anthology for College Students, 1938, rev. ed. 1959; Night Rider, 1939; Eleven Poems on the Same Theme, 1942; (with C. Brooks) Understanding Fiction, 1943, rev. ed. 1959; At Heaven's Gate, 1943; Selected Poems 1923-1943, 1944; Blackberry Winter (short stories), 1946; All the King's Men (Pulitzer Prize for fiction), 1946, play, 1959; A Poem of Pure Imagination; An Experiment in Reading, 1946; Proud Flesh (verse play), 1947, rev. prose version, 1948; The Circus in the Attic and Other Stories, 1947; (with C. Brooks) Modern Rhetoric: With Readings, 1949, rev. ed. 1958; (with C. Brooks) Fundamentals of Good Writing: A Handbook of Modern Rhetoric, 1950, rev. ed. 1956; World Enough and Time: A Romantic Novel, 1950; Brother to Dragons: A Tale in Verse and Voices, 1953; (ed. with C. Brooks) Anthology of Stories from the Southern Review, 1953; (ed. with A. Erskine) Short Story Masterpieces, 1954; (ed. with A. Erskine) Six Centuries of Great Poetry, 1955; Band of Angels, 1955; Segregation: The Inner Conflict in the South, 1956; Promises: Poems, 1954–55 (Pulitzer Prize for poetry), 1957; (ed. with A. Erskine) A New Southern Harvest, 1957; Remember the Alamo!, 1958; Selected Essays, 1958; The Gods of Mount Olympus, 1959; The Cave, 1959; You, Emperors and Others: Poems 1957-1960, 1960; Wilderness: A Tale of the Civil War, 1961; The Legacy of the Civil War: Meditations on the Centennial, 1961; (ed. with Allen Tate) Selected Poems by Denis Devlin, 1963; Flood: A Romance of Our Times, 1964; Who Speaks for the Negro?, 1965; Selected Poems: New and Old 1923-1966, 1966 (National Book Award); (ed.) Faulkner: A Collection of Critical Essays, 1967; (ed. with Robert Lowell and Peter Taylor) Randall Jarrell 1914-1965, 1967; Incarnations: Poems 1966-1968, 1968; Audubon: A Vision (poetry), 1969; Meet Me in the Green Glen, 1971; Homage to John Dreiser, 1971; (ed.) Selected Poems of Herman Melville, 1971; (ed.) Selected Poems of John Greenleaf Whittier, 1971; Democracy and Poetry, 1975; Selected Poems 1923-76, 1976; A Place to Come To, 1977; Now and Then: Poems 1976-77, 1978 (Pulitzer Prize for poetry); (ed.) Katherine Anne Porter: A Collection of Critical Essays, 1979; Being Here, 1980; Rumor Verified, 1981; New and Selected Poems 1923-1985, 1985; (ed.) The Essential Melville, 1987; A Robert Penn Warren Reader, 1987; Portrait of a Father, 1988; New and Selected Essays, 1989. Died, 1989.

WARREN, Sidney. American, b. 1916. History, Politics/Government Prof. of Political Science, United States Intnl. Univ., 1952–81; now retired. *Publs:* American Freethought, 1943; Farthest Frontier, 1949; The President as World Leader, 1964; (ed.) The American President, 1967; The Battle for the Presidency, 1968. Add: 1325 Alexandria Dr., San Diego, Calif 92107, U.S.A.

WARREN, Wilfred Lewis. British, b. 1929. History, Biography. Prof. of Modern History, Queen's Univ. of Belfast, since 1973 (Asst. Lectr., 1955–68; Lectr., 1958–68; Warden, Alanbrooke Hall, 1963–70; Reader, 1968–73) Member of the Bd., Arts Council of Northern Ireland, 1976–81, and since 1984; Member, Arts Sub-Cttee., Univ. Grants Cttee., since 1984. *Publs:* King John, 1961, 1978; 1066: The Year of the Three Kings, 1966; Henry II, 1973, 1977; The Governance of Norman and Angevin England 1086-1272, 1987. Add: Dept. of Modern History, The Queen's Univ., Belfast BT7 1NN, Northern Ireland.

WARSH, Lewis. American, b. 1944. Poetry, Translations. Ed., United Artists Books, since 1977. *Publs:* The Suicide Rates, 1967; Highjacking, 1968; Moving Through Air, 1968; (with T. Clark) Chicago, 1969; Two Poems, 1971; Dreaming as One, 1971; Long Distance, 1972; Part of My History, 1972; (trans.) Night of Loveless Nights, by Robert Desnos, 1973; Immediate Surrounding, 1974; Blue Heaven, 1978; Hives, 1979; Methods of Birth Control, 1983; Agnes and Sally (novel), 1984; The Corset, 1987; Information from the Surface of Venus, 1987; A Free Man (novel), 1989 Add: 40 Clinton St., New York, N.Y. 10002, U.S.A.

WARTOFSKY, William Victor. American, b. 1931. Novels/Short stories, Plays/Screenplays. Dir, Public Affairs, Fairfax County, Va. Dept. of Housing and Community Development, since 1988. Corresp., United Press Intnl., Washington, D.C., 1954–59; Writer-Publicist, B'nai B'rith, Washington, D.C., 1959; Information Officer, 1960–80, and Education Program Officer, 1980–85, National Insts. of Health, Bethesda, Md; Public Relations Coordinator, National Assn. of Social Workers, Silver Springs, Md., 1985–88. *Publs:* Mr. Double (short stories), 1968; Meeting the Pieman, 1971; Year of the Yahoo, 1972; The Passage, 1980; Death Be My Destiny (screenplay), 1982; The Hellbox (screenplay), 1983; Feathers (screenplay), 1984; Prescription for Justice, 1987; Terminal Justice, 1988. Add: 8507 Wild Olive Dr., Potomac, Md. 20854, U.S.A.

WARWICK, Roger. British, b. 1912. Anthropology, Biology, Medicine. Hon. Secty., Intnl. Anatomical Nomenclature Cttee., since 1970. House Surgeon, Professional Unit, Royal Infirmary, Manchester, 1938–39; Asst. Physician, Cheadle Royal Mental Hosp., Cheshire, 1939; Demonstrator and Lectr., Dept. of Anatomy, Univ. of Manchester, 1945–55; Head, Dept. of Anatomy, Guy's Hosp. Medical Sch., London, 1955–85. *Publs:* (ed.) Whillis' Elementary Anatomy and Physiology, 4th ed. 1957; Introduction to Anatomy, 1965; (ed.) Johnston's Synopsis of Anatomy, 1963, 10th ed. 1968; (co.-ed.) Gray's Anatomy, 35th ed. 1973, 36th ed. 1980, 37th ed. 1989; (ed.) Wolff's Anatomy of the Eye and Orbit, 7th ed., 1976; Nomina Anatomica, 4th ed. 1977, 5th ed. 1983. Add: 85 Hall Dr., London SE26 6XL, England

WASHINGTON, Joseph R., Jr. American, b. 1930. Race relations, Theology/Religion. Prof. of Religious Studies, and Chmn. of Afro-American Studies, Univ. of Virginia, Charlottesville, since 1970. Asst. Prof. of Religious Studies, Dillard Univ., 1960–63, and Dickinson Coll., 1963–66; Assoc. Prof., Albion Coll., Michigan, 1966–69; Prof., Beloit Coll., Wisconsin, 1969–70. *Publs:* Black Religion: The Negro and Christianity in the U.S., 1964; The Politics of God, 1967; Black and White Power Subreption, 1969; Marriage in Black White, 1970; Black Sects and Cults, 1972; (ed.) Jews in Black Perspective, 1984; Anti-Blackness in English Religion, 1985; Puritan Race Virtue, Vice, and Values 1620-1820, 1988. Add: B-12 Cocke Hall, Univ. of Virginia, Charlottesville, Va. 22901, U.S.A.

WASIOLEK, Edward. American, b. 1924. Literature. Prof. and Chmn., Dept. of Comparative Literature, Univ. of Chicago, since 1955. Editorial Bd. Member, Studies in the Novel, Essays in Literature, Critical Inquiry, and The International Fiction Review. *Publs:* (with R. Bauer) Nine Soviet Portraits, 1955; (ed.) Crime and Punishment and the Critics, 1961; Dostoevsky, the Major Fiction, 1964; (ed. and trans.) The Notebooks for Crime and Punishment, 1967; (ed.) The Brothers Karamazov and the Critics, 1967; (ed.) The Notes for The Idiot, 1968; (ed.) The Notebooks for The Possessed, 1968; (ed.) The Notebooks for A Raw Youth, 1969; (ed. and trans.) The Notebooks for The Brothers Karamazov, 1970; (ed.) The Gambler and Polina Suslova's Diary, 1972; Tolstoy's Major Fiction, 1978; L.N. Tolstoy: Work, Life and Criticism, 1984; (ed.) Critical Essays on Tolstoy, 1986. Add: Butterfield Lane, Flossmoor, Ill. 60422, U.S.A.

WASSERMAN, Dale. American, b. 1917. Plays/Screenplays. *Publs:* Elisha and the Long Knives, 1954; The Fog, 1957; (with B. Geller) Livin' the Life, 1957; I, Don Quixote, 1960; The Pencil of God, 1961; The Lincoln Murder Case, 1961; (adaptor) K. Kesey's One Flew Over the Cuckoo's Nest (play), 1963; screenplays—World Strangers, 1955; The Vikings, 1958; Two Faces to Go, 1959; Aboard the Flying Swan, 1962; Jangadeiro, 1962; Cleopatra, 1963; Quick Before it Melts, 1964; Mr. Buddwing, 1965; A Walk with Love and Death, 1969; Man of La Mancha, 1972; Play with Fire, 1978. Add: c/o Random House, 201 E. 50th St., New York, N.Y. 10022. U.S.A.

WASSERMAN, Paul. American, b. 1924. Administration/Management, Education, Information science/Computers, Librarianship. Prof., Sch. of Library and Information Services, Univ. of Maryland, since 1970 (Dean, 1965–70). Member, Editorial Advisory Bd., Social Sciences Citation Index, since 1972; Member, Editorial Bd., Journal of Library Administration, since 1979, and Social Science Information Studies, since 1979. Asst. to Business Librarian to Chief, Science and Industry Div., Brooklyn Public Library, N.Y., 1949–53; Librarian and Asst. Prof., to Librarian and Prof., Grad. Sch. of Business and Public Admin., Cornell Univ., Ithaca, N.Y., 1953–65; Part-time Lectr., Sch. of Library Science, Western Reserve Univ., Cleveland, Ohio, 1963–64. Book Review Ed., Administrative Science quarterly, 1956–61; Chmn., Education and Training Cttee., Intnl. Federation for Documentation, 1979–82; Managing Ed., Newsletter on Education and Training Programs for Specialized Information Personnel, 1979–82. *Publs:* (managing ed.) Commodity Prices, 1960, 1974; (ed.) Directory of University Research Bureaus and Institutes, 1960; Sources for Hospital Administrators, 1961; (co-ed.) Directory of Health Organizations of the United States, Canada, and Internationally, 1961, 4th ed. 1977; (ed.) Statistics Sources, 1962, 7th ed. 1982; (managing ed.) Executive's Guide to Information Sources, 3 vols., 1965; The Librarian and the Machine, 1965; (managing ed.) Consultants and Consulting Organizations, 1966, 5th ed. 1982; (managing ed.) Who's Who in Consulting, 1968, 1973; (ed. with Bundy) Reader in Library Administration, 1968; (managing ed.) Awards, Honors and Prizes: A Source Book and Directory, 1969, 5th ed. 1982; (ed.) Reader in Research Methods for Librarianship, 1970; (managing ed.) Encyclopedia of Business Information Science Today, 1971; The New Librarianship, 1972; (ed. with Esther Herman) Museum Media, 1973, 1979; (managing ed.) Consumer Sourcebook, 1974, 3rd ed. 1981; (ed. with Esther Herman) Library Bibliographies and Indexes, 1975; (managing ed.) Ethnic Information Sources in the United States, 1976, 1982; (with Rizzo) Outline for a Course in Administration for Managers of Information Sciences and Centers (in French), 1977; Training and Development Organizations Directory, 1977; (ed. with Esther Herman) Festivals Sourcebook, 1977; (ed.) Training and Development Organizations, 1978, 1980; (managing ed.) Speakers and Lecturers: How to Find Them, 1978, 1981; (ed.) Recreation and Outdoor Life Directory, 1979; (ed.) Learning Independently Directory, 1979, 1982; (managing ed.) Law and Legal Information Directory, 1980, 3rd ed. 1984; (ed. with Steven R. Wasserman) Lively Arts Information Directory, 1982; (ed.) Festivals Sourcebook, 1984; (managing ed.) Encyclopedia of Health Information Services, 1986. Add: Coll. of Library and Information Services, Univ. of Maryland, College Park, Md. 20742, U.S.A.

WASSERSTEIN, Wendy. American. Plays/Screenplays. *Publs:* Uncommon Women and Others, 1979; Isn't It Romantic, 1985; The Man in Case (in Orchards), 1986. Add: c/o Luis Sanjurgo, ICM, 40 W. 57th St., New York, N.Y. 10019, U.S.A.

WATERHOUSE, Keith (Spencer). British, b. 1929. Novels/Short stories, Plays/Screenplays, History, Social commentary/phenomena, Humour/Satire. Columnist, Daily Mirror, London; Gov., Leeds Theatre Trust. *Publs:* (with Guy Deghy as Harold Froy) The Cafe Royal: Ninety Years of Bohemia, 1955; (with G. Deghy) How to Avoid Matrimony, 1957; (with P. Cave) Britain's Voice Abroad, 1957; There Is a Happy Land, 1957; (ed.) The Future of Television, 1958; (with G. Deghy as Lee Gibb) The Joneses: How to Keep Up with Them, 1959; Billy Liar, 1959, play with Willis Hall, 1960; (with G. Deghy as Lee Gibb) The Higher Joneses, 1961; (with W. Hall) Celebration, 1961; (with W. Hall) England, Our England, 1962; (with W. Hall) The Sponge Room, and Squat Betty, 1963; (with W. Hall) All Things Bright and Beautiful, 1963; Jubb, 1963; (with W. Hall) Come Laughing Home, 1965; (with W. Hall) Say Who You Are (in U.S. as Help Stamp Out Marriage), 1965; (ed. with W. Hall) Writer's Theatre, 1967; Whoops-a-Daisy, 1968; The Bucket Shop (in U.S. as Everything Must Go), 1968; (with W. Hall) Pretty Polly, 1968; (with W. Hall) Who's Who, 1971; (with W. Hall) Saturday, Sunday, Monday (adaption), 1973; Passing of the Third-Floor Buck, 1974; Billy Liar on the Moon, 1975; Mondays, Thursdays, 1976; (with W. Hall) Filumena (adaptation), 1977; Office Life, 1979; Rhubarb, Rhubarb, 1979; (with W. Hall) Worzel Gummidge (juvenile), 1981; Thinks, 1984; Waterhouse at Large, 1985; The Collected Letters of a Nobody, 1986; The Theory and Practice of Lunch, 1986; Our Song, 1987. Add: 29 Kenway Rd., London SW5, England.

WATERMAN, Andrew (John). British, b. 1940. Poetry. Sr. Lectr. in English, New University of Ulster, Coleraine, since 1978 (Lectr., 1968–78). *Publs:* Living Room, 1974; From the Other Country, 1977; Over the Wall, 1980; Out for the Elements, 1981; (ed.) The Poetry of Chess, 1981; Selected Poems, 1986. Add: 15 Hazelbank Rd., Coleraine, Northern Ireland.

WATERS, David Watkin. British, b. 1911. History, Marine science/Oceanography, Travel/Exploration/Adventure. Retired Lieutenant-Comdr., Royal Navy, 1925–50; Admiralty Historian, 1950–60; Head, Dept. of Navigation and Astronomy, 1960–76, Secty, 1968–71, Deputy Dir., 1971–78, and Caird Research Fellow, 1979–84, National Maritime Museum, London. Pres., British Soc. for the History of Science, 1976–78. *Publs:* The True and Perfecte Newes of Syr Frauncis Drake, 1955; (with F. Barley) Naval Staff History, Second World War: The Defeat of the Enemy Attack upon Shipping 1939-1945, 1957; The Art of Navigation in England in Elizabethan and Early Stuart Times, 1958, 1978; The Sea: or, Mariner's Astrolabe, 1966; The Rutter of the Sea, 1967; (with H. Waters) The Saluki in History, Art and Sport, 1969, 1983; Science and the Techniques of Navigation in the Renaissance, 1974; (with G.P.B. Naish) The Elizabethan Navy and the Armada of Spain, 1975. Add: Robin Hill, Bury, nr. Pulborough, Sussex, England.

WATERS, Frank (Joseph). American, b. 1902. Novels/Short stories, Westerns/Adventure, Anthropology/Ethnology, History, Biography. Engineer in Los Angeles, riverside, and Imperial Valley, Southern California Telephone Co., 1926–35; Propaganda Analyst, Office of Inter-American Affairs, Washington, D.C., 1943–46; Ed., El Crepusculo newspaper, Taos, N.M., 1949–51; Information Advisor, Los Alamos Scientific Lab., N.M., 1952–56; Writer-in-Residence, Colorado State Univ., Fort Collins, 1966; Dir., New Mexico Arts Commn., Santa Fe, 1966–68. Book Reviewer, Saturday Review of Literature, NYC, 1950–56. *Publs:* western novels—Fever Pitch, 1930; The Wild Earth's Novility: A Novel of the Old West, 1935, Below Grass Roots, 1937, Dust Within the Rock, 1940, in 1 vol. as Pike's Peak: A Mining Saga, 1971; People of the Valley, 1941; The Man Who Killed the Deer, 1942; (with Houston Branch) River Lady, 1942; The Yogi of Cockroach Court, 1947; (with Houston Branch) Diamond Head, 1948; The Woman at Otowi Crossing, 1966; other—Midas of the Rockies: The Story of Stratton and Cripple Creek, 1937; The Colorado, 1946; Masked Gods: Navajo and Pueblo Ceremonialism, 1950; The Earp Brothers of Tombstone: The Story of Mrs. Virgil Earp, 1960; Book of the Hopi, 1963; Leon Gaspard, 1964; Pumpkin Seed Point, 1969; Conversations with Frank Waters, by John R. Milton, 1971; (ed.) Rocks and Minerals, 1971; To Possess the Land: A Biography of Arthur Rochford Manby, 1974: Mexico Mystique: The Coming Sixth World of Consciousness, 1975; Mountain Dialogues, 1981; (ed.) Cuchama and Sacred Mountains, by W.Y. Evans-Wentz, 1981; Flights from Fiesta, 1986. Add: Box 1127, Taos, N.M. 87571, U.S.A.

WATERS, John F(rederick). American, b. 1930. Children's fiction, Biology, Children's non-fiction, Natural history. Reporter, Cape Cod Standard Times, Massachusetts, 1959–60; Teacher, elementary sch., Falmouth, Massachusetts, 1960–66. *Publs:* Marine Animal Collectors, 1970; Saltmarshes and Shifting Dunes, 1970; The Crab from Yesterday, 1970; What Does an Oceanographer Do?, 1970; The Sea Farmers, 1970; Turtles, 1971; Neighborhood Puddle, 1971; The Royal Potwasher, 1972; Green Turtle Mysteries, 1972; Some Mammals Live in the Sea, 1972; The Mysterious Eel, 1973; Giant Sea Creatures, 1973; Seal Harbor, 1973; Hungry Sharks, 1973; Camels, Ships of the Desert, 1974; Exploring New England Shores, 1974; Creatures of Darkness, 1974; Carnivorous Plants, 1974; Hungry Sharks, 1974; Maritime Careers, 1977; Fishing, 1978; Summer of the Seals, 1978; A Jellyfish Is Not a Fish, 1979. Add: c/o Harper and Row Junior Books, 10 E. 53rd St., New York, N.Y. 10022, U.A.

WATHEN, Richard. American, b. 1917. Novels/Short stories. Indiana State Rep., since 1970. *Publs:* The Only Yankee, 1970; Hangups of Politician, 1980; Wathen's Law, 1981. Add: Utica Pike, Jeffersonville, Ind. 47130, U.S.A.

WATKINS, Alan (Rhun). British, b. 1933. Politics/Government. Political Columnist, The Observer, London, since 1976. Rugby Corresp., Field mag., London, since 1984. Called to the Bar, Lincoln's Inn, London, 1957; Member of the Editorial Staff, Sunday Express, London, 1959–64; Political Corresp./Columnist, Spectator, 1964–67, New Statesman, 1967–76, Sunday Mirror, 1968–69, and Evening Standard, 1974–75, all in London; Dir., Statesman and National Publishing Co. Ltd., 1973–76. *Publs:* The Liberal Dilemma, 1966; (with others) The Left, 1966; (co-author) The Making of the Prime Minister, 1970; Brief Lives, 1982; The Queen Observed, 1986. Add: 54 Barnsbury St., London N1 1ER, England.

WATKINS, Floyd C. American, b. 1920. Cultural/Ethnic topics, Language/Linguistics, Literature. Candler Prof. Emeritus of American Literature, Emory Univ., Atlanta, Ga. (joined faculty, 1949). *Publs:* (co-

author) The Literature of the South, 1952; Thomas Wolfe's Characters, 1957; (co-author) Writer to Writer, 1961; Practical English Handbook, 1961, 8th ed. 1989; Yesterday in the Hills, 1963; The Death of Art; The Flesh and the Word: Eliot, Hemingway, Faulkner, 1971; In Time and Place, 1977; Robert Penn Warren Talking, 1980; Then and Now, 1982; (co-author) Some Poems and Some Talk About Poetry, 1985. Add: Dept. of English, Emory Univ., Atlanta, Ga. 30322, U.S.A.

WATKINS, Gerrold. *See* **MALZBERG,** Barry.

WATKINS, John Goodrich. American, b. 1913. Psychology. Prof. of Psychology, Univ. of Montana, Missoula, 1964–84, now Emeritus (Dir. of Clinical Training, 1964–80). High sch. teacher, 1933–39; Chief Clinical Psychologist, U.S. Army's Welch Hosp., Daytona Beach, fla., 1945–46; Assoc. Prof. of Psychology, Washington State Coll., Pullman, 1946–49; Chief Clinical Psychologist, Veterans Admin. Mental Hygiene Clinic, Chicago, 1950–53; Chief, Psychology Service, Veterans Admin. Hosp., Portland, Ore., 1953–64. *Publs:* Objective Measurement of Instrumental Performance, 1942; Hypnotherapy of War Neuroses, 1949; General Psychotherapy, 1960; The Therapeutic Self, 1978; We, The Divided Self, 1982; Hypnotherapeutic Techniques, 1987; Hypnoanalytic Techniques, 1989. Add: 413 Evans St., Missoula, Mont. 59801, U.S.A.

WATKINS, Ronald. British, b. 1904. Theatre. Lectr. on Shakespeare in U.K. and U.S.A. Staff member, Harrow Sch., Middx., U.K., 1932–64. *Publs:* Moonlight at the Globe, 1946; On Producing Shakespeare, 1950; (ed. with J. Lemmon) The Harrow Shakespeare: Macbeth, 1964; (with J. Lemmon) In Shakespeare's Playhouse, 4 vols., 1974; Shakespeare Study Series (cassettes), 1980; The Importance of Peter Quince (cassettes), 1988. Add: Lobswood, South Hill Ave., Harrow-on-the-Hill, Middx. HA1 3NX, England.

WATKINS, Wiliam John. American, b. 1942. Science fiction/Fantasy, Children's fiction, Plays, Poetry, Urban studies. Prof. of Humanities, Brookdale Community Coll., Lincroft, N.J., since 1979 (Instr., 1969–70; Asst. Prof., 1970–71; Assoc. Prof., 1971–79). Instr., Delaware Valley Coll., Doylestown, Pa., 1965–68; Teacher, Asbury Park High Sch., N.J., 1968–69. *Publs:* Five Poems, 1968; The Judas Wheel (play), 1969; (with Gene Snyder) Ecodeath, 1972; Clickwhistle, 1973; The God Machine, 1973; A Fair Advantage (juvenile), 1975; (with Gene Snyder) The Litany of Sh'reev, 1976; The Thacker, 1978; The Psychic Experiment Book, 1980; What Rough Beast, 1980; Suburban Wilderness (non-fiction), 1981; Centrifugal Rickshaw Dancer, 1985; Going to See the End of the Sky, 1986; The Last Deathship off Antanus, 1989. Add: 1406 Garven Ave., Ocean, N.J. 07712, U.S.A.

WATKINS-PITCHFORD, D(enys) J(ames). Also writes as "BB". British, b. 1905. Children's fiction, Animals/Pets, Sports. *Publs:* Countryman's Bedside Book, 1936; Sportman's Bedside Book, 1936; Fisherman's Bedside Book, 1936; Wild Lone, 1939; Manka, 1939; Little Grey Men, 1942; Down the Bright Stream, 1944; Brendon Chase, 1944; The Wayfaring Tree, 1945; Tides Ending, 1950; Confessions of a Carp Fisher, 1950; Letter from Compton Deverell, 1950; Dark Estuary, 1953; The Forest of Boland Light Railway, 1955; Alexander, 1957; Bill Badger's Big Mistake, 1957; The Wind in the Wood, 1958; The Autumn Road to the Isles, 1959; The Spring Road to Wales, 1959; Lepus the Brown Hare, 1961; The White Road Westwards, 1961; A Summer of the Nene, 1967; The Tyger Tray, 1971; Bill Badger's Voyage to the World's End, 1972; Pool of the Black Witch, 1974; Lord of the Forest, 1975; Mr. Bumstead, 1975; Recollections of a Longshore Gunner, 1976; A Child Alone, 1978; Ramblins of a Sportsman Naturalist, 1979; The Naturalist's Bedside Book, 1980; The Quiet Fields, 1981; The Best of "BB" (anthology), 1985. Add: The Round House, Sudborough, Kettering, Northants., England.

WATMOUGH, David. Canadian, b. 1926. Novels/Short stories. Jr. Reporter, Cornish Guardian, Bodmin, Cornwall, England, 1943–44; Ed., Holy Cross Press, NYC, 1953–54; Talks Producer, BBC Third Programme, London, 1955; Ed., Ace Books, London, 1956; Feature Writer/Critic, The Examiner newspaper, San Francisco, 1957–60; Music and Theatre Critic, CBC, Vancouver, 1960–64; Arts and Theatre Critic, The Vancouver Sun, 1964–67; Music and Theatre Critic, 1967–80, and Host of Artslib weekly TV prog., 1979–80, CBC, Vancouver. *Publs:* A Church Renascent: A Study in Modern French Catholicism, 1951; Ashes for Easter (short stories), 1972; From a Cornish Landscape (short stories), 1975; Love and the Waiting Game (short stories), 1975; No More into the Garden (novel), 1978; The Connecticut Countess (short stories), 1984; Fury (short stories), 1984; The Unlikely Pioneer (history), 1985; (ed.) The Vancouver Fiction Book, 1985; Vibrations in Time (short stories), 1986; The Year of Fears (novel), 1987; Families (novel), 1989. Add:

3358 W. First Ave., Vancouver, B.C. V6R 1G4, Canada.

WATNEY, John Basil. British. Novels/Short stories, History, Autobiography/Memoirs/Personal, Biography. *Publs:* The Enemy Within, 1946; The Unexpected Angel, 1949; Common Love, 1954; Leopard with a Thin Skin, 1959; The Quarrelling Room, 1960; The Glass Façade, 1963; He Also Served, 1971; Clive of India, 1974; Beer Is Best, 1974; Lady Hester Stanhope, 1975; Mervyn Peake, 1975; Mother's Ruin, 1976; The Churchills, 1977. Add: Flat 36, 5 Elm Park Gardens, London SW10 9QQ, England.

WATSON, Alan. British, b. 1933. Classics, Law. Fellow, Oriel Coll., Oxford, 1960–65; former Douglas Prof. of Civil Law, Univ. of Glasgow; Prof. of Civil Law, Univ. of Edinburgh, 1968–69; Prof. of Law and Classics, 1979–84, and N.F. Gallicho Prof. of Law, 1984–86, Univ. of Pennsylvania, Philadelphia. *Publs:* Contract of Mandate in Roman Law, 1961; Law of Obligations in Later Roman Republic, 1965; Law of Persons in Later Roman Republic, 1967; Law of Property in Later Roman Republic, 1968; Law of the Ancient Romans, 1970; Law of Succession in Later Roman Republic, 1971; Roman Private Law Around 200 BC, 1971; Law Making in the Later Roman Republic, 1974; (ed.) Daube Noster, 1974; Rome of the XII Tables, 1975; Society and Legal Change, 1977; Nature of Law, 1977; Making of the Civil Law, 1981; Sources of Law, Legal Change and Ambiguity, 1984; The Evolution of Law, 1985. Roman Slave Law, 1987; Failures of the Legal Imagination, 1988. Add: c/o Law Sch., Univ. of Pennsylvania, 3400 Chestnut St., Philadelphia, Pa. 19104, U.S.A.

WATSON, Clyde. American, b. 1947. Children's fiction. Freelance writer, and composer. *Publs:* (composer) Fisherman Lullabies, 1968; Father Fox's Pennyrhymes, 1971; Tom Fox and the Apple Pie, 1972; Quips and Quirks, 1975; Hickory Stick Rag, 1976; Binary Numbers, 1977; Catch Me and Kiss Me and Say It Again, 1978; How Brown Mouse Kept Christmas, 1979; Midnight Moon, 1979; Applebet: an abc, 1982; Father Fox's Feast of Songs, 1983; Valentine Foxes, 1989. Add: c/o Curtis Brown Ltd., Ten Astor Pl., New York, N.Y. 10003, U.S.A.

WATSON, George (Grimes). British, b. 1927. Literature. Univ. Lectr. in English, and Fellow, St. John's Coll., Cambridge Univ., since 1959. *Publs:* (ed.) Coleridge, Biographia Literaria, 1956; (ed.) The Unservile State, 1957; (ed.) Concise Cambridge Bibliography of English Literature, 1958; The Literary Critics, 1962, 1986; (ed.) Radical Alternative, 1962; (ed.) The English Mind: Studies in the English Moralists Presented to Basil Willey, 1964; (ed.) Maria Edgeworth, Castle Rackrent, 1964; Coleridge the Poet, 1966; (ed.) The English Petrarchans, 1967; The Study of Literature, 1969; (ed.) New Cambridge Bibliography of English Literature, Vols. I-III, 1969–74, shorter edition, 1981; The English Ideology: Studies in the Language of VIctorian Politics, 1973; Politics and Literature in Modern Britain, 1977; The Discipline of English, 1978; Modern Literary Thought, 1978; The Story of the Novel, 1979; The Idea of Liberalism, 1985; Writing a Thesis, 1987; The Certainty of Literature, 1989. Add: St. John's Coll., Cambridge, England.

WATSON, Ian. British, b. 1943. Science fiction/Fantasy, Area studies. Features Ed., and contrib., Foundation mag., London. Lectr., University Coll., Dar es Salaam, Tanzania, 1965–67, and Tokyo Univ. of Education, 1967–70; Lectr., 1970–75, and Sr. Lectr. in Complementary Studies, 1975–76, Birmingham Polytechnic Art and Design Centre. *Publs:* Japan: A Cat's Eye View (non-fiction), 1969; The Embedding, 1973; The Jonah Kit, 1975; The Martian Inca, 1977; Japan Tomorrow (non-fiction), 1977; Alien Embassy, 1977; Miracle Visitors, 1978; God's World, 1979; The Very Slow Time Machine (short stories), 1979; The Gardens of Delight, 1980; (with Michael Bishop) Under Heaven's Bridge, 1980; Deathhunter, 1981; Sunstroke and Other Stories, 1982; Chekhov's Journey, 1983; The Book of the River, 1984; Converts, 1984; The Book of the Stars, 1984; The Book of Being, 1985; Slow Birds and Other Stories, 1985; Queenmagic, Kingmagic, 1986; (co-ed) Afterlives, 1986; Evil Water, 1987; The Power, 1987; The Fire Worm, 1988; Salvage Rites, 1989. Add: Bay House, Banbury Rd., Moreton Pinkney, nr. Daventry, Northants. NN11 6SQ, England.

WATSON, James. British, b. 1936. Novels/Short stories, Plays/Screenplays, Communications media/Broadcasting, Education. Lectr. in Communications, West Kent Coll. of Further Education, since 1965. Former journalist. *Publs:* Sign of the Swallow, 1967; The Bull Leapers, 1970; Gilbert Makepeace Lives!, 1972; Legion of the White Tiger, 1973; Liberal Studies in Further Education—An Informal Survey, 1973; The Freedom Tree, 1976; Venus Rising from the Sea, 1977; A Slight Insurrection, 1979; The Loneliness of a Long Distance Innovation:

General Studies in a College of Further Education, 1980; What a Little Moonlight Can Do, 1982; Talking in Whispers, 1983; (with Anne Hill) A Dictionary of Communication and Media Studies, 1984; What is Communication Studies?, 1985; When Nobody Sees, 1987; Make Your Move (stories), 1988. Add: 9 Farmcombe Close, Tunbridge Wells, Kent TN2 5DG, England.

WATSON, James D(ewey). American, b. 1928. Biology. Dir., Cold Spring Harbor Lab., Cold Spring Harbor, N.Y., since 1968. Fellow, Cavendish Lab., Cambridge, 1951–53; Sr. Research Fellow in Biology, California Inst. of Technology, Pasadena, 1953–55; Asst. Prof., 1955–58, Assoc. Prof., 1958–61, and Prof. of Biology, 1961–76, Harvard Univ., Cambridge, Mass. Recipient, with F.H.C. Crick and M.H.F. Wilkins, Nobel Prize in Medicine, 1962. *Publs:* Molecular Biology of the Gene, 1965, 3rd ed. 1976; The Double Helix: A Personal Account of the Discovery of the Structure of DNA, 1968; (ed. with others) Origins of Human Cancer, 1977; (with John Tooze) The DNA Story: A Documentary History of Gene Cloning, 1981; (with John Tooze) Recombinant DNA: A Short Course, 1983; Recognition and Regulation in Cell-Mediated Immunity, 1985. Add: Cold Spring Harbor Lab., P.O. Box 100, Cold Spring Harbor, N.Y. 11724, U.S.A.

WATSON, James Wreford. Writes poetry as James Wreford. Canadian/British, b. 1915. Poetry, Geography, Social sciences. Chief Geographer, Canada, 1948–54; Prof. of Geography, 1954–82, and Dir. of the Centre of Canadian Studies, 1972–82, Univ. of Edinburgh. *Publs:* (co-author as James Wreford) Unit of 5, 1949; (as James Wreford) Of Time and the Lover, 1954; (as James Wreford) Scotland, the Great Upheaval, 1962; North America, Its Countries and Regions, 1963, 1968; (with J.B. Sissons) The British Isles: A Systematic Geography, 1964; (co-author with C.H. Foggs and J. Oliver) A Geography of Bermuda, 1965; Canada: Problems and Prospects, 1968; (ed. with T. O'Riordan) The American Environment: Perceptions and Policies, 1975; (with Jessie Watson) The Canadians: How They Live and Work, 1977; A Social Geography of the United States, 1978; (as James Wreford) Cross-Country Canada, 1979; The U.S.A.: Habitation of Hope, 1983. Add: Broomhill, Kippford, Galloway, Scotland.

WATSON, J(ohn) R(ichard). British, b. 1934. Literature. Prof. of English, Univ. of Durham, since 1978. Asst., then Lectr., Univ. of Glasgow, 1962–66; Lectr., then Sr. Lectr. in English, Univ. of Leicester, 1966–78. *Publs:* Picturesque Landscape and English Romantic Poetry, 1970; (ed., with N.P. Messenger) Victorian Poetry, 1974; (ed.) Browning: Men and Women, 1974; A Leicester Calendar, 1976; (ed.) Everyman's Book of Victorian Verse, 1982; Wordsworth's Vital Soul, 1983; English Poetry of the Romantic Period 1789–1830, 1985; The Poetry of Gerard Manley Hopkins, 1987; (co-ed.) Companion to Hymns and Psalms, 1988. Add: 3 Victoria Terrace, Durham, England.

WATSON, Lyall. South African/British, b. 1939. Anthropology/Ethnology, Zoology. Formerly apprenticed to Desmond Morris, London Zoo; worked in archaeology with American Sch. of Oriental Research, Jordan, and Saudi Arabia; anthropological work in Northern Nigeria; Dir. of Johannesburg Zoo; Television producer, BBC, London; Founder of life science consultancy, Biologic of London; expeditions in marine biology, Indian Ocean. *Publs:* Omnivore, 1971; Supernature, 1973; The Romeo Error, 1975; Gifts of Unknown Things, 1977; Lifetide, 1979; Whales of the World, 1981; Lightning Bird, 1982; Heaven's Breath, 1984; Earthworks, 1985; Beyond Supernature, 1986; The Water Planet, 1987. Add: c/o Murray Pollinger, 4 Garrick St., London WC2E 9BH, England.

WATSON, Nancy Dingman. American. Children's fiction. Columnist, Brattleboro Daily Reformer, 1960–85. *Publs:* What Is One?, 1954; Whose Birthday Is It, 1954; Toby and Doll, 1955; When Is Tomorrow, 1955; What Is Tomorrow?, 1955; What Does A Begin With?, 1956; Annie's Spending Spree, 1957; Picture Book of Fairy Tales, 1957; The Arabian Nights Picture Book, 1959; Sugar on Snow, 1964; Katie's Chickens, 1965; Carol to a Child, 1969; New Under the Stars, 1970; Tommy's Mommy's Fish, 1971; The Birthday Goat, 1974; Muncus Agruncus, 1976; Blueberries Lavender, 1977. Add: c/o Harper and Row, 10 E. 53rd St., New York, N.Y. 10022, U.S.A.

WATSON, Robert (Winthrop). American, b. 1925. Novels/Short stories, Plays, Poetry. Prof. of English, Univ. of North Carolina, Greensboro, since 1965 (member of faculty, 1953–65). Instr., Johns Hopkins Univ., Baltimore, Md., 1950–52, and Williams Coll. Williamstown, Mass., 1952–53; Visiting Poet, San Fernando Valley State Coll., Los Angeles, Calif., 1968–69. *Publs:* A Paper Horse, 1962; A Plot in the Palace (play), 1964; (ed. with G. Ruark) The Greensboro Reader, 1964; Advantages of Dark: Poems, 1966; Three Sides of the Mirror (novel), 1966; Christmas in Las Vegas, 1971; Watson on the Beach, 1972; Selected Poems, 1974; Lily Lang (novel), 1977; Island of Bones, 1977; Night Blooming Cactus, 1980. Add: 9-D Fountain Dr., Greensboro, N.C. 27403, U.S.A.

WATSON, Roderick. British, b. 1943. Poetry, Literature. Sr. Lectr. in English, Univ. of Stirling since 1987. Gen. Ed., Canongate Classics, since 1987. Lectr. in English, Univ.of Victoria, B.C., 1965–66. *Publs:* (with J. Rankin) 28 Poems, 1964; Poems, 1970; (with V. Simmons and P. Mills) Trio: New Poets from Edinburgh, 1971; (co-ed.) Scottish Poetry Seven, Eight and Nine, 3 vols., 1974–76; Hugh MacDiarmid, 1976; True History on the Walls, 1976; (with Martin Gray) The Penguin Book of the Bicycle, 1978; (ed. with Angus Ogilvy and George Sutherland) Birds: An Anthology of New Poems, 1978; The Literature of Scotland, 1984; MacDiarmid, 1985; The Poetry of Norman MacCaig, 1989. Add: 19 Millar Pl., Stirling FK8 1XD, Scotland.

WATSON, Will. *See* FLOREN, Lee.

WATT, Ian (Pierre). British, b. 1917. History, Literature. Prof. of English since 1964, and Dir. of Stanford Humanities Center since 1980, Stanford Univ., Calif. Advisory Ed., Nineteenth-Century Fiction journal since 1958, Novel journal since 1966, and Style journal since 1967. Asst. Prof. 1952–55, Assoc. Prof. 1955–59, and Prof. 1959–62, Dept. of English, Univ. of Calfornia, Berkeley; Advisory Ed., Victorian Studies journal, 1960–72; Prof. of English, and Dean, Sch. of English Studies, Univ. of East Anglia, Norwich, 1962–64; Advisory Ed., Eighteenth Century Literature journal, 1966–74. *Publs:* The Rise of the Novel: Studies in Defoe, Richardson and Fielding, 1957; (ed. and contrib.) Jane Austen: A Collection of Critical Essays, 1963; (ed.) Tristram Shandy, 1965; (ed.) The Victorian Novel: Modern Essays in Criticism, 1971; (ed. and contrib.) Conrad: The Secret Agent, a Casebook, 1973; (compiler) From Scott to Hardy, 1973; Conrad in the Nineteenth Century, 1980; The Humanities on the River Kwai, 1981; Conrad: Nostromo, 1988. Add: c/o Cambridge Univ. Press, 32 E. 57th St., New York, N.Y. 10022, U.S.A.

WATT, W(illiam) Montgomery. British, b. 1909. History, Sociology, Theology/Religion. Asst. Lectr. in Moral Philosophy, 1934–38, Lectr. in Ancient Philosophy, 1946–47, Lectr. in Arabic, 1955–64, and Prof. of Arabic and Islamic Studies, 1964–79, Univ. of Edinburgh. Arabic Specialist, Anglican Bishopric, Jerusalem, 1943–46. *Publs:* Free Will and Predestination in Early Islam, 1949; The Faith and Practice of Al-Ghazali, 1953; Muhammad at Mecca, 1953; Muhammad at Medina, 1956; The Reality of God, 1958; The Cure for Human Troubles, 1959; Islam and the Integration of Society, 1961; Muhammad, Prophet and Statesman, 1961; Islamic Philosophy and Theology, 1962, 1986; Muslim Intellectual, 1963; Truth in the Religions, 1963; (with P.J.E. Cachia) Islamic Spain, 1965; A Companion to the Qur'an, 1967; What is Islam?, 1968; Islamic Political Thought, 1968; Islamic Revelation and the Modern World, 1970; Bell's Introduction to the Qur'an, 1970; The Influence of Islam on Medieval Europe, 1972; The Formative Period of Islamic Thought, 1973; The Majesty That Was Islam, 1974; (co-author) Der Islam, 2 vols., 1980–85; Islam and Christianity Today, 1984; Muhammad's Mecca: History from the Qur'an, 1988; Islamic Fundamentalism and Modernity, 1988. Add: The Neuk, Dalkeith, Midlothian EH22 1JT, Scotland.

WATTENBERG, Ben J. American, b. 1933. Social commentary/phenomena. Sr. Fellow, American Enterprise Inst. Co-Ed., Public Opinion Mag.; Co-Founder and Co-Chmn., Coalition for a Democratic Majority. Asst. to President Johnson, 1966–68; Aide to Senator Hubert H. Humphrey, 1970; Advisor to Senator Henry M. Jackson, 1972, 1976. *Publs:* This U.S.A., 1965; (with R. Scammon) The Real Majority, 1970; The Real America, 1974; (with E. Duggan) Against All Enemies; (with R. Whalen) The Wealth Weapon, 1980; The Good News Is the Bad News Is Wrong, 1984; Are World Population Trends a Problem?, 1985; The Birth Dearth, 1987. Add: 1150 17th St. N.W., Washington, D.C. 20036, U.S.A. Washington, D.C. 20037, U.S.A.

WATTS, Alan (James). British, b. 1925. Meteorology/Atmospheric sciences, Recreation, Sciences (general). Lectr. in Physics, Colchester Inst., since 1957. Ed. and Originator, Science Slide Folios, The Slide Centre, since 1970. Weather Adviser, British Olympic Yachting Team, 1966–68. *Publs:* Wind and Sailing Boats, 1965; Weather Forecasting Ashore and Afloat, 1968; Instant Weather Forecasting, 1968, 1988; The Wind Pilot, 1975; Instant Wind Forecasting, 1975; Basic Windcraft, 1976; The Course Builder's Handbook, 1979; Cruising Weather, 1982; Dinghy and Board Sailing Weather, 1984; Home Course Building and Jumping, 1984; Reading the Weather: Modern Techniques for Yachtsmen, 1987.

Add: Ryelands, Elmstead Market, Colchester, Essex, England.

WATTS, Anthony John. British, b. 1942. History, Military/Defence. Ed., Navy Intertional, since 1978. Freelance naval publishing consultant, since 1968. Engineer, 1961–64, and Studio Mgr., 1964–78, BBC, London. *Publs:* Japanese Warships of World War II, 1966; Pictorial History of the Royal Navy 1816-1880, vol. I, 1970, 1880-1914, vol. II, 1971; The Loss of the Scharnhorst, 1970; (with B.G. Gordon) The Imperial Japanese Navy, 1971; (ed.) Warships and Navies 1973, 1972; (ed.) The Russian Fleet 1914-17, 1972; (ed.) Scapa Flow 1919, 1973; (ed.) Chronology of the War at Sea 1939-45, 2 vols., 1972–74; (ed.) Warships and Navies 1974, 1974; Source Book of Submarines, 1976; Source Book of Aircraft Carriers and Their Aircraft, 1977; Fact File on Submarines, 2 vols., 1977; Source Book on Hovercraft and Hydrofoils, 1978; Fact File on Battleships, 1978; Fact File on Cruisers, 2 vols., 1979; Source Book of Helicopters and Vertical Take-off Aircraft, 1982; (with A. English) Battle for the Falklands, 1982. Add: Hunters Moon, Hogspudding Lane, Newdigate, Dorking, Surrey RH5 5DS, England.

WATTS, Harold H. American, b. 1906. Plays/Screenplays, Literature, Theology/Religion. Instr., to Prof. of English, Purdue Univ., Indiana, 1929–72. *Publs:* Witches Go Silently (play), 1941; The Modern Reader's Guide to the Bible, 1949, 1959; Ezra Pound and the Cantos, 1951; Hound and Quarry, 1953; The Modern Reader's Guide to Religions, 1964; Aldous Huxley, 1969; (with Lilly Lessing) I Was His Wife, 1981. Add: 2020 N. River Rd., West Lafayette, Ind. 47906, U.S.A.

WATTS, John Francis. British, b. 1926. Children's fiction, Education. Headmaster, Les Quennevais Sch., Jersey, 1964–69; former Lectr., Univ. of London Inst. of Education; Principal, Countesthorpe Colol., Leics., 1972–81. Chmn., National Assn. for the Teaching of English, 1974–76. *Publs:* Year with the Slaters, 1965; Point of Departure, 1965; Encounters, vols. I-IV, 1966–68; Early Encounters, 1969; Encounters International, 1970; Twentieth Century Encounters, 1970; (with W. Grono) Contact, vols. I-III, 1970–71; Interplay One to Three, 3 vols, 1972–79; Teaching, 1974; Towards an Open School, 1980. Add: 106 Kineton Green Rd., Olton, Solihull, W. Midlands B92 7EE, England.

WAUGH, Auberon (Alexander). British, b. 1939. Novels/Short stories, Politics/Government, Autobiography/Memoirs/Personal, Documentaries/Reportage, Essays. Columnist, Political Corresp., and Literary Ed., Private Eye, London, since 1970. Contrib., Books and Bookmen, since 1972; Chief Reviewer, Daily Mail, London, since 1981; Columnist, Spectator, London, since 1976. Reporter, Daily Telegraph, London, 1960–63; Special Writer, Intnl. Publs. Corp., London, 1963–67; Chief Political Corresp., 1967–70, and Chief Fiction Reviewer, 1970–73, The Spectator, London; Columnist, News of the World and The Sun, 1969–70, The Times, 1970, and New Statesman, 1973–75, London; Chief Fiction Reviewer, Evening Standard, London, 1973–81. *Publs:* The Foxglove Saga, 1960; Path of Dalliance, 1963; Who Are the Violets Now? 1965; Consider the Lilies, 1968; (with S. Crowje) Biafra: Britain's Shame, 1969; Bed of Flowers: or As You Like It, 1973; Country Topics, 1974; Four Crowded Years (diaries), 1976; In the Lion's Den (essays), 1978; The Last Word: An Eye-Witness Account of the Thorpe Trial, 1980; Auberon Waugh's Yearbook, 1981; The Diaries of Auberon Waugh: A Turbulent Decade 1976-85, 1985; Waugh on Wine, 1986; Another Voice (essays), 1986. Add: 124 Rotherfield St., Islington, London N1 3DA, England.

WAUGH, Dorothy. American. Homes/Gardens, Biography. Freelance writer, illustrator, designer. *Publs:* Among the Leaves and Grasses, 1931; Warm Earth, 1943; Muriel Saves String, 1956; Handbook of Christmas Decoration, 1958; Festive Decoration the Year Round, 1962; Emily Dickinson's Beloved, 1976. Add: 38 E. 38th St., New York, N.Y. 10016, U.S.A.

WAUGH, Hillary (Baldwin). Also writes as Elissa Grandower (in the U.S.; Grandower books published by Hillary Waugh in the U.K.), H. Baldwin Taylor, and Harry Walker. American, b. 1920. Mystery/Crime/Suspense. Free-lance cartoonist and song writer. Teacher of mathematics and physics, Hamden Hall Country Day Sch., Connecticut, 1956–57; Ed., of the Review, Branford, Conn., 1961–62. Past Pres., and currently Exec.Vice-Pres., Mystery Writers of America. *Publs:* Madame Will Not Dine Tonight, 1947; Hope to Die, 1948; The Odds Run Out, 1949; Last Seen Wearing . . ., 1952; A Rag and a Bone, 1954; (as Harry Walker) The Case of the Missing Gardener, 1954; Rich Man, Dead Man (in U.K. as Rich Man, Murder), 1956 (in U.S. paperback, The Case of the Brunette Bombshell, 1957); The Eighth Mrs. Bluebeard, 1958; The Girl Who Cried Wolf, 1958; Sleep Long, My Love, 1959 (in U.K. paperback, Jigsaw), 1962; Road Block, 1960; That Night It Rained,

1961; Murder on the Terrace, 1961; The Late Mrs. D., 1962; Born Victim, 1962; Death and Circumstances, 1963; Prisoner's Plea, 1963; The Missing Man, 1964; (as H. Baldwin Taylor) The Duplicate, 1964; End of a Party, 1965; Girl on the Run, 1965; Pure Poisin, 1966; (as H. Baldwin Taylor) The Triumvirate, 1966; (as H. Baldwin Taylor) The Trouble with Tycoons (in U.K. as The Missing Tycoon), 1967; The Con Game, 1968; "30" Manhattan East, 1968; Run When I Say Go, 1969; The Young Prey, 1969; (ed.) Merchants of Menace, 1969; Finish Me Off, 1970; The Shadow Guest, 1971; Parrish for the Defense, 1974 (in U.S. paperback, Doctor on Trial, 1977); A Bride for Hampton House, 1975; (as Elissa Grandower) Seaview Manor, 1976; (as Elissa Grandower) The Summer at Raven's Roost, 1976; (as Elissa Grandower) The Secret Room of Margate House, 1977; Madman at My Door, 1978; (as Elissa Grandower) Blackbourne Hall, 1979; (as Elissa Grandower) Rivergate house, 1980; The Glenna Powers Case, 1980; The Doria Rafe Case, 1980; The Billy Cantrell Case, 1981; The Nerissa Claire Case, 1983; The Veronica Dean Case, 1984; The Priscilla Copperwaite Case, 1985; Murder on Safari, 1987; Death in a Town, 1988. Add: c/o Ann Elmo Agency, 60 E. 42nd St., New York, N.Y. 10017, U.S.A.

WAX, Murray L. American, b. 1922. Anthropology/Ethnology, Education, Sociology. Prof. of Sociology, Washington Univ., St. Louis, since 1973 (Chmn., 1973–76). Instr. in Philosophy, Temple Univ., Philadelphia, 1946–47; Instr. in Social Science, Univ. of Chicago, 1948–49, and Univ. of Illinois, Chicago, 1953–54; Project Dir., Science Research Assocs., Chicago, 1954–56; Sr. Analyst, 1956–58, and Research Supvr., 1958–59, Gillette Corp., Chicago; Asst. Prof. of Sociology and Anthropology, Univ. of Miami, 1959–62; Assoc. Prof. of Sociology, Emory Univ., Atlanta, 1962–64; Dir., Oglala Sioux Education Research Project, 1962–63; Assoc. Prof., 1964–67, Prof. of Sociology, 1967–73, Vice-Chmn., and Dir. of Grad. Studies, 1969–72, and Chmn., 1972–73, Univ. of Kansas, Lawrence. *Publs:* (ed. with C.W. Churchman and R.L. Ackoff) The Measure of Consumer Interest, 1947; Indian Americans: Unity and Diversity, 1971; (ed. with S. Diamona and F.O. Gearing) Anthropological Perspectives on Education, 1971; (ed. with Robert Buchanan) Solving the Indian Problem: The White Man's Burdensome Business, 1975; (ed. with Joan Cassell) Federal Regulations: Ethical Issues and Social Research, 1979. Add: 7106 Westmoreland Dr., University City, Mo. 63130, U.S.A.

WAY, Margaret. Historical/Romance/Gothic. *Publs:* Blaze of Silk, 1970; King Country, 1970; The Time of the Jacaranda, 1970; Return to Belle Amber, 1971; Summer Magic, 1971; Bauhinia Junction, 1971; The Man from Bahl Bahla, 1971; Noonfire, 1972; Ring of Jade, 1972; A Man Like Daintree, 1972; Copper Moon, 1972; The Rainbow Bird, 1972; Storm over Mandargi, 1973; Sweet Sundown, 1974; The Love Theme, 1974; McCabe's Kingdom, 1974; Wind River, 1974; Reeds of Honey, 1975; Storm Flower, 1975; A Lesson in Loving, 1975; Flight into Yesterday, 1976; The Man on Half-Moon, 1976; Red Cliffs of Malpara, 1976; Swans' Reach, 1977; One Way Ticket, 1977; The Awakening Flame, 1978; Wake the Sleeping Tiger, 1978; The Wild Swan, 1978; Ring of Fire, 1978; Portrait of Jaime, 1978; Mutiny in Paradise, 1978; Black Ingo, 1978; Blue Lotus, 1979; The Butterfly and the Baron, 1979; Valley of the Moon, 1979; White Magnolia, 1979; The Winds of Heaven, 1979; The Golden Puma, 1980; Flamingo Park, 1980; Lord of the High Valley, 1980; Temple of Fire, 1980; Shadow Dance, 1981; A Season for Change, 1981. Add: c/o Mills and Boon Ltd., 15-16 Brooks Mews, London W1A 1DR, England.

WAY, Peter (Howard). British, b. 1936. Novels/Short stories, Poetry, Military/Defence. Consultant publisher to The War Papers. Features Ed., Readers Digest, London, 1962; Ed., Mind Alive, 1968. *Publs:* The Kietzmer Syndrome, 1970; A Perfect State of Health, 1972; Pieces of a Game (poetry), 1974; Codes and Ciphers, 1977; Super-Celeste (novel), 1977; Sunrise (novel), 1980; Icarus (novel), 1981; Belshazzar's Feast (novel), 1982. Add: 5 Egerton Dr., London SE10, England.

WAYMAN, Tom. Canadian, b. 1945. Poetry. Instr., Kwantlen Coll., Surrey B.C., since 1988. Writer-in-Residence, Univ. of Windsor, Ont., 1975–76; Asst. Prof. of English, Wayne State Univ., Detroit, 1976–77; Writer-in-Residence, Univ. of Alberta, Edmonton, 1978–79; Instr., David Thompson Univ. Centre, Nelson, B.C., 1980–82; Writer-in-Residence, Simon Fraser Univ., Burnaby, B.C., 1983; Instr., Kootenay Sch. of Writing. Vancouver 1984–87. *Publs:* (with others) Mindscapes, 1971; Waiting for Wayman, 1973; For and Against the Moon: Blues, Yells and Chuckles, 1974; (ed.) Beaton Abbott's Got the Contract: An Anthology of Working Poems, 1974; Money and Rain: Tom Wayman Live!, 1975; Routines, 1976; Transport, 1976; (ed.) A Government Job at Last: An Anthology of Working Poems, Mainly Canadian, 1976;

Kitchener/Chicago/Saskatoon, 1977; Free Time: Industrial Poems, 1977; A Planet Mostly Sea, 1979; Living on the Ground: Tom Wayman Country, 1980; Introducing Tom Wayman: Selected Poems 1973-1980, 1980; (ed.) Going for Coffee: Poetry on the Job, 1981; The Nobel Prize Acceptance Speech, 1981; Counting the Hours: City Poems, 1983; Inside Job: Essays on the New Work Writing, 1983; The Face of Jack Monro, 1986. Add: c/o 17 Noel Ave., Toronto, Ont. M4G 1B2, Canada.

WAYMAN, Vivienne. British, b. 1926. Children's fiction. *Publs:* The Rose Boy at Penny Spring, 1968; Emma of Lark Water Hall, 1969; The Alabaster Princess, 1970; A Cage in the Apple Orchard, 1972; The Seventh Bull Maiden, 1974; Panchit's Secret, 1975. Add: 42 Old Church Lane, Stanmore, Middx., England.

WAYNE, Donald. *See* **DODD,** Wayne D.

WAYNE, Joseph. *See* **OVERHOLSER,** Wayne D.

WEALE, Anne. Also writes as Andrea Blake. British. Historical/Romance. Staff Reporter, Eastern Evening News, Western Daily Press, and Yorkshire Evening Press. *Publs:* Winter is Past, 1955; The Lonely Shore, 1956; The House of Seven Fountains, 1957; Never to Love, 1958; Sweet to Remember, 1958; Castle in Corsica, 1959; Hope for Tomorrow, 1959; A Call for Nurse Templar, 1960; Until We Met, 1961; The Doctor's Daughters, 1962; The House on Flamingo Cay, 1962; If This Is Love, 1963; The Silver Dolphin, 1963; (as Andrea Blake) September in Paris, 1963; All I Ask, 1964; Islands of Summer, 1964; Three Weeks in Eden, 1964; (as Andrea Blake) Now and Always, 1964; Doctor in Malaya, 1965; Girl about Town, 1965; The Feast of Sara, 1965; (as Anddrea Blake) Whisper of Doubt, 1965; (as Andrea Blake) Night of the Hurricane, 1965; Christina Comes to Town, 1966; Terrace in the Sun, 1966; The Sea Waif, 1967; South from Sounion, 1968; The Man in Command, 1969; Sullivan's Reef, 1970; That Man Simon, 1971; A Treasure for Life, 1972; The Fields of Heaven, 1974; Lord of the Sierras, 1975; Frangipani, 1975; Girl in a Golden Bed, 1975; The Sun in Splendour, 1975; Now or Never, 1978; The River Room, 1978; Separate Bedrooms, 1979; Stowaway, 1979; The Girl from the Sea, 1979; The First Officer, 1980; The Last Night at Paradise, 1980; Touch of the Devil, 1980; Blue Days at Sea, 1981; Passage to Paxos, 1981; Rain of Diamonds, 1981; Bed of Roses, 1981; Antigua, 1982; Portrait of Bethany, 1982; Wedding of the Year, 1982; All That Heaven Allows, 1983; Ecstasy, 1983; Flora, 1983; Yesterday's Island, 1983; Summer's Awakening, 1984; All My Worldly Goods, 1987; Lost Lagoon, 1987; Night Train, 1987; Neptune's Daughter, 1987; Catalan Christmas, 1988; Do You Remember Babylon?, 1989; Time and Chance, 1989. Add: Apartado 150, San Carlos de la Rapitá, Tarragona, Spain.

WEALES, Gerald. American, b. 1925. Novels/Short stories, Children's fiction, Literature, Theatre. Prof. Emeritus of English, Univ. of Pennsylvania, Philadelphia, since 1987 (Asst. Prof., 1958–63; Assoc. Prof., 1963–67; Prof., 1967–87). Instr. in English, Georgia Inst. of Technology, Atlanta, 1951–53, Newark Coll. of Engineering, New Jersey, 1953–55, and Wayne State Univ., Detroit, 1955–56; Asst. Prof. of English, Brown Univ., Providence, R.I., 1957–58. *Publs:* Miss Grimsbee Is a Witch, 1957; Tale for the Bluebird, 1960; Religion in Modern English Drama, 1961; American Drama since World War II, 1962; (ed.) Edwardian Plays, 1962; A Play and Its Parts, 1964; (ed.) Eleven Plays, 1964; Miss Grimsbee Takes a Vacation, 1965; (ed.) The Complete Plays of William Wycherley, 1966; (ed.) Death of a Salesman, by Arthur Miller: Text and Criticism, 1967; The Jumping-Off Place: American Drama in the 1960's, 1969; Clifford Odets, Playwright, 1971, 1985; (ed.) The Crucible, by Arthur Miller, 1971; (ed. with R.J. Nelson) Revolution (collection of plays), 1975; (ed. with R.J. Nelson) Enclosure (collection of plays), 1975; Canned Goods as Caviar: American Film Comedy of the 1930's, 1985. Add: Dept. of English, Univ. of Pennsylvania, Philadelphia, Pa. 19104, U.S.A.

WEARIN, Otha Donner. American, b. 1903. Agriculture/Forestry, Art, History, Politics/Government, Biography. Farm Mgr. and Joint Owner, Brazelton & Wearin Farms, Hastings, Iowa, since 1939. Member of Iowa State Legislature, 1928–32, U.S. House of Reps., 1932–39, and Iowa State Commn. on Ageing, 1962–66. *Publs:* An Iowa Farmer Abroad, 1928; A Century on an Iowa Farm, 1959; Statues that Pour, 1965; I Remember Hastings, 1965; Clarence Arthur Ellsworth: Artist of the Old West, 1967; Political Americana: Political Campaign Buttons in Color, 1967; Before the Colors Fade, 1971; I Remember Yesteryear, 1974; Heinhold's First and Last Chance Saloon, 1974; Country Roads to Washington, 1976; Along Our Country Road, 1976; Grass Grown Trails, 1977; Paul Raymond Rowe: Tracker of Ancient Indians, 1977. Add: Hastings, Iowa 51540,

U.S.A.

WEART, Spencer R(ichard). American, b. 1942. Physics. Dir., Center for the History of Physics, American Inst. of Physics, NYC. Research Fellow, Mount Wilson and Palomar Observatories, Pasadena, Calif., 1968–70; Research Asst. in the History Dept., Univ. of California, Berkeley, from 1971. *Publs:* Light: A Key to the Universe (juvenile), 1968; How to Build a Sun (juvenile), 1970; (ed, with Gertrud W. Szilard) Leo Szilard: His Version of the Facts, 1978; Scientists in Power, 1979; (ed. with Melba Phillips) History of Physics, 1987; Nuclear Fear: A History of Images, 1988. Add: c/o Harvard Univ. Press, 79 Garden St., Cambridge, Mass. 02138, U.S.A.

WEARY, Ogdred. *See* **GOREY,** Edward.

WEATHERHEAD, A(ndrew) Kingsley. American, b. 1923. Literature, Biography. Prof. of English, Univ. of Oregon, Eugene, since 1960; Editorial Bd. of Twentieth Century Literature, since 1968. *Publs:* A Reading of Henry Green, 1961; The Edge of the Image, 1967; (ed. with S. Greenfield) The Poem, 1967; Stephen Spender and the Thirties, 1975; Leslie Weatherhead: A Personal Portrait, 1975; The British Dissonance, 1983. Add: 2698 Fairmount Blvd., Eugene, Ore. 97403, U.S.A.

WEATHERS, Philip. British, b. 1908. Plays/Screenplays. Freelance writer and producer. Suprv. to His Grace the Duke of Northumberland, since 1968. *Publs:* The Weary Heart, 1938; Arms and the Woman, 1947; (with F.L.S. Cary) Madam Tic-Tac, 1951; Tell-Tale Murder, 1952; (with F.L.S. Cary) The Shadow Witness, 1954; (with F.L.S. Cary) The Proof of the Poison, 1955; This Is My Life, 1957; Murder Isn't a Cricket, 1959; Once Upon a Crime, 1961; Permit to Kill, 1968; Syon House (guidebook), 1968; Home or Away?, 1969; Three Shots in the Dark, 1970; The Nuns of Syon, 1975; O Mistress Mine, 1977. Add: Charterhouse, London EC1M 6AN, England.

WEAVER, Carl Harold. American, b. 1910. Psychology, Speech/Rhetoric. Asst. Prof., Dept. of Speech, Central Michigan Univ., Mt. Pleasant, 1955–60; Assoc. Prof., and Dir. of Gen. Speech, Univ. of Maryland, College Park, 1960–66; Prof. of Interpersonal Communication, Ohio Univ., Athens, 1966–74, now Emeritus. *Publs:* (with W.L. Strausbaugh) The Fundamentals of Speech Communications, 1964; Speaking in Public, 1966; Human Listening: Behavior and Processes, 1972; The Story of the International Communication Association. Add: R.R. 2, Box 334, Eutawville, S.C. 29048, U.S.A.

WEAVER, Kitty D. American, b. 1910. Education. *Publs:* Lenin's Grandchildren, 1971; Russia's Future, 1981. Add: c/o Praeger Publishers, One Madison Ave., New York, N.Y. 10010, U.S.A.

WEBB, Bernice (Larson). American. Poetry, Biography. Ed., Louisiana Poets, since 1970. Prof. of English, Univ. of Southwestern Louisiana, Lafayette, since 1980–87 (Asst. Prof., 1961–67; Assoc. Prof., 1967–80). *Publs:* The Basketball Man, 1973; Beware of Ostriches, 1978; Poetry on the Stage, 1979; Lady Doctor on a Homestead, 1987. Add: 159 Whittington Dr., Lafayette, La. 70503, U.S.A.

WEBB, Charles. American, b. 1939. Novels/Short stories. *Publs:* The Graduate, 1963; Love, Roger, 1967; The Marriage of a Young Stockbroker, 1969; Orphans and Other Children (novellas), 1974; The Abolitionist of Clark Gable Place, 1975; Elsinor, 1976; The Nose Collector, 1985. Add: c/o New American Library, 1633 Broadway, New York, N.Y. 10019, U.S.A.

WEBB, G(odfrey) E(dward) C(harles). British, b. 1914. Novels/Short stories, Anthropology/Ethnology. Civil Servant, Ordnance Survey Office, Southampton, 1936–75, now retired. *Publs:* Gypsies: The Secret People, 1960; Tom Hathaway, 1963. Add: 11 Shirley Ave., Southampton, Hants, England.

WEBB, Harri. Welsh, b. 1920. Poetry. Former librarian in Dowlais and Mountain Ash, Glamorgan. *Publs:* Dic Penderyn and the Merthyr Rising in 1831, 1956; (with P. Gruffydd and Meic Stephens) Triad: Thirty-Three Poems, 1963; Our National Anthem: Some Observations on "Hen wlad fy nhadau", 1964; The Green Desert, 1969; A Crown for Branwen, 1973; Rampage and Revel, 1977; Poems and Points, 1983; Tales from Wales (for children), 1983. Add: c/o Granada Collins, 8 Grafton St., London WIX 3LA, England.

WEBB, James (Edwin). American, b. 1906. Business/Trade/Industry. Attorney-at-Law, Washington; Dir., Kerr Consolidated, since 1979; Member, National Academy of Public Administration, since 1969. Trustee: Meridian House Foundn., Washington (Chmn. of Trustees), Urban Studies Inc., Washington (Chmn. of Trustees and Pres.), Cttee. for Economic Development, NYC, National Geographic Soc., Washington, etc.; Member of Council, American Soc. for Public Admin., Washington. Dir., U.S. Bureau of the Budget, Washington, 1946–49; U.S. Under Secty. of State, and Alternate Gov., World Bank and Intnl. Monetary Fund, Washington, 1949–52; Dir. and Asst. to the Pres., Kerr-McGee Oil Industries, Inc., Oklahoma City, 1952–61; Pres., 1953–58, and Chmn., 1958; Republic Supply Co., Oklahoma City (Dir., 1952–58); Pres., 1958–61, and Chmn., 1959, Educational Services, Inc., Watertown, Mass. (Dir., 1958–63); Administrator, NASA, Washington, 1961–68; Dir., Gannett Co., 1969–79, Sperry Rand Corp., 1969–77, and McGraw-Hill Inc., 1972–81; Dir., Computer Data Systms Inc., 1977–87; Dir., Kerr Foundn. Inc., 1977–85 (Chmn., 1980–81). Member: Exec. Cttee., U.S. Cttee. for the U.N., 1955–60; President's Cttee. to Study the U.S. Military Assistance Program (Draper Cttee.), 1958–59; National Aeronautics and Space Council, and Federal Council for Science and Technology, 1961–68; President's Cttee. of Equal Employment Opportunity, 1961–65; President's Cttee. on Manpower, and President's Advisory Cttee. on Supersonic Transport, 1964–68. *Publs:* (with Corson) Governmental Manpower for Tomorrow's Cities, 1962; Space Age Management, 1968; NASA as an Adaptive Organization, 1968; Leadership Evaluation in Large-Scale Efforts, 1972; Management Leadership and Relationships, 1972. Add: 2800 36th St. N.W., Washington, D.C. 20007, U.S.A.

WEBB, Jean Francis. Also writes as Ethel Hamill, Ian Kavanaugh, Roberta Morrison, and Roswell Brown. American, b. 1910. Mystery/Crime/Suspense, Historical/Romance/Gothic, Western/Adventure, Children's fiction History, Theatre, Biography. Member, Bd. of Dirs., Mystery Writers of America, since 1976. Trustee, South Salem Library, 1946–71. *Publs:* Love They Must, 1933; Forty Brothers (short stories), 1934; No Match for Murder, 1942; (with N. Webb) Chick Carter: Boy Detective (radio series), 1944–45; (as Ethel Hamill) Challenge to Love, 1946; (as Ethel Hamill) Reveille for Romance, 1946; Little Women (novelization of screenplay), 1949; Anna Lucasta (novelization of screephlay), 1949; King Solomon's Mines (novelization of screenplay), 1950; (as Ethel Hamill) Honeymoon in Honolulu, 1950; (as Ethel Hamill) Tower in the Forest, 1951, in U.K. as Tower of Dreams, 1961; (as Ethel Hamill) The Dancing Mermaid, 1952, as All for Love, 1965; (as Ethel Hamill) Nurse on Horseback, 1952; (as Ethel Hamill) Bluegrass Doctor, 1953; (as Ethel Hamill) The Minister's Daughter, 1953; (as Ethel Hamill) The Nurse Comes Home, 1954; (as Ethel Hamill) Gloria and the Bullfighter, 1954; (with N. Webb) Golden Feathers (juvenile), 1954; (as Ethel Hamill) A Nurse Comes Home, 1954, in U.K. as Nurse Elizabeth Comes Home, 1955; (as Ethel Hamill) Runaway Nurse, 1955; (with N. Webb) The Hawaiian Islands, 1956, 1963; (as Ethel Hamill) A Nurse for Galleon Key, 1957; (as Ethel Hamill) The Golden Image, 1959; (as Ethel Hamill) Aloha Nurse, 1961; (as Ethel Hamill) Sudden Love, 1962; (with N. Webb) Kaiulani, Crown Princess of Hawaii, 1962; (with N. Webb) Will Shakespeare and His America, 1964; (as Ethel Hamill) The Nurse from Hawaii, 1964; (as Roberta Morrison) Tree of Evil, 1966; The Craigshaw Curse, 1968; Carnavaron's Castle, 1969; Roses from a Haunted Garden, 1971; Somewhere Within this House, 1973; The Bride of Cairngore, 1974; Is This Coffin Taken?, 1978; (as Lee Davis Willoughby) The Cajuns, 1981; (as Ian Kavanaugh) A Waltz on the Wind, 1983; The Empty Attic, 1983; Revenge of the Heart, 1986; (with N. Webb) Plots and Pans: A Mystery Writers of America Cookbook, 1989. Add: 242 East 72nd St., New York, N.Y. 10021, U.S.A.

WEBB, Kempton Evans. American, b. 1931. Geography. Prof. since 1971, and Chmn. since 1974, Dept. of Geography, Columbia Univ., NYC (Asst., to Assoc. Prof. of Geography, 1961–71; Asst., to Dir. of Latin American Studies, 1961–73). Contrib. Ed., Handbook of Latin American Studies, since 1959. Asst. Prof. of Geography, Indiana Univ., Bloomington, 1958–61; Member of First Exec. Council, Latin American Studies Assn., 1965–68; Gen. Ed. of Cultural geography series of schs. texts, 1967–71. *Publs:* Suprimento dos Generos Alimenticios Basicos para a Cidade de Fortaleza, 1957; Geography of Food Supply in Central Minas Gerais, 1959; Brazil, 1964; (ed.) Latin America: A Geographical Commentary, 1966; (with D. Grossman) Geography, 1967; Latin America, 1972; The Changing Face of Northeast Brazil, 1974; All Possible Worlds, 1980. Add: c/o Columbia Univ. Press, 562 W. 113th St., New York, N.Y. 10025, U.S.A.

WEBB, Phyllis. Canadian, b. 1927. Poetry. Prog. Organizer, 1964–67, and Exec. Producer, 1967–69, CBC, Toronto. Visiting Asst. Prof., 1978–79, and Part-time Lectr., 1982–85, Creative Writing Dept., Univ. of Victoria, B.C.; Writer-in-Residence, Univ. of Alberta, Edmonton,

1980–81; Guest Lectr., Banff Centre, Alta., 1981. *Publs:* (with G. Turnbull and E. Mandel) Trio, 1954; Even Your Right Eye, 1956; The Sea Is Also a Garden: Poems, 1962; Naked Poems, 1965; Selected Poems 1954-1965, 1971; Wilson's Bowl, 1980; Talking, 1982; The Vision Tree (selected poems), 1982; Sunday Water: Thirteen Anti Ghazals, 1982; Water and Light, 1984. Add: Box 11, Fulford, B.C. V0S 1C0, Canada.

WEBB, Sharon. American, b. 1936. Science fiction. Freelance writer, 1959–65, and since 1979. Registered nurse, South Miami Hosp., Miami, 1972–73, and in Blairsville, Ga., 1973–81. *Publs:* R.N. (non-fiction), 1982; Earthchild, 1982; Earth Song, 1983; Ram Song, 1984; The Adventures of Terra Tarkington, 1985; Pestis 18, 1987; The Halflife, 1989. Add: Route 2, Box 2600, Blairsville, Ga. 30512, U.S.A.

WEBB, (Edward) Timothy. Irish, b. 1942. Classics, Intellectual history, Literature. Prof. of English, Univ. of Bristol, since 1989. Ed., Keats-Shelley Review, since 1978. Lectr., Sch. of English, Univ. of Leeds, 1967–75; Lectr., 1976–82, Reader, 1982–85, and Prof., 1985–89, Dept. of English and Related Literature, Univ of York. *Publs:* (ed.) The Black Prophet by Wiliam Carleton, 1972; (ed.) Letters Concerning Poetical Translation by William Benson, 1976; The Violet in the Crucible: Shelley and Translation, 1976; (ed.) Selected Poems by Shelley, 1977; Shelley: A Voice Not Understood, 1977; (ed.) English Romantic Hellenism 1700-1824 (annotated anthology), 1982; (with David Pirie) Shelley, 1984. Add: Dept. of English, Univ. of Bristol, Bristol, England.

WEBBER, E. Ronald. British, b. 1915. History, Horticulture, Biography. *Publs:* The Early Horticulturists, 1968; Covent Garden: Mud Salad Market, 1969; The Village Blacksmith, 1971; Market Gardening: The History of Commercial Flower, Fruit and Vegetable Growing, 1972; Percy Cane, Garden Designer, 1975; The Devon and Somerset Blackdowns, 1976; (co-author) Percy Thrower: My Lifetime in Gardening, 1977; The Peasants Revolt, 1980. Add: 6 Ribblesdale, Roman Rd., Dorking, Surrey, England.

WEBBER, Ross A. American, b. 1934. Administration/Management. Prof. of Mgmt., Wharton Sch., Univ. of Pennsylvania, Philadelphia (joined faculty, 1964). *Publs:* (with D. Hampton and C. Summer) Organizational Behavior and Practice of Management, 1968, 4th ed. 1986; (ed.) Culture and Management: Text and Readings in Comparative Management, 1969; Time and Management, 1972; Management: Basic Elements of Managing Organizations, 1975, 3rd ed. 1984; (ed.) Management Pragmatics: Cases and Readings on Managing Organizations, 1979; Time Is Money, 1980; To Be a Manager, 1981; A Manager's Guide to Getting Things Done, 1984; The Procrastinator's Guide to Getting Things Done, 1986. Add: 574 Warwick R., Haddonfield, N.J. 08033, U.S..

WEBER, Brom. American, b. 1917. Literature. Prof. of English, Univ. of California, Davis, 1963–86. *Publs:* Hart Crane: A Biographical and Critical Study, 1948; (ed.) The Letters of Hart Crane 1916–1932, 1952; (with C. Glicksberg) American Vanguard, 1952; (ed.) Sut Lovingood, Selected works by G. Harris, 1954; (ed.) The Art of American Humor, 1962; (ed.) The Story of a Country Town, novel by E. Howe, 1964; Sherwood Anderson, 1964; (ed.) Complete Poems and Selected Letters and Prose of Hart Crane, 1966; (ed. with H.T. Meserole and W. Sutton) American Literature: Tradition and Innovation, 1969; (ed.) Sense and Sensibility in Twentieth-Century Writing, 1970; Our Multi-Ethnic Origins and American Literary Studies, 1975. Add: 48 Brookside, Missoula, Mont. 59802, U.S.A.

WEBER, David Joseph. American, b. 1940. History. Prof. of History, Southern Methodist Univ., Dallas, since 1976. Asst. Prof., 1967–70, Assoc. Prof., 1970–73, and Prof. of History, 1973–76, San Diego State Univ., California. *Publs:* (ed.) The Extranjeros: Selected Documents from the Mexican Side of the Santa Fe Trail 1825-1828, 1967; The Taos Trappers: The Fur Trade in the Far Southwest 1540-1846, 1971; (ed.) Foreigners in Their Native Land: Historical Roots of the Mexican Americans, 1973; (ed.) Northern Mexico on the Eve of the United States Invasion: Rare Imprints Concerning California, New Mexico and Texas, 1976; (ed. with Duane Smith) Fortunes Are for the Few, by Charles W. Churchill, 1976; (ed.) New Spain's Far Northern Frontier: Essays on Spain in the American West, 1979; The Mexican Frontier 1821-1846: The American Southwest Under Mexico, 1982; Richard H. Kern: Expeditionary Artist in the Far Southwest 1848-1853, 1985; Myth and the History of the Hispanic Southwest: Essays, 1988. Add: 6292 Mercedes, Dallas, Tex. 75214, U.S.A.

WEBER, Eugen. American, b. 1925. History. Prof. of History, Univ. of California, Los Angeles, since 1956 (Dean, Coll. of Letters and Scien-

ces, 1977–82). Member, Editorial Bd., Journal of Contemporary History, London, since 1966. *Publs:* The Nationalist Revival in France 1905-1914, 1959; (ed.) The Western Tradition, 1959, 4th ed. 1989; Paths to the Present, 1960; Action Française, 1962; Satan Franc-Maçon, 1964; Varieties of Fascism, 1964; (with H. Rogger) The European Right, 1965; (ed.) Jean Barois, by R.M. du Gard, 1969; A Modern History of Europe, 1971; Europe since 1715, 1972; Peasants into Frenchman, 1976; (ed.) The Life of a Simple Man, by Emile Guillaumin, 1982; France, Fin de Siècle, 1986. Add: Dept. of History, Univ. of California, Los Angeles, Calif. 90024, U.S.A.

WEBER, Nancy. Also writes as Olivia Harmston, Lindsay West and Jennifer Rose. American, b. 1942. Novels/Short stories, Autobiography/Memoirs/Personal. *Publs:* Star Fever, 1971; The Life Swap, 1974; $500, 1976; (as Lindsay West) Empire of the Ants (novelization), 1977; Lily, Where's Your Daddy?, 1980; (as Jennifer Rose) Blueprint for Ecstasy, 1981; The Playgroup, 1982; (as Jennifer Rose) Shamrock Season, 1982; (as Jennifer Rose) Twilight Embrace, 1982; A Taste of Heaven, 1983; (as Jennifer Rose) Kisses Sweeter Than Wine, 1983; (as Jennifer Rose) Keys to the Heart, 1984; (as Jennifer Rose) Pennies from Heaven, 1984; (as Jennifer Rose) Suddenly that Summer, 1985; (as Nancy Weber) Brokenhearted, 1989. Add: c/o Jane Rotrosen Agency, 318 E. 51st St., New York, N.Y. 10022, U.S.A.

WEBER, Ralph E. American, b. 1926. History, International relations/Current affairs, Biography. Prof. of History, Marquette Univ., since 1969 (Asst. to the Dean, 1954–57; Asst. Prof., 1956–63; Registrar and Dir. of Admissions, 1958–61; Assoc. Prof., 1963–69). Membership Chmn., Soc. for Historians of American Foreign Relations, since 1976. Instr., Univ. of Notre Dame, 1953–54. Member, Exec. Council, American Catholic Historians Assn., 1972–75. *Publs:* Notre Dame's John Zahm, 1961; (with J. Arnold) Admission to College, 1964; (ed.) As Others See Us, 1972, rev. ed. as From the Foreign Press, 1979; (co-ed.) Voices of Revolution, 1972; United States Diplomatic Codes and Ciphers 1775-1938, 1979; (co-ed.) The Awakening of a Sleeping Giant, 1980; (co-ed.) European Ideologies since 1789, 1980; (co-ed.) American Dissent from Thomas Jefferson to Cesar Chavez, 1980; (ed.) The Final Memoranda: General Ralph Van Deman, The Father of U.S. Military Intelligence, 1988. Add: Marquette Univ., History Dept., Milwaukee, Wisc. 53233, U.S.A.

WEBER, Richard. Irish, b. 1932. Poetry. Visiting Lectr., Mount Holyoke Coll., South Hadley, Mass., since 1967. Former Advisory Ed., Icarus, Journal of Trinity Coll., Dublin: Poetry Ed., Poetry Ireland, Dublin; Asst. Warden in boys' clubs, Dublin, 1957–58; Lamplighter, London, 1959; Bookseller's Asst., London, 1959; Dublin, 1961; Asst. Ed., Bookseller, London, 1961; Librarian, Chester Beatty Library, Dublin, 1961–65. *Publs:* O'Reilly: Poems, 1957; The Time Being: A Poem in Three Parts: Autumn to Winter, Winter to Spring, Spring to Summer, 1957; Lady and Gentleman, 1963; Stephen's Green Revisited: Poems, 1968; A Few Small Ones, 1971. Add: Dept. of English, Mount Holyoke Coll., South Hadley, Mass. 01075, U.S.A.

WEBER, Sarah Appleton. *See* **APPLETON,** Sarah.

WEBSTER, Alan Brunskill. British, b. 1918. Theology/Religion. Former Warden of Lincoln Theological Coll., and Canon of Lincoln Cathedral; Dean of Norwich, 1970–78; Dean of St. Paul's, London, 1978–87. *Publs:* Joshua Watson, 1954; Broken Bones May Joy, 1968; Julian of Norwich, 1974, 1980. Add: 20 Beechbank, Norwich NR2 2AL, England.

WEBSTER, Jan. British, b. 1924. Novels/Short stories. *Publs:* Colliers Row, 1977; Saturday City, 1978; Beggarman' Country, 1979; Due South, 1982; Muckle Annie (novel), 1985; One Little Room, 1987; The Rags of Time, 1987; A Different Woman, 1989. Add: c/o Hale, 45–47 Clerkenwell Green, London EC1R 0HT, England.

WEBSTER, Noah. *See* **KNOX,** William.

WEBSTER, Norman William. British, b. 1920. History, Transportation, Biography. Retired from the Scientific Civil Service, Ministry of Defence, U.K. *Publs:* Joseph Locke, Railway Revolutionary, 1970; Britain's First Trunk Line: The Grand Junction Railway, 1972; The Great North Road, 1974. Add: 15 Hillcrest Dr., Slackhead, Cumbria LA7 7BB, England.

WEDDE, Ian. New Zealander, b. 1946. Novels/Short stories, Poetry, Translations. Former forester, factory worker, gardener, and postman; British Council teacher, Jordan, 1969–70; Poetry Reviewer, London mag.,

1970–71. *Publs:* Homage to Matisse, 1971; Made Over, 1974; (trans. with F. Tuqan) Selected Poems, by Mahmud Darwich, 1974; Earthly: Sonnets for Carlos, 1975; Castaly, 1981; The Shirt Factory and Other Stories, 1981; Tales of Gotham City, 1984; Georgicon, 1984; Symmes Hole (novel), 1986; (ed. with Harvey MC Queen) The Penguin Book of New Zealand Verse, 1986; Driving into the Storm, 1988; Survival Arts, 1988. Add: 118-A Maidavale Rd., Roseneath, Wellington, New Zealand.

WEDDELL, Martin. *See* **SEFTON,** Catherine.

WEDELL, Eberhard George. British, b. 1927. Communications media/ Broadcasting, Education. Prof. of Communications Policy and Dir., European Inst. for the Media, Univ. of Manchester, since 1983 (Prof. of Adult Education, 1964–75; Hon. Prof. of Employment Policy, 1975–83). With Ministry of Education, London, 1950–60; Secty., Independent Television Authority, 1960–64; Sr. Official and Adviser, E.E.C. Commn., Brussels, 1973–82. *Publs:* The Use of Television in Education, 1963; Broadcasting and Public Policy, 1968; (with H.D. Perraton) Teaching at a Distance, 1968; (ed. and contrib.) Structures of Broadcasting, 1970; (with R. Glatter) Study by Correspondence, 1971; Correspondence Education in Europe, 1971; Teachers and Educational Development in Cyprus, 1971; (ed. and contrib.) Education and the Development of Malawi, 1973; (with E. Katz) Broadcasting in the Third World, 1978; Making Broadcasting Useful, 1986; (with R. Leonard) Mass Communications in Western Europe, 1986; (co-author) Media in Competition, 1986. Add: 18 Cranmer Rd., Manchester M2O 0AW, England.

WEDGWOOD, (Dame) C(icely) V(eronica). British, b. 1910. Art, History, Literature, Biography, Translations. Hon. Fellow, Lady Margaret Hall, Oxford, since 1962; London Sch. of Economics; University Coll., London. Pres., English Centre of Intnl. P.E.N. 1950–57, and the English Assn. 1955–56; Member, Royal Commn. on Historical Manuscripts, 1952–78, Inst. for Advanced Study, Princeton, N.J., 1953–68, Advisory Council, Victoria & Albert Museum, 1959–69, and Arts Council Literature Panel 1965–67; London; Trustee, National Gallery, London, 1960–67, 1970–77. *Publs:* Strafford, 1936; The Thirty Years War, 1938; (trans.) The Emperor Charles V, by Karl Brandi, 1939; William the Silent, 1944; (trans.) Die Blendung, by Elias Canetti (in U.K. as Auto da Fe, in U.S. as Tower of Babel), 1946; Velvet Studies, 1946; Richelieu and the French Monarchy, 1949; Seventeenth Century English Literature, 1950; Montrose, 1952; The King's Peace, 1955; The King's War, 1958; Poetry and Politics, 1960; Truth and Opinion, 1960; Thomas Wentworth: A Revaluation, 1961; Trial of Charles I (in U.S. as A Coffin for King Charles), 1964; The World of Rubens, 1967; Milton and His World, 1970; Oliver Cromwell, 1973; The Political Career of Peter Paul Rubens, 1975; The Spoils of Time: A History of the World, vol. 1, 1984; History and Hope, 1987. Add: c/o William Collins Ltd., 8 Grafton St., London W1X 3LA, England.

WEEKS, Jeffrey. British, b. 1945. History, Politics/Government, Sex, Sociology. Research Fellow, Social Work Studies, Univ. of Southampton, since 1983. Research Officer, London Sch. of Economics, 1970–77; Fellow, Univ. of Essex, Colchester, 1978–79; Lectr. in Sociology, Kent Univ., Canterbury, 1980–83. *Publs:* (ed., with C. Cook and others) Sources in British Political History, 5 vols., 1974–78; (with Sheila Rowbotham) Socialism and the New Life: The Personal and Sexual Politics of Edward Carpenter and Havelock Ellis, 1977; Coming Out: Homosexual Politics in Britain from the 19th Century to the Present, 1977; Sex, Politics, and Society, 1981; Sexuality and Its Discontents, 1985; Sexuality, 1986; (ed.) Family Directory, 1986; Family Studies, 1986. Add: 26 Dresden Rd., London N19 3BD, England.

WEEMS, John Edward. American, b. 1924. Children's non-fiction, History, Travel/Exploration/Adventure, Biography. Member, National Book Critics Circle. Asst. Dir., Univ. of Texas Press, Austin, 1958–68; Prof. of English, Baylor Univ., Waco, Tex., 1968–71. *Publs:* A Weekend in September, 1957; The Fate of the Maine, 1958; Race for the Pole, 1960; Peary: The Explorer and the Man, 1967; Men Without Countries, 1969; Dream of Empire: A Human History of the Republic of Texas 1836-1846, 1971; To Conquer a Peace: The War Between the United States and Mexico, 1974; Death Song: The Last of the Indian Wars, 1976; Tornado, 1977; Black Art in Houston: The Texas Southern University Experience, 1978; (ed.) A Texas Christmas, 1986; The Story of Texas (for children), 4 vols., 1986. Add: 2012 Collins Dr., Waco, Tex. 76710, U.S.A.

WEGELIN, Christof (Andreas). American/Swiss, b. 1911. Literature. Prof. Emeritus of English, Univ. of Oregon, Eugene, since 1977 (Asst. Prof. to Prof. of English, 1952–77). Jr. Instr. of English, Johns Hopkins Univ., Baltimore, 1945–46; Instr., then Asst. Prof. of English, Princeton Univ., New Jersey, 1946–52. res., Philological Assn. of the Pacific Coast, 1972; Chmn., 20th Century American Literature Section, Modern Language Assn., 1973; Member, PMLA Advisory Bd., 1974–78; Member, Bd. of Editors, American Literature, Durham, N.C., 1981–85. Publs: The Image of Europe in Henry James, 1958; (ed.) The American Novel: Background Readings and Criticism, 1972; (ed.) Tales of Henry James, 1984. Add: Dept. of English, Univ. of Oregon, Eugene, Ore. 97403, U.S.A.

WEHEN, Joy DeWeese. Also writes as Jennifer Wade. American, b. 1936. Historical/Romance/Gothic, Children's fiction. California Ed., Antique Monthly, Horizon, and The Gray Letter, since 1976. *Publs:* Stairway to a Secret, 1953; The Tower in the Sky, 1955; Stranger at Golden Hill, 1961, in paperback as The Golden Hill Mystery; The Silver Cricket, 1966; So Far from Malabar, 1970; (as Jennifer Wade) The Singing Wind (romance), 1977. Add: 1931 Funston Ave., San Francisco, Calif. 94116, U.S.A.

WEIDENBAUM, Murray. American, b. 1927. Business/Trade/Industry, Economics, Politics/Government. Mallinckrodt Distinguished Univ. Prof., since 1971, and Dir. of Center for the Study of American Business, since 1975, Washington Univ., St. Louis, Mo., (Assoc. Prof., 1964-66, Chmn., Dept. of Economics, 1966–69). Asst. Secty. of the Treasury for Economic Policy, 1969–71; Chmn., U.S. Council of Economic Advisers, 1981–82. *Publs:* The Military Market, 1963; Federal Budgeting, 1964; Economic Impact of the Vietnam War, 1967; Prospects for Reallocating Public Resources, 1967; The Modern Public Sector, 1969; The Defense Budget, 1972; Fiscal Responsibility, 1973; Matching Needs and Resources, 1973; Political Economy of the Military-Industrial Complex, 1973; Econ-mics of Peacetime Defense, 1974; Government Mandated Price Increases, 1975; Business, Government and the Public, 1977, 4th ed. 1989; The Future of Business Regulation, 1979; (co-ed.) Two Revolutions in Economic Policy, 1988; (co-ed.) Public Policy Toward Corporate Takeovers, 1988; Rendezvous with Reality, 1988. Add: Washington Univ., Center for the Study of American Business, St. Louis, Mo. 63130, U.S.A.

WEIDMAN, Jerome. American, b. 1913. Novels/Short stories, Plays/Screenplays, Travel/Exploration/Adventure, Essays, Autobiography. Pres., Authors League of America, since 1967. *Publs:* I Can Get It for You Wholesale, 1937, as musical play, 1962; What's in It for Me?, 1938; The Horse that Could Whistle "Dixie" and Other Stories, 1939; Letter of Credit (on travel), 1940; I'll Never Go There Anymore, 1941; The Lights Around the Shore, 1942; (ed.) A Somerset Maugham Reader, 1943; Too Early to Tell, 1946; The Captain's Tiger (short stories), 1947; The Price Is Right, 1949; Give Me Your Love, 1949; The Damned Don't Cry (screenplay), 1950; The Hand of the Hunter, 1951; The Third Angel, 1953; (ed.) Traveler's Cheque, 1954; Your Daughter, Iris, 1955; House of Strangers (screenplay), 1955; A Dime a Throw (short stories), 1957; Slander (screenplay), 1957; The Enemy Camp, 1958; (with George Abbott) Fiorello! (play), 1959; (with G. Abbott) Tenderloin (play), 1960; Before You Go, 1960; Nine Stories, 1960; My Father Sits in the Dark and Other Selected Stories, 1961; (co-ed.) The First College Bowl Question Book, 1961; The Sound of Bow Bells, 1962; Back Talk (essays), 1963; Where the Sun Never Sets and Other Stories, 1964; Word of Mouth, 1964; Cool Off! (play), 1964; The Death of Dickie Draper and Nine Other Stories, 1965; Pousse Café (play), 1966; Other People's Money, 1967; (with J. Yaffe) Ivory Tower (play), 1968; The Mother Lover (play), 1969; Asterisk! A Comedy of Terrors (play), 1969; The Center of the Action, 1969; Fourth Street East, 1971; Last Respects, 1972; Tiffany Street, 1974; The Temple, 1975; A Family Fortune, 1978; Counselors at Law, 1980; Praying for Rain (autobiography), 1986. Add: c/o Brandt & Brandt, 1501 Broadway, New York, N.Y. 10036, U.S.A.

WEINBERG, Florence M(ay). American, b. 1933. Literature. Prof., St. John Fisher Coll., Rochester, N.Y., since 1975 (Instr., 1967; Asst. Prof., 1967–71; Assoc. Prof., 1971–75; Chmn., Div. of Modern Languages and Classical Studies, 1972–79). *Publs:* The Wine and the Will: Rabelais's Bacchic Christianity, 1972; Gargantua in a Convex Mirror, 1986; The Cave, 1987. Add: 290 Forest Hills Rd., Rochester, N.Y. 14625, U.S.A.

WEINBERG, Kerry. American. Literature, Essays. Member of the faculty, Fairleigh Dickinson Univ., Madison, N.J., since 1979. Secondary Sch. Teacher in English, Latin, French, German and Hebrew, East Ramapo Central Sch. District, Spring Valley, N.Y., 1956–78. *Publs:* T.S. Eliot and Charles Baudelaire, 1969; (co-author) Emuna/Horizonte, 1972. Add: P.O. Box 342, Spring Valley, N.Y. 10977, U.S.A.

WEINBERG, Meyer. American, b. 1920. Education, History, Social sciences. Prof. Dept. of Afro-American Studies, Univ. of Massachusetts, Amherst, since 1978. Teacher, City Coll. of Chicago, 1945-78. *Publs:* (with others) Society and Man, 1956, 1965; (ed.) Issues in Social Science, 1959; TV in America, 1962; Desegregation Research: An Appraisal, 1968, 1970; Race and Place: A Legal History of the Neighborhood School, 1968; (ed.) W.E.B. DuBois: A Reader, 1970; A Chance to Learn: A History of Race and Schools, 1977; Minority Students: A Research Appraisal, 1977; (compiler) The Education of Poor and Minority Children: A World Bibliography, 2 vols., 1981; America's Economic Heritage, 2 vols., 1983; The Search for Quality Integrated Education, 1983; Because They Were Jews: A History of Anti-Semitism, 1986. Add: 7 Winston Ct., Amherst, Mass. 01002, U.S.A.

WEINBERG, Steven. American, b. 1933. Astronomy, Physics. Josey Regental Prof. of Science, Univ. of Texas, Austin, since 1982. Instr., Columbia Univ., NYC, 1957-59; member of the faculty, 1960-69, and Prof., 1964-69, Univ. of California, Berkeley; Prof., Massachusetts Inst. of Technology, Cambridge, 1969-73; Higgins Prof. of Physics, Harvard Univ., Cambridge, Mass., and Sr. Scientist, Smithsonian Astrophysical Observatory, 1973-83. *Publs:* Gravitation and Cosmology: Principles and Applications of the General Theory of Relativity, 1972; The First Three Minutes: A Modern View of the Origin of the Universe, 1977; The Discovery of the Subatomic Particles, 1982; (with R.P. Feynman) Elementary Particles and the Laws of Physics, 1987. Add: Physics Dept., Univ. of Texas, Austin, Tex. 78712, U.S.A.

WEINER, Henri. *See* **LONGSTREET,** Stephen.

WEINMAN, Irving. American, b. 1937. Novels/Short stories, Poetry. *Publs:* Eye of the Storm, 1978; Tailor's Dummy, 1986; Hampton Heat, 1988. Add: c/o Writers House Inc., 21 W. 26th St., New York, N.Y. 10010, U.S.A.

WEINRICH, A(nna) K(atharina) H(ildegard). (Sister Mary Aquinas). German, b. 1933. Anthropology/Ethnology, Race relations, Women, Psychology. Analytical psychologist, London, since 1986. Sr. Lectr. in Social Anthropology, Univ. of Rhodesia, Salisbury, 1966-75; Unesco staff, London, 1975-77; Prof. of Sociology, Univ. of Dar es Salaam, 1977-80. *Publs:* Chiefs and Councils in Rhodesia, 1971; Black and White Elites in Rural Rhodesia, 1973; African Farmers in Rhodesia, 1975; Mucheke: Race, Status, and Power in a Rhodesian Provincial Town, 1977; Women and Racial Discrimination in Rhodesia, 1979; African Marriage in Zimbabwe, 1982; Der Kelch und die Schlange, 1989. Add: 115 Dunfield Rd., London SE6 3RD, England.

WEINSTEIN, Allen. American, b. 1937. History, Politics/Government. Univ. Prof. of History, Boston Univ., and Pres., Center for Democracy, Washington, D.C., since 1985. Prof., Smith Coll., Northampton, Mass., 1966-81; Prof., Georgetown Univ., Washington, D.C., and Exec. Ed., Washington Quarterly, 1981-83; Pres., Robert Maynard Hutchins CDSI, Santa Barbara, Calif., 1984. Exec. Dir., The Democracy Program, Washington, D.C., 1982-83; Acting Pres., National Endowment for Democracy, Washington, D.C., 1983-84. *Publs:* (ed. with F.O. Gatell) American Themes: Essays in Historiography, 1968; (ed. with F.O. Gatell) American Negro Slavery: A Modern Reader, 1968, 3rd ed. 1979; (ed. with F.O. Gatell) The Segregation Era 1863-1954, 1970; (gen. ed.) Random House Readings in American History, 6 vols., 1970; Prelude to Populism: Origins of the Silver Issue, 1970; (co-ed.) The Growth of American Politics, vols., 1972; Freedom and Crisis: An American History, 1974, 3rd ed. 1981; Between the Wars: American Foreign Policy from Versailles to Pearl Harbor, 1978; Perjury: The Hiss-Chambers Case, 1978; (ed. with Moshe Maoz) Harry S. Truman and the Founding of Israel, 1981. Add: Center for Democracy, 1101 15th St. N.W., Washington D.C., 20005, U.S.A.

WEINSTEIN, Arnold. American, b. 1927. Plays/Screenplays, Poetry. Co-Dir., Second City improvisational group, Chicago; Dir., Free Theatre, Chicago, Actors Studio, NYC and Los Angeles, RockTheatre and Guerilla Theatre, Los Angeles. Visiting Lectr., New York Univ., NYC, 1955-56; United States Information Service Lectr., Italy, 1958-60; Prof. of Dramatic Literature, New Sch. for Social Research, NYC, 1957-66; Visiting Prof., Hollins Coll., Va., 1964-65; Chmn., Dept. of Playwriting, Yale Univ., New Haven, Conn., 1966-69; Chmn., Dept. of Drama, Columbia Coll., Chicago, 1969-. *Publs:* Red Eye of Love, 1958; Different Poems by the Same Author, 1960; Dynamite Tonite, 1964. Add: c/o Audrey Wood, ICM, 40 W. 57th St., New York, N.Y. 10019, U.S.A.

WEINSTEIN, Mark Allen. American, b. 1937. Literature, Biography. Prof. of English, Univ. of Nevada, Las Vegas, since 1974 (Assoc. Prof.

of English, 1970-74). Asst. Prof. of English, Brooklyn Coll., N.Y., 1968-70. *Publs:* William Edmondstoune Aytoun and the Spasmodic Controversy, 1968; (ed.) The Prefaces to the Waverly Novels, by Sir Walter Scott, 1978. Add: 2933 Natalie, Las Vegas, Nev. 89121, U.S.A.

WEINTRAUB, Dov. Israeli, b. 1926. Regional/Urban planning, Sociology. Prof. of Sociology, Hebrew Univ., Jerusalem, since 1979 (joined faculty, 1963). *Publs:* (with S.N. Eisenstadt and N. Toren) Analysis of Processes of Role Change, 1968; (with M. Lissak and Y. Azmon) Moshava, Kibbutz, Moshav: Jewish Rural Settlement and Development in Palestine, 1969; Immigration and Social Change: Agricultural Settlement of New Immigrants in Israel, 1971; (with M. Shapiro and B. Aquino) Agrarian Modernization and Development in the Philippines, 1972; (ed. with A. Shahar, I. Shelach and E. Cohen) Town and City in Israel: A Reader, 1973; Social Modernization in the Philippines: The Problem of Change in a Context of Social Stability and Continuity, 1973; (with M. Shapiro) Rural Reconstruction in Greece: Differential Social Prerequisites in the Development Process, 1975; (with J. Cohen) Land Tenure and Peasant Production in Ethiopia: The Social and Institutional Background to a Revolution, 1975; (with Julia Margulies) Basic Social Diagnosis for IRRD Planning Conceptual Framework, 1985. Add: Dept. of Sociology, Hebrew Univ., Jerusalem, Israel.

WEINTRAUB, Stanley. American, b. 1929. Art, Intellectual history, Literature, Biography. Research Prof. and Dir. of the Inst. for the Arts and Humanistic Studies, Pennsylvania State Univ., University Park (joined faculty, 1956). *Publs:* (ed.) An Unfinished Novel, by George Bernard Shaw, 1958; (ed.) C.P. Snow: A Spectrum, 1963; Private Shaw and Public Shaw: A Dual Portrait of Lawrence of Arabia and George Bernard Shaw, 1963; The Ward in the Wards: Korea's Forgotten Battle, 1964, 1977; (ed.) The Yellow Book: Quintessence of the Nineties, 1964; (with B.S. Oldsey) The Art of William Golding, 1965; Reggie: A Portrait of Reginald Turner, 1965; (ed.) The Savoy: Nineties Experiment, 1966; (ed.) The Court Theatre, 1966; Beardsley: A Biography, 1967; The Last Great Cause: The Intellectuals and the Spanish Civil War, 1968; (with R. Weintraub) Evolution of a Revolt: Early Postwar Writings of T.E. Lawrence, 1968; (ed.) Biography and Truth, 1968; (ed.) Cashel Byron's Profession, by Shaw, 1968; (ed.) The Literary Criticism of Oscar Wilde, 1968; (ed.) Shaw: An Autobiography, 2 vols., 1969-70; (ed.) The Green Carnation, by Robert Hichens, 1970; (ed.) Saint Joan, by Shaw, 1971; Journey to Heartbreak: The Crucible Years of Bernard Shaw 1914-1918, 1971; (ed.) Bernard Shaw's Nondramatic Literary Criticism, 1972; (ed. with Philip Young) Directions in Literary Criticism, 1973; (ed.) Saint Joan: Fifty Years After, 1973; Whistler: A Biography, 1974; (with R. Weintraub) Lawrence of Arabia: The Literary Impulse, 1975; Aubrey Beardsley: Imp of the Perverse, 1976; Four Rossettis: A Victorian Biography, 1977; (ed.) The Portable Bernard Shaw, 1977; The London Yankees: Portraits of American Writers and Artists in London 1894-1914, 1979; (ed.) The Portable Oscar Wilde, 1981; (ed. with Anne Wright) Heartbreak House: A Facsimile of the Revised Typescript, 1981; (ed.) Modern British Dramatists 1900-1945, 2 vols., 1982; (ed.) The Playwright and the Pirate: Bernard Shaw and Frank Harris, a Correspondence, 1982; The Unexpected Shaw: Biographical Approaches to G.B.S. and His Work, 1982; (ed.) British Dramatists since World War II, 2 vols., 1982; The End of the Great War, 1985; Bernard Shaw: The Diaries 1885-1897, 1986; Victoria: An Intimate Biography, 1987. Add: 105 Ihlseng Cottage, University Park, Pa. 16802, U.S.A.

WEIR, La Vada. American. Children's fiction, Children's non-fiction. Freelance travel writer; writes travel column "Going Like Go!". *Publs:* (with J. Weir) Hic Away Henry, 1967; Little Pup, 1969; Howdy!, 1971; Laurie Newman Adventures: The New Girl, A Long Distance, Edge of Fear, Men!, The Chaotic Kitchen, Breaking Point, The Horse Flambeau, Laurie Loves a Horse, 1974; Skateboards and Skateboarding: A Complete Beginner's Guide, 1977, 6th ed. 1979; Aviation Reading Kit, 1978; Advanced Skateboarding: A Complete Guide to Skatepark Riding, 1979; The Roller Skating Book, 1979; The First Book of Grass Skiing, 1981. Add: 760 W. 30th St. 8, San Pedro, Calif. 90731, U.S.A.

WEIR, Molly. British, b. 1920. Cookery/Gastronomy/Wine, Autobiography/ Memoirs/Personal. Freelance scriptwriter, and journalist. *Publs:* Molly Weir's Recipes, 1960, 1980; Shoes Were for Sunday, 1970; Best Foot Forward, 1972; A Toe on the Ladder, 1973; Stepping into the Spotlight, 1975; Walking into the Lyons' Den, 1977; One Small Footprint, 1980; Spinning Like a Peerie, 1983. Add: 26 Moss Lane, Pinner, Middx. HA5 3AX, England.

WEIR, Ronald Blackwood. British, b. 1944. Economics. Lectr. in

Economic and Social History, since 1969, and Provost, Derwent Coll., since 1980, Univ. of York. *Publs:* The History of the North of Scotland Malt Distillers Association 1874-1926, 1970; A History of the Scottish American Investment Company 1873-1893, 1973; (with A. Peacock) The Composer in the Market Place, 1975; The History of the Malt Distillers Association of Scotland, 1975. Add: Derwent House, University Rd., York YO1 5DD, England.

WEIR, Rosemary. Also writes as Catherine Bell. British, b. 1905. Children's fiction. Has worked as an actress, farmer, and teacher. *Publs:* The Secret Journey, 1957; The Secret of Cobbetts Farm, 1957; No. 10 Green Street, 1958; The Off-White Elephant (radio play), 1958; Island of Birds, 1959; The Honeysuckle Line (in U.S. as Robert's Rescued Railway), 1959; The Hunt for Harry, 1959; Great Days in Green Street, 1960; Pineapple Farm, 1960; Little Lion's Real Island, 1960; A Dog of Your Own, 1960; The House in the Middle of the Road, 1961; Albert the Dragon, 1961; What a Lark, 1961; Tania Takes the Stage, 1961; Top Secret, 1962; The Star and the Flame, 1962; Soap Box Derby, 1962; Black Sheep (in U.S. as Mystery of the Black Sheep), 1963; The Smallest Dog on Earth, 1963; The Young David Garrick, 1963; Further Adventures of Albert the Dragon, 1964; Mike's Gang, 1965; A Patch of Green, 1965; (as Catherine Bell) Devon Venture, 1965; The Real Game (in U.S. as The Heirs of Ashton Manor), 1965; The Boy from Nowhere, 1966; High Courage, 1967; Pyewacket, 1967; Boy on a Brown Horse, 1967; The Fox-wood Flyer, 1968; Albert the Dragon and the Centaur, 1968; No Sleep for Angus, 1969; Summer of the Silent Hands, 1969; The Lion and the Rose, 1970; The Man Who Built a City: A Life of Sir Christopher Wren, 1971; The Red Herrings, 1972; Blood Royal, 1973; Uncle Barney and the Sleep Destroyer, 1974; Uncle Barney and the Shrink-Drink, 1977; Albert and the Dragonettes, 1977; Albert's World Tour, 1979; Pyewacket and Son, 1980. Add: Ford Farm, Holcombe Rogus, Wellington, Somerset, England.

WEISBERG, Joseph. American, b. 1937. Earth sciences, Marine science/Oceanography, Meterology/Atmospheric sciences. Prof. and Chmn., Dept. of Geoscience and Geography, Jersey City State Coll., since 1964; Dean, Sch. of Arts and Sciences, since 1983. Councilman, Parsippany, N.J., since 1988; Chmn., Jersey City Environmental Cttee.; Commissioner, Hudson River Planning, Study and Development Commn.; Vice-Pres., Parsippany Bd. of Education; Dir., North Jersey Computer Academy. Teacher, Wayne Township Public Schools, New Jersey, 1960–64. First Vice-Pres., New Jersey State Alliance for Environmental Education, 1976–78. *Publs:* (co-author) InvestiGuide Series, 12 books, 1967–68; (co-author) From Generation to Generation, 1970; (co-author) Earth Science, 1971; (with Parish) Introductory Oceanography, 1974; Meteorology: The Earth and Its Weather, 1976, 1981. Add: 4 Camelot Way, Parsippany, N.J. 07054, U.S.A.

WEISMANN, Donald L. American, b. 1914. Poetry, Art, Humanities (general). Univ. Prof. of the Arts, Emeritus, Grad. Faculty, Univ. of Texas, Austin, since 1982 (Chmn., Dept. of Art, 1954–58; Prof. of Art, Grad. Faculty, 1958–64; Chmn., Comparative Studies, 1967–72; Univ. Prof. of Arts, 1972–82). Prof. of Art, Grad. Faculty, Dir. of Grad. Studies in Art, and Head of the Dept. of Art, Univ. of Kentucky, Lexington, 1951–54; Member, National Council on the Arts, 1966–72. *Publs:* Some Folks Went West, 1960; Jelly Was the Word, 1965; Language and Visual Form: The Personal Record of a Dual Creative Process, 1968; (with A. Christ-Janer, H. Carruth and H.D. Williams) Forms, 1968; The Visual Arts and Human Experience, 1970; Why Draw?, 1974; The 12 Cadavers of Joe Mariner, 1977; Follow the Bus with the Greek License Plates, 1981; Duncan Phyfe and Drum with Notes for the Bugle Corps, 1984; Frank Reaugh, Painter to the Longhorns, 1985. Add: Rt. 2, Box 2622, Cedar Creek, Tex. 78612, U.S.A.

WEISS, Paul. American, b. 1901. Art, Philosophy, Politics/Government, Sports. Prof. of Philosophy Emeritus, Yale Univ., New Haven, Conn., since 1969 (Prof., 1946–62; Sterling Prof., 1962–69); Heffer Prof. of Philosophy, Catholic Univ. of America, Washington, D.C., since 1969. Member, Bd. of Govs., Hebrew Univ., Jerusalem, and Advisory Bd., Luce Foundn., U.S.A. *Publs:* Reality, 1938; Nature and Man, 1947; Man's Freedom, 1950; Philosophy in Process, 11 vols., 1955–88; Modes of Being, 1958; Our Public Life, 1959; World of Art, 1961; Nine Basic Arts, 1961; History: Written and Lived, 1962; Religion and Art, 1963; The God We Seek, 1964; The Making of Men, 1967; Sport: A Philosophic Inquiry, 1969; (co-ed.) Collected Papers of C.S. Peirce, 6 vols.; (co-author) Right and Wrong: A Philosophic Dialogue Between Father and Son, 1967; Beyond All Appearances, 1974; Cinematics, 1975; First Considerations, 1977; You, I, and the Others, 1980; Privacy, 1982; Toward a Perfected State, 1986. Add: 2000 N St. N.W., Washington, D.C. 20036,

U.S.A.

WEISS, Theodore (Russell). American, b. 1916. Poetry, Literature. Prof. Emeritus of Ancient and Creative Literature, Princeton Univ., N.J., since 1987 (Poet-in-Residence, 1966–67; Prof. English and Creative Writing, 1968–77; Paton Prof., 1977–87). Ed. and Owner, Quarterly Review of Literature, Annandale-on-Hudson, N.Y., later, Princeton, since 1943; Hon. Fellow, Ezra Stiles Coll., Yale Univ., New Haven, Conn., since 1964. Asst. Prof., 1947–52, Assoc. Prof., 1952–55, and Prof. of English, 1955–56, Bard Coll., Annandale-on-Hudson, N.Y.; Lectr., New Sch. for Social Research, NYC, 1955–56; Visiting Prof. of Poetry, Massachusetts Inst. of Technology, Cambridge, 1961–62; Lectr., New York City Young Men's Hebrew Assn., 1965–67; Visiting Fellow, Inst. for Advanced Study, Princeton, N.J., 1986–87. *Publs:* (ed.) Selections from the Note-books of Gerard Manley Hopkins, 1945; The Catch, 1951; Outlanders, 1960; Gunsight, 1962; The Medium: Poems, 1965; The Last Day and the First: Poems, 1968; The World Before Us: Poems 1950-1970, 1970; The Breath of Clowns and Kings: A Study of Shakespeare, 1971; Fireweeds: Poems, 1976; Views and Spectacles: New Poems and Selected Shorter Poems, 1979; Recoveries: A Long Poem, 1982; The Man from Porlock: Selected Essays, 1982; A Slow Fuse: Poems, 1984; From Princeton One Autumn Afternoon: Collected Poems, 1987. Add: 26 Haslet Ave., Princeton, N.J. 08540, U.S.A.

WEISSBORT, Daniel. British, b. 1935. Poetry, Translations. Dir., Translation Workshop, Univ. of Iowa, since 1974. Ed., Modern Poetry in Trans. Mag., and Gen. Ed., Persea Series of Poetry in Trans. Advisory Dir., Poetry Intnl., 1969–73; Member, Exec. Bd., American Literary Translators Assn., 1980–85. *Publs:* (trans.) The Soviet People and Their Society, 1969; (trans.) Guerilas in Latin America, 1969; (trans. and ed.) Scrolls: Selected Poems of Nikolai Zabolotsky, 1970; (trans.) A History of the Peoples' Democracies, 1971; (trans.) The Trial of the Four, 1971; The Leaseholder, 1971; (trans. and ed.) Natalya Gorbanevskaya, 1972; (trans.) The History of Holy Russia, 1972; (trans. and ed.) Nose! Nose? No-se! and Other PLays by Andrei Amalrik, 1972; In an Emergency, 1972; (trans. and ed.) Post-War Russian Poetry, 1974; (trans.) The War Is Over, 1976; Soundings, 1977; (trans. and ed.) Russian Poetry: The Modern Period, 1978; (trans.) Ivan the Terrible and Ivan the Fool, 1979; (trans.) Missing Person, by Patrick Modiano, 1980; (trans.) The World About Us, by Claude Simon, 1983; Leaseholder: New and Collected Poems 1965-1985, 1986; Translating Poetry, 1988. Add: Dept. of Comparative Literature, Univ. of Iowa, Iowa City, Iowa 52242, U.S.A.

WEISSTEIN, Ulrich W(erner). American, b. 1925. Literature, Music, Translations. Prof. of German and Comparative Literature, Indiana Univ., Bloomington, since 1966 (Asst. Prof., 1959–62; Assoc. Prof., 1962–66). *Publs:* Heinrich Mann: Eine historisch-kritisch Einführung in sein dichterisches Werk, 1962; (trans.) The Grotesque in Art and Literature, by Wolfgang Kayser, 1963; (ed. and trans.) The Essence of Opera, 1964; Max Frisch, 1967; Einführung in die vergleichende Literaturwissenschaft (in U.S. as Comparative Literature and Literary Theory: Survey and Introduction), 1968; (co-ed.) Texte und Kontexte: Studien zur deutschen und vergleichenden Literaturwissenschaft, 1973; (ed.) Expressionism as an International Literary Phenomenon: Twenty-One Essays and A Bibliography, 1973; Vergleichende Literaturwissenschaft: Erster Bericht 1968-1977, 1982; (ed.) Literature and the Other Arts (vol. III of Proceedings of IXth ICLA Congress), 1981; Links und links gesellt sich nicht: Gesammelte Aufsatze zum Werk Heinrich Manns und Bertolt Brechts, 1985. Add: c/o Peter Land Publishing, 62 W. 45th St., 4th floor, New York, N.Y. 10036, U.S.A.

WEISSTUB, David N(orman). Canadian, b. 1944. Poetry, Law. Prof. of Law, Osgoode Hall Law Sch., York Univ., Ontario. Ed.-in-Chief, Intnl. Journal of Law and Psychiatry; Special Lectr., Univ. of Toronto; Special Consultant to the Federal Govt. of Canada. *Publs:* Heaven Take My Hand (poetry), 1968; (ed.) Law and Psychiatry, 3 vols., 1978–80; Law and Psychiatry in the Canadian Context, 1981; Law and Mental Health, 1984. Add: Osgoode Hall Law Sch., York Univ., 4700 Keele St., Downsview 463, Ont., Canada.

WELBURN, Vivienne C. British. Plays/Screenplays, Women. *Publs:* The Drag, and Johnny So Long, 1967; Clearway, 1967; The Treadwheel, and Coil Without Dreams, 1975; Postnatal Depression, 1980; Below the Belt, 1982. Add: c/o Anthony Sheil Assocs., 43 Doughty St., London WC1N 2LF, England.

WELCH, Ann Courtenay. British, b. 1917. Children's fiction, Meteoraology/ Atmospheric sciences, Recreation/Leisure/Hobbies, Autobiography/Memoirs/Personal. Ed., Annual Bulletin Federation

Aeronautique Internationale; Royal Aero Club Gazette. *Publs:* Silent Flight, 1937; Cloud Reading for Pilots, 1943; (with P. Wills and A.E. Slater) Gliding and Advanced Soaring, 1947; (with L. Welch) Flying Training in Gliders, 1952; Come Gliding with Me, 1955; (with L. Welch and F. Irving) The Soaring Pilot, 1955; Go Gliding, 1960; John Goes Gliding, 1962; Glider Flying, 1963; Laws and Rules for Glider Pilots, 1967; The Woolacombe Bird, 1964; (with L. Welch) The Story of Gliding, 1965, 1980; Pilots Weather, 1973; (co-author) The New Soaring Pilot, 1976; KTG Gliding, 1976; (with G. Breen) Hang Glider Pilot, 1977; The Book of Airsports, 1978; Accidents Happen, 1978; KTG Hang Gliding, 1978; (with Roy Hill) Soaring Hang Gliders, 1981; Complete Microlight Guide, 1983; Happy to Fly (autobiography), 1983; Complete Soaring Guide, 1986. Add: 14 Upper Old Park Lane, Farnham, Surrey GU9 0AS, England.

WELCH, James. American, b. 1940. Novels/Short stories, Poetry. *Publs:* Riding the Earthboy 40, 1971, 1975; Winter in the Blood (novel), 1974; The Death of Jim Loney (novel), 1979; Fools Crow (novel), 1986; (co-ed.) The Real West Marginal Way: A Poet's Autobiography, by Richard Hugo, 1986. Add: Roseacres Farm, Rt. 6, Missoula, Mont. 59801, U.S.A.

WELCHER, Rosalind. American, b. 1922. Children's fiction, Poetry, Humor/Satire. Formerly, Art Dir., Fisher Hill Studios, Fitzwilliam, N.H. *Publs:* The Runaway Angel, 1963; The Split-Level Child, 1963; The Magic Top, 1965; It's Wonderful to Be in Love, 1966; Somebody's Thinking of You, 1966; Do You Ever Feel Lonely?, 1967; I Wish You a Merry Christmas (poetry), 1967; Please Don't Feel Blue, 1967; It Must Be Hard to Be a Mother, 1968; There Is Nothing Like a Cat, 1968; Squeaking By, 1969; Do You Believe in Magic, 1969; Wouldn't You Like to Run Away?, 1969; When You're Away, 1969; Moonlight, Cobwebs and Shadows (poetry), 1970; Maybe the Sky Is Falling, 1970; This Could Be Such a Beautiful World . . ., 1970; The Wonderful Season (poetry), 1970; The Watergate Coloring FIle, 1974; I Want to Be Somebody's Cat, 1987; My Brother Says There's a Monster Living in Our Toilet, 1988; Dear Tabby, 1989. Add: Fisher Hill, Fitzwilliam, N.H. 03447, U.S.A.

WELCOME, John. Pseud. for John Brennan. Irish, b. 1914. Novels/ Short stories, Mystery/Crime/Suspense, Sports. Principal, Huggard and Brennan, solicitors, Wexford, Ireland. *Publs:* novels—Red Coats Galloping, 1949; Mr. Merston's Money, 1951; Mr. Merston's Hounds, 1953; Grand National, 1976; Bellary Bay, 1979; mystery novels—Run for Cover, 1958; Stop at Nothing, 1959; Beware of Midnight, 1961; Hard to Handle, 1964; Wanted for Killing, 1965; Hell Is Where You Find It, 1968; On the Stretch, 1969; Go for Broke, 1972; A Call to Arms, 1985; A Painted Devil, 1988; other—(ed. with V.R. Orchard) Best Hunting Stories, 1954; The Cheltenham Gold Cup: The Story of a Great Steeplechase, 1957, 1973; (ed.) Best Motoring Stories, 1959; (ed.) Best Secret Service Stories, 2 vols., 1960–65; (ed.) Best Gambling Stories, 1961; (ed.) Best Legal Stories, 2 vols., 1962–70; Cheating at Cards: The Cases in Court, 1963 (in U.S. as Great Scandals of Cheating at Cards: Famous Court Cases, 1964); (ed.) Best Crime Stories, 3 vols., 1964–68; (ed. with Dick Francis) Best Racing and Chasing Stories, 2 vols., 1966–69; (ed.) Best Smuggling Stories, 1967; (ed.) Best Spy Stories, 1967; Fred Archer: His Life and Times, 1967; (ed. with Dick Francis) The Racing Man's Bedside Book, 1969; (ed.) Ten of the Best: Selected Short Stories, 1969; Neck or Nothing: The Extraordinary Life and Times of Bob Sievier, 1970; (ed.) The Welcome Collection: Fourteen Racing Stories, 1972; The Sporting Empress: The Story of Elizabeth of Austria and Bay Middleton, 1975; A Light-Hearted Guide to British Racing, 1975; Infamous Occasions, 1980; The Sporting World of R.S. Surtees, 1982; Irish Racing: An Illustrated History, 1982; Great Racing Disasters, 1985; (with Rupert Collens) Snuffles: The Life and Work of Charlie Johnson Payne, 1987; Snuffles on Racing and Point to Pointing, 1988; Great Racing Stories, 1989. Add: c/o John Johnson, 45–47 Clerkenwell Green, London EC1R 0HT, England.

WELDON, Fay. British. Novels/Short stories, Plays/Screenplays. *Publs:* The Fatwoman's Joke (in U.S. as And the Wife Ran Away), 1967; Down Among the Women, 1970; Female Friends, 1973; Poor Baby (television play), 1975; Words of Advice (play), 1975; Remember Me, 1976; Little Sisters (in U.S. as Words of Advice), 1978; Praxis, 1979; Puffball, 1980; Pride and Prejudice (adaptation for TV), 1980; The President's Child, 1982; Life and Loves of a She Devil, 1984; Letters to Alice, on First Reading Jane Austen, 1984; Polaris and Other Stories, 1985; Rebecca West, 1985; The Shrapnel Academy, 1986; The Heart of the Country, 1987; The Hearts and Lives of Men, 1987; The Rules of Life, 1987; Leader of the Band, 1988; Wolf the Mechanical Dog, 1988; The Cloning of Joanna May, 1988. Add: c/o Anthony Sheil and Assocs.,

43 Doughty St., London WC1N 2LF, England.

WELK, Lawrence. American, b. 1903. Autobiography/Memoirs/Personal. Orchestra Leader: orchestra has appeared throughout the U.S. since 1927. *Publs:* (with Bernice McGeehan) Wunnerful, Wunnerful!, 1971; (with Bernice McGeehan) Ah One, Ah Two, 1974; (with Bernice McGeehan) My America, Your America (memoirs), 1976; (with Bernice McGeehan) Musical Family Album, 1977; (with Bernice McGeehan) Bunny Rabbit Story, 1977; (with Bernice McGeehan) This I Believe, 1979; (with Bernice McGeehan) You're Never Too Young, 1981. Add: Teleklew Productions, Inc., 1299 Ocean Ave., Suite 800, Santa Monica, Calif. 90401, U.S.A.

WELLEK, René. American, b. 1903. Intellectual history, Literature, Philosophy. Prof. of Comparative Literature, Yale Univ., New Haven, Conn., 1946–72. Pres., Intnl. Comparative Literature Assn., 1961–64, and Modern Humanities Research Assn., 1974. *Publs:* Immanuel Kant in England, 1931; The Rise of English Literary History, 1941; (with A. Warren) Theory of Literature, 1948; A History of Modern Criticism, 6 vols., 1955–86; (ed.) Dostoevsky: A Collection of Essays, 1962; Concepts of Criticism, 1963; Essays in Czech Literature, 1963; Confrontations, 1965; Discriminations, 1970; Four Critics: Croce, Valéry, Lukacs, Ingarden, 1981; The Attack on Literature and Other Essays, 1982; (ed. with Nonna Wellek) Chekhov: Twentieth-Century Views, 1984. Add: 45 Fairgrounds Rd., Woodbridge, Conn. 06525, U.S.A.

WELLER, George Anthony. American, b. 1907. Novels/Short stories, Plays/Screenplays, History, Autobiography/Memoirs/Personal. Corresp. in Greece for the New York Times, 1932-36; Dir., Homeland Foundn., NYC, 1937–40; Foreign Corresp., Chicago Daily News, 1940–72. Recipient: Pulitzer Prize for foreign correspondence, 1943. *Publs:* Not to Eat, Not for Love, 1933; Clutch and Differential, 1936; (trans.) Fontamara, by Ignazio Silone, 1936; Singapore is Silent, 1943; Bases Overseas, 1944; Crack in the Column, 1949; The Paratroops, 1958; Second Saint of Cyprus, 1960; Story of Submarines, 1962. Add: Stampa Estera, Via della Mercede 55, Rome, Italy.

WELLER, Michael. American, b. 1942. Plays/Screenplays. *Publs:* Cancer (in U.S. as Moonchildren), 1971; The Bodybuilders, and Tira Tells Everything There Is to Know about Herself, 1972; Grant's Movie, and Tira, 1972; Fishing, 1975; Split, 1979; Loose Ends, 1980; Five Plays, 1982; The Ballad of Soapy Smith, 1983; Ghost on Fire, 1986; Spoils of War, 1989. Add: 215 E. 5th St., New York, N.Y. 10003, U.S.A.

WELLES, Elizabeth. *See* **ROBY,** Mary Linn.

WELLES, Samuel P(aul). American, b. 1907. Biology, Children's non-fiction, Earth sciences. Former Lectr. and Principal Museum Paleontologist, Univ. of California, Berkeley; Fulbright Scientist to New Zealand, 1969–70. *Publs:* (with W. Fox) Bones to Bodies, 1959; (with C. Camp) Bibliography of Fossil Vertebrates 1934-1938, 1942; (with C. Camp and M. Green) Bibliography of Fossil Vertebrates 1939-1943, 1948; Jurassic Dinosaur from Arizona, 1954; (with R.A. Long) All New Dinosaurs, 1975. Add: Museum of Paleontology, Univ. of California, Berkeley, Calif. 94720, U.S.A.

WELLESLEY, Kenneth. British, b. 1911. Classics.Reader in Humanity, Univ. of Edinburgh, 1967–81, now retired (Lectr., 1949-63; Sr. Lectr., 1963–67). Asst. Master, Bede Sch., Sunderland, 1934–36, and Cambridgeshire High Sch., 1936–48. *Publs:* Tacitus, The Histories: A New Translation, 1964; Tacitus: The Histories, Book III: Text and Commentary, 1972; The Long Year AD 69, 1975; Tacitus, Annals XI-XVI, 1986; Histories, 1989. Add: 125 Trinity Rd., Edinburgh EH5 3LB, Scotland.

WELLINGTON, Kate. *See* **SCHULZE,** Hertha.

WELLINGTON, Richard Anthony. British, b. 1919. Business/Trade/Industry, Economics, Travel/Exploration/Adventure. Air Attaché, H.M. Embassy, Lisbon, 1944–46; Officer, H.M. Diplomatic Service, 1951–73. *Publs:* The Brazilians: How They Live and Work, 1974. Add: c/o National Westminster Bank Ltd., 36 St. James's St., London SW1, England.

WELLMAN, Carl Pierce. American, b. 1926. Civil liberties/Human rights, Philosophy. Prof. of Philosophy, Washington Univ., St. Louis, Mo., since 1968. Instr., 1953–57, Asst. Prof., 195719662, Assoc. Prof., 1962–66, and Prof. and Chmn. of Philosophy, 1966–68, Lawrence Univ., Appleton, Wisc. *Publs:* The Language of Ethics, 1961; Challenge and

Response: Justification in Ethics, 1971; Morals and Ethics, 1975; Welfare Rights, 1982; A Theory of Rights, 1985. Add: 6334 S. Rosebury, 2W, St. Louis, Mo. 63105, U.S.A.

WELLS, A(lexander F(rank). British, b. 1912. Chemistry. Emeritus Prof. of Chemistry, Univ. of Conneticut, Storrs, since 1980 (Prof., 1968–80). Researcher at Cambridge and Birmingham Univs., England, 1937–44; Sr. Research Assoc., Imperial Chemical Industries Ltd., Manchester, 194468. *Publs:* Structural Inorganic Chemistry, 1945, 5th ed. 1983; The Third Dimension in Chemistry, 1956; Models in Structural Inorganic Chemistry, 1970; Three-Dimensional Nets and Polyhedra, 1977; Further Studies of Three-Dimensional Nets, 1979. Add: 19 Pleasant Valley Rd., Willimantic, Conn. 06226, U.S.A.

WELLS, Charles (Alexander). British, b. 1898. Medicine/Health. Ed., Scientific Foundn. Series, William Heinemann Medical Books Ltd., London, since 1967. Prof. of Surgery, Univ. of Liverpool, 1945–63. *Publs:* Surgery for Nurses, 1930; Prostatectomy, 1952; (co-author) Peptic Ulceration, 1960; (ed.) Scientific Foundations of Surgery, 1967, 1973. Add: c/o 21 Canynge Rd., Bristol BS8 3J2, England.

WELLS, Joel Freeman. American, b. 1930. Novels/Short stories. Ed., Thomas More Press since 1971, and Vice-Pres. and Dir., Thomas More Assn., Chicago (Promotion Dir., 1955–64). Lectr. in English, Grad. Sch. of Loyola Univ., Chicago. Lectr., Rosary Coll., River Forest, Ill., 1963–65. Ed., The Critic Mag., 1964–79. *Publs:* (ed with Dan Herr) Bodies and Souls, 1961; (ed. with Dan Herr) Blithe Spirits, 1962; (ed. with Dan Herr) Bodies and Spirits, 1964; (ed. with Dan Herr) Through Other Eyes, 1965; (ed.) Moments of Truth, 1966; Grim Fairy Tales for Adults, 1967; (ed.) A Funny Thing Happened to the Church, 1969; Under the Spreading Heresy, 1971; The Bad Children's Book, 1972; (ed.) Contrasts, 1972; Second Collection, 1973; Here's to the Family, 1979; How to Survive Your Teenager, 1982; Coping in the 80's: Eliminating Needless Stress and Guilt, 1986; No Rolling in the Aisles, 1987. Add: 827 Colfax St., Evanston, Ill. 60201, U.S.A.

WELLS, John (Campbell). British, b. 1936. Novels/Short stories, Plays/Screenplays, Essays. Actor and Journalist. *Publs:* (with R. Ingrams) Mrs. Wilson's Diary, 1967; (with J. Fortune) A Melon for Ecstasy (novel), 1971; The Exploding Present (essays), 1971; (with R. Ingram) Dear Bill, 1980; Anyone for Denis? (play), 1981; The Other Half: Further Letters of Denis Thatcher, 1981; One for the Road: Further Letters of Denis Thatcher, 1982; My Round! Denis Thatcher's Letters to Bill, 1984; 50 Glorious Years, 1984. Add: 1A Scarsdale Villas, London W8 6PT, England.

WELLS, Martin John. British, b. 1928. Biology, Zoology. Fellow, Churchill Coll., Cambridge, and Reader, Dept. of Zoology, Cambridge Univ., since 1976 (Demonstrator, 1959–64; Lectr., 1964–76). Asst., Naples Zoological Station, 1953–56; Fellow, Trinity Coll., Cambridge, 1956–59. *Publs:* Brain and Behaviour in Cephalopods, 1962; You, Me and the Animal World, 1965; Lower Animals, 1968; Octopus: Physiology and Behaviour of an Advanced Invertebrate, 1978. Add: The Bury, Home End, Fulbourn, Cambridge, England.

WELLS, Peter Frederick. New Zealander, b. 1918. Language/Linguistics. Sr. Lectr., Language Methodology, Auckland Secondary Teachers' Coll., 1953–60; Head of Language Studies Dept., Univ. of Waikato, Hamilton, N.Z., 1961–73; Dir., Inst. of Modern Languages, James Cook Univ. of North Queensland, 1974–83. *Publs:* Let's Learn French, 1963; Let's Teach French, 1964; French, 1964, 1966; Les Quatre Saisons, 1966; Let's Learn Japanese, 1968, 1971; Nihongo no Kakikata, 1971; French for Adult Beginners, 1975. Add: 3 Portree Pl., Hamilton, New Zealand.

WELLS, Rosemary. American, b. 1943. Children's fiction. Freelance illustrator and writer since 1968. Worked in a store in Austin, Mass., and in publishing in Boston and New York. *Publs:* John and the Rarey, 1969; Michael and the Mitten Test, 1969; The First Child, 1970; Martha's Birthday, 1970; Miranda's Pilgrims, 1970; The Fog Comes on Little Pig Feet, 1972; Unfortunately Harriet, 1972; Noisy Nora (verse), 1973; Benjamin and Tulip, 1973; None of the Above, 1974; Abdul, 1975; Morris's Disappearing Bag: A Christmas Story, 1975; Leave Well Enough Alone, 1977; Don't Spill It Again, James (verse), 1977; Stanley and Rhoda, 1978; Max's series, 10 vols., 1979–86; When No One Was Looking, 1980; Timothy Goes to School, 1981; Good Night, Fred, 1981; A Lion for Lewis, 1982; Peabody, 1983; The Man in the Woods, 1984; Hazel's Amazing Mother, 1985; Through the Hidden Door, 1987; Forest of Dreams, 1988; Shy Charles, 1988. Add: c/o Dial Press, 1 Dag Hammarskjold Plaza, New York, N.Y. 10017, U.S.A.

WELLS, Stanley (William). British, b. 1930. Literature, Theatre. Prof. of Shakespeare Studies, and Dir. of the Shakespeare Inst., Univ. of Birmingham, since 1988. Gen. Ed., Oxford Shakespeare, since 1978; Ed., Shakespeare Survey, since 1981. Gov., Royal Shakespeare Theatre, since 1974. Reader in English, and Fellow, Shakespeare Inst., Univ. of Birmingham, 1962–77; Sr. Research Fellow, Balliol Coll., Oxford, 1980–88. *Publs:* (ed.) Thomas Nashe: Selected Writings, 1964; (ed.) A Midsummer Night's Dream, 1967; (ed.) Richard II, 1969; Shakespeare: A Reading Guide, 1969, 1970; Literature and Drama, 1970; (ed.) The Comedy of Errors, 1972; (ed.) Select Bibliographical Guides: Shakespeare, 1973, and English Drama Excluding Shakespeare, 1975; Royal Shakespeare, 1977; Shakespeare: An Illustrated Dictionary, 1978; Shakespeare: The Writer and His Work, 1978; (ed. with R.L. Smallwood) The Shoemaker's Holiday, 1979; Re-Editing Shakespeare for the Modern Reader, 1984; (gen. ed. with G. Taylor) The Complete Oxford Shakespeare, 1986; (with others) William Shakespeare: A Textual Companion, 1987; (ed.) The Cambridge Companion to Shakespeare Studies, 1986; The Oxford Anthology of Shakespeare, 1987. Add: Shakespeare Inst., Church St. Stratford-upon-Avon CV37 2DP, England.

WELLS, Susan Jocelyn. British, b. 1920. Crafts. Self-employed in china repair business, Sussex. Tutor in China Mending, Women's Inst., Marcham. *Publs:* Mend Your Own China and Glass, 1975. Add: Longmeadow, Boxgrove, nr. Chichester, Sussex, England.

WELLS, Tobias. *See* FORBES, Stanton.

WELLS, Walter. American, b. 1937. Literature, Writing/Journalism. Member, English and American Studies Faculties, California State Univ., Dominguez Hills, since 1967. Instr. in Language Arts, California State Polytechnic Coll., Pomona, 1963–66. *Publs:* Communications in Business, 1968, 5th ed. 1988; Tycoons and Locusts: A Regional Look at Hollywood Fiction of the 1930s, 1973; Mark Twain's Guide to Backgrounds in American Literature, 1977; (with Alain Robbe-Grillet) Djinn; or, The Evanescent English Teacher, 1983. Add: 19442 Sierra Nuevo, Irvine, Calif. 92715, U.S.A.

WELLWARTH, George E. American, b. 1932. Literature, Translations. Prof. of Theatre and Comparative Literature, State Univ. of New York at Binghamton, since 1970. Co-Ed., Modern Intnl. Drama mag., since 1967. *Publs:* (trans.) Concise Encyclopaedia of the Modern Drama, 1964; The Theatre of Protest and Paradox, 1964, 1971; (co-ed.) Modern French Theatre, 1964; (co-ed.) Post War German Theatre, 1967; (co-ed.) Modern Spanish Theatre, 1968; (ed.) The New Wave Spanish Drama, 1970; (ed.) German Drama Between the Wars, 1972; (ed.) Themes of Drama, 1972; Spanish Underground Drama, 1972; (ed.) New Generation Spanish Drama, 1974; (ed.) 3 Catalan Dramatists, 1974; Modern Drama and the Death of God, 1986. Add: Dept. of Theatre, State Univ. of New York, Binghamton, N.Y. 13901, U.S.A.

WELSH, Alexander. American, b. 1933. Literature. Prof. of English, Univ. of California at Los Angeles, since 1972. Instr., Asst. Prof., and Assoc. Prof., Yale Univ., New Haven, Conn., 1960–67; Prof. of English, Univ. of Pittsburgh, Pa., 1967–72. Ed., Nineteenth Century Fiction, 1975–81. *Publs:* The Hero of the Waverley Novels, 1963; (ed.) Thackeray: A Collection of Critical Essays, 1968; The City of Dickens, 1971; Reflections on the Hero as Quixote, 1981; George Eliot and Blackmail, 1985; From Copyright to Copperfield, 1987. Add: Dept. of English, Univ. of California, Los Angeles, Calif. 90024, U.S.A.

WELTER, Rush (Eastman). American, b. 1923. Intellectual history. Prof. of History, Bennington Coll., Vermont, since 1952 (Dean of Studies, 1985–87). Fulbright Lectr. in American Studies, Univ. of Manchester, U.K., 1964–65. *Publs:* Bennington, Vermont: An Industrial History, 1959; Problems of Scholarly Publication in the Humanities and Social Sciences, 1959; Popular Education and Democratic Thought in America, 1962; (ed.) American Writings on Popular Education: The 19th Century, 1972; The Mind of America 1820-1860, 1975. Add: Dept. of History, Bennington Coll., Bennington, Vt. 05201, U.S.A.

WELTY, Eudora. American, b. 1909. Novels/Short stories, Children's fiction, Literature. *Publs:* A Curtain of Green (short stories), 1941; The Robber Bridegroom, 1942; The Wide Net and Other Stories, 1943; Delta Wedding, 1946; Music from Spain, 1948; Short Stories, 1949; The Golden Apples (short stories), 1949; The Ponder Heart, 1954; Selected Stories, 1954; The Bride of the Innisfallen and Other Stories, 1955; Place in Fiction, 1957; Three Papers on Fiction, 1962; The Shoe Bird, 1964; Thirteen Stories, 1965; A Sweet Devouring, 1969; Losing Battles, 1970; One Time, One Place: Mississippi in the Depression: A Snapshot Album, 1971; The

Optimist's Daughter, 1972; A Pageant of Birds, 1974; The Eye of the Story, 1978; Ida M'toy, 1979; Collected Stories, 1980; Conversations with Eudora Welty, 1984; One Writer's Beginnings, 1984. Add: 1119 Pinehurst St., Jackson, Miss. 39202, U.S.A.

WENDT, Albert. Western Samoan, b. 1939. Novels/Short stories, Poetry. Prof. of Pacific Literature, Univ. of the South Pacific, since 1980 (Sr. Lectr., 1974–75, Asst. Dir. of Extension Services, 1976–77, and Dir. of the USP Centre, 1978–80). Principal, Samoa Coll., Western Samoa, 1969–73. *Publs:* Sons for the Return Home (novel), 1973; Flying Fox in a Freedom Tree (short stories), 1974; (ed.) Some Modern Poetry from Fiji, 1974; (ed.) Some Modern Poetry from Western Samoa, 1975; (ed.) Some Modern Poetry from the New Hebrides, 1975; (ed.) Some Modern Poetry from the Solomons, 1975; Inside Us the Dead (verse), 1976; Pouliuli (novel), 1977; Leaves of the Banyan Tree (novel), 1979; (ed.) Lali: A Pacific Anthology, 1980; Shaman of Visions (verse), 1984; The Birth and Death of the Miracle Man (short stories), 1986. Add: School of Humanities, University of the South Pacific, Box 1168, Suva, Fiji.

WENGER, J(ohn) C(hristian). American, b. 1910. Theology/Religion. Ordained, Deacon, 1943, Minister, 1944, Bishop, 1951. Member, Mennonite Bd. of Education, 1935–39; Prof. of Historical Theology, Goshen Biblical Seminary, Elkhart, Ind., 1938–85; Bishop, North Goshen Mennonite Church, Ind., 1970–85 (Deacon, 1943–44; Assoc. Pastor, 1944–49); Acting Pastor, 1949–50, and Bishop, 1951–64, Olive Mennonite Church, Elkhart, Ind.; Bishop, Hudson Lake Mennonite Church, 1951–64, Holdeman Mennonite Church, 1956–58, and Maple Grove Mennonite Church, 1962–64. *Publs:* Franconia History, 1937, 1985; Glimpses of Mennonite History, 1940; Christ the Redeemer and Judge, 1942; Glimpses of Mennonite History and Doctrine, 1947, 3rd ed. 1959; Doctrines of the Mennonites, 1950, 1952; Separated unto God, 1951, 4th ed. 1974; Introduction to Theology, 1954, 4th ed. 1976; (ed.) Mennonite Handbook: Indiana-Michigan Mennonite Conference, 1956; (ed.) Complete Writings of Menno Simons, 1956, 5th ed. 1986; Even unto Death, 1961; The Mennonites in Indiana and Michigan, 1961; The Church Nurtures Faith, 1963; (ed.) They Met God, 1964; (ed.) Bless the Lord, O My Soul, 1964; God's Word Written, 1966; Mennonite Church in America, 1966; (ed.) Conrad Grebel's Programmatic Letters of 1524, 1970; The Christian Faith: Glimpses of Church History, 1971; Our Christ-Centered Faith, 1973; How Mennonites Came to Be, 1977; What Mennonites Believe, 1977; The Way to New Life, 1977; The Way of Peace, 1977; Disciples of Jesus, 1977; Faithfully, Geo. R., 1978; The Book We Call the Bible, 1980; A Faith to Live By, 1980; (ed.) A Cloud of Witnesses, 1981; A Lay Guide to Romans, 1983; The Yellow Creek Mennonites, 1985. Add: 1300 Greencroft Drive, Apt. 1, Goshen, Ind. 46526, U.S.A.

WERSBA, Barbara. American, b. 1932. Children's fiction, Poetry. Stage and television actress, 1944–59. *Publs:* The Boy Who Loved the Sea, 1961; The Brave Balloon of Benjamin Buckley, 1963; The Land of Forgotten Beasts, 1964; A Song for Clowns, 1965; Do Tigers Ever Bite Kings? (verse), 1966; The Dream Watcher, 1968; Run Softly, Go Fast, 1970; Let Me Fall Before I Fly, 1971; Amanda Dreaming, 1973; The Country of the Heart, 1975; The Dream Watcher (play), 1975; Tunes for a Small Harmonica, 1976; Twenty-Six Starlings Will Fly Through Your Mind (verse), 1980; Footfalls, 1982; The Crystal Child, 1982; The Carnival in My Mind, 1982; Crazy Vanilla, 1986; Fat: A Love Story, 1987; Love Is the Crooked Thing, 1987; Beautiful Losers, 1988; Just Be Gorgeous, 1988, Wonderful Me, 1989. Add: c/o Harper and Row Junior Books, 10 E. 53rd St., New York, N.Y. 10022, U.S.A.

WERT, Jonathan (Maxwell, Jr.). American, b. 1939. Education, Environmental science/Ecology. Pres., Management Diagnostics, since 1981. Member, Advisory Bd., Environmental Education Report, Washington, D.C., since 1974; Bd. of Eds., Journal of Environmental Education, Washington, D.C., since 1975; and HEW's National Advisory Council on Environmental Education, Washington, D.C., since 1975. Chief of Interpretive Services, Dept. of Environmental Education Program Dir., Bays Mountain Park, Kingsport, Tenn., 1969–71; Supervisor, Environmental Education Section, 1971–74, and Energy Conservation Education Section and Energy Resource Materials Center (ERMC), 1974–75, Tennessee Valley Authority, Knoxville; Consultant, Univ. of Tennessee, Knoxville, 1975, and Pennsylvania State Univ., College Park, 1977–81. *Publs:* Environmental Education Study Projects for College Students and for High School Students, 2 vols., 1974; Developing Environmental Education Curriculum Material, 1974; Developing Environmental Study Areas, 1974; Energy: Selected Resource Materials for Developing Energy Education/Conservation Programs, 1975; (co-author) Energy Conservation Education in the Public Schools of Tennessee, 1975; Assessing an Issue in Relation to Environmental, Economic and Social

Impact: A Process Guide, 1976; Energy Education/Conservation: A Selected Annotated Bibliography, 1976; Selected Energy Conservation Options for the Home, 1978; Selected Energy Management Options for Small Business and Local Government, 1978. Add: Box 194, Port Royal, Pa. 17082, U.S.A.

WERTENBAKER, Lael Tucker. American, b. 1909. Novels/Short stories, Art, Medicine/Health, Biography. *Publs:* Lament for Four Virgins, 1951; Festival (in U.K. as The Deeper Strings), 1953; Death of a Man, 1957; Mister Junior, 1958; Tip and Dip, 1960; (with S. Gleaves) You and the Armed Services, 1961; Mercy, Percy, 1962; (ed.) To Light a Candle, 1962; The Eye of the Lion, 1964; The Afternoon Women, 1964; Rhyming Word Games, 1964; (ed.) A Ship Called Hope, 1964; Portrait of Hotchkiss, 1965; (co-author) The World of Pablo Picasso, 1967; (with J. Rosenthal) The Magic of Light, 1972; Unbidden Guests, 1974; Perilous Voyage, 1975; To Mend the Heart, 1980. Add: 369 Roxbury St., Keene, N.H. 03431, U.S.A.

WERTENBAKER, Timberlake. British/American. Plays/Screenplays. Journalist in London and New York, and French teacher in Greece; resident writer, Shared Experience, 1983, and Royal Court Theatre, 1985, both London. *Publs:* New Anatomies (in Plays Introduction), 1984; The Grace of Mary Traverse, 1985; Léocadia (in Anouilh: Five Plays), 1987; The Love of the Nightingale, 1989. Add: c/o Michael Imison Playwrights Ltd., 28 Almeida St., London N1 1TD, England.

WESCOTT, Jan (née Vlachos). American, b. 1912. Historical/Romance. *Publs:* The Border Lord, 1946; Captain for Elizabeth, 1948; The Hepburn, 1050; Captain Barney, 1951; The Walsingham Woman, 1953; The Queen's Grace, 1959; Condottiere, 1962, in U.K. as The Mercenary, 1963; The White Rose, 1969, in U.K. as The Lion's Share, 1972; Set Her on a Throne, 1972; The Tower and the Dream, 1974; A Woman of Quality, 1978. Add: c/o Harold Matson Co., 276 Fifth Ave., New York, N.Y. 10001, U.S.A.

WESKER, Arnold. British, b. 1932. Novels/Short stories, Plays/Screenplays, Essays. Dir., Centre 42: Centre for the Arts, London, 1961– 70; Chmn., British Section, 1978–85, and Pres., Playwrights Permanent Cttee., 1980–85, Intnl. Theatre Inst. *Publs:* Chicken Soup with Barley, 1959; Roots, 1959; I'm Talking About Jerusalem, 1960; The Kitchen, 1961; Chips with Everything, 1962; Their Very Own Golden City, 1966; The Four Seasons, 1966; The Friends, 1970; Fears of Fragmentation, 1970; Six Sundays in January, 1971; The Old Ones, 1972; Love Letters on Blue Paper, 1974, as play, 1978; Say Goodbye, You May Never See Them Again, 1974; The Journalists, 1975; The Plays of Arnold Wesker, 2 vols., 1976–77; Words as Definitions of Experience, 1977; Journey into Journalism, 1977; The Merchant, 1977; Fatlips (juvenile), 1978; Said the Old Man to the Young Man (stories), 1978; The Journalists: A Triptych, 1979; The Journalists, The Wedding Feast, The Merchant, 1980; Collected Plays and Stories, 5 vols., 1980; Caritas, 1981; Annie Wobbler, 1983; Distinctions (essays), 1985; Yardsale and Whatever Happened to Betty Lemon, 1987; Four Portraits, 1987. Add: 37 Ashley Rd., London N19 3AG, England.

WESLEY, Elizabeth. *See* **McELFRESH**, Adeline.

WESLEY, James. *See* **RIGONI**, Orlando.

WESLEY, Mary. British, b. 1912. Novels/Short stories. Staff Member, War Office, 1939–41. *Publs:* The Sixth Seal, 1969; Speaking Terms, 1969; Haphazard House, 1983; Camomile Lawn, 1984; Jumping the Queue, 1984; Harnessing Peacocks, 1985; The Vacillations of Polly Carew, 1986; Not That Sort of Girl, 1988. Add: c/o Viking Penguin Inc., 40 W. 23rd St., New York, N.Y. 10010, U.S.A.

WESLEY, Richard (Errol). American, b. 1945. Plays/Screenplays. Worked for United Airlines, Newark, 1967–69; ed., Black Theatre, NYC, 1969–73; founding member, Frank Silvera Writers Workshop, NYC, 1973; taught at Manhattanville Coll., Purchase, N.Y., and Wesleyan Univ., Middletown, Conn., 1973–74; Manhattan Community Coll., NYC, 1980–83, and Rutgers Univ., New Brunswick, N.J., 1984. *Publs:* The Black Terror (in The New Lafayette Theatre Presents), 1974; The Sirens, 1975; The Mighty Gents, 1979; The Past Is the Past, and Gettin' It Together, 1979. Add: c/o Jay C. Kramer, 135 E. 55th St., New York, N.Y. 10022, U.S.A.

WESSEL, Helen S. American, b. 1924. Medicine/Health, Theology/Religion. Pres., Bookmates Intnl. Inc., since 1969. Pres., Intnl. Childbirth Education Assn., 1964–68. *Publs:* Natural Childbirth and the Christian Family, 1963, 5th ed. 1985; (ed. with H. Ellis) Childbirth

1976; Under the Apple Tree, 1981. Add: c/o Bookmates Intl., P.O. Box 9883, Fresno, Calif. 93795, U.S.A.

WESSON, Robert G. American, b. 1920. International relations/Current affairs, Politics/Government. Prof., Univ. of California, Santa Barbara, since 1964; Sr. Research Fellow, Hoover Instn., Stanford Univ., California, since 1978; Sr. Fellow, Center for the Study of Democratic Institutions. *Publs:* Soviet Communes, 1963; The American Problem, 1963; The Imperial Order, 1967; Soviet Foreign Policy in Perspective, 1969; The Soviet Russian State, 1972; The Russian Dilemma, 1974, 1985; Why Marxism?, 1976; Foreign Policy for a New Age, 1977; Communism and Communist Systems, 1978; Lenin's Legacy, 1978; State Systems, 1978; (ed.) The Soviet Union: Looking to the 1980's, 1980; The Aging of Communism, 1980; The United States and Brazil: Limits of Influence, 1981; Modern Government: Three Worlds of Politics, 1981; Democracy in Latin America, 1982; (ed.) Communism in Central America and the Caribbean, 1982; (ed.) The New Military Politics in Latin America, 1982; (ed.) U.S. Influence in Latin America in the 1980's, 1982; (ed.) Yearbook on Internationl Communist Affairs, 1982; (co-ed.) Brazil in Transition, 1983; (ed.) Politics, Policies and Economic Development in Latin America, 1984; (ed.) The Latin American Military Institution, 1986; (ed.) Latin American Views of U.S. Policy, 1986; Democracy: A Worldwide Survey, 1987; Democracy 1987, 1988; Politics: Individual and State, 1988; Coping with the Latin American Debt, 1988. Add: Hoover Instn., Stanford, Calif. 94305, U.S.A.

WEST, Anthony C. Irish, b. 1910. Novels/Short stories. *Publs:* River's End and Other Stories, 1957; The Native Moment, 1959; Rebel to Judgement, 1962; The Ferret Fancier, 1962, 1984; As Towns with Fire, 1968, 1984; All the King's Horses and Other Stories, 1981. Add: c/o Midland Bank Ltd., Castle St., Beaumaris, Anglesey, Gwynedd LL58 8AR, Wales.

WEST, Donald James. British, b. 1924. Criminology/Law enforcement/Prisons, Sex. Prof. Emeritus of Clinical Criminology, Univ. of Cambridge. Hon. Consultant Psychiatrist, Cambridge Psychiatric Service. *Publs:* Eleven Lourdes Miracles, 1957; Psychical Research Today, 1963; The Habitual Prisoner, 1963; Murder Followed by Suicide, 1965; The Young Offender, 1967; Homosexuality, 1968; Present Conduct and Future Delinquency, 1969; (ed.) The Future of Parole, 1972; Who Becomes Delinquent?, 1973; The Delinquent Way of Life, 1977; Homosexuality Re-Examined, 1977; Understanding Sexual Attacks, 1978; Delinquency, 1982; Sexual Victimisation, 1985; Sexual Crimes and Confrontations, 1987; Children's Sexual Contacts with Adults, 1989. Add: Inst. of Criminology, 7 West Rd., Cambridge CB3 9DT, England.

WEST, Francis James. British, b. 1927. History, Human relations, Politics/Government, Biography. Pro-Vice-Chancellor, Deakin Univ., Geelong, Australia, since 1986 (Dean of Social Sciences, 1976–83). Research Fellow, British Academy, 1970–71; Pro-Principal, Dean of Arts, and Prof. of History, Univ. Coll., Buckingham, 1973–75; Professorial Fellow, Inst. of Advanced Studies, Australian National Univ., Canberra, 1964–76; Fellow, Churchill Coll., Cambridge, 1982–85. *Publs:* Political Advancement in the South Pacific, 1961; The Justiciarship in England 1066-1232, 1966; Hubert Murray: The Australian Pro-Council, 1968; (ed.) Selected Letters of Hubert Murray, 1970; Biography as History, 1973; University House, 1980; Gilbert Murray: A Life, 1984. Add: c/o Deakin Univ., Geelong, Australia.

WEST, Gertrude (Trudy). British. Architecture, Biography. *Publs:* The Dental Assistants Handbook, 1948; The Young Charles Lamb, 1964; The Young Wordsworth, 1965; The Timber-Frame House in England, 1971; The Fireplace in the English Home, 1975; New Life for an Old House, 1984. Add: 6 Hunter Rd., Wimbledon, London SW20 8NZ, England.

WEST, John Frederick. British, b. 1929. History, Translations. Sr. Lectr., Trent Polytechnic, Nottingham, 1969–1985 (Lectr., 1967–69). *Publs:* The Great Intellectual Revolution, 1965; (trans.) Hedin Bru: The Old Man and His Sons, 1970; (ed.) The Journals of the Stanley Expedition to the Faroe Islands and Iceland in 1789, 3 vols., 1970–76; Faroe: The Emergence of a Nation, 1973; (trans.) Faroese Folktales and Legends, 1980; The History of the Faroe Islands 1709-1816, 1985. Add: 86 Washington Rd., Woodthorpe, Nottingham NG5 4NR, England.

WEST, Lindsay. *See* **WEBER,** Nancy.

WEST, Morris (Langlo). Also writes as Michael East and Julian Morris. Australian, b. 1916. Novels/Short stories, Plays/Screenplays, Social commentary/phenomena. Film and dramatic writer for Shell Co. and Australian Broadcasting Network, and freelance commentator and feature writer, since 1954. Former member, Christian Brothers Order, 1933, until left order before final vows, 1939; Publicity Mgr., Radio Station 3 DB, Melbourne, 1944–45; Founder and later Managing Dir., Australian Radio Productions Pty. Ltd., Melbourne, 1945–54. *Publs:* (as Julian Morris) Moon in My Pocket, 1945; Gallows on the Sand, 1956; Kundu, 1956; The Big Story (in U.S. as The Crooked Road), 1957; Children of the Sun (in U.S. as Children of the Shadows: The True Story of the Street Urchins of Naples), 1957; The Second Victory (in U.S. as Backlash), 1958; (as Michael East) McCreary Moves In, 1958; reissued under real name as The Concubine, 1973; The Devil's Advocate, 1959; (as Michael East) The Naked Country, 1960; Daughter of Silence (novel and play), 1961; The Shoes of the Fisherman, 1963; The Ambassador, 1965; The Tower of Babel, 1968; (with R. Francis) Scandal in the Assembly: The Matrimonial Laws and Tribunals of the Roman Catholic Church, 1980; Summer of the Red Wolf, 1971; The Salamander, 1973; Harlequin, 1974; The Navigator, 1976; Proteus, 1979; The Clowns of God, 1981; The World Is Made of Glass, 1983; Cassidy, 1986; Masterclass, 1988. Add: c/o Greenbaum, 575 Madison Ave., New York, N.Y. 10022, U.S.A.

WEST, Owen. *See* **KOONTZ,** Dean R.

WEST, Paul. American, b. 1930. Novels/Short stories, Science fiction/Fantasy, Literature, Essays. Prof. of English and Comparative Literature, since 1962, and Sr. Fellow, Inst. for the Arts, since 1969, Pennsylvania State Univ., University Park. Novelist in Residence, Visiting Prof. of English, Cornell Univ., since 1987. Crawshaw Prof. of Literature, Colgate Univ., Hamilton, New York, 1970; Writer-in-Residence, Wichita State Univ., 1982, and Univ. of Arizona, 1984. *Publs:* The Growth of the Novel, 1959; Byron and the Spoiler's Art, 1960; A Quality of Mercy, 1961; I, Said the Sparrow (autobiography), 1963; The Modern Novel, 1963, 3rd ed. 1967; (ed.) Byron: 20th Century Views, 1963; The Snow Leopard (poems), 1964; Tenement of Clay, 1965; The Wine of Absurdity, 1966; Alley Jaggers, 1966; I'm Expecting to Live Quite Soon, 1970; Words for a Deaf Daughter, 1970; Caliban's Filibuster, 1971; Bela Lugosi's White Christmas, 1972; Colonel Mint, 1972; Gala, 1976; The Very Rich Hours of Count von Stauffenberg, 1989; Out of My Depths: A Swimmer in the Universe, 1983; Rat Man of Paris (novel), 1986; Sheer Fiction (essays), 1987; The Universe and Other Fictions, 1988; The Place in Flowers Where Pollen Rests, 1988; Lord Byron's Doctor (novel), 1989. Add: 117 Burrowes Bldg., University Park, Pa. 16802, U.S.A.

WEST, Wallace (George). American, b. 1900. Science fiction/Fantasy, Children's fiction, Children's non-fiction, Environmental science/Ecology, International relations/Current affairs. Farmer, barber, and telegrapher; Lawyer, Calvin and West, in the 1920's; Journalist, United Press; Publicity officer, Paramount Pictures; Ed., ROTO, Voice of Experience, Song Hits, and Movie Mirror mags.; Publicity Writer for CBS Radio, and News Writer and Commentator for ABC, NBC, and Mutual Radio; Pollution Control Expert, American Petroleum Inst., 1947–58; Consultant, Pollution Control Administration, now retired. *Publs:* Betty Boop in Snow-White (adaptation of screenplay; juvenile), 1934; Alice in Wonderland (novelization of screenplay, juvenile), 1934; Paramount Newsreel Men with Admiral Byrd in Little America, 1934; Jimmy Allen in The Sky Parade (novelization of screenplay), 1936; Thirteen Hours by Air (novelization of screenplay), 1936; Our Good Neighbors in Latin America, 1942; (with James P. Mitchell) Our Good Neighbors in Soviet Russia, 1945; Down to the Sea in Ships, 1947; Find a Career in Electronics, 1959; The Birds of Time (science fiction), 1959; Lords of Atlantis (science fiction), 1960; The Memory Bank (science fiction), 1961; Clearing the Air, 1961; Outposts in Space (short stories), 1962; River of Time (science fiction), 1963; The Time-Lockers (science fiction), 1964; Conserving Our Waters, 1964; The Everlasting Exiles (science fiction), 1967; The Amazing Inventor from Laurel Creek (juvenile non-fiction), 1967. Add: c/o Avalon Books, Thomas Bouregy and Co, 401 Lafayette St., New York, N.Y. 10003, U.S.A.

WESTALL, Robert. British, b. 1929. Children's fiction. Head of Art since 1960, and Head of Careers since 1970, Sir John Deane's Coll., Northwich, now retired. Art Critic, Chester Chronicle, since 1962. Art Master, Erdington Hall Secondary Modern Sch., Birmingham, 1957–58, and Keighley Boys' Grammar Sch., Yorkshire, 1958–60; Writer, Whitehorn Press, Manchester, 1968–71; Northern Art Critic, Guardian, London, 1970, 1980. Dir., Telephone Samaritans of Mid-Cheshire, 1966–75. *Publs:* The Machine-Gunners, 1975; The Wind Eye, 1976; The Watch House, 1977; The Devil on the Road, 1978; Fathom Five, 1979; Scarecrows, 1981; Break of Dark, 1982; Futuretrack Five, 1983; The

Haunting of Chas McGill, 1983; The Cats of Seroster, 1984; The Children of the Blitz, 1985; Rachel and the Angel, 1986; The Witness, 1986; Urn Burial, 1987; Rosalie, 1987; Ghosts and Journeys, 1987; The Creature in the Dark, 1988; Ghost Abbey, 1989; Blitzcat, 1989; Old Man on a Horse, 1989; Antique Dust, 1989; Echoes of War, 1989; A Walk on the Wild Side, 1989; The Call and Other Stories, 1990. Add: 2 Dyar Terr., Winnington, Northwich, Cheshire CW8 4DN, England.

WESTBROOK, Perry D. American. Novels, History, Literature, Biography. Prof. Emeritus of English, State Univ. of New York, Albany, since 1983. (Prof. of English, 1945–83). Instr. of English, Univ. of Kansas, Lawrence, 1938–41; Faculty member, Georgia Inst. of Technology, Atlanta, 1941–43, and Univ. of Maine, Orono, 1943–44; Teacher, Orono High Sch., Me., 1944–45. *Publs:* Happy Deathday, 1947; The Red Herring Murder, 1949; Infra Blood, 1950; Acres of Flint: Writers of Rural New England, 1870-1900, 1951; It Boils Down to Murder, 1953; The Sting of Death, 1955; Biography of an Island, 1958; The Greatness of Man: An Essay on Whitman and Dostoyevsky, 1961; (with A. Westbrook) Trail Horses and Trail Riding, 1963; Mary Ellen Chase, 1966; Mary Wilkins Freeman, 1969; (ed.) Pembroke, by Mary Wilkins Freeman, 1971; (ed.) Seacoast and Upland: A New England Anthology, 1972; John Burroughs, 1974; William Bradford, 1978; Free Will and Determinism in American Literature, 1979; (ed. with Arlen Westbrook) The Writing Women of New England 1630-1900, 1982; The New England Town in Fact and Fiction, 1982; A Literary History of New England, 1988. Add: R.D. 4, Box 84, Voorheesville, N.Y. 12186, U.S.A.

WESTCOTT, Jan (née Vlachos). American, b. 1912. Novels, Historical/Romance, Mystery/Crime/Suspense. Freelance writer and journalist, Philadelphia. *Publs:* The Border Lord, 1946; Captain for Elizabeth,1948; The Hepburn,1950; Captain Barney,1951; The Walsingham Woman, 1953; The Queen's Grace, 1959; Condottiere, 1962 (in U.K. as The Mercenary, 1963); The White Rose, 1969 (in U.K. as The Lion's Share, 1972); Set Her on a Throne, 1972; The Tower and the Dream, 1974; A Woman of Quality, 1978. Add: c/o Harold Matson Company, 276 Fifth Avenue, New York, NY 10001, U.S.A.

WESTCOTT, Joanna (Kimberley). British, b. 1957. Novels/Short stories, Children's fiction, Historical/Romance. Lecturer in Creative Writing, Polytechic of Central London, since 1986. Copy writer, Laurie Advertising, London, 1982–84; freelance writer, 1985–86. *Publs:* The Amazing Teddy Bear (juvenile), 1984; The Amazing Teddy Bear Meets Assistant Dog (juvenile), 1984; Abandoned to Moonlight, 1985; Clipper Ship to Tahiti, 1987. Add: 3 Percy Street, London W1P9FA, England.

WESTCOTT JONES, Kenneth. British, b. 1921. Business/Trade/Industry, Transportation, Travel/Exploration/Adventure. Travel Corresp., East Anglian Daily Times Series, since 1951, and freelance journalist. Travel Consultant to Uganda Govt., 1959–66; Focus Columnist, Business Travel World, 1962–85. *Publs:* To the Polar Sunrise, 1957; America Beyond the Bronx, 1961; Great Railway Journeys of the World, 1964; (co-author) Business Air Travellers Guide, 1970; Romantic Railways, 1971; Steam in the Landscape, 1971; (co-author) The Great Trains, 1974; (co-author) Fodor's Railways of the World, 1976; Railways for Pleasure, 1980; Scenic America, 1985. Add: Hillswick, Michael Rd., London SE25 6RN, England.

WESTERN, Mark. *See* **CRISCUOLO,** Anthony Thomas.

WESTFALL, Richard S(amuel). American, b. 1924. History, Biography. Distinguished Prof. of History and Philosophy of Science, Indiana Univ., Bloomington, since 1976 (Prof. of History of Science, 1963, and Prof. of History, 1966). Instr. and Asst. Prof. of History, State Univ. of Iowa, 1953–57; Asst. and Assoc. Prof. of History, Grinnell Coll., Iowa, 1957–63. *Publs:* Science and Religion in Seventeenth Century England, 1958, rev. ed. 1970; Force in Newton's Physics: The Science of Dynamics in the Seventeenth Century, 1971; The Construction of Modern Science: Mechanisms and Mechanics, 1971; Never at Rest: A Biography of Isaac Newton, 1980. Add: 2222 Browncliff Rd., Bloomington, Ind. 47408, U.S.A.

WESTGATE, John. *See* **BLOOMFIELD,** Anthony John Westgate.

WESTHEIMER, David. American, b. 1917. Novels/Short stories, Plays/Screenplays. *Publs:* Summer on the Water, 1948; The Magic Fallacy (in U.K. as The Long Bright Days), 1950; Watching Out for Dulie, 1960; Von Ryan's Express, 1964; My Sweet Charlie, 1965, as play, 1966; Song of the Young Sentry, 1968; Lighter Than a Feather, 1971; Over the Edge, 1972; Going Public, 1973; The Olmec Head, 1974; The Avila

Gold, 1974; Rider on the Wind, 1979; Von Ryan's Return, 1980; (with John Sherlock) The Most Dangerous Gamble, 1982. Add: 11722 Darlington, Apt. 2, Los Angeles, Calif. 90049, U.S.A.

WESTHEIMER, (Karola) Ruth. American, b. 1928. Sex counseling, Psychology, Autobiography. Own radio show, Sexually Speaking, New York, since 1980, syndicated nationally since 1984; own TV show, The Doctor Ruth Show, since 1985 (as Good Sex With Dr. Westheimer, 1984–85); Ask Dr. Ruth, syndicated TV show, since 1987. In private practice as a psychologist and family counselor, New York. Born in Germany, educated in Switzerland, moved to Palestine after WWII; member of Haganah, Jewish underground movement for creation of Jewish Homeland; taught kindergarten on a kibbutz; in Paris, 1950 until move to New York, 1956; Project Dir., Planned Parenthood clinic, Harlem, New York, 1967–70; Assoc. Prof., Dept. of Sex Counseling, Lehman Coll., Bronx, N.Y., 1970–77; taught briefly at Brooklyn Coll., N.Y.; own TV show, Dr. Ruth, New York, 1982; contributor, Playgirl mag. *Publs:* Dr. Ruth's Guide to Good Sex, 1983; First Love: A Young People's Guide to Sexual Information, 1985; Dr. Ruth's Guide for Married Lovers, 1986; All in a Lifestyle: An Autobiography, 1987: (with Nathan Kravetz) First Love: A Young People's Guide to Sexual Information, 1988; (with Louis Leiberman) Sex and Morality: Who Is Teaching Our Sex Standards?, 1988. Add:c/o Metromedia, 205 East 67th St., New York, N.Y. 10021, U.S.A.

WESTLAKE, Donald E. Also writes as Curt Clark, Tucker Coe, Timothy J. Culver, and Richard Stark. American, b. 1933. Novels/Short stories, Mystery/Crime/Suspense, Documentaries/Reportage, Humor Satire. *Publs:* The Mercenaries, 1960; Killing Time, 1961; 361, 1962; (as Richard Stark) The Hunter, 1962; (as Richard Stark) The Man with the Getaway Face, 1963; (as Richard Stark) The Outfit, 1963; (as Richard Stark) The Mourner, 1963; Killy, 1963; Pity Him Afterwards, 1964; (as Richard Stark) The Score, 1964; (as Richard Stark) The Jugger, 1965; The Fugitive Pigeon, 1965; The Busy Body, 1966; The Spy in the Ointment, 1966; (as Tucker Coe) Kinds of Love, Kinds of Death, 1966; (as Richard Stark) The Handle, 1966; (as Richard Stark) The Seventh, 1966; (as Curt Clark) Anarchaos, 1967; (as Richard Stark) The Rare Coin Score, 1967; (as Richard Stark) The Green Eagle Score, 1967; (as Richard Stark) The Damsel, 1967; (as Tucker Coe) Murder among Children, 1967; Philip, 1967; God Save the Mark, 1967; (ed. with W. Tenn) Once Against the Law, 1968; The Curious Facts Preceding My Execution, 1968; (as Richard Stark) The Black Ice Score, 1968; (as Richard Stark) The Sour Lemon Score, 1969; (as Richard Stark) The Dame, 1969; (as Richard Stark) The Blackbird, 1969; Who Stole Sassi Manoon?, 1969; Somebody Owes Me Money, 1969; Up Your Banners, 1969; The Hot Rock, 1970; Adios, Scheherezade, 1970; (as Timothy J. Culver) Ex Officio, 1970; (as Tucker Coe) Wax Apple, 1970; (as Tucker Coe) A Jade in Aries, 1971; (as Richard Stark) Slayground, 1971; (as Richard Stark) Deadly Edge, 1971; (as Richard Stark) Lemons Never Lie, 1971; I Gave at the Office, 1971; Bank Shot, 1972; Under an English Heaven, 1972; Cops and Robbers, 1972; (as Tucker Coe) Don't Lie to Me, 1972; (as Richard Stark) Plunder Squad, 1972; Comfort Station, 1973; (with B. Garfield) Gangway, 1973; Help I Am Being Held Prisoner, 1974; (as Richard Stark) Butcher's Moon, 1974; Jimmy the Kid, 1974; Brothers Keepers, 1975; Two Much, 1975; Dancing Aztecs (in U.K. as A New York Dance), 1976; Enough, 1977; Nobody's Perfect, 1977; Castle in the Air, 1980; Kahawa, 1982; Why Me?, 1983; Levine, 1984; A Likely Story, 1984; High Adventure, 1985; Good Behavior, 1986; Trust Me on This, 1988; Sacred Monster, 1989. Add: c/o Knox Burger, 391 Washington Sq. South, New York, N.Y. 10012, U.S.A.

WESTOFF, Charles F. American, b. 1927. Demography. Prof. of Demographic Studies and Sociology since 1962, and Dir. of Office of Population Research since 1976, Princeton Univ., N.J. (Research Assoc., 1955–62; Chmn., Dept. of Sociology, 1965–70). Sr. Technical Adviser, Demographic Health Surveys, since 1985. Research Assoc., Milbank Memorial Fund, NYC, 1953–55; Assoc. Prof. of Sociology, New York Univ., 1958–62; Exec. Dir., Commn. on Population Growth and the American Future, Washington, D.C., 1970–72. Pres., Population Assn. of America, 1974–75; Chmn., National Cttee. for Research on the 1980 Census, 1980. *Publs:* Family Growth in Metropolitan America, 1961; The Third Child, 1963; College Women and Fertility Values, 1967; The Later Years of Childbearing, 1970; (ed.) Aspects of Population Growth Policy, 1972; (ed.) Demographic and Social Aspects of Population Growth, 1972; Reproduction in the U.S.: 1965, 1971; From Now to Zero, 1971; (ed.) Toward the End of Growth, 1973; The Contraceptive Revolution, 1977. Add: 537 Drake's Corner Rd., Princeton, N.J. 08540, U.S.A.

WESTON, Allen. *See* **HOGARTH,** Grace.

WESTON, Burns H. American, b. 1933. Law, International relations/Current affairs. Bessie Dutton Murray Prof. of Law, Univ. of Iowa, Iowa City (joined faculty, 1966; Dir., Center for World Order Studies, 1972–76). Assoc., Paul, Weiss, Rifkind, Wharton & Garrison, law firm, NYC, 1961–64. *Publs:* International Claims: Postwar French Practice, 1971; (with Richard B. Lillich) International Claims: Their Settlement by Lump Sum Agreements, 1974; (ed. with Michael Reisman) Toward World Order and Dignity, 1976; (ed. with Richard A. Falk and Anthony A. D'Amato) International Law and World Order: A Problem-Oriented Coursebook, 1980; 1990; (ed. with Richard A. Falk and Anthony A. D'Amato) Basic Documents in International Law and World Order, 1980; 1990; (ed. with Richard B. Lillich) International Claims: Contemporary European Practice, 1982; Toward Nuclear Disarmament and Global Security: A Search for Alternatives, 1984; (ed. with Richard P. Claude) Human Rights in the World Community: Issue and Action, 1989. Add: Coll. of Law, Univ. of Iowa, Iowa City, Ia. 52242, U.S.A.

WESTON, Corinne Comstock. American, b. 1919. History, Law, Politics/Government. Prof. of History, Herbert H. Lehman Coll., since 1969, and Doctoral Prog., since 1965, City Univ. of New York. Lectr., Columbia Univ. Sch. of Gen. Studies, NYC, 1947–48, 1949–51; Asst. Prof. then Prof., Univ. of Houston, Tex., 1952–63; Assoc. Prof., Hunter Coll., NYC, 1965–68. *Publs:* (with R.L. Schuyler) British Constitutional History since 1832, 1957; (with R.L. Schuyler) Cardinal Documents British History, 1961; English Constitutional Theory and the House of Lords, 1556-1832, 1965; (with Janelle Greenberg) Subjects and Sovereigns: The Grand Controversy over Legal Sovereignty in Stuart England, 1981. Add: 200 Central Park South, New York, N.Y. 10019, U.S.A.

WESTON, Helen Gray. *See* **DANIELS,** Dorothy.

WESTON, Susan. American, b. 1943. Novels, Literature. Free-lance writer. Instr., to Asst. Prof. of English, Univ. of Hawaii, Honolulu, 1972–79. *Publs:* Wallace Stevens: An Introduction to the Poetry, 1977; Children of the Light (novel) 1985. Add: 2548 Mary St., Evanston, Ill. 60201, U.S.A.

WESTON, William. *See* **MILSOM,** Charles Henry.

WESTWOOD, Gwen. British, b. 1915. Historical/Romance/Gothic, Children's fiction. *Publs:* Monkey Business (juvenile), 1965; The Gentle Dolphin (juvenile), 1965; The Red Elephant Blanket (juvenile), 1966; The Pumpkin Year (juvenile), 1966; Narni of the Desert (juvenile), 1967; A Home for Digby (juvenile), 1968; Keeper of the Heart, 1969; Bright Wilderness, 1969; The Emerald Cuckoo, 1970; Castle of the Unicorn, 1971; Pirate of the Sun, 1972; Citadel of Swallows, 1973; Sweet Roots and Honey, 1974; Blossoming Gold, 1976; Bride of Bonamour, 1977; A Place for Lovers, 1978; Forgotten Bride, 1980; Zulu Moon, 1980; Dangerous to Live 1981; Secondhand Bride, 1983; Bitter Deception, 1987. Add: 422 Blackburn Rd., Durban, Natal, South Africa.

WESTWOOD, John Norton. British, b. 1931. History, Transportation. Hon. Research Fellow, Birmingham Univ., since 1976. Assoc. Prof. of History, Florida State Univ., Tallahassee, 1967–69; Sr. Lectr., Sydney Univ., N.S.W., 1970–71. *Publs:* Soviet Railways Today, 1963; A History of Russian Railways, 1964; Russia 1917-1964, 1966; Witnesses of Tsushima, 1971; Endurance and Endeavour: Russian History, 1812-1971, 1973; Illustrated History of the Russo-Japanese War, 1973; Railways of India, 1974; Fighting Ships of World War II, 1975; Locomotive Designers in the Age of Steam, 1977; All Colour World of Trains, 1978; Trains, 1979; Railways at War, 1980; Russia since 1917, 1980; St. Michael Book of Steam, 1980; Soviet Locomotive Technology, 1982; History of the Middle East Wars, 1984; The Eastern Front, 1984; Railway Data Book, 1983; Russia Against Japan 1904-05, 1986; Pictorial History of Railroads, 1988. Add: 9 Whitefriars Meadow, Sandwich, Kent CT13 9AS, England.

WETTENHALL, Roger. Australian, b. 1931. Administration/Management, Institutions/Organizations, Politics/Government, Public/Social administration. College Fellow in Admin. Studies, Canberra Coll. of Advanced Education, since 1985 (Head., Sch. of Admin. Studies, 1971–85). Personnel Officer, Australian Commonwealth Public Service, 1948–59; Research Scholar, Australian National Univ., 1959–61; Hallsworth Research Fellow, Univ. of Manchester, 1964–65; Lectr., Sr. Lectr., and Reader, Political Science Dept., Univ. of Tasmania, 1961–71; Visiting Scholar, State Univ. of New York at Albany, 1979; Visiting Scholar, Univ. of Southern Calif., 1985. *Publs:* Railway Management and Politics in Victoria 1856-1906, 1961; Evolution of a Departmental System, 1967; A Guide to Tasmanian Government Administration, 1968; The Iron Road

and the State: W.M. Acworth as Scholar, Critic and Reformer, 1970; Bushfire Disaster: An Australian Community in Crisis, 1975; (co-ed.) The First Thousand Days of Labor, 1975; (co-ed.) Local Government Systems of Australia, 1981; (co-ed.) Understanding Public Administration, 1981; (co-ed.) Australian Commonwealth Administration, 1983, 1984; Organising Government: The Uses of Ministries and Departments, 1986; Public Enterprise and National Development: Selected Essays, 1987; (co-ed.) Public Enterprise: The Management Challenge, 1987; (co-ed.) Getting Together in Public Enterprise, 1987. Add: Canberra Coll. of Advanced Education, Belconnen, A.C.T. 2616, Australia.

WHALE, John (Hilary). British, b. 1931. Politics/Government, Theology/Religion, Writing/Journalism. Ed. Church Times, London, since 1989. Television, since 1984. Sub-Ed., Section Anglaise, French radio, Paris, 1958–59; Scriptwriter and Reporter, London, 1960–63, Political Corresp., London, 1963–67, and U.S. Corresp., Washington, D.C., 1967–69, Independent Television News; Leader Writer, 1969–84, and Religious Affairs Corresp., 1979–84, The Sunday Times, London. Head of Religious Programmes, BBC Television 1984–89. *Publs:* The Half-Shut Eye: Television and Politics in Britain and America, 1969; Journalism and Government, 1972; (co-author) Ulster, 1972; (contrib.) Lessons from America, 1974; The Politics of the Media, 1977, 1980; One Church, One Lord, 1979; (ed.) The Pope from Poland: An Assessment, 1980; Put It in Writing, 1984; The Future of Anglicanism, 1988. Add: 28 St. James's Walk, London EC1R 0AP, England.

WHALEN, Philip (Glenn). American, b. 1923. Novels/Short stories, Children's fiction, Poetry. Part-time lectr. and teacher, since 1955. *Publs:* Three Satires, 1951; Self-Portrait, from Another Direction, 1959; Like I Say, 1960; Memoirs of an Interglacial Age, 1960; Monday in the Evening: 26 viii 61, 1963; Every Day: Poems, 1965; Highgrade: Doodles, Poems, 1966; The Education Continues Along, 1967; You Didn't Even Try (novel), 1967; The Invention of the Letter: A Beastly Morality, 1967; On Bear's Head: Selected Poems, 1969; Severance Pay: Poems 1967-69, 1970; Scenes of Life at the Capital, 1971; Imaginary Speeches for a Brazen Head (novel), 1972; The Kindness of Strangers, 1975; Selected Poems, 1976; (with others) On Bread and Poetry, 1976; Decompressions, 1977; Off the Wall, edited by Donald Allen, 1977; The Diamond Noodle, 1979; Enough Said: Fluctuat nec Mergitur: Poems 1974-1979, 1980; Heavy Breathing, 1983. Add: c/o Four Seasons Foundn., P.O. Box 31190, San Francisco, Calif. 94131, U.S.A.

WHALEN, Richard James. American, b. 1935. Social commentary. Chmn., Worldwide Information Resources Ltd., Washington, D.C., since 1971. Visiting Fellow, American Enterprise Inst., since 1980. Assoc. Ed., Richmond News Leader, Va., 1957–59; Contrib. Ed., Time mag., NYC, 1959–60; Editorial Writer, Wall Street Journal, NYC, 1960–62; Assoc. Ed., 1962–66, and Sr. Ed., 1966, Fortune mag., NYC; Writer-in-Residence, Center for Strategic and Intnl. Studies, Georgetown Univ., Washington, D.C., 1966–71. *Publs:* The Founding Father: A Story of Joseph P. Kennedy, 1964; New York: A City Destroying Itself, 1965; Catch the Falling Flag: A Republican's Challenge to His Party, 1972; Taking Sides, 1974; The Wealth Weapon: U.S. Foreign Policy and Multinational Corporations, 1980; Trade Warriors, 1986. Add: 3220 Volta Pl. N.W., Washington, D.C. 20007, U.S.A.

WHALLEY, Joyce Irene. British. Art, Crafts, History. With Victoria and Albert Museum, London, 1950–81. *Publs:* English Handwriting, 1540-1843, 1969; Cobwebs to Catch Flies: Illustrated Books for the Nursery and Schoolroom, 1700-1900, 1974; Writing Implements and Accessories, 1975; The Pen's Excellencie: Calligraphy in Western Europe and America, 1980; Pliny's Historia Naturalis, 1982; Beatrix Potter's Derwentwater Sketchbook (facsimile), 1984; A Student's Guide to Western Calligraphy, 1984; Beatrix Potter: The V & A Collections (catalogue), 1985; Two Victorian Railway Alphabets, 1986; (with J. Taylor and others) Beatrix Potter 1866-1945: The Artist and Her World, 1987; (with W. Bartlett) Beatrix Potter's Derwentwater, 1988; (with T.R. Chester) A History of Children's Book Illustration, 1988. Add: High Banks, Stoneborough Lane, Budleigh Salterton, Devon EX9 6HL, England.

WHALLEY, Peter. British, b. 1946. Mystery/Crime/Suspense. Writer, Coronation Street, Granada TV, Manchester. School teacher, 1969–80. *Publs:* Post Mortem, 1982; The Mortician's Birthday Party, 1983; Old Murders, 1984; Love and Murder, 1985; Robbers, 1985; Bandits, 1986; Villains, 1987; Blackmailer's Summer, 1989. Add: Holly House, Green Lane, Lancaster, England.

WHARTON, William. American, b. 1925. Novels/Short stories. *Publs:* Birdy, 1978; Dad, 1981; A Midnight Clear, 1982; Scumbler, 1984;

Pride, 1985; Tidings, 1988. Add: B.P. 18 Port Harly, France.

WHEATCROFT, John Stewart. American, b. 1925. Novels/Short stories, Plays/Screenplays, Poetry. Presidential Prof. of English, and Dir., The Stadlen Center for Poetry, Bucknell Univ., Lewisburg, Pa., since 1979 (Instr. 1952–58; Asst. Prof., 1958–62; Assoc. Prof., 1962–66; Prof. of English, since 1966). Instr., Univ. of Kansas, Lawrence, 1950–52. *Publs:* Death of a Clown, 1964; Prodigal Son, 1967; Ofoti (play) 1967; Edie Tells (novel), 1975; A Voice from the Hump (poetry), 1977; Ordering Demons (poetry), 1981; Catherine, Her Book (novel), 1984; Slow Exposures, 1985; The Beholder's Eye (novel), 1987. Add: 55 N. 8th St., Apt. 5, Lewisburg, Pa. 17837, U.S.A.

WHEELER, Helen Rippier. American, b. 1926. Education, Librarianship, Media, Social sciences, Women. Consultant in media, bibliographic instruction, and affirmative action with emphasis on gender equity; Visiting Lectr., Univ of California at Berkeley. Provides nonprofit research-support service, known as Womanhood Media. Library Dir., Hicksville, N.Y., 1951–53; Asst. Librarian, Univ of Chicago Lab. Sch., 1953–55; Teacher and librarian, Chicago high schs., 1955–56; Librarian, Agnes Russell Center, Teachers Coll., Columbia Univ., NYC, 1956–58; Head Librarian and Audio-Visual Coordinator, Chicago City Jr. Coll., 1958–62; Latin American Specialist, Columbia Univ. Libraries, NYC, 1962–64; Assoc. Prof., Grad. Library Sch., Univ. of Hawaii, Honolulu, 1965–66; Assoc. Prof., Dept. of Library Science, Indiana State Univ., Terre Haute, and Louisiana State Univ., Baton Rouge. *Publs:* The Community College Library: A Plan for Action, 1965; A Basic Book Collection for the Community College Library, 1968; Womanhood Media, 1972, supplement, 1975; The Bibliographic Instruction-course Handbook, 1988; Getting Published in Women's Studies, 1989. Add: 2701 Durant Ave., Box 14, Berkeley, Calif. 94704, U.S.A.

WHEELER, John Archibald. American, b. 1911. Physics, Sciences. Prof. of Physics, Emeritus, Princeton Univ. since 1976, and Univ. of Texas, Austin, since 1978. Member of U.S. Gen. Advisory Cttee. on Arms Control and Disarmament, under Presidents Nixon and Ford. Asst. Prof., 1938–44, Assoc. Prof., 1945–46, Prof., 1947–76, and Joseph Henry Prof. of Physics, 1966–76, Princeton Univ., New Jersey. *Publs:* Geometrodynamics, 1962; (with E. Taylor) Spacetime Physics, 1963; Einstein's Vision, 1968; (with C. Misner and K. Thorne) Gravitation, 1973; (with M. Rees and R. Ruffini) Black Holes, Gravitational Waves and Cosmology, 1974; Frontiers of Time, 1979; (with W. H. Zurek) Quantum Theory and Measurement, 1983. Add: Physics Dept., Princeton Univ., Princeton, N.J. 08544, U.S.A.

WHEELER, Penny Estes. American, b. 1943. Novels/Short stories, Plays/Screenplays, Education, Medicine/Health, Theology/Religion. Acquisitions Ed.; Ed., Guide mag. Teacher of second grade, Nashville, Tenn., 1967–68. *Publs:* Your Career in Elementary Education, 1970; A Time of Tears and Laughter, 1971; (ed.) Good Foods for Good Health, 1972; (ed.) Journal of a Happy Woman, 1973; Don't Be Lonely, 1973; Three for the Show, 1973; VD, 1974; Alcohol, 1974; With Long Life, 1978; The Appearing, 1979; The Beginning, 1981; More Than Harps of Gold, 1981. Add: c/o Review and Herald Publ. Assoc., 55 W. Oak Ridge Dr., Hagerstown, Md. 21740, U.S.A.

WHEELWRIGHT, Edward Lawrence. British, b. 1921. Economics, Politics/Government. Lectr., 1952–57, Sr. Lectr., 1957–65, and Assoc. Prof., 1965–86, Univ. of Sydney. *Publs:* Ownership and Control of Australian Companies, 1957; Industrialisation in Malaysia, 1965; (ed.) Higher Education in Australia, 1965; (with B. Fitzpatrick) The Highest Bidder: A Citizen's Guide to Problems of Foreign Investment in Australia, 1965; (with J. Miskelly) Anatomy of Australian Manufacturing Industry, 1967; (with B. McFarlane) The Chinese Road to Socialism, 1970; Radical Political Economy: Collected Essays, 1974; (ed. with K. Buckley) Essays in the Political Economy of Australian Capitalism, 5 vols., 1975–82; (ed. with F.J.B. Stilwell) Readings in Political Economy, 2 vols., 1976; Capitalism, Socialism, or Barbarism?, 1978; (ed. with G.J. Crough and T. Wilshire) Australian and World Capitalism, 1980; (with G.J. Crough) Australia: A Client State, 1982; (ed.) Consumers, Transnational Corporations and Development, 1985; (ed. with K. Buckley) Communications and the Media in Australia, 1986; Capitalism and the Common People in Australia, vol. I 1788-1914, 1988; (with Abe David) Asian Capitalism and Australia, 1989. Add: 14 Somerset St., Mosman, Sydney, N.S.W., Australia 2088.

WHISTLER, Laurence. British, b. 1912. Poetry, Architecture, Crafts, Autobiography/Memoirs/Personal, Biography. Freelance writer, and glass engraver. *Publs:* Sir John Vanbrugh, 1938; The English Festivals,

1947; Rex Whistler: His Life and His Drawing, 1948; The World's Room, 1949; The Engraved Glass of Laurence Whistler, 1952; The Imagination of Vanbrugh, 1954; The View from This Window, 1956; Engraved Glass 1952-1958, 1959; (with Ronald Fuller) The Work of Rex Whistler, 1960; Audible Silence, 1961; The Initials in the Heart (autobiography), 1964; To Celebrate Her Living, 1967; Pictures on Glass, 1972; The Image on the Glass, 1975; AHA: Verses to Reversible Faces by Rex Whistler, 1978; Scenes and Signs on Glass, 1985, The Laughter and the Urn (life of Rex Whistler), 1985; Enter (poems), 1987. Add: c/o F. Section, Lloyds Bank Ltd., 6 Pall Mall, London SW1Y 5NH, England.

WHITAKER, Ben(jamin Charles George). British, b. 1934. Civil liberties/Human rights, Criminology/Law enforcement/Prisons, Sociology. Dir., Gulbenkian Foundn. (U.K.), since 1988. Called to the Bar, 1959; Extra-Mural Lectr. in Law, Univ. of London, 1963–64; Labour Member of Parliament (U.K.) for Hampstead, London, 1966–70: Parliamentary Secty., Ministry of Overseas Development, 1969–70. Exec. Dir., Minority Rights Group, 1971–88. U.K. Member, U.N. Human Rights Subcommn., 1975–88; Chmn. Defence of Literature and the Arts Soc., 1976–82; Member, U.K. National Commn. for Unesco, 1978–85. *Publs:* The Police, 1964; Crime and Society, 1967; (ed.) A Radical Future, 1967; (with K. Browne) Parks for People, 1971; (ed.) The Fourth World, 1972; The Foundations (in U.S. as The Philanthropoids), 1974; The Police in Society, 1979; U.N. Report on Slavery, 1982; A Bridge of People, 1983; (ed.) Minorities: A Question of Human Rights, 1984; U.N. Report on Genocide, 1985; The Global Connection, 1987. Add: 13 Elsworthy Rd., London NW3, England.

WHITAKER, Gilbert R(iley), Jr. American, b. 1931. Economics. Prof. of Business Economics, and Dean, Grad. Sch. of Business Admin., Univ. of Michigan, Ann Arbor, since 1979. Assoc. Prof. of Business Economics, Northwestern Univ., Evanston, Ill., 1960–66; Assoc. Prof., 1966–67, Prof., 1967–76, and Assoc. Dean, Grad. Sch. of Business Admin., 1969–76, Washington Univ., St. Louis; Prof. and Dean, Neeley Sch. of Business, Texas Christian Univ., Fort Worth, 1976–78. *Publs:* (with M. Colberg and D. Forbush) Business Economics: Principles and Cases, 1964, 6th ed. 1981; (with R. Chisholm) Forecasting Methods, 1971. Add: Grad. Sch. of Business Admin., Univ. of Michigan, Ann Arbor, Mich. 48109, U.S.A.

WHITAKER, Rod. *See* **TREVANIAN**.

WHITBY, Sharon. *See* **PETERS**, Maureen.

WHITCOMB, John C(lement). American, b. 1924. Astronomy, Earth sciences, History, Theology/Religion. Prof. of Theology and Old Testament, Grace Theological Seminary, Winona Lake, Ind., since 1951 (Dir. of Post-Graduate Studies, 1961–86). Pres. of the Bd., Spanish-World Gospel Mission Inc., since 1962; Ed., Grace Theological Journal, since 1980. Member, Bd. of Trustees, Foreign Missionary Soc. of the Brethren Church, 1966–86. *Publs:* Darius the Mede, 1959; (with H.M. Morris) The Genesis Flood, 1961; The Origin of the Solar System, 1964; Chronology Charts of the Old Testament: Solomon to the Exile, 1971; (with Donald J. Young) The Moon, 1978; Esther: The Triumph of God's Sovereignty, 1979; (with John J. Davis) A History of Israel, 1980; The Bible and Astionomy, 1984; Daniel, 1985; The Early Earth: An Introduction to Biblical Creationism, 1986; The World That Perished: An Introduction to Biblical Catastrophism, 1988. Add: Grace Theological Seminary, 200 Seminary Dr., Winona Lake, Ind. 46590, U.S.A.

WHITE, Alan Richard. British, b. 1922. Philosophy. Ferens Prof. of Philosophy, Univ. of Hull, since 1961. *Publs:* G.E. Moore, 1958; Attention, 1964; The Philosophy of Mind, 1967; (ed.) The Philosophy of Action, 1968; Truth, 1970; Modal Thinking, 1975; The Nature of Knowledge, 1982; Rights, 1984; Grounds of Liability, 1985; Methods of Metaphysics, 1987. Add: Dept. of Philosophy, Univ. of Hull, Hull, Yorks., England.

WHITE, Christopher (John). British, b. 1930. Art. Dir., Ashmolean Museum, Oxford, and Follow of Worcester Coll., Oxford, since 1985. Asst. Keeper, Dept. of Prints and Drawings, British Museum, London, 1954–65; Dir., P. and D. Colnaghi, London, 1965–71; Curator of Graphic Arts, Natl. Gallery of Art, Washington, D.C., 1971–73; Dir. of Studies, Paul Mellon Centre for Studies in British Art, 1973–85, Adjunct Prof. of History of Art, 1976–85, and Assoc. Dir., Yale Center for British Art, 1976–85, Yale Univ., New Haven, Conn. Reviews Ed., Master Drawings, 1967–80. *Publs:* Rembrandt and His World, 1964; The Flower Drawings of Jan van Huysum, 1965; Rubens and His World, 1968; Rembrandt as an Etcher, 1969; (co-author) Rembrandt's Etchings: A Catalogue

Raisonné, 1970; Dürer: The Artist and His Drawings, 1972; English Landscape 1630-1850, 1977; The Dutch Paintings in the Collection of H.M. the Queen, 1982; (ed.) Rembrandt in Eighteenth Century England, 1983; Peter Paul Rubens: Man and Artist, 1987; (with others) Drawing in England from Hilliard to Hogarth, 1987; also exhibition catalogues. Add: 14 S. Villas, London NW1 9BS, England.

WHITE, Edmund. American, b. 1940. Novels/Short stories, Essays. Contributing Ed., Vogue mag., NYC. Formerly Instr. of Literature and Creative Writing, Yale Univ., New Haven, Conn., Johns Hopkins Univ., Baltimore, Md., and George Mason Univ., Fairfax, Va.; Visiting Writer, Columbia Univ., NYC, 1981–82; Exec. Dir., New York Inst. for the Humanities, 1982–83. *Publs:* Forgetting Elena, 1973; Nocturnes for the King of Naples, 1978; States of Desire (non-fiction), 1980; A Boy's Own Story, 1982; Caracole, 1985; (co-author) The Darken Proof, 1987; The Beautiful Room Is Empty, 1988. Add: 8 rue Poulletier, Paris 75004, France.

WHITE, Edward M. American, b. 1933. Literature, Writing. Prof. of English, California State Univ., San Bernardino, since 1965. Instr., and subsequently Asst. Prof., Wellesley Coll., Mass., 1960–65. *Publs:* The Writer's Control of Tone, 1970; The Pop Culture Tradition, 1972; Comparison and Contrast: The California State University English Equivalency Examination, 8 vols., 1974–81; Teaching and Assessing Writing, 1985; Developing Successful College Writing Programs, 1989. Add: 933 West Edgehill Rd., San Bernardino, Calif. 92405, U.S.A.

WHITE, Gillian Mary. British, b. 1936. Law. Prof. of Intnl. Law, Univ. of Manchester, since 1975 (Lectr., 1967–71; Sr. Lectr., 1971–73; Reader, 1973–75). Gen. Ed., Melland Schill Monographs on Intnl. Law, since 1983. Editorial and Research Asst., Intnl. Law Reports, and British Practice in Intnl. Law, 1961–67; Research Fellow, New Hall, Cambridge, 1964–67. *Publs:* Nationalization of Foreign Property, 1961; The Use of Experts by International Tribunals, 1965. Add: Faculty of Law, Univ. of Manchester, Manchester M13 9PL, England.

WHITE, Ivan. British, b. 1929. Poetry. Tutor-Organizer, Workers' ucational Assn., in Lancashire and Cumbria. *Publs:* Cry Wolf: A Poem of Urgency, 1962; Crow's Fall, 1969; Removal of an Exhibition, 1976. Add: Park Cottage, Tanpits Lane, Burton, Camforth, Lancs., England.

WHITE, James. British, b. 1928. Science fiction/Fantasy. Retired Publicity Officer, Short Brothers & Harland Ltd. *Publs:* The Secret Visitors, 1957; Hospital Station, 1962; Second Ending, 1963; Star Surgeon, 1962; Deadly Litter, 1964; Open Prison, 1965; The Watch Below, 1966; All Judgement Fled, 1968; The Aliens Among Us, 1969; Tomorrow is Too Far, 1971; Major Operation, 1971; Dark Inferno, 1972; The Dream Millennium, 1974; Monsters and Medics, 1977; Underkill, 1979; Ambulance Ship, 1980; Futures Past, 1982; Sector General, 1983; Star Healer, 1985; Code Blue—Emergency, 1987; Federation World, 1988. Add: 2 West Dr., Portstewart, Co. Londonderry BT55 7ND, Northern Ireland.

WHITE, James Floyd. American, b. 1932. Architecture, Theology/Religion. Prof. of Liturgy, Univ. of Notre Dame, South Bend, Ind., since 1983. Instr. in Religion, Ohio Wesleyan Univ., Delaware, Ohio, 1959–61; Prof. of Christian Worship, Perkins Sch. of Theology, Southern Methodist Univ., Dallas, Tex., 1961–83. *Publs:* The Cambridge Movement, 1962, 1979; Protestant Worship and Church Architecture, 1964; (coauthor) Celebration of the Gospel, 1964; Architecture at SMU, 1966; The Worldliness of Worship, 1967; New Forms of Worship, 1971; Christian Worship in Transition, 1976; Seasons of the Gospel, 1979; Introduction to Christian Worship, 1980; Sacraments as God's Self Giving, 1983; John Wesley's Sunday Service, 1984; (co-author) Church Architecture, 1988; Protestant Worship, 1989. Add: 17840 Ponader Dr., South Bend, Ind. 46635, U.S.A.

WHITE, John (Sylvester). American, b. 1919. Plays/Screenplays. Former actor. *Publs:* Bugs, and Veronica, 1966. Add: c/o Greenvine Agency, 9021 Melrose Ave., Los Angeles, Calif. 90069, U.S.A.

WHITE, John Edward (Clement Twarowski). British, b. 1924. Architecture, Art. Durning-Lawrence Professor of the History of Art, University Coll., London, since 1971. Trustee, Whitechapel Art Gallery, London, since 1976. Lectr., 1952–58, and Reader, 1958–59, Courtauld Inst., London; Pilkington Prof. of the History of Art, and Dir., Whitworth Art Gallery, Univ. of Manchester, 1959–66; Prof. of the History of Art, Johns Hopkins Univ., Baltimore, 1966–71. Member, Advisory Council, Victoria and Albert Museum, London, 1973–76; Member of the Exec. Cttee., 1974–81, and Chmn., 1976–80, Assn. of Art Historians; Member

of the Art Panel, Arts Council, 1974–78; Member, 1975–82, and Chmn., 1976–82, Reviewing Cttee. on Export of Works of Art. *Publs:* Perspective in Ancient Drawings and Painting, 1956; The Birth and Rebirth of Pictorial Space, 1957, 3rd ed., 1987; Art and Architecture in Italy 1250-1400, 1966, 1987; Duccio, 1980; Studies in Renaissance Art, 1983; Studies in Late Medieval Italian Art, 1984. Add: Dept. of the History of Art, University College, Gower St., London WC1H 0PD England.

WHITE, Jon Manchip. British, b. 1924. Novels/Short stories, Poetry, History, Biography. Lindsay Young Prof. of English, Univ. of Tennessee, Knoxville, since 1977. Story Ed., BBC, London, 1950–51; Sr. Exec. Officer, U.K. Foreign Service, 1952–56; freelance writer, 1956–67; Prof. of English, Univ. of Texas, El Paso, 1967–77. *Publs:* Dragon, 1943; Salamander, 1943; The Rout of San Romano, 1952; Ancient Egypt, 1952, 1970; Mask of Dust (in U.S. as The Last Race), 1953; Build Us a Dam, 1954; Anthropology, 1954; The Girl from Indiana, 1955; (ed.) The Glory of Egypt, by Samivel, 1955; No Home But Heaven, 1956; The Mercenaries, 1958; Hour of the Rat, 1962; Marshal of France: The Life and Times of Maurice, Conte de Saxe, 1962, Everyday Life in Ancient Egypt, 1963; The Rose in the Brandy Glass, 1965; Nightclimber, 1968; Diego Velazquez: Painter and Courtier, 1969; The Land God Made in Anger: Reflections on a Journey Through South West Africa, 1969; Cortes and the Downfall of the Aztec Empire, 1971; (ed.) Life in Ancient Egypt by Adolf Erman; 1971; (ed.) Tomb of Tutankhamen, by Howard Carter, 1971; The Game of Troy, 1971; The Mountain Lion, 1971; (ed.) Manners and Customs of the Modern Egyptians, by E.W. Lane, 1972; The Garden Game, 1973; Send for Mr. Robinson, 1974; A World Elsewhere: One Man's Fascination with the American Southwest, 1975, in U.K. as The Great American Desert, 1977; Everyday Life of the North American Indian, 1979; The Moscow Papers, 1979; Death by Dreaming, 1981; Chills and Fevers: Three Extravagant Tales, 1983; The Last Grand Master: A Novel of Revolution, 1985. Add: Dept. of English, Univ. of Tennessee, Knoxville, Tenn. 37916, U.S.A.

WHITE, Jonathan. *See* **HARVEY,** John B.

WHITE, Jude Gilliam. *See* **DEVERAUX,** Jude.

WHITE, Kenneth. British, b. 1936. Poetry, Autobiography/Memoirs/Personal, Essays, Translations. Matre de Conférences, Univ. of Paris, since 1973 (Lectr. in English, 1969–73). Lectr., Sorbonne, Paris, 1962–63; Lectr. in French Language and Literature, Univ. of Glasgow, 1963–67; Lectr., Univ. of Bordeaux at Pau, 1967–68. *Publs:* En toute Candeur, 1964; The Cold Wind of Dawn, 1966; Letters from Gourgounel (autobiography), 1966; The Most Difficult Area, 1968 (trans.) Selected Poems by André Breton, 1969; (trans.) Ode to Charles Fourier, by André Breton, 1969; Travels in the Drifting Dawn, 1972; The Tribal Dharma, 1974; One the Haiku Path, 1975; A Walk along the Shore, 1977; Dérives (fiction), 1978; The Life-Technique of John Cowper Powys, 1978; Segalen: Théorie et pratique du voyage, 1979; Mahamudra, 1979; Ode Fragmente a la Bretagne, 1980; Le Grand Rivage, 1980; L'Ecosse avec Kenneth White, 1980; Le Visage du vent d'est, 1980; La Figure du dehors, 1982; Scè nes d'un monde flottant, 1983; La Route bleue, 1983; The Bird Bath: Collected Longer Poems, 1989; Travels in the Drifting Dawn, 1989. Add: Gwenved, Chemin du Goaquer, 22560 Trebeurden, France.

WHITE, Lawrence J. American, b. 1943. Business/Trade/Industry, Economics. Prof. of Economics, Grad Sch. of Business Admin., New York Univ., since 1979 (Assoc. Prof., 1976–78). Consultant to U.S. Dept. of Justice, U.S. Senate Subcttee. on Antitrust and Monopoly, U.S. Agency for Intnl. Development, U.S. Environmental Protection Agency, U.S. Dept. of Housing and Urban Development, U.S. Small Business Admin., and Office on Technology Assessment, U.S. Congress. Economic Adviser and Consultant, Harvard Development Advisory Service, 1969–70; Asst. Prof. of Economics, Princeton Univ., New Jersey, 1970–76; Sr. Staff Economist, U.S. Council of Economic Advisers, 1978–79; Chief Economist, Antitrust Division, U.S. Dept. of Justice, 1981–82. North American Ed., Journal of Industrial Economics, 1984–87; Bd. member, Federal Home Loan Bank Bd., 1986–80. *Publs:* The Automobile Industry since 1945, 1971; Industrial Concentration and Economic Power in Pakistan, 1974; Reforming Regulation: Processes and Problems, 1981; The Regulation of Air Pollutant Emissions from Motor Vehicles, 1982; The Public Library in the 1980's: The Problems of Choice, 1983; International Trade in Ocean Shipping Services: The United States and the World, 1988. Add: Grad. Sch. of Business Admin., New York Univ., 90 Trinity Pl., New York, N.Y. 10006, U.S.A.

WHITE, Lionel. American, b. 1905. Mystery/Crime/Suspense. *Publs:* The Snatchers, 1953; To Find a Killer, 1954 (in U.S. paperback,

Before I Die, 1964); Love Trap, 1955; The Big Caper, 1955; Clean Break, 1955 (in U.S. paperback, The Killing, 1964); Flight into Terror, 1955; Operation—Murder, 1956; The House Next Door, 1956; Right for Murder, 1957; Death Takes the Bus, 1957; Hostage for a Hood, 1957; Too Young to Die, 1958; Coffin for a Hood, 1958; Invitation to Violence, 1958; The Merriweather File, 1959; Rafferty, 1959; Run, Killer, Run, 1959; Lament for a Virgin, 1960; Steal Big, 1960; The Time of Terror, 1960; Marilyn

on K Street, 1965; A Party to Murder, 1966; Thath At Sea, 1961; Ob 1967; The Crimshaw Memorandum, 1967; Hijack, 1969; Death of a City, 1970; The Mexico Run, 1974; A Rich and Dangerous Game, 1974; Protect Yourself, Your Family, and Your Property in an Unsafe World (non-fiction), 1974; Jailbreak, 1976; The Walked Yard, 1978. Add: P.O. Box 1737, Cullowhee, S.C. 28723, U.S.A.

WHITE, Morton (Gabriel). American, b. 1917. Philosophy. Prof., Inst. for Advance Study, Princeton. Instr., of Philosophy, Columbia Univ., NYC, 1942–46; Asst. Prof. of Philosophy, Univ. of Pennsylvania, Philadelphia, 1946–48; Asst. Prof. to Prof. of Philosophy, Harvard Univ., Cambridge, Mass., 1948–70. *Publs:* The Origin of Dewey's Instrumentalism, 1943; Social Thought in America, 1949; (ed.) The Age of Analysis, 1955; Toward Reunion in Philosophy, 1956; Religion, Politics and the Higher Learning, 1959; (with Lucia White) The Intellectual Versus the City, 1962; (ed. with Schlesinger) Paths of American Thought, 1963; Foundations of Historical Knowledge, 1965; Science and Sentiment in America, 1972; (ed.) Documents in the History of American Philosophy, 1972; Pragmatism and the American Mind, 1973; The Philosophy of the American Revolution, 1978; What Is and What Ought to Be Done, 1981; (with Julia White) Journeys to the Japanese 1952-1979, 1986; Philosophy, the Federalist, and the Constitution, 1987. Add: Inst. for Advanced Study, Princeton, N.J. 08540, U.S.A.

WHITE, Patrick (Victor Martindale). Australian, b. 1912. Novels/Short stories, Plays/Screenplays, Poetry, Autobiography/Memoirs/Personal. *Publs:* The Ploughman and Other Poems, 1935; Happy Valley, 1939; The Living and the Dead, 1941; The Aunt's Story, 1948; The Tree of Man, 1955; Voss, 1957; Riders in the Chariot, 1961; The Burnt Ones, 1964; Four Plays, 1965; The Solid Mandala, 1966; The Vivisector, 1970; The Eye of the Storm, 1974; The Cockatoos: Shorter Novels and Stories, 1974; A Fringe of Leaves, 1976; Big Toys (play), 1977; The Night of the Prowler (screenplay), 1978; The Twyborn Affair, 1979; Flaws in the Glass: A Self-Portrait, 1981; Memoirs of Many in One, 1986. Add: 20 Martin Rd., Centennial Park, Sydney, N.S.W., 2021, Australia.

WHITE, Ray Lewis. American, b. 1941. Literature, Biography, Essays. Distinguished Prof. of English, Illinois State Univ., Normal, since 1973 (Asst. Prof., 1968– 70, Assoc. Prof., 1970–73). Instr., North Carolina State Univ., 1965–68. *Publs:* (ed.) Achievement of Sherwood Anderson, 1966; (ed.) Return to Winesburg, 1967; Gore Vidal, 1968; (ed.) A Story Teller's Story, 1968; (ed.) Sherwood Anderson's Memoirs, 1969; (ed.) Tar: A Midwest Childhood, 1069; (ed.) Checklist of Sherwood Anderson, 1969; (ed.) Studies in Winesburg, Ohio, 1971; (ed.) Marching Men, 1972; (ed.) Sherwood Anderson/Gertrude Stein, 1972; Sherwood Anderson: A Reference Guide, 1977; Heinrich Boll in America, 1979; Par Lagerkvist in America, 1979; Gunter Grass in America, 1981; R.K. Narayan: The American Reception, 1983; Gertrude Stein/Alice B. Toklas, 1984; Arnold Zweig in the U.S.A., 1986; Index to Best American Short Stories and O. Henry Prize Stories, 1988; (ed.) Sherwood Anderson: Early Writings, 1989. Add: Dept. of English, Illinois State Univ., Normal, Ill. 61761, U.S.A.

WHITE, Reginald (Ernest Oscar). British, b. 1914. Theology/Religion. Lectr., 1966–67, and Principal, 1968–79, Baptist Theological Coll. of Scotland. *Publs:* Into the Same Image, 1957; They Teach Us to Pray, 1957; Prayer is the Secret, 1958; Beneath the Cross of Jesus, 1959; Stranger of Galilee, 1960; Biblical Doctrine of Initiation, 1960; The Upward Calling, 1961; Apostle Extraordinary, 1962; 52 Seed Thoughts, 1963; A Relevant Salvation, 1963; Open Letter to Evangelicals, 1964; Sermon Suggestions I, 1965–66; Sermon Suggestions II, 1967; Five Minutes with the Master, 1966; Exploration of Faith, 1969; 52 Stories for Children, 1970; Guide to Preaching, 1973; In Him the Fullness, 1973; Contemporary Sermon Outline, 1974; Guide to Pastoral Care, 1976; The Changing Continuity of Christian Ethics, 2 vols., 1979–80; The Answer Is the Spirit, 1980; Matthew Lays It on the Line (in U.S. as The Mind of Matthew), 1980; 52 More Stories for Children, 1981; Interpreting the Bible Today, 1982; 52 Personality Profiles from the Bible, 1983; The Night He Was Betrayed, 1983; Christian Handbook to the Psalms, 1984;

Luke's Case for Christianity, 1987. Add: 72 Great George St., Glasgow G12 8RU, Scotland.

WHITE, Robert Lee. American, b. 1928. Literature. Prof., Dept. of English, York Univ., Downsview, Ont., since 1967. Ed., Canadian Review of American Studies, 1969–76. *Publs:* John Peale Bishop, 1966. Add: Dept. of English, York Univ., North York, Ont., Canada.

WHITE, Stanhope. British, b. 1913. Novels/Short stories, History, Autobiography/Memoirs/Personal, Biography. Freelance writer, lectr. for Workers Educational Assn. and N. Yorks. Education Authority. With Colonial Admin. Service, Nigeria, 1935–54 (with final position as Dir., Dept. of Local Industries, Northern Region); Exec., I.C.I., and Fisons Ltd., 1954–74. *Publs:* Descent from the Hills, 1963; Dan Bana, 1966; Lost Empire on the Nile, 1971; The North York Moors: An Introduction, 1979; Standing Stones and Earth works, North York Moors, 1987; Newtondale, the Forge Valley, and Other Gorges in the North Yorkshire Moors, 1984. Add: 40 The Glade, Scarborough, N. Yorks. YO11 2ST, England.

WHITE, Ted. (Theodore Edwin White). Also writes as Ron Archer and Norman Edwards. American, b. 1938. Science fiction/Fantasy, Children's fiction. Head of Foreign Dept., Scott Meredith Literary Agency, 1963; Asst. Ed., 1963–67, and Assoc. Ed., 1967–68, Fantasy and Science Fiction mag.; Assoc. Ed., Lancer Books, 1966; Managing Ed., 1969, and Ed., 1970–78, Amazing and Fantastic mags. Ed., Void fan mag., 1959–68. *Publs:* (as Norman Edwards, with Terry Carr) Invasion from 2500, 1964; Android Avenger, 1965; Phoenix Prime, 1966; The Sorceress of Qar, 1966; The Jewels of Elsewhen, 1967; (as Ron Archer, with Dave Van Arnam) Lost in Space (novelization of TV play), 1967; (with Dave Van Arnam) Sideslip, 1968; Captain America: The Great Gold Steal, 1968; The Spawn of the Death Machine, 1968; No Time Like Tomorrow (juvenile), 1969; By Furies Possessed, 1970; Star Wolf!, 1971; Trouble on Project Ceres (juvenile), 1971; (ed.) The Best from Amazing Stories, 1973; (ed.) The Best from Fantastic, 1973; (with David Bischoff) Forbidden World, 1978. Add: c/o Henry Morrison Inc., 320 McLain St., Bedford Hills, N.Y. 10705, U.S.A.

WHITE, (Herbert) Terence de Vere. Irish, b. 1912. Novels/Short stories, History, Travel/Exploration/Adventure, Biography. Literary Ed., The Irish Times, 1961–77; Dir., The Gate Theatre, Dublin, 1969–81; Solicitor and Sr. Partner, McCann Fitzgerald Roche Dudley, until 1962. *Publs:* The Road of Excess: A Life of Isaac Butt, 1945; Kevin O'Higgins, 1948; The Story of the Royal Dublin Society, 1955; A Fretful Midge: An Autobiography, 19 7; (ed.) Letters and Diaries of George Egerton, 1958; A Leaf from the Yellow Book, 1958; An Affair with the Moon, 1959; Prenez Garde, 1962; The Remainder Man, 1963; Lucifer Falling, 1965; The Parents of Oscar Wilde, 1967; Tara, 1967; Leinster, 1968; Ireland, 1968; The Lambert Mile, 1969; The March Hare, 1970; Mr. Stephen, 1971; The Anglo-Irish, 1972; The Distance and the Dark, 1973; The Radish Memoirs, 1974; Big Fleas and Little Fleas, 1976; Tom Moon, 1977; Chimes at Midnight and Other Stories, 1977; My Name Is Norval, 1978; Birds of Prey, 1980; Johnny Cross, 1983; Chat Show, 1987. Add: c/o Allied Irish Banks, 100 Grafton St., Dublin 2, Ireland.

WHITE, William. American, b. 1910. Literature. Taught at Wayne State Univ., 1947–80; Dir., Journalism Prog., Oakland Univ., Rochester, Mich., 1974–81. *Publs:* A Henry David Throeau Bibliography, 1908-1937, 1939; (ed.) Three Comic Poems, by A.E. Housman, 1941; John Donne since 1900, 1942; (ed.) Annual Bibliography of English Language and Literature, 1947–63; D.H. Lawrence: A Checklist, 1931-1950, 1950; (ed.) This Is Detroit 1701-1951: 250 Years in Pictures, 1951; Sir William Osler: Historian and Literary Essayist, 1951; John Ciardi: A Bibliography, 1959; (ed. with H.W. Blodgett) Walt Whitman: An 1855-1856 Notebook, 1959; (ed.) A.E. Housman: A Centennial Memento, 1959; (ed.) A.E. Housman to Joseph Ishill: Five Unpublished Letters, 1959; W.D. Snodgrass: A Bibliography, 1960, 1960; Karl Shapiro: A Bibliography, 1960; (ed.) The People and John Quincy Adams, by Walt Whitman, 1961; Ernest Hemingway: Guide to a Memorial Exhibition, 1961; (with Z.G. Zeke) George Orwell: A Selected Bibliography, 1962; (ed.) A Shropshire Lad, by A.E. Housman, 1962; Wilfred Owen 1893-1918: A Bibliography, 1967; (ed.) By-Line: Ernest Hemingway, 1967; Walt Whitman's Journalism: A Bibliography, 1969; (ed.) Studies in the Sun Also Rises, by Ernest Hemingway, 1969; Guide to Ernest Hemingway, 1969; Checklist of Ernest Hemingway, 1970; (ed.) Walt Whitman in Our Time: Four Essays, 1970; Edwin Arlington Robinson: A Supplementary Bibliography, 1971; (ed. with R. Asselineau) Walt Whitman in Europe Today: A Collection of Essays, 1972; (ed.) Kai Lung: Six Uncolected Stories from Punch, by Ernest Bramah, 1974; Nathanael West: A Bibliography, 1975; (ed.) The Bicentennial Walt Whitman, 1976; (ed.) The Daybooks and Notebooks of Walt

Whitman, 1978; (with H.W. Blodgett and Sculley Bradley) Variorum Edition of Walt Whitman's Leaves of Grass, 1979; (with Gertrude Traubel) With Walt Whitman in Camden, vol. 6, 1982; A.E. Housman: A Bibliography, 1982; (ed.) Ernest Hemingway, Dateline, 1986. Add: c/o Kent State Univ. Press, Kent, Ohio 44242, U.S.A.

WHITE, William, Jr. American, b. 1934. Novels/Short stories, Poetry, Children's non-fiction, Sciences (general), Translations. Publisher, The Franklin Inst. Press, Philadelphia, since 1976. Instr. in Ancient History, Temple Univ., Philadelphia, 1963–68; Asst. Prof., Univ. of North Carolina, Greenville, 1968–70; Assoc. Prof., Philadelphia Coll. of Textiles and Science, 1970–71; Editorial Dir., Reference Books, North American Publishing Co., Philadelphia, 1970–72; Science Writer and Managing Ed., The Emergency Care Research Inst., 1972–75. *Publs:* Enuma Elish and the Old Testament, 1963; (trans.) A Babylonian Anthology, 1966; Studies in Akkadian Medical Texts, 1968; (ed. and contrib.) The New Woman, 1972; (ed. with F. Little) The North American Reference Encyclopedia of Ecology and Pollution, 1972; A Frog Is Born, 1972; A Turtle Is Born, 1973; (ed. with R.F. Albano) Symposium on Drugs and Drug Abuse, 1974; The Guppy, 1974; The Siamese Fighting Fish, 1974; The Angelfish, 1975; An Earthworm Is Born, 1975; The Edge of the Pond, 1976; The Forest and Garden, 1976; The Cycle of the Seasons, 1977; The Edge of the Ocean, 1977; (with S.J. White) A Terrarium in Your Home, 1977; The American Chameleon, 1977; A Mosquito Is Born, 1978; The First New Testament, 1978; Cornelius Van Til: Defender of the Faith, 1979; Theological and Grammatical Phrasebook of the Bible, 1984; Photomacrography, 1987; The Subminiature Camera, 1987. Add: The Franklin Inst. Press, Philadelphia, Pa. 19103, U.S.A.

WHITE, William Luther. American, b. 1931. Literature, Theology/Religion. Chaplain and Prof. of Religion, Wesleyan Univ., Bloomingon, Ill., since 1963. Asst. Pastor, St. Paul Methodist Church, Chicago, 1953–56; Minister of Christian Education, Methodist Temple, Evansville, Ind., 1957–62. *Publs:* The Image of Man in C.S. Lewis, 1969. Add: Illinois Wesleyan Univ., Bloomington, Ill. 61701, U.S.A.

WHITEHEAD, Frank. British, b. 1916. Education, Literature. Reader in English and Education, Univ. of Sheffield, 1973–81, now retired (Sr. Lectr., 1962–73). Lectr., Univ. of London Inst. of Education, 1948–62; Ed., The Use of English, 1969–75. *Publs:* (ed.) George Crabbe: Selections from His Poetry, 1955; The Disappearing Dais: A Study of the Principles and Practice of English Teaching, 1966; Creative Experiment: Writing and the Teacher, 1970; (co-author) Children's Reading Interests, 1974; (co-author) Children and Their Books, 1977. Add: 26 Victoria Rd., Broomhall, Sheffield S10 2DL, England.

WHITEHEAD, Geoffrey Michael. British, b. 1921. Business/Trade/Industry. Formerly, Sr. Lectr. and Head, Professional Studies Dept., Thurrock Technical Coll., Essex Education Cttee., and Chief Examiner, Principles of Accounts, East Anglian Examination Bd. *Publs:* Economics: Commerce, Office Practice, Bookkeeping, Secretarial Practice, Money and Banking, Business Law, Elements of Banking, Made Simple, 8 vols., 1968–87; The Story of Money, 1975; (ed.) Ridley's Law of Carriage of Goods by Land, Sea, and Air, 1975; The Simplex Teachers' Series of Record Books, 7 vols., 1976; Test Yourself on the Highway Code, 1977; Simplified Bookkeeping for Small Businesses, 1979; Choosing Options for Your Future in the World of Work, 1981; Working for Yourself Is Also a Career, 1981; Success in Principles of Accounting (Business Calculations, Accounting and Costing), 3 vols., 1982; Elements of Cargo Insurance (International Trade and Payments, Freight Forwarding, Transportation and Documentation), 4 vols., 1982; Pitman Business Correspondence, 1982; Statistics for Business, 1984; Professional Competence for Road Haulage Operation, 1985; Test Yourself on Road Haulage Operation, 1985; Revise and Test Series (business studies), 16 vols., 1986–87; Office in Every Home, 1988; Organization and Administration for Business, 1989. Add: 15 Camside, Church St., Chesterton, Cambridge CB4 1PQ, England.

WHITEHEAD, James. American, b. 1936. Novels/Short stories, Poetry. Prof. of English, Univ. of Arkansas, Fayetteville. Member of faculty, Millsaps Coll., Jackson, Miss., 1960–63. *Publs:* Domains: Poems, 1966; Joiner (novel), 1971; Local Men (poetry), 1979; Actual Size (poetry), 1985. Add: Dept. of English, Univ. of Arkansas, Fayetteville, Ark. 72701, U.S.A.

WHITEHEAD, Ted. British, b. 1933. Plays/Screenplays. *Publs:* The Foursome, 1972; Alpha Beta, 1972; The Sea Anchor, 1975; Old Flames, 1976; Mecca, 1977; World's End (novel), 1981; The Man Who Fell in Love with His Wife, 1984. Add: c/o Judy Daish Associates Ltd., 83

Eastbourne Mews, London W2 6LQ, England.

WHITEHORN, Katharine (Elizabeth). British. Cookery/Gastonomy/Wine, Social commentary/phenomena, Essays. Columnist, The Observer, London, since 1963 (Fashion Ed., 1960–63). Staff Writer, Picture Post, 1956–57, and Woman's Own, 1958, both London; Member of Editorial Staff, Spectator, London, 1959–61. *Publs:* Cooking in a Bedsitter, 1960; Roundabout, 1961; Only on Sundays, 1966; Social Survival, 1968; Observations, 1970; How to Survive in Hospital, 1972; How to Survive Children, 1975; Sunday Best, 1976; How to Survive in the Kitchen, 1979; View from a Column, 1981; How to Survive Your Money Problems, 1983. Add: The Observer, Chelsea Bridge House, Queenstown Rd., London SW8 4NN, England.

WHITEHOUSE, Walter Alexander. British, b. 1915. Theology/Religion. Prof. of Theology, Univ. of Kent, Canterbury, 1965–77, now Emeritus. Reader in Divinity, Univ. of Durham, 1947–65. *Publs:* (co-author) Reformation Old and New, 1947; Christian Faith and the Scientific Attitude, 1952; (with H.H. Schrey and H.H. Walz) Biblical Doctrine of Justice and Law, 1955; Order, Goodness, Glory, 1960; The Authority of Grace, 1981. Add: 37 Cotswold Green, Stonehouse, Glos., England.

WHITEMAN, (Joseph Hilary) Michael. British/South African, b. 1906. Paranormal (mysticism), Philosophy, Sciences. Assoc. Prof. Emeritus, Univ. of Cape Town, since 1972 (Lectr. in Applied Mathematics, 1941–43, 1946–53; Sr. Lectr., 1954–1961; Assoc. Prof., 1962–71). Ed., The South African Music Teacher, since 1941. *Publs:* The Mystical Life, 1961; Philosophy of Space and Time, 1967; Old and New Evidence on the Meaning of Life, 1986. Add: 20 Erica Pl., Bergvliet, South Africa 7945.

WHITEMORE, Hugh (John). British, b. 1936. Plays/Screenplays, Communications media (television and film scrpts) *Publs:* (co-author) Elizabeth R, 1972; Stevie, 1977; Pack of Lies, 1983; Breaking the Code, 1987. Add: c/o Judy Daish Assocs., 83 Eastbourne Mews, London W2 6LQ, England.

WHITFIELD, George (Joshua Newbold). British, b. 1909. Education, Literature, Philosophy, Theology/Religion. Chief Examiner in English, Univ. of Durham Sch. Examinations Bd., 1940–43; Headmaster, Tavistock Grammar Sch., 1943–46, Stockport Sch., 1946–50, and Hampton Sch., 1950–68; Pres., Headmasters' Assn., 1967; Gen. Secty., Church of England Bd. of Education, 1969–74. *Publs:* (ed. and author with K. Muir, W.R. Niblett and A.A. Le M. Simpson) Teaching Poetry, 1937; An Introduction to Drama, 1938; God and Man in the Old Testament, 1949; (co-ed.) Poetry in the Sixth Form, 1950; Philosophy and Religion, 1955; (co-author) Christliche Erziehung in Europa: England, 1975. Add: Bede Lodge, 31A Rolle Rd., Exmouth, Devon EX8 2AW, England.

WHITFIELD, John Humphreys. British, b. 1906. Classics, Literature, Translations. Univ. Lectr. in Italian, Oxford Univ., 1936–46; Ed., 1962–74 and Chief Ed., 1967–74, Italian Studies, Heffer, Cambridge; Serena Prof. of Italian Language and Literature, Univ. of Birmingham, 1947–74; Fellow, Inst. for Advanced Research in the Humanities, Univ. of Birmingham, 1985. *Publs:* Petrarch and the Renascence, 1943; Machiavelli, 1947; Dante and Virgil, 1949; Giacomo Leopardi, 1954; Barlow Lectures on Dante, 1960; A Short History of Italian Literature, 1960, 5th ed. 1980; (trans.) The Canti of Leopardi in English Verse, 1962; (ed.) Canti, by Leopardi, 1966; Discourses on Machiavelli, 1969; (ed.) The Charlecote Manuscript of Machiavelli's The Prince, 1970; (ed.) The Courtier, by Castiglione, 1974; (bilingual ed.) Il Pastor Fido, by Guarini, 1976. Add:Woodbourne Rd., Edgbaston, Birmingham 15, England.

WHITING, Robert. American, b. 1942. Social commentary. Pres., Creative Resources Group, Tokyo, since 1977. *Publs:* The Chrysanthemum and the Bat, 1977; You Gotta Have Wa, 1989. Add: c/o Macmillan, 866 Third Ave., New York, N.Y. 10022, U.S.A.

WHITINGTON, Richard (Smallpiece). Australian, b. 1912. Sports/Fitness, Biography. Lawyer, Adelaide, 1935–40;Officer, Australian Imperial Force, 1940–46; Journalist, Australia, England and South Africa, 1946–69. *Publs:* (with K.R. Miller) Cricket Caravan, 1951; (with K.R. Miller) Catch, 1952; (with K.R. Miller) Straight Hit, 1953; (with K.R. Miller) Bumper, 1953; (with K.R. Miller) Gods or Flanneled Fools?, 1954; (with K.R. Miller) Cricket Typhoon, 1955; Keith Miller, Cricket Companion, 1956; (with J.H.B. Waite) Perchance to Bowl, 1961; John Reid's Kiwis, 1962; Bradman, Benaud and Goddard's Cinderellas, 1963; (with V.Y. Richardson) Vic Richardson Story, 1966; The Quiet Australian, 1967; Simpson's Safari, 1967; Fours Galore, 1969; Time of the Tiger, 1970; Sir Frank, 1971; Captains Outrageous?, 1972;

Illustrated History of Australian Cricket, 1972; Bodyline Umpire, 1974; Courage Book of Australian Test Cricket, 1974; Great Moments of Australian Sport, 1974; Illustrated History of Australian Tennis, 1975; Keith Miller: The Golden Nugget, 1983. Add: Polgeto di Umbertide 06019, Italy.

WHITLAM, (Edward) Gough. Australian, b. 1916. Politics/Government. Member, Exec. Bd. of Unesco, since 1985; Chmn., Australia-China Council, since 1986, and Australian National Gallery Council, since 1987; Fellow, Sydney Univ. Senate, 1981–83 and since 1986. Labor Party Member of Parliament (Aus.) for Werriwa, N.S.W., 1952–78: Deputy Leader, Labor Party, 1960–67; Leader of the Opposition, 1967–72, 1975–77; Leader of the Australian Labor Party, 1967–77; Prime Minister of Australia, 1972–75, also Foreign Minister, 1972–73. Visting Fellow, 1978–79 and First National Fellow, 1980–81, Australian National Univ., Canberra; Visiting Prof. of Australian Studies, Harvard Univ., Cambridge, Mass., 1979–80. Member, Independent Commn. on Intnl. Humanitarian Issues, 1983–87; Australian Ambassador to Unesco, 1983–86; Member, Australian Constitutional Commn., 1986–88. *Publs:* The Constitution Versus Labor, 1957; Australian Foreign Policy, 1963; Socialism Within the Constitution, 1965; Australia: Base or Bridge, 1966; Beyond Vietnam: Australia's Regional Responsibility, 1968; Australia: An Urban Nation, 1970; A New Federalism, 1971; Australian Public Administration, 1973; Australia's Foreign Policy, 1973; Road to Reform, 1975; The New Federalism, 1976; On Australia's Constitution, 1977; Reform During Recession, 1978; The Truth of the Matter, 1979; The Italian Inspiration in English Literature, 1980; A Pacific Community (Harvard lectures), 1981; Australian Federalism in Crisis, 1983; The Whitlam Government, 1985. Add: 100 William St., Sydney, N.S.W. 2011, Australia.

WHITLOCK, Ralph. Also writes as John Reynolds and Madge Reynolds. British, b. 1914. Children's non-fiction, Country life/Rural societies, History, Mythology/Folklore, Natural history, Autobiography/Memoirs/Personal, Biography. Columnist and Feature Writer, Western Gazette Group, since 1932; Columnist, The Guardian Weekly, since 1981; television and radio personality, and freelance lectr. Agricultural Consultant, Methodist Missionary Soc., 1968–73; Farming Corresp., The Field, 1946–74. *Publs:* Round Roundbarrow Farm, 1946; Peasant's Heritage, 1947;Cowleaze Farm, 1948; Common British Birds, 1948; Wiltshire, 1949; The Other Side of the Fence, 1950; Harvest at Cowleaze Farm, 1951; Winter at Cowleaze Farm, 1952; Rare and Extinct British Birds, 1953; The Land First, 1954; Salisbury Plain, 1955; Farming as a Career, 1959; (as Madge Reynolds) The Farmer's Wife, 1960; A Year on Cowleaze Farm, 1964; Short History of British Farming, 1965; Farming from the Road, 1967; The Great Cattle Plague, 1968; A Family and a Village, 1969; (ed.) Agricultural Records, 1969, 1978; Feast or Famine?, 1974; Squirrels, 1974; Deer, 1974; Spiders, 1974; Otters, 1974; Rats and Mice, 1974; Stoats and Weasels, 1974; (as John Reynolds) Bees and Wasps, 1974; Birds of Prey, 1974; Rabbits and Hares, 1974; My World of the Past, 1975; Somerset, 1975; Wessex, 1975; Wildlife in Wersex, 1975; Gentle Giants, 1976; Wiltshire, 1976; Everyday Life of the Maya, 1976; Folklore of Wiltshire, 1976; Exploring Rivers, Lakes and Canals, 1976; A Closer Look at Butterflies and Moths, 1977; Chimpanzees, 1977; Penguins, 1977; Folklore of Devon, 1977; Bulls Through the Ages, 1977; Warrior Kings of Saxon England, 1977; Pond Life, 1978; Growing Unusual Vegetables, 1978; Thinking About Rural Development, 1978; A Calendar of Country Customs, 1978; The Shaping of the Countryside, 1979; Historic English Forests, 1979; In Search of Lost Gods, 1979; Eels, 1979; Ducks, 1979; Wild Cats, 1979; (trans.) The Tree Frog (children's book), 1980; Crabs, 1980; Ants, 1980; Dragonflies, 1980, Snails, 1980; Grasshoppers and Crickets, 1980; Thinking about Food, 1980; Royal Farmers, 1980; Hyenas and Jackals, 1981; Yaks and Llamas, 1981; Sheep, 1981; Dairy Cows, 1981; The Countryside: Random Gleamings, 1981; Birds at Risk, 1981; Clara's Country Year, 1981; Water Divining, 1982; Bird Watch in an English Village, 1982; Pigs, 1982; Poultry, 1982; Insects, 1982; Farming in Dorset, 1982; The English Farm, 1983; Here Be Dragons, 1983; Working on a Farm, 1983; Farming in History, 1983; Landscape in History, 1984; Harvest and Thanksgiving, 1984; Weather, 1985; British Birds from Nature, 1985; The Oak, 1985; In the Town, 1985; The Weather, 1985; In the Soil, 1986; In the Park, 1986; The Seasons: Summer, 1986; Roots in the Soil: The Biography of Sir Joseph Nickerson, 1987; The Lost Village, 1988; Letters from an English Village, 1988. Add: The Penchet, Tytherley Rd., Winterslow, Salisbury, Wilts. SP5 1PY, England.

WHITMAN, Marina (von Neumann). American, b. 1935. Economics. Vice-Pres., General Motors, since 1979. Distinguished Public Service Prof. of Economics, Univ. of Pittsburgh, 1973–79 (Lectr., 1962–64; Asst.Prof., 1964–66; Assoc. Prof., 1966–71; Prof., 1971–73). *Publs:* The United States Investment Guaranty Program and Private Foreign Investment, 1959; Government Risk-Sharing in Foreign Investment, 1965; International and Interregional Payment Adjustment: A Synthetic View, 1967; Special Bibliography in International Economics, 1967; Economic Goals and Policy Instruments: Policies for Internal and External Balance, 1970; Reflections of Interdependence: Issues for Economic Theory and U.S. Policy, 1979; (with M. Shubik) The Aggressive Conservative Investor, 1979; International Trade and Investment, 1981. Add: General Motors Corp., 767 Fifth Ave., New York, N.Y. 10022, U.S.A.

WHITMAN, Ruth. American, b. 1922. Poetry, Translations. Instr. in Poetry, Radcliffe Coll., Cambridge, Mass., since 1970 (Scholar-in-Poetry, Radcliffe Inst., 1968–70). Ed. Asst., 1941–42, and Educational Ed., 1944–45, Houghton Mifflin Co., publrs., Boston; Ed., Harvard Univ. Press, 1945–60; Poetry Ed., Audience, Cambridge, Mass., 1958–63; Dir., Cambridge Center for Adult Education Poetry Workshop, 1964–68; Dir., Massachusetts Schs. Poetry Writing Prog., 1971–74; Instr. in Poetry, Harvard Writing Prog., Harvard Univ., Cambridge, Mass. 1979–84; Writer-in-Residence: Hamden-Sydney Coll., 1974; Trin ty Coll., 1976; Univ. of Denver, 1976, Holy Cross Coll., 1978, Massachusetts Inst. of Technology, 1979, 1989, Centre Coll., 1980, 1987, Univ. of Massachusetts, 1980; and Kentucky Arts Commn., 1981; Sr. Fulbright Writer-in-Residence, Hebrew Univ., Jerusalem, 1984–85. *Publs:* Blood and Milk Poems, 1963; (ed. and trans.) An Anthology of Modern Yiddish Poetry, 1966; The Marriage Wig and Other Poems, 1968; (trans.) Selected Poems, by Jacob Glatstein, 1972; The Passion of Lizzie Borden: New and Selected Poems, 1973; Tamsen Donner:Woman's Journey, 1977; Permanent ddress: New Poems 1973-1980, 1980; Becoming a Poet: Source, Process, and Practice, 1982; The Testing of Hanna Senesh, 1986; (trans.) The Fiddle Rose, by Abraham Sutckeuer, 1989; Laughing Gas: Poems New and Selected, 1990. Add: 40 Tuckerman Ave., Middletown, R.I. 02840, U.S.A.

WHITMORE, Cilla. *See* **GLADSTONE,** Arthur M.

WHITMORE, Raymond Leslie. British, b. 1920. Earth sciences, History, Medicine/Health. Prof. of Mining and Metallurgical Engineering, Univ. of Queensland, 1967–85, now Emeritus (Dean of Engineering, 1974–76). Head of Mechanical Sciences Dept., Ferodo Ltd., Stockport, 1951–53; Reader in Mining Engineering, Univ. of Nottingham, 1953–67. *Publs:* Rheology of the Circulation, 1968; (ed. and co-author) The Future of Australia's Mineral Industry, 1974; Coal in Queensland, 3 vols., 1981–89; Total Recovery of the Energy Resource, 1983; Eminent Queensland Engineers, 1984. Add: 297 Indooroopilly Rd., Brisbane, Qld. 4068, Australia.

WHITNAH, Donald Robert. American, b. 1925. History, Meteorology/ Atmospheric sciences, Transportation. Prof. since 1966, and Head since 1968, Dept. of History, Univ. of Northern Iowa, Cedar Falls (Asst. Prof., 1959; Assoc. Prof., 1962). *Publs:* A History of the United States Weather Bureau, 1961; Safer Skyways: U.S. Control of Aviation, 1926-66, 1966; (ed.) Government Agencies, 1983; The American Occupation of Austria: Planning and Early Years, 1985. Add: Dept. of History, Univ. of Northern Iowa, Cedar Falls, Iowa 50614, U.S.A.

WHITNEY, Hallam. *See* **WHITTINGTON,** Harry.

WHITNEY, Phyllis A(yame). American, b. 1903. Mystery/Crime/Suspense, Historical/Romance/Gothic, Children's fiction, Writing/Journalism. Children's Book Ed., Chicago Sun (now Chicago Sun Times), 1942–46, and Philadephia Inquirer, 1946–48; Instr. in Juvenile Fiction Writing, Northwestern Univ., Evanston, Ill., 1945–46, and New York Univ., 1947–58. Pres., Mystery Writers of America, 1975. *Publs:* children's fiction—A Place for Ann, 1941; A Star for Ginny, 1942; A Window for Julie, 1943; The Silver Inkwell, 1945; Willow Hill, 1947; Ever After, 1948; Mystery of the Gulls, 1949; Linda's Homecoming, 1950; The Island of Dark Woods, 1951, as Mystery of the Strange Traveler, 1967; Love Me, Love Me Not, 1952; Mystery of the Black Diamonds, 1954, in U.K. as Black Diamonds, 1957; Step to the Music, 1952; A Long Time Coming, 1954; Mystery on the Isle of Skye, 1955; The Fire and the Gold, 1956; The Highest Dream, 1956; Mystery of the Green Cat, 1957; Secret of the Samurai Sword, 1958; Creole Holiday, 1959; Mystery of the Haunted Pool, 1960; Secret of the Tiger's Eye, 1961; Mystery of the Golden Horn, 1962; Mystery of the Hidden Hand, 1963; Secret of the Emerald Star, 1964; Mystery of the Angry Idol, 1965; Secret of the Spotted Shell, 1967; Secret of Goblin Glen, 1968; The Mystery of the Crimson Ghost, 1969; Secret of the Missing Footprint, 1969; The Vanishing Scarecrow, 1971; Nobody Likes Trina, 1972; Mystery of the Scowling Boy, 1973; Secret of the Haunted Mesa, 1975; Secret of the Stone Face,

1977; romance and mystery novels—Red Is for Murder, 1943, as The Red Carnelian, 1968; The Quicksilver Pool, 1955; The Trembling Hills, 1956; Skye Cameron, 19 7; The Moonflower, 1958, in U.K. as The Mask and the Moonflower, 1960; Thunder Heights, 1960; Blue Fire, 1961; Window on the Square, 1962; Seven Tears for Apollo, 1963; Black Amber, 1964; Sea Jade, 1964; Columbella, 1966; Silverhill, 1967; Hunter's Green 1968; The Winter People, 1969; Lost Island, 1970; Listen for the Whisperer, 1972; Snowfire, 1973; The Turquoise Mask, 1974; Spindrift, 1975; The Golden Unicorn, 1976; The Stone Bull, 1977; The Glass Flame, 1978; Domino, 1979; Poinciana, 1980; Vermilion, 1981; Emerald, 1983; on writing—Writing Juvenile Fiction, 1947, 1960; Writing Juvenile Stories and Novels, 1976; Guide to Fiction Writing, 1982; Rainsong, 1984; Dream of Orchids, 1985; Flaming Tree, 1986; Silversword, 1987; Feather on the Moon, 1988, Rainbow in the Mist, 1989; Grand Master award for lifetime achievement, Mystery Writers of America, 1988. Add: c/o McIntosh and Otis Inc., 310 Madison Ave., New York, N.Y. 10017, U.S.A.

WHITTEMORE, (Edward) Reed (Jr.). American, b. 1919. Poetry, Literature, Essays. Prof. of English, Univ. of Maryland, College Park, since 1968. Ed., Furioso, 1939–53, and Carleton Miscellany, 1960–64, both in Northfield, Minn.; Member of faculty, 1947–62, Chmn. of the English Dept., 1962–64, and Prof. of English, 1962–67, Carleton Coll., Northfield, Minn.; Consultant in Poetry, Library of Congress, Washington, D.C., 1964–65; Bain-Swiggett Lectr., Princeton Univ., N.J., 1967–68; Literary Ed., New Republic mag., Washington, D.C. 1969–73. Consultant in Poetry, Library of Congress, 1984–85. Publs: Heroes and Heroines: Poems, 1947; An American Takes a Walk and Other Poems, 1956; The Self-Made Man and Other Poems, 1959; (ed.) Browning, 1960; The Boy from Iowa: Poems and Essays, 1962; Little Magazines, 1963; The Fascination of the Abomination: Poems, Stories and Essays, 1963; Return, Alpheus: A Poem for the Literary Elders of Phi Beta Kappa, 1965; Ways of Misunderstanding Poetry, 1965; Poems, New and Selected, 1967; From Zero to the Absolute: Essays, 1968; 50 Poems 50, 1970; The Mother's Breast and the Father's House, 1974; William Carlos Williams: Poet from Jersey, 1974; The Poet as Journalist: Life at the New Republic, 1976; The Feel of Rock: Poems of Three Decades, 1982; Pure Lives: The Early Biographers, 1988. Add: 4326 Albion Rd., College Park, Md. 20740, U.S.A.

WHITTEN, Leslie Hunter, Jr. American, b. 1928. Novels/Short stories, Children's fiction, Poetry, Biography, Translations. Senior Investigator, Washington Merry-Go-Round, since 1978 (Chief Asst. to columnist Jack Anderson, 1969–78). With Radio Free Europe, 1951–57, Intnl. News Service, 1957, United Press Intnl., 1958, and Washington Post, Washington, D.C., 1958–63; Asst. Bureau Chief, Washington, D.C., Hearst Newspapers, 1963–69. Publs: Progeny of the Adder, 1965; Moon of the Wolf (in U.K. as Death of the Nurse), 1967; Pinion, the Golden Eagle, 1968; (trans.) The Abyss, by Baudelaire, 1970; F. Lee Bailey, 1971; The Alchemist, 1973; Conflict of Interest, 1976; Sometimes a Hero, 1979; A Washington Cycle, 1979; A Killing Pace, 1983; A Day Without Sunshine, 1985; The Lost Disciple, 1989. Add: 114 Eastmoor Dr., Silver Spring, Md. 20901, U.S.A.

WHITTEN, Norman E., Jr. American, b. 1937. Anthropology/Ethnology. Prof. of Anthropology, Univ. of Illinois, Urbana, since 1970 (Dept Chmn., 1983–86). Asst. Prof., and Assoc. Prof., Washington Univ., St. Louis, 1965–70. Ed., American Ethnologist, 1979–84. Publs: Class, Kinship and Power in an Ecuadorian Town, 1965; (ed. with J.F. Szwed) Afro-American Anthropology, 1970; Black Frontiersmen: A South American Case, 1974; Sacha Runa: Ethnicity and Adaptation of Ecuadorian Jungle Quichua, 1976; Cultural Transformations and Ethnicity in Modern Ecuador, 1981; Transformaciones Culturales y Etnicidad en al Ecuador Contemporaneo, 1982; Temas sobre la Continuidad y Adaptacion Cultural Ecuatoriana, 1984; Amazonia Ecuatoriana: La Otra Cara del Progreso, 1985; (with Dorothea S. Whitten) Art, Knowledge and Health, 1985; Sicnanga Runa: The Other Side of Development in the Amazonian Ecuador, 1985; (with Dorthea S. Whitten) From Myth to Creation: Art of Amazonian Ecuador, 1988. Add: Dept. of Anthropology, Univ. of Illinois, 109 Darenport Hall, 607 S. Mathews, Urbana, Ill. 61801, U.S.A.

WHITTINGHAM, Charles Percival. British, b. 1922. Agriculture/Forestry, Biology, Botany. Prof. of Botany and Dir. of Agricultural Research Council's Unit of Plant Physiology, Imperial Coll., London, 1964–71 (Dean of Royal Coll. of Science, 1968–71); Head of Botany Dept., Rothamstead Experimental Station, Harpenden, Herts., 1971–82. Publs: (with R. Hill) Photosynthesis, 1955, 1977; Chemistry of Plant Processes, 1964; The Mechanism of Photosynthesis, 1974. Add: Red

Cottage, The Green, Brisley, Dereham, Norfolk, England.

WHITTINGTON, Geoffrey. British, b. 1938. Money/Finance. Price Waterhouse Prof. of Financial Accounting, Cambridge Univ., since 1988. Former Sr. Research Officer, Dept. of Applied Economics, and former Fellow and Dir. of studies, Fitzwilliam Coll., Cambridge; Prof. of Accountancy and Finance, Univ. of Edinburgh, 1972–75; Prof. of Accounting and Finance, Dept. of Economics, Univ. of Bristol, 1975–88. Publs: (with A. Singh) Growth, Profitability and Valuation, 1968; Prediction of Profitability, 1971; Inflation Accounting, 1983; (with D. Tweedie) The Debate on Inflation Accounting, 1984; (ed. with R.H. Parker and G.C. Harcourt) Readings in the Concept and Measurement of Income, 1986. Add: Faculty of Economics and Politics, Austin Robinson Bldg., Sidgwick Ave., Cambridge CB3 9DD, England.

WHITTINGTON, Harry (Benjamin). Also writes as Ashley Carter, Tabor Evans, Whit Harrison, Blaine Stevens, and Hallam Whitney. American, b. 1915. Mystery/Crime/Suspense, Westerns/Adventure. Advertising Coywriter, 1933–35; with U.S. Post Office, 1936–45; Ed., Advocate mag., 1938–45; Freelance writer, 1949–68; Screenwriter, Warner Brothers, 1957; Ed./Writer, Rural Electric Admin., U.S. Dept. of Agriculture, 1968–75. Publs: Vengeance Valley, 1945; Slay Ride For a Lady, 1950; Lady Was a Tramp, 1950; Call Me Killer, 1951; Murder Is My Mistress, 1951; Mourn the Hangman, 1951; Swamp Kill, 1951; Married to Murder, 1951; Fires That Destroy, 1951; So Dead My Love, 1952; You'll Die Next, 1953; This Woman Is Mine, 1953; Saddle the Storm, 1954; Naked Island, 1954; Desire in the Dust, 1955; One Got Away, 1955; A Woman on the Place, 1955; Across That River, 1956; Humming Box, 1956; Backwoods Tramp, 1956; Brute in Brass, 1956; Saturday Night Town, 1956; Web of Murder, 1957; Strangers on Friday, 1957; Play for Keeps, 1957; One Deadly Dawn, 1957; Valerie, 1957; Man in the Shadow, 1957; Vengeance Is the Spur, 1958; Ticket to Hell, 1958; Desert Stake-Out, 1958; Heat of Night, 1958; Trouble Rides Tall, 1958; Devil Wears Wings, 1959; Rebel Woman, 1959; Strange Bargain, 1959; Face of the Phantom (screenplay), 1960; Journey into Violence, 1960; Guerrila Girls, 1960; A Night for Screaming, 1960; Hell Can Wait, 1960; Connolly's Woman, 1960; Haven for the Damned, 1961; God's Back Was Turned, 1961; Searching Rider, 1961; Wild Sky, 1962; Don't Speak to Strange Girls, 1963; Fall of the Roman Empire, 1964; High Fury, 1964; Wild Lonesome, 1965; Pain and Pleasure (screenplay), 1966; Doomsday Mission, 1967; Doomsday Affair, 1967; Burden's Mission, 1968; Charro, 1969; as Whit Harrison—Swamp Kill, 1951; Violent Night, 1952; Body and Passion, 1952; Nature Girl, 1952; Sailor's Weekend, 1952; Army Girl, 1952; Girl on Parole, 1952; Rapture Alley, 1952; Shanty Road, 1953; Strip the Town Nakes, 1953; Any Woman He Wanted, 1960; A Woman Possessed, 1960; as Hallam Whitney—Backwoods Hussy, 1952; as Lisa, 1965; Shack Road, 1953; Sinners Club, 1953; City Girl, 1953; Backwoods Shack, 1954; The Wild Seed, 1954; as Ashley Carter—(with Lance Horner) Golden Stud, 1975; Master of Black Oaks, 1976; The Sword of the Golden Stud, 1977; Secret of Blackoaks, 1978; Panama, 1978; Taproots of Falconhurst, 1978; Scandal of Falconhurst, 1980; Heritage of Blackoaks, 1981; Against All Gods, 1982; Rogue of Falconhurst, 1983; Road to Falconhurst, 1983; Farewell to Blackoaks, 1984; as Blaine Stevens—The Outlanders, 1979; Embrace the Wind, 1982; as Tabor Evans—Longarm series, 6 vols., 1981–82. Add: 426-N. Harbor Dr. Indian Rocks Beach, Fla. 34635, U.S.A.

WHITTINGTON, Peter. See MACKAY, James Alexander.

WHITTLE, Peter. New Zealander, b. 1927. Mathematics/Statistics. Churchill Prof. of Mathematics, Univ. of Cambridge, since 1967 (Lectr., 1959–61). Prof. of Mathematical Statistics, Univ. of Manchester, 1961–67. Publs: Hypothesis Testing in Time Series Analysis, 1951; Prediction and Regulation, 1963, 1984; Probability, 1970; Optimisation under Constraints, 1971; Optimisation over Time, 2 vols., 1982–83; Systems in Stochastic Equilibrium, 1986. Add: 268 Queen Edith's Way, Cambridge CB1 4NL, England.

WHITTLE, Tyler. See TYLER-WHITTLE, Michael.

WHITWORTH, John McKelvie. Canadian, b. 1942. Sociology, Theology/Religion. Assoc. Prof. of Sociology, Simon Fraser Univ., Burnaby, B.C., since 1967. Publs: God's Blueprints: A Sociological Study of Three Utopian Sects, 1974. Add: c/o Sociology and Anthropology Dept., Simon Fraser Univ., Burnaby, B.C., Canada.

WHITWORTH, Rex. (Reginald Henry Whitworth). British, b. 1916. History, Biography. Regular Army Officer, 1939–70 (retired as Major Gen.); Bursar and Official Fellow, Exeter Coll., Oxford, 1970–81.

Publs: Field Marshal Lord Ligonier, 1958; The Grenadier Guards, 1974; (ed.) Gunner at Large, 1988. Add: Abbey House Farm, Goosey, Faringdon, Oxon, England.

WHONE, Herbert. British, b. 1925. Poetry, Architecture, Music, Photography. Professional violinist and teacher. *Publs:* The Simplicity of Playing the Violin, 1972; The Hidden Face of Music, 1974; The Essential West Riding, 1975, 1987; The Integrated Violinist, 1976; Church, Monastery, Cathedral, 1977; Nursery Rhymes for Adult Children (poems), 1985; Fountain Abbey, 1987; A Journey among Trees, 1989. Add: 46 Duchy Rd., Harrogate, Yorks., England.

WIAT, Phillippa. Pseud. for Phillippa Ferridge (née Wyatt). British. Historical/Romance. *Publs:* Like as the Roaring Waves, 1972; The Heir of Allington, 1973; The Master of Blandeston Hall, 1973; The Knight of Allington, 1974; The Rebel of Allington, 1974; Lord of the Black Boar, 1975; Sword of Woden, 1975; Lion Without Claws, 1976; The Queen's Fourth Husband, 1976; Tree of Vortigern, 1976; My Lute Be Still, 1977; Sound Now the Passing-Bell, 1977; The Atheling, 1977; Maid of Gold, 1978; Raven in the Wind, 1979; Yet a Lion, 1978; The Four-Poster, 1979; The Golden Chariot, 1979; Westerfalca, 1979; Lord of the Wolf, 1980; Shadow of Samain, 1980; The King's Vengeance, 1981; The Mistletoe Bough, 1981; Bride in Darkness, 1982; Wychwood, 1982; Children of the Spring, 1983; Five Gold Rings, 1983; Carismandua, 1984; Prince of the White Rose, 1984; Queen-Gold;, 1985; Fair Rosamond, 1985; The Grey Goose Wing, 1986; The Whyte Swan, 1986; Wear a Green Kirtle, 1987; The Cloister and the Flame, 1988; Phantasmagoria, 1988. Add: 19 Normandale, Bexhill-on-Sea, East Sussex, TN39 3LU, England.

WICK, Carter. *See* **WILCOX,** Collin.

WICKENS, Peter Charles. Australian, b. 1912. Law. Gen. Mgr., City Mu ual Life Assurance Soc. Ltd., 1970–77, now retired (Assoc. Actuary, 1942–61; Actuary, 1961–70). *Publs:* Law of Life Insurance in Australia, 1948, 5th ed. 1979; The City Mutual Story, 1978; Insurance Institutes in Australia 1884-1984, 1984. Add: 20 Pearl Bay Ave., Mosman, N.S.W. 2088, Australia.

WICKER, Brian John. British, b. 1929. International relations (peace studies), Literature, Philosophy, Theology/Religion. Corresp., Commonweal, NYC, since 1971. Careers Advisory Officer, L.C.C., 1953–56; Asst. Secty., Univ. Appointments Bd., 1956–60, and Sr. Lectr. in English, 1960–68, Univ. of Birmingham; Columnist, The Guardian, 1963–68; Principal, Fircroft Coll., Birmingham, 1930–88. *Publs:* Culture and Liturgy, 1963; God and Modern Philosophy, 1964; Work and the Christian Community, 1964; Culture and Theology (in U.S. as Towards a Contemporary Christianity), 1966; First the Political Kingdom, 1967; (co-ed. and contrib.) From Culture to Revolution, 1968; The Story-Shaped World, 1976; Nuclear Deterrence: What Does the Church Teach?, 1986. Add: "Chimney Pots," 33 Westcroft Rd., Carshalton, Surrey SM5 2TG, England.

WICKER, Tom. (Thomas Grey Wicker). Also writes as Paul Connolly. American, b. 1926. Novels/Short stories, Politics/Government, Social commentary/phenomena, Biography. Columnist, New York Times (Chief, Washington Bureau, 1964–68; Assoc. Ed., 1968–85). Ed., North Carolina Journal, Winston-Salem, 1951–59; Ed., Nashville Tennessean, 1950–60. *Publs:* as Paul Connolly—Get Out of Town, 1951; Tears Are for Angels, 1952; So Fair, So Evil, 1955; as Tom Wicker—The Kingpin, 1953; The Devil Must, 1957; The Judgement, 1961; Kennedy Without Tears, 1964; JFK and LBJ: The Influence of Personality Upon Politics, 1968; Facing the Lions (novel), 1973; A Time to Die, 1975; On Press, 1978; One of Us: The Age of Nixon, 1989. Add: c/o The New York Times, 229 W. 43rd St., New York, N.Y. 10036, U.S.A.

WICKHAM, Edward Ralph. British, b. 1911. Sociology, Theology/Religion, Urban studies. Asst. Bishop, Diocese of Manchester, since 1982. Chaplain, Royal Ordnance Factory, 1941–45; Dir., Sheffield Industrial Mission, 1945–59; Bishop Suffragan of Middleton, 1959–82. *Publs:* Church and People in an Industrial City, 1959; (co-author) The English Church: A New Look, 1966; Encounter with Modern Society, 1964; (co-author) Religion, Culture and Society, 1967; (co-author) All One Body, 1969; Growth and Inflation, 1975; (co-author) Urban Harvest, 1977; Economic Growth, Unemployment, and the Future of Work, 1985. Add: 12 Westminster Rd., Eccles, Manchester, England.

WICKHAM, Glynne (William Gladstone). British, b. 1922. Communications media/Broadcasting, Theatre. Prof. of Drama, Univ. of Bristol, 1960–82, now Emeritus (Asst. Lectr., 1948–51; Lectr., 1951–55; Sr. Lectr., 1955–60). Member, Editorial Cttee., Shakespeare Survey, since

1974; Pres., British Soc. for Theatre Research, since 1978; Trustee, St. Deiniol's Residential Library, Hawthornden, s nce 1985. Gov., Bristol Old Vic Trust, 1963–83; Chmn., Radio West, 1979–84; Member, Culture Advisory Panel, U.K. National Commn. to Unesco, 1984–86. *Publs:* (ed.) The Relationship Between Universities and Radio, Film and Television, 1956; Early English Stages, vol. I, 1959, 1963, vol. 2 (part I), 1963, vol. 2 (part 2), 1972, 1980, vol. 3, 1981; Drama in a World of Science, 1962; Shakespeare's Dramatic Heritage, 1969; The Medieval Theatre, 1974, 3rd ed., 1986; English Moral Interludes, 1975, 1985; (Chmn., Ed. Bd.) The Theatre in Europe: Documents and Sources, 1979; A History of the Theatre, 1985. Add: 6 College Rd., Bristol 8, England.

WICKRAMASINGHE, Nalin Chandra. British, b. 1939. Astronomy, Mathematics, Physics. Prof. of Applied Mathematics and Astronomy, Univ. of Wales, Coll. of Cardiff, since 1988. (joined faculty, 1973). Fellow, 1963–73, and Tutor, 1971–73, Jesus Coll., Cambridge. *Publs:* Interstellar Grains, 1967; Light Scattering Functions with Applications in Astronomy, 1973; The Cosmic Laboratory, 1975; (with D.J. Morgan) Solid State Astrophysics, 1976; Is Life a Cosmic Phenomenon?, 1982; Fundamental Studies and the Future of Science, 1984; with Fred Hoyle—Lifecloud, 1978; Diseases from Space, 1979; Evolution from Space, 1981; Space Travellers, The Bringers of Life, 1981; Why Neo-Darwinism Does Not Work, 1982; Proofs That Life Is Cosmic, 1983; From Grains to Bacteria, 1984; (ed.) Living Comets, 1985; (with J. Watkins) Viruses from Space, 1985; Archaeopteryx—The Primordial Bird: A Case of Fossil Forgery, 1986; Cosmic Life Force, 1988. Add: 24 Llwynypia Rd., Lisvane, Cardiff CF4 5SY, Wales.

WIDEMAN, John Edgar. American, b. 1941. Novels/Short stories, Memoirs. Prof. of English, Univ. of Wyoming, Laramie, since 1975. Member of the English Dept., Howard Univ., Washington, D.C., 1965; Instr. to Assoc. Prof. of English, 1966–74; Asst. Basketball Coach, 1968–72, and Dir. of the Afro-American Studies Program, 1971–73, Univ. of Pennsylvania, Philadelphia. *Publs:* A Glance Away (novel), 1967; Hurry Home (novel), 1970; The Lynchers (novel), 1973; Hiding Place (novel), 1981; Damballah (short stories), 1981; Sent for You Yesterday (novel), 1983; Brothers and Keepers (memoirs), 1984; Reuben, 1987. Add: Dept. of English, Univ. of Wyoming, Laramie, Wyo. 82071, U.S.A.

WIDGERY, Jan. Pseud. for Jeanne-Anna Widgery. American, b. 1920. Novels/Short stories. Instr. of English, Chatham Coll., Pittsburgh, 1947–50; Teacher of Speech, and Dir. of Drama, Ellis Sch., Pittsburgh, 1956–60; Chmn., English Dept., Winchester-Thurston Sch., Pittsburgh, 1960–75; Lectr., Univ. of Houston, Texas, 1976; Staff, Southwest Writers Conference, Houston, 1976. Pres., Houston Harpischord Soc., 1981–82; Vice-Pres., American Assn. of Univ. Women, West Harris, 1981–83. *Publs:* The Adversary, 1966; Trumpet at the Gates, 1970. Add: Dept. of English, Univ. of Alberta, Edmonton, Canada.

WIEBE, Rudy. Canadian, b. 1934. Novels/Short stories. Prof. of English, Univ. of Alberta, Edmonton (joined faculty, 1967). Ed., The Mennonite Brethren Herald, Winnipeg, 1962–63; Asst. Prof. of English, Goshen Coll., Ind., 1963–67. *Publs:* Peace Shall Destroy Many, 1962; First and Vital Candle, 1966; The Blue Mountains of China, 1970; (ed.) The Story-Makers: A Collection of Modern Short Stories, 1970; (ed.) Stories from Western Canada: A Selection, 1972; The Temptations of Big Bear, 1973; Where Is the Voice Coming From? (short stories), 1974; (ed.) Double Vision (short story anthology), 1976; The Scorched-Wood People, 1977; As Far as the Eye Can See (play), 1977; Alberta: A Celebration (short stories), 1979; The Mad Trapper, 1980; A Voice in the Land, 1981; The Angel of the Tar Sands and Other Stories, 1982; My Lovely Enemy, 1983. Add: 5315-143 St., Edmonton, Alta. T6H 4E3 Canada.

WIEGAND, William (George). American, b. 1928. Novels/Short stories, Mystery/Crime/Suspense. Prof. of English and Creative Writing, San Francisco State Univ., since 1972 (Asst. Prof., 1962–67; Assoc. Prof., 1967–72). *Publs:* At Last, Mr. Tolliver (mystery novel), 1950; The Treatment Man (novel), 1959; The School of Soft Knocks (novel), 1968; (ed., with Richard Kraus) Student's Choice, 1970; The Chester A. Arthur Conspiracy (novel), 1983. Add: Dept. of Creative Writing, San Francisco State Univ., 1600 Holloway Ave., San Francisco, Calif. 94132, U.S.A.

WIENER, Joel Howard. American, b. 1937. History. Prof. of History, City Coll. of New York, since 1967. *Publs:* The War of the Unstamped, 1969; A Descriptive Finding List of Unstamped British Periodicals, 1970; (ed.) Great Britain: Foreign Policy and the Span of Empire, 4 vols., 1972; (ed.) Great Britain: The Lion at Home, 4 vols., 1974; Radicalism and Freethought in Nineteenth-Century Britain, 1983; (ed.) Innovators and Preachers: The Role of the Editor in Victorian

England, 1985; (ed.) Papers for the Millions: The New Journalism in Britain 1850s to 1914, 1988; William Lovett, 1989. Add: 267 Glen Ct., Teaneck, N.J., U.S.A.

WIENER, Philip Paul. American, b. 1905. Philosophy. Prof. of Philosophy, Temple Univ., Philadelphia. Exec. Ed. Emeritus, Journal of the History of Ideas; Ed.-in-Chief, Dictionary of the History of Ideas. Chmn., Philosophy Dept., City Coll. of New York, 1959–65. *Publs:* Evolution and the Founders of Pragmatism, 1949; Leibniz, 1951; Readings in the Philosophy of Science, 1953; (trans.) Duhem's Aim and Structure of Physical Theory, 1954; (ed.) Roots of Scientific Thought, 1957; (ed.) Nakamura's Ways of Thinking of Eastern Peoples, 1965; (ed.) Charles S. Peirce: Selected Writings, 1966; (co-author) Basic Problems of Philosophy, 4th ed. 1972; (co-ed.) Violence and Aggression in the History of Ideas, 1974; (ed.) Dictionary of the History of Ideas, 1980. Add: 7608 Louise Lane, Wyndmoor, Pa. 19118, U.S.A.

WIENERS, John (Joseph). American, b. 1934. Plays/Screenplays, Poetry, Literature. Co-Founding Ed., Measure, Boston, since 1957. Library Clerk, Lamont Library, Harvard Univ., Cambridge, Mass., 1955–57; Actor and Stage Mgr., Poets Theater, Cambridge, 1956; Asst. Bookkeeper, 8th St. Bookshop, NYC, 1962–63; Subscriptions Ed., Jordon Marsh Co., Boston, 1963–65. *Publs:* The Hotel Wentley Poems, 1958, rev. ed. 1965; Still-Life (play), 1961; Asphodel in Hell's Despite (play), 1963; Ace of Pentacles, 1964; Chinoiserie, 1965; Hart Crane, Harry Crosby, I See You Going over the Edge, 1966; Anklesox and Five Shoelaces (play), 1966; King Solomon's Magnetic Quiz, 1967; Pressed Water, 1967; Selected Poems, 1968; Unhired, 1968; A Letter to Charles Olson, 1968; Asylum Poems, 1969; Untitled Essay on Frank O'Hara, 1969; A Memory of Black Mountain College, 1969; Nerves, 1970; Youth, 1970; Selected Poems, 1972; Woman, 1972; The Lanterns along the Wall, 1972; Playboy, 1972; We Were There!, 1972; Holes, 1974; Behind the State Capitol; or, Cincinnati Pike: A Collection of Poetry, 1975; Collected Poems 1950-1984, 1985; Cultural Affairs in Boston: Poetry and Prose 1956-85, 1988. Add: Raymond Foye Editions, Chelsea Hotel, 222 W. 23rd St., No. 807, New York, N.Y. 10011, U.S.A.

WIER, Ester (Alberti). American, b. 1910. Children's fiction, social commentary/phenomena. *Publs:* The Answer Book on Naval (and Air Force) Social Customs, 2 vols., 1956–57; Army Social Customs, 1958; What Every Air Force Wife Should Know, 1958; The Loner, 1963; Gift of the Mountains, 1963; The Rumptydoolers, 1964; Easy Does It, 1965; The Barrel, 1966; The Wind Chasers, 1967; The Winners, 1967; The Space Hut, 1967; Action at Paradise Marsh, 1968; The Long Year, 1969; The Straggler, 1970; The White Oak, 1971; The Partners, 1972; The Hunting Trail, 1974; The King of the Mountain, 1975. Add: 2534 S.W. 14th Drive, Gainesville, Fla., 32608, U.S.A.

WIESEL, Elie. American (born Rumanian), b. 1928. Novels/Short stories, Plays/Screenplays, Theology/Religion, Documentaries/Reportage, Essays. Andrew W. Mellon Prof. in the Humanities, Univ. Prof., and Prof. of Religion, Boston Univ., since 1976; also, Journalist for Israeli, French and American newspapers, Chmn., President's Commn. on the Holocaust, and U.S. Holocaust Memorial Council; Member, Bd. of Dirs., National Cttee. on American Foreign Policy; Member, Bd. of Govs., Oxford Centre for Postgrad. Hebrew Studies, Ben-Gurion Univ. of the Negev, Haifa Univ., Tel-Aviv Univ., and Bar-Ilan Univ.; Trustee, Yeshiva Univ.; Honorary Chmn., National Jewish Resource Center. Distinguished Prof. of Judaic Studies, City Coll., City Univ. of New York, 1972–76; Henry Luce Visiting Scholar in the Humanities and Social Thought, Whitney Humanities Center, Yale Univ., New Haven, Conn., 1982–83. Recipient, Congressional Gold Medal, 1984. *Publs:* Night (memoir), 1960; Dawn (novel), 1961; The Accident (novel), 1962; The Town Beyond the Wall (novel), 1964; The Gates of the Forest (novel), 1966; The Jews of Silence (personal testimony), 1966; Legends of Our Time (essays and stories), 1968; A Beggar in Jerusalem (novel), 1970; One Generation After (essays and stories), 1971; Souls on Fire: Portraits and Legends of the Hasidic Masters, 1972; The Oath (novel), 1973; Ani Maamin (cantata), 1973; Zalmen; or, The Madness of God (play), 1975; Messengers of God: Portraits and Legends of Biblical Heroes, 1976; Four Hasidic Masters, 1978; A Jew Today (essays; stories; dialogues), 1978; The Trial of God (play), 1979; The Testament (novel), 1980; Images from the Bible, 1980; Five Biblical Portraits, 1981; So ewhere a Master (Hasidic tales), 1982; Paroles d'étranger (essays; stories; dialogues), 1982; The Golem (retelling of legend), 1983; Le Cinquigme File (novel), 1983; The Fifth Son, 1984; Twilight, 1988. Add: 745 Commonwealth Ave., Boston, Mass. 02215, U.S.A.

WIESENFARTH, Joseph (John). American, b. 1933. Literary

criticism (theory). Prof. of English, Univ. of Wisconsin, Madison, since 1976 (Assoc. Prof., 1970–76; Dept. Chmn., 1983–86). Asst. Prof., La Salle Coll., Philadelphia, Pa., 1962–64; Asst. Prof., 1964–67, and Assoc. Prof., 1967–70, Manhattan Coll., Bronx, N.Y. *Publs:* Henry James and the Dramatic Analogy, 1963; The Errand of Form (on Jane Austen's novels), 1967; George Eliot's Mythmaking, 1977; George Eliot: A Writer's Notebook 1854-1879, 1981; Gothic Manners and the Classic English Novel, 1988. Add: Dept. of English, 600 N. Park St., Univ. of Wisconsin, Madison, Wisc. 53706, U.S.A.

WIEST, Grace L. *See* **DELOUGHERY,** Grace L.

WIGAN, Christopher. *See* **BINGLEY,** David Ernest.

WIGGINS, David. British, b. 1933. Philosophy. Fellow, and Praelector in Philosophy, University Coll., Oxford, since 1981. Asst. Principal, Colonial Office, 1957–58; Lectr. and Fellow, New Coll., Oxford, 1959–67; Prof. of Philosophy, Bedford Coll., London, 1967–80. *Publs:* Identity and Spatio-Temporal Continuity, 1967; Truth, Invention, and the Meaning of Life, 1977; Sameness and Substance, 1980; Needs, Values, Truth, 1987. Add: University Coll., Oxford, England.

WIGHAM, Eric (Leonard). British, b. 1904. Industrial relations. Reporter, North Mail, and the Newcastle Chronicle, 1925–29, and the Evening World, Newcastle-upon-Tyne, 1929–32; Reporter, Film Critic, Literary Ed., and Leader Writer, Manchester office, 1932–40, and London Office, 1940–44, Manchester Evening News; War Corresp. in Northern Europe for Manchester Evening News, and The Observer, 1944–45; Labour Corresp., Manchester Guardian, 1945–46, and The Times, London, 1946–69. Member, Royal Commn. on Trade Union and Employers' Assn., 1965–68. *Publs:* Trade Unions, 1956, 1969; What's Wrong With the Unions?, 1961; The Power to Manage: A History of the Engineering Employers' Federation, 1973; Strikes and the Government 1893-1974, 1976; From Humble Petition to Militant Action: A History of the Civil and Public Services Association, 1980; Strikes and the Government 1893-1981, 1982. Add: 29 Priory Lodge, 49a Glebeway, West Wickham, Kent BR4 9HP, England.

WIKE, Edward L. American, b. 1922. Mathematics/Statistics, Psychology. Prof. Emeritus of Psychology, Univ. of Kansas, Lawrence, since 1987 (Asst. Prof., 1952–57; Assoc. Prof., 1957–62; Prof., 1962–87). Visiting Assoc. Prof., Univ.of California, Los Angeles, 1958. *Publs:* Secondary Reinforcement: Selected Experiments, 1966; Data Analysis: A Statistical Primer for Psychology Students, 1971; Numbers: A Primer of Data Analysis, 1985. Add: 3411 W. 8th St., Lawrence, Kans. 66044, U.S.A.

WILBER, Donald Newton. American, b. 1907. Area studies. *Publs:* Iran Past and Present, 1948, 9th ed. 1981; The Architecture of Islamic Iran: The Il Khanid Period, 1955; (ed. and contrib.) Afghanistan, 2 vols., 1956; Annotated Bibliography of Afghanistan, 1956, 3rd ed. 1968; (trans.) Iran Past and Present, 1958; (ed. and contrib.) Afghanistan: Its People, Its Society, Its Culture, 1962; Persian Gardens and Garden Pavilions, 1962, 1979; Contemporary Iran, 1963; The Land and People of Ceylon, 1963, 1972; Pakistan Yesterday and Today, 1964; (ed. and contrib.) Pakistan: Its People, Its Society, Its Culture, 1964; (ed. and contrib.) The Nations of Asia, 1966; (trans.) The Land and People of Ceylon, 1967; Persepolis: The Archaeology of Parsa, Seat of the Persian Kings, 1969, 1989; (ed. and contrib.) UAR (Egypt): Its People, Its Society, Its Culture, 1969; (trans.) Persian Gardens and Garden Pavilions, 1969; Four Hundred Forty-Six Kings of Iran, 1972; (with M. Dimand) L'Arte dell'Islam, 1972; The Bronze Makers, 1974; Riza Shah Pahlavi: The Resurrection and Reconstruction of Iran, 1975; (with L. Golombek) The Timurid Architecture of Iran and Turan, 1986; Adventures in the Middle East, 1986. Add: 41-10 Meadow Lakes, Hightstown, N.J. 08520, U.S.A.

WILBUR, Richard (Purdy). American, b. 1921. Songs, lyrics and libretti, Poetry, Literature, Translations. Gen. Ed., Laurel Poets series, Dell Publishing Co., NYC. Member of the Soc. of Fellows, 1947–50, and Asst. Prof. of English, 1950–54, Harvard Univ., Cambridge, Mass.; Assoc. Prof. of English, Wellesley Coll., Mass., 1955–57; Prof. of English, Wesleyan Univ., Middleton, Conn., 1957–77; Writer-in-Residence, Smith Coll., Northampton, Mass., 1977–86. Former Pres. and Chancellor, American Academy of Arts and Letters. *Publs:* The Beautiful Changes and Other Poems, 1947; Ceremony and Other Poems, 1950; (trans.) The Misanthrope, by Molière, 1955; (ed. with Louis Untermeyer and Karl Shapiro) Modern American and Modern British Poetry, 1955; (ed.) A Bestiary (anthology), 1955; (with Lillian Hellman) Candide (comic operetta), 1956; Things of This World: Poems, 1956, one section reprinted as Digging to China, 1970; Poems 1943-1956, 1957; (ed.) Complete Poems of Poe, 1959; (with L. Bogan and Archibald MacLeish) Emily Dickinson, 1960; Advice to a Prophet and Other Poems, 1961; The Poems of Richard Wilbur, 1963; The Pelican from a Bestiary of 1120, 1963; Prince Souvanna Phouma: An Exchange Between Richard Wilbur and William Jay Smith, 1963; (trans.) Tartuffe, by Molière, 1963; Loudmouse, 1963; (ed. with A. Harbage) Poems of Shakespeare, 1966, rev. ed. as The Narrative Poems, and Poems of Doubtful Authenticity, 1974; Complaint, 1968; Walking to Sleep: New Poems and Translations, 1969; Opposites, 1973; (trans.) School for Wives, by Molière, 1971; Seed Leaves, 1974; The Mind Reader (poems), 1976; Responses: Prose Pieces 1953-1976, 1976; (trans.) The Learned Ladies, by Molière, 1978; (ed.) Selected Poems of Witter Bynner, 1978; (with William Jay Smith) Verses on the Times, 1978; Seven Poems, 1981; (trans.) Andromache, by Racine, 1982; (trans.) Molière: Four Comedies, 1982; (trans.) The Whale, 1982; (trans.) Phaedra, by Racine, 1986; New and Collected Poems, 1988. Recipient of: National Book Award, 1957; Pulitzer Prize, 1957; Harriet Monroe Poetry Prize, 1978; PEN Translation Prize, 1983. Add: R.R.1, Box 82, Dodwells Rd., Cummington, Mass. 01026, U.S.A.

WILBY, Basil Leslie. Also writes as Gareth Knight. British, b. 1930. Paranormal. Publishing Mgr., Longman Group Ltd., Harlow, since 1976 (Univ. Sales Mgr., 1970–76). *Publs:* (as Gareth Knight) A Practical Guide to Qabalistic Symbolism, 1965; (ed.) The New Dimensions Red Book, 1968; (as Gareth Knight) The Practice of Ritual Magic, 1969; (as Gareth Knight) Occult Exercises and Practices, 1969; Meeting the Occult, 1973; (as Gareth Knight) Experience of the Inner Worlds, 1975; (as Gareth Knight) The Occult—An Introduction, 1975; (as Gareth Knight) A History of White Magic, 1979; (as Gareth Knight) The Secret Tradition in Arthurian Legend, 1983; (as Gareth Knight) The Rose Cross and the Goddess, 1985; (as Gareth Knight) The Gareth Knight Tarot Deck, 1985; (as Gareth Knight) The Treasure House of Images, 1986. Add: 8 Acorn Ave., Braintree, Essex, England.

WILCOX, Collin. Also writes as Carter Wick. American, b. 1924. Mystery/Crime/Suspense. Full-time writer since 1970. Teacher at the Town Sch., San Francisco, 1950–53; Partner, Amthor and Co., furniture store, San Francisco, 1953–55; Owner, Collin Wilcox Lamps, San Francisco, 1955–70. Regional Vice-Pres., 1975, and Member, Bd. of Dirs., 1976, Mystery Writers of America. *Publs:* The Black Door, 1967; The Third Figure, 1968; The Lonely Hunter, 1969; The Disappearance, 1970; Dead Aim, 1971; Hiding Place, 1973; McCloud, 1973; Long Way Down, 1974; The New Mexico Connection, 1974; Aftershock, 1975; (as Carter Wick) The Faceless Man, 1975; The Third Victim, 1976; Doctor, Lawyer..., 1977; The Watcher, 1978; (with Bill Pronzini) Twospot, 1978; Power Plays, 1979; Mankiller, 1980; Spellbinder, 1980; Stalking Horse, 1981; Dark House, Dark Road, 1982; Swallow's Fall, 1983; Victims, 1985; Night Games, 1986; The Pariah, 1988; Bernhardt's Edge, 1988. Add: 4174 26th St., San Francisco, Calif. 94131, U.S.A.

WILD, Peter. American, b. 1940. Poetry. Assoc. Prof. to Prof. of English, Univ. of Arizona, Tucson, since 1971. Asst. Prof. of English, Sul Ross State Univ., Alpine, Tex., 1969–71. *Publs:* The Good Fox, 1967; Sonnets, 1967; The Afternoon in Dismay, 1968; Mica Mountain Poems, 1968; Joining Up and Other Poems, 1968; Mad Night with Sunflowers, 1968; Love Poems, 1969; Three Nights in Chiricahuas, 1969; Poems, 1969; Fat Man Poems, 1970; Terms and Renewals, 1970; Grace, 1971; Wild's Magical Book of Cranial Effusions, 1971; Peligros, 1972; New and Selected Poems, 1973; Cochise, 1973; The Cloning, 1974; Tumacacori, 1974; Chihuahua, 1976; House Fires, 1977; Barn Fires, 1978; Pioneer Conservationists of Western America, 1979; Jeanne d'Arc: A Collection of New Poems, 1979; The Lost Tribe, 1971; Enos Mills, 1979; Wilderness, 1980; Getting Ready for a Date, 1984. Add: 1547 East Lester, Tucson, Ariz. 85719, U.S.A.

WILDEN, Anthony. Canadian, b. 1935. Communications/Media, Language/Linguistics, Philosophy, Psychology, Social sciences. Prof. of Communications, Simon Fraser Univ., Burnaby, since 1974; also television scriptwriter and producer. Corresponding Ed., Dialectical Anthropology, New York, since 1976; Assoc., The Behavioral and Brain Sciences, Princeton, N.J., since 1978; Member, Intnl. Advisory Bd., Recherches Sémiotiques/Semiotic Inquiry, Toronto, since 1980. Asst. Prof. of Literature, Univ. of California, San Diego, 19680–74; Visiting Prof., Ecole Pratique des Hautes Etudes, Univ. of Paris, France, 1971–72; Research Assoc., National Science Foundn., Michigan State Univ., East Lansing, 1973–74; Visiting Prof. in Ecology and Society, Western Washington State Coll., Bellingham, 1976; Visiting Prof. of Comparative Literature, Univ. of British Columbia, Vancouver, 1977. *Publs:* (with Jacques Lacan) The Language of the Self, 1968, as Speech and Language

in Psychoanalysis, 1981; System and Structure: Essays in Communication and Exchange, 1972, 1980, 3rd ed. (in French), 1983; Le Canada Imaginaire, 1979; The Imaginary Canadian, An Examination for Discovery, 1980; Greetings from Canada: This Is a Talking Picture, 1980; The Rules Are No Game: The Strategy of Communication, 1985; Man and Woman, War and Peace: The Strategist's Companion, 1985. Add: Dept. of Communications, Simon Fraser Univ., Burnaby B.C. V5A 1S6, Canada.

WILDER, Cherry. Pseud. for Cherry Barbara Lockett Grimm. New Zealander, b. 1930. Science fiction/Fantasy, Children's fiction. Lived in Australia, 1954–76: high sch. teacher, editorial asst., theatre dir., regular reviewer for Sydney Morning Herald, and The Australian newspapers, 1964–74. *Publs:* The Luck of Brin's Five, 1977; The Nearest Fire, 1980; Second Nature, 1982; The Tapestry Warriors, 1983; A Princess of the Chameln, 1984; Yorath the Wolf, 1984; The Summer's Kings, 1985; Cruel Designs, 1988. Add: Egelsbacher Str., 6070 Langen/Hessen, West Germany.

WILDING, Griseda. *See* MCCUTCHEON, Hugh Davie-Martin.

WILDING, Michael. British, b. 1942. Novels/Short stories, Literature. Reader in English, Univ. of Sydney, since 1972 (Lectr., 1963–66; Sr. Lectr., 1969–72). Asst. Lectr. then Lectr., Dept. of English, Univ. of Birmingham, 1967–68. Ed., Tabloid Story, 1972–76; Dir., Wild & Woolley Pty. Ltd., 1974–79. *Publs:* (ed. with Charles Higham) Australians Abroad, 1967; (ed.) Three Tales, by Henry James, 1967; Milton's Paradise Lost, 1969; (ed.) Marvell: Modern Judgments, 1969; (with Michael Green and Richard Hoggart) Cultural Policy in Great Britain, 1970; (ed.) The Tragedy of Julius Caesar and Marcus Brutus, by John Sheffield, 1970; (ed. with Shirley Cass, Ros Cheney and David Malouf) We Took Their Orders and Are Dead, 1971; Aspects of the Dying Process, 1972; Living Together, 1974; The Short Story Embassy, 1975; The West Midland Underground, 1975; Scenic Drive, 1976; (ed.) The Portable Marcus Clarke, 1976; Marcus Clarke, 1977; (co-ed.) The Radical Reader, 1977; The Phallic Forest, 1978; (ed.) The Tabloid Story Pocket Book, 1978; Political Fictions, 1980; Pacific Highway, 1982; Reading the Signs, 1984; The Paraguayan Experiment, 1985; The Man of Slow Feeling, 1985; Dragons Teeth: Literature in the English Revolution, 1987; Under Saturn, 1988. Add: Dept. of English, Univ. of Sydney, Sydney, N.S.W. 2006, Australia.

WILES, Maurice Frank. British, b. 1923. Theology/Religion. Regius Prof. of Divinity, Univ. of Oxford, since 1970. Lectr. in Divinity, and Dean, Clare Coll., Cambridge, 1959–67; Prof. of Christian Doctrine, King's Coll., Univ. of London, 1967–70. *Publs:* The Spiritual Gospel, 1960; The Christian Fathers, 1966; The Divine Apostle, 1967; The Making of Christian Doctrine, 1967; The Remaking of Christian Doctrine, 1974; (with M. Santer) Documents in Early Christian Thought, 1975; What Is Theology?, 1976; Working Papers in Doctrine, 1976; Theological Explorations 4, 1979; Faith and the Mystery of God, 1982; God's Action in the World, 1986. Add: Christ Church, Oxford, England.

WILEY, Margaret L. *See* MARSHALL, Margaret Lenore.

WILGUS, D. K. American, b. 1918. Language/Linguistics, Literature, Music, Mythology/Folklore. Prof. of English and Anglo-American Folksong, Univ. of Califor ia, Los Angeles, since 1962. Assoc. Prof., 1950–60, Prof. of English and Folklore, 1960–62, Western Kentucky Univ., Bowling Green. *Publs:* Anglo-American Folksong Scholarship since 1898, 1959; Folklore International, 1967; (ed.) Folk-Songs of the Southern United States, by Josiah Combs, 1967. Add: Folklore and Mythology Prog., Univ. of California, Los Angeles, Calif. 90024, U.S.A.

WILHELM, Kate. American, b. 1928. Novels/Short stories, Science fiction/Fantasy. Lectr., Clarion Fantasy Workshop, Tulane Univ., New Orleans, 1968–80; Co-Dir., Milford Science Fiction Writers Conference, 1963–72. *Publs:* The Mile-Long Spaceship (anthology), 1963 (in U.K. as Andover and the Android, 1966); More Bitter Than Death, 1963; (with Theodore Thomas) The Clone, 1965; The Nevermore Affair, 1966; The Killer Thing, 1967 (in U.K. as The Killing Thing); The Downstairs Room and Other Speculative Fiction (anthology), 1968; Let the Fire Fall, 1969; (with Theodore L. Thomas) The Year of the Cloud, 1970; Abyss: Two Novellas, 1971; City of Cain, 1974; (ed.) Nebula Award Stories Nine, 1974; The Infinity Box (anthology), 1975; The Clewiston Test, 1976; Where Late the Sweet Birds Sang, 1976; Fault Lines, 1977; (ed.) Clarion SF (anthology), 1977; Somerset Dreams and Other Fictions, 1978; Juniper Time, 1979; (with Damon Knight) Better Than One (anthology), 1980; A Sense of Shadow, 1981; Listen, Listen, 1981; Oh, Susannah!, 1982; Welcome, Chaos, 1983; Huysmans' Pets, 1986; The Hamlet Trap, 1987; Crazy Time, 1988; Dark Door, 1988; Smart House, 1989. Add: 1645

Horn Lane, Eugene, Ore. 97404, U.S.A.

WILKINSON, (J.) Burke. American, b. 1913. Novels/Short stories, Biography. Contributing Reviewer, Christian Science Monitor, since 1972. Deputy Asst. Secty. of State, 1956–58; Public Affairs Adviser, SHAPE, 1958–62. *Publs:* Proceed at Will, 1948; Run, Mongoose, 1950; Last Clear Chance, 1954; By Sea and Stealth (awarded Italian Order of Merit), 1956; Night of the Short Knives, 1962; The Helmet of Navarre, 1965; The Adventures of Geoffrey Mildmay, 1969; Cardinal in Armor, 1966; Young Louis XIV, 1969; (ed.) Cry Spy!, 1969; Francis in All His Glory, 1972; (ed.) Cry Sabotage!, 1972; The Zeal of the Convert, 1976; Uncommon Clay: The Life and Works of Augustus Saint Gaudens, 1985. Add: 3210 Scott Pl. N.W., Washington, D.C. 20007, U.S.A.

WILKINSON, (Sir) Denys (Haigh). British, b. 1922. Physics. Ed., Oxford Studies in Physics (formerly Oxford Library of the Physical Sciences), since 1957, and Intnl. Monographs on Physics, since 1960. Demonstrator, 1947–51, Lectr., 1951–56, and Reader in Nuclear Physics, 1956–57, Cambridge Univ.; Prof. of Experimental Physics and Head of Nuclear Physics Lab., Oxford Univ., 1957–76; Vice-Chancellor, Univ. of Sussex, 1976–87. Ed., Progress in Particle and Nuclear Physics, 1976–84; Vice-Chancellor, Univ. of Sussex, 1976–87. *Publs:* Ionization Chambers and Counters, 1950; (ed.) Isospin in Nuclear Physics, 1969; (ed.) Mesons in Nuclei, 1979. Add: Univ. of Sussex, Falmer, Brighton, Sussex BN1 9QH, England.

WILKINSON, John (Donald). British, b. 1929. Archaeology/Antiquities, Theology/Religion. Fellow, Dumbarton Oaks Center for Byzantine Studies, since 1985. Former Gen. Ed., United Soc. for the Propagation of the Gospel, U.K.; Tutor, 1961–63, and Dean of Studies, 1969, St. George's Coll., Jerusalem; Bishops' Dir. of Clergy Training, London Diocese, 1975–79; Dir., British Sch. of Archaeology, Jerusalem, 1979–85. *Publs:* No Apology, 1961; Interpretation and Community, 1963; (ed.) Mutual Responsibility, Questions and Answers, 1964; The Supper and the Eucharist, 1965; (ed.) Catholic Anglicans Today, 1968; (trans.) Egeria's Travels, 1971, as Egeria's Travels to the Holy Land, 1981; Jerusalem Pilgrims Before the Crusades, 1978; Jerusalem as Jesus Knew it, 1978; Health and Healing: Studies in New Testament Principles, 1980. Add: 1703 32nd St. N.W., Washington D.C. 20007, U.S.A.

WILKINSON, Paul. British, b. 1937. International relations/Current affairs, Politics/Government, Social commentary/phenomena, Sociology. Prof. of Intnl. Relations, since 1979, and Head of Dept. of Politics and Intnl. Relations, Univ. of Aberdeen. Ed., Terrorism and Political Violence, since 1988. Regular officer, R.A.F., 1959–65; Asst. Lectr., Lectr., then Sr. Lectr. in Politics, University Coll., Cardiff, 1966–77; Reader, Univ. of Wales, 1978–79. Editorial Adviser, Contemporary Review, since 1980; Member, Editorial Bd., Conflict Quarterly, since 1980; Civilian Consultant, Police Staff Coll., Bramshill; Special Consultant, CBS, New York, since 1986; Chmn. of Trustees, Research Foundn. for the Study of Terrorism, since 1986; Member, Academic Advisory Council, Hughenden Foundn., since 1986; Hon. Fellow, University Coll., Swansea, since 1986. *Publs:* Social Movement, 1971; Political Terrorism, 1974; Terrorism versus Liberal Democracy, 1976; Terrorism and the Liberal State, 1977, 1986; (co-author) Terrorism: Theory and Practice, 1978; (ed.) British Perspectives on Terrorism, 1981; The New Fascists, 1981, 1983; One Last Chance, 1987; (ed.) Contemporary Research on Terrorism, 1988; (ed.) Product Adulteration and Extortion, 1989; Defence of the West, 1989. Add: Univ. of Aberdeen, Edward Wright Bldg., Dunbar St., Old Aberdeen AB9 2UB, Scotland.

WILKINSON, Sylvia J. American, b. 1940. Novels/Short stories, Education, Sports (antomobiles, racing). Writer-in-Residence, Sweet Briar Coll., Hollins Coll., and Richmond Humanities Center, all Va., since 1970. Instr. in English, Art, and Drama, Univ. of North Carolina, Asheville, 1963–65; Instr. in English and Creative Writing, Coll. of William & Mary, 1966–67; Lectr. in Creative Writing and Visiting Writer, Univ. of North Carolina, Chapel Hill, 1967–70; Visiting Writer, Washington Coll., 1984, and Univ. of Wisconsin, Milwaukee, 1985. *Publs:* Moss on the North Side, 1966; A Killing Frost, 1967; Cale, 1970; Change, 1971; The Stainless Steel Carrot, 1973; Shadow of the Mountain, 1977; Bone of My Bones, 1980; Dirt Tracks to Glory, 1983; World of Racing, 10 vols., 1981–85; Automobiles, 1982. Add: 514 Arena St., El Sequndo, Calif. 90245, U.S.A.

WILKINSON, Tim. (Percy Francis Hamilton Wilkinson). British, b. 1912. Recreation/Leisure/Hobbies, Autobiography/Memoirs/Personal. Licensed Victualler in Cornwall and Berks., 1950–62. *Publs:* Hold on

a Minute, 1965; We Ran A Cornish Pub, 1967; Motor Caravanning, 1968. Add: 6 Hartland Rd., Hampton Hill, Middx. TW12 1DT, England.

WILKINSON, Winifred. *See* **HAUSMANN,** Winifred Wilkinson.

WILKINSON-LATHAM, Robert John. British, b. 1943. Antiques/Furnishings, History. Asst. Advertising Mgr., 1963–66, and Mgr., West End Showroom, London, 1966–67, Wilkinson Sword Ltd.; Dir., Regimental, military antique shop, London, 1967–68; Group Editorial Dir., Hobgate Group, 1978–79. *Publs:* British Military Bayonets, 1967; (with C. Wilkinson-Latham) Cavalry Uniforms of Britain and the Commonwealth, 1969; (with C. Wilkinson-Latham) Infantry Uniforms of Britain and the Commonwealth, Book I, 1969, Book II, 1970; (with C. Wilkinson-Latham) Home Service Helmet, 1970; Discovering Artillery, 1972; Discovering British Military Badges and Buttons, 1973; Discovering Famous Battles: The Peninsula War, 1973; Life Lines: Lord Kitchener, 1973; Pictorial History of Swords and Bayonets, 1973; British Artillery on Land and Sea 1790-1820, 1973; Crimean Uniforms No. 2: British Artillery, 1974; Napoleon's Artillery, 1974; Scottish Uniforms, 1975; Sudan, 1976; Royal Navy, 1976; North West Frontier, 1976; History of Cycles, 1978; Swords and Edged Weapons, 1978; Antique Guns 1265-1865, 1978; From Our Special Correspondent: Victorian War Correspondents and Their Campaigns, 1979; Uniforms and Weapons of the Crimean War, 1980; Guide to Antique Weapons and Armour, 1981; Artillery, 1987. Add: c/o Phaidon Press, Musterlin House, Jordan Hill Rd., Oxford OX2 8DP, England.

WILL, George F. American, b. 1941. Politics/Government, Social commentary. Washington Ed., National Review, since 1972, and Political Columnist, Washington Post and Newsweek magazine. *Publs:* (ed.) Press, Politics and Popular Government, 1972; The Pursuit of Happiness and Other Sobering Thoughts, 1979; The Pursuit of Virtue and Other Tory Notions, 1982; Statecraft as Soulcraft: What Government Does, 1984. Recipient, Pulitzer Prize for Commentary, 1977. Add: c/o Washington Post, 1150 15th St. N.W., Washington, D.C. 20071, U.S.A.

WILLARD, Barbara. British, b. 1909. Novels/Short stories, Children's fiction. *Publs:* novels—(with Elizabeth Helen Devas) Love in Ambush, 1930; Ballerina, 1931; Candle Flame, 1932; Name of Gentleman, 1933; Joy Befall Thee, 1934; As Far as in Me Lies, 1936; The Dogs Do Bark, 1938; Set Piece, 1938; Personal Effects, 1939; Portrait of Philip, 1950; Proposed and Seconded, 1951; Celia Scarfe, 1951; Echo Answers, 1952; He Fought for His Queen, 1954; Winter in Disguise, 1958; children's fiction—Snail and the Pennithornes, 1957; Snail and the Pennithornes Next Time, 19587; Son of Charlemagne, 1959; The House with Roots, 1959; Snail and the Pennithornes and the Princess, 1960; The Dippers and Jo, 1960; Eight for a Secret, 1960; The Penny Pony, 1961; If All the Swords in England, 1961; The Pram Race, 1961; Stop the Train, 1961; The Summer with Spike, 1961; Duck on a Pond, 1962; Hetty, 1962; Augustine Came to Kent, 1963; The Battle of Wednesday Week, 1963 (in U.S. as Storm from the West, 1964); The Dippers and the High-Flying Kite, 1963; The Suddenly Gang, 1963; A Dog and a Half, 1964; Three and One to Carry, 1964; The Wild Idea, 1965; Charity at Home, 1965; Surprise Island, 1966; The Richleighs of Tantamount, 1966; The Grove of Green Holly (in U.S. as Flight to the Forest), 1967; The Pet Club, 1967; To London! To London!, 1968; Hurrah for Rosie!, 1968; Royal Rosie, 1968; The Family Tower, 1968; The Toppling Towers, 1969; The Pocket Mouse, 1969; Mantlemass—The Lark and the Laurel, 1970, The Sprig of Broom, 1971, A Cold Wind Blowing, 1972, The Iron Lily, 1973, Harrow and Harvest, 1974, The Miller's Boy, 1976, The Eldest Son, 1977, A Flight of Swans, 1980, and The Keys of Mantlemass, 1981; Priscilla Pentecost, 1970; The Reindeer Slippers, 1970; The Dragon Box, 1972; Jubilee!, 1973; Bridesmaid, 1976; The Convent Cat, 1976; The Country Maid, 1978; The Gardener's Grandchildren, 1978; Spell Me a Witch, 1979; Summer Season, 1981; Famous Rowena Lamont, 1983; The Queen of the Pharisees' Children, 1983; Smiley Tiger, 1984; Ned Only, 1985. Add: Forest Edge, Nutley, Uckfield, Sussex, England.

WILLENSKY, Elliot. American, b. 1933. Architecture, Urban studies. Commissioner, NYC Landmarks Commn., since 1979, and Vice-Chmn. since 1984; Borough Historian, Brooklyn, N.Y., since 1979. Assoc. Prof. of Architecture, and Dir., NYC Prog., Cornell Univ., N.Y., 1963–68; Deputy Administrator, NYC Parks, Recreation and Cultural Affairs Admin., 1968–70; Dir., High Rock Park Conservation Center, N.Y., 1971–76; Adjunct Prof. of Architecture and Planning, Columbia Univ., NYC, 1981–83. *Publs:* (with Norval White) AIA Guide to New York City, 1967, 3rd ed. 1988; Guide to Developing a Neighborhood Marker System, 1972; An Urban Information System for New York City, 1972; Grand Central: Shaper of a City, 1982; When Brooklyn Was the World 1920-

1957, 1986. Add: 52 Clark St., Brooklyn, N.Y. 11201, U.S.A.

WILLETT, Frank. British, b. 1925. Anthropology/Ethnology, Art. Dir., and Prof., Hunterian Museum and Art Gallery, Univ. of Glasgow, since 1976. Keeper of Ethnology and Gen. Archaeology, Manchester Museum, U.K., 1950–58; Govt. Archaeologist, Nigeria, 1958–63; Research Fellow, Nuffield Coll., Oxford, 1964–66; Prof. of Art History, Northwestern Univ., Evanston, Ill., 1966–76; Visiting Fellow, Clare Hall, Cambridge, 1970–71. *Publs:* Ife in the History of West African Sculpture, 1967; African Art: An Introduction, 1971; (with E. Eyo) Treasures of Ancient Nigeria, 1980. Add: Hunterian Museum, The Univ., Glasgow G12 8QQ, Scotland.

WILLETT, John (William Mills). British, b. 1917. Art, Intellectual history, Biography, Translations. Joint Ed., Methuen and Random House eds. of works of Bertolt Brecht. Leader-writer, Manchester Guardian, 1948–51; Asst. Ed., 1960–69 and Planning Ed., 1969–71, Times Literary Supplement, London; Visiting Teacher, California Inst. of the Arts, 1972–73; Visiting Prof., Univ. of New South Wales, 1979. Member, Art Panel, Arts Council of G.B., 1980–84; Visiting Prof., Univ. of Giessen, 1986–87. *Publs:* Popski: A Biography of Lt.-Col. Vladimir Peniakoff, 1954; The Theatre of Bertolt Brecht, 1959; (ed.and trans.) Brecht on Theatre, 1964; (trans.) Brecht: The Messingkauf Dialogues, 1965; Art in a City, 1967; Expressionism, 1970; (co-ed. and part-trans.) Brecht: Collected Plays, 1970; (co-ed. and co-trans.) Brecht Poems 1913-1956, 1976; The Theatre of Erwin Piscator, 1978; The New Sobriety: Art and Politics in the Weimar Period, 1978; (co-ed. and co-trans.) Brecht, Short Stories, 1983; The Weimar Years: A Culture Cut Short, 1984; Brecht in Context, 1984; Casper Neher, Brecht's Designer, 1986; The Theatre of the Weimar Republic, 1988. Add: Volta House, Windmill Hill, London NW3 6SJ, England.

WILLETTS, Ronald Frederick. British, b. 1915. Poetry, Area Studies (Cypriot studies), Classics, History. Language/Linguistics (philology, textual criticism). Prof. of Greek, Univ. of Birmingham, since 1970–81, now Emeritus (Lectr., 1946–57; Sr. Lectr., 1957–63; Reader, 1963–69; Public Orator, 1975–80); Hon. Fellow, Inst. for Advanced Research in the Humanities, since 1984. Gen. Ed., States and Cities of Ancient Greece series, Routledge & Kegan Paul, London, since 1970; Editorial Bd., Cretan Studies. *Publs:* Aristocratic Society in Ancient Crete, 1955, 1980; (trans.) The Ion of Euripides, 1958; The Trobriand Islanders (poetry), 1960; Cretan Cults and Festivals, 1962, 1980; Ancient Crete: A Social History, 1965; (trans.) The Plutus of Aristophanes, 1965; (co-author) New Poems, 1965; The Law Code of Gortyn, 1967; Everyday Life in Ancient Crete, 1969, 1988; Blind Wealth and Aristophanes, 1970; The Civilization of Ancient Crete, 1977; The Baths of Aphrodite (poetry), 1979; Argo (poetry), 1984; Selected Papers, 2 vols., 1986–87; Pale Moonlight (poetry), 1987; (co-author) Early Greek in Cyprus, 1987. Add: 95 Selly Park Rd., Birmingham B29 7LH, England.

WILLEY, Peter Robert Everard. British, b. 1922. Anthropology/Ethnology, Archaeology, Architecture, Literature, Travel/Exploration/Adventure. Lectr. in Fine Arts, Bristol Univ.; Chmn., Educational Experience in Europe. Formerly Head of German Dept., Wellington Coll., Crowthorne, Berks. (Asst. Master, 1947; Housemaster, 1954–75; Sr. German Tutor, 1957). *Publs:* Guten Tag, 1961; Castles of the Assassins, 1963; Drugs and Slavery in Afghanistan, 1971; Achievements in German Literature; The Assassins of Central Asia. Add: 17 Fairfield, Upavon, Pewsey, Wilts. SN9 6D2, England.

WILLHELM, Sidney McLarty. American, b. 1934. Sociology. Prof., Dept. of Sociology, State Univ. of New York, Buffalo, since 1962. Asst. Prof., Dept. of Sociology, San Francisco State Univ., Calif., 1960–62. *Publs:* Urban Zoning and Land-Use Theory, 1962; Who Needs the Negro?, 1971; Black in a White America, 1983; Racial Separation in an Equal America, 1989. Add: Dept. of Sociology, State Univ. of New York, Buffalo, N.Y. 14261, U.S.A.

WILLIAM, Vera B. American, b. 1927. Children's fiction. Author and illustrator of children's books, since 1975. Political activist. Co-founder, Gate Hill Cooperative and Collaberg Sch., Stony Point, N.Y. Emigrated to Canada, 1970. *Publs:* The Great Watermelon Birthday, 1980; Three Days on a River in a Red Canoe, 1981; A Chair for My Mother, 1981; Something Special For Me, 1983; Music, Music for Everyone, 1984; Cherries and Cherry Pits, 1986; Stringbean's Trip to the Shining Sea, 1988; (with Grace Paley) Three Hundred Sixty-Five Reasons Not to Have Another War, 1989; Peace Calendar, 1988. Add: c/o Greenwillow Books, 105 Madison Ave., New York, N.Y. 10016, U.S.A.

WILLIAMS, Alan. British, b. 1935. Sciences. Livesey Prof. of Fuel and Combustion Science, Leeds Univ. (previously Lectr., and Sr. Lectr.). *Publs:* Combustion of Sprays of Liquid Fuels, 1976. Add: Dept. of Fuel and Energy, Univ. of Leeds, Leeds LS2 9JT, Yorks., England.

WILLIAMS, Alan Lee, OBE. British, b. 1930. Military/Defence, Politics/Government. Warden and Chief Exec., Toynbee Hall, London, since 1986. Labour M.P. (U.K.) for Hornchurch, Essex, 1966–79, 1974–76; Parliamentary Private Secty. to Secty. of State for Defence, 1969–70, 1976; Leader of H.M. Govt. Delegation to 24th Gen. Assembly of the U.N., 1969; Deputy Dir. of the European Movement, 1970–72; Dir., British Atlantic Cttee., 1972–74; PPS to Secty. of State for Northern Ireland, 1976–79; Dir.-Gen., English-Speaking Union, 1979–86. *Publs:* The Future of the Labour Party: A Book of Radical Essays, 1966; Europe or the Open Sea, 1970; Crisis in European Defence, 1974; The European Defence Initiative: Europe's Bid for Equality, 1985; Labour's Decline and the Social Democrat's Fall, 1989. Add: Toynbee Hall, 28 Commercial St., London E1 6LS, England.

WILLIAMS, Barry. British, b. 1932. Education, History. Head of history side and univ. advisor, Sherborne Sch. for Girls, Dorset, since 1972. Series Ed., Nelson's Advanced History Series, London, since 1979. Former History Advisor to Education Div., Rank Film Org., London; Research Fellow, Pembroke Coll., Oxford, 1980. *Publs:* Struggle for Canada, 1967; Modern Japan, 1968; Struggle for North America, 1969; Emerging Japan, 1969; Modern Africa 1870-1970, 1970; Making of Modern World: Asia, 1970; Making of Modern World: Africa, 1972; (ed.) The First Industrial Revolution, 1973; (ed.) Transport, 1974; Modern France (film strip), 1974; (co-author) The Teaching of History, 1975; Modern France 1870-1976, 1979; Elusive Settlement: England's Revolutionary Years 1637-1701, 1984. Add: Little Orchard, South Cadbury, Yeovil, Somerset, England.

WILLIAMS, Bernard (Arthur Owen). British, b. 1929. Philosophy. Prof. of Philosophy, Univ. of California, Berkeley, since 1988. Fellow of New Coll., Oxford, 1954–59; Lectr. in Philosophy, University Coll., 1959–64, and Prof. of Philosophy, Bedford Coll., 1964–67, Univ. of London; Fellow of King's Coll., and Knightsbridge Porf. of Philosophy, Cambridge Univ., 1967–79, and Provost of King's Coll., 1979–87. *Publs:* (co-ed., with Montefiore) British Analytical Philosophy, 1966; Morality: An Introduction to Ethics, 1972; Problems of the Self, 1973; Utilitarianism: For and Against, 1973; Descartes, 1978; Moral Luck, 1981; (co-ed.) Utilitarianism and Beyond, 1982; Ethics and the Limits of Philosophy, 1985. Add: Dept. of Philosophy, Univ. of California, Berkeley, Calif. 94720, U.S.A.

WILLIAMS, Bert (Nolan). Canadian, b. 1930. Novels/Short stories, Historical/Romance/Gothic, Plays/Screenplays. Teacher, Scarborough Bd. of Education, Ontario, since 1953. *Publs:* Food for the Eagle, 1970; Master of Ravenspur, 1970; The Rocky Mountain Monster, 1973; Son of Egypt, 1977; Brumaire (play), 1977. Add: 10 Muirhead Rd., Apt. 504, Willowdale, Ont. M2J 4P9, Canada.

WILLIAMS, Bronwyn. *See* **BROWNING,** Dixie Burrus.

WILLIAMS, (Sir) Bruce Rodda. British, b. 1919. Economics, Education. Robert Otley Prof. of Economics, 1959–63, and Stanley Jevons Prof. of Political Economy, 1963–67, Univ. of Manchester; Member, U.K. National Bd. for Prices and Incomes, 1966–67; Economic Adviser to U.K. Minister of Technology, 1966–67; Vice-Chancellor and Principal, Univ. of Sydney, 1967–81; Dir., Technical Change Centre, and Visiting Prof., Imperial Coll. of Science and Technology, London, 1981–86; Visiting Fellow, and Chmn. of Review of the Engineering Disciplines, Australian National Univ., 1987–88. Member, Bd. of Reserve Bank of Australia, 1969–81; Chmn., National Cttee. of Inquiry into Education and Training, 1976–79. *Publs:* (with C.F. Carter) Industry and Technical Progress, 1957; (with C.F. Carter) Investment in Innovation, 1958; (with C.F. Carter) Science in Industry, 1959; International Report on Factors in Investment Behaviour, 1962; (with W.P. Scott) Investment Proposals and Decisions, 1965; Investment, Technology and Growth, 1967; (ed.) Science and Technology in Economic Growth, 1973; Systems of Higher Education: Australia, 1978; Education, Training and Employment, 1979; Disappointed Expectations, 1982; Living with Technology, 1982; Knowns and Unknowns in Technical Change, 1985; National Attitudes in Technology, 1986; Technological Change and Higher Education, 1987. Add: 106 Grange Rd., London W5 3PJ, England.

WILLIAMS, C. Arthur, Jr. American, b. 1924. Business/Trade/Industry, Economics. Prof., Sch. of Mgmt., Univ. of Minnesota, Minneapolis, since 1958 (Asst. Prof., 1952–55; Assoc. Prof., 1955–58; Dean, 1972–78). Lectr. in Statistics and Insurance, Univ. of Buffalo, N.Y., 1950–52. *Publs:* (with J.G. Turnbull and E.F. Cheit) Economic and Social Security, 1957, 5th ed. 1982; (with R.M. Heins) Risk Management and Insurance, 1964, 6th ed. 1989; (ed. with P.S. Barth) Compendium on Workmen's Compensation, 1973; (with R. Riegel and J. Miller) Insurance Principles and Practices: Property and Liability, 6th ed. 1976; (with G.L. Head and G.W. Glendenning) Principles of Risk Management and Insurance, 1978, 1981; (With A.E. Brunck and V.P. Simone) Ocean Marine Insurance, 1988. Add: 1984 Shryer Ave. W., St. Paul, Minn. 55113, U.S.A.

WILLIAMS, C(harles) K(enneth). American, b. 1936. Poetry, Translations. Prof. of English, George Mason Univ., since 1982. Visiting Prof., Franklin and Marshall Coll., Lancaster, Pa., 1977, and Univ. of California at Irvine, 1978, Boston Univ., 1979–80, and Brooklyn Coll., 1982–83; Lectr., Columbia Univ., 1982–85; Holloway Lectr., Univ. of Calif., Berkeley, 1986. *Publs:* A Day for Anne Frank, 1968; Lies, 1969; I Am the Bitter Name, 1972; The Sensuous President, 1972; With Ignorance, 1977; (co-trans.) The Women of Trachis, 1978; The Lark, The Thrush, The Starling, 1983; Tar, 1983; Flesh and Blood, 1987, Poems 1963-1983, 1988. Add: 82, Rue d'Hauteville, 75010 Paris, France.

WILLIAMS, C(hristopher) J(ohn) F(ardo). British, b. 1930. Philosophy. Reader in Philosophy, Univ. of Bristol, since 1972 (Lectr., 1966–72). Former Member, Analysis Cttee. (Ed., Analysis, 1971–76). Asst. Lectr. in Philosophy, 1962–64, and Lectr., 1964–66, Univ. of Hull. *Publs:* (trans.) The Problem of Evil, by François Petit, 1959; What Is Truth?, 1976; What Is Existence?, 1981; Aristotle's De Generatione et Corruptione, 1982; What is Identity?, 1989. Add: 1 Fossefield Rd., Midsomer Norton, Bath BA3 4AS, England.

WILLIAMS, Claudette. Historical/Romance/Gothic. *Publs:* Spring Gambit, 1976; Sassy, 1977; Sunday's Child, 1977; After the Storm, 1977; Blades of Passion, 1978; Cotillion for Mandy, 1978; Myriah, 1978; Cassandra, 1979; Jewelene, 1979; Lacey, 1979; Mary, Sweet Mary, 1980; Naughty Lady Ness, 1980; Passion's Pride, 1980; Desert Rose, English Moon, 1981; Song of Silkie, 1984; Fire and Desire, 1985; Sweet Disorder, 1981; Lady Magic, 1983; Regency Star, 1985; Lady Bell, 1986; Wild Dawn Fever, 1986. Add: c/o Fawcett, 1515 Broadway, New York, N.Y. 10036, U.S.A.

WILLIAMS, Clifford Glyn. American, b. 1928. Business/Trade/Industry, Economics. Prof. of Economics, Univ. of South Carolina, since 1974 (Assoc. Prof. 1969–74). Asst. Prof., Univ. of Alberta, Edmonton, 1961–63, Indiana Univ., Bloomington, 1963–66, and Boston Coll., Mass., 1966–69. *Publs:* Technological Changes in the Railway Industry, 1967; Labor Economics, 1970; Inter-Industry Redistribution of Employment in South Carolina 1960-70, 1974; Urban Labor Markets, 1978; Unions and Inflation, 1980; Labor Productivity, 1981; Price Equations, 1982; Collective Bargaining Models, 1982; Economics of Older Workers, 1985; Vocational Education, Technological Change, 1988. Add: Dept. of Economics, Univ. of South Carolina, Columbia, S.C. 29208, U.S.A.

WILLIAMS, David. British, b. 1926. Mystery/Crime/Suspense. Gov., Pusey House, Oxford, since 1965. Managing Dir., David Williams and Partners, London, 1958–68; Chmn., David Williams and Ketchum, London, 1968–78; Dir., Ketchum Communications, Pittsburgh, 1968–86; Vice-Chmn., Ketchum Group Holdings, London, 1978–86. *Publs:* Advertising and Social Conscience (non-fiction), 1972; Unholy Writ, 1976; Treasure by Degrees, 1977; Treasure Up in Smoke, 1978; Murder for Treasure, 1980; Copper, Gold and Treasure, 1982; Treasure Preserved, 1983; Advertise for Treasure, 1984; Wedding Treasure, 1985; Murder in Advent, 1985; Treasure in Roubles, 1986; Divided Treasure, 1987; Treasure in Oxford, 1988; Holy Treasure!, 1989. Add: Blandings, Pinewood Rd., Virginia Water, Surrey GU25 4PA, England.

WILLIAMS, Emmett. American, b. 1925. Plays, Poetry, Essays, Translations. Artist-in-Residence and Guest Prof., Hochschule der Künste, Berlin, and Hochschule fur Bildende Künste, Hamburg, since 1981. Associated with the Darmstadt group of concrete poets; Founding member of the Domaine Poetique, Paris, and the intnl. Fluxus group. Ed., Something Else Press, NYC, 1966–70; Prof. of Critical Studies, California Inst. of Arts, Valencia, 1970–72; Visiting Prof. of Art, Nova Scotia Coll. of Art and Design, Halifax, 1972–74; Visiting Artist, Mount Holyoke Coll., South Hadley, Mass., 1975–77; Visiting Artist, Research Fellow, Carpenter Center for the Visual Arts, Harvard Univ., Cambridge, Mass., 1977–80. *Publs:* Konkretionen, 1958; (trans.) Anecdoted Topography of Chance, by Daniel Spoerri, 1966; (ed.) An Anthology of Concrete

Poetry, 1967; (ed.) Claes Oldenburg's Store Days, 1967; Sweethearts, 1967; The Book of Thorn and Eth, 1968; The Boy and the Bird, 1969; A Valentine for Noël, 1973; Selected Shorter Poems 1950-1970, 1974; The Voyage, 1975; Schemes and Variations, 1981; (with Keith Godard) Holdup, 1981; (with Keith Godard) A Little Nightbook, 1983; Faustzeichnungen, 1983; Chicken Feet, Duck Limbs and Dada Handshakes, 1984; Altmodische Gedichte und Neumodische Lichtsculpturen, 1987. Add: Koblenzerstrasse 17, D-1000 Berlin 31, West Germany.

WILLIAMS, Glanville (Llewelyn). British, b. 1911. Law. Fellow, Jesus Coll., Cambridge, since 1955 (Research Fellow, St. John's Coll., 1936–42; Reader, 1957–65, Prof., 1966, and Rouse Ball Prof. of English Law, 1968–78, Cambridge Univ.). Hon. Bencher, Middle Temple, London, since 1966. Reader in English Law, and successively Prof. of Public Law and Quain Prof. of Jurispridence, Univ. of London, 1945–55. *Publs:* Liability for Animals, 1939; (contrib.) Impossibility of Performance, 1941; The Law Reform (Frustrated Contracts) Act (1943), 1944; Learning the Law, 1945, 11th ed. 1982; Crown Proceedings, 1948; Joint Obligations, 1949; Joint Torts and Contributory Negligence, 1950; Criminal Law: The General Part, 1953, 1961; The Proof of Guilt, 1955, 3rd ed. 1963; The Sanctity of Life and the Criminal Law, 1956; The Mental Element in Crime, 1965; (with B.A. Hepple) Foundations of the Law of Tort, 1976; Textbook of Criminal Law, 1978, 1983; Shorthand, 8th ed., 1980. Add: Merrion Gate, Gazeley Rd., Cambridge CB2 2HB, England.

WILLIAMS, Gordon. Has also written, with Terry Venables, as P.B. Yuill. British, b. 1934. Novels/Short stories, Mystery/Crime/Suspense. *Publs:* The Last Day of Lincoln Charles, 1965; The Camp, 1966; The Man Who Had Power over Women, 1967; From Scenes Like These, 1969; The Siege of Trenchers Farm, 1969; The Upper Pleasure Garden, 1970; (with Terry Venables) They Used to Play on Grass, 1971; Walk Don't Walk, 1972; Big Morning Blues, 1974; The Duellists (novelization of screenplay), 1977; The Micronauts, 1978; The Microcolony, 1979, in U.K. as Micronaut World, 1979; Revolt of the Micronauts, 1981; Pomeroy, 1981; as P.B. Yuill (with Terry Venables)—Hazell Plays Solomon, 1974; Hazell and the Three Card Trick, 1975; Hazell and the Menacing Jester, 1976. Add: c/o John Farquharson Ltd., 162-168 Regent St., London W1R 5TA, England.

WILLIAMS, Guy R(ichard Owen). British, b. 1920. Children's nonfiction, Criminology/Law enforcement/Prisons, Recreation/Leisure/Hobbies, Travel/Exploration/Adventure. Sch. Master, Parmiter's Sch., London, since 1950. Advisory Ed., Dramascripts series, Macmillan, London. *Publs:* Use Your Hands!, 1945; Use Your Leisure! 1958; Instructions to Young Collectors, 1959; Instructions to Young Model-Makers, 1960; Making a Miniature House, 1964; Let's Look at London!, 1965; Let's Look at Wales!, 1965; Collecting Pictures, 1967; The World of Model Trains, 1970; The World of Model Ships and Boats, 1971; The Hidden World of Scotland Yard, 1972; The Black Treasures of Scotland Yard, 1973; The World of Model Aircraft, 1973; The Age of Agony, 1976; The Royal Parks of London, 1978; London Walks, 1981; The Age of Miracles, 1981; Guide to the Magical Places of England, Wales, and Scotland, 1987. Add: 1a Earl Rd., London SW14 7JH, England.

WILLIAMS, (David) Gwyn. British, b. 1904. Novels/Short stories, Poetry, Literature, Travel/Exploration/Adventure, Autobiography/-Memoirs/Personal, Translations. Freelance writer since 1969. *Publs:* (with others) Personal Landscape, 1945; (trans.) The Rent That's Due to Love, 1950; An Introduction to Welsh Poetry from the Beginning to the Sixteenth Century, 1953; (trans.) The Burning Tree: Poems from the First Thousand Years of Welsh Verse, 1956, rev. ed. as Welsh Poems: Sixth Century to 1600, 1973; (ed.) Presenting Welsh Poetry: An Anthology of Welsh Verse in Translation and of English Verse by Welsh Poets, 1959; (trans.) In Defence of Woman: A Welsh Poem, by William Cynwal, 1960; This Way to Lethe (novel), 1962; Green Mountain: An Informal Guide to Cyrenaica and Jebel Akhdar, 1963; Turkey: A Traveller's Guide and History, 1967; Inns of Love: Selected Poems, 1970; The Avocet (novel), 1970; Eastern Turkey, 1972; Foundation Stock, 1974; Two Sketches of Womanhood (fiction), 1975; To Look for a Word (collected translations), 1976; The Land Remembers: A View of Wales, 1977; An Introduction to Welsh Literature, 1978; Choose Your Stranger, 1979; Y Ddefod Goll, 1981; Person and Persona, 1981; ABC of (D)GW: A Kind of Autobiography, 1981; Y Cloc Ty wod (novel), 1984; Collected Poems, 1989. Add: 40 Queen St., Aberystwyth, Dyfed SY23 1PU, Wales.

WILLIAMS, Harold (Claude Noel). British, b. 1914. Music, Theology/Religion. Chaplain, Community of the Cross of Nails, since 1981. Principal, St. Matthew's Coll., S. Africa; Vicar of Hyde, Winchester; Rector of St. Mary's, Southampton; Provost of Coventry, 1958–81. *Publs:*

African Folk Songs, 1946; Vision of Duty, 1962; Coventry Cathedral, 1962; Twentieth Century Cathedral, 1962; Nothing to Fear, 1963; Coventry Cathedral—Its Ministry, 1964; Cathedral in Action, 1966; Basics and Variables, 1969; The Latter Glory, 1979; Order My Steps in Thy Way, 1982. Add: 96 Stoney Rd., Coventry CV3 6HY, England.

WILLLIAMS, Heathcote. British, b. 1941. Plays/Screenplays, Poetry. Freelance playwright. *Publs:* The Speakers, 1964, adapted as play, 1974; AC/DC, and The Local Stigmatic: Two Plays, 1973; Manifestoes, Manifesten, 1975; Hancock's Last Half-Hour, 1977; The Immortalist, 1977; Severe Joy, 1979; Remember the Truth Dentist, and The Speakers, 1980; Elephants, 1981; Autogeddon, 1981; At It, 1983; What the Dickens (TV play) 1983; Whale Nation (poetry), 1988; Falling for a Dolphin, 1988. Add: c/o Curtis Brown, 168 Regent St., London W1R 5TB, England.

WILLIAMS, Herbert (Lloyd). British, b. 1932. Novels/Short stories, Poetry, History. Former Radio Producer, BBC Wales, and Sub-Ed., Birmingham Evening Mail. *Publs:* Too Wet for the Devil, 1962; The Dinosaurs, 1966; The Trophy, 1967; A Lethal Kind of Love, 1968; Battles in Wales, 1975; Stage Coaches in Wales, 1977; The Welsh Quiz Book, 1978; Come Out Wherever You Are, 1978; Railways in Wales, 1981; Pembrokeshire Coast National Park Guide, 1987. Add: 28 Le Sor Hill, Peterstan-Suru-Gly, S. Glam, Wales.

WILLIAMS, Hugo. British, b. 1942. Poetry, Travel. TV Critic and Poetry Ed., New Statesman, London. Asst. Ed., London Mag., 1966–1970. *Publs:* Symptoms of Loss: Poems, 1965; All the Time in the World (travel), 1966; (ed.) "London Magazine" Poems 1961-1966, 1966; Poems, 1969; Sugar Daddy, 1970; Cherry Blossom, 1972; Some Sweet Day, 1975; Love-Life, 1979; No Particular Place to Go (travel), 1981; Writing Home, 1985; Selected Poems, 1989. Add: 3 Raleigh St., London W1, England.

WILLIAMS, Ioan M(iles). British, b. 1941. Literature. Sr. Lectr. in English, Univ. of Warwick, since 1967. Asst. Lectr., Univ. of Exeter, Devon, 1964–66. *Publs:* Browning, 1967; (ed.) Sir Walter Scott, 1968; Thackeray, 1968; (ed.) Novel and Romance, 1970; (ed.) The Criticism of Henry Fielding, 1970; George Meredith: The Critical Heritage, 1971; The Realist Novel in England, 1974; Idea of the Novel in Europe, 1979; Emyr Humphreys, 1980. Add: 2 Fishponds Rd., Kenilworth, Warwicks., England.

WILLIAMS, J.R. See **WILLIAMS**, Jeanne.

WILLIAMS, Jeanne. Also writes as Jeanne Crecy, Deirdre Rowan, J.R. Williams, Kristin Michaels, Jeanne Foster, and Megan Castell. American, b. 1930. Novels/Short stories, Children's fiction. Past Pres., Western Writers of America. *Publs:* To Buy a Dream, 1958; Promise of Tomorrow, 1959; (as J.R. Williams) Mission in Mexico, 1960; (as J.R. Williams) The Horsetalker, 1961; (as J.R. Williams) The Confederate Fiddle, 1962; (as J.R. Williams) River Guns, 1962; (as J.R. Williams) Oh Susanna!, 1963; Coyote Winter, 1965; Beasts with Music, 1967; (as J.R. Williams) Tame the Wild Stallion, 1967; Oil Patch Partners, 1968; New Medicine, 1971; Trails of Tears, 1972; (as Jeanne Crecy) Hands of Terror (in U.K. as Lady Gift), 1972; Freedom Trail, 1973; (as Jeanne Crecy) The Lightning Tree, 1972; (as Deirdre Rowan) Dragon's Mount, 1973; (as Deirdre Rowan) Silver Wood, 1974; (as Deirdre Rowan) Shadow of the Volcano, 1975; (as Jeanne Crecy) My Face Beneath the Stone, 1975; (as Jeanne Crecy) The Winter Keeper, 1975; (as Jeanne Crecy) The Night Hunters, 1975; Winter Wheat, 1975; (as Kristin Michaels) To Begin with Love, 1975; (as Kristin Michaels) Enchanted Twilight, 1975; (as Kristin Michaels) A Special Kind of Love, 1976; (as Deirdre Rowan) Time of the Burning Mask, 1976; (as Deirdre Rowan) Ravensgate, 1976; (as Jeanne Williams) A Lady Bought with Rifles, 1977; (as Kristin Michaels) Enchanted Journey, 1977; (as Kristin Michaels) Song of the Heart, 1977; (as Kristin Michaels) Make Believe Love, 1978; Voyage to Love, 1978; (as Jeanne Williams) A Woman Clothed in Sun, 1978; (as Jeanne Williams) Bride of Thunder, 1978; (as Jeanne Williams) Daughter of the Sword, 1979; (as Megan Castell) The Queen of a Lonely Country, 1980; (as Jeanne Foster) Deborah Leigh, 1981; (as Jeanne Williams) The Valiant Women, 1981; (as Jeanne Williams) Harvest of Fury, 1982; (as Jeanne Foster) Eden Richards, 1982; (as Jeanne Williams) The Heaven Sword, 1983; (as Jeanne Williams) A Mating of Hawks, 1984; (as Jeanne Foster) Woman of Three Worlds, 1984; (as Jeanne Williams) The Cave Dreamers, 1985; The Heaven Sword, 1985; So Many Kingdom, 1986; Texas Pride, 1987; Lady of No Man's Land, 1988. Add: Box 335, Portal, Ariz. 85632, U.S.A.

WILLIAMS, John. American, b. 1922. Novels, Poetry, Literature.

Prof. of English, Univ. of Denver, Colo., since 1964 (Dir., Workshop for Writers 1954–59, and Creative Writing Prog. 1954–74; Asst. Prof., 1954–60; Assoc. Prof., 1960–64); retired, 1986. Instr., Univ. of Missouri, 1950–54; Ed., Twentieth Century Literature: A Scholarly and Critical Journal, 1954–56, and Univ. of Denver Quarterly: A Journal of Modern Culture, 1965–70. *Publs:* Nothing But the Night, 1948; The Broken Landscape (poetry), 1949; Butcher's Crossing, 1960; (ed.) English Renaissance Poetry, 1963; Stoner, 1965; The Necessary Lie (poetry), 1965; Augustus (winner of National Book Award), 1972. Add: 853 Highland Ave., Fayetteville, Ark. 72701, U.S.A.

WILLIAMS, John A(lfred). American, b. 1925. Novels/Short stories, Science fiction, History, Autobiography/Memoirs/Personal, Biography Prof. of English, Rutgers Uhiv., New Brunswick, N.J., since 1979. Public Relations Officer, Doug Johnson Assocs., Syracuse, N.Y., 1952–54; with CBS Radio-Television Special Events, Hollywood and NYC, 1954–55; Publicity Dir., Comet Press Books, NYC, 1955–56; Ed. and Publr., Negro Market Newsletter, NYC, 1956–57; Asst. to Publr., Abelard-Schuman Inc., NYC, 1957–58; European Corresp., Ebony mag. and Jet Mag., 1958–59; Corresp., Newsweek mag., Africa, 1964–65. *Publs:* The Angry Ones, 1960; Night Song, 1961; Africa: Her History, Lands and People, 1963; (ed.) The Angry Black, 1962; Sissie (in U.K. as Journey Out of Anger), 1963; The Protectors, 1964; This Is My Country, Too, 1965; The Man Who Cried I Am, 1967; (ed.) Beyond the Angry Black, 1967; Sons of Darkness, Sons of Light: A Novel of Some Probability, 1969; The Most Native of Sons, 1970; The King God Didn't Save, 1970; (ed.) Amistad I and II, 1970, 1971; The Ordeal of Abraham Blackman, The Negro Soldier, 1971; Captain Blackman, 1971; Romare Bearden, 1973; Flashbacks: A Twenty-Year Diary of Article Writing, 1972; Mothersill and the Foxes, 1975; Minorities in the City, 1975; The Junior Bachelor Society, 1976; Click Song, 1982; The Berhama Account, 1985; Jacob's Ladder, 1987. Add: 693 Forest Ave., Teaneck, N.J. 07666, U.S.A.

WILLIAMS, John Stuart. British, b. 1920. Poetry. Head, Dept. of Communications, South Glamorgan Inst. of Higher Education from 1977, now retired. Head, English and Drama Dept., Cardiff Coll. of Education, 1956, 1956–77. Co-opted Member, Welsh Arts Council Literature Cttee., 1973, 1973–77. *Publs:* (ed. with Richard Milner) Dragons and Daffodils, 1960; Last Fall, 1962; Green Rain, 1967; (ed. with Meic Stephens) The Lilting House, 1969; (ed.) Poems 1969, 1969; Dic Penderyn and Other Poems, 1970; Banna Strand, 1975. Add: 52 Dan-Y-Coed Rd., Cyncoed, Cardiff, Wales.

WILLIAMS, Jonathan (Chamberlain). American, b. 1929. Poetry, Photography, Essays. Exec. Dir., The Jargon Soc., Highlands, N.C., since 1951. Scholar-in-Residence, Aspen Inst. for Humanistic Studies, 1962, and 1967–68; Poet-in-Residence, Maryland Inst. Coll. of Art, 1968–69, and Univ. of Kansas, 1971. *Publs:* (with Basil Bunting) Descent on Rawthey's Madrigal, 1968; An Ear in Bartram's Tree: Selected Poems 1957-67, 1969; Mahler, 1969; (ed.) Edward Dahlberg: A Tribute, 1970; The Appalachian Photographs of Doris Ulmann, 1971; Blues and Roots—Rue and Bluets, 1971; The Loco Logodaedalist in Situ: Selected Poems 1968-70, 1972; (ed.) Epitaphs for Lorine: Lorine Niedecker, 1973; Clarence John Laughlin: The Personal Eye, 1973; Imaginary Postcards, 1974; (ed.) Bunting at 75, 1975; Letter to the Great Dead, 1975; Selected Essays, 1975; Elite Elate Poems: Poems 1971-75, 1979; Portrait Photographs, 1979; St. Swithin's Swivet, 1979; Get Hot or Get Out: A Selection of Poems 1957-1981, 1982; The Magpie's Bagpipe (essays), 1982. Add: Corn Close, Dentdale, Sedbergh, Cumbria, England.

WILLIAMS, Joy. American, b. 1944. Novels/Short stories, Travel. Researcher and data analyst, U.S. Navy, Mate Marine Laboratory, Siesta Key, Fla., 1967–69; Visiting Instructor, Univ. of Houston, 1982, Univ. of Florida, 1983, Univ. of California, Irvine, 1984, Univ. of Iowa, 1984, and Univ. of Arizona, 1987. National Endowment for the Arts grant, 1973; Guggenheim fellowship, 1974. *Publs:* State of Grace, 1973; The Changling, 1978; Taking Care (short stories), 1982; The Florida Keys: A History and Guide, 1986; Breaking and Entering, 1988. Add: c/o Random House, 201 E. 50th St., New York, N.Y. 10022, U.S.A.

WILLIAMS, Miller. American, b. 1930. Poetry, Translations. Prof. of English since 1973, and Dir., Univ. Press, since 1980, Univ. of Arkansas, Fayetteville (Assoc. Prof., 1973–73; Chmn., Comparative Literature Prog., 1978–80). Member, Advisory Council, Sch. for Classical Studies, since 1985. Visiting Prof. of American Literature, Univ. of Chile, Santiago, 1963–64; Assoc. Prof. of English, Loyola Univ., New Orleans, La., 1966–69; Fulbright Prof. of American Studies, National Univ. of Mexico, Mexico City, 1970–71. *Publs:* A Circle of Stone, 1964; Recital, 1965; (ed.) 19 Poetas de hoy en Los Estados Unidos, 1966; (with J.W. Corrington) Southern Writing in the Sixties: Poetry, 1966; (with J.W. Corrington) Southern Writing in the Sixties: Fiction, 1966; (trans.) Poems and Antipoems, by N. Parra, 1967; So Long at the Fair, 1968; Chile: An Anthology of New Writing, 1968; The Achievement of John Ciardi, 1968; The Only World There Is, 1971; The Poetry of John Crowe Ransom, 1971; (trans.) Emergency Poems, by N. Parra, 1972; (ed.) Contemporary Poetry in America, 1972; Halfway from Hoxie: New and Selected Poems, 1973; (with John Ciardi) How Does a Poem Mean?, 1974; (with James Alan McPherson) Railroad: Trains and Train People in American Culture, 1976; Why God Permits Evil: New Poems, 1977; A Roman Collection, 1980; Distractions, 1981; (ed.) Ozark, Ozark: A Hillside Reader, 1981; (ed.) Sonnets of Giuseppe Bell, 1981; The Boys on Their Bony Mules, 1983; Patterns of Poetry, 1986; Imperfect Love, 1986; Living on the Surface: New and Selected Poems, 1989. Add: Univ. of Arkansas Press, Fayetteville, Ark. 72701, U.S.A.

WILLIAMS, Nigel. British, b. 1948. Novels/Short stories, Plays/Screenplays. *Publs:* My Life Closed Twice (novel), 1977; Class Enemy, 1978; Jack Be Nimble (novel), 1980; Sugar and Spice, and Trial Run, 1981; W.C.P.C., 1983; Johnny Jarvis (novel), 1983; Charlie (novel), 1984; Star Turn (novel), 1985; My Brother's Keeper, 1985; Witchcraft (novel), 1987; Country Dancing, 1987; Black Magic, 1988; Breaking Up, 1988. Add: C/O Judy Daish Assocs. Ltd., 83 Eastbourne Mews, London W2 6LQ, England.

WILLIAMS, Paul O(sborne). American, b. 1935. Science fiction. Cornelius and Muriel Wood Prof. of Humanities, Principia Coll., Elsah, Ill; 1981–86 (Asst. Prof., 1964–68; Assoc. Prof., 1968–77; Prof. of English, 1977–81). Trustee, Village of Elsah, 1969–75; Pres., Greater St. Louis Literature Assn., 1975; and Thoreau Soc., 1977. *Publs:* science fiction—The Breaking of Northwall, 1981; The Ends of the Circle, 1981; The Dome in the Forest, 1981; The Fall of the Shell, 1982; An Ambush of Shadows, 1983; The Song of the Axe, 1984; The Sword of Forbearance, 1985; The Gifts of the Gorboduc, Vandal, 1989; other—(with Charles B. Hosmer) Elsah: A Historic Guidebook, 1967; The McNair Family of Elsah, Illinois, 1982; Fredrick Oakes Sylvester: The Artist's Encounter With Elsah, 1986. Add: 2718 Monserat Ave., Belmont, Calif. 94002, U.S.A.

WILLIAMS, Roland. British, b. 1910. Zoology. Partner, N.M. Rothschild & Sons, London, 1930–70. *Publs:* Where the World Is Quiet, 1965. Add: Denby Lodge, Denne Park, Horsham, West Sussex RH13 7AY, England.

WILLIAMS, Thomas. American, b. 1926. Novels/Short stories, Poetry, Literature, Essays. Prof. of English, Univ. of New Hampshire, Durham, since 1967 (Instr., 1958–61; Asst. Prof., 1961–64; Assoc. Prof., 1964–67). *Publs:* Ceremony of Love, 1955; Town Burning, 1959, 3rd ed. 1988; The Night of Trees, 1961, 3rd ed. 1989; A High New House, 1963; Whipple's Castle, 1969, 1988; The Hair of Harold Roux, 1974, 1988; Tsuga's Children, 1977; The Followed Man, 1978; The Moon Pinnace, 1986, 1988. Add: 13 Orchard Dr., Durham, N.H. 03824, U.S.A.

WILLIAMS, Trevor Illtyd. British, b. 1921. History, Sciences, Technology. Scientific Ed., Endeavour, since 1974 (Deputy Ed., 1945–54; Ed., 1954–74); Ed., Outlook on Agriculture, since 1981. *Publs:* An Introduction to Chromatography, 1946; Drugs from Plants, 1947; (ed.) The Soil and the Sea, 1949; The Chemical Industry Past and Present, 1953; The Elements of Chromatography, 1954; (co-ed.) A History of Technology, 8 vols., 1954–84; (with T.K. Derry) A Short History of Technology, 1960; (ed.) 100 Years of Chemistry, 1965; (ed.) A Biographical Dictionary of Scientists, 1969; Alfred Nobel, 1974; James Cook, 1974; Man the Chemist, 1976; (ed.) A History of Technology: The Twentieth Century, 1978; A History of the British Gas Industry, 1981; A Short History of 20th Century Technology, 1982; Howard Florey: Penicillin and After, 1984; The Triumph of Invention, 1987. Add: 20 Blenheim Dr., Oxford OX2 8DG, England.

WILLIAMS, Ursula Moray. See **MORAY WILLIAMS,** Ursula.

WILLIAMS, Walter E(dward). American, b. 1936. Mathematics/ Statistics, Politics/Government, Public/Social administration, Race relations. John M. Olin Distinguished Prof. of Economics, Geroge Mason Univ., Fairfax, Va., since 1980. Economics Instr., Los Angeles City Coll., 1967–68; Asst. Prof., California State Univ., Los Angeles, 1969–71; Member, Research Staff, Urban Inst., 1971–73; Assoc. Prof. of Economics, Temple Univ., Philadelphia, 1973–80. Ford Foundn. Fellow, 1970; Hoover Inst. Fellow, 1976. *Publs:* Youth and Minority Unemployment, 1977; (with James H. Reed) Fundamentals of Business Mathematics

(textbook), 1977; Government by Agency: Lessons From the Grants-in-Aid Experience, 1980; The Implementation Perspective: A Guide for Managing Social Service Delivery Programs, 1980; America: A Minority Viewpoint, 1982; The State Against Blacks, 1982; All It Takes Is Guts: A Minority View, 1987. Add: c/o Dept. of Economics, George Mason Univ., 4400 Univ. Dr., Fairfax, Va. 22030, U.S.A.

WILLIAMS, William A(ppleman). American, b. 1921. History. Prof. of History, Oregon State Univ., Corvalis. *Publs:* American-Russian Relations 1784-1947, 1950; The Shaping of American Diplomacy 1763-1970, 1956; The Tragedy of American Diplomacy, 1960, 1986; The Contours of American History, 1961; The United States, Cuba and Castro, 1962; The Great Evasion, 1964; The Roots of the Modern American Empire, 1969; Some Presidents: From Wilson to Nixon, 1972; America Confronts a Revolutionary World 1776-1976, 1976; Americans in a Changing World, 1978; Empire as a Way of Life, 1980; (ed. with others) America in Vietnam: A Documentary History, 1985. Add: History Dept., Oregon State Univ., Corvalis, Ore. 97331, U.S.A.

WILLIAMSON, Alan (Bacher). American, b. 1944. Literary Criticism. Member of the English faculty, Univ. of Virginia, Charlottesville. *Publs:* Pity the Monsters: The Political Vision of Robert Lowell, 1974; Introspection and Contemporary Poetry, 1984; The Muse of Distance, 1988. Add: c/o Knopf, 201 E. 50th St., New York, N.Y. 10022, U.S.A.

WILLIAMSON, David (Keith). Australian, b. 1942. Plays/ Screenplays. Former Lectr., Swinburne Coll. of Technology. *Publs:* The Removalists, 1972; Don's Party, 1973; The Coming of Stork, Juggler's Three, and What if You Died Tomorrow, 1974; The Department, 1975; The Club, 1978; Travelling North, 1980; The Perfectionist, 1982; Sons of Cain, 1985; Collected Plays: 1986; Emerald City, 1987. Add: c/o Anthony Williams Mgmt., 55 The Basement, Victoria St., Potts Point, N.S.W. 2011, Australia.

WILLIAMSON, Jack. (John Stewart Williamson). Also writes as Will Stewart. American, b. 1908. Science fiction/Fantasy, Literature. Prof. of English, Eastern New Mexico Univ., Portales, 1960–77. Pres., Science Fiction Writers of America, 1978–80. *Publs:* The Legion of Space, 1947; Darker Than You Think, 1948; The Humanoids, 1949; The Green Girl, 1950; The Cometeers, and One Against the Legion, 1950; (as Will Stewart) Seetee Shock, 1950; (as Will Stewart) Seetee Ship, 1951; Dragon's Island, 1951; The Legion of Time, and After World's End, 1952; (with F. Pohl) Undersea Quest, 1954; Dome Around America, 1955; (with James E. Gunn) Star Bridge, 1955; (with F. Pohl) Undersea Fleet, 1955; (with F. Pohl) Undersea City, 1956; The Trial of Terra, 1962; Golden Blood, 1964; (with F. Pohl) The Reefs of Space, 1964; (with F. Pohl) Starchild, 1965; The Reign of Wizardry, 1965; Bright New Universe, 1967; Trapped in Space, 1968; The Pandora Effect, 1969; (with F. Pohl) Rogue Star, 1969; People Machines, 1971; The Moon Children, 1972; H.G. Wells: Critic of Progress, 1973; (with F. Pohl) The Farthest Star, 1975; The Early Williamson, 1975; The Power of Blackness, 1976; The Best of Jack Williamson, 1978; Brother to Demons, Brothers to Gods, 1979; The Humanoid Touch, 1980; (ed.) Teaching Science Fiction: Education for Tomorrow, 1980; Manseed, 1982; The Queen of the Legion, 1983; (with F. Pohl) Wall Around a Star, 1983; Lifeburst, 1984; Wonder's Child: My Life in Science Fiction, 1984; Firechild, 1986; (with F. Pohl) Land's End, 1988. Add: Box 761, Portales, N.M. 88130, U.S.A.

WILLIAMSON, Joel. American, b. 1930. History, Race Relations (and Southern culture). Lineberger Prof. in The Humanities, Univ. of North Carolina, since 1985 (Instr.of History 1960–64; Asst. Prof., 1964–66; Assoc. Prof., 1966–69; Prof., 1969–85). *Publs:* After Slavery: The Negro in South Carolina During Reconstruction 1861-1877, 1965; The Origins of Segregation, 1968; New People: Miscegenation and Mulattoes in the United States, 1980; The Crucible of Race: Black-White Relations in the American South since Emancipation, 1984; A Rage for Order, 1986. Add: Dept. of History, Univ. of North Carolina, Chapel Hill, N.C. 27514, U.S.A.

WILLIAMSON, Richard. British, b. 1935. Novels/Short stories, Natural history, Autobiography/Memoirs/Personal Land Mgr. of the Nature Conservancy Council, since 1964. Columnist, Nature Trails, and Nature Diary, Portsmouth & Sunderland Newspapers, since 1964, and In the Country, Daily Mail, London; Scripwriter, BBC Television, since 1974. *Publs:* The Dawn is My Brother (autobiography); Capreol: The Story of a Roebuck, 1974; The Great Yew Forest, 1978; (ed.) Tarka the Otter, by Henry Williamson, 1978. Add: West Dean Woods, Chichester, Sussex PO18 0RU, England.

WILLIAMSON, Robert C(lifford). American, b. 1916. Sociology. Prof. of Sociology and Psychology, Los Angeles City Coll., Calif., 1946–60; Prof. of Sociology, Lehigh Univ., Bethlehem, Pa., 1963–84. *Publs:* (with S. Sargent) Social Psychology, 3rd ed. 1966, 4th ed. (with P. Swingle and S. Sargent) 1982; (ed. with C.H. Seward) Sex Roles in a Changing Society, 1970; Marriage and Family Relations, 2nd ed. 1972. Add: 100 Woodland Dr. Bethlehem, Pa. 18015, U.S.A.

WILLIAMSON, Robin (Duncan Harry). British, b. 1943. Novels/Short stories, Poetry, Songs, lyrics and libretti. Composer of television, theatre and movie scores. Musician, songwriter, and recorder producer with the "Incredible String Band," U.K., 1966–74, as "Robin Williamson and His Merry Band," Los Angeles, 1977–79, and as a solo performer, since 1979; also, Principal, Robin Williamson Productions, and Pig's Whisker Music, both Los Angeles, since 1975. *Publs:* (with Mike Heron) Incredible String Band Song Book (lyrics and music), 1968; Home Thoughts from Abroad (verse), 1972; (with Mike Heron) Incredible String Band: A Second Songbook (lyrics and music), 1973; (with Dan Sherman) Glory Trap (novel), 1976; Fiddle Tunes: English, Welsh, Scottish, and Irish, 1976; The Penny Whistle Book (music), 1977; Five Denials on Merlin's Grave (verse), 1979; Selected Writings 1980-83 (poetry), 1983; The Crane Skin Bag (Celtic stories), 1989. Add: Robin Williamson Productions, P.O. Box 27522, Los Angeles, Calif. 90027, U.S.A.

WILLIAMSON, Tony. (Anthony George Williamson). Also writes as Steven Cade. British, b. 1932. Novels/Short stories, Plays/Screenplays. Journalist, Kemsley/Thomson newspapers, 1954–60, and CBC-TV, Montreal, 1960–63; Story Ed., BBC, London, 1966. *Publs:* Night Watch (screenplay), 1972; The Connector (novel), 1976; Counter Strike: Entebe (non-fiction), 1976; The Fabulous Assassin (screenplay), 1977; Doomsday Contract (novel), 1977; Technicians of Death (novel), 1978; Breakthrough (screenplay), 1979; Samson Strike (novel), 1979, TV adaption, 1985; Night Without End (screenplay), 1980; (as Steven Cade) Slade's Marauders, 1980; Warhead, 1981; (as Steven Cade) Barrington's Women, 1982; television plays—Ask Any Neighbour; Cage of Canvas; Victim; television series—The Avengers; The Persuaders; Jason King; The Champions; Department S; Randall and Hopkirk; Z Cars; The Spies; Mask of Janus; Codename; Dr. Finlay's Casebook; The Revenue Men; Spy Trap; Dixon of Dock Green; Counter-strike; The Adventurer; (screenplay) Strike the Devil, 1985; (stageplay) The Cabinet Mole, 1985. Add: c/o Robin Lowe, M.L. Representation, 194 Old Brompton Rd., London, England.

WILLINGHAM, Calder (Baynard, Jr.). American, b. 1922. Novels/Short stories, Plays/Screenplays. *Publs:* End as a Man, 1947, play, 1953, screenplay, 1958; Geraldine Bradshaw, 1950; Reach to the Stars, 1951; The Gates of Hell (short stories), 1951; To Eat a Peach, 1955; Paths of Glory (screenplay), 1957; The Vikings (screenplay), 1960; One-Eyed Jacks (screenplay), 1962; Eternal Fire, 1963; The Graduate (screenplay), 1967; Providence Island, 1969; Little Big Man (screenplay), 1970; Rambling Rose, 1972; The Big Nickel, 1975; The Building of Venus Four, 1977. Add: c/o Vanguard Press, 424 Madison Ave., New York, N.Y. 10017, U.S.A.

WILLIS, Connie. (Constance E. Willis). American, b. 1945. Science fiction. Full-time writer since 1982. Teacher in elementary and jr. high schs., Branford, Conn., 1967–69. *Publs:* (with Cynthia Felice) Water Witch (novel), 1982; Fire Watch (short stories), 1985; Lincoln's Dreams, 1987; (with Cynthia Felice) Light Raid, 1989. Add: 1716 13th Ave., Greeley, Colo. 80631, U.S.A.

WILLIS, Edgar E(rnest). American. Media. Prof. Emeritus, Dept. of Communication, Univ. of Michigan, Ann Arbor, since 1957 (Assoc. Prof., 1952–57). Writer, Detroit Public Schs. Radio Dept., 1935–38, 1940–43; News Analyst, Station WWJ-TV, Detroit, Mich., 1953–54; Prog. Assoc., National Educational Television, 1958–59. *Publs:* Foundations in Broadcasting, 1951; A Radio Directors Manual, 1961; Writing Television and Radio Programs, 1967; (with G. Chester and G. Garrison) Television and Radio, 1978; (with C. D'Arienzo) Writing Scripts for Television, Radio, and Film, 1981. Add: 1112 Clair Circle, Ann Arbor, Mich. 48103, U.S.A.

WILLIS, James. British, b. 1928. Psychiatry. Consultant Psychiatrist, Guy's Hosp., King's Coll. Hosp., and Bexley Hosp., London, since 1967. Consultant Psychiatrist, Waringham Park Hosp., 1967. *Publs:* Lecture Notes in Psychiatry, 1964, 6th ed. 1984; Drug Dependence, 1969; Addicts: Drugs and Alcohol Re-examined, 1973; Clinical Psychiatry, 1976. Add: Dept. of Psychiatry, Guy's Hosp., London SE1, England.

WILLIS, John A(lvin). American, b. 1916. Film, Media, Theatre. Ed., Theatre World and Screen World yearbooks, since 1964, and Dance World yearbook, since 1965, all NYC. *Publs:* Great Stars of the American Stage, 1952; A Pictorial History of the Silent Screen, 1953; A Pictorial History of the Talkies, 1958; A Pictorial History of Television, 1959; A Pictorial Treasury of Opera in America, 1960; (with D. Blum) A Pictorial History of the American Theatre 1860-1950, 1970, 4th ed. 1985. Add: 190 Riverside Dr., New York, N.Y. 10024, U.S.A.

WILLIS, Ted. (Edward Henry Willis; Baron Willis of Chislehurst). British, b. 1918. Novels/Short stories, Mystery/Crime/Suspense, Plays/Screenplays, Autobiography/Memoirs/Personal. Dir., World Wide Pictures, London, since 1967; Dir., Capital Radio, London. Life Pres., Writers Guild of Great Britain, since 1976 (Chmn., 1958–63; Pres., 1963–68). Exec. Member, League of Dramatists, London, 1948–74; Pres., Intnl. Writers Guild, 1967–69; Gov., National Film Sch., London, 1970–73. *Publs:* God Bless the Guv'nor, 1945; The Lady Purrs, 1950; George Comes Home, 1955; Doctor in the House (adaptation of the novel by Richard Gordon), 1957; Hot Summer Night, 1959; Woman in a Dressing Gown and Other Television Plays, 1959; (with Henry Cecil) Brothers-in-Law (adaptation of the novel by Cecil), 1959; The Eyes of Youth, 1960; Doctor at Sea (adaptation of the novel by Richard Gordon), 1961; The Little Goldmine, 1962; Dead on Saturday, 1970; Stardust, 1987; Tommy Boy, 1988; Doctor on the Boil, 1989; It Takes Two to Make a Murder, 1989; novels—The Blue Lamp, 1950; The Devil's Churchyard, 1957; (with Charles Hatton) Dixon of Dock Green: My Life, 1960; (with Paul Graham) Dixon of Dock Green: A Novel, 1961; Black Beauty, 1972; Death May Surprise Us, 1974 (in U.S. as Westminster One, 1975); The Left-Handed Sleeper, 1975; Man-Eater, 1976; The Churchill Commando, 1977; The Buckingham Palace Connection, 1978; The Lions of Judah, 1979; The Naked Sun, 1980; The Most Beautiful Girl in the World, 1981; Spring at the Winged House, 1983; The Green Leaves of Summer, 1988. other—Fighting Youth of Russia, 1942; The Devil's Churchyard (juvenile), 1957; Seven Gates to Nowhere (juvenile) 1958; Whatever Happened to Tom Mix? The Story of One of My Lives, 1970; Mother Christmas (juvenile), 1986. Add:t 5 Shepherds Green, Chislehurst, Kent BR7 6PB, England.

WILLMER, Edward Nevill. British, b. 1902. Biology, Zoology. Prof. of Histology Emeritus, Univ. of Cambridge (Reader, 1948–65; Prof., 1965–69). Ed., Biological Reviews, Cambridge Philosophical Soc., 1969–80. *Publs:* Tissue Culture, 1935, 3rd ed. 1958; Retinal Structure and Colour Vision, 1946; Cytology and Evolution, 1960, 1970; (ed.) Cells and Tissues in Culture, vols. I-III, 1965–66; Old Grantchester, 1976; The River Cam, 1979; Waen and the Willmens, 1988. Add: Yew Garth, Grantchester, Cambridge CB3 9ND, England.

WILLMOTT, Peter. British, b. 1923. Sociology. Sr. Fellow, Policy Studies Inst., since 1983. Research Officer, 1954–60, Deputy Dir., 1960–64, and Co-Dir., 1964–78, Inst. of Community Studies; Dir., Centre for Environmental Studies, 1978–80; Head, Central Policy Unit, Greater London Council, 1981–83. *Publs:* (with M. Young) Family and Kinship in East London, 1957; (with M. Young) Family and Class in a London Suburb, 1960; Evolution of a Community, 1963; Adolescent Boys of East London, 1966; (with M. Young) The Symmetrical Family: A Study of Work and Leisure in the London Region, 1974; (with Graeme Shankland and David Jordon) Inner London, 1977; (with C. Madge) Inner City Poverty in Paris and London, 1981; Community in Social Policy, 1984; Social Networks, Informal Care, and Public Policy, 1986; Friendship Networks and Social Support, 1987; Polarization and Social Housing, 1988. Add: Kingsley Place, London N6 5EA, England.

WILLOCK, Colin (Dennistoun). British, b. 1919. Novels/Short stories, Mystery/Crime/Suspense, Animals/Pets, Natural history, Sports, Travel/Exploration/Adventure, Autobiography/Memoirs/Personal, iography. Dir., Survival Anglia Ltd. (Head, Anglia Television Natural History Unit, 1961–72). Former Ed., Lilliput, and Angling Times; Asst. Ed., Picture Post; Deputy Ed., This Week television programme. *Publs:* Come Fishing with Me, 1952; Come Fly Fishing with Me, 1953; (ed.) In Praise of Fishing 1943; Coarse Fishing, 1955; Death at Flight, 1956; Death at the Strike, 1957; The Gun Punt Adventure, 1958; Rod, Pole or Perch, 1958; The Angler's Encyclopaedia, 1960; (ed.) The Man's Book, 1961; (ed.) The Farmer's Book of Field Sports, 1961; Death in Covert, 1961; Kenzie, The Wild Goose Man, 1962; Duck Shooting, 1962; Look at African Animals, 1963; (ed.) The ABC of Fishing, 1964; (ed.) The Survival Series of Books, 1964; The Enormous Zoo, 1964; The Animal Catchers, 1964; (ed.) The Bedside Wildfowler, 1966; (ed.) The Penguin Guide to Fishing, 1966; Landscape with Solitary Figure, 1966; Hazanda, 1968; The Coast of Loneliness, 1971; The Fighters, 1973; Town Gun,

1973; (ed.) The ABC of Shooting, 1974; The Great Rift Valley, 1974; Gorilla; The Worst Dog in the World, 1977; The World of Survival, 1978; Town Gun 2, 1981; In the Rut, 1982; The Complete Dudley, 1988. Add: 17 Ashley D., Walton-on-Thames, Surrey, England.

WILLOUGHBY, Cass. See **OLSEN,** T.V.

WILLOUGHBY, Hugh. See **HARVEY,** Nigel.

WILLOUGHBY, Lee Davis. See **AVALLONE,** Michael.

WILLOUGHBY, Lee Davis. See **DeANDREA,** William L.

WILLOUGHBY-HIGSON, Philip. See **HIGSON,** Philip.

WILLRICH, Mason. American, b. 1933. Engineering/Technology, International relations/Current affairs, Politics/Government, Public/Social administration. Sr. Vice-Pres. of Corporate Planning and Information Systems, Pacific Gas and Electric Co., San Francisco, since 1984 (Vice-Pres., 1979–84). Consultant, Rand Corp., Ford Foundn., and U.S. Arms Control and Disarmament Agency. Assoc., Pillsbury, Madison and Sutro, San Francisco, 1960–62; Asst. Gen Counsel, U.S. Arms Control and Disarmament Agency, Washington, 1962–65; Prof. of Law, Univ. of Virginia, Charlottesville, 1965–76; Dir. of Intnl. Relations, Rockefeller Foundn., NYC, 1976–79. *Publs:* Non-Proliferation Treaty: Framework for Nuclear Arms Control, 1969; (ed. with Boskey) Nuclear Proliferation: Prospects for Control, 1970; (ed.) Civil Nuclear Power and International Security, 1971; Global Politics of Nuclear Energy, 1971; (ed. and co-author) International Safeguards and Nuclear Industry, 1973; (ed. with J.B. Rhinelander, and co-author with others) SALT: The Moscow Agreements and Beyond, 1974; (with T.B. Taylor) Nuclear Theft: Risks and Safeguards, 1974; Energy and World Politics, 1976; (with R.K. Lester) Radioactive Waste: Management and Regulation, 1977; Administration of Energy Shortages, 1977. Add: Pacific Gas and Electric Co., 77 Beale St., San Francisco, Calif. 94106, U.S.A.

WILLS, Alfred J(ohn). British, b. 1927. History. Asst. Master, Norwich Sch., since 1964. Education Officer, Northern Rhodesia Govt., 1951–58; Asst. Lectr., Northwestern Polytechnic, London, 1960–63. *Publs:* An Introduction to the History of Central Africa, 1964, 4th ed. 1985; The Story of Africa—Books I and II, 1968–69. Add: 28 Players Way, Norwich, Norfolk NR6 7AU, England.

WILLS, Garry. American, b. 1934. Literature, Social commentary/phenomena, Theology/Religion. Luce Prof. of American Culture, Northwestern Univ., Evanston, Ill., since 1980. Asst. Prof., Johns Hopkins Univ., Baltimore, 1962–81. *Publs:* Chesterton, Man and Mask, 1961; Politics and Catholic Freedom, 1964; Roman Culture, 1966; (ed.) Values Americans Live By, 1975; Inventing America, 1978; At Buttons (novel), 1979; Confessions of a Conservative, 1979; Explaining America, 1980; Cincinnatus, 1982; Lead Time, 1983; Reagan's America: The Innocents at Home, 1987. Add: Dept. of History, Northwestern Univ., Evanston, Ill. 60201, U.S.A.

WILLS, Walter J. American, b. 1915. Agriculture/Forestry, Business/Trade/Industry, Marketing. Prof. Emeritus, Agricultural Industries Dept., Southern Illinois Univ. (joined faculty, 1956). *Publs:* Introduction to Grain Marketing, 1972; Introduction to Agri-Business Management, 1973, 1979; Introduction to Agricultural Sales, 1982. Add: Agribusiness Economics Dept., Sch. of Agriculture, Southern Illinois Univ., Carbondale, Ill. 62901, U.S.A.

WILLY, Margaret (Elizabeth). British, b. 1919. Poetry, Literature. British Council Lectr. since 1950. Publishers' copywriter, 1936–42; Ed., English, journal, 1954–75; Lectr., City Literary Inst., London, 1956–85, Goldsmiths' Coll., London, 1959–75, St. Marylebone Literary Inst., London, 1966–72, and Morley Coll., London, 1973–85. *Publs:* The Invisible Sun (poetry), 1946; Life Was Their Cry (biographical studies of Chaucer, Traherne, Fielding and Browning), 1950; Every Star a Tongue (poetry), 1951; The South Hams, 1955; Three Metaphysical Poets: Richard Crashaw, Henry Vaughan, Thomas Traherne, 1961; (ed.) Two Plays of Goldsmith, 1962; English Diarists: Evelyn and Pepys, 1963; (ed.) Poems of Today: Fifth Series, 1963; Three Women Diarists: Celia Fiennes, Dorothy Wordsworth, Katherine Mansfield, 1964; A Critical Commentary on Emily Brontë's "Wuthering Heights", 1966; A Critical Commentary on Browning's "Men and Women", 1968; (ed.) The Metaphysical Poets, 1971. Add: 19 Hillview Rd., Findon Valley, Worthing, Sussex, England.

WILMER, Clive. British, b. 1945. Poetry. Teacher of English as a foreign language; also freelance university teacher and journalist. Co-Founder-Ed., Numbers mag., since 1986. *Publs:* (with Dick Davis and Robert Wells) Shade Mariners, 1970; The Dwelling-Place, 1977; (trans., with George Gomori) Forced March: Selected Poems, by Miklos Radnoti, 1979; (ed.) The Occasions of Poetry: Essays in Criticism and Autobiography, by Thom Gunn, 1982; Devotions, 1982; (ed.) Unto This Last and Other Writings, by John Ruskin, 1985; A Catalogue of Flowers, 1986. Add: 3 Norfolk Terr., Cambridge CB1 2NG, England.

WILMER, Dale. See **WADE,** Robert.

WILMERDING, John. American, b. 1938. Art. Deputy Dir., National Gallery of Art, Washington, D.C., since 1983 (Curator and Sr. Curator of American Art, 1977–82). Taught at Dartmouth Coll., Hanover, N.H., 1965–77; Vice-Pres., Shelburne Museum, Vermont, 1966–76. *Publs:* Fitz Hugh Lane, 1971; Winslow Homer, 1972; American Art, 1976; American Masterpieces from the National Gallery of Art, 1980; Important Information Inside, 1983; (ed.) Essays in Honor of Paul Mellon, Collector and Benefactor, 1986; American Marine Painting, 1987; (with others) Frank W. Benson: The Impressionist Years 1898-1920, 1988. Add: National Gallery of Art, Washington, D.C. 20565, U.S.A.

WILSON, A(lfred) Jeyaratnam. Sri Lankan, b. 1928. Politics/Government. Prof. of Political Science, Univ. of New Brunswick, Fredericton, since 1972. Member of Editorial Bd., The Round Table. Leverhulme Research Scholar, London Sch. of Economics, 1955; Research Fellow in Politics, Univ. of Leicester, 1964–65; Research Assoc., McGill Univ., Montreal, 1970–71; Prof. of Political Science, and Head, Dept. of Economics and Political Science, Univ. of Ceylon, 1970–72; Simon Sr. Fellow, Manchester Univ., 1971–72; Sr. Assoc. Member, St. Antony's Coll., Oxford, 1976–77; Simon Prof. in Government, Victoria Univ. of Manchester, 1986–86. *Publs:* Politics in Sri Lanka 1947-73, 1974, 1979; Electoral Politics in an Emergent State: The Ceylon General Election of May 1970, 1975; The Gaullist System in Asia, 1980; (ed. and contrib. with Dennis Dalton) The States of South Asia: Problems of National Integration, 1982; (ed. with Robert Goldmann) From Independence to Statehood: Managing Ethnic Conflict in Five African and Asian States, 1984; The Break-up of Sri Lanka: The Sinhalese-Tamil Conflict, 1989. Add: Dept. of Political Science, Univ. of New Brunswick, Fredericton, N.B., Canada.

WILSON, Andrew. British, b. 1923. International relations/Current affairs, Military/Defence. Assoc. Ed., since 1982, and Moscow Corresp., since 1986, The Observer newspaper, London (Defence and Aviation Corresp. 1963–79; Foreign Ed., 1979–82). *Publs:* Flame Thrower, 1956; (trans. with Eva Wilson) The Schlieffen Plan, 1957; North from Kabul, 1961; The Bomb and the Computer, 1969, reissued as War Gaming, 1970; (ed.) The Observer Atlas of World Affairs, 1971; The Concorde Fiasco, 1973; The Aegean Question, 1980; The Disarmer's Handbook, 1983; (with Nina Bachkatov) living with Glasnost, 1988. Add: 44 Fitzalan Rd., London N3, England.

WILSON, A(ndrew) N. British, b. 1950. Children's fiction, Novels/Short stories, Literature, Theology/Religion, Biography. Lectr., St. Hugh's Coll., Oxford, 1976–82, and New Coll., Oxford, 1977–81; Literary Ed., Spectator, London, 1981–83. *Publs:* The Sweets of Pimlico (novel), 1977; Unguarded Hours (novel), 1978; Kindly Light (novel), 1979; The Laird of Abbotsford, 1980; The Healing Art (novel), 1980; Who Was Oswald Fish (novel), 1981; Wise Virgin (novel), 1982; A Life of John Milton, 1983; Scandal (novel), 1983; Hilaire Belloc, 1984; How Can We Know? An Essay on the Christian Religion, 1985; Gentlemen in England (novel), 1985; Love Unknown (novel), 1986; (with C. Moore and G. Stamp) The Church in Crisis, 1986; (ed.) Essays by Divers Hands 44, 1986; (ed.) The Lion and the Honeycombe: Tolstoy's Religious Writings, 1987; Stray (novel), 1987; Landscape in France, 1987; Incline Our Hearts (novel), 1988; Penfriends from Porlock: Essays and Reviews 1977-1986, 1988; Tolstoy: A Biography, 1988; Tabitha (for children), 1989. Add: c/o A.D. Peters, The Chambers, Chelsea Harbour, Lots Rd., London SW10 0XF, England.

WILSON, (Sir) Angus (Frank Johnstone). British, b. 1913. Novels/Short stories, Literature. Prof. of English Literature, Univ. of East Anglia, Norwich, 1966–78, now Emeritus (Lectr., 1963–66). Pres., Royal Soc. of Literature, and Kipling Soc. Staff member, British Museum, London, 1937–55 (Deputy Supt. of the Reading Room, 1949–55); Leslie Stephen Lectr., Cambridge Univ., 1962–63; Member, Arts Council of Great Britain, 1966–69; Chmn., National Book League, London, 1971–75. *Publs:* The Wrong Set and Other Stories, 1950; Such Darling Dodos and Other Stories, 1950; Hemlock and After, 1952; Emile

Zola: An Introductory Study of His Novels, 1952, rev. ed. 1965; For Whom the Cloche Tolls:Scrapbook of the Twenties, 1953; Anglo-Saxon Attitudes, 1956; The Mulberry Bush (play), 1956; A Bit off the Map and Other Stories, 1957; The Middle Age of Mrs. Eliot, 1959; The Old Men at the Zoo, 1961; The Wild Garden: or, Speaking of Writing, 1963; Late Call, 1965; Tempo: The Impact of Television on the Arts, 1966; (ed.) A Maugham Twelve, by W. Somerset Maugham, 1966; (ed.) Cakes and Ale, and Twelve Short Stories, by W. Somerset Maugham, 1967; No Laughing Matter, 1967; Death Dance: 25 Stories, 1969; The World of Charles Dickens, 1970; As If By Magic, 1973; The Strange Ride of Rudyard Kipling, 1977; (ed.) Writers of East Anglia, 1977; Setting the World on Fire, 1980; (ed.) The Portable Dickens, 1983; Diversity and Depth in Fiction: Selected Critical Writings, 1983; Reflections in a Writer's Eye: Writings on Travel, 1986. Add: 7 Place de la République, Apt. 61, 13210 St. Remy de Provence, France.

WILSON, Arthur James Cochran. British, b. 1914. Physics. Emeritues Fellow, Crystallographic Data Centre, Univ. of Cambridge, since 1983. Ed., Intnl. Tables for Crystallography, since 1982. Prof. of Physics, Univ. Coll. of South Wales and Monmouthshire, 1954–65; Prof. of Crystallography, Univ. of Birmingham, 1965–82. Ed., Structure Reports, 1948–59; Ed., Acta Crystallograpohica, 1960–77. *Publs:* X-Ray Optics, 1949, 1962; (ed. with H.S. Peiser and H.P. Rooksby) X-ray Diffraction by Polycrystalline Materials, 1955, 1960; Mathematical Theory of X-ray Powder Diffractometry, 1963; Elements of X-ray Crystallography, 1970; (co-ed) Crystallographic Statistics, 1982; (ed.) Structure and Statistics in Crystallography, 1985. Add: Univ. Chemical Lab., Lensfield Rd., Cambridge CB2 1EW, England.

WILSON, August. American, b. 1945. Plays. Founder, Black Horizons Theatre Co., St. Paul, 1968. *Publs:* Ma Rainey's Black Bottom, 1985; Fences, 1986; Joe Turner's Come and Gone, 1988. Add: c/o Playwrights Center, 2301 Franklin Ave. E., Minneapolis, Minn. 55406, U.S.A.

WILSON, Barbara. See **JANIFER,** Laurence M.

WILSON, Barbara Ker. British. b, 1929. Children's fiction, Children's non-fiction, Mythology/Folklore. Children's Book Ed., Bodley Head, publrs., London, 1956–61, William Collins, publrs., London, 1961–64, Angus & Robertson, publrs., Sydney, 1965–72, and Hodder and Stoughton, Sydney, 1973–76. *Publs:* Scottish Folk-Tales and Legends, 1954; Path Through the Woods, 1958; Lovely Summer, 1960; Look at Books, 1960; Writing for Children, 1960; Noel Streatfeild: A Monograph, 1961; (ed.) The Young Eve-2, 1962; Last Year's Broken Toys (in U.S. as In Love and War), 1962; A Story to Tell, 1964; Beloved of the Gods (in U.S. as In the Shadow of Vesuvius), 1965; A Family Likeness (in U.S. as The Biscuit-Tin Family), 1967; Animal Folk Tales, 1968; (ed.) Australian Kaleidoscope, 1968; Australia: Wonderland Down Under, 1969; Hiccups, 1971; Tales Told to Kabbarli, 1972; The Magic Fishbones, 1974; The Magic Bird, 1974; (ed.) Handful of Ghosts, 1976; The Turtle and the Island, 1978; The Willow Pattern Story, 1979; The Persian Carpet Story, 1982; Kelly the Sleepy Koala, 1983; Kevin the Kookaburra, 1983; Jane Austen in Australia (adult novel), 1984, in U.S. as Antipodes Jane, 1985; (ed.) The Illustrated Treasury of Australian Stories and Verse for Children, 1987; Acacia Terrace, 1988; The Quade Inhoritance (adult novel), 1988. Add: 1/10 Harnett Ave., Mosman Bay, N.S.W. 2088, Australia.

WILSON, Bryan R. British. Education, History, Sociology, Theology/Religion. Reader in Sociology since 1962, and Fellow, All Souls Coll., since 1963, Univ. of Oxford. Pres., Conference Intnl. de Sociologie Religieuse, 1971–75. *Publs:* Sects and Society, 1961; Religion in Secular Society, 1966; (ed.) Rationality, 1970; Religious Sects, 1971; Magic and the Millennium, 1973; The Noble Savages, 1975; (ed.) Education, Equality and Society, 1975; Contemporary Transformations of Religious Consciousness, 1976; (ed.) The Social Impact of the New Religious Movements, 1981; Religion in Sociological Perspective, 1982; (with Daisaku Ikeda) Human Values in a Changing World, 1984; (co-ed.) Values: A Symposium, 1988. Add: All Souls Coll., Oxford, England.

WILSON, Carter. American, b. 1941. Novels/Short stories; Screenplays. Prof. of Community Studies, and Fellow of Merrill Coll., Univ. of California, Santa Cruz, since 1974 (Asst. Prof., 1972–74). Lectr. in English, Stanford Univ., Calif., 1965–66; Briggs-Copeland Lectr. in English and Gen. Education, Harvard Univ., Cambridge, Mass., 1966–69; Lectr., and Asst. Prof. of English, Tufts Univ., Medford, Mass., 1969–72. *Publs:* Crazy February, 1966; I Have Fought the Good Fight, 1967;

Appeals to Santiago (film narration), 1967; On Firm Ice, 1970; A Green Tree and a Dry Tree, 1972; (trans. with Mario L. Davila) Canek: Legend and History of a Mayan Hero, by Ermilo Abreu Gomez, 1979; Treasures on Earth, 1981; (with Judith Coburn) The Times of Harvey Milk (film narration), 1984 (Oscar for best feature-length documentary), 1984. Add: Community Studies Bd., Univ. California, Santa Cruz, Calif. 95064, U.S.A.

WILSON, Christine. See **GEACH,** Christine.

WILSON, Colin (Henry). British, b. 1931. Novels/Short stories, Criminology, Psychology, Paranormal. *Publs:* The Outsider, 1956; Religion and the Rebel, 1957; The Age of Defeat (in U.S. as The Stature of Man), 1959; Ritual in the Dark, 1960; (with P. Pitman) Encyclopaedia of Murder, 1961; Adrift in Soho, 1961; The Strength to Dream, 1962; The World of Violence (in U.S. as The Violent World of Hugh Greene), 1963; Origins of the Sexual Impulse, 1963; Man Without a Shadow (in U.S. as The Sex Diary of Gerard Sorme), 1963; Necessary Doubt, 1964; Rasputin and the Fall of the Romanovs, 1964; The Brandy of the Damned (in U.S. as Chords and Dischords), 1964; Beyond the Outsider, 1965; Eagle and Earwig, 1965; Sex and the Intelligent Teenager, 1966; The Glass Cage, 1966; Introduction to the New Existentialism, 1966; The Mind Parasites, 1967; Voyage to a Beginning, 1968; Bernard Shaw and Reassessment, 1969; Poetry and Mysticism, 1969; Case Book of Murder, 1969; The Philosopher's Stone, 1969; Poetry and Mysticism, 1970; The Killer (in U.S. as Lingard), 1970; The God of the Labyrinth (in U.S. as The Hedonists), 1970; (with J.B. Pick and E.H. Visiak) The Strange Genius of David Lindsay, 1970; L'Amour: The Ways of Love, 1970; The Occult, 1971; The Black Room, 1971; Strindberg (play), 1972; New Pathways in Psychology, 1972; Order of Assassins, 1972; Strange Powers, 1973; Tree by Tolkien, 1973; Reich, Borges, Hesse, 1973; The Schoolgirl Murder Case, 1974; The Return of the Lloigor, 1974; A Book of Booze, 1974; The Craft of the Novel, 1975; The Space Vampires, 1975; Men of Strange Powers, 1976; Enigmas and Mysteries, 1976; The Geller Phenomenon, 1976; Mysteries, 1976; Science Fiction as Existentialism, 1978; Starseekers, 1980; Frankenstein's Castle, 1980; The War Against Sleep, 1980; The Quest for Wilhelm Reich, 1981; (ed. with J. Grant) The Directory of Possibilities, 1981; Poltergeist!, 1981; Anti-Sartre, 1981; Access to Inner Worlds, 1982; The Criminal History of Mankind, 1983; (with Donald Seaman) Modern Encyclopaedia of Murder, 1983; Psychic Detectives, 1983; The Janus Murder Case, 1984; JUNG: The Lord of the Underworld, 1984; Afterlife, 1985; Rudolf Steiner: The Man and His Work, 1985; The Personality Surgeon, 1985; Existential Essays, 1985; The Essential Colin Wilson, 1985; (with Donald Seaman) An Encyclopaedia of Scandal, 1986; (ed. with Christopher Evans) Great Mysteries, 1986; Aleister Crowley: The Man and the Myth, 1987; Spider World—The Tower, 1987; (ed. with Ronald Duncan) Marx Refuted, 1987; (with R. Odell) Jack the Ripper, 1987, Spider World—The Delta, 1988; The Misfits, 1988; Beyond the Occult, 1988; The Magician from Siberia, 1988. Add: Tetherdown, Gorran Haven, Cornwall, England.

WILSON, Dave. See **FLOREN,** Lee.

WILSON, David Henry. British, b. 1937. Novels/Short stories, Children's fiction, Plays, Translations. Univ. Lectr., Univ. of Constance, W. Germany, since 1967, and Bristol Univ., since 1972. *Publs:* (trans.) The Cathedral of Monreale, 1965; All the World's a Stage, 1968; (trans.) Nepal: Art Treasures from the Himalayas, 1969; Der Elefant Auf Papas Auto, 1972; The Make-Up Artist, 1973; (trans.) The Implied Reader, 1974; On Stage, Mr. Smith, 1975; Elephants Don't Sit on Cars, 1977; Jeremy James, 1978; The Fastest Gun Alive, and Other Night Adventures, 1978; (trans.) Act of Reading, 1978; (trans.) New Perspectives in German Literary Criticism, 1979; Wenn Schweine Flugel Hatten, 1979; Getting Rich with Jeremy James, 1979; Beside the Sea with Jeremy James, 1980; Monster Man, 1981; Ich bin ein Superhund, 1981; Gas and Candles and Other Plays, 1983; Are You Normal, Mr. Norman and Other Plays, 1984; How to Stop a Train with One Finger, 1984; Superdog, 1984; Do Goldfish Play the Violin, 1985; Asmadi, 1985; Superdog the Hero, 1986; There's A Wolf in My Pudding, 1986; Shylock's Revenge, 1986; (trans.) Walter Pater, 1987; Yuchy and Ducky, 1988; Superdog in Trouble, 1988; (trans.) Sterne's Tristram Shandy, 1988; Gander of the Yard, 1989; The Coachman Rat, 1989. Add: c/o ACTAC Ltd., 16 Cadogan Lane, London SW1, England.

WILSON, (Sir) David M(ackenzie). British, b. 1931. Archaeology, Art, Crafts, Engineering, History. Dir., British Museum, London, since 1977 (Asst. Keeper, 1954–64). Reader, 1964–71, and Prof. of Medieval Archaeology, 1971–76, Univ. of London, and Jt. Head of Dept. of Scandinavian Studies, University Coll., London, 1973–76. Pres., British Archaeological Assn., 1962–68, and Viking Soc., 1968–70. *Publs:* The Anglo-Saxons, 1960, 3rd ed., 1981; Anglo-Saxon Medalwork 700-1100 in the British Musuem, 1964; (with O. Klindt-Jensen) Viking Art, 1966 (with G. Bersu) Three Viking Graves in the Isle of Man, 1969; The Vikings and Their Origins, 1970, 1980; (with P.G. Foote) The Viking Achievement, 1970; (co-author) St. Ninian's Isle and Its Treasure, 1975; The Viking Age in the Isle of Man, 1974; (ed.) Anglo-Saxon Archaeology, 1976; Civil and Military Engineering in Viking Age Scandinavia, 1978; (ed.) The Northern World, 1980; Anglo-Saxon Art, 1984; The Bayeux Tapestry, 1985. Add: British Museum, London WC1, England.

WILSON, David S(cofield). American, b. 1931. Art, Folklore, Natural history. Assoc. Prof. of American Studies, Univ. of California, Davis, since 1968. English teacher in Morris and Forest Lake, Minn., 1957–62; Instr., Univ. of Minnesota, Minneapolis, 1962–64, 1967–68; Asst. Prof. of English, State Univ. of New York, Cortland, 1964–67. *Publs:* In the Presence of Nature, 1978; (with others) American Wildlife in Symbol and Story, 1978; Beyond Mediation, 1979; (with J. Mechling and R. Merideth) Morning Work, 1979; (with D. Robertson) Signs of Life in the Valley, 1981. Add: Rte. 1, Box 1758, Davis, Calif. 95616, U.S.A.

WILSON, Des. New Zealander, b. 1941. Politics/Government, Sociology. Chmn., Campaign for Freedom of Information, since 1984.Journalist/Broadcaster, 1957–67; Dir., Shelter: National Campaign for the Homeless, 1967–71; Head of Public Affairs, Royal Shakespeare Company, London, 1974–76; Ed., Social Work Today, 1976–79; Chmn., CLEAR (Campaign for Lead-Free Air), 1981–85, and Friends of the Earth 1982–86; Pres., Liberal Party, 1986–87. Columnist, The Guardian, 1968–70, and The Observer, 1971–75; Deputy Ed., Illustrated London News, 1979–81. *Publs:* I Know It Was the Place's Fault, 1970; Des Wilson's Minority Report: A Diary of Protest, 1973; So You Want to Be Prime Minister: A Personal View of British Politics, 1979; The Lead Scandal, 1982; Pressure: The A to Z of Campaigning in Britain, 1984; The Environmental Crisis, 1984; The Secrets File, 1984; Battle for Power, 1987. Add: 46 Arundel St., Brighton, Sussex, England.

WILSON, Doric. American, b. 1939. Plays/Screenplays. Playwright-in-Residence, The Glines, NYC, since 1978. Member, Bd. of Advisers, Hibbs Gallery and Visual Arts Center, NYC, since 1981. Founding Member and Playwright-in-Residence, New Playwrights Unit Workshop, NYC, 1963–65; Artistic Dir., Ensemble Project, NYC, 1965–68; Founding Member and Playwright-in-Residence, Circle Repertory Co., NYC, 1969–71; Founding Artistic Dir., TOSOS Theatre Co., NYC, 1973–77. *Publs:* Two Plays: The West Street Gang, and A Perfect Relationship, 1979; Forever After: A Vivisection of Gaymale Love, Without Intermission, 1980; Street Theatre, 1981. Add: c/o J.H. Press, P.O. Box 294, Village Station, New York, N.Y. 10014, U.S.A.

WILSON, Dorothy Clarke. American, b. 1904. Novels/Short stories, Children's fiction, Plays/Screenplays, Autobiography/Memoirs/Personal, Biography. *Publs:* Twelve Months of Drama for the Average Church, 1933; The Brother: A Story of James, the Brother of Jesus, 1944; The Herdsman: A Story of Amos, 1946; Prince of Egypt: Story of Moses, 1949; House of Earth, 1952; Fly With Me to India, 1954; Jezebel, 1955; The Gifts, 1957; Dir. Ida: Story of Dr. Ida Scudder, 1959; Take My Hands: Story of Dr. Mary Verghese, 1963; Ten Fingers for God: Story of Dr. Brand, 1965; The Journey, 1962; The Three Gifts, 1963; Handicap Race, 1967; Palace of Healing, 1968; Lone Woman: Story of Elizabeth Blackwell, 1970; The Big-Little World of Doc Pritham, 1971; Hilary: Story of Hilary Pole, 1972; Bright Eyes: Story of an Omaha Indian, 1973; Stranger and Traveler: Story of Dorothea Dix, 1975; Climb Every Mountain, 1976; Granny Brand, 1976; Twelve Who Cared (autobiography), 1977; Apostle of Sight: Story of Dr. Victor Rambo, Surgeon to India's Blind, 1980; Lincoln's Mothers: The Story of Nancy and Sally, 1981; Lady Washington: The Story of Our First First Lady. 1984; Queen Dolley: The Life and Times of Dolley Madison, 1987. Add: 114 Forest Ave., Orono, Me. 04473, U.S.A.

WILSON, Edward O(sborne). American, b. 1929. Biology, Sciences, Zoology. Curator of Entomology since 1973, and Frank B. Baird Jr. Prof. of Science since 1976, Harvard Univ., Cambridge (Asst. Prof., of Biology, 1956–58; Assoc. Prof. of Zoology, 1958–64; Prof. of Zoology, 1964–76). Member, World Wild Life Fund, since 1984 (Member, Advisory Council, 1977–84); Member, Editorial Bd., Behavioral Ecology and Sociobiology, Biological Bulletin, and Psyche. Tarner Lectr., Cambridge Univ., 1979–82. *Publs:* (with R.H. MacArthur) The Theory of Island Biogeography, 1967; The Insect Societies, 1971; Sociobiology: The New Synthesis, 1975; On Human Nature, 1978; Biophilia, 1984. Recipient of National Medal of Science, 1977, and Pulitzer Prize for Non-Fiction, 1979. Add:

Museum of Comparative Zoology, Harvard Univ., Cambridge, Mass. 02138, U.S.A.

WILSON, Elizabeth. British, b. 1936. Women, Autobiography/Memoirs/ Personal. Sr. Lectr. in Social Studies, Polytechnic of N. London, since 1973. Member of Ed. Bd., Feminist Review, since 1977. *Publs:* Women and the Welfare State, 1977; Only Halfway to Paradise: Women in Postwar Britain, 1980; Mirror Writing (autobiography), 1982; Adorned in Dreams, 1985; Hidden Agendas, 1986; Prisoners of Glass, 1986; Fifty Years of Association Work among Women, 1987. Add: Dept. of Applied Social Studies, Polytechnic of N. London, Ladbroke House, Highbury Grove, London N5 2AD, England.

WILSON, F(rancis) Paul. American, b. 1946. Science fiction Physician: associated with the Cedar Bridge Medical Group, Bricktown, N.J., since 1974. *Publs:* Healer, 1976; Wheels Within Wheels, 1979; An Enemy of the State, 1980; The Keep, 1981; The Tomb, 1984; The Touch, 1986; Black Wind, 1988; Soft and Others, 1989; Dydeetown World, 1989. Add: c/o Albert Zuckerman, Writers House, 21 W. 26th St., New York, N.Y. 10010, U.S.A.

WILSON, (Brian) Geoffrey. British, b. 1920. Lyrics and libretti, History, Transportation. Asst. Ed., The Railway Gazette, 1938–39, 1946–56 (served in British Armed Forces, 1939–46); Ed., Railway World, 1956–61; Ed., U.K. Staff, World Book Encyclopedia, London, 1961–63; Ed., U.K., International Railway Journal, 1963–68; Member, British Government Information Service, serving as Press Officer, Ministry of Public Building and Works, Press Officer, Dept. of the Environment, Press and Publications Officer, Countryside Commn., and Publications Officer, Dept. of the Environment, 1968–82. *Publs:* (as B.G. Wilson; with V.S. Haram) The Central London Railway, 1950; (as B.G. Wilson, with J.R. Day) Famous Railways of the World, 1956; (as B.G. Wilson, with J.R. Day) Unusual Railways, 1958; London United Tramways, 1970; Ba-ta-clan (unpublished libretto), 1973; The Old Telegraphs, 1976; The Drum Major's Daughter (libretto), 1976; The Bells of Corneville (libretto), 1978; Genevieve of Brabant (unpublished libretto), 1980; Monsieur Choufleuri's At-Home (unpublished libretto), 1980; Love Apple (unpublished libretto), 1980; The Two Anglers (unpublished libretto), 1982; (with Christopher Spencer) Elbow Room: The Story of John Sydney Brocklesby, 1984. Add: 34 Melrose Rd., Merton Park, London SW19 3HG, England.

WILSON, George Wilton. American, b. 1928. Business/Trade/Industry, Economics, Sociology, Transportation. Distinguished Prof. of Business Admin. and Prof. of Economics, Indiana Univ. Sch. of Business, Bloomington, since 1966 (Chmn., Dept. of Economics, 1966–70; Dean, Coll. of Arts and Sciences, 1970–73). Project Dir., Study of Transport and Economic Development of Indochina, and Study of Rail Freight Rates and Economic Development of Western Canada, both since 1974. Asst. Prof. of Economics, Middlebury Coll., Vt., 1955–57. *Publs:* Output and Employment Relations, 1957; (with Bass) Mathematical Models and Methods in Marketing, 1961; Essays on Some Unsettled Questions in the Economics of Transportation, 1962; (ed.) Classics of Economic Theory, 1964; (with Gordon, Judek and Breton) Canada: An Appraisal of Its Needs and Resources, 1965; (with Willbern and Breneman) Growth and Change at Indiana University, 1966; (with Bergman, Hirsch and Klein) The Impact of Highway Investment on Development, 1966; (with Doxey, Edwards, Gainer, Moore and Sargent) Tripartite Economic Survey of the Eastern Caribbean, 1967; (with Myrdal, Wightman, Streeten and Barber) Asian Drama, 1968; (with Darby) Transportation on the Prairies, 1968; (ed. and contrib. with Gehrels and Oliver) Essays in Economic Analysis Policy, 1970; (ed. and contrib.) Technological Development and Economic Growth, 1972; (with A.D. Little) Southeast Asian Regional Transportation Survey, 1972; (with Banks, Menzies and Ross) Rail Freight Rates and the Future Development of Western Canada, 1974; (with Orr and the staff of SEA-TAC) Regional Transport Survey for the Khmer Republic, the Kingdom of Laos and the Republic of Vietnam, 1975; Economic Analysis of Intercity Freight Transportation, 1980; Inflation: Causes, Consequences and Cures, 1982. Add: Sch. of Business, Indiana Univ., Bloomington, Ind. 47405, U.S.A.

WILSON, Gina. British, b. 1943. Children's fiction (including poetry). Full-time writer. Asst. Ed., Scottish National Directory, 1967–73, and the Dictionary of the Older Scottish Tongue, 1972–73, Edinburgh. *Publs:* Cora Ravenwing, 1980; A Friendship of Equals, 1981; The Whisper, 1982; All Ends Up, 1984; Family Feeling, 1986; Just Us, 1988; Polly Pipes Up, 1989; I Hope You know..., 1989; Jim-Jam Pyjamas, 1990; Wompus Galumpus, 1990. Add: c/o Faber and Faber Ltd., 3 Queen Square, London WC1N 3AU, England.

WILSON, Harold. (Baron Wilson of Kirklees in the County of West Yorkshire). British, b. 1916. Politics/Government, Memoirs. Chmn., British Screen Advisory Council, since 1985. Dir. of Economics and Statistics, Ministry of Fuel and Power, 1943–44; Labour Member of Parliament (U.K.) for Ormskirk Div. of Lancashire, 1945–50; Parliamentary Secty. to Ministry of Works, 1945–47; Secty. for Overseas Trade, 1947; Pres., Bd. of Trade, 1947–51; M.P. for Huyton div. of Lancashire, from 1950; Chmn., Public Accounts Cttee., 1959–63, and Labour Party Exec. Cttee., 1961–62; Leader, Labour Party, 1963–76; Leader of the Opposition, 1963–64, and 1970–74; Prime Minister and First Lord of the Treas, 1964–70, and 1974–76. Chancellor, Bradford Univ., 1966–85. Pres., Royal Statistical Soc., 1972–73. *Publs:* New Deal for Coal, 1945; In Place of Dollars, 1952; The War on World Poverty: An Appeal to the Conscience of Mankind, 1953; The Relevance of British Socialism, 1964; Purpose in Politics: Selected Speeches, 1964; The New Britain: Labour's Plan, 1964; Purpose in Power: Selected Speeches, 1966 (in U.S. as Purpose and Power: Selected Speeches); The Labour Government 1964-1970: A Personal Record, 1971; The Governance of Britain, 1976; A Prime Minister on Prime Ministers, 1977; Final Term: The Labour Government 1974-76, 1979; Memoirs 1916-64, 1986. Add: House of Lords, London SW1, England.

WILSON, Harriett C(harlotte). British, b. 1916. Sociology. Visiting Scholar, Inst. of Criminology, Univ. of Cambridge, since 1983. Sr. Research Assoc., Univ. of Birmingham, 1968–72; Sr. Research Fellow, Univ. of Warwick, 1976–82. *Publs:* Delinquency and Child Neglect, 1962, 1964; (with R. Holman, F. Lafitte and K. Spencer) Socially Deprived Families in Britain, 1970, 1973; (with G. W. Herbert) Parents and Children in the Inner City, 1978. Add: 25 Kings Rd., Cambridge CB3 9DY, England.

WILSON, Jacqueline (née Aitken). British, b. 1945. Mystery/Crime/Suspense, Children's fiction. Freelance writer since 1965. Journalist, Thomson Newspapers, Dundee, Scotland, 1963–65. *Publs:* mystery novels—Hide and Seek, 1972; Truth or Dare, 1973; Snap, 1974; Let's Pretend, 1976; Making Hate, 1977; children's fiction—Nobody's Perfect, 1982; Waiting for the Sky to Fall, 1983; The Other Side, 1984; The School Trip, 1984; The Killer Tadpole, 1984; How to Survive Summer Camp, 1985; Amber, 1986; The Monster in the Cupboard, 1986; The Power of the Shade, 1987; Glubbslyme, 1987; Stevie Day Supersleuth, 1987; Stevie Day Lonelyhearts, 1987; Stevie Day Ratrace, 1988; Stevie Day Vampire, 1988; This Girl, 1988. Add: Gina Pollinger, Murray Pollinger, 4 Garrick St., London WC2E 9BH, England.

WILSON, James Quinn. American, b. 1931. Politics/Government, Urban studies. Collins Prof. of Management, Univ. of California, Los Angeles, since 1987. Prof., Harvard Univ., Cambridge, Mass., 1961–87; Chmn., The Police Foundn. Dir. of the Joint Center for Urban Studies of Massachusetts Inst. of Technology and Harvard Univ., 1963–68. *Publs:* Negro Politics, 1960; The Amateur Democrat, 1961; City Politics, 1963; Urban Renewal, 1966; City Politics, and Public Policy, 1967; Varieties of Police Behavior, 1968; The Metropolitan Enigma, 1968; Political Organizations, 1973; Thinking About Crime, 1975; The Investigators, 1978; American Government, 1980; Crime and Human Nature, 1985. Add: Grad. Sch. of Management, U.C.L.A., Los Angeles, Calif. 90024, U.S.A.

WILSON, John (Boyd). British, b. 1928. Education, Philosophy, Psychology, Theology/Religion. Lectr. and Tutor, Dept. of Educational Studies, Oxford Univ., since 1970. Housemaster and Second Master, King's Sch., Canterbury, 1954–61; Prof. of Religious Knowledge, Trinity Coll., Univ. of Toronto, 1961–62; Lectr. in Philosophy, Univ. of Sussex, 1962–70; Dir., Farmington Trust Research Unit, Oxford, 1965–70. *Publs:* Thinking with Concepts; Reason and Morals; Language and the Pursuit of Truth; Equality; Education and the Concept of Mental Health; Introduction to Moral Education; A Teacher's Guide to Moral Education; Education in Religion and the Emotions; Practical Methods of Moral Education; Moral Thinking, 1970; Religion, 1972; Ideals, 1972; Philosophy and Practical Education, 1977; Preface to the Philosophy of Education, 1979; (with R. Straughan) Philosophizing about Education, 1983; what Philosophy Can Do, 1986; (co-ed.) Philosophers on Education, 1987. Add: Dept. of Educational Studies, Oxford Univ, Oxford, England.

WILSON, John Burgess. See **BURGESS,** Anthony.

WILSON, (Sir) John (Foster). British, b. 1919. Medicine/Health, Sociology, Autobiography/Memoirs/Personal. Sr. Consultant, U.N. Development Programme; Vice-Pres., Royal Commonwealth Soc. for the Blind. Formulated Asian Plan for the Blind, 1962, African Plan for the Blind, 1966, and Caribbean Plan for the Blind, 1968; Pres., Intnl. Agency for the Prevention of Blindness, since 1975–83. *Publs:* Blindness in British African and Near East Territories, 1947; Ghana's Handicapped Citizens, 1960; Travelling Blind (autobiography), 1962; (ed.) World Blindness and Its Prevention, vol. I, 1980, vol. II, 1984; Disability Prevention: The Global Challenge, 1983. Add: 22 The Cliff, Roedean, Brighton, Sussex BN2 4RE, England.

WILSON, John Stuart Gladstone. Australian, b. 1916. Economics. Prof. of Economics and Commerce, Univ. of Hull, 1959–82, now Emeritus (Head of Dept., 1959–71, and 1974–77; Dean of Social Sciences and Law, 1962–65). Gvr., SOAS, London, since 1963. Lectr. in Economics, Univ. of Tasmania, 1941–43, Univ. of Sydney, 1944–45, Univ. Coll. of Canberra, 1946–47, and London Sch. of Economics, 1948–49; Reader in Economics, Univ. of London, 1950–59; Ed., Yorkshire Bulletin of Economic and Social Research, 1964–67. Member, Editorial Advisory Bd., Modern Asian Studies, 1966–89; Secty.-Gen., Soc. Univ. Européene de Recherches Financieres (SUERF), 1968–72 (Pres., 1973–75; Vice-Pres., 1977–83; Editorial Cttee., 1971–81). *Publs:* French Banking Structure and Credit Policy, 1957; Economic Environment and Development Programmes, 1960; Economic Survey of the New Hebrides, 1966; Monetary Policy and the Development of Money Markets, 1966; (ed. with C.R. Whittlesey) Essays in Money and Banking, 1968; Availability of Capital and Credit to United Kingdom Agriculture, 1973; (ed. with C.F. Scheffer) Multinational Enterprises: Financial and Monetary Aspects, 1974; Credit to Agriculture: United Kingdom, 1975; The London Money Markets, 1976; (co-ed.) The Development of Financial Institutions in Europe 1956–76, 1977; Industrial Banking: A Comparative Study, 1978 Banking Policy and Structure: A Comparative Analysis, 1986; (ed.) Managing Bank Assets and Liabilities, 1988. Add: Dept. of Economics and Commerce, Univ. of Hull, Hull HU6 7RX, England.

WILSON, June. See **BADENI,** June.

WILSON, Keith. American, b. 1927. Poetry. Prof. Emeritus, and Resident Poet, New Mexico State Univ., Las Cruces. *Publs:* Sketches for a New Mexico Hill Town, 1966; The Old Car and Other Blackpoems, 1968; Il Sequences, 1968; Graves Registry, 1968; The Shadow of Our Bones, 1969; Graves Registry, 1969; Psalms for Various Voices, 1969; Homestead, 1970; The Old Man and Others, 1970; Rocks, 1970; (ed.) The Dance Book: An Anthology of Southwestern Poems, 1970; Midwatch, 1972; While Dancing Feet Shatter the Earth, 1978; Thantog, 1978; The Streets of San Miguel, 1978; Desert Cenote, 1978; The Shaman Deer, 1978; Stone Roses: Poems from Transylvania, 1983; (with T. Enslin) Meeting in Jal, 1985; Lion's Gate: Selected Poems, 1988; The Winds of Pentecost, 1989; The Way of the Grey Bird, 1989.. Add: 1500 S. Locust, Las Cruces, N.M. 88003, U.S.A.

WILSON, Lanford. American, b. 1937. Plays/Screenplays. Dir., and designer, Caffe Cino and Cafe La Mama theatres, NYC, and others. Co-Founder, Circle Repertory Theatre Co., 1969. *Publs:* Balm in Gilead and Other Plays, 1965; The Rimers of Eldritch and Other Plays, 1967; The Gingham Dog, 1968; Home Free!, and The Madness of Lady Bright, 1968; Lemon Sky, 1970; Serenading Louie, 1970; The Sand Castle and Three Other Plays, 1970; (adaptor) Summer and Smoke, 1971; The Great Nebula in Orion and Three Other Plays, 1972; The Hot L Baltimore, 1972; The Mound Builders, 1975; The 5th of July, 1978; Talley's Folly, 1980 (Pulitzer Prize); A Tale Told, 1981; Angels Fall, 1982; (trans.) The Three Sisters by Chekhov, 1984; Talley and Son, 1985; Burn This, 1987. Add: c/o Bridget Aschenberg, ICM, 40 W. 57th St., New York, N.Y. 10019, U.S.A.

WILSON, Mary. See **ROBY,** Mary Linn.

WILSON, Pat(ricia Elsie). British, b. 1910. Plays/Screenplays, Poetry. Part-time Lectr., Longlands Coll. of Further Education, since 1956. *Publs:* No, My Darling Daughter; The Re-Union; Thy Kingdom Come; Little Miracle; A Summer's Tale, 1969; 3 Sheep 2-1/2 Kangaroos (in U.S. as One More Time); Four for a Boy, 1972; Jan Adamant, 1972; Rectors' Return, 1973; Enchanted Pantomime, 1973; The Snow Queen, 1973; Ballet Who, 1973; New Broom, 1973; Mixed Bag, 1973; The Tektite, 1973; Fairies at the Bottom of the Garden, 1973; Send Us Victorias, 1973; Funeral Tea, 1974; Hogmanay Hurrah!, 1974; Get it All Together, 1974; The Rummage Rip-Off, 1974; Silver Wedding, 1974; Hairy Holiday, 1974; Queen Bee, 1975; Christmas Eve at the Mortuary, 1975; Ashes to Ashes, Crust to Crust, 1976; Christmas Cake and Chuppaties, 1976; Look Both Ways, 1976; I Was Here Before You, So Shove Up, 1977; You Too Can Be a Glamorous Gran, 1978; I Wish I'd Never Asked Them to Come,

1978; What Shall We Call the Baby?, 1978; There Is a Fairy Upstairs in Our Attic, 1979; Things That Go Bump in the Night, 1979; Hi Jiminy!, 1979; Medium Rare, 1980; Anybody Seen My Body?, 1980; Back Door to Heaven (in U.S. as Heavenly Highrise), 1980; A Midsummer Nightmare, 1981; The Wok, 1982; (with O. Wilson) Hurrah for Algie's Wedding!, 1986. Add: 66 Marwood Dr., Great Ayton, Cleveland TS9 6PD, England.

WILSON, Phillip (John). New Zealander, b. 1922. Novels/Short stories, Biography. Staff member, New Zealand Listener, 1947–56. *Publs:* Some Are Lucky, 1960; The Maorilander, 1961; Beneath the Thunder, 1963; Pacific Flight, 1964; The Outcasts, 1965; William Satchell, 1968; New Zealand Jack, 1973; Pacific Star, 1976. Add: 12 Bank Rd., Wellington 5, New Zealand.

WILSON, Richard. American, b. 1920. Science fiction/Fantasy, History. Reporter, Copy Reader, and Asst. Drama Critic, Fairchild publs., NYC, 1941–42; Chief of Bureau, Transradio Press, Chicago, Washington, D.C., and NYC, 1946–51; Reporter, and Deputy to the North American Ed., Reuters, NYC, 1951–64; Dir., Syracuse Univ. News Bureau, N.Y., 1964–80; Univ. Ed., Syracuse Univ., 1980–82. *Publs:* The Girls from Planet 5, 1955; Those Idiots from Earth (short stories), 1957; And Then the Town Took Off, 1960; 30-Day Wonder, 1960; Time Out for Tomorrow (short stories), 1962; The Critical Years: History of Syracuse Univ., vol. 3, 1984. Add: c/o Syracuse Univ. Press, 1600 Jamesville Ave., Syracuse, N.Y. 13244, U.S.A.

WILSON, Robert Anton. American, b. 1932. Novels/Short stories, Science fiction/Fantasy, Medicine/Health, Sex, Autobiography/Memoirs Personal. Astrology Columnist, National Mirror; Ed., Jaguar mag. Engineering Aide, Ebasco Inc., NYC, 1950–56; Salesman, Doubleday Publs., 1957; Copywriter, Popular Club, Passaic, N.J., 1959–62; Sales Mgr., Antioch Bookplate, Yellow Springs, Ohio, 1962–65; Assoc. Ed., Playboy mag., Chicago, 1966–71. *Publs:* Playboy's Book of Forbidden Words, 1972; Sex and Drugs, 1973; The Book of the Breast, 1974; The Sex Magician (novel), 1974; (with Robert Shea) Illuminatus! (SF novel trilogy The Eye in the Pyramid, The Golden Apple, Leviathan), 3 vols., 1975; Cosmic Trigger: The Final Secret of the Illuminati (reflections), 1977; (with Timothy Leary) Neuropolitics, 1977; The Schrodinger's Cat trilogy: The Universe Next Door, The Trick Top Hat, and The Homing Pigeons, 3 vols., 1979–81; Masks of the Illuminati, 1981; The Earth Will Shake, 1982; Right Where You Are Sitting Now, 1982; Prometheus Rising, 1983; The Widow's Son, 1985; The New Inquisition, 1987, Wilhelm Reich in Hell, 1987; Coincidance, 1988; Nature's God, 1989; Ishtar Rising, 1989. Add: c/o Al Zuckerman, Writers House, 21 W. 26th St., New York, N.Y. 10001, U.S.A.

WILSON, Robert McLachlan. British, b. 1916. Theology/Religion. Minister, Rankin Church, Strathaven, Lanarkshire, 1946–54; Lectr., 1954–64, Sr. Lectr., 1964–69, Prof. of New Testament, 1969–78, Prof. of Biblical Criticism, 1978–83, Univ. of St. Andrews. Assoc. Ed., 1967–77, Ed., 1977–83, New Testament Studies. *Publs:* The Gnostic Problem, 1958; Studies in the Gospel of Thomas, 1960; The Gospel of Philip, 1962; (trans. ed.) New Testament Apocrypha, 2 vols., by Hennecke-Schneemelcher, 1963–65; (trans. ed.) The Acts of the Apostles, by Haenchen, 1971; (trans. ed.) Gnosis, 2 vols., by Foerster, 1972–74; Gnosis and the New Testament, 1968; (ed.) Nag Hammadi and Gnosis, 1978; (ed.) The Future of Coptology, 1978; (trans. and ed.) Gnosis, by Kurt Rudolph, 1983; Commentary on Hebrews, 1987. Add: 10 Murrayfield Rd., St. Andrews, Fife, Scotland.

WILSON, Robert Neal. American, b. 1924. Literature, Medicine/Health, Sociology. Prof. of Sociology, Univ. of North Carolina, Chapel Hill, since 1963 (Prof. of Epidemiology, Sch. of Public Health, 1963–66; Prof. and Chmn., Dept. of Mental Health, 1966–72). *Publs:* Man Made Plain: The Poet in Contemporary Society, 1958; (ed. and co-author) The Arts in Society, 1964; Coming Home: The Problem of After-Care, 1965; Community Structure and Health Action, 1968; The Sociology of Health, 1970; (co-author and co-ed.) Further Explorations in Social Psychiatry, 1976; The Writer as Social Seer, 1979; Experiencing Creativity, 1986. Add: 213 Hamilton Hall, Univ. of North Carolina, Chapel Hill, N.C. 27514, U.S.A.

WILSON, Sandra. Also writes as Sandra Heath. British, b. 1944. Historical/Romance/Gothic. With British Civil Service until 1969. *Publs:* Less Fortunate than Fair, 1973; The Queen's Sister, 1974; The Lady Cicely, 1974; Wife to the Kingmaker, 1974; Alice, 1976; The Penrich Dragon, 1977; as Sandra Heath—Mannerby's Lady, 1977; The Whispering Rocks, 1978; Mally, 1982; Unwilling Heiress, 1983. Add:

c/o Bolt Assocs., 12 Heath Dr., Send, Surrey, GU23 7EP, England.

WILSON, Sandy. British, b. 1924. Songs, lyrics and libretti, Autobiography/Memoirs/Personal, Humour/Satire. *Publs:* This Is Sylvia, 1954; The Boy Friend (libretto), 1955; The Buccaneer, 1955; Who's Who for Beginners, 1957; Valmouth, 1958; The Poodle from Rome (short stories), 1962; Divorce Me, Darling, 1965; His Monkey Wife, 1971; I Could Be Happy (autobiography), 1975; Ivor, 1975; Caught in the Act, 1976; The Roaring Twenties, 1976; The Clapham Wonder, 1978; Aladdin, 1979. Add: 2 Southwell Gardens, London SW7 4SB, England.

WILSON, Sloan. American, b. 1920. Novels/Short stories. Reporter, Providence Journal, R.I., 1946–47; Writer, Time Inc., NYC, 1947–49; Asst. Dir., National Citizans Commn. for the Public Schs., NYC, 1949–52; Dir. of Information Services, Univ. of Buffalo, N.Y., 1952–55; Asst. Dir., White House Conference on Education, Washington, D.C., 1956; Education Ed., New York Herald Tribune, NYC, 1956–58. *Publs:* Voyage to Somewhere, 1947; The Man in the Gray Flannel Suit, 1955; A Summer Place, 1958; A Sense of Values, 1960; Georgie Winthrop, 1963; Janus Island, 1967; Away from It All, 1969; All the Best People, 1970; What Shall We Wear to This Party? (autobiography), 1976; Small Town, 1978; Ice Brothers, 1979; The Greatest Crime, 1980; Pacific Interlude, 1982; The Man in the Gray Flannel Suit II, 1984. Add: c/o Arbor House, 105 Madison Ave., New York, N.Y. 10016, U.S.A.

WILSON, Snoo. British, b. 1948. Novels, Plays/Screenplays. Assoc. Dir., Portable Theatre, London, 1969–71; Script Ed., Play for Today, BBC TV, 1972; Dramaturge, Royal Shakespeare Co., 1975–76; Dir., Scarab Theatre, 1975–80. *Publs:* (with others) Lay By, 1971; The Pleasure Principle, 1974; Pignight, and Blow Job, 1975; Soul of the White Ant, 1978; The Glad Hand, 1978; A Greenish Man, 1978; Vampire, 1979; Space Ache (novel), 1984; Inside Babel (novel), 1985. Add: 41 The Chase, London SW4 0NP, England.

WILSON, Thomas. British, b. 1916. Economics, Money/Finance. Adam Smith Prof. of Political Economy, Univ. of Glasgow, 1958–82. Civil Servant, Ministry of Economic Warfare, Ministry of Aircraft Production, and Prime Minister's Statistical Branch, 1940–46; Fellow, Univ. Coll. and Lectr., Univ. of Oxford, and Ed., Oxford Economic Papers, 1946–58. *Publs:* Fluctuations in Income and Employment, 1942; Oxford Studies in the Price Mechanism, 1951; Inflation, 1961; Planning and Growth, 1964; (ed.) Pensions, Inflation and Growth, 1974; (ed.) Essays on Adam Smith, 1975; (ed.) The Market and the State, 1976; (with D.J. Wilson) The Political Economy of the Welfare State, 1982; Inflation, Unemployment, and the Market, 1984; Unemployment and the Labour Market, 1987; Ulster: Conflict or Consent, 1989. Add: 1 Chatford House, The Promenade, Clifton Down, Bristol, England.

WILSON, Trevor Frederick. Australian. Cookery/Gastronomy/Wine, Design (general), Photography, Travel/Exploration. Proprietor, Trevor Wilson Pty. Ltd., Advertising Agents, since 1975. Member, Industrial Design Council of Australia (Chmn., 1980–82). Pres., Australian Commercial and Industrial Artists Assn., 1956–64. *Publs:* Ski Trails of Australia and New Zealand, 1968; Best of the Bake-Off Recipes, 1969; Great Rice Dishes of the World, 1970; Great Chicken Dishes of the World, 1974; The Luck of the Draw, 1980; Tasmanian Essay, Lord Snowdon, 1982; Sixth Wish, 1985. Add: 24 Airlie St., South Yarra, Vic. 3141, Australia.

WILSON, Trevor Gordon. New Zealander, b. 1928. History. Prof. of History, Univ. of Adelaide, since 1968 (Lectr., then Sr. Lectr. in History, 1960–67). Asst. Lectr. in History, Canterbury Univ., 1952, and Auckland Univ., 1953–55; Research Asst., Manchester Univ., 1957–59; Nuffield Dominion Travelling Fellow, 1964–65; Commonwealth Fellow, St. John's Coll., Cambridge, 1972. *Publs:* The Downfall of the Liberal Party 1914-1935, 1966; (ed.) The Political Diaries of C.P. Scott 1911-1928, 1970; The Myriad Faces of War: Britain and the Great War 1914-1918, 1986. Add: Dept. of History, Univ. of Adelaide, S.A. 5001, Australia.

WILSON, Wesley M. American, b. 1927. International relations/Current affairs, Law. Labor Relations Attorney, since 1970. Attorney, National Labor Relations Bd., 1960–69. *Publs:* Labor Law Handbook and Cumulative Pocket Supplements, 1963, 9th ed. 1985; Labor Relations Primer, 1973; Know Your Job Rights, 1976. Add: 3300 Carpenter Rd. S.E., #113E, Olympia, Wash. 98503, U.S.A.

WILTGEN, Ralph (Michael). American, b. 1921. History, Theology/Religion. Roman Catholic Priest; Member, Soc. of the Divine Word (S.V.D.). Publicity and Public Relations Dir., Techny, Ill., 1953–58,

Alexishafen, Papua New Guinea, 1958–60, and Rome, Italy, 1960–63; Ed., Arnoldus, Rome, 1960–63; Ed. and Dir. of Council News Service, Rome, 1962–65. *Publs:* Gold Coast Mission History 1471-1880, 1956; The Rhine Flows Into the Tiber: A History of Vatican II, 1967; The Religious Life Defined, 1970; The Founding of the Roman Catholic Church in Oceania 1825 to 1850, 1979; (ed.) A History of the Divine Word Missionaries, 1981; (ed.) Online Union Catalog of Periodicals of the Theological Library Network (TLN), 1982; How to Use a Computer in Ten Easy Lessons, 1983. Add: Collegio del Verbo Divino, Via Verbiti 1, 00154 Rome, Italy.

WINCH, Michael Bluett. British, b. 1907. Travel/Exploration/Adventure. Antique exporter, since 1960. Foreign Corresp., Christian Science Monitor and Reuters, 1933–39; with Foreign Service, 1930–31, and 1941–54. *Publs:* Republic for a Day: An Eye-Witness Account of the Carpatho-Ukraine Incident, 1939; Introducing Germany, 1957; Introducing Belgium, 1964; The World in Colour: Austria. Add: Boughton Monchelsea Pl., nr. Maidstone, Kent, England.

WINCH, Peter (Guy). British, b. 1926. Philosophy, Social sciences. Prof. of Philosophy, Univ. of Illinois, Urbana, since 1985; Prof. of Philosophy, Univ. of London, King's Coll., 1967–84, now Emeritus. Lectr. in Philosophy, Univ. of Coll. of Swansea, 1951–64; Reader, Univ. of London, Birkbeck Coll., 1964–67; Ed., Analysis, 1965–71. *Publs:* The Idea of a Social Science, 1958; (ed.) Studies in the Philosophy of Wittgenstein, 1969; Ethics and Action, 1972; (trans.) Culture and Value, by L. Wittgenstein, 1980; Trying to Make Sense, 1987; Simone Weil: "The Just Balance," 1989. Add: Dept. of Philosophy, Univ. of Illinois, Urbana, Ill. 61801, U.S.A.

WINCHESTER, Simon. British, b. 1944. Documentaries/Reportage. Corresp., The Sunday Times, since 1981. Corresp., Guardian, 1972–81. Reporter, The Journal, Newcastle upon Tyne, 1967–70. *Publs:* In Holy Terror, 1974; American Heartbeat: Notes from a Midwestern Journey, 1976; Their Noble Lordships, 1981; (with Jan Morris) Stones of Empire, 1984; Prison Diary, Argentina, 1984; The Sun Never Sets, 1986; Korea, 1988. Add: c/o Wallace Agency, 177 E. 70th St., New York, N.Y. 10021, U.S.A.

WINDER, Mavis Areta. Also writes as Mavis Areta and Mavis Areta Wynder. New Zealander, b. 1907. Novels/Short stories. *Publs:* (as Mavis Areta) A Reed Shaken, 1949; (as Mavis Areta) Badge of Bondage, 1953; (as Mavis Areta) As We Forgive Them, 1954; The Things Temporal, 1955; Shadowed Journey, 1955; The Stubble Field, 1956; (as Mavis Areta) Nest Among the Stars, 1956; Safer Than a Known Way, 1956; Stranger to Mercy, 1957; (as Mavis Areta) The Silvers of Silverstream, 1957; Render Unto Caesar, 1957; (as Mavis Areta) Faint Is the Bliss, 1958; The Gulf Between, 1958; Vain Is the Glory, 1959; Reap the Whirlwind, 1961; (as Mavis Areta) No Easy Path, 1961; (as Mavis Areta) Memory's Yoke, 1962; (as Mavis Areta) How Great a Fire, 1963; (as Mavis Areta) Love Keeps No Score, 1964; Scent of the Woods, 1965; River in the Valley, 1965; The Glitter and the Gold, 1967; (as Mavis Areta Wynder) Smile at the Storm, 1967; The Fanned Flame, 1968; Life Is for Living, 1968; (as Mavis Areta Wynder) The Lamp in the Window, 1969; Folly Is Joy, 1973. Add: F1-22 Longfellow St., Christchurch 2, New Zealand.

WINDHAM, Donald. American, b. 1920. Novels/Short stories, Plays/Screenplays, Autobiography/Memoirs/Personal. Ed., Dance Index mag., NYC, 1943–45. *Publs:* (with Tennessee Williams) You Touched Me (play), 1947; The Hitchhiker (short story), 1950; The Dog Star, 1950; The Hero Continues, 1960; The Warm Country (short stories), 1960; Emblems of Conduct (autobiography), 1964; Two People, 1965; Tanaquil: or, The Hardest Thing of All, 1972, 1977; (ed.) E.M. Forster's Letters to Donald Windham, 1975; (ed.) Tennessee Williams' Letters to Donald Windham 1940-1965, 1976; Stone in the Hourglass, 1981; Footnote to a Friendship (memoirs of Truman Capote), 1983; As If . . . (memoirs of Tennessee Williams), 1985; Lost Friendships, 1987; (ed.) The Roman Spring of Alice Toklas. 44 Letters by Alice Toklas in a Reminiscence by Donald Windham, 1987. Add: 230 Central Park South, New York, N.Y. 10019, U.S.A.

WINDSOR, Patricia. American, b. 1938. Also writes as Colin Daniel. Novels/Short stories, Children's fiction. Dir., Wordspring Writing Consultants. Member of the faculty, Inst. of Children's Literature. Formerly, Writer, producer and director, American Telephone and Telegraph, Washington, D.C.; Instr., Univ. of Maryland Writer's Inst./Open Univ., Washington, D.C.; Correspondent, National Council of Social Services, London. Formerly, Ed.-in-Chief, Easterner. *Publs:* The Summer Before, 1973; Something's Waiting for You, Baker D, 1974; Old Coat's

Cat, 1974; Home Is Where Your Feet Are Standing, 1975; Diving for Roses, 1976; Mad Martin, 1976; Killing Time, 1980; (as Colin Daniel) Demon Tree, 1983; The Sandman's Eyes, 1985; How a Weirdo and a Ghost Can Change Your Life, 1986; The Hero, 1988. Add: c/o Writer's House, 21 W. 26th St., New York, N.Y. 10010, U.S.A.

WINE, Dick. See **POSNER,** Richard.

WINEGARTEN, Renee. British, b. 1922. Literature. *Publs:* French Lyric Poetry in the Age of Malherbe, 1954; Writers and Revolution: The Fatal Lure of Action, 1974; The Double Life of George Sand: Woman and Writer, 1978; Mme. de Staël, 1985; Simone de Beauvoir: A Critical View, 1988. Add: 12 Heather Walk, Edgware, Middx. HA8 9TS, England.

WINETROUT, Kenneth. American, b. 1912. Philosophy, Biography. Instr. in Creative Writing, 1946–48, and Chmn., Education Dept., 1948–69, Stephens Coll., Columbia, Mo.; Margaret C. Ells Prof., American Intnl. Coll., Springfield, Mass., 1968–78. *Publs:* (with R. Bohlke) Bureaucrats and Intellectuals: A Critique of C. Wright Mills, 1963; F.C.S. Schiller and the Dimensions of Pragmatism, 1967; Arnold Toynbee: The Ecumenical Vision, 1975; After One Is Dead: Arnold Toynbee as Prophet, 1989. Add: 10 Hickory Lane, Hampden, Mass. 01036, U.S.A.

WING, John K. British, b. 1923. Psychiatry. Dir., Medical Research Council Psychiatry Unit, and Prof. of Social Psychiatry, Inst. of Psychiatry, London. Hon. Consultant Psychiatrist, Maudsley and Bethlem Royal Hosps., London. *Publs:* (with G.W. Brown, Margaret Bone and Bridget Dalison) Schizophrenia and Social Care, 1966; (ed.) Early Childhood Autism, 1966; (with G.W. Brown) Institutionalism and Schizophrenia, 1970; (ed. with E.H. Hare) Psychiatric Epidemiology, 1970; (ed. with Anthea Hailey) Evaluating a Community Psychiatric Service, 1972; (ed. with H. Häfner) Roots of Evaluation, 1973; (with J.E. Cooper and N. Sartorius) Measurement and Classification of Psychiatric Symptoms, 1974; (ed.) Schizophrenia: Towards a New Synthesis, 1978; Reasoning about Madness, 1978; (co-ed.) Community Care for the Mentally Disabled, 1979; (with J. Leach) Helping Destitute Men, 1980; (co-ed.) What Is a Case?, 1980; (co-ed.) Psychoses of Uncertain Aetiology, 1982. Add: MRC Social Psychiatry Unit, Inst. of Psychiatry, De Crespigny Park, London SE5 8AF, England.

WINGATE, John (Allan). British, b. 1920. Novels/Short stories, Children's fiction, History. With Royal Navy, 1933–46, 1951–52; Housemaster, Milton Abbey Sch., 1957–65; Warden, Calshot Activities Centre, 1965–70. *Publs:* Submariner Sinclair, 1959; Jimmy-the-One, 1960; Sinclair in Command, 1961; Nuclear Captain, 1962; Sub-Zero, 1963; Torpedo Strike, 1964; Never So Proud, 1966; Full Fathom Five, 1967; Last Ditch, 1970; In Trust for the Nation: H.M.S. Belfast, 1972; In the Blood, 1973; (ed.) Warships in Profile, vols. II and III, 1973–74; Below the Horizon, 1974; Oil Strike, 1975; The Sea Above Them, 1976; Avalanche, 1977; Red Mutiny, 1978; Target Risk, 1979; Seawaymen, 1979; Frigate, 1980; Carrier, 1980; Submarine, 1981; William, The Conqueror, 1982; Go Deep, 1985; The Windship Race, 1987; The Fighting Tenth: A History of the 10th Submarine Flotilla, Malta 1940-1944, 1987. Add: c/o Lloyds Bank Intnl., 43 Blvd. des Capucines, Paris, France.

WINGFIELD, Sheila. (Sheila, Viscountess Powerscourt). British, b. 1906. Poetry, Autobiography/Memoirs/Personal. *Publs:* Poems, 1938; Beat Drum, Beat Heart, 1946; A Cloud Across the Sun, 1949; Real People (autobiography), 1952; A Kite's Dinner: Poems 1938–1954, 1954; The Leaves Darken, 1964; (as Sheila Powerscourt) Sun Too Fast, 1974; Her Storms: Selected Poems, 1974; Admissions, 1977; Cockatrice and Basilisk, 1982; Collected Poems 1938-83, 1983. Add: c/o Rawlinson and Hunter, 1 Hanover Sq., London W1A 4SR, England.

WINGO, Glenn Max. American, b. 1913. Education. Prof. Emeritus of Education, Sch. of Education, Univ. of Michigan, Ann Arbor, since 1979 (Asst. Prof., 1945–49; Assoc. Prof., 1949–54; Prof., 1954–79). Elementary sch. principal, New London, 1941–43, and Darien, 1943–45, both Conn. *Publs:* (with R. Schorling) Elementary School Student Teaching, 1950, 3rd ed. 1960; (with W.C. Morse) Psychology and Teaching, 1955, 3rd ed. 1969; (ed. with W.C. Morse) Readings in Educational Psychology, 1962; The Philosophy of American Education, 1965; (with W.C. Morse) Classroom Psychology, 3rd ed. 1971; Philosophies of Education: An Introduction, 1974. Add: 3490 E. Huron River Dr., Ann Arbor, Mich. 48104, U.S.A.

WINGREN, Gustaf Fredrik. Swedish, b. 1910. Theology/Religion. Prof. of Systematic Theology, Univ. of Lund, since 1951 (Docent, 1944–

50). *Publs:* Luther on Vocation, 1957; Theology in Conflict: Nygren-Barth-Bultmann, 1958; Man and the Incarnation: A Study in the Biblical Theology of Irenaenus, 1959; Creation and Law, 1961; Gospel and Church, 1964; The Living Word, 2nd ed. 1965; An Exodus Theology, 1969; The Flight from Creation, 1971; Creation and Gospel, 1979; Credo: The Christian View of Faith and Life, 1981. Add: Warholms Vag 6B, S-22365 Lund, Sweden.

WINKLER, Anthony C. Jamaican, b. 1942. Novels/Short stories, Writing/Journalism. Adjunct Prof., Dekalb Community Coll., North Campus, Atlanta. Field Rep., Appleton-Century-Crofts, NYC, 1968–70, and for Scott Foresman and Co., Chicago, 1971–75; English Tutor, Moneague Teachers Coll., Moneague, Jamaica, 1975–76. *Publs:* Poetry as System, 1971; (with JoRay McCuen) Rhetoric Made Plain, 1974; (with JoRay McCuen) Readings for Writers, 1974; (with JoRay McCuen) From Idea to Essay, 1977; (with Don Ochs) A Brief Introduction to Speech, 1979; (with JoRay McCuen) Writing the Research Paper: A Handbook, 1979; (with JoRay McCuen) Writing Sentences, Paragraphs, and Essays, 1981; The Painted Canoe, 1983; (with JoRay McCuen) Rewriting Writing, 1987; The Lunatic, 1987. Add: c/o Lyle Stuart Inc., 120 Enterprise Ave., Secaucus, N.J. 07094 U.S.A.

WINKLER, Henry Ralph. American, b. 1916. History. Univ. Prof. of History Emeritus, Univ. of Cincinnati (Pres., 1977–84). Asst. Prof., 1947–52, Assoc. Prof., 1952–58, Prof., 1958–77, Dean of the Faculty of Liberal Arts, 1967–70, Vice-Provost, 1968–70, Vice Pres. for Academic Affairs, 1970–72, Sr. Vice-Pres. for Academic Affairs, 1972–76, Acting Pres., 1976, and Exec. Vice-Pres., 1976–77, Rutgers Univ., New Brunswick, N.J. *Publs:* The League of Nations Movement in Great Britain 1914-1919, 1952, 1967; Great Problems in European Civilization, 1954, 1965; Great Britain in the Twentieth Century, 1960, 1967; Twentieth-Century Britain: National Power and Social Welfare, 1976. Add: Dept. of History, Univ. of Cincinnati, Cincinnati, Ohio 45221, U.S.A.

WINKLER, John. British, b. 1935. Marketing. Managing Dir., Winkler Marketing Ltd., Brighton, since 1969. *Publs:* Marketing for the Developing Company, 1969; Winkler on Marketing Planning, 1972; Company Survival During Inflation, 1975; Bargaining for Results, 1981; Pricing for Results, 1984; Winning Tactics, 1989. Add: 17 Surrenden Park, Brighton, Sussex, England.

WINNIFRITH, T(homas) J(ohn). British, b. 1938. Literature. Asst. Master, Eton Coll., 1961–66; E.K. Chambers Student, Corpus Christi Coll., Oxford, 1966–68; Lectr., 1970–77, and Sr. Lectr., 1977–88, Dept. of English and Comparative Literary Studies, Univ. of Warwick. *Publs:* The Brontës and Their Background, 1973; The Brontës, 1977; (trans. with J. O'Malley) Streets, by J. Nyiri, 1979; (ed. with P. Murray) Greece Old and New, 1983; (ed. with P. Murray and K. Gransden) Aspects of the Epic, 1983; (ed.) The Poems of Branwell Brontë, 1983; (ed.) The Poems of Charlotte Brontë, 1984; (with E. Chitham) Brontë Facts and Problems, 1984; (with W.V. Whitehead) 1984 and All's Well?, 1984; (ed. with E. Chiltham) Selected Brontë Poems, 1985; A New Life of Charlotte Brontë 1987; (co-ed.) The Philosophy of Leisure, 1989; (with E. Chitham) Charlotte and Emily Brontë: A Literary Life, 1989. Add: 10 Grove St., Leamington Spa CV32 5AJ, England.

WINNIKOFF, Albert. American (born Canadian), b. 1930. Money/Finance. *Publs:* The Land Game—Or How to Make a Fortune in Real Estate, 1970; (with Burt Prelutsky) Sell, Sell, Sell; or, How to Make $100,000 a Year, 1977. Add: 29046 Cliffside Dr., Malibu, Calif, 90265, U.S.A.

WINSLOW, Pauline Glen. Also writes as Jane Sheridan. British-American. Mystery/Crime/Suspense, Romance. Court reporter, NYC and Federal Govt., 1963–64; freelance court reporter, NYC, 1964–73. *Publs:* novels—The Strawberry Marten, 1973, in U.S. as Gallows Child, 1978; (as Jane Sheridan) Damaris, 1978; The Windsor Plot, 1981; (as Jane Sheridan) My Lady Hoyden, 1981; I, Martha Adams, 1982; (as Jane Sheridan) Love at Sunset, 1982; The Kindness of Strangers, 1983; Judgement Day, 1984; mystery novels—Death of an Angel, 1975; The Brandenburg Hotel, 1976; The Witch Hill Murder, 1977; Coppergold, 1978; The Counsellor Heart, 1980, in U.K. paperback as Sister Death, 1982; The Rockefeller Gift, 1981. Add: 210 Sixth Ave., New York, N.Y. 10014, U.S.A.

WINSOR, Kathleen. American, b. 1919. Historical/Romance/Gothic. Reporter and Receptionist, Oakland Tribune, Calif., 1937–38; Story Consultant, Dreams in the Dust TV series, 1971. *Publs:* Forever Amber, 1944; Star Money, 1950; The Lovers, 1952; America, With Love, 1957;

Wanderers Eastward, Wanderers West, 1965; Calais, 1979; Jacintha, 1983; Robert and Arabella, 1986. Add: c/o Roslyn Targ Literary Agency, Inc., 105 W. 13th St., New York, N.Y. 10011, U.S.A.

WINSTON, Daoma. American, b. 1922. Mystery/Crime/Suspense, Historical/Romance/Gothic. *Publs:* Tormented Lovers, 1962; Love Her, She's Yours, 1963; The Secrets of Cromwell Crossing, 1965; Sinister Stone, 1966; The Wakefield Witches, 1966; The Mansion of Smiling Masks, 1967; The Castle of Closing Doors, 1967; Shadow of an Unknown Woman, 1967; The Carnaby Curse, 1967; Shadow on Mercer Mountain, 1967; Pity My Love, 1967; The Traficante Treasure, 1968; Moderns, 1968; The Long and Living Shadow, 1968; Braken's World, 1969; Mrs. Berrigan's Dirty Book, 1970; Beach Generation, 1970; Wild Country, 1970; Dennison Hill, 1970; House of Mirror Images, 1970; Sound Stage, 1970; The Love of Lucifer, 1970; The Vampire Curse, 1971; Flight of a Fallen Angel, 1971; The Devil's Daughter, The Devil's Princess, 1971; Seminar in Evil, 1972; The Victim, 1972; The Return, 1972; The Inheritance, 1972; Kingdom's Castle, 1972; Skeleton Key, 1972, as The Mayeroni Myth, 1979; Moorhaven, 1973; The Trap, 1973; The Unforgotten, 1973; The Haversham Legacy, 1974; Mills of the Gods, 1974; Emerald Station, 1974; The Golden Valley, 1975; Death Watch, 1975; A Visit after Dark, 1975; Walk Around the Square, 1975; Gallows Way, 1976; The Dream Killers, 1976; The Adventuress, 1978; The Lotteries, 1980; A Sweet Familiarity, 1981; Mira, 1982; The Fall River Line, 1984; Maybe This Time, 1988. Lives in Washington, D.C. Add: c/o Jay Garon-Brooke Assocs., 415 Central Park W., New York, N.Y. 10025, U.S.A.

WINSTON, Sarah. Also writes as Sarah E. Lorenz. American, b. 1912. Novels/Short stories, Poetry, Psychology. *Publs:* (as Sarah E. Lorenz) And Always Tomorrow, 1963, in paperback as Our Son, Ken, 1969; Everything Happens for the Best (biographical fiction), 1969, 1970; Not Yet Spring (poetry), 1976; (ed. and contrib.) V . . .—Mail: Letters of a World War II Combat Medic, 1985. Add: 1838 Rose Tree Lane, Havertown, Pa. 19083, U.S.A.

WINSTONE, Reece. British, b. 1909. History (photographic histories), Urban studies (local). Freelance photographer, writer and publr. *Publs:* Bristol As It Was 1845–1962, 22 vols.; Bristol Today; Bristol Fashion; Bristol Blitzed; Bristol's Earliest Photographs; Bristol Tradition; Bristol's Trams; (ed.) Bristol's History, 2 vols.; (ed.) Miss Ann Green; History of Bristol's Suburbs; Bristol's Suburbs in the 1920's and 1930's; Bath as It Was; Bristol's Suburbs Long Ago; Changes in the Face of Bristol. Add: Ilex House, Front St., Churchill, Bristol BS19 5LZ, England.

WINTER, David Brian. British, b. 1929. Theology/Religion, Biography. Ed., Crusade, 1959–71; Producer, 1971–82, Head of Religious Programmes, 1982–87, and Head of Religious Broadcasting, 1987–89, BBC Radio. *Publs:* The Christian's Guide to Church Membership, 1963; Ground of Truth, 1964; Old Faith, Young World, 1966; For All the People, 1966; New Singer, New Song, 1967; (with S. Linden) Two a Penny, 1969; How to Walk with God, 1969; Laurie, The Happy Man (in U.S. as Closer than a Brother), 1971; (with J. Bryant) Well God, Here We Are Again, 1971; Hereafter, 1972; (ed.) Matthew Henry's Commentary, 2 vols., 1975; After the Gospels, 1978; But This I Can Believe, 1980; The Search for the Real Jesus, 1982; Living Through Loss, 1983; Truth in the Son, 1985; Walking in the Light, 1986; Believing the Bible, 1987; Battered Bride?, 1988. Add: 6 Standlake Rd., Ducklington, Witney, Oxon, England.

WINTER, Elmer. American, b. 1912. Business/Trade/Industry, Children's non-fiction, Women. Chief Price Attorney for Wisconsin, Office of Price Admin., 1942–44; Pres., Intnl. Franchise Assn., 1963–64; Past Pres., Manpower Inc.; Past Pres., American Jewish Cttee; past Dir., Haifa Univ., Israel; Chmn., Cttee. for Economic Growth of Israel. *Publs:* A Woman's Guide to Earning a Good Living, 1961; A Complete Guide to Making a Public Stock Offering, 1962, 1973; Cutting Costs Through the Effective Use of Temporary and Part-time Help, 1964; How to Be an Effective Secretary, 1965; Your Future in Your Own Business, 1966; Women at Work: Every Woman's Guide to Successful Employment, 1967; 1,015 Ways to Save Time, Trouble and Money in the Operation of Your Business, 1967; Your Future in Jobs Abroad, 1968; Your Future as a Temporary Office Worker, 1969; How to Get and Keep a Job, 1982; A Complete Guide to Preparing a Corporate Annual Report, 1985. Add: 8014 N. Lake Dr., Fox Point, Wisc. 53217, U.S.A.

WINTER, John (Anthony). British, b. 1930. Architecture. Principal of John Winter and Assocs., London, since 1960. Asst. Architect, Stillman and Eastwick-Field, London, 1953–54, Skidmore Owings and Merrill, San Francisco, 1957–59, and Ernö Goldfinger, London, 1959–60;

Instr., Yale Univ., New Haven, Conn., 1956–57, Architectural Assn., London, 1960–64, University Coll., London, 1976–79, and Cambridge Univ., 1977–78; Visiting Prof., Toronto Univ., 1962, and Syracuse Univ., N.Y., 1978. *Publs:* Modern Building, 1968; Industrial Architecture, 1969; (part author) The Open Hand: Essays on Le Corbusier, 1977; (part author) Architecture: Style, Structure, and Design, 1982. Add: 80 Lamble St., London NW5 4AB, England.

WINTER, Michael Morgan. British, b. 1930. History, Theology/Religion. Catholic Chaplain to the Univ. of London. Former Lectr. in Fundamental Theology, St. John's Seminary, Surrey, and Lectr. in Dogmatic Theology, Beda Coll., Rome. *Publs:* St. Peter and the Popes, 1960; Mission or Maintenance, 1973; A Concordance to the Peshitta Version of Ben Sira, 1975; Mission Resumed?, 1978; What Ever Happened to Vatican II?, 1985. Add: c/o Sheed and Ward, 2 Creechurch Lane, London EC3A 5AQ, England.

WINTERBOTHAM, Frederick William. British, b. 1897. History, International relations/Current affairs, Military/Defence. With Cavalry and Royal Flying Corps, 1915–18, British Air Staff and Foreign Office, 1930–45; Exec., British Overseas Aircraft Corp., 1945–49, and Commonwealth Development Corp., 1949–52. *Publs:* Secret and Personal, 1969; The Ultra Secret, 1974; The Nazi Connection, 1979; From Victoria to Ultra, 1984. Add: Westwinds, Tarrant Gunville, nr. Blandford, Dorset DT11 8JW, England.

WINTERBOTTOM, Michael. British, b. 1934. Classics. Fellow and Tutor in Classics, Worcester Coll., Oxford, since 1967. Lectr. in Latin and Greek, University Coll. London, 1962–67. *Publs:* (ed.) Quintilian, 1970; (with D.A. Russell) Ancient Literary Criticism, 1972; Three Lives of English Saints, 1972; (ed. and trans.) The Elder Seneca, 1974; (ed. with R.M. Ogilvie) Tacitus: Opera Minora, 1975; (ed. and trans.) Gildas, 1978; Roman Declamation, 1980; (ed. with commentary) The Minor Declamations Ascribed to Quintilian, 1984; (with D.C. Innes) Sopatros the Rhetor, 1988. Add: Worcester Coll., Oxford, England.

WIRTH, Arthur. American, b. 1919. Education, Philosophy. Prof., Grad. Inst. of Education, Washington Univ., St. Louis, Mo., since 1961. Member of faculty, Ohio State Univ., Columbus, 1947–49, and Brooklyn Coll., City Univ. of New York, N.Y., 1949–61. *Publs:* John Dewey as Educator, 1966; Education and the Technological Society, 1972; Productive Work in Industry and Schools, 1984; Beyond Acceptance: Parents of Gays Tell Their Story, 1986. Add: Grad. Inst. of Education, Box 1183, Washington Univ., St. Louis, Mo. 63130, U.S.A.

WISE, Charles Conrad, Jr. American, b. 1913. Poetry, Songs, lyrics and libretti, Theology/Religion. Instr. in Philosophy and Thanatology, Blue Ridge Community Coll., Weyers Cave, Va., since 1973. Chief Dept. Counsel, Security Policy, Dept. of Defense, Washington, D.C., 1962–73 (began U.S. Govt. Service in 1933). *Publs:* Windows on the Passion, 1967; Windows on the Master, 1968; (ed.) Chanticleer, 1968; 1970; Ruth and Naomi (libretto), 1971; Mind Is It: Meditation, Prayer, Healing, and the Psychic, 1978; Picture Windows on the Christ, 1979; The Magian Gospel, 1979; Thus Saith the Lord: The Autobiography of God, 1983; The Holy Families, 1989. Add: Solon-Lair, Cross Keys, Penn Laird, Va. 22846, U.S.A.

WISE, David. American, b. 1930. Politics/Government. Reporter, 1951–66, and Chief of Washington Bureau, 1963–66, New York Herald Tribune; Fellow of the Woodrow Wilson Intnl. Center for Scholars, Washington, D.C., 1970–71; Lectr. in Political Science, Univ. of California at Santa Barbara, 1977–79. *Publs:* (with T.B. Ross) The U-2 Affair, 1962; The Invisible Government, 1964; The Espionage Establishment, 1967; (with M. Cummings) Democracy Under Pressure: An Introduction to the American Political System, 1971, 5th ed. 1985; The Politics of Lying: Government Deception, Secrecy, and Power, 1973; The American Police State, 1976; Spectrum, 1981; The Children's Game, 1983; The Spy Who Got Away, 1988. Add: c/o Sterling Lord Agency, One Madison Ave., New York, N.Y. 10010, U.S.A.

WISE, Leonard (Christian). American. Novels/Short stories. *Publs:* The Big Biazarro, 1977; The Diggstown Ringers, 1978; Dumachas and Sheba, 1979; Doc's Legacy, 1986. Add: c/o Doubleday & Co. Inc., 666 Fifth Ave., New York, N.Y. 10103, U.S.A.

WISE, Terence. British, b. 1935. Genealogy/Heraldry, History, Recreation/Leisure/Hobbies. *Publs:* Introduction to Battle Gaming, 1969, 4th ed. 1975; Guide to Military Museums, 1969, 6th ed. 1988; To Catch a Whale, 1970; Military Vehicle Markings, 2 vols., 1972–73; Bat-

tles for Wargamers, 6 vols., 1972–74; American Military Camouflage and Markings, 1973; Forts and Castles, 1973; European Edged Weapons, 1974; Polar Exploration, 1974; Medieval Warfare 1300-1500, 1974; Men at Arms series, 13 vols., 1974–84; Guide to American Civil War Wargaming, 1977; Military Flags of the World 1618-1900, 1977; Wars of the Crusades, 1978; D-Day to Berlin: WW2 Vehicle Camouflage, 1979; 1066, Year of Destiny, 1979; Military Vehicle Markings of World War II, 1980. Add: 20 St. Mary's Rd., Wheatley, Doncaster, S. Yorks, DN1 2NP, England.

WISEMAN, Adele. Canadian, b. 1928. Novels/Short stories, Plays. Head of the Writing Program, Banff Sch. of Fine Arts. Former teacher of English, MacDonald Coll., McGill Univ., Montreal. *Publs:* The Sacrifice, 1956; Old Markets, New World, 1964; Crackpot, 1974; Testimonial Dinner (play), 1976; Old Woman at Play, 1978; Canadian Woman Writers Calendar 1985, 1986; Memoirs of a Book Molesting Childhood, 1987. Add: c/o Oxford Univ. Press, 70 Wynford Dr., Don Mills, Ont. M3C 1J9, Canada.

WISEMAN, Alan. British, b. 1936. Biology. Sr. Lectr. in Biochemistry, Univ. of Surrey, since 1978. Ed., Topics in Enzyme and Fermentation Biotechnology Series, since 1977. *Publs:* Organization for Protein Biosynthesis, 1965; (with B.J. Gould) Enzymes: Their Nature and Role, 1971; (ed. and contrib.) Handbook of Enzyme Biotechnology, 1975, 1985. Add: Dept. of Biochemistry, Univ. of Surrey, Guildford, England.

WISEMAN, Bernard. American, b. 1922. Children's fiction, Children's non-fiction, Humor/Satire. Cartoonist, New Yorker mag., NYC, and Punch mag., London, both 1947–59; Cartoonist and Ed., McNaught Syndicate, 1965–66, and Spadea Syndicate, 1967–69. *Publs:* Cartoon Countdown, 1959; Morris and Boris series, 13 vols., 1959–83; The Log and Admiral Frog, 1960; Boatniks, 1961; Irwin the Interne, 1962; The Hat That Grew, 1965; 96 Cats, 1969; Sex-Ed, 1971; Detective Dog, 1972; Hats and Coats, Cows and Goats, 1972; Nutty Nature Book, 1972; Silly Science Book, 1972; Little New Kangaroo, 1973; Billy Learns Karate, 1976; Iglook's Seal, 1977; Quick Quackers, 1979; The Lucky Runner, 1979; Tails Are Not for Painting, 1980; Hooray for Patsy's Oink!, 1980; Oscar Is a Mama, 1980; Penny's Poodle Puppy, 1980; Don't Make Fun, 1982; Cats! Cats! Cats!, 1984; Doctor Duck and Nurse Swan, 1984; Dolly Dodo, 1986. Add: c/o Little, Brown and Co., 34 Beacon St., Boston, Mass. 02108, U.S.A.

WISEMAN, Donald John. British, b. 1918. Archaeology/Antiquities, History, Literature, Theology/Religion. Vice Pres., British Sch. of Archaeology in Iraq; Trustee, British Sch. of Archaeology in Jerusalem. Asst. Keeper, Dept. of Western Asiatic Antiquities, British Museum, London, 1948–61; Ed., Iraq, 1953–78; Prof. of Assyriology, Univ. of London, 1961-82. Co-Ed., Reallexikon der Assyriologie, De Gruyter, Berlin, 1966-82. *Publs:* The Alalakh Tablets, 1953; Chronicles of Chaldaean Kings, 1956; Cylinder Seals of Western Asia, 1958; The Vassal Treaties of Esarhaddon, 1958; Illustrations from Biblical Archaeology, 1958; The Expansions of Assyrian Studies, 1962; Catalogue of Western Asiatic Seals in the British Museum I, 1963; (ed.) Peoples of Old Testament Times, 1973; Archaeology and the Bible, 1979; Essays on the Patriarchal Narratives, 1980; (co-ed.) Illustrated Bible Dictionary, 1980; Nebuchadrezzar and Babylon, 1985. Add: 26 Downs Way, Tadworth, Surrey KT20 5DZ, England.

WISER, William. American, b. 1929. Novels/Short stories. Writer-in-Residence, Queen's Univ. of Belfast. *Publs:* K, 1971; The Wolf Is Not Native to the South of France, 1978; Disappearances, 1980; Ballads, Blues, and Swan Songs, 1982; Crazy Years: Paris in the Twenties, 1983; The Circle Tour, 1988. Add: Quartier le ribas, Cabris, 06530 Peymeinade, France.

WISLER, G(ary) Clifton. American, b. 1950. Westerns/Adventure, Children's fiction. Teacher, Ben C. Jackson Middle Sch., Texas, since 1974. *Publs:* My Brother, The Wind, 1979; A Cry of Angry Thunder, 1980; Winter of the Wolf (for young adults), 1981; The Trident Brand, 1982; Sunrise, 1982; Thunder on the Tennessee (for children), 1983; The Chicken Must Have Died Laughing, 1983; A Special Gift, 1983; Buffalo Moon (for children), 1984; Starr's Showdown, 1985; The Raid (for children), 1985; Antelope Springs, 1986; The Antrian Messenger (for children), 1986; Comanche Crossing, 1987; Comanche Summer, 1987; Texas Brazos, 1987; This New Land, 1987; Avery's Law, 1988; The Seer, 1988; South Pass Ambush, 1988; Return of Canlfield Blake, 1989. Add: Ben C. Jackson Middle Sch., Garland, Tex., U.S.A.

WITEMEYER, Hugh Hazen. American, b. 1939. Literature. Prof. of

English, Univ. of New Mexico, Albuquerque, since 1973. Asst. Prof. of English, Univ. of California at Berkeley, 1966–73. *Publs:* The Poetry of Ezra Pound: Forms and Renewal 1908-1920, 1969; George Eliot and the Visual Arts, 1979; (ed.) William Carlos Williams and James Laughlin: Selected Letters, 1989; (co-ed.) W.B. Yeats, Letters to the New Island: A New Edition, 1989. Add: Dept. of English, Univ. of New Mexico, Albuquerque, N.M. 87131, U.S.A.

WITHEFORD, Hubert. New Zealander, b. 1921. Poetry. Dir., Reference Div., Central Office of Information, London, 1978–81, now retired (joined staff, 1954; Head of Overseas Section, 1968–78). Staff member, New Zealand Prime Minister's Office, 1939–45, and New Zealand War History Branch, 1945–53. *Publs:* Shadow of the Flame: Poems 1942-1947, 1949; The Falcon Mask, 1951; The Lightning Makes a Difference: Poems, 1962; A Native, Perhaps Beautiful, 1967; A Possible Order, 1980. Add: 88 Roxborough Rd., Harrow, Middx., England.

WITKE, Roxane. American, b. 1938. Area studies. Adjunct Prof., of Oriental Languages and Cultures, Columbia Univ., NYC, since 1987. Asst. Prof., 1971–72, Assoc. Prof., 1972–78, and Prof. of History, 1978–79, State Univ. of New York at Binghamton. *Publs:* (with R. Rinden) The Red Flag Waves: A Guide to the Hung-Ch'i P'iao-P'iao Collection, 1968; (ed. with Margery Wolf) Women in Chinese Society, 1975; Comrade Chiang Ch'ing, 1977. Add: Columbia Coll., Intnl. Affairs Building, Columbia Univ., New York, N.Y. 10027, U.S.A.

WITT, Harold Vernon. American, b. 1923. Poetry. Consulting Ed., Poet Lore, since 1976; Co-Ed., Blue Unicorn, since 1977. Reference Librarian, Washoe County Library, Reno, Nev., 1953–55; Reference Librarian, San Jose State Coll., Calif., 1956–59. *Publs:* Family in the Forest, 1956; Superman Unbound, 1956; The Death of Venus, 1958; Beasts in Clothes, 1961; Winesburg by the Sea: A Preview, 1970; Pop, by 1940: 40,000, 1971; Now, Swim, 1974; Surprised by Others at Fort Cronkhite, 1975; Winesburg by the Sea, 1979; The Snow Prince, 1982; Flashbacks and Reruns, 1985. Add: 39 Claremont Ave., Orinda, Calif. 94563, U.S.A.

WITTENBACH, Henry August. British, b. 1900. Children's fiction, International relations/Current affairs, Theology/Religion. Ordained Anglican Priest, since 1923. Canon Emeritus, Hong Kong Cathedral, since 1941. Asia Secty., 1947–61, and Secty., 1961–65, Church Missionary Soc., London; Asst. Dir., Coll. of Preaachers, London, 1965–70. *Publs:* Forward, 1948; Christianity and Communism in China, 1949; Communist China: What of the Church, 1950; China: An Object Lesson, 1951; Eastern Horizons, 1954; Missionaries Are Our Business, 1963; The Donkey Who Learned to Sing, 1975; The First Easter Egg, 1975; I Meet the Japanese, 1989. Add: 30 Halstead Rd., Enfield, Middx. EN1 1QB, England.

WITTLIN, Thaddeus (Andrew). Has also written as Janusz Karniewski. American (born Polish), b. 1909. Novels/Short stories, Plays, Poetry, History, Biography. Scriptwriter and Ed., Polish desk, Radiodiffusion Francaise, Paris, 1950–51; freelance writer for Voice of America and Radio Free Europe, and trans.-narrator for Motion Picture Service Branch, U.S. Information Agency, NYC, 1952–58; Ed., America Illustrated monthly mag., U.S. Information Agency, Washington, D.C., 1958–71; Lectr. In Polish Literature, George Washington Univ., Washington, D.C., 1969–70. *Publs:* Trasa na Parnas, 1929; Marzyciel i Goscie, 1933; (as Janusz Karniewski) Zlamane Skrzydla, 1934; (as Janusc Karniewski) Przekreslony Czlowiek, 1935; Romans z Urzedem Skarbowym, 1938; Pieta Achillesa, 1939; Radosne Dni, 1946; Wyspa Zakochanych, 1950; Diabel w Raju, 1951, trans. as A Reluctant Traveler in Russia, 1952, paperback as An Unwilling Traveler in Russia, 1966; Modigliani: Prince of Montparnasse, 1964; Time Stopped at 6:30, 1965; Commissar: The Life and Death of Lavrenty Pavlovich Beria, 1972; Ostatnia Cyganeria, 1979; Piesniarka Warszawy, 1985; An Evening with Anton Chekhov and Maxim Gorky, 1987. Add: 2020 F St. N.W., Washington, D.C. 20006, U.S.A.

WITTNER, Lawrence Stephen. American, b. 1941. History, Politics/Government. Prof. of History, State Univ. of New York at Albany, since 1983 (Lectr. 1974–76; Asst. Prof., 1976–77; Assoc. Prof., 1977–83). Asst. Prof., Hampton Inst., Va., 1967–68; Asst. Prof., Vassar Coll., Poughkeepsie, N.Y., 1968–73; Sr. Fulbright Lectr., Japan, 1973–74. Pres., Conference on Peace Research in History, 1977–79; Co-Exec. Ed., Peace and Change, 1984–87. *Publs:* Rebels Against War: The American Peace Movement 1941-60, 1969; (ed.) MacArthur, 1971; Cold War America: From Hiroshima to Watergate, 1974, 1978; American Intervention in Greece 1943-1949, 1982; Rebels Against War: The American Peace Movement 1933-1983, 1984. Add: Dept. of History, State Univ. of New York at Albany, Albany, N.Y. 12222, U.S.A.

WITTON-DAVIES, Carlyle. British, b. 1913. Theology/Religion, Translations. Archdeacon of Oxford, and Canon of Christ Church, Oxford, 1957–82, now retired. Dean of St. Davids, 1950–57. *Publs:* (trans. with M. Wittio-Davies) Hasidism, by Martin Buber, 1948; (trans.) The Prophetic Faith, by Martin Buber, 1949; Journey of a Lifetime, 1962. *Publs:* Hill Rise, 199 Divinity Rd., Oxford OX4 1LS, England.

WODHAMS Jack. Australian (b. British), b. 1931. Science fiction/Fantasy. Mailvan driver, Brisbane; also freelance writer, mainly of science fiction short stories. Has worked as a weighing-machine mechanic, brush salesman, porter in a mental hosp., taxi and truck driver, bartender, welder, and magician's asst. *Publs:* The Authentic Touch, 1971; Looking for Blucher, 1980; Ryn, 1982; Future War (stories), 1982. Add: P.O. Box 48, Caboolture, Qld. 4510, Australia.

WOGAMAN, J(ohn) Philip. American, b. 1932. Sociology, Theology/Religion. Prof. of Christian Social Ethics, Wesley Theological Seminary, Washington, D.C., since 1966 (Dean, 197–83); Assoc. Prof., Bible and Social Ethics, Univ. of the Pacific, and Dir., Pacific Center for the Study of Social Issues, 1961–66. Pres., American Soc. of Christian Ethics, 1976–77. *Publs:* Methodism's Challenge in Race Relations: A Study of Strategy, 1960; Protestant Faith and Religious Liberty, 1967; Guaranteed Annual Income: The Moral Issues, 1968; (ed.) The Population Crisis and Moral Responsibility, 1973; A Christian Method of Moral Judgment, 1977; The Great Economic Debate, 1977; (with Paul McCleary) Quality of Life in a Global Society, 1978; Faith and Fragmentation: Christianity for a New Age, 1985; Economics and Ethics, 1986; Christian Perspectives on Politics, 1988. Add: 4500 Masachusetts Ave. N.W., Washington, D.C. 20016, U.S.A.

WOHLGELERNTER, Maurice. American, b. 1921. Literature. Prof. of English, Baruch Coll., City Univ. of New York, since 1972. Taught at Yeshiva Univ., NYC, 1955–70, and the New Sch. for Social Research, NYC, 1966–68. *Publs:* Israel Zangwill: A Study, 1964; (ed.) The King of Schnorrers, by Israel Zangwill, 1964; Frank O'Connor: An Introduction, 1977; (ed.) History, Religion and Spiritual Democracy: Essays in Honor of Joseph Leon Blau, 1980; (ed.) The Great Hatred, by Maurice Samuel, 1988. Add: Box 411, Dept. of English, Baruch Coll., CUNY, 17 Lexington Ave., New York, N.Y. 10010, U.S.A.

WOIWODE, Larry (Alfred). American, b. 1941. Novels/Short stories, Poetry. Writer-in-Residence, Univ. of Wisconsin, Madison, 1973–74. Member, Exec. Bd., P.E.N., 1972; Visiting Prof., SUNY Binghamton, 1983–85; Prof. and Dir. of Creative Writing Prog., SUNY Binghamton, 1985–88. Publs What I'm Going to Do, I Think, 1969; (with others) Poetry North, 1970; Beyond the Bedroom Wall, 1975; Even Tide (verse), 1977; Poppa John, 1981; Born Brothers, 1988. Add: c/o Michael di Capua Books, Farrar Straus & Giroux, 19 Union Sq. W., New York, N.Y. 10003, U.S.A.

WOJCIECHOWSKA, Maia (Teresa). American (b. Polish), b. 1927. Novels/Short stories, Children's fiction, Poetry, Translations. Professional tennis instr., since 1949. Trans., Radio Free Europe, 1949–51; worked for William Burns Detective Agency, 1951–69; Asst. Ed., Retail Wholesale and Dept. Store Union Record, NYC, 1953–55; Copy girl, Newsweek mag., NYC, 1953–55; Asst. Ed., American Hairdresser mag., NYC, 1955–57; Agent and Ed., Kurt Hellmer Literary Agency, NYC, 1958–61; Publicity Mgr., Hawthorn Books, NYC, 1961–65. *Publs:* Market Day for Ti Andre, 1952; Shadow of a Bull, 1964; The International Loved Look, 1964; A Kingdom in a Horse, 1965; Odyssey of Courage: The Story of Alvar Nunez Cabeza de Vaca, 1965; The Hollywood Kid, 1966; A Single Light, 1968; Turned Out, 1968; All at Sea (play), 1968; Hey, What's Wrong with This One?, 1969; Don't Play Dead Before You Have To, 1970; (trans.) The Bridge to the Other Side, by Monika Kotowska, 1970; The Rotten Years, 1971; The Life and Death of a Brave Bull, 1972; Through the Broken Mirror with Alice, 1972; Till the Break of Day, 1972; Winter Tales from Poland, 1973; The People in His Life, 1980; How God Got Christian into Trouble, 1984. Add: c/o Westminister/John Knox Press, 100 Witherspoon St., Lovisville, Ky. 40202, U.S.A.

WOLCOTT, Leonard Thompson. American. Theology/Religion. Freelance writer, lectr.; writer of curriculum for the United Methodist Church. *Publs:* Twelve Modern Disciples, 1963; Meditation on Ephesians, 1965; (with C. Wolcott) Religions Around the World, 1967; La Iglesia en el Mundo, 1972; (with C. Wolcott) Through the Moongate, 1978; A New Testament Odyssey, 1979; Introduction à l'étude du Nouveau

Testament et de son Message, 1982; (with C. Wolcott) Wilderness Rider, 1984; (with C. Wolcott) We Go Forward, 1984; Commentary on Hebrews, 1988; Commentary on I and II Chronicles, 1988. Add: 3372 Mimosa Dr., Nashville, Tenn. 37211, U.S.A.

WOLCOTT, Patty. American, b. 1929. Children's fiction. Elementary sch. teacher in public schs., 1952–56; Ed., Elementary Sch. Textbooks, Houghton Mifflin Co., Boston, Mass., 1956–59; Ed., Juvenile Trade Books, Artists and Writers Press., 1960–61; Elementary Sch. Teacher, Agnes Russell Center, Columbia Univ. Teachers Coll., NYC, 1963–66. *Publs:* The Reef of Coral, 1969; The Marvelous Mud Washing Machine, 1974; The Cake Story, 1974; Where Did That Naughty Little Hamster Go?, 1974; The Forest Fire, 1974; I'm Going to New York to Visit the Queen, 1974; Tunafish Sandwiches, 1975; Beware of a Very Hungry Fox, 1975; Super Sam and the Salad Garden, 1975; My Shadow and I, 1975; Pickle Pickle Pickle Juice, 1975; The Dragon and the Wild Fandango, 1980; Double-Decker Double-Decker Double-Decker Bus, 1980; Pirates, Pirates over the Salt, Salt Sea, 1981; Eeeeeek!, 1981; The Dragon and the Gold, 1983; This Is Wierd, 1985. Add: 140 Jennie Dugan Rd., Concord, Mass. 01742, U.S.A.

WOLF, Gary K. American, b. 1951. Science fiction/Fantasy. *Publs:* Killerbowl, 1975; A Generation Removed, 1977; The Resurrectionist, 1979; Who Censored Roger Rabbit?, 1981. Add: Box 436, Harvard, Mass. 01451, U.S.A.

WOLFBEIN, Seymour L(ouis). American, b. 1915. Economics, International relations/Current affairs. Pres., TWO Consulting, since 1985. Dir., Jewish Employment and Vocational Service, Philadelphia. Formerly associated with the U.S. Dept. of Labor, Washington: Economist, Bureau of Labor Statistics, 1942–45; Chief, Occupational Outlook Div., 1946–49; Chief, Div. of Manpower and Productivity, 1949–50; Chief, Div. of Manpower and Employment, 1950–59; Deputy Asst. Secty. of Labor, 1959–62; Dir., Office of Manpower, Automation and Training, 1962–67, and Economic Adviser to the Secty. of Labor, 1965–67; Dean, 1967–78, and Boettner Prof. of Business Admin., 1978–84, Temple Univ., Philadelphia. Pres., Washington Statistical Soc., 1958. *Publs:* Decline of a Cotton Textile City, 1944; Our World of Work, 1951; Employment and Unemployment in the U.S., 1964; Employment, Unemployment and Public Policy, 1965; Education and Training for Full Employment, 1967; Occupational Information, 1968; (ed.) Emerging Sectors of Collective Bargaining, 1970; Work in American Society, 1971; (ed.) Manpower Policy: Perspective and Prospects, 1973; Labor Market Information for Youth, 1975; Men in the Pre-Retirement Years, 1977; Establishment Reporting in the U.S., 1978; America's Service Economy, 1988; The Temporary Employment Industry, 1989. Add: E706 Parktowne, 2200 Benjamin Franklin Parkway, Philadelphia, Pa. 19130, U.S.A.

WOLFE, Burton H. American, b. 1932. Social commentary/Phenomena, Biography, Humor/Satire. Specialist in writing legal papers. Reporter, Intnl. News Service, 1957–58; Ed. and Publr., The Californian, 1960–62; Ed. and Writer, Civic Education Service, 1965–66. *Publs:* The Hippies, 1968; Hitler and the Nazis, 1970; The Devil and Dr. Noxin, 1973; Pileup on Death Row, 1973; The Devil's Avenger: A Biography of Anton Szandor La Vey, 1974. Add: P.O. Box 1199, San Francisco, Calif. 94101, U.S.A.

WOLFE, Gene (Rodman). American, b. 1931. Novels/Short stories, Science fiction/Fantasy, Children's fiction. Project Engineer, Procter and Gamble 1956–72; Sr. Ed., Plant Engineering mag., Barrington, Ill., 1972–84. *Publs:* Operation ARES, 1970; The Fifth Head of Cerberus (SF short stories), 1972; Peace (novel), 1975; The Devil in a Forest (juvenile novel), 1976; The Island of Doctor Death and Other Stories and Other Stories, 1980; The Shadow of the Torturer, 1980; The Claw of the Conciliator, 1981; Gene Wolfe's Book of Days (short stories), 1981; The Sword of the Lictor, 1981; The Citadel of the Autarch, 1984; Free Live Free, 1984; Soldier of the Mist, 1986; The Urth of the New Sun, 1987; There Are Doors, 1988; Storeys from the Old Hotel, 1988; For Rosemary, 1988; Endangered Species, 1989. Add: P.O. Box 69, Barrington, Ill. 60011, U.S.A.

WOLFE, Michael. American, b. 1945. Novels/Short stories, Poetry, Travel/Exploration. Ed. and Publisher, Tombouctou Books, Bolinas, Calif., since 1976. English teacher, private sch., Andover, Mass., 1968–69; Journalist, Alpha Photojournalists Cooperative, Mill Valley, Calif., 1969–70; Owner, Purple Heron Bookstore, 1975–77; Owner, Fastback Book Bindery, 1978–80. *Publs:* How Love Gets Around, 1974; World Your Own, 1976; In Moroco, 1980; No, You Wore Red, 1980; Invisible Weapons, 1986; The Chinese Fire Drill, 1986. Add: c/o Thomas Dyja,

17 Portsmouth St., Cambridge, Mass. 02141, U.S.A.

WOLFE, Peter. American, b. 1933. Literature. Prof. of English, Univ. of Missouri, St. Louis, since 1967. Pres., Modern Literature Section, Modern Language Assn., 1971, 1975. *Publs:* The Disciplined Heart: Iris Murdoch and Her Novels, 1966; Mary Renault, 1969; Rebecca West: Artist and Thinker, 1971; Graham Greene and the Art of Entertainment, 1972; John Fowles: Magus and Moralist, 1976, 1978; Dreamers Who Live Their Dreams: The Novels of Ross Macdonald, 1977; Beams Falling: The Art of Dashiell Hammett, 1980; Jean Rhys, 1980; Laden Choirs: The Novels of Patrick White, 1983; Something More Than Night: The Case of Raymond Chandler, 1985; Corridors of Deceit: The World of John le Carré, 1987; (ed.) Essays in Graham Greene, 1987, 1989; Yukio Mishima, 1989; (ed.) Patrick White, 1990. Add: Dept. of English, Univ. of Missouri, St. Louis, Mo. 63121, U.S.A.

WOLFE, Tom. (Thomas Kennerly Wolfe, Jr.). American, b. 1930. Novels, Social commentary/phenomena. Contrib. Artist, Harper's mag., NYC, since 1977; Contrib. Ed., Esquire mag., NYC, since 1977. Reporter, Springfield, Mass. Union, 1956–59; Reporter and Latin American Corresp., Washington Post, 1959–62; Reporter and Mag. Writer, New York Herald Tribune, 1962–66; Mag. Writer, New York World Journal Tribune, 1966–67. *Publs:* The Kandy-Kolored Tangerine-Flake Streamline Baby, 1965; The Pump House Gang, 1968; The Electric Kool-Aid Acid Test, 1968; Radical Chic and Mau-Mauing the Flak Catchers, 1970; The New Journalism, 1973; The Painted Word, 1975; Mauve Gloves and Madmen, Clutter and Vine, 1976; The Right Stuff, 1979; In Our Time, 1980; From Bauhaus to Our House, 1981; The Purple Decades: A Reader, 1982; The Bonfire of the Vanities, 1987. Add: c/o Farrar Straus and Giroux, 19 Union Sq. W., New York, N.Y. 10003, U.S.A.

WOLFF, Geoffrey. American, b. 1937. Novels/Short stories, Biography. Writer-in-Residence, Brandeis Univ., Waltham Mass., since 1982. Contrib. Ed., Esquire mag., NYC, since 1979. Lectr. in Literature, Robert Coll., Istanbul, Turkey, 1961–63; Lectr. in American Literature, Istanbul Univ., 1962–63; Book Critic, The Washington Post, Washington, D.C., 1964–69; Literary Critic, Newsweek, NYC, 1969–71; Resident Writer, Princeton Univ., New Jersey, 1970–74; Literary Ed., New Times, NYC, 1974–79; Lectr., Middlebury Coll., Vermont, 1976. Lectr., Columbia Univ., NYC, 1979; Ferris Prof., Princeton Univ., New Jersey, 1980; Lectr., Brown Univ., Providence, R.I., 1981. *Publs:* Bad Debts, 1969; The Sightseer, 1974; Black Sun (biography), 1976; Inklings, 1978; The Duke of Deception, 1979; Providence, 1986. Add: c/o Viking Penguin Inc., 40 West 23rd St., New York, N.Y. 10010, U.S.A.

WOLFF, Konrad. American (b. German), b. 1907. Music. Contrib. Ed., Piano Quarterly, and Journal of American Liszt Society. Asst. Music Dir., New Friends of Music, NYC, 1942–50; Teacher of Piano, Westchester Conservatory of Music, White Plains, N.Y., 1949–54, Drew Univ., Madison, N.J., 1956–62, Peabody Conservatory, Baltimore, 1963–74, and Smith Coll., Northampton, Mass., 1975–76; Prof. of Music History, Rutgers Univ., New Brunswick, N.J., 1974–75; Teacher of Piano, Montclair State Coll., New Jersey, 1976–82. *Publs:* (ed.) On Music and Musicians, by Robert Schumann, 1946, 1952; The Teaching of Artur Schnabel, 1972, 1979; Masters of the Keyboard, 1983, 1990. Add: 210 Riverside Dr., New York, N.Y. 10025, U.S.A.

WOLFF, Kurt H. American (b. German), b. 1912. Sociology, Translations. Emeritus Yellen Prof. of Social Relations, Brandeis Univ., since 1982 (Prof., 1959–69; Chmn., Dept. of Sociology, 1959–62; Yellen Prof., 1969–82). Asst. Prof., 1945–52, and Assoc. Prof., 1952–59, Ohio State Univ., Columbus. *Publs:* (ed. and trans.) The Sociology of Georg Simmel, 1950; (trans.) Conflict, by Georg Simmel, 1955; (ed. and trans.) Georg Simmel 1858-1918, 1959; (ed. and trans.) Emile Durkheim 1858-1917, 1960; (ed.) The Sociology of Knowledge, 1961; (ed.) Wissenssoziologie, by Karl Mannheim, 1964; (co-ed. and contrib.) The Critical Spirit: Essays in Honor of Herbert Marcuse, 1967; Versuch zu einer Wissenssoziologie, 1968; Hingebung und Begriff, 1968; (ed., contrib. and trans.) From Karl Mannheim, 1971; Trying Sociology, 1974; Surrender and Catch, 1976; Vorgang und immerwährende Revolution, 1978; Beyond the Sociology of Knowledge, 1983; Das Unumgängliche, 1988. Add: 58 Lombard St., Newton, Mass. 02158, U.S.A.

WOLFF, Robert P(aul). American, b. 1933. Education, Philosophy, Politics/Government, Social commentary. Prof. of Philosophy, Univ. of Massachusetts, Amherst, since 1971. Instr., Harvard Univ., Cambridge, Mass., 1958–61; Asst. Prof. of Philosophy, Univ. of Chicago, 1961–63; Visiting Lectr., Wellesley Coll., Mass., 1963–64; Prof. of Philosophy, Columbia Univ., NYC, 1964–71. *Publs:* Kant's Theory of Mental Activity, 1962; (with H. Marcuse and B. Moore) Critique of Pure Tolerance, 1965; (ed.) Political Man and Social Man, 1965; (ed.) Kant: A Collection of Critical Essays, 1967; The Poverty of Liberalism, 1968; (ed.) Kant's Foundations: Text and Commentary, 1968; The Ideal of the University, 1969; (ed.) The Essential Hume, 1969; (ed.) Ten Great Works of Philosophy, 1969; In Defence of Anarchism, 1970; (ed.) Philosophy: A Modern Encounter, 1971; (ed.) The Rule of Law, 1971; (ed.) Styles of Political Action in America, 1972; (ed.) 1984 Revisited: Prospects for American Politics, 1973; The Autonomy of Reason, 1973; About Philosophy, 1976, 4th ed. 1989; Understanding Rawls, 1977; (ed.) Introductory Philosophy, 1979; Understanding Marx, 1985; Moneybags Must Be So Lucky, 1988. Add: c/o Dept. of Philosophy, Univ. of Massachusetts, Amherst, Mass. 01003, U.S.A.

WOLFF, Sonia. See **LEVITIN**, Sonia.

WOLFF, Tobias (Jonathan Ansell). American, b. 1945. Novels/Short stories. Has served as a member of the faculty at Stanford Univ., California; Goddard Coll., Plainvield, Vt.; Arizona State Univ., Tempe; Syracuse Univ., Syracuse, N.Y.; and as a reporter for the Washington Post. *Publs:* In the Garden of the North American Martyrs (short stories), 1981, in U.K. as Hunters in the Snow, 1982; (ed.) Matters of Life and Death: New American Stories, 1983; The Barracks Thief (novella), 1984; Back in the World (short stories), 1985; This Boy's Life: A Memoir, 1989. Add: c/o Atlantic Monthly Press, 19 Union Sq. W., New York, N.Y. 10003, U.S.A.

WOLFLE, Dael. American, b. 1906. Administration/Management, Politics/Government, Sciences. Prof. Emeritus of Public Affairs, Univ. of Washington, Seattle, since 1976 (Prof., 1970–76). Asst. Prof., and subsequently Assoc. Prof., Univ. of Chicago, 1936–45; Exec. Secty., American Psychological Assn., 1946–50, Dir., Commn. on Human Resources and Advanced Training 1950–54, and Exec. Officer, American Assn. for the Advancement of Science, 1954–70, all in Washington, D.C. *Publs:* Factor Analysis to 1940 (statistics); (ed.) Human Factors in Military Efficiency; (co-author) Improving Undergraduate Instruction in Psychology; America's Resources of Specialized Talent, 1954; (ed.) Symposium on Basic Research, 1959; Science and Public Policy, 1959; (co-author) The Graduate Education of Physicians; (ed.) The Discovery of Talent; The Uses of Talent, 1971; The Home of Science: The Role of the University, 1972. Add: Grad. Sch. of Public Affairs, Univ. of Washington, Seattle, Wash. 98195, U.S.A.

WOLITZER, Hilma. American, b. 1930. Novels/Short stories, Children's fiction. Visiting Lectr., Bread Loaf Writers Conference, Middlebury Coll., Vermont, 1975–78; Distinguished Writer-in-Residence, Wichita State Univ., Kansas, 1979; also former Lectr. in Writing, Iowa State Univ., Iowa City, and Columbia Univ., NYC. *Publs:* Ending, 1974; Introducing Shirley Braverman (juvenile), 1975; Out of Love (juvenile), 1976; In the Flesh, 1977; Toby Lived Here (juvenile), 1978; Hearts, 1980; In the Palomar Arms, 1983; Wish You Were Here (juvenile), 1985; Silver, 1988. Add: 11 Ann Dr., Syosset, N.Y. 11791, U.S.A.

WOLL, Peter. American, b. 1933. Administration/Management, Law, Politics/Government. Prof., Brandeis Univ., Waltham, Mass., since 1976 (Assoc. Prof., 1964–76). Instr., 1958–60, and Asst. Prof., 1960–64, Univ. of California, Los Angeles. *Publs:* American Bureaucracy, 1963, 1977; Administrative Law: The Informal Process, 1963, 1974; (ed.) Public Administration and Policy, 1966; Public Policy, 1974; (co-author) America's Political System, 3rd ed. 1979; (co-author) America's Political System: State and Local, 3rd ed. 1979; (ed.) American Government: Readings and Cases, 1962, 10th ed., 1990; (ed.) Behind the Scenes in American Government, 1977, 7th ed. 1989; (co-author) The Private World of Congress, 1979; Constitutional Law, 1981; Congress, 1985; American Government: The Core, 1989. Add: 43 Oxbow Rd., Weston, Mass. 02193, U.S.A.

WOLLASTON, Nicholas. British, b. 1926. Novels/Short stories, Travel. *Publs:* Handles of Chance, 1956; China in the Morning, 1960; Red Rumba, 1962; Winter in England, 1965; Jupiter Laughs, 1967; Pharoah's Chicken, 1969; The Tale Bearer, 1972; Eclipse, 1974; The Man on the Ice Cap, 1980; Mr. Thistlewood, 1985; The Stones of Bau, 1987; Cafe de Paris, 1988. Add: c/o Gillon Aitken, 29 Fernshaw Rd., London SW10 0TG, England.

WOLLHEIM, Donald A(llen). American, b. 1914. Science fiction/Fantasy. Ed., World's Best Science Fiction anthologies, since 1965; Ed. and Publr., DAW Books, NYC, since 1971. Ed., Ace Books, NYC, 1952–71. *Publs:* The Secret of Saturn's Rings, 1954; The Secret of the Martian Moons, 1955; One Against the Moon, 1956; Across Time, 1957;

Edge of Time, 1958; The Secret of the Ninth Planet, 1959; The Martian Missile, 1959; Mike Mars, 1961; Mike Mars Flies the X-15, 1961; Mike Mars at Cape Canaveral, 1961; Mike Mars in Orbit, 1961: Destiny's Orbit, 1961; Mike Mars Flies the Dyna-Soar, 1962; South Pole Spaceman, 1962; Mike Mars Around the Moon, 1964; The Universe Makers, 1971; Two Dozen Dragon Eggs, 1974; The Men from Ariel, 1982. Add: c/o DAW Books, 1633 Broadway, New York, N.Y. 10019, U.S.A.

WOLMAN, Benjamin B. American. Pyschiatry, Psychology. In private practice of psychoanalysis and psychotherapy, since 1939; Prof., Doctoral Prog. in Clinical Psychology, Long Island Univ., NYC, since 1965; Ed.-in-Chief, Intnl. Journal of Group Tensions, and Intnl. Encyclopedia of Neurology, Psychiatry, Pschoanalysis and Psychology; Assoc. Ed., American Imago. *Publs:* Freedom and Discipline in Education, 1948; (co-ed. and contrib.) Encyclopedia Hebraica, 1949; Contemporary Theories and Systems in Psychology, 1960; Handbook of Clinical Psychology, 1965; (with E. Nagel) Scientific Psychology, 1965; Vectoriasis Praecox or the Group of Schizophrenias, 1966; The Unconscious Mind, 1967; Psychoanalytic Techniques, 1968; Historical Roots of Contemporary Psychology, 1968; Children Without Childhood: A Study of Childhood Schizophrenia, 1970; Success and Failure in Psychoanalysis and Psychotherapy, 1972; Manual of Child Psychopatholoy, 1972; Handbook of General Psychology, 1973; Handbook of Child Psychoanalysis, 1973; (ed.) Dictionary of Behavioral Science, 1973; Call No Man Normal, 1973; Victims of Success, 1973; Between Survival and Suicide, 1976; Psychoanalysis and Catholicism, 1976; The Therapist's Handbook, 1976; Handbook of Parapsychology, 1977; Children's Fears, 1978; Handbook of Treatment of Mental Disorders in Childhood and Adolescence, 1978; Clinical Diagnosis of Mental Disorders, 1978; Psychological Aspects of Gynecology and Obstetrics, 1978; Handbook of Dreams, 1979; International Directory of Psychology, 1979; Handbook of Human Sexuality, 1980; Contemporary Theories and Systems in Psychology, 1981; Psychological Aspects of Obesity: A Handbook, 1982; Handbook of Developmental Psychology, 1982; The Therapist's Handbook (rev.), 1983; The Logic of Science in Psychoanalysis, 1984; Handbook of Family and Marital Therapy, 1984; Interactional Psychotherapy, 1984; Problems of Modern Living, 1984; The Diary of Mordekhai Ben-Yosef, 1984; (ed.) Handbook of Intelligence, 1985; (with M. Ullman) Handbook of States of Consciousness, 1986; The Sociopathic Personality, 1987. Add: c/o Brunner/Mazel, Inc., 19 Union Sq., W., New York, N.Y. 10003, U.S.A.

WOLOCH, Isser. American, b. 1937. History. Prof. of History, Columbia Univ., since 1975 (Assoc. Prof. 1969–75). Lectr., 1963–64, and Asst. Prof., 1964–66, Indiana Univ., Bloomington; Asst. Prof., Univ. of California, Los Angeles, 1966–69. *Publs:* Jacobin Legacy, 1970; (ed.) The Peasantry in the Old Regime, 1970; (with M. Chambers, R. Grew, D. Herlihy and T. Rabb) The Western Experience, 1974, 1987; The French Veteran from the Revolution to the Restoration, 1979; Eighteenth-Century Europe: Tradition and Progress, 1982. Add: History Dept., Columbia Univ., New York, N.Y. 10027, U.S.A.

WOLPE, Joseph. American, b. 1915. Psychiatry. Prof. of Psychiatry, Temple Univ. Sch. of Medicine, Philadelphia, since 1965. Lectr. in Psychiatry, Univ. of Witwatersrand, Johannesburg, 1950–59; Prof. of Psychiatry, Univ. of Virginia Sch. of Medicine, 1960–65. *Publs:* Psychotherapy by Reciprocal Inhibition, 1958; (ed. with Salter and Reyna) Conditioning Therapies, 1964; The Practice of Behavior Therapy, 1973, 3rd ed. 1982; Theme and Variations, 1975; Our Useless Fears, 1981; Life Without Fear, 1988. Add: Dept. of Psychiatry, Medical Coll. of Pennsylvania, Philadelphia, Pa. 19129, U.S.A.

WOLPERT, Stanley Albert. American, b. 1927. Novels/Short stories. History. Prof. of History, Univ. of California, Los Angeles, since 1968 (Instr., 1958–60; Asst. Prof., 1960–64; Assoc. Prof., 1964–68). *Publs:* Aboard the Flying Swan, 1954; Nine Hours to Rama, 1962; Tilak and Gokhale, 1962, 1978; India, 1965; Morley and India 1906-1910, 1967; The Expedition, 1968; An Error of Judgment, 1971; A New History of India, 1977, 1982; Roots of Confrontation in South Asia: Afghanistan, Pakistan, India and the Superpowers, 1982; Jinnah of Pakistan: A Life, 1984; Massacre of Jallianwala Bagh, 1988. Add: History Dept., Univ. of California, Los Angeles, Calif. 90024, U.S.A.

WOLRIGE GORDON, Anne. British, b. 1936. Plays/Screenplays, Biography. *Publs:* Peter Howard, Life and Letters, 1969; Blindsight, 1970; Dame Flora, 1974. Add: Ythan Lodge, Newburgh, Aberdeenshire AB4 0AD, Scotland.

WOLSELEY, Roland E. American, b. 1904. Travel/Exploration/Adventure, Writing/Journalism, Biography. Emeritus Prof. of Journalism,

Syracuse Univ., N.Y., since 1972 (Assoc. Prof., 1946–47; Prof., 1947–72). Book Review Ed., Quill and Scroll Mag., since 1933. With Daily News-Index, Evanston, Ill., 1934–37; Instr., and Asst. Prof. of Journalism, Northwestern Univ., Evanston, Ill., 1938–46. *Publs:* (with L.D. Case) Around the Copy Desk, 1934, 1946; (with H.F. Harrington) The Copyreader's Work Shop, 1934; The Journalist's Bookshelf, 1939, (with Isabel Wolseley) 8th ed. 1986; (with L.R. Campbell) Exploring Journalism, 1943, 3rd ed. 1957; (with L.R. Campbell) Newsmen at Work, 1949; Interpreting the Church Through Press and Radio, 1951; (ed. and contrib.) Journalism in Modern India, 1953, 1964; Face to Face with India, 1954; Careers in Religious Communications, 1955, 3rd ed. 1977; (ed.) Writing for the Religious Market, 1956; Critical Writing for the Journalist, 1959; (with L.R. Campbell) How to Report and Write the News, 1961; Understanding Magazines, 1965, 1969; (with P.D. Tandon) Gandhi: Warrior of Non-Violence, 1969; The Low Countries, 1969; The Black Press, U.S.A.: The Changing Magazine, 1972, 1989; (with P.D. Tandon) Three Women to Remember, 1975; Four Flames of Lamps (in Hindi), 1982; Still in Print, 1985. Add: Sch. of Public Communications, Syracuse Univ., Syracuse, N.Y. 13244, U.S.A.

WOLSTEIN, Benjamin. American, b. 1922. Philosophy, Psychology. In private practide of psychoanalysis, NYC, since 1951; Clinical Prof. of Psychology, Adelphi Uniuv., Garden City, Long Island, N.Y., since 1963; Training and Supervising Analyst, W.A. White Inst. of Psychiatry, Psychoanalysis, and Psychology, NYC, since 1969 (joined faculty, 1960); Clinical Prof. of Psychology, New York Univ., NYC, since 1975. Lectr., New Sch. for Social Research, NYC, 1958–72; Supvr. of Psychotherapy, Yeshiva Univ., 1964–79. *Publs:* Experience and Valuation, 1949; Transference, 1954, 1964; Countertransference, 1959; Irrational Despair, 1962; Freedom to Experience, 1964; Theory of Psychoanalytic Therapy, 1967; Human Psyche in Psychoanalysis, 1971; (ed.) Essential Papers on Countertransference, 1988. Add: 2 West 67th St., New York, N.Y. 10023, U.S.A.

WOLTERS, Oliver William. British, b. 1915. History. Goldwin Smith Prof. of South East Asian History, Cornell Univ., Ithaca, N.Y., since 1975 (Prof., 1964–75), retired 1985. With Malayan Civil Service, 1938–57; Lectr. in South East Asian History, Sch. of Oriental and African Studies, London Univ., 1957–63. *Publs:* Early Indonesian Commerce,1967; The Fall of Srivijaya in Malay History, 1970; South East Asian History and Historiography: Essays Presented to D.G.E. Hall, 1975; Culture, History, and Region in Southeast Asian Perspectives, 1983; Two Essays on Fai-Viêl in the Fourteenth Century, 1988. Add: 112 Comstock Rd., Ithaca, N.Y. 14850, U.S.A.

WOLTERS, Raymond. American, b. 1938. History. Prof. of History, Univ. of Delaware, since 1975 (Instr., 1965–67; Asst. Prof., 1967–70; Assoc. Prof., 1970–75). *Publs:* Negroes and the Great Depression: The Problem of Economic Recovery, 1970; The New Negro on Campus: Black College Rebellions of the 1920s, 1974; The Burden of Brown: Thirty Years of School Desegregation, 1984. Add: Dept. of History, Univ. of Delaware, Newark, Del. 19711, U.S.A.

WOLTERS, Richard A. American, b. 1920. Animals/Pets, Sports/Physical education/Keeping fit. Freelance writer and photographer, Richard A. Wolters & Assoc., since 1971. *Publs:* Gun Dog, 1961; Family Dog, 1963; Water Dog, 1964; Beau, 1966; Instant Dog, 1968; The Art and Technique of Soaring, 1971; Living on Wheels, 1973; City Dog, 1975; The Kid's Dog, 1978; The Labrador Retriever, 1981; Game Dog, 1983; House Dog, 1984. Add: c/o Petersen Publ. Co., 8490 Sunset Blvd., Los Angeles, Calif. 90069, U.S.A.

WOLTERSTORFF, Nicholas (Paul). American, b. 1932. Art, Education, Philosophy. Consultant, National Endowment for the Humanities, since 1968; Prof. of Philosophy, Yale Univ., Divinity Sch. New Haven, Conn., since 1989. member of the Bd., Urban Inst. for Contemporary Art, since 1975. Prof. of Philosophy, Calvin Coll., Grand Rapids, Mich., 1959–89. Visiting Prof.: Univ. of Chicago, 1964; Univ. of Texas, 1969; Univ. of Michigan, 1972; Temple Univ., 1977; Notre Dame Univ., 1979; Free Univ. of Amsterdam, 1981; Princeton Univ., 1985. *Publs:* Religion and the Schools, 1956; On Universals: An Essay in Ontology, 1970; Reason Within the Bounds of Religion, 1976; Art in Action, 1980; Works and Worlds of Art, 1980; Educating for Responsible Action, 1980; Until Justice and Peace Embrace, 1983; (with A. Phantinga) Faith and Rationality, 1983. Add: Yale Univ. Divinity School, New Haven, Conn. 06519, U.S.A.

WOLVERTON, Robert E. American, b. 1925. Education, Language/Linguistics, Literature, Mythology/Folklore. Prof. of Classics,

Mississippi State Univ. (Vice-Pres. for Academic Affairs, 1977–86). Dean ofGrad. Sch. and Research, Miami Univ., Oxford, Ohio, 1969–72; Pres., Coll. of Mt. St. Joseph on the Ohio, 1972–77. Pres., American Classical League, 1972–76; Ed. Adviser, The National Forum of Phi Kappa Phi, 1984–87. *Publs:* Classical Elements in English Words, 1965; An Outline of Classical Mythology, 1966. Add: P.O. Drawer FL, Mississippi State, Miss. 39762, U.S.A.

WONG, May. Singaporean, b. 1944. Poetry, Translations. *Publs:* A Bad Girl's Book of Animals, 1969; Reports, 1972; Wannsee Poems (bilingual ed.), 1975; (trans. with H. Buch) Lu Hsün; Superstition: Poems 1971-1976, 1978. Add: c/o Harcourt Brace Jovanovich, 1250 Sixth Ave., San Diego, Calif. 92101, U.S.A.

WONNACOTT, Paul. American, b. 1933. Economics. Prof. of Economics, Univ. of Maryland, College Park, since 1967 (Assoc. Prof., 1962–67). Asst. Prof. of Economics, Columbia Univ., NYC, 1959–62; Staff member, Council of Economic Advisers, 1968–70, Bd. of Govs. of the Federal Reserve, 1974–75, and U.S. Treasury, 1980. *Publs:* The Canadian Dollar, Sciences 1961, 1965; (with R. Wonnacott) Free Trade Between the United States and Canada, 1967; (with H. Johnson and Hirofumi Shibata) Harmonization of National Economic Politics under Free Trade, 1968; Macroeconomics, 1974, 1984; (with R. Wonnacott) Economics, 1979, 4th ed. 1990; U.S. Intervention in the Exchange Market for DM, 1982; The United States and Canada: The Quest For Free Trade, 1987. Add: Dept. of Economics, Univ. of Maryland, College Park, Md. 20742, U.S.A.

WONNACOTT, Ronald Johnston. Canadian, b. 1930. Economics. Prof. of Economics, Univ. of Western Ontario, London, since 1965 (Asst. Prof., 1958–61; Assoc. Prof., 1962–65; Chmn., Dept. of Economics, 1969–72). Consultant, Resources for the Future, 1963–66, Private Planning Assn. of Canada, 1967–68, Economic Council of Canada, 1972–75, and Ontario Economic Council, 1985; Pres., Canadian Economics Assn., 1981. *Publs:* Canadian-American Dependence: An Inter-industry Analysis, 1961; (with G.L. Reuber) Cost of Capital in Canada, 1961; (with P. Wonnacott) Free Trade Between the United States and Canada: The Potential Economic Effects, 1967; (with T. Wonnacott) Introductory Statistics, 1969; (with T. Wonnacott) Econometrics, 1970; (with T. Wonnacott) Introductory Statistics for Business and Economics, 1972; Canada's Trade Options, 1975; (with P. Wonnacott) Economics, 1979; (with T. Wonnacott) Regression, 1981; Canada-U.S. Free Trade: Problems and Opportunities, 1985; (with R. Hill) Canadian and U.S. Adjustment Policies in a Bilateral Trade Ageement, 1987. Add: 171 Wychwood Park, London, Ont., Canada.

WOOD, Arthur Skevington. British, b. 1916. History, Theology/Religion, Biography. Methodist Circuit Minister, 1940–62; Travelling Lectr., Movement for World Evangelization, 1962–70; Sr. Lectr. in Theology, 1970–77, Principal, 1977–83, Cliff. Coll., Derbyshire. *Publs:* Thomas Haweis 1734–1820, 1957; And with Fire: Messages on Revival, 1958; The Inextinguishable Blaze: Spiritual Renewal in the Eighteenth Century, 1960; Luther's Principles of Biblical Interpretation, 1961; Paul's Pentecost, 1963; Life by the Spirit, 1963; Heralds of the Gospel: Message, Method and Motive in Preaching, 1963; Prophecy in the Space Age, 1963; William Grimshaw of Haworth, 1963; The Art of Preaching, 1964; Evangelism: Its Theology and Practice, 1966; Designed by Love, 1966; The Burning Heart: John Wesley, Evangelist, 1967; The Principles of Biblical Interpretation, 1967; Captive to the Word: Martin Luther, Doctor of Sacred Scripture, 1969; Signs of the Times: Biblical Prophecy and Current Events, 1970; (with E.M. Blaiklock) Man and Sin, 1972; The Evangelical Understanding of the Gospel, 1974; The Nature of Man, 1978; For All Seasons: Sermons for the Christian Year, 1979; The Call of God: Studies in Prophetic Vocation, 1980; What the Bible Says about God, 1980; Baptized with Fire, 1981; Studying Theology, 1981; Let Us Go On, 1985; Love Excluding Sin: Wesley's Doctrine of Sanctification, 1986; Revival: Biblical Principles in Historical Perspective, 1986; The Gift of Love: Daily Readings with John Wesley, 1987. Add: 17 Dalewood Rd., Sheffield S8 0EB, England.

WOOD, Barbara (née Lewandowski). Also writes as Kathryn Harvey. American, b. 1947 (born in England). Historical/Romance. Instr., Univ. of California at Riverside. Surgical Teachnician, Santa Monica Hospital, Calif., 1973–77. *Publs:* The Magdalane Scrolls, 1978; Hounds and Jackals, 1978; Curse This House, 1978; (with Gareth Wootton) Night Trains, 1979; Yesterday's Child, 1979; The Watchgods, 1980; Childsong, 1981; Domina, 1983; Vital Signs, 1985; Soul Flame, 1987; Green City in the Sun, 1988; (as Kathryn Harvey) Butterfly, 1988. Add: c/o Random House, 210 E. 50th St., New York, N.Y. 10022, U.S.A.

WOOD, Charles (Gerald). British, b. 1933. Plays/Screenplays. Designer and scenic artist; stage mgr., 1957–62. *Publs:* Cockade, 1967; Dingo, 1969; Fill the Stage with Happy Hours, 1969; H: Being Monologues in Front of Burning Cities, 1970; Veterans, 1972; Has "Washington" Legs?, and Dingo, 1978; Tumbledown, 1987. Add: c/o Fraser and Dunlop, 91 Regent St., London W1R 8RU, England.

WOOD, Charles Tuttle. American, b. 1933. History. Daniel Webster Prof. of History, Dartmouth Coll., Hanover, N.H., since 1980 (Asst. Prof., 1964–67; Assoc. Prof., 1967–71; Prof., 1971–80; Dept. Chmn., 1976–79). Instr. in History, Harvard Univ., Cambridge, Mass., 1961–64. *Publs:* The French Apanages and the Capetian Monarchy, 1224-1328, 1966; (ed. and trans.) Philip the Fair and Boniface VIII, 1967, 1976; The Age of Chivalry: Manners and Morals, 1000-1450, 1970; (trans.) Thomas Hobbes: Man and Citizen, 1972; The Quest for Eternity, 1983; Joan of Arc and Richard III: Sex, Saints, and Government in the Middle Ages, 1988; (ed. with David Lagomarsiho) The Trial of Charles I: A Documentry History, 1989. Add: Dept. of History, Dartmouth Coll., Hanover, N.H. 03755, U.S.A.

WOOD, David. British, b. 1944. Children's fiction, Plays/Screenplay. *Publs:* Musical plays for children—The Owl and the Pussycat Went to See..., 1970; The Plotters of Cabbage Patch Corner, 1972; Flibberty and the Penguin, 1974; Hijack over Hygenia, 1974; Old Mother Hubbard, 1976; The Papertown Paperchase, 1976; Larry the Lamb in Toytown, 1977; Rock Nativity (for adults), 1977; The Gingerbread Man, 1977; Old Father Time, 1977; Tickle (for adults), 1978; Mother Goose's Golden Christmas, 1978; Babes in the Magic Wood, 1979; Cinderella, 1980; There Was an Old Woman, 1980; Nutcracker Sweet, 1981; Aladdin, 1981; The Ideal Gnome Expedition, 1982; Dick Whittington and Wondercat, 1983; Meg and Mog Show, 1984; Robin Hood, 1985; The Selfish Shellfish, 1986; children's fiction—The Operats of Rodent Garden, 1984; The Discorats, 1985; The Gingerbread Man, 1985; Playtheatres, 1987; Sidney the Monster, 1988. Add: c/o Margaret Ramsay Ltd., 14a Goodwin's Court, London WC2N 4LL, England.

WOOD, Derek Harold. British, b. 1930. Air/Space topics, History, Military/Defence. Publisher, Jane's Defence Weekly, since 1987 (Ed.-in-Chief 1984–87). Air Corresp., Liverpool Daily Post, 1952–60, Westminster Newspapers, 1954–60 and the Sunday Telegraph, London, 1961–86; Managing Dir. and London Ed., Interavia (U.K.) Ltd., 1953–83. *Publs:* (with Derek Dempster) The Narrow Margin, 1961; Project Cancelled, 1975; Attack Warning Red, 1976; Jane's World Aircraft Recognition Handbook, 1979; Target England, 1980. Add: Stroods, Whitemans Green, Cuckfield, Sussex, England.

WOOD, Fergus James. American, b. 1917. Astronomy, Earth Sciences, Documentaries/Reportage. Geophysical consultant (tidal dynamics), since 1978. Asst. Prof. of Physics, Univ. of Maryland, College Park, 1949–50; Assoc. Physicist, Applied Physics Lab., Johns Hopkins Univ., Silver Spring, Md., 1950–55; Science Ed., Encyclopedia Americana, 1955–60; Scientific Asst. to the Dir., Office of Space Flight Progs., NASA, 1960–61; Prog. Dir., Foreign Science Information, National Science Found., 1961–62; Physical Scientist, 1962–73, and Research Assoc. 1973–77, National Oceanic and Atmospheric Admin., Rockville, Md. *Publs:* (ed.-in-chief, vols. 1 and 2A; scientific coordinator, vols. 2B, 2C and 3) The Prince William Sound, Alaska, Earthquake of 1964 and Aftershocks, 3 vols., 1966–69; Pathfinders from the Stars (screenplay), 1967; The Strategic Role of Perigean Spring Tides in Nautical History and North American Coastal Flooding 1635-1976, 1978; Tidal Dynamics: Coastal Flooding and Cycles of Gravitational Force, 1986. Add: 3103 Casa Bonita Dr., Bonita, Calif. 92002, U.S.A.

WOOD, Kerry. Pseud. for Edgar Allardyce Wood. Canadian, b. 1907. Children's fiction, History, Natural history, Autobiography/Memoirs/Personal, Biography. Federal Migratory Bird Officer, since 1924. Corresp. and Columnist for newspapers including Edmonton Bulletin, Edmonton Journal, Calgary Herald, and Calgary Albertan, 1926–73. Member of the Bd., Alberta Natural History Soc., 1936–64. *Publs:* Robbing the Roost: The Marquis of Roostburg Rules Governing the Ancient and Dishonourable Sport, 1939; I'm a Gaggle Man, Myself, 1940; Three Mile Bend, 1945; Birds and Animals in the Rockies, 1946; A Nature Guide for Farmers, 1947; The Magpie Menace, 1949; Cowboy Yarns for Young Folk, 1951; The Sanctuary, 1952; A Letter from Alberta, 1954; A Letter from Calgary, 1954; Wild Winter (autobiography), 1954; The Map-Maker: The Story of David Thompson, 1955; Willowdale, 1956; The Great Chief: Maskepetoon, Warrior of the Crees, 1957; The Queen's Cowboy: Colonel Macleod of the Mounties, 1960; Great Horned MacOwl (fiction), 1961; The Boy and the Buffalo, 1963; Mickey the Beaver and Other Stories, 1964; A Lifetime of Service: George Moon, 1966; A Corner of Canada:

A Personalized History of the Red Deer River Country, 1966; A Time for Fun, 1967; The Medicine Man, 1968; Samson's Long Ride, 1968; The Creek, 1970; The Icelandic-Canadian Poet Stephan G. Stephansson: A Tribute, 1974; Red Deer, A Love Story, 1975; Bessie, The Coo, 1975; A Legacy of Laughter, 1986. Add: Site 3, R.R. 2, Red Deer, Alta. T4N 5E2, Canada.

WOOD, Laura Newbold. *See* **ROPER, Laura Wood.**

WOOD, Leonard C. American, b. 1923. History. Prof. Emeritus of History, Eastern Illinois Univ., Charleston. Freelance writer for educational publrs., especially Harcourt Brace Jovanovich, NYC. Ed., McGraw-Hill, 1951–54, Holt Rinehart & Winston, 1955–58, and Macmillan, 1958–60, NYC. *Publs:* The Soviet Army, 1953; The Satellite Armies, 1954; Sir Edmund Monson, 1960; (with Ralph Gabriel) America: Its People and Values, 1971, Heritage Ed. 1986; (with Carol Berkin) Land of Promise: A History of the United States, 1985. Add: Old State Rd., R.R.2, Box 153, Charleston, Ill. 61920, U.S.A.

WOOD, Lorna. British, b. 1913. Novels/Short stories, Children's fiction. Worked for BBC Monitoring Service, 1942–75. *Publs:* for adults—The Crumb-Snatchers, 1933; Gilded Sprays, 1935; The Hopeful Travellers, 1936; for children—The Smiling Rabbit, 1939; The Travelling Tree, 1943; Ameliaranne Goes Digging, 1948; The Finicky Mouse, 1949; The Handkerchief Man, 1951; The People in the Garden, 1954; Rescued by Broomstick, 1954; Hags series, 4 vols., 1957–70; Holiday on Hot Bricks, 1958; Seven-League Ballet Shoes, 1959; Climb by Candlelight, 1959; The Golden-Haired Family, 1961; The Dogs of Pangers, 1970; Pangers Pup, 1972. Add: Mrs. L.M. Swire, c/o Dent, 33 Welbeck St., London, W1M 8LX, England.

WOOD, Marguerite N. British. Poetry, Literature. Chartered Physiotherapist (non-practising). Justice of the Peace, since 1968; Member, Editorial Panel, Envoi, since 1974; Chmn., Suffolk Poetry Soc., 1976–88; Member, Gen. Council, Poetry Soc., U.K. 1963–69. *Publs:* Stone of Vision, 1964; Windows Are Not Enough, 1971; Crack Me the Shell, 1975; A Line Drawn in Water, 1980. Add: 12 Castle Rd., Hadleigh, Ipswich, Suffolk, England.

WOOD, Maurice Arthur Ponsonby. British, b. 1916. Theology/Religion. Proctor in Convocation of Canterbury, and member, House of Clergy of Church Assembly, and Gen. Synod, since 1954; Asst. Bishop, Diocese of London, since 1985. Vicar and Rural Dean of Islington, and Pres. of Islington Clerical Conference, 1952–61; Principal, Oak Hill Theological Coll., Southgate, London, 1961–71; Prebendary of St. Paul's Cathedral, London, 1969–71; Bishop of Norwich, 1971–85. *Publs:* Like a Mighty Army, 1956; Comfort in Sorrow, 1957; Your Suffering, 1959; To Every Man's Door, 1960; Christian Stability, 1968; Into the Way of Peace, 1982; This Is Our Faith, 1985. Add: c/o Hodder and Stoughton, 47 Bedford Sq., London WC1B 3DP, England.

WOOD, Neal. Canadian, b. 1922. History. Politics/Government. Prof. Emeritus of Political Science, York Univ., Toronto, since 1988 (Prof., 1966–88). Asst. Prof. of Govt., Columbia Univ., NYC, 1957–63; Asst. Prof. of Political Science, 1963–65, and Assoc. Prof., 1966, Univ. of California, Los Angeles. *Publs:* Communism and British Intellectuals, 1959; (ed.) N. Machiavelli: The Art of War, 1965; (with Ellen Meiksins Wood) Class Ideology and Ancient Political Theory, 1978; The Politics of Locke's Philosophy, 1983; John Locke and Agrarian Capitalism, 1984; Cicero's Social and Political Thought, 1988. Add: Dept. of Political Science, York Univ., Toronto, Ont., Canada.

WOOD, Phyllis Anderson. American, b. 1923. Children's fiction. High sch. teacher, Jefferson Union High Sch. District, Daly City, Calif., since 1966. *Publs:* Andy, 1971; Your Bird Is Here, Tom Thompson, 1972; I've Missed a Sunset or Three, 1973; Song of the Shaggy Canary, 1974; A Five-Color Buick and a Blue-Eyed Cat, 1975; I Think This Is Where We Came In, 1976; Win Me and You Lose, 1977; Get a Little Lost, Tia, 1978; This Time Count Me In, 1980; Pass Me a Pine Cone, 1982; Meet Me in the Park, Angie, 1983; Then I'll Be Home Free, 1986; Nelson's Own Choice, 1989. Add: 65 Capay Circle, South San Francisco, Calif. 94080, U.S.A.

WOOD, Robert (Coldwell). American, b. 1923. Politics/Government. Henry Luce Prof. of Democratic Instns. and the Society Order, Wesleyan Univ., Middletown, Conn., since 1983. Asst. Prof. of Political Science, 1957–59, Assoc. Prof., 1959–62, Prof., 1962–66, and Head of the Dept., 1965–66, Massachusetts Inst. of Technology, Cambridge; Under Secty. and Secty., U.S. Dept. of Housing and Urban Development, Washington,

1966–69; Head, Dept. of Political Science, M.I.T., and Dir., M.I.T.-Harvard Univ. Joint Center for Urban Studies, 1969–70; Chmn., Bd. of Dirs., Metropolitan Bay Transit Authority, Boston, 1969–70; Superintendent, Boston Public Schools, 1978–80; Pres., Univ., of Massachusetts, 1970–77, and Prof. of Political Science, Univ. of Massachusetts at Boston, 1980–83. *Publs:* Suburbia: Its People and Their Politics, 1958; Metropolis Against Itself, 1959; 1400 Governments: The Political Economy of the New York Region, 1960; (co-author) Schoolmen and Politics, 1962; (co-author) The Government and Politics of the U.S., 1965; The Necessary Majority: Middle America and the Urban Crisis, 1972. Add: c/o Wesleyan Univ., High St., Middletwon, Conn. 06457, U.S.A.

WOOD, Robin. British, b. 1931. Film. Chmn., Dept. of Fine Arts, Atkinson Coll., York Univ., Toronto, since 1977. Lectr. in Film Studies, Queen's Univ., Canada, 1969–72, and Univ. of Warwick, England, 1973–77. *Publs:* Hitchcock's Films, 1965; Howard Hawks, 1967, 1981; Arthur Penn, 1968; (with Ian Cameron) Antonioni, 1968; Ingmar Bergman, 1969; (with Michael Walker) Claude Chabrol, 1971; The Apu Trilogy, 1972; Personal Views: Explorations in Film, 1975; (ed. with Richard Lippe, and contrib.) The American Nightmare: Essays on the Horror Film, 1979; Hollywood from Vietnam to Reagan, 1986. Add: Atkinson Coll., York Univ., Toronto, Ont., Canada.

WOOD, Ursula. *See* **VAUGHAN WILLIAMS,** Ursula.

WOODBERRY, Joan Merle. Australian, b. 1921. Novels/Short stories, Children's fiction, Plays/Screenplays, History. Former Lectr., Univ. of Tasmania, Hobart; Justice of the Peace. *Publs:* Rafferty series, 4 vols., 1959–62; Come Back Peter, 1968; Ash Tuesday, 1968; The Cider Duck, 1969; A Garland of Gannets, 1969; Little Black Swan, 1970; Andrew Bent, 1972; Historic Hobart (Richmond, Tasmania, New Norfolk, Battery Point), 5 vols., 1975–78. Add: 657 Nelson Rd., Mt. Nelson, Tas. 7007, Australia.

WOODCOCK, George. Canadian, b. 1912. Poetry, History, Travel/Exploration/Adventure, Biography. Ed., Now mag., 1940–47; Asst. Prof. of English, 1956–60, Ed., Canadian Literature, 1959–77, Assoc. Prof., 1961–63, 1966–67, and Lectr. in Asian Studies, 1966–67, Univ. of British Columbia. *Publs:* The White Island (poetry), 1940; The Centre Cannot Hold (poetry), 1943; Railways and Society, 1943; Anarchy or Chaos, 1944; Homes or Hovels: the Housing Problem and its Solutions, 1944; William Godwin, 1946; The Basis of Communal Living, 1947; Imagine the South (poetry), 1947; (ed.) A Hundred Years of Revolution: 1948 and After, 1948; The Imcomparable Aphra, 1948; The Writer and Politics, 1948; The Paradox of Oscar Wilde, 1949; (with I. Avakumovic) The Anarchist Prince, 1950; British Poetry Today, 1950; (ed.) The Letters of Charles Lamb, 1950; Ravens and Prophets: An Account of Journeys in British Columbia and Alberta, 1952; Pierre Joseph Proudhon, 1956; To the City of the Dead: An Account of Travels in Mexico, 1957; Incas and Other Men: Travels in Andes, 1960; Anarchism: A History of Libertarian Ideas and Movements, 1962; Faces of India: A Travel Narrative, 1964; Asia, Gods, and Cities, 1966; (ed.) A Choice of Critics: Selections from Canadian Literature, 1966; The Crystal Spirit: A Study of George Orwell, 1966; The Greeks in India, 1966; (compiler) Variations on a Human Theme, 1966; Kerala: A Portrait of the Malabar Coast, 1967; Selected Poems, 1967; (with L. Avakumovic) The Doukhobors, 1968; Civil Disobedience, 1969; The British in the Far East, 1969; Henry Walter Bates: Naturalist of the Amazons, 1969; Hugh MacLennan, 1969; (ed.) The Sixties: Writers and Writing of the Decade, 1969; Canada and the Canadians, 1970; The Hudson's Bay Company, 1970; Mordecai Richler, 1970; Odysseus Ever Returning: Essays on Canadian Writers and Writing, 1970; Into Tibet: The Early British Explorers, 1971; (ed.) Malcolm Lowry: The Man and His Work, 1971; Ghandi, 1971; (ed.) Wyndham Lewis in Canada, 1971; Dawn and the Darkest Hour: A Study of Aldous Huxley, 1972; Herbert Read, 1972; The Rejection of Politics and Other Essays, 1972; Who Killed the British Empire, 1974; Gabriel Dumont, 1975; Notes on Visitations, 1975; South Sea Journey, 1976; Peoples of the Coast, 1977; Two Plays, 1977; Thomas Merton, Monk and Poet, 1978; Faces from History, 1978; A George Woodcock Reader, 1980; The Mountain Road, 1980; The World of Canadian Writing, 1980; Confederation Betrayed, 1981; Ivan Eyre, 1981; Letter to the Past, 1982; Letters From Sooke, 1982; Collected Poems, 1983; Orwell's Message, 1984; Strange Bedfellows, 1985; The Walls of India, 1985; The University of British Columbia, 1986; Northern Spring, 1987; Beyond the Blue Mountain, 1987; Cares in the Desert, 1988; Social History of Canada, 1988; The Marvelous Century, 1988. Add: 6429 McCleery St., Vancouver, B.C. V6N 1G5, Canada.

WOODCOTT, Keith. *See* **BRUNNER,** John.

WOODFORD, (Irene) Cecile. Also writes as Jane Barrie, Veronica Lee, and Vicki Strauss. British. Children's fiction, Travel/Exploration/Adventure. Founded Crown Books, 1968; Ed., Eastbourne Civic Soc. Newsletter, 1967–69. *Publs:* A Sip from any Goblet, 1965; Jane-Anne's Story Book, 1965; A Devil in Paradise; The Art of Inning; Yuletide Festival; In the High Wood; Stir the Witches Cauldron, 1967; Sussex Ways and Byways, 1967; Portrait of Sussex, 1972, 4th ed. 1984; The Life and Loves of Caroline (BBC serial), 1979; By the Crown Divided, 1983; Caroline's Kingdom, 1984. Add: Crown Quality Books, 19 Carmen Ct., Willingdon, Sussex BN20 9NP, England.

WOODFORD, Peggy. British, b. 1937. Novels/Short stories, History, Music, Biography. *Publs:* Abraham's Legacy, 1963; Mozart, 1963; Schubert, 1966; Please Don't Go, 1972; Backwater War, 1975; Mozart: His Life and Times, 1977; (ed. and contrib.) The Real Thing (stories), 1977; Schubert: His Life and Times, 1978; Rise of the Raj, 1978; See You Tomorrow, 1979; (contrib.) New Stories 5, 1980; (ed. and contrib.) You Can't Keep Out the Darkness, 1980; The Girl with a Voice, 1981; Love Me, Love Rome, 1984; (ed. and contrib.) Misfits, 1984; The Monster in Our Midst, 1987. Add: c/o Murray Pollinger, 4 Garrick St., London WC1E 9BH, England.

WOODFORDE, John (Edward) Ffooks. British, b. 1925. Antiques/Furnishings, Architecture, Country life/Rural societies. *Publs:* Observer's Book of Furniture, 1964; The Strange Story of False Teeth, 1968; The Truth about Cottages, 1969; The Story of the Bicycle, 1970; The Strange Story of False Hair, 1971; Furnishing a Country Cottage, 1972; Bricks to Build a House, 1976; Georgian Houses for All, 1978; Observer's Book of Kitchen Antiques, 1982; Farm Buildings in England and Wales, 1983. Add: New Hall, High St., Lydd, Kent, England.

WOODHOUSE, Emma. *See* **HARROD-EAGLES,** Cynthia.

WOODHOUSE, Martin (Charlton). Also writes as John Charlton. British, b. 1932. Novels/Short stories, Plays/Screenplays. *Publs:* Tree Frog (novel), 1966, screenplay 1967; Rock Baby, 1968; Phil and Me, 1970; Mama Doll, 1972; Blue Bone, 1973; (with Robert Ross) The Medici Emerald, 1976; Moon Hill, 1976; (as John Charlton) The Remington Set, 1976; Traders, 1980. Add: c/o A.D. Peters & Co. Ltd., 5th Floor, The Chambers, Chelsea Harbour, Lots Rd., London SW10 0XF, England.

WOODHOUSE, (Christopher) Montague. British, b. 1917. History, Biography. Visiting Prof., Dept. of Modern Greek, King's Coll., London Univ., since 1978. Dir.-Gen., Royal Inst. of Intnl. Affairs, London, 1955–59; Conservative M.P. for Oxford, 1959–66 and 1970–74: Parliamentary Secty., Ministry of Aviation, 1961–62 and Joint Under Secty. of State, Home Office, 1962–64; Dir. of Education and Training, Confedn. of British Industry, 1966–70. Pres., Classical Assn., 1968; Chmn. of the Council, Royal Soc. of Literature, 1977–86. *Publs:* Apple of Discord, 1948; One Sciences Omen, 1950; Dostoievsky, 1951; The Greek War of Independence, 1952; Britain and the Middle East, 1959; British Foreign Policy since the Second World War, 1962; (with Lockhart) Rhodes, 1963; The New Concert of Nations, 1964; The Battle of Navarino, 1965; Post-War Britain, 1966; The Story of Modern Greece, 1968; The Philhellenes, 1969; Capodistria, 1973; The Struggle for Greece, 1976; Modern Greece, 1977; Karamanlis, 1982; Something Ventured, 1982; The Rise and Fall of the Greek Colonels, 1985; Gemistos Plethon, 1986. Add: Willow Cottage, Latimer, Bucks., England

WOODIWISS, Kathleen E. American. Historical/Romance/Gothic. *Publs:* The Flame and the Flower, 1972; The Wolf and the Dove, 1974; Shanna, 1977; Ashes in the Wind, 1979; A Rose in Winter, 1982; Come Love a Stranger, 1984. Add: c/o Avon Books, 105 Madison Ave., New York, N.Y. 10016, U.S.A.

WOODMAN, Harold David. American, b. 1928. History. Prof. of History, since 1971, and Chmn., Cttee. on American Studies, since 1981, Purdue Univ., W. Lafayette, Ind. Pres., Business History Conference, 1980; Vice-Pres., 1982, and Pres., 1983, Agricultural History Soc. *Publs:* Conflict and Consensus in American History, 1966, 7th ed., 1988; (ed.) Slavery and the Southern Economy, 1966; King Cotton and His Retainers, 1968; (ed.) The Legacy of the American Civil War, 1973. Add: 1100 N. Grant St., West Lafayette, Ind. 47906, U.S.A.

WOODRESS, James (Leslie, Jr.) American, b. 1916. Literature. Prof. of English, Univ. of California, Davis, since 1966; now Emeritus. Asst. News Ed., KWK radio, St. Louis, 1939–40; Rewrite Man, U.P.I., NYC, 1941–43; Instr., Grinnell Coll., Iowa, 1949–50; Asst. then Assoc. Prof., Butler Univ., Indianapolis, 1950–58; Prof. of English, 1958–66, and Dean, 1963–64, San Fernando Valley State Coll., Northridge, Calif. Advisory Ed., College English, 1961–63. *Publs:* Howells and Italy, 1952; Booth Tarkington: Gentleman from Indiana, 1955; Disertations in American Literature 1891-1955, 1957, 1962; A Yankee's Odyssey: The Life of Joel Barlow, 1958; (ed., with Richard B. Morris) Voices from America's Past series, 1962–63, 1975; (ed.) American Literary Scholarship: An Annual: 1963, 1965 (and later vols.); Willa Cather: Her Life and Art, 1970; (ed.) Eight American Authors, 1971; American Fiction 1900-1950, 1974; Willa Cather: A Literary Life, 1987. Add: Dept. of English, Univ. of California, Davis, Calif. 95616, U.S.A.

WOODRING, Carl. American, b. 1919. Literature. Woodberry Prof. of Literature Emeritus, Columbia Univ., NYC. Instr. to Prof., Univ. of Wisconsin, Madison, 1948–61. Pres., Assn. of Depts. of English, 1971. *Publs:* Victorian Samplers, 1952; Politics in the Poetry of Coleridge, 1961; (ed.) Prose of the Romantic Period, 1961; Wordsworth, 1965; Virginia Woolf, 1966; Politics in English Romantic Poetry, 1970; Nature into Art: Cultural Transformations in Nineteenth-Century Britain, 1989. Add: 2838 Montebello Rd., No. 20, Austin, Tex. 78746, U.S.A.

WOODRING, Paul. American, b. 1907. Education. Distinguished Service Prof., Western Washington Univ., Bellingham, since 1962, now Emeritus. Ed., Professional Education for Teachers series, Harcourt Brace Jovanovich, publrs. Education Ed., 1960–66, and Ed.-at-Large, 1966–70, Saturday Review mag. *Publs:* Let's Talk Sense about Our Schools, 1953; A Fourth of a Nation, 1957; New Directions in Teacher Education, 1957; (with R. Gustavson and P. Viereck) Education in a Free Society, 1958; (with J. Scanlon) American Education Today, 1962; Introduction to American Education, 1965; The Higher Learning in America: A Reassessment, 1968; Investment in Innovation: An Historical Appraisal of the Fund for the Advancement of Education, 1970; The Persistent Problems of Education, 1983. Add: Dept. of Psychology, Western Washington Univ., Bellingham, Wash. 98225, U.S.A.

WOODRUFF, (Sir) Michael (Francis Addison). British, b. 1911. Medicine/Health, Sciences. Prof. Emeritus of Surgery, Univ. of Edinburgh, since 1977 (Prof., 1957–77). Prof. of Surgery, Univ. of Otago, NZ, 1952–57. *Publs:* Surgery for Dental Students, 1954, 4th ed. (with H. Berry) 1984; Transplantation of Tissues and Organs, 1960; The Edwin Stevens Lectures for the Laity, 1970; On Science and Surgery, 1977; The Interaction of Cancer and Host, 1981. Add: 506 Lanark Rd., Juniper Green, Edinburgh EH14 5DH, Scotland.

WOODRUFF, Philip. *See* **MASON,** Philip.

WOODS, (Sister) Frances Jerome. American, b. 1913. Sociology. Prof. Emerita of Sociology, Our Lady of the Lake Univ., San Antonio, Tex. (Vice-Pres., 1964–67). Research Consultant, San Antonio Housing Authority, and Hogg Foundn., Univ. of Texas, 1959–62; Research Asst., District Office of Congressman Henry B. Gonzalez (20th District), Texas, 1978–81. *Publs:* Mexican Ethnic Leadership in San Antonio, Texas, 1949, 1976; Cultural Values of American Ethnic Groups, 1956; The American Family System, 1959; (with A. Calverley) A Community Experiment in Establishing a Senior Center, 1964; Introductory Sociology, 1966; Marginality and Identity: A Coloured Creole Family Through 10 Generations, 1972; The Model Cities Program in Perspective: The San Antonio, Texas Experience, 1982. Add: 411 S.W 24th St., San Antonio, Tex. 78285, U.S.A.

WOODS, Frederick. British, b. 1932. Mystery/Crime/Suspense, Music, Biography. Ed., Folk Review, 1971–79; Gen. Ed., Collected Works of Sir Winston Churchill, Library of Imperial History, 1974–76. *Publs:* A Blbliography of the Works of Sir Winston Churchill, 1963, 4th ed. 1979; (ed.) Young Winston's Wars, 1972; (compiler) Catalogue to the Centenary Exhibition of Sir Winston Churchill, 1974; Folk Revival: The Rediscovery of a National Music, 1979; Observer Book of Folksong in Britain, 1980; Rundown (novel), 1982; Legends and Traditions of Cheshire, 1982; Further Legends and Traditions of Cheshire, 1983; (ed.) The Oxford Book of English Traditional Verse, 1983; Cheshire in Camera, 1983; Shooting Star (novel), 1984. Add: c/o Hale, 45-47 Clerkenwell Green, London EC1R 0HT, England.

WOODS, John (Warren). American, b. 1926. Poetry. Prof. of English, Western Michigan Univ., Kalamazoo, since 1965 (Asst. Prof., 1955–60; Assoc. Prof., 1961–64). *Publs:* The Deaths at Paragon, Indiana, 1955; On the Morning of Color, 1961; The Cutting Edge, 1966; Keeping Out of Trouble, 1968; Turning to Look Back: Poems, 1955-1970, 1972; The Knees of Widows, 1972; (with F. Pollack and J. Hearst)

Voyages to the Inland Sea II: Essays and Poems, 1972; Alcohol, 1973; A Bone Flicker, 1973; Striking the Earth, 1978; Thirty Years on the Force, 1979; The Night of the Game, 1982; The Valley of Minor Animals, 1982; The Salt Stone: Selected Poems, 1985. Add: Dept. of English, Western Michigan Univ., Kalamazoo, Mich. 49001, U.S.A.

WOODS, L(eslie) C(olin). New Zealander, b. 1922. Mathematics. Fellow, Balliol Coll., Oxford, and Prof. of Mathematics (Theory of Plasma), Oxford Univ., since 1970 (Fellow and Tutor in Engineering Science, 1960–70; Reader in Applied Mathematics, 1964–70); Chmn., Mathematical Inst., Oxford, since 1984. Scientist, National Physical Laboratory, 1951–54; Sr. Lectr. in Applied Mathematics, Sydney Univ., 1954–56; Nuffield Research Prof. of Engineering, Univ. of New South Wales, 1956–60. *Publs:* The Theory of Subsonic Plane Flow, 1961; Introduction to Neutron Distribution Theory, 1964; The Thermodynamics of Fluid Systems, 1975; Principles of Magnetoplasma Dynamics, 1987. Add: Balliol College, Oxford, England.

WOODS, Richard (John Francis). American, b. 1941. Sex, Theology/Religion. Roman Catholic Priest, Dominican Order; Assoc. Prof., Loyola Univ., Chicago. Dir., Center for Religion and Society, Chicago. *Publs:* The Media Maze, 1969; The Occult Revolution, 1971; The Devil, 1973; (ed.) Heterodoxy, 1974; (ed.) The Pastoral Dimension, 1977; Another Kind of Love, 1978; (ed.) Understanding Mysticism, 1979; Mysterion, 1980; Symbion: Spirituality for a Possible Future, 1983; Eckhart's Way, Christian Spirituality, 1989. Add: Center for Religion and Society, 7200 W. Division St., River Forest, Ill. 60305, U.S.A

WOODS, Stockton. *See* **FORREST,** Richard.

WOODWARD, Bob. (Robert Upshur Woodward). American, b. 1943. Politics/Government. Asst. Managing Ed., Washington Post. since 1981 (Reporter, 1971–79; Metropolitan Ed., 1979–81).Reporter, Montgomery County Sentinel, Md., 1970–71. *Publs:* (with Carl Bernstein) All the President's Men, 1974; The Final Days, 1976; (with Scott Armstrong) The Brethren, 1979; Wired: The Short Life and Fast Times of John Belushi, 1984; The Secret Wars of the CIA, 1987. Add: 3027 Q St. N.W., Washington, D.C. 20007, U.S.A.

WOODWARD, C(omer) Vann. American, b. 1908. History. Emeritus Prof. of History, Yale Univ., New Haven, since 1977 (Sterling Prof., 1961–77). Ed., Oxford History of the United States, since 1981. Prof. of History, Johns Hopkins Univ., Baltimore, 1946–61. Pres., Org. of American Historians, 1968; American Historical Assn., 1969. Add: Tom Watson: Agrarian Rebel, 1938; The Battle for Leyte Gulf, 1947; Reunion and Reaction, 1951; Origins of the New South, 1951; The Strange Career of Jim Crow, 1955, 3rd ed. 1974; The Burden of Southern History, 1960, 1968; (ed.) The Comparative Approach to American History, 1968; American Counterpoint, 1971; (ed.) Responses of the Presidents to Charges of Misconduct, 1974; (ed.) Mary Chesnut's Civil War, 1981; Thinking Back, 1986; The Future of the Past, 1989. Add: 104 Hall of Grad. Studies, Yale Univ., New Haven, Conn. 06520, U.S.A.

WOODWARD, John. British, b. 1945. Medicine/Health. Sr. Lectr. in Economic and Social History, Univ. of Sheffield, since 1981 (Lectr., 1970–81). *Publs:* To Do the Sick No Harm: A Study of the British Voluntary Hospital System to 1875, 1974; (co-ed.) Health Care and Popular Medicine in Nineteenth Century England, 1977; (co-ed.) Urban Disease and Mortality in Nineteenth-Century England, 1984. Add: Dept. of History, The University, Sheffield S10 2TN, England.

WOODWARD, Ralph Lee, Jr. American, b. 1934. History. Prof. of History, Tulane Univ., New Orleans, La., since 1970 (Head, Dept. of History, 1973–75, 1986–88). Asst. Prof. of History, Univ. of Wichita, Kans., 1961–62, and Univ. of Southwestern Louisiana, Lafayette, 1962–63; Assoc. Prof. of History, Univ. of North Carolina, Chapel Hill, 1963–67. Visiting Prof., U.S.A. Military Acadamy, West Point, 1989. *Publs:* Political Economy in Guatemala, 1962; Class Privilege and Economic Development, 1966; Robinson Crusoe's Island, 1969; (ed.) Positivism in Latin America, 1971; (with M. Rodriguez, M. Williford, and W.J. Griffith) Applied Englightenment: 19th Century Liberalism, 1972; Central America: A Nation Divided, 1976, 1985; Tribute to Don Bernardo de Galvez, 1979; Belize, 1980; Nicaragua, 1983; (ed.) Research Guide to Central America and the Caribbean, 1985; (ed.) Central America: Historical Perspectives on the Contemporary Crises, 1988; El Salvador, 1988. Add: Dept. of History, Tulane Univ., New Orleans, La. 70118, U.S.A.

WOODWARD, Robert H. American, b. 1925. Literature. Prof. of English since 1954, and Assoc. Dean, Sch. of Humanities and the Arts,

1972–74, and since 1975, San Jose State Univ., Calif. (Chmn., Dept. of English, 1962–66; Acting Dean, Sch. of Humanities and the Arts, 1974–75). Member, Advisory Cttee., Steinbeck Research Center, San Jose State Univ., Calif., since 1971; Secty., Bd. of Trustees, San Jose Studies, since 1974; Bibliography Ed., Magic Lantern Soc. of the U.S. and Canada, since 1982. Columnist, American Collector, 1973–84. *Publs:* The Craft of Prose, 1963, 5th ed., 1980; (ed. with J.J. Clark) Success in America, 1966; (ed. with J.J. Clark) The Social Rebel in American Literature, 1968; (with F. Howell and C. Woodward) The Craft of Pottery, 1975; (with T.F. O'Donnell and S. Garner) A Bibliography of Writings by and about Harold Frederic, 1975; (ed. with G. Fortenberry and S. Garner) The Correspondence of Harold Frederic, 1977; Jack London and the Amateur Press, 1983; The Steinbeck Research Center at San Jose State University: A Descriptive Catalogue, 1985; San Jose State University Faculty Reference Book, 1985. Add: Dept. of English, San Jose State Univ., San Jose, Calif. 95192, U.S.A.

WOOLF, Douglas. American, b. 1922. Novels/Short stories. Freelance writer, and itinerant worker in western U.S., NYC, Canada, Wales, France and Mexico, since 1950. *Publs:* The Hypocritic Days, 1955; Fade Out, 1959; Wall to Wall, 1962; Signs of a Migrant Worrier (short stories), 1965; John-Juan, 1967; Ya! & John-Juan, 1971; The Spring of the Lamb, 1972; On Us, 1977; HAD, 1977; Future Preconditional (short stories), 1978; The Timing Chain, 1985; Loving Ladies, 1986. Add: c/o Wolf Run Books, P.O. Box 215, Tacoma, Wash. 98401, U.S.A.

WOOLF, Harry. American, b. 1923. History (history of science). Prof., Inst. for Advanced Study, Princeton, N.J., since 1987 (Dir., 1976–87). Series Ed., The Sources of Science, since 1964; Assoc. Ed., Dictionary of Scientific Biography. Willis K. Shepard Prof., Dept. of History of Science, 1961–76, Chmn., 1961–72, and Provost, 1972–76, Johns Hopkins Univ., Baltimore. Ed., ISIS: An Intnl. Review Devoted to the History of Science and Its Cultural Influences, 1958–64. *Publs:* The Transits of Venus: A Study in Eighteenth-Century Science, 1959; (ed.) Quantification: Essays in the History of Measurement in the Natural and Social Sciences, 1961; (ed.) Science as a Cultural Force, 1964; (ed.) Scientific Memoirs, Selected from The Transactions of Foreign Academies of Science and Learned Societies, and from Foreign Journals, 7 vols, 1966; (ed.) History of Physical Astronomy, by Robert Grant, 1966; (ed. with S. Toulmin) What I Do Not Believe and Other Essays, 1971; (ed. and contrib.) Some Strangeness in the Proportion: A Centennial Symposium to Celebrate the Achievements of Albert Einstein, 1980; (ed.) The Analytic Spirit: Essays in the History of Science, 1981. Add: Inst. for Advanced Study, Princeton, N.J. 08540, U.S.A.

WOOLF, Stuart Joseph. British, b. 1936. Economics, History, Politics/ Government. Prof. of History, Univ. of Essex, Colchester, since 1975, and European Univ. Inst., Florence, since 1983. Fellow and Asst. Dir. of Studies in History, Pembroke Coll., Cambridge, 1961–65; Reader in Italian History, 1965–74, and Dir., Centre for the Advanced Study of Italian Soc., 1965–74, Univ. of Reading. *Publs:* Studi sulla nobilta piemontese nell'epoca dell' assolutismo, 1963; (trans.) If This is a Man, by P. Levi, 1961; (trans.) The Truce, by P. Levi, 1965; (with M.V. Posner) Italian Public Enterprise, 1967; (ed.) European Fascism, 1968; (trans./reviser) Medieval Parliaments, A Comparative Study, by A. Marongiu, 1968; (ed.) The Nature of Fascism, 1968; The Italian Risorgimento, 1969; (ed. with E. Jones) Agrarian Change and Economic Development: The Historical Problems, 1969; (ed.) The Rebirth of Italy, 1943-50, 1972; (ed.) Italy and the Enlightenment, Studies in a Cosmopolitan Century, by F. Venturi, 1972; (co-author) Storia d'Italia: Dal primo Settecento all'-Unita; La Storia Politica e Sociale, 1973; L'Epoca della Reazione: Fascismo e Nazismo, 1978; A History of Italy 1700-1860: The Social Constraints of Political Change, 1979; (ed.) Fascism in Europe, 1981; (with J.C. Perrot) State and Statistics in France 1789-1815, 1984; The Poor in Western Europe, 1986. Add: Dept. of History, Univ. of Essex, Wivenhoe Pk., Colchester CO4 3SQ, England.

WOOLLCOMBE, Robert. British, b. 1922. History, Military/ Defence. Freelance historical researcher and writer. *Publs:* Lion Rampant, 1955; The Campaigns of Wavell, 1959; The Winds of March, 1962; The First Tank Battle: Cambrai 1917, 1967; All the Blue Bonnets: The History of the King's Own Scottish Borderers, 1980. Add: Stone Cottage, Byworth, Petworth, Sussex, England.

WOOLRYCH, Austin Herbert. British, b. 1918. History. Lectr., then Sr. Lectr., Univ. of Leeds, 1949–64; Prof. of History, Univ. of Lancaster, 1964–85. *Publs:* Battles of the English Civil War, 1961; Oliver Cromwell, 1964; Complete Prose Works of John Milton, Vol. 7, 1974, 1980; Commonwealth to Protectorate, 1982; Soldiers and Statesmen, 1987.

Add: Patchetts, Caton, Lancaster LA2 9QN, England.

WOOTTON, (John) Graham (George). British, b. 1917. History, Politics/Government, Sociology. Prof. of Political Science, Tufts Univ., Medford, Mass. (Visiting Prof. of Gov., 1965–66; Head of Dept., 1979–82, 1983–84). Sr. Staff Tutor, Rewley House, Oxford Univ., 1951–69. *Publs:* Official History of the British Legion, 1956; The Politics of Influence: British Ex-Servicemen, Cabinet Decisions and Cultural Change 1917-57, 1963; Workers, Unions and the State, 1966; Interest Groups, 1970; Pressure Groups in Britain 1720-1970, 1975; Pressure Politics in Contemporary Britain, 1978; (with S. Ehrlich) Three Faces of Pluralism: Political, Ethnic, Religious, 1980; Interest Groups: Policy and Politics in America, 1985. Add: 26 Grove St., Winchester, Mass. 01890, U.S.A.

WORBOYS, Anne. (Annette Isobel Worboys). Also writes as Annette Eyre, Vicky Maxwell, and Anne Eyre Worboys. British. Mystery/ Crime/Suspense, Historical/Romance/Gothic. *Publs:* as Anne Eyre Worboys—Dream of Petals Whim, 1961; Palm Rock and Paradise, 1961; Call from a Stranger, 1962; as Annette Eyre—Three Strings to a Fortune, 1962; Visit to Rata Creek, 1964; The Valley of Yesterday, 1965; A Net to Catch the Wind, 1966; Return to Bellbird Country, 1966; The House of Five Pines, 1967; The River and Wilderness, 1967, in U.S. as Give Me Your Love, 1975; A Wind from the Hill, 1968; Thorn-Apple, 1968; Tread Softly in the Sun, 1969; The Little Millstones, 1970; Dolphin Bay, 1970; Rainbow Child, 1971; The Magnolia Room, 1972; Venetian Inheritance, 1973; as Vicky Maxwell—Chosen Child, 1973; Flight to the Villa Mistra, 1973; The Way of the Tamarisk, 1974, in U.S. as Anne Worboys, 1975; High Hostage, 1976; The Other Side of Summer, 1977; as Anne Worboys—The Lion of Delos, 1974; Every Man a King, 1975, in U.S. paperback as Rendezvous with Fear, 1977; The Barrancourt Destiny, 1977; The Bhunda Jewels, 1980; Run, Sara, Run, 1981; A Kingdom for the Bold, 1986, in U.S. as Aurora Rose, 1988. Add: The White House, Leigh, nr. Tonbridge, Kent, England.

WORCESTER, Donald E. American, b. 1915. Children's fiction, Chil-dren's non-fiction, History. Ida and Cecil Green Emeritus Prof. of History, Texas Christian Univ., Fort Worth, since 1980 (Chmn., Dept. of History, 1963–72; Lorin A. Boswell Prof., 1971–80). Member, Editorial Advisory Bd., Red River Valley Historical Review and the American Indian Quarterly, since 1973. Managing Ed., Hispanic American Historical Review, 1960–65; Chmn., Bd. of Univ. Press Mgrs., Univ. of Florida, 1961–63; Pres., Western Writers of America, 1973–74, Western History Assn., 1974–75, and Westerners Intnl., 1978–79. *Publs:* Lone Hunter's Gray Pony, 1956; (with W.G. Schaffer) The Growth and Culture of Latin America, 1956, 1971; Lone Hunter and the Cheyenne, 1957; Lone Hunter's First Buffalo Hunt, 1958; Lone Hunter and the Wild Horses, 1959; Kit Carson: Mountain Scout, 1959; John Paul Jones: Soldier of the Sea, 1961; War Pony, 1961; (ed. and trans.) Instructions for Governing the Interior Provinces of New Spain 1786, 1951; Sea Power and Chilean Independence, 1962; The Three Worlds of Latin America, 1963; (with M. Boyd) American Civilization, 1964, 1968; (with R. and K. Foster) Man and Civilization, 1965; The Makers of Latin America, 1966; (ed. with M. Boyd) Contemporary America: Issues and Problems, 1968; Brazil: From Colony to World Power, 1973; (ed.) Forked Tongues and Broken Treaties, 1975; Bolivar, 1977; The Apaches: Eagles of the Southwest, 1979; The Chisholm Trail: High Road of the Cattle Kingdom, 1981; (co-ed.) Kiowa Voices, 2 vols., 1981, 1983; (ed.) Pioneer Trails West, 1985; The Texas Cowboy, 1986; The Spanish Mustang: From the Plains of Andalusia to the Prairies of Texas, 1986; The Texas Longhorn: Relic of the Past, Asset of the Future, 1987; The War in the Nueces Strip (novel), 1989. Add: Dept. of History, Texas Christian Univ., Fort Worth, Tex. 76129, U.S.A.

WORKMAN, William D(ouglas), Jr. American, b. 1914. History, Politics/ Government, Race relations. Research Fellow, Inst. for Southern Studies, Univ. of South Carolina, since 1981. Capital Corresp., Columbia, S.C., 1946–62; Radio-TV Commentator, WIS and WIS-TV, Columbia, S.C., 1950–52; Assoc. Ed., 1963–66, Ed., 1966–72, and Editorial Analyst, 1972–79, The State, Columbia Newspapers. *Publs:* (co-author) With All Deliberate Speed, 1957; (co-author) This Is the South, 1959; (co-author) Southern Schools: Progress and Problems, 1959; The Case for the South, 1960; The Bishop from Barnwell, 1963; (co-author) Charles E. Daniel: His Philosophy and Legacy, 1981. Add: 915 Belt Line Blvd., Columbia, S.C. 29205, U.S.A.

WORKS, John. American, b. 1949. Novels/Short stories. Attorney, Idaho Legal Services, Caldwell, Idaho, 1975–76. *Publs:* Thank You, Queen Isabella, 1986. Add: 1600 Forest Trail, Austin, Tex. 78703, U.S.A.

WORLOCK, Derek (John Harford). British, b. 1920. Theology/Religion. Roman Catholic Archbishop of Liverpool. Formerly Bishop of Portsmouth. Vice-Pres., Bishops' Conference of England and Wales; Member, Holy See's Laity Council. *Publs:* (ed.) Seek Ye First, 1949; (ed.) Take One at Bedtime, 1963; English Bishops at the Council, 1965; (ed.) Turn and Turn Again, 1971; Give Me Your Hand, 1977; Better Together. Add: Archbishop's House, 87 Green Lane, Mossley Hill, Liverpool L18 2EP, England.

WORNER, Philip (Arthur Incledon). Has written as Philip Sylvester and Philip Incledon. British, b. 1910. Plays/Screenplays, Poetry. School-master, Simon Langton Sch., Canterbury, 1936–40; Tutor, The Coll. of Education, Worcester, 1949–70. *Publs:* Eros or Psyche, 1933; (as Philip Sylvester) The Little Mermaid, 1938; (as Philip Sylvester) All Dreaming Gone, 1940; (as Philip Sylvester) Freedom Is My Fame, 1942; (as Philip Incledon) The Cactus Hedge, 1951; The Calling of Wenceslas, 1960; Wrack (verse), 1971; Way Out (verse), 1975; His Star Returns (play), 1978; Rainbow Returning (verse), 1987. Add: The Rookery, 216 Henwick Rd., Worcester, England.

WORRALL, Ralph Lyndal. Australian, b. 1903. History, Human relations, Sciences. Medical Statistician, Epidemic Control Branch of the Health Div., U.N. Relief and Rehabilitation Admin., London, 1946–47; Medical Consultant, Concept Pharmaceuticals Ltd., 1971–78. *Publs:* Footsteps of Warfare, 1936; The Outlook of Science, 2nd ed. 1946; Energy and Matter, 1948. Add: 31 Braeside Ave., Sevenoaks, Kent, England.

WORTH, Helen, (Mrs. Arthur M. Gladstone). American, b. 1913. Food/Wine. Newspaper and magazine contrib., since 1949; Food/wine/equipment consultant to national corporations and assns., since 1968. Dir., Helen Worth Enterprises and Cooking Sch., NYC, 1945–80, and Virginia, 1980–82; Adjunct Prof., Food and wine appreciation course, Columbia Univ., 1978, and Univ., of Virginia, Charlottesville, 1985–87. *Publs:* Down-On-the-Farm Cookbook, 1943; Shrimp Cookery, 1952; Cooking Without Recipes, 1965, 1980; Hostess Without Help, 1971; Damm Yankee in a Southern Kitchen, 1973. Add: 1701 Owensville Rd., Charlottesville, Va. 22901, U.S.A.

WORTHINGTON, Edgar Barton. British, b. 1905. Biology/Environmental science/Ecology, Travel/Exploration/Adventure. Environmental consultant. Dir., Freshwater Biological Assn., 1937–46; Secty., Colonial Research Cttee., 1946–50; Secty. Gen., Scientific Council of Africa, 1952–57; Deputy Dir. Gen., Nature Conservancy, 1957–64; Scientific Dir., Intnl. Biological Prog., London, 1964–74. *Publs:* Inland Waters of Africa, 1932; Science in Africa, 1937; Middle East Science, 1946; Development Plan for Uganda, 1946; (with T.T. Macan) Life in Lakes and Rivers, 1951, 1972; Science in the Development of Africa 1958; The Evolution of International Biological Programme, 1975; Arid Land Irrigation in Developing Countries, 1977; The Nile, 1978; The Ecological Century, 1983. Add: Colin Godmans, Furners Green, nr. Uckfield, Sussex, England.

WORTLEY, Ben Atkinson. British, b. 1907. Law. Prof. of Jurisprudence and Intnl. Law, Univ. of Manchester, 1946–75, now Emeritus (Reader in Jurisprudence, 1936–46). Appointed Queen's Counsel, 1969; Hon. Bencher, Gray's Inn, 1989. *Publs:* Expropriation in Public International Law, 1958; Jurisprudence, 1967; (co-author and ed.) An Introduction to the Law of the E.E.C., 1972, and The Law of the Common Market, 1974. Add: 24 Gravel Lane, Wilmslow SK9 6LA, England.

WOUK, Herman. American, b. 1915. Novels/Short stories, Plays/Screenplays. Member, National Advisory Bd., Center for the Book, Library of Congress, Washington, D.C. Visiting Prof. of English, Yeshiva Univ., NYC, 1953–57; Scholar-in-Residence, Aspen Inst. for Humanistic Studies, Colo., 1973–74. Trustee, Coll. of the Virgin Islands, 1961–69; Dir., Washington National Symphony, 1969–71, and Kennedy Center Productions, Washington, D.C., 1974–75. *Publs:* Aurora Dawn, 1947; City Boy, 1948; The Traitor, 1949; The Caine Mutiny, 1951, play as The Caine Mutiny Court Martial, 1953; Marjorie Morningstar, 1955; Nature's Way, 1957; This Is My God, 1959; Youngblood Hawke, 1962; Don't Stop the Carnival, 1965; The Winds of War, 1971 (television screenplay, 1983), War and Remembrance, 1978; (co-author, television screenplay, 1986), Inside, Outside, 1985. Add: BSW Literary Agency, 3255 N St., N.W. Washington D.C. 20007, U.S.A.

WRAGG, David W(illiam). British, b. 1946. Air/Space topics, History. City Air Corresp., Sunday Telegraph, London, 1966–73; Defence and Transport Corrresp., The Spectator, London, 1973–76; in Public Relations Dept., Peninsular & Oriental Steam Navigation Co., 1974–79. *Publs:* World's Air Fleets, 1967, 1969; (with Richard Gardner) Plane Talk, 1970; World's Air Forces, 1971; A Dictionary of Aviation, 1974; Flight Before Flying, 1974; Speed in the Air, 1974; Flight with Power, 1978; Wings over the Sea, 1979; Publicity and Customer Relations in Transport Management, 1982; Boats of the Air, 1984; Airlift: History of Military Air Transport, 1986; Offensive Weapon: Strategy of Bombing, 1986. Add: 25 Midhope Close, Woking, Surrey GU22 7UF, England.

WRAGG, Edward Conrad. British, b. 1938. Education. Prof. of Education and Dir. of the Sch. of Education, Univ. of Exeter, since 1978. Chmn., School Broadcasting Council for the U.K., since 1981. Asst. Master, Queen Elizabeth Grammar Sch., Wakefield, Yorks., 1960–64; Head of German, Wyggeston Boys' Sch., Leicester, 1964–66; Lectr. in Education, Univ. of Exeter, 1966–73; Prof. of Education, Univ. of Nottingham, 1973–78. Pres., British Educational Research Assn., 1971–82. *Publs:* Teaching Teaching, 1974; Teaching Mixed Ability Groups, 1976; Classroom Interaction, 1976; A Handbook for School Governors, 1980; Class Management and Control, 1981; A Review of Teacher Education, 1982; Swineshead Revisited, 1982; Classroom Teaching Skills, 1984; Pearls from Swineshire, 1984; The Domesday Project, 1985; Education: An Action Guide for Parents, 1986; Teacher Appraisal, 1987; Education in the Market Place, 1988; The Wragged Edge, 1988; Schools and Parents, 1989. Add: 14 Doriam Close, Exeter, Devon EX4 4RS, England.

WREFORD, James. *See* **WATSON,** James Wreford.

WREN, Christopher G(ove). American, b. 1950. Law, Librarianship. Asst. Attorney-Gen., Wisconsin Dept. of Justice, Madison, since 1984. Police Officer, District of Columbia Metropolitan Police Dept., 1971–72; Research Assoc., Douglas A. Danner, Boston, 1979–80; Judicial Law Clerk, U.S. District Court Judge James E. Doyle, Madison, 1980–81; Assoc. Attorney, Michael, Best and Friedrich, Madison, 1981–84. *Publs:* (with Jill Robinson Wren) The Legal Research Manual: A Game Plan for Legal Research and Analysis, 1983, 1986; (with Jill Robinson Wren) The Teaching of Legal Research, 1988. Add: 702 Emerson St., Madison, Wisc. 53715, U.S.A.

WREN, Jill Robinson. American, b. 1954. Law, Librarianship. Sr. Ed., Adams and Ambrose Publishing (Formerly American Academic Press), Madison, since 1986. Law Clerk, Wisconsin Attorney Gen., Madison, 1979; Asst. Ed., Food Service Marketing mag., Madison, 1980–81; Judicial Law Clerk, Dane County Circuit Judge P. Charles Jones, Madison, 1981, and Judge Angela B. Bartell, 1981–83, Ed., State Bar of Wisconsin Continuing Legal Education Div., Madison, 1984–86. *Publs:* (with Christopher G. Wren) The Legal Research Manual: A Game Plan for Legal Research and Analysis, 1983, 1986; (with Christopher G. Wren) The Teaching of Legal Research, 1988. Add: P.O. Box 9684, Madison, Wisc. 53715, U.S.A.

WRIGHT, A(mos) J(asper). American, b. 1952. Poetry, Criminology. Clinical Librarian, Dept. of Anesthesiology, Univ. of Alabama at Birmingham, since 1983. Paraprofessional Librarian, Ralph Brown Draughon Library, Auburn Univ., Ala., 1973–81; Cataloger, Tuscaloosa Public Library, 1982–83. *Publs:* (with D.M. Petrizzi) Proposal for Implementation of Office of Educational Radio Services, 1977; Frozen Fruit, 1978; Right Now I Feel Like Robert Johnson, 1981; Criminal Activity in the Deep South, 1989. Add: 617 Valley View Dr., Pelham, Ala. 35124, U.S.A.

WRIGHT, Austin M. American, b. 1922. Novels/Short stories, Literature. Prof. of English, Univ. of Cincinnati, Ohio, since 1969 (Asst. Prof., 1962–66; Assoc. Prof., 1966–69). Instr. of English, Augustana Coll., Rock Island, Ill., 1948–50; Lectr. in Humanities, 1953–55, and Asst. Prof. of English, 1960–62, Univ. of Chicago; Instr., Wright Jr. Coll., Chicago, 1955–60. *Publs:* The American Short Story in the Twenties, 1961; Camden's Eyes, 1969; (co-ed.) The Art of the Short Story, 1969; First Persons, 1973; The Morley Mythology, 1977; The Formal Principle in the Novel, 1982. Add: Dept. of English, Univ. of Cincinnati, Ohio 45221, U.S.A.

WRIGHT, Celeste Turner. American, b. 1906. Poetry, Literature, Autobiography/Memoirs/Personal. Emeritus Prof. of English, Univ. of California, Davis, since 1973 (Instr., Asst. Prof., Assoc. Prof., 1928–48; Chmn. of English Dept., 1928–55; Prof., 1948–73). *Publs:* Anthony

Mundy: An Elizabethan Man of Letters, 1928; Etruscan Princess and Other Poems, 1964; A Sense of Place, 1973; Seasoned Timber (poetry), 1977; University Woman (memoirs), 1981.   Add: Dept. of English, Univ. of California, Davis, Calif. 95616, U.S.A.

WRIGHT, Charles (P. Jr.).   American, 1935.   Poetry.   Prof. of English, Univ. of Virginia, Charlottesville, since 1983.   Member of the English Dept., Univ. of California at Irvine, 1966–83.   Visiting Lectr., Univ. of Iowa, Iowa City, 1974–75, Princeton Univ., New Jersey, 1978, and Columbia Univ., NYC, 1978.   *Publs:* The Voyage, 1963; 6 Poems, 1965; The Dream Animal, 1968; Private Madrigals, 1969; The Grave of the Right Hand, 1970; The Venice Notebook, 1971; Backwater, 1973; Hard Freight, 1973; Bloodlines, 1975; Colophons, 1977; China Trace, 1977; (trans.) The Storm and Other Poems, by Eugenio Montale, 1978; Wright: A Profile, 1979; Dead Color, 1980; The Southern Cross, 1981; Country Music: Selected Early Poems, 1982; The Other Side of the River, 1984; (trans.) Orphic Songs, 1984; 5 Journals, 1986; Zone Journals, 1988; Halflife, 1988.   Add: 940 Locust Ave., Charlottesville, Va. 22901, U.S.A.

WRIGHT, Charles (Stevenson).   American, b. 1932.   Novels/Short stories, Poetry.   Freelance writer.   Former Columnist, Wright's World, Village Voice, NYC.   *Publs:* The Messenger, 1963; The Wig: A Mirror Image, 1966; Black Studies, 1972; Absolutely Nothing to Get Alarmed About, 1973; Bloodlines (poetry), 1975.   Add: c/o Farrar, Straus & Giroux Inc., 19 Union Sq. West, New York, N.Y. 10003, U.S.A.

WRIGHT, Christopher.   British, b. 1924.   History, Theology/Religion.   Housemaster, Aldenham Sch., Elstree, Herts., 1956–67; Councillor, Herts. County Council, 1965–68; Sr. History Master, Archway Comprehensive Sch., London, 1967–68, and Kent Coll., Canterbury, 1968–84.   *Publs:* The Working Class, 1972; Kent Through the Years, 1975; The Welfare State, 1981; The Christian Church, 1982; Child's History of Britain, 1986.   Add: 1 Pond Cottages, Adisham, near Canterbury, Kent, England.

WRIGHT, (Charles) Conrad.   American, b. 1917.   Theology/Religion.   Prof. of American Church History, Harvard Divinity Sch., Cambridge, Mass., since 1969, now Emeritus (Lectr., 1954–69; Registrar, 1955–67).   Faculty member, Massachusetts Inst. of Technology, Cambridge, 1946–54.   *Publs:* The Beginnings of Unitarianism in America, 1955; (ed.) Three Prophets of Religious Liberalism, 1961; The Liberal Christians, 1970; (ed.) Religion in American Life, 1972; (co-author) A Stream of Light, 1975.   Add: 983 Memorial Dr., Cambridge, Mass. 02138, U.S.A.

WRIGHT, David (John Murray).   British, b. 1920.   Poetry, Literature, Travel/Exploration/Adventure, Autobiography/Memoirs/Personal, Translations.   Staff member, Sunday Times, London, 1942–47; Ed., Nimbus, London, 1955–56; Ed., X mag., London, 1959–62.   *Publs:* Poems, 1949; (ed. with John Heath-Stubbs) The Forsaken Garden: An Anthology of Poetry 1824-1909, 1950; Moral Stories, 1952; (ed. with J. Heath-Stubbs) The Faber Book of Twentieth Century Verse, 1953, 1975; Moral Stories, 1954; (trans.) Beowulf, 1957; Monologue of a Deaf Man, 1958; Roy Campbell, 1960; (trans.) The Canterbury Tales, by Geoffrey Chaucer, 1964; Adam at Evening, 1965; (with P. Swift) Algarve, 1965, 1971; (ed.) The Mid-Century English Poetry 1940-60, 1965; Poems, 1966; (ed.) Longer Contemporary Poems, 1966; (with P. Swift) Minho and North Portugal: A Portrait and a Guide, 1968; (ed.) The Penguin Book of English Romantic Verse, 1968; Nerve Ends, 1969; Deafness: A Personal Account, 1969; (ed.) Recollections of the Lakes and the Lake Poets, by Thomas de Quincey, 1970; (with P. Swift) Lisbon: A Portrait and a Guide, 1971; (ed.) Records of Shelley, Byron, and the Author, by Edward Trelawny, 1973; A South African Album, 1975; A View of the North, 1976; To the Gods the Shades: New and Collected Poems, 1976; (ed.) The Penguin Book of Everyday Verse, 1976; (ed.) Under the Greenwood Tree, by Hardy, 1978; (ed.) Selected Poems, by Hardy, 1979; Metrical Observations, 1980; Selected Poems, 1980; (ed.) Edward Thomas: Selected Poems and Prose, 1981; The Canterbury Tales, by Chaucer (verse trans.) 1985; (co-ed.) An Anthology from X, 1988.   Add: c/o A.D. Peters Ltd., 10 Buckingham St., Adelphi, London WC2N 6BU, England.

WRIGHT, Dorothy (Mrs. C.B. Dix).   British, b. 1910.   Novels/Short stories, Plays/Screenplays, Crafts.   *Publs:* The Gentle Phoenix, 1938; Queens Wilde, 1950; Advance in Love, 1953; Laurian and the Wolf, 1956; Among the Cedars, 1959; A Cradle of Willow, 1952; The Nightingale, 1954; Baskets and Basketry, 1959; A Caneworker's Book, 1970; Beginning Patchwork, 1971; The Complete Book of Baskets and Basketry, 1977.   Add: Long Whitstone, Bovey Tracey, South Devon, England.

WRIGHT, Esmond.   British, b. 1915.   History, International relations/Current affairs, Biography.   Prof. of Modern History, Univ. of Glas-

gow, 1957–67; Conservative Member of Parliament (UK) for the Pollok Div. of Glasgow, 1967–70; Dir. and Prof., Inst. of United States Studies, Univ. of London, 1971–84.   *Publs:* Washington and the American Revolution, 1957; Fabric of Freedom, 1961, 1978; Benjamin Franklin and American Independence, 1966; (ed.) Causes and Consequences of the American Revolution, 1966; (ed.) Benjamin Franklin: A Profile, 1966; The World Today, 4th ed. 1975; A Tug of Loyalties, 1975; (co-author) Europe, Today, 1980; The Fire of Liberty, 1983; Franklin of Philadelphia, 1986; Benjamin Franklin: His Life as He Wrote It, 1989.   Add: 31 Tavistock Sq., London WC1, England.

WRIGHT, George Thaddeus.   American, b. 1925.   Literature, Translations.   Prof. of English since 1968, and Chmn. of Dept. since 1974, Univ. of Minnesota, Minneapolis.   Instr., and Asst. Prof. of English, Univ. of Kentucky, Lexington, 1957–60; Asst. Prof. of English, San Francisco State Coll., 1960–61; Assoc. Prof. of English, Univ. of Tennessee, 1961–68; Fulbright Lectr. in American Literature, Université d'Aix-Marseille, 1964–66.   *Publs:* The Poet in the Poem, 1960; W.H. Auden, 1969, 1981; (ed.) Seven American Literary Stylists from Poe to Mailer: An Introduction, 1973.   Add: 1205 Upton Ave. N., Minneapolis, Minn. 55411, U.S.A.

WRIGHT, Helen L(ouise).   American, b. 1932.   Cultural/Ethnic Topics, Music.   Writer and Pres., Helen L. Wright, Inc.   *Publs:* Metropolitan Opera House, 1980; News for Opera Lovers: The Met Is Still There, 1980; The Art, Power and Technique of Writing, 1984; Panic in New York, 1985; Unlimited Powers, 1985.   Add: P.O. Box 2451, Westport, Conn. 06880, U.S.A.

WRIGHT, Judith Arundell.   Australian, b. 1915.   Novels/Short stories, Children's fiction, Poetry, Biography, Essays.   Councillor, Australian Soc. of Authors.   *Publs:* The Moving Image, 1946; (ed.) Australian Poetry 1948; Woman to Man, 1950; The Gateway, 1953; The Two Fires, 1955; The Generations of Men, 1955; (ed.) A Book of Australian Verse, 1956; Kings of the Dingoes, 1958; Birds, 1960; The Day the Mountains Played, 1960; Range the Mountains High, 1962; (ed.) New Land New Language, 1962; Five Senses, 1963; Charles Harpur, 1963; (ed.) Shaw Neilson, 1963; Preoccupations in Australian Poetry, 1964; The Other Half, 1966; The Nature of Love, 1966; The River and the Road, 1966; Henry Lawson, 1967; Collected Poems, 1971; Alive, 1972; Because I Was Invited (essays), 1976; Fourth Quarter, 1977; The Coral Battleground, 1977; Charles Harpur, 1977; The Double Tree: Selected Poems 1942-1976, 1978; The Cry for the Dead, 1981; We Call for a Treaty, 1985; Phantom Dwelling, 1985.   Add: P.O. Box 93, Braidwood, N.S.W. 2622, Australia.

WRIGHT, Kenneth.   *See* **del REY,** Lester.

WRIGHT, Kit. (Christopher Wright).   British, b. 1944.   Poetry.   Education Secty., Poetry Soc., London, 1970–75; Fellow-Commoner in Creative Arts, Trinity Coll., Cambridge, 1977–79.   *Publs:* (with Stephen Miller and Elizabeth Maslen) Treble Poets 1, 1974; (ed.) Soundings: A Selection of Poems for Speaking Aloud, 1975; The Bear Looked over the Mountain, 1977; Arthur's Father (Granny, Sister, Uncle), 4 vols. (juvenile), 1978; Rabbiting On and Other Poems (juvenile), 1978; Hot Dog (juvenile), 1981; The Day Room, 1983; Bump-Starting the Hearse, 1983; (ed.) Poems for 9-Year Olds and Under Over 10-Year Olds, 2 vols., 1984; Cat Among the Pigeons (juvenile), 1987; Poems 1974-1983, 1988; Real Rags and Red, 1988.   Add: 27 Wrights Ln., London W8 5TZ, England.

WRIGHT, Nicholas.   British, b. 1940.   Plays.   Dir., Theatre Upstairs Royal Court Theatre, London, 1970–75; joint artistic dir., Royal Court Theatre, 1976–77; Literary Mgr., National Theatre, 1988–89.   *Publs:* The Crimes of Vautrin, 1983; The Custom of the Country, 1983; The Desert Air, 1985; La Double Inconstance, and Slave Island (adaptations), 1987.   Add: Judy Daish Assocs., 83 Eastbourne Mews, London W2 6LQ, England.

WRIGHT, (Mary) Patricia.   Also writes as Mary Napier.   British, b. 1932.   Historical/Romance (including modern romantic thrillers), History.   Teacher, 1965–79; Surveyor and Land Agent, 1955–60; County Councillor, 1981; District Councillor, 1983.   *Publs:* (as Mary Napier) Woman's Estate (sketches), 1959; Conflict on the Nile: Study of Fashoda Incident 1897-1900, 1972; Space of the Heart, 1976 (in paperback as Ilena, 1977); Journey into Fire, 1977; Shadow of the Rock, 1978; Storm Harvest (in U.S. As Heart of the Storm), 1979; Blind Chance, 1980; This, My City, 1981; (as Mary Napier) Forbidden Places, 1981; While Paris Danced, 1982; History of Frant, 1982; (as Mary Napier) State of Fear, 1984; I Am England, 1987; (as Mary Napier) Heartsearch, 1988; That Near and Distant Place, 1988.   Add: Whitehill House, Frant, Sussex,

England.

WRIGHT, Philip Arthur. British, b. 1908. Agriculture/Forestry, Engineering/Technology, History, Theology/Religion. Agricultural Corresp., Essex Countryside mag., since 1954. Vicar of Littlebury, 1945–54, of Woodford Bridge, 1954–65, and of Roxwell, 1965–78. *Publs:* Ploughshare and Pulpit; Padre Calling; Traction Engines; Old Farm Implements; Old Farm Tractors; Salute the Carthorse; Country Padre, 1980; Day after Day, 1984; Rustic Rhymes, 1985. *Publs:* Queen Anne Cottage, Greensted, near Ongar, Essex CM5 9LA, England.

WRIGHT, Robert Lee. American, b. 1920. Cultural/Ethnic topics, History, Mythology/Folklore. Prof. of American Thought and Language, and Comparative Literature, Michigan State Univ., East Lansing, from 1961, now Emeritus. Instr. in English, Univ. of Minnesota, Minneapolis, 1946–48; Instr. in English, Columbia Univ. Teachers Coll., NYC, 1953–54. *Publs:* Writing without Rules, 1951, rev. ed. 1955; (ed., trans. and collector) Swedish Emigrant Ballads, 1965; (co-author) University College and the Decade Ahead: General Education in a Changing University, 1969; (co-author) The Dark and Tangled Path, 1971; (ed. and collector) Irish Emigrant Ballads and Songs, 1975; Composition; (anthologist) Ballads and Songs of Emigration from Europe to America; (contrib.) Ballads and Ballad Research, 1978; (co-ed., trans. and collector) Danish Emigrant Ballads and Songs, 1983; (with Rochelle Wright) Danish Epigrams, Ballads, and Songs, 1983. Add: 274 Oakland Dr., East Lansing, Mich. 48823, U.S.A.

WRIGHT, The Very Reverend R(onald W.V.) Selby. British, b. 1908. Sociology, Theology/Religion. Emeritus Minister of the Canongate (The Kirk of Holyrood House), and Edinburgh Castle (Minister, 1936–77). Chaplain to H.M. the Queen, since 1961; Chaplain to the Queen's Bodyguard, Scotland, since 1973; Fellow, Royal Soc. of Edinburgh. Moderator, The Presbytery of Edinburgh, 1963, and Church of Scotland, 1972–73. *Publs:* (ed.) Asking Them Questions, 6 vols.; (ed.) Fathers of the Kirks; (ed.) Manual of Church Doctrine; Take Up God's Armour; The Kirk in the Canongate; Our Club; Seven Sevens, 1977; Another Home, 1980. Add: The Queen's House, Moray Pl., Edinburgh EH3 6BX, Scotland.

WRIGHT, Stephen. American, b. 1922. Novels/Short stories, Plays/Screenplays, Essays. Free-lance writer and authors' representative. *Publs:* Crime in the Schools (novel), 1959; (ed.) Different: An Anthology of Homosexual Short Stories, 1974; Brief Encyclopedia of Homosexuality (essays), 1978; The Greatest Thrill (mystery play), 1980; Stephen Wright's Mystery Notebook, 13 vols., 1984–87; The Adventures of Sandy West, Private Eye (novel), 1986. Add: P.O. Box 1341, F.D.R. Station, New York, N.Y. 10150, U.S.A.

WRIGHT, Theodore Paul, Jr. American, b. 1926. Area studies, International relations/Current affairs, Politics/Government. Prof. of Political Science, State Univ. of New York, Albany, since 1971 (Assoc. Prof., 1965–71). Instr., 1955–57, Asst. Prof., 1957–64, and Assoc. Prof., 1964–65, Bates Coll., Lewiston, Me. *Publs:* American Support of Free Elections Abroad, 1964; The Muslim Minority in India, 1975. Add: 27 Vandenburg Lane, Latham, N.Y. 12110, U.S.A.

WRIGHT, Walter F(rancis). American, b. 1912. Literature. Emeritus Marie Kotouc Roberts Prof. of English, Univ. of Nebraska, Lincoln, since 1982 (Asst. Prof., Assoc. Prof., and Prof., 1945–65; Marie Kotouc Roberts Prof., 1965–82). Member of faculty, North Dakota State Univ., Fargo, 1934–35, Doane Coll., Crete, Nebr., 1935–38, and Washington State Univ., Pullman, 1938–45. *Publs:* Sensibility in English Prose Fiction 1760-1814, 1937; Romance and Tragedy in Joseph Conrad, 1949; Art and Substance in George Meredith, 1953; The Madness of Art: A Study of Henry James, 1962; The Shaping of the Dynasts: A Study in Thomas Hardy, 1967; Arnold Bennett: Romantic Realist, 1971. Add: 1021 Robert Rd., Lincoln, Nebr. 68510, U.S.A.

WRIGHT, William David. British, b. 1906. Sciences (general). Former Prof. of Applied Optics, Imperial Coll. of Science and Technology, London. *Publs:* The Perception of Light, 1938; The Measurement of Colour, 1944, 4th ed. 1969; Researches on Normal and Defective Colour Vision, 1946; Photometry and the Eye, 1949; The Rays are Not Coloured, 1967. Add: 68 Newberries Ave., Radlett, Herts. WD7 7EP, England.

WRIGHT, William Edward. American, b. 1926. History. Prof. of History, Univ. of Minnesota, Minneapolis, since 1972 (Instr., 1957–59; Asst. Prof., 1959–62; Assoc. Prof., 1962–66; Dir., Center for Immigration Studies, 1966–67; Dir., Grad. History Studies, 1967–69; Assoc. Dean,

Intnl. Progs., 1969–70; Assoc. to the Vice-Pres. for Intnl. Progs., 1970–76; Dir., Center for Austrian Studies, 1977–88). Ed., Austrian History Yearbook, since 1982. *Publs:* Serf, Seigneur, and Sovereign: Agrarian Reform in Eighteenth-Century Bohemia, 1966; (ed.) Austria since 1945, 1982. Add: 18200 Honeysuckle Lane, Deephaven, Minn. 55391, U.S.A.

WRIGHTSMAN, Lawrence S(amuel). American, b. 1931. Human relations, Psychology, Sociology. Prof. of Psychology, George Peabody Coll. for Teachers, Nashville, Tenn., since 1966 (Asst. Prof., 1958–59; Exec. Officer and Assoc. Prof., 1959–64; Assoc. Prof. of Psychology, 1964–66). Member, Bd. of Eds., Soundings: An Interdisciplinary Journal, since 1972; Member, Bd. of Editorial Consultants, Journal of Personality, since 1973; Editorial Bd. Member, Journal of Applied Social Psychology, since 1973. Member, APA Cttee. on Intnl. Relations in Psychology, 1968–71. *Publs:* (ed.) Contemporary Issues in Social Psychology, 1968, 2nd ed. with J.C. Brigham, 1973; (with F.H. Sanford) Psychology: A Scientific Study of Man, 3rd ed. 1970, 5th ed. as Psychology: A Scientific Study of Human Behavior, 1978; (with F.H. Sanford) Student Workbook for Psychology: A Scientific Study of Man, 3rd ed. 1970, 4th ed. as Student Workbook for Psychology: A Scientific Study of Human Behavior, 1975; (ed. with J. O'Connor and N.J. Baker) Cooperation and Competition: Readings on Mixed-Motive Games, 1972; Social Psychology in the Seventies, 1972, 1975; Social Psychology in the Seventies: Brief Edition, 1973; Assumptions About Human Nature: A Social Psychological Approach, 1974. Add: c/o Brooks-Cole, 511 Forest Lodge Rd., Pacific Grove, Calif. 93950, U.S.A.

WRIGHTSON, (Alice) Patricia. Australian, b. 1921. Children's fiction. Secty. and Admin., Bonalbo District Hosp., 1946–60, and Sydney District Nursing Assn., 1960–64; Asst. Ed., 1964–70, and Ed., 1970–75, School Magazine, Sydney. *Publs:* The Crooked Snake, 1955; The Bunyip Hole, 1958; The Rocks of Honey, 1960; The Feather Star, 1962; Down to Earth, 1965; I Own the Racecourse! (in U.S. as A Racecourse for Andy), 1968; An Older Kind of Magic, 1972; (ed.) Beneath the Sun: An Australian Collection for Children, 1972; The Nargun and the Stars, 1973; The Ice is Coming, 1977; (ed.) Emu Stew (anthology), 1977; The Dark Bright Water, 1979; Behind the Wind (in U.S. as Journey Behind the Wind), 1981; A Little Fear, 1983; Night Outside, 1985; Moon-Dark, 1987; Balyet, 1989. Add: P.O. Box 91, Maclean, N.S.W. 2463, Australia.

WRIGLEY, Gordon. British, b. 1923. Agriculture. Ed., Tropical Agriculture Assn. UK Newsletter; Ed., Longman Tropical Agriculture Series. Worked in the Colonial Agriculture Service, Uganda, 1945–54; Development Mgr., Fisons Pest Control Ltd., Cambridge, 1954–64; Sr. Agronomist, British Petroleum, London, 1964–83. *Publs:* Tropical Agriculture: The Development of Production, 1962, 4th ed. 1982; Coffee, 1987. Add: 2 Church Lane, Linton, Cambridge CB1 6JX, England.

WROTTESLEY, (Arthur) John Francis. British, b. 1908. Transportation (railways), Law. Barrister-at-Law, Inner Temple, London (called to the bar, 1932), and on Oxford Circuit, 1932–39, 1945–53, and 1973–79; part-time Lectr. in Law, City of London Coll., 1937–39, and 1945–46; British Army, 1939–45; Legal Adviser, London Express Newspapers, 1946–53; Special Asst., Office of Chief Solicitor, British Transport Commn., 1953–62; with British Railways Bd., 1962–73. *Publs:* (with Sir Samuel Bosanquet) A Magistrates Handbook, 1949; You and the Law, 1951; Famous Underground Railways of the World, 1955; The Midland and Great Northern Joint Railway, 1970, 1981; The Great Northern Railway, 3 vols., 1979–81. Add: 54 Warrington Cres., London W9 1EP, England.

WROUGHTON, John Presbury. British, b. 1934. History. Headmaster, King Edward Sch., Bath, since 1982 (Head of History Dept., 1965–74; Second Master, 1974–82). *Publs:* Cromwell and the Roundheads, 1969; Plots, Traitors and Spies 1953-1985, 1970; (with J. Paxton) Smuggling, 1971; Documents on British Political History, 3 vols., 1971–72; (ed.) Bath in the Age of Reform 1830-41, 1972; The Civil War in Bath and North Somerset, 1973; (with D. Cook) Documents on World History, 2 vols., 1976; Documents and Debates, 17th Century Britain, 1980; (with C. Cook) English Historical Facts 1603-1689, 1980; King Edward's School at Bath 1552-1982, 1982. Add: 6 Ormonde House, Sion Hill, Bath BA1 2UN, England.

WUNDERLICH, Ray Charles. Jr. American, b. 1929. Education, Medicine/Health, Psychology. Pediatrician in private practice, St. Petersburg, Fla., since 1961: currently practicing preventive and nutritional medicine. *Publs:* Kids, Brains, and Learning, 1970; Allergy,

Brains, and Children Coping, 1973; Improving Your Diet, and Fatigue, 1976; Sugar and Your Health, 1982; Nourishing Your Child, 1984; Help for New Parents and Parents-to-Be, 1989. Add: 666-6th St. S., St. Petersburg, Fla. 33701, U.S.A.

WUNSCH, Josephine M. Also writes as J. Sloan McLean. American, b. 1914. Novels/Short stories, Children's fiction. *Publs:* Flying Skis, 1962; Passport to Russia, 1965; Summer of Decision, 1968; Lucky in Love, 1970; (with Virginia Gillette as J. Sloan McLean) The Aerie, 1974; Girl in the Rough, 1981; Class Ring, 1983; Free as a Bird, 1984; Breaking Away, 1985; The Perfect Ten, 1986; Lucky in Love, 1987; Between Us, 1989. Add: 830 Bishop Rd., Grosse Pointe Park, Mich. 48230, U.S.A.

WURLITZER, Rudolph. American, b. 1938. Novels/Short stories, Screenplays. *Publs:* Nog (in U.K. as The Octopus), 1969; Flats, 1970; (with Will Corry) Turo-Lane Blacktop (screenplay), 1971; Quake, 1972; Slow Fade, 1984. Add: c/o Knopf Inc., 201 E. 50th St., New York, N.Y. 10022, U.S.A.

WYATT, Lord, of Weeford; Woodrow Lyle Wyatt. British, b. 1918. Children's fiction, International relations/Current affairs, Autobiography. Chmn. of the Horserace Totaliser Bd., since 1976. Politician: Labour Member of Parliament (U.K.) for the Aston Div. of Birmingham, 1945–55, and the Bosworth Div. of Leicester, 1959–70. Columnist, the Times and News of the World. *Publs:* The Jews at Home, 1950; Southwards from China, 1952; Into the Dangerous World, 1952; The Peril in Our Midst, 1956; Distinguished for Talent, 1958; Turn Again, Westminster, 1973; Mr. Saucy Squirrel, 1976; The Further Exploits of Mr. Saucy Squirrel, 1977; What's Left of the Labour Party?, 1977; To the Point, 1981; Confessions of an Optimist (autobiography), 1985. Add: 19 Cavendish Ave., London NW8, England.

WYBOURNE, Brian Garner. New Zealander, b. 1935. Mathematics, Physics. Prof. of Physics, Univ. of Canterbury, since 1966. Asst. Prof., Johns Hopkins Univ., Baltimore, Md., 1960–62; Assoc. Physicist, Argonne National Lab., Ill., 1963–66. *Publs:* Spectroscopic Properties of Rare Earths, 1965; Symmetry Principles and Atomic Spectroscopy, 1970; (ed.) The Structure of Matter: Rutherford Centennial Symposium, 1972; Classical Groups for Physicists, 1974. Add: Physics Dept., Univ. of Canterbury, Christchurch, New Zealand.

WYKEHAM, (Sir) Peter. British, b. 1915. History, Biography. Export Consultant. Former Pilot, R.A.F., 1932–69. *Publs:* Fighter Command, 1960; Santos-Dumont, 1963. Add: Green Place, Stockbridge, Hants., England.

WYKES, Alan. British, b. 1914. Novels/Short stories, History, Literature, Recreation/Leisure/Hobbies, Sociology, Biography. Fiction Ed., Strand Mag., London, 1947–49; Fiction Exec., Hulton Press, 1953–61. *Publs:* Pursuit Till Morning, 1947; The Music Sleeping, 1948; The Pen Friend, 1950; Happyland, 1952; A Concise Survey of American Literature, 1955; (ed.) The Brabazon Story, 1965; (with J.A. Hunter) Hunter's Tracks, 1957; (compiler) A Sex By Themselves, 1958; (with W.H. Scott-Shawe) Mariner's Tale, 1959; Snake Man, 1960; Nimrod Smith, 1961; Party Games, 1963; Gambling, 1964; The Doctor and His Enemy, 1964; Handbook of Amateur Dramatics, 1965, 1966; (with D.A. Rayner) The Great Yacht Race, 1966; An Eye on the Thames, 1966; Air Atlantic, 1967; Siege of Leningrad, 1968; The Royal Hampshire Regiment, 1968; Doctor Cardano, 1969; The Nuremberg Rallies, 1970; Reading: Biography of a Town, 1970; Lucrezia Borgia, 1970; Hitler, 1970; Goebbels, 1971; Himmler, 1972; Heydrich, 1972; 1942: The Turning Point, 1972; (compiler) Abroad, 1973; Hitler's Bodyguards, 1974; Not So Savage, 1975; Saucy Seaside

Postcards, 1976; Circus, 1977; H.G. Wells in the Cinema, 1978; Ale and Hearty, 1979; Eisenhower, 1983. Add: 382 Tilehurst Rd., Reading RG3 2NG, England.

WYLIE, Laura. *See* **MATTHEWS,** Patricia.

WYLLIE, Peter J(ohn). British, b. 1930. Earth sciences. Prof. of Geology, Division of Geological and Planetary Sciences, California Inst. of Technology, Pasadena, since 1987 (Chmn., 1983–87); Member of the Commn., CIMP (formerly CEPHT): Intnl. Union of Geological Sciences (Chmn., 1976–80); Pres., Intnl. Mineralogical Assn., since 1986 (Vice Pres., 1978–86). Assoc. Prof. of Geochemistry, Pennsylvania State Univ., University Park, 1961–65; Prof., 1965–83, Homer J. Livingston Prof. of Geology, 1978–83, and Chmn., Dept. of Geophysical Sciences,

1979–82, Univ. of Chicago. Pres, Mineralogical Soc. of America, 1977–78. *Publs:* Ultramafic and Related Rocks, 1967; The Dynamic Earth: Textbook in Geosciences, 1971; The Way the Earth Works: Introduction to the New Global Geology and Its Revolutionary Development, 1975. Add: Divison of Geological and Planetary Sciences, California Inst. of Technology, Pasadena, Calif. 91125, U.S.A.

WYMARK, Olwen (Margaret). American. Plays/Screenplays. *Publs:* Three Plays, 1967; The Gymnasium and Other Plays, 1971; Find Me, 1977; Loved, 1980; Female Parts: One Woman Plays (adaptation of Plays by Dario Fo and Franca Rame), 1981; Best Friends and Other Plays, 1984; Lessons and Lovers: D.H. Lawrence in New Mexico, 1985; Nana, 1987. Add: c/o Harvey Unna and Stephen Durbridge Ltd., 24 Pottery Lane, London W11 4LZ, England.

WYND, Oswald. Also writes as Gavin Black. Scottish, b. 1913. Novels/Short stories, Mystery/Crime/Suspense. *Publs:* Black Fountains, 1947; When Ape Is King (in U.S. as Red Sun South), 1948; The Stubborn Flower (in U.S. as Friend of the Family), 1950; Moon of the Tiger, 1958; Summer Can't Last, 1959; The Devil Came on Sunday, 1961; A Walk in the Long Dark Night, 1962; Death the Red Flower, 1965; Walk Softly, Men Praying, 1967; Sumatra Seven Zero, 1968; The Hawser Pirates, 1970; The Forty Days, 1972; The Ginger Tree, 1977; The Blazing Air, 1981; as Gavin Black—Suddenly at Singapore, 1960; Dead Man Calling, 1962; A Dragon for Christmas, 1963; The Eyes Around Me, 1964; You Want to Die, Johnny?, 1966; A Wind of Death, 1967; The Cold Jungle, 1969; A Time for Pirates, 1971; The Bitter Tea, 1972; The Golden Cockatrice, 1974; A Big Wind for Summer, 1975; A Moon for Killers, 1976; Night Run from Java, 1979; The Fatal Shadow, 1983, The Sleeping Partner, 1989. Add: St. Adrian's Crail, Fife FY10 3SU, Scotland.

WYNDER, Mavis Areta. *See* **WINDER,** Mavis Areta.

WYNDHAM, Esther. *See* **LUTYENS,** Mary.

WYNES, Charles E. American, b. 1929. History, Race relations, Essays. Prof. of History, Univ. of Georgia, Athens, now retired.. *Publs:* Race Relations in Virginia 1870-1902, 1961, 1971; (ed.) Southern Sketches from Virginia 1881-1901, 1964; (ed.) The Negro in The South since 1865, 1965; (ed.) Forgotten Voices, 1967; (co-author) A History of Georgia, 1977, Charles Richard Drew: The Man and the Myth, 1988. Add: Dept. of History, Univ. of Georgia, Athens, Ga. 30602, U.S.A.

WYNN, Dale Richard. American, b. 1918. Administration/Management, Education, Institutions/Organizations. Emeritus Prof. of Education, Univ. of Pittsburgh, since 1984 (Assoc. Dean, Sch. of Education, 1960–65; Chmn., Dept. of Educational Admin., 1967–74; Prof., 1960–84). Editorial Bd. Member, Educational Admin. Quarterly, 1966–68; Member, Bd. of Trustees, Univ. Council for Educational Admin., 1966–69. *Publs:* Careers in Education, 1960; (with D. Griffiths, D. Clark and L.Lannaecone) Organizing Schools for Effective Education, 1962; Organizations of Public Schools, 1964; (with H. NcNally and W. Elsbree) Elementary School Administration and Supervision, 3rd ed. 1967; Administrative Responses to Conflict, 1972; Instructional Methods and Materials for Preparing Educational Administrations, 1972; Theory and Practice of the Administrative Team, 1973; (with J. Wynn) American Education, 9th ed. 1987; Collective Gaining, 1983; (with C. Guditus) The Administrative Team: Leadership Through Consensus Management, 1983. Add: 4514 Bucktail Dr., Allison Park, Pa. 15101, U.S.A.

WYNN, J(ohn) C(harles). American, b. 1920. Sex, Theology/Religion. Prof. of Pastoral Theology, Colgate Rochester Divinity Sch., Rochester,

N.Y., 1959–85, now Emeritus (Dir. of Studies, 1965–70); Member of faculty, Univ. Coll., Univ. of Rochester. Dir. of Family Education Research, United Presbyterian Church in the U.S., 1950–59. *Publs:* How Christian Parents Face Family Problems, 1955; (ed.) Sermons on Marriage and Family, 1956; Pastoral Ministry to Families, 1957; (co-author) Families in the Church: A Protestant Survey, 1961; (ed.) Sex, Family, and Society in Theological Focus, 1966; (ed.) Sexual Ethics and Christian Responsibility, 1971; Christian Education for Liberation and Other Upsetting Ideas, 1977; Family Therapy in Pastoral Ministry, 1982; The Family Therapist, 1987. Add: 5663-102 Columbia Pike, Columbia, Md. 21044, U.S.A.

WYNNE, Brian. *See* **GARFIELD,** Brian.

WYNNE, Frank. *See* **GARFIELD,** Brian.

WYSOR, Bettie. American, b. 1928. Novels/Short stories, Essays. Consultant for advertising and promotion. Art and Antiques Ed., Town Country Mag., 1970–72; Founder and Ed., Dramatists Guild Newsletter, 1976. *Publs:* The Lesbian Myth: Insights & Conversations, 1974; To Remember Tina (novel), 1975; A Stranger's Eyes (novel), 1980; Echos (novel), 1983. Add: P.O. Box 103, Wainscott, L.I., N.Y. 11975, U.S.A.

WYTRWAL, Joseph A. American, b. 1924. Cultural/Ethnic topics, History. Principal, Wilson Middle Sch., Detroit Public Schs., since 1973 (Counselor, Chadsey High Sch., 1963–70; Asst. Principal, Mumford High Sch., 1970–73). Coordinator, Wayne County Community Coll., Detroit, 1968–70. *Publs:* America's Polish Heritage, 1961; Poles in American History and Tradition, 1969; Poles in America, 1969; American Poles, 1974; Behold! the Polish-Americans, 1977; Polish-Black Encounters, 1982. Add: 5695 Lumley St., Detroit, Mich. 48210, U.S.A.

Y

YAFFE, James. American, b. 1927. Novels/Short stories, Plays/Screenplays. Prof. of English, Colorado Coll., Colorado Springs, since 1968. *Publs:* Poor Cousin Evelyn, 1950; The Good-for-Nothing, 1953; What's the Big Hurry?, 1954; Nothing but the Night, 1957; The Deadly Game (play), 1960; Mister Margolies, 1962; This Year's Genie (play), 1965; Nobody Does You Any Favors, 1966; The American Jews, 1968; (with J.Weidman) Ivory Tower (play), 1969; The Voyage of the Franz Joseph, 1970; So Sue Me! The Story of a Community Court, 1972; Saul and Morris, World's Apart, 1982; Cliffhanger (play), 1985; A Nice Murder for Mom, 1988. Add: 1215 North Cascade, Colorado Springs, Colo. 80903, U.S.A.

YANDELL, Keith Edward. American, b. 1938. Philosophy, Theology/Religion. Prof. of Philosophy and South Asian Studies, Univ. of Wisconsin, Madison, since 1974 (Asst. Prof. of Philosophy, 1966–71; Assoc. Prof. of Philosophy, 1971–74). Member, Center for South Asian Studies, since 1972. Instr. in Philosophy, Kings Coll., Briarcliff Manor, N.Y. 1961–63; Instr. in Philosophy, Ohio State Univ., Columbus, 1965–66. *Publs:* Basic Issues in the Philosophy of Religion, 1971; (ed. with J.R. Weinberg) Problems in Philosophical Inquiry, 1971; (ed.) God, Man, and Religion, 1973; Christianity and Philosophy, 1983; Hume's Inevitable Mystery, 1989; The Epistemology of Religious Experience, 1990. Add: 5185 Helen C. White Hall, Dept. of Philosophy, Univ. of Wisconsin, Madison, Wisc. 53706, U.S.A.

YANKOWITZ, Susan. American, b. 1941. Novels/Short stories, Plays. *Publs:* Silent Witness (novel), 1976. Add: 205 W. 89th St., 8F, New York, N.Y. 10024, U.S.A.

YARBRO, Chelsea Quinn. Also writes as Vanessa Pryor. American, b. 1942. Historical/Romance/Gothic, Science fiction/Fantasy, Western, Paranormal. Theatre Mgr., and playwright, Mirthmakers Children's Theatre, San Francisco, 1961-64; children's counsellor, 1963; Cartographer, C.E. Erick-son and Assocs., Oakland, Calif., 1963–70; composer, card and palm reader, 1974–78. Secty., Science Fiction Writers of America, 1970–72; Pres., Horror Writes of America, 1988–89. *Publs:* (ed. with Thomas N. Scortia) Two Views of Wonder, 1973; Time of the Fourth Horseman (science fiction), 1976; Ogilvie, Tallant, and Moon, 1976; Hotel Transylvania, 1978; False Down (science fiction), 1978; Cautionary Tales (SF short stories), 1978, 1980; Music When Sweet Voices Die, 1979; The Palace, 1979; Messages from Michael (occult), 1979; Blood Games, 1980; Sins of Omission, 1980; Ariosto, 1980; Dead and Buried, 1980; Path of the Eclipse, 1981; Tempting Fate, 1982; (as Vanessa Pryor) A Taste of Wine, 1982; The Saint-Germain Chronicles (short stories), 1983; The Godforsaken (novel), 1983; Hyacinths (science fiction), 1983; The Making of Australia #5: The Outback, 1983; Locadio's Apprentice (juvenile fiction), 1984; Nomads (novelization), 1984; Signs and Portents (short stories), 1984; Four Horses for Tishtry (juvenile fiction), 1985; A Mortal Glamour (novel), 1985; To the High Redoubt (novel), 1985; More Messages from Michael, 1986; A Baroque Fable (novel with music), 1986; Floating Illusions (juvenile fiction), 1986; Firecode (novel), 1987; A Flame in Byzantium (novel), 1987; Crusader's Torch (novel), 1988; Michael's People (novelization), 1988; Taji's Syndrome (novel), 1988; The Law in Charity (western), 1989; Candles for D'Artagnan (novel), 1989; Beastnights (novel), 1989; Chiaroscuro (short stories), 1990; Out of the House of Life (novel), 1990. Add: P.O. Box 7568, Berkeley, Calif. 94707, U.S.A.

YARMOLINSKY, Adam. American, b. 1922. Military/Defence, So-cial commentary/phenomena. Provost, Univ. of Maryland, Baltimore County. Member, Cttee. for National Security, since 1985; Bd. Chmn., Bennington Coll., Vermont, since 1986; Bd. Member, Vera Inst. of Justice since 1967 (Chmn., 1986–88); Member, Council on Foreign Relations. Law Clerk to Justice Charles E. Clark, U.S. Court of Appeals, 1948–49, and Justice Reed, U.S. Supreme Court, 1950–51; Law Practice, Cleary, Gottlieb, Friendly & Ball, Washington, D.C., 1951–55; Secty., Fund for the Republic, 1955–57; Special Correspondent, The Economist, London, 1956–60; Public Affairs Ed., Doubleday and Co., NYC, 1957–59; Kennedy Presidential Campaign and Talent Hunt, 1960; Special Asst. to the U.S. Secty. of Defense, 1961–64; Deputy Dir., President's Task Force on the War Against Poverty, 1964; Chief, U.S. Emergency Relief Mission to the Dominican Republic, 1965; Principal Deputy Asst. Secty. of Defence, 1965–66; Prof. of Law, and Member of the Inst. of Politics, J.F. Kennedy Sch. of Govt., Harvard Univ., Cambridge, Mass., 1966–72; Emerson Univ. Prof., Univ. of Massachusetts, Boston, 1972–79. Adjunct Prof., Georgetown Univ. Law Center, 1984–85. *Publs:* (ed.) Case Studies in Personnel Security, 1955; Recognition of Excellence, 1960; The Military Establishment, 1971; (co-ed.) The Military and American Society, 1973; (ed.) Race and Schooling in the City, 1981; Paradoxes of Power, 1983. Add: Admin. Bldg., Univ. of Maryland, Baltimore, Md. 21228, U.S.A.

YARROW, Philip John. British, b. 1917. Literature, Translations. Sr. French Master, Royal Masonic Sch., Bushey, 1938–39; Modern Language Master, Sedbergh Sch., 1939–47; Lectr. in French, 1948–60, and Sr. Lectr., 1960–63, Univ. of Exeter; Prof. of French, Univ. of Newcastle upon Tyne, 1963–83. *Publs:* (trans.) Agostino Bassi, Del Mal del Segno, 1958; (ed.) Moliere, L'Avare, 1959; (with Jacques Petit) Barbey d'-Aurevilly journaliste et critique, 1959; La Pensée politique et religieuse de Barbey d'Aurevilly, 1961; Corneille, 1963; A Literary History of France, Vol. II: The Seventeenth Century, 1967; (ed.) Pierre Corneille, Horace, 1967; (ed. with Elizabeth Suddaby) Lady Morgan in France, 1971; (ed.) Thomas Corneille and Donneau de Visé, La Devineresse, 1971; (ed.) Chatiments, by Hugo, 1975; Racine, 1978. Add: 50 Moorside South, Newcastle upon Tyne NE4 9BB, England.

YARSHATER, Ehsan (Ollah). Persian (American resident), b. 1920. Area studies, International Relations/Current affairs. Hagop Kevorkian Prof. of Iranian Studies, and Dir. of the Center for Iranian Studies, Columbia Univ., NYC, since 1961 (Chmn., Dept. of Middle East Languages and Cultures, 1968–73). Member, Bd. of Eds., Iranica Antiqua, Leiden, since 1961; Ed., Persian Heritage series, since 1962; Trustee, American Inst. of Iranian Studies, since 1968; Ed., Encyclopaedia Iranica, since 1974. Secty., Unesco Council of Philosophy and Humanistic Sciences, in Iran, 1954–58. Founding Ed., Rahnema-ye Ketab, literary and book review journal, 1975–79. *Publs:* (ed.) Theorems and Remarks, by Ibn Sina, 1953; (ed.) Five Treaties in Arabic and Persian, by Ibn Sina, 1953; Persian Poetry Under Shah-Rukh: Fifteenth Century, 1955; Old Iranian Myths and Legends, 1957, 1964; Legends of the Epic of Kings, 1957, 4th ed. 1982; A Grammar of Southern Tati Dialects, 1969; (ed.) Iran Faces the Seventies, 1971; (ed.) Sadeq Hedayat: An Anthology, 1971; (ed. with D. Bivar) The Inscriptions of Eastern Mazandaran, 1979; (ed. with R. Ettinghausen) Highlights of Persian Art, 1980; (ed.) Cambridge History of Iran, vol. III, 1982; (ed.) Persian Literature, 1988. Add: 450 Riverside Dr., New York, N.Y. 10027, U.S.A.

YARWOOD, Doreen. British, b. 1918. Architecture, Fashion/Costume, Homes/Gardens, Biography. Freelance writer and artist, since

1949. *Publs:* English Costume, 1952, 5th ed. 1979; The English Home, 1956, 1979; The Architecture of England, 1963, 1967; Outline of English Architecture, 1965, 1977; English Houses, 1966; Outline of English Costume, 1967, 4th ed. 1977; The Architecture of Italy, 1970; Robert Adam, 1970; The Architecture of Europe, 1974, 3rd ed. 1987; European Costume, 1975; The Architecture of Britain, 1976, 3rd ed. 1980; The Encyclopedia of World Costume, 1978, 3rd ed. 1988; Costume of the Western World, 1981; The British Kitchen, 1981; 500 Years of Technology in the Home, 1982; English Interiors, 1984; Encyclopaedia of Architecture, 1985; Chronology of Western Architecture, 1987; Science and the Home, 1987. Add: 18 Herontye Dr., E. Grinstead RH19 4LR, England.

YASHIMA, Taro. Pseud. for Jun Atsushi Iwamatsu. American, b. 1908. Children's Fiction, Translations. Free-lance artist, illustrator, and writer; several one-man shows; collections include Phillips Memorial Museum, Washington, D.C. Dir., Yashima Art Institute, Los Angeles, in the 1950's. *Publs:* The New Sun, 1943; Horizon Is Calling, 1947; The Village Tree, 1953; (with Mitsu Yashima) Plenty to Watch, 1954; Crow Boy, 1955; Umbrella, 1958; (trans.) The Golden Footprints, by Hatoju Muku, 1960; (with Mitsu Yashima) Momo's Kitten, 1961; The Youngest One, 1962; Seashore Story, 1967. Add: c/o Viking Press, 40 W. 23rd St., New York, N.Y. 10010, U.S.A.

YATES, Alfred. British, b. 1917. Education. Consultant, National Foundn. for Eductional Research in England and Wales, since 1983 (Dir., 1972–83). Sr. Tutor, Dept. of Educational Studies, Oxford Univ., 1959–72. *Publs:* (with Watts and Pidgeon) Secondary School Entrance Examinations, 1952; (with Pidgeon) Admission to Grammar Schools, 1957; (ed.) Grouping in Education, 1966; (with Pidgeon) An Introduction to Educational Measurement, 1968; (ed.) Current Problems of Teacher Education, 1970; (ed.) The Role of Research in Educational Change, 1971; The Organisation of Schooling, 1971. Add: 14 Craighall Rd., Bolton, England.

YATES, Aubrey James. Australian, b. 1925. Psychiatry, Psychology. Prof. of Psychology, Univ. of New England, 1965–67; Sr. Lectr., 1960–63, Reader, 1964–65, and Prof. of Psychology, 1967–87, Univ. of Western Australia, Nedlands. *Publs:* Frustration and Conflict, 1962; Frustration and Conflict: Readings, 1965; Behavior Therapy, 1970; Theory and Practice in Behavior Therapy, 1975; Biofeedback and the Modification of Behavior, 1980. Add: c/o Dept. of Psychology, Univ. of Western Australia, Nedlands, W.A. 6004, Australia.

YATES, Elizabeth. American, b. 1905. Novels/Short stories, Children's fiction, Autobiography/Memoirs/Personal, Biography. *Publs:* High Holiday, 1938; (ed.) Gathered Grace: A Short Selection of George MacDonald's Poems, 1938; Hans and Frieda in the Swiss Mountains, 1939; Climbing Higher (in U.S. as Quest in the North-land), 1939; (ed.) Piskey Folk: A Book of Cornish Legends, by Enys Tregarthen, 1940; Haven for the Brave, 1941; Under the Little Fir and Other Stories, 1942; Around the Year in Iceland, 1942; (ed.) The Doll Who Came Alive, by Enys Tregarthen, 1942; Patterns on the Wall, 1943; Mountain Born, 1943; Wind of Spring, 1945; Nearby, 1947; Once in the Year, 1947; Joseph, 1947; The Young Traveller in the U.S.A., 1948; Beloved Bondage, 1948; (ed.) The White Ring, by Enys Tregarthen, 1949; The Christmas Story, 1950; Children of the Bible, 1950; Amos Fortune, Free Man, 1950; Guardian Heart, 1950; Brave Interval, 1952; A Place for Peter, 1952; David Livingstone, 1952; Hue and Cry, 1953; Rainbow 'round the World: A Story of UNICEF, 1954; (ed.) Your Prayers and Mine, 1954; Prudence Crandall, Woman of Courage, 1955; The Carey Girl, 1956; Gifts of True Love, 1958; Pebble in a Pool: The Widening Circles of Dorothy Canfield Fisher's Life, 1958, rev. ed. as The Lady from Vermont, 1971; The Lighted Heart (autobiographical), 1960; The Next Fine Day, 1962; Someday You'll Write, 1962; (ed.) Sir Gibbie, by George MacDonald, 1963; Sam's Secret Journal, 1964; Carolina's Courage (in U.K. as Carolina and the Indian Doll), 1964; Howard Thurman: Portrait of a Practical Dreamer, 1964; Up the Golden Stair, 1966; Is There a Doctor in the Barn? A Day in the Life of Forest F. Tenney, D.V.M, 1966; An Easter Story, 1967; With Pipe, Paddle, and Song, 1968; New Hampshire, 1969; On That Night, 1969; Sarah Whitcher's Story, 1971; Skeezer, Dog with a Mission, 1973; The Road Through Sandwich Notch, 1973; A Book of Hours, 1976; Call it Zest, 1977; The Seventh One, 1978; My Diary—My World, 1981; Silver Lining, 1981; My Widening World, 1983; One Writer's Way, 1984; Sound Friendships, 1987. Add: 381 Old Street Rd., Peterborough, N.H. 03458, U.S.A.

YATES, Frank. British, b. 1902. Design (general), Mathematics/Statistics. Head, Dept. of Statistics, 1933–68, and Deputy Dir., 1958–68, Rothamsted Experimental Station, Herts. *Publs:* (with R.A. Fisher)

Statistical Tables for Biological, Argricultural and Medical Research, 1938, 6th ed. 1963; Sampling Methods for Censuses and Surveys, 1949, 4th ed. 1981; Experimental Design: Selected Papers, 1970. Add: Rothamsted Experimental Station, Harpenden, Herts. AL5 2JQ, England.

YATES, J. Michael. Canadian, b. 1938. Novels/Short stories, Plays/Screenplays, Poetry. Pres., Sono Nis Press, Vancouver, since 1971. Promotional Dir., Public Radio Corp., Houston, Tex., 1961–62; Teaching Fellow, Univ. of Michigan, Ann Arbor, 1962–63; Instr. in English and Creative Writing, Ohio Univ., Athens, 1964–65; Special Lectr. in Literature and Creative Writing, Univ. of Alaska, Fairbanks, 1965–66; Assoc. Prof. of Creative Writing, Univ. of British Columbia, Vancouver, 1966–71; Ed.-in-Chief, 1966–67, and Poetry Ed., 1966–71, Prism Intnl., and a member of the Editorial Bd., Prism Intnl. Press, Mission, B.C. 1966–71. *Publs:* Subjunction (play), 1965; The Grand Edit (screenplay), 1966; Spiral of Mirrors, 1967; Hunt in an Unmapped Interior and Other Poems, 1967; Canticle for Electronic Music, 1967; (with B. Frick) Parallax, 1968; Night Freight (play), 1968; Man in the Glass Octopus (short stories), 1968; The Great Bear Lake Meditations, 1970; (ed. with A. Schroder) Contemporary Poetry of British Columbia, 2 vols., 1970, 1972; The Abstract Beast, 1971; (ed. with C. Lillard) Volvox: Poetry from the Unofficial Languages of Canada in English Translations, 1971; (ed.) Contemporary Fiction of British Columbia, 1971; Exploding (novel), 1972; Nothing Speaks for the Blue Moraines: New and Selected Poems, 1973; Breath of the Snow Leopard, 1974; The Qualicum Physics, 1975; Quarks (radio plays), 1975; Fazes in Elsewhen: New and Selected Fiction, 1977; Esex Nobilion non Esox Lucius, 1978; Fugue Brancusi, 1983; Insel: The Queen Charlotte Islands Meditations, 1983; Completely Collapsible Portable Man, 1984; Oita Poems, 1984; Schedules of Silence, 1986; Torque, 1987; Torpor, 1989. Add: 6890 Mac Pherson, Barnaby, B.C., V5J 4NI, Canada.

YEE, Min S. American, b. 1938. Criminology/Law enforcement/Prisons, Sports/Physical education/Keeping fit, Travel/Exploring/Adventure. Ed. and Publr., The Great Escape, since 1973. With Time Mag., and New York Times, 1964–66, Boston Globe, 1966–68, Newsweek, 1968–71, and Washington Post, 1971–72; Ed., Ramparts mag., 1972–73. *Publs:* The Melancholy History of Soledad Prison, 1973; (with Don K. Wright) The Great Escape, 1974; The Driver's Companion, 1975; (with Don K. Wright) The Sports Book, 1975; (with T.N. Layton) In My Father's House, 1981. Add: c/o Holt Rinehart and Winston, 1250 Sixth Ave., San Diego, Calif. 92101, U.S.A.

YEP, Laurence (Michael). American, b. 1948. Science fiction/Fantasy, Children's fiction. Part-time Instr. of English, Foothill Coll., Mountain View, Calif., 1975, and San Jose City Coll., Calif., 1975–76; Lectr., Creative writing, Univ. of Calif., Berkeley, 1987–89. *Publs:* Sweetwater (juvenile science fiction), 1973; Dragonwings (juvenile), 1975; Child of the Owl (juvenile), 1977; Seademons (adult SF novel), 1977; Liar, Liar, 1983; Tom Sawyer Fires, 1984; Dragon Steel, 1985; Mountain Light, 1985; Shadow Lord, 1985; Rainbow People, 1989. Add: 921 Populus Pl., Sunnyvale, Calif. 94086, U.S.A.

YERBY, Frank (Garvin). American, b. 1916. Historical/Romance/Gothic. Full-time writer since 1945. Instr. in English, Florida A & M. Coll., Baton Rouge, La., 1939–41; Lab. Technician, Ford Motor Co., Dearborn, Mich., 1941–44; Magnaflux Insp., Ranger (Fairchild) Aircraft, Jamaica, N.Y., 1944–45. *Publs:* The Foxes of Harrow, 1946; The Vixens, 1947; The Golden Hawk, 1948; Pride's Castle, 1949; Floodtide, 1950; A Woman Called Fancy, 1951; The Sacracen Blade, 1952; The Devil's Laughter, 1953; Benton's Row, 1954; Bride of Liberty, 1954; The Treasure of Pleasant Valley, 1955; Captain Rebel, 1956; Fairoaks, 1957; The Serpent and the Staff, 1958; Jarrett's Jade, 1959; Gillian, 1960; The Garfield Honor, 1961; Griffin's Way, 1962; The Old Gods Laugh: A Modern Romance, 1964; An Odor of Sanctity, 1965; Goat Song: A Novel of Ancient Greece, 1968; Judas, My Brother: The Story of the Thirteenth Disciple, 1968; Speak Now, 1969; The Dahomean (in U.K. as the Man from Dahomey), 1971; The Girl from Storyville: A Victorian Novel, 1972; The Voyage Unplanned, 1974; Tobias and the Angel, 1975; A Rose for Ann Marie, 1976; Hail the Conquering Hero, 1977; A Darkness at Ingraham's Crest, 1979; Western: A Saga of the Great Plains, 1982; Devilseed, 1984; Mackenzie's Hundred, 1985. Add: Avenida de America 37, Apt. 710, Madrid 2, Spain.

YERMAKOV, Nicholas. Also writes as Simon Hawke. American, b. 1951. Novels, Science fiction. Has worked as a musician, broadcaster, journalist, salesman, bartender, and factory worker. *Publs:* Journey from Flesh, 1981; Last Communion, 1981; Fall into Darkness, 1982; Clique, 1982; Epiphany, 1982; (with Glen A. Larson) Battlestar Galactica 6: The

Living Legend, 1982; (with Glen A. Larson) Battlestar Galactica 7: War of the Gods, 1982; Jehad, 1984; novels as Simon Hawkes—The Ivanhoe Gambit, 1984; The Timekeeper Conspiracy, 1984; The Pimpernel Plot, 1984; The Zenda Vendetta, 1985; The Nautilus Sanction, 1985. Add: c/o Ace Books, 200 Madison Ave., New York, N.Y. 10016, U.S.A.

YGLESIAS, Helen. American, b. 1915. Novels/Short stories, Autobiography/Memoirs/Personal. Adjunct Prof., Columbia Sch. of Arts, NYC, Spring 1973; Adjunct Prof., Univ. of Iowa Writing Division, Fall 1980. Literary Ed., Nation, 1965–69. *Publs:* How She Died, 1972; Family Feeling, 1976; Starting (memoirs), 1978; Sweetsir, 1981; The Saviors, 1987; Isabel Bishop, 1989. Add: N. Brooklin, Me. 04661, U.S.A.

YGLESIAS, José. American, b. 1919. Novels/Short stories, Politics/Government, Translations. Film Critic, Daily Worker, NYC, 1948–50; Asst. to Vice-Pres., Merck, Sharp & Dohme Intnl., 1953–63. *Publs:* (trans.) Villa Milo, by Zaveir Domingo, 1962; (trans.) Island of Women, by Juan Goytisolo, 1962; (trans.) Sands of Torremolinos, by J. Goytisolo, 1962; A Wake in Ybor City, 1963; (trans.) The Party's Over, by J. Goytisolo, 1966; The Goodbye Land, 1967; In the Fist of the Revolution: Life in a Cuban Country Town (in U.K. as In the Fist of the Revolution: Life in Castro's Cuba), 1968; An Orderly Life, 1968; Down There, 1970; The Truth About Them, 1971; Double, Double, 1974; The Kill Price, 1976; The Franco Years, 1977; (with Leonard Barkin) The Raptors, 1986; Home Again, 1987; Tristan and the Hispanics, 1989. Add: 13 W. 13th St., New York, N.Y. 10011, U.S.A.

YIANNOPOULOS, A(thanassios) N. American, b. 1928. Law. Prof. of Law, Tulane Univ. Law Sch., New Orleans, since 1979. Reporter, Louisiana State Law Inst., Civil Code Revision. Prof. of Law, Louisiana State Univ. Law Sch., Baton Rouge, 1958–79. *Publs:* Negligence Clauses in Ocean Bills of Lading, 1964; Civil Law Property, 1966, 1980; Personal Servitudes, 1968, 1979; Predial Servitudes, 1982. Add: 662 Sunset Blvd., Baton Rouge, La. 70808, U.S.A.

YODER, Glee. American, b. 1916. Recreation/Leisure/Hobbies, Theology/Religion. Freelance lectr. and workshop leader. *Publs:* The Church and Infants and Toddlers, 1966; Who Is God?, 1969; The Christian Faces His World, 1970; All That Is Within Me, 1970; The Gospel of Luke, 1971; A World Wide Fellowship, 1972; Why Not Peace?, 1972; Foundations for Life, 1972; Take It From Here, 1973; Christian Sign Language, 1974; Handle with Care, 1975; Take It From Here, Series Two, 1975; To Be Like Jesus, 1976; The Unfolding World, 1976; Good News, Everybody, 1977; The Lord Is King, 1977; Older Children: Manual for Christian Education, 1977; Passing on the Gift, 1978; Design for Centers for Developing Christian Leadership, 1978; March Wind, 1983. Add: 300 Willow Valley Lakes Dr., Apt. A-417, Willow Street, Pa. 17584, U.S.A.

YOLEN, Jane. American, b. 1939. Science fiction/Fantasy, Children's fiction, Poetry. Asst. Ed., Gold Medal Books, NYC, 1960–61; Assoc. Ed., Rutledge Books, NYC, 1961–62; Asst. Ed., Alfred A. Knopf Juvenile Books, NYC, 1962–65. Member, Bd. of Dirs., Soc. of Children's Book Writers, and Children's Literature Assn.Pres., Science Fiction Writers of America, 1986–88. *Publs:* See This Little Line? (verse), 1963; Pirates in Petticoats, 1963; The Witch Who Wasn't, 1964; Gwinellen, The Princess Who Could Not Sleep, 1965; Trust a City Kid, 1966; Isabel's Noel, 1967; The Emperor and the Kite, 1967; Robin Hood (musical play), 1967; World on a String: The Story of Kites, 1968; The Minstrel and the Mountain, 1968; Greyling, 1968; The Longest Name on the Block, 1968; The Wizard of Washington Square, 1969; The Inway Investigators; or, The Mystery at McCracken's Place, 1969; It All Depends (verse), 1969; The Seventh Mandarin, 1970; Hobo Toad and the Motorcycle Gang, 1970; The Bird of Time, 1971; The Girl Who Loved the Wind, 1972; Friend: The Story of George Fox and the Quakers, 1972; (ed.) The Fireside Song Book of Birds and Beasts, 1972; (ed.) Zoo 2000: Twelve Stories of Science Fiction and Fantasy Beasts, 1973; The Wizard Islands, 1973; Writing Books for Children, 1973; The Girl Who Cried Flowers and Other Tales, 1974; The Rainbow Rider, 1974; The Adventures of Eeka Mouse, 1974; The Boy Who Had Wings, 1974; The Magic Three of Solatia, 1974; The Little Spotted Fish, 1975; The Transfigured Hart, 1975; Ring Out!, 1975; A Book of Bells, 1975; Moon Ribbon and Other Tales, 1976; Milweed Days, 1976; Simple Gifts, 1976; The Sultan's Perfect Tree, 1977; The Seeing Stick, 1977; The Hundredth Dove and Other Tales, 1977; The Giant's Farm, 1977; Hannah Dreaming, 1977; An Invitation to the Butterfly Ball (verse), 1977; (ed.) Rounds about Rounds, 1977; The Seeing Stick, 1977; (ed.) Shape Shifters, 1978; The Simple Prince, 1978; The Mermaid's Three Wisdoms, 1978; Spider Jane, 1978; No Bath Tonight,

1978; The Grants Go Gamping, 1979; Dream Weaver, 1979; All in the Woodland Early (verse), 1979; Spider Jane on the Move, 1980; Mice on Ice, 1980; How Beastly! (verse), 1980; Dragon Night and Other Lullabies (verse), 1980; Commander Toad in Space, 1980; The Robot and Rebecca: The Mystery of the Code-Carrying Kids, 1980; Sleeping Ugly, 1981; Uncle Lemon's Spring, 1981; Brothers of the Wind, 1981; The Boy Who Spoke Chimp, 1981; The Gift of Sarah Barker, 1971; Shirlick Holmes and the Case of the Wandering Wardrobe, 1981; The Robot and Rebecca and the Missing Owser, 1981; Touch Magic, 1971; Dragons Blood, 1982; Commander Toad and the Planet of the Grapes, 1982; Neptune Rising, 1982; Commander Toad and the Big Black Hole, 1983; Cards of Grief, 1984; Children of the Wolf, 1974; Heart's Blood, 1984; The Stone's Silenus, 1984; Dragonfield and Other Stories, 1985; Commander Toad and the Dis-Asteroid, 1985; Dragons and Dreams, 1986; The Lullaby Songbook, 1986; Commander Toad and the Inter-Galactic Spy, 1986; Merlin's Booke, 1986; Ring of Earth, 1986; Favorite Folktales from Around the World, 1986; Piggins, 1987; Three Bear Rhyme Book, 1987; A Sending of Dragons, 1987; Owl Moon, 1987; Sister Light, Sister Dark, 1988; The Devil's Arithmetic, 1988; Picnic with Piggins, 1988; Werewolves, 1988; Piggins and the Royal Wedding, 1989; Dove Isabeau, 1989; Things that Go Bump in the Night, 1989; Best Witches, 1989; Laptime Song and Play Book, 1989; White Jenna, 1989; The Faery Flag, 1989. Add: Phoenix Farm, 31 School St., Box 27, Hatfield, Mass. 01038, U.S.A.

YORBURG, Betty. American, b. 1926. Social commentary, Sociology. Assoc. Prof. of Sociology, City Coll., City Univ. of New York, since 1974 (Lectr., 1967–68; Asst. Prof., 1969–73). *Publs:* Utopia and Reality: A Collective Portrait of American Socialists, 1969; The Changing Family, 1973; Sexual Identity, Sex Roles and Social Change, 1974; (co-author) The New Women, 1976; Introduction to Sociology, 1982; Families and Societies, 1983. Add: c/o Columbia Univ. Press, 562 W. 113 St., New York, N.Y. 10025, U.S.A.

YORK, Andrew. *See* **NICOLE,** Christopher.

YORK, Helen. American. Mystery/Crime/Suspense. *Publs:* Malverne Manor, 1974; Tremorra Towers, 1976; Venetian Charade, 1978; Pennhaven, 1978. Add: 11 Scenery Rd., Pittsburgh, Pa. 15221, U.S.A.

YORK, Herbert (Frank). American, b. 1921. International relations/Current affairs, Military/Defence. Prof. of Physics, and Dir. of the Inst. on Global Conflict and Cooperation, Univ. of California at San Diego, since 1961 (Physicist, 1943–58, and Assoc. Dir., 1954–58, Univ. of California Radiation Lab., Berkeley; Dir., Lawrence Livermore Lab., 1952–58, Asst. Prof., 1951–54, Assoc. Prof., 1954–59, and Prof. of Physics, 1959–61, Univ. of California, Berkeley; Chancellor, Univ. of California at San Diego, 1961–64, 1970–72; Prof. of Physics and Dean of Grad. Studies and Research, Univ. of California at San Diego, 1964–70). Trustee, Aerospace Corp., El Segundo, Calif.; Trustee, Inst. for Defense Analyses; Assoc., Center for the Study of Democratic Instns.; Member, Exec. Cttee., Fedn. of American Scientists. Dir. of Research, Advanced Research Projects Div., Inst. for Defense Analyses, 1958, Chief Scientist, Advanced Research Projects Agency, 1958, and Dir. of Defence Research and Engineering, 1958–61, U.S. Dept. of Defense. Member, U.S. Air Force Science Advisory Bd., 1953–58, U.S. Army Science Advisory Panel, 1955–58, President's Science Advisory Commn., 1957–58, 1964–68, and Gen. Advisory Cttee. on Arms Control and Disarmament, 1962–69; U.S. Ambassador, Comprehensive Test Ban Negotiations, 1978–81. *Publs:* Race to Oblivion, 1970; Readings on Arms Control, 1973; The Advisers, 1976, 1989; Making Weapons, Talking Peace, 1987; Does Strategic Defense Breed Offense, 1987; (with S. Lakoff) A Shield in Space?, 1989. Add: 6110 Camino de la Costa, La Jolla, Calif. 92037, U.S.A.

YORKE, Katherine. *See* **ELLERBECK,** Rosemary.

YORKE, Margaret. Pseud. for Margaret Beda Nicholson. British, b. 1924. Novels/Short stories, Mystery/Crime/Suspense. Chmn., Crime Writer's Assn., 1979–80. Asst. Librarian, St. Hilda's Coll., Oxford, 1959–60; Library Asst., Christ Church, Oxford, 1963–65. *Publs:* Summer Flight, 1957; Pray Love Remember, 1958; Christopher, 1959; Deceiving Mirror, 1960; The China Doll, 1961; Once a Stranger, 1962; The Birthday, 1963; Full Circle, 1965; No Fury, 1967; The Apricot Bed, 1968; The Limbo Ladies, 1969; Dead in the Morning, 1970; Silent Witness, 1972; Grave Matters, 1973; No Medals for the Major, 1974; Mortal Remains, 1974; The Small Hours of the Morning, 1975; Cast for Death, 1976; The Cost of Silence, 1977; The Point of Murder, 1978; Death on Account, 1979; The Scent of Fear, 1980; The Hand of Death, 1981; Devil's Work, 1982; Find Me a Villain, 1983; The Smooth Face of Evil,

1984; Intimate Kill, 1985; Safely to the Grave, 1986; Evidence to Destroy, 1987; Speak for the Dead, 1988; Crime in Question, 1989. Add: c/o Curtis Brown, 162–168 Regent St., London W1R 5TA, England.

YORKE, Ritchie Ian. Australian, b. 1944. Music. Music Columnist, Toronto Telegram, 1967, 1970, and Toronto Globe and Mail, 1968–69. *Publs:* Lowdown on the English Pop Scene, 1967; Axes, Chops, and Hot Licks, 1971; Into the Music: The Van Morrison Biography, 1975; The Led Zeppelin Biography, 1976; The History of Rock 'n Roll, 1976. Add: c/o Routledge, Chapman and Hall Ltd., 11 New Fetter Ln., London EC 4P 4EE, England.

YORKE, Roger. *See* **BINGLEY,** David Ernest.

YOST, Nellie Snyder. American, b. 1905. History, Biography. Member, Bd. of Dirs., Nebraska State Historical Soc. Writer and Researcher for Centennial Ed., on the staff of North Platte Telegraph, 1960–67. Past Pres., Nebraska Writers Guild, and Nebraska State Historical Soc.; Secty.-Treas., Western Writers of America, 1971–79; Member, Bd. of Dirs., Westerners Intnl., Tucson, Ariz., 1981–87. *Publs:* (with Albert Benton Snyder) Pinnacle Jake, 1951; (with John Leakey) The West That Was: From Texas to Montana, 1958; (with Grace McCance Snyder) No Time On My Hands (biography), 1963, 1974; Call of the Range: Story of the Nebraska Stock Growers Assocation, 1966; (ed.) Boss Cowman: The Recollections of Ed Lemmon 1857-1946, 1969; Medicine Lodge: The Story of a Kansas Frontier Town, 1970; Before Today, 1977; Buffalo Bill: His Family, Friends, Fame, Failures and Fortunes, 1978; A Man as Big as the West, 1979; (ed.) Women Who Made the West, 1980; (ed.) Backtrailing an Old Cowboys, 1983; Keep On Keeping On, 1983. Add: 1505 West D St., North Platte, Nebr. 69101, U.S.A.

YOUD, C.S. *See* **CHRISTOPHER,** John.

YOUNG, Al. American, b. 1939. Novels/Short stories, Plays/Screenplays, Poetry. Co-Ed., Yardbird Reader, Berkeley, Calif., since 1972; Contrib. Ed., Changes, NYC, since 1972, and Umoja, N.M., since 1973. Freelance Musician, 1958–64; Disk Jockey, KJAZ-FM, San Francisco, Calif., 1961–65; Instr. and Linguistic Consultant, San Francisco, Neighborhood Youth Corps Writing Workshops, 1968–69; Writing Instr., Teenage Workshop, San Francisco Museum of Art, 1968–69; Jones Lectr. in Creative Writing, Stanford Univ., Calif., 1969–76. *Publs:* Dancing: Poems, 1969; Snakes (novel), 1970; The Song Turning Back into Itself, 1971; Nigger (screenplay), 1972; Sparkle (screenplay), 1972; Who Is Angelina? (novel), 1975; Geography of the Near East (poetry), 1976; Untitled Sidney Poitier Comedy (screenplay), 1976; Sitting Pretty (novel and screenplay), 1977; (ed. with Ishmael Reed) Yardbird Lives!, 1978; (co-ed) Calafia: The California Poetry, 1979; Ask Me Now, 1980; Bodies and Soul: Musical Memoirs, 1981; Kinds of Blue: Musical Memoirs, 1984; Seduction by Night (novel), 1988. Add., c/o Dell Publishing Co., 666 Fifth Ave., New York, N.Y. 10103, U.S.A.

YOUNG, Bernice Elizabeth. American, b. 1931. Children's non-fiction, Biography. Asst. to Dir. of Advertising, Charles of the Ritz, 1961–64; Dir., Beatles (U.S.A.) Ltd., 1964–67; Protestant Adviser/Media Adviser, Girl Scouts of the U.S.A., 1968; Account Exec., Addison, Goldstein & Walsh, 1969–70. *Publs:* Harlem: The Story of a Changing Community, 1972; The Picture Story of Hank Aaron, 1974; Tribes of Africa, 1975; The Story of Frank Robinson, 1977. Add: 333 East 34th St., Apt. 17H, New York, N.Y. 10016, U.S.A.

YOUNG, Carter Travis. *See* **CHARBONNEAU,** Louis.

YOUNG, Chesley Virginia (Barnes). Also edits as C.V. Barnes. American, b. 1919. Psychology. Teacher, New York City Bd. of Education, 1955–68. *Publs:* (ed. as C.V. Barnes) W. Jonson's Magic Tricks, 1952; (ed. as C.V. Barnes) W. Jonson's Card Tricks, 1952; (with M.N. Young) How to Read Faster and Remember More, 1965, 1972; Magic of a Mighty Memory, 1971; The Magic of a Powerful Memory, 1986. Add: 2 Fifth Ave., New York, N.Y. 10011, U.S.A.

YOUNG, David (Pollock). American, b. 1936. Poetry, Literature. Prof. of English, Oberlin Coll., Ohio, since 1973 (Instr., 1961–65; Asst. Prof., 1965–68; Assoc. Prof., 1969–73); Ed., Field: Contemporary Poetry and Poetics, Oberlin, since 1969. *Publs:* Something of Great Constancy: The Art of "A Midsummer Night's Dream", 1966; (ed.) Twentieth Century Interpretations of "Henry IV, Part Two": A Collection of Critical Essays, 1968; Sweating Out the Winter: Poems, 1969; Six Poems from Wang Wei, 1969; Thoughts of Chairman Mao, 1970; The Heart's Forest: A Study of Shakespeare's Pastoral Plays, 1972; Boxcars, 1973; Work Lights; 32

Prose Poems, 1977; (trans.) Rilke's Duino Elegies, 1978; The Names of a Hare in English: Poems, 1979; (trans.) Four T'ng Poets, 1980; (co-ed.) A Field Guide to Contemporary Poetry and Poetics, 1980; (co-trans.) Valuable Nail: Selected Poems of Gunter Eich, 1981; (co-ed.) Longman Anthology of Contemporary American Poetry, 1982, 1988; (co-trans.) Interferon, or On Theatre: Poems by Miroslav Holub, 1982; (co-ed.) Magical Realist Fiction, 1984; Foraging: Poems, 1986; Troubled Mirror: A Study of Yeats' "The Tower," 1987; (trans.) The Heights of Macchu Picchu, 1987; Earthshine, 1988; The Action to the Word: Style and Structure in Shakespeare's Tragedies, 1990. Add: 220 Shepherd Circle, Oberlin, Ohio 44074, U.S.A.

YOUNG, Donald. American, 1933. Natural history, Politics/Government. Sr. Ed., American History and Political Science, Encyclopedia Americana, Grolier Inc., NYC, 1967–77; Managing Ed., Aperture Foundn., 1986–87. *Publs:* American Roulette: The History and Dilemma of the Vice Presidency, 1965, 1972; (ed. and contrib.) Adventure in Politics: The Memoirs of Philip La Follette, 1970; (author and photographer) The Great American Desert, 1980; (ed.) The Sierra Club Guides to the National Parks, Vols. 3-5, 1984–86; (contr.) The World Almanac, 1984–90; The Sierra Club Book of Our National Parks, 1989. Add: 166 E. 61st St., New York, N.Y. 10021, U.S.A.

YOUNG, Elizabeth. British. Poetry, International relations/Current affairs. Member, Advisory Bd. for Redundant Churches, since 1980. *Publs:* (with W. Young) Old London Churches, 1956; Time Is as Time Does (poetry), 1958; (co-ed. and contrib.) Quiet Enjoyment: Arms Control and Police Forces for the Ocean, 1971; A Farewell to Arms Control?, 1972; (with Brian Johnson) Law of the Sea, 1973; (with Peter Fricke) Sea-Use Planning, 1975; (with W. Kennet) Neither Red nor Dead: The Case for Disarmament, 1981; Men and Women: Equal But Not Interchangeable, 1982; (with W. Young) London's Churches, 1986; The Gorbachev Phenomenon, 1987. Add: 100 Bayswater Rd., London W2, England.

YOUNG, Eric William. British, b. 1915. Geography. Geography specialist in public, grammar and secondary modern schs., 1937–61; Headmaster, Royston Secondary Sch., 1954–61. *Publs:* (with J. Mosby) Our World—Books 1-4, 1949–52; (with J.H. Lowry) A Course in World Geography—Books 1-11, 1960–83; Basic Studies in Geography—Books S1-S7, 1968–73; Places and People—Books 1-3, 1975; Pan Study Aids: Geography I and II, 1980. Add: 29 Alexandra Rd., Sheringwood, Sheringham, Norfolk, England.

YOUNG, Ian. Canadian (b. British), b. 1945. Poetry, Translations. Dir., The Magic Word (Communications), since 1988. *Publs:* White Garland: 9 Poems for Richard, 1969; Year of the Quiet Sun, 1969; Double Exposure, 1970; (with Richard Phelan) Cool Fire, 1970; (trans.) Curieux d'Amour, by Count Jacques Fersen, 1970; (with Richard Phelan) Lions in the Stream, 1971; Some Green Moths, 1972; (ed.) The Male Muse: A Gay Anthology, 1973; Yuletide Story, 1973; The Male Homosexual in Literature: A Bibliography, 1975; Common or Garden Gods, 1976; (ed.) The Son of the Male Muse, 1983; Gay Resistance: Homosexuals in the Anti-Nazi Underground, 1985; Sex Magick, 1986. Add: 2483 Gerrard St. E., Scarborough, Ont. M1N 1W7, Canada.

YOUNG, James S(terling). American, b. 1927. Politics/Government. Prof. of Govt., Columbia Univ., NYC (member of the faculty, since 1964) Fellow, Brookings Instn., Washington, D.C., 1966–67. *Publs:* The Washington Community 1800-1828, 1966; (with Perry Goldman) U.S. Congressional Directories 1789-1840, 1974; (ed.) Problems and Prospects of Presidential Leadership in the 1980's, 3 vols., 1982–84. Add: Dept. of Political Science, Columbia Univ., New York, N.Y. 10027, U.S.A.

YOUNG, Jan. *See* **YOUNG,** Janet Randall.

YOUNG, Janet Randall. Also writes as Janet Randall and Jan Young. American, b. 1919. Novels/Short stories, Children's fiction, History, Biography, *Publs:* (with B. and J. Young) Across the Tracks, 1958; (as Janet Randall) Miracle of Sage Valley, 1958; (with B. and J. Young) Run Sheep Run, 1959; (as Janet Randall) Tumbleweed Heart, 1959; (with B. and J. Young) One Small Voice, 1961; (as Janet Randall) Saddles for Breakfast, 1961; (as Janet Randall) Girl from Boothill, 1962; (with B. and J. Young) Sunday Dreamer, 1962; (with B. and J. Young) Goodbye Amigos, 1963; (as Janet Randall) Pony Girl, 1963; (as Janet Randall) Desert Venture, 1963; (as Janet Randall) Jellyfoot, 1964; (as Janet Randall) Burro Canyon, 1964; (as Janet Randall) Seeing Heart, 1965; (with B. and J. Young) Anza: Hard Riding Captain, 1966; (with B. and J. Young) The Forty-Niners, 1966; (with B. & J. Young) Plant Detective, 1966; (with B. and J. Young) Fifty-Four Forty or Fight!, 1967; (with B. and J. Young)

Empire Builder, 1967; (with B. and J. Young) Where Tomorrow?, 1967; (with B. and J. Young) Forged in Silver, 1968; (with B. and J. Young) Frontier Scientist, 1968; (with B. and J. Young) Simon Bolivar, 1968; (with B. and J. Young) Mr. Polk's War, 1968; (as Janet Randall) Topi Forever, 1968; (as Janet Randfall) Buffalo Boy, 1969; (as Janet Randall) Brave Young Warriors, 1969; (with B. and J. Young) Story of the Rocky Mountains, 1969; (with B. and J. Young) The Liberators of South America, 1969; (with B. and J. Young) The Last Emperor, 1969; (with B. and J. Young) Seven Faces West, 1969; (with B. and J. Young) Pikes Peak or Bust, 1970; (with B. and J. Young) Old Rough and Ready, 1970; (as Janet Randall) Island Ghost, 1970; (as Janet Randall) To Save a Tree, 1971; Reluctant Warrior, 1971; Chavez and the Migrant Workers, 1972. Add: P.O. Box 607, Ferndale, Calif. 95536, U.S.A.

YOUNG, Jock. British, b. 1942. Communications media/Broadcasting, Criminology/Law enforcement/Prisons. Prof. of Sociology and Dir. of the Centre for Criminology, Middlesex Polytechnic. *Publs:* The Zookeepers of Deviancy, 1970; The Drugtakers, 1971; (with I. Taylor and P. Walton) The New Criminology, 1972; (ed. with S. Cohen) The Manufacture of News, 1973, 1981; (ed. with R. Bailey) Contemporary Social Problems in Britain, 1973; (ed. with I. Taylor and P. Walton) Critical Criminology, 1974; (with V. Greenwood) Abortion in Demand, 1976; (ed.) Capitalism and the Rule of Law, 1979; (ed.) Permissiveness and Control, 1980; (with M. Fitzgerald) Know Your Own Society, 1981; (co-ed.) Policing the Riots, 1982; (with J. Lea) What Is to Be Done about Law and Order, 1984; (with R. Kinsey and J. Lea) Losing the Fight Against Crime, 1986; (ed.) Confronting Crime, 1986; Islington Crime Survey, 1986; Realist Criminology, 1989. Add: c/o Middlesex Polytechnic, Enfield Coll., Queensway, Enfield, Middx., England.

YOUNG, J(ohn) Z(achary). British, b. 1907. Biology, Marine science/ Oceanography, Psychology, Zoology. Prof. Emeritus of Anatomy, University Coll. London, since 1974 (Prof., 1945–74). Fellow, Magdalen Coll., Oxford, 1931–45. Pres., Marine Biological Assn. of Great Britain, 1976–86. *Publs:* Life of Vertebrates, 1950, 3rd ed., 1982; Doubt and Certainty in Science, 1951; Life of Mammals, 1955, 1972; A Model of the Brain, 1960; An Introduction to the Study of Man, 1971; The Anatomy of the Nervous System of "Octopus Vulgaris," 1971; Programs of the Brain, 1978; Philosophy and the Brain, 1987. Add: 1 The Crossroads, Brill, Bucks, HP18 9TL, England.

YOUNG, Louise B. American, b. 1919. Sciences. Dir., Open Lands Project, since 1973, and Citizens for a Better Environment, since 1977. Research Assoc., Radiation Lab., Massachusetts Inst. of Technology, Cambridge, 1942–44; Science Ed., American Foundn. for Continuing Education, 1962–73; Dir., Lake Michigan Fedn., 1974–78. *Publs:* (ed.) Exploring the Universe, 1963, rev. ed. 1971; (ed.) The Mystery of Matter, 1965; (ed.) Population in Perspective, 1968; Best Foot Forward, 1968; (ed.) Evolution of Man, 1970; Power Over People, 1973; Earth's Aura, 1977; The Blue Planet, 1983; The Unfinished Universe, 1986. Add: 1420 Sheridan Rd., Apt. 3-F, Wilmette, Ill. 60091, U.S.A.

YOUNG, Marguerite (Vivian). American, b. 1909. Novels/Short stories, Poetry, History. Teacher, Univ. of Iowa, Iowa City, 1955–57, New Sch. for Social Research, NYC, 1958–67, and Fairleigh Dickinson Univ., Rutherford, N.J. 1960–62. *Publs:* Prismatic Ground (poetry), 1937; Moderate Fable (poetry), 1944; Angel in the Forest: A Fairy Tale of Two Utopias, 1945; Miss MacIntosh, My Darling, 1965. Add: 375 Bleecker St., New York, N.Y. 10014, U.S.A.

YOUNG, Matt Norvel, Jr. American, b. 1915. Theology/Religion. Chancellor Emeritus, Pepperdine Univ., Malibu, Calif., since 1984 (Pres., 1957–71; Chancellor, 1971–84). Ed., 20th Century Christian mag., and Power for Today Mag. *Publs:* History of Christian Colleges, 1949; The Church Is Building, 1956; Great Preachers of Today, 1963; (ed.) Preachers of Today, vol. I, 1952, vol. II, 1959, vol. III, 1964, vol. IV, 1970, vol. V, 1982; Churches of Today, vol. I, 1960, vol. II, 1970; Poison Stress Is a Killer, 1978. Add: 24420 Tiner Ct., Malibu, Calif. 90265, U.S.A.

YOUNG, Michael (Dunlop). (Lord Young of Dartington). British, b. 1915. Science fiction/Fantasy, Economics, Education, Sociology. Dir., Inst. of Community Studies, London, since 1953. Trustee, Dartington Hall, since 1942; Chmn., 1956–65, and Pres., since 1965, Consumer's Assn; Chmn., 1962–71, and Pres., since 1971 National Extension Coll. Dir. of Political and Economic Planning, 1941–45; Secty., Research Dept., Labour Party, 1945–51. Chmn., Social Science Research Council, 1965–68; Chmn., National Consumer Council, 1975–77. *Publs:* (with Henry Bunbury) Will the War Make Us Poorer?, 1943; Civil Aviation, 1944; (with Theodore Prager) There's Work for All, 1945; Labour's Plan for

Plenty, 1947; What Is Socialised Industry?, 1947; Small Man, Big World: A Discussion of Socialist Democracy, 1949; Fifty Million Unemployed (on India), 1952; (with Peter Willmott) Family and Kinship in East London, 1957, 1962; The Rise of the Meritocracy 1870-2033: An Essay on Education and Equality (science fiction), 1958; (with Peter Willmott) Family and Class in a London Suburb, 1960; (with Michael Armstrong) New Look at Comprehensive Schools, 1964; Innovation and Research in Education, 1965; (with Patrick McGeeney) Learning Begins at Home, 1968; (ed.) Forecasting and the Social Sciences, 1968; Is Equality a Dream (lecture), 1972; (with Peter Willmott) The Symmetrical Family: A Study of Work and Leisure in the London Region, 1973; (ed.) Poverty Report 1974 (and 1975), 2 vols., 1974–75; (with others) Distance Teaching for the Third World, 1980; The Elmhirsts of Dartington: The Creation of a Utopian Community, 1982; (with Marianne Rigge) Revolution from Within, 1985; (ed. with Tom Schuller) The Rhythms of Society, 1988; The Metronomic Society: Natural Rhythms and Human Time tables, 1988. Add: Inst. of Community Studies, 18 Victoria Park Sq., London E2 9PF, England.

YOUNG, Morris N. American, b. 1909. Education, Medicine/Health, Sciences. Ophthalmologist in private practice, NYC, since 1940. Hon. Consultant in the Literature of Magic, Library of Congress, since 1975. Ed., NYAMSUS Newsletter, N.Y. Chapter, Assn. of Military Surgeons of the U.S., 1968–70. *Publs:* (co-author) The Lion's Loose Again (song), 1938; (ed.) Magicol (serial), 1949–52; Hobby Magic, 1950; The Story of Blackstone's Party Magic on Records, 1950; (ed. with W.B. Gibson) Houdini on Magic, 1953; (with W.B. Gibson) Houdini's Fabulous Magic, 1961; Bibliography of Memory, 1961; (with W.B. Gibson) How to Develop an Exceptional Memory, 1962; (with C.V. Young) How to Read Faster and Remember More, 1965, 1972; (with J. Stoltzfus) The Complete Guide to Science Fair Competition, 1972. Add: 150 Broadway, New York, N.Y. 10038, U.S.A.

YOUNG, Philip. American, b. 1918. Literature, Biography. Research Prof. of English, Pennsylvania State Univ., University Park, since 1959. *Publs:* Ernest Hemingway, 1952; Ernest Hemingway: A Reconsideration, 1966; (co-author) The Hemingway Manuscripts: An Inventory, 1969; Three Bags Full: Essays in American Fiction, 1970; Revolutionary Ladies, 1977; Hawthorne's Secret, 1984. Add: Dept. of English, Pennsylvania State Univ., University Park, Pa. 16801, U.S.A.

YOUNG, Rose. *See* HARRIS, Marion Rose.

YOUNG, Scott (Alexander). Canadian, b. 1918. Novels/Short stories, Children's fiction, Screenplays, Biography. Sports Columnist, Winnipeg Free Press, 1937–40; Writer, Maclean's mag., Toronto, 1945–48; Columnist, Toronto Globe and Mail, 1957–69, 1971–80; Sports Ed., Toronto Telegram, 1970–71. *Publs:* Red Shield in Action: A Record of Canadian Savation Army War Services in the Second Great War, 1949; Scrubs on Skates, 1952; Boy on Defense, 1953; The Flood (novel), 1956; The Clue of the Dead Duck, 1962; A Boy at the Leaf's Camp, 1963; (with Astrid Young) Big Cityoffice Junior, 1964; Sports Stories, 1965; The Leafs I Knew (sports columns), 1966; (with Astrid Young) O'Brien (biography of Michael John O'Brien), 1967; We Won't Be Needing You, Al: Stories of Men and Sport, 1968; (with Punch Imlach) Hockey Is A Battle: Punch Imlach's Own Story, 1969; (with George Robertson) Face-Off (novel), 1971; Face-Off Series (Face-Off in Moscow, Learning to Be Captain, The Moscow Challenger, The Silent One Speaks Up), 4 vols., 1973; (with Leo Cahill) Goodbye Argos, 1973; (with Astrid Young) Silent Frank Cochrane: The North's First Great Politician, 1973; Hockey Heroes Series (Bobby Hull, Superstar; Frank Mahovlich, The Big M; Gil Perreault Makes It Happen; Stan Mikita, Tough Kid Who Grew Up), 4 vols., 1974; War on Ice (Canada-Russia hockey series), 1976; Canada Cup, 1976; (with Margaret Hogan) Best Talk in Town, 1980; (with Conn Smythe) If You Can't Beat 'Em in the Alley, 1981; That Old Gang of Mine (novel), 1982; (with Punch Imlach) Heaven and Hell in the NHL, 1982; Neil and Me (memoir about son, Neil Young), 1984; Hello, Canada: The Life and Times of Foster Hewitt, 1985; Lori (screenplay), 1986; Gordon Sinclair: A Life and Then Some., 1987; Murder in a Cold Climate (novel), 1988; Home for Christmas (short stories), 1989. Add: R.R. 2, Cavan, Ont. LOA 1CO, Canada.

YOUNG, Sheila. British, b. 1943. Art. Assoc., Trinity Coll. of Music, London, 1965. *Publs:* The Queen's Jewellery, 1968. Add: 23 Towers Ave., Jesmond, Newcastle upon Tyne NE2 3QE, England.

YOUNG, T(homas) D(aniel). American, b. 1919. Literature, Autobiography/Memoirs. Gertrude Conaway Vanderbilt Prof. Emeritus, Vanderbilt Univ., Nashville, since 1985 (Prof. of English, 1961–85; Chmn. of the Dept., 1966–72). Pres., Soc. for the Study of Southern Literature; member, Editorial Bd., South Atlantic Bulletin, since 1975, and Mississippi Quarterly, since 1976. Chmn., Dept. of English, Univ. of Southern Mississippi, 1950–57; Academic Dean, Delta State Coll., 1957–61. Chmn., American Literature Section, 1966–68, and Literary Criticism Section, 1967, South Atlantic Modern Language Assn. *Publs:* (ed. with Floyd C. Watkins) The Literature of the South, 1951, 1968; Donald Davidson: An Essay and a Bibliography, 1965; (ed.) John Crowe Ransom: Critical Essays and a Bibliography, 1968; (with M. Thomas Inge) Donald Davidson, 1970; John Crowe Ransom, 1971; (ed.) The Literary Correspondence of Allen Tate and Donald Davidson, 1974; Gentleman in a Dustcoat: A Biography of John Crowe Ransom, 1976; (ed.) The New Criticism and After, 1976; (ed., with John Hindle) The Tate-Bishop Correspondence, 1980; The Past Is the Present: A Thematic Study of Modern Southern Fiction, 1980; Tennessee Writers, 1980; John Crowe Ransom: An Annotated Bibliography, 1981; (ed. with George Core) Selected Letters of John Crowe Ransom, 1985; (ed.) John Crowe Ransom: Selected Essays, 1984; (ed. with Louis D. Rubin, Lewis Simpson, et al) The History of Southern Literature, 1985; (ed.) Conversations with Malcolm Cowley, 1986; (ed. with Elizabeth Sarcone) The Lytle-Tate Letters, 1987; Fabulovs Provinces: A memoir, 1988; (ed.) Modern American Fiction: Form and Function, 1989. Add: Box 31, Rose Hill, Miss. 39356, U.S.A.

YOUNG, Wayland. (Lord Kennet). British, b. 1923. Novels/Short stories, International relations/Current affairs, Politics/Government, Social commentary/Phenomena, Travel. Member, House of Lords: Social Democratic Party Spokesman on Foreign Affairs and Defence, since 1981 (Parliamentary Secty., Ministry of Housing and Local Govt., 1966–70; Opposition Spokesman on Foreign Affairs and Science Policy, 1971–74; Chief Whip, SDP, 1981–83). Ed., Disarmament and Arms Control, 1962–65; Chmn., Council for the Protection of Rural England, 1970–72. *Publs:* The Italian Left, 1949; The Deadweight, 1952; Now or Never, 1953; (with E. Young) Old London Churches, 1956; The Montesi Scandal, 1957; Still Alive Tomorrow, 1958; Strategy for Survival, 1959; (with E. Young) The Socialist Imagination, 1960; (with E. Young) Disarmament: Finnegan's Choice, 1961; The Profumo Affair, 1963; Eros Denied, 1965; Thirty-four Articles, 1965; (ed.) Existing Mechanics of Arms Control, 1965; Preservation, 1972; (ed.) The Futures of Europe, 1976; (with E. Young) Neither Red Nor Dead: The Case for Disarmament, 1981; The Rebirth of Britain, 1982; (with E. Young) London's Churches, 1986. Add: 100 Bayswater Rd., London W2, England.

YOUNG, William (Curtis). American, b. 1928. Film, Theatre. Member, Dept. of English, Univ. of Kansas, Lawrence. Lectr., Lincoln Univ., Oxford, Pa., 1957–59, and Paterson State Coll., Wayne, N.J., 1959–61; Assoc. Prof., Wagner Coll., Staten Island, and Adjunct Prof., C.W. Post Coll., Brookville, N.Y., 1961–63; Prof., and Dir. of Theater, Rose Polytechnic Inst., and Dir. of Community Theater, Terre Haute, Ind, 1964–67; Prof., and Curriculum Coordinator, Baker Univ., Baldwin, Kans., 1967–68; Educational Adviser to Govt. of Iran, Jundi Shapur Univ., Ahwaz, Iran, 1969–71; Prof., and Dir., of Graduate Studies in Drama, Univ. of Nebraska, Omaha, 1974–75. *Publs:* American Theatrical Arts, 1971; Famous American Playhouses, 2 vols., 1973; Famous Actors and Actresses on the American Stage, 2 vols., 1975; A Guide to the Outstanding Books on Drama and the Performing Arts 1967–1975, 1976. Add: P.O. Box 313, Lawrence, Kans. 66044, U.S.A.

YOUNGBLOOD, Ronald Fred. American, b. 1931. History, Theology/Religion. Prof. of Old Testament and Hebrew, Bethel Theological Seminary (West Campus), since 1982 (Asst. Prof., 1961–65, Assoc. Prof., 1965–70, and Prof., 1970–78). Prof. of Old Testament, 1978–81, and Dean of the Grad. Sch., 1980–81, Wheaton Coll., Ill. (Assoc. Dean, 1978–80); Prof. of Old Testament and Semitic Languages, Trinity Evangelical Divinity Sch., 1981–82. *Publs:* Great Themes of the Old Testament, 1968, red. ed. as The Heart of the Old Testament, 1971; Special Day Sermons, 1973; Faith of Our Fathers, 1976; How It All Began, 1980; (co-ed. with Morris Inch) The Living and Active Word of God, 1983; Exodus, 1983; Themes from Isaiah, 1983; (with Merrill C. Tenney) What the Bible Is All About (revision), 1983; (assoc. ed.) New International Version Study Bible, (ed.) Evangelicals and Inerrancy, 1985; (ed. with Walter C. Kaiser, Jr.) A Tribute to Gleason Archer, 1986; (ed.) The Genesis Debate: Persistent Questions about Creation and the Flood, 1986. Add: 4747 College Ave., San Diego, Calif. 92115, U.S.A.

YOUNG-BRUEHL, Elisabeth. American, b. 1946. Novels/Short

stories, Philosophy, Biography, Essays. Prof. of Letters, Wesleyan Univ., Middletown, Conn., since 1974. *Publs:* Freedom and Karl Jaspers's Philosophy, 1981; Hannah Arendt: For Love of the World (biography), 1982; Vigil (novel), 1983; Anna Frend (biography), 1988; Mind and the Body Politic (essays), 1989. Add: Coll. of Letters, Wesleyan Univ., Middletown, Conn. 06412, U.S.A.

YOUNGS, Betty F. American, b. 1928. Education, Writing/Journalism. Consultant, Measurement Inc., Dorham, N.C., since 1988. Style Ed., Vocational Guidance Consultant, and Ed. of Vocational Guidance Materials, Baptist Bd., Nashville, Tenn., 1958–66; Instr., Humanities Dept., Grand Conyon Coll., Phoenix, 1976–88, former Columnist, Accent mag. *Publs:* Let's Explore Jobs, 1971; What's Bugging You?, 1973. Add: 2720 Oberlin Dr., Durham, N.C. 27705, U.S.A.

YOUNIE, William J(ohn). American, b. 1932. Education. Prof. of Special Education, and Chmn. of the Dept., William Paterson Coll. of New Jersey, Wayne, since 1971; Consultant, Elwyn Inst., since 1965. Dir. of Education, Southbury Training Sch., Conn., 1959–64; Assoc. Prof. of Special Educatioin, Columbia Univ., NYC, 1964–70. *Publs:* Guidelines for Establishing School Work Study Programs, 1966; (ed.) Preparation of Work Study Teachers of the M.R., 1966; Instructional Approaches to Slow Learning, 1966; (with H. Rusalem) The World of Rehabilitation, 1971; Basic Speech Improvement, 1976; Marking Time, 1978. Add: 307 South Dr., Paramus, N.J. 07652, U.S.A.

YOUNT, John Alonzo. American, b. 1935. Novels/Short stories. Prof. of English, Univ. of New Hampshire, Durham, since 1973 (Assoc. Prof., 1967–73). *Publs:* Wolf at the Door, 1967; The Trapper's Last Shot, 1973; Hardcastle, 1980; Toots in Solitude, 1982. Add: c/o St. Martin's Press, 175 Fifth Ave., New York, N.Y. 10010, U.S.A.

YOUSUF, Ahmed. *See* **ESSOP,** Ahmed.

YOXEN, Edward (John). British, b, 1950. Biology, Sciences, Techonology. Lectr. in Science and Techonology Policy, Univ. of Manchester, since 1976. *Publs:* The Gene Business: Who Should Control Biotechnology?, 1983; Unnatural Selection?: Coming to Terms with the New Genetics, 1986. Add: c/o A P. Watt Ltd., 20 John St., London WC1N 2DL, England.

YUDKIN, John. British, b. 1910. Medicine/Health. Freelance writer, and consultant in nutrition. Prof. of Physiology, 1945–54, and Prof. of Nutrition, 1954–71, Univ. of London. *Publs:* This Slimming Business (in U.S. as Lose Weight, Feel Great), 1958; (with G. Chappell) The Slimmer's Cookbook, 1961; (with J.C. McKenzie) Changing Food Habits, 1964; (with T.C. Barker and J.C. McKenzie) Our Changing Fare, 1966; (with T.C. Barker and D.J. Oddy) The Dietary Surveys of Edward Smith, 1970; (ed. with T.C. Barker) Fish in Britain, 1971; Pure White and Deadly (in U.S. as Sweet and Dangerous), 1972, 1986; This Nutrition Business, 1976; A-Z of Slimming, 1977; Diet of Man, 1978; East Well, Slim Well, 1982; Eat, 1982; The Penguin Encyclopaedia of Nutrition, 1985. Add: 20 Wellington Ct., London NW8 9TA, England.

YUDKIN, Leon Israel. British, b. 1939. Literary criticism, Translations. Lectr., Univ. of Manchester, since 1966. *Publs:* Isaac Lamdan: A Study in Twentieth-Century Hebrew Poetry, 1971; (co-ed.) Meetings with the Angel (short story anthology), 1973; Escape into Siege, 1974; U.Z. Greenberg: On the Anvil of Hebrew Poetry, 1980, 1987; Jewish Writing and Identity in the Twentieth Century, 1982; 1948 and After: Aspects of Israeli Fiction, 1984; (ed.) Modern Hrbrew Literature in English Translation, 1986; (ed.) Agnon. Texta and Contexts in English Transalation, 1988. Add: 51 Hillside Ct., 409 Finchley Rd., London NW3 6HQ, England.

YUILL, P.B. *See* **WILLIAMS,** Gordon.

YURICK, Sol. American, b. 1925. Novels/Short stories. Librarian, New York Univ., NYC, 1945–53; Social Investigator, NYC Dept. of Welfare, 1954–59. *Publs:* The Warriors, 1965; Fertig, 1966; The Bag, 1968; Someone Just Like You (short stories) 1973; (ed.) Voices of Brooklyn: An Anthology, 1973; An Island Death, 1975; Richard A, 1981; The Big Green-Out, 1983. Add: c/o Morrow, 105 Madison Ave., New York. N.Y. 10016, U.S.A.

Z

ZACEK, Joseph Frederick. American, b. 1930. History, Politics/Government, Biography, Translations. Prof. of History, since 1971, and Chmn. of Intnl. Research, Ed. and Development, since 1984, State Univ. of New York, Albany (Assoc. Prof., 1968–71; Dept. Chmn., 1974–77). Member of Editorial Bd., Canadian-American Slavic Studies, since 1968, East Central Europe, since 1972, Canadian Review of Studies in Nationalism, since 1973, and Kosmas: Journal of Czechoslovak and Central European Studies, since 1981; Ed., Central and East European Series Academic Intnl. Press; Member, National Bd. of Consultants, National Endowment for the Humanities, since 1975. Asst. Prof. of History, Occidental Coll., Los Angeles, Calif., 1962–65; Asst. Prof. of History, Univ. of California, Los Angeles, 1965–68; IREX Sr. Scholar Exchange with Czechoslovakia, 1973, and Member, National Screening Cttee. for Eastern Europe, 1978–81; Visiting—Scholar, Columbia Univ., NYC, 1977–78; Fellow, Russian Research Center, Harvard University, Cambridge; Mass., 1986–88. *Publs:* (with P.F. Sugar and I.J. Lederer) Nationalism in Eastern Europe, 1969; Palacky: The Historian as Scholar and Nationalist, 1970; (with P. Brock and H.G. Skilling) The Czech Renascence of the Nineteenth Century, 1970; (with P.F. Sugar) Native Fascism in the Successor States, 1918-1945, 1971; (with A. Vantuch and L. Holotik) Der Osterreichisch-Ungarische Ausgleich 1968, 1971; (ed. and contrib.) Frantisek Palacky 1798-1876: A Centennial Appreciation, 1981; (ed. and contrib.) The Enlightenment and the National Revivals in Eastern Europe, 1983; (ed. and contrib.) The Intimate Palacky, 1984. Add: Dept. of History, State Univ. of New York, Albany, N.Y. 12222, U.S.A.

ZACHARY, Elizabeth. American, b. 1928. Novels/Short stories. *Publs:* (with Hugh Zachary) The Landrushers, 1978; (with Hugh Zachary) Dynasty of Desire, 1978; (with Hugh Zachary) Hotel Destiny, 1980; (with Hugh Zachary) Blitz Hotel, 1980; (with Hugh Zachary) The Golden Dynasty, 1980; Blazing Vixen, 1980; (with Hugh Zachary) Of Love and Battle, 1981. Add: 7 Pebble Beach Dr., Yaupon Beach, N.C. 28461, U.S.A.

ZACHARY, Hugh. Also writes as Ginny Gorman, Elizabeth Hughes, Zach Hughes (science fiction), Peter Kanto, Derral Pilgrim, Olivia Rangely, and Marcus van Heller. American, b. 1928. Mystery/Crime/Suspense, Historical/Romance/Gothic, Science fiction/Fantasy. Radio and TV broadcaster, Okla., Tenn., N.C., and Fla., 1951–62. *Publs:* One Day in Hell, 1961; (as Derral Pilgrim) Lolila, 1964; (as Olivia Rangely) The Bashful Lesbian, 1965; (as Peter Kanto) A Man Called Sex, 1965; (as Derral Pilgrim) Lust Addict, 1965; (as Derral Pilgrim) Battalion Broads, 1965; (as Peter Kanto) Call Me Gay, 1965; (as Peter Kanto) Two Way Beach Girl, 1965; (as Peter Kanto) Too Young to Wait, 1966; (as Peter Kanto) Bedroom Touchdown, 1966; (as Peter Kanto) Beach Wife, 1966; (as Peter Kanto) One Lonely Summer, 1966; (as Peter Kanto) License to Prowl, 1966; (as Peter Kanto) Gold in Her Eyes, 1966; (as Peter Kanto) Glamor Boy, 1966; (as Peter Kanto) Color Her Willing, 1967; (as Peter Kanto) Matinee in Three Scenes, 1967; (as Ginny Gorman) Flames of Joy, 1967; (as Peter Kanto) The Bedroom Beat, 1967; (as Peter Kanto) Playboy's Lament, 1967; (as Peter Kanto) The Girl with the Action, 1967; (as Peter Kanto) Tomcat, 1967; (as Peter Kanto) The Love Standard, 1967; (as Peter Kanto) The Johnson Girls, 1967; (as Peter Kanto) The Love Boat, 1967; (as Peter Kanto) Wallins' Wantons, 1967; (as Peter Kanto) Neighborly Lover, 1967; (as Peter Kanto) Black and White, 1967; (as Peter Kanto) The Girls Upstairs, 1968; (as Peter Kanto) Suddenly, Wonderfully Gay, 1968; (as Peter Kanto) Moonlighting Wives, 1968; (as Peter Kanto) The Sullied Virgin, 1968; (as Peter Kanto) Two Beds for Liz, 1968; (as Peter Kanto) A Small Slice of War, 1968; A Feast of Fat Things, 1968; (as Peter Kanto) The Snake Room, 1968; (as Peter Kanto) Angel Baby, 1968; (as Peter Kanto) Taste of Evil, 1969; (as Peter Kanto) First Experiences, 1969; (as Peter Kanto) World Where Sex Was Born, 1969; (as Peter Kanto) Nest of Vixens, 1969; (as Peter Kanto) Unnatural Urges, 1969; (as Peter Kanto) The Coupling Game, 1970; (as Peter Kanto) Back Way In, 1970; The Beachcombers Handbook of Seafood Cookery, 1970; (as Peter Kanto) Naked Joy, 1970; (as Peter Kanto) Das Drachennest, 1970; (as Peter Kanto) Green Thumb and Silver Tongue, 1970; (as Peter Kanto) Sexpo, Danish Style, 1970; (as Peter Kanto) Rake's Junction, 1970; (as Peter Kanto) On Campus, 1970; (as Peter Kanto) A Dick for All Seasons, 1970; (as Peter Kanto) Das Grosse Sexspiel, 1970; (as Peter Kanto) Der Sexplanet, 1971; (as Peter Kanto) Her Husband's Best Friend, 1971; (as Peter Kanto) The Sex Experiment at Diddle U, 1971; The Competition for Alan, 1971; (as Peter Kanto) Super Sex Stars, 1971; (as Peter Kanto) Doing It with Daughter, 1972; (as Peter Kanto) Lustful Nights, 1972; (as Peter Kanto) Lay-A-Day, 1972; (as Peter Kanto) Girl in Revolt, 1972; (as Peter Kanto) Try Me!, 1973; (as Elizabeth Hughes) The Legend of the Deadly Doll, 1973; (as Peter Kanto) Make the Bride Blush, 1973; (as Zach Hughes) Book of Rack the Healer, 1973; (as Zach Hughes) Legend of Miaree, 1974; Gwen, In Green, 1974; (as Zach Hughes) Seed of the Gods, 1974; (as Zach Hughes) Tide, 1974; (as Zach Hughes) The Stork Factor, 1975; How to Win at Wild Card Poker, 1975; (as Zach Hughes) For Texas and Zed, 1976; (as Zach Hughes) Tiger in the Stars, 1976; (as Zach Hughes) The St. Francis Effect, 1976; Second Chance, 1976; (with Elizabeth Zachary) Dynasty of Desire, 1978; (with Elizabeth Zachary) The Land Rushers, 1978; (with Elizabeth Zachary) The Golden Dynasty, 1980; (with Elizabeth Zachary) Hotel Destiny, 1980; (with Elizabeth Zachary) Blitz Hotel, 1980; (as Zach Hughes) Killbird, 1980; To Guard the Right, 1980; (as Zach Hughes) Pressure, Man, 1980; (with Elizabeth Zachary) Of Love and Battle, 1981; Bloodrush, 1981; Murder in White, 1981; Top Level Death, 1981; (as Zachary Hughes) The Hotel Destiny Series: The Adlon Link, Fortress London, The Fires of Paris, Tower of Treason, 1981; The Sierra Leone Series: Flight to Freedom, Freedom's Passion, Treasure of Hope, Freedom's Victory, 1981–82; (as Zach Hughes) Thunderworld, 1982; The Venus Venture, 1986; The Revenant, 1988. Add: 7 Pebble Beach Dr., Yaupon Beach, N.C. 28461, U.S.A.

ZACHER, Robert Vincent. American, b. 1917. Administration/Management, Advertising/Public relations. Prof. of Business Admin., Arizona State Univ., Tempe, since 1947. Assoc. Prof. of Business Admin., Univ. of Southern California, Los Angeles, 1951–52. *Publs:* Advertising Techniques and Management, 1961, 1967. Add: 2625 E. Southern, C-141, Tempe, Ariz. 85282, U.S.A.

ZADE, Hans Peter. British, b. 1907. Engineering/Technology. Freelance consultant and writer. Designer of Welding equipment, Arc Mfg. Co. Ltd., 1937–46; Development Engineer, Rediffusion Ltd., 1946–51; Former Gen. Mgr., Rediweld Ltd. Member, Inst. of Plastics; Delegate, British Delegation to the Intnl. Inst. of Welding; Member, Instn. of Electrical Engineers. *Publs:* (with G. Haim) The Welding of Plastics, 1947; Heatsealing and High-Frequency Welding of Plastics, 1959; Welding Transformers and Rectifiers, 1967. Add: 16 Oak Way, Northgate, Crawley, Sussex, England.

ZAHN, Gordon C(harles). American, b. 1918. History, Sociology, Theology/Religion, Biography. Prof. Emeritus of Sociology, Univ. of Massachusetts, Boston, since 1981 (Prof. of Sociology, 1968–81). Prof. of Sociology, Loyola Univ., Chicago, 1953–67. *Publs:* (ed.) Readings in Sociology, 1961; German Catholics and Hitler's Wars, 1962, 1989; In Solitary Witness, 1964, 1986; What is Society?, 1964; The Military Chaplaincy (in U.K. as Chaplains of the R.A.F.), 1969; Thomas Merton on Peace, 1971; Another Part of the War: The Camp Simon Story, 1979. Add: 780 Boylston, Apt. 26D, Boston, Mass. 02199, U.S.A.

ZAHN, Timothy. American, b. 1951. Science fiction. Full-time writer since 1980. *Publs:* The Blackcollar, 1983; A Coming of Age, 1985; Cobra, 1985; Spinneret, 1985; The Backlash Mission, 1986; Cascade Point and Other Stories, 1986; Cobra Bargain, 1988; Time Bomb and Zahndry Others, 1988. Add: c/o Baen Books, 260 Fifth Ave., New York, N.Y. 10001, U.S.A.

ZALBEN, Jane Breskin. American. Children's fiction. Freelance book designer. Asst. to the Art Dir. of Children's Books, Dial Press, NYC, 1971–72; Dir., T.Y. Crowell, 1974–75; Art Dir., Charles Scribners, 1975–76. *Publs:* Cecilia's Older Brother, 1973; Lyle and Humus, 1974; Basil and Hillary, 1975; Penny and the Captain, 1978; Will You Count the Stars with Me?, 1979; Norton's Nighttime, 1979; Oliver and Alison's Week, 1980; A Perfect Nose for Ralph, 1980; Oh, Simple, 1981; Maybe It Will Rain Tomorrow, 1982; Here's Looking at You, Kid, 1984; The Walrus and the Carpenter, 1986; Water from the Moon, 1987; Beni's First Chanukah, 1988; Earth to Andrew O. Blechman, 1989; Happy Passover, Rosie, 1990. Add: c/o Farrar Straus and Giroux, 19 Union Sq. W., New York, N.Y. 10003, U.S.A.

ZALD, Mayer Nathan. American, b. 1931. Institutions/Organizations, Sociology. Prof. of Sociology and Social Work, Univ. of Michigan, Ann Arbor, since 1977 (Chmn., 1981–86). Assoc. Prof., 1964–71, Prof., 1968–77, and Chmn., 1971–75, Dept. of Sociology, Vanderbilt Univ., Nashville. *Publs:* (ed.) Social Welfare Institutions, 1965; (ed.) Organizing for Community Welfare, 1967; (ed.) Power in Organizations, 1970; Organizational Change: The Political Economy of the YMCA, 1970; Occupations and Organizations in American Life, 1971; (with G. Wamsley) The Political Economy of Public Organizations, 1973; (with J. McCarthy) Social Movements in an Organizational Society, 1987. Add: Dept. of Sociology, Univ. of Michigan, Ann Arbor, Mich. 48109, U.S.A.

ZALL, Paul M. American, b. 1922. Literary criticism, Biography, Writing/Journalism. Prof. of English, California State Univ., Los Angeles, 1957–87, now Emeritus. *Publs:* Elements of Technical Report Writing, 1962; (compiler) A Hundred Merry Tales, 1963; (ed.) Literary Criticism of William Wordsworth, 1966; Coleridge's Sonnets from Various Authors, 1967; (with J. Durham) Plain Style, 1967; (with J.R. Trevor) Proverb to Poem, 1969; (ed.) Simple Cobler of Agawam in America, 1969; (compiler) A Nest of Ninnies, 1970; (ed.) Peter Pindar's Poems, 1970; (ed.) Comical Spirit of '76, 1976; Ben Franklin Laughing, 1980; (with J.A.L. Lemay) Genetic Text of Franklin's Autobiography, 1981; Abe Lincoln Laughing, 1982; Mark Twain Laughing, 1985; (with Eric Birdsall) Wordsworth's Descriptive Sketches, 1985; George Washington Laughing, 1989. Add: Huntington Library, San Marino, Calif. 91108, U.S.A.

ZANTS, Emily. American, b. 1937. Literature. Prof., Univ. of Hawaii, Manoa, since 1972. Instr. in Gen. Studies, Columbia Univ., NYC, 1960–62; Instr. in French Literature, City Coll., City Univ. of New York, NYC, 1962–67; Asst. Prof., Univ. of California, Davis, 1967–72. *Publs:* The Aesthetics of the New Novel in France, 1968. Add: Dept. of Eurpoean Languages, Univ. of Hawaii, Honolulu 96822, U.S.A.

ZAPOLEON, Marguerite Wykoff. American, b. 1907. Economics, Education, Women, Biography. Labor economist, U.S. Govt., Washington, D.C., 1935–59. Founder and Supvr., Outlook for Women series, Women's Bureau, U.S. Dept. of Labor, 1944–51; Ed., Current Information on Occupational Outlook, U.S. Dept. of Labour Bureau of Statistics, 1951–55; Ed., Vocational Guidance Quarterly, 1953–54. *Publs:* Community Occupational Surveys, 1942; The College Girl Looks Ahead to Her Career Opportunities, 1956; Occupational Planning for Women, 1961; Girls and Their Futures, 1962, rev. ed. 1978; Everyone Needs a Mountain, 1985. Add: 816 S.E. Riviera Isle, Ft. Lauderdale, Fla. 33301, U.S.A.

ZARNOWITZ, Victor. American, b, 1919. Economics. Prof. of Economics and Finance, Grad. Sch. of Business, Univ. of Chicago, since 1965 (Assoc. Prof., 1955–64); Member, Research Staff, National Bureau of Economic Research, NYC, since 1952. Dir., Study of Cyclical Indicators, Bureau of Economic Analysis, U.S. Dept. of Commerce, Washington, 1972–75. *Publs:* Die Theorie of Einkommens-verteilung (Theory of Income Distribution), 1951; Unfilled Orders, Price Changes, and Business Fluctuations, 1962; Forecasting Business Conditions: A Critical View, 1965; An Appraisal of Short-term Economic Forecasts, 1967; (co-author and ed.) The Business Cycle Today, 1972; Orders, Production, and Investment: A Cyclical and Structural Analysis, 1974; An Analysis of Forecasts of Aggregate Income, Output, and the Price level, 1979; Business Cycle Analysis and Experimental Survey Data, 1984; Recent Work on Business Cycles in Historical Perspective, 1985; Rational Expectation and Macroeconomic Forecasts, 1985. Add: Grad. Sch. of Business, Univ. of Chicago, Chicago, Ill. 60637, U.S.A.

ZAWODNY, J(anusz) K. American, b. 1921. International relations/Current affairs. Consultant, National Security Council, since 1979. Fellow, Center for Advanced Study in the Behavioral Sciences, Stanford, Calif., 1961–62; Assoc. Prof., 1962–63, and Prof. of Intnl. Relations, 1965–75, Univ. of Pennsylvania, Philadelphia. Research Assoc., Harvard Univ. Center for Intnl. Affairs, Cambridge, Mass., 1968; Sr. Assoc. Member, St. Antony's Coll., Oxford Univ., 1968–69; Member, Inst. for Advanced Study, Princeton, N.J., 1971–72. Prof. of Intnl. Relations, Claremont Grad. Sch. and Pomona Coll., Claremont, Calif., 1975–82. *Publs:* Death in the Forest: Responsibility for the Katyn Forest Massacre, 1962, 5th ed. 1989; (ed. and contrib.) Unconventional Warfare, 1962; (ed. and contrib.) Man and International Relations: Contributions of the Social Sciences to the Study of Human Conflict, 2 vols., 1967; Guide to the Study of International Relations, 1967; Nothing But Honor: The Story of the Warsaw Uprising 1944, 1978; Katyn, 1989. Add: Brush Prairie, Wash. 98606, U.S.A.

ZEBROWSKI, George. American (b. Austrian), b. 1945. Science fiction/Fantasy. Freelance writer and lectr. Copy Ed., Binghamton Evening Press, 1967; filtration plant operator, NYC, 1969–70; Lectr. in Science Fiction, State Univ. of New York at Binghamton, 1971; Ed., SFWA Bulletin, 1970–75. *Publs:* The Omega Point, 1972; The Star Web, 1975; (ed.) Tomorrow Today, 1975; (ed. with Thomas N. Scortia) Human-Machines: An Anthology of Stories about Cyborgs, 1975; (ed. with Jack Dann) Faster Than Light: An Anthology of Stories about Interstellar Trave, 1976; Ashes and Stars, 1977; The Monadic Universe and Other Stories, 1977; Macrolife, 1979; The Omega Point Trilogy, 1983; Sunspacer, 1984; The Stars Will Speak (juvenile), 1985; (ed.) Nebula Awards 20 (21, 22), 3 vols., 1985–88; (ed.) Synergy 1 (2, 3), 3 vols., 1987–88. Add: Box 486, Johnson City, N.Y. 13790, U.S.A.

ZEIGRIED, Karl. *See* **FANTHORPE,** R. Lionel.

ZEILIK, Michael. American, b. 1946. Astronomy. Prof. of Astronomy, since 1985, and Dir., Center for Graduate Studies at Los Alamos, since 1987, Univ. of New Mexico, Albuquerque (Asst. Prof., 1975–79; Assoc. Prof., 1979–85; Assoc. Dir., Inst. for Astrophysics, 1985–88). Instr. in Astronomy, Harvard Univ., Cambridge, Mass., 1974–75, and Southern Connecticut State Coll., New Haven, 1969–72. *Publs:* Astronomy: The Evolving Universe, 1976, 5th ed. 1988; (with J. Gaustaud) Astronomy: The Cosmic Perspective, 1983, 1989; (with E.V.P. Smith) Introductory Astronomy and Astrophysics, 1987. Add: Dept. of Physics and Astronomy, Univ. of New Mexico, 800 Yale Blvd. N.E., Albuquerque, N.M. 87131, U.S.A.

ZELAZNY, Roger (Joseph Christopher). American, b. 1937. Science fiction/Fantasy. *Publs:* This Immortal, 1966; The Dream Master, 1966; Four for Tomorrow (in U.K. as A Rose for Ecclesiastes), 1967; Lord of Light, 1967; Isle of the Dead, 1969; Creatures of Light and Darkness, 1969; Damnation Alley, 1969; Nine Princes in Amber, 1970; The Doors of His Face, The Lamps of His Mouth, and Other Stories, 1971; Jack of Shadows, 1971; The Guns of Avalon, 1972; Today We Choose Faces, 1973; To Die in Italbar, 1973; Sign of the Unicorn, 1975; (with Philip K. Dick) Deus Irae, 1976; Bridge of Ashes, 1976; Doorways in the Sand, 1976; My Name Is Legion, 1976; The Hand of Oberon, 1977; Courts of Chaos, 1978; Roadmarks, 1979; Coils, 1980; The Changing Land, 1981; Eye of the Cat, 1982; Dilvish, The Damned, 1982; Unicorn Variations (short stories), 1983; Trumps of Doom, 1985; Blood of Amber, 1986; A Dark Traveling, 1987; Sign of Chaos, 1987. Add: c/o Kirby McCauley Ltd., 432 Park Ave. S., Suite 1509, New York, N.Y. 10016, U.S.A.

ZELDIN, Theodore. British, b. 1933. History, Biography. Sr. Tutor, and Dean, St. Antony's Coll., Oxford, since 1963 (Research Fellow, 1957–

63); Univ. Lectr., Oxford Univ., and Lectr., Christ Church, Oxford, since 1959. *Publs:* The Political System of Napoleon III, 1958, 1970; (ed.) Emile Ollivier: Journal 1846-69, 2 vols., 1961; Emile Ollivier and the Liberal Empire of Napoleon III, 1963; (ed. and contrib.) Conflicts in French Society: Anticlericalism, Education and Morals in the 19th Century, 1970; France 1848-1945, 4 vols., 1973–81; The French, 1983. Add: c/o St. Antony's Coll., Oxford, England.

ZELDIS, Chayym. American, b. 1927. Novels/short stories, Poetry, Translations. National Publicity Dir., Women's American Org. for Rehabilitation Through Training (ORT), NYC, since 1960. *Publs:* Streams in the Wilderness, 1962; Seek Haven, 1968; (ed.) May My Words Feed Others, 1974; Golgotha, 1974; Brothers, 1976; The Marriage Bed, 1978; The Brothel, 1979; A Forbidden Love, 1983. Add: c/o Shapolsky Publishers, 136 W. 22nd St., New York, N.Y. 10017, U.S.A.

ZELINGER, Geza. Canadian, b. 1911. Engineering/Technology, Mathematics/Statistics. Independent Consultant, since 1982. Staff member, Canadian Marconi Co., Montreal, 1958–64, De Havilland Aircraft of Canada Ltd., Toronto, 1969–71; Lectr., Humber Coll., Technology Div., Toronto, Ont., 1971–82. *Publs:* Basic Matrix Algebra and Transistor Circuits, 1963; Basic Matrix Analysis and Synthesis, 1966; Optoelectronics Fundamentals, 1978; Fundamentals of Optoelectronics, Lasers and Lightwave Communications, 1983. Add: 92 Prince George Dr., Islington, Ont. M9B 2X8, Canada.

ZELINSKY, Wilbur. American, b. 1921. Geography. Prof. of Geography, Pennsylvania State Univ., University Park, since 1963. Prof., Univ. of Georgia, Athens, 1948–52, Univ. of Wisconsin, Madison, 1952–54, and Southern Illinois Univ., Carbondale, 1959–63. *Publs:* A Bibliographic Guide to Population Geography, 1962; A Prologue to Population Geography, 1966; (co-ed.) A Basic Geographical Library, 1966; (co-ed.) Geography and a Crowding World, 1970; The Cultural Geography of the United States, 1973; (co-ed.) This Remarkable Continent, 1982; Nation Into State, 1988. Add: Dept. of Geography, Pennsylvania State Univ., University Park, Pa. 16802, U.S.A.

ZELLNER, Arnold. American, b. 1927. Economics, Mathematics/Statistics. H.G.B. Alexander Prof. of Economics and Statistics, Univ. of Chicago, Grad. Sch. of Business, since 1966. Co-Ed., Journal of Econometrics. Asst. and Assoc. Prof. of Economics, Univ. of Washington, Seattle, 1955–60; Assoc. and Prof. of Economics, Univ. of Wisconsin, Madison, 1960–66. *Publs:* (with J.A. Crutchfield) Economic Aspects of the Pacific Halibut Fishery, 1963; (ed.) Readings in Economic Statistics and Econometrics, 1968; (with H.R. Hamilton, E. Roberts, A.J. Pugh, J. Milliman and S. Goldstone) Systems Simulation for Regional Analysis: An Application to River-Basin Planning, 1969; (with T.C. Lee and G.G. Judge) Estimating the Parameters of the Markov Probability Model from Aggregate Time Series Data, 1970; An Introduction to Bayesian Inference in Econometrics, 1971; (ed. with S.E. Fienberg) Studies in Bayesian Econometrics and Statistics in Honor of Leonard J. Savage; (ed.) Seasonal Analysis of Economic Time Series, 1978; (ed.) Bayesian Analysis in Econometrics and Statistics: Essays in Honor of Harold Jeffreys, 1980; Basic Issues in Econometrics, 1984. Add: Grad. Sch. of Business, Univ. of Chicago, Chicago, Ill. 60637, U.S.A.

ZENTNER, Peter. British, b. 1932. Business/Trade/Industry, Politics/Government. Mgmt. consultant and journalist. *Publs:* East West Trade: A Practical Guide to Selling in Eastern Europe, 1967; Social Democracy in Britain—Must Labour Lose?, 1982. Add: 38 Woodland Gardens, London N10 3UA, England.

ZETTERLING, Mai (Elisabeth). Swedish, b. 1925. Novels/Short stories, Plays/Screenplays, Autobiography. Film Dir. and Actress. *Publs:* (co-author) The War Game (screenplay), 1963; (co-author) Loving Couples (screenplay), 1965; (with David Hughes) The Cat's Tale, 1965; Night Games (novel), 1966, and co-author of screenplay, 1966; (co-author) Dr. Glas (screenplay), 1968; (co-author) The Girls (screenplay), 1968; (co-author) Flickorna (screenplay), 1968; Shadow of the Sun (novel), 1974; Bird of Passage (novel), 1976; Ice Island (children's novel), 1980; All Those Tomorrows (autobiography), 1985. Add: c/o Douglas Rae Management Ltd., 28 Charing Cross Rd., London WC2H 0DB, England.

ZIEGLER, Philip (Sandeman). British, b. 1929. History, Biography. Staff Member, William Collins Sons & Co. Ltd., London, since 1966. Chmn., Soc. of Authors, since 1988. Served in Vientiane, Pretoria, Paris,

and Bogota, British Diplomatic Service, 1952–66. *Publs:* The Duchess of Dino, 1962; Addington, 1965; The Black Death, 1968; William IV, 1971; Omdurman, 1974; Melbourne, 1976; Crown and People, 1978; Diana Cooper, 1981; Mountbatten, 1985; Elizabeth's Britain, 1986; The Sixth Great Power: Borings 1782-1929, 1988. Add: 22 Cottesmore Gardens, London W8 5PR, England.

ZIEMKE, Earl F. American, b. 1922. History, Military/Defence. Prof. of History, Univ. of Georgia, Athens, since 1967. Researcher, Columbia Univ. Bureau of Applied Social Science, Alexandria, Va., 1951–55; Historian, Office of the Chief of Military History, Dept. of U.S. Army, Washington, D.C., 1955–67. *Publs:* The German Northern Theater of Operations, 1959; Stalingrad to Berlin, 1964; (with K.K. Greenfield) Command Decisions, 1964; (with V.C. Esposito) A Concise History of World War II, 1964; The Soviet Partisan Movement in World War II, 1964; Battle for Berlin, 1968. Add: Dept. of History, Univ. of Georgia, Athens, Ga. 30604, U.S.A.

ZIETLOW, E(dward) R(obert). American, b. 1932. Novels/Short stories, Literature. Prof. of English, Univ. of Victoria, B.C., since 1965. *Publs:* These Same Hills, 1960; A Country for Old Men and Other Stories, 1977; Transhominal Criticism, 1978; The Indian Maiden's Captivity and The Heart of the Country, 1978. Add: Dept. of English, Univ. of Victoria, Victoria, B.C., Canada.

ZIFF, Larzer. American, b. 1927. Cultural/Ethnic topics, History, Literature. Caroline Donovan Prof. of English, The Johns Hopkins Univ., Baltimore, since 1981. Asst. Prof. to Prof. of English, 1956–73, and Chmn. of Grad. Studies and Vice-Chmn. of the Dept. of English, 1965–69, Univ. of California, Berkeley; Fellow of Exeter Coll. and Univ. Lectr., Oxford Univ., 1973–78; Prof. of English, Univ. of Pennsylvania, Philadelphia, 1978–81. Chmn., Literature and Soc. Group, Modern Language Assn., 1965; Chmn., Criticism and History Section, English Inst., 1966; Member, U.S.-U.K. Educational Commn., 1969–71; Member, Editorial Bd., PMLA, 1979–82. *Publs:* (ed.) Walden, by Thoreau, 1961; (ed.) The Scarlet Letter, by Hawthorne, 1962; The Career of John Cotton, 1962; (ed.) The Genius, by Dreiser, 1967; (ed.) The Financier, by Dreiser, 1967; The American 1890's, 1968; (ed.) John Cotton on the Churches of New England, 1969; (ed.) The Literature of America: Colonial Period, 1970; (ed. with Robie Macauley) America and Its Discontents, 1971; Puritanism in America, 1973; (ed.) Selected Writings of Benjamin Franklin, 1979; Literary Democracy, 1981; (ed.) Selected Essays of Emerson, 1982. Add: Dept. of English, Johns Hopkins Univ., Baltimore, Md. 21218, U.S.A.

ZILIOX, Marc. *See* **FICHTER,** George S.

ZIM, Herbert S(pencer). American, b. 1909. Natural history. Adjunct Prof. of Education, Univ. of Miami, since 1967; Editorial Consultant, Individualized Science Instructional System, since 1972. Assoc. Prof. of Education, 1950–54, Prof., Univ. of Illinois, Urbana. Ed., Golden Guides Series, 1949–69, Ed.-in-Chief, Our Wonderful World Encyclopedia, 1952–63, and Ed.-in-Chief, Golden Encyclopedia of Natural History, 1962–75. *Publs:* Author/co-author of about 100 books since 1942, including: The Universe, 1961; (with A. Sprunt) Gamebirds, 1961; Fossils, 1962; The Rock Mountains, 1964; Butterflies and Moths, 1964; Sharks, 1966; Corals, 1966; Non-Flowering Plants, 1967; Mexico, 1969; Machine Tools, 1969; Trucks, 1970; Life and Death, 1970; (ed.) How Things Work, 10 vols., 1968-75; (with J. Skelly) Armored Animals, 1971; Your Stomach, 1973; Medicine, 1974; (with L. Krantz) Crabs, 1974; (with L. Krantz) Snails, 1975; (with L. Krantz) Sea Stars and Their Kin, 1977; Caves, 1979; Little Cats, 1978; Your Skin, 1979; The New Moon, 1980; Quartz, 1981. Add: 88835 Old Highway, Tavernier, Fla. 33070, U.S.A.

ZIMBARDO, Philip. American, b. 1933. Psychology. Prof., Stanford Univ., Calif. Writer, Host, PBS-TV Series, "Discovering Psychology," 1990. *Publs:* (ed.) The Cognitive Control of Motivation, 1969; (with F. Ruch) Psychology and Life, 8th ed. 1971, sole author of 12th ed. 1987; (with E. Ebbesen and C. Maslach) Influencing Attitudes and Changing Behavior, 1970, 1977; Shyness: What It Is, What To Do About It, 1977; (with S. Radl) The Shyness Workbook, 1980; (with S. Radl) The Shy Child, 1981. Add: 25 Montclair Terr., San Francisco, Calif. 94109, U.S.A.

ZIMMER, Paul J. American, b. 1934. Poetry. Dir., Univ. of Iowa Press, since 1984. Macy's Book Dept. Mgr., San Francisco, Calif., 1961–63; Mgr., San Francisco News Co., 1963–65; Mgr., U.C.L.A. Bookstore,

Los Angeles, Calif., 1965–67; Asst. Dir., Univ. of Pittsburgh Press, and Ed., Pitt Poetry Series, 1967–78; Dir., Univ. of Georgia Press, 1978–84. *Publs:* A Seed on the Wind: Poems, 1960; The Ribs of Death, 1967; The Republic of Many Voices, 1969; The Zimmer Poems, 1976; With Wanda: Town and Country Poems, 1979; The Ancient Wars, 1981; Family Reunion: Selected and New Poems, 1983; The American Zimmer, 1984; Live with Animals, 1987; The Great Bird of Love, 1989. Add: 204 Lexington Ave., Iowa City, Ia. 52246, U.S.A.

ZIMMERMAN, Franklin (Bershir). American, b. 1923. Music. Prof. of Music, Dir. of Pro Musica, and Chmn., Dept. of Music, since 1968, and Lectr., Coll. of Gen. Studies, since 1969, Univ. of Pennsylvania, Philadelphia. Asst. Prof., State Univ. of New York, Potsdam, 1958–59; Assoc. Prof., and Chmn., Dept. of History, Music and Literature, Univ. of Southern California, Los Angeles, 1959–64; Prof. of Music, Dartmouth Coll., Hanover, N.H., and Dir., Dartmouth Collegium Musicum, 1964–67; Prof. of Music, Dir. of Pro Musica, Dir., Div. of Music History and Musicology, and Dir., Collegium Musicum, Univ. of Kentucky, Lexington, 1967–68. *Publs:* Henry Purcell 1659-1695: An Analytical Catalogue of His Music, 1963; Henry Purcell, His Life and Times, 1967; (ed.) Introduction to the Skill of Music, 12th ed. 1972; Henry Purcell 1695-1695: Melodic and Intervallic Indexes to His Complete Works, 1972; (ed.) The William Kennedy Gostling Manuscript (facsimile ed.), 1973; Henry Purcell: A Guide to Research. Add: Dept. of Music, Univ. of Pennsylvania, Philadelphia, Pa. 19174, U.S.A.

ZIMMERMAN, Joseph Francis. American, b. 1928. Politics/Government, Public/Social administration, Transportation. Prof. of Political Science, State Univ. of New York, Albany, since 1965 (Dir., Local Govt. Studies Center, 1965–68; Chmn., Dept. of Political Science, 1973–74). Research Dir., New York State Legislative Commn. on Critical Transportation Choices, since 1982; Contrib. Ed., National Civic Review, since 1968. Prof. of Political Science, Worcester Polytechnic Inst., Mass., 1954–65. Staff Dir., New York State Joint Legislative Cttee. on Mass Transportation, 1967–68; Research Dir., New York State Select Legislative Cttee. on Transportation, 1967–76; and New York State Senate Cttee. on Transportation, 1976–82. *Publs:* State and Local Government, 1962, 3rd ed. 1978; (ed.) Readings in State and Local Government, 1964; The Massachusetts Town Meeting: A Tenacious Institution, 1967; (ed.) Metropolitan Charters, 1967; (ed.) The Government of the Metropolis, 1968; (ed.) Subnational Politics, 1970; (ed.) The Crisis in Mass Transportation, 1971; The Federated City: Community Control in Large Cities, 1972; Pragmatic Federalism: The Reassignment of Functional Responsibility, 1976; (with Frank W. Prescott) The Politics of the Veto of Legislation in New York, 2 vols., 1980; The Government and Politics of New York State, 1981; State-Local Relations: A Partnership Approach, 1983; Participatory Democracy: Populism Revived, 1986. Add: Grad. Sch. of Public Affairs, State Univ. of New York, 135 Western Ave., Albany, N.Y. 12222, U.S.A.

ZIMMERMAN, Naoma. American, b. 1914. Children's fiction. Psychiatric Social Worker, Consultant and Lectr. in Family Therapy, Family Service of South Lake Co., Highland Park, Ill., since 1958. *Publs:* Sleepy Forest, 1943; Timothy Tick-Tock, 1943; The Party Dress, 1943; The Sleepy Village, 1944; The New Comer, 1944; Baby Animals, 1955; Little Deer, 1956; (with R. Schuyler) Corky Meets a Spaceman, 1960; (with R. Schuyler) Corky in Orbit, 1962. Add: 465 Drexel Ave., Glencoe, Ill. 60022, U.S.A.

ZIMMERMANN, Arnold Walter. British, b. 1913. Education, Geography, History, Theology/Religion. Gen. Secty. and Dir., Summer Schs. Dir. of Studies, Educational Development Assn. Intnl. Sch. Head Teacher, Horsenden Jr. Sch., 1949–56, and Newport Jr. Schs., London, 1957–72; Leader, Waltham Forest Teachers Centre, 1972–74. *Publs:* (with F.M. Meade) Time and Progress Histories-Books 1-6; (with F.M. Meade) School Study Bible Books 1-7; Write Me a Story; (with F.M. Meade) Spotlight on Geography; (with F.M. Meade) Panorama Readers; (with F.M. Meade) New English Study Bible; (with F.M. Meade) Religions of the World; (with F.M. Meade) Illustrated Study Bible; (with F.M. Meade) Integrated Studies; (with F. Whaling) Religions of the World. Add: 8 Windmill Gardens, Enfield, Middx. EN2 7DU, England.

ZIMPEL, Lloyd. American, b. 1929. Novels/Short stories, Business/Trade/Industry, Cultural/Ethnic topics, Social sciences. Advertising Dir., West Coast Life Insurance Co., San Francisco, 1959–63; Education Dir., Fair Employment Practice Commn., State Dept. of Industrial Rela-

tions, San Francisco, 1964–81. *Publs:* (with Daniel Panger) Business and the Hardcore Unemployed, 1970; Meeting the Bear: Journal of the Black Wars, 1971; (ed.) The Disadvantaged Worker, 1971; (ed.) Man Against Work, 1974; Foundry Foreman, 1980. Add: 38 Liberty St., San Francisco, Calif. 94110, U.S.A.

ZINDEL, Paul. American, b. 1936. Children's fiction, Plays/Screenplays. Chemistry teacher, Tottenville, N.Y., 1960–69. *Publs:* The Pigman, 1968; My Darling, My Hamburger, 1969; I Never Loved Your Mind, 1970; The Effects of Gamma Rays on Man-in-the-Moon Marigolds (play), 1971; And Miss Reardon Drinks a Little (play), 1972; The Secret Affairs of Mildred Wild (play), 1973; Let Me Hear You Whisper (play), 1974; I Love My Mother, 1975; Pardon Me, You're Stepping on My Eyeball!, 1976; Confessions of a Teenage Baboon, 1977; The Undertaker's Gone Bananas, 1978; The Ladies Should Be in Bed (play), 1978; The Pigman's Legacy, 1980; (with Bonnie Zindel) A Star for the Latecomer, 1980; The Girl Who Wanted a Boy, 1981; (with Crescent Dragonwagon) To Take a Dare, 1982; When a Darkness Falls, 1984; Harry and Hortense at Hormone High, 1984; The Amazing and Death-Defying Diary of Eugene Dingman, 1987. Add: c/o Harper and Row, 10 E. 53rd St., New York, N.Y. 10022, U.S.A.

ZINKIN, Taya. British, b. 1918. Anthropology/Ethnology, Children's non-fiction, History, Autbiography/Memoirs/Personal. Chief Corresp. in India: Economist, Manchester Guardian and New Commonwealth, 1950–60, and for Le Monde, 1954–60. *Publs:* India Changes, 1958; Rishi, 1960; Rishi Returns, 1961; Caste Today, 1962; Reporting India, 1962; India, 1964; (with M. Zinkin) Britain and India, 1964; Life of Gandhi, 1965; Challenges in India, 1966; India and Her Neighbours, 1967; The Faithful Parrot, 1967; Tales Told Round the World, 1968; The Heartland of Asia, 1971; Odious Child, 1971; Weeds Grow Fast, 1973; Write Right, 1980; French Mensahib, 1989. Add: 6 Kensington Ct. Gardens, London W8 5QE, England.

ZINN, Howard. American, b. 1922. History, Plays, Politics/Government. Prof. of Political Science, Boston Univ., Mass., since 1964. Chmn., Dept. of History, Spelman Coll., Atlanta, Ga., 1956–63. *Publs:* LaGuardia in Congress, 1959; The Southern Mystique, 1964; SNCC: The New Abolitionists, 1964; (ed.) New Deal Thought, 1965; Vietnam: The Logic of Withdrawal, 1967; Disobedience and Democracy, 1968; The Politics of History, 1970; (ed. with Noam Chomsky) The Pentagon Papers: Critical Essays, 1972; Post-war America, 1973; (ed.) Justice in Everyday Life, 1974; Emma (play), 1976; A People's History of the United States, 1980; Daughter of Venus (play), 1985; Rebel in Paradise (play), 1987. Add: 29 Fern St., Auburndale, Mass. 02166, U.S.A.

ZINNES, Harriet. American. Short stories, Poetry. Prof. of English, Queens Coll., City Univ. of New York, Flushing, 1949–53, and since 1962. Ed., Publs. Div., Raritan Arsenal, Metuchen, N.J., 1942–43; Assoc. Ed., Harper's Bazaar mag., 1944–46; Tutor, Hunter Coll., 1946–49; Lectr., Rutgers Univ., New Brunswick, N.J., 1960–62; Art Critic, Pictures on Exhibit, 1971–81; Poetry Consultant, Great Neck Library, N.Y., 1972–82. *Publs:* Waiting and Other Poems, 1964; An Eye for an I, 1966; I Wanted to See Something Flying, 1976; Entropisms, 1978; (ed.) Ezra Pound and the Visual Arts, 1980; Book of Ten, 1981; (trans.) Blood and Feathers: Selected Poems of Jacques Prévert, 1988; Lover: A Collection of Short Stories, 1989. Add: 25 W. 54th St., New York, N.Y. 10019, U.S.A.

ZIOLKOWSKI, Theodore. American, b. 1932. Literature, Translations. Prof. of German and Comparative Literature since 1964, and Dean of the Grad. Sch. since 1979, Princeton Univ., N.J. Instr. and Asst. Prof., Yale Univ., New Haven, Conn., 1956–62; Assoc. Prof., Columbia Univ., NYC, 1962–64. *Publs:* Hermann Broch, 1964; The Novels of Hermann Hesse, 1965; Hermann Hesse, 1966; (trans. with Y. Ziolkowski) Herman Meyer, The Poetics of Quotation in the European Novel, 1968; Dimensions of the Modern Novel, 1969; (ed.) Hermann Hesse: Stories of Five Decades, 1972; (ed.) Hermann Hesse: Autobiographical Writings, 1972; Fictional Transfigurations of Jesus, 1972; (ed.) Hesse: A Collection of Critical Essays, 1973; (ed.) Hermann Hesse, My Belief: Essays of Art and Life, 1974; (trans. with Y. Ziolkowski) Hermann Hesse: A Pictorial Biography, 1975; (ed.) Hermann Hesse, Student Stories, 1975; Disenchanted Images: A Literary Iconology, 1977; Der Schriftsteller Hermann Hesse, 1979; The Classical German Elegy, 1980; (ed.) Hermann Hesse, Pictor's Metamorphoses and other Fantasies, 1982; Varieties of Literary Thematics, 1983; German Romanticism and Its Institution, 1989. Add: Wyman House, 50 Springdale Rd., Princeton, N.J. 08540, U.S.A.

ZOCHERT, Donald (Paul, Jr.). American, b. 1938. Novels, Biography. Freelance writer since 1978. Reporter, United Press Intnl., Chicago, 1961–66, and Chicago Daily News, 1966–78. *Publs:* (ed.) Walking in America, 1974; Laura: The Life of Laura Ingalls Wilder, 1976; Murder in the Hellfire Club (novel), 1979; Yellow Dogs, 1989. Add: c/o Atlantic Monthly Press, 19 Union Sq. W., New York, N.Y. 10003, U.S.A.

ZOHN, Harry. American, b. 1923. History, Language/Linguistics, Literature, Biography, Translations. Prof. of German, Brandeis Univ. (joined faculty as Instr., 1951). Exec. Dir., Goethe Soc. of New England, 1963–68. *Publs:* (co-ed.) Wie sie es sehen, 1952; (ed.) Liber Amicorum Friderike Maria Zweig, 1952; (trans.) Sigmund Freud: Delusion and Dream, 1956; (ed. and trans.) The World Is a Comedy: A Kurt Tucholsky Anthology, 1957; (trans.) Jacob Burckhardt: Judgments on History and Historians, 1958; (ed.) Stefan Zweig: Schachnovelle, 1960; (trans.) The Complete Diaries of Theodor Herzl, 5 vols., 1960–61; Wiener Juden in der deutschen Literatur, 1964; (ed. and trans. with K.F. Ross) Tucholsky: What If?, 1968; (ed. and trans. with E.W. Rollins) Men of Dialogue: Martin Buber and Albrecht Goes, 1969; (trans.) Walter Benjamin: Illuminations, 1969; (trans.) Herzl: The Jewish State, 1970; Karl Kraus, 1971; (ed.) Der farbenvolle Untergang, 1971; (ed.) Friderike Zweig: Greatness Revisited, 1972, 1982; (trans.) Herzl: Zionist Writings, 1973; (trans.) Walter Benjamin: Charles Baudelaire, 1973; (trans. and ed.) Marianne Weber: Max Weber, 1975; (trans. and ed.) In These Great Times: A Karl Kraus Reader, 1976; Kraus: Half-Truths and One-and-a-Half Truths, 1976; (trans. and ed.) Rudolf Kayser: The Saints of Oumran, 1977; (trans.) Gershom Scholem: From Berlin to Jerusalem, 1980; Walter Benjamin: The Story of a Friendship, 1982; Ich bin ein Sohn der deutschen Sprache nur . . ., 1986; (trans.) My European Heritage, by Brigitte Fischer, 1986; (trans.) The Hebrew Vowels and Consonants, by Ernst Ettisch, 1986; (trans.) The Jewish Question, by Alex Bein, 1989; (trans.) The Austrian Resistance 1938-45, by Fritz Molden, 1989. Add: Shiffman Humanities Center, Brandeis Univ., Waltham, Mass. 02154, U.S.A.

ZOLOTOW, Charlotte. American, b. 1915. Children's fiction, Poetry. Editorial Consultant and Editorial Dir., Charlotte Zolotow Books, Harper and Row, since 1981 (Sr. Ed., 1962–76; Vice-Pres., Assoc. Publr., and Editorial Dir., Harper Jr. Books Div., Harper and Row, 1976–81). *Publs:* The Park Book, 1944; But Not Billy, 1944; The Storm Book, 1952; The Magic Word, 1952; The City Boy and the Country Horse, 1952; Indian, Indian, 1952; The Quiet Mother and the Noisy Little Boy, 1953; One Step, Two . . ., 1955; Over and Over, 1957; Not a Little Monkey, 1957; The Night Mother Was Away, 1958, as The Summer Night, 1974; The Park Book, 1958; Do You Know What I'll Do?, 1958, Sleepy Book, 1958; Bunny Who Found Easter, 1959; Aren't You Glad, 1960; Big Brother, 1960; The Three Funny Friends, 1961; The Sky Was Blue, 1963; The Quarreling Book, 1963; The White Marble, 1963; A Tiger Called Thomas, 1963; I Have a Horse of My Own, 1964; The Poodle Who Barked at the Moon, 1964; A Rose, a Bridge, and a Wild Black Horse, 1964; Mr. Rabbit and the Lovely Present, 1964; When the Wind Stops, 1964; 1975; Flocks of Birds, 1965; Someday, 1965; When I Have a Little Girl, 1965; If it Weren't for You, 1966; Big Sister and Little Sister, 1966; I Want to Be Little, 1966; Summer Is . . ., 1967; WhenI Have a Son, 1967; All That Sunlight, 1967; The New Friend, 1968; Some Things Go Together, 1969; A Week in Yoni's World: Greece, 1969; The Hating Book, 1969; (as Sara Abbot) Here Is Where I Begin, 1970; River Winding, 1970, 1978; A Week in Lateef's World: India, 1970; You and Me, 1971; A Father Like That, 1971; Wake Up and Goodnight, 1971; William's Doll, 1972; Hold My Hand, 1972; The Beautiful Christmas Tree, 1972; Janey, 1973; My Grandson Lew, 1974; (ed.) An Overpraised Season, 1974; The Unfriendly Book, 1975; The Little Black Pony, 1975; It's Not Fair, 1976; May I Visit, 1976; Someone New, 1978; If You Listen, 1980; Say It!, 1980; The Song, 1982; I Know a Lady, 1984; Everything Glistens and Everything Sings: New and Selected Poems, 1987; I Like to Be Little, 1987; Something Is Going to Happen, 1988. Add: c/o Charlotte Zolotow Books, Harper & Row, 10 East 53rd St., New York, N.Y. 10022, U.S.A.

ZOLOTOW, Maurice. American, b. 1913. Biography. Contributing Ed., Los Angeles Mag. *Publs:* Never Whistle in a Dressing Room, 1944; The Great Balsamo, 1946; No People Like Show People, 1951; It Takes All Kinds, 1952; Oh Careless Love, 1959; Marilyn Monroe: A Biography, 1960; Stagestruck: The Romance of Alfred Lunt and Lynn Fontanne, 1965; (with A. Sherman) A Gift of Laughter, 1965; Shooting Star: The Life of John Wayne, 1974; Billy Wilder in Hollywood, 1978; Confessions of a Racetrack Fiend, 1983. Add: c/o Los Angeles Mag., 1888 Century Park E., of Angeles, Calif. 90067, U.S.A.

ZORNOW, William Frank. American, b. 1920. History, Biography. Prof. of History, Kent State Univ., Ohio, since 1958. Clerk of Probate

Court, Cuyahoga County, Ohio, 1941–43; Production Planning Engineer, Hickok Electrical Instrument Co., Cleveland, Ohio, 1943–46; Instr., in History, Univ. of Akron, 1946–47, and Case Inst. of Technology, Cleveland, 1947–50; Asst. Prof. of History, Kansas State Univ., Manhattan, 1951–58. *Publs:* Lincoln and the Party Divided, 1954, 1972; Kansas: A History of the Jayhawk State, 1957, 1972; America at Mid-Century, 1959. Add: Kent State Univ., 305 Bowman Hall, Kent, Ohio 44242, U.S.A.

ZUBIN, Joseph. American. b. 1900. Psychiatry, Psychology. Prof. Distinguished Research Prof. of Psychiatry, School of Medicine, Univ. of Pittsburgh, Penn., since 1977; Adjunct Prof./Gregory Razran Prof. of Psychology, Queens Coll., NYC, since 1970; Prof. Emeritus of Psychology and Special Lectr. in Psychiatry, Dept. of Psychology and Coll. of Physicians and Surgeons, Columbia Univ., NYC, since 1969 (Asst. in Ed. Psychology, Teachers Coll., 1930–31; Instr. in Psychometrics, Coll. of Physicians and Surgeons, 1932–33; Instr. in Psychiatry, 1939–47; Asst. Prof. of Psychology, 1947–50; Adjunct Prof. of Psychology, 1950–56; Prof. of Psychology, 1956–69). Research Career Scientist, since 1978, and Coord. of Research and Development, since 1984, VA Medical Center, Pittsburgh, Penn.; Attending Biometrician, New York State Psychiatric Inst., since 1976. Asst. Psychologist, Mental Hospital Survey Cttee., National Cttee. for Mental Hygiene, 1936–38; Assoc. Research Psychologist, New York State Psychiatric Inst. and Hospital, 1938–56; Visiting Prof., Univ. of Wisconsin, Madison, Summer 1948; Visiting Prof., Univ. of California, Los Angeles, Summer 1951; Consultant, VA National Inst. of Mental Health, National Research Council, 1956–69; Principal Research Scientist of Biometrics, New York State Dept. of Mental Hygiene, 1956–76; Research Psychologist, VA Medical Center, Pittsburgh, 1976–78. *Publs:* Some Effects of Incentives: A Study of Individual Differences in Rivalry, 1932; Choosing a Life Work, 1937; Sorting Tests in Relation to Drug Therapy in Schizophrenia, 1941; Handwriting Analysis: A Series of Scales for Evaluating Dynamic Aspects of Handwriting, 1942; Quantitative Techniques and Methods in Abnormal Psychology, 1950; An Experimental Approach to Projective Techniques, 1965; (ed. with Fritz A. Freyan) Disorders of Mood, 1972; Contemporary Sexual Behavior: Critical Issues in the 1970s, 1973; Experimental Approaches to Psychopathology, 1975. Add: 190 Highwood Ave., Leonia, N.J. 07605, U.S.A.

ZUCKER, Norman Livingston. American, b. 1933. History, Politics/Goverment. Prof. of Political Science, Univ. of Rhode Island, Kingston, since 1969. Consultant, Select Commn. on Immigration and Refugee Policy, 1980. *Publs:* George W. Norris: Gentle Knight of American Democracy, 1966; (ed.) The American Party Process: Readings and Comments, 1968; The Coming Crisis in Israel: Private Faith and Public Policy, 1973; The Voluntary Agencies and Refugee Resettlement in the United States, 1981; The Guarded Gate: The Reality of American Refugee Policy, 1987. Add: 25 Locust Dr., Kingston, R.I. 02881, U.S.A.

ZUCKERMAN, Edward (Ben). American, b. 1948. Sciences, Technology. Contributing Ed., Spy. English Instr., Harrisburg Area Community Coll. Harrisburg, Pa., 1970–71; Ed., Independent Press, Harrisburg, 1971–72; Tour Operator, Transtrek Ltd., Kemmel, Belgium, 1973; Columnist, "City Rites," The Real Paper, 1975–77; Contributing Ed., Rolling Stone, 1978–80. *Publs:* The Day After World War III: The U.S. Government's Plans for Surviving a Nuclear War, 1984. Add: 1410 Astoria Park S., Astoria, N.Y. 11102, U.S.A.

ZUCKERMAN, Lord. *See* **ZUCKERMAN,** Solly.

ZUCKERMAN, Michael. American, b. 1939. History, Politics/Government. Prof. of History, Univ. of Pennsylvania, Philadelphia, since 1984 (Instr., 1965–67; Asst. Prof., 1967–70, Assoc. Prof., 1970–84). *Publs:* Peaceable Kingdoms: New England Towns in the Eighteenth Century, 1970; Friends and Neighbors: Group Life in America's First Plural Society, 1982. Add: Dept. of History, Univ. of Pennsylvania, Philadelphia, Pa. 19104, U.S.A.

ZUCKERMAN, Solly. (Lord Zuckerman). British, b. 1904. Environmental science/Ecology, Sciences. Staff member, Oxford Univ. 1934–45; Scientific Adviser on Air Planning to Supreme Command, 1943–45; Sands Cox Prof. of Anatomy, Univ. of Birmingham, 1943–68; Chief Scientific Adviser to H.M. Govt., 1964–71. *Publs:* The Social Life of Monkeys and Apes, 1932, 1981; Functional Affinities of Man, Monkeys and Apes, 1933; A New System of Anatomy, 1961, 1981; (ed.) The Ovary, 1962, 1977; Scientists and War, 1966; Beyond the Ivory Tower, 1970; Cancer Research, 1972; Advice and Responsibility, 1975; From Apes to Warlords, 1978; Nuclear Illusion and Reality, 1982; Star Wars in a Nuclear World, 1986; Monkeys, Men, and Missiles, 1988. Add: Univ. of East

Anglia, Norwich NR4 7TJ, England.

ZURNDORFER, Lotte. British, b. 1929. Poetry. Lectr. in English, Univ. of Helsinki. *Publs:* (Poems), 1952; Poems, 1960. Add: Myotale 5, Mankans, Finland.

ZWINGER, Ann Haymond. American, b. 1925. Environmental science/Ecology, Natural history. Former Instr. in History of Art, Smith Coll., Northampton, Mass. *Publs:* (author and illustrator) Beyond the Aspen Grove, 1970; (with Beatrice Willard) Land Above the Trees, 1972; (author and illustrator) Run, River, Run, 1975; Wind in the Rock, 1978; (with Edwin Way Teale) A Conscious Stillness, 1982; A Desert Country Near the Sea, 1983; John Xantus: The Fort Tejon Letters 1857-1859, 1986. Add: c/o Univ. of Arizona Press, 1230 N. Park Ave., Suite 102, Tucson, Ariz. 85719, U.S.A.